A TENNYSON CONCORDANCE

A CONCORDANCE

TO THE

POETICAL AND DRAMATIC WORKS

OF

ALFRED, LORD TENNYSON

INCLUDING THE POEMS CONTAINED IN
THE "LIFE OF ALFRED, LORD TENNYSON,"
AND THE "SUPPRESSED POEMS," 1830-1868.

By ARTHUR E. BAKER, F.R.Hist.S., F.L.A.

SECRETARY AND LIBRARIAN, TAUNTON.

AUTHOR OF

"A BRIEF ACCOUNT OF THE PUBLIC LIBRARY MOVEMENT IN TAUNTON," ETC.

Routledge & Kegan Paul Ltd.

ROUTLEDGE & KEGAN PAUL LTD.
BROADWAY HOUSE, 68-74 CARTER LANE,
LONDON, E.C.4

First published 1914
by Kegan Paul, Trench, Trubner & Co. Ltd.
reissued 1965
by Routledge & Kegan Paul Ltd,
Broadway House, 68-74 Carter Lane,
London, E.C.4

Printed in Great Britain
by The Compton Printing Works Ltd.
London, N.1

TO THE MEMORY

OF

MY MOTHER,

MY FIRST AND BEST TEACHER,

THIS BOOK IS

AFFECTIONATELY DEDICATED.

" Until the day break, and the shadows flee away."

PREFATORY NOTE

It may, perhaps, not be out of place to say a word or two as to how I came to undertake the compilation of this work. Some years ago, when occupying the position of Deputy-Librarian in a public library in the North of England, I received numerous enquiries from readers at that institution for a Concordance to the Works of Tennyson. Realising that here was a distinct *desideratum* in the library of the student of English Literature, I there and then decided to undertake the compilation of such a Work. Taking from one of the Book-presses a copy of the poet's Works, and opening it, my eyes fell on the following quotation :—

Origin of the Work.

> " Make knowledge circle with the winds ;
> But let her herald, Reverence, fly
> Before her to whatever sky
> Bear seed of men and growth of minds."
> *—Love thou thy land.*

I jotted down the lines under their respective key-words, and thus the work was commenced.

Shortly afterwards it happened that I removed to my present position in the South of England ; consequently the matter was for some time "shelved"; but at the end of 1907 I returned to the subject, and after about eight years of what has been to me a labour of love, I present my humble labour to the public, with a sincere hope that students, and lovers of Tennyson, and others, will find it of interest and utility.

The volume consists of Verbal Indexes to the Poetical and Dramatic Works of the author comprised in the *Complete Edition*, published by Messrs Macmillan & Co., to the *Poems* contained in the *Life of Lord Tennyson* by his son, and published by the same publishers; also to the *Suppressed Poems*, edited by J. C. Thomson, and published by Messrs Sands & Co.

Contents.

The Concordance has been arranged in strict alphabetical sequence ; the different senses or grammatical functions of a word are frequently distinguished under separate headings ; the dialect words are paraphrased ; all proper names are included, and occasionally some indication has been added of their identity.

Arrangement.

Line-references are given, thereby greatly facilitating the finding of a quotation or reference, particularly in the larger poems.

Line-references.

vii

As each one has to number the lines for himself in all but school editions of Tennyson's Works, I must

Method of numbering Lines.

explain the method, or rather methods, of numbering for the purpose of this Concordance. In the *Poems* the lines have been numbered without regard to the typographical peculiarities of the standard edition, which has two columns to a page. The following lines, here reprinted as they stand in that edition, were numbered 1-6, thus :—

1 THESE to His Memory—since he held
   them dear,
2 Perchance as finding there unconsciously
3 Some image of himself—I dedicate,
4 I dedicate, I consecrate with tears—
5 These Idylls.
6   And indeed He seems to me
   —*Idylls of the King. Dedication.*

That is to say, a line broken into two by the printer was counted as one; a line broken by the poet was counted as two.

In the *Dramatic Works*, another and merely mechanical system was adopted. There every line of print as it occurs in Macmillan's one-volume edition of the *Complete Works* was numbered separately, even if only containing a single word. Thus :—

1 *Cranmer.* To Strasburg, Antwerp,
2   Frankfort, Zurich, Worms,
3 Geneva, Basle—our Bishops from their
4   sees
5 Or fled, they say, or flying—Poinet,
6   Barlow,
   —*Queen Mary, Act i., Scene ii.*

Metrically, of course, there are only three lines here, not six. A method of numbering that is not to be avoided in the prose portions of the plays has intentionally been extended also to the blank verse in order to facilitate rapid reference to copies of the text in which the lines are not already numbered. On receiving a reference, say to line 560 of *The Falcon*, a reader using Macmillan's standard edition in one volume can quickly reckon out the page and even the column in which the quotation appears, by remembering that the column contains approximately fifty lines of print. Had the lines been numbered metrically he would have had to count from the beginning of the piece. Only the lines of the text proper, not the stage-directions, have been numbered.

Cross-references.

Cross-references are supplied in the case of compounds and dialect forms—*e.g.,* **Life** (*See also* **After-life, Loife**).

In the *Collected Works*, two poems appear bearing the same title—viz., *To the Queen.* The one which

Duplicate Titles and Headings of Poems.

appears on page 474, immediately preceding the *Lover's Tale,* has been described as *To the Queen ii,* in contradistinction to the one which appears on page 1. Then there are a few poems with no distinct titles, but simply headed thus : *To ——, Song, Sonnet,* etc. To avoid confusion, these are referred to in the Concordance by the first two or three words of each poem.

Omitted Words. No quotations are furnished for the following words. A few quotations, however, may be found under those marked with an asterisk (*Poetical Works*) or dagger (*Dramatic Works*) but they are there to illustrate some especial use, and by no means represent every occurrence of the word :—

A	But	†If	Ourself	Too
About	By	In	Out	'Twas
Above	Can	*Indeed	Over	'Twere
Adown	Cannot	Into	Perchance	'Twill
†After	Canst	Is	*Round	*Under
Again	†Could	It	*Scarce	Until
Against	Couldst	Its	Scarcely	Unto
Ago	Did	Itself	Seldom	Up
Ah	Didst	Lest	Shall	Upon
Albeit	*Do	Let	Shalt	Us
†All	Does	May	She	*†Very
Almost	Done	May'st	Should	*†Was
*Along	Dost	Me	Shouldst	Wast
Aloof	Doth	*Mid	Since	We
Already	Down	Might	So	*†Well
Also	†Downward	Might'st	*†Some	Were
Although	Each	†Mine	*†Something	Wert
Alway	E'er	More	Soon	What
Always	*Either	Most	Still (adv.)	Whate'er
Am	Else	Must	*†Such	Whatsoever
Among	Ere	My	Than	*†When
An	Even	Myself	That	Whence
And	†Ever	Near	The	Whene'er
†Any	*Every	Nearly	Thee	Where
Are	For	*Need	Their	Whereat
Around	Forth	Ne'er	Theirs	Whether
Art	From	†Neither	Them	Which
As	'Gainst	*Never	*Then	Whicheve
At	Had	*No	Thence	While
Athwart	Hadst	*None	There	Who
Atwain	Has	Nor	Therefore	Whom
Atween	Hast	Not	These	†Whose
Away	Have	Nothing	They	Why
*Ay	Having	†Now	Thine	*Will
Back	He	O	†This	Wilt
Be	Hence	O'er	Tho'	With
Because	Henceforth	Of	Those	Within
Been	Her	Off	Thou	Without
*Before	Here	Oft	Though	Would
Behind	Herself	Often	Thro'	Wouldst
Being	Him	Oh	Through	Ye
Below	Himself	On	Thus	Yea
Beneath	His	Once	Thy	Yes
Beside	*How	*†Only	Thyself	Yet
Between	Howe'er	*Onward	Till	You
Betwixt	However	Or	'Tis	Your
Beyond	Howsoe'er	Our	To	Yours
Both	*I	Ours	Together	Yourself

A*

It was originally intended, in order to curtail the heavy expenditure entailed in publication, to omit various adjectives and other words; but as enquiries were made regarding their omission, it was decided later to insert these words as far as it was possible. As, however, the letters A-D (*Poetical Works* only) had already been printed, it was impossible to make these entries, consequently many ordinary adjectives under the above letters are omitted.

Poems in Duplicate. The following poems in the *Life* occur also in the *Collected Works*, or in the *Suppressed Poems*, and are, of course, treated only once :—

As when a man that sails in a balloon. (See *Suppressed Poems* under *Dream of Fair Women*.)

Check every outflash, every ruder sally. (See *Suppressed Poems*.)

Farewell, Macready, since to-night we part. (See *Collected Works* under *To W. C. Macready*.)

First drink a health, this solemn night. (See *Suppressed Poems* under *Hands all Round*.) A few readings peculiar to the *Life* are, however, recorded in their place.

God bless our Prince and Bride ! (See *Suppressed Poems*.)

Grave mother of majestic works. (See *Collected Works* under *Of old sat Freedom*.)

Helen's Tower, here I stand. (See *Collected Works*, under *Helen's Tower*.) The sole variant is duly recorded, however.

Here often when a child I lay reclined. (See *Suppressed Poems* under *Mablethorpe*.) Important variants in the *Life* are recorded.

Me my own Fate to lasting sorrow doometh. (See *Suppressed Poems*.)

Rise, Britons, rise, if manhood be not dead. (See *Suppressed Poems* under *Britons, guard your own*.) Important variants in the *Life* are recorded.

Row us out from Desenzano, to your Sirmione row ! (See *Collected Works* under *Frater Ave Atque Vale*.)

The North wind fall'n in the new-starréd night. (See *Suppressed Poems* under *The Hesperides*.)

Therefore your Halls, your ancient Colleges. (See *Suppressed Poems* under *Cambridge*.) The significant variants are all recorded.

Thy prayer was "Light — more Light — while time shall last !" (See *Collected Works* under *Epitaph on Caxton*.)

The poem *Lover's Tale* appears in the *Collected Works* and also in the *Suppressed Poems*. The portion common to both versions have not been indexed twice; they have been neglected in making the Concordance to the *Suppressed Poems*.

The volume contains approximately 150,000 quotations and references; and as each quotation or **Alphabetizing and Checking.** reference was written on a separate slip, which was then placed in its alphabetical order, and afterwards classified according to the sense or grammatical function of the key-word, it can better be imagined than described what an immense amount of labour and time was thus bestowed upon the work.

In this respect my acknowledgments are due, and are hereby tendered, to Miss Beatrice Hewlett (the hon. librarian of the Crewe Green Parish Library, Cheshire), and to my two sisters, Miss Mary **Appreciation.** E. Baker and Miss Miriam Maud Mary Baker, for their valuable assistance in this portion of the work. At the same time, I beg to tender my hearty thanks to those who have from time to time written me encouraging letters, which have greatly assisted me in my arduous task, and in this respect I would specially mention Mr Lionel R. M. Strachan, English Lecturer in Heidelberg University, for the great interest he has invariably evinced in the compilation of the work—particularly for his valuable help in the checking of the proofs—and for his readiness at all times to render assistance.

A. E. B.

TAUNTON,
1914.

CORRIGENDA

Page 132 Dawn (verb) *Tiresias* 206 *read* Dawn (s).
  ,,   252 Gave (*See also* Gied, Giv) *read* Gave (*See also* Gev, Gied, Giv).
  ,,   256 Gev (give) *read* Gev (gave).
  ,,   258 Give (*See also* Gev, Gie) *read* Give (*See also* Gie).
  ,,   334 Hope (verb) *Supp. Confessions* 31 *read* Hope (s).
  ,,   832 Alight (lighted) *read* Alight.
  ,,   832 Alighted.   *See* Lighted—*delete*.

CONTENTS

LIST OF SHORT TITLES AND ABBREVIATIONS

Achilles over the T.	Achilles over the Trench.
(adj.)	adjective.
(adv.)	adverb.
A gate and a field	A gate and a field half ploughed.
Akbar's D., Hymn	Akbar's Dream. Hymn.
Akbar's D., Inscrip.	Akbar's Dream. Inscription.
Along this glimmering	Along this glimmering gallery.
Arabian Nights	Recollections of the Arabian Nights.
Are those the far-famed	Are those the far-famed Victor Hours ?
A spirit haunts	A spirit haunts the year's last hours.
A surface man	A surface man of many theories.
Batt. of Brunanburh	Battle of Brunanburh.
Beauty, Good, etc.	Beauty, Good, and Knowledge are three sisters.
Because she bore	Because she bore the iron name.
Blow ye the trumpet	Blow ye the trumpet, gather from afar.
Bold Havelock	Bold Havelock march'd.
Bright is the moon	Bright is the moon on the deep.
Britons, guard	Britons, guard your own.
By an Evolution	By an Evolutionist.
Check every outflash	Check every outflash, every ruder sally.
Church-warden, etc.	Church-warden and the Curate.
Com. of Arthur	Coming of Arthur.
Come not, when, etc.	Come not, when I am dead.
(compar.)	comparative.
Could I outwear	Could I outwear my present state of woe.
D. of F. Women	Dream of Fair Women.
D. of the Duke of C.	Death of the Duke of Clarence and Avondale.
D. of the O. Year	Death of the Old Year.
Day-Dm., Pro.	Day-Dream, Prologue.
" *Sleep. P.*	" Sleeping Palace.
" *Sleep. B.*	" Sleeping Beauty.
" *Depart.*	" Departure.
" *Ep.*	" Epilogue.
Ded." of Idylls	Idylls of the King. Dedication.
Ded. Poem Prin. Alice	Dedicatory Poem to the Princess Alice.
Deep glens I found	Deep glens I found, and sunless gulfs.
Def. of Lucknow	Defence of Lucknow.
Demeter and P.	Demeter and Persephone.
De Prof., Two G.	De Profundis : The Two Greetings.
" *Human C.*	" The Human Cry.
Early-wise	Early-wise, and pure, and true.
England and Amer.	England and America.
Epit. on Caxton	Epitaph on Caxton.
Epit. on Gordon	Epitaph on General Gordon.
Epit. on Stratford	Epitaph on Lord Stratford de Redcliffe.
Every day, etc.	Every day hath its night.
Faded ev'ry violet	Faded ev'ry violet, all the roses.
Far off in the dun	Far off in the dun, dark occident.
First drink a health	First drink a health, this solemn night.
Flow. in cran. wall	Flower in the crannied wall.
Frater Ave, etc.	Frater Ave atque Vale.
Frenchman, etc.	Frenchman, a hand is thine !
From shape to shape	From shape to shape at first within the womb
Full light aloft	Full light aloft doth the laverock spring.
G. of Swainston	In the Garden at Swainston.
Gardener's D.	Gardener's Daughter.
Gareth and L.	Gareth and Lynette.
Geraint and E.	Geraint and Enid.
God and the Univ.	God and the Universe.
God bless our Prince	God bless our Prince and Bride.
Gone into Darkness	Gone into darkness that full light.
He was too good	He was too good and kind and sweet.
Hear you the sound	Hear you the sound of wheels ?
Heavy Brigade	Charge of the Heavy Brigade at Balaclava.
Here, I that stood	Here, I that stood in On beside the flow.
Here often when a child	Here often when a child I lay reclined.
High. Pantheism	Higher Pantheism.
Hither, when all	Hither, when all the deep, unsounded skies
Hold thou, my friend	Hold thou, my friend, no lesser life in scorn.
Home they brought him	Home they brought him slain with spears.
How glad am I	How glad am I to walk.
How is it that men	How is it that men have so little grace ?
How strange it is	How strange it is, O God, to wake.
I keep no more	I keep no more a lone distress.
I, loving Freedom	I, loving Freedom for herself.
In Mem., Pro.	In Memoriam, Prologue.
" *Con.*	" Conclusion.
" *W. G. Ward*	" William George Ward.
I met in all	I met in all the close green ways.
(interj.)	interjection.
In the Child. Hosp.	In the Children's Hospital.
(intrans.)	intransitive.
June Bracken, etc.	June Bracken and Heather.
L. C. V. de Vere	Lady Clara Vere de Vere.
L. of Burleigh	Lord of Burleigh.
L. of Shalott	Lady of Shalott.
Lancelot and E.	Lancelot and Elaine.
Leonine Eleg.	Leonine Elegiacs.
Life of the Life	Life of the Life within my blood.
Light Brigade	Charge of the Light Brigade.
Lit. Squabbles	Literary Squabbles.
Little Aubrey	Little Aubrey in the West !
Locksley H., Sixty	Locksley Hall, Sixty Years after.
Long as the heart	Long as the heart beats life within the breast.
Lotos-Eaters, C. S.	Lotos-Eaters. Choric Song.
Love, Pride, etc.	Love, Pride, and Forgetfulness.
Mariana in the S.	Mariana in the South.
Marr. of Geraint	Marriage of Geraint.
May Queen, N. Y.'s E.	May Queen, New Year's Eve.
" *Con.*	" Conclusion.
M. d"Arthur	Morte d'Arthur.

xv

M. d'Arthur, Ep.	Morte d'Arthur, Epilogue.
Me my own fate	Me my own fate to lasting sorrow doometh.
Merlin and the G.	Merlin and the Gleam.
Merlin and V.	Merlin and Vivien.
Methought I saw	Methought I saw a face whose every line.
Miller's D.	Miller's Daughter.
Move eastward	Move eastward, happy earth, and leave.
My life is full	My life is full of weary days.
N. Farmer, N. S.	Northern Farmer, New Style.
O. S.	,, Old Style.
New 'Timon	The New Timon and the Poets.
North. Cobbler	Northern Cobbler.
Not a whisper	Not a whisper stirs the gloom.
Not such were those	Not such were those whom Freedom claims.
Not to Silence	Not to Silence would I build.
Ode on Well.	Ode on the Death of the Duke of Wellington.
Ode Inter. Exhib.	Ode sung at the Opening of the International Exhibition.
O God, make this age	O God, make this age great that we may be.
Oh, Beauty	Oh, beauty, passing beauty.
O leave not thou	O leave not thou thy son forlorn.
Of old sat Freedom	Of old sat Freedom on the heights.
Old ghosts	Old ghosts whose day was done ere mine began
On Jub. Q. Victoria	On the Jubilee of Queen Victoria.
On One who effec. E. M.	On One who affected an Effeminate Manner.
One was the Tishbite	One was the Tishbite, whom the raven fed.
Open. I. and C. Exhib.	Opening of the Indian and Colonial Exhibition by the Queen.
Oriana	Ballad of Oriana.
O sad No more!	O sad *No more!* O sweet *No more!*
Pallid thunderstricken (part.)	The pallid thunderstricken sigh for gain. participle.
Pass. of Arthur	Passing of Arthur.
Pelleas and E.	Pelleas and Ettarre.
Poets and their B.	Poets and their Bibliographies.
Popular, Popular	Popular, Popular, Unpopular!
Pref. Poem. Broth. S. (prep.)	Prefatory Poem to my Brother's Sonnets. preposition.
Prin. Beatrice	To H.R.H. Princess Beatrice.
Princess, Pro.	Princess, Prologue.
Con.	,, Conclusion.
Pro. to Gen. Hamley	Prologue to General Hamley.
Prog. of Spring	Progress of Spring.
Prom. of May	Promise of May.
(pron.)	pronoun.
Remember you	Remember you the clear moonlight?
Remembering him	Remembering him who waits thee far away.
Rise, Britons, rise	Rise, Britons, rise, if manhood be not dead.
Romney's R.	Romney's Remorse.
Roses on the T.	Roses on the Terrace.
(s.)	substantive.
St. S. Stylites	St. Simeon Stylites.
Shall the hag	Shall the hag Evil die.
Sir J. Franklin	Sir John Franklin.
Sir J. Oldcastle	Sir John Oldcastle, Lord Cobham.
Sir L. and Q. G.	Sir Launcelot and Queen Guinevere.
Sisters (E. and E.)	Sisters (Evelyn and Edith).
Speak to me	Speak to me from the stormy sky!
Spec. of Iliad	Specimen of a Translation of the Iliad in Blank Verse.
Spinster's S's	Spinster's Sweet-Arts.
Spurge with fairy	Spurge with fairy crescent set.
Steersman	Steersman, be not precipitate in thine act.
Sugg. by Reading	Suggested by reading an article in a newspaper.
Supp. Confessions	Supposed Confessions of a Second-rate Sensitive Mind.
Take, Lady	Take, Lady, what your loyal nurses give.
That is his portrait	That is his portrait, painted by himself.
That the voice	That the voice of a satisfied people may keep.
The child was sitting	The child was sitting on the bank.
The form, the form	The form, the form alone is eloquent.
The lamps were bright	The lamps were bright and gay.
The lintwhite	The lintwhite and the throstlecock.
The night, etc.	The night with sudden odour reel'd.
The noblest men	The noblest men methinks are bred.
The winds, etc.	The winds, as at their hour of birth.
There are three things	There are three things that fill my heart with sighs.
Therefore your Halls	Therefore your Halls, your ancient Colleges.
They say, etc.	They say some foreign powers have laid their heads together.
They wrought, etc.	They wrought a work which time reveres.
Third of Feb.	Third of February, 1852.
Thou may'st remember	Thou may'st remember that I said.
Though night	Though Night hath climbed.
Thy soul is like	Thy soul is like a landskip, friend.
'Tis not alone	'Tis not alone the warbling woods.
To a Lady Sleep.	To a Lady Sleeping.
To A. Tennyson	To Alfred Tennyson, My Grandson.
To C. North	To Christopher North.
To F. D. Maurice	To the Rev. F. D. Maurice.
To J. M. K.	Sonnet To J. M. K.
To One who ran down Eng.	To One who ran down the English.
To Prof. Jebb	To Professor Jebb.
To Marq. of Dufferin	To the Marquis of Dufferin and Ava.
To Master of B.	To the Master of Balliol.
To Prin. F. of H.	To the Princess Frederica of Hanover on her Marriage.
To thee with whom	To thee with whom my true affections dwell.
To W. H. Brookfield	To the Rev. W. H. Brookfield.
Townsmen, etc.	Townsmen, or of the hamlet, young or old.
(trans.)	transitive.
Trans. of Homer	On Translations of Homer.
V. of Cauteretz	In the Valley of Cauteretz.
V. of Maeldune	Voyage of Maeldune.
Vicar of this	Vicar of this pleasant spot.
Voice and the P.	Voice and the Peak.
Voice spake, etc.	A Voice spake out of the Skies.
W. to Alexandra	A Welcome to Alexandra.
W. to Marie Alex.	A Welcome to Her Royal Highness Marie Alexandrovna, Duchess of Edinburgh.
Walk. to the Mail	Walking to the Mail.
Wan Sculptor	Wan sculptor, weepest thou.
We lost you	We lost you for how long a time.
Well, as to Fame	Well, as to Fame, who strides the earth.
What rustles	What rustles hither in the dark?
What time I wasted	What time I wasted youthful hours.
Wherever evil	Wherever evil customs thicken.
While I live	While I live, the owls!
Why suffers	Why suffers human life so soon eclipse?
Will Water	Will Waterproof's Lyrical Monologue.
Window. At the W.	Window. At the Window.
Marr. Morn	,, Marriage Morning.
Woman of noble	Woman of noble form and noble mind!
Yon huddled cloud	Yon huddled cloud his motion shifts.
You ask me, why,	You ask me, why, tho' ill at ease.
You might have won	You might have won the Poet's name.
Young is the grief	Young is the grief I entertain.
Youth, lapsing	Youth, lapsing thro' fair solitudes.

A CONCORDANCE to the POETICAL WORKS

OF

ALFRED, LORD TENNYSON.

A mouthing out his hollow oes and *aes*,	*The Epic* 50
Aäge (age) owd *a* as 'appy as iver I can,	*Owd Roä* 3
'Aäir (hair) an' cryin' and teärin' 'er '*a*	*North. Cobbler* 34
Aäle (ale) Says that I moänt 'a naw moor *a*:	*N. Farmer, O. S.*, 3
Git ma my *a*, (repeat)	,, 4, 36, 68
I've 'ed my point o' *a* ivry noight	,, 7
an' doesn bring ma the *a*?	,, 65
an' droonk wi' the farmer's *a*,	*Village Wife* 77
An' the taäble staäin'd wi' 'is *a*,	*Spinster's S's.* 99
tha mun nobbut hev' one glass of *a*.	*Owd Roä* 20
'Aäpoth (half-pennyworth) Joänes, as 'ant not a '*a* o'	
sense,	*N. Farmer, O. S.*, 49
Aäste (haste) thaw summun said it in '*a*:	,, 27
Abaddon *A* and Asmodeus caught at me.	*St. S. Stylites* 172
Abase *A* those eyes that ever loved	*Princess ii* 427
Abash'd so forlorn As I am!' half *a* him;	*Enoch Arden* 288
Enid, all *a* she knew not why,	*Marr. of Geraint* 765
man of thine to-day *A* us both,	*Balin and Balan* 71
A Lavaine, whose instant reverence,	*Lancelot and E.* 418
beauty of her flesh *a* the boy,	*Pelleas and E.* 78
Abate *A* the stride, which speaks of man	*Princess ii* 429
Abbess Our simple-seeming *A* and her nuns,	*Guinevere* 309
till in time their *A* died.	,, 692
Was chosen *A*, there, an *A*, lived For three brief	
years, and there, an *A*, past	,, 696
Abbey 'Come out,' he said, 'To the *A*:	*Princess, Pro.*, 51
But we went back to the *A*,	,, *Con.*, 106
fellow hath broken from some *A*,	*Gareth and L.* 456
The helmet in an *a* far away	*Holy Grail* 6
Abbey-ruin Carved stones of the *A-r*	*Princess, Pro.*, 14
Abbey-wall I see the moulder'd *A-w's*,	*Talking Oak* 3
Abbot An *a* on an ambling pad,	*L. of Shalott ii* 20
Abdiel Titan angels, Gabriel, *A*,	*Milton* 5
A-beälin' (bellowing) An' thou was *a-b* likewise,	*Owd Roä* 89
Abeär (bear) for I couldn *a* to see it.	*N. Farmer, O. S.*, 64
An' I can't *a* 'em, I can't,	*Church-warden, etc.*, 13
Abeat Eats scarce enow to keep his pulse *a*;	*Balin and Balan* 456
A-begging I never came *a-b* for myself,	*Dora* 141
Abeyance Those winters of *a* all worn out,	*Princess iv* 440
Abhor I hate, *a*, spit, sicken at him;	*Lucretius* 199
Abhorr'd they fell and made the glen *a*:	*Lancelot and E.* 42
Abhorrent *A* of a calculation crost,	*Enoch Arden* 473
Abide 'Trust me, in bliss I shall *a*	*Palace of Art* 18
Tho' much is taken, much *a's*;	*Ulysses* 65
In whose least act *a's* the nameless charm	*Princess v* 70
you failing, I *a* What end soever:	,, 405
hate me not, but *a* your lot,	*Spiteful Letter* 11
A: thy wealth is gather'd in,	*In Mem. lii* 15
A a little longer here,	,, *lviii* 11
Dare I bid her *a* by her word?	*Maud I xvi* 25
but *a* Without, among the cattle	*Gareth and L.* 273
A: take counsel; for this lad	,, 730
shalt *a* her judgment on it;	*Marr. of Geraint* 584
'I will *a* the coming of my lord,	*Geraint and E.* 131
thou art man, and canst *a* a truth,	*Balin and Balan* 501
Yet better if the King *a*,	*Last Tournament* 109
Abide (*continued*) the wife Whom he knows false, *a*	*Guinevere* 515
which thou wilt *a*, if thou be wise,	*Ancient Sage* 35
Wretch you must *a* it . . .	*Forlorn* 52
Abidest *a* lame and poor, Calling thyself	*Two Voices* 197
Abiding *A* with me till I sail To seek thee	*In Mem. cxxv* 13
Able-bodied Grew plump and *a-b*;	*The Goose* 18
Abler A quarter-sessions chairman, *a* none;	*Princess, Con.*, 90
Abode at the farm *a* William and Dora.	*Dora* 1
those four *a* Within one house	,, 169
Wherein the younger Charles *a*	*Talking Oak* 297
she *a* his coming, and said to him	*Geraint and E.* 139
stately Queen *a* For many a week,	*Guinevere* 146
mightiest of my knights, *a* with me,	,, 430
Clave to him, and *a* in his own land.	,, 440
Time and Grief *a* too long with Life,	*Lover's Tale i* 107
Abodest While thou *a* in the bud.	*Two Voices* 158
Abolish Caught at the hilt, as to *a* him:	*Marr. of Geraint* 210
Abominable The *A*, that uninvited came	*Œnone* 224
shapes of lust, unspeakable, *A*,	*Lucretius* 158
and shatter it, hold it *a*,	*Boädicea* 65
Abreast One walk'd *a* with me,	*Lover's Tale ii* 86
Abruptly broke the sentence in his heart *A*,	*Geraint and E.* 42
Absence she mourn'd his *a* as his grave,	*Enoch Arden* 247
in his *a* full of light and joy,	*Lover's Tale i* 425
Absolution A sort of *a* in the sound	*Sea Dreams* 61
Absolution-seller *a-s's*, monkeries	*Sir John Oldcastle* 93
Absorb in its onward current it *a's*	*Isabel* 31
Absorbing *A* all the incense of sweet thoughts	*Lover's Tale i* 469
Abstraction They do so that affect *a*	*Princess ii* 359
A-buried I'll hev 'im *a-b* wi'mma	*North. Cobbler* 106
Abû Saïd (Sufee Poet) him *A S*—a sun but dimly	
seen	*Akbar's Dream* 94
Abuse (s) 'lest from the *a* of war,	*Princess v* 126
bore without *a* The grand old name	*In Mem. cxi* 21
Perchance from some *a* of Will	*Epilogue* 24
Abuse (verb) wayward grief *a* The genial hour	*In Mem. cv* 9
my Leonard, use and not *a* your day,	*Locksley H., Sixty*, 265
Abused God's great gift of speech *a*	*A Dirge* 44
Abysm fell into the *a* Of forms outworn,	*Lover's Tale i* 796
weigh'd him down into the *a*—	*Columbus* 37
into the *a*, The *A* of all *A's*,	*Ancient Sage* 39
downward too into the *a*.	*Locksley H., Sixty*, 146
Abyss and the waste wide Of that *a*,	*Two Voices* 120
to sound the *a* Of science,	*Princess ii* 176
lighten thro' The secular *a* to come,	*In Mem. lxxvi* 6
O, from the distance of the end	,, *xciii* 11
upheaven from the *a* By fire, to sink into the *a*	
again;	*Pass. of Arthur* 82
bubble bursts above the *a* Of Darkness,	*Romney's R.* 52
Acacia Was lispt about the *a's*,	*Princess vii* 251
The slender *a* would not shake	*Maud I xxii* 45
Academe The softer Adams of your *A*,	*Princess ii* 197
this your *A*, Whichever side be Victor,	,, 230
A-callin' *a-c* ma 'hugly' mayhap to my faäce	*Spinster's S's.* 91
kep *a-c* o' Roä till 'e waggled 'is taäil	*Owd Roä* 105
Acanthus-wreath many a wov'n *a-w* divine!	*Lotos-Eaters, C. S.*, 97

Accent an *a* very low In blandishment, — *Isabel 19*
  She replies, in *a*'s fainter, — *L. of Burleigh 5*
  With nearing chair and lower'd *a*) — *Aylmer's Field 267*
Accept God *a* him, Christ receive him. — *Ode on Well. 281*
  do *a* my madness, and would die — *Maud I xviii 44*
  to *a* this cloth of gold, — *Gareth and L. 398*
  that I *a* thee aught the more — *,, 766*
  a thee aught the more, Scullion, — *,, 839*
  a this old imperfect tale, — *To the Queen ii 36*
  dark lord *a* and love the Sun, — *Demeter and P. 137*
Acceptance Blithe would her brother's *a* be. — *Maud I x 27*
Access closed her *a* to the wealthier farms, — *Aylmer's Field 503*
  down the lane of *a* to the King, — *Gareth and L. 661*
Acclaim tumult of their *a* is roll'd — *Dying Swan 33*
  And follow'd with *a*'s, — *Will Water. 138*
  let a people's voice In full *a*, — *Ode on Well. 143*
  Is wrought with tumult of *a*, — *In Mem. lxxv 20*
Accompanied and oft a By Averill: — *Aylmer's Field 137*
Accompanying brethren slowly with bent brows *A*, — *Lancelot and E. 1139*
Accomplice The *a* of your madness unforgiven, — *Princess vi 276*
Accomplish 'Which did *a* their desire, — *Two Voices 217*
  A thou my manhood and thyself; — *Princess vii 365*
  A that blind model in the seed, — *Prog. of Spring 114*
Accomplish'd (*See also* **All-accomplish'd**, **Full-accomplished**)
  Who, thro' their own desire *a*, — *Aylmer's Field 776*
  I have *a* what I came to do. — *Columbus 65*
  My mission be *a*!' — *Akbar's Dream 199*
Accomplishment win all eyes with all *a*: — *The form, the form 4*
  Miss the full flower of this *a*.' — *Gareth and L. 1297*
Accord (s) when both were brought to full *a*, — *Last Tournament 722*
  Faith and Work were bells of full *a*, — *In Mem. W. G. Ward 2*
Accord (verb) I *a* it easily as a grace. — *Gareth and L. 975*
Accorded Prince *A* with his wonted courtesy, — *Lancelot and E. 638*
According That mind and soul, *a* well, — *In Mem., Pro., 27*
  would work *a* as he will'd. — *Holy Grail 784*
  lady's love, *A* to her promise, — *Pelleas and E. 162*
  A to the Highest in the Highest. — *Ancient Sage 90*
  for my sake, *A* to my word?' — *Romney's R. 130*
  To pray, to do *a* to the prayer, — *Akbar's Dream 8*
Account (s) dodged me with a long and loose *a*. — *Sea Dreams 149*
  may show In some fifth *A*'s, — *,, 162*
  of the crowd you took no more *a* — *Lancelot and E. 105*
Account (verb) Eat and be glad, for I
  a you mine' — *Geraint and E. 647*
  whatsoever he *a*'s Of all his treasures — *Lover's Tale iv 233*
Accounted Is thy white blamelessness *a* blame!' — *Merlin and V. 799*
Accoutrement Among piled arms and rough *a*'s, — *Princess v 55*
Accrue Delight a hundredfold *a*, — *In Mem. cxvii 8*
Accurate your fine epithet Is *a* too, — *Merlin and V. 533*
Accurst-Accursed Thro' you, my life will be *accurst*.' — *The Letters 36*
  Accursed, who from the wrongs — *Gareth and L. 347*
  Accursed, who strikes nor lets the hand — *,, 435*
  Accursèd were she!' (repeat) — *Kapiolani 21, 24*
Accusation Like bitter *a* ev'n to death, — *Love and Duty 81*
  people's talk And *a* of uxoriousness — *Marr. of Geraint 83*
  breathe but *a* vast and vague, — *Merlin and V. 701*
Accuse sent for Blanche to *a* her — *Princess iv 239*
  A her of the least immodesty: — *Geraint and E. 111*
Accused You never once *a* me, — *Happy 69*
Achæan nor join'd The *A*'s— — *Achilles over the T. 16*
Ache (s) (*See also* **Finger-ache**, **Haäche**)
  In coughs, *a*'s, stitches, — *St. S. Stylites 13*
  And ills and *a*'s, and teethings, — *Holy Grail 554*
Ache (verb) would not let your little finger *a* — *Godiva 22*
  The sight that throbs and *a*'s — *Lover's Tale i 33*
  a's in the grasp of an idiot power, — *Despair 43*
Achievable if our end were less a — *Princess iii 283*
Achieve Gone! He will *a* his greatness — *Tiresias 168*
  spoken true Of all we shall *a*, — *Mechanophilus 26*
Achieved sword and golden circlet were *a*. — *Pelleas and E. 170*
  a, The loneliest ways are safe — *Last Tournament 101*
Achieving some have striven, *A* calm, — *Two Voices 209*
Achilles see the great *A*, whom we knew. — *Ulysses 64*
  Then rose *A* dear to Zeus — *Achilles over the T. 2*
Acknowledge in my heart of hearts I did *a* nobler. — *Lancelot and E. 1211*

A-cleänin' as we was *a-c* the floor, — *Spinster's S's. 49*
Aconite Their rich ambrosia tasted *a*. — *Demeter and P. 105*
Acorn An *a* in her breast. — *Talking Oak 228*
  nor yet Thine *a* in the land. — *,, 260*
Acorn-ball wear Alternate leaf and *a-b* — *,, 287*
Acquiescing the Queen But coldly *a*, — *Last Tournament 23*
A-crawin' (crowing) cocks kep *a-c* an' crawin' — *Owd Roä 106*
Acre (*See also* **Five-acre**, **Haäcre**) dinner To
  the men of many *a*'s, — *Maud I xx 32*
Acreage No coarse and blockish God of *a* — *Aylmer's Field 651*
A-creeäpin (creeping) wur *a-c* about my waäist; — *Spinster's S's. 26*
Acrimony flow'd in shallower *acrimonies*: — *Aylmer's Field 563*
A-cryin' then I seed 'er *a-c*, I did. — *Owd Roä 80*
Act (s) A saying, hard to shape in *a*; — *Love thou thy land 49*
  swift mind, In *a* to throw: — *M. d'Arthur 61*
  king demand An *a* unprofitable, — *,, 96*
  In *a* to render thanks. — *Gardener's D. 162*
  which I clothed in *a*, — *Princess i 195*
  a tiger-cat In *a* to spring — *,, ii 451*
  by single *a* Of immolation — *,, iii 284*
  And all creation in one *a* at once, — *,, 325*
  One *a* a phantom of succession: — *,, 329*
  makes Such head from *a* to *a*, — *,, iv 452*
  least *a* abides the nameless charm — *,, v 70*
  creatures native unto gracious *a*, — *,, vii 27*
  How much of *a* at human hands — *In Mem. lxxxv 38*
  bold in heart and *a* and word was he, — *Com. of Arthur 176*
  graced the lowliest *a* in doing it. — *Gareth and L. 490*
  dream she could be guilty of foul *a*, — *Marr. of Geraint 120*
  hearts who see but *a*'s of wrong: — *,, 438*
  So splendid in his *a*'s and his attire, — *,, 620*
  Balin graspt, but while in *a* to hurl, — *Balin and Balan 368*
  FROM noiseful arms, and *a*'s of prowess — *Holy Grail 1*
  one last *a* of knighthood shalt thou see. — *Pass. of Arthur 163*
  the swift mind, In *a* to throw: — *,, 229*
  king demand An *a* unprofitable, — *,, 264*
  beautiful in Past of *a* or place, — *Lover's Tale i 135*
  with her highest *a* the placid face — *,, 216*
  power on thine own *a* and on the world. — *De Prof. Two G. 56*
  A first, this Earth, a stage — *The Play 1*
  may show In some fifth *A* — *,, 4*
Act (verb) up and *a*, nor shrink For fear — *Princess iii 265*
  For who can always *a*? — *In Mem. cxi 9*
  be born and think, And *a* and love, — *,, Con., 127*
  Not he, not yet! and time to *a*— — *The Flight 73*
Acted weaker grows thro' *a* crime, — *Will 12*
  If more and *a* on, what follows? — *Princess ii 229*
  after madness *a* question ask'd: — *Geraint and E. 813*
  thro' the journey home, *A* her hest, — *Pelleas and E. 203*
Acting (*See also* **Over-acting**) *A* the law we
  live by without fear; — *Œnone 148*
Action 'Which in all *a* is the end of all; — *,, 122*
  until endurance grow Sinew'd with *a*, — *,, 165*
  enough of *a*, and of motion we, — *Lotos-Eaters, C. S., 105*
  I myself must mix with *a*, — *Locksley Hall 98*
  A life in civic *a* warm, — *In Mem. cxxiii 9*
  shape His *a* like the greater ape, — *,, cxxx 11*
  unfathom'd woe Reflex of *a*. — *Lover's Tale i 747*
  mould it into *a* pure as theirs. — *Tiresias 129*
Acton (**Sir Roger**) *See* **Roger Acton**
Actor let the dying *a* mouth his last — *Locksley H., Sixty, 152*
Adair (**Ellen**) *See* **Ellen Adair**
A-dallackt (overdrest) An' hallus *a-d* an' dizen'd out, — *Village Wife 37*
Adam The gardener *A* and his wife — *L. C. V. de Vere 51*
  when *A* first embraced his Eve — *Day-Dm., L'Envoi 41*
  The softer *A*'s of your Academe, — *Princess ii 197*
  there be Two *A*'s, two mankinds, — *Columbus 54*
Adam's wine I a' nowt but *A w*: — *North. Cobbler 5*
  an' a beslings-puddin' an' *A w*; — *,, 112*
Add *a* A crimson to the quaint Macaw, — *Day-Dm., Pro., 15*
  Nor *a* and alter, many times, — *Will Water. 15*
  a my diamonds to her pearls; — *Lancelot and E. 1224*
  months will *a* themselves and make — *Guinevere 625*
Added set the words, and *a* names I knew. — *Audley Court 61*
  'Swear' *a* Enoch sternly 'on the book.' — *Enoch Arden 842*

Added (*continued*) Put on more calm and *a*
  suppliantly; — *Princess vi 215*
  Had surely *a* praise to praise. — *In Mem. xxxi 8*
  faith, I fain had *a*—Knight, — *Gareth and L. 1162*
  weight is *a* only grain by grain, — *Marr. of Geraint 526*
  Then Balan *a* to their Order — *Balin and Balan 91*
  a, of her wit, A border fantasy — *Lancelot and E. 10*
  a plain Sir Torre, 'Yea, since I cannot — ,, 198
  'A fair large diamond, *a* plain Sir Torre, — ,, 230
  a wound to wound, And ridd'n away — ,, 567
  Were *a* mouths that gaped, — ,, 1249
  a to the griefs the great must bear, — *Guinevere 205*
  each other They should have *a*), — *Lover's Tale i 263*
  Your viceregal days Have *a* fulness — *To Marq. of Dufferin 11*
Adder I thought it was an *a's* fold, — *Lover's Tale i 691*
  harm an *a* thro' the lust for harm, — *Ancient Sage 271*
Addition Balin, ' the Savage'—that *a* — *Balin and Balan 53*
Addle (**earn**) Mun be a guvness, lad, or summut,
  and *a* her breäd : — *N. Farmer, N. S., 26*
Address Began to *a* us, and was moving on — *Princess ii 184*
Address'd-Addrest faces toward us and *address'd* Their
  motion : — ,, iv 551
  now *address'd* to speech—Who spoke few words — ,, *Con.*, 93
  suddenly *addrest* the hoary Earl : — *Marr. of Geraint 402*
  address'd More to the inward than the outward — *Lover's Tale i 720*
Adeline Faintly smiling *A*, — *Adeline 10, 39*
  Shadowy, dreaming *A* ? (repeat) — ,, 22, 64
  Spiritual *A* ? (repeat) — ,, 24
  Who talketh with thee, *A* ? — ,, 48
  Thou faint smiler, *A* ? — ,, 48
  Than your twin-sister, *A* — *Margaret 48*
Adieu uttered it, And bade *a* for ever — *Love and Duty 83*
  What more ? we took our last *a*, — *The Daisy 85*
  'A, a,' for evermore. — *In Mem. lvii 16*
  For tho' my lips may breathe *a*, — ,, cxxiii 11
Adit yourself and yours shall have Free *a* ; — *Princess vi 302*
Adjust *a* My vapid vegetable loves — *Talking Oak 182*
Admiral Chains for the *A* of the Ocean ! — *Columbus 19*
  Chains ! we are *A's* of the Ocean, — ,, 28
  Ocean—of the Indies—A's we— — ,, 31
Admire *a* Joints of cunning workmanship — *Vision of Sin 185*
  not to desire or *a*, if a man — *Maud I iv 41*
Admired which when now *a* By Edith — *Aylmer's Field 231*
Admiring sat beside the couch, *A* him, — *Marr. of Geraint 80*
  the two Were turning and *a* it, — ,, 637
Admission beat a in a thousand years, — *Princess iii 155*
Admit Nor other thought her mind *a's* — *In Mem. xxxii 2*
  The time *a's* not flowers or leaves — ,, cvii 5
Ado why make we such *a* ? — *May Queen, Con.*, 56
Adoration Meet *a* to my household gods, — *Ulysses 42*
  shaken voice, And flutter'd *a*, — *Merlin and V. 158*
Adore How many measured words *a* — *Eleänore 45*
  To stand apart, and to *a*, — ,, 79
  on the meadow grass, and *a*, — *Maud I v 26*
  Strong in the power that all men *a*, — ,, x 14
Adored was *a* ; He, loved for her — *Aylmer's Field 178*
  A her, as the stateliest and the best — *Marr. of Geraint 20*
  Call'd on the Power *a* by the Christian, — *Kapiolani 32*
Adoring *A* That who made, and makes, — *Akbar's Dream 123*
  Kneel *a* Him the Timeless — ,, *D. Hymn* 8
Adorn brought to *a* her with, The jewels, — *Last Tournament 715*
Adorn'd her I loved, *a* with fading flowers. — *Lover's Tale iii 40*
A-dressin' an' jessmine *a-d* it greeän, — *Spinster's S's. 105*
A-drooping locks *a-d* twined Round thy neck — *Adeline 57*
Adulation golden eloquence And amorous *a*, — *Lancelot and E. 650*
Adulterer My knights are all *a's* like his own, — *Last Tournament 84*
  'A, Go back to thine adulteress and die !' — *Death of Œnone 48*
Adulteress Go back to thine *a* and die !' — ,, 48
Adultery mother of the foul *adulteries* — *Aylmer's Field 376*
  adulteries, Wife-murders, — *Romney's R. 133*
Advance (**s**) But these are the days of *a*, — *Maud I i 25*
Advance (**verb**) 'The years with change *a* : — *Two Voices 52*
  How gain in life, as life *a's* — *To F. D. Maurice 39*
  Let all my genial spirits *a* — *In Mem., Con.*, 77
  'A and take, as fairest of the fair, — *Marr. of Geraint 553*

Advance (**verb**) (*continued*) 'A and take thy prize
  The diamond'; — *Lancelot and E. 503*
  wreaths of all that would *a*, — *To Victor Hugo 5*
Advanced Something far *a* in State, — *Ode on Well. 275*
  a The monster, and then paused, — *Gareth and L. 1384*
  who *a*, Each growling like a dog, — *Geraint and E. 558*
  the King himself *A* to greet them, — ,, 879
Advancing up and down *A* nor retreating. — *Sisters (E. and E.) 179*
Advantage He took *a* of his strength to be — *Princess ii 152*
  Forebore his own *a*, (repeat) — *Guinevere 331, 333*
Advent Wink at our *a* : help my prince — *Princess iii 160*
  dividing clove An *a* to the throne? — ,, iv 284
  Expecting still his *a* home ; — *In Mem. vi 21*
Adventure battle, bold *a*, dungeon, wreck, — *Aylmer's Field 98*
  mad for strange *a*, dash'd away — *Balin and Balan 289*
  then, with small *a* met, Sir Bors — *Holy Grail 660*
  Bound upon solitary *a*, saw — *Pelleas and E. 275*
Adversary robbers mock at a barbarous *a*. — *Boädicea 18*
  hearing her tumultuous *adversaries* — ,, 78
Advice he wouldn't take my *a*. — *Grandmother 4*
Adviser Horace, you the wise *A* — *Poets and their B. 6*
A-dying For the old year lies *a-d*. — *D. of the O. Year 5*
Æakidês So rang the clear voice of Æ ; — *Achilles over the T. 21*
  cry of Æ Was heard among the Trojans, — ,, 22
Ægis Pallas flung Her fringed *æ*, — ,, 4
Æolian Æ harp that wakes No certain air, — *Two Voices 436*
  Scarce living in the Æ harmony, — *Lover's Tale i 477*
Æon the great Æ sinks in blood, — *In Mem. cxxvii 16*
  Whirl'd for a million *æ's* — *De Prof. Two G. 3*
  Many an Æ moulded earth before her highest, — *Locksley H., Sixty, 205*
  Many an Æ too may pass — ,, 206
  Shall not *æ* after *æ* pass and touch — *Making of Man 4*
Æonian Draw down Æ hills, and sow — *In Mem. xxxv 11*
  Æ music measuring out The steps — ,, xcv 41
  Æ Evolution, swift or slow, — *The Ring 44*
Aërially And less *a* blue, — *Margaret 51*
  a murmur heard *a*, — *Boädicea 24*
Ætna as Æ does The Giant of Mythology — *Lover's Tale iv 17*
  and Æ kept her winter snow — *Demeter and P. 115*
Afear'd (**afraid**) But Squire wur *a* o' 'is son, — *Village Wife 63*
  allus *a* of a man's gittin' ower fond, — *Spinster's S's. 27*
  I wasn't *a*, or I thinks leästwaäys as I wasn't *a* ; — *Owd Roä 86*
Affair For I never whisper'd a private *a*— — *Maud II v 47*
  kinsman travelling on his own *a* — *Merlin and V. 717*
Affect They do so that *a* abstraction — *Princess ii 359*
Affection The still *a* of the heart — *Miller's D. 225*
  he spoke, Part banter, part *a* — *Princess, Pro.*, 167
  old and strange *a* of the house. — ,, i 13
  cared not for the *a* of the house ; — ,, 26
  like a flash the weird *a* came : — ,, v 477
  wing'd *a's* clipt with crime : — ,, vii 316
  My old *a* of the tomb, (repeat) — *In Mem. lxxxv 75, 77*
  With what divine *a's* bold — ,, xciv 2
  A, and the light of victory, — *Gareth and L. 331*
  a mood Of over-strain'd *a*, — *Merlin and V. 522*
  'Stabb'd through the heart's *a's* — ,, 868
  with full *a* said, 'Lancelot, — *Lancelot and E. 1355*
  if *A* Living slew Love, — *Lover's Tale ii 30*
Affiance when I dwelt upon your old *a*, — *Princess iii 139*
  in whom I have Most joy and most *a*, — *Lancelot and E. 1357*
Affianced *a* years ago To the Lady Ida : — *Princess ii 215*
  A, Sir ? love-whispers may not — ,, 221
  with Melissa Florian, I With mine *a*. — ,, iii 356
Affirm *A's* your Psyche thieved her theories, — ,, 92
Affirm'd she *a* not, or denied : — ,, iv 234
Affirming *A* each his own philosophy— — *Lucretius 216*
  A that his father left him gold, — *Marr. of Geraint 451*
  A that as long as either lived, — *Lover's Tale iv 277*
Affluence (*See also* **Heart-Affluence**) You, that
  wanton in *a*, — *On Jub. Q. Victoria 28*
Affright nothing there her maiden grace *a* ! — *Maud I xviii 71*
  like a man in a mortal *a* ; — *V. of Maeldune 74*
Affrighted Round *a* Lisbon drew — *Ode on Well. 103*
Affronted *A* with his fulsome innocence ? — *Pelleas and E. 266*
Afire (**on fire**) the house is *a*,' she said. — *Owd Roä 68*

Afire (*continued*) 'But the stairs is *a*,' she said ;   *Owd Roä* 80
A-flyin' wool of a thistle *a-f* an' seeädin'   *Spinster's S's.* 79
Afraid   *See* **Afear'd, Half-afraid.**
Afric On capes of *A* as on cliffs of Kent,   *W. to Marie Alex.* 17
African Indian, Australasian, *A*,   *On Jub. Q. Victoria* 61
After-age Thro' *a-a's* in the love of Truth,   *Akbar's Dream* 101
After-beauty that *a-b* makes Such head   *Princess iv* 451
After-days It grows to guerdon *a-d* :   *Love thou thy land* 27
After-dinner It seems in *a-d* talk   *Miller's D.* 31
   'Twas but an *a-d's* nap.   *Day-Dm., Revival* 24
After-fulness from the *a-f* of my heart,   *Lover's Tale i* 146
After-hands whence *a-h* May move the world,   *Princess iii* 263
After-heat It might have drawn from *a-h.*'   *In Mem. lxxxi* 12
After-life my dead face would vex her *a-l.*   *Enoch Arden* 891
   she will pass me by in *a-l*   *Princess v* 91
After-love *A-l's* of maids and men   *Window, No Answer* 25
Aftermath a sweep Of meadow smooth from *a*   *Audley Court* 14
After-morn Which left my *a-m* content.   *In Mem. ciii* 4
   That man can have no *a-m*,   *Epilogue* 73
Afternoon In the *a* they came unto a land   *Lotos-Eaters* 3
   In which it seemed always *a*.   ,,   4
   Bright was that *a*, Sunny but chill ;   *Enoch Arden* 669
   Half-sickening of his pension'd *a*,   *Aylmer's Field* 461
   'That *a* the Princess rode   *Princess iii* 169
   all That *a* a sound arose   ,,   *vi* 379
   in the all-golden *a* A guest,   *In Mem. lxxxix* 25
   But in the falling *a* return'd   *Geraint and E.* 591
   It made the laughter of an *a*   *Merlin and V.* 163
   Here in the never-ended *a*,   *Last Tournament* 584
   For brief repast or *a* repose   *Guinevere* 395
   and yester *a* I dream'd,—   *Akbar's Dream* 169
Aftertime I am sung or told In *a*,   *M. d'Arthur* 35
   relic of my lord Should be to *a*,   ,,   99
   some old man speak in the *a*   ,,   107
   a, And that full voice which circles   *Princess ii* 44
   sole men we shall prize in the *a*,   ,,   *v* 412
   I am sung or told In *a*,   *Pass. of Arthur* 203
   relic of my lord Should be to *a*,   ,,   267
   some old man speak in the *a*   ,,   275
After-years *a-y* Will learn the secret of our
   Arthur's birth.'   *Com. of Arthur* 158
Agape A rabbit mouth that is ever *a*—   *Maud I x* 31
   ye seem *a* to roar !   *Gareth and L.* 1306
Agaric learned names of *a*, moss and fern,   *Edwin Morris* 17
   as one That smells a foul-flesh'd *a*   *Gareth and L.* 747
Agate Turkis and *a* and almondine   *The Merman* 32
   bottom *a's* seen to wave and float   *Princess ii* 327
Agave One tall *A* above the lake.   *The Daisy* 84
A-gawin' (*going*) I beänt *a-g* to breäk my rule.   *N. Farmer, O. S.,* 4
A-gawinin' (*staring*) an' foälk stood *a-g* in,   *North. Cobbler* 81
Age (*See also* **Aäge, After-age, Mother-age**) There
   hath he lain for *a's* and will lie.   *The Kraken* 11
   'I know that *a* to *a* succeeds,   *Two Voices* 205
   makes me talk too much in *a*.   *Miller's D.* 194
   And the great *a's* onward roll.   *To J. S.* 72
   Now the most blessed memory of mine *a*.   *Gardener's D.* 279
   thrifty too beyond her *a*.   *Dora* 16
   until he grows Of *a* to help us.'   ,,   127
   old sore breaks out from *a* to *a*   *Walk. to the Mail* 79
   Of different *a's*, like twin-sisters   *Edwin Morris* 32
   suffer'd long For *a's* and for *a's* !'   *St. S. Stylites* 100
   float about the threshold of an *a*,   *Golden Year* 16
   an *a*, when every hour Must sweat   ,,   68
   Old *a* hath yet his honour   *Ulysses* 50
   Immortal *a* beside immortal youth,   *Tithonus* 22
   thro' the *a's* one increasing purpose   *Locksley Hall* 137
   I the heir of all the *a's*,   ,,   178
   As all were order'd, *a's* since.   *Day-Dm., Sleep. P.,* 54
   'Tis vain ! in such a brassy *a*   *Amphion* 65
   found My spirits in the golden *a*.   *To E. L.* 12
   tonsured head in middle *a* forlorn,   *The Brook* 200
   when *this* Aylmer came of *a*,   *Aylmer's Field* 407
   huge cathedral fronts of every *a*,   *Sea Dreams* 218
   palsy, death-in-life, And wretched *a*—   *Lucretius* 155
   every clime and *a* Jumbled together ;   *Princess, Pro.,* 16

Age (*continued*) 'The climax of his *a* !   *Princess, Pro., ii* 50
   Amazon As emblematic of a nobler *a* ;   *Princess ii* 127
   some *a's* had been lost ;   ,,   153
   second-sight of some Astræan *a*,   ,,   443
   reasons drawn from *a* and state,   ,,   *v* 357
   you got a friend of your own *a*,   ,,   *vi* 251
   To such a name for *a's* long,   *Ode on Well.* 76
   For many and many an *a* proclaim   ,,   226
   tho' the Giant *A's* heave the hill   ,,   259
   at your *a*, Annie, I could have wept (repeat)   *Grandmother* 20, 100
      ,,   97
   And *a* is a time of peace,   ,,
   I hear the roll of the *a's*.   *Spiteful Letter* 8
   Milton, a name to resound for *a's* ;   *Milton* 4
   to-morrow, And that's an *a* away.'   *Window, When* 14
   left for human deeds In endless *a* ?   *In Mem. lxxiii* 12
   take the print Of the golden *a*—   *Maud I i* 30
   many a million of *a's* have gone   ,,   *iv* 35
   Wretchedest *a*, since Time began,   ,,   *II v* 21
   His *a* hath slowly droopt,   *Gareth and L.* 79
   sadder *a* begins To war against ill uses   ,,   1129
   suffering thus he made Minutes an *a* :   *Geraint and E.* 115
   flatter his own wish in *a* for love,   *Merlin and V.* 185
   Who paced it, *a's* back :   ,,   553
   more fitly yours, not thrice your *a* :   *Lancelot and E.* 953
   Built by old kings, *a* after *a*,   *Holy Grail* 340
   I found Only one man of an exceeding *a*.   ,,   431
   In the white winter of his *a*,   *Pass. of Arthur* 4
   weight as if of *a* upon my limbs,   *Lover's Tale i* 125
   she, my love, is of an *a* with me   ,,   196
   poisons of his heart In his old *a*.'   ,,   357
   the fool this *A* that doubts of all—   *Sisters (E. and E.)* 141
   in that flight of *a's* which are God's   *Columbus* 202
   but thine *a*, by *a* as winter-white   *Tiresias* 19
   And oldest *a* in shadow from the night,   ,,   104
   and the human heart, and the *A*.   *Despair* 40
   For these are the new dark *a's*,   ,,   88
   And cap our *a* with snow ?'   *Ancient Sage* 98
   The poet whom his *A* would quote   *Locksley H., Sixty,* 10
   well might fool a dotard's *a*.   ,,   46
   Some thro' *a* and slow diseases,   ,,   81
   A's after, while in Asia,   ,,   83
   an *a* of noblest English names,   ,,   108
   When was *a* so cramm'd with menace ?   ,,   137
   Bring the old dark *a's* back without the faith,   ,,   151
   well, it scarce becomes mine *a*—   ,,   281
   Gone at eighty, mine own *a*,   *Epilogue* 71
   tho', in this lean *a* forlorn,   *To Virgil* 25
   Light among the vanish'd *a's* ;   *Open. I. and C. Exhib.* 11
   May we find, as *a's* run,   *On Jub. Q. Victoria* 71
   darkness Dawns into the Jubilee of the *A's*.   *The Ring* 77
   the morning when you came of *a*   ,,   160
   girls of equal *a*, but one was fair,   ,,   289
   My ring too when she comes of *a*,   *Happy* 46
   For *A* will chink the face,   *Romney's R.* 64
   gloom of *A* And suffering cloud   *Parnassus* 3
   And over the flight of the *A's* !   *By an Evolution.* 9
   What hast thou done for me, grim Old *A*,   *St. Telemachus* 41
   I have climb'd to the snows of *A*,   *Making of Man* 3
   all but deaf thro' *a* and weariness,   *The Dreamer* 7
   and ere the crowning *A* of *a's*,   *Poets and Critics* 2
   When I make for an *A* of gold,   *Love thou thy land* 39
   Helter-skelter runs the *a* ;
Agent (*See also* **Agint**) Thro' many *a's* making strong,
Aghast (*See also* **Half-Aghast**) all that mark'd him
   were *a*   *Gareth and L.* 1399
   not a word !' and Enid was *a* ;   *Geraint and E.* 18
   men and women staring and *a*,   ,,   804
   a the maiden rose, White as her veil,   *Guinevere* 362
Agincourt 'this,' he said, 'was Hugh's at *A* ;   *Princess, Pro.,* 25
Agint (**Agent**) Yer Honour's own *a*, he says to me   *Tomorrow* 63
Agitated people around the royal chariot *a*,   *Boädicea* 73
Aglaïa a double April old, *A* slept.   *Princess ii* 111
   my sweet *A*, my one child :   ,,   *v* 101
   Came Psyche, sorrowing for *A*.   ,,   *vi* 29
A-glare all the Hells *a-g* in either eye,   *Akbar's Dream* 115

Aglow ' *My* Rose' set all your face *á*, — *Roses on the T.* 3
Agned-Cathregonion And up in *A-C* too, — *Lancelot and E.* 300
Agoän (gone) whoy, Doctor's abeän an' *a*: — *N. Färmer, O. S.,* 2
Agony ancient melody Of an inward *a*, — *Claribel* 7
   one voice an *a* Of lamentation, — *M. d'Arthur* 200
   kill'd with some luxurious *a*, — *Vision of Sin* 43
   modest bosom prest In *a*, — *Aylmer's Field* 417
   as cried Christ ere His *a* — " 793
   wail of women and children, multitudinous *agonies*. — *Boädicea* 26
   Roman slaughter, multitudinous *agonies*. — " 84
   With *agonies*, with energies, — *In Mem. cxiii* 18
   Travail, and throes and *agonies* of the life, — *Com. of Arthur* 76
   into wastes and solitudes For *a*, — *Lancelot and E.* 253
   up the side, sweating with *a*, — " 494
   Brain-feverous in his heat and *a*, — " 854
   one voice, an *a* Of lamentation, — *Pass. of Arthur* 368
   All joy, to whom my *a* was a joy. — *Lover's Tale i* 656
   and in his *a* conceives A shameful sense — " 793
   these in my *a* Did I make bare — " ii 47
   my dull *a*, Ideally to her transferr'd, — " 136
   Dead of some inward *a*—is it so ? — *To W. H. Brookfield* 10
   Twisted hard in mortal *a* — *Locksley H., Sixty,* 98
A-grawin' (growing) hes now be *a-g* sa howd, — *Village Wife* 107
Agreed *a* That much allowance must be made — *Aylmer's Field* 409
   so it was *a* when first they came ; — *Princess iii* 36
   A to, this, the day fled on — " 176
   his wish, whereto the Queen *a* — *Lancelot and E.* 1169
   then they were *a* upon a night — *Guinevere* 96
   he sent, an' the father *a* ; — *First Quarrel* 18
   An' Molly an' me was *a*, — *Spinster's S's.* 49
Agrin His visage all *a* as at a wake, — *Princess v* 93
Agrippina and the Roman brows Of *A* — " ii 85
Agypt (Egypt) Thim ould blind nagers in *A*, — *Tomorrow* 69
A-hawking We ride *a-h* with Sir Lancelot — *Merlin and V.* 95
Ahead he rode on *a*, as he waved his blade — *Heavy Brigade* 9
Aid (s) knew not whither he should turn for *a*. — *Com. of Arthur* 40
   for lack of gentle maiden's *a*. — *Lancelot and E.* 765
   He needs no *a* who doth his lady's will.' — *Pelleas and E.* 281
   following thy true counsel, by thine *a*, — *Akbar's Dream* 154
Aid (verb) Us, who stand now, when we should *a* the right— — *Poland* 13
   O Lord, *A* all this foolish people ; — *St. S. Stylites* 223
   a me, give me strength Not to tell her, — *Enoch Arden* 785
   a me Heaven when at mine uttermost, — *Marr. of Geraint* 502
Aiding serve them both in *a* her— — *Princess vii* 268
Aidless to leave thee thus, *A*, alone, — *M. d'Arthur* 41
   to leave thee thus, *A*, alone, — *Pass. of Arthur* 209
Aidoneus car Of dark *A* rising rapt thee — *Demeter and P.* 39
Ail mother thought, What *a*'s the boy ? — *Miller's D.* 93
   What *a*'s us, who are sound, — *Walk. to the Mail* 105
Ail'd What *a* her then, that ere she enter'd, — *Enoch Arden* 518
   told his gentle wife What *a* him, — *Geraint and E.* 504
Aileth What *a* thee ? whom waitest thou — *Adeline* 45
Ailing 'Anything *a*,' I ask'd her, 'with baby?' — *The Wreck* 61
   only—you Were always *a*. — *The Ring* 311
Ailment Yours has been a slighter *a*, — *Locksley H., Sixty,* 17
Aim (s) Embrace our *a*'s : work out your freedom. — *Princess i* 89
   For fear our solid *a* be dissipated — " iii 266
   works Without a conscience or an *a*. — *In Mem. xxxiv* 8
   so I wake to the higher *a*'s — *Maud III vi* 38
   he kept his mind on one sole *a*, — *Merlin and V.* 626
   a's Were sharpen'd by strong hate — *Guinevere* 19
   Because all other Hope had lower *a* ; — *Lover's Tale i* 455
   Ready ! take *a* at their leaders— — *Def. of Lucknow* 42
   Look to your butts, and take good *a*'s ! — *Riflemen form !* 16
Aim (verb) one would *a* an arrow fair, — *In Mem. lxxxvii* 25
Aim'd fairy arrows *a* All at one mark, — *Aylmer's Field* 94
   Nay, but she *a* not at glory, — *Wages* 4
   A at the helm, his lance err'd ; — *Geraint and E.* 157
   better *a* are your flank fusillades— — *Def. of Lucknow* 57
Aiming near storm, and *a* at his head, — *Aylmer's Field* 727
   In *a* at an all but hopeless mark — *The Ring* 346
Aimless three days, *a* about the land, — *Pelleas and E.* 391
Air (atmosphere) Till the *a* And the ground — *Nothing will Die* 27
   Or breathe into the hollow *a*, — *Supp. Confessions* 58

Air (atmosphere) (*continued*) fires and fluid range Of lawless *a*'s, — *Supp. Confessions* 148
   The living *a*'s of middle night — *Arabian Nights* 69
   a is damp, and hush'd, and close, — *A spirit haunts* 13
   Life in dead stones, or spirit in *a* ; — *A Character* 9
   Wide, wild, and open to the *a*, — *Dying Swan* 2
   Or when little *a*'s arise, — *Adeline* 33
   With melodious *a*'s lovelorn, — " 55
   reveal'd themselves to English *a*, — *Eleänore* 2
   a Sleepeth over all the heaven, — " 38
   Like softened *a*'s that blowing steal, — *Two Voices* 406
   The very *a* about the door — *Miller's D.* 108
   earth and *a* seem only burning fire.' — *Œnone* 268
   the summer *a*'s blow cool — *May Queen, N. Y's. E.* 27
   the languid *a* did swoon, — *Lotos-Eaters* 5
   Falls, and floats adown the *a*. — " *C. S.,* 31
   warm *a*'s lull us, blowing lowly**)** — " 89
   was no motion in the dumb dead *a*, — *D. of F. Women* 65
   round them sea and *a* are dark — *Love thou thy land* 63
   made the *a* Of Life delicious, — *Gardener's D.* 69
   murmur broke the stillness of that *a* — " 147
   Felt earth as a beneath me, — " 212
   A soft *a* fans the cloud apart ; — *Tithonus* 32
   deep *a* listen'd round her as she rode, — *Godiva* 54
   I yearn to breathe the *a*'s of heaven — *Sir Galahad* 63
   Are touch'd, are turn'd to finest *a*. — " 72
   And clouds are highest up in *a*, — *Lady Clare* 2
   All the *a* was torn in heaven, — *The Captain* 43
   Like Fancy made of golden *a*, — *The Voyage* 66
   green From draughts of balmy *a*. — *Sir L. and Q. G.* 9
   black yew gloom'd the stagnant *a*, — *The Letters* 3
   sweet half-English Neilgherry *a* — *The Brook* 17
   breath Of tender *a* made tremble — " 202
   at a touch of light, an *a* of heaven, — *Aylmer's Field* 5
   rush of the *a* in the prone swing, — " 86
   to flush his blood with *a*, — " 459
   Drank the large *a*, and saw, — *Sea Dreams* 34
   towering o'er him in serenest *a*, — *Lucretius* 178
   flushing the guiltless *a*, Spout — " 239
   soul flies out and dies in the *a*.' — " 274
   sweet as English *a* could make her, — *Princess, Pro.,* 155
   each light *a* On our mail'd heads: — " v 244
   'for this wild wreath of *a*, — " 318
   went The enamour'd *a* sighing — " vi 79
   with a tender foot, light as on *a*, — " 88
   shake To the same sweet *a*, — " vii 69
   Naked, a double light in *a* and wave, — " 167
   like a broken purpose waste in *a* : — " 214
   In that fine *a* I tremble, — " 354
   Thro' the long-tormented *a* Heaven — *Ode on Well.* 128
   Flash'd as they turn'd in *a* — *Light Brigade* 28
   Clash, ye bells, in the merry March *a* ! — *W. to Alexandra* 18
   diviner *a* Breathe thro' the world — *W. to Marie Alex.* 43
   And snowy dells in a golden *a*. — *The Daisy* 68
   bird in *a*, and fishes turn'd — *The Victim* 19
   cloud in my heart, and a storm in the *a* ! — *Window, Gone* 6
   no ruder *a* perplex Thy sliding keel, — *In Mem. ix* 9
   Calm and deep peace in this wide *a*, — " xi 13
   And circle moaning in the *a* : — " xii 15
   Was as the whisper of an *a* — " xvii 3
   As light as carrier-birds in *a* ; — " xxv 6
   seem to have reach'd a purer *a*, — " xxxiii 2
   Sweet after showers, ambrosial *a*, — " lxxxvi 1
   And shook to all the liberal *a* — " lxxxix 7
   drink the cooler *a*, and mark — " 15
   The memory like a cloudless *a*, — " xciv 11
   With summer spice the humming *a* ; — " ci 8
   the stirring *a* The life re-orient — " cxvi 5
   Thy voice is on the rolling *a* ; — " cxxx 1
   ruin'd woodlands drove thro' the *a*. — *Maud I i* 12
   essences turn'd the live *a* sick — " xiii 11
   fed With honey'd rain and delicate *a*, — " xviii 21
   Melody on branch, and melody in mid *a*. — *Gareth and L.* 183
   solid turrets topsy-turvy in *a* : — " 255
   under one long lane of cloudless *a* — *Bálin and Balan* 461

Air (atmosphere) (*continued*)   their foreheads felt

the cooling *a*,	*Balin and Balan* 589
for God's love, a little *a*!	*Lancelot and E.* 505
a that smites his forehead is not *a*	*Holy Grail* 914
choice from *a*, land, stream, and sea,	*Pelleas and E.* 149
my rose, that sweeten'd all mine *a*—	„ 403
started thro' mid *a* Bearing an eagle's nest:	*Last Tournament* 14
stump Pitch-blacken'd sawing the *a*,	„ 67
heather-scented *a*, Pulsing full man;	„ 691
spouting from a cliff Fails in mid *a*,	*Guinevere* 609
could not breathe in that fine *a*	„ 645
outward circling *a* wherewith I breathe	*Lover's Tale i* 167
seem'd a gossamer filament up in *a*,	„ 413
moon, Half-melted into thin blue *a*,	„ 421
flowing odour of the spacious *a*,	„ 478
to all that draw the wholesome *a*,	„ 500
the gentlest *a's* of Heaven Should kiss	„ 738
A morning, sweet after rain,	„ iii 3
Bore her free-faced to the free *a's*	„ iv 38
veil, that seemed no more than gilded *a*,	„ 290
and horrible fowls of the *a*,	*Rizpah* 39
'O diviner *A*.' (repeat)	*Sisters (E. and E.)* 4
Breathe, diviner *A*!	„ 13
but as welcome as free *a's* of heaven	„ 197
God's free *a*, and hope of better things.	*Sir J. Oldcastle* 10
jewell'd throne thro' the fragrant *a*,	*V. of Maeldune* 59
where the water is clearer than *a*:	„ 77
all that suffers on land or in *a* or the deep,	*Despair* 45
Yon summit half-a-league in *a*—	*Ancient Sage* 11
And now one breath of cooler *a*	„ 117
side by side in God's free light and *a*,	*The Flight* 81
The woods with living *a's*	*Early Spring* 19
Light *a's* from where the deep,	„ 21
there In haunts of jungle-poison'd *a*	*To Marq. of Dufferin* 31
pierce the glad and songful *a*,	*Demeter and P.* 45
we will feed her with our mountain *a*,	*The Ring* 319
up the tower—an icy *a* Fled by me.—	„ 445
marvel how in English *a* My yucca,	*To Ulysses* 20
her bare To breaths of balmier *a*;	*Prog. of Spring* 13

Air (strain of music)

Æolian harp that wakes No certain *a*,	*Two Voices* 437
With the *a* of the trumpet round him,	*Princess v* 162
slightest *a* of song shall breathe	*In Mem. xlix* 7
She is singing an *a* that is known to me,	*Maud I v* 3
while I past he was humming an *a*,	„ xiii 17
playest that *a* with Queen Isolt,	*Last Tournament* 263
hum An *a* the nuns had taught her;	*Guinevere* 163
play That *a* which pleased her first.	*Lover's Tale i* 21
amid eddies of melodious *a's*,	„ 450
'*A* and Words,' Said Hubert,	*The Ring* 24

Air (manner)   I KNOW her by her angry *a*,   *Kate* 1

A cold *a* pass'd between us,	*The Ring* 380

'Air (hair)   was stroäkin ma down wi' the '*a*,   *Spinster's S's.* 19

An' 'is '*a* coom'd off i' my 'ands	*Owd Roä* 100

Air'd   into the world, And *a* him there: *Aylmer's Field* 468

Airing   A *a* snowy hand and signet gem,   *Princess i* 121

Airm (arm)   blacksmith 'e strips me the thick ov 'is *a*,   *North. Cobbler* 85

Airth   But *a* was at pace nixt mornin',   *Tomorrow* 25

Aisle   'Dark porch,' I said, 'and silent *a*,   *The Letters* 47

but in the middle *a* Reel'd,	*Aylmer's Field* 818
ambrosial *a's* of lofty lime	*Princess, Pro.,* 87
giant *a's*, Rich in model and design;	*Ode Inter. Exhib.* 12
sombre, old, colonnaded *a*,	*The Daisy* 56
often I and Amy in the mouldering *a* have stood,	*Locksley H., Sixty,* 31

Ajalon   like Joshua's moon in *A*!   *Locksley Hall* 180

Ajar   THEY have left the doors *a*;   *Sisters (E. and E.)* 7

A-joompin' (jumping)   An' hallus *a-j'* about ma   *Spinster's S's.* 89

Akbar (Mogul Emperor)   ask'd his Chronicler Of *A*   *Akbar's Dream* 2

turning slowly toward him, *A* said	„ 4

Akin   (*See also* **Half-akin**)   Maud to him is nothing *a*:   *Maud I xiii* 38

lawful and lawless war Are scarcely even *a*.	„ II v 95
swallow and the swift are near *a*,	*Com. of Arthur* 313

Akrokeraunian   The vast *A* walls,   *To E. L.* 4

A-laäid (lying)   fun 'um theer *a-l* on 'is faäce   *N. Farmer, O. S.,* 33

Alarm   when fresh from war's *a's*,   *D. of F. Women* 149

Alarm (*continued*) I shook her breast with vague *a's*—   *The Letters* 38

our sallies, their lying *a's*,	*Def. of Lucknow* 75
a's Sounding 'To arms! to arms!'	*Prog. of Spring* 103

Alas   with many a vain '*A*!'   *Doubt and Prayer* 2

Albert   'And with him *A* came on his.   *Talking Oak* 105

Albert (Prince Consort)   Hereafter, thro' all times, *A* the Good.   *Ded. of Idylls* 43

Albion   laborious, Patient children of *A*   *On Jub. Q. Victoria* 9

Alcestis   The true *A* of the time.   *Romney's R.* 91

Alchemise   *a* old hates into the gold Of Love,   *Akbar's Dream* 163

Alcor   Red-pulsing up thro' Alioth and *A*,   *Last Tournament* 480

Alder   blowing over meadowy holms And *a's*,   *Edwin Morris* 96

Came wet-shod *a* from the wave,	*Amphion* 41
But here will sigh thine *a* tree,	*A Farewell* 9
Balin's horse Was fast beside an *a*,	*Balin and Balan* 29

Ale   (*See also* **Aäle**) mellow'd all his heart with *a*,   *The Brook* 155

A mockery to the yeomen over *a*,	*Aylmer's Field* 497

A-leaning   Weak Truth *a-l* on her crutch,   *Clear-headed friend* 18

Ale-house   Jack on his *a-h* bench   *Maud I iv* 9

Alexandra   SEA-KING'S daughter from over the sea, *A*!   *W. to Alexandra* 2

Danes in our welcome of thee, *A*!	„ 5
all Dane in our welcome of thee, *A*!	„ 34

Alexandrovna   (*See also* **Marie, Marie Alexandrovna**) Prince his own imperial Flower, *A*.   *W. to Marie Alex.* 5

sultry palms of India known, *A*.	„ 15
gives its throne a wife, *A*!	„ 25
thy young lover hand in hand *A*!	„ 35
and change the hearts of men, *A*?	„ 45
Alfred—*A*!	„ 50

Alfred (King of England)   Truth-teller was our England's *A* named;   *Ode on Well.* 188

Alfred (Duke of Edinburgh, 1844-1900)   *A*—Alexandrovna!   *W. to Marie Alex.* 50

Alice   My own sweet *A*, we must die.   *Miller's D.* 18

Pray, *A*, pray, my darling wife,	„ 23
But, *A*, what an hour was that,	„ 57
Sweet *A*, if I told her all?'	„ 120
Go fetch your *A* here,' she said:	„ 143
But, *A*, you were ill at ease;	„ 146
foolish song I gave you, *A*, on the day	„ 162
none so fair as little *A*	*May Queen* 7
In there came old *A* the nurse,	*Lady Clare* 13
said *A* the nurse, (repeat)	*Lady Clare* 17, 23, 33, 41, 45

Alien   I am but an *a* and a Genovese.   *Columbus* 243

Alif   The *A* of Thine alphabet of Love.'   *Akbar's Dream* 31

A-liggin' (lying)   wheere thou was *a-l*, my lad,   *Owd Roä* 87

Alighted   (*See also* **Lighted**) To Francis just *a* from the boat,   *Audley Court* 7

Alioth   Red-pulsing up thro' *A* and Alcor,   *Last Tournament* 480

Alive   That thou, if thou wert yet *a*,   *Supp. Confessions* 100

Joying to feel herself *a*,	*Palace of Art* 178
pass away before, and yet *a* I am;	*May Queen, Con.,* 1
palace-front *A* with fluttering scarfs	*Princess v* 509
not always certain if they be *a*	*Grandmother* 84
there's none of them left *a*;	„ 85
strive To keep so sweet a thing *a*:'	*In Mem. xxxv* 7
Dark bulks that tumble half *a*,	*lxx* 11
at fifty Should Nature keep me *a*,	*Maud I vi* 32
with beatings in it, as if *a*,	*Holy Grail* 118
marvel among us that one should be left *a*,	*Def. of Lucknow* 78
And doom'd to burn *a*.	*Sir J. Oldcastle* 183
But we old friends are still *a's*,	*To E. Fitzgerald* 42
The love that keeps this heart *a*	*The Flight* 35
the dead are not dead but *a*.	*Vastness* 36

'All (hall)   sin fust *a* coom'd to the '*A*;   *N. Farmer, O. S.,* 55

walks down fro' the '*A* to see,	*North. Cobbler* 91

Alla   both, to worship *A*, but the prayers,   *Akbar's Dream* 9

are faint And pale in *A's* eyes	„ 11
A be my guide!	„ 16
'Mine is the one fruit *A* made for man.'	„ 40
pulse of *A* beats Thro' all His world.	„ 41
Yet '*A*,' says their sacred book, 'is Love,	„ 73
Yea, *A* here on earth, who caught	„ 84
was not *A* call'd In old Irân	„ 86

Alla (*continued*) Who all but lost himself in *A*,   *Akbar's Dream* 93
  One *A* ! one Kalifa !   " 167
  ' All praise to *A* by whatever hands   " 198
All-accomplish'd modest, kindly, *a-a*, wise   *Ded. of Idylls* 18
All-amorous Brushing his instep, bow'd the *a-a* Earl   *Geraint and E.* 360
Allan WITH Farmer *A* at the farm   *Dora* 1
  a day When *A* call'd his son,   " 10
  bells were ringing, *A* call'd His niece   " 41
  said *A*, 'did I not Forbid you, Dora ?'   " 91
  A said, 'I see it is a trick   " 95
  seal, that hung From *A's* watch,   " 136
  A set him down, and Mary said :   " 139
All-arm'd *A-a* I ride, whate'er betide,   *Sir Galahad* 83
All-assuming The *a-a* months and years   *In Mem. lxxxv* 67
All-comprehensive express *A-c* tenderness,   " 47
Allegiance from all neighbour crowns Alliance and *a*,   *Œnone* 125
  my rose, there my a due.   *Sir J. Oldcastle* 59
  One full voice of *a*,   *On Jub. Q. Victoria* 22
Allegory I SEND you here a sort of *a*,   *To——— With Pal. of Art* 1
  the third fool of their *a*.'   *Gareth and L.* 1085
  four fools have suck'd their *a*   " 1199
Allen (Francis) *See* **Francis, Francis Allen**
All-enduring like the *a-e* camel,   *Lover's Tale i* 136
Alley From the long *a's* latticed shade   *Arabian Nights* 112
  plaited *a's* of the trailing rose,   *Ode to Memory* 106
  a's falling down to twilight grots,   " 107
  every hollow cave and *a* lone   *Lotos-Eaters, C. S.,* 103
  And *a's*, faded places,   *Amphion* 86
  firefly-like in copse And linden *a*:   *Princess i* 209
  as she rode The woodland *a's*,   *Balin and Balan* 439
  There among the glooming *a's*   *Locksley H., Sixty,* 219
All-fragrant slip at once *a-f* into one.   *Princess vii* 70
All-generating *a-g* powers and genial heat Of Nature,   *Lucretius* 97
All-golden in the *a-g* afternoon A guest,   *In Mem. lxxxix* 25
All-graceful *A-g* head, so richly curl'd,   *Day-Dm., L'Envoi* 38
All-heal with a bunch of *a-h* in her hand,   *Vastness* 12
Alliance from all neighbour crowns A   *Œnone* 125
  longs For this *a* :   *Sisters (E. and E.)* 29
Allied However when she came to be so *a*.   *Maud I xiii* 36
Allies backward reel'd the Trojans and *a* ;   *Achilles over the T.* 31
All-in-all Is like another, *a i a*.'   *Two Voices* 36
  with that mood or this, Is *a-i-a* to all :   *Will Water.* 108
  Philip was her children's *a-i-a* ;   *Enoch Arden* 348
  her good Philip was her *a-i-a*,   " 525
  take them *a-i-a*, Were we ourselves   *Princess v* 200
  'trust me not at all or *a i a* ' (repeat)   *Merlin and V.* 384, 398, 449
  Love Were not his own imperial *a-i-a*.   *Sisters (E. and E.)* 227
  Out of His whole World-self and *a-i-a*—   *De Prof. Two G.* 49
  What England is, and what her *a-i-a*,   *The Fleet* 2
  fleet of England is her *a-i-a* ;   " 13
  been till now each other's *a-i-a*.   *The Ring* 53
  Within us, as without, that *A-i-a*,   *Akbar's Dream* 146
All-kindled *A-k* by a still and sacred fire,   *Enoch Arden* 71
Allot The sphere thy fate *a's* :   *Will Water.* 218
Allotted (part.) quit the post *A* by the Gods: *Lucretius* 149
  show'd an empty tent *a* her,   *Geraint and E.* 885
Allow one of less desert *a's* This laurel   *To the Queen* 6
  fly no more : I *a* thee for an hour.   *Gareth and L.* 892
  A me for mine hour, and thou wilt find   " 902
  our true King Will then *a* your pretext,   *Lancelot and E.* 153
  answer for a noble knight? *A* him !   " 202
  Will well *a* my pretext,   " 586
Allowance much *a* must be made for men.   *Aylmer's Field* 410
  Made more and more *a* for his talk ;   *Sea Dreams* 75
  To make *a* for us all.   *In Mem. li* 16
Allow'd leave To see the hunt, *a* it easily.   *Marr. of Geraint* 155
  loyal worship is *a* Of all men: *Lancelot and E.* 110
  Lightly, her suit *a*, she slipt away,   " 778
  Scorn was *a* as part of his defect,   *Guinevere* 43
  thro' his cowardice *a* Her station,   " 516
Allowing (*See also* **Half-allowing**) *A* it, the Prince
  and Enid rode,   *Marr. of Geraint* 43
Alloy Bright metal all without *a*   *Rosalind* 21
All-perfect *A-p*, finish'd to the finger nail.   *Edwin Morris* 22
All-puissant noble breast and *a-p* arms,   *Marr. of Geraint* 86

All-seeing or of older use *A-s* Hyperion—   *Lucretius* 126
All-shamed I rode *a-s*, hating the life   *Geraint and E.* 852
All-silent Sigh fully, or *a-s* gaze upon him   *Merlin and V.* 182
All-subtilising *A-s* intellect :   *In Mem. lxxxv* 48
All-too-full *a-t-f* in bud For puritanic stays: *Talking Oak* 59
Allure beacon-blaze *a's* The bird of passage,   *Enoch Arden* 728
Allured *A* him, as the beacon-blaze allures   " 728
  a The glance of Gareth   *Gareth and L.* 1315
  the sweet name *A* him first,   *Last Tournament* 399
Allusion phrases of the hearth, And far *a*,   *Princess ii* 316
Ally (Alfred). GOLDEN-HAIR'D *A* whose name is one   *To A. Tennyson* 1
Ally (s) True we have got—*such* a faithful *a*   *Riflemen form !* 24
Ally (verb) *à* Your fortunes, justlier balanced,   *Princess ii* 65
Almesbury sat There in the holy house at *A*   *Guinevere* 2
  she to *A* Fled all night long   " 127
  when she came to *A* she spake   " 138
  As even here they talk at *A*   " 208
  saw One lying in the dust at *A*,   *Pass. of Arthur* 77
Almighty (*See also* **Amoighty**) O God *A*, blessed
  Saviour, Thou   *Enoch Arden* 782
  SIR AYLMER-AYLMER, that *a* man,   *Aylmer's Field* 13
Almond-blossom The sunlit a-b shakes—   *To the Queen* 16
Almondine Turkis and agate and *a* :   *The Merman* 32
Alms set himself, Scorning an *a*, to work   *Enoch Arden* 812
  free of *a* her hand—The hand that   *Aylmer's Field* 697
  life of prayer, Praise, fast and *a* ;   *Holy Grail* 5
  She gave herself, to fast and *a*.   " 77
  cripple, one that held a hand for *a*—   *Pelleas and E.* 542
  fling free *a* into the beggar's bowl,   *Ancient Sage* 260
  From the golden *à* of Blessing   *Locksley H., Sixty,* 87
Almsdeed wear out in *a* and in prayer   *Guinevere* 687
Aloän (**alone**) an' if Sally be left *a*,   *North. Cobbler* 105
  Hallus a wi' 'is boooks,   *Village Wife* 27
  one night I wur sittin' *a*,   *Owd Roä* 29
Aloe Of olive, *a*, maize and vine.   *The Daisy* 4
Alone (*See also* **Aloän**) moon cometh, And looketh down *a*.   *Claribel* 14
  While I do pray to Thee *a*,   *Supp. Confessions* 12
  A and warming his five wits, (repeat)   *The Owl, I.* 6, 13
  My friend, with you to live *a*,   *Ode to Memory* 119
  Death, walking all *a* beneath a yew,   *Love and Death* 5
  A I wander to and fro,   *Oriana* 8
  A merman bold, Sitting *a*, Singing *a*   *The Merman* 3
  mermaid fair, Singing *a*,   *The Mermaid* 3
  Springing *a* With a shrill inner sound,   " 19
  For sure thou art not all *a*.   *Adeline* 25
  broad river rushing down *a*,   *Mine be the strength* 2
  ' Ah,' she sang, 'to be all *a*, (repeat)   *Mariana in the S.* 11, 23
  'but I wake *a*, I sleep forgotten,   " 35
  She thought, ' My spirit is here *a*,   " 47
  ' Sweet Mother, let me not here *a*   " 59
  So be *a* for evermore.'   " 68
  Is this the end to be left *a*,   " 71
  ' But thou shalt be *a* no more.'   " 76
  And day and night I am left *a*   " 83
  When I shall cease to be all *a*,   " 95
  And you and I were all *a*.   *Miller's D.* 136
  Came up from reedy Simois all *a*.   *Œnone* 52
  from that time to this I am *a*,   " 193
  And I shall be *a* until I die.   " 194
  I will not die *a*, (repeat)   *Œnone* 246, 257
  some one pacing there *a*,   *Palace of Art* 66
  Nor these *a*, but every landscape fair,   " 89
  Nor these *a* : but every legend   " 125
  prolong Her low preamble all *a*,   " 174
  Flash'd thro' her as she sat *a*,   " 214
  And all *a* in crime :   " 272
  But I shall lie *a*, mother,   *May Queen, N. Y's. E.* 20
  why should we toil *a*,   *Lotos-Eaters, C. S.,* 15
  Let us *a*. Time driveth onward   " 43
  Let us *à*. What is it that will last ?   " 45
  Let us *a*. What pleasure can we have   " 48
  ' Not so, nor once *a* ;   *D. of F. Women* 203
  That standeth there *a*,   *D. of the O. Year* 50
  Falls off, and love is left *a*.   *To J. S.* 16
  leave thee thus, Aidless, *a*,   *M. d'Arthur* 41

Alone (*continued*) For not *a* this pillar-
punishment, Not this *a* — *St. S. Stylites* 60
I might be more *a* with thee, — " 85
In which we sat together and *a*, — *Love and Duty* 60
both with those That loved me, and *a* ; — *Ulysses* 9
About the hall, among his dogs, *a*, — *Godiva* 17
She lying on her couch *a*, — *Day-Dm., Sleep. B.,* 2
Ah, let the rusty theme *a* ! — *Will Water.* 177
fell Sun-stricken, and that other lived *a* — *Enoch Arden* 570
who speaks with Him, seem all *a*, — " 620
'*A*,' I said, 'from earlier than I know, — *Princess vii* 311
When ill and weary, *a* and cold, — *The Daisy* 96
A, *a*, to where he sits, — *In Mem. xxiii* 3
When I contemplate all *a* — " *lxxxiv* 1
light Went out, and I was all *a*, — " *xcv* 20
Which not *a* had guided me, — " *cxiii* 3
she will let me *a*. — *Maud I i* 74
For am I not, am I not, here *a* — " *vi* 65
I am here at the gate *a* ; — " *xxii* 4
When will the dancers leave her *a* ? — " 21
That thou art left for ever *a* : — " *II iii* 4
a And all the world asleep, — *Com. of Arthur* 118
sought The King *a*, and found, and told — *Gareth and L.* 541
and they were left *a*. — *Geraint and E.* 244
endured Strange chances here *a* ;' — " 810
I was all *a* upon the flood, — *Lancelot and E.* 1046
shaped, it seems, By God for thee *a*, — " 1367
leave me all *a* with Mark and hell. — *Last Tournament* 536
leave thee thus, Aidless, *a*, — *Pass. of Arthur* 209
didst sit *a* in the inner house, — *Lover's Tale i* 112
To me *a*, Push'd from his chair — " 117
Our general mother meant for me *a*, — " 245
They tell me we would not be *a*,— — " 252
many weary moons I lived *a—A*, — " *ii* 2
day waned ; *A* I sat with her : — " 140
I will be all *a* with all I love, — " *iv* 47
Found, as it seem'd, a skeleton *a*, — " 139
dark eyes ! and not her eyes *a*, — " 166
I am all *a* in the world, — *First Quarrel* 8
go, go, you may leave me *a*— — *Rizpah* 79
I was there *a* : The phantom — *Sisters (E. and E.)* 113
I lying here bedridden and *a*, — *Columbus* 164
when I left my darling *a*.' — *The Wreck* 97
a on that lonely shore— — *Despair* 33
I am left *a* on the land, she is all *a* — " 63
Nor canst not prove that thou art body *a*, — *Ancient Sage* 59
Nor canst thou prove that thou art spirit *a*, — " 60
when I Sat all *a*, revolving — " 230
but we were left *a* : — *The Flight* 77
sitting on the wreck *a*. — *Locksley H., Sixty,* 16
Thou *a*, my boy, of Amy's kin — " 56
wearying to be left *a*, — " 57
first dark hour of his last sleep *a*. — " 238
gazing from this height *a*, — *Pro. to Gen. Hamley* 9
he dash'd up a Thro' the great gray slope — *Heavy Brigade* 16
Or Might must rule *a* ; — *Epilogue* 29
And he sung not *a* of an old sun set, — *Dead Prophet* 41
To forage for herself *a* ; — *Open. I. and C. Exhib.* 29
I parted from her, and I went *a*. — *The Ring* 437
would he live and die *a* ? — *Happy* 5
but I wept *a*, and sigh'd — " 69
Listen ! we three were *a* in the dell — *Bandit's Death* 19
of that Power which *a* is great, — *God and the Univ.* 5
Along six tall men haling a seventh *a*, — *Gareth and L.* 811
Alongside if t'one stick *a* t'uther — *Church-warden, etc.,* 10
A-loving When I was *a-l* you all along — *First Quarrel* 65
Alphabet The Alif of Thine *a* of Love.' — *Akbar's Dream* 31
Alphabet-of-heaven-in-man *A-o-h-i-m* Made vocal— — " 136
Alpine In gazing up an *A* height, — *Two Voices* 362
an *A* harebell hung with tears — *Princess vii* 115
Alps Sun-smitten *A* before me lay. — *The Daisy* 62
Alraschid *See* Haroun Alraschid
Altar (*See also* Isle-altar, Mountain-altars) Leads her
to the village *a*, — *L. of Burleigh* 11
And saw the *a* cold and bare. — *The Letters* 4

Altar (*continued*) 'Cold *a*, Heaven and earth shall meet — *The Letters* 7
fire, That burn'd as on an *a*. — *Enoch Arden* 72
at the *a* the poor bride Gives her harsh groom — *Princess v* 377
The Priest in horror about his *a* — *The Victim* 7
Burnt and broke the grove and *a* — *Boädicea* 2
sacred *a* blossom'd white with May, — *Com. of Arthur* 461
Beheld before a golden *a* lie — *Balin and Balan* 410
from the *a* glancing back upon her, — *Sisters (E. and E.)* 210
to pray Before *that a*—so I think ; — " 239
There, brooding by the central *a*, — *Ancient Sage* 33
Tower and *a* trembling — *Forlorn* 34
fire from off a pure Pierian *a*, — *Parnassus* 17
Altar-cloth Fair gleams the snowy *a-c*, — *Sir Galahad* 33
as thine *a-c* From that best blood — *Gareth and L.* 599
Altar-fashion'd smooth rock Before it, *a-f*, — *Tiresias* 147
Altar-fire As mounts the heavenward *a-f*, — *In Mem. xli* 3
Altar-flame made my life a perfumed *a-f* ; — *Maud I xviii* 24
Altar-shrine before The stateliest of her *a-s's*, — *Com. of Arthur* 455
Altar-stairs Upon the great world's *a-s* — *In Mem. lv* 15
Altar-stone To the *a-s* she sprang alone, — *The Victim* 67
Alter Sequel of guerdon could not *a* me — *Will Water.* 15
Nor add and *a*, many times, — *Aylmer's Field* 418
Persuasion, no, nor death could *a* her : — *Princess v* 262
as the fiery Sirius *a's* hue, — *Miller's D.* 94
Alter'd For I was *a*, and began — *Princess ii* 306
tho' you have grown You scarce have *a* : — *Maud I i* 39
Alum chalk and *a* and plaster are sold — *Œnone* 97
Amaracus Violet, and asphodel, — *Lotos-Eaters, C. S.,* 88
Amaranth propt on beds of *a* and moly, — *Romney's R.* 111
in heaven With Milton's *a*. — *The Daisy* 16
Amaryllis A milky-bell'd *a* blew. — *Guinevere* 23
A-maying Had been, their wont, *a-m*
Amaze (*See also* **Half-amaze**) In much *a* he stared
On eyes — *The Brook* 205
Up went the hush'd *a* of hand and eye. — *Princess iii* 138
Suddenly honest, answer'd in *a*, — *Geraint and E.* 410
sister's vision, fill'd me with *a* ; — *Holy Grail* 140
And some of us, all in *a*, — *Heavy Brigade* 35
a Our brief humanities ; — *Epilogue* 56
set the mother waking in *a* — *Demeter and P.* 57
Amazed (*See also* **Half-amazed, Part-amazed**) *A*
and melted all who listen'd — *Enoch Arden* 649
Averill solaced as he might, *a* : — *Aylmer's Field* 343
half *a* half frighted all his flock : — " 631
A he fled away Thro' the dark land, — *Princess v* 48
'*A* am I to hear Your Highness — " *vi* 324
a They glared upon the women, — " 360
brake on him, till, *a*, He knew not — *Com. of Arthur* 39
those who went with Gareth were *a*, — *Gareth and L.* 197
and all hearers were *a*. — " 655
Enid ask'd, *a*, 'If Enid errs, — *Marr. of Geraint* 131
the armourer turning all *a* — " 283
plover's human whistle *a* Her heart, — *Geraint and E.* 49
when he found all empty, was *a* ; — " 216
A am I, Beholding how ye butt — " 676
He much *a* us ; after, when we sought — *Balin and Balan* 115
A were these ; 'Lo there' she cried— — " 465
more *a* Than if seven men had set — *Lancelot and E.* 350
the Queen *a*, 'Was he not with you ? — " 572
He *a*, 'Torre and Elaine ! why here ? — " 795
So that the angels were *a*, — *Holy Grail* 451
ye look *a*, Not knowing they were lost — *Last Tournament* 41
babble about his end *A* me ; — " 671
I sware, Being *a* : but this went by— — " 674
dead world's winter dawn *A* him, — *Pass. of Arthur* 443
nor lights nor feast Dazed or *a*, — *Lover's Tale iv* 311
mask that I saw so *a* me, — *The Wreck* 117
I stood there, naked, *a* — *Despair* 77
still in her cave, *A*, — *Death of Œnone* 70
Amazement stood Stock-still for sheer *a*. — *Will Water.* 136
all the guests in mute *a* rose— — *Lover's Tale iv* 305
which made the more, — " 334
Amazing *See* Maäzin'
Amazon Glanced at the legendary *A* — *Princess ii* 126
Ambassador My father sent *a's* with furs — " *i* 42

Ambassador (*continued*) Sir Lancelot went *a,* at first,	*Merlin and V.* 774	
A, to lead her to his lord	*Guinevere* 383	
Ambassadress 'are you *a'es* From him to me?	*Princess iii* 203	
Amber (*adj.*) lights, rose, *a,* emerald, blue,	*Palace of Art* 169	
Purple or *a,* dangled a hundred fathoms	*V. of Maeldune* 56	
Like the tender *a* round,	*Margaret* 19	
and the *a* eves When thou and I, Camilla,	*Lover's Tale i* 52	
Ran *a* towards the west, and nigh the sea	,, 432	
Amber (s) fans Of sandal, *a,* ancient rosaries,	*Princess, Pro.,* 19	
Ambition No madness of *a,* avarice, none:	*Lucretius* 212	
lawless perch Of wing'd *a's,*	*Ded. of Idylls* 23	
Down with *a,* avarice, pride,	*Maud I x* 47	
Ambrosia Hebes are they to hand *a,*	*Princess iii* 113	
Their rich *a* tasted aconite.	*Demeter and P.* 105	
Ambrosial oak-tree sigheth, Thick-leaved, *a,*	*Claribel* 5	
her deep hair *A,* golden	*Œnone* 178	
Sweet after showers, *a* air,	*In Mem. lxxxvi* 1	
Ambrosially fruit of pure Hesperian gold, That smelt *a,*	*Œnone* 67	
Ambrosius fellow-monk among the rest, *A,*	*Holy Grail* 9	
monk *A* question'd Percivale:	,, 17	
Then spake the monk *A,* asking him,	,, 203	
I told him all thyself hast heard, *A,*	,, 737	
Ambuscade In every wavering brake an *a.*	*Geraint and E.* 51	
Ambush (*See also* **Lilac-ambush**) Lances in a set;	*D. of F. Women* 28	
Ambush'd meanings *a* under all they saw,	*Tiresias* 5	
Ambushing poisonous counsels, wayside *a's*—	*Gareth and L.* 432	
Amen yet I take it with *A.*	*Lancelot and E.* 1223	
A! Nay, I can burn,	*Sir J. Oldcastle* 172	
Amend might *a* it by the grace of Heaven,	*Geraint and E.* 53	
Amends Can thy love, Thy beauty, make *a,*	*Tithonus* 24	
She made me divine *a*	*Maud I vi* 13	
Well, we will make *a.*'	*Gareth and L.* 300	
A hereafter by some gaudy-day,	*Marr. of Geraint* 818	
Courteous—*a* for gauntness—	*Merlin and V.* 104	
our *a* for all we might have done—	*Columbus* 34	
Amethyst chrysoprase, Jacynth, and *a*—	,, 86	
Amid gap they had made—Four *a* thousands!	*Heavy Brigade* 24	
Golden branch *a* the shadows,	*To Virgil* 27	
Why not bask *a* the senses	*By an Evolution.* 6	
bracken *a* the gloom of the heather.	*June Bracken, etc.,* 1	
Amiss There's somewhat in this world *a*	*Miller's D.* 19	
Kind to Maud? that were not *a.*	*Maud I xix* 82	
pray you check me if I ask *a*—	*Guinevere* 324	
Amity idioted By the rough *a* of the other,	*Aylmer's Field* 591	
Ammon my race Hew'd *A,* hip and thigh,	*D. of F. Women* 238	
Ammonian *A* Oasis in the waste.	*Alexander* 8	
Ammonite Huge *A's,* and the first bones of Time;	*Princess, Pro.,* 15	
Amo 'Io t'*a*'—and these diamonds—	*The Ring* 70	
This very ring Io t'*a*?	,, 134	
This ring 'Io t'*a*' to his best beloved,	,, 210	
cried 'I see him, Io t'*a,* Io t'*a.*'	,, 223	
call thro' this 'Io t'*a*' to the heart Of Miriam;	,, 234	
'Io t'*a,* all is well then.' Muriel fled.	,, 271	
You love me still 'Io t'*a.*'—	,, 291	
'Io t'*a,*'' flung herself	,, 397	
even that 'Io t'*a,*' those three sweet Italian words,	,, 406	
Amoighty (**Almighty**) 'The *a's* a taäkin o'		
you to 'issén, (repeat)	*N. Farmer, O. S.,* 10, 26	
Amorous (*See also* **All-amorous, Human-amorous**)		
with argent-lidded eyes *A,*	*Arabian Nights* 136	
Of temper *a,* as the first of May,	*Princess i* 2	
High nature *a* of the good,	*In Mem. cix* 9	
Amorously kiss Thy taper fingers *a,*	*Madeline* 44	
shall we dandle it *a?*	*Boädicea* 33	
A-mountin' we 'eärd 'im *a-m* oop 'igher an' 'igher,	*North. Cobbler* 47	
Amourist your modern *a* is of easier, earthlier		
make.	*Locksley H., Sixty,* 18	
Amphion In days of old *A,*	*Amphion* 10	
Amuck Ran a Malayan *a* against the times,	*Aylmer's Field* 463	
Amulet What a drew her down	,, 507	
kept it as a sacred *a* About me,—	*The Ring* 442	
Amurath (**Turkish Emperor**) Or *A* of the East?	*Sir J. Oldcastle* 97	
Amy I said, 'My cousin *A,* speak,	*Locksley Hall* 23	
O my *A,* mine no more!	,, 39	
A's arms about my neck—	*Locksley H., "Sixty,"* 13	

Amy (*continued*) *A* loved me, *A* fail'd me, *A* was		
a timid child;	*Locksley H., Sixty,* 19	
often I and *A* in the mouldering aisle have stood,	,, 31	
Lies my *A* dead in child-birth,	,, 36	
Here to-day was *A* with me,	,, 53	
of *A's* kin and mine art left to me.	,, 56	
our latest meeting—*A*—sixty years ago—	,, 177	
Amygdaloid trap and tuff, *A* and trachyte,	*Princess iii* 363	
Ana Ere days, that deal in *a,*	*Will Water.* 199	
Anadem Lit light in wreaths and *a's,*	*Palace of Art* 186	
A-naggin' Moother 'ed beän *a-n* about the gell	*Owd Roä* 69	
Anakim I felt the thews of *A,*	*In Mem. ciii* 37	
Analyse and *a* Our double nature,	*Supp. Confessions* 174	
Anarch wearied of Autocrats, *A's,* and Slaves,	*The Dreamer* 10	
Anathema Thunder '*A,*' friend, at you;	*To F. D. Maurice* 8	
Anatolian Ghost Crag-cloister; *A G*;	*To Ulysses* 43	
Anatomic not found among them all One *a.*'	*Princess iii* 307	
Ancestor those fixt eyes of painted *a's*	*Aylmer's Field* 832	
Anchor (s) with silver *a* left afloat,	*Arabian Nights* 93	
there was no *a,* none, To hold by.'	*The Epic* 20	
Nor *a* dropt at eve or morn;	*The Voyage* 82	
A's of rusty fluke, and boats	*Enoch Arden* 18	
Cast all your cares on God; that *a* holds.	,, 222	
lay At *a* in the flood below;	*In Mem. ciii* 20	
my love Waver'd at *a* with me,	*Lover's Tale i* 65	
Anchor (verb) Why not yet *A* thy frailty there,	*Supp. Confessions* 124	
To *a* by one gloomy thought?	*Two Voices* 459	
Anchor'd Tho' *a* to the bottom, such is he.'	*Princess iv* 257	
A tawny pirate *a* in his port,	*Merlin and V.* 558	
Half-swallow'd in it, *a* with a chain;	*Holy Grail* 803	
Anchorite *a* Would haunt the desolated fane,	*St. Telemachus* 12	
Ancients (s) For we are *A's* of the earth,	*Day-Dm., L'Envoi* 19	
Ancle *See* **Ankle**		
'And (hand) an' thy muther coom to '*a,*	*N. Farmer, N. S.,* 21	
But I puts it inter 'er '*a's*	*North. Cobbler* 72	
an' poonch'd my '*a* wi' the hawl,	,, 78	
Fur I couldn't 'owd '*a's* off gin,	,, 84	
An' 'e spanks 'is '*a* into mine,	,, 92	
new Squire's coom'd wi' 'is taäil in 'is '*a,* (repeat) *Village Wife* 14, 121		
'e 'ed hallus a booök i' 'is '*a,*	,, 26	
an' our Nelly she gied me 'er '*a,*	,, 111	
An' that squeedg'd m t'*a* i' the shed,	*Spinster's S's.* 39	
Or sits wi' their '*a's* afoor 'em,	,, 86	
An' 'is 'air coom'd off i' my '*a's*	*Owd Roä* 100	
Anemone (*See also* **'Enemies**) burn'd The red *a.*	*D. of F. Women* 72	
Crocus, *a,* violet,	*To F. D. Maurice* 44	
among the gardens, auriculas, *a's,*	*City Child* 4	
'Ang'd (hanged) Noäks wur '*a* for it oop at 'soize—	*N. Farmer, O. S.,* 36	
Angel (*adj.*) So sweet a face, such *a* grace,	*Beggar Maid* 13	
With books, with flowers, with *A* offices,	*Princess vii* 26	
a dearer being, all dipt In *A* instincts,	,, 321	
Rings to the roar of an *a* onset—	*Milton* 8	
And be found of *a* eyes	*Helen's Tower* 11	
The toll of funeral in an *A* ear	*D. of the Duke of C.* 10	
Angel (s) (*See also* **Earth-Angel, Hangel**)		
When *a's* spake to men aloud,	*Supp. Confessions* 25	
once by man and *a's* to be seen,	*The Kraken* 14	
Like that strange *a* which of old,	*Clear-headed friend* 24	
thyself a little lower 'Than *a's.*	*Two Voices* 199	
temper'd with the tears Of *a's*	*To—— With Pal. of Art* 19	
slept St. Cecily; An *a* look'd at her.	*Palace of Art* 100	
a's rising and descending met	,, 143	
March-morning I heard the *a's* call;	*May Queen, Con.,* 25	
saw An *a* stand and watch me,	*St. S. Stylites* 35	
Is that the *a* there That holds	,, 203	
Three *a's* bear the holy Grail:	*Sir Galahad* 42	
And, stricken by an *a's* hand,	,, 69	
been as God's good *a* in our house.	*Enoch Arden* 423	
Fair as the *A* that said 'Hail!'	*Aylmer's Field* 681	
himself Were that great *A*;	*Sea Dreams* 27	
devil in man, there is an *a* too,	,, 278	
His *a* broke his heart.	,, 280	
'lest some classic *A* speak In scorn	*Princess iii* 70	
the woman's *A* guards you,	,, v 410	
No *A,* but a dearer being,	,, vii 320	

Angel (s) *(continued)* **Whose** Titan *a's*, Gabriel, Abdiel,   *Milton* 5
My guardian *a* will speak out   *In Mem. xliv* 15
I found an *a* of the night ;   ,, *lxix* 14
An *a* watching an urn Wept   *Maud I viii* 3
ship and sail and *a's* blowing on it :   *Balin and Balan* 365
a's of our Lord's report.   *Merlin and V.* 16
I pray him, send a sudden *A* down   *Lancelot and E.* 1424
So that the *a's* were amazed,   *Holy Grail* 451
a's, awful shapes, and wings and eyes.   ,, 848
I, and Arthur and the *a's* hear,   *Last Tournament* 350
we are not *a's* here Nor shall be :   ,, 698
face, Which then was as an *a's*,   *Guinevere* 596
I to her became Her guardian and her *a*,   *Lover's Tale i* 393
Come like an *a* to a damned soul,   ,, 673
like the waft of an *A's* wing ;   *In the Child. Hosp.* 38
Till you find the deathless *A*   *Locksley H., Sixty,* 278
mountain-walls Young *a's* pass.   *Early Spring* 12
hear a death-bed *A* whisper 'Hope.'   *Romney's R.* 148

Angelo   The bar of Michael *A*.   *In Mem. lxxxvii* 40

Anger (s)   Delicious spites and darling *a's*,   *Madeline* 6
Then wax'd her *a* stronger.   *The Goose* 30
as with a kind of *a* in him,   *Enoch Arden* 392
his *a* reddens in the heavens ;   *Princess iv* 386
their ravening eagle rose In *a*,   *Ode on Well.* 120
troubled, as if with *a* or pain :   *Grandmother* 65
all their *a* in miraculous utterances,   *Boädicea* 23
an *a*, not by blood to be satiated.   ,, 52
The bitter springs of *a* and fear ;   *Maud I x* 49
Till I with as fierce an *a* spoke,   ,, *II i* 17
vassals of wine and *a* and lust,   ,, 43
strength of *a* thro' mine arms,   *Gareth and L.* 948
And when his *a* tare him,   ,, 1340
ruth began to work Against his *a*   *Geraint and E.* 102
or hot, God's curse, with *a*—   ,, 661
beast, whose *a* was his lord.   *Balin and Balan* 488
As some wild turn of *a*,   *Merlin and V.* 531
turn of *a* born Of your misfaith ;   ,, 531
Vivien, frowning in true *a*,   ,, 691
breaths of *a* puff'd Her fairy nostril   ,, 848
his *a* slowly died Within him,   ,, 891
too faint and sick am I For *a* :   *Lancelot and E.* 1087
first her *a*, leaving Pelleas   *Pelleas and E.* 289
storm of *a* brake From Guinevere,   *Guinevere* 361
as *a* falls aside And withers   *Lover's Tale i* 9
so fluster'd with *a* were they   *V. of Maeldune* 25
and in *a* we sail'd away.   ,, 54
great God, Arês, burns in *a* still   *Tiresias* 11
climbing from the bath In *a* ;   ,, 41
And *a's* of the Gods for evil done   ,, 62
and quench The red God's *a*,   ,, 158
And who, when his *a* was kindled,   *The Wreck* 17
moment's *a* of bees in their hive ?—   *Vastness* 35
sound of *a* like a distant storm.   *The Ring* 119
wild horse, *a*, plunged To fling me,   *Akbar's Dream* 118
Rolling her *a* Thro' blasted valley   *Kapiolani* 11

Anger (verb)   *A's* thee most, or *a's* thee at all ?   *Lucretius* 75

Anger-charm'd   Sat *a-c* from sorrow,   *Aylmer's Field* 728

Anger'd (adj.)   *(See also* **Half-anger'd**) The flush
of *a* shame O'erflows   *Madeline* 32
Those dragon eyes of *a* Eleanor   *D. of F. Women* 255
Gareth spake *A*, 'Old Master,   *Gareth and L.* 280
Sick ? or for any matter *a* at me ?'   *Balin and Balan* 276
most of these were mute, some *a*,   *Last Tournament* 210
I was jealous, *a*, vain,   *Happy* 66

Anger'd (verb)   jealousies Which *a* her.   Who *a*
James ?   *The Brook* 100
'So Merlin riddling *a* me ;   *Com. of Arthur* 412
a saying that *a* her.   *Last Tournament* 628
But he *a* me all the more,   *First Quarrel* 64
an' he *a* me more and more.   ,, 66
Eh ! how I *a* Arundel asking me   *Sir J. Oldcastle* 135

Angerly   Again thou blushest *a* ;   *Madeline* 45

Angle (corner)   We rub each other's *a's* down,   *In Mem. lxxxix* 40

Angle (race of people)   Saxon and *A* from
Over the broad billow   *Batt. of Brunanburh* 118

Angled   But *a* in the higher pool.   *Miller's D.* 64
a with them for her pupil's love :   *Princess iii* 93

Angling   left That *a* to the mother.   *The Ring* 356

Angrier   I never ate with *a* appetite   *Geraint and E.* 233

Angry   Hungry for honour, *a* for his king.   *Princess v* 314
Hortensia pleading : *a* was her face.   ,, *vii* 132
—it makes me *a* now.   *Grandmother* 44
makes me *a* yet to speak of it—   *Lover's Tale iv* 135

Anguisant (King of Erin)   With *A* of Erin,
Morganore,   *Com. of Arthur* 115

Anguish   Life, *a*, death, immortal love,   *Arabian Nights* 73
'Thine *a* will not let thee sleep,   *Two Voices* 49
'Or that this *a* fleeting hence,   ,, 235
down in hell Suffer endless *a*,   *Lotos-Eaters, C. S.,* 124
Beauty and *a* walking hand in hand   *D. of F. Women* 15
She loveth her own *a* deep   *To J. S.* 42
Shall I heed them in their *a* ?   *Boädicea* 9
My deeper *a* also falls,   *In Mem. xix* 15
My *a* hangs like shame.   *Maud II iv* 74
in her *a* found The casement :   *Guinevere* 586
Sweat, writhings, *a*, labouring   *Pass. of Arthur* 116
in the sudden *a* of her heart   *Lover's Tale i* 702
became *A* intolerable.   ,, *ii* 138
Life with its *a*, and horrors, and errors—   *Despair* 48

Animal (adj.)   With *a* heat and dire insanity ?   *Lucretius* 163

Animal (s)   The single pure and perfect *a*,   *Princess vii* 306

Animalism   Hetairai, curious in their art,
Hired *a's*,   *Lucretius* 53

Ankle-Ancle   From head to *ancle* fine,   *Talking Oak* 224
One praised her *ancles*, one her eyes,   *Beggar Maid* 11
At last I hook'd my *ankle* in a vine,   *Princess iv* 268
Behind his *ankle* twined her hollow feet   *Merlin and V.* 240

Ankle-bells   To make her smile, her golden *a-b.*   ,, 579

Ankle-bones   feet unmortised from their *a-b*   ,, 552

Ankle-deep   And brushing *a-d* in flowers,   *In Mem. lxxxix* 49

Ankle-wing   as it were with Mercury's *a-w*,   *Lucretius* 201

Anlaf (Danish King)   Sparing not any of Those
that with *A*,   *Batt. of Brunanburh* 46
Earls of the army of *A* Fell   ,, 53
nor had *A* With armies so broken   ,, 81

Annal-book   Merlin did In one great *a-b.*   *Com. of Arthur* 158

Annals   Holding the folded *a* of my youth ;   *Gardener's D.* 244
Told him, with other *a* of the port,   *Enoch Arden* 702
with a day Blanch'd in our *a*,   *Princess vi* 63
Read the wide world's *a*, you,   *Locksley H., Sixty,* 104
glorious *a* of army and fleet,   *Vastness* 7

Anne   is gone, you say, little *A* ?   *Grandmother* 1
I had not wept, little *A*, not since   ,, 63

Annie   *(See also* **Annie Lee**, **Hannie**) While *A*
still was mistress ;   *Enoch Arden* 26
and make a home For *A* :   ,, 48
a home For *A*, neat and nestlike,   ,, 59
Enoch and *A*, sitting hand-in-hand,   ,, 69
set *A* forth in trade With all that seamen   ,, 138
moving homeward came on *A* pale,   ,, 149
to break his purposes To *A*,   ,, 156
A fought against his will :   ,, 158
Bought *A* goods and stores,   ,, 169
A seem'd to hear Her own death-scaffold   ,, 174
would work for *A* to the last,   ,, 180
A's fears, Save, as his *A's*,   ,, 183
'*A*, this voyage by the grace of God   ,, 190
A, come, cheer up before I go.'   ,, 200
A, the ship I sail in passes here   ,, 214
'*A*, my girl, cheer up, be comforted,   ,, 218
When *A* would have raised him   ,, 232
A from her baby's forehead clipt   ,, 235
same week when *A* buried it,   ,, 271
but *A*, seated with her grief,   ,, 280
'*A*, I came to ask a favour of you.'   ,, 285
A, now—Have we not known each other   ,, 305
A—for I am rich and well-to-do.   ,, 311
A with her brows against the wall   ,, 314
ask'd 'Then you will let me, *A* ?'   ,, 323
for *A's* sake, Fearing the lazy gossip   ,, 334

Annie (*continued*) Philip did not fathom
A's mind : *Enoch Arden* 344
one evening A's children long'd To go ,, 362
And A would go with them ; ,, 364
For was not A with them ? , 371
'Listen, A, How merry they are ,, 388
Tired, A ?' for she did not speak ,, 390
And A said 'I thought not of it : ,, 395
'A, there is a thing upon my mind, ,, 399
O A, It is beyond all hope, ,, 402
answer'd A ; tenderly she spoke : ,, 422
'A, as I have waited all my life ,, 435
fearing night and chill for A, ,, 443
At A's door he paused and gave ,, 447
'A, when I spoke to you, ,, 448
A weeping answer'd 'I am bound.' ,, 451
'Take your own time, A, take ,, 466
A could have wept for pity of him ; ,, 467
chanced That A could not sleep, ,, 490
never merrily beat A's heart. ,, 513
The babes, their babble, A, ,, 606
home Where A lived and loved him, ,, 685
His gazing in on A, his resolve, ,, 863
tell my daughter A, whom I saw ,, 882
For, A, you see, her father was not the man *Grandmother* 5
I cannot cry for him, A : ,, 15
Why do you look at me, A ? ,, 17
at your age, A, I could have wept (repeat) ,, 20, 100
I mean your grandfather, A : ,, 23
But soiling another, A, ,, 36
Shadow and shine is life, little A, ,, 60
children, A, they're all about me yet. ,, 76
my A who left me at two, ,, 77
my own little A, an A like you : ,, 78
in this Book, little A, the message ,, 96
Get me my glasses, A : ,, 106
Hall but Miss A, the heldest, *Village Wife* 8
but Miss A she said it wur draäins, ,, 11
Hoänly Miss A were saw stuck oop, ,, 59
An' es for Miss A es call'd me afoor ,, 105
taäke it kindly ov owd Miss A ,, 109
O A, what shall I do ?' *In the Child.' Hosp.* 47
A consider'd. 'If I,' said the wise little A, ,, 48
That was a puzzle for A. ,, 55

Annie Lee (*See also* **Annie**) A L, The prettiest little
damsel *Enoch Arden* 11
A later but a loftier A L, ,, 748

Annihilate eagle's beak and talon a us ? *Boädicea* 11

Announced A the coming doom, and fulminated *Sea Dreams* 22

Annulet And into many a listless, a, *Geraint and E.* 258

Answer (s) Our thought gave a each to each, *Sonnet To——* 10
The sullen a slid betwixt : *Two Voices* 226
There must be a to his doubt, ,, 309
I spoke, but a came there none : ,, 425
To which my soul made a readily : *Palace of Art* 17
Not rendering true a, *M. d'Arthur* 74
some sweet a, tho' no a came, *Gardener's D.* 159
let me have an a to my wish ; *Dora* 30
before thine a given Departest, *Tithonus* 44
an a peal'd from that high land, *Vision of Sin* 221
Rejoicing at that a to his prayer. *Enoch Arden* 127
such a voluble a promising all, ,, 903
And Leolin's horror-stricken a, *Aylmer's Field* 318
hush'd itself at last Hopeless of a : ,, 543
therewithal an a vague as wind : *Princess i* 45
In this report, this a of a king, ,, 70
Her a was 'Leave me to deal with that.' ,, iii 149
a which, half-muffled in his beard, ,, v 234
oozed All o'er with honey'd a ,, 242
I lagg'd in a loth to render up ,, 299
shall have her a by the word.' ,, 327
Last, Ida's a, in a royal hand, ,, 371
what a should I give ? ,, vii 6
The noblest a unto such Is perfect *Lit. Squabbles* 19
it seem'd that an a came. *The Victim* 24

Answer (s) (*continued*) Bark an a, Britain's raven ! *Boädicea* 13
doubts and a's here proposed, *In Mem. xlviii* 3
What hope of a, or redress ? ,, lvi 27
But Death returns an a sweet : ,, lxxxi 9
A faithful a from the breast, ,, lxxxv 14
win An a from my lips, ,, ciii 50
Make a, Maud my bliss, *Maud I xviii* 57
old Seer made a playing on him *Gareth and L.* 252
said your say ; Mine a was my deed. ,, 1175
being still rebuked, would a still ,, 1249
Made a sharply that she should not *Marr. of Geraint* 196
So moving without a to her rest ,, 530
He made a wrathful a : 'Did I wish *Geraint and E.* 76
he flung a wrathful a back : ,, 146
Made a, either eyelid wet *Merlin and V.* 379
Is that an a for a noble knight ? *Lancelot and E.* 201
Full simple was her a, 'What know I ? ,, 671
all their a's were as one : *Holy Grail* 284
And when his a chafed them, ,, 673
Percivale made a not a word. *Pelleas and E.* 534
Well then, what a ?' *Last Tournament* 713
voice about his feet Sent up an a ,, 761
when she drew No a, by and by *Guinevere* 162
a mournful a made the Queen : ,, 341
Not rendering true a, *Pass. of Arthur* 242
Had made a silent a : *Lover's Tale iv* 96
to that passionate a of full heart *Sisters (E. and E.)* 259
an a came Not from the nurse— *The Wreck* 143
all the night an a shrill! *Demeter and P.* 61

Answer (verb) And a's to his mother's calls *Supp. Confessions* 159
I shall know Thy voice, and a *My life is full* 10
Or a should one press his hands ? *Two Voices* 245
He a's not, nor understands. ,, 246
'But thou canst a not again. ,, 310
Or thou wilt a but in vain. ,, 312
O will she a if I call ? *Miller's D.* 118
you dare to a thus ! *Dora* 26
To that man My work shall a, *Love and Duty* 29
He will a to the purpose, *Locksley Hall* 55
Scarce a to my whistle ? *Amphion* 68
in gentle murmur, When they a *L. of Burleigh* 50
could a him, If question'd, *Enoch Arden* 653
to a, Madam, all those hard things *Princess ii* 345
Madam, *you* should a, *we* would ask) ,, 353
told me she would a us to-day, ,, iii 166
a, echoes, dying, dying, dying. (repeat) ,, iv 6, 12
a, echoes, a, dying, dying, dying. ,, iv 18
(A, O a) We give you his life.' *The Victim* 15
'O wife, what use to a now ? *In Mem.' xxviii* 4
A each other in the mist. ,, xxxv 13
Love would a with a sigh, *Maud I i* 4
whatever is ask'd her, a's 'Death.' ,, xviii 59
wilt thou not a this ? *Com. of Arthur* 426
musing 'Shall I a yea or nay ?' *Gareth and L.* 953
but a scorn with scorn. *Merlin and V.* 386
it shall a for me. Listen to it. ,, 397
But shall it ? a, darling, a, no. *Holy Grail* 12
To a that which came : ,, 434
he had Scarce any voice to a, *Lover's Tale i* 277
Doth question'd memory a not, ,, iv 161
if my neighbour whistle a's him— *Def. of Lucknow* 99
Highlanders a with conquering cheers, *Columbus* 213
Who then will have to a, *Bandit's Death* 27
'give it to me,' but he would not a me— *Two Voices* 37

Answer'd To which he a scoffingly ; *Gardener's D.* 231
in that time and place she a me, *Dora* 22
But William a short ; ,, 33
William a madly ; bit his lips, *Edwin Morris* 24
he a me ; And well his words *Talking Oak* 20
plagiarised a heart, And a *Golden Year* 53
in mimic cadence a James— *Will Water.* 106
She a to my call, *Aylmer's Field* 465
A all queries touching those at home *Princess, Pro.,* 66
Echo a in her sleep From hollow fields : ,, iii 140
a sharply that I talk'd astray.

Answer'd (*continued*) I *a* nothing, doubtful in myself   *Princess* iii 272
    when have I *a* thee?   " vii 4
Gods have a; We give them the wife!'   *The Victim* 78
Doubt not ye the Gods have *a*,   *Boädicea* 22
The 'wilt thou' *a*, and again   *In Mem. Con.*, 54
and *a* me In riddling triplets   *Com. of Arthur* 401
Gareth *a* them With laughter   *Gareth and L.* 208
Sir Gareth *a*, laughingly,   " 1007
thou hast ever *a* courteously,   " 1167
reviled, hast *a* graciously,   " 1269
A Sir Gareth graciously to one   " 1414
ask'd it of him, Who *a* as before ;   *Marr. of Geraint* 205
a with such craft as women use,   *Geraint and E.* 352
not dead !' she *a* in all haste.   " 542
Enid *a*, harder to be moved   " 694
truest eyes that ever *a* Heaven,   " 842
I am *a*, and henceforth   *Merlin and V.* 879
ever well and readily *a* he :   *Lancelot and E.* 269
Lancelot spoke And *a* him at full,   " 286
in her heart she *a* it and said,   " 786
he *a* not, Or short and coldly,   " 886
whom she *a* with all calm.   " 997
He *a* with his eyes upon the ground,   " 1352
Lancelot *a* nothing, but he went,   " 1387
a not, but, sharply turning,   *Holy Grail* 739
she *a*, and she laugh'd,   *Pelleas and E.* 132
Gawain *a* kindly tho' in scorn,   " 333
a them Even before high God.   " 462
he *a* not, ' Or hast thou other griefs?   " 598
was *a* softly by the King   *Guinevere* 44
I should have *a* his farewell.   " 615
To all their queries *a* not a word,   *Lover's Tale* iv 333
Julian, sitting by her, *a* all :   " 340
he *a* her wail with a song—   *The Dreamer* 16
Answering *a* under crescent brows ;   *Princess* ii 428
a now my random stroke   *In Mem.* xxxix 2
a not one word, she led the way.   *Geraint and E.* 495
to the court of Arthur *a* yea.   *Com. of Arthur* 446
Ant one whose foot is bitten by an *a*,   *Pelleas and E.* 184
What is it all but a trouble of *a*'s   *Vastness* 4
Antagonism in the teeth of clench'd *a*'s   *Princess* iv 465
And toppling over all *a*,   *Marr. of Geraint* 491
And, toppling over all *a*,   *Geraint and E.* 834
Anthem *a* sung, is charm'd and tied   *D. of F. Women* 193
sound of the sorrowing *a* roll'd   *Ode on Well.* 60
Anther With *a*'s and with dust: *Talking Oak* 184
Antibabylonianism And loud-lung'd *A*'s   *Sea Dreams* 252
Antichrist He leans on *A* ; or that his mind,   *Sir J. Oldcastle* 74
    That mock-meek mouth of utter *A*,   " 170
Antiquity A front of timber-crost *a*,   *Enoch Arden* 692
Anton (a knight) This is the son of A, not the King.'   *Com. of Arthur* 74
Arthur born of Gorloïs, Others of *A* ?   " 171
And gave him to Sir *A*,   " 222
else the child of *A*, and no king,   " 233
Antony (Mark) *See* **Mark Antony**
Anvil silver hammers falling On silver *a*'s,   *Princess* i 217
iron-clanging *a* bang'd With hammers ;   " v 504
Anything He never meant us *a* t but good.   *Enoch Arden* 887
Behold, we know not *a* ;   *In Mem.* liv 13
can see elsewhere, *a* so fair.   *Marr. of Geraint* 499
Henceforth in all the world at *a*,   *Geraint and E.* 649
Apartment died Of fright in far *a*'s.   *Princess* vi 371
Ape (s) In bed like monstrous *a*'s   *St. S. Stylites* 174
And let the *a* and tiger die.   *In Mem.* cxviii 28
His action like the greater *a*,   " cxx 11
moods of tiger, or of *a* ?   *Making of Man* 2
Ape (verb) should *a* Those monstrous males   *Princess* iii 309
as far As I could *a* their treble,   " iv 92
Aphroditè Herè comes to-day, Pallas and *A*,   *Œnone* 86
Idalian *A* beautiful,   " 174
Apocalyptic as if he held The *A* millstone,   *Sea Dreams* 26
Apollo strange song I heard *A* sing,   *Tithonus* 62
another of our Gods, the Sun, *A*,   *Lucretius* 125
Apology But ended with a so sweet,   *Geraint and E.* 394
No less than one divine *a*.   *Lover's Tale* iv 169

Apostle shrive myself No, not to an *A*.'   *Sir J. Oldcastle* 147
Apothegm My curse upon the Master's *a*,   *Romney's R.* 37
Appal *A* me from the quest.'   *Gareth and L.* 1331
Appall'd cliff-side, *a* them, and they said,   *Lancelot and E.* 1253
In our most need, *a* them,   *Columbus* 71
Apparel in her hand A suit of bright *a*,   *Marr. of Geraint* 678
store of rich *a*, sumptuous fare,   " 709
a as might well beseem His princess,   " 758
clothed her in *a* like the day.   *Geraint and E.* 948
Appeal (s) She the *a* Brook'd not,   *Princess* vi 139
'Thou makest thine *a* to me :   *In Mem.* lvi 5
tho' it spake and made *a*   " xcii 4
she lifted up A face of sad *a*,   *Merlin and V.* 234
Appeal (verb) *a* Once more to France or England ;   *Columbus* 57
Appeal'd *a* To one that stood beside.   *D. of F. Women* 99
And with a larger faith *a*   *Talking Oak* 15
Appealing *A* to the bolts of Heaven ;   *Princess* iv 372
Appear Shadows of the world *a*.   *L. of Shalott* ii 12
made *a* Still-lighted in a secret shrine,   *Mariana in the S.* 17
Falling have let *a* the brand of John—   *Aylmer's Field* 509
things *a* the work of mighty Gods,   *Lucretius* 102
Thy marble bright in dark *a*'s,   *In Mem.* lxvii 5
Which makes *a* the songs I made   " Con., 21
Shall I *a*, O Queen, at Camelot,   *Lancelot and E.* 142
beauties of the work *a* The darkest faults :   *Sisters (E. and E.)* 105
and now the morn *a*'s   *The Flight* 137
Miriam your Mother might *a* to me.   *The Ring* 137
Appear'd The very graves *a* to smile,   *The Letters* 45
now that shadow of mischance *a*   *Enoch Arden* 128
blew and blew, but none *a* :   *Princess* v 336
the work To both *a* so costly,   *Marr. of Geraint* 638
a, low-built but strong ;   *Balin and Balan* 333
never yet Had heaven *a* so blue,   *Holy Grail* 365
Appearing *A* ere the times were ripe,   *In Mem. Con.*, 139
dark in the golden grove *A*,   *Last Tournament* 380
Appeased holy Gods, they must be *a*,   *The Victim* 47
Appertain all That *a*'s to noble maintenance.   *Marr. of Geraint* 712
Appetite I never ate with angrier *a*   *Geraint and E.* 233
Applauded mildly, that all hearts *A*,   " 958
Applause (*See also* **Self-applause**) might reap
the *a* of Great,   *Princess* iii 262
the Trojans roar'd *a* ;   *Spec. of Iliad* 1
Shall he for whose *a* I strove,   *In Mem.* li 5
To laughter and his comrades to *a*.   *Geraint and E.* 296
Apple full-juiced *a*, waxing over-mellow,   *Lotos-Eaters, C. S.*, 33
swung an *a* of the purest gold,   *Marr. of Geraint* 170
a's by the brook Fallen, and on the lawns.   *Holy Grail* 384
and ate The goodly *a*'s,   " 388
The warm white *a* of her throat,   *Last Tournament* 717
peak of the mountain was *a*'s,   *V. of Maeldune* 63
Apple-arbiter beardless *a-a* Decided fairest.   *Lucretius* 91
Apple-blossom Fresh *a-b*, blushing for a boon.   *The Brook* 90
cheek of *a-b*, Hawk-eyes?   *Gareth and L.* 589
Apple-cheek'd a bevy of Eroses *a-c*,   *The Islet* 11
Apple-tree and o'er the brook Were *a-t*'s,   *Holy Grail* 384
Appliances With half a night's *a*,   *Lover's Tale* iv 93
Application And liberal *a*'s lie In Art   *Day-Dm.*, Moral 13
Appraised *A* his weight, and fondled   *Enoch Arden* 154
A the Lycian custom,   *Princess* ii 128
Apprehend And thro' thick veils to *a*   *Two Voices* 296
Approach (s) less achievable By slow *a*'es,   *Princess* iii 284
Preserve a broad *a* of fame,   *Ode on Well.* 78
Approach (verb) and let him presently *A*,   *St. S. Stylites* 216
a To save the life despair'd of,   *Enoch Arden* 830
A and fear not ;   *Princess* vii 353
Morning-Star, *a*, Arm me,'   *Gareth and L.* 924
' *A* and arm me !'   " 1112
Approach'd *a* Melissa, tinged with wan   *Princess* iii 24
A between them toward the King,   *Gareth and L.* 441
as the great knight *A* them :   *Lancelot and E.* 180
A him, and with full affection said,   " 1355
Approaching *A*, press'd you heart to heart.   *Lancelot and E.* 1000
A thro' the darkness, call'd ;   *Maud* I xix 71
Approve And wishes me to *a* him,   *The Letters* 16
Approved She wore the colours I *a*.

Approved (*continued*) *A* him, bowing at their own
deserts | *The Brook* 128
and all the knights *A* him, | *Balin and Balan* 210
Approven he by miracle was *a* King: | *Guinevere* 296
Approvingly often talk'd of him *A*, | *Aylmer's Field* 474
'Appy (happy) as *'a* as *'art* could think, | *North. Cobbler* 15
I loovs tha to maäke thysen *'a*, | *Spinster's S's.* 57
maäke *'is owd* aäge as *'a* as iver I can, | *Owd Roä* 3
A-preächin' Fur *they*'ve bin *a-p mea* down, | *Church-warden, etc.*, 53
Apricot blanching *a* like snow in snow. | *Prog. of Spring* 30
April (adj.) When *A* nights began to blow, | *Miller's D.* 106
A hopes, the fools of chance ; | *Vision of Sin* 164
And breathes in *A* autumns. | *The Brook* 196
clad her like an *A* daffodilly | *Princess* ii 324
Can trouble live with *A* days, | *In Mem. lxxxiii* 7
Thro' all the years of *A* blood ; | ,, *cix* 12
and my regret Becomes an *A* violet, | ,, *cxv* 19
For all an *A* morning, till the ear | *Lancelot and E.* 897
gustful *A* morn That puff'd | *Holy Grail* 14
Green prelude, *A* promise, glad new-year | *Lover's Tale i* 281
April (s) ('Twas *A* then), I came and sat | *Miller's D.* 59
And *A's* crescent glimmer'd cold, | ,, 107
balmier than half-opening buds Of *A*, | *Tithonus* 60
May or *A*, he forgot, The last of *A* | *The Brook* 151
Her maiden babe, a double *A* old, | *Princess* ii 110
To rain an *A* of ovation round Their statues, | ,, *vi* 66
From *A* on to *A* went, | *In Mem. xxii* 7
Make *A* of her tender eyes ; | ,, *xl* 8
That keenlier in sweet *A* wakes, | ,, *cxvi* 2
(For then was latter *A*) | *Com. of Arthur* 451
in *A* suddenly Breaks from a coppice | *Marr. of Geraint* 338
With *A* and the swallow. | *The Ring* 60
Apt supple, sinew-corded, *a* at arms ; | *Princess v* 535
a at arms and big of bone | *Marr. of Geraint* 489
A-raägin' (raging) fire was *a-r* an' raävin' | *Owd Roä* 110
Arab delicate *A* arch of her feet | *Maud I xvi* 15
Arâbi (Leader of Egyptian Revolt, 1882) And
Wolseley overthrew *A*, | *Pro. to Gen. Hamley* 31
Arabian nodding together In some *A* night ? | *Maud I vii* 12
I know not, your *A* sands ; | *To Ulysses* 35
plunge old Merlin in the *A* sea : | *Gareth and L.* 211
Arac (Prince) Not ev'n her brother *A*, | *Princess i* 153
rumour of Prince *A* hard at hand. | ,, *v* 112
speak with *A* : *A's* word is thrice | ,, 226
midmost and the highest Was *A* : | ,, 257
The genial giant, *A*, roll'd himself | ,, 274
but we will send to her,' Said *A*, | ,, 325
whereas I know Your prowess, *A*, | ,, 404
Down From those two bulks at *A's* side, | ,, 499
From *A's* arm, as from a giant's flail, | ,, 500
but *A* rode him down : | ,, 532
A, satiate with his victory. | ,, *vii* 90
Arbaces *A*, and Phenomenon, and the rest, | *The Brook* 162
Arbiter *See* **Apple-arbiter**
Arbitrate to-morrow, *a* the field ; | *Last Tournament* 104
,, 162
Arbitration Before his throne of *a* | ,, *Amphion* 85
Arbour They read in *a's* clipt and cut, | *Amphion* 85
Arbutus there ? yon *a* Totters. | *Lucretius* 184
Arc thro' a little *a* Of heaven, | *To J. S.* 26
Bear had wheel'd Thro' a great *a* | *Princess iv* 213
sine and *a*, spheroïd and azimuth, | ,, *vi* 256
Run out your measured *a's*, | *In Mem. cv* 27
bridge of single *a* Took at a leap ; | *Gareth and L.* 908
Arcady To many a flute of *A*. | *In Mem. xxiii* 24
Arch (s) (*See also* **Innocent-arch, Portal-arch**) Thro'
little crystal *a'es* low | *Arabian Nights* 49
shadow'd grots of *a'es* interlaced, | *Palace of Art* 51
Many an *a* high up did lift, | ,, 142
round and round, and whirl'd in an *a*, | *M. d'Arthur* 138
to three *a'es* of a bridge Crown'd | *Gardener's D.* 43
Yet all experience is an *a* wherethro' Gleams | *Ulysses* 19
we past an *a*, Whereon a woman-statue | *Princess i* 209
Or under *a'es* of the marble bridge | ,, *ii* 458
bloom profuse and cedar *a'es* Charm, | *Milton* 11
the delicate Arab *a* of her feet | *Maud I xvi* 15

Arch (s) (*continued*) round and round, and
whirl'd in an *a*, | *Pass. of Arthur* 306
Straining his eyes beneath an *a* of hand, | ,, 464
thro' the *a* Down those loud waters, | *Lover's Tale i* 58
Arch (verb) fires that *a* this dusky dot— | *Epilogue* 52
Archbishop *A*, Bishop, Priors, Canons, | *Sir J. Oldcastle* 159
Arched *See* **High-arched**
Arching (*See also* **Slow-arching**) now *a*
leaves her bare To breaths | *Prog. of Spring* 12
Architect You, the Patriot *A*, | *On Jub. Q. Victoria* 42
Archives of crimeful record all My mortal *a*. | *St. S. Stylites* 159
Archway Gleam thro' the Gothic *a* in the wall. | *Godiva* 64
so thou pass Beneath this *a*, | *Gareth and L.* 268
a shatter'd *a* plumed with fern ; | *Marr. of Geraint* 316
While I shelter'd in this *a* | *Locksley H., Sixty,* 259
Arctic would dare Hell-heat or *A* cold, | *Ancient Sage* 116
Arden (surname) (*See also* **Enoch, Enoch Arden**)
'You *A*, you ! nay,—sure he was a foot Higher | *Enoch Arden* 854
Eh, let me fetch 'em, *A*,' | ,, 871
Arden face again, My Rosalind
in this *A*— | *Sisters (E. and E.)* 119
'Are (hare) An' 'e niver not shot one *'a*, | *Village Wife* 42
Arês great God, *A*, burns in anger still | *Tiresias* 11
hail of *A* crash Along the sounding walls. | ,, 96
yesternight, To me, the great God *A*, | ,, 111
Argent The polish'd *a* of her breast | *D. of F. Women* 158
To yonder *a* round ; | *St. Agnes' Eve* 16
Argent-lidded Serene with *a-l* eyes Amorous, | *Arabian Nights* 135
Argive On *A* heights divinely sang, | *In Mem. xxiii* 22
Argosy argosies of magic sails, | *Locksley Hall* 121
Arguing A boundless forbearance :
seem As *a* love of knowledge and of power ; | *Aylmer's Field* 1
| *Princess ii* 57
Argument Half-buried in some weightier *a*, | *Lucretius* 9
A-rilin' thowt she was nobbut *a-r* ma then. | *Owd Roä* 74
Arimathæan Joseph *See* **Joseph**
A-ringing we heard them *a-r* the bell, | *First Quarrel* 21
Arise Scarce outward signs of joy *a*, | *Supp. Confessions* 49
Come forth, I charge thee, *a*, | *Ode to Memory* 46
I feel the tears of blood *a* | *Oriana* 77
Or when little airs *a*, | *Adeline* 33
Many suns *a* and set. | *Miller's D.* 205
A, and let us wander forth, | ,, 239
I will *a* and slay thee with my hands.' | *M. d'Arthur* 132
yearning for thy yoke, *a*, | *Tithonus* 40
mighty wind *a's*, roaring seaward, | *Locksley Hall* 194
Expecting when a fountain should *a* : | *Vision of Sin* 8
The thoughts that *a* in me. | *Break, break, etc.* 4
pillars of the hearth *A* to thee ; | *Princess vii* 217
'*A*, and get thee forth and seek | *In Mem. lxxxv* 79
A and fly The reeling Faun, | ,, *cxxviii* 25
Morning *a's* stormy and pale, | *Maud I vi* 1
And ah for a man to *a* in me, | ,, *x* 67
A, my God, and strike, for we hold | ,, *II i* 45
war would *a* in defence of the right, | *Maud III vi* 19
saw the dreary phantom *a* and fly | ,, 36
saying, '*A*, and help us thou ! | *Com. of Arthur* 44
A And quickly pass to Arthur's hall, | *Gareth and L.* 983
these from all his life *a*, and cry, | ,, 1131
Until my lord *a* and look upon me ?' | *Geraint and E.* 650
Till yonder man upon the bier *a*, | ,, 657
my dear lord *a* and bid me do it, | ,, 665
Until himself *a* a living man, | ,, 706
And by the great Queen's name, *a* | *Balin and Balan* 482
A, go forth and conquer as of old.' | *Pass. of Arthur* 64
I will *a* and slay thee with my hands.' | ,, 300
A in open prospect—heath and hill, | *Lover's Tale i* 397
A, my own true sister, come forth ! | *The Flight* 96
Arisen (*See also* **Half-arisen**) mountains have *a*
since With cities | *Merlin and V.* 675
Arising at Bible meetings, o'er the rest *A*, | *Sea Dreams* 195
from the floor, Tusklike, *a*, | *Balin and Balan* 316
horse, *A* wearily at a fallen oak, | ,, 425
goblet with a priceless wine *A*, | *Lover's Tale iv* 228
Ilion falling, Rome *a*, | *To Virgil* 3
Aristocrat what care I, *A*, democrat, autocrat— | *Maud I x* 65

Ark sought'st to wreck my mortal *a*,   *Two Voices* 389
I leave this mortal *a* behind,   *In Mem. xii* 6
Rich *a*'s with priceless bones   *Balin and Balan* 110

Arm (s) (*See also* **Airm, Hairm**) enormous polypi
Winnow with giant *a*'s   *The Kraken* 10
And with a sweeping of the *a*,   *A Character* 16
Of wrath her right *a* whirl'd,   *The Poet* 54
Sweet faces, rounded *a*'s,   *Sea Fairies* 3
Fold thine *a*'s, turn to thy rest.   *A Dirge* 3
right *a* debased The throne of Persia,   *Alexander* 1
A glowing *a*, a gleaming neck,   *Miller's D.* 78
When, *a* in *a*, we went along,   ,, 163
Round my true heart thine *a*'s entwine   ,, 216
The kiss, The woven *a*'s, seem   ,, 232
Puts forth an *a*, and creeps   *Œnone* 4
when I look'd, Paris had raised his *a*,   ,, 189
that my *a*'s Were wound about thee,   ,, 202
Sat smiling, babe in *a*.   *Palace of Art* 96
my *a* was lifted to hew down   *D. of F. Women* 45
humid *a*'s festooning tree to tree,   ,, 70
mailed Bacchus leapt into my *a*'s,   ,, 151
kneeling, with one *a* about her king,   ,, 270
He held a goose upon his *a*,   *The Goose* 5
He took the goose upon his *a*,   ,, 41
an *a* Rose up from out the bosom   *M. d'Arthur* 29
rose an *a* Clothed in white samite,   ,, 143
behold an *a*, Clothed in white samite,   ,, 158
with pain, reclining on his *a*,   ,, 168
One *a* aloft—Gown'd in pure white,   *Gardener's D.* 125
in the circle of his *a*'s Enwound us both ;   ,, 216
thrust him in the hollows of his *a*,   *Dora* 132
To Francis, with a basket on his *a*,   *Audley Court* 6
Sleep, Ellen, folded in thy sister's *a*,   ,, 63
sleeping, haply dream her *a* is mine.   ,, 64
'Sleep, Ellen, folded in Emilia's *a*,   ,, 65
in my weak, lean *a*'s I lift the cross,   *St. S. Stylites* 118
leg and *a* with love-knots gay,   *Talking Oak* 65
She sank her head upon her *a*   ,, 207
close and dark my *a*'s I spread,   ,, 225
I wither slowly in thine *a*'s,   *Tithonus* 6
Roll'd in one another's *a*'s,   *Locksley Hall* 58
Glows forth each softly-shadow'd *a*   *Day-Dm. Sleep. B.* 13
AND on her lover's *a* she leant,   ,, *Depart.* 1
Mute with folded *a*'s they waited—   *The Captain* 39
HER *a*'s across her breast she laid   *Beggar Maid* 1
We rush'd into each other's *a*'s   *The Letters* 40
laid the feeble infant in his *a*'s ;   *Enoch Arden* 152
strong *a*'s about his drooping wife,   ,, 228
babe, who rear'd his creasy *a*'s,   ,, 751
he rose, he spread his *a*'s abroad   ,, 912
grovelike, each huge *a* a tree,   *Aylmer's Field* 510
a's stretch'd as to grasp a flyer :   ,, 588
sideways up he swung his *a*'s,   *Sea Dreams* 24
waved my *a* to warn them off ;   ,, 132
raised your *a*, you tumbled down   ,, 141
soft *a*, which, like the pliant bough   ,, 290
roll thy tender *a*'s Round him,   *Lucretius* 82
her *a* lifted, eyes on fire,   *Princess, Pro.,* 41
long *a*'s and hands Reach'd out,   ,, *i* 28
lapt In the *a*'s of leisure,   ,, *ii* 168
holding out her lily *a*'s Took both his hands,   ,, 303
Herself and Lady Psyche the two *a*'s ;   ,, *iii* 35
then Oaring one *a*, and bearing in my left   ,, *iv* 183
drew My burthen from mine *a*'s ;   ,, 192
A Niobëan daughter, one *a* out,   ,, 371
She stretch'd her *a*'s and call'd   ,, 496
From Arac's *a*, as from a giant's flail,   ,, *v* 500
Ida stood With Psyche's babe in *a*:   ,, *vi* 31
on every side A thousand *a*'s,   ,, 37
glittering axe was broken in their *a*'s,   ,, 51
a's were shatter'd to the shoulder blade.   ,, 52
and with the babe yet in her *a*'s,   ,, 74
reach its fatling innocent *a*   ,, 138
in your own *a*'s To hold your own,   ,, 177
breast that fed or *a* that dandled you,   ,, 181

Arm (s) (*continued*) from mine *a*'s she rose Glowing   *Princess vii* 159
and Jenny hung on his *a*.   *Grandmother* 42
he turn'd and claspt me in his *a*'s,   ,, 55
So dear a life your *a*'s enfold   *The Daisy* 93
She cast his *a*'s about the child.   *The Victim* 32
He stay'd his *a*'s upon his knee: ,, 54
And moves his doubtful *a*'s, and feels   *In Mem. xiii* 3
When Science reaches forth her *a*'s   ,, *xxi* 18
Laid their dark *a*'s about the field. (repeat)   ,, *xcv* 16, 52
They mix in one another's *a*'s   *In Mem. cii* 23
That watch'd her on her nurse's *a*,   ,, *Con.* 46
To find the *a*'s of my true love   *Maud II iv* 3
So well thine *a* hath wrought for me to-day.'   *Com. of Arthur* 127
a's Stretch'd under all the cornice   *Gareth and L.* 218
with a kindly hand on Gareth's *a*   ,, 578
bears a skeleton figured on his *a*'s,   ,, 640
lifted either *a*, 'Fie on thee, King !   ,, 657
His *a*'s, the rosy raiment, and the star.   ,, 938
Sun Heaved up a ponderous *a*,   ,, 1045
writhed his wiry *a*'s Around him,   ,, 1150
Lifted an *a*. and softly whisper'd,   ,, 1361
a's on which the standing muscle sloped,   *Marr. of Geraint* 76
'O noble breast and all-puissant *a*'s,   ,, 86
Not to be folded more in these dear *a*'s,   ,, 99
Claspt the gray walls with hairy-fibred *a*'s,   ,, 323
Down by the length of lance and *a*   *Geraint and E.* 463
and she cast her *a*'s About him,   ,, 761
His *a* half rose to strike again, but fell :   *Balin and Balan* 223
If *a* of flesh could lay him.'   ,, 299
either lock'd in either's *a*.   ,, 632
woven paces and with waving *a*'s,   *Merlin and V.* 207
curved an *a* about his neck,   ,, 241
made her lithe *a* round his neck Tighten,   ,, 614
gentle wizard cast a shielding *a*.   ,, 908
rose, Her *a*'s upon her breast across,   ,, 910
sloping down to make *A*'s for his chair,   *Lancelot and E.* 438
battle-writhen *a*'s and mighty hands   ,, 812
innocently extending her white *a*'s,   ,, 932
armlet for the roundest *a* on earth,   ,, 1183
an *a* to which the Queen's Is haggard,   ,, 1226
Caught from his mother's *a*'s—   ,, 1405
often in her *a*'s She bare me,   ,, 1410
milky *a* Red-rent with hooks of bramble,   *Holy Grail* 210
she rose Opening her *a*'s to meet me,   ,, 395
Open'd his *a*'s to embrace me as he came,   ,, 417
every moment glanced His silver *a*'s   ,, 493
Hold her a wealthy bride within thine *a*'s,   ,, 621
in her white *a*'s Received,   *Last Tournament* 23
Why ye not wear on *a*, or neck, or zone   ,, 36
Right *a* of Arthur in the battlefield,   ,, 202
wert lying in thy new leman's *a*'s.'   ,, 625
For feel this *a* of mine—   ,, 690
milkwhite *a*'s and shadowy hair   *Guinevere* 416
while yet Sir Lancelot, my right *a*   ,, 429
Then she stretch'd out her *a*'s and cried   ,, 606
an *a* Rose up from out the bosom   *Pass. of Arthur* 197
rose an *a* Clothed in white samite,   ,, 311
behold an *a*, Clothed in white samite,   ,, 326
with pain, reclining on his *a*,   ,, 336
on one *a* The flaxen ringlets of our infancies   *Lover's Tale i* 233
Bent o'er me, and my neck his *a* upstay'd.   ,, 690
Love's *a*'s were wreath'd about the neck of Hope,   ,, 815
I wound my *a*'s About her :   ,, *ii* 200
softly put his *a* about her neck   ,, *iv* 71
Holding his golden burthen in his *a*'s,   ,, 89
To greet us, her young hero in her *a*'s !   ,, 171
bearing high in *a*'s the mightly babe,   ,, 295
bearing on one *a* the noble babe,   ,, 370
sisters closed in another's *a*'s,   *Sisters (E. and E.)* 155
'Emmie, you put out your *a*'s,   *In the Child. Hosp.* 56
It's the little girl with her *a*'s lying out   ,, 58
little *a*'s lying out on the counterpane ;   ,, 70
I spread mine *a*'s, God's work, I said,   *Sir J. Oldcastle* 136
As I lean'd away from his *a*'s—   *The Wreck* 102

Arm (s) (*continued*) 'Woman'—he graspt at my *a*—   *The Wreck* 120
Ah, clasp me in your *a's*, sister,   *The Flight* 5
O would I were in Edwin's *a's*—   ,, 45
I feel'd thy *a* es I stood   *Spinster's S's.* 26
Amy's *a's* about my neck—   *Locksley H., Sixty*, 13
'Mother!' and I was folded in thine *a's*,   *Demeter and P.* 22
here, my child, tho' folded in thine *a's*,   ,, 40
And dying rose, and rear'd her *a's*,   *The Ring* 222
happy had I died within thine *a's*,   *Death of Œnone* 31
and Rome was a babe in *a's*,   *The Dawn* 9
'O what an *a*,' said the king.   *The Tourney* 12
Arm (verb) to *a* in proof, and guard about   *Supp. Confessions* 65
Morning-star, approach, *A* me,'   *Gareth and L.* 925
'Approach and *a* me!'   ,, 1112
Arm-chair Her father left his good *a-c*,   *Talking Oak* 103
small goodman Shrinks in his *a-c*   *Princess v* 454
When asleep in this *a-c*?   *Maud I vii* 4
So I sits i' my oän *a-c*   *Spinster's S's.* 9
Arm'd (*See also* **All-arm'd, Full-arm'd, Plump-armed**)
one that *a* Her own fair head,   *Princess, Pro.*, 32
Sleep must lie down *a*, for the villainous   *Maud I i* 41
fair, strong, *a*—But to be won by force—   *Gareth and L.* 104
who alway rideth *a* in black,   ,, 636
These *a* him in blue arms, and gave   ,, 931
damsel came, And *a* him in old arms,   ,, 1115
wholly *a*, behind a rock In shadow,   *Geraint and E.* 57
horsemen waiting, wholly *a*,   ,, 121
And each of them is wholly *a*,   ,, 143
issuing *a* he found the host and cried,   ,, 407
he *a* himself and went,   *Balin and Balan* 22
There two stood *a*, and kept the door;   *Lancelot and E.* 1247
and we ride, *A* as ye see,   *Pelleas and E.* 65
knights *A* for a day of glory before the King.   *Last Tournament* 55
a by day and night Against the Turk;   *Montenegro* 3
Armlet *a* for the roundest arm on earth,   *Lancelot and E.* 1183
a for an arm to which the Queen's   ,, 1226
Armour And as he rode his *a* rung,   *L. of Shalott iii* 17
This mortal *a* that I wear,   *Sir Galahad* 70
His own forefathers' arms and *a* hung.   *Princess, Pro.*, 24
Your very *a* hallow'd, and your statues   ,, *v* 413
When *a* clash'd or jingled,   ,, *vi* 363
he had ask'd For horse and *a*:   *Gareth and L.* 474
so ye cleave His *a* off him,   ,, 1095
hew'd great pieces of his *a* off him,   ,, 1142
youth who scour'd His master's *a*;   *Marr. of Geraint* 258
slay him and will have his horse And *a*,   *Geraint and E.* 63
and possess your horse And *a*,   ,, 75
three gay suits of *a* which they wore,   ,, 95
bound the suits Of *a* on their horses,   ,, 97
Their three gay suits of *a*, each from each,   ,, 181
heap'd The pieces of his *a* in one place,   ,, 374
glimmer'd on his *a* in the room.   ,, 386
'Take Five horses and their *a's*;'   ,, 409
palfrey heart enough To bear his *a*?   ,, 490
Bled underneath his *a* secretly,   ,, 502
A light of *a* by him flash,   *Balin and Balan* 326
moved Among us in white *a*, Galahad.   *Holy Grail* 135
one that on me moved In golden *a*   ,, 410
horse In golden *a* jewell'd everywhere: ,, 412
In silver *a* suddenly Galahad shone   ,, 458
In silver-shining *a* starry-clear;   ,, 511
Wherefore now thy horse And *a*:   *Pelleas and E.* 355
Behold his horse and *a*.   ,, 373
he that hath His horse and *a*:   ,, 378
In blood-red *a* sallying,   *Last Tournament* 443
and all her *a* golden *a* on the grass,   *Tiresias* 45
Armour'd And *a* all in forest green,   *Last Tournament* 170
Armourer riding further past an *a's*, Who,   *Marr. of Geraint* 266
Whereat the *a* turning all amazed   ,, 283
Armoury from Jehovah's gorgeous *armouries*,   *Milton* 6
Arms (weapons) *a*, or *power of brain, or birth*   *To the Queen* 3
Those men thine *a* withstood,   *England and Amer.* 7
one might show it at a joust of *a*,   *M. d'Arthur* 102
broke a close with force and *a*:   *Edwin Morris* 131
His own forefathers' *a* and armour hung.   *Princess, Pro.*, 24

Arms (weapons) (*continued*) clash'd in *a*, By glimmering lanes   *Princess, Pro., v* 5
piled *a* and rough accoutrements,   ,, 55
horses yell'd; they clash'd their *a*;   ,, 250
two armies and the noise Of *a*;   ,, 346
none to trust Since our *a* fail'd—   ,, 427
supple, sinew-corded, apt at *a*;   ,, 535
whose *a* Champion'd our cause and won it   ,, *vi* 61
Roll of cannon and clash of *a*,   *Ode on Well.* 116
Arthur yet had done no deed of *a*,   *Com. of Arthur* 46
many of these in richer *a* than he,   ,, 52
Closed in her castle from the sound of *a*.   *Gareth and L.* 163
his *a* Clash'd; and the sound was good   ,, 311
A for her son, and loosed him from his vow.   ,, 530
Gareth ere he parted flash'd in *a*.   ,, 689
Mounted in *a*, threw up their caps   ,, 697
'Bound upon a quest With horse and *a*—   ,, 709
few goodlier than he) Shining in *a*,   ,, 745
These arm'd him in *a*,   ,, 931
strength of anger thro' mine *a*,   ,, 948
and take his horse And *a*,   ,, 956
Hath overthrown thy brother, and hath his *a*.'   ,, 1037
damsel came, And arm'd him in old *a*,   ,, 1115
His *a* are old, he trusts the harden'd skin—   ,, 1139
on a nightblack horse, in nightblack *a*,   ,, 1381
a On loan, or else for pledge;   *Marr. of Geraint* 219
a, *a*, *a* to fight my enemy?   ,, 282
A? truth! I know not: ,, 289
thought to find *A* in your town,   ,, 418
if ye know Where I can light on *a*,   ,, 422
heard me praise Your feats of *a*,   ,, 435
true heart,' replied Geraint, 'but *a*,   ,, 474
'*A*, indeed, but old And rusty,   ,, 477
Who being apt at *a* and big of bone   ,, 489
Yniol's rusted *a* Were on his princely person,   ,, 543
will not fight my way with gilded *a*,   *Geraint and E.* 21
Three horses and three goodly suits of *a*,   ,, 124
Two sets of three laden with jingling *a*,   ,, 188
take A horse and *a* for guerdon;   ,, 218
one with *a* to guard his head and yours,   ,, 427
paid with horses and with *a*;   ,, 486
loosed the fastenings of his *a*,   ,, 511
grow In use of *a* and manhood,   *Lancelot and E.* 64
while she watch'd their *a* far-off Sparkle,   ,, 395
earth shake, and a low thunder of *a*.   ,, 460
glittering in enamell'd *a* the maid   ,, 619
From noiseful *a*, and acts of prowess   *Holy Grail* 1
a Hack'd, and their foreheads grimed   ,, 264
Lend me thine horse and *a*,   *Pelleas and E.* 345
Pelleas lent his horse and all his *a*,   ,, 358
one might show it at a joust of *a*,   *Pass. of Arthur* 270
Gold, jewels, *a*, whatever it may be.   *Lover's Tale iv* 235
and shoutings and soundings to *a*,   *Def. of Lucknow* 76
The warrior hath forgot his *a*,   *Ancient Sage* 138
alarms Sounding 'To *a*! to *a*!'   *Prog. of Spring* 104
clatter of *a*, and voices, and men passing   *Bandit's Death* 24
Arms (ensigns armorial) His *a* were carven only;   *Gareth and L.* 412
but if twain His *a* were blazon'd also;   *Merlin and V.* 474
then was painting on it fancied *a*,   *Lancelot and E.* 17
guess'd a hidden meaning in his *a*,   ,,
quartering your own royal *a* of Spain,   *Columbus* 115
Arm's-length Paris held the costly fruit Out at *a-l*,   *Œnone* 136
Army crying there was an *a* in the land,   *Princess iv* 484
compassed by two *armies* and the noise   ,, *v* 345
Charging an *a*, while All the world   *Light Brigade* 30
To preach our poor little *a* down,   *Maud I x* 38
councils thinn'd, And *armies* waned,   *Merlin and V.* 573
Earls of the *a* of Anlaf Fell   *Batt. of Brunanburh* 53
nor had Anlaf With *armies* so broken   ,, 82
Her dauntless *a* scatter'd, and so small,   *The Fleet* 11
glorious annals of *a* and fleet,   *Vastness* 7
Arno unfamiliar *A*, and the dome   *The Brook* 189
Arnon from Aroer On *A* unto Minneth.'   *D. of F. Women* 239
Aroer from *A* On Arnon unto Minneth.'   ,, 238
Aromat from the blessed land of *A*—   *Holy Grail* 48

Arose *a*, and I releas'd The casement,	*Two Voices* 403
a wind *a*, And overhead the wandering ivy	*Œnone* 98
THE rain had fallen, the Poet *a*,	*Poet's Song* 1
and *a* Eager to bring them down,	*Enoch Arden* 871
not to die a listener, I *a*,	*The Brook* 163
a the labourers' homes,	*Aylmer's Field* 147
footstool from before him, and *a*;	" 327
wind *a* and rush'd upon the South,	*Princess* i 97
a Once more thro' all her height,	" vi 159
That afternoon a sound *a* of hoof And chariot,	" 379
Star after star, *a* and fell;	" vii 50
on one side *a* The women up in wild revolt,	" 122
Then thorpe and byre *a* in fire,	*The Victim* 3
Thro' four sweet years *a* and fell,	*In Mem.*, *xxii* 3
Since our first Sun *a* and set.	" *xxiv* 8
Till at the last *a* the man;	" *cxxviii* 12
till I could bear it no more, But *a*,	*Maud I iii* 10
Nor ever *a* from below,	" *II ii* 36
on the further side A *a* silk pavilion,	*Gareth and L.* 910
a, and raised Her mother too,	*Marr. of Geraint* 535
in their halls *a* The cry of children,	*Geraint and E.* 964
damsel bidden *a* And stood with folded hands	*Merlin and V.* 68
with smiling face *a*,	*Lancelot and E.* 552
and all the knights *a*, And staring	*Holy Grail* 192
King *a* and went To smoke the	" 213
words of Arthur flying shriek'd, *a*,	*Last Tournament* 139
She clear'd her sight, she *a*,	*Dead Prophet* 31
call'd *a*, and, slowly plunging down	*St. Telemachus* 28
from the ruin *a* The shriek and curse	*Akbar's Dream* 189
Aroused So sleeping, so *a* from sleep	*Day-Dm., L'Envoi* 21
A the black republic on his elms,	*Aylmer's Field* 529
a Lancelot, who rushing outward	*Guinevere* 106
Arrange Dispute the claims, *a* the chances;	*To F. D. Maurice* 31
A the board and brim the glass;	*In Mem., cvii* 16
Arranged *a* Her garden, sow'd her name	*Aylmer's Field* 87
men and maids *A* a country dance,	*Princess, Pro.*, 84
A the favour, and assumed the Prince.	" *iv* 602
Arras (adj.) In Arthur's *a* hall at Camelot:	*Merlin and V.* 250
Arras (s) hung with *a* green and blue,	*Palace of Art* 61
Array (s) Singing of men that in battle *a*,	*Maud I v* 8
Array'd *a* with her own white hands A	*Marr. of Geraint* 17
took them, and *a* herself therein,	" 139
took it, and *a* herself therein.	" 849
there the Queen *a* me like the sun:	*Geraint and E.* 701
Arraying morn by morn, *a* her sweet self	*Lancelot and E.* 906
Arrival will harangue The fresh *a's* of the week	*Princess* ii 96
Arrive *A* at last the blessed goal,	*In Mem. lxxxiv* 41
Arrived *A* and found the sun of sweet content	*The Brook* 168
a, by Dubric the high saint,	*Com. of Arthur* 453
Arriving *A* all confused among the rest	*Princess iv* 224
A at a time of golden rest,	*Merlin and V.* 142
Arrogance They said with such heretical *a*	*Sir J. Oldcastle* 15
Arrow viewless *a's* of his thoughts were headed	*The Poet* 11
The bitter *a* went aside,	*Oriana* 37
The false, false *a* went aside,	" 39
The damned *a* glanced aside,	" 41
Within thy heart my *a* lies,	" 80
shoot into the dark *A's* of lightnings.	*To J. M. K.* 14
A random *a* from the brain.	*Two Voices* 345
look'd a flight of fairy *a's* aim'd	*Aylmer's Field* 94
Fly twanging headless *a's* at the hearts,	*Princess ii* 402
When one would aim an *a* fair,	*In Mem. lxxxvii* 25
Or into silver *a's* break The sailing	" *ci* 15
Before an ever-fancied *a*, made	*Geraint and E.* 531
a whizz'd to the right, one to the left,	*Balin and Balan* 419
lest an *a* from the bush Should leave me	*Last Tournament* 535
jingle of bits, Shouts, *a's*,	*Tiresias* 94
Struck by a poison'd *a* in the fight,	*Death of Œnone* 26
Arrowing *a* light from clime to clime,	*Akbar's D. Hymn* 5
Arrowlet blows a globe of after *a's*,	*Gareth and L.* 1029
Arrow-seed like the *a-s's* of the field flower,	*The Poet* 19
Arrow-slain With loss of half his people *a-s*;	*Merlin and V.* 565
Arrow-wounded your *a-w* fawn Came flying	*Princess ii* 270
Arsenic *A*, *a*, sure, would do it,	*Maud II v* 62
Art discovery And newness of thine *a* so pleased	*Ode to Memory* 88
Art (*continued*) knowledge of his *a* Held me	*D. of F. Women* 9
words, tho' cull'd with choicest *a*,	" 285
I and he, Brothers in *A*;	*Gardener's D.* 4
'will you climb the top of *A*.	" 169
liberal applications lie In *A* like Nature,	*Day-Dm. Moral* 14
Her *a*, her hand, her counsel	*Aylmer's Field* 151
Hetairai, curious in their *a*,	*Lucretius* 52
At wine, in clubs, of *a*, of politics;	*Princess, Pro.*, 161
in *a's* of government Elizabeth and others; *a's* of war The peasant Joan and others; *a's* of grace Sappho and others	" *ii* 161
with inmost terms Of *a* and science:	" 447
Two great statues, *A* And Science,	" *iv* 200
Science, *A*, and Labour have outpour'd	*Ode Inter. Exhib.* 1
shapes and hues of *A* divine!	" 22
piece of inmost Horticultural *a*,	*Hendecasyllabics* 20
And owning but a little *a*	*In Mem. xxxvii* 1
From *a*, from nature, from the schools,	" *xlix* 1
on mind and *a*, And labour,	" *lxxxvii* 22
The graceful tact, the Christian *a*;	" *cx* 16
That all, as in some piece of *a*,	" *cxxviii* 14
letters, dear to Science, dear to *A*,	*Ded. of Idylls* 40
served King Uther thro' his magic *a*;	*Com. of Arthur* 152
Knowing all *a's*, had touch'd,	*Gareth and L.* 307
knew the range of all their *a's*,	*Merlin and V.* 167
since ye seem the Master of all *A*,	" 468
Or *A* with poisonous honey stol'n from France,	*To the Queen ii* 56
Heirlooms, and ancient miracles of *A*,	*Lover's Tale iv* 192
Repell'd by the magnet of *A*.	*The Wreck* 22
with the living hues of *A*.	*Locksley H., Sixty,* 140
A and Grace are less and less:	" 245
And here the Singer for his *A*	*Epilogue* 79
You see your *A* still shrined in	*Poets and their B.* 11
a nation purer through their *a*,	*To W. C. Macready* 8
the fault is less In me than *A*.	*Romney's R.* 9
A! Why should I so disrelish	" 10
seem'd my lodestar in the Heaven of *A*,	" 39
Of ancient *A* in Paris, or in Rome.	" 87
This *A*, that harlot-like	" 115
I replied 'Nay, Lord, for *A*,'	" 131
'Art (heart) as 'appy as '*a* could think,	*North. Cobbler* 15
Artemisia (Carian) *See* **Carian Artemisia**	
Arthur (Epic poem) 'he burnt His epic, his King *A*,	*The Epic* 28
Arthur (King) Until King *A's* table, man by man,	*M. d'Arthur* 3
fallen in Lyonnesse about their Lord, King *A*:	" 5
spake King *A* to Sir Bedivere: (repeat)	" 13, 66
replied King *A*, faint and pale:	" 72
'King *A's* sword, Excalibur,	" 103
spoke King *A*, breathing heavily:	" 113
replied King *A*, much in wrath:	" 118
Then spoke King *A*, drawing thicker breath:	" 148
answer made King *A*, breathing hard:	" 162
as he walk'd, King *A* panted hard,	" 176
murmur'd *A*, 'Place me in the barge,'	" 204
like that *A* who, with lance in rest,	" 222
my Lord *A*, whither shall I go?	" 227
slowly answer'd *A* from the barge:	" 239
sail with *A* under looming shores,	" *Ep.* 17
King *A*, like a modern gentleman	" 22
cried '*A* is come again: he cannot die.'	" 24
For many a petty king ere *A* came	*Com. of Arthur* 5
man was less and less, till *A* came.	" 12
after this King *A* for a space,	" 16
for he heard of *A* newly crown'd,	" 41
A yet had done no deed of arms,	" 46
A, looking downward as he past,	" 55
A, passing thence to battle,	" 75
When *A* reach'd a field-of-battle	" 96
till by main might, And mightier	" 109
A call'd to stay the brands	" 120
in the heart of *A* joy was lord.	" 124
A said, 'Man's word is God in man:	" 133
'Knowest thou aught of *A's* birth?'	" 147
learn the secret of our *A's* birth?'	" 159
By this King *A* as by thee to-day,	" 162

B

A-singin' Theer wur a lark *a-s* 'is best — *North. Cobbler* 46
Ask *A* the sea At midnight, — *Supp. Confessions* 125
  When I *a* her if she love me, — *Lilian* 3
  A's what thou lackest, — *Two Voices* 98
  a thou not my name: — *D. of F. Women* 93
  You *a* me, why, tho' ill at ease, — *You ask me, why,* 1
  he has a mint of reasons: *a.* — *The Epic* 33
  'Annie, I came to *a* a favour of you.' — *Enoch Arden* 285
  " 313
  what is it that you *a?*' — " 427
  O then to *a* of my shares, — *Sea Dreams* 115
  That Sheba came to *a* of Solomon.' — *Princess ii* 346
  you should answer, *we* would *a)* — " 353
  'O *a* me nothing,' I said: — " *iii* 59
  a for him Of your great head— — " *vi* 313
  A me no more: (repeat) — *Princess vii* 1, 5, 6, 9, 10, 11, 15
  would but *a* you to fulfil yourself : — *Princess vii* 146
  I *a* you nothing : only, if a dream, — " 148
  A her to marry me by and by ? — *Window', Letter* 6
  And *a* a thousand things of home ; — *In Mem. xiv* 12
  Let no one *a* me how it came to pass; — *Maud I xviii* 49
  If one should *a* me whether The habit, — " *xx* 17
  I will not *a* thee why — " *II iii* 2
  Or if I *a* thee why, — " 6
  Or to a her, 'Take me, sweet, — " *iv* 87
  Before thou *a* the King to make thee knight, — *Gareth and L.* 145
  and loathe to *a* thee aught. — " 356
  I scarce can *a* it thee for hate, — " 361
  or thyself be mad, I *a* not: — " 877
  'So this damsel *a* it of me Good— — " 974
  'I charge thee, *a* not, but obey.' — *Marr. of Geraint* 133
  'Then will I *a* it of himself, — " 197
  I swear I will not *a* your meaning in it: — *Geraint and E.* 743
  I am silent then, And *a* no kiss : — *Merlin and V.* 254
  a your boon, for boon I owe you — " 306
  wherefore *a* ; And take this boon — " 309
  will ye never *a* some other boon? — " 375
  Who feels no heart to *a* another boon. — " 382
  has tript a little : *a* thyself. — " 602
  never could undo it : *a* no more : — " 686
  I *a* you, is it clamour'd by the child, — " 771
  a me not Hereafter ye shall know me— — *Lancelot and E.* 191
  a you not to see the shield he left, — " 653
  should *a* some goodly gift of him — " 912
  '*A* me not, for I may not speak of it: — *Holy Grail* 758
  yield me sanctuary, nor *a* Her name — *Guinevere* 141
  and they spared To *a* it. — " 145
  pray you check me if I *a* amiss— — " 324
  Ye *a* me, friends, When I began to love. — *Lover's Tale i* 144
  Ye know not what ye *a.* — " 150
  I'*a* you now, should this first master — " *iv* 265
  let me *a* you then, Which voice — *Sisters (E. and E.)* 181
  Edith wrote: 'My mother bids me *a*' — " 181
  Did *he* believe it? did you *a* him? — *The Ring* 225
  a 'Why left you wife and children ?' — *Romney's R.* 128

Ask'd (*See also* **Hax'd**) for I *a* him, and he said, — *Dora* 145
  once I *a* him of his early life, — *Edwin Morris* 23
  I *a* him half-sardonically. — " 59
  she knew it not, And would if *a* deny it. — *Enoch Arden* 44
  till I *a* If James were coming. — *The Brook* 105
  To learn the price and what the price he *a,* — " 142
  a her 'Are you from the farm ?' — " 209
  wonder'd at her strength, and *a* her of it: — *Sea Dreams* 113
  And *a* ; but not a word ; — " 116
  and *a* That which I *a* the woman — " 146
  her we *a* of that and this, — *Princess i* 231
  and when I *a* her 'how,' — " *iii* 29
  'Tell us,' Florian *a,* 'How grew this feud — " 76
  mutual pardon *a* and given — " *v* 46
  a but space and fairplay for her scheme ; — " 282
  Ay or no, if *a* to her face ? — *Window, Letter* 9
  again The 'wilt thou' *a,* — *In Mem. Con.* 55
  whatever is *a* her, answers 'Death.' — *Maud I i* 4
  therefore Arthur's sister ?' *a* the King. — *Com. of Arthur* 317
  a him if these things were truth— — " 398

Ask'd (*continued*) *A* me to tilt with him, — *Gareth and L.* 27
  he had *a* For horse and armour : — " 473
  I *a* for thy chief knight, — " 658
  bound to thee for any favour *a* !' — " 977
  a it of him, Who answer'd as before ; — *Marr. of Geraint* 204
  after madness acted question *a* : — *Geraint and E.* 813
  a her not a word, But went apart — " 880
  Arthur seeing *a* 'Tell me your names ; — *Balin and Balan* 49
  Balin was bold, and *a* To bear — " 199
  at feast Sir Galon likewise *a* — " 347
  a this very boon, Now *a* again: — *Merlin and V.* 323
  died Thrice than have *a* it once— — " 919
  proof of trust—so often *a* in vain ! — " 920
  they *a* of court and Table Round, — *Lancelot and E.* 268
  when he *a* 'Is it for Lancelot. — " 1104
  and eyes that *a* 'What is it?' — " 1249
  a us, knight by knight, if any Had seen it, — *Holy Grail* 283
  'O brother,' *a* Ambrosius,—'for in sooth — " 540
  then he *a,* 'Where is he ? — " 638
  scarce had pray'd or *a* it for myself— — " 691
  sharply turning, *a* Of Gawain. — " 739
  Lancelot,' *a* the King, 'my friend, — " 764
  'Dead, is it so?' she *a.* 'Ay, ay,' said he, — *Pelleas and E.* 384
  'Have ye fought?' She *a* of Lancelot. — " 593
  a, 'Why skipt ye not, Sir Fool ?' — *Last Tournament* 256
  she *a,* I know not what, and *a,* — *Lover's Tale i* 706
  and *a* If I would see her burial : — " *ii* 70
  in his fantasy, I never *a* : — " *iv* 13
  she rais'd an eye that *a* 'Where ?' — " 94
  then he suddenly *a* her if she were. — " 328
  once my prattling Edith *a* him 'why ?' — *Sisters (E. and E.)* 58
  'Anything ailing,' I *a,* 'with baby ?' — *The Wreck* 61
  a the waves that moan about the world — *Demeter and P.* 64
  and I *a* About my Mother, — *The Ring* 102
  'Why weird ?' I *a* him, — " 197
  Had *a* us to their marriage, — " 430
  paused—and then *a* Falteringly, — *Death of Œnone* 94
  a 'Is earth On fire to the West ? — *St. Telemachus* 18
  of the nations' *a* his Chronicler Of Akbar — *Akbar's Dream* 1
  her name ? what was it ? I *a* her. — *Charity* 35
Askew all his conscience and one eye *a*'—(repeat) — *Sea Dreams* 180, 184
Asking (*See also* **Haxin'**) grant mine *a* with a smile, — *Tithonus* 16
  Nor *a* overmuch and taking less, — *Enoch Arden* 252
  a, one Not fit to cope your quest. — *Gareth and L.* 1173
  therefore at thine *a,* thine. — *Marr. of Geraint* 479
  not so strange as my long *a* it, — *Merlin and V.* 312
  braved a riotous heart in *a* for it. — *Lancelot and E.* 359
  a him, 'What said the King ? — *Holy Grail* 203
  a whence Had Arthur right to bind — *Last Tournament* 683
  Arundel *a* me To worship Holy Cross ! — *Sir J. Oldcastle* 135
A-sleeäpin' (sleeping) cat wur *a-s* alongside Roäver, — *Owd Roä* 33
Asleep (*See also* **Deep-asleep, Half-asleep, Warm-asleep**)
  smiling *a,* Slowly awaken'd, — *Eleänore* 84
  but I fall *a* at morn ; — *May Queen, N. Y's. E.* 50
  Falling *a* in a half-dream ! — *Lotos-Eaters, C.S.* 56
  Since that dear soul hath fall'n *a.* — *To J. S.* 34
  To fall *a* with all one's friends ; — *Day-Dm., L'Envoi* 4
  If e'er when faith had fall'n *a,* — *In Mem. cxxiv* 9
  When *a* in this arm-chair ? — *Maud I vii* 4
  But come to her waking, find her *a,* — " *II ii* 81
  himself alone And all the world *a,* — *Com. of Arthur* 119
  vext his day, but blesses him *a*— — *Gareth and L.* 1286
  half *a* she made comparison — *Marr. of Geraint* 651
  fell *a* again ; And dreamt herself — " 653
  He fell *a,* and Enid had no heart — *Geraint and E.* 369
  not seem as dead, But fast *a,* — *Lancelot and E.* 1161
  when they fall *a* Into delicious dreams, — *Lover's Tale i* 161
  First falls *a* in swoon, wherefrom awaked, — " 791
  I have done it, while you were *a*— — *'Rizpah* 19
  we believed her *a* again— — *In the Child. Hosp.* 69
  ere the dotard fall *a* ? — *Locksley H., Sixty,* 153
  fall of water lull'd the noon *a.* — *Romney's R.* 83
  But such a tide as moving seems *a,* — *Crossing the Bar* 5
A-smilin' An' Squire wur hallus *a-s,* — *Village Wife* 33
Asmodeus Abaddon and *A* caught at me. — *St. S. Stylites* 172

Aspasia　not for all *A's* cleverness,　　*Princess ii* 344
Aspect　Of pensive thought and *a* pale,　　*Margaret* 6
　　More bounteous *a's* on me beam,　　*Sir Galahad* 21
　　Under the selfsame *a* of the stars,　　*Lover's Tale i* 199
Aspen　(*See also* **Aspen-tree**) Willows whiten, *a's* quiver,　　*L. of Shalott i* 10
　　And here thine *a* shiver ;　　*A Farewell* 10
Aspen-tree　in the meadows tremulous *a-t's*　　*Lancelot and E.* 410
　　showers, And ever-tremulous *a-t's*,　　,, 524
Asphodel　Violet, amaracus, and *a*,　　*Œnone* 97
　　weary limbs at last on beds of *a*.　　*Lotos-Eaters, C. S.* 125
　　Along the silent field of *A*.　　*Demeter and P.* 153
Aspick　Showing the *a's* bite.)　　*D. of F. Women* 160
A-squeälin'　an' *a-s*, as if tha was bit,　　*Owd Roä* 89
　　and thou was *a-s'* thysen,　　,, 107
Ass (**an animal**)　whisper'd ' *A'es* ears,' among the sedge,　　*Princess ii* 113
　　one of thy long *a'es* ears,　　*Last Tournament* 273
　　swine, goats, *a'es*, rams and geese　　,, 321
　　' Then were swine, goats, *a'es*, geese　　,, 325
Ass (**a stupid fellow**)　Sam, thou's an *a* for thy paaïns :　*N. Farmer, N.S.* 3
　　we boäth on us thinks tha an *a*. (repeat)　　,, 12, 38
　　an *a* as near as mays nowt—　　,, 39
Assail　To *a* this gray preëminence of man !　　*Princess iii* 234
Assail'd　brother king, Urien, *A* him :　　*Com. of Arthur* 36
　　They that *a*, and they that held　　*Lancelot and E.* 455
Assassin　earls, and caitiff knights, *A's*,　　*Marr. of Geraint* 36
　　Sanctuary granted To bandit, thief, *a*—　　*Sir J. Oldcastle* 113
Assault　Sharp is the fire of *a*,　　*Def. of Lucknow* 57
　　Ever the mine and *a*, our sallies,　　,, 75
Assay　' I shall *a*,' said Gareth　　*Gareth and L.* 783
　　A it on some one of the Table Round,　　*Merlin and V.* 689
Assaye　Against the myriads of *A*　　*Ode on Well.* 99
Assemble　plans, And phantom hopes *a* ;　　*Will Water.* 30
Assembled　Narrowing in to where they sat *a*　　*Vision of Sin* 16
Assent　I gave *a* : Yet how to bind　　*Princess, Con.* 7
Assented　Enoch all at once *a* to it,　　*Enoch Arden* 126
Assert　*a* None lordlier than themselves　　*Princess ii* 143
　　a's his claim In that dread sound　　*Ode on Well.* 70
Assign'd　purpose of God, and the doom *a*.　　*Maud III vi* 59
　　quest *A* to her not worthy of it,　　*Lancelot and E.* 825
　　kiss the child That does the task *a*,　　,, 829
Assize　*See* **'Soize**
Association　A fresh *a* blow,　　*In Mem. ci* 18
Assoil'd　And the Holy man he *a* us,　　*V. of Maeldune* 126
Assume　law The growing world *a*,　　*England and Amer.* 17
　　lose the child, *a* The woman :　　*Princess i* 137
Assumed　Arranged the favour, and *a* the Prince.　　,, *iv* 602
　　A from thence a half-consent　　,, *vii* 82
　　A that she had thank'd him,　　*Geraint and E.* 646
Assuming　*See* **All-assuming**
Assumption　heart In its *a's* up to heaven ;　　*In Mem. lxiii* 4
　　quench'd herself In that *a* of the bridesmaid—　*Sisters (E. and E.)* 234
Assurance　*A* only breeds resolve.'　　*Two Voices* 315
Assure　may now *a* you mine ;　　*Merlin and V.* 549
Assured　*See* **Half-assured**
Assyrian　oil'd and curl'd *A* Bull Smelling of musk　　*Maud I vi* 44
　　A kings would flay Captives　　*Locksley H., Sixty,* 79
A-stanning (**standing**)　'What's i' tha bottle *a's* theer ?'　*North. Cobbler* 7
A-steppin'　yon laädy *a-s* along the streeät,　　,, 107
Astolat　(*See also* **Lord of Astolat, Maid of Astolat**)
　　Elaine, the lily maid of *A*,　　*Lancelot and E.* 2
　　Ran to the Castle of *A*,　　,, 167
　　And issuing found the Lord of *A*　　,, 173
　　then the Lord of *A* : 'Whence comest thou,　　,, 180
　　said the Lord of *A*, 'Here is Torre's :　　,, 195
　　And came at last, tho' late, to *A* :　　,, 618
　　came The Lord of *A* out, to whom the Prince　　,, 627
　　the Lord of *A*, 'Bide with us,　　,, 632
　　About the maid of *A*, and her love.　　,, 723
　　'The maid of *A* loves Sir Lancelot,　　,, 725
　　Sir Lancelot loves the maid of *A*.'　　,, 726
　　But far away the maid in *A*,　　,, 745
　　To *A* returning rode the three.　　,, 905
　　Then spake the lily maid of *A* :　　,, 1085
　　So that day there was dole in *A*.　　,, 1136
　　the lily maid of *A* Lay smiling,　　,, 1242

Astolat (*continued*)　I, sometime call'd the maid of *A*,　*Lancelot and E.* 1273
Astride　men and boys *a* On wyvern,　　*Holy Grail* 349
A-stroäkin' (**stroking**)　as I be *a-s* o' you,　　*Spinster's S's.* 19
Astræan　second-sight of some *A* age,　　*Princess ii* 443
Astrology　brought to understand *A* sad *a*,　　*Maud I xviii* 36
Astronomy　their cosmogonies, their *astronomies* :　　*Columbus* 42
　　Dead the new *a* calls her . . .　　*Locksley H., Sixty,* 175
　　A and Geology, terrible Muses !　　*Parnassus* 16
Asunder　each as each, Not to be pluck'd *a* ;　　*Holy Grail* 777
　　They might be pluck'd *a*.　　,, 780
　　save they could be pluck'd *a*,　　,, 782
　　To tear the twain *a* in my heart,　　,, 786
　　As if 'twere drawn *a* by the rack.　　*Lover's Tale ii* 57
　　shook us *a*, as if she had struck　　*The Wreck* 108
'At (**hat**)　doesn not touch thy '*a* to the Squire ;'　　*North. Cobbler* 25
　　says Parson, and laäys down 'is '*a*,　　,, 89
A-taäkin' (**taking**)　what a's doing *a-t* o' meä ?　　*N. Farmer, O.S.* 45
A-talkin'　Me an' thy muther, Sammy, 'as　　,, *N.S.* 9
　　beän *a-t* o' thee ;　　,, 9
Atar　infuse Rich *a* in the bosom of the rose,　　*Lover's Tale i* 270
Ate　*A* with young lads his portion　　*Gareth and L.* 480
　　Sat down beside him, *a* and then began.　　,, 872
　　Sir Gareth drank and *a*, and all his life　　,, 1280
　　let the horses graze, and *a* themselves.　　*Geraint and E.* 211
　　Geraint *A* all the mowers' victual　　,, 215
　　I never *a* with angrier appetite　　,, 233
　　a with tumult in the naked hall,　　,, 605
　　That ever among ladies *a* in hall,　　*Lancelot and E.* 255
　　drank the brook, and *a* The goodly apples,　　*Holy Grail* 387
　　our solemn feast—we *a* and drank,　　*Lover's Tale iv* 221
Atheist　Authors—essayist, *a*,　　*Locksley H., Sixty,* 139
　　On whom the women shrieking ' *A*'　　*Akbar's Dream* 91
Atheling　(*See also* **Edmund Atheling**)　Also the
　　brethren, King and *A*　　*Batt. of Brunanburh* 100
Athelstan (**King of England**)　*A* King, Lord
　　among Earls,　　,, 1
Athene (**Pallas**)　*See* **Pallas, Pallas Athene**
Athens　when *A* reign'd and Rome,　　*Freedom* 9
Athlete　Until she be an *a* bold,　　*Clear-headed friend* 21
　　an *a*, strong to break or bind　　*Palace of Art* 153
Athos　Tomohrit, *A*, all things fair,　　*To E. L.* 5
Atlantic　waste *A* roll'd On her and us　　*Third of Feb.* 21
　　I wish they were a whole *A* broad.'　　*Princess, Con.* 71
　　same bones back thro' the *A* sea,　　*Columbus* 214
Atmosphere　Floating thro' an evening *a*,　　*Eleänore* 100
　　For love possess'd the *a*,　　*Miller's D.* 91
　　Cold in that *a* of Death,　　*In Mem. xx* 14
Atom　If all be *a's*, how then should the Gods　　*Lucretius* 114
　　Vanishing, *a* and void, *a* and void,　　,, 258
　　Boundless inward, in the *a*,　　*Locksley H., Sixty,* 212
Atomic　Being *a* not be dissoluble,　　*Lucretius* 115
Atom-stream　I saw the flaring *a-s's* And torrents　　,, 38
Atomy　Crowded with driving *atomies*,　　*Lover's Tale ii* 174
Atonement　morning shine So rich in *a* as this　　*Maud I xix* 6
Attach　phantasm of the form It should *a* to ?　　*Lover's Tale i* 647
Attain　*A* the wise indifference of the wise ;　　*A Dedication* 8
Attain'd　(*See also* **Half-attained**)　have *a* Rest in a happy place　*Œnone* 130
Attempt　Vivien should *a* the blameless King.　　*Merlin and V.* 164
Attend　each ear was prick'd to *a* A tempest,　　*Princess vi* 280
　　And in his presence I *a* To hear　　*In Mem. cxxvi* 2
Attendance　And make her dance *a* ;　　*Amphion* 62
　　You come with no *a*, page or maid,　　*Geraint and E.* 322
Attended　So she goes by him *a*,　　*L. of Burleigh* 25
Attest　*A* their great commander's claim　　*Ode on Well.* 148
Attic　And round the *a's* rumbled,　　*The Goose* 46
　　single sordid *a* holds the living and the dead.　*Locksley H., Sixty,* 222
Attire　She in her poor *a* was seen :　　*Beggar Maid* 10
　　So splendid in his acts and his *a*,　　*Marr. of Geraint* 620
Attired　women who *a* her head,　　,, 62
　　than Geraint to greet her thus *a* ;　　,, 772
Attorney　*See* **'Turney**
Attracted　*a*, won, Married, made one with,　　*Lover's Tale i* 133
Attribute　all the gentle *a's* Of his lost child,　　*Aylmer's Field* 730
　　Or, crown'd with *a's* of woe　　*In Mem. cxviii* 18
A-tuggin'　Roäver *a-t* an' teärin' my slieäve.　　*Owd Roä* 60

Awaked (*See also* **Half-awaked**) myself have *a*, as it seems,   *Maud III vi* 56
falls asleep in swoon, wherefrom *a*,   *Lover's Tale i* 791
Awaken if the King *a* from his craze,   *Gareth and L.* 724
Awaken'd (*See also* **Half-awaken'd**) Slowly *a*, grow so full and deep   *Eleänore* 85
Awaking *A* knew the sword, and turn'd   *Pelleas and E.* 489
A-walkin' murnin' when we was *a-w* togither,   *Spinster's S's.* 23
Award would seem to *a* it thine,   *Œnone* 73
Aware After a lingering,—ere she was *a*,—   *Enoch Arden* 268
Enid was *a* of three tall knights   *Geraint and E.* 56
she by tact of love was well *a*   *Lancelot and E.* 984
Awe springs of life, the depths of *a*,   *Two Voices* 140
shall hold a fretful realm in *a*,   *Locksley Hall* 129
heart beat thick with passion and with *a*;   *Princess iii* 190
To feel once more, in placid *a*,   *In Mem. cxxii* 5
but all in *a*, For twenty strokes   *Lancelot and E.* 719
he wellnigh kiss'd her feet For loyal *a*,   ,, 1173
tenderness of manner, and chaste *a*,   *Pelleas and E.* 110
with the excess of sweetness and of *a*,   *Lover s Tale ii* 155
Awearied For I was much *a* of the Quest: *Holy Grail* 744
Aweary She said, 'I am *a, a*, (repeat)   *Mariana* 11, 23, 35, 47, 59, 71
She wept, 'I am *a, a*,   *Mariana* 83
And I am all *a* of my life.   *Œnone* 33
Awed *a* and promise-bounden she forbore,   *Enoch Arden* 869
Still It *a* me.'   *Sea Dreams* 205
And my dream *a* me:—well—   ,, 247
eyes *A* even me at first, thy mother—   *Demeter and P.* 24
Awe-stricken hold *A-s* breaths at a work divine,   *Maud I x* 17
Awful But all she is and does is *a*;   *Princess i* 140
Awl *See* **Hawl**
Awning ample *a's* gay Betwixt the pillars,   *Princess ii* 25
A blood-red *a* waver overhead,   *St. Telemachus* 52
Awoke And last with these the king *a*,   *Day-Dm. Revival* 17
night-light flickering in my eyes *A* me.'   *Sea Dreams* 104
desire that *a* in the heart of the child,   *Maud I xix* 48
Leodogran *a*, and sent Ulfius,   *Com. of Arthur* 444
these *a* him, and by great mischance   *Marr. of Geraint* 112
Refused her to him, then his pride *a*;   ,, 448
strongly striking out her limbs *a*;   *Geraint and E.* 380
every evil deed I ever did, *A*   *Holy Grail* 374
mantle clung, And pettish cries *a*,   *Last Tournament* 214
owl-whoop and dorhawk-whirr *A* me not,   *Lover's Tale ii* 117
Awry wherefore do we grow *a* From roots   *Supp. Confessions* 77
To woman, superstition all *a*:   *Princess ii* 137
Stampt into dust—tremulous, all *a*,   *Romney's R.* 113
Axe (*See also* **Battle-axe**) ere the falling *a* did part   *Margaret* 38
see the woodman lift His *a* to slay my kin.   *Talking Oak* 236
Nor wielded *a* disjoint,   ,, 262
hammer and *a*, Auger and saw,   *Enoch Arden* 173
The woodmen with their *a's*:   *Princess vi* 44
glittering *a* was broken in their arms,   ,, 51
train of dames: by *a* and eagle sat,   ,, *vii* 128
'Churl, thine *a*!' he cried,   *Balin and Balan* 295
Axelike That *a* edge unturnable,   *Princess ii* 203
Axle war Rides on those ringing *a's*!   *Tiresias* 93
Ay Why? For its *a, a, a*.   *Window. Ay.* 18
A-year my two 'oonderd *a-y* to mysen;   *Spinster's S's.* 12
but my two 'oonderd *a-y*.   ,, 22
fro' my oän two 'oonderd *a-y*.   ,, 58
Aylmer (*See also* **Lawrence Aylmer**)
Sir *A A* that almighty man,   *Aylmer's Field* 13
A followed *A* at the Hall   ,, 36
like an *A* in his Aylmerism,   ,, 123
Sir *A* half forgot his lazy smile   ,, 197
Sir *A* past, And neither loved   ,, 249
did Sir *A* know That great pock-pitten   ,, 255
had Sir *A* heard—Nay, but he must—   ,, 261
did Sir *A* (deferentially With nearing chair   ,, 266
Sir *A A* slowly stiffening spoke: ,, 273
They parted, and Sir *A A* watch'd.   ,, 277
Things in an *A* deem'd impossible,   ,, 305
Sir *A* reddening from the storm within,   ,, 322
To shame these mouldy *A's* in their graves: ,, 396
when *this A* came of age—   ,, 407

Aylmer (*continued*) and Sir *A* watch'd them all,   *Aylmer's Field* 552
and with her the race of *A*, past.   ,, 577
Aylmer-Averill There was an *A-A* marriage once.   ,, 49
Aymerism like an Aylmer in his *A*,   ,, 123
A-yowlin' *a-y* an' yaupin' like mad;   *Owd Roä* 88
An' the dogs was *a-y* all round,   ,, 107
Azimuth sine and arc, spheroid and *a*,   *Princess vi* 256
Azores AT FLORES in the *A* Sir Richard Greville lay,   *The Revenge* 1
Azrael the black-wing'd *A* overcame,   *Akbar's Dream* 186
Azure Her eyes *a* bashful *a*, and her hair   *The Brook* 71
he stared On eyes *a* bashful *a*,   ,, 206
Immingled with Heaven's *a* waveringly,   *Gareth and L.* 936
A, an Eagle rising or, the Sun   *Merlin and V.* 475
Shallow skin of green and *a*—   *Locksley H., Sixty*, 208
and, men, below the dome of *a*   *Akbar's D. Hymn* 7
Azure-circled High over all the *a-c* earth,   *Lover's Tale i* 390

B

Baäcon (**bacon**) *B* an' taätes, an' a beslings puddin'   *North. Cobbler* 112
Baäked (**baked**) fever 'ed *b* Jinny's eäd as bald   *Village Wife* 102
Baäl and honour thy brute *B*,   *Aylmer's Field* 644
came a Lord in no wise like to *B*.   ,, 647
Babble (s) the *b* of the stream Fell,   *Mariana in the S.* 51
The babes, their *b*, Annie,   *Enoch Arden* 606
night goes In *b* and revel and wine.   *Maud I xxii* 28
But *b*, merely for *b*.   *II v* 46
Merlin's mystic *b* about his end   *Last Tournament* 670
laughter and *b* and earth's new wine,   *To A. Tennyson* 2
And you liken—boyish *b*—   *Locksley H., Sixty*, 6
B, b; our old England may go down in *b*   ,, 8
—words, Wild *b*.   *Romney's R.* 32
Babble (verb) by the poplar tall rivulets *b* and fall.   *Leonine Eleg.* 4
I *b* on the pebbles.   *The Brook* 42
Howe'er you *b*, great deeds cannot die;   *Princess iii* 254
brook shall *b* down the plain,   *In Mem. ci* 10
Began to scoff and jeer and *b* of him   *Marr. of Geraint* 58
because ye dream they *b* of you.'   *Merlin and V.* 690
ye set yourself To *b* about him,   *Last Tournament* 340
Babbled *b* for the golden seal, that hung   *Dora* 135
b for you, as babies for the moon,   *Princess iv* 428
Had *b* 'Uncle' on my knee;   *In Mem. lxxxiv* 13
He moving homeward *b* to his men,   *Geraint and E.* 362
While thus they *b* of the King,   *Lancelot and E.* 1260
their tongues may have *b* of me—   *The Wreck* 41
I myself have often *b* doubtless   *Locksley H., Sixty*, 7
she said, I *b*, Mother, Mother—   *The Ring* 115
Babbler garrulously given, A *b* in the land.   *Talking Oak* 24
she, like many another *b*, hurt   *Guinevere* 354
mothers with their *b's* of the dawn,   *Tiresias* 103
Babbling runlets *b* down the glen.   *Mariana in the S.* 44
his wheat-suburb, *b* as he went.   *The Brook* 123
My words are like the *b's* in a dream Of nightmare, when the *b's* break the dream.   *Ancient Sage* 106
Babby (*See also* **Babe, Baby**) An' then the *b* wur burn,   *North. Cobbler* 16
an' she an' the *b* beäl'd,   ,, 37
An' the *b's* faäce wurn't wesh'd   ,, 42
Thou's rode of 'is back when a *b*,   *Owd Roä* 5
Babe (*See also* **Babby, Baby**) Sat smiling, *b* in arm.   *Palace of Art* 96
With his first *b's* first cry,   *Enoch Arden* 85
Nursing the sickly *b*, her latest-born.   ,, 150
Pray'd for a blessing on his wife and *b's*   ,, 188
be comforted, Look to the *b's*,   ,, 219
To give his *b's* a better bringing-up   ,, 299
know his *b's* were running wild Like colts   ,, 304
A gilded dragon, also, for the *b's*.   ,, 540
The *b's*, their babble, Annie,   ,, 606
lived and loved him, and his *b's*   ,, 685
rosy, with his *b* across his knees;   ,, 746
and a ring To tempt the *b*,   ,, 751
mother glancing often toward her *b*,   ,, 754
saw the *b* Hers, yet not his,   ,, 759

Babe (*continued*) I shall see him, My *b* in bliss: *Enoch Arden* 898
The *b* shall lead the lion.   *Aylmer's Field* 648
the *b* Too ragged to be fondled   ,,   685
One *b* was theirs, a Margaret,   *Sea Dreams* 3
the *b*, Their Margaret cradled near   ,,   56
Her maiden *b*, a double April old,   *Princess* ii 110
Father will come to his *b* in the nest,   ,,   iii 13
vassals to be beat, nor pretty *b's*   ,,   iv 146
my *b*, my blossom, ah, my child,   ,,   v 82
My *b*, my sweet Aglaïa, my one child :   ,,   101
With Psyche's *b*, was Ida watching us,   ,,   512
Ida stood With Psyche's *b* in arm :   ,,   vi 31
with the *b* yet in her arms,   ,,   74
b that by us, Half-lapt in glowing gauze   ,,   133
burst The laces toward her *b*;   ,,   149
Laid the soft *b* in his hard-mailed hands.   ,,   208
Not tho' he built upon the *b* restored ;   ,,   vii 75
'Here's a leg for a *b* of a week !'   *Grandmother* 11
for the *b* had fought for his life.   ,,   64
bring her *b*, and make her boast,   *In Mem.* xl 26
From youth and *b* and hoary hairs :   ,, lxix 10
Mammonite mother kills her *b* for a burial fee,   *Maud* I i 45
red man's *b* Leap, beyond the sea.   ,, xvii 19
now we poison our *b's*, poor souls !   ,, II v 63
in the flame was borne *A* naked *b*, and rode
   to Merlin's feet, Who stoopt and caught
   the *b*,   *Com. of Arthur* 384
naked *b*, of whom the Prophet spake,   *Gareth and L.* 501
lad and girl—yea, the soft *b* !   ,, 1341
ye men of Arthur be but *b's*.'   *Balin and Balan* 361
As clean as blood of *b's*,   *Merlin and V.* 344
his wife And two fair *b's*,   ,, 707
seven-months' *b* had been a truer gift.   ,, 711
broken shed, And in it a dead *b* ;   *Holy Grail* 399
brought A maiden *b* ; which Arthur
   pitying took,   *Last Tournament* 21
But the sweet body of a maiden *b*.   ,, 48
cursed The dead *b* and the follies   ,, 163
In honour of poor Innocence the *b*,   ,, 292
bearing high in arms the mighty *b*,   *Lover's Tale* iv 295
And over all her *b* and her the jewels   ,, 298
bearing on one arm the noble *b*,   ,, 370
Whereat the very *b* began to wail ;   ,, 375
a truth the *b* Will suck in with his milk   *Columbus* 37
b in lineament and limb Perfect,   *De Prof. Two G.* 11
and the wail Of a beaten *b*,   *The Wreck* 123
Saving women and their *b's*,   *Locksley H., Sixty,* 64
a cotter's *b* is royal-born by right divine ;   ,, 125
many a time ranged over when a *b*.   *The Ring* 151
senseless, worthless, wordless *b*,   ,, 304
all her talk was of the *b* she loved ;   ,, 353
She used to shun the wailing *b*,   ,, 358
In your sweet *b* she finds but you—   ,, 365
bending by the cradle of her *b*.   ,, 415
linger, till her own, the *b* She lean'd to   ,, 483
found Paris, a naked *b*, among the woods   *Death of Œnone* 54
I was lilting a song to the *b*,   *Bandit's Death* 20
Screams of a *b* in the red-hot palms   *The Dawn* 2
and Rome was a *b* in arms,   ,, 9

Babe-faced He came with the *b-f* lord ;   *Maud* II i 13
Babel let be Their cancell'd *B's* :   *Princess* iv 77
clamour grew As of a new-world *B*,   ,, 487
Baby (**adj.**) Moulded thy *b* thought.   *Eleänore* 5
Baby (**s**) in her bosom bore the *b*, Sleep.   *Gardener's D.* 268
As ruthless as a *b* with a worm,   *Walk. to the Mail* 108
Then lightly rocking *b's* cradle   *Enoch Arden* 194
from her *b's* forehead clipt A tiny curl,   ,, 235
His *b's* death, her growing poverty,   ,, 705
What does little *b* say,   *Sea Dreams* 301
B says, like little birdie,   ,, 303
B, sleep a little longer,   ,, 305
B too shall fly away.   ,, 308
babies roll'd about Like tumbled fruit   *Princess, Pro.,* 82
babbled for you, as *babies* for the moon,   ,, iv 428
I knew them all as *babies*,   *Grandmother* 88

Baby (**s**) (*continued*) The *b* new to earth and sky,   *In Mem.* xlv 1
I cannot bide Sir *B*.   *Pelleas and E.* 190
I have gather'd my *b* together—   *Rizpah* 20
My *b*, the bones that had suck'd me,   ,, 53
kill Their *babies* at the breast   *Columbus* 180
'Anything ailing,' I asked her, 'with *b* ?'   *The Wreck* 61
Baby-germ gamboll'd on the greens A *b-g*,   *Talking Oak* 78
Baby-girl a *b-g*, that had never look'd on the light :   *Despair* 71
Babyism In *b's*, and dear diminutives   *Aylmer's Field* 539
Babylon Shall *B* be cast into the sea ;   *Sea Dreams* 28
and life Pass in the fire of *B* !   *Sir J. Oldcastle* 124
For *B* was a child new-born,   *The Dawn* 9
Babylonian The foundress of the *B* wall,   *Princess* ii 80
Baby-oak magnetise The *b-o* within.   *Talking Oak* 256
Baby-rose The *b-r's* in her cheeks ;   *Lilian* 17
Baby-sole tender pink five-beaded *b-s's*,   *Aylmer's Field* 186
Baby-wife nor wail of *b-w*, Or Indian widow ;   *Akbar's Dream* 196
Bacchanal like wild *B's* Fled onward   *Lover's Tale* iii 25
Bacchante *B*, what you will ;   *Romney's R.* 6
Bacchus mailed *B* leapt into my arms,   *D. of F. Women* 151
Back wear an undress'd goatskin on my *b* ;   *St. S. Stylites* 116
How she mouths behind my *b*.   *Vision of Sin* 110
Read rascal in the motions of his *b*   *Sea Dreams* 167
hear my father's clamour at our *b's*   *Princess* i 105
Her *b* against a pillar, her foot   ,, iii 180
Them as 'as coäts to their *b's* an' taäkes   *N. Farmer, N.S.* 46
The daily burden for the *b*.   *In Mem.* xxv 4
b turn'd, and bow'd above his work,   *Marr. of Geraint* 302
brutes of mountain *b* That carry kings   *Merlin and V.* 576
long *b's* of the bushless downs, (repeat)   *Lancelot and E.* 400, 789
Look at the cloäths on 'er *b*,   *North. Cobbler* 109
Backbiter Face-flatterer and *b* are the same.   *Merlin and V.* 824
Back'd *See* **Bow-back'd**
Bacon (**Francis**) *See* **Verulam**
Bacon *See* **Baäcon**
Bad (**adj.**) O base and *b* ! what comfort ?   *Princess* v 78
for she wur a *b* un, sheä.   *N. Farmer, O.S.* 22
the poor in a loomp is *b*.   ,, *N.S.* 48
What is she now ? My dreams are *b*.   *Maud* I i 73
And here beneath it is all as *b*,   ,, II v 14
good ye are and *b*, and like to coins,   *Holy Grail* 25
Ya was niver sa *b* as that.   *Church-warden, etc.* 26
Bad (**s**) I fear to slide from *b* to worse.   *Two Voices* 231
sa o' coorse she be gone to the *b* !   *Village Wife* 98
I wur gawin' that waäy to the *b*,   *Owd Roä* 71
Bad-bade (**verb**) I made a feast : I *bad* him come ;   *The Sisters* 13
and do the thing I *bad* thee,   *M. d'Arthur* 81
utter'd it, And *bade* adieu for ever.   *Love and Duty* 83
bade him cry, with sound of trumpet,   *Godiva* 36
bad him with good heart sustain himself—   *Aylmer's Field* 544
He *bad* you guard the sacred coasts.   *Ode on Well.* 172
my three brethren *bad* me do it,   *Gareth and L.* 1410
'Fair Sir, they *bad* me do it.'   ,, 1417
Thro' which he *bad* her lead him on,   *Geraint and E.* 29
bad the host Call in what men   ,, 285
Prince *bad* him a loud good-night.   ,, 361
In this poor gown he *bad* me clothe myself,   ,, 702
Nor waved his hand, Nor *bad* farewell,   *Lancelot and E.* 987
who *bad* a thousand farewells to me,   ,, 1056
Lancelot, who coldly went, nor *bad* me one :   ,, 1057
So Arthur *bad* the meek Sir Percivale   ,, 1264
I left her and I *bad* her no farewell ;   ,, 1304
when he saw me, rose, and *bad* me hail,   *Holy Grail* 725
and do the thing I *bade* thee,   *Pass. of Arthur* 249
bad them to a banquet of farewells.   *Lover's Tale* iv 186
bad his menials bear him from the door,   ,, 260
We *bad* them no farewell,   ,, 386
bad them remember my father's death,   *V. of Maeldune* 70
bad his trumpeter sound To the charge,   *Heavy Brigade* 8
I *bad* her keep, Like a seal'd book,   *The Ring* 122
bad the man engrave 'From Walter' on the ring,   ,, 235
Badger live like an old *b* in his earth,   *Holy Grail* 629
Badon broke the Pagan yet once more on *B* hill.'   *Lancelot and E.* 280
on the mount Of *B* I myself beheld   ,, 303
Baffle 'Thy glory *b's* wisdom.   *Akbar's Dream* 28

B*

Barrier (*continued*) Russia bursts our
    Indian *b*,   *Locksley H., Sixty*, 115
    b that divided beast from man Slipt,   *St. Telemachus* 60
Barring out graver than a schoolboy's *b o*;   *Princess Con.* 66
Barrow grassy *b's* of the happier dead.   *Tithonus* 71
    behind it a gray down With Danish *b's*;   *Enoch Arden* 7
    Pass from the Danish *b* overhead ;   " 442
Barter not being bred To *b*,   " 250
Base (adj.) *him that utter'd nothing* b :   *To the Queen* 8
    Counts nothing that she meets with *b*,   *On a Mourner* 4
    ' Ungenerous, dishonourable, *b*,   *Aylmer's Field* 292
    O *b* and bad ! what comfort?   *Princess v* 78
    is he not too *b*?   *Maud I v* 36
    And myself so languid and *b*.   " *v* 18
    And therefore splenetic, personal, *b*,   " *x* 33
    Nor know I whether I be very *b*   *Marr. of Geraint* 468
    Not only to keep down the *b* in man,   *Guinevere* 480
    spared the flesh of thousands, the coward and
    the *b*,   *Happy* 17
Base (s) (*See also* **Meadow-bases**) Wrapt in dense
    cloud from *b* to cope.   *Two Voices* 186
    The seas that shock thy *b*!   *England and Amer.* 15
    Upon the hidden *b's* of the hills.'   *M. d'Arthur* 106
    people hum About the column's *b*,   *St. S. Stylites* 39
    The broken *b* of a black tower,   *Aylmer's Field* 511
    a pillar'd porch, the *b's* lost In laurel :   *Princess i* 230
    He has a solid *b* of temperament :   " *iv* 254
    roots of earth and *b* of all ;   " *v* 446
    fangs Shall move the stony *b's* of the world.   " *vi* 58
    roar that breaks the Pharos from his *b*   " 339
    great the crush was, and each *b*,   " 353
    It sees itself from thatch to *b*   *Requiescat* 3
    drown The *b's* of my life in tears.   *In Mem. xlix* 16
    a hundred feet Up from the *b* :   *Balin and Balan* 171
    lash'd it at the *b* with slanting storm ;   *Merlin and V.* 635
    at the *b* we found On either hand,   *Holy Grail* 497
    earthquake shivering to your *b* Split you,   *Pelleas and E.* 465
    gathering at the *b* Re-makes itself,   " 609
    Upon the hidden *b's* of the hills.'   *Pass. of Arthur* 274
    iceberg splits From cope to *b*—   *Lover's Tale i* 604
    wander round the *b's* of the hills,   *ii* 121
    plunge to the *b* of the mountain walls,   *V. of Maeldune* 14
Baseborn Call him *b*, and since his ways   *Com. of Arthur* 180
    and no king, Or else he.'   " 234
Based (*See also* **Broad-based, Firm-based**) *b* His
    feet on juts of slippery crag   *M. d'Arthur* 188
    b His feet on juts of slippery crag   *Pass. of Arthur* 356
Basement Modred brought His creatures to the *b*   *Guinevere* 104
Baseness ' He knows a *b* in his blood   *Two Voices* 301
    equal *b* lived in sleeker times   *Princess v* 385
    Is there no *b* we would hide?   *In Mem. li* 3
    She finds the *b* of her lot,   " *lx* 6
    there is no *b* in her.'   *Merlin and V.* 127
    To leave an equal *b* ;   " 830
    Puts his own *b* in him by default   *Pelleas and E.* 81
Basest ALTHO' I be the *b* of mankind,   *St. S. Stylites* 1
    The *b*, far into that council-hall   *Lucretius* 171
    All that is noblest, all that is *b*,   *Vastness* 32
Bashful reddens, cannot speak, So *b*,   *Balin and Balan* 520
Bashfulness His *b* and tenderness at war,   *Enoch Arden* 289
    His broken utterances and *b*,   *Pelleas and E.* 111
Basilisk hornless unicorns, Crack'd *b's*,   *Holy Grail* 718
Basis All but the *b* of the soul.   *Love thou thy land* 44
Bask or to *b* in a summer sky :   *Wages* 9
    To you that *b* below the Line,   *To Ulysses* 5
    Why not *b* amid the senses   *By an Evolution.* 6
Bask'd *b* and batten'd in the woods.   *In Mem. xxxv* 24
    wealthy enough to have *b*   *The Wreck* 45
Basket To Francis, with a *b* on his arm,   *Audley Court* 6
    holiday, With bag and sack and *b*,   *Enoch Arden* 63
    set down His *b*, and dismounting   *Geraint and E.* 210
    skin Clung but to crate and *b*,   *Merlin and V.* 625
Basking city Of little Monaco, *b*, glow'd.   *The Daisy* 8
    summer *b* in the sultry plains   *Prog. of Spring* 77
Bassa by the shore Of Duglas ; that on *B* ;   *Lancelot and E.* 290

Bassoon (*continued*) liquid treble of that *b*, my throat ;   *Princess ii* 426
Bassoon heard The flute, violin, *b* ;   *Maud I xxii* 14
Basting be for the spit, Larding and *b*.   *Gareth and L.* 1083
Bastion A looming *b* fringed with fire.   *In Mem. xv* 20
Bastion'd from the *b* walls Like threaded spiders,   *Princess i* 107
Bat After the flitting of the *b's*,   *Mariana* 17
    this Mock-Hymen were laid up like winter *b's*   *Princess iv* 144
    b's wheel'd, and owls whoop'd,   *Princess, Con.,* 110
    b's went round in fragrant skies,   *In Mem. xcv* 9
    For the black *b*, night, has flown,   *Maud I xxii* 2
    A home of *b's*, in every tower an owl.   *Balin and Balan* 336
    When the *b* comes out of his cave.   *Despair* 89
Batchelor Molly Magee wid her *b*, Danny O'Roon—   *Tomorrow* 10
Bath the *b's* Of all the western stars,   *Ulysses* 60
    His wife a faded beauty of the *B's*,   *Aylmer's Field* 27
    Balmier and nobler from her *b* of storm,   *Lucretius* 175
    dipt in *b's* of hissing tears,   *In Mem. cxviii* 23
    Pallas Athene climbing from the *b* In anger ;   *Tiresias* 40
    fuse themselves to little spicy *b's*,   *Prog. of Spring* 33
    The *B's*, the Forum gabbled of his death,   *St. Telemachus* 74
Bathe Balm-dews to *b* thy feet !   *Talking Oak* 268
    Coldly thy rosy shadows *b* me,   *Tithonus* 66
    Soft lustre *b's* the range of urns   *Day-Dm., Sleep. P.,* 19
    she *b's* the Saviour's feet   *In Mem. xxxii* 11
Bathed (*See also* **New-bathed**) lying *b* In the
    green gleam   *Princess i* 93
    Vivien *b* your feet before her own ?   *Merlin and V.* 284
    So *b* we were in brilliance.   *Lover's Tale i* 313
    So fair in southern sunshine *b*,   *Freedom* 5
    B in that lurid crimson—   *St. Telemachus* 18
Batin' (**beating**) set me heart *b* to music wid ivery
    word !   *Tomorrow* 34
Batten And *b* on her poisons ?   *Lover's Tale i* 777
Batten'd bask'd and *b* in the woods.   *In Mem. xxxv* 24
Battenest Thou *b* by the greasy gleam   *Will Water.* 221
Battening lie *B* upon huge seaworms   *The Kraken* 12
Batter some one *b's* at the dovecote-doors,   *Princess iv* 169
Batter'd (*See also* **Bone-batter'd**) flints *b* with
    clanging hoofs ;   *D. of F. Women* 21
    He *b* at the doors ; none came :   *Princess v* 337
    Cyril, *b* as he was, Trail'd himself   " *vi* 154
    And *b* with the shocks of doom   *In Mem. cxviii* 24
    and so left him bruised And *b*,   *Pelleas and E.* 547
Battering *B* the gates of heaven   *St. S. Stylites* 7
Battery-smoke Plunged in the *b's*   *Light Brigade* 32
Battle (s) (*See also* **Field-of-battle, Mahratta-battle**)
    We heard the steeds to *b* going,   *Oriana* 15
    The *b* deepen'd in its place,   " 51
    The distant *b* flash'd and rung.   *Two Voices* 126
    Peal after peal, the British *b* broke,   *Buonaparte* 7
    all day long the noise of *b* roll'd   *M. d'Arthur* 1
    drunk delight of *b* with my peers,   *Ulysses* 16
    boyish histories Of *b*, bold adventure,   *Aylmer's Field* 98
    That beat to *b* where he stands   *Princess iv* 578
    And gives the *b* to his hands :   " 580
    prove Your knight, and fight your *b*,   " 595
    Breathing and sounding beauteous *b*,   " *v* 161
    doing *b* with forgotten ghosts,   " 480
    I and mine have fought Your *b* :   " *vi* 225
    From talk of *b's* loud and vain,   *Ode on Well.* 247
    Some ship of *b* slowly creep,   *To F. D. Maurice* 26
    War with a thousand *b's*,   *Maud I i* 48
    months ran on and rumour of *b* grew,   " *III vi* 29
    Far into the North, and *b*,   " 37
    hail once more to the banner of *b* unroll'd !   " 42
    Arthur, passing thence to *b*, felt   *Com. of Arthur* 75
    long-lanced *b* let their horses run.   " 104
    like a painted *b* the war stood Silenced,   " 122
    in twelve great *b's* overcame The heathen hordes,   " 518
    Grant me some knight to do the *b* for me,   *Gareth and L.* 362
    King had saved his life In *b* twice,   " 494
    thou send To do the *b* with him,   " 619
    To bring thee back to do the *b*   " 1294
    loving the *b* as well As he that rides him.'   " 1301
    ride with him to *b* and stand by,   *Marr. of Geraint* 94

Battle (s) (continued) 'Do *b* for it then,' no more ; *Marr. of Geraint* 561
   In the great *b* fighting for the King.   " 596
   soldiers wont to hear His voice in *b*, *Geraint and E.* 175
   In *b*, fighting for the blameless King.   " 970
   banners of twelve *b's* overhead stir, *Balin and Balan* 88
   My father died in *b* for thy King, *Merlin and V.* 72
   ever-moaning *b* in the mist,   " 192
   after furious *b* turfs the slain   " 657
   In *b* with the love he bare his lord, *Lancelot and E.* 246
   in the four loud *b's* by the shore Of Duglas ;   " 289
   hast been in *b* by my side,   " 1358
   twelve great *b's* of our King. *Holy Grail* 250
   Knights that in twelve great *b's*   " 311
   with one Who gets a wound in *b*, *Pelleas and E.* 529
   Fought in her father's *b's*? wounded *Last Tournament* 592
   Isolt?—I fought his *b's*, for Isolt !   " 604
   In open *b* or the tilting-field (repeat) *Guinevere* 330, 332
   In twelve great *b's* ruining   " 432
   Far down to that great *b* in the west,   " 571
   ere he goes to the great *B* ?   " 652
   ere that last weird *b* in the west, *Pass. of Arthur* 29
   is this *b* in the west Whereto we move,   " 66
   last, dim, weird *b* of the west.   " 94
   old ghosts Look in upon the *b* ;   " 104
   King glanced across the field Of *b* :   " 127
   held the field of *b* was the King :   " 138
   all day long the noise of *b* roll'd   " 170
   The darkness of that *b* in the West, *To the Queen ii* 65
   In *b* with the glooms of my dark will, *Lover's Tale i* 744
   God of *b's*, was ever a *b* like this *The Revenge* 62
   Floated in conquering *b* or flapt *Def. of Lucknow* 2
   kings Of Spain than all their *b's* ! *Columbus* 23
   And we took to playing at *b*, *V. of Maeldune* 95
   For the passion of *b* was in us,   " 96
   Till the passion of *b* was on us,   " 111
   Gaining a lifelong Glory in *b*, *Batt. of Brunanburh* 8
   That they had the better In perils of *b*   " 85
   himself Blood-red from *b*, *Tiresias* 113
   flay Captives whom they caught in *b*— *Locksley H.. Sixty*, 80
   mad for the charge and the *b* were we, *Heavy Brigade* 41
   Stately purposes, valour in *b*, *Vastness* 7
   crimson with *b's*, and hollow with graves, *The Dreamer* 12
   Storm of *b* and thunder of war ! *Riflemen form !* 3
Battle (verb) For them I *b* till the end, *Sir Galahad* 15
Battle-axe Bloodily, bloodily fall the *b-a*, *Boädicea* 56
   fall *b* upon helm, Fall *b*, *Com. of Arthur* 486
   Clang *b* and clash brand ! (repeat) *Com. of Arthur* 493, 496, 499
   crash Of *b's* on shatter'd helms, *Pass. of Arthur* 110
Battle-bolt *b-b* sang from the three-decker *Maud I i* 50
Battle-club *b-c's* From the isles of palm : *Princess, Pro.*, 21
Battle-cry battle or flapt to the *b-c* ! *Def. of Lucknow* 2
   and could raise such a *b-c* *V. of Maeldune* 23
Battled (adj.) glow Beneath the *b* tower. *D. of F. Women* 220
Battled (verb) Who *b* for the True, the Just, *In Mem. lvi* 18
Battle-field Be shot for sixpence in a *b-f*, *Audley Court* 41
   Descends upon thee in the *b-f* : *Com. of Arthur* 129
   Arthur mightiest on the *b-f*— *Gareth and L.* 496
   Right arm of Arthur in the *b*, *Last Tournament* 202
   A galleried palace, or a *b*, *The Ring* 246
Battle-flag and the *b-f's* were furl'd *Locksley Hall* 127
Battlement The *b* overtopt with ivytods, *Balin and Balan* 335
Battle-plain springs Of Dircè laving yonder *b-p*, *Tiresias* 139
Battleshield Hack'd the *b*, *Batt. of Brunanburh* 13
Battle-song hear again The chivalrous *b-s* *Maud I x* 54
Battle-thunder thine the *b-t* of God,' *Boädicea* 44
   the *b-t* broke from them all. *The Revenge* 49
   with her *b-t* and flame ;   " 59
Battle-twig (earwig) 'Twur es bad es a *b-t* 'ere *Spinster's S's.* 80
Battle-writhen *b-w* arms and mighty hands *Lancelot and E.* 812
Baulk (beam) 'eärd the bricks an' the *b's* *Owd Roä* 109
Bawl throats of Manchester may *b*, *Third of Feb.* 43
   Millions of throats would *b* for civil rights, *Princess v* 387
   shamed to *b* himself a kitchen-knave. *Gareth and L.* 717
   b's this frontless kitchen-knave.   " 860
Bawl'd you *b* the dark side of your faith *Despair* 39

Bay (arm of the sea) (*See also* **Lover's Bay**) spangle
   dances in bight and *b*, *Sea-Fairies* 24
   glassy *b's* among her tallest towers.' *Œnone* 119
   where the *b* runs up its latest horn. *Audley Court* 11
   farmer's son, who lived across the *b*,   " 75
   lower down The *b* was oily calm ;   " 86
   That he sings in his boat on the *b* ! *Break, break, etc.* 8
   I bubble into eddying *b's*, *The Brook* 41
   By *b*, the peacock's neck in hue ; *The Daisy* 14
   In caves about the dreary *b*, *Sailor Boy* 10
   long waves that roll in yonder *b* ? *Maud I xviii* 63
   pleasant breast of waters, quiet *b*, *Lover's Tale i* 6
   borne about the *b* or safely moor'd   " 54
   growing holier as you near'd the *b*,   " 338
   into the sympathy Of that small *b*,   " i 435
   curving round The silver-sheeted *b* :   " ii 76
   Moved with one spirit round about the *b*,   " iii 17
   their gloom, the mountains and the *B*,   " iv 16
   After their marriage lit the lover's *B*,   " 28
   I with our lover to his native *B*.   " 155
   and flung them in bight and *b*, *V. of Maeldune* 53
   that dropt to the brink of his *b*, *The Wreck* 73
   that *b* with the colour'd sand—   " 135
Bay (a tree) the boar hath rosemaries and *b*. *Gareth and L.* 1074
   that wear a wreath of sweeter *b*, *Poets and their B.* 7
Bay (at bay) Where he greatly stood at *b*, *Ode on Well.* 106
   heard The noble hart at *b*, *Marr. of Geraint* 233
Bay (verb) Not less, tho' dogs of Faction *b*, *Love thou thy land* 85
Baying chiefly for the *b* of Cavall, *Marr. of Geraint* 185
Bay-window from some *b-w* shake the night ; *Princess i* 106
   lands in your view From this *b-w* *Sisters (E. and E.)* 52
Beach rib and fret The broad-imbased *b*, *Supp. Confessions* 128
   To watch the crisping ripples on the *b*, *Lotos-Eaters, C.S.* 61
   rounded by the stillness of the *b* *Audley Court* 10
   Here about the *b* I wander'd, *Locksley Hall* 11
   on this *b* a hundred years ago, *Enoch Arden* 10
   here and there, on sandy *b'es* *The Daisy* 15
   The breaker breaking on the *b*. *In Mem. lxxi* 16
   the scream of a madden'd *b* *Maud I iii* 12
   shore-cliff's windy walls to the *b*, *Geraint and E.* 164
   leaving Arthur's court he gain'd the *b* ; *Merlin and V.* 197
   tremulously as foam upon the *b* *Guinevere* 364
   the narrow fringe Of curving *b*— *Lover's Tale i* 39
   the fig ran up from the *b* *V. of Maeldune* 58
Beacon (s) like a *b* guards thee home. *In Mem. xvii* 12
   prophet's *b* burn'd in vain, *Ancient Sage* 142
Beacon (verb) Not in vain the distance *b's*. *Locksley Hall* 181
Beacon-blaze *b-b* allures The bird of passage, *Enoch Arden* 728
Beacon-star Each with a *b-s* upon his head, *Guinevere* 241
Beacon-tower Fixt like a *b-t* above the wayes *Princess iv* 493
Bead (*See also* **Frost-bead**) And number'd *b*, and shrift, *Talking Oak* 46
Beaded (*See also* **Black-beaded**, **Five-beaded**) And woolly breasts and *b* eyes ; *In Mem. xcv* 12
Beak hawk stood with the down on his *b*, *Poet's Song* 11
   swoops The vulture, *b* and talon, *Princess v* 383
   ever-ravening eagle's *b* and talon *Boädicea* 11
   And all unscarr'd from *b* or talon, *Last Tournament* 20
Beaker *b* brimm'd with noble wine. *Day-Dm., Sleep. P.*, 36
Beäl'd (bellowed) she *b* 'Ya mun saäve little Dick, *Owd Roä* 81
   an' she an' the babby *b*, *North. Cobbler* 37
   an' 'e *b* to ya 'Lad coom hout' *Church-warden, etc.* 28
Beam (ray) So many minds did gird their orbs with *b's* *The Poet* 29
   ' Or will one *b* be less intense, *Two Voices* 40
   into two burning rings All *b's* of Love, *D. of F. Women* 175
   deep-blue gloom with *b's* divine :   " 186
   the white dawn's creeping *b's*,   " 261
   fresh *b* of the springing east ; *M. d'Arthur* 214
   like a lane of *b's* athwart the sea, *Golden Year* 50
   b's, that thro' the Oriel shine, *Day-Dm., Sleep. P.*, 34
   Pure spaces clothed in living *b's*, *Sir Galahad* 66
   b of Heaven Dawn'd sometime *Aylmer's Field* 684
   Was it the first *b* of my latest day ? *Lucretius* 59

Beam (ray) (*continued*)   a *b* Had slanted forward,   *Princess ii* 138
' Fresh as the first *b* glittering on a sail,   ,,   *iv* 44
b Of the East, that play'd upon them,   ,,   *v* 258
A *b* in darkness: let it grow.   *In Mem. Pro.*, 24
A chequer-work of *b* and shade   ,,   *lxxii* 15
Pale with the golden *b* of an eyelash   *Maud I iii* 3
Like a *b* of the seventh Heaven,   ,,   *xiv* 21
smitten by the dusty sloping *b*,   *Marr. of Geraint* 262
Stream'd thro' my cell a cold and silver *b*,   *Holy Grail* 116
down the long *b* stole the Holy Grail, (repeat)   ,,   117, 188
Grail Past, and the *b* decay'd,   ,,   122
A crimson grail within a silver *b* ;   ,,   155
b of light seven times more clear than day :   ,,   187
Smote by the fresh *b* of springing east ;   *Pass. of Arthur* 382
crown of *b*'s about his brows—   *Lover's Tale i* 672
And solid *b* of isolated light,   ,,   *ii* 173
Beam (timber) (*See also* **Baulk, Rigtree**) shape
   it plank and *b* for roof   *Princess vi* 46
Beam (verb)   More bounteous aspects on me *b*,   *Sir Galahad* 21
Beam'd   Love's white star *B* thro'   *Gardener's D.* 166
b, Beneath a manelike mass   *Aylmer's Field* 67
ghostly grace *B* on his fancy,   *Lancelot and E.* 886
Beän   'ere a *b* an' yonder a peä ;   *N. Farmer, O.S.* 46
Bear (an animal)   grosser than your native *b*'s—
   dog, and wolf and boar and *b*   *Princess iv* 537
Albeit grizzlier than a *b*, to ride   *Com. of Arthur* 23
      Pelleas and E. 193
Bear (constellation)   *B* had wheel'd Thro' a great arc   *Princess iv* 212
Bear (verb) (*See also* **Abeär, Bore**)   That *b*'s relation
   to the mind.   *Two Voices* 177
' His sons grow up that *b* his name,   ,,   256
how canst thou *b* my weight?   *Œnone* 237
I know you proud to *b* your name,   *L. C. V. de Vere* 10
whatever sky *B* seed of men   *Love thou thy land* 20
As we *b* blossom of the dead ;   ,,   94
I will not *b* it longer.'   *The Goose* 32
And *b* me to the margin ;   *M. d'Arthur* 165
Less burthen, by ten-hundred-fold, to *b*,   *St. S. Stylites* 24
B witness, if I could have found   ,,   55
in truth (thou wilt *b* witness mine)   ,,   129
that which *b*'s but bitter fruit ?   *Locksley Hall* 65
and he *b*'s a laden breast,   ,,   143
Three angels *b* the holy Grail :   *Sir Galahad* 42
Which *b*'s a season'd brain about,   *Will Water.* 85
b me with thee, smoothly borne,   *Move eastward* 9
beseech you by the love thou *b* Him   *Enoch Arden* 307
' Too hard to *b* ! why did they take me   ,,   781
boat that *b*'s the hope of life   ,,   830
thought to *b* it with me to my grave ;   ,,   896
b's about A silent court of justice   *Sea Dreams* 173
jam the doors, and *b* The keepers down,   *Lucretius* 169
not he, who *b*'s one name with her   ,,   235
The king would *b* him out ;'   *Princess i* 182
Earth Should *b* a double growth   ,,   *ii* 180
think I *b* that heart within my breast,   ,,   334
much I *b* with her :   ,,   *iii* 81
hear me, for I *b*, Tho' man, yet human,   ,,   *iv* 424
if thou needs must *b* the yoke,   ,,   *vi* 205
skater on ice that hardly *b*'s him,   *Hendecasyllabics* 6
But help thy foolish ones to *b* ;   *In Mem. Pro.*, 31
Help thy vain worlds to *b* thy light.   ,,   32
To *b* thro' Heaven a tale of woe,   ,,   *xii* 2
Come then, pure hands, and *b* the head   ,,   *xviii* 9
I loved the weight I had to *b*,   ,,   *xxv* 7
A life that *b*'s immortal fruit   ,,   *xl* 18
To that ideal which he *b*'s ?   ,,   *lii* 10
She often brings but one to *b*,   ,,   *lv* 12
He *b*'s the burthen of the weeks   ,,   *lxxx* 11
growing, till I could *b* it no more,   *Maud I iii* 9
b's a skeleton figured on his arms,   *Gareth and L.* 640
heart enough To *b* his armour ?   *Geraint and E.* 490
b him hence out of this cruel sun ?   ,,   544
take him up, and *b* him to our hall :   ,,   552
pray the King To let me *b* some token   *Balin and Balan* 188
said ' What wilt thou *b* ?'   ,,   199
and ask'd To *b* her own crown-royal   ,,   200

Bear (verb) (*continued*)   ladies living gave me this to *b*.'   *Balin and Balan* 340
best and purest, granted me To *b* it !'   ,,   351
Thee will I *b* no more,'   ,,   432
b's, with all Its stormy crests   *Lancelot and E.* 483
Then will I *b* it gladly ;'   ,,   1106
But I myself must *b* it.'   ,,   1108
seize me by the hair and *b* me far,   ,,   1425
see thou, that it may *b* its flower.   *Holy Grail* 887
cannot *b* to dream you so forsworn :   *Pelleas and E.* 300
added to the griefs the great must *b*,   *Guinevere* 205
B with me for the last time   ,,   454
And *b* me to the margin ;   *Pass. of Arthur* 333
B witness, that rememberable day,   *To the Queen ii* 3
that perfectness Which I do *b* within me :   *Lover's Tale i* 89
bade his menials *b* him from the door,   ,,   *iv* 260
How could I *b* with the sights and the loathsome smells   *In the Child. Hosp.* 25
Him, who should *b* the sword Of Justice—   *Sir J. Oldcastle* 87
Why should we *b* with an hour of torture,   *Despair* 81
sorrow that I *b* is sorrow for *his* sake.   *The Flight* 64
and I and you will *b* the pall ;   *Locksley H., Sixty,* 281
B witness you, that yesterday   *To Prof. Jebb* 2
younger kindlier Gods to *b* us down,   *Demeter and P.* 131
creed and race Shall *b* false witness,   *Akbar's Dream* 98
The flood may *b* me far,   *Crossing the Bar* 14
Beard   *b* Was tagg'd with icy fringes   *St. S. Stylites* 31
His *b* a foot before him, and his hair   *Godiva* 18
' By holy rood, a royal *b* !'   *Day-Dm., Revival* 20
My *b* has grown into my lap.'   ,,   22
paw'd his *b*, and muttered ' catalepsy.'   *Princess i* 20
answer which, half-muffled in his *b*,   ,,   *v* 234
father's face and reverend *b*   ,,   *vi* 103
b That looks as white as utter truth,   *Gareth and L.* 280
Broad-faced with under-fringe of russet *b*,   *Geraint and E.* 537
took his russet *b* between his teeth ;   ,,   713
one curl of Arthur's golden *b*.   *Merlin and V.* 58
to part The lists of such a *b*   ,,   245
shaggy mantle of his *b* Across her neck   ,,   256
no more sign of reverence than a *b*.   ,,   279
b that clothed his lips with light—   *Last Tournament* 668
and his white *b* fell to his feet,   *V. of Maeldune* 118
we kiss'd the fringe of his *b*   ,,   125
Beard-blown   *b-b* goat Hang on the shaft,   *Princess iv* 78
Bearded (*See also* **Black-bearded, Bush-bearded, Lichen-
   Bearded, Long-bearded, Parcel-bearded, Russet-
   bearded**)   In among the *b* barley,   *L. of Shalott i* 29
Some *b* meteor, trailing light,   ,,   *iii* 26
the *b* grass Is dry and dewless.   *Miller's D.* 245
tho' you were not then So *b*.   *Columbus* 9
Beardless   *b* apple-arbiter Decided fairest.   *Lucretius* 91
Bearer   Save under pall with *b*'s.   *Aylmer's Field* 827
Bearest   love thou *b* The first-born   *Ode to Memory* 91
Bearing (part.)   *b* on My shallop thro'   *Arabian Nights* 35
B a lifelong hunger in his heart.   *Enoch Arden* 79
b hardly more Than his own shadow   *Aylmer's Field* 29
and, as *b* in myself the shame   ,,   355
Oaring one arm, and *b* in my left   *Princess iv* 183
as underhand, not openly *b* the sword.   *Maud I i* 28
B all down in thy precipitancy—   *Gareth and L.* 8
b in their common bond of love,   *Balin and Balan* 150
sent him to the Queen *B* his wish,   *Lancelot and E.* 1169
started thro' mid air *B* an eagle's nest :   *Last Tournament* 15
b round about him his own day,   *Lover's Tale i* 510
b high in arms the mighty babe,   ,,   *iv* 295
b on one arm the noble babe,   ,,   370
from our fiery beech Were *b* off the mast,   *Pro. to Gen. Hamley* 4
Bearing (mien)   face nor *b*, limbs nor voice,   *Com. of Arthur* 71
thro' these Princelike his *b* shone ;   *Marr. of Geraint* 545
And all her *b* gracious ;   *Holy Grail* 394
gazed upon the man Of princely *b*,   *Pelleas and E.* 306
I dream'd the *b* of our knights   *Last Tournament* 120
Bearing (bringing forth)   *b* and the training of a child   *Princess v* 465
Bearing (armorial)   gateway she discerns With
   armorial *b*'s   *L. of Burleigh* 43
Bearing (force)   To change the *b* of a word,   *In Mem. cxxviii* 16

Beat (verb) (continued) tho' there b a heart in either eye ; *Lover's Tale i* 34
Death drew nigh and b the doors of Life ;   ,, 111
noons B from the concave sand ;   ,, 140
felt the blast B on my heated eyelids :   ,, *iii* 28
Hearts that had b with such a love   ,, *iv* 69
It b—the heart—it b : Faint—but it b :   ,, 80
They b me for that, they b me— *Rizpah* 48
and b Thro' all the homely town *Columbus* 82
heart alive b's on it night and day— *The Flight* 35
heart that once had b beside her own. *Locksley H., Sixty*, 58
when life has ceased to b. *Happy* 52
' B, little heart—I give you this and this ' *Romney's R.* 1
' B upon mine, little heart ! b, b !   ,, 94
' B upon mine ! you are mine, my sweet !   ,, 95
' B little heart ' on this fool brain   ,, 155
pulse of Alla b's Thro' all His world. *Akbar's Dream* 41
b back The menacing poison   ,, 164
Harmony Whereto the worlds b time, *D. of the Duke of C.* 16
Beät (verb) An' it b's ma to knaw wot
   she died on, *Church-warden, etc.* 6
Beaten (*See also* **Barren-beaten, Breaker-beaten, Hollow-beaten, Thrice-beaten, Weather-beaten**)
B with some great passion at her heart, *Princess iv* 388
B I had been for a little fault *Com. of Arthur* 341
seems no bolder than a b hound ; *Geraint and E.* 61
forward by a way which, b broad,   ,, 436
b back, and b back Settles. *Merlin and V.* 371
took To bitter weeping like a b child,   ,, 855
Of every dint a sword had b in it, *Lancelot and E.* 19
lance had b down the knights, *Holy Grail* 363
There was I b down by little men   ,, 789
a traitor proven, or hound B, *Pelleas and E.* 440
save for dread of thee had b me, *Last Tournament* 525
many a heathen sword Had b thin ; *Pass. of Arthur* 167
Drooping and b by the breeze, *Lover's Tale i* 700
better ha' b me black an' blue *First Quarrel* 72
Havelock baffled, or b, *Def. of Lucknow* 91
thus was I b back, *Columbus* 55
Beating (*See also* **Batin**) When will the heart
   be aweary of b ? *Nothing will Die* 6
in joyance is b Full merrily ; *All Things will Die* 6
Do b hearts of salient springs *Adeline* 26
music in his ears his b heart did make. *Lotos-Eaters* 36
heard with b heart The Sweet-Gale *Edwin Morris* 109
bosom b with a heart renew'd. *Tithonus* 36
B it in upon his weary brain, *Enoch Arden* 796
b up thro' all the bitter world,   ,, 802
two-cell'd heart b, with one full stroke, *Princess vii* 307
B from the wasted vines *Ode on Well.* 109
Rose-red with b's in it, as if alive, *Holy Grail* 118
own steps, and his own heart B, *Pelleas and E.* 417
Heart b time to heart, *Lover's Tale i* 260
found her b the hard Protestant doors. *Sisters (E. and E.)* 240
warriors to have the swarm Of Turkish *Montenegro* 10
O the deathwatch b ! *Forlorn* 24
Beatitude Fulfils him with b. *Supp. Confessions* 62
Beauteous The reflex of a b form, *Miller's D.* 77
To find my heart so near the b breast, *The form, the form* 7
when the b hateful isle Return'd *Enoch Arden* 617
Breathing and sounding b battle, *Princess v* 161
In whispers b the world. *In Mem. lxxix* 12
Come, b in thine after form,   ,, *xci* 15
the b beast Scared by the noise *Merlin and V.* 421
Paris, himself as b as a God. *Death of Œnone* 18
Paris, no longer b as a God,   ,, 25
Beautiful spirit-thrilling eyes so keen and b : *Ode to Memory* 39
And said the earth was b. *A Character* 12
Her b bold brow, *The Poet* 38
B Paris, evil-hearted Paris, *Œnone* 50
Idalian Aphroditè b,   ,, 174
How b a thing it was to die For God *D. of F. Women* 231
Twin-sisters differently b. *Edwin Morris* 33
ever thus thou growest b In silence, *Tithonus* 43
' She is more b than day.' *Beggar Maid* 8
his own children tall and b, *Enoch Arden* 762

Beautiful (continued) the stars about the moon Look b, *Spec. of Iliad* 12
made His darkness b with thee. *In Mem. lxxiv* 12
Perfectly b ; let it be granted her : *Maud I ii* 4
pride flash'd over her b face.   ,, *iv* 16
Silence, b voice !   ,, *v* 19
O b creature, what am I   ,, *xvi* 10
Not b now, not even kind ;   ,, *II v* 66
He had not dream'd she was so b. *Lancelot and E.* 353
Beyond my knowing of them, b, *Holy Grail* 103
B in the light of holiness.   ,, 105
' God make thee good as thou art b,'   ,, 136
' Is Guinevere herself so b ? ' *Pelleas and E.* 70
And enter it, and make it b ? *Pass. of Arthur* 17
Forgetting how to render b Her countenance *Lover's Tale i* 96
The b in Past of act or place,   ,, 135
Of all his treasures the most b,   ,, *iv* 234
cries about the banquet—' B !   ,, 239
That which is thrice as b as these,   ,, 248
Of all my treasures the most b,   ,, 318
pity, if one so b Prove,   ,, 338
both are b : Evelyn is gayer, *Sisters (E and E)* 35
Both b alike, nor can 1 tell   ,, 276
So b, vast, various, *Ancient Sage* 84
one was dark, and both were b. *The Ring* 161
Bountiful, b, apparell'd gay, *Prog. of Spring* 62
Beautiful-brow'd B-b Œnone, my own soul, *Œnone* 71
Beautifully So lightly, b built : *Palace of Art* 294
dress her b and keep her true'— *Geraint and E.* 40
that beauty should go b : (repeat)   ,, 681, 684
Beauty (*See also* **After-beauty**) solid form
   Of constant b. *Supp. Confessions* 150
He spake of b : that the dull *A Character* 7
I see thy b gradually unfold, *Eleänore* 70
Light Hope at B's call would perch *Caress'd or chidden* 3
they live with B less and less,   ,, 9
' But now thy b flows away, *Mariana in the S.* 67
I loved his b passing well. *The Sisters* 33
love B only (B seen In all varieties *To—— With Pal. of Art* 6
And Knowledge for its b ;   ,, 8
Good only for its b, seeing not That B, Good,
   and Knowledge, are three sisters   ,, 9
B and anguish walking hand in hand *D. of F. Women* 15
' I had great b : ask not my name :   ,, 93
B such a mistress of the world. *Gardener's D.* 58
Her b grew ; till Autumn brought   ,, 207
many a group Of *beauties*, *Talking Oak* 62
glorious in his b and thy choice, *Tithonus* 12
Can thy love, Thy b, make amends,   ,, 24
Thou wilt renew thy b morn by morn ;   ,, 74
Her constant b doth inform Stillness *Day-Dm. Sleep. B.* 15
His wife a faded b of the Baths, *Aylmer's Field* 27
Edith, whose pensive b, perfect else,   ,, 70
made pleasant the baits Of gold and b,   ,, 487
sank down shamed At all that b ; *Lucretius* 64
murmurs of her b from the South. *Princess i* 36
All b compass'd in a female form,   ,, *ii* 34
beauties every shade of brown and fair   ,, 437
underneath the crag, Full of all b.   ,, *iii* 337
brief the moon of b in the South.   ,, *iv*. 113
Another kind of b in detail   ,, 448
We hunt them for the b of their skins ;   ,, *v* 156
became Her former b treble ;   ,, *vii* 25
All of b, all of use, *Ode. Inter. Exhib.* 23
Willy, my b, my eldest-born, *Grandmother* 9
So Willy has gone, my b, my eldest-born,   ,, 101
She's a b thou thinks— *N. Farmer, N. S.* 14
—wot's a b ?—the flower as blaws.   ,, 15
Maäybe she warn't a b :—   ,, 23
His b still with his years increased, *The Victim* 34
this orb of flame, Fantastic b ; *In Mem. xxxiv* 6
Who shall rail Against her b ?   ,, *cxiv* 2
of the singular b of Maud *Maud I i* 67
Done but in thought to your b,   ,, *iii* 6
O child, you wrong your b,   ,, *iv* 17
and B fair in her flower ;   ,, 25

Beauty (*continued*) dream of her *b* with
tender dread,   *Maud I xvi* 14
To know her *b* might half undo it.   „ 19
The *b* would be the same.   „ *II ii* 12
Remembering all the *b* of that star   *Ded. of Idylls* 46
gazed on all earth's *b* in their Queen,   *Com. of Arthur* 463
To make her *b* vary day by day,   *Marr. of Geraint* 9
The prize of *b* for the fairest there.   „ 485
having seen all *beauties* of our time,   „ 498
won for thee, The prize of *b*.'   „ 555
Your *b* is no *b* to him now ;   *Geraint and E.* 330
put your *b* to this flout and scorn   „ 675
that *b* should go beautifully : (repeat)   „ 681, 684
thine The wreath of *b*, thine the crown   *Merlin and V.* 79
Guinevere, The pearl of *b* :   *Lancelot and E.* 114
Your *b* is your *b*, and I sin   „ 1186
b of her flesh abash'd the boy,   *Pelleas and E.* 78
As tho' it were the *b* of her soul :   „ 79
so did Pelleas lend All the young *b*   „ 83
And title, 'Queen of B,' in the lists   „ 116
the sight Of her rich *b* made him   „ 238
cannot brook to see your *b* marr'd   „ 298
Queen of *B* and of love, behold This
day my Queen of *B*   *Last Tournament* 208
great Queen My dole of *b* trebled ?'   „ 558
'Her *b* is her *b*, and thine thine,   „ 559
her *b*, grace and power, Wrought   *Guinevere* 143
b such as never woman wore,   „ 549
In giving so much *b* to the world,   *Lover's Tale i* 212
A *b* which is death ;   „ *ii* 190
did he know her worth, Her *b* even ?   „ *iv* 151
Who could desire more *b* at a feast ?'   „ 240
b that is dearest to his heart—   „ 249
veriest *beauties* of the work appear   *Sisters (E. and E.)* 105
One bloom of youth, health, *b*,   „ 120
Ineffable *b*, out of whom, at a glance,   *Tiresias* 55
A *b* with defect—till That which knows,   *Ancient Sage* 86
Science grows and *B* dwindles   *Locksley H., Sixty,* 246
Like worldly *beauties* in the Cell,   *The Ring* 143
that only doats On outward *b*,   „ 164
You would not mar the *b* of your bride   *Happy* 24
give place to the *b* that endures,   „ 36
b that endures on the Spiritual height,   „ 37
A *b* came upon your face,   „ 51
My b marred by you ? by you !   „ 57
lose it and myself in the higher *b*,   „ 58
b lured that falcon from his eyry on the fell.   „ 59
never caught one gleam of the *b* which endures—   „ 60

Became Therefore revenge *b* me well.   *The Sisters* 5
And well his words *b* him :   *Edwin Morris* 25
And one *b* head-waiter.   *Will Water.* 144
crime of sense *b* The crime of malice,   *Vision of Sin* 215
b Her former beauty treble ;   *Princess vii* 24
B no better than a broken shed,   *Holy Grail* 398
Thereon her wrath *b* a hate ;   *Pelleas and E.* 224
courtesies of household life, *B* her bane ;   *Guinevere* 87
'Sir Lancelot, as *b* a noble knight,   „ 328
I to her *b* Her guardian and her angel,   *Lover's Tale i* 392
Italian words, *b* a weariness,   *The Ring* 407
Her Past *b* her Present,   *Death of Œnone* 14
in the mist at once *B* a shadow,   „ 50
dream *b* a deed that woke the world,   *St. Telemachus* 70

Beck (Brook) (*See also* **Howlaby beck, Wrigglesby beck**)
Within the dark and dimpled *b*.   *Miller's D.* 80
Thou's coom'd oop by the *b* ;   *Village Wife* 79
thaw the banks o' the *b* be sa high,   „ 83
fur 'e lost 'is taäil i' the *b*.   „ 86
An' 'cos o' thy farm by the *b*,   *Spinster's S's.* 73
Fur I seed the *b* coomin' down   *Owd Roä* 40
slushin' down fro' the bank to the *b*,   „ 41
An' ya stood oop naäkt i' the *b*,   *Church-warden, etc.* 29

Beck (call) move, my friend, At no man's *b*,   *Princess iii* 227
Beckon Time and Grief did *b* unto Death,   *Lover's Tale i* 110
Beckon'd She ended here, and *b* us :   *Princess ii* 182
Beckoning And *b* unto those they know ;   *In Mem. xiv* 8

Become *B's* dishonour to her race—   *Two Voices* 255
B the master of a larger craft,   *Enoch Arden* 144
it *b's* no man to nurse despair,   *Princess iv* 464
then wilt thou *b* A thrall to his enchantments,   *Gareth and L.* 268
B's the sea-cliff pathway broken short,   *Merlin and V.* 882
had the boat *B* a living creature   *Holy Grail* 519
tilt with a lance *B's* thee well—   *Last Tournament* 637
well, it scarce *b's* mine eye—   *Locksley H., Sixty,* 151

Bed (*See also* **Bulrush-bed, Death-bed, Moss-bed,
River-bed**) Upon her *b*, across her brow.   *Mariana* 56
Thou wilt not turn upon thy *b* ;   *A Dirge* 15
And after supper, on a *b*,   *The Sisters* 16
I blest him, as he knelt beside my *b*.   *May Queen, Con.* 16
But sit beside my *b*, mother,   „ 23
and I listened in my *b*,   „ 33
propt on *b's* of amaranth and moly,   *Lotos-Eaters, C. S.* 88
limbs at last on *b's* of asphodel.   „ 125
Like one that feels a nightmare on his *b*   *M. d'Arthur* 177
so to *b* : where yet in sleep   „ *Ep.* 16
farmer vext packs up his *b's* and chairs,   *Walk. to the Mail* 39
had pack'd the thing among the *b's*,)   „ 44
to the college tower From her warm *b*,   „ 90
In *b* like monstrous apes   *St. S. Stylites* 174
See that sheets are on my *b* ;   *Vision of Sin* 68
Started from *b*, and struck herself a light,   *Enoch Arden* 494
with yet a *b* for wandering men.   „ 698
kept the house, his chair, and last his *b*.   „ 826
then homeward and to *b* :   *Sea Dreams* 40
In her *b* at peep of day ?   „ 302
then to *b*, where half in doze   *Princess i* 246
hall glitter'd like a *b* of flowers.   „ *ii* 439
Half-naked as if caught at once from *b*   „ *iv* 285
I took it for an hour in mine own *b*   „ *v* 434
they hover about my *b*—   *Grandmother* 83
an' a sittin' 'ere o' my *b*.   *N. Farmer, O. S.* 9
An' 'e maäde the *b* as e' ligs on   „ *N. S.* 28
flush'd the *b* Of silent torrents,   *The Daisy* 33
along the valley, down thy rocky *b*,   *V. of Cauteretz* 7
When on my *b* the moonlight falls,   *In Mem. lxvii* 1
From off my *b* the moonlight dies ;   „ 10
And tends upon *b* and bower,   *Maud I xiv* 4
Hung over her dying *b*—   „ *xix* 36
On a *b* of daffodil sky,   „ *xxii* 10
Were it earth in an earthy *b* ;   „ 70
By the curtains of my *b*   „ *II iv* 54
hurl'd his huge limbs out of *b*,   *Marr. of Geraint* 124
brook o'er a shingley *b* Brawling,   „ 248
now get you hence to *b* :'   *Lancelot and E.* 388
Full lowly by the corners of his *b*,   „ 826
Then take the little *b* on which I died   „ 1117
on the black decks laid her in her *b*,   „ 1147
but creatures of the board and *b*,   *Pelleas and E.* 267
drier than a fountain *b* In summer :   „ 507
that feels a nightmare on his *b*   *Pass. of Arthur* 345
they fasten'd me down on my *b*.   *Rizpah* 46
I blubber'd awaäy o' the *b*—   *North. Cobbler* 61
such a lot of *b's* in the ward !'   *In the Child. Hosp.* 54
you leave 'em outside on the *b*—   „ 56
women who tended the hospital *b*,   *Def. of Lucknow* 87
I have hung them by my *b*,   *Columbus* 200
an' my oän *b* o' sparrow-grass,   *Spinster's S's.* 104
when Moother 'ed gotten to *b*,   *Owd Roä* 53
Too laäte, tha mun git tha to *b*,   „ 117
I am fitter for my *b*, or for my grave,   *The Ring* 433
leech forsake the dying *b* for terror of his life ?   *Happy* 98
she sat day and night by my *b*,   *Charity* 33
Brings the Dreams about my *b*,   *Silent Voices* 2

Bedded With all its casements *b*,   *Audley Court* 18
Bedivere (**A Knight of the Round Table**) The bold
Sir *B* uplifted him,   *M. d'Arthur* 6
Sir *B*, the last of all his knights,   „ 7
spake King Arthur to Sir *B* : (repeat)   „ 13, 66
To him replied the bold Sir *B* :   „ 39
answer made the bold Sir *B* : (repeat)   *M. d'Arthur* 69, 115, 151
Then went Sir *B* the second time   *M. d'Arthur* 82

Beggar (s) (*continued*)   I am a *b* born,' she said,   *Lady Clare* 71
her, he loved, a *b* : then he pray'd   *Enoch Arden* 117
tho' she were a *b* from the hedge,   *Marr. of Geraint* 230
fling free alms into the *b*'s bowl,   *Ancient Sage* 260
And a *b* began to cry, ' Food, food   *Voice spake, etc.* 5

Beggar'd   and I fell *B* for ever—   *Lover's Tale i* 670

Beggar Maid   Bare-footed came the *b m*   *Beggar Maid* 3
' This *b m* shall be my queen !'   " 16

Beggar-Woman   silken rag, the *b-w*'s weed :   *Geraint and E.* 680

Begged   then they *b* For Father Philip   *Enoch Arden* 364
At last she *b* a boon,   *Princess i* 146

Begin   fret Of that sharp-headed worm *b*'s   *Supp. Confessions* 186
And rugged barks *b* to bud,   *My life is full* 18
That to *b* implies to end ;   *Two Voices* 339
When meres *b* to uncongeal,   " 407
call me loud when the day *b*'s to break :   *May Queen* 10
O look ! the sun *b*'s to rise,   *May Queen, Con.*, 49
lights *b* to twinkle from the rocks :   *Ulysses* 54
B's to move and tremble.   *Will Water.* 32
Till the graves *b* to move, And the dead *b* to dance.   *Vision of Sin* 165
B's the scandal and the cry :   *You might have won* 16
Which made a selfish war *b* ;   *To F. D. Maurice* 30
The noise of life *b*'s again,   *In Mem. vii* 10
From whence clear memory may *b*,   " *xlv* 10
overhead *B*'s the clash and clang   " *Con.* 61
sadder age *b*'s To war against   *Gareth and L.* 1129
b's to play That air which pleased her   *Lover's Tale i* 20
an' saw she *b*'s to cry,   *North. Cobbler* 71
Evelyn *b*'s it ' O diviner Air.'   *Sisters (E. and E.)* 4
listen how the birds *B* to warble   *The Flight* 61

Beginner   fair *b*'s of a nobler time,   *Com. of Arthur* 457

Beginning (part.)   world's great work is heard *B*,   *In Mem. cxxi* 11
B to faint in the light that she loves   *Maud I xxii* 9
B at the sequel know no more.   *Lover's Tale iv* 158
And he *b* languidly—   " 274
The boat was *b* to move,   *First Quarrel* 21

Beginning (s)   end and the *b* vex His reason :   *Two Voices* 298
blind *b*'s that have made me man,   *Lucretius* 246
break The low *b*'s of content.   *In Mem. lxxxiv* 48
And be the fair *b* of a time.   *Guinevere* 466

Begone   ' You must *b*,' said Death,   *Love and Death* 7
B : we will not look upon you more.   *Princess iv* 547
B ! my knave !—belike and like   *Gareth and L.* 713
thou *b*, take counsel, and away,   " 1002

Begotten   (*See also* **Want-begotten**)   My father hath *b* me in his wrath.   *Balin and Balan* 283

Beguile   To *b* her melancholy ;   *Maud I xx* 3

Beguil'd   well, well, well, I *may* be *b*   " *vi* 89

Begun   help me as when life *b* :   *Locksley Hall* 185
into my heart, and *b* to darken my eyes.   *Rizpah* 16
My brain had *b* to reel—   *In the Child. Hosp.* 60
A juster epoch has *b*.   *Epilogue* 6
The light of days when life *b*,   *Pref. Poem Broth. S.* 23
Altho' the months have scarce *b*,   *To Ulysses* 22
this bare dome had not *b* to gleam   *To Mary Boyle* 41
O weary one, has it *b* ?   *The Dreamer* 26

Beheld   *b* Thy mild deep eyes upraised,   *Supp. Confessions* 73
I *b* great Here's angry eyes,   *Œnone* 190
Since I *b* young Laurence dead.   *L. C. V. de Vere* 28
ere a star can wink, *b* her there.   *Gardener's D.* 122
I *b* her ere she knew my heart,   " 276
when the boy *b* His mother,   *Dora* 137
B the dead flame of the fallen day   *Enoch Arden* 441
b His wife his wife no more,   " 758
Turning *b* the Powers of the House   *Aylmer's Field* 287
I *b* her, when she rose The yesternight,   *Princess v* 175
The Priest *b* him, And cried   *The Victim* 37
And what I am *b* again   *In Mem. cxxiv* 21
b The death-white curtain drawn ;   *Maud I xiv* 33
I *b* From eye to eye thro' all their Order   *Com. of Arthur* 269
likewise I *b* Excalibur   " 295
when her son *B* his only way to glory   *Gareth and L.* 159
b Far over heads in that long-vaulted   " 318
B the long street of a little town   *Marr. of Geraint* 242

Beheld (*continued*)   Geraint *B* her first in field,   *Marr. of Geraint* 540
Turn'd, and *b* the four, and all   " 558
b A little town with towers,   *Geraint and E.* 196
I never yet *b* a thing so pale.   " 615
Have I *b* a lily like yourself.   " 620
true eyes *B* the man you loved   " 847
b Balin and Balan sitting Statuelike,   *Balin and Balan* 23
B before a golden altar lie   " 410
B the Queen and Lancelot get to horse.   *Merlin and V.* 102
b the King Charge at the head   *Lancelot and E.* 303
Arthur, who *b* his cloudy brows,   " 1354
every knight *b* his fellow's face   *Holy Grail* 191
Another hath *b* it afar off,   " 897
b That victor of the Pagan   *Last Tournament* 664
b three spirits mad with joy   *Guinevere* 252
B at noon in some delicious dale   " 393
glancing up *b* the holy nuns All round her,   " 666
some *b* the faces of old ghosts   *Pass. of Arthur* 103
When I *b* her weep so ruefully ;   *Lover's Tale i* 773
b All round about him that which   " *iv* 53
never yet *b* **a** thing so strange,   " 303
when before have Gods or men *b* The Life   *Demeter and P.* 29
b A blood-red awning waver   *St. Telemachus* 51

Behest   Then not to disobey her lord's *b*,   *Geraint and E.* 129

Behold   Where'er they fell, *b*, Like to   *The Poet* 22
' *B*, it is the Sabbath morn.'   *Two Voices* 402
B this fruit, whose gleaming rind   *Œnone* 72
Mayst well *b* them unbeheld,   " 89
when I look'd again, *b* an arm,   *M. d'Arthur* 158
B her there, As I beheld her   *Gardener's D.* 275
' Who is this ? *b* thy bride,'   *Love and Duty* 49
some one spake : ' *B* ! it was a crime   *Vision of Sin* 213
In such a shape dost thou *b* thy God.   *Aylmer's Field* 657
in me *b* the Prince Your countryman,   *Princess ii* 214
B your father's letter.'   " *iv* 468
reverent people *b* The towering car,   *Ode on Well.* 54
' *B* the man that loved and lost,   *In Mem. i* 15
B me, for I cannot sleep,   " *vii* 6
B a man raised up by Christ !   " *xxxi* 13
An inner trouble I *b*,   " *xli* 18
B, we know not anything ;   " *liv* 13
B their brides in other hands ;   " *xx* 14
B, I dream a dream of good,   " *cxxix* 11
O happy hour, *b* the bride   " *Con.* 69
Arthur said, ' *B* thy doom is mine.   *Com. of Arthur* 467
' *B*, for these have sworn To wage my wars,   " 507
did Enid, keeping watch, *b*   *Geraint and E.* 118
B me overturn and trample on him.   " 843
b me come To cleanse this common   " 894
father, I *b* him in my dreams   *Lancelot and E.* 763
B it, crying, ' We have still **a** King.'   *Holy Grail* 245
b a woman at a door Spinning ;   " 391
when they led me into hall, *b*,   " 577
looking up, *B*, the enchanted towers   " 813
' In happy time *b* our pilot-star !   *Pelleas and E.* 63
' *B* me, Lady, A prisoner,   " 240
B his horse and armour.   " 373
b This day my Queen of Beauty   *Last Tournament* 208
Till the High God *b* it from beyond,   *Pass. of Arthur* 16
B, I seem but King among the dead.'   " 146
when I look'd again, *b* an arm,   " 326
in her *b* Of all my treasures   *Lover's Tale iv* 317
Behind this darkness, I *b* her still,   *Tiresias* 52
when these *b* their Lord,   *Akbar's Dream* 142

Beholden   But being so *b* to the Prince,   *Marr. of Geraint* 623
shame the Prince To whom we are *b* ;   " 727

Beholding   *B* how the years which are not Time's   *Aylmer's Field* 601
B one so bright in dark estate,   *Marr. of Geraint* 786
B how ye butt against my wish,   *Geraint and E.* 677
B it was Edyrn son of Nudd,   " 781
b her Tho' pale, yet happy,   " 879
b him so strong, she thought   *Pelleas and E.* 117

Behoof   break them more in their *b*,   *Princess vi* 61
To mask, tho' but in his own *b*,   *Maud I vi* 48

Being   changes should control Our *b*,   *Love thou thy land* 42

Being (*continued*) all the current of my *b* sets to thee.' — *Locksley Hall* 24
and spoils **My** bliss in *b* ; — *Lucretius* 222
No Angel, but a dearer *b*, — *Princess* vii 320
Her peaceful *b* slowly passes by — *Requiescat* 7
And all the wheels of *B* slow. — *In Mem. l* 4
His *b* working in mine own, — *In Mem. lxxxv* 43
And strike his *b* into bounds, — „ *Con.* 124
b he loved best in all the world, — *Geraint and E.* 103
and he felt his *b* move In music — *Balin and Balan* 211
glad new-year Of *B*, which with earliest — *Lover's Tale i* 282
Beknaved Gareth following was again *b*. — *Gareth and L.* 786
Bel Till the face of *B* be brighten'd, — *Boädicea* 16
Belabour'd so *b* him on rib and cheek — *Princess v* 341
Belaud blush to *b* myself a moment— — *Hendecasyllabics* 18
Beldam Then glided a vulturous *B* forth, — *Dead Prophet* 25
Beleaguerer Blown by the fierce *b's* of a town, — *Achilles over the T.* 20
Belfry white owl in the *b* sits. (repeat) — *The Owl* I. 7, 14
Low breezes fann'd the *b* bars, — *The Letters* 43
Belied liars *b* in the hubbub of lies : — *Maud I iv* 51
Belief Think my *b* would stronger grow ! — *Supp. Confessions* 13
but my *b* In all this matter— — *Com. of Arthur* 183
Beyond mine old *b* in womanhood, — *Lancelot and E.* 955
I am quicker of *b* Than you believe me, — „ 1204
and he believed in her *b*. — *Holy Grail* 165
or that which most Enchains *b*, — *Lover's Tale ii* 134
Believable that he sinn'd is not *b* ; — *Merlin and V.* 760
Believe (*See also* **Make-believes**) Why not *b* then ? — *Supp. Confessions* 123
But I *b* she wept. — *Talking Oak* 164
I *b*, if you were fast my wife, — *Enoch Arden* 414
Save Christ as we *b* him— — *Aylmer's Field* 573
Gods there are, for all men so *b*. — *Lucretius* 117
there is iron in the blood, And I *b* it. — *Princess vi* 231
we *b* him Something far advanced — *Ode on Well.* 274
nor *b* me Too presumptuous, — *Hendecasyllabics* 15
I heard a voice, '*b* no more' — *In Mem. cxxiv* 10
you wrong your beauty, *b* it, — *Maud I iv* 17
Shall I *b* him ashamed to be seen ? — „ *xiii* 25
I well *b* You be of Arthur's Table,' — *Gareth and L.* 835
I do *b* yourself against yourself, — *Geraint and E.* 744
world will not *b* a man repents: — „ 900
I well *b* this damsel, and the one — *Balin and Balan* 612
we *b* all evil of thy Mark— — *Merlin and V.* 93
and half *b* her true : — „ 186
I well *b* that all about this world — „ 541
I well *b* she tempted them and fail'd, — „ 819
I might *b* you then, Who knows ? — „ 922
noble it is, I well *b*, the noblest— — *Lancelot and E,* 361
if I could *b* the things you say — „ 1097
I may not well *b* that you *b*.' — „ 1196
I am quicker of belief Than you *b* me, — „ 1205
with him, to *b* as he believed. — *Holy Grail* 487
Our Lady says it, and we well *b* : — „ 604
greatest hardly will *b* he saw ; — „ 896
lie to me : I *b*. Will ye not lie ? — *Last Tournament* 645
I should all as soon *b* that his, — *Guinevere* 350
to *b* it—'tis so sweet a thought, — *Lover's Tale i* 275
can well *b*, for he look'd so coarse — *In the Child. Hosp.* 7
'O soul of little faith, slow to *b* ! — *Columbus* 147
who *b* These hard memorials — „ 195
speak the truth that no man may *b*.' — *Tiresias* 50
were used to *b* everlasting would die : — *Despair* 54
Did *he b* it ? did you ask him ? — *The Ring* 225
That no man would *b*. — *Mechanophilus* 28
Believed The woman cannot be *b*. — *The Letters* 32
b This filthy marriage-hindering — *Aylmer's Field* 373
when he came again, his flock *b*— — „ 600
and saw, but scarce *b* — *Sea Dreams* 34
often she *b* that I should die : — *Princess vii* 100
I *b* that in the living world My spirit — „ 157
Queen *b* that when her son — *Gareth and L.* 158
Not less Geraint *b* it ; — *Marr. of Geraint* 28
I *b* myself Unconquerable, — *Geraint and E.* 835
He spoke, and Enid easily *b*, — „ 874
and half *b* her true, (repeat) — *Merlin and V.* 400, 893

Believed (*continued*) and he *b* in her belief. — *Holy Grail* 165
One with him, to believe as he *b*. — „ 487
in vows when men *b* the King ! — *Last Tournament* 649
every knight *B* himself a greater — „ 677
we *b* her asleep again— — *In the Child. Hosp.* 69
And if I *b* in a God, I would — *Despair* 70
Believing *B* where we cannot prove ; — *In Mem., Pro.* 4
own soul to hers, *B* her ; — *Pelleas and E.* 84
B, 'lo mine helpmate, one to feel — *Guinevere* 485
Only, *b* I loved Edith, — *Sisters (E. and E.)* 138
b that the girl's Lean fancy, — *The Ring* 335
people *b* that Peelè the Goddess — *Kapiolani* 8
Bell (*See also* **Ankle-bells, Bindweed-bell, Chapel Bell, Church-bell, Flower-bells, Marriage-bell**) Nine — *All Things will Die* 35
times goes the passing *b* : — *Arabian Nights* 62
dropping low their crimson *b's* Half-closed, — *Sea-Fairies* 14
with white *b's* the clover-hill swells — *L. of Shalott iii* 13
The bridle *b's* rang merrily — *Two Voices* 72
The foxglove cluster dappled *b's*.' — „ 408
The sweet church *b's* began to peal. — *D. of F. Women* 247
in the towers I placed great *b's* that swung, — *Palace of Art* 129
those great *b's* Began to chime. — „ 157
midnight *b's* cease ringing suddenly. — *M. d'Arthur, Ep.,* 29
At this a hundred *b's* began to peal, — *Gardener's D.* 36
sound of funeral or of marriage *b's* ; — „ 221
from them clash'd The *b's* ; we listen'd ; — *Dora* 41
when the *b's* were ringing, Allan call'd — *Edwin Morris* 56
I do not hear the *b's* upon my cap, — *Talking Oak* 272
blow The sound of minster *b's*. — *Sir Galahad* 35
shrill *b* rings, the censer swings, — *The Letters* 48
There comes a sound of marriage *b's*. — *Enoch Arden* 80, 511
were wed, and merrily rang the *b's*, (repeat) — „ 512
Merrily rang the *b's* and they were wed — „ 615
heard the pealing of his parish *b's* ; — *Princess ii* 432
hark the *b* For dinner, let us go !' — „ 470
the chapel *b's* Call'd us : we left — „ *vi* 193
half open'd *b* of the woods ! — „ 331
like a *b* Toll'd by an earthquake — *Ode on Well.* 53, 58
Let the *b* be toll'd : (repeat) — *W. to Alexandra* 18
Clash, ye *b's*, in the merry March air ! — *N. Farmer, N. S.* 13
Saäint's daäy—they was ringing the *b's*. — *In Mem. viii* 3
'lights and rings the gateway *b*, — „ *x* 2
I hear the *b* struck in the night: — „ *xxviii* 3
The Christmas *b's* from hill to hill — „ 16
Before I heard those *b's* again : — „ 20
The merry merry *b's* of Yule. — „ *lvii* 10
One set slow *b* will seem to toll — „ *civ* 5
A single peal of *b's* below, — „ 8
That these are not the *b's* I know. — „ *cvi* 1
Ring out, wild *b's*, to the wild sky, — „ 6
Ring, happy *b's*, across the snow : — „ *Con.* 64
The dead leaf trembles to the *b's*. — *Maud I vi* 62
Is cap and *b's* for a fool. — *II v* 24
Not a *b* was rung, not a prayer was read ; — *Merlin and V.* 131
she tower'd ; her *b's*, Tone under tone, — *Holy Grail* 298
ye, that follow but the leader's *b*' — *Lover's Tale ii* 83
thence at intervals A low *b* tolling. — „ *iii* 10
came on me The hollow tolling of the *b*, — „ 13
by slow degrees the sullen *b* Toll'd quicker, — „ 20
Four *b's* instead of one began to ring, — „ 21
Four merry *b's*, four merry marriage-bells, — „ 29
b's Lapsed into frightful stillness ; — „ 52
again the *b's* Jangled and clang'd : — „ *iv* 2
the *b's*, Those marriage-bells, — „ 29
Heard yet once more the tolling *b*, — *First Quarrel* 21
we heard them a-ringing the *b*, — *V. of Maeldune* 108
butted each other with clashing of *b's*, — „ 110
the clash and boom of the *b's* rang — *Tiresias* 192
The tolling of his funeral *b* — *Early Spring* 41
Ring little *b's* of change — *The Ring* 411
b's that rang without a hand, — „ 482
where the loyal *b's* Clash welcome— — *Forlorn* 70
Bridal *b's* with tolling ! . . . . — *To Ulysses* 24
A spike of half-accomplish'd *b's*— — *Far-far-away* 5
lin-lan-lone of evening *b's* Far-far-away. — *Far-far-away* 5

Bell (*continued*) Faith and Work were *b's* of full
    accord,   *In Mem., W. G. Ward* 2
    many a pendent *b* and fragrant star,   *Death of Œnone* 13
    people ring the *b* from love to Thee.   *Akbar's Dream, Inscrip.* 4
    in praise of Whom The Christian *b,*   *Akbar's Dream* 149
    Twilight and evening *b,*   *Crossing the Bar* 9
Bell'd *See* **Milky-Bell'd**
Bellerophon White Rose, B, the Jilt,   *The Brook* 161
Bellicent (Queen) the Queen of Orkney, B,
    (repeat)   *Com. of Arthur* 190, 245
    last tall son of Lot and B,   *Gareth and L.* 1
    Then B bemoan'd herself and said,   ,,   72
    son Of old King Lot and good Queen B,   ,, 1231
Belling Last in a roky hollow, *b,* heard   *Last Tournament* 502
Bell-like many a deep-hued *b-l* flower   *Eleänore* 37
Bell-mouth'd whom the *b-m* glass had wrought,   *Princess iv* 155
Bellow'd (*See also* **Beäl'd**) ever overhead   *Merlin and V.* 957
    B the tempest,
Bellowing (*See also* **A-bealin', Hollower-bellowing**)
    B victory, *b* doom :   *Ode on Well.* 66
    b thro' the darkness on to dawn,   *Gareth and L.* 177
    Hell burst up your harlot roofs B,   *Pelleas and E.* 467
Bellringer Friars, *b's,* Parish-clerks—   *Sir J. Oldcastle* 160
Belong'd boooks, I ha' see'd 'em, *b* to the Squire,   *Village Wife* 71
    an' 'is gells es *b* to the land ;   ,, 112
    my Fathers *b* to the church of old,   *The Wreck* 1
Belonging things *b* to thy peace and ours !   *Aylmer's Field* 740
    I knew it—Of and *b* to me,   *Lucretius* 44
Beloved (*See also* **Much-beloved, Well-beloved**)
    Revered, *b*—O you that hold   *To the Queen* 1
    O this world's curse,—*b* but hated—   *Love and Duty* 47
    For love reflects the thing *b* ;   *In Mem. lii* 2
    Maud the *b* of my mother,   *Maud I i* 72
    the liquid note *b* of men Comes   *Marr. of Geraint* 336
    friend, the neighbour, Lionel, the *b,*   *Lover's Tale i* 653
    b for a kindliness Rare in Fable   *On Jub. Q. Victoria* 4
    This ring ' Io t'amo' to his best *b,*   *The Ring* 210
Belt (s) (*See also* **Blossom-belt, Sword-belt**) A
    gleaming crag with *b's* of pines.   *Two Voices* 189
    Unclasp'd the wedded eagles of her *b,*   *Godiva* 43
    glories of the broad *b* of the world,   *Enoch Arden* 579
    A *b,* it seem'd, of luminous vapour,   *Sea Dreams* 209
    ridge Of breaker issued from the *b,*   ,, 212
    same as that Living within the *b)*   ,, 216
    past into the *b* and swell'd again   ,, 222
    Half-lost in *b's* of hop and breadths of wheat ;   *Princess, Con.,* 45
    From *b* to *b* of crimson seas   *In Mem. lxxxvi* 13
    By summer *b's* of wheat and vine   ,, *xcviii* 4
    a mighty purse, Hung at his *b,*   *Geraint and E.* 23
    seem a sword beneath a *b* of three,   *Merlin and V.* 441
    faltering sideways downward to her *b,*   ,, 850
    crimson in the *b* a strange device,   *Holy Grail* 154
    round thee, maiden, bind my *b.*   ,, 159
Belt (verb) woods that *b* the gray hill-side,   *Ode to Memory* 55
    and from the woods That *b* it rise   *Lover's Tale i* 536
    deeps that *b* the changeful West,   *Prog. of Spring* 98
Belt (built) an' *b* long afoor my daäy   *Owd Roä* 21
Belted with puff'd cheek the *b* hunter blew   *Palace of Art* 63
    B his body with her white embrace,   *Last Tournament* 513
Bemoan'd Then Bellicent *b* herself and said,   *Gareth and L.* 72
Bench Jack on his ale-house *b* has as many   *Maud I iv* 9
    I saw, No *b* nor table, painting   *Holy Grail* 829
    Down on a *b,* hard-breathing.   *Pelleas and E.* 592
Bench'd stately theatres B crescent-wise.   *Princess ii* 370
Bencher wrinkled *b's* often talk'd of him   *Aylmer's Field* 473
Bend chafes me that I could not *b* One will ;   *D. of F. Women* 137
    How sweet are looks that ladies *b*   *Sir Galahad* 13
    fathers *b* Above more graves,   *In Mem. xcviii* 15
    On me she *b's* her blissful eyes   ,, *Con.* 29
    tyranny now should *b* or cease,   *Maud III vi* 20
    O ay—the winds that *b* the brier !   *Last Tournament* 731
Bending erect, but *b* from his height   *Aylmer's Field* 119
    b by the cradle of her babe.   *The Ring* 415
Bengal For which, in branding summers of B,   *The Brook* 16
Bent lowly *b* With melodious airs   *Adeline* 54

Bent (*continued*) From yon blue heavens above us *b*   *L. C. V. de Vere* 50
    b or broke The lithe reluctant boughs   *Enoch Arden* 380
    b as he was To make disproof of scorn,   *Aylmer's Field* 445
    Nor *b,* nor broke, nor shunn'd   *Princess, Pro.,* 38
    seal was Cupid *b* above a scroll,   ,, *i* 242
    B their broad faces toward us   ,, *iv* 551
    Her head a little *b* ; and on her mouth   ,, *vi* 269
    The King *b* low, with hand on brow,   *The Victim* 53
    a straight staff *b* in a pool :   *High. Pantheism* 16
    thrice as large as man he *b* To greet   *In Mem. ciii* 42
    either spear B but not brake,   *Gareth and L.* 964
    b he seem'd on going the third day,   *Marr. of Geraint* 604
    B as he seem'd on going this third day,   ,, 625
    since her mind was *b* On hearing,   *Pelleas and E.* 114
    round him *b* the spirits of the hills   *Guinevere* 283
    but he *B* o'er me, and my neck   *Lover's Tale i* 690
    so feeble : she *b* above me, too ;   ,, 693
    the mast *b* and the ravin wind   ,, *ii* 170
    And the pikes were all broken or *b,*   *The Revenge* 80
    Bow'd the spoiler, B the Scotsman,   *Batt. of Brunanburh* 21
    The plowman passes, *b* with pain,   *Ancient Sage* 144
Bequeath'd This ring *b* you by your mother,   *The Ring* 75
Bereave nothing can *b* him Of the force   *Ode on Well.* 272
Berg goes, like glittering *b's* of ice,   *Princess iv* 71
Berkshire weed the white horse on the B hills   *Geraint and E.* 936
Berried about my feet The *b* briony fold.'   *Talking Oak* 148
Berry With bunch and *b* and flower   *Œnone* 102
    red *berries* charm the bird,   *Gareth and L.* 85.
    With ever-scattering *berries,* and on   *Last Tournament* 173
    Married among the red *berries,*   *First Quarrel* 40
    and the branch with *berries* on it,   *Columbus* 73
    And the crimson and scarlet of *berries*   *V. of Maeldune* 61
    But in every *b* and fruit was the   ,, 62
    Clomb the mountain, and flung the *berries,*   *Kapiolani* 6
    handle or gather the *berries* of Peelè !   ,, 20
    Into the flame-billow dash'd the *berries,*   ,, 33
Beryl sardius, Chrysolite, *b,* topaz,   *Columbus* 85
Beseech I do *b* you by the love you bear   *Enoch Arden* 307
Beseem might well *b* His princess,   *Marr. of Geraint* 758
Beseem'd true answer, as *b* Thy fëalty,   *M. d'Arthur* 74
    true answer, as *b* Thy fëalty,   *Pass. of Arthur* 242
Besiege so *b's* her To break her will,   *Gareth and L.* 616
Besieged (*See also* **Strait-Besieged**) *b* Ygerne
    within Tintagil,   *Com. of Arthur* 198
Besotted A drowning life, *b* in sweet self,   *Princess vii* 314
    So far *b* that they fail to see   *Balin and Balan* 359
Besought *B* him, supplicating, if he cared   *Enoch Arden* 163
    the knight *b* him, 'Follow me,   *Geraint and E.* 807
    B Lavaine to write as she devised   *Lancelot and E.* 1103
    B me to be plain and blunt,   ,, 1301
Bess (horse) Black *B,* Tantivy, Tallyho,   *The Brook* 160
Bess (Christian name) MILK for my sweet-'arts, B !   *Spinster's S's.* 1
    Mew ! mew !—*B* wi' the milk !   ,, 113
    I says ' I'd be good to tha, B,   *Owd Roä* 75
Bessy Marris 'bout *B M's* barne.   *N. Farmer, O. S.* 14
    B M's barne ! tha knaws she laäid   ,, 21
Best (*See also* **Earthly-best, Heavenly-best**) at *b*
    A vague suspicion of the breast :   *Two Voices* 335
    they say : Kind nature is the *b:*   *Walk to the Mail* 64
    b That ever came from pipe.   *Will Water.* 75
    He gave the people of his *b* :   *You might have won* 25
    His worst he kept, his *b* he gave.   ,, 26
    You chose the *b* among us—a strong man :   *Enoch Arden* 293
    Their *b* and brightest, when they dwelt   *Aylmer's Field* 69
    so true that second thoughts are *b*?   *Sea Dreams* 65
    Arising, did his holy oily *b,*   ,, 195
    sit the *b* and stateliest of the land ?   *Lucretius* 172
    who love *b* have *b* the grace to know   *W. to Marie Alex.* 28
    I could have wept with the *b.* (repeat)   *Grandmother* 20, 100
    fur them as 'as it's the *b.*   *N. Farmer, N. S.* 44
    And do their little *b* to bite   *Lit. Squabbles* 6
    And cancell'd nature's *b:*   *In Mem. lxxii* 6
    Fair words were *b* for him who fights   *Gareth and L.* 946
    as the stateliest and the *b*   *Marr. of Geraint* 20
    my dear child is set forth at her *b,*   ,, 728

Best (*continued*) arms for guerdon ; choose the *b*.' — *Geraint and E.* 218
desired the humbling of their *b*, — " 637
fairest and the *b* Of ladies living — *Balin and Balan* 339
I, and all, As fairest, *b* and purest, — " 350
I have seen ; but *b*, B, purest ? — " 356
From homage to the *b* and purest, — " 376
women, worst and *b*, as Heaven and Hell. — *Merlin and V.* 815
Win shall I not, but do my *b* to win : — *Lancelot and E.* 221
Young as I am, yet would I do my *b*.' — " 222
with meats and vintage of their *b* — " 266
Lives for his children, ever at its *b* — " 336
when they love their *b*, Closest — " 869
she deem'd she look'd her *b*, — " 907
having loved God's *b* And greatest, — " 1093
'Let love be free ; free love is for the *b* : — " 1381
What should be *b*, if not so pure a love — " 1383
Arthur kept his *b* until the last ; — *Holy Grail* 763
'Then,' I said, 'I'm none o' the *b*.' — *First Quarrel* 61
he would have been one of his *b*. — *Rizpah* 28
our Lawrence the *b* of the brave : — *Def. of Lucknow* 11
their marksmen were told of our *b*, — " 19
sees the B that glimmers thro' the Worst, — *Ancient Sage* 72
an' I knaws it be all fur the *b*. — *Spinster's S's.* 52
Is girlish talk at *b* ; — *Epilogue* 43
rank with the *b*, Garrick — *To W. C. Macreday* 6
so fickle are men—the *b* ! — *The Ring* 392
and body is foul at *b*. — *Happy* 28
Phra-Chai, the Shadow of the *B*, — *To Ulysses* 41
The *b* in me that sees the worst in me, — *Romney's R.* 44
the Highest is the wisest and the *b*, — *Faith* 1
Bestial Courteous or *b* from the moment, — *Gareth and L.* 631
Best-natured 'Which was prettiest, *B-n* ?' — *Princess i* 234
Bestrode he *b* my Grandsire, when he fell, — " *ii* 242
Bethink *B* thee, Lord, while thou and all — *St. S. Stylites* 105
Bethlehem Not least art thou, thou little *B* In Judah, — *Sir J. Oldcastle* 24
Bethought Then she *b* her of a faded silk, — *Marr. of Geraint* 134
and *b* her of her promise given — " 602
b her how she used to watch, — " 647
Betide All-arm'd I ride, whate'er *b*, — *Sir Galahad* 83
I meet my fate, whatever ills *b* ! — *The Flight* 95
Betray wouldst *b* me for the precious hilt ; — *M. d'Arthur* 126
Break lock and seal : *b* the trust : — *You might have won* 18
They know me not. I should *b* myself. — *Enoch Arden* 789
and said, ' *B* me not, but help— — *Pelleas and E.* 360
Simpler than any child, *b's* itself. — *Guinevere* 371
wouldst *b* me for the precious hilt ; — *Pass. of Arthur* 294
you knew that he meant to *b* me— — *Charity* 12
Betray'd 'Thou hast *b* thy nature and thy name, — *M. d'Arthur* 73
B my secret penance, so that all — *St. S. Stylites* 68
let them know themselves *b* ; — *Aylmer's Field* 524
b her cause and mine— — *Princess v* 76
' Thou hast *b* thy nature and thy name, — *Pass. of Arthur* 241
Betraying statesman there, *b* His party-secret, — *Maud II v* 34
Betrothed (*See also* **Long-betroth'd**) her far-off cousin and *b*, — *The Brook* 75
b To one, a neighbouring Princess : — *Princess i* 32
I spake of why we came, And my *b*. — " 120
B us over their wine, — *Maud I ix* 39
Betrothment how the strange *b* was to end : — *Princess v* 474
Betted they *b* ; made a hundred friends, — *Princess, Pro.* 163
Better how much *b* than to own A crown, — *Ode to Memory* 120
Were it not *b* not to be ?' — *Two Voices* 3
Is boundless *b*, boundless worse. — " 27
Surely 'twere *b* not to be. — " 48
'Twere *b* not to breathe or speak, — " 94
A murmur, ' Be of *b* cheer.' — " 429
'Twere *b* I should cease Although — *To J. S.* 66
are men *b* than sheep or goats — *M. d'Arthur* 250
Something *b* than his dog, — *Locksley Hall* 50
B thou wert dead before me, — " 56
B thou and I were lying, — " 57
held it *b* men should perish one by one, — " 179
B to me the meanest weed — *Amphion* 93

Better (*continued*) griefs Like his have worse or *b*, — *Enoch Arden* 741
B not be at all Than not be noble. — *Princess ii* 93
B to clear prime forests, — " *iii* 127
Methinks he seems no *b* than a girl ; — " 218
You hold the woman is the *b* man ; — " *iv* 410
Almost our maids were *b* at their homes, — " *v* 428
b or worse Than the heart of the citizen — *Maud I i* 23
peace or war ? *b*, war ! loud war — " 47
far *b* to be born To labour — *Maud I xviii* 33
myself have awaked, as it seems, to the *b* mind ; — " *III vi* 56
It is *b* to fight for the good — " 57
A worse were *b* ; yet no worse would I. — *Gareth and L.* 17
But truly foul are *b*, for they send — " 947
b were I laid in the dark earth, — *Marr. of Geraint* 97
sigh'd ' Was I not *b* there with him ?' — *Balin and Balan* 292
b have died Thrice than have ask'd — *Merlin and V.* 918
B the King's waste hearth and — *Guinevere* 524
are men *b* than sheep or goats — *Pass. of Arthur* 418
b that than his, than he The friend, — *Lover's Tale i* 652
B have sent Our Edith thro' — *Sisters (E. and E.)* 224
B a rotten borough or so — *Riflemen form !* 17
Go, therefore, thou ! thy *b's* went — *Will Water.* 185
Thine elders and thy *b's*. — " 192
Thy *b* born unhappily from thee, — *Aylmer's Field* 675
in the distance pealing news Of *b*, — *Princess iv* 82
My brother and my *b*, this man here, — *Balin and Balan* 54
By striking at her *b*, miss'd, — *Merlin and V.* 499
That they had the *b* In perils of battle — *Batt. of Brunanburh* 84
And then I will let you a *b*.' — *By an Evolution.* 4
ever cared to *b* his own kind, — *Sea Dreams* 201
his work, That practice *b's* ?' — *Princess iii* 299
voice that—you scarce could *b* that. — *Sisters (E. and E.)* 14
B fifty years of Europe than a cycle — *Locksley Hall* 184
for I love him all the *b* for it— — *Enoch Arden* 196
B the waste Atlantic roll'd On her — *Third of Feb.* 21
For himself has done much *b*. — *Spiteful Letter* 4
I loved him *b* than play ; — *First Quarrel* 14
an' I loved him *b* than all. — " 14
I had *b* ha' put my naked hand in a hornets' nest. — " 50
you had *b* ha' beaten me black an' blue — " 72
Bettering ill for him who, *b* not with time, — *Will* 10
Beugh (bough) togither like birds on a *b* ; — *North. Cobbler* 54
Beverley Burnt too, my faithful preacher, *B* ! — *Sir J. Oldcastle* 80
Bevy a *b* of Eroses apple-cheek'd, — *The Islet* 11
Bewail Let golden youth *b* the friend, — *To Mary Boyle* 53
Bewail'd maidens with one mind *B* their lot ; — *In Mem. ciii* 46
Beware *b* Lest, where you seek — *Princess, vi* 171
Bewitch'd thaw it wur summat *b* — *North. Cobbler* 82
Bib their bottles o' pap, an' their mucky *b's*, — *Spinster's S's.* 87
Bible oft at *B* meetings, o'er the rest — *Sea Dreams* 194
read me a *B* verse of the Lord's good will — *Rizpah* 61
But as a Latin *B* to the crowd ; — *Sir J. Oldcastle* 18
Bicker To *b* down a valley. — *The Brook* 26
And *b's* into red and emerald, — *Princess v* 263
men may *b* with the things they love, — *Geraint and E.* 325
and the points of lances *b* in it. — " 449
Bicker'd Flicker'd and *b* From helmet — *Merlin and the G.* 70
Bid Friends, I was *b* to speak of such a one — *Aylmer's Field* 677
of him I was not *b* to speak— — " 710
lest I should *b* thee live ; — *Princess vii* 9
Dare I *b* her abide by her word ? — *Maud I xvi* 25
b him bring Charger and palfrey.' — *Geraint and E.* 400
my dear lord arise and *b* me do it, — " 665
And *b* me cast it. — " 707
we shall never *b* again Goodmorrow— — *Balin and Balan* 622
I *b* the stranger welcome. — *Merlin and V.* 270
She needs must *b* farewell to sweet Lavaine. — *Lancelot and E.* 341
and *b* call the ghostly man Hither, — " 1099
Send ! *b* him come ;' but Lionel was away— — *Lover's Tale iv* 101
when he came to *b* me goodbye. — *First Quarrel* 78
I had *b* him my last goodbye ; — *Rizpah* 41
Edith wrote : ' My mother *b's* me ask ' — *Sisters (E. and E.) i* 181
Not there to *b* my boy farewell, — *To Marq. of Dufferin* 42
as 'ull hallus do as 'e's *b*.' — *Owd Roä* 79
B him farewell for me, and tell him— — *Romney's R.* 147

Bidden I knock'd and, *b*, enter'd ; — *Princess iii* 130
Rise !' and the damsel *b* rise arose — *Merlin and V.* 68
The foot that loiters, *b* go,— — *Last Tournament* 117
Bidding *b* him Disband himself, and scatter — *Geraint and E.* 797
And in my vision *b* me dream on, — *Lover's Tale ii* 119
Bide 'Were this not well, to *b* mine hour, — *Two Voices* 76
Will you not *b* your year as I *b* mine ?' — *Enoch Arden* 438
Philip answer'd 'I will *b* my year.' — " 439
why she should *B* by this issue : — *Princess v* 326
bound am I to *b* with thee. — *Gareth and L.* 805
B ye here the while. — *Merlin and V.* 97
'Go ! I *b* the while.' — " 99
To whom the Lord of Astolat, '*B* with us, — *Lancelot and E.* 632
if I *b*, lo ! this wild flower for me !' — " 644
B,' answer'd he : 'we needs must hear — " 756
I cannot *b* Sir Baby. — *Pelleas and E.* 190
yourselves : how can ye *b* at peace, — " 265
But never let me *b* one hour at peace.' — " 387
thou canst not *b*, unfrowardly, — " 597
will draw me into fresher life, — *Guinevere* 122
I *b* no more, I meet my fate, — *The Flight* 95
Bided ever *b* tryst at village stile, — *Merlin and V.* 378
They heard, they *b* their time. — *Bandit's Death* 14
Bideford Men of *B* in Devon, — *The Revenge* 17
Biding leave Thine easeful *b* here, — *Gareth and L.* 128
Bier (*See also* **Chariot-bier**, **Litter-bier**) This truth
came borne with *b* and pall, — *In Mem. lxxxv* 1
cast him and the *b* in which he lay — *Geraint and E.* 572
Till yonder man upon the *b* arise, — " 657
Wreathed round the *b* with garlands : — *Lover's Tale ii* 79
those six virgins which upheld the *b*, — " 84
and all The vision of the *b*. — " *iii* 11
those that held the *b* before my face, — " 16
on the sand Threw down the *b* ; — " 33
She from her *b*, as into fresher life, — " 42
I stood stole beside the vacant *b*. — " 58
I hate the black negation of the *b*, — *Ancient Sage* 204
Who saw you kneel beside your *b*, — *Happy* 54
THE bridal garland falls upon the *b*, — *D. of the Duke of C.* 1
Big being apt at arms and *b* of bone — *Marr. of Geraint* 489
Cried out with a *b* voice, 'What, is he dead ?' — *Geraint and E.* 541
as *b* i' the mouth as a cow, — *Village Wife* 103
Bigger With me, Sir, enter'd in the *b* boy, — *Princess ii* 404
No *b* than a glow-worm under the tent — " *iv* 25
Bight the spangle dances in *b* and bay, — *Sea-Fairies* 24
and flung them in *b* and bay, — *V. of Maeldune* 53
Bill (**beak**) With that gold dagger of thy *b* — *The Blackbird* 11
A golden *b* ! the silver tongue, — " 13
Bill (**parliamentary measure**) I had heard it was
this *b* that past, — *Walk. to the Mail* 67
My lord, and shall we pass the *b* — *Day-Dm., Revival* 27
Bill (**an account**) But 'e niver looökt ower a *b*, — *Village Wife* 51
Bill of Sale (A *b o s* gleam'd thro' the drizzle) — *Enoch Arden* 688
Billow (*See also* **Flame-billow**) to the *b* the fountain
calls : — *Sea-Fairies* 9
a *b*, blown against, Falls back, — *Two Voices* 316
the wanton *b* wash'd Them over, — *Lover's Tale ii* 9
the upblown *b* ran Shoreward — " 178
flow'd away To those unreal *b*'s: — " 196
jarring breaker, the deep-sea *b*, — *Batt. of Brunanburh* 97
Saxon and Angle from over the broad *b* — " 119
Billow'd heard The voice that *b* round — *Last Tournament* 167
Billowing Blanching and *b* in a hollow of it, — *Lucretius* 31
Enring'd a *b* fountain in the midst ; — *Princess ii* 28
and his river *b* ran, — *Maud I iv* 32
Billy (**horse**) '*B*,' says 'e, 'hev a joomp !'— — *Village Wife* 83
But *B* fell bakkuds o' Charlie, — " 85
Billy-rough-un (**horse**) Fur he ca'd 'is 'erse *B-r-u*, — " 84
Bin (*See also* **Corn-bin**) In musty *b*'s and chambers, — *Will Water.* 102
Bind cords that *b* and strain The heart — *Clear-headed friend* 4
We must *b* And keep you fast, — *Rosalind* 42
We'll *b* you fast in silken cords, — " 49
b with bands That island Queen — *Buonaparte* 2
an athlete, strong to break or *b* — *Palace of Art* 153
Life, that, working strongly, *b*'s— — *Love thou thy land* 34

Bind (*continued*) rent The woodbine wreaths that *b* her, — *Amphion* 34
Faster *b*'s a tyrant's power ; — *Vision of Sin* 128
dream That Love could *b* them closer — *Aylmer's Field* 41
my vow *B*'s me to speak, — *Princess ii* 203
Psyche, wont to *b* my throbbing brow, — " 250
b the scatter'd scheme of seven — " *Con.* 8
he may read that *b*'s the sheaf, — *In Mem. xxxvi* 13
the frame that *b*'s him in His isolation — " *xlv* 11
I took the thorns to *b* my brows, — " *lxix* 6
May *b* a book, may line a box, — " *lxxvii* 6
King Will *b* thee by such vows, — *Gareth and L.* 270
would *b* The two together ; — *Marr. of Geraint* 790
what is worthy love Could *b* him, — *Lancelot and E.* 1379
yet thee She fail'd to *b*, — " 1385
round thee, maiden, *b* my belt. — *Holy Grail* 159
'*B* him, and bring him in.' — *Pelleas and E.* 232
B him as heretofore, and bring him in : — " 271
Far less to *b*, your victor, and thrust him — " 293
let my lady *b* me if she will, — " 334
vow that *b*'s too strictly snaps itself— — *Last Tournament* 657
Had Arthur right to *b* them to himself ? — " 684
To *b* them by inviolable vows, — " 688
B me to one ? The wide world laughs — " 695
What ! shall I *b* him more ? — *Lover's Tale iv* 346
b the maid to love you by the ring ; — *The Ring* 202
Binding *b* his good horse To a tree, — *Pelleas and E.* 30
Bindweed-bell fragile *b*-*b*'s and briony rings ; — *The Brook* 203
Bine When burr and *b* were gather'd ; — *Aylmer's Field* 113
berries that flamed upon *b* and vine, — *V. of Maeldune* 61
Binn beeswing from a *b* reserved For banquets, — *Aylmer's Field* 405
Birch (*See also* **Birk**) OUR *b*'es yellowing and from
each — *Pro. to Gen. Hamley* 1
Bird (*See also* **Birdie**, **Wild-bird**, **Carrier-bird**, **Sea-bird**) voice of the *b* Shall no more be heard, — *All Things will Die* 24
heart of the garden the merry *b* chants. — *Poet's Mind* 22
b would sing, nor lamb would bleat, — *Mariana in the S.* 37
Not any song of *b* or sound of rill ; — *D. of F. Women* 66
singing clearer than the crested *b* — " 179
lusty *b* takes every hour for dawn. — *M. d'Arthur, Ep.* 11
Sang loud, as tho' he were the *b* of day. — *Gardener's D.* 96
These *b*'s have joyful thoughts. — " 99
Slides the *b* o'er lustrous woodland, — *Locksley Hall* 162
every *b* of Eden burst In carol, — *Day-Dm., L'Envoi* 7
Like long-tail'd *b*'s of Paradise — *Ep.* 7
fly, like a *b*, from tree to tree ; — *Edward Gray* 31
b that pipes his lone desire — *You might have won* 31
Like the caged *b* escaping suddenly, — *Enoch Arden* 269
lightning flash of insect and of *b*, — " 575
beacon-blaze allures The *b* of passage, — " 729
Philip chatter'd more than brook or *b* ; — *The Brook* 51
'The *b*'s were warm, (repeat) — *Aylmer's Field* 260
Returning, as the *b* returns, at night, — *Sea Dreams* 43
and every *b* that sings : — " 102
b Makes his heart voice amid — *Lucretius* 100
b or fish, or opulent flower : — " 249
the *b*, the fish, the shell, the flower, — *Princess ii* 383
As flies the shadow of a *b*, she fled. — " *iii* 96
not see The *b* of passage flying south — " 210
earliest pipe of half-awaken'd *b*'s — " *iv* 50
wild *b*'s on the light Dash themselves dead. — " 495
b's that piped their Valentines, — " *v* 239
a *b*, That early woke to feed — " *vii* 251
Make music, O *b*, in the new-budded — *W. to Alexandra* 11
There is but one *b* with a musical throat, — *The Islet* 27
And *b* in air, and fishes turn'd — *The Victim* 19
B's' love, and *b*'s' song — *Window, Spring* 1
B's' song and *b*'s' love, (repeat) — " 3, 5
We'll be *b*'s of a feather, — " 14
Be merry, all *b*'s, to-day, — *Ay.*
Like *b*'s the charming serpent draws, — *In Mem. xxxiv* 14
Wild *b*, whose warble, liquid sweet, — " *lxxxviii* 1
Flits by the sea-blue *b* of March ; — " *xci* 1
So loud with voices of the *b*'s, — " *xcix* 1
low love-language of the *b* — " *cii* 11
happy *b*'s, that change their sky — " *cxv* 15

Bird (*continued*) I hear a chirp of *b*'s ; — *In Mem. cxix* 5
  Beginning, and the wakeful *b* ; — ,, *cxxi* 11
  B's in the high Hall-garden (repeat) — *Maud I xii* 1, 25
  B's in our wood sang — ,, 9
  And the *b* of prey will hover, — ,, *xx* 28
  Till a silence fell with the waking *b*, — ,, *xxii* 17
  My *b* with the shining head, — *II iv* 45
  red berries charm the *b*, — *Gareth and L* 85
  b's made Melody on branch, — ,, 182
  ' O *b*'s, that warble to the morning sky, O *b*'s that
    warble as the day goes by, — ,, 1075
  ' What knowest thou of *b*'s, — ,, 1078
  and as the sweet voice of a *b*, — *Marr. of Geraint* 329
  Moves him to think what kind of *b* it is — ,, 331
  by the *b*'s song ye may learn the nest,' — ,, 359
  Among the dancing shadows of the *b*'s, — ,, 601
  all about were *b*'s Of sunny plume — ,, 658
  we will live like two *b*'s in one nest. — *Geraint and E.* 627
  than all shriek of *b* or beast, — *Balin and Balan* 545
  the *b* Who pounced her quarry — *Merlin and V.* 134
  took his brush and blotted out the *b*, — ,, 478
  foul *b* of rapine whose whole prey — ,, 728
  Then as a little helpless innocent *b*, — *Lancelot and E.* 894
  b's of passage piping up and down, — *Holy Grail* 146
  once the shadow of a *b* Flying, — *Pelleas and E.* 38
  Beneath the shadow of some *b* of prey ; — ,, 608
  head all night, like *b*'s of prey, — *Last Tournament* 138
  like wild *b*'s that change Their season — *Pass. of Arthur* 38
  sent his soul Into the songs of *b*'s, — *Lover's Tale i* 321
  the *b* That will not hear my call, — ,, *iv* 159
  togither like *b*'s on a beugh ; — *North. Cobbler* 54
  And a pinnace, like a flutter'd *b*, — *The Revenge* 2
  b's make ready for their bridal-time — *Sisters (E. and E.)* 71
  Some *b*'s are sick and sullen when they moult. — ,, 73
  not arter the *b*'s wi' 'is gun, — *Village Wife* 41
  a score of wild *b*'s Cried — *V. of Maeldune* 27
  And the shouting of these wild *b*'s — ,, 33
  And we left the dead to the *b*'s — ,, 36
  flight of *b*'s, the flame of sacrifice, — *Tiresias* 6
  b with a warble plaintively sweet — *The Wreck* 81
  b's could make This music in the *b* ? — *Ancient Sage* 21
  shell must break before the *b* can fly. — ,, 154
  listen how the *b*'s Begin to warble — *The Flight* 60
  whishper was sweet as the lilt of a *b* ! — *Tomorrow* 33
  av the *b* 'ud come to me call, — ,, 45
  thy chuckled note, Thou twinkling *b*, — *Early Spring* 38
  The summer *b* is still, — *Pref. Poem Broth. S.* 18
  FAINT as a climate-changing *b* that flies — *Demeter and P.* 1
  I envied human wives, and nested *b*'s, — ,, 53
  my ravings hush'd The *b*, — ,, 109
  b's that circle round the tower — *The Ring* 85
  B's and brides must leave the nest. — ,, 89
  bright *b* that still is veering thro' — ,, 332
  My *b*'s would sing, You heard not. — *To Mary Boyle* 18
  scaled the buoyant highway of the *b*'s, — *Prog. of Spring* 80
  Sing like a *b* and be happy, — *Parnassus* 14
  waked a *b* of prey that scream'd and past ; — *Death of Œnone* 87
  Warble *b*, and open flower, — *Akbar's D., Hymn* 7
Birdie Sleep, little *b*, sleep ! — *Sea Dreams* 282
  Without her ' little *b* '? well then, — ,, 283
  sleep, And I will sing you '*b*.' — ,, 284
  What does little *b* say — ,, 293
  Let me fly, says little *b*, — ,, 295
  B, rest a little longer, — ,, 297
  Baby says, like little *b*, — ,, 303
Bird's-eye-view *b-e-v* of all the ungracious past — *Princess ii* 125
Birk Shadows of the silver *b* — *A Dirge* 5
  ere thy maiden *b* be wholly clad, — *Prog. of Spring* 50
Birth *arms, or power of brain, or b* — *To the Queen* 3
  The old earth Had a *b*, — *All Things will Die* 38
  Her temple and her place of *b*, — *Supp. Confessions* 53
  winds, as at their hour of *b*, — *The Winds, etc.* 1
  At the moment of thy *b*, — *Eleänore* 15
  range of evil between death and *b*, — *If I were loved* 3
  hadst not between death and *b* — *Two Voices* 169

Birth (*continued*) From that first nothing ere his *b* — *Two Voices* 332
  Would God renew me from my *b* — *Miller's D.* 27
  slew him with your noble *b*. — *L. C. V. de Vere* 48
  Titanic forces taking *b* In divers — *Day-Dm., L'Envoi* 17
  'He does not love me for my *b*, — *Lady Clare* 9
  marriage, and the *b* Of Philip's child : — *Enoch Arden* 708
  one act at once, The *b* of light : — *Princess iii* 326
  The time draws near the *b* of Christ : — *In Mem. xxviii* 1
  Beyond the second *b* of Death. — ,, *xlv* 16
  Who breaks his individous bar, — ,, *lxiv* 5
  Evil haunts The *b*, the bridal ; — ,, *xcviii* 14
  Memories of bridal, or of *b*, — ,, *xcix* 15
  The time draws near the *b* of Christ ; — ,, *civ* 1
  Becoming, when the time has *b*, — ,, *cxiii* 14
  shaping an infant ripe for his *b*, — *Maud I iv* 34
  mine by a right, from *b* till death. — ,, *xix* 42
  By the home that gave me *b*, — ,, *II iv* 7
  ' Knowest thou aught of Arthur's *b* ?' — *Com. of Arthur* 147
  learn the secret of our Arthur's *b*.' — ,, 159
  the cloud that settles round his *b* — *Gareth and L.* 130
  had tended on him from his *b*, — ,, 179
  creatures voiceless thro' the fault of *b*, — *Geraint and E.* 266
  that weird legend of his *b*, — *Last Tournament* 669
  mystery From all men, like his *b* ; — *Guinevere* 298
  govern a whole life from *b* to death, — *Lover's Tale i* 76
  like each other was the *b* of each ! (repeat) — ,, 197, 201
  Gives *b* to a brawling brook, — ,, 526
  Rose of Lancaster, Red in thy *b*, — *Sir J. Oldcastle* 53
  Have I not been about thee from thy *b* ? — *Columbus* 148
  and was noble in *b* as in worth, — *V. of Maeldune* 3
  sweet mother land which gave them *b* — *Tiresias* 122
  Youth and Health, and *b* and wealth, — *By an Evolution.* 8
  how far' from o'er the gates of B, — *Far-far-away* 13
  the *b* of a baseborn child. — *Charity* 28
Birthday Each month, a *b-d* coming on, — *Will Water.* 93
  the night Before my Enid's *b*, — *Marr. of Geraint* 458
  given her on the night Before her *b*, — ,, 633
  I send a *b* line Of greeting ; — *To E. Fitzgerald* 45
  on your third September *b* — *The Ring* 130
  And sent it on her *b*. — ,, 211
  She in wrath Return'd it on her *b*, — ,, 212
  And on your Mother's *b*—all but yours— — ,, 248
  This *b*, death-day, and betrothal ring, — ,, 276
  Your *b* was her death-day. — ,, 301
  forgotten it was your *b*, child— — ,, 378
  Your fifth September *b*. — ,, 423
  Every morning is thy *b* — *Akbar's D., Hymn* 2
  b came of a boy born happily dead. — *Charity* 34
Biscay The *B*, roughly ridging eastward, — *Enoch Arden* 529
Bishop Archbishop, *B*, Priors, Canons, — *Sir J. Oldcastle* 159
  Ay, an' ya seed the *B*. — *Church-warden, etc.* 17
  an' sits o' the *B*'s throän. — ,, 20
  an' thou'll be a *B* yit. — ,, 50
Bit (*s*) or *b*'s of roasting ox Moan — *Lucretius* 131
  Nobbut a *b* on it's left, — *N. Farmer, O.S.* 41
  an' a nicetish *b* o' land. — *N. S.* 22
  Vext me a *b*, till he told me — *First Quarrel* 36
  I am going to leave you a *b*— — ,, 80
  ' tha mun breäk 'im off *b* by *b*.' — *North. Cobbler* 88
  jingle of *b*'s, Shouts, arrows, — *Tiresias* 93
  like a *b* of yisther-day in a dhrame— — *Tomorrow* 8
  Now I'll tha tha a *b* o' my mind — *Church-warden, etc.* 21
  if tha wants to git forrads a *b*, — ,, 49
Bit (*verb*) *b* his lips, And broke away. — *Dora* 33
  crack'd the helmet thro', and *b* the bone, — *Marr. of Geraint* 573
  clench'd her fingers till they *b* the palm, — *Lancelot and E.* 611
  an' a-squeälin, as if tha was *b*, — *Owd Roä* 89
Bite (*s*) Showing the aspick's *b*.) — *D. of F. Women* 160
  An' it wasn't a *b* but a burn, — *Owd Roä* 90
Bite (*verb*) *b*'s it for true heart and not for harm, — *Princess, Pro.* 174
  And do their little best to *b* — *Lit. Squabbles* 6
  B, frost, *b* ! (repeat) — *Window, Winter* 7, 13
  b far into the heart of the house, — ,, 11
Biting *b* laws to scare the beasts of prey — *Princess v* 393
  Modred *b* his thin lips was mute, — *Gareth and L.* 31

Bitten (*See also* **Root-bitten**) *b* the heel of the
  going year.   *Window, Winter* 6
b into the heart of the earth,   ,, 18
one whose foot is *b* by an ant,   *Pelleas and E.* 184
Scratch'd, *b*, blinded, marr'd me *Last Tournament* 526
Bitter (*See also* **Seeming-bitter, Wormwood-**
  bitter) Failing to give the *b* of the sweet,   *D. of F. Women* 286
O sweet and *b* in a breath,   *In Mem. iii* 3
My own less *b*, rather more :   ,, *vi* 6
If I find the world so *b*   *Maud I vi* 33
Then the world were not so *b* (repeat) ,, 38, 94
canst abide a truth, Tho' *b*. *Balin and Balan* 502
she tempted them and fail'd, Being so *b*: *Merlin and V.* 820
b death must be : Love, thou art *b* ; *Lancelot and E.* 1010
Bitterer Yet *b* from his readings. *Aylmer's Field* 553
Bitterly *B* weeping I turn'd away: (repeat) *Edward Gray* 6, 34
 '*B* wept I over the stone :   ,, 33
long and *b* meditating,   *Boädicea* 35
spake the Queen and somewhat *b*, *Guinevere* 271
Bittern *See* **Butter-bump**
Bitterness Sweet in their utmost *b*, *Supp. Confessions* 117
Have fretted all to dust and *b*.' *Princess vi* 264
wake The old *b* again,   *In Mem. lxxxiv* 13
By reason of the *b* and grief *Com. of Arthur* 210
they were, A *b* to me !—   *Last Tournament* 41
his spirit From *b* of death. *Lover's Tale i* 143
Bivouac Gone the comrades of my *b*, *Locksley H., Sixty,* 45
Blabbing physician, *b* The case of his patient— *Maud II v* 36
Prophet, curse me the *b* lip,   ,, 57
Black (*See also* **Coal-black, Jet-black**) *B* the
  garden-bowers and grots *Arabian Nights* 78
In the yew-wood *b* as night,   *Oriana* 19
foreground *b* with stones and slags, *Palace of Art* 81
that hair More *b* than ashbuds *Gardener's D.* 28
in its coarse *b*'s or whites, *W. to the Mail* 107
The streets were *b* with smoke *In Mem. lxix* 3
To *b* and brown on kindred brows. ,, *lxxix* 16
who alway rideth arm'd in *b*, *Gareth and L.* 636
B, with *b* banner, and a long *b* horn ,, 1366
ready on the river, clothed in *b*. *Lancelot and E.* 1123
Part *b*, part whiten'd with the bones *Holy Grail* 500
B as the harlot's heart— *Pelleas and E.* 468
Wear *b* and white, and be a nun *Guinevere* 677
stoled from head to foot in flowing *b* ; *Lover's Tale ii* 85
bars Of *b* and bands of silver, ,, *iv* 59
better ha' beaten me *b* an' blue *First Quarrel* 72
An' yer hair as *b* as the night, *Tomorrow* 32
b in white above his bones. *Locksley H., Sixty,* 44
B with bridal favours mixt ! *Forlorn* 69
B was the night when we crept away *Bandit's Death* 25
the dumb Hour, clothed in *b*, *Silent Voices* 1
Black (**Sea**) side of the *B* and the Baltic deep, *Maud III vi* 51
Black-beaded Glancing with *b-b* eyes, *Lilian* 15
Black-bearded stern *b-b* kings with wolfish eyes, *D. of F. Women* 111
Black Bess (**Horse**) *B B*, Tantivy, Tallyho, *The Brook* 160
Blackbird (*See also* **Merle**) O *B* ! sing me some-
  thing well :   *The Blackbird* 1
while the *b* on the pippin hung *Audley Court* 38
The *b*'s have their wills, (repeat) *Early Spring* 5, 47
Black-blue *b-b* Irish hair and Irish eyes *Last Tournament* 404
Blackcap The *b* warbles, and the turtle purrs, *Prog. of Spring* 55
Black'd *B* with thy branding thunder, *St. S. Stylites* 76
Blacken pierces the liver and *b*'s the blood ; *The Islet* 35
bark and *b* innumerable,   *Boädicea* 14
B round the Roman carrion,   ,, 14
upon a throne, And *b*'s every blot : *Ded. of Idylls* 28
City children soak and *b* *Locksley H., Sixty,* 218
b round The corpse of every man *Romney's R.* 122
Blacken'd (*See also* **Pitch-blacken'd**) So *b* all her world
  in secret,   *Princess vii* 42
the walls *B* about us,   ,, *Con* 110
His countenance *b*, and his forehead *Balin and Balan* 391
Blackening *b* over heath and holt, *Locksley Hall* 191
And *b* in the sea-foam sway'd *Holy Grail* 802
B against the dead-green stripes *Pelleas and E.* 554

Blackening (*continued*) *b*, swallow'd all the land, *Guinevere* 82
Was *b* on the slopes of Portugal, *Sisters (E. and E.)* 62
Blackest lie which is half a truth is ever the *b* of lies, *Grandmother* 30
To lie, to lie—in God's own house—the *b* of all lies ! *The Flight* 52
Black-heart unnetted *b-h*'s ripen dark, *The Blackbird* 7
Black-hooded Black-stoled, *b-h*, like a dream *M. d'Arthur* 197
Black-stoled, *b-h*, like a dream *Pass. of Arthur* 365
Blackness In the gross *b* underneath. *Supp. Confessions* 187
With *b* as a solid wall, *Palace of Art* 274
The *b* round the tombing sod, *On a Mourner* 27
dark was Uther too, Wellnigh to *b* ; *Com. of Arthur* 330
she make My darkness *b* ? *Balin and Balan* 193
Blackshadow'd there, *b* nigh the mere *Gareth and L.* 809
Blacksmith *b* border-marriage—one they knew— *Aylmer's Field* 263
b 'e strips me the thick ov 'is airm, *North. Cobbler* 85
Black-stoled *B-s*, black-hooded, like a dream *M. d'Arthur* 197
B-s, black-hooded, like a dream *Pass. of Arthur* 365
Blackthorn never see The blossom on the *b*, *May Queen, N. Y's. E.* 8
Blackthorn-blossom *b-b* fades and falls and leaves
  the bitter sloe,   *The Flight* 15
Black-wing'd the *b-w* Azrael overcame, *Akbar's Dream* 186
Blade (**of grass**) varying year with *b* and
  sheaf   *Day-Dm., Sleep. P.* 1
In bud or *b*, or bloom, may find, *Moral* 10
While life was yet in bud and *b*, *Princess i* 32
while the sun yet beat a dewy *b*, *Geraint and E.* 446
voice clings to each *b* of grass, *Lancelot and E.* 107
From buried grain thro' springing *b*, *Demeter and P.* 146
Blade (**of sword**) pure and true as *b*'s of steel. *Kate* 15
MY good *b* carves the casques of men, *Sir Galahad* 1
She bore the *b* of Liberty. *The Voyage* 72
struck out and shouted ; the *b* glanced, *Princess v* 540
Geraint's, who heaved his *b* aloft, *Marr. of Geraint* 572
b so bright That men are blinded *Com. of Arthur* 300
but turn the *b* and ye shall see, ,, 303
these will turn the *b*.' *Gareth and L.* 1095
the *b* flew Splintering in six, *Balin and Balan* 395
waved his *b* To the gallant three hundred *Heavy Brigade* 9
drove the *b* that had slain my husband *Bandit's Death* 34
Blade (**of dagger**) with the *b* he prick'd his hand, *Aylmer's Field* 239
 'From Edith' was engraven on the *b*. ,, 598
Blade (**shoulder-bone**) (*See also* **Shoulder blade**)
  arms were shatter'd to the shoulder *b*. *Princess vi* 52
Blain I face deform'd by lurid blotch and *b*— *Death of Œnone* 72
Blame (**s**) But he is chill to praise or *b*. *Two Voices* 258
Joyful and free from *b*. *D. of F. Women* 214
Shall smile away my maiden *b* ,, 214
The crime of malice, and is equal *b*.' *Vision of Sin* 216
Nor yours the *b*—for who beside *Aylmer's Field* 735
Which he has worn so pure of *b*, *Ode on Well.* 72
I had such reverence for his *b*, *In Mem. li* 6
white blamelessness accounted *b* !' *Merlin and V.* 799
mine the *b* that oft I seem as he *Last Tournament* 115
Received unto himself a part of *b*, *Lover's Tale i* 786
lines I read Nor utter'd word of *b*, *Pro. to Gen. Hamley* 18
Blame (**verb**) In truth You must *b* Love. *Miller's D.* 192
 'I have been to *b*—to *b*. *Dora* 159
I have been to *b*. Kiss me, my children.' ,, 161
Am I to *b* for this, *St. S. Stylites* 124
she had **a** will ; was he to *b* ? *Princess i* 48
yet I *b* you not so much for fear ; ,, *iv* 506
'Ida—'sdeath ! you *b* the man ; ,, *vi* 221
'*b* not thyself too much,' I said, 'nor *b* ,, *vii* 255
They are all to *b*, they are all to *b*. *Sailor Boy* 20
knot thou the winds that make *In Mem. xlix* 10
b not thou thy plaintive song,' ,, *lii* 5
Nor *b* I Death, because he bare ,, *lxxxii* 9
Nor count me all to *b* if I *Con.* 85
She did not wish to *b* him— *Maud I xx* 5
'Damsel,' he said, 'you be not all to *b*, *Gareth and L.* 1171
who should *b* me then ?' *Merlin and V.* 661
'To *b*, my lord Sir Lancelot, much to *b* ! *Lancelot and E.* 97
the girl was the most to *b*. *First Quarrel* 26
An' I felt I had been to *b* ; ,, 90
You praise when you should *b* *Épilogue* 4

Blame (verb) (continued) the Priest is not to b,	Happy 105
Blamed Shall love be b for want of faith ?	In Mem. li 10
Let love be b for it, not she, nor I :	Gareth and L. 299
b herself for telling hearsay tales :	Merlin and V. 951
Blameless b is he, centred in the sphere	Ulysses 39
Wearing the white flower of a b life.	Ded. of Idylls 25
Fearing the mild face of the b King,	Geraint and E. 812
Yourself were first the b cause	,, 826
The b King went forth and cast	,, 932
fighting for the b King.	,, 970
Arthur the b, pure as any maid,	Balin and Balan 479
Vivien should attempt the b King.	Merlin and V. 164
Arthur, b King and stainless man ?'	,, 779
And I myself, myself not b,	Columbus 185
Blamelessness thy white b accounted blame !'	Merlin and V. 799
Blanch breakers boom and b on the precipices,	Boädicea 76
b the bones of whom she slew,	Tiresias 150
ripple would hardly b into spray	The Wreck 137
Blanche Two widows, Lady Psyche, Lady B ;	Princess i 128
who were tutors. 'Lady B'	,, 232
brought a message here from Lady B.'	,, ii 319
we saw The Lady B's daughter	,, 321
Lady B alone Of faded form	,, 447
sent for B to accuse her face to face ;	,, iv 239
Lady B erect Stood up and spake,	,, 290
but B At distance follow'd :	,, vi 82
With kisses, ere the days of Lady B :	,, 114
she had authority—The Lady B :	,, 239
'Ay so?' said B : 'Amazed am I	,, 324
B had gone, but left Her child	,, vii 56
Not tho' B had sworn That after that dark night	,, 72
Blanched (See also **Summer-blanched**) Upon the b	
tablets of her heart ;	Isabel 17
B with his mill, they found ;	Enoch Arden 367
won it with a day B in our annals,	Princess vi 63
How b with darkness must I grow !	In Mem. lxi 8
wave, That b upon its side.	Lover's Tale i 45
Blanching Or scatter'd b on the grass.	Day-Dm., Arrival 12
confluence of watercourses B and	Lucretius 31
chanted on the b bones of men ?'	Princess ii 199
b apricot like snow in snow.	Prog. of Spring 30
Bland Shakespeare b and mild ;	Palace of Art 134
small his voice, But b the smile	Princess i 115
And bless thee, for thy lips are b,	In Mem. cxix 9
like the bountiful season b,	Maud I iv. 3
Blandishment an accent very low In b,	Isabel 20
Blank made b of crimeful record	St. S. Stylites 158
As b as death in marble ;	Princess i 177
b And waste it seem'd and vain ;	,, vii 42
rain On the bald street breaks the b day.	In Mem. vii 12
some but carven, and some b,	Gareth and L. 406
shield was b and bare without a sign	,, 414
B, or at least with some device	Lancelot and E. 194
God wot, his shield is b enough.	,, 197
he roll'd his eyes Yet b from sleep,	,, 820
one to the west, and counter to it, And b :	Holy Grail 255
the world as b as Winter-tide.	Last Tournament 221
the goodly view Was now one b,	Death of Œnone 4
Blanket When a b wraps the day,	Vision of Sin 80
Blankly Had gazed upon her b and gone by :	Merlin and V 161
Blare (s) With b of bugle, clamour of men,	Ode on Well. 115
Lured by the glare and the b,	V. of Maeldune 73
Blare (verb) Warble, O bugle, and trumpet, b !	W. to Alexandra 14
To b its own interpretation—	Lancelot and E. 943
Blared trumpet b At the barrier	Princess v 485
Blaspheme So they b the muse !	,, iv 137
O God, I could b, for he fought	Happy 15
Blasphemy troops of devils, mad with b,	St. S. Stylites 4
filth, and monstrous blasphemies,	Pass. of Arthur 114
B ! whose is the fault ?	Despair 107
B ! ay, why not,	,, 109
B ! true ! I have scared you	,, 111
But the b to my mind lies	,, 112
Blast (s) (See also **Trumpet-blast**) burst thro'	
with heated b's	D. of F. Women 29

Blast (s) (continued) The b was hard and harder.	The Goose 50
a b of sparkles up the flue :	M. d' Arthur, Ep. 15
desires, like fitful b's of balm	Gardener's D. 68
Cramming all the b before it,	Locksley Hall 192
b's would rise and rave and cease,	The Voyage 85
like the b of doom, Would shatter	Enoch Arden 769
a b of trumpets from the gate,	Princess, Pro. 42
the b and bray of the long horn	v 252
storm and b Had blown the lake	The Daisy 70
To break the b of winter, stand ;	To F. D. Maurice 22
b's that blow the poplar white,	In Mem. lxxii 3
Fiercely flies The b of North and East,	,, cvii 7
and a b, and overhead Thunder,	Holy Grail 184
in the b there smote along the hall	,, 186
such a b, my King, began to blow,	,, 795
So loud a b along the shore and sea,	,, 796
could not hear the waters for the b,	,, 797
That turns its back on the salt b,	Pelleas and E. 544
felt the b Beat on my heated eyelids :	Lover's Tale iii 27
The b and the burning shame	Rizpah 18
the b of that underground thunderclap	Def. of Lucknow 32
a sudden b blew us out and away	V. of Maeldune 10
to put forth and brave the b ;	Pref. Son. 19th. Cent. 8
with a howl and a hoot of the b	The Wreck 91
still'd the b and strown the wave,	Freedom 34
Blast (verb) I heard them b The steep slate-quarry,	Golden Year 75
like a poisonous wind I pass to b	Pelleas and E. 569
Blasted a sunbeam by the b Pine,	Princess vii 196
'was b with a curse :	D. of F. Women 103
years which are not Time's Had b him—	Aylmer's Field 602
B and burnt, and blinded as I was,	Holy Grail 844
So—your happy suit was b—	Locksley H., Sixty 5
And sent him charr'd and b	Happy 84
laurel is b by more than lightning !	Parnassus 12
Blasting b the long quiet of my breast	Lucretius 162
Blatant O b Magazines, regard me rather—	Hendecasyllabics 17
One still strong man in a b land,	Maud I x 63
Blaw (blossom) —wot's a beauty ?'—the	
flower as b's.	N. Farmer, N.S. 15
Blawin' (blowing) wind b hard tother waäy,	Owd Roä 104
Blaze (s) (See also **Beacon-blaze**) The b upon the	
waters to the east ; The b upon his island over-	
head ; The b upon the waters to the west ;	Enoch Arden 594
distant b of those dull banquets,	Aylmer's Field 489
voice amid the b of flowers :	Lucretius 101
Sat fifty in the b of burning fire ;	Spec. of Iliad 20
Her shadow on the b of kings :	In Mem. xcviii 19
wayside blossoms open to the b.	Balin and Balan 449
The incorporate b of sun and sea.	Lover's Tale i 409
vast sun-clusters' gather'd b,	Epilogue 54
betwixt the whitening sloe And kingcup b,	To Mary Boyle 26
Made by the noonday b without,	St. Telemachus 50
Blaze (verb) B upon her window, sun,	Window, When 15
the sun b on the turning scythe,	Geraint and E. 252
b the crime of Lancelot and the Queen.'	Pelleas and E. 570
smouldering scandal break and b	Guinevere 91
B by the rushing brook or silent well.	,, 400
B, making all the night a steam	,, 599
Blazed many a fire before them b :	Spec. of 'Iliad 10
b before the towers of Troy,	,, 18
joy that b itself in woodland wealth	Balin and Balan 82
thing was b about the court,	Merlin and V. 743
B the last diamond of the nameless king.	Lancelot and E. 444
heart's sad secret b itself	,, 836
heavens Open'd and b with thunder	Holy Grail 508
the heavens open'd and b again	,, 516
in a moment when they b again	,, 523
The sunset b along the wall of Troy.	Death of Œnone 77
Blazing See **Far-blazing**	
Blazon B your mottos of blessing	W. to Alexandra 12
twelve great windows b Arthur's wars,	Holy Grail 248
who shall b it ? when and how ?—	,, 255
Blazon'd from his b baldric slung	L. of Shalott iii 15
Sweat on his b chairs ;	Walk. to the Mail 76
No b statesman he, nor king.	You might have won 24

Blazon'd (*continued*)   b lions o'er the imperial tent   *Princess v 9*
Bright let it be with its b deeds,   *Ode on Well.* 56
The giant windows' b fires,   *The Daisy* 58
b fair In diverse raiment   *Palace of Art* 167
Some b, some but carven,   *Gareth and L.* 406
if twain His arms were b also;   " 413
all true hearts be b on her tomb   *Lancelot and E.* 1344
purple b with armorial gold.   *Godiva* 52
lamps b like Heaven and Earth   *Princess i* 223
monsters b what they were,   " *iv* 345
The prophet b on the panes;   *In Mem. lxxxvii* 8
shield of Gawain b rich and bright,   *Gareth and L.* 416
All the devices b on the shield   *Lancelot and E.* 9
  " 1149
Blazoning silken case with braided b's,   *Akbar's Dream* 137
banners b a Power That is not seen   *Merlin and V.* 597
Bleach'd wizard brow b on the walls: *Lancelot and E.* 43
lay till all their bones were b,   *Ode to Memory* 65
Bleat b Of the thick-fleeced sheep   *Mariana in the S.* 37
bird would sing, nor lamb would b,   *In the Child. Hosp.* 64
motherless b of a lamb in the storm   *May Queen, Con.* 2
Bleating I hear the b of the lamb.   *Princess iv* 392
Sent out a bitter b for its dam;   *Alexander* 2
Bled when her Satrap b At Issus   *Geraint and E.* 502
B underneath his armour secretly,   *Clear-headed friend* 5
Bleed strain The heart until it b's,   *Epilogue* 35
For which her warriors b,   *To J. S.* 63
Bleedeth my true breast B for both;   *Merlin and V.* 832
Blemish stain or b in a name of note,   *Dead Prophet* 66
'Small b upon the skin!   *In Mem. lxii* 2
Blench make thee somewhat b or fail,   *Making of Man* 7
Blend all their voices b in choric Hallelujah   *Princess vii* 30
Blent hatred of her weakness, b with shame.   *Miller's D.* 235
Bless But that God b thee, dear—   *Dora* 70, 94
And b him for the sake of him (repeat)   " 149
'God b him!' he said, 'and may he   *Lady Clare* 56
And b me, mother, ere I go.'   *Enoch Arden* 197
b him, he shall sit upon my knees   " 424
God b you for it, God reward you   *Aylmer's Field* 187
softly whisper 'B, God b 'em: " 372
And forty blest ones b him,   *Princess, Con.* 51
God b the narrow sea which keeps   " 70
God b the narrow seas!   *In Mem. lvi* 26
O for thy voice to soothe and b!   " *cxix* 9
And b thee, for thy lips are bland,   " *cxxiv* 1
That which we dare invoke to b;   *Gareth and L.* 698
And cried, 'God b the King,   " 1286
vext his day, but b'es him asleep—   *First Quarrel* 22
God b you, my own little Nell.'   *Rizpah* 64
the Saviour lives but to b.   *De Prof. Two G.* 17
that men May b thee as we b thee,   *To W. H. Brookfield* 14
dream of a shadow, go—God b you.   *To Prin. F. of H.* 4
He b'es the wife.   *Locksley H., Sixty* 85
Love your enemy, b your haters,   *Demeter and P.* 146
and b Their garner'd Autumn also,   *Akbar's Dream* 76
and 'b' Whom? even 'your persecutors'!   *Charity* 4
a woman, God b her, kept me from Hell.

Blessed *See* **Blest**
Blessedness Or is there b like theirs?   *In Mem. xxxii* 16
Blessin' for a b 'ud come wid the green!'   *Tomorrow* 64
Blessing tell her that I died B her,   *Enoch Arden* 879
spent in b her and praying for her.   " 884
tell my son that I died b him.   " 885
b those that look on them.   *Princess iii* 256
B the wholesome white faces   *Def. of Lucknow* 101
B his field, or seated in the dusk   *Demeter and P.* 125
With b's beyond hope or thought,   *Miller's D.* 237
With b's which no words can find.   " 238
O b's on his kindly voice   *May Queen, Con.* 13
And b's on his whole life long,   " 14
O b's on his kindly heart   " 15
be tended by My b!   *Love and Duty* 88
God's b on the day!   *Lady Clare* 8
Pray'd for a b on his wife and babes   *Enoch Arden* 188
calling down a b on his head   " 327
And b's on the falling out   *Princess ii* 6

Blessing (*continued*)   from Heaven A b on her labours   *Princess ii* 479
Blazon your mottoes of b and prayer!   *W. to Alexandra* 12
My b, like a line of light,   *In Mem. xvii* 10
We yield all b to the name   " *xxxvi* 3
crown'd with b she doth rise   " *xl* 5
Why do they prate of the b's of Peace?   *Maud I i* 21
she was deaf To b or to cursing   *Geraint and E.* 579
Thy b, stainless King!   *Merlin and V.* 54
take withal Thy poet's b,   *To the Queen ii* 46
hold the hand of b over them,   *Lover's Tale i* 754
saved by the b of Heaven!   *Def. of Lucknow* 104
'Bread—Bread left after the b?'   *Sir J. Oldcastle* 154
From the golden alms of B   *Locksley H., Sixty* 87
Blest-Blessed And forty blest ones bless him,   *Aylmer's Field* 372
Sammy, I'm blest If it isn't the saäme oop yonder,   *N. Farmer, N.S.* 43
soul laments, which hath been blest,   *D. of F. Women* 281
fruit of thine by Love is blest,   *Talking Oak* 249
Thy name was blest within the narrow door;   *W. to Marie Alex.* 38
Marie, shall thy name be blest,   " 39
As if the quiet bones were blest   *In Mem. xviii* 38
what may count itself as blest,   " *xxvii* 8
Thrice blest whose lives are faithful prayers,   " *xxxii* 13
my heart more blest than heart can tell,   *Maud I. xviii* 8
Blest, but for some dark undercurrent   "
'Blessed be thou, Sir Gareth,   *Gareth and L.* 1258
They might as well have blest her: *Geraint and E.* 578
blest be Heaven That brought thee   *Holy Grail* 616
Blessed are Bors, Lancelot and Percivale,   " 874
blessed be the King, who hath forgiven   *Guinevere* 634
Blest be the voice of the Teacher   *Kapiolani*
fancy made me for a moment blest   *The form, the form* 6
She desires no isles of the blest,   *Wages* 8
As she looks among the blest,   *Maud II iv* 84
in a dream from a band of the blest,   " *III vi* 10
fellowship Would make me wholly blest: *Balin and Balan* 148
follow Edwin to those isles, those islands of the Blest!   *The Flight* 42
I blest them, and they wander'd on: *Two Voices* 424
A thousand times I blest him,   *May Queen, Con.* 16
bless'd herself, and cursed herself,   *The Goose* 15
say to Philip that I blest him too;   *Enoch Arden* 886
Perceived the waving of his hands that blest.   *Guinevere* 584
saw not his daughter—he blest her: *To Prin. F. of H.* 20
And they blest him in their pain,   *The Revenge* 20
Blew breeze of a joyful dawn b free   *Arabian Nights*
B his own praises in his eyes,   *A Character* 22
hunter b His wreathed bugle-horn.   *Palace of Art*
sweet Europa's mantle b unclasp'd,   " 117
The glass b in, the fire b out,   *The Goose* 49
Her cap b off, her gown b up,   " 51
full-fed with perfume, b Beyond us,   *Gardener's D.* 113
The hedge broke in, the banner b,   *Day-Dm., Revival* 9
A light wind b from the gates of the sun,   *Poet's Song* 3
from the tiny pitted target b,   *Aylmer's Field* 93
the wind b; The rain of heaven,   " 427
b the swoll'n cheek of a trumpeter,   *Princess ii* 364
bush-bearded Barons heaved and b,   " *v* 21
he b and b, but none appear'd: " 336
stood four-square to all the winds that b!   *Ode on Well.* 127
Last, the Prussian trumpet b;   "
A milky-bell'd amaryllis b.   *The Daisy* 16
all the bugle breezes b Reveillée   *In Mem. lxviii* 7
Altho' the trumpet b so loud.   " *xcvi* 24
cloth of gold, the trumpets b,   *Com. of Arthur* 480
other b A hard and deadly note   *Gareth and L.* 1110
that ye b your boast in vain?'   " 1229
and lights, and once again he b;   " 1371
O'er the four rivers the first roses b,   *Geraint and E.* 764
and anon The trumpets b;   *Lancelot and E.* 454
trumpets b Proclaiming his the prize,   " 500
sun Shone, and the wind b, thro' her,   *Holy Grail* 99
And b my merry maidens all about   " 748
to the summit, and the trumpets b.   *Pelleas and E.* 167
ever the wind b, and yellowing leaf   *Last Tournament* 154
Far off a solitary trumpet b.   *Guinevere* 529

Blew (continued) from the North, and b The mist aside,

and b Fresh fire into the sun, *Pass. of Arthur* 124

and b Coolness and moisture and all smells *Lover's Tale i* 318

and b it far Until it hung, ,, iii 4

ever that evening ended a great gale b, ,, 35

topmost roof our banner of England b. (repeat) *The Revenge* 114

topmost roof our banner in India b. *Def. of Lucknow* 6, 30, 45, 60, 94

the old banner of England b. ,, 72

a sudden blast b us out and away ,, 106

whirlwind blow these woods, as never b before. *V. of Maeldune* 10

All at once the trumpet b, *The Flight* 12

Bleys (Merlin's master) (so they call him) B, *Happy* 75

B Laid magic by, and sat him down, *Com. of Arthur* 153

B, our Merlin's master, as they say, ,, 155

 ,, 360

Blight (s) B and famine, plague and earthquake, *Lotos-E's., C. S.,* 115

The b of low desires— *Aylmer's Field* 673

b Of ancient influence and scorn. *Princess ii* 168

And b and famine on all the lea : *The Victim* 46

like a b On my fresh hope, *Maud I xix* 102

b Lives in the dewy touch of pity *Lover's Tale i* 694

if the blossom can doat on the b, *The Wreck* 19

Blight (verb) Which would b the plants. *Poet's Mind* 18

Shall sharpest pathos b us, *Love and Duty* 85

b thy hope or break thy rest, *Faith* 2

Blighted 'your pretty bud, So b here, *The Ring* 317

Blind (sightless) (*See also* **Half-blind, Hoodman-blind**)

All night long on darkness b. *Adeline* 44

this dreamer, deaf and b, *Two Voices* 175

men, whose reason long was b, ,, 370

parch'd and wither'd, deaf and b, *Fatima* 6

those, not b, who wait for day, *Love thou thy land* 15

almost b, And scarce can recognise *St. S. Stylites* 39

mate is b and captain lame, *The Voyage* 91

b or lame or sick or sound, ,, 93

for he groped as b, and seem'd *Aylmer's Field* 821

wept her true eyes b for such a one, *Princess iv* 134

b with rage she miss'd the plank, ,, 177

I cried myself well-nigh b, *Grandmother* 37

And shall I take a thing so b, *In Mem. iii* 13

He would not make his judgment b, ,, xcvi 14

not b To the faults of his heart *Maud I xix* 67

He mark'd not this, but b and deaf *Balin and Balan* 318

were I stricken b That minute, *Lancelot and E.* 426

one hath seen, and all the b will see. *Holy Grail* 313

on the splendour came, flashing me b ; ,, 413

thrice as b as any noonday owl, ,, 866

Being too b to have desire to see. ,, 872

Mute, b and motionless as then I lay ; *Lover's Tale i* 607

B, for the day was as the night ,, 610

Almost b With ever-growing cataract, *Sisters (E. and E.)* 191

'Henceforth be b, for thou hast seen *Tiresias* 49

Or power as of the Gods gone b *Ancient Sage* 80

leave him, b of heart and eyes, ,, 113

For wert thou born or b or deaf, ,, 175

no man halt, or deaf or b ; *Locksley H., Sixty,* 163

Fur the dog's stoän-deäf, an' e's b, *Owd Roä* 2

an' seeäm'd as b as a poop, ,, 101

A barbarous people, B to the magic, *Merlin and the G.* 26

Blind (screen) (*See also* **Lattice-blind**) Sometimes your shadow cross'd me b. *Miller's D.* 124

Blind (verb) lest the gems Should b my purpose, *M. d'Arthur* 153

Ere yet they b the stars, *Tithonus* 39

To b the truth and me : *Princess iii* 112

He shall not b his soul with clay.' ,, vii 331

good King means to b himself, *Merlin and V.* 783

b's himself and all the Table Round ,, 784

lest the gems Should b my purpose, *Pass. of Arthur* 321

b your pretty blue eyes with a kiss ! *Romney's R.* 101

Blinded (*See also* **Half-blinded, Self-blinded**)

those whom passion hath not b, *Ode to Memory* 117

blissful tears b my sight *Oriana* 23

and b With many a deep-hued *Eleänore* 36

Droops b with his shining eye : *Fatima* 38

Blinded (continued) I, b with my tears, 'Still strove *D. of F. Women* 108

Not with b eyesight poring *Locksley Hall* 172

so bright That men are b by it— *Com. of Arthur* 301

Blasted and burnt, and b as I was, *Holy Grail* 844

Scratch'd, bitten, b, marr'd me *Last Tournament* 526

Too early b by the kiss of death— *Romney's R.* 103

May leave the windows b, ,, 146

He stumbled in, and sat B ; *St. Telemachus* 49

Blinder Nature made them b motions *Locksley Hall* 150

'Gawain, and b unto holy things *Holy Grail* 870

Blind Fate Rail at ' B F ' with many *Doubt and Prayer* 2

Blindfold Drug down the b sense of wrong *In Mem. lxxi* 7

from what side The b rummage *Balin and Balan* 416

Blinding Struck up against the b wall. *Mariana in the S.* 56

Dash'd together in b dew : *Vision of Sin* 42

his fire is on my face B, *Lucretius* 145

raised the b bandage from his eyes : *Princess i* 244

suck the b splendour from the sand, ,, vii 39

all in mail Burnish'd to b, *Gareth and L.* 1027

Are b desert sand ; we scarce can *Akbar's Dream* 30

Blindless the b casement of the room, *Marr. of Geraint* 71

Blindly That read his spirit b wise, *Two Voices* 287

And, while now she wonders b, *L. of Burleigh* 53

'The stars,' she whispers, 'b run ; *In Mem. iii* 5

And staggers b ere she sink ? ,, xvi 14

muffled motions b drown ,, xlix 15

b rush'd on all the rout behind. *Geraint and E.* 466

Blindness That in this b of the frame *In Mem. xciii* 15

for talk Which lives with b, *Sisters (E. and E.)* 249

curse Of b and their unbelief, *Tiresias* 59

Blink those that did not b the terror, *Gareth and L.* 1402

Blinkt B the white morn, sprays grated, *Balin and Balan* 385

Bliss Then in madness and in b, *Madeline* 42

Weak symbols of the settled b, *Miller's D.* 233

Above the thunder, with undying b *Œnone* 132

'Trust me, in b I shall abide *Palace of Art* 18

move Me from my b of life, *D. of F. Women* 210

I rose up Full of his b, *Gardener's D.* 211

A man had given all other b, *Sir L. and Q. G.* 42

I shall see him, My babe in b : *Enoch Arden* 898

and spoils My b in being ; *Lucretius* 222

A central warmth diffusing b *In Mem. lxxxiv* 6

I triumph in conclusive b, ,, lxxxv 91

O b, when all in circle drawn ,, lxxxix 21

With gods in unconjectured b, ,, xciii 10

A wither'd violet is her b : ,, xcvii 26

For fuller gain of after b : ,, cxvii 4

Nor have I felt so much of b ,, Con. 5

Make answer, Maud my b, *Maud I xviii* 57

My dream? do I dream of b? ,, xix 3

Sun, that wakenest all to b or pain, *Gareth and L.* 1060

thrills of b That strike across the soul *Lover's Tale i* 363

b stood round me like the light of Heaven,— ,, 495

tell him of the b he had with God— ,, 674

sunder'd With smiles of tranquil b, ,, ii 143

O b, what a Paradise there ! *V. of Maeldune* 78

whose one b Is war, and human sacrifice— *Tiresias* 111

Twelve times in the year Bring me b, *The Ring* 6

'Sleep, little blossom, my honey, my b ! *Romney's R.* 99

I had one brief summer of b. *Bandit's Death* 9

Blissful here are the b downs and dales, *Sea-Fairies* 22

While b tears blinded my sight *Oriana* 23

As from some b neighbourhood, *Two Voices* 430

sleep down from the b skies. *Lotos-Eaters, C.S.* 7

With b treble ringing clear. *Sir L. and Q. G.* 22

b palpitations in the blood, *Princess iv* 28

B bride of a b heir, *W. to Alexandra* 27

led him thro' the b climes, *In Mem. lxxxv* 25

On me she bends her b eyes ,, Con. 29

Blister'd B every word with tears, *Forlorn* 81

Blistering bared her forehead to the b sun, *Geraint and E.* 515

Blithe New-year b and bold, my friend, *D. of the O. Year* 35

B would her brother's acceptance be. *Maud I x* 27

Bloat b himself, and ooze All over *Sea Dreams* 154

Blood (*continued*)   stream of life, one stream, one life,
     one *b*,   *Lover's Tale i* 239
As mountain streams Our *b's* ran free :   ,,   327
I was as the brother of her *b*,   ,,   559
my *b* Crept like marsh drains   ,,   *ii* 52
I weänt shed a drop on 'is *b*,   *North. Cobbler* 114
Now reddest with the *b* of holy men,   *Sir J. Oldcastle* 54
a cross of flesh and *b* And holier.   ,,   137
Blue *b* of Spain,   *Columbus* 114
blue *b* and black *b* of Spain,   ,,   116
innocent hospitalities quench'd in *b*,   ,,   176
and the boast of our ancient *b*,   *V. of Maeldune* 88
red with *b* the Crescent reels   *Montenegro* 6
All the field with *b* of the fighters Flow'd,   *Batt. of Brunanburh* 24
wholesome heat the *b* had lost,   *To E. Fitzgerald* 24
crowd would roar For *b*, for war,   *Tiresias* 65
Spain in his *b* and the Jew—   *The Wreck* 15
are both of them turn'd into *b*,   *Despair* 91
Her *b* is in your bloom.   *Ancient Sage* 166
evil thought may soil thy children's *b* ;   ,,   275
yer Honour's the thrue ould *b*   *Tomorrow* 5
on that founder of our *b*.   *Locksley H., Sixty* 32
shriek'd and slaked the light with *b*.   ,,   90
Like drops of *b* in a dark-gray sea,   *Heavy Brigade* 43
O follow, leaping *b*,   *Early Spring* 25
Their idol smear'd with *b*,   *Freedom* 28
crescent moon, and changed it into *b*.   *Happy* 44
Diffuse thyself at will thro' all my *b*,   *Prog. of Spring* 24
hopes, which race the restless *b*,   ,,   115
herb or balm May clear the *b* from poison,   *Death of Œnone* 36
as he yell'd of yore for Christian *b*,   *St. Telemachus* 46
dust send up a steam of human *b*,   ,,   53
hour Dark with the *b* of man   ,,   80
warms the *b* of Shiah and Sunnee,   *Akbar's Dream* 107
gentleman, heart, *b* and bone,   *Bandit's Death* 2
For he reek'd with the *b* of Piero ;   ,,   13
a ray red as *b* Glanced on the strangled face—   ,,   31
Rang the stroke, and sprang the *b*,   *The Tourney* 9
Blood-eagle   red '*B-e*' of liver and heart ;   *Dead Prophet* 71
Blooded   *See* **Cold-blooded, Pale-blooded**
Bloodier   the hands of power Were *b*,   *Aylmer's Field* 453
Bloodily   *B* flow'd the Tamesa rolling   *Boädicea* 27
B, *b* fall the battle-axe,   ,,   56
Bloodless   now, the *b* point reversed,   *The Voyage* 71
b east began To quicken to the sun,   *Marr. of Geraint* 534
Blood-red   dabbled with *b-r* heath,   *Maud I i* 2
flames The *b-r* blossom of war   ,, *III vi* 53
the *b-r* light of dawn Flared   *Lancelot and E.* 1025
but always in the night *B-r*, and sliding down
    the blacken'd marsh *B-r*, and on the naked
    mountain top *B-r*, and in the sleeping mere
    below *B-r*.   *Holy Grail* 473
In *b-r* armour sallying,   *Last Tournament* 443
himself *B-r* from battle,   *Tiresias* 113
Bloodshed   hold were all as free From cursed *b*,   *Gareth and L.* 599
Bloody   shovell'd up into some *b* trench   *Audley Court* 42
see the raw mechanic's *b* thumbs   *Walk. to the Mail* 75
Where the *b* conduit runs,   *Vision of Sin* 144
take such *b* vengeance on you both ?—   *Princess iv* 534
Bloom (s) (*See also* **Chestnut-bloom, Milk-bloom,**
    Orange-bloom)   inlay Of braided *b's* unmown,   *Arabian Nights* 29
lovely freight Of overflowing *b's*,   *Ode to Memory* 17
throng with stately *b's* the breathing spring   *The Poet* 27
Whence that aery *b* of thine,   *Adeline* 11
violet eyes. and all her Hebe *b*,   *Gardener's D.* 137
In bud or blade, or *b*, may find,   *Day-Dm., Moral* 10
many a slope was rich in *b*   *To E. L.* 20
fair in our sad world's best *b*,   *The Brook* 218
scatter'd, each a nest in *b*.   *Aylmer's Field* 150
cheek and bosom brake the wrathful *b*   *Princess iv* 383
bud ever breaks into *b* on the tree,   *The Islet* 32
The chestnut towers in his *b* ;   *Voice and the P.* 18
b profuse and cedar arches Charm,   *Milton* 11
not for thee the glow, the *b*,   *In Mem.*   *ii* 9
And every spirit's folded *b*   ,,   *xliii* 2

Bloom (s) (*continued*)   Which sicken'd every living *b*,   *In Mem. lxxii* 7
over brake and *b* And meadow,   ,, *lxxxvi* 3
And passion pure in snowy *b*   ,, *cix* 11
azure *b* of a crescent of sea,   *Maud I iv* 5
wild-wood hyacinth and the *b* of May.   *Balin and Balan* 271
and her *b* A rosy dawn kindled   *Pelleas and E.* 71
ribb'd And barr'd with *b* on *b*.   *Lover's Tale i* 416
We was busy as beeäs i' the *b*   *North. Cobbler* 15
Edith—all One i' youth,   *Sisters (E. and E.)* 120
' How far thro' all the *b* and brake   *Ancient Sage* 19
wake The *b* that fades away ?   ,,   94
Her blood is in your *b*.   ,,   166
lifts her buried life from gloom to *b*,   *Demeter and P.* 98
rounder cheek had brighten'd into *b*.   *The Ring* 351
vernal *b* from every vale and plain   *To Mary Boyle* 9
Bloom (verb)   She saw the water-lily *b*,   *L. of Shalott iii* 39
Lotos *b's* below the barren peak :   *Lotos-Eaters, C.S.* 100
b's the garden that I love.   *Gardener's D.* 34
That if it can it there may *b*,   *In Mem.*   *viii* 23
from marge to marge shall *b* the eternal landscape   ,,   *xlvi* 7
Will *b* to profit, otherwhere.   ,,   *lxxxii* 12
hearts are warm'd and faces *b*,   ,, *Con.* 82
my white heather only *b's* in heaven   *Romney's R.* 110
B's in the Past, but close to me to-day   *Roses on the T.* 6
Bloomed   thro' The low and *b* foliage,   *Arabian Nights* 13
Blooming   The maid-of-honour *b* fair ;   *Day-Dm., Sleep. P.* 28
By Cupid-boys of *b* hue—   ,, *Ep.* 10
her *b* mantle torn.   *Princess vi* 145
Blossom (s) (*See also* **Almond-blossom, Apple-**
    blossom, Blackthorn-blossom, Lake-blossom,
    May-blossom, Orange-blossom)   Atween the
    b's, 'We are free.'   *The Winds, etc.* 8
Bursts into *b* in his sight.   *Fatima* 35
He prest the *b* of his lips to mine,   *Œnone* 78
The *b* on the blackthorn, the leaf   *May Queen, N. Y's.* 8
As we bear *b* of the dead   *Love thou thy land* 94
b fades, and they that loved   *Walk. to the Mail* 57
The maiden *b's* of her teens   *Talking Oak* 79
break In full and kindly *b*.   *Will Water.* 24
as Nature packs Her *b* or her seedling,   *Enoch Arden* 179
With here a *b* sailing,   *The Brook* 56
Gather'd the *b* that rebloom'd,   *Aylmer's Field* 142
Into a land all sun and *b*,   *Sea Dreams* 101
caught the *b* of the flying terms,   *Princess, Pro.* 164
Perch'd on the pouted *b* of her lips :   ,,   199
Fruit, *b*, viand, amber wine, and gold.   ,, *iv* 35
my babe, my *b*, ah, my child,   ,, *v* 82
lay my little *b* at my feet,   ,,   100
the *b* wavering fell,   ,, *vi* 80
Scatter the *b* under her feet !   *W. to Alexandra* 9
Or rosy *b* in hot ravine,   *The Daisy* 32
they tumble the *b*, the mad little tits !   *Window, Ay.* 9
The tender *b* flutter down,   *In Mem. ci* 2
flames The blood-red *b* of war   *Maud III vi* 53
sun, and rain ! and the free *b* flows :   *Com. of Arthur* 409
near her, like a *b* vermeil-white,   *Marr. of Geraint* 364
tints the *b* of the quince   *Balin and Balan* 267
wayside *b's* open to the blaze.   ,,   449
that will strike my *b* dead.   *Lancelot and E.* 971
blood beats, and the *b* blows,   *Holy Grail* 671
groves that look'd a paradise Of *b*,   *Guinevere* 390
little *b*, O mine, and mine   *To A. Tennyson* 4
Had set the *b* of her health again,   *Sisters (E. and E.)* 151
And starr'd with a myriad *b*   *V. of Maeldune* 40
B and *b*, and promise of *b*,   ,,   51
if the *b* can doat on the blight,   *The Wreck* 19
tastes the fruit before the *b* falls,   *Ancient Sage* 75
Jet upward thro' the mid-day *b*.   *Demeter and P.* 47
hillock, Would break into *b* ;   *Merlin and the G.* 108
' Sleep, little *b*, my honey, my bliss '   *Romney's R.* 99
From each fair plant the *b* choicest-grown   *Akbar's Dream* 22
Blossom (verb)   A little garden *b*.   *Amphion* 104
wilderness shall *b* as the rose.   *Aylmer's Field* 649
buds and *b's* like the rest.   *In Mem. cxv* 20
And *b* in purple and red.   *Maud I xxii* 74

Blossom (**verb**) (*continued*) where the winter thorn *B*'s at
Christmas,   *Holy Grail* 52
b an' spring from the grass,   *Tomorrow* 89
B again on a colder isle.   *To Prof. Jebb* 12
Blossom-ball Made *b-b* or daisy-chain,   *Aylmer's Field* 87
Blossom-belt Above the garden's glowing *b-b*'s,   *Princess* v 363
Blossom-dust like the working bee in *b-d*,   *Enoch Arden* 366
  Foot-gilt with all the *b-d*   *Merlin and V.* 282
Blossom'd (**adj.**) (*See also* **Daisy-blossomed, Heavy-**
blossom'd) white robe like a *b* branch   *Princess* iv 179
  On the *b* gable-ends   *Maud* I vi 9
  O *b* portal of the lonely house,   *Lover's Tale* i 280
Blossom'd (**verb**) branch'd And *b* in the zenith,   *Enoch Arden* 586
  b up From out a common vein   *Princess* iii 313
  when the wreath of March has *b*,   *To F. D. Maurice* 43
  Great garlands swung and *b* ;   *Lover's Tale* iv 191
Blossom-flake elmtree's ruddy-hearted *b-f*   *To Mary Boyle* 3
Blossom-fragrant *b-f* slipt the heavy dews   *Princess* v 243
Blossoming (*See also* **Many-blossoming**) and the
happy *b* shore ?   *Sea-Fairies* 8
Blot (**s**) With *b*'s of it about them,   *Aylmer's Field* 620
  'Tis the *b* upon the brain   *Maud* II iv 60
  a throne, And blackens every *b* :   *Ded. of Idylls* 28
  Gareth's eyes had flying *b*'s   *Gareth and L.* 1031
  square of text that looks a little *b*,   *Merlin and V.* 671
  Far-off, a *b* upon the stream,   *Lancelot and E.* 1392
  A *b* in heaven, the Raven,   *Guinevere* 133
Blot (**verb**) *B* out the slope of sea   *Princess* vii 38
Blotch face deform'd by lurid *b* and blain—   *Death of Œnone* 72
Blotted (*See also* **Mist-blotted**) took his brush
and *b* out the bird,   *Merlin and V.* 478
Blow (**s**) (*See also* **Death-blow, Head-blow**) O cursed
hand ! O cursed *b* !   *Oriana* 82
  stood like one that had received a *b* :   *Sea Dreams* 161
  red-hot iron to be shaped with *b*'s.   *Princess* v 209
  clench'd his purpose like a *b* !   " 306
  b's rain'd, as here and everywhere   " 501
  With their own *b*'s they hurt themselves,   " vi 49
  Back to France with countless *b*'s,   *Ode on Well.* 111
  knife uprising toward the *b*   *The Victim* 66
  Phantom sound of *b*'s descending,   *Boädicea* 25
  breasts the *b*'s of circumstance,   *In Mem.* lxiv 7
  But in the present broke the *b*,   " lxxxv 56
  shocks of Chance—The *b*'s of Death.   " xcv 43
  That must have life for a *b*.   *Maud* II i 27
  red life spilt for a private *b*—   " v 93
  mightier of his hands with every *b*,   *Com. of Arthur* 110
  Three with good *b*'s he quieted,   *Gareth and L.* 813
  mightful hand striking great *b*'s   *Marr. of Geraint* 564
  lash'd at each So often and with such *b*'s,   *Balin and Balan* 296
  Descended, and disjointed it at a *b* :   *Merlin and V.* 870
  Kill'd with a word worse than a life of *b*'s !   *Lancelot and E.* 41
  each had slain his brother at a *b* ;   " 1165
  hardly won with bruise and *b*,   *Pass. of Arthur* 167
  while Arthur at one *b*, Striking   *The Revenge* 95
  live to fight again and to strike another *b*.'   *Heavy Brigade* 32
  Rode flashing *b* upon *b*,
Blow (**verb**) (*See also* **Blaw**) The stream flows,
The wind *b*'s,   *Nothing will Die* 10
  make the winds *b* Round and round,   " 23
  The wind will cease to *b* ;   *All Things will Die* 10
  loud the Norland whirlwinds *b*,   *Oriana* 6
  Round thee *b*, self-pleached deep,   *A Dirge* 29
  And tell me if the woodbines *b*.   *My life is full* 25
  Gazing where the lilies *b*   *L. of Shalott* i 7
  That all about the thorn will *b*   *Two Voices* 59
  When April nights began to *b*,   *Miller's D.* 106
  gales, as from deep gardens, *b* Before him,   *Fatima* 24
  the wind *b*'s the foam, and all my heart   *Œnone* 62
  by the meadow-trenches the faint sweet cuckoo-flowers;   *May Queen* 30
  from the dry dark wold the summer airs *b*
cool   *May Queen, N. Y's. E.* 27
  and all the flowers that *b*,   *Con.* 7
  Lotos *b*'s by every winding creek :   *Lotos-Eaters, C. S.* 101
  b's More softly round the open wold,   *To J. S.* 1

Blow (**verb**) (*continued*) Nor ever wind *b*'s loudly ;   *M. d'Arthur* 261
  or then While the gold-lily *b*'s,   *Edwin Morris* 146
  I saw Your own Olivia *b*,   *Talking Oak* 76
  light as any wind that *b*'s So fleetly   " 129
  The full south-breeze around thee *b*   " 271
  winds from all the compass shift and *b*,   *Godiva* 33
  wildweed-flower that simply *b*'s ?   *Day-Dm., Moral* 6
  B, flute, and stir the stiff-set sprigs,   *Amphion* 63
  weed That *b*'s upon its mountain,   " 94
  she makes The violet of a legend *b*   *Will Water.* 147
  IT was the time when lilies *b*,   *Lady Clare* 1
  And the wind did *b* ;   *The Captain* 34
  To *b* these sacrifices thro' the world—   *Aylmer's Field* 758
  Low, low, breathe and *b*,   *Princess* iii 3
  and *b*, *B* him again to me ;   " 6
  B, bugle, *b*, set the wild echoes flying, (repeat)   " iv 5 17
  B, bugle ; answer, echoes, dying, (repeat)   " 6 12
  B, let us hear the purple glens replying :   " 11
  A moment, while the trumpets *b*,   " 581
  let the mournful martial music *b* ;   *Ode on Well.* 17
  To Britain, when her flowers begin to *b* !   *W. to Marie Alex.* 7
  Wet west wind how you *b*, you *b* !   *Window, No Answer* 14
  B then, *b*, and when I am gone,   " 17
  And make them pipes whereon to *b*.   *In Mem.* xxi 4
  With blasts that *b* the poplar white,   " lxxii 1
  fan my brows and *b* The fever from my cheek,   " lxxxvi 8
  from the garden and the wild A fresh association *b*,   " ci 18
  There in due time the woodbine *b*'s,   " cv 4
  By ashen roots the violets *b*,   " cxv 4
  And all the breeze of Fancy *b*'s,   " cxxii 17
  woodland lilies, Myriads *b* together.   *Maud* I xii 8
  lily and rose That *b* by night,   " II v 75
  and rain ! and the free blossom *b*'s :   *Com. of Arthur* 409
  ' *B* trumpet, for the world is white with May ;   " 482
  B trumpet, the long night hath roll'd away !   " 483
  B thro' the living world—   " 484
  ' *B* trumpet ! he will lift us from the dust.   " 491
  B trumpet ! live the strength and die the lust !   " 492
  ' *B*, for our Sun is mighty in his May !   " 497
  B, for our Sun is mightier day by day !   " 498
  flower, That *b*'s a globe of after arrowlets,   *Gareth and L.* 1029
  flowers that close when day is done, *B* sweetly :   " 1068
  King gave order to let *b* His horns   *Marr. of Geraint* 152
  we *b* with breath, or touch with hand,   *Holy Grail* 114
  blood beats, and the blossom *b*'s,   " 671
  But such a blast, my King, began to *b*,   " 795
  clash the shield, and *b* the horn.   *Last Tournament* 436
  I hear the trumpet *b* : They summon me   *Guinevere* 569
  Nor ever wind *b*'s loudly ;   *Pass. of Arthur* 429
  trust that Heaven Will *b* the tempest   *To the Queen* ii 47
  whirlwind *b* these woods, as never blew before.   *The Flight* 12
  gather the roses whenever they *b*,   *Romney's R.* 107
  Let *b* the trumpet strongly while I pray,   *Doubt and Prayer* 10
Blower ' O hunter, and O *b* of the horn, Harper,   *Last Tournament* 542
Blowing (*See also* **Blawin'**, **Equal-blowing, Merrily-**
blowing, Trumpet-blowings) When will the
wind be aweary of *b* Over the sky ?   *Nothing will Die* 3
  south winds are *b* Over the sky.   *All Things will Die* 3
  myrrh-thickets *b* round The stately cedar,   *Arabian Nights* 104
  Winds were *b*, waters flowing,   *Oriana* 17
  Aloud the hollow bugle,   *Two Voices* 206
  B a noise of tongues and deeds,   " 406
  Like soften'd airs that *b* steal,   *The Sisters* 3, 33
  wind is *b* in turret and tree. (repeat)   *Lotos-Eaters, C. S.* 89
  (while warm airs lull us, *b* lowly)   *M. d'Arthur, Ep.* 21
  a bark that, *b* forward, bore King Arthur,   *Edwin Morris* 95
  wind *b* over meadowy holms And alders,   *Golden Year* 44
  and *b* havenward With silks, and fruits,   *L. of Burleigh* 19
  Summer woods, about them *b*,   *Sir L. and Q. G.* 39
  B the ringlet from the braid :   *Princess* i 111
  and *b* bosks of wilderness,   " iv 10
  The horns of Elfland faintly *b* !   *Boädicea* 38
  ' Fear not, isle of *b* woodland,   *In Mem.* xxxviii 5
  No joy the *b* season gives,   *Maud* I xvii 13
  Over glowing ships ; Over *b* seas,

Blowing (*continued*) south-west that *b* Bala lake Fills	*Geraint and E.* 929
ship and sail and angels *b* on it :	*Balin and Balan* 365
he waits below the wall, *B* his bugle	*Pelleas and E.* 381
Brake with a wet wind *b*,	*Last Tournament* 137
breezes of May *b* over an English field,	*Def. of Lucknow* 83
Wild flowers *b* side by side in God's	*The Flight* 81
Fame *b* out from her golden trumpet	*Vastness* 21
When the storms are *b*.	*Forlorn* 6

Blown (*See also* **Beard-blown, Broad-blown, Full-blown**) your branching limes have *b*

Since I beheld	*L. C. V. de Vere* 27
petals from *b* roses on the grass,	*Lotos-Eaters, C. S.* 2
round the spicy downs the yellow Lotos-dust is *b*.	" 104
Death is *b* in every wind ;'	*To J. S.* 46
and roughly set His Briton in *b* seas	*Ode on Well.* 155
The golden news along the steppes is *b*,	*W. to Marie Alex.* 11
The rooks are *b* about the skies ;	*In Mem. xv* 4
Be *b* about the dearer dust,	" *lvi* 19
Nor harp be touch'd, nor flute be *b* ;	" *cv* 22
far-off sail is *b* by the breeze	*Maud I iv* 4
And the musk of the rose is *b*.	" *xxii* 6
when the Prince Three times had *b*—	*Gareth and L.* 1378
the face, as, when a gust hath *b*,	*Last Tournament* 368
her father left us just before The daffodil was *b*?	*Lover's Tale i* 294
The wind had *b* above me,	" 622
ghost of Gawain *b* Along a wandering wind,	*Pass. of Arthur* 31
I am *b* along a wandering wind,	" 36
we came to the Isle we were *b* from,	*V. of Maeldune* 127
thy fame Is *b* thro' all the Troad,	*Death of Œnone* 37
Like Indian reeds *b* from his silver tongue,	*The Poet* 13
when a billow, *b* against, Falls back,	*Two Voices* 316
And trumpets *b* for wars ;	*D. of F. Women* 20
gale had caught, And *b* across the walk.	*Gardener's D.* 125
b by baffling winds,	*Enoch Arden* 628
gale That *b* about the foliage underneath,	" 661
from inmost south And *b* to inmost north ;	*Princess iii* 121
B from over every main,	" *iv* 432
Had *b* the lake beyond his limit,	*Ode Inter. Exhib.* 26
after trumpet *b*, Spake to the lady	*The Daisy* 71
by strong storm *B* into shelter at Tintagil,	*Marr. of Geraint* 551
Her bright hair *b* about the serious face	*Merlin and V.* 10
silver horn from o'er the hills *B*,	*Lancelot and E.* 392
after trumpet *b*, her name And title,	*Holy Grail* 110
night, a rumour wildly *b* about Came,	*Pelleas and E.* 115
all their dewy hair *b* back like flame :	*Guinevere* 153
B by the fierce beleaguerers of a town,	" 284
B into glittering by the popular breath,	*Achilles over the T.* 20
	Romney's R. 49
	Princess iv 279
	North. Cobbler 61

Blowzed Huge women *b* with health,

Blubber'd *b* awääy o' the bed—

Blue (adj.) (*See also* **Black-blue, Dark-blue, Dead-blue, Deep-blue, Faint-blue, June-blue, Light-blue, Sea-blue, Steel-blue, Warm-blue**) And less aërially *b*,

the lights, rose, amber, emerald, *b*,	*Margaret* 51
and gave a shield *B* also,	*Palace of Art* 169
never yet Had heaven appear'd so *b*,	*Gareth and L.* 932
better ha' beaten me black an' *b*	*Holy Grail* 365
ship stood still, and the skies were *b*,	*First Quarrel* 72
Some far *b* fell,	*The Wreck* 115

Blue (s) clove The citron-shadows in the *b* :

Were glistening to the breezy *b* ;	*Early Spring* 34
star Shook in the stedfast *b*,	*Arabian Nights* 15
While yon sun prospers in the *b*,	*Miller's D.* 61
navies grappling in the central *b* ;	*D. of F. Women* 56
And sweet the vapour-braided *b*,	*Blackbird* 22
B's and reds They talk'd of : *b*'s were	*Locksley Hall* 124
such a star of morning in their *b*,	*The Letters* 42
years That breathed beneath the Syrian *b* :	*Aylmer's Field* 251
The little speedwell's darling *b*,	" 692
And drown'd in yonder living *b*	*In Mem. lii* 12
morning star that smilest in the *b*,	" *lxxxiii* 10
like a shoaling sea the lovely *b* Play'd	" *cxv* 7
but under open *b* Came on the hoarhead woodman	*Gareth and L.* 999
	Geraint and E. 688
	Balin and Balan 293

Blue (s) (*continued*) Venus ere she fell Would often loiter in her balmy *b*,	*Lover's Tale i* 62
little star Were drunk into the inmost *b*,	" 309
from the sky to the *b* of the sea ;	*V. of Maeldune* 46
sign of aught that lies Behind the green and *b* ?	*Ancient Sage* 26
b of sky and sea, the green of earth,	" 41
Green Sussex fading into *b*,	*Pro. to Gen. Hamley* 7
domes the red-plow'd hills With loving *b* ;	*Early Spring* 4
moon of heaven, Bright in *b*,	*The Ring* 2
Broaden the glowing isles of vernal *b*.	*Prog. of Spring* 60
Glows in the *b* of fifty miles away.	*Roses on the T.* 8
Sing the new year in under the *b*.	*The Throstle* 5
round me and over me June's high *b*,	*June Bracken, etc.* 2

Bluebell frail *b* peereth over Rare broidry	*A Dirge* 37
merry *b* rings To the mosses underneath ?	*Adeline* 34
Rose-campion, *b*, kingcup,	*Last Tournament* 234

Blue-eyed A Prince I was, *b-e*, and fair — *Princess i* 1

Bluff (adj.) *B* Harry broke into the spence — *Talking Oak* 47

Bluff (s) echo flap And buffet round the hills,	*Golden Year* 77
shadowing *b* that made the banks,	*In Mem. ciii* 22
from *b* to *b*.	

Blunder'd the soldier knew Some one had *b* : — *Light Brigade* 12

Blunt (adj.) So *b* in memory, so old at heart,	*Gardener's D.* 53
felt so *b* and stupid at the heart :	*Geraint and E.* 747
Besought me to be plain and *b*,	*Lancelot and E.* 1301

Blunt (verb) discourtesy To *b* or break her passion.'	" 974
b the curse Of Pallas, hear,	*Tiresias* 154

Blunted being rudely *b*, glanced and shot	*Holy Grail* 75
Being *b* in the Present, grew at length	*Lover's Tale ii* 131

Blur but for one black *b* of earth — *Demeter and P.* 37

Blurr'd (adj. and part.) one was patch'd and *b* and lustreless	*Marr. of Geraint* 649
light betwixt them burn'd *B* by the creeping mist,	*Guinevere* 5
And *b* in colour and form,	*Dead Prophet* 22
B like a landskip in a ruffled pool,—	*Romney's R.* 114

Blurr'd (verb) And *b* the splendour of the sun ; — *In Mem. lxxii* 8

Blurt they *b* Their furious formalisms, — *Akbar's Dream* 56

Blush (s) She look'd : but all Suffused with *b*'es—	*Gardener's D.* 154
The *b* is fix'd upon her cheek.	*Day-Dm., Sleep. P.* 32
loose A flying charm of *b*'es o'er this cheek,	*Princess ii* 430
'What pardon, sweet Melissa, for a *b* ?'	" *iii* 66
b and smile, a medicine in themselves	" *vii* 62
And the sick man forgot her simple *b*,	*Lancelot and E.* 864
Quick *b*'es, the sweet dwelling of her eyes	*Sisters (E. and E.)* 165
the *b* Of millions of roses that sprang	*V. of Maeldune* 43
Solved in the tender *b*'es of the peach ;	*Prog. of Spring* 34
That *b* of fifty years ago, my dear,	*Roses on the T.* 5

Blush (verb) As it were with shame she *b*'es,	*L. of Burleigh* 63
Said Cyril : 'Pale one, *b* again : than wear Those lilies, better *b* our lives away.	*Princess iii* 67
Since I *b* to belaud myself a moment—	*Hendecasyllabics* 18
Pass and *b* the news Over glowing ships ;	*Maud I xvii* 11
B it thro' the West ; (repeat)	" 16 24
B from West to East, *B* from East to West,	" 21
You should have seen him *b* ;	*Merlin and V.* 481
The linnet's bosom *b*'es at her gaze,	*Prog. of Spring* 17

Blush'd Katie laugh'd, and laughing *b*,	*The Brook* 214
how pretty Her blushing was, and how she *b* again,	*Princess iii* 100
suddenly, sweetly, strangely *b*	*Maud I viii* 6
She neither *b* nor shook,	*Lancelot and E.* 965
Then *b* and brake the morning	*Pelleas and E.* 157

Blushest Again thou *b* angerly ; — *Madeline* 45

Blushing (adj.) On a *b* mission to me, — *Maud I xxi* 11

Blushing (part.) Fresh apple-blossom, *b* for a boon.	*The Brook* 90
B upon them *b*, and at once He rose	*Merlin and V.* 741

Blushing (s) how pretty Her *b* was, and how she blush'd again, — *Princess iii* 100

Bluster *B* the winds and tides the self-same way,	*D. of F. Women* 38
'tis well that I should *b* !—	*Locksley Hall* 63
And *b* into stormy sobs and say,	*Lancelot and E.* 1067

Blustering *b* I know not what Of insolence and love,	*Princess v* 396
Sir Kay, the seneschal, would come *B* upon them,	*Gareth and L.* 514

Boädicea (British Queen) *B*, standing loftily charioted, (repeat) — *Boädicea* 3, 70

Boän (bone) an' 'e got a brown pot an' a *b*, — *Village Wife* 48

Boane (bone) when an' wheere to bury his *b*. — *Owd Roä* 8
Boanerges Our *B* with his threats of doom, — *Sea Dreams* 251
Boar dog, and wolf and *b* and bear Came — *Com. of Arthur* 23
  wherewithal deck the *b*'s head ? Flowers ? nay,
  the *b* hath rosemaries and bay. — *Gareth and L.* 1073
Board (table) 'This was cast upon the *b*, — *Œnone* 79
  cast the golden fruit upon the *b*, — ,, 226
  I pledge her silent at the *b* ; — *Will Water.* 25
  cups and silver on the burnish'd *b* — *Enoch Arden* 742
  There at a *b* by tome and paper sat, — *Princess ii* 32
  And on the *b* the fluttering urn : — *In Mem. xcv* 8
  Arrange the *b* and brim the glass ; — ,, *cvii* 16
  seating Gareth at another *b*, Sat down — *Gareth and L.* 871
  boil'd the flesh, and spread the *b*, — *Marr. of Geraint* 391
  knife's haft hard against the *b*, — *Geraint and E.* 600
  bare her by main violence to the *b*, — ,, 654
  Along the walls and down the *b* ; — *Balin and Balan* 84
  A goblet on the *b* by Balin, — ,, 362
  all the light that falls upon the *b* — *Holy Grail* 249
  Who spake so low and sadly at our *b* ; — ,, 701
  left me gazing at a barren *b*, — ,, 893
  Are ye but creatures of the *b* and bed, — *Pelleas and E.* 267
  Before the *b*, there paused and stood, — *Lover's Tale iv* 307
Board (ship) he served a year On *b* a merchantman, — *Enoch Arden* 53
  Am I so like her ? so they said on *b*. — *The Brook* 223
  I leap on *b* : no helmsman steers— — *Sir Galahad* 39
Board (for a game) That pushes us off from the *b*, — *Maud I iv* 27
Board (floor) Pattering over the *b*'s, (repeat) — *Grandmother* 77, 79
Board (list, register) hastily subscribed, We enter'd on
  the *b*'s : — *Princess ii* 74
Boarding *B*'s and rafters and doors— — *Def. of Lucknow* 67
Boast (s) To shame the *b* so often made, — *Love thou thy land* 71
  And bring her babe, and make her *b*, — *In Mem. xl* 26
  that ye blew your *b* in vain ? ' — *Gareth and L.* 1229
  to mar the *b* Thy brethren of thee make— — ,, 1242
  Abash'd us both, and brake my *b*. — *Balin and Balan* 71
  and the *b* of our ancient blood, — *V. of Maeldune* 88
  crime, of her eldest-born, her glory, her *b*, — *Despair* 73
Boast (verb) you know it—I will not *b* : — *Princess iv* 353
  the clipt palm of which they *b* ; — *The Daisy* 26
  and *b*, 'Behold the man that loved and lost, — *In Mem i* 14
  heard them *b* That they would slay you, — *Geraint and E.* 73
  b's his life as purer than thine own ; — *Balin and Balan* 104
Boasted each of them *b* he sprang from the
  oldest race — *V. of Maeldune* 4
Boastful ruled the hour, Tho' seeming *b*: — *Aylmer's Field* 195
Boat (*See also* **Pleasure-boat**) leaping lightly
  from the *b*, — *Arabian Nights* 92
  Down she came and found a *b* — *L. of Shalott iv* 6
  Francis just alighted from the *b*, — *Audley Court* 7
  B, island, ruins of a castle, built — *Edwin Morris* 6
  That he sings in his *b* on the bay ! — *Break, break, etc.* 8
  Anchors of rusty fluke, and *b*'s updrawn ; — *Enoch Arden* 18
  To purchase his own *b*, and make a home — ,, 47
  He purchased his own *b*, and made a home For Annie, — ,, 58
  sell the *b*—and yet he loved her well— — ,, 134
  The horse he drove, the *b* he sold, — ,, 609
  b that bears the hope of life approach — ,, 830
  till as when a *b* Tacks, — *Princess ii* 185
  b's and bridges for the use of men. — ,, *vi* 47
  The *b* is drawn upon the shore ; — *In Mem. cxxxi* 6
  The market *b* is on the stream, — ,, 13
  There found a little *b*, and stept into it ; — *Merlin and V.* 198
  the *b* Drave with a sudden wind across — ,, 200
  He saw two cities in a thousand *b*'s — ,, 561
  Up the great river in the boatman's *b*. — *Lancelot and E.* 1038
  with exceeding swiftness ran the *b*, If *b* it were— — *Holy Grail* 514
  or had the *b* Become a living creature — ,, 518
  blackening in the sea-foam sway'd a *b*, — ,, 802
  I burst the chain, I sprang into the *b*. — ,, 807
  And felt the *b* shock earth, — ,, 812
  Then from the *b* I leapt, — ,, 819
  be yon dark Queens in yon black *b*, — *Pass. of Arthur* 452
  The *b* was beginning to move, — *First Quarrel* 21
  an' go to-night by the *b*.' — ,, 88

Boat (*continued*) the *b* went down that night—(repeat) — *First Quarrel* 92
  till I saw that a *b* was nearing us— — *The Wreck* 12?
  and there in the *b* I lay With sad eyes — ,, 12?
  his *b* was on the sand ; — *The Flight* 37
  And lay on that funereal *b*, — *To Marq. of Dufferin* 34
  Had parted from his comrade in the *b*, — *The Ring* 30?
  b's of Dahomey that float upon human blood ! — *The Dawn* 5
Boated I *b* over, ran My craft aground, — *Edwin Morris* 108
  They *b* and they cricketed ; — *Princess, Pro.* 160
Boat-head did I turn away The *b-h* — *Arabian Nights* 25
  as the *b-h* wound along The willowy hills — *L. of Shalott iv* 24
Boatman wrought To make the *boatmen* fishing-nets, — *Enoch Arden* 278
  By the great river in a *b*'s hut. — ,, 1038
  Up the great river in a *b*'s boat. — ,,
Boatswain China-bound, and wanting yet a *b*. — *Enoch Arden* 123
Boboli Or walks in *B*'s ducal bowers. — *The Daisy* 44
Bode thither wending there that night they *b*. — *Lancelot and E.* 412
  And Lancelot *b* a little, till he saw — ,, 461
  There *b* the night : but woke with dawn, — ,, 846
  And *b* among them yet a little space — ,, 921
  And there awhile it *b* ; and if a man — *Holy Grail* 54
  spake not any word, But *b* his hour, — *Last Tournament* 386
Bodied Is *b* forth the second whole. — *Love thou thy land* 66
Bodily were she the prize of *b* force, — *Marr. of Geraint* 541
Body I wrapt his *b* in the sheet, — *The Sisters* 34
  A *b* slight and round, and like a pear — *Walk. to the Mail* 5?
  I was strong and hale of *b* then ; — *St. S. Stylites* 29
  touch my *b* and be heal'd, and live : — ,, 79
  bodies and the bones of those That strove — *Day-Dm., Arrival* 9
  'Here lies the *b* of Ellen Adair ; — *Edward Gray* 9
  There lies the *b* of Ellen Adair ! — ,, 35
  Bore to earth her *b*, drest In the dress — *L. of Burleigh* 98
  He cast his *b*, and on we swept. — *The Voyage* 80
  Like that long-buried *b* of the king, — *Aylmer's Field* 3
  adulteries That saturate soul with *b*. — ,, 377
  His *b* half flung forward in pursuit, — ,, 587
  as not passing thro' the fire *Bodies*, but souls— — ,, 672
  that break *B* toward death, and palsy, — *Lucretius* 154
  unlaced my casque And grovell'd on my *b*, — *Princess vi* 28
  and to dance Its *b*, and reach — ,, 138
  There lay the sweet little *b* — *Grandmother* 62
  I look'd at the still little *b*— — ,, 66
  this weight of *b* and tomb, — *High. Pantheism* 5
  phantom *bodies* of horses and men ; — *Boädicea* 7
  and back return To where the *b* sits, — *In Mem. xii* 19
  cheeks drop in ; the *b* bows Man dies: — ,, *xxxv* 3
  Bare of the *b*, might it last, — ,, *xliii* 4
  in the ghastly pit long since a *b* was found, — *Maud I i* 5
  sworn to bury All this dead *b* of hate, — ,, *xix* 97
  Hath *b* enow to hold his foemen down ?' — *Com. of Arthur* 253
  blood Of their strong *bodies*, flowing, — *Marr. of Geraint* 569
  And let the *bodies* lie, but bound — *Geraint and E.* 42
  And being weak in *b* said no more ; — *Lancelot and E.* 839
  'Faith of my *b*,' he said, ' and art thou not— — *Pelleas and E.* 318
  But the sweet *b* of a maiden babe. — *Last Tournament* 48
  Belted his *b* with her white embrace, — ,, 513
  A *b* journeying onward, sick with toil. — *Lover's Tale i* 124
  breathless *b* of her good deeds past. — ,, 217
  soul and heart and *b* are all at ease : — ,, 556
  had the ghastliest That ever lusted for a *b*, — ,, 648
  She took the *b* of my past delight, — ,, 681
  '*b* and soul And life and limbs, — ,, *iv* 282
  sank his *b* with honour down into the deep, — *The Revenge* 109
  He veils His flesh in bread, *b* and bread
    together; — *Sir J. Oldcastle* 157
  'No bread, no bread. God's *b* !' — ,, 159
  Thou canst not prove that thou art *b* alone, — *Ancient Sage* 59
  they laid this *b* they foun' an' the grass — *Tomorrow* 73
  nurse of ailing *b* and mind, — *Locksley H., Sixty* 5?
  lustier *b*, larger mind ? — ,, 164
  out of his *b* she drew The red 'Blood-eagle' — *Dead Prophet* 5?
  You say your *b* is so foul— — *Happy* 25
  Your *b* is not foul to me, and *b* is foul at best. — ,, 28
  If my *b* come from brutes, (repeat) — *By an Evolution.* 5, 13
  Where I sank with the *b* at times — ,, 18

C

Bone (*continued*) in these spasms that grind *B* against *b*.   *Columbus* 221
the white North has thy *b's*,   *Sir J. Franklin* 1
There blanch the *b's* of whom she slew,   *Tiresias* 150
black in white above his *b's*.   *Locksley H., Sixty* 44
moulder'd nest On its barkless *b's*,   *Dead Prophet* 19
honest Poverty, bare to the *b*,   *Vastness* 19
save breaking my *b's* on the rack ?   *By an Evolution.* 9
gentleman, heart, blood and *b*,   *Bandit's Death* 2
Bone-batter'd being all *b-b* on the rock, Yielded ;   *Gareth and L.* 1050
Bonnet Or the frock and gipsy *b*   *Maud I xx* 19
Bonny Doon Whistling a random bar of *B D*,   *The Brook* 82
Book (*See also* **Annal-book, Booök, Statute-book**)
Take, Madam, this poor *b* of song ;   *To the Queen* 17
burnt His epic, his King Arthur, some twelve *b's*—   *The Epic* 28
these twelve *b's* of mine Were faint   ,, 38
old Sir Robert's pride, His *b's*—   *Audley Court* 59
faces grow between me and my *b* ;   *St. S. Stylites* 176
eyesight poring over miserable *b's*,   *Locksley Hall* 172
prose O'er *b's* of travell'd seamen,   *Amphion* 82
Nor yet the fear of little *b's*   *Will Water.* 195
the priest, above his *b* Leering   *Vision of Sin* 117
And bought them needful *b's*,   *Enoch Arden* 332
Then desperately seized the holy *B*,   ,, 495
she closed the *B* and slept :   ,, 499
swear upon the *b* Not to reveal it,   ,, 838
'on the *b*.' And on the *b*, half-frighted,   ,, 842
After his *b's*, to flush his blood with air, Then to   his *b's* again.   *Aylmer's Field* 459
'Show me the *b's* !'   *Sea Dreams* 148
'The *b's* ! the *b's* !' but he, he could not   ,, 150
great *B's* (see Daniel seven and ten)   ,, 152
'O miracle of women,' said the *b*,   *Princess, Pro.* 35
(I kept the *b* and had my finger in it)   ,, 53
which brought My *b* to mind :   ,, 120
on lattice edges lay Or *b* or lute ;   ,, ii 30
'can he not read—no *b's* ?   ,, iii 214
but brooding turn The *b* of scorn,   ,, v 142
rout of saucy boys Brake on us at our *b's*,   ,, 395
to and fro With *b's*, with flowers,   ,, vii 26
was cramm'd with theories out of *b's*,   ,, Con. 35
in this *B*, little Annie, the message   *Grandmother* 96
Still in the little *b* you lent me,   *The Daisy* 99
May bind a *b*, may line a box,   *In Mem. lxxvii* 6
One lesson from one *b* we learn'd,   ,, lxxix 14
Discuss'd the *b's* to love or hate,   ,, lxxxix 34
With festal cheer, With *b's* and music,   ,, cvii 22
in their hand Is Nature like an open *b* ;   ,, Con. 132
She sits by her music and *b's*   *Maud I xiv* 13
a palm As glitters gilded in thy *B* of Hours.   *Gareth and L.* 46
Read but one *b*, and ever reading   *Merlin and V.* 622
and his *b* came down to me.'   ,, 650
'Ye have the *b*: the charm is written in it: ,, 652
'Thou read the *b*, my pretty Vivien !   ,, 667
cities on their flanks—thou read the *b* !   ,, 676
'From our old *b's* I know That Joseph   *Holy Grail* 59
For so they say, these *b's* of ours,   ,, 65
'for in sooth These ancient *b's*—   ,, 541
Of Geoffrey's *b*, or him of Malleor's,   *To the Queen ii* 42
gie fur a howry owd *b* thutty pound an' moor,   *Village Wife* 45
An' 'e'd wrote an owd *b*, his awn sen,   ,, 46
I am written in the Lamb's own *B* of Life   *Columbus* 88
dipt In some forgotten *b* of mine   *To E. Fitzgerald* 47
He would open the *b's* that I prized,   *The Wreck* 21
We had read their know-nothing *b's*   *Despair* 55
their knowing and know-nothing *b's*   ,, 93
knows not ev'n the *b* he wrote,   *Ancient Sage* 148
knew no *b's* and no philosophies,   ,, 218
there were *b's* and dresses—left to me,   *The Ring* 113
I bad her keep, Like a seal'd *b*,   ,, 123
scarce have learnt the title of your *b*,   ,, 126
'The *b's*, the miniature, the lace are hers,   ,, 288
my friend, To prize your various *b*,   *To Ulysses* 47
thought to myself I would offer this *b* to you,   *June Bracken, etc.* 4
'Alla,' says their sacred *b*, 'is Love,'   *Akbar's Dream* 73

Booklearned *See* **Boooklarn'd.**

Booklearning *See* **Boooklarnin'.**
Bookless Your flight from out your *b* wilds   *Princess ii* 56
Boom (s) air was torn in sunder, Crashing went the *b*   *The Captain* 44
clash and *b* of the bells rang   *V. of Maeldune* 110
Boom (verb) His captain's-ear has heard them *b*   *Ode on Well.* 65
b and blanch on the precipices,   *Boädicea* 76
Boometh At eve the beetle *b*   *Claribel* 9
Booming Listens the muffled *b* indistinct   *Lover's Tale i* 637
Boon (adj.) Fled all the *b* companions of the Earl,   *Geraint and E.* 477
Boon (s) *b* from me, From me, Heaven's Queen,   *Œnone* 126
Fresh apple-blossom, blushing for a *b*.   *Princess i* 146
At last she begg'd a *b*,   *Gareth and L.* 334
widow crying to the King, 'A *b*, Sir King !   ,, 345
No *b* is here, But justice,   ,, 351
'A *b*, Sir King ! Thine enemy, King, am I.   ,, 365
'A *b*, Sir King ! I am her kinsman, I.   ,, 368
came Sir Kay, the seneschal, and cried, 'A *b*, Sir King !   ,, 370
the wholesome *b* of gyve and gag.'   ,, 442
b, Sir King (his voice was all ashamed),   ,, 449
youth and worth a goodlier *b* !   ,, 647
'A *b*, Sir King—this quest !' then—   ,, 94
'To what request for what strange *b*,'   *Merlin and V.* 264
B, ay, there was a *b*, one not so strange—   ,, 287
ask your *b*, for *b* I owe you thrice,   ,, 306
take this *b* so strange and not so strange.'   ,, 310
Whenever I have ask'd this very *b*,   ,, 323
Yield my *b*, Till which I scarce can yield   ,, 351
Why will ye never ask some other *b* ?   ,, 375
Who feels no heart to ask another *b*.   ,, 382
Not ever be too curious for a *b*,   ,, 486
Lo, there my *b* ! What other ?   ,, 494
To snare her royal fancy with a *b*   *Lancelot and E.* 71
tale of diamonds for his destined *b*)   ,, 91
Booök (book) 'e 'ed hallus a *b* i' 'is 'and,   *Village Wife* 26
Hallus aloän wi' 'is *b's*,   ,, 28
An' *b's*, what's *b's* ?   ,, 69
niver knawd nowt but *b's*, an' *b's*,   ,, 70
why shouldn't thy *b's* be sowd ?   ,, 71
I hears es soom o' thy *b's* mebbe worth   ,, 73
Heäps an' heäps o' *b's*, I ha' see'd 'em,   ,, 87
moäst on 'is owd big *b's* fetch'd   ,, 113
Sa 'is taäil wur lost an' 'is *b's* wur gone   ,, 23
B's, es I said afoor, thebbe neyther 'ere nor theer !   ,, 24
Boooklarn'd (booklearned) An' I 'oäps es 'e beänt *b* :   ,, 13
Boooklarnin' (booklearning) an' we haätes *b* 'ere.   ,, 94
Booöt (boot) I could fettle and clump owd *b's*   *North. Cobbler* 13
And browt me the *b's* to be cobbled   ,, 87
Boor-tree (elder-tree) in wan grave be the dead *b-t*,   *Tomorrow* 19
Boot (*See also* **Booöt**) Leisurely tapping a glossy *b*   *Maud I xiii* 99
an' the mud o' 'is *b's* o' the stairs,   *Spinster's S's.* 1005
Boot (in addition) Will pay thee all thy wages,   and to *b*.   *Gareth and L.* 28
Booth sport and song, in *b* and tent,   *In Mem. xcviii* 34
Bootless proxy-wedded with a *b* calf   *Princess i* 565
Booty chance of *b* from the morning's raid,   *Geraint and E.* 11
Border (adj.) A *b* fantasy of branch and flower,   *Lancelot and E.* 265
Border (s) Morn broaden'd on the *b's* of the dark,   *D. of F. Women* 24
From out the *b's* of the morn,   *On a Mourner* 34
Close on the *b's* of a territory,   *Marr. of Geraint* 101
on the *b* of her couch they sat   *Guinevere* 116
There on the *b* Of boundless Ocean,   *Lotos-Eaters* 22
Border'd the yellow down *B* with palm,   *Merlin and the G.* 116
Border-marriage land was ringing of it—This   blacksmith *b-m*—   *Aylmer's Field* 263
Border-race such counter-terms, my son, Are *b-r's*,   *Ancient Sage* 251
Bore (to burrow) hedgehog underneath the   plaintain *b's*,   *Aylmer's Field* 850
Bore (to bear) winds which *b* Them earthward till   they lit ;   *The Poet* 17
The broad stream *b* her far away,   *L. of Shalott iv* 17
B and forbore, and did not tire.   *Two Voices* 218
That *b* a lady from a leaguer'd town ;   *D. of F. Women* 47
Branches they *b* of that enchanted stem,   *Lotos-Eaters* 28
b him to a chapel nigh the field.   *M. d'Arthur* 8
And rising *b* him thro' the place of tombs.   ,, 175

Bore (to bear) (*continued*)   blowing forward, *b* King
  Arthur,   *M. d'Arthur, Ep.* 21
in her bosom *b* the baby, Sleep.   *Gardener's D.* 268
But Dora *b* them meekly,   *Dora* 36
knowest I *b* this better at the first,   *St. S. Stylites* 28
Not this alone I *b* :   ,,   61
I *b*, whereof, O God, thou knowest all.   ,,   70
and love her for the love she *b* ?   *Locksley Hall* 73
she Not less thro' all *b* up, till,   *Godiva* 62
Right down by smoky Paul's they *b*,   *Will Water.* 141
Three fair children first she *b* him,   *L. of Burleigh* 87
B to earth her body, drest In the dress   ,,   98
She *b* the blade of Liberty.   *The Voyage* 72
A light-green tuft of plumes she *b*   *Sir L. and Q. G.* 26
B him another son, a sickly one :   *Enoch Arden* 109
grieving held his will, and *b* it thro'.   ,,   167
do the thing he will'd, and *b* it thro'.   ,,   295
weight of the dead leaf *b* it down :   ,,   678
And Enoch *b* his weakness cheerfully.   ,,   827
To be the ghost of one who *b* your name   *The Brook* 219
yet she *b* it : yet her cheek   *Aylmer's Field* 505
loneliness of grief *B* down in flood,   ,,   633
her own people *b* along the nave Her pendent hands,   ,,   812
motion of the boundless deep *B* thro' the cave,   *Sea Dreams* 92
motion of the great deep *b* me on,   ,,   111
They *b* her back into the tent ;   *Princess iv* 193
Yet I *b* up in part from ancient love,   ,,   303
Yet I *b* up in hope she would be known :   ,,   320
b down a Prince, And Cyril, one.   ,,   *v* 518
me they *b* up the broad stairs,   ,,   *vi* 374
He *b* but little game in hand ;   *The Victim* 42
And *b* thee where I could not see   *In Mem. xxii* 17
And thus he *b* without abuse   ,,   *cxi* 21
In either hand he *b* What dazzled all,   *Gareth and L.* 386
And he that *b* The star, when mounted,   ,,   950
with a costrel *b* The means of goodly welcome,   *Marr. of Geraint* 386
best by her that *b* her understood.   ,,   511
b Down by the length of lance and arm   *Geraint and E.* 462
b him to the naked hall of Doorm,   ,,   570
She *b* me there, for born from death was I   *Merlin and V.* 44
He *b* a knight of old repute to the earth,   *Lancelot and E.* 492
he *b* the prize and could not find The victor,   ,,   629
thus they *b* her swooning to her tower.   ,,   968
reverently they *b* her into hall.   ,,   1266
b them down, And broke thro' all,   *Holy Grail* 479
b him to a chapel nigh the field,   *Pass. of Arthur* 176
And rising *b* him thro' the place of tombs.   ,,   343
she that *b* Camilla close beneath   *Lover's Tale i* 202
converse sweet, In which our voices *b* least part.   ,,   542
A whirlwind caught and *b* us ;   ,,   *ii* 197
so they *b* her (for in Julian's land   ,,   *iv* 36
B her free-faced to the free airs   ,,   38
So *b* her thro' the solitary land   ,,   90
Sir Richard *b* in hand all his sick men   *The Revenge* 15
stately Spanish men to their flagship *b* him   ,,   97
She *b* a child, whom reverently we call'd   *Sisters (E. and E.)* 268
and the love I *b* them both—   ,,   281
we, who *b* the Cross Thither,   *Columbus* 191
And so, when I *b* him a girl,   *The Wreck* 33
Nature who knew not that which she *b* !   *Despair* 34
on an earth that *b* not a flower ;   ,,   44
wheat Of Egypt *b* a grain as sweet   *To Prof. Jebb* 6
As we *b* down the Gods before us ?   *Demeter and P.* 132
yesterday They *b* the Cross before you   *Happy* 48
In a while I *b* him a son,   *Bandit's Death* 15
Borest   Ah little rat that *b* in the dyke   *Merlin and V.* 112
Boring   *B* a little auger-hole in fear,   *Godiva* 68
Born (*See also* **Burn, Devil-born, Eldest-born,
  Equal-born, First-born, Gentle-born, King-
  born, Lame-born, Latest-born, New-born,
  Royal - born, Sickly-born, Spleen - born**)
Nothing was *b* ; Nothing will die ;   *Nothing will Die* 36
All things were *b*.   *All Things will Die* 47
And Thou and peace to earth were *b*.   *Supp. Confessions* 26
THE poet in a golden clime was *b*,   *The Poet* 1

Born (*continued*)   Two children in one hamlet *b* and bred ;   *Circumstance* 8
Thou wert *b*, on a summer morn,   *Eleänore* 7
Truth is *b* Beyond the polar gleam   *Two Voices* 181
features of her child Ere it is *b* :   *Œnone* 253
never child be *b* of me, Unblest,   ,,   254
which mood was *b* Scorn of herself ;   *Palace of Art* 230
call me before the day is *b*.   *May Queen, N. Y's. E.* 49
thousand times I would be *b* and die.   *D. of F. Women* 204
Was never *b* into the earth.   *To J. S.* 32
With that fair child betwixt them *b*.   *On a Mourner* 25
B out of everything I heard and saw,   *Gardener's D.* 66
days went on, there was *b* a boy To William ;   *Dora* 48
sinful man, conceived and *b* in sin :   *St. S. Stylites* 122
group Of beauties, that were *b* In teacup-times of hood   *Talking Oak* 62
'But I was *b* too late : the fair new forms,   *Golden Year* 15
glimpse of that dark world where I was *b*.   *Tithonus* 33
And thought and time be *b* again,   *Day-Dm., Sleep. P.* 50
serving-man As any *b* of woman.   *Will Water.* 152
I'm a beggar *b*,' she said,   *Lady Clare* 37
I am a beggar *b*,' she said,   ,,   71
' If you are not the heiress *b*, (repeat)   ,,   83, 85
honour Unto which she was not *b*.   *L. of Burleigh* 80
Every moment dies a man, Every moment one
  is *b*. (repeat)   *Vision of Sin* 98, 122
but when her child was *b*,   *Enoch Arden* 686
In those far-off seven happy years were *b* ;   ,,   686
B of a village girl, carpenter's son,   *Aylmer's Field* 668
Thy better *b* unhappily from thee,   ,,   675
A CITY clerk, but gently *b* and bred ;   *Sea Dreams* 1
chiefly you were *b* for something great,   *Princess iv* 307
Ere you were *b* to vex us ?   ,,   *vi* 248
dead before he was *b*, (repeat)   *Grandmother* 59, 68
naw, naw, tha was not *b* then ;   *N. Farmer, O. S.* 29
The linnet *b* within the cage,   *In Mem. xxvii* 3
The light that shone when Hope was *b*.   ,,   *xxx* 32
In these brief lays, of Sorrow *b*,   ,,   *xlviii* 1
In that dark house where she was *b*.   ,,   *lx* 12
It is the day when he was *b*,   ,,   *cvii* 1
And, *b* of love, the vague desire   ,,   *cx* 19
But I was *b* to other things.   ,,   *cxx* 12
Result in man, be *b* and think,   ,,   *Con.* 126
it seem'd far better to be *b* To labour   *Maud I xviii* 33
On the day when Maud was *b* ;   ,,   *xix* 40
O Rivulet, *b* at the Hall,   ,,   *xxi* 8
Is a juggle *b* of the brain ?   ,,   *II ii* 42
tickle the maggot *b* in an empty head,   ,,   *v* 38
Some calling Arthur *b* of Gorloïs, Others of
  Anton ?   *Com. of Arthur* 170
all before his time Was Arthur *b*,   ,,   212
Or *b* the son of Gorloïs, after death, Or Uther's
  son, and *b* before his time,   ,,   240
Else, wherefore *b* ? '   *Gareth and L.* 119
saying thou wert basely *b*.   ,,   355
God wot, so thou wert nobly *b*,   ,,   1064
Stript from the three dead wolves of woman *b*   *Geraint and E.* 94
creatures gently *b* But into bad hands   ,,   191
B with the blood, not learnable,   *Balin and Balan* 175
We two were *b* together, and we die   ,,   629
bore me there, for *b* from death was I   *Merlin and V.* 44
turn of anger *b* Of your misfaith ;   ,,   531
but *b* of sickness, could not live :   *Lancelot and E.* 880
sons *B* to the glory of thy name and fame,   ,,   1372
Well is it that no child is *b* of thee.   *Guinevere* 424
children *b* of thee are sword and fire,   ,,   425
Like the last echo *b* of a great cry,   *Pass. of Arthur* 459
Life knows not when young Life was *b*,   *Lover's Tale i* 156
falsehood of all starcraft !) we were *b*.   ,,   200
So were we *b*, so orphan'd.   ,,   218
Because my grief as yet was newly *b*   ,,   613
Back to the mother's house where she was *b*.   ,,   *iv* 91
b Not from believing mind,   ,,   104
and that day a boy was *b*, Heir   ,,   128
But the boy was *b* i' trouble,   *First Quarrel* 2
The boy was *b* in wedlock,   ,,   6
For the lawyer is *b* but to murder—   *Rizpah* 64

Born (*continued*) all my doubts were fools *B* of
the fool   *Sisters* (*E. and E.*) 141
in the second year was *b* A second—   ,, 269
fatal kiss, *B* of true life and love,   *Ded. Poem Prin. Alice* 3
In Judah, for in thee the Lord was *b* ;   *Sir J. Oldcastle* 25
for in thee the word was *b* again.   ,, 27
slain my father the day before I was *b*.   *V. of Maeldune* 8
who wailest being *b* And banish'd into mystery,   *De Prof. Two G.* 41
grief for ever *b* from griefs to be,   *Tiresias* 80
as if she were basely *b* !   *The Wreck* 36
B of the brainless Nature who knew not   *Despair* 34
For wert thou *b* or blind or deaf,   *Ancient Sage* 175
a bitter word, not once since we were *b* ;   *The Flight* 86
She the worldling *b* of worldlings—   *Locksley H., Sixty* 25
Stronger ever *b* of weaker,   ,, 164
before her highest, man, was *b*,   ,, 205
you my Miriam *b* within the year ;   *The Ring* 285
As we forget our wail at being *b*.   ,, 465
You will live till *that* is *b*,   *Forlorn* 63
For on a tropic mountain was I *b*,   *Prog. of Spring* 67
words ! Words only, *b* of fever,   *Romney's R.* 30
and him, and the day I was *b*.   *Charity* 24
birthday came of a boy *b* happily dead.   ,, 34
WHERE is one that, *b* of woman,   *Making of Man* 1

Borne (*See also* **Eagle-borne**, **Fancy-borne**)
Adown the Tigris I was *b*,   *Arabian Nights* 6
From off her shoulder backward *b* :   *Palace of Art* 118
And many a merry wind was *b*,   *Day-Dm., Depart* 14
When on my goodly charger *b*   *Sir Galahad* 49
bear me with thee, smoothly *b*,   *Move Eastward* 9
Enoch lives : that is *b* in on me.   *Enoch Arden* 319
I have *b* it with me all these years.   ,, 895
ovation round Their statues, *b* aloft,   *Princess vi* 67
Now to glorious burial slowly *b*,   *Ode on Well.* 193
B down by gladness so complete,   *In Mem. xxxii* 10
This truth came *b* with bier and pall,   ,, lxxxv 1
And daughters had she *b* him,—   *Com. of Arthur* 189
but a son she had not *b*.   ,, 192
Before him at his crowning *b*,   ,, 296
down the wave and in the flame was *b* A naked babe,   ,, 383
wild Limours, *B* on a black horse,   *Geraint and E.* 458
B by some high lord-prince of Arthur's hall,   *Balin and Balan* 466
Else never had he *b* her crown,   ,, 566
Across the silent seeded meadow-grass *B*, clash'd :   *Pelleas and E.* 562
b about the bay or safely moor'd   *Lover's Tale i* 54
my name was *b* Upon her breath.   ,, 443
B into alien lands and far away.   ,, 802
I, too, was *b* along and felt the blast   ,, iii 27
great love they both had *b* the dead,   ,, iv 181
we had always *b* a good name.   *Rizpah* 35
You never have *b* a child—   ,, 80
thou wouldst have her flag *B* on thy
coffin—   *Ded. Poem Prin. Alice* 17
great flame-banner *b* by Teneriffe,   *Columbus* 69
B in the bark's-bosom,   *Batt. of Brunanburh* 49
wail came *b* in the shriek of a growing wind,   *The Wreck* 87
nurse Who had *b* my flower on her hireling heart ;   ,, 143
b in white To burning or to burning,   *Ancient Sage* 207
earth has never *b* a nobler man.   *Epit. on Gordon* 4
b along by that full stream of men,   *St. Telemachus* 43
I have *b* Rain, wind, frost,   *St. S. Stylites* 15
think that I have *b* as much as this—   ,, 92
bearing in myself the shame The woman should
have *b*,   *Aylmer's Field* 356
That a calamity hard to be *b* ?   *Maud I xiii* 3
likewise for the high rank she had *b*,   *Guinevere* 695
b With more than mortal swiftness,   *Lover's Tale ii* 72
The love they both have *b* me,   *Sisters* (*E. and E.*) 280
heathen men have *b* as much as this,   *Sir J. Oldcastle* 185
Born-unborn with their offspring, *b-u*,   *Locksley H., Sixty* 98
Borough half The neighbouring *b* with their Institute   *Princess, Pro.* 5
may they see Beyond the *b* and the shire !   *Hands all Round* 28
Better a rotten *b* or so Than a rotten fleet   *Riflemen form !* 17
Borrow'd *B* a glass, but all in vain :   *Enoch Arden* 240
A cap of Tyrol *b* from the hall,   *Princess iv* 601

Bors (**a knight**) Sir *B*, our Lancelot's cousin, sware,   *Holy Grail* 200
The pelican on the casque of our Sir *B*   ,, 635
Once,' Said good Sir *B*, ' he dash'd across me   ,, 640
' Then Sir *B* had ridden on Softly,   ,, 647
to *B* Beyond the rest :   ,, 652
Sir *B* Rode to the lonest tract of all the realm,   ,, 660
Said good Sir *B*, ' beyond all hopes of mine,   ,, 690
Sir *B* it was Who spake so low   ,, 700
Ay, ay, Sir *B*, who else ?   ,, 707
for Sir *B*, on entering, push'd Athwart   ,, 752
saying to him, ' Hail, *B* ! if ever loyal man   ,, 756
and *B*, ' Ask me not for I may not speak   ,, 757
Blessed are *B*, Lancelot and Percivale,   ,, 874
Bos thundering shores of Bude and *B*,   *Guinevere* 291
Boscage to thee, green *b*, work of God,   *Sir J. Oldcastle* 129
Bosk and blowing *b's* of wilderness,   *Princess i* 111
Boskage Thridding the sombre *b* of the wood,   *D. of F. Women* 243
Bosom (*See also* **Bark's-bosom**) *b's* prest To little
harps of gold ;   *Sea-Fairies* 3
woodpecker From the *b* of a hill.   *Kate* 5
From brow and *b* slowly down   *Mariana in the S.* 14
rising, from her *b* drew Old letters,   ,, 61
long to fall and rise Upon her balmy *b*,   *Miller's D.* 183
fingers backward drew From her warm brows and *b*   *Œnone* 177
an arm Rose up from out the *b* of the lake,   *M. d'Arthur* 30
in her *b* bore the baby, Sleep.   *Gardener's D.* 268
and fall about thy neck, And on thy *b*   *Love and Duty* 42
and *b* beating with a heart renew'd.   *Tithonus* 36
her *b* shaken with a sudden storm of sighs—   *Locksley Hall* 27
I will pluck it from my *b*,   ,, 66
moral shut Within the *b* of the rose ?   *Day-Dm., Moral* 8
I will not vex my *b* :   *Amphion* 102
snowdrop of the year That in my *b* lies.   *St. Agnes' Eve* 12
charm have power to make New lifeblood warm the *b*,   *Will Water.* 22
Him, to her meek and modest *b* prest In agony,   *Aylmer's Field* 416
fondled on her lap, Warm'd at her *b* ?   ,, 687
sun their milky *b's* on the thatch,   *Princess ii* 103
an erring pearl Lost in her *b*,   ,, iv 61
lay me on her *b*, and her heart Would rock   ,, 103
over brow And cheek and *b* brake the wrathful bloom   ,, 383
half The sacred mother's *b*, panting,   ,, vi 148
And hid her *b* with it ;   ,, 214
And slips into the *b* of the lake :   ,, vii 187
and slip Into my *b* and be lost in me.'   ,, 189
The *b* with long sighs labour'd ;   ,, 225
Slide from the *b* of the stars.   *In Mem. xvii* 10
sword That rose from out the *b* of the lake,   *Com. of Arthur* 297
Yniol's heart Danced in his *b*,   *Marr. of Geraint* 505
his beard Across her neck and *b* to her knee,   *Merlin and V.* 257
and in her *b* pain was lord.   *Last Tournament* 239
arm Rose up from out the *b* of the lake,   *Pass. of Arthur* 198
our baby lips, Kissing one *b*,   *Lover's Tale i* 238
infuse Rich atar in the *b* of the rose,   ,, 270
Cast the poison from your *b*,   *Locksley H., Sixty* 241
The linnet's *b* blushes at her gaze,   *Prog. of Spring* 17
Bosom'd and *b* the burst of the spray,   *V. of Maeldune* 103
Bosom-friend My *b-f* and half of life ;   *In Mem. lix* 3
Bosom-peak And budded *b-p's*—who this way   *Lucretius* 191
Bosom-sepulchre Sympathy hew'd out The *b-s*
of Sympathy ?   *Lover's Tale ii* 32
Bosom-throne Had nestled in this *b-t* of Love,   ,, i 624
Boss the silver *b* Of her own halo's   *The Voyage* 31
Boss'd *b* with lengths Of classic frieze,   *Princess ii* 24
goblet on the board by Balin, *b* With holy
Joseph's legend,   *Balin and Balan* 362
Botanic They read *B* Treatises,   *Amphion* 77
Bottle ' What's i' tha *b* a-stanning theer ?'   *North. Cobbler* 1
Thou gits naw gin fro' the *b* theer,   ,, 10
yon big black *b* o' gin.   ,, 70
An' 'e points to the *b* o' gin,   ,, 90
Smash the *b* to smithers, the Divil's in 'im,   ,, 104
And 'a taïen to the *b* beside,   *Spinster's S's.* 56
their *b's* o' pap, an' their mucky bibs,   ,, 87
Bottom (**adj.**) As *b* agates seem to wave and float   *Princess ii* 327
Bottom (**s**) creation pierce Beyond the *b* of his eye.   *A Character* 6

Bottom (s) (*continued*) made a plunge To the *b*, and dispersed, — *Enoch Arden* 380
fox—where started—kill'd In such a *b* : — *Aylmer's Field* 254
Tho' anchor'd to the *b*, such is he.' — *Princess iv* 257
the sand danced at the *b* of it. — *Balin and Balan* 27
b of the well, Where Truth is hidden. — *Merlin and V.* 47
glances from the *b* of the pool, — *The Ring* 371

Bough (*See also* **Beechen-bough, Beugh**) beneath the dome Of hollow *b's*. — *Arabian Nights* 42
garlanding the gnarled *b's* With bunch — *Œnone* 101
Whose thick mysterious *b's* in the dark morn — " 213
came To rest beneath thy *b's.*—(repeat) — *Talking Oak* 36, 156
Olivia came To sport beneath thy *b's*. — " 100
till thy *b's* discern The front of Sumner-place. — " 247
bent or broke The lithe reluctant *b's* — *Enoch Arden* 381
one soft arm, which, like the pliant *b* — *Sea Dreams* 290
grasping down the *b's* I gain'd the shore. — *Princess iv* 189
and while the holly *b's* Entwine — *In Mem. xxix* 9
I found a wood with thorny *b's*, — " *lxix* 6
And sow the sky with flying *b's*, — " *lxxii* 24
Unwatch'd, the garden *b* shall sway, — " *ci* 1
Came on the hoarhead woodman at a *b* Wearily hewing. — *Balin and Balan* 294
He burst his lance against a forest *b*, — " 329
canker'd *b's* without Whined in the wood ; — " 345
and old *b's* Whined in the wood. — " 385
made him quickly dive Beneath the *b's*, — " 423
and on the *b's* a shield Showing — *Last Tournament* 432
and the wind among the *b's*. — " 489
shot forth *B's* on each side, — *Lover's Tale i* 230
beechen *b's* Of our New Forest. — *Sisters (E. and E.)* 112
Look, he stands, Trunk and *b*, — *The Oak* 14

Bought (*See also* **Bowt**) have *b* A mansion incorruptible. — *Deserted House* 20
B Annie goods and stores, and set — *Enoch Arden* 169
b them needful books, and everyway, — " 332
b Quaint monsters for the market of those times, — " 538
We *b* the farm we tenanted before. — *The Brook* 222
B? what is it he cannot buy ? — *Maud I x* 32
sold and sold had *b* them bread : — *Marr. of Geraint* 641
who *b* me for his slave? — *The Flight* 19

Boulder found a glen, gray *b* and black tarn. — *Lancelot and E.* 36

Bound (adj.) (*See also* **China-bound, Seaward-bound**)
B on a matter he of life and death : — *Sea Dreams* 151
'Was he so *b*, poor soul ?' — " 169
B for the Hall, I am sure was he : — *Maud I x* 25
B for the Hall, and I think for a bride. — " 26
'*B* upon a quest With horse and arms— — *Gareth and L.* 708
B on a foray, rolling eyes of prey, — *Geraint and E.* 538
B upon solitary adventure, — *Pelleas and E.* 275
Whither are you ? For Naples — *The Ring* 57

Bound (limit) *make The* b's *of freedom wider yet* — *To the Queen* 32
Transgress his ample *b* to some new crown :— — *Poland* 8
And mete the *b's* of hate and love— — *Two Voices* 135
Beyond the utmost *b* of human thought. — *Ulysses* 32
You that have dared to break our *b*, — *Princess iv* 539
And music in the *b's* of law, — *In Mem. lxxxvii* 34
And strike his being into *b's*, — " *Con.* 124
b's of heaven and earth were lost— — *Com. of Arthur* 372
shun to break those *b's* of courtesy — *Lancelot and E.* 1220
Drew from before Sir Tristram to the *b's*, — *Last Tournament* 185
Back to the sunset *b* of Lyonnesse— — *Pass. of Arthur* 81
charged the winds With spiced May-sweets from *b* to *b*, — *Lover's Tale i* 318
Nor understandest *b* nor boundlessness, — *Ancient Sage* 48
and the *b's* Determining concession ; — *To Duke of Argyll* 2
Narrowing the *b's* of night.' — *Prog. of Spring* 91
all the *b's* of earth, Far-far-away ? — *Far-far-away* 14
I spy nor term nor *b*. — *Mechanophilus* 20

Bound (spring) but a single *b*, and with a sweep — *Geraint and E.* 727

Bound (verb) wild winds *b* within their cell, — *Mariana* 54
Two lives *b* fast in one — *Circumstance* 5
Sleep had *b* her in his rosy band, — *Caress'd or chidden* 6
Art thou so *b* To men, — *Two Voices* 109
Which only to one engine *b* — " 347

Bound (verb) (*continued*) In front they *b* the sheaves. — *Palace of Art* 78
earth is every way *B* by gold chains — *M. d'Arthur* 255
'I am *b* : you have my promise— — *Enoch Arden* 437
I am always *b* to you, but you are free.' — " 450
Annie weeping answer'd 'I am *b*.' — " 451
she knew that she was *b*— — " 462
B in an immemorial intimacy, — *Aylmer's Field* 39
nor *b* plight or broken ring *B*, — " 136
you think me *b* In some sort, — *Princess i* 158
given us letters, was he *b* to speak ? — " 181
I b by precontract Your bride, — " *iv* 541
each beside his chariot *b* his own ; — *Spec. of Iliad* 3
lost the links that *b* Thy changes ; — *In Mem. xli* 6
Had *b* us one to the other, — *Maud I xix* 38
B them by so strait vows to his own self, — *Com. of Arthur* 262
vows, as is a shame A man should not be *b* by, — *Gareth and L.* 271
b my lord to cast him in the mere.' — " 803
'*B* am I to right the wrong'd, — " 804
straitlier *b* am I to bide with thee.' — " 805
I *b* to thee for any favour ask'd !' — " 977
b the suits Of armour on their horses, — *Geraint and E.* 96
b them on their horses, each on each, — " 182
B are they To speak no evil. — *Balin and Balan* 145
Arthur *b* them not to singleness — *Merlin and V.* 28
They b to holy vows of chastity ! — " 695
then he *b* Her token on his helmet, — *Lancelot and E.* 373
but free love will not be *b*.' — " 1379
'Free love, so *b*, were freëst,' — " 1380
bright boy-knight, and *b* it on him, — *Holy Grail* 156
'All men, to one so *b* by such a vow, — " 565
Seized him, and *b* and plunged him into a cell — " 675
Give ye the slave mine order to be *b*, — *Pelleas and E.* 270
rose up, and *b*, and brought him in. — " 288
Not to be *b*, save by white bonds — " 353
and *b* his horse Hard by the gates. — " 413
B on her brow, were Gawain and Ettarre. — " 435
the King hath *b* And sworn me to this brotherhood ; — " 448
earth is every way *B* by gold chains — *Pass. of Arthur* 423
So to be *b* by common love and loss— — *Lover's Tale iv* 345
Harry was *b* to the Dorsetshire farm — *First Quarrel* 19
only done my duty as a man is *b* to do : — *The Revenge* 102
I had not *b* myself by words, — *Sisters (E. and E.)* 137
I was *b* to her ; I could not free myself — " 160
b Not by the sounded letter of the word, — " 161
broken chain that *b* me to my kind. — *Locksley H., Sixty* 52
the laughing shepherd *b* with flowers ; — *To Virgil* 16
b to follow, wherever she go Stark-naked, — *Dead Prophet* 45
for twenty years *B* by the golden cord — *The Ring* 429

Bound *See also* **Brow-bound, Charm-bound**

Boundary Close at the *b* of the liberties ; — *Princess i* 172

Bounded motions in a shallower brain : — *Locksley Hall* 150
a spirit *b* and poor ; — *Maud I iv* 38
Death's dark war-horse *b* forward — *Gareth and L.* 1401
Then *b* forward to the castle walls, — *Pelleas and E.* 363
b forth and vanish'd thro' the night. — " 487
Seeing it is not *b* save by love.' — *Last Tournament* 703

Bounden (*See also* **Long-bounden, Promise-bounden**)
and lying *b* there In darkness — *Holy Grail* 676
those he overthrew Be *b* straight, — *Pelleas and E.* 236
but thrust him *b* out of door. — " 314
Thus to be *b*, so to see her face, — " 326
tho' she hath me *b* but in spite, — " 329
Let me be *b*, I shall see her face ; — " 331

Bounding *b* forward 'Leave them to the wolves.' — *Balin and Balan* 588

Boundless Feels that the deep is *b*, — *Ancient Sage* 192
Sent the shadow of Himself, the *b*, — *Locksley H., Sixty* 211
B inward, in the atom, *b* outward, — " 212

Boundlessness Nor understandest bound nor *b*, — *Ancient Sage* 48

Bounteous Of whom were any *b*, merciful, — *Gareth and L.* 423

Bounteous Isle And we came to the *B I*, — *V. of Maeldune* 83
Till we hated the *B I* and the sunbright hand — " 92

Bounteously *b* made, And yet so finely, — *Aylmer's Field* 74

Bountiful Spare not now to be *b*, — *On Jub. Q. Victoria* 29
B, beautiful, apparell'd gay, — *Prog. of Spring* 62

Bounty God only thro' his *b* hath thought fit,   *St. S. Stylites* 186
Here he lives in state and *b*,   *L. of Burleigh* 57
Or Heaven in lavish *b* moulded, grew.   *Aylmer's Field* 107
Bourg Ye think the rustic cackle of your *b*   *Marr. of Geraint* 276
They take the rustic murmur of their *b*   " 419
Bourn-Bourne and rang Beyond the *bourn* of sunset;   *Princess, Con.* 100
from out our *bourne* of Time and Place   *Crossing the Bar* 13
Bovadilla *B,* one As ignorant and impolitic   *Columbus* 127
Bow (respectful inclination) O the formal mocking *b*,   *The Flight* 29
Bow (an instrument) spirit ever strung Like a new *b*,   *Kate* 11
Bow (rainbow) great *b* will waver in the sun,   *Palace of Art* 43
And every dew-drop paints a *b*,   *In Mem. cxxxii* 18
For there beyond a bridge of treble *b*,   *Gareth and L.* 1086
Bow (part of a ship) figure-head Stared o'er the ripple feathering from her *b's*:   *Enoch Arden* 544
huge sea-castles heaving upon the weather *b*.   *The Revenge* 24
Bow (s) *See* **Foam-bow, Saddle-bow, Torrent-bow**
Bow (verb) *B* myself down, where thou hast knelt,   *Supp. Confessions* 80
B down one thousand and two hundred   *St. S. Stylites* 111
gay domestic *B's* before him at the door.   *L. of Burleigh* 48
as when a field of corn *B's* all its ears   *Princess i* 237
She *b's,* she bathes the Saviour's feet   *In Mem. xxxii* 11
cheeks drop in ; the body *b's* Man dies: " *xxxv* 3
made him flush, and *b* Lowly, to kiss his hand,   *Gareth and L.* 548
O ay—the winds that *b* the grass !   *Last Tournament* 735
To thee, dead wood, I *b* not head nor knees.   *Sir J. Oldcastle* 128
Bow-back'd supporters on a shield, *B-b* with fear: *Princess vi* 359
Bow'd Like Thine own mother's when she *b* Above Thee,   *Supp. Confessions* 23
A group of Houris *b* to see The dying Islamite,   *Palace of Art* 102
power in his eye That *b* the will.   *M. d'Arthur* 123
She *b* upon her hands,   *Dora* 103
She *b* down her head,   " 105
She *b* down And wept in secret ;   " 107
My knees are *b* in crypt and shrine :   *Sir Galahad* 18
Enoch as a brave God-fearing man *B* himself down,   *Enoch Arden* 186
Enoch was so brown, so *b,* So broken—   " 703
'My God has *b* me down to what I am ;   " 856
b her state to them, that they might grow   *Princess ii* 166
She *b* as if to veil a noble tear ;   " *iii* 289
handmaid on each side *B* toward her,   " *iv* 276
B on her palms and folded up from wrong,   " 288
She *b,* she set the child on the earth ;   " *vi* 120
thine own land has *b* to Tartar hordes   *W. to Marie Alex.* 23
save Thy sailor,—while thy head is *b,*   *In Mem. vi* 14
When have I *b* to her father,   *Maud I iv* 13
not to her brother I ; I *b* to his lady-sister   " 14
the budded peaks of the wood are *b*   " *vi* 4
redden'd her cheek When I *b* to her   " *xix* 66
Gareth *b* himself With all obedience   *Gareth and L.* 487
Low *b* the tributary Prince,   *Marr. of Geraint* 174
with back turn'd, and *b* above his work,   " 267
lifted adoring eyes, *B* at her side   *Geraint and E.* 305
b the all-amorous Earl,   " 360
low *b* the Prince, and felt His work   " 920
b black knees Of homage,   *Merlin and V.* 577
then *b* his homage, bluntly saying,   *Last Tournament* 206
he *b* to kiss the jewell'd throat,   " 751
and *b* down upon her hands Silent,   *Guinevere* 158
and *b* her head nor spake.   " 310
power in his eye That *b* the will.   *Pass. of Arthur* 291
B the spoiler, Bent the Scotsman,   *Batt. of Brunanburh* 20
b myself down as a slave to his intellectual throne,   *The Wreck* 66
Edith *b* her stately head,   *The Tourney* 13
Edith Montfort *b* her head,   " 15
Bower (*See also* **Garden-bower, Tree-bower**) Creeping thro' blossomy rushes and *b's* of rose-blowing bushes,   *Leonine Eleg.* 3
day Was sloping toward his western *b*.   *Mariana* 80
Dwelling amid these yellowing *b's*:   *A spirit haunts* 2
Youngest Autumn, in a *b* Grape-thicken'd   *Eleänore* 35
Then to the *b* they came,   *Œnone* 94
they came to that smooth-swarded *b*,   " 95
And I was left alone within the *b* ;   " 192
honeysuckle round the porch has wov'n its wavy *b's*,   *May Queen* 29

Bower (*continued*) Leaving the promise of my bridal *b*,   *D. of F. Women* 218
bulk Of mellow brickwork on an isle of *b's*.   *Edwin Morris* 12
Pursue thy loves among the *b's*   *Talking Oak* 199
Droops the heavy-blossom'd *b*,   *Locksley Hall* 163
Then fled she to her inmost *b*,   *Godiva* 42
but even then she gain'd Her *b* ;   " 77
The peacock in his laurel *b*,   *Day-Dm., Sleep. P.* 15
From havens hid in fairy *b's*,   *The Voyage* 54
she moved To meet me, winding under woodbine *b's*,   *The Brook* 88
from a *b* of vine and honeysuckle :   *Aylmer's Field* 156
broader-grown the *b's* Drew the great night   *Princess vii* 48
music, O bird, in the new-budded *b's* !   *W. to Alexandra* 11
Or walks in Boboli's ducal *b's*.   *The Daisy* 44
and make her a *b* All of flowers,   *Window, At the W.* 5
out of her *b* All of flowers,   " 12
light Dies off at once from *b* and hall,   *In Mem. viii* 6
That sweeps with all its autumn *b's*,   " *xi* 10
have clothed their branchy *b's* With fifty Mays,   " *lxxvi* 13
With thy lost friend among the *b's*,   " *cii* 15
glowing like the moon Of Eden on its bridal *b* :   " *Con.* 28
And tends upon bed and *b*,   *Maud I xiv* 4
out of *b* and casement shyly glanced   *Gareth and L.* 313
walk of lilies crost it to the *b*:   *Balin and Balan* 243
long white walk of lilies toward the *b*.   " 249
and Balin started from his *b*.   " 280
Remembering that dark *b* at Camelot,   " 526
' Had ye not held your Lancelot in your *b*,   *Pelleas and E.* 182
spied not any light in hall or *b*,   " 419
In her high *b* the Queen, Working a tapestry,   *Last Tournament* 128
then slowly to her *b* Parted,   " 238
Thro' many a league-long *b* he rode.   " 374
saw The great Queen's *b* was dark,—   " 758
in thy *b's* of Camelot or of Usk   *Guinevere* 503
vanish'd from my sight Beneath the *b*   *Lover's Tale ii* 43
they were swallow'd in the leafy *b's*,   " *iii* 57
All the *b's* and the flowers,   *Sisters (E. and E.)* 10
Fainting flowers, faded *b's*,   " 11
Over all the woodland's flooded *b's*,   " 20
piping underneath his beechen *b's* ;   *To Virgil* 14
wealth of tropic *b* and brake.   *To Ulysses* 37
Bower'd (*See also* **Close-bower'd**) garden *b* close With plaited alleys of the trailing rose,   *Ode to Memory* 105
Bower-eaves Look out below your *b-e,*   *Margaret* 66
A **BOW-SHOT** from her *b-e,*   *L. of Shalott iii* 1
Boweth Earthward he *b* the heavy stalks   *A spirit haunts* 7
Bowing Approved him, *b* at their own deserts :   *The Brook* 128
and *b* o'er the brook A tonsured head   " 199
She spoke, and *b* waved Dismissal :   *Princess ii* 99
b over him, Low to her own heart   *Marr. of Geraint* 84
b lowly down before thee,   *Akbar's D., Hymn* 3
Bowl (*See also* **Wassail-bowl**) Nor robb'd the farmer of his *b* of cream :   *Princess v* 223
Nor *b* of wassail mantle warm ;   *In Mem. cv* 18
fling free alms into the beggar's *b*,   *Ancient Sage* 260
Bowl'd a herd of boys with clamour *b*   *Princess, Pro.* 81
Bowl-shaped saw, *B-s,* thro' tops of many thousand pines   *Gareth and L.* 796
Bowman *See* **Master-bowman**
Bow-shot A *B-s* from her bower-eaves,   *L. of Shalott iii* 1
Bow-string His *b-s* slacken'd, languid Love,   *Eleänore* 117
Bowt (**bought**) An' 'e *b* owd money, es wouldn't goä,   *Village Wife* 49
An' 'e *b* little statues all-naäkt   " 50
Box (a case) (*See also* **Deal-box**) A long green *b* of mignonette,   *Miller's D.* 83
and the *b* of mignonette.   *May Queen, N. Y's. E.* 48
May bind a book, may line a *b*,   *In Mem. lxxvii* 6
Box (compartment) Old *b'es,* larded with the steam   *Will Water.* 223
Shall call thee from the *b'es.*   " 240
Box (boxful) 'e snifft up a *b* in a daäy,   *Village Wife* 40
Box (a shrub) breath Of the fading edges of *b* beneath,   *A spirit haunts* 19
Boy (*See also* **Cupid-boys, Orphan-boy**) A merry *b* in sun and shade ?   *Two Voices* 321
' A merry *b* they call'd him then,   " 322

Bracket statuette Of my dear Mother on your *b* here—	*The Ring* 110
Brag (s) Said Gareth, 'Old, and over-bold in *b*!	*Gareth and L.* 1107
Brag (verb) *b* to his fellow rakes of his conquest	*Charity* 18
Bragging armies so broken A reason for *b*	*Batt. of Brunanburh* 83
Brahmin B, and Buddhist, Christian, and Parsee,	*Akbar's Dream* 25
Braid wound Her looser hair in *b*,	*Gardener's D.* 158
fire-flies tangled in a silver *b*.	*Locksley Hall* 10
Forth streaming from a *b* of pearl :	*Day-Dm., Sleep. B.* 6
Blowing the ringlet from the *b* :	*Sir L. and Q. G.* 39
the *b* Slipt and uncoil'd itself,	*Merlin and V.* 888
Braided (*See also* **Vapour-braided**) *b* thereupon All	
the devices blazon'd	*Lancelot and E.* 8
precious crystal into which I *b* Edwin's hair !	*The Flight* 34
Brain (*See also* **Braäin, Full-brain, Half-brain**) arms,	
or power of *b*, or birth	*To the Queen* 3
Right to the heart and *b*, tho' undescried,	*Isabel* 22
From the *b* of the purple mountain	*Poet's Mind* 29
falling axe did part The burning *b* from the true heart,	*Margaret* 39
A random arrow from the *b*.	*Two Voices* 345
From some odd corner of the *b*.	*Miller's D.* 68
In my dry *b* my spirit soon,	*Fatima* 26
Devil, large in heart and *b*,	*To—With Pal. of Art* 5
great thought strikes along the *b*,	*D. of F. Women* 43
dawn's creeping beams, Stol'n to my *b*,	262
Drawn from the spirit thro' the *b*,	*"To J. S.* 38
nourish a blind life within the *b*,	*M. d'Arthur* 251
Simeon, whose *b* the sunshine bakes ;	*St. S. Stylites* 164
Better the narrow *b*, the stony heart,	*Love and Duty* 15
mist of tears, that weigh'd Upon my *b*,	44
that his *b* is overwrought.	*Locksley Hall* 53
blinder motions bounded in a shallower *b* :	150
On secrets of the *b*, the stars,	*Day-Dm., L'Envoi* 11
Which bears a season'd *b* about,	*Will Water.* 85
were scatter'd Blood and *b*'s of men.	*The Captain* 48
Beating it in upon his weary *b*,	*Enoch Arden* 796
tickling the brute *b* within the man's	*Lucretius* 21
but as his *b* Began to mellow,	*Princess i* 179
Besides the *b* was like the hand,	*" ii* 150
Then while I dragg'd my *b*'s for such a song,	*" iv* 154
Whose *b*'s are in their hands and in their heels,	*" 518
upon whose hand and heart and *b*	*Ode on Well.* 239
Perchance, to charm a vacant *b*,	*The Daisy* 106
dash the *b*'s of the little one out,	*Boädicea* 68
But, for the unquiet heart and *b*,	*In Mem. v* 5
And marvel what possess'd my *b* ;	*" xiv* 16
I make a picture in the *b* ;	*" lxxx* 9
As but the canker of the *b* ;	*" xcii* 3
Pallas from the *b* Of Demons ?	*" cxiv* 12
I think we are not wholly *b*,	*" cxx* 2
And like is darken'd in the *b*.	*" cxxi* 8
would not marvel at either, but keep a temperate *b* ;	*Maud I iv* 40
What was it ? a lying trick of the *b* ?	*" II i* 37
Is a juggle born of the *b* ?	*" ii* 42
'Tis the blot upon the *b* That *will* show	*" iv* 60
Beat into my scalp and my *b*,	*" v* 10
So dark a forethought roll'd about his *b*,	*Merlin and V.* 230
may make My scheming a cinder,	*" 933*
Skip to the broken music of my *b*'s	*Last Tournament* 258
'Save for that broken music in thy *b*'s,	*" 267*
and clove him thro' the *b*.	*" 754*
nourish a blind life within the *b*,	*Pass. of Arthur* 419
springing from her fountains in the *b*,	*Lover's Tale i* 83
clear brow, bulwark of the precious *b*,	*" 130*
Past thro' into his citadel, the *b*,	*" 631*
O'erbore the limits of my *b* :	*" 689*
meaning of the letters shot into My *b* ;	*" ii* 9
In my *b* The spirit seem'd to flag	*" 50*
thro' my eyes into my innermost *b*,	*" 95*
Flatter'd the fancy of my fading *b* ;	*" 107*
love is of the *b*, the mind, the soul ;	*" iv* 156
her *b* broke With over-acting,	*Sisters (E. and E.)* 235
My *b* had begun to reel—	*In the Child. Hosp.* 60
brute bullet broke thro' the *b*	*Def. of Lucknow* 20
For I am emptier than a friar's *b*'s ;	*Sir J. Oldcastle* 7
rang into the heart and the *b*,	*V. of Maeldune* 110

Brain (*continued*) My *b* is full of the crash of wrecks,	*The Wreck* 4
for my *b* was drunk with the water,	*Despair* 65
statesman's *b* that sway'd the past	*Ancient Sage* 134
Set the feet above the *b* and swear the *b* is in	
the feet.	*Locksley H., Sixty* 136
oust the madness from your *b*.	241
Works of subtle *b* and hand,	*Open. I. and C. Exhib.* 7
'Beat little heart' on this fool *b* of mine.	*Romney's R.* 155
Who was a shadow in the *b*,	*Mechanophilus* 15
Brain-feverous *B-f* in his heat and agony,	*Lancelot and E.* 854
Brain-labour And prodigal of all *b-l* he,	*Aylmer's Field* 447
Brainless Insolent, *b*, heartless !	*"*
Brainpan Than if my *b* were an empty hull,	*Princess ii* 398
Brake (s) Close-matted, bur and *b* and briar,	*Day-Dm., Sleep. P.* 46
gloom Of evening over *b* and bloom And meadow,	*In Mem. lxxxvi* 3
And bristles all the *b*'s and thorns	*cvii* 9
In every wavering *b* an ambuscade.	*Geraint and E.* 51
'How far thro' all the bloom and *b*	*Ancient Sage* 19
wealth of tropic bower and *b* ;	*To Ulysses* 37
downy drift against the *b*'s,	*Prog. of Spring* 27
Brake (verb) at their feet the crocus *b* like fire,	*Œnone* 96
B with a blast of trumpets from the gate,	*Princess, Pro.* 42
from my breast the involuntary sigh *B*,	*" iii* 192
over brow And cheek and bosom *b* the wrathful bloom	*" iv* 383
titter, out of which there *b* On all sides,	*" v* 16
a rout of saucy boys *B* on us at our books,	*" 395*
then *b* out my sire, Lifting his grim head	*" vi* 271
For on them *b* the sudden foe ;	*" The Victim* 4
Suddenly from him *b* his wife,	*" 70*
No spirit ever *b* the band That stays him	*In Mem. xciii* 2
fires of Hell *b* out of thy rising sun,	*Maud II i* 9
b on him, till, amazed, He knew not whither	*Com. of Arthur* 39
they swerved and *b* Flying,	*" 119*
great lords Banded, and so *b* out in open war.'	*" 237*
neither clomb, nor *b* his neck, But *b* his very heart	
in pining for it,	*Gareth and L.* 56
That lookt half-dead, *b* bright,	*" 685*
there *b* a servingman Flying from out of the black wood,	*" 801*
either spear Bent but not *b*,	*" 964*
Clash'd his, and *b* it utterly to the hilt.	*" 1148*
and thrice they *b* their spears.	*Marr. of Geraint* 562
then *b* short, and down his enemy roll'd,	*Geraint and E.* 160
Abash'd us both, and *b* my boast. Thy will ?'	*Balin and Balan* 71
I *b* upon thy rest, And now full loth	*" 499*
the storm *B* on the mountain and I cared not	*Merlin and V.* 503
and the skull *B* from the nape,	*Lancelot and E.* 50
b a sudden-beaming tenderness Of manners	*" 328*
then out she *b* : 'Going ?	*" 925*
when the next sun *b* from underground,	*" 1137*
B from the vast oriel-embowering vine	*" 1198*
Stoopt, took, *b* seal, and read it ;	*" 1271*
'But when the next day *b* from under ground—	*Holy Grail* 338
Then blush'd and *b* the morning of the jousts,	*Pelleas and E.* 157
comes again'—there she *b* short ;	*" 295*
Reel'd in the smoke, *b* into flame, and fell.	*" 519*
It chanced that both *B* into hall together,	*" 587*
and the Red Knight *B* in upon me	*Last Tournament* 137
B with a wet wind blowing,	*" 238*
B up their sports, then slowly to her bower	*Guinevere* 160
maid, who brook'd No silence, but *b* it,	*" 361*
storm of anger *b* From Guinevere,	*" 607*
there her voice *b* suddenly,	*Pass. of Arthur* 68
b the petty kings, and fought with Rome,	*" 130*
wan wave *B* in among dead faces,	*" 158*
while they *b* them, own'd me King.	*Batt. of Brunanburh* 11
B the shield-wall,	*Last Tournament* 568
Brakest *b* thro' the scruple of my bond,	*Holy Grail* 211
Bramble arm Red-rent with hooks of *b*,	*Pelleas and E.* 422
and *b*'s mixt And overgrowing them,	*A Dirge* 30
Bramble Rose *B r*'s, faint and pale,	
Branch (s) (*See also* **Willow-branches**) Like to some	
b of stars we see	*L. of Shalott iii* 11
B'es they bore of that enchanted stem,	*Lotos-Eaters* 28
With winds upon the *b*,	*" C. S.* 27
curved *b*'es, fledged with clearest green,	*D. of F. Women* 59

Branch (s) *(continued)* paused, And dropt the *b* she held,   *Gardener's D.* 157
  Whose topmost *b'es* can discern The roofs   *Talking Oak* 31
  And from thy topmost *b* discern The roofs   ,, 190
  From spray, and *b*, and stem,   ,, 190
  Stagger'd and shook, holding the *b*,   *Enoch Arden* 767
  whirl'd her white robe like a blossom'd *b*   *Princess iv* 179
  the *b'es* thereupon Spread out at top,   ,, 205
  and shook the *b'es* of the deer   ,, *Con.* 98
  That makes the barren *b'es* loud ;   *In Mem. xv* 13
  On all the *b'es* of thy blood ;   ,, *lxxxiv* 8
  lie, while these long *b'es* sway,   *Maud I xviii* 29
  Melody on *b*, and melody in mid air.   *Gareth and L.* 183
  high on a *b* Hung it,   *Balin and Balan* 432
  Tore from the *b*, and cast on earth,   ,, 539
  and the rotten *b* Snapt in the rushing   *Merlin and V.* 957
  A border fantasy of *b* and flower,   *Lancelot and E.* 11
  puff'd the swaying *b'es* into smoke   *Holy Grail* 15
  were our mothers' *b'es* of one stem ?   *Lover's Tale ii* 25
  and the *b* with berries on it,   *Columbus* 73
  Golden *b* amid the shadows,   *To Virgil* 27
  Who lops the moulder'd *b* away.   *Hands all round* 8
  gliding thro' the *b'es* over-bower'd   *Death of Œnone* 6
Branch (verb) But *b'es* current yet in kindred veins.'   *Princess ii* 245
  o'er the friths that *b* and spread   *In Mem., Con.* 115
  a name that *b'es* o'er the rest,   *Balin and Balan* 182
Branch'd cloisters, *b* like mighty woods,   *Palace of Art* 26
  whisper of huge trees that *b* And blossom'd in
    the zenith,   *Enoch Arden* 585
  that *b* itself Fine as ice-ferns   *Aylmer's Field* 221
  throve and *b* from clime to clime,   *In Mem. cxviii* 13
  dress All *b* and flower'd with gold,   *Marr. of Geraint* 631
  forehead veins Bloated, and *b* ;   *Balin and Balan* 392
Branching empires *b*, both, in lusty life !—   *W. to Marie Alex.* 21
  trace On paler heavens the *b* grace Of leafless elm,   *To Ulysses* 15
Branch-work Beneath *b-w* of costly sardonyx   *Palace of Art* 95
Brand (a mark) a part Falling had let appear
    the *b* of John—   *Aylmer's Field* 509
Brand (a sword) *(See also* **Levin-brand)** The *b*, the
    buckler, and the spear—   *Two Voices* 129
  Thou therefore take my *b* Excalibur,   *M. d'Arthur* 95
  There drew he forth the *b* Excalibur,   ,, 52
  ' And if indeed I cast the *b* away,   ,, 88
  The great *b* Made lightnings in the splendour   ,, 136
  So flash'd and fell the *b* Excalibur :   ,, 142
  The hard *b's* shiver on the steel,   *Sir Galahad* 6
  And, ringing, springs from *b* and mail ;   ,, 54
  —*b*, mace, and shaft, and shield—   *Princess v* 503
  Arthur call'd to stay the *b's*   *Com. of Arthur* 120
  So this great *b* the king Took,   ,, 308
  Flash *b* and lance, fall battleaxe   ,, 486
  Fall battleaxe, and flash *b* ! (repeat)   ,, 487, 490, 502
  Clang battleaxe and clash *b* ! (repeat)   ,, 493, 496, 499
  Gareth lash'd so fiercely with his *b*   *Gareth and L.* 968
  Sir Gareth's *b* Clash'd his,   ,, 1147
  neither hunting-dress Nor weapon, save a
    golden-hilted *b*,   *Marr. of Geraint* 166
  Swung from his *b* a windy buffet out Once,   *Geraint and E.* 90
  and tearing out of sheath The *b*,   *Balin and Balan* 393
  Where Arthur finds the *b* Excalibur.   *Holy Grail* 253
  The *b* Excalibur will be cast away.   ,, 257
  Shield-breakings, and the clash of *b's*,   *Pass. of Arthur* 109
  b's that once had fought with Rome,   ,, 133
  There drew he forth the *b* Excalibur,   ,, 220
  ' And if indeed I cast the *b* away,   ,, 256
  The great *b* Made lightnings in the splendour   ,, 304
  So flash'd and fell the *b* Excalibur :   ,, 310
  Sons of Edward with hammer'd *b's*.   *Batt. of Brunanburh* 14
Brand (verb) power to burn and *b* His nothingness
    into man.   *Maud I xviii* 39
  b us, after, of whose fold we be :   *Merlin and V.* 764
  Earth and Hell will *b* your name,   *Forlorn* 51
Brandagoras King *B* of Latangor,   *Com. of Arthur* 114
Brandish'd caught him by the hilt, and *b*
    him (repeat)   *M. d'Arthur* 145, 160
  caught him by the hilt, and *b* him (repeat)   *Pass. of Arthur* 313, 328

C*

Brandishing *B* in her hand a dart   *Boädicea* 71
Brass crag-platform smooth as burnish'd *b* I chose.   *Palace of Art* 5
  Two handfuls of white dust, shut in an urn
    of *b* !   *Lotos-Eaters C.S.* 68
  A flying splendour out of *b* and steel,   *Princess vi* 365
  Among the knightly *b'es* of the graves,   *Merlin and V.* 752
Brastias (a knight) Ulfius, and *B*, and Bedivere,
    (repeat)   *Com. of Arthur* 136, 165, 445
  Ulfius and *B* answer'd, ' Ay.'   *Com. of Arthur* 173
Brat I hevn't naw likin' fur *b's* ;   *Spinster's S's.* 84
Brave (adj.) *B* the Captain was :   *The Captain* 5
  few his knights, however *b* they be—   *Com. of Arthur* 252
  but all *b*, all of one mind with him ;   ,, 255
  Truth-speaking, *b*, good livers,   *Gareth and L.* 424
  till she left Not even Lancelot *b*,   *Merlin and V.* 805
  All *b*, and many generous, and some chaste.   ,, 817
  Each was as *b* in the fight   *V. of Maeldune* 5
  being true as he was *b* ;   *Locksley H., Sixty* 59
Brave (s) our Lawrence the best of the *b* :   *Def. of Lucknow* 11
  Follow'd by the *b* of other lands,   *Ode on Well.* 194
  whatsoe'er He wrought of good or *b*   *Epilogue* 76
Brave (verb) never : here I *b* the worst :'   *Edwin Morris* 118
  However we *b* it out, we men are a little breed.   *Maud I iv* 30
Braved She *b* a riotous heart in asking for it.   *Lancelot and E.* 359
Bravery Lancelot, the flower of *b*,   ,, 113
Bravest Fought with the *b* among us,   *Def. of Lucknow* 71
Brawl (s) creature wholly given to *b's* and wine,   *Marr. of Geraint* 441
Brawl (verb) Cease to wail and *b* !   *Two Voices* 199
  I care not what the sects may *b*.   *Palace of Art* 210
  left the drunken king To *b* at Shushan   *Princess iii* 230
  b Their rights or wrongs like potherbs   ,, *v* 458
  our free press should cease to *b*,   *Third of Feb.* 3
  Is perfect stillness when they *b*.   *Lit. Squabbles* 20
Brawler ' What fear ye, *b's* ?   *Princess iv* 498
Brawling brook o'er a shingly bed *B*,   *Marr. of Geraint* 249
  Romans *b* of their monstrous games ;   *St. Telemachus* 40
Bray loud rung out the bugle's *b's*,   *Oriana* 48
  in the blast and *b* of the long horn   *Princess v* 252
Brazen-headed O'erthwarted with the *b-h* spear   *Œnone* 139
Breach One has leapt up on the *b*,   *Def. of Lucknow* 64
Breach'd *b* the belting wall of Cambalu,   *Columbus* 108
Bread *(See also* **Breäd)** I speak the truth, as I live by *b* !   *Lady Clare* 26
  Taking her *b* and theirs :   *Enoch Arden* 111
  wine And *b* from out the houses brought,   *Spec. of Iliad* 6
  chalk and alum and plaster are sold to the poor for *b*,   *Maud I i* 39
  Where *b* and baken meats and good red wine   *Gareth and L.* 1190
  in her veil enfolded, manchet *b*.   *Marr. of Geraint* 389
  sold and sold had bought them *b* :   ,, 641
  smote itself into the *b*, and went ;   *Holy Grail* 467
  But, *b*, merely for *b*.   *Sir J. Oldcastle* 14
  ' *B*—*B* left after the blessing ?'   ,, 153
  now He veils His flesh in *b*, body and *b*   ,, 157
  ' No *b*, no *b*. (repeat)   ,, 159, 161
  Hast thou brought *b* with thee ?   ,, 198
  I have not broken *b* for fifty hours.   ,, 199
  For holding there was *b* where *b* was none—No *b*.   ,, 201
  I am not like to die for lack of *b*.   ,, 205
  B enough for his need till the labourless day   *V. of Maeldune* 86
  dream, now and then, of a hand giving *b* and wine,   *The Wreck* 114
  Master scrimps his haggard sempstress of her
    daily *b*,   *Locksley H., Sixty* 221
Breäd Mun be a guvness, lad, or summut, and addle
    her *b* :   *N. Farmer, N. S.* 26
Breadth *B's* of tropic shade and palms in cluster,   *Locksley Hall* 160
  left but narrow *b* to left and right   *Enoch Arden* 674
  shattering on black blocks A *b* of thunder.   *Princess iii* 292
  whence they need More *b* of culture :   ,, *v* 188
  a *b* Of Autumn, dropping fruits of power :   ,, *vi* 54
  She mental *b*, nor fail in childward care,   ,, *vii* 283
  tower Half-lost in belts of hop and *b's* of wheat ;   *In Mem. lxxxix* 3
  with all thy *b* and height Of foliage,   ,, *Con.* 45
  highway running by it leaves a *b* Of sward to left
    and right,   *Sisters (E. and E.)* 80
  from over the *b* of a street,   *Def. of Lucknow* 23
  she with all the *b* of man,   *Locksley H., Sixty* 48

Break (s) Across a *b* on the mist-wreathen isle   *Enoch Arden* 632
  At *b* of day the College Portress came :   *Princess ii* 15
  I climb'd the roofs at *b* of day ;   *The Daisy* 61
Break (verb) (*See also* **Breāk**) passion fann'd, About
  thee *b's* and dances :   *Madeline* 30
  breaking heart that will not *b*,   *Oriana* 64
  athlete, strong to *b* or bind All force   *Palace of Art* 153
  ' No voice *b's* thro' the stillness   259
  You thought to *b* a country heart   *L. C. V. de Vere* 3
  Nor would I *b* for your sweet sake   ,, 13
  call me loud when the day begins to *b* :   *May Queen* 10
  lest a cry Should *b* his sleep by night,   *Walk. to the Mail* 74
  same old sore *b's* out from age to age   ,, 79
  Faltering, would *b* its syllables,   *Love and Duty* 39
  He *b's* the hedge : he enters there :   *Day-Dm., Arrival* 18
  But *b* it. In the name of wife,   ,, *L'Envoi* 53
  B up the heavens, O Lord !   *St. Agnes' Eve* 21
  barren commonplaces *b* In full and kindly blossom.   *Will Water.* 23
  B lock and seal : betray the trust :   *You might have won* 18
  B, b, b, On thy cold gray stones,   *Break, break, etc.* 1
  B, b, b, At the foot of thy crags,   ,, 13
  But had no heart to *b* his purposes To Annie,   *Enoch Arden* 155
  I think your kindness *b's* me down ;   ,, 318
  Help me not to *b* in upon her peace.   ,, 787
  Which *b's* all bonds but ours ;   *Aylmer's Field* 425
  Who broke the bond which they desired to *b*,   ,, 778
  trifle makes a dream, a trifle *b's.*   *Sea Dreams* 144
  that *b* Body toward death,   *Lucretius* 153
  which *b's* As I am breaking now !   ,, 241
  In iron gauntlets : *b* the council up.'   *Princess i* 89
  wherefore *b* her troth ?   ,, 95
  To *b* my chain, to shake my mane :   ,, *ii* 424
  Kill up with pity, *b* us with ourselves—   ,, *iii* 258
  tho' the rough kex *b* The starr'd mosaic,   ,, *iv* 77
  did I *b* Your precinct ;   ,, 421
  On me, me, me, the storm first *b's* :   ,, 499
  You that have dared to *b* our bound,   ,, 539
  she's yet a colt—Take, *b* her :   ,, *v* 456
  takes, and *b's*, and cracks, and splits,   ,, 527
  fear we not To *b* them more in their behoof,   ,, *vi* 61
  Nemesis *B* from a darken'd future,   ,, 175
  We *b* our laws with ease,   ,, 323
  your Highness *b's* with ease The law   ,, 325
  roar that *b's* the Pharos from his base   ,, 339
  sorrowing in a pause I dared not *b* ;   ,, *vii* 249
  b the shore, and evermore Make and *b*,   *Ode on Well.* 260
  War, who *b's* the converse of the wise ;   *Third of Feb.* 8
  Tho' all the storm of Europe on us *b* ;   ,, 14
  B, happy land, into earlier flowers !   *W. to Alexandra* 10
  everywhere, The blue heaven *b*,   *W. to Marie Alex.* 43
  To *b* the blast of winter, stand ;   *To F. D. Maurice* 22
  the bud ever *b's* into bloom on the tree,   *The Islet* 32
  b the works of the statuary,   *Boädicea* 64
  immeasurable heavens *B* open to their highest,   *Spec. of Iliad* 15
  Must I take you and *b* you,   *Window, The Answer* 3
  I must take you, and *b* you,   ,, 5
  take—*b, b—B*—you may *b* my heart.   ,, 7
  B, and all's done.   ,, 10
  B, thou deep vase of chilling tears,   *In Mem. iv* 11
  To evening, but some heart did *b*.   ,, *vi* 8
  On the bald street *b's* the blank day.   ,, *vii* 12
  B's hither over Indian seas,   ,, *xxvi* 14
  that my hold on life would *b* Before I heard   ,, *xxviii* 15
  That *b's* about the dappled pools :   ,, *xlix* 4
  Who *b's* his birth's invidious bar,   ,, *lxiv* 5
  and *b* The low beginnings of content.   ,, *lxxxiv* 47
  And *b* the livelong summer day   ,, *lxxxix* 31
  b's The rocket molten into flakes Of crimson   ,, *xcviii* 30
  Or into silver arrows *b* The sailing moon   ,, *ci* 15
  the rolling brine That *b's* the coast.   ,, *cvii* 15
  Will let his coltish nature *b*   ,, *cxi* 7
  And every thought *b's* out a rose.   ,, *cxxii* 20
  million emeralds *b* from the ruby-budded lime   *Maud I iv* 1
  Can *b* her word were it even for me ?   ,, *xvi* 29
  B not, O woman's-heart,   *Ded. of Idylls* 44

Break (verb) (*continued*) *B* not, for thou art Royal, but
  endure,   *Ded. of Idylls* 45
  ' Climb not lest thou *b* thy neck,   *Gareth and L.* 54
  To *b* him from the intent to which he grew,   ,, 140
  so besieges her To *b* her will, and make her wed   ,, 617
  Running too vehemently to *b* upon it.   *Marr. of Geraint* 78
  Here often they *b* covert at our feet.'   ,, 183
  Then will I fight him, and will *b* his pride,   ,, 221
  and in April suddenly *B's* from a coppice   ,, 339
  That lightly *b's* a faded flower-sheath,   ,, 365
  fight and *b* his pride and have it of him.   ,, 416
  I will *b* his pride, and learn his name,   ,, 424
  In next day's tourney I may *b* his pride.'   ,, 476
  b perforce Upon a head so dear in thunder,   *Geraint and E.* 12
  as a man upon his tongue May *b* it,   ,, 43
  chance That *b's* upon them perilously,   ,, 354
  nature's prideful sparkle in the blood *B* into
  furious flame :   828
  b Into some madness ev'n before the Queen ?'   *Balin and Balan* 229
  and *b* the King And all his Table.'   ,, 458
  knight, we *b* on thy sweet rest,   ,, 470
  now full loth am I to *b* thy dream,   ,, 500
  Began to *b* her sports with graver fits,   *Merlin and V.* 180
  in the slippery sand before it *b's* ?   ,, 293
  fled from Arthur's court To *b* the mood.   ,, 298
  that wave about to *b* upon me And sweep me   ,, 302
  tiny-trumpeting gnat can *b* our dream When
  sweetest ;   *Lancelot and E.* 137
  crying Christ and him, And *b* them ;   ,, 306
  Would he *b* faith with one I may not name ?   ,, 685
  discourtesy To blunt or *b* her passion.'   ,, 974
  (He meant to *b* the passion in her)   ,, 1079
  Would shun to *b* those bounds of courtesy   ,, 1220
  To *b* her passion, some discourtesy   ,, 1302
  I needs must *b* These bonds that so defame me :   ,, 1420
  b thro' all, till one will crown thee king   *Holy Grail* 161
  ' I never heard his voice But long'd to *b* away.   *Pelleas and E.* 256
  said Tristram, ' I would *b* thy head.   *Last Tournament* 268
  and after the great waters *b* Whitening   ,, 464
  make the smouldering scandal *b* and blaze   *Guinevere* 91
  Stands in a wind, ready to *b* and fly,   ,, 365
  b the heathen and uphold the Christ,   ,, 470
  —let my heart *B* rather—   *Lover's Tale i* 738
  Not to *b* in on what I say by word   ,, *iv* 352
  B, diviner light !   *Sisters (E. and E.)* 23
  one of those who would *b* their jests on the
  dead,   *In the Child. Hosp.* 8
  B thro' the yews and cypress of thy grave,   *Ded. Poem Prin. Alice* 12
  would *b* down and raze The blessed tomb   *Columbus* 98
  Years that make And *b* the vase of clay,   *Ancient Sage* 92
  B into ' Thens ' and ' Whens '   ,, 104
  when the babblings *b* the dream.   ,, 107
  Scarce feels the senses *b* away   ,, 152
  shell must *b* before the bird can fly.   ,, 154
  B the State, the Church, the Throne,   *Locksley H., Sixty* 138
  thro' this midnight *b's* the sun   *Pref. Poem Broth. S.* 21
  Might *b* thro' clouded memories   *Demeter and P.* 10
  And *b* into the crocus-purple hour   ,, 50
  b The sunless halls of Hades into Heaven ?   ,, 135
  b's her latest earthy link With me to-day.   *The Ring* 47
  Your ' Miriam *b's*'—is making   ,, 99
  No pliable idiot I to *b* my vow ;   ,, 402
  made one barren effort to *b* it at the last.   *Happy* 72
  groundflame of the crocus *b's* the mould,   *Prog. of Spring* 1
  The mortal hillock, Would *b* into blossom ;   *Merlin and the G.* 108
  blight thy hope or *b* thy rest,   *Faith* 2
Breäk (verb) fur I beänt a-gawin' to *b* my rule.   *N. Farmer, O. S.* 4
  I weänt *b* rules fur Doctor,   ,, 67
  B me a bit o' the esh for his 'eäd,   ,, *N. S.* 41
  Tis'n them as 'as munny as *b's* into 'ouses   ,, 45
  an' sweär'd as I'd *b* ivry stick   *North. Cobbler* 35
  ' tha mun *b* 'im off bit by bit.'   ,, 88
  runs out when ya *b's* the shell.   *Village Wife* 4
Breaker (one who breaks) A *b* of the bitter news
  from home,   *Aylmer's Field* 594

Breaker (one who breaks) (*continued*) Nor those horn-
handed *b*'s of the glebe, | *Princess ii* 159
Breaker (wave) long swells of *b* sweep The nutmeg
rocks | *The Voyage* 39
following up And flying the white *b*, | *Enoch Arden* 21
hard upon the cry of ' *b*'s ' came | ,, 548
a ridge Of *b* issued from the belt, | *Sea Dreams* 212
The mellow *b* murmur'd Ida. | *Princess iv* 436
roaring *b*'s boom and blanch on the precipices, | *Boädicea* 76
The *b* breaking on the beach. | *In Mem. lxxi* 16
And the fringe Of that great *b*, | *Com. of Arthur* 387
And steps that met the *b* ! | *Holy Grail* 816
chafed *b*'s of the outer sea Sank powerless, | *Lover's Tale i* 8
the *b*'s on the shore Sloped into louder surf : | ,, iii 14
Javelins over The jarring *b*, | *Batt. of Brunanburh* 97
came thro' the roar of the *b* a whisper, | *Despair* 13
The *b*'s lash the shores : | *Pref. Poem Broth. S.* 2
Breaker-beaten For leagues along that *b-b* coast | *Enoch Arden* 51
Breakest so thou *b* Arthur's music too.' | *Last Tournament* 266
Breaking (part) (*See also* **Ever-breaking**) Just
b over land and main ? | *Two Voices* 84
heart is *b*, and my eyes are dim, | *Œnone* 32
They say his heart is *b*, mother— | *May Queen* 22
The thunders *b* at her feet : | *Of old sat Freedom* 2
while on all sides *b* loose Her household fled | *The Goose* 53
Old elms came *b* from the vine, | *Amphion* 45
LONG lines of cliff *b* have left a chasm ; | *Enoch Arden* 1
Nor let him be, but often *b* in, | ,, 701
he saw An end, a hope, a light *b* upon him. | *Aylmer's Field* 480
b that, you made and broke your dream : | *Sea Dreams* 143
which breaks As I am *b* now ! | *Lucretius* 241
nation weeping, and *b* on my rest ? | *Ode on Well.* 82
B their mailed fleets and armed towers, | *Ode Inter. Exhib.* 39
Or *b* into song by fits, | *In Mem. xxiii* 2
The breaker *b* on the beach. | ,, lxxi 16
And *b* let the splendour fall | ,, Con. 119
why come you so cruelly meek, *B* a slumber | *Maud I iii* 2
B up my dream of delight. | ,, xix 2
and *b* into song Sprang out, | *Com. of Arthur* 320
heard The world's loud whisper *b* into storm, | *Marr. of Geraint* 27
Then *b* his command of silence given, | *Geraint and E.* 390
Vivien *b* in upon him, said : | *Merlin and V.* 600
Outram and Havelock *b* their way through | *Def. of Lucknow* 96
O young life *B* with laughter | *De. Prof. Two G.* 18
Who *b* in upon us yestermorn, | *Akbar's Dream* 114
Breaking (s) (*See also* **Shield-breaking**) Until the *b*
of the light, | *Clear-headed friend* 25
Yours came but from the *b* of a glass, | *Sea Dreams* 248
crave His pardon for thy *b* of his laws. | *Gareth and L.* 986
Red ruin, and the *b* up of laws, | *Guinevere* 426
making a new link *B* an old one ? | *The Ring* 51
save *b* my bones on the rack ? | *By an Evolution.* 9
Breast (s) Naiad Throbbing in mild unrest holds him
beneath in her *b*. | *Leonine Eleg.* 12
Showering thy gleaned wealth into my open *b* | *Ode to Memory* 23
Fold thy palms across thy *b*, | *A Dirge* 2
Take the heart from out my *b*. | *Adeline* 8
To find my heart so near the beauteous *b* | *The form, the form* 7
Dominion in the head and *b*.' | *Two Voices* 21
' His palms are folded on his *b* : | ,, 247
A vague suspicion of the *b* : | ,, 336
fill'd the *b* with purer breath. | *Miller's D.* 92
I crush'd them on my *b*, my mouth ; | *Fatima* 12
Over her snow-cold *b* and angry cheek | *Œnone* 142
His ruddy cheek upon my *b*, | *The Sisters* 20
hundred winters snow'd upon his *b*. | *Palace of Art* 139
as I lie upon your *b*— | *May Queen, Con.* 59
polish'd argent of her *b* to sight | *D. of F. Women* 158
and my true *b* Bleedeth for both ; | *To J. S.* 62
So muscular he spread, so broad of *b*. | *Gardener's D.* 8
wave of such a *b* As never pencil drew. | ,, 139
breathing health and peace upon her *b* : | *Audley Court* 68
An acorn in her *b*. | *Talking Oak* 228
crimson comes upon the robin's *b* ; | *Locksley Hall* 17
press me from the mother's *b*. | ,, 90

Breast (s) (*continued*) and he bears a laden *b*, | *Locksley Hall* 143
in its *b* a thunderbolt. | ,, 192
old Earl's daughter died at my *b* ; | *Lady Clare* 25
HER arms across her *b* she laid ; | *Beggar Maid* 1
I shook her *b* with vague alarms— | *The Letters* 38
silent court of justice in his *b*, | *Sea Dreams* 174
stood out the *b*'s, The *b*'s of Helen, | *Lucretius* 60
blasting the long quiet of my *b* | ,, 162
Beat *b*, tore hair, cried out upon herself | ,, 277
think I bear that heart within my *b*, | *Princess ii* 334
Rest, rest, on mother's *b*, | ,, iii 11
My secret, seem'd to stir within my *b* ; | ,, 44
from my *b* the involuntary sigh Brake, | ,, 191
I smote him on the *b* ; | ,, iv 164
now her *b*, Beaten with some great passion | ,, 387
Her noble heart was molten in her *b* ; | ,, vi 119
if you loved The *b* that fed or arm | ,, 181
Thy helpless warmth about my barren *b* | ,, 202
something wild within her *b*, | ,, vii 237
Sent from a dewy *b* a cry for light : | ,, 253
Chop the *b*'s from off the mother, | *Boädicea* 68
And dead calm in that noble *b* | *In Mem. xi* 19
And onward drags a labouring *b*, | ,, xv 18
Be tenants of a single *b*, | ,, xvi 3
Against the circle of the *b*, | ,, xlv 3
A faithful answer from the *b*, | ,, lxxxv 14
That warms another living *b*. | ,, 116
They haunt the silence of the *b*, | ,, xciv 9
And woolly *b*'s and beaded eyes ; | ,, xcv 12
A single murmur in the *b*, | ,, civ 7
and in my *b* Spring wakens too ; | ,, cxv 17
And enter in at *b* and brow, | ,, cxxii 11
A warmth within the *b* would melt | ,, cxxiv 13
opulence jewel-thick Sunn'd itself on his *b* | *Maud I xiii* 13
Lord of the pulse that is lord of her *b*, | ,, xvi 13
ruddy shield on the Lion's *b*. | ,, III vi 14
o'er her *b* floated the sacred fish ; | *Gareth and L.* 223
The massive square of his heroic *b*, | *Marr. of Geraint* 75
' O noble *b* and all-puissant arms, | ,, 86
weep True tears upon his broad and naked *b*, | ,, 111
thro' his manful *b* darted the pang | ,, 121
Sank her sweet head upon her gentle *b* ; | ,, 527
fell'd him, and set foot upon his *b*, | ,, 574
Drave the long spear a cubit thro' his *b* | *Geraint and E.* 86
Her arms upon her *b* across, | *Merlin and V.* 910
pleasant *b* of waters, quiet bay, | *Lover's Tale i* 6
anger falls aside And withers on the *b* of peaceful love ; | ,, 10
Her *b* as in a shadow-prison, | ,, iv 58
her *b* Hard-heaving, and her eyes upon her feet, | ,, 307
her thin hands crost on her *b*— | *In the Child. Hosp.* 39
kill Their babies at the *b* | *Columbus* 180
And from her virgin *b*, and virgin eyes | *Tiresias* 46
ah, fold me to your *b* ! | *The Flight* 5
pluck from this true *b* the locket that I wear, | ,, 33
well-used to move the public *b*. | *To W. C. Macready* 3
gave Thy *b* to ailing infants in the night, | *Demeter and P.* 56
my loving head upon your leprous *b*. | *Happy* 26
let me lean my head upon your *b*. | *Romney's R.* 154
blade that had slain my husband thrice thro' his *b*. | *Bandit's Death* 34
Breast (verb) *b*'s the blows of circumstance, | *In Mem. lxiv* 7
Breast-bone white *b-b*, and barren ribs of Death, | *Gareth and L.* 1382
Breast-deep all night long *b-d* in corn, | *Princess ii* 387
Breasted *See* **Full-breasted, Man-breasted, White-
breasted.**
Breast-high *B-h* in that bright line | *Pelleas and E.* 56
Breath (*See also* **Morning-breath**) Her subtil, warm,
and golden *b*, | *Supp. Confessions* 60
b Of the fading edges of box beneath, | *A spirit haunts* 18
There is frost in your *b* | *Poet's Mind* 17
the *b* Of the lilies at sunrise ? | *Adeline* 36
I lose my colour, I lose my *b*, | *Eleänore* 137
No life that breathes with human *b* | *Two Voices* 395
fill'd the breast with purer *b*. | *Miller's D.* 92
As half-asleep his *b* he drew, | *The Sisters* 28
Long labour unto aged *b*, | *Lotos-Eater's, C. S.* 85

Breath (*continued*) Dan Chaucer, the first warbler,
    whose sweet *b* — *D. of F. Women* 5
Drew forth the poison with her balmy *b*, — " 271
but empty *b* And rumours of a doubt? — *M. d'Arthur* 99
spoke King Arthur, drawing thicker *b*: — " 148
Clothed with his *b*, and looking, — " 182
my ears could hear Her lightest *b*; — *Edwin Morris* 65
but ever at a *b* She linger'd, — *Godiva* 44
My *b* to heaven like vapour goes: — *St. Agnes' Eve* 3
'Greet her with applausive *b*, — *Vision of Sin* 135
While we keep a little *b*! — " 192
The *b* of heaven came continually — *Enoch Arden* 535
my latest *b* Was spent in blessing her — " 883
a low *b* Of tender air made tremble — *The Brook* 201
ice-ferns on January panes Made by a *b*. — *Aylmer's Field* 223
on a sudden rush'd Among us, out of *b*, — *Princess iv* 375
b of life; O more than poor men wealth, — " 459
body that never had drawn a *b*. — *Grandmother* 62
O sweet and bitter in a *b*, — *In Mem. iii* 3
And scarce endure to draw the *b*, — " *xx* 15
And so the Word had *b*, and wrought — " *xxxvi* 9
This use may lie in blood and *b*, — " *xlv* 13
spirit does but mean the *b* I know no more.' — " *lvi* 7
Death's twin-brother, times my *b*; — " *lxviii* 2
new life that feeds thy *b* Throughout — *In Mem. lxxxvi* 10
East and West, without a *b*, — *In Mem. xcv* 62
To where he breathed his latest *b*, — " *xcviii* 5
Who wakenest with thy balmy *b* — " *xcix* 13
I trust I have not wasted *b*: — " *cxx* 1
Be quicken'd with a livelier *b*, — " *cxxii* 13
Awe-stricken *b*'s at a work divine, — *Maud I x* 17
Prickle my skin and catch my *b*, — " *xiv* 36
Catch not my *b*, O clamorous heart, — " *xvi* 31
Not die; but live a life of truest *b*, — *Maud I xviii* 53
Seal'd her mine from her first sweet *b*. — " *xix* 41
mix'd my *b* With a loyal people shouting — " *III vi* 34
with the might and *b* of twenty boys.' — *Gareth and L.* 1106
Sent all his heart and *b* thro' all the horn. — " 1369
Here ceased the kindly mother out of *b*; — *Marr. of Geraint* 732
fits of prayer, at every stroke a *b*. — *Geraint and E.* 155
Sweet lady, never since I first drew *b* — " 619
and the *b* Of her sweet tendance — " 925
b's of anger puff'd Her fairy nostril — *Merlin and V.* 848
At last he got his *b* and answer'd, 'One, — *Lancelot and E.* 422
whereat she caught her *b*; — " 623
blow with *b*, or touch with hand, — *Holy Grail* 114
She felt the King's *b* wander o'er her neck, — *Guinevere* 582
but empty *b* And rumours of a doubt? — *Pass. of Arthur* 267
spoke King Arthur, drawing thicker *b*: — " 316
Clothed with his *b*, and looking, — " 350
I feel thy *b*; I come, great Mistress — *Lover's Tale i* 21
Thy *b* is of the pinewood; — " 23
faints, and hath no pulse, no *b*— — " 268
rose as it were *b* and steam of gold, — " 402
my name was borne Upon her *b*. — " 444
by that name I moved upon her *b*; — " 560
Love drew in her *b* In that close kiss, — " 816
about my brow Her warm *b* floated — " *ii* 141
at once, soul, life And *b* and motion, — " 195
And parted lips which drank her *b*, — " 204
Took the *b* from our sails, and we stay'd. — *The Revenge* 42
but never a murmur, a *b*— — *V. of Maeldune* 19
their *b* met us out on the seas, — " 37
thro' life to my latest *b*; — *The Wreck* 79
thro' the roar of the breaker a whisper, a *b*, — *Despair* 13
And now one *b* of cooler air — *Ancient Sage* 117
A *b*, a whisper—some divine farewell— — " 225
to feel his *b* Upon my cheek— — *The Flight* 45
b that past With all the cold of winter. — *The Ring* 32
and felt An icy *b* play on me, — " 131
an icy *b*, As from the grating of a sepulchre, — " 399
leaves her bare To *b*'s of balmier air; — *Prog. of Spring* 13
Blown into glittering by the popular *b*, — *Romney's R.* 49
a *b* From some fair dawn beyond — *Far-far-away* 10
open-door'd To every *b* from heaven, — *Akbar's Dream* 180

Breathe in her first sleep earth *b*'s stilly: — *Leonine Eleg.* 7
Or *b* into the hollow air, — *Supp. Confessions* 58
odorous wind *B*'s low between the sunset — *Eleänore* 124
But *b* it into earth and close it up — *Wan Sculptor* 12
'Twere better not to *b* or speak, — *Two Voices* 94
'To *b* and loathe, to live and sigh, — " 104
No life that *b*'s with human breath — " 395
I least should *b* a thought of pain. — *Miller's D.* 26
wind *b*'s low with mellower tone: — *Lotos-Eaters, C. S.* 102
How hard he *b*'s! — *D. of the O. Year* 37
to sit, to sleep, to wake, to *b*.' — *Edwin Morris* 40
I do not *b*, Not whisper, any murmur — *St. S. Stylites* 21
When that, which *b*'s within the leaf, — *Talking Oak* 187
As tho' to *b* were life. — *Ulysses* 24
I yearn to *b* the airs of heaven — *Sir Galahad* 63
A carefuller in peril, did not *b* — *Enoch Arden* 50
And *b*'s in April-autumns. — *The Brook* 196
love-whispers may not *b* Within this vestal limit, — *Princess ii* 221
Low, low, *b* and blow, — " *iii* 3
let us *b* for one hour more in Heaven' — " 69
'Alas your Highness *b*'s full East,' — " 231
Where shall I *b*? — " *v* 77
that each May *b* himself, and quick! — " 316
b upon my brows; — " *vii* 353
To let the people *b*? — " *Con.* 104
diviner air *B* thro' the world and change — *W. to Marie Alex.* 44
To *b* thee over lonely seas. — *In Mem. xvii* 4
That *b* a thousand tender vows, — " *xx* 2
The slightest air of song shall *b* — " *xlix* 7
And *b*'s a novel world, the while — " *lxii* 9
And, while we *b* beneath the sun, — " *lxxv* 14
To *b* my loss is more than fame, — " *lxxvii* 15
summer's hourly-mellowing change May *b*, — " *xci* 10
I find no place that does not *b* Some gracious
    memory — " *c* 3
Nor landmark *b*'s of other days, — " *civ* 11
Thro' which the spirit *b*'s no more? — " *cv* 20
For tho' my lips may *b* adieu, — " *cxxiii* 11
Left the still King, and passing forth to *b*, — *Com. of Arthur* 369
only *b* Short fits of prayer, — *Geraint and E.* 154
'You *b* but accusation vast and vague, — *Merlin and V.* 701
No keener hunter after glory *b*'s. — *Lancelot and E.* 156
there *b*'s not one of you Will deem this prize — " 540
'Look, He haunts me—I cannot *b*— — *Pelleas and E.* 227
thought I could not *b* in that fine air — *Guinevere* 645
B but a little on me, — *Lover's Tale i* 26
outward circling air wherewith I *b*, — " 167
b with her as if in heaven itself; — " 391
Which pass with that which *b*'s them? — " 481
B, diviner Air! — *Sisters (E. and E.)* 13
none could *b* Within the zone of heat; — *Columbus* 52
can I *b* divorced from the Past? — *Despair* 113
And all that *b* are one Slight ripple — *Ancient Sage* 188
who *b* the balm Of summer-winters — *To Ulysses* 10

Breathed *B* low around the rolling earth — *The Winds, etc.* 3
She *b* in sleep a lower moan, — *Mariana in the S.* 45
Rose slowly to a music slowly *b*, — *Œnone* 41
B, like the covenant of a God, — *Gardener's D.* 209
I *b* In some new planet: — *Edwin Morris* 114
I *b* upon her eyes Thro' all the summer — *Talking Oak* 210
the low wind hardly *b* for fear. — *Godiva* 55
on him *b* Far purelier in his rushings — *Aylmer's Field* 457
while I *b* in sight of haven, he, Poor fellow, — *The Brook* 157
he had *b* the Proctor's dogs; — *Princess, Pro.* 113
And look on Spirits *b* away, — *In Mem. xl* 2
That *b* beneath the Syrian blue: — " *lii* 12
Where all things round me *b* of him. — " *lxxxv* 32
To where he *b* his latest breath, — " *xcviii* 5
He *b* the spirit of the song; — " *cxxv* 10
living words of life *B* in her ear. — " *Con.* 53
Whenever slander *b* against the King— — *Com. of Arthur* 177
God hath *b* a secret thing. — " 501
twice they fought, and twice they *b*, — *Marr. of Geraint* 567
Queen's fair name was *b* upon, — *Geraint and E.* 951
B in a dismal whisper 'It is truth.' — *Balin and Balan* 527

Breathed (*continued*)   emerald center'd in a sun Of silver
  rays, that lighten'd as he *b*;   *Lancelot and E.* 296
  Whereof the chill, to him who *b* it,   *Pass. of Arthur* 96
  Has *b* a race of mightier mountaineers.   *Montenegro* 14
  No sound is *b* so potent to coerce,   *Tiresias* 120
  warm winds had gently *b* us away from the land—   *The Wreck* 63
Breather   those we call the dead Are *b*'s of an ampler
  day   *In Mem. cxviii* 6
Breathing   (*See also* **Hard-breathing**)   *B* Light
  against thy face,   *Adeline* 56
  Old letters, *b* of her worth,   *Mariana in the S.* 62
  A hint, a whisper *b* low,   *Two Voices* 434
  B like one that hath a weary dream.   *Lotos-Eaters* 6
  spoke King Arthur, *b* heavily :   *M. d'Arthur* 113
  answer made King Arthur, *b* hard :   ,, 162
  alighted from the boat, And *b* of the sea.   *Audley Court* 8
  'Sleep, *b* health and peace upon her breast :   ,, 68
  Sleep, *b* love and trust against her lip :   ,, 69
  her *b*'s are not heard In palace chambers   *Day-Dm., Sleep. B.* 17
  warm-blue *b*'s of a hidden hearth Broke   *Aylmer's Field* 155
  like a beast hard-ridden, *b* hard.   ,, 291
  b down From over her arch'd brows,   *Princess ii* 38
  B and sounding beauteous battle,   ,, *v* 161
  In Angel instincts, *b* Paradise.   ,, *vii* 321
  Closer is He than *b*, and nearer than hands   *High. Pantheism* 12
  Would *b* thro' his lips impart   *In Mem. xviii* 15
  slowly *b* bare The round of space,   ,, *lxxxvi* 4
  By meadows *b* of the past,   ,, *xcix* 7
  Bright English lily, *b* a prayer   *Maud 1 xix* 55
  hear him *b* low and equally.   *Geraint and E.* 372
  she glided out Among the heavy *b*'s of the house,   ,, 402
  Beside the placid *b*'s of the King,   *Guinevere* 69
  spoke King Arthur, *b* heavily :   *Pass. of Arthur* 281
  answer made King Arthur, *b* hard :   ,, 330
  b on each other, Dreaming together   *Lover's Tale i* 261
  and joy In *b* nearer heaven ;   ,, 389
  b hard at the approach of Death,—   ,, 585
  Is *b* in his sleep,   *Early Spring* 23
  changest, *b* it, the sullen wind,   *Prog. of Spring* 110
Breathing-space   ballad or a song To give us *b-s.*'   *Princess, Pro.* 242
Breathing-while   Except when for a *b-w* at eve,   *Aylmer's Field* 449
Bred   (*See also* **Home-bred**, **Wisdom-bred**)   Two
  children in one hamlet born and *b* ;   *Circumstance* 8
  upon the board, And *b* this change ;   *Œnone* 227
  for his sake I *b* His daughter Dora :   *Dora* 19
  not being *b* To barter,   *Enoch Arden* 249
  A CITY clerk, but gently born and *b* ;   *Sea Dreams* 1
  her will *B* will in me to overcome   *Princess v* 351
  From out the doors where I was *b*,   *In Mem. ciii* 2
  'e wur burn an' *b* i' the 'ouse,   *Spinster's S.'s* 69
  opiate then *B* this black mood ?   *Romney's R.* 62
Brede   in glowing gauze and golden *b*,   *Princess vi* 134
Breed (s)   looks not like the common *b* That with the
  napkin dally ;   *Will Water.* 117
  In doubt if you be of our Barons' *b*—   *Third of Feb.* 32
  we men are a little *b*.   *Maud 1 iv* 30
Breed (verb)   Assurance only *b*'s resolve.'   *Two Voices* 315
  graze and wallow, *b* and sleep ;   *Palace of Art* 202
  like *b*'s like, they say :   *Walk. to the Mail* 63
  could he understand how money *b*'s,   *The Brook* 6
  much loth to *b* Dispute betwixt myself   *Princess i* 156
  in thunderstorms, And *b* up warriors !   ,, *v* 440
  earth's embrace May *b* with him,   *In Mem. lxxxii* 4
Breeding   Softness *b* scorn of simple life,   *To the Queen ii* 53
Breeze   (*See also* **River-breeze**, **South-breeze**)   The
  b's pause and die,   *Claribel* 2
  LOW-FLOWING *b*'s are roaming the broad valley   *Leonine Eleg.* 1
  WHEN the *b* of a joyful dawn blew free   *Arabian Nights* 1
  fann'd With *b*'s from our oaken glades,   *Eleänore* 10
  Coming in the scented *b*,   ,, 24
  Little *b*'s dusk and shiver   *L. of Shalott i* 11
  And heard her native *b*'s pass,   *Mariana in the S.* 43
  A *b* thro' all the garden swept,   *Day-Dm., Revival* 6
  Warm broke the *b* against the brow,   *The Voyage* 9
  Low *b*'s fann'd the belfry bars,   *The Letters* 43

Breeze (*continued*)   Made noise with bees and *b* from
  end to end.   *Princess, Pro.* 88
  long *b*'s rapt from inmost south   ,, *iv* 431
  roll'd With music in the growing *b* of Time,   ,, *vi* 56
  such a *b* Compell'd thy canvas,   *In Mem. xvii* 1
  all the bugle *b*'s blew Reveillée   ,, *lxviii* 7
  And round thee with the *b* of song   ,, *lxxv* 11
  A *b* began to tremble o'er The large leaves   ,, *xcv* 54
  And all the *b* of Fancy blows,   ,, *cxxii* 17
  tells The joy to every wandering *b* ;   ,, *Con.* 62
  blown by the *b* of a softer clime,   *Maud I iv* 4
  sighing for Lebanon In the long *b*   ,, *xviii* 16
  For a *b* of morning moves,   ,, *xxii* 7
  Drooping and beaten by the *b*,   *Lover's Tale i* 700
  Thoughts of the *b*'s of May blowing   *Def. of Lucknow* 83
  sat each on the lap of the *b* ;   *V. of Maeldune* 38
  a balmier *b* curl'd over a peacefuller sea,   *The Wreck* 133
  lark has past from earth to Heaven upon the
  morning *b* !   *The Flight* 62
  Flies back in fragrant *b*'s to display   *Prog. of Spring* 64
Brendan (**Irish Saint**)   who had sail'd with St. *B*
  of yore,   *V. of Maeldune* 115
Brethren   (*See also* **Brother**)   so that all My *b*
  marvell'd greatly.   *St. S. Stylites* 69
  And of her *b*, youths of puissance ;   *Princess i* 37
  Not ev'n her brother Arac, nor the twins Her *b*,   ,, 154
  The *b* of our blood and cause,   ,, *vi* 71
  To where her wounded *b* lay ;   ,, 90
  O let me have him with my *b* here   ,, 123
  bite And pinch their *b* in the throng,   *Lit. Squabbles* 7
  grieve Thy *b* with a fruitless tear ?   *In Mem. lviii* 10
  till Doubt and Death, Ill *b*,   ,, *lxxxvi* 12
  both my *b* are in Arthur's hall,   *Gareth and L.* 82
  b, and a fourth And of that four the mightiest,   ,, 614
  younger *b* have gone down Before this youth ;   ,, 1102
  to mar the boast Thy *b* of thee make—   ,, 1243
  my three *b* bad me do it,   ,, 1410
  Among his burnish'd *b* of the pool ;   *Marr. of Geraint* 650
  B, to right and left the spring,   *Balin and Balan* 25
  Arthur lightly smote the *b* down,   ,, 41
  Thy chair, a grief to all the *b*,   ,, 78
  My *b* have been all my fellowship ;   *Lancelot and E.* 672
  came her *b* saying, 'Peace to thee,   ,, 996
  those two *b* slowly with bent brows Accompanying,   ,, 1138
  So those two *b* from the chariot took   ,, 1146
  friends in testimony, Her *b*, and her father,   ,, 1300
  Where all the *b* are so hard,   *Holy Grail* 618
  Also the *b*, King and Atheling,   *Batt. of Brunanburh* 100
Breton   on the *B* strand ! *B*, not Briton ;   *Maud II ii* 29
  Back from the *B* coast,   ,, 43
  touching *B* sands, they disembark'd.   *Merlin and V.* 202
  cried the *B*, ' Look, her hand is red !   *Last Tournament* 412
Breviary   read but on my *b* with ease,   *Holy Grail* 545
Brew'd   found a witch Who *b* the philtre   *Lucretius* 16
Brewer   gloomy Oak's soul Went by me,   *Talking Oak* 55
Brewis   The kitchen *b* that was ever supt   *Gareth and L.* 781
Briar   (*See also* **Brier**)   bur and brake and *b*,   *Day-Dm., Sleep. P.* 46
Bribe   a costly *b* To guerdon silence,   *Princess i* 203
  which for *b* had wink'd at wrong,   *Geraint and E.* 939
Bribed   *B* with large promises the men   *Marr. of Geraint* 453
Brick   When we made *b*'s in Egypt.   *Princess iv* 128
  mantles all the mouldering *b*'s—   *Locksley H., Sixty* 257
  as graw'd hall ower the *b* ;   *Owd Roä* 26
  'eärd the *b*'s an' the baulks ;   ,, 109
Brickwork   Tudor-chimnied bulk Of mellow *b*   *Edwin Morris* 12
Bridal (adj.)   Leapt lightly clad in *b* white—   *Lover's Tale iii* 44
  Thy Soldier-brother's *b* orange-bloom Break   *Ded. Poem Prin. Alice* 11
  THE *b* garland falls upon the bier.   *D. of the Duke of C.* 1
Bridal (s)   Then reign the world's great *b*'s,   *Princess vii* 294
  Evil haunts The birth, the *b* ;   *In Mem. xcviii* 14
  Memories of *b*, or of birth,   ,, *xcix* 15
  Will clothe her for her *b*'s like the sun.'   *Marr. of Geraint* 231
  clothed her for her *b*'s like the sun ;   ,, 836
Bridal-gift   poor bride Gives her harsh groom for *b-g*
  a scourge ;   *Princess v* 378

Brief (continued) B, b is a summer leaf, — *Spiteful Letter* 21
if Thou willest, let my day be b, — *Doubt and Prayer* 13

Brier (See also **Briar**) whom Gideon school'd with b's. — *Buonaparte* 14
The little life of bank and b, — *You might have won* 30
drench'd with ooze, and torn with b's. — *Princess* v 28
I have heard of thorns and b's. — *Window, Marr. Morn.* 20
Over the thorns and b's, — " 21
the winds that bend the b ! — *Last Tournament* 731
wild b had driven Its knotted thorns — *Lover's Tale* i 619
rough b tore my bleeding palms ; — " ii 18

Brig (bridge) An' I'll run oop to the b, — *N. Farmer, N. S.* 55

Brigade Glory to all the three hundred, and all the B ! — *Heavy Brigade* 66

Brigade, Heavy See **Heavy Brigade**
Brigade, Light See **Light Brigade**

Bright (adj.) See also **Over-bright, Rosy-bright, Summer-bright.**
Clear and b it should be ever, — *Poet's Mind* 5
B as light, and clear as wind. — " 7
met with two so full and b—Such eyes ! — *Miller's D.* 86
I made my dagger sharp and b. — *The Sisters* 26
but none so b as mine ; — *May Queen* 5
Make b our days and light our dreams, — *Of old sat Freedom* 22
B was that afternoon, Sunny but chill ; — *Enoch Arden* 669
B with the sun upon the stream — *Sea Dreams* 97
b and fierce and fickle is the South, — *Princess* iv 97
B let it be with its blazon'd deeds, — *Ode on Well.* 56
Phosphor, b As our pure love, — *In Mem.* ix 10
Thy marble b in dark appears, — " lxvii 5
The voice was low, the look was b ; — " lxix 15
And b the friendship of thine eye ; — " cxix 10
To-day the grave is b for me, — " Con. 73
b and light as the crest Of a peacock, — *Maud* I xvi 16
soft splendours that you look so b ? — " xviii 79
dawn of Eden b over earth and sky, — " II i 8
in a weary world my one thing b ; — " III vi 17
Geraint with eyes all b replied, — *Marr. of Geraint* 494
strange b and dreadful thing, a court, — " 616
she knew That all was b ; — " 658
Beholding one so b in dark estate, — " 786
keep him b and clean as heretofore, — *Geraint and E.* 937
She with a face, b as for sin forgiven, — *Lancelot and E.* 1102
her look B for all others, — *Pelleas and E.* 177
our eyes met : hers were b, and mine Were dim — *Lover's Tale* i 441
an' I keeäps 'im cleän an' b, — *North. Cobbler* 97
Far from out a sky for ever b, — *Sisters (E. and E.)* 19
an' yer eyes as b as the day ! — *Tomorrow* 32
How b you keep your marriage-ring ! — *Romney's R.* 59
morning that looks so b from afar ! — *By an Evolution.* 10
When I look'd at the bracken so b — *June Bracken, etc.* 3

Bright (s) level lake with diamond-plots Of dark and b. — *Arabian Nights* 86
Remaining betwixt dark and b : — *Margaret* 28
Of this flat lawn with dusk and b ; — *In Mem.* lxxxix 2
B and Dark have sworn that I, — *Demeter and P.* 96
Beyond the darker hour to see the b, — *Prog. of Spring* 88

Brighten cheek brighten'd as the foam-bow b's — *Œnone* 61
stars above them seem to b as they pass ; — *May Queen* 34
Thy sweet eyes b slowly close to mine, — *Tithonus* 38
it b's and darkens down on the plain. — *Window, On the Hill* 2
it b's and darkens and b's like my hope, And it darkens and b's and darkens like my fear, — 18
And b like the star that shook — *In Mem., Con.* 31
b's at the clash of 'Yes' and 'No,' — *Ancient Sage* 71
b's thro' the Mother's tender eyes, — *Prin. Beatrice* 4

Brighten'd cheek b as the foam-bow brightens — *Œnone* 61
For so mine own was b : — *Aylmer's Field* 683
Till the face of Bel be b, — *Boädicea* 16
Your pretty sports have b all again. — *Merlin and V.* 305
The rounder cheek had b into bloom. — *The Ring* 351

Brightening (See also **Ever-brightening**) Like sheet lightning, Ever b — *Poet's Mind* 26
B the skirts of a long cloud, — *M. d'Arthur* 54
Unseen, is b to his bridal morn. — *Gardener's D.* 73

Brightening (continued) Enid listen'd b as she lay : — *Marr. of Geraint* 733
B the skirts of a long cloud, — *Pass. of Arthur* 222
And slowly b Out of the glimmer, — *Merlin and the G.* 88

Brighter broader and b The Gleam flying onward, — " 95

Brightest Their best and b, when they dwelt on hers, — *Aylmer's Field* 69

Brightly Enoch faced this morning of farewell B — *Enoch Arden* 183

Brightness as babies for the moon, Vague b ; — *Princess* iv 429
false sense in her own self Of my contrasting b, overbore — *Marr. of Geraint* 801
set apart Their motions and their b from the stars, — *Lover's Tale* i 174
The b of a burning thought, — " 743

Brilliance star The black earth with b rare. — *Ode to Memory* 20
So bathed we were in b. — *Lover's Tale* i 313

Brim (s) By garden porches on the b, — *Arabian Nights* 16
He froth'd his bumpers to the b ; — *D. of the O. Year* 19
New stars all night above the b — *The Voyage* 25

Brim (verb) I b with sorrow drowning song. — *In Mem.* xix 12
Arrange the board and b the glass ; — cvii 16

Brimful heart, B of those wild tales, — *D. of F. Women* 12

Brimm'd (See also **Broad-brimm'd**) B with delirious draughts of warmest life. — *Eleänore* 139
And beaker b with noble wine. — *Day-Dm., Sleep. P.* 36

Brine Lulling the b against the Coptic sands. — *Buonaparte* 8
Fresh-water springs come up through bitter b. — *If I were loved* 8
hear and see the far-off sparkling b, — *Lotos-Eaters, C. S.* 98
Gloom'd the low coast and quivering b — *The Voyage* 42
Should gulf him fathom-deep in b — *In Mem.* x 18
To darken on the rolling b That breaks — cvii 14

Bring b me my love, Rosalind. — *Leonine Eleg.* 14
'B this lamb back into Thy fold, — *Supp. Confessions* 105
Music that b's sweet sleep down — *Lotos-Eaters, C. S.* 7
And in its season b the law ; — *Love thou thy land* 32
Certain, if knowledge b the sword, That knowledge takes — 87
For nature b's not back the Mastodon, — *The Epic* 36
Watch what thou seëst, and lightly b me word.' — *M. d'Arthur* 38
Watch what I see, and lightly b thee word.' — " 44
I bad thee, watch, and lightly b me word.' — " 81
A word could b the colour to my cheek ; — *Gardener's D.* 196
I will have my boy, and b him home ; — *Dora* 122
b me offerings of fruit and flowers : — *St. S. Stylites* 128
Love himself will b The drooping flower — *Love and Duty* 23
sweet hours that b us all things good, — " 57
sad hours that b us all things ill, — " 58
Nay, but Nature b's thee solace ; — *Locksley Hall* 87
my latest rival b's thee rest. — " 89
B truth that sways the soul of men ? — *Day-Dm., Sleep. P.* 52
And b the fated fairy Prince. — " 56
'B the dress and put it on her, — *L. of Burleigh* 95
B me spices, b me wine ; — *Vision of Sin* 76
Will b fair weather yet to all of us. — *Enoch Arden* 191
I warrant, man, that we shall b you round.' — " 841
and arose Eager to b them down, — " 872
b Their own gray hairs with sorrow to the grave— — *Aylmer's Field* 776
And b her in a whirlwind : — *Princess* i 65
b's our friends up from the underworld, — " iv 45
an' doesn b ma the aäle ? — *N. Farmer, O. S.* 65
The seasons b the flower again, — *In Mem.* ii 5
And b the firstling to the flock ; — " 6
So b him : we have idle dreams : — " x 9
And not the burthen that they b. — " xiii 20
If one should b me this report, — " xiv 1
And all was good that Time could b, — " xxiii 18
They b me sorrow touch'd with joy, — " xxviii 19
Which b's no more a welcome guest — " xxix 5
And b her babe, and make her boast, — " xl 26
She often b's but one to bear, — " lv 12
I b to life, I b to death : — " lvi 6
Then b an opiate trebly strong, — " lxxi 6
In verse that b's myself relief, — " lxxv 2
B orchis, b the foxglove spire, — " lxxxiii 9
Demanding, so to b relief — " lxxxv 6
Ah, take the imperfect gift I b, — " 117

Brok (broke) an' Charlie 'e *b* 'is neck, — *Village Wife* 85
Broke (*See also* **Brok**) Peal after peal, the British battle *b*, — *Buonaparte* 7
A nobler yearning never *b* her rest — *The Form, the form* 2
What time the foeman's line is *b*, — *Two Voices* 155
From out my sullen heart a power, *B*, — ,, 444
thro' wavering lights and shadows *b*, — *Lotos-Eaters* 12
love the gleams of good that *b* From either side, — *Love thou thy land* 89
murmur *b* the stillness of that air — *Gardener's D.* 147
bit his lips, And *b* away. — *Dora* 34
She *b* out in praise To God, — ,, 112
I *b* a close with force and arms : — *Edwin Morris* 131
Bluff Harry *b* into the spence — *Talking Oak* 47
struck his staff against the rocks And *b* it,— — *Golden Year* 60
The hedge *b* in, the banner blew, — *Day-Dm., Revival* 9
The linden *b* her ranks and rent — *Amphion* 33
Warm *b* the breeze against the brow, — *The Voyage* 9
When you came in my sorrow *b* me down ; — *Enoch Arden* 317
with jubilant cries *B* from their elders, — ,, 378
bent or *b* The lithe reluctant boughs — ,, 380
long-winded tale, and *b* him short ; — *The Brook* 109
tide of youth *B* with a phosphorescence — *Aylmer's Field* 116
B from a bower of vine and honeysuckle : — ,, 156
Then *b* all bonds of courtesy, — ,, 323
B into nature's music when they saw her. — ,, 694
Who *b* the bond which they desired to break, — ,, 778
you tumbled down and *b* The glass — *Sea Dreams* 141
you made and *b* your dream : — ,, 143
on those cliffs *B*, mixt with awful light, — ,, 215
ever when it *b* The statues, — ,, 223
on the crowd *B*, mixt with awful light — ,, 235
His angel *b* his heart. — ,, 280
nor *b*, nor shunn'd a soldier's death, — *Princess, Pro.* 49
when the council *b*, I rose and past — ,, i 90
dances *b* and buzz'd in knots of talk ; — ,, 133
she *b* out interpreting my thoughts, — ,, iii 275
b the letter of it to keep the sense. — ,, iv 338
in the furrow *b* the ploughman's head, — ,, v 221
at our disguise *B* from their lips, — ,, 272
cloud that dimm'd her *b* A genial warmth and light — ,, vi 281
courts of twilight *b* them up Thro' all the — ,, Con. 113
even if they *b* In thunder, silent ; — *Ode on Well.* 176
We *b* them on the land, we drove them — *Third of Feb.* 30
Right thro' the line they *b* ; — *Light Brigade* 33
Burnt and *b* the grove and altar — *Boädicea* 2
Who *b* our fair companionship, — *In Mem. xxii* 13
idly *b* the peace Of hearts that beat — ,, lviii 5
But in the present *b* the blow. — ,, lxxxv 56
And strangely on the silence *b* — ,, xcv 25
Has *b* the bond of dying use. — ,, cv 12
And the sunlight *b* from her lip ? — *Maud I vi* 86
million horrible bellowing echoes *b* — ,, II i 24
light laugh *B* from Lynette, — *Gareth and L.* 837
there he *b* the sentence in his heart — *Geraint and E.* 41
b the bandit holds and cleansed the land. — ,, 944
Balin the stillness of a minute *b* — *Balin and Balan* 51
but God *B* the strong lance, — *Lancelot and E.* 26
She *b* into a little scornful laugh : — ,, 120
till our good Arthur *b* The Pagan — ,, 279
when the next day *b* from underground, — ,, 413
heard mass, *b* fast, and rode away : — ,, 415
But sin *b* out. Ah, Christ, — *Holy Grail* 93
when the sun *b* next from under ground, — ,, 328
bore them down, And *b* thro' all, — ,, 480
fairy-circle wheel'd and *b* Flying, and link'd again, and wheel'd and *b* Flying, — *Guinevere* 257
after tempest, when the long wave *b* — ,, 290
wicked one, who *b* The vast design — ,, 669
Gleams of the water-circles as they *b*, — *Lover's Tale* i 67
light methought *b* from her dark, dark eyes, — ,, 368
bliss, which *b* in light Like morning — ,, ii 143
softly as his mother *b* it to him— — ,, iv 31
all The guests *b* in upon him — ,, 238
the battle-thunder *b* from them all. — *The Revenge* 49
her brain *b* With over-acting, — *Sisters (E. and E.)* 235

Broke (*continued*) mother *b* her promise to the dead, — *Sisters (E. and E.)* 252
the brute bullet *b* thro' the brain — *Def. of Lucknow* 20
I have *b* their cage, no gilded one, — *Sir J. Oldcastle* 3
silent ocean always *b* on a silent shore, — *V. of Maeldune* 12
and the dwelling *b* into flame ; — ,, 32
B into Britain with Haughty war-workers — *Batt. of Brunanburh* 120
funeral bell *B* on my Pagan Paradise, — *Tiresias* 163
For I *b* the bond. — *The Wreck* 59
a tone so rough that I *b* into passionate tears, — ,, 122
And we *b* away from the Christ, — *Despair* 25
heart of the mother, and *b* it almost ; — ,, 74
B thro' the mass from below, — *Heavy Brigade* 29
then the tear fell, the voice *b*. — *The Ring* 367
light of happy marriage *b* Thro' all — *Death of Œnone* 102
B the Taboo, Dipt to the crater, — *Kapiolani* 30

Broken (*See also* **Bridge-broken, Brokken, Heart-broken**) Half shown, are *b* and withdrawn. — *Two Voices* 306
Each morn my sleep was *b* thro' — *Miller's D.* 39
Let what is *b* so remain. — *Lotos-Eaters, C. S.* 80
all the man was *b* with remorse ; — *Dora* 165
Oh, his. He was not *b*. — *Walk. to the Mail* 17
The clouds are *b* in the sky, — *Sir Galahad* 73
Spars were splinter'd ; decks were *b* : — *The Captain* 49
Mine was *b*, When that cold vapour — *Vision of Sin* 57
A limb was *b* when they lifted him ; — *Enoch Arden* 107
I seem so foolish and so *b* down. — ,, 316
every day The sunrise *b* into scarlet shafts — ,, 592
Enoch was so brown, so bow'd, So *b*— — ,, 704
My grief and solitude have *b* me ; — ,, 857
The tented winter-field was *b* up — *Aylmer's Field* 110
A creeper when the prop is *b*, — ,, 810
Then the great Hall was wholly *b* down, — ,, 846
Till like three horses that have *b* fence, — *Princess ii* 386
Your oath is *b* : we dismiss you : — ,, iv 360
glittering axe was *b* in their arms, — ,, vi 51
sanctuary Is violate, our laws *b* : — ,, 60
Her iron will was *b* in her mind ; — ,, 118
'Our laws are *b* : let him enter too.' — ,, 317
It will never be *b* by Maud, — *Maud I ii* 2
This fellow hath *b* from some Abbey, — *Gareth and L.* 456
Because my means were somewhat *b* into — *Marr. of Geraint* 455
My pride is *b* : men have seen my fall.' — ,, 578
my pride Is *b* down, for Enid sees my fall !' — ,, 590
each of whom had *b* on him A lance — *Geraint and E.* 88
From which old fires have *b*, — ,, 822
There was I *b* down ; — ,, 851
hast *b* shell, Art yet half-yolk, — *Balin and Balan* 568
the high purpose *b* by the worm. — *Merlin and V.* 196
these have *b* up my melancholy.' — ,, 267
false voice made way, *b* with sobs ; — ,, 857
Becomes the sea-cliff pathway *b* short, — ,, 882
cried 'They are *b*, they are *b* !' — *Lancelot and E.* 310
It can be *b* easier. — ,, 1208
and so full, So many lances *b*— — *Holy Grail* 331
lance *B*, and his Excalibur a straw.' — *Last Tournament* 88
saw the laws that ruled the tournament *B*, — ,, 161
what music have I *b*, fool ?' — ,, 261
B with Mark and hate and solitude, — ,, 643
Not to be loudly *b* in upon. — *Lover's Tale i* 687
the Spanish fleet with *b* sides lay round — *The Revenge* 71
And the pikes were all *b* or bent, — ,, 80
My sleep was *b* besides with dreams — *In the Child. Hosp.* 65
I have not *b* bread for fifty hours. — *Sir J. Oldcastle* 199
With armies so *b* A reason for bragging — *Batt. of Brunanburh* 82
And Hope will have *b* her heart, — *Despair* 92
that poor link With earth is *b*, — *The Ring* 476
wait on one so *b*, so forlorn ? — *Romney's R.* 17
We return'd to his cave—the link was *b*— — *Bandit's Death* 29

Broken-kneed *See* **Brokken-kneeäd**

Broken-wise Peering askance, and muttering *b-w*, — *Merlin and V.* 100

Brokken (broken) as if 'e'd 'a *b* 'is neck, — *Owd Roä* 63

Brokken-kneeäd (broken-kneed) an' the mare *b-k*, — *Church-warden, etc.* 4

Bronze on his right Stood, all of massiest *b* : — *Balin and Balan* 364

Bronzed   on the cheek, And bruised and *b*,   *Lancelot and E.* 259
Brooch   Pull off, pull off, the *b* of gold,   *Lady Clare* 39
   read and earn our prize, A golden *b* :   *Princess iii* 301
Brood (s)   If there were many Lilias in the *b*,   ,, *Pro.* 146
   tell her, Swallow, that thy *b* is flown :   ,, *iv* 108
   He sees his *b* about thy knee :   ,, 582
   Because her *b* is stol'n away.   *In Mem. xxi* 28
   O sound to rout the *b* of cares,   ,, *lxxxix* 17
   Her own *b* lost or dead,   *Com. of Arthur* 28
   Heathen, the *b* by Hengist left ;   *Guinevere* 16
Brood (verb)   with downcast eyes we muse and *b*,   *Sonnet to—* 1
   About him *b's* the twilight dim :   *Two Voices* 263
   To muse and *b* and live again in memory,   *Lotos-Eaters, C. S.* 65
   That *b's* above the fallen sun,   *To J. S.* 51
   happy birds, that change their sky To build and *b* ;   *In Mem. cxv* 16
   nevermore to *b* On a horror of shatter'd limbs   *Maud I i* 55
   sunshine seem'd to *b* More warmly on the heart   *Lover's Tale i* 327
   What use to *b* ? this life of mingled pains   *To Mary Boyle* 49
Brooded   stillness of that air Which *b* round about her :   *Gardener's D.* 148
   while she *b* thus And grew half-guilty   *Guinevere* 407
   tender love Of him she *b* over.   *Lover's Tale i* 617
   B one master-passion evermore,   ,, *ii* 60
Broodeth   But where the sunbeam *b* warm,   *In Mem. xxi* 14
Brooding   ragged rims of thunder *b* low,   *Palace of Art* 75
   Sit *b* in the ruins of a life,   *Love and Duty* 12
   Across my fancy, *b* warm,   *Day-Dm., Pro.* 10
   but *b* turn The book of scorn,   *Princess v* 141
   wordless *b's* on the wasted cheek—   ,, *vii* 112
   But *b* on the dear one dead,   *In Mem. xxxvii* 17
   But over all things *b* slept   ,, *lxxviii* 7
   felt that tempest *b* round his heart,   *Geraint and E.* 11
   There, *b* by the central altar,   *Ancient Sage* 33
   She that in her heart is *b*   *Locksley H., Sixty* 23
Brook (s)   (*See also* **Beck, Mountain-brook, Yabbok brook**)   Past Yabbok *b* the livelong night,   *Clear-headed friend* 27
   b that loves To purl o'er matted cress   *Ode to Memory* 58
   deep *b* groan'd beneath the mill ;   *Miller's D.* 113
   I thirsted for the *b's*, the showers :   *Fatima* 10
   long *b* falling thro' the clov'n ravine   *Œnone* 8
   O mountain *b's*, I am the daughter   ,, 37
   'The torrent *b's* of hallow'd Israel   *D. of F. Women* 181
   and leap the rainbows of the *b's*,   *Locksley Hall* 171
   HERE, by this *b*, we parted ;   *The Brook* 1
   yet the *b* he loved,   ,, 15
   ' O *b*,' he says, ' O babbling *b*,'   ,, 20
   and the *b*, why not ? replies.   ,, 22
   Philip's farm where *b* and river meet.   ,, 38
   Philip chatter'd more than *b* or bird ;   ,, 51
   Beyond the *b*, waist-deep in meadow-sweet.   ,, 118
   and bowing o'er the *b* A tonsured head   ,, 199
   Little about it stirring save a *b* !   *Aylmer's Field* 32
   where the *b* Vocal, with here and there a silence,   ,, 145
   part were drown'd within the whirling *b* :   *Princess, Pro.* 47
   Cataract *b's* to the ocean run,   *The Islet* 17
   b's of Eden mazily murmuring,   *Milton* 10
   Oh is it the *b*, or a pool,   *Window, On the Hill* 4
   Spring that swells the narrow *b's*,   *In Mem. lxxxv* 70
   The *b* alone far-off was heard,   ,, *xcv* 7
   On yon swoll'n *b* that bubbles fast   ,, *xcix* 6
   The *b* shall babble down the plain,   ,, *ci* 10
   slopes a wild *b* o'er a little stone,   *Marr. of Geraint* 77
   a broad *b* o'er a shingly bed Brawling,   ,, 248
   And at the inrunning of a little *b*   *Lancelot and E.* 1388
   By grove, and garden-lawn, and rushing *b*,   *Holy Grail* 230
   saw deep lawns, and then a *b*,   ,, 380
   and o'er the *b* Were apple-trees, and apples by the *b* Fallen,   ,, 383
   But even while I drank the *b*,   ,, 387
   Stay'd in the wandering warble of a *b* :   *Last Tournament* 254
   Blaze by the rushing *b* or silent well.   *Guinevere* 400
   blue valley and the glistening *b's*,   *Lover's Tale i* 331
   With falling *b* or blossom'd bush—   ,, 405
   Gives birth to a brawling *b*,   ,, 526
   echoes of the hollow-banked *b's*   ,, 566
   the chillness of the sprinkled *b* Smote   ,, 633
   black *b's* Of the midforest heard me—   ,, *ii* 11

Brook (s) (*continued*)   I cast them in the noisy *b* beneath,   *Lover's Tale ii* 41
   moanings in the forest, the loud *b*,   ,, 114
   b's glitter'd on in the light without sound,   *V. of Maeldune* 13
   I found these cousins often by the *b*,   *The Ring* 158
   b that feeds this lakelet murmur'd ' debt,'   ,, 171
   following her old pastime of the *b*,   ,, 354
   the secret splendour of the *b's*.   *Prog. of Spring* 21
   Sounded ' Œnone ';   *Death of Œnone* 23
Brook (verb)   I must *b* the rod And chastisement   *Supp. Confessions* 107
   I would not *b* my fear Of the other :   *D. of F. Women* 154
   We *b* no further insult but are gone.'   *Princess vi* 342
   shall I *b* to be supplicated ?   *Boädicea* 9
   I scarce could *b* the strain and stir   *In Mem. xv* 12
   Who cannot *b* the shadow of any lie.'   *Gareth and L.* 293
   I cannot *b* to gaze upon the dead.'   *Balin and Balan* 586
   I cannot *b* to see your beauty marr'd   *Pelleas and E.* 298
   thine eyes not *b* in forest-paths,   *Prog. of Spring* 31
Brook'd   *B* not the expectant terror of her heart,   *Enoch Arden* 493
   but she *b* no more :   *Aylmer's Field* 57
   She *b* it not ; but wrathful,   *Lucretius* 14
   She the appeal *B* not, but clamouring out   *Princess vi* 140
   until the little maid, who *b* No silence,   *Guinevere* 159
Brooking   *b* not the Tarquin in her veins,   *Lucretius* 237
   peculiar treasure, *b* not Exchange or currency :   *Lover's Tale i* 447
Brooks   *B*, for they call'd you so that knew you best,   *To W. H. Brookfield* 1
   Old *B*, who loved so well to mouth   *Princess, Pro.* 184
Broom   walks were stript as bare as *b's*,   *Lover's Tale i* 400
   Gilded with *b*, or shatter'd into spires,   *Lucretius* 19
Broth   wicked *b* Confused the chemic labour   *Lucretius* 19
Brother   (*See also* **Brethren, Soldier-brother, Twin-brother**)   my *b's* they : *B's* in Christ—   *Supp. Confessions* 28
   vexed eddies of its wayward *b* :   *Isabel* 29
   Each to each is dearest *b* ;   *Madeline* 7
   Oh rest ye, *b* mariners,   *Lotos-Eaters, C. S.* 128
   I knew your *b* : his mute dust I honour   *To J. S.* 29
   Who miss the *b* of your youth ?   ,, 59
   Thy *b's* and immortal souls.   *Love thou thy land* 8
   I and he, *B's* in Art ;   *Gardener's D.* 4
   She is my *b's* daughter :   *Dora* 1
   Come, blessed *b*, come.   *St. S. Stylites* 204
   Sun flies forward to his *b* Sun ;   *Golden Year* 23
   Men, my *b's*, men the workers,   *Locksley Hall* 117
   b's of the weather stood Stock-still   *Will Water.* 135
   Hob-and-nob with *b* Death !   *Vision of Sin* 194
   My dearest *b*, Edmund, sleeps,   *The Brook* 187
   My *b* James is in the harvest-field :   ,, 227
   Leolin, his *b*, living oft With Averill,   *Aylmer's Field* 138
   his, a *b's* love, that hung With wings   ,, 341
   thro' the bright lawns to his *b's* ran,   ,, 351
   ' *B*, for I have loved you more as son Than *b*,   ,, 364
   b, where two fight The strongest wins,   ,, 398
   ' O *b*, I am grieved to learn your grief—   ,, 404
   How low his *b's* mood had fallen,   ,, 607
   Sent to the harrow'd *b*, praying him   ,, 667
   shall thy *b* man, the Lord from Heaven,   *Princess i* 153
   they see no men, Not ev'n her *b* Arac.   ,, *ii* 188
   ' My *b* !' ' Well, my sister.'   ,, 208
   Here lies a b by a sister slain,   ,, 275
   That was fawn's blood, not *b's*,   ,, 291
   be swerved from right to save A prince, a *b* ?   ,, 308
   I give thee to death My b !   ,, *v* 302
   Till, one of those two *b's*, half aside   ,, 374
   ' O *b*, you have known the pangs we felt,   ,, 410
   B's, the woman's Angel guards you,   ,, *vi* 108
   ' He saved my life : my *b* slew him for it.'   ,, 299
   to wait upon him, Like mine own *b*.   ,, 305
   Help, father, *b*, help ;   ,, 313
   ' Your *b*, Lady,—Florian,—ask for him   ,, 345
   but the Prince Her *b* came ;   ,, *vii* 89
   Did those twin *b's*, risen again   *In Mem. ix* 16
   My friend, the *b* of my love ;   ,, 20
   More than my *b's* are to me.   ,, *xxxi* 5
   ' Where wert thou, *b*, those four days ?'   ,, *xxxii* 7
   Roves from the living *b's* face,

Brother (*continued*) 'More than my *b*'s are to me,'—   *In Mem. lxxix* 1
I met her to-day with her *b*, but not to her *b* I bow'd :   *Maud I iv* 14
and chuckle, and grin at a *b*'s shame ;   ,,   29
Her *b*, from whom I keep aloof,   ,,   *vi* 46
Blithe would her *b*'s acceptance be.   ,,   *x* 27
All, all upon the *b*.   ,,   *xiii* 43
her *b* lingers late With a roystering company)   ,,   *xiv* 14
Her *b* is coming back to-night,   ,,   *xix* 1
only Maud and the *b* Hung over her dying bed—   ,,   35
This *b* had laugh'd her down,   ,,   60
her *b* comes, like a blight On my fresh hope,   ,,   102
her *b* ran in his rage to the gate,   ,,   *II i* 12
A cry for a *b*'s blood :   ,,   34
'O that ye had some *b*, pretty one,   *Com. of Arthur* 335
my husband's *b* had my son Thrall'd in his castle,   *Gareth and L.* 357
Our noblest *b*, and our truest man,   ,,   565
second *b* in their fool's parable—   ,,   1004
'What doest thou, *b*, in my marches here ?'   ,,   1034
Hath overthrown thy *b*, and hath his arms.'   ,,   1037
the third *b* shouted o'er the bridge,   ,,   1096
My *b* and my better, this man here,   *Balin and Balan* 54
Embracing Balin, 'Good my *b*, hear !   ,,   139
on his dying *b* cast himself Dying ;   ,,   593
'*B*, I dwelt a day in Pellam's hall :   ,,   605
'O *b*' answer'd Balin 'woe is me !   ,,   618
darken thine, Goodnight, true *b*.'   ,,   626
'Goodnight, true *b* here !.goodmorrow there !   ,,   628
two *b*'s, one a king, And fought   *Lancelot and E.* 39
each had slain his *b* at a blow ;   ,,   41
brought the yet-unblazon'd shield, His *b*'s ;   ,,   380
rosy-kindled with her *b*'s kiss—   ,,   393
Sir Modred's *b*, and the child of Lot,   ,,   558
Came on her *b* with a happy face   ,,   791
Full ill then should I quit your *b*'s love,   ,,   944
the *b*'s heard, and thought With shuddering,   ,,   1021
'Sweet *b*'s, yesternight I seem'd   ,,   1034
'Fret not yourself, dear *b*, nor be wroth,   ,,   1074
'O *b*, I have seen this yew-tree smoke,   *Holy Grail* 18
what drove thee from the Table Round, My *b* ?   ,,   29
'Sweet *b*, I have seen the Holy Grail :   ,,   107
b, fast thou too and pray, And tell thy *b* knights to fast
   and pray,   ,,   125
and himself her *b* more than I.   ,,   142
'Sister or *b* none had he ;   ,,   143
b, In our great hall there stood   ,,   166
b, had you known our mighty hall,   ,,   225
b, had you known our hall within,   ,,   246
b, when I told him what had chanced,   ,,   271
(*B*, the King was hard upon his knights)   ,,   299
O *b*, had you known our Camelot,   ,,   339
'O *b*,' ask'd Ambrosius,—   ,,   540
O *b*, saving this Sir Galahad,   ,,   561
my *b*, Why wilt thou shame me to confess   ,,   566
was the one, *B*, and that one only,   ,,   579
O me, my *b* ! but one night my vow   ,,   607
For, *b*, so one night, because they roll   ,,   685
'And that can I, *B*, and truly ;   ,,   712
B, I need not tell thee foolish words,—   ,,   855
Art thou the purest, *b* ?   *Last Tournament* 192
b, thou nor I have made the world ;   ,,   203
is the King thy *b* fool ?'   ,,   352
ay, my *b* fool, the king of fools !   ,,   354
A goodly *b* of the Table Round   ,,   431
Slain was the *b* of my paramour   ,,   448
So *b*, pluck and spare not.'   *Lover's Tale i* 351
'*B*,' she said, 'let this be call'd   ,,   461
I was as the *b* of her blood,   ,,   559
deem'd I wore a *b*'s mind : she call'd me *b* :   ,,   741
Deem that I love thee but as *b*'s do,   ,,   767
Praise to our Indian *b*'s,   *Def. of Lucknow* 69
Drove me and my good *b*'s home in chains,   *Columbus* 134
He with his *b*, Edmund Atheling   *Batt. of Brunanburh* 5
Christ, our human *b* and friend,   *Despair* 25
the tears, O *b*, mine or thine,   *Ancient Sage* 186
Sisters, *b*'s—and the beasts—   *Locksley H., Sixty* 102

Brother (*continued*) Rip your *b*'s' voices open,   *Locksley H., Sixty* 141
True *b*, only to be known By those who love   *Pref. Poem Broth. S.* 7
Sons and *b*'s that have sent,   *Open. I. and C. Exhib.* 3
B's, must we part at last ?   ,,   32
Is *b* of the Dark one in the lowest,   *Demeter and P.* 95
He, the *b* of this Darkness,   ,,   116
Will my Indian *b* come ?   *Romney's R.* 143
Well spake thy *b* in his hymn to heaven   *Akbar's Dream* 27
Meanwhile, my *b*'s, work, and wield   *Mechanophilus* 29
Father, and my *B*, and my God !   *Doubt and Prayer* 8
Brother-brute ever butted his rough *b-b* For lust   *Lucretius* 197
Brother-hands I, clasping *b-h*, aver I could not,   *In Mem. lxxxv* 102
Brotherhood And all men work in noble *b*,   *Ode Inter. Exhib.* 38
To fight the *b* of Day and Night—   *Gareth and L.* 857
hast thou so defamed Thy *b*   *Pelleas and E.* 322
hath bound And sworn me to this *b* ;'   ,,   449
Unlawful and disloyal *b*—   *Sisters (E. and E.)* 174
Brother-in-law that mock-sister there—*B-i-l*   ,,   173
Brother-knight Lo ! he hath slain some *b-k*,   *Balin and Balan* 549
Brother-like kiss'd her with all pureness, *b-l*,   *Geraint and E.* 884
Brother-oak honours that, Thy famous *b-o*,   *Talking Oak* 296
Brother-sister are you That *b-s* Psyche,   *Princess ii* 254
Brother-slayer Not from the skeleton of a *b-s*,   *Last Tournament* 47
Brother-star *b-s*, why shine ye here so low ?   *Gareth and L.* 1097
Brother-worm and its last *b-w* will have fled   *Despair* 85
Brought (*See also* **Browt, Far-brought**) Is not my
   human pride *b* low ?   *Supp. Confessions* 14
from the outward to the inward *b*,   *Eleänore* 4
The oriental fairy *b*,   ,,   14
I marvell'd how the mind was *b* To anchor   *Two Voices* 458
slowly was my mother *b* To yield consent   *Miller's D.* 137
Although the loss had *b* us pain,   ,,   229
light-foot Iris *b* it yester-eve,   *Œnone* 83
I won his love, I *b* him home.   *The Sisters* 14
and *b* Into the gulfs of sleep.   *D. of F. Women* 51
Where'er I came I *b* calamity.'   *The Epic* 48
then at my request He *b* it ;   ,,   48
every morning *b* a noble chance, And every chance
   b out a noble knight.   *M. d'Arthur* 230
till Autumn *b* an hour For Eustace,   *Gardener's D.* 207
B out a dusky loaf that smelt of home,   *Audley Court* 22
his bailiff *b* A Chartist pike.   *Walk. to the Mail* 70
b the night In which we sat together   *Love and Duty* 59
all the mothers *b* Their children,   *Godiva* 14
The pint, you *b* me, was the best   *Will Water.* 75
Lord Ronald *b* a lily-white doe   *Lady Clare* 3
lily-white doe Lord Ronald had *b*   ,,   61
then with what she *b* Buy goods and stores—   *Enoch Arden* 137
b the stinted commerce of those days ;   ,,   817
letter which he *b*, and swore besides   *Aylmer's Field* 522
She *b* strange news.   *Sea Dreams* 267
which he *b*, and I Dived in a hoard of tales   *Princess, Pro.* 28
which *b* My book to mind :   ,,   119
these *b* back A present, a great labour   ,,   *i* 43
He *b* it, and himself, a sight to shake   ,,   200
She *b* us Academic silks,   ,,   *ii* 16
'I *b* a message here from Lady Blanche.'   ,,   319
from the Queen's decease she *b* her up.   ,,   *iii* 86
—or *b* her chain'd, a slave,   ,,   *v* 139
Home they *b* her warrior dead :   ,,   *vi* 1
B from under every star,   *Ode Inter. Exhib.* 25
And bread from out the houses *b*,   *Spec. of Iliad* 6
As tho' they *b* but merchants' bales,   *In Mem. xiii* 19
Such precious relics *b* by thee ;   ,,   *xviii* 18
And he that *b* him back is there.   ,,   *xxxii* 4
He *b* an eye for all he saw ;   ,,   *lxxxix* 9
she *b* the harp and flung A ballad   ,,   27
And *b* a summons from the sea :   ,,   *ciii* 16
Large elements in order *b*,   ,,   *cxii* 13
and *b* to understand A sad astrology,   *Maud I xviii* 35
B Arthur forth, and set him in the hall,   *Com. of Arthur* 229
Or *b* by Merlin, who, they say,   ,,   347
B down a momentary brow.   *Gareth and L.* 653
champion thou hast *b* from Arthur's hall ?   ,,   916
ere his horse was *b*, Glorying ;   ,,   934

Brought (*continued*) *b* a helm With but a drying	
evergreen	*Gareth and L.* 1115
Gareth *b* him grovelling on his knees,	" 1124
Enid *b* sweet cakes to make them cheer,	*Marr. of Geraint* 388
and he *b* me to a goodly house ;	" 713
like a madman *b* her to the court,	" 725
promise, that whatever bride I *b,*	" 783
b a mantle down and wrapt her in it,	" 824
Prince had *b* his errant eyes Home	*Geraint and E.* 245
And wine and food were *b,*	" 289
as they *b* upon their forays out	" 567
men *b* in whole hogs and quarter beeves,	" 602
they *b* report 'we hardly found,	*Balin and Balan* 94
who first *B* the great faith to Britain	" 103
b By holy Joseph hither,	" 112
b report of azure lands and fair,	" 168
as he That *b* her hither.	" 187
To save thy life, have *b* thee to thy death.	" 600
miss'd, and *b* Her own claw back,	*Merlin and V.* 499
He lightly scatter'd theirs and *b* her off,	" 564
He *b,* not found it therefore :	" 719
I by mere mischance have *b,* my shield.	*Lancelot and E.* 189
red sleeve Broider'd with pearls,' and *b* it :	" 373
Returning *b* the yet-unblazon'd shield,	" 379
And *b* his horse to Lancelot where he lay.	" 493
the shield was *b,* and Gawain saw	" 662
have *b* thee, now a lonely man Wifeless	" 1370
saw the barge that *b* her moving down,	" 1391
Joseph, journeying *B* to Glastonbury,	*Holy Grail* 51
b thee here to this poor house of ours	" 617
they fell from, *b* us to the hall.	" 720
Joseph of old to Glastonbury ?'	" 735
bounden straight, and so they *b* him in.	*Pelleas and E.* 236
rose up, and bound, and *b* him in.	" 288
Waited, until the third night *b* a moon	" 393
b A maiden babe ; which Arthur pitying took,	*Last Tournament* 20
b to adorn her with, The jewels,	" 715
when both were *b* to full accord,	" 722
And hither *b* by Tristram for his last	" 747
Modred *b* His creatures to the basement	*Guinevere* 103
and my tears have *b* me good :	" 202
he that *b* The heathen back among us,	*Pass. of Arthur* 151
every morning *b* a noble chance, And every	
chance *b* out a noble knight.	" 398
Looking on her that *b* him to the light :	*Lover's Tale* i 160
the shuddering moonlight *b* its face	" 650
rare or fair Was *b* before the guest :	" iv 204
He slowly *b* them back to Lionel.	" 371
caught and *b* him in To their charm'd circle,	" 376
For we *b* them all aboard,	*The Revenge* 19
On whom I *b* a strange unhappiness,	*Sisters (E. and E.)* 89
So took her thence, and *b* her here,	" 267
He had *b* his ghastly tools :	*In the Child. Hosp.* 69
Hast thou *b* bread with thee ?	*Sir J. Oldcastle* 198
b out a broad sky Of dawning over—	*Columbus* 77
Whatever wealth I *b* from that new world	" 101
I had *b* your Princes gold enough	" 105
I *b* From Solomon's now-recover'd Ophir	" 111
This creedless people will be *b* to Christ	" 189
That day my nurse had *b* me the child.	*The Wreck* 59
Dead ! 'Is it *he* then *b* so low ?'	*Dead Prophet* 6
Until I *b* thee hither.	*Demeter and P.* 8
I *b* you to that chamber on your	*The Ring* 129
I *b* you, you remember, these roses,	*Happy* 73
b you down A length of staghorn-moss,	*Romney's R.* 78
'hast *thou b* us down a new Korân	*Akbar's Dream* 116
when I met you first—when *he b* you !—	*Charity* 9
Brow *This laurel greener from the b's*	*To the Queen* 7
Among the thorns that girt Thy *b,*	*Supp. Confessions* 6
when with *b's* Propt on thy knees,	" 69
An image with profulgent *b's,*	" 145
Upon her bed, across her *b.*	*Mariana* 56
Falsehood shall bare her plaited *b* :	*Clear-headed friend* 11
Frowns perfect-sweet along the *b*	*Madeline* 15
o'er black *b's* drops down A sudden-curved frown : (repeat)	" 34, 46

Brow (*continued*) a *b* of pearl Tressed with	
redolent ebony,	*Arabian Nights* 137
Even as a maid, whose stately *b*	*Ode to Memory* 13
Her beautiful bold *b,*	*The Poet* 38
With thy soften'd, shadow'd *b,*	*Adeline* 46
wearing on my swarthy *b's* The garland	*Kate* 23
His broad clear *b* in sunlight glow'd ;	*L. of Shalott* iii 28
From *b* and bosom slowly down	*Mariana in the S.* 14
Look up, the fold is on her *b.*	*Two Voices* 192
blow Before him, striking on my *b.*	*Fatima* 25
and the charm of married *b's.*'	*Œnone* 76
drew From her warm *b's* and bosom her deep hair	" 177
steep our *b's* in slumber's holy balm ;	*Lotos-Eaters, C. S.* 21
Whereto the other with a downward *b* :	*D. of F. Women* 117
lying dead, my crown about my *b,*	" 162
dropping bitter tears against his *b*	*M. d'Arthur* 211
But the full day dwelt on her *b's,*	*Gardener's D.* 136
Love with knit *b's* went by,	" 245
whose bald *b's* in silent hours become	*St. S. Stylites* 165
I waited long ; My *b's* are ready.	" 206
glimmer steals From thy pure *b's,*	*Tithonus* 35
Her sweet face from *b* to chin :	*L. of Burleigh* 62
Warm broke the breeze against the *b,*	*The Voyage* 9
A band of pain across my *b* ;	*The Letters* 6
sleepy light upon their *b's* and lips—	*Vision of Sin* 9
we know the hue Of that cap upon her *b's.*	" 142
And gain'd a laurel for your *b*	*You might have won* 3
Annie with her *b's* against the wall	*Enoch Arden* 314
o'er his bent *b's* linger'd Averill,	*Aylmer's Field* 625
often placed upon the sick man's *b*	" 700
breathing down From over her arch'd *b's,*	*Princess* ii 39
and the Roman *b's* Of Agrippina,	" 84
gaunt old baron with his beetle *b* Sun-shaded	" 240
Psyche, wont to bind my throbbing *b,*	" 250
Star-sisters answering under crescent *b's* ;	" 428
lilylike Melissa droop'd her *b's* ;	" iv 161
manlike, but his *b's* Had sprouted,	" 204
With hooded *b's* I crept into the hall,	" 225
made the single jewel on her *b* Burn	" 273
till over *b* And cheek and bosom brake	" 382
raised the cloak from *b's* as pale and smooth	" v 73
veil'd her *b's,* and prone she sank,	" 107
she laid A feeling finger on my *b's,*	" vi 121
With *b* to *b* like night and evening	" 131
fear not ; breathe upon my *b's* ;	" vii 353
King bent low, with hand on *b,*	*The Victim* 53
gladness even crown'd The purple *b's* of Olivet.	*In Mem.* xxxi 12
Urania speaks with darken'd *b* :	" xxxvii 1
I took the thorns to bind my *b's,*	" lxix 7
Lift as thou may'st thy burthen'd *b*	" lxxii 21
So, dearest, now thy *b's* are cold,	" lxxiv 5
turn'd To black and brown on kindred *b's.*	" lxxix 16
fan my *b's* and blow The fever from my cheek,	" lxxxvi 8
Be large and lucid round thy *b.*	" xci 8
And enter in at breast and *b,*	" cxxii 11
Broad *b's* and fair, a fluent hair and fine,	*Gareth and L.* 464
a *b* May-blossom, and a cheek of apple-blossom,	" 588
Brought down a momentary *b.*	" 653
Then seeing cloud upon the mother's *b,*	*Marr. of Geraint* 777
with droopt *b* down the long glades he rode ;	*Balin and Balan* 311
drawing down the dim disastrous *b*	" 597
a wizard *b* bleach'd on the walls :	*Merlin and V.* 597
two brethren slowly with bent *b's*	
Accompanying,	*Lancelot and E.* 1138
kiss'd her quiet *b's,* and saying	" 1150
Arthur, who beheld his cloudy *b's,*	" 1354
the circlet of the jousts Bound on her *b,*	*Pelleas and E.* 435
circlet of the tourney round her *b's,*	" 454
under her black *b's* a swarthy one Laugh'd	*Last Tournament* 216
laid His *b's* upon the drifted leaf and dream'd.	" 406
a *b* Like hillsnow high in heaven,	" 666
dropping bitter tears against a *b*	*Pass. of Arthur* 379
To pass my hands across my *b's,*	*Lover's Tale* i 31
clear, bulwark of the precious brain,	" 130
brood More warmly on the heart than on the *b.*	" 328

Brow (continued) for her *b's* And mine made garlands   *Lover's Tale i* 342
   Beyond the nearest mountain's bosky *b's*,   ,, 396
   knotted thorns thro' my unpaining *b's*,   ,, 620
   sprinkled brook Smote on my *b's*,   ,, 634
   great crown of beams about his *b's*—   ,, 672
   walk'd abreast with me, and veil'd his *b*,   ,, ii 86
   and from his *b* drew back His hand to push   ,, 92
   about my *b* Her warm breath floated   ,, 140
   Upon my fever'd *b's* that shook and throbb'd   ,, iii 7
   walk'd behind with one who veil'd his *b*.   ,, 12
   Cold were his *b's* when we kiss'd him—   *Def. of Lucknow* 12
   in your raised *b's* I read Some wonder   *Columbus* 1
   Why, what a *b* was there !   *The Wreck* 48
   The broad white *b* of the Isle—   ,, 135
   dreamer stoopt and kiss'd her marble *b*.   *Locksley H., Sixty* 38
   out of the field, And over the *b* and away.   *Heavy Brigade* 64
   Unfurnish'd *b's*, tempestuous tongues—   *Freedom* 38
   But seen upon the silent *b* when life   *Happy* 52
   when I let him kiss my *b* ;   ,, 65
   round her *b's* a woodland culver flits,   *Prog. of Spring* 18
   till the heat Smote on her *b*,   *Death of Œnone* 98
   Me they front With sullen *b's*.   *Akbar's Dream* 52
Brow-beat while the worn-out clerk *B-b's* his desk below.   *To J. M. K.* 12
Brow-bound eyes, *B-b* with burning gold.   *D. of F. Women* 128
Brow'd *See* **Beautiful-brow'd**, **Dark-brow'd**, **Large-brow'd**
Brow-high the hemlock, *B-h*, did strike my forehead   *Lover's Tale ii* 19
Brown in a silent shade of laurel *b* Apart   *Alexander* 9
   Her streaming curls of deepest *b*   *Mariana in the S.* 16
   B, looking hardly human, strangely clad,   *Enoch Arden* 638
   Enoch was so *b*, so bow'd,   ,, 703
   beauties every shade of *b* and fair   *Princess ii* 437
   all her autumn tresses falsely *b*,   ,, 449
   I watch the twilight falling *b*   *To F. D. Maurice* 14
   To black and *b* on kindred brows.   *In Mem. lxxix* 16
   park and suburb under *b* Of lustier leaves ;   ,, xcviii 24
   Unloved, that beech will gather *b*,   ,, ci 3
   bracken so bright and the heather so *b*,   *June Bracken, etc.* 3
Browsed *b* by deep-udder'd kine,   *Gardener's D.* 46
Browt (brought) I *b* what tha seeäs stannin' theer,   *North. Cobbler* 70
   b me the booöts to be cobbled   ,, 94
   So I *b* tha down, an' I says   *Owd Roä* 97
   I *b* 'im down, an' we got to the barn,   ,, 103
   An' I *b* Roä round, but Moother   ,, 113
Bruise Hard-won and hardly won with *b* and blow,   *Lancelot and E.* 1165
Bruised cursed and scorn'd, and *b* with stones :   *Two Voices* 222
   that there Lie *b* and maim'd,   *Princess vi* 72
   Had *b* the herb and crush'd the grape,   *In Mem. xxxv* 23
   swordcut on the cheek, And *b* and bronzed,   *Lancelot and E.* 259
   and so left him *b* And batter'd,   *Pelleas and E.* 546
   Nor *b* the wildbird's egg.   *Lover's Tale i* 21
   b and butted with the shuddering War-thunder   *Tiresias* 99
Brunanburh Slew with the sword-edge There *b*,   *Batt. of Brunanburh* 10
Brunelleschi Arno, and the dome Of *B* ;   *The Brook* 190
Brunette A quick *b*, well-moulded,   *Princess ii* 106
Brush (pencil) took his *b* and blotted out the bird,   *Merlin and V.* 478
Brush (tail of fox) ' Peter had the *b*, My Peter, first :'   *Aylmer's Field* 254
Brush (verb) to *b* the dew From thine own lily,   *Supp. Confessions* 84
Brush'd *b* Thro' the dim meadow toward his   *Aylmer's Field* 530
   when, this gad-fly *b* aside,   *Princess v* 414
   and *b* My fallen forehead in their to and fro,   *Lover's Tale i* 700
Brushing And *b* ankle-deep in flowers,   *In Mem. lxxxix* 49
   with his brandish'd plume *B* his instep,   *Geraint and E.* 360
Brushwood elm-tree-boles did stoop and lean Upon the dusky *b*   *D. of F. Women* 58
Brute (*See also* **Brother-brute**) Take my *b*, and lead him in,   *Vision of Sin* 65
   Thou madest Life in man and *b*;   *In Mem., Pro.* 6
   No longer half-akin to *b*,   ,, Con. 133
   he had not been a Sultan of *b's*,   *Maud II v* 81
   b's of mountain back That carry kings   *Merlin and V.* 576
   O great and sane and simple race of *b's*   *Pelleas and E.* 480
   Come from the *b*, poor souls—   *Despair* 36

Brute (continued) no souls—and to die with the *b*—   *Despair* 36
   and burn the kindlier *b's* alive.   *Locksley H., Sixty* 96
   B's, the *b's* are not your wrongers—   ,, 97
   let the house of a *b* to the soul of a man,   *By an Evolution.* 1
   If my body come from *b's*, (repeat)   ,, 5, 13
   I, the finer *b* rejoicing in my hounds,   ,, 7
   and rule thy Province of the *b*.   ,, 16
   these Are like wild *b's* new-caged—   *Akbar's Dream* 50
   The Ghost of the *B* that is walking   *The Dawn* 23
Brutus (**Lucius Junius**) *See* **Lucius Junius Brutus**
Bubble (s) watch'd Or seem'd to watch the dancing *b*,   *Princess iii* 24
   colour'd *b* bursts above the abyss   *Romney's R.* 52
Bubble (verb) I *b* into eddying bays,   *The Brook* 41
   On yon swoll'n brook That *b's* fast   *In Mem. xcix* 6
   And yet *b's* o'er like a city, with gossip,   *Maud I iv* 8
Bubbled at mine ear *B* the nightingale   *Princess iv* 266
   The milk that *b* in the pail,   *In Mem. lxxxix* 51
   oilily *b* up the mere.   *Gareth and L.* 816
Bubbling *See* **Life-bubbling**
Bublin' (young unfledged bird) An' haäfe on 'im bare as a *b*.'   *Owd Roä* 102
Bucket rope that haled the *b's* from the well,   *St. S. Stylites* 64
   helpt to pass a *b* from the well   *To Mary Boyle* 39
Buckled *B* with golden clasps before ;   *Sir L. and Q. G.* 25
Buckler The brand, the *b*, and the spear—   *Two Voices* 129
   Clash the darts and on the *b* beat   *Boädicea* 79
   snatch'd a sudden *b* from the Squire   *Balin and Balan* 554
Bud (s) (*See also* **Chestnut-bud**, **Sea-bud**) While thou abodest in the *b*.   *Two Voices* 158
   chestnuts, when their *b's* Were glistening   *Miller's D.* 60
   flowers, and *b's* and garlands gay,   *May Queen* 11
   folded leaf is woo'd from out the *b*   *Lotos-Eaters, C. S.* 26
   Sweet as new *b's* in Spring.   *D. of F. Women* 272
   all-too-full in *b* For puritanic stays :   *Talking Oak* 59
   kisses balmier than half-opening *b's* Of April,   *Tithonus* 59
   In *b* or blade, or bloom, may find,   *Day-Dm., Moral* 10
   burst In carol, every *b* to flower,   ,, *L'Envoi* 44
   While life was yet in *b* and blade,   *Princess i* 32
   ' Pretty b ! Lily of the vale !   ,, vi 192
   b ever breaks into bloom on the tree,   *The Islet* 32
   longs to burst a frozen *b* And flood   *In Mem. lxxxiii* 15
   O when her life was yet in *b*,   ,, Con. 33
   flower tell What sort of *b* it was,   *Lover's Tale i* 152
   from within Burst thro' the heated *b's*,   ,, 320
   No *b*, no leaf, no flower, no fruit   ,, 725
   and all smells of *b* And foliage from the dark   ,, iii 5
   spies the summer thro' the winter *b*,   *Ancient Sage* 74
   fleets the shower, And burst the *b's*,   *Early Spring* 14
   ' your pretty *b*, So blighted here,   *The Ring* 316
   Thy warmths from *b* to *b* Accomplish   *Prog. of Spring* 113
Bud (verb) And rugged barks begin to *b*,   *My life is full* 18
   times, when some new thought can *b*,   *Golden Year* 27
   out of tyranny tyranny *b's*.   *Boädicea* 83
   And *b's* and blossoms like the rest.   *In Mem. cxv* 20
Budded *See* **New-budded**, **Ruby-budded**
Buddhist Brahmin, and *B*, Christian, and Parsee,   *Akbar's Dream* 25
Bude the thundering shores of *B* and Bos,   *Guinevere* 291
Buffet (s) with a stronger *b* he clove the helm   *Gareth and L.* 1406
   Swung from his brand a windy *b*   *Geraint and E.* 90
Buffet (verb) echo flap And *b* round the hills,   *Golden Year* 77
   Strove to *b* to land in vain.   *Princess iv* 185
Buffeted *See* **Tempest-buffeted**
Bugle (adj.) all the *b* breezes blew Reveillée   *In Mem. lxviii* 7
Bugle (s) Aloud the hollow *b* blowing,   *Oriana* 17
   Loud, loud rung out the *b's* brays,   ,, 48
   A mighty silver *b* hung,   *L. of Shalott iii* 16
   Blow, *b*, blow, set the wild echoes (repeat)   *Princess iv* 5, 17
   Blow, *b* ; answer, echoes, dying, (repeat)   ,, 6, 12
   and bray of the long horn And serpent-throated *b*,   ,, v 253
   With blare of *b*, clamour of men,   *Ode on Well.* 115
   Warble, O *b*, and trumpet, blare !   *W. to Alexandra* 14
   March with banner and *b* and fife   *Maud I v* 10
   raised a *b* hanging from his neck,   *Pelleas and E.* 364
   waits below the wall, Blowing his *b*   ,, 381
   and on shield A spear, a harp, a *b*—   *Last Tournament* 174

Bugle (s) (continued) B's and drums in the darkness, *Def. of Lucknow* 76
Bugle-horn belted hunter blew His wreathed *b-h.* *Palace of Art* 64
when you want me, sound upon the *b-h.* *Locksley Hall* 2
call me, sounding on the *b-h,* " 145
Œnone 39
Build *b* up all My sorrow with my song, *Edwin Morris* 7
built When men knew how to *b,* *Princess, Pro.* 134
I would *b* Far off from men a college " ii 145
She had founded ; they must *b.* " iv 351
I, that have lent my life to *b* up yours, " v 230
b some plan Foursquare to opposition.' *Ode on Well.* 266
On God and Godlike men we *b* our trust. *In Mem.* xxxvi 14
b's the house, or digs the grave, " cxv 16
change their sky To *b* and brood ; *"Holy Grail* 62
Gave him an isle of marsh whereon to *b* ; *Pelleas and E.* 555
he groan'd, 'ye *b* too high.' *Lover's Tale* i 176
b a wall betwixt my life and love, *Ancient Sage* 83
none but Gods could *b* this house *Deserted House* 15
Builded The house was *b* of the earth, *Gareth and L.* 276
Building like enow They are *b* still,
Built (*See also* **Belt, Half-built, Low-built, Sand-built, Woman-built**) *b* up everywhere An
under-roof *Dying Swan* 3
I *B* my soul a lordly pleasure-house, *Palace of Art* 1
Thereon I *b* it firm. " 9
In this great mansion, that is *b* for me, " 19
' My spacious mansion *b* for me, " 234
palace towers, that are So lightly, beautifully *b* : " 294
b When men knew how to build, *Edwin Morris* 6
And *b* herself an everlasting name. *Godiva* 79
B for pleasure and for state. *L. of Burleigh* 32
b their castles of dissolving sand *Enoch Arden* 19
b, and thatch'd with leaves of palm, " 559
Rhodope, that *b* the pyramid, *Princess* ii 82
vapour streak the crowned towers *B* to the Sun :' " iii 345
' The plan was mine. I *b* the nest' " iv 365
conscious of what temper you are *b,* " 400
Far off from men I *b* a fold for them : " v 390
tho' he *b* upon the babe restored " vii 75
And towers fall'n as soon as *b—* *In Mem.* xxvi 8
Who *b* him fanes of fruitless prayer, " lvi 12
New as his title, *b* last year, *"Maud* I x 19
city of Enchanters, *b* By fairy Kings.' *Gareth and L.* 199
and whether this be *b* By magic, " 247
Fairy Queens have *b* the city, son ; " 259
And *b* it to the music of their harps. " 262
seeing the city is *b* To music, therefore never
b at all, " 276
And therefore *b* for ever.' " 278
B that new fort to overawe my friends, *Marr. of Geraint* 460
that low church he *b* at Glastonbury. *Balin and Balan* 367
Had *b* the King his havens, ships, *Merlin and V.* 168
there he *b* with wattles from the marsh *Holy Grail* 63
Which Merlin *b* for Arthur long ago ! " 226
Climbs to the mighty hall that Merlin *b.* " 231
B by old kings, age after age, " 340
some ancient king Had *b* a way, " 502
saw High up in heaven the hall that Merlin *b,* *Pelleas and E.* 553
B for a summer day with Queen Isolt *Last Tournament* 378
There be some hearts so airily *b,* that they, *Lover's Tale* i 803
Timur *b* his ghastly tower of eighty thousand *Locksley H., Sixty* 82
Served the poor, and *b* the cottage, " 268
Son's love *b* me, and I hold Mother's love *Helen's Tower* 3
b their shepherd-prince a funeral pile ; *Death of Œnone* 63
whose pious hand had *b* the cross, *St. Telemachus* 9
Bulbul Died round the *b* as he sung ; *Arabian Nights* 70
'O *B,* any rose of Gulistan Shall burst *Princess* iv 122
Bulge cheek *B* with the unswallow'd piece, *Geraint and E.* 631
Bulk Tudor-chimnied *b* Of mellow brickwork *Edwin Morris* 11
bones of some vast *b* that lived and roar'd *Princess* iii 294
Down From those two *b's* at Arac's side, " v 499
and grown a *b* Of spanless girth, " vi 35
Dark *b's* that tumble half alive, *In Mem.* lxx 11
strike him, overbalancing his *b,* *Last Tournament* 460
Bulk'd an old-world mammoth *b* in ice, *Princess* v 148
Bull grasp'd The mild *b's* golden horn. *Palace of Art* 120

Bull (*continued*) oil'd and curl'd Assyrian *B* Smelling
of musk *Maud* I vi 44
Kay near him groaning like a wounded *b—* *Gareth and L.* 648
whom his shaking vassals call'd the *B,* *Geraint and E.* 439
brainless *b's,* Dead for one heifer !' *Balin and Balan* 578
like a *b* gotten loose at a faär. *North. Cobbler* 33
and the *b* couldn't low, and the dog *V. of Maeldune* 18
Bull (**Inn Sign**) 'THE *B,* the Fleece are cramm'd, *Audley Court* 1
Bull (**Edward**) *See* **Edward Bull**
Bullet (*See also* **Cannon-bullet, Musket-bullet, Rifle-bullet**) *B's* fell like rain ; *The Captain* 46
b struck him that was dressing it *The Revenge* 67
And caught the laming *b.* *Sisters (E. and E.)* 65
the brute *b* broke thro' the brain *Def. of Lucknow* 20
B's would sing by our foreheads, and *b's* would rain " 21
Bulrush sword-grass, and the *b* in the pool. *May Queen, N. Y's. E.* 28
mid-thigh-deep in *b'es* and reed, *Gareth and L.* 810
Bulrush-bed plunged Among the *b-b's,* and clutch'd
the sword, *M. d'Arthur* 135
plunged Among the *b-b's,* and clutch'd the sword, *Pass. of Arthur* 303
Bulwark now they saw their *b* fallen, *Geraint and E.* 168
Bummin' (**buzzing**) *b'* awaäy loike a buzzard-clock *N. Farmer, O. S.* 18
Bump'd I *b* the ice into three several stars, *The Epic* 12
Bumper He froth'd his *b's* to the brim ; *D. of the O. Year* 19
Bunch (*See also* **Fruit-bunches, Vine-bunches**) With *Œnone* 102
b and berry and flower
grapes with *b'es* red as blood ; *Day-Dm., Sleep. P.* 44
Craft with a *b* of all-heal in her hand, *Vastness* 12
Bundle now hastily caught His *b,* waved his hand, *Enoch Arden* 238
Buoy (*See also* **Harbour-buoy**) WE left behind the
painted *b* *The Voyage* 1
The *b* that rides at sea, and dips *Gareth and L.* 1146
Buoy'd range Of vapour *b* the crescent-bark, *Day-Dm., Depart.* 22
B upon floating tackle and broken *Enoch Arden* 551
Bur (*See also* **Burr**) *b* and brake and briar, *Day-Dm., Sleep. P.* 46
like a wall of *b's* and thorns ; *Sea Dreams* 119
Burden (*See also* **Burthen**) people here, a beast
of *b* slow, *Palace of Art* 149
prepared The daily *b* for the back. *In Mem.* xxv 4
Burdock eft and snake, In grass and *b,* *Holy Grail* 571
Burgeon space to *b* out of all Within her— *Princess* vii 271
Now *b's* every maze of quick *In Mem.* cxv 2
Burgher Knight and *b,* lord and dame, *L. of Shalott* iv 43
Burial (**adj.**) Mammonite mother kills her babe for a *b* fee, *Maud* I i 45
Burial (**s**) at a *b* to hear The creaking cords *Supp. Confessions* 35
Fresh from the *b* of her little one, *Enoch Arden* 281
A summer *b* deep in hollyhocks ; *Aylmer's Field* 164
That hears his *b* talk'd of by his friends, *Princess* vii 193
Now to glorious *b* slowly borne, *Ode on Well.* 193
Pray for my soul, and yield me *b.* *Lancelot and E.* 1280
place of *b* Far lovelier than their cradle ; *Lover's Tale* i 529
and ask'd If I would see her *b* : " ii 71
At some precipitance in her *b.* " iv 107
Past thro' his visions to the *b,* " 357
borne in white To *b* or to burning, *Ancient Sage* 208
Those that in barbarian *b's* kill'd the slave, *Locksley Hall, Sixty* 67
Beyond our *b* and our buried eyes, *The Ring* 296
Buried (*See also* **A-buried, Half-buried, Long-buried**)
I *b* her like my own sweet child, *Lady Clare* 27
that same week when Annie *b* it, *Enoch Arden* 271
And when they *b* him the little port " 916
Old scandals *b* now seven decads deep *Aylmer's Field* 442
Half *b* in some weightier argument, *Lucretius* 122
have they not *b* me deep enough ? *Maud* II v 96
Dead, whom we *b* ; more than one of us *Balin and Balan* 122
rummage in the walls Might echo, " 416
see that she be *b* worshipfully.' *Lancelot and E.* 1329
maiden *b,* not as one unknown, " 1334
I kiss'd 'em, *b* 'em all— *Rizpah* 55
She died and she was *b* ere we knew. *Sisters (E. and E.)* 241
So feyther an' son was *b* togither, *Village Wife* 90
as God's truer images Are daily *b.'* *Sir J. Oldcastle* 141
I will have them *b* in my grave. *Columbus* 201
his Riverence *b* thim both in wan grave *Tomorrow* 87
There, there ! he *b* you, the Priest ; *Happy* 105

Burleigh *See* **Lord of Burleigh**
Burleigh-house *B-h* by Stamford-town. *L. of Burleigh* 92
Burlesque Had ever seem'd to wrestle with *b*, *Princess, Con.* 16
Burn (stream) Over the pools in the *b* water-gnats *Leonine Eleg.* 8
  tall firs and our fast-falling *b's* ; *Gareth and L.* 91
Burn (burnt place) An' it was'nt a bite but a *b*, *Owd Roä* 90
Burn (verb) cricket chirps: the light *b's* low : *D. of the O. Year* 40
  While the stars *b*, the moons increase, *To J. S.* 71
  And *b* a fragrant lamp before my bones, *St. S. Stylites* 196
  And *b* the threshold of the night, *The Voyage* 18
  but my cheek Began to *b* and *b*, *Princess iii* 46
  b's Above the unrisen morrow :'   ,, *iv* 82
  made the single jewel on her brow *B*   ,, 274
  Wherefore in me *b's* an anger, *Boädicea* 52
  Burst the gates, and *b* the palaces,   ,, 64
  fires *b* clear, And frost is here *Window, Winter* 4
  And with the thought her colour *b's* ; *In Mem. vi* 34
  And calm that let the tapers *b*   ,, *xcv* 5
  This maple *b* itself away ;   ,, *ci* 4
  Cold fires, yet with power to *b* *Maud I xviii* 39
  beneath there *b's* A jewell'd harness, *Gareth and L.* 687
  Made her cheek *b* and either eyelid fall. *Marr. of Geraint* 775
  Made her cheek *b* and either eyelid fall. *Geraint and E.* 434
  sin that practice *b's* into the blood, *Merlin and V.* 762
  Made my tears *b*—is also past— *Guinevere* 542
  Amen ! Nay, I can *b*, so that the Lord *Sir J. Oldcastle* 173
  And doom'd to *b* alive.   ,, 183
  So, caught, I *b*. *B*?   ,, 184
  God willing, I will *b* for Him.   ,, 193
  for the bright-eyed goddess made it *b*. *Achilles over the T.* 29
  great God, Arês, *b's* in anger still *Tiresias* 11
  noonday crag made the hand *b* ;   ,, 35
  —but how my temples *b* ! *The Flight* 73
  and *b* the kindlier brutes alive. *Locksley H., Sixty* 96
  fur the barn wouldn't *b* *Owd Roä* 103
  What star could *b* so low ? not Ilion yet. *Death of Œnone* 83
  ' Who *b's* upon the pyre ?'   ,, 99
Burn (born) Cooms of a gentleman *b* : *N. Farmer, N. S.* 38
  Gentleman *b* ! what's gentleman *b*?   ,, 42
  An' then the babby wur *b*, *North. Cobbler* 16
  For 'e warn't not *b* to the land, *Village Wife* 44
  'e wur *b* an' bred i' the 'ouse, *Spinster's S's.* 69
Burn'd (*See also* **Burnt**) *B* like one burning flame
  together, *L. of Shalott iii* 22
  green grasses *b* The red anemone. *D. of F. Women* 71
  Or *b* in fire, or boil'd in oil, *St. S. Stylites* 52
  that, which in me *b*, The love, *Talking Oak* 10
  eye, That *b* upon its object thro' such tears *Love and Duty* 63
  At times the whole sea *b*, *The Voyage* 51
  sacred fire, That *b* as on an altar. *Enoch Arden* 72
  But still the foeman spoil'd and *b*, *The Victim* 17
  Last night, when the sunset *b* *Maud I vi* 8
  b Full on her knights in many an evil name *Pelleas and E.* 289
  one low light betwixt them *b* *Guinevere* 4
  great light of heaven *B* at his lowest *Pass. of Arthur* 91
  And *b* alive as heretics ! *Sir J. Oldcastle* 48
  o'er the great Peleïon's head *B*, *Achilles over the T.* 29
  The prophet's beacon *b* in vain, *Ancient Sage* 142
Burning A love still *b* upward, *Isabel* 18
  All earth and air seem only *b* fire.' *Œnone* 268
  Larger constellations *b*, mellow moons *Locksley Hall* 159
  The tapers *b* fair. *Sir Galahad* 32
  with life-long injuries *b* unavenged, *Geraint and E.* 696
  On *them* the smell of *b* had not past. *Sir J. Oldcastle* 177
  borne in white To burial or to *b*, *Ancient Sage* 208
Burnish to scream, to *b*, and to scour, *Princess* 520
Burnish'd sitting, *b* without fear The brand, *Two Voices* 128
  That glitter *b* by the frosty dark ; *Princess v* 261
  and all in mail *B* to blinding, *Gareth and L.* 1027
Burnt (*See also* **Burn'd**) *B* like a fringe of fire. *Palace of Art* 48
  he *b* His epic, his King Arthur, *The Epic* 27
  Mere chaff and draff, much better *b*.'   ,, 40
  B in each man's blood. *The Captain* 16
  and *b*, Now chafing at his own great self *Aylmer's Field* 536
  the good Sir Ralph had *b* them all— *Princess, Pro.* 236

Burnt (*continued*) grandsire *b* Because he cast no
  shadow, *Princess i* 6
  Nor *b* the grange, nor buss'd the milking-maid,   ,, *v* 222
  other thoughts than Peace *B* in us,   ,, 246
  B and broke the grove and altar *Boädicea* 2
  the rest Slew on and *b*, crying, *Com. of Arthur* 439
  So *b* he was with passion, *Marr. of Geraint* 560
  smoulder'd wrong that *b* him all within ; *Geraint and E.* 107
  many of those who *b* the hold, *Holy Grail* 264
  but one night my vow *B* me within,   ,, 608
  Blasted and *b*, and blinded as I was,   ,, 844
  B as a living fire of emeralds, *Pelleas and E.* 35
  and in it Far cities *b*, *Guinevere* 83
  took and hang'd, Took, hang'd and *b*— *Sir J. Oldcastle* 46
  B—good Sir Roger Acton, my dear friend !   ,, 79
  B too, my faithful preacher, Beverley !   ,, 80
  B, it may be, while this mitred Arundel   ,, 104
  Not *b* were they. On *them* the smell of burning   ,, 176
  b at midnight, found at morn, *Locksley H., Sixty* 97
  the smoke, The pyre he *b* in.'— *The Ring* 340
Burr (*See also* **Bur**) When *b* and bine were gather'd ; *Aylmer's Field* 113
Burrowing I have ferreted out their *b's*, *Merlin and V.* 55
Burst (s) Preluded those melodious *b's* *D. of F. Women* 264
  Caught in a *b* of unexpected storm, *Aylmer's Field* 285
  more than mortal in the *b* Of sunrise, *Princess, Pro.* 40
  but given to starts and *b's* Of revel ;   ,, *i* 54
  B's of great heart and slips in sensual mire,   ,, *v* 199
  after some quick *b* of sudden wrath, *Balin and Balan* 216
  now the storm, its *b* of passion spent, *Merlin and V.* 961
  interspaces gush'd in blinding *b's* The
  incorporate blaze of sun *Lover's Tale i* 408
  and bosom'd the *b* of the spray, *V. of Maeldune* 103
Burst (verb) *B's* into blossom in his sight. *Fatima* 35
  shrine-doors *b* thro' heated blasts *D. of F. Women* 264
  all at once the old man *b* in sobs :— *Dora* 158
  with hoggish whine They *b* my prayer. *St. S. Stylites* 178
  Or to *b* all links of habit— *Locksley Hall* 157
  every bird of Eden *b* In carol, *Day-Dm., L'Envoi* 43
  All heaven *b's* her starry floors, *St. Agnes' Eve* 27
  Now high on waves that idly *b* *The Voyage* 69
  b away In search of stream or fount, *Enoch Arden* 634
  B his own wyvern on the seal, *Aylmer's Field* 516
  the great organ almost *b* his pipes, *Princess ii* 474
  rose of Gulistan Shall *b* her veil :   ,, *iv* 123
  Ready to *b* and flood the world with foam :   ,, 474
  clad in iron *b* the ranks of war,   ,, 504
  in the saddle, then *b* out in words.   ,, *v* 275
  Descending, *b* the great bronze valves,   ,, *vi* 75
  b The laces toward her babe ;   ,, 148
  made the serf a man, and *b* his chain— *W. to Marie Alex.* 3
  B the gates, and *burn* the palaces, *Boädicea* 64
  That longs to *b* a frozen bud *In Mem. lxxxiii* 15
  fiery-hot to *b* All barriers   ,, *cxiv* 13
  And yearn'd to *b* the folded gloom,   ,, *cxxxii* 3
  Ready to *b* in a colour'd flame ; *Maud I vi* 19
  should *b* and drown with deluging storms   ,, *II i* 42
  should make your Enid *b* Sunlike *Marr. of Geraint* 788
  pavement echoing, *b* Their drowse ; *Geraint and E.* 271
  fringe of coppice round them *b* A sprangled
  pursuivant, *Balin and Balan* 46
  b his lance against a forest bough,   ,, 329
  pearl-necklace of the Queen, That *b* *Merlin and V.* 452
  And half his blood *b* forth, *Lancelot and E.* 517
  b away To weep and wail in secret ;   ,, 1244
  almost *b* the barriers in their heat, *Holy Grail* 336
  I *b* the chain, I sprang into the boat.   ,, 807
  Hell *b* up your harlot roofs Bellowing *Pelleas and E.* 466
  from within *B* thro' the heated buds, *Lover's Tale i* 320
  Methought a light *B* from the garland   ,, 366
  b through the cloud of thought Keen,   ,, *ii* 164
  B vein, snap sinew, and crack heart, *Sir J. Oldcastle* 123
  wish yon moaning sea would rise and *b* the shore, *The Flight* 11
  Russia *b's* our Indian barrier, *Locksley H., Sixty* 115
  B like a thunderbolt, Crash'd like a hurricane, *Heavy Brigade* 27
  fleets the shower, And *b* the buds, *Early Spring* 14

Burst (verb) (*continued*)   Sun *B* from a swimming fleece   *Demeter and P.* 20
   smoke of war's volcano *b* again   *Prog. of Spring* 97
   colour'd bubble *b*'s above the abyss   *Romney's R.* 52
Bursting   thistle *b* Into glossy purples,   *Ode on Well.* 206
Burthen (load)   (*See also* **Burden**)   Less *b*, by ten-hundred-fold,   *St. S. Stylites* 24
   Or seem to lift a *b* from thy heart   *Love and Duty* 96
   vapours weep their *b* to the ground,   *Tithonus* 2
   With the *b* of an honour   *L. of Burleigh* 79
   No *b*, save my care for you and yours :   *Enoch Arden* 419
   breathless *b* of low-folded heavens   *Aylmer's Field* 612
   One *b* and she would not lighten it ?   „ 703
   reaching forward drew My *b* from mine arms ;   *Princess* iv 192
   We flung the *b* of the second James.   *Third of Feb.* 28
   And not the *b* that they bring.   *In Mem.* xiii 20
   He bears the *b* of the weeks But turns his *b* into gain.   „ lxxx 11
   Were all a *b* to her, and in her heart   *Pelleas and E.* 112
   now yearn'd to shake The *b* off his heart   *Last Tournament* 180
   friends—your love Is but a *b*:   *To the Queen* ii 17
   careful *b* of our tender years Trembled   *Lover's Tale* i 222
   Holding his golden *b* in his arms,   „ iv 89
Burthen (refrain)   (*See also* **Ballad-Burthen**)   Again they shriek'd the *b*—' Him !'   *Edwin Morris* 123
   As tho' it were the *b* of a song,   *Enoch Arden* 797
   Again and like a *b*, ' Him or death.'   *Lancelot and E.* 903
Bury   You'll *b* me, my mother, just beneath   *May Queen, N. Y's. E.* 29
   b me beside the gate, And cut this epitaph   *Princess* ii 206
   B the Great Duke With an empire's   *Ode on Well.* 1
   Let us *b* the Great Duke To the noise   „ 3
   I will *b* myself in myself,   *Maud I* i 76
   have sworn to *b* All this dead body of hate,   „ xix 96
   They cannot even *b* a man ;   „ *II* v 22
   some kind heart will come To *b* me, *b* me Deeper,   „ 103
   when an' wheere to *b* his boane.   *Owd Roä* 8
Burying   Driving, hurrying, marrying, *b*,   *Maud II* v 12
Bush   (*See also* **Myrrh-bush, Rose-bush**)   rushes and bowers of rose-blowing *b*'es,   *Leonine Eleg.* 3
   girls all kiss'd Beneath the sacred *b*   *The Epic* 3
   ' Hear how the *b*'es echo !   *Gardener's D.* 98
   Holding the *b*, to fix it back,   „ 127
   What ?—that the *b* were leafless ?   *Lucretius* 206
   in the *b* beside me chirrupt the nightingale.   *Grandmother* 40
   Or underneath the barren *b*   *In Mem.* xci 3
   He dragg'd his eyebrow *b*'es down,   *Merlin and V.* 807
   Above the *b*'es, gilden-peakt :   *Pelleas and E.* 429
   lest an arrow from the *b* Should leave me   *Last Tournament* 535
   With falling brook or blossom'd *b*—   *Lover's Tale* i 405
   sprang without leaf or a thorn from the *b* ;   *V. of Maeldune* 44
   sick For shadow—not one *b* was near—   *Tiresias* 36
   from the *b* we both had set—   *Happy* 102
   low *b*'es dip their twigs in frost,   *Prog. of Spring* 51
Bush-bearded   huge *b-b* Barons heaved and blew,   *Princess* v 21
Bush'd   So *b* about it is with gloom,   *Balin and Balan* 95
Business   her *b* often call'd her from it,   *Enoch Arden* 264
   Two in the tangled *b* of the world,   *Princess* ii 174
Buss   *B* me, thou rough sketch of man,   *Vision of Sin* 189
Buss'd   nor *b* the milking-maid.   *Princess* v 222
Bust   show'd the house, Greek, set with *b*'s :   „ *Pro.* 11
   There stood a *b* of Pallas for a sign,   „ i 222
Busted   *See* **Full-busted**
Busying   *B* themselves about the flowerage   *Aylmer's Field* 203
Butcher'd   or *b* for all that we knew—   *Def. of Lucknow* 91
Butler   Here sits the *B* with a flask   *Day-Dm., Sleep. P.* 25
   The *b* drank, the steward scrawl'd,   *Revival* 10
Butt (cask)   woman like a *b*, and harsh as crabs.   *Walk. to the Mail* 49
   drew, from *b*'s of water on the slope,   *Princess, Pro.* 60
   straddling on the *b*'s While the wine   *Guinevere* 268
Butt (target)   Look to your *b*'s, and take good aims !   *Riflemen form !* 16
Butt (verb)   Beholding how ye *b* against my wish,   *Geraint and E.* 677
   b each other here, like brainless bulls,   *Balin and Balan* 578
   cow shall *b* the ' Lion passant '   *Locksley H., Sixty* 248
Butted   *b* his rough brother-brute For lust   *Lucretius* 197
   b each other with clashing of bells,   *V. of Maeldune* 108
   bruised and *b* with the shuddering War-thunder   *Tiresias* 99

Butter   *B* an' heggs—yis—yis.   *Village Wife* 2
   B I warrants be prime,   „ 3
   But I sarved 'em wi' an' heggs   „ 114
   An' I niver puts saäme i' *my b*,   „ 119
Butter-bump (bittern)   Moäst loike a *b-b*, for I 'eärd 'um   *N. Farmer, O. S.* 31
Butterfly   Hast thou heard the *butterflies*   *Adeline* 28
   flutter'd round her lip Like a golden *b* ;   *Talking Oak* 220
Buttoned   *See* **Close-buttoned**
Buy   *B* goods and stores—set Annie forth   *Enoch Arden* 138
   b strange shares in some Peruvian mine.   *Sea Dreams* 15
   Bought ? what is it he cannot *b* ?   *Maud I* x 32
   Go to the town and *b* us flesh   *Marr. of Geraint* 372
   scarce a coin to *b* a meal withal,   *Columbus* 169
Buying   sold her wares for less Than what she gave in *b*   *Enoch Arden* 256
Buzz   It *b*'es fiercely round the point ;   *Merlin and V.* 432
   vermin voices here May *b* so loud—   *Lancelot and E.* 139
   shake off the bee that *b*'es at us ;   „ 785
Buzzard-clock (Cockchafer)   bummin' awaäy loike a *b-c*   *N. Farmer, O. S.* 33
Buzz'd   palace bang'd, and *b* and clackt,   *Day-Dm., Revival* 14
   dances broke and *b* in knots of talk ;   *Princess* i 133
   b abroad About the maid of Astolat,   *Lancelot and E.* 722
Buzzing   (*See also* **Bummin'**)   And *b*'s of the honied hours.   *In Mem.* lxxxix 52
By-and-by   I will show it you *b-a-b*.   *Bandit's Death* 8
Bygones   trim our sails, and let old *b* be,   *Princess* iv 69
   ' Let *b* be !'   ' *B* !   *First Quarrel* 67
   ' *B-g* ma' be come-agains ;   „ 69
By-lane   Till the filthy *b-l* rings to the yell   *Maud I* i 38
Byre (cow-house)   Then thorpe and *b* arose in fire,   *The Victim* 3
Byway   where this *b* joins The turnpike ?   *Walk. to the Mail* 4
Byword   fatal *b* of all years to come,   *Godiva* 67

C

Caäke (cake)   Doänt maäke thysen sick wi' the *c*.   *Owd Roä* 34
Cabin   all day long till Enoch's last at home, Shaking their pretty *c*,   *Enoch Arden* 173
   And down in the *c* were we,   *The Wreck* 89
   lay like the dead by the dead on the *c* floor,   „ 112
   Call'd from her *c* an' 'ould her to come away   *Tomorrow* 20
Cabin'd   Be *c* up in words and syllables,   *Lover's Tale* i 480
Cabinet   And moving toward a cedarn *c*,   *Marr. of Geraint* 136
Cabin-window   I see the *c-w* bright ;   *In Mem.* x 3
Cackle   With *c* and with clatter.   *The Goose* 12
   rustic *c* of your bourg The murmur of the world !   *Marr. of Geraint* 276
   The *c* of the unborn about the grave,   *Merlin and V.* 507
Cackled   It clack'd and *c* louder.   *The Goose* 24
Cadence   a hand, a foot Lessening in perfect *c*,   *Walk. to the Mail* 55
   in mimic *c* answer'd James—   *Golden Year* 53
   but when the preacher's *c* flow'd   *Aylmer's Field* 729
   In clanging *c* jangling peal on peal—   *Lover's Tale* iii 229
Cadmean   sprang No dragon warriors from *C* teeth,   *Lucretius* 13
Cadmus   Our *C*, out of whom thou art,   *Tiresias* 13
   for I loathe The seed of *C*—   „ 117
   Thou, one of these, the race of *C*—   „ 134
Caer-Eryri   On *C-E's* highest found the King,   *Gareth and L.* 500
Caerleon   Held court at old *C* upon Usk.   *Marr. of Geraint* 146
   When late I left *C*, our great Queen,   „ 781
   And all that week was old *C* gay,   „ 837
   longer time Than at *C* the full-tided Usk,   *Geraint and E.* 116
   they past With Arthur to *C* upon Usk.   „ 946
   Dost thou remember at *C* once—A year ago—   *Balin and Balan* 503
   By the great tower—*C* upon Usk—   „ 506
   Who never sawest *C* upon Usk—   „ 570
   dealt him at Caerlyle ; That at *C* ; this at Camelot ;   *Lancelot and E.* 23
   And at *C* had he help'd his lord,   „ 297
   A minstrel of *C* by strong storm   *Merlin and V.* 9

Caerleon (*continued*) as he sat In hall at old *C*, the
    high doors   *Pelleas and E.* 3
    to find *C* and the King, had felt the sun   ,,   22
    to tilt against the knights There at *C*,   ,,   66
    but will ye to *C*? I Go likewise: ,,   106
    when they reach'd *C*, ere they past to lodging,   ,,   125
    Then at *C* for a space—her look Bright   ,,   176
Caerlyle this dealt him at *C*; That at Caerleon ;   *Lancelot and E.* 22
Cæsar tame and tutor with mine eye That dull cold-
    blooded *C*.   *D. of F. Women* 139
    Roman legions here again, And *C's* eagle: *Com. of Arthur* 35
    for whose love the Roman *C* first Invaded
    Britain,   *Marr. of Geraint* 745
    Rome of *C*, Rome of Peter,   *Locksley H., Sixty* 88
    fallen every purple *C's* dome—   *To Virgil* 30
    Lightning may shrivel the laurel of *C*,   *Parnassus* 4
Cage (s) Lay silent in the muffled *c* of life :   *Princess vii* 47
    The linnet born within the *c*,   *In Mem. xxvii* 3
    I have broke their *c*, no gilded one,   *Sir J. Oldcastle* 3
    I took it, he made it a *c*,   *The Wreck* 83
    the narrower The *c*, the more their fury.   *Akbar's Dream* 51
Cage (verb) Ye *c* a buxom captive here and there.   *Merlin and V.* 542
Caged *See* **New-caged, Newly-caged**
Cageling as the *c* newly-flown returns,   ,,   901
Caiaphas-Arundel These Pharisees, this *C-A*   *Sir J. Oldcastle* 179
Cain lust of gain, in the spirit of *C*,   *Maud I i* 23
    Daughter of the seed of *C*,   *Forlorn* 39
    And set a crueller mark than *C's* on him,   *Happy* 18
Cairn And cleaves to *c* and cromlech still ;   *To the Queen ii* 41
Cairn'd And the *c* mountain: was a shadow,   *Merlin and V.* 638
Caitiff (adj.) bandit earls, and *c* knights,   *Marr. of Geraint* 35
    I will tell him all their *c* talk ;   *Geraint and E.* 66
Caitiff (s) hand striking great blows At *c's*   *Marr. of Geraint* 96
    I would track this *c* to his hold,   ,,   415
    In shadow, waiting for them, *c's* all ;   *Geraint and E.* 58
    The *c's* !' 'Nay,' said Pelleas, but forbear ;   *Pelleas and E.* 280
    As let these *c's* on thee work their will ?'   ,,   323
Cajole and juggle, and lie and *c*,   *Charity* 29
Cake (*See also* **Caäke**) brought sweet *c's* to make
    them cheer,   *Marr. of Geraint* 388
    'Have I not earn'd my *c* in baking of it ?   *Gareth and L.* 575
Calaber (Quintus) *See* **Quintus Calaber**
Calamity Where'er I came I brought *c*.'   *D. of F. Women* 96
    His heart foreshadowing all *c*,   *Enoch Arden* 683
    Nor all *C's* hughest waves confound,   *Will* 5
    That a *c* hard to be borne ?   *Maud I xiii* 3
Calculated mind Mine ; worse, cold, *c*.   *Romney's R.* 152
Calculation Abhorrent of a *c* crost,   *Enoch Arden* 473
Calendar'd names Are register'd and *c* for saints.   *St. S. Stylites* 132
Calf (of the leg) proxy-wedded with a bootless *c*   *Princess i* 34
Calf (young of the cow) *See* **Cauf**
Caliphat I came upon the great Pavilion of the *C*.   *Arabian Nights* 114
Call (s) And answers to his mother's *c's*   *Supp. Confessions* 159
    Hope at Beauty's *c* would perch and stand,   *Caress'd or chidden* 3
    At length I saw a lady within *c*,   *D. of F. Women* 85
    Whistle back the parrot's *c*,   *Locksley Hall* 171
    She answer'd to my *c*,   *Will Water.* 106
    When they answer to his *c*,   *L. of Burleigh* 50
    a stable wench Came running at the *c*,   *Princess i* 227
    A martial song like a trumpet's *c* !   *Maud I v* 5
    But heard the *c*, and came :   *Com. of Arthur* 47
    Then at his *c*, 'O daughters of the Dawn,   *Gareth and L.* 923
    yet I say the bird That will not hear my *c*,   *Lover's Tale iv* 160
    An' Parson as hesn't the *c*, nor the mooney,   *Village Wife* 91
    av the bird 'ud come to me *c*,   *Tomorrow* 45
    we couldn't ha' 'eärd tha *c*,   *Owd Roä* 49
    in his heart he cried, 'The *c* of God !'   *St. Telemachus* 27
    muttering to himself, 'The *c* of God'   ,,   42
    And one clear *c* for me !   *Crossing the Bar* 2
Call (verb) *And thro' wild March the throstle c's*,   *To the Queen* 14
    Yet, my God, Whom *c* I Idol ?   *Supp. Confessions* 180
    Day and night to the billow the fountain *c's* :   *Sea-Fairies* 9
    She saw me fight, she heard me *c*,   *Oriana* 32
    We would *c* aloud in the dreamy dells,   *The Merman* 25
    C to each other and whoop and cry   ,,   26

Call (verb) (*continued*) if any came near I would *c*,
    and shriek,   *The Mermaid* 38
    O will she answer if I *c*?   *Miller's D.* 118
    You must wake and *c* me early, *c* me early, (repeat) *May Queen* 1, 41
    If you do not *c* me loud when the day begins to
    break ;   ,,   10
    They *c* me cruel-hearted, but I care not what
    they say,   ,,   19
    IF you're waking *c* me early, *c* me early,
    (repeat)   *May Queen, N. Y's. E.* 1, 52
    c me before the day is born.   ,,   49
    in the wild March-morning I heard the angels *c* ; *May Queen, Con.* 25
    in the wild March-morning I heard them *c* my soul.   ,,   28
    I am that Rosamond, whom men *c* fair,   *D. of F. Women* 251
    for themselves and those who *c* them friend ?   *M. d'Arthur* 253
    Or change a word with her he *c's* his wife,   *Dora* 44
    Father !—if you let me *c* you so—   ,,   140
    'They *c* me what they will,' he said :   *Golden Year* 14
    as of old, the curlews *c*,   *Locksley Hall* 3
    Hark, my merry comrades *c* me,   ,,   3
    Yet say the neighbours when they *c*,   *Amphion* 5
    guest, Shall *c* thee from the boxes.   *Will Water.* 240
    But when he *c's*, and thou shalt cease   ,,   241
    What do they *c* you ?' 'Katie.'   *The Brook* 211
    the voice that *c's* Doom upon kings,   *Aylmer's Field* 741
    do not *c* him, love, Before you prove him,   *Sea Dreams* 170
    From childly wont and ancient use I *c*—   *Lucretius* 209
    I—would *c* them masterpieces ?   *Princess i* 145
    Brutus of my kind ? Him you *c* great: ,, *ii* 285
    Should I not *c* her wise, who made me wise ?   ,,   396
    c down from Heaven A blessing on her labours   ,,   478
    She *c's* her plagiarist ;   ,, *iii* 94
    'There sinks the nebulous star we *c* the Sun,   ,, *iv* 19
    And *c* her Ida, tho' I knew her not, And *c* her sweet,
    as if in irony, And *c* her hard and cold which
    seem'd a truth :   ,, *vii* 96
    the children *c*, and I Thy shepherd pipe,   ,,   217
    again the people *C* it but a weed.   *The Flower* 24
    c us Britain's barbarous populaces,   *Boädicea* 7
    and *c* To what I feel is Lord of all,   *In Mem. lv* 18
    To clap their cheeks, to *c* them mine.   *In Mem. lxxxiv* 18
    c The spirits from their golden day,   ,, *xciv* 5
    To whom a thousand memories *c*,   ,, *cxi* 10
    But trust that those we *c* the dead   ,, *cxviii* 5
    you may *c* it a little too ripe,   *Maud I ii* 9
    Whatever they *c* him, what care I,   ,, *x* 64
    Who shall *c* me ungentle, unfair,   ,, *xiii* 14
    Scarcely, now, would I *c* him a cheat ;   ,,   29
    That heard me softly *c*,   ,, *II iv* 76
    Merlin's master (so they *c* him) Bleys,   *Com. of Arthur* 153
    those who hate him in their hearts, *C* him baseborn,   ,,   180
    And there was none to *c* to but himself.   ,,   202
    Than make him knight because men *c* him
    king.   *Gareth and L.* 420
    Look therefore when he *c's* for this in hall,   ,,   583
    Proud in their fantasy *c* themselves the Day,   ,,   633
    But that I heard thee *c* thyself a knave,—   ,,   1163
    O damsel, be you wise To *c* him shamed,   ,,   1260
    And tho' I heard him *c* you fairest fair,   *Marr. of Geraint* 720
    his own ear had heard *C* herself false :   *Geraint and E.* 114
    C for the woman of the house,'   ,,   263
    bad the host *C* in what men soever were his friends,   ,,   286
    Yet fear me not : I *c* mine own self wild,   ,,   311
    For, *c* it lovers' quarrels, yet I know   ,,   324
    C the host and bid him bring Charger and palfrey.'   ,,   400
    whom her ladies loved to *c* Enid the Fair,   ,,   962
    The people *c* you prophet: let it be: *Merlin and V.* 317
    she will *c* That three-days-long presageful gloom   ,,   319
    I *c* it,—well, I will not *c* it vice :   ,,   368
    Know well that Envy *c's* you Devil's son,   ,,   467
    And then did Envy *c* me Devil's son :   ,,   497
    Master, shall we *c* him overquick To crop   ,,   724
    Could *c* him (were it not for womanhood)   ,,   786
    Could *c* him the main cause of all their crime ;   ,,   788
    For fear our people *c* you lily maid In earnest,   *Lancelot and E.* 386

Call (verb) (*continued*)

'Me you *c* great: mine is the firmer seat,	*Lancelot and E.* 446
'Father, you *c* me wilful, and the fault Is yours	,, 750
Would *c* her friend and sister, sweet Elaine,	,, 865
I needs must follow death, who *c's* for me ; *C* and I follow, I follow! let me die.'	,, 1017
I know not what you *c* the highest ;	,, 1080
and bid *c* the ghostly man Hither,	,, 1099
To this I *c* my friends in testimony,	,, 1299
Art thou not he whom men *c* light-of-love?'	*Pelleas and E.* 361
We *c* the harp of Arthur in heaven?'	*Last Tournament* 333
strike against the man they *c* My sister's son—	*Guinevere* 572
how dare I *c* him mine? The shadow of another	,, 617
Nor shun to *c* me sister, dwell with you ;	,, 676
But *c* not thou this traitor of my house	*Pass. of Arthur* 155
Both for themselves and those who *c* them friend?	,, 421
we came To what our people *c* 'The Hill of Woe.'	*Lover's Tale i* 374
Why should he *c* me to-night,	*Rizpah* 3
and you, will you *c* it a theft?—	,, 52
he used but to *c* in the dark,	,, 83
he *c's* to me now from the church	,, 84
Good-night. I am going. He *c's*.	,, 86
An' Doctor 'e *c's* o' Sunday	*North. Cobbler* 87
Their favourite—which I *c* 'The Tables Turned.'	*Sisters (E. and E.)* 3
An' 'e *c's* fur 'is son,	*Village Wife* 62
'but then if I *c* to the Lord,	*In the Child. Hosp.* 53
if what we *c* The spirit flash not all at once	*Ded. Poem Prin. Alice* 4
Without a roof that I can *c* mine own,	*Columbus* 168
the waters—you hear them *c*!	*Despair* 47
c on that Infinite Love that has served us	,, 95
set The lamps alight, and *c* For golden music,	*Ancient Sage* 196
My Edwin loved to *c* us then	*The Flight* 80
What did they *c* her, yer Honour?	*Tomorrow* 4
I *c's* 'em arter the fellers	*Spinster's S's.* 4
while I heard the curlews *c*,	*Locksley H., Sixty* 3
curse your fellow-victim? *c* him dotard in your rage	,, 9
used to *c* the very flowers Sisters, brothers—	,, 101
Dead the new astronomy *c's* her . . .	,, 175
Britain's myriad voices *c*,	*Open. I. and C. Exhib.* 35
C your poor to regale with you,	*On Jub. Q. Victoria* 30
you used to *c* me once The lonely maiden-Princess	*The Ring* 64
I Would *c* thro' this 'Io t'amo'	,, 234
There! I heard Our cuckoo *c*.	*To Mary Boyle* 6
Down to the haven, *C* your companions,	*Merlin and the G.* 125
the palm *C* to the cypress 'I alone am fair'?	*Akbar's Dream* 38
Teacher who *c's* to them 'Set yourselves free!'	*Kapiolani* 2
C me not so often back,	*Silent Voices* 3
C me rather, silent voices,	,, 7

Call'd

We are *c*—we must go.	*All Things will Die* 20
Old voices *c* her from without.	*Mariana* 68
'A merry boy they *c* him then,	*Two Voices* 322
Far-off the torrent *c* me from the cleft :	*Œnone* 54
Which men *c* Aulis in those iron years :	*D. of F. Women* 106
And *c* him by his name, complaining loud,	*M. d'Arthur* 210
C to me from the years to come,	*Gardener's D.* 180
came a day When Allan *c* his son, and said,	*Dora* 10
bells were ringing, Allan *c* His niece and said :	,, 41
c him Crichton, for he seem'd All-perfect,	*Edwin Morris* 21
her business often *c* her from it,	*Enoch Arden* 264
play'd with him And *c* him, Father Philip.	,, 354
For Father Philip (as they *c* him) too :	,, 365
'After the Lord has *c* me she shall know,	,, 810
He *c* aloud for Miriam Lane and said	,, 836
and *c* old Philip out To show the farm :	*The Brook* 120
C to the bar, but ever *c* away	*Aylmer's Field* 59
C all her vital spirits into each ear To listen :	,, 201
the great Sicilian *c* Calliope to grace his golden verse	*Lucretius* 93
enter'd an old hostel, *c* mine host To council,	*Princess i* 173
Above an entry : riding in, we *c* ;	,, 225
the chapel bells *C* us : we left the walks ;	,, ii 471
Girl after girl was *c* to trial :	,, iv 228
she *c* For Psyche's child to cast it from the doors ;	,, 237

Call'd (*continued*)

stretch'd her arms and *c* Across the tumult	*Princess iv* 496
pique at what she *c* The raillery, or grotesque,	,, 587
C him worthy to be loved,	,, vi 6
prest Their hands, and *c* them dear deliverers,	,, 92
or *c* On flying Time from all their silver tongues—	,, vii 104
They *c* me in the public squares	*In Mem. lxix* 11
They *c* me fool, they *c* me child :	,, 13
and Arthur *c* to stay the brands	*Com. of Arthur* 120
and *c* A hoary man, his chamberlain,	,, 144
And one—they *c* her Fame ; and one,—	*Gareth and L.* 114
they *c* To Gareth, 'Lord, the gateway is alive.'	,, 234
Sir Gareth *c* from where he rose,	,, 645
Of any save of him whom I *c*—	,, 859
Why came ye not, when *c*? and wherefore now Come ye, not *c*?	,, 1247
And *c* her like that maiden in the tale,	*Marr. of Geraint* 742
c For Enid, and when Yniol made report	,, 755
Or hasty judger would have *c* her guilt,	*Geraint and E.* 433
whom his shaking vassals *c* the Bull,	,, 439
And *c* for flesh and wine to feed his spears.	,, 601
They *c* him the great Prince and man of men.	,, 961
wherefore Arthur *c* His treasurer,	*Balin and Balan* 4
The people *c* him Wizard ;	*Merlin and V.* 170
And *c* herself a gilded summer fly	,, 258
So Vivien *c* herself, But rather seem'd	,, 261
Who *c* her what he *c* her—	,, 864
C her to shelter in the hollow oak,	,, 894
Since, if I be what I am grossly *c*,	,, 915
And *c* him dear protector in her fright,	,, 946
she *c* him lord and liege, Her seer, her bard,	,, 953
Lancelot Would, tho' he *c* his wound a little hurt	*Lancelot and E.* 852
Approaching thro' the darkness, *c* ;	,, 1000
And *c* her song 'The Song of Love and Death,'	,, 1005
and *c* The father, and all three in hurry	,, 1023
I, sometime *c* the maid of Astolat,	,, 1273
Whom Arthur and his knighthood *c* The Pure,	*Holy Grail* 3
but some *C* him a son of Lancelot,	,, 144
And Merlin *c* it 'The Siege perilous,'	,, 172
Shrilling along the hall to Arthur, *c*,	,, 289
Across the forest *c* of Dean, to find Caerleon	*Pelleas and E.* 21
And this was *c* 'The Tournament of Youth :'	,, 158
She *c* them, saying, 'There he watches yet,	,, 262
he *c*, 'I strike upon thy side—The cailiffs!'	,, 279
the poor Pelleas whom she *c* her fool?	,, 474
rider, who *c* out from the dark field,	,, 575
And when I *c* upon thy name as one	*Last Tournament* 73
By these in earnest those in mockery *c*	,, 135
'Isolt Of the white hands' they *c* her :	,, 398
Who *c* the false son of Gorloïs :	*Guinevere* 288
he, the King, *C* me polluted ;	,, 620
His hope he *c* it ; but he never mocks,	,, 632
Arthur woke and *c*, 'Who spake? A dream.	*Pass. of Arthur* 45
And *c* him by his name, complaining loud,	,, 378
'let this be *c* henceforth The Hill of Hope ;'	*Lover's Tale i* 461
I wore a double name : she *c* me brother :	,, 741
he *c* me his own little wife ;	*First Quarrel* 10
he *c* in the dark to me year after year—	*Rizpah* 47
one of those about her knowing me *C* me to join them ;	*Sisters (E. and E.)* 123
She bore a child, whom reverently we *c* Edith ;	,, 268
An' es for Miss Annie es *c* me afoor	*Village Wife* 105
OUR doctor had *c* in another,	*In the Child. Hosp.* 1
Softly she *c* from her cot to the next,	,, 46
how many—thirty-nine—*C* it revellion—	*Sir J. Oldcastle* 4
I changed the name ; San Salvador I *c* it ;	*Columbus* 76
BROOKS, for they *c* you so that knew you best,	*To W. H. Brookfield* 1
standing, shouted, and Pallas far away *C* ;	*Achilles over the T.* 18
our trembling fathers *c* The God's own son.	*Tiresias* 16
and he *c* to me 'Kiss me !' and there—	*The Wreck* 104
On me, when boy, there came what then I *c*,	*Ancient Sage* 217
They *c* her Molly Magee.	*Tomorrow* 4
C from her cabin an' tould her to come	,, 20

Call'd (*continued*) Thin a slip of a gossoon *c*,
  Tomorrow 78
c me es pretty es ony lass i' the Shere ;
  Spinster's S's. 13
poet *c* the Bringer home of all good things.
  Locksley H., Sixty 185
he *c* ' Left wheel into line ! '
  Heavy Brigade 6
They *c* her ' Reverence ' here upon earth,
  Dead Prophet 27
Then I *c* out Roä, Roä, Roä,
  Owd Roä 91
I raised her, *c* her ' Muriel,
  The Ring 449
and *c* arose, and, slowly plunging down
c ' Forbear In the great name of Him who
  died for men,
  St. Telemachus 28
     62
Alla *c* In old Irán the Sun of Love ?
  Akbar's Dream "
An' ya *c* 'im a clown, ya did,
  Church-Warden, etc. 30
C on the Power adored by the Christian,
  Kapiolani 32
Callest *C* thou that thing a leg ?
  Vision of Sin 89
Callin o' use to be *c* 'im Roä, Roä, Roä,
  Owd Roä 1
Calling (*See also* **A-callin'**, **Callin'**) Hark !
  death is *c* While I speak
  All Things will Die 28
C thyself a little lower ' Than angels.
  Two Voices 198
To hear the dewy echoes *c* From cave to cave
  Lotos-Eaters, C. S. 94
Then *c* down a blessing on his head
  Enoch Arden 327
And *c*, here and there, about the wood.
  " 383
Maud, Maud, They were crying and *c*,
  Maud I xii 4
Were crying and *c* to her, Where is Maud,
  " 26
Some *c* Arthur born of Gorloïs, Others of Anton ?
  Com. of Arthur 170
c two That still had tended on him
  Gareth and L. 178
and *c* ' Damsel, is this he, The champion
  " 915
And chafing his pale hands, and *c* to him.
  Geraint and E. 582
And chafing his faint hands, and *c* to him ;
  " 585
Moaning and *c* out of other lands,
  Merlin and V. 962
But he pursued her, *c* ' Stay a little !
  Lancelot and E. 683
the King Look'd up, *c* aloud, ' Lo, there !
  Holy Grail 219
named us each by name, *C* ' God speed ! '
  " 352
And *c* me the greatest of all knights,
  " 595
Then *c* her three knights, she charged them,
  Pelleas and E. 219
C me thy white hind, and saying to me
  Last Tournament 569
rollers on the cliffs Clash'd, *c* to each other,
  Lover's Tale i 58
And voices in the distance *c* to me
  ii 118
cuckoo of a joyless June Is *c* out of doors :
  Pref. Poem Broth. S. 4
cuckoo of a worse July Is *c* thro' the dark :
  " 12
Are *c* to each other thro' a dawn
  The Ring 37
all Stood round it, hush'd, or *c* on his name.
  Death of Œnone 66
very well just now to be *c* me darling and sweet,
  Charity 7
Calling (s) There came so loud a *c* of the sea,
  Enoch Arden 910
Calliope called *C* to grace his golden verse—
  Lucretius 94
Calm (adj.) reign the world's great bridals, chaste and *c* :
  Princess vii 294
C is the morn without a sound, *C* as to suit a
  calmer grief,
  In Mem. xi 1
if calm at all, If any calm, a *c* despair :
  " 16
His eye was *c*, and suddenly she took
  Merlin and V. 854
' May her life be as blissfully *c*,
  The Wreck 139
The night was *c*, the morn is *c*,
  The Flight 10
Calm (s) The summer *c* of golden charity,
  Isabel 8
No tranced summer *c* is thine,
  Madeline 2
My shallop through the star-strown *c*,
  Arabian Nights 36
I cannot hide that some have striven, Achieving *c*,
  Two Voices 209
' There is no joy but *c* ! '
  Lotos-Eaters, C. S. 23
lower down The bay was oily *c* ;
  Audley Court 86
star of phosphorescence in the *c*,
  " 87
Then follow'd *c*'s, and then winds variable,
  Enoch Arden 545
That mock'd him with returning *c*,
  Lucretius 25
fain Would follow, center'd in eternal *c*.
  " 79
to mar Their sacred everlasting *c* !
  " 110
Not all so fine, nor so divine a *c*,
  " 111
Put on more *c* and added suppliantly :
  Princess vi 215
C and deep peace on this high wold,
  In Mem. xi 5
C and still light on yon great plain
  " 9
C and deep peace in this wide air,
  " 13
if *c* at all, If any *c*, a calm despair :
  " 15
C on the seas, and silver sleep,
  " 17
And dead *c* in that noble breast
  " 19
The touch of change in *c* or storm ;
  " xvi 6
And *c* that let the tapers burn Unwavering :
  " xcv 5
And tracts of *c* from tempest made,
  In Mem. cxii 14
And moulded in colossal *c*.
  " Con. 16
Long have I sigh'd for a *c* :
  Maud I ii 1

Calm (s) (*continued*) And presently thereafter
  follow'd *c*,
  Com. of Arthur 391
whom she answer'd with all *c*.
  Lancelot and E. 997
sway and whirl Of the storm dropt to windless *c*,
  Lover's Tale ii 207
Calming *C* itself to the long-wish'd-for end,
  Maud I xviii 5
Calpe From *C* unto Caucasus they sung,
  The Poet 15
Calumet celts and *c*'s, Claymore and snowshoe,
  Princess, Pro. 18
Calumny Sweeter tones than *c* ?
  A Dirge 17
Calve *See* **Cauve**
Cama throne of Indian *C* slowly sail'd
  Palace of Art 115
Cambalu breach'd the belting wall of *C*,
  Columbus 108
Came (*See also* **Coom'd**, **Kem**) From the dark fen
  the oxen's low *C* to her :
  Mariana 29
In marvel whence that glory *c* Upon me,
  Arabian Nights 94
I *c* upon the great Pavilion of the Caliphat.
  " 113
It would fall to the ground if you *c* in.
  Poet's Mind 23
It would shrink to the earth if you *c* in.
  " 37
But if any *c* near I would call,
  The Mermaid 38
Fancy *c* and at her pillow sat,
  Caress'd or chidden 5
A moment *c* the tenderness of tears,
  The form, the form 9
C two young lovers lately wed ;
  L. of Shalott ii 34
The sun *c* dazzling thro' the leaves,
  " iii 3
Down she *c* and found a boat Beneath a willow
  " iv 6
Out upon the wharfs they *c*,
  " 42
There *c* a sound as of the sea ;
  Mariana in the S. 86
C out clear plates of sapphire mail.
  Two Voices 12
' Or if thro' lower lives I *c*—
  " 364
I spoke, but answer *c* there none :
  " 425
I *c* and sat Below the chestnuts,
  Miller's D. 59
That went and *c* a thousand times.
  " 72
From off the wold I *c*, and lay
  " 111
From my swift blood that went and *c*
  Fatima 16
Hither *c* at noon Mournful Œnone,
  Œnone 15
C up from reedy Simois all alone.
  " 52
Went forth to embrace him coming ere he *c*.
  " 63
river of speech *C* down upon my heart.
  " 69
Then to the bower they *c*, Naked they *c*
  " 94
They *c*, they cut away my tallest pines,
  " 208
in the dark morn The panther's roar *c* muffled,
  " 214
The Abominable, that uninvited *c*,
  " 224
On corpses three-months-old at noon she *c*,
  Palace of Art 243
Too proud to care from whence I *c*.
  L. C. V. de Vere 12
As I *c* up the valley whom think ye should I see,
  May Queen 13
Till Charles's Wain *c* out above the tall white
  chimney-tops.
  May Queen, N. Y's. E. 12
To die before the snowdrop *c*,
  May Queen, Con. 4
There *c* a sweeter token when the night
  " 22
up the valley *c* a swell of music on the wind.
  " 32
And up the valley *c* again the music
  " 36
once again it *c*, and close beside the window-bars,
  " 39
In the afternoon they *c* unto a land
  Lotos-Eaters 3
mild-eyed melancholy Lotos-eaters *c*.
  " 27
Where'er I *c* I brought calamity.'
  D. of F. Women 95
Strength *c* to me that equall'd my desire.
  " 230
You *c* to us so readily,
  D. of the O. Year 7
mighty voice *C* rolling on the wind.
  Of old sat Freedom 8
(for so we held it then), What *c* of that ?'
  The Epic 27
C on the shining levels of the lake.
  M. d'Arthur 51
And to the barge they *c*.
  " 205
Then *c* a bark that, blowing forward,
  " Ep. 21
Artist he than all, *C*, drew your pencil from you,
  Gardener's D. 26
C voices of the well-contented doves.
  " 89
some sweet answer, tho' no answer *c*,
  " 159
little words, More musical than ever *c*
  " 233
while I mused *c* Memory with sad eyes,
  " 243
farewells—Of that which *c* between,
  " 252
Then there *c* a day When Allan call'd his son,
  Dora 9
then distresses *c* on him ;
  " 49
Dora *c* and said : ' I have obey'd my uncle
  " 58
all thro' me This evil *c* on William at the first.
  " 61
Far off the farmer *c* into the field
  " 74
when the morrow *c*, she rose and took The child
  " 80
c and said : ' Where were you yesterday ?
  " 87
the boy's cry *c* to her from the field,
  " 104
Remembering the day when first she *c*,
  " 106

Came (*continued*) when she *c* From barren deeps to conquer
all with love ;   *Princess vii* 163
when we ceased There *c* a minute's pause,   ,, *Con.* 4
C thro' the jaws of Death,   *Light Brigade* 46
Remember how we *c* at last To Como ;   *The Daisy* 69
Up there *c* a flower,   *The Flower* 3
at last it seem'd that an answer *c*.   *The Victim* 24
'I murmur'd, as I *c* along,   *In Mem. xxxiii* 7
The path we *c* by, thorn and flower,   ,, *xxxvii* 21
c In whispers of the beauteous world.   ,, *xlvi* 2
This truth *c* borne with bier and pall,   ,, *lxxix* 11
But if they *c* who past away,   ,, *lxxxv* 1
c on that which is, and caught The deep pulsations   ,, *xc* 13
c at length To find a stronger faith his own ;   ,, *xcv* 39
And out of darkness *c* the hands   ,, *xcvi* 16
they went and *c*, Remade the blood   ,, *cxxiv* 23
if an enemy's fleet *c* yonder round the hill,   ,, *Con.* 10
when the morning *c* In a cloud, it faded,   *Maud I i* 49
C out of her pitying womanhood,   ,, *vi* 20
She *c* to the village church,   ,, 64
Last week *c* one to the county town,   ,, *viii* 1
However she *c* to be so allied.   ,, *x* 37
snow-limb'd Eve from whom she *c*.   ,, *xiii* 36
Let no one ask me how it *c* to pass ;   ,, *xviii* 28
And at last, when each *c* home,   ,, 49
He *c* with the babe-faced lord ;   ,, *xix* 61
hard mechanic ghost That never *c* from on high   ,, *II i* 13
C glimmering thro' the laurels At the quiet evenfall,   ,, *ii* 35
Everything *c* to be known.   ,, *iv* 77
for he *c* not back From the wilderness,   ,, *v* 51
know not whether he *c* in the Hanover ship,   ,, 53
man was less and less, till Arthur *c*.   ,, 59
wolf and boar and bear *C* night and day,   *Com. of Arthur* 12
But heard the call, and *c*:   ,, 24
when they *c* before him, the King said,   ,, 47
c to Cameliard, With Gawain and young Modred,   ,, 166
I know not whether of himself he *c*,   ,, 243
Why, Gawain, when he *c* With Modred hither   ,, 346
c an ancient man, Long-bearded,   *Gareth and L.* 25
They *c* from out a sacred mountain-cleft   ,, 240
Then *c* a widow crying to the King,   ,, 260
C yet another widow crying to him,   ,, 333
Then *c* Sir Kay, the seneschal, and cried,   ,, 350
Then *c* in hall the messenger of Mark,   ,, 367
suppliant crying *c* With noise of ravage   ,, 384
out of kitchen *c* The thralls in throng,   ,, 436
Out of the smoke he *c*, and so my lance Hold,   ,, 694
'Well that Ye *c*, or else these caitiff rogues   ,, 722
Wherethro' the serpent river coil'd, they *c*.   ,, 819
three fair girls in gilt and rosy raiment *c* :   ,, 906
Then when he *c* upon her, spake 'Methought,   ,, 927
The savour of thy kitchen *c* upon me   ,, 991
damsel *c*, And arm'd him in old arms,   ,, 993
unhappiness Of one who *c* to help thee,   ,, 1114
Why *c* ye not, when call'd ?   ,, 1238
a page Who *c* and went, and still reported   ,, 1247
anon *C* lights and lights, and once again he blew ;   ,, 1338
Remembering when first he *c* on her   *Marr. of Geraint* 140
Before him *c* a forester of Dean,   ,, 148
C quickly flashing thro' the shallow ford   ,, 167
And thither *c* Geraint, and underneath   ,, 241
C forward with the helmet yet in hand   ,, 285
c again with one, A youth,   ,, 385
thither *c* the twain, and when Geraint Beheld her   ,, 539
and errant knights And ladies *c*,   ,, 546
There *c* a clapping as of phantom hands.   ,, 566
and *c* to loathe His crime of traitor,   ,, 593
c A stately queen whose name was Guinevere,   ,, 666
therewithal one *c* and seized on her,   ,, 673
C one with this and laid it in my hand,   ,, 699
I *c* among you here so suddenly,   ,, 794
Remembering how first he *c* on her,   ,, 842
from the place There *c* a fair-hair'd youth,   *Geraint and E.* 201
when the fair-hair'd youth *c* by him, said,   ,, 205

Came (*continued*) *c* upon him, and he sigh'd ;   *Geraint and E.* 249
Crost and *c* near, lifted adoring eyes,   ,, 304
I thought, but that your father *c* between,   ,, 314
Suddenly *c*, and at his side all pale Dismounting,   ,, 510
She rested, and her desolation *c* Upon her,   ,, 518
C riding with a hundred lances up ;   ,, 539
ere he *c*, like one that hails a ship,   ,, 540
out of her there *c* a power upon him ;   ,, 613
Neigh'd with all gladness as they *c*,   ,, 755
C purer pleasure unto mortal kind   ,, 765
o'er her meek eyes *c* a happy mist   ,, 769
And you *c*—But once you *c*,—   ,, 845
thither *c* The King's own leech to look   ,, 922
For whatsoever knight against us *c*   *Balin and Balan* 35
and *c* To learn black magic, and to hate his kind   ,, 126
the great Queen *C* with slow steps,   ,, 245
under open blue *C* on the hoarhead woodman at a
bough   ,, 294
scream of that Wood-devil I *c* to quell !'   ,, 548
a wanton damsel *c*, And sought for Garlon   ,, 609
no quest *c*, but all was joust and play,   *Merlin and V.* 145
turn'd to tyrants when they *c* to power)   ,, 518
They said a light *c* from her when she moved :   ,, 567
and his book *c* down to me.'   ,, 650
C to her old perch back, and settled there.   ,, 903
Her eyes and neck glittering went and *c* ;   ,, 960
How *c* the lily maid by that good shield Of
Lancelot,   *Lancelot and E.* 28
Arthur *c*, and labouring up the pass,   ,, 47
Then *c* an old, dumb, myriad-wrinkled man,   ,, 170
across him *c* a cloud Of melancholy severe,   ,, 324
Past inward, as she *c* from out the tower.   ,, 346
Then *c* on him a sort of sacred fear,   ,, 354
Then *c* the hermit out and bare him in,   ,, 519
C round their great Pendragon, saying   ,, 528
since the knight *C* not to us,   ,, 544
c at last, tho' late, to Astolat :   ,, 618
c The Lord of Astolat out,   ,, 626
One old dame *C* suddenly on the Queen   ,, 730
C on her brother with a happy face   ,, 791
She *c* before Sir Lancelot, for she thought   ,, 908
Then *c* her father, saying in low tones,   ,, 994
c her brethren saying, 'Peace to thee,   ,, 996
the King *C* girt with knights :   ,, 1261
c the fine Gawain and wonder'd at her, And
Lancelot later *c* and mused at her,   ,, 1267
To answer that which *c* :   *Holy Grail* 12
I know That Joseph *c* of old to Glastonbury,   ,, 60
And when she *c* to speak, behold her eyes   ,, 102
touch with hand, Was like that music as it *c* ;   ,, 115
'Then *c* a year of miracle :   ,, 166
'Then on a summer night it *c* to pass,   ,, 179
Had Camelot seen the like, since Arthur *c* ;   ,, 332
to the Gate of the three Queens we *c*,   ,, 358
C like a driving gloom across my mind.   ,, 370
And on the splendour *c*, flashing me blind ;   ,, 413
Open'd his arms to embrace me as he *c*,   ,, 417
I saw not whence it *c*.   ,, 515
return'd To whence I *c*, the gate of Arthur's wars.'   ,, 539
C ye on none but phantoms in your quest,   ,, 562
And now I *c* upon her once again,   ,, 585
c a night Still as the day was loud ;   ,, 682
My madness *c* upon me as of old,   ,, 787
I *c* All in my folly to the naked shore,   ,, 792
But if indeed there *c* a sign from heaven,   ,, 873
out of those to whom the vision *c*   ,, 895
and the sunshine *c* along with him.   *Pelleas and E.* 6
And as he *c* away, The men who met him   ,, 141
strange knights From the four winds *c* in :   ,, 148
out they *c*, But Pelleas overthrew them   ,, 220
Then when he *c* before Ettarre,   ,, 237
from a tiny cave *C* lightening downward,   ,, 426
c the village girls And linger'd talking,   ,, 508
Then a long silence *c* upon the hall,   ,, 609
C Tristram, saying, 'Why skip ye so,   *Last Tournament* 9

Camelot (*continued*) That eat in Arthur's hall at C. *Marr. of Geraint* 432
Adown the crystal dykes at *C* — *Geraint and E.* 470
strange knights Who sit near C at a fountain-side, — *Geraint and E.* 470
'Too high this mount of *C* for me : — *Balin and Balan* 11
Remembering that dark bower at *C*, — ,, 226
But Vivien, into *C* stealing, lodged — *Merlin and V.* 63
In Arthur's arras hall at *C* : — ,, 250
this dealt him at Caerlyle ; That at Caerleon ; this at *C*: — *Lancelot and E.* 23
let proclaim a joust At *C*, — ,, 77
Shall I appear, O Queen, at *C*, — ,, 142
go to joust as one unknown At *C* for the diamond, — ,, 191
To ride to *C* with this noble knight : — ,, 220
knew there lived a knight Not far from *C*, — ,, 402
when they reach'd the lists By *C* in the meadow, — ,, 429
'What news from *C*, lord ? — ,, 620
To *C*, and before the city-gates Came on her brother — ,, 790
His own far blood, which dwelt at *C* ; — ,, 803
helmet in an abbey far away From *C*, — *Holy Grail* 7
o'er the plain that then began To darken under *C*: — ,, 218
For all the sacred mount of *C*, — ,, 227
never yet Had *C* seen the like, since Arthur came ; — ,, 332
O brother had you known our *C*, — ,, 339
Lancelot slowly rode his warhorse back To *C*, — *Pelleas and E.* 584
mock-knight of Arthur's Table Round, At *C*, — *Last Tournament* 3
trumpet-blowings ran on all the ways From *C*, — ,, 53
At *C*, ere the coming of the Queen.' — *Guinevere* 223
And when at last he came to *C*, — ,, 260
And in thy bowers of *C* or of Usk — ,, 503
Walking about the gardens and the halls Of *C*, — *Pass. of Arthur* 189
Shot thro' the lists at *C*, — ,, 392
Clouds and darkness Closed upon *C* ; — *Merlin and the G.* 76
Camest Come not as thou *c* of late, — *Ode to Memory* 8
Whilome thou *c* with the morning mist, (repeat) — ,, 12, 21
friend, who *c* to thy goal So early, — *In Mem. cxiv* 23
but thee, When first thou *c*— — *Holy Grail* 22
can no more, thou *c*, O my child, — *Demeter and P.* 4
Camilla thou and I, *C*, thou and I Were borne — *Lover's Tale i* 53
bore *C* close beneath her beating heart, — ,, 203
What marvel my *C* told me all ? (repeat) — ,, 557, 579
C, my *C*, who was mine No longer in the dearest sense — ,, 586
And as for me, *C*, as for me,— — ,, 764
Sometimes I thought *C* was no more, — ,, ii 69
An hour or two, *C's* travail came Upon her, — ,, iv 127
To bring *C* down before them all. — ,, 285
Camp Thro' the courts, the *c's*, the schools, — *Vision of Sin* 104
And at her head a follower of the *c*, — *Princess v* 60
a murmur ran Thro' all the *c* and inward raced — ,, 111
Back rode we to my father's *c*, — ,, 331
'See that there be no traitors in your *c*: — ,, 425
King, *c* and college turn'd to hollow shows ; — ,, 478
'Follow me, Prince, to the *c*, — *Geraint and E.* 808
when they reach'd the *c* the King himself — ,, 878
Campanili What slender *c* grew By bays, — *The Daisy* 13
Campion *See* **Rose-campion**
Cámulodúne near the colony *C*, — *Boädicea* 5
Lo their colony half-defended ! lo their colony, *C*! — ,, 17
lo the colony *C*, (repeat) — ,, 31, 53
city, and citadel, London, Verulam, *C*. — ,, 86
Can 'Tis but a steward of the *c*, — *Will Water.* 149
truth, that flies the flowing *c*, — ,, 171
'Fill the cup, and fill the *c* : (repeat) — *Vision of Sin* 95, 119, 203
'Fill the *c*, and fill the cup: (repeat) — ,, 131, 167
Cana like him of *C* in Holy Writ, — *Holy Grail* 762
Canada loyal pines of *C* murmur thee, — *W. to Marie Alex.* 19
To *C* whom we love and prize, — *Hands all Round* 19
Canadian *C*, Indian, Australasian, African, — *On Jub. Q. Victoria* 60
Canal The boat-head down a broad *c* — *Arabian Nights* 25
the clear *c* Is rounded to as clear a lake. — ,, 45
Cancel Hours That *c* weal with woe, — *Ancient Sage* 96
Cancell'd Is *c* in the world of sense ?' — *Two Voices* 42
Powers, who wait On noble deeds, *c* a sense misused ; — *Godiva* 72
And *c* nature's best : — *In Mem. lxxii* 20
At length my trance Was *c*, — ,, xcv 44

Cancer Cured lameness, palsies, *c's*. — *St. S. Stylites* 82
Candle an' just as *c's* was lit, — *North. Cobbler* 87
Candle-light and with solemn rites by *c-l*— — *Princess v* 292
Cane court-Galen poised his gilt-head *c*, — ,, i 19
home in the *c's* by the purple tide, — *The Wreck* 71
Your *c*, your palm, tree-fern, bamboo, — *To Ulysses* 36
in the sultry plains About a land of *c's* ; — *Prog. of Spring* 78
Canker (s) As but the *c* of the brain ; — *In Mem. xcii* 3
Canker (verb) No lapse of moons can *c* Love, — ,, xxvi 3
Canker'd *See* **Worm-canker'd**
Canning Or stow'd, when classic *C* died, — *Will Water.* 101
THOU third great *C*, stand among our best — *Epit. on Stratford* 1
Cannon with knobs and wires and vials fired A *c*, — *Princess, Pro.* 66
the volleying *c* thunder his loss ; — *Ode on Well.* 62
Roll of *c* and clash of arms, — ,, 116
Your *c's* moulder on the seaward wall ; — ,, 173
C to right of them, *C* to left (repeat) — *Light Brigade* 18, 39
C in front of them Volley'd and thunder'd ; — ,, 20
C behind them Volley'd and thunder'd ; — ,, 41
cobweb woven across the *c's* throat Shall shake — *Maud III vi* 27
Cannonade In the crash of the *c's* — *The Revenge* 78
Hark *c*, fusillade ! is it true what was told — *Def. of Lucknow* 95
Cannon-ball and death from their *c-b's*, — ,, 14
musket-bullets, and thousand of *c-b's*— — ,, 93
Cannon-bullet Nor the *c-b* rust on a slothful shore, — *Maud III vi* 26
Cannon-shot *C's*, musket-shot, volley on volley, — *Def. of Lucknow* 34
Fell like a *c*, Burst like a thunderbolt, — *Heavy Brigade* 26
Canon Archbishop, Bishop, Priors, *C's*, — *Sir J. Oldcastle* 160
Canonized *See* **Half-canonized**
Canopus and lit Lamps which out-burn'd *C*. — *D. of F. Women* 146
Canopy in the costly *c* o'er him set, — *Lancelot and E.* 443
Canter 'ear my 'erse's legs, as they *c's* awaäy. — *N. Farmer, N. S.* 1
proputty, proputty—*c* an' *c* awaäy ? — ,, 60
Canterbury-bell Roses and lilies and *C-b's*.' — *City Child* 5
Canvas In the north, her *c* flowing, — *The Captain* 27
By glimmering lanes and walls of *c* — *Princess v* 6
such a breeze Compell'd thy *c*, — *In Mem. xvii* 2
Launch your vessel, And crowd your *c*, — *Merlin and the G.* 127
Could make pure light live on the *c* ? — *Romney's R.* 10
Canvass Doubtless our narrow world must *c* it: — *Aylmer's Field* 774
And so last night she fell to *c* you : — *Princess iii* 40
Canvass'd He *c* human mysteries, — *A Character* 20
Canzonet A rogue of *c's* and serenades. — *Princess iv* 135
Cap (s) Nor wreathe thy *c* with doleful crape, — *My life is full* 14
Her *c* blew off, her gown blew up, — *The Goose* 51
I do not hear the bells upon my *c*, — *Edwin Morris* 56
we know the hue Of that *c* upon her brows. — *Vision of Sin* 142
knightlike in his *c* instead of casque, — *Princess iv* 600
man's own angry pride Is *c* and bells for a fool. — *Maud I vi* 62
Mounted in arms, threw up their *c's* — *Gareth and L.* 697
put on the black *c* except for the worst — *Rizpah* 65
staghorn-moss, and this you twined About her *c*. — *Romney's R.* 80
Cap (verb) 'That *c's* owt, says Sally, — *North. Cobbler* 71
And *c* our age with snow ?' — *Ancient Sage* 98
Capability love for him have drain'd My *capabilities* of love : — *In Mem. lxxxv* 12
Capable neither *c* of lies, Nor asking overmuch — *Enoch Arden* 251
Cape (headland) tower, and hill, and *c*, and isle, — *Mine be the strength* 6
So they past by *c's* and islands, — *The Captain* 21
We past long lines of Northern *c's* — *The Voyage* 35
By grassy *c's* with fuller sound — *Sir L. and Q. G.* 14
lake and lawn, and isles and *c's*— — *Vision of Sin* 11
Then after a long tumble about the *C* — *Enoch Arden* 532
fold to fold, of mountain or of *c* ; — *Princess vii* 3
On *c's* of Afric as on cliffs of Kent, — *W. to Marie Alex.* 17
Or olive-hoary *c* in ocean ; — *The Daisy* 31
would not pass beyond the *c* That has the poplar on it : — *Lancelot and E.* 1039
round from the cliffs and the *c's*, — *V. of Maeldune* 55
stood on each of the loftiest *c's* — ,, 100
set me climbing icy *c's* And glaciers, — *To E. Fitzgerald* 25
From isle and *c* and continent, — *Open. I. and C. Exhib.* 4
Cape (a covering) with ermine *c's* And woolly breasts — *In Mem. xcv* 11
Caper Making a roan horse *c* and curvet — *Lancelot and E.* 792
Capital North to gain Her *c* city, — *The Ring* 482

Capitol the pillar'd Parthenon, The glittering *C* ;   *Freedom* 4
Caprera which here The warrior of *C* set,   *To Ulysses* 26
Captain melting the mighty hearts Of *c*'s and of
    kings.   *D. of F. Women* 176
    The *c* of my dreams Ruled in the eastern sky.   " 263
    Brave the *C* was :   *The Captain* 5
    harsh and cruel Seem'd the *C*'s mood.   " 14
    Then the *C*'s colour heighten'd,   " 29
    beneath the water Crew and *C* lie ;   " 68
    Now mate is blind, and *c* lame,   *The Voyage* 91
    He got it ; for their *c* after fight,   *Aylmer's Field* 226
    Without the *c*'s knowledge.   " 717
    Communing with his *c*'s of the war.   *Princess i* 67
    young *c*'s flash'd their glittering teeth,   " *v* 20
    to meet us lightly pranced Three *c*'s out ;   " 255
    every *c* waits Hungry for honour,   " 313
    Foremost *c* of his time,   *Ode on Well.* 31
    those deep voices our dead *c* taught The tyrant,   " 69
    To a lord, a *c*, a padded shape,   *Maud I x* 29
    the crew were gentle, the *c* kind ;   *The Wreck* 129
    band will be scatter'd now their gallant *c* is dead,   *Bandit's Death* 41
Captain's-ear His *c-e* has heard them boom   *Ode on Well.* 65
        Princess v 277
Captive 'sdeath ! and he himself Your *c*,   *In Mem. xxxvii* 2
    The *c* void of noble rage,   *Merlin and V.* 542
    Ye cage a buxom *c* here and there.   *Columbus* 131
    seized upon my papers, loosed My *c*'s,   *Tiresias* 102
    void of joy, Lest she be taken *c*—   *Locksley H., Sixty* 80
    flay *C*'s whom they caught in battle—   *Ode on Well.* 55
Car reverent people behold The towering *c*,   *Spec. of Iliad* 22
    Fixt by their *c*'s, waited the golden dawn.   *Demeter and P.* 38
    thro' which the *c* Of dark Aïdoneus rising   *Last Tournament* 206
    round the gallery made his horse *C* ;   *Com. of Arthur* 112
Caracole *C*, Urien, Cradlemont of Wales,   *Columbus* 140
Carádos (**King**)   *Holy Grail* 813
Caravel frailer *c*, With what was mine,   *Adeline* 59
Carbonek the enchanted towers of *C*,   *Last Tournament* 6
Carcanet Make a *c* of rays,   " 28
    a *c* Of ruby swaying to and fro,   " 419
    c Vext her with plaintive memories of the child :   " 740
    Because the twain had spoil'd her *c*.   *Boädicea* 14
    Tristram show'd And swung the ruby *c*.   *Batt. of Brunanburh* 105
Carcase make the *c* a skeleton,   *Aylmer's Field* 28
    Many a *c* they left to be carrion,   *To the Queen* 9
Card Insipid as the Queen upon a *c* ;   *Supp. Confessions* 48
Care (**s**) and *the c That yokes with empire,*   " 63
    He hath no *c* of life or death ;   *A Dirge* 8
    sure it is a special *c* Of God,   *L. of Shalott ii* 8
    Thee nor carketh *c* nor slander ;   *Lotos-Eaters, C. S.* 28
    And little other *c* hath she,   *D. of F. Women* 249
    Grows green and broad, and takes no *c*,   *M. d'Arthur* 173
    a low voice, full of *c*, Murmur'd   *Day-Dm., Sleep. P.* 55
    took with *c*, and kneeling on one knee,   *Will Water.* 227
    Come, *C* and Pleasure, Hope and Pain,   *Enoch Arden* 222
    Thy *c* is, under polish'd tins,   " 263
    Cast all your *c*'s on God ;   " 418
    mother cared for it With all a mother's *c* ;   *Aylmer's Field* 688
    no kin, no *c*, No burthen, save my *c* for you   " 814
    The common *c* whom no one cared for,   *Princess, Pro.* 173
    Seam'd with the shallow *c*'s of fifty years :   " *iii* 19
    takes a lady's finger with all *c*,   " 85
    each by other drest with *c* Descended   " *v* 85
    She had the *c* of Lady Ida's youth,   " *vii* 101
    either she will die from want of *c*,   " 283
    out of long frustration of her *c*,   *To F. D. Maurice* 1
    mental breadth, nor fail in childward *c*,   *In Mem.*   *viii* 16
    COME, when no graver *c*'s employ,   " *xii* 14
    Which once she foster'd up with *c* ;   " *xxxviii* 9
    Is this the end of all my *c* ?'   " *xlviii* 5
    If any *c* for what is here Survive   " *lv* 14
    Her *c* is not to part and prove ;   " *lxxxix* 17
    And falling with my weight of *c*'s   " *xcix* 10
    O sound to rout the brood of *c*'s,   " *cv* 13
    A song that slights the coming *c*,   " *cvi* 17
    Let *c*'s that petty shadows cast,   " *cxxv* 9
    Ring out the want, the *c*, the sin,
    And if the song were full of *c*,

Care (**s**) (*continued*) Shall I not take *c* of all that I think,   *Maud I xv* 7
    Forgetful of his princedom and its *c*'s.   *Marr. of Geraint* 54
    he thought, 'In spite of all my *c*,   " 115
    Told him that her fine *c* had saved his life.   *Lancelot and E.* 863
    so forgot herself A moment, and her *c*'s :   *Last Tournament* 26
    took with *c*, and kneeling on one knee,   *Pass. of Arthur* 341
    offices Of watchful *c* and trembling tenderness.   *Lover's Tale i* 226
    But there from fever and my *c* of him   " *iv* 143
    the Lord has look'd into my *c*,   " *Rizpah* 75
    lad will need little more of your *c*.'   *In the Child. Hosp.* 17
    days' of fever, and want of *c* !   *The Wreck* 147
    Muriel nursed you with a mother's *c* ;   *The Ring* 349
    made you leper in His loving *c* for both,   *Happy* 91
    With politic *c*, with utter gentleness.   *Akbar's Dream* 128
Care (**verb**) You *c* not for another's pains,   *Rosalind* 19
    random eyes, That *c* not whom they kill,   " 38
    Nor *c*'s to lisp in love's delicious creeds ;   *Caress'd or chidden* 11
    She still will take the praise, and *c* no more.   *The form, the form* 14
    Nor *c* to sit beside her where she sits—   *Wan Sculptor* 10
    I *c* not what the sects may brawl.   *Palace of Art* 210
    Too proud to *c* from whence I came.   *L. C. V. de Vere* 13
    but I *c* not what they say,   *May Queen* 19
    I *c* not if I go to-day.   " *Con.* 43
    But if you *c* indeed to listen, hear   *Golden Year* 20
    Like wealthy men who *c* not how they give.   *Tithonus* 17
    be happy ! wherefore should I *c* ?   *Locksley Hall* 97
    To choose your own you did not *c* ;   *Day-Dm., L'Envoi* 30
    And that for which I *c* to live.   " 56
    I *c* no longer, being all unblest :   *Come not, when etc.* 8
    What I *c* for any name ?   *Vision of Sin* 85
    ' His head is low, and no man *c*'s for him.   *Enoch Arden* 850
    if my children *c* to see me dead,   " 888
    Would *c* no more for Leolin's walking   *Aylmer's Field* 124
    Slight was his answer ' Well—I *c* not for it :'   " 238
    I *c* not for it either ;'   " 240
    wherefore need he *c* Greatly for them,   *Lucretius* 150
    '*C* not thou ! Thy duty ? What is duty ?   " 280
    c not while we hear A trumpet in the distance   *Princess iv* 80
    myself, what *c* I, war or no ?   " *v* 278
    And, right or wrong, I *c* not :   " 290
    nor *c*'s to walk With Death and Morning   " *vii* 203
    Him who *c*'s not to be great,   *Ode on Well.* 199
    what do I *c* for Jane, let her speak of you   *Grandmother* 51
    shall we *c* to be pitiful ?   *Boädicea* 32
    Nor *c*'s to fix itself to form,   *In Mem. xxxiii* 4
    I *c* for nothing, all shall go.   " *lvi* 9
    I *c* not in these fading days   " *lxxv* 9
    Whatever they call him, what *c* I,   *Maud I x* 64
    But now shine on, and what *c* I,   " *xviii* 41
    C not thou to reply :   " *II iii* 7
    C not for shame : thou art not knight but knave.'   *Gareth and L.* 1006
    ' And *c* not for the cost ; the cost is mine.'   *Geraint and E.* 288
    Nor did I *c* or dare to speak with you,   " 871
    He *c*'s not for me : only here to-day   *Lancelot and E.* 126
    nor *c*'s For triumph in our mimic wars,   " 311
    she cried, ' I *c* not to be wife,   " 937
    I *c* not howsoever great he be,   *Holy Grail* 615
    And this am I, so that ye *c* for me   " 899
    C's but to pass into the silent life.   *Pelleas and E.* 77
    And pass and *c* no more.   *Last Tournament* 105
    wherefore shouldst thou *c* to mingle with it,   " 314
    since I *c* not for thy pearls.   " 607
    C not for her ! patient, and prayerful,   *Guinevere* 452
    I the King should greatly *c* to live ;   " 495
    Not greatly *c* to lose ;   *Pass. of Arthur* 58
    And *c* not thou for dreams from him,   *Rizpah* 78
    Do you think that I *c* for *my* soul if my boy   *Sisters (E. and E.)* 77
    I *c* not for a name—no fault of mine.   *Village Wife* 98
    Not es I *c*'s fur to hear ony harm,   *In the Child. Hosp.* 71
    Ah why should we *c* what they say ?'   *The Wreck* 98
    heart of the father will *c* for his own.   *The Ring* 89
    Fly—*c* not. Birds and brides must leave   *Parnassus* 18
    their music here be mortal need the singer greatly *c* !   *L. C. V. de Vere* 32
Cared Which you had hardly *c* to see.   *Edwin Morris* 138
    nor heard of her, nor *c* to hear. Nor *c* to hear ?

Cared (*continued*) Nor *c* for seed or scion !   *Amphion* 12
if he *c* For her or his dear children,   *Enoch Arden* 163
Yet sicklier, tho' the mother *c* for it   ,, 262
C not to look on any human face,   ,, 282
question'd, aught of what he *c* to know.   ,, 654
Held his head high, and *c* for no man,   ,, 848
prov'n or no, What *c* he ?   *Aylmer's Field* 55
Me ?—but I *c* not for it.   ,, 244
slowly lost Nor greatly *c* to lose, her hold on life.   ,, 568
The common care whom no one *c* for,   ,, 688
Nor ever *c* to better his own kind,   *Sea Dreams* 201
c not for the affection of the house ;   *Princess* i 26
And some they *c* not ; till a clamour grew   ,, iv 486
but she nor *c* Nor knew it,   ,, vi 149
Which little *c* for fades not yet.   *In Mem.* viii 20
Nor *c* the serpent at thy side   ,, cx 7
Now I thought that she *c* for me,   *Maud I* xiv 25
Nor *c* a broken egg-shell for her lord.   *Geraint and E.* 364
Was *c* as much for as a summer shower :   ,, 523
storm Brake on the mountain and I *c* not for it.   *Merlin and V.* 503
cackle of the unborn about the grave, I *c* not for it :   ,, 508
C not for her, nor anything upon earth.'   *Holy Grail* 612
I *c* not for the thorns ;   *Pelleas and E.* 404
who *c* Only to use his own,   *Lover's Tale* iv 311
For I *c* so much for my boy that the Lord   *Rizpah* 75
meller 'e mun be by this, if I *c* to taäste,   *North. Cobbler* 101
he *c* not for his own ;   *The Flight* 78
Fur I niver *c* nothink for neither—   *Spinster's S's.* 62
Nor ever *c* to set you on her knee,   *The Ring* 386
Careful At you, so *c* of the right,   *To F. D. Maurice* 10
All in quantity, *c* of my motion,   *Hendecasyllabics* 5
So *c* of the type she seems,   *In Mem.* lv 7
'So *c* of the type ?' but no.   ,, lvi 1
And that which knows, but *c* for itself,   *To the Queen* ii 57
Carefuller A *c* in peril, did not breathe   *Enoch Arden* 50
Careless *C* both of wind and weather,   *Rosalind* 7
To wait for death—mute—*c* of all ills,   *If I were loved* 10
like Gods together, *c* of mankind.   *Lotos-Eaters, C. S.* 110
And Enoch's comrade, *c* of himself,   *Enoch Arden* 568
Where *c* of the household faces near,   *Aylmer's Field* 575
but he that holds The Gods are *c*,   *Lucretius* 150
O ye Gods, I know you *c*,   ,, 208
Rapt in her song, and *c* of the snare.   *Princess* i 221
So *c* of the single life ;   *In Mem.* lv 8
Now with slack rein and *c* of himself,   *Balin and Balan* 309
eats And uses, *c* of the rest ;   *Merlin and V.* 463
Then answer'd Merlin *c* of her words :   ,, 700
Merlin answer'd *c* of her charge,   ,, 754
C of all things else, led on with light   *Lover's Tale* i 77
C of our growing kin,   *Open I. and C. Exhib.* 23
Careless-order'd All round a *c-o* garden   *To F. D. Maurice* 15
Caress (s) The trance gave way To those *c'es*,   *Love and Duty* 66
Or for chilling his *c'es*   *Maud I* xx 12
white hand whose ring'd *c* Had wander'd   *Balin and Balan* 512
Thy hurt and heart with unguent and *c*—   *Last Tournament* 595
that no *c* could win my wife   *Sisters (E. and E.)* 258
at home if I sought for a kindly *c*,   *The Wreck* 31
Caress (verb) 'Thrice-happy he that may *c* The ringlet's waving balm—   *Talking Oak* 177
be not wrathful with your maid ; *C* her :   *Merlin and V.* 381
Caress'd *C* or chidden by the slender hand,   *Caress'd or chidden* 1
Carest *c* not How roughly men may woo   *Lucretius* 272
Careworn contracting grew *C* and wan ;   *Enoch Arden* 487
Carian Artemisia The *C A* strong in war,   *Princess* ii 81
Caring not for his own self *c* but her,   *Enoch Arden* 165
No longer *c* to embalm In dying songs   *In Mem., Con.* 13
Carketh Thee nor *c* care nor slander ;   *A Dirge* 8
Carnage Leaving his son too Lost in the *c*,   *Batt. of Brunanburh* 73
Could we dream of wars and *c*,   *Locksley H., Sixty* 189
Carnation *See* **Rose-carnation**
Carnival Love in the sacred halls Held *c*   *Princess* vii 85
Carol (s) Flow'd forth on a *c* free and bold ;   *Dying Swan* 30
Heard a *c*, mournful, holy,   *L. of Shalott* iv 28
She, as her *c* sadder grew,   *Mariana in the S.* 13
Losing her *c* I stood pensively,   *D. of F. Women* 245

Carol (s) (*continued*) swan That, fluting a wild *c* ere her death,   *M. d'Arthur* 267
every bird of Eden burst In *c*,   *Day-Dm., L'Envoi* 44
The hall with harp and *c* rang.   *In Mem.* ciii 9
swan That, fluting a wild *c* ere her death,   *Pass. of Arthur* 435
And lavish *c* of clear-throated larks   *Lover's Tale* i 283
Carol (verb) merrily, merrily *c* the gales,   *Sea-Fairies* 23
The balm-cricket *c's* clear In the green   *A Dirge* 47
if I should *c* aloud, from aloft All things   *The Mermaid* 52
Or *c* some old roundelay,   *Gareth and L.* 506
That you should *c* so madly ?   *The Throstle* 8
Caroline Margaret and Mary, there's Kate and *C*:   *May Queen* 6
Carolleth the grasshopper *c* clearly ;   *Leonine Eleg.* 5
Carolling (*See also* **Down-carolling**) and beside The *c* water set themselves again,   *Balin and Balan* 44
and *c* as he went A true-love ballad,   *Lancelot and E.* 704
Carouse 'O Soul, make merry and *c*,   *Palace of Art* 3
Where long and largely we *c*   *Will Water.* 91
Carp Near that old home, a pool of golden *c* ;   *Marr. of Geraint* 648
Carpenter Cooper he was and *c*,   *Enoch Arden* 814
Born of a village girl, *c's* son,   *Aylmer's Field* 668
Carpet *c* es fresh es a midder o' flowers i' Maäy—   *Spinster's S's.* 45
Carriage as I found when her *c* past,   *Maud I* ii 3
Carried see me *c* out from the threshold of the door ;   *May Queen, N. Y's. E.* 42
But him she *c*, him nor lights nor feast   *Lover's Tale* iv 310
Carrier-bird As light as *c-b's* in air ;   *In Mem.* xxv 6
Carrion For whom the *c* vulture waits To tear his heart   *You might have won* 35
Blacken round the Roman *c*,   *Boädicea* 14
And deems it *c* of some woodland thing,   *Gareth and L.* 748
troop of *c* crows Hung like a cloud   *Merlin and V.* 598
Many a carcase they left to be *c*,   *Batt. of Brunanburh* 105
Carry the king of them all would *c* me,   *The Mermaid* 45
Warriors *c* the warrior's pall,   *Ode on Well.* 6
brutes of mountain back That *c* kings in castles,   *Merlin and V.* 577
Fur 'e'd fetch an' *c* like owt,   *Owd Roä* 6
Carrying always came to meet me *c* you,   *The Ring* 352
She came no more to meet me, *c* you,   ,, 385
Cart *See* **Go-cart**
Carve to *c* out Free space for every human doubt,   *Two Voices* 136
you may *c* a shrine about my dust,   *St. S. Stylites* 195
My good blade *c's* the casques of men,   *Sir Galahad* 1
monstrous males that *c* the living hound,   *Princess* iii 310
c's A portion from the solid present,   *Merlin and V.* 461
Beyond all work of those who *c* the stone,   *Tiresias* 53
Carved Caucasian mind *C* out of Nature for itself,   *Palace of Art* 127
A million wrinkles *c* his skin ;   ,, 138
for if I *c* my name Upon the cliffs   *Audley Court* 48
thou, whereon I *c* her name, (repeat)   *Talking Oak* 33, 97
read the name I *c* with many vows   ,, 154
Wept over her, *c* in stone ;   *Maud I* viii 4
Had *c* himself a knightly shield of wood,   *Merlin and V.* 473
our Lady's Head, *C* of one emerald   *Lancelot and E.* 295
her scarlet sleeve, Tho' *c* and cut,   ,, 807
Scribbled or *c* upon the pitiless stone ;   *Sir J. Oldcastle* 5
one *c* all over with flowers,   *V. of Maeldune* 106
Homer's fame, Tho' *c* in harder stone—   *Epilogue* 59
Carven (*See also* **Crag-carven**) Some blazon'd, some but *c*, and some blank,   *Gareth and L.* 406
His arms were *c* only ;   ,, 412
shield of Lancelot at her feet Be *c*,   *Lancelot and E.* 1342
And *c* with strange figures ;   *Holy Grail* 169
Carven-work from the *c-w* behind him crept   *Lancelot and E.* 436
Caryatid great statues, Art And Science, *C's*,   *Princess* iv 201
Cascinè What drives about the fresh *C*,   *The Daisy* 43
Case (covering) (*See also* **Wing-case**) And warm'd in crystal *c's*.   *Amphion* 88
fearing rust or soilure fashion'd for it A *c* of silk,   *Lancelot and E.* 8
entering barr'd her door, Stript off the *c*,   ,, 16
meekly rose the maid, Stript off the *c*,   ,, 979
shield was gone ; only the *c*, Her own poor work,   ,, 990
The silken *c* with braided blazonings,   ,, 1149
Case (circumstance) profits it to put An idle *c* ?   *In Mem.* xxxv 18
blabbing The *c* of his patient—   *Maud II* v 37

D

Case (circumstance) (*continued*) it was all but a
  hopeless *c*: — *In the Child. Hosp.* 14
And it was but a hopeless *c*, — ,, 16
Casement (*See also* **Chancel-casement**) Or at the
  c seen her stand? — *L. of Shalott* i 25
I arose, and I released The *c*, — *Two Voices* 404
And all the *c* darken'd there. — *Miller's D.* 128
And fires your narrow *c* glass, — ,, 243
As one that from a *c* leans his head, — *D. of F. Women* 246
gardener's lodge, With all its *c*'s bedded, — *Audley Court* 18
Many a night from yonder ivied *c*, — *Locksley Hall* 7
Flew over roof and *c*: — *Will Water.* 134
and he clamour'd from a *c*, 'Run' — *The Brook* 85
The *c* slowly grows a glimmering square; — *Princess* iv 52
All night has the *c* jessamine stirr'd — *Maud* I xxii 15
Down from the *c* over Arthur, smote Flame-colour, — *Com. of Arthur* 274
out of bower and *c* shyly glanced Eyes — *Gareth and L.* 313
Beat thro' the blindless *c* of the room, — *Marr. of Geraint* 71
rang Clear thro' the open *c* of the hall, — ,, 328
Push'd thro' an open *c* down, — *Balin and Balan* 413
royal rose In Arthur's *c* glimmer'd chastely — *Merlin and V.* 740
Unclasping flung the *c* back, — *Lancelot and E.* 981
Down in a *c* sat, A low sea-sunset glorying — *Last Tournament* 507
and in her anguish found The *c*: — *Guinevere* 587
From that *c* where the trailer mantles — *Locksley H., Sixty* 257
Close beneath the *c* crimson with the shield — ,, 34
Casement-curtain She drew her *c-c* by, — *Mariana* 19
Casement-edge That morning, on the *c-e* — *Miller's D.* 82
Cask when their *c*'s were fill'd they took aboard: — *Enoch Arden* 646
Casket since The key to that weird *c*, — *Ancient Sage* 254
Casque And loosed the shatter'd *c*, and chafed his hands, — *M. d'Arthur* 209
My good blade carves the *c*'s of men, — *Sir Galahad* 1
knightlike in his cap instead of *c*, — *Princess* iv 600
unlaced my *c* And grovell'd on my body, — ,, vi 27
This bare a maiden shield, a *c*; — *Gareth and L.* 680
jangling, the *c* Fell, and he started up — *Geraint and E.* 388
dismount and loose their *c*'s — *Balin and Balan* 573
there first she saw the *c* Of Lancelot on the wall: — *Lancelot and E.* 805
a crown of gold About a *c* all jewels; — *Holy Grail* 411
I saw The pelican on the *c* of our Sir Bors — ,, 635
I remember now That pelican on the *c*: — ,, 700
That ware their ladies' colours on the *c*, — *Last Tournament* 184
And loosed the shatter'd *c*, and chafed his hands, — *Pass. of Arthur* 377
C's were crack'd, and hauberks hack'd — *The Tourney* 7
Cassandra Talk with the wild *C*, — *Œnone* 263
C, Hebe, Joan, — *Romney's R.* 4
Cassia turning round a *c*, full in view, — *Love and Death* 4
Cassiopëia had you been Sphered up with *C*, — *Princess* iv 438
Cássívëlaún (British king) hear it, Spirit of *C*! — *Boädicea* 20
sweeter then the bride of *C*, Flur, — *Marr. of Geraint* 744
Cast (mould) take the *c* Of those dead lineaments — *Wan Sculptor* 1
Not only cunning *c*'s in clay: — *In Mem.* cxx 5
Cast (vomit) Lies the hawk's *c*, — *Aylmer's Field* 849
Cast (throw) Jephtha vows his child . . . to one *c*
  of the dice. — *The Flight* 26
Cast (verb) Low on her knees herself she *c*, — *Mariana in the S.* 27
'Let me not *c* in endless shade — *Two Voices* 5
I *c* me down, nor thought of you, — *Miller's D.* 63
'This was *c* upon the board, — *Œnone* 79
And *c* the golden fruit upon the board, — ,, 226
those That are *c* in gentle mould. — *To J. S.* 4
Memory standing near *C* down her eyes, — ,, 54
'And if indeed I *c* the brand away, — *M. d'Arthur* 88
Dora *c* her eyes upon the ground, — *Dora* 89
who would *c* and balance at a desk, — *Audley Court* 44
'Yet, since I first could *c* a shade, — *Talking Oak* 85
Had *c* upon its crusty side — *Will Water.* 103
overboard one stormy night He *c* his body, — *The Voyage* 80
C all your cares on God; — *Enoch Arden* 222
C his strong arms about his drooping wife, — ,, 228
'Enoch, poor man, was *c* away and lost, — ,, 713
Repeated muttering '*c* away and lost;' — ,, 715
she *c* back upon him A piteous glance, — *Aylmer's Field* 283
But they that *c* her spirit into flesh, — ,, 481
He had *c* the curtains of their seat aside— — ,, 803

Cast (verb) (*continued*) Shall Babylon be *c* into the sea; — *Sea Dreams* 28
The mountain there has *c* his cloudy slough, — *Lucretius* 177
grandsire burnt Because he *c* no shadow, — *Princess* i 7
entering here, to *c* and fling The tricks, — ,, ii 62
eddied into suns, that wheeling *c* The planets: — ,, 118
Psyche's child to *c* it from the doors, — ,, iv 238
turn'd her face, and *c* A liquid look on Ida, — ,, 368
But a *c* oop, thot a did, — *N. Farmer, O. S.* 14
in a golden hour I *c* to earth a seed. — *The Flower* 2
She *c* her arms about the child. — *The Victim* 32
Or *c* as rubbish to the void, — *In Mem.* liv 7
And if thou *c* thine eyes below, — ,, lxi 5
Tho' if an eye that's downward *c* — ,, lxii 1
To chances where our lots were *c* — ,, xcii 5
Let cares that petty shadows *c*, — ,, cv 13
I seem to *c* a careless eye On souls, — ,, cxii 7
Uther *c* upon her eyes of love: — *Com. of Arthur* 193
written in the speech ye speak yourself, '*C* me
  away!" — ,, 305
time to *c* away Is yet far-off.' — ,, 307
rend In pieces, and so *c* it on the hearth. — *Gareth and L.* 401
rend the cloth and *c* it on the hearth. — ,, 418
cloth of roughest web, and *c* it down, — ,, 683
bound my lord to *c* him in the mere. — ,, 803
rough dog, to whom he *c* his coat, — ,, 1011
but straining ev'n his uttermost *C*, — ,, 1153
saw That Death was *c* to ground, — ,, 1403
Who, moving, *c* the coverlet aside, — *Marr. of Geraint* 73
At this she *c* her eyes upon her dress, — ,, 609
And *c* it on the mixen that it die.' — ,, 672
she could *c* aside A splendour dear to women, — ,, 807
she *c* about For that unnoticed failing — *Geraint and E.* 46
c him and the bier in which he lay — ,, 572
c his lance aside, And doff'd his helm: — ,, 595
this poor gown I will not *c* aside — ,, 705
arise a living man, And bid me *c* it. — ,, 707
and she *c* her arms About him, — ,, 761
c his eyes On each of all whom Uther left — ,, 932
Stumbled headlong, and *c* his face to ground. — *Balin and Balan* 426
And there in gloom *c* himself all along, — ,, 434
Tore from the branch, and *c* on earth, the shield, — ,, 539
on his dying brother *c* himself Dying; — ,, 593
As Love, if Love be perfect, *c*'s out fear, So Hate, — *Merlin and V.* 40
  if Hate be perfect, *c*'s out fear. — ,, 66
C herself down, knelt to the Queen, — ,, 430
Where children *c* their pins and nails, — ,, 908
The gentle wizard *c* a shielding arm. — *Lancelot and E.* 313
For if his own knight *c* him down, — ,, 640
stay'd; and *c* his eyes on fair Elaine? — ,, 1199
Leaf after leaf, and tore, and *c* them off, — *Holy Grail* 257
The brand Excalibur will be *c* away. — ,, 622
all but hold, and then—*c* her aside, — *Pelleas and E.* 31
binding his good horse To a tree, *c* himself down; — ,, 515
c himself down, And gulf'd his griefs — ,, 591
but *c* himself Down on a bench, hard-breathing, — *Last Tournament* 161
a knight *c* down Before his throne of arbitration — ,, 196
Like a dry bone *c* to some hungry hound? — ,, 232
So dame and damsel *c* the simple white, — ,, 711
and *c* thee back Thine own small saw, — *Guinevere* 35
And *c* him as a worm upon the way; — *Pass. of Arthur* 256
'And if indeed I *c* the brand away, — *To the Queen* ii 64
Are morning shadows huger than the shapes
  That *c* them, — *Lover's Tale* i 295
we found The dead man *c* upon the shore? — ,, ii 41
I *c* them in the noisy brook beneath, — ,, iv 4
But *c* a parting glance at me, — ,, 103
'He *c*'s me out,' she wept, 'and goes' — ,, 329
She shook, and *c* her eyes down, — ,, 366
Yet *c* her not away so suddenly, — *North. Cobbler* 3
'*C* awaäy on a disolut land wi' a vartical soon!' — *Columbus* 111
And *c* it to the Moor: — ,, 158
I heard his voice, 'Be not *c* down. — ,, 165
C off, put by, scouted by court and king— — *To Dante* 7
C at thy feet one flower that fades — *To E. Fitzgerald* 36
A planet equal to the sun Which *c* it, —

ast (verb) (*continued*) To *c* wise words among the multitude *Tiresias* 66

when he *c* a contemptuous glance *The Wreck* 25

the crew should *c* me into the deep,   ,,   94

But the blind wave *c* me ashore, *Despair* 61

curb the beast would *c* thee in the mire, *Ancient Sage* 276

Crime and hunger *c* our maidens *Locksley H., Sixty* 220

C the poison from your bosom,   ,,   241

shadows which that light would *c*, *Epit. on Caxton* 3

The roses that you *c* aside— *Happy* 22

Which, *c* in later Grecian mould, *To Master of B.* 6

And *c* aside, when old, for newer,— *Akbar's Dream* 134

vanish'd in the shadow *c* by Death. *D. of the Duke of C.* 3

astalies I led you then to all the *C*; *Princess iv* 294

astanet The starling claps his tiny *c's. Prog. of Spring* 56

aste Which stamps the *c* of Vere de Vere. *L. C. V. de Vere* 40

I hate the rancour of their *c's* and creeds, *Akbar's Dream* 65

astile The noble and the convict of *C*, *Columbus* 117

astillano Weigh'd nigh four thousand *C's*   ,,   136

asting (*See also* **Shadow-Casting**) by two yards in

c bar or stone Was counted best ; *Gareth and L.* 518

unhooded *c* off The goodly falcon free ; *Merlin and V.* 130

astle (adj.) She stood upon the *c* wall, *Oriana* 28

Atween me and the *c* wall,   ,,   35

The splendour falls on *c* walls *Princess iv* 1

Guinevere Stood by the *c* walls to watch him

pass ; *Com. of Arthur* 48

Then from the *c* gateway by the chasm Descending   ,,   370

Then rode Geraint into the *c* court, *Marr of Geraint* 312

And while he waited in the *c* court,   ,,   326

met The scorner in the *c* court, *Balin and Balan* 387

Moving to meet him in the *c* court ; *Lancelot and E.* 175

Then bounded forward to the *c* walls, *Pelleas and E.* 363

astle (s) (*See also* **Sea-castle**) *c*, built When men

knew how to build, *Edwin Morris* 6

See the lordly *c's* stand : *L. of Burleigh* 18

And built their *c's* of dissolving sand *Enoch Arden* 19

The lady of three *c's* in that land : *Princess iii* 1

Well, Are *c's* shadows ? Three of them ?   ,,   *ii* 414

Shall those three *c's* patch my tatter'd coat ?   ,,   416

dear are those three *c's* to my wants,   ,,   417

To that fair port below the *c The Daisy* 79

Seeing his gewgaw *c* shine, *Maud I x* 18

he that held Tintagil *c* by the Cornish sea, *Com. of Arthur* 187

Closed in her *c* from the sound of arms. *Gareth and L.* 163

husband's brother had my son Thrall'd in his *c*,   ,,   358

And saddening in her childless *c*,   ,,   528

holds her stay'd In her own *c*,   ,,   616

And on one side a *c* in decay, *Marr. of Geraint* 245

And keeps me in this ruinous *c* here,   ,,   462

till the *c* of a King, the hall Of Pellam, *Balin and Balan* 331

from the *c* a cry Sounded across the court,   ,,   399

brutes of mountain back That carry kings in *c's*, *Merlin and V.* 577

Ran to the *C* of Astolat, *Lancelot and E.* 167

and again By *c* Gurnion, where the glorious King   ,,   293

The Princess of that *c* was the one, *Holy Grail* 578

A *c* like a rock upon a rock,   ,,   814

when she gain'd her *c*, upsprang the bridge, *Pelleas and E.* 206

Catlike thro' his own *c* steals my Mark, *Last Tournament* 516

And fly to my strong *c* overseas : *Guinevere* 113

Round that strong *c* where he holds the Queen ;   ,,   194

astle-bridge until he stood There on the *c-b Pelleas and E.* 443

astle-gate sought for Garlon at the *c-g's*, *Balin and Balan* 610

astle Perilous She lives in *C P* : *Gareth and L.* 611

pitch'd Beside the *C P* on flat field,   ,,   1363

astle-wall her orchard underneath Her *c-w's*, *Holy Grail* 594

astle-well pool or stream, The *c-w*, belike ; *Lancelot and E.* 215

asualty Howbeit ourself, foreseeing *c*, *Princess iii* 317

at (*See also* **Tiger-cat**) WHEN *c's* run home and light

is come, *The Owl i* 1

yelp'd the cur, and yawl'd the *c* ; *The Goose* 33

like dove and dove were *c* and dog. *Walk. to the Mail* 58

Her gay-furr'd *c's* a painted fantasy, *Princess iii* 186

the two great *c's* Close by her,   ,,   *vi* 357

Within the hearing of *c* or mouse, *Maud II v* 48

I will be deafer than the blue-eyed *c*, *Holy Grail* 865

Cat (*continued*) an' scratted my faäce like a *c*, *North. Cobbler* 22

they kep the *c* an' the dog, *Tomorrow* 71

a *c* may loöök at a king thou knaws but the *c*

mun be cleän. *Spinster's S's.* 34

fond o' thy bairns es I be mysen o' my *c's*,   ,,   83

till the Lion look no larger than the *C*, Till the *C*

thro' that mirage *Locksley H., Sixty* 112

c wur a-sleeäpin alongside Roäver, *Owd Roä* 33

to-daäy, when she hurl'd a plaäte at the *c Church-warden, etc.* 25

Catacomb water falls In vaults and *c's*, *In Mem. lviii* 4

Catalepsy paw'd his beard, and mutter'd '*c.*' *Princess i* 20

Catalonian Minorite By him, the *C M*, *Columbus* 194

Catapult Your cities into shards with *c's*, *Princess v* 138

Hurl'd as a stone from out of a *c Gareth and L.* 965

Cataract (a fall of water) (*See also* **Sea-cataract**)

In *c* after *c* to the sea. *Œnone* 9

snowy peak and snow-white *c* Foster'd   ,,   211

ocean-ridges roaring into *c's*. *Locksley Hall* 6

stream of life Dashed downward in a *c. Day-Dm., Revival* 16

Beyond the darkness and the *c*, *Vision of Sin* 49

we came to where the river sloped To plunge in *c*, *Princess iii* 291

And the wild *c* leaps in glory.   ,,   *iv*   4

c and the tumult and the kings Were shadows ;   ,,   564

Set in a *c* on an island-crag,   ,,   *v* 347

C brooks to the ocean run, *The Islet* 17

The *c* flashing from the bridge, *In Mem. lxxi* 15

senseless *c*, Bearing all down in thy precipitancy— *Gareth and L.* 7

thro' the crash of the near *c* hears *Geraint and E.* 172

the sea Drove like a *c*, and all the sand *Holy Grail* 799

and swept in a *c* off from her sides, *The Wreck* 90

hollow ridges roaring into *c's*, *Locksley H., Sixty* 2

Or *c* music Of falling torrents, *Merlin and the G.* 46

Hear my *c's* Downward thunder *To Master of B.* 15

in blood-red *c's* down to the sea ! *Kapiolani* 12

Cataract (a disease of the eye) Almost blind With

ever-growing *c*, *Sisters (E. and E.)* 192

Catch (s) 'but 'tis eating dry To dance without a *c. Last Tournament* 250

Catch (verb) Whereof I *c* the issue, as I hear Dead sounds *Œnone* 248

C me who can, and make the catcher crown'd— *Golden Year* 18

C the wild goat by the hair, *Locksley Hall* 170

C her, goatfoot : nay, Hide, *Lucretius* 203

To *c* a dragon in a cherry net, *Princess v* 169

I would *c* Her hand in wild delirium,   ,,   *vii* 92

c The far-off interest of tears ? *In Mem. i* 7

And *c* at every mountain head, *In Mem. Con.* 114

Prickle my skin and *c* my breath, *Maud I xiv* 36

C not my breath, O clamorous heart,   ,,   *xvi* 31

To *c* a friend of mine one stormy day ;   ,,   *II v* 85

for my wont hath ever been To *c* my thief, *Gareth and L.* 822

'Overquick art thou To *c* a loathly plume *Merlin and V.* 727

cheek did *c* the colour of her words. *Lover's Tale i* 569

The hope I *c* at vanishes and youth *The Flight* 16

Prophet-eyes may *c* a glory slowly gaining *Making of Man* 6

Catcher and make the *c* crown'd— *Golden Year* 18

Catching Seem'd *c* at a rootless thorn, *Geraint and E.* 378

Cate many a viand left, And many a costly *c*, *Gareth and L.* 849

Caterpillar Picks from the colewort a green *c*, *Guinevere* 32

Cat-footed *C-f* thro' the town and half in dread *Princess i* 104

Cathay Better fifty years of Europe than a

cycle of *C. Locksley Hall* 184

Cathedral sunshine laves The lawn by some *c*, *D. of F. Women* 190

gray *c* towers, Across a hazy glimmer *Gardener's D.* 218

But huge *c* fronts of every age, *Sea Dreams* 218

And in the vast *c* leave him. *Ode on Well.* 280

Catherine *C*, *C*, in the night, *Forlorn* 13

Catholic Cross I cling to the *C C* once more, *The Wreck* 3

Catholic Faith hope was mine to spread the *C f*, *Columbus* 230

Catieuchlanian Hear Icenian, *C*, hear Coritanian,

(repeat) *Boädicea* 10, 34, 47

Gods have answer'd, *C*, Trinobant.   ,,   22

Shout Icenian, *C*, shout Coritanian,   ,,   57

Catlike *C* thro' his own castle steals *Last Tournament* 516

Princess vii 126

Sea Dreams 190

Cato A dwarf-like *C* cower'd.

Catspaw Him his *c* and the Cross his tool, *Lucretius* 99

Cattle strikes thro' the thick blood Of *c*,

Cattle (*continued*) And *c* died, and deer in wood, — *The Victim* 18
The *c* huddled on the lea, — *In Mem. xv* 6
abide Without, among the *c* of the field. — *Gareth and L.* 274
half of the *c* went lame, — *V. of Maeldune* 31
drive Innocent *c* under thatch, — *Locksley H., Sixty* 96
Catullus All composed in a metre of *C*, — *Hendecasyllabics* 4
Thro' this metrification of *C*, — „ 10
Sweet *C*'s all-but-island, — *Frater Ave, etc.* 9
C, whose dead songster never dies; — *Poets and their B.* 8
Caucasian Which the supreme *C* mind Carved — *Palace of Art* 126
Where our *C*'s let themselves be sold. — *Aylmer's Field* 349
Caucasus From Calpe unto *C* they sung, — *The Poet* 15
Elburz and all the *C* have heard; — *W. to Marie Alex.* 13
Cauf (*calf*) 'Cushie wur craäzed fur 'er *c*' — *Spinster's S's.* 115
'thank God that I hevn't naw *c* o' my oän.' — „ 116
Caught (*See also* **Cotch'd**) eddying of her garments *c* from
thee The light — *Ode to Memory* 31
And there a vision *c* my eye; — *Miller's D.* 76
C in the frozen palms of Spring. — *The Blackbird* 24
She *c* the white goose by the leg, — *The Goose* 9
She dropt the goose, and *c* the pelf, — „ 13
c him by the hilt, and brandish'd him Three times,
(repeat) — *M. d'Arthur* 145, 160
the last night's gale had *c*, — *Gardener's D.* 124
And there he *c* the younker tickling trout— — *Walk. to the Mail* 33
C in flagrante—what's the Latin word? — „ 34
Thou wouldst have *c* me up into thy rest, — *St. S. Stylites* 18
Abaddon and Asmodeus *c* at me. — „ 172
C up the whole of love and utter'd it, — *Love and Duty* 82
Like truths of Science waiting to be *c*— — *Golden Year* 17
The page has *c* her hand in his: — *Day-Dm., Sleep P.* 29
Lady's-head upon the prow *C* the shrill salt, — *The Voyage* 12
C the sparkles, and in circles, — *Vision of Sin* 30
C each other with wild grimaces, — „ 35
now hastily *c* His bundle, waved his hand, — *Enoch Arden* 237
C at his hand, and wrung it passionately, — „ 328
C at and ever miss'd it, and they laugh'd; — „ 752
about the fields you *c* His weary daylong chirping, — *The Brook* 52
great pock-pitten fellow had been *c*? — *Aylmer's Field* 256
C in a burst of unexpected storm, — „ 285
And *c* the blossom of the flying terms, — *Princess, Pro.* 164
and the flood drew: yet I *c* her; — „ *iv* 182
Right on this we drove and *c*, — „ 188
And falling on my face was *c* and known. — „ 270
as if *c* at once from bed And tumbled — „ 285
On one knee Kneeling, I gave it, which she *c*, — „ 470
Like tender things that being *c* feign death, — „ *v* 108
Were *c* within the record of her wrongs, — „ 143
Came sallying thro' the gates, and *c* his hair, — „ 340
not less one glance he *c* Thro' open doors — „ 342
And reach'd the ship and *c* the rope, — *Sailor Boy* 3
He *c* her away with a sudden cry; — *The Victim* 69
And Fancy light from Fancy *c*, — *In Mem. xxiii* 14
And *c* once more the distant shout, — „ *lxxxvii* 9
c The deep pulsations of the world, — „ *xcv* 39
C and cuff'd by the gale: — *Maud I vi* 5
and *c* By that you swore to withstand? — „ 79
Last year, I *c* a glimpse of his face, — „ *xiii* 27
For how often I *c* her with eyes all wet, — „ *xix* 23
Who stoopt and *c* the babe, and cried — *Com. of Arthur* 385
c And stay'd him, 'Climb not lest thou break — *Gareth and L.* 53
The listening rogue hath *c* the manner of it. — „ 778
C at the hilt, as to abolish him: — *Marr. of Geraint* 210
Yniol *c* His purple scarf, and held, — „ 376
Edyrn's men had *c* them in their flight, — „ 642
Her by both hands he *c*, and sweetly said, — „ 778
he sharply *c* his lance and shield, — *Balin and Balan* 287
'And passing gentle' *c* his hand away — „ 371
C in a great old tyrant spider's web, — *Merlin and V.* 259
one of Satan's shepherdesses *c* And meant to
stamp him — „ 758
plunged, and *c* And set it on his head, — *Lancelot and E.* 54
The heathen *c* and reft him of his tongue. — „ 273
and him they *c* and maim'd; — „ 275
whereat she *c* her breath; — „ 623

Caught (*continued*) Lady of the Lake *C* from his
mother's arms— — *Lancelot and E.* 140
the holy cup Was *c* away to Heaven, — *Holy Grail* 1
c his hand, Held it, and there, half-hidden by him, — „ 75
she *c* the circlet from his lance, — *Pelleas and E.* 17
C his unbroken limbs from the dark field, — „ 58
Then Tristram laughing *c* the harp, — *Last Tournament* 7
c him by the hilt, and brandish'd him Three times,
(repeat) — *Pass. of Arthur* 313, 32
round and round A whirlwind *c* and bore us; — *Lover's Tale ii* 19
they turn'd, and *c* and brought him in — „ *iv* 37
old Sir Richard *c* at last, — *The Revenge* 9
And *c* the laming bullet. — *Sisters (E. and E.)* 6
Had *c* her hand, and her eyelids fell— — „ 14
C in a mill and crush'd— — *In the Child. Hosp.* 1
So, *c*, I burn, Burn? heathen men have borne — *Sir J. Oldcastle* 18
I *c* the wreath that was flung. — *The Wreck* 4
flay Captives whom they *c* in battle— — *Locksley H., Sixty* 8
And his eloquence *c* like a flame — *Dead Prophet* 1
And *c* her chaplet here—and there — *To Marg. of Dufferin* 1
woman came And *c* me from my nurse. — *The Ring* 11
C by the flower that closes on the fly, — „ 34
Who never *c* one gleam of the beauty — *Happy* 1
c and held His people by the bridle-rein — *Akbar's Dream* 8
And he *c* my little one from me: — *Bandit's Death* 2
died of a fever *c* when a nurse — *Charity* 4
Cause embattail and to wall about thy *c* — *To J. M. K.*
more *c* to weep have I: My tears, no tears of love, — *Wan Sculptor* 1
Nor in a merely selfish *c*— — *Two Voices* 14
'In some good *c*, not in mine own, — „ 14
This woman was the *c*. — *D. of F. Women* 10
only love were *c* enough for praise.' — *Gardener's D.* 10
no *c*; James had no *c*: but when I prest the *c*, — *The Brook* 9
who most have *c* to sorrow for her— — *Aylmer's Field* 67
such extremes, I told her, well might harm The
woman's *c*. — *Princess iii* 14
Or, falling, protomartyr of our *c*, Die: — „ *iv* 50
twice I sought to plead my *c*, — „ 55
betray'd her *c* and mine— — „ *v* 7
and storming in extremes, Stood for her *c*, — „ 17
why, the *c*'s weigh'd, Fatherly fears— — „ 21
in our noble sister's *c*? More, more,—for honour: — „ 31
I would not aught of false—Is not our *c* pure? — „ 40
you The sole men to be mingled with our *c*, — „ 41
our side was vanquish'd and my *C* For ever lost, — „ *vi* 2
whose arms Champion'd our *c* and won it — „ 7
The brethren of our blood and *c*, — „ 20
To dream thy *c* embraced in mine, — „ *vii* 23
She pray'd me not to judge their *c* from her — „ 22
that know The woman's *c* is man's: — *In Mem. xxix*
With such compelling *c* to grieve — „ *cvi* 1
Ring out a slowly dying *c*, — *Maud I x* 4
can he tell Whether war be a *c* or a consequence? — *Maud III vi* 3
I cleaved to a *c* that I felt to be pure — „ 5
We have proved we have hearts in a *c*, — *Gareth and L.* 82
good *c* is theirs To hate me, — „ 128
'Sound sleep be thine! sound *c* to sleep hast thou. — „
Am I the *c*, I the poor *c* that men Reproach you, — *Marr. of Geraint* 8
I *am* the *c*, because I dare not speak — „ 8
'Graver *c* than yours is mine, To curse — „ 30
you that most had *c* To fear me, fear no longer, — *Geraint and E.* 82
Yourself were first the blameless *c* — „ 82
And made her good man jealous with good *c*. — *Merlin and V.* 60
Some *c* had kept him sunder'd from his wife— — „ 71
Could call him the main *c* of all their crime; — „ 78
now remains But little *c* for laughter: — *Lancelot and E.* 59
that I gave No *c*, not willingly, for such a love— — „ 129
hither had she fled, her *c* of flight Sir Modred; — *Guinevere*
come my way! to twit me with the *c*! — *Lover's Tale i* 66
So much God's *c* was fluent in it— — *Sir J. Oldcastle* 1
some less *c*, some *c* far less than mine; — „ 18
For every other *c* is less than mine. — „ 18
To this great *c* of Freedom drink, my friends,
(repeat) — *Hands all Round* 11, 3
Death for the right *c*, death for the wrong *c*, — *Vastness*

Cedar (*continued*) bloom profuse and *c* arches Charm,   *Milton* 11
   Sighing for Lebanon, Dark *c*,   *Maud I xviii* 18
Cedar-tree A voice by the *c t* In the meadow   ,,   *v* 1
   red man dance By his red *c-t*,   ,,   *xvii* 18
Cedar-wood A mile beneath the *c-w*.   *Eleänore* 8
Cede learn if Ida yet would *c* our claim,   *Princess v* 333
Ceiling (*See also* **Hall-ceiling**) men Walk'd like the
   fly on *c's?*   *Columbus* 51
Celandine in varnish'd glory shine Thy stars of *c*.   *Prog. of Spring* 39
Celebrate To *c* the golden prime   *Arabian Nights* 131
Celebrated thine the deeds to be *c*,   *Boädicea* 41
Celibacy Into the suburb—their hard *c*,   *Sir J. Oldcastle* 107
Celidon gloomy skirts Of *C* the forest;   *Lancelot and E.* 292
Cell From many a wondrous grot and secret *c*   *The Kraken* 8
   And wild winds bound within their *c*,   *Mariana* 54
   'Not less the bee would range her *c's*,   *Two Voices* 70
   From *c's* of madness unconfined,   ,,   371
   Made havock among those tender *c's*,   *Lucretius* 22
   And weave their petty *c's* and die.   *In Mem. l* 12
   track Suggestion to her inmost *c*.   ,,   *xcv* 32
   The tiny *c* is forlorn,   *Maud II* ii 13
   Thro' *c's* of madness, haunts of horror   ,,   *III vi* 2
   in your frosty *c's* ye feel the fire!   *Balin and Balan* 446
   c's and chambers: all were fair and dry;   *Lancelot and E.* 407
   When they gain'd the *c* wherein he slept,   ,,   811
   Across the iron grating of her *c* Beat,   *Holy Grail* 81
   Stream'd thro' my *c* a cold and silver beam,   ,,   116
   Till all the white walls of my *c* were dyed   ,,   119
   I never stray'd beyond the *c*,   ,,   628
   bound and plunged him into a *c* Of great piled stones;   ,,   675
   such a craziness as needs A *c* and keeper),   *Lover's Tale iv* 165
   They had fasten'd the door of his *c*.   *Rizpah* 42
   Like worldly beauties in the *C*,   *The Ring* 143
Cellar in the *c's* merry bloated things   *Guinevere* 267
Celled *See* **Full-celled, Two-cell'd**
Celt (race of people) Teuton or *C*, or whatever
   we be,   *W. to Alexandra* 32
   The blind hysterics of the *C*;   *In Mem. cix* 16
Celt (stone implement) *c's* and calumets, Claymore and
   snowshoe,   *Princess, Pro.* 17
Censer incense free From one *c* in one shrine,   *Eleänore* 59
   The shrill bell rings, the *c* swings,   *Sir Galahad* 35
   A *c*, either worn with wind and storm;   *Gareth and L.* 222
Censure England's honest were too far;   *Third of Feb.* 2
   It might be safe our *c's* to withdraw;   ,,   11
Cent mellow metres more than *c* for *c*;   *The Brook* 5
Center'd *See* **Centred**
Centre Earth is dry to the *c*,   *Nothing will Die* 20
   Till toward the *c* set the starry tides,   *Princess ii* 117
   thoughts that On you, their *c*:   ,,   *iv* 444
   in the *c* stood The common men with rolling eyes;   ,,   *vi* 359
   Whose faith has *c* everywhere,   *In Mem. xxxiii* 3
   The *c* of a world's desire;   ,,   *lxiv* 16
   In the *c* stood A statue veil'd,   ,,   *ciii* 11
   Safe, damsel, as the *c* of this hall.   *Gareth and L.* 604
   To *c* in this place and time.   *Lover's Tale i* 552
   the *c* and crater of European confusion,   *Beautiful City* 1
Centre-bit *c-b's* Grind on the wakeful ear   *Maud I i* 41
Centred-Center'd music *centred* in a doleful
   song   *Lotos-Eaters, C. S.* 117
   centred in the sphere Of common duties,   *Ulysses* 39
   Would follow, *center'd* in eternal calm.   *Lucretius* 79
   one emerald *center'd* in a sun Of silver rays,   *Lancelot and E.* 295
Century When the *centuries* behind me like a fruitful
   land   *Locksley Hall* 13
   A maiden of our *c*, yet most meek;   *The Brook* 68
   thro' the *centuries* let a people's voice   *Ode on Well.* 142
   Had I lain for a *c* dead,   *Maud I xxii* 72
   years will roll into the *centuries*,   *Guinevere* 626
   speak to the *centuries*, All the *centuries*,   *On Jub. Q. Victoria* 48
   The *c's* three strong eights have met   *To Ulysses* 7
Ceremonial Hail the fair *C* Of this year of her
   Jubilee.   *On Jub. Q. Victoria* 23
   in his heart rejoice At this glad *C*,   ,,   37
   Of this great *C*,   ,,   50

Ceremony Long summers back, a kind of *c*—   *Princess i* 12
   in the darkness, at the mystical *c*,   *Boädicea* 3
   suit of fray'd magnificence, Once fit for feasts
   of *c*)   *Marr. of Geraint* 29?
   And there be wedded with all *c*.   ,,   60?
   They twain were wedded with all *c*.   ,,   83?
Chaänge (change) I thowt shall I *c* my staäte?   *Spinster's S's.* 4?
Chaänged (changed) But arter I *c* my mind,   *North. Cobbler* 10?
Chaängin' (changing) all the while I wur *c* my gown,   *Spinster's S's.* 4?
Chace-Chase (*See also* **Sumner-chace**) That stand
   within the *chace*.   *Talking Oak* 9?
   And overlook the *chace*   ,,   9?
   Look further through the *chace*,   ,,   24?
   Then crost the common into Darnley *chase*   *The Brook* 13?
Chafe yet it *c's* me that I could not bend   *D. of F. Women* 13?
   Began to *c* as at a personal wrong.   *Enoch Arden* 47?
Chafed *c* his hands, And call'd him by his name,   *M. d'Arthur* 20?
   And when his answer *c* them,   *Holy Grail* 67?
   c his hands, And call'd him by his name,   *Pass. of Arthur* 37?
   I took And *c* the freezing hand.   *The Ring* 45?
Chaff Mere *c* and draff, much better burnt.'   *The Epic* 35?
   will be *c* For every gust of chance,   *Princess iv* 35?
   And vacant *c* well meant for grain.   *In Mem. vi* ?
   and grope, And gather dust and *c*,   ,,   *lv* 1?
Chaffering *C's* and chatterings at the market-cross,   *Holy Grail* 55?
Chafing *c* at his own great self defied,   *Aylmer's Field* 53?
   But *c* me on fire to find my bride)   *Princess i* 1?
   and the squire *C* his shoulder;   *Geraint and E.* 2?
   c his pale hands, and calling to him.   ,,   58?
   c his faint hands, and calling to him;   ,,   58?
Chain (s) (*See also* **Daisy-chain, Ruby-chain**) to chain
   with *c's*, and bind with bands   *Buonaparte* ?
   loosed the *c*, and down she lay;   *L. of Shalott iv* 1?
   such a *c* Of knitted purport,   *Two Voices* 16?
   Bound by gold *c's* about the feet of God.   *M. d'Arthur* 25?
   But dallied with his golden *c*,   *Day-Dm., Revival* 3?
   Twofooted at the limit of his *c*,   *Aylmer's Field* 12?
   To break my *c*, to shake my mane: *Princess ii* 42?
   From growing commerce loose her latest *c*,   *Ode Inter. Exhib.* 3?
   made the serf a man, and burst his *c*—   *W. to Marie Alex.* ?
   boat, Half-swallow'd in it, anchor'd with a *c*;   *Holy Grail* 80?
   I burst the *c*, I sprang into the boat.   ,,   80?
   Bound by gold *c's* about the feet of God.   *Pass. of Arthur* 42?
   seem'd as tho' a link Of some tight *c*   *Lover's Tale i* 59?
   sat as if in *c's*—to whom he said: ,,   *iv* 36?
   He workt me the daisy *c*—   *First Quarrel* 1?
   but am led by the creak of the *c*,   *Rizpah* ?
   They hang'd him in *c's* for a show—   ,,   3?
   C's, my good lord: in your raised brows   *Columbus* ?
   C's for the Admiral of the Ocean! *c's* For him who gave
   a new heaven,   ,,   1?
   c's for him Who push'd his prows   ,,   2?
   C's! we are Admirals of the Ocean,   ,,   2?
   Drove me and my good brothers home in *c's*,   ,,   13?
   the *c's*, what do *they* mean—the *c's*?'   ,,   21?
   'These same *c's* Bound these same bones   ,,   21?
   wept with me when I return'd in *c's*,   ,,   23?
   She that link'd again the broken *c*   *Locksley H., Sixty* 5?
   c's of mountain, grains of sand   ,,   20?
   The slave, the scourge, the *c*;   ,,*Freedom* 1?
   all the gold from each laburnum *c*   *To Mary Boyle* 1?
   Down hill 'Too-quick,' the *c*.   *Politics* 1?
Chain (verb) to *c* with chains, and bind with bands   *Buonaparte* ?
   And *c's* regret to his decease,   *In Mem. xxix* ?
Chain'd My right leg *c* into the crag,   *St. S. Stylites* ?
   —or brought her *c*, a slave,   *Princess v* 13?
   so *c* and coupled with the curse Of blindness   *Tiresias* 5?
   dog: it was *c*, but its horrible yell   *Bandit's Death* 3?
Chaining But *c* fancy now at home   *To Ulysses* 3?
Chair (*See also* **Arm-chair, Elbow-chair**) If one
   but speaks or hems or stirs his *c*,   *Sonnet To—* ?
   In yonder *c* I see him sit,   *Miller's D.* ?
   And the long shadow of the *c*   ,,   12?
   Two years his *c* is seen Empty   *To J. S.* 2?
   farmer vext packs up his beds and *c's*,   *Walk. to the Mail* 3?

Chair (*continued*) Sweat on his blazon'd *c's*; — *Walk. to the Mail* 76
And in his *c* himself uprear'd, — *Day-Dm., Revival* 18
But kept the house, his *c*, and last his bed. — *Enoch Arden* 826
With nearing *c* and lower'd accent) — *Aylmer's Field* 267
I cry to vacant *c's* and widow'd walls, — ” 720
They come and sit by my *c*, — *Grandmother* 83
spirits sink To see the vacant *c*, — *In Mem. xx* 19
The *c's* and thrones of civil power? — ” *xxi* 16
He plays with threads, he beats his *c* — ” *lxvi* 13
Why sits he here in his father's *c*? — *Maud I xiii* 23
Gareth went, and hovering round her *c* Ask'd, — *Gareth and L.* 33
pushing could move The *c* of Idris. — *Marr. of Geraint* 543
in their *c's* set up a stronger race — *Geraint and E.* 940
Thy *c*, a grief to all the brethren, — *Balin and Balan* 78
sloping down to make Arms for his *c*, — *Lancelot and E.* 438
In our great hall there stood a vacant *c*, — *Holy Grail* 167
Merlin sat In his own *c*, and so was lost; — ” 176
Galahad would sit down in Merlin's *c*. — ” 181
now his *c* desires him here in vain, — ” 901
fill'd his double-dragon'd *c*. — *Last Tournament* 144
Push'd from his *c* of regal heritage, — *Lover's Tale i* 118
Led his dear lady to a *c* of state. — ” *iv* 321
I mash'd the taäbles an' *c's*, — *North. Cobbler* 37
an' the mark o' 'is 'eäd o' the *c's*! — *Spinster's S's.* 100
An' I slep i' my *c* hup-on-end, — *Owd Roä* 54
An' I slep' i' my *c* ageän — ” 65
Sa I kep i' my *c*, fur I thowt she was nobbut — ” 74
she skelpt ma haäfe ower i' the *c*, — ” 76
Chairman A quarter-sessions *c*, abler none; — *Princess, Con.* 90
Chaise Within the low-wheel'd *c*, — *Talking Oak* 110
Chalcedony *C*, emerald, sardonyx, sardius, — *Columbus* 84
Chalice The *c* of the grapes of God; — *In Mem. x* 16
C and salver, wines that, Heavens knows when, — *Lover's Tale iv* 193
Chalk all his joints Are full of *c*? — *Audley Court* 47
Tumbles a billow on *c* and sand; — *To F. D. Maurice* 24
c and alum and plaster are sold to the poor — *Maud I i* 39
Chalk'd *c* her face, and wing'd Her transit — *Princess iv* 377
Chalk-hill On the *c-h* the bearded grass Is dry — *Miller's D.* 245
Chalk-quarry white *c-q* from the hill Gleam'd — ” 115
Challenge madness made thee *c* the chief knight — *Gareth and L.* 1416
a jubilant *c* to Time and to Fate; — *Vastness* 21
Challenging *c* And overthrowing every knight — *Balin and Balan* 12
Chamber (*See also* **Chaumber**) faults were thick
as dust In vacant *c's*, — *To the Queen* 19
thick-moted sunbeam lay Athwart the *c's*, — *Mariana* 79
door that bar The secret bridal *c's* of the heart, — *Gardener's D.* 249
breathings are not heard In palace *c's* far
apart. — *Day-Dm., Sleep B.* 18
till he find The quiet *c* far apart. — ” *Arrival* 28
In musty bins and *c's*, — ” *Will Water.* 102
till the comrade of his *c's* woke, — *Aylmer's Field* 583
To one deep *c* shut from sound, — *Princess vi* 376
all The *c's* emptied of delight: — *In Mem. viii* 8
The field, the *c* and the street, — ” 11
Moved in the *c's* of the blood; — ” *xxiii* 20
About its echoing *c's* wide, — *Maud I vi* 74
In the *c* or the street, — ” *II iv* 83
But hire us some fair *c* for the night, — *Geraint and E.* 238
the boy return'd And told them of a *c*, — ” 261
the two remain'd Apart by all the *c's* width, — ” 265
High in her *c* up a tower to the east — *Lancelot and E.* 3
cells and *c's*: all were fair and dry; — ” 407
Past to her *c*, and there flung herself — ” 609
The lucid *c's* of the morning star, — *Lover's Tale i* 28
Shut in the secret *c's* of the rock. — ” 521
Death in our innermost *c*, — *Def. of Lucknow* 15
read Some wonder at our *c* ornaments. — *Columbus* 2
That *c* in the tower. — *The Ring* 94
What *c*, child? Your nurse is here? — ” 95
You took me to that *c* in the tower, — ” 111
I brought you to that *c* — ” 129
Chamber-door (*See also* **Chaumber-door**) As
lightly as a sick man's *c-d*, — *Enoch Arden* 776
Chamberlain call'd A hoary man, his *c*, — *Com. of Arthur* 145
Then spake the hoary *c* and said, — ” 148

Chamian Apart the *C* Oracle divine — *Alexander* 10
Champaign river-sunder'd *c* clothed with corn, — *Œnone* 114
high Above the empurpled *c*, drank the gale — *Princess iii* 120
shadowing down the *c* till it strikes On a wood, — ” *v* 526
Champion My *c* from the ashes of his hearth.' — *Gareth and L.* 899
c thou hast brought from Arthur's hall? — ” 916
but have ye slain The damsel's *c*? — ” 1099
Lady Lyonors Had sent her coming *c*, — ” 1192
Champion'd *C* our cause and won it — *Princess vi* 62
Chance (s) I shut my life from happier *c*. — *Two Voices* 54
Many a *c* the years beget. — *Miller's D.* 31
For that is not a common *c* — *To J. S.* 47
every morning brought a noble *c*, And every *c* brought
out a noble knight. — *M. d'Arthur* 230
April hopes, the fools of *c*; — *Vision of Sin* 164
'Drink to Fortune, drink to *C*, — ” 191
It is beyond all hope, against all *c*, — *Enoch Arden* 403
He gave them line: and how by *c* — *The Brook* 150
rate your *c* Almost at naked fortune.' — *Princess i* 160
With open eyes, and we must take the *c*. — ” *iii* 143
dread His wildness, and the *c's* of the dark.' — ” *iv* 244
will be chaff For every gust of *c*, — ” 356
my flitting *c* Were caught within the record — ” *v* 142
she's comely; there's the fairer *c*: — ” 460
or was it *c*, She past my way. — ” *vi* 97
Dispute the claims, arrange the *c's*; — *To F. D. Maurice* 5
And grasps the skirts of happy *c*, — *In Mem. lxiv* 6
To *c's* where our lots were cast — ” *xcii* 5
steps of Time—the shocks of *C*— — ” *xcv* 2
And leaps into the future *c*, — ” *cxiv* 7
can a sweeter *c* ever come to me here? — *Maud I i* 62
if it had not been For a *c* of travel, — ” *ii* 8
an often *c* In those brain-stunning shocks, — *Gareth and L.* 88
some *c* to mar the boast Thy brethren — ” 1242
good *c* that we shall hear the hounds: — *Marr. of Geraint* 182
What *c* is this? how is it I see you — *Geraint and E.* 309
A common *c*—right well I know it— — ” 331
Guilty or guiltless, to stave off a *c* — ” 353
Their *c* of booty from the morning's raid, — ” 565
ye surely have endured Strange *c's* here alone;' — ” 810
Queen demanded as by *c* 'Know ye the stranger
woman?' — *Merlin and V.* 128
This *c* of noble deeds will come and go Unchallenged, — *Holy Grail* 318
Our fear of some disastrous *c* for thee On hill, — ” 727
Ready to spring, waiting a *c*: — *Guinevere* 12
Some evil *c* Will make the smouldering scandal — ” 90
c and craft and strength in single fights, — *Pass. of Arthur* 106
every morning brought a noble *c*, And every *c*
brought out a noble knight. — ” 398
Above the perilous seas of Change and *C*; — *Lover's Tale i* 806
c's of dividend, consol, and share— — *The Wreck* 30
Like a clown—by *c* he met me— — *Locksley H., Sixty* 256
Chance (verb) when did Arthur *c* upon thee first?' — *Com. of Arthur* 338
However that might *c*! — *Gareth and L.* 458
boast Thy brethren of thee make—which could
not *c*— — ” 1243
Chance-comer You set before *c-c's*, — *Will Water.* 6
Chanced It *c* one evening Annie's children — *Enoch Arden* 362
At last one night it *c* That Annie could not sleep, — ” 489
Now it *c* that I had been, — *Princess i* 31
and if their *c* a joust, — *Gareth and L.* 519
then by what thereafter *c*, — ” 1214
At last, it *c* that on a summer morn — *Marr. of Geraint* 69
It *c* the song that Enid sang was one — ” 345
with her mind all full of what had *c*, — *Geraint and E.* 778
King's own ear Speak what has *c*; — ” 809
Then *c*, one morning, that Sir Balin sat — *Balin and Balan* 240
All that had *c*, and Balan moan'd again. — ” 604
And as it *c* they are happy, being pure.' — *Merlin and V.* 745
'These jewels, whereupon I *c* Divinely, — *Lancelot and E.* 58
one morn it *c* He found her in among the garden
yews, — ” 922
I told him what had *c*, My sister's vision, — *Holy Grail,* 271
And then I *c* upon a goodly town — ” 573
It *c* that both Brake into hall together — *Pelleas and E.* 586

Chanced (*continued*) For thus it *c* one morn when all
the court,   *Guinevere* 21
c that, when half of the short summer night was gone, *The Revenge* 65
and it *c* on a day Soon as the blast   *Def. of Lucknow* 31
Chance-gift eating not, Except the spare *c-g* *St. S. Stylites* 78
Chancel A broken *c* with a broken cross,   *M. d'Arthur* 9
I peer'd athwart the *c* pane   *The Letters* 3
A broken *c* with a broken cross,   *Pass. of Arthur* 177
and mute below the *c* stones,   *Locksley H., Sixty* 43
Chancel-casement Upon the *c-c*, and upon that
grave   *May Queen, N. Y's. E.* 21
Chancellor The *c*, sedate and vain,   *Day-Dm., Revival* 29
C, or what is greatest would he be—   *Aylmer's Field* 397
Chance-met cross-lightnings of four *c-m* eyes   " 129
Change (s) Truth may stand forth unmoved of *c*, *Supp. Confessions* 144
oxen's low Came to her : without hope of *c*,   *Mariana* 29
And airy forms of flitting *c*.   *Madeline* 7
run thro' every *c* of sharp and flat ;   *Caress'd or Chidden* 4
I said, 'The years with *c* advance :   *Two Voices* 52
'Then comes the check, the *c*, the fall,   " 163
upon the board, And bred this *c* ;   *Œnone* 227
fit for every mood And *c* of my still soul. *Palace of Art* 60
Full-welling fountain-heads of *c*,   " 166
but all hath suffer'd *c* :   *Lotos-Eaters, C.S.* 71
'I govern'd men by *c*, and so I sway'd *D. of F. Women* 130
thro' all *c* Of liveliest utterance.   " 167
Lie still, dry dust, secure of *c*.   " *To J. S.* 76
Meet is it *c's* should control Our being, *Love thou thy land* 41
So let the *c* which comes be free   " 45
Of many *c's*, aptly join'd,   " 65
And sick of home went overseas for *c*. *Walk. to the Mail* 24
And fear of *c* at home, that drove him hence.   " 68
With all the varied *c's* of the dark,   *Edwin Morris* 36
shrivelling thro' me, and a cloudlike *c*, *St. S. Stylites* 199
Changed with thy mystic *c*,   *Tithonus* 55
spin for ever down the ringing grooves of *c*. *Locksley Hall* 182
And, rapt thro' many a rosy *c*,   *Day-Dm., Depart* 23
The flower and quintessence of *c*.   *L'Envoi* 24
voice grew faint : there came a further *c* : *Vision of Sin* 207
came a *c*, as all things human change. *Enoch Arden* 101
So much to look to—such a *c*—   " 461
and the *c* and not the *c*,   *Aylmer's Field* 831
dismal lyrics, prophesying *c* Beyond all reason : *Princess i* 142
woman wed is not as we, But suffers *c* of frame. " *v* 463
Then came a *c* : for sometimes I would catch " *vii* 92
Till notice of a *c* in the dark world   " 250
the *c*, This truthful *c* in thee has kill'd it. " 349
I perceived no touch of *c*,   *In Mem. xiv* 17
The touch of *c* in calm or storm ;   " *xvi* 6
Each voice four *c's* on the wind,   " *xxviii* 9
I have lost the links that bound Thy *c's* ; here upon
the ground No more partaker of thy *c*.   " *xli* 7
we talk'd Of men and minds, the dust of *c*, " *lxxi* 10
There cannot come a mellower *c*,   " *lxxxi* 3
For *c's* wrought on form and face ;   " *lxxxii* 2
Recalls, in *c* of light or gloom,   " *lxxxv* 74
Or touch'd the *c's* of the state,   " *lxxxix* 35
When summer's hourly-mellowing *c* May breathe, " *xci* 9
abyss Of tenfold-complicated *c*,   " *xciii* 12
For *c* of place, like growth of time,   " *cv* 11
O earth, what *c's* hast thou seen !   " *cxxiii* 2
His very face with *c* of heart is changed. *Geraint and E.* 899
in *c* of glare and gloom Her eyes and neck *Merlin and V.* 959
Naked of glory for His mortal *c*,   *Holy Grail* 448
with living waters in the *c* Of seasons : *Pelleas and E.* 511
Above the perilous seas of *C* and Chance, *Lover's Tale i* 806
In marvel at that gradual *c*, I thought   " *iii* 19
their bridal-time By *c* of feather : *Sisters (E. and E.)* 72
Glance at the wheeling Orb of *c*,   *To E. Fitzgerald* 3
Over the range and the *c* of the world *The Wreck* 70
After all the stormy *c's* shall we find *Locksley H., Sixty* 156
Far away beyond her myriad coming *c's*   " 231
Ring little bells of *c* From word to word. *Early Spring* 41
By *c's* all too fierce and fast   *Freedom* 22
c of the tide—what is all of it worth ? *Vastness* 30

Change (s) (*continued*) glimmer of relief In *c* of place. *To Mary Boyle* 48
That after many *c's* may succeed Life, *Prog. of Spring* 116
Change (verb) (*See also* **Chaänge**) All things will
c Thro' eternity.   *Nothing will Die* 15
It will *c*, but it will not fade   " 31
All things will *c*.   " 38
Not swift nor slow to *c*, but firm : *Love thou thy land* 31
Or *c* a word with her he calls his wife, *Dora* 44
'It cannot be : my uncle's mind will *c* !'   " 47
full music seem'd to move and *c*   *Edwin Morris* 35
iris *c's* on the burnish'd dove ;   *Locksley Hall* 19
She *c's* with that mood or this,   *Will Water.* 107
'*C*, reverting to the years,   *Vision of Sin* 159
Then came a change, as all things human *c*. *Enoch Arden* 101
If our old halls could *c* their sex, *Princess, Pro.* 140
you began to *c*—I saw it and grieved—   " *iv* 298
one that wishes at a dance to *c* The music—   " 589
When your skies *c* again :   " *vi* 278
Some patient force to *c* them when we will,   " *Con.* 56
and *c* the hearts of men, *W. to Marie Alex.* 44
But hearts that *c* not, love that cannot cease,   " 46
Nor *c* to us, although they *c* ; *In Mem. xxx* 24
Will *c* my sweetness more and more,   " *xxxv* 15
And every winter *c* to spring.   " *liv* 16
Thy ransom'd reason *c* replies   " *lxi* 2
fly The happy birds, that *c* their sky   " *cxv* 15
To *c* the bearing of a word,   " *cxxviii* 16
the wind will never *c* again.' *Gareth and L.* 1140
Let Gareth, an he will, *C* his for mine,   " 1300
and the wine will *c* your will.' *Geraint and E.* 663
The music in him seem'd to *c*, *Balin and Balan* 217
Must our true man *c* like a leaf at last ? *Lancelot and E.* 686
The twain together well might *c* the world. *Guinevere* 301
like wild birds that *c* Their season in the night *Pass. of Arthur* 38
Nevertheless, we did not *c* the name. *Lover's Tale i* 464
Yet must you *c* your name : *Sisters (E. and E.)* 226
To *c* with her horizon,   " 226
A wish in you To *c* our dark Queen-city, *To Mary Boyle* 65
Changed (*See also* **Chaänged**, **Autumn-changed**,
Counter-changed) Till all the crimson *c*,
and past   *Mariana in the S.* 25
'O cruel heart,' she *c* her tone,   " 69
You *c* a wholesome heart to gall. *L. C. V. de Vere* 44
but ere my flower to fruit *C*, *D. of F. Women* 208
thy flute-notes are *c* to coarse,   *The Blackbird* 18
We all are *c* by still degrees, *Love thou thy land* 43
flower of knowledge *c* to fruit Of wisdom. *Love and Duty* 24
C with thy mystic change,   *Tithonus* 55
And her spirit *c* within.   *L. of Burleigh* 64
the rim *C* every moment as we flew. *The Voyage* 28
Moved with violence, *c* in hue, *Vision of Sin* 34
but that name has twice been *c*— *Enoch Arden* 859
my mind is *c*, for I shall see him,   " 897
tost on thoughts that *c* from hue to hue, *Princess iv* 210
Our mind is *c* : we take it to ourself.'   " 362
and her hue *c*, and she said :   " *vi* 107
Walk'd at their will, and everything was *c*.   " 384
And one is sad ; her note is *c*, *In Mem. xxi* 27
crying, How *c* from where it ran   " *xxiii* 9
A grief, then *c* to something else,   " *lxxvii* 16
O grief, can grief be *c* to less ?   " *lxxviii* 16
Thy place is *c* ; thou art the same.   " *cxxi* 20
Remade the blood and *c* the frame,   " *Con.* 16
Of her whose gentle will has *c* my fate, *Maud 1 xviii* 23
mood is *c*, for it fell at a time of year   " *III vi* 4
Till with a wink his dream was *c*, *Com. of Arthur* 441
but the wind hath *c* : *Gareth and L.* 994
'Hath not the good wind, damsel, *c* again ?'   " 1054
being young, he *c* and came to loathe His crime *Marr. of Geraint* 593
To fear me, fear no longer, I am *c*. *Geraint and E.* 825
But kept myself aloof till I was *c* ; And fear not,
cousin ; I am *c* indeed.'   " 872
have ye seen how nobly *c* ?   " 897
His very face with change of heart is *c*.   " 899
her hue *C* at his gaze : *Balin and Balan* 279

Changed (*continued*)   And *c* itself and echo'd in her
    heart,   *Lancelot and E.* 782
    I doubt not that however *c*,   1218
    I was *c* to wan And meagre,   *Holy Grail* 571
    find thy favour *c* and love thee not '—   *Last Tournament* 500
    Denouncing judgment, but tho' *c*,   *Guinevere* 421
    I *c* the name ; San Salvador I call'd it ;   *Columbus* 75
    And *c* her into dust.   *Ancient Sage* 162
    We never *c* a bitter word,   *The Flight* 86
    And then had *c* ! so fickle are men—   *The Ring* 392
    clove the Moslem crescent moon, and *c* it into blood.   *Happy* 44
    I that heard, and *c* the prayer   ,, 55
    A man who never *c* a word with men,   *St. Telemachus* 10
Changeless   thee the *c* in thine ever-changing skies.   *Akbar's D., Hymn* 4
Changeling   Or sorrow such a *c* be ?   *In Mem.* xvi 4
    like a fairy *c* lay the mage ;   *Com. of Arthur* 363
    But only *c* out of Fairyland,   *Gareth and L.* 203
Changest   Who *c* not in any gale,   *In Mem.* ii 10
    And *c*, breathing it, the sullen wind,   *Prog. of Spring* 110
Changeth   old order *c*, yielding place to new,   *M. d'Arthur* 240
    old order *c*, yielding place to new ;   *Com. of Arthur* 509
    old order *c*, yielding place to new.   *Pass. of Arthur* 408
Changing (*See also* **Chaängin'**, **Ever-changing**,
    Never-changing)   In *c*, chime with never-
    changing Law.   *To Duke of Argyll* 11
Channel (*See also* **Mid-channel**) Tho' every *c* of the
    State Should fill   *You ask me, why* 23
    the hoary *C* Tumbles a billow on chalk and
    sand ;   *To F. D. Maurice* 23
    brooks Are fashion'd by the *c* which they keep),   *Lover's Tale* i 567
    We seem'd like ships i' the *C*   *First Quarrel* 42
    may The fated *c* where thy motion lives   *De Prof. Two G.* 19
Chant   In the heart of the garden the merry bird *c's*.   *Poet's Mind* 4
    ' *C* me now some wicked stave,   *Vision of Sin* 151
    c the history Of that great race,   *In Mem.* ciii 34
    From prime to vespers will I *c* thy praise   *Pelleas and E.* 349
    to the *c* of funeral hymns.   *Happy* 48
Chanted   *C* loudly, *c* lowly,   *L. of Shalott* iv 29
    C from an ill-used race of men that cleave   *Lotos-Eaters, C. S.* 120
    And *c* a melody loud and sweet,   *Poet's Song* 6
    c on the blanching bones of men ?'   *Princess* ii 199
    So they *c*: how shall Britain light   *Boädicea* 45
    So they *c* in the darkness,   ,, 46
    whose hymns Are *c* in the minster,   *Merlin and V.* 766
    She *c* snatches of mysterious hymns   *Lancelot and E.* 1407
    Had *c* on the smoky mountain-tops,   *Guinevere* 282
    and *c* the triumph of Finn,   *V. of Maeldune* 48
    And we *c* the songs of the Bards   ,, 90
Chanter   *C* of the Pollio,   *To Virgil* 17
Chanting   But mine own phantom *c* hymns ?   *In Mem.* cviii 10
    murmur of their temples *c*, Me, me,   *Demeter and P.* 72
Chaos   *C*, Cosmos ! Cosmos, *C* ! (repeat)   *Locksley H., Sixty* 103, 127
Chapel   bore him to a *c* nigh the field,   *M. d'Arthur* 8
    To *c*: where a heated pulpiteer,   *Sea Dreams* 20
    The portal of King Pellam's *c*   *Balin and Balan* 405
    In the white rock a *c* and a hall   *Lancelot and E.* 405
    where the vale Was lowest, found a *c*,   *Holy Grail* 442
    bore him to a *c* nigh the field,   *Pass. of Arthur* 176
    Is it, you, that preach'd in the *c*   *Despair* 1
    We have knelt in your know-all *c*   ,, 94
    Yonder in that *c*, slowly sinking   *Locksley H., Sixty* 27
Chapel bell   the *c b's* Call'd us: we left the walks ;   *Princess* ii 470
    when they toll the *C b* !   *Locksley H., Sixty* 261
Chapel-door   and against the *c d* Laid lance,   *Holy Grail* 459
    I touch'd The *c-d's* at dawn I know ;   ,, 536
    meet you again tomorra,' says he, ' be the *c-d.*'   *Tomorrow* 16
    this body they foun' an the grass Be the *c-d*,   ,, 74
Chapel-green   she stept an the *c-g*,   ,, 27
Chapel-yard   in the precincts of the *c-y*,   *Merlin and V.* 751
    Then paced for coolness in the *c-y* ;   ,, 757
Chap-fallen   The *c-f* circle spreads ;   *Vision of Sin* 172
Chaplet   And caught her *c* here—   *To Marq. of Dufferin* 30
Char   Nor ever lightning *c* thy grain,   *Talking Oak* 277
Character'd   laws of marriage *c* in gold   *Isabel* 16
    How dimly *c* and slight,   *In Mem.* lxi 6

D*

Charade   *C's* and riddles as at Christmas   *Princess, Pro.* 189
Charge (imputation)   Redeem'd it from the *c* of
    nothingness—   *M. d'Arthur, Ep.* 7
    Set up the *c* ye know,   *Merlin and V.* 703
    Merlin answer'd careless of her *c*,   ,, 754
Charge (care)   father left him gold, And in my *c*,   *Marr. of Geraint* 452
    And all in *c* of whom ? a girl :   *Geraint and E.* 125
    whom Uther left in *c* Long since,   ,, 933
    Modred whom he left in *c* of all,   *Guinevere* 195
Charge (directions)   he gave them *c* about the Queen,   ,, 591
    thy *c* Is an abounding pleasure to me.   *Gareth and L.* 981
Charge (attack)   surging *c's* foam'd themselves away ;   *Ode on Well.* 126
    O the wild *c* they made !   *Light Brigade* 51
    Honour the *c* they made !   ,, 53
    Plunged in the last fierce *c* at Waterloo,   *Sisters (E. and E.)* 64
    The crash of the *c's*,   *Batt. of Brunanburh* 89
    THE *c* of the gallant three hundred,   *Heavy Brigade* 1
    bad his trumpeter sound To the *c*,   ,, 9
    The trumpet, the gallop, the *c*,   ,, 13
    O mad for the *c* and the battle were we,   ,, 41
    Glory to each and to all, and the *c* that they made !   ,, 65
Charge (to enjoin)   Come forth, I *c* thee, arise,   *Ode to Memory* 46
    I *c* thee, quickly go again   *M. d'Arthur* 79
    I *c* you now, When you shall see her,   *Enoch Arden* 877
    I *c* thee by my love,'   *Gareth and L.* 55
    ' I *c* thee, ask not, but obey.'   *Marr. of Geraint* 133
    c the gardeners now To pick the faded creature   ,, 670
    I *c* thee ride before,   *Geraint and E.* 14
    I *c* thee, on thy duty as a wife,   ,, 16
    I *c* you, Enid, more especially,   ,, 414
    I count it of small use To *c* you)   ,, 417
    I *c* thee by that crown upon thy shield,   *Balin and Balan* 481
    I *c* you, follow me not.'   *Lancelot and E.* 507
    I *c* you that you get at once to horse.   ,, 539
    Leave me that, I *c* thee, my last hope.   *Guinevere* 568
    I *c* thee, quickly go again,   *Pass. of Arthur* 247
    I *c* you never to say that I laid him   *Rizpah* 58
    ' Never surrender, I *c* you,   *Def. of Lucknow* 10
Charge (to impute)   if he did that wrong you *c*
    him with,   *Sea Dreams* 279
Charge (to rush)   *C* for the guns ! ' he said :   *Light Brigade* 6
    I myself beheld the King *C* at the head   *Lancelot and E.* 304
Charge (to load)   See **Double-charge**
Charged (ordered)   Then Arthur *c* his warrior whom
    he loved   *Com. of Arthur* 447
    c by Valence to bring home the child.   *Merlin and V.* 718
    calling her three knights, she *c* them,   *Pelleas and E.* 219
Charged (attacked)   *c* Before the eyes of ladies and
    of kings.   *M. d'Arthur* 224
    down we swept and *c* and overthrew.   *Ode on Well.* 130
    c Before the eyes of ladies and of kings.   *Pass. of Arthur* 392
Charged (filled)   *C* both mine eyes with tears.   *D. of F. Women* 13
    and *c* the winds With spiced May-sweets   *Lover's Tale* i 317
Charged (loaded)   It is *c* and we fire, and they run.   *Def. of Lucknow* 68
Charged (entrusted)   so much wealth as God had
    c her with—   *Lover's Tale* i 213
Charger   When on my goodly *c* borne   *Sir Galahad* 49
    on my *c's*, trample them under us.'   *Boädicea* 69
    and take my *c*, fresh,   *Gareth and L.* 1300
    At once Sir Lancelot's *c* fiercely neigh'd,   ,, 1400
    cried, ' My *c* and her palfrey ; '   *Marr. of Geraint* 126
    His *c* trampling many a prickly star   ,, 313
    So Enid took his *c* to the stall ;   ,, 382
    Call the host and bid him bring *C* and palfrey.'   *Geraint and E.* 401
    Who saw the *c's* of the two that fell   ,, 481
    While the great *c* stood, grieved like a man.   ,, 535
    See ye take the *c* too, A noble one.'   ,, 555
    (His gentle *c* following him unled)   ,, 571
    fly, your *c* is without,   ,, 749
    When Edyrn rein'd his *c* at her side,   ,, 820
    found His *c*, mounted on him and away.   *Balin and Balan* 418
    glad, Knightlike, to find his *c* yet unlamed,   ,, 428
    so they overbore Sir Lancelot and his *c*, and
    a spear Down-glancing lamed the *c*,   *Lancelot and E.* 487
    from his *c* down he slid, and sat,   ,, 510

Chasm (*continued*)   Thro' one wide *c* of time and frost   *Princess, Pro.* 93
By every coppice-feather'd *c* and cleft,   " *iv* 23
from the castle gateway by the *c*   *Com. of Arthur* 370
little elves of *c* and cleft Made answer,   *Guinevere* 248
clash'd his harness in the icy caves And barren *c*'s,   *Pass. of Arthur* 355
The yawning of an earthquake-cloven *c*.   *Lover's Tale i* 377
Flies with a shatter'd foam along the *c*.   " 383
Clove into perilous *c*'s our walls   *Def. of Lucknow* 55
black passes and foam-churning *c*'s—   *Sir J. Oldcastle* 9
blur of earth Left by that closing *c*,   *Demeter and P.* 38
of the *c* between Work and Ideal?   *Romney's R.* 63
Chasm-like   With *c-l* portals open to the sea,   *Holy Grail* 815
Chaste   world's great bridals, *c* and calm: *Princess, vii* 294
All brave, and many generous, and some *c*.   *Merlin and V.* 817
Chasten   we love the Heaven that *c*'s us.   *Geraint and E.* 789
Chastisement   brook the rod And *c* of human pride;   *Supp. Confessions* 108
May not that earthly *c* suffice?   *Aylmer's Field* 784
Chastity   With the clear-pointed flame of *c*,   *Isabel* 2
she rode forth, clothed on with *c*:   *Godiva* 53
she rode back, clothed on with *c*:   " 65
They bound to holy vows of *c*!   *Merlin and V.* 695
To lead sweet lives in purest *c*,   *Guinevere* 474
Chatelet   The last wild thought of C,   *Margaret* 37
Chattel   Live *c*'s, mincers of each other's fame,   *Princess, iv* 515
Chatter   Would *c* with the cold, and all my beard   *St. S. Stylites* 31
I *c* over stony ways,   *The Brook* 39
I *c*, *c*, as I flow To join the brimming river,   " 47
crane,' I said, 'may *c* of the crane,   *Princess iii* 104
then to hear a dead man *c* Is enough   *Maud II v* 19
Chatter'd   Philip *c* more than brook or bird;   *The Brook* 51
They *c* trifles at the door: *In Mem. lxix* 4
Chatterer   Begotten by enchantment—*c*'s they,   *Holy Grail* 145
Chattering (*part.*)   *c* stony names Of shale and hornblende,'   *Princess iii* 361
Chattering (*s*)   Chafferings and *c*'s at the market-cross,   *Holy Grail* 558
Chaucer (Dan)   *See* **Dan Chaucer**
Chaumber (chamber)   i' my oän blue *c* to me.   *Spinster's S's.* 80
Thou slep i' the *c* above us,   *Owd Roä* 49
Roäver was theere i' the *c*   " 88
Chaumber door (chamber door)   thy *c d* wouldn't sneck;   " 88
Chaunt (*See also* **Chant**)   I would mock thy *c* anew;   *The Owl ii* 8
And solemn *c*'s resound between.   *Sir Galahad* 36
Chaunteth   C not the brooding bee   *A Dirge* 16
Cheap   had holden the power and glory of Spain so *c*   *The Revenge* 106
Cheat (*s*)   Yet, if she were not a *c*, (repeat)   *Maud I vi* 35, 91
Scarcely, now, would I call him a *c*;   " *xiii* 29
Cheat (*verb*)   love to *c* yourself with words: *Princess vii* 334
C and be cheated, and die: *Maud I i* 32
Cheated (*See also* **Half-cheated**)   Cheat and be *c*, and die: " 32
Cheating   *c* the sick of a few last gasps,   " 43
Check (*s*)   'Then comes the *c*, the change,   *Two Voices* 163
With motions, *c*'s, and counterchecks.   " 300
Check (*verb*)   too noble' he said 'to *c* at pies,   *Merlin and V.* 126
the good nuns would *c* her gadding tongue   *Guinevere* 313
c me too Nor let me shame my father's memory,   " 317
pray you *c* me if I ask amiss—   " 324
Check'd   and *c* His power to shape: *Lucretius* 22
Here the King's calm eye Fell on, and *c*,   *Gareth and L.* 548
there he *c* himself and paused.   *Pelleas and E.* 527
Cheek (*See also* **Maiden-cheek**)   The red *c* paling, The strong limbs failing,   *All things will Die* 31
laughters dimple The baby-roses in her *c*'s;   *Lilian* 17
then the tears run down my *c*,   *Oriana* 69
That dimples your transparent *c*,   *Margaret* 15
Tie up the ringlets on your *c*:   " 57
And your *c*, whose brilliant hue   *Rosalind* 39
Leaning his *c* upon his hand,   *Eleänore* 118
Returning with hot *c* and kindled eyes.   *Alexander* 14
Tho' one should smite him on the *c*,   *Two Voices* 251
c Flush'd like the coming of the day,   *Miller's D.* 131
Her *c* had lost the rose, and round her neck   *Œnone* 18
his *c* brighten'd as the foam-bow brightens   " 61
eye Over her snow-cold breast and angry *c* Kept watch,   " 142

Cheek (*continued*)   His ruddy *c* upon my breast.   *The Sisters* 20
with puff'd *c* the belted hunter blew   *Palace of Art* 63
From *c* and throat and chin.   " 140
along the brain, And flushes all the *c*.   *D. of F. Women* 44
with swarthy *c*'s and bold black eyes,   " 127
A word could bring the colour to my *c*;   *Gardener's D.* 196
clapt him on the hands and on the *c*'s,   *Dora* 133
laughter dimpled in his swarthy *c*;   *Edwin Morris* 61
and pat The girls upon the *c*,   *Talking Oak* 44
'Then flush'd her *c* with rosy light,   " 165
Thy *c* begins to redden thro' the gloom,   *Tithonus* 37
and thy tears are on my *c*.   " 45
Then her *c* was pale and thinner   *Locksley Hall* 21
On her pallid *c* and forehead came a colour   " 25
the barking cur Made her *c* flame: *Godiva* 58
While, dreaming on your damask *c*,   *Day-Dm., Pro.* 3
The blush is fix'd upon her *c*.   *Day-Dm., Sleep. P.* 32
The colour flies into his *c*'s: *Day-Dm., Arrival* 19
C by jowl, and knee by knee: *Vision of Sin* 84
Flamed in his *c*; and eager eyes,   *Aylmer's Field* 66
Cooling her false *c* with a featherfan,   " 289
yet her *c* Kept colour: wondrous!   " 505
On glassy water drove his *c* in lines;   *Princess i* 116
when the king Kiss'd her pale *c*,   " *ii* 264
blew the swoll'n *c* of a trumpeter;   " 364
flying charm of blushes o'er this *c*,   " 430
but my *c* Began to burn and burn,   " *iii* 45
till over brow And *c* and bosom brake   " *iv* 383
my Sire, his rough *c* wet with tears,   " *v* 23
And so belabour'd him on rib and *c*   " 341
wan was her *c* With hollow watch,   " *vi* 144
I love not hollow *c* or faded eye: " *vii* 7
wordless broodings on the wasted *c*—   " 112
'The *c*'s drop in; the body bows   *In Mem. xxxv* 3
A touch of shame upon her *c*:   " *xxxvii* 10
Come; let us go: your *c*'s are pale;   " *lvii* 5
To clap their *c*'s, to call them mine.   " *lxxxiv* 18
fan my brows and blow The fever from my *c*,   " *lxxxvi* 9
beam of an eyelash dead on the *c*,   *Maud I iii* 3
Roses are her *c*'s, And a rose her mouth (repeat)   *Maud I xvii* 7, 21
but speak Of my mother's faded *c*   " *xix* 19
this was what had redden'd her *c*   " 65
and a *c* of apple-blossom, Hawk-eyes;   *Gareth and L.* 589
Struck at him with his whip, and cut his *c*.   *Marr. of Geraint* 207
Whom first she kiss'd on either *c*,   " 517
Made her *c* burn and either eyelid fall,   " 775
Made her *c* burn and either eyelid fall.   *Geraint and E.* 434
so there lived some colour in your *c*,   " 621
spearman let his *c* Bulge with the unswallow'd piece,   " 630
However lightly, smote her on the *c*.   " 718
White was her *c*: sharp breaths of anger puff'd   *Merlin and V.* 848
Seam'd with an ancient swordcut on the *c*,   *Lancelot and E.* 258
c did catch the colour of her words.   *Lover's Tale i* 569
bent above me, too; Wan was her *c*;   " 694
c's as bright as when she climb'd the hill.   " *iii* 47
As well as the plump *c*—   *Sisters (E. and E.)* 184
kiss fell chill as a flake of snow on the *c*:   *The Wreck* 32
to feel his breath Upon my *c*—   *The Flight* 46
Yet tho' this *c* be gray,   *Epilogue* 7
Each poor pale *c* a momentary rose—   *The Ring* 315
rounder *c* had brighten'd into bloom.   " 351
her lips Were warm upon my *c*,   " 399
From off the rosy *c* of waking Day.   *Akbar's Dream* 202
Cheek'd   *See* **Apple-cheek'd**
Cheep   *c* and twitter twenty million loves.   *Princess iv* 101
Cheeping   birds that circle round the tower Are *c* to each other   *The Ring* 86
Cheer (*s*)   flowers would faint at your cruel *c*.   *Poet's Mind* 15
Died the sound of royal *c*;   *L. of Shalott iv* 48
Naked I go, and void of *c*:   *Two Voices* 239
A murmur, 'Be of better *c*.'   " 429
Welcome her, thundering *c* of the street!   *W. to Alexandra* 7
With festal *c*, With books and music,   *In Mem. cvii* 21
And I make myself such evil *c*,   *Maud I xv* 2

Cheer (s) (continued) With all good c, He spake and | Gareth and L. 301
laugh'd, |
Enid brought sweet cakes to make them c, | Marr. of Geraint 388
cried Geraint for wine and goodly c | Geraint and E. 283
lily maid had striven to make him c, | Lancelot and E. 327
Yet with good c he spake, | Pelleas and E. 240
Highlanders answer with conquering c's, | Def. of Lucknow 99
hard rocks, hard life, hard c, or none, | Sir J. Oldcastle 6
guest may make True c with honest wine— | Pro. to Gen. Hamley 16
men gallop up with a c and a shout, | Heavy Brigade 61

Cheer (verb) Annie, come, c up before I go.' | Enoch Arden 200
'Annie, my girl, c up, be comforted, | „ 218
Cheer'd And he c her soul with love. | L. of Burleigh 68
But he c me, my good man, | Grandmother 69
And we with singing c the way, | In Mem. xxii 5
Be c with tidings of the bride, | „ xl 23
he spake and c his Table Round | Com. of Arthur 267
Nor ever c you with a kindly smile, | The Ring 388
Cheerful It wellnigh made her c; | Geraint and E. 443
grew so c that they deem'd her death | Lancelot and E. 1131
Cheerfully Enoch bore his weakness c. | Enoch Arden 827
Cheerful-minded Be c-m, talk and treat Of all things | In Mem. cvii 19
Cheerfulness hold out the lights of c; | Lover's Tale i 807
Cheque violates virgin Truth for a coin or a c. | The Dawn 15
Chequer-work A c-w of beam and shade | In Mem. lxxii 15
Cherish c that which bears but bitter fruit? | Locksley Hall 65
The love of all Thy daughters c Thee, | Ded. of Idylls 53
grace Thy climbing life, and c my prone year, | Gareth and L. 95
Cherish'd fed, and c, and saved his life. | Lover's Tale iv 264
Cherry To catch a dragon in a c net, | Princess v 169
Cherub There is no being pure, My c; | Merlin and V. 52
Chess our wine and c beneath the planes, | Princess vi 246
Chest (part of body) like monstrous apes they | St. S. Stylites 174
crush'd my c: |
Live long, nor feel in head or c | Will Water. 237
big voice, big c, big merciless hands! | In the Child. Hosp. 4
The tiger spasms tear his c, | Ancient Sage 123
Chest (box) She took the little ivory c, | The Letters 17
For keep it like a puzzle c in c, With each c |
lock'd and padlock'd | Merlin and V. 654
—a c there, by which you knelt— | The Ring 112
There, the c was open—all The sacred relics | „ 446
Chested See Deep-chested
Chestnut (tree) Or three or three c's near, that hung | Miller's D. 55
I came and sat Below the c's, | „ 60
While those full c's whisper by, | „ 168
in the c shade I found the blue Forget-me-not. | „ 201
Parks with oak and c shady, | L. of Burleigh 29
I see the slowly-thickening c towers | Prog. of Spring 42
Chestnut (fruit) c, when the shell Divides threefold | The Brook 72, 207
(repeat) | In Mem. xi 4
The c pattering to the ground! |
Chestnut-bloom that islet in the c-b Flamed in | Aylmer's Field 65
his cheek; |
Chestnut-bud drooping c-b's began To spread | Sir L. and Q. G. 16
Chew'd c The thrice-turn'd cud of wrath, | Princess i 65
Chick Sir C, that scarce hast broken shell | Balin and Balan 568
Or else Sir C—dismount and loose their casques | „ 573
Chid be friends, like children being c! | Princess vi 289
C her, and forbid her to speak To me, | Maud I xix 63
Chidden CARESS'D or c by the slender hand, | Caress'd or Chidden 1
Chief answer'd Lancelot, the c of knights: | Lancelot and E. 140, 187
(repeat) | „ 183
guess thee c of those, After the King, | Aylmer's Field 763
heads of c's and princes fall so fast, | Merlin and V. 476
an Eagle rising or, the Sun In dexter c; | Pelleas and E. 62
she that seem'd the c among them said, |
Child (See also Bairn, Childer, Children) Fed thee, a |
c, lying alone, | Eleänore 25
A glorious c, dreaming alone, | „ 27
One walk'd between his wife and c, | Two Voices 412
features of her c Ere it is born: her c! | Œnone 252
never c be born of me, Unblest, | „ 254
You should not fret for me, mother, you have |
another c, | May Queen, N. Y's. E. 36

Child (continued) She'll be a better c to you than ever |
I have been. | May Queen, N. Y's. E. 44
dream of Fatherland, Of c, and wife, | Lotos-Eaters 40
With that fair c betwixt them born. | On a Mourner 25
Dora took the c, and went her way | Dora 71
none of all his men Dare tell him Dora waited with the c; | „ 76
she rose and took The c once more, | „ 81
Whose c is that? What are you doing here? | „ 88
answer'd softly, 'This is William's c!' | „ 90
take the c, And bless him for the sake of him that's gone!' | „ 93
work for William's c, until he grows Of age | „ 126
a-begging for myself, Or William, or this c; | „ 142
three hours he sobb'd o'er William's c | „ 167
cling About the darling c: | Talking Oak 128
O, the c too clothes the father | Locksley Hall 91
barbarian lower than the Christian c. | „ 174
that c's heart within the man's Begins | Will Water. 31
'I speak the truth: you are my c. | Lady Clare 24
I buried her like my own sweet c, And put my c in her |
stead.' | „ 27
'Nay now, my c,' said Alice the nurse, (repeat) | „ 33, 41
Alas, my c, I sinn'd for thee.' | „ 50
C, if it were thine error or thy crime | Come not, when, etc. 7
from the palace came a c of sin, | Vision of Sin 5
And give his c a better bringing-up | Enoch Arden 87
how should the c Remember this?' | „ 233
the third c was sickly-born and grew Yet sicklier, | „ 261
fears were common to her state, Being with c: but |
when her c was born, Then her new c | „ 522
marriage, and the birth Of Philip's c: | „ 709
darling Katie Willows, his one c! | The Brook 67
His only c, his Edith whom he loved | Aylmer's Field 23
Nursing a c, and turning to the warmth | „ 185
—who could trust a c? | „ 264
Their c.' 'Our c!' 'Our heiress!' | „ 297
and because I love their c They hate me: | „ 423
and read Writhing a letter from his c, | „ 517
Of such a love as like a chidden c, | „ 541
He seldom crost his c without a sneer; | „ 562
praying him To speak before the people of her c, | „ 608
The poor c of shame The common care | „ 687
all the gentle attributes Of his lost c, | „ 731
Is not our own c on the narrow way, | „ 743
The childless mother went to seek her c; | „ 829
in the narrow gloom By wife and c, | „ 841
His wife, an unknown artist's orphan c— | Sea Dreams 2
Virgin Mother standing with her c | „ 242
the c Clung to the mother, and sent out a cry | „ 244
And mine but from the crying of a c.' | „ 249
'C? No!' said he, 'but this tide's roar, | „ 250
Good man, to please the c. | „ 267
voice (You spoke so loud) has roused the c again. | „ 281
flock'd at noon His tenants, wife and c, | Princess, Pro. 4
Half c half woman as she was, | „ 101
they must lose the c, assume The woman: | „ i 137
odes About this losing of the c; | „ 141
when we came where lies the c We lost in other years, | „ ii 10
Your language proves you still the c. | „ 58
At her left, a c, In shining draperies, | „ 108
turn'd to go, but Cyril took the c, | „ 362
the c Push'd her flat hand against his face | „ 365
call'd For Psyche's c to cast it from the doors; | „ iv 238
on the purple footcloth, lay The lily-shining c; | „ 287
For this lost lamb (she pointed to the c) | „ 361
and a hope The c of regal compact, | „ 421
live, dear lady, for your c!' | „ v 80
my babe, my blossom, ah, my c, My one sweet c, whom |
I shall see no more! | „ 82
when they say The c is hers—for every little fault, The |
c is hers; | „ 87
My babe, my sweet Aglaïa, my one c: | „ 101
Who gave me back my c?' | „ 105
You have spoilt this c; she laughs at you | „ 116
Our chiefest comfort is the little c | „ 430
c shall grow To prize the authentic mother | „ 432

Child (*continued*) the training of a c Is woman's wisdom.'   *Princess* v 465
Set his c upon her knee—   ,,   vi 14
'Sweet my c, I live for thee.'   ,,   16
Knelt on one knee,—the c on one,—   ,,   91
She bow'd, she set the c on the earth ;   ,,   120
not yours, but mine : give me the c'   ,,   141
The mother, me, the c ;   ,,   153
give her the c ! (repeat)   *Princess* v 168, 179, 183
twilight mellowing, dwelt Full on the c ;   *Princess* v 192
Ida spoke not, rapt upon the c.   ,,   220
Blanche had gone, but left Her c among us,   ,,   vii 57
old world of ours is but a c Yet in the go-cart.   ,, *Con.* 77
love not this French God, the c of Hell,   *Third of Feb.* 7
But I wept like a c that day,   *Grandmother* 64
wept like a c for the c that was dead   ,,   68
King is happy In c and wife ;   *The Victim* 26
She cast her arms about the c.   ,,   32
The c was only eight summers old,   ,,   33
'They have taken the c To spill his blood   ,,   43
Poor c, that waitest for thy love !   *In Mem.* vi 28
They call'd me fool, they call me c :   ,, *lxix* 13
find in c and wife An iron welcome   ,, *xc* 7
Familiar to the stranger's c ;   ,, *ci* 20
c would twine A trustful hand, unask'd, in thine,   ,, *cix* 18
Half-grown as yet, a c, and vain—   ,, *cxiv* 9
With wisdom, like the younger c :   ,,   20
No, like a c in doubt and fear :   ,, *cxxiv* 17
Then was I as a c that cries,   ,,   19
I play'd with the girl when a c ;   *Maud* I i 68
O c, you wrong your beauty,   ,, *iv* 17
I have play'd with her when a c ;   ,, *vi* 87
For then, perhaps, as a c of deceit,   ,, *xiii* 30
Made her only the c of her mother,   ,,   40
desire that awoke in the heart of the c,   ,, *xix* 48
one fair daughter, and none other c ;   *Com. of Arthur* 2
split the mother's heart Spitting the c,   ,,   39
surely would have torn the c Piecemeal among them,   ,,   217
Wherefore Merlin took the c,   ,,   221
Or else the c of Anton, and no king,   ,,   233
Arthur were the c of shamefulness,   ,,   239
dried my tears, being a c with me.   ,,   350
So that the c and he were clothed in fire.   ,,   390
same c,' he said, 'Is he who reigns ;   ,,   392
The shining dragon and the naked c   ,,   399
this King thine only c, Guinevere :   ,,   413
the good mother holds me still a c !   *Gareth and L.* 15
'Mother, tho' ye count me still the c, Sweet mother,
   do ye love the c ?'   ,,   34
'Then, mother, an ye love the c,'   ,,   37
Hear the c's story.'   ,,   39
'An ye hold me yet for c, Hear yet once more the story
   of the c.   ,,   99
all day long hath rated at her c,   ,,   1285
'My fair c, What madness made thee challenge   ,,   1415
Had married Enid, Yniol's only c,   *Marr. of Geraint* 4
dear c hath often heard me praise   ,,   434
O noble host, For this dear c,   ,,   497
'See here, my c, how fresh the colours   ,,   680
Look on it, c, and tell me if ye know it.'   ,,   684
worn My faded suit, as you, my c,   ,,   706
my dear c is set forth at her best,   ,,   728
your fair c shall wear your costly gift   ,,   819
wail ye for him thus ? ye seem a c.   *Geraint and E.* 547
Make knight or churl or c or damsel seem   *Balin and Balan* 162
plumed with green replied, 'Peace, c !   *Merlin and V.* 90
neither eyes nor tongue—O stupid c !   ,,   251
Your pardon, c. Your pretty sports have brighten'd
   all again.   ,,   304
In you, that are no c, for still I find Your face   ,,   366
a mere c Might use it to the harm of anyone,   ,,   684
One c they had ; it lived with her :   ,,   716
charged by Valence to bring home the c.   ,,   718
I ask you, is it clamour'd by the c,   ,,   771
bitter weeping like a beaten c,   ,,   855
moral c without the craft to rule,   *Lancelot and E.* 146

Child (*continued*) 'True, my c. Well, I will wear
   it :   *Lancelot and E.* 370
' Do me this grace, my c, to have my shield   ,,   382
Sir Modred's brother, and the c of Lot,   ,,   558
the diamond : wit ye well, my c,   ,,   771
kiss the c That does the task assign'd,   ,,   828
Meeker than any c to a rough nurse,   ,,   857
Milder than any mother to a sick c,   ,,   858
'O my c, ye seem Light-headed,   ,,   1062
Yet, seeing you desire your c to live,   ,,   1095
kiss'd me saying, "Thou are fair, my c,   ,,   1409
I saw the fiery face as of a c   *Holy Grail* 466
winding wall of rock Heard a c wail.   *Last Tournament* 12
thro' the wind Pierced ever a c's cry :   ,,   17
Vext her with plaintive memories of the c :   ,,   29
that unhappy c Past in her barge :   ,,   44
Queen White-robed in honour of the stainless c,   ,,   147
whimpering of the spirit of the c,   ,,   418
Arthur make me pure As any maiden c ?   ,,   693
'Will the c kill me with her innocent talk ?'   *Guinevere* 214
'Will the c kill me with her foolish prate ?'   ,,   225
They found a naked c upon the sands   ,,   293
'The simple, fearful c Meant nothing,   ,,   369
too-fearful guilt, Simpler than any c,   ,,   371
' Liest thou here so low, the c of one I honour'd,   ,,   422
Well is it that no c is born of thee.   ,,   424
wife and c with wail Pass to new lords ;   *Pass. of Arthur* 44
Or Cowardice, the c of lust for gold,   *To the Queen* ii 54
Which to the imprison'd spirit of the c,   *Lover's Tale* i 204
Had thrust his wife and c and dash'd himself   ,,   380
you may hear The moaning of the woman and the c,   ,,   520
at last he freed himself From wife and c,   ,, *iv* 380
I was a c, an' he was a c, an' he came   *First Quarrel* 23
told it me all at once, as simple as any c,   ,,   58
You'll have her to nurse my c,   ,,   70
when he was but a c—   *Rizpah* 25
The wind that 'ill wail like a c   ,,   72
You never have borne a c—   ,,   80
My father with a c on either knee, A hand upon the
   head of either c,   *Sisters (E. and E.)* 54
Here's to your happy union with my c !   ,,   68
widow with less guile than many a c.   ,,   182
desire that her lost c Should earn   ,,   250
here She bore a c, whom reverently we call'd Edith ;   ,,   268
gratefullest heart I have found in a c of her
   years—   *In the Child. Hosp.* 32
the c didn't see I was there.   ,,   44
I had sat three nights by the c—   ,,   59
and we went to see to the c.   ,,   68
I sorrow for that kindly c of Spain   *Columbus* 212
OUT of the deep, my c, (repeat)   *De Prof. Two G.* 1, 5, 26, 29
I am roused by the wail of a c,   *The Wreck* 7
The c that I felt I could die for—   ,,   36
That day my nurse had brought me the c.   ,,   59
I thought of the c for a moment,   ,,   84
I shall look on the c again.   ,,   124
'O c, I am coming to thee.'   ,,   134
I pray'd—'my c'—for I still could pray—   ,,   138
Was it well with the c ?   ,,   141
Godless Jeptha vows his c . . .   *The Flight* 26
that smiles at her sleepin' c—   *Tomorrow* 26
Amy was a timid c ;   *Locksley H., Sixty* 19
dead the mother, dead the c.   ,,   36
Edith but a c of six—   ,,   258
wife and his c stood by him in tears,   *Dead Prophet* 57
And warms the c's awakening world   *Prin. Beatrice* 7
from her household orbit draws the c   ,,   7
the c Is happy—ev'n in leaving *her* !   ,,   11
can no more, thou camest, O my c.   *Demeter and P.* 4
Queen of the dead no more—my c !   ,,   18
C, those imperial, disimpassion'd eyes   ,,   23
here, my c, tho' folded in thine arms,   ,,   40
C, when thou wert gone, I envied human *wives*,   ,,   52
do ye make your moaning for my c ?'   ,,   65
the c Of thee, the great Earth-Mother,   ,,   96

Chime (s) speak for noise Of clocks and c's,	*Princess i* 216
oft we two have heard St. Mary's c's!	*To W. H. Brookfield* 3
Chime (verb) the blue river c's in its flowing	*All Things will Die* 1
and those great bells Began to c.	*Palace of Art* 158
Set her sad will no less to c with his,	*Enoch Arden* 248
changing, c with never changing Law.	*To Duke of Argyll* 11
Chimera C's, crotchets, Christmas solecisms,	*Princess, Pro.* 203
Chimley (Chimney) haäfe o' the c's a-twizzen'd	*Owd Roä* 22
Chimney (*See also* **Chimley, Chimney-top**) And half the c's	*The Goose* 48
tumbled.	
And c's muffled in the leafy vine.	*Audley Court* 19
For now her father's c glows	*In Mem. vi* 29
Chimney-top above the tall white c-t's.	*May Queen, N. Y's. E.* 12
Chin smooth'd his c and sleek'd his hair,	*A Character* 11
His double c, his portly size,	*Miller's D.* 2
From cheek and throat and c.	*Palace of Art* 140
Close up his eyes: tie up his c:	*D. of the O. Year* 48
Her sweet face from brow to c:	*L. of Burleigh* 62
reddening in the furrows of his c,	*Princess vi* 228
many-winter'd fleece of throat and c.	*Merlin and V.* 841
China laws Salique And little-footed C,	*Princess ii* 134
China-bound Reporting of his vessel C-b,	*Enoch Arden* 122
Chink (sound) Even in dreams to the c of his pence,	*Maud I x* 43
Chink (crevice) walls Were full of c's and holes;	*Godiva* 60
Found in a c of that old moulder'd floor!'	*The Ring* 280
Chink (verb) For Age will c the face,	*Happy* 46
Chink'd C as you see, and seam'd,	*Lover's Tale i* 131
Chirp (s) (*See also* **Matin-chirp**) I hear a c of birds;	*In Mem. cxix* 5
Chirp (verb) The cricket c's: the light burns low:	*D. of the O. Year* 40
Chirping about the fields you caught His weary daylong c,	*The Brook* 53
Chirpt gray cricket c of at our hearth—	*Merlin and V.* 110
Chirr'd not a cricket c:	*In Mem. xcv* 6
Chirrup The sparrow's c on the roof,	*Mariana* 73
titmouse hope to win her With his c at her ear.	*Maud I xx* 30
Chirrupt beside me c the nightingale.	*Grandmother* 40
Chivalry came to c: When some respect,	*Princess ii* 135
urged All the devisings of their c	*Gareth and L.* 1349
Choice wherefore rather I made c To commune	*Two Voices* 460
Teach that sick heart the stronger c,	*On a Mourner* 18
And told him of my c,	*Talking Oak* 18
glorious in his beauty and thy c,	*Tithonus* 12
But you have made the wiser c,	*You might have won* 5
Which weep the comrade of my c,	*In Mem. xiii* 9
your sweetness hardly leaves me a c	*Maud I v* 24
c from air, land, stream, and sea,	*Pelleas and E.* 149
her c did leap forth from his eyes!	*Lover's Tale i* 657
Choicest-grown blossom c-g To wreathe a crown	*Akbar's Dream* 22
Choke Should fill and c with golden sand—	*You ask me, why* 24
'A quinsy c thy cursed note!'	*The Goose* 29
yellow vapours c The great city	*Maud II iv* 63
Chok'd I c. Again they shriek'd the burthen—	*Edwin Morris* 123
Heaven, and Earth, and Time are c.	*St. S. Stylites* 104
Her voice c, and her forehead sank	*Princess vii* 247
hopes are mine,' and saying that, she c,	*Lancelot and E.* 607
His mercy c me.	*Guinevere* 616
C all the syllables, that strove to rise	*Lover's Tale i* 711
Choler old, but full Of force and c,	*Golden Year* 61
Cholera C, scurvy, and fever,	*Def. of Lucknow* 84
Chooch (church) An' I allus comed to 's c	*N. Farmer, O. S.* 17
Choorch (church) voäted wi' Squoire an' c an' staäte,	15
Choose To c your own you did not care;	*Day-Dm., L'Envoi* 30
'Twere hardly worth my while to c	*In Mem. xxxiv* 10
arms for guerdon; c the best.'	*Geraint and E.* 218
of overpraise and overblame We c the last.	*Merlin and V.* 91
Chop (s) His proper c to each.	*Will Water.* 116
Among the c's and steaks!	148
Chop (verb) C the breasts from off the mother,	*Boädicea* 68
Chop-house Head-waiter of the c-h here,	*Will Water.* 209
Chord (*See also* **Master-chord**) clear twang of the golden c's	*Sea-Fairies* 38
note From that deep c which Hampden smote	*England and Amer.* 19
and smote on all the c's with might;	*Locksley Hall* 33
Chord (*continued*) 'Screw not the c too sharply lest it snap.'	*Aylmer's Field* 469
Consonant c's that shiver to one note;	*Princess iii* 90
The deepest measure from the c's:	*In Mem. xlviii* 12
Will flash along the c's and go.	" *lxxxviii* 12
speak His music by the framework and the c;	*Holy Grail* 879
Sweeps suddenly all its half-moulder'd c's	*Lover's Tale i* 19
would drop from the c's or the keys,	*The Wreck* 27
Chorus Go' (shrill'd the cotton-spining c);	*Edwin Morris* 122
O you c of indolent reviewers,	*Hendecasyllabics* 1
All that c of indolent reviewers,	" 12
whereupon Their common shout in c, mounting,	*Balin and Balan* 87
Chose crag-platform, smooth as burnish'd brass I c.	*Palace of Art* 6
That sober-suited Freedom c,	*You ask me, why* 6
for your sake, the woman that he c,	*Dora* 63
You c the best among us—	*Enoch Arden* 293
C the green path that show'd the rarer foot,	*Lancelot and E.* 162
Chosen Who madest him thy c,	*Tithonus* 13
Gods,' he said, 'would have c well;	*The Victim* 58
'Had I c to wed, I had been wedded earlier,	*Lancelot and E.* 934
Was c Abbess, there, an Abbess,	*Guinevere* 696
happy to be c Judge of Gods,	*Death of Œnone* 16
Chousin' an' I wur c the wife,	*North. Cobbler* 83
Christ (*See also* **Christ Jesus, Jesus, Lamb**) Brothers in C—a world of peace	*Supp. Confessions* 29
C, the Virgin Mother, and the saints;	*St. S. Stylites* 112
So I clutch it. C! 'Tis gone:	" 207
Save C as we believe him—	*Aylmer's Field* 573
as cried C ere His agony to those that swore	" 793
Not preaching simple C to simple men,	*Sea Dreams* 21
C the bait to trap his dupe and fool;	" 191
God accept him, C receive him.	*Ode on Well.* 281
The time draws near the birth of C:	*In Mem. xxviii* 1
Behold a man raised up by C!	" *xxxi* 13
The time draws near the birth of C;	" *civ* 1
Ring in the C that is to be.	" *cvi* 32
Ah C, that it were possible For one short hour	*Maud II ii* 1
As the churches have kill'd their C.	" *v* 29
Sware at the shrine of C a deathless love:	*Com. of Arthur* 466
'The King will follow C, and we the King	" 500
we that fight for our fair father C,	" 510
Follow the deer? follow the C, the King,	*Gareth and L.* 117
Hath prosper'd in the name of C,	*Balin and Balan* 99
the Roman pierced the side of C.	" 114
scarce could spy the C for Saints,	" 409
saintly youth, the spotless lamb of C,	*Merlin and V.* 749
all his legions crying C and him,	*Lancelot and E.* 305
Ah, C, that it would come,	*Holy Grail* 93
C kill me then But I will slice him	*Pelleas and E.* 337
'My churl, for whom C died,	*Last Tournament* 62
Have everywhere about this land of C	*Guinevere* 431
To break the heathen and uphold the C,	" 470
And so thou lean on our fair father C,	" 562
God my C—I pass but shall not die.'	*Pass. of Arthur* 28
and shrieks After the C,	" 111
wrinkled children that are C's	*Sisters (E. and E.)* 183
ears for C in this wild field of Wales—	*Sir J. Oldcastle* 19
and raze The blessed tomb of C;	*Columbus* 99
This creedless people will be brought to C	" 189
And we broke away from the C,	*Despair* 25
A thousand summers ere the time of C	*Ancient Sage* 1
transfigured, like C on Hermon hill,	*Happy* 38
In that four-hundredth summer after C,	*St. Telemachus* 4
Christian C's with happy countenances—	*Supp. Confessions* 20
barbarian lower than the C child.	*Locksley Hall* 174
she, who kept a tender C hope,	*Sea Dreams* 41
The graceful tact, the C art;	*In Mem. cx* 16
Nor any cry of C heard thereon,	*Pass. of Arthur* 128
C conquerors took and flung the conquered C into flames.	*Locksley H., Sixty* 84
That ever wore a C marriage-ring.	*Romney's R.* 36
at length he touch'd his gaol, The C city.	*St. Telemachus* 35
as he yell'd of yore for C blood.	" 46
eighty thousand C faces watch Man murder man.	" 55
Brahmin, and Buddhist, C, and Parsee,	*Akbar's Dream* 25

Circle (s) (*continued*) Scarce housed within the *c* of this Earth, *Lover's Tale i* 479
caught and brought him in To their charm'd *c*, *iv* 377
Whirling their sabres in *c's* of light ! *Heavy Brigade* 34
Circle (verb) Make knowledge *c* with the winds ; *Love thou thy land* 17
tho' I *c* in the grain Five hundred rings *Talking Oak* 83
We *c* with the seasons. *Will Water.* 64
full voice which *c's* round the grave, *Princess ii* 45
And *c* moaning in the air : *In Mem. xii* 15
It *c's* round, and fancy plays, " *Con.* 81
birds that *c* round the tower Are cheeping *The Ring* 85
Circled (*See also* **Azure-circled, Crimson-circled, Musky-circled, Ruby-circled**) *C* thro' all experiences, pure law, *Œnone* 166
I prosper, *c* with thy voice ! *In Mem. cxxx* 15
c with her maids, The Lady Lyonors *Gareth and L.* 1374
and settling *c* all the lists. *Marr. of Geraint* 547
Circlet prize A golden *c* and a knightly sword, *Pelleas and E.* 12
Pelleas for his lady won The golden *c*, " 14
he will fight for me, And win the *c* : " 119
And win me this fine *c*, Pelleas, " 128
The sword and golden *c* were achieved. " 170
she caught the *c* from his lance, " 173
yea and he that won The *c* ! " 321
their wills are hers For whom I won the *c* ; " 325
the *c* of the jousts Bound on her brow, " 434
The *c* of the tourney round her brows, " 454
—on her head A diamond *c*, *Lover's Tale iv* 289
Circling past her feet the swallow *c* flies, *Prog. of Spring* 44
Circuit The *c's* of thine orbit round *In Mem. lxiii* 11
Circumstance strong Against the grief of *c* *Supp. Confessions* 92
saw The hollow orb of moving *C* *Palace of Art* 255
And breasts the blows of *c*, *In Mem. lxiv* 7
This ever-changing world of *c*, *To Duke of Argyll* 10
Cirque Within the magic of *c* of memory, *Lover's Tale ii* 159
Citadel Troas and Ilion's column'd *c*, *Œnone* 118
Mast-throng'd beneath her shadowing *c* "
A moulder'd *c* on the coast, *The Daisy* 28
Fell the colony, city, and *c*, *Boädicea* 86
Past thro' into his *c*, the brain, *Lover's Tale i* 631
Citadel-crown'd Tempest-buffeted, *c-c.* *Will* 9
Cited Some *c* old Lactantius : *Columbus* 49
Citizen (*See also* **Fellow-citizen**) gravest *c* seems to lose his head, *Princess, Con.* 59
heart of the *c* hissing in war *Maud I i* 24
like a statue, rear'd To some great *c*, *Tiresias* 83
Citron-shadow clove The *c-s's* in the blue : *Arabian Nights* 15
City (*See also* **Mother-city, Queen-city, Soldier-city**)
Full of the *c's* stilly sound, " 103
a *c* glorious—A great and distant *c*— *Deserted House* 19
Thro' the open gates of the *c* afar, *Dying Swan* 34
Below the *c's* eastern towers : *Fatima* 9
Or in a clear-wall'd *c* on the sea, *Palace of Art* 97
When I and Eustace from the *c* went *Gardener's D.* 2
grew The fable of the *c* where we dwelt. " 6
News from the humming *c* comes to it " 35
O'er the mute *c* stole with folded wings, " 186
in the dust and drouth Of *c* life ! *Edwin Morris* 4
Beyond the lodge the *c* lies, *Talking Oak* 5
cities of men And manners, climates, *Ulysses* 13
I shaped The *c's* ancient legend into this :— *Godiva* 4
Mammon made The harlot of the *cities* : *Aylmer's Field* 375
A *C* clerk, but gently born and bred ; *Sea Dreams* 1
There rose a shriek as of a *c* sack'd ; *Princess iv* 165
we dash'd Your *cities* into shards with catapults, *v* 138
cross of gold That shines over *c* and river, *Ode on Well.* 50
when the long-illumined *cities* flame, " 228
Flash, ye *cities*, in rivers of fire ! *W. to Alexandra* 19
c Of little Monaco, basking, glow'd. *The Daisy* 7
the *c* glitter'd, Thro' cypress avenues, " 47
Yet here to-night in this dark *c*, " 95
The *c* sparkles like a grain of salt. *Will* 20
they rioted in the *c* of Cúnobelíne ! *Boädicea* 60
Fell the colony, *c*, and citadel, " 86
And oxen from the *c*, and goodly sheep *Spec. of Iliad* 4

City (*continued*) breathed his latest breath, That *C.* *In Mem. xcviii* 6
I come once more : the *c* sleeps ; " *cxix* 3
bubbles o'er like a *c*, with gossip, *Maud I iv* 8
For a tumult shakes the *c*, " *II iv* 50
vapours choke The great *c* sounding wide ; " 64
paced a *c* all on fire With sun and cloth of gold, *Com. of Arthur* 479
At times the summit of the high *c* flash'd ; *Gareth and L.* 192
the whole fair *c* had disappear'd. " 196
Here is a *c* of Enchanters, " 199
' Lord, there is no such *c* anywhere, " 206
Out of the *c* a blast of music peal'd. " 238
(Your *c* moved so weirdly in the mist) " 245
there be any *c* at all, Or all a vision ? " 249
Fairy Queens have built the *c*, son ; " 259
hold The King a shadow, and the *c* real : " 266
seeing the *c* is built To music, " 276
a *c* of shadowy palaces And stately, " 303
nay, the King's—Descend into the *c* : ' " 540
thro' silent faces rode Down the slope *c*, " 735
Vivien, into Camelot stealing, lodged Low in the *c*, *Merlin and V.* 64
upon far-off *cities* while they dance— " 114
He saw two *cities* in a thousand boats " 561
heads should moulder on the *c* gates. " 594
arisen since With *cities* on their flanks— " 676
Past up the still rich *c* to his kin, *Lancelot and E.* 802
Far up the dim rich *c* to her kin ; " 845
thro' the dim rich *c* to the fields, " 847
across the fields Far into the rich *c*, " 891
crown thee king Far in the spiritual *c* : ' *Holy Grail* 162
all the dim rich *c*, roof by roof, " 228
And on the top, a *c* wall'd : " 422
I past Far thro' a ruinous *c*, " 429
crown me king Far in the spiritual *c* ; " 483
I saw the spiritual *c* and all her spires " 526
from the star there shot A rose-red sparkle to the *c*, " 530
But when ye reach'd The *c*, " 708
O, when we reach'd The *c*, " 716
And follow'd to the *c*. *Pelleas and E.* 586
Down the slope *c* rode, and sharply turn'd *Last Tournament* 127
And down the *c* Dagonet danced away ; " 359
and in it Far *cities* burnt, *Guinevere* 83
saw the King Ride toward her from the *c*, " 404
As of some lonely *c* sack'd by night, *Pass. of Arthur* 43
Sounds, as if some fair *c* were one voice " 460
the full *c* peal'd Thee and thy Prince ! *To the Queen ii* 26
The *c* deck'd herself To meet me, *Columbus* 9
when a smoke from a *c* goes to heaven *Achilles over the T.* 7
men contend in grievous war From their own *c*, " 10
The madness of our *cities* and their kings. *'Tiresias* 71
from within The *c* comes a murmur void of joy, " 101
All day long far-off in the cloud of the *c*, *The Wreck* 29
From out his ancient *c* came a Seer *Ancient Sage* 2
I am wearied of our *c*, son, " 15
But some in yonder *c* hold, my son, " 82
night enough is there In yon dark *c* : " 253
storms Of Autumn swept across the *c*, *Demeter and P.* 71
North to gain Her capital *c*, *The Ring* 482
ruin, this little *c* of sewers, *Happy* 34
To the *c* and palace Of Arthur the king ; *Merlin and the G.* 65
passing it glanced upon Hamlet or *c*, " 104
BEAUTIFUL *c*, the centre and crater *Beautiful City* 1
at length he touch'd his goal, The Christian *c.* *St. Telemachus* 35
war dashing down upon *cities* and blazing farms, *The Dawn* 8
press of a thousand *cities* is prized " 14
Than a rotten fleet and a *c* in flames ! *Riflemen, Form !* 18
City-gate before the *c-g's* Came on her brother *Lancelot and E.* 790
City-gloom Droopt in the giant-factoried *c-g*, *Sea Dreams* 5
City-house this pretty house, this *c-h* of ours ? *City Child* 7
City-roar a shout More joyful than the *c-r* that hails Premier or king ! *Princess, Con.* 101
Civility But keep a touch of sweet *c* *Geraint and E.* 312
Civilisation Or an infant *c* be ruled with rod *Maud I iv* 47
Claäy (clay) hoïckt my feet wi' a flop fro' the *c.* *Spinster's S's.* 30
it wur clatted all ower wi' *c.* " 46

Clack'd-Clackt It *clack'd* and cackled louder. — *The Goose* 24
The palace bang'd, and buzz'd and *clackt*, — *Day-Dm., Revival* 14

Clad (*See also* Ivy-clad, Lady-clad, Vine-clad, Winter-clad) Or long-hair'd page in crimson *c*, — *L. of Shalott* ii 22
She *c* herself in a russet gown, — *Lady Clare* 57
looking hardly human, strangely *c*, — *Enoch Arden* 638
c her like an April daffodilly — *Princess* ii 324
Six hundred maidens *c* in purest white, — " iv 472
c in iron burst the ranks of war, — " iv 504
Mixt with myrtle and *c* with vine, — *The Islet* 19
three were *c* like tillers of the soil. — *Gareth and L.* 181
boat Become a living creature *c* with wings? — *Holy Grail* 519
Leapt lightly *c* in bridal white— — *Lover's Tale* iii 44
ere thy maiden birk be wholly *c*, — *Prog. of Spring* 50

Claim (s) *A thousand c's to reverence closed* — *To the Queen* 27
Smile at the *c's* of long descent. — *L. C. V. de Vere* 52
she will not: waive your *c*: — *Princess* v 296
To learn if Ida yet would cede our *c*, — " 333
sware to combat for my *c* till death. — " 360
With *c* on *c* from right to right, — " 417
Nor did her father cease to press my *c*, — " vii 87
asserts his *c* In that dread sound — *Ode on Well.* 70
Attest their great commander's *c* — " 148
From our first Charles by force we wrung our *c's*. — *Third of Feb.* 26
Dispute the *c's*, arrange the chances; — *To F. D. Maurice* 31
And each prefers his separate *c*, — *In Mem* cii 18
crush'd in the clash of jarring *c's*, — *Maud III* vi 44
Lays *c* to for the lady at his side, — *Marr. of Geraint* 487
Who had a twofold *c* upon my heart, — *Lover's Tale* i 210
their *c* to be thy peers; — *To Victor Hugo* 6
I am bankrupt of all *c* On your obedience; — *Romney's R.* 70
single star Should shriek its *c* — *Akbar's Dream* 43

Claim (verb) Of sounder leaf than I can *c*; — *You might have won* 4
in his walks with Edith, *c* A distant kinship — *Aylmer's Field* 61
much that Ida *c's* as right Had ne'er been mooted, — *Princess* v 202
Who but *c's* her as his due? — *Maud* I xx 11
Came not to us, of us to *c* the prize, — *Lancelot and E.* 544
Wilt spring to me, and *c* me thine, — *Guinevere* 565
should this first master *c* His service, — *Lover's Tale* i 265
—one has come to *c* his bride, — *Locksley H., Sixty* 263
I may *c* it without a lie. — *Bandit's Death* 7

Claim'd So *c* the quest and rode away, — *Balin and Balan* 138
Muriel *c* and open'd what I meant For Miriam, — *The Ring* 242

Claiming *c* each This meed of fairest. — *Œnone* 86
stood once more before her face, O her promise. — *Enoch Arden* 458
Nay, but I am not *c* your pity; — *Despair* 37

Clamber'd *c* half way up The counter side; — *Golden Year* 6
narrow street that *c* toward the mill. — *Enoch Arden* 60
I *c* o'er at top with pain, — *Princess* iv 208
fall'n from off the crag we *c* up in play, — *The Flight* 22

Clambering and *c* on a mast In harbour, — *Enoch Arden* 105
vessel in mid-ocean, her heaved prow *C*, — *Lover's Tale* ii 170

Clamour (s) And fill'd the house with *c*. — *The Goose* 36
With peals of genial *c* sent — *Will Water.* 187
and fill'd the shores With *c*. — *Enoch Arden* 636
a herd of boys with *c* bowl'd and stump'd — *Princess, Pro.* 81
To hear my father's *c* at our backs — " i 105
A *c* thicken'd, mixt with inmost terms — " ii 446
till a *c* grew As of a new-world Babel, — " iv 486
trampling the flowers With *c*: — " v 248
With blare of bugle, *c* of men, — *Ode on Well.* 115
But that blind *c* made me wise; — *In Mem* cxxiv 18
Far-off from me a *c* of liars belied — *Maud* I iv 51
C and rumble, and ringing and clatter, — " II v 13
or like a *c* of the rooks At distance, — *Marr. of Geraint* 249
And all the windy *c* of the daws — *Geraint and E.* 255

Clamour (verb) and to *c*, mourn, and sob, — *St. S. Stylites* 6
Yet cease I not to *c* and to cry, — " 42
Nor ever ceased to *c* for the ring; — *The Ring* 389
every splinter'd fraction of a sect Will *c* — *Akbar's Dream* 34

Clamour'd 'Dead' *c* the good woman, — *Enoch Arden* 840
and he *c* from a casement, 'Run' — *The Brook* 85
'Take Lilia, then, for heroine,' *c* he, — *Princess, Pro.* 223
Melissa *c* 'Flee the death;' — " iv 166
And while the people *c* for a king — *Com. of Arthur* 235

Clamour'd (*continued*) I ask you, is it *c* by the child, — *Merlin and V.* 771

Clamouring *c*, 'If we pay, we starve!' — *Godiva* 15
c etiquette to death, Unmeasured mirth; — *Princess* v 17
but *c* out 'Mine—mine—not yours, — " vi 140
c on, till Ida heard, Look'd up, — " 150
pulses at the *c* of her enemy fainted — *Boädicea* 82
the damsel *c* all the while, — *Gareth and L.* 1134

Clan beyond the passions of the primal *c*? — *Locksley H., Sixty* 93

Clang (s) overhead Begins the clash and *c* — *In Mem., Con.* 61

Clang (verb) An eagle *c* an eagle to the sphere. — *Princess* iii 106
wildswan in among the stars Would *c* it, — " iv 435
the wood which grides and *c's* — *In Mem.* cvii 11
C battleaxe, and clash brand! (repeat) — *Com. of Arthur* 493, 496, 499
ring thy name To every hoof that *c's* it, — *Tiresias* 138

Clang'd left and right The bare black cliff *c* round him, — *M. d'Arthur* 188
knell to my desires, *C* on the bridge; — *Princess* iv 175
left and right The bare black cliff *c* round him, — *Pass. of Arthur* 356
again the bells Jangled and *c*: — *Lover's Tale* iii 53

Clanging (*See also* Iron-Clanging) you hear The windy *c* of the minster clock; — *Gardener's D.* 38

Clap (s) Dead *c's* of thunder from within — *Sea Dreams* 55
stammering cracks and *c's* that follow'd, — *Merlin and V.* 942

Clap (verb) *C's* her tiny hands above me, — *Lilian* 4
crested bird That *c's* his wings at dawn. — *D. of F. Women* 180
c their cheeks, to call them mine. — *In Mem.* lxxxiv 18
The starling *c's* his tiny castanets. — *Prog. of Spring* 56

Clapper Than in a *c* clapping in a garth, — *Princess* ii 227

Clapping Laughing and *c* their hands between, — *The Merman* 29
Than in a clapper *c* in a garth, — *Princess* ii 227
all within was noise Of songs, and *c* hands, — *In Mem.* lxxxvii 19
from distant walls There came a *c* as of phantom hands. — *Marr. of Geraint* 566

Clapt and *c* her hands and cried, 'I marvel — *Palace of Art* 189
c his hand On Everard's shoulder, — *The Epic* 21
c him on the hands and on the cheeks, — *Dora* 133
c his hand in mine and sang— — *Audley Court* 109
And feet that ran, and doors that *c*, — *Day-Dm., Revival* 3
c her hands and cried for war, — *Princess* iv 590
Lancelot'—and she *c* her hands— — *Gareth and L.* 1290
mused a little, and then *c* her hands — *Merlin and V.* 866
Dagonet *c* his hands and shrill'd, — *Last Tournament* 353
Sa I hain't *c* eyes on 'im yit, — *Village Wife* 123
I *c* my hands. — *Happy* 83

Clara Vere de Vere (*See also* Vere de Vere) LADY *C V d V*, (repeat) — *L. C. V. de Vere* 1, 9, 17, 25, 33, 41
Trust me, *C V d V*, — *L. C. V. de Vere* 49
I know you, *C V d V* — " 57
C, C V d V, — " 65

Clare To give his cousin, Lady *C*. — *Lady Clare* 4
And that is well,' said Lady *C*. — " 12
'It was my cousin,' said Lady *C*, — " 15
And you are *not* the Lady *C*.' — " 20
Said Lady *C*, 'that ye speak so wild?' — " 22
She was no longer Lady *C*: — " 58
Lady *C*, you shame your worth! — " 66
beggar born,' she said, 'And not the Lady *C*.' — " 72
And you shall still be Lady *C*.' — " 88

Clariance Claudias, and *C* of Northumberland, — *Com. of Arthur* 113

Claribel Where *C* low-lieth (repeat) — *Claribel* 1, 8, 21

Clarion shouts, and *c's* shrilling unto blood, — *Com. of Arthur* 103

Clash (s) I heard the *c* so clearly. — *Sea Dreams* 136
Roll of cannon and *c* of arms, — *Ode on Well.* 116
overhead Begins the *c* and clang — *In Mem., Con.* 61
crush'd in the *c* of jarring claims, — *Maud III* vi 44
Shield-breakings, and the *c* of brands, — *Last. of Arthur* 109
long loud *c* of rapid marriage-bells. — *Lover's Tale* iii 23
by their *c*, And prelude on the keys, — *Sisters (E. and E.)* 11
And the *c* and boom of the bells — *V. of Maeldune* 110
reasons had He to be glad of The *c* of the war-glaive— — *Batt. of Brunanburh* 78
brightens at the *c* of 'Yes' and 'No,' — *Ancient Sage* 71
struck from out the *c* of warring wills; — *Prog. of Spring* 95
hear The *c* of tides that meet in narrow seas.— — *Akbar's Dream* 58
and your fiery *c* of meteorites? — *God and the Univ.* 3

Clash (verb) Fly on to *c* together again, — *Lucretius* 41

Clash (verb) (*continued*)   O hard, when love and duty *c* !   *Princess ii* 293
but you *c* them all in one,   " *v* 180
C, ye bells, in the merry March air !   *W. to Alexandra* 18
C' the darts and on the buckler   *Boädicea* 79
Clang battleaxe, and *c* brand ! (repeat)   *Com. of Arthur* 493, 496, 499
C like the coming and retiring wave,   *Gareth and L.* 522
each would *c* the shield, and blow the horn.   *Last Tournament* 436
at her girdle *c* The golden keys   *To Marq. of Dufferin* 3
where the loyal bells *C'* welcome—   *The Ring* 483
And I *c* with an iron Truth,   *The Dreamer* 6
Clash'd   Dry *c* his harness in the icy caves   *M. d'Arthur* 186
from them *c* The bells ; we listen'd ,   *Gardener's D.* 220
shameless noon Was *c* and hammer'd,   *Godiva* 75
Touch'd, clink'd, and *c*, and vanish'd,   *Sea Dreams* 135
and one, that *c* in arms,   *Princess v* 5
they *c* their arms ; the drum Beat ;   " 250
he *c* His iron palms together with a cry ;   " 353
all silent, save When armour *c* or jingled,   " *vi* 363
C with his fiery few and won ;   *Ode on Well.* 100
As the music *c* in the hall ;   *Maud I xxii* 34
his arms *C* ; and the sound was good   *Gareth and L.* 312
Sir Gareth's brand *C* his, and brake it utterly   " 1148
thrice They *c* together, and thrice they brake their spears.   *Marr. of Geraint* 562
they sat, And cup *c* cup ;   *Balin and Balan* 85
when they *c*, Rolling back upon Balin,   " 561
table of our Arthur closed And *c*   *Holy Grail* 330
And *c* with Pagan hordes, and bore them down   " 479
meadow-grass Borne, *c*:   *Pelleas and E.* 562
Dry *c* his harness in the icy caves   *Pass. of Arthur* 354
slowly-ridging rollers on the cliffs *C*,   *Lover's Tale i* 58
Two trains *c*: then and there he was crush'd   *Charity* 21
Clashing (*See also* **Iron-clashing**) there were cries and *c's* in the nest,   *Gareth and L.* 70
Enid heard the *c* of his fall,   *Geraint and E.* 509
With all her golden thresholds *c*,   *Lover's Tale i* 605
butted each other with *c* of bells,   *V. of Maeldune* 108
Clasp (fastening) Buckled with golden *c's* before ;   *Sir L. and Q. G.* 25
Clasp (embrace) In glance and smile, and *c* and kiss,   *In Mem. lxxxiv* 7
Clasp (verb)   I'd *c* it round so close and tight.   *Miller's D.* 180
He *c's* the crag with crooked hands ;   *The Eagle* 1
but everywhere Some must *c* Idols.   *Supp. Confessions* 179
c These idols to herself ?   *Lucretius* 164
c it once again, And call her Ida,   *Princess vii* 95
C' her window, trail and twine !   *Window. At the W.* 2
Trail and twine and *c* and kiss,   " 4
Let Love *c* Grief lest both be drown'd,   *In Mem. i* 9
Some landing-place, to *c* and say,   " *xlvii* 15
Thy passion *c's* a secret joy :   " *lxxxviii* 8
and *c* the hands and murmur,   *Locksley H., Sixty* 192
Ah, *c* me in your arms, sister,   *The Flight* 5
Clasp'd-Claspt (*See also* **Ivy-claspt**) *claspt* hand-in-hand with thee,   *If I were loved* 9
Die, dying *clasp'd* in his embrace.   *Fatima* 42
I saw her, who *clasp'd* in her last trance   *D. of F. Women* 266
Are *clasp'd* the moral of thy life,   *Day-Dm., L'Envoi* 55
But he *clasp'd* her like a lover,   *L. of Burleigh* 67
Claspt hands and that petitionary grace fell on him, *Clasp'd*, kiss'd him, wail'd :   *The Brook* 112
That *clasp't* the feet of a Mnemosyne,   *Lucretius* 280
in hands so lately *clasp't* with yours,   *Princess vi* 269
But he turn'd and *clasp't* me in his arms,   " *184*
Claspt on her seal, my sweet !   *Grandmother* 55
A hand that can be *clasp'd* no more—   *Window. The Answer* 2
And hands so often *clasp'd* in mine,   *In Mem. vii* 5
Of comfort *clasp'd* in truth reveal'd ;   " *x* 19
land Where first he walk'd when *clasp't* in clay ?   " *xxxvii* 22
He is *clasp't* by a passion-flower.   " *xciii* 4
ivy-stems *Claspt* the gray walls with hairy-fibred arms,   *Maud I xiv* 8
clasp't and kiss'd her, and they rode away.   *Marr. of Geraint* 323
flinging round her neck, *Clasp't* it,   " 825
but I *clasp'd* her without fear :   *Last Tournament* 750
And *clasp't* her hand in his :   *Lover's Tale ii* 202
   " *iii* 52

Clasp'd-Claspt (*continued*) round him closed and *claspt* again.   *Lover's Tale iv* 378
she that *clasp'd* my neck had flown ;   *Locksley H., Sixty* 15
Here we stood and *claspt* each other,   " 180
Who might have chased and *claspt* Renown   *To Marq. of Dufferin* 29
You *claspt* our infant daughter,   *Romney's R.* 77
Clasping   That round me, *c* each in each,   *Talking Oak* 143
I, *c* brother-hands, aver I could not,   *In Mem. lxxxv* 102
Claspt   *See* **Clasp'd**
Class   Of Knowledge fusing *c* with *c*,   *Freedom* 17
Clat (mess)   But wa boäth was i' sich a *c*   *Spinster's S's.* 33
their mucky bibs, an' the *c's* an' the clouts,   " 87
Clatted (soiled)   it wur *c* all ower wi' clääy.   " 46
Clatter   With cackle and with *c*.   *The Goose* 12
Clamour and rumble, and ringing and *c*,   *Maud II v* 13
and a *c* of hail on the glass,   *In the Child. Hosp.* 62
c of arms, and voices, and men passing   *Bandit's Death* 24
Claudias   Urien, Cradlemont of Wales, *C*,   *Com. of Arthur* 113
Claum (climb)   I *c's* an' I mashes the winder hin,   *Owd Roä* 83
Claumb'd (climbed)   I *c* up ageän to the winder,   " 99
Clause   lead my Memmius in a train Of flowery *c's*   *Lucretius* 120
the little *c* 'take not his life :'   *Princess v* 470
Clave   loved one only and who *c* to her—'   *Ded. of Idylls* 11
c Like its own mists to all the mountain side ;   *Lancelot and E.* 37
and all his kith and kin *C* to him,   *Guinevere* 440
c To Modred, and a remnant stays with me.   " 442
Claw   Nature, red in tooth and *c* With ravine,   *In Mem. lvi* 15
miss'd, and brought Her own *c* back,   *Merlin and V.* 500
what evil beast Hath drawn his *c's*   *Last Tournament* 63
Naäy, but the *c's* o' tha ! quiet !   *Spinster's S's.* 36
mun be fools to be hallus a-shawin' your *c's*,   " 61
Clay (*See also* **Clääy**)   grave Was deep, my mother, in the *c* ?   *Supp. Confessions* 86
They should have trod me into *c*,   *Oriana* 62
And on my *c* her darnel grow ;   *My life is full* 22
Doing dishonour to my *c*.'   *Two Voices* 102
common *c* ta'en from the common earth   *To—— With Pal. of Art.* 17
growing coarse to sympathize with *c*.   *Locksley Hall* 46
And the leaf is stamp'd in *c*.   *Vision of Sin* 82
Rose from the *c* it work'd in as she past,   *Aylmer's Field* 170
He shall not blind his soul with *c*.'   *Princess vii* 331
Half-conscious of their dying *c*,   *In Mem. lviii* 7
land Where first he walk'd when *claspt* in *c* ?   " *xciii* 4
Not only cunning casts in *c*:   " *cxx* 5
judge all nature from her feet of *c*,   *Merlin and V.* 835
death, that seems to make us loveless *c*,   *Lancelot and E.* 1014
From the same *c* came into light   *Lover's Tale i* 194
make And break the vase of *c*,   *Ancient Sage* 92
Claymore   *C* and snowshoe, toys in lava,   *Princess, Pro.* 18
Clean (*See also* **Cleän**)   As *c* and white as privet when it flowers.   *Walk. to the Mail* 56
whole, and *c*, and meet for Heaven,   *St. S. Stylites* 213
will never make oneself *c*.   *Grandmother* 36
make all *c*, and plant himself afresh.   *Geraint and E.* 905
keep him bright and *c* as heretofore,   " 937
As *c* as blood of babes, as white as milk :   *Merlin and V.* 344
I decreed That even the dog was *c*,   *Akbar's Dream* 53
Cleän   as a flower fro' 'eäd to feeät :   *North. Cobbler* 44
an' I keeäps 'im *c* an' bright,   " 97
but the cat mun be *c*.   *Spinster's S's.* 34
es *c* a shillin' fresh fro' the mint   " 75
An' thy farmin' es *c* es thysen,'   " 77
Clean-cut   There were some for the *c-c* stone,   *V. of Maeldune* 112
Cleaner   house with all its hateful needs no *c* than the beast,   *Happy* 32
Cleaner-fashion'd   fork of thine Is *c-f*—   *Merlin and V.* 60
Cleaning   *See* **A-cleanin'**
Cleanse   working out his will, To *c* the world.   *Gareth and L.* 25
c this common sewer of all his realm,   *Marr. of Geraint* 39
c this common sewer of all my realm,   *Geraint and E.* 895
Cleansed   broke the bandit holds and *c* the land.   " 944
Cleanser   saved a life Worth somewhat as the *c* of this wood.   *Gareth and L.* 828
Cleän-wud (clean-mad)   An' I thowt as 'e'd goan *c-w*,   *Owd Roä* 61
Clear (adj.)   (*See also* **Silver-clear**, **Starry-clear**)   *C*, without heat, undying,   *Isabel* 3

Clear (adj.) *(continued)* With chisell'd features *c* and sleek. *A Character* 30
C and bright it should be ever, *Poet's Mind* 5
Bright as light, and *c* as wind. " 7
so *c* and bold and free As you, *Rosalind* 17
C as the twanging of a harp, *Kate* 8
So healthy, sound, and *c* and whole, *Miller's D.* 15
Make Thou my spirit pure and *c* *St. Agnes' Eve* 9
O hark, O hear! how thin and *c*, *Princess* iv 7
nobbut a curate, an' weänt niver git hissen *c*, *N. Farmer, N. S.* 27
I feel so free and so *c* *Maud* I xix 98
world Was all so *c* about him, that he saw *Com. of Arthur* 98
C as a lark, high o'er me as a lark, *Holy Grail* 833
Name, surname, all as *c* as noon, *The Ring* 237
a faith as *c* as the heights of the June-blue
heaven, *June-Bracken, etc.* 7
Clear (adv.) came A bitter wind, *c* from the North, *Pass. of Arthur* 124
That sings so delicately *c*, *Marr. of Geraint* 332
long es she lived she kep 'em all *c*, *Village Wife* 53
Clear (verb) Better to *c* prime forests, *Princess* iii 127
Will *c* away the parasitic forms " vii 269
balm May *c* the blood from poison, *Death of Œnone* 36
Clear-cut But a cold and *c-c* face, *Maud* I ii 3
Cold and *c-c* face, why come you so cruelly meek, " iii 1
Clear'd And a whirlwind *c* the larder: *The Goose* 52
flash of semi-jealousy *c* it to her. *Aylmer's Field* 189
moving everywhere *C* the dark places *Geraint and E.* 943
She *c* her sight, she arose, *Dead Prophet* 31
Clearer like a light that grows Larger and *c*, *Œnone* 109
The fires are all the *c*, *Window. Winter* 16
every turn and depth Between is *c* in my life *Lover's Tale* i 149
Clearest Yet *c* of ambitious crime, *Ode on Well.* 28
Clear-faced Until they found the *c-f* King, *Lancelot and E.* 432
Clear-featured that *c-f* face Was lovely, " 1159
Clear-headed *C-h* friend, whose joyful scorn, *Clear-headed friend* 1
Clearness 'are like the rest; No certain *c*, *Two Voices* 335
The starry *c* of the free? *In Mem.* lxxxv 86
The critic of *c* an eye, " cix 3
c of his fame hath gone Beneath the shadow *Lover's Tale* i 789
no shade of doubt, But utter *c*, *Ancient Sage* 236
Clear-pointed fed With the *c-p* flame of chastity, *Isabel* 2
Clear-stemm'd *c-s* platans guard The outlet, *Arabian Nights* 23
Clear-voiced The *c-v* mavis dwelleth, *Claribel* 16
Clear-wall'd Or in a *c-w* city on the sea, *Palace of Art* 97
Cleave (to adhere) love thee well and *c* to thee, *Œnone* 160
'The man will *c* unto his right.' *Lady Clare* 46
C to your contract: *Princess* iv 409
if I fall, *c* to the better man.' *Geraint and E.* 152
To love one maiden only, *c* to her, *Guinevere* 475
The shadow of another *c's* to me, " 618
c's to cairn and cromlech still; *To the Queen* ii 41
The lecher would *c* to his lusts, *Despair* 100
C ever to the sunnier side of doubt, *Ancient Sage* 68
C to one another still? *Open. I and C. Exhib.* 34
Cleave (to divide) Clear Love would pierce and *c*, *If I were loved* 6
ill-used race of men that *c* the soil, *Lotos-Eaters, C. S.* 120
To *c* the rift of difference deeper yet; *Princess* v 301
When mighty Love would *c* in twain *In Mem.* xxv 10
master-bowman, he, Would *c* the mark. " lxxxvii 30
To *c* a creed in sects and cries, " cxxviii 15
and so ye *C* His armour off him, *Gareth and L.* 1094
May this hard earth *c* to the Nadir hell *Merlin and V.* 349
Cleaved (For I *c* to a cause that I felt *Maud* III vi 31
ever like a loyal sister *c* To Arthur, *Com. of Arthur* 191
some she *c* to, but they died of her. *Gareth and L.* 113
So to this king I *c*: my friend was he, *Sir J. Oldcastle* 61
Cleaving The fruitful wit *C*, took root, *The Poet* 21
Cleft (s) *(See also* **Mountain-cleft**) Far-off the
torrent call'd me from the *c*: *Œnone* 54
thro' mountain *c's* the dale Was seen *Lotos-Eaters* 20
every coppice-feather'd chasm and *c*, *Princess* iv 23
gather'd trickling dropwise from the *c*, *Merlin and V.* 274
little elves of chasm and *c* Made answer, *Guinevere* 248
saw The *c's* and openings in the mountains *Lover's Tale* i 330
Cleft (verb) He *c* me thro' the stomacher; *Princess* ii 407
spire of land that stands apart *C* from the main, " iv 282

Cleft (verb) *(continued)* Has risen and *c* the soil, and
grown a bulk *Princess* vi 35
Which *c* and *c* again for evermore, *Ancient Sage* 43
Clelia *C*, Cornelia, with the Palmyrene *Princess* ii 83
Clematis O'erflourish'd with the hoary *c*: *Golden Year* 63
among the meadows, the clover and the *c*, *City Child* 9
Rose, rose and *c*, (repeat) *Window. At the W.* 3, 10
and the dark-blue *c*, clung, *V. of Maeldune* 39
Clemm'd (clutched) an' *c* owd Roä by the 'eäd, *Owd Roä* 99
Clench those, who *c* their nerves to rush *Love and Duty* 77
Clench'd *(See also* **Half-clench'd**) taunt that *c* his
purpose like a blow! *Princess* v 306
c her fingers till they bit the palm, *Lancelot and E.* 611
c His hands, and madden'd with himself *Pelleas and E.* 459
Muriel *c* The hand that wore it, *The Ring* 261
Cleopatra-like *C-l* as of old To entangle me *Maud* I vi 27
Clergyman that good man, the *c*, has told me
words of peace, *May Queen, Con.* 12
Clerk *(See also* **Parish-clerks**) worn-out *c* Brow-
beats his desk below. *To J. M. K.* 13
now we left The *c* behind us, I and he, *Edwin Morris* 97
That was a God, and is a lawyer's *c*, " 102
A CITY *c*, but gently born and bred; *Sea Dreams* 1
mitre-sanction'd harlot draws his *c's* Into the
suburb— *Sir J. Oldcastle* 106
Cletch (brood of chickens) But Nelly, the last of the *c*, *Village Wife* 9
Cleverness not for all Aspasia's *c*, *Princess* ii 344
Click merry milkmaids *c* the latch, *The Owl* I 8
C with the pick, coming nearer *Def. of Lucknow* 1
Cliff *(See also* **Sea-cliff, Shore-cliff**) light upon the
wall Of purple *c's*, *Ode to Memory* 54
mountain-shade Sloped downward to her seat from
the upper *c*. *Œnone* 22
Along the *c* to fall and pause and fall *Lotos-Eaters* 9
bare black *c* clang'd round him, *M. d'Arthur* 188
Upon the *c's* that guard my native land, *Audley Court* 49
girt the region with high *c* and lawn: *Vision of Sin* 47
lines of *c* breaking have left a chasm: *Enoch Arden* 1
A narrow cave ran in beneath the *c*: " 23
sand and *c* and deep-inrunning cave, *Sea Dreams* 17
on sand they walk'd, and now on *c*, " 37
claps of thunder from within the *c's* " 90
enter'd one Of those dark caves that run beneath
the *c's*. " 214
on those *c's* Broke, mixt with awful light " 217
those lines of *c's* were *c's* no more, *Princess* iii 360
we wound About the *c's*, the copses, " iv 9
O sweet and far from *c* and scar " 524
A stroke of cruel sunshine on the *c*, *W. to Marie Alex.* 17
On capes of Afric as on *c's* of Kent, *In Mem.* xii 8
And leave the *c's*, and haste away " lvi 2
From scarped *c* and quarried stone *Marr. of Geraint* 318
like a crag that tumbles from the *c*, *Guinevere* 280
Between the steep *c* and the coming wave; " 608
as a stream that spouting from a *c* Fails *Pass. of Arthur* 356
left and right The bare black *c* clang'd round him, *Lover's Tale* i 1
HERE far away, seen from the topmast *c*, " 57
slowly-ridging rollers on the *c's* Clash'd, *V. of Maeldune* 39
the red passion-flower to the *c's*, " 55
all round from the *c's* and the capes, *The Wreck* 73
And *c's* all robed in lianas that dropt
blanch into spray At the feet of the *c*; " 138
I climb'd on all the *c's* of all the seas, *Demeter and P.* 63
Cliff-side broken rocks On some *c-s*, *Lancelot and E.* 1253
Climate manners, *c's*, councils, governments, *Ulysses* 14
Climax and he: 'The *c* of his age!' *Princess* ii 50
Climb *(See also* **Claum**) Where he was wont to leap
and *c*, *Supp. Confessions* 165
'Cry, faint not, *c*: the summits slope *Two Voices* 184
could she *c* Beyond her own material prime? " 377
You seem'd to hear them *c* and fall *Palace of Art* 70
'will you *c* the top of Art. *Gardener's D.* 169
long day wanes: the slow moon *c's*; *Ulysses* 55
I leave the plain, I *c* the height; *Sir Galahad*, 57
street *c's* to one tall-tower'd mill; *Enoch Arden* 5

Climb (*continued*) stairs That *c* into the windy halls of heaven :	*Lucretius* 136
but we Set forth to *c* ;	*Princess iii* 354
as one that *c*'s a peak to gaze O'er land and main,	,, *vii* 35
Be near us when we *c* or fall :	*In Mem. li* 13
C thy thick noon, disastrous day ;	,, *lxxii* 26
I *c* the hill : from end to end	,, *c* 1
I could *c* and lay my hand upon it,	*Gareth and L.* 50
'*C* not lest thou break thy neck,	,, 54
felt the knot *C* in her throat,	*Lancelot and E.* 741
C's to the mighty hall that Merlin built.	*Holy Grail* 231
'There rose a hill that none but man could *c*,	,, 489
in a dream I seem'd to *c* For èver :	,, 836
I would not or I could not *c*—	*Guinevere* 644
clomb Ev'n to the highest he could *c*,	*Pass of Arthur* 463
C first and reach me down thy hand.	*Sir J. Oldcastle* 204
sister of the sun Would *c* from out the dark,	*Tiresias* 31
And *c* the Mount of Blessing,	*Ancient Sage* 280
wounded warrior *c*'s from Troy to thee.	*Death of Œnone* 39
if ever a woman should *c* to the dwelling	*Kapiolani* 22
Climb'd (*See also* **Claumb'd**) They *c* as quickly, for the rim Changed	*The Voyage* 27
as he *c* the hill, Just where the prone edge	*Enoch Arden* 66
he had *c* across the spikes,	*Princess, Pro.* 111
we *c* The slope to Vivian-place,	,, *Con.* 39
I *c* to the top of the garth,	*Grandmother* 38
I *c* the roofs at break of day ;	*Daisy* 40
And thither I *c* at dawn	*Maud I xiv* 5
I have *c* nearer out of lonely Hell.	,, *xviii* 80
sweet son, had risk'd himself and *c*,	*Gareth and L.* 60
And *c* upon a fair and even ridge,	*Marr. of Geraint* 239
Guinevere had *c* The giant tower,	,, 826
on his foot She set her own and *c* ;	*Geraint and E.* 760
For one from out his village lately *c*	*Balin and Balan* 167
c That eastern tower, and entering barr'd	*Lancelot and E.* 14
Then to her tower she *c*,	,, 397
I *c* a thousand steps With pain :	*Holy Grail* 835
came Arthur home, and while he *c*,	*Last Tournament* 755
C to the high top of the garden-wall	*Guinevere* 25
cheeks as bright as when she *c* the hill.	*Lover's Tale iii* 47
heard a groaning overhead, and *c* The moulder'd stairs	,, *iv* 136
c one step beyond Our village	*Ancient Sage* 206
I *c* on all the cliffs of all the seas,	*Demeter and P.* 63
I *c* the hill with Hubert yesterday,	*The Ring* 152
I have *c* to the snows of Age,	*By an Evolution.* 17
c from the dens in the levels below,	*The Dawn* 17
Climbing In ever *c* up the *c* wave ?	*Lotos-Eater's, C. S.* 50
And ever *c* higher ;	*D. of F. Women* 32
And *c* up into my airy home,	*St. S. Stylites* 217
valleys underneath Came little copses *c*.	*Amphion* 32
A lily-avenue *c* to the doors ;	*Aylmer's Field* 162
Was *c* up the valley ; at whom he shot :	,, 228
then, *c*, Cyril kept With Psyche,	*Princess iii* 354
turn'd his face And kiss'd her *c*,	*Geraint and E.* 761
Cried to me *c*, 'Welcome, Percivale !	*Holy Grail* 425
over all the great wood rioting And *c*,	*Lover's Tale i* 404
set me *c* icy capes And glaciers,	*To E. Fitzgerald* 25
Pallas Athene *c* from the bath In anger :	*Tiresias* 144
Evolution ever *c* after some ideal good,	*Locksley H., Sixty* 199
saw Him, *c* toward her with the golden	*Death of Œnone* 15
Climbing Maud with her venturous *c*'s	*Maud I i* 69
Clime THE poet in a golden *c* was born,	*The Poet* 1
thro' mine ears in that unblissful *c*,	*D. of F. Women* 82
Put forth and feel a gladder *c*.'	*On a Mourner* 15
—what to me were sun or *c* ?	*Locksley Hall* 177
In divers seasons, divers *c*'s ;	*Day-Dm., L'Envoi* 18
O hundred shores of happy *c*'s,	*The Voyage* 49
Again to colder *c*'s we came,	,, 89
on the tables every *c* and age a Jumbled together ;	*Princess, Pro.* 16
For many a time in many a *c*	*Ode on Well.* 64
And led him through the blissful *c*'s,	*In Mem. lxxxv* 25
who throve and branch'd from *c* to *c*,	,, *cxviii* 13
blown by the breeze of a softer *c*,	*Maud I iv* 4
prayer of many a race and creed, and *c*—	*To the Queen ii* 11
Clime (*continued*) arrowing light from *c* to *c*,	*Akbar's D., Hymn* 5
Cling As close as might be would he *c*	*Talking Oak* 127
They *c* together in the ghastly sack—	*Aylmer's Field* 764
'My mother *c*'s about my neck,	*Sailor Boy* 17
flower that *c*'s To the turrets and the walls ;	*Maud II iv* 33
all night long a cloud *c*'s to the hill,	*Geraint and E.* 691
voice *c*'s to each blade of grass,	*Lancelot and E.* 107
glory *c* To all high places like a golden cloud	*Pass. of Arthur* 53
I *c* to the Catholic Cross once more,	*The Wreck* 3
c to Faith beyond the forms of Faith !	*Ancient Sage* 69
Who *c*'s to earth, and once would dare	,, 115
That we might *c* together,	,, *Happy* 92
Clinging Not *c* to some ancient saw ;	*Love thou thy land* 29
Unshaken, *c* to her purpose,	*Princess v* 344
necks Of dragons *c* to the crazy walls,	*Holy Grail* 347
C to the silent mother !	*Locksley H., Sixty* 99
Clink (s) the tinsel *c* of compliment.	*Princess ii* 55
Clink (verb) Thou hear'st the village hammer *c*,	*In Mem. cxxi* 15
Clink'd Touch'd, *c*, and clash'd and vanish'd,	*Sea Dreams* 135
Clinking Hammering and *c*, chattering stony names	*Princess iii* 361
Clinkt blade flew Splintering in six, and *c* upon the stones.	*Balin and Balan* 396
Clip And *c* your wings, and make you love :	*Rosalind* 45
Tho' fortune *c* my wings,	*Will Water.* 50
Clipt They read in arbours *c* and cut,	*Amphion* 85
from her baby's forehead *c* A tiny curl, and gave it :	*Enoch Arden* 235
many thousand days Were *c* by horror	*Aylmer's Field* 603
Or keeps his wing'd affections *c* with crime :	*Princess vii* 316
had *c* free manhood from the world—	*Last Tournament* 446
a sample, *c* out of the 'deaths' in a paper, fell.	*The Wreck* 146
Cloak (s) And the red *c*'s of market girls,	*L. of Shalott ii* 17
Pitiful sight, wrapp'd in a soldier's *c*,	*Princess v* 56
raised the *c* from brows as pale and smooth	,, 73
Wrapt in a *c*, as I saw him,	*Maud I i* 59
Sir Gareth loosed A *c* that dropt	*Gareth and L.* 682
wrapping her all over with the *c* He came in,	*Lover's Tale iv* 86
Cloak (verb) wife-worship *c*'s a secret shame ?	*Balin and Balan* 360
c's the scar of some repulse with lies ;	*Merlin and V.* 818
Cloak'd The Shadow *c* from head to foot,	*In Mem. xxiii* 4
Cloäths (clothes) Sally she wesh'd foälks ' *c*	*North. Cobbler* 29
Look at the *c* on 'er back,	,, 109
Cloäthes (clothes) an' a-buyin' new *c*,	*Village Wife* 37
Clock The slow *c* ticking, and the sound	*Mariana* 74
The windy clanging of the minster *c* ;	*Gardener's D.* 38
The heavy *c*'s knolling the drowsy hours.	,, 184
There rose a noise of striking *c*'s,	*Day-Dm., Revival* 2
speak for noise Of *c*'s and chimes,	*Princess i* 216
the dark, when *c*'s Throbb'd thunder	,, *vii* 103
c Beats out the little lives of men.	*In Mem. ii* 7
And hark the *c* within,	*Maud I xviii* 64
lights the *c* ! the hand points five—	*The Flight* 94
Clock-work little *c-w* steamer paddling plied	*Princess, Pro.* 71
Clod before the heavy *c* Weighs on me,	*Supp. Confessions* 184
and the *c*, Less dull than thou,	*Gareth and L.* 1391
Clog (s) A *c* of lead was round my feet,	*The Letters* 5
To lighten this great *c* of thanks,	*Princess vi* 126
Clog (verb) fulsome Pleasure *c* him, and drown	*Maud I xvi* 4
Cloister (*See also* **Crag-cloister**) row Of *c*'s, branch'd like mighty woods,	*Palace of Art* 26
while our *c*'s echo'd frosty feet,	*Princess, Pro.* 183
world-old yew-tree, darkening half The *c*'s,	*Holy Grail* 14
Walk your dim *c*, and distribute dole	*Guinevere* 683
Sometimes I frequent the Christian *c*,	*Akbar's D., Inscrip.* 5
Clomb Imprisoning sweets, which, as they *c*	*Arabian Nights* 40
C to the roofs, and gazed alone for hours	*Princess vii* 32
neither *c*, nor brake his neck,	*Gareth and L.* 56
And glad was I and *c*, but found at top	*Holy Grail* 427
turn'd and slowly *c* The last hard footstep	*Pass. of Arthur* 446
c Ev'n to the highest he could climb,	,, 462
C the mountain, and flung the bierries,	*Kapiolani* 6
Close (an enclosure) I broke a *c* with force and arms :	*Edwin Morris* 131
I lay Pent in a roofless *c* of ragged stones ;	*S. St. Stylites* 74
Are wither'd in the thorny *c*,	*Day-Dm., Arrival* 11
Close (an end) sweet *c* of his delicious toils—	*Palace of Art* 185

Close (an end) (*continued*) The c, ' Your Letty, only
yours ;'   *Edwin Morris* 106
OF love that never found his earthly c,   *Love and Duty* 1
Death dawning on him, and the c of all.   *Enoch Arden* 832
At c of day ; slept, woke, and went the next,   *Sea Dreams* 18
Then comes the c.'   " 29
and the bitter c of all,   *Princess vi* 117
drove us, last to quite a solemn c—   " *Con.* 17
all, they said, as earnest as the c ?   " 21
Such a war had such a c.   *Ode on Well.* 118
HERE ; it is here, the c of the year,   *Spiteful Letter* 1
Here is the golden c of love,   *Window. Marr. Morn.* 3
To such a stern and iron-clashing c,   *Merlin and V.* 419
Perchance, because we see not to the c ;—   *Pass. of Arthur* 21
Restrain'd himself quite to the c—   *Lover's Tale iv* 10
Laud me not Before my time, but hear me to the c.   " 243
My c of earth's experience May prove   *Tiresias* 216
gloom of the evening, Life at a c ;   *Vastness* 15
were alone in the dell at the c of the day.   *Bandit's Death* 19

Close (adj. and adv.) order'd all Almost as neat and c   *Enoch Arden* 178
princedom lay C on the borders of a territory,   *Marr. of Geraint* 33
So c are we, dear Mary,   *To Mary Boyle* 59
but c to me to-day As this red rose,   *Roses on the T.* 6
I was c on that hour of dishonour,   *Charity* 28
my hot lips prest C, c to thine   *Œnone* 204
I never can be c with her,   *Balin and Balan* 186
c upon it peal'd A sharp quick thunder.'   *Holy Grail* 695
C beneath the casement crimson   *Locksley H., Sixty* 34
they stood So c together   *The Ring* 258
Now wraps her c, now arching leaves her bare   *Prog. of Spring* 12

Close (verb) C the door, the shutters c,   *Deserted House* 9
breathe it into earth and c it up   *Wan Sculptor* 12
In love with thee forgets to c His curtains,   *Adeline* 42
C up his eyes : tie up his chin :   *D. of the O. Year* 48
With one wide Will that c's thine.   *On a Mourner* 20
To c the interests of all.   *Love thou thy land* 36
And this be true, till Time shall c,   " 79
Death c's all : but something ere the end,   *Ulysses* 51
till he heard the ponderous door C,   *Aylmer's Field* 338
to c with Cyril's random wish :   *Princess iii* 101
hearts So gentle, so employ'd, should c in love,   " *vii* 67
before his journey c's, He shall find   *Ode on Well.* 205
and the daisy c Her crimson fringes   *In Mem. lxxii* 11
Until we c with all we loved,   " *cxxxi* 11
' O dewy flowers that c when day is done,   *Gareth and L.* 1067
To c with her lord's pleasure.   *Geraint and E.* 214
—so that fate and craft and folly c,   *Merlin and V.* 57
Down, down, and c again, and nip me flat,   " 350
and c the hand Upon it   *Lancelot and E.* 1114
but he that c's both Is perfect, he is Lancelot—   *Last Tournament* 708
And who shall escape if they c ?   *Heavy Brigade* 16
Both the days Now c in one.   *The Ring* 79
closed her eyes, which would not c,   " 299
Caught by the flower that c's on the fly,   " 344
his fresh life may c as it began,   *Prog. of Spring* 89

Close-bower'd Sir Balin sat C-b in that garden   *Balin and Balan* 241
Close-button'd turned once more, c-b to the storm ;   *Edwin Morris* 136
Closed (*See also* **Half-closed**) A thousand claims to
reverence c   *To the Queen* 27
I c mine eyelids, lest the gems   *M. d'Arthur* 152
all grace Summ'd up and c in little ;—   *Gardener's D.* 13
She turn'd, we c, we kiss'd,   *Edwin Morris* 114
I had hoped that ere this period c   *St. S. Stylites* 17
for the promise that it c :   *Locksley Hall* 14
C in a golden ring   *Sir L. and Q. G.* 27
she c the Book and slept :   *Enoch Arden* 499
when she c ' Enoch, poor man, was cast away   " 712
Crept to the gate, and open'd it, and c,   " 775
Until they c a bargain, hand in hand.   *The Brook* 156
c her access to the wealthier farms,   *Aylmer's Field* 503
fain had she c them now,   " 805
c by those who mourn a friend in vain,   *Lucretius* 142
And thus our conference c.   *Princess ii* 367
until they c In conflict with the crash   " *v* 490
darkness c me ; and I fell.   " 542

Closed (*continued*) My spirit c with Ida's at the lips ;   *Princess vii* 158
So c our tale, of which I give you all   " *Con.* 1
the gates were c At sunset,   " 36
few words and pithy, such as a c Welcome, farewell,   " 94
where warm hands have prest and c,   *In Mem. xiii* 7
such as c Grave doubts and answers   " *xlviii* 2
whose dying eyes Were c with wail,   " *xc* 6
pulses c their gates with a shock   *Maud I i* 15
gates of Heaven are c, and she is gone.   " *xviii* 12
now by this my love has c her sight   " 67
C in her castle from the sound of arms.   *Gareth and L* 163
But when they c—in a moment—   " 1222
Dash'd on Geraint, who c with him,   *Geraint and E.* 462
while he spoke C his death-drowsing eyes,   *Balin and Balan* 631
C in the four walls of a hollow tower,
(repeat)   *Merlin and V.* 209, 543
and the thicket c Behind her,   " 973
And c the hand upon it, and she died.   *Lancelot and E.* 1135
great table of our Arthur c And clash'd   *Holy Grail* 329
and then a fawn ; and his eyes c.   *Pelleas and E.* 39
Drew back a space, and when they c,   " 573
' O c about by narrowing nunnery-walls,   *Guinevere* 342
On the waste sand by the waste sea they c.   *Pass. of Arthur* 92
' Sir King, I c mine eyelids, lest the gems   " 320
Ideal manhood c in real man,   *To the Queen ii* 38
round him c and claspt again.   *Lover's Tale iv* 378
I c my heart to the gloom ;   *The Wreck* 38
If utter darkness c the day,   *Ancient Sage* 199
c her eyes, which would not close,   *The Ring* 299
Clouds and darkness C upon Camelot ;   *Merlin and the G.* 76
kiss'd his hand, another c his eyes,   *Death of Œnone* 58

Close-latticed C-l to the brooding heat,   *Mariana in the S.* 3
Close-lapt c-l in silken folds.   *Lover's Tale i* 153
Closelier once mine, now thine, is c mine,   *Merlin and V.* 446
Close-matted a wall of green C-m,   *Day-Dm., Sleep P.* 46
Closeness such a c, but apart there grew,   *Holy Grail* 884
Closer C is He than breathing,   *High. Pantheism* 12
But thou art c to this noble prince,   *Com. of Arthur* 314
C on the Sun, perhaps a world   *Locksley H., Sixty* 184
Close-set wore A c-s robe of jasmine   *Aylmer's Field* 158
Betwixt the c-s ivies came a broad   *Lover's Tale ii* 172
Closet not to myself in the c alone,   *Maud II v* 49
Closeted (*See also* **Long-closeted**) with that woman c
for hours !'   *Princess iii* 56
Closing (part) There—c like an individual life—   *Love and Duty* 79
And c eaves of wearied eyes   *In Mem. lxvii* 11
As c in himself the strength of ten,   *Gareth and L.* 1339
c round him thro' the journey home,   *Pelleas and E.* 202
Closing (s) And at the c of the day   *L. of Shalott iv* 15
Clot Is a c of warmer dust,   *Vision of Sin* 113
Cloth (*See also* **Altar-cloth, Cloth of Gold, Face-cloth**)
a c of palest gold, Which down he laid   *Gareth and L.* 389
Arthur cried to rend the c, (repeat)   " 400, 418
we should lap him up in c of lead,   " 430
c of roughest web, and cast it down,   " 683
sparkle of a c On fern and foxglove.   *Sisters (E. and E.)* 117
What have I here in the c ?   *Bandit's Death* 8
Clothe That c the wold and meet the sky ;   *L. of Shalott i* 3
O, the child too c's the father   *Locksley Hall* 91
C's and reclothes the happy plains,   *Day-Dm., Sleep P.* 2
often toil'd to c your little ones ;   *Aylmer's Field* 699
lingereth she to c her heart with love,   *Princess iv* 105
tender ash delays To c herself,   " 107
Will c her for her bridals like the sun.'   *Marr. of Geraint* 231
So c yourself in this, that better fits   " 717
Herself would c her like the sun in Heaven.   " 784
In this poor gown he bad me c myself,   *Geraint and E.* 702
' And lo, I c myself with wisdom,   *Merlin and V.* 255
her love did c itself in smiles About his lips !   *Lover's Tale i* 658
earth-baldness c's itself afresh,   *Demeter and P.* 49
Clothed river-sunder'd champaign c with corn,   *Œnone* 114
C in white samite, mystic, wonderful,
(repeat)   *M. d'Arthur* 31, 144, 159
ridge to ridge, C with his breath,   " 182
she rode forth, c on with chastity :   *Godiva* 53

Clothed (*continued*) she rode back, *c* on with chastity :   *Godiva* 65
Pure spaces *c* in living beams,   *Sir Galahad* 66
with thy worst self hast thou *c* thy God.   *Aylmer's Field* 646
thought flash'd thro' me which I *c* in act,   *Princess i* 195
these have *c* their branchy bowers With fifty Mays,   *In Mem. lxxvi* 13
C in white samite, mystic, wonderful.   *Com. of Arthur* 285
So that the child and he were *c* in fire.   ,, 390
And truth or *c* or naked let it be,   ,, 408
see her now, *C* with my gift,   *Marr. of Geraint* 753
And *c* her for her bridals like the sun ;   ,, 836
And *c* her in apparel like the day.   *Geraint and E.* 948
barge Be ready on the river, *c* in black.   *Lancelot and E.* 1123
a love *C* in so pure a loveliness?   ,, 1384
C in white samite or a luminous cloud.   *Holy Grail* 513
golden beard that *c* his lips with light—   *Last Tournament* 668
C in white samite, mystic, wonderful,
(repeat)   *Pass. of Arthur* 199, 312, 327
ridge to ridge, *C* with his breath,   *Pass. of Arthur* 350
c with living light, They stood before his
throne   454
When he *c* a naked mind with the wisdom   *The Wreck* 65
But *c* with The Gleam,   *Merlin and the G.* 94
WHEN the dumb Hour, *c* in black,   *Silent Voices* 1

Clothes (*See also* **Cloäthes, Cloäths**) wholesome
food, And wear warm *c*,   *St. S. Stylites* 109
And *c* they gave him and free passage   *Enoch Arden* 650
Like coarsest *c* against the cold :   *In Mem. v* 10
She is not fairer in new *c* than old.   *Marr. of Geraint* 722

Clothing upbearing parasite, *C* the stem,   *Isabel* 35
Cloth of Gold With inwrought flowers, a *c o g.*   *Arabian Nights* 149
city all on fire With sun and *c o g*,   *Com. of Arthur* 480
pray'd him well to accept this *c o g*,   *Gareth and L.* 398
seeing he hath sent us *c o g*,   ,, 428
children of the King in *c o g* Glanced   *Marr. of Geraint* 664
all the children in their *c o g* Ran to her,   ,, 668
all the coverlid was *c o g* Drawn to her waist,   *Lancelot and E.* 1157

Clotted Or, *c* into points and hanging loose,   *M. d'Arthur* 219
Or, *c* into points and hanging loose,   *Pass. of Arthur* 387

Cloud (s) (*See also* **Thunder-cloud**) When will the
c's be aweary of fleeting ?   *Nothing will die* 5
The *c* fleets, The heart beats,   ,, 11
One after another the white *c's* are fleeting ;   *All Things will die* 5
The *c's* will cease to fleet ;   ,, 11
Like little *c's* sun-fringed,   *Madeline* 17
with the evening *c*, Showering thy gleaned wealth   *Ode to Memory* 22
morn Forth gushes from beneath a low-hung *c*.   ,, 71
while Slowly, as from a *c* of gold,   *Eleänore* 73
Nor any *c* would cross the vault,   *Mariana in the S.* 38
Wrapt in dense *c* from base to cope.   *Two Voices* 186
Embracing *c*, Ixion-like ;   ,, 195
That every *c*, that spreads above And veileth love,   ,, 446
A *c* that gather'd shape :   *Œnone* 42
one silvery *c* Had lost his way between   ,, 92
o'er him flow'd a golden *c*, and lean'd   ,, 105
As she withdrew into the golden *c*,   ,, 191
narrow moon-lit slips of silver *c*,   ,, 218
death, death, thou ever-floating *c*,   ,, 238
A *c* of incense of all odour steam'd   *Palace of Art.* 39
All barr'd with long white *c* the scornful crags,   ,, 83
c's are lightly curl'd Round their golden
houses,   *Lotos-Eaters, C. S.* 112
Hold swollen *c's* from raining,   *D. of F. Women* 11
'The light white *c* swam over us.   ,, 221
Brightening the skirts of a long *c*,   *M. d'Arthur* 54
as one large *c* Drew downward :   *Gardener's D.* 78
The light *c* smoulders on the summer crag.   *Edwin Morris* 147
sign betwixt the meadow and the *c*,   *St. S. Stylites* 14
A soft air fans the *c* apart ;   *Tithonus* 32
looking like a summer moon Half-dipt in *c* :   *Godiva* 46
The *c's* are broken in the sky,   *Sir Galahad* 73
And *c's* are highest up in air,   *Lady Clare* 2
made the wild-swan pause in her *c*,   *Poet's Song* 7
c Cuts off the fiery highway of the sun,   *Enoch Arden* 129
Sailing along before a gloomy *c*   *Sea Dreams* 124
Where never creeps a *c*, or moves a wind,   *Lucretius* 106

Cloud (s) (*continued*) and molten on the waste Becomes a *c*:   *Princess iv* 73
As of some fire against a stormy *c*,   ,, 384
Settled a gentle *c* of melancholy ;   ,, 570
As comes a pillar of electric *c*,   ,, v 524
thro' the *c* that dimm'd her broke A genial warmth   ,, vi 281
The *c* may stoop from heaven and take the shape   ,, vii 2
sees a great black *c* Drag inward from the deeps,   ,, 36
C's that are racing above,   *Window. On the Hill* 6
Gone, and a *c* in my heart,   ,, *Gone* 6
No is trouble and *c* and storm,   ,, *No Answer* 8
Such *c's* of nameless trouble cross   *In Mem. iv* 13
dote and pore on yonder *c* That rises upward   ,, xv 16
A rainy *c* possess'd the earth,   ,, xxx 3
With fruitful *c* and living smoke,   ,, xxxix 3
Thro' *c's* that drench the morning star,   ,, lxxii 22
'Can *c's* of nature stain The starry clearness   ,, lxxxv 85
But in the darkness and the *c*,   ,, xcvi 21
We steer'd her toward a crimson *c*   ,, ciii 55
The flying *c*, the frosty light ;   ,, cvi 2
Like *c's* they shape themselves and go.   ,, cxxiii 8
high in heaven the streaming *c*,   ,, Con. 107
man walks with his head in a *c* of poisonous flies.   *Maud I iv* 54
In fold upon fold of hueless *c*,   ,, vi 3
when the morning came In a *c*, it faded,   ,, 21
sun look'd out with a smile Betwixt the *c* and the moor   ,, ix 4
till the *c* that settles round his birth   *Gareth and L.* 130
In counter motion to the *c's*,   ,, 1315
under *c* that grew To thunder-gloom palling
all stars,   ,, 1358
Turn thy wild wheel thro' sunshine, storm,
and *c* ;   *Marr. of Geraint* 348
wheel and thou are shadows in the *c* ;   ,, 357
and by and by Slips into golden *c*,   ,, 736
Then seeing *c* upon the mother's brow,   ,, 777
make your Enid burst Sunlike from *c*—   ,, 789
all night long a *c* clings to the hill,   *Geraint and E.* 691
Hung like a *c* above the gateway towers.'   *Merlin and V.* 599
Drew the vast eyelid of an inky *c*,   ,, 634
across him came a *c* Of melancholy severe,   *Lancelot and E.* 324
Dispersed his resolution like a *c*.   ,, 884
All over cover'd with a luminous *c*,   *Holy Grail* 189
'Lo now,' said Arthur, 'have ye seen a *c* ?   ,, 286
Clothed in white samite or a luminous *c*.   ,, 513
—a smile beneath a *c*, But heaven had meant it   ,, 705
o'er it crost the dimness of a *c* Floating,   *Pelleas and E.* 37
colours like the *c* Of sunset and sunrise,   ,, 53
upward-rushing storm and *c* Of shriek and
plume,   *Last Tournament* 440
Far over sands marbled with moon and *c*,   ,, 466
they cannot weep behind a *c* :   *Guinevere* 207
and wail their way From *c* to *c*,   *Pass. of Arthur* 40
glory cling To all high places like a golden *c*
For ever: ,, 54
Brightening the skirts of a long *c*,   ,, 222
Streams like a *c*, man-shaped,   *To the Queen ii* 40
sails, White as white *c's*, floated from sky to sky.   *Lover's Tale i* 5
Moved from the *c* of unforgotten things,   ,, 48
Stay'd on the *c* of sorrow ;   ,, 255
daylight of your minds But *c* and smoke,   ,, 297
would have flung himself From *c* to *c*,   ,, 302
Shading his eyes till all the fiery *c*,   ,, 306
Held for a space 'twixt *c* and wave,   ,, 417
Into a clearer zenith, pure of *c*,   ,, 514
Diffused and molten into flaky *c*.   ,, 641
life, burst through the *c* of thought Keen,   ,, ii 164
billow ran Shoreward beneath red *c's*,   ,, 179
a little silver *c* Over the sounding seas :   ,, iii 36
Willy—the moon's in a *c*—   *Rizpah* 86
melted like a *c* in the silent summer heaven ;   *The Revenge* 14
San Philip hung above us like a *c*   ,, 43
c that roofs our noon with night,   *Sisters (E. and E.)* 17
days Of doubt and *c* and storm,   *Columbus* 156
at dawn from the *c* glitter'd o'er us   *V. of Maeldune* 84
ridges drew the *c* and brake the storm   *Montenegro* 13
glorious goddess wreath'd a golden *c*,   *Achilles over the T.* 5

Cloud (s) (continued) All day long far-off in the *c* of the city, *The Wreck* 29
c of the mother's shame will enfold her   "   100
only a *c* and a smoke who was once a pillar   *Despair* 29
and higher, The *c* that hides it—higher still, the
    heavens Whereby the *c* was moulded, and
    whereout The *c* descended.   *Ancient Sage* 12
beacon burn'd in vain, And now is lost in *c*:   "   143
past into the Nameless, as a *c* Melts into Heaven.   "   233
But still the *c*'s remain ;' The *c*'s themselves are
    children of the Sun.   "   241
A *c* between the Nameless and thyself,   "   278
An' the sun kem out of a *c*   *Tomorrow* 37
And roll'd them around like a *c*,—   *Heavy Brigade* 40
One year without a storm, or even a *c* ;   *The Ring* 284
Would Earth tho' hid in *c* not be follow'd   *Happy* 97
C's and darkness Closed upon Camelot ;   *Merlin and the G.* 75
Or does the gloom of Age And suffering *c*   *Romney's R.* 65
my reign Was redden'd by that *c* of shame   *Akbar's Dream* 64
methought The *c* was rifted by a purer gleam   "   78
Cloud (verb) ever swarm about And *c* the highest heads,   *Columbus* 120
Clouded So spake he, *c* with his own conceit,   *M. d'Arthur* 110
    (For all my mind is *c* with a doubt)—   "   258
Being so *c* with his grief and love,   *Holy Grail* 656
So spake he, *c* with his own conceit,   *Pass. of Arthur* 278
    (For all my mind is *c* with a doubt)—   "   426
c with the grateful incense-fume   " *Tiresias* 183
all the Thrones are *c* by your loss,   *D. of the Duke of C.* 6
Cloudier *c* on her knight—Linger'd Ettarre :   *Pelleas and E.* 177
Cloudlet From little *c*'s on the grass,   *In Mem., Con.* 94
Cloud-pavilion'd The *c-p* element, the wood,   *Lover's Tale ii* 199
Cloud-tower *C-t*'s by ghostly masons wrought,   *In Mem. lxx* 5
Cloud-weaver *C-w* of phantasmal hopes and fears,   *To Victor Hugo* 2
Cloudy made him look so *c* and so cold ;   *Geraint and E.* 48
Clout an' the clats an' the *c*'s,   *Spinster's S*'s. 87
Clove (s) nutmeg rocks and isles of *c*.   *The Voyage* 40
Clove (verb) *C* the citron-shadows in the blue: *Arabian Nights* 14
the crowd dividing *c* An advent to the throne :   *Princess iv* 283
Laid him that *c* it grovelling on the ground.   *Gareth and L.* 972
with a stronger buffet he *c* the helm   "   1406
said Mark, and *c* him thro' the brain.   *Last Tournament* 754
C into perilous chasms our walls   *Def. of Lucknow* 55
And *c* the Moslem crescent moon,   *Happy* 44
Cloven (*See also* **Earthquake-cloven, Furrow-cloven**)
    Was *c* with the million stars   *Ode to Memory* 35
That not a worm is *c* in vain ;   *In Mem. liv* 9
Till Gareth's shield was *c* ;   *Gareth and L.* 971
earth beneath me yawning *c* With such a sound   *Lover's Tale i* 602
My heart was *c* with pain ;   " *ii* 200
       A Dirge 38
Clover Rare broidry of the purple *c*.   *City Child* 9
among the meadows, the *c* and the clematis,   *Sea-Fairies* 14
Clover-hill with white bells the *c-h* swells   *Locksley Hall* 47
Clown thou art mated with a *c*,   "   27
knave nor *c* Shall hold their orgies   *You might have won* 11
Shakespeare's curse on a knave and knave   "   27
this is proper to the *c*, Tho' smock'd, or furr'd and
    purpled, still the *c*,   *Princess iv* 246
turnspits for the *c*, The drunkard's football,   "   516
Glorifying *c* and satyr ;   " *v* 187
By blood a king, at heart a *c* ;   *In Mem. cxi* 4
Not all mismated with a yawning *c*,   *Geraint and E.* 426
not worthy to be knight ; A churl, a *c* !'   *Balin and Balan* 286
Like a *c*—by chance he met me—   *Locksley H., Sixty* 256
An' ya call'd 'im a *c*, ya did,   *Church-warden, etc.* 30
Club (*See also* **Battle-club**) talk'd At wine, in *c*'s,
    of art,   *Princess, Pro.* 161
Clump (mend) I could fettle and *c* owd booöts   *North. Cobbler* 13
Clung You should have *c* to Fulvia's waist,   *D. of F. Women* 259
Then they *c* about The old man's neck,   *Dora* 163
friendly mist of morn *C* to the lake.   *Edwin Morris* 108
When I *c* to all the present   *Locksley Hall* 14
evil fancies *c* Like serpent eggs together,   *Enoch Arden* 479
from the beetling crag to which he *c*   *Aylmer's Field* 229
sootflake of so many a summer still *C* to their fancies)   *Sea Dreams* 36
and the child *C* to the mother,   "   245
then, a moment after, *c* About him,   *Princess ii* 312

Clung (continued) about his motion *c* The shadow of his
    sister,   *Princess v* 257
Late the little children *c*:   *Ode on Well.* 237
C to the shield that Lancelot lent him,   *Gareth and L.* 1320
dawn ascending lets the day Strike where it *c*:   *Geraint and E.* 693
but that other *c* to him, Fixt in her will,   *Merlin and V.* 187
c about her lissome limbs,   "   223
curved an arm about his neck, *C* like a snake ;   "   242
while the skin *C* but to crate and basket,   "   625
c to him and hugg'd him close ;   "   945
to his crown the golden dragon *c*,   *Lancelot and E.* 434
knightly in me twined and *c* Round that one sin,   *Holy Grail* 774
fell thick rain, plume droopt and mantel *c*,   *Last Tournament* 213
A voice *c* sobbing till he question'd it,   "   759
C to the dead earth, and the land was still.   *Guinevere* 8
for crest the golden dragon *c* Of Britain ;   "   594
c In utter silence for so long,   *Sisters (E. and E.)* 216
from the ladders to which they had *c*,   *Def. of Lucknow* 58
C closer to us for a longer term   *Columbus* 197
and the dark-blue clematis, *c*,   *V. of Maeldune* 39
I *c* to the sinking form,   *The Wreck* 105
She *c* to me with such a hard embrace,   *The Ring* 435
Cluster (s) (*See also* **Sun-cluster**) Below the starry
    c's bright,   *L. of Shalott iii* 25
tropic shade and palms in *c*,   *Locksley Hall* 160
red roofs about a narrow wharf In *c* ;   *Enoch Arden* 4
lithe reluctant boughs to tear away Their tawny *c*'s,   "   382
Came men and women in dark *c*'s   *Sea Dreams* 226
Cluster (verb) The foxglove *c* dappled bells.'   *Two Voices* 72
Clustered sunny hair *C* about his temples   *Œnone* 60
Clutch So I *c* it. Christ ! 'Tis gone :   *St. S. Stylites* 207
And lives to *c* the golden keys,   *In Mem. lxiv* 10
Clutch'd (*See also* **Clemm'd**) *c* the sword, And strongly
    wheel'd and threw it.   *M. d'Arthur* 135
stoop'd and *c* him, fair and good,   *Will Water.* 133
So my mother *c* The truth at once,   *Princess iii* 27
He, standing still, was *c* ;   " *iv* 260
wakening, fiercely *c* the shield,   *Gareth and L.* 1304
C at the crag, and started thro' mid air   *Last Tournament* 14
c the sword, And strongly wheel'd and threw it.   *Pass. of Arthur* 303
Or *c* the sacred crown of Prester John,   *Columbus* 110
Clutter'd If *c* here, it chuckled there ;   *The Goose* 110
       St. S. Stylites 169
Coal On the *c*'s I lay, A vessel full of sin :   *Maud I x* 11
left his *c* all turn'd into gold   *Romney's R.* 1
c's of fire you heap upon my head   *L. of Shalott iii* 31
Coal-black flow'd His *c-b* curls as on he rode,   *Village Wife* 76
Coämb (comb) raäke out Hell wi' a small-tooth *c*—   *Church warden, etc.* 32
Coämb'd (combed) theer an' then I *c* 'im down,   *Talking Oak* 163
Coarse sense of touch is something *c*,   *Locksley Hall* 46
growing *c* to sympathise with clay.   *The Brook* 69
daughter of our meadows, yet not *c* ;   *Geraint and E.* 208
thou, My lord, eat also, tho' the fare is *c*,   *In the Child. Hosp.* 7
and I can well believe, for he lock'd so *c*
Coarseness According to the *c* of their kind,   *Princess iv* 346
Coast show'd an iron *c* and angry waves.   *Palace of Art* 69
All round the *c* the languid air   *Lotos-Eaters* 5
all in shade, Gloom'd the low *c*   *The Voyage* 42
leagues along that breaker-beaten *c*   *Enoch Arden* 51
Then moving up the *c* they landed him,   "   665
seaward-bound for health they gain'd a *c*,   *Sea Dreams* 16
she told it, having dream'd Of that same *c*.   "   207
He bad you guard the sacred *c*'s.   *Ode on Well.* 172
left the last free race with naked *c*'s !   *Third of Feb.* 40
A moulder'd citadel on the *c*,   *The Daisy* 28
A lucid veil from *c* to *c*,   *In Mem. lxvii* 14
rolling brine That breaks the *c*.   " *cvii* 15
shipwreck'd man on a *c* Of ancient fable and fear—   *Maud II ii* 31
Back from the Breton *c*,   "   43
province with a hundred miles of *c*, (repeat)   *Merlin and V.* 588, 647
about a stone On the bare *c*.   *Guinevere* 52
After the sunset, down the *c*,   "   238
All down the lonely *c* of Lyonnesse,   "   240
mountains ended in a *c* Of ever-shifting sand,   *Pass. of Arthur* 85
while we roam'd along the dreary *c*,   *Lover's Tale iv* 145
while I wander'd down the *c*,   *Locksley H., Sixty* 53

Coast (*continued*) Phra-bat the step ; your Pontic *c* ; — *To Ulysses* 42

Coasted *See* **Silver-coasted**

Coat (*See also* **Coät**) three castles patch my tatter'd *c*? — *Princess ii* 416
rough dog, to whom he cast his *c*, — *Gareth and L.* 1011
And such a *c* art thou, — ,, 1013

Coät Them as 'as *c's* to their backs — *N. Farmer, N. S.* 46

Coat-of-arms Is worth a hundred *c's-o-a*. — *L. C. V. de Vere* 16

Coax'd kept and *c* and whistled to— — *Gareth and L.* 14

Coäx'd An' *c* an' coodled me oop — *North. Cobbler* 80

Cobbled browt me the booöts to be *c* — ,, 94

Cobham Some cried on *C*, on the good Lord *C* ; — *Sir J. Oldcastle* 43

Cobra Those *c's* ever setting up their hoods— — *Akbar's Dream* 166

Cobweb The petty *c's* we have spun : — *In Mem. cxxiv* 8
the *c* woven across the cannon's throat — *Maud III vi* 27
I well could wish a *c* for the gnat, — *Merlin and V.* 370
Seems but a *c* filament to link — *Lover's Tale i* 376

Cobweb'd *See* **Many-cobweb'd**

Cock The *c* sung out an hour ere light : — *Mariana* 27
the *c* hath sung beneath the thatch — *The Owl I* 10
At midnight the *c* was crowing, — *Oriana* 12
Before the red *c* crows from the farm — *May Queen, N. Y's. E.* 23
I heard just now the crowing *c*. — *D. of the O. Year* 38
sitting, as I said, The *c* crew loud ; — *M. d'Arthur, Ep.* 10
And barking dogs, and crowing *c's* ; — *Day-Dm., Revival* 4
The *c* crows ere the Christmas morn, — *Sir Galahad* 51
O PLUMP head-waiter at The *C*, — *Will Water.* 1
The *C* was of a larger egg — ,, 121
Which was the red *c* shouting to the light, — *Geraint and E.* 384
And the *c* couldn't crow, — *V. of Maeldune* 18
The *c* has crow'd already once, — *The Flight* 3
c's kep a-crawin' an' crawin' — *Owd Roä* 106

Cockatrice basilisks, and splinter'd *c's*, — *Holy Grail* 718

Cockchafer *See* **Buzzard-Clock**

Cock-eyed I loöök'd *c-e* at my noäse — *North. Cobbler* 26

Cockney (Look at it) pricking a *c* ear. — *Maud I x* 22

Coco slender *c's* drooping crown of plumes, — *Enoch Arden* 574

Cocoon Spins, toiling out his own *c*. — *Two Voices* 180
we as rich as moths from dusk *c's*, — *Princess ii* 19

Coco-palm some dark dweller by the *c-p* — *Prog. of Spring* 84

Code Christless *c*, That must have life — *Maud II i* 26

Codlin fresh as a *c* wesh'd i' the dew. — *North. Cobbler* 110

Coerce No sound is breathed so potent to *c*, — *Tiresias* 120

Coffin (*See also* **Corpse-coffin**) in his *c* the Prince of courtesy lay. — *G. of Swainston* 10
thou wouldst have her flag Borne on thy *c*— *Ded. Poem Prin. Alice* 17
That within the *c* fell, Fell— — *To Marq. of Dufferin* 43
brother come ? to find Me or my *c*? — *Romney's R.* 144

Cognizance Some goodly *c* of Guinevere. — *Balin and Balan* 195
memory of that *c* on shield Weighted it down, — ,, 224
Stared at the priceless *c*, — ,, 430
one that hath defamed The *c* she gave me : — ,, 485

Cogoletto I stay'd the wheels at *C*, — *The Daisy* 23

Coil Hard *c's* of cordage, swarthy fishing-nets, — *Enoch Arden* 17
roots like some black *c* of carven snakes, — *Last Tournament* 13

Coil'd convolvuluses That *c* around the stately stems, — *Enoch Arden* 577
long loops Wherethro' the serpent river *c*, — *Gareth and L.* 906
serpent *c* about his broken shaft, — *Demeter and P.* 77

Coin Light *c*, the tinsel clink of compliment. — *Princess ii* 55
Him that made them current *c* ; — *In Mem. xxxvi* 4
and like to *c's*, Some true, some light, — *Holy Grail* 25
With scarce a *c* to buy a meal withal, — *Columbus* 169
All the chosen *c* of fancy flashing — *To Virgil* 7
violates virgin Truth for a *c* or a cheque. — *The Dawn* 15

Coinage Ringing like proven golden *c* true, — *Aylmer's Field* 182
strown With gold and scatter'd *c*, — *Geraint and E.* 26

Coin'd When he *c* into English gold some treasure — *The Wreck* 67
man had *c* himself a curse : — *Locksley H., Sixty* 87

Cold (*adj.*) (*See also* **Snow-cold, Cowd**) All *c*, and dead, and corpse-like grown? — *Supp. Confessions* 17
And dew is *c* upon the ground, — *The Owl I* 2
Quiet, dispassionate, and *c*, — *A Character* 28
Ere the placid lips be *c*? — *Adeline* 13
Because my memory is so *c*, — *Two Voices* 341
Is not more *c* to you than I. — *L. C. V. de Vere* 24
surely now our household hearts are *c* : — *Lotos-Eaters, C. S.* 72

Cold (*adj.*) (*continued*) Night is starry and *c*, my friend, — *D. of the O. Year* 34
c Are all thy lights, and *c* my wrinkled feet — *Tithonus* 66
'Shy she was, and I thought her *c* ; — *Edward Gray* 13
And saw the altar *c* and bare. — *The Letters* 4
Full *c* my greeting was and dry ; — ,, 13
round him ere he scarce be *c*, Begins the scandal — *You might have won* 15
LUCILIA, wedded to Lucretius, found Her master *c* ; — *Lucretius* 2
The loyal warmth of Florian is not *c*, — *Princess ii* 244
motionlessly pale, *C* ev'n to her, — ,, *vi* 102
And call her hard and *c* which seem'd a truth : — ,, *vii* 98
you think I am hard and *c* ; — *Grandmother* 17
We loved that hall, tho' white and *c*, — *The Daisy* 37
When ill and weary, alone and *c*, — ,, 96
C in that atmosphere of Death, — *In Mem. xx* 14
A spectral doubt which makes me *c*, — ,, *xli* 19
So, dearest, now thy brows are *c*, — ,, *lxxiv* 5
Is *c* to all that might have been. — ,, *lxxv* 16
He looks so *c* : she thinks him kind. — ,, *xcvii* 24
And smile as sunny as *c*, — *Maud I vi* 24
she was kind Only because she was *c*. — ,, *xiv* 27
made him look so cloudy and so *c* ; — *Geraint and E.* 48
'Poor men, when yule is *c*, — *Holy Grail* 613
glanced at him, thought him *c*, High, self-contain'd, — *Guinevere* 405
till all his heart was *c* With formless fear ; — *Pass. of Arthur* 97
subject of thy power, be *c* in her, — *Lover's Tale i* 782
in the hold were most of them stark and *c*, — *The Revenge* 79
C were his brows when we kiss'd him— — *Def. of Lucknow* 12
of the mind Mine ; worse, *c*, calculated. — *Romney's R.* 152

Cold (*s*) (*See also* **Cowd**) I fear My wound hath taken *c*, — *M. d'Arthur* 166
and in thirsts, fevers and *c*, — *St. S. Stylites* 166
Would chatter with the *c*, — ,, 31
In height and *c*, the splendour of the hills? — *Princess vii* 194
Like coarsest clothes against the *c* : — *In Mem. v.* 10
How dwarf'd a growth of *c* and night, — ,, *lxi* 7
fire of Heav'n has kill'd the barren *c*, — *Balin and Balan* 440
smitten in mid heaven with mortal *c* Past from her ; — *Last Tournament* 27
hour of *c* Falls on the mountain in midsummer snows, — ,, 227
I fear My wound hath taken *c*, — *Pass. of Arthur* 334
the *c* Without, and warmth within me, — *To E. Fitzgerald* 28
would dare Hell-heat or Arctic *c*, — *Ancient Sage* 116
thaws the *c*, and fills the flower — *Early Spring* 45
a breath that past With all the *c* of winter — *The Ring* 33

Cold-blooded That dull *c-b* Cæsar. — *D. of F. Women* 139

Coldness The faithless *c* of the times ; — *In Mem. cvi* 18
By the *c* of her manners, — *Maud I xx* 13

Cold-white white against the *c-w* sky, — *Dying Swan* 12

Colewort Picks from the *c* a green caterpillar, — *Guinevere* 32

Collar A grazing iron *c* grinds my neck ; — *St. S. Stylites* 117
She cried, 'The *c* of some Order, which — *Last Tournament* 741

Collar-bone cloak that dropt from *c-b* to heel, — *Gareth and L.* 682

Collatine made her blood in sight of *C* — *Lucretius* 238

Colleaguing *C* with a score of petty kings, — *Com. of Arthur* 67

College 'we knew your gift that way At *c* : — *The Epic* 25
For I remember'd Everard's *c* fame — ,, 46
I was at school—a *c* in the South : — *Walk. to the Mail* 83
By night we dragg'd her to the *c* tower — ,, 89
My *c* friendships glimmer. — *Will Water.* 40
I was there From *c*, visiting the son,— — *Princess, Pro.* 7
but we, unworthier, told Of *c* : — ,, 111
build Far off from men a *c* like a man's, — ,, 135
swore he long'd at *c*, only long'd, — ,, 158
A talk of *c* and of ladies' rights, — ,, 233
when the *c* lights Began to glitter — ,, *i* 207
At break of day the *C* Portress came : — ,, *ii* 15
A rosy blonde, and in a *c* gown, — ,, 323
Her *c* and her maidens, empty masks, — ,, *iii* 187
King, camp and *c* turn'd to hollow shows ; — ,, *v* 478
So their fair *c* turn'd to hospital ; — ,, *vii* 17
'Look there, garden !' said my *c* friend, — ,, *Con.* 49
And heard once more in *c* fanes — *In Mem. lxxxvii* 5

College-council Should eighty-thousand *c-c's* — *To F. D. Maurice* 7

College-time save for *c-t's* Or Temple-eaten terms, *Alymer's Field* 104
Colon (Columbus) *See* **Christopher Colon**
Colony near the *c* Cámulodúne, *Boädicea* 5
  Lo their *c* half-defended ! lo their *c*, ,, 17
  Then a phantom *c* smoulder'd on the refluent estuary ; ,, 28
  Lo the *c*, there they rioted in the city of Cúnobelíne ! ,, 60
  silent *c* hearing her tumultuous adversaries ,, 78
  Fell the *c*, city and citadel, ,, 86
Colossal Let his great example stand *C*, *Ode on Well.* 221
Colosseum Gain'd their huge *C.* *St. Telemachus* 45
Colour (*See also* **Flame-colour**) sweet is the *c* of cove
  and cave, *Sea-Fairies* 30
  I lose my *c*, I lose my breath, *Eleänore* 137
  A magic web with *c's* gay. *L. of Shalott* ii 2
  A word could bring the *c* to my cheek ; *Gardener's D.* 196
  came a *c* and a light, *Locksley Hall* 25
  The *c* flies into his cheeks : *Day-Dm., Arrival* 19
  Then the Captain's *c* heighten'd, *The Captain* 29
  the *c* flushes Her sweet face from brow to chin : *L. of Burleigh* 61
  She wore the *c's* I approved. *The Letters* 16
  a rough piece Of early rigid *c*, *Aylmer's Field* 281
  yet her cheek Kept *c* : wondrous ! ,, 506
  sense of wrong had touched her face With *c*) *Princess, Pro.* 220
  April daffodilly (Her mother's *c*) ,, ii 325
  In *c's* gayer than the morning mist, ,, 438
  shook the woods, And danced the *c*, ,, iii 293
  'Sir Ralph has got your *c* : ,, iv 594
  With Psyche's *c* round his helmet, ,, v 534
  But such as gather'd *c* day by day. ,, vii 118
  But distant *c*, happy hamlet, *The Daisy* 27
  And with the thought her *c* burns ; *In Mem.* vi 34
  Be all the *c* of the flower ? ,, xliii 8
  The *c's* of the crescent prime ? ,, cxvi 4
  Saying in odour and *c*, 'Ah, be Among the roses *Maud* I xxi 12
  O rainbow with three *c's* after rain, *Gareth and L.* 1160
  my child, how fresh the *c's* look, How fast they
  hold like *c's* of a shell *Marr. of Geraint* 680
  and play'd upon it, And made it of two *c's* ; *Geraint and E.* 292
  And so there lived some *c* in your cheek, ,, 621
  In *c* like the satin-shining palm *Merlin and V.* 224
  With *c's* of the heart that are not theirs. ,, 822
  Took gayer *c's*, like an opal warm'd. ,, 950
  And lichen'd into *c* with the crags : *Lancelot and E.* 44
  The low sun makes the *c* : ,, 134
  The shape and *c* of a mind and life, ,, 335
  let me bring your *c* back ; ,, 387
  secret blazed itself In the heart's *c's* ,, 837
  But did not love the *c* ; ,, 840
  cell were dyed With rosy *c's* leaping on the wall ; *Holy Grail* 120
  In *c* like the fingers of a hand Before a burning taper, ,, 693
  Damsels in divers *c's* like the cloud *Pelleas and E.* 53
  That ware their ladies' *c's* on the casque, *Last Tournament* 184
  With all the kindlier *c's* of the field.' ,, 224
  And glowing in all *c's*, the live grass, ,, 233
  I yearn'd for warmth and *c* which I found In
  Lancelot— *Guinevere* 647
  The *c* and the sweetness from the rose, *Lover's Tale* i 172
  Her cheek did catch the *c* of her words. ,, 569
  shadowing pencil's naked forms *C* and life : ,, ii 181
  And blurr'd in *c* and form, *Dead Prophet* 22
  concentrate into form And *c* all you are, *Romney's R.* 8
Colour'd *See* **Emerald-colour'd**, **Leaden-coloured**,
  Vary-coloured
Colourless for all his face was white And *c*, *M. d'Arthur* 213
  for all his face was white And *c*, *Pass. of Arthur* 381
Colt 'Then ran she, gamesome as the *c*, *Talking Oak* 121
  babes were running wild Like *c's* about the waste. *Enoch Arden* 305
  He pointed out a pasturing *c*, *The Brook* 136
  Squire had seen the *c* at grass, ,, 139
  the *c* would fetch its price ; ,, 149
  she's yet a *c*—Take, break her : *Princess* v 455
  Ran like a *c*, and leapt at all he saw : *Com. of Arthur* 322
  never *c* would more delight To roll *Romney's R.* 13
Colt-like *c-l* whinny and with hoggish whine *St. S. Stylites* 177
Columbus How young *C* seem'd to rove, *The Daisy* 17

Column Six *c's*, three on either side, *Arabian Nights* 144
  So like a shatter'd *c* lay the King ; *M. d'Arthur* 221
  people hum About the *c's* base, *St. S. Stylites* 39
  The watcher on the *c* till the end ; ,, 163
  And in we stream'd Among the *c's*, *Princess* ii 435
  To left and right, of those tall *c's* ,, vi 354
  bared the knotted *c* of his throat, *Marr. of Geraint* 74
  massive *c's*, like a shorecliff cave, *Lancelot and E.* 406
  So like a shatter'd *c* lay the King ; *Pass. of Arthur* 389
  masses Of thundershaken *c's* indistinct, *Lover's Tale* ii 66
  From *c* on to *c*, as in a wood, ,, iv 189
  names, Graven on memorial *c's*, *Tiresias* 124
Co-mate one of my *c-m's* Own'd a rough dog, *Gareth and L.* 1010
  true *c-m's* regather round the mast ; *Pref. Son. 19th Cent.* 5
Comb (s) *See* **Coämb, Comb of Pearl, Hornet-comb**
Comb (valley) they past a narrow *c* wherein *Gareth and L.* 1193
Comb (verb) With a comb of pearl I would *c* my hair ; *The Mermaid* 11
  I would *c* my hair till my ringlets ,, 14
Combat (s) And when the tide of *c* stands, *Sir Galahad* 10
  To prick us on to *c* 'Like to like ! *Princess* v 304
  Not dare to watch the *c*, *Geraint and E.* 154
  In *c* with the follower of Limours, ,, 501
Combat (verb) sware to *c* for my claim till death. *Princess* v 360
  a knight To *c* for my sister, Lyonors, *Gareth and L.* 608
  he needs must *c* might with might, *Epilogue* 28
Comb'd (*See also* **Coämb'd**) as I *c* I would sing and
  say, *The Mermaid* 12
  I curl'd and *c* his comely head, *The Sisters* 31
Combing *C* her hair Under the sea, *The Mermaid* 4
  c out her long black hair damp from the river ; *Princess* iv 276
Comb of Pearl With a *c o p*, On a throne ? *The Mermaid* 7
  With a *c o p* I would comb my hair ; ,, 11
  Made with her right a *c o p* *Merlin and V.* 244
Come (*See also* **Coom, To-come**) Spring will *c*
  never more. *All Things will die* 15
  Ye will *c* never more, ,, 48
  He will not *c*,' she said ; *Mariana* 82
  WHEN cats run home and light is *c*, *The Owl* i 1
  C not as thou camest of late, *Ode to Memory* 8
  C forth, I charge thee, arise, ,, 46
  C from the woods that belt the gray hill-side, ,, 55
  Dark-brow'd sophist, *c* not anear ; *Poet's Mind* 8
  Hollow smile and frozen sneer *C* not here. ,, 11
  O hither, *c* hither and furl your sails, *Sea-Fairies* 16
  C hither to me and to me ; Hither, *c* hither and frolic
  and play ; ,, 17
  Hither, *c* hither and see ; ,, 28
  O hither, *c* hither, and be our lords, ,, 32
  C away : no more of mirth Is here *Deserted House* 13
  C away : for Life and Thought Here no longer
  dwell ; ,, 17
  How could I rise and *c* away, *Oriana* 57
  I dare not die and *c* to thee, ,, 96
  Lull'd echoes of laborious day *C* to you, *Margaret* 30
  C down, *c* down, and hear me speak : ,, 56
  C down, *c* home, My Rosalind, *Rosalind* 33
  C's out thy deep ambrosial smile. *Eleänore* 74
  Thought seems to *c* and go In thy large eyes, ,, 96
  C only, when the days are still, *My life is full* 23
  Fresh-water springs *c* up through bitter brine. *If I were loved* 8
  The knights *c* riding two and two ; *L. of Shalott* ii 25
  'The curse is *c* upon me,' ,, iii 44
  night a *c* that knows not morn, *Mariana in the S.* 94
  I saw the dragon-fly *C* from the wells *Two Voices* 9
  'Then *c's* the check, the change, the fall, ,, 163
  In days that never *c* again. ,, 324
  Here *c's* to-day, Pallas and Aphrodìtè, *Œnone* 85
  Should *c* most welcome, seeing men, ,, 129
  (power of herself Would *c* uncall'd for) ,, 147
  sounds at night *c* from the inmost hills, ,, 249
  her child !—a shudder *c's* Across me : ,, 253
  Lest their shrill happy laughter *c* to me ,, 258
  the stars *c* forth Talk with the wild Cassandra, ,, 262
  I made a feast ; I bad him *c* ; *The Sisters* 13
  There *c's* no murmur of reply. *Palace of Art* 286

Come (*continued*) shepherd lads on every side 'ill *c* from
  far away,   *May Queen* 27
The night-winds *c* and go, mother,   ,,   33
I only wish to live till the snowdrops *c*
  again :   *May Queen, N. Y's. E.* 14
and the sun *c* out on high :   ,,   ,,   15
And the swallow, 'ill *c* back again   ,,   ,,   19
When the flowers *c* again, mother,   ,,   ,,   25
And you'll *c* sometimes and see me   ,,   ,,   30
If I can I'll *c* again, mother,   ,,   ,,   37
Don't let Effie *c* to see me   ,,   ,,   43
sweet is the new violet, that *c's* beneath the
  skies,   ,,   *Con.*   5
if it *c* three times, I thought,   ,,   ,,   38
to wait a little while till you and Effie *c*—   ,,   58
we should *c* like ghosts to trouble joy.   *Lotos-Eaters, C. S.* 74
' *C* here, That I may look on thee.'   *D. of F. Women* 123
C's up to take his own.   *D. of the O. Year* 36
And gently *c's* the world to those   *To J. S.* 3
Nothing *c's* to thee new or strange.   ,,   74
So let the change which *c's* be free   *Love thou thy land* 45
The Spirit of the years to *c*   55
keep a thing, its use will *c*.   *The Epic* 42
Merlin sware that I should *c* again   *M. d'Arthur* 23
land, where no one *c's*, Or hath *c*,   ,,   202
' Arthur is *c* again : he cannot die.'   ,,   *Ep.* 24
' *C* again, and thrice as fair ;   ,,   26
' *C* With all good things, and war shall be no more.'   ,,   27
News from the humming city *c's* to it In sound
  of funeral   *Gardener's D.* 35
Nor heard us *c*, nor from her tendance   ,,   144
Call'd to me from the years to *c*,   ,,   180
the time Is *c* to raise the veil.   ,,   274
for this orphan, I am *c* to you :   *Dora* 64
His mother, he cried out to *c* to her :   ,,   138
but now I *c* For Dora : take her back ;   ,,   142
I go to-night : I *c* to-morrow morn.   *Audley Court* 70
And when does this *c* by ?   *Walk. to the Mail* 7
and here it *c's* With five at top :   112
For that the evil ones *c* here,   *St. S. Stylites* 98
That here *c* those that worship me ?   ,,   125
I do not say But that a time may *c*—   ,,   190
C, blessed brother, *c*.   ,,   204
And down the way you use to *c*,   *Talking Oak* 115
Spun round in station, but the end had *c*.   *Love and Duty* 76
O might it *c* like one that looks content,   93
slow and sure *c's* up the golden year.   *Golden Year* 31
The fatal byword of all years to *c*,   *Godiva* 67
C, my friends, 'Tis not too late to seek   *Ulysses* 56
Man *c's* and tills the field and lies   *Tithonus* 3
there *c's* A glimpse of that dark world   32
crimson *c's* upon the robin's breast ;   *Locksley Hall* 17
tho' my mortal summers to such length of years
  should *c*   ,,   67
Slowly *c's* a hungry people,   ,,   135
Knowledge *c's*, but wisdom lingers, (repeat)   ,, 141, 143
Never *c's* the trader, never floats   ,,   161
C's a vapour from the margin,   ,,   191
Faint murmurs from the meadows *c*,   *Day-Dm., Sleep P.* 6
C, Care and Pleasure, Hope and Pain,   ,,   55
He *c's*, scarce knowing what he seeks :   ,,   *Arrival* 17
The flashes *c* and go ;   *St. Agnes' Eve* 26
' Love may *c*, and love may go,   *Edward Gray* 29
Till Ellen Adair *c* back to me.   ,,   32
she *c's* and dips Her laurel in the wine,   *Will Water.* 17
earth of light and shade *C's* out a perfect round.   ,,   68
To *c* and go, and *c* again,   ,,   229
' That all *c's* round so just and fair :   *Lady Clare* 18
Why *c* you drest like a village maid,   ,,   67
' If I *c* drest like a village maid.'   ,,   69
When beneath his roof they *c*.   *L. of Burleigh* 40
C not, when I am dead,   *Come not, when, etc.* 1
There *c's* a sound of marriage bells.   *The Letters* 48
Here is custom *c* your way ;   *Vision of Sin* 64
Therefore *c's* it we are wise.   ,,   100

Come (*continued*) day that is dead Will never *c* back
  to me.   *Break, break, etc.* 16
' Save them from this, whatever *c's* to me.'   *Enoch Arden* 118
(Sure that all evil would *c* out of it)   ,,   162
make him merry, when I *c* home again.   ,,   199
C, Annie, *c*, cheer up before I go.   ,,   200
Look to the babes, and till I *c* again   ,,   219
if he *c* again, vext will he be To find   ,,   301
when Enoch *c's* again Why then he shall repay me—   ,,   309
' *C* with us Father Philip '   ,,   368
If Enoch *c's*—but Enoch will not *c*—   ,,   431
C out and see.' But she—she put him off—   ,,   460
when the dead man *c* to life beheld His wife   ,,   758
let them *c*, I am their father ; but she must not *c*,
  For my dead face would vex her after-life.   ,,   889
' Whence *c* you ?' and the brook, why not ? replies.
  I *c* from haunts of coot and hern,   *The Brook* 22
men may *c* and men may go, (repeat)   *The Brook* 33, 49, 65, 184
Yes, men may *c* and go ; and these are gone,   *The Brook* 186
days That most she loves to talk of, *c* with me.   ,,   226
you will be welcome—O, *c* in !'   ,,   228
Cries ' *C* up hither,' as a prophet to us ?   *Aylmer's Field* 745
link'd their race with times to *c*—   ,,   779
Then *c's* the close,'   *Sea Dreams* 29
Too ripe, too late ! they *c* too late for use.   ,,   67
then *c's* what *c's* Hereafter ?   ,,   177
' His deeds yet live, the worst is yet to *c*.   ,,   314
recollect the dreams that Just ere the waking :   *Lucretius* 35
' *C* out,' he said, ' To the Abbey :   *Princess, Pro.* 177
' *C*, listen ! here is proof that you were miss'd :   ,,   177
No matter : we will say whatever *c's*.   ,,   239
Should *c* to fight with shadows and to fall.   ,,   i 10
what, if these weird seizures *c* Upon you   ,,   82
ye *c*, The first-fruits of the stranger :   ,,   ii 43
For Solomon may *c* to Sheba yet.'   ,,   349
C from the dying moon, and blow,   ,,   iii 6
Father will *c* to thee soon ; (repeat)   ,, 10, 12
Father will *c* to his babe in the nest,   ,,   13
Then *c's* the feebler heiress of your plan,   ,,   237
Nor willing men should *c* among us,   ,,   318
Would rather we had never *c* !   ,,   iv 243
there are those to avenge us and they *c* :   ,,   501
Thy face across his fancy *c's*,   ,,   579
in the night Had *c* on Psyche weeping :   ,,   v 50
c's With the air of the trumpet round him,   ,,   161
You did but *c* as goblins from the fire,   ,,   220
(our royal word upon it, He *c's* back safe)   ,,   225
As *c's* a pillar of electric cloud,   ,,   524
' *C* hither, O Psyche,' she cried out, ' embrace me,
  c, Quick while I melt ;   ,,   vi 284
C to the hollow heart they slander so !   ,,   288
C down, O maid, from yonder mountain   ,,   vii 192
And *c*, for Love is of the valley, *c*, For Love is of the
  valley, *c* thou down And find him ;   ,,   198
but *c* ; for all the vales Await thee ;   ,,   215
When *c's* another such ? never, I think,   ,,   244
Then *c's* the statelier Eden back to men :   ,,   293
trust in all things high *C's* easy to him,   ,,   330
the new day *c's*, the light Dearer for night,   ,,   346
I love thee: *c*, Yield thyself up :   ,,   363
But yonder, whiff ! there *c's* a sudden heat,   ,, *Con.* 58
To thee the greatest soldier *c's* ;   *Ode on Well.* 88
C to us, love us and make us your own :   *W. to Alexandra* 30
Jenny, my cousin, had *c* to the place,   *Grandmother* 25
she *c's* and goes at her will,   ,,   79
Often they *c* to the door in a pleasant kind of a dream.
  They *c* and sit by my chair,   ,,   82
neighbours *c* and laugh and gossip,   ,,   91
summun 'ull *c* ater meä mayhap   *N. Farmer, O. S.* 61
C, when no graver cares employ, Godfather, *c* and
  see your boy :   *To F. D. Maurice* 1
(Take it and *c*) to the Isle of Wight :   ,,   12
C, Maurice, *c* : the lawn as yet Is hoar with rime,   ,,   41
Nor pay but one, but *c* for many,   ,,   47
I *c* to the test, a tiny poem   *Hendecasyllabics* 3

Come (continued) every height c's out, and jutting peak   *Spec. of Iliad* 13
my heart is there before you are c, and gone,   *Window. On the Hill* 14
Take my love, for love will c, Love will c but
   once a life.   ,,   *No Answer* 20
Sun c's, moon c's, Time slips away.   ,,   *When* 1
Flash, I am coming, I c,   ,,   *Marr. Morn.* 13
And yet we trust it c's from thee,   *In Mem., Pro.* 23
From out waste places c's a cry,   ,,   *iii* 7
Or ' here to-morrow will he c.'   ,,   *vi* 24
A happy lover who has c   ,,   *viii* 1
saying ; ' C's he thus, my friend ?   ,,   *xii* 13
C Time, and teach me, many years,   ,,   *xiii* 13
C stepping lightly down the plank,   ,,   *xiv* 7
c The man I held as half-divine ;   ,,   *xvii* 8
C quick, thou bringest all I love.   ,,   *xviii* 9
C then, pure hands, and bear the head   ,,   11
And c, whatever loves to weep,   ,,   *xxi* 12
The praise that c's to constancy.'   ,,   *xxxix* 6
To thee too c's the golden hour   ,,   *xl* 7
And hopes and light regrets that c   ,,   *xli* 22
The wonders that have c to thee,   ,,   *lvii* 1
Peace ; c away: the song of woe   ,,   3
Peace ; c away: we do him wrong   ,,   5
let us go. C ; let us go: your cheeks are pale ;   ,,   *lix* 14
With so much hope for years to c,   ,,   *lx* 13
The foolish neighbours c and go,   ,,   *lxvii* 4
There c's a glory on the walls :   ,,   *lxxiv* 4
likeness, hardly seen before, C's out—   ,,   *lxxxi* 3
There cannot c a mellower change,   ,,   *xc* 21
Ah dear, but c thou back to me :   ,,   *xciii* 6
But he, the Spirit himself, may c   ,,   *cv* 8
The violet c's, but we are gone.   ,,   *cxiii* 17
With thousand shocks that c and go,   ,,   *cxix* 3
I c once more ; the city sleeps ;   ,,   *cxxi* 12
Behind thee c's the greater light :   ,,   *cxxxi* 9
With faith that c's of self-control,   ,,   *Con.* 100
And back we c at fall of dew.   *Maud I i* 62
can a sweeter chance ever c to me here ?   ,,   *iii* 1
Cold and clear-cut face, why c you so cruelly meek   ,,   *vi* 85
C sliding out of her sacred glove,   ,,   *xi* 5, 12
Then let c what c may, (repeat)   ,,   *xii* 28
One is c to woo her.   ,,   *xiii* 24
That old man never c's to his place :   ,,   *xviii* 10
shook my heart to think she c's once more ;   ,,   *xix* 102
her brother c's, like a blight On my fresh hope,   ,,   *xx* 44
And then, oh then, c out to me For a minute,   ,,   46
C out to your own true lover,   ,,   *xxii* 1, 3
C into the garden, Maud, (repeat)   ,,   54
C hither, the dances are done,   *II ii* 81
But c to her waking, find her asleep,   ,,   *iv* 56
Get thee hence, nor c again,   ,,   *v* 65
The day c's, a dull red ball   ,,   44
Has c to pass as foretold ;   ,,   70
c's from another stiller world of the dead,   ,,   88
he c's to the second corpse in the pit ?   ,,   102
some kind heart will c To bury me,   *III vi* 3
I c to be grateful at last for a little thing :   *Com. of Arthur* 249
Ye c from Arthur's court.   ,,   422
will not die, But pass, again to c ;   *Gareth and L.* 243
c to see The glories of our King :   ,,   246
King be King at all, or c From Fairyland,   ,,   469
Lest he should c to shame thy judging of him.'   ,,   513
the seneschal, would c Blustering upon them,   ,,   623
Now therefore have I c for Lancelot.   ,,   644
And therefore am I c for Lancelot.'   ,,   752
And look who c's behind,   ,,   957
C, therefore, leave thy lady lightly   ,,   1211
Look, Who c's behind ?'   ,,   1248
and wherefore now C ye, not call'd ?   *Marr. of Geraint* 179
I but c like you to see the hunt,   ,,   219
To find, at some place I shall c at,   ,,   337
C's flying over many a windy wave To Britain,   ,,   716
Constrain'd us, but a better time has c ;   ,,   832
By the flat meadow, till she saw them c ;   *Geraint and E.* 60
Look, Here c's a laggard hanging down his head,

Come (continued) C, we will slay him and will have
   his horse   *Geraint and E.* 62
said the second, 'yonder c's a knight.'   ,,   126
And if he want me, let him c to me.   ,,   237
You c with no attendance, page or maid,   ,,   322
c with morn, And snatch me from him as by violence ;   ,,   356
C slipping o'er their shadows on the sand,   ,,   471
And now their hour has c ;   ,,   697
I c the mouthpiece of our King to Doorm   ,,   796
' If he will not go To Arthur, then will Arthur c to you,'   ,,   815
sometime you would c To these my lists   ,,   839
now behold me c To cleanse this common sewer   ,,   894
overthrowing ever knight who c's.   *Balin and Balan* 13
My violence, and my villainy, c to shame.'   ,,   492
Art yet half-yolk, not even c to down—   ,,   569
and now The night has c.   ,,   621
' C from the storm,' and having no reply,   *Merlin and V.* 895
to have my shield In keeping till I c.'   *Lancelot and E.* 383
who will c to all I am And overcome it ;   ,,   448
' Is it Lancelot who hath c Despite the wound   ,,   565
This will he send or c for :   ,,   635
when the ghostly man had c and gone,   ,,   1101
Or c to take the King to Fairyland ?   ,,   1257
C, for you left me taking no farewell,   ,,   1274
phantom of a cup that c's and goes ?'   *Holy Grail* 44
thought That now the Holy Grail would c again ; But
   sin broke out. Ah, Christ, that it would c,   ,,   92
might it c To me by prayer and fasting ?'   ,,   95
we know not whence they c ;   ,,   147
chance of noble deeds will c and go   ,,   318
madness has c on us for our sins.'   ,,   357
And hither am I c ;   ,,   468
fail'd from my side, nor c Cover'd,   ,,   470
and in the strength of this C victor.   ,,   481
and c thou too, For thou shalt see the vision   ,,   483
and the vision had not c ;   ,,   572
C, as they will ; and many a time they c,   ,,   911
But lately c to his inheritance,   *Pelleas and E.* 18
For out of the waste islands had he c,   ,,   86
So that he could not c to speech with her.   ,,   205
if he c's again '—there she brake short ;   ,,   295
C, ye know nothing : here I pledge my troth,   ,,   341
Then, when I c within her counsels,   ,,   348
they c no more Till the sweet heavens have fill'd it   ,,   509
and say his hour is c,   *Last Tournament* 86
C—let us gladden their sad eyes,   ,,   222
Tristram, waiting for the quip to c,   ,,   260
C, thou art crabb'd and sour !   ,,   272
as the water Moab saw C round by the East,   ,,   483
C, I am hunger'd and half-anger'd—   ,,   719
And out beyond into the dream to c.'   ,,   721
Traitor c out, ye are trapt at last,'   *Guinevere* 106
then she, 'The end is c, And I am shamed   ,,   110
For if there ever c a grief to me   ,,   200
knowest thou now from whence I c—   ,,   433
think not that I c to urge thy crimes,   ,,   532
I did not c to curse thee, Guinevere,   ,,   533
But hither shall I never c again,   ,,   578
Merlin sware that I should c again To rule   *Pass. of Arthur* 191
waste land, where no one c's, Or hath c,   ,,   370
He c's again ; but—if he c no more—   ,,   451
I c, great Mistress of the ear and eye :   *Lover's Tale i* 22
O Love, O Hope ! They c,   ,,   47
Death gave back, and would no further c.   ,,   115
throning fancies c To boys and girls   ,,   554
seas upon my head To c my way !   ,,   661
should he not c my way if he would ?   ,,   667
why *should* he c my way Robed in those robes   ,,   670
C like an angel to a damned soul,   ,,   673
C like a careless and a greedy heir   ,,   675
C's in upon him in the dead of night,   ,   *ii* 154
thought His dreams had c again.   ,   *iv* 78
Send ! bid him c ;' but Lionel was away—   ,,   101
To c and revel for one hour with him   ,,   182
' you are sure it 'll all c right,'   *First Quarrel* 1

Come (*continued*) I'll *c* for an hour to-morrow, | *First Quarrel* 46
C, c, little wife, let it rest ! | ,, 62
I am sure it 'll all *c* right.' (repeat) | ,, 74, 91
'O mother, *c* out to me !' | *Rizpah* 2
what are *you*? do you *c* as a spy? | ,, 11
C! Here's to your happy union with my child ! | *Sisters* (*E. and E.*) 67
Pray *c* and see my mother. | ,, 191
'Pray *c* and see my mother, and farewell.' | ,, 196
know they *c*, They smile upon me, | ,, 278
when I saw him *c* in at the door, | *In the Child. Hosp.* 2
Had ? has it *c* ? It has only dawn'd. It will be by | and by.
' Little children should *c* to me.' | ,, 23
women and children *c* out, | ,, 50
He might be kindlier : happily *c* the day ! | *Def. of Lucknow* 100
might have *c* to learn Our Wiclif's learning : | *Sir J. Oldcastle* 23
who will *c*, God willing, to outlearn the filthy friar. | ,, 64
He that thirsteth, *c* and drink ! | ,, 117
Who *c's* ? A thousand marks are set upon my head. | ,, 134
he unchain'd for all the world to *c*.' | ,, 194
'*C* to us, O *c, c*' | *Columbus* 215
that also has *c* from Thee ; | *V. of Maeldune* 98
from within The city *c's* a murmur void of joy, | *De Prof. Human C.* 7
C from the brute, poor souls— | *Tiresias* 101
When the bat *c's* out of his cave, | *Despair* 36
' And idle gleams will *c* and go, | ,, 89
C, speak a little comfort ! | *Ancient Sage* 240
he *c's*, and finds me dead ! | *The Flight* 17
my own true sister, *c* forth ! the world is wide. | ,, 72
That matters not : let *c* what will ; | ,, 96
an' told her to *c* away from the man, | ,, 103
whin Dan didn't *c* to the fore, | *Tomorrow* 20
av the bird 'ud *c* to me call, | ,, 43
for a blessin' 'ud *c* wid the green !' | ,, 45
to-morrow—you, you *c* so late, | ,, 64
one has *c* to claim his bride, | *Locksley H., Sixty* 214
I that loathed, have *c* to love him. | ,, 263
On you will *c* the curse of all the land, | ,, 280
C's at last to the bounteous | *The Fleet* 3
far-off friendship that he *c's* no more, | *On Jub. Q. Victoria* 10
She *c's* to dress me in my bridal veil. | *Demeter and P.* 90
My ring too when she *c's* of age, | *The Ring* 98
Let her *c*! And we will feed her with our mountain air, | ,, 289
There will *c* a witness soon | ,, 318
Dreadful ! has it *c* to this, | *Forlorn* 25
C back, nor let me know it ! | ,, 43
wall of solid flesh that *c's* between your soul | *Happy* 5
May I *c* a little nearer, | ,, 35
' I *c* with your spring-flowers.' | ,, 55
C, Spring, for now from all the dripping eaves | *To Mary Boyle* 17
She *c's* ! The loosen'd rivulets run ; | *Prog. of Spring* 5
C, Spring ! She *c's* on waste and wood, | ,, 9
C, Spring ! She *c's*, and Earth is glad | ,, 22
Will my Indian brother *c*? | ,, 48
If my body *c* from brutes, (repeat) | *Romney's R.* 143
ghostly murmur floated, ' *C* to me, Œnone ! | *By an Evolution.* 5, 13
But *c*, My noble friend, | *Death of Œnone* 79
Or makes a friend where'er he *c*, | *Akbar's Dream* 17
But seldom *c's* the poet here, | *The Wanderer* 6
c's a gleam of what is higher. | *Poets and Critics* 15
| *Faith* 6
Come-agains By-gones ma' be *c-a* ; | *First Quarrel* 69
Comelier comely, yea, and *c* than myself. | *Gareth and L.* 610
taller indeed, Rosier and *c*, thou— | *Last Tournament* 710
Comeliness a broad-blown *c*, red and white, | *Maud I xiii* 9
Comely '*C*, too, by all that's fair,' | *Princess ii* 114
say she's *c* ; there's the fairer chance : | ,, *v* 460
c, yea, and comelier than myself. | *Gareth and L.* 610
Yet, since the face *is c*— | *Geraint and E.* 551
Comer (*See also* **Chance-comer, New-comer**) But | spring, a new *c*, A spring rich | *Nothing will die* 21
Comest Thou *c* morning or even ; | *Leonine Eleg.* 15
Thou *c* not with shows of flaunting vines | *Ode to Memory* 48
Thou *c* atween me and the skies, | *Oriana* 75
Thou *c*, much wept for : | *In Mem. xvii* 1
' Whence *c* thou, my guest, | *Lancelot and E.* 181

Comest (*continued*) thou *c*, darling boy ; (repeat) | *De Prof. Two G.* 10, 34
Cometh At midnight the moon *c*, | *Claribel* 13
she *c* not morning or even. | *Leonine Eleg.* 15
He *c* not,' she said ; (repeat) | *Mariana* 22, 34, 46, 58
I know He *c* quickly ; | *Fatima* 23
he that *c*, like an honour'd guest, | *Ode on Well.* 80
and there *c* a victory now. | *Boädicea* 46
Comfort (s) (*See also* **Coomfut**) The *c*, I have found in | thee : | *Miller's D.* 234
dreadful eternity, No *c* anywhere ; | *Palace of Art* 268
Comfort thyself : what *c* is in me ? | *M. d'Arthur* 243
Then follow'd counsel, *c*, | *Love and Duty* 69
Where is *c*? in division of the records of the mind ? | *Locksley Hall* 69
C? *c* scorned of devils ; | ,, 75
' I may see her now, May be some little *c* ;' | *Enoch Arden* 276
Why, that would be her *c* ;' | ,, 809
but a voice Of *c* and an open hand of help, | *Aylmer's Field* 174
they talk'd, Poor children, for their *c* : | ,, 427
what *c* ? none for me !' | *Princess v* 78
Take *c* : live, dear lady, | ,, 80
I think Our chiefest *c* is the little child | ,, 430
Sole of my dark hour, | ,, *vi* 194
That out of words a *c* win ; | *In Mem. xx* 10
Of *c* clasp'd in truth reveal'd ; | ,, *xxxvii* 22
And find his *c* in thy face ; | ,, *cix* 20
take again That *c* from their converse | *Geraint and E.* 950
saying in low tones, ' Have *c*,' | *Lancelot and E.* 995
If here be *c*, and if ours be sin, | *Last Tournament* 575
Comfort thyself : what *c* is in me ? | *Pass. of Arthur* 411
Come, speak a little *c*! | *The Flight* 17
And yet no *c* came to me, | ,, 18
' Take *c* you have won the Painter's fame,' | *Romney's R.* 43
groans to see it, finds no *c* there. | ,, 45
Comfort (verb) (*See also* **Coomfut**) They *c* him by | night and day ; | *Supp. Confessions* 45
But, Effie, you must *c* her | *May Queen, Con.* 44
' It *c's* me in this one thought to dwell, | *D. of F. Women* 233
C thyself : what comfort is in me ? | *M. d'Arthur* 243
Take, give her this, for it may *c* her : | *Enoch Arden* 899
said the kindly wife to *c* him, | *Sea Dreams* 140
Reach out dead hands to *c* me. | *In Mem. lxxx* 16
C her, *c* her, all things good, | *Maud II ii* 75
And *c* her tho' I die. | ,, 83
The love of all Thy people *c* Thee, | *Ded. of Idylls* 54
' *C* thyself,' said Arthur, ' I nor mine Rest : | *Gareth and L.* 601
Because I saw you sad, to *c* you. | *Merlin and V.* 441
C your sorrows ; for they do not flow | *Guinevere* 188
C thyself : what comfort is in me ? | *Pass. of Arthur* 411
C yourself, for the heart of the father | *The Wreck* 98
Comfortable Nor wholly *c*, I sit, | *Will Water.* 158
Comforted ' Annie, my girl, cheer up, be *c*, | *Enoch Arden* 218
look up : be *c* : Sweet is it to have done the thing | *Princess v* 66
' Be *c* : have I not lost her too, | ,, 69
' Be *c*,' Said Cyril, ' you shall have it :' | ,, 105
and *c* my heart, And dried my tears, | *Com. of Arthur* 349
let me go : be *c* : | *Pelleas and E.* 355
He answer'd, ' O my soul, be *c* ! | *Last Tournament* 573
after these had *c* the blood With meats | ,, 724
Queen Smiles on me, saying, ' Be thou *c* ! | *Columbus* 188
Let the weary be *c*, | *On Jub. Q. Victoria* 34
Yet be *c* ; For if this earth be ruled | *D. of the Duke of C.* 7
Comforting An image *c* the mind, | *In Mem. lxxxv* 51
Comic Too *c* for the solemn things they are, | *Princess, Con.* 67
Comin' remimbers wan night *c* down be the | sthrame, | *Tomorrow* 7
Coming (*See also* **Comin', Coomin'**) *C* in the scented | breeze, | *Eleänore* 24
heart Went forth to embrace him *c* ere he came. | *Œnone* 63
C thro' Heaven, like a light that grows | *May Queen, N. Y's. E.* 7
the New-year's *c* up, mother, | ,, 108
A noise of some one *c* thro' the lawn, | *D. of F. Women* 178
Each month, a birth-day *c* on, | *Will Water.* 93
Philip *c* somewhat closer spoke. | *Enoch Arden* 398
' Ay, ay, I mind him *c* down the street ; | ,, 847
His wreck, his lonely life, his *c* back. | ,, 862

Coming (*continued*) If James were *c*. '*C* every day.' — *The Brook* 106
Leolin, *c* after he was gone, — *Aylmer's Field* 234
and *c* fitfully Like broken music, — " 476
A crippled lad, and *c* turn'd to fly, — " 519
like swallows *c* out of time Will wonder — *Princess ii* 431
Or at thy *c*, Princess, everywhere, — *W. to Marie Alex.* 42
she to be *c* and slandering me, — *Grandmother* 27
Flash, I am *c*, I come, — *Window. Marr. Morn.* 13
they are *c* back from abroad ; — *Maud I i* 65
I see my Oread *c* down, — " *xvi* 8
Her brother is *c* back to-night — " *xix* 1
She is *c*, my dove, my dear ; She is *c*, my life, my fate ; — " *xxii* 61
She is *c*, my own, my sweet ; — " 67
But *c* back he learns it, — *Geraint and E.* 498
And *c* up close to her, said at last : — " 670
c up quite close, and in his mood — " 714
So *c* to the fountain-side beheld — *Balin and Balan* 23
A STORM was *c*, but the winds were still, — *Merlin and V.* 1
C and going, and he lay as dead — " 213
Such trumpet-blowings in it, *c* down — " 418
C and going, and she lay as dead, — " 644
C upon me—O never harp nor horn, — *Holy Grail* 113
and *c* out of gloom Was dazzled by the sudden light, — *Pelleas and E.* 104
but a sound Of Gawain ever *c*, and this lay— — " 396
feet Thro' the long gallery from the outer doors Rang *c*, — *Guinevere* 414
To guard thee in the wild hour *c* on, — " 446
for wasn't he *c* that day ? — *First Quarrel* 47
it is *c*—shaking the walls— — *Rizpah* 85
c nearer and nearer again than before— — *Def. of Lucknow* 28
c down on the still-shatter'd walls — " 92
hands, when I heard him *c* would drop — *The Wreck* 27
'I am *c* to thee in thine Ocean-grave.' — " 132
'O child, I am *c* to thee.' — " 134
light of a Sun that was *c* would scatter — *Despair* 23
But a sun *c* up in his youth ! — *Dead Prophet* 42
Silver crescent-curve, *C* soon, — *The Ring* 14
c home—And on your Mother's birthday— — " 247
c nearer—Muriel had the ring— — " 259
she sees Her maiden *c* like a Queen, — " 480
he was *c* down the fell— — *Happy* 82
C in the cold time, — *The Snowdrop* 5
'SUMMER is *c*, summer is *c*. — *The Throstle* 1
Summer is *c*, is *c*, my dear, — " 15
in *c* near, Across the downward thunder — *Death of Œnone* 22
Flush'd like the *c* of the day ; — *Miller's D.* 132
Narrow'd her goings out and *c's* in ; — *Aylmer's Field* 501
Half-blinded at the *c* of a light. — *Com. of Arthur* 266
himself Had told her, and their *c* to the court. (repeat) — *Marr. of Geraint* 144, 846
She look'd on ere the *c* of Geraint. — " 614
'I will abide the *c* of my lord, — *Geraint and E.* 131
And she abode his *c*, and said to him — " 139
Would listen for her *c* and regret Her parting step, — *Lancelot and E.* 866
ere the *c* of the Queen.' (repeat) — *Guinevere* 223, 233
Before the *c* of the sinful Queen.' — " 270
(My friend is long in *c*.) — *Sir J. Oldcastle* 148
you have dared Somewhat perhaps in *c* ? — *Columbus* 242
kiss so sad, no, not since the *c* of man ! — *Despair* 60

Command (s) He, that ever following her *c's*, — *Ode on Well.* 211
under whose *c* Is Earth and Earth's, — *In Mem., Con.* 130
Thy life is thine at her *c*. — *Gareth and L.* 983
gave *c* that all which once was ours — *Marr. of Geraint* 696
one *c* I laid upon you, not to speak to me, — *Geraint and E.* 77
Debating his *c* of silence given, — " 366
Then breaking his *c* of silence given, — " 390
Wroth that the King's *c* to sally forth — *Lancelot and E.* 560
That only seems half-loyal to *c*,— — *Last Tournament* 118
lifted up a voice Of shrill *c*, — *Death of Œnone* 99

Command (*verb*) 'Will he obey when one *c's* ? — *Two Voices* 244
Man to *c* and woman to obey ; — *Princess v* 450
I cannot all *c* the strings ; — *In Mem. lxxxviii* 10
strength of the race to *c*, to obey, — *Def. of Lucknow* 47

Commander Attest their great *c's* claim With honour ; — *Ode on Well.* 148
Commeasure *C* perfect freedom.' — *Œnone* 167
Commenced However then *c* the dawn : — *Princess ii* 138
c A to-and-fro, so pacing till she paused — " 301
Comment thoughts in rubric thus For wholesale *c*,' — " *iii* 51
and heard in thought Their lavish *c* — *Merlin and V.* 151
crost, and cramm'd With *c*, — " 678
And none can read the *c* but myself ; And in the *c* did I find the charm. — " 682
like the critic's blurring *c* make — *Sisters (E. and E.)* 104
Six foot deep of burial mould Will dull their *c's* ! — *Romney's R.* 126
Commerce Saw the heavens fill with *c*, — *Locksley Hall* 121
brought the stinted *c* of those days ; — *Enoch Arden* 817
two crowned twins, *C* and conquest, — *Princess v* 421
From growing *c* loose her latest chain, — *Ode Inter. Exhib.* 33
So hold I *c* with the dead, — *In Mem. lxxxv* 93
No more shall *c* be all in all, — *Maud III vi* 23
that *c* with the Queen, I ask you, — *Merlin and V.* 770
Fifty years of ever-broadening *C* ! — *On Jub. Q. Victoria* 52
Commercing *c* with himself, He lost the sense — *Walk. to the Mail* 21
Commingled *C* with the gloom of imminent war, — *Ded. of Idylls* 13
Commission A bought *c*, a waxen face, — *Maud I x* 30
c one of weight and worth To judge between — *Columbus* 124
Commissioner See **Church-commissioner**
Common (*adj.*) and fears were *c* to her state, — *Enoch Arden* 521
'Loss is *c* to the race'—And *c* is the commonplace, — *In Mem. vi* 2
That loss is *c* would not make My own less bitter, — " 5
Too *c* ! Never morning wore To evening, — " 7
Their *c* shout in chorus, mounting, — *Balin and Balan* 87
but love's first flash in youth, Most *c* : — *Lancelot and E.* 950
Common (s) crost the *c* into Darnley chase — *The Brook* 132
Commonplace barren *c's* break In full and kindly blossom. — *Will Water.* 23
And common is the *c*, And vacant chaff — *In Mem. vi* 3
To lift us as it were from *c*, — *Sisters (E. and E.)* 223
shrunk by usage into commonest *c* ! — *Locksley H., Sixty* 76
Common-sense Rich in saving *c-s*, — *Ode on Well.* 32
crown'd Republic's crowning *c-s*, — *To the Queen ii* 61
Priests Who fear the king's hard *c-s* — *Sir J. Oldcastle* 66
Commonwealth from it sprang the *C*, which breaks — *Lucretius* 241
Commune (s) For days of happy *c* dead ; — *In Mem. cxvi* 14
Held *c* with herself, — *Geraint and E.* 368
Commune (*verb*) To *c* with that barren voice, — *Two Voices* 461
Communed I *c* with a saintly man, — *Holy Grail* 742
But *c* only with the little maid, — *Guinevere* 150
And while I *c* with my truest self, — *The Ring* 181
Communicate We two *c* no more.' — *In Mem. lxxxv* 84
Communing *C* with herself : 'All these are mine, — *Palace of Art* 181
C with his captains of the war. — *Princess i* 67
Communion An hour's *c* with the dead. — *In Mem. xciv* 4
was a very miracle Of fellow-feeling and *c*. — *Lover's Tale i* 251
Como Remember how we came at last To *C* ; — *The Daisy* 70
past From *C*, when the light was gray, — " 73
Compact (*adj.*) churl, *c* of thankless earth, — *Godiva* 66
issued in a court *C* of lucid marbles, — *Princess ii* 24
Compact (s) He said there was a *c* ; — " *i* 47
there did a *c* pass Long summers back, — " 123
Our formal *c*, yet, not less — " 165
and a hope The child of regal *c*, — " *iv* 421
'that our *c* be fulfill'd — " *v* 115
she would not keep Her *c*.' — " 324
Companion on her bridal morn before she past From all her old *c's*, — " *ii* 263
Too harsh to your *c* yestermorn ; — " *iii* 199
When wine and free *c's* kindled him, — *Geraint and E.* 293
Fled all the boon *c's* of the Earl, — " 477
Meanwhile the new *c's* past away — *Lancelot and E.* 399
My boon *c*, tavern-fellow— — *Sir J. Oldcastle* 90
Kindly landlord, boon *c*— — *Locksley H., Sixty* 240
Down to the haven, Call your *c's*, — *Merlin and the G.* 125
Companionless I, the last, go forth *c*, — *M. d'Arthur* 236
I, the last, go forth *c*, — *Pass. of Arthur* 404
Companionship Who broke our fair *c*, — *In Mem. xxii* 13

Company   Where sat a *c* with heated eyes,   *Vision of Sin* 7
   The little wife would weep for *c*,   *Enoch Arden* 34
   yes !—but a *c* forges the wine.   *Maud I i* 36
   her brother lingers late With a roystering *c*)
   twos and threes, or fuller *companies*,   ,, *xiv* 15
   ' Where is that goodly *c*,' said I,   *Marr. of Geraint* 57
   Spread the slow smile thro' all her *c*.   *Holy Grail* 432
   ' Belike for lack of wiser *c* ;   *Pelleas and E.* 95
   A glorious *c*, the flower of men,   *Last Tournament* 245
   in *companies* Troubled the track of the host   *Guinevere* 464
Comparison   And half asleep she made *c*   *Batt. of Brunanburh* 39
Compass (s)   And in the *c* of three little words,   *Marr. of Geraint* 651
   winds from all the *c* shift and blow,   *Gardener's D.* 232
   Might lie within their *c*,   *Godiva* 33
   And his *c* is but of a single note,   *Aylmer's Field* 485
   sorrow of my spirit Was of so wide a *c*   *The Islet* 28
   The *c*, like an old friend false   *Lover's Tale ii* 135
Compass (verb)   To *c* our dear sisters' liberties.'   *Columbus* 70
   To *c* her with sweet observances,   *Princess iii* 288
   you should only *c* her disgrace,   *Geraint and E.* 39
   made him leper to *c* him with scorn—   *The Fleet* 17
Compass'd   *And c by the inviolate sea.'*   *Happy* 16
   With what dull pain C,   *To the Queen* 36
   Then *c* round by the blind wall of night   *D. of F. Women* 278
   All beauty *c* in a female form,   *Enoch Arden* 492
   Sat *c* with professors;   *Princess ii* 34
   Tho' *c* by two armies and the noise   ,, 444
   That, *c* round with turbulent sound,   ,, *v* 345
   And *c* by the fires of Hell ;   *Will* 7
   So, *c* by the power of the King,   *In Mem. cxxvii* 17
   He *c* her with sweet observances   *Com. of Arthur* 203
Compassion   ' Full of *c* and mercy—(repeat)   *Marr. of Geraint* 48
Compel   I *c* all creatures to my will.' (repeat)   *Rizpah* 62, 63
Compell'd   such a breeze C thy canvas.   *Geraint and E.* 629, 673
Compensated   For often fineness *c* size :   *In Mem. xvii* 2
Compensating   nor *c* the want By shrewdness,   *Princess ii* 149
Competence   Seven happy years of health and *c*,   *Enoch Arden* 250
   gracious children, debtless *c*, golden mean ;   ,, 82
Complaining   broad stream in his banks *c*,   *Vastness* 24
   C, 'Mother, give me grace To help me   *L. of Shalott iv* 3
   call'd him by his name, *c* loud,   *Mariana in the S.* 29
   call'd him by his name, *c* loud,   *M. d'Arthur* 210
Complaint   Not whisper, any murmur of *c*.   *Pass. of Arthur* 378
   What end is here to my *c*?   *St. S. Stylites* 22
Completer   gipsy bonnet Be the neater and *c* ;   *In Mem. lxxxi* 6
Completion   awaits C in a painful school ;   *Maud I xx* 20
   fulfill'd itself, Merged in *c*?   *Love thou thy land* 58
Complexity   many-corridor'd *complexities* Of Arthur's   *Gardener's D.* 239
   palace :   *Merlin and V.* 732
Complicated   *See* **Tenfold-complicated**
Compliment   Light coin, the tinsel clink of *c*.   *Princess ii* 55
Composed   All *c* in a metre of Catullus,   *Hendecasyllabics* 4
Compound   ' No *c* of this earthly ball   *Two Voices* 35
Comprehensive   *See* **All-comprehensive**
Comprest   rais'd her head with lips *c*,   *The Letters* 19
Comrade   C's, leave me here a little,   *Locksley Hall* 1
   Hark, my merry *c's* call me,   ,, 145
   And Enoch's *c*, careless of himself,   *Enoch Arden* 568
   His *c's* having fought their last below,   *Aylmer's Field* 227
   till the *c* of his chambers woke,   ,, 583
   Which weep the *c* of my choice,   *In Mem. xiii* 9
   Is *c* of the lesser faith   ,, cxxviii 3
   labour him Beyond his *c* of the hearth,   *Gareth and L.* 485
   and then against his brace Of *c's*,   *Geraint and E.* 88
   His craven pair Of *c's* making slowlier   ,, 167
   To laughter and his *c's* to applause.   ,, 296
   —thy shame, and mine, Thy *c*—   *Sir J. Oldcastle* 102
   And some are wilder *c's*, sworn to seek   *Pref. Son. 19th Cent.* 12
   Gone the *c's* of my bivouac,   *Locksley H., Sixty* 45
   parted from his *c* in the boat,   *The Ring* 308
Conceal   she knows too, And she *c's* it.'   *Princess iii* 60
   And half *c* the Soul within.   *In Mem. v* 4
   Marriage will *c* it . . .   *Forlorn* 10
Conceal'd   it seem'd Better to leave Excalibur *c*   *M. d'Arthur* 62
   it seem'd Better to leave Excalibur *c*   *Pass. of Arthur* 230

Concealment   maiden-meek I pray'd C: *Princess iii* 135
Conceit (s)   (*See also* **Self-conceit**) So spake he, clouded
   with his own *c*,   *M. d'Arthur* 110
   So spake he, clouded with his own *c*,   *Pass. of Arthur* 278
Conceit (verb)   C's himself as God that he can   *Last Tournament* 355
   make
Conceive   and in his agony *c's* A shameful sense   *Lover's Tale i* 793
Conceived   sinful man, *c* and born in sin :   *St. S. Stylites* 122
Concentrate   if I fail To conjure and *c*   *Romney's R.* 7
Concession   and the bounds Determining *c* ;   *To Duke of Argyll* 3
Conciliate   so potent to coerce, And to *c*,   *Tiresias* 121
Concluded   At last a solemn grace C,   *Princess ii* 453
   dreamt Of some vast charm *c* in that star   *Merlin and V.* 512
Conclusion   To those *c's* when we saw   *In Mem. lxxxvii* 35
   a semi-smile As at a strong *c*—   *Lover's Tale iv* 282
Concourse   banquet, and *c* of knights and kings.   *Lancelot and E.* 562
Concubine   Sent like the twelve-divided *c*   *Aylmer's Field* 759
   wives and children Spanish *c's*,   *Columbus* 175
Condemn'd   prisoner at the bar, ever *c* :   *Sea Dreams* 176
Condensation   cramm'd With comment, densest *c*,   *Merlin and V.* 678
Condition   with sound of trumpet, all The hard *c* ;   *Godiva* 37
   Hear my *c's* : promise (otherwise You perish)   *Princess ii* 295
   And these were the *c's* of the King :   *Gareth and L.* 107
Conditioning   ebb and flow *c* their march,   *Golden Year* 30
Condole   *See* **Condowl**
Condoned   treacheries—wink'd at, and *c*—   *Columbus* 226
Condowl (**condole**)   frinds 'ud consowl an' *c* wid her,   *Tomorrow* 47
Conduct (verb)   C by paths of growing powers,   *In Mem. lxxiv* 31
Conduit   Where the bloody *c* runs,   *Vision of Sin* 144
Cone   (*See also* **Cypress-cone**, **Mountain-cones**) In
   masses thick with milky *c's*.   *Miller's D.* 56
Confederacy   between her daughters o'er a wild *c*.   *Boädicea* 6
Conference   And thus our *c* closed.   *Princess ii* 367
Confess   I *c* with right) you think me bound   ,, *i* 158
   As I *c* it needs must be ;   *In Mem. lix* 4
   Why wilt thou shame me to *c* to thee   *Holy Grail* 567
   I will find the Priest and *c*.   *Bandit's Death* 18
Confessed   thunders often have *c* Thy power,   *To W. C. Macready* 2
Confidence   In *c* of unabated strength,   *Lover's Tale i* 511
Confined   C on points of faith,   ,, *ii* 150
Conflict   *c* with the crash of shivering points,   *Princess v* 491
   Folk and his friends that had Fallen in *c*.   *Batt. of Brunanburh* 71
Confluence   A riotous *c* of watercourses   *Lucretius* 30
Confound   did all *c* Her sense ;   *Mariana* 76
   Nor all Calamity's hugest waves *c*,   *Will* 5
   On whom the victor, to *c* them more,   *Geraint and E.* 169
   God the traitor's hope *c*! (repeat)   *Hands all Round* 10, 22, 34
Confounded (*See also* **Worse-confounded**) Shame and
   wrath his heart *c*,   *The Captain* 61
   Saw them lie *c*,   *The Tourney* 14
Confuse   Nor thou with shadow'd hint *c* A life   *In Mem. xxxiii* 7
   pass on ! the sight *c's*—   *Parnassus* 15
Confused   Makes thy memory *c* :   *A Dirge* 45
   Remaining utterly *c* with fears,   *Palace of Art* 269
   wicked broth C the chemic labour of the blood,   *Lucretius* 20
   Arriving all *c* among the rest   *Princess iv* 224
   C by brainless mobs and lawless Powers ;   *Ode on Well.* 153
   C me like the unhappy bark   *In Mem. xvi* 12
   Thro' all that crowd *c* and loud,   *Maud II iv* 71
   ' C, and illusion, and relation,   *Gareth and L.* 287
   Enid look'd, but all *c* at first,   *Marr. of Geraint* 685
   Those twelve sweet moons *c* his fatherhood.'   *Merlin and V.* 712
Confusion   The airy hand *c* wrought,   *Palace of Art* 226
   Is there *c* in the little isle ?   *Lotos-Eaters, C.S.* 79
   There *is c* worse than death,   ,, 83
   Unsubject to *c*, Tho' soak'd and saturate   *Will Water.* 86
   Man to command and woman to obey ; All else *c*.   *Princess v* 451
   At first with all *c* : by and by Sweet order lived   ,, *vii* 18
   C's of a wasted youth ;   *In Mem., Pro.* 42
   yet-loved sire would make C worse than death,   ,, *xc* 19
   Once for wrong done you by *c*,   *Merlin and V.* 307
   Thieves, bandits, leavings of *c*,   *Last Tournament* 95
   From flat *c* and brute violences,   ,, 124
   disloyal life Hath wrought *c* in the Table Round   *Guinevere* 220
   and ev'n on Arthur fell C,   *Pass. of Arthur* 99

Confusion (*continued*) for on my heart hath fall'n C, — *Pass. of Arthur* 144
centre and crater of European c, — *Beautiful City* 1
Confuted come a witness soon Hard to be c, — *Forlorn* 26
Conjecture (s) make C of the plumage and the form ; — *Marr. of Geraint* 333
Conjecture (verb) C's of the features of her child — *Œnone* 252
count me all to blame if I C of a stiller guest, — *In Mem., Con.* 86
Conjecturing C when and where : this cut is fresh ; — *Lancelot and E.* 21
Conjure if I fail To c and concentrate — *Romney's R.* 7
Conquer From barren deeps to call — *Princess vii* 164
Is rack'd with pangs that c trust ; — *In Mem. l* 6
you are Lancelot ; your great name, This c's : — *Lancelot and E.* 151
Arise, go forth and c as of old,' — *Pass. of Arthur* 64
lake and mountain c's all the day. — *Sisters (E. and E.)* 100
Love will c at the last. — *Locksley H., Sixty* 280
That only c's men to c peace, — *Akbar's Dream* 15
Conquer'd (*See also* **Woman-conquer'd**) A cry above the c years — *In Mem. cxxxi* 7
At last she let herself be c by him, — *Merlin and V.* 900
knowing he was Lancelot ; his great name C : — *Lancelot and E.* 580
Conqueror (*See also* **Woman-conqueror**) Christian c's took and flung — *Locksley H., Sixty* 84
Conquest two crowned twins, Commerce and c, — *Princess v* 421
brag to his fellow rakes of his c — *Charity* 18
Conscience A little grain of c made him sour.' — *Vision of Sin* 218
' With all his c and one eye askew'—(repeat) — *Sea Dreams* 180, 184
My c will not count me fleckless ; — *Princess ii* 294
' Who reverenced his c as his king ; — *Ded. of Idylls* 8
To whom a c never wakes ; — *In Mem. xxvii* 8
Without a c or an aim. — *,, xxxiv* 8
The c as a c at rest : — *,, xciv* 12
Their c, and their c as their King, — *Guinevere* 469
as is the c of a saint Among his warring senses, — *,, 639*
Conscious (*See also* **Half-conscious**) nor c of a bar Between them, — *Aylmer's Field* 134
Slowly and c of the rageful eye That watch'd him, — *,, 336*
c of ourselves, Perused the matting ; — *Princess ii* 67
And partly c of my own deserts, — *,, iv* 305
We, c of what temper you are built, — *,, 400*
am I c, more Than other Masters, — *Romney's R.* 62
Consecrate I dedicate, I confer with tears— — *Ded. of Idylls* 4
be c to lead A new crusade against the Saracen. — *Columbus* 102
Consent (*See also* **Half-consent**) To yield c to my desire : — *Miller's D.* 138
his long wooing her, Her slow c, and marriage, — *Enoch Arden* 708
Was handed over by c of all To one who had not spoken, — *Lover's Tale iv* 271
Consequence Were wisdom in the scorn of c.' — *Œnone* 150
And duty duty, clear of c's. — *Princess iii* 152
can he tell Whether war be a cause or a c ? — *Maud I x* 45
Conservative That man's the true C — *Hands all Round* 7
Consider 'C well,' the voice replied, — *Two Voices* 241
C, William : take a month to think, — *Dora* 29
c them, and all Their bearing in their common bond — *Balin and Balan* 149
Consider'd Again she c and said : — *In the Child. Hosp.* 55
Considering c everywhere Her secret meaning — *In Mem. lv* 9
Consistent liberal-minded, great, C ; — *,, Con.* 39
Consol chances of childhood, c, and share— — *The Wreck* 30
Consolable A long, long weeping, not c. — *Merlin and V.* 856
Console *See* **Consowl**
Consolidate became C in mind and frame— — *Two Voices* 366
Consort And a gentle c made he, — *L. of Burleigh* 73
Consowl (console) 'ud c an' condowl wid her, — *Tomorrow* 47
Constancy The praise that comes to c.' — *In Mem. xxi* 12
may yours for ever be That old strength and c — *Open. I. and C. Exhib.* 14
Constantinus Also the crafty one, C, — *Batt. of Brunanburh* 63
Constellation Larger c's burning, mellow moons and happy skies, — *Locksley Hall* 159
With c and with continent, — *Princess i* 224
Sphere-music of stars and of c's. — *Parnassus* 8
Constrain'd thro' that young traitor, cruel need C us, — *Marr. of Geraint* 716

Constraining C it with kisses close and warm, — *Lover's Tale i* 468
Consume Me only cruel immortality C's : — *Tithonus* 6
Consumed utterly c with sharp distress, — *Lotos-Eaters, C. S.* 13
Contained *See* **Self-contained**
Contemplate When I c all alone — *In Mem. lxxxiv* 1
C all this work of Time, — *,, cxviii* 1
c The torment of the damn'd' — *Akbar's Dream* 48
Contemplating no form of creed, But c all.' — *Palace of Art* 212
but lay C her own unworthiness ; — *Marr. of Geraint* 533
Contemplation And luxury of c : — *Eleänore* 107
Contempt (*See also* **Self-contempt**) touch'd on Mahomet With much c, — *Princess ii* 135
Contend C for loving masterdom. — *In Mem. cii* 8
Content (adj.) (*See also* **Ill-content**, **Well-content**) I had been c to perish, — *Locksley Hall* 103
might it come like one that looks c, — *Love and Duty* 93
' I am c' he answer'd 'to be loved — *Enoch Arden* 428
Which left my after-morn c. — *In Mem. ciii* 4
He rested well c that all was well. — *Geraint and E.* 952
Nor rested thus c, but day by day, — *Lancelot and E.* 13
' Queen, she would not be c Save that I wedded her, — *Holy Grail* 614
Must be c to sit by little fires. — *,, 653*
he well had been c Not to have seen, — *Pelleas and E.* 243
C am I so that I see thy face But once a day : — *The Revenge* 51
that had left her ill c ; — *Sisters (E. and E.)* 126
was I c ? Ay—no, not quite ; — *,, 132*
Not findable here—c, and not c, — *Locksley H., Sixty* 25
born of worldlings—father, mother—be c — *Happy* 27
I shall hardly be c Till I be leper — *To Mary Boyle* 63
He rests c, if his young music wakes — *,,*
Content (s) (*See also* **Self-content**) breast That once had power to rob it of c. — *The form, the form* 8
With meditative grunts of much c, — *Walk. to the Mail* 87
found the sun of sweet c Re-risen — *The Brook* 168
and break The low beginnings of c. — *In Mem. lxxxiv* 48
nor more c, He told me, lives in any crowd, — *,, xcviii* 12
Contented (*See also* **Well-contented**) leapt into my arms, C there to die ! — *D. of F. Women* 152
Continent With constellation and with c, — *Princess i* 224
Maoris and that Isle of C, — *W. to Marie Alex.* 18
From isle and cape and c, — *Open. I and C. Exhib.* 4
and sow The dust of c's to be ; — *In Mem. xxxv* 8
Continue you saw, As who should say 'C.' — *Lover's Tale iv* 53
Contradiction seem'd to live A c on the tongue, — *In Mem. cxxv* 4
Contract Cleave to your c : — *Princess iv* 409
Contracting Philip's rosy face c grew — *Enoch Arden* 486
Contrast love will go by c, as by likes. — *Sisters (E. and E.)* 64
Contrivance With great c's of Power. — *Love thou thy land* 64
Contrived where the two c their daughter's good— — *Aylmer's Field* 848
Contriving c their dear daughter's good— — *,, 781*
Control (s) (*See also* **Half-control**, **Self-control**) keep it ours, O God, from brute c ; — *Ode on Well.* 159
O friendship, equal-poised c, — *In Mem. lxxxv* 33
Control (verb) changes should c Our being, — *Love thou thy land* 41
Controll'd For they c me when a boy ; — *In Mem. xxviii* 18
Controlleth C all the soul and sense Of Passion — *Eleänore* 115
Convent (*See also* **Hill-convent**) while I lived In the white c down the valley — *St. S. Stylites* 62
Convention but c beats them down : — *Princess, Pro.* 128
Dwell with these, and lose C, — *,, ii* 511
to-morrow morn We hold a great c : — *,, iv* 511
Convent-roof DEEP on the c-r the snows — *St. Agnes' Eve* 5
Convent-tower shadows of the c-t's Slant down — *,,*
Converse (s) (*See also* **Honey-converse**) We may hold c with all forms — *Ode to Memory* 115
War, who breaks the c of the wise ; — *Third of Feb.* 8
But open c is there none, — *In Mem. xx* 17
Thy c drew us with delight, — *,, cx* 1
rode In c till she made her palfrey halt, — *Gareth and L.* 1360
he suspends his c with a friend, — *Marr. of Geraint* 340
told her all their c in the hall, — *,, 520*
Edyrn, whom he held In c for a little, — *Geraint and E.* 882
That comfort from their c which he took — *,, 950*
c sweet and low—low c sweet, — *Lover's Tale i* 541
Am not thyself in c with thyself, — *Ancient Sage* 171

Converse (verb) Hears him lovingly *c*, — *L. of Burleigh* 26
Convert That was a miracle to *c* the king. — *Sir J. Oldcastle* 178
Convey'd *c* them on their way And left them — *Gareth and L.* 889
Convict The noble and the *c* of Castile. — *Columbus* 117
Convolution saturate, out and out, Thro' every *c*. — *Will Water.* 88
Convolvulus The lustre of the long *c'es* — *Enoch Arden* 576
   with a myriad blossom the long *c* hung ; — *V. of Maeldune* 40
Cony Or *conies* from the down, — *Enoch Arden* 340
Coo Deeply the wood-dove *c's* ; — *Leonine Eleg.* 6
Coodled (cuddled) An' coäx'd an' *c* me oop — *North. Cobbler* 80
Coo'd it *c* to the Mother and smiled. — *The Wreck* 60
Cook'd *c* his spleen, Communing with his captains — *Princess i* 66
Cool (adj.) while she wept, and I strove to be *c*, — *Maud II i* 15
   fair days—not all as *c* as these, — *Balin and Balan* 273
   Is all as *c* and white as any flower.' — *Last Tournament* 416
Cool (s) as we enter'd in the *c*. — *Gardener's D.* 114
Cool (verb) 'Drink to lofty hopes that *c*— — *Vision of Sin* 147
   saw it and grieved—to slacken and to *c* ; — *Princess iv* 299
Cool'd placed upon the sick man's brow *C* it, — *Aylmer's Field* 701
   Or *c* within the glooming wave ; — *In Mem. lxxxix* 45
   ere his cause Be *c* by fighting, — *Gareth and L.* 703
Cooling *C* her false cheek with a featherfan, — *Aylmer's Field* 289
Coolness paced for *c* in the chapel-yard ; — *Merlin and V.* 757
   blew *C* and moisture and all smells of bud — *Lover's Tale iii* 5
Coom (come) But Parson a *c's* an' a goäs, — *N. Farmer, O. S.* 25
   an' thy muther *c* to 'and, — ,, *N. S.* 21
   C's of a gentleman burn: — ,, 38
   Wrigglesby beck *c's* out by the 'ill ! — ,, 53
   C oop, proputty, proputty— — ,, 59
   Waäit till our Sally *c's* in, — *North. Cobbler* 1
   one night I *c's* 'oäm like a bull — ,, 33
   'My lass, when I *c's* to die, — ,, 103
   C thou 'eer—yon laädy a-steppin' — ,, 107
   but 'e dosn' not *c* fro' the shere ; — *Village Wife* 23
   sa I knaw'd es 'e'd *c* to be poor ; — ,, 46
   C ! *c* ! feyther,' 'e says, — ,, 69
   fur they weänt niver *c* to naw good. — ,, 96
   When Molly *c's* in fro' the far-end close — *Spinster's S's.* 2
   Rob, *c* oop 'ere o' my knee. — ,, 11
   C give hoäver then, weant ye ? — ,, 63
   let Steevie *c* oop o' my knee. — ,, 67
   Dick, when 'e *c's* to be deäd, — *Owd Roä* 11
   'ud *c* at the fall o' the year, — ,, 23
   I'll *c* an' I'll squench the light, — ,, 117
   an' 'e beal'd to ya ' Lad *c* hout' — *Church-warden, etc.* 28
Coom'd (came) An' I hallus *c* to 's chooch — *N. Farmer, O. S.* 17
   said what a owt to 'a said an' I *c* awaäy. — ,, 20
   afoor I *c* to the plaäce. — ,, 34
   sin fust a *c* to the 'All ; — ,, 55
   afoor 'e *c* to the shere. — ,, *N.S.* 28
   'e *c* to the parish wi' lots o' Varsity debt, — ,, 29
   An' I *c* neck-an-crop soomtimes, — *North. Cobbler* 20
   An' when we *c* to Meeätin', — ,, 53
   fur New Squire *c* last night. — *Village Wife* 1
   new Squire's *c* wi' 'is taäil in 'is 'and, (repeat) — ,, 14, 121
   Thou's *c* oop by the beck ; — ,, 79
   fur he *c* last night so laäte— — ,, 123
   But 'e c thruf the fire wi' my bairn — *Owd Roä* 92
   He *c* like a Hangel o' marcy — ,, 93
   An' 'is 'air *c* off i' my 'ands — ,, 100
   fur a lot on 'em *c* ta-year— — *Church-warden, etc.* 13
   They says 'at he *c* fra nowt— — ,, 17
   an' *c* to the top o' the tree, — ,, 38
Coomfut (s) (comfort) But she wur a power o' *c*, — *North. Cobbler* 79
   Fur she hedn't naw *c* in 'er, — *Village Wife* 12
Coomfut (verb) When I goäs fur to *c* the poor — *Spinster's S's.* 108
Coomin' (coming) upo' *c* awaäy Sally gied me a kiss — *North. Cobbler* 56
   Fur I seed that Steevie wur *c*,' — *Spinster's S's.* 40
   but, O Lord, upo' *c* down— — ,, 44
   'cep' it wur at a dog *c* in, — ,, 60
   By a man *c* in wi' a hiccup — ,, 98
   Fur I seed the beck *c* down — *Owd Roä* 40
   an' the times 'at was *c* on ; — ,, 44
Coontryside (Countryside) booöts to be cobbled
   fro' hafe the *c*. — *North. Cobbler* 94

E

Cooper *C* he was and carpenter, — *Enoch Arden* 814
Cöoperant Is toil *c* to an end. — *In Mem. cxxviii* 24
Coortin (courting) gied tha a raätin that sattled thy
   c o' me, — *Spinster's S's.* 48
Coostom (custom) Foälks' *c* flitted awaäy — *North. Cobbler* 28
   An' *c* ageän draw'd in like a wind — ,, 93
Coot I come from haunts of *c* and hern, — *The Brook* 23
Cope *c* Of the half-attain'd futurity, — *Ode to Memory* 32
   Wrapt in dense cloud from base to *c*. — *Two Voices* 186
   one Not fit to *c* your quest. — *Gareth and L.* 1174
   slinks from what he fears To *c* with, — *Pelleas and E.* 439
   sound as when an iceberg splits From *c* to base— — *Lover's Tale i* 604
   the *c* and crown Of all I hoped and fear'd ?— — ,, *ii* 27
Cophetua came the beggar maid Before the king *C*. — *Beggar Maid* 4
   C sware a royal oath ; — ,, 15
Coppice in April suddenly Breaks from a *c* — *Marr. of Geraint* 339
   scour'd into the *c's* and was lost, — *Geraint and E.* 534
   from the fringe of *c* round them burst — *Balin and Balan* 46
Coppice-feather'd every *c-f* chasm and cleft, — *Princess iv* 23
Copse danced about the may-pole and in the
   hazel *c*, — *May Queen, N. Y's. E.* 11
   shadowy pine above the woven *c*. — *Lotos-Eaters* 18
   did we hear the *c's* ring, — *Locksley Hall* 35
   Came little *c's* climbing. — *Amphion* 32
   Then move the trees, the *c's* nod, — *Sir Galahad* 77
   In *c* and fern Twinkled the innumerable ear — *The Brook* 133
   firefly-like in *c* And linden alley : — *Princess i* 208
   we wound About the the cliffs, the *c's*, — ,, *iii* 360
   Here is the *c*, the fountain and— — *Sir J. Oldcastle* 127
   seas leaning on the mangrove *c*, — *Prog. of Spring* 76
Coptic Lulling the brine against the *C* sands. — *Buonaparte* 8
Coquette the slight *c*, she cannot love, — *The form, the form* 12
Coquette-like or half *c-l* Maiden, — *Hendecasyllabics* 20
Coquetting *C* with young beeches ; — *Amphion* 28
Cord The creaking *c's* which wound and eat — *Supp. Confessions* 36
   The wounding *c's* that bind and strain — *Clear-headed friend* 4
   We'll bind you fast in silken *c's*, — *Rosalind* 49
   Lower'd softly with a threefold *c* of love — *D. of F. Women* 211
   Bound by the golden *c* of their first love— — *The Ring* 429
   while she stared at those dead *c's* — *Death of Œnone* 10
   A silken *c* let down from Paradise, — *Akbar's Dream* 139
Cordage coils of *c*, swarthy fishing-nets, — *Enoch Arden* 17
Corded *See* **Sinew-corded**
Cordon draw The *c* close and closer — *Aylmer's Field* 500
Core Else earth is darkness at the *c*, — *In Mem. xxxiv* 3
   To make a solid *c* of heat ; — ,, *cvii* 18
Corinna wrought With fair *C's* triumph ; — *Princess iii* 349
Coritanian hear *C*, Trinobant ! (repeat) — *Boädicea* 10, 34, 47
   Gods have heard it, O Icenian, O *C* ! — *Boädicea* 21
   Shout Icenian, Catieuchlanian, shout *C*, Trinobant, — ,, 57
Corkscrew up the *c* stair With hand and rope — *Walk. to the Mail* 90
Corn (*See also* **Curn**) river-sunder'd champaign clothed with *c*, *(Œnone* 114
   land of hops and poppy-mingled *c*, — *Aylmer's Field* 31
   Ruth among the fields of *c*, — ,, 680
   when a field of *c* Bows all its ears — *Princess i* 236
   glutted all night long breast-deep in *c*, — ,, *ii* 387
   Steel and gold, and *c* and wine, — *Ode Inter. Exhib.* 17
   sweating underneath a sack of *c*, — *Marr. of Geraint* 263
   Take him to stall, and give him *c*, — ,, 371
   fell Like flaws in Summer laying lusty *c* : — ,, 764
   spice and her vintage, her silk and her *c* ; — *Vastness* 13
   A thousand squares of *c* and meadow, — *The Ring* 149
Corn-bin horse That hears the *c-b* open, — *The Epic* 45
Cornelia Clelia, *C*, with the Palmyrene — *Princess ii* 83
Corner 'Sometimes a little *c* shines, — *Two Voices* 187
   From some odd *c* of the brain. — *Miller's D.* 68
   in dark *c's* of her palace stood Uncertain shapes ; — *Palace of Art* 237
   crow shall tread The *c's* of thine eyes : — *Will Water.* 236
   sitting-room With shelf and *c* for the goods — *Enoch Arden* 171
   From distant *c's* of the street they ran — ,, 349
   or Ralph Who shines so in the *c* ; — *Princess, Pro.* 145
   my own sad name in *c's* cried, — *Maud I vi* 72
   Found Enid with the *c* of his eye, — *Geraint and E.* 281
   A damsel drooping in a *c* of it. — ,, 611
   folded hands and downward eyes Of glancing *c*, — *Merlin and V.* 70

Corner (*continued*) Or whisper'd in the *c*? do ye know it?' *Merlin and V.* 772
    knelt Full lowly by the *c's* of his bed, *Lancelot and E.* 826
    dragon, griffin, swan, At all the *c's*, *Holy Grail* 351
    deal-box that was push'd in a *c* away, *First Quarrel* 48
Cornice Now watching high on mountain *c*, *The Daisy* 19
    Stretch'd under all the *c* and upheld : *Gareth and L.* 219
Cornish held Tintagil castle by the *C* sea, *Com. of Arthur* 187
    name of evil savour in the land, The *C* king. *Gareth and L.* 386
    Mark her lord had past, The *C* King, *Last Tournament* 382
    sands Of dark Tintagil by the *C* sea ; *Guinevere* 294
Corn-laws And struck upon the *c-l*, *Audley Court* 35
Coronach Prevailing in weakness, the *c* stole *Dying Swan* 26
Coronal My *c* slowly disentwined itself *Lover's Tale i* 361
    dost uphold Thy *c* of glory like a God,   „ 488
Coroner *c* doubtless will find it a felo-de-se, *Despair* 115
Coronet Kind hearts are more than *c's*, *L. C. V. de Vere* 55
Corp (**corpse**) a *c* lyin' undher groun'. *Tomorrow* 62
Corpse (*See also* **Corp**) On *c's* three-months-old at
    noon she came, *Palace of Art* 243
    C's across the threshold ; *D. of F. Women* 25
    Step from the *c*, and let him in *D. of the O. Year* 49
    he comes to the second *c* in the pit ? *Maud II v* 88
    A yet-warm *c*, and yet unburiable, *Gareth and L.* 80
    My mother on his *c* in open field ; (repeat) *Merlin and V.* 43, 73
    night with its coffinless *c* to be laid *Def. of Lucknow* 80
    I'd sooner fold an icy *c* dead of some *The Flight* 54
    She tumbled his helpless *c* about. *Dead Prophet* 65
    Pain, that has crawl'd from the *c* of Pleasure, *Vastness* 17
    And found a *c* and silence, *The Ring* 217
    lies, that blacken round The *c* of every man *Romney's R.* 123
Corpse-coffin end but in being our own *c-c's* at last, *Vastness* 33
Correspond Not for three years to *c* with home ; *Princess ii* 70
Corridor Full of long-sounding *c's* it was, *Palace of Art* 53
Corridor'd *See* **Many-corridor'd**
Corrientes and flowers, From *C* to Japan, *To Ulysses* 4
Corrupt Plenty *c's* the melody That made thee famous
    once, *The Blackbird* 15
    Lest one good custom should *c* the world. *M. d'Arthur* 242
    C's the strength of heaven-descended *Will* 11
    Lest one good custom should *c* the world. *Pass. of Arthur* 410
Corruption *c* crept among his knights, *Merlin and V.* 154
Corselet thro' the bulky bandit's *c* home, *Geraint and E.* 159
Cosmogony their *cosmogonies*, their astronomies : *Columbus* 42
Cosmopolite That man's the best *C* *Hands all Round* 3
Cosmos Chaos, *C*! *C*, Chaos ! (repeat) *Locksley H., Sixty* 103, 127
Cossack *C* and Russian Reel'd *Light Brigade* 34
Cost (s) care not for the *c* ; the *c* is mine.' *Geraint and E.* 288
Cost (verb) story that *c* me many a tear. *Grandmother* 22
    it *c* me a world of woe,   „ 23
    They still remember what it *c* them here, *The Ring* 201
Costliest. Black velvet of the *c*— *Aylmer's Field* 804
Costly the work To both appear'd so *c*, *Marr. of Geraint* 658
    'Let her tomb Be *c*, *Lancelot and E.* 1340
Costly-broider'd Laid from her limbs the *c-b* gift, *Marr. of Geraint* 769
Costly-made half-cut-down, a pasty *c-m*, *Audley Court* 23
Costrel youth, that following with a *c* bore *Marr. of Geraint* 386
Cot and kiss'd him in his *c*. *Enoch Arden* 234
    Here is the *c* of our orphan, *In the Child. Hosp.* 28
    Softly she call'd from her *c* to the next,   „ 46
    Thro' many a palace, many a *c*, *Demeter and P.* 55
Cotch'd (**caught**) but Charlie 'e *c* the pike, *Village Wife* 43
    Thou'd niver 'a *c* ony mice *Spinster's S's.* 55
    An' 'e *c* howd hard o' my hairm, *Owd Roä* 58
    c 'er death o' cowd that night,   „ 114
    I *c* tha wonst i' my garden, *Church-warden, etc.* 33
Coterie Came yews, a dismal *c* ; *Amphion* 42
Cottage Or even a lowly *c* whence we see *Ode to Memory* 100
    ' Make me a *c* in the vale,' she said, *Palace of Art* 291
    Love will make our *c* pleasant, *L. of Burleigh* 15
    she seems to gaze On that *c* growing nearer,   „ 35
    FAIR is her *c* in its place, *Requiescat* 1
    Served the poor, and built the *c*, *Locksley H., Sixty* 268
    sound ran Thro' palace and *c* door, *Dead Prophet* 38
Cottager She was the daughter of a *c*, *Walk. to the Mail* 59
Cottage-walls robed your *c-w* with flowers *Aylmer's Field* 698

Cotter a *c's* babe is royal-born by right divine ; *Locksley H., Sixty* 125
Cotton (s) Whose ear is cramm'd with his *c*, *Maud I x* 42
Cotton (verb) If tha *c's* down to thy betters, *Church-warden, etc.* 48
Cotton-spinner We are not *c-s's* all, *Third of Feb.* 45
Cotton-spinning Go' (shrill'd the *c-s* chorus) ; *Edwin Morris* 122
Co-twisted New things and old *c-t*, *Gareth and L.* 226
Couch Kings have no such *c* as thine, *Dirge* 40
    She lying on her *c* alone, *Day-Dm., Sleep B.* 2
    And flung her down upon a *c* of fire, *Aylmer's Field* 574
    light of healing, glanced about the *c*, *Princess vii* 59
    Rolling on their purple *c'es* *Boädicea* 62
    And Enid woke and sat beside the *c*, *Marr. of Geraint* 79
    which she laid Flat on the *c*, and spoke exultingly :   „ 679
    left her maiden *c*, and robed herself,   „ 737
    wearied out made for the *c* and slept, *Merlin and V.* 736
    flung herself Down on the great King's *c*, *Lancelot and E.* 610
    Low on the border of her *c* they sat *Guinevere* 101
    And the crowded *c* of incest in the warrens *Locksley H., Sixty* 224
Couchant *c* with his eyes upon the throne, *Guinevere* 11
Couch'd (*See also* **Low-couch'd**) tame leopards *c* beside
    her throne, *Princess ii* 33
    c behind a Judith, underneath The head   „ *iv* 226
    The wine-flask lying *c* in moss, *In Mem. lxxxix* 44
    c at ease, The white kine glimmer'd, (repeat)   „ *xcv* 14, 50
    c at night with grimy kitchen-knaves. *Gareth and L.* 481
    They *c* their spears and prick'd their steeds, *Lancelot and E.* 479
    at her will they *c* their spears, Three against one : *Pelleas and E.* 273
    Lancelot passing by Spied where he *c*, *Guinevere* 31
Cough *c's*, aches, stitches, ulcerous throes *St. S. Stylites* 13
Council (*See also* **College-council**) 'And statesmen at
    her *c* met *To the Queen* 29
    manners, climates, *c's*, governments, *Ulysses* 14
    In iron gauntlets : break the *c* up.' *Princess i* 89
    But when the *c* broke, I rose and past   „ 90
    enter'd an old hostel, call'd mine host To *c*,   „ 174
    'everywhere Two heads in *c*,   „ *ii* 173
    Great in *c* and great in war, *Ode on Well.* 30
    c's thinn'd, And armies waned, *Merlin and V.* 572
Council-hall The basest, far into that *c-h* *Lucretius* 171
    His voice is silent in your *c-h* *Ode on Well.* 174
Counsel (**advice**) silver flow Of subtle-paced *c* *Isabel* 21
    Then follow'd *c*, comfort, and the words *Love and Duty* 69
    Her art, her hand, her *c* all had wrought *Aylmer's Field* 151
    Nor dealing goodly *c* from a height   „ 172
    You prized my *c*, lived upon my lips : *Princess iv* 293
    In part It was ill *c* had misled the girl   „ *vii* 241
    to whom He trusted all things, and of him required
    His *c*: *Com. of Arthur* 147
    man of plots, Craft, poisonous *c's*, *Gareth and L.* 432
    Abide : take *c* : for this lad is great   „ 730
    thou begone, take *c*, and away,   „ 1002
    take my *c* : let me know it at once : *Merlin and V.* 653
    he turn'd Her *c* up and down within his mind, *Lancelot and E.* 369
    Then, when I come within her *c's*, *Pelleas and E.* 348
    I would not spurn Good *c* of good friends, *Sir J. Oldcastle* 146
    My *c* that the tyranny of all Led backward *Tiresias* 75
    And following thy true *c*, *Akbar's Dream* 154
    mix the wines of heresy in the cup Of *c*—   „ 175
Counsel (**advocate**) a sound Like sleepy *c* pleading ; *Amphion* 74
    A man is likewise *c* for himself, *Sea Dreams* 182
Counsel (verb) Speak to me, sister ; *c* me ; *The Flight* 75
Counsell'd but old Merlin *c* him, *Com. of Arthur* 306
Counsellor He play'd at *c's* and kings, *In Mem. lxiv* 23
    My noble friend, my faithful *c*, *Akbar's Dream* 18
    and bravest soul for *c* and friend.   „ 69
Count (title) *c's* and kings Who laid about them *Princess, Pro.* 30
    C, baron—whom he smote, he overthrew. *Lancelot and E.* 465
    C who sought to snap the bond *Happy* 61
Count (reckoning) 'Heaven heads the *c* of crimes *D. of F. Women* 201
Count (verb) I can but *c* thee perfect gain, *Palace of Art* 198
    or touch Of pension, neither *c* on praise : *Love thou thy land* 26
    C's nothing that she meets with base, *On a Mourner* 13
    but *c* not me the herd ! *Golden Year* 13
    But I *c* the gray barbarian lower *Locksley Hall* 174
    Deep as Hell I *c* his error. *The Captain* 3

Count (verb) *(continued)* C the more base idolater of
the two ;
conscience will not c me fleckless ; *Aylmer's Field 670*
what every woman c's her due, Love, children, *Princess ii 294*
Nor, what may c itself as blest, ,, iii 244
Shall c new things as dear as old : *In Mem. xxvii 9*
I c it crime To mourn for any ,, xl 28
To c their memories half divine ; ,, lxxxv 61
Thy likeness, I might c it vain ,, xc 12
To-day they c as kindred souls ; ,, xcii 2
Nor c me all to blame if I ,, xcix 19
'Mother, tho' ye c me still the child, ,, Con. 85
I c it of small use To charge you) *Gareth and L. 34*
be he dead, I c you for a fool ; *Geraint and E. 416*
'I c it of no more avail, Dame, ,, 548
may c The yet-unbroken strength ,, 715
I should c myself the coward if I left them, *Holy Grail 325*
You c the father of your fortune, *The Revenge 11*
The gells they c's fur nowt, *Sisters (E. and E.) 28*
Thy frailty c's most real, *Village Wife 18*
I c them all My friends *Ancient Sage 51*
I c you kind, I hold you true ; *Epilogue 18*
Counted casting bar or stone Was c best ; *The Wanderer 11*
So died Earl Doorm by him he c dead. *Gareth and L. 519*
And only queens are to be c so, *Geraint and E. 730*
Countenance Christians with happy c's— *Lancelot and E. 238*
With a glassy c Did she look to Camelot. *Supp. Confessions 20*
If I make dark my c, I shut my life *L. of Shalott iv 13*
Then her c all over Pale again as death *Two Voices 53*
o'er his c No shadow past, nor motion : *L. of Burleigh 65*
Else I withdraw favour and c From you *Enoch Arden 709*
She sets her forward c *Aylmer's Field 307*
His c blacken'd, and his forehead veins *In Mem. cxiv 6*
his face Shone like the c of a priest *Balin and Balan 391*
Forgetting how to render beautiful Her c *Pelleas and E. 144*
to see the settled c Of her I loved, *Lover's Tale i 97*
Counter rogue would leap from his c ,, ii 39
one to the west, and c to it, And blank : *Maud I i 51*
My knights have sworn the c to it— *Holy Grail 254*
We run more c to the soul thereof *Last Tournament 80*
Counterchange Witch-elms that c the floor ,, 659
Counter-changed c 'The level lake with diamond- *In Mem. lxxxix 1*
plots
half-disfame, And c with darkness ? *Arabian Nights 84*
Countercharm c of space and hollow sky, *Merlin and V. 466*
Countercheck With motions, checks, and c's. *Maud I xviii 43*
Countermarch would fight and march and c, *Two Voices 300*
Counterpane girl with her arms lying out on *Audley Court 40*
the c.
little arms lying out on the c ; *In the Child Hosp. 58*
Counterpressure But c's of the yielded hand ,, 70
Counter-scoff fiery-short was Cyril's c-s, *Sisters (E. and E.) 163*
Counter-term such c't's, my son, Are border-races, *Princess v 307*
Counter-yell yells and c-y's of feud And faction, *Ancient Sage 250*
Countest See thou, that c reason ripe *To Duke of Argyll 5*
Counting C the dewy pebbles, fix'd in thought ; *In Mem. xxxiii 13*
C the dewy pebbles, fix'd in thought. *M. d'Arthur 84*
Country His c's war-song thrill his ears : *Pass. of Arthur 252*
None of these Came from his c, *Two Voices 153*
O Prince, I have no c none : *Enoch Arden 653*
If love of c move thee there at all, *Princess ii 218*
neither court nor c, tho' they sought *Ode on Well. 140*
Who loves his native c best. *Marr. of Geraint 729*
Countryman and in me behold the Prince Your c, *Hands all Round 4*
Country-side *(See also* **Coontryside)** tree by tree, The *Princess ii 215*
c-s descended :
Countrywoman countrywomen ! she did not envy *Amphion 52*
gives the manners of your countrywomen ?' *Princess iii 41*
A foreigner, and I your c, ,, iv 151
County Not a lord in all the c ,, 317
that almighty man, The c God— *L. of Burleigh 59*
County Member not the C M's with the vane : *Aylmer's Field 14*
County Town Last week came one to the c t, *Walk. to the Mail 12*
Couple (s) a c, fair As ever painter painted, *Maud I x 37*
then, the c standing side by side, *Aylmer's Field 105*
The Bridesmaid 5

Couple (verb) then let men c at once with wolves. *Pelleas and E. 536*
Coupled No power—so chain'd and c with the curse *Tiresias 58*
Courage A c to endure and to obey ; *Isabel 25*
'C !' he said, and pointed toward the land, *Lotos-Eaters 1*
C, St Simeon ! This dull chrysalis *St. S. Stylites 155*
Till thy drooping c rise, *Vision of Sin 152*
C, poor heart of stone ! *Maud II iii 1*
C, poor stupid heart of stone.— ,, 5
if dynamite and revolver leave you c to be
wise : *Locksley H., Sixty 107*
Courier Which every hour his c's bring. *In Mem. cxxvi 4*
By c's gone before ; *Guinevere 396*
Course (s) *(See also* **Water-course)** Their c, till thou
wert also man : *Two Voices 327*
You held your c without remorse, *L. C. V. de Vere 45*
winds variable, Then baffling, a long c of them ; *Enoch Arden 546*
Like the Good Fortune, from her destined c, ,, 629
Or baser c's, children of despair.' *Princess iii 213*
outran The hearer in its fiery c ; *In Mem. cix 8*
And roll it in another c, ,, cxiii 10
And all the c's of the suns. ,, cxvii 12
move his c, and show That life is not as idle ore, ,, cxviii 19
faith That sees the c of human things. ,, cxxviii 4
Fill'd all the genial c's of his blood *Geraint and E. 927*
The c of life that seem'd so flowery to me *Merlin and V. 880*
Paused in their c to hear me, *Lover's Tale ii 14*
and sway thy c Along the years of haste *De Prof. Two G. 20*
Three that were next in their fiery c, *Heavy Brigade 21*
Course (verb) To c and range thro' all the world, *Sir J. Oldcastle 120*
Coursed we c about The subject most at heart, *Gardener's D. 222*
C one another more on open ground *Marr. of Geraint 522*
Court Her c was pure ; her life serene ; *To the Queen 25*
Four c's I made, East, West, and South and North, *Palace of Art 21*
round the cool green c's there ran a row Of cloisters, ,, 25
I earth in earth forget these empty c's, *Tithonus 75*
'O seek my father's c with me, *Day-Dm., Depart. 27*
old-world trains, upheld at c By Cupid-boys ,, Ep. 9
in a c he saw A something-pottle-bodied boy *'Will Water. 130*
Thro' the c's, the camps, the schools, *Vision of Sin 104*
A silent c of justice in his breast, *Sea Dreams 174*
often, in that silent c of yours— ,, 183
'I have a sister at a foreign c, *Princess i 75*
I stole from c With Cyril and with Florian, ,, 102
In masque or pageant at my father's c. ,, 198
a c Compact of lucid marbles, ,, ii 23
'We of the c,' said Cyril. 'From the c' ,, 48
we crost the c To Lady Psyche's : ,, 100
rolling thro' the c A long melodious thunder ,, 475
Descended to the c that lay three parts In shadow, ,, iii 20
So saying from the c we paced, ,, 117
there rose A hubbub in the c ,, iv 476
push'd us, down the steps and thro' the c, ,, 555
Deepening the c's of twilight broke them up ,, Con. 113
pleased him, fresh from brawling c's *In Mem. lxxxix 11*
I keep Within his c on earth, ,, cxxvi 7
Ye come from Arthur's c. *Com. of Arthur 249*
to the c of Arthur answering yea. ,, 446
Merlin's hand, the Mage at Arthur's c, *Gareth and L. 306*
then will I to c again, And shame the King ,, 897
brave Geraint, a knight of Arthur's c, *Marr. of Geraint 1*
Next after her own self, in all the c. ,, 18
himself Had told her, and their coming to the c. ,, 144, 846
(repeat)
Held c at old Caerleon upon Usk. ,, 146
with the morning all the c were gone. ,, 156
rode Geraint into the castle c, ,, 312
while he waited in the castle c, ,, 326
the good knight's horse stands in the c ; ,, 370
Shalt ride to Arthur's c, and coming there, ,, 582
rising up, he rode to Arthur's c, ,, 591
ride with him this morning to the c, ,, 606
bright and dreadful thing, a c. ,, 616
her own faded self And the gay c, ,, 653
lord and ladies of the high c went In silver tissue ,, 662
like a madman brought her to the c, ,, 725

Court (*continued*) neither *c* nor country, though they
 sought *Marr. of Geraint* 729
I can scarcely ride with you to *c*, ,, 749
such a sense might make her long for *c* ,, 803
In this poor gown I rode with him to *c*, *Geraint and E.* 700
A knight of Arthur's *c*, who laid his lance In rest, ,, 775
Was but to rest awhile within her *c* ; ,, 855
we be mightier men than all In Arthur's *c* ; *Balin and Balan* 34
c and King And all the kindly warmth ,, 235
stall'd his horse, and strode across the *c*, ,, 341
He rose, descended, met The scorner in the castle *c*, ,, 387
from the castle a cry Sounded across the *c*, ,, 400
the mask of pure Worn by this *c*, *Merlin and V.* 36
because that foster'd at *thy c* I savour ,, 38
narrow *c* and lubber King, farewell ! ,, 119
thro' the peaceful *c* she crept And whisper'd : ,, 139
wily Vivien stole from Arthur's *c*. ,, 149
leaving Arthur's *c* he gained the beach ; ,, 197
I rose and fled from Arthur's *c* ,, 297
the thing was blazed about the *c*, ,, 743
the *c*, the king, dark in your light, ,, 875·
Arthur, holding then his *c* Hard on the river *Lancelot and E.* 74
Moving to meet him in the castle *c* ; ,, 175·
great knight, the darling of the *c*, ,, 261·
much they ask'd of *c* and Table Round, ,, 268
she heard Sir Lancelot cry in the *c*, ,, 344
Above her, graces of the *c*, and songs, Sighs, ,, 648
we two May meet at *c* hereafter : ,, 698
ye will learn the courtesies of the *c*, ,, 699
Thence to the *c* he past ; ,, 706
So ran the tale like fire about the *c*, ,, 734
And all the gentle *c* will welcome me, ,, 1060
I go in state to *c*, to meet the Queen. ,, 1124
I hear of rumours flying thro' your *c*. ,, 1190·
Nun as she was, the scandal of the *C*, *Holy Grail* 78
'Gawain am I, Gawain of Arthur's *c*, *Pelleas and E.* 371
Gawain of the *c*, Sir Gawain— ,, 379
Then he crost the *c*, And spied not any light ,, 418
Creep with his shadow thro' the *c* again, ,, 441
My tower is full of harlots, like his *c*, *Last Tournament* 81
tonguesters of the *c* she had not heard. ,, 393
QUEEN GUINEVERE had fled the *c*, *Guinevere* 1
one morn when all the *c*, Green-suited, ,, 21
lissome Vivien, of her *c* The wiliest and the worst ; ,, 28
Lured by the crimes and frailties of the *c*, ,, 136
I came into *c* to the Judge and the lawyers. *Rizpah* 33
showing *c*'s and kings a truth *Columbus* 37
Fonseca my main enemy at their *c*, ,, 126
Cast off, put by, scouted by *c* and king— ,, 165
Than any friend of ours at *C* ? ,, 198
You move about the *C*, I pray you tell King Ferdinand ,, 222
Courted a well-worn pathway *c* us To one green
 wicket *Gardener's D.* 109
Courteous And mighty *c* in the main— *Aylmer's Field* 121
Sir, I was *c*, every phrase well oil'd, *Princess iii* 133
C or bestial from the moment, *Gareth and L.* 631
C—amends for gauntness— *Merlin and V.* 104
Gawain, surnamed The *C*, fair and strong, *Lancelot and E.* 555
' Too *c* truly ! ye shall go no more ,, 716
Too *c* are ye, fair Lord Lancelot. ,, 972
some one thrice as *c* as thyself— *Last Tournament* 706
Courtesy To greet the sheriff, needless *c* ! *Edwin Morris* 133
Then broke all bonds of *c*, *Aylmer's Field* 323
With garrulous ease and oily *courtesies* *Princess i* 164
in his coffin the Prince of *c* lay. *G. of Swainston* 10
men have I known In *c* like to thee : ,, 12
amends For a *c* not return'd. *Maud I vi* 14
stout knaves with foolish *courtesies* : ' *Gareth and L.* 733
waving to him White hands, and *c* ; ,, 1377
Geraint, from utter *c*, forbore. *Marr. of Geraint* 381
Host and Earl, I pray your *c* ; ,, 403
' I pray you of your *c*, He being as he is, *Geraint and E.* 641
I see ye scorn my *courtesies*, ,, 671
such a grace Of tenderest *c*, ,, 862
To learn what Arthur meant by *c*, *Balin and Balan* 158

Courtesy (*continued*) high-set *courtesies* are not for
 me. *Balin and Balan* 227
Whom all men rate the king of *c*. ,, 257
' Is this thy *c*—to mock me, ha ? ,, 495
wonted *c*, *C* with a touch of traitor in it, *Lancelot and E.* 638
ye will learn the *courtesies* of the court, ,, 699
Deeming our *c* is the truest law, ,, 712
Obedience is the *c* due to kings.' ,, 718
myself Would shun to break those bounds of *c* ,, 1220
And loved thy *courtesies* and thee, ,, 1363
such a *c* Spake thro' the limbs and in the voice— *Holy Grail* 22
one Murmuring, ' All *c* is dead,' *Last Tournament* 211
King by *c*, Or King by right— ,, 341
The greater man, the greater *c*. ,, 633
For *c* wins woman all as well As valour ,, 707
trustful *courtesies* of household life, *Guinevere* 86
And of the two first-famed for *c*— ,, 323
Had yet that grace of *c* in him left ,, 436
Yield thee full thanks for thy full *c* *To Victor Hugo* 13
Court-favour willing she should keep *C-f* : *Princess vii* 58
Court-Galen *c-G* poised his gilt-head cane, ,, i 19
Court-lady And should some great *c-l* say, *Marr. of Geraint* 723
Courtliness He moving up with pliant *c*, *Geraint and E.* 278
thought, and amiable words And *c*, *Guinevere* 482
Courting *See* Coortin
Courtly Not her, who is neither *c* nor kind, *Maud I v* 27
looking at her, Full *c*, yet not falsely, *Lancelot and E.* 236
Courtship Discussing how their *c* grew, *In Mem., Con.* 97
Cousin a silent *c* stole Upon us and departed : *Edwin Morris* 115
Trust me, *c*, all the current of my being *Locksley Hall* 24
Saying, ' Dost thou love me, *c* ? ' ,, 30
O my *c*, shallow-hearted ! ,, 39
To give his *c*, Lady Clare. *Lady Clare* 4
' It was my *c*,' said Lady Clare, ,, 15
Her and her far-off *c* and betrothed, *The Brook* 75
My lady's *c*, Half-sickening of his pension'd *Aylmer's Field* 460
And had a *c* tumbled on the plain, *Princess vi* 319
Jenny, my *c*, had come to the place, *Grandmother* 25
Had made his goodly *c*, Tristram, knight, *Gareth and L.* 394
' O *c*, slay not him who gave you life.' *Geraint and E.* 783
' Fair and dear *c*, you that most had ,, 824
poor *c*, with your meek blue eyes, ,, 841
fear not, *c* ; I am changed indeed.' ,, 873
My sister, and my *c*, and my love, *Lover's Tale iii* 43
c of his and hers—O God, so like ! ' ,, iv 327
' Take my free gift, my *c*, for your wife ; ,, 363
And Muriel Erne—the two were *c*'s— *The Ring* 147
I found these *c*'s often by the brook, ,, 158
Cove dimple in the dark of rushy *c*'s, *Ode to Memory* 60
sweet is the colour of *c* and cave, *Sea-Fairies* 30
And shadow'd *c*'s on a sunny shore, *Eleänore* 18
waves that up a quiet *c* Rolling slide, ,, 108
And steering, now, from a purple *c*, *The Daisy* 20
curl'd Thro' all his eddying *c*'s ; *In Mem. lxxix* 10
The sailing moon in creek and *c* ; ,, ci 16
then the two Dropt to the *c*, *Com. of Arthur* 378
Sat by the river in a *c*, and watch'd *Lancelot and E.* 1389
Covenant Breathed, like the *c* of a God, *Gardener's D.* 209
Coventry *I waited for the train at* C ; *Godiva* 1
wife to that grim Earl, who ruled In *C* : ,, 13
Cover (**s**) I slide by hazel *c*'s ; *The Brook* 171
Cover (**verb**) Have mercy, mercy ! *c* all my sin. *St. S. Stylites* 84
C the lions on thy shield, *Gareth and L.* 585
Cover'd His blue shield-lions *c*— ,, 1217
All over *c* with a luminous cloud, *Holy Grail* 189
fail'd from my side, nor come *C*, ,, 471
what I saw was veil'd And *c* ; ,, 852
Coverlet Across the purple *c*, *Day-Dm., Sleep. B.* 3
Who, moving, cast the *c* aside, *Marr. of Geraint* 73
Coverlid The silk star-broider'd *c* *Day-Dm., Sleep. B.* 9
And all the *c* was cloth of gold *Lancelot and E.* 1157
Covert Rode thro' the *c*'s of the deer, *Sir L. and Q. G.* 21
Here often they break *c* at our feet.' *Marr. of Geraint* 183
Coverture In closest *c* upsprung, *Arabian Nights* 68
Cow He praised his ploughs, his *c*'s, his hogs, *The Brook* 125

Cow (continued) theer warn't not feeäd for a c ; — *N. Farmer, O. S.* 37
Wi' aäf the c's to cauve — " 52
as big i' the mouth as a c, — *Village Wife* 103
wi' her paäils fro' the c. — *Spinsters S's.* 2
peasant c shall butt the 'Lion passant' — *Locksley H., Sixty* 248
an' wa lost wer Haldeny c, — *Church-warden, etc.* 5
an' I doubts they poison'd the c. — " 16
an' it poison'd the c. — " 54

Coward The fear of men, a c still. — *Two Voices* 108
Where idle boys are c's to their shame, — *Princess v* 309
dwell On doubts that drive the c back, — *In Mem. xcv* 30
were he not crown'd King, c, and fool.' — *Merlin and V.* 789
a c slinks from what he fears To cope with, — *Pelleas and E.* 438
'Fore God I am no c : — *The Revenge* 4
'I know you are no c ; — " 8
I should count myself the c if I left them, — " 11
spared the flesh of thousands, the c and the base, — *Happy* 17

Cowardice full of c and guilty shame, — *Princess iv* 348
being thro' his c allow'd Her station, — *Guinevere* 516
Or c, the child of lust for gold, — *To the Queen II* 54

Cowd (cold) sa c !—hev another glass ! Straänge an' c fur the time ! — *Village Wife* 20
Of a Christmas Eäve, an' as c as this, — *Owd Roä* 31
but the barn was as c as owt, — " 111
she cotch'd 'er death o' c that night, — " 114

Cower'd A dwarf-like Cato c. — *Princess vii* 126
Had often truckled and c When he rose — *Dead Prophet* 62

Cowering *See* Low-cowering

Cowl And turn'd the c's adrift : — *Talking Oak* 48
leaving for the c The helmet in an abbey — *Holy Grail* 5

Cowl'd Some c, and some bare-headed, — *Princess vi* 77
Beside that tower where Percivale was c, — *Pelleas and E.* 501

Cowslip Spring Letters c's on the hill? — *Adeline* 62
To stoop the c to the plains, — *Rosalind* 16
c and the crowfoot are over all the hill, — *May Queen* 38
As c unto oxlip is, — *Talking Oak* 107
The little dells of c, fairy palms, — *Aylmer's Field* 91
what joy can be got from a c out of the field ; — *In the Child. Hosp.* 36

Cowslip Ball he made me the c b, — *First Quarrel* 13

Cowslip Wine hev a glass o' c w ! — *Village Wife* 5

Craädle (cradle) An' I tummled athurt the c — *North. Cobbler* 35
Nelly wur up fro' the c — *Village Wife* 103
bring tha down, an' thy c an' all ; — *Owd Roä* 50

Craäzed (crazed) Warn't I c fur the lasses mysén — *N. Farmer, N. S.* 18
'Cushie wur c fur 'er cauf' — *Spinster's S's.* 115

Crab like a butt, and harsh as c's. — *Walk. to the Mail* 49

Crabb'd Thro' solid opposition c and gnarl'd. — *Princess iii* 126
Come, thou are c and sour : — *Last Tournament* 272

Crack (s) deafen'd with the stammering c's — *Merlin and V.* 942
c of earthquake shivering to your base — *Pelleas and E.* 465

Crack (verb) chrysalis C's into shining wings, — *St. S. Stylites* 156
splinter'd spear-shafts c and fly, — *Sir Galahad* 7
earthquake in one day C's all to pieces,— — *Lucretius* 252
living hearts that c within the fire — *Princess v* 379
and takes, and breaks, and c's, and splits, — " 527
whelp to c ; C them now for yourself, — *Maud II v* 55
Burst vein, snap sinew, and c heart, — *Sir J. Oldcastle* 123

Crack'd The mirrow c from side to side ; — *L. of Shalott iii* 43
all her bonds C ; and I saw the flaring atom-streams — *Lucretius* 38
The forest c, the waters curl'd, — *In Mem. xv* 5
And c the helmet thro', and bit the bone, — *Marr. of Geraint* 573
And once the laces of a helmet c, — *Last Tournament* 164
whin I c his skull for her sake, — *Tomorrow* 41
Casques were c and hauberks hack'd — *The Tourney* 7

Crackle The tempest c's on the leads, — *Sir Galahad* 53

Crackling His hair as it were c into flames, — *Aylmer's Field* 586
heard A c and a rising of the roofs, — *Holy Grail* 183

Cradle (*See also* **Craädle**) To deck thy c, Eleänore. — *Eleänore* 21
Then lightly rocking baby's c — *Enoch Arden* 194
sway'd The c, while she sang this baby song. — *Sea Dreams* 292
on my c shone the Northern star. — *Princess i* 4
rock the snowy c till I died. — " *iv* 104
Love, Warm in the heart, his c, — *Lover's Tale i* 158
we slept In the same c always, — " 259
place of burial Far lovelier than its c ; — " 530

Cradle (continued) bending by the c of her babe. — *The Ring* 415
paler then Than ever you were in your c, moan'd, — " 432

Cradled (*See also* **Lily-cradled**) Their Margaret c near them, — *Sea Dreams* 57
half-embraced the basket c-h — " 289

Cradle-head half-embraced the basket c-h — *Sea Dreams* 289

Cradle-time Familiar up from c-t, so wan, — *Balin and Balan* 591

Cradlemont Urien, C of Wales, Claudias, — *Com. of Arthur* 112

Craft (art, etc.) before we came, This c of healing. — *Princess iii* 320
less from Indian c Than beelike instinct — " *iv* 198
Yet Merlin thro' his c, — *Com. of Arthur* 234
man of plots, C, poisonous counsels, — *Gareth and L.* 432
answer'd with such c as women use, — *Geraint and E.* 352
Nor left untold the c herself had used ; — " 393
moral child without the c to rule, — *Lancelot and E.* 146
The c of kindred and the Godless hosts — *Guinevere* 427
chance and c and strength in single fights, — *Pass. of Arthur* 106
c and madness, lust and spite, — *Locksley H., Sixty* 189
Had never served for c or fear, — *To Marq. of Dufferin* 27
C with a bunch of all-heal in her hand, — *Vastness* 17
O the flattery and the c — *Forlorn* 3
Then you that drive, and know your C, — *Politics* 5

Craft (vessel) I boated over, ran My c aground, — *Edwin Morris* 109
At times a carven c would shoot — *The Voyage* 53
Become the master of a larger c, — *Enoch Arden* 144
pushing his black c among them all, — *Merlin and V.* 563
seamen made mock at the mad little c — *The Revenge* 38
Of others their old c seaworthy still, — *Pref. Son. 19th Cent.* 3

Crag (*See also* **Island-crag**) And the c that fronts the Even, — *Eleänore* 40
A gleaming c with belts of pines. — *Two Voices* 189
barr'd with long white cloud the scornful c's, — *Palace of Art* 83
All night the splinter'd c's that wall the dell — *D. of F. Women* 187
And the wild water lapping on the c.' — *M. d'Arthur* 71
'I heard the water lapping on the c, — " 116
based His feet on juts of slippery c — " 189
when the bracken rusted on their c's, — *Edwin Morris* 100
The light cloud smoulders on the summer c. — " 147
My right leg chain'd into the c, I lay — *St. S. Stylites* 73
still hearth, among these barren c's, — *Ulysses* 2
swings the trailer from the c ; — *Locksley Hall* 162
He clasps the c with crooked hands ; — *The Eagle* 1
At the foot of thy c's, O Sea ! — *Break, break, etc.* 14
from the beetling c to which he clung — *Aylmer's Field* 229
came On flowery levels underneath the c, — *Princess iii* 336
like a jewel set In the dark c : — " 359
find the toppling c's of Duty scaled — *Ode on Well.* 215
They tremble, the sustaining c's : — *In Mem. cxxvii* 11
like a c that tumbles from the cliff, And like a c was gay with wilding flowers : — *Marr. of Geraint* 318
And lichen'd into colour with the c's : — *Lancelot and E.* 44
And found a people there among their c's, — *Holy Grail* 662
Clutch'd at the c, and started thro' mid air — *Last Tournament* 14
and c and tree Scaling, Sir Lancelot — " 17
And the wild water lapping on the c.' — *Pass. of Arthur* 239
'I heard the water lapping on the c, — " 284
based His feet on juts of slippery c — " 357
last hard footstep of that iron c ; — " 447
path was perilous, loosely strown with c's : — *Lover's Tale i* 384
issuing from his portals in the c — " 430
Revenge herself went down by the island c's — *The Revenge* 118
the pine shot along from the c — *V. of Maeldune* 16
down the c's and thro' the vales. — *Montenegro* 8
The noonday c made the hand burn ; — *Tiresias* 35
When I had fall'n from off the c we clamber'd — *The Flight* 22

Crag-carven left c-c o'er the streaming Gelt— — *Gareth and L.* 1203

Crag-cloister C-c ; Anatolian Ghost ; — *To Ulysses* 43

Crag-platform huge c-p, smooth as burnish'd brass — *Palace of Art* 5

Crake (*See also* **Meadow-crake**) flood the haunts of hern and c ; — *In Mem. ci* 14

Cram green Christmas c's with weary bones. — *Wan Sculptor* 14
'Give, C us with all,' — *Golden Year* 13
c him with the fragments of the grave, — *Princess iii* 311
Well needs it we should c our ears with wool — " *iv* 65
Like any pigeon will I c his crop, — *Gareth and L.* 459

Cramm'd (*See also* **Furze-cramm'd**) 'THE Bull, the Fleece are c, — *Audley Court* 1

Cramm'd (*continued*) And *c* a plumper crop ; — *Will Water.* 124
Not like your Princess *c* with erring pride, — *Princess iii* 102
Titanic shapes, they *c* The forum, — ,, *vii* 124
she was *c* with theories out of books, — ,, *Con.* 35
Whose ear is *c* with his cotton, — *Maud I x* 42
every margin scribbled, crost, and *c* With comment, — *Merlin and V.* 677
When was age so *c* with menace ? — *Locksley H., Sixty* 108
Cramming *C* all the blast before it, — *Locksley Hall* 192
Cramp (s) stitches, ulcerous throes and *c*'s, — *St. S. Stylites* 13
Cramp (verb) *c* its use, if I Should hook it — *Day-Dm., Moral* 15
I will not *c* my heart, nor take Half-views — *Will Water.* 51
To *c* the student at his desk, — *In Mem. cxxviii* 18
Cramp'd (*See also* **Iron-cramp'd**) for women, up till this *C* under worse — *Princess iii* 278
weakness or necessity have *c* Within themselves, — *Tiresias* 87
Crane *c*,' I said, ' may chatter of the *c*, — *Princess iii* 104
steaming marshes of the scarlet *c*'s, — *Prog. of Spring* 75
Crannied FLOWER in the *c* wall, — *Flow. in Cran. wall* 1
Cranny I pluck you out of the *crannies*, — ,, 2
In an ancient mansion's *crannies* and holes : — *Maud II v* 61
A light was in the *crannies*, — *Holy Grail* 838
Crape Nor wreathe thy cap with doleful *c*, — *My life is full* 14
Crash (s) came The *c* of ruin, and the loss of all — *Enoch Arden* 549
In conflict with the *c* of shivering points, — *Princess v* 491
There at his right with a sudden *c*, — *The Islet* 8
thro' the *c* of the near cataract hears — *Geraint and E.* 172
c Of battleaxes on shatter'd helms, — *Pass. of Arthur* 109
maim'd for life In the *c* of the cannonades — *The Revenge* 78
The *c* of the charges, — *Batt. of Brunanburh* 89
My brain is full of the *c* of wrecks, — *The Wreck* 4
then came the *c* of the mast. — ,, 92
the *c* was long and loud— — *Happy* 80
Crash (verb) The fortress *c*'es from on high, — *In Mem. cxxvii* 14
I thought the great tower would *c* — *Balin and Balan* 515
hail of Arês *c* Along the sounding walls. — *Tiresias* 96
Crash'd boys That *c* the glass and beat the floor ; — *In Mem. lxxxvii* 20
and so they *c* In onset, — *Balin and Balan* 555
the stormy surf *C* in the shingle : — *Lover's Tale iii* 54
as if she had struck and *c* on a rock ; — *The Wreck* 108
C like a hurricane, Broke thro' the mass — *Heavy Brigade* 28
Crashing *C* went the boom, — *The Captain* 44
c with long echoes thro' the land, — *Aylmer's Field* 338
c thro' it, their shot and their shell, — *Def. of Lucknow* 18
Crass (cross) as ye did—over yer *C* ! — *Tomorrow* 90
An shure, be the *C*, that's betther nor cuttin' — ,, 94
Crasst (crossed) ' niver *c* over say to the Sassenach whate ; — ,, 48
Crate the skin Clung but to *c* and basket, — *Merlin and V.* 625
Crater the centre and *c* of European confusion, — *Beautiful City* 1
Broke the Taboo, Dipt to the *c* — *Kapiolani* 31
Crathur' (whisky) been takin' a dhrop o' the *c* — *Tomorrow* 11
Crave household shelter *c* From winter rains — *Two Voices* 260
I *c* your pardon, O my friend ; — *In Mem. lxxxv* 100
damsel back To *c* again Sir Lancelot of the King. — *Gareth and L* 882
See thou *c* His pardon for thy breaking — ,, 985
C pardon for that insult done the Queen, — *Marr. of Geraint* 583
stay'd to *c* permission of the King, — *Balin and Balan* 288
dazzled by the sudden light, and *c* Pardon : — *Pelleas and E.* 105
Might I *c* One favour ? — *Romney's R.* 69
Craved He *c* a fair permission to depart, — *Marr. of Geraint* 40
Lancelot at the palace *c* Audience of Guinevere, — *Lancelot and E.* 1162
Craven Silenced for ever—*c*—a man of plots, — *Gareth and L.* 431
' A *c* ; how he hangs his head.' — *Geraint and E.* 127
c, weakling, and thrice-beaten hound — *Pelleas and E.* 291
my *c* seeks To wreck thee villainously : — *Last Tournament* 548
c shifts, and long crane legs of Mark— — ,, 729
Craw (crow) theer's a *c* to pluck wi' tha, Sam : — *N. Farmer, N. S.* 5
Crawin' (crowing) cocks kep a-crawin' an' *c'* — *Owd Roä* 106
Crawl Why inch by inch to darkness *c*? — *Two Voices* 200
The wrinkled sea beneath him *c*'s ; — *The Eagle* 4
But into some low cave to *c*, — *Merlin and V.* 884
Crawl'd (*See also* **Scaped**) *C* slowly with low moans to where she lay, — *Balin and Balan* 592
Pain, that has *c* from the corpse of Pleasure, — *Vastness* 17
But 'e creeäpt an' 'e *c* along, — *Church-warden, etc.* 19

Crawling scorpion *c* over naked skulls ;— — *Demeter and P.* 78
Crayon Mary, my *c*'s! if I can, I will. — *Romney's R.* 88
Craze if the King awaken from his *c*, — *Gareth and L.* 724
Crazed (*See also* **Craäzed**, **Half-crazed**) I saw her (and I thought him *c*, — *Lover's Tale iv* 163
so *c* that at last There were some leap'd — *V. of Maeldune* 75
arrogant opulence, fear I myself turned *c*, — *Despair* 78
I *c* myself over their horrible infidel writings ? — ,, 87
for War's own sake Is fool, or *c*, or worse ; — *Epilogue* 31
coals of fire you heap upon my head Have *c* me. — *Romney's R.* 142
I was all but *c* With the grief — *Bandit's Death* 38
Craziness such a *c* as needs A cell and keeper), — *Lover's Tale iv* 164
For such a *c* as Julian's look'd — ,, 168
Crazy when I were so *c* wi' spite, — *First Quarrel* 73
Never a prophet so *c* ! — *The Throstle* 10
Creak but am led by the *c* of the chain, — *Rizpah* 7
Creak'd The doors upon their hinges *c* ; — *Mariana* 62
Cream fruits and *c* Served in the weeping elm ; — *Gardener's D.* 194
robb'd the farmer of his bowl of *c* : — *Princess v* 223
Cream-white Her *c-w* mule his pastern set : — *Sir L. and Q. G.* 31
Crease (weapon) cursed Malayan *c*, and battle clubs — *Princess, Pro.* 21
Create Life eminent *c*'s the shade of death ; — *Love and Death* 13
Creation Yet could not all *c* pierce — *A Character* 5
And all *c* in one act at once, — *Princess iii* 325
serene *C* minted in the golden moods — ,, *v* 194
And love *C*'s final law— — *In Mem. lvi* 14
To which the whole *c* moves. — ,, *Con.* 144
Creature Did never *c* pass So slightly, — *Talking Oak* 86
But not a *c* was in sight : — ,, 167
happy as God grants To any of his *c*'s, — *Enoch Arden* 417
As hunters round a hunted *c* draw — *Aylmer's Field* 499
the gentle *c* shut from all Her charitable use, — ,, 565
The *c* laid his muzzle on your lap, — *Princess ii* 272
Like some wild *c* newly-caged, — ,, 301
So stood that same fair *c* at the door. — ,, 329
The sleek and shining *c*'s of the chase, — ,, *v* 155
The lovely, lordly *c* floated on — ,, *vi* 89
Like *c*'s native unto gracious act, — ,, *vii* 27
Thy *c*, whom I found so fair. — *In Mem., Pro.* 38
leave at times to play As with the *c* of my love ; — ,, *lix* 12
O beautiful *c*, what am I — *Maud I xvi* 12
A *c* wholly given to brawls and wine, — *Marr. of Geraint* 441
To pick the faded *c* from the pool, — ,, 671
they themselves, like *c*'s gently born — *Geraint and E.* 191
c's voiceless thro' the fault of birth, — ,, 266
I compel all *c*'s to my will.' (repeat) — ,, 629, 673
To chase a *c* that was current then — *Merlin and V.* 408
There sat the lifelong *c* of the house. — *Lancelot and E.* 1143
or had the boat Become a living *c* clad with wings ? — *Holy Grail* 519
Are ye but *c*'s of the board and bed, — *Pelleas and E.* 267
His *c*'s to the basement of the tower — *Guinevere* 104
and his *c*'s took and bare him off, — ,, 109
Had I but loved thy highest *c* here ? — ,, 656
but the *c*'s had worked their will. — *Rizpah* 50
glorious *c* Sank to his setting. — *Batt. of Brunanburh* 29
O unhappy *c* ? — *Forlorn* 44
diseaseful *c* which in Eden was divine, — *Happy* 33
I worship all too well this *c* of decay, — ,, 45
like a *c* frozen to the heart Beyond all hope — *Death of Œnone* 73
tenderest Christ-like *c* that ever stept — *Charity* 32
Credible I almost think That idiot legend *c*. — *Princess v* 153
Credit (s) Hadst thou such *c* with the soul ? — *In Mem. lxxi* 5
His *c* thus shall set me free ; — ,, *lxxx* 13
Credit (verb) The world which *c*'s what is done — ,, *lxxv* 13
Credited *See* **Scarce-credited**
Creditor They set an ancient *c* to work : — *Edwin Morris* 130
Credulous *c* Of what they long for, — *Geraint and E.* 875
Credulousness darken, as he cursed his *c*, — *Sea Dreams* 13
Creeäp (creep) But *c* along the hedge-bottoms, — *Church-warden, etc.* 19
Creeäpt (crept) But 'e *c* an' 'e crawl'd along, — ,, 19
Creed compare All *c*'s till we have found the one, — *Supp. Confessions* 176
The knots that tangle human *c*'s, — *Clear-headed friend* 3
And other than his form of *c*, — *A Character* 29
cares to lisp in love's delicious *c*'s : — *Caress'd or Chidden* 11
A dust of systems and of *c*'s. — *Two Voices* 207

Creed (*continued*)   I sit as God holding no form of *c*,   *Palace of Art* 211
Against the scarlet woman and her *c* ;   *Sea Dreams* 23
Who keeps the keys of all the *c's*,   *In Mem. xxiii* 5
wrought With human hands the *c* of *c's*   ,,   *xxxvi* 10
shriek'd against his *c*—   ,,   *lvi* 16
Believe me, than in half the *c's.*   ,,   *xcvi* 12
To cleave a *c* in sects and cries,   ,,   *cxxviii* 15
The prayer of many a race and *c*, and clime—   *To the Queen ii* 11
drear night-fold of your fatalist *c*,   *Despair* 21
cramping *c's* that had madden'd the peoples   ,,   24
Despite of very Faith and *C*,   *To Mary Boyle* 51
I hate the rancour of their castes and *c's*,   *Akbar's Dream* 65
when *c* and race Shall bear false witness,   ,,   97
Like calming oil on all their stormy *c's*,   ,,   160
Neither mourn if human *c's* be lower   *Faith* 5
Creedless   This *c* people will be brought to Christ   *Columbus* 189
Creek   marish-flowers that throng The desolate *c's* and
pools among,   *Dying Swan* 41
The Lotos blows by every winding *c*:   *Lotos-Eaters, C. S.* 101
The sailing moon in *c* and cove ;   *In Mem. ci* 19
Creep (*See also* **Creeäp**)   Wind *c* ; dews fall chilly :   *Leonine Eleg.* 7
These in every shower *c*   *A Dirge* 33
a languid fire *c's* Thro' my veins   *Eleänore* 130
c's from pine to pine, And loiters,   *Œnone* 4
And thro' the moss the ivies, *c*,   *Lotos-Eaters C. S.* 9
lost their edges, and did *c* Roll'd on each other,   *D. of F. Women* 50
C's to the garden water-pipes beneath,   ,,   206
c's on, Barge-laden, to three arches of a bridge   *Gardener's D.* 42
The slow-worn *c's*, and the thin weasel   *Aylmer's Field* 852
Where never *c's* a cloud, or moves a wind,   *Lucretius* 106
Could dead flesh *c*, or bits of roasting ox   ,,   131
Some ship of battle slowly *c*,   *To F. D. Maurice* 26
And like a guilty thing I *c*   *In Mem. vii* 7
When the blood *c's*, and the nerves prick   ,,   *l* 2
Must I *c* to the hollow and dash myself   *Maud I i* 54
Felt a horror over me *c*,   ,,   *xiv* 35
Always I long to *c* Into some still cavern deep,   ,,   *II iv* 95
The slow tear *c* from her closed eyelid   *Merlin and V.* 906
C with his shadow thro' the court again,   *Pelleas and E.* 441
like a new disease, unknown to men, *C's*,   *Guinevere* 519
down, down ! and *c* thro' the hole !   *Def. of Lucknow* 25
who *c* from thought to thought,   *Ancient Sage* 103
he—some one— this way *c's* !   *The Flight* 70
fire of fever *c's* across the rotted floor,   *Locksley H., Sixty* 223
c down to the river-shore,   *Charity* 15
Creeper   as falls A *c* when the prop is broken,   *Aylmer's Field* 810
With *c's* crimsoning to the pinnacles,   *The Ring* 82
Creeping (*See also* **A-creeäpin**, **Forward-creeping**,
Silent-creeping)   *C* thro' blossomy rushes and
bowers   *Leonine Eleg.* 3
And crystal silence *c* down,   *Two Voices* 86
Upon the tortoise *c* to the wall ;   *D. of F. Women* 27
c on from point to point :   *Locksley Hall* 134
comes a hungry people, as a lion *c* nigher,   ,,   135
Still *c* with the *c* hours   *St. Agnes' Eve* 7
Crept (*See also* **Creeäpt**)   The cluster'd marish-mosses *c*.   *Mariana* 40
deep inlay Of braided blooms unmown, which *c*
Adown   *Arabian Nights* 29
' From grave to grave the shadow *c* :   *Two Voices* 274
And out I stept, and up I *c* :   *Edwin Morris* 111
And down my surface *c*.   *Talking Oak* 162
C down into the hollows of the wood ;   *Enoch Arden* 76
Another hand *c* too across his trade   ,,   110
He *c* into the shadow : at last he said,   ,,   387
c Still downward thinking ' dead   ,,   688
C to the gate, and open'd it,   ,,   775
With hooded brows I *c* into the hall,   *Princess iv* 225
As on The Lariano *c* To that fair port   *The Daisy* 78
a gentler feeling *c* Upon us: *In Mem. xxx* 17
till he *c* from a gutted mine   *Maud I x* 9
MY life has *c* so long on a broken wing   ,, *III vi* 1
thro' the peaceful court she *c* And whisper'd :   *Merlin and V.* 139
some corruption *c* among his knights,   ,,   154
from the carven-work behind him *c*   *Lancelot and E.* 436
C to her father, while he mused alone,   ,,   748

Crept (*continued*)   all that walk'd, or *c*, or perch'd,
or flew.   *Last Tournament* 367
in the pause she *c* an inch Nearer,   *Guinevere* 527
my blood *C* like marsh drains thro' all my languid
limbs ;   *Lover's Tale ii* 53
the night has *c* into my heart,   *Rizpah* 16
C to his North again, Hoar-headed hero !   *Batt. of Brunanburh* 64
Black was the night when we *c* away   *Bandit's Death* 25
Crescent (*adj.*) (*See also* **De-crescent**, **In-crescent**)
many a youth Now *c*, who will come   *Lancelot and E.* 448
Crescent (*s*)   Hundreds of *c's* on the roof   *Arabian Nights* 129
And April's *c* glimmer'd cold,   *Miller's D.* 107
beneath a moon, that, just In *c*,   *Audley Court* 81
When down the stormy *c* goes,   *Sir Galahad* 25
As when the sun, a *c* of eclipse,   *Vision of Sin* 10
A downward *c* of her minion mouth,   *Aylmer's Field* 533
To which thy *c* would have grown ;   *In Mem. lxxxiv* 4
To yon hard *c*, as she hangs   ,,   *cvii* 10
Half-lost in the liquid azure bloom of a *c* of sea,   *Maud I iv* 5
With this last moon, this *c*—   *De Prof. Two G.* 9
red with blood the *C* reels from fight   *Montenegro* 6
Crescent-bark   range Of vapour buoy'd the *c-b*,   *Day-Dm., Depart.* 22
Crescent-curve   Set in a gleaming river's *c-c*,   *Princess i* 171
Silver *c-c*, Coming soon,   *The Ring* 13
Crescent-lit   while the balmy glooming, *c-l*,   *Gardener's D.* 263
Crescent-moon   And clove the Moslem *c-m*,   *Happy* 44
Crescent-wise   thro' stately theatres Bench'd *c-w*.   *Princess ii* 370
Cress   brook that loves To purl o'er matted *c*   *Ode to Memory* 59
I loiter round my *c'es* ;   *The Brook* 181
Crest   She watch'd my *c* among them all,   *Oriana* 30
lapwing gets himself another *c* ;   *Locksley Hall* 18
and light as the *c* Of a peacock,   *Maud I xvi* 16
With but a drying evergreen for *c*,   *Gareth and L.* 1116
The giant tower, from whose high *c*, they say,   *Marr. of Geraint* 827
stormy *c's* that smoke against the skies,   *Lancelot and E.* 484
And wearing but a holly-spray for *c*,   *Last Tournament* 172
while he mutter'd, ' Craven *c's* ! O shame !   ,,   187
Fall, as the *c* of some slow-arching wave,   ,,   462
To which for *c* the golden dragon clung   *Guinevere* 594
c of the tides Plunged on the vessel   *The Wreck* 89
' A warrior's *c* above the cloud of war '—   *The Ring* 338
Crete   Had rest by stony hills of *C*.   *On a Mourner* 35
Crevice   shriek'd, Or from the *c* peer'd about.   *Mariana* 65
fretful as the wind Pent in a *c*:   *Princess iii* 81
Crew (*s*)   the seamen Made a gallant *c*,   *The Captain* 6
beneath the water *C* and Captain lie ;   ,,   68
And half the *c* are sick or dead,   *The Voyage* 92
They sent a *c* that landing burst away   *Enoch Arden* 634
And ever as he mingled with the *c*,   ,,   643
a *c* that is neither rude nor rash,   *The Islet* 10
mann'd the Revenge with a swarthier alien *c*,   *The Revenge* 110
harass'd by the frights Of my first *c*,   *Columbus* 68
ran into the hearts of my *c*,   *V. of Maeldune* 33
the *c* should cast me into the deep,   *The Wreck* 94
the *c* were gentle, the captain kind ;   ,,   129
Crew (*verb*)   sitting, as I said, The cock *c* loud ;   *M. d'Arthur, Ep.* 10
Crichton   I call'd him *C*, for he seem'd   *Edwin Morris* 21
Cricket (*See also* **Balm-cricket**)   The *c* chirps ; the
light burns low :   *D. of the O. Year* 40
not a *c* chirr'd :   *In Mem. xcv* 6
As that gray *c* chirpt of at our hearth—   *Merlin and V.* 110
Than of the myriad *c* of the mead,   *Lancelot and E.* 106
And each was as dry as a *c*,   *V. of Maeldune* 50
Cricketed   They boated and they *c* ;   *Princess, Pro.* 160
Cried   he took the boy that *c* aloud   *Dora* 101
when the boy beheld His mother he *c* out   ,,   138
Leolin *c* out the more upon them—   *Aylmer's Field* 367
mock'd him with returning calm, and *c*:   *Lucretius* 25
c out upon herself As having fail'd in duty   ,,   277
clapt her hands and *c* for war,   *Princess iv* 590
So thrice they *c*, I likewise,   ,, *Con.* 104
I *c* myself well-nigh blind,   *Grandmother* 37
Like those who *c* Diana great ;   *Lit. Squabbles* 16
So thick they died the people *c*,   *The Victim* 5
And *c* with joy, ' The Gods have answer'd :   ,,   38

Cried (*continued*) my own sad name in corners *c*, — *Maud I vi* 72
Arthur *c* to rend the cloth (repeat) — *Gareth and L.* 400, 417
when mounted, *c* from o'er the bridge, — *Gareth and L.* 951
Then *c* the fall'n, 'Take not my life: — " 973
C out with a big voice, 'What, is he dead?' — *Geraint and E.* 541
Here the huge Earl *c* out upon her talk, — " 651
had you *c*, or knelt, or pray'd to me, — " 844
more than one of us *C* out on Garlon, — *Balin and Balan* 123
lost itself in darkness, till she *c*— — " 514
I *c* because ye would not pass Beyond it, — *Lancelot and E.* 1042
So many knights that all the people *c*, — *Holy Grail* 335
'That so *c* out upon me?' — " 433
left alone once more, and *c* in grief, — " 437
'Queen of Beauty,' in the lists *C*— — *Pelleas and E.* 117
his helpless heart Leapt, and he *c*, — " 131
from the tower above him *c* Ettarre, — " 231
'And oft in dying *c* upon your name.' — " 385
And woke again in utter dark, and *c*, — *Last Tournament* 623
We *c* when we were parted: — *Lover's Tale i* 253
the bones that had laughed and had *c*— — *Rizpah* 53
Sir Richard *c* in his English pride, — *The Revenge* 82
An' I *c* along wi' the gells, — *Village Wife* 96
Fur, lawks! 'ow I *c* when they went, — " 111
Some *c* on Cobham, on the good Lord Cobham; — *Sir J. Oldcastle* 43
a score of wild birds *C* from the topmost summit — *V. of Maeldune* 28
Once in an hour they *c*, — " 29
An' I could *c* a ammost, — *Spinster's S's.* 47
c the king of sacred song; — *Locksley H., Sixty* 201
And the Muses *c* with a stormy cry — *Dead Prophet* 2
till I *c* again: 'O Miriam, if you love me — *The Ring* 262
I *c* for nurse, and felt a gentle hand — " 418
I *c* to the Saints to avenge me. — *Bandit's Death* 14
that the boy never *c* again. — " 28
Crime thorough-edged intellect to part Error from *c*; — *Isabel* 15
And all alone in *c*: — *Palace of Art* 272
'Heaven heads the count of *c*'s — *D. of F. Women* 201
When single thought is civil *c*, — 'You ask me, why, 19
if it were thine error or thy *c* — *Come not, when, etc.* 7
it was a *c* Of sense avenged by sense — *Vision of Sin* 213
'The *c* of sense became The *c* of malice, — " 215
keeps his wing'd affections clipt with *c*: — *Princess vii* 316
Yet clearest of ambitious *c*, — *Ode on Well.* 28
to dodge and palter with a public *c*? — *Third of Feb.* 24
And ever weaker grows thro' acted *c*, — *Will* 12
Unfetter'd by the sense of *c*, — *In Mem. xxvii* 7
Day, mark'd as with some hideous *c*, — " *lxxii* 18
I count it *c* To mourn for any overmuch; — " *lxxxv* 61
Perhaps from madness, perhaps from *c*, — *Maud I xvi* 22
came to loathe His *c* of traitor, — *Marr. of Geraint* 594
call him the main cause of all their *c*; — *Merlin and V.* 788
that most impute a *c* Are pronest to it, — " 825
all her *c*, All—all—the wish to prove him — " 864
blaze the *c* of Lancelot and the Queen.' — *Pelleas and E.* 570
Lured by the *c*'s and frailties of the court, — *Guinevere* 136
think not that I come to urge thy *c*'s, — " 532
A shameful sense as of a cleaving *c*— — *Lover's Tale i* 794
or such *c*'s As holy Paul— — *Sir J. Oldcastle* 109
curbing *c*'s that scandalised the Cross, — *Columbus* 193
But the *c*, if a *c*, of her eldest-born, — *Despair* 73
crown'd for a virtue, or hang'd for a *c*? — " 76
C and hunger cast our maidens — *Locksley H., Sixty* 220
'Who was witness of the *c*? — *Forlorn* 7
His *c* was of the senses: — *Romney's R.* 151
Whose *c* had half unpeopled Ilion, — *Death of Œnone* 61
his kisses were red with his *c*, — *Bandit's Death* 13
Crimson (*adj.*) (*See also* **Silvery-crimson**) above, *C*,
  a slender banneret fluttering. — *Gareth and L.* 913
c in the belt of strange device, A *c* grail — *Holy Grail* 154
All pall'd in *c* samite, — " 847
We steer'd her toward a *c* cloud, — *In Mem. ciii* 55
c with battles, and hollow with graves, — *The Dreamer* 12
Crimson (*s*) long-hair'd page in *c* clad, — *L. of Shalott ii* 22
Till all the *c* changed, and past — *Mariana in the S.* 25
In the Spring a fuller *c* comes — *Locksley Hall* 17
add A *c* to the quaint Macaw, — *Day-Dm., Pro.* 16

Crimson (*s*) (*continued*) rocket molten into flakes Of *c* — *In Mem. xcviii* 32
Sunder the glooming *c* on the marge, — *Gareth and L.* 1365
In *c*'s and in purples and in gems. — *Marr. of Geraint* 10
the *c* and scarlet of berries that flamed — *V. of Maeldune* 61
Close beneath the casement *c* — *Locksley H., Sixty* 34
Was all ablaze with *c* to the roof, — *The Ring* 250
but—when now Bathed in that lurid *c*— — *St. Telemachus* 18
Crimson (*verb*) *C*'s over an inland mere, — *Eleänore* 42
Crimson-circled Before the *c-c* star — *In Mem. lxxxix* 47
Crimson'd glow that slowly *c* all Thy presence — *Tithonus* 56
Crimson-hued *c-h* the stately palmwoods Whisper — *Milton* 15
Crimson-rolling when the *c-r* eye Glares ruin, — *Princess iv* 494
Crimson-threaded When from *c-t* lips Silver-treble
  laughter trilleth: — *Lilian* 23
Cripple a story which in rougher shape Came from a
  grizzled *c*, — *Aylmer's Field* 8
he met A *c*, one that held a hand for alms— — *Pelleas and E.* 542
Crisp To make the sullen surface *c*. — *In Mem. xlix* 7
Crispeth The babbling runnel *c*, — *Claribel* 19
Critic No *c* I—would call them masterpieces: — *Princess i* 145
Musician, painter, sculptor, *c*, — " *ii* 178
And like the *c*'s blurring comment — *Sisters (E. and E.)* 104
And the *C*'s rarer still. — *Poets and Critics* 16
Critic-pen Unboding *c-p*. — *Will Water.* 12
Croak *c* thee sister, or the meadow-crake — *Princess iv* 124
When did a frog coarser *c* upon our Helicon? — *Trans. of Homer* 4
For a raven ever *c*'s, at my side, — *Maud I vi* 19
Once at the *c* of a Raven who crost it, — *Merlin and the G.* 24
Croak'd A blot in heaven, the Raven, flying high, *C*, — *Guinevere* 134
Crocodile *C*'s wept tears for thee: — *A Dirge* 22
Crocus at their feet the *c* brake like fire, — *Œnone* 96
From one hand droop'd a *c*: — *Palace of Art* 119
C, anemone, violet, — *To F. D. Maurice* 44
And we roll'd upon capes of *c* — *V. of Maeldune* 47
in this roaring moon of daffodil And *c*, — *Pref. Son. 19th Cent.* 8
groundflame of the *c* breaks the mould, — *Prog. of Spring* 1
Croft Thro' *c*'s and pastures wet with dew — *Two Voices* 14
Started a green linnet Out of the *c*; — *Minnie and Winnie* 18
an' thy windmill oop o' the *c*, — *Spinster's S's.* 73
Cromlech And cleaves to cairn and *c* still; — *To the Queen ii* 41
Crone rhymes and scraps of ancient *c*'s, — *Lover's Tale i* 289
Garrulous old *c*, — *The Ring* 120
Crook *C* and turn upon itself — *Locksley H., Sixty* 236
Crooked Lame, *c*, reeling, livid, — *Death of Œnone* 27
Crop (*of a bird*) And cramm'd a plumper *c*; — *Will Water.* 124
Like any pigeon will I cram his *c*, — *Gareth and L.* 459
Crop (*verb*) call him overquick To *c* his own sweet rose — *Merlin and V.* 725
Cropt They might have *c* the myriad flower of May, — *Balin and Balan* 577
Cross (*s*) (*See also* **Catholic Cross, Crass, Market-Cross**)
A broken chancel with a broken *c*, — *M. d'Arthur* 9
I lift the *c*, and strive and wrestle — *St. S. Stylites* 118
I smote them with the *c*; — " 173
Fly happy with the mission of the *C*; — *Golden Year* 43
Made Him his catspaw and the *C* his tool, — *Sea Dreams* 190
They mark'd it with the red *c* to the fall, — *Princess vi* 41
Under the *c* of gold That shines — *Ode on Well.* 49
roll'd Thro' the dome of the golden *c*; — " 61
the *c* And those around it and the Crucified, — *Com. of Arthur* 272
like the *c* her great and goodly arms Stretch'd — *Gareth and L.* 358
Thorns of the crown and shivers of the *c*, — *Balin and Balan* 111
beat the *c* to earth, and break the King — " 458
lone woman, weeping near a *c*, Stay'd him. — *Last Tournament* 493
A broken chancel with a broken *c*, — *Pass. of Arthur* 177
the copse, the fountain and—a *C*! — *Sir J. Oldcastle* 127
how I anger'd Arundel asking me To worship Holy *C*! — " 136
I said, a *c* of flesh and blood And holier. — " 137
we, who bore the *C* Thither, were excommunicated — *Columbus* 191
curbing crimes that scandalised the *C*, — " 193
He that has nail'd all flesh to the *C*, — *Vastness* 28
My soldier of the *C*? it is he and he — *Happy* 12
My warrior of the Holy *C* and of the conquering sword, — " 21
yesterday They bore the *C* before you — " 48
Touch'd at the golden *C* of the churches, — *Merlin and the G.* 68
under the *C*'es The dead man's garden, — " 105
sunset glared against a *c* — *St. Telemachus* 5

Cross (verb) Nor any cloud would *c* the vault — *Mariana in the S.* 38
he was wrong to *c* his father thus : — *Dora* 148
Should my Shadow *c* thy thoughts Too sadly — *Love and Duty* 88
Should it *c* thy dreams, O might it come — „ 92
the lonely seabird *c'es* With one waft of the wing. — *The Captain* 71
Not for three years to *c* the liberties ; — *Princess* ii 71
It *c'es* here, it *c'es* there, — *Maud* II iv 70
never shadow of mistrust can *c* Between us. — *Marr. of Geraint* 815
shadow of mistrust should never *c* — *Geraint and E.* 248
Your leave, my lord, to *c* the room, — „ 298
He shall not *c* us more ; — „ 342
I forbear you thus : *c* me no more. — „ 678
To *c* our mighty Lancelot in his loves ! — *Lancelot and E.* 688
To *c* between their happy star and them ? — *Lover's Tale* i 730
Cross-bones carved *c-b*, the types of Death, — *Will Water.* 245
Cross'd-Crost (*See also* **Crasst**) And they *cross'd* themselves for fear, — *L. of Shalott* iv 49
Sometimes your shadow *cross'd* the blind. — *Miller's D.* 124
And *cross'd* the garden to the gardener's lodge, — *Audley Court* 7
then we *crost* Between the lakes, and clamber'd — *Golden Year* 5
And seldom *crost* her threshold, — *Enoch Arden* 337
Abhorrent of a calculation *crost*, — „ 473
crost By that old bridge which, half in ruins — *The Brook* 78
where the waters marry—*crost*, Whistling a random bar — „ 81
Then *crost* the common into Darnley chase — „ 132
He seldom *crost* his child without a sneer ; — *Aylmer's Field* 562
then we *crost* To a livelier land ; — *Princess* i 109
back again we *crost* the court To Lady Psyche's : — „ ii 100
We *cross'd* the street and gain'd a petty mound — „ iv 557
But when we *crost* the Lombard plain — *The Daisy* 49
The shade by which my life was *crost*, — *In Mem.* lxvi 5
little thumb, That *crost* the trencher — *Marr. of Geraint* 396
Crost and came near, lifted adoring eyes, — *Geraint and E.* 304
A walk of lilies *crost* it to the bower : — *Balin and Balan* 243
every margin scribbled, *crost*, and cramm'd With comment, — *Merlin and V.* 677
was it earthly passion *crost*? ' — *Holy Grail* 29
with the bones of men, Not to be *crost*, — „ 501
every bridge as quickly as he *crost* Sprang into fire — „ 505
crost the dimness of a cloud Floating, — *Pelleas and E.* 37
Then he *crost* the court, And spied not any light — „ 418
her thin hands *crost* on her breast— — *In the Child. Hosp.* 39
Wiclif-preacher whom I *crost* In flying hither ? — *Sir J. Oldcastle* 38
Cross'd! for once he sailed the sea — *Locksley H., Sixty* 29
at the croak of a Raven who *crost* it, — *Merlin and the G.* 24
shadowy fighters *crost* The disk, — *St. Telemachus* 23
When I have *crost* the bar. — *Crossing the Bar* 16
Crossing (part) And, *c*, oft we saw the glisten — *The Daisy* 35
I past him, I was *c* his lands ; — *Maud* I xiii 6
Rivulet *c* my ground, — „ xxi 1
Guinevere was *c* the great hall Cast herself down, — *Merlin and V.* 65
c her own picture as she came, — *Lover's Tale* iv 286
we saw your soldiers *c* the ridge, — *Bandit's Death* 21
Crossing (s) Who sweep the *c's*, wet or dry, — *Will Water.* 47
Cross-lightnings *c-l* of four chance-met eyes — *Aylmer's Field* 129
Cross-pipes carved *c-p*, and, underneath, — *Will Water.* 247
Cross-road stake and the *c-r*, fool, if you will, — *Despair* 116
Crost *See* **Cross'd**
Crotchet Chimeras, *c's*, Christmas solecisms, — *Princess*, Pro. 203
Crouch'd with playful tail *C* fawning in the weed. — *Œnone* 201
I *c* on one that rose Twenty by measure ; — *St. S. Stylites* 88
I *c* upon deck— — *The Wreck* 120
She *c*, she tore him part from part, — *Dead Prophet* 69
heard as we *c* below, The clatter of arms, — *Bandit's Death* 23
Crow (s) (*See also* **Craw**) Perch'd like a *c* upon a three-legg'd stool, — *Audley Court* 45
many-winter'd *c* that leads — *Locksley Hall* 68
ere the hateful *c* shall tread The corners — *Will Water.* 235
a troop of carrion *c's* Hung like a cloud — *Merlin and V.* 598
sober rook And carrion *c* cry ' Mortgage.' — *The Ring* 174
Crow (verb) she heard the night-fowl *c* : — *Mariana* 26
Before the red cock *c's* from the farm — *May Queen, N. Y's. E.* 23
The cock *c's* ere the Christmas morn, — *Sir Galahad* 51
And the cock couldn't *c*, — *V. of Maeldune* 18
and *c's* to the sun and the moon, — *Despair* 90

Crow (verb) *continued* he *c's* before his time ; — *The Flight* 3
Crowd (s) I saw *c's* in columned sanctuaries : — *D. of F. Women* 22
The *c's*, the temples, waver'd — „ 114
To me, methought, who waited with a *c*, — *M. d'Arthur*, Ep. 20
A *c* of hopes, That sought to sow themselves — *Gardener's D.* 64
To tear his heart before the *c* ! — *You might have won* 36
those that held their heads above the *c*, — *The Brook* 10
Among the honest shoulders of the *c*, — *Sea Dreams* 166
while none mark'd it, on the *c* Broke, — „ 234
c's that in an hour Of civic tumult — *Lucretius* 168
they gave The park, the *c*, the house ; — *Princess*, Pro. 94
preach'd An universal culture for the *c*, — „ 109
as we came, the *c* dividing clove An advent — „ iv 283
I know Your faces there in the *c*— — „ 510
thereat the *c* Muttering, dissolved : — „ 522
the *c* were swarming now, To take their leave, — „ Con. 37
civic manhood firm against the *c*— — „ 57
For me, the genial day, the happy *c*, — „ 75
let the sorrowing *c* about it grow, — *Ode on Well.* 16
Till *c's* at length be sane and crowns be just. — „ 169
dark *c* moves, and there are sobs and tears ; — „ 268
c's that stream from yawning doors, — *In Mem.* lxx 9
more content, He told me, lives in any *c*, — „ xcviii 26
To fool the *c* with glorious lies, — „ cxxviii 14
Thro' all that *c* confused and loud, — *Maud* II iv 71
turn thy wheel above the staring *c* ; — *Marr. of Geraint* 356
such blows, that all the *c* Wonder'd, — „ 564
and in this Are harlots like the *c*, — *Merlin and V.* 831
c Will murmur, ' Lo the shameless ones, — *Lancelot and E.* 99
Then of the *c* ye took no more account — „ 105
And by the gateway stirr'd a *c* ; — *Holy Grail* 424
rough *c*, Hearing he had a difference with their priests, — „ 673
no precaution used, among the *c*, — *Guinevere* 519
But as a Latin Bible to the *c* ; — *Sir J. Oldcastle* 18
And then in Latin to the Latin *c*, — „ 31
a *c* Throng'd the waste field about the city gates : — „ 39
I saw your face that morning in the *c*. — *Columbus* 7
the *c* would roar For blood, for war, — *Tiresias* 64
the heart of a listening *c*— — *The Wreck* 47
dark-muffled Russian *c* Folded its wings — *Heavy Brigade* 38
That all the *c* might stare. — *Dead Prophet* 16
lawless crown As of the lawless *c* ; — *Freedom* 32
there past a *c* With shameless laughter, — *St. Telemachus* 38
draw The *c* from wallowing in the mire — *Akbar's Dream* 141
Crowd (verb) They come, they *c* upon me all at once — *Lover's Tale* i 47
Launch your vessel, And *c* your canvas, — *Merlin and the G.* 127
Crowded *C* with driving atomies, — *Lover's Tale* ii 174
Crow'd *C* lustier late and early, — *Will Water.* 126
maid, That ever *c* for kisses.' — *Princess* ii 280
The cock has *c* already once, — *The Flight* 3
Crowfoot cowslip and the *c* are over all the hill, — *May Queen* 38
Crowing (*See also* **A-crawin'**, **Crawin'**) At midnight the cock was *c*, — *Oriana* 12
Came *c* over Thames. — *Will Water.* 140
Crown (diadem, etc.) Revered Isabel, the *c* and head, — *Isabel* 10
better than to own A *c*, a sceptre, — *Ode to Memory* 121
With a *c* of gold, On a throne? — *The Merman* 6
under my starry sea-bud *c* Low adown — *The Mermaid* 16
Gliding with equal *c's* two serpents led — *Alexander* 6
his ample bound to some new *c* :— — *Poland* 8
from his cold *c* And crystal silence — *Two Voices* 85
Ilion's column'd citadel, The *c* of Troas. — *Œnone* 14
from all neighbour *c's* Alliance and allegiance, — „ 124
rolling to and fro The heads and *c's* of kings ; — *Palace of Art* 152
Last May we made a *c* of flowers : — *May Queen, N. Y's. E.* 9
only toil, the roof and *c* of things ? — *Lotos-Eaters*, C. S. 24
soldier found Me lying dead, my *c* about my brows, — *D. of F. Women* 162
And, King-like, wears the *c* : — *Of old sat Freedom* 16
Three Queens with *c's* of gold— — *M. d'Arthur* 198
those moments when we met, The *c* of all, — *Edwin Morris* 70
the angel there That holds a *c* ? — *St. S. Stylites* 204
'tis here again ; the *c* ! the *c* ! — „ 208
That a sorrow's *c* of sorrow is — *Locksley Hall* 76
The mountain stirr'd its bushy *c*, — *Amphion* 25
In robe and *c* the King stept down, — *Beggar Maid* 5

E*

Crown (diadem, etc.) (continued)   doom Of those

that wear the Poet's c:	You might have won 10
slender coco's drooping c of plumes,	Enoch Arden 574
And so she wears her error like a c	Princess iii 111
gold That veins the world were pack'd to make your c,	„ iv 543
one that sought but Duty's iron c	Ode on Well. 122
crowds at length be sane and c's be just.	„ 169
he wears a truer c Than any wreath	„ 276
It wore a c of light,	The Flower 10
And you my wren with a c of gold,	Window. Spring 1
flit like the king of the wrens with a c of fire.	„ Ay. 16
I wore them like a civic c:	In Mem. lxix 8
The fool that wears a c of thorns:	„ 12
He look'd upon my c and smiled:	„ 16
But ill for him that wears a c,	„ cxxvii 9
has past and leaves The C a lonely splendour.	Ded. of Idylls 49
More like are we to reave him of his c	Gareth and L. 419
Thorns of the c and shivers of the cross,	Balin and Balan 111
'Thou shalt put the c to use. The c is but the shadow of the King,	„ 202
Balin bare the c, and all the knights Approved him,	„ 209
Before another wood, the royal c Sparkled,	„ 462
'Lo there' she cried—'a c—	„ 465
I charge thee by that c upon thy shield,	„ 481
Drove his mail'd heel athwart the royal c,	„ 540
Else never had he borne her c,	„ 566
Trampled ye thus on that which bare the C?'	„ 602
wreath of beauty thine the c of power,	Merlin and V. 79
he, that once was king, had on a c Of diamonds,	Lancelot and E. 45
from the skull the c Roll'd into light,	„ 50
he had the gems Pluck'd from the c,	„ 57
Since to his c the golden dragon clung,	„ 434
statue in the mould Of Arthur, made by Merlin, with a c,	Holy Grail 239
the c And both the wings are made of gold,	„ 241
a c of gold About a casque all jewels ;	„ 410
And from the c thereof a carcanet Of ruby	Last Tournament 6
high on land, A c of towers.	„ 506
then this c of towers So shook to such a roar	„ 620
Three queens with c's of gold :	Pass. of Arthur 366
The loyal to their c Are loyal to their own far sons,	To the Queen ii 27
great c of beams about his brows—	Lover's Tale i 672
the cope and c Of all I hoped and fear'd ?	„ ii 27
clutch'd the sacred c of Prester John,	Columbus 110
feed the rebels of the c,	„ 131
A c the Singer hopes may last,	Epilogue 38
I should wear my c entire	Helen's Tower 9
Thou loather of the lawless c	Freedom 31
Wilt neither quit the widow'd C	Prin. Beatrice 15
To wreathe a c not only for the king	Akbar's Dream 23
The shadow of a c, that o'er him hung,	D. of the Duke of C. 2

Crown (five shillings) (See also Half-crown) and

he gave the ringers a c.	Grandmother 58

Crown (verb)

this high dial, which my sorrow c's—	St. S. Stylites 95
C thyself, worm, and worship thine own lusts !—	Aylmer's Field 650
you fair stars that c a happy day	Maud I xviii 30
c thee king Far in the spiritual city :'	Holy Grail 161
and one will c me king Far in the spiritual city ;	„ 482
However they may c him otherwhere.	„ 902
To c it with herself.	Lover's Tale i 63
who c's himself Above the naked poisons	„ 355
It still were right to c with song	Epilogue 36

Crown'd (See also Citadel-crown'd, Fire-crown'd, Glory-crown'd)

'The simple senses c his head :	Two Voices 277
night divine C dying day with stars,	Palace of Art 184
A name for ever !—lying robed and c,	D. of F. Women 163
I shall be saved ; Yea, c a saint.	St. S. Stylites 153
Catch me who can, and make the catcher c—	Golden Year 18
reissuing, robed and c, To meet her lord,	Godiva 77
Like Heavenly hope she c the sea,	The Voyage 70
and true love C after trial ;	Aylmer's Field 100
two fair images, Both c with stars	Sea Dreams 241
C with a flower or two,	Lucretius 229
and c with all her flowers.	Ode Inter. Exhib. 41
And, c with all the season lent,	In Mem. xxii 6
c The purple brows of Olivet.	„ xxxi 11

Crown'd (continued)

When c with blessing she doth rise	In Mem. xl 5
I see thee sitting c with good,	„ lxxxiv 5
Or, c with attributes of woe	„ cxviii 18
for he heard of Arthur newly c,	Com. of Arthur 41
clamour'd for a king, Had Arthur c ;	„ 236
Arthur sat C on the daïs,	„ 258
the King stood out in heaven, C.	„ 444
And c with fleshless laughter—	Gareth and L. 1383
he c A happy life with a fair death,	Geraint and E. 967
had I c With my slain self the heaps	Balin and Balan 177
were he not c King, coward, and fool.'	Merlin and V. 789
Her godlike head c with spiritual fire,	„ 837
Arthur, long before they c him King,	Lancelot and E. 34
Lancelot's azure lions, c with gold,	„ 663
the gilded parapets were c With faces,	Pelleas and E. 165
there before the people c herself :	„ 174
c the state pavilion of the King,	Guinevere 399
dying thus, C with her highest act	Lover's Tale i 216
with my work thus C her clear forehead.	„ 345
where that day I c myself as king,	„ 592
Julian, who himself was c With roses,	„ iv 296
There c with worship—	Tiresias 175
whether c for a virtue, or hang'd for a crime ?	Despair 76
Her shadow c with stars—	Ancient Sage 201
songs in praise of death, and c with flowers !	„ 209
C with sunlight—over darkness—	Locksley H., Sixty 92
C so long with a diadem Never worn by a worthier,	On Jub. Q. Victoria 7
Love for the maiden, c with marriage,	Vastness 23
maiden-Princess, c with flowers,	The Ring 485
the c ones all disappearing !	Parnassus 13
C her knights, and flush'd as red As poppies when she c it.	The Tourney 16

Crowning

Knighted by Arthur at his c—	Com. of Arthur 175
And c's and dethronements :	To the Queen ii 45

Crown-farm   Sold the c-f's for all but nothing,   Columbus 132

Crown-royal

bear her own c-r upon shield,	Balin and Balan 200
Why wear ye this c-r upon shield ?'	„ 338
'Why wear ye that c-r ?'	„ 348

Crown-scandalous   wear ye still that same c-s ?'   „ 390

Crowsfoot   Made wet the crafty c round his eye ;   Sea Dreams 187

Crucified

either they were stoned or c,	St. S. Stylites 51
the cross And those around it and the C,	Com. of Arthur 273

Crucifix   Or the maid-mother by a c,   Palace of Art 93

Cruel

c as a schoolboy ere he grows To Pity—	Walk. to the Mail 109
'C, the words I said !	Edward Gray 17
more harsh and c Seem'd the Captain's mood.	The Captain 13
no tenderness—Too hard, too c :	Princess v 516
O c, there was nothing wild or strange,	Merlin and V. 860

Cruel-hearted   They call me c-h, but I care not   May Queen 19

Crueller

C : as not passing thro' the fire	Aylmer's Field 671
'O c than was ever told in tale,	Merlin and V. 858
which was c ? which was worse ?	Locksley H., Sixty 88

Cruelty   Infinite c rather that made everlasting Hell,   Despair 96

Cruet   gentlemen, That trifle with the c.   Will Water. 232

Crumble

touch it, it will c into dust.'	Holy Grail 439
and they c into dust.	Locksley H., Sixty 72

Crumbled

Till public wrong be c into dust,	Ode on Well. 167
Fell into dust, and c in the dark—	Lover's Tale i 95

Crumpled

More than a poppy from the sheath,	Princess v 29
the rest Were c inwards.	The Ring 454

Crupper

Beyond his horse's c and the bridge,	Gareth and L. 966
length of lance and arm beyond The c,	Geraint and E. 464

Crusade

to lead A new c against the Saracen,	Columbus 103
lead One last c against the Saracen,	„ 239

Crush (s)   great the c was, and each base,   Princess vi 353

Crush (verb)

Like a rose-leaf I will c thee,	Lilian 29
Will c her pretty maiden fancies dead	Princess i 88
Or c her, like a vice of blood,	In Mem. iii 15
this Order lives to c All wrongers	Gareth and L. 625
when I thought he meant To c me,	Holy Grail 416
he sail'd the sea to c the Moslem in his pride ;	Locksley H., Sixty 29

Crush'd (See also Half-crushed)

I c them on my breast, my mouth ;	Fatima 12
sin, that c My spirit flat before thee.	St. S. Stylites 25
like monstrous apes they c my chest :	„ 174

Cry (verb) (*continued*) rose *cries*, 'She is near, she is near;' *Maud I xxii* 63
I will *c* to the steps above my head   " *II v* 101
A *c* from out the dawning of my life, *Com. of Arthur* 333
Who will *c* shame? *Gareth and L.* 942
and *c*, 'Thou hast made us lords, " 1131
mother-maidenhood of Heaven, *C* out upon her. *Balin and Balan* 522
children cast their pins and nails, and *c*, *Merlin and V.* 430
she heard Sir Lancelot *c* in the court, *Lancelot and E.* 344
I *c* my cry in silence, *Guinevere* 201
'O mother!' I heard him *c*. *Rizpah* 42
an' saw she begins to *c*, *North. Cobbler* 71
I should *c* to the dear Lord Jesus to help me, *In the Child. Hosp.* 49
Before thy light, and *c* continually—*C* *Sir J. Oldcastle* 85
that men *C* out against thee : *Columbus* 153
So dark that men *c* out against the Heavens. *Ancient Sage* 172
weep my fill once more, and *c* myself to rest ! *The Flight* 6
Cries to Weakest as to Strongest, *Locksley H., Sixty* 110
Nay, your pardon, *c* your 'forward,' " 225
Too many a voice may *c* That man *Epilogue* 72
Far off a phantom cuckoo *cries* *Pref. Poem Broth. S.* 19
sober rook And carrion crow *c* 'Mortgage.' *The Ring* 174
Nor even a Sir Joshua, some will *c*, *Romney's R.* 47
some *c* 'Quick' and some *c* 'Slow,' *Politics* 9
Shall the rose *C* to the lotus *Akbar's Dream* 37
And a beggar began to *c* 'Food, food *Voice spake, etc.* 5
Cryin' (part) an' *c* and teärin' 'er 'aäir, *North. Cobbler* 34
but we hard it *c*, 'Ochone!' *Tomorrow* 84
Crying (part) (*See also* **A-cryin', Cryin', Keenin'**) *c* to
each other And calling, *Enoch Arden* 382
C with a loud voice 'A sail ! " 913
And *c* upon the name of Leolin, *Aylmer's Field* 576
Some *c* there was an army in the land, *Princess iv* 484
An infant *c* in the night : An infant *c* for the light : *In Mem. liv* 18
But, *c*, knows his father near ; " *cxxiv* 20
They were *c* and calling. *Maud I xii* 4
Were *c* and calling to her, " 26
many another suppliant *c* came With noise *Gareth and L.* 436
Then came a widow *c* to the King, " 333
Came yet another widow *c* to him, " 350
Gareth *c* prick'd against the cry ; " 1221
flying back and *c* out, 'O Merlin, *Merlin and V.* 943
And all his legions *c* Christ and him, *Lancelot and E.* 305
c that his prize is death.' " 531
maiden sprang into the hall *C* on help : *Holy Grail* 209
c with full voice 'Traitor, come out, *Guinevere* 105
Whereat the novice *c*, with clasp'd hands, " 311
Two friars *c* that if Spain should oust *Columbus* 96
c after voices that have fled ! *Locksley H., Sixty* 251
Crying (s) mine but from the *c* of a child.' *Sea Dreams* 249
Whose *c* is a cry for gold ? *The Daisy* 94
and *c's* for the light, *Pass. of Arthur* 116
Or at my *c* 'Mother ?' *The Ring* 141
Crypt My knees are bow'd in *c* and shrine : *Sir Galahad* 18
And fall'n into the dusty *c* *Will Water.* 183
those cold *c's* where they shall cease. *In Mem. lviii* 8
Crystal And down the streaming *c* dropt ; *Princess vii* 165
In a shallop of *c* ivory-beak'd, *The Islet* 12
Became a *c*, and he saw them thro' it, *Merlin and V.* 630
c into which I braided Edwin's hair ! *The Flight* 34
Cube hard-grain'd Muses of the *c* and square *Princess, Pro.* 180
Cubit lived upon a pillar, high Six *c's*, *St. S. Stylites* 87
numbers forty *c's* from the soil. " 91
Drave the long spear a *c* thro' his breast *Geraint and E.* 86
Cuckoo The *c* told his name to all the hills *Gardener's D.* 93
I built the nest,' she said, 'To hatch the *c*. *Princess iv* 366
'*C*! *c*!' was ever a May so fine ? *Window. Ay* 10
'I have seen the *c* chased by lesser fowl, *Com. of Arthur* 167
Than the gray *c* loves his name, *Lover's Tale i* 257
The *c* of a joyless June Is calling out of doors : *Pref Poem Broth. S.* 3
The *c* of a worse July Is calling thro' the dark : " 11
a phantom *c* cries From out a phantom hill ; " 19
There ! I heard Our *c* call. *To Mary Boyle* 6
A clamorous *c* stoops to meet her hand ; *Prog. of Spring* 45
Cuckoo-flower As perfume of the *c-f*? *Margaret* 8
blow the faint sweet *c-f's* ; *May Queen* 30

Cud chew'd The thrice-turn'd *c* of wrath, *Princess i* 66
Cuddle as good to *c* an' kiss as a lass as 'ant nowt ? *N. Farmer, N. S.* 24
Cuddled (*See also* **Coodled**) An' we *c* and huddled together, *Owd Roä* 112
Cuff'd Caught and *c* by the gale : *Maud I vi* 5
Cuirass on his *c* work our Lady's Head, *Lancelot and E.* 294
and a spear Prick'd sharply his own *c*, " 489
Cuisses and *c* dash'd with drops Of onset ; *M. d'Arthur* 215
and *c* dash'd with drops Of onset ; *Pass. of Arthur* 383
Cull I *c* from every faith and race *Akbar's Dream* 68
Cull'd whitest honey in fairy gardens *c*— *Eleänore* 26
Because all words, *c* with choicest art, *D. of F. Women* 285
but one, by those fair fingers *c*, *Gardener's D.* 150
In mine own lady palms I *c* the spring *Merlin and V.* 273
Culminate lead The new light up, and *c* in peace, *Princess ii* 348
Culmination All starry *c* drop Balm-dews *Talking Oak* 267
Cultivation months of toil, And years of *c*, *Amphion* 98
Culture An universal *c* for the crowd, *Princess, Pro.* 109
whence they need More breadth of *c* : " *v* 188
Culver round her brows a woodland *c* flits, *Prog. of Spring* 18
Cunning-simple So innocent-arch, so *c-s*, *Lilian* 13
Cúnobeline rioted in the city of *C* ! *Boädicea* 60
Cup I drink the *c* of a costly death, *Eleänore* 138
I pledge her not in any cheerful *c*, *Wan Sculptor* 2
Three fingers round the old silver *c*— *Miller's D.* 10
incense of all odour steam'd From out a golden *c*. *Palace of Art* 40
That was the last drop in the *c* of gall. *Walk. to the Mail* 90
My little oakling from the *c*, *Talking Oak* 231
Will haunt the vacant *c* : *Will Water.* 172
'Fill the *c*, and fill the can : (repeat) *Vision of Sin* 95, 119, 203
'Fill the can, and fill the *c* : (repeat) " 131, 167
c's and silver on the burnish'd board Sparkled *Enoch Arden* 742
The magic *c* that fill'd itself anew. *Aylmer's Field* 143
Only such *c's* as left us friendly-warm, *Lucretius* 215
There they drank in *c's* of emerald, *Boädicea* 64
The crowning *c*, the three-times-three, *In Mem. Con.* 104
they sat, And *c* clash'd *c* ; *Balin and Balan* 85
to hurl his *c* Straight at the speaker, *Merlin and V.* 30
Except indeed to drink : no *c* had we : " 272
made a pretty *c* of both my hands " 275
phantom of a *c* that comes and goes ?' *Holy Grail* 44
'The *c*, the *c* itself, from which our Lord " 46
the holy *c* Was caught away to Heaven, " 57
Lancelot might have seen, The Holy *C* of healing ; " 655
hast thou seen the Holy *C*, " 734
children sat in white with *c's* of gold, *Last Tournament* 142
And them that round it sat with golden *c's* " 289
white slips Handed her *c* and piped, " 296
the *c* was gold, the draught was mud.' " 298
c's Where nymph and god ran ever round *Lover's Tale iv* 196
Warm as the crocus *c*, *Early Spring* 29
wines of heresy in the *c* Of counsel— *Akbar's Dream* 174
Cupid The rentroll *C* of our rainy isles. *Edwin Morris* 103
The modish *C* of the day, *Talking Oak* 67
The seal was *C* bent above a scroll, *Princess i* 242
Cupid-boys By *C-b* of blooming hue— *Day-Dm., Ep.* 10
Cur yelp'd the *c*, and yawl'd the cat ; *The Goose* 33
the barking *c* Made her cheek flame : *Godiva* 57
c Pluckt from the *c* he fights with, *Gareth and L.* 701
Curate and with Edward Bull The *c* ; *Edwin Morris* 15
said the fat-faced *c* Edward Bull, (repeat) " 42, 90
'e's nobbut a *c*, an' weänt niver git hissen clear, *N. Farmer, N. S.* 27
An' thou'll be 'is *C* 'ere, *Church-warden, etc.* 45
Curb 'Wild natures need wise *c's*. *Princess v* 173
mine the voice to *c* The madness *Tiresias* 70
c the beast would cast thee in the mire, *Ancient Sage* 276
Curb'd strongly groom'd and straitly *c* *Princess v* 456
Curdled half the wolf's-milk *c* in their veins, " *vii* 130
Cure (curacy) The curate ; he was fatter than his *c*. *Edwin Morris* 15
Cure (remedy) declined, And trusted any *c*. *Palace of Art* 156
Wonderful *c's* he had done, O yes, *In the Child. Hosp.* 5
Cured *C* lameness, palsies, cancers. *St. S. Stylites* 82
And *c* some halt and maim'd ; " 137
could only be *c*, if *c*, by the surgeon's knife, *Despair* 80
Curious Hetairai, *c* in their art, *Lucretius*

Curious (*continued*) Too *c* Vivien, tho' you talk of trust, *Merlin and V.* 358
Not ever be too *c* for a boon,   ,, 486
You are *c*. How should I tell?   *Despair* 3
Curiousness In children a great *c* be well, *Merlin and V.* 364
Curl (s) his ridges are not *c's* And ripples *Supp. Confessions* 130
In many a dark delicious *c*, *Arabian Nights* 139
In a golden *c* With a comb of pearl, *The Mermaid* 6
flow'd His coal-black *c's* as on he rode, *L. of Shalott* iii 31
fingers drew Her streaming *c's* of deepest brown *Mariana in the S.* 16
and the light and lustrous *c's*— *M. d'Arthur* 216
dim *c's* kindle into sunny rings; *Tithonus* 54
And moves not on the rounded *c*. *Day-Dm., Sleep. B.* 8
took him by the *c's*, and led him in, *Vision of Sin* 6
from his baby's forehead clipt A tiny *c*, and gave it: *Enoch Arden* 236
The hand that play'd the patron with her *c's*. *Princess, Pro.* 138
Melissa shook her doubtful *c's*,   ,, iii 75
From the flaxen *c* to the gray lock   ,, iv 426
on their *c's* From the high tree the blossom wavering fell,   ,, vi 79
And down dead-heavy sank her *c's*,   ,, 147
And winds their *c's* about his hand: *In Mem. lxvi* 12
little head, sunning over with *c's*, *Maud I xxii* 57
Perchance, one *c* of Arthur's golden beard. *Merlin and V.* 58
and the light and lustrous *c's*— *Pass. of Arthur* 384
One golden *c*, his golden gift, *The Flight* 36
begun to gleam Thro' youthful *c's*, *To Mary Boyle* 42
Curl (verb) *c* round my silver feet silently, *The Mermaid* 50
May serve to *c* a maiden's locks, *In Mem. lxxvii* 7
Began to move, seethe, twine and *c*: *Gareth and L.* 234
Curl'd about His dusty forehead drily *c*, *Miller's D.* 6
I *c* and comb'd his comely head, *The Sisters* 31
on herself her serpent pride had *c*. *Palace of Art* 257
the clouds are lightly *c* Round their golden houses, *Lotos-Eaters, C. S.* 112
Faint shadows, vapours lightly *c*, *Day-Dm., Sleep. P.* 5
All-graceful head, so richly *c*,   ,, *L'Envoi* 38
The forest crack'd, the waters *c*, *In Mem. xv* 5
For us the same cold streamlet *c*   ,, lxxix 9
a mist Of incense *c* about her, *Com. of Arthur* 288
breeze *c* over a peacefuller sea. *The Wreck* 133
Curlew all around it, as of old, the *c's* call, *Locksley Hall* 3
while I heard the *c's* call, *Locksley H., Sixty* 3
Curn (Corn) Till I gied 'em Hinjian *c*, *Village Wife* 118
Currency brooking not Exchange or *c*: *Lover's Tale i* 448
Current (*See also* **Full-current, Main-current, Sea-current**) Till in its onward *c* it absorbs *Isabel* 31
From those four jets four *c's* in one swell *Palace of Art* 33
The ever-shifting *c's* of the blood *D. of F. Women* 133
'all the *c* of my being sets to thee.' *Locksley Hall* 34
upward runs The *c* of my days: *Will Water.* 26
turn'd The *c* of his talk to graver things *Enoch Arden* 203
Fast flow'd the *c* of her easy tears,   ,, 865
then the motion of the *c* ceased, *Sea Dreams* 117
crystal *c's* of clear morning seas. *Princess ii* 328
You turn'd your warmer *c's* all to her,   ,, iv 301
glowing in the broad Deep-dimpled *c* underneath, *Gareth and L.* 1089
and driven My *c* to the fountain whence it sprang, *Lover's Tale i* 503
But in the onward *c* of her speech,   ,, 565
Noises of a *c* narrowing, *Locksley H., Sixty* 154
alchemise old hates into the gold Of Love, and make it *c*; *Akbar's Dream* 164
Curse (s) A *c* is on her if she stay *L. of Shalott* ii 4
She knows not what the *c* may be,   ,, 6
'The *c* is come upon me,' cried The Lady   ,, iii 44
I said, 'I toil beneath the *c*, *Two Voices* 229
'My youth,' she said, ' was blasted with a *c*: *D. of F. Women* 103
This is the *c* of time. *To J. S.* 17
this world's *c*,—beloved but hated— *Love and Duty* 47
My Shakespeare's *c* on clown and knave *You might have won* 27
And left their memories a world's *c*— *Aylmer's Field* 796
A *c* in his God-bless-you: *Sea Dreams* 164
I remember'd that burnt sorcerer's *c* *Princess v* 475
when she turn'd, the *c* Had fallen, *In Mem. vi* 37
we have made them a *c*, *Maud I i* 21

Curse (s) (*continued*) She may bring me a *c*. *Maud I i* 73
the sparrow-hawk, My *c*, my nephew *Marr. of Geraint* 445
God's *c*, it makes me mad to see you weep. *Geraint and E.* 616
Thy *c*, and darken'd all thy day; *Balin and Balan* 620
'That is love's *c*; pass on, *Lancelot and E.* 1353
woman-worshipper? Yea, God's *c*, and I! *Last Tournament* 447
Until it came a kingdom's *c* with thee— *Guinevere* 550
their *c's* and their groans. *Columbus* 68
chain'd and coupled with the *c* Of blindness and their unbelief, *Tiresias* 58
blunt the *c* Of Pallas, hear,   ,, 154
never gloom'd by the *c* Of a sin, *The Wreck* 139
If a *c* meant ought, I would curse you *Despair* 64
follies, furies, *c's*, passionate tears, *Locksley H., Sixty* 39
man had coin'd himself a *c*:   ,, 87
And 'The *C* of the Prophet' in Heaven. *Dead Prophet* 28
On you will come the *c* of all the land, *The Fleet* 3
stings him back to the *c* of the light; *Vastness* 18
My *c* upon the Master's apotheosis, *Romney's R.* 37
arose The shriek and *c* of trampled millions, *Akbar's Dream* 190
I sent him a desolate wail and a *c*, *Charity* 14
Curse (verb) I *c* not nature, no, nor death; *In Mem. lxxiii* 7
c me the blabbing lip, And *c* me *Maud II v* 57
I *c* the tongue that all thro' yesterday *Gareth and L.* 1322
To *c* this hedgerow thief, *Marr. of Geraint* 309
I did not come to *c* thee, Guinevere, *Guinevere* 533
I would *c* you for not having let me be. *Despair* 64
may the Great God *c* him and bring him   ,, 106
'*C* him!' *c* your fellow-victim? *Locksley H., Sixty* 9
Cursed *c* and scorn'd, and bruised with stones: *Two Voices* 222
And bless'd herself, and *c* herself, *The Goose* 15
C be the social wants that sin against the strength of youth! *C* be the social lies that warp us from the living truth! *C* be the sickly forms that err from honest Nature's rule! *C* be the gold that gilds *Locksley Hall* 59
face Would darken, as he *c* his credulousness, *Sea Dreams* 13
C me and my flower. *The Flower* 8
I have *c* him even to lifeless things) *Maud I xix* 15
and *c* the tale, The told-of, and the teller. *Balin and Balan* 542
c The dead babe and the follies, of the King; *Last Tournament* 162
'I had sooner be *c* than kiss'd!'— *First Quarrel* 83
I, Earth-Goddess, *c* the Gods of Heaven. *Demeter and P.* 102
Snarl'd at and *c* me. *Merlin and the G.* 28
he sobb'd and he wept, And *c* himself; *Bandit's Death* 30
I had *c* the woman he married, *Charity* 24
I had *c* her as woman and wife,   ,, 31
Cursing (part.) I stood With Florian, *c* Cyril, *Princess iv* 171
I was *c* them and my doom, *Maud I xix* 51
And *c* their lost time, and the dead man, *Geraint and E.* 576
Cursing (s) she was deaf To blessing or *c*   ,, 579
Curtain (*See also* **Casement-curtain**) In the white *c*, to and fro, She saw *Mariana* 51
with thee forgets to close His *c's*, *Adeline* 43
haunted with a jolly ghost, that shook The *c's*, *Walk. to the Mail* 37
He had cast the *c's* of their seat aside— *Aylmer's Field* 803
I beheld The death-white *c* drawn; *Maud I xiv* 34
the death-white *c* meant but sleep,   ,, 37
By the *c's* of my bed   ,, II iv 54
at one end of the hall Two great funereal *c's*, *Lover's Tale iv* 214
drama's closing *c* is the pall! *Locksley H., Sixty* 62
Curtain-fold from out the silken *c-f's* *Gareth and L.* 925
Curtsey made me a mocking *c* and went. *Grandmother* 46
Curtseying *c* her obeisance, let us know The Princess Ida waited: *Princess ii* 20
Curve (s) (*See also* **Crescent-curve**) the rainbow lives in the *c* of the sand; *Sea-Fairies* 27
c's of mountain, bridge, Boat, island, *Edwin Morris* 5
In *c's* the yellowing river ran, *Sir L. and Q. G.* 15
With many a *c* my banks I fret *The Brook* 43
To left and right thro' meadowy *c's*, *In Mem. c* 15
Or the least little delicate aquiline *c* *Maud I ii* 10
in kindly *c's*, with gentlest fall, *De Prof., Two G.* 23
turn upon itself in many a backward streaming *c*. *Locksley H., Sixty* 236

Curve (verb) And out again I *c* and flow   *The Brook* 182
Curved (*See also* **Sudden-curved**) *c* an arm about
   his neck,   *Merlin and V.* 241
Curvet Making a roan horse caper and *c*   *Lancelot and E.* 792
Curving And *c* a contumelious lip,   *Maud I xiii* 20
   a procession, *c* round The silver-sheeted bay :   *Lover's Tale ii* 75
Cushie ' *C* wur craäzed fur 'er cauf '   *Spinster's S's.* 115
Cushion On silken *c*'s half reclined ;   *Eleänore* 126
   The *c*'s of whose touch may press   *Talking Oak* 179
   Tom, lig theere o' the *c*,   *Spinster's S's.* 94
Custom (habit) one good *c* should corrupt the world.   *M. d'Arthur* 242
   Appraised the Lycian *c*,   *Princess ii* 128
   Disyoke their necks from *c*,   ,, 143
   And moved beyond his *c*, Gama said :   ,, *vi* 229
   For this was Arthur's *c* in his hall ;   *Gareth and L.* 410
   And reverencing the *c* of the house   *Marr. of Geraint* 380
   pick the vicious quitch Of blood and *c*   *Geraint and E.* 904
   I rode, Shattering all evil *c*'s   *Holy Grail* 477
   one good *c* should corrupt the world.   *Pass. of Arthur* 410
   ' There is a *c* in the Orient, friends—   *Lover's Tale iv* 230
   This *c*—' Pausing here a moment,   ,, 236
   This *c* steps yet further when the guest   ,, 244
Cutsom (business) *See* **Coostom**
Cut (s) this *c* is fresh ; That ten years back ;   *Vision of Sin* 64
   Here is *c* come your way ;   *Lancelot and E.* 21
Cut (verb) *c*'s atwain The knots that tangle   *Clear-headed friend* 2
   they *c* away my tallest pines,   *Œnone* 208
   I was *c* off from hope in that sad place,   *D. of F. Women* 105
   C Prejudice against the grain :   *Love thou thy land* 22
   where the hedge-row *c*'s the pathway, stood,   *Gardener's D.* 86
   some little cloud *C*'s off the fiery highway   *Enoch Arden* 130
   C off the length of highway on before,   ,, 673
   ,, 894
   This hair is his : she *c* it off and gave it,   *Princess ii* 207
   And *c* this epitaph above my bones ;   *Boädicea* 66
   C the Roman boy to pieces   *In Mem. cxiv* 11
   What is she, *c* from love and faith,   *Maud I x* 48
   c off from the mind The bitter springs   *Marr. of Geraint* 207
   Struck at him with his whip, and *c* his cheek.   *Village Wife* 30
   es he couldn't *c* down a tree !   ,, 64
   ' Lad, thou mun *c* off thy taäil,   ,, 66
   thou'll 'gree to *c* off thy taäil   ,, 74
   to git 'im to *c* off 'is taäil.   ,, 78
   an' 'e wouldn't *c* off the taäil.   *Tomorrow* 14
   ' Goin' to *c* the Sassenach whate '   ,, 65
   c his bit o' turf for the fire ?
Cut *See also* **Clean-cut, Clear-cut**
Cuttin' betther nor *c* the Sassenach whate   *Tomorrow* 94
Cutting (*See also* **Cuttin'**) *c* eights that day upon the
   pond,   *The Epic* 10
Cycle (s) Young Nature thro' five *c*'s ran,   *Two Voices* 17
   plann'd With *c*'s of the human tale,   *Palace of Art* 146
   Better fifty years of Europe than a *c* of Cathay.   *Locksley Hall* 184
   together at her will Thro' all her *c*'s—   *Lucretius* 248
   But when their *c* is o'er,   *Voice and the P.* 26
   lead The closing *c* rich in good.   *In Mem. cv* 28
Cycle (verb) Falls off, but *c*'s always round.   *Two Voices* 348
Cycle-year Will mould him thro' the *c-y*   *Epilogue* 77
Cygnet the swan's Is tawnier than her *c*'s :   *Lancelot and E.* 1185
Cymbal people rejoice With shawms, and with *c*'s,   *Dying Swan* 32
Cypress With *c* promenaded,   *Amphion* 38
   Nor waves the *c* in the palace walk ;   *Princess vii* 177
   watch'd awake A *c* in the moonlight shake,   *The Daisy* 82
   Made *c* of her orange flower,   *In Mem. lxxxiv* 15
   rise three dark, tall *c*'es,—Three *c*'es,   *Lover's Tale i* 536
   The mountain, the three *c*'es, the cave,   ,, *ii* 109
   Break thro' the yews and *c* of thy grave,   *Ded. Poem Prin. Alice* 12
   the poplar and *c* unshaken by storm   *V. of Maeldune* 15
   the palm Call to the *c* ' I alone am fair ?'   *Akbar's Dream* 38
Cypress-cone *c-c*'s That spired above the wood ;   *Lover's Tale ii* 38
Cyril I stood With *C* and with Florian,   *Princess i* 52
   C whisper'd : ' Take me with you too.'   ,, 81
   I stole from court With *C* and with Florian,   ,, 103
   ' We of the court ' said *C*. ' From the court   ,, *ii* 48
   ' Comely, too, by all that's fair,' said *C*.   ,, 115
   ' Let me die too,' said *C*, ' having seen   ,, 210

Cyril (*continued*) ' You are that Psyche,' *C* said,
   (repeat)   *Princess ii* 256, 278
   Said *C*, ' Madam, he the wisest man   ,, 350
   C took the child, And held her round   ,, 362
   Said *C* : ' Pale one, blush again :   ,, *iii* 67
   As if to close with *C*'s random wish :   ,, 101
   Hither came *C*, and yawning ' O hard task,'   ,, 124
   then, climbing, *C* kept With Psyche,   ,, 354
   C, with whom the bell-mouth'd glass had wrought   ,, *iv* 155
   I stood With Florian, cursing *C*,   ,, 171
   And where are Psyche, *C* ? both are fled :   ,, 241
   for *C*, howe'er He deal in frolic, as to-night—   ,, 249
   Go : *C* told us all.'   ,, *v* 36
   C met us. A little shy at first,   ,, 44
   To whom remorseful *C*, ' Yet I pray Take comfort :   ,, 79
   such as her ! if *C* spake her true,   ,, 168
   fiery-short was *C*'s counter-scoff,   ,, 307
   and bore down a Prince, And *C*, one.   ,, 519
   C seeing it, push'd against the Prince,   ,, 533
   Beside us, *C*, batter'd as he was,   ,, *vi* 154
   When *C* pleaded, Ida came behind   ,, *vii* 78
Cyrus And what she did to *C* after fight,   ,, *v* 366
Czar Jack on his ale-house bench has as many lies as a *C* ;   *Maud I iv* 9

D

Daäle (dale) (*See also* **Howlaby Daäle**) an' the *d* was
   all of a thaw,   *Owd Roä* 39
Daäy (day) 'e shall stan to my dying *d* ;   *North. Cobbler* 95
   'e snifft up a box in a *d*,   *Village Wife* 40
   I'll tell tha some o' these *d*'s.   ,, 58
   niver 'a liked tha sa well, as I did that *d*,   *Spinster's S.'s* 29
   I warrant ye soom fine *d*—   ,, 63
   Thaw thou was es soäber es *d*,   ,, 75
   an' belt long afoor my *d*   *Owd Roä* 21
   Eh ? good *d* ! good *d* ! thaw it beän't not mooch
   of a *d*,   *Church-warden, etc.* 1
   I minds when i' Howlaby beck won *d*   ,, 27
Dabbled all *d* with the blood Of his own son,   *Princess vi* 104
   Its lips in the field above are *d* with blood-red heath,   *Maud I i* 2
Dabbling *d* in the fount of fictive tears,   *The Brook* 93
   D a shameless hand with shameful jest,   *Princess iii* 314
Daffodil (*See also* **Daffodilly**) and found The
   shining *d* dead,   *Maud I iii* 14
   On a bed of *d* sky,   ,, *xxii* 10
   And the shining *d* dies,   ,, *III vi* 6
   left us just before The *d* was blown ?   *Lover's Tale i* 294
   in this roaring moon of *d* And crocus,   *Pref. Son. 19th Cent.* 7
Daffodilly That clad her like an April *d*   *Princess iv* 324
Dagger I made my *d* sharp and bright.   *The Sisters* 26
   and thrust The *d* thro' her side.'   *D. of F. Women* 260
   With that gold *d* of thy bill   *The Blackbird* 11
   A *d*, in rich sheath with jewels on it   *Aylmer's Field* 220
   Tumbled the tawny rascal at his feet, This *d* with him,   ,, 231
   left alone he pluck'd her *d* forth   ,, 470
   and the *d* which himself Gave Edith,   ,, 596
   Shot sidelong *d*'s at us,   *Princess ii* 450
   had she found a *d* there   *Merlin and V.* 851
   Sir, do you see this *d* ?   *Bandit's Death* 5
   one day He had left his *d* behind him.   ,, 12
   felt I could end myself too with the *d*—   ,, 37
   I with this *d* of his—do you doubt me ?   ,, 42
Dagonet *D*, the fool, whom Gawain in his mood   *Last Tournament* 1
   And little *D* on the morrow morn,   ,, 240
   D replied, ' Belike for lack of wiser company ;   ,, 244
   while he twangled little *D* stood Quiet   ,, 252
   And little *D*, skipping, ' Arthur, the King's ;   ,, 262
   but lean me down, Sir *D*,   ,, 273
   D with one foot poised in his hand,   ,, 285
   And little *D* mincing with his feet,   ,, 311
   D, turning on the ball of his foot,   ,, 329
   D answer'd, ' Ay, and when the land Was freed,   ,, 338
   D, ' Nay, nor will : I see it and hear.   ,, 348

Damsel (*continued*) And down they ran, Her *d's*, crying to
  their lady, *Pelleas and E.* 376
  Froz'n by sweet sleep, four of her *d's* lay: " 433
  Dame, *d*, each thro' worship of their Queen *Last Tournament* 146
  'Fair *d's*, each to him who worships each " 207
  dame and *d* glitter'd at the feast Variously gay: " 225
  So dame and *d* cast the simple white, " 232
  dame or *d* have ye kneel'd to last?' " 550
Damsel-errant A *d-e*, warbling, as she rode *Balin and Balan* 438
  Youth, we are *d's-e*, and we ride, *Pelleas and E.* 64
Dan that had no likin' for *D*, *Tomorrow* 19
  An' *D* stood there for a minute, " 22
  whin *D* didn't come to the fore, " 43
Dan Chaucer *D C*, the first warbler, *D. of F. Women* 5
Danaë lies the Earth all *D* to the stars, *Princess* vii 182
Danaïd prove The *D* of a leaky vase, " ii 340
Dance (s) (*See also* **Devil's-dances**) echoing *d* Of
  reboant whirlwinds, *Supp. Confessions* 96
  Yet in the whirling *d's* as we went, *The form, the form* 5
  star that with the choral starry *d* Join'd not, *Palace of Art* 253
  Leaving the *d* and song, *D. of F. Women* 216
  men and maids Arranged a country *d*, *Princess*, Pro. 84
  d's broke and buzz'd in knots of talk; " i 133
  Like one that wishes at a *d* to change The music— " iv 589
  In *d* and song and game and jest? *In Mem.* xxix 8
  And *d* and song and hoodman-blind. " lxxviii 12
  wheels the circled *d*, and breaks The rocket " xcviii 30
  No *d*, no motion, save alone What lightens " cv 30
  And last the *d*;—till I retire: " Con. 105
  A dinner and then a *d* For the maids and marriage-
  makers, *Maud* I xx 34
  She is weary of *d* and play.' " xxii 22
  Come hither, the *d's* are done, " 54
  with *d* And revel and song, made merry over Death, *Gareth and L.* 1422
  Rush'd into *d*, and like wild Bacchanals *Lover's Tale* iii 25
  whirling rout Led by those who rush'd into *d*, " 55
  An' the fall of yer foot in the *d* *Tomorrow* 36
Dance (verb) About thee breaks and *d's*: *Madeline* 30
  And the spangle *d's* in bight and bay, *Sea-Fairies* 24
  but to *d* and sing, be gaily drest, *The form, the form* 3
  for she says A fire *d's* before her, *Œnone* 264
  And make her *d* attendance; *Amphion* 62
  And the dead begin to *d*. *Vision of Sin* 166
  I make the netted sunbeam *d* *The Brook* 176
  But fit to flaunt, to dress, to *d*, to thrum, *Princess* iv 519
  to *d* Its body, and reach its fatling innocent arms " vi 137
  let the torrent *d* thee down To find him in the valley; " vii 209
  To *d* with death, to beat the ground, *In Mem.* i 12
  Now *d* the lights on lawn and lea, " cxv 9
  Till the red man *d* By his red cedar-tree, *Maud* I xvii 17
  flickering in a grimly light *D* on the mere. *Gareth and L.* 827
  Down upon far-off cities while they *d*— *Merlin and V.* 114
  eating dry To *d* without a catch, a roundelay
  To *d* to.' *Last Tournament* 250
  D to the pibroch!—saved! *Def. of Lucknow* 103
  D in a fountain of flame with her devils, *Kapiolani* 10
Danced we *d* about the may-pole and in the
  hazel copse, *May Queen*, N'Y's E. 11
  Till all the tables *d* again, *The Goose* 47
  d The greensward into greener circles, *Gardener's D.* 133
  D into light, and died into the shade; " 203
  And madly *d* our hearts with joy, *The Voyage* 23
  the gilded ball *D* like a wisp; *Princess*, Pro. 64
  O'er it shook the woods, And *d* the colour, " iii 293
  For I *d* her on my knee, *In Mem.*, Con. 45
  Yniol's heart *D* in his bosom, *Marr. of Geraint* 505
  and the sand *d* at the bottom of it. *Balin and Balan* 27
  For all my blood *d* in me, and I knew *Holy Grail* 366
  D like a wither'd leaf before the hall. (repeat) *Last Tournament* 4, 242
  And down the city Dagonet *d* away; " 359
  as *d* in 'er pratty blue eye; *North. Cobbler* 50
Dancer To the *d's* dancing in tune; *Maud* I xxii 16
  When will the *d's* leave her alone? " 21
  A wreath of airy *d's* hand-in-hand *Guinevere* 261
Dancing Tho' if, in *d* after Letty Hill, *Edwin Morris* 55

Dancing (*continued*) that keeps A thousand pulses *d*, *In Mem.* cxxv 16
  To the dancers *d* in tune; *Maud* I xxii 16
  burst in *d*, and the pearls were spilt; *Merlin and V.* 452
  Till the *d* will be over; *Maud* I xx 43
  d of Fairies In desolate hollows, *Merlin and the G.* 41
Dandle shall we *d* it amorously? *Boädicea* 33
  I bore him a son, and he loved to *d* the child, *Bandit's Death* 15
Dandled nor pretty babes To be *d*, *Princess* iv 147
  breast that fed or arm that *d* you, " vi 181
Dandy-despot What if that *d-d*, he, *Maud* I vi 42
Dane Saxon and Norman and *D* are we, But all of
  us *D's* in our welcome of thee, *W. to Alexandra* 3
  For Saxon or *D* or Norman we, " 31
  We are each all *D* in our welcome of thee, " 33
Dang'd (**damned**) an' be *d* if I iver let goä! *Village Wife* 68
Danger like of shocks, *D's*, and deeds, *Œnone* 164
  Her household fled the *d*, *The Goose* 54
  I take my part Of *d* on the roaring sea, *Sailor Boy* 22
  I see the *d* which you cannot see: *Geraint and E.* 421
Dangled *D* a length of ribbon and a ring *Enoch Arden* 750
  when my father *d* the grapes, *Maud* I i 71
  d a hundred fathom of grapes, *V. of Maeldune* 56
Dangling one with shatter'd fingers *d* lame, *Last Tournament* 60
Dangtha (**damn you**) Woä then, wiltha? *d*! *N. Farmer, N.S.* 40
Daniel great Books (see *D* seven and ten) *Sea Dreams* 152
Danish behind it a gray down With *D* barrows; *Enoch Arden* 7
  Pass from the *D* barrow overhead; " 442
Danny (*See also* **Danny O'Roon**) an' *D* says 'Troth,
  an' I been Dhrinkin' *Tomorrow* 11
  for *D* was not to be foun', " 28
  For the Divil a *D* was there, " 30
  'Your *D*,' they says, 'niver crasst over " 48
Danny O'Roon (*See also* **Danny**) Molly Magee wid her
  batchelor, *D O'R*— " 10
  meet your paärints agin an' yer *D O'R* afore God " 57
  young man *D O'R* wid his ould woman, " 88
  about Molly Magee an' her *D O'R*, " 92
Dante there the world-worn *D* grasp'd his song, *Palace of Art* 135
Danube The *D* to the Severn gave *In Mem.* xix 1
  Let her great *D* rolling fair Enwind her isles, " xcviii 9
Dare why *d* Paths in the desert? *Supp. Confessions* 78
  d to kiss Thy taper fingers amorously, *Madeline* 43
  I *d* not think of thee, Oriana, *Oriana* 93
  I *d* not die and come to thee, " 96
  'The doubt would rest, I *d* not solve. *Two Voices* 313
  'You will not, boy! you *d* to answer thus! *Dora* 26
  none of all his men *D* tell him Dora waited " 76
  Then not to *d* to see! *Love and Duty* 38
  'I will speak out, for I *d* not lie. *Lady Clare* 38
  But I must go: I *d* not tarry,' *Princess* iii 95
  '*D* we dream of that,' I ask'd, " 297
  I *d* All these male thunderbolts: " iv 499
  he that does the thing they *d* not do, " v 160
  What *d's* not Ida do that she should prize " 174
  d not ev'n by silence sanction lies. *Third of Feb.* 10
  How *d* we keep our Christmas-eve; *In Mem.* xxix 4
  Nor *d* she trust a larger lay, " xlviii 13
  And *d* we to this fancy give, " liii 5
  By which we *d* to live or die. " lxxxv 40
  D I say No spirit ever brake the band " xciii 1
  That which we *d* invoke to bless; " cxxiv 1
  Who can rule and *d* not lie. *Maud* I x 66
  That I *d* to look her way; " xvi 11
  D I bid her abide by her word? " 25
  Who *d's* foreshadow for an only son *Ded. of Idylls* 29
  not once *d* to look him in the face.' *Gareth and L.* 782
  I *am* the cause, because I *d* not speak *Marr. of Geraint* 89
  yet not *d* to tell him what I think, " 105
  How should I *d* obey him to his harm? *Geraint and E.* 136
  Not *d* to watch the combat, " 154
  Nor did I care or *d* to speak with you, " 871
  'What *d* the full-fed liars say of me? *Merlin and V.* 692
  And no man there will *d* to mock at me; *Lancelot and E.* 1053
  What rights are his that *d* not strike for them? *Last Tournament* 527
  how *d* I call him mine? *Guinevere* 617

Dare (*continued*) They swore that he *d* not rob the mail, | *Rizpah* 30
names who *d* For that sweet mother land | *Tiresias* 122
but if thou *d*—Thou, one of these, | " 133
would *d* Hell-heat or Arctic cold, | *Ancient Sage* 115
I *d* without your leave to head | *Pro. to Gen. Hamley* 19
For *d* we dally with the sphere | *Epilogue* 44
Mother, *d* you kill your child ? | *Forlorn* 37
crying ' I *d* her, let Peelè avenge herself '! | *Kapiolani* 32

Dared 'He *d* not tarry,' men will say, | *Two Voices* 101
But when at last I *d* to speak, | *Miller's D.* 129
I had not *d* to flow In these words toward you, | *To J. S.* 6
my word was law, and yet you *d* To slight it. | *Dora* 98
Yet I *d* not stir to do it, | *Aylmer's Field* 806
d To leap the rotten pales of prejudice, | *Princess ii* 141
You that have *d* to break our bound, | " *iv* 539
sorrowing in a pause I *d* not break ; | " *vii* 249
D not to glance at her good mother's face, | *Marr. of Geraint* 766
Nor *d* to waste a perilous pity on him : | *Geraint and E.* 525
she thought, 'He had not *d* to do it, | " 720
'They *d* me to do it,' he said, | *Rizpah* 24
'The farmer *d* me to do it,' he said ; | " 26
But they *d* not touch us again, | *The Revenge* 72
d her with one little ship and his English few ; | " 107
you have *d* Somewhat perhaps in coming ? | *Columbus* 242
and flung the berries, and *d* the Goddess, | *Kapiolani* 6

Darest Who scarcely *d* to inquire, | *In Mem. iv* 7
How *d* thou, if lover, push me even In fancy | *Last Tournament* 638

Daring But now it were too *d*. | *Guinevere* 654
Not *d* yet to glance at Lionel. | *Lover's Tale iv* 309

Dark (*See also* **Derk, Dewy-dark**) In the *d* we
   must lie. | *All Things will Die* 22
drive Thro' utter *d* a full-sail'd skiff, | *Supp. Confessions* 95
I am void, *D*, formless, | " 121
When thickest *d* did trance the sky, | *Mariana* 18
Which upon the *d* afloat, | *The Owl ii* 3
level lake with diamond-plots Of *d* and bright. | *Arabian Nights* 86
twisted silvers look'd to shame The hollow-vaulted *d*, | " 126
Or dimple in the *d* of rushy coves, | *Ode to Memory* 60
thro' the wreaths of floating *d* upcurl'd, | *The Poet* 35
All within is *d* as night : | *Deserted House* 5
Ere the light on *d* was growing, | *Oriana* 10
Remaining betwixt *d* and bright : | *Margaret* 28
shoot into the *d* Arrows of lightnings. | *To J. M. K.* 14
If I make *d* my countenance, | *Two Voices* 53
'If all be *d*, vague voice,' I said, | " 265
seem'd all *d* and red—upon a tract of sand, | *Palace of Art* 65
moon was setting, and the *d* was over all ; | *May Queen, Con.* 26
brides of ancient song Peopled the hollow *d*, | *D. of F. Women* 18
Morn broaden'd on the borders of the *d*, | " 265
The unnetted black-hearts ripen *d*, | *The Blackbird* 7
Shot on the sudden into *d*. | *To J. S.* 28
And round them sea and air are *d* | *Love thou thy land* 63
A length of bright horizon rimm'd the *d*. | *Gardener's D.* 181
the sun fell, and all the land was *d*. (repeat) | *Dora* 79, 109
all the varied changes of the *d*, | *Edwin Morris* 36
Till now the *d* was worn, | *Love and Duty* 71
spirit deeply dawning in the *d* of hazel eyes— | *Locksley Hall* 28
'Love, if thy tresses be so *d*, How *d* those hidden
   eyes must be!' | *Day-Dm., Arrival* 31
The twilight died into the *d*. | " *Depart.* 24
As these white robes are soil'd and *d*, | *St Agnes' Eve* 13
I float till all is *d*. | *Sir Galahad* 40
But o'er the *d* a glory spreads, | " 55
With wakes of fire we tore the *d* ; | *The Voyage* 52
And *d* and true and tender is the North. | *Princess iv* 98
I dread His wildness, and the chances of the *d*.' | " 244
Slipt round and in the *d* invested you, | " 404
That glitter burnish'd by the frosty *d* ; | " *v* 261
little seed they laugh'd at in the *d*, | " *vi* 34
like night and evening mixt Their *d* and gray, | " 132
And watches in the dead, the *d*, | " *vii* 103
D in its funeral fold. | *Ode on Well.* 57
D is the world to thee : | *High. Pantheism* 7
My will is bondsman to the *d* ; | *In Mem. iv* 2
And all the place is *d*, and all The chambers | " *viii* 7

Dark (*continued*) For all is *d* where thou art not. | *In Mem. viii* 12
balmy drops in summer *d* Slide from the bosom | " *xvii* 15
Thy marble bright in *d* appears, | " *lxvii* 5
Immantled in ambrosial *d*, | " *lxxxix* 14
A shade falls on us like the *d* | " *Con.* 93
For the drift of the Maker is *d*, | *Maud I iv* 43
Thro' the livelong hours of the *d* | " *vi* 17
Then returns the *d* With no more hope of light. | " *ix* 15
For *d* my mother was in eyes and hair, And *d*
   in hair and eyes am I ; and *d* Was Gorloïs,
   yea and *d* was Uther too, | *Com. of Arthur* 327
And tho' she lay *d* in the pool, she knew | *Marr. of Geraint* 657
All round her prest the *d*, | *Balin and Balan* 262
D my doom was here, and *d* It will be there. | " 623
D in the glass of some presageful mood, | *Merlin and V.* 295
the court, the King, *d* in your light, | " 875
Arthur to the banquet, *d* in mood, | *Lancelot and E.* 564
Was I too *d* a prophet when I said | *Holy Grail* 889
Sprang from the door into the *d*. | *Pelleas and E.* 603
d in the golden grove Appearing, | *Last Tournament* 379
The night was *d* ; the true star set. Isolt ! The
   name was ruler of the *d*—Isolt? | " 605
Mark's way to steal behind one in the *d*— | " 618
That here in utter *d* I swoon'd away, And woke
   again in utter *d*, and cried, | " 622
Out of the *d*, just as the lips had touch'd, | " 752
look'd and saw The great Queen's bower was *d*,— | " 758
so late ! and *d* the night and chill ! | *Guinevere* 168
so late ! and *d* and chill the night ! | " 174
Fell into dust, and crumbled in the *d*— | *Lover's Tale i* 95
in the *d* of mine Is traced with flame. | " 297
We past from light to *d*. | " 516
All thro' the livelong hours of utter *d*, | " 810
spray wind-driven Far thro' the dizzy *d*. | " *ii* 199
Down welter'd thro' the *d* ever and ever. | " 208
the nightingale's hymn in the *d*. | *First Quarrel* 34
call'd in the *d* to me year after year— | *Rizpah* 47
I have been with God in the *d*— | " 79
he used but to call in the *d*, | " 83
I came on lake Llanberris in the *d*, | *Sisters (E. and E.)* 95
D thro' the smoke and the sulphur | *Def. of Lucknow* 33
D with the smoke of human sacrifice. | *Sir J. Oldcastle* 84
Breaking with laughter from the *d* ; | *De Prof., Two G.* 18
I cannot laud this life, it looks so *d* : | *To W. H. Brookfield* 12
sister of the sun Would climb from out the *d*, | *Tiresias* 31
till mine grew *d* For ever, | " 47
in the *d* of his wonderful eyes. | *The Wreck* 55
thy world Might vanish like thy shadow in the *d*. | *Ancient Sage* 52
When all is *d* as night.' | " 170
the world is *d* with griefs and graves, So *d* that
   men cry out against the Heavens. | " 171
an' thin wint into the *d*. | *Tomorrow* 22
Bright and *D* have sworn that I, | *Demeter and P.* 96
Voices of the day Are heard across the Voices of the *d*. | *The Ring* 40
but one was fair, And one was *d*, | " 161
one betwixt the *d* and light had seen *Her*, | " 414
Stark and *d* in his funeral fire. | *To Master of B.* 20
dead cords that ran *D* thro' the mist, | *Death of Œnone* 11
festal hour *D* with the blood of man who
   murder'd man. | *St. Telemachus* 80
Thro' a dream of the *d* ? | *The Dreamer* 16
D no more with human hatreds | *Faith* 8
Must my day be *d* by reason, | *God and the Univ.* 2
And after that the *d* ! | *Crossing the Bar* 10

Dark-blue *D-b* the deep sphere overhead, | *Arabian Nights* 89
Hateful is the *d-b* sky, Vaulted o'er the *d-b* sea. | *Lotos-Eaters, C. S.* 39
and the *d-b* clematis, clung, | *V. of Maeldune* 39

Dark-brow'd *D-b* sophist, come not anear ; | *Poet's Mind* 8

Dark-dawning For my *d-d* youth, Darken'd watching | *Maud I xix* 7

Darken the days *d* round me, and the years, | *M. d'Arthur* 237
And never more *d* my doors again.' | *Dora* 32
shores that *d* with the gathering wolf, | *Aylmer's Field* 767
face Would *d*, as he cursed his credulousness, | *Sea Dreams* 13
And sorrow *d*'s hamlet and hall. | *Ode on Well.* 7
it brightens and *d*'s down on the plain. | *Window. On the Hill* 2

Darken (*continued*) *d's* and brightens like my hope,
  And it *d's* and brightens and *d's* like my
    fear,   *Window. On the Hill* 18
drifts that pass To *d* on the rolling brine   *In Mem. cvii* 14
Not close and *d* above me   *Maud I xi* 9
Tho' many a light shall *d*   " *III vi* 43
I would not mine again should *d* thine,   *Balin and Balan* 625
May yon just heaven, that *d's* o'er me,   *Merlin and V.* 931
flash of youth, would *d* down To rise hereafter *Lancelot and E.* 1318
o'er the plain that then began To *d* under Camelot; *Holy Grail* 218
deed seem'd to be done in vain, *D*;   " 275
the days *d* round me, and the years,   *Pass. of Arthur* 405
And why was I to *d* their pure love,   *Lover's Tale i* 727
into my heart, and begun to *d* my eyes.   *Rizpah* 16
as I saw the white sail run, And *d*,   *The Flight* 40
lost in the gloom of doubts that *d* the schools ; *Vastness* 11
Storm in the South that *d's* the day !   *Riflemen form !* 2
His shadow *d's* earth :   *D. of the Duke of C.* 13

Darken'd (*See also* **Derken'd, Self-darken'd**) And
  her eyes were *d* wholly,   *L. of Shalott iv* 31
And all the casement *d* there.   *Miller's D.* 128
pines That *d* all the northward of her Hall.   *Aylmer's Field* 415
all the sails were *d* in the west,   *Sea Dreams* 39
You stood in your own light and *d* mine.   *Princess iv* 314
And *d* sanctities with song.'   *In Mem. xxxvii* 24
And life is *d* in the brain.   " *cxxi* 8
D watching a mother decline   " *Maud I xix* 8
He had *d* into a frown,   " 62
And *d* from the high light in his eyes,   *Marr. of Geraint* 100
Till his eye *d* and his helmet wagg'd ;   *Geraint and E.* 505
So when his moods were *d*, court and King   *Balin and Balan* 235
Thy curse, and *d* all thy day ;   " 620
his face *D*, as I have seen it more than once,   *Holy Grail* 273
D the common path :   *Pelleas and E.* 550
when the outer lights are *d* thus,   *Lover's Tale i* 35
Because my own was *d* ?   " 729
And all my life was *d*,   *The Flight* 39
The landskip *d*, The melody deaden'd,   *Merlin and the G.* 31
' what has *d* thee to-night ? '   *Akbar's Dream* 2
d with doubts of a Faith that saves,   *The Dreamer* 11

Darkening *d* thine own To thine own likeness ; *Aylmer's Field* 673
swarms of men *D* her female field :   *Princess vii* 34
And *d* the dark graves of men,—   *In Mem. xxxix* 9
shadow of His loss drew like eclipse, *D* the world. *Ded. of Idylls* 15
world-old yew-tree, *d* half The cloisters,   *Holy Grail* 13
D the wreaths of all that would advance,   *To Victor Hugo* 5
And, *d* in the light,   *Ancient Sage* 151

Darker Your hair is *d*, and your eyes   *Margaret* 49
made those eyes *D* than darkest pansies,   *Gardener's D.* 27
lonelier, *d*, earthlier for my loss.   *Aylmer's Field* 750
loved to make men *d* than they are,   *Merlin and V.* 876

Dark-eyed She was dark-haired, *d-e* :   *Lover's Tale i* 74
Dark-green spread his *d-g* layers of shade.   *Gardener's D.* 116
Dark-hair'd She was *d-h*, dark-eyed :   *Lover's Tale i* 74
Darkling name Went wandering somewhere *d* in his
  mind.   *Last Tournament* 457
Darkness something in the *d* draws His forehead
    earthward,   *Supp. Confessions* 167
somehow which possess'd The *d* of the world,   *Arabian Nights* 72
and lashes like to rays Of *d*,   *Adeline* 44
All night long on *d* blind.   *My life is full* 11
When in the *d* over me The four-handed mole   *Two Voices* 200
Why inch by inch to *d* crawl?   " 273
And *d* in the village yew.   *To ——, With Pal. of Art* 16
on her threshold lie Howling in outer *d.*   *D. of F. Women* 67
Gross *d* of the inner sepulchre   *M. d'Arthur, Ep.* 2
Had wink'd and threaten'd *d*,   *Audley Court* 72
I would I were The pilot of the *d*   *Tithonus* 41
shake the *d* from their loosen'd manes,   *Godiva* 70
were shrivell'd into *d* in his head,   *Vision of Sin* 49
Beyond the *d* and the cataract,   *Aylmer's Field* 431
as they kiss'd each other In *d*,   " 643
worshipt their own *d* in the Highest ?   " 771
May Pharaoh's *d*, folds as dense   *Sea Dreams* 93
and I was heaved upon it In *d* :

Darkness (*continued*) Muses' heads were touch'd Above
    the *d*   *Princess iii* 22
d closed me ; and I fell.   " *v* 542
So much the gathering *d* charm'd :   " *Con.* 107
There I heard them in the *d*,   " *Boädicea* 36
So they chanted in the *d*,   " 46
A beam in *d* : let it grow.   *In Mem., Pro.* 24
Let *d* keep her raven gloss :   " *i* 10
Else earth is *d* at the core,   " *xxxiv* 3
drop head-foremost in the jaws Of vacant *d*   " 16
That slope thro' *d* up to God,   " *lv* 16
How blanch'd with *d* must I grow !   " *lxi* 7
Death has made His *d* beautiful with thee.   " *lxxiv* 12
matin songs, that woke The *d* of our planet,   " *lxxvi* 10
which makes the *d* and the light,   " *xcvi* 19
But in the *d* and the cloud,   " 21
A treble *d*, Evil haunts The birth,   " *xcviii* 13
Ring out the *d* of the land,   " *cvi* 31
The Power in whom we guess ;   " *cxxiv* 4
out of *d* came the hands That reach thro' nature,   " 23
over whom thy *d* must have spread   *Maud I xviii* 25
many a *d* into the light shall leap,   " *III vi* 46
Swept bellowing thro' the *d* on to dawn,   *Gareth and L.* 177
would she make My *d* blackness ?   *Balin and Balan* 193
mark'd not on his right a cavern-chasm Yawn over *d*, " 313
And lost itself in *d*, till she cried—   " 514
He walk'd with dreams and *d*,   *Merlin and V.* 190
And counterchanged with *d* ?   " 466
Approaching thro' the *d*, call'd ;   *Lancelot and E.* 1000
After the day of *d*, when the dead   *Holy Grail* 49
and lying bounden there In *d*   " 677
d falling, sought A priory not far off,   *Pelleas and E.* 213
their own *d*, throng'd into the moon.   " 458
She made her face a *d* from the King :   *Guinevere* 417
And in the *d* o'er her fallen head,   " 583
forego The *d* of that battle in the West,   *To the Queen ii* 65
far on within its inmost halls, The home of *d* ;   *Lover's Tale i* 524
and the *d* of the grave, The *d* of the grave and utter night, " 597
And vex them with my *d* ?   " 732
in the end, Opening on *d*,   " *ii* 125
so those fair eyes Shone on my *d*,   " 158
Seem'd stepping out of *d* with a smile.   " *iv* 220
What end but *d* could ensue from this   *Sisters (E. and E.)* 175
bleat of a lamb in the storm and the *d* without ;   *In the Child. Hosp.* 76
Bugles and drums in the *d*,   *Def. of Lucknow* 76
he past away From the *d* of life—   *To Prin. F. of H.* 2
world of sight, that lives Behind this *d*,   *Tiresias* 52
Stood out before a *d*, crying,   " 115
not to plunge Thy torch of life in *d*,   " 159
and the master gone. Gone into *d*,   " 202
fountain pour'd From *d* into daylight,   *Ancient Sage* 8
Who knows but that the *d* is in man ?   " 173
and forget The *d* of the pall.'   " 198
If utter *d* closed the day, my son—   " 199
Crown'd with sunlight—over *d*—   *Locksley H., Sixty* 92
Flare from Tel-el-Kebir Thro' *d*,   *Pro. to Gen. Hamley* 29
and griefs, and deaths, Were utter *d*—   *Prin. Beatrice* 3
Are there spectres moving in the *d* ?   *On Jub. Q. Victoria* 67
the *d* Dawns into the Jubilee of the Ages.   " 70
bird that flies All night across the *d*,   *Demeter and P.* 82
following out A league of labyrinthine *d*,   " 100
and for evermore The Bride of *D.*'   " 116
Then He, the brother of this *D*,   *Merlin and the G.* 75
Clouds and *d* Closed upon Camelot ;   " 81
For out of the *d* Silent and slowly   *Romney's R.* 53
bubble bursts above the abyss Of *D*,

Dark-purple lying in *d-p* spheres of sea.   *Locksley Hall* 164
Dark-splendid the face before her lived, *D-s*, *Lancelot and E.* 338
Darlin' wid a heart and a half, me *d*,   *Tomorrow* 39
Darling (*See also* **Darlin'**) The *d* of my manhood, and,
    alas !   *Gardener's D.* 278
how pale she had look'd *D*, to-night !   *Aylmer's Field* 380
Seventy years ago, my *d*, (repeat)   *Grandmother* 24, 56
'Me, not my *d*, no !'   *The Victim* 68
Her feet, my *d*, on the dead ;   *In Mem., Con.* 50

Darling (*continued*) the moon-faced *d* of all,— *Maud I i* 72
  You are not her *d*.   *" xii* 32
  and render All homage to his own *d*, *" xx* 49
  But shall it ? answer, *d*, answer, no. *Merlin and V.* 397
  Then the great knight, the *d* of the court, *Lancelot and E.* 261
  our orphan, our *d*, our meek little maid ; *In the Child. Hosp.* 28
  not a mother's heart, when I left my *d* alone.' *The Wreck* 97
  All very well just now to be calling me *d* *Charity* 7

Darnel And on my clay her *d* grow ; *My life is full* 22

Darnley There is *D* bridge, It has more ivy ; *The Brook* 36
  Then crost the common into *D* chase *"* 132

Dart (s) with their fires Love tipt his keenest *d's* ; *D. of F. Women* 173
  Brandishing in her hand a *d* *Boädicea* 71
  Madly dash'd the *d's* together, *" * 74
  Clash the *d's* and on the buckler *" * 79
  dying now Pierced by a poison'd *d*. *Death of Œnone* 34

Dart (verb) forward *d* again, and play About the prow, *In Mem. xii* 17

Darted thro' his manful breast *d* the pang *Marr. of Geraint* 121

Darter (daughter) the Squire an' 'is *d's* an' me, *Village Wife* 7
  talkt o' my *d* es died o' the fever at fall: *" * 10
  ivry *d* o' Squire's hed her awn ridin-erse *" * 35
  niver hed none of 'er *d's* 'ere ; *" * 54
  'Er an' 'er blessed *d*— *" * 60
  Then 'e married a greät Yerl's *d*, *Church-warden, etc.* 20

Dash *D* them anew together at her will *Lucretius* 247
  birds on the light *D* themselves dead. *Princess iv* 496
  Waves on a diamond shingle *d*, *The Islet* 16
  d the brains of the little one out, *Boädicea* 68
  and *d* myself down and die *Maud I i* 54
  upon all things base, and *d* them dead, *Gareth and L.* 23
  each at either *d* from either end— *" * 535
  To *d* against mine enemy and to win. *" * 1355
  D back that ocean with a pier, *Mechanophilus* 5

Dash'd (rushed) *D* downward in a cataract. *Day-Dm., Revival* 16
  Again we *d* into the dawn ! *The Voyage* 24
  d Into the chronicle of a deedful day, *Aylmer's Field* 195
  uttering a dry shriek, *D* on Geraint, *Geraint and E.* 462
  But, mad for strange adventure, *d* away, *Balin and Balan* 289
  'he *d* across me—mad, And maddening what he rode ; *Holy Grail* 641
  Pelleas overthrew them as they *d* Against him one
    by one ; *Pelleas and E.* 221
  d up alone Thro' the great gray slope *Heavy Brigade* 16

Dash'd (flung, hurled) As *d* about the drunken leaves *Amphion* 55
  D together in blinding dew ; *Vision of Sin* 42
  grief Bore down in flood, and *d* his angry heart *Aylmer's Field* 633
  or into rhythm have *d* The passion of the prophetess ; *Princess iv* 139
  and *d* Unopen'd at her feet ; *" * 470
  roll The torrents, *d* to the vale ; *" v* 350
  Then came a postscript *d* across the rest. *" * 424
  D on every rocky square Their surging charges *Ode on Well.* 125
  Roll as a ground-swell *d* on the strand, *W. to Alexandra* 23
  And wildly *d* on tower and tree *In Mem. xv* 7
  Christless foe of thine as ever *d* Horse against
    horse ; *Balin and Balan* 97
  He *d* the pummel at the foremost face, *" * 402
  with violence The sword was *d* from out my hand, *Holy Grail* 826
  Isolt of Britain *d* Before Isolt *Last Tournament* 588
  and *d* himself Into the dizzy depth below. *Lover's Tale i* 380
  and *d* herself Dead in her rage ; *Tiresias* 152
  And *d* half dead on barren sands, *The Ring* 309
  Into the flame-billow *d* the berries, *Kapiolani* 33

Dash'd (struck) Madly *d* the darts together, *Boädicea* 74
  He *d* the rowel into his horse, *Pelleas and E.* 486
  sudden fire from Heaven had *d* him dead, *Happy* 83

Dash'd (broke) we *d* Your cities into shards with
    catapults, *Princess v* 137

Dash'd (bespattered) his greaves and cuisses *d* with drops
    Of onset ; *M. d'Arthur* 215
  And where it *d* the reddening meadow, *Lucretius* 49
  d with death He reddens what he kisses : *Princess v* 164
  d with wandering isles of night. *In Mem. xxiv* 4
  That life is *d* with flecks of sin. *" lii* 14
  Deep tulips *d* with fiery dew, *" lxxxiii* 11
  his greaves and cuisses *d* with drops Of onset ; *Pass. of Arthur* 383

Dashing *d* down on a tall wayside flower, *Guinevere* 253

Dashing (*continued*) *D* the fires and the shadows of
  dawn *V. of Maeldune* 99
  the bolt of war *d* down upon cities *The Dawn* 8

Date but when his *d* Doubled her own, *Aylmer's Field* 80
  Beyond the common *d* of death— *The Ring* 108

Dating *d*, many a year ago, Has hit on this, *To E. Fitzgerald* 49

Daughter (*See also* **Darter**) His little *d*, whose sweet
  face He kiss'd, *Two Voices* 253
  It is the miller's *d*, *Miller's D.* 169
  I am the *d* of a River-God, *Œnone* 38
  WE were two *d's* of one race : *The Sisters* 1
  The *d* of a hundred Earls, *L. C. V. de Vere* 7
  A *d* of the gods, divinely tall, *D. of F. Women* 87
  The *d* of the warrior Gileadite, *" * 197
  Eustace from the city went To see the Gardener's *D* ; *Gardener's D.* 3
  Go and see The Gardener's *d* : *" * 30
  Who had not heard Of Rose, the Gardener's *d* ? *" * 52
  The *d's* of the year, One after one, *" * 200
  She is my brother's *d* : *Dora* 17
  for his sake I bred His *d* Dora : *" * 20
  woo'd and wed A labourer's *d*, Mary Morrison. *" * 40
  d of a cottager, Out of her sphere, *Walk. to the Mail* 59
  Cry, like the *d's* of the horseleech, 'Give, *Golden Year* 12
  preaching down a *d's* heart. *Locksley Hall* 94
  'The old Earl's *d* died at my breast ; *Lady Clare* 25
  With children ; first a *d*. *Enoch Arden* 84
  evermore the *d* prest upon her To wed the man *" * 483
  tell my *d* Annie, whom I saw So like her mother, *" * 882
  A *d* of our meadows, yet not coarse ; *The Brook* 69
  And how it was the thing his *d* wish'd, *" * 140
  sons of men *D's* of God ; *Aylmer's Field* 45
  Averill walk So freely with his *d* ? *" * 270
  Pale as the Jephtha's *d*, *" * 280
  He never yet had set his *d* forth *" * 347
  Grossly contriving their dear *d's* good— *" * 781
  devising their own *d's* death ! *" * 783
  where the two contrived their *d's* good, *" * 848
  knowledge, so my *d* held, Was all in all : *Princess i* 135
  His *d* and his housemaid were the boys ; *" * 190
  turning round we saw The Lady Blanche's *d* *" ii* 321
  d's of the plough, stronger than men, *" iv* 278
  A Niobëan *d*, one arm out, *" * 371
  'Fair *d*, when we sent the Prince your way *" * 398
  Then those eight mighty *d's* of the plough *" * 550
  I would he had our *d* : *" v* 214
  vainlier than a hen To her false *d's* in the pool ; *" * 329
  those eight *d's* of the plough Came *" * 339
  SEA-KINGS' *d* from over the sea, *W. to Alexandra* 1
  The sea-kings' *d* as happy as fair, *" * 26
  Yell'd and shriek'd between her *d's*, (repeat) *Boädicea* 6, 72
  he loved A *d* of our house ; *In Mem., Con.* 7
  love of all Thy *d's* cherish Thee, *Ded. of Idylls* 53
  Had one fair *d*, and none other child ; *Com. of Arthur* 2
  Give me thy *d* Guinevere to wife.' *" * 139
  Give my one *d* saving to a king, *" * 143
  And *d's* had she borne him,— *" * 189
  '*D* of Gorloïs and Ygerne am I ;' *" * 316
  Then at his call, 'O *d's* of the Dawn, *Gareth and L.* 923
  were the the *d* of a king, *Marr. of Geraint* 229
  The voice of Enid, Yniol's *d*, rang Clear *" * 327
  fair Enid, all in faded silk, Her *d*. *" * 367
  after, turn'd her *d* round, and said, *" * 740
  I doubted whether *d's* tenderness, Or easy nature, *" * 797
  behind them stept the lily maid Elaine, his *d* : *Lancelot and E.* 177
  But I, my sons, and little *d* fled *" * 276
  D, I know not what you call the highest ; *" * 1080
  Isolt, the *d* of the King ? *Last Tournament* 397
  The mother fell about the *d's* neck, *Sister's (E. and E.)* 154
  told the living *d* with what love *" * 253
  England's England-loving *d*—thou *Ded. Poem 'Prin. Alice* 15
  He saw not his *d*—he blest her : *To Prin. F. of H.* 3
  d yield her life, heart, soul to one— *The Flight* 28
  hold the Present fatal *d* of the Past, *Locksley H., Sixty* 105
  Her maiden *d's* marriage ; *Prin. Beatrice* 10
  True *d*, whose all-faithful, filial eyes *" * 13

Day (*continued*)   But sometimes in the falling *d*   *Mariana in the S.* 73
From heat to heat the *d* decreased,   ,,   78
'The *d* to night,' she made her moan, 'The *d* to night, the night to morn, And *d* and night I am left alone   ,,   81
Would sweep the tracts of *d* and night.   *Two Voices* 69
How grows the *d* of human power?'   ,,   78
One hope that warm'd me in the *d*'s   ,,   122
In *d*'s that never come again.   ,,   324
Whose troubles number with his *d*'s: ,,   330
That we may die the self-same *d*.   *Miller's D.* 24
Flush'd like the coming of the *d*;   ,,   132
song I gave you, Alice, on the *d* When, arm in arm,   ,,   162
For hid in ringlets *d* and night,   ,,   173
And all *d* long to fall and rise   ,,   182
The *d*, when in the chestnut shade I found   *Œnone* 267
wheresoe'er I am by night and *d*,   ,,
And, while *d* sank or mounted higher,   *Palace of Art.* 46
Thro' which the livelong *d* my soul did pass,   ,,   55
young night divine Crown'd dying *d* with stars,   ,,   184
Of all the glad New-year, mother, the maddest merriest *d*;   *May Queen* 3
call me loud when the *d* begins to break: ,,   10
many a bolder lad 'ill woo me any summer *d*,   ,,   23
drop of rain the whole of the livelong *d*,   ,,   35
To-morrow 'ill be of all the year the maddest merriest *d*,   ,,   43
we had a merry *d*;   *May Queen, N.Y's. E.* 9
I long to see a flower so before the *d* I die.   ,,   16
Good-night, sweet mother: call me before the *d* is born.   ,,   49
ere this *d* is done The voice, that now is speaking,   *Con.* 53
All its allotted length of *d*'s,   *Lotos-Eaters, C. S.* 35
Eating the Lotos *d* by *d*,   ,,   60
All *d* the wind breathes low with mellower tone: ,,   102
eyes of anger'd Eleanor Do hunt me, *d* and night.'   *D. of F. Women* 256
He will not see the dawn of *d*.   *D. of the O. Year* 11
Make bright our *d*'s and light our dreams,   *Of old sat Freedom* 22
From those, not blind, who wait for *d*,   *Love thou thy land* 15
cutting eights that *d* upon the pond,   *The Epic* 10
Looks freshest in the fashion of the *d*:   ,,   32
So all *d* long the noise of battle roll'd   *M. d'Arthur* 1
the halls Of Camelot, as in the *d*'s that were.   ,,   21
In those old *d*'s, one summer noon,   ,,   29
And the *d*'s darken round me, and the years,   ,,   237
Rise like a fountain for me night and *d*.   ,,   249
Begin to feel the truth and stir of *d*,   ,, *Ep.* 19
THIS morning is the morning of the *d*   *Gardener's D.* 1
memory folds For ever in itself the *d* we went To see her.   ,,   75
Sang loud, as tho' he were the bird of *d*.   ,,   96
But the full *d* dwelt on her brows,   ,,   136
I, that whole *d*, Saw her no more.   ,,   163
d by *d*, Like one that never can be wholly known,   ,,   205
chambers of the heart, Let in the *d*.'   ,,   250
May not be dwelt on by the common *d*.   ,,   271
came a *d* When Allan called his son,   *Dora* 9
d's went on, and there was born a boy To William;   ,,   48
And *d* by *d* he pass'd his father's gate,   ,,   50
Remembering the *d* when first she came,   ,,   106
And either twilight and the *d* between;   *Edwin Morris* 37
I spoke her name alone. Thrice-happy *d*'s!   ,,   68
seems a part of those fresh *d*'s to me;   ,,   142
leap'd and laugh'd The modish Cupid of the *d*,   *Talking Oak* 67
ah! my friend, the *d*'s were brief   ,,   185
'Tis little more: the *d* was warm;   ,,   205
Some happy future *d*.   ,,   252
staring eye glazed o'er with sapless *d*'s,   *Love and Duty* 16
we that *d* had been Up Snowdon;   *Golden Year* 3
A tongue-tied Poet in the feverous *d*'s,   ,,   10
Happy *d*'s Roll onward, leading up the golden year.   ,,   40
The long *d* wanes: the slow moon climbs: *Ulysses* 55
strength which in old *d*'s Moved earth and heaven;   ,,   66
a saying learnt, In *d*'s far-off,   *Tithonus* 48
with what another heart In *d*'s far-off,   ,,   51
thou shalt lower to his level *d* by *d*,   *Locksley Hall* 45

Day (*continued*)   turn to, lighting upon *d*'s like these?   *Locksley Hall* 99
When I heard my *d*'s before me,   ,,   110
island unto island at the gateways of the *d*.   ,,   158
we sweep into the younger *d*:   ,,   183
Stillness with love, and *d* with light.   *Day-Dm., Sleep. B.* 16
That strove in other *d*'s to pass,   *Arrival* 10
And deep into the dying *d*   *Depart.* 7
Beyond the night, across the *d*,   ,,   31
song was great In *d*'s of old Amphion,   *Amphion* 10
fountain upward runs The current of my *d*'s: *Will Water.* 36
draws me down Into the common *d*?   ,,   154
Ere *d*'s, that deal in ana,   ,,   199
Thy latter *d*'s increased with pence   ,,   219
God's blessing on the *d*!   *Lady Clare* 8
D by *d* more harsh and cruel   *The Captain* 13
On a *d* when they were going O'er the lone expanse,   ,,   25
Where they twain will spend their *d*'s   *L. of Burleigh* 36
Down the waste waters *d* and night,   *The Voyage* 58
'She is more beautiful than *d*.'   *Beggar Maid* 8
When a blanket wraps the *d*,   *Vision of Sin* 80
the tender grace of a *d* that is dead   *Break, break, etc.* 15
Enoch was host one *d*, Philip the next,   *Enoch Arden* 25
And pass his *d*'s in peace among his own.   ,,   147
Many a sad kiss by *d* by night renew'd   ,,   161
So all *d* long till Enoch's last at home,   ,,   172
ship I sail in passes here (He named the *d*)   ,,   215
the *d*, that Enoch mention'd, came,   ,,   239
in *d*'s of difficulty And pressure,   ,,   254
Beheld the dead flame of the fallen *d*   ,,   441
Thro' many a fair sea-circle, *d* by *d*,   ,,   542
or all *d* long Sat often in the seaward-gazing gorge,   ,,   588
No sail from *d* to *d*, but every *d*   ,,   591
There Enoch rested silent many *d*'s.   ,,   699
the dull November *d* Was growing duller twilight,   ,,   721
brought the stinted commerce of those *d*'s;   ,,   817
meet the *d* When Enoch had return'd,   ,,   822
I have not three *d*'s more to live;   ,,   851
Coming every *d*,' She answer'd,   *The Brook* 106
five *d*'s after that He met the bailiff   ,,   145
if you knew her in her English *d*'s,   ,,   224
the *d*'s That most she loves to talk of,   ,,   225
Thinn'd, or would seem to thin her in a *d*,   *Aylmer's Field* 76
dash'd Into the chronicle of a deedful *d*,   ,,   196
Slept thro' the stately minuet of those *d*'s: ,,   207
The next *d* came a neighbour.   ,,   251
second *d*, My lady's Indian kinsman rushing in,   ,,   592
many thousand *d*'s Were clipt by horror   ,,   602
Darkly that *d* rose: ,,   609
At close of *d*; slept, woke,   *Sea Dreams* 18
birdie say, In her nest at peep of *d*?   ,,   294
baby say, In her bed at peep of *d*?   ,,   302
Was it the first beam of my latest *d*?   *Lucretius* 59
Whether I mean this *d* to end myself,   ,,   146
Shatter'd into one earthquake in one *d*   ,,   251
all a summer's *d* Gave his broad lawns   *Princess, Pro.* 1
Took this fair *d* for text,   ,,   108
On a sudden in the midst of men and *d*,   ,, *i* 15
the *d*'s drew nigh that I should wed,   ,,   41
three *d*'s he feasted us, And on the fourth   ,,   118
At break of *d* the College Portress came: ,, *ii* 15
In gentler *d*'s, your arrow-wounded fawn   ,,   270
then *d* droopt; the chapel bells Call'd   ,,   470
the *d* fled on thro' all Its range of duties   ,, *iii* 176
and mould The woman to the fuller *d*.'   ,,   332
thinking of the *d*'s that are no more.   ,, *iv* 43
So sad, so fresh, the *d*'s that are no more.   ,,   48
So sad, so strange, the *d*'s that are no more.   ,,   53
O Death in Life, the *d*'s that are no more.'   ,,   58
was not thus, O Princess, in old *d*'s: ,,   292
yet this *d* (tho' you should hate me for it)   ,,   341
won it with a *d* Blanch'd in our annals,   ,, *vi* 62
a *d* Rose from the distance on her memory,   ,,   111
With kisses, ere the *d*'s of Lady Blanche: ,,   114
while the *d*, Descending, struck athwart the hall,   ,,   363
till on a *d* When Cyril pleaded,   ,, *vii* 77

Day (*continued*) Alas for me then, my good *d*'s are done.' *Lancelot and E.* 947
And in those *d*'s she made a little song,	,,	1004
So that *d* there was dole in Astolat.	,,	1136
That *d* Sir Lancelot at the palace craved	,,	1162
After the *d* of darkness, when the dead	*Holy Grail* 49
A little lonely church in *d*'s of yore,	,,	64
For on a *d* she sent to speak with me.	,,	101
beam of light seven times more clear than *d* :	,,	187
ride A twelvemonth and a *d* in quest of it,	,,	197
early that same *d*, Scaped thro' a cavern	,,	206
' But when the next *d* brake from under ground—	,,	338
but moving with me night and *d*, Fainter by *d*, but always in the night	,,	471
when the *d* began to wane, we went.	,,	488
while I tarried, every *d* she set A banquet richer than the *d* before	,,	588
then came a night Still as the *d* was loud ;	,,	683
twelvemonth and a *d* were pleasant to me.'	,,	750
Seven *d*'s I drove along the dreary deep,	,,	808
Let visions of the night or of the *d* Come,	,,	910
Riding at noon, a *d* or twain before,	*Pelleas and E.* 20
and slowly Pelleas drew To that dim *d*,	,,	30
all *d* long Sir Pelleas kept the field	,,	168
but rose With morning every *d*,	,,	215
Full-arm'd upon his charger all *d* long Sat by the walls,	,,	216
I see thy face But once a *d* :	,,	244
Give me three *d*'s to melt her fancy,	,,	356
So those three *d*'s, aimless about the land,	,,	391
risen against me in their blood At the last *d*?	,,	462
And each foresaw the dolorous *d* to be :	,,	606
Arm'd for a *d* of glory before the King.	*Last Tournament* 55
behold This *d* my Queen of Beauty is not here.'	,,	209
wan *d* Went glooming down in wet and weariness :	,,	214
Our one white *d* of Innocence hath past,	,,	218
new life—the *d*'s of frost are o'er : New life, new love, to suit the newer *d* :	,,	278
I have had my *d*.	,,	316
I have had my *d* and my philosophies—	,,	319
King Was victor wellnigh *d* by *d*,	,,	335
fool,' said Tristram, 'not in open *d*.'	,,	347
So on for all that *d* from lawn to lawn	,,	373
Built for a summer *d* with Queen Isolt	,,	378
Then pressing *d* by *d* thro' Lyonesse	,,	501
he went To-day for three *d*'s' hunting,—	,,	530
There came a *d* as still as heaven,	*Guinevere* 292
golden *d*'s In which she saw him first,	,,	380
and every *d* Beheld at noon in some delicious dale	,,	392
in the golden *d*'s before thy sin.	,,	500
The *d*'s will grow to weeks,	,,	624
The sombre close of that voluptuous *d*,	,,	688
that *d* when the great light of heaven Burn'd	*Pass. of Arthur* 90
when the dolorous *d* Grew drearier	,,	122
The voice of old and *d*'s to be.	,,	135
whiter than the mist that all *d* long	,,	137
So all *d* long the noise of battle roll'd	,,	170
the halls Of Camelot, as in the *d*'s that were.	,,	189
In those old *d*'s, one summer noon,	,,	197
the *d*'s darken round me, and the years,	,,	405
Rise like a fountain for me night and *d*.	,,	417
the three whereat we gazed On that high *d*,	,,	454
Bear witness, that rememberable *d*,	*To the Queen ii* 3
make it wholly thine on sunny *d*.	*Lover's Tale i* 14
d's Of dewy dawning and the amber eves	,,	51
when *d* hung From his mid-dome in Heaven's	,,	65
all her flowers, And length of *d*'s,	,,	105
with the growths Of vigorous early *d*'s,	,,	133
Before he saw my *d* my father died,	,,	191
I said to her, ' A *d* for Gods to stoop,'	,,	304
for that *d* Love, rising, shook his wings,	,,	316
d which did enwomb that happy hour, Thou art blessed in the years, divinest !	,,	485
Then had he stemm'd my *d* with night,	,,	502
Yet bearing round about him this own *d*,	,,	510
come To boys and girls when summer *d*'s are new,	,,	555
where that *d* I crown'd myself as king,	,,	592

Day (*continued*) for the *d* was as the night to me ! The night to me was kinder than the *d* ; The night in pity took away my *d*, *Lover's Tale* 610
All *d* I watch'd the floating isles of shade,	,,	ii 5
All *d* I sat within the cavern-mouth.	,,	37
The *d* waned ; Alone I sat with her :	,,	139
From the outer *d*, Betwixt the close-set ivies	,,	171
I CAME one *d* and sat among the stones	,,	iii 1
what height The *d* had grown I know not.	,,	9
had lain three *d*'s without a pulse :	,,	iv 34
till the great *d* Peal'd on us with that music	,,	64
that *d* a boy was born, Heir to his face and land,	,,	128
for wasn't he coming that *d*?	*First Quarrel* 47
For the down's are as bright as *d*,	*Rizpah* 4
you were only made for the *d*.	,,	19
past away with five ships of war that *d*,	*The Revenge* 13
drew away From the Spanish fleet that *d*,	,,	47
fought such a fight for a *d* and a night	,,	83
And a *d* less or more At sea or ashore,	,,	86
tho' I loiter'd there The full *d* after,	*Sisters (E. and E.)* 98
lake and mountain conquers all the *d*.	,,	100
my crowning hour, my *d* of *d*'s.	,,	124
Then came the *d* when I, Flattering myself	,,	139
Not I that *d* of Edith's love or mine—	,,	142
Edith would be bridesmaid on the *d*. But on that *d*, not being all at ease,	,,	208
Thro' dreams by night and trances of the *d*,	,,	274
but the good Lord Jesus has had his *d*.'	*In the Child. Hosp.* 22
Say that His *d* is done !	,,	71
for fifteen *d*'s or for twenty at most.	*Def. of Lucknow* 9
it chanced on a *d* Soon as the blast	,,	31
we were every *d* fewer and fewer.	,,	49
to be a soldier all *d* and be sentinel	,,	74
Ever the *d* with its traitorous death	,,	79
Then *d* and night, *d* and night,	,,	92
' Hold it for fifteen *d*'s !'	,,	105
might be kindlier : happily come the *d* !	*Sir J. Oldcastle* 23
so spurn'd, so baited two whole *d*'s—	,,	163
more than once in *d*'s Of doubt and cloud	*Columbus* 155
To whom I send my prayer by night and *d*—	,,	233
slain my father the *d* before I was born.	*V. of Maeldune* 8
And we stay'd three *d*'s, and we gorged	,,	67
till the labourless *d* dipt under the West ;	,,	86
thunder of God peal'd over us all the *d*,	,,	113
I shall join you in a *d*.	*To W. H. Brookfield* 14
arm'd by *d* and night Against the Turk ;	*Montenegro* 3
All *d* the men contend in grievous war	*Achilles over the T.* 9
I, wearing but the garland of a *d*,	*To Dante* 6
When, in our younger London *d*'s,	*To E. Fitzgerald* 54
A clearer *d* Than our poor twilight	*Tiresias* 205
All *d* long far-off in the cloud of the city,	*The Wreck* 29
the sun of the soul made *d* in the dark	,,	55
That *d* my nurse had brought me the child.	,,	59
Ten long sweet summer *d*'s upon deck,	,,	64
the sons of a winterless *d*.	,,	74
Ten long *d*'s of summer and sin—if it must be so— But *d*'s of a larger light than I ever again shall know—*D*'s that will glimmer, I fear,	,,	77
little one found me at sea on a *d*,	,,	86
the storm and the *d*'s went by, but I knew no more—	,,	111
' Ten long sweet summer *d*'s ' of fever,	,,	147
And gone—that *d* of the storm—	,,	148
Three *d*'s since, three more dark *d*'s	*Despair* 6
to the glare of a drearier *d* ;	,,	28
What rulers but the *D*'s and Hours	*Ancient Sage* 95
The *d*'s and hours are ever glancing by,	,,	99
But with the Nameless is nor *D* nor Hour ;	,,	102
For man has overlived his *d*	,,	150
If utter darkness closed the *d*,	,,	199
sight and night to lose themselves in *d*.	,,	203
When only *D* should reign.'	,,	244
D and Night are children of the Sun,	,,	245
No night no *d* !—I touch thy world again—	,,	249
And send the *d* into the darken'd heart ;	,,	261
dawn of more than mortal *d* Strike on the Mount of Vision !	,,	284

Day (*continued*)   morning brings the *d* I hate and fear;   *The Flight* 2
the morn is calm, and like another *d*;   "   10
on that summer *d* When I had fall'n   "   21
love that keeps his heart alive beats on it night and *d*—   "   35
an' yer eyes as bright as the *d*!   *Tomorrow* 32
paäirints had inter'd glory, an' both in wan *d*,   "   53
sleeps the gleam of dying *d*.   *Locksley H., Sixty* 42
watching till the *d* begun—   "   91
force to guide us thro' the *d*'s I shall not see?   "   158
On this *d* and at this hour,   "   175
planets whirling round them, flash a million miles a *d*.   "   204
I shelter'd in this archway from a *d* of driving showers—   "   259
my Leonard, use and not abuse your *d*,   "   265
stood like a rock In the wave of a stormy *d*;   *Heavy Brigade* 57
I that loved thee since my *d* began,   *To Virgil* 38
The light of *d*'s when life begun, The *d*'s that
    seem to-day,   *Pref. Poem Broth. S.* 23
now thy long *d*'s work hath ceased,   *Epit. on Stratford* 2
maintain The *d* against the moment, and the
    year Against the *d*;   *To Duke of Argyll* 6
live With stronger life from *d* to *d*;   *Hands all round* 6
Two Suns of Love make *d* of human life,   *Prin. Beatrice* 1
light and genial warmth of double *d*.   "   22
Men that in a narrower *d*—   *Open I. and C. Exhib.* 25
lavish all the golden *d* To make them wealthier *Poets and their B.* 3
Your viceregal *d*'s Have added fulness *To Marq. of Dufferin* 10
My memories of his briefer *d* Will mix   "   51
that the *d*, When here thy hands let fall *Demeter and P.* 8
And robed thee in his *d* from head to feet—   "   21
a worm which writhes all *d*,   *Vastness* 17
Voices of the *d* Are heard across the Voices of the dark. *The Ring* 39
when you came of age Or on the *d* you married. Both
    the *d*'s Now close in one.   "   78
made The rosy twilight of a perfect *d*.   "   187
on her birthday, and that *d* His death-day,   "   212
one *d* came And saw you, shook her head,   "   312
I came, I went, was happier *d* by *d*;   "   348
on that *d* Two lovers parted by no scurrilous tale—   "   426
In summer if I reach my *d*—   *To Ulysses* 9
When frost is keen and *d*'s are brief—   "   19
years ago, In rick-fire *d*'s, When Dives loathed
    the times,   *To Mary Boyle* 28
O'er his uncertain shadow droops the *d*. *Prog. of Spring* 8
While the long *d* of knowledge grows and warms,   "   101
Thy scope of operation, *d* by *d*,   "   111
stumbled back again Into the common *d*,   *Romney's R.* 33
To you my *d*'s have been a life-long lie,   "   41
To flame along another dreary *d*.   "   58
And on this white midwinter *d*—   *To Master of B.* 9
d long labour'd, hewing the pines,   *Death of Œnone* 62
vanish'd like a ghost Before the *d*,   "   68
more than he that sang the Works and *D*'s,   *To Virgil* 6
d by *d*, thro' many a blood-red eve,   *St. Telemachus* 3
off the rosy cheek of waking *D*.   *Akbar's Dream* 202
one *d* He had left his dagger behind him. *Bandit's Death* 11
alone in the dell at the close of the *d*.   "   19
and the *d* I was born.   *Charity* 24
she sat *d* and night by my bed,   "   33
Dawn not *D*! (repeat)   *The Dawn* 11, 16
Storm in the South that darkens the *d*! *Riflemen, form!* 2
if Thou willest, let my *d* be brief, So Thou wilt
    strike Thy glory thro' the *d*. *Doubt and Prayer* 13
Must my *d* be dark by reason,   *God and the Univ.* 2
after his brief range of blameless *d*'s, *D. of the Duke of C.* 9

Daylight   Ind to Ind, but in fair *d* woke, *Buonaparte* 4
Flood with full *d* glebe and town?   *Two Voices* 87
Seems to the quiet *d* of your minds *Lover's Tale i* 296
Long as the *d* Lasted,   *Batt. of Brunanburh* 38
d made itself Ruddy thro' both the roofs of sight, *Tiresias* 2
whence an affluent fountain pour'd From darkness into *d*, *Ancient Sage* 8
vapour in *d* Over the mountain Floats,   *Kapiolani* 16
Daylong   you caught His weary *d* chirping, *The Brook* 53
Dayshine   Naked in open *d*?' 'Nay,' she cried, *Gareth and L.* 1092
Dazed   the sudden light *D* me half-blind: *Princess v* 12
And *d* all eyes, till Arthur by main might, *Com. of Arthur* 109

Dazed (*continued*)   Some flush'd, and others *d*, *Com. of Arthur* 265
nor lights nor feast *D* or amazed, *Lover's Tale iv* 311
d and dumb With passing thro' at once *Demeter and P.* 6
end myself too with the dagger—so deafen'd and *d*— *Bandit's Death* 37
Dazing   from the lava-lake *D* the starlight, *Kapiolani* 15
Dazzle   not shown To *d* all that see them? *The Ring* 144
Dazzled   both his eyes were *d*, as he stood, *M. d'Arthur* 59
The rhymes are *d* from their place *Day-Dm., Pro.* 19
boyish dream involved and *d* down *Princess iv* 450
Be *d* by the wildfire Love to sloughs   "   *v* 441
In either hand be bore What *d* all, *Gareth and L.* 387
And *d* by the livid-flickering fork, *Merlin and V.* 941
So that his eyes were *d* looking at it. *Pelleas and E.* 36
Was *d* by the sudden light,   "   105
both his eyes were *d* as he stood, *Pass. of Arthur* 227
Dazzling   The sun came *d* thro' the leaves, *L. of Shalott iii* 3
Dead (*adj.*) (*See also* **Deäd, Half-dead**) All cold, and
    d, and corpse-like grown? *Supp. Confessions* 17
I would that I were *d*!' (repeat) *Mariana* 12, 24, 36, 48, 60, 72
Oh God, that I were *d*!'   *Mariana* 84
Nor canst thou show the dead are *d*. *Two Voices* 267
like a shadow, and the winds are *d*. *Œnone* 28
He look'd so grand when he was *d*. *The Sisters* 32
Since I beheld young Laurence *d*. *L. C. V. de Vere* 28
Roman soldier found Me lying *d*, *D. of F. Women* 162
And the old year is *d*.   "   248
But he'll be *d* before. *D. of the O. Year* 32
I see the true old times are *d*, *M. d'Arthur* 229
who was *d*, Who married, who was like to be, *Audley Court* 29
I hope my end draws nigh: half *d* I am, *St. S. Stylites* 37
this wonder, *d*, become Mere highway dust? *Love and Duty* 10
Better thou wert *d* before me, *Locksley Hall* 56
Can I think of her as *d*, and love her   "   73
And half the crew are sick or *d*, *The Voyage* 92
Come not, when I am *d*, *Come not, when, etc.* 1
She talk'd as if her love were *d* *The Letters* 27
tender grace of a day that is *d* *Break, break, etc.* 15
Still downward thinking '*d* or *d* to me!' *Enoch Arden* 689
If you could tell her you had seen him *d*,   "   808
Not to reveal it, till you see me *d*.' '*D*,'   "   839
But if my children care to see me *d*,   "   888
Were *d* to him already; bent as he was *Aylmer's Field* 445
D for two years before his death was he;   "   837
We *must* forgive the dead.' 'Dead! who is *d*?' *Sea Dreams* 270
He suddenly dropt *d* of heart-disease.' '*D*? he?
    of heart-disease? what heart had he To die of? *d*!'   "   274
crush her pretty maiden fancies *d* *Princess i* 88
Peace be with her. She is *d*.   "   *iv* 136
And strikes him *d* for thine and thee.   "   584
cold reverence worse than were she *d*.   "   *v* 92
I would the old God of war himself were *d*,   "   145
Home they brought her warrior *d*:   "   *vi* 1
she said, 'he lives: he is not *d*:   "   122
he is *d*, Or all as *d*:   "   169
Till the Sun drop, *d*, from the signs.'   "   *vii* 245
lift thine eyes; my doubts are *d*,   "   348
if to-night our greatness were struck *d*, *Third of Feb.* 17
was *d* before he was born, (repeat) *Grandmother* 59, 68
not always certain if they be alive or *d*.   "   84
And when I am there and *d* and gone, *Window. No Answer* 11
Where lies the master newly *d*; *In Mem. xx* 4
But, he was *d*, and there he sits,   "   *xxxii* 3
'But brooding on the dear one *d*' *In Mem. xxxvii* 17
Nor can I dream of thee as *d*:   "   *lxviii* 4
Regret is *d*, but love is more   "   *Con.* 17
and found The shining daffodil *d*, *Maud I iii* 14
Had I lain for a century *d*;   "   *xxii* 72
Strike *d* the whole weak race of venomous worms,   "   *II i* 46
Who knows if he be *d*?   "   *ii* 71
She is but *d*, and the time is at hand   "   *iii* 8
There is some one dying or *d*,   "   *iv* 48
D, long *d*, Long *d*!   "   *v* 1
And wept, and wish'd that I were *d*; *Com. of Arthur* 345
Thrall'd in his castle, and hath starved him *d*; *Gareth and L.* 358
Emrys would have scourged thee *d*,   "   375

Dead (adj.) (*continued*) Fell, as if *d*; but quickly rose

and drew,	*Gareth and L.* 967
and all wing'd nothings peck him *d*!	*Marr. of Geraint* 275
be he *d* I know not, but he past to the wild land.	” 442
once without remorse to strike her *d*,	*Geraint and E.* 109
and so left him stunn'd or *d*,	” 464
'What, is he *d*?' 'No, no, not *d*!'	” 541
sure am I, quite sure, he is not *d*.'	” 545
if he be not *d*, Why wail ye for him thus?	” 546
And be he *d*, I count you for a fool; Your wailing will not quicken him: *d* or not,	” 548
yet lay still, and feign'd himself as *d*,	” 588
were I *d* who is it would weep for me?	” 618
Take warning: yonder man is surely *d*;	” 672
Except he surely knew my lord was *d*,'	” 721
died Earl Doorm by him be counted *d*.	” 730
D, whom we buried; more than one of us	*Balin and Balan* 122
yonder lies one *d* within the wood. Not *d*;	” 468
like brainless bulls, *D* for one heifer!'	”
Coming and going, and he lay as *d*	*Merlin and V.* 213
Coming and going, and she lay as *d*,	” 644
And in the hollow oak he lay as *d*,	” 969
I fear me, that will strike my blossom *d*.	*Lancelot and E.* 971
Give me good fortune, I will strike him *d*,	” 1071
she did not seem as *d*, But fast asleep,	” 1160
broken shed, And in it a *d* babe;	*Holy Grail* 399
dry old trunks about us, *d*, Yea, rotten	” 495
And one had wedded her, and he was *d*,	” 586
'Lo! Pelleas is *d*—he told us—	*Pelleas and E.* 377
'*D*, is it so?' she ask'd. 'Ay, ay,' said he,	” 384
I to your *d* man have given my troth,	” 389
one Murmuring, 'All courtesy is *d*,'	*Last Tournament* 211
The leaf is *d*, the yearning past away:	” 277
Is all the laughter gone *d* out of thee?—	” 300
High on a grim *d* tree before the tower,	” 430
Heard in *d* night along that table-shore,	” 463
'my man Hath left me or is *d*;'	” 495
child of one I honour'd, happy, *d* before thy shame?	*Guinevere* 423
strike him *d*, and meet myself Death,	” 575
strikes them *d* is as my death to me.	*Pass. of Arthur* 74
That quick or *d* thou holdest me for King.	” 161
I see the true old times are *d*,	” 397
Hope was not wholly *d*, But breathing hard	*Lover's Tale* i 584
I had lain as *d*, Mute, blind and motionless	” 606
D, for henceforth there was no life for me!	” 608
but mine was wholly *d*,	” 724
Some one had told me she was *d*,	” ii 70
low knell tolling his lady *d*— *D*—	” iv 33
All that look'd on her had pronounced her *d*.	” 35
but after my man was *d*;	*First Quarrel* 6
an' I wish I was *d*—	” 52
hear that cry of my boy that was *d*,	*Rizpah* 45
bullet struck him that was dressing it suddenly *d*,	*The Revenge* 67
nay, murder'd, doubtless *d*.	*Sir J. Oldcastle* 60
Some *d* of hunger, some beneath the scourge,	*Columbus* 177
he had stricken my father *d*—	*V. of Maeldune* 1
men dropt *d* in the valleys	” 31
D of some inward agony—is it so?	*To W. H. Brookfield* 10
the winds were *d* for heat;	*Tiresias* 34
and dash'd herself *D* in her rage:	” 153
D to the death beside me,	*The Wreck* 113
I would thank him, the other is *d*,	*Despair* 70
From the *d* fossil skull that is left in the rocks of an earth that is *d*?	” 86
Would fain that he were *d*;	*Ancient Sage* 126
Found, fear'd me *d*, and groan'd,	*The Flight* 23
an icy corpse *d* of some foul disease:	” 54
he comes, and finds me *d*.	” 72
'Ud 'a shot his own sowl *d* for a kiss	*Tomorrow* 40
her wits wor *d*, an' her hair was as white	” 60
an' dhropt down *d* an the dead.	” 80
D the warrior, *d* his glory, *d* the cause	*Locksley H., Sixty* 30
Lies my Amy *d* in child-birth, *d* the mother, *d* the child. *D*—and sixty years ago, and *d* her aged husband now—	” 36

Dead (adj.) (*continued*) earth be *d* as yon *d* world the moon? *D* the new astronomy calls

her. . . .	*Locksley H., Sixty* 174
D, but now her living glory lights the hall,	” 181
D! And the Muses cried with a stormy cry	*Dead Prophet* 1
D! 'Is it *he* then brought so low?'	” 5
D, who had served his time,	” 9
somewhere *d* far in the waste Soudan,	*Epit. on Gordon* 2
Tho' *d* in its Trinacrian Enna,	*To Prof. Jebb* 11
The dead are not *d* but alive.	*Vastness* 36
she my Miriam *d* within the year.	*The Ring* 286
D! I took And chafed the freezing hand.	” 451
D!—and maybe stung With some remorse,	” 454
—but *d* so long, gone up so far,	” 462
In fright, and fallen *d*.	” 471
'HE is fled—I wish him *d*—	*Forlorn* 1
He is fled, or he is *d*,	” 9
and when The Priest pronounced you *d*,	*Happy* 50
fire from Heaven had dash'd him *d*,	” 83
As *d* from all the human race as if beneath the mould; If you be *d*, then I am *d*,	” 95
D with the dead?	*To Mary Boyle* 14
mountain rolls into the plain, Fell headlong *d*;	*Death of Œnone* 52
then a shower of stones that stoned him *d*,	*St. Telemachus* 68
rabble in half-amaze Stared at him *d*,	” 72
band will be scatter'd now their gallant captain is *d*,	*Bandit's Death* 41
birthday came of a boy born happily *d*.	*Charity* 34
when all but the winds were *d*,	*The Dreamer* 1

Dead (s) (*See also* **Living-dead**). Ev'n in the charnels

of the *d*,	*Two Voices* 215
Nor canst thou show the *d* are dead.	” 267
'We find no motion in the *d*.'	” 279
And of the rising from the *d*,	*Palace of Art* 206
Once heard at *d* of night to greet	*On a Mourner* 32
As we bear blossom of the *d*;	*Love thou thy land* 94
And grassy barrows of the happier *d*.	*Tithonus* 71
He gazes on the silent *d*:	*Day-Dm., Arrival* 13
'O love, thy kiss would wake the *d*!'	” *Depart.* 20
was deadly wounded Falling on the *d*.	*The Captain* 64
And the *d* begin to dance.	*Vision of Sin* 166
Yes, as the *d* we weep for testify—	*Aylmer's Field* 747
We *must* forgive the *d*.' 'D'! who is dead?'	*Sea Dreams* 270
shine among the *d* Hereafter; tales!	*Lucretius* 129
Sat watching like a watcher by the *d*.	*Princess* v 62
And watches in the *d*, the dark,	” vii 103
Thy living voice to me was as the voice of the *d*,	*V. of Cauteretz* 8
voice of the *d* was a living voice to me.	” 10
And scratch the very *d* for spite:	*Lit. Squabbles* 8
That name the under-lying *d*,	*In Mem.* ii 2
And hear the ritual of the *d*.	” xviii 12
But Sorrow—fixt upon the *d*,	” xxxix 8
How fares it with the happy *d*?	” xliv 1
Do we indeed desire the *d* Should still be near	” li 1
The *d* shall look me thro' and thro'.	” li 12
Eternal greetings to the *d*;	” lvii 14
So hold I commerce with the *d*;	” lxxxv 93
Or so methinks the *d* would say;	” 94
That could the *d*, whose dying eyes	” xc 5
hold An hour's communion with the *d*.	” xciv 4
The noble letters of the *d*:	” xcv 24
And woodlands holy to the *d*;	” xcix 8
I dream'd a vision of the *d*,	” ciii 3
But trust that those we call the *d*	” cxviii 5
Should pile her barricades with *d*.	” cxxvii 8
Her feet, my darling, on the *d*;	*Con.* 50
I hear the *d* at midday moan,	*Maud* I vi 70
For I thought the *d* had peace,	” II v 15
which makes us loud in the world of the *d*	” 25
For it is but a world of the *d*;	” 40
comes from another stiller world of the *d*,	” 70
the living quiet as the *d*,	*Com. of Arthur* 123
I cannot brook to gaze upon the *d*.'	*Balin and Balan* 586
Among the *d* and sown upon the wind—	*Merlin and V.* 45
And by the cold Hic Jacets of the *d*!'	” 753
and the *d*, Oar'd by the dumb,	*Lancelot and E.* 1153

Dearest (*continued*) Of all things upon earth the *d* to me.'   *Lover's Tale iv* 319
which of all things is the *d* to me,   ,, 348
What sound was *d* in his native dells?   *Far-far-away* 4
Dearness with a *d* not his due.   *Locksley Hall* 91
A distant *d* in the hill,   *In Mem. lxiv* 19
Death   Oh! vanity! *D* waits at the door.   *All Things will Die* 17
Hark! *d* is calling While I speak to ye,   ,, 28
Patient of ill, and *d*, and scorn,   *Supp. Confessions* 4
To hold a common scorn of *d*!   ,, 34
He hath no care of life or *d*;   ,, 48
stooping low Unto the *d*, not sunk!   ,, 98
Shall we not look into the laws Of life and *d*,   ,, 172
O weary life! O weary *d*!   ,, 188
A gentler *d* shall Falsehood die,   *Clear-headed friend* 16
Life, anguish, *d*, immortal love,   *Arabian Nights* 73
when he taketh repose An hour before *d*;   *A Spirit haunts* 15
He saw thro' life and *d*,   *The Poet* 5
In your eye there is *d*,   *Poet's Mind* 16
D, walking all alone beneath a yew,   *Love and Death* 5
' You must begone,' said *D*,   ,, 7
Life eminent creates the shade of *d*;   ,, 13
I drink the cup of a costly *d*,   *Eleänore* 138
With secret *d* for ever, in the pits   *Wan Sculptor* 13
And range of evil between *d* and birth,   *If I were loved* 3
wait for *d*—mute—careless of all ills,   ,, 10
' Thou hadst not between *d* and birth   *Two Voices* 169
Know I not *D*? the outward signs?   ,, 270
Has ever truly long'd for *d*.   ,, 396
Oh life, not *d*, for which we pant;   ,, 398
That I should die an early *d*:   *Miller's D.* 90
O *d*, *d*, *d*, thou ever-floating cloud,   *Œnone* 238
Walking the cold and starless road of *D*   ,, 259
And *d* and life she hated equally,   *Palace of Art* 265
And sweeter far is *d* than life to me   *May Queen, Con.* 8
D is the end of life;   *Lotos-Eaters, C. S.* 41
Give us long rest or *d*, dark *d*, or dreamful ease.   ,, 53
There *is* confusion worse than *d*,   ,, 83
The downward slope to *d*.   *D. of F. Women* 16
bright *d* quiver'd at the victim's throat;   ,, 115
I was ripe for *d*.   ,, 208
who knew that Love can vanquish *D*,   ,, 269
Once thro' mine own doors *D* did pass;   *To J. S.* 19
D is blown in every wind;'   ,, 46
fluting a wild carol ere her *d*,   *M. d'Arthur* 267
But Dora lived unmarried till her *d*.   *Dora* 172
suit had wither'd, nipt to *d* by him   *Edwin Morris* 101
did not all thy martyrs die one *d*?   *St. S. Stylites* 50
and whole years long, a life of *d*.   ,, 54
hope ere *d* Spreads more and more and more,   ,, 156
Like *D* betwixt thy dear embrace and mine,   *Love and Duty* 48
Like bitter accusation ev'n to *d*,   ,, 81
every hour Must sweat her sixty minutes to the *d*,   *Golden Year* 69
D closes all : but something ere the end,   *Ulysses* 51
Till mellow *D*, like some late guest,   *Will Water.* 239
No carved cross-bones, the types of *D*,   ,, 245
Pale again as *d* did prove: *L. of Burleigh* 66
gray and gap-tooth'd man as lean as *d*,   *Vision of Sin* 60
Let us hob-and-nob with *D*.   ,, 74
' *D* is king, and Vivat Rex!   ,, 179
Hob-and-nob with brother *D*!   ,, 194
In those two *d's* he read God's warning   *Enoch Arden* 571
His baby's *d*, her growing poverty,   ,, 705
than he saw *D* dawning on him,   ,, 832
.peace which each had prick'd to *d*.   *Aylmer's Field* 52
no force, Persuasion, no, nor *d* could alter her: ,, 418
cordon close and closer toward the *d*,   ,, 500
a letter edged with *d* Beside him,   ,, 595
Averill went and gazed upon his *d*.   ,, 599
for the second *d* Scarce touch'd her   ,, 604
hapless loves And double *d* were widely murmur'd,   ,, 617
wounded to the *d* that cannot die;   ,, 662
from the people's eyes Ere the great *d*,   ,, 773
devising their own daughter's *d*!   ,, 783
Stumbling across the market to his *d*,   ,, 820
Dead for two years before his *d* was he;   ,, 837

Death (*continued*) dark retinue reverencing *d* At golden thresholds;   *Aylmer's Field* 842
Bound on a matter he of life and *d*:   *Sea Dreams* 151
gout and stone, that break Body toward *d*,   *Lucretius* 154
nor shunn'd a soldier's *d*,   *Princess, Pro.* 38
I would make it *d* For any male thing   ,, 151
As blank as *d* in marble;   ,, *i* 177
LET NO MAN ENTER IN ON PAIN OF *D*?   ,, *ii* 195
I give thee to *d* My brother!   ,, 307
To give three gallant gentlemen to *d*.'   ,, 335
I spoke of war to come and many *d's*,   ,, *iii* 150
you will shock him ev'n to *d*,   ,, 212
act Of immolation, any phase of *d*,   ,, 285
Sun Grew broader toward his *d* and fell,   ,, 364
' Dear as remember'd kisses after *d*,   ,, *iv* 54
O *D* in Life, the days that are no more.'   ,, 58
Melissa clamour'd ' Flee the *d*;'   ,, 166
On all sides, clamouring etiquette to *d*,   ,, *v* 17
those that mourn half-shrouded over *d*   ,, 74
record of her wrongs, And crush'd to *d*:   ,, 144
dash'd with *d* He reddens what he kisses: ,, 164
and had not shunn'd the *d*,   ,, 178
sware to combat for my claim till *d*.   ,, 360
trust that there is no one hurt to *d*,   ,, *vi* 242
think that you might mix his draught with *d*,   ,, 277
well-nigh close to *d* For weakness;   ,, *vii* 119
Leapt fiery Passion from the brinks of *d*;   ,, 156
nor cares to walk With *D* and Morning   ,, 204
Or pines in sad experience worse than *d*,   ,, 315
All in the valley of *D* Rode the six hundred.   *Light Brigade* 3
Into the valley of *D* Rode the six hundred. (repeat)   ,, 7, 16
Into the jaws of *D*,   ,, 24
Came thro' the jaws of *D*,   ,, 46
first time, too, that ever I thought of *d*.   *Grandmother* 61
' *d* is sure To those that stay and those that roam,   *Sailor Boy* 13
My father raves of *d* and wreck,   ,, 19
Far worse than any *d* to me.'   ,, 24
The wages of sin is *d*:   *Wages* 6
Thou madest *D*; and lo, thy foot   *In Mem., Pro.* 7
To dance with *d*, to beat the ground,   ,, *i* 12
O Priestess in the vaults of *D*,   ,, *iii* 2
No hint of *d* in all his frame,   ,, *xiv* 14
Cold in that atmosphere of *D*,   ,, *xx* 14
If *D* were seen At first as *D*,   ,, *xxxv* 18
To that vague fear implied in *d*;   ,, *xli* 14
If Sleep and *D* be truly one,   ,, *xliii* 1
(If *D* so taste Lethean springs),   ,, *xliv* 10
Beyond the second birth of *D*.   ,, *xlv* 16
There must be wisdom with great *D*:   ,, *li* 11
I bring to life, I bring to *d*:   ,, *lvi* 6
Sleep, *D's* twin-brother, times my breath; Sleep, *D's* twin-brother, knows not *D*,   ,, *lxviii* 2
Sleep, kinsman thou to *d* and trance   ,, *lxxi* 1
I curse not nature, no, nor *d*;   ,, *lxxiii* 7
knowing *D* has made His darkness beautiful   ,, *lxxiv* 11
That holy *D* ere Arthur died   ,, *lxxx* 2
But *D* returns an answer sweet: ,, *lxxxi* 9
I wage not any feud with *D*   ,, *lxxxii* 1
Nor blame I *D*, because he bare   ,, 9
For this alone on *D* I wreak   ,, 13
till Doubt and *D*, Ill brethren,   ,, *lxxxvi* 11
sire would make Confusion worse than *d*,   ,, *xc* 19
shocks of Chance—The blows of *D*.   ,, *xcv* 43
Mixt their dim lights, like life and *d*,   ,, 63
gleams On Lethe in the eyes of *D*.   ,, *xcviii* 8
And unto myriads more, of *d*.   ,, *xcix* 16
As one would sing the *d* of war,   ,, *ciii* 33
Or dive below the wells of *D*?   ,, *cviii* 8
on the depths of *d* there swims The reflex   ,, 11
She cannot fight the fear of *d*.   ,, *cxiv* 10
Like Paul with beasts, I fought with *D*;   ,, *cxx* 4
I slip the thoughts of life and *d*;   ,, *cxxii* 16
Unpalsied when he met with *D*,   ,, *cxxviii* 2
whatever is ask'd her, answers ' *D*.'   *Maud I i* 4
To the *d*, for their native land.   ,, *v* 11

Dedicate (continued) Shut in from Time, and d to thee: | *Lover's Tale i* 438
Dee Bala lake Fills all the sacred D. | *Geraint and E.* 930
Deed Fruitful of further thought and d, | *Two Voices* 144
Blowing a noise of tongues and d's, | " 206
a life of shocks, Dangers, and d's, | *Œnone* 164
' I take possession of man's mind and d. | *Palace of Art* 209
our great d's, as half-forgotten things. | *Lotos-Eaters, C. S.* 78
Would serve his kind in d and word, | *Love thou thy land* 86
Delight our souls with talk of knightly d's, | *M. d'Arthur* 19
the Powers, who wait On noble d's, | *Godiva* 72
' They perish'd in their daring d's.' | *Day-Dm., Arrival* 14
I am yours in word and in d. | *Lady Clare* 74
Divorce the Feeling from her mate the D. | *The Brook* 95
Nor d's of gift, but gifts of grace | *Sea Dreams* 192
' His d's yet live, the worst is yet to come. | " 314
and your great d's For issue, | *Princess iii* 242
Howe'er you babble, great d's cannot die; | " 254
on the highest Foam of men's d's— | " v 320
Bright let it be with its blazon'd d's, | *Ode on Well.* 56
thine the d's to be celebrated, | *Boädicea* 41
In loveliness of perfect d's, | *In Mem. xxxvi* 11
Her secret meaning in her d's, | " lv 10
What fame is left for human d's | " lxxiii 11
On songs, and d's, and lives, | " lxxvii 3
O true in word, and tried in d, | " lxxxv 5
Perplext in faith, but pure in d's, | " xcvi 9
Flow thro' our d's and make them pure, | " cxxxi 4
some good knight had done one noble d, | *Gareth and L.* 411
And the d's sake my knighthood do the d, | " 572
My d's will speak : it is but for a day.' | " 577
for the d's sake have I done the d, | " 832
' Say thou thy say, and I will do my d. | " 901
said your say ; Mine answer was my d. | " 1175
far-sounded among men For noble d's ? | *Marr. of Geraint* 428
So grateful is the noise of noble d's | " 437
Because I knew my d's were known, | *Geraint and E.* 858
doubtless, all unearn'd by noble d's. | *Balin and Balan* 471
love of God and men And noble d's, | *Merlin and V.* 413
And each incited each to noble d's, | " 414
the great d's Of Lancelot, and his prowess | *Lancelot and E.* 81
do and almost overdo the d's Of Lancelot, | " 469
some brave d seem'd to be done in vain, | *Holy Grail* 274
This chance of noble d's will come and go | " 318
every evil I I ever did, Awoke and cried, | " 373
honour and all noble d's Flash'd, | *Pelleas and E.* 278
flower Waits to be solid fruit of golden d's, | *Last Tournament* 100
uprear'd By noble d's at one with noble vows, | " 123
Did mightier d's than elsewhere he had done, | " 680
here and there a d Of prowess done | *Guinevere* 458
And worship her by years of noble d's, | " 476
miss to hear high talk of noble d's | " 499
she, for her good d's and her pure life, | " 693
and in the mist Was many a noble d, | *Pass. of Arthur* 105
Delight our souls with talk of knightly d's, | " 187
breathless body of her good d's past. | *Lover's Tale i* 217
Love and Longing dress thy d's in light, | *Ded. Poem Prin. Alice* 9
this ballad of the d's Of England, | " 20
Virtue must shape itself in d, | *Tiresias* 86
light upon the ways of men As one great d. | " 162
crown with song The warrior's noble d— | *Epilogue* 37
For so the d endures ; | " 39
And d and song alike are swept Away, | " 67
nation's heart, Is in itself a d.' | " 82
His dream became a d that woke the world, | *St. Telemachus* 70
prayers, That have no successor in d, | *Akbar's Dream* 10
By d's a light to men ? | " 111
Deem who d him not, Or will not d him, | *Gareth and L.* 120
And d's it carrion of some woodland thing, | " 748
But d not I accept thee aught the more, | " 839
who d this maid Might wear as fair a jewel | *Lancelot and E.* 239
d this prize of ours is rashly given : | " 541
damsel, for I d you know full well | " 689
I d As of the visions that he told— | *Lover's Tale iv* 22
If I should d it over nice— | *Tiresias* 191
And d me grateful, and farewell ! | *The Wanderer* 16

Deem'd she d no mist of earth could dull | *Ode to Memory* 38
well had d he felt the tale Less than the teller : | *Enoch Arden* 711
Things in an Aylmer d impossible, | *Aylmer's Field* 305
the peace, that I d no peace, is over | *Maud III vi* 50
Smile at him, as he d, presumptuously : | *Balin and Balan* 222
wherein she d she look'd her best, | *Lancelot and E.* 907
they d her death Was rather in the fantasy | " 1131
wellnigh d His wish by hers was echo'd ; | *Pelleas and E.* 120
I loved you and I d you beautiful, | " 297
I d him fool ? yea so ? | " 309
She d I wore a brother's mind : | *Lover's Tale i* 740
Deeming Vivien, d Merlin overborne By instance, | *Merlin and V.* 800
D our courtesy is the truest law, | *Lancelot and E.* 712
Deem'st D thou that I accept thee | *Gareth and L.* 766
Deep (adj. and adv.) (*See also* Ankle-deep, Breast-deep, Elbow-deep, Fathom-deep, Knee-deep, Love-deep, Mellow-deep, Mid-thigh-deep, Waist-deep)
Tho' d not fathomless, | *Ode to Memory* 34
grow so full and d In thy large eyes | *Eleänore* 85
So full, so d, so slow, | " 95
King Arthur : then, because his wound was d, | *M. d'Arthur* 5
rain, That makes thee broad and d ! | *Talking Oak* 280
And d into the dying day | *Day-Dm., Depart.* 7
One sabbath d and wide— | *St. Agnes' Eve* 34
D as Hell I count his error. | *The Captain* 3
King Arthur. Then, because his wound was d, | *Pass. of Arthur* 174
Love lieth d : Love dwells not in lip-depths. | *Lover's Tale i* 466
I can't dig, I am old— | *Rizpah* 56
look you here—the shadows are too d, | *Sisters (E. and E.)* 103
I heard that voice,—as mellow and d As a psalm | *The Wreck* 52
Six foot d of burial mould Will dull | *Romney's R.* 125
thou knowest how d a well of love | *Akbar's Dream* 170
Deep (s) (*See also* Forest-deeps) BELOW the thunders of the upper d ; | *The Kraken* 1
Until the latter fire shall heat the d ; | " 13
drove The fragrant, glistening d's, | *Arabian Nights* 14
Round thee blow, self-pleached d, | *A Dirge* 29
From his coiled sleeps in the central d's | *The Mermaid* 24
And drives them to the d.' | *Palace of Art* 204
The abysmal d's of Personality, | " 223
roaring d's and fiery sands, | *Lotos-Eaters," C. S.* 115
Nine years she wrought it, sitting in the d's | *M. d'Arthur* 105
He heard the d behind him, | " 184
the d Moans round with many voices. | *'Ulysses* 55
Where either haven open'd on the d's, | *Enoch Arden* 671
Trembled in perilous places o'er a d : | *Sea Dreams* 11
I from out the boundless outer d | " 88
I thought the motion of the boundless d | " 91
motion of the great d bore me on, | " 111
To the waste d's together. | " 238
great black cloud Drag inward from the d's, | *Princess vii* 37
From barren d's to conquer all with love ; | " 164
Glimmer away to the lonely d, | *To F. D. Maurice* 28
But they—they feel the desire of the d— | *Voice and the P.* 19
The d has power on the height, And the height has power on the d ; | " 21
A d below the d, | " 33
Which heaves but with the heaving d. | *In "Mem. xi* 20
That stir the spirit's inner d's, | " xlii 10
A higher height, a deeper d. | " lxiii 12
and we to draw From d to d, | " ciii 39
cloud That landlike slept along the d. | " 56
There rolls the d where grew the tree. | " cxxiii 1
That tumbled in the Godless d ; | " cxxiv 12
To seek thee on the mystic d's, | " cxxv 14
Powers of the height, Powers of the d, | *Maud II ii* 82
by the side of the Black and the Baltic d, | *III vi* 51
high upon the dreary d's It seem'd in heaven, | *Com. of Arthur* 373
gathering half the d And full of voices, | " 380
From the great d to the great d he goes.' | " 411
in the d's whereof a mere, | *Gareth and L.* 798
by night to let the boundless d Down | *Merlin and V.* 113
boat Drave with a sudden wind across the d's, | " 201
On some wild down above the windy d, | " 658
fell the floods of heaven drowning the d. | *Holy Grail* 533

Deep (s) *(continued)*   Seven days I drove along the dreary *d*,   *Holy Grail* 808

From the great *d* to the great *d* he goes.'   *Last Tournament* 133

wash'd up from out the *d* ?   " 685

Nine years she wrought it, sitting in the *d's*   *Pass. of Arthur* 273

He heard the *d* behind him, and a cry   " 352

From the great *d* to the great *d* he goes.'   " 445

Down that long water opening on the *d*   " 466

sank his body with honour down into the *d*,   *The Revenge* 109

Out of the *d*, my child, out of the *d*, (repeat)   *De Prof., Two G.* 1, 5, 26, 29.

To that last *d* where we and thou are still.   *De Prof., Two G.* 25

From that great *d*, before our world begins,   " 27

Out of the *d*, Spirit, out of the *d*,   " 32

rolls the heavens, and lifts, and lays the *d*,   *Tiresias* 22

word of the Poet by whom the *d's* of the world are stirr'd,   *The Wreck* 23

the crew should cast me into the *d*,   " 94

between me and the *d* and my doom,   *Despair* 5

suffers on land or in air or the *d*,   " 45

Slight ripple on the boundless *d*   *Ancient Sage* 189

that one ripple on the boundless *d* Feels that the *d* is boundless,   " 191

One with the boundless motion of the *d*.   " 194

Noises of a current narrowing, not the music of a *d* ?   *Locksley H., Sixty* 154

Light airs from where the *d*,   *Early Spring* 21

she peers along the tremulous *d*,   *Demeter and P.* 14

drown'd in the *d's* of a meaningless Past ?   *Vastness* 34

far As the gray *d*, a landscape   *The Ring* 150

hoary *d's* that belt the changeful West,   *Prog. of Spring* 98

Not the Great Voice not the true *D*.   *Akbar's Dream* 59

D under *d* for ever goes,   *Mechanophilus* 35

wholly vanish in your *d's* and heights ?   *God and the Univ.* 1

which drew from out the boundless *d*   *Crossing the Bar* 7

Deep-asleep   *d–a* he seem'd, yet all awake,   *Lotos-Eaters* 35

Deep-blue   Floods all the *d–b* gloom   *D. of F. Women* 186

Deep-chested   *D–c* music, and to this result.   *The Epic* 51

Deep-domed   as the *d–d* empyrean Rings   *Milton* 7

Deepen   *d's* on and up ! the gates Roll back,   *St Agnes' Eve* 29

same old rut would *d* year by year ;   *Aylmer's Field* 34

Ay me, the sorrow *d's* down,   *In Mem. xlix* 14

the gloom Of twilight *d's* round it,   *Balin and Balan* 233

Deepen'd *(See also* **Ever-deepen'd***)*   The battle *d* in its place,   *Oriana* 51

and in him gloom on gloom *D* :   *Balin and Balan* 287

Deepening *(See also* **Down-deepening***)*   *d* thro' the silent spheres Heaven over Heaven   *Mariana in the S.* 91

D the courts of twilight broke them up   *Princess, Con.* 113

D thy voice with the *d* of the night,   *V. of Cauteretz* 2

Deeper   bury me *D*, ever so little *d*.   *Maud II v* 104

plunges thro' the wound again, And pricks it *d* :   *Pelleas and E.* 531

D than any yearnings after thee   *Last Tournament* 586

Tho' one is somewhat *d* than the other,   *Sisters (E. and E.)* 25

Deep-hued   With many a *d–h* bell-like flower   *Eleänore* 91

garden rose *D–h* and many-folded !   *Balin and Balan* 270

Deep-inrunning   sand and cliff and *d–i* cave,   *Sea Dreams* 17

Deeply-wounded   Or mythic Uther's *d–w* son   *Palace of Art* 105

Deep-meadow'd   it lies *D–m*, happy, fair with orchard-lawns   *M. d'Arthur* 262

it lies *D–m*, happy, fair with orchard-lawns   *Pass. of Arthur* 430

Deep-seated   *D–s* in our mystic frame,   *In Mem. xxxvi* 2

Deep-set   the *d–s* windows, stain'd and traced,   *Palace of Art* 49

Deep-tranced   they dwelt *D–t* on hers,   *Balin and Balan* 278

Deep-udder'd   dewy-fresh, browsed by *d–u* kine,   *Gardener's D.* 46

Deep-wooded   on the *d–w* mountain-side,   *The Wreck* 72

Deer   To chase the *d* at five ;   *Talking Oak* 52

Rode thro' the coverts of the *d*,   *Sir L. and Q. G.* 21

To show Sir Arthur's *d*.   *The Brook* 133

Like flies that haunt a wound, or *d*,   *Aylmer's Field* 571

Betwixt the monstrous horns of elk and *d*,   *Princess, Pro.* 23

and shook the branches of the *d*   " *Con.* 98

And cattle died, and *d* in wood,   *The Victim* 18

follow the *d* By these tall firs   *Gareth and L.* 90

Follow the *d* ? follow the Christ, the King,   " 117

Deer *(continued)*   There tript a hundred tiny silver *d*,   *Last Tournament* 171

But at the slot or fewmets of a *d*,   " 371

The *d*, the dews, the fern, the founts,   " 727

Defacement   royal crown, Stampt all into *d*,   *Balin and Balan* 541

Defacing   Defaming and *d*, till she left   *Merlin and V.* 804

Defamed   *D* by every charlatan,   *In Mem. cxi* 23

one that hath *d* The cognizance she gave me :   *Balin and Balan* 484

hast thou so *d* Thy brotherhood   *Pelleas and E.* 321

Defaming   *D* and defacing, till she left   *Merlin and V.* 804

Default   own baseness in him by *d* Of will and nature,   *Pelleas and E.* 81

Defeat   Whether ye wish me victory or *d*,   *Geraint and E.* 80

I must not dwell on that *d* of fame.   *Guinevere* 628

trumpets of victory, groans of *d*,   *Vastness* 8

Defect   each fulfils *D* in each, and always thought in thought,   *Princess vii* 304

D's of doubt, and taints of blood ;   *In Mem. liv* 4

an hour's *d* of the rose,   *Maud I ii* 8

have in it an absoluter trust To make up that *d* :   *Lancelot and E.* 1193

Scorn was allow'd as part of his *d*,   *Guinevere* 43

A beauty with *d*—till That which knows,   *Ancient Sage* 86

Defence   war would arise in *d* of the right,   *Maud III vi* 19

and my squire Hath in him small *d* ;   *Balin and Balan* 477

on all the *d's* our myriad enemy fell.   *Def. of Lucknow* 35

Clean from our lines of *d* ten or twelve   " 62

Defend   thou might'st *d* The thesis which thy words   *Two Voices* 337

and three knights *D* the passings,   *Gareth and L.* 614

And there *d* his marches ;   *Marr. of Geraint* 41

and there *d* Your marches,   *Geraint and E.* 889

And would *d* his judgment well,   *Tiresias* 190

Defended *(See also* **Half-defended***)*   works that *d* the hold we held with our lives—   *Def. of Lucknow* 7

Deferentially   Sir Aylmer *(d* With nearing chair   *Aylmer's Field* 266

Defiance   With one smile of still *d* Sold him   *The Captain* 59

and flung *d* down Gagelike to man,   *Princess v* 177

With message and *d*, went and came ;   " 370

Defiant   Sullen, *d*, pitying, wroth,   *Aylmer's Field* 492

Deficiency   Who'll weep for thy *d* ?   *Two Voices* 39

Defied   chafing at his own great self *d*,   *Aylmer's Field* 537

Defileth   he *d* heavenly things With earthly uses '—   *Balin and Balan* 442

Define   Hold thou the good : *d* it well :   *In Mem. liii* 13

Defined   His isolation grows *d*.   " *xlv* 12

Deform'd   Vext with unworthy madness, and *d*.   *Aylmer's Field* 335

His face *d* by lurid blotch and blain—   *Death of Œnone* 72

Defying   We drink *d* trouble,   *Will Water.* 94

Was love's dumb cry *d* change   *In Mem. xcv* 27

Degrade   And throned races may *d* ;   " *cxxviii* 7

Degree   and by *d's* May into uncongenial spirits   *Mine be the strength* 10

But by *d's* to fullness wrought,   *You ask me, why,* 14

We all are changed by still *d's*,   *Love thou thy land* 43

and thro' soft *d's* Subdue them to the useful   *Ulysses* 37

What for order or *d* ?   *Vision of Sin* 86

More than is of man's *d* Must be with us,   *Ode on Well.* 242

by slow *d's* of the sullen bell Toll'd   *Lover's Tale iii* 13

Deign'd   Arthur *d* not use of word or sword,   *Last Tournament* 458

Deity   lays that will outlast thy *D* ? ' *D* ?' nay,   *Lucretius* 72

D false in human-amorous tears ;   " 90

Such is Rome, and this her *d* :   *Boädicea* 20

Nor take thy dial for thy *d*,   *Ancient Sage* 109

Delay (s)   Raw Haste, half-sister to *D*.   *Love thou thy land* 96

And dull the voyage was with long *d's*,   *Enoch Arden* 655

winning easy grace, No doubt, for slight *d*,   *Princess iv* 331

' Ah, the long *d*.'   *Window. When* 10

Delay (verb)   now *d* not : take Excalibur, And fling him   *M. d'Arthur* 36

tender ash *d's* To clothe herself,   *Princess iv* 106

Delaying long, *d* no more.   *In Mem. lxxxiii* 4

but *d's* his purport till thou send   *Gareth and L.* 618

D not thou for ought, but let them sit,   *Balin and Balan* 18

'*D* no longer, speak your wish,   *Lancelot and E.* 924

now *d* not : take Excalibur, And fling him   *Pass. of Arthur* 204

While you still *d* to take Your leave of Town,   *To Mary Boyle* 1

Delay'd   —*d* at first Thro' helping back   *Gareth and L.* 1212

till *d* By their mountain-like San Philip   *The Revenge* 39

Delayest   *D* the sorrow in my blood,   *In Mem. lxxxiii* 14

Delaying   *D* as the tender ash delays To clothe herself,   *Princess iv* 106

A sweet new-year *d* long ;   *In Mem. lxxxiii* 2

Delaying (continued)   D long, delay no more.   *In Mem. lxxxiii* 4
   O thou, new-year, d long,   " 13
Delayingly   And yet she held him on d   *Enoch Arden* 468
Delegate   she send her d to thrall These fighting hands   *Pelleas and E.* 336
Delicacy   But could not out of bashful d ;   *Marr. of Geraint* 66
Delicate   (*See also* **Fairily-delicate**)   Fair speech was his, and d of phrase,   *Lover's Tale iv* 273
Delicate-handed   dilettante, D-h priest intone ;   *Maud I viii* 11
Delicately   Most d hour by hour He canvass'd   *A Character* 19
   And Enid took a little d,   *Geraint and E.* 212
Delicious   made the air Of Life d,   *Gardener's D.* 70
   Were not his words d,   *Edwin Morris* 71
Delicto   what's the Latin word ?—D: *Walk. to the Mail* 35
Delight (s)   triple-mailèd trust, and clear D,   *Supp. Confessions* 67
   So took echo with d, (repeat)   *The Owl ii* 4
   d, Life, anguish, death, immortal love,   *Arabian Nights* 72
   and feedeth The senses with a still d   *Margaret* 17
   Whose free d, from any height of rapid flight,   *Rosalind* 3
   seeming-bitter From excess of swift d.   " 32
   And that d of frolic flight,   " 47
   Falling into a still d,   *Eleänore* 106
   I die with my d, before I hear what I would hear   " 140
   ' Some vague emotion of d   *Two Voices* 361
   My heart, pierced thro' with fierce d,   *Fatima* 34
   ' I marvel if my still d   *Palace of Art* 190
   great d and shuddering took hold of all my mind,   *May Queen, Con.* 35
   When she made pause I knew not for d ;   *D. of F. Women* 169
   The sole d is, sitting still,   *The Blackbird* 10
   The common mouth, So gross to express d,   *Gardener's D.* 56
   drunk d of battle with my peers,   *Ulysses* 16
   To shape the song for your d   *Day-Dm., Ep.* 6
   and all The chambers emptied of d :   *In Mem. viii* 8
   And was the day of my d As pure   " *xxiv* 1
   With shower'd largess of d In dance   " *xxix* 7
   And what d's can equal those   " *xlii* 9
   Thy converse drew us with d,   " *cx* 1
   when we meet, D a hundredfold accrue,   " *cxviii* 8
   Maud the d of the village,   *Maud I i* 70
   and seems But an ashen-gray d.   " *vi* 22
   echo of something Read with a boy's d,   " *vii* 10
   and my D Had a sudden desire,   " *xiv* 19
   darkness must have spread With such d as theirs   " *xviii* 26
   My bride to be, my evermore d,   " 73
   Breaking up my dream of d,   " *xix* 2
   I sorrow after The d of early skies ;   " *II iv* 25
   The d of happy laughter, the d of low replies.   " 29
   a dream, yet it yielded a dear d   " *III vi* 15
   Guinevere, and in her his one d.   *Com. of Arthur* 4
   He, reddening in extremity of d,   *Geraint and E.* 219
   Inflate themselves with some insane d,   *Merlin and V.* 834
   Sprang to her face and fill'd her with d ;   *Lancelot and E.* 377
   shrilling, ' Hollow, hollow all d !   *Pass. of Arthur* 33
   And hollow, hollow all d.'   " 37
   She took the body of my past d,   *Lover's Tale i* 681
   without hope, without any d In anything   *Despair* 7
Delight (verb)   in her web she still d's To weave   *L. of Shalott ii* 28
   D our souls with talk of knightly deeds,   *M. d'Arthur* 19
   how the sun d's To glance and shift about   *Lucretius* 188
   nor deals in that Which men d in,   *Princess iii* 216
   D myself with gossip and old wives,   *Holy Grail* 553
   D our souls with talk of knightly deeds,   *Pass. of Arthur* 187
   and d thyself To make it wholly thine   *Lover's Tale i* 13
   never colt would more d To roll himself   *Romney's R.* 13
Delighted   D with the freshness and the sound.   *Edwin Morris* 99
   I am all as well d,   *Maud I xx* 40
Delighteth   nightingale d to prolong Her low preamble   *Palace of Art* 173
Delirium   I would catch Her hand in wild d,   *Princess vii* 93
Delius   the Sun, Apollo, D, or of older use   *Lucretius* 125
Deliver   D not the tasks of might To weakness,   *Love thou thy land* 13
   D me the blessed sacrament ;   *St. S. Stylites* 218
   Thy tribute wave d :   *A Farewell* 2
   Ignorance D's brawling judgments,   *Merlin and V.* 665
   Rise and take This diamond, and d it,   *Lancelot and E.* 546
Deliver'd   D at a secret postern-gate   *Com. of Arthur* 213
Deliverer   and call'd them dear d's,   *Princess vi* 92

Delivering   D, that to me, by common voice   *Œnone* 84
   D seal'd dispatches which the Head   *Princess iv* 379
   D, that his lord, the vassal king,   *Gareth and L.* 391
   So she, d it to Arthur, said,   *Last Tournament* 30
Dell   Out of the live-green heart of the d's   *Sea-Fairies* 12
   We would call aloud in the dreamy d's,   *The Merman* 25
   diamond-ledges that jut from the d's ;   *The Mermaid* 40
   The furzy prickle fire the d's,   *Two Voices* 39
   all night long, in falling thro' the d,   *D. of F. Women* 183
   the splinter'd crags that wall the d   " 187
   The little d's of cowslip, fairy palms,   *Aylmer's Field* 91
   How richly down the rocky d   *The Daisy* 9
   And snowy d's in a golden air.   " 68
   moved in the hollows under the d's,   *V. of Maeldune* 107
   What sound was dearest in his native d's ?   *Far-far-away* 4
   were alone in the d at the close of the day.   *Bandit's Death* 19
   rang out all down thro' the d,   " 36
Deluge   some new d from a thousand hills   *If I were loved* 13
   Pour with such sudden d's of light   *Lover's Tale i* 315
   or a d of cataract skies,   *Def. of Lucknow* 84
   In the common d drowning old political common-sense !   *Locksley H., Sixty* 250
Delver   careful robins eye the d's toil,   *Marr. of Geraint* 774
   careful robins eye the d's toil;   *Geraint and E.* 431
Demand (s)   To make d of modern rhyme   *To the Queen* 11
   obedience make d Of whom ye gave me to,   *Gareth and L.* 558
Demand (verb)   if a king d An act unprofitable,   *M. d'Arthur* 95
   The sense of human will d's   *In Mem. lxxxv* 30
   D not thou a marriage lay ;   " *Con.* 2
   thy love to me, Thy mother,—I d.'   *Gareth and L.* 147
   sent Her maiden to d it of the dwarf,   *Marr. of Geraint* 193
   Sent her own maiden to d the name,   " 411
   Garlon, mine heir, Of him d it,'   *Balin and Balan* 118
   if a king d An act unprofitable,   *Pass. of Arthur* 263
Demanded   she d who we were, And why we came ?   *Princess iii* 135
   And then, d if her mother knew,   " *iv* 233
   Was this d—if he yearn'd To hear   *In Mem. xxxi* 3
   when the Queen d as by chance   *Merlin and V.* 128
   And when the King d how she knew,   *Lancelot and E.* 317
Demanding   And then to me d why ?   *The Epic* 29
   D, so to bring relief   *In Mem. lxxxv* 6
Demigod   Elysian lawns, Where paced the D's of old,   *Princess iii* 343
Democrat   what care I, Aristocrat, d,   *Maud I x* 25
Demon   Pallas from the brain Of D's ?   *In Mem. cxiv* 23
   some d in the woods Was once a man,   *Balin and Balan* 124
   who will hunt for me This d of the woods ? '   " 137
   Whereout the D issued up from Hell.   " 317
   Celtic Demos rose a D,   *Locksley H., Sixty* 90
   A d vext me,   *Merlin and the G.* 29
   and drove the d from Hawa-i-ee.   *Kapiolani* 90
Demon-god   is the d-g Wroth at his fall?'   *St. Telemachus* 19
Demonstration   rounded under female hands With flawless d :   *Princess ii* 373
Demos   Celtic D rose a Demon,   *Locksley H., Sixty* 90
   D end in working its own doom.   " 114
Demur   He yielded, wroth and red, with fierce d :   *Princess v* 358
Demure   The little maiden walk'd d,   *Two Voices* 419
Den   We heard the lion roaring from his d ;   *D. of F. Women* 222
   ' Trooping from their mouldy d's   *Vision of Sin* 171
   and the children, housed In her foul d,   *Com. of Arthur* 17
   climb'd from the d's in the levels below,   *The Dawn* 17
Denial   Or by d flush her babbling wells   *Princess v* 334
   Who will not hear d, vain and rude   *Lover's Tale i* 628
Denied   He oft d his heart his dearest wish,   *Enoch Arden* 336
   ' Come with us Father Philip ' he d ;   " 368
   at first Was silent ; closer prest, d it not,   *Princess iv* 234
   she affirm'd not, or d :   *Lancelot and E.* 1112
   ' ye never yet D my fancies—   *Sir J. Oldcastle* 114
   d to him, Who finds the Saviour   *Guinevere* 421
Denouncing   like a Ghost's D judgment,   *M. d'Arthur* 196
Dense   the decks were d with stately forms   *Aylmer's Field* 771
   folds as d as those Which hid the Holiest   *Balin and Balan* 424
   race thro' many a mile Of d and open,   *Pass. of Arthur* 19
   But that these eyes of men are d and dim,   " 364
   all the decks were d with stately forms,

Deny What! *d* it now? Nay, draw, and cry For that which all *d* them— *St. S. Stylites* 206

And would if ask'd *d* it. *Will Water.* 46

To hold your own, *d* not hers to her *Enoch Arden* 44

father, tender and true, D me not,' *Princess vi* 178

you will not *d* my sultry throat *Lancelot and E.* 1111

Denying D not these weather-beaten limbs *Romney's R.* 22

Denyingly How hard you look and how *d*! *St. S. Stylites* 19

Depart He craved a fair permission to *d*, *Merlin and V.* 338

friend, too old to be so young, *d*, *Marr. of Geraint* 40

and still *d* From death to death *Balin and Balan* 17

Departed a silent cousin stole Upon us and *d*: *De Prof., Two G.* 51

She watch'd it, and *d* weeping for him; *Edwin Morris* 116

James *d* vext with him and her.' *Enoch Arden* 246

then, hot in haste to join Their luckier mates, *The Brook* 110

So these *d*. Early, one fair dawn, *Geraint and E.* 574

And thence *d* every one his way. *Balin and Balan* 246

Departest then before thine answer given D, *Holy Grail* 360

Departing With frequent smile and nod *d* *Tithonus* 45

Deplore Where shall we lay the man whom we *d*? *Marr. of Geraint* 515

Such was he whom we *d*. *Ode on Well.* 8

Still mine, that cannot but *d*, *"* 40

Depress'd With lips *d* as he were meek, *In Mem. lxxxv* 109

Depth (*See also* **Love-depths**) The springs of life, the *d's* of awe, *A Character* 25

Tears from the *d* of some divine despair *Two Voices* 140

on the *d's* of death there swims The reflex *Princess iv* 40

You cannot find their *d*; for they go back, *In Mem. cviii* 11

tho' every turn and *d* Between is clearer *Lover's Tale i* 80

dash'd himself Into the dizzy *d* below. *"* 148

dwelling on the light and *d* of thine, *"* 381

There on the *d* of an unfathom'd woe *"* 492

Derive D's it not from what we have *"* 746

Derk (**dark**) thowt it wur Charlie's ghoäst i' the *d*, *In Mem. lv* 3

Derken'd (**darkened**) —they niver *d* my door. *Village Wife* 82

Desave (**deceive**) an' she didn't intind to *d*, *"* 60

Descend *d*, and proffer these The brethren *Tomorrow* 59

D below the golden hills *Princess vi* 70

D, and touch, and enter; *In Mem. lxxxiv* 28

Why then my scorn might well *d* On you *"* xciii 13

Would the happy spirit *d*, *"* cxxviii 21

fire of God D's upon thee in the battle-field: *Maud II iv* 81

nay, the King's—D into the city:' *Com. of Arthur* 129

The Holy Grail, *d* upon the shrine: *Gareth and L.* 540

Descendant On him their last, *d*, *Holy Grail* 465

Descended (*See also* **Heaven-descended**) tree by tree, The *Aylmer's Field* 834

country-side *d*; *Amphion* 52

Then all *d* to the port, *Enoch Arden* 446

D to the court that lay three parts *Princess iii* 20

As we *d* following Hope, *In Mem. xxii* 11

his dream was changed, the haze D, *Com. of Arthur* 442

The Sun of May *d* on their King, *"* 462

the stream D, and the Sun was wash'd away. *Gareth and L.* 1047

robed them in her ancient suit again, And so *d*. *Marr. of Geraint* 771

finds himself *d* from the Saint Arimathæan Joseph; *Balin and Balan* 101

D, and disjointed it at a blow: *"* 296

He rose, *d*, met The scorner in the castle court, *"* 386

setting, when Even *d*, the very sunset *V. of Maeldune* 66

and whereout The cloud *d*. *Ancient Sage* 14

beheld The Life that had *d* re-arise, *Demeter and P.* 30

Descending angels rising and *d* met *Palace of Art* 143

d they were ware That all the decks *M. d'Arthur* 195

Once she lean'd on me, D, *Princess iv* 27

D, burst the great bronze valves, *"* vi 75

the day, D, struck athwart the hall, *"* 364

Phantom sound of blows *d*, *Boädicea* 25

D thro' the dismal night— *Com. of Arthur* 371

D in the glory of the seas— *"* 400

And then *d* met them at the gates, *Marr. of Geraint* 833

d they were ware That all the decks *Pass. of Arthur* 363

D from the point and standing both, *Lover's Tale i* 411

some, *d* from the sacred peak Of hoar *Pref. Son. 19th Cent.* 9

Self-darken'd in the sky, *d* slow! *Prog. of Spring* 28

Descent Smile at the claims of long *d*. *L. C. V. de Vere* 52

Descent (*continued*) She might by a true *d* be untrue; *Maud I xiii* 31

Fierce in the strength of far *d*, *Lover's Tale i* 382

farm can teach us there is something in *d*. *Locksley H., Sixty* 26

Descried wall Of purple cliffs, aloof *d*: *Ode to Memory* 54

Descry I could *d* The stern black-bearded kings *D. of F. Women* 110

Desenzano Row us out from D, *Frater Ave, etc.* 1

Desert (**merit**) *Royal grace To one of less* d *allows*, *To the Queen* 6

bowing at their own *d's*: *The Brook* 128

And partly conscious of my own *d's*, *Princess iv* 305

Desert (**waste**) why dare Paths in the *d*? *Supp. Confessions* 79

Of that long *d* to the south. *Fatima* 14

Which makes a *d* in the mind, *In Mem. lxvi* 6

every blazing *d* till'd, *Locksley H., Sixty* 168

science making toward Thy Perfectness Are blinding *d* sand, *Akbar's Dream* 30

the Star that lights a *d* pathway, *Locksley H., Sixty* 275

Deserve *d* That we this night should pluck what might that man not *d* of me, *Princess iv* 413

" v 104

Deserved Since we *d* the name of friends, *In Mem. lxv* 9

Design wherein were wrought Two grand *d's*; *Princess vii* 122

the vast *d's* Of his labour'd rampart-lines, *Ode on Well.* 104

giant aisles, Rich in model and *d*; *Ode Inter. Exhib.* 13

A miracle of *d*! *Maud II ii* 8

learnt and warn'd me of their fierce *d* *Lancelot and E.* 274

found The new *d* wherein they lost themselves, *"* 441

broke The vast *d* and purpose of the King. *Guinevere* 670

Design'd was there Not less than truth *d*. *Palace of Art* 92

Not less than life, *d*. *"* 128

Desire (**s**) oh, haste, Visit my low *d*! *Ode to Memory* 4

flow'd upon the soul in many dreams Of high *d*. *The Poet* 32

'Which did accomplish their *d*, *Two Voices* 217

To yield consent to my *d*: *Miller's D.* 138

The skies stoop down in their *d*; *Fatima* 32

my *d* is but to pass to Him that died for me. *May Queen, Con.* 20

things have ceased to be, with my *d* of life. *"* 48

Strength came to me that equall'd my *d*. *D. of F. Women* 230

vague *d's*, like fitful blasts of balm *Gardener's D.* 68

to say That my *d*, like all strongest hopes, *"* 237

this gray spirit yearning in *d* To follow *Ulysses* 30

The bird that pipes his lone *d* *You might have won* 31

thro' the smoke The blight of low *d's*— *Aylmer's Field* 673

thro' their own *d* accomplish'd, *"* 776

That lent my knee *d* to kneel, *Princess iii* 193

fail so far In high *d*, they know not, *"* 280

And every hoof a knell to my *d's*, *"* iv 174

Melt into stars for the land's *d*! *W. to Alexandra* 21

welcome her, welcome the land's *d*, *"* 25

But they—they feel the *d* of the deep— *Voice and the P.* 19

sparrow and throstle, and have your *d*! *Window, Ay* 14

That thou should'st fail from thy *d*, *In Mem. iv* 6

That not a moth with vain *d* Is shrivell'd *"* liv 10

The centre of a world's *d*; *"* lxiv 16

If any vague *d* should rise, *"* lxxx 1

I seem to meet their least *d*, *"* lxxxiv 17

born of love, the vague *d* That spurs *"* cx 19

Submitting all things to *d*. *"* cxiv 8

might ensue D of nearness doubly sweet; *"* cxvii 6

Dear friend, far off, my lost *d*, *"* cxxix 1

and my Delight Had a sudden *d*, *Maud I xiv* 20

A *d* that awoke in the heart of the child, *"* xix 48

but the deathbed *d* Spurn'd by this heir *"* 77

the heart of a people beat with one *d*; *"* III vi 49

d To close with her lord's pleasure; *Geraint and E.* 213

monk and nun, ye scorn the world's *d*, *Balin and Balan* 445

low *d* Not to feel lowest makes them level all; *Merlin and V.* 827

Suddenly flash'd on her a wild *d*, *Lancelot and E.* 357

but you work against your own *d*; *"* 1096

her hand is hot With ill *d's*, *Last Tournament* 415

when old and gray, And past *d*!' *"* 628

love me ev'n when old, Gray-hair'd, and past *d*, *"* 653

Ay, ay, O ay—a star was my *d*, *"* 733

words And courtliness, and the *d* of fame, *Guinevere* 482

or *d* that her lost child Should earn *Sisters (E. and E.)* 250

O therefore that the unfulfill'd *d*, *Tiresias* 79

sank with the body at times in the sloughs of a low *d*, *By an Evolution.* 18

F

Desire (s) (*continued*) Till, led by dream and vague *d*, *To Master of B.* 17
creeds be lower than the heart's *d* ! *Faith* 5
and woke *D* in me to infuse my tale of love *Princess* v 240
save *my* soul, that is all your *d* : *Rizpah* 77
d to keep So skilled a nurse about you always— *The Ring* 373
Desire (verb) IF I were loved, as I *d* to be, *If I were loved* 1
Her open eyes *d* the truth. *Of old sat Freedom* 17
Why should a man *d* in any way To vary *Tithonus* 28
And I *d* to rest. *Come not, when, etc.* 10
not of those that men *d*, Sleek Odalisques, *Princess* ii 76
d you more Than growing boys their manhood ; " iv 456
She *d's* no isles of the blest, *Wages* 8
Do we indeed *d* the dead *In Mem. li* 1
not to *d* or admire, if a man could learn *Maud I iv* 41
Rich in the grace all women *d*, " x 13
save yourself *d* it, We will not touch *Marr. of Geraint* 310
Yet, seeing you *d* your child to live, *Lancelot and E.* 1095
now his chair *d's* him here in vain, *Holy Grail* 901
howsoever much they may *d* Silence, *Guinevere* 206
Who could *d* more beauty at a feast ? ' *Lover's Tale iv* 240
more than one Here sitting who *d's* it. " 242
Wan, but as pretty as heart can *d*, *In the Child. Hosp.* 40
Desired You are not one to be *d*. *L. C. V. de Vere* 8
long *d* A certain miracle of symmetry, *Gardener's D.* 10
they hated, Had what they *d* : *The Captain* 38
broke the bond which they *d* to break, *Aylmer's Field* 778
—and many men *D* her ; one, good lack, no man *d*. *Gareth and L.* 106
needs Must wed that other, whom no man *d*, " 109
d his name, and sent Her maiden to demand it *Marr. of Geraint* 192
But now the humbling of their best, *Geraint and E.* 637
Desiring *D* what is mingled with past years, *D. of F. Women* 282
D to be join'd with Guinevere ; *Com. of Arthur* 77
Wasted and pined, *d* him in vain. *Pelleas and E.* 496
And I, *d* that diviner day, *To Victor Hugo* 12
Desk worn-out clerk Brow-beats his *d* below. *To J. M. K.* 12
'Oh ! who would cast and balance at a *d*, *Audley Court* 44
Erect behind a *d* of satin-wood, *Princess* ii 105
To cramp the student at his *d*, *In Mem. cxxviii* 18
Deskwork a dozen years Of dust and *d* : *Sea Dreams* 78
Desolate O spirit and heart made *d* ! *Supp. Confessions* 189
Your house is left unto you *d* ! ' (repeat) *Aylmer's Field* 629, 797
' My house is left unto me *d*.' " 721
' Our house is left unto us *d* ' ? " 737
became Imbecile ; his one word was ' *d* ; ' " 836
D ? yes ! *D* as that sailor, *The Ring* 306
Desolation Against the *d's* of the world. *Aylmer's Field* 634
No *d* but by sword and fire ? " 748
and her *d* came Upon her, and she wept *Geraint and E.* 518
wind of the Night shrilling out *D* and wrong *The Dreamer* 15
Despair Plagued her with sore *d*. *Palace of Art* 224
And nothing saw, for her *d*, " 266
must mix with action, lest I wither by *d*. *Locksley Hall* 98
Whisper'd ' Listen to my *d* : *Edward Gray* 22
shake The midriff of *d* with laughter, *Princess* i 201
Or baser courses, children of *d*.' " iii 213
Tears from the depth of some divine *d* " iv 40
hold That it becomes no man to nurse *d*, " 464
A day of onsets of *d* ! *Ode on Well.* 124
If any calm, a calm *d* : *In Mem. xi* 16
Can calm *d* and wild unrest Be tenants " xvi 2
D of Hope, and earth of thee. " lxxxiv 16
and ever wann'd with *d*, *Maud I i* 10
was but a dream, yet it lighten'd my *d* " III vi 18
He half *d's* ; so Gareth seem'd to strike *Gareth and L.* 1133
Gray-hair'd, and past desire, and in *d*.' *Last Tournament* 653
Despair'd approach To save the life of *d*, *Enoch Arden* 831
Despise my flesh, which I *d* and hate, *St. S. Stylites* 58
whom the strong sons of the world *d* ; *The Brook* 3
But that his pride too much *d's* me : And I myself
sometimes *d* myself ; *Marr. of Geraint* 464
Despised *See* **Half-despised**
Despite *D* of Day and Night and Death and Hell.' *Gareth and L.* 887
till he felt, *d* his mail, Strangled, " 1151
Lancelot who hath come *D* the wound *Lancelot and E.* 566
many a year have done *d* and wrong To one " 1209

Despite (*continued*) *d* All fast and penance. *Holy Grail* 630
the Gods, *d* of human prayer, Are slower to forgive *Tiresias* 9
D of every Faith and Creed, *To Mary Boyle* 51
Despondence Listless in all *d*,—read ; *Aylmer's Field* 534
Despot (*See also* **Dandy-despot**) the fire Where smoulder
their dead *d's* ; *Princess* v 380
Nothing of the lawless, of the *D*, *On Jub. Q. Victoria* 12
How can a *d* feel with the Free ? *Riflemen form!* 11
Destined opposite Of all my heart had *d* *Guinevere* 492
Destiny No one can be more wise than *d*. *D. of F. Women* 94
hung their heavy hands, The weight of *d* : *Princess* iv 554
Destitute All the lowly, the *d*, *On Jub. Q. Victoria* 31
Destroyed void, Dark, formless, utterly *d*. *Supp. Confessions* 122
And this *d* him ; for the wicked broth *Lucretius* 19
That not one life shall be *d*, *In Mem. liv* 6
Destructive was as a boy *D*, *Walk. to the Mail* 82
Detaching *d*, fold by fold, From those still heights *Vision of Sin* 51
Detail Another kind of beauty in *d* *Princess* iv 448
" v 215
Detention for the rest, Our own *d*, why, "
Determined Thus Enoch in his heart *d* all : *Enoch Arden* 148
Detestable She might not rank with those *d* *Princess* v
Dethronement And crownings and *d's* : *To the Queen ii* 45
Develop'd (*See also* **Slow-developed**) Beyond all
grades *d*, *Gardener's D.* 241
Development present The world with some *d*. *Two Voices* 75
And new *d's*, whatever spark Be struck *Prog. of Spring* 94
Device our *d* ; wrought to the life *Princess* iii 303
Were Arthur's wars in weird *d's* done, *Gareth and L.* 225
by some *d* Full cowardly, or by mere unhappiness, " 767
Or some *d*, hast foully overthrown ? " 998
D and sorcery and unhappiness— " 1235
All the *d's* blazon'd on the shield *Lancelot and E.* 9
Blank, or at least with some *d* not mine.' " 194
thread And crimson in the belt a strange *d* ; *Holy Grail* 154
Among the strange *d's* of our kings : " 730
Restrain'd him with all manner of *d*, *Pelleas and E.* 204
Devil (*See also* **Divil**, **Wood-devil**) What *D* had the
heart to scathe Flowers *Supp. Confessions* 83
That pride, the sin of *d's*, " 109
A glorious *d*, large in heart and brain, *To ——, With Pal. of Art* 5
And oft some brainless *d* enters in, *Palace of Art* 203
Quoth she, ' The *D* take the goose, *The Goose* 55
Vex'd with a morbid *d* in his blood *Walk. to the Mail* 51
let him go ; his *d* goes with him, " 77
scarce meet For troops of *d's*, *St. S. Stylites* 4
D's pluck'd my sleeve, " 171
Comfort ? comfort scorn'd of *d's* ! *Locksley Hall* 75
glaring, by his own stale *d* spurr'd, *Aylmer's Field* 290
True *D's* with no ear, they howl in tune With
nothing but the *D* ! ' *Sea Dreams* 260
if there be A *d* in man, there is an angel too, " 278
A *d* rises in my heart, *Sailor Boy* 23
and the *D* may pipe to his own. *Maud I i* 76
thou could'st lay the *D* of these woods *Balin and Balan* 298
Balin cried ' Him, or the viler *d* who plays his part,
To lay that *d* would lay the *D* in me.' ' Nay,'
said the churl, ' our *d* is a truth, " 300
Or *d* or man Guard thou thine head.' " 552
Know well that Envy calls you *D's* son : *Merlin and V.* 467
And then did Envy call me *D's* son : " 497
and stirs the pulse With *d's* leaps, *Guinevere* 522
dogs of Seville, the children of the *d*, *The Revenge* 30
I never turn'd my back upon Don or *d* yet.' " 31
Was he *d* or man ? He was *d* for aught they knew, " 108
Are we *d's* ? are we men ? *Locksley H., Sixty* 99
Dance in a fountain of flame with her *d's*, *Kapiolani* 10
only the *D* can tell what he means. *Riflemen form!* 25
Devil-born You tell me, doubt is *D-b*. *In Mem. xcvi* 4
Devil's-dances bagpipes, revelling, *d-d*. *Sir J. Oldcastle* 149
Devised Besought Lavaine to write as she *d* *Lancelot and E.* 1103
Then he wrote The letter she *d* ; " 1109
her lips, Who had *d* the letter, moved again. " 1288
Devising And moist and dry, *d* long, *Love thou thy land* 38
d their own daughter's death ! *Aylmer's Field* 783
urged All the *d's* of their chivalry *Gareth and L.* 1349

Die (*continued*) He will not love me: how then?

must I *d*?	*Lancelot and E.* 893
half the night repeating, 'Must I *d*?'	„ 899
I must *d* for want of one bold word.'	„ 927
I love you: let me *d*.'	„ 930
O Love, if death be sweeter, let me *d*.	„ 1012
Call and I follow, I follow! let me *d*.'	„ 1018
she shrilling, 'Let me *d*!'	„ 1026
I should but *d* the sooner;	„ 1098
and let me shrive me clean, and *d*.'	„ 1100
lay the letter in my hand A little ere I *d*,	„ 1114
some do hold our Arthur cannot *d*,	„ 1258
Not knowing he should *d* a holy man.	„ 1429
In moments when he feels he cannot *d*,	*Holy Grail* 916
I *d* thro' mine unhappiness.'	*Pelleas and E.* 332
One rose, my rose; a rose that will not *d*,—	„ 408
He *d's* who loves it,—if the worm be there.'	„ 409
but here, Here let me rest and *d*,'	„ 515
help it from the death that cannot *d*,	*Guinevere* 66
I, whose vast pity almost makes me *d*	„ 534
I waged His wars, and now I pass and *d*.	*Pass. of Arthur* 12
God my Christ—I pass but shall not *d*.'	„ 28
Nor shall see, here or elsewhere, till I *d*,	„ 322
I fear My wound hath taken cold, and I shall *d*.'	„ 334
I fear it is too late, and I shall *d*.'	„ 348
Where all of high and holy *d's* away.	*To the Queen* ii 66
To *d* in gazing on that perfectness	*Lover's Tale* i 88
And cannot *d*, and am, in having been—	„ 121
I died then, I had not seem'd to *d*,	„ 494
Love would *d* when Hope was gone,	„ 818
I seem'd to faint and fall, To fall and *d* away.	„ ii 97
What did he then? not *d*: he is here and hale—	„ iv 40
And leave him in the public way to *d*.	„ 261
if I *d* o' my lying in!	*First Quarrel* 70
I kiss'd my boy in the prison, before he went out to *d*.	*Rizpah* 23
'My lass, when I cooms to *d*,	*North. Cobbler* 103
For to fight is but to *d*!	*The Revenge* 27
We *d*—does it matter when?	„ 88
With a joyful spirit I Sir Richard Grenville *d*!'	„ 103
I am sure that some of our children would *d*	*In the Child. Hosp.* 11
every man *d* at his post!' (repeat)	*Def. of Lucknow* 10, 13, 52
Kill or be kill'd, live or *d*,	„ 41
I am not like to *d* for lack of bread,	*Sir J. Oldcastle* 205
I woke, and thought—death—I shall *d*—	*Columbus* 87
would rush on a thousand lances and *d*—	*V. of Maeldune* 24
Nobly to do, nobly to *d*.	*Tiresias* 123
The child that I felt I could *d* for—	*The Wreck* 36
I would fling myself over and *d*!	„ 118
no souls—and to *d* with the brute—	*Despair* 36
we were used to believe everlasting would *d*:	„ 54
If every man *d* for ever,	„ 82
With him, where summer never *d's*, with Love,	*The Flight* 44
I will wander till I *d* about the barren moors.	„ 56
war will *d* out late then.	*Locksley H., Sixty* 173
gallant three hundred whose glory will never *d*—	*Heavy Brigade* 10
for evermore. Let the people *d*.'	*Dead Prophet* 4
Catullus, whose dead songster never *d's*;	*Poets and their B.* 8
Thine is it that our drama did not *d*,	*To W. C. Macready* 9
why The sons before the fathers *d*,	*To Marq. of Dufferin* 47
And all the Shadow *d* into the Light,	*Demeter and P.* 138
Do not *d* with a lie in your mouth,	*Forlorn* 57
No—you will not *d* before,	„ 61
Tell him all before you *d*, Lest you *d* for ever . . .	„ 75
would he live and *d* alone?	*Happy* 5
d with him side by side?	„ 8
I will live and *d* with you.	„ 108
They lose themselves and *d* On that new life	*Prog. of Spring* 35
king who loved me, And cannot *d*;	*Merlin and the G.* 80
And can no longer, But *d* rejoicing,	„ 112
To win her back before I *d*—	*Romney's R.* 118
Go back to thine adulteress and *d*!'	*Death of Œnone* 48
his dying words, Which would not *d*,	*St. Telemachus* 76
Form, be ready to do or *d*!	*Riflemen form!* 22
beggar began to cry 'Food, food or I *d*'!	*Voice spake, etc.* 6

Died   *D* round the bulbul as he sung;   *Arabian Nights* 70

Died (*continued*) Singing in her song she *d*,

D the sound of royal cheer;	*L. of Shalott* iv 35
'His face, that two hours since hath *d*;	„ 48
She *d*: she went to burning flame:	*Two Voices* 242
desire is but to pass to Him that *d* for me.	*The Sisters* 7
The dim red morn had *d*,	*May Queen, Con.* 20
Many drew swords and *d*.	*D. of F. Women* 61
Myself for such a face had boldly *d*,'	„ 95
Contented there to *d*! 'And there he *d*:	„ 98
'I *d* a Queen. The Roman soldier found Me	„ 152
her that *d* To save her father's vow;	„ 161
To whom the Egyptian; 'O, you tamely *d*!	„ 195
And when the zoning eve has *d*	„ 258
And on the mere the wailing *d* away.	*On a Mourner* 21
Danced into light, and *d* into the shade;	*M. d'Arthur* 272
Had once hard words, and parted, and he *d*	*Gardener's D.* 203
and in harvest time he *d*.	*Dora* 18
when William *d*, he *d* at peace With all men;	„ 55
like endless welcome, lived and *d*.	„ 144
The twilight *d* into the dark.	*Love and Duty* 68
Or stow'd, when classic Canning *d*,	*Day-Dm., Depart.* 24
old Earl's daughter *d* at my breast;	*Will Water.* 101
Then before her time she *d*.	*Lady Clare* 25
Then the music touch'd the gates and *d*:	*L. of Burleigh* 88
When the years have *d* away.'	*Vision of Sin* 23
And that mysterious instinct wholly *d*.	*Poet's Song* 16
Surely the man had *d* of solitude.	*Enoch Arden* 526
tell her that I *d* Blessing her, praying for her,	„ 621
And tell my son that I *d* blessing him.	„ 878
he *d* at Florence, quite worn out,	„ 885
knolls That dimpling *d* into each other,	*The Brook* 35
scandals that have lived and *d*,	*Aylmer's Field* 149
Remembering her dear Lord who *d* for all,	„ 443
(I thought I could have *d* to save it)	*Sea Dreams* 47
a low musical note Swell'd up and *d*;	„ 134
the first embrace had *d* Between them,	„ 211
laid about them at their wills and *d*;	*Lucretius* 3
teaching him that *d* Of hemlock; our device;	*Princess, Pro.* 31
her heart Would rock the snowy cradle till I *d*—	„ iii 302
Better have *d* and spilt our bones in the flood—	„ iv 104
My dream had never *d* or lived again.	„ 532
Ida has a heart'—just ere she *d*—	„ vi 17
and *d* Of fright in far apartments.	„ 235
And he *d*, and I could not weep—	„ 370
God's *d*, will that I, too, then could have *d*:	*Grandmother* 72
an' 'e *d* a good 'un, 'e did.	„ 73
So thick they *d* the people cried,	*N. Farmer, N. S.* 52
And cattle *d*, and deer in wood,	*The Victim* 5
That holy Death ere Arthur *d*	„ 18
And He that *d* in Holy Land	*In Mem.* lxxx 2
'The dawn, the dawn,' and *d* away;	„ lxxxiv 42
So many a summer since she *d*,	„ xcv 61
Whose old grandfather has lately *d*,	*Maud* I vi 66
past in bridal white, And *d* to live,	„ x 5
Aurelius lived and fought and *d*, And after him	„ xviii 66
King Uther fought and *d*,	*Com. of Arthur* 13
King Uther *d* himself, Moaning and wailing	„ 206
the savage yells Of Uther's peerage *d*,	„ 257
D but of late, and sent his cry to me,	„ 361
served about the King, Uther, before he *d*;	„ 366
some she cleaved to, but they *d* of her.	*Gareth and L.* 113
King Who lived and *d* for men,	„ 383
but, overtaken, *d* the death Themselves	*Geraint and E.* 177
So *d* Earl Doorm by him he counted dead.	„ 730
and the spiteful whisper *d*:	„ 958
when he *d*, his soul Became a Fiend,	*Balin and Balan* 128
The whole day *d*, but, dying, gleam'd	„ 314
'I hold them happy, so they *d* for love:	„ 581
I that fain had *d* To save thy life,	„ 599
My father *d* in battle against the King,	*Merlin and V.* 42
My father *d* in battle for thy King,	„ 72
One child they had: it lived with her: she *d*:	„ 716
while his anger slowly *d* Within him,	„ 891
better have *d* Thrice than have ask'd it once—	„ 918
the living smile *D* from his lips,	*Lancelot and E.* 324

Died (continued) d the death In any knightly fashion *Lancelot and E.* 870
Then take the little bed on which I d ,, 1117
And closed the hand upon it, and she d. ,, 1135
I dreamt the damsel would have d, ,, 1305
this she would not, and she d.' ,, 1325
From Camelot, there, and not long after, d. *Holy Grail* 7
ere the summer when he d, ,, 16
The rosy quiverings d into the night. ,, 123
And all talk d, as in a grove all song *Pelleas and E.* 607
'My churl, for whom Christ d, *Last Tournament* 62
and he d, Kill'd in a tilt, *Guinevere* 320
till in time their Abbess d. ,, 692
My dead, as tho' they had not d for me?— *Pass. of Arthur* 142
And on the mere the wailing d away. ,, 440
Trust me, long ago I should have d, *Lover's Tale i* 87
I had d, But from my farthest lapse, ,, 89
Before he saw my day my father d, ,, 191
Had I d then, I had not seem'd to die, ,, 494
Had I d then, I had not known the death; ,, 496
So d that hour, and fell into the abysm ,, 796
So that hour d Like odour rapt ,, 800
Had d almost to serve them any way, ,, iv 124
His master would not wait until he d, ,, 259
An' I almost d o' your going away, *First Quarrel* 54
And he fell upon their decks, and he d. *The Revenge* 104
She d and she was buried ere we knew. *Sisters (E. and E.)* 241
my darter es d o' the fever at fall: *Village Wife* 10
But arter she d we was all es one, ,, 55
each of them liefer had d than have done *V. of Maeldune* 6
and the harvest d from the field, ,, 30
twelve of their noblest d Among their spears *Achilles over the T.* 32
prayer for a soul that d in his sin, *The Wreck* 10
But it d, and I thought of the child ,, 84
perhaps, perhaps, if we d, if we d; *Despair* 56
dead the cause in which he d. *Locksley H., Sixty* 30
Rain-rotten d the wheat, *Demeter and P.* 112
d in the doing it, flesh without mind; *Vastness* 27
till Self d out in the love of his kind; ,, 28
she did not grow, she d. *Romney's R.* 105
happy had I d within thine arms, *Death of Œnone* 31
In the great name of Him who d for men, *St. Telemachus* 63
An' it beäts ma to knaw wot she d on, *Church-warden, etc.* 6
he was crush'd in a moment and d, *Charity* 21
She d of a fever caught when a nurse ,, 41
Diest if thou d, The King is King, *Com. of Arthur* 494
two things shalt thou do, or else thou d. *Marr. of Geraint* 580
Diet D and seedling, jesses, leash and lure. *Merlin and V.* 125
As if they knew your d spares *To E. Fitzgerald* 10
Differ Or do my peptics d? *Will Water.* 80
men at most d as Heaven and earth, *Merlin and V.* 814
Difference When thy peculiar d Is cancell'd *Two Voices* 41
Might I not tell Of d, reconcilement, *Gardener's D.* 257
girl and boy, Sir, know their d's!' *Aylmer's Field* 274
when some heat of d sparkled out, ,, 705
That have as many d's as we. *Princess v* 181
To cleave the rift of d deeper yet; ,, 301
Not like to like, but like in d. ,, vii 278
Ay me, the d I discern! *In Mem. xl* 21
Hearing he had a d with their priests, *Holy Grail* 674
Difficulty in days of d And pressure, had she sold *Enoch Arden* 254
With d in mild obedience Driving them on: *Geraint and E.* 104
Diffuse D thyself at will thro' all my blood, *Prog. of Spring* 24
Diffused Thy God is far d in noble groves *Aylmer's Field* 653
D the shock thro' all my life, *In Mem. lxxxv* 55
D and molten into flaky cloud. *Lover's Tale i* 641
Diffusing A central warmth d bliss *In Mem. lxxxiv* 6
Dig builds the house, or d's the grave, ,, xxxvi 14
d, pick, open, find and read the charm: *Merlin and V.* 660
I can't d deep, I am old— *Rizpah* 56
Digg'd An' 'e d up a loomp i' the land *Village Wife* 48
Diggin' last month they wor d the bog, *Tomorrow* 61
Digging *See* **Diggin', Half-digging**
Dignity maiden *dignities* of Hope and Love— *Lover's Tale i* 580
Dilate in a day, A joyous to d, as toward the light. *Aylmer's Field* 77
That now d, and now decrease, *In Mem. xxviii* 10

Dilating wind of prophecy D on the future; *Princess ii* 172
Dilation her eye with slow d roll'd Dry flame, ,, vi 189
Dilettante snowy-banded, d, Delicate-handed *Maud I viii* 10
Dim (adj.) eyes are d with glorious tears, *Two Voices* 151
About him broods the twilight d: ,, 263
My heart is breaking, and my eyes are d, *Œnone* 32
eyes grown d with gazing on the pilot-stars. *Lotos-Eaters, C. S.* 87
Till all the paths were d, *Talking Oak* 298
He saw not far: his eyes were d: *The Voyage* 75
Perhaps her eye was d, hand tremulous; *Enoch Arden* 242
We sung, tho' every eye was d, *In Mem. xxx* 14
Is d, or will be d, with weeds: ,, lxxiii 10
I remain'd, whose hopes were d, ,, lxxxv 29
Thou watches't all things ever d And dimmer, ,, cxxi 3
Myself would work eye d, *Marr. of Geraint* 628
the hall was d with steam of flesh: *Geraint and E.* 603
and d thro' leaves Blinkt the white morn, *Balin and Balan* 384
So strange, and rich, and d; *Holy Grail* 342
these eyes of men are dense and d, *Pass. of Arthur* 19
and mine Were d with floating tears, *Lover's Tale i* 442
Dim (verb) work in hues to d The Titianic Flora. *Gardener's D.* 170
Dim-gray Now and then in the d-g dawn; *Maud I xiv* 32
Diminutive In babyisms, and dear d's, *Aylmer's Field* 539
Dim-lit while he past the d-l woods, *Guinevere* 251
Dimm'd broad valley d in the gloaming: *Leonine Eleg.* 1
thro' the cloud that d her broke *Princess vi* 281
trust in things above Be d of sorrow, *In Mem. lxxxv* 10
and the sorrow d her sight, *Lancelot and E.* 889
Thy glorious eyes are d with pain *Freedom* 11
Dimmer all things ever dim And d, *In Mem. cxxi* 4
Dimness o'er it crost the d of a cloud Floating, *Pelleas and E.* 37
Dimple Till the lightning laughters d *Lilian* 16
Or d in the dark of rushy coves, *Ode to Memory* 60
That d's your transparent cheek, *Margaret* 15
Dimpled laughter d in his swarthy cheek; *Edwin Morris* 61
Dimpling knolls That d died into each other, *Aylmer's Field* 149
Upon the dappled d's of the wave, *Lover's Tale i* 44
Dim Saesneg with his hard 'D S' passes, *Sir J. Oldcastle* 21
Dim-yellow With her fair head in the d-y light, *Marr. of Geraint* 600
Din From the groves within The wild-bird's d. *Poet's Mind* 21
The dust and d and steam of town: *In Mem. lxxxix* 8
But when the heart is full of d ,, xciv 13
for me that sicken at your lawless d, *Locksley H., Sixty* 149
Dine You'll have no scandal while you d, *To F. D. Maurice* 17
shall we fast, or d? *Geraint and E.* 490
an' we be a-goin to d, *North. Cobbler* 111
Dinner (*See also* **After-dinner**) with the steam Of thirty thousand d's. *Will Water.* 224
hark the bell For d, let us go!' *Princess ii* 433
A grand political d To half the squirelings *Maud I xx* 25
A grand political d To the men of many acres, ,, 31
A d and then a dance For the maids ,, 34
Man with his brotherless d *The Dawn* 3
Dinnerless when I left your mowers d. *Geraint and E.* 234
The lusty mowers labouring d, ,, 251
Dint Sharp-smitten with the d of armed heels— *M. d'Arthur* 190
every d a sword had beaten in it, *Lancelot and E.* 19
Sharp-smitten with the d of armed heels— *Pass. of Arthur* 358
Dinted and crush'd, and d into the ground: *Maud I i* 7
his strong hands gript And d the gilt dragons *Last Tournament* 182
Diotima beneath an emerald plane Sits D, *Princess iii* 302
Dip (s) the last d of the vanishing sail *Enoch Arden* 245
The d of certain strata to the North. *Princess iii* 170
Dip (verb) the prime swallow d's his wing, *Edwin Morris* 145
and d's Her laurel in the wine, *Will Water.* 17
D forward under starry light, *Move eastward* 10
d Their wings in tears, and skim away. *In Mem. xlviii* 15
D down upon the northern shore, ,, lxxxiii 1
and d's and springs For ever; *Gareth and L.* 1146
these low bushes d their twigs in foam, *Prog. of Spring* 51
Dippest And d toward the dreamless head, *In Mem. xxxix* 5
Dipping d his head low beneath the verge, *Lover's Tale i* 509
ships from out the West go d thro' the foam, *The Flight* 91
Dipt (*See also* **Half-dipt**) the sky D down to sea and sands. *Palace of Art* 32

Dipt (*continued*) But ere he *d* the surface, rose an arm — *M. d'Arthur* 143
d, And mix'd with shadows of the common ground ! — *Gardener's D.* 134
one green sparkle ever and anon *D* by itself, — *Audley Court* 89
d and rose, And turn'd to look at her. — *Talking Oak* 131
When I *d* into the future (repeat) — *Locksley Hall* 15, 119
with her *d* Against the rush of the air — *Aylmer's Field* 85
d in all That treats of whatsoever is, — *Princess* ii 379
and *d* Beneath the satin dome and enter'd in, — „ iv 30
a dearer being, all *d* In Angel instincts, — „ vii 320
I sleep till dusk is *d* in gray; — *In Mem.* lxvii 12
And *d* in baths of hissing tears, — „ cxviii 23
Beneath a low door *d*, and made his feet — *Balin and Balan* 403
Sparkle, until they *d* below the downs. — *Lancelot and E.* 396
But ere he *d* the surface, rose an arm — *Pass. of Arthur* 311
till the labourless day *d* under the West ; — *V. of Maeldune* 86
son, who *d* In some forgotten book of mine — *To E. Fitzgerald* 46
dark hull *d* under the smiling main, — *The Wreck* 127
never yet hath *d* into the abysm, — *Ancient Sage* 39
we *d* down under the bridge — *Bandit's Death* 22
Broke the Taboo, *D* to the crater, — *Kapiolani* 31
Dircê who found Beside the springs of *D*, — *Tiresias* 14
and the springs Of *D* laving yonder battle-plain, — „ 139
Direct Now over and now under, now *d*, — *Lucretius* 62
Dirt these, tho' fed with careful *d*, — *Amphion* 89
Disappear earth yawns: the mortal *d's*; — *Ode on Well.* 269
and as the phantom *d's*, — *Locksley Hall, Sixty* 253
Disappear'd the whole fair city had *d*. — *Gareth and L.* 196
And up the rocky pathway, *d*, — *Gareth and E.* 243
cup Was caught away to Heaven, and *d*.' — *Holy Grail* 58
as he spoke Fell into dust, and *d*, — „ 436
Became a shadow, sank and *d*, — *Death of Œnone* 50
Disarm'd The proud was half *d* of pride, — *In Mem.* cz 6
Who let him into lodging and *d*. — *Lancelot and E.* 171
Thither I made, and there was I *d* . • — *Holy Grail* 575
Disarray Drove it in wild *d*, — *Heavy Brigade* 60
Disarray'd found, Half *d* as to her rest, — *Marr. of Geraint* 516
Disaster all *d* unto thine and thee! — *Gareth and L.* 1101
Disband bidding him *D* himself, and scatter — *Geraint and E.* 798
Discaged Until she let me fly *d* to sweep — *Gareth and L.* 20
Discern The roofs Of Sumner-place ! (repeat) — *Talking Oak* 31, 95, 151
till thy bough *d* The front of Sumner-place. — „ 247
Till a gateway she *d's* With armorial bearings — *L. of Burleigh* 42
Ay me, the difference I *d*! — *In Mem.* xl 21
I wake, and I *d* the truth; — „ lxviii 14
Discerned into my inmost ring A pleasure I *d*, — *Talking Oak* 174
Discerning *d* to fulfil This labour, — *Ulysses* 35
Disciple and yet Was no *d*, richly garb'd, — *Ancient Sage* 4
Disclaim'd each *D* all knowledge of us: — *Princess* iv 229
Disclosed *D* a fruit of pure Hesperian gold, — *Œnone* 66
Discomfort this *d* he hath done the house.' — *Lancelot and E.* 1072
blew my merry maidens all about With all *d*; — *Holy Grail* 749
Disconsolate On the nigh-naked tree the robin piped *D*, — *Enoch Arden* 677
Discontent lent The pulse of hope to *d*. — *Two Voices* 450
She look'd with *d*. — *Talking Oak* 116
muttering *d* Cursed me and my flower. — *The Flower* 7
Discord soul Of *D* race the rising wind; — *Love thou thy land* 68
too like The *d's* dear to the musician. — *Sea Dreams* 258
A monster then, a dream, A *d*. — *In Mem.* lvi 22
Discordance no *d* in the roll And march — *D. of the Duke of C.* 14
Discouraged I grew, Sir ; but since I knew — *Princess* iii 80
Discourse In such *d* we gain'd the garden rails, — „ Con. 80
Discourtesy 'Meseems, that here is much *d*, — *Gareth and L.* 853
I pray you, use some rough *d* — *Lancelot and E.* 973
This was the one *d* that he used. — „ 988
some *d* Against my nature: — „ 1302
Discover'd ALL precious things, *d* late, — *Day-Dm., Arrival* 1
Discoverer The first *d* starves—his followers, — *Columbus* 166
Discovery For the *d* And newness of thine art — *Ode to Memory* 87
Discredit heaven, how much I shall *d* him ! — *Marr. of Geraint* 621
Far liefer than so much *d* him.' — „ 629
Discuss We might *d* the Northern sin — *To F. D. Maurice* 29
Discuss'd *d* the farm, The fourfield system, — *Audley Court* 33
D his tutor, rough to common men, — *Princess*, Pro. 114
D a doubt and tost it to and fro: — „ ii 445
D the books to love or hate, — *In Mem.* lxxxix 34

Discussing *D* how their courtship grew, — *In Mem.*, Con. 97
Discussion That from *D's* lip may fall With — *Love thou thy land* 33
Disdain (*See also* **Half-disdain**) And my *d* is my reply. — *L. C. V. de Vere* 22
with some *d* Answer'd the Princess, — *Princess* iv 61
With some surprise and thrice as much *d* Turn'd, — *Marr. of Geraint* 557
not with half *d* Hid under grace, — *Lancelot and E.* 263
Sir Lancelot leant, in half *d* At love, — „ 1238
Disdain'd if the Queen *d* to grant it ! — *Balin and Balan* 191
Tolerant of what he half *d*, and she, Perceiving
that she was but half *d*, — *Merlin and V.* 178
Disease (*See also* **Heart-disease, Mock-disease**) But
sickening of a vague *d*, — *L. C. V. de Vere* 62
wretched age—and worst *d* of all, — *Lucretius* 155
Ring out old shapes of foul *d*; — *In Mem.* cvi 25
A *d*, a hard mechanic ghost That never came — *Maud* II ii 34
She like a new *d*, unknown to men, — *Guinevere* 518
and the loathsome smells of *d* — *In the Child. Hosp.* 25
I'd sooner fold an icy corpse dead of some foul *d*: — *The Flight* 54
Some thro' age and slow *d's*, — *Locksley H., Sixty* 46
All *d's* quench'd by Science, — „ 163
mar the beauty of your bride with your *d*. — „ *Happy* 24
Diseased (*See also* **Half-diseased**) But ours he swore
were all *d*. — *The Voyage* 76
The land is sick, the people *d*, — *The Victim* 45
You thought my heart too far *d*; — *In Mem.* lxvi 1
Disedge served a little to *d* The sharpness — *Geraint and E.* 189
But here will I *d* it by thy death.' — *Pelleas and E.* 578
Disembark'd touching Breton sands, they *d*. — *Merlin and V.* 202
Disengage I strove to *d* myself, but fail'd, — *Lover's Tale* i 692
Disentwined My coronal slowly *d* itself — „ 361
Disfame *See* **Half-disfame**.
Disgraäded (**disgraced**) I'd feäl mysen cleän *d*. — *North. Cobbler* 102
black Sal, es 'ed been *d*? — *Spinster's S's.* 25
Disgrace Alone might hint of my *d*; — *Two Voices* 360
lying, hidden from the heart's *d*, — *Locksley Hall* 57
why, the greater their *d*! — *Aylmer's Field* 384
Heap'd on her terms of *d*, — *Maud* II i 14
an' often at home in *d*, — *First Quarrel* 15
If you should only compass her *d*, — *The Fleet* 17
Disgraced (*See also* **Disgraäded**) Memmian naphtha-
pits, *d* For ever— — *Alexander* 1
d, Dishonour'd all for trial of true love— — *Pelleas and E.* 474
Disguise common light of smiles at our *d* — *Princess* v 276
Disguised thou shalt go *d* to Arthur's hall, — *Gareth and L.* 152
For hence will I, *d*, and hire myself — „ 169
Thou art so well *d*, I knew thee not. — *Sir J. Oldcastle* 197
Dish harpies miring every *d*, — *Lucretius* 159
And those that hand the *d* across the bar. — *Gareth and L.* 155
Think ye this fellow will poison the King's *d*? — „ 471
thrust the *d* before her, crying, ' Eat.' — *Geraint and E.* 655
Dishallow 'Ye, that so *d* the holy sleep, — *Pelleas and E.* 446
Dishelm'd she saw me lying stark, *D* and mute, — *Princess* vi 101
Dishonour Doing *d* to my clay.' — *Two Voices* 102
Becomes *d* to her race— — „ 255
So loathed the bright *d* of his love, — *Com. of Arthur* 195
His honour rooted in *d* stood, — *Lancelot and E.* 876
knights At that *d* done the gilded spur, — *Last Tournament* 435
I was close on that hour of *d*, — *Charity* 28
Dishonourable 'Ungenerous, *d*, base, — *Aylmer's Field* 292
Dishonour'd *D* all for trial of true love— — *Pelleas and E.* 477
Dishorsed each, *d* and drawing, lash'd at each — *Marr. of Geraint* 563
D himself, and rose again, and fled — *Balin and Balan* 330
Dish-washer *D-w* and broach-turner, loon !— — *Gareth and L.* 770
Disjoint Nor wielded axe *d* — *Talking Oak* 262
Disjointed Descended, and *d* it at a blow: — *Balin and Balan* 296
Disk studded wide With *d's* and tiars, — *Arabian Nights* 64
Ray round with flames her *d* of seed, — *In Mem.* ci 6
flight of shadowy fighters crost The *d*, — *St. Telemachus* 24
Dislink'd *D* with shrieks and laughter: — *Princess*, Pro. 70
But she *d* herself at once and rose, — *Merlin and V.* 909
Dislodging heroes tall *D* pinnacle and parapet — *D. of F. Women* 26
Dismay were the words Mutter'd in our *d*; — *Heavy Brigade* 47
Dismay'd Was there a man *d*? — *Light Brigade* 10
we turn'd to each other, whispering, all *d*, — *Heavy Brigade* 44
Dismember May never saw *d* thee, — *Talking Oak* 261

Divine (adj.) (continued)   Thou seemest human and d,   *In Mem., Pro.* 13
To count their memories half d;   "   xc 12
Known and unknown; human, d;   "   cxxix 5
not learnable, d, Beyond my reach.   *Balin and Balan* 175
see the highest Human Nature is d.   *Locksley H., Sixty* 276
creature which in Eden was d,   *Happy* 33
she the faultless, the d;   *Locksley H., Sixty* 5
Divine (verb)   A deeper tale my heart d's.   *Two Voices* 269
Nor the meaning can d,   *L. of Burleigh* 54
She is not of us, as I d;   *Maud II v* 69
Divinely   D thro' all hindrance finds the man   *Lancelot and E.* 333
Some warning—sent d—as it seem'd   *Lover's Tale iv* 21
Divinity   the dull Saw no d in grass,   *A Character* 8
If gazing on d disrobed Thy mortal eyes   *Œnone* 157
lift the woman's fall'n d Upon an even pedestal   *Princess iii* 223
Division   in d of the records of the mind?   *Locksley Hall* 69
'betwixt these two D smoulders hidden;   *Princess iii* 79
Are they not sign and symbol of thy d from Him?   *High. Pantheism* 6
Made strange d of its suffering With her,   *Lover's Tale ii* 128
Divorce   D the Feeling from her mate the Deed.   *The Brook* 95
d thee not From earthly love and life—   *Ded. Poem Prin.*
Divorced   I prophesy your plan, D from my experience,   *Princess iv* 355
can I breathe d from the Past?   *Despair* 113
Do   'Ye d it to me, when ye d it to these'?   *In the Child. Hosp.* 26
Doat   sisters That d upon each other,   *To ——. With Pal. of Art* 11
A heart that d's on truer charms.   *L. C. V. de Vere* 14
if the blossom can d on the blight,   *The Wreck* 19
eye, that only d's On outward beauty,   *The Ring* 163
and d's On this of yours.'   "   358
Dock'd   For which his gains were d,   *Sea Dreams* 7
Doctor   lilted out By violet-hooded D's,   *Princess ii* 376
then the D's!   O to hear The D's!   "   421
'Here's a leg for a babe of a week!' says d;   *Grandmother* 11
whoy, D's abeän an' agoän;   *N. Farmer, O. S.* 2
D's, they knaws nowt,   "   5
D's a 'toättler, lass,   "   66
I weänt breäk rules fur D,   "   67
D, if you can wait, I'll tell you the tale   *First Quarrel* 9
An' D 'e calls o' Sunday   *North. Cobbler* 87
OUR d had call'd in another,   *In the Child. Hosp.* 1
—so quiet, our d said 'Poor little dear,   "   41
I walk'd with our kindly old d   "   43
And the d came at his hour,   "   68
Doctrine   if we held the d sound   *In Mem. liii* 9
Dodge   to d and palter with a public crime?   *Third of Feb.* 24
Dodged   He d me with a long and loose account.   *Sea Dreams* 149
Doe   Lord Ronald brought a lily-white d   *Lady Clare* 3
The lily-white d Lord Ronald had brought   "   61
And follow'd up by a hundred airy d's,   *Princess vi* 87
Doff'd   Until the grave churchwarden d,   *The Goose* 19
cast his lance aside, And d his helm: *Geraint and E.* 596
Dog (See also **Shepherd-dog**)   I did not hear the d howl, mother,   *May Queen, Con.* 21
Not less, tho' d's of Faction bay,   *Love thou thy land* 85
At first like dove and dove were cat and d.   *Walk. to the Mail* 58
Something better than his d,   *Locksley Hall* 50
Like a d, he hunts in dreams,   "   79
he strode About the hall, among his d's,   *Godiva* 17
He parted, with great strides among his d's.   "   31
And barking d's, and crowing cocks!   *Day-Dm., Revival* 4
He praised his ploughs, his cows, his hogs, his d's;   *The Brook* 125
My men shall lash you from them like a d;   *Aylmer's Field* 325
the d With inward yelp and restless forefoot   *Lucretius* 44
he had breathed the Proctor's d's;   *Princess, Pro.* 113
swine were sows, and all the d's'—   "   i 193
wild d, and wolf and boar and bear Came   *Com. of Arthur* 23
'D, thou liest. I spring from loftier lineage   *Gareth and L.* 960
one of my co-mates Own'd a rough d,   "   1011
a d, am I, To worry, and not to flee—   "   1014
advanced, Each growling like a d—   *Geraint and E.* 559
Vivien, tho' ye beat me like your d,   *Balin and Balan* 582
I better prize The living d than the dead lion: "   585
There like a d before his master's door!   *Pelleas and E.* 263
Trembled and quiver'd, as the d,   "   284
these Inquisition d's and the devildoms of Spain.'   *The Revenge* 12

F*

Dog (continued)   Let us bang these d's of Seville,   *The Revenge* 30
shook 'em off as a d that shakes his ears   "   54
And mangle the living d that had loved him   *In the Child." Hosp.* 9
and the d couldn't bark.   *V. of Maeldune* 18
they kep the cat an' the d,   *Tomorrow* 71
sweär 'cep' it wur at a d coomin' in,   *Spinster's S's.* 60
Eighty winters leave the d too lame   *Locksley H., Sixty* 226
Fur the d's stoän-deäf, an' e's blind,   *Owd Roä* 2
Roä was the d as knaw'd when an' wheere   "   8
An' the d's was a-yowlin' all round,   "   107
I decreed That even the d was clean,   *Akbar's Dream* 53
He was loved at least by his d: *Bandit's Death* 35
Dogg'd   and d us, and drew me to land?   *Despair* 2
Dogwhip-weals   From ear to ear with d-w,   *Last Tournament* 58
Doing   See here, my d: *Edwin Morris* 5
their own d; this is none of mine;   *St. S. Stylites* 123
With all its d's had and had not been,   *Princess iv* 566
No, no, you are d me wrong!   *First Quarrel* 4
died in the d it, flesh without mind;   *Vastness* 27
Dole (mourning)   that day there was d in Astolat.   *Lancelot and E.* 1136
Dole (gift)   distribute d To poor sick people,   *Guinevere* 683
hath not our great Queen My d of beauty trebled?'   *Last Tournament* 558
Dole (verb)   I mete and d Unequal laws   *Ulysses* 3
Domain   See **World-domain**.
Dome (s)   (See also **Mid-dome**)   stay'd beneath the d Of hollow boughs.   *Arabian Nights* 41
stream'd Upon the mooned d's aloof   "   127
Arno, and the d Of Brunelleschi;   *The Brook* 189
and dipt Beneath the satin d   *Princess iv* 31
roll'd Thro' the d of the golden cross;   *Ode on Well.* 61
Save that the d was purple,   *Gareth and L.* 912
fallen every purple Cæsar's d—   *To Virgil* 30
this bare d had not begun to gleam   *To Mary Boyle* 41
roll her North below thy deepening d,   *Prog. of Spring* 49
and men, below the d of azure Kneel   *Akbar's D., Hymn* 7
Dome (verb)   d's the red-plow'd hills With loving blue;   *Early Spring* 9
Domed   See **Deep-domed**.
Domestic   Many a gallant gay d Bows   *L. of Burleigh* 47
Domine   'Libera me, D!' you sang the Psalm,   *Happy* 49
'Libera nos, D'—you knew not one was there   "   53
Dominion   D in the head and breast.'   *Two Voices* 21
Think I may hold d sweet,   *Maud I xvi* 12
Thro' all the vast d which a sword,   *Akbar's Dream* 14
Don   I never turn'd my back upon D or devil yet.'   *The Revenge* 31
Done   See **Ill-done**.
Donjon   The ruinous d as a knoll of moss,   *Balin and Balan* 334
And if thou keep me in thy d here,   *Pelleas and E.* 242
Donn'd   Then as he d the helm,   *Gareth and L.* 690
Donovan's   back wid the best he could give at ould D's wake—   *Tomorrow* 42
Doom (s)   chord which Hampden smote Will vibrate to the d.   *England and Amer.* 20
Hard is my d and thine: *Love and Duty* 54
thunder Roaring out their d;   *The Captain* 42
you have miss'd the irreverent d   *You might have won* 9
in their eyes and faces read his d;   *Enoch Arden* 73
his lonely d Came suddenly to an end.   "   626
like the blast of d, Would shatter all   "   769
the voice that calls D upon kings,   *Aylmer's Field* 742
Announced the coming d,   *Sea Dreams* 22
Boanerges with his threats of d,   "   251
death-blow struck the dateless d of kings,   *Lucretius* 236
But lies and dreads his d.   *Princess vii* 154
Bellowing victory, bellowing d: *Ode on Well.* 66
thou fulfillest thy d Making him   *High. Pantheism* 9
Fall, and follow their d.   *Voice and the P.* 20
On souls, the lesser lords of d,   *In Mem. cxii* 8
And batter'd with the shocks of d   "   cxviii 24
While I rose up against my d,   "   cxxii 2
I was cursing them and my d,   *Maud I xix* 51
I embrace the purpose of God, and the d assign'd.   "   III vi 59
and striking found his d.   *Com. of Arthur* 325
Arthur said, 'Behold thy d is mine.   "   467
the King Throned, and delivering d—   *Gareth and L.* 321
own false d, That shadow of mistrust   *Geraint and E.* 247
My madness all thy life has been thy d,   *Balin and Balan* 619

Doom (s) *(continued)* Dark my *d* was here, and dark It
 will be — *Balin and Balan* 623
born together, and we die Together by one *d* :' — " 630
A *d* that ever poised itself to fall, — *Merlin and V.* 191
loved him, with that love which was her *d*. — *Lancelot and E.* 260
Galahad, when he heard of Merlin's *d*, Cried, — *Holy Grail* 177
draw me into sanctuary, And bide my *d*.' — *Guinevere* 122
Pray for him that he scape the *d* of fire, And weep
 for her who drew him to his *d*.' — " 347
that I march to meet my *d*. — " 450
The *d* of treason and the flaming death, — " 538
that my *d* is, I love thee still. — " 559
I know not what mysterious *d*. — " 576
became as mist Before her, moving ghostlike to his *d*. — " 605
Ill *d* is mine To war against my people — *Pass. of Arthur* 70
'My house hath been my *d*. — " 154
On that sharp ridge of utmost *d* ride — *Lover's Tale i* 805
whose issue was their *d*, — *Tiresias* 65
echo shall not tongue thy glorious *d*, — " 136
uncall'd, between me and the deep and my *d*, — *Despair* 5
Demos end in working its own *d*. — *Locksley H., Sixty* 114
for man can half-control his *d* — " 277
at the doubtful *d* of human kind ; — *To Virgil* 24
the dead, who wait the *d* of Hell — *Romney's R.* 132

Doom (verb) King will *d* me when I speak.' — *Gareth and L.* 324

Doom'd *D* them to the lash. — *The Captain* 12
kings of old had *d* thee to the flames, — *Gareth and L.* 374
d to be the bride of Night and Death ; — " 1396
Who rose and *d* me to the fire. — *Sir J. Oldcastle* 172
And *d* to burn alive. — " 183
Fell the shipcrews *D* to the death. — *Batt. of Brunanburh* 23
Drew to this island : *D* to the death. — " 51

Doomsday as grand as *d* and as grave : — *Princess i* 187
To and thro' the *D* fire, — *Helen's Tower* 10

Doon (Bonny) *See* **Bonny Doon.**

Door *(See also* **Chamber-door, Chapel-door, Chaumber door, Dovecote - doors, Shrine - doors, Tavern-door)** Oh ! vanity ! Death waits at
 the *d*. — *All Things will Die* 17
The *d's* upon their hinges creak'd ; — *Mariana* 62
Old faces glimmer'd thro' the *d's*, — " 66
The costly *d's* flung open wide — *Arabian Nights* 17
Right to the carven cedarn *d's*, — " 115
poplars four That stand beside my father's *d*, — *Ode to Memory* 57
Leaving *d* and windows wide : — *Deserted House* 3
And no murmur at the *d*, — " 7
Close the *d*, the shutters close, — " 9
An image seem'd to pass the *d*, (repeat) — *Mariana in the S.* 65, 74
The very air about the *d* Made misty — *Miller's D.* 103
As near this *d* you sat apart, — " 158
The guilt of blood is at your *d* : — *L. C. V. de Vere* 43
carried out from the threshold of the *d* ; — *May Queen, N. Y's. E.* 42
thro' the *d* Hearing the holy organ — *D. of F. Women* 190
standeth there alone, And waiteth at the *d*. — *D. of the O. Year* 51
a new face at the *d*, my friend, A new face at the *d*. — " 53
thro' mine own *d's* Death did pass ; — *To J. S.* 19
There strode a stranger to the *d*, (repeat) — *The Goose* 3, 39
d's that bar The secret bridal chambers of the heart, — *Gardener's D.* 248
And never more darken my *d's* again.' — *Dora* 32
The *d* was off the latch : they peep'd, — " 130
whined in lobbies, tapt at *d's*, — *Walk. to the Mail* 37
I say, that time is at the *d's* — *St. S. Stylites* 192
This same grand year is ever at the *d's*.' — *Golden Year* 74
Every *d* is barr'd with gold, — *Locksley Hall* 100
all Should keep within, *d* shut, — *Godiva* 41
And feet that ran, and *d's* that clapt, — *Day-Dm., Revival* 3
He lifts me to the golden *d's* ; — *St. Agnes' Eve* 25
The stalls are void, the *d's* are wide, — *Sir Galahad* 31
One fix'd for ever at the *d*, — *Will Water.* 143
gay domestic Bows before him at the *d*. — *L. of Burleigh* 48
Paused for a moment at an inner *d*, — *Enoch Arden* 278
there At Annie's *d* he paused and gave his hand, — " 447
when they follow'd us from Philip's *d*, — *The Brook* 167
A lily-avenue climbing to the *d's* ; — *Aylmer's Field* 162
Withdrawing by the counter *d* — " 282

Door *(continued)* should I find you by my *d's* again, — *Aylmer's Field* 324
till he heard the ponderous *d* Close, — " 337
month by month the noise about their *d's*, — " 488
oaken finials till he touch'd the *d* ; — " 823
jam the *d's*, and bear The keepers down, — *Lucretius* 169
stood that same fair creature at the *d*. — *Princess ii* 329
call'd For Psyche's child to cast it from the *d's* ; — " iv 238
came a little stir About the *d's*, — " 374
I will go and sit beside the *d's*, — " v 96
He batter'd at the *d's* ; none came : — " 337
one glance he caught Thro' open *d's* of Ida — " 343
'Fling our *d's* wide ! all, all, — " vi 334
bare Straight to the *d's* : to them the *d's* — " 349
long-laid galleries past a hundred *d's* — " 375
roll the torrent out of dusky *d's* : — " vii 208
Thy name was blest within the narrow *d* ; — *W. to Marie Alex.* 38
Often they come to the *d* — *Grandmother* 82
D's, where my heart was used to beat — *In Mem. vii* 8
I creep At earliest morning to the *d*. — " 8
as if a *d* Were shut between me and the sound : — " xxviii 7
Shall enter in at lowly *d's*. — " xxxvi 8
They chatter'd trifles at the *d* : — " lxix 4
crowds that stream from yawning *d's*, — " lxx 9
Another name was on the *d*. — " lxxxvii 17
From out the *d's* where I was bred, — " ciii 2
D's, where my heart was used to beat — " cxix 1
Thou listenest to the closing *d*, — " cxxi 7
And touch with shade the bridal *d's*, — " Con. 117
Look, a horse at the *d*, — *Maud I xii* 29
even then I heard her close the *d*, — " xviii 11
Did he stand at the diamond *d* — " II ii 16
Modred laid his ear beside the *d's*, — *Com. of Arthur* 323
shone the fields of May thro' open *d*, — " 460
Ate with young lads his portion by the *d*, — *Gareth and L.* 480
saw without the *d* King Arthur's gift, — " 676
so Sir Kay beside the *d* Mutter'd in scorn — " 705
broken into Thro' open *d's* and hospitality ; — *Marr. of Geraint* 456
Glanced at the *d's* or gambol'd down — " 665
d, Push'd from without, drave backward — *Geraint and E.* 272
thought she heard the wild Earl at the *d*, — " 381
A walk of roses ran from *d* to *d* ; — *Balin and Balan* 242
And all in shadow from the counter *d* — " 246
Beneath a low *d* dipt, and made his feet — " 403
found a *d*, And darkling felt the sculptured
 ornament — *Merlin and V.* 733
and entering barr'd her *d*, — *Lancelot and E.* 15
guide me to that palace, to the *d's*.' — " 1129
There two stood arm'd, and kept the *d* ; — " 1247
rose And pointed to the damsel, and the *d's*. — " 1263
lords and dames And people, from the high *d* streaming, — " 1347
behold a woman at a *d* Spinning ; — *Holy Grail* 391
against the chapel *d* Laid lance, and enter'd, — " 459
Pass not from *d* to *d* and out again, — " 714
at the last I reach'd a *d*, — " 837
in my madness I essay'd the *d* ; — " 841
the high *d's* Were softly sunder'd, — *Pelleas and E.* 3
Unbind him now, And thrust him out of *d's* ; — " 257
There like a dog before his master's *d* ! — " 263
but thrust him bounden out of *d*. — " 314
straight on thro' open *d* Rode Gawain, — " 382
Pelleas, leaping up, Ran thro' the *d's* — " 539
Sprang from the *d* into the dark. — " 603
And while they stood within the *d's*, — *Last Tournament* 113
machicolated tower That stood with open *d's*, — " 425
but sprang Thro' open *d's*, — " 473
Flush'd, started, met him at the *d's*, — " 512
Like to some doubtful noise of creaking *d's*, — *Guinevere* 72
There rode an armed warrior to the *d's*. — " 409
Thro' the long gallery from the outer *d's* Rang — " 413
waiting by the *d's* the warhorse neigh'd — " 530
lo, he sat on horseback at the *d* ! — " 589
open'd on the pines with *d's* of glass, — *Lover's Tale i* 41
Death drew nigh and beat the *d's* of Life, — " 111
had Heaven from all her *d's*, — " 604
To stand a shadow by their shining *d's*, — " 731

Door (*continued*) bad his menials bear him from the *d*,   *Lover's Tale* iv 260
There were our horses ready at the *d's*—   " 385
They had fasten'd the *d* of his cell.   " *Rizpah* 42
to keep the wolf fro' the *d*,   *North. Cobbler* 29
our Sally as kep the wolf fro' the *d*,   " 59
THEY have left the *d's* ajar;   *Sisters (E. and E)* 1
and a noise of welcome at the *d's*—   " 149
found her beating the hard Protestant *d's*.   " 240
they niver derken'd my *d*.   *Village Wife* 60
when I saw him come in at the *d*,   *In the Child. Hosp.* 2
Boardings and rafters and *d's*—   *Def. of Lucknow* 67
what a *d* for scoundrel scum I open'd   *Columbus* 170
The *d's* of Night may be the gates of Light;   *Ancient Sage* 174
let them spurn me from the *d's*,   *The Flight* 55
A *d* was open'd in the house—   " 69
but she put him all to the *d*.   *Tomorrow* 44
sound ran Thro' palace and cottage *d*,   *Dead Prophet* 38
Opens a *d* in Heaven;   *Early Spring* 7
cuckoo of a joyless June Is calling out of *d's*:   *Pref. Poem Broth. S.* 4
Door-handles turn'd when none was at the *d*, And bolted
   d's that open'd of themselves :   *The Ring* 412
The *d* is open. He ! is he standing at the *d*,   *Happy* 11
some fair dawn beyond the *d's* of death   *Far-far-away* 11
—a widow came to my *d* :   *Charity* 26
Door'd *See* **Open-door'd**
Door-handle *D-h's* turn'd when none was at the door,   *The Ring* 412
Doorm *D*, whom his shaking vassals call'd the Bull,   *Geraint and E.* 439
we may meet the horsemen of Earl *D*,   " 492
One took him for a victim of Earl *D*,   " 524
Another, flying from the wrath of *D*   " 530
at the point of noon the huge Earl *D*,   " 536
said Earl *D* : 'Well, if he be not dead,   " 546
And bore him to the naked hall of *D*,   " 570
return'd The huge Earl *D* with plunder to the hall.   " 592
Earl *D* Struck with a knife's haft hard   " 599
But when Earl *D* had craven'd the would,   " 609
So died Earl *D* by him he counted dead.   " 730
I took you for a bandit knight of *D* ;   " 786
I come the mouthpiece of our King to *D*   " 796
'and lo, the powers of *D* Are scatter'd,'   " 801
Door-poorch (door-porch) my oän *d-p* wi' the
   woodbine   *Spinster's S's.* 105
to pictur the *d-p* theere.   *Owd Roä* 24
Doorwaäy (doorway) An' then as I stood i' the *d*,   " 42
Doorway (*See also* **Doorwaäy, Palace-doorway**) Dawn'd
   sometime thro' the *d*—   *Aylmer's Field* 685
God shut the *d's* of his head.   *In Mem.* xliv 4
out by this main *d* past the King.   *Gareth and L.* 671
Doost (dust) Loovs 'im, an' roobs 'im, an' *d's* 'im,   *North. Cobbler* 98
Dora at the farm abode William and *D*.   *Dora* 2
Now *D* felt her uncle's will in all,   " 5
Thought not of *D*.   " 8
Now therefore look to *D* ;   " 15
for his sake I bred His daughter *D* :   " 20
'I cannot marry *D* ; by my life, I will not marry *D*.'   " 23
his ways were harsh ; But *D* bore them meekly.   " 36
And *D* promised, being meek.   " 46
D stored what little she could save,   " 52
Then *D* went to Mary.   " 56
and thought Hard things of *D*. *D* came and said :   " 58
D took the child, and went her way   " 71
none of all his men Dare tell him *D* waited with the child ;   " 76
D would have risen and gone to him,   " 77
D cast her eyes upon the ground,   " 89
'did I not Forbid you, *D* ?' *D* said again :   " 92
The wreath of flowers fell At *D's* feet.   " 103
Then *D* went to Mary's house,   " 110
Mary saw the boy Was not with *D*.   " 112
D said, 'My uncle took the boy ;   " 114
now I come For *D* : take her back ;   " 143
take *D* back And let all this be as it was   " 154
and *D* hid her face By Mary.   " 156
But *D* lived unmarried till her death.   " 172
Dorhawk-whirr and *d-w* Awoke me not,   *Lover's Tale* ii 116
Dormouse blue wood-louse, and the plump *d*,   *Window, Winter* 9

Dorset-Dorsetshire There was a farmer in *Dorset* of
   Harry's kin,   *First Quarrel* 17
So Harry was bound to the *Dorsetshire* farm   " 19
Dose fumes Of that dark opiate *d* you gave me,—   *Romney's R.* 31
Dot hull Look'd one black *d* against the verge   *M. d'Arthur* 271
hull Look'd one black *d* against the verge   *Pass. of Arthur* 439
The fires that arch this dusky *d*—   *Epilogue* 52
Dotage Cries of unprogressive *d*   *Locksley H., Sixty* 153
Dotard call him *d* in your rage   " 9
ere the *d* fell asleep ?   " 153
Dote *d* and pore on yonder cloud   *In Mem.* xv 16
Double (adv.) And then we drank it *d* ;   *Will Water.* 96
Double (verb) wind And *d* in and out the boles,   *Princess* iv 262
Double-charge Now *d-c* it with grape !   *Def. of Lucknow* 68
Doubled *d* his own warmth against her lips,   *Gardener's D.* 138
old man Was wroth, and *d* up his hands,   *Dora* 25
but when his date *D* her own,   *Aylmer's Field* 81
Double-dragon'd fill'd his *d-d* chair.   *Last Tournament* 144
Doubling *d* all his master's vice of pride,   *Marr. of Geraint* 195
Doubt (s) a special care Of God, to fortify from *d*,   *Supp. Confessions* 64
Moved from beneath with *d* and fear.   " 138
If so be that from *d* at length,   " 143
Roof'd the world with *d* and fear,   *Eleänore* 99
carve out Free space for every human *d*,   *Two Voices* 137
These things are wrapt in *d* and dread,   " 266
There must be answer to his *d*.   " 309
'The *d* would rest, I dare not solve.   " 313
The *d* my mother would not see ;   *Miller's D.* 154
In *d* and great perplexity,   *Palace of Art* 278
but empty breath And rumours of a *d* ?   *M. d'Arthur* 100
(For all my mind is clouded with a *d*)   " 258
lying thus inactive, *d* and gloom.   *Enoch Arden* 113
Such *d's* and fears were common to her state,   " 521
One spiritual *d* she did not soothe ?   *Aylmer's Field* 704
Discuss'd a *d* and tost it to and fro :   *Princess* ii 445
Disturb'd me with the *d* 'if this were she,'   " iv 217
came On a sudden the weird seizure and the *d* :   " 560
for spite of *d's* And sudden ghostly shadowings   " 571
Deeper than those weird *d's* could reach me,   " vii 51
I have heard Of your strange *d's* :   " 336
my *d's* are dead, My haunting sense of hollow shows :   " 348
In *d* if you be of our Barons' breed—   *Third of Feb.* 32
A spectral *d* which makes me cold,   *In Mem.* xliv 14
O turn thee round, resolve the *d* ;   " xliv 14
such as closed Grave *d's* and answers   " xlviii 3
What slender shade of *d* may flit,   " 7
Defects of *d*, and taints of blood ;   " liv 4
Nor can my dream resolve the *d*   " lxviii 12
D and Death, Ill brethren, let the fancy fly   " lxxxvi 11
And *d* beside the portal waits,   " xciv 9
bold to dwell On *d's* that drive the coward back,   " xcv 30
trance Was cancell'd, stricken thro' with *d*.   " 44
You tell me, *d* is Devil-born.   " xcvi 4
There lives more faith in honest *d*,   " 11
He fought his *d's* and gather'd strength,   " 13
To seize and throw the *d's* of man ;   " cix 6
Our dearest faith ; our ghastliest *d* ;   " cxxiv 2
No, like a child in *d* and fear :   " 17
Mix not memory with *d*,   *Maud* II iv 57
A *d* that ever smoulder'd in the hearts   *Com. of Arthur* 64
in daily *d* Whether to live or die,   *Lancelot and E.* 520
Lost in a *d*, Pelleas wandering Waited,   *Pelleas and E.* 392
This tender rhyme, and evermore the *d*,   " 410
fault and *d*—no word of that fond tale—   *Last Tournament* 578
but empty breath And rumours of a *d* ?   *Pass. of Arthur* 268
(For all my mind is clouded with a *d*)—   " 426
'But solve me first a *d*.   *Lover's Tale* iv 254
Naw *d* : But I liked a bigger feller to fight   *North. Cobbler* 99
fluttering in a *d* Between the two—   *Sisters (E. and E.)* 33
raise the full High-tide of *d*   " 178
in days Of *d* and cloud and storm,   *Columbus* 156
And *D* is the lord of this dunghill   *Despair* 90
Cleave ever to the sunnier side of *d*,   *Ancient Sage* 68
and yet no shade of *d*, But utter clearness,   235
lost in the gloom of *d's* that darken the schools ;   *Vastness* 11

Doubt (s) (*continued*) after hours of search and *d* and threats, *The Ring* 278
Still—at times A *d*, a fear,— *Akbar's Dream* 169
darken'd with *d's* of a Faith that saves, *The Dreamer* 11
Doubt (verb) It is man's privilege to *d*, *Supp. Confessions* 142
I fear All may not *d*, " 178
evidence, By which he *d's* against the sense ? *Two Voices* 285
I *d* not thro' the ages *Locksley Hall* 137
'True,' she said, 'We *d* not that. *Princess, Pro.* 169
'*D* my word again!' he said. " 176
Until we *d* not that for one so true *Ode on Well.* 255
D not ye the Gods have answer'd, *Boädicea* 22
For can I *d*, who knew thee keen *In Mem. cxiii* 5
I *d* not what thou wouldst have been : " cxiii 8
Who *d's* thee victor ? *Gareth and L.* 1296
I do not *d* To find, at some place *Marr. of Geraint* 218
Henceforward I will rather die than *d*. *Geraint and E.* 738
And will henceforward rather die than *d*. " 745
nor did he *d* her more, But rested in her fealty, " 966
I *d* not that however changed, *Lancelot and E.* 1218
To *d* her fairness were to want an eye, To *d* her
  pureness were to want a heart— " 1376
heard a voice, '*D* not, go forward ; if thou *d*,
  the beasts Will tear thee piecemeal.' *Holy Grail* 824
enow To make one *d* if ever the great Queen *Last Tournament* 564
never *d* each other more. *Happy* 92
I with this dagger of his—do you *d* me ? *Bandit's Death* 42
an' I *d's* they poison'd the cow. *Church-warden, etc.* 16
D no longer that the Highest is the wisest *Faith* 1
Doubted *D*, and drowsed, nodded and slept, *Com. of Arthur* 427
and *d* him No more than he, himself ; *Gareth and L.* 125
I *d* whether daughter's tenderness, *Marr. of Geraint* 797
Doubtful I answer'd nothing, *d* in myself *Princess iii* 272
the old man, Tho' *d*, felt the flattery, *Merlin and V.* 184
some were *d* how the law would hold, *Lover's Tale iv* 270
Doubting thought To sift his *d's* to the last, *Com. of Arthur* 311
Doubtless '*D*—ay, but ever since In all the world *The Ring* 363
Dove (*See also* **Ringdove, Wood-dove**) Let Thy *d*
  Shadow me over, *Supp. Confessions* 180
And oft I heard the tender *d* *Miller's D.* 41
Came relics of the well-contented *d's*. *Gardener's D.* 89
Like *d's* about a dovecote, wheeling round " 224
they that loved At first like *d* and *d* *Walk. to the Mail* 58
iris changes on the burnish'd *d* ; *Locksley Hall* 19
I would not one of thine own *d's*, *Lucretius* 68
morning *d's* That sun their milky bosoms *Princess ii* 102
The *d* may murmur of the *d*, " iii 105
A troop of snowy *d's* athwart the dusk, " iv 168
The moan of *d's* in immemorial elms, " vii 221
O merry the linnet and *d*, *Window, Ay* 13
O somewhere, meek, unconscious *d*, *In Mem. vi* 25
as a *d* when up she springs To bear " xii 1
then flew in a *d* And brought a summons " ciii 15
She is coming, my *d*, my dear ; *Maud I xxii* 61
My own *d* with the tender eye ? " II iv 6
And while your *d's* about you flit, *To E. Fitzgerald* 7
round her forehead wheels the woodland *d*, *Prog. of Spring* 57
Dovecote Like doves about a *d*, wheeling round *Gardener's D.* 224
Dovecote-doors some one batters at the *d-d*, *Princess iv* 169
Dowager prudes for proctors, *d's* for deans, " Pro. 141
Do-well *D-w* will follow though, *Ancient Sage* 273
Dower lent you, love, your mortal *d* Of pensive thought *Margaret* 5
Dower'd *D* with the hate of hate, *The Poet* 3
Dowerless but both Were *d*, and myself, *The Ring* 167
Down (hill) here are the blissful *d's* and dales, *Sea-Fairies* 22
the yellow *d* Border'd with palm, *Lotos-Eaters* 21
Round and round the spicy *d's* " C. S. 104
She went by dale, and she went by *d*, *Lady Clare* 59
behind it a gray *d* With Danish barrows ; *Enoch Arden* 6
Green in a cuplike hollow of the *d*, " 9
But in the leafy lanes behind the *d*, " 97
early roses from his wall, Or conies from the *d*, " 340
after scaling half the weary *d*, " 372
November dawns and dewy-glooming *d's*, " 610
Close to the ridge of a noble *d*. *To F. D. Maurice* 16
And on the *d's* a rising fire : *In Mem., Con.* 108

Down (hill) (*continued*) And rise, O moon, from
  yonder *d*, *In Mem., Con.* 109
Till over *d* and over dale " 110
face of night is fair on the dewy *d's*, *Maud III vi* 5
some wild *d* above the windy deep, *Merlin and V.* 658
And there among the solitary *d's*, *Lancelot and E.* 163
O'er these waste *d's* whereon I lost myself, " 225
Sparkle, until they dipt below the *d's*. " 396
the long backs of the bushless *d's*, (repeat) " 400, 789
For the *d's* are as bright as day, *Rizpah* 4
and the storm rushing over the *d*, " 6
when the storm on the *d's* began, " 71
lived With Muriel's mother on the *d*, *The Ring* 148
Among the quarried *d's* of Wight, *To Ulysses* 32
THERE on the top of the *d*, *June Bracken, etc.* 1
Down (feathery substance) silk-soft folds, upon yielding *d*, *Eleänore* 28
rosy thigh Half-buried in the Eagle's *d*, *Palace of Art* 122
wild hawk stood with the *d* on his beak, *Poet's Song* 11
in broider'd *d* we sank Our elbows : *Princess iv* 32
When in the *d* I sink my head, *In Mem. lxviii* 1
Art yet half-yolk, not even come to *d*— *Balin and Balan* 569
Down-carolling *D-c* to the crisped sea, *The Winds, etc.* 6
Downcast her eyes were *d*, not to be seen) *Maud I ii* 5
Down-deepening *D-d* from swoon to swoon, *Fatima* 27
Down-droop'd-Down-dropt EYES not *down-dropt* nor over-bright, *Isabel* 1
Down-droop'd, in many a floating fold, *Arabian Nights* 147
With *down-dropt* eyes I sat alone : *Œnone* 56
Downfall 'tween the spring and *d* of the light, *St. S. Stylites* 110
Down-glancing a spear *D-g* lamed the charger *Lancelot and E.* 488
Down-lapsing fancies, by *d-l* thought Stream'd onward, *D. of F. Women* 49
Down-streaming the dread sweep of the *d-s* seas : *Enoch Arden* 55
Down-way Pleasure who flaunts on her wide *d-w* *Vastness* 16
Dowry Large *dowries* doth the raptured eye *Ode to Memory* 72
Doy (die) But sin' I mun *d* I mun *d*, *N. Farmer, O. S.* 64
an' if I mun *d* I mun *d*. " 68
Doze Fell in a *d* ; and half-awake I heard *The Epic* 13
half in *d* I seem'd To float about *Princess i* 94
Did I hear it half in a *d* Long since, *Maud I vii* 1
In a wakeful *d* I sorrow For the hand, " II iv 26
Dozed Miriam watch'd and *d* at intervals, *Enoch Arden* 909
As the pimpernel *d* on the lea ? *Maud I xxii* 48
Then *d* awhile herself, but overtoil'd *Geraint and E.* 376
I *d* ; I woke. An open landaulet Whirl'd *Sisters (E. and E.)* 85
Dozing Lay, *d* in the vale of Avalon, *Palace of Art* 107
Draäin (drain) Miss Annie she said it wur *d's*, *Village Wife* 11
Draff chaff and *d*, much better burnt.' *The Epic* 40
Drag will have weight to *d* thee down. *Locksley Hall* 48
And that *d's* down his life : *Sea Dreams* 177
poor Psyche whom she *d's* in tow.' *Princess iii* 103
Should *d* you down, and some great Nemesis " vi 174
and *d's* me down From my fixt height " 307
a great black cloud *D* inward from the deeps, " vii 37
That seem to keep her up but *d* her down— " 270
And onward *d's* a labouring breast, *In Mem. xv* 18
To *d* me down to seventy-nine. *To Ulysses* 8
wife and children *d* an Artist down ! *Romney's R.* 38
if the rebel subject seek to *d* me from the throne, *By an Evolution.* 15
Dragg'd we *d* her to the college tower *Walk. to the Mail* 89
What Roman would be *d* in triumph thus ? *Lucretius* 234
I *d* my brains for such a song, *Princess iv* 154
a madden'd beach *d* down by the wave, *Maud I iii* 12
D him, and struck, but from the castle *Balin and Balan* 399
so by force they *d* him to the King. *Merlin and V.* 640
He *d* his eyebrow bushes down, " 807
d me up there to his cave in the mountain, *Bandit's Death* 11
and the weight that *d* at my hand ; " 39
Dragging Grimy nakedness *d* his trucks *Maud I x* 7
a dream Of *d* down his enemy made them move. *Lancelot and E.* 814
Reversion ever *d* Evolution in the mud. *Locksley H., Sixty* 200
Draggle An' Sally wur sloomy an' *d* *North. Cobbler* 41
Draggled Tho' somewhat *d* at the skirt. *Last Tournament* 219
Dragon The golden gorge of *d's* spouted forth *Palace of Art* 23
A gilded *d*, also, for the babes. *Enoch Arden* 540
To catch a *d* in a cherry net, *Princess v* 169
D's of the prime, That tare each other *In Mem. lvi* 22

Dream (s) (*continued*)   Yet feels, as in a pensive *d*,   *In Mem.* lxiv 17
Nor can my *d* resolve the doubt: „ lxviii 12
Or threaded some Socratic *d*;   „ lxxxix 36
And dream my *d*, and hold it true;   „ cxxiii 10
Behold, I dream a *d* of good,   „ cxxix 11
What is she now?   My *d's* are bad.   *Maud* I i 73
Kept itself warm in the heart of my *d's*,   „ vi 18
Even in *d's* to the chink of his pence,   „ x 43
Breaking up my *d* of delight.   „ xix 2
My *d*? do I dream of bliss?   „ 3
Half in *d's* I sorrow after The delight   „ II iv 24
And I wake, my *d* is fled;   „ 51
divide in a *d* from a band of the blest,   *Maud* III vi 10
it was but a *d*, yet it yielded a dear delight To have
   look'd, tho' but in a *d*, upon eyes so fair,   „ 15
but a *d*, yet it lighten'd my despair   „ 18
Vext with waste *d's*?   *Com. of Arthur* 85
Till with a wink his *d* was changed,   „ 441
O star, my morning *d* hath proven true,   *Gareth and L.* 1000
And heated the strong warrior in his *d's*;   *Marr. of Geraint* 72
lay late into the morn, Lost in sweet *d's*,   „ 158
All overshadow'd by the foolish *d*,   „ 675
Could scarce divide it from her foolish *d*;   „ 686
And ears to hear you even in his *d's.*'   *Geraint and E.* 429
D's ruling when wit sleeps!   *Balin and Balan* 143
Let be: ye stand, fair lord, as in a *d*.'   „ 258
Lancelot with his hand among the flowers ' Yea—
   for a *d*.   „ 260
poisoning all his rest, Stung him in *d's*.   „ 384
And now full loth am I to break thy *d*,   „ 500
As one that labours with an evil *d*,   *Merlin and V.* 101
ride, and dream The mortal *d* that never yet was
   mine—   „ 117
He walk'd with *d's* and darkness,   „ 190
Ev'n in the jumbled rubbish of a *d*,   „ 347
tiny-trumpeting gnat can break our *d*   *Lancelot and E.* 137
I behold him in my *d's* Gaunt   „ 763
a *d* Of dragging down his enemy made them move.   „ 813
plagued with *d's* of something sweet   *Holy Grail* 625
in a *d* I seem'd to climb For ever—   „ 836
damsel,' answer'd he, ' I woke from *d's*;   *Pelleas and E.* 104
so lay, Till shaken by a *d*,   „ 517
Or art thou mazed with *d's*?   „ 525
The sudden trumpet sounded as in a *d*   *Last Tournament* 151
Tristram waking, the red *d* Fled with a shout,   „ 487
And out beyond into the *d* to come.'   „ 721
if she slept, she dream'd An awful *d*;   *Guinevere* 76
down the long wind the *d* Shrill'd;   *Pass. of Arthur* 40
Arthur woke and call'd ' Who spake?   A *d*.   „ 46
And care not thou for *d's* from him,   „ 58
Black-stoled, black-hooded, like a *d*—   „ 365
they fall asleep Into delicious *d's*,   *Lover's Tale* i 162
As from a dismal *d* of my own death,   „ 748
One golden *d* of love, from which may death   „ 760
Were wrought into the tissue of my *d*;   „ ii 113
Like sounds without the twilight realm of *d's*,   „ 120
thought His *d's* had come again.   „ iv 78
Thro' *d's* by night and trances of the day,   *Sisters* (E. and E.) 274
broken besides with *d's* of the dreadful knife   *In the Child. Hosp.* 65
Not yet—not all—last night a *d*—   *Columbus* 66
The Lord had sent this bright, strange *d* to me   „ 91
wrought To mould the *d*;   *To E. Fitzgerald* 30
Beyond all *d's* of Godlike womanhood,   *Tiresias* 54
And mixt the *d* of classic times   „ 194
And all the phantoms of the *d*,   „ 195
With a dim *d*, now and then,   *The Wreck* 114
quiet at length out of pleasant *d's*,   *Despair* 66
words are like the babblings in a *d* Of nightmare,
   when the babblings break the *d*.   *Ancient Sage* 106
brainless will May jar thy golden *d*   *Freedom* 16
d's that scarce will let me be,   *To Marq. of Dufferin* 41
Led upward by the God of ghosts and *d's*,   *Demeter and P.* 5
he, the God of *d's*, who heard my cry,   „ 91
saw the world fly by me like a *d*,   *The Ring* 180
Or is it some half memory of a *d*?   „ 422

Dream (s) (*continued*)   O foolish *d's*, that you, that I,   *Happy* 89
you were then a lover's fairy *d*,   *To Mary Boyle* 43
Till, led by *d* and vague desire,   *To Master of B.* 17
thro' her *d* A ghostly murmur floated,   *Death of Œnone* 78
and the *d* Wail'd in her,   „ 81
His *d* became a deed that woke the world,   *St. Telemachus* 70
shadow of a *d*—an idle one It may be.   *Akbar's Dream* 5
I pray'd against the *d*.   „ 7
I vow'd Whate'er my *d's*, I still would do the right   „ 13
And yet so wild and wayward that my *d*—   „ 172
Desolation and wrong Thro' a *d* of the dark?   *The Dreamer* 16
Brings the *D's* about my bed,   *Silent Voices* 2
d of a shadow, go—God bless you.   *To W. H. Brookfield* 13
Dream (verb)   As a young lamb, who cannot *d*,   *Supp. Confessions* 170
And did not it was a dream;   *Two Voices* 213
sweet it was to *d* of Fatherland,   *Lotos-Eaters* 39
To *d* and *d*, like yonder amber light,   „ C. S. 57
More things are wrought by prayer Than this world
   d's of.   *M. d'Arthur* 248
Ellen Aubrey, sleep, and *d* of me: *Audley Court* 62
And sleeping, haply *d* her arm is mine.   „ 64
Ellen Aubrey, love, and *d* of me.'   „ 73
borne as much as this—Or else I *d*—   *St. S. Stylites* 93
She sleeps, nor *d's*, but ever dwells   *Day-Dm., Sleep B.* 23
D's over lake and lawn, and isles   *Vision of Sin* 11
to *d* That love could bind them closer   *Aylmer's Field* 41
Indeed, We *d* not of him: *Princess* ii 59
' Dare we *d* of that,' I ask'd,   „ iii 297
We shudder but to *d* our maids should ape   „ 309
To *d* myself the shadow of a dream: „ v 481
To *d* thy cause embraced in mine,   „ vi 200
Let us *d* our dream to-day.   *Ode Open. Exhib.* 31
Perchance, to *d* you still beside me,   *The Daisy* 107
D in the sliding tides.   *Requiescat* 4
That made me *d* I rank'd with him.   *In Mem.* xlii 4
Nor can I *d* of thee as dead: „ lxviii 4
rather *d* that there, A treble darkness,   „ xcviii 12
Nor *d* of human love and dust,   „ cxviii 3
And *d* my dream, and hold it true;   „ cxxiii 10
Behold, I *d* a dream of good,   „ cxxix 11
Did I *d* it an hour ago,   *Maud* I vii 1
And *d* of her beauty with tender dread,   „ xvi 14
My dream? do I *d* of bliss?   „ xix 3
And *d* he dropt from heaven: *Com. of Arthur* 183
what *d* ye when they utter forth May-music   *Gareth and L.* 1079
d's Of goodly supper in the distant pool,   „ 1186
To *d* she could be guilty of foul act,   *Marr. of Geraint* 120
I full oft shall *d* I see my princess   „ 751
d That any of these would wrong thee,   *Balin and Balan* 143
Or *d*—of thee they dream'd not—   *Merlin and V.* 115
ride, and *d* The mortal dream that never yet   „ 116
Ride, ride and *d* until ye wake—   „ 118
' Man *d's* of Fame while woman wakes to love.'   „ 460
because ye *d* they babble of you.'   „ 690
I cannot bear to *d* you so forsworn: *Pelleas and E.* 300
Too wholly true to *d* untruth in thee,   *Guinevere* 541
Let no man *d* but that I love thee still.   „ 560
Let no one *d* but that he loves me   „ 674
More things are wrought by prayer Than this
   world *d's* of.   *Pass. of Arthur* 416
Or if thou *d* aught farther, *d* but how   *Lover's Tale* i 769
And in my vision bidding me *d* on,   „ ii 119
But who could *d* that we, who bore the Cross   *Columbus* 191
Indian warriors *d* of ampler hunting grounds   *Locksley H., Sixty* 69
but *d* not that the hour will last.   „ 106
Could we *d* of wars and carnage,   „ 189
He *d's* of that long walk   *To Mary Boyle* 55
Dream'd   Till I *d* 'at Squire walkt in,   *Owd Roä* 55
Dream'd-Dreamt (*See also* **Dreäm'd**)   In midst of knowledge,
   dream'd not yet.   *Two Voices* 90
Before I *dream'd* that pleasant dream—   *Miller's D.* 46
sweeter than the dream *Dream'd* by a happy man,   *Gardener's D.* 72
I too *dream'd*, until at last   *Day-Dm., Pro.* 9
' I *dream'd* Of such a tide swelling   *Sea Dreams* 86
I *dream'd* that still The motion of the great deep   „ 110

Dream'd-Dreamt (*continued*)   told it, having *dream'd* Of that
same coast.   *Sea Dreams* 206
Sphere-music such as that you *dream'd* about,   "   256
it seem'd a dream, I *dream'd* Of fighting.   *Princess* v 492
I *dream'd* there would be Spring no more,   *In Mem. lxix* 1
I *dream'd* a vision of the dead,   " *ciii* 3
And her smile were all that I *dream'd*,   *Maud I vi* 37
her smile had all that I *dream'd*,   " 93
They never *dream'd* the passes would be past,'   *Gareth and L.* 1413
They never *dream'd* the passes could be past.'   " 1420
dreamt herself was such a faded form   *Marr. of Geraint* 654
Or dream—of thee they *dream'd* not—   *Merlin and V.* 115
I *dream'd* Of some vast charm concluded   " 511
the maiden *dreamt* That some one put this diamond   *Lancelot and E.* 211
He had not *dream'd* she was so beautiful.   " 353
Who *dream'd* my knight the greatest knight   " 667
' And if I *dream'd*,' said Gawain,   " 668
this night I *dream'd* That I was all alone   " 1045
I *dream'd* the damsel would have died,   " 1305
for he *dream'd* His lady loved him,   *Pelleas and E.* 152
I *dream'd* the bearing of our knights   *Last Tournament* 120
laid His brows upon the drifted leaf and *dream'd*.   " 406
He *dream'd*; but Arthur with a hundred spears   " 420
if she slept, she *dream'd* An awful dream;   *Guinevere* 75
such a feast As never man had *dream'd*;   " 264
and as yet no sin was *dream'd*,)   " 388
Had I not *dream'd* I loved her yestermorn ?   *Sisters (E. and E.)* 169
I *dream'd* last night of that clear summer noon,   *Romney's R.* 74
sphere-music as the Greek Had hardly *dream'd* of.   *Akbar's Dream* 45
and yester afternoon I *dream'd*,   " 170
I *dream'd* That stone by stone I rear'd   " 176
he *dream'd* that a Voice of the Earth went   *The Dreamer* 3
Dreamer ' Much less this *d*, deaf and blind,   *Two Voices* 175
fools they,—we forward : *d's* both :   *Golden Year* 67
visions in the Northern *d's* heavens,   *Aylmer's Field* 161
white-headed *d* stoopt and kiss'd her   *Locksley H., Sixty* 38
heard an answer ' Wake Thou deedless *d*,   *St. Telemachus* 21
Dreaming A glorious child, *d* alone,   *Eleänore* 27
In *d* of my lady's eyes.   *Kate* 28
D, she knew it was a dream :   *Mariana in the S.* 49
While, *d* on your damask cheek,   *Day-Dm., Pro.* 3
To see you *d*—and, behind,   " 7
wrathful, petulant, *D* some rival,   *Lucretius* 15
' What are they *d* of ?   Who can tell ?'   *Minnie and Winnie* 15
For pastime, *d* of the sky ;   *In Mem. lxvi* 14
Or how should England *d* of *his* sons   *Ded. of Idylls* 31
nodded and slept, and saw, *D*,   *Com. of Arthur* 428
glance of Gareth *d* on his liege.   *Gareth and L.* 1316
and *d* of her love For Lancelot,   *Marr. of Geraint* 158
he pray'd for both he slept *D* of both :   *Lover's Tale i* 228
D together (*d* of each other They should have added),   " 262
What is this you're *d* ?   *Forlorn* 14
Dreamlike *D*, should on the sudden vanish,   *Holy Grail* 260
Dream-world thou be wise in this *d-w* of ours,   *Ancient Sage* 108
Dreamt *See* **Dream'd**
Dreary She only said, ' My life is *d*, (repeat)   *Mariana* 9, 45, 69
She only said, ' The night is *d*, (repeat)   " 21, 57
She only said, ' The day is *d*,   " 33
Then, said she, ' I am very *d*,   " 81
Dregs *D* of life, and lees of man :   *Vision of Sin* 205
Drench stoop'd To *d* his dark locks   *Princess iv* 187
And on these dews that *d* the furze,   *In Mem. xi* 6
Thro' clouds that *d* the morning star,   " *lxxii* 22
Drench'd long, rank, dark wood-walks *d* in dew,   *D. of F. Women* 75
For I was *d* with ooze, and torn with briers,   *Princess v* 28
So *d* it is with tempest, to the sun,   " *vii* 142
I find myself *d* with the rain.   *Rizpah* 8
D with the hellish oorali—   *In the Child. Hosp.* 10
Dress (s) (*See also* **Hunting-dress**) This *d* and that by
turns you tried,   *Miller's D.* 147
' Bring the *d* and put it on her,   *L. of Burleigh* 95
drest In the *d* that she was wed in,   " 99
' What do you here ? and in this *d* ?   *Princess ii* 189
you look well too in your woman's *d* :   " *iv* 529
Nay, the plainness of her *d's* ?   *Maud I xx* 14

Dress (s) (*continued*) all her *d* Wept from her sides   *Gareth and L.* 216
put on thy worst and meanest *d*   *Marr. of Geraint* 130
he came on her Drest in that *d*, (repeat)   " 141, 843
And all her foolish fears about the *d*, (repeat)   " 142, 844
(His *d* a suit of fray'd magnificence,   " 296
At this she cast her eyes upon her *d*,   " 609
The *d* that now she look'd on to the *d*   " 613
Enid fell in longing for a *d*   " 630
Put on your worst and meanest *d*,'   " 848
your wretched *d*, A wretched insult on you,   *Geraint and E.* 327
there were books and *d'es*—left to me,   *The Ring* 113
D'es and laces and jewels and never a ring   *Charity* 6
Dress (verb) *d* the victim to the offering up.   *Princess iv* 130
to flaunt, to *d*, to dance, to thrum,   " 519
d her beautifully and keep her true '—   *Geraint and E.* 40
Love and Longing *d* thy deeds in light,   *Ded. Poem Prin. Alice* 9
Pretty anew when ya *d'es* 'em oop,   *Spinster's S's.* 85
She comes to *d* me in my bridal veil.   *The Ring* 98
Dressed *See* **Drest**
Dressing (*See also* **A-dressin'**) *D* their hair with
the white sea-flower ;   *The Merman* 13
flout and scorn By *d* it in rags ?   *Geraint and E.* 676
bullet struck him that was *d* it suddenly dead,   *The Revenge* 67
I am *d* the grave of a woman with flowers.   *Charity* 2
I am *d* her grave with flowers.   " 44
Drest-Dressed to dance and sing, be gaily *drest*,   *The form, the form* 3
Why come you *drest* like a village maid,   *Lady Clare* 67
' If I come *drest* like a village maid,   " 69
her body, *drest* In the dress that she was wed in,   *L. of Burleigh* 98
each by other *drest* with care Descended   *Princess iii* 19
' What, if you *drest* it up poetically !'   " *Con.* 6
Are but dainties *drest* again :   *Window, No Answer* 26
he came on her *Drest* in that dress, (repeat)   *Marr. of Geraint* 141, 843
A tribe of women, *dress'd* in many hues,   *Geraint and E.* 598
With a grisly wound to be *drest*   *The Revenge* 66
Drew She *d* her casement-curtain by,   *Mariana* 19
Thro' rosy taper fingers *d* Her streaming curls   *Mariana in the S.* 15
rising, from her bosom *d* Old letters,   " 61
once he *d* With one long kiss my whole soul   *Fatima* 19
With rosy slender fingers backward *d*   *Œnone* 176
As half-asleep his breath he *d*,   *The Sisters* 28
as morn from Memnon, *d* Rivers of melodies.   *Palace of Art* 171
Many *d* swords and died.   *D. of F. Women* 95
they *d* into two burning rings All beams of Love,   " 174
D forth the poison with her balmy breath,   " 271
There *d* he forth the brand Excalibur,   *M. d'Arthur* 52
and *d* him under in the mere. (repeat)   " 146, 161
O'er both his shoulders *d* the languid hands,   " 174
Came, *d* your pencil from you,   *Gardener's D.* 26
as one large cloud *D* downward :   " 79
wave of such a breast As never pencil *d*.   " 140
Light pretexts *d* me ;   " 192
and *d* My little oakling from the cup,   *Talking Oak* 230
As homeward by the church I *d*.   *The Letters* 44
as their faces *d* together, groan'd,   *Enoch Arden* 74
thro' all his blood *D* in the dewy meadow   " 660
talking from the point, he *d* him in,   *The Brook* 154
What amulet *d* her down to that old oak,   *Aylmer's Field* 507
the great ridge *d*, Lessening to the lessening music,   *Sea Dreams* 220
One rear'd a font of stone And *d*,   *Princess, Pro.* 60
the days *d* nigh that I should wed,   " *i* 41
I *d* near ; I gazed.   " *iii* 182
the flood *d* ; yet I caught her ;   " *iv* 182
One reaching forward *d* My burthen from mine arms ;   " 191
roll'd on the earth and rose again and *d* :   " *v* 497
D from my neck the painting and the tress,   " *vi* 110
he *d* Her robe to meeting his lips,   " 155
Whence *d* you this steel temper ?   " 232
D the great night into themselves,   " *vii* 49
voice from which their omens all men *d*,   *Ode on Well.* 36
Round affrighted Lisbon *d* The treble works,   " 103
And up the snowy Splugen *d*,   *The Daisy* 86
Thy converse *d* us with delight,   *In Mem. cx* 1
D in the expression of an eye,   " *cxi* 19
The shadow of His loss *d* like eclipse,   *Ded. of Idylls* 14

Drew (*continued*) D all their petty princedoms under

him,	*Com. of Arthur* 18
those great lords D back in wrath,	" 514
King D in the petty princedoms under him,	" 517
To whom Sir Gareth d (And there were none	*Gareth and L.* 743
Fell, as if dead; but quickly rose and d,	" 967
d him home; but he that fought no more,	" 1049
lighted, d, There met him drawn,	" 1121
softly d Behind the twain, and when he saw the star	" 1217
d himself Bright from his old dark life,	*Marr. of Geraint* 594
d from those dead wolves Their three gay suits	*Geraint and E.* 180
Sweet lady, never since I first d breath	" 619
these her emblems d mine eyes—	*Balin and Balan* 265
Balin d the shield from off his neck,	" 429
D the vague glance of Vivien,	" 464
and d down from out his night-black hair	" 511
d The vast and shaggy mantle of his beard	*Merlin and V.* 255
magnet-like she d The rustiest iron	" 573
d back, and let her eyes Speak for her,	" 615
D the vast eyelid of an inky cloud,	" 634
when the time d nigh Spake (for she had been sick)	*Lancelot and E.* 77
she d Nearer and stood.	" 349
draw—Draw,'—and Lavaine d,	" 515
D near, and sigh'd in passing, 'Lancelot,	" 1350
D me, with power upon me, till I grew	*Holy Grail* 486
The heads of all her people d to me,	" 601
There d my sword.	" 820
slowly Pelleas d To that dim day,	*Pelleas and E.* 29
find a nest and feels a snake, he d :	" 437
and d the sword, and thought, 'What!	" 447
and either knight D back a space,	" 573
D from before Sir Tristram to the bounds,	*Last Tournament* 185
and when she d No answer, by and by	*Guinevere* 161
weep for her who d him to his doom.'	" 348
kings who d The knighthood-errant of this realm	" 460
d Down with his blood, till all his heart	*Pass. of Arthur* 96
There d he forth the brand Excalibur,	" 220
and d him under in the mere. (repeat)	" 314, 329
O'er both his shoulders d the languid hands,	" 342
Death d nigh and beat the doors of Life;	*Lover's Tale* i 111
ever d from thence The stream of life,	" 238
and Love d in her breath In that close kiss,	" 816
upon the sands Insensibly I d her name,	" ii 7
fed we from one fountain? d one sun?	" 24
from his brow d back His hand to push me	" 92
She d it long ago Forthgazing on the waste	" 176
Four galleons d away From the Spanish fleet	*The Revenge* 46
d back with her dead and her shame.	" 60
one quick peal Of laughter d me thro'	*Sisters (E. and E.)* 116
But I d them the one from the other,	*V. of Maeldune* 35
every one d His sword on his fellow to slay him,	" 67
D to this shore lit by the suns	*De Prof., Two G.* 38
D to this island: Doom'd to the death.	*Batt. of Brunanburh* 50
Omar d Full-handed plaudits from our best	*To E. Fitzgerald* 37
as we d to the land;	*The Wreck* 136
and dogg'd us, and d me to land?	*Despair* 2
horsemen, d to the valley—and stay'd;	*Heavy Brigade* 3
d The foe from the saddle and threw	" 53
d perchance a happier lot Than ours,	*Epilogue* 50
out of his body she d The red 'Blood-eagle'	*Dead Prophet* 70
And d him over sea to you—	*To Marq. of Dufferin* 92
D from thyself the likeness of thyself	*Demeter and P.* 92
d down before his time Sickening,	" 114
d the ring From his dead finger,	*The Ring* 217
Unclosed the hand, and from it d the ring,	" 269
D to the valley Named of the shadow,	*Merlin and the G.* 86
that which d from out the boundless deep	*Crossing the Bar* 7
Dried Her tears fell ere the dews were d;	*Mariana* 14
'D his wings: like as gauze they grew;	*Two Voices* 13
all his juice is d, and all his joints	*Audley Court* 46
comforted my heart, And d my tears,	*Com. of Arthur* 350
Drier but felt his eyes Harder and d	*Pelleas and E.* 507
Drift (*See also* **Diamond-drift**) city lies, Beneath its d	
of smoke;	*Talking Oak* 6
Thro' scudding d's the rainy Hyades	*Ulysses* 10

Drift (*continued*) Together, in the d's that pass To darken

	In Mem. cvii 13
For the d of the Maker is dark,	*Maud I iv* 43
Wrapt in d's of lurid smoke	" *II iv* 66
In d's of smoke before a rolling wind,	*Com. of Arthur* 434
and sank Down on a d of foliage	*Last Tournament* 388
with his d Of flickering spectres,	*Demeter and P.* 26
a downy d against the brakes,	*Prog. of Spring* 27
Drifted These d, stranding on an isle	*Enoch Arden* 552
Drifting d up the stream In fancy,	*Sea Dreams* 108
Drill d the raw world for the march of mind,	*Ode on Well.* 168
Drink (s) sometimes Sucking the damps for d,	*St. S. Stylites* 77
this, at times, she mingled with his d,	*Lucretius* 18
Yea ev'n o' wretched meat and d,	*Maud I xv* 8
hire thyself to serve for meats and d's	*Gareth and L.* 153
grant me to serve For meat and d	" 445
Kay, The master of the meats and d's	" 451
mellow master of the meats and d's!	" 560
And mighty thro' thy meats and d's am I, (repeat)	" 650, 862
with meats and d's And forage for the horse,	" 1276
pinch a murderous dust into her d,	*Merlin and V.* 610
and then I taäkes to the d.	*North. Cobbler* 16
she druv me to d the moor,	" 30
All along o' the d, fur I loov'd her	" 60
'Pilgrimages?' 'D, bagpipes,	*Sir J. Oldcastle* 149
Drink (verb) (*See also* **Dhrink**) I d the cup of a costly	
death,	*Eleänore* 138
I will d Life to the lees:	*Ulysses* 6
'I am old, but let me d;	*Will Water.* 94
'D, and let the parties rave	*Vision of Sin* 75
'D to lofty hopes that cool—	" 123
D we, last, the public fool,	" 147
'D to Fortune, d to Chance,	" 149
D to heavy Ignorance!	" 191
D deep, until the habits of the slave,	" 193
To d the cooler air, and mark	*Princess ii* 91
Will d to him, whate'er he be,	*In Mem. lxxxix* 15
'D, then,' he answer'd. 'Here!'	" *cvii* 23
D therefore and the wine will change your will.'	*Geraint and E.* 658
I will not d Till my dear lord arise and bid me do it,	" 663
And d with me;	" 664
Not eat nor d? And wherefore wail for one,	" 674
you never open'd lip, Except indeed to d:	*Merlin and V.* 272
Forgot to d to Lancelot and the Queen,	*Lancelot and E.* 737
'D, d, Sir Fool,' and thereupon I drank,	*Last Tournament* 297
Nor d: and when thou passest any wood	" 534
'Summat to d—sa' 'ot ?'	*North. Cobbler* 5
He that thirsteth, come and d!	*Sir J. Oldcastle* 134
Then d to England, every guest;	*Hands all Round* 2
To this great cause of Freedom d, my friends, (repeat)	" 11, 35
To this great name of England d,	" 23
men may taste Swine-flesh, d wine;	*Akbar's Dream* 54
Drinketh as sunlight d away.	*Fatima* 21
Drinkin' thaw theer's naw d i' Hell;	*North. Cobbler* 58
Drinking (*See also* **Dhrinkin'**, **Drinkin'**) As d health	
to bride and groom	*In Mem., Con.* 83
Men were d together, D and talking of me;	*Maud I vii* 5
Drinking-song why should Love, like men in d-s's,	" *xviii* 55
Drip woodbine and eglatere D sweeter dews	*A Dirge* 24
When the rotten woodland d's,	*Vision of Sin* 81
red-ribb'd ledges d with a silent horror of blood,	*Maud I i* 3
I feeäld it d o' my neck.	*Owd Roä* 42
Dripping (*See also* **Autumn-dripping**) D with Sabæan	
spice On thy pillow,	*Adeline* 53
Dript belike the lance hath d upon it—	*Last Tournament* 200
Drive (s) What d's about the fresh Cascine,	*The Daisy* 43
Drive (verb) and seest me d Thro' utter dark	*Supp. Confessions* 94
And d's them to the deep.	*Palace of Art* 204
Nature's evil star D men in manhood,	*Love thou thy land* 74
And shoals of pucker'd faces d;	*In Mem. lxx* 10
On doubts that d the coward back,	" *xcv* 30
Is enough to d one mad.	*Maud II v* 20
sword, Whereby to d the heathen out:	*Com. of Arthur* 287
To d the heathen from your Roman wall,	" 512
and d them all apart.	*Gareth and L.* 515

Drive (verb) (continued) ' *D* them on Before you ; '
  (repeat) — *Geraint and E.* 99, 184
d The Heathen, who, some say, shall rule the land — *Lancelot and E.* 64
' Out ! And *d* him from the walls.' — *Pelleas and E.* 220
And *d* him from my walls.' — " 229
from the ditch where they shelter we *d* them — *Def. of Lucknow* 59
and *d* Innocent cattle under thatch, — *Locksley H., Sixty* 95
Then you that *d*, and know your Craft, — *Politics* 5
Or you may *d* in vain, — " 8
To *d* A people from their ancient fold — *Akbar's Dream* 60
Driv'n-Driven (*See also* **O'er-driven, Wind-driven**)
morning *driv'n* her plow of pearl Far furrowing — *Love and Duty* 99
the herd was *driven*, Fire glimpsed ; — *Com. of Arthur* 432
' O King, for thou hast *driven* the foe without, — *Gareth and L.* 593
driven by evil tongues From all his fellows, — *Balin and Balan* 125
Their plumes *driv'n* backward by the wind — *Lancelot and E.* 480
Thy holy nun and thou have *driven* men mad, — *Holy Grail* 862
camel, *driven* Far from the diamond fountain — *Lover's Tale i* 136
driven My current to the fountain whence it sprang,— " 502
the wild brier had *driven* Its knotted thorns — " 619
driven by one angel face, And all the Furies. — *Sisters (E. and E.)* 158
I am *driven* by storm and sin and death — *The Wreck* 2
she had never *driven* me wild. — *Locksley H., Sixty* 20
the foe was *driven*, And Wolseley overthrew — *Pro. to Gen. Hamley* 29
shrillings of the Dead When *driven* to Hades, — *Death of Œnone* 22
Driveth Let us alone. Time *d* onward fast, — *Lotos-Eaters, C. S.* 43
Driving The sunlight *d* down the lea, — *Rosalind* 13
blood by Sylla shed Came *d* rainlike — *Lucretius* 48
D, hurrying, marrying, burying, — *Maud II v* 12
difficulty in mild obedience *D* them on : — *Geraint and E.* 105
Drizzle Thicker the *d* grew, deeper the gloom ; — *Enoch Arden* 679
(A bill of sale gleam'd thro' the *d*) — " 688
drank the dews and *d* of the North, — *Prog. of Spring* 81
Drone *See* **Pulpit-drone**
Droned *d* her lurdane knights Slumbering, — *Pelleas and E.* 430
Droonk (drunk) hallus as *d* as a king, — *North. Cobbler* 27
D wi' the Quoloty's wine, an' *d* wi' the farmer's aäle, — *Village Wife* 77
Droop Fair-fronted Truth shall *d* not now — *Clear-headed friend* 12
I cannot veil, or *d* my sight, — *Eleänore* 87
D's both his wings, regarding thee, — " 119
D's blinded with his shining eye : — *Fatima* 38
The purple flower *d*'s : — *Œnone* 29
D's the heavy-blossom'd bower, — *Locksley Hall* 163
Here *d*'s the banner on the tower, — *Day-Dm., Sleep P.* 13
mantles from the golden pegs *D* sleepily : — " 20
Where on the double rosebud *d*'s — *L'Envoi* 47
his own head Began to *d*, to fall ; — *Aylmer's Field* 835
d's the milkwhite peacock like a ghost, — *Princess vii* 180
left hand *D* from his mighty shoulder — *Merlin and V.* 243
and seeing Pelleas *d*, Said Guinevere, — *Pelleas and E.* 178
O'er his uncertain shadow *d*'s the day. — *Prog. of Spring* 8
Droop'd-Droopt a leopard-skin *Droop'd* from his shoulder, — *Œnone* 59
From one hand *droop'd* a crocus, — *Palace of Art* 119
So she *droop'd* and *droop'd* before him, — *L. of Burleigh* 85
thinking that her clear germander eye *Droopt* — *Sea Dreams* 5
then day *droopt* ; the chapel bells Call'd — *Princess ii* 470
The lilylike Melissa *droop'd* her brows ; — " iv 161
above her *droop'd* a lamp, And made — " 272
And how my life had *droop'd* of late, — *In Mem. xiv* 14
His age hath slowly *droopt*, and now lies — *Gareth and L.* 79
he let them glance At Enid, where she *droopt* : — *Geraint and E.* 247
plume *droopt* and mantle clung, — *Last Tournament* 213
Drooping (*See also* **A-drooping, Half-drooping, Low-drooping**) found A damsel *d* in a corner of it. — *Geraint and E.* 611
answer'd in low voice, her meek head yet *D*, — " 641
D and beaten by the breeze, — *Lover's Tale i* 700
Droopt *See* **Droop'd.**
Drop (s) (*See also* **Dhrop**) There will not be a *d* of rain — *May Queen* 35
and, dew'd with showery *d*'s, — *Lotos-Eaters* 17
greaves and cuisses dash'd with *d*'s Of onset ; — *M. d'Arthur* 215
That was the last *d* in the cup of gall. — *Walk. to the Mail* 69
Thro' glittering *d*'s on her sad friend. — *Princess vi* 283
And balmy *d*'s in summer dark — *In Mem. xvii* 15
As *d* by *d* the water falls In vaults and catacombs, — " lviii 3
than the sward with *d*'s of dew, — *Geraint and E.* 690

Drop (s) (continued) Thicker than *d*'s from thunder, — *Holy Grail* 348
greaves and cuisses dash'd with *d*'s Of onset ; — *Pass. of Arthur* 383
Like water, *d* by *d*, upon my ear Fell ; — *Lover's Tale i* 576
few *d*'s of that distressful rain Fell on my face, — " 698
hoard of happiness distill'd Some *d*'s of solace ; — " 715
I weänt shed a *d* on 'is blood, — *North. Cobbler* 114
wi' hoffens a *d* in 'is eye. — *Village Wife* 34
Taäste another *d* o' the wine— — " 120
ye shant hev a *d* fro' the paäil. — *Spinster's S.'s* 65
Like *d*'s of blood in a dark-gray sea, — *Heavy Brigade* 43
The falling *d* will make his name — *Epilogue* 36
you spill The *d*'s upon my forehead. — *Romney's R.* 24
Drop (verb) that grace Would *d* from his o'er-brimming love, — *Supp. Confessions* 113
o'er black brows *d*'s down (repeat) — *Madeline* 34, 46
D's in a silent autumn night. — *Lotos-Eaters, C. S.* 34
Till all my limbs *d* piecemeal from the stone, — *St. S. Stylites* 11
All starry culmination *d* Balm-dews — *Talking Oak* 267
a larger egg Than modern poultry *d*, — *Will Water.* 122
To *d* thy foolish tears upon my grave, — *Come not, when, etc.* 2
And *d*'s at Glory's temple-gates, — *You might have won* 34
And the lark *d* down at his feet. — *Poet's Song* 8
Till the Sun *d*, dead, from the signs.' — *Princess vii* 245
d me a flower, *D* me a flower. — *Window, At the W.* 6
D me a flower, a flower, to kiss, — "
D's in his vast and wandering grave. — *In Mem. vi* 16
To *d* head-foremost in the jaws — " xxxiv 15
' The cheeks *d* in ; the body bows Man dies : — " xxxv 7
D's flat, and after the great waters break — *Last Tournament* 464
would *d* from the chords or the keys, — *The Wreck* 27
till I feäld mysen ready to *d*. — *Owd Roä* 71
gold from each laburnum chain *D* to the grass. — *To Mary Boyle* 11
Dropp'd-Dropt (*See also* **Dhropt, Down-drooped, Down-dropt, Half-dropt, Low-dropt**) before my eyelids *dropt* their shade, — *D. of F. Women* 1
a tear *Dropt* on the letters as I wrote. — *To J. S.* 56
She *dropt* the goose, and caught the pelf, — *The Goose* 13
And *dropt* the branch she held, and turning — *Gardener's D.* 157
tho' my teeth, which now are *dropt* away, — *St. S. Stylites* 30
' Her eyelids *dropp'd* their silken eaves. — *Talking Oak* 209
Dropt dews upon her golden head, — " 227
shrivell'd into darkness in his head, And *dropt* before him. — *Godiva* 71
Down they *dropt*—no word was spoken— — *The Captain* 51
Nor anchor *dropt* at eve or morn ; — *The Voyage* 82
Dropt her head in the maiden's hand, — *Lady Clare* 63
He suddenly *dropt* dead of heart-disease.' — *Sea Dreams* 274
And *dropt* a fairy parachute and past : — *Princess, Pro.* 76
Like threaded spiders, one by one, we *dropt*, — " i 108
We *dropt* with evening on a rustic town — " 170
Two plummets *dropt* for one to sound the abyss — " ii 176
Dropt thro' the ambrosial gloom to where below — " iv 24
I clamber'd o'er at top with pain, *Dropt* on the sward, — " 209
And down the streaming crystal *dropt* ; — " vii 165
Nor find him *dropt* upon the firths of ice, — " 206
a flower, a flower, *Dropt*, a flower. — *Window, At the W.* 14
And *dropt* the dust on tearless eyes ; — *In Mem. lxxx* 4
Dropt off gorged from a scheme that had left — *Maud I i* 20
And dream he *dropt* from heaven : — *Com. of Arthur* 183
then the two *Dropt* to the cove, — "
A cloak that *dropt* from collar-bone to heel, — *Gareth and L.* 682
' And thence I *dropt* into a lowly vale, — *Holy Grail* 440
Dropt down from heaven ? — *Last Tournament* 685
with his head below the surface *dropt* — *Lover's Tale i* 636
And the men *dropt* dead in the valleys — *V. of Maeldune* 31
it open'd and *dropt* at the side of each man, — " 85
that *dropt* to the brink of his bay, — *The Wreck* 73
She *dropt* the gracious mask of motherhood, — *The Ring* 384
Dropping (*See also* **Slow-dropping**) Some *d* low their crimson bells — *Arabian Nights* 62
lean'd Upon him, slowly *d* fragrant dew. — *Œnone* 106
d bitter tears against his brow — *M. d'Arthur* 211
d down with costly bales ; — *Locksley Hall* 122
D the too rough H in Hell and Heaven, — *Sea Dreams* 196
a breadth Of Autumn, *d* fruits of power ; — *Princess vi* 55
d bitter tears against a brow — *Pass. of Arthur* 379

Dropping-wells   Laburnums, *d-w* of fire.   *In Mem. lxxxiii* 12

Dropt   *See* **Dropp'd**

Dropwise   gather'd trickling *d* from the cleft,   *Merlin and V.* 274

Dross   scurf of salt, and scum of *d*,   *Vision of Sin* 211

Drought   On stony *d* and steaming salt ;   *Mariana in the S.* 40

Drouth   (*See also* **Drowth**)   I look'd athwart the burning *d*   *Fatima* 13
My one Oasis in the dust and *d* Of city life !   *Edwin Morris* 3
in the dust and *d* of London life She moves   ,, 143

Drove (s)   I watch the darkening *d's* of swine   *Palace of Art* 199
Not one of all the *d* should touch me: swine!'   *Merlin and V.* 699

Drove (verb)   (*See also* **Druv**)   foliage, *d* The fragrant, glistening deeps.   *Arabian Nights* 13
His own thought *d* him, like a goad.   *M. d'Arthur* 185
d his heel into the smoulder'd log,   ,, Ep. 14
fear of change at home, that *d* him hence.   *Walk. to the Mail* 68
Across the boundless east we *d*,   *The Voyage* 38
But whence were those that *d* the sail   ,, 86
Storm, such as *d* her under moonless heavens   *Enoch Arden* 547
The horse he *d*, the boat he sold,   ,, 609
thought Haunted and harass'd him, and *d* him forth,   ,, 720
d The footstool from before him, and arose ;   *Aylmer's Field* 326
D in upon the student once or twice,   ,, 462
and round me *d* In narrowing circles   *Lucretius* 56
With that he *d* the knife into his side: ,, 275
tale of her That *d* her foes with slaughter   *Princess, Pro.* 123
On glassy water *d* his cheek in lines;   ,, i 116
Right on this we *d* and caught,   ,, iv 188
And *d* us, last, to quite a solemn close—   ,, Con. 17
We broke them on the land, we *d* them on the seas.   *Third of Feb.* 30
and goodly sheep In haste they *d*,   *Spec. of Iliad* 5
gold of the ruin'd woodlands *d* thro' the air.   *Maud I* i 12
and she *d* them thro' the waste.   *Geraint and E.* 100
and she *d* them thro' the wood.   ,, 185
He *d* the dust against her veilless eyes: ,, 529
D his mail'd heel athwart the royal crown,   *Balin and Balan* 540
Whom Pellam *d* away with holy heat.   ,, 611
And *d* him into wastes and solitudes   *Lancelot and E.* 252
Tell me, what *d* thee from the Table Round,   *Holy Grail* 286
D me from all vainglories, rivalries,   ,, 32
heapt in mounds and ridges all the sea *D* like a cataract,   ,, 799
Seven days I *d* along the dreary deep, And with me *d* the moon and all the stars,   ,, 808
His own thought *d* him like a goad.   *Pass. of Arthur* 353
I flung him the letter that *d* me wild,   *First Quarrel* 57
and *d* them, and smote them, and slew,   *Def. of Lucknow* 71
D me and my good brothers home   *Columbus* 134
D thro' the midst of the foe,   *Heavy Brigade* 30
D it in wild disarray,   ,, 60
D from out the mother's nest   *Open. I. and C. Exhib.* 27
I *d* the blade that had slain my husband   *Bandit's Death* 34
and *d* the demon from Hawa-i-ee.   *Kapiolani* 33

Drown   her sacred blood doth *d* The fields,   *Poland* 4
Whose muffled motions blindly *d*   *In Mem. xlix* 15
d His heart in the gross mud-honey   *Maud I* xvi 4
they should burst and *d* with deluging storms   ,, II i 42
Might *d* all life in the eye,—   ,, ii 61
A stone about his neck to *d* him in it.   *Gareth and L.* 812
and then like vermin here *D* him,   ,, 823
melody That *d's* the nearer echoes.   *Lover's Tale i* 533
Nor *d* thyself with flies   *Ancient Sage* 268

Drownded (**drowned**)   Wheer the poor wench *d* hersen,   *Spinster's S's.* 25

Drown'd   (*See also* **Dhrownded, Drowndid**)   I *d* the whoopings of the owl   *St. S. Stylites* 33
part were *d* within the whirling brook :   *Princess, Pro.* 47
the glens are *d* in azure gloom   ,, iv 525
tall columns *d* In silken fluctuation   ,, vi 354
Love clasp Grief lest both be *d*,   *In Mem. i* 9
Was *d* in passing thro' the ford,   ,, vi 39
And *d* in yonder living blue   ,, cxv 7
in which all spleenful folly was *d*,   *Maud I* iii 3
Would she had *d* me in it,   *Lancelot and E.* 1412
rest of her *D* in the gloom and horror   *Lover's Tale iv* 62
such a vehemence that it *d* The feebler motion   ,, 82
d in the deeps of a meaningless Past ?   *Vastness* 34

Drowning   I brim with sorrow *d* song,   *In Mem. xix* 12

Drowning (*continued*)   fell the floods of heaven *d* the deep.   *Holy Grail* 533
and the transient trouble of *d*—   *Despair* 67
d old political common-sense !   *Locksley H., Sixty* 250
Thousands of voices *d* his own   *Vastness* 6

Drowse   Let not your prudence, dearest, *d*,   *Princess ii* 339
heel against the pavement echoing, burst Their *d*;   *Geraint and E.* 272

Drowsed   Doubted, and *d*, nodded and slept,   *Com. of Arthur* 427
ravine Which *d* in gloom, seld-darken'd   *Death of Œnone* 76

Drowsing   *See* **Death-drowsing**

Drowth   (*See also* **Drouth**)   Thro' the heat, the *d*, the dust,   *Sisters (E. and E.)* 6

Drug (s)   'What *d* can make A wither'd palsy   *Two Voices* 56

Drug (verb)   *D* thy memories, lest thou learn it,   *Locksley Hall* 77
D down the blindfold sense of wrong   *In Mem. lxxi* 7

Druid   Each was like a *D* rock ;   *Princess iv* 280
grove and altar of the *D* and Druidess,   *Boädicea* 2

Druidess   grove and altar of the Druid and *D*,   ,, 2

Drum   (*See also* **War-drum**)   The murmurs of the *d* and fife   *Talking Oak* 215
Thy voice is heard thro' rolling *d's*   *Princess iv* 577
they clash'd their arms ; the *d* Beat ;   ,, v 250
Now, to the roll of muffled *d's*,   *Ode on Well.* 87
Bugles and *d's* in the darkness,   *Def. of Lucknow* 76

Drunk   (*See also* **Droonk, Sow-droonk**)   And *d* delight of battle with my peers,   *Ulysses* 16
Ah, sweeter to be *d* with loss,   *In Mem. i* 11
D even when he woo'd ;   *Marr. of Geraint* 442
Till, *d* with its own wine, and overfull   *Lover's Tale i* 271
Were *d* into the inmost blue,   ,, 309
D in the largeness of the utterance Of Love ;   ,, 472
for my brain was *d* with the water,   *Despair* 65

Drunkard   Shaking a little like a *d's* hand,   *Enoch Arden* 465
The *d's* football, laughing-stocks of Time,   *Princess iv* 517
let the *d*, as he stretch'd from horse   *Last Tournament* 459

Drunken   (*See also* **Love-drunken**)   Before I well have *d*, scarce can eat :   *Geraint and E.* 662

Druv (drove)   she *d* me to drink the moor,   *North. Cobbler* 30
But the heät *d* hout i' my heyes   *Owd Roä* 84

Dry (adj.)   (*See also* **Dusty-dry**)   Earth is *d* to the centre,   *Nothing will Die* 20
the bearded grass Is *d* and dewless.   *Miller's D.* 246
the silver tongue, Cold February loved, is *d* :   *The Blackbird* 14
youth Keep *d* their light from tears ;   *Of old sat Freedom* 20
And moist and *d*, devising long,   *Love thou thy land* 38
passion sweeping thro' me left me *d*,   *Locksley Hall* 131
Full cold my greeting was and *d* ;   *The Letters* 13
Whose pious talk, when most his heart was *d*,   *Sea Dreams* 186
I found, tho' crush'd to hard and *d*,   *The Daisy* 97
Be near me when my faith is *d*,   *In Mem. l* 9
But with long use her tears are *d*.   ,, lxxviii 20
For underfoot the herb was *d* ;   ,, xcv 2
cells and chambers ; all were fair and *d* ;   *Lancelot and E.* 407
and moist or *d*, Full-arm'd upon his charger   *Pelleas and E.* 215
I never said 'on wi' the *d*,'   *First Quarrel* 77
but thaw tha was iver sa *d*,   *North. Cobbler* 9
And each was as *d* as a cricket,   *V. of Maeldune* 50

Dry (verb)   'The sap *dries* up: the plant declines.   *Two Voices* 268
if thou be'st Love, *d* up these tears   *Lover's Tale i* 780

Dryad-like   *D-l*, shall wear Alternate leaf   *Talking Oak* 286

Dry-tongued   the *d-t* laurels' pattering talk   *Maud I* xviii 8

Dubb'd   Said Arthur, when he *d* him knight;   *Holy Grail* 137

Dubric   To whom arrived, by *D* the high saint,   *Com. of Arthur* 453
holy *D* spread his hands and spake,   ,, 471
D said ; but when they left the shrine   ,, 476
For by the hands of *D*, the high saint,   *Marr. of Geraint* 838
oft I talk'd with *D*, the high saint,   *Geraint and E.* 865

Duck   grew So witty that ye play'd at *d's* and drakes   *Last Tournament* 344

Duct   'Before the little *d's* began   *Two Voices* 325

Due (adj.)   feud, with question unto whom 'twere *d* :   *Œnone* 82
Up in one night and *d* to sudden sun ;   *Princess iv* 312
and *d* To languid limbs and sickness ;   ,, vi 376
one so saved was *d* All to the saver—   *Lover's Tale iv* 279

Due (s)   little *d's* of wheat, and wine and oil ;   *Lotos-Eaters, C. S.* 122
clothes the father with a dearness not his *d*.   *Locksley Hall* 91
So many years from his *d*.'   *Lady Clare* 32

Due (s) (continued) what every woman counts her d, Love, — Princess iii 244
but as frankly theirs As d's of Nature. — " v 204
Who give the Fiend himself his d, — To F. D. Maurice 6
they miss their yearly d Before their time? — In Mem. xxix 15
And render human love his d's; — " xxxvii 16
Which else were fruitless of their d, — " xlv 14
lazy lover Who but claims her as his d? — Maud I xx 11
and let the dark face have his d! — Def. of Lucknow 69
Tho' a prophet should have his d, — Dead Prophet 50

Dug (See also **New-dug**) falling prone he d His fingers
into the wet earth, — Enoch Arden 779
But iron d from central gloom, — In Mem. cxviii 21

Duglas loud battles by the shore Of D; — Lancelot and E. 290

Duke BURY the Great D With an empire's lamentation,
Let us bury the Great D — Ode on Well. 1
Truth-lover was our English D; — " 189
King, d, earl, Count, baron— — Lancelot and E. 464

Dull (adj.) the d Saw no divinity in grass, — A Character 7
You never would hear it; your ears are so d; — Poet's Mind 35
How d it is to pause, to make an end, — Ulysses 22
And d the voyage was with long delays, — Enoch Arden 655
d and self-involved, Tall and erect, — Aylmer's Field 118

Dull (verb) d Those spirit-thrilling eyes — Ode to Memory 38
'Weep, weeping d's the inward pain.' — To J. S. 40
burial mould Will d their comments! — Romney's R. 126

Dull'd And d the murmur on thy lip, — In Mem. xxii 16

Duller something d than at first, — Will Water. 157

Dumb (See also **Death-dumb**) And the far-off stream is d, — The Owl i 3
in a little while our lips are d. — Lotos-Eaters, C. S. 44
The streets are d with snow. — Sir Galahad 52
Winds are loud and you are d, — Window, No Answer 19
ran Thro' lands where not a leaf was d; — In Mem. xxiii 10
lo, thy deepest lays are d — " lxxvi 7
D is that tower which spake so loud, — Con. 106
Then I cannot be wholly d; — Maud II v 100
and the dead, Oar'd by the d, went upward — Lancelot and E. 1154
one hath sung and all the d will sing — Holy Grail 301
and cast her eyes down, and was d. — Lover's Tale iv 329
I almost dread to find her, d!' — " 339
'She is but d, because in her you see — " 341
'Now all be d, and promise all of you — " 351
D on the winter heath he lay. — Dead Prophet 13
dazed and d With passing thro' — Demeter and P. 6

Dumb'd the wholesome music of the wood Was d — Balin and Balan 437
O they to be d by the charm!— — V. of Maeldune 25

Dune (See also **Sea-dune**) long low d, and lazy-
plunging sea. — Last Tournament 484
glory lights the hall, the d, the grass! — Locksley H., Sixty 181

Dung round and round In d and nettles! — Pelleas and E. 471

Dungeon histories Of battle, bold adventure, d, — Aylmer's Field 98
In damp and dismal d's underground, — Lover's Tale ii 149
airs of heaven After a d's closeness. — Sisters (E. and E.) 198
rib-grated d of the holy human ghost, — Happy 31

Dunghill Upon an ampler d trod, — Will Water. 125
And Doubt is the lord of this d — Despair 90

Duomo Of tower or d, sunny-sweet, — The Daisy 46

Dupe Christ the bait to trap his d — Sea Dreams 191

Dusk (s) Beam'd thro' the thicken'd cedar in the d. — Gardener's D. 166
A troop of snowy doves athwart the d, — Princess iv 168
And in the d of thee, the clock Beats out — In Mem. ii 7
I sleep till d is dipt in gray: — " lxvii 12
this flat lawn with d and bright; — " lxxxix 2
shapes That haunt the d, with ermine capes — " xcv 11
now the doubtful d reveal'd The knolls — " 49
So till the d that follow'd evensong — Gareth and L. 793
Till the points of the foam in the d came — Despair 50
or seated in the d Of even, — Demeter and P. 125

Dusk (verb) Little breezes d and shiver — L. of Shalott i 11

Dusky-rafter'd The d-r many-cobweb'd hall, — Marr. of Geraint 362

Dust (See also **Blossom-dust, Doost, Lotos-dust, Touch-wood-dust**) tho' the faults were thick as d In
vacant chambers, — To the Queen 18
right ear, that is fill'd with d, Hears little — Two Voices 116
soil'd with noble d, he hears His country's war-song — " 152
A d of systems and of creeds. — " 207

Dust (continued) Two handfuls of white d, shut in an urn
of brass! — Lotos-Eaters, C. S. 68
I knew your brother: his mute d I honour — To J. S. 29
Lie still, dry d, secure of change. — " 76
parch'd with d; Or, clotted into points — M. d'Arthur 218
The pillar'd d of sounding sycamores, — Audley Court 16
My one Oasis in the d and drouth Of city life! — Edwin Morris 3
For in the d and drouth of London Life — " 143
you may carve a shrine about my d, — St. S. Stylites 195
With anthers and with d: — Talking Oak 184
dead, become Mere highway d? — Love and Duty 11
And vex the unhappy d thou wouldst not save. — Come not, when, etc. 4
Is a clot of warmer d, — Vision of Sin 113
Are but d that rises up, (repeat) — " 133, 169
D are our frames; and, gilded d, — Aylmer's Field 1
scrapings from a dozen years Of d and deskwork: — Sea Dreams 78
Have fretted all to d and bitterness.' — Princess vi 264
Till public wrong be crumbled into d, — Ode on Well. 167
Ashes to ashes, d to d; — " 270
if the wages of Virtue be d, — Wages 6
Thou wilt not leave us in the d: — In Mem., Pro. 9
The d of him I shall not see — " xvii 19
Ye never knew the sacred d: — " xxi 22
And d and ashes all that is; — " xxxiv 4
Man dies: nor is there hope in d:' — " xxxv 4
sow The d of continents to be; — " 12
And Time, a maniac scattering d, — " l 7
grope, And gather d and chaff, — " lv 18
Be blown about the desert d, — " lvi 19
we talk'd Of men and minds, the d of change, — " lxxi 10
To stir a little d of praise. — " lxxv 12
And dropt the d on tearless eyes; — " lxxx 4
The d and din and steam of town: — " lxxxiii 8
Our father's d is left alone — " cv 5
The life re-orient out of d, — " cxvi 6
That we may lift from out of d A voice — " cxxxi 1
who knows? we are ashes and d. — Maud I i 32
Spice his fair banquet with the d of death? — " xviii 56
My d would hear her and beat, — " xxii 71
That sting each other here in the d; — " II i 47
And my heart is a handful of d, — " v 3
he will lift us from the d. — Com. of Arthur 491
who swept the d of ruin'd Rome — Gareth and L. 449
turning round she saw D, and the points of lances — Geraint and E. 449
held Her finger up, and pointed to the d. — " 453
He drove the d against her veilless eyes: — " 529
Or pinch a murderous d into her drink, — Merlin and V. 610
in the d of half-forgotten kings, — Lancelot and E. 1338
Fell into d, and I was left alone, (repeat) — Holy Grail 389, 400, 419
she, too, Fell into d and nothing, — " 397
Fell into d, and disappear'd, — " 436
And touch it, it will crumble into d.' — " 439
whirl the d of harlots round and round — Pelleas and E. 470
he knew the Prince tho' marr'd with d, — Guinevere 36
I saw One lying in the d at Almesbury, — Pass. of Arthur 77
parch'd with d; Or, clotted into points — " 386
heart of Hope Fell into d, and crumbled — Lover's Tale i 95
Down in the dreadful d that once was man, D, — " iv 67
Raving of dead men's d and beating hearts. — " 140
D to d—low down—let us hide! — Rizpah 37
Thro' the heat, the drowth, the d, the glare, — Sisters (E. and E.) 6
The guess of a worm in the d — Despair 30
And changed her into d. — Ancient Sage 162
Her d is greening in your leaf, — " 165
and burns the feet would trample it to d. — The Flight 68
and they crumble into d. — Locksley H., Sixty 72
Only 'd to d' for me that sicken — " 150
D in wholesome old-world d — Dead Prophet 32
she swept The d of earth from her knee. — Vastness 9
may roll with the d of a vanish'd race. — Romney's R. 113
Stampt into d—tremulous, all awry, — St. Telemachus 53
The d send up a steam of human blood, — Akbar's D., Inscrip. 53
d of the rose-petal belongs to the heart — Lucretius 32

Dusty-dry all but yester-eve was d-d. — Lucretius 32

Dusty-white The river-bed was d-w; — Mariana in the S. 54

Dutch sometimes a *D* love For tulips; — *Gardener's D.* 192
Duty for a man may fail in *d* twice, — *M. d'Arthur* 129
  I must be taught my *d*, and by you! — *Dora* 97
  and *D* loved of Love— — *Love and Duty* 46
  centred in the sphere Of common *duties*, — *Ulysses* 40
  Go to him: it is thy *d*: kiss him: — *Locksley Hall* 52
  To all *duties* of her rank: — *L. of Burleigh* 72
  Like one who does his *d* by his own, — *Enoch Arden* 333
  Swerve from her *d* to herself and us— — *Aylmer's Field* 304
  As having fail'd in *d* to him, — *Lucretius* 278
  Thy *d*? What is *d*? Fare thee well!' — " 281
  O hard, when love and *d* clash! — *Princess ii* 293
  My brother! it was *d* spoke, not I. — " 308
  she replied, her *d* was to speak, And *d d*, clear of consequences. — " iii 151
  day fled on thro' all Its range of *duties* — " 177
  they That love their voices more than *d*, — " iv 512
  Some sense of *d*, something of a faith, — " *Con.* 54
  Till one that sought but *D's* iron crown — *Ode on Well.* 122
  path of *d* was the way to glory: (repeat) — " 202, 210
  find the toppling crags of *D* scaled — " 215
  The path of *d* be the way to glory: — " 224
  I done moy *d* boy 'um, (repeat) — *N. Farmer, O. S.* 12, 24
  I done moy *d* by Squoire an' I done moy *d* — " 56
  As it were a *d* done to the tomb, — *Maud I xix* 49
  I charge thee, on thy *d* as a wife, — *Geraint and E.* 16
  It was my *d* to have loved the highest: — *Guinevere* 657
  for a man may fail in *d* twice, — *Pass. of Arthur* 297
  I have only done my *d* as a man is bound to do: — *The Revenge* 102
Dwarf (s) *D's* of the gynæceum, fail so far — *Princess iii* 279
  after seen The *d's* of presage: — " iv 447
  there rode Full slowly by a knight, lady, and *d*; — *Marr. of Geraint* 187
  Whereof the *d* lagg'd latest, — " 193
  sent Her maiden to demand it of the *d*; — " 198
  my faith, thou shalt not,' cried the *d*; — " 204
  Made sharply to the *d*, and ask'd it of him,' — " 412
  His *d*, a vicious under-shapen thing, — " 581
  thou thyself, with damsel and with *d*, — *Sisters (E. and E.)* 199
  Selfish, strange! What *d's* are men! — *The Wreck* 42
  for all but a *d* was he, — *Merlin and V.* 492
Dwarf (verb) *d's* the petty love of one to one. — *Princess vii* 260
Dwarf'd rise or sink Together, *d* or godlike, — *In Mem. lxi* 7
  How *d* a growth of cold and night, — *Their ever-rising life has d* Or lost — *Pelleas and E.* 543
  their ever-rising life has *d* Or lost — *The Ring* 463
Dwarf-elm like an old *d-e* That turns its back — *Princess vii* 126
Dwarf-like among the rest A *d-l* Cato cower'd. — *Supp. Confessions* 54
Dwell Where she would ever wish to *d*, — *Deserted House* 18
  Life and Thought Here no longer *d*; — *Miller's D.* 189
  His light upon the letter *d's*, — " 220
  May those kind eyes for ever *d*! — *Palace of Art* 2
  Wherein at ease for aye to *d*. — " 196
  My Gods, with whom I *d*! — *Lotos-Eaters C. S.* 124
  others in Elysian valleys *d*, — *D. of F. Women* 233
  'It comforts me in this one thought to *d*, — *The Blackbird* 4
  thou may'st warble, eat and *d*. — *To J. S.* 52
  And *d's* in heaven half the night. — *Love and Duty* 36
  would *d* One earnest, earnest moment — *Tithonus* 21
  To *d* in presence of immortal youth, — *Day-Dm., Sleep B.,* 23
  d's A perfect form in perfect rest. — *L. of Burleigh* 24
  Where the wealthy nobles *d*.' — *Princess ii* 85
  D with these, and lose Convention, — *City Child* 2
  pretty home, the home where mother *d's*? — *Boädicea* 63
  there—there—they *d* no more. — *In Mem., Pro.* 26
  But more of reverence in us *d*; — " xcv 29
  the vigour, bold to *d* On doubts that drive — " xcvi 20
  And *d's* not in the light alone, — " xcvii 35
  She *d's* on him with faithful eyes, — " cxxiii 9
  But in my spirit will I *d*, — *Maud I xv* 1
  So dark a mind within me *d's*, — " xviii 69
  wastes where footless fancies *d* — *Com. of Arthur* 291
  for she *d's* Down in a deep; calm, — *Balin and Balan* 485
  I *d* Savage among the savage woods, — " 614
  'She *d's* among the woods' he said — *Lancelot and E.* 449
  and in me there *d's* No greatness, — " 1027
  As when we *d* upon a word we know,

Dwell (continued) Why did the King *d* on my name to me? — *Lancelot and E.* 1402
  I must not *d* on that defeat of fame. — *Guinevere* 628
  d with you; Wear black and white, — " 676
  Love *d's* not in lip-depths. — *Lover's Tale i* 466
  Shakespeare's bland and universal eye *D's* pleased, — *To W. C. Macready* 14
  thou should'st *d* For nine white moons — *Demeter and P.* 120
  thou shalt *d* the whole bright year with me, — " 139
  noble Ulric *d's* forlorn. — *Happy* 10
Dweller some dark *d* by the coco-palm — *Prog. of Spring* 68
Dwelleth The clear-voiced mavis *d*, — *Claribel* 16
Dwelling *D* amid these yellowing bowers: — *A spirit haunts* 2
  d on his boundless love, — *Marr. of Geraint* 63
  Her fancy *d* in this dusky hall: — " 802
  thus he spake, his eye, *d* on mine, — *Holy Grail* 485
  their eyes are dim With *d* on the light — *Lover's Tale i* 492
  Unto the *d* she must sway. — *Ode to Memory* 79
  Philip's *d* fronted on the street, — *Enoch Arden* 731
  How mend the *d's*, of the poor; — *To F. D. Maurice* 38
  With one great *d* in the middle of it; — *Holy Grail* 574
  This is a charmed *d* which I hold;' — *Lover's Tale i* 114
  the sweet *d* of her eyes Upon me — *Sisters (E. and E.)* 165
  who sack'd My *d*, seized upon my papers, — *Columbus* 130
  and the *d* broke into flame; — *V. of Maeldune* 32
  Old Empires, *d's* of the kings of men; — *Prog. of Spring* 99
  climb to the *d* of Peelè the Goddess! — *Kapiolani* 22
Dwelling-place So unproportion'd to the *d-p*,) — *Lover's Tale i* 187
Dwelt The fable of the city where we *d*. — *Gardener's D.* 6
  But the full day of *d* on her brows, — " 136
  keep me from that Eden where she *d*. — " 191
  May not be *d* on by the common day. — " 271
  And *d* a moment on his kindly face, — *Enoch Arden* 326
  Ev'n as she *d* upon his latest words, — " 454
  Her hand *d* lingeringly on the latch, — " 519
  D with eternal summer, ill-content. — " 562
  best and brightest, when they *d* on hers, — *Aylmer's Field* 69
  But when I *d* upon your old affiance, — *Princess iii* 139
  There *d* an iron nature in the grain: — " vi 50
  mournful twilight mellowing, *d* Full on the child; — " 191
  A doubtful smile *d* like a clouded moon — " 270
  the dew *D* in her eyes, — " vii 136
  There they *d* and there they rioted; — *Boädicea* 63
  I past To see the rooms in which he *d*. — *In Mem. lxxxvii* 16
  These two—they *d* with eye on eye, — " xcvii 9
  Methought I *d* within a hall, — " ciii 5
  From which he sallies, and wherein he *d*. — *Balin and Balan* 132
  they *d* Deep-tranced on hers, — " 277
  'Brother, I *d* a day in Pellam's hall:' — " 605
  Lifted her eyes, and they *d* languidly On Lancelot, — *Lancelot and E.* 84
  and *d* among the woods By the great river — " 277
  His own far blood, which *d* at Camelot; — " 803
  Yet larger thro' his leanness, *d* upon her, — " 835
  So *d* the father on her face, — " 1030
  happy as when we *d* among the woods, — " 1036
  I saw That man had once *d* there; — *Holy Grail* 430
  shot A rose-red sparkle to the city, and there *D*, — " 531
  D with them, till in time their Abbess died. — *Guinevere* 692
  to those With whom he *d*, new faces, — *Pass. of Arthur* 5
  fragments of forgotten peoples *d*, — " 84
  Who hath but *d* beneath one roof with me. — " 156
  And heaven pass too, *d* on my heaven, — *Lover's Tale i* 72
  the sudden wail his lady made *D* in his fancy: — " iv 150
  he *d* and whence he roll'd himself — *Tiresias* 145
  while we *d* Together in this valley— — *Death of Œnone* 29
  Love and Justice came and *d* therein; (repeat) — *Akbar's Dream* 181, 194
Dwindle Thou shalt wax and he shall *d*, — *Boädicea* 40
  Science grows and Beauty *d's*— — *Locksley H., Sixty* 246
Dwindled *d* down to some odd games In some odd nooks — *The Epic* 8
Dwindling *See* **Daily-Dwindling**
Dyed walls of my cell were *d* With rosy colours leaping — *Holy Grail* 119
  splash'd and *d* The strong White Horse — " 311
Dyeing blood spirted upon the scarf, *D* it; — *Marr. of Geraint* 209
Dyflen Shaping their way toward *D* again, — *Batt. of Brunanburh* 98

Dying (*See also* **Slowly-dying**) I *would* be *d* evermore,

So *d* ever,	*Eleänore* 143
Then *d* of a mortal stroke,	*Two Voices* 154
Die, *d* clasp'd in his embrace.	*Fatima* 42
They say he's *d* all for love,	*May Queen* 21
When Ellen Adair was *d* for me.	*Edward Gray* 16
as they lay *d*, Did they smile on him.	*The Captain* 55
foretold, *D*, that none of all our blood	*Princess i* 8
He, *d* lately, left her, as I hear,	" 78
Blow, bugle; answer, echoes, *d, d, d.* (repeat)	" iv 6, 12
And answer, echoes, answer, *d, d, d.*	" 18
Or *d*, there at least may die.	*In Mem. viii* 24
The year is *d* in the night;	" *cvi* 3
I felt she was slowly *d* Vext with lawyers	*Maud I xix* 21
D abroad and it seems apart	" 29
When he lay *d* there,	" II ii 67
There is some one *d* or dead,	" iv 48
d, gleam'd on rocks Roof-pendent, sharp;	*Balin and Balan* 314
laughter *d* down as the great knight Approach'd	*Lancelot and E.* 179
methought I spied A *d* fire of madness	*Holy Grail* 768
' And oft in *d* cried upon your name.'	*Pelleas and E.* 385
Moans of the *d*, and voices of the dead.	*Pass. of Arthur* 117
d thus, Crown'd with her highest act	*Lover's Tale i* 215
And the lion there lay *d*,	*The Revenge* 96
D so English thou wouldst have her flag	*Ded. Poem Prin. Alice* 16
Death to the *d*, and wounds to the wounded,	*Def. of Lucknow* 17
women in travail among the *d* and dead,	" 88
glory and shame *d* out for ever	" *Despair* 75
and *d* while they shout her name.	*Locksley H., Sixty* 128
D, 'Unspeakable' he wrote 'Their kindness,'	*To Marq. of Dufferin* 35
but then A kinsman, *d*, summon'd me to Rome—	*The Ring* 178
And *d* rose, and rear'd her arms,	" 222
I sat beside her *d*, and she gaspt:	" 287
You that know you're *d* . . .	*Forlorn* 58
I am Merlin, And *I* am *d*,	*Merlin and the G.* 8
worn-out Reason *d* in her house May leave the windows	*Romney's R.* 145
I am *d* now Pierced by a poison'd dart.	*Death of Œnone* 33
D in childbirth of dead sons.	*Akbar's Dream* 12

Dyke
Adown the crystal *d's* at Camelot	*Geraint and E.* 470
Ah little rat that borest in the *d*	*Merlin and V.* 112
From wall to wall he stood,	*Achilles over the T.* 15
Thrice from the *d* he sent his mighty shout,	" 30

Dynamite if *d* and revolver leave you courage   *Locksley H., Sixty* 107

E

Each
E month is various to present the world	*Two Voices* 74
E morn my sleep was broken thro'	*Miller's D.* 39
And steal you from *e* other!	*Aylmer's Field* 707
Who hate *e* other for a song,	*Lit. Squabbles* 5
scarce could hear *e* other speak for noise Of clocks and chimes,	*Princess i* 215
with *e* light air On our mail'd heads:	" *v* 244
while *e* ear was prick'd to attend A tempest,	" *vi* 280
and *e* base, To left and right,	" 353
Christmas bells from hill to hill Answer *e* other in the mist.	*In Mem. xxviii* 4
E voice four changes on the wind,	" 9
and prey By *e* cold hearth,	" *xcviii* 18
That will not yield *e* other way.	" *cii* 20
and join'd *E* office of the social hour	" *cxi* 14
Where *e* man walks with his head in a cloud of poisonous flies.	*Maud I iv* 54
hiss'd *e* at other's ear What shall not be recorded—	*Geraint and E.* 634
With *e* chest lock'd and padlock'd thirty-fold,	*Merlin and V.* 655
the knights, Glorying in *e* new glory,	*Last Tournament* 336
Do *e* low office of your holy house;	*Guinevere* 682
How like *e* other was the birth of *e* !	*Lover's Tale i* 197
E way from verge to verge a Holy Land,	" 337
No sisters ever prized *e* other more.	*Sisters (E. and E.)* 43
Sway'd by *e* Love, and swaying to *e* Love,	*Prin. Beatrice* 19
birds that circle round the tower Are cheeping to *e* other	*The Ring* 86

'Eäd (head) bummin' awaäy loike a buzzard-clock

ower my *'e*,	*N. Farmer, O. S.* 18
Breäk me a bit o' the esh for his *'e*	" *N. S.* 41
cleän as a flower fro' *'e* to feeät:	*North. Cobbler* 44
' When theer's naw *'e* to a 'Ouse	*Village Wife* 17
but *'e* niver not lift oop *'is 'e*:	" 88
fever *'ed* baäked Jinny's *'e* as bald as one o' them heggs,	" 102
wi' a bran-new *'e* o' the Queeän,	*Spinster's S's.* 76
an' the mark o' *'is 'e* o' the chairs !	" 100
an' the Freeä Traäde runn'd *'i* my *'e*,	*Owd Roä* 54
an' clemm'd owd Roä by the *'e*,	" 99

Eager
and arose *E* to bring them down,	*Enoch Arden* 872
e eyes, that still Took joyful note of all things joyful,	*Aylmer's Field* 66
But Edith's *e* fancy hurried with him	" 208
rising race were half as *e* for the light.	*Locksley H., Sixty* 228
they lifted up Their *e* faces, wondering at the strength,	*Merlin and V.* 133
But *e* to follow, I saw,	*Merlin and the G.* 101

Eager-hearted *E-h* as a boy when first he leaves his father's field,   *Locksley Hall* 112

Eagerness in his heat and *e* Trembled and quiver'd,   *Pelleas and E.* 283

Eagle (*See also* **Blood-eagle, Heagle**) Half-buried in the

E's down,	*Palace of Art* 122
Shall *e's* not be *e's* ? wrens be wrens ?	*Golden Year* 37
wonder of the *e* were the less, But he not less the *e*.	" 39
Unclasp'd the wedded *e's* of her belt,	*Godiva* 43
An *e* clang an *e* to the sphere.	*Princess iii* 106
a poising *e*, burns Above the unrisen morrow:'	" *iv* 82
A train of dames : by axe and *e* sat,	" *vii* 128
Lean-headed *E's* yelp alone,	" 211
Till o'er the hills her *e's* flew	*Ode on Well.* 112
Again their ravening *e* rose In anger,	" 119
Must their ever-ravening *e's* beak and talon	*Boädicea* 11
Tho' the Roman *e* shadow thee,	" 39
Or *e's* wing, or insect's eye?	*In Mem. cxxiv* 6
Roman legions here again, And Cæsar's *e*:	*Com. of Arthur* 35
For this an *E*, a royal *E*,	*Gareth and L.* 44
an *E* rising or, the Sun In dexter chief;	*Merlin and V.* 475
and started thro' mid air Bearing an *e's* nest:	*Last Tournament* 15
Follow'd a rush of *e's* wings,	" 417
THEY rose to where their sovran *e* sails,	*Montenegro* 11
Left for the white-tail'd *e* to tear it,	*Batt. of Brunanburh* 107
rose as it were on the wings of an *e*	*The Wreck* 69
That young *e* of the West To forage for herself	*Open. I. and C. Exhib.* 28

Eagle-borne ' Peace to thine *e-b* Dead nestling,   *Last Tournament* 33

Eagle-circle sweep In ever-highering *e-c's*   *Gareth and L.* 21

Eagle-like *e-l* Stoop at thy will on Lancelot   *Balin and Balan* 535

Eagle-owl Round as the red eye of an *E-o*,   *Gareth and L.* 799

Eagle-peak I stared from every *e-p*,   *Demeter and P.* 68

Eaglet Foster'd the callow *e*—   *Œnone* 212

Ear (organ of hearing) (*See also* **Captain's-ear, Ear-stunning**) Pour round mine *e's* the livelong bleat

	Ode to Memory 65
You never would hear it; your *e's* are so dull;	*Poet's Mind* 35
at first to the *e* The warble was low,	*Dying Swan* 23
With dinning sound my *e's* are rife,	*Eleänore* 135
The right *e*, that is fill'd with dust,	*Two Voices* 116
His country's war-song thrill his *e's*:	" 153
A second voice was at mine *e*,	*Miller's D.* 172
the jewel That trembles in her *e*:	*Œnone* 186
drawing nigh Half-whisper'd in his *e*,	" 265
a sound Rings ever in her *e's* of armed men.	*Palace of Art* 109
Or hollowing one hand against his *e*,	" 219
Like Herod, when the shout was in his *e's*,	*Lotos-Eaters* 36
music in his *e's* his beating heart did make.	*D. of F. Women* 82
a clear under-tone Thrill'd thro' mine *e's*	*The Epic* 45
horse That hears the corn-bin open, prick'd my *e's*;	*M. d'Arthur* 179
murmuring at his *e* ' Quick, Quick !	*Gardener's D.* 85
Rings in mine *e's*. The steer forgot to graze,	*Edwin Morris* 64
my *e's* deafen'd Her lightest breath;	*St. S. Stylites* 185
pits of fire, that still Sing in mine *e's*.	*Talking Oak* 82
(And hear me with thine *e's*,)	

Ear (organ of hearing) (*continued*) If the sense is hard

To alien *e's*,	*Love and Duty* 52
song from out the distance in the ringing of thine *e's*;	*Locksley Hall* 84
Then fillip'd at the diamond in her *e*;	*Godiva* 25
And whisper'd voices at his *e*.	*Day-Dm., Arrival* 24
In her *e* he whispers gaily,	*L. of Burleigh* 1
Worried his passive *e* with petty wrongs	*Enoch Arden* 352
a whisper on her *e*, She knew not what;	,, 515
likewise, in the ringing of his *e's*,	,, 613
Twinkled the innumerable *e* and tail.	*The Brook* 134
Call'd all her vital spirits into each *e*	*Aylmer's Field* 201
And foam'd away his heart at Averill's *e*:	,, 342
His message ringing in thine *e*,	,, 666
won mysterious way Thro' the seal'd *e*	,, 696
True Devils with no *e*, they howl in tune	*Sea Dreams* 260
Or lend an *e* to Plato where he says,	*Lucretius* 147
twinn'd as horse's *e* and eye.	*Princess* i 57
my very *e's* are hot To hear them:	,, 134
no livelier than the dame That whisper'd ' Asses' *e's*,'	,, ii 113
To dying *e's*, when unto dying eyes	,, iv 51
we should cram our *e's* with wool And so pace by:	,, 65
at mine *e* Bubbled the nightingale and heeded not,	,, 265
Each hissing in his neighbour's *e*;	,, v 15
infuse my tale of love In the old king's *e's*,	,, 241
while each *e* was prick'd to attend A tempest,	,, vi 280
the Dead March wails in the people's *e's*:	*Ode on Well.* 267
And the *e* of man cannot hear,	*High. Pantheism* 17
But I should turn mine *e's* and hear	*In Mem.* xxxv 8
Not all ungrateful to thine *e*.	,, xxxviii 12
Yet in these *e's*, till hearing dies,	,, lvii 9
Till on mine *e* this message falls,	,, lxxxv 18
A willing *e* We lent him.	,, lxxxvii 30
heart and *e* were fed To hear him,	,, lxxxix 22
words of life Breath'd in her *e*.	*Con.* 53
centre-bits Grind on the wakeful *e*	*Maud* I i 42
(Look at it) pricking a cockney *e*.	,, x 22
Whose *e* is cramm'd with his cotton,	,, 42
With the evil tongue and the evil *e*,	,, 51
hope to win her With his chirrup at her *e*.	,, xx 30
It will ring in my heart and my *e's*, till I die.	,, II i 35
An old song vexes my *e*;	,, ii 47
Modred laid his *e* beside the doors,	*Com. of Arthur* 323
weary her *e's* with one continuous prayer,	*Gareth and L.* 19
and the sound was good to Gareth's *e*.	,, 312
felt his young heart hammering in his *e's*,	,, 322
He sow'd a slander in the common *e*,	*Marr. of Geraint* 450
she *could* speak whom his own *e* had heard	*Geraint and E.* 113
prick'd their light *e's*, and felt Her low firm voice	,, 193
And *e's* to hear you even in his dreams.'	,, 429
a heavily-galloping hoof Smote on her *e*,	,, 448
hiss'd each at other's *e* What shall not be recorded—	,, 634
tho' mine own *e's* heard you yestermorn—	,, 740
in the King's own *e* Speak what has chanced;	,, 808
Then hand at *e*, and hearkening from what side	*Balin and Balan* 415
Woods have tongues, As walls have *e's*:	,, 531
And sowing one ill hint from *e* to *e*,	*Merlin and V.* 143
That glorious roundel echoing in our *e's*,	,, 426
All *e's* were prick'd at once,	*Lancelot and E.* 724
Her father's latest word humm'd in her *e*,	,, 780
till the *e* Wearies to hear it,	,, 897
the world, the world, All *e* and eye,	,, 941
a stupid heart To interpret *e* and eye,	,, 942
And took both *e* and eye;	*Holy Grail* 383
by mine eyes and by mine *e's* I swear,	,, 864
From *e* to *e* with dogwhip-weals,	*Last Tournament* 58
' A sound is in his *e's*'?	,, 116
trumpet sounded as in a dream To *e's* but half-awaked.	,, 152
one of thy long asses' *e's*,	,, 273
Modred still in green, all *e* and eye,	*Guinevere* 24
To vex an *e* too sad to listen to me,	,, 315
and past his *e* Went shrilling, ' Hollow,	*Pass. of Arthur* 32
murmuring at his *e*, ' Quick, Quick !	,, 347
I come, great Mistress of the *e* and eye:	*Lover's Tale* i 22
drop by drop, upon my *e* Fell;	,, 576

Ear (organ of hearing) (*continued*) And thro' the hasty

notice of the *e*	*Lover's Tale* i 615
address'd More to the inward than the outward *e*,	,, 721
marriage-bells, echoing in *e* and heart—	,, iv 3
A crueller reason than a crazy *e*,	,, 32
Flying by each fine *e*, an Eastern gauze	,, 291
we shook 'em off as a dog that shakes his *e's*	*The Revenge* 54
But Charlie 'e sets back 'is *e's*,	*Village Wife* 67
pibroch of Europe is ringing again in our *e's* !	*Def. of Lucknow* 97
lyre Is ever sounding in heroic *e's* Heroic hymns,	*Tiresias* 181
Nor lend an *e* to random cries,	*Politics* 7
at his *e* he heard a whisper ' Rome '	*St. Telemachus* 26
But Death had *e's* and eyes;	*Akbar's Dream* 187
The toll of funeral in an Angel *e*	*D. of the Duke of C.* 10

Ear (as of corn)

Bows all its *e's* before the roaring East;	*Princess* i 237
And pluck'd the ripen'd *e's*,	,, ii 2
For now is love mature in *e*.'	*In Mem.* lxxxi 4
some scatter'd *e's*, Some *e's* for Christ	*Sir J. Oldcastle* 12

'Ear (hear)

Dosn't thou 'e my 'erse's legs,	*N. Farmer, N. S.* 1
that's what I 'e's 'em saäy.	,, 8
woä then woä—let ma 'e mysén speäk.	,, 59
that's what I 'e's 'im saäy—	,,
But I 'e's es 'e'd gie fur a howry owd book	*Village Wife* 45
An' I liked to 'e it I did,	*Spinster's S's* 18
ye knawed it wur pleasant to 'e,	,, 21
so es all that I 'e's be true;	,, 56
wait till tha 'e's it be strikin' the hour.	*Owd Roä* 18
thaw I didn't haäfe think as 'e'd 'e,	,, 91
an' I 'e's 'em yit;	,, 106
An' Parson 'e 'e's on it all,	*Church-warden, etc.* 37

'Eärd (heard)

An 'e 'um a bummin' awaäy	*N. Farmer, O. S.* 18
Theer wur a boggle in it, I often 'e 'um mysen ;	
Moäst like a butter-bump, fur I 'e 'um about an' about,	,, 30
we 'e 'im a-mountin' oop 'igher an' 'igher,	*North. Cobbler* 47
An' nawbody 'e on 'er sin,	*Village Wife* 98
Ye niver 'e Steevie sweär	*Spinster's S's.* 60
I 'e 'er a maäkin' 'er moän,	,, 115
we couldn't ha' 'e tha call,	*Owd Roä* 49
tummled up stairs, fur I 'e 'im,	,, 63
as soon as 'e 'e 'is naäme,	,, 93
An' I *'e* the bricks an' the baulks	,, 109

Earl (*See also* Yerl)

O the *E* was fair to see ! (repeat)	*The Sisters* 6, 12, 18, 24, 30, 36
The daughter of a hundred *E's*,	*L. C. V. de Vere* 7
that grim *E*, who ruled In Coventry:	*Godiva* 12
eagles of her belt, The grim *E's* gift;	,, 44
' The old *E's* daughter died at my breast;	*Lady Clare* 25
Wherein were bandit *e's*, and caitiff knights,	*Marr. of Geraint* 35
There musing sat the hoary-headed *E*,	,, 295
Then sigh'd and smiled the hoary-headed *E*,	,, 307
But none spake word except the hoary *E*:	,, 369
while the Prince and *E* Yet spoke together,	,, 384
Then suddenly addrest the hoary *E*: ' Fair Host and *E*, I pray your courtesy;	,, 402
So spake the kindly-hearted *E*,	,, 514
' *E*, entreat her by my love,	,, 760
fetch Fresh victual for these mowers of our *E*;	*Geraint and E.* 225
And into no *E's* palace will I go.	,, 235
And feast with these in honour of their *E*;	,, 287
' *E*, if you love me as in former years,	,, 355
bow'd the all-amorous *E*,	,, 360
thought she heard the wild *E* at the door,	,, 381
To the waste earldom of another *e*,	,, 438
Fled all the boon companions of the *E*,	,, 477
Rode on a mission to the bandit *E*;	,, 527
And their own *E*, and their own souls,	,, 577
the huge *E* cried out upon her talk,	,, 651
Then strode the brute *E* up and down his hall,	,, 712
I knew this *E*, when I myself Was half a bandit	,, 794
the huge *E* lay slain within his hall.	,, 806
King, duke, *e*, Count, baron—	*Lancelot and E.* 464
Athelstan King, Lord among *E's*,	*Batt. of Brunanburh* 2
Seven strong *E's* of the army of Anlaf	,, 53
E's that were lured by the Hunger	,, 123

Earldom   From mine own *e* foully ousted me;   *Marr. of Geraint* 459
   Thou shalt give back their *e* to thy kin.   „   585
   'This noble prince who won our *e* back,   „   619
   Because we have our *e* back again.   „   701
   To the waste *e* of another earl,   *Geraint and E.* 438
   ye shall share my *e* with me, girl,   „   626

Earlier   (*See also* **Season-earlier**)   I will turn that *e*   *Locksley Hall* 107
   page.
   Break, happy land, into *e* flowers!   *W. to Alexandra* 10
   But that was in her *e* maidenhood,   *Holy Grail* 73

Earliest   Because they are the *e* of the year).   *Ode to Memory* 27
   The *e* pipe of half-awaken'd birds ·   *Princess* iv 50
   like a guilty thing I creep At *e* morning to the door.   *In Mem.* vii 8
   With one that was his *e* mate;   „   *lxiv* 24
   The roofs, that heard our *e* cry,   „   *cii* 3
   she placed where morning's *e* ray Might strike it,   *Lancelot and E.* 5
   So what was *e* mine in *e* life,   *Lover's Tale* i 247
   nor tell Of this our *e*, our closest-drawn,   „   278
   with *e* violets And lavish carol of clear-throated larks   „   282
   first gray streak of *e* summer-dawn,   *Ancient Sage* 220
   A soul that, watch'd from *e* youth,   *To Marq. of Dufferin* 25

Early   (*See also* **Rathe**)   gaze On the prime labour   *Ode to Memory* 94
   of thine *e* days:
   Make thy grass hoar with *e* rime.   *Two Voices* 66
   love dispell'd the fear That I should die an *e* death: *Miller's D.* 90
   His *e* rage Had force to make me rhyme in youth,   „   192
   Whole weeks and months, and *e* and late,   *The Sisters* 10
   In the *e e* morning the summer sun 'ill shine,   *May Queen, N. Y's. E.* 22
   And once I ask'd him of his *e* life,   *Edwin Morris* 23
   leave me here a little, while as yet 'tis *e* morn: *Locksley Hall* 1
   Faint as a figure seen in *e* dawn   *Enoch Arden* 357
   mate had seen at *e* dawn Across a break   „   631
   a rough piece Of *e* rigid colour,   *Aylmer's Field* 281
   Some pleasure from thine *e* years.   *In Mem.* iv 10
   e light Shall glimmer on the dewy decks.   „   ix 11
   Her *e* Heaven, her happy views;   „   *xxxiii* 6
   to him she sings Of *e* faith and plighted vows;   „   *xcvii* 30
   A light-blue lane of *e* dawn, And think of *e* days and thee,   „   *cxix* 7
   Half in dreams I sorrow after The delight of *e* skies;   *Maud* II iv 25
   Enid, my *e* and my only love,   *Geraint and E.* 307
   soul twines and mingles with the growths Of   *Lover's Tale* i 133
   vigorous *e* days,
   I was then in *e* boyhood, Edith but a child   *Locksley H., Sixty* 258
   of six—
   When over the valley, In *e* summers,   *Merlin and the G.* 18

Early-silvering   Thus over Enoch's *e-s* head   *Enoch Arden* 622

Earn   (*See also* **Addle**)   *E* well the thrifty months,   *Love thou thy land* 95
   lease Of life, shalt *e* no more;   *Will Water.* 244
   metaphysics! read and *e* our prize,   *Princess* iii 300
   popular name such manhood *e's*,   *Merlin and V.* 787
   child Should *e* from both the praise of heroism,   *Sisters (E. and E.)* 251

Earn'd   Thus *e* a scanty living for himself: *Enoch Arden* 818
   Has *e* himself the name of sparrow-hawk.   *Marr. of Geraint* 492
   'Have I not *e* my cake in baking of it?   *Gareth and L.* 575

Earnest (adj.)   (*See also* **Too-earnest**)   all, they said,   *Princess, Con.* 21
   as *e* as the close?
   her full and *e* eye Over her snow-cold breast   *Œnone* 141
   dwell One *e*, *e* moment upon mine,   *Love and Duty* 37

Earnest (seriousness)   words were half in *e*, half in jest,)   *Gardener's D.* 23
   take it—*e* wed with sport,   *Day-Dm., Ep.* 11
   jest and *e* working side by side,   *Princess* iv 563
   By these in *e* those in mockery call'd   *Last Tournament* 135

Earnest (pledge)   *e* of the things that they shall do: *Locksley Hall* 118
   Are *e* that he loves her yet,   *In Mem.* xcvii 15
   blood Hath *e* in it of far springs to be.   *Merlin and V.* 557

Earning   save all *e's* to the uttermost   *Enoch Arden* 86

Ear-stunning   *e-s* hail of Arès crash Along the sounding   *Tiresias* 96
   walls.'

Earth   O you that hold A nobler office upon *e* Than arms,   *To the Queen* 2
   E is dry to the centre,   *Nothing will Die* 20
   The old *e* Had a birth,   *All Things will Die* 37
   And the old *e* must die.   „   41
   in her first sleep *e* breathes stilly: *Leonine Eleg.* 7
   And Thou and peace to *e* were born.   *Supp. Confessions* 26
   whene'er *E* goes to *e*, with grief,   „   38

Earth (*continued*)   Hating to wander out on *e*,   *Supp. Confessions* 57
   To the *e*—until the ice would melt   „   81
   Breathed low around the rolling *e*   *The Winds, etc.* 3
   star The black *e* with brilliance rare.   *Ode to Memory* 20
   sure she deem'd no mist of *e* could dull   „   38
   Over the dark dewy *e* forlorn,   „   69
   Over its grave i' the *e* so chilly; (repeat)   *A spirit haunts* 10, 22
   And said the *e* was beautiful.   *A Character* 12
   spirit of man, Making *e* wonder,   *The Poet* 52
   It would shrink to the *e* if you came in.   *Poet's Mind* 37
   The house was builded of the *e*,   *Deserted House* 15
   Adeline, Scarce of *e* nor all divine,   *Adeline* 3
   The choicest wealth of all the *e*,.   *Eleanore* 19
   But breathe it into *e* and close it up   *Wan Sculptor* 12
   What is there in the great sphere of the *e*,   *If I were loved* 2
   true, To what is loveliest upon *e*.'   *Mariana in the S.* 64
   Dissolved the riddle of the *e*,   *Two Voices* 170
   To that last nothing under *e*!'   „   333
   Have I not found a happy *e*?   *Miller's D.* 25
   Hear me, O *E*, hear me, O Hills,   *Œnone* 36
   O happy *e*, how canst thou bear my weight?   „   237
   There are enough unhappy on this *e*,   „   239
   All *e* and air seem only burning fire.'   „   268
   common clay ta'en from the common *e*   *To ——, With Pal. of Art* 17
   Lord of the visible *e*,   *Palace of Art* 179
   oft the riddle Of the painful *e* Flash'd thro' her   „   213
   mouldering with the dull *e's* mouldering sod,   „   261
   Was never born into the *e*.   *To J. S.* 32
   note, Should thus be lost for ever from the *e*,   *M. d'Arthur* 20
   round *e* is every way Bound by gold chains   „   254
   Felt *e* as air beneath me,   *Gardener's D.* 212
   Unfit for *e*, unfit for heaven,   *St. S. Stylites* 3
   Heaven, and *E*, and Time are choked.   „   104
   men on *e* House in the shade of comfortable roofs,   *Talking Oak* 273
   The fat *e* feed thy branchy root,   *Golden Year* 24
   dark *E* follows wheel'd in her ellipse;   *Ulysses* 67
   strength which in old ·days Moved *e* and heaven;   *Tithonus* 48
   In days far-off, on that dark *e*,   „   75
   I *e* in *e* forget these empty courts,   *Locksley Hall* 130
   And the kindly *e* shall slumber,   „   180
   perish one by one, Than that *e* should stand at gaze   *Godiva* 66
   one low churl, compact of thankless *e*,   *Day-Dm., L'Envoi* 19
   For we are Ancients of the *e*,   *Will Water.* 65
   This *e* is rich in man and maid;   „   67
   This whole wise of *e* of light and shade Comes out   „   202
   Like all good things on *e*!   *Lady Clare* 68
   That are the flower of the *e*?'   *L. of Burleigh* 98
   Bore to *e* her body, drest In the dress   *Move Eastward* 1
   Move eastward, happy *e*, and leave   *The Letters* 7
   'Cold altar, Heaven and *e* shall meet   *You might have won* 23
   No public life was his on *e*,   *Enoch Arden* 780
   he dug His fingers into the wet *e*,   *Aylmer's Field* 160
   this, a milky-way on *e*, Like visions   „   557
   one kiss Was Leolin's one strong rival upon *e*;   „   635
   Never since our bad *e* became one sea,   „   760
   e Lightens from her own central Hell—   *Sea Dreams* 99
   All over earthy, like a piece of *e*,   *Lucretius* 48
   blood by Sylla shed Came driving rainlike down again on *e*,   „   130
   never yet on *e* Could dead flesh creep,   *Princess* i 223
   two sphere lamps blazon'd like Heaven and *E*   „   ii 37
   close upon the Sun, Than our man's *e*;   „   179
   broad and bounteous *E* Should bear a double growth   „   iii 259
   there is nothing upon *e* More miserable   „   v 43
   Leapt from the dewy shoulders of the *E*,   „   192
   sweet influences Of *e* and heaven?   „   446
   fixt As are the roots of *e* and base of all;   „   497
   Part roll'd on the *e* and rose again   „   528
   twists the grain with such a roar that *E* Reels,   „   vi 120
   she set the child on the *e*;   „   vii 182
   lies the *E* all Danaë to the stars,   *Ode on Well.* 269
   black *e* yawns: the mortal disappears;   *Ode Inter. Exhib.* 2
   wide hall with *e's* invention stored,   „   41
   And gathering all the fruits of *e*   *The Daisy* 102
   The gloom that saddens Heaven and *E*,   *The Flower* 2
   I cast to *e* a seed.

Earth (*continued*) throbs Thro' *e*, and all her graves,   *Romney's R.* 128
Sounding for ever and ever thro' *E*   *Parnassus* 7
e's green stole into heaven's own hue,   *Far-far-away* 2
all the bounds of *e*, Far-far-away ?   " 14
ACT first, this *E*, a stage so gloom'd   *The Play* 1
In silence wept upon the flowerless *e*.   *Death of Œnone* 9
' Is *e* On fire to the West ?   *St. Telemachus* 18
Yea, Alla here on *e*, who caught and held   *Akbar's Dream* 84
mists of *e* Fade in the noon of heaven,   " 96
Let the Sun, Who heats our *e* to yield us grain   " 105
draw The crowd from wallowing in the mire of *e*,   " 141
' The meek shall inherit the *e* '   *The Dreamer* 2
dream'd that a Voice of the *E* went wailingly past   " 3
Moaning your losses, O *E*,   " 17
The Reign of the Meek upon *e*,   " 25
Minds on this round *e* of ours   *Poets and Critics* 3
For if this *e* be ruled by Perfect Love,   *D. of the Duke of C.* 8
His shadow darkens *e* :   " 13
Earth-angel O Heaven's own white *E-a*,   *Merlin and V.* 81
Earth-baldness *e-b* clothes itself afresh,   *Demeter and P.* 49
Earthen Drawing into his narrow *e* urn,   *Ode to Memory* 61
Earth-Goddess I, *E-G*, cursed the Gods of Heaven.   *Demeter and P.* 102
I, *E-G*, am but ill-content With them,   " 128
Earthlier myself Am lonelier, darker, *e* for my loss   *Aylmer's Field* 750
your modern amourist is of easier, *e* make.   *Locksley H., Sixty* 18
smiling downward at this *e* earth of ours,   " 183
Earthly Or love that never found his *e* close,   *Love and Duty* 1
As this pale taper's *e* spark,   *St. Agnes' Eve* 15
So in mine *e* house I am,   " 19
May not that *e* chastisement suffice ?   *Aylmer's Field* 784
Lay your *e* fancies down,   *Ode on Well.* 279
For I am but an *e* Muse,   *In Mem. xxxvii* 13
May some dim touch of *e* things Surprise thee   " *xliv* 11
the song of woe Is after all an *e* song :   " *lvii* 2
The head hath miss'd an *e* wreath :   " *lxxiii* 6
Till slowly worn her *e* robe,   " *lxxxiv* 33
For she is *e* of the mind,   " *cxiv* 21
he defileth heavenly things With *e* uses '—   *Balin and Balan* 422
was it *e* passion crost ? '   *Holy Grail* 29
e heats that spring and sparkle out   " 33
how should *E* measure mete The Heavenly-unmeasured   *Lover's Tale i* 473
divorce thee not From *e* love and life—   *Ded. Poem Prin. Alice* 4
happier voyage now Toward no *e* pole.   *Sir J. Franklin* 4
Trusting no longer that *e* flower would be heavenly fruit—   *Despair* 35
filial eyes Have seen the loneliness of *e* thrones,   *Prin. Beatrice* 14
Miriam, breaks her latest *e* link With me to-day.   *The Ring* 47
Earthly-best or if she gain her *e-b*,   *Locksley H., Sixty* 233
Earthly-heavenliest Most loveliest, *e-h* harmony ?   *Lover's Tale i* 279
Earthly-wise blessed Lord, I speak too *e*,   *Holy Grail* 627
Earthly-worst Earth may reach her *e-w*,   *Locksley H., Sixty* 233
Earth-Mother child Of thee, the great *E-M*,   *Demeter and P.* 97
reap with me, *E-m*, in the harvest hymns   " 148
Earth-narrow whether this *e-n* life Be yet but yolk,   *Ancient Sage* 129
Earthquake (*See also* **World's-earthquake**) Blight and famine, plague and *e*,   *Lotos-Eaters, C. S.* 115
flood, fire, *e*, thunder, wrought Such waste   *Aylmer's Field* 639
wholly out of sight, and sink Past *e*—   *Lucretius* 153
Shatter'd into one *e* in one day   " 251
like a bell Toll'd by an *e* in a trembling tower,   *Princess vi* 332
crack of *e* shivering to your base Split you,   *Pelleas and E.* 465
An *e*, my loud heart-beats,   *Lover's Tale ii* 193
a wave like the wave that is raised by an *e* grew,   *The Revenge* 115
another wild *e* out-tore Clean from our lines   *Def. of Lucknow* 61
an *e* always moved in the hollows under the dells,   *V. of Maeldune* 107
Shrine-shattering *e*, fire, flood, thunderbolt,   *Tiresias* 61
Gone like fires and floods and *e*'s   *Locksley H., Sixty* 40
Thunder, or the rending *e*, or the famine,   *Faith* 4
Earthquake-cloven yawning of an *e-c* chasm.   *Lover's Tale i* 377
Earth-shock'd Above some fair metropolis, *e-s*,—   " *ii* 62
Earth-sweeping upbare A broad *e-s* pall of whitest lawn   " 78
Earthy Were it earth in an *e* bed ;   *Maud I xxii* 70
All over *e*, like a piece of earth,   *Sea Dreams* 99
Earwig See **Battle-Twig**

Ease Two lives bound fast in one with golden *e* ;   *Circumstance* 5
' Why, if man rot in dreamless *e*,   *Two Voices* 280
Alice, you were ill at *e* ;   *Miller's D.* 146
Wherein at *e* for aye to dwell,   *Palace of Art* 2
long rest or death, dark death, or dreamful *e*.   *Lotos-Eaters, C. S.* 53
You ask me, why, tho' ill at *e*,   *You ask me,* 1
control Our being, lest we rust in *e*.   *Love thou thy land* 42
Seeing with how great *e* Nature can smile,   *Lucretius* 174
With garrulous *e* and oily courtesies   *Princess i* 164
We break our laws with *e*,   " *vi* 323
but your Highness breaks with *e* The law   " 325
I would set their pains at *e*.   *In Mem. lxiii* 8
wrought All kind of service with a noble *e*   *Gareth and L.* 489
Drank till he jested with all *e*,   *Geraint and E.* 290
She lied with *e* ; but horror-stricken he,   *Balin and Balan* 525
he let his wisdom go For *e* of heart,   *Merlin and V.* 893
Them surely I can silence with all *e*.   *Lancelot and E.* 109
they lost themselves, Yet with all *e*,   " 442
And found no *e* in turning or in rest ;   " 901
Who read but on my breviary with *e*,   *Holy Grail* 545
ruffians at their *e* Among their harlot-brides,   *Last Tournament* 427
But on that day, not being all at *e*,   *Sister's (E. and E.)* 209
And yet my heart is ill at *e*,   *The Flight* 97
Eased And *e* her heart of madness . . .   *Forlorn* 82
Easeful wilt thou leave Thine *e* biding here,   *Gareth and L.* 128
Easier With fuller profits lead an *e* life,   *Enoch Arden* 193
But evermore it seem'd an *e* thing   *Geraint and E.* 108
your modern amourist is of *e*, earthlier make.   *Locksley H., Sixty* 18
East Till that o'ergrown Barbarian in the *E*   *Poland* 1
And slowly rounded to the *e*   *Mariana in the S.* 79
light increased With freshness in the dawning *e*.   *Two Voices* 405
Four courts I made, *E*, West and South and North,   *Palace of Art* 21
Smote by the fresh beam of the springing *e* ;   *M. d'Arthur* 214
dark *E*, Unseen, is brightening to his bridal morn.   *Gardener's D.* 72
went To greet their fairer sisters of the *E*.   " 188
The ever-silent spaces of the *E*,   *Tithonus* 9
Yet hold me not for ever in thine *E* :   " 64
Across the boundless *e* we drove,   *The Voyage* 38
The blaze upon the waters to the *e* ;   *Enoch Arden* 594
I to the *E* And he for Italy—   *The Brook* 1
darken'd in the west, And rosed in the *e* :   *Sea Dreams* 40
King of the *E* altho' he seem,   *Lucretius* 133
Bows all its ears before the roaring *E* ;   *Princess i* 237
Nor stunted squaws of West or *E* ;   " *ii* 78
touch'd Above the darkness from their native *E*.   " *iii* 22
' Alas your Highness breathes full *E*,'   " 231
beam Of the *E*, that play'd upon them,   " *v* 259
a feast Of wonder, out of West and *E*,   *Ode Inter. Exhib.* 21
The bitter *e*, the misty summer And gray metropolis   *The Daisy* 103
voices go To North, South, *E*, and West ;   *Voice and the P.* 14
Far in the *E* Boädicéa, standing loftily charioted,   *Boädicea* 3
Flown to the *e* or the west,   *Window, Gone* 7
O Father, touch the *e*, and light   *In Mem. xxx* 31
heaved a windless flame Up the deep *E*,   " *lxxii* 19
E and West, without a breath,   " *xcv* 62
What lightens in the lucid *e*   " *cv* 24
Fiercely flies The blast of North and *E*,   " *cvii* 7
Blush from West to *E*, Blush from *E* to West, Till the West is *E*,   *Maud I xvii* 21
breeze that streams to thy delicious *E*,   " *xviii* 16
there be dawn in West and eve in *E* ?   *Gareth and L.* 712
pale and bloodless *e* began To quicken   *Marr. of Geraint* 534
There lived a king in the most Eastern *E*,   *Merlin and V.* 555
in her chamber up a tower to the *e*   *Lancelot and E.* 3
star Led on the gray-hair'd wisdom of the *e* ;   *Holy Grail* 453
' One night my pathway swerving *e*,   " 634
Let the fierce *e* scream thro' your eyelet-holes,   *Pelleas and E.* 469
water Moab saw Come round by the *E*,   *Last Tournament* 483
Smote by the fresh beam of the springing *e* ;   *Pass. of Arthur* 382
deeds Of England, and her banner in the *E* ?   *Ded. Poem Prin. Alice* 21
Or Amurath of the *E* ?   *Sir J. Oldcastle* 97
made West *E*, and sail'd the Dragon's mouth,   *Columbus* 25
our most ancient *E* Moriah with Jerusalem ;   " 80
Up from the *E* hither Saxon and Angle   *Batt. of Brunanburh* 117
Who wert the voice of England in the *E*.   *Epit. on Stratford* 4

East (*continued*)   clash The golden keys of *E* and
    West.   *To Marq. of Dufferin* 4
    she lent The sceptres of her West, her *E*,   „   6
Easterday   For it was past the time of *E*.   *Gareth and L.* 186
Eastern   Below the city's *e* towers: *Fatima* 9
    captain of my dreams Ruled in the *e* sky.   *D. of F. Women* 264
    Far up the porch there grew an *E* rose,   *Gardener's D.* 123
    Beyond the fair green field and *e* sea.   *Love and Duty* 101
    'There lived a king in the most *E* East,   *Merlin and V.* 555
    an *E* gauze With seeds of gold—   *Lover's Tale iv* 291
    Who reads your golden *E* lay,   *To E. Fitzgerald* 32
    e flowers large, Some dropping low   *Arabian Nights* 61
    But she was sharper than an *e* wind,   *Audley Court* 53
    The foaming grape of *e* France.   *In Mem., Con.* 80
    climb'd That *e* tower, and entering barr'd her door,   *Lancelot and E.* 15
    at the *e* end, Wealthy with wandering lines   *Holy Grail* 251
Eastward   Past *e* from the falling sun.   *Balin and Balan* 320
    singing in the topmost tower To the *e*:   *Holy Grail* 835
East-wind   In the stormy *e-w* straining,   *L. of Shalott iv* 1
Easy   (*See also* **Eäsy**)   For it's *e* to find a rhyme.
    (repeat)   *Window, Ay* 6, 12
    sleepless nights Of my long life have made it
    e to me.   *Merlin and V.* 680
    He will answer to the purpose, *e* things to
    understand—   *Locksley Hall* 55
    Fast flow'd the current of her *e* tears,   *Enoch Arden* 865
    Were no false passport to that *e* realm,   *Aylmer's Field* 183
    I said no, Yet being an *e* man, gave it: *Princess i* 149
    winning *e* grace, No doubt, for slight delay,   „   *iv* 330
    If *e* patrons of their kin Have left the last free race   *Third of Feb.* 39
    doubted whether daughter's tenderness, Or
    e nature,   *Marr. of Geraint* 798
    down the highway moving on With *e* laughter   *Tiresias* 200
    Flowing with *e* greatness and touching   *The Wreck* 50
Eäsy   an' a says it *e* an' freeä   *N. Farmer, O. S.* 25
    Lets them inter 'eaven *e* es leäves their debts to
    be paäid.   *Village Wife* 94
    but they wasn't that *e* to pleäse,   „   117
Eat   The creaking cords which wound and *e*   *Supp. Confessions* 36
    princes over-bold Have *e* our substance,   *Lotos-Eaters, C. S.* 76
    thou may'st warble, *e* and dwell,   *The Blackbird* 4
    we sat and *e* And talk'd old matters over;   *Audley Court* 28
    e wholesome food, And wear warm clothes,   *St. S. Stylites* 108
    I will not *e* my heart alone,   *In Mem. cviii* 3
    'A thousand pips *e* up your sparrow-hawk!   *Marr. of Geraint* 274
    I will enter, I will *e* With all the passion   „   305
    those That *e* in Arthur's hall at Camelot.   „   432
    'Friend, let her *e*; the damsel is so faint.'   *Geraint and E.* 206
    My lord, *e* also, tho' the fare is coarse,   „   208
    And rising on the sudden he said, '*E*!   „   614
    it makes me mad to see you weep. *E*!   „   617
    E and be glad, for I account you mine.'   „   647
    thrust the dish before her, crying, '*E*.'   „   655
    'No, no,' said Enid, vext, 'I will not *e*   „   656
    man upon the bier arise, And *e* with me.'   „   658
    Before I well have drunken, scarce can *e*:   „   662
    Not *e* nor drink? And wherefore wail for one,   „   674
    E's scarce enow to keep his pulse abeat;   *Balin and Balan* 105
    And one said '*E* in peace! a liar is he,   „   607
    Who meant to *e* her up in that wild wood   *Merlin and V.* 260
    e's And uses, careless of the rest;   „   462
    After the king, who *e* in Arthur's halls.   *Lancelot and E.* 184
    I knew For one of those who *e* in Arthur's hall;   *Holy Grail* 24
    but *e* not thou with Mark,   *Last Tournament* 532
    Is it worth his while to *e*,   *Voice spake, etc.* 7
'Eät (heat)   What's the '*e* of this 'illside to the '*e*   *North. Cobbler* 6
Eaten   (*See also* **Temple-eaten, Worm-eaten**)   after all
    had *e*, then Geraint,   *Marr. of Geraint* 397
    'Boy,' said he, 'I have *e* all,   *Geraint and E.* 217
    when Earl Doorm had *e* all he would,   „   609
    And myself, I had *e* but sparely,   *V. of Maeldune* 69
Eater   *See* **Lotos-Eaters**
Eating   *E* the Lotos day by day,   *Lotos-Eaters, C. S.* 60
    Until the ulcer, *e* thro' my skin,   *St. S. Stylites* 67
    and *e* not, Except the spare chance-gift   „   77

Eating (*continued*)   And *e* hoary grain and pulse the
    steeds,   *Spec. of Iliad.* 21
    And a morbid *e* lichen fixt On a heart   *Maud I vi* 77
    the village boys Who love to vex him *e*,   *Geraint and E.* 561
    'tis *e* dry To dance without a catch,   *Last Tournament* 249
Eavedrops   Then I rise, the *e* fall,   *Maud II iv* 62
'Eaven (heaven)   Lets them inter *'e* eäsy es leäves   *Village Wife* 94
Eaves   (*See also* **Bower-eaves, Mountain-eaves**)   Her eyelids
    dropp'd their silken *e*.   *Talking Oak* 209
    One, almost to the martin-haunted *e*   *Aylmer's Field* 163
    Fly to her, and fall upon her gilded *e*,   *Princess iv* 94
    closing at last of wearied eyes I sleep till dusk   *In Mem. lxvii* 11
    Who murmurest in the foliaged *e*   „   *xcix* 9
    Makes daggers at the sharpen'd *e*,   „   *cvii* 8
    With hands for *e*, uplooking and almost Waiting   *Lover's Tale i* 311
    And murmur at the low-dropt *e* of sleep,   „   *ii* 122
    now from all the dripping *e* The spear of ice   *Prog. of Spring* 5
Ebb (s)   We left the dying *e* that faintly lipp'd   *Audley Court* 12
    Have *e* and flow conditioning their march,   *Golden Year* 30
    float or fall in endless *e* and flow;   *W. to Marie Alex.* 27
    I could rest, a rock in *e*'s and flows,   *Marr. of Geraint* 812
    from my farthest lapse, my latest *e*,   *Lover's Tale i* 90
    Sway'd by vaster *e*'s and flows   *Locksley H., Sixty* 194
Ebb (verb)   brood, And *e* into a former life,   *Sonnet To ——* 2
    According to my humour *e* and flow.   *D. of F. Women* 134
    When the tide *e*'s in sunshine,   *Princess vi* 162
Ebb'd   sat round the wassail-bowl, Then half-way *e*:   *The Epic* 6
    (possibly He flow'd and *e* uncertain,   *Aylmer's Field* 218
    'O mine have *e* away for evermore,   *Merlin and V.* 439
Ebbing   felt them slowly *e*, name and fame.'   „   437
Ebony   brow of pearl Tress'd with redolent *e*,   *Arabian Nights* 138
    cups of emerald, there at tables of *e* lay,   *Boädicea* 61
Echo (s)   So mutch *e* with delight, (repeat)   *The Owl ii* 4
    Lull'd *e* of laborious day Come to you,   *Margaret* 29
    An *e* from a measured strain,   *Miller's D.* 66
    To hear the dewy *e*'es calling From cave to cave   *Lotos-Eaters, C. S.* 94
    Were faint Homeric *e*'es, nothing-worth,   *The Epic*.39
    the great *e* flap And buffet round the hills,   *Golden Year* 76
    Like hints and *e*'es of the world   *Day-Dm., Sleep. P.* 7
    Like *e*'es from beyond a hollow,   *Aylmer's Field* 298
    crashing with long *e*'es thro' the land,   „   338
    E answer'd in her sleep From hollow fields: *Princess, Pro.* 66
    An *e* like a ghostly woodpecker,   „   217
    Blow, bugle, blow, set the wild *e*'s flying, (repeat)   „   *iv* 5, 17
    Blow, bugle; answer, *e*'es, dying, dying, dying. (repeat)   „   6, 12
    Our *e*'es roll from soul to soul,   „   15
    And answer, *e*'es, answer, dying, dying,   „   18
    A step Of lightest *e*,   „   215
    barrier like a wild horn in a land Of *e*'es,   „   *v* 487
    And now and then an *e* started up,   „   *vi* 369
    The proof and *e* of all human fame,   *Ode on Well.* 145
    E on *e* Dies to the moon,   *Minnie and Winnie* 11
    A hollow *e* of my own—   *In Mem. iii* 11
    Like *e*'es in sepulchral halls,   „   *lviii* 2
    As *e*'es out of weaker times,   „   *Con.* 22
    E there, whatever is ask'd her,   *Maud I i* 4
    an *e* of something Read with a boy's delight,   „   *vii* 9
    a million horrible bellowing *e*'es broke   „   *II i* 24
    And the woodland *e* rings;   „   *iv* 38
    great Queen, In words whose *e* lasts,   *Marr. of Geraint* 782
    old *e*'es hidden in the wall Rang out   *Pelleas and E.* 366
    Like the last *e* born of a great cry,   *Pass. of Arthur* 459
    And mellow'd *e*'es of the outer world—   *Lover's Tale i* 208
    melody That drowns the nearer *e*'es.   „   533
    e'es of the hollow-banked brooks Are fashion'd   „   566
    If so be that the *e* of that name Ringing   „   644
    Whose *e* shall not tongue thy glorious doom,   *Tiresias* 136
    A dying *e* from a falling wall;   *Ancient Sage* 263
    Silent *e*'es! You, my Leonard,   *Locksley H., Sixty* 265
Echo (verb)   Hear a song that *e*'s clearly,   *L. of Shalott i* 30
    The haunts of memory *e* not.   *Two Voices* 369
    With sounds that *e* still.   *D. of F. Women* 8
    'Hear how the bushes *e*!   *Gardener's D.* 98
    Then made his pleasure *e*, hand to hand,   *Aylmer's Field* 257
    E round his bones for evermore.   *Ode on Well.* 12

Echo (verb) (*continued*) The last wheel *e'es* away. — *Maud I xxii* 26
the great wave that *e'es* round the world; — *Marr. of Geraint* 420
rummage buried in the walls Might *e*, — *Balin and Balan* 417
Echo'd (adj.) hear her *e* song Throb thro' the ribbed stone; — *Palace of Art* 175
Echo'd (verb) further inland, voices *e*—' Come — *M. d'Arthur, Ep.* 27
For while our cloisters *e* frosty feet, — *Princess, Pro.* 183
And *e* by old folk beside their fires — *Com. of Arthur* 417
second *e* him, 'Lord, we have heard from our wise man — *Gareth and L.* 200
E the walls; a light twinkled; — " 1370
and the forest *e* 'fool.' — *Merlin and V.* 974
And changed itself and *e* in her heart, — *Lancelot and E.* 782
he wellnigh deem'd His wish by hers was *e*; — *Pelleas and E.* 121
That timorously and faintly *e* mine, — *Sisters (E. and E.)* 164
that underground thunderclap *e* away, — *Def. of Lucknow* 32
a song Which often *e* in me, — *Romney's R.* 85
All her harmonies *e* away?— — *To Master of B.* 12
would not die, but *e* on to reach Honorius, — *St. Telemachus* 76
Echoing (*See also* **Ever-echoing**) the *e* dance Of reboant whirlwinds, — *Supp. Confessions* 96
with *e* feet he threaded The secretest walks — *The Poet* 9
And the wave-worn horns of the *e* bank, — *Dying Swan* 39
was thrown From his loud fount upon the *e* lea:— — *Mine be the strength* 4
shiver of dancing leaves is thrown About its *e* chambers wide, — *Maud I vi* 74
E all night to that sonorous flow — *Palace of Art* 27
ILLYRIAN woodlands, *e* falls Of water, — *To E. L.* 1
e me you cry 'Our house is left unto us desolate'? — *Aylmer's Field* 736
And heel against the pavement *e*, — *Geraint and E.* 271
That glorious roundel *e* in our ears, — *Merlin and V.* 426
the father answer'd, *e* 'highest?' — *Lancelot and E.* 1078
e yell with yell, they fired the tower, — *Last Tournament* 478
Or ghostly footfall *e* on the stair. — *Guinevere* 507
Echo-like Then *e-l* our voices rang; — *In Mem. xxx* 13
Eclipse Gaiety without *e* Wearieth me, — *Lilian* 20
As when the sun, a crescent of *e*, — *Vision of Sin* 10
The shadow of His loss drew like *e*, — *Ded. of Idylls* 14
Ecliptic Sear'd by the close *e*, — *Aylmer's Field* 193
Ecstasy So tranced, so rapt in *ecstasies*, — *Eleänore* 78
the boy Was half beyond himself for *e*. — *Gareth and L.* 524
To holy virgins in their *ecstasies*, — *Holy Grail* 867
Eddied *e* into suns, that wheeling cast — *Princess ii* 118
Eddy (s) vexed *eddies* of its wayward brother: — *Isabel* 33
There the river *e* whirls, — *L. of Shalott ii* 15
In crystal *eddies* glance and poise, — *Miller's D.* 52
I cannot keep My heart an *e* — *Princess vi* 322
The fancy's tenderest *e* wreathe, — *In Mem. xlix* 6
No doubt vast *eddies* in the flood — " *cxxviii* 5
Charm'd amid *eddies* of melodious airs, — *Lover's Tale i* 450
Eddy (verb) those that *e* round and round? — *In Mem. liii* 12
Eddying (part) (*See also* **Multitudinous-eddying**) Were flooded over with *e* song. — *Dying Swan* 42
I bubble into *e* bays, — *The Brook* 41
cold streamlet curl'd Thro' all his *e* coves; — *In Mem. lxxix* 10
Eddying (s) The *e* of her garments caught from thee — *Ode to Memory* 31
Eden Saw distant gates of *E* gleam, — *Two Voices* 212
Could keep me from that *E* where she dwelt. — *Gardener's D.* 191
Summer isles of *E* lying in dark-purple spheres — *Locksley Hall* 164
And every bird of *E* burst In carol, — *Day-Dm., L'Envoi* 43
Set in this *E* of all plenteousness, — *Enoch Arden* 561
Then comes the statelier *E* back to men: — *Princess vii* 293
a sweet little *E* on earth that I know, — *The Islet* 14
The brooks of *E* mazily murmuring, — *Milton* 10
Rings *E* thro' the budded spheres — *In Mem. lxxxviii* 5
the moon Of *E* on its bridal bower: — " *Con.* 28
O dawn of *E* bright over earth and sky, — *Maud II i* 8
Like that which kept the heart of *E* green — *Geraint and E.* 770
And all the separate *E's* of this earth, — *Lover's Tale i* 551
diseaseful creature which in *E* was divine, — *Happy* 33
Eden-isle Your Oriental *E-i's*, — *To Ulysses* 38
Edge (*See also* **Casement-edge, Sword-edge**) the fading *e's* of box beneath, — *A spirit haunts* 19
bright and sharp As *e's* of scymetar. — *Kate* 12

Edge (*continued*) Stream'd onward, lost their *e's*, — *D. of F. Women* 50
three times slipping from the outer *e*, — *The Epic* 11
where the prone *e* of the wood began (repeat) — *Enoch Arden* 67, 373
here and there on lattice *e's* lay — *Princess ii* 29
That axelike *e* unturnable, our Head, — " 203
grass There growing longest by the meadow's *e*, — *Geraint and E.* 257
The memory's vision hath a keener *e*. — *Lover's Tale i* 36
sweeping down Took the *e's* of the pall, — " *iii* 35
Edged (*See also* **Shrill-edged, Thorough-edged**) scorn, *E* with sharp laughter, — *Clear-headed friend* 2
Found a dead man, a letter *e* with death Beside him, — *Aylmer's Field* 595
Edge-tools ill jesting with *e-t*! — *Princess ii* 201
Edict waiting still The *e* of the will — *Lover's Tale ii* 161
Edith (*See also* **Edith Montfort**) his *E*, whom he loved As heiress — *Aylmer's Field* 23
often, in his walks with *E*, claim A distant kinship — " 61
shook the heart of *E* hearing him. — " 63
E, whose pensive beauty, perfect else, — " 70
and roll'd His hoop to pleasure *E*, — " 85
make-believes For *E* and himself: — " 96
the labourers' homes, A frequent haunt of *E*, — " 148
Each, its own charm; and *E's* everywhere; and *E* ever visitant with him, He but less loved than *E*, of her poor: — " 165
But *E's* eager fancy hurried with him — " 208
oriental gifts on everyone And most on *E*: — " 215
E whom his pleasure was to please, — " 232
was *E* that same night; Pale as the Jephtha's daughter, — " 279
its worth Was being *E's*. — " 379
would go, Labour for his own *E*, and return — " 420
remembering His former talks with *E*, — " 457
the keen shriek 'Yes love, yes *E*, yes,' — " 582
dagger which himself Gave *E*, redden'd with no bandit's blood: 'From *E*' was engraven on the blade. — " 597
many too had known *E* among the hamlets round, — " 615
Now follows *E* echoing Evelyn. — *Sisters (E. and E.)* 15
one is somewhat graver than the other—*E* than Evelyn. — " 27
but the paler and the graver, *E*. — " 38
once my prattling *E* ask'd him 'why?' — " 58
memorial Of *E*—no, the other—both — " 108
E—all One bloom of youth, healthy, — " 119
haze to magnify The charm of *E*— — " 130
believing I loved *E*, made *E* love *me*. — " 138
Not I that day of *E's* love or mine— — " 142
E wrote: 'My mother bids me ask' — " 180
simple mother work'd upon By *E* pray'd me not to whisper of it. And *E* would be bridesmaid on the day. — " 207
when we parted, *E* spoke no word, — " 215
Our *E* thro' the glories of the earth, — " 225
she That loved me—our true *E*— — " 235
daily want Of *E* in the house, the garden, — " 246
E had welcomed my brief wooing of her, — " 254
scarce as great as *E's* power of love, — " 261
bore a child whom reverently we call'd *E*; — " 269
But *you* love *E*; and her own true eyes — " 284
I think *I* likewise love your *E* most. — " 293
E, yet so lowly-sweet, — *Locksley H., Sixty* 49
Near us *E's* holy shadow, — " 54
E but a child of six— — " 258
Peept the winsome face of *E* — " 260
RALPH would fight in *E's* sight, For Ralph was *E's* lover, — *The Tourney* 1
E bow'd her stately head, — " 13
Edith Montfort (*See also* **Edith**) *E M* bow'd her head, — " 15
Educated Sir Robert with his watery smile And *e* whisker. — *Edwin Morris* 129
Have all his pretty young ones *e*, — *Enoch Arden* 146
Edmund 'O babbling brook,' says *E* in his rhyme, — *The Brook* 21
the week Before I parted with poor *E*; — " 78
My dearest brother, *E*, sleeps, — " 187

Edmund Atheling (*See also* **Atheling**) He with his
    brother, *E A*, *Batt. of Brunanburh* 6
Edward (the Elder, King of the English, 901-925)
    Sons of *E* with hammer'd brands.   ,,   14
    they play'd with The children of *E*.   ,,   92
Edward (III., King of England) Gray with distance
    E's fifty summers, *On Jub. Q. Victoria* 40
Edward (Christian name) Then, and here in *E*'s
    time, *Locksley H., Sixty* 83
Edward Bull With Edwin Morris and with *E B* *Edwin Morris* 14
    Then said the fat-faced curate *E B*, (repeat)   42, 90
Edward Gray ' And are you married yet, *E G* ? ' *Edward Gray* 4
    love no more Can touch the heart of *E G*.   ,,   8
    ' To trouble the heart of *E G* '   ,,   20
    And here the heart of *E G* ! '   ,,   28
    And there the heart of *E G* ! '   ,,   36
Edward Head Sir *E H*'s : But he's abroad : *Walk. to the Mail* 15
Edwin (*See also* **Edwin Morris**) ' Friend *E*, do not
    think yourself alone *Edwin Morris* 77
    And I and *E* laugh'd ;   ,,   93
    So left the place, left *E*,   ,,   137
    crystal into which I braided *E*'s hair ! *The Flight* 34
    follow *E* to those isles, those islands of the Blest !   ,,   42
    O would I were in *E*'s arms—   ,,   45
    —on *E*'s ship, with *E*, ev'n in death,   ,,   46
    My *E* loved to call us then   ,,   80
    flowers of the secret woods, when *E* found us there,   ,,   82
    sail at last which brings our *E* home.   ,,   92
Edwin Morris (*See also* **Edwin**) With *E M* and with
    Edward Bull *Edwin Morris* 14
    But *E M*, he that knew the names,   ,,   16
Edyrn answer, groaning, ' *E*, son of Nudd ! *Marr. of Geraint* 576
    ' Then, *E*, son of Nudd,' replied Geraint,   ,,   579
    E answer'd, ' These things will I do,   ,,   587
    night of fire, when *E* sack'd their house,   ,,   634
    rose a cry That *E*'s men were on them,   ,,   639
    E's men had caught them in their flight,   ,,   642
    Beholding it was *E* son of Nudd, *Geraint and E.* 781
    E moving frankly forward spake :   ,,   784
    Till *E* crying, ' If ye will not go To Arthur,   ,,   814
    And one from *E*. Every now and then, When *E* rein'd
    his charger at her side,   ,,   819
    went apart with *E*, whom he held In converse   ,,   881
    E and with others : have ye look'd At *E* ?   ,,   896
    E has done it, weeding all his heart   ,,   906
    This work of *E* wrought upon himself   ,,   912
Eerie My people too were scared with *e* sounds, *The Ring* 408
Eery elfin prancer springs By night to *e* warblings, *Sir L. and Q. G.* 34
Effect (s) And thine *e* so lives in me, *In Mem. lxv* 10
    Thro' manifold *e* of simple powers— *Prog. of Spring* 86
Effect (verb) tho' she herself *e* But little : *Princess iii* 264
Effeminacy Rolling on their purple couches in their
    tender *e*. *Boädicea* 62
    all his force Is melted into mere *e* ? *Marr. of Geraint* 107
Effeminate ' *E* as I am, I will not fight my way *Geraint and E.* 20
Effie Little *E* shall go with me tomorrow *May Queen* 25
    Don't let *E* come to see me *May Queen, N. Y.'s. E.* 43
    And *E* on the other side,   ,,   *Con.* 24
    I thought of you and *E* dear ;   ,,   29
    But, *E*, you must comfort *her*   ,,   44
    there to wait a little while till you and *E* come—   ,,   58
Effluence perennial *e*'s, Whereof to all that draw *Lover's Tale i* 499
Effort I made one barren *e* to break it at the last. *Happy* 72
Eft A monstrous *e* was of old the Lord *Maud I iv* 31
    A bedmate of the snail and *e* and snake, *Holy Grail* 570
Egalities That cursed France with her *e* ! *Aylmer's Field* 265
Egbert doing nothing Since *E*—why,   ,,   384
Egg (*See also* **Hegg**) ·The goose let fall a golden *e* *The Goose* 11
    we stole his fruit, His hens, his *e*'s ; *Walk. to the Mail* 85
    Roof-haunting martins warm their *e*'s : *Day-Dm., Sleep. P.* 17
    The Cock was of a larger *e* *Will Water.* 121
    evil fancies clung Like serpent *e*'s *Enoch Arden* 480
    Sleeps in the plain *e*'s of the nightingale. *Aylmer's Field* 103
    lay their *e*'s, and sting and sing *In Mem. l* 11
    'twere but of the goose and golden *e*'s.' *Gareth and L.* 40

Egg (*continued*) good mother, but this *e* of mine Was finer
    gold *Gareth and L.* 42
    even in their hens and in their *e*'s— *Holy Grail* 560
    Nor bruised the wildbird's *e*. *Lover's Tale ii* 21
    She hears the lark within the songless *e*, *Ancient Sage* 76
Egg-shell Nor cared a broken *e-s* for her lord. *Geraint and E.* 364
Eglantine Vine, vine and *e*, (repeat) *Window, At the W.* 1, 8
    presently received in a sweet grave Of *e*'s, *Lover's Tale i* 529
    Beneath the bower of wreathed *e*'s   ,,   *ii* 43
Eglatere woodbine and *e* Drip sweeter dews *A Dirge* 23
Egypt (*See also* **Agypt**) O my life In *E* ! *D. of F. Women* 147
    the time When we made bricks in *E*. *Princess iv* 128
    fierce Soldan of *E*, would break down *Columbus* 98
    torpid mummy wheat Of *E* bore a grain as sweet *To Prof. Jebb* 6
Egyptian To whom the *E*: ' O, you tamely died ! *D. of F. Women* 258
Egypt-plague our arms fail'd—this *E-p* of men ! *Princess v* 427
Eight (adj.) (*See also* **Height**) Was proxy-wedded with
    a bootless calf At *e* years old !   ,,   *i* 35
    close behind her stood *E* daughters of the plough,   ,,   *iv* 278
    Then those *e* mighty daughters of the plough   ,,   550
    those *e* daughters of the plough Came sallying thro'   ,,   *v* 339
    And *e* years past, *e* jousts had been, *Lancelot and E.* 67
    E that were left of all her purer world— *Aylmer's Field* 638
    The child was only *e* summers old *The Victim* 33
Eight (s) cutting *e*'s that day upon the pond, *The Epic* 10
Eighteen Pass me then A term of *e* years. *Lover's Tale i* 287
    E long years of waste, seven in your Spain, *Columbus* 36
Eighty Whose *e* winters freeze with one rebuke *Ode on Well.* 186
    Timur built his ghastly tower of *e* thousand human
    skulls, *Locksley H., Sixty* 82
    E winters leave the dog too lame to follow   ,,   226
    Forward far and far from here is all the hope of
    e years.   ,,   254
    starved the wild beast that was linkt with thee *e*
    years back *By an Evolution.* 11
    e thousand Christian faces watch Man murder man. *St. Telemachus* 55
Eighty-thousand Should *e-t* college-councils *To F. D. Maurice* 7
Eight-year-old *See* **Height-year-old**
Either *e* hand, Or voice, or else a motion of the mere. *M. d'Arthur* 76
    On *e* side All round about the fragrant marge *Arabian Nights* 58
    And *e* twilight and the day between ; *Edwin Morris* 37
    Powers of the House On *e* side the hearth, *Aylmer's Field* 288
    with his hopes in *e* grave.   ,,   624
    familiar with her, Easily gather'd *e* guilt. *Princess iv* 236
    seeing *e* sex alone Is half itself,   ,,   *vii* 301
    For groves of pine on *e* hand, *To F. D. Maurice* 21
    And drops of water fell from *e* hand ; *Gareth and L.* 220
    In *e* hand he bore What dazzled all,   ,,   386
    And each at either dash from *e* end—   ,,   535
    she lifted *e* arm, ' Fie on thee, King !   ,,   657
    and *e* spear Bent but not brake, and *e* knight
    at once,   ,,   963
    at *e* end whereof There swung an apple *Marr. of Geraint* 169
    Whom first she kiss'd on *e* cheek, and then On *e*   ,,   517
    Made her cheek burn and *e* eyelid fall.   ,,   775
    day by day she past In *e* twilight ghost-like *Lancelot and E.* 849
    at the base we found On *e* hand, *Holy Grail* 498
    yell'd the youth, and *e* knight Drew back a space, *Pelleas and E.* 572
    Wheel'd round on *e* heel, Dagonet replied, *Last Tournament* 244
    At once from *e* side, with trumpet-blast, *Com. of Arthur* 102
    e hand, Or voice, or else a motion of the mere. *Pass. of Arthur* 244
    As tho' there beat a heart in *e* eye ; *Lover's Tale i* 34
    Love wraps his wings on *e* side the heart,   ,,   467
    My father with a child on *e* knee, A hand upon
    the head of *e* child, *Sisters (E. and E.)* 54
    He joins us once again, to his *e* office true : *Happy* 106
    Thy elect have no dealings with *e* heresy or
    orthodoxy ; *Akbar's D., Inscrip.* 7
    With all the Hells a-glare in *e* eye, *Akbar's Dream* 115
    And each at *e* dash from either end— *Gareth and L.* 535
Elaborately Who read me rhymes *e* good, *Edwin Morris* 20
Elaine *E* the fair, *E* the loveable, *E*, the lily maid *Lancelot and E.* 1
    behind them stept the lily maid *E*,   ,,   177
    E, and heard her name so tost about,   ,,   233
    lily maid *E*, Won by the mellow voice   ,,   242

Elaine (*continued*) Who parted with his own to
    fair *E*:   *Lancelot and E.* 381
  stay'd; and cast his eyes on fair *E*:   ,,   640
  'So be it,' cried *E*, And lifted her fair face   ,,   681
  'Torre and *E*! why here?   ,,   796
  Then rose *E* and glided thro' the fields,   ,,   843
  call her friend and sister, sweet *E*,   ,,   865
  I had been wedded earlier, sweet *E*:   ,,   935
  on her face, and thought 'Is this *E*?'   ,,   1031
Elbow In every *e* and turn,   *Ode to Memory* 62
  deep in broider'd down we sank Our *e's*:   *Princess iv* 33
Elbow-chair She shifted in her *e-c*,   *The Goose* 27
Elbow-deep Or *e-d* in sawdust, slept,   *Will Water.* 99
Elbowed *See* **Half-elbowed**
Elburz *E* and all the Caucasus have heard;   *W. to Marie Alex.* 13
Elder (s) led The holy *E's* with the gift of myrrh.   *M. d'Arthur* 233
  Thine *e's* and thy betters.   *Will Water.* 192
  with jubilant cries Broke from their *e's*,   *Enoch Arden* 378
  passion of youth Toward greatness in its *e*,   *Lancelot and E.* 283
  led The holy *E's* with the gift of myrrh   *Pass. of Arthur* 400
Elder (adj.) The Tory member's *e* son,   *Princess, Con.* 50
Elderly I knew them all as babies, and now they're *e* men.   *Grandmother* 88
Elder-thicket saw The white-flower'd *e-t* from the field   *Godiva* 63
Elder-tree *See* **Boor-tree**
Eldest-born Whatever *e-b* of rank or wealth   *Aylmer's Field* 484
  AND Willy, my *e-b*, is gone, you say,   *Grandmother* 1, 87
  Willy, my beauty, my *e-b*, the flower of the flock;   ,,   9
  Willy, my *e-b*, at nigh threescore and ten;   ,,   87
  Willy has gone, my beauty, my *e-b*, my flower;   ,,   101
  her *e-b*, her glory, her boast,   *Despair* 73
Eleanor Those dragon eyes of anger'd *E*   *D. of F. Women* 255
Eleänore To deck thy cradle, *E*.   *Eleänore* 21
  Crimsons over an inland mere, *E*!   ,,   43
  Of thy swan-like stateliness, *E*?   ,,   48
  Of thy floating gracefulness, *E*?   ,,   51
  Every lineament divine, *E*.   ,,   54
  Who may express thee, *E*?   ,,   68
  I stand before thee, *E*;   ,,   69
  Serene, imperial *E*! (repeat)   ,, 81, 121
  In thy large eyes, imperial *E*.   ,,   97
  So dying ever, *E*.   ,,   144
Elect (chosen) Thy *e* have no dealings with either
  heresy or orthodoxy;   *Akbar's D., Inscrip.* 7
Elected by common voice *E* umpire,   *Œnone* 85
Election *E*, *E* and Reprobation—   *Rizpah* 73
Electric *e* shock Dislink'd with shrieks and laughter: *Princess, Pro.* 69
  E, chemic laws, and all the rest,   ,, *ii* 384
  came As comes a pillar of *e* cloud,   ,, *v* 524
  this *e* force, that keeps A thousand pulses dancing,   *In Mem. xcv* 15
  with some *e* thrill A cold air pass'd between us,   *The Ring* 379
Elegant *See* **Illigant**
Elegy *elegies* And quoted odes,   *Princess ii* 376
Element The *e's* were kindlier mix'd.'   *Two Voices* 228
  may to soul Strike thro' a finer *e*   *Aylmer's Field* 579
  And in their own clear *e*, they moved.   *Princess vii* 28
  Large *e's* in order brought,   *In Mem. cxii* 13
  One God, one law, one *e*,   ,, *Con.* 142
  I saw The holy *e's* alone;   *Holy Grail* 463
  I am not made of so slight *e's*.   *Guinevere* 510
  The cloud-pavilion'd *e*, the wood,   *Lover's Tale i* 108
Elemental And learnt their *e* secrets,   *Merlin and V.* 632
Eleusis Who laid thee at *E*, dazed and dumb   *Demeter and P.* 6
Eleventh when the *e* moon After their marriage lit the
  lover's Bay,   *Lover's Tale iv* 27
Elf the little *elves* of chasm and cleft Made   *Guinevere* 248
  Elves, and the harmless glamour of the field;   *Pass. of Arthur* 52
  and glancing at *E* of the woodland,   *Merlin and the G.* 38
Elf-god 'I saw the little *e-g* eyeless once   *Merlin and V.* 249
Elfin rich With jewels, or Urim, on the hilt,   *Com. of Arthur* 298
  whose *e* prancer springs By night   *Sir L. and Q. G.* 33
Elfland The horns of *E* faintly blowing!   *Princess iv* 10
Elizabeth (Queen) The spacious times of great *E*   *D. of F. Women* 7
  in arts of government *E* and others;   *Princess ii* 162
Elizabeth (Aunt) there is Aunt *E* And sister Lilia   ,, *Pro.* 51
  And here we lit on Aunt *E*   ,,   96

Elk the monstrous horns of *e* and deer,   *Princess, Pro.* 23
Ellen (*See also* **Ellen Adair, Ellen Aubrey**) Sleep,
  E, folded in thy sister's arm,   *Audley Court* 63
  'Sleep, *E*, folded in Emilia's arm;   ,,   65
  By *E's* grave, on the windy hill.   *Edward Gray* 12
  'You said that you hated me, *E*,   *First Quarrel* 79
Ellen Adair (*See also* **Ellen**) '*E A* she loved me well,   *Edward Gray* 9
  When *E A* was dying for me.   ,,   16
  Speak a little, *E A*!'   ,,   24
  'Here lies the body of *E A*;   ,,   27
  Till *E A* come back to me.   ,,   32
  There lies the body of *E A*!   ,,   35
Ellen Aubrey (*See also* **Ellen**) *E A*, sleep, and dream
  of me: *Audley Court* 62
  Sleep, *E A*, love, and dream of me.'   ,,   73
Elle vous suit sent a note, the seal an *E v s*,   *Edwin Morris* 105
Ellipse Earth follows wheel'd in her *e*;   *Golden Year* 24
Elm (*See also* **Dwarf-elm, Witch-elm**) The seven *e's*,
  the poplars four   *Ode to Memory* 56
  The mellow ouzel fluted in the *e*;   *Gardener's D.* 94
  fruits and cream Served in the weeping *e*;   ,,   195
  Old *e's* came breaking from the vine,   *Amphion* 45
  Aroused the black republic on his *e's*,   *Aylmer's Field* 529
  always friends, none closer, *e* and vine: *Princess ii* 337
  varies from the lily as far As oak from *e*:   ,, *v* 183
  The moan of doves in immemorial *e's*,   ,, *vii* 221
  approaching rookery swerve From the *e's*,   ,, *Con.* 97
  Rock'd the full-foliaged *e's*,   *In Mem. xcv* 58
  swaying upon a restless *e* Drew the vague glance   *Balin and Balan* 463
  in Julian's land They never nail a dumb head
  up in *e*),   *Lover's Tale iv* 37
  in yon arching avenue of old *e's*,   *The Ring* 172
  Of leafless *e*, or naked lime,   *To Ulysses* 16
  few lanes of *e* And whispering oak.   *To Mary Boyle* 67
Elm-tree rook 'ill caw from the windy tall *e-t*,   *May Queen, N.Y's. E.* 17
  topmost *e-t* gather'd green From draughts   *Sir L. and Q. G.* 8
  e's ruddy-hearted blossom-flake Is fluttering   *To Mary Boyle* 3
Elm-tree-boles Enormous *e-t-b* did stoop and lean   *D. of F. Women* 57
Eloquence A full-cell'd honeycomb of *e*   *Edwin Morris* 26
  and golden *E* And amorous adulation,   *Lancelot and E.* 649
  his *e* caught like a flame From zone to zone   *Dead Prophet* 34
Eloquent THE form, the form alone is *e*!   *The form, the form* 1
  her *e* eyes, (As I have seen them many a hundred
  times)   *Lover's Tale ii* 144
'Elp (help) es I oäps es thou'll '*e* me a bit,   *Village Wife* 65
Elsewise Did mightier deeds than *e* he had done,   *Last Tournament* 233
Elsinore when *E* Heard the war moan   *Buonaparte* 9
Elusion *E*, and occasion, and evasion'?   *Gareth and L.* 288
Elvish dragon-boughts and emblemings Began to move,   ,,   233
Elysian others in *E* valleys dwell,   *Lotos-Eaters, C. S.* 124
  fields Are lovely, lovelier not The *E* lawns,   *Princess iii* 342
Elysium dimly-glimmering lawns Of that *E*,   *Demeter and P.* 151
Emancipation on whom The secular *e* turns   *Princess ii* 289
Embalm In dying songs a dead regret,   *In Mem., Con.* 13
Embark 'I will *e* and I will lose myself,   *Holy Grail* 805
  may there be no sadness of farewell, When I *e*;   *Crossing the Bar* 12
Embassage till their *e* return'd.   *Balin and Balan* 93
Embassy Such touches are but *embassies* of love,   *Gardener's D.* 18
Embathing *E* all with wild and woeful hues,   *Lover's Tale ii* 64
Embattail To *e* and to wall about thy cause   *To J. M. K.* 8
Embattled when we saw the *e* squares,   *Princess v* 246
  Till this *e* wall of unbelief My prison,   *Doubt and Prayer* 11
Embellish overflowing revenue Wherewith to *e* state,   *Œnone* 113
Emblem Graven with *e's* of the time,   *Arabian Nights* 108
  Like *e's* of infinity,   *Ode to Memory* 103
  Caryatids, lifted up A weight of *e*,   *Princess iv* 202
  rich in *e* and the work Of ancient kings   *Gareth and L.* 304
  Half-tarnish'd and half-bright, his *e*, shone.   ,,   1118
  these her *e's* drew mine eyes—away;   *Balin and Balan* 40
Emblematic Amazon As *e* of a nobler age;   *Princess ii* 127
Embleming and elvish *e's* Began to move,   *Gareth and L.* 233
Embodied When truth *e* in a tale   *In Mem. xxxvi* 7
Emboss'd bronze valves, *e* with Tomyris   *Princess v* 365
Embower However deep you might *e* the nest,   ,, *Pro.* 147
Embowering *See* **Oriel-embowering**

Endure (*continued*) Love, that *e's* not sordid ends, — *Love thou thy land* 6
But while the races of mankind *e*, — *Ode on Well.* 219
I will nevermore *e* To sit with empty hands — *Sailor Boy* 15
Would she have heart to *e* for the life of the worm — *Wages* 7
That dies not, but *e's* with pain, — *In Mem. xviii* 17
And scarce *e* to draw the breath, — ,, *xx* 15
Whose loves in higher love *e*; — ,, *xxxii* 14
O living will that shalt *e* — ,, *cxxxi* 1
Let the sweet heavens *e*, — *Maud I xi* 8
As long as my life *e's* I feel I shall owe you — ,, *xix* 86
Break not, O woman's-heart, but still *e*; Break not, for thou art Royal, but *e*, — *Ded. of Idylls* 44
E's not that her guest should serve — *Marr. of Geraint* 379
But can *e* it all most patiently.' — ,, 473
canst *e* To mouth so huge a foulness— — *Balin and Balan* 378
thought to do while he might yet *e*, — *Lancelot and E.* 495
strength of the race to command, to obey, to *e*, — *Def. of Lucknow* 47
E! thou hast done so well for men, — *Columbus* 152
every heart that loves with truth is equal to *e*. — *The Flight* 104
For so the deed *e's*, — *Epilogue* 39
But while my life's late eve *e's*, — *To Marq. of Dufferin* 49
vanish and give place to the beauty that *e's*, The — *Happy* 36
beauty that *e's* on the Spiritual height, — ,, 60
caught one gleam of the beauty which *e's*— — ,, 60

Endured Have all in all *e* as much, — *St. S. Stylites* 130
Nor yet *e* to meet her opening eyes, — *Princess iv* 195
they knew her; *they e*, Long-closeted with her — ,, 321
ye surely have *e* Strange chances here alone;' — *Geraint and E.* 809
Nor yet *e* in presence of His eyes — *Lover's Tale i* 423
while I mused nor yet *e* to take So rich a prize, — ,, *iii* 49

Enduring (*See also* **All-enduring, Long-enduring**) 'Yet hadst thou, thro' *e* pain, — *Two Voices* 166
Sow the seed, and reap the harvest with *e* toil, — *Lotos-Eaters, C. S.* 121
'Enemies (anemones) Down i' the woild '*e* — *N. Farmer, O. S.* 34
Enemy (*See also* **Hennemy**) 'Our *enemies* have fall'n, but this shall grow — *Princess vi* 53
'Our *enemies* have fall'n, have fall'n: (repeat) *Princess vi* 33, 38, 43, 48
moan of an *e* massacred, — *Boädicea* 25
tho' the gathering *e* narrow thee, — ,, 39
pulses at the clamouring of her *e* fainted — ,, 82
I trust if an *e's* fleet came yonder — *Maud I i* 49
'A boon, Sir King! Thine *e*, King, am I. — *Gareth and L.* 351
He drave his *e* backward down the bridge, — ,, 969
being but knave, I throw thine *enemies*.' — ,, 1023
To dash against mine *e* and to win. — ,, 1355
arms, arms, arms to fight my *e*? — *Marr. of Geraint* 282
down his *e* roll'd, And there lay still; — *Geraint and E.* 160
an *e* that has left Death in the living waters, — *Merlin and V.* 147
roll'd his *e* down, And saved him; — *Lancelot and E.* 26
the knights Are half of them our *enemies*, — ,, 99
a dream Of dragging down his *e* made them move. — ,, 814
and said, 'Mine *enemies* Pursue me, — *Guinevere* 139
Ev'n in the presence of an *e's* fleet, — ,, 279
on all the defences our myriad *e* fell. — *Def. of Lucknow* 35
in a moment two mines by the *e* sprung — ,, 54
Fonseca my main at their court, — *Columbus* 126
For there was not an *e* near, — *V. of Maeldune* 93
so often in Strife with their *enemies* — *Batt. of Brunanburh* 18
Love your *e*, bless your haters, — *Locksley H., Sixty* 18
'Kill your *e*, for you hate him,' still, 'your *e* — ,, 94
Energy spurr'd at heart with fieriest *e* — *To J. M. K.* 7
By its own *e* fulfill'd itself, — *Gardener's D.* 238
suit The full-grown *energies* of heaven. — *In Mem. xl* 20
come and go, With agonies, with *energies*, — ,, *cxiii* 18
To those still-working *energies* I spy — *Mechanophilus* 19
Enfold So dear a life your arms *e* — *The Daisy* 93
that large grief which these *e* — *In Mem. v* 11
mother's shame will *e* her and darken — *The Wreck* 100
Enfolded Two mutually *e*; Love, the third, — *Gardener's D.* 215
And in her veil *e*, manchet bread. — *Marr. of Geraint* 389
Enfolding *E* that dark body which had lain — *Death of Œnone* 93
Enforced *E* she was to wed him in her tears, — *Com. of Arthur* 204
Engarlanded *E* and diaper'd With inwrought flowers, — *Arabian Nights* 148
Engine Which only to one *e* bound Falls off, — *Two Voices* 347
Enginery Loom and wheel and *e*, — *Ode Inter. Exhib.* 15

G

Engirt *E* with many a florid maiden-cheek, — *Princess iii* 350
England And more than that, — *Talking Oak* 295
show you slips of all that grows From *E* to Van Diemen. — *Amphion* 84
dewy meadowy morning-breath Of *E*, — *Enoch Arden* 661
thanks to the Giver, *E*, for thy son. — *Ode on Well.* 45
For this is *E's* greatest son, — ,, 95
And *E* pouring on her foes. — ,, 117
keep our noble *E* whole, — ,, 161
Truth-teller was our *E's* Alfred named; — ,, 188
E's honest censure went too far; — *Third of Feb.* 2
What *E* was, shall her *true* sons forget? — ,, 44
some love *E* and her honour yet. — ,, 46
Harold's *E* fell to Norman swords; — *W. to Marie Alex.* 22
It told of *E* then to me, — *The Daisy* 89
harsher sound ever heard, ye Muses, in *E*? — *Trans. of Homer* 3
God-gifted organ-voice of *E*, — *Milton* 3
freedom in her regal seat Of *E*; — *In Mem. cix* 15
Or how should *E* dreaming of *his* sons — *Ded. of Idylls* 31
boundless homes For ever-broadening *E*, — *To the Queen ii* 30
Thou—*E's* England-loving daughter—thou — *Ded. Poem Prin. Alice* 21
this ballad of the deeds Of *E*, — ,, 21
BANNER of *E*, not for a season, — *Def. of Lucknow* 1
upon the topmost roof our banner of *E* blew. (repeat) — *Def. of Lucknow* 6, 30, 45, 60, 94
the old banner of *E* blew. — ,, 106
appeal Once more to France or *E*; — *Columbus* 58
Who dost not love our *E*— — *To Victor Hugo* 9
E, France, all man to be Will make one people — ,, 10
To younger *E* in the boy my son. — ,, 14
E may go down in babble at last. — *Locksley H., Sixty* 8
Yet know you, as your *E* knows — *Pro. to Gen. Hamley* 23
Who wert the voice of *E* in the East. — *Epit. on Stratford* 4
Then drink to *E*, every guest; — *Hands all Round* 2
New *E* of the Southern Pole! — ,, 16
the great name of *E*, round and round. (repeat) — ,, 12, 36
To *E* under Indian skies, — ,, 17
To this great name of *E* drink, — ,, 23
if you shall fail to understand What *E* is, — *The Fleet* 2
Should this old *E* fall Which Nelson left — ,, 4
The fleet of *E* is her all-in-all; — ,, 13
that which gilds the glebe of *E*, — *To Prof. Jebb.* 7
a valorous weapon in olden *E*! — *Kapiolani* 4
England-loving England's *E-l* daughter—thou — *Ded. Poem Prin. Alice* 15
English (*See also* **Half-English**) first reveal'd themselves to *E* air, — *Eleänore* 2
one, an *E* home—gray twilight pour'd — *Palace of Art* 85
E natures, freemen, friends, — *Love thou thy land* 7
Who sprang from *E* blood! — *England and Amer.* 10
Gallant sons of *E* freemen, — *The Captain* 7
if you knew her in her *E* days, — *The Brook* 224
sweet as *E* air could make her, she: — *Princess, Pro.* 155
Nor ever lost an *E* gun; — *Ode on Well.* 97
Truth-lover was our *E* Duke; — ,, 189
since *E* Harold gave its throne a wife, — *W. to Marie Alex.* 24
we may stand Where he in *E* earth is laid, — *In Mem. xviii* 2
feet like sunny gems on an *E* green, — *Maud I v* 14
I see her there, Bright *E* lily, — ,, *xix* 55
Sir Richard cried in his *E* pride, — *The Revenge* 82
dared her with one little ship and his *E* few; — ,, 107
Dying so *E* thou wouldst have her flag — *Ded. Poem Prin. Alice*
we were *E* in heart and in limb, — *Def. of Lucknow* 46
When he coin'd into *E* gold some treasure — *The Wreck* 67
no version done In *E* more divinely well; — *To E. Fitzgerald* 34
an age of noblest *E* names, — *Locksley H., Sixty* 83
who long To keep our *E* Empire whole! — *Hands all Round* 14
Or marvel how in *E* air My yucca, — *To Ulysses* 20
All flaming, made an *E* homestead Hell— — *To Mary Boyle* 37
Englishman A great broad-shoulder'd genial *E*, — *Princess, Con.* 85
The last great *E* is low. — *Ode on Well.* 18
'We be all good *English* men. — *The Revenge* 29
held his own Like an *E* there and then; — *Heavy Brigade* 19
Engrail'd over hills with peaky tops *e*, — *Palace of Art* 113
Engrain'd walk with vary-colour'd shells Wander'd *e*. — *Arabian Nights* 58
Engrave I bad the man *e* 'From Walter' on the ring, — *The Ring* 235
Engraven 'From Edith' was *e* on the blade. — *Aylmer's Field* 598

Enoch Arden (*See also* **Arden, Enoch**) *E A*, a rough
    sailor's lad   *Enoch Arden* 14
    Did you know *E A* of this town ? '   "   845
    Proclaiming *E A* and his woes: "   868
Enormous   *e* polypi Winnow with giant arms   *The "Kraken* 9
    Stretch'd wide and wild the waste *e* marsh,   *Ode to Memory* 101
    E elm-tree-boles did stoop and lean   *D. of F. Women* 57
Enrich   *E* the markets of the golden year.   *Golden Year* 46
    thoughts *e* the blood of the world.'   *Princess ii* 181
    To *e* the threshold of the night   *In Mem. xxix* 6
Enring'd   *E* a billowing fountain in the midst ;   *Princess ii* 28
Enroll   Your Highness would *e* them with your own,   "   *i* 239
    In many a figured leaf *e*'s   *In Mem. xliii* 11
Enroll'd   good livers, them we *e* Among us,   *Gareth and L.* 424
Ensample   drawing foul *e* from fair names,   *Guinevere* 490
Ensepulchre   let the wolves' black maws *e*   *Balin and Balan* 487
Enshrouded   cold worm Fretteth thine *e* form.—   *A Dirge* 10
Ensign   drowsy folds of our great *e* shake   *Princess v* 8
Enskied   seem'd at first 'a thing *e*'   *To E. Fitzgerald* 16
Ensue   that which might *e* With this old soul   *Two Voices* 392
    out of distance might *e* Desire of nearness   *In Mem. cxvii* 5
Ensued   then *e* A Martin's summer of his faded love,   *Aylmer's Field* 559
Entail   *See* **Taäil**
Entangle   To *e* me when we met,   *Maud I vi* 28
Entangled   The girl might be *e* ere she knew.   *Aylmer's Field* 272
Entanglest   All my bounding heart *e*   *Madeline* 40
Enter   But *e* not the toil of life.   *Margaret* 24
    oft some brainless devil *e*'s in,   *Palace of Art* 203
    He breaks the hedge : he *e*'s there :   *Day-Dm., Arrival* 18
    lingeringly on the latch, Fearing to *e* :   *Enoch Arden* 520
    LET NO MAN *E* IN ON PAIN OF DEATH ?   *Princess ii* 195
    ' Our laws are broken : let him *e* too.'   "   *vi* 317
    friend or foe, Shall *e*, if he will.   "   337
    in a tale Shall *e* in at lowly doors.   *In Mem. xxxvi* 8
    She *e*'s other realms of love ;   "   *xl* 12
    Descend, and touch, and *e* ;   "   *xciii* 13
    ' *E* likewise ye And go with us : '   "   *ciii* 51
    And *e* in at breast and brow,   "   *cxxii* 11
    She *e*'s, glowing like the moon   "   *Con.* 27
    Slain by himself, shall *e* endless night.   *Gareth and L.* 642
    Then Yniol, ' *E* therefore and partake   *Marr. of Geraint* 300
    I will *e*, I will eat With all the passion   "   305
    Said Yniol ; ' *e* quickly.'   "   360
    nor lets Or dame or damsel *e* at his gates   *Balin and Balan* 107
    There will I *e* in among them all,   *Lancelot and E.* 1052
    Late, late, so late ! but we can *e* still.   *Guinevere* 169
    too late ! ye cannot *e* now. (repeat)   *Guinevere* 170, 173, 176, 179
    And *e* it, and make it beautiful ?   *Pass. of Arthur* 17
    but *e* also here, Diffuse thyself at will   *Prog. of Spring* 23
Enter'd (*See also* **Newly-enter'd**)   another night in night
    I *e*,   *Arabian Nights* 38
    Each *e* like a welcome guest.   *Two Voices* 411
    blew Beyond us, as we *e* in the cool.   *Gardener's D.* 114
    struck it thrice, and, no one opening, *E* ;   *Enoch Arden* 280
    What ail'd her then, that ere she *e*,   "   518
    e one Of those dark caves that run beneath the cliffs.   *Sea Dreams* 89
    e an old hostel, call'd mine host To council,   *Princess i* 173
    hastily subscribed, We *e* on the boards :   "   *ii* 74
    as we *e* in, There sat along the forms,   "   101
    With me, Sir, *e* in the bigger boy,   "   404
    I knock'd and, bidden, *e* ;   "   *iii* 130
    dipt Beneath the satin dome and *e* in,   "   *iv* 31
    we *e* in, and there Among piled arms   "   *v* 54
    Empanoplied and plumed We *e* in,   "   484
    ' Enter likewise ye And go with us : ' they *e* in.   *In Mem. ciii* 52
    Left her and fled, and Uther *e* in,   *Com. of Arthur* 201
    when I *e* told me that himself And Merlin   "   364
    then *e* with his twain Camelot,   *Gareth and L.* 302
    And *e*, and were lost behind the walls.   *Marr. of Geraint* 252
    E, the wild lord of the place, Limours.   *Geraint and E.* 277
    Thereafter, when Sir Balin *e* hall,   *Balin and Balan* 80
    Laid lance, and *e*, and we knelt in prayer.   *Holy Grail* 460
    The younger sister, Evelyn, *e*—   *Sisters (E. and E.)* 152
    Muriel *e* with it, ' See !—   *The Ring* 279
    Has *e* on the larger woman-world   "   486

Entering (*See also* **Half-entering**)   *e* fill'd the house with
    sudden light.   *Aylmer's Field* 682
    for on *e* He had cast the curtains of their seat aside—   "   802
    You likewise will do well, Ladies, in *e* here,   *Princess ii* 62
    E, the sudden light Dazed me half-blind :   "   *v* 11
    E then, Right o'er a mount of newly-fallen stones,   *Marr. of Geraint* 360
    and *e* barr'd her door, Stript off the case,   *Lancelot and E.* 15
    e, loosed and let him go.'   *Holy Grail* 698
    Sir Bors, on *e*, push'd Athwart the throng to Lancelot,   "   752
    E all the avenues of sense Past thro' into his citadel,   *Lover's Tale i* 630
    and *e* the dim vault, And, making there a sudden light,   "   *iv* 52
Enterprise   Far-famed for well-won *e*,   *Kate* 22
    Here on the threshold of our *e*.   *Gareth and L.* 298
Entertain'd   talk and minstrel melody *e*.   *Lancelot and E.* 267
Entertainment   the slender *e* of a house Once rich,   *Marr. of Geraint* 301
Enthroned   or the *e* Persephonè in Hades,   *Princess iv* 438
Entranced   *E* with that place and time,   *Arabian Nights* 97
Entreat   ' Earl, *e* her by my love,   *Marr. of Geraint* 760
Entreaty   manifold *entreaties*, many a tear,   *Enoch Arden* 160
Entry   Above an *e* : riding in, we call'd ;   *Princess i* 225
    A column'd *e* shone and marble stairs,   "   *v* 364
    in the Vestal *e* shriek'd The virgin marble   "   *vi* 350
    two great *entries* open'd from the hall,   *Gareth and L.* 665
    by this *e* fled The damsel in her wrath,   "   674
    a lion on each side That kept the *e*,   *Holy Grail* 818
    Strewn in the *e* of the moaning cave ;   *Lover's Tale iii* 2
Entry-gates   Stood from his walls and wing d his *e g*   *Aylmer's Field* 18
Entwine   Round my true heart thine arms *e*   *Miller's D.* 216
    E the cold baptismal font,   *In Mem. xxix* 10
Envied   I *e* your sweet slumber,   *The Flight* 9
Envious   *See* **Half-envious**
Envy (s)   far aloof From *e*, hate and pity,   *Lucretius* 77
    No lewdness, narrowing *e*, monkey-spite,   "   211
    Know well that *E* calls you Devil's son,   *Merlin and V.* 467
    then did *E* call me Devil's son :   "   497
    E wears the mask of Love,   *Locksley H., Sixty* 109
Envy (verb)   *Her* countrywomen ! she did not *e*   *Princess iii* 41
    I *e* not in any moods The captive void   *In Mem. xxvii* 1
    I *e* not the beast that takes His license   "   5
Envying   Leolin, I almost sin in *e* you :   *Aylmer's Field* 360
    And *e* all that meet him there.   *In Mem. lx* 8
Enwind   Danube rolling fair *E* her isles,   *In Mem. xcviii* 10
Enwomb   O day which did *e* that happy hour,   *Lover's Tale i* 485
Enwound   the circle of his arms *E* us both ;   *Gardener's D* 217
    E him fold by fold, and made him gray   *Guinevere* 603
Epic (adj.)   Princess, six feet high, Grand, *e*,   *Princess, Pro.* 225
Epic (s)   ' he burnt His *e*, his King Arthur,   *The Epic* 28
    With scraps of thundrous *E* lilted out   *Princess i* 375
Epicurean (adj.)   majesties Of settled, sweet, *E* life.   *Lucretius* 218
Epicurean (s)   like a stoic, or like A wiser *e*,   *Maud I iv* 21
Epitaph (*See also* **Hepitaph**)   cut this *e* above my bones ;   *Princess ii* 207
Epithet   And pelted with outrageous *e*'s,   *Aylmer's Field* 286
    and your fine *e* Is accurate too,   *Merlin and V.* 532
Epoch   A juster *e* has begun.   *Epilogue* 6
Equal (adj.)   Gliding with *e* crowns two serpents led   *Alexander* 6
    who wrought Two spirits to one *e* mind—   *Miller's D.* 236
    Let us swear an oath, and keep it with an *e* mind, *Lotos-Eaters, C. S.* 108
    we are ; One *e* temper of heroic hearts,   *Ulysses* 68
    crime of sense became The crime of malice, and is
    e blame.'   *Vision of Sin* 216
    Maintaining that with *e* husbandry   *Princess i* 130
    Toward that great year of *e* mights and rights,   "   *iv* 74
    I saw That *e* baseness lived in sleeker times   "   *v* 385
    scorn'd to help their *e* rights Against the sons of men,   "   *vii* 233
    the track Whereon with *e* feet we fared ;   *In Mem. xxv* 2
    But lives to wed an *e* mind,   "   *lxii* 8
    First love, first friendship, *e* powers,   "   *lxxxv* 107
    Faith and unfaith can ne'er be *e* powers :   *Merlin and V.* 388
    To leave an *e* baseness   "   830
    As Love and I do number *e* years,   *Lover's Tale i* 195
    A planet *e* to the sun Which cast it,   *To E. Fitzgerald* 35
    The girls of *e* age, but one was fair,   *The Ring* 160
    every heart that loves with truth is *e* to endure.   *The Flight* 104
    your passionate shriek for the rights of an *e* humanity, *Beautiful City* 2
    For all they rule—by *e* law for all ?   *Akbar's Dream* 110

Equal (s) The woman were an *e* to the man.   *Princess i* 131
and this proud watchword rest Of *e* ;   ,, *vii* 301
in true marriage lies Nor *e*, nor unequal :   ,, 303
' Ye are *e*'s, equal-born.'   *Locksley H., Sixty* 110
Each religion says, ' Thou art one, without *e*.'   *Akbar's D., Inscrip.* 3
Equal (verb) what delights can *e* those   *In Mem. xlii* 9
   Gardener's D. 77
Equal-blowing Beneath a broad and *e-b* wind,   *Locksley H., Sixty* 110
Equal-born ' Ye are equals, *e-b* ' E-b ?   *D. of F. Women* 230
Equall'd Strength came to me that *e* my desire.   *In Mem. lxxxv* 33
Equal-poised O friendship, *e-p* control,   *Lover's Tale iv* 190
Equatorial Not such as here—an *e* one,   *Will Water.* 238
Equinox feel in head or chest Our changeful *e*'es,
Erased *See* **Sand-erased**
Erect Tall and *e*, but bending from his height   *Aylmer's Field* 119
anger-charm'd from sorrow, soldierlike, *E* :   ,, 729
Tall and *e*, but in the middle aisle Reel'd,   ,, 818
Strode from the porch, tall, and *e* again.   ,, 825
E behind a desk of satin-wood,   *Princess ii* 105
Lady Blanche *e* Stood up and spake,   ,, *iv* 290
E and silent, striking with her glance   ,, *vi* 152
Erin With Anguisant of *E*, Morganore,   *Com. of Arthur* 115
Ermine with *e* capes And woolly-breasts and beaded
eyes ;   *In Mem. xcv* 11
Erne (Miriam) *See* **Miriam, Miriam Erne**
Erne (Muriel) *See* **Muriel, Muriel Erne**
Eros a bevy of *E*'es, apple-cheek'd,   *The Islet* 11
Err forms that *e* from honest Nature's rule !   *Locksley Hall* 61
O my princess ! true she *e*'s,   *Princess iii* 107
she that has a son And sees him *e* :   ,, 261
For nothing is that *e*'s from law.   *In Mem. lxxiii* 8
' If Enid *e*'s, let Enid learn her fault.'   *Marr. of Geraint* 132
Errant (*See also* **Damsel-errant, Knighthood-errant**)
and *e* knights And ladies came,   *Marr. of Geraint* 545
To lead an *e* passion home again.   *Lucretius* 17
Prince had brought his *e* eyes Home from the rock,   *Geraint and E.* 245
Errantry *See* **Knight-errantry**
Err'd Aim'd at the helm, his lance *e* ;   *Geraint and E.* 157
if ancient prophecies Have *e* not,   *Guinevere* 450
Errest ' Nay—but thou, Lancelot :   *Holy Grail* 881
Erring an *e* pearl Lost in her bosom :   *Princess iv* 60
Error intellect to part *E* from crime ;   *Isabel* 15
Shall *E* in the round of time Still father Truth ?   *Love and Duty* 4
Deep as Hell I count his *e*.   *The Captain* 3
Dismal *e* ! fearful slaughter !   ,, 65
Child, if it were thine *e* or thy crime   *Come not, when, etc.* 7
some gross *e* lies In this report,   *Princess i* 69
so she wears her *e* like a crown   ,, *iii* 111
The damsel's headlong *e* thro' the wood—   *Gareth and L.* 1215
When he flouted a statesman's *e*,   *The Wreck* 68
Life with its anguish, and horrors, and *e*'s   *Despair* 48
'Erse (horse) DOSN'T thou 'ear my '*e*'s legs,   *N. Farmer, N. S.* 1
Fur he ca'd 'is '*e* Billy-rough-un,   *Village Wife* 84
Esau a heart as rough as *E*'s hand,   *Godiva* 28
Escape (s) and tumbles and childish *e*'s,   *Maud I i* 69
From which was no *e* for evermore ;   *Merlin and V.* 210
From which is no *e* for evermore.'   ,, 544
Escape (verb) who scarce would *e* with her life ;   *In the Child. Hosp.* 66
if they be bold enough, who shall *e* ?   *Def. of Lucknow* 40
if I do not *e* you at last.   *Despair* 114
And who shall *e* if they close ?   *Heavy Brigade* 16
can *e* From the lower world within him,   *Making of Man* 1
Escaped (*See also* **'Scaped**) when the second Christmas
came, *e* His keepers,   *Aylmer's Field* 838
From which I *e* heart-free,   *Maud I i* 11
Escaping Like the caged bird *e* suddenly,   *Enoch Arden* 269
Esh (ash) Breäk me a bit o' the *e* for his 'eäd,   *N. Farmer, N. S.* 41
Eshcol vines with grapes Of *E* hugeness ;   *To E. Fitzgerald* 28
Espalier *e*'s and the standards all Are thine ;   *The Blackbird* 5
Espied stood, Until the King *e* him,   *Holy Grail* 755
Essay must thou dearly love thy first *e*,   *Ode to Memory* 83
Essay'd *e*, by tenderest-touching terms,   *Merlin and V.* 898
Then in my madness I *e* the door ;   *Holy Grail* 841
Essayist Authors—*e*, atheist, novelist,   *Locksley H., Sixty* 139
Essence I floated free, As naked *e*,   *Two Voices* 374
O sacred *e*, other form,   *In Mem. lxxxv* 35

Essence (*continued*) his *e*'s turn'd the live air sick,   *Maud I xiii* 11
In thine own *e*, and delight thyself   *Lover's Tale i* 13
Estate (condition) Whose life in low *e* began   *In Mem. lxiv* 3
Day, when my crown'd *e* begun To pine   ,, *lxxii* 5
Beholding one so bright in dark *e*,   *Marr. of Geraint* 786
Estate (lands) (*See also* **'Staäte**) now lord of the broad *e*
and the Hall,   *Maud I i* 19
This lump of earth has left his *e*   ,, *xvi* 1
an orphan with half a shire of *e*,   *Charity* 13
Estate (verb) *E* them with large land and territory   *Lancelot and E.* 1322
Esteem talk kindlier : we *e* you for it—   *Princess v* 212
Esteem'd we trust that you *e* us not Too harsh   ,, *iii* 198
Esther those of old That lighted on Queen *E*,   *Marr. of Geraint* 731
Estuary colony smoulder'd on the refluent *e* ;   *Boädicea* 28
Ethereal over those *e* eyes The bar of Michael Angelo.   *In Mem. lxxxvii* 39
Eternal (adj.) Lay there exiled from *e* God,   *Palace of Art* 263
every hour is saved From that *e* silence,   *Ulysses* 27
Pure lilies of *e* peace,   *Sir Galahad* 67
Or that *e* want of pence,   *Will Water.* 43
Dwelt with *e* summer, ill-content.   *Enoch Arden* 562
center'd in *e* calm.   *Lucretius* 79
E honour to his name. (repeat)   *Ode on Well.* 150, 231
Nor palter'd with *E* God for power ;   ,, 180
shall bloom The *e* landscape of the past ;   *In Mem. xlvi* 7
E form shall still divide The *e* soul from all beside ;   ,, *xlvii* 6
on the low dark verge of life The twilight of *e* day.   ,, *l* 16
E greetings to the dead ;   ,, *lvii* 14
E process moving on,   ,, *lxxii* 5
Which masters Time indeed, and is *E*,   ,, *lxxxv* 66
To bare the *e* Heavens again,   ,, *cxxii* 4
Lo ! I forgive thee, as *E* God Forgives :   *Guinevere* 544
quiet fields of *e* sleep !   *V. of Maeldune* 86
bawl'd the dark side of your faith and a God of *e* rage,   *Despair* 39
pity for our own selves till we long'd for *e* sleep.   ,, 46
march of that *E* Harmony Whereto the worlds beat
time,   *D. of the Duke of C.* 15
Eternal (s) Shiah and Sunnee, Symbol the *E* !   *Akbar's Dream* 108
Eternity All things will change Thro' *e*.   *Nothing will Die* 10
even and morn Ever will be Thro' *e*.   ,, 35
even and morn Ye will never see Thro' *e*.   *All Things will Die* 10
So in the light of great *e*   *Love and Death* 13
He names the name *E*.   *Two Voices* 29
But dreadful time, dreadful *e*,   *Palace of Art* 26
The sabbaths of *E*,   *St Agnes' Eve* 32
Music's golden sea Setting toward *e*,   *Ode on Well.* 253
O skill'd to sing of Time or *E*,   *Milton* 1
girth of Time Inswathe the fullness of *E*,   *Lover's Tale i* 48
You that shape for *E*,   *On Jub. Q. Victoria* 4
Seem'd nobler than their hard *Eternities*.   *Demeter and P.* 10
Etiquette clamouring *e* to death,   *Princess v* 1
Ettarre for the lady was *E*, And she was a great lady   *Pelleas and E.* 10
Linger'd *E* : and seeing Pelleas droop,   ,, 17
from the tower above him cried *E*,   ,, 23
Then when he came before *E*,   ,, 23
Bound on her brow, were Gawain and *E*.   ,, 43
Eunuch-hearted art thou not that *e-h* King   *Last Tournament* 44
whine And snivel, being *e-h* too,   ,, 45
Europa sweet *E*'s mantle blew unclasp'd,   *Palace of Art* 11
Europe Better fifty years of *E* than a cycle of Cathay.   *Locksley Hall* 18
guard the eye, the soul Of *E*,   *Ode on Well.* 16
Once the weight and fate of *E* hung.   ,, 24
Tho' all the storm of *E* on us break ;   *Third of Feb.* 1
But the one voice in *E* : we *must* speak ;
avenging rod Shall lash all *E* into blood ;   *To F. D. Maurice* 2
Surely the pibroch of *E* is ringing   *Def. of Lucknow* 9
gain'd a freedom known to *E*, known to all ;   *Locksley H., Sixty* 12
European never floats an *E* flag,   *Locksley Hall* 16
the centre and crater of *E* confusion,   *Beautiful City* 2
Europe-shadowing wheel'd on *E*'s wings,   *Ode on Well.* 15
Eustace I and *E* from the city went   *Gardener's D.*
My *E* might have sat for Hercules ;   ,,
E painted her, And said to me,   ,,
E turn'd, and smiling said to me,   ,,
' *E*,' I said, ' this wonder keeps the house.'   ,, 1
With solemn gibe did *E* banter me.   ,, 1

Eustace (*continued*) till Autumn brought an hour For *E*,   *Gardener's D.* 208
Evangel Heaven-sweet *E*, ever-living word,   *Sir J. Oldcastle* 28
Evangelist something seal'd The lips of that *E*.   *In Mem. xxxi* 16
Evasion Elusion, and occasion, and *e* '?   *Gareth and L.* 288
Eve (*See also* **Christmas Eäve, Christmas-eve, Yester-eve**)
    At *e* the beetle boometh   *Claribel* 9
    At *e* a dry cicala sung,   *Mariana in the S.* 85
    And when the zoning *e* has died   *On a Mourner* 21
    Nor anchor dropt at *e* or morn ;   *The Voyage* 82
    From fringes of the faded *e*,   *Move eastward* 3
    Except when for a breathing-while at *e*,   *Aylmer's Field* 449
    As thro' the land at *e* we went,   *Princess ii* 1
    at *e* and dawn With Ida, Ida, Ida, rang the woods ;   „ *iv* 432
    sitting at home in my father's farm at *e* :   *Grandmother* 90
    Will there be dawn in West and *e* in East ?   *Gareth and L.* 712
    No later than last *e* to Prince Geraint—   *Marr. of Geraint* 603
    Her seer, her bard, her silver star of *e*,   *Merlin and V.* 954
    Heard on the winding waters, *e* and morn   *Lancelot and E.* 1408
    days Of dewy dawning and the amber *e*'s   *Lover's Tale i* 549
    while my life's late *e* endures,   *To Marq. of Dufferin* 49
    star of *e* was drawing light From the dead sun,   *Death of Œnone* 64
    day by day, thro' many a blood-red *e*,   *St. Telemachus* 3
    E after *e* that haggard anchorite Would haunt   „ 12
Eve (proper name) since the time when Adam first
    Embraced his *E*   *Day-Dm., L'Envoi* 42
    Shadowing the snow-limb'd *E*   *Maud I xviii* 28
Evelyn *E* begins it ' O diviner Air.'   *Sisters (E. and E.)* 4
    Now follows Edith echoing *E*.   „ 15
    graver than the other—Edith than *E*.   „ 27
    E is gayer, wittier, prettier,   „ 36
    The younger sister, *E*, enter'd—   „ 152
    told your wayside story to my mother And *E*.   „ 190
    For *E* knew not of my former suit,   „ 205
    round my *E* clung In utter silence for so long,   „ 216
    bright quick smile of *E*, that had sunn'd   „ 243
    this I named from her own self, *E* :   „ 271
    traitors to her ; our quick *E*—   „ 285
Even (adj.) Upon a pedestal with man.'   *Princess iii* 224
    And climb'd upon a fair and *e* ridge,   *Marr. of Geraint* 239
Even (s) (*See also* **Yester-even**) For *e* and morn
    Ever will be Thro' eternity.   *Nothing will Die* 33
    For *e* and morn Ye will never see Thro' eternity.   *All Things will Die* 44
    Thou comest morning or *e*; she cometh not morning or *e*. *Leonine Eleg.* 15
    Her tears fell with the dews at *e* ;   *Mariana* 14
    And the crag that fronts the *E*,   *Eleänore* 40
    Whisper in odorous heights of *e*.   *Milton* 16
    gave a shield whereon the Star of *E*   *Gareth and L.* 1117
    setting, when *E* descended, the very sunset   *V. of Maeldune* 66
    Light the fading gleam of *E* ?   *Locksley H., Sixty* 229
    or seated in the dusk Of *e*,   *Demeter and P.* 126
Evenfall thro' the laurels At the quiet *e*,   *Maud II iv* 78
Evening (adj.) (*See also* **Evening-Star**) And with the *e* cloud, *Ode to Memory* 22
    To the shepherd who watcheth the *e* star.   *Dying Swan* 35
    You are the *e* star,   *Margaret* 27
    Floating thro' an *e* atmosphere,   *Eleänore* 100
    Eyed like the *e* star, with playful tail   *Œnone* 200
    same strength which threw the Morning Star Can
      throw the *E*,'   *Gareth and L.* 1109
    We should see the Globe we groan in, fairest of
      their *e* stars.   *Locksley H., Sixty* 188
    The mellow lin-lan-lone of *e* bells   *Far-far-away* 5
    SUNSET and *e* star,   *Crossing the Bar* 1
    Twilight and *e* bell,   „ 9
Evening (s) in stillest *e*'s With what voice   *Adeline* 30
    Many an *e* by the waters did we watch   *Locksley Hall* 37
    It chanced one *e* Annie's children long'd   *Enoch Arden* 362
    At *e* when the dull November day   „ 721
    We dropt with *e* on a rustic town   *Princess i* 170
    With brow to brow like night and *e* mixt   „ *vi* 131
    it was *e* : silent light Slept on the painted walls,   „ *vii* 120
    all of an *e* late I climb'd to the top   *Grandmother* 37
    Never morning wore To *e*,   *In Mem. vi* 8
    air, That rollest from the gorgeous gloom Of *e*   „ *lxxxvi* 3
    It leads me forth at *e*,   *Maud II iv* 17
    knight, That named himself the Star of *E*,   *Gareth and L.* 1090

Evening (s) (*continued*) mixt Her fancies with the
    sallow-rifted glooms Of *e*,   *Lancelot and E.* 1003
    or ever that *e* ended a great gale blew,   *The Revenge* 114
    gloom of the *e*, Life at a close ;   *Vastness* 15
Evening-lighted From the *e-l* wood,   *Margaret* 10
Evening-Star call themsleves the Day, Morning-Star,
    and Noon-Sun, and *E-S*,   *Gareth and L.* 634
Evenness I lost myself and fell from *e*,   *Sir J. Oldcastle* 164
Even-sloping Near him a mound of *e-s* side,   *Pelleas and E.* 25
Evensong I know At matins and at *e*,   *Supp. Confessions* 99
    till the dusk that follow'd *e*   *Gareth and L.* 793
Event such refraction of *e*'s As often rises   *In Mem. xcii* 15
    And one far-off divine *e*,   „ *Con.* 143
    Enid stood aside to wait the *e*,   *Geraint and E.* 153
    thou remaining here wilt learn the *e* ;   *Guinevere* 577
    Move with me to the *e*.   *Lover's Tale i* 298
    there, my latest vision—then the *e* !   „ *iii* 59
    HE flies the *e* : he leaves the *e* to me :   „ *iv* 1
    the *e* Glanced back upon them in his after life,   „ 23
Eventide Either at morn or *e*.   *Mariana* 16
    For at *e*, listening earnestly,   *A spirit haunts* 4
    Then, on a golden autumn *e*,   *Enoch Arden* 61
Everard (*See also* **Everard Hall, Hall**) clapt his hand On
    E's shoulder, and, ' I hold by him.' And I,' quoth *E*, *The Epic* 22
    For I remember'd *E*'s college fame   „ 46
Everard Hall (*See also* **Everard, Hall**) parson Holmes, the
    poet *E H*,   „ 4
Ever-breaking heard an *e-b* shore That tumbled   *In Mem. cxxiv* 11
Ever-brightening Fifty years of *e-b* Science !   *On Jub. Q. Victoria* 53
Ever-broadening Fifty years of *e-b* Commerce !   „ 52
    ocean-empire with her boundless homes For *e-b*
      England,   *To the Queen ii* 30
Ever-changing a power to make This *e-c* world of
    circumstance,   *To Duke of Argyll* 10
    the never-changing One And *e-c* Many,   *Akbar's Dream* 148
    thee the changeless in thine *e-c* skies.   *Akbar's D., Hymn* 4
Ever-climbing but that *e-c* wave, Hurl'd back again   *Last Tournament* 92
Ever-deepen'd By the long torrent's *e-d* roar,   *Death of Œnone* 85
Ever-echoing And *e-e* avenues of song.   *Ode on Well.* 79
Ever-fancied Before an *e-f* arrow, made   *Geraint and E.* 531
Ever-fleeting And rippled like an *e-f* wave,   *Gareth and L.* 215
Ever-floating death, death, thou *e-f* cloud,   *Œnone* 238
Evergreen (adj.) that *e* laurel is blasted by more than
    lightning !   *Parnassus* 12
Evergreen (s) And in it throve an ancient *e*,   *Enoch Arden* 735
    O hollies and ivies and *e*'s,   *Spiteful Letter* 23
    With but a drying *e* for crest,   *Gareth and L.* 1116
Ever-growing Almost blind With *e-g* cataract,   *Sisters (E. and E.)* 192
    How long thine *e-g* mind Hath still'd   *Freedom* 33
Ever-heightening And every phase of *e-h* life,   *De Prof., Two G.* 7
Ever-highering In *e-h* eagle-circles up To the great Sun *Gareth and L.* 21
Everlasting The marvel of the *e* will,   *The Poet* 7
    she took the tax away And built herself an *e* name.   *Godiva* 79
    Nor sound of human sorrow mounts to mar Their sacred
      e calm !   *Lucretius* 110
    Lamp of the Lord God Lord *e*,   *Batt. of Brunanburh* 28
    Knowing the Love we were used to believe *e* would die : *Despair* 54
    Infinite cruelty rather than make *e* Hell,   „ 96
    In the name Of the *e* God, I will live and die with you.   *Happy* 108
Ever-living Heaven-sweet Evangel, *e-l* word,   *Sir J. Oldcastle* 28
Ever-loyal Their *e-l* iron leader's fame,   *Ode on Well.* 229
Ever-moaning An *e-m* battle in the mist,   *Merlin and V.* 192
Evermore My bride to be, my *e* delight,   *Maud I xviii* 73
Ever-murder'd *e-m* France, By shores that darken   *Aylmer's Field* 766
Ever-ravening *e-r* eagle's beak and talon   *Boädicea* 11
Ever-rising A hundred *e-r* mountain lines,   *Ancient Sage* 282
    now their *e-r* life has dwarf'd   *The Ring* 463
Ever-scattering wearing but a holly-spray for crest,
    With *e-s* berries,   *Last Tournament* 173
Ever-shifting *e-s* currents of the blood   *D. of F. Women* 133
    long mountains ended in a coast Of *e-s* sand,   *Pass of Arthur* 86
Ever-showering And rode beneath an *e-s* leaf,   *Last Tournament* 492
Ever-silent The *e-s* spaces of the East,   *Tithonus* 9
    passive sailor wrecks at last In *e-s* seas ;   *Ancient Sage* 137
Ever-tremulous falling showers, And *e-t* aspen-trees,   *Lancelot and E.* 524

Eye (s) (*continued*) *E's* with idle tears are wet. *Miller's D.* 211
Look thro' mine *e's* with thine.   "   215
May those kind *e's* for ever dwell!   They have not
   shed a many tears, Dear *e's*,   "   220
Droops blinded with his shining *e*: *Fatima* 38
My *e's* are full of tears, my heart of love, My heart
   is breaking, and my *e's* are dim, *Œnone* 31
With down-dropt *e's* I sat alone: "   56
The while, above, her full and earnest *e*   "   141
Thy mortal *e's* are frail to judge of fair,   "   158
She with a subtle smile in her mild *e's*,   "   184
And I beheld great Here's angry *e's*,   "   190
to vex me with his father's *e's*!   "   255
gaze upon My palace with unblinded *e's*, *Palace of Art* 42
hand and *e's* That said, We wait for thee.   "   103
Flush'd in her temples and her *e's*,   "   170
all things fair to sate my various *e's*!   "   193
Oh your sweet *e's*, your low replies: *L. C. V. de Vere* 29
The languid light of your proud *e's*   "   59
There's many a black *e*, they say, *May Queen* 5
Than tir'd eyelids upon tir'd *e's*; *Lotos-Eaters, C. S.* 6
With half-shut *e's* ever to seem Falling   "   55
e's grown dim with gazing on the pilot-stars.   "   87
Charged both mine *e's* with tears. *D. of F. Women* 13
The star-like sorrows of immortal *e's*,   "   91
stern black-bearded kings with wolfish *e's*,   "   111
with swarthy cheeks and bold black *e's*,   "   127
nor tame and tutor with mine *e*   "   138
Those dragon *e's* of anger'd Eleanor   "   255
But tho' his *e's* are waxing dim, *D. of the O. Year* 21
Close up his *e's*: tie up his chin: "   48
And tho' mine own *e's* fill with dew, *To J. S.* 37
Memory standing near Cast down her *e's*,   "   54
Her open *e's* desire the truth. *Of old sat Freedom* 17
broke From either side, nor veil his *e's*: *Love thou thy land* 90
both his *e's* were dazzled, as he stood, *M. d'Arthur* 59
might have pleased the *e's* of many men.   "   91
Laid widow'd of the power in his *e*   "   122
Valuing the giddy pleasure of the *e's*.   "   128
' Now see I by thine *e's* that this is done.   "   149
looking wistfully with wide blue *e's* As in a picture,   "   169
charged Before the *e's* of ladies and of kings.   "   225
shall I hide my forehead and my *e's*?   "   228
made those *e's* Darker than darkest pansies, *Gardener's D.* 26
Her violet *e's*, and all her Hebe bloom,   "   137
A thought would fill my *e's* with happy dew;   "   197
following her dark *e's* Felt earth as air   "   211
while I mused came Memory with sad *e's*,   "   243
this whole hour your *e's* have been intent   "   269
Make thine heart ready with thine *e's*:   "   273
And I will set him in my uncle's *e* *Dora* 67
To make him pleasing in her uncle's *e*.   "   84
Dora cast her *e's* upon the ground,   "   89
like a pear In growing, modest *e's*, *Walk. to the Mail* 54
his nice *e's* Should see the raw mechanic's   "   74
film made thick These heavy, horny *e's*. *St. S. Stylites* 201
with what delighted *e's* I turn to yonder oak. *Talking Oak* 7
I breathed upon her *e's*   "   210
sunbeam slip, To light her shaded *e*;   "   218
Streaming *e's* and breaking hearts? *Love and Duty* 2
staring *e* glazed o'er with sapless days,   "   16
When *e's*, love-languid thro' half tears   "   36
Gave utterance by the yearning of an *e*,   "   62
With quiet *e's* unfaithful to the truth,   "   94
Shines in those tremulous *e's* *Tithonus* 26
sweet *e's* brighten slowly close to mine,   "   38
with what other *e's* I used to watch—   "   51
I dipt into the future far as human *e* could see;
   (repeat) *Locksley Hall* 15, 119
And her *e's* on all my motions   "   22
dawning in the dark of hazel *e's*—   "   28
What is this? his *e's* are heavy: "   51
an *e* shall vex thee, looking ancient kindness   "   85
and left me with the jaundiced *e*; *E*, to which all
   order festers,   "   132

Eye (s) (*continued*) No *e* look down, she passing; *Godiva* 40
heads upon the spout Had cunning *e's* to see: "   57
but his *e's*, before they had their will,   "   69
Nor look with that too-earnest *e*— *Day-Dm., Pro.* 18
A fairy Prince, with joyful *e's*,   " *Arrival* 7
How dark those hidden *e's* must be!'   "   32
' O *e's* long laid in happy sleep!'   " *Depart.* 17
So much your *e's* my fancy take—   " *L'Envoi* 26
That I might kiss those *e's* awake!   "   28
What *e's*, like thine, have waken'd hopes,   "   45
this heart and *e's*, Are touch'd, *Sir Galahad* 71
crow shall tread The corners of thine *e's*: *Will Water.* 236
She look'd into Lord Ronald's *e's*, *Lady Clare* 79
gladness lighten'd In the *e's* of each. *The Captain* 32
He saw not far: his *e's* were dim: *The Voyage* 75
One praised her ancles, one her *e's*, *Beggar Maid* 11
To glass herself in dewy *e's* That watch me *Move eastward* 7
I saw with half-unconscious *e* She wore the colours *The Letters* 15
Where sat a company with heated *e's*, *Vision of Sin* 7
Hair, and *e's*, and limbs, and faces,   "   39
Glimmer in thy rheumy *e's*.   "   154
I cannot praise the fire In your *e*—   "   184
then would Philip, his blue *e's* All flooded *Enoch Arden* 31
Enoch set A purpose evermore before his *e's*,   "   45
His large gray *e's* and weather-beaten face   "   70
And in their *e's* and faces read his doom;   "   73
She could not fix the glass to suit her *e*; Perhaps her *e*
   was dim, hand tremulous;   "   241
rose, and fixt her swimming *e's* upon him,   "   325
his *e's* Full of that lifelong hunger,   "   463
His *e's* upon the stones, he reach'd   "   684
Enoch rolling his gray *e's* upon her,   "   844
That once again he roll'd his *e's* upon her   "   904
Her *e's* a bashful azure, and her hair *The Brook* 71
Katie snatch'd her *e's* at once from mine,   "   101
sweet content Re-risen in Katie's *e's*,   "   169
he stared On *e's* a bashful azure,   "   206
Whose *e's* from under a pyramidal head *Aylmer's Field* 20
eager *e's*, that still Took joyful note   "   66
the cross-lightnings of four chance-met *e's*   "   129
Till Leolin ever watchful of her *e*,   "   210
conscious of the rageful *e* That watch'd him,   "   336
With a weird bright *e*, sweating and trembling,   "   585
her fresh and innocent *e* Had such a star of morning   "   691
hid the Holiest from the people's *e's*   "   772
Then their *e's* vext her;   "   802
And those fixt *e's* of painted ancestors   "   832
thinking that her clear germander *e* Droopt *Sea Dreams* 4
night-light flickering in my *e's* Awoke me.'   "   103
then my *e's* Pursued him down the street,   "   164
all his conscience and one *e* askew'—(repeat)   " 180, 184
Made wet the crafty crowsfoot round his *e*;   "   187
Grave, florid, stern, as far as *e* could see,   "   219
show'd their *e's* Glaring, and passionate looks,   "   235
I fixt My wistful *e's* on two fair images,   "   240
' Dead! who is dead?' ' The man your *e* pursued.   "   272
And here he glances on an *e* new-born, *Lucretius* 137
her arm lifted, *e's* on fire— *Princess, Pro.* 41
turns Up thro' gilt wires a crafty loving *e*,   "   172
twinn'd as horse's ear and *e*.   " *i* 57
raised the blinding bandage from his *e's*:   "   244
such *e's* were in her head,   " *ii* 37
all her thoughts as fair within her *e's*,   "   326
Abase those *e's* that ever loved to meet   "   427
wander from his wits Pierced thro' with *e's*,   "   441
glowing round her dewy *e's* The circled Iris   " *iii* 26
her lynx *e* To fix and make me hotter,   "   46
settled in her *e's* The green malignant light   "   131
Up went the hush'd amaze of hand and *e*.   "   138
we had limed ourselves With open *e's*,   "   143
as she smote me with the light of *e's*   "   192
She spake With kindled *e's*:   "   334
Rise in the heart, and gather to the *e's*,   " *iv* 41
unto dying *e's* The casement slowly grows   "   51
Stared with great *e's*, and laugh'd with alien lips,   "   119

Eye (s) (*continued*) She wept her true *e's* blind for such

a one,	*Princess iv* 134
with *e's* Of shining expectation fixt on mine.	,, 152
Not yet endured to meet her opening *e's*,	,, 195
an *e* like mine, A lidless watcher of the public weal,	,, 324
Fear Stared in her *e's*, and chalk'd her face,	,, 377
gems and gemlike ; And gold and golden heads ;	,, 480
the crimson-rolling *e* Glares ruin,	,, 494
slink From ferule and the trespass-chiding *e*,	,, v 38
Alive with fluttering scarfs and ladies' *e's*,	,, 509
loved me closer than his own right *e*,	,, 531
old lion, glaring with his whelpless *e*,	,, vi 99
grief and mother's hunger in her *e*,	,, 146
her *e* with slow dilation roll'd Dry flame,	,, 189
meet it, with an *e* that swum in thanks ;	,, 210
So she, and turn'd askance a wintry *e*:	,, 330
The common men with rolling *e's*;	,, 360
I love not hollow cheek or faded *e* :	,, vii 7
Nor knew what *e* was on me,	,, 53
the dew Dwelt in her *e's*,	,, 136
I on her Fixt my faint *e's*, and utter'd	,, 144
with shut *e's* I lay Listening ; then look'd.	,, 223
and mild the luminous *e's*,	,, 226
yearlong poring on thy pictured *e's*,	,, 340
lift thine *e's* ; my doubts are dead,	,, 348
guard the *e*, the soul Of Europe,	*Ode on Well.* 160
he turn'd, and I saw his *e's* all wet,	*Grandmother* 49
thank God that I keep my *e's*.	,, 106
and the *e* of man cannot see ;	*High. Pantheism* 17
A jewel, a jewel dear to a lover's *e* !	*Window, On the Hill* 3
fine little feet—Dewy blue *e*.	,, *Letter* 4
Tell my wish to her dewy blue *e* :	,, ,, 14
lighten into my *e's* and my heart,	*Marr. Morn.* 15
cross All night below the darken'd *e's* ;	*In Mem. iv* 14
But since it pleased a vanish'd *e*,	,, viii 21
Mine *e's* have leisure for their tears ;	,, xiii 16
Paradise It never look'd to human *e's*	,, xxiv 7
if that *e* which watches guilt And goodness,	,, xxvi 9
Oh, if indeed that *e* foresee Or see	,, 9
We sung, tho' every *e* was dim,	,, xxx 14
Her *e's* are homes of silent prayer,	,, xxxii 1
those wild *e's* that watch the wave	,, xxxvi 15
Make April of her tender *e's* ;	,, xl 8
See with clear *e* some hidden shame	,, li 7
With larger other *e's* than ours,	,, 15
Such splendid purpose in his *e's*,	,, lvi 10
That ever look'd with human *e's*.	,, lvii 12
And if thou cast thine *e's* below,	,, lxi 5
Tho' if an *e* that's downward cast	,, lxii 1
Or in the light of deeper *e's*	,, 11
And closing eaves of wearied *e's*	,, lxvii 11
I find a trouble in thine *e*,	,, lxviii 10
him, who turns a musing *e* On songs,	,, lxxvii 2
And dropt the dust on tearless *e's* ;	,, lxxx 4
And over those ethereal *e's*	,, lxxxii 39
He brought an *e* for all he saw ;	,, lxxxix 9
dying *e's* Were closed with wail,	,, xc 5
And woolly breasts and beaded *e's* ;	,, xcv 12
whose light-blue *e's* Are tender over drowning flies,	,, xcvi 2
These two—they dwelt with *e* on *e*,	,, xcvii 9
She dwells on him with faithful *e's*,	,, xcvii 35
gleams On Lethe in the *e's* of Death.	,, xcviii 8
But each has pleased a kindred *e*,	,, c 17
The critic clearness of an *e*,	,, cix 3
and thee mine *e's* Have look'd on :	,, 21
Drew in the expression of an *e*,	,, cxi 19
I, who gaze with temperate *e's*,	,, cxii 7
I seem to cast a careless *e* On souls,	,, 7
And bright the friendship of thine *e* ;	,, cxix 10
Or eagle's wing, or insect's *e* ;	,, cxxiv 6
She did but look thro' dimmer *e's* ;	,, cxxv 6
Sweet human hand and lips and *e* ;	,, cxxix 6
On me she bends her blissful *e's*	*Con.* 29
By village *e's* as yet unborn ;	,, 59
e to *e*, shall look On knowledge ;	,, 129

G*

Eye (s) (*continued*) (for her *e's* were downcast, not to be seen)

	Maud I ii 5
An *e* well-practised in nature,	,, iv 38
her *e* seem'd full Of a kind intent to me,	,, vi 40
And a moist mirage in desert *e's*,	,, 53
once, but once, she lifted her *e's*,	,, viii 5
Let not my tongue be a thrall to my *e*,	,, xvi 32
Innumerable, pitiless, passionless *e's*,	,, xviii 38
often I caught her with *e's* all wet,	,, xix 23
every *e* but mine will glance At Maud	,, xx 36
In violets blue as your *e's*,	,, xxii 42
Was it he lay there with a fading *e* ?	*II i* 29
But only moves with the moving *e*,	,, ii 37
it well Might drown all life in the *e*,—	,, 61
I sorrow For the hand, the lips, the *e's*,	,, iv 27
My own dove with the tender *e* ?	,, 46
look'd, tho' but in a dream, upon *e's* so fair,	,, *III vi* 16
O passionate heart and morbid *e*,	,, 32
Felt the light of her *e's* into his life	*Com. of Arthur* 56
And dazed all *e's*, till Arthur by main might,	,, 109
From *e* to *e* thro' all their Order flash	,, 270
Bewildering heart and *e*—	,, 300
Fixing full *e's* of question on her face,	,, 312
dark my mother was in *e's* and hair, And dark in hair and *e's* am I ;	,, 327
the Queen replied with drooping *e's*,	,, 469
Gareth answer'd her with kindling *e's*, (repeat)	*Gareth and L.* 41, 62
Nor fronted man or woman, *e* to *e*—	,, 112
The mother's *e* Full of the wistful fear	,, 172
Gareth likewise on them fixt his *e's*	,, 236
shyly glanced *E's* of pure women,	,, 314
the listening *e's* Of those tall knights,	,, 327
the field was pleasant in our *e's*,	,, 337
The field was pleasant in my husband's *e*.'	,, 342
Return, and meet, and hold him from our *e's*,	,, 429
the King's calm *e* Fell on, and check'd,	,, 547
A head with kindling *e's* above the throng,	,, 646
Round as the red *e* of an Eagle-owl,	,, 799
Gareth's *e's* had flying blots Before them	,, 1031
And Enid, but to please her husband's *e*,	*Marr. of Geraint* 11
this she gather'd from the people's *e's* :	,, 61
darken'd from the high light in his *e's*,	,, 100
maybe pierced to death before mine *e's*,	,, 104
with fixt *e* following the three.	,, 237
Let his *e* rove in following,	,, 399
To whom Geraint with *e's* all bright replied,	,, 494
Nor did she lift an *e* nor speak a word,	,, 528
At this she cast her *e's* upon her dress,	,, 609
Myself would work *e* dim, and finger lame,	,, 628
Help'd by the mother's careful hand and *e*,	,, 738
the Prince had brought his errant *e*	*Geraint and E.* 245
Found Enid with the corner of his *e*,	,, 281
Crost and came near, lifted adoring *e's*,	,, 304
would not make them laughable in all *e's*,	,, 326
Made his *e* moist ; but Enid fear'd his *e's*,	,, 350
With *e's* to find you out however far,	,, 428
his *e* darken'd and his helmet wagg'd ;	,, 505
let her true hand falter, nor blue *e* Moisten,	,, 512
drove the dust against her veilless *e's* :	,, 529
Bound on a foray, rolling *e's* of prey,	,, 538
Half-bold, half-frighted, with dilated *e's*,	,, 597
He roll'd his *e's* about the hall,	,, 610
o'er her meek blue *e's*, came a happy mist	,, 769
Yet not so misty were her meek blue *e's*	,, 772
with your meek *e's*, The truest *e's*	,, 841
with your own true *e's* Beheld the man	,, 846
having look'd too much thro' alien *e's*,	,, 892
King went forth and cast his *e's* On each	,, 932
Sent me a three-years' exile from thine *e's*.	*Balin and Balan* 59
Sir Lancelot with his *e's* on earth,	,, 253
Lo ! these her emblems drew mine *e's*—	,, 265
Then Lancelot lifted his large *e's* ;	,, 277
hast thou *e's*, or if, are these So far besotted	,, 358
Then fiercely to Sir Garlon ' *E's* have I That saw	,, 372
E's too that long have watch'd how Lancelot	,, 375
The longest lance his *e's* had ever seen,	,, 411

Eye (s) *(continued)*   he lifted faint *e's*; he felt One near
him ;   *Balin and Balan* 594
Closed his death-drowsing *e's*, and slept   ,,   631
stood with folded hands and downward *e's* Of
   glancing corner,   *Merlin and V.* 69
her slow sweet *e's* Fear-tremulous,   ,,   85
With reverent *e's* mock-loyal,   ,,   157
neither *e's* nor tongue—O stupid child !   ,,   251
sweetly gleam'd her *e's* behind her tears   ,,   402
isle-nurtured *e's* Waged such unwilling tho' successful war   ,,   570
lady never made *unwilling* war With those fine *e's* :   ,,   604
Not one to flirt a venom at her *e's*,   ,,   609
let her *e's* Speak for her, glowing on him,   ,,   615
So lean his *e's* were monstrous ;   ,,   624
often o'er the sun's bright *e* Drew the vast eyelid   ,,   633
densest condensation, hard To mind and *e* ;   ,,   679
A snowy penthouse for his hollow *e's*,   ,,   808
Without the will to lift their *e's*,   ,,   836
His *e* was calm, and suddenly she took To bitter weeping   ,,   854
He raised his *e's* and saw The tree that shone   ,,   938
Her *e's* and neck glittering went and came :   ,,   960
Queen Lifted her *e's*, and they dwelt   *Lancelot and E.* 84
gleam'd a vague suspicion in his *e's* :   ,,   127
she, who held her *e's* upon the ground,   ,,   232
Lifted her *e's*, and read his lineaments.   ,,   244
And noblest, when she lifted up her *e's*.   ,,   256
she lifted up her *e's* And loved him,   ,,   259
let his *e's* Run thro' the peopled gallery   ,,   429
stay'd ; and cast his *e's* on fair Elaine :   ,,   640
O damsel, in the light of your blue *e's* ;   ,,   660
he roll'd his *e's* Yet blank from sleep,   ,,   819
His *e's* glisten'd : she fancied ' Is it for me ? '   ,,   822
his large black *e's*, Yet larger thro' his leanness,   ,,   834
' Nay, the world, the world, All ear and *e*, with such
   a stupid heart To interpret ear and *e*,   ,,   941
Speaking a still good-morrow with her *e's*.   ,,   1033
old servitor, on deck, Winking his *e's*,   ,,   1145
saw with a sidelong *e* The shadow of some piece   ,,   1173
Close underneath his *e's*, and right across   ,,   1240
and *e's* that ask'd ' What is it ? '   ,,   1249
men Shape to their fancy's *e* from broken rocks   ,,   1252
From the half-face to the full *e*,   ,,   1262
raised his head, their *e's* met and hers fell,   ,,   1312
He answer'd with his *e's* upon the ground,   ,,   1352
Seeing the homeless trouble in thine *e's*,   ,,   1365
To doubt her fairness were to want an *e*,   ,,   1376
lifted up his *e's* And saw the barge that brought   ,,   1390
I trust We are green in Heaven's *e's*   *Holy Grail* 38
her *e's* Beyond my knowing of them, beautiful,   ,,   102
His *e's* became so like her own,   ,,   141
sent the deathless passion in her *e's* Thro' him,   ,,   163
lifting up mine *e's*, I found myself Alone,   ,,   375
And took both ear and *e* ;   ,,   383
And kind the woman's *e's* and innocent,   ,,   393
' While thus he spake, his *e*, dwelling on mine,   ,,   485
On either hand, as far as *e* could see,   ,,   498
Which never *e's* on earth again shall see.   ,,   532
like bright *e's* of familiar friends,   ,,   688
his *e's*, An out-door sign of all the warmth   ,,   703
' A welfare in thine *e* reproves Our fear   ,,   726
I saw it ; ' and the tears were in his *e's*.   ,,   759
A dying fire of madness in his *e's*.   ,,   768
angels, awful shapes, and wings and *e's*.   ,,   848
by mine *e's* and by mine ears I swear,   ,,   864
light that strikes his *e* is not light,   ,,   913
So that his *e's* were dazzled looking at it.   *Pelleas and E.* 36
and his *e's* closed. And since he loved all maidens,   ,,   39
For large her violet *e's* look'd,   ,,   71
for those large *e's*, the haunts of scorn,   ,,   75
while they rode, the meaning in his *e's*,   ,,   109
green wood-ways, and *e's* among the leaves ;   ,,   139
in mid-banquet measuring with his *e's*   ,,   150
tower fill'd with *e's* Up to the summit,   ,,   166
glory fired her face ; her *e* Sparkled,   ,,   172
but felt his *e's* Harder and drier   ,,   506

Eye (s) *(continued)*   hard his *e's* ; harder his heart
Seem'd,   *Peleas and E.* 512
Rolling his *e's*, a moment stood, then spake :   ,,   581
Pelleas lifted up an *e* so fierce She quail'd ;   ,,   601
nose Bridge-broken, one *e* out, and one hand off,   *Last Tournament* 59
He look'd but once, and vail'd his *e's*   ,,   150
Come—let us gladden their sad *e's*,   ,,   222
Made dull his inner, keen his outer *e*   ,,   366
The black-blue Irish hair and Irish *e's*   ,,   404
steel-blue *e's*, The golden beard that clothed   ,,   667
Lay couchant with his *e's* upon the throne,   *Guinevere* 11
Modred still in green, all ear and *e*,   ,,   24
Heart-hiding smile, and gray persistent *e* :   ,,   64
Hands in hands, and *e* to *e*.   ,,   100
Makes wicked lightnings of her *e's*,   ,,   520
her hand Grasp'd, made her vail her *e's* :   ,,   663
richer in His *e's* Who ransom'd us,   ,,   684
these *e's* of men are dense and dim,   *Pass. of Arthur* 19
both his *e's* were dazzled as he stood,   ,,   227
might have pleased the *e's* of many men.   ,,   259
Laid widow'd of the power in his *e*   ,,   290
Valuing the giddy pleasure of the *e's*.   ,,   296
' Now see I by thine *e's* that this is done.   ,,   317
looking wistfully with wide blue *e's* As in a picture.   ,,   337
charged Before the *e's* of ladies and of kings.   ,,   393
shall I hide my forehead and my *e's* ?   ,,   396
Straining his *e's* beneath an arch of hand,   ,,   464
I come, great Mistress of the ear and *e* :   *Lover's Tale i* 22
tho' there beat a heart in either *e* ;   ,,   34
Leapt like a passing thought across her *e's* ;   ,,   70
Oh, such dark *e's* ! a single glance of them   ,,   75
a common light of *e's* Was on us as we lay :   ,,   236
Shading his *e's* till all the fiery cloud,   ,,   306
down to sea, and far as *e* could ken,   ,,   336
light methought broke from her dark, dark *e's*,   ,,   368
endured in presence of His *e's* To indue his lustre ;   ,,   423
our *e's* met : hers were bright,   ,,   441
gaze upon thee till their *e's* are dim   ,,   491
still I kept my *e's* upon the sky.   ,,   572
Of *e's* too weak to look upon the light ;   ,,   614
Leaning its roses on my faded *e's*.   ,,   621
And what it has for *e's* as close to mine   ,,   651
how her choice did leap forth from his *e's* !   ,,   657
e's—I saw the moonlight glitter on their tears—   ,,   696
And could I look upon her tearful *e's* ?   ,,   735
Fixing my *e's* on those three cypress-cones   *ii* 38
Flash'd thro' my *e's* into my innermost brain,   ,,   95
Like morning from her *e's*—her eloquent *e's*,   ,,   144
All unawares before his half-shut *e's*   ,,   153
so those fair *e's* Shone on my darkness,   ,,   157
and the *e* Was riveted and charm-bound,   ,,   187
over my dim *e's*, And parted lips which drank her breath,   ,,   203
—her *e's* And cheeks as bright as when she climb'd   *iii* 46
she rais'd an *e* that ask'd ' Where ? '   *iv* 94
dark *e's* of hers—Oh ! such dark *e's* ! and not her *e's* alone,   ,,   165
Wonder'd at some strange light in Julian's *e's*   ,,   205
Have jested also, but for Julian's *e's*,   ,,   223
breast Hard-heaving, and her *e's* upon her feet,   ,,   308
Dazed or amazed, nor *e's* of men ;   ,,   311
She shook, and cast her *e's* down,   ,,   329
and begun to darken my *e's*.   *Rizpah* 16
sun as danced in 'er pratty blue *e* ;   *North. Cobbler* 50
sweet *e's* frown : the lips Seem but a gash.   *Sisters (E. and E.)* 106
the sweet dwelling of her *e's* Upon me   ,,   165
her own true *e's* Are traitors to her ;   ,,   284
wi' hoffens a drop in 'is *e*.   *Village Wife* 34
Sa I han't clapt *e's* on 'im yit,   ,,   123
and the smile, and the comforting *e*—   *In the Child.'' Hosp.* 12
and his *e's* were sweet,   *V. of Maeldune* 117
you that were *e's* and light to the King   *To Prin. F. of H.* 1
and woke, These *e's*, now dull, but then so keen   *Tiresias* 4
And from her virgin breast, and virgin *e's*   ,,   46
Menœceus, thou hast *e's*, and I can hear   ,,   90
These eyeless *e's*, that cannot see thine own,   ,,   108
these *e's* will find The men I knew,   ,,   175

F

Face *(continued)* O silent *f's* of the Great and Wise, *Palace of Art* 195
I shall look upon your *f*; *May Queen, N. Y's. E.* 38
round about the keel with *f's* pale, Dark *f's* pale
against that rosy flame, *Lotos-Eaters* 25
With those old *f's* of our infancy ,, *C. S.* 66
turning on my *f* The star-like sorrows *D. of F. Women* 90
Myself for such a *f* had boldly died,' ,, 98
My father held his hand upon his *f*; ,, 107
Here her *f* Glow'd, as I look'd at her. ,, 239
His *f* is growing sharp and thin. *D. of the O. Year* 46
a new *f* at the door, my friend, A new *f* at the door. ,, 53
Imitates God, and turns her *f* To every land *On a Mourner* 2
reveal'd The fullness of her *f*— *Of old sat Freedom* 12
Lift up thy rocky *f*, *England and Amer.* 12
all his *f* was white And colourless, *M. d'Arthur* 212
Among new men, strange *f's*, other minds.' ,, 238
If thou should'st never see my *f* again, ,, 246
Then he turn'd His *f* and pass'd— *Dora* 151
and Dora hid her *f* By Mary. ,, 156
came again together on the king With heated *f's*; *Audley Court* 37
hid his *f* From all men, *Walk. to the Mail* 20
A pretty *f* is well, and this is well, *Edwin Morris* 45
saw Their *f's* grow between me and my book ; *St. S. Stylites* 176
I know thy glittering *f*. ,, 205
before my *f* I see the moulder'd Abbey-walls, *Talking Oak* 2
seen some score of those Fresh *f's*, ,, 50
Turn your *f*, Nor look with that too-earnest eye— *Day-Dm., Pro.* 17
Grave *f's* gather'd in a ring. ,, *Sleep. P.* 38
And yawn'd, and rubb'd his *f*, and spoke, ,, *Revival* 19
'There I put my *f* in the grass— *Edward Gray* 21
the dusty crypt Of darken'd forms and *f's*. *Will Water.* 184
Were their *f's* grim. *The Captain* 54
colour flushes Her sweet *f* from brow to chin: *L. of Burleigh* 62
Her *f* was evermore unseen, *The Voyage* 61
So sweet a *f*, such angel grace, *Beggar Maid* 13
Panted hand-in-hand with *f's* pale, *Vision of Sin* 19
Hair, and eyes, and limbs, and *f's*, ,, 39
Every *f*, however full, Padded round ,, 176
His large gray eyes and weather-beaten *f* *Enoch Arden* 70
And in their eyes and *f's* read his doom ; Then, as
their *f's* drew together, groan'd, ,, 73
his *f*, Rough-redden'd with a thousand winter gales, ,, 94
I shall look upon your *f* no more.' ,, 212
Spy out my *f*, and laugh at all your fears.' ,, 216
Cared not to look on any human *f*, ,, 282
'I cannot look you in the *f* I seem so foolish ,, 315
And dwelt a moment on his kindly *f*, ,, 326
but her *f* had fall'n upon her hands; ,, 391
stood once more before her *f*, Claiming her promise. ,, 457
Philip's rosy *f* contracting grew Careworn and wan; ,, 486
He could not see, the kindly human *f*, ,, 581
Enoch yearn'd to see her *f* again; 'If I might look
on her sweet *f* again ,, 717
my dead *f* would vex her after-life. ,, 891
With half a score of swarthy *f's* came. *Aylmer's Field* 191
a hoary *f* Meet for the reverence of the hearth, ,, 332
her sweet *f* and faith Held him from that: ,, 392
mixt Upon their *f's*, as they kiss'd each other ,, 430
f to *f* With twenty months of silence, ,, 566
careless of the household *f's* near, ,, 575
His *f* magnetic to the hand from which ,, 626
the wife, who watch'd his *f*, Paled ,, 731
he veil'd His *f* with the other, ,, 809
pendent hands, and narrow meagre *f* ,, 813
The rabbit fondles his own harmless *f*, ,, 851
sitting all alone, his *f* Would darken, *Sea Dreams* 12
altho' his fire is on my *f* Blinding, *Lucretius* 144
sown With happy *f's* and with holiday. *Princess, Pro.* 56
(A little sense of wrong had touch'd her *f* ,, 219
prince I was, blue-eyed, and fair in *f*, ,, *i* 1
I saw my father's *f* Grow long and troubled ,, 58
keep your hoods about the *f*; ,, *ii* 358
Push'd her flat hand against his *f* ,, 366
She sent for Blanche to accuse her *f* to *f*; ,, *iv* 239
And falling on my *f* was caught and known. ,, 270

Face *(continued)* Half-drooping from her, turn'd her *f*, *Princess, iv.* 368
Stared in her eyes, and chalk'd her *f*, ,, 377
I know Your *f's* there in the crowd— ,, 510
Bent their broad *f's* toward us and address'd ,, 551
so from her *f* They push'd us, down the steps, ,, 554
Thy *f* across his fancy comes, ,, 579
And every *f* she look'd on justify it) ,, *v* 134
therefore I set my *f* Against all men, ,, 388
Took the face-cloth from the *f*; ,, *vi* 11
The haggard father's *f* and reverend beard ,, 103
then once more she look'd at my pale *f*: ,, 115
And turn'd each *f* her way: ,, 144
when she learnt his *f*, Remembering his ill-omen'd song, ,, 158
thro' the parted silks the tender *f* Peep'd, ,, *vii* 60
at which her *f* A little flush'd, ,, 80
Hortensia pleading : angry was her *f*. ,, 132
all for languor and self-pity ran Mine down my *f*, ,, 140
Pale was the perfect *f*; ,, 224
His dear little *f* was troubled, *Grandmother* 65
Before the stony *f* of Time, *Lit. Squabbles* 3
His *f* was ruddy, his hair was gold, *The Victim* 35
Till the *f* of Bel be brighten'd, *Boädicea* 16
they hide their *f's*, miserable in ignominy ! ,, 51
are you flying over her sweet little *f*? *Window, On the Hill* 13
Ay or no, if ask'd to her *f*? ,, *Letter* 9
Whom we, that have not seen thy *f*, *In Mem., Pro.* 2
Roves from the living brother's *f*, ,, *xxxii* 7
And tears are on the mother's *f*, ,, *xl* 10
I strive to paint The *f* I know; ,, *lxx* 3
And shoals of pucker'd *f's* drive; ,, 10
Looks thy fair *f* and makes it still. ,, 16
As sometimes in a dead man's *f*, ,, *lxxiv* 1
And in a moment set thy *f*, ,, *lxxvi* 2
For changes wrought on form and *f*; ,, *lxxxii* 2
I see their unborn *f's* shine ,, *lxxxiv* 19
saw The God within him light his *f*, ,, *lxxxvii* 36
swims The reflex of a human *f*. ,, *cviii* 12
And find his comfort in thy *f*; ,, *cix* 20
Not all regret: the *f* will shine Upon me, ,, *cxvi* 9
Many a merry *f* Salutes them— ,, *Con.* 66
And hearts are warm'd and *f's* bloom, ,, 82
make my heart as a millstone, set my *f* as a flint, *Maud I i* 31
But a cold and clear-cut *f*, ,, *ii* 3
Cold and clear-cut *f*, why come you so cruelly meek, ,, *iii* 1
Passionless, pale, cold *f*, star-sweet ,, 4
pride flash'd over her beautiful *f*. ,, *iv* 16
Maud with her exquisite *f*, ,, *v* 12
A *f* of tenderness might be feign'd, ,, *vi* 52
A bought commission, a waxen *f*, ,, *x* 30
His *f*, as I grant, in spite of spite, ,, *xiii* 8
Last year, I caught a glimpse of his *f*, ,, 27
And he struck me, madman, over the *f*, ,, *II i* 18
And the *f's* that one meets, ,, *iv* 93
the *f* of night is fair on the dewy downs, ,, *III vi* 5
One among many, tho' his *f* was bare. *Com. of Arthur* 54
find nor *f* nor bearing, limbs nor voice, ,, 71
And ere it left their *f's*, ,, 272
gazing on him, tall, with bright Sweet *f's*, ,, 279
her *f* Wellnigh was hidden in the minster ,, 288
And sad was Arthur's *f* Taking it, ,, 305
Fixing full eyes of question on her *f*, ,, 312
Southward they set their *f's* Down the slope city, *Gareth and L.* 182
on thro' silent *f's* rode Down the slope city, ,, 734
not once dare to look him in the *f*.' ,, 782
And cipher *f* of rounded foolishness, ,, 1039
Slab after slab, their *f's* forward all, ,, 1206
'Follow the *f's*, and we find it. ,, 1210
nor rough *f*, or voice, Brute bulk of limb, ,, 1329
'God wot, I never look'd upon the *f*, ,, 1333
Issued the bright *f* of a blooming boy ,, 1408
the sweet *f* of her Whom he loves most, *Marr. of Geraint* 122
knight Had vizor up, and show'd a youthful *f*, ,, 189
Guinevere, not mindful of his *f*, ,, 191
kept her off and gazed upon her *f*, ,, 519
Across the *f* of Enid hearing her ; ,, 524

Fail (*continued*) Could make thee somewhat blench or *f*,   *In Mem. lxii* 2
Thy spirit should *f* from off the globe;   ,, *lxxxiv* 36
that keeps A thousand pulses dancing, *f*.   ,, *cxxv* 16
shall I shriek if a Hungary *f*?   *Maud I iv* 46
solid ground Not *f* beneath my feet   ,, *xi* 2
fill up the gap where force might *f*   *Gareth and L.* 1352
Like him who tries the bridge he fears may *f*,   *Geraint and E.* 303
they *f* to see This fair wife-worship   *Balin and Balan* 359
fine plots may *f*, Tho' harlots paint   *Merlin and V.* 820
if ye *f*, Give ye the slave mine order   *Pelleas and E.* 269
spouting from a cliff *F*'s in mid air,   *Guinevere* 609
for a man may *f* in duty twice,   *Pass. of Arthur* 297
That saved her many times, not *f*—   *To the Queen ii* 62
scales Their headlong passes, but his footstep *f*'s,   *Montenegro* 5
Pray God our greatness may not *f*   *Hands all Round* 31
if you shall *f* to understand What England is,   *The Fleet* 1
should those *f*, that hold the helm,   *Prog. of Spring* 100
if I *f* To conjure and concentrate   *Romney's R.* 6
When fine Philosophies would *f*,   *Akbar's Dream* 140
And let not Reason *f* me,   *Doubt and Prayer* 5
Fail'd sweet incense rose and never *f*,   *Palace of Art* 45
her heart *f* her; and the reapers reap'd,   *Dora* 78
She *f* and sadden'd knowing it;   *Enoch Arden* 257
all her force *F* her; and sighing,   ,, 375
thought and nature *f* a little,   ,, 792
As having *f* in duty to him,   *Lucretius* 278
the year in which our olives *f*.   *Princess i* 125
none to trust Since our arms *f*—   ,, *v* 427
Old studies *f*: seldom she spoke: ,, *vii* 31
she had *f* In sweet humility; had *f* in all;   ,, 228
for a vast speculation had *f*,   *Maud I i* 9
either *f* to make the kingdom one.   *Com. of Arthur* 15
ever *f* to draw The quiet night into her blood,   *Marr. of Geraint* 531
f of late To send his tribute;   *Balin and Balan* 3
But on all those who tried and *f*,   *Merlin and V.* 590
many tried and *f*, because the charm   ,, 595
I well believe she tempted them and *f*,   ,, 819
f to find him, tho' I rode all round   *Lancelot and E.* 531
yet thee She *f* to bind, tho' being,   ,, 1385
This Holy Thing, *f* from my side, nor come Cover'd,   *Holy Grail* 470
'Hath Gawain *f* in any quest of thine?   ,, 859
the great heart of knighthood in thee *f*   *Pelleas and E.* 596
They *f* to trace him thro' the flesh and blood   *Last Tournament* 686
the purport of my throne hath *f*,   *Pass. of Arthur* 160
strove to disengage myself, but *f*, Being so feeble: *Lover's Tale i* 692
But ever I *f* to please him,   *The Wreck* 28
Amy loved me, Amy *f* me,   *Locksley H., Sixty* 19
Britain *f*; and never more,   *Open I. and C. Exhib.* 22
I *f* To send my life thro' olive-yard   *Demeter and P.* 109
All her splendour *f* To lure those eyes   *St. Telemachus* 35
wild horse, anger, plunged To fling me, and *f*.   *Akbar's Dream* 119
Failing (*part.*) The strong limbs *f*;   *All Things will Die* 32
F to give the bitter of the sweet,   *D. of F. Women* 286
utterance *f* her, She whirl'd them on to me,   *Princess iv* 395
you *f*, I abide What end soever: ,, *v* 405
When the mind is *f*!   *Forlorn* 36
Failing (s) that unnoticed *f* in herself,   *Geraint and E.* 47
Fain how *f* was I To dream thy cause embraced   *Princess vi* 199
'Sir,—and, good faith, I *f* had added—Knight,   *Gareth and L.* 1162
'*F* would I still be loyal to the Queen.'   *Balin and Balan* 254
and *f*, For hate and loathing, would have past   ,, 387
I *f* would know what manner of men they be.'   ,, 574
Balin, Balin, I that *f* had died To save thy life,   ,, 599
f Have all men true and leal,   *Merlin and V.* 793
Lionel, who *f* had risen, but fell again,   *Lover's Tale iv* 361
Would *f* that he were dead;   *Ancient Sage* 126
one of those I *f* would meet again,   *Pro. to Gen. Hamley* 22
Faint (*adj.*) Bramble roses, *f* and pale,   *A Dirge* 30
Wherefore those *f* smiles of thine,   *Adeline* 21
Wherefore that *f* smile of thine,   ,, 38
Thou *f* smiler, Adeline?   ,, 48
And *f*, rainy lights are seen,   *Margaret* 60
by the meadow-trenches blow the *f* sweet
   cuckoo-flowers;   *May Queen* 30
these twelve books of mine Were *f* Homeric echoes,   *The Epic* 39

Faint (*adj.*) (*continued*) To whom replied King Arthur, *f*
   and pale: *M. d'Arthur* 72
with slow steps, With slow, *f* steps,   *St. S. Stylites* 183
F shadows, vapours lightly curl'd, *F* murmurs
   from the meadows come,   *Day-Dm., Sleep. P.* 5
sketches rude and *f*.   *Aylmer's Field* 100
I on her Fixt my *f* eyes,   *Princess vii* 144
F heart never won—   *Window, Answer* 9
The *f* horizons, all the bounds of earth,   *Far-far-away* 14
F she grew, and ever fainter,   *L. of Burleigh* 81
The voice grew *f*: there came a further change: *Vision of Sin* 207
F as a figure seen in early dawn   *Enoch Arden* 357
the hues are *f* And mix with hollow masks   *In Mem. lxx* 3
This haunting whisper makes me *f*,   ,, *lxxxi* 7
let her eat; the damsel is so *f*.'   *Geraint and E.* 206
chafing his *f* hands, and calling to him;   ,, 585
seem'd to change, and grow *F* and far-off.   *Balin and Balan* 218
F in the low dark hall of banquet: ,, 343
dying brother cast himself Dying; and *he* lifted *f* eyes;   ,, 594
I was *f* to swooning, and you lay Foot-gilt   *Merlin and V.* 281
all too *f* and sick am I For anger: *Lancelot and E.* 1086
To whom replied King Arthur, *f* and pale: *Pass. of Arthur* 240
there came, but *f* As from beyond the limit of the world,   ,, 457
the heart—it beat: *F*—but it beat: *Lover's Tale iv* 81
faint-stomach'd! *f* as I am,   *Sir J. Oldcastle* 192
F as a climate-changing bird that flies   *Demeter and P.* 1
are *f* And pale in Alla's eyes,   *Akbar's Dream* 10
Faint (*verb*) I *f*, I fall. Men say that thou   *Supp. Confessions* 2
I *f* in this obscurity, (repeat)   *Ode to Memory* 6, 44, 123
My very heart *f*'s and my whole soul grieves   *A spirit haunts* 16
flowers would *f* at your cruel cheer.   *Poet's Mind* 15
'Cry, *f* not: either Truth is born   *Two Voices* 181
'Cry, *f* not, climb: the summits slope   ,, 184
F's like a dazzled morning moon.   *Fatima* 28
and the heart *F*'s, faded by its heat.   *D. of F. Women* 288
They *f* on hill or field or river: *Princess iv* 14
Beginning to *f* in the light that she loves   *Maud I xxii* 9
To *f* in the light of the sun she loves, To *f* in his
   light, and to die.   ,, 11
my whole soul languishes And *f*'s,   *Lover's Tale i* 268
at his feet I seem'd to *f* and fall,   ,, *ii* 96
Faint-blue A *f-b* ridge upon the right,   *Mariana in the S.* 5
Fainted at the clamouring of her enemy *f*   *Boädicea* 82
sick with love, *F* at intervals,   *Lover's Tale i* 546
Fainter Wears all day a *f* tone.   *The Owl ii* 7
She replies, in accents, *f*,   *L. of Burleigh* 5
Faint she grew and ever *f*,   ,, 81
F by day, but always in the night Blood-red,   *Holy Grail* 472
f onward, like wild birds that change   *Pass. of Arthur* 38
Our voices were thinner and *f*   *V. of Maeldune* 99
slower and *f*, Old and weary,   *Merlin and the G.* 99
Is it turning a *f* red?   *The Dawn* 22
Faintest *f* sunlights flee About his shadowy sides: *The Kraken* 4
The smallest rock far on the *f* hill,   *Com. of Arthur* 99
Has push'd toward our *f* sun   *To Ulysses* 23
Faint-heart'd *F-h*? tut!—faint-stomach'd!   *Sir J. Oldcastle* 192
Fainting *F* flowers, faded bowers,   *Sisters (E. and E.)* 11
Faintlier Then laugh'd again, but *f*,   *Guinevere* 58
savour of thy kitchen came upon me A little *f*:   *Gareth and L.* 994
Faintly Tho' *f*, merrily—far and far away—   *Enoch Arden* 614
F smiling Adeline,   *Adeline* 2
Faintly-flush'd How *f-f*, how phantom-fair,   *The Daisy* 65
Faintly-shadow'd as he traced a *f-s* track,   *Lancelot and E.* 165
Faintly-venom'd smiles, and *f-v* points Of slander,   *Merlin and V.* 172
Faint-stomach'd '*f-s*! faint as I am,   *Sir J. Oldcastle* 192
Fair (*adj., s., adv.*) (*See also* **Full-fair, Phantom-fair, Silver-fair,**
   Starry-fair) But beyond expression *f*   *Adeline* 5
gleaming rind ingrav'n, 'For the most *f*,'   *Œnone* 73
Thy mortal eyes are frail to judge of *f*,   ,, 158
Fairest—why fairest wife? am I not *f*?   ,, 196
Methinks I must be *f*, for yesterday,   ,, 198
uninvited came Into the *f* Peleïan banquet-hall,   ,, 225
O the Earl was *f* to see! (repeat)   *The Sisters* 6, 12, 18,
   24, 30, 36
divinely tall, And most divinely *f*.   *D. of F. Women* 88

Fair (adj., s., adv.) *(continued)*   who deem this maid

Might wear as *f* a jewel	*Lancelot and E.* 240
'Save your great self, *f* lord;'	,, 320
'*F* lord, whose name I know not—	,, 360
'*F* lady, since I never yet have worn	,, 363
Who parted with his own to *f* Elaine:	,, 381
cells and chambers: all were *f* and dry;	,, 407
Gawain, surnamed The Courteous, *f* and strong,	,, 555
And stay'd; and cast his eyes on *f* Elaine:	,, 640
And lifted her *f* face and moved away:	,, 682
'Nay, for near you, *f* lord, I am at rest.'	,, 833
a faith once *f* Was richer than these diamonds—	,, 1228
F lord, as would have help'd her from her death.'	,, 1311
Delicately pure and marvellously *f*,	,, 1369
'*F* she was, my King, Pure,	,, 1374
Farewell too—now at last—Farewell, *f* lily.	,, 1397
kiss'd me saying, 'Thou art *f*, my child,	,, 1409
and *f* the house whereby she sat,	*Holy Grail* 392
disarm'd By maidens each as *f* as any flower!	,, 576
till one *f* morn, I walking to and fro beside a stream	,, 591
For *f* thou art and pure as Guinevere,	*Pelleas and E.* 44
have the Heavens but given thee a *f* face,	,, 101
'Ay,' thought Gawain, 'and you be *f* enow:	,, 388
A rose, one rose, and this was wondrous *f*,	,, 401
Let be thy *f* Queen's fantasy.	*Last Tournament* 197
Be happy in thy *f* Queen as I in mine.'	,, 204
'*F* damsels, each to him who worships each	,, 207
In that *f* Order of my Table Round,	*Guinevere* 463
And be the *f* beginning of a time.	,, 466
And drawing foul ensample from *f* names,	,, 490
And so thou lean on our *f* father Christ,	,, 562
What might I not have made of thy *f* world,	,, 655
Or else as if the world were wholly *f*,	*Pass. of Arthur* 18
f with orchard-lawns And bowery hollows	,, 430
Sounds, as if some *f* city were one voice	,, 460
Ye cannot shape Fancy so *f* as is this memory.	*Lover's Tale i* 548
F speech was his and delicate of phrase,	,, 719
Above some *f* metropolis, earth-shock'd,—	,, *ii* 62
Oftentimes The vision has *f* prelude,	,, 124
so those *f* eyes Shone on my darkness,	,, 157
rare or *f* Was brought before the guest:	,, *iv* 203
F speech was his, and delicate of phrase.	,, 273
Making fresh and *f* All the bowers and the flowers,	*Sisters (E. and E.)* 9
the great things of Nature and the *f*,	,, 222
what is *f* without Is often as foul within.'	*Dead Prophet* 67
all that is filthy with all that is *f*?	*Vastness* 32
one was *f*, And one was dark,	*The Ring* 160
WHO would be A mermaid *f*,	*The Mermaid* 2
I would be a mermaid *f*;	,, 9
From Ind to Ind, but in *f* daylight woke,	*Buonaparte* 4
Not these alone, but every landscape *f*,	*Palace of Art* 89
In some *f* space of sloping greens Lay,	,, 106
but every legend *f* Which the supreme Caucasian mind	,, 126
Above, the *f* hall-ceiling stately-set	,, 141
'O all things *f* to sate my various eyes!	,, 193
none so *f* as little Alice in all the land they say,	*May Queen* 7
With that *f* child betwixt them born.	*On a Mourner* 25
That her *f* form may stand and shine,	*Of old sat Freedom* 21
happy, *f* with orchard-lawns And bowery hollows	*M. d'Arthur* 262
by those *f* fingers cull'd,	*Gardener's D.* 150
Pontius and Iscariot by my side Show'd like *f* seraphs.	*St. S. Stylites* 169
Beyond the *f* green field and eastern sea.	*Love and Duty* 101
the *f* new forms, That float about the threshold	*Golden Year* 15
The maid-of-honour blooming *f*;	*Day-Dm., Sleep. P.* 28
He trusts to light on something *f*;	*Arrival* 20
So keep I *f* thro' faith and prayer A virgin heart	*Sir Galahad* 23
With *f* horizons bound:	*Will Water.* 66
Nor for my lands so broad and *f*;	*Lady Clare* 10
Lord of Burleigh, *f* and free,	*L. of Burleigh* 58
Three *f* children first she bore him,	,, 87
For one *f* Vision ever fled Down the waste waters	*The Voyage* 57
Like Virtue firm, like Knowledge *f*,	,, 68
Will bring *f* weather yet to all of us.	*Enoch Arden* 191

Fair (adj., s., adv.) *(continued)*   Thro' many a *f* sea-circle,

day by day,	*Enoch Arden* 542
'Then I fixt My wistful eyes on two *f* images,	*Sea Dreams* 240
The marvel of that *f* new nature—	*Columbus* 79
It was all of it *f* as life, it was all of it quiet as death,	*V. of Maeldune* 20
F Florence honouring thy nativity,	*To Dante* 3
And earth as *f* in hue!	*Ancient Sage* 24
'Earth is *f*' When all is dark as night.'	,, 169
And show us that the world is wholly *f*.	,, 182
O THOU in summers gone,	*Freedom* 1
So *f* in southern sunshine bathed,	,, 5
Our own *f* isle, the lord of every sea—	*The Fleet* 7
as honouring your *f* fame Of Statesman,	*To Marq. of Dufferin* 14
Hail the *f* Ceremonial Of this year	*On Jub. Q. Victoria* 23
F things are slow to fade away,	*To Prof. Jebb* 1
I loved you first when young and *f*,	*Happy* 29
F Spring slides hither o'er the Southern sea,	*Prog. of Spring* 2
a breath From some *f* dawn beyond the doors of death	*Far—far—away* 11
f mothers they Dying in childbirth of dead sons.	*Akbar's Dream* 11
From each *f* plant the blossom choicest-grown	,, 22
palm Call to the cypress 'I alone am *f*'?	,, 38
F garments, plain or rich, and fitting close	,, 131
loosen, stone from stone, All my *f* work;	,, 189
Fair (s) (*See also* **Faäir**) the *f* Was holden at the town;	*Talking Oak* 101
Fairer guerdon could not alter me To *f*.	*Œnone* 154
Emilia, *f* than all else but thou, For thou art *f* than all else that is.	*Audley Court* 66
F his talk, a tongue that ruled the hour,	*Aylmer's Field* 194
F than Rachel by the palmy well, *F* than Ruth among the fields of corn,	,, 679
And *f* she, but ah how soon to die!	*Requiescat* 5
Stiller, not *f* than mine.	*Maud II v* 71
F than aught in the world beside,	,, 73
She is not *f* in new clothes than old.	*Marr. of Geraint* 722
O as much *f*—as a faith once fair	*Lancelot and E.* 1228
To greet their *f* sisters of the East.	*Gardener's D.* 188
Where *f* fruit of Love may rest Some happy future day.	*Talking Oak* 251
there's the *f* chance:	*Princess v* 460
F thy fate than mine, if life's best end	*Tiresias* 130
She that finds a winter sunset *f* than a morn of Spring	*Locksley H., Sixty* 22
Fairest That all which thou hast drawn of *f*	*Ode to Memory* 89
(Tho' all her *f* forms are types of thee,	*Isabel* 39
claiming each This meed of *f*.	*Œnone* 87
So shalt thou find me *f*.	,, 155
I promise thee The *f* and most loving wife in Greece,'	,, 187
F—why *f* wife? am I not fair?	,, 196
She was the *f* in the face:	*The Sisters* 1
rose the tallest of them all And *f*,	*M. d'Arthur* 208
beardless apple-arbiter Decided *f*.	*Lucretius* 92
her that was *f* under heaven,	*Com. of Arthur* 86
The prize of beauty for the *f* there,	*Marr. of Geraint* 485
'Advance and take, as *f* of the fair,	,, 553
For tho' ye won the prize of *f* fair, And tho' I heard him call you *f* fair,	,, 719
f and the best Of ladies living gave me	*Balin and Balan* 339
I, and all, As *f*, best and purest,	,, 350
'*F* I grant her: I have seen;	,, 356
rose the tallest of them all And *f*,	*Pass. of Arthur* 376
f of their evening stars.	*Locksley H., Sixty* 188
f flesh at last is filth on which the worm will feast;	*Happy* 30
Fairest-spoken That art the *f-s* tree	*Talking Oak* 263
Fair-fronted *F-f* Truth shall droop not now	*Clear-headed friend* 12
Fair-hair'd a loftier Annie Lee, *F-h* and tall,	*Enoch Arden* 749
F-h and redder than a windy morn;	*Princess, Con.* 91
came a *f-h* youth, that in his hand Bare	*Geraint and E.* 201
when the *f-h* youth came by him, said,	,, 205
Fair-hands Sir Fine-face, Sir *F-h*?	*Gareth and L.* 475
Fairily Made so *f* well With delicate spire	*Maud II ii* 5
Fairily-delicate *F-d* palaces shine	*The Islet* 18
Fair-maid many welcomes, February *f-m*, (repeat)	*The Snowdrop* 2, 10
Fairness To doubt her *f* were to want an eye,	*Lancelot and E.* 1376

Fairplay ask'd but space and *f* for her scheme;	*Princess v* 282
Fair-spoken stranger that hath been To thee *f-s* ?'	*Gareth and L.* 284
Fairy (adj.) AIRY, *f* Lilian, Flitting, *f* Lilian,	*Lilian* 1
Like a rose-leaf I will crush thee, F Lilian,	,, 30
A *f* shield your Genius made	*Margaret* 41
With whitest honey in *f* gardens cull'd—	*Eleänore* 26
And woke her with a lay from *f* land.	*Caress'd or chidden* 8
'Tis the *f* Lady of Shalott.'	*L. of Shalott i* 35
heavens between their *f* fleeces pale	*Gardener's D.* 261
With the *f* tales of science,	*Locksley Hall* 12
And bring the fated *f* Prince.	*Day-Dm., Sleep P.* 56
A *f* Prince, with joyful eyes,	,, *Arrival* 7
As wild as aught of *f* lore;	,, *L'Envoi* 12
From havens hid in *f* bowers,	*The Voyage* 54
many a *f* foreland set With willow-weed	*The Brook* 45
Show'd her the *f* footings on the grass, The little dells of cowslip, *f* palms, The petty marestail forest, *f* pines,	*Aylmer's Field* 90
What look'd a flight of *f* arrows aim'd	,, 94
And dropt a *f* parachute and past:	*Princess, Pro.* 76
golden foot or a *f* horn Thro' his dim water-world?	*Maud II ii* 19
Here is a city of Enchanters, built By *f* Kings.'	*Gareth and L.* 200
whether this be built By magic, and by *f* Kings and Queens?	,, 248
a F King And F Queens have built the city,	,, 258
Shrunk like a *f* changeling lay the mage;	*Com. of Arthur* 363
Until they vanish'd by the *f* well That laughs at iron—	*Merlin and V.* 428
sharp breaths of anger puff'd Her *f* nostril out;	,, 849
Look how she sleeps—the F Queen, so fair!	*Lancelot and E.* 1255
we chanted the songs of the Bards and the glories of *f* kings;	*V. of Maeldune* 90
The *f* fancies range,	*Early Spring* 39
but now Your *f* Prince has found you,	*The Ring* 69
And you were then a lover's *f* dream,	*To Mary Boyle* 43
Fairy (s) The oriental *f* brought,	*Eleänore* 14
'For as to *fairies*, that will flit	*Talking Oak* 89
dancing of *Fairies* In desolate hollows,	*Merlin and the G.* 41
Fairy-circle flickering *f-c* wheel'd and broke	*Guinevere* 257
Fairy-fine Fabric rough, or *f-f*,	*Ode Inter. Exhib.* 18
Fairyland (*See also* **Fairy**) But only changeling out of F,	*Gareth and L.* 203
if the King be King at all, or come From F ;	,, 247
Or come to give the King to F?	*Lancelot and E.* 1257
Fairy-tale (*See also* **Fairy**) told her *f-t's*, Show'd her the fairy	*Aylmer's Field* 89
Faith (*See also* **Catholic Faith**) left to me, but Thou, And *f* in Thee?	*Supp. Confessions* 19
How sweet to have a common *f*!	,, 33
that knew The beauty and repose of *f*,	,, 75
Great in *f*, and strong Against the grief	,, 91
And simple *f* than Norman blood.	*L. C. V. de Vere* 56
F from tracts no feet have trod,	*On a Mourner* 29
settled down Upon the general decay of *f*	*The Epic* 18
run My *f* beyond my practice into his :	*Edwin Morris* 54
we closed, we kiss'd, swore *f*,	,, 114
with a larger *f* appeal'd Than Papist unto Saint.	*Talking Oak* 15
Wait: my *f* is large in Time,	*Love and Duty* 25
So keep I fair thro' *f* and prayer	*Sir Galahad* 23
I will know If there be any *f* in man.' 'Nay now, what *f*?' said Alice the nurse,	*Lady Clare* 44
His resolve Upbore him, and firm *f*,	*Enoch Arden* 800
her sweet face and *f* Held him from that:	*Aylmer's Field* 392
Have *f*, have *f*! We live by *f*,' said he;	*Sea Dreams* 157
why kept ye not your *f*?	*Princess v* 77
their sinless *f*, A maiden moon that sparkles	,, 185
f in womankind Beats with his blood,	,, *vii* 328
Some sense of duty, something of a *f*,	,, *Con.* 54
The sport half-science, fill me with a *f*,	,, 76
honouring your sweet *f* in him,	*A Dedication* 5
By *f*, and *f* alone, embrace,	*In Mem., Pro.* 3
We have but *f*: we cannot know;	,, 21
Whose *f* has centre everywhere,	,, *xxxiii* 3
Her *f* thro' form is pure as thine,	,, 9
This *f* has many a purer priest,	,, *xxxvii* 3

Faith (*continued*) Is *f* as vague as all unsweet:	*In. Mem. xlvii* 5
Be near me when my *f* is dry,	,, *l* 9
Shall love be blamed for want of *f*?	,, *li* 10
I stretch lame hands of *f*, and grope,	,, *lv* 17
May breed with him, can fright my *f*.	,, *lxxxii* 4
The *f*, the vigour, bold to dwell	,, *xcv* 29
Perplext in *f*, but pure in deeds,	,, *xcvi* 9
There lives more *f* in honest doubt,	,, 11
To find a stronger *f* his own ;	,, 17
to him she sings Of early *f* and plighted vows ;	,, *xcvii* 30
Her *f* is fixt and cannot move,	,, 33
What profit lies in barren *f*	,, *cviii* 5
What is she, cut from love and *f*,	,, *cxiv* 11
Our dearest *f* ; our ghastliest doubt;	,, *cxxiv* 2
If e'er when *f* had fall'n asleep,	,, *cxxiv* 9
all is well, tho' *f* and form Be sunder'd	,, *cxxvii* 1
Is comrade of the lesser *f*	,, *cxxviii* 3
With *f* that comes of self-control,	,, *cxxxi* 9
have *f* in a tradesman's ware or his word ?	*Maud I i* 26
and *f* in their great King,	*Gareth and L.* 330
good *f*, I fain had added—Knight,	,, 1162
'Nay, by my *f*, thou shalt not,' cried	*Marr. of Geraint* 198
a rock in ebbs and flows, Fixt on her *f*.	,, 813
Brought the great *f* to Britain over seas ;	*Balin and Balan* 103
F and unfaith can ne'er be equal powers : Unfaith in aught is want of *f* in all.	*Merlin and V.* 388
break *f* with one I may not name ?	*Lancelot and E.* 685
And *f* unfaithful kept him falsely true.	,, 877
f once fair Was richer than these diamonds— heal'd at once, By *f*, of all his ills.	,, 1228
a maid, Who kept our holy *f* among her kin	*Holy Grail* 56
those who love them, trials of our *f*.	,, 697
all these pains are trials of my *f*,	*Pelleas and E.* 210
'F of my body,' he said, 'and art thou not—	,, 246
f have these in whom they sware to love ?	,, 318
here the *f* That made us rulers ?	*Last Tournament* 188
fierce or careless looseners of the *f*,	*To the Queen ii* 18
Confined on points of *f*,	,, 52
'I have fought for Queen and F	*Lover's Tale ii* 150
In matters of the *f*, alas the while !	*The Revenge* 101
Lest the false *f* make merry over them !	*Sir J. Oldcastle* 76
'O soul of little *f*, slow to believe !	,, 82
the sacred peak Of hoar high-templed F,	*Columbus* 147
to the F that saves,	*Pref. Poem 19th Cent.* 10
Where you bawl'd the dark side of your *f*	*The Wreck* 3
away from your *f* and your face !	*Despair* 39
cling to F beyond the forms of F !	,, 110
Bring the old dark ages back without the *f*,	*Ancient Sage* 69
wars and filial *f*, and Dido's pyre ;	*Locksley H., Sixty* 137
F at her zenith, or all but lost	*To Virgil* 4
Despite of every F and Creed,	*Vastness* 11
Whose F and Works were bells of full accord,	*To Mary Boyle* 51
With a *f* as clear as the heights	*In Mem. G. W. Ward* 2
And mood of *f* may hold its own,	*June Bracken, etc.* 7
A people from their ancient fold of F,	*Akbar's Dream* 56
I cull from every *f* and race the best	,, 61
shook Those pillars of a moulder'd *f*,	,, 68
and to spread the Divine F	,, 81
darken'd with doubts of a F that saves,	,, 159
Faithful (*See also* **Faäithful**) Lean'd on him, *f*, gentle, good,	*The Dreamer* 11
And shaping *f* record of the glance	*Two Voices* 416
'O just and *f* knight of God !	*Gardener's D.* 177
I, falling on his *f* heart,	*Sir Galahad* 79
Thrice blest whose lives are *f* prayers,	*In Mem. xviii* 14
A *f* answer from the breast,	,, *xxxii* 13
She dwells on him with *f* eyes,	,, *lxxxv* 14
sleep Encompass'd by his *f* guard,	,, *xcvi* 35
And fair without, *f* within,	,, *cxxvi* 8
She is not *f* to me, and I see her Weeping	*Maud I xiii* 37
Hath push'd aside his *f* wife,	*Marr. of Geraint* 117
He had a *f* servant, one who loved His master	*Balin and Balan* 106
in her you see That *f* servant whom we spoke about,	*Lover's Tale iv* 256
Thanks to the kindly dark faces who fought with us, *f* and few,	,, 342
	Def. of Lucknow 70

Faithful (*continued*) Burnt too, my *f* preacher,
Beverley !   *Sir J. Oldcastle* 80
My noble friend, my *f* counsellor,   *Akbar's Dream* 18
True we have got—*such a f* ally   *Riflemen form!* 24
Faithfulness loving, utter *f* in love,   *Gareth and L.* 554
Faithless Lest I be found as *f* in the quest   *Lancelot and E.* 761
Whate'er the *f* people say.   *In Mem. xcvii* 16
The *f* coldness of the times ;   " *cvi* 18
Falcon (adj.) bold and free As you, my *f* Rosalind.   " *Rosalind* 18
Falcon (s) My frolic *f*, with bright eyes,   " 2
My bright-eyed, wild-eyed *f*,   " 6
If all the world were *f*'s, what of that ?   *Golden Year* 38
Forgetful of the *f* and the hunt,   *Marr. of Geraint* 51
given us a fair *f* which he train'd ;   *Merlin and V.* 96
unhooded casting off The goodly *f* free ;   " 131
No surer than our *f* yesterday,   *Lancelot and E.* 656
beauty lured that *f* from his eyry on the fell,   *Happy* 59
Falcon (name of ship) every soul from the decks of The
F but one ;   *The Wreck* 109
Falcon-eyed quick brunette, well-moulded, *f-e*,   *Princess ii* 106
Fall (s) (*See also* **Foot-fall, Tourney-fall**) many a *f* Of
diamond rillets musical,   *Arabian Nights* 47
comes the check, the change, the *f*,   *Two Voices* 163
Came in a sun-lit *f* of rain.   *Sir L. and Q. G.* 4
ILLYRIAN woodlands, echoing *f*'s Of water,   *To E. L.* 1
like the flakes In a *f* of snow,   *Lucretius* 167
and the river made a *f* Out yonder :   *Princess iii* 172
blossom'd branch Rapt to the horrible *f* :   " *iv* 180
They mark'd it with the red cross to the *f*,   " *vi* 41
That huddling slant in furrow-cloven *f*'s   " *vii* 207
as the rapid of life Shoots to the *f*—   *A Dedication* 4
These leaves that redden to the *f* ;   *In Mem. xi* 14
And back we come at *f* of dew.   " *Con.* 100
Here at the head of a tinkling *f*,   *Maud I xxi* 6
My pride is broken : men have seen my *f*.'   *Marr. of Geraint* 578
my pride Is broken down, for Enid sees my *f* !'   " 590
The drumming thunder of the huger *f*   *Geraint and E.* 173
Enid heard the clashing of his *f*,   *Lancelot and E.* 509
never woman yet, since man's first *f*,   *Pelleas and E.* 859
hear the manner of thy fight and *f* ;   " 347
bide, unfrowardly, A *f* from *him* ?'   " 598
laugh'd Lightly, to think of Modred's dusty *f*,   *Guinevere* 55
a *f* fro' a kiss to a kick like Saätan as fell   *North. Cobbler* 57
we may happen a *f* o' snaw—   *Village Wife* 21
kindly curves, with gentlest *f*,   *De. Prof., Two G.* 23
Following a torrent till his myriad *f*'s   *Tiresias* 37
and mine was the deeper *f* ;   *The Wreck* 11
An' the *f* of yer foot in the dance   *Tomorrow* 36
A *f* of water lull'd the noon asleep.   *Romney's R.* 83
is the Demon-god Wroth at his *f* ?'   *St. Telemachus* 20
he, That other, prophet of their *f*,   *Akbar's Dream* 82
Fall (autumn) an' I mean'd to 'a stubb'd it at *f*,   *N. Farmer, O. S.* 41
we talkt o' my darter es died o' the fever at *f* :   *Village Wife* 10
'ud coom at the *f* o' the year,   *Owd Roä* 23
An' my pigs didn't sell at *f*,   *Church-warden, etc.* 5
Fall (verb) (*See also* **Fall out**) Letting the rose-leaves *f* :   *Claribel* 3
Down by the poplar tall rivulets babble and *f*.   *Leonine Eleg.* 4
Winds creep ; dews *f* chilly ;   " 7
I faint, I *f*, Men say that Thou Didst die   *Supp. Confessions* 2
on his light there *f*'s A shadow ;   " 163
Place it, where sweetest sunlight *f*'s   *Ode to Memory* 85
It would *f* to the ground if you came in.   *Poet's Mind* 23
And shall *f* again to ground.   *Deserted House* 16
The shadow passeth when the tree shall *f*,   *Love and Death* 14
my ringlets would *f* Low adown,   *The Mermaid* 14
Then did my response clearer *f* :   *Two Voices* 34
when a billow, blown against, *F*'s back,   " 317
Which only to one engine bound *F*'s off,   " 348
Until they *f* in trance again.   " 354
And all day long to *f* and rise   *Miller's D.* 182
You seem'd to hear them climb and *f*   *Palace of Art* 70
to hear the dully sound Of human footsteps *f*.   " 276
Along the cliff to *f* and pause and *f* did seem.   *Lotos-Eaters* 9
THERE is sweet music here that softer *f*'s   " *C. S.* 1
turning yellow *F*'s, and floats adown the air.   " 31
Ripens and fades, and *f*'s, and hath no toil,   " 37

Fall (verb) (*continued*) In silence : ripen, *f* and cease :   *Lotos-Eaters* 52
thunder-drops *f* on a sleeping sea :   *D. of F. Women* 122
f down and glance From tone to tone,   " 166
F into shadow, soonest lost :   *To J. S.* 11
that on which it throve *F*'s off,   " 16
That from Discussion's lip may *f* With Life,   *Love thou thy land* 33
The goose let *f* a golden egg   *The Goose* 11
Where *f*'s not hail, or rain, or any snow,   *M. d'Arthur* 260
'*F* down, O Simeon : thou hast suffer'd long   *St. S. Stylites* 99
and oft I *f*, Maybe for months,   " 102
ONCE more the gate behind me *f*'s ;   *Talking Oak* 1
And when my marriage morn may *f*,   " 285
not leap forth and *f* about thy neck,   *Love and Duty* 41
THE woods decay, the woods decay and *f*,   *Tithonus* 1
and the shadows rise and *f*,   *Locksley Hall* 80
now for me the roof-tree *f*.   " 190
Let it *f* on Locksley Hall,   " 193
I'll take the showers as they *f*,   *Amphion* 101
Perfume and flowers *f* in showers,   *Sir Galahad* 11
On whom their favours *f* !   " 14
Swells up, and shakes and *f*'s.   " 76
F from his Ocean-lane of fire,   *The Voyage* 19
And like a thunderbolt he *f*'s.   *The Eagle* 6
A footstep seem'd to *f* beside her path,   *Enoch Arden* 514
F back upon a name ! rest, rot in that !   *Aylmer's Field* 385
heads of chiefs and princes *f* so fast,   " 763
as *f*'s A creeper when the prop is broken,   " 809
and seem'd Always about to *f*,   " 822
his own head Began to droop, to *f* ;   " 835
'Set them up ! they shall not *f* !'   *Sea Dreams* 227
ever *f*'s the least white star of snow,   *Lucretius* 107
She heard him raging, heard him *f* ;   " 276
come to fight with shadows and to *f*.   *Princess i* 10
but perchance : I speak ; it *f*'s.'   " *ii* 224
the gracious dews Began to glisten and to *f* :   " 317
The splendour *f*'s on castle walls   " *iv* 1
Fly to her, and *f* upon her gilded eaves,   " 94
Bred will in me to overcome it or *f*.   " *v* 351
one should fight with shadows and should *f* ;   " 476
Yea, let her see me *f* !   " 517
tho' he trip and *f* He shall not blind his soul   " *vii* 330
Mourning when their leaders *f*,   *Ode on Well.* 5
float or *f*, in endless ebb and flow ;   *W. to Marie Alex.* 27
I roar and rave for I *f*.   *Voice and the P.* 12
F, and follow their doom.   " 20
Bloodily, bloodily *f* the battle-axe,   *Boädicea* 56
she felt the heart within her *f*   " 81
I *f* unawares before the people,   *Hendecasyllabics* 7
Her place is empty, *f* like these ;   *In Mem xiii* 4
When fill'd with tears that cannot *f*,   " *xix* 11
My deeper anguish also *f*'s,   " 15
If such a dreamy touch should *f*,   " *xliv* 13
should *f* Remerging in the general Soul,   " *xlvii* 3
Be near us when we climb or *f* :   " *li* 13
I can but trust that good shall *f*   " *liv* 14
As drop by drop the water *f*'s   " *lviii* 3
When on my bed the moonlight *f*'s,   " *lxvii* 1
Till on mine ear this message *f*'s,   " *lxxxv* 18
And lightly does the whisper *f* ;   " 89
And strangely *f*'s our Christmas-eve.   " *cv* 4
A shade *f*'s on us like the dark From little cloudlets   " *Con.* 93
And breaking let the splendour *f*   " 119
Shall I weep if a Poland *f* ?   *Maud I iv* 46
and *f* before Her feet on the meadow grass,   " *v* 25
For I heard your rivulet *f*   " *xxii* 36
the heavens *f* in a gentle rain,   " *II i* 41
a dewy splendour *f*'s On the little flower   " *iv* 32
Then I rise, the eavedrops *f*,   " 62
and watch'd the great sea *f*, Wave after wave,   *Com. of Arthur* 378
f battleaxe upon helm, *F* battleaxe,   " 486
See that he *f* not on thee suddenly,   *Gareth and L.* 921
'Lo,' said Gareth, ' the foe *f*'s !'   " 1317
And if I *f* her name will yet remain   *Marr. of Geraint* 500
While slowly falling as a scale that *f*'s,   " 525
Made her cheek burn and either eyelid *f*,   " 775
Before he turn to *f* seaward again,   *Geraint and E.* 117

Fall (verb) (*continued*)   Wait here, and when he passes *f*

upon him.'	*Geraint and E.* 129
And they will *f* upon him unawares.	,, 134
they will *f* upon you while ye pass.'	,, 145
And if I *f*, cleave to the better man.'	,, 152
Made her cheek burn and either eyelid *f*.	,, 434
a dreadful loss F's in a far land and he knows it not,	,, 497
and made as if to *f* upon him.	,, 776
fear not, Enid, I should *f* upon him,	,, 787
see He do not *f* behind me:	*Balin and Balan* 135
Deep-tranced on hers, and could not *f*:	,, 278
A doom that ever poised itself to *f*,	*Merlin and V.* 191
Had I for three days seen, ready to *f*.	,, 296
Set up the charge ye know, to stand or *f*!'	,, 703
the victim's flowers before he *f*.'	*Lancelot and E.* 910
women watch Who wins, who *f's*;	*Holy Grail* 35
all the light that *f's* upon the board	,, 249
King himself had fears that it would *f*,	,, 341
F on him all at once, And if ye slay him	*Pelleas and E.* 268
' Would rather you had let them *f*,'	*Last Tournament* 39
cold F's on the mountain in midsummer snows,	,, 228
F, as the crest of some slow-arching wave,	,, 462
Where *f's* not hail, or rain, or any snow,	*Pass. of Arthur* 428
as anger *f's* aside And withers on the breast	*Lover's Tale i* 9
Or as men know not when they *f* asleep	,, 161
It *f* on its own thorns—if this be true—	,, 273
my raised eyelids would not *f*,	,, i 571
First *f's* asleep in swoon, wherefrom awaked,	,, 791
faint and *f*, To *f* and die away.	,, ii 96
nay—what was there left to *f*?	*Rizpah* 9
F's? what *f's*? who knows? As the tree *f's* so must it lie.	,, 12
the thunderbolt will *f* Long and loud,	*The Revenge* 44
F into the hands of God, not into the hands of Spain!'	,, 90
Better to *f* by the hands that they love, than to *f*	*Def. of Lucknow* 53
Mark him—he *f's*! then another,	,, 65
I knew we should *f* on each other,	*V. of Maeldune* 104
Have heard this footstep *f*,	*Tiresias* 27
Thy Thebes shall *f* and perish,	,, 116
I felt one warm tear *f* upon it.	,, 167
My Shelley would *f* from my hands	*The Wreck* 25
She tastes the fruit before the blossom *f's*,	*Ancient Sage* 75
The blackthorn-blossom fades and *f's*	*The Flight* 15
thro' the tonguesters we may *f*.	*Locksley H., Sixty* 130
Kingdoms and Republics *f*,	,, 159
Jacob's ladder *f's* On greening grass,	*Early Spring* 9
Should this old England *f*	*The Fleet* 4
and at dawn F's on the threshold	*Demeter and P.* 3
thy hands let *f* the gather'd flower,	,, 9
flowers that brighten as thy footstep *f's*,	,, 36
felt a gentle hand *F* on my forehead,	*The Ring* 419
my strongest wish F's flat before your least unwillingness.	*Romney's R.* 72
Thou, thou—I saw thee *f* before me,	*Akbar's Dream* 185
the chuch weänt happen a *f*.	*Church-warden, etc.* 10
your shadow *f's* on the grave.	*Charity* 20
My prison, not my fortress, *f* away!	*Doubt and Prayer* 12
THE bridal garland *f's* upon the bier,	*D. of the Duke of C.* 1

Fallen (*See also* **Chap-fallen, Half-fallen, New-fallen, Newly-fallen**) legend of a *f* race Alone might hint

	Two Voices 359
mournful light That broods above the *f* sun,	*To J. S.* 51
To trample round my *f* head,	*Come not, when* 3
Philip glancing up Beheld the dead flame of the *f* day	*Enoch Arden* 441
The two remaining found a *f* stem;	,, 567
To lift the woman's *f* divinity	*Princess iii* 223
So those two foes above my *f* life,	,, vi 130
O *f* nobility, that, overawed,	*Third of Feb.* 35
In those *f* leaves which kept their green,	*In Mem. xcv* 23
saw the chargers of the two that fell Start from their *f* lords,	*Geraint and E.* 482
Arising wearily at a *f* oak,	*Balin and Balan* 425
Then leapt her palfrey o'er the *f* oak,	,, 587
And in the darkness o'er her *f* head,	*Guinevere* 583
Or ev'n a *f* feather, vanish'd again.	*Last Tournament* 372
My *f* forehead in their to and fro,	*Lover's Tale i* 701

Fallen (*continued*) Were she . . . a *f* state?   *The Fleet* 10

I saw the tiger in the ruin'd fane Spring from his *f* God,	*Demeter and P.* 80
stem, which else had *f* quite With cluster'd flower-bells	*Isabel* 35
F silver-chiming, seem'd to shake	*Arabian Nights* 51
dews, that would have *f* in tears,	*Miller's D.* 151
She ceased in tears, *f* from hope and trust:	*D. of F. Women* 257
Had *f* in Lyonnesse about their Lord,	*M. d'Arthur* 4
half has *f* and made a bridge;	*Walk. to the Mail* 32
f into the dusty crypt Of darken'd forms	*Will. Water* 183
THE rain had *f*, the Poet arose,	*Poet's Song* 1
but her face had *f* upon her hands;	*Enoch Arden* 391
on her the thunders of the house Had *f* first	*Aylmer's Field* 279
How low his brother's mood had *f*,	,, 404
' Let them lie, for they have *f*.'	*Sea Dreams* 228
And here upon a yellow eyelid *f*	*Lucretius* 141
When *f* in darker ways.'	*Princess v* 68
' Our enemies have *f*, have *f*: (repeat)	*Princess vi* 33, 38, 43, 48
would have strown it, and are *f* themselves.	*Princess vi* 42
Our enemies have *f*, but this shall grow	,, 53
O *f* at length that tower of strength	*Ode on Well.* 38
when she turn'd, the curse Had *f*,	*In Mem. vi* 13
What words are these have *f* from me?	,, xvi 1
And towers *f* as soon as built—	,, xxvi 8
Had *f* into her father's grave,	,, lxxxix 13
There has *f* a splendid tear From the passion-flower	*Maud I xxii* 59
Then cried the *f*, ' Take not my life:	*Gareth and L.* 973
I have not *f* so low as some would wish.	*Marr. of Geraint* 129
So that I be not *f* in fight. Farewell.'	,, 223
And here had *f* a great part of a tower,	,, 317
now they saw their bulwark *f*, stood;	*Geraint and E.* 168
creatures gently born But into bad hands *f*,	,, 192
catch a loathly plume *f* from the wing	*Merlin and V.* 727
Lay like a rainbow *f* upon the grass,	*Lancelot and E.* 431
Where these had *f*, slowly past the barge	,, 1241
apples by the brook *F*, and on the lawns.	*Holy Grail* 385
Lancelot, with his heel upon the *f*,	*Pelleas and E.* 580
A manner somewhat *f* from reverence—	*Last Tournament* 119
And shouted and leapt down upon the *f*—	,, 469
Ye twain had *f* out about the bride Of one—	,, 545
wonders, what has *f* upon the realm?	*Guinevere* 275
turn'd, and reel'd, and would have *f*,	,, 304
Tumbling the hollow helmets of the *f*,	*Pass. of Arthur* 132
for on my heart hath *f* Confusion,	,, 143
Had *f* in Lyonnesse about their lord,	,, 173
if she knows And dreads it we are *f*.—	*To the Queen ii* 33
And *f* away from judgment.	*Lover's Tale i* 103
pillars which from earth uphold Our childhood, one had *f* away,	,, 221
that shock of gloom had *f* Unfelt,	,, 505
and the rain Had *f* upon me, and the gilded snake	,, 623
I had *f* Prone by the dashing runnel on the grass.	,, ii 100
Anything *f* again? nay—	*Rizpah* 9
and his friends that had *F* in conflict,	*Batt. of Brunanburh* 71
When I had *f* from off the crag	*The Flight* 22
but now to silent ashes *f* away.	*Locksley H., Sixty* 41
f every popular Cæsar's dome—	*To Virgil* 30
Fifty times the golden harvest *f*,	*On Jub. Q. Victoria* 2
torn the ring In fright, and *f* dead.	*The Ring* 471
All his leaves *F* at length,	*The Oak* 12

Falling (*See also* **Fast-falling, Half-falling, Quick-falling, Slow-falling**) The jaw is *f*, The red cheek paling,

	All Things will Die 30
Long alleys *f* down to twilight grots,	*Ode to Memory* 107
F into a still delight, And luxury	*Eleänore* 106
The leaves upon her *f* light—	*L. of Shalott iv* 21
Lo, *f* from my constant mind,	*Fatima* 5
The long brook *f* thro' the clov'n ravine	*Œnone* 8
watch the emerald-colour'd water *f*	*Lotos-Eaters, C. S.* 96
Sound all night long, in *f* thro' the dell,	*D. of F. Women* 183
content to perish, *f* on the foeman's ground,	*Locksley Hall* 103
himself was deadly wounded *F* on the dead.	*The Captain* 64
Rising, *f*, like a wave,	*Vision of Sin* 125
Like moonlight on a *f* shower?	*Margaret* 4
Just ere the *f* axe did part The burning brain	,, 38

Fame (*continued*) And one—they call'd her F ; and one,— — *Gareth and L.* 113
And lost to life and use and name and f. (repeat) — *Merlin and V.* 214, 970
such fire for f, Such trumpet-blowings in it, — „ 417
My use and name and f. — „ 304
Upon my life and use and name and f, — „ 374
And into such a song, such fire for f, — „ 417
felt them slowly ebbing, name and f.' — „ 437
touching f, howe'er ye scorn my song, — „ 444
For f, could f be mine, that f were thine, — „ 447
'Man dreams of F while woman wakes to love.' — „ 460
F, The F that follows death is nothing — „ 463
what is F in life but half-disfame, — „ 465
the scroll ' I follow f.' — „ 476
this for motto, ' Rather use than f.' — „ 480
F with men, Being but ampler means to serve — „ 488
Use gave me F at first, and F again — „ 493
Right well know I that F is half-disfame, — „ 504
That other f, To one at least, who hath not children, — „ 505
concluded in that star To make f nothing. — „ 513
I rather dread the loss of use than f ; — „ 519
Born to the glory of thy name and f, — *Lancelot and E.* 1372
May not your crescent fear for name and f — „ 1400
' I am wrath and shame and hate and evil f, — *Pelleas and E.* 568
courtliness, and the desire of f, — *Guinevere* 482
I must not dwell on that defeat of f. — „ 628
now much honour and much f were lost.' — *Pass. of Arthur* 277
all the clearness of his f hath gone — *Lover's Tale* i 789
As heir of endless f— — *Ancient Sage* 147
patriot—soldier take His meed of f in verse ; — *Epilogue* 33
And so does Earth ; for Homer's f, — „ 58
Her ancient f of Free— — *The Fleet* 9
honouring your fair f Of Statesman, — *To Marq. of Dufferin* 14
F blowing out from her golden trumpet — *Vastness* 21
' Take comfort you have won the Painter's f,' — *Romney's R.* 43
What f ? I am not Raphaël, — „ 46
Wrong there ! The painter's f ? — „ 48
Her sad eyes plead for my own f with me — „ 55
thy f Is blown thro' all the Troad, — *Death of Œnone* 36
Famed *See* **Far-famed, First-famed**
Fame-lit Bard whose f-l laurels glance — *To Victor Hugo* 4
Familiar And pace the sacred old f fields, — *Enoch Arden* 625
like bright eyes of f friends, — *Holy Grail* 688
till the things f to her youth Had made a silent answer : — *Lover's Tale* iv 95
Surely his King and most f friend — *Lancelot and E.* 592
whence the Royal mind, f with her, — *Princess* iv 235
bones are blest Among f names to rest — *In Mem.* xviii 7
grow F to the stranger's child ; — „ ci 20
F up from cradle-time, so wan, — *Balin and Balan* 591
Familiarity Such dear *familiarities* of dawn ? — *Aylmer's Field* 131
Family the f tree Sprang from the midriff of a prostrate king— — „ 15
A fiery f passion for the name Of Lancelot, — *Lancelot and E.* 477
Famine Blight and f, plague and earthquake, — *Lotos-Eaters, C. S.* 115
A f after laid them low, — *The Victim* 2
' Help us from f And plague and strife ! — „ 9
And blight and f on all the lea : — „ 46
shipwrecks, f's, fevers, fights, Mutinies, — *Columbus* 225
when I spake of f, plague, Shrine-shattering earthquake, — *Tiresias* 60
to stay, Not spread the plague, the f ; — *Demeter and P.* 134
earthquake, or the f, or the pest ! — *Faith* 4
Famishing f populace, wharves forlorn ; — *Vastness* 14
Famous Plenty corrupts the melody That made thee f once, — *Blackbird* 16
fellowship of f knights Whereof this world holds record. — *M. d'Arthur* 15
Thy f brother-oak. — *Talking Oak* 296
That many a f man and woman, — *Princess* iv 445
Thine island loves thee well, thou f man, — *Ode on Well.* 85
rather proven in his Paynim wars Than f jousts ; — *Balin and Balan* 39
the most f man of all those times, — *Merlin and V.* 166
lance had beaten down the knights, So many and f names ; — *Holy Grail* 364
I will make thee with my spear and sword As f— — *Pelleas and E.* 46

Famous (*continued*) fellowship of f knights Whereof this world holds record. — *Pass. of Arthur* 183
And mingled with the f kings of old, — *Tiresias* 171
Fan (s) To spread into the perfect f, — *Sir L. and Q. G.* 17
toys in lava, f's Of sandal, amber, — *Princess, Pro.* 18
Fan (verb) A soft air f's the cloud apart ; — *Tithonus* 32
f my brows and blow The fever from my cheek, — *In Mem.* lxxxvi 8
Fancied (*See also* **Ever-fancied**) I had f it would be fair. — *Maud* I vi 6
she f ' Is it for me ? ' — *Lancelot and E.* 822
I f that my friend For this brief idyll — *Tiresias* 187
In impotence of f power. — *A Character* 24
Beneath all f hopes and fears Ay me, — *In Mem.* xlix 13
And then was painting on it f arms, — *Merlin and V.* 474
Fancy (s) And a f as summer-new As the green — *June Bracken, etc.* 8
Would that my gloomed f were As thine, — *Supp. Confessions* 68
With youthful f re-inspired, — *Ode to Memory* 114
F came and at her pillow sat, — *Caress'd or chidden* 5
F watches in the wilderness, Poor F sadder than a single star, — „ 12
My f made me for a moment blest — *The form, the form* 6
my life with f play'd Before I dream'd — *Miller's D.* 45
I thought that it was f, and I listen'd — *May Queen, Con.* 33
those sharp *fancies*, by down-lapsing thought — *D. of F. Women* 49
And if I said that F, led by Love, — *Gardener's D.* 59
In the Spring a young man's f lightly turns — *Locksley Hall* 20
Falser than all f fathoms, — „ 41
Soothe him with thy finer *fancies*, — „ 54
I have but an angry f : — „ 102
Fool, again the dream, the f ! — „ 173
founts of inspiration well thro' all my f yet. — „ 188
Across my f, brooding warm, — *Day-Dm., Pro.* 10
So much your eyes my f take— — „ *L'Envoi* 26
My f, ranging thro' and thro', — „ 34
But whither would my f go ? — *Will Water.* 145
she gleam'd Like F made of golden air, — *The Voyage* 66
Set thy hoary *fancies* free ; — *Vision of Sin* 156
evil *fancies* clung Like serpent eggs together, — *Enoch Arden* 479
His f fled before the lazy wind Returning, — „ 657
Prattling the primrose *fancies* of the boy, — *The Brook* 19
But Edith's eager f hurried with him — *Aylmer's Field* 208
many a summer still Clung to their *fancies*) — *Sea Dreams* 36
drifting up the stream In f, till I slept again, — „ 109
maiden *fancies* ; loved to live alone — *Princess* i 49
crush her pretty maiden *fancies* dead — „ 88
What were those *fancies* ? — „ 95
fair philosophies That lift the f ; — „ iii 341
sweet as those by hopeless f feign'd — „ iv 55
thine are *fancies* hatch'd In silken-folded — „ 66
Which melted Florian's f as she hung, — „ 370
Thy face across his f comes, — „ 579
understanding all the foolish work Of F, — „ vi 117
fancies like the vermin in a nut Have fretted — „ 263
Lay your earthly *fancies* down, — *Ode on Well.* 279
My f fled to the South again. — *The Daisy* 108
flatters thus Our home-bred *fancies* : — *In Mem.* x 11
My *fancies* time to rise on wing, — „ xiii 17
And but for *fancies*, which aver — „ xv 9
delirious man Whose f fuses old and new, — „ xvi 18
And F light from F caught, — „ xxiii 14
I vex my heart with *fancies* dim : — „ xlii 1
The f's tenderest eddy wreathe, — „ xlix 6
And dare we to this f give, — „ liii 5
I lull a f trouble-tost — „ lxv 2
You wonder when my *fancies* play — „ lxvi 2
Take wings of f, and ascend, — „ lxxvi 1
Then f shapes, as f can, The grief my loss — „ lxxx
backward f, wherefore wake The old bitterness again, — „ lxxxiv 46
Ill brethren, let the f fly. — „ lxxxvi 12
Or villain f fleeting by, — „ cxi 18
And all the breeze of F blows, — „ cxxii 17
It circles round, and f plays, — „ Con. 81
The f flatter'd my mind, — *Maud* I xiv 23
dreamful wastes where footless *fancies* dwell — „ xviii 69
these be for the snare (So runs thy f) — *Gareth and L.* 1082
Then let her f flit across the past, — *Marr. of Geraint* 645

Fancy (s) *(continued)* Her *f* dwelling in this dusky
  hall ; — *Marr. of Geraint* 802
And sweet self-pity, or the *f* of it, — *Geraint and E.* 349
fabler, these be *fancies* of the churl, — *Balin and Balan* 307
mood as that, which lately gloom'd Your *f* — *Merlin and V.* 326
So fixt her *f* on him : let them be. — ,, 777
what was once to me Mere matter of the *f*, — ,, 924
To snare her royal *f* with a boon — *Lancelot and E.* 71
Rapt in this *f* of his Table Round, — ,, 129
Full often lost in *f*, lost his way ; — ,, 164
that ghostly grace Beam'd on his *f*, — ,, 886
Her *fancies* with the sallow-rifted glooms — ,, 1002
' ye never yet Denied my *fancies*— — ,, 1112
Not for me ! For her ! for your new *f*. — ,, 1216
men Shape to their *f*'s eye from broken rocks — ,, 1252
Give me three days to melt her *f*, — *Pelleas and E.* 356
her ever-veering *f* turn'd To Pelleas, — ,, 493
Appearing, sent his *f* back to where — *Last Tournament* 380
push me even In *f* from thy side, — ,, 639
Made all our tastes and *fancies* like, — *Lover's Tale i* 242
graceful thought of hers Grav'n on my *f* ! — ,, 358
Ye cannot shape *F* so fair as in this memory. — ,, 548
thronging *fancies* come To boys and girls — ,, 554
Ringing within the *f* had updrawn A fashion — ,, 645
Flatter'd the *f* of my fading brain ; — ,, *ii* 107
The *f* stirr'd him so He rose and went, — ,, *iv* 51
the sudden wail his lady made Dwelt in his *f*: — ,, 150
And idle *fancies* flutter me, — *The Flight* 74
Set the maiden *fancies* wallowing — *Locksley H., Sixty* 145
All the chosen coin of *f* flashing out — *To Virgil* 7
The fairy *fancies* range, — *Early Spring* 39
till I believing that the girl's Lean *f*, — *The Ring* 336
For one monotonous *f* madden'd her, — ,, 404
But chaining *f* now at home — *To Ulysses* 31
Fancy (verb) I *f* her sweetness only due To the sweeter
  blood — *Maud I xiii* 33
What thing soever ye may hear, or see, Or *f* — *Geraint and E.* 416
Hope ! O yes, I hope, or *f* that, — *Romney's R.* 158
Fancy-borne Or *f-b* perhaps upon the rise — *Lucretius* 10
Fancy-fed And pining life be *f-f*. — *In Mem. lxxxv* 96
Fancy-flies we that love the mud, Rising to no *f-f*. — *Vision of Sin* 102
Fancying *f* that her glory would be great — *Merlin and V.* 217
Fane translucent *f* Of her still spirit ; — *Isabel* 4
hopes and hates, his homes and *f*'s, — *Lucretius* 255
wise humility As befits a solemn *f*: — *Ode on Well.* 250
Who built him *f*'s of fruitless prayer, — *In Mem. lvi* 12
And heard once more in college *f*'s — ,, *lxxxvii* 5
I saw the tiger in the ruin'd *f* — *Demeter and P.* 79
an old *f* No longer sacred to the Sun, — *St. Telemachus* 6
anchorite Would haunt the desolated *f*, — ,, 12
stone by stone, I rear'd a sacred *f*, — *Akbar's Dream* 177
Fang the *f*'s Shall move the stony bases — *Princess vi* 57
Fann'd sudden flame, By veering passion *f*, — *Madeline* 29
Thy bounteous forehead was not *f* — *Eleänore* 9
A summer *f* with spice. — *Palace of Art* 116
Low breezes *f* the belfry bars, — *The Letters* 43
river-breeze, Which *f* the gardens of that rival rose — *Aylmer's Field* 455
The woods with living airs How softly *f*, — *Early Spring* 20
Fantastic overhead *F* gables, crowding, stared : — *Godiva* 61
That lute and flute *f* tenderness, — *Princess iv* 129
long *f* night With all its doings — ,, 565
round of green, this orb of flame, *F* beauty ; — *In Mem. xxxiv* 6
spreading made *F* plume or sable pine ; — *The Voyage* 44
Fantastical So *f* is the dainty metre. — *Hendecasyllabics* 14
Albeit I know my knights *f*, — *Lancelot and E.* 594
Fantasy Her gay-furr'd cats a painted *f*, — *Princess iii* 186
Proud in their *f* call themselves the Day, — *Gareth and L.* 633
Or whether it be the maiden's *f*, — ,, 874
A border *f* of branch and flower, — *Lancelot and E.* 11
And saved him : so she lived in *f*. — ,, 27
There kept it, and so lived in *f*. — ,, 398
death Was rather in the *f* than the blood. — ,, 1132
Let be thy fair Queen's *f*. — *Last Tournament* 197
Or prophets of them in his *f*, — *Lover's Tale iv* 12
Far Thoro' the black-stemm'd pines only the *f* river shines. *Leonine Eleg.* 2

Far *(continued)* Sadly the *f* kine loweth : — *Leonine Eleg.* 9
overtakes *F* thought with music that it makes : — *Two Voices* 438
Going before to some *f* shrine, — *On a Mourner* 17
I cannot sink So *f*—*f* down, — *My life is full* 9
And fixt upon the *f* sea-line ; — *The Voyage* 62
Down at the *f* end of an avenue, — *Enoch Arden* 358
phrases of the hearth, And *f* allusion, — *Princess ii* 316
O sweet and *f* from cliff and scar — ,, *iv* 9
and died Of fright in *f* apartments. — ,, *vi* 371
Thro' the long gorge to the *f* light — *Ode on Well.* 213
' *F* and *f* away,' said the dainty little maiden,
  (repeat) — *City Child* 3, 8
He seems so near and yet so *f*, — *In Mem. xcvii* 23
Falls in a *f* land and he knows it not, — *Geraint and E.* 497
my blood Hath earnest in it of *f* springs — *Merlin and V.* 557
His own *f* blood, which dwelt at Camelot ; — *Lancelot and E.* 803
flame At sunrise till the people in *f* fields, — *Holy Grail* 243
loyal to their crown Are loyal to their own *f* sons, — *To the Queen ii* 28
Fierce in the strength of *f* descent, — *Lover's Tale i* 382
Then at the *f* end of the vault he saw His lady — ,, *iv* 56
On one *f* height in one far-shining fire, — *Tiresias* 185
Some *f* blue fell, — *Early Spring* 34
Watch'd my *f* meadow zoned with airy morn ; — *Prog. of Spring* 69
Desolate sweetness—*f* and *f* away— — *Ancient Sage* 226
Far-blazing *F-b* from the rear of Philip's house, — *Enoch Arden* 727
Far-brought love *f-b* From out the storied Past, — *Love thou thy land* 1
Farce ' Ah fool, and made myself a Queen of *f* ! — *Princess vii* 243
For by and by she sicken'd of the *f*, — *The Ring* 383
Fare (s) Friday *f* was Enoch's ministering. — *Enoch Arden* 100
With store of rich apparel, sumptuous *f*, — *Marr. of Geraint* 709
My lord, eat also, tho' the *f* is coarse, — *Geraint and E.* 208
And serve thee costlier than with mowers' *f*.' — ,, 231
    Then said Geraint, ' I wish no better *f*: — ,, 231
That Lenten *f* makes Lenten thought, — *To E. Fitzgerald* 31
Fare (verb) So *f*'s it since the years began, — *Will Water.* 169
F's richly, in fine linen, not a hair — *Aylmer's Field* 659
Thy duty ? What is duty ? *F* thee well !' — *Lucretius* 281
O heart, how *f*'s it with thee now, — *In Mem. iv* 5
How *f*'s it with the happy dead ? — ,, *xliv* 1
bring us where he is, and how he *f*'s, — *Lancelot and E.* 547
F you well A thousand times !— — ,, 695
How *f*'s my lord Sir Lancelot ?' — ,, 795
Fared so *f* she gazing there ; — *Princess vii* 41
Whereon with equal feet we *f*; — *In Mem. xxv* 2
So *f* it with Geraint, who thought and said, — *Marr. of Geraint* 343
So *f* it with Geraint, (repeat) — *Geraint and E.* 8, 500
Then *f* it with Sir Pelleas as with one — *Pelleas and E.* 528
Far-end When Molly cooms in fro' the *f-e* close — *Spinster's S's.* 2
Farewell Ye merry souls, — *All Things will Die* 36
But now *f*. I am going a long way With these
  thou seëst— — *M. d'Arthur* 256
might I tell of meetings, of *f*'s— — *Gardener's D.* 251
F, like endless welcome, lived and died. — *Love and Duty* 68
a long *f* to Locksley Hall ! — *Locksley Hall* 189
Enoch faced this morning of *f* Brightly — *Enoch Arden* 182
she said : ' *f*, Sir—and to you. — *Princess ii* 235
he reach'd White hands of *f* to my sire, — ,, *v* 233
The wrath I nursed against the world : *f*.' — ,, 437
Pledge of a love not to be mine, *f*, — ,, *vi* 197
few words and pithy, such as closed Welcome, *f*, — *Con.* 95
landing-place, to clasp and say ' *F* ! — *In Mem. xlvii* 16
In those sad words I took *f*: — ,, *lviii* 1
I cannot think the thing *f*. — ,, *cxxiii* 12
F, we kiss, and they are gone. — *Con.* 92
own heart's heart, my ownest own, *f*; — *Maud I xviii* 74
Thy shield is mine— — *Gareth and L.* 988
So that I be not fall'n in fight. *F*.' ' *F*, fair
  Prince,' answer'd the stately Queen. — *Marr. of Geraint* 223
narrow court and lubber King, *f* ! — *Merlin and V.* 119
F; think gently of me, for I fear My fate or folly, — ,, 926
She needs must bid *f* to sweet Lavaine. — *Lancelot and E.* 341
A thousand times !—a thousand times *f* ! — ,, 696
Nor bad *f*, but sadly rode away. — ,, 987
Gawain, who bad a thousand *f*'s to me, — ,, 1056
' Sister, *f* for ever,' and again ' *F*, — ,, 1151

Farewell (*continued*)   Come, for you left me taking no *f*,
   Hither, to take my last *f* of you.   *Lancelot and E.* 1274
I left her and I bad her no *f*;   „   1304
F too—now at last—*F*, fair lily.   „   1396
Than to be loved again of you—*f*;   *Pelleas and E.* 302
It was their last hour, A madness of *f*'s.   *Guinevere* 103
Nay, friend, for we have taken our *f*'s.   „   117
see thee no more—*F*!'   „   580
F? I should have answer'd his *f*.   „   615
F! there is an isle of rest for thee.   *Pass. of Arthur* 35
But now *f*. I am going a long way With these
   thou seëst.   „   424
And bad them to a banquet of *f*'s.   *Lover's Tale iv* 186
We bad them no *f*, but mounting these He past   „   386
She remembers you. *F*.   *Sisters (E. and E.)* 190
thinks She sees you when she hears. Again *f*.'   „   193
'Pray come and see my mother, and *f*.'   „   196
for ever and ever, for ever and ever *f*,   *Despair* 58
a whisper—some divine *f*—   *Ancient Sage* 225
Strike on the Mount of Vision! So, *f*.   „   286
F, Macready, since to-night we part;   *To W. C. Macready* 1
F, Macready, since this night we part;   „   5
F, Macready; moral, grave, sublime;   „   12
Not there to bid my boy *f*,   *To Marq. of Dufferin* 42
if so, Bid him *f* for me,   *Romney's R.* 147
F, whose living like I shall not find,   *In Mem. W. G. Ward* 1
F!—You will not speak, my friends,   *The Wanderer* 3
deem me grateful, and *f*!   „   16
And may there be no sadness of *f*,   *Crossing the Bar* 11
Far-famed   *F-f* for well-won enterprise,   *Kate* 22
Far-fleeted   *F-f* by the purple island-sides,   *Princess vii* 166
Far-folded   *F-f* mists, and gleaming halls of morn.   *Tithonus* 10
Far-heard   *F-h* beneath the moon.   *D. of F. Women* 184
Farm   (*See also* **Crown-farm**)   red cock crows from
   the *f* upon the hill,   *May Queen, N. Y's. E.* 23
WITH farmer Allan at the *f* abode   *Dora* 1
and set out, and reach'd the *f*.   „   129
discuss'd the *f*, The four-field system,   *Audley Court* 33
Till last by Philip's *f* I flow   *The Brook* 31
Philip's *f* where brook and river meet.   „   38
and call'd old Philip out To show the *f*:   „   121
how he sent the bailiff into the *f* To learn   „   141
He found the bailiff riding by the *f*,   „   153
ask'd her 'Are you from the *f*?'   „   209
We bought the *f* we tenanted before.   „   222
closed her access to the wealthier *f*'s,   *Aylmer's Field* 503
princely halls, and *f*'s, and flowing lawns,   „   654
the broad woodland parcell'd into *f*'s;   „   847
Willy had not been down to the *f*   *Grandmother* 33
there past by the gate of the *f*, Willy,—   „   41
sitting at home in my father's *f* at eve: „   90
Feyther run oop to the *f*,   *N. Farmer, N. S.* 54
And crowded *f*'s and lessening towers,   *In Mem. xi* 11
To leave the pleasant fields and *f*'s;   „   *cii* 22
had need Of a good stout lad at his *f*;   *First Quarrel* 18
Harry was bound to the Dorsetshire *f*   „   19
that workt with him up at the *f*,   „   24
they does it at Willis's *f*,   *Village Wife* 119
An' 'cos o' thy *f* by the beck,   *Spinster's S's.* 73
Ev'n the homely *f* can teach us   *Locksley H., Sixty* 26
Fur the gell o' the *f* 'at slep wi' tha   *Owd Roä* 51
Moother 'ed beän a-naggin' about the gell o' the *f*,   „   69
mine the hall, the *f*, the field;   *The Ring* 169
on waste and wood, On *f* and field: *Prog. of Spring* 23
How be the *f* gittin on? noäways.   *Church-warden, etc.* 3
war dashing down upon cities and blazing *f*'s,   *The Dawn* 8
Farmer   WITH *f* Allan at the farm abode   *Dora* 1
Far off the *f* came into the field And spied her not;   „   74
when the *f* pass'd into the field He spied her,   „   85
Francis Hale, The *f*'s son, who lived across the bay,   *Audley Court* 75
The *f* vext packs up his beds and chairs,   *Walk. to the Mail* 39
robb'd the *f* of his bowl of cream: *Princess v* 223
There was a *f* in Dorset of Harry's kin,   *First Quarrel* 17
'The *f* dared me to do it,' he said;   *Rizpah* 26
Howiver was British *f*'s to stan' ageän   *Owd Roä* 46

Farmin'   An' thy *f*' es cleän es thysen,'   *Spinster's S's.* 77
Farmstead   he, by *f*, thorpe and spire,   *Will Water.* 137
Far-off   And the *f-o* stream is dumb,   *The Owl i* 3
F-o the torrent call'd me from the cleft: *Œnone* 54
I dimly see My *f-o* doubtful purpose,   „   251
In those *f-o* seven happy years were born;   *Enoch Arden* 686
her *f-o* cousin and betrothed,   *The Brook* 75
sorcerer, whom a *f-o* grandsire burnt   *Princess i* 6
to catch The *f-o* interest of tears?   *In Mem. i* 8
The brook alone *f-o* was heard,   „   *xcv* 7
And one *f-o* divine event,   „ *Con.* 143
the *f-o* sail is blown by the breeze   *Maud I iv* 4
some *f-o* touch Of greatness to know   *Lancelot and E.* 450
The storm, you hear *F-o*, is Muriel—   *The Ring* 139
Only to hear and see the *f-o* sparkling brine,   *Lotos-Eaters, C. S.* 98
In days *f-o*, on that dark earth, be true?   *Tithonus* 48
deep Down upon *f-o* cities while they dance—   *Merlin and V.* 114
from him flits to warn A *f-o* friendship   *Demeter and P.* 90
For have the *f-o* hymns of May,   *To Master of B.* 10
Farran'd (fashioned)   *See* Owd-farran'd
Far-renowned   *f-r* brides of ancient song   *D. of F. Women* 17
Far-rolling   Seem'd those *f-r*, westward-smiling
   seas,   *Last Tournament* 587
Far-seen   Amid thy melancholy mates *f-s*,   *Lover's Tale i* 489
Far-shadowing   half in light, and half *F-s*   *Princess, Con.* 42
Far-shining   On one far height in one *f-s* fire.   *Tiresias* 186
'One height and one *f-s* fire'   „   186
Far-sighted   *F-s* summoner of War and Waste   *Ded. of Idylls* 37
Far-sounded   Amid *f-s*, a name *f-s* among men   *Marr. of Geraint* 427
Farther   With *f* lookings on.   *Miller's D.* 231
Farthest   But from my *f* lapse, my latest ebb,   *Lover's Tale i* 90
Far-welter'd (overthrown)   Woorse nor a *f-w* yowe: *N. Farmer, N. S.* 32
Fashion (s)   After the *f* of the time,   *Arabian Nights* 119
Looks freshest in the *f* of the day: *The Epic* 32
I know your sex, From the *f* of your bones.   *Vision of Sin* 182
In sailor *f* roughly sermonizing   *Enoch Arden* 204
Fire-hollowing this in Indian *f*,   „   569
No more in soldier *f* will he greet   *Ode on Well.* 21
veil His want in forms for *f*'s sake,   *In Mem. cxi* 6
What the *f* of the men?' 'They be of foolish *f*,   *Gareth and L.* 627
O Sir King, The *f* of that old knight-errantry   *Geraint and E.* 285
and sumptuously According to his *f*,   *Lancelot and E.* 871
In any knightly *f* for her sake.   *Pelleas and E.* 100
Knowest thou not the *f* of our speech?   *Lover's Tale i* 645
had updrawn A *f* and a phantasm of the form   *Sisters (E. and E.)* 133
In some such *f* as a man may be   *In Mem. cxiii* 7
Fashion (verb)   skill To strive, to *f*, to fulfil—
Fashion'd   (*See also* **Altar-fashion'd, Cleaner-fashion'd, Noblier-fashion'd, Owd-farran'd**)   holy hand hath
   f on the rock   *Gareth and L.* 1197
f for it A case of silk, and braided   *Lancelot and E.* 7
F by Merlin ere he past away,   *Holy Grail* 168
brooks Are *f* by the channel which they keep),   *Lover's Tale i* 567
a people have *f* and worship a Spirit   *Kapiolani* 1
F after certain laws;   *Poets and Critics* 5
Fast (adj.)   my friend was he, Once my *f* friend: *Sir J. Oldcastle* 62
By changes all too fierce and *f*   *Freedom* 22
Fast (s)   all the passion of a twelve hours' *f*.'   *Marr. of Geraint* 306
heard mass, broke *f*, and rode away: *Lancelot and E.* 415
life of prayer, Praise, *f* and alms.   *Holy Grail* 5
She gave herself, to *f*, and alms.   „   77
about him everywhere, despite All *f* and penance.   „   631
Fast with your *f*'s, not feasting   *Guinevere* 678
Penance?' 'F, Hairshirt and scourge—   *Sir J. Oldcastle* 141
Fast (adv.)   Two lives bound *f* in one   *Circumstance* 5
And I believe, if you were *f* my wife,   *Enoch Arden* 414
We must bind And keep you *f*, my Rosalind, *F*, *f*,
   my wild-eyed Rosalind,   *Rosalind* 43
We'll bind you *f* in silken cords,   „   49
'Lead, and I follow,' and *f*.away she fled.
   (*repeat*)   *Gareth and L.* 760, 990
Fast (verb)   If it may be, *f* Whole Lents,   *St. S. Stylites* 181
bear his armour? shall we *f*, or dine?   *Geraint and E.* 490
brother, *f* thou too and pray, And tell thy brother
   knights to *f* and pray,   *Holy Grail* 125

Father (s) (*continued*) O *F*, touch the east, and light *In Mem. xxx* 31
And doubtful joys the *f* move, ,, *xl* 9
How many a *f* have I seen, ,, *liii* 1
star Had fall'n into her *f's* grave, ,, *lxxxix* 48
f's bend Above more graves, ,, *xcviii* 15
Our *f's* dust is left alone And silent ,, *cv* 5
But crying, knows his *f* near; ,, *cxxiv* 20
O *f*! O God! was it well?— *Maud I i* 6
raging alone as my *f* raged in his mood ? ,, 53
sweet purse-mouth when my *f* dangled the grapes, ,, 71
When have I bow'd to her *f*, ,, *iv* 13
Your *f* has wealth well-gotten, ,, 18
Your *f* is ever in London, ,, 59
Why sits he here in his *f's* chair ? ,, *xiii* 23
Not touch on her *f's* sin: ,, *xix* 17
That Maud's dark *f* and mine Had bound ,, 37
Mine, mine—our *f's* have sworn. ,, 43
Thou noble *F* of her Kings to be, *Ded. of Idylls* 34
'Her *f* said That there between the man *Com. of Arthur* 78
we that fight for our fair *f* Christ, ,, 510
thy *f* Lot beside the hearth Lies like a log, *Gareth and L.* 74
Thy *f*, Uther, reft From my dead lord ,, 334
who from the wrongs his *f* did Would shape ,, 347
Affirming that his *f* left him gold, *Marr. of Geraint* 451
I thought, but that your *f* came between, *Geraint and E.* 314
And loved me serving in my *f's* hall ,, 699
I should have slain your *f*, seized yourself. ,, 838
My *f* hath begotten me in his wrath. *Balin and Balan* 283
My *f* died in battle against the King, *Merlin and V.* 42
My *f* died in battle for thy King, ,, 72
Leaving her household and good *f*, *Lancelot and E.* 14
Here laugh'd the saying 'Fie,' ,, 200
Nay, *f*, nay good *f*, shame me not ,, 207
But, *f*, give me leave, an if he will, ,, 219
Crept to her *f*, while he mused alone, ,, 748
'*F*, you call me wilful, and the fault Is yours ,, 750
Sweet *f*, will you let me lose my wits ?' ,, 752
Sweet *f*, I behold him in my dreams ,, 763
My *f*, to be sweet and serviceable ,, 767
Then her *f* nodding said, 'Ay, ay, ,, 770
Her *f's* latest word humm'd in her ear, ,, 780
brother's love, And your good *f's* kindness.' ,, 945
her *f*: 'Ay, a flash, I fear me, ,, 970
Then came her *f*, saying in low tones, ,, 994
call'd The *f*, and all three in hurry ,, 1024
So dwelt the *f* on her face, and thought ,, 1030
'Peace,' said her *f*, 'O my child, ,, 1062
'Highest ?' the *f* answer'd, echoing 'highest ?' ,, 1078
'Sweet *f*, all too faint and sick am I ,, 1086
so let me pass, My *f*, howsoe'er I seem to you, ,, 1092
wherefore cease, Sweet *f*, and bid call ,, 1099
sweet *f*, tender and true, Deny me not,' ,, 1110
She ceased: her *f* promised ,, 1130
Her *f* laid the letter in her hand, ,, 1134
in testimony, Her brethren, and her *f*, ,, 1300
'O *F*!' ask'd the maiden, *Holy Grail* 95
A slender page about her *f's* hall ,, 581
Fought in her *f's* battles ? wounded *Last Tournament* 592
So said my *f*, and himself was knight *Guinevere* 234
So said my *f*—yea, and furthermore, ,, 250
Not even thy wise *f* with his signs ,, 274
one, a bard; of whom my *f* said, ,, 277
So said my *f*—and that night the bard ,, 285
and the tales Which my good *f* told me, check me too
    Nor let me shame my *f's* memory, ,, 317
And so thou lean on our fair *f* Christ, ,, 562
Before he saw my day my *f* died, *Lover's Tale i* 191
She was motherless And I without a *f*. ,, 219
what use To know her *f* left us just before ,, 293
that same nearness Were *f* to this distance, ,, *ii* 29
His other *f* you! Kiss him, ,, *iv* 174
he sent, an' the *f* agreed; *First Quarrel* 18
You count the *f* of your fortune, *Sisters (E. and E.)* 28
My *f* with a child on either knee, ,, 54
he had stricken my *f* dead— *V. of Maeldune* 1

Father (s) (*continued*) slain my *f* the day before I was
    born. *V. of Maeldune* 8
I bad them remember my *f's* death, ,, 70
His *f's* have slain thy *f's* in war or in single strife,
    Thy *f's* have slain his *f's*, each taken a life for
    a life, Thy *f* had slain his *f*, ,, 121
The man that had slain my *f*. ,, 128
trembling *f's* call'd The God's own son *Tiresias* 16
my *F's* belong'd to the church of old, *The Wreck* 1
the heart of the *f* will care for his own.' ,, 98
'The heart of the *f* will spurn her,' ,, 99
one son had forged on his *f* and fled, *Despair* 69
Some say, the Light was *f* of the Night, And some,
    the Night was *f* of the Light, *Ancient Sage* 247
This *f* pays his debt with me, *The Flight* 20
What *f*, this or mine, was he, ,, 21
I loved him then; he *was* my *f* then.   No *f* now,
    the tyrant vassal of a tyrant vice ! ,, 24
My *f's* madness makes me mad— ,, 59
And tho' these *f's* will not hear, ,, 67
who ? who ? my *f* sleeps ! ,, 69
she knew this *f* well; ,, 87
f, mother,—be content, *Locksley H., Sixty* 25
Gone our sailor son thy *f*, *Open I. and C. Exhib.* 15
constancy Which has made your *f's* great ,, 24
Shall we sin our *f's* sin, *To Marq. of Dufferin* 47
why The sons before the *f's* die, *The Ring* 59
No! *f*, Spain, but Hubert brings me home ,, 175
F's fault Visited on the children ! ,, 303
you, poor desolate *F*, and poor me, *Romney's R.* 104, 106
'*F* and Mother will watch you grow'—(repeat) *Bandit's Death* 33
and the murderous *f* at rest, . . . *Mechanophilus* 21
As we surpass our *f's* skill, *Doubt and Prayer* 8
My *F*, and my Brother, and my God ! *Love and Duty* 5
Father (verb) in the round of time Still *f* Truth ?
Father'd See **Re-father'd**
Father-fool Thwarted by one of these old *f-f's*, *Aylmer's Field* 390
Father-grape *f-g* grew fat On Lusitanian summers. *Will Water.* 7
Fatherhood twelve sweet moons confused his *f*.' *Merlin and V.* 712
Fatherland sweet it was to dream of *F*, *Lotos-Eaters* 39
Fatherless this earth is a *f* Hell— *Despair* 57
Fatherlike Appraised his weight and fondled *f*, *Enoch Arden* 154
Fathom For thou canst not *f* it. *Poet's Mind* 4
Falser than all fancy *f's*, *Locksley Hall* 41
Philip did not *f* Annie's mind : *Enoch Arden* 344
'Tis hard for thee to *f* this; *In Mem. lxxxv* 90
dangled a hundred *f* of grapes, *V. of Maeldune* 56
Fathom-deep Should gulf him *f-d* in brine; *In Mem. x* 18
Fathom'd Which none have *f*. *Lover's Tale i* 518
Fathomless half-attain'd futurity, Tho' deep not *f*, *Ode to Memory* 34
Fatling reach its *f* innocent arms And lazy lingering fingers. *Princess vi* 138
Fatten many streams to *f* lower lands, *Golden Year* 34
Fatter he was *f* than his cure. *Edwin Morris* 15
No, there is *f* game on the moor; *Maud I i* 74
Fault *tho' the f's were thick as dust* *To the Queen* 18
'Proclaim the *f's* he would not show: *You might have won* 17
Nor mine the *f*, if losing both of these *Aylmer's Field* 719
gentleman of broken means (His father's *f*) *Princess i* 54
'My *f*' she wept 'my *f*! and yet not mine; ,, *iii* 30
The child is hers—for every little *f*, ,, *v* 87
her one *f* The tenderness, not yours, ,, *vi* 185
as dearer thou for *f's* Lived over: ,, *vii* 347
Not ours the *f* if we have feeble hosts— *Third of Feb.* 38
Or seeming-genial venial *f*, *Will* 13
let it be granted her: where is the *f*? *Maud I ii* 4
blind To the *f's* of his heart and mind, ,, *xix* 61
'THE *f* was mine, the *f* was mine'— ,, *II i* 1
'The *f* was mine,' he whisper'd, 'fly!' ,, 30
a little *f* Whereof I was not guilty; *Com. of Arthur* 341
wayside ambushings—No *f* of thine: *Gareth and L.* 433
'If Enid errs, let Enid learn her *f*.' *Marr. of Geraint* 132
creatures voiceless thro' the *f* of birth, *Geraint and E.* 266
and for her *f* she wept Of petulancy; *Merlin and V.* 952
He is all *f* who hath no *f* at all: *Lancelot and E.* 132
you call me wilful, and the *f* Is yours ,, 750

Fear (s) (*continued*) And *f*'s for our delicate Emmie — *In the Child. Hosp.* 66
Cloud-weaver of phantasmal hopes and *f*'s, — *To Victor Hugo* 2
fail Thro' craven *f*'s of being great. — *Hands all Round* 32
Had never swerved for craft or *f*, — *To Marq. of Dufferin* 27
as Gods against the *f* Of Death and Hell; — *Demeter and P.* 141
that worship which is *F*, Henceforth, — " 143
and paced his land In *f* of worse, — *To Mary Boyle* 30
May your *f*'s be vain! — *To one who ran down Eng.* 2
Still—at times A doubt, a *f*,— — *Akbar's Dream* 169
'Twere joy, not *f*, claspt hand-in-hand with thee, — *If I were loved* 9

Fear (verb) I *f* All may not doubt, — *Supp. Confessions* 177
I *f* to slide from bad to worse. — *Two Voices* 231
What is it that I may not *f*?' — " 240
That I should *f*,—if I were loved — *If I were loved* 4
I *f* My wound hath taken cold, — *M. d'Arthur* 165
I *f* it is too late, and I shall die.' — " 180
I *f* That we shall miss the mail: — *Walk. to the Mail* 111
'*F* not thou to loose thy tongue; — *Vision of Sin* 155
f no more for me; or if you *f* Cast all your cares — *Enoch Arden* 221
I *f*, If there were many Lilias in the brood, — *Princess, Pro.* 145
Let them not *f*: some said their heads were less: — " ii 147
I *f* My conscience will not count me fleckless; — " 293
But, dearest Lady, pray you *f* me not, — " 333
'Ah, *f* me not' Replied Melissa, — " 342
'What *f* ye, brawlers? am not I your Head? — " iv 498
what is it ye *f*? Peace! — " 500
'We *f*, indeed, you spent a stormy time — " v 121
f we not To break them more in their behoof, — " vi 60
Sighing she spoke 'I *f* They will not.' — " vii 297
Approach and *f* not;' breathe upon my brows; — " 353
Shall we *f* him? our own we never fear'd. — *Third of Feb.* 25
I *f* you'll listen to tales, be jealous — *Grandmother* 54
'*F* not, isle of blowing woodland, — *Boädicea* 38
We mock thee when we do not *f*: — *In Mem., Pro.* 30
She *f*'s not, or with thee beside — " Con. 43
And me behind her, will not *f*. — " 44
I *f*, the new strong wine of love, — *Maud I vi* 82
some one else may have much to *f*; — " xv 4
I should grow light-headed, I *f*, — " 100
Should I *f* to greet my friend — " II iv 85
I almost *f* they are not roses, but blood; — " v 78
F not to give this King thine only child, — *Com. of Arthur* 413
I *f* that I am no true wife.' — *Marr. of Geraint* 108
Like him who tries the bridge he *f*'s may fail, — *Geraint and E.* 303
Yet *f* me not: I call mine own self wild, — " 311
he *f*'s To lose his bone, and lays his foot — " 561
f not, Enid, I should fall upon him, — " 787
men may *f* Fresh fire and ruin. — " 822
you that most had cause To *f* me, *f* no longer, — " 825
f not, cousin; I am changed indeed.' — " 873
O Vivien, save ye *f* The monkish manhood, — *Merlin and V.* 34
Vivien answer'd, smiling scornfully, 'Why *f*? — " 38
I savour of thy—virtues? *f* them? no. — " 39
loathe, *f*—but honour me the more.' — " 122
make me *f* still more you are not mine, — " 327
Wherefore, if I *f*, Giving you power upon me — " 513
for I *f* My fate or folly, — " 926
a flash, I *f* me, that will strike my blossom dead, — *Lancelot and E.* 971
as a coward slinks from what he *f*'s To cope with, — *Pelleas and E.* 438
'*F* God: honour the King— — *Last Tournament* 302
Because he hates thee even more than *f*'s; — " 533
F not: thou shalt be guarded till my death. — *Guinevere* 448
I *f* My wound hath taken cold, — *Pass. of Arthur* 333
I *f* it is too late, and I shall die.' — " 348
tho' sometimes I *f* You may be flickering, — *Sisters (E. and E.)* 32
she'll never live thro' it, I *f*.' — *In the Child. Hosp.* 42
Priests Who *f* the king's hard common-sense — *Sir J. Oldcastle* 66
And a man men *f* is a man to be loved — *The Wreck* 18
Days that will glimmer, I *f*, — " 79
'Do you *f*?' and there came thro' the roar of the breaker a whisper, a breath, '*F*? am I not with you? — *Despair* 13
morning brings the day I hate and *f*; — *The Flight* 2
lurks, listens, *f*'s his victim may have fled— — " 71

Fear (verb) (*continued*) and what is it that you *f*? — *Happy* 1
an' thou'll git along, niver *f*, — *Church-warden, etc.* 7
F not thou the hidden purpose of that Power — *God and the Univ.* 5

Fear'd *f* To send abroad a shrill and terrible cry, — *Enoch Arden* 767
I *f* Lest the gay navy there should splinter — *Sea Dreams* 130
I *f* To meet a cold 'We thank you, — *Princess iv* 327
but *f* To incense the Head once more; — " vii 76
she *f* that I should lose my mind, — " 99
Shall we fear him? our own we never *f*. — *Third of Feb.* 25
I say, we *never f*! — " 29
There sat the Shadow *f* of man; — *In Mem. xxii* 12
And that she *f* she was not a true wife. — *Marr. of Geraint* 114
she *f* In every wavering brake an ambuscade. — *Geraint and E.* 50
Enid *f* his eyes, Moist as they were, — " 350
I ever *f* ye were not wholly mine; — *Merlin and V.* 315
ridd'n away to die?' So *f* the King, — *Lancelot and E.* 568
cope and crown Of all I hoped and *f*?— — *Lover's Tale ii* 27
he was *f* to look at me now. — *First Quarrel* 38
they *f* that we still could sting, — *The Revenge* 72
I *f* The very fountains of her life were chill'd; — *Sisters (E. and E.)* 265
I be *f* fur to tell tha 'ow much— — *Village Wife* 47
f myself turning crazed, — *Despair* 78
Found, *f* me dead, and groan'd, — *The Flight* 23
They was all on 'em *f* o' the Ghoäst — *Owd Roä* 37
She *f* I had forgotten her, — *The Ring* 102

Fearful (*See also* **Too-fearful**) Too *f* that you should not please. — *Miller's D.* 148
Half *f* that, with self at strife, — *Will Water.* 161
If you be *f*, then must we be bold. — *Third of Feb.* 19
Dismal error! *f* slaughter! — *The Captain* 65
the sea roars Ruin: a *f* night!' 'Not *f*; — *Sea Dreams* 81
'The simple, *f* child Meant nothing, — *Guinevere* 369

Fearing (*See also* **God-fearing**) hid my feelings, *f* they should do me wrong, — *Locksley Hall* 29
F the lazy gossip of the port, — *Enoch Arden* 335
Then *f* night and chill for Annie, — " 443
dwelt lingeringly on the latch, *F* to enter: — " 520
And *f* waved my arm to warn them off; — *Sea Dreams* 132
fling whate'er we felt, not *f*, into words. — *Third of Feb.* 6
F to lose, and all for a dead man, — *Geraint and E.* 564
Then, *f* for his hurt and loss of blood, — " 777
F the mild face of the blameless King, — " 812
But Vivien, *f* heaven had heard her oath, — *Merlin and V.* 940
f rust or soilure fashion'd for it — *Lancelot and E.* 7
Still hoping, *f* 'is it yet too late?' — *Guinevere* 691
f not to plunge Thy torch of life — *Tiresias* 158

Fear-tremulous her slow sweet eyes *F*-t, — *Merlin and V.* 86

Feast (s) Rise from the *f* of sorrow, lady, — *Margaret* 62
scare church-harpies from the master's *f*; — *To J. M. K.* 3
I made a *f*; I bad him come; — *The Sisters* 13
while Audley *f* Humm'd like a hive — *Audley Court* 4
No larger *f* than under plane or pine — *Lucretius* 213
near his tomb a *f* Shone, silver-set; — *Princess, Pro.* 105
Nymph, or Goddess, at high tide of *f*, — " i 197
Blanch'd in our annals, and perpetual *f*, — " vi 63
a *f* Of wonder, out of West and East, — *Ode Inter. Exhib.* 20
And we shall sit at endless *f*, — *In Mem. xlvii* 9
Be neither song, nor game, nor *f*; — " cv 21
The reeling Faun, the sensual *f*; — " cxviii 25
Who stay to share the morning *f*, — " Con. 75
Again the *f*, the speech, the glee, — " 101
the King Made *f* for, saying, as they sat at meat, — *Com. of Arthur* 247
that day a *f* had been Held in high hall, — *Gareth and L.* 847
suit of fray'd magnificence, Once fit for *f*'s of ceremony) — *Marr. of Geraint* 297
eyes, Moist as they were, wine-heated from the *f*; — *Geraint and E.* 351
Till when at *f* Sir Garlon likewise ask'd — *Balin and Balan* 347
our knights at *f* Have pledged us in this union, — *Lancelot and E.* 114
So dame and damsel glitter'd at the *f* — *Last Tournament* 225
such a *f* As never man had dream'd — *Guinevere* 263
Fast with your fasts, not feasting with your *f*'s; — " 678
And Julian made a solemn *f*: — *Lover's Tale iv* 187
such a *f*, ill-suited as it seem'd To such a time, — " 207
such a *f* So rich, so strange, — " 210
our solemn *f*—we ate and drank, — " 221

Feast (s) *(continued)* And when the *f* was near an end, he said: — *Lover's Tale iv* 229
Who could desire more beauty at a *f*?' — " 240
him nor lights nor *f* Dazed or amazed, — " 310
I would not mingle with their *f's*; — *Demeter and P.* 103
mouthing a bloodless name at *her* cannibal *f*, — *The Dawn* 12
Feast (verb) *f* with these in honour of their Earl; — *Geraint and E.* 287
a man Will honour those who *f* with him, — *Lover's Tale iv* 232
fairest flesh at last is filth on which the worm will *f*; — *Happy* 30
Feasted three days he *f* us, And on the fourth — *Princess i* 118
he the wisest man *F* the woman wisest then, — " *ii* 351
having there so oft with all his knights *F*, — *Holy Grail* 224
Feastful Singing and murmuring in her *f* mirth, — *Palace of Art* 177
Feasting Fast with your fasts, not *f* with your feasts; — *Guinevere* 678
Feat often heard me praise Your *f's* of arms, — *Marr. of Geraint* 435
Feather (s) *(See also* **Helmet-feather**) All grass of silky *f* grow— — *Talking Oak* 269
I did but shear a *f*, and dream and truth — *Princess v* 541
We'll be birds of a *f*, — *Window, Spring* 14
ask me whether The habit, hat, and *f*, — *Maud I xx* 18
Or ev'n a fall'n *f*, vanish'd again. — *Last Tournament* 372
ready for their bridal-time By change of *f*: — *Sisters (E. and E.)* 72
Feather (verb) all about the large lime *f's* low, — *Gardener's D.* 47
wood began To *f* toward the hollow, (repeat) — *Enoch Arden* 68, 374
Feather'd *See* **Coppice-feather'd**
Featherfan Cooling her false cheek with a *f*, — *Aylmer's Field* 289
Feathering the ripple *f* from her bows: — *Enoch Arden* 544
Feature chisell'd *f's* clear and sleek. — *A Character* 30
Conjectures of the *f's* of her child — *Œnone* 252
Reading her perfect *f's* in the gloom, — *Gardener's D.* 175
I cannot see the *f's* right, — *In Mem. lxx* 1
that small charm of *f* mine, pursued— — *Merlin and V.* 76
Featured *(See also* **Clear-featured**) The mother *f* in the son; — *Open I. and C. Exhib.* 12
February (adj.) Many many welcomes F fair- maid, (repeat) — *The Snowdrop* 2, 10
February (s) silver tongue, Cold *F* loved, is dry; — *The Blackbird* 14
Fed *(See also* **Dew-fed, Fancy-fed, Fountain-fed, Full-fed**) *f* With the clear-pointed flame of chastity, — *Isabel* 1
f the time With odour — *Arabian Nights* 64
F thee, a child, lying alone, — *Eleänore* 25
these, tho' *f* with careful dirt, — *Amphion* 89
By dancing rivulets *f* his flocks — *To E. L.* 22
They *f* her theories, in and out of place — *Princess i* 129
I *f* you with the milk of every Muse; — " *iv* 295
breast that *f* or arm that dandled you, — " *vi* 181
heart and ear were *f* To hear him, — *In Mem. lxxxix* 2
distant hills From hidden summits *f* with rills — " *ciii* 7
You have but *f* on the roses — *Maud I iv* 60
f With honey'd rain and delicate air, — " *xviii* 20
Memory *f* the soul of Love with tears. — *Lover's Tale i* 822
Why *f* we from one fountain ? — " *ii* 24
f and cherish'd him, and saved his life. — " *iv* 264
island-myriads *f* from alien lands— — *The Fleet* 12
She watch'd me, she nursed me, she *f* me, — *Charity* 33
Federation the *F* of the world. — *Locksley Hall* 128
The *F's* and the Powers; — *Day-Dm., L'Envoi* 16
Fee To hold the costliest love in *f*. — *In Mem. lxxix* 4
Mammonite mother kills her babe for a burial *f*, — *Maud I i* 45
Feeäd (feed) theer warn't not *f* for a cow; — *N. Farmer, O. S.* 37
an' now theer's lots o' *f*, — " 39
Feeäl (feel) '*F* thou this! thou can't graw — *North. Cobbler* 86
Feeäld (felt) I *f* it drip o' my neck. — *Owd Roä* 42
till 'e *f* 'e could howd 'is oän, — *Church-warden, etc.* 19
Feeät (feet) cleän as a flower fro' 'eäd to *f*: — *North. Cobbler* 44
Wi' Roäver athurt my *f*, — *Owd Roä* 30
British farmers to stan' ageän o' their *f*. — " 46
Feeble Now am I *f* grown; — *St. S. Stylites* 36
And laid the *f* infant in his arms; — *Enoch Arden* 152
his knees Were *f*, so that falling prone — " 779
frail at first And *f*, all unconscious of itself, — *Princess vii* 117
disengage myself, but fail'd, Being so *f*: — *Lover's Tale i* 693
wild hearts and *f* wings That every sophister can lime. — *Love thou thy land* 11
Not ours the fault if we have *f* hosts— — *Third of Feb.* 38

Feeble *(continued)* The *f* soul, a haunt of fears, — *In Mem. cx* 3
f vassals of wine and anger and lust, — *Maud II i* 43
thro' the *f* twilight of this world Groping, — *Geraint and E.* 5
and Pellam's *f* cry, 'Stay, stay him!' — *Balin and Balan* 420
Feebler Is *f* than his knees; — *Ancient Sage* 135
Then comes the *f* heiress of your plan, — *Princess iii* 237
it drown'd The *f* motion underneath his hand. — *Lover's Tale iv* 83
Feed *(See also* **Feeäd**) For the Ox *F's* in the herb, — *Supp. Confessions* 151
Thy kingly intellect shall *f*, — *Clear-headed friend* 20
Upon himself himself did *f*: — *A Character* 27
Some honey-converse *f's* thy mind, — *Adeline* 40
little ducts began To *f* thy bones with lime, — *Two Voices* 326
Nor *f* with crude imaginings The herd, — *Love thou thy land* 10
The fat earth *f* thy branchy root, — *Talking Oak* 273
That hoard, and sleep, and *f*, — *Ulysses* 5
That early woke to *f* her little ones, — *Princess vii* 252
The full new life that *f's* thy breath — *In Mem. lxxxvi* 10
That *f* the mothers of the flock — " *c* 16
a rose-carnation *f* With summer spice — " *ci* 7
Nor *f* with sighs a passing soul: — " *cviii* 4
goodly cheer To *f* the sudden guest, — *Geraint and E.* 284
call'd for flesh and wine to *f* his spears. — " 601
Feeding like horses when you hear them *f*; — " 606
and *f's* their downward flow. — *Lover's Tale i* 784
f the rebels of the crown, — *Columbus* 131
F the budding rose of boyhood — *Locksley H., Sixty* 143
brook that *f's* this lakelet murmur'd 'debt,' — *The Ring* 171
we will *f* her with our mountain air, — " 319
Feedeth *f* The senses with a still delight — *Margaret* 16
Feeding water-pipes beneath, *F* the flower; — *D. of F. Women* 207
And *f* high, and living soft, — *The Goose* 17
F like horses when you hear them feed; — *Geraint and E.* 606
Feel *(See also* **Feäl, Feeäl**) and I *f* as thou hast felt = — *Supp. Confessions* 82
I *f* the tears of blood arise — *Oriana* 77
f their immortality Die in their hearts — *The Mermaid* 29
For Kate no common love will *f*; — *Kate* 14
To *f*, altho' no tongue can prove, — *Two Voices* 445
Joying to *f* herself alive, — *Palace of Art* 175
Put forth and *f* a gladder clime.' — *On a Mourner* 15
Like one that *f's* a nightmare on his bed — *M. d'Arthur* 177
Begin to *f* the truth and stir of day, — " *Ep.* 19
make a man *f* strong in speaking truth; — *Love and Duty* 70
I *f* about my feet The berried briony — *Talking Oak* 147
my heart so slow To *f* it! — *Love and Duty* 35
unto him who works, and *f's* he works. — *Golden Year* 73
guinea helps the hurt that Honour *f's*, — *Locksley Hall* 105
Make me *f* the wild pulsation — " 109
the master-chord Of all I felt and *f*. — *Will Water.* 28
Live long, nor *f* in head or chest — " 237
Their voices make me *f* so solitary.' — *Enoch Arden* 397
f's a glimmering strangeness in his dream. — *The Brook* 216
Were living nerves to *f* the rent; — *Aylmer's Field* 536
And *f* myself the shadow of a dream. — *Princess i* 18
f, at least, that silence here were sin, — *Third of Feb.* 37
which has power to *f* 'I am I'? — *High. Pantheism* 8
But they—they *f* the desire of the deep— — *Voice and the P.* 19
As one who *f's* the immeasurable world, — *A Dedication* 7
To put in words the grief I *f*; — *In Mem. v* 2
and *f's* Her place is empty, — " *xiii* 3
I should not *f* it to be strange. — " *xiv* 20
reaches forth her arms To *f* from world to world, — " *xxi* 19
I *f* it, when I sorrow most; — " *xxvii* 14
and call To what I *f* is Lord of all, — " *lv* 19
Yet *f's*, as in a pensive dream, — " *lxiv* 17
I felt and *f*, tho' left alone, — " *lxxxv* 42
Canst thou *f* for me Some painless sympathy — " 87
My Ghost may *f* that thine is near. — " *xciii* 16
She darkly *f's* him great and wise, — " *xcvii* 34
To *f* once more, in placid awe, — " *cxxii* 5
I *f* There is a lower and a higher; — " *cxxix* 3
To *f* thee some diffusive power, — " *cxxx* 7
I *f* with thee the drowsy spell. — *Maud I xviii* 72
I *f* I shall owe you a debt, — " *xix* 87
I *f* so free and so clear By the loss — " 98

Feel (continued) loved with that full love I *f* for thee,   *Gareth and L.* 84
the plant that *f's* itself Root-bitten   „ 453
in your frosty cells ye *f* the fire!   *Balin and Balan* 446
Caress her: let her *f* herself forgiven Who *f's* no heart to ask another boon.   *Merlin and V.* 381
Might *f* some sudden turn of anger born   „ 531
low desire Not to *f* lowest makes them level all;   „ 828
In moments when he *f's* he cannot die,   *Holy Grail* 916
find a nest and *f's* a snake, he drew: *Pelleas and E.* 437
For *f* this arm of mine—   *Last Tournament* 690
' lo mine helpmate, do to *f* My purpose   *Guinevere* 485
find or *f* a way Thro' this blind haze,   *Pass. of Arthur* 75
Like one that *f's* a nightmare on his bed   „ 345
I *f* thy breath; I come, great Mistress   *Lover's Tale i* 21
flaw In his throne's title make him *f* so frail,   *Sir J. Oldcastle* 73
We *f* we are nothing—   *De Prof., Human C.* 6
We *f* we are something—   „ 7
What did I *f* that night?   *Despair* 3
She *f's* the Sun is hid but for a night,   *Ancient Sage* 73
we *f* Within ourselves is highest,   „ 87
Scarce *f's* the senses break away To mix   „ 152
F's that the deep is boundless,   „ 192
to *f* his breath Upon my cheek—   *The Flight* 45
these would *f* and follow Truth   *Locksley H., Sixty* 119
I *f* the deathless heart of motherhood   *Demeter and P.* 41
Who *f* no touch of my temptation,   *Romney's R.* 121
Polytheism and Islám *f* after thee.   *Akbar's D., Inscrip.* 2
Feel'd (felt) till ageän I *f* mysen free.   *North. Cobbler* 80
I *f* thy arm es I stood wur a-creeäpin   *Spinster's S's.* 26
Feeling *f* all along the garden-wall,   *Enoch Arden* 773
She laid A *f* finger on my brows,   *Princess vi* 121
And often *f* of the helpless hands,   „ *vii* 111
When flower is *f* after flower;   *In Mem. xxxix* 7
The blind wave *f* round his long sea-hall   *Merlin and V.* 232
I, *f* that you felt me worthy trust,   „ 334
sideways downward to her belt, And *f*;   „ 851
Feeling (s) (*See also* **Fellow-feeling**) embassies of love,   *Gardener's D.* 19
To tamper with the *f's*,   *Locksley Hall* 29
Saying ' I have hid my *f's*,   „ 44
to decline On a range of lower *f's*   „ 95
' They were dangerous guides the *f's*—   *The Brook* 95
Divorce the *F* from her mate the Deed.   *In Mem. xx* 5
Who speak their *f* as it is,   „ *xxx* 17
We ceased: a gentler *f* crept Upon us: *Princess v* 108
Feign things that being caught *f* death,   „ *iv* 55
Feign'd sweet as those by hopeless fancy *f*   *Maud I vi* 52
A face of tenderness might be *f*,   *Geraint and E.* 588
yet lay still, and *f* himself as dead,   *Lancelot and E.* 842
and *f* a sleep until he slept.   *Princess iv* 587
Feigning *f* pique at what she call'd The raillery,
Fell (adj.) Outram and Havelock breaking their way through the *f* mutineers?   *Def. of Lucknow* 96
the bees is as *f* as owt.   *N. Farmer, N. S.* 40
Fell (hair) Half-suffocated in the hoary *f*   *Merlin and V.* 840
Fell (mountain) ye meanwhile far over moor and *f*   *Maud I xviii* 76
gleam from yonder vale, Some far blue *f*,   *Early Spring* 34
lured that falcon from his eyry on the *f*,   *Happy* 59
he was coming down the *f*—   „ 82
Fell (verb) (*See also* **Fell out**) rusted nails *f* from the knots   *Mariana* 3
Her tears *f* with the dews at even;   „ 13
Her tears *f* ere the dews were dried;   „ 14
The shadow of the poplar *f* Upon her bed,   „ 55
springing forth anew Where'er they *f*,   *The Poet* 22
the babble of the stream *F*,   *Mariana in the S.* 52
I kiss'd away before they *f*.   *Miller's D.* 152
They were together, and she *f*;   *The Sisters* 4
folds, that floating as they *f* Lit up a torrent-bow.   *Palace of Art* 35
on the fourth she *f*, Like Herod,   „ 218
and loathing of her solitude *F* on her,   „ 230
because the kiss he gave me, ere I *f*,   *D. of F. Women* 235
F in a doze; and half-awake I heard   *The Epic* 13
So flash'd and *f* the brand Excalibur: *M. d'Arthur* 142
and threaten'd darkness, flared and *f*;   „ *Ep.* 2
the sun *f*, and all the land was dark. (repeat)   *Dora* 79, 109
The wreath of flowers *f* At Dora's feet.   „ 102

Fell (verb) (continued) in wild Mahratta-battle *f* my father   *Locksley Hall* 155
Bullets *f* like rain;   *The Captain* 46
The silver lily heaved and *f*;   *To E. L.* 19
by mischance he slipt and *f*:   *Enoch Arden* 106
on him *f*, Altho' a grave and staid God-fearing man,   „ 111
these things *f* on her Sharp as reproach.   „ 487
f Sun-stricken, and that other lived alone.   „ 569
and so *f* back and spoke no more.   „ 914
Tho' Leolin flamed and *f* again,   *Aylmer's Field* 409
f The woman shrieking at his feet,   „ 810
and *f* In vast sea-cataracts   *Sea Dreams* 53
The statues, king or saint, or founder *f*;   „ 224
f on him, Clasp'd, kiss'd him, wail'd: *Lucretius* 279
he bestrode my Grandsire, when he *f*,   *Princess ii* 242
Grew broader toward his death and *f*,   „ *iii* 364
Stirring a sudden transport rose and *f*.   „ *iv* 29
the tear, She sang of, shook and *f*,   „ 60
wing'd Her transit to the throne, whereby she *f*   „ 378
but *f* Into his father's hands,   „ 401
call'd Across the tumult and the tumult *f*.   „ 497
' then we *f* Into your father's hand,   „ *v* 50
darkness closed me; and I *f*.   „ 542
From the high tree the blossom wavering *f*,   „ *vi* 80
But sadness on the soul of Ida *f*,   „ *vii* 29
Star after star, arose and *f*;   „ 50
back I *f*, and from mine arms she rose   „ 159
She moved, and at her feet the volume *f*.   „ 254
While horse and hero *f*,   *Light Brigade* 44
Yet Harold's England *f* to Norman swords;   *W. to Marie Alex.* 22
The torrent vineyard streaming *f*   *The Daisy* 10
A PLAGUE upon the people *f*,   *The Victim* 1
down their statue of Victory *f*.   *Boädicea* 30
F the colony, city, and citadel,   „ 86
Thro' four sweet years arose and *f*,   *In Mem. xxii* 3
And sadly *f* our Christmas-eve.   „ *xxx* 4
In vaults and catacombs, they *f*;   „ *lviii* 4
And calmly *f* our Christmas-eve: „ *lxxviii* 4
And *f* in silence on his neck: „ *ciii* 44
rock that *f* with him when he *f*.   *Maud I i* 8
a silence *f* with the waking bird,   „ *xxii* 17
The white lake-blossom *f* into the lake   „ 47
mood is changed, for it *f* at a time of year   „ *III vi* 4
sword rose, the hind *f*, the herd was driven,   *Com. of Arthur* 432
A slender-shafted Pine Lost footing, *f*,   *Gareth and L.* 4
And drops of water *f* from either hand;   „ 220
the King's calm eye *F* on, and check'd,   „ 548
they shock'd, and Kay *F* shoulder-slipt,   „ 759
F, as if dead; but quickly rose and drew,   „ 967
Went sliding down so easily, and *f*,   „ 1224
there *f* A horror on him, lest his gentle wife,   *Marr. of Geraint* 28
He spoke and *f* to work again.   „ 292
f at last In the great battle fighting   „ 595
it *f* Like flaws in summer laying lusty corn: „ 763
jangling, the casque *F*, and he started   *Geraint and E.* 389
saw the chargers of the two that *f*   „ 481
Prince, without a word, from his horse *f*.   „ 508
a fair death, and *f* Against the heathen   „ 968
His arm half rose to strike again, but *f*:   *Balin and Balan* 223
Garlon, reeling slowly backward, *f*,   „ 397
and either *f*, and swoon'd away.   „ 563
Then *f* on Merlin a great melancholy;   *Merlin and V.* 189
they *f* and made the glen abhorr'd;   *Lancelot and E.* 42
slipt and *f* into some pool or stream,   „ 214
Treroit, Where many a heathen *f*;   „ 302
when he *f* From talk of war to traits of pleasantry—   „ 320
' Of all this will I nothing; ' and so *f*,   „ 967
back the maiden *f*, Then gave a languid hand   „ 1031
raised his head, their eyes met and hers *f*,   „ 1312
showers of flowers *F* as we past;   *Holy Grail* 349
F into dust, and I was left alone, (repeat)   *Holy Grail* 389, 400, 419
she too, *F* into dust and nothing,   *Holy Grail* 397
The plowman left his plowing, and *f* down Before it;   „ 404
milkmaid left her milking, and *f* down Before it,   „ 406
as he spoke *F* into dust, and disappear'd,   „ 436
Then *f* the floods of heaven drowning the deep.   „ 533

Felt (*continued*)   transfer The whole I *f* for him to you.   *In Mem. lxxxv* 104
and *f* The same, but not the same ;   „ *lxxxvii* 13
I *f* the thews of Anakim,   „ *ciii* 31
A love of freedom rarely *f*,   „ *cix* 13
And *f* thy triumph was as mine ;   „ *cx* 14
Stood up and answer'd, ' I have *f*.'   „ *cxxiv* 16
Because he *f* so fix'd in truth :   „ *cxxv* 8
Nor have I *f* so much of bliss   „ *Con.* 5
f himself in his force to be Nature's crowning race.   *Maud I iv* 33
F a horror over me creep,   „ *xiv* 35
I *f* she was slowly dying Vext with lawyers   „ *xix* 21
Strange, that I *f* so gay,   „ *xx* 1
I cleaved to a cause that I *f* to be pure   „ *III vi* 31
I have *f* with my native land,   „ 58
His love, unseen but *f*, o'ershadow Thee,   *Ded. of Idylls* 51
F the light of her eyes into his life   *Com. of Arthur* 56
but *f* him more, Of closest kin to me :   *Gareth and L.* 126
f his young heart hammering in his ears,   „ 322
he *f*, despite his mail, Strangled,   „ 1151
I *f* Thy manhood thro' that wearied lance   „ 1265
Lancelot thro' his warm blood *f* Ice strike,   „ 1398
F ye were somewhat, yea, and by your state   *Marr. of Geraint* 430
He *f*, were she the prize of bodily force,   „ 541
I *f* That I could rest, a rock in ebbs and flows,   „ 811
f that tempest brooding round his heart,   *Geraint and E.* 11
f Her low firm voice and tender government.   „ 193
f the warm tears falling on his face ;   „ 586
She *f* so blunt and stupid at the heart :   „ 747
And *f* him hers again : she did not weep,   „ 768
f His work was neither great nor wonderful,   „ 920
and he *f* his being move In music with his order,   *Balin and Balan* 211
He *f* the hollow-beaten mosses thud   „ 321
when their foreheads *f* the cooling air,   „ 589
he lifted faint eyes ; he *f* One near him ;   „ 594
old man, Tho' doubtful, *f* the flattery,   *Merlin and V.* 184
I, feeling that you *f* me worthy trust,   „ 334
I *f* as tho' I knew this cursed charm,   „ 435
that I lay And *f* them slowing ebbing,   „ 437
darkling *f* the sculptured ornament   „ 734
Thro' her own side she *f* the sharp lance go ;   *Lancelot and E.* 624
f the knot Climb in her throat,   „ 740
And *f* the boat shock earth,   *Holy Grail* 812
f the sun Beat like a strong knight on his helm,   *Pelleas and E.* 22
she, that *f* the cold touch on her throat,   „ 488
but *f* his eyes Harder and drier than a fountain bed   „ 506
and *f* the goodly hounds Yelp at his heart,   *Last Tournament* 503
My soul, I *f* my hatred for my Mark Quicken   „ 519
f the King's breath wander o'er her neck,   *Guinevere* 582
f the blast Beat on my heated eyelids,   *Lover's Tale iii* 27
Thrice in a second, *f* him tremble too,   „ *iv* 324
I *f* that my heart was hard,   *First Quarrel* 76
An' I *f* I had been to blame ;   „ 90
I *f* I could do it no more.   *In the Child. Hosp.* 60
I *f* one warm tear fall upon it.   *Tiresias* 167
The child that I *f* I could die for—   *The Wreck* 36
till I *f* myself ready to weep   „ 51
With the first great love I had *f*   „ 76
Does it matter so much what I *f*?   *Despair* 4
but *f* thro' what we feel   *Ancient Sage* 87
F within us as ourselves, the Powers of Good,   *Locksley H., Sixty* 273
I *f* On a sudden I know not what,   *The Ring* 31
and *f* An icy breath play on me,   „ 130
and *f* a gentle hand Fall on my forehead,   „ 418
I *f* for what I could not find, the key,   „ 440
And sanguine Lazarus *f* a vacant hand   *To Mary Boyle* 31
I *f* I could end myself too with the dagger—   *Bandit's Death* 37
Female The stately flower of *f* fortitude,   *Isabel* 11
A random string Your finer *f* sense offends.   *Day-Dm., L'Envoi* 2
We sent mine host to purchase *f* gear ;   *Princess i* 199
All beauty compass'd in a *f* form,   „ *ii* 34
The circle rounded under *f* hands   „ 372
tender ministries Of *f* hands and hospitality.'   „ *vi* 73
and served With *f* hands and hospitality.'   „ 96
and the swarm Of *f* whisperers :   „ 356
swarms of men Darkening her *f* field :   „ *vii* 34

Female (*continued*)   manhood fused with *f* grace   *In Mem. cix* 17
In such a sort,   *On one who affec. E. M.* 3
Which types all Nature's male and *f* plan,   „
then a loftier form Than *f*,   *Princess iv* 216
Fen From the dark *f* the oxen's low Came   *Mariana* 28
Fly o'er waste *f*'s and windy fields.   *Sir Galahad* 60
raised the school, and drain'd the *f*.   *Locksley H., Sixty* 268
somewheers i' the Wowd or the *F*,   *Church-warden, etc.* 47
Fence three horses that have broken *f*,   *Princess ii* 386
Robins—a niver mended a *f*:   *N. Farmer, O. S.* 50
Break me a bit o' the esh for his 'eäd, lad, out o' the *f*!   „ *N. S.* 41
An' the *f*'s all on 'em bolster'd oop   *Owd Roä* 32
Fenced (**fought**) voice with which I *f* A little ceased,   *Two Voices* 317
Fenced (**hedged**) I *f* it round with gallant institutes,   *Princess v* 392
Ferdinand *F* Hath signed it and our Holy Catholic queen   *Columbus* 29
I pray you tell King *F* who plays with me,   „ 223
Fere And raceth freely with his *f*,   *Supp. Confessions* 158
Fern (*See also* **Ice-ferns, Lady-fern, Tree-fern**) learned names of agaric, moss and *f*,   *Edwin Morris* 17
Hail, hidden to the knees in *f*,   *Talking Oak* 29
Oh, hide thy knotted knees in *f*,   „ 93
O muffle round thy knees with *f*,   „ 149
O flourish, hidden deep in *f*,   „ 201
Step deeper yet in herb and *f*,   „ 245
Among the palms and *f*'s and precipices ;   *Enoch Arden* 593
And sparkle out among the *f*,   *The Brook* 25
In copse and *f* Twinkled the innumerable   „ 133
From slope to slope thro' distant *f*'s,   *Princess, Con.* 99
stood a shatter'd archway plumed with *f*;   *Marr. of Geraint* 316
all round was open space, And *f* and heath :   *Pelleas and E.* 29
f without Burnt as a living fire of emeralds,   „ 34
The deer, the dews, the *f*, the founts,   *Last Tournament* 727
sparkle of a cloth On *f* and foxglove.   *Sisters (E. and E.)* 118
Ferreted I have *f* out their burrowings,   *Merlin and V.* 55
Ferule As boys that slink From *f*   *Princess v* 74
Fervent With such a *f* flame of human love,   *Holy Grail* 74
Fescue Sweeping the frothfly from the *f*   *Aylmer's Field* 530
Festal With music and sweet showers Of *f* flowers,   *Ode to Memory* 78
On the hall-hearths the *f* fires,   *Day-Dm., Sleep. P.* 14
With *f* cheer, With books and music,   *In Mem. cvii* 21
on a *f* day When Guinevere was crossing   *Merlin and V.* 4
' If I be loved, these are my *f* robes,   *Lancelot and E.* 909
make her *f* hour Dark with the blood of man   *St. Telemachus* 79
Fester Eye, to which all order *f*'s,   *Locksley Hall* 133
Festival Two strangers meeting at a *f*;   *Circumstance* 11
illuminate All your towns for a *f*,   *On Jub. Q. Victoria* 19
Festoon in many a wild *f* Ran riot,   *Œnone* 100
Festooning Their humid arms *f* tree to tree,   *D. of F. Women* 70
Fetch Go *f* your Alice here,' she said :   *Miller's D.* 143
And down I went to *f* my bride :   „ 145
Go *f* a pint of port :   *Will Water.* 4
Eh, let me *f* 'em, Arden,'   *Enoch Arden* 871
the colt would *f* its price :   *The Brook* 149
with furs And jewels, gifts, to *f* her :   *Princess i* 43
f the wine, Arrange the board and brim the glass ;   *In Mem. cvii* 15
f Fresh victual for these mowers of our Earl ;   *Geraint and E.* 628
I will *f* you forage from all fields,   „
Lancelot went ambassador, at first, To *f* her,   *Merlin and V.* 775
Well, I will wear it : *f* it out to me :   *Lancelot and E.* 371
Fur 'e'd *f* an' carry like owt,   *Owd Roä* 6
Fetch'd-Fetch *fetch'd* His richest beeswing from a binn   *Aylmer's Field* 404
booöks *fetch'd* nigh to nowt at the saäle,   *Village Wife* 73
I *fetcht* 'im a kick an' 'e went.   *Owd Roä* 62
Fettle I could *f* and clump owd booöts   *North. Cobbler* 13
Feud Rose *f*, with question unto whom 'twere due :   *Œnone* 82
New and Old, disastrous *f*,   *Love thou thy land* 77
how they mar this little by their *f*'s.   *Sea Dreams* 49
' How grew this *f* betwixt the right and left.'   *Princess iii* 77
Then rose a little *f* betwixt the two,   „ *Con.* 23
I wage not any *f* with Death   *In Mem. lxxxii* 1
Ring out the *f* of rich and poor,   „ *cvi* 11
And ever mourning over the *f*,   *Maud I xix* 31
splinter it into *f*'s Serving his traitorous end;   *Guinevere* 18

Feud (*continued*)   counter-yells of *f* And faction,   *To Duke of Argyll* 8
    Before the *f* of Gods had marr'd our peace,   *Death of Œnone* 32
Feudal   above their heads I saw The *f* warrior lady-clad;   *Princess, Pro.* 119
    A *f* knight in silken masquerade,   "   234
    And tuft with grass a *f* tower;   *In Mem.* cxxviii 20
Fever   till at last a *f* seized On William,   *Dora* 54
    In hungers and in thirsts, *f*'s and cold,   *St. S. Stylites* 12
    some low *f* ranging round to spy The weakness   *Aylmer's Field* 569
    mix the foaming draught Of *f*,   *Princess* ii 252
    fan my brows and blow The *f* from my cheek,   *In Mem.* lxxxvi 9
    There *f* seized upon him: *Lover's Tale* iv 132
    there from *f* and my care of him Sprang up   "   143
    we talkt o' my darter es died o' the *f* at fall: *Village Wife* 10
    f'ed baäked Jinny's 'eäd as bald as one o' them heggs,   "   102
    Cholera, scurvy, and *f*,   *Def. of Lucknow* 84
    f's, fights, Mutinies, treacheries—   *Columbus* 225
    summer days' of *f*, and want of care !   *The Wreck* 147
    fire of *f* creeps across the rotted floor,   *Locksley H., Sixty* 223
    born of *f*, or the fumes Of that dark opiate dose   *Romney's R.* 30
    She died of a *f* caught when a nurse   *Charity* 41
Fever'd   so hot, So *f*! never colt would more delight   *Romney's R.* 13
    Upon my *f* brows that shook and throbb'd   *Lover's Tale* iii 7
Feverous (*See also* **Brain-feverous**)   A tongue-tied Poet
    in the *f* days,   *Golden Year* 10
    who slept After a night of *f* wakefulness,   *Enoch Arden* 231
    or laid his *f* pillow smooth !   *Aylmer's Field* 701
Fever-worn   When, pale as yet, and *f-w*,   *To the Queen* ii 4
Few (adj.)   Sharp and *f*, but seeming-bitter   *Rosalind* 31
    ' I found him when my years were *f*;   *Two Voices* 271
    Who spoke *f* words and pithy,   *Princess, Con.* 94
    For those are *f* we hold as dear;   *To F. D. Maurice* 46
    While another is cheating the sick of a *f* last gasps,   *Maud* I i 43
    f, F, but all brave, all of one mind with him;   *Com. of Arthur* 254
    so *f* words, and seem'd So justified   *Geraint and E.* 395
    That has but one plain passage of *f* notes,   *Lancelot and E.* 895
    Thanks to the kindly dark faces who fought with
    us, faithful and *f*,   *Def. of Lucknow* 70
    these *f* lanes of elm And whispering oak.   *To Mary Boyle* 67
    some *f* drops of that distressful rain Fell on my face,   *Lover's Tale* i 698
Few (s)   Clash'd with his fiery *f* and won;   *Ode on Well.* 100
    that honest *f*, Who give the Fiend   *To F. D. Maurice* 5
    F at first will place thee well;   *Poets and Critics* 10
Fewer   we were every day *f* and *f*.   *Def. of Lucknow* 49
    albeit their glorious names Were *f*,   *Princess* ii 156
Fewmet   But at the slot or *f*'s of a deer,   *Last Tournament* 371
Feyther (father)   Them or thir *f*'s, tha sees,   *N. Farmer, N. S.* 49
    F 'ad ammost nowt;   "   51
    F run oop to the farm,   "   54
    Coom ! coom ! *f*,' 'e says,   *Village Wife* 69
    Sa *f* an' son was buried together,   "   90
    F 'ud saäy I wur ugly es sin,   *Spinster's S's.* 15
    Fur if iver thy *f*'ed riled me   *Church-Warden, etc.* 41
Fiat   This *f* somewhat soothed himself   *Aylmer's Field* 26
Fibre   Thy *f*'s net the dreamless head,   *In Mem.* ii 3
Fibred   *See* **Hairy-fibred**
Fibrous   pale and *f* as a wither'd leaf,   *Lover's Tale* i 422
Fickle   ' You're too slight and *f*,' I said,   *Edward Gray* 19
    bright and fierce and *f* is the South,   *Princess* iv 97
    Whatever *f* tongues may say.   *In Mem.* xxvi 4
    ' Rapt from the *f* and the frail   "   xxx 25
    so *f* are men—the best !   *The Ring* 392
Fictive   Who dabbling in the fount of *f* tears,   *The Brook* 93
Fiddle   And ta'en my *f* to the gate, (repeat)   *Amphion* 11, 15
    Twang out, my *f*! shake the twigs !   "   61
    wa 'greed as well as a *f* i' tune: *North. Cobbler* 12
Fiddled   And *f* in the timber !   *Amphion* 16
Fie   she lifted either arm, ' F on thee, King !   *Gareth and L.* 658
Field (adj.)   (*See also* **Field-flower**)   like the arrow-seeds
    of the *f* flower,   *The Poet* 19
Field (s)   (*See also* **Autumn-fields, Battle-field, Feäld,
    Field-of-battle, Four-field, Harvest-field, War-
    field, Winter-field**) the high *f* on the bushless Pike,   *Ode to Memory* 96
    Whither away from the high green *f*,   *Sea-Fairies* 8
    f and wood Grow green beneath the showery gray,   *My life is full* 16
    her sacred blood doth drown The *f*'s,   *Poland* 5

Field (s) (*continued*)   Long *f*'s of barley and of rye,   *L. of Shalott* i 2
    And thro' the *f* the road runs by   "   4
    That sparkled on the yellow *f*,   "   iii 8
    The willowy hills and *f*'s among,   "   iv 25
    thy father play'd In his free *f*,   *Two Voices* 320
    And forth into the *f*'s I went,   "   448
    see me more in the long gray *f*'s at night;   *May Queen, N. Y's. E.* 26
    in the *f*'s all round I hear the bleating of
    the lamb.   "   *Con.* 2
    He shines upon a hundred *f*'s,   "   50
    Weary the wandering *f*'s of barren foam.   *Lotos-Eaters* 42
    in fair *f* Myself for such a face had boldly died,'   *D. of F. Women* 97
    Then stept she down thro' town and *f*   *Of old sat Freedom* 9
    And bore him to a chapel nigh the *f*,   *M. d'Arthur* 8
    The *f*'s between Are dewy-fresh,   *Gardener's D.* 45
    Leaning his horns into the neighbour *f*,   "   87
    hired himself to work within the *f*;   *Dora* 38
    Far off the farmer came into the *f*   "   74
    when the farmer pass'd into the *f*   "   85
    the boy's cry came to her from the *f*,   "   104
    And scarce can recognise the *f*'s I know;   *St. S. Stylites* 40
    To yonder oak within the *f* I spoke   *Talking Oak* 13
    Beyond the fair green *f* and eastern sea.   *Love and Duty* 101
    Man comes and tills the *f* and lies beneath,   *Tithonus* 3
    the steam Floats up from those dim *f*'s   "   69
    a boy when first he leaves his father's *f*,   *Locksley Hall* 112
    white-flower'd elder-thicket from the *f*   *Godiva* 63
    Fly o'er waste fens and windy *f*'s.   *Sir Galahad* 60
    The houseless ocean's heaving *f*,   *The Voyage* 30
    And pace the sacred old familiar *f*'s,   *Enoch Arden* 625
    I fret By many a *f* and fallow,   *The Brook* 44
    all about the *f*'s you caught His weary daylong chirping,   "   52
    Sunning himself in a waste *f* alone—   *Aylmer's Field* 9
    became in other *f*'s A mockery to the yeomen   "   496
    Fairer than Ruth among the *f*'s of corn,   "   680
    That all neglected places of the *f*   "   693
    Follows the mouse, and all is open *f*.   "   853
    woman heard his foot Return from pacings in the *f*,   *Lucretius* 6
    makes Thy glory fly along the Italian *f*,   "   71
    answer'd in her sleep From hollow *f*'s: *Princess, Pro.* 67
    when a *f* of corn Bows all its ears   "   i 236
    First in the *f*: some ages had been lost;   "   ii 153
    for indeed these *f*'s Are lovely,   "   iii 341
    They faint on hill or *f* or river: "   iv 14
    waive your claim: If not, the foughten *f*,   "   v 297
    ran the *f* Flat to the garden-wall: "   361
    Man for the *f* and woman for the hearth: "   447
    Thro' open *f* into the lists they wound Timorously;   "   vi 84
    swarms of men Darkening her female *f*:   "   vii 34
    after that dark night among the *f*'s   "   73
    ' The *f*'s are fair beside them,   *Voice and the P.* 17
    The *f*, the chamber and the street,   *In Mem.* viii 11
    beast that takes His license in the *f* of time,   "   xxvii 6
    And loiter'd in the master's *f*,   "   xxxvii 23
    My paths are in the *f*'s I know,   "   xl 31
    The howlings from forgotten *f*'s;   "   xli 12
    And those five years its richest *f*.   "   xlvi 12
    A bounded *f*, nor stretching far;   "   14
    And hill and wood and *f* did print   "   lxxix 7
    trees Laid their dark arms about the *f*. (repeat)   "   xcv 16, 52
    set To leave the pleasant *f*'s and farms;   "   cii 22
    Its lips in the *f* above are dabbled   *Maud* I i 2
    Go not, happy day, From the shining *f*'s,   "   xvii 2
    Came night and day, and rooted in the *f*'s,   *Com. of Arthur* 24
    Sware on the *f* of death a deathless love.   "   132
    from the foughten *f* he sent Ulfius,   "   135
    F after *f*, up to a height, the peak Haze-hidden,   "   429
    Far shone the *f*'s of May thro' open door,   "   460
    mount That rose between the forest and the *f*.   *Gareth and L.* 191
    gate shone Only, that open'd on the *f* below: "   195
    abide Without, among the cattle of the *f*.   "   274
    Uther, reft From my dead lord a *f* with violence: "   335
    Yet, for the *f* was pleasant in our eyes,   "   337
    reft us of it Perforce, and left us neither gold nor *f*.'   "   339
    ' Whether would ye ? gold or *f* ? '   "   340

H

Field (s) (*continued*)   The *f* was pleasant in my husband's
eye.'   And Arthur, 'Have thy pleasant *f* again,   *Gareth and L.* 342
shone far-off as shines A *f* of charlock   ,,   388
paused without, beside The *f* of tourney,   ,,   664
But by the *f* of tourney lingering yet   ,,   736
Silent the silent *f* They traversed.   ,,   1313
pitch'd Beside the Castle Perilous on flat *f*,   ,,   1363
what knight soever be in *f* Lays claim   *Marr. of Geraint* 486
Geraint Beheld her first in *f*, awaiting him,   ,,   540
For these are his, and all the *f* is his,   *Geraint and E.* 226
I will fetch you forage from all *f's*,   ,,   628
Are scatter'd,' and he pointed to the *f*,   ,,   802
One from the bandit scatter'd in the *f*,   ,,   818
My mother on his corpse in open *f*; (repeat)   *Merlin and V.* 43, 73
in the *f* were Lancelot's kith and kin,   *Lancelot and E.* 466
spoke, and vanish'd suddenly from the *f*   ,,   508
So that he went sore wounded from the *f*:   ,,   600
crown'd with gold, Ramp in the *f*,   ,,   664
For pleasure all about a *f* of flowers :   ,,   793
Then rose Elaine and glided thro' the *f's*,   ,,   843
past Down thro' the dim rich city to the *f's*,   ,,   847
And drave her ere her time across the *f's*   ,,   890
Death, like a friend's voice from a distant *f*   ,,   999
Past like a shadow thro' the *f*,   ,,   1140
flame At sunrise till the people in far *f's*,   *Holy Grail* 243
in one full *f* Of gracious pastime,   ,,   323
where it smote the plowshare in the *f*,   ,,   403
But found a silk pavilion in a *f*,   ,,   745
And whipt me into the waste *f's* far away ;   ,,   788
I stinted stroke in foughten *f* ?   ,,   860
Who may not wander from the allotted *f*   ,,   908
and the sweet smell of the *f's* Past,   *Pelleas and E.* 5
the flat *f* by the shore of Usk Holden :   ,,   164
all day long Sir Pelleas kept the *f* With honour :   ,,   168
And he was left alone in open *f*.   ,,   208
flung His rider, who call'd out from the dark *f*,   ,,   575
Caught his unbroken limbs from the dark *f*,   ,,   585
in among the faded *f's* To furthest towers ;   *Last Tournament* 53
Enchair'd tomorrow, arbitrate the *f*,   ,,   104
With all the kindlier colours of the *f*.'   ,,   224
' Free love—free *f*—we love (repeat)   ,,   275, 281
Showing a shower of blood in a *f* noir,   ,,   433
she thought ' He spies a *f* of death ;   *Guinevere* 134
I mark'd Him in the flowering of His *f's*,   *Pass. of Arthur* 10
and the harmless glamour of the *f* ;   ,,   52
the pale King glanced across the *f* Of battle :   ,,   126
Had held the *f* of battle was the King;   ,,   138
And bore him to a chapel nigh the *f*.   ,,   176
For I heard it abroad in the *f's*   *First Quarrel* 32
Hard was the frost in the *f*,   ,,   39
what joy can be got from a cowslip out of the *f* ;   *In the Child. Hosp.* 36
breezes of May blowing over an English *f*,   *Def. of Lucknow* 83
ears for Christ in this wild *f* of Wales—   *Sir J. Oldcastle* 13
a crowd Throng'd the waste *f* about the city gates :   ,,   40
and the harvest past from the *f*,   *V. of Maeldune* 30
Silent palaces, quiet *f's* of eternal sleep !   ,,   80
By quiet *f's*, a slowly-dying power,   *De Prof., Two G.* 24
the *f* with blood of the fighters Flow'd,   *Batt. of Brunanburh* 24
hear the voices from the *f*.   *Locksley H., Sixty* 116
cow shall butt the ' Lion passant ' from his *f*.   ,,   248
out of the *f*, And over the brow and away.   *Heavy Brigade* 63
a careless people flock'd from the *f's*   *Dead Prophet* 7
Produce of your *f* and flood,   *Open. I. and C. Exhib.* 5
in this pleasant vale we stand again, The *f* of Enna,   *Demeter and P.* 35
Blessing his *f*, or seated in the dusk Of even,   ,,   125
glide Along the silent *f* of Asphodel.   ,,   153
mine the hall, the farm, the *f* ;   *The Ring* 169
She comes on waste and wood, On farm and *f*:   *Prog. of Spring* 23
and I gaze at a *f* in the Past,   *By an Evolution.* 17
WHAT sight so lured him thro' the *f's*   *Far-far-away* 1
waste and *f* and town of alien tongue,   *St. Telemachus* 30
I reap No revenue from the *f* of unbelief.   *Akbar's Dream* 67
And laughs upon thy *f* as well as mine,   ,,   106
Nor in the *f* without were seen or heard   ,,   195
And plow the Present like a *f*,   *Mechanophilus* 31

Field-flower (See also **Field (adj.)**) would they grew Like
f-f's everywhere !   *Princess iii* 252
Field-of-battle   Arthur reach'd a *f-o-b*   *Com. of Arthur* 96
Fiend   Who give the *F* himself his due,   *To F. D. Maurice* 6
the *f* best knows whether woman or man   *Maud I i* 75
when he died, his soul Became a *F*,   *Balin and Balan* 129
hold them outer *f's*, Who leap at thee to tear thee ;   ,,   141
but in him His mood was often like a *f*,   *Lancelot and E.* 251
drawn his claws athwart thy face ? or *f* ?   *Last Tournament* 63
In fuming sulphur blue and green, a *f*—   ,,   617
like so many *f's* in their hell ;   *Def. of Lucknow* 33
we have sent them very *f's* from Hell ;   *Columbus* 184
The *F* would yell, the grave would yawn,   *The Flight* 51
the night, While the *F* is prowling.   *Forlorn* 66
Fierce   Kate loves well the bold and *f* ;   *Kate* 29
My heart, pierced thro' with *f* delight,   *Fatima* 34
Twisted hard in *f* embraces,   *Vision of Sin* 40
f old man Follow'd, and under his own lintel   *Aylmer's Field* 330
Methought I never saw so *f* a fork—   *Lucretius* 28
I urged the *f* inscription on the gate,   *Princess iii* 141
That bright and *f* and fickle is the South,   ,, *iv* 97
a tide of Invective seem'd to wait   ,,   471
He yielded, wroth and red, with *f* demur :   ,, *v* 358
I felt my veins Stretch with *f* heat ;   ,,   538
half the wolf's-milk curdled in their veins, The *f*
triumvirs ;   ,, *vii* 131
He heard a *f* mermaiden cry,   *Sailor Boy* 6
Mad and maddening all that heard her in her *f* volubility,   *Boädicea* 4
Yell'd and shriek'd between her daughters in her *f* volubility.   ,,   72
f extremes employ Thy spirits in the darkening
leaf,   *In Mem. lxxxviii* 5
Till I with as *f* an anger spoke,   *Maud II i* 17
In that *f* light which beats upon a throne,   *Ded. of Idylls* 27
Her own brood lost or dead, lent her *f* teat   *Com. of Arthur* 28
the lords Of that *f* day were as the lords of this,   ,,   216
When I was kitchen-knave among the rest *F* was the
hearth,   *Gareth and L.* 1010
flash'd the *f* shield, All sun ;   ,,   1030
When I that knew him *f* and turbulent Refused
her   *Marr. of Geraint* 447
Thy too *f* manhood would not let thee lie.   *Balin and Balan* 74
In those *f* wars, struck hard—   ,,   177
Nor ever touch'd *f* wine, nor tasted flesh,   *Merlin and V.* 627
' He learnt and warn'd me of their *f* design   *Lancelot and E.* 274
So *f* a gale made havoc here of late   *Holy Grail* 729
Let the *f* east scream thro' your eyelet-holes,   *Pelleas and E.* 469
But Pelleas lifted up an eye so *f* She quail'd ;   ,,   601
wrath which forced my thoughts on that *f* law,   *Guinevere* 537
And *f* or careless looseners of the faith,   *To the Queen ii* 52
Hued with the scarlet of a *f* sunrise,   *Lover's Tale i* 353
F in the strength of far descent,   ,,   382
Plunged in the *f* charge at Waterloo,   *Sisters (E. and E.)* 64
he, the *f* Soldan of Egypt,   *Columbus* 97
HAD the *f* ashes of some fiery peak Been hurl'd   *St. Telemachus* 1
Blown by the *f* beleaguerers of a town,   *Achilles over the T.* 20
because the *f* beast found A wiser than herself,   *Tiresias* 151
By changes all too *f* and fast   *Freedom* 22
Fierceness   With such a *f* that I swoon'd   *Holy Grail* 845
Fierier   *F* and stormier from restraining,   *Balin and Balan* 229
Fieriest   But spurr'd at heart with *f* energy   *To J. M. K.* 7
Fiery   for *f* thoughts Do shape themselves within me,   *Œnone* 246
roaring deeps and *f* sands,   *Lotos-Eaters, C. S.* 115
To make my blood run quicker, Used all her *f* will,   *Will Water.* 111
cloud Cuts off the *f* highway of the sun,   *Enoch Arden* 130
chance-met eyes Flash into *f* life from nothing,   *Aylmer's Field* 130
Or down the *f* gulf as talk of it,   *Princess iii* 287
And as the *f* Sirius alters hue,   ,, *v* 262
shower the *f* grain Of freedom broadcast   ,,   421
And into *f* splinters leapt the lance,   ,,   494
Leapt *f* Passion from the brinks of death ;   ,, *vii* 156
Clash'd with his *f* few and won ;   *Ode on Well.* 100
Not sting the *f* Frenchman into war.   *Third of Feb.* 4
Deep tulips dash'd with *f* dew,   *In Mem. lxxxiii* 11
here and there A *f* finger on the leaves ;   ,, *xcix* 12
which outran The hearer in its *f* course ;   ,, *cix* 8

Fiery (*continued*) all at *f* speed the two Shock'd on the
  central bridge,   *Gareth and L.* 962
Sir Balin with a *f* 'Ha!   *Balin and Balan* 393
But follow Vivien thro' the *f* flood!   "   454
A *f* family passion for the name Of Lancelot, *Lancelot and E.* 477
All in a *f* dawning wild with wind   " 1020
I saw the *f* face as of a child   *Holy Grail* 466
For every *f* prophet in old times,   " 876
Shading his eyes till all the *f* cloud,   *Lover's Tale i* 306
Like to a low-hung and a *f* sky   " *ii* 61
Brother-in-law—the *f* nearness of it— *Sisters (E. and E.)* 173
A *f* scroll written over with lamentation and woe. *Despair* 20
To vex the noon with *f* gems,   *Ancient Sage* 265
and Suns along their *f* way,   *Locksley H., Sixty* 203
While squirrels from our *f* beech Were bearing off
  the mast,   *Pro. to Gen. Hamley* 3
Three that were next in their *f* course, *Heavy Brigade* 21
lighted from below By the red race of *f* Phlegethon; *Demeter and P.* 28
' A *f* phœnix rising from the smoke,   *The Ring* 339
And you spurr'd your *f* horse,   *Happy* 76
would wallow in *f* riot and revel On Kilauëä, *Kapiolani* 8
Quail not at the *f* mountain,   *Faith* 3
and your *f* clash of meteorites?   *God and the Univ.* 3
Fiery-hot *f-h* to burst All barriers *In Mem. cxiv* 13
Fiery-new yet unkept, Had relish *f-n*, *Will Water.* 98
Fiery-short *f-s* was Cyril's counter-scoff, *Princess v* 307
Fife The murmurs of the drum and *f*   *Talking Oak* 215
merrily-blowing shrill'd the martial *f*;   *Princess v* 251
March with banner and bugle and *f*   *Maud I v* 10
Fifteen I ha' work'd for him *f* years,   *First Quarrel* 7
and for *f* days or for twenty at most. *Def. of Lucknow* 9
' Hold it for *f* days!'   " 105
and his winters were *f* score,   *V. of Maeldune* 116
beän chuch-warden mysen i' the parish fur *f* year. *Church-warden, etc.* 8
mountain-like San Philip that, of *f* hundred tons, *The Revenge* 40
Fifth To slant the *f* autumnal slope, *In Mem. xxii* 10
Your *f* September birthday.   *The Ring* 423
Our Playwright may show In some *f* Act *The Play* 4
Fifty Better *f* years of Europe than a cycle
  of Cathay.   *Locksley Hall* 184
Seam'd with the shallow cares of *f* years: *Aylmer's Field* 814
Her that talk'd down the *f* wisest men; *Princess v* 294
finding that of *f* seeds She often brings *In Mem. lv* 11
these have clothed their branchy bowers With *f* Mays, " *lxxvi* 14
And *f* knights rode with them,   *Marr. of Geraint* 44
Was wont to glance and sparkle like a gem Of
  f facets;   *Geraint and E.* 295
f knights rode with them to the shores Of Severn, " 954
I have not broken bread for *f* hours. *Sir J. Oldcastle* 199
F times the rose has flower'd and faded, F times
  the golden harvest fallen,   *On Jub. Q. Victoria* 1
Henry's *f* years are all in shadow, Gray with
  distance Edward's *f* summers,   " 39
F years of ever-broadening Commerce! F years
  of ever-brightening Science! F years of ever-
  widening Empire!   " 52
Rose, on this terrace *f* years ago, *Roses on the T.* 1
That blush of *f* years ago, my dear,   " 5
on our terrace here Glows in the blue of *f* miles away. " 8
Ah, what shall I be at *f*   *Maud I vi* 31
Fifty-fold ' My lord, you overpay me *f-f*.' *Geraint and E.* 220
Fifty-three We are six ships of the line; can we
  fight with *f-t*? '   *The Revenge* 7
Fig *F's* out of thistles, silk from bristles, *Last Tournament* 356
the *f* ran up from the beach and rioted over the
  land,   *V. of Maeldune* 58
Are *f's* of thistles? or grapes of thorns? *Riflemen form!* 10
Fight (s) Ere I rode into the *f*,   *Oriana* 21
Laid by the tumult of the *f*.   *Margaret* 26
pierce The blackest files of clanging *f*, *Kate* 26
Clanging *f's*, and flaming towns, *Lotos-Eaters, C. S.* 116
He got it; for their captain after *f*, *Aylmer's Field* 226
Sun-shaded in the heat of dusty *f's*) *Princess ii* 44
some grand *f* to kill and make and end: " *iv* 591
And what she did to Cyrus after *f*,   " *v* 366

Fight (s) (*continued*) something real, A gallant *f*, a noble
  princess—   *Princess, Con.* 19
He that gain'd a hundred *f's*,   *Ode on Well.* 96
For each had warded either in the *f*, *Com. of Arthur* 131
So that I be not fall'n in *f*.   *Marr. of Geraint* 223
My lord is weary with the *f* before, *Geraint and E.* 133
pleased To find him yet unwounded after *f*, " 371
I, myself, when flush'd with *f*,   " 660
free to stretch his limbs in lawful *f*,   " 754
having been With Arthur in the *f* *Lancelot and E.* 287
hear the manner of thy *f* and fall; *Pelleas and E.* 347
Nor ever yet had Arthur fought a *f* Like this *Pass. of Arthur* 93
chance and craft and strength in single *f's*, " 106
But never a moment ceased the *f*   *The Revenge* 57
fought such a *f* for a day and a night   " 83
fevers, *f's*, Mutinies, treacheries— *Columbus* 225
Each was as brave in the *f*   *V. of Maeldune* 5
red with blood the Crescent reels from *f* *Montenegro* 6
some in *f* against the foe, *Locksley H., Sixty* 45
the charge, and the might of the *f*! *Heavy Brigade* 13
Who were held for a while from the *f*, " 36
for he fought Thy *f* for Thee,   *Happy* 15
Struck by a poison'd arrow in the *f*, *Death of Œnone* 26
The gladiators moving toward their *f*, *St. Telemachus* 54
Ralph went down like a fire to the *f* *The Tourney* 3
Fight (verb) She saw me *f*, she heard me call, *Oriana* 32
who would *f* and march and countermarch, *Audley Court* 40
brother, where two *f* The strongest wins, *Aylmer's Field* 364
one Should come to *f* with shadows and to fall. *Princess i* 10
Nor would I *f* with iron laws,   " *iv* 75
I prove Your knight, and *f* your battle,   " 595
' F ' she said, ' And make us all we would be, " 598
make yourself a man to *f* with men.   " *v* 35
I was pledged To *f* in tourney for my bride, " 353
what mother's blood You draw from, *f*; " 405
F and well strike and strike home.   " 409
one should *f* with shadows and should fall; " 476
she sees me *f*, Yea, let her see me fall! " 516
I would sooner *f* thrice o'er than see it.' " *vi* 226
king is scared, the soldier will not *f*, " *Con.* 60
a lie which is part a truth is a harder matter to *f*. *Grandmother* 32
Glory of Virtue, to *f*, to struggle,   *Wages* 3
She cannot *f* the fear of death.   *In Mem. cxiv* 10
teach true life to *f* with mortal wrongs. *Maud I xviii* 54
It is better to *f* for the good than to rail " *III vi* 57
we that *f* for our fair father Christ, *Com. of Arthur* 510
Hereafter I will *f*.'   *Gareth and L.* 447
the cur Pluckt from the cur he *f's* with, " 702
F, an thou canst: I have missed the only way.' " 792
To *f* the brotherhood of Day and Night— " 857
Far liefer had I *f* a score of times   " 944
Fair words were best for him who *f's* for thee; " 946
Such *f* not I, but answer scorn with scorn. " 953
nor meet To *f* for gentle damsel,   " 1177
thou goest, he will *f* thee first;   " 1295
yield him this again: 'tis he must *f*:   " 1321
Said Gareth laughing, ' An he *f* for this, " 1345
will I *f* him, and will break his pride, *Marr. of Geraint* 221
arms, arms to *f* my enemy?   " 282
And *f* and break his pride, and have it of him. " 416
this nephew, *f* In next day's tourney   " 475
thou, that hast no lady, canst not *f*.'   " 493
I will not *f* my way with gilded arms, *Geraint and E.* 21
he will *f* for me, And win the circlet: *Pelleas and E.* 118
look at mine! but wilt thou *f* for me, " 127
' F therefore,' yell'd the youth,   " 572
The king who *f's* his people *f's* himself. *Pass. of Arthur* 72
I liked a bigger feller to *f* wi' *North. Cobbler* 100
can we *f* with fifty-three?   *The Revenge* 7
fly them for a moment to *f* with them again. " 9
only a hundred seamen to work the ship and to *f*, " 22
' Shall we *f* or shall we fly?   " 25
For to *f* is but to die!   " 27
many were shatter'd, and so could *f* us no more— " 61
he said ' F on! *f* on! (repeat)   " 63, 69

Fight (verb) (*continued*) We shall live to *f* again and to
    strike another blow.'   *The Revenge* 95
  We can *f*! But to be soldier all day   *Def. of Lucknow* 73
  shall we *f*? shall we yield?   *Locksley H., Sixty* 115
  he needs must *f* To make true peace his own,   *Epilogue* 26
  'e'd *f* wi' a will *when* 'e fowt;   *Owd Roä* 7
  RALPH would *f* in Edith's sight,   *The Tourney* 1
Fighter rustiest iron of old *f's* hearts;   *Merlin and V.* 574
  With her hundred *f's* on deck,   *The Revenge* 34
  the field with blood of the *f's* Flow'd,   *Batt. of Brunanburh* 24
  a flight of shadowy *f's* crost The disk,   *St. Telemachus* 23
Fighting 'No *f* shadows here!   *Princess iii* 125
  Yet it seem'd a dream, I dream'd Of *f*.   " *v* 493
  ere his cause Be cool'd by *f*,   *Gareth and L.* 703
  In the great battle *f* for the King.   *Marr. of Geraint* 596
  In battle, *f* for the blameless King.   *Geraint and E.* 970
  All *f* for a woman on the sea.   *Merlin and V.* 562
  send her delegate to thrall These *f* hands of mine—   *Pelleas and E.* 337
Figtree wild *f* split Their monstrous idols,   *Princess iv* 79
Figure Faint as a *f* seen in early dawn   *Enoch Arden* 357
  Some *f* like a wizard pentagram   *The Brook* 103
  Tall as a *f* lengthen'd on the sand   *Princess vi* 161
  for so long a space Stared at the *f's*,   *Gareth and L.* 232
  comb wherein Were slabs of rock with *f's*,   " 1194
  beneath five *f's*, armed men,   " 1205
  carven with strange *f's*; and in out The *f's*,   *Holy Grail* 169
  So the sweet *f* folded round with night   *Lover's Tale iv* 219
Figured bears a skeleton *f* on his arms,   *Gareth and L.* 640
  In many a leaf enrolls The total world   *In Mem. xliii* 11
Figure-head full-busted *f-h* Stared o'er the ripple   *Enoch Arden* 543
Filament Seems but a cobweb *f* to link   *Lover's Tale i* 376
  Had seem'd a gossamer *f* up in air,   " 413
File The blackest *f's* of clanging fight,   *Kate* 26
  in the foremost *f's* of time—   *Locksley Hall* 178
Filed grated down and *f* away with thought,   *Merlin and V.* 623
Filial wars, and *f* faith, and Dido's pyre;   *To Virgil* 4
  f eyes Have seen the loneliness of earthly thrones,   *Prin. Beatrice* 13
Fill (verb) or *f's* The horned valleys all about,   *Supp. Confessions* 151
  f the sea-halls with a voice of power;   *The Merman* 10
  Yet *f* my glass: give me one kiss: *Miller's D.* 17
  bursts that *f* The spacious times of great Elizabeth   *D. of F. Women* 6
  And tho' mine own eyes *f* with dew,   *To J. S.* 37
  F's out the many quickset-screens,   *On a Mourner* 6
  Should *f* and choke with golden sand—   *You ask me, why* 24
  A thought would *f* my eyes with happy dew;   *Gardener's D.* 197
  those tremulous eyes that *f* with tears To hear me?   *Tithonus* 26
  Saw the heavens *f* with commerce.   *Locksley Hall* 121
  Heard the heavens *f* with shouting,   " 123
  '*F* the cup, and *f* the can: (repeat)   *Vision of Sin* 95, 119, 203
  '*F* the can, and *f* the cup: (repeat)   " 131, 167
  Musing on him that used to *f* it for her,   *Enoch Arden* 208
  from all the provinces, And *f* the hive.'   *Princess ii* 98
  sport half-science, *f* me with a faith,   " *Con.* 76
  There twice a day the Severn *f's*;   *In Mem. xix* 5
  prosperous labour *f's* The lips of men   " *lxxxiv* 25
  so *f* up the gap where force might fail   *Gareth and L.* 1352
  Bala lake *F's* all the sacred Dee.   *Geraint and E.* 930
  in this heathen war the fire of God *F's* him: *Lancelot and E.* 316
  KING ARTHUR made new knights to *f* the gap   *Pelleas and E.* 1
  and *f's* The flower with dew;   *Early Spring* 45
  felt a vacant hand *F* with *his* purse.   *To Mary Boyle* 32
  F out the spaces by the barren tiles.   *Prog. of Spring* 43
  The kingcup *f's* her footprint,   " 59
  f the hollows between wave and wave;   *Akbar's Dream* 161
Fill (s) weep my *f* once more, and cry myself to rest!   *The Flight* 6
Fill'd the ground Shall be *f* with life anew.   *Nothing will Die* 29
  The right ear, that is *f* with dust,   *Two Voices* 116
  The woods were *f* so full with song,   " 455
  And *f* the breast with purer breath.   *Miller's D.* 92
  and *f* with light The interval of sound.   *D. of F. Women* 171
  And *f* the house with clamour.   *The Goose* 36
  F I was with folly and spite,   *Edward Gray* 15
  They are *f* with idle spleen;   *Vision of Sin* 124
  and *f* the shores With clamour.   *Enoch Arden* 635
  when their casks were *f* they took aboard: " 646

Fill'd (*continued*) drank The magic cup that *f* itself
    anew.   *Aylmer's Field* 143
  entering *f* the house with sudden light.   " 682
  F thro' and thro' with Love, a happy sleep.   *Princess vii* 172
  When *f* with tears that cannot fall,   *In Mem. xix* 11
  The streets were *f* with joyful sound,   " *xxxi* 10
  f a horn with wine and held it to her,)   *Geraint and E.* 659
  F all the genial courses of his blood   " 927
  Sprang her face and *f* her with delight;   *Lancelot and E.* 377
  great tower *f* with eyes Up to the summit,   *Pelleas and E.* 166
  Till the sweet heavens have *f* it   " 510
  Ascending, *f* his double-dragon'd chair.   *Last Tournament* 144
  and the ways Were *f* with rapine,   *Guinevere* 458
  larks *F* all the March of life!—   *Lover's Tale i* 284
  openings in the mountains *f* With the blue valley   " 330
  F all with pure clear fire,   " *ii* 146
Fillest thou, that *f* all the room Of all my love,   *In Mem. cxii* 5
Filling *F* with light And vagrant melodies   *The Poet* 16
Fillip'd *f* at the diamond in her ear;   *Godiva* 25
Film with a grosser *f* made thick These heavy, horny
    eyes.   *St. S. Stylites* 200
Filmed Floats from his sick and *f* eyes,   *Supp. Confessions* 166
Filmy wheel'd or lit the *f* shapes That haunt the dusk,   *In Mem. xcv* 10
Filter'd The *f* tribute of the rough woodland,   *Ode to Memory* 63
Filth shown the truth betimes, That old true *f*,   *Merlin and V.* 47
  poach'd *f* that floods the middle street,   " 798
  insult, *f*, and monstrous blasphemies,   *Pass. of Arthur* 114
  fairest flesh at last is *f* on which the worm will feast;   *Happy* 30
  women shrieking 'Atheist' flung *F* from the roof,   *Akbar's Dream* 92
Filthy In *f* sloughs they roll a prurient skin,   *Palace of Art* 201
  He believed This *f* marriage-hindering Mammon   *Aylmer's Field* 374
  monster lays His vast and *f* hands upon my will,   *Lucretius* 220
  Till the *f* by-lane rings to the yell of the trampled wife,   *Maud I i* 38
  to outlearn the *f* friar.   *Sir J. Oldcastle* 118
  all that is *f* with all that is fair?   *Vastness* 32
Fin winks the gold *f* in the porphyry font: *Princess vii* 178
  There is not left the twinkle of a *f*   *Geraint and E.* 474
Finance poring over his Tables of Trade and *F*;   *The Wreck* 26
Final we trust that somehow good Will be the *f* goal of ill,   *In Mem. liv* 2
  trusted God was love indeed And love Creation's *f* law—   " *lvi* 1
Find She cannot *f* a fitting mate.   *Kate* 31
  for a moment blest To *f* my heart so near   *The form, the form* 7
  Could *f* no statelier than his peers   *Two Voices* 29
  And seem to *f*, but still to seek.   " 96
  but to seem to *f* Asks what thou lackest,   " 97
  Named man, may hope some truth to *f*,   " 176
  I shall not fail to *f* her now.   " 191
  seeking to undo One riddle, and to *f* the true,   " 233
  Wilt thou *f* passion, pain or pride?   " 243
  'We *f* no motion in the dead.'   " 279
  In Nature can he nowhere *f*.   " 293
  Could his dark wisdom *f* it out,   " 308
  'As here we *f* in trances, men Forget the dream   " 352
  With blessings which no words can *f*.   *Miller's D.* 238
  So shalt thou *f* me fairest.   *Œnone* 155
  Some meeker pupil you must *f*,   *L. C. V. de Vere* 18
  f my garden-tools upon the granary floor: *May Queen, N. Y's. E.* 45
  it can't be long before I *f* release;   " *Con.* 11
  But they smile, they *f* a music centred   *Lotos-Eaters, C. S.* 117
  To strive, to seek, to *f*, and not to yield.   *Ulysses* 70
  till he *f* The quiet chamber far apart.   *Day-Dm., Arrival* 27
  And if you *f* no moral there,   " *Moral* 2
  In bud, or blade, or bloom, may *f*,   " 10
  f's a closer truth than this All-graceful head,   " *L'Envoi* 37
  And, if you *f* a meaning there,   " *Ep.* 2
  on lonely mountain-meres I *f* a magic bark;   *Sir Galahad* 38
  Until I *f* the holy Grail.   " 84
  f the precious morning hours were lost.   *Enoch Arden* 302
  Suddenly set it wide to *f* a sign,   " 496
  you *f* That you meant nothing—   *Aylmer's Field* 312
  should I *f* you by my doors again,   " 324
  And being used to *f* her pastor texts,   " 606
  To *f* a deeper in the narrow gloom   " 840
  and *f* A sort of absolution in the sound   *Sea Dreams* 60
  I should *f* he meant me well;   " 153

Fine (*continued*) Cuck-oo!' was ever a May so *f*? — *Window, Ay* 10
hair Is golden like thy Mother's, not so *f*.' — *The Ring* 104
From head to ancle *f*, — *Talking Oak* 224
in *f* linen, not a hair Ruffled upon the scarfskin, — *Aylmer's Field* 659
In that *f* air I tremble, all the past — *Princess vii* 354
This *f* old world of ours is but a child — " *Con.* 77
Broad brows and fair, a fluent hair and *f*, High nose, a nostril large and *f*, and hands Large, fair and *f*!— — *Gareth and L.* 464
fair and *f*, forsooth! Sir Fine-face, Sir Fair-hands? but see thou to it That thine own fineness, Lancelot, some *f* day — " 474
Such *f* reserve and noble reticence, — *Geraint and E.* 860
and your *f* epithet Is accurate too, — *Merlin and V.* 532
lady never made *unwilling* war With those *f* eyes: — " 604
for *f* plots may fail, — " 820
Told him that her *f* care had saved his life. — *Lancelot and E.* 863
But there the *f* Gawain will wonder at me, — " 1054
Then came the *f* Gawain and wonder'd at her, — " 1267
And win me this *f* circlet, Pelleas, — *Pelleas and E.* 128
a wire as musically as thou Some such *f* song— — *Last Tournament* 324
I thought I could not breathe in that *f* air — *Guinevere* 645
Flying by each *f* ear, an Eastern gauze — *Lover's Tale* iv 291
F an' meller 'e mun be by this, — *North. Cobbler* 101
I warrant ye soom *f* daäy— — *Spinster's S's.* 63
An' my oän *f* Jackman i' purple — " 106
'This model husband, this *f* Artist'! — *Romney's R.* 124
When *f* Philosophies would fail, — *Akbar's Dream* 140
Fine-face Sir *F-f*, Sir Fair-hands? — *Gareth and L.* 475
Fineness some pretext of *f* in the meal — *Enoch Arden* 341
For often *f* compensated size; — *Princess ii* 149
That thine own *f*, Lancelot, — *Gareth and L.* 476
force might fail With skill and *f*. — " 1352
Finer Soothe him with thy *f* fancies, — *Locksley Hall* 54
A random string Your *f* female sense offends. — *Day-Dm., L'Envoi* 2
may soul to soul Strike thro' a *f* element of her own? — *Aylmer's Field* 579
And like a *f* light in light. — *In Mem. xci* 16
Who wants the *f* politic sense To mask, — *Maud I vi* 47
this egg of mine Was *f* gold than any goose can lay; — *Gareth and L.* 43
I, the *f* brute rejoicing in my hounds, — *By an Evolution.* 7
tho' somewhat *f* than their own, — " 13
Finest because he was The *f* on the tree. — *Talking Oak* 238
Are touch'd, are turn'd to *f* air. — *Sir Galahad* 72
Of *f* Gothic lighter than a fire, — *Princess, Pro.* 92
Finger (*adj.*) seem'd All-perfect, finish'd to the *f* nail. — *Edwin Morris* 22
Finger (s) lets his rosy *f's* play About his mother's neck, — *Supp. Confessions* 42
weary with a *f's* touch Those writhed limbs — *Clear-headed friend* 22
dare to kiss Thy taper *f's* amorously, — *Madeline* 44
Kate snaps her *f's* at my vows; — *Kate* 19
Thro' rosy taper *f's* drew Her streaming curls — *Mariana in the S.* 15
Three *f's* round the old silver cup— — *Miller's D.* 10
With rosy slender *f's* backward drew — *Œnone* 176
And on thy heart a *f* lays, — *On a Mourner* 11
One rose, but one, by those fair *f's* cull'd, — *Gardener's D.* 150
And with a flying *f* swept my lips, — " 246
To save her little *f* from a scratch — *Edwin Morris* 63
Baby *f's*, waxen touches, — *Locksley Hall* 90
'You would not let your little *f* ache — *Godiva* 22
f's steal And touch upon the master-chord — *Will Water.* 26
Enoch's golden ring had girt Her *f*, — *Enoch Arden* 158
Suddenly put her *f* on the text, — " 497
he dug His *f's* into the wet earth, — " 780
My lady with her *f's* interlock'd, — *Aylmer's Field* 199
(I kept the book and had my *f* in it) — *Princess, Pro.* 53
And takes a lady's *f* with all care, — " 173
now a pointed *f*, told them all; — " *v* 270
she laid A feeling *f* on my brows, — " *vi* 121
innocent arms And lazy lingering *f's*. — " 139
With trembling *f's* did we weave The holly — *In Mem. xxx* 1
God's *f* touch'd him, and he slept. — " *lxxxv* 20
A fiery *f* on the leaves; — " *xcix* 12
With petulant thumb and *f*, shrilling, — *Gareth and L.* 750

Finger (s) (*continued*) Myself would work eye dim, and *f* lame, — *Marr. of Geraint* 628
He sits unarm'd; I hold a *f* up; — *Geraint and E.* 337
moving back she held Her *f* up; — " 453
clench'd her *f's* till they bit the palm, — *Lancelot and E.* 611
In colour like the *f's* of a hand Before a burning taper, — *Holy Grail* 693
one with shatter'd *f's* dangling lame, — *Last Tournament* 60
had let one *f* lightly touch The warm white apple — " 716
Touch'd by the adulterous *f* of a time — *To the Queen* iv 43
placed My ring upon the *f* of my bride. — *Sisters (E. and E.)* 214
Death at the glimpse of a *f* — *Def. of Lucknow* 23
nor voice Nor *f* raised against him— — *Sir J. Oldcastle* 45
drew the ring From his dead *f*, — *The Ring* 218
His *f's* were so stiffen'd by the frost — " 239
mark ran All round one *f* pointed straight, — " 453
worn the ring—Then torn it from her *f*, — " 456
Finger-ache Who never knewest *f-a*, — *Gareth and L.* 87
Fingering *f* at the hair about his lip, — *Princess v* 303
F at his sword-handle until he stood — *Pelleas and E.* 442
Finger-nail (*See also* **Finger (adj.)**) crush'd with a tap Of my *f-n* on the sand, — *Maud II* ii 22
Fingers an' toäs (**a disease in turnips**) tonups was haäfe on 'em *f a t*, — *Church-warden, etc.* 4
Finger-tips she sway'd The rein with dainty *f-t*, — *Sir L. and Q. G.* 41
Finials grasping the pews And oaken *f* — *Aylmer's Field* 823
Finish I leave not till I *f* this fair quest, — *Gareth and L.* 774
'Ay, wilt thou *f* it? Sweet lord, — " 776
Finished when four years were wholly *f*, — *Palace of Art* 289
Of such a *f* chasten'd purity. — *Isabel* 41
seem'd All-perfect, *f* to the finger-nail. — *Edwin Morris* 22
'It is *f*. Man is made.' — *Making of Man* 8
Finite-infinite wrought Not Matter, nor the *f-i*, — *De Prof., Two G.* 1
Sun, sun, and sun, thro' *f-i* space In *f-i* Time— — " 45
Finn And we sang the triumph of *F*, — *V. of Maeldune* 48
And we sang the triumphs of *F*, — " 88
Go back to the Isle of *F* — " 124
I landed again, with a tithe of my men, on the Isle of *F*. — " 130
Fir tall *f's* and our fast-falling burns; — *Gareth and L.* 91
glories of the moon Below black *f's*, — *Lover's Tale* ii 111
Fire (s) (*See also* **Afire, Altar-fire, Hell-fire, Idol-fires, Rick-fire**) a bolt of *f* Would rive the slumbrous summer noon — *Supp. Confessions* 10
the storm Of running *f's* and fluid range — " 147
Until the latter *f* shall heat the deep; — *The Kraken* 13
THOU who stealest *f*, From the fountains — *Ode to Memory* 1
Tho' one did fling the *f*. — *The Poet* 30
Losing his *f* and active might — *Eleänore* 104
a languid *f* creeps Thro' my veins — " 130
with sudden *f's* Flamed over: — *Buonaparte* 11
Like Stephen, an unquenched *f*, — *Two Voices* 219
O Love, O *f*! once he drew With one long kiss — *Fatima* 19
from beyond the noon a *f* Is pour'd upon the hills, — " 30
at their feet the crocus brake like *f*, — *Œnone* 96
for she says A *f* dances before her, — " 264
All earth and air seem only burning *f*.' — " 268
Burnt like a fringe of *f* — *Palace of Art* 48
slow-flaming crimson *f's* From shadow'd grots — " 50
And highest, snow and *f*. — " 84
She howl'd aloud, 'I am on *f* within. — " 285
wild marsh-marigold shines like *f* — *May Queen* 31
blasts That run before the fluttering tongues of *f*; — *D. of F. Women* 30
their *f's* Love tipt his keenest darts; — " 173
The glass blew in, the *f* blew out, — *The Goose* 49
hung From Allan's watch, and sparkled by the *f*. — *Dora* 136
Or burn'd in *f*, or boil'd in oil, — *St. S. Stylites* 52
Sit with their wives by *f's*, — " 108
Have scrambled past those pits of *f*, — " 184
beat the twilight into flakes of *f*. — *Tithonus* 42
and winks behind a slowly-dying *f*. — *Locksley Hall* 136
with rain or hail, or *f* or snow; — " 193
On the hall-hearths the festal *f's*, — *Day-Dm., Sleep. P.* 14
The *f* shot up, the martin flew, — *Revival* 11
But in my words were seeds of *f*. — *The Letters* 28
Fall from his Ocean-lane of *f*, — *The Voyage* 19

Fire (s) (*continued*) With wakes of *f* we tore the dark; *The Voyage* 52
'No, I cannot praise the *f* In your eye— *Vision of Sin* 183
All-kindled by a still and sacred *f*, *Enoch Arden* 71
Keep a clean hearth and a clear *f* for me, " 192
And flung her down upon a couch of *f*, *Aylmer's Field* 574
flood, *f*, earthquake, thunder, wrought " 639
as not passing thro' the *f* Bodies, but souls— " 671
No desolation but by sword and *f*? " 748
a *f*, The *f* that left a roofless Ilion, *Lucretius* 64
altho' his *f* is on my face Blinding, " 144
her arm lifted, eyes on *f*— *Princess*, Pro. 41
Of finest Gothic lighter than a *f*, " 92
made to kill Time by the *f* in winter.' " 205
But chafing me on *f* to find my bride) " i 166
Burnt like the mystic *f* on a mast-head, " iv 274
bloom As of some *f* against a stormy cloud, " 384
The next, like *f* he meets the foe, " 583
red-faced war has rods of steel and *f*; " v 118
living hearts that crack within the *f* " 379
the *f*'s of Hell Mix with his hearth; " 454
out of stricken helmets sprang the *f*. " 495
Break from a darken'd future, crown'd with *f*, " vi 175
Flash, ye cities, in rivers of *f*! *W. to Alexander* 19
the tongue is a *f* as you know, my dear, the tongue
    is a *f*. *Grandmother* 28
moon like a rick on *f* was rising over the dale, " 39
The giant windows' blazon'd *f*'s, *The Daisy* 58
Then thorpe and byre arose in *f*, *The Victim* 83
At his highest with sunrise *f*; *Voice and the P.* 30
Thunder, a flying *f* in heaven, *Boädicea* 24
many a *f* before them blazed; *Spec. of Iliad* 10
many a *f* between the ships and stream " 17
Sat fifty in the blaze of burning *f*; " 20
And *f*'s burn clear, And frost is here *Window, Winter* 4
The *f*'s are all the clearer, " 16
king of the wrens with a crown of *f*. " Ay 16
A looming bastion fringed with *f*. *In Mem.* xv 20
Is shrivell'd in a fruitless *f*, " liv 11
Laburnums, dropping-wells of *f*. " lxxxiii 12
shine Beside the never-lighted *f*. " lxxxiv 20
But on her forehead sits a *f*: " cxiv 5
And compass'd by the *f*'s of Hell; " cxxvii 17
And on the downs a rising *f*: " Con. 108
f of a foolish pride flash'd over *Maud* I iv 16
Cold *f*'s, yet with power to burn and brand " xviii 39
f's of Hell brake out of thy rising sun, The *f*'s of
    Hell and of Hate; " II i 9
blood-red blossom of war with a heart of *f*. " III vi 53
f of God Descends upon thee in the battle-field: *Com. of Arthur* 128
And all at once all round him rose in *f*, " 389
the child and he were clothed in *f*. " 390
echo'd by old folk beside their *f*'s For comfort " 417
the herd was driven, *F* glimpsed " 433
a city all on *f* With sun and cloth of gold, " 479
I will walk thro' *f*, Mother, to gain it— *Gareth and L.* 133
'Will ye walk thro' *f*? Who walks thro' *f* will
    hardly heed the smoke. " 142
f, That lookt half-dead, brake bright, " 684
For an your *f* be low ye kindle mine! " 711
But up like *f* he started: " 1123
forage for the horse, and flint for *f*. " 1277
Glow'd like the heart of a great *f* at Yule, *Marr. of Geraint* 559
night of *f*, when Edyrn sack'd their house, " 634
loosed in words of sudden *f* the wrath *Geraint and E.* 106
In a hollow land, From which old *f*'s have broken,
    men may fear Fresh *f* and ruin. " 822
f of Heaven has kill'd the barren cold, *Balin and Balan* 440
f of heaven is not the flame of Hell. (repeat) " 443, 447,
    451, 455
Yet in your frosty cells ye feel the *f*! " 446
'The *f* of Heaven is on the dusty ways. " 448
'The *f* of Heaven is lord of all things good, And
    starve not thou this *f* within thy blood, " 452
'This *f* of heaven, This old sun-worship, " 456
into such a song, such *f* for fame, *Merlin and V.* 417

Fire (s) (*continued*) Rage like a *f* among the noblest
    names, *Merlin and V.* 802
Her godlike head crown'd with spiritual *f*, " 837
in this heathen war the *f* of God Fills him: *Lancelot and E.* 315
shot red *f* and shadows thro' the cave, " 414
So ran the tale like *f* about the court, " 734
F in dry stubble a nine-days' wonder flared: " 735
wrapt In unremorseful folds of rolling *f*. *Holy Grail* 261
while ye follow wandering *f*'s Lost in the quagmire! " 319
most of us would follow wandering *f*'s, (repeat) " 369, 599
years of death, Sprang into *f*: " 497
Sprang into *f* and vanish'd, " 506
Must be content to sit by little *f*'s. " 614
A mocking *f*: 'what other *f* than he, " 670
methought I spied A dying *f* of madness " 768
most of them would follow wandering *f*'s, " 891
Burnt as a living *f* of emeralds, *Pelleas and E.* 35
A vision hovering on a sea of *f*, " 52
a sacrifice Kindled by *f* from heaven; " 146
thro' his heart The *f* of honour and all noble deeds Flash'd, " 278
maiden snow mingled with sparks of *f*. *Last Tournament* 149
Who sits and gazes on a faded *f*, " 157
Arthur's vows on the great lake of *f*. " 345
one was water and one star was *f*, " 736
Pray for him that he scape the doom of *f*, *Guinevere* 347
The children born of thee are sword and *f*, " 425
making all the night a steam of *f*. " 599
land of old unheaven from the abyss By *f*, *Pass. of Arthur* 83
and blew Fresh *f* into the sun, *Lover's Tale* i 319
Thy *f*'s from heaven had touch'd it, " 439
dragonfly Shot by me like a flash of purple *f*. " ii 17
Fill'd all with pure clear *f*, " 146
Had suck'd the *f* of some forgotten sun, " iv 194
and all *f* again Thrice in a second, " 323
if my boy be gone to the *f*? *Rizpah* 78
an' I seeäd 'im a-gittin' o' *f*; *North. Cobbler* 26
an' 'e shined like a sparkle o' *f*. " 48
leaves i' the middle to kindle the *f*; *Village Wife* 72
F from ten thousand at once of the rebels *Def. of Lucknow* 22
Sharp is the *f* of assault, " 57
thou bringest Not peace, a sword, a *f*. *Sir J. Oldcastle* 36
and life Pass in the *f* of Babylon! " 124
Who rose and doom'd me to the *f*. " 172
How now, my soul, we do not heed the *f*? " 191
For I must live to testify by *f*. " 206
Thro' the *f* of the tulip and poppy, *V. of Maeldune* 43
And we came to the Isle of *F*: " 71
For the peak sent up one league of *f* " 72
There were some leap'd into the *f*; " 76
Dashing the *f*'s and the shadows of dawn " 99
with set of sun Their *f*'s flame thickly, *Achilles over the T.* 11
To see the dread, unweariable *f* " 27
Shrine-shattering earthquake, *f*, flood, thunderbolt, *Tiresias* 61
On one far height in one far-shining *f*. " 185
'One height and one far-shining.' " 186
Flashing with *f*'s as of God, *Despair* 16
and a smoke who was once a pillar of *f*, " 29
Love is *f*, and burns the feet *The Flight* 68
cut his bit o' turf for the *f*? *Tomorrow* 65
Gone the *f*'s of youth, the follies, *Locksley H., Sixty* 39
Gone like *f*'s and floods and earthquakes " 40
F's that shook me once, but now to silent ashes " 41
f of fever creeps across the rotted floor, " 223
The *f*'s that arch this dusky dot— *Epilogue* 52
Ilion's lofty temples robed in *f*, *To Virgil* 2
One shriek'd 'The *f*'s of Hell!' *Dead Prophet* 80
To and thro' the Doomsday *f*, *Helen's Tower* 10
all the hateful *f*'s Of torment, *Demeter and P.* 151
'e coom'd thruf the *f* wi' my bairn i' 'is mouth *Owd Roä* 92
the *f* was a-raägin' an' raävin' " 110
Fur we moänt 'ev naw moor *f*'s— " 118
vows that are snapt in a moment of *f*; *Vastness* 26
f from Heaven had dash'd him dead, *Happy* 83
blasted to the deathless *f* of Hell. " 84
lured me from the household *f* on earth. *Romney's R.* 40

Fire (s) (*continued*)   The coals of *f* you heap upon my head   *Romney's R.* 141
If the lips were touch'd with *f*   *Parnassus* 17
the *f* within him would not falter ;   „ 19
Stark and dark in his funeral *f.*   *To Master of B.* 20
mixt herself with *him* and past in *f.*   *Death of Œnone* 106
' Is earth On *f* to the West ?   *St. Telemachus* 19
were seen or heard *F's* of Suttee,   *Akbar's Dream* 196
passing souls thro' *f* to the *f,*   *The Dawn* 4
Ralph went down like a *f* to the fight   *The Tourney* 3
in the glare of deathless *f* !   *Faith* 8
f—thro' one that will not shame   *Gareth and L.* 1310
Fire (verb)   The furzy prickle *f* the dells,   *Two Voices* 71
And *f's* your narrow casement glass,   *Miller's D.* 243
I, by Lionel sitting, saw his face *F,*   *Lover's Tale iv* 323
Now let it speak, and you *f,*   *Def. of Lucknow* 29
It is charged and we *f,* and they run.   „ 68
Fire-balloon   a *f-b* Rose gem-like up   *Princess, Pro.* 74
Firebrand   this *f*—gentleness To such as her !   „ *v* 167
Fire-crown'd   The *f-c* king of the wrens,   *Window, Ay.* 8
Fired   Not a gun was *f.*   *The Captain* 40
man with knobs and wires and vials *f* A cannon ;   *Princess, Pro.* 65
Now *f* an angry Pallas on the helm,   „ *vi* 367
HE rose at dawn and, *f* with hope,   *Sailor Boy* 1
he saw *F* from the west, far on a hill,   *Lancelot and E.* 168
the heat Of pride and glory *f* her face ;   *Pelleas and E.* 172
that Gawain *f* The hall of Merlin,   „ 517
echoing yell with yell, they *f* the tower,   *Last Tournament* 478
F all the pale face of the Queen,   *Guinevere* 357
Fire-fly   Glitter like a swarm of *fire-flies*   *Locksley Hall* 10
The *f-f* wakens : waken thou with me.   *Princess vii* 179
Firefly-like   glitter *f-l* in copse And linden alley :   „ *i* 208
Fire-hollowing   *F-h* this in Indian fashion, fell   *Enoch Arden* 569
Fireside   her old *f* Be cheer'd with tidings of the bride,   *In Mem. xl* 22
at your own *f,* With the evil tongue   *Maud I x* 50
Firewood   heap'd Their *f,* and the winds   *Spec. of Iliad* 7
Firm (adj. and adv.)   Not swift nor slow to change,
    but *f* :   *Love thou thy land* 31
With measured footfall *f* and mild,   *Two Voices* 413
Thereon I built it *f.*   *Palace of Art* 9
Like Virtue *f,* like Knowledge fair,   *Voyage* 68
His resolve Upbore him, and *f* faith,   *Enoch Arden* 800
f upon his feet, And like an oaken stock   *Golden Year* 61
Not one stroke *f.*   *Romney's R.* 115
he stood *f* ; and so the matter hung ; (repeat)   *The Brook* 144, 148
Her *f* will, her fix'd purpose.   *The Ring* 293
f Tho' compass'd by two armies   *Princess v* 344
Some civic manhood *f* against the crowd—   „ *Con.* 57
keep the soldier *f,* the statesman pure :   *Ode on Well.* 222
Met his full frown timidly *f,* and said ;   *Geraint and E.* 71
felt Her low *f* voice and tender government.   „ 194
Firm (s)   Head of all the golden-shafted *f,*   *Princess ii* 405
Firmament   Shoot your stars to the *f,*   *On Jub. Q. Victoria* 17
Firm-based   stand *F-b* with all her Gods.   *Tiresias* 142
Firmer   Stept forward on a *f* leg,   *Will Water.* 123
And slowly forms the *f* mind,   *In Mem. xviii* 18
mine is the *f* seat,   *Lancelot and E.* 446
Firmly   Will *f* hold the rein,   *Politics* 6
Firmness   and said to him With timid *f,*   *Geraint and E.* 140
Firry   heard the tender dove In *f* woodlands making moan ;   *Miller's D.* 42
First (adj.) (*See also* **Fust**)   in her *f* sleep earth breathes stilly :   *Leonine Eleg.* 7
When the *f* matin-song hath waken'd loud   *Ode to Memory* 68
In setting round thy *f* experiment   „ 81
Needs must thou dearly love thy *f* essay,   „ 83
The *f* house by the water-side,   *L. of Shalott iv* 34
From that *f* nothing ere his birth   *Two Voices* 332
For is not our *f* year forgot ?   „ 368
foundation-stones were laid Since my *f* memory ? '   *Palace of Art* 236
Dan Chaucer, the *f* warbler, whose sweet breath   *D. of F. Women* 5
Love at *f* sight, first-born, and heir to all,   *Gardener's D.* 189
beheld her ere she knew my heart, My *f,* last love ;   „ 277
once I ask'd him of his early life, And his *f* passion ;   *Edwin Morris* 24
when the *f* low matin-chirp hath grown Full quire,   *Love and Duty* 98
Or this *f* snowdrop of the year   *St. Agnes' Eve* 11
' Tell me tales of thy *f* love—   *Vision of Sin* 163
In him woke, With his *f* babe's *f* cry,   *Enoch Arden* 85

First (adj.) (*continued*)   Has she no fear that her *f* husband
    lives ? '   *Enoch Arden* 806
Leolin's *f* nurse was, five years after, hers :   *Aylmer's Field* 79
and the *f* embrace has died Between them,   *Lucretius* 3
Was it the *f* beam of my latest day ?   „ 59
Huge Ammonites, and the *f* bones of Time ;   *Princess, Pro.* 15
took advantage of his strength to be *F* in the field :   „ *ii* 153
' Fresh as the *f* beam glittering on a sail,   „ *iv* 44
Deep as *f* love, and wild with all regret ;   „ 57
lines of green that streak the white Of the *f* snowdrop's
    inner leaves ;   „ *v* 197
From our *f* Charles by force we wrung our claims.   *Third of Feb.* 26
That was the *f* time, too,   *Grandmother* 61
Since our *f* Sun arose and set.   *In Mem. xxiv* 8
Where thy *f* form was made a man ;   „ *lxi* 10
F love, *f* friendship, equal powers,   „ *lxxxv* 107
Seal'd her mine from her *f* sweet breath.   *Maud I xix* 41
But those *f* days had golden hours for me,   *Com. of Arthur* 357
let my name Be hidd'n, and give me the *f* quest,   *Gareth and L.* 545
' I have given him the *f* quest :   „ 582
In the *f* shallow shade of a deep wood,   *Geraint and E.* 119
O'er the four rivers the *f* roses blew,   „ 764
who held and lost with Lot In that *f* war,   *Balin and Balan* 2
which ruin'd man Thro' woman the *f* hour :   *Merlin and V.* 363
Hurt in his *f* tilt was my son, Sir Torre.   *Lancelot and E.* 196
never woman yet, since man's *f* fall,   „ 859
This is not love : but love's *f* flash in youth,   „ 949
Embraced me, and so kiss'd me the *f* time,   *Holy Grail* 596
O the pity To find thine own *f* love once more—   „ 620
But I and the *f* daisy on his grave   *Lover's Tale i* 193
should this *f* master claim His service,   „ *iv* 265
As I of mine, and my *f* passion.   *Sisters (E. and E.)* 67
Love at *f* sight May seem—   „ 91
at *f* glimpse and for a face Gone in a moment—   „ 93
I sail'd On my *f* voyage, harass'd by the frights Of
    my *f* crew,   *Columbus* 67
scouted by court and king—The *f* discoverer starves—   „ 166
Who fain had pledged her jewels on my *f* voyage,   „ 229
With the *f* great love I had felt for the *f* and greatest of
    men ;   *The Wreck* 76
The *f* gray streak of earliest summer-dawn,   *Ancient Sage* 220
Leave the Master in the *f* dark hour of his last
    sleep alone.   *Locksley H., Sixty* 238
Bound by the golden cord of their *f* love—   *The Ring* 429
First (s)   And these had been together from the *f* ;   *Aylmer's Field* 713
First-born   love thou bearest The *f-b* of thy genius.   *Ode to Memory* 92
Love at first sight, *f-b,* and heir to all,   *Gardener's D.* 189
meal she makes On the *f-b* of her sons.   *Vision of Sin* 146
First-famed   of the two *f-f* for courtesy—   *Guinevere* 323
First-fruits   The *f-f* of the stranger :   *Princess ii* 44
Firstling   And bring the *f* to the flock ;   *In Mem. ii* 6
Ever as of old time, Solitary, *f,*   *The Snowdrop* 4
Firth   find him dropt upon the *f's* of ice,   *Princess vii* 206
By *f* and loch thy silver sister grow,   *Sir J. Oldcastle* 58
Fish   *F* are we that love the mud,   *Vision of Sin* 101
beast or bird or *f,* or opulent flower :   *Lucretius* 249
the bird, the *f,* the shell, the flower,   *Princess ii* 383
bird in air, and *f'es* turn'd And whiten'd   *The Victim* 19
o'er her breast floated the sacred *f* ;   *Gareth and L.* 223
' If we have *f* at all Let them be gold ;   *Marr. of Geraint* 669
vanish'd panic-stricken, like a shoal Of darting *f,*   *Geraint and E.* 469
an' ya thraw'd the *f* i' 'is faäce,   *Church-warden, etc.* 30
Fish'd   An' 'e niver not *f* 'is awn ponds,   *Village Wife* 43
Fisherman   O well for the *f's* boy,   *Break, break, etc.* 5
A luckier or a bolder *f,*   *Enoch Arden* 49
Fishing-nets   coils of cordage, swarthy *f-n,*   „ 17
and wrought To make the boatmen *f-n,*   „ 815
Fist   tiny *f* Had graspt a daisy from your Mother's grave—   *The Ring* 322
Fit (adj.)   I scarce am *f* for your great plans :   *Princess vi* 218
Becoming as is meet and *f* A link   *In Mem. xl* 14
asking, one Not *f* to cope your quest.   *Gareth and L.* 1174
ye that scarce are *f* to touch,   *Pelleas and E.* 292
O happy he, and *f* to live,   *The Wanderer* 9
Fit (s)   Gleam'd to the flying moon by *f's.*   *Miller's D.* 116
in a *f* of frolic mirth She strove to span my waist :   *Talking Oak* 137

Fit (s) (*continued*) Or breaking into song by *f*'s, | *In Mem. xxiii* 2
only breathe Short *f*'s of prayer, | *Geraint and E.* 155
Began to break her sports with graver *f*'s, | *Merlin and V.* 180
the riotous *f*'s Of wine and harlotry— | *Sir J. Oldcastle* 100

Fit (verb) *f* us like a nature second-hand; | *Walk. to the Mail* 65
f their little streetward sitting-room | *Enoch Arden* 170
sad and slow, As *f*'s an universal woe, | *Ode on Well.* 14
harden'd skins That *f* him like his own ; | *Gareth and L.* 1094
better *f*'s Our mended fortunes and a Prince's bride : | *Marr. of Geraint* 717

Fitful like *f* blasts of balm To one that travels quickly, | *Gardener's D.* 68

Fitly yield your flower of life To one more *f* yours, | *Lancelot and E.* 953

Fitted Power I to the season; wisdom-bred | *Œnone* 123
Gown'd in pure white, that *f* to the shape— | *Gardener's D.* 126
So now 'tis *f* on and grows to me, | *St. S. Stylites* 209
old and formal, *f* to thy petty part, | *Locksley Hall* 93
As his unlikeness *f* mine. | *In Mem. lxxix* 20
No stone is *f* in yon marble girth | *Tiresias* 135
Who *f* stone to stone again, | *Akbar's Dream* 193

Fitter a villain *f* to stick swine Than ride abroad | *Gareth and L.* 865
I am *f* for my bed, or for my grave, | *The Ring* 433

Fitting expert In *f* aptest words to things, | *In Mem. lxxv* 6
and *f* close Or flying looselier, | *Akbar's Dream* 131
Whence shall she take a *f* mate ? | *Kate* 13
She cannot find a *f* mate. | " 31

Fitz OLD *F*, who from your suburb grange, | *To E. Fitzgerald* 1
which you will take My *F*, and welcome, | " 51

Five Alone and warming his *f* wits, (repeat) | *The Owl i* 6, 13
Young Nature thro' *f* cycles ran, | *Two Voices* 17
Lord of the senses *f*; | *Palace of Art* 180
You know there has not been for these *f* years | *Dora* 65
and here it comes With *f* at top: | *Walk. to the Mail* 113
Leolin's first nurse was, *f* years after, hers : | *Aylmer's Field* 79
son A Walter too,—with others of our set, *F* others : | *Princess, Pro.* 9
And those *f* years its richest field. | *In Mem. xlvi* 12
beneath *f* figures, armed men, | *Gareth and L.* 1205
'Take *F* horses and their armours ;' | *Geraint and E.* 409
and hath overborne *F* knights at once, | *Holy Grail* 303
f summers back, And left me ; | *Guinevere* 321
So Lord Howard past away with *f* ships of war | *The Revenge* 13
swarm Of Turkish Islam for *f* hundred years, | *Montenegro* 11
F young kings put asleep by the sword-stroke, | *Batt. of Brunanburh* 52

Five-acre While Harry is in the *f-a* | *Grandmother* 80

Five-beaded The tender pink *f-b* baby-soles, | *Aylmer's Field* 186

Five-fold *f-f* thy term Of years, I lay ; | *Tiresias* 33

Five-words-long quoted odes, and jewels *f-w-l* | *Princess ii* 337

Fix Holding the bush, to *f* it back, she stood, | *Gardener's D.* 127
'Twere all as one to *f* our hopes on Heaven | *Golden Year* 57
She could not *f* the glass to suit her eye ; | *Enoch Arden* 241
and her lynx eye To *f* and make me hotter, | *Princess iii* 47
Sun sets, moon sets, Love, *f* a day. | *Window, When* 4
wait a little, You shall *f* a day.' | " 12
Nor cares to *f* itself to form, | *In Mem. xxxiii* 4
And *f* my thoughts on all the glow | " *lxxiv* 3
Who shall *f* Her pillars ? | " *cxiv* 3

Fixed-Fixt there like a sun remain *Fix'd*— | *Eleänore* 93
' Not that the grounds of hope were *fix'd*, | *Two Voices* 227
Be *fix'd* and froz'n to permanence : | " 237
And, last, you *fix'd* a vacant stare, | *L. C. V. de Vere* 47
Counting the dewy pebbles, *fix'd* in thought ; | *M. d'Arthur* 84
The blush is *fix'd* upon her cheek. | *Day-Dm., Sleep. P.* 32
One *fix'd* for ever at the door, | *Will Water.* 143
And *fix't* upon the far sea-line ; | *The Voyage* 62
Were *fixed* shadows of thy *fixed* mood, | *Isabel* 9
orb of moving Circumstance Roll'd round by one *fix'd* law. | *Palace of Art* 256
True love turn'd round on *fixed* poles, | *Love thou thy land* 5
my fresh but *fixt* resolve To pass away | *Holy Grail* 737
either *fixt* his heart On that one girl ; | *Enoch Arden* 39
where he *fixt* his heart he set his hand | " 294
and *fixt* her swimming eyes upon him, | " 325
fixt the Sabbath. Darkly that day rose : | *Aylmer's Field* 609
And those *fixt* eyes of painted ancestors, | " 832
I *fixt* My wistful eyes on two fair images, | *Sea Dreams* 239

Fixed-Fixt (*continued*) eyes Of shining expectation *fixt* on mine. | *Princess iv* 153
Fixt like a beacon-tower above the waves | " 493
this is *fixt* As are the roots of earth | " *v* 445
Fix'd in yourself, never in your own arms | " *vi* 177
drags me down From my *fixt* height to mob me | " 308
I on her *Fixt* my faint eyes, and utter'd whisperingly : | " *vii* 144
she *fixt* A showery glance upon her aunt, | *Con.* 32
Fixt by their cars, waited the golden dawn. | *Spec. of Iliad* 22
But Sorrow—*fixt* upon the dead, | *In Mem. xxxix* 8
Her faith is *fixt* and cannot move, | " *xcvii* 3
Because he felt so *fix'd* in truth : | " *cxxv* 8
And a morbid eating lichen *fixt* On a heart | *Maud I vi* 77
Gareth likewise on them *fixt* his eyes | *Gareth and L.* 236
with *fixt* eye following the three. | *Marr. of Geraint* 237
Two forks are *fixt* into the meadow ground, | " 482
there they *fixt* the forks into the ground, | " 548
a rock in ebbs and flows, *Fixt* on her faith. | " 813
humbly hopeful, rose *Fixt* on her hearer's, | *Merlin and V.* 87
or all-silent gaze upon him With such a *fixt* devotion, | " 183
but that other clung to him, *Fixt* in her will, | " 188
So *fixt* her fancy on him : let them be. | " 777
ye *fixt* Your limit, oft returning with the tide. | *Lancelot and E.* 1040
Counting the dewy pebbles, *fix'd* in thought ; | *Pass. of Arthur* 252
and virgin eyes Remaining *fixt* on mine, | *Tiresias* 47
With sad eyes *fixt* on the lost sea-home, | *The Wreck* 126
' *That* should be *fix'd*,' she said ; | *The Ring* 316
But after ten slow weeks her *fix'd* intent, | " 345
Her firm will, her *fix'd* purpose. | " 293

Fixing warm blood mixing ; The eyeballs *f*. | *All Things will Die* 34
F full eyes of question on her face, | *Com. of Arthur* 312
F my eyes on those three cypress-cones | *Lover's Tale ii* 38

Fixt See **Fixed**

Flaäme (flame) ' at summun seed i' the *f*, | *Owd Roä* 94

Flaccid a scheme that had left us *f* and drain'd. | *Maud I i* 20

Flag never floats an European *f*, | *Locksley Hall* 161
F's, flutter out upon turrets and towers ! | *W. to Alexander* 15
their sails and their masts and their *f*'s, | *The Revenge* 116
thou would'st have her *f* Borne on thy coffin— | *Ded. Poem Prin. Alice* 16
But one—he was waving a *f*— | *The Wreck* 119
wherever her *f* fly, Glorying between sea and sky, | *Open I. and C. Exhib.* 17
One life, one *f*, one fleet, one Throne ! ' | " 39

Flag-flower tall *f-f*'s when they sprung | *Miller's D.* 53

Flagrante Caught *in f*—what's the Latin word ?— | *Walk. to the Mail* 34

Flagship stately Spanish men to their *f* bore him | *The Revenge* 97

Flail From Arac's arm, as from a giant's, *f*, | *Princess v* 500
A thresher with his *f* had scatter'd them. | *Gareth and L.* 842

Flake (*See also* **Blossom-flake, Foam-flakes**) sea-wind sang Shrill, chill, with *f*'s of foam. | *M. d'Arthur* 49
beat the twilight into *f*'s of fire. | *Tithonus* 42
here and there a foamy *f* Upon me, | *The Brook* 59
thicker, like the *f*'s In a fall of snow, | *Lucretius* 166
Before me shower'd the rose in *f*'s ; | *Princess iv* 264
This *f* of rainbow flying on the highest | " 319
rocket molten into *f*'s Of crimson | *In Mem. xcviii* 31
sea-wind sang Shrill, chill, with *f*'s of foam. | *Pass. of Arthur* 217
gladly see I thro' the wavering *f*'s | *Prog. of Spring* 29

Flaky Diffused and molten into *f* cloud. | *Lover's Tale i* 641

Flame (s) (*See also* **Altar-flame, Flaäme, Martyr-flames, Sun-flame, Under-flame**) With the clear-pointed *f* of chastity, | *Isabel* 2
A subtle, sudden *f*, By veering passion fann'd, | *Madeline* 28
alight As with the quintessence of *f*, | *Arabian Nights* 123
arrows of his thoughts were headed And wing'd with *f*, | *The Poet* 12
in her raiment's hem was traced in *f* WISDOM, | " 45
Burn'd like one burning *f* together, | *L. of Shalott iii* 22
A thousand little shafts of *f* | *Fatima* 17
She died : she went to burning *f*: | *The Sisters* 7
thro' the topmost Oriels' coloured *f* | *Palace of Art* 161
hollow shades enclosing hearts of *f*, | " 241
Dark faces pale against that rosy *f*, | *Lotos-Eaters* 26
' Saw God divide the night with flying *f*, | *D. of F. Women* 225
Beheld the dead *f* of the fallen day | *Enoch Arden* 441

H*

Flash'd (*continued*) A thought *f* thro' me which I clothed
in act,   *Princess* i 195
young captains *f* their glittering teeth,   " *v* 20
Heaven *f* a sudden jubilant ray,   *Ode on Well.* 129
F all their sabres bare, F as they turn'd   *Light Brigade* 27
The living soul was *f* on mine,   *In Mem.* xcv 36
pride *f* over her beautiful face.   *Maud* I iv 16
Something *f* in the sun,   " *ix* 10
Barons of his realm F forth and into war: *Com. of Arthur* 66
At times the summit of the high city *f*;   *Gareth and L.* 192
and *f* as those Dull-coated things,   " 685
So Gareth ere he parted *f* in arms.   " 689
madden'd her, and away she *f* again   " 784
f the fierce shield, All sun;   " 1030
Whereat Geraint *f* into sudden spleen: *Marr. of Geraint* 273
out he *f*, And into such a song,   *Merlin and V.* 416
F the bare-grinning skeleton of death!   " 847
Suddenly *f* on her a wild desire,   *Lancelot and E.* 357
Then *f* into wild tears, and rose again,   " 613
and down they *f*, and smote the stream.   " 1235
f, as it were, Diamonds to meet them,   " 1236
Then *f* a yellow gleam across the world,   *Holy Grail* 402
a stream That *f* across her orchard underneath   " 593
The fire of honour and all noble deeds F,   *Pelleas and E.* 279
For so the words were *f* into his heart   " 503
Then *f* a levin-brand; and near me stood,   *Last Tournament* 616
So *f* and fell the brand Excalibur: *Pass. of Arthur* 310
A mystic light *f* ev'n from her white robe   *Lover's Tale* i 370
all my wealth F from me in a moment   " 669
face and form of Lionel F thro' my eyes   " ii 95
jewels Of many generations of his house Sparkled and *f*,   " iv 300
one lightning-fork F out the lake;   *Sisters (E. and E.)* 97
bright face was *f* thro' sense and soul   " 109
And all the heavens *f* in frost;   *To E. Fitzgerald* 22
upon me *f* The power of prophesying—   *Tiresias* 56
and *f* into the Red Sea,   *To Marq. of Dufferin* 44
and *f* into a frolic of song And welcome;   *Demeter and P.* 12
F on the Tournament, Flicker'd and bicker'd   *Merlin and the G.* 69

Flashest ALL along the valley, stream that *f* white,   *V. of Cauteretz* 1
Flashing She, *f* forth a haughty smile, began   *D. of F. Women* 129
f round and round, and whirl'd in an arch,   *M. d'Arthur* 138
The cataract *f* from the bridge,   *In Mem.* lxxi 15
Came quickly *f* thro' the shallow ford   *Marr. of Geraint* 167
Was all the marble threshold *f*,   *Geraint and E.* 25
on the splendour came, *f* me blind;   *Holy Grail* 413
f round and round, and whirl'd in an arch,   *Pass. of Arthur* 306
the whole isle-side *f* down from the peak   *V. of Maeldune* 45
F with fires as of God,   *Despair* 16
Rode *f* blow upon blow,   *Heavy Brigade* 32
coin of fancy *f* out from many a golden phrase;   *To Virgil* 8

Flask (*See also* **Wine-flask**) A *f* of cider from his
father's vats,   *Audley Court* 27
Here sits the Butler with a *f*   *Day-Dm., Sleep.* P. 25
I leave an empty *f*:   *Will Water.* 164

Flat (adj. and adv.) and so this earth was *f*:   *Columbus* 48
dying ebb that faintly lipp'd The *f* red granite;   *Audley Court* 13
sin, that crush'd My spirit *f* before thee.   *St. S. Stylites* 26
child Push'd her *f* hand against his face   *Princess* ii 366
on this side the palace ran the field F   " *v* 362
Of this *f* lawn with dusk and bright;   *In Mem.* lxxix 2
pitch'd Beside the Castle Perilous on *f* field,   *Gareth and L.* 1363
up the vale of Usk, By the *f* meadow,   *Marr. of Geraint* 832
Take my salute,' unknightly with *f* hand,   *Geraint and E.* 717
Arthur had the jousts Down in the *f* field   *Pelleas and E.* 164
From *f* confusion and brute violences,   *Last Tournament* 124
in dead night along that table-shore, Drops *f*,   " 464
A *f* malarian ground of reed and rush!   *Lover's Tale* iv 142
Strow yonder mountain *f*,   *Mechanophilus* 6
leaves Laid their green faces *f*   *Balin and Balan* 344
To lay the sudden heads of violence *f*,   *Holy Grail* 310
teeth of Hell *f*ay bare and gnash thee *f*!—   *Last Tournament* 444
and my strongest wish Falls *f*   *Romney's R.* 72

Flat (a level) And glanced athwart the glooming *f's*.   *Mariana* 20
By sands and steaming *f's*, and floods   *The Voyage* 45
here upon the *f* All that long morn   *Princess v* 367

Flat (a level) (*continued*) all about The same gray *f's*
again,   *In Mem.* lxxxvii 13
Wide *f's*, where nothing but coarse grasses grew;   *Holy Grail* 794
if yonder hill be level with the *f*.   *Locksley H., Sixty* 111
Flat (note in music) run thro' every change of
sharp and *f*;   *Caress'd or chidden* 4
Flatten'd Mangled, and *f*, and crush'd,   *Maud* I i 7
Flatter (*See also* **Face-flatter**) They would sue me,
and woo me, and *f* me,   *The Mermaid* 43
To *f* me that I may die?   *Two Voices* 204
F myself that always everywhere I know   *Princess* ii 412
This look of quiet *f's* thus Our home-bred fancies: *In Mem.* x 10
at times Would *f* his own wish in age for love,   *Merlin and V.* 185
Softly laugh'd Isolt; 'F me not,   *Last Tournament* 557
F me rather, seeing me so weak,   " 642
O you that can *f* your victims,   *Charity* 29
Flatter'd Teach your *f* kings that only those   *Locksley H., Sixty* 132
thought of power F his spirit   *Œnone* 137
Be *f* to the height.   *Palace of Art* 192
snares them by the score F and fluster'd,   *Princess* v 164
The fancy *f* my mind,   *Maud* I xiv 23
therefore *f* him, Being so gracious,   *Pelleas and E.* 119
F the fancy of my fading brain;   *Lover's Tale* ii 107
Flattering But *f* the golden prime   *Arabian Nights* 76
f childish thought The oriental fairy brought,   *Eleänore* 13
A splendid presence *f* the poor roofs   *Aylmer's Field* 175
I, that *f* my true passion, saw The knights,   *Merlin and V.* 874
Half-envious of the *f* hand,   *Lancelot and E.* 349
F myself that all my doubts were fools   *Sisters (E. and E.)* 140
Flattery the wit, The *f* and the strife,   *D. of F. Women* 148
Nor speak I now from foolish *f*;   *Marr. of Geraint* 433
the old man, Tho' doubtful, felt the *f*,   *Merlin and V.* 184
F gilding the rift in a throne;   *Vastness* 20
O the *f* and the craft Which were my undoing . . .   *Forlorn* 3
Flaunt Was this a time for these to *f* their pride?   *Aylmer's Field* 770
and *f* With prudes for proctors,   *Princess, Pro.* 140
to *f*, to dress, to dance, to thrum,   " iv 519
Pleasure who *f's* on her wide downway   *Vastness* 16
Flaunted took the ring, and *f* it Before that other   *The Ring* 243
Flaunting Thou comest not with shows of *f* vines   *Ode to Memory* 48
Flaw Like *f's* in summer laying lusty corn: *Marr. of Geraint* 764
heirless F In his throne's title make him feel so frail,   *Sir. J. Oldcastle* 72
Flawless circle rounded under female hands With *f*
demonstration: *Princess* ii 373
Flax Touch *f* with flame—a glance will serve   *Merlin and V.* 111
Flaxen With thy floating *f* hair;   *Adeline* 6
From the *f* curl to the gray lock   *Princess* iv 426
Ere childhood's *f* ringlet turn'd To black and brown   *In Mem.* lxxix 15
on one arm The *f* ringlets of our infancies   *Lover's Tale* i 234
Flay teeth of Hell *f* bare and gnash thee   *Last Tournament* 444
f Captives whom they caught in battle—   *Locksley H., Sixty* 79
Flayflint There lived a *f* near; we stole   *Walk. to the Mail* 84
Flaying The roofs and sucking up the drains,   *Princess* v 525
Flea text no larger than the limbs of *f's*;   *Merlin and V.* 672
Fleck slid, a sunny *f*, From head to ancle   *Talking Oak* 223
That life is dash'd with *f's* of sin.   *In Mem.* lii 14
Fleckless My conscience will not count me *f*;   *Princess* ii 294
Fled *f* Beyond the Memmian naphtha-pits,   *Alexander* 3
Her household *f* the danger,   *The Goose* 54
Her voice *f* always thro' the summer land;   *Edwin Morris* 67
I read, and *f* by night, and flying turn'd: " 134
Then *f* she to her inmost bower,   *Godiva* 42
'O happy sleep, that lightly *f*!'   *Day-Dm., Depart.* 18
Thought her proud, and *f* over the sea;   *Edward Gray* 14
For one fair Vision ever *f* Down the waste waters   *The Voyage* 57
As fast she *f* thro' sun and shade,   *Sir L. and Q. G.* 37
F forward, and no news of Enoch came.   *Enoch Arden* 361
His fancy *f* before the lazy wind Returning,   " 657
For maidens, on the spur she *f*;   *Princess* i 151
when he fell, And all else *f*?   " ii 243
They *f*, who might have shamed us: " 299
As flies the shadow of a bird, she *f*.   " iii 96
the day *f* on thro' all Its range of duties   " 176
and *f*, as flies A troop of snowy doves   " iv 167
Amazed he *f* away Thro' the dark land,   " v 48

Fled (*continued*) And shuddering *f* from room to room,   *Princess* vi 370
My fancy *f* to the South again.   *The Daisy* 108
Less yearning for the friendship *f*,   *In Mem. cxvi* 15
Were it not wise I *f* from the place   *Maud I i* 64
Whether I need have *f*?   „ *II ii* 72
And I wake, my dream is *f*;   „ *iv* 51
Left her and *f*, and Uther enter'd in,   *Com. of Arthur* 201
F down the lane of access to the King,   *Gareth and L.* 661
by this entry *f* The damsel in her wrath,   „ 674
'Lead, and I follow,' and fast away she *f*. (repeat)   „ 760, 990
but three *F* thro' the pines;   „ 814
a Shape that *f* With broken wings,   „ 1207
they *f* With little save the jewels they had on,   *Marr. of Geraint* 639
F all the boon companions of the Earl,   *Geraint and E.* 477
and *f* Yelling as from a spectre,   „ 732
women staring and aghast, While some yet *f*;   „ 805
Dishorsed himself, and rose again, and *f* Far,   *Balin and Balan* 330
f from Arthur's court To break the mood.   *Merlin and V.* 297
F like a glittering rivulet to the tarn: *Lancelot and E.* 52
But I, my sons, and little daughter *f*   „ 276
F ever thro' the woodwork, till they found The new design   „ 440
But on that day when Lancelot *f* the lists,   „ 525
Galahad *f* along them bridge by bridge,   *Holy Grail* 504
Burnt me within, so that I rose and *f*,   „ 608
Ran thro' the doors and vaulted on his horse And *f*:   *Pelleas and E.* 540
left him bruised And batter'd, and *f* on,   „ 547
Before him *f* the face of Queen Isolt   *Last Tournament* 363
Tristram waking, the red dream *F* with a shout,   „ 488
QUEEN GUINEVERE had *f* the court,   *Guinevere* 9
hither had she *f*, her cause of flight Sir Modred;   „ 128
F all night long by glimmering waste   „ 130
Moan as she *f*, or thought she heard   „ 367
Queen had added ' Get thee hence,' *F* frighted.   *Pass. of Arthur* 89
he that *f* no further fly the King;   *Lover's Tale iii* 26
like wild Bacchanals *F* onward to the steeple   „ 55
f Wind-footed to the steeple in the woods,   *Sisters (E. and E.)* 158
in the thick of question and reply I *f* the house,   „ 236
she rose and *f* Beneath a pitiless rush   *Batt. of Brunanburh* 59
Few were his following, *F* to his warship: *The Wreck* 62
and turn'd in her haste and *f*,   *Despair* 69
one son had forged on his father and *f*,   „ 85
and its last brother-worm will have *f*   *The Flight* 71
listens, fears his victim may have *f*—   *Locksley H., Sixty* 251
crying after voices that have *f*!   *Demeter and P.* 15
F wavering o'er thy face, and chased away and turn'd, And *f* by many a waste,   „ 74
Muriel *f*. Poor Muriel ! Ay, poor Muriel   *The Ring* 271
up the tower—an icy air *F* by me—   „ 446
' HE is *f*—I wish him dead—   *Forlorn* 1
He is *f*, or he is dead,   „ 9
have you lost him, is he *f*?   *Happy* 2
If *f*. I was all but crazed With the grief   *Bandit's Death* 38

Fledged curved branches, *f* with clearest green,   *D. of F. Women* 59
F as it were with Mercury's ankle-wing,   *Lucretius* 201
lightlier move The minutes *f* with music :'   *Princess iv* 37
pines that *f* The hills that watch'd thee,   *Lover's Tale i* 11

Flee faintest sunlights *f* About his shadowy sides :   *The Kraken* 4
with increasing might doth forward *f* By town,   *Mine be the strength* 5
if I *f* to these Can I go from Him ?   *Enoch Arden* 224
Melissa clamour'd ' *F* the death ;'   *Princess iv* 166
What time mine own might also *f*,   *In Mem. lxxiv* 37
I *f* from the cruel madness of love,   *Maud I iv* 55
F down the valley before he get to horse.   *Gareth and L.* 941
a dog am I, To worry, and not to *f*—   „ 1015
' I will *f* hence and give myself to God '—   *Last Tournament* 624
I would *f* from the storm within,   *The Wreck* 9

Fleece heavens between their fairy *f*'s pale   *Gardener's D.* 261
many-wintered *f* of throat and chin.   *Merlin and V.* 841
Burst from a swimming *f* of winter gray,   *Demeter and P.* 20

Fleece (an inn) ' THE Bull, the *F* are cramm'd,   *Audley Court* 1

Fleeced *See* **Thick-fleeced**

Fleecy Moving thro' a *f* night.   *Margaret* 21

Fleet (adj.) *f* I was of foot: Before me shower'd   *Princess iv* 263

Fleet (s) all the *f* Had rest by stony hills   *On a Mourner* 34
a *f* of glass, That seem'd a *f* of jewels   *Sea Dreams* 122
An idle signal, for the brittle *f*   „ 133
my poor venture but a *f* of glass   „ 138
Breaking their mailed *f*'s and armed towers,   *Ode Inter. Exhib.* 39
Welcome her, thunders of fort and of *f*!   *W. to Alexandra* 6
I trust if an enemy's *f* came yonder   *Maud I i* 49
Ev'n in the presence of an enemy's *f*,   *Guinevere* 279
For half of their *f* to the right   *The Revenge* 35
the Spanish *f* with broken sides lay round   „ 71
The *f* of England is her all-in-all ; Her *f* is in your hands, And in her *f* her Fate.   *The Fleet* 13
you, that have the ordering of her *f*,   „ 16
One life, one flag, one *f*, one Throne !'   *Open I. and C. Exhib.* 39
valour in battle, glorious annals of army and *f*,   *Vastness* 7
Than a rotten *f* and a city in flames !   *Riflemen form !* 18

Fleet (verb) The cloud *f*'s, The heart beats,   *Nothing will Die* 11
The clouds will cease to *f*;   *All Things will Die* 11
And the light and shadow *f*,   *Maud II iv* 36
And the shadow flits and *f*'s   „ 90
Before them *f*'s the shower,   *Early Spring* 13

Fleeted (*See also* **Far-fleeted**) As fast we *f* to the South: *The Voyage* 4
THOSE that of late had *f* far and fast   *Pref. Son. 19th Cent.* 1
F his vessel to sea with the king in it,   *Batt. of Brunanburh* 60

Fleeter know Whether smile or frown be *f*?   *Madeline* 12

Fleeting (*See also* **Ever-fleeting**) When will the clouds be aweary of *f*?   *Nothing will Die* 5
Sow'd all their mystic gulfs with *f* stars ;   *Gardener's D.* 262
One after another the white clouds are *f*;   *All Things will Die* 5
' Or that this anguish *f* hence,   *Two Voices* 235
And *f* thro' the boundless universe,   *Lucretius* 161
Or villain fancy *f* by, Drew in the expression   *In Mem. cxi* 18
in the night, When the ghosts are *f*.   *Forlorn* 18
F betwixt her column'd palace-walls,   *St. Telemachus* 37

Flesh (*See also* **Swine-flesh**) my *f*, which I despise and hate,   *St. S. Stylites* 58
Mortify Your *f*, like me, with scourges   „ 180
But far too spare of *f*.'   *Talking Oak* 92
Padded round with *f* and fat,   *Vision of Sin* 177
But they that cast her spirit into *f*,   *Aylmer's Field* 481
Thou wilt not gash thy *f* for *him*,   „ 658
and swept away The men of *f* and blood,   *Sea Dreams* 237
never yet on earth Could dead *f* creep,   *Lucretius* 131
Oh, sacred be the *f* and blood   *In Mem. xxxiii* 11
All knowledge that the sons of *f*   „ lxxxv 27
O heart of stone, are you *f*,   *Maud I vi* 79
And she was fairest of all *f* on earth,   *Com. of Arthur* 3
Some hold that he hath swallow'd infant *f*,   *Gareth and L.* 1342
Go to the town and buy us *f*   *Marr. of Geraint* 372
means of goodly welcome, *f* and wine.   „ 387
boil'd the *f*, and spread the board,   „ 391
call'd for *f* and wine to feed his spears.   *Geraint and E.* 601
all the hall was dim with steam of *f*:   „ 603
If arm of *f* could lay him.'   *Balin and Balan* 299
shield of Balan prick'd The hauberk to the *f*;   „ 560
World-war of dying *f* against the life,   *Merlin and V.* 193
Nor ever touch'd fierce wine, nor tasted *f*,   „ 627
how pale ! what are they ? *f* and blood ?   *Lancelot and E.* 1256
The beauty of her *f* abash'd the boy,   *Pelleas and E.* 78
the world Is *f* and shadow—I have had my day.   *Last Tournament* 316
They fail'd to trace him thro' the *f* and blood   „ 686
Which *f* and blood perforce would violate: „ 689
I cannot take thy hand ; that too is *f*,   *Guinevere* 553
in the *f* thou hast sinn'd ; and mine own *f*,   „ 554
My love thro' *f* hath wrought into my life   „ 558
F of my *f* was gone, but bone of my bone was left—   *Rizpah* 51
a cross of *f* and blood And holier.   *Sir J. Oldcastle* 137
' He veil'd Himself in *f*, and now He veils His *f* in bread,   „ 156
Chill'd, till I tasted *f* again   *To E. Fitzgerald* 20
keep their haithen kings in the *f* for the Jidgemint day,   *Tomorrow* 70
died in the doing it, *f* without mind ;   *Vastness* 28
He that has nail'd all *f* to the Cross,   „ 28
Hast spared the *f* of thousands,   *Happy* 17
fairest *f* at last is filth on which the worm   „ 30
This wall of solid *f* that comes between   „ 35

Flesh (*continued*)   If man and wife be but one *f*,   *Happy* 94
Flesh'd   *See* **Foul-flesh'd**
Fleshless   crown'd with *f* laughter—   *Gareth and L.* 1383
     like a barren ghost From out the *f* world of spirits,   *The Ring* 228
Fleshly   this *f* sign That thou art thou—   *De Prof., Two G.* 40
Fleurs-de-lys   sink Thy *f-d-l* in slime again,   *Sir J. Oldcastle* 99
Flew   Out *f* the web and floated wide;   *L. of Shalott* iii 42
     That loosely *f* to left and right—   *iv* 20
     A living flash of light he *f*.'   *Two Voices* 15
     The goose *f* this way and *f* that,   *The Goose* 35
     The fire shot up, the martin *f*,   *Day-Dm., Revival* 11
     F over roof and casement: *Will Water.* 134
     'Chase,' he said: the ship *f* forward,   *The Captain* 33
     the rim Changed every moment as we *f*.   *The Voyage* 28
     till they *f*, Hair, and eyes, and limbs,   *Vision of Sin* 38
     a country dance, and *f* thro' light And shadow,   *Princess, Pro.* 84
     f kite, and raced the purple fly,   *ii* 248
     Till o'er the hills her eagles *f*   *Ode on Well.* 112
     The gust that round the garden *f*,   *In Mem. lxxix* 19
     then *f* in a dove And brought a summons   *"" ciii* 15
     and the blade *f* Splintering in six,   *Balin and Balan* 395
     all that walk'd, or crept, or perch'd, or *f*.   *Last Tournament* 367
     its shadow *f* Before it, till it touch'd her,   *Guinevere* 79
     And the daws *f* out of the Towers   *V. of Maeldune* 109
Flexile   So youthful and so *f* then,   *Amphion* 59
Flicker   The shadows *f* to and fro: *D. of the O. Year* 39
     Where the dying night-lamp *f*'s,   *Locksley Hall* 80
     wisp that *f*'s where no foot can tread.'   *Princess iv* 358
     To *f* with his double tongue.   *In Mem. cx* 8
     seem to *f* past thro' sun and shade,   *Ancient Sage* 100
     Nor *f* down to brainless pantomime,   *To W. C. Macready* 10
Flicker'd   high masts *f* as they lay afloat;   *D. of F. Women* 113
     F like doubtful smiles about her lips,   *Lover's Tale i* 68
     in the heaven above it there *f* a songless lark,   *V. of Maeldune* 17
     Lightnings *f* along the heath;   *Dead Prophet* 79
     F and bicker'd From helmet to helmet,   *Merlin and the G.* 70
Flickering   (*See also* **Livid-flickering**)   night-light *f*
     in my eyes Awoke me.   *Sea Dreams* 103
     and *f* in a grimly light Dance on the mere.   *Gareth and L.* 826
     lark Shot up and shrill'd in *f* gyres,   *Princess vii* 46
     f fairy-circle wheel'd and broke   *Guinevere* 257
     Draw downward into Hades with his drift Of *f*
     spectres,   *Demeter and P.* 27
     Prince Who scarce had pluck'd his *f* life   *To the Queen ii* 5
     Might find a *f* glimmer of relief In change of place.   *To Mary Boyle* 47
     sometimes I fear You may be *f*,   *Sisters (E. and E.)* 33
Flight (*flying*)   (*See also* **Swallow-flight**)   And of so
     fierce a *f*, From Calpe unto Caucasus   *The Poet* 14
     Love wept and spread his sheeny vans for *f*;   *Love and Death* 8
     free delight, from any height of rapid *f*,   *Rosalind* 3
     And that delight of frolic *f*,   *"" 47*
     Rapt after heaven's starry *f*,   *Two Voices* 68
     summits slope Beyond the furthest *f*'s of hope,   *"" 185*
     she led, In hope to gain upon her *f*.   *The Voyage* 60
     What look'd a *f* of fairy arrows aim'd   *Aylmer's Field* 94
     F's, terrors, sudden rescues,   *"" 99*
     Your *f* from out your bookless wilds   *Princess ii* 56
     Edyrn's men had caught them in their *f*,   *Marr. of Geraint* 642
     she fled, her cause of *f* Sir Modred;   *Guinevere* 9
     prone *F* By thousands down the crags   *Montenegro* 7
     f of birds, the flame of sacrifice,   *Tiresias* 6
     cheeping to each other of their *f* To summer lands!   *The Ring* 86
     And over the *f* of the Ages!   *Parnassus* 3
     once a *f* of shadowy fighters crost The disk,   *St. Telemachus* 23
Flight (*of stairs*)   Broad-based *f*'s of marble stairs   *Arabian Nights* 117
     And up a *f* of stairs into the hall.   *Princess ii* 31
Fling (s)   Give me my *f*, and let me say my say.'   *Aylmer's Field* 399
Fling (verb)   to *f* The winged shafts of truth,   *The Poet* 25
     f one did *f* the fire.   *"" 30*
     f on each side my low-flowing locks,   *The Mermaid* 32
     take Excalibur, And *f* him far into the middle mere: *M. d'Arthur* 37
     But, if thou spare to *f* Excalibur,   *"" 131*
     good luck Shall *f* her old shoe after.   *Will Water.* 216
     And *f* the diamond necklace by.'   *Lady Clare* 40
     'Can I not *f* this horror off me again,   *Lucretius* 173

Fling (verb) (*continued*)   will she *f* herself, Shameless
     upon me?   *Lucretius* 202
     f The tricks, which make us toys of men,   *Princess ii* 62
     all prophetic pity, *f* Their pretty maids   *"" v* 381
     '*F* our doors wide! all, all, not one,   *"" vi* 334
     And *f* it like a viper off, and shriek   *"" vii* 94
     f whate'er we felt, not fearing, into words.   *Third of Feb.* 6
     Never a man could *f* him: *Grandmother* 10
     f This bitter seed among mankind: *In Mem. xc* 3
     sadness *f*'s Her shadow on the blaze of kings: *"" xcviii* 18
     Did he *f* himself down? who knows?   *Maud I i* 9
     I swear thou canst not *f* the fourth.'   *Gareth and L.* 1327
     And *f* me deep in that forgotten mere.   *Lancelot and E.* 1426
     an ye *f* those rubies round my neck In lieu of
     hers,   *Last Tournament* 312
     take Excalibur, And *f* him far into the middle
     mere: *Pass. of Arthur* 205
     But, if thou spare to *f* Excalibur,   *"" 299*
     That *f*'s a mist behind it in the sun—   *Lover's Tale iv* 294
     and *f* Thy royalty back into the riotous fits   *Sir J. Oldcastle* 99
     I would *f* myself over and die!   *The Wreck* 118
     earth's dark forehead *f*'s athwart the heavens   *Ancient Sage* 200
     And *f* free alms into the beggar's bowl,   *"" 260*
     What? *f* them to you?—well—   *Happy* 103
     Mussulman Who *f*'s his bowstrung Harem   *Romney's R.* 135
     horse, anger, plunged To *f* me, and fail'd.   *Akbar's Dream* 119
Flinging   *F* the gloom of yesternight On the white day;   *Ode to Memory* 9
     f round her neck, Claspt it, and cried   *Last Tournament* 749
     like the wave *f* forward again,   *Def. of Lucknow* 43
     Was *f* fruit to lions?   *Tiresias* 67
Flint   shake The sparkling *f*'s beneath the prow.   *Arabian Nights* 52
     clattering *f*'s batter'd with clanging hoofs;   *D. of F. Women* 21
     Is there no stoning save with *f* and rock?   *Aylmer's Field* 746
     own one port of sense not *f* to prayer,   *Princess vi* 182
     out upon you, *f*! You love nor her,   *"" 229*
     heart as a millstone, set my face as a *f*,   *Maud I i* 31
     But then what a *f* is he!   *"" xix* 57
     forage for the horse, and *f* for fire.   *Gareth and L.* 1277
Flippant   The *f* put himself to school   *In Mem. cx* 10
Flirt   Not one to *f* a venom at her eyes,   *Merlin and V.* 609
Flit   will *f* To make the greensward fresh,   *Talking Oak* 89
     Let our girls *f*, Till the storm die!   *Princess vi* 337
     Look, look, how he *f*'s,   *Window, A y* 7
     f like the king of the wrens with a crown of fire.   *"" 16*
     Or like to noiseless phantoms *f*:   *In Mem. xx* 16
     What slender shade of doubt may *f*,   *"" xlviii* 7
     F's by the sea-blue bird of March;   *"" xci* 4
     A shadow *f*'s before me,   *Maud II iv* 11
     shadow *f*'s and fleets And will not let me be;   *"" 90*
     Then let her fancy *f* across the past,   *Marr. of Geraint* 645
     And while your doves about you *f*,   *To E. Fitzgerald* 7
     from him *f*'s to warn A far-off friendship   *Demeter and P.* 89
     round her brows a woodland culver *f*'s,   *Prog. of Spring* 18
Flitted   *F* across into the night,   *Miller's D.* 127
     The little innocent soul *f* away.   *Enoch Arden* 270
     unawares they *f* off, Busying themselves about   *Aylmer's Field* 202
     left me in shadow here! Gone—*f* away!   *Window, Gone* 4
     f I know not where!   *"" 7*
     Foälks' coostom *f* awaäy like a kite   *North. Cobbler* 28
     music Of falling torrents, *F* The Gleam.   *Merlin and the G.* 48
Flittermouse-shriek   fainter than any *f-s*;   *V. of Maeldune* 22
Flitteth   The shallop *f* silken-sail'd   *L. of Shalott i* 22
Flitting (*part.*)   'What! You're *f*!' 'Yes, we're *f*,'   *Walk. to the Mail* 43
     says he, 'you *f* with us too—   *"" 45*
     F, fairy Lilian,   *Lilian* 2
     And airy forms of *f* change.   *Madeline* 7
     till all my *f* chance Were caught within the record   *Princess v* 142
Flitting (s)   After the *f* of the bats,   *Mariana* 17
     Plagued with a *f* to and fro,   *Maud II ii* 33
Float   *F*'s from his sick and filmed eyes,   *Supp. Confessions* 166
     F by you on the verge of night.   *Margaret* 31
     languors of thy love-deep eyes *F* on to me.   *Eleänore* 77
     as the warm gulf-stream of Florida *F*'s   *Mine be the strength* 13
     Floated her hair or seem'd to *f* in rest.   *Œnone* 19
     Falls, and *f*'s adown the air.   *Lotos-Eaters, C. S.* 31

Float (*continued*)   forms, That *f* about the threshold of an
    age,   *Golden Year* 16
    steam *F*'s up from those dim fields about the homes   *Tithonus* 69
    never *f*'s an European flag,   *Locksley Hall* 161
    f thro' Heaven, and cannot light?   *Day-Dm., Ep.* 8
    I *f* till all is dark.   *Sir Galahad* 40
    I seem'd To *f* about a glimmering night,   *Princess i* 247
    bottom agates seem to wave and *f*   „ *ii* 327
    the streams that *f* us each and all   „ *iv* 70
    And *f* or fall, in endless ebb and flow;   *W. to Marie Alex.* 27
    airy-light To *f* above the ways of men,   *To E. Fitzgerald* 18
    She *f*'s across the hamlet.   *Prog. of Spring* 40
    May *f* awhile beneath the sun,   *Romney's R.* 50
    vapour in daylight Over the mountain *F*'s,   *Kapolani* 18
    boats of Dahomey that *f* upon human blood!   *The Dawn* 5

Floated   Adown it *f* a dying swan,   *Dying Swan* 6
    Out flew the web and *f* wide;   *L. of Shalott iii* 42
    She *f* down to Camelot: „ *iv* 23
    A gleaming shape she *f* by,   „ 39
    if first I *f* free, As naked essence,   *Two Voices* 373
    F her hair or seem'd to float in rest.   *Œnone* 19
    F the glowing sunlights, as she moved.   „ 182
    she *f* to us and said: 'You have done well   *Princess iv* 526
    lordly creature *f* on To where her wounded brethren lay;   „ *vi* 89
    And o'er her breast *f* the sacred fish;   *Gareth and L.* 223
    She might have risen and *f* when I saw her.   *Holy Grail* 100
    White as white clouds, *f* from sky to sky.   *Lover's Tale i* 5
    Waver'd and *f*—which was less than Hope,   „ 452
    And *f* on and parted round her neck,   „ 704
    about my brow Her warm breast *f* in the utterance   „ *ii* 141
    f in—While all the guests in mute amazement   „ *iv* 304
    F in conquering battle or flapt to the battle-cry!   *Def. of Lucknow* 2
    Had *f* in with sad reproachful eyes,   *The Ring* 469
    Moving to melody, *F* The Gleam,   *Merlin and the G.* 23
    and thro' her dream A ghostly murmur *f*,   *Death of Œnone* 79

Floating (*See also* **Ever-floating**)   And *f* about the under-
    sky,   *Dying Swan* 25
    F thro' an evening atmosphere,   *Eleänore* 100
    misty folds, that *f* as they fell Lit up   *Palace of Art* 35
    With thy *f* flaxen hair;   *Adeline* 6
    Down-droop'd, in many a *f* fold,   *Arabian Nights* 147
    Stays on her *f* locks the lovely freight   *Ode to Memory* 16
    thro' the wreaths of *f* dark upcurl'd,   *The Poet* 35
    land Of lavish lights, and *f* shades;   *Eleänore* 12
    luxuriant symmetry Of thy *f* gracefulness,   „ 50
    Made misty with the *f* meal.   *Miller's D.* 104
    Buoy'd upon *f* tackle and broken spars,   *Enoch Arden* 551
    Came *f* on for many a month and year,   *Vision of Sin* 54
    o'er it crost the dimness of a cloud *F*,   *Pelleas and E.* 38
    and mine Were dim with *f* tears,   *Lover's Tale i* 442
    All day I watch'd the *f* isles of shade,   „ *ii* 5
    in their *f* folds They past and were no more: „ 99

Flock   And in the *f*'s The lamb rejoiceth   *Supp. Confessions* 156
    By dancing rivulets fed his *f*'s   *To E. L.* 22
    when he came again, his *f* believed—   *Aylmer's Field* 600
    half amazed half frighted all his *f*:   „ 631
    my eldest-born, the flower of the *f*;   *Grandmother* 9
    And bring the firstling to the *f*;   *In Mem. ii* 6
    meadowy curves, That feed the mothers of the *f*;   „ *c* 16
    The *f*'s are whiter down the vale,   „ *cxv* 10

Flock'd   thither *f* at noon His tenants,   *Princess, Pro.* 3
    a careless people *f* from the fields   *Dead Prophet* 7

Flood (s) (*See also* **Fountain-flood**)   From the westward-
    winding *f*,   *Margaret* 9
    island queen who sways the *f*'s and lands   *Buonaparte* 3
    They past into the level *f*,   *Miller's D.* 75
    dragons spouted forth A *f* of fountain-foam.   *Palace of Art* 24
    and takes the *f* With swarthy webs.   *M. d'Arthur* 268
    By sands and steaming flats, and *f*'s   *The Voyage* 45
    his passions all in *f* And masters of his motion,   *Aylmer's Field* 339
    Bore down in *f*, and dash'd his angry heart   „ 633
    f, fire, earthquake, thunder, wrought Such waste   „ 639
    the *f* drew; yet I caught her;   *Princess iv* 182
    Better have died and spilt our bones in the *f*—   „ 532
    fling Their pretty maids in the running *f*,   „ *v* 382

Flood (s) (*continued*)   And whiten'd all the rolling *f*;   *The Victim* 20
    lead Thro' prosperous *f*'s his holy urn.   *In Mem. ix* 8
    Summer on the steaming *f*'s,   „ *lxxxv* 69
    shadowing down the horned *f* In ripples,   „ *lxxxvi* 7
    lay At anchor in the *f* below;   „ *ciii* 20
    And roll'd the *f*'s in grander space,   „ 26
    And molten up, and roar in *f*;   „ *cxxvii* 13
    No doubt vast eddies in the *f* Of onward time   „ *cxxviii* 5
    have isled together, knave, In time of *f*.   *Gareth and L.* 894
    follow Vivien thro' the fiery *f*!   *Balin and Balan* 454
    when ye used to take me with the *f*   *Lancelot and E.* 1037
    far up the shining *f* Until we found the palace   „ 1043
    I was all alone upon the *f*,   „ 1046
    Beyond the poplar and far up the *f*,   „ 1050
    Oar'd by the dumb, went upward with the *f*—   „ 1154
    Then fell the *f*'s of heaven drowning the deep.   *Holy Grail* 533
    and takes the *f* With swarthy webs.   *Pass. of Arthur* 436
    booming indistinct Of the confused *f*'s,   *Lover's Tale i* 638
    Saving his life on the fallow *f*.   *Batt. of Brunanburh* 61
    Shrine-shattering earthquake, fire, *f*, thunderbolt,   *Tiresias* 61
    Gone like fires and *f*'s and earthquakes   *Locksley H., Sixty* 40
    shine the level lands, And flash the *f*'s;   *Early Spring* 16
    Produce of your field and *f*,   *Open. I. and C. Exhib.* 5
    From under rose a muffled moan of *f*'s;   *Prog. of Spring* 7
    The *f* may bear me far,   *Crossing the Bar* 14

Flood (verb)   *F* with full daylight glebe and town?   *Two Voices* 87
    F's all the deep-blue gloom with beams   *D. of F. Women* 186
    Ready to burst and *f* the world with foam   *Princess iv* 474
    And *f* a fresher throat with song.   *In Mem. lxxxiii* 16
    the haunts of hern and crake;   „ *ci* 14
    poach'd filth that *f*'s the middle street,   *Merlin and V.* 798
    f's with redundant life Her narrow portals.   *Lover's Tale i* 84

Flooded   Were *f* over with eddying song.   *Dying Swan* 42
    risen before his time And *f* at our nod.   *D. of F. Women* 144
    eyes All *f* with the helpless wrath of tears,   *Enoch Arden* 32
    Over all the woodland's *f* bowers,   *Sisters (E. and E.)* 20
    the lake beyond his limit, And all was *f*;   *The Daisy* 72

Flooding   *f*, leaves Low banks of yellow sand;   *Lover's Tale i* 534
    On hill, or plain, at sea, or *f* ford.   *Holy Grail* 728

Floor   Old footsteps trod the upper *f*'s,   *Mariana* 67
    Flung inward over spangled *f*'s,   *Arabian Nights* 116
    The meal-sacks on the whiten'd *f*,   *Miller's D.* 101
    find my garden-tools upon the granary *f*:   *May Queen, N. Y's.* 45
    rolling waves Of sound on roof and *f* Within,   *D. of F. Women* 192
    There's a new foot on the *f*, my friend,   *D. of the O. Year* 52
    As head and heels upon the *f* They flounder'd   *The Goose* 37
    All heaven bursts her starry *f*,   *St. Agnes' Eve* 27
    thou shalt cease To pace the gritted *f*,   *Will Water.* 242
    shape it plank and beam for roof and *f*,   *Princess vi* 46
    Throbb'd thunder thro' the palace *f*'s,   „ *vii* 104
    crash'd the glass and beat the *f*;   *In Mem. lxxxvii* 20
    Witch-elms that counterchange the *f*   „ *lxxxix* 1
    But let no footstep beat the *f*,   „ *cv* 17
    russet-bearded head roll'd on the *f*.   *Geraint and E.* 729
    others from the *f*, Tusklike, arising,   *Balin and Balan* 315
    Crush'd the wild passion out against the *f*   *Lancelot and E.* 742
    once she slipt like water to the *f*.   „ 830
    grovell'd with her face against the *f*:   *Guinevere* 415
    Parted a little ere they met the *f*,   *Lover's Tale iv* 215
    like the dead by the dead on the cabin *f*,   *The Wreck* 112
    as we was a-cleänin' the *f*,   *Spinster's S's.* 49
    fire of fever creeps across the rotted *f*,   *Locksley H., Sixty* 223
    wi' my hairm hingin' down to the *f*,   *Owd Roä* 65
    Found in a chink of that old moulder'd *f*!'   *The Ring* 280
    The sacred relics tost about the *f*—   „ 447

Flop   hoickt my feet wi' a *f* fro' the claäy.   *Spinster's S's.* 30

Flora (**Christian name**)   work in hues to dim The Titianic *F*.   *Gardener's D.* 171
    O, LADY *F*, let me speak: *Day-Dm., Pro.* 1
    So, Lady *F*, take my lay,   „ *Moral* 1
    So, Lady *F*, take my lay,   „ *Ep.* 1

Florence (**town**)   'Poor lad, he died at *F*,   *The Brook* 35
    At *F* too what golden hours,   *The Daisy* 41
    Abroad, at *F*, at Rome,   *Maud I xix* 58
    Fair *F* honouring thy nativity, Thy *F* now the
    crown of Italy,   *To Dante* 3

Flores AT F in the Azores Sir Richard Grenville lay,   *The Revenge* 1
   And he sailed away from F   ,,   23
Florian I stood With Cyril and with F,   *Princess* i 52
   F said : I have a sister at the foreign court,   ,,   74
   I stole from court With Cyril and with F,   ,,   103
   F, but no livelier than the dame   ,, ii 112
   'The fifth in line from that old F,   ,,   238
   The loyal warmth of F is not cold,   ,,   244
   'Are you that Psyche,' F added ;   ,,   246
   'Are you that Psyche,' F ask'd,   ,,   269
   so pacing till she paused By F;   ,,   303
   I am sad and glad To see you, F.   ,,   307
   'Ungracious !' answer'd F; 'have you learnt   ,,   392
   What think you of it, F?   ,,   408
   'Tell us,' F ask'd, 'How grew this feud   ,, iii 76
   Then murmur'd F gazing after her,   ,,   97
   Cyril kept With Psyche, with Melissa F,   ,,   355
   F nodded at him, I frowning ;   ,, iv 159
   Alone I stood With F, cursing Cyril,   ,,   171
   the doubt ' if this were she,' But it was F.   ,,   218
   prayer, Which melted F's fancy as she hung,   ,,   370
   Then F knelt, and 'Come' he whisper'd to her,   ,, v 63
   F, he That loved me closer than his own right eye,   ,,   530
   'Your brother, Lady,—F,—ask for him   ,, vi 313
   But Psyche tended F: ,, vii 55
Florid f, stern, as far as eye could see,   *Sea Dreams* 219
   Engirt with many a f maiden-cheek,   *Princess* iii 350
Florida as the warm gulf-stream of F Floats   *Mine be the strength* 12
Flounce dimpled f of the sea-furbelow flap,   *Sea Dreams* 266
Flounder began to move, And f into hornpipes.   *Amphion* 24
   Should I f awhile without a tumble   *Hendecasyllabics* 9
Floundered They f all together,   *The Goose* 38
Floundering The weary steed of Pelleas f   *Pelleas and E.* 574
   Part stumbled mixt with f horses.   *Princess* v 498
Flour f From his tall mill that whistled   *Enoch Arden* 342
Flourish (s) In the mid might and f of his May,   *Lancelot and E.* 554
Flourish (verb) O f high, with leafy towers,   *Talking Oak* 197
   O f, hidden deep in fern,   ,,   201
   f'es Green in a cuplike hollow of the down.   *Enoch Arden* 8
   life in him Could scarce be said to f,   *The Brook* 12
   Out of evil evil f'es,   *Boädicea* 83
   She said, 'The evil f in the world.'   *Lover's Tale* i 348
Flourish'd F a little garden square and wall'd :   *Enoch Arden* 734
   They f then or then ; but life in him   *The Brook* 11
   From all a closer interest f up,   *Princess* vii 113
   poplar and cypress unshaken by storm f up beyond sight,   *V. of Maeldune* 15
   You should be jubilant that you f here   *Poets and their B.* 12
Flourishing cave Of touchwood, with a single f spray.   *Aylmer's Field* 512
   thence they wasted all the f territory,   *Boädicea* 54
Flout put your beauty to this f and scorn   *Geraint and E.* 675
   And all to f me, when they bring me in,   *Pelleas and E.* 330
Flouted When he f a statesman's error,   *The Wreck* 68
Flow (s) Low-tinkled with a bell-like f   *The winds, etc.* 7
   silver Of subtle-paced counsel in distress,   *Isabel* 20
   Down from the central fountain's f   *Arabian Nights* 50
   sonorous f Of spouted fountain-floods,   *Palace of Art* 27
   that f Of music left the lips of her that died   *D. of F. Women* 194
   Have ebb and f conditioning their march,   *Golden Year* 30
   float or fall, in endless ebb and f ;   *W. to Marie Alex.* 27
   a rock in ebbs and f's, Fixt on her faith.   *Marr. of Geraint* 812
   clearer in my life than all Its present f.   *Lover's Tale* i 150
   With its true-touch'd pulses in the f   ,,   205
   source Of these sad tears, and feeds their downward f.   ,,   784
   Sway'd by vaster ebbs and f's   *Locksley H., Sixty* 194
Flow (verb) The stream f's, The wind blows,   *Nothing will Die* 9
   The stream will cease to f;   *All Things will Die* 9
   till his own blood f's About his hoof.   *Supp. Confessions* 155
   All night the silence seems to f   *Oriana* 86
   Motions f To one another,   *Eleänore* 61
   May into uncongenial spirits f;   *Mine be the strength* 11
   But now thy beauty f's away.   *Mariana in the S.* 67
   There's somewhat f's to us in life,   *Miller's D.* 21
   They saw the gleaming river seaward f   *Lotos-Eaters* 14
   According to my humour ebb and f.   *D. of F. Women* 134

Flow (verb) *(continued)* I had not dared to f In these words toward you,   *To J. S.* 6
   thro' such tears As f but once a life.   *Love and Duty* 64
   F down, cold rivulet, to the sea,   *A Farewell* 1
   F, softly f, by lawn and lea,   ,,   5
   Till last by Philip's farm I f   *The Brook* 31
   and f To join the brimming river, (repeat)   ,, 63, 182
   your great name f on with broadening time   *Princess* iii 164
   let the turbid streams of rumour f   *Ode on Well.* 181
   All along the valley, where thy waters f,   *V. of Cauteretz* 3
   The tide f's down, the wave again Is vocal   *In Mem.* xix 13
   The double tides of chariots f   ,, xcviii 23
   The hills are shadows, and they f   ,, cxxiii 5
   F thro' our deeds and make them pure,   ,, cxxxi 4
   And all we f from, soul in soul.   ,,   12
   they do not f From evil done;   *Guinevere* 188
   F back again unto my slender spring   *Lover's Tale* i 147
Flow'd tide of time f back with me,   *Arabian Nights* 3
   Heaven f upon the soul in many dreams   *The Poet* 31
   Rare sunrise f.   ,,   36
   F forth on a carol free and bold ;   *Dying Swan* 30
   From underneath his helmet f   *L. of Shalott* iii 30
   o'er him f a golden cloud, and lean'd Upon him,   *Œnone* 105
   Thus far he f, and ended ;   *Golden Year* 52
   Fast f the current of her easy tears,   *Enoch Arden* 865
   (possibly He f and ebb'd uncertain,   *Aylmer's Field* 218
   The mother f in shallower acrimonies: ,,   563
   but when the preacher's cadence f   ,,   729
   and dream and truth F from me ;   *Princess* v 542
   Bloodily f the Tamesa rolling phantom bodies   *Boädicea* 27
   ladies came, and by and by the town F in,   *Marr. of Geraint* 547
   light upon her silver face F from the spiritual lily   *Balin and Balan* 264
   in that hour A hope f round me,   *Lover's Tale* i 449
   that life I heeded not F from me,   ,,   597
   Loosed from their simple thrall they had f abroad,   ,,   703
   past and f away To those unreal billows: ,, ii 195
   the grape from whence it f Was blackening   *Sisters (E. and E.)* 61
   the field with blood of the fighters F,   *Batt. of Brunanburh* 25
Flower (s) (*See also* **Cuckoo-flower, Field-flower, Flag-flower, Hearth-flower, Heather-flower, Honey-suckle-flower, Marish-flowers, Passion-flower, Poison-flowers, Orange-flower, Sea-flower, Spring-flowers, Wild-flower, Wildweed-flower**)
   the heart to scathe F's thou hadst rear'd—   *Supp. Confessions* 84
   The stately f of female fortitude,   *Isabel* 11
   In order, eastern f's large,   *Arabian Nights* 61
   Engarlanded and diaper'd With inwrought f's,   ,,   149
   (Those peerless f's which in the rudest wind   *Ode to Memory* 24
   and sweet showers Of festal f's,   ,,   78
   the heavy stalks Of the mouldering f's :   *A spirit haunts* 8
   like the arrow-seeds of the field f,   *The Poet* 19
   mother plant in semblance, grew A f all gold,   ,,   24
   water will I pour Into every spicy f   *Poet's Mind* 13
   The f's would faint at your cruel cheer.   ,,   15
   With many a deep-hued bell-like f   *Eleänore* 37
   Overlook a space of f's,   *L. of Shalott* i 16
   About the opening of the f,   *Two Voices* 161
   You scarce could see the grass for f's.   ,,   453
   and you were gay With bridal f's—   *Miller's D.* 165
   I roll'd among the tender f's :   *Fatima* 11
   meadow-ledges midway down Hang rich in f's,   *Œnone* 7
   purple f droops : the golden bee Is lily-cradled :   ,,   29
   With bunch and berry and f thro' and thro'.   ,,   102
   A simple maiden in her f Is worth   *L. C. V. de Vere* 15
   But I must gather knots of f's,   *May Queen* 11
   Last May we made a crown of f's :   *May Queen, N. Y's. E.* 9
   There's not a f on all the hills :   ,,   13
   I long to see a f so before the day I die.   ,,   16
   When the f's come again, mother,   ,,   25
   the land about, and all the f's that blow,   ,, Con. 7
   Wild f's in the valley for other hands   ,,   52
   enchanted stem, Laden with f and fruit,   *Lotos-Eaters* 29
   in the stream the long-leaved f's weep,   ,, C. S. 10
   The f ripens in its place,   ,,   36
   I knew the f's, I knew the leaves,   *D. of F. Women* 73

Flower (s) (continued) Cast at thy feet one *f* that fades
  away.   *To Dante* 7
one snowy knee was prest Against the margin *f*'s; *Tiresias* 43
And him the last; and laying *f*'s, " 212
speaking aloud To women, the *f* of the time, *The Wreck* 49
Who had borne my *f* on her hireling heart; " 143
Trusting no longer that earthly *f* *Despair* 35
on an earth that bore not a *f*; " 44
And wind the front of youth with *f*'s, *Ancient Sage* 97
songs in praise of death, and crown'd with *f*'s! " 209
a *f* Had murmurs 'Lost and gone and lost and gone!' " 223
'His two wild woodland *f*'s.' Wild *f*'s blowing side
  by side *The Flight* 80
Wild *f*'s of the secret woods, " 82
May all the *f*'s o' Jeroosilim blossom *Tomorrow* 89
An' the lark fly out o' the *f*'s " 91
carpet es fresh es a midder o' *f*'s i' Maäy— *Spinster's S's.* 45
used to call the very *f*'s Sisters, *Locksley H., Sixty* 101
perhaps a world of never fading *f*'s. " 184
face of Edith like a *f* among the *f*'s. " 260
Or Love with wreaths of *f*'s. *Epilogue* 17
the laughing shepherd bound with *f*'s; *To Virgil* 16
and fills The *f* with dew; *Early Spring* 46
where the purple *f*'s grow, *Frater Ave, etc.* 4
here thy hands let fall the gather'd *f*, *Demeter and P.* 9
now once more ablaze With *f*'s that brighten " 36
All *f*'s—but for one black blur of earth " 37
My quick tears kill'd the *f*, " 108
Caught by the *f* that closes on the fly, *The Ring* 344
lonely maiden-Princess, crown'd with *f*'s, " 485
Her tribes of men, and trees, and *f*'s, *To Ulysses* 3
the bloodless heart of lowly *f*'s *Prog. of Spring* 84
No louder than a bee among the *f*'s, *Romney's R.* 82
the rose Cry to the lotus 'No *f* thou'? *Akbar's Dream* 37
Warble bird, and open *f*, and, men, " *Hymn* 7
I am dressing the grave of a woman with *f*'s. *Charity* 2
I am dressing her grave with *f*'s. " 44
Vary like the leaves and *f*'s, *Poets and Critics* 4
Draw from my death Thy living *f* and grass, *Doubt and Prayer* 6
Flower (verb) white as privet when it *f*'s. *Walk. to the Mail* 56
but as poets' seasons when they *f*, *Golden Year* 28
his followers, all *F* into fortune; *Columbus* 167
So blighted here, would *f* into full health *The Ring* 317
while the races *f* and fade, *Making of Man* 5
Flowerage Busying themselves about the *f* *Aylmer's Field* 203
Flower-bells cluster'd *f-b* and ambrosial orbs *Isabel* 36
Flower'd (*See also* **Freshly-flowered, White-flower'd**)
a dress All branch'd and *f* with gold, *Marr. of Geraint* 631
answers to his mother's calls From the *f*
  furrow. *Supp. Confessions* 160
FIFTY times the rose has *f* and faded, *On Jub. Q. Victoria* 1
A rhyme that *f* betwixt the whitening sloe *To Mary Boyle* 25
Flowering (part. and adj.) A spacious garden full
  of *f* weeds, *To —— With Pal. of Art* 4
there grew an Eastern rose, That, *f* high, *Gardener's D.* 124
burgeons every maze of quick About the *f* squares, *In Mem. cxv* 3
The snowdrop only, *f* thro' the year, *Last Tournament* 220
f grove Of grasses Lancelot pluck'd him *Guinevere* 33
And we hated the *F* Isle, *V. of Maeldune* 52
charm of all the Muses often *F* in a lonely word; *To Virgil* 12
Flowering (s) I mark'd Him in the *f* of his fields, *Pass. of Arthur* 10
Flowerless In silence wept upon the *f* earth. *Death of Œnone* 9
Flower-plot WITH blackest moss the *f-p*'s *Mariana* 1
Flower-sheath lightly breaks a faded *f-s*, *Marr of Geraint* 365
Flowery rivulet in the *f* dale 'll merrily glance and
  play. *May Queen* 39
I turning saw, throned on a *f* rise, *D. of F. Women* 125
All the land in *f* squares, *Gardener's D.* 76
lead my Memmius in a train Of *f* clauses *Lucretius* 120
came On *f* levels underneath the crag, *Princess iii* 336
Thy partner in the *f* walk Of letters, *In Mem. lxxxiv* 22
Witness their *f* welcome. *Balin and Balan* 145
course of life that seem'd so *f* to me *Merlin and V.* 880
Floweth From thy rose-red lips MY name *F*; *Eleänore* 134
from whose left hand *f* The Shadow of Death, *Lover's Tale i* 498

Flowing (*See also* **Forward-flowing, Full-flowing,**
  Low-flowing) stream be aweary of *f* Under
  my eye? *Nothing will Die* 1
the blue river chimes in its *f* *All Things will Die* 1
A clear stream *f* with a muddy one, *Isabel* 30
f rapidly between Their interspaces, *Arabian Nights* 83
F beneath her rose-hued zone, " 140
lordly music *f* from The illimitable years. *Ode to Memory* 41
F like a crystal river; *Poet's Mind* 6
Winds were blowing, waters *f*, *Oriana* 14
My tears, no tears of love, are *f* *Wan Sculptor* 7
island in the river *F* down to Camelot *L. of Shalott i* 14
her canvas *f*, Rose a ship of France. *The Captain* 27
hung to hear The rapt oration *f* free *In Mem. lxxxvii* 32
the blood Of their strong bodies, *f*, *Marr. of Geraint* 569
F with easy greatness and touching *The Wreck* 50
A land of promise *f* with the milk And honey *Lover's Tale i* 334
Were stoled from head to foot in *f* black; *ii* 85
And holding them back by their *f* locks *The Merman* 14
But pledge me in the *f* grape. *My life is full* 15
And o'er them many a *f* range *Day-Dm., Depart.* 21
The truth, that flies the *f* can, *Will Water.* 171
princely halls, and farms, and *f* lawns, *Aylmer's Field* 654
Dragon's cave Half hid, they tell me, now in *f* vines— *Tiresias* 144
Flown as tho' it were The hour just *f*, *Gardener's D.* 83
He rode a horse with wings, that would have *f*, *Vision of Sin* 3
Had tost his ball and *f* his kite, *Aylmer's Field* 84
tell her, Swallow, that thy brood is *f*: *Princess iv* 108
F to the east or the west, *Window, Gone* 7
love is more Than in the summers that are *f*, *In Mem., Con.* 18
For the black bat, night, has *f*, *Maud I xxii* 2
as the cageling newly *f* returns, *Merlin and V.* 901
life had *f*, we sware but by the shell— *Last Tournament* 270
she that clasp'd my neck had *f*; *Locksley H., Sixty* 15
Floy (fly) a knaws naw moor nor a *f*; *N. Farmer, O. S.* 67
Fluctuate And *f* all the still perfume, *In Mem. xcv* 56
Fluctuated *F*, as flowers in storm, some red, *Princess iv* 482
Fluctuation tall columns drown'd In silken *f* " *vi* 355
world-wide *f* sway'd In vassal tides *In Mem. cxii* 15
Flue sent a blast of sparkles up the *f*: *M. d'Arthur, Ep.* 15
Fluent In tracts of *f* heat began, *In Mem. cxviii* 9
Broad brows and fair, a *f* hair and fine, *Gareth and L.* 464
Fluid and *f* range Of lawless airs, *Supp. Confessions* 147
'This world was once a *f* haze of light, *Princess ii* 116
Fluke Anchors of rusty *f*, and boats updrawn; *Enoch Arden* 18
Flung (*See also* **Broad-flung**) The costly doors *f* open wide, *Arabian Nights* 17
F inward over spangled floors, " 116
F leagues of roaring foam into the gorge *If I were loved* 13
Backward the lattice-blind she *f*, *Mariana in the S.* 87
Then with both hands I *f* him, *M. d'Arthur* 157
And *f* him in the dew. *Talking Oak* 232
F the torrent rainbow round; *Vision of Sin* 32
And *f* her down upon a couch of fire, *Aylmer's Field* 574
His body half *f* forward in pursuit, " 587
F ball, flew kite, and raced the purple fly, *Princess ii* 248
She took it and she *f* it. 'Fight' she said, " *iv* 598
and *f* defiance down Gagelike to man, " *v* 177
She *f* it from her, thinking: " *Con.* 32
We *f* the burthen of the second James. *Third of Feb.* 28
and *f* A ballad to the brightening moon: *In Mem. lxxxix* 27
and *f* The lilies to and fro, and said " *xcv* 59
I ran And *f* myself down on a bank of heath, *Com. of Arthur* 343
here is glory enow In having *f* the three: *Gareth and L.* 1326
To which he *f* a wrathful answer back: *Geraint and E.* 146
f herself Down on the great King's couch, *Lancelot and E.* 609
Unclasping *f* the casement back, " 981
F them, and down they flash'd, " 1235
A stone is *f* into some sleeping tarn, *Pelleas and E.* 93
nipt the hand, and *f* it from her; " 133
And *f* them o'er the walls; " 316
steed of Pelleas floundering *f* His rider, " 574
I have *f* thee pearls and find thee swine.' *Last Tournament* 310
Then with both hands I *f* him, *Pass. of Arthur* 325
would have *f* himself From cloud to cloud, *Lover's Tale i* 301
I *f* myself upon him In tears and cries: " *ii* 89

Flung (*continued*)   I, groaning, from me *f* Her empty phantom,   *Lover's Tale ii* 205
This question, so *f* down before the guests,   " *iv* 268
I *f* him the letter that drove me wild,   *First Quarrel* 57
when all was done He *f* it among his fellows—   *Rizpah* 32
the Priest's pearl, *f* down to swine—   *Sir J. Oldcastle* 116
and *f* them in bight and bay,   *V. of Maeldune* 53
Pallas *f* Her fringed ægis,   *Achilles over the T.* 3
I am *f* from the rushing tide of the world   *The Wreck* 6
I caught the wreath that was *f*.   " 40
Till you *f* us back on ourselves,   *Despair* 40
Christian conquerors took and *f*   *Locksley H., Sixty* 84
from their hands *F* thro' the woods,   *Early Spring* 18
f herself Against my heart,   *The Ring* 397
and *f* the mould upon your feet,   *Happy* 50
f himself between The gladiatorial swords,   *St. Telemachus* 61
women shrieking 'Atheist' *f* Filth from the roof,   *Akbar's Dream* 91
I *f* myself down at her feet,   *Charity* 38
Clomb the mountain, and *f* the berries,   *Kapiolani* 6
Wait till Death has *f* them open,   *Faith* 7
Flur   *F*, for whose love the Roman Cæsar   *Marr. of Geraint* 745
Flurried   the little fowl were *f* at it,   *Gareth and L.* 69
Flush (s)   *f* of anger'd shame O'erflows thy calmer glances,   *Madeline* 32
for when the morning *f* Of passion   *Lucretius* 2
As light a *f* As hardly tints the blossom   *Balin and Balan* 266
For here a sudden *f* of wrathful heat   *Guinevere* 356
opposite The *f* and dawn of youth,   *Lover's Tale i* 189
Her husband in the *f* of youth and dawn,   *Death of Œnone* 17
Flush (verb)   strikes along the brain, And *f'es* all the cheek.   *D. of F. Women* 44
colour *f'es* Her sweet face from brow to chin: *L. of Burleigh* 61
After his books, to *f* his blood with air,   *Aylmer's Field* 459
Or by denial *f* her babbling wells   *Princess v* 334
madness *f'es* up in the ruffian's head,   *Maud I i* 37
and made him *f*, and bow Lowly,   *Gareth and L.* 548
Flush'd   (*See also* **Faintly-flushed, New-flush'd, Sun-flush'd**)   *F* all the leaves with rich gold-green,   *Arabian Nights* 82
F like the coming of the day;   *Miller's D.* 132
f Ganymede, his rosy thigh Half-buried   *Palace of Art* 121
F in her temples and her eyes,   " 170
'Then *f* her cheek with rosy light,   *Talking Oak* 165
Psyche *f* and wann'd and shook;   *Princess iv* 160
When first she came, all *f* you said to me   " *vi* 250
her face A little *f*, and she past on;   " *vii* 81
Where oleanders *f* the bed Of silent torrents,   *The Daisy* 33
The Peak is high and *f* At his highest   *Voice and the P.* 29
Some *f*, and others dazed,   *Com. of Arthur* 265
when *f* with fight, or hot, God's curse,   *Geraint and E.* 660
that other *f*, And hung his head,   " 810
Upright and *f* before him: *Merlin and V.* 912
F slightly at the slight disparagement   *Lancelot and E.* 234
beyond them *f* The long low dune,   *Last Tournament* 483
F, started, met him at the doors,   " 512
The small sweet face was *f*,   *The Wreck* 60
and *f* as red As poppies when she crown'd it.   *The Tourney* 16
Flushing   rosy red *f* in the northern night.   *Locksley Hall* 26
let my query pass Unclaim'd, in *f* silence,   *The Brook* 105
f the guiltless air, Spout from the maiden fountain   *Lucretius* 239
Fluster'd   him that *f* his poor parish wits   *Aylmer's Field* 521
snares them by the score Flatter'd and *f*,   *Princess v* 164
But once in life was *f* with new wine,   *Merlin and V.* 756
so *f* with anger were they, They almost fell   *V. of Maeldune* 25
Flute (s)   Blow, *f*, and stir the stiff-set sprigs,   *Amphion* 63
thicket rang To many a *f* of Arcady.   *In Mem. xxiii* 24
Nor harp be touch'd, nor *f* be blown;   " *cv* 22
the roses heard The *f*, violin, bassoon;   *Maud I xxii* 14
To the sound of dancing music and *f's*:   " *II v* 76
Flute (verb)   lute and *f* fantastic tenderness;   *Princess iv* 129
Fluted   The mellow ouzel *f* in the elm;   *Gardener's D.* 94
From *f* vase, and brazen urn In order,   *Arabian Nights* 24
And *f* to the morning sea.   *To E. L.* 24
Flute-notes   thy *f-n* are changed to coarse,   *The Blackbird* 18
Fluting   swan That, *f* a wild carol ere her death,   *M. d'Arthur* 267
swan That, *f* a wild carol ere her death,   *Pass. of Arthur* 435
Flutter   His spirit *f's* like a lark,   *Day-Dm., Arrival* 29

Flutter (*continued*)   Wings *f*, voices hover clear: *Sir Galahad* 78
Flags, *f* out upon turrets and towers!   *W. to Alexandra* 15
heart within her fall and *f* tremulously,   *Boädicea* 81
There *f's* up a happy thought,   *In Mem. lxv* 7
The tender blossom *f* down,   " *ci* 2
idle fancies *f* me, I know not where to turn;   *The Flight* 74
Flutter'd   *F* about my senses and my soul: *Gardener's D.* 67
A second *f* round her lip Like a golden butterfly;   *Talking Oak* 219
melody *F* headlong from the sky.   *Vision of Sin* 45
A little *f*, with her eyelids down,   *The Brook* 89
there *f* in, Half-bold, half-frighted,   *Geraint and E.* 596
And *f* adoration, and at last With dark sweet hints   *Merlin and V.* 158
The footstep *f* me at first: *Last Tournament* 515
And a pinnace, like a *f* bird,   *The Revenge* 2
Fluttering (*part.*)   voice Faltering and *f* in her throat,   *Princess ii* 187
Alive with *f* scarfs and ladies' eyes,   " *v* 509
above, Crimson, a slender banneret *f*.   *Gareth and L.* 913
f in a doubt Between the two—   *Sisters (E. and E.)* 33
F the hawks of this crown-lusting line—   *Sir J. Oldcastle* 57
and then fell *f* down at my feet;   *The Wreck* 82
elmtree's ruddy-hearted blossom-flake Is *f* down.   *To Mary Boyle* 4
blasts That run before the *f* tongues of fire;   *D. of F. Women* 30
And on the board the *f* urn: *In Mem. xcv* 15
With half a night's appliances, recall'd Her *f* life: *Lover's Tale iv* 94
Fluttering (s)   I watch'd the little *f's*,   *Miller's D.* 153
Fly (s)   (*See also* **Dragon-fly, Fancy-flies, Fire-fly, Floy, Gad-fly**)   The blue *f* sung in the pane;   *Mariana* 63
Kate saith 'the men are gilded *flies*.'   *Kate* 18
The swallow stopt as he hunted the *f*,   *Poet's Song* 9
Like *flies* that haunt a wound,   *Aylmer's Field* 571
flew kite, and raced the purple *f*,   *Princess ii* 248
In lieu of many mortal *flies*,   " *iii* 268
endure for the life of the worm and the *f*?   " *Wages* 7
bees are still'd, and the *flies* are kill'd,   *Window, Winter* 10
And men the *flies* of latter spring,   *In Mem. l* 10
eyes Are tender over drowning *flies*,   " *xcvi* 3
his head in a cloud of poisonous *flies*.   *Maud I iv* 54
And call'd herself a gilded summer *f*   *Merlin and V.* 258
since you name yourself the summer *f*,   " 369
gape for *flies*—we know not whence they come;   *Holy Grail* 147
and infinite torment of *flies*,   *Def. of Lucknow* 5
men Walk'd like the *f* on ceilings?   *Columbus* 51
for you know The *flies* at home,   " 119
Nor drown thyself with *flies* in honied wine;   *Ancient Sage* 268
Miriam sketch'd and Muriel threw the *f*;   *The Ring* 159
She threw the *f* for me;   " 355
black *f* upon the pane May seem the black ox   *To one who ran down Eng.* 3
Fly (verb)   Then away she *flies*.   *Lilian* 18
whither away, whither away? *f* no more.   *Sea-Fairies* 7
rainbow forms and *flies* on the land   " 25
mariner, mariner, *f* no more.   " 42
Whither *f* ye, what game spy ye,   *Rosalind* 8
'Here sits he shaping wings to *f*:   *Two Voices* 289
let her herald, Reverence, *f* Before her   *Love thou thy land* 18
To ingroove itself with that which *flies*;   " 46
Sun *flies* forward to his brother Sun;   *Golden Year* 23
'*F*, happy happy sails, and bear the Press; *F* happy with the mission of the Cross;   " 42
And order'd words asunder *f*.   *Day-Dm., Pro.* 20
The colour *flies* into his cheeks: " *Arrival* 19
splinter'd spear-shafts crack and *f*,   *Sir Galahad* 7
F o'er waste fens and windy fields.   " 60
And *f*, like a bird, from tree to tree;   *Edward Gray* 30
The truth, that *flies* the flowing can,   *Will Water.* 171
We follow that which *flies* before;   *The Voyage* 94
to *f* sublime Thro' the courts, the camps,   *Vision of Sin* 103
A crippled lad, and coming turn'd to *f*,   *Aylmer's Field* 519
Let me *f*, says little birdie,   *Sea Dreams* 295
rests a little longer, Then she *flies* away.   " 300
Let me rise and *f* away.   " 304
Baby too shall *f* away.   " 308
F on to clash together again,   *Lucretius* 41
Thy glory *f* along the Italian field,   " 71
do they *f* Now thinner, and now thicker,   " 165
the soul *flies* out and dies in the air.'   " 274

Fly (verb) (*continued*) baby loves F twanging headless arrows
at the hearts,   *Princess ii* 402
f,' she cried, 'O f, while yet you may!   "   *iii* 28
But you may yet be saved, and therefore f: "   64
As *flies* the shadow of a bird, she fled.   "   96
F to her, and fall upon her gilded eaves,   "   *iv* 94
F to her, and pipe and woo her,   "   115
and fled, as *flies* A troop of snowy doves,   "   167
I grant in her some sense of shame, she *flies*;   "   349
She *flies* too high, she *flies* too high!   "   *v* 281
I say she *flies* too high, 'sdeath!   "   286
peacemaker f To happy havens under all the sky, *Ode Inter. Exhib.* 34
THE lights and shadows f!   *Window, On the Hill* 1
F; F to the light in the valley below—   "   *Letter* 12
As *flies* the lighter thro' the gross.   *In Mem. xli* 4
Ill brethren, let the fancy f   "   *lxxxvi* 12
Fiercely *flies* The blast of North and East,   "   *cvii* 6
and f The happy birds, that change their sky   "   *cxv* 14
Arise and f The reeling Faun,   "   *cxviii* 25
Wild Hours that f with Hope and Fear,   "   *cxxviii* 9
'The fault was mine,' he whisper'd, 'f!'   *Maud I i* 30
I saw the dreary phantom arise and f   "   *III vi* 36
Until she let me f discaged to sweep   *Gareth and L.* 20
A jewell'd harness, ere they pass and f.   "   688
But after sod and shingle ceased to f   "   761
'I f no more: I allow thee for an hour.   "   892
Larded thy last, except thou turn and f.   "   1084
all about it *flies* a honeysuckle.   "   1278
and wildly f, Mixt with the flyers.   *Geraint and E.* 482
'F, they will return And slay you; f, your charger
is without,   "   748
Behold, I f from shame, A lustful King,   *Balin and Balan* 473
I f to thee. Save, save me thou—   *Merlin and V.* 77
When did not rumours f?   *Lancelot and E.* 1194
if he f us, Small matter! let him.'   *Pelleas and E.* 199
And f to my strong castle overseas: *Guinevere* 113
yet rise now, and let us f,   "   120
Stands in a wind, ready to break and f,   "   365
And he that fled no further f the King;   *Pass. of Arthur* 89
stream *Flies* with a shatter'd foam   *Lover's Tale i* 383
HE *flies* the event: he leaves the event   "   *iv* 1
I must f, but follow quick.   *The Revenge* 6
You f them for a moment to fight with them again.   "   9
'Shall we fight or shall we f?   "   25
and aloft the glare *Flies* streaming, *Achilles over the T.* 12
shell must break before the bird can f.   *Ancient Sage* 154
and now I f from Hell, And you with me;   *The Flight* 88
An' the lark f out o' the flowers   *Tomorrow* 91
stormy moment f and mingle with the Past. *Locksley H., Sixty* 279
And wherever her flag f,   *Open I. and C. Exhib.* 17
bird that *flies* All night across the darkness, *Demeter and P.* 1
F—care not. Birds and brides must leave the nest. *The Ring* 89
And saw the world f by me like a dream,   "   180
And *flies* above the leper's hut,   *Happy* 4
Now past her feet the swallow circling *flies*, *Prog. of Spring* 44
Flies back in fragrant breezes to display   "   64

Flyer arms stretch'd as to grasp a f: *Aylmer's Field* 588
and all f's from the hand Of Justice,   *Marr. of Geraint* 36
and wildly fly, Mixt with the f's.   *Geraint and E.* 483
brands That hack'd among the f's,   *Com. of Arthur* 121
Fiercely we hack'd at the f's before us. *Batt. of Brunanburh* 42

Flyin' Molly Magee kem f acrass me,   *Tomorrow* 21

Flying (*See also* **A-Flyin', Flyin'**) fled by night, and
f turn'd: *Edwin Morris* 134
Dreary gleams about the moorland f   *Locksley Hall* 4
in the f of a wheel Cry down the past,   *Godiva* 6
Or f shone, the silver boss Of her own halo's
dusky shield;   *The Voyage* 31
following up And f the white breaker,   *Enoch Arden* 21
And caught the blossom of the f terms,   *Princess, Pro.* 164
we dropt, And f reach'd the frontier: "   *i* 109
your arrow-wounded fawn Came f   "   *ii* 271
and loose A f charm of blushes o'er this cheek,   "   430
he could not see The bird of passage f south   "   *iii* 210
Blow, bugle, blow, set the wild echoes f, (repeat)   "   *iv* 5, 17

Flying (*continued*) 'O Swallow, Swallow, f, f South,   *Princess iv* 93
'O Swallow, f from the golden woods,   "   114
A woman-post in f raiment.   "   376
f on the highest Foam of men's deeds—   "   *v* 319
shot A f splendour out of brass and steel,   "   *vi* 365
f struck With showers of random sweet   "   *vii* 85
or call'd On f Time from all their silver tongues—   "   105
Paid with a voice f by to be lost   " *Wages* 2
are you f over her sweet little face?   *Window, On the Hill* 13
and birds' song F here and there,   "   *Spring* 2
f gold of the ruin'd woodlands drove thro' the air.   "   *Maud I i* 12
F along the land and the main—   "   *II ii* 38
they swerved and brake F,   *Com. of Arthur* 120
follow'd by his f hair Ran like a colt,   "   321
servingman F from out of the black wood, *Gareth and L.* 802
Gareth's eyes had f blots Before them   "   1031
Comes f over many a windy wave To Britain, *Marr. of Geraint* 337
And white sails f on the yellow sea;   "   829
F, but, overtaken, died the death Themselves *Geraint and E.* 530
Another, f from the wrath of Doorm   "   *Merlin and V.* 943
f back and crying out, 'O Merlin,   *Lancelot and E.* 1190
I hear of rumours f thro' your court.   *Pelleas and E.* 39
and once the shadow of a bird F,   *Guinevere* 133
A blot in heaven, the Raven, f high,   "   258
wheel'd and broke F, and link'd again, and wheel'd
and broke F,   *Lover's Tale i* 69
Quiver'd a f glory on her hair,   "   *iv* 291
F by each fine ear, an Eastern gauze   *The Revenge* 2
pinnace, like a flutter'd bird, came f from far away: *Def. of Lucknow* 4
F at top of the roofs in the ghastly siege   "   44
F and foil'd at the last by the handful *Sir J. Oldcastle* 39
Wiclif-preacher whom I crost In f hither? *Vastness* 13
Trade f over a thousand seas with her spice   "   16
with her f robe and her poison'd rose; *Merlin and the G.* 96
and brighter The Gleam f onward,   *Akbar's Dream* 132
and fitting close Or f looselier,   *Miller's D.* 116
Gleam'd to the f moon by fits.   *Palace of Art* 123
Sole as a f star shot thro' the sky   *D. of F. Women* 225
'Saw God divide the night with f flame, *Love thou thy land* 75
To follow f steps of Truth Across the brazen
bridge of war—   *Gardener's D.* 60
Would play with f forms and images,   "   246
And with a f finger swept my lips,   *Boädicea* 24
Thunder, a f fire in heaven,   "   37
Loosely robed in f raiment,   *In Mem. lxii* 12
Is matter for a f smile.   "   *lxxii* 24
And sow the sky with f boughs,   "   *cvi* 2
The f cloud, the frosty light: *Holy Grail* 452
like a f star Led on the gray-hair'd wisdom

Foälk (folk) F's coostom flitted awaäy   *North. Cobbler* 28
an' f stood a-gawmin' in,   "   81
call'd me afoor my awn f's to my faäce *Village Wife* 105
that the f be sa scared at,   *Spinster's S's.* 24
Fur to goä that night to 'er f by cause   *Owd Roä* 52

Foam (s) (*See also* **Fountain-foam, Ocean-foam, Sea-foam**) the green brink and the running f,   *Sea-Fairies* 2
Flung leagues of roaring f into the gorge *If I were loved* 13
brightens When the wind blows the f,   *Œnone* 62
Aphroditè beautiful, Fresh as the f,   "   175
Rolling a slumbrous sheet of f below.   *Lotos-Eaters* 13
Weary the wandering fields of barren f.   "   42
I would the white cold heavy-plunging f, *D. of F. Women* 118
sea-wind sang Shrill, chill, with flakes of f. *M. d'Arthur* 49
in the chasm are f and yellow sands;   *Enoch Arden* 2
And scaled in sheets of wasteful f,   *Sea Dreams* 53
burst and flood the world with f: *Princess iv* 474
flying on the highest F of men's deeds—   "   *v* 320
sang from the three-decker out of the f,   *Maud I i* 50
Hurl'd back again so often in empty f, *Last Tournament* 93
As tremulously as f upon the beach   *Guinevere* 364
sea-wind sang Shrill, chill, with flakes of f. *Pass. of Arthur* 217
Flies with a shatter'd f along the chasm. *Lover's Tale i* 383
the points of the f in the dusk came playing *Despair* 50
ships from out the West go dipping thro' the f, *The Flight* 91
On broader zones beyond the f,   *To Ulysses* 30

Foam (s) (*continued*) And these low bushes dip their twigs
in *f*,   *Prog. of Spring* 51
Too full for sound and *f*,   *Crossing the Bar* 6
Foam (verb) Should all our churchmen *f* in spite
forward-creeping tides Began to *f*,   *In Mem. ciii* 38
Foam-bow his cheek brighten'd as the *f-b* brightens   *Œnone* 61
Foam-churning These wet black passes and *f-c* chasms— *Aylmer's Field* 342
Foam'd *f* away his heart at Averill's ear;   *Ode on Well.* 126
Their surging charges *f* themselves away;   *Ode on Well.* 126
raved And thus *f* over at a rival name: *Balin and Balan* 567
Foam-flakes Crisp *f-f* scud along the level sand,   *D. of F. Women* 39
Foam-fountains monster spouted his *f-f* in the sea. *Lotos-Eaters, C. S.* 107
Foaming horse across the *f's* of the ford,   *Gareth and L.* 1040
To smoothe my pillow, mix the *f* draught Of fever,   *Princess ii* 251
The *f* grape of eastern France.   *In Mem., Con.* 80
Foamy here and there a *f* flake Upon me,   *The Brook* 59
Foe tho' his *f's* speak ill of him, He was a friend
to me.   *D. of the O. Year* 22
The land, where girt with friends or *f's*   *You ask me, why* 7
Must ever shock, like armed *f's*,   *Love thou thy land* 78
went she Norward, Till she near'd the *f*.   *The Captain* 36
divine to warn them of their *f's*:   *Sea Dreams* 69
Had beat her *f's* with slaughter   *Princess, Pro.* 34
drove her *f's* with slaughter from her walls,   „ 123
The next, like fire he meets the *f*,   „ iv 583
The general *f*. More soluble is this knot,   „ v 135
Truest friend and noblest *f*,   „ vi 7
those two *f's* above my fallen life,   „ 130
friend or *f*, Shall enter, if he will.   „ 336
His *f's* were thine; he kept us free;   *Ode on Well.* 91
And England pouring on her *f's*.   „ 117
Who never spoke against a *f*;   „ 185
For on them brake the sudden *f*;   *The Victim* 4
Friend, to be struck by the public *f*,   *Maud II v* 89
bright With pitch'd pavilions of his *f*,   *Com. of Arthur* 97
thou hast driven the *f* without, See to the *f* within! *Gareth and L.* 593
thou hast wreak'd his justice on his *f's*,   „ 1268
'Lo,' said Gareth, 'the *f* falls!'   „ 1317
second was your *f*, the sparrow-hawk,   *Marr. of Geraint* 444
what they long for, good in friend or *f*,   *Geraint and E.* 876
Pellam, once A Christless *f* of thine   *Balin and Balan* 97
He makes no friend who never made a *f*.   *Lancelot and E.* 1089
I hold that man the worst of public *f's*   *Guinevere* 512
friend and *f* were shadows in the mist,   *Pass. of Arthur* 100
Revenge ran on sheer into the heart of the *f*,   *The Revenge* 33
and they yielded to the *f*.   „ 96
the *f* sprung his mine many times,   *Def. of Lucknow* 31
and the *f* may outlive us at last—   „ 52
Friend?—*f* perhaps—a tussle for it then!   *Sir J. Oldcastle* 196
Far off from out an island girt by *f's*,   *Achilles over the T.* 8
and a boundless panic shook the *f*.   „ 18
where'er they ran, Have ended mortal *f's*;   *Ancient Sage* 158
some in fight against the *f*,   *Locksley H., Sixty* 45
the *f* was driven, And Wolseley overthrew
Arâbi,   *Pro. to Gen. Hamley* 29
Drove thro' the midst of the *f*,   *Heavy Brigade* 30
drew The *f* from the saddle and threw   „ 54
WARRIOR of God, man's friend, and tyrant's *f*,   *Epit. on Gordon* 1
hand Which fell'd the *f's* before you   *Happy* 42
Foeman forth there stept a *f* tall,   *Oriana* 33
What time the *f's* line is broke,   *Two Voices* 155
to perish, falling on the *f's* ground,   *Locksley Hall* 103
But they heard the *f's* thunder   *The Captain* 41
still the *f* spoil'd and burn'd,   *The Victim* 17
body enow to hold his *foemen* down?'   *Com. of Arthur* 253
and by this will beat his *foemen* down.'   „ 309
foemen scared, like that false pair who turn'd   *Geraint and E.* 176
f surged, and waver'd, and reel'd Up the hill,   *Heavy Brigade* 62
Fog the white *f* vanish'd like a ghost   *Death of Œnone* 67
Foil'd Flying and *f* at the last by the handful   *Def. of Lucknow* 44
Fold (thing folded) Down-droop'd, in many a floating *f*, *Arabian Nights* 147
In silk-soft *f's*, upon yielding down,   *Eleänore* 28
Look up, the *f* is on her brow.   *Two Voices* 192
Winds all the vale in rosy *f's*,   *Miller's D.* 242
In misty *f's*, that floating as they fell   *Palace of Art* 35

Fold (thing folded) (*continued*) detaching, *f* by *f*, From
those still heights,   *Vision of Sin* 51
f's as dense as those Which hid the Holiest   *Aylmer's Field* 771
The drowsy *f's* of our great ensign shake   *Princess v* 8
With *f* to *f*, of mountain or of cape;   „ vii 3
Dark in its funeral *f*.   *Ode on Well.* 57
And wrapt thee formless in the *f*,   *In Mem. xxii* 15
In *f* upon *f* of hueless cloud,   *Maud I vi* 3
Thro' twenty *f's* of twisted dragon,   *Gareth and L.* 510
sprigs of summer laid between the *f's*,   *Marr. of Geraint* 138
Thro' knots and loops and *f's* innumerable   *Lancelot and E.* 439
wrapt In unremorseful *f's* of rolling fire.   *Holy Grail* 221
a streetway hung with *f's* of pure White samite,   *Last Tournament* 140
Enwound him *f* by *f*, and made him gray And grayer,   *Guinevere* 603
I wish that somewhere in the ruin'd *f's*,   *Œnone* 221
Thro' all its *f's* the multitudinous beast,   *Tiresias* 15
close-lapt in silken *f's*,   *Lover's Tale i* 153
There is no shade or *f* of mystery   „ 182
I thought it was an adder's *f*,   „ 691
Hung round with ragged rims and burning *f's*,—   „ ii 63
in their floating *f's* They past and were no more :   „ 99
Fold (as for sheep) (*See also* **Night-fold**) 'Bring this
lamb back into Thy *f*,   *Supp. Confessions* 105
the thick-fleeced sheep from wattled *f's*,   *Ode to Memory* 66
very whitest lamb in all my *f* Loves you: *Aylmer's Field* 361
who are these? a wolf within the *f*!   *Princess ii* 190
Far off from men I built a *f* for them: „ v 390
No gray old grange, or lonely *f*,   *In Mem. c* 5
some black wether of St. Satan's *f*.   *Merlin and V.* 750
brand us, after, of whose *f* we be: „ 764
if the tigers leap into the *f* unawares—   *Def. of Lucknow* 51
driven by storm and sin and death to the ancient *f*,   *The Wreck* 2
ranged from the narrow warmth of your *f*,   *Despair* 38
A people from their ancient *f* of Faith,   *Akbar's Dream* 61
Fold (verb) *F* thy palms across thy breast, *F* thine
arms, turn to thy rest.   *A Dirge* 2
the green that *f's* thy grave. (repeat) *A Dirge* 6, 13, 20, 27, 34, 41, 48
'High up the vapours *f* and swim: *Two Voices* 262
f our wings, And cease from wanderings,   *Lotos-Eaters, C. S.* 19
sure this orbit of the memory *f's*   *Gardener's D.* 74
about my feet The berried briony *f*.'   *Talking Oak* 148
round her waist she felt it *f*,   *Day-Dm., Depart.* 2
Now *f's* the lily all her sweetness up,   *Princess vii* 186
So *f* thyself, my dearest, thou,   „ 188
or *f* Thy presence in the silk of sumptuous   *Ancient Sage* 265
ah, *f* me to your breast !   *The Flight* 5
I'd sooner *f* an icy corpse dead of some foul disease : „ 54
Fold *See also* **Five-fold, Hundred-fold, Fifty-fold, Ten-
hundred-fold, Thousand-fold**
Folded (*See also* **Far-folded, Heavy-folded, Many-folded,
Silken-folded**) Thought *f* over thought, smiling
asleep,   *Eleänore* 84
'His palms are *f* on his breast: *Two Voices* 247
Sleep, Ellen, *f* in thy sister's arm,   *Audley Court* 63
'Sleep, Ellen, *f* in Emilia's arm;   „ 65
To spirits *f* in the womb,   *Day-Dm., Sleep P.* 8
Bow'd on her palms and *f* up from wrong,   *Princess iv* 288
She heard, she moved, She moan'd, a *f* voice;   „ v 72
And every spirit's *f* bloom   *In Mem. xliii* 2
Is pealing, *f* in the mist.   „ civ 4
And yearn'd to burst the *f* gloom,   „ cxxii 3
Not to be *f* more in these dear arms,   *Marr. of Geraint* 99
Wherein she kept them *f* reverently With sprigs
of summer   „ 137
letter she devised; which being writ And *f*,   *Lancelot and E.* 1110
Hath *f* in the passes of the world.'   *Pass. of Arthur* 78
on the horizon of the mind Lies *f*,   *Lover's Tale i* 50
the sweet figure *f* round with night   „ iv 219
F her lion paws, and look'd to Thebes.   *Tiresias* 149
Russian crowd *F* its wings from the left   *Heavy Brigade* 39
and I was *f* in thine arms.   *Demeter and P.* 22
here, my child, tho' *f* in thine arms,   „ 40
The *f* leaf is woo'd from out the bud   *Lotos-Eaters, C. S.* 26
dissolved the mystery Of *f* sleep.   *D. of F. Women* 263
O'er the mute city stole with *f* wings,   *Gardener's D.* 186

Folded (*continued*)   Holding the *f* annals of my youth ;   *Gardener's D.* 244
   With *f* feet, in stoles of white,   *Sir Galahad* 43
   Mute with *f* arms they waited—   *The Captain* 39
   stood with *f* hands and downward eyes   *Merlin and V.* 69
Folding   black *f*'s, that which housed therein.   *Gareth and L.* 1380
   F each other, breathing on each other,   *Lover's Tale* i 261
   F his hands, deals comfortable words   "   717
Foliage   rustling thro' The low and bloomed *f*,   *Arabian Nights* 13
   gale That blown about the *f* underneath,   *Princess* iii 121
   all thy breadth and height Of *f*,   *In Mem.* lxxxix 4
   sank Down on a drift of *f* random-blown ;   *Last Tournament* 389
   moisture and all smells of bud And *f*   *Lover's Tale* iii 6
Foliaged   (*See also* **Full-foliaged**)   Who murmurest
   in the *f* eaves   *In Mem.* xcix 9
Folk   (*See also* **Foälk**)   *f* that knew not their own minds,   *Enoch Arden* 478
   And echo'd by old *f* beside their fires   *Com. of Arthur* 417
   mingle with our *f*; And knowing every honest face   *Holy Grail* 549
   slay the *f*, and spoil the land.'   *Guinevere* 137
   He that was reft of his *F* and his friends   *Batt. of Brunanburh* 70
Foller (*follow*)   tha'll *f* 'im slick into Hell.'   *North. Cobbler* 66
Foller'd (*followed*)   fur the 'turney's letters they *f* sa
   fast ;   *Village Wife* 62
Follow   (*See also* **Foller**)   lightning to the thunder
   Which *f*'s it,   *The Poet* 51
   because right is right, to *f* right   *Œnone* 149
   To *f* flying steps of Truth   *Love thou thy land* 75
   What good should *f* this, if this were done ?   *M. d'Arthur* 92
   dark Earth *f*'s wheel'd in her ellipse ;   *Golden Year* 24
   f knowledge like a sinking star,   *Ulysses* 31
   The vine stream'd out to *f*,   *Amphion* 46
   May my soul *f* soon !   *St. Agnes' Eve* 4
   I *f* till I make thee mine.'   *The Voyage* 64
   We *f* that which flies before :   "   94
   f Such dear familiarities of dawn ?   *Aylmer's Field* 130
   One who cried, 'Leave all and *f* me.'   "   664
   the thin weasel there *F*'s the mouse,   "   853
   which all our greatest fain Would *f*,   *Lucretius* 79
   not be dissoluble, Not *f* the great law ?   "   116
   A satyr, a satyr, see, *F*'s ;   "   193
   The rest would *f*, each in turn ;   *Princess*, Pro. 201
   'Then *f* me, the Prince,' I answer'd,   "   227
   Voice Went with it, '*F*, *f*, thou shalt win.'   "   i 100
   falling in a land Of promise ; fruit would *f*.   "   ii 140
   If more and acted on, what *f*'s ?   "   229
   Whence *f*'s many a vacant pang ;   "   403
   bird of passage flying south but long'd To *f*:   "   iii 211
   'O Swallow, Swallow, if I could *f*,   "   iv 99
   And tell her, tell her, that I *f* thee.'   "   116
   I cannot cease to *f* you,   "   455
   To *f* up the worthiest till he die :   "   466
   F us : who knows ? we four may build some plan   "   v 230
   And on the '*F*, *f*, thou shalt win :   "   472
   But *f*; let the torrent dance thee down   "   vii 209
   farewell, and welcome for the year To *f*:   *Con.* 96
   Fall, and *f* their doom.   *Voice and the P.* 20
   F, *f* the chase !   *Window, On the Hill* 11
   F them down the slope ! And I *f* them down
   to the window-pane   "   16
   Nor *f*, tho' I walk in haste,   *In Mem.* xxii 18
   'The King will *f* Christ, and we the King   *Com. of Arthur* 599
   f the deer By these tall firs and our fast-falling
   burns ;   *Gareth and L.* 90
   F the deer ? *f* the Christ, the King, Live pure,
   speak true, right wrong, *f* the King—   "   117
   Thou get to horse and *f* him far away.   "   584
   f's, being named, His owner,   "   703
   Lead, and I *f*.' (repeat)   *Gareth and L.* 746, 760, 807, 891,
     990, 1053, 1155
   '*F*, I lead !' so down among the pines He plunged ;   *Gareth and L.* 808
   'Full pardon, but I *f* up the quest,   "   886
   '*F* the faces, and we find it.   "   1210
   the Prince, as Enid past him, fain To *f*,   *Marr. of Geraint* 376
   the knight besought him, '*F* me,   *Geraint and E.* 807
   'Enough,' he said, 'I *f*,' and they went.   "   816
   and crying 'Sirs, Rise, *f*!'   *Balin and Balan* 48

Follow (*continued*)   But *f* Vivien thro' the fiery flood !   *Balin and Balan* 454
   Help, for he *f*'s ! take me to thyself !   *Merlin and V.* 82
   The Fame that *f*'s death is nothing to us ;   "   464
   the scroll 'I *f* fame.'   "   476
   I charge you, *f* me not.'   *Lancelot and E.* 507
   serve you, and to *f* you thro' the world.'   "   939
   'I fain would *f* love, if that could be ; I needs
     must *f* death, who calls for me ; Call and I
     f, I *f*! let me die.'   "   1016
   Then might she *f* me thro' the world,   "   1316
   I sware a vow to *f* it till I saw.'   *Holy Grail* 282
   Galahad, and O Galahad, *f* me.'   "   292
   But ye, that *f* but the leader's bell '   "   298
   while ye *f* wandering fires Lost in the quagmire !   "   319
   most of us would *f* wandering fires, (repeat)   "   369, 599
   and vanish'd, tho' I yearn'd To *f*;   "   507
   most of them would *f* wandering fires,   "   891
   the gloom, That *f*'s on the turning of the world,   *Pelleas and E.* 549
   after wail Of suffering, silence *f*'s,   *Pass. of Arthur* 119
   What good should *f* this, if this were done ?   "   260
   I could not rise Albeit I strove to *f*.   *Lover's Tale* ii 98
   I must fly, but *f* quick.   *The Revenge* 6
   Now *f*'s Edith echoing Evelyn.   *Sisters* (E. and E.) 15
   crying out : '*F* me, *f* me !'—   *Def. of Lucknow* 64
   Do-well will *f* thought,   *Ancient Sage* 273
   f Edwin to those isles, those islands of the Blest !   *The Flight* 42
   these would feel and *f* Truth if only you and
     you,   *Locksley H., Sixty* 119
   leave the dog too lame to *f* with the cry,   "   226
   know them, *f* him who led the way,   "   266
   F you the Star that lights a desert pathway,   "   275
   F Light, and do the Right—   "   277
   '*F*,' and up the hill, up the hill,   *Heavy Brigade* 11
   bound to *f*, wherever she go Stark-naked,   *Dead Prophet* 45
   O *f*, leaping blood,   *Early Spring* 25
   poor Muriel when you hear What *f*'s !   *The Ring* 274
   I am Merlin Who *f* The Gleam.   *Merlin and the G.* 10
   The Master whisper'd '*F* the Gleam.'   "   34
   But eager to *f*, I saw,   "   101
   After it, *f* it, *F* the Gleam.   "   130
   I whirl, and I *f* the Sun.'   *The Dreamer* 14
   Whirl, and *f* the Sun ! (repeat)   *The Dreamer* 20, 24, 28, 32
   But what may *f* who can tell ?   *The Wanderer* 14
Follow'd   (*See also* **Foller'd**)   For surer sign had *f*, either
   hand,   *M. d'Arthur* 76
   Then *f* counsel, comfort, and the words   *Love and Duty* 69
   The happy princess *f* him.   *Day-Dm., Depart.* 8
   Thro' all the world she *f* him.   "   32
   And *f* with acclaims,   *Will Water.* 138
   And *f* her all the way.   *Lady Clare* 64
   still we *f* where she led, (repeat)   *The Voyage* 59, 90
   Then *f* calms, and then winds variable,   *Enoch Arden* 545
   when they *f* us from Philip's door,   *The Brook* 167
   Where Aylmer *f* Aylmer at the Hall   *Aylmer's Field* 36
   the fierce old man *F*, and under his own lintel stood   "   331
   Seconded, for my lady *f* suit,   "   558
   f out Tall and erect, but in the middle aisle Reel'd,   "   817
   I *f*: and at top She pointed seaward :   *Sea Dreams* 121
   I began, And the rest *f*:   *Princess*, Pro. 244
   We *f* up the river as we rode,   "   i 206
   f then A classic lecture, rich in sentiment,   "   ii 373
   resolder'd peace, whereon *F* his tale.   "   v 48
   but Blanche At distance *f*: so they came :   "   vi 83
   And *f* up by a hundred airy does,   "   87
   Passionate tears *F*: the king replied not :   "   312
   F up in valley and glen With blare of bugle,   *Ode on Well.* 114
   F by the brave of other lands,   "   194
   the day that the day she was wed,   *The Islet* 4
   And silence *f*, and we wept.   *In Mem.* xxx 20
   In vassal tides that *f* thought.   "   cxii 16
   f by his flying hair Ran like a colt,   *Com. of Arthur* 321
   thereafter *f* calm, Free sky and stars !   "   391
   But in the weeks that *f*, the good Queen,   *Gareth and L.* 526
   The two that out of north had *f* him :   "   679
   till the dusk that *f* evensong Rode on the two,   "   793

Follow'd (*continued*) He *f* nearer : ruth began to work *Geraint and E.* 101
He *f* nearer still ; the pain she had " 186
And overthrew the next that *f* him, " 465
His lusty spearmen *f* him with noise : " 593
ye be sent for by the King,' They *f* ; *Balin and Balan* 49
F the Queen ; Sir Balin heard her " 250
and *f* this, But all so blind in rage " 327
' And is the fair example *f*, Sir, *Merlin and V.* 19
Vivien *f*, but he mark'd her not. " 199
And then she *f* Merlin all the way, " 203
Dear feet, that I have *f* thro' the world, " 227
You *f* me unask'd ; " 298
the stammering cracks and claps That *f*, " 943
F, and in among bright faces, ours, *Holy Grail* 266
and she *F* Him down, and like a flying star " 452
Told him he *f*—almost Arthur's words— " 669
knights all set their faces home, Sir Pelleas *f*. *Pelleas and E.* 188
And *f* to the city. " 586
Arthur rose and Lancelot *f* him, *Last Tournament* 112
F a rush of eagle's wings, " 417
For surer sign had *f*, either hand, *Pass. of Arthur* 244
in weeping and in praise Of her, we *f*: *Lover's Tale ii* 88
it seem'd By that which *f*— " *iv* 22
F us too that night, and dogg'd us, *Despair* 2
From wasteful living, *f*— *Ancient Sage* 5
Good, for Good is Good, he *f*, *Locksley H., Sixty* 60
up the hill, *F* the Heavy Brigade. *Heavy Brigade* 12
All in a moment *f* with force " 20
f up by her vassal legion of fools ; *Vastness* 12
hid in cloud not be *f* by the Moon ? *Happy* 97
Thro' which I *f* line by line Your leading hand, *To Ulysses* 45
A silence *f* as of death, *St. Telemachus* 65
those that *f*, loosen, stone from stone, *Akbar's Dream* 188
Follower tho' thou numberest with the *f*'s *Aylmer's Field* 663
And at her head a *f* of the camp, *Princess v* 60
my *f*'s ring him round : He sits unarm'd ; *Geraint and E.* 336
With all his rout of random *f*'s, " 382
Went Enid with her sullen *f* on. " 440
prick'd In combat with the *f* of Limours, " 501
one true knight—Sole *f* of the vows '— *Last Tournament* 303
And every *f* eyed him as a God, " 678
his *f*'s, all Flower into fortune— *Columbus* 166
O *f* of the Vision, still In motion to the distant gleam, *Freedom* 13
Following *f* her dark eyes Felt earth as air *Gardener's D.* 211
or *f* flying the white breaker, *Enoch Arden* 20
f our own shadows thrice as long *The Brook* 166
f thro' the porch that sang All round with laurel, *Princess ii* 22
Went forth in long retinue *f* up The river " *iii* 195
ever *f* those two crowned twins, " *v* 420
He, that ever *f* her commands, *Ode on Well.* 211
As we descended *f* Hope, *In Mem. xxii* 11
Tho' *f* with an upward mind The wonders " *xli* 21
And Gareth *f* was again beknaved, *Gareth and L.* 786
with fixt eye *f* the three. *Marr. of Geraint* 237
A youth, that *f* with a costrel bore " 386
Let his eye rove in *f*, or rest On Enid " 399
(His gentle charger *f* him unled) *Geraint and E.* 571
and Vivien *f* him, Turn'd to her : *Merlin and V.* 32
And when I look'd, and saw you *f* still, " 299
gloom'd Your fancy when ye saw me *f* you, " 326
f you to this wild wood, Because I saw you sad, " 440
and this honour after death, *F* thy will ! *Last Tournament* 489
f these my mightiest knights, *Guinevere* 489
Few were his *f*, Fled to his warship : *Batt. of Brunanburh* 58
F a torrent till its myriad falls *Tiresias* 37
and, *f* out A league of labyrinthine darkness, *Demeter and P.* 81
So, *f* her old pastime of the brook, *The Ring* 354
How loyal in the *f* of thy Lord ! *In Mem. W. G. Ward* 6
f lighted on him there, And shouted, *Death of Œnone* 55
f, as in trance, the silent cry. " 86
F a hundred sunsets, and the sphere *St. Telemachus* 31
And *f* thy true counsel, by thine aid, *Akbar's Dream* 154
Folly ' Ah, *f*!' in mimic cadence answer'd James— *Golden Year* 53
' Ah, *f*! for it lies so far away, " 53
Fill'd I was with *f* and spite, *Edward Gray* 15

Folly (*continued*) And others' *follies* teach us not, *Will Water.* 173
f taking wings Slipt o'er those lazy limits *Aylmer's Field* 494
brace Of twins may weed her of her *f*. *Princess v* 464
How I hate the spites and the *follies* ! *Spiteful Letter* 24
Deep *f*! yet that this could be— *In Mem. xli* 9
slumber in which all spleenful *f* was drown'd, *Maud I iii* 2
heart of the poet is whirl'd into *f* and vice. " *iv* 39
perplext her With his worldly talk and *f*: " *xx* 7
thy much *f* hath sent thee here His kitchen-knave : *Gareth and L.* 919
for I fear My fate or *f*, *Merlin and V.* 927
I came All in my *f* to the naked shore, *Holy Grail* 793
dead babe and the *follies* of the King ; *Last Tournament* 163
But then what *f* had sent him overseas " 394
Gone the fires of youth, the *follies*, *Locksley H., Sixty* 39
Fond But O too *f*, when have I answer'd *Princess vii* 4
no word of that *f* tale— *Last Tournament* 578
Fonder man of science himself is *f* of glory, *Maud I iv* 37
Fondle rabbit *f*'s his own harmless face, *Aylmer's Field* 851
Fondled Appraised his weight and *f* fatherlike, *Enoch Arden* 154
Too ragged to be *f* on her lap, *Aylmer's Field* 686
And all this morning when I *f* you : *Merlin and V.* 286
we *f* it, Stephen and I, But it died, *The Wreck* 83
Fondling *f* all her hand in his he said, *Marr. of Geraint* 509
Tristram, *f* her light hands, replied, *Last Tournament* 601
Fonseca *F* my main enemy at their court, *Columbus* 126
Font One rear'd a *f* of stone And drew, *Princess, Pro.* 59
Nor winks the gold fin in the porphyry *f*: " *vii* 178
Entwine the cold baptismal *f*, *In Mem. xxix* 10
Food eat wholesome *f*, And wear warm clothes, *St. S. Stylites* 108
wine and *f* were brought, and Earl Limours *Geraint and E.* 289
a beggar began to cry ' *F*, or I die '! *Voice spake, etc.* 6
Fool (*adj.*) What, if she be fasten'd to this *f* lord, *Maud I xvi* 24
' Beat little heart' on this *f* brain of mine. *Romney's R.* 155
Fool (s) (*See also* **Father-fool**) an absent *f*, I cast
me down, *Miller's D.* 62
we should mimic this raw *f* the world, *Walk. to the Mail* 106
while we stood like *f*'s Embracing, *Edwin Morris* 118
push'd the happy season back,—The more *f*'s they,— *Golden Year* 67
gilds the straiten'd forehead of the *f*! *Locksley Hall* 62
F, again the dream, the fancy ! " 173
' A ship of *f*'s,' he shriek'd in spite, ' A ship of
f's,' he sneer'd and wept. *The Voyage* 77
Bandied by the hands of *f*'s. *Vision of Sin* 106
Drink we, last, the public *f*, " 149
April hopes, the *f*'s of chance ; " 164
f's, With such a vantage-ground for nobleness ! *Aylmer's Field* 386
Went further, *f*! and trusted him with all, *Sea Dreams* 76
Christ the bait to trap his dupe and *f*; " 191
(God help her) she was wedded to a *f*; *Princess iii* 83
slaves at home and *f*'s abroad.' " *iv* 521
' Ah *f*, and made myself a Queen of farce ! " *vii* 243
Ah, there's no *f* like the old one— *Grandmother* 44
but I beänt a *f*: *N. Farmer, O. S.* 3
' *F*,' he answer'd, ' death is sure To those that stay *Sailor Boy* 13
AH God ! the petty *f*'s of rhyme *Lit. Squabbles* 1
no God at all, says the *f*; *High. Pantheism* 15
We are *f*'s and slight ; *In Mem., Pro.* 29
' Thou shalt not be the *f* of loss.' " *iv* 16
O to us, The *f*'s of habit, " *x* 12
The *f* that wears a crown of thorns : " *lxix* 2
They call'd me *f*, they call'd me child : " 13
and the brazen *f* Was soften'd, " *cx* 11
who but a *f* would have faith in a tradesman's ware *Maud I i* 26
angry pride Is cap and bells for a *f*. " *vi* 62
F that I am to be vext with his pride ! " *xiii* 5
thought like a *f* of the sleep of death. " *xiv* 38
Struck me before the languid *f*, " *II i* 19
betraying His party-secret, *f*, to the press ; " *v* 34
and Evening-Star, Being strong *f*'s ; *Gareth and L.* 635
all these four be *f*'s, but mighty men, " 643
Back with thou, *f*? For hard by here is one " 895
The second brother in their *f*'s parable— " 1004
this strong *f* whom thou, Sir Knave, " 1058
There stands the third *f* of their allegory.' " 1085
yon four *f*'s have suck'd their allegory " 1199

Foot (*continued*) push'd alone on *f* (For since her horse
    was lost   *Princess iv* 196
fleet I was of *f*: Before we shower'd the rose   ,,   263
a vine, That claspt the *feet* of a Mnemosyne,   ,,   269
their mask was patent, and my *f* Was to you: ,,   326
wisp that flickers where no *f* can tread.'   ,,   358
lost lamb at her *feet* Sent out a bitter bleating   ,,   391
and dash'd Unopen'd at her *feet*:   ,,   471
some sweet sculpture draped from head to *f*,   ,, *v* 57
lay my little blossom at my *feet*,   ,,   100
those that iron-cramp'd their women's *feet*;   ,,   376
We plant a solid *f* into the Time,   ,,   415
they came, Their *feet* in flowers, her loveliest: ,, *vi* 78
Steps with a tender *f*, light as on air,   ,,   88
See, your *f* is on our necks, We vanquish'd,   ,,   166
felt it sound and whole from head to *f*,   ,,   211
on her *f* she hung A moment, and she heard,   ,, *vii* 79
She moved, and at her *feet* the volume fell.   ,,   254
And the *feet* of those he fought for,   *Ode on Well.* 11
myriad horns of plenty at our *feet*.   *Ode Inter. Exhib.* 6
Scatter the blossom under her *feet*.   *W. to Alexandra* 9
Thro' cypress avenues, at our *feet*.   *The Daisy* 48
and nearer than hands and *feet*.   *High. Pantheism* 12
Fine little hands, fine little *feet*—   *Window, Letter* 3
f Is on the skull which thou hast made.   *In Mem., Pro.* 7
The Shadow cloak'd from head to *f*,   ,, *xxiii* 4
Whereon with equal *feet* we fared ;   ,, *xxv* 2
She bows, she bathes the Saviour's *feet*   ,, *xxxii* 11
On thy Parnassus set thy *feet*,   ,, *xxxvii* 6
That nothing walks with aimless *feet*;   ,, *liv* 5
Whose *feet* are guided thro' the land,   ,, *lxvi* 9
Thy *feet* have stray'd in after hours   ,, *cii* 14
my *feet* are set To leave the pleasant fields   ,, 21
Her *feet*, my darling, on the dead ;   ,, *Con.* 50
feet like sunny gems on an English green,   *Maud I v* 14
fall before Her *feet* on the meadow grass,   ,, 26
And fawn at a victor's *feet*.   ,, *vi* 30
solid ground Not fail beneath my *feet*   ,, *xi* 2
For her *feet* have touch'd the meadows   ,, *xii* 23
Gorgonised me from head to *f*   ,, *xiii* 21
the delicate Arab arch of her *feet*   ,, *xvi* 15
her light *f* along the garden walk,   ,, *xviii* 9
He sets the jewel-print of your *feet* In violets   ,, *xxii* 41
Would start and tremble under her *feet*,   ,, 73
A shadow there at my *feet*,   ,, *II i* 39
Lying close to my *f*, Frail, but a work divine,   ,, *ii* 3
A golden *f* or a fairy horn   ,, 19
the rivulet at her *feet* Ripples on   ,, *iv* 41
never an end to the stream of passing *feet*,   ,, *v* 11
mock their foster-mother on four *feet*,   *Com. of Arthur* 31
in the flame was borne A naked babe, and rode to
    Merlin's *feet*,   ,, 384
their *feet* were planted on the plain   *Gareth and L.* 187
I leap from Satan's *f* to Peter's knee—   ,, 538
loosed his bonds and on free *feet* Set him,   ,, 817
their *feet* In dewy grasses glisten'd ;   ,, 927
The gay pavilion and the naked *feet*,   ,, 937
do him further wrong Than set him on his *feet*,   ,, 955
often they break covert at our *feet*.'   *Marr. of Geraint* 183
Worn by the *feet* that now were silent,   ,, 321
fell'd him, and set *f* upon his breast,   ,, 574
rose Limours, and looking at his *feet*,   *Geraint and E.* 302
lays his *f* upon it, Gnawing and growling :   ,, 562
on his *f* She set her own and climb'd ;   ,, 759
set his *f* upon me, and give me life.   ,, 850
Hath hardly scaled with help a hundred *feet*   *Balin and Balan* 170
made his *feet* Wings thro' a glimmering gallery,   ,, 403
At Merlin's *feet* the wily Vivien lay.   *Merlin and V.* 5
all the heathen lay at Arthur's *feet*,   ,, 144
kiss'd his *feet*, As if in deepest reverence   ,, 219
Dear *feet*, that I have follow'd thro' the world,   ,, 227
Behind his ankle twined her hollow *feet* Together,   ,, 240
Vivien bathed your *feet* before her own ?   ,, 284
Scared by the noise upstarted at our *feet*,   ,, 422
The *feet* unmortised from their ankle-bones   ,, 552

Foot (*continued*) judge all nature from her *feet* of clay,   *Merlin and V.* 835
the green path that show'd the rarer *f*,   *Lancelot and E.* 162
her shape From forehead down to *f*, perfect—
    again From *f* to forehead exquisitely turn'd :   ,, 642
with her *feet* unseen Crush'd the wild passion   ,, 741
he wellnigh kiss'd her *feet* For loyal awe,   ,, 1172
let the shield of Lancelot at her *feet* Be carven,   ,, 1341
made a silken mat-work for her *feet*;   *Holy Grail* 151
how my *feet* recrost the deathful ridge   ,, 534
—yea, his very hand and *f*—   ,, 915
one whose *f* is bitten by an ant,   *Pelleas and E.* 184
there three squires across their *feet* :   ,, 431
The *f* that loiters, bidden go,—   *Last Tournament* 117
Dagonet with one *f* poised in his hand,   ,, 285
little Dagonet mincing with his *feet*,   ,, 311
Dagonet, turning on the ball of his *f*,   ,, 329
when she heard the *feet* of Tristram grind   ,, 510
Her light *feet* fell on our rough Lyonnesse,   ,, 554
his *f* was on a stool Shaped as a dragon;   ,, 671
about his *feet* A voice clung sobbing till he question'd it,   ,, 758
voice about his *feet* Sent up an answer,   ,, 760
broadening from her *feet*, And blackening,   *Guinevere* 81
let us in, tho' late, to kiss his *feet*!   ,, 178
with a wild sea-light about his *feet*, He saw them—   ,, 242
when armed *feet* Thro' the long gallery   ,, 412
in the darkness heard his armed *feet* Pause by her;   ,, 418
and laid her hands about his *feet*.   ,, 528
My pride in happier summers, at my *feet*.   ,, 536
And while she grovell'd at his *feet*,   ,, 581
based His *feet* on juts of slippery crag   *Pass. of Arthur* 357
Bound by gold chains about the *feet* of God.   ,, 423
To stay his *feet* from falling,   *Lover's Tale i* 142
she saw Beneath her *feet* the region far away,   ,, 395
at her *feet*, Ev'n the *feet* of her I loved,   ,, 599
Were stoled from head to *f* in flowing black ;   ,, *ii* 85
at his *feet* I seem'd to faint and fall,   ,, 96
Hard-heaving, and her eyes upon her *feet*,   ,, *iv* 308
I lay At thy pale *feet* this ballad   *Ded. Poem Prin. Alice* 20
and bullets would rain at our *feet*—   *Def. of Lucknow* 21
was pollen'd from head to *f*   *V. of Maeldune* 49
and his white beard fell to his *feet*,   ,, 118
Cast at thy *feet* one flower that fades away.   *To Dante* 7
Or on your head their rosy *feet*,   *To E. Fitzgerald* 41
one glittering *f* disturb'd The lucid well ;   *Tiresias* 41
I will sit at your *feet*, I will hide my face,   *The Wreck* 12
then fell fluttering down at my *feet*;   ,, 82
blanch into spray At the *feet* of the cliff ;   ,, 138
foam in the dusk came playing about our *feet*.   *Despair* 50
And Love is fire, and burns the *feet*   *The Flight* 68
A stealthy *f* upon the stair !   ,, 70
fall of yer *f* in the dance was as light as snow   *Tomorrow* 36
an' laid himself undher yer feet,   ,, 38
I plumpt *f* fust i' the pond ;   *Spinster's S's.* 28
tha' hoickt my *feet* wi' a flop fro' the claäy.   ,, 30
forefather, with his *feet* upon the hound.   *Locksley H., Sixty* 28
and woman to her tender *feet*,   ,, 50
Set the *feet* above the brain and swear the brain is
    in the *feet*.   ,, 136
Progress halts on palsied *feet*,   ,, 219
We needs must scan him from head to *feet*   *Dead Prophet* 55
wild mob's million *feet* Will kick you   *The Fleet* 18
robed thee in his day from head to *feet*—   *Demeter and P.* 21
For, see, thy *f* has touch'd it ;   ,, 48
see beneath our *feet* The mist of autumn   *The Ring* 328
and flung the mould upon your *feet*,   *Happy* 50
past her *feet* the swallow circling flies,   *Prog. of Spring* 44
f to *f* With your own shadow in the placid lake,   *Romney's R.* 75
mine from your pretty blue eyes to your *feet*,   ,, 96
Six *f* deep of burial mould Will dull their
    comments !   ,, 125
vines Which on the touch of heavenly *feet*   *Death of Œnone* 5
The mango spurn the melon at his *f*?   *Akbar's Dream* 39
I flung myself down at her *feet*,   *Charity* 38
Football drunkard's *f*, laughing-stocks of Time,   *Princess iv* 517
Footcloth and tumbled on the purple *f*,   ,, 286

Footed *See* **Bare-footed, Cat-footed, Four-footed, Lighter-footed, Little-footed, Wind-footed**

Foot-fall With measured *f* firm and mild, *Two Voices* 413
 list a *f-f*, ere he saw The wood-nymph, *Palace of Art* 110
 her palfrey's *f* shot Light horrors *Godiva* 58
 Or ghostly *f* echoing on the stair. *Guinevere* 507

Foot-gilt lay *F-g* with all the blossom-dust *Merlin and V.* 282

Footing Show'd her the fairy *f*'s on the grass, *Aylmer's Field* 90
 A slender-shafted Pine Lost *f*, fell, *Gareth and L.* 4
 hath o'erstept The slippery *f* of his narrow wit, *Lover's Tale i* 102

Footless where *f*ancies dwell Among the fragments *Maud I* xviii 44

Foot-lights By the low *f-l* of the world— *The Wreck* 40

Footprint left The little *f* daily wash'd away. *Enoch Arden* 22
 May only make that *f* upon sand *Princess* iii 239
 watch The sandy *f* harden into stone.' " 271
 The kingcup fills her *f*, *Prog. of Spring* 59

Foot-sore Reel'd as a *f* ox in crowded ways *Aylmer's Field* 819
 F-s, way-worn, at length he touch'd his goal, *St. Telemachus* 34

Footstep Old *f*'s trod the upper floors, *Mariana* 67
 night come from the inmost hills, Like *f*'s upon wool. *Œnone* 250
 hear the dully sound Of human *f*'s fall. *Palace of Art* 276
 his *f*'s smite the threshold stairs Of life— *St. S. Stylites* 191
 More close and close his *f*'s wind: *Day-Dm., Arrival* 25
 While he treads with *f* firmer, *L. of Burleigh* 51
 A *f* seem'd to fall beside her path, *Enoch Arden* 514
 I prest my *f*'s into his, *Lucretius* 118
 He seems as one whose *f*'s halt, *Will* 15
 The *f*'s of his life in mine; *In Mem.* lxxxv 44
 But at his *f* leaps no more, " 112
 But let no *f* beat the floor, " cv 17
 guide Her *f*'s, moving side by side " cxiv 19
 The *f* flutter'd me at first: *Last Tournament* 515
 clomb The last hard *f* of that iron crag; *Pass. of Arthur* 44
 and fell about My *f*'s on the mountains. *Lover's Tale i* 372
 scales Their headlong passes, but his *f* fails, *Montenegro* 5
 Have heard this *f* fall, *Tiresias* 27
 flowers that brighten as thy *f* falls, *Demeter and P.* 36
 A *f*, a low throbbing in the walls, *The Ring* 409

Footstool drove The *f* from before him, and arose; *Aylmer's Field* 327

Forage for the horse, and flint for fire. *Gareth and L.* 1277
 I will fetch you *f* from all fields, *Geraint and E.* 628
 To *f* for herself alone; *Open I. and C. Exhib.* 29

Forager they found—his *f*'s for charms— *Merlin and V.* 619

Foray Bound on a *f*, rolling eyes of prey, *Geraint and E.* 538
 Such as they brought upon their *f*'s out " 567

Forbad *F* her first the house of Averill, *Aylmer's Field* 502

Forbear '*F*,' the Princess cried; '*F*, Sir' I; *Princess* iv 162
 caught His purple scarf, and held, and said, '*F*! *Marr. of Geraint* 377
 '*F*: there is a worthier,' " 556
 That I *f* you thus: cross me no more. *Geraint and E.* 678
 'Nay,' said Pelleas, ' but *f*. *Pelleas and E.* 280
 call'd ' *F* In the great name of Him who died for men, *St. Telemachus* 62

Forbearance Arguing boundless *f*: *Aylmer's Field* 317

Forbid ' did I not *F* you, Dora?' *Dora* 92
 Chid her, and *f* her to speak To me, *Maud I* xix 63
 And batten on her poisons? Love *f*! *Lover's Tale i* 777

Forbore Bore and *f*, and did not tire, *Two Voices* 218
 But awed and promise-bounden she *f*, *Enoch Arden* 869
 Geraint, from utter courtesy, *f*. *Marr. of Geraint* 381
 hurl his cup Straight at the speaker, but *f*: *Merlin and V.* 31
 the meek maid Sweetly *f* him ever, *Lancelot and E.* 856
 looking at the villainy done, *F*, *Pelleas and E.* 283
 F his own advantage, (repeat) *Guinevere* 331, 333

Force (s) Had *f* to make me rhyme in youth, *Miller's D.* 193
 All *f* in bonds that might endure, *Palace of Art* 154
 I broke a close with *f* and arms: *Edwin Morris* 131
 you know him,—old, but full Of *f* and choler, *Golden Year* 61
 his passion shall have spent its novel *f*, *Locksley Hall* 49
 Titanic *f*'s taking birth In divers seasons, *Day-Dm., L'Envoi* 17
 I spoke with heart, and heat and *f*, *The Letters* 37
 toward the hollow, all her *f* Fail'd her; *Enoch Arden* 374
 she promised that no *f*, Persuasion, no, *Aylmer's Field* 417
 Is duer unto freedom, *f* and growth Of spirit *Princess* iv 141
 felt the blind wildbeast of *f*, " v 266

Force (s) *(continued)* Ida stood nor spoke, drain'd of her *f* *Princess* vi 266
 Some patient *f* to change them when we will, " Con. 56
 can bereave him Of the *f* he made his own *Ode on Well.* 273
 From our first Charles by *f* we wrung our claims. *Third of Feb.* 26
 Who makes by *f* his merit known *In Mem.* lxiv 9
 Of *f* that would have forged a name. " lxxiii 16
 I know thee of what *f* thou art " lxxix 3
 Seraphic intellect and *f* To seize and throw " cix 5
 with *f* and skill To strive, to fashion, " cxiii 6
 Should licensed boldness gather *f*, " 13
 this electric *f*, that keeps A thousand pulses dancing, " cxxv 15
 in his *f* to be Nature's crowning race. *Maud I* iv 33
 but of *f* to withstand, Year upon year, " II ii 24
 That save he won the first by *f*, *Gareth and L.* 107
 his great self, Hath *f* to quell me.' " 1183
 so fill up the gap where *f* might fail " 1352
 Reproach you, saying all your *f* is gone? *Marr. of Geraint* 88
 all his *f* Is melted into mere effeminacy? " 106
 He felt, were she the prize of bodily *f*, " 541
 blood Of their strong bodies, flowing, drain'd their *f*. " 569
 But either's *f* was match'd till Yniol's cry, " 805
 could I someway prove such *f* in her *Merlin and V.* 633
 elemental secrets, powers And *f*'s; " 640
 so by *f* they dragg'd him to the King. *Lancelot and E.* 471
 I do not mean the *f* alone, " 1063
 for what *f* is yours to go So far, *Last Tournament* 540
 Drain'd of her *f*, again she sat, *Pass. of Arthur* 15
 But had not *f* to shape it as he would, *Ancient Sage* 14
 F is from the heights. *Locksley H., Sixty* 158
 f to guide us thro' the days I shall not see? *Freedom* 15
 Howe'er blind *f* and brainless will May jar *Mechanophilus* 30
 my brothers, work, and wield The *f*'s of to-day, *Vision of Sin* 130

Force (verb) cruel glee *F*'s on the freer hour. *Princess, Pro.* 37
 this wild king to *f* her to his wish, " iii 125

Forced If a way Thro' solid opposition " vii 343
 f Sweet love on pranks of saucy boyhood: *Merlin and V.* 744
 brute world howling *f* them into bonds, *Guinevere* 537
 wrath which *f* my thoughts on that fierce law, *Rizpah* 41, 44
 the jailer *f* me away. (repeat) *Spinster's S's.* 39
 fur theere we was *f* to 'ide, *Lucretius* 245

Forcing *f* far apart Those blind beginnings *Sir Galahad* 82

Ford By bridge and *f*, by park and pale, *In Mem.* vi 39
 her future Lord Was drown'd in passing thro' the *f*, *Gareth and L.* 594
 bridge, *f*, beset By bandits, " 1003
 hard by here is one that guards a *f*— " 1040
 Push'd horse across the foamings of the *f*, " 1048
 Gareth laid his lance athwart the *f*; " 1056
 There lies a ridge of slate across the *f*; " 1232
 And victor of the bridges and the *f*, *Marr. of Geraint* 167
 quickly flashing thro' the shallow *f* *Holy Grail* 728
 hill, or plain, at sea, or flooding *f*.

Forded Took horse, and *f* Usk, and gain'd the wood; *Marr. of Geraint* 161

Fore when Dan didn't come to the *f*, *Tomorrow* 43

Forebode His heart *f*'s a mystery: *Two Voices* 290

Foreboding *f* ' what would Enoch say?' *Enoch Arden* 253

Forecast But who shall so *f* the years *In Mem.* i 5

Foredoom'd Made us, foreknew us, *f* us, *Despair* 91

Foredooming *F* all his trouble was in vain, *Gareth and L.* 1127

Forefather His own *f*'s' arms and armour hung. *Princess, Pro.* 24
 thy great *F*'s of the thornless garden, *Maud I* xviii 27
 Lies the warrior, my *f*, with his feet upon the hound. *Locksley H., Sixty* 28
 that same path our true *f*'s trod; *Doubt and Prayer* 4

Forefinger on the stretch'd *f* of all Time Sparkle *Princess* ii 378

Forefoot With inward yelp and restless *f* plies *Lucretius* 45

Forego which *f* The darkness of that battle *To the Queen* iv 64

Foregoing *F* all her sweetness, like a weed. *Holy Grail* 623

Foregone ' But could I, as in times *f*, *Talking Oak* 189
 have quite *f* All matters of this world: *Balin and Balan* 116

Foreground a *f* black with stones and slags, *Palace of Art* 81

Forehead (adj.) and his *f* veins Bloated, and branch'd; *Balin and Balan* 391

Forehead (s) draws His *f* earthward, and he dies. *Supp. Confessions* 168

Forehead (s) (continued) Thy bounteous f was not fann'd With
  breezes   Eleänore 9
  about His dusty f drily curl'd,   Miller's D. 6
  And, with dim fretted f's all,   Palace of Art 242
  curls—That made his f like a rising sun   M. d'Arthur 217
  Where shall I hide my f and my eyes?   „ 228
  and opposed Free hearts, free f's—   Ulysses 49
  f, eyelids, growing dewy-warm With kisses   Tithonus 58
  On her pallid cheek and f came a colour   Locksley Hall 25
  gilds the straiten'd f of the fool!   „ 62
  I, to herd with narrow f's,   „ 175
  Annie from her baby's f clipt A tiny curl,   Enoch Arden 235
  at last he said, Lifting his honest f,   „ 388
  We turn'd our f's from the falling sun,   The Brook 165
  With that she kiss'd His f,   Princess iii 312
  and o'er her f past A shadow,   „ vi 106
  With all their f's drawn in Roman scowls,   „ vii 129
  and her f sank upon her hands,   „ 247
  But on her f sits a fire: In Mem. cxiv 5
  But on the damsel's f shame,   Gareth and L. 656
  Had bared her f to the blistering sun,   Geraint and E. 515
  when their f's felt the cooling air,   Balin and Balan 589
  her shape From f to foot, perfect—again
  From foot to f exquisitely turn'd?   Lancelot and E. 642
  Clean from her f all that wealth of hair   Holy Grail 150
  their f's grimed with smoke, and sear'd,   „ 265
  Met f's all along the street of those Who watch'd
    us pass;   „ 344
  This air that smites his f is not air   „ 914
  Glanced from the rosy f of the dawn.   Pelleas and E. 502
  Pure on the virgin f of the dawn!'   „ 505
  curls—That made his f like a rising sun   Pass. of Arthur 385
  Where shall I hide my f and my eyes?   „ 396
  with my work thus Crown'd her clear f.   Lover's Tale i 345
  holdeth his undimmed f far Into a clearer zenith, „ 513
  brush'd My fallen f in their to and fro,   „ 701
  Brow-high, did strike my f as I past;   „ ii 19
  Bullets would sing by our f's,   Def. of Lucknow 21
  earth's dark f flings athwart the heavens   Ancient Sage 200
  f vapour-swathed In meadows ever green;   Freedom 7
  felt a gentle hand Fall on my f,   The Ring 419
  round her f wheels the woodland dove,   Prog. of Spring 57
  And last on the f Of Arthur the blameless   Merlin and the G. 72
  you spill The drops upon my f.   Romney's R. 24

Foreign and he died In f lands;   Dora 19
  And I will tell him tales of f parts,   Enoch Arden 198
  'I have a sister at the f court,   Princess i 75
  And travell'd men from f lands;   In Mem. x 6
  often abroad in the fragrant gloom Of f churches— Maud I xix 54
  Display'd a splendid silk of f loom,   Geraint and E. 687
  some other question'd if she came From f lands,   Lover's Tale iv 331
  they praised him to his face with their courtly f grace; Revenge 99
  Urge him to f war.   Sir J. Oldcastle 68
Foreigner (See also Furriner) A f, and I your country-
    woman,   Princess iv 317
Foreknew Made us, f us, foredoom'd us,   Despair 97
Foreland many a fairy f set With willow-weed   The Brook 45
Forelock Are taken by the f. Let it be.   Golden Year 19
Foremost (See also Head-foremost) f in thy various
    gallery Place it,   Ode to Memory 84
  And being ever f in the chase,   Geraint and E. 959
  I the heir of all the ages, in the f files of time— Locksley Hall 178
  which, on the f rocks Touching,   Sea Dreams 51
  F captain of his time,   Ode on Well. 31
  He dash'd the pummel at the f face,   Balan and Balan 402
Foreran So much the boy f;   Aylmer's Field 80
Forerun F thy peers, thy time, and let Thy feet,   Two Voices 88
  in the cold wind that f's the morn   Guinevere 132
Foresaw (See also Half-foresaw) The fame is quench'd
    that I f,   In Mem. lxxiii 5
  what doubt that he f This evil work   Guinevere 306
  And each f the dolorous day to be: Pelleas and E. 606
Foresee Oh, if indeed that eye f   In Mem. xxvi 9
  could none of them f, Not even thy wise father   Guinevere 273
Foreseeing Howbeit ourself, f casualty,   Princess iii 317

Foreshadow Who dares f for an only son A lovelier life, Ded. of Idylls 29
  What omens may f fate to man And woman,   Tiresias 7
Foreshadowing His heart f all calamity,   Enoch Arden 683
  Immersed in rich f's of the world,   Princess vii 312
Foreshorten'd lie F in the tract of time?   In Mem. lxxvii 4
Foresight Whose f preaches peace,   Love and Duty 34
  Take wings of f; lighten thro' The secular abyss In Mem. lxxvi 5
Forest (adj.) And armour'd all in f green,   Last Tournament 170
  his good warhorse left to graze Among the f greens, „ 491
  He burst his lance against a f bough,   Balin and Balan 329
  hurl'd it from him Among the f weeds,   „ 542
Forest (s) (See also Mid-forest, New Forest) so deadly
    still As that wide f.   D. of F. Women 69
  Between dark stems the f glows,   Sir Galahad 27
  The petty marestail f, fairy pines,   Aylmer's Field 92
  Better to clear prime f's, heave and thump   Princess iii 127
  While I roved about the f,   Boädicea 35
  The f crack'd, the waters curl'd,   In Mem. xv 5
  and pitch'd His tents beside the f.   Com. of Arthur 58
  slew the beast, and fell'd The f,   „ 60
  mount That rose between the f and the field.   Gareth and L. 191
  A mile beneath the f, challenging And over-
    throwing   Balin and Balan 12
  the harlot leapt Adown the f, and the thicket
    closed Behind her, and the f echo'd 'fool.'   Merlin and V. 973
  the gloomy skirts Of Celidon the f;   Lancelot and E. 292
  Across the f call'd of Dean, to find Caerleon   Pelleas and E. 21
  Alone, and in the heart of the great f.   Lover's Tale ii 3
  moanings in the f, the loud brook,   „ 114
  On icy fallow And faded f,   Merlin and the G. 85
  Thro' blasted valley and flaring f   Kapiolani 12
Forest-deeps And far, in f-d unseen,   Sir L. and Q. G. 7
Forester How once the wandering f at dawn,   Gareth and L. 498
  Down on a rout of craven f's.   „ 841
  Before him came a f of Dean,   Marr. of Geraint 148
Forest-path thine eyes not brook in f-p's,   Prog. of Spring 31
Forest-shadow and through the f-s borne   Lover's Tale ii 12
Forethought So dark a f roll'd about his brain,   Merlin and V. 230
Foretold f, Dying, that none of all our blood   Princess i 7
  He too f the perfect rose.   In Mem., Con. 34
  Has come to pass as f;   Maud II v 44
Forfeits game of f done—the girls all kiss'd   The Epic 2
  magic music, f, all the rest.   Princess, Pro. 195
Forgave there the Queen f him easily.   Marr. of Geraint 592
  And he f me, and I could not speak.   Guinevere 614
Forge yes!—but a company f's the wine.   Maud I i 36
  f a life-long trouble for ourselves,   Geraint and E. 3
Forged 'Who f that other influence,   Two Voices 283
  f a thousand theories of the rocks,   Edwin Morris 18
  he f, But that was later, boyish histories   Aylmer's Field 96
  Nor deeds of gift, but gifts of grace he f,   Sea Dreams 192
  and so We f a sevenfold story.   Princess, Pro. 202
  thou hast f at last A night-long Present   In Mem. lxxi 2
  results Of force that would have f a name.   „ lxxiii 16
  Whereof they f the brand Excalibur,   Gareth and L. 67
  one son had f on his father and fled,   Despair 69
Forget rose In love with thee f's to close His curtains, Adeline 42
  men F the dream that happens then,   Two Voices 353
  'I might f my weaker lot;   „ 367
  who that knew him could f The busy wrinkles   Miller's D. 3
  Can he pass, and we f?   „ 204
  What is love? for we f: „ 213
  I shall not f you, mother,   May Queen, N. Y's. E. 31
  And God f the stranger!'   The Goose 56
  Authority f's a dying king,   M. d'Arthur 121
  I earth in earth f these empty courts,   Tithonus 75
  Perplext her, made her half f herself,   Aylmer's Field 303
  Swear by St something—If her name—   Princess v 293
  all men else their nobler dreams f,   Ode on Well. 152
  What England was, shall her true sons f?   Third of Feb. 44
  ten years back, or more, if I don't f: Grandmother 75
  Could we f the widow'd hour   In Mem. xl 1
  But he f's the days before   „ xliii 3
  Nor can it suit me to f The mighty hopes   „ lxxxv 59
  The days she never can f   „ xcvii 14

Forget (*continued*) I should *f* That I owe this debt to you — *Maud I xix* 89
shall I say?—If ever I *should f*, — " 93
the lone hern *f's* his melancholy, — *Gareth and L.* 1185
f My heats and violences? live afresh? — *Balin and Balan* 189
ye *f* Obedience is the courtesy due to kings.' — *Lancelot and E.* 717
Authority *f's* a dying king, — *Pass. of Arthur* 289
Men will *f* what we suffer and not what we do. — *Def. of Lucknow* 73
and *f* The darkness of the pall.' — *Ancient Sage* 197
As we *f* our wail at being born. — *The Ring* 465
A name that earth will not *f* — *To Ulysses* 27
but thou forgive, *F* it. — *Death of Œnone* 44

Forgetful *F* how my rich prœmion makes Thy glory fly — *Lucretius* 70
F of Maud and me, — *Maud I xxi* 4
F of his promise to the King, — *Marr. of Geraint* 50
F of the falcon and the hunt, — " 51
F of the tilt and tournament, *F* of his glory and his name, *F* of his princedom and its cares. — " 52
'The sound of that *f* shore — *In Mem. xxxv* 14
dreaming of her love For Lancelot, and *f* of the hunt; — *Marr. of Geraint* 159
F of their troth and fealty, — *Guinevere* 442
f of the man, Whose crime had half unpeopled Ilion, — *Death of Œnone* 60

Forgetfulness falling into Lot's *f* I know not thee, — *Gareth and L.* 96
And this *f* was hateful to her. — *Marr. of Geraint* 55

Forget-me-not I found the blue *F-m-n*. — *Miller's D.* 202
f-m-n's That grow for happy lovers. — *The Brook* 172

Forgetteth The place he knew *f* him. — *Two Voices* 264

Forgetting *F* how to render beautiful Her countenance — *Lover's Tale i* 96
O the night, Where there's no *f*. — *Forlorn* 78

Forgive Us, O Just and Good, *F*, — *Poland* 12
I have been wild and wayward, but you'll *f* me now; You'll kiss me, my own mother, and *f* me ere I go; — *May Queen N. Y's. E.* 33
May God *f* me!—I have been to blame. — *Dora* 161
And easily *f's* it as his own, — *Aylmer's Field* 401
'Love, *f* him:' but he did not speak; — *Sea Dreams* 45
'*F*! How many will say, '*f*,' — " 60
neither God nor man can well *f*, — " 63
Before you prove him, rogue, and proved, *f*. — " 171
We *must f* the dead. — " 270
f him, dear, And I shall sleep the sounder!' — " 311
I do *f* him!' 'Thanks, my love,' — " 316
F me, I waste my heart in sighs: — *Princess vii* 358
F what seem'd my sin in me; — *In Mem., Pro.* 33
F my grief for one removed, — " 37
F these wild and wandering cries, — " 41
F them where they fail in truth, — " 43
hearts that know not how to *f*: — *Maud II i* 44
Or to say '*F* the wrong,' — " iv 86
F me; mine was jealousy in love.' — *Lancelot and E.* 1351
I *f* thee, as Eternal God *F's*: — *Guinevere* 544
Kiss him, and then *F* him, — *Lover's Tale iv* 175
Are slower to *f* than human kings. — *Tiresias* 10
All his virtues—I *f* them— — *Locksley H., Sixty* 44
For you *f* me, you are sure of that— — *Romney's R.* 160
but thou *f*, Forget it. — *Death of Œnone* 43

Forgiven not easily *f* Are those, who setting — *Gardener's D.* 247
Say one soft word and let me part *f*.' — *Princess iv* 219
Caress her! let her feel herself — *Merlin and V.* 381
She with a face, bright as for sin *f*, — *Lancelot and E.* 1102
pass on, my Queen, *f*.' — " 1353
blessed be the King, who hath *f* My wickedness — *Guinevere* 634
'Yea, little maid, for am *I* not *f*?' — " 665
And has he not *f* me yet, — *Happy* 1
trust myself *f* by the God to whom I kneel. — " 86
Reflected, sends a light on the *f*. — *Romney's R.* 161

Forgiveness I seem no more: I want *f* too: — *Princess vi* 290
we embrace you yet once more With all *f*, — " 295
thro' this ring Had sent his cry for her *f*, — *The Ring* 233
Could kneel for your *f*. — *Romney's R.* 26
Human *f* touches heaven, and thence— — " 159

Forgiving I had set my heart on your *f* him — *Sea Dreams* 269

Forgot For is not our first year *f*? — *Two Voices* 368
having seen, *f*? The common mouth, — *Gardener's D.* 55

Forgot (*continued*) The steer *f* to graze, — *Gardener's D.* 85
Philip sitting at her side *f* Her presence, — *Enoch Arden* 384
might be May or April, he *f*, — *The Brook* 151
Sir Aylmer half *f* his lazy smile — *Aylmer's Field* 197
And I *f* the clouded Forth, — *The Daisy* 101
F his weakness in thy sight. — *In Mem. cx* 4
Nor yet *f* her practice in her fright, — *Merlin and V.* 947
F to drink to Lancelot and the Queen, — *Lancelot and E.* 737
And the sick man *f* her simple blush, — " 864
so *f* herself A moment, and her cares; — *Last Tournament* 25
when their faces are *f* in the land— — *Lover's Tale i* 759
that I might ha' *f* him somehow— — *First Quarrel* 37
The warrior hath *f* his arms, — *Ancient Sage* 138
But I clean *f* tha, my lad, — *Owd Roä* 53
An' I'd clear *f*, little Dicky, — " 64

Forgotten (*See also* **Half-forgotten, Long-forgotten**)
To live *f*, and love forlorn.' (repeat) — *Mariana in the S.* 24, 84, 96
I sleep *f*, I wake forlorn. — " 36
Walks *f*, and is forlorn.' — " 48
Live *f* and die forlorn.' (repeat) — " 60, 72
not to be *f*—not at once—Not all *f*. — *Love and Duty* 91
I meant? I have *f* what I meant: — *Lucretius* 122
F, rusting on his iron hills, — *Princess v* 146
And doing battle with *f* ghosts, — " 480
'I had *f* all in my strong joy To see thee— — *Last Tournament* 582
My God, thou hast *f* me in my death: — *Pass. of Arthur* 27
Where fragments of *f* peoples dwelt, — " 84
Are you sleeping? have you *f*? — *The Flight* 1
Ev'n her grandsire's fifty half *f*. — *On Jub. Q. Victoria* 41
She fear'd I had *f* her, and I ask'd About my Mother, — *The Ring* 102
I had *f* it was your birthday, child— — " 378
f mine own rhyme By mine own self, As I shall be *f* by old Time, — *To Mary Boyle* 21
Like glimpses of *f* dreams— — *Two Voices* 381
wasting his *f* heart, — *Aylmer's Field* 689
The howlings from *f* fields; — *In Mem. xli* 16
And fling me deep in that *f* mere, — *Lancelot and E.* 1426
Had suck'd the fire of some *f* sun, — *Lover's Tale iv* 194
who dipt In some *f* book of mine — *To E. Fitzgerald* 47

Fork (*See also* **Lightning-fork**) Who, God-like, grasps the triple *f's*, — *Of old sat Freedom* 15
Ruin'd trunks on wither'd *f's*, — *Vision of Sin* 93
I never saw so fierce a *f*— — *Lucretius* 28
A double hill ran up his furrowy *f's* — *Princess iii* 174
Two *f's* are fixt into the meadow ground, — *Marr. of Geraint* 482
there they fixt the *f's* into the ground, — " 548
To me this narrow grizzled *f* of thine — *Merlin and V.* 59
And dazzled by the livid-flickering *f*, — " 941

Forked things that are *f*, and horned, and soft, — *The Mermaid* 53
f Of the near storm, and aiming at his head, — *Aylmer's Field* 726

Forlorn In sleep she seem'd to walk *f*, — *Mariana* 30
To live forgotten, and love *f*.' (repeat) — *Mariana in the S.* 24, 84, 96
I sleep forgotten, I wake *f*.' — " 36
Walks forgotten, and is *f*.' — " 48
Live forgotten and die *f*.' (repeat) — " 60, 72
I am too *f*, Too shaken: — *Supp. Confessions* 135
Over the dark dewy earth *f*, — *Ode to Memory* 69
in a lonely grove He set up his *f* pipes, — *Amphion* 22
I ceased, and sat as one *f*. — *Two Voices* 400
Mournful Œnone, wandering *f* Of Paris, — *Œnone* 16
Yet we will not die *f*, — *Vision of Sin* 206
'Favour from one so sad and so *f* — *Enoch Arden* 287
A tonsured head in middle age *f*, — *The Brook* 200
The little village looks *f*; — *In Mem. lx* 9
I walk as ere I walk'd *f*, — " lxviii 5
purple-frosty bank Of vapour, leaving night *f*. — " cvii 4
Who am no more so all *f*, — *Maud I xviii* 32
speak of the mother she loved As one scarce less *f*, — " xix 28
The tiny cell is *f*, — " II ii 13
thus in grief to wander forth *f*; — *The Flight* 85
may pass when earth is manless and *f*, — *Locksley H., Sixty* 206
tho', in this lean age *f*, — *Epilogue* 71
And fled by many a waste, *f* of man, — *Demeter and P.* 74
Where noble Ulric dwells *f*, — *Happy* 10
To wait on one so broken, so *f*? — *Romney's R.* 17

Form (s) This excellence and solid *f* Of constant
  beauty. — *Supp. Confessions* 149
(Tho' all her fairest *f*'s are types of thee, — *Isabel* 39
And airy *f*'s of flitting change. — *Madeline* 7
converse with all *f*'s Of the many-sided mind, — *Ode to Memory* 115
And other than his *f* of creed, — *A Character* 29
rites and *f*'s before his burning eyes Melted — *The Poet* 39
Fretteth thine enshrouded *f*. — *A Dirge* 10
The *f*, the *f* alone is eloquent! — *The form, the form* 1
'Is this the *f*,' she made her moan, — *Mariana in the S.* 33
The reflex of a beauteous *f*, — *Miller's D.* 77
o'er her rounded *f* Between the shadows — *Œnone* 180
I sit as God holding no *f* of creed, — *Palace of Art* 211
f's that pass'd at windows and on roofs — *D. of F. Women* 23
That her fair *f* may stand and shine, — *Of old sat Freedom* 21
Matures the individual *f*. — *Love thou thy land* 40
Phantoms of other *f*'s of rule, — ″ 59
all the decks were dense with stately *f*'s — *M. d'Arthur* 196
play with flying *f*'s and images, — *Gardener's D.* 60
fair new *f*'s, That float about the threshold — *Golden Year* 15
Cursed be the sickly *f*'s that err — *Locksley Hall* 61
And loosely settled into *f*. — *Day-Dm., Pro.* 12
On either side her tranced *f* Forth streaming — ″ *Sleep B.* 5
ever dwells A perfect *f* in perfect rest. — ″ 24
But blessed *f*'s in whistling storms — *Sir Galahad* 59
dusty crypt Of darken'd *f*'s and faces. — *Will Water.* 184
And slowly quickening into lower *f*'s; — *Vision of Sin* 210
All beauty compass'd in a female *f*, — *Princess ii* 34
since to look on noble *f*'s Makes noble — ″ 86
There sat along the *f*'s, like morning doves — ″ 102
Of faded *f* and haughtiest lineaments, — ″ 448
then a loftier *f* Than female, — ″ *iv* 215
I saw the *f*'s: I knew not where I was: — ″ *vii* 133
Will clear away the parasitic *f*'s — ″ 269
And other *f*'s of life than ours, — *Ode on Well.* 264
A hollow *f* with empty hands.' — *In Mem. iii* 12
A late-lost *f* that sleep reveals, — ″ *xiii* 2
But knows no more of transient *f* — ″ *xvi* 7
Nor cares to fix itself to *f*, — ″ *xxxiii* 4
Her faith thro' *f* is pure as thine, — ″ *xlvii* 6
Eternal *f* shall still divide The eternal soul — ″ *lxi* 10
Where thy first *f* was made a man; — ″ *lxxix* 8
print The same sweet *f*'s in either mind. — ″ *lxxxii* 2
For changes wrought on *f* and face; — ″ *lxxxv* 35
O sacred essence, other *f*, — ″ *lxxxvii* 37
And seem to lift the *f*, and glow — ″ *lxxxix* 41
'And merge,' he said, 'in *f* and gloss — ″ *xci* 5
wear the *f* by which I know Thy spirit — ″ 15
Come, beauteous in thine after *f*, — ″ *xcv* 46
frame In matter-moulded *f*'s of speech, — ″ *cv* 19
For who would keep an ancient *f* — ″ *cvi* 14
And ancient *f*'s of party strife; — ″ *cxi* 6
he veil His want in *f*'s for fashion's sake, — ″ *cxviii* 10
And grew to seeming-random *f*, — ″ *cxxiii* 6
flow From *f* to *f*, and nothing stands; — ″ *cxxvii* 1
tho' faith and *f* Be sunder'd in the night — *Gareth and L.* 1200
these damp walls, and taken but the *f*. — *Marr. of Geraint* 333
Conjecture of the plumage and the *f*; — ″ 654
And dreamt herself was such a faded *f* — *Holy Grail* 450
all her *f* shone forth with sudden light — *Guinevere* 548
O imperial-moulded *f*, — *Pass. of Arthur* 548
all the decks were dense with stately *f*'s, — *Lover's Tale i* 646
a phantasm of the *f* It should attach to? — ″ 705
Mantling her *f* halfway. — ″ 797
fell into the abysm Of *f*'s outworn, — ″ *ii* 94
very face and *f* of Lionel Flash'd thro' my eyes — ″ 158
f's which ever stood Within the magic cirque — ″ 180
pencil's naked *f*'s Colour and life: — *Sisters (E. and E.)* 171
Grew after marriage to full height and *f*? — *De Prof., Two G.* 13
face and *f* are hers and mine in one, — *The Wreck* 105
I clung to the sinking *f*, — *Ancient Sage* 193
and itself For ever changing *f*, — *Dead Prophet* 22
And blurr'd in colour and *f*, — *The Ring* 184
The *f* of Muriel faded, and the face Of Miriam — *Romney's R.* 7
concentrate into *f* And colour all you are,

Form (s) (*continued*) crown'd *f*'s high over the sacred
  fountain? — *Parnassus* 1
all else *F*, Ritual, varying with the tribes of men, — *Akbar's Dream* 124
thou knowest I hold that *f*'s Are needful: — ″ 126
And what are *f*'s? Fair garments, — ″ 130
*F*s! The Spiritual in Nature's market-place— — ″ 134
Who shaped the *f*'s, obey them, — ″ 143
And is a living *f*? — *Mechanophilus* 16
Form (verb) the rainbow *f*'s and flies on the land — *Sea-Fairies* 25
slowly *f*'s the firmer mind, — *In Mem. xviii* 18
Storm, Storm, Riflemen *f*! (repeat) — *Riflemen form!* 5, 19
Riflemen, Riflemen, Riflemen, *f*! (repeat) — ″ 7, 14, 21, 28
F, *F*, Riflemen *F*! (repeat) — ″ 12, 26
F, be ready to do or die! *F* in Freedom's name
  and the Queen's! — ″ 22
Formal O the *f* mocking bow, — *The Flight* 29
His *f* kiss fell chill as a flake of snow — *The Wreck* 32
O, I see thee old and *f*, — *Locksley Hall* 93
Formalism they blurt Their furious *f*'s, — *Akbar's Dream* 57
Former And ebb into a *f* life, — *Sonnet, To* — 2
remembering His *f* talks with Edith, — *Aylmer's Field* 457
became Her *f* beauty treble; — *Princess vii* 25
Makes *f* gladness loom so great? — *In Mem. xxiv* 10
As in the *f* flash of joy, — ″ *cxxii* 15
In *f* days you saw me favourably. — *Geraint and E.* 315
'Earl, if you love me as in *f* years, — ″ 355
that I began To glance behind me at my *f* life, — ″ 863
Because his *f* madness, — *Holy Grail* 649
For Evelyn knew not of my *f* suit, — *Sisters (E. and E.)* 205
Forming The lucid outline *f* round thee; — *Tithonus* 53
Be yet but yolk, and *f* in the shell? — *Ancient Sage* 130
Formless I am void, Dark, *f*, utterly destroyed. — *Supp. Confessions* 122
A vapour heavy, hueless, *f*, cold, — *Vision of Sin* 53
And wrapt thee *f* in the fold, — *In Mem. xxii* 15
till all his heart was cold With *f* fear; — *Pass. of Arthur* 98
Forrards (forwards) if tha' wants to git *f* a bit, — *Church-warden, etc.* 49
Forsake Ah yet, tho' all the world *f*, — *Will Water.* 49
what a heart was mine to *f* her — *The Wreck* 95
leech *f* the dying bed for terror — *Happy* 98
Forsaken O my *f* heart, with thee And this poor flower — *In Mem. viii* 18
We saw far off an old *f* house, — *The Ring* 155
Forsaking See! our friends are all *f* — *All Things will Die* 18
Forsworn I cannot bear to dream you so *f*: — *Pelleas and E.* 300
I swore to the great King, and am *f*. — *Last Tournament* 661
I swear and swear *f* To love him most, — *The Flight* 49
Fort (*See also* **Hill-fort**) Welcome her, thunders of
  f and of fleet! — *W. to Alexandra* 6
Built that new *f* to overawe my friends, — *Marr. of Geraint* 460
Forth And I forgot the clouded *F*, — *The Daisy* 101
Forthgazing *F* on the waste and open sea, — *Lover's Tale ii* 177
Fortitude stately flower of female *f*, — *Isabel* 11
Fortress The *f*, and the mountain ridge, — *In Mem. lxxi* 14
The *f* crashes from on high, — ″ *cxxvii* 14
deathful-grinning mouths of the *f*, — *Maud III vi* 52
White from the mason's hand, a *f* rose; — *Marr. of Geraint* 244
And onward to the *f* rode the three, — ″ 251
Ride into that new *f* by your town, — ″ 407
be thy heart a *f* to maintain The day — *To Duke of Argyll* 5
My prison, not my *f*, fall away! — *Doubt and Prayer* 12
Fortunate You, the Mighty, the *F*, — *On Jub. Q. Victoria* 55
Fortune I rode sublime On *F*'s neck: — *D. of F. Women* 142
Tho' *f* clip my wings, I will not cramp my heart, — *Will Water.* 50
I am but as my *f*'s are: — *Lady Clare* 70
'Drink to *F*, drink to Chance, — *Vision of Sin* 191
mark me! for your *f*'s are to make. — *Aylmer's Field* 300
Name, *f* too: the world should ring of him — ″ 395
Thro' which a few, by wit or *f* led, — ″ 438
besides Their slender household *f*'s — *Sea Dreams* 9
ally Your *f*'s, justlier balanced, — *Princess ii* 66
affluent *F* emptied all her horn. — *Ode on Well.* 197
Becomes on *F*'s crowning slope, — *In Mem. lxiv* 14
My *f*'s all as fair as hers who lay — *Gareth and L.* 903
loved her in a state Of broken *f*'s, — *Marr. of Geraint* 13
song that Enid sang was one Of *F* and her wheel, — ″ 346
'Turn, *F*, turn thy wheel and lower the proud; — ″ 347

Fortune (*continued*) 'Turn, *F*, turn thy wheel with
  smile or frown;   *Marr. of Geraint* 350
since our *f* slipt from sun to shade,   ,, 714
that better fits Our mended *f*'s   ,, 718
Give me good *f*, I will strike him dead,   *Lancelot and E.* 1071
You count the father of your *f*,   *Sisters (E. and E.)* 28
his followers, all Flower into *f*—   *Columbus* 167
Forty (*See also* **Foorty**) That numbers *f* cubits
  from the soil.   *St. S. Stylites* 91
And *f* blest one bless him,   *Aylmer's Field* 372
for *f* years A hermit, who had pray'd,   *Lancelot and E.* 402
Divil a Danny was there, yer Honour, for *f* year,   *Tomorrow* 30
Gone with whom for *f* years my life in golden
  sequence ran,   *Locksley H., Sixty* 47
Forum Titanic shapes, they cramm'd The *f*.   *Princess vii* 125
Now thy *F* roars no longer,   *To Virgil* 29
The Baths, the *F* gabbled of his death,   *St. Telemachus* 74
Forward (*See also* **Forrards**) with increasing might
  doth *f* flee   *Mine be the strength* 5
F, *f* let us range,   *Locksley Hall* 181
'*F*, the Light Brigade! (repeat)   *Light Brigade* 5, 9
She sets her *f* countenance   *In Mem. cxiv* 6
To right? to left? straight *f*?   *Pelleas and E.* 67
Then bounded *f* to the castle walls,   ,, 363
Gone the cry of '*F*, *F*,'   *Locksley H., Sixty* 73
'*F*' rang the voices then,   ,, 77
f—naked—let them stare.   ,, 78
F, *f*, ay and backward,   ,, 142
F, backward, backward, *f*,   ,, 146
Nay, your pardon, cry your '*f*,'   ,, 193
F then, but still remember how the course of Time
  will swerve,   ,, 225
F far and far from here is all the hope of eighty years.   ,, 235
F, till you see the highest Human Nature is divine.   ,, 254
F, let the stormy moment fly and mingle with the Past.   ,, 276
moving quickly *f* till the heat Smote on her brow,   *Death of Œnone* 97
F to the starry track Glimmering up   *Silent Voices* 8
Forward-creeping *f-c* tides Began to foam,   *In Mem. ciii* 37
Forward-flowing The *f-f* tide of time;   *Arabian Nights* 4
Fossil lark and leveret lay, Like *f*'s of the rock,   *Audley Court* 25
Foster guard and *f* her for evermore.   *Guinevere* 592
Foster'd *F* the callow eaglet—
  Which once she *f* up with care—   *Œnone* 212
because that *f thy* court I savour of thy—virtues?   *In Mem. viii* 16
that was Arthur; and they *f* him   *Merlin and V.* 38
OLD poets *f* under friendlier skies,   *Guinevere* 295
Foster-mother mock their *f-m* on four feet,   *Poets and their B.* 1
Foster-sister She was my *f-s*:   *Com. of Arthur* 37
Fought (*See also* **Fowt**) And in thy spirit with   *Lover's Tale i* 233
  thee *f*   *England and Amer.* 9
Annie *f* against his will: *Enoch Arden* 158
His comrades having *f* their last below,   *Aylmer's Field* 227
F with what seem'd my own uncharity;   *Sea Dreams* 73
with the Palmyrene That *f* Aurelian,   *Princess ii* 84
And nursed by those for whom you *f*,   ,, *vi* 95
I and mine have *f* Your battle.   ,, 224
And the feet of those he *f* for,   *Ode on Well.* 11
those great men who *f*, and kept it ours.   ,, 158
Than when he *f* at Waterloo,   ,, 257
have we *f* for Freedom from our prime,   *Third of Feb.* 23
Were those your sires who *f* at Lewes?   ,, 33
They that had *f* so well Came thro' the jaws   *Light Brigade* 45
may be met and *f* with outright,   *Grandmother* 31
for the babe had *f* for his life.   ,, 64
He *f* his doubts and gather'd strength,   *In Mem. xcvi* 13
Like Paul with beasts, I *f* with Death;   ,, *cxx* 4
Aurelius lived and *f* and died, And after him King
  Uther *f* and died,   *Com. of Arthur* 13
F, and in twelve great battles overcame   ,, 518
He *f* against him in the Barons' war,   *Gareth and L.* 77
Lot and many another rose and *f* Against thee,   ,, 354
but he that *f* no more, As being all bone-batter'd   ,, 1049
thy foul sayings *f* for me: ,, 1180
twice they *f*, and twice they breathed,   *Marr. of Geraint* 567

Fought (*continued*) *f* Hard with himself, and seem'd
  at length in peace,   *Balin and Balan* 238
f in her name, Sware by her—   *Merlin and V.* 13
two brothers, one a king, had met And *f*   *Lancelot and E.* 40
if I went and if I *f* and won it   ,, 216
'you have *f*. O tell us—for we live apart—   ,, 283
it seem'd half-miracle To those he *f* with,—   ,, 498
name Of greatest knight? I *f* for it,   ,, 1414
'Have ye *f*?' She ask'd of Lancelot.   *Pelleas and E.* 592
whatever knight of thine I *f* And tumbled.   *Last Tournament* 453
F in her father's battles? wounded there?   ,, 592
Isolt?—I *f* his battles, for Isolt!   ,, 604
brake the petty kings, and *f* with Rome,   *Pass. of Arthur* 68
Nor ever yet had Arthur *f* a fight Like this   ,, 93
fell Confusion, since he saw not whom he *f*.   ,, 99
shiver'd brands that once had *f* with Rome,   ,, 133
He *f* the boys that were rude,   *First Quarrel* 14
and they *f* us hand to hand,   *The Revenge* 52
And we had not *f* them in vain,   ,, 74
'We have *f* such a fight for a day and a night As
  may never be *f* again!   ,, 83
'I have *f* for Queen and Faith   ,, 101
Each of us *f* as if hope for the garrison   *Def. of Lucknow* 48
Thanks to the kindly dark faces who *f* with us,
  faithful and few, *F* with the bravest among us,   ,, 70
and *f* till I sunder'd the fray,   *V. of Maeldune* 69
F for their lives in the narrow gap   *Heavy Brigade* 23
Britain *f* her sons of yore—   *Open I. and C. Exhib.* 21
He wildly *f* a rival suitor— him The causer of
  that scandal, *f* and fell;   *The Ring* 214
for he *f* Thy fight for Thee,   *Happy* 15
Foughten the lords Have *f* like wild beasts   *Com. of Arthur* 226
had I *f*—well—In those fierce wars,   *Balin and Balan* 176
the *f* field, what else, at once Decides it,   *Princess v* 297
Then quickly from the *f* field he sent   *Com. of Arthur* 135
When have I stinted stroke in *f* field?   *Holy Grail* 860
Foul (*adj*.) keep where you are: you are *f* with sin;   *Poet's Mind* 36
Kill the *f* thief, and wreak me for my son.'   *Gareth and L.* 363
But if their talk were *f*,   ,, 504
But truly *f* are better,   ,, 947
thy *f* sayings fought for me: ,, 1180
F are their lives; *f* are their lips;   *Balin and Balan* 616
Of that *f* bird of rapine whose whole prey   *Merlin and V.* 728
as false and *f* As the poach'd filth   ,, 797
what is fair without *f* is often as *f* within.'   *Dead Prophet* 68
You say your body is so *f*—   *Happy* 25
Your body is not *f* to me, and body is *f* at best.   ,, 28
F! *f*! the word was yours not mine,   ,, 41
'I So *f* a traitor to myself and her,   *Aylmer's Field* 319
nature crost Was mother of the *f* adulteries   ,, 376
Ring out old shapes of *f* disease;   *In Mem. cvi* 25
housed in her *f* den, there at their meat would
  growl,   *Com. of Arthur* 30
As one that let *f* wrong stagnate and be,   *Geraint and E.* 891
And drawing *f* ensample from fair names,   *Guinevere* 490
sucking The *f* steam of the grave to thicken by it,   *Lover's Tale i* 649
I'd sooner fold an icy corpse dead of some *f* disease: *The Flight* 54
Fright and *f* dissembling,   *Forlorn* 32
strip your own *f* passions bare;   *Locksley H., Sixty* 141
Foul (*s*) frequent interchange of *f* and fair,   *Enoch Arden* 533
Foul'd Experience, in her kind Hath *f* me—   *Last Tournament* 318
Foulest Or the *f* sewer of the town—   *Dead Prophet* 48
Foul-flesh'd as one That smells a *f-f* agaric in the holt,   *Gareth and L.* 747
Foully phantom husks of something *f* done,   *Lucretius* 160
Foulness canst endure To mouth so huge a *f*—   *Balin and Balan* 379
This fellow hath wrought some *f*   ,, 565
And of the horrid *f* that he wrought,   *Merlin and V.* 748
To all the *f* that they work.   ,, 785
Foun' for Danny was not to be *f*,   *Tomorrow* 28
they *f* Dhrownded in black bog-wather   ,, 61
they laid this body they *f* an the grass   ,, 73
Found (find) (*See also* **Foun'**, **Fun**) compare All
  creeds till we have *f* the one,   *Supp. Confessions* 176
Down she came and *f* a boat   *L. of Shalott iv* 6
'I *f* him when my years were few;   *Two Voices* 271

Found (find) (continued) to be *f* Long after, as it seem'd, — *Sisters (E. and E.)* 110
seen And lost and *f* again, — " 147
They *f* her beating the hard Protestant doors. — " 240
gratefullest heart I have *f* in a child — *In the Child. Hosp.* 32
(Hath he been here—not *f* me—gone — *Sir J. Oldcastle* 152
He would be *f* a heretic to Himself, — " 182
the harmless people whom we *f* — *Columbus* 181
You *f* some merit in my rhymes, — *To E. Fitzgerald* 55
who *f* Beside the springs of Dircê, smote, — *Tiresias* 13
the fierce beast *f* A wiser than herself, — " 151
little one *f* me at sea on a day, — *The Wreck* 86
I *f* myself moaning again 'O child, — " 134
We never had *f* Him on earth, — *Despair* 57
F, fear'd me dead, and groan'd, — *The Flight* 23
when Edwin *f* us there, — " 82
burnt at midnight *f* at morn, — *Locksley H., Sixty* 97
Shepherds, have I *f*, and more than once, — " 121
poet, surely to be *f* When Truth is *f* again. — *Pref. Poem" Broth. S.* 15
be *f* of angel eyes In earth's recurring Paradise. — *Helen's Tower* 11
now Your fairy Prince has *f* you, — *The Ring* 69
I *f* these cousins often by the brook, — " 158
And *f* a corpse and silence, — " 217
F in a chink of that old moulder'd floor!' — " 280
laugh'd a little and *f* her two— — " 337
I *f* her not in house Or garden— — " 444
F yesterday—forgotten mine own rhyme — *To Mary Boyle* 21
Wizard Who *f* me at sunrise Sleeping, — *Merlin and the G* 12
and the same who first had *f* Paris, — *Death of Œnone* 53
He had left his dagger behind him. I *f* it. — *Bandit's Death* 12
She *f* my letter upon him, — *Charity* 31
I *f* The tenderest Christ-like creature — "

Found (establish) All wild to *f* an University — *Princess i* 150
ere he *f* Empire for life? — *Gardener's D.* 19

Foundation-stone Whereof the strong *f-s's* were laid — *Palace of Art* 235

Founded She had *f*; they must build. — *Princess ii* 145
I Have *f* my Round Table in the North, — *Last Tournament* 78
some Order, which our King Hath newly *f*, — " 742
Table Round Which good King Arthur *f*, — *Guinevere* 221
We *f* many a mighty state; — *Hands all Round* 30

Founder statues, king or saint, or *f* fell; — *Sea Dreams* 224
on that *f* of our blood. — *Locksley H., Sixty* 32

Founding About the *f* of a Table Round, — *Merlin and V.* 411
knight Of the great Table—at the *f* of it; — *Guinevere* 235

Foundress The *f* of the Babylonian wall, — *Princess ii* 80
Some say the third—the authentic *f* you. — " iii 158

Fount he was thrown From his loud *f* — *Mine be the strength* 4
Ancient *f's* of inspiration well — *Locksley Hall* 188
burst away In search of stream or *f*, — *Enoch Arden* 635
Who dabbling in the *f* of fictive tears, — *The Brook* 93
Not past the living *f* of pity in Heaven. — *Aylmer's Field* 752
There while we stood beside the *f*, — *Princess iii* 23
The very source and *f* of Day — *In Mem. xxiv* 3
deer, the dews, the fern, the *f's*, the lawns; — *Last Tournament* 727

Fountain (adj.) Harder and drier than a *f* bed In summer; — *Pelleas and E.* 507

Fountain (s) (See also **Foam-fountains**) Life of the *f* there, beneath Its salient springs, — *Supp. Confessions* 55
from the central *f's* flow Fall'n silver-chiming, — *Arabian Nights* 50
stealest fire, From the *f's* of the past, — *Ode to Memory* 2
In the middle leaps a *f* — *Poet's Mind* 24
Day and night to the billow the *f* calls: — *Sea-Fairies* 2
I should look like a *f* of gold — *The Mermaid* 18
let thy voice Rise like a *f* for me — *M. d'Arthur* 249
The *f* to his place returns — *Day-Dm., Sleep. P.* 11
And sixty feet the *f* leapt. — "
runs to seed Beside its native *f*. — *Revival* 8
Against its *f* upward runs The current — *Amphion* 96
Expecting when a *f* should arise: — *Will Water.* 35
Till the *f* spouted, showering wide — *Vision of Sin* 8
Like *f's* of sweet water in the sea, — " 21
Spout from the maiden *f* in her heart. — *Enoch Arden* 803
The *f* of the moment, playing now — *Lucretius* 240
the splash and stir Of *f's* spouted up — *Princess, Pro.* 61
Enring'd a billowing *f* in the midst; — " i 218
— " ii 28

Fountain (s) (continued) Knowledge is now no more a *f* seal'd: — *Princess i;* 90
and race By all the *f's*: fleet I was of foot: — " iv 263
And tears that at their *f* freeze; — *In Mem. xx* 12
And show'd him in the *f* fresh — " lxxxv 26
From household *f's* never dry; — " cix 2
saw The *f* where they sat together, — *Balin and Balan* 291
and by *f's* running wine, — *Last Tournament* 141
'Friend, did ye mark that *f* yesterday — " 286
let thy voice Rise like a *f* for me — *Pass. of Arthur* 417
springing from her *f's* in the brain, — *Lover's Tale i* 83
from the diamond *f* by the palms, — " 137
A draught of that sweet *f* that he loves, — " 141
whate'er is *f* to the one Is *f* to the other; — " 179
My current to the *f* whence it sprang,— — " 503
Why fed we from one *f*? drew one sun? — " ii 24
I fear'd The very *f's* of her life were chill'd; — *Sisters (E. and E.)* 266
Here is the copse, the *f* and—a Cross! — *Sir J. Oldcastle* 127
f pour'd From darkness into daylight, — *Ancient Sage* 7
She finds the *f* where they wail'd 'Mirage'! — " 77
Send the drain into the *f*, — *Locksley H., Sixty* 144
shedding poison in the *f's* of the Will. — " 274
The *f* pulses high in sunnier jets, — *Prog. of Spring* 54
WHAT be those crown'd forms high over the sacred *f*? — *Parnassus* 1
What be those two shapes high over the sacred *f*, — " 9
Dance in a *f* of flame with her devils, — *Kapiolani* 10

Fountain'd See **Many-fountain'd**

Fountain-fed *f-f* Ammonian Oasis in the waste. — *Alexander* 7

Fountain-flood sonorous flow Of spouted *f-f's*. — *Palace of Art* 28

Fountain-foam dragons spouted forth A flood of *f-f*. — " 24

Fountain-head The murmur of the *f-h*— — *Two Voices* 216
Full-welling *f-h's* of change, — *Palace of Art* 166

Fountain-jets others tost a ball Above the *f-j*, — *Princess ii* 461

Fountain-side sit near Camelot at a *f-s*, — *Balin and Balan* 11
So coming to the *f-s* beheld Balin and Balan — " 23

Fountain-urns Gods at random thrown By *f-u*; — *To E. L.* 16

Four The seven elms, the poplars *f* — *Ode to Memory* 56
F gray walls, and *f* gray towers, — *L. of Shalott i* 15
From those *f* jets *f* currents in one swell — *Palace of Art* 33
From *f* wing'd horses dark against the stars; — *Princess i* 211
Thro' *f* sweet years arose and fell, — *In Mem. xxii* 3
F voices of *f* hamlets round, — " xxviii 5
Each voice *f* changes on the wind, — " 9
'Where wert thou, brother, these *f* days?' — " xxxi 5
And mock their foster-mother on *f* feet, — *Com. of Arthur* 31
And all these *f* be fools, but mighty men, — *Gareth and L.* 643
f strokes they struck With sword — " 1042
yon *f* fools have suck'd their allegory — " 1199
O'er the *f* rivers the first roses blew, — *Geraint and E.* 764
Closed in the *f* walls of a hollow tower, (repeat) — *Merlin and V.* 209, 543
in the *f* loud battles by the shore Of Duglas; — *Lancelot and E.* 289
and strange knights From the *f* winds came in: — *Pelleas and E.* 148
I thought *F* bells instead of one began to ring, *F* merry bells, *f* merry marriage-bells, — *Lover's Tale iii* 20
F galleons drew away From the Spanish fleet — *The Revenge* 46
a single piece Weigh'd nigh *f* thousand Castillanos — *Columbus* 136
An' noän o' my *f* sweet-arts 'ud 'a let me 'a hed my oän waäy, — *Spinster's S's.* 101
upo' *f* short legs ten times fur one upo' two. — *Owd Roä* 16
bird that still is veering there Above his *f* gold letters) — *The Ring* 333

Four-field The *f-f* system, and the price of grain; — *Audley Court* 34

Four-footed no slaves of a *f-f* will? — *The Dawn* 18

Four-handed The *f-h* mole shall scrape, — *My life is full* 12

Four-hundredth In that *f-h* summer after Christ, — *St. Telemachus* 1

Four-in-hand as quaint a *f-i-h* As you shall see— — *Walk. to the Mail* 113

Foursquare build some plan *F* to opposition.' — *Princess v* 231
stood *f* to all the winds that blew! — *Ode on Well.* 39

Four-year-old 'That was the *f-y-o* I sold the Squire.' — *The Brook* 137

Fowl (See also **Night-fowl, Ocean-fowl, Water-fowl**) To scare the *f* from fruit: — *Princess ii* 228
I have seen the cuckoo chased by lesser *f*, — *Com. of Arthur* 167
all the little *f* were flurried at it, — *Gareth and L.* 69
and horrible *f's* of the air, — *Rizpah* 39

Fowt (fought) An' once I *f* wi' the Taäilor— feller to fight wi' an' *f* it out. — *North. Cobbler* 21
— " 100
'e'd fight wi' a will when 'e *f*; — " *Owd Roä* 7

Fox   whole hill-side was redder than a *f*.   *Walk. to the Mail* 3
   And lighter-footed than the *f*.   *Day-Dm., Arrival* 8
   Then of the latest *f*—where started—   *Aylmer's Field* 253
   Let the *f* bark, let the wolf yell.   *Pelleas and E.* 472
   An' 'e niver runn'd arter the *f*,   *Village Wife* 41

Foxglove   The *f* cluster dappled bells.'   *Two Voices* 72
   Bring orchis, bring the *f* spire,   *In Mem. lxxxiii* 9
   snowlike sparkle of a cloth On fern and *f*.   *Sisters (E. and E.)* 118

Foxlike   Or *f* in the vine;   *Princess vii* 203

Foxy   Modred's narrow *f* face,   *Guinevere* 63

Fraction   Some niggard *f* of an hour,   *Aylmer's Field* 450
   For every splinter'd *f* of a sect Will clamour   *Akbar's Dream* 33

Fragile   pressure thrice as sweet As woodbine's *f* hold,   *Talking Oak* 146
   The *f* bindweed-bells and briony rings;   *The Brook* 203

Fragment   leaning on *f* twined with vine,   *Œnone* 20
   Among the *f*'s tumbled from the glens,   " 222
   But *f*'s of her mighty voice Came   *Of old sat Freedom* 7
   The silver *f*'s of a broken voice,   *Gardener's D.* 234
   cram him with the *f*'s of the grave,   *Princess iii* 311
   Among the *f*'s of the golden day.   *Maud I xviii* 70
   He heard but *f*'s of her later words,   *Marr. of Geraint* 113
   Among the tumbled *f*'s of the hills.'   *Lancelot and E.* 1427
   Where *f*'s of forgotten peoples dwelt,   *Pass. of Arthur* 84
   And all the *f*'s of the living rock   *Lover's Tale ii* 44
   Spurning a shatter'd *f* of the God,   *St. Telemachus* 16

Fragrance   girt With song and flame and *f*,   *Lucretius* 134
   f and the green Of the dead spring: *Lover's Tale i* 723

Fragrant   (*See also* **All-fragrant, Blossom-fragrant**)
   drove The *f*, glistening deeps,   *Arabian Nights* 14
   All round about the *f* marge   " 59
   blinded With many a deep-hued bell-like flower Of *f* trailers,   *Eleänore* 38
   slowly dropping *f* dew.   *Œnone* 106
   mingled with her *f* toil,   *Gardener's D.* 143
   And burn a *f* lamp before my bones,   *St. S. Stylites* 196
   The *f* tresses are not stirr'd That lie   *Day-Dm., Sleep B.* 19
   Yet in a heart remembering His former talks   *Aylmer's Field* 456
   on a tripod in the midst A *f* flame rose,   *Princess iv* 34
   And bats went round in *f* skies,   *In Mem. xcv* 9
   often abroad in the *f* gloom Of foreign churches—   *Maud I xix* 53
   mountain arose like a jewell'd throne thro' the *f* air,   *V. of Maeldune* 59
   Flies back in *f* breezes to display A tunic   *Prog. of Spring* 64
   With many a pendent bell and *f* star,   *Death of Œnone* 13

Frail (adj.)   Thy mortal eyes are *f* to judge of fair,   *Œnone* 158
   nor shrink For fear our solid aim be dissipated By *f* successors.   *Princess iii* 267
   f at first And feeble, all unconscious of itself,   *vii* 116
   O life as futile, then, as *f*!   *In. Mem. lvi* 25
   F, but a work divine,   *Maud II ii* 4
   F, but of force to withstand,   " 24
   The *f* bluebell peereth over Rare broidry   *A Dirge* 37
   Your melancholy sweet and *f* As perfume   *Margaret* 7
   Friends, this *f* bark of ours, when sorely tried,   *Aylmer's Field* 715
   F Life was startled from the tender love   *Lover's Tale i* 616
   And sympathies, how *f*, In sound and smell!   *Early Spring* 35
   F were the works that defended the hold   *Def. of Lucknow* 73
   In his throne's title make him feel so *f*,   *Sir J. Oldcastle* 73

Frail (s)   'Rapt from the fickle and the *f*   *In Mem. xxx* 25

Frailer   the *f* caravel, With what was mine,   *Columbus* 140

Frailty   Why not yet Anchor thy *f* there,   *Supp. Confessions* 124
   Nor human *f* do me wrong.   *In Mem. lii* 8
   Lured by the crimes and *frailties* of the court,   *Guinevere* 136
   Thy *f* counts most real,   *Ancient Sage* 51

Frame (s)   (*See also* **Broidery-frame**)   creeps Thro my veins to all my *f*,   *Eleänore* 131
   A healthy *f*, a quiet mind.'   *Two Voices* 99
   Consolidate in mind and *f*—   " 366
   shafts of flame Were shiver'd in my narrow *f*.   *Fatima* 18
   Pour'd back into my empty soul and *f*   *D. of F. Women* 78
   Dust are our *f*'s; and, gilded dust,   *Aylmer's Field* 1
   Another and another *f* of things   *Lucretius* 42
   The morals, something of the *f*, the rock,   *Princess ii* 382
   woman wed is not as we, But suffers change of *f*.   *v* 463
   A man of well-attemper'd *f*.   *Ode on Well.* 74
   No hint of death in all his *f*,   *In Mem. xiv* 18

Frame (s) (*continued*)   Deep-seated in our mystic *f*.   *In Mem. xxxvi* 2
   As thro' the *f* that binds him in His isolation   " *xlv* 11
   Be near me when the sensuous *f* Is rack'd   " *l* 5
   No—mixt with all this mystic *f*,   " *lxxviii* 18
   new life that feeds thy breath Throughout my *f*,   " *lxxxvi* 11
   That in this blindness of the *f*   " *xciii* 15
   Remade the blood and changed the *f*,   *Con.* 11
   I steal, a wasted *f*, It crosses here,   *Maud II iv* 69
   my inmost *f* Was riven in twain: *Lover's Tale i* 595
   shook me, that my *f* would shudder,   " *ii* 56
   taken Some years before, and falling hid the *f*.   " *iv* 217

Frame (verb)   Vague words! but ah, how hard to *f*   *In Mem. xcv* 45

Framed   Neither modell'd, glazed, nor *f*:   *Vision of Sin* 188

Framework   With royal *f-w* of wrought gold;   *Ode to Memory* 82
   yet with such a *f* scarce could be.   *Princess, Con.* 22
   And all the *f* of the land;   *In Mem. lxxxvii* 24
   speak His music by the *f* and the chord;   *Holy Grail* 879

Framing   (*See also* **Sea-framing**)   *F* the mighty landscape to the west,   *Lover's Tale i* 406

France   Joan of Arc, A light of ancient *F*;   *D. of F. Women* 268
   Rose a ship of *F*.   *The Captain* 28
   That cursed *F* with her egalities!   *Aylmer's Field* 265
   Had golden hopes for *F* and all mankind,   " 464
   ever-murder'd *F*, By shores that darken   " 766
   Imagined more than seen, the skirts of *F*.   *Princess, Con.* 48
   Back to *F* her banded swarms, Back to *F* with countless blows,   *Ode on Well.* 110
   In which we went thro' summer *F*.   *In Mem. lxxi* 4
   The foaming grape of eastern *F*.   " *Con.* 80
   Art with poisonous honey stol'n from *F*,   *To the Queen ii* 56
   Fresh from the surgery-schools of *F*   *In the Child. Hosp.* 3
   appeal Once more to *F* or England;   *Columbus* 58
   Stormy voice of *F*! Who dost not love our England—   *To Victor Hugo* 8
   England, *F*, all man to be Will wake one people   " 10
   F had shown a light to all men,   *Locksley H.," Sixty* 89
   Her fuller *f*—what would that be worth—   *The Fleet* 8

Franchise   Her fuller *f*—what would that be worth—

Francis   (*See also* **Francis Allen**)   *F*, laughing, clapt his hand On Everard's shoulder,   *The Epic* 21
   'But I,' said *F*, 'pick'd the eleventh   " 41
   F, muttering like a man ill-used,   *M. d'Arthur, Ep.* 12
   To *F*, with a basket on his arm, To *F* just alighted from the boat,   *Audley Court* 6
   'With all my heart,' Said *F*.   " 9
   F laid A damask napkin wrought with horse and hound,   " 20

Francis Allen   (*See also* **Francis**)   At *F A*'s on the Christmas-eve,—   *The Epic* 1

Francis Hale   *F H*, The farmer's son,   *Audley Court* 74

Francis of Assisi   Sweet St *F o A*, would that he   *Locksley H., Sixty* 100

Frank   'You know,' said *F*, 'he burnt His Epic,   *The Epic* 27

Frankincense   sweet! spikenard, and balm, and *f*.   *St. S. Stylites* 211

Frantic   *F* love and *f* hate.   *Vision of Sin* 150
   For while the *f* rabble in half-amaze Stared at him dead,   *St. Telemachus* 71

Frater Ave atque Vale   '*F A a V*'—as we wander'd   *Frater Ave, etc.* 7

Fraud   whispers of this monstrous *f*!   *Third of Feb.* 36

Fraught   when *f* With a passion so intense   *Maud II ii* 58

Fray   and fought till I sunder'd the *f*,   *V. of Maeldune* 79
   and threw Underfoot there in the *f*—   *Heavy Brigade* 55

Fray'd   (His dress a suit of *f* magnificence,   *Marr. of Geraint* 296

Free (adj.)   (*See also* **Freeä, Heart-free**)   With mellow preludes, 'We are *f*.'   *The Winds, etc.* 4
   Atween the blossoms, 'We are *f*.'   " 8
   so clear and bold and *f* As you,   *Rosalind* 17
   to have been Joyful and *f* from blame.   *D. of F. Women* 80
   So let the change which comes be *f*   *Love thou thy land* 45
   I am always bound to you, but you are *f*.'   *Enoch Arden* 450
   clothes they gave him and *f* passage home;   " 650
   —*f* of alms her hand—   *Aylmer's Field* 697
   'King, you are *f*! We did but keep you surety for our son,   *Princess v* 24
   Knowledge in our own land make her *f*,   " 419
   yourself and yours shall have *F* adit;   " *vi* 302
   dwarf'd or godlike, bond or *f*:   " *vii* 260
   His foes were thine; he kept us *f*;   *Ode on Well.* 91

Free (adj.) (continued) all too f For such a wise humility — *Ode on Well.* 248
peace, so it be f from pain, — *Grandmother* 97
Survive in spirits render'd f, — *In Mem. xxxviii* 10
Whose jest among his friends is f, — " *lxvi* 10
Ring in the valiant man and f, — " *cvi* 29
I feel so f and so clear By the loss — *Maud I xix* 98
unhooded casting off The goodly falcon; — *Merlin and V.* 131
Flow'd forth a carol f and bold; — *Dying Swan* 30
Whose f delight, from any height of rapid flight, — *Rosalind* 3
Like two streams of incense f — *Eleänore* 58
MINE be the strength of spirit, full and f, — *Mine be the strength* 1
'Where wert thou when thy father play'd In his f field, — *Two Voices* 320
and opposed F hearts, f foreheads— — *Ulysses* 49
Lord of Burleigh, fair and f, — *L. of Burleigh* 58
Set thy hoary fancies f; — *Vision of Sin* 156
That our f press should cease to brawl, — *Third of Feb.* 3
Have left the last f race with naked coasts ! — " 40
presently thereafter follow'd calm, F sky and stars; — *Com. of Arthur* 392
crush'd The Idolaters, and made the people f? Who should be King save him who makes us f?' — *Gareth and L.* 137
'The thrall in person may be f in soul, — " 165
Till ev'n the lonest hold were all as f — " 598
Gareth loosed his bonds and on f feet Set him, — " 817
'I take it as f gift, then,' said the boy. — *Geraint and E.* 222
told F tales, and took the word and play'd upon it, — " 291
When wine and f companions kindled him, — " 293
'My f leave,' he said ; ' Get her to speak : — " 300
But f to stretch his limbs in lawful fight, — " 754
f flashes from a height Above her, — *Lancelot and E.* 647
but f love will not be bound.' ' F love, so bound, were freëst,' said the King. ' Let love be f; f love is for the best: — " 1379
' F love—f field—we love but while we may : (repeat) — *Last Tournament* 275, 281
It frighted all f fool from out thy heart ; — " 307
King Who fain had clipt f manhood from the world— — " 446
tide within Red with f chase and heather-scented air, — " 691
Was not the land as f thro' all her ways — *Lover's Tale i* 662
Bore her free-faced to the f airs of heaven, — " *iv* 38
'Take my f gift, my cousin, for your wife; — " 363
An' coäx'd an' coodled me oop till ageän I feel'd mysen f. — *North. Cobbler* 80
Cold, but as welcome as f airs of heaven — *Sisters (E. and E.)* 197
'What, will she never set her sister f?' — " 218
And God's f air, and hope of better things. — *Sir J. Oldcastle* 10
gave All but f leave for all to work the mines, — *Columbus* 133
when thou sendest thy f soul thro' heaven, — *Ancient Sage* 47
And fling f alms into the beggar's bowl, — " 260
Wild flowers blowing side by side in God's f light and air, — *The Flight* 81
But Moother was f of 'er tongue, — *Owd Roä* 73
they know too that whene'er In our f Hall, — *Akbar's Dream* 55
Till every Soul be f; — *Freedom* 20
Her ancient fame of F— — *The Fleet* 9
With earth is broken, and has left her f, — *The Ring* 476
calls to them ' Set yourselves f !' — *Kapiolani* 3
walking and haunting us yet, and be f? — *The Dawn* 23

Free (s) The starry clearness of the f? — *In Mem. lxxv* 86
How can a despot feel with the F? — *Riflemen form!* 11

Freeä (free) Parson a cooms an' a goäs, an' a says it easy an' f — *N. Farmer, O. S.* 25
an' the F Traäde runn'd i' my 'ead, — *Owd Roä* 54

Freed Well hast thou done ; for all the stream is f, — *Gareth and L.* 1267
the land Was f, and the Queen false, — *Last Tournament* 339
he f himself From wife and child, — *Lover's Tale iv* 379
and f the people Of Hawa-i-ee ! — *Kapiolani* 6

Freedom and make The bounds of i wider yet — *To the Queen* 32
And F rear'd in that august sunrise — *The Poet* 37
pure law, Commeasure perfect f.' — *Œnone* 167
That sober-suited F chose, — *You ask me, why, etc.* 6
F slowly broadens down From precedent to precedent : — " 11

Freedom (continued) And individual f mute ; — *You ask me, why, etc.* 20
OF old sat F on the heights, — *Of old sat Freedom* 1
shout For some blind glimpse of f — *Love and Duty* 6
F, gaily doth she tread ; — *Vision of Sin* 136
Embrace our aims : work out your f. — *Princess ii* 89
for song Is duer unto f, — " *iv* 141
shower the fiery grain Of f broadcast — " *v* 422
bear the yoke, I wish it Gentle as f'— — " *vi* 206
And save the one true seed of f sown — *Ode on Well.* 162
That sober f out of which there springs — " 164
we fought for F from our prime, — *Third of Feb.* 23
A love of f rarely felt, — *In Mem. cix* 13
Of f in her regal seat Of England ; — " 14
white bonds and warm, Dearer than f. — *Pelleas and E.* 354
For f, or the sake of those they loved, — *Sir J. Oldcastle* 186
They kept their faith, their f, — *Montenegro* 2
rough rock-throne Of F ! — " 10
F, free to slay herself, — *Locksley H., Sixty* 128
we gain'd a f known to Europe, — " 129
To this great cause of F drink, my friends, (repeat) — *Hands all Round* 11, 35
Thraldom who walks with the banner of F, — *Vastness* 10
Form in F's name and the Queen's ! — *Riflemen form!* 23

Free-faced Bore her f-f to the free airs — *Lover's Tale iv* 38

Freeing any knight Toward thy sister's f.' — *Gareth and L.* 1018

Freeman It is the land that *freemen* till, — *You ask me, why, etc.* 5
For English natures, *freemen*, friends, — *Love thou thy land* 7
Gallant sons of English *freemen*, — *The Captain* 1
and the Rome of *freemen* holds her place, — *To Virgil* 34
To mark in many a f's home The slave, — *Freedom* 11

Freër leave thee f, till thou wake refresh'd — *Love and Duty* 97
But smit with f light shall slowly melt — *Golden Year* 33
tyrant's cruel glee Forces on the f hour. — *Vision of Sin* 130
noble thought be f under the sun, — *Maud III vi* 48

Free-spoken or being one Of our f-s Table — *Pelleas and E.* 526

Freëst ' Free love, so bound, were f,' — *Lancelot and E.* 1380

Freewill joy I had in my f All cold, — *Supp. Confessions* 16

Freeze eighty winters f with one rebuke — *Ode on Well.* 186
tears that at their fountain f; — *In Mem. xx* 12
tho' every pulse would f, — *The Flight* 53
Death will f the supplest limbs— — *Happy* 46

Freezing here he stays upon a f orb — *Lucretius* 139
The f reason's colder part, — *In Mem. cxxiv* 14
I took And chafed the f hand. — *The Ring* 452

Freight lovely f Of overflowing blooms, — *Ode to Memory* 16
And, thy dark f, a vanish'd life. — *In Mem. x* 8

French We love not this F God, the child of Hell, — *Third of Feb.* 7
F of the F, and Lord of human tears ; — *To Victor Hugo* 3

Frenchman Not sting the fiery F into war. — *Third of Feb.* 4

Frenzied See **Half-frenzied**

Frequence Not in this f can I lend full tongue, — *Princess iv* 442
Staled by f, shrunk by usage — *Locksley H., Sixty* 76

Frequent (adj.) So f on its hinge before. — *Deserted House* 8
I was f with him in my youth, — *Gareth and L.* 124
Where from the f bridge, — *Ode to Memory* 102
And f interchange of foul and fair, — *Enoch Arden* 533
A f haunt of Edith, on low knolls — *Aylmer's Field* 148
she With f smile and nod departing found, — *Marr. of Geraint* 515

Frequent (verb) Sometimes I f the Christian cloister, — *Akbar's D., Inscrip.* 5

Fresh (See also **Dewy-fresh**, **Frish**, **Sparkling-fresh**)
Keeps his blue waters f for many a mile. — *Mine be the strength* 8
Aphroditè beautiful, F as the foam, — *Œnone* 175
All the valley, mother, 'ill be f — *May Queen* 37
How f the meadows look Above the river, — *Walk. to the Mail* 1
I have seen some score of those F faces, — *Talking Oak* 50
flit To make the greensward f, — " 90
Oh, nature first was f to men, — *Amphion* 57
moon Smote by the f beam of the springing east; — *M. d'Arthur* 214
My sweet, wild, f three quarters of a year, — *Edwin Morris* 2
She seems a part of those f days to me; — " 142
her f and innocent eyes Had such a star — *Aylmer's Field* 691
What drives about the f Cascinè, — *The Daisy* 43
her brother comes, like a blight On my f hope, — *Maud I xix* 103
take my charger, f, Not to be spurr'd, — *Gareth and L.* 1300
and fetch F victual for these mowers of our Earl; — *Geraint and E.* 225

I

Fresh (*continued*)   men may fear *F* fire and ruin.   *Geraint and E.* 823
my *f* but fixt resolve To pass away   *Holy Grail* 737
moon Smote by the *f* beam of the springing east ;   *Pass. of Arthur* 382
evermore *F* springing from her fountains in the brain,   *Lover's Tale* i 83
and blew *F* fire into the sun,   ,,   319
an' es clean Es a shillin' *f* fro' the mint   *Spinster's S's.* 76
While yet thy *f* and virgin soul   *Freedom* 2
There no one came, the turf was *f*,   *Prog. of Spring* 72
flowers To work old laws of Love to *f* results,   ,,   85
That his *f* life may close as it began,   ,,   89
How *f* was every sight and sound   *The Voyage* 5
So *f* they rose in shadow'd swells   *The Letters* 46
F from the burial of her little one,   *Enoch Arden* 281
'Too happy, *f* and fair, Too *f*   *The Brook* 217
Lady Psyche will harangue The *f* arrivals of the week   *Princess* ii 96
F as the first beam glittering on a sail,   ,,   iv 44
So sad, so *f*, the days that are no more.   ,,   48
f young captains flash'd their glittering teeth,   ,,   v 20
When all our path was *f* with dew,   *In Mem.* lxviii 6
And show'd him in the fountain *f*   ,,   lxxv 26
If not so *f*, with love as true,   ,,   101
pleased him, *f* from brawling courts   ,,   lxxxix 11
from the garden and the wild A *f* association blow,   ,,   ci 18
daily fronted him In some *f* splendour ;   *Marr. of Geraint* 14
my child, how *f* the colours look,   ,,   680
this cut is *f* ; That ten years back ;   *Lancelot and E.* 21
Tommy's faäce be as *f* as a codlin   *North. Cobbler* 110
Making *f* and fair All the bowers and the flowers,   *Sisters (E. and E.)* 9

Freshen   They *f* the silvery-crimson shells,   *Sea-Fairies* 13
They *f* and sweeten the wards   *In the Child. Hosp.* 38

Fresher   And flood a *f* throat with song.   *In Mem.* lxxxiii 16
Bright Phosphor, *f* for the night,   ,,   cxxi 9
She from her bier, as into *f* life,   *Lover's Tale* iii 42

Freshest   a truth Looks *f* in the fashion of the day :   *The Epic* 32

Freshlier   And gathering *f* overhead,   *In Mem.* xcv 57

Freshly-flower'd   and lay Upon the *f-f* slope.   *Miller's D.* 112

Freshmen   Everard's college fame When we were *F*:   *The Epic* 47

Freshness   The unsunn'd *f* of my strength,   *Supp. Confessions* 140
increased With *f* in the dawning east.   *Two Voices* 405
Delighted with the *f* and the sound.   *Edwin Morris* 99
Yet so did I let my *f* die.   *Maud* I xix 11
immortality Of thought, and *f* ever self-renew'd.   *Lover's Tale* i 106

Fresh-wash'd   *f-w* in coolest dew The maiden splendours   *D. of F. Women* 54

Fresh-water   *F-w* springs come up through bitter brine.   *If I were loved* 8

Fret (s)   busy *f* Of that sharp-headed worm   *Supp. Confessions* 185
Love is hurt with jar and *f*.   *Miller's D.* 209
(all *f's* But chafing me on fire to find   *Princess* i 165

Fret (verb)   rib and *f* The broad-imbased beach,   *Supp. Confessions* 127
You should not *f* for me, mother,   *May Queen, N. Y's. E.* 36
say to Robin a kind word, and tell him not to *f*;   ,, Con. 45
The changing market *f's* or charms   *Ancient Sage* 140
To *f* the summer jenneting.   *The Blackbird* 12
We *f*, we fume, would shift our skins,   *Will Water.* 225
With many a curve my banks I *f*   *The Brook* 43
'So *f* not, like an idle girl,   *In Mem.* lii 13
Is that a matter to make me *f* ?   *Maud* I xiii 2
'*F* not yourself, dear brother,   *Lancelot and E.* 1074

Fretful   *f* as the wind Pent in a crevice :   *Princess* iii 80
common sense of most shall hold a *f* realm in awe,   *Locksley Hall* 129

Fretted (adj.)   By Bagdat's shrines of *f* gold,   *Arabian Nights* 7
And, with dim *f* foreheads all,   *Palace of Art* 242

Fretted (verb)   Have *f* all to dust and bitterness.'   *Princess* vi 264

Fretteth   *F* thine enshrouded form.   *A Dirge* 10

Fretwork   holds a stately *f* to the Sun,   *Princess* vi 86

Friar   For I am emptier than a *f's* brains ;   *Sir J. Oldcastle* 7
at Pardoners, Summoners, *F's*, absolution-sellers,   ,,   93
God willing, to outlearn the filthy *f*.   ,,   118
poor man's money gone to fat the *f*.   ,,   150
F's, bellringers, Parish-clerks—   ,,   160
Two *f's* crying that if Spain should oust   *Columbus* 96

Friday   Whose *F* fare was Enoch's ministering.   *Enoch Arden* 100
we sail'd on a *F* morn—   *V. of Maeldune* 7

Friend   (*See also* **Bosom-friend, Frind, Sea-friend**)
our *f's* are all forsaking The wine   *All Things will Die* 18

Friend (*continued*)   CLEAR-HEADED *f*, whose joyful scorn,   *Clear-headed friend* 1
My *f*, with you to live alone,   *Ode to Memory* 119
So, *f*, when first I look'd upon your face,   *Sonnet To* ——— 9
painting some dead *f* from memory ?   *Wan Sculptor* 4
'He seems to hear a Heavenly *F*,   *Two Voices* 295
f's to man, Living together under the same roof,   *To* —— *With Pal. of Art* 11
Prythee, *f*, Where is Mark Antony ?   *D. of F. Women* 139
He gave me a *f*, and a true true-love,   *D. of the O. Year* 13
He was a *f* to me.   ,,   23
The night is starry and cold, my *f*, And the New-Year blithe and bold, my *f*,   ,,   34
Alack ! our *f* is gone.   ,,   47
There's a new foot on the floor, my *f*, And a new face at the door, my *f*,   ,,   52
he too was a *f* to me : Both are my *f's*,   *To J. S.* 61
The land, where girt with *f's* or foes   *You ask me, why, etc.* 7
English natures, freemen, *f's*,   *Love thou thy land* 7
Both for themselves and those who call them *f* ?   *M. d'Arthur* 253
who lived across the bay, My *f*;   *Audley Court* 76
'*F* Edwin, do not think yourself alone   *Edwin Morris* 77
Sets out, and meets a *f* who hails   *Walk. to the Mail* 93
my *f*, the days were brief Whereof the poets talk,   *Talking Oak* 185
Come, my *f's*, 'Tis not too late to seek   *Ulysses* 56
In Art like Nature, dearest *f*,   *Day-Dm., Moral* 1
To fall asleep with all one's *f's*;   ,, *L'Envoi* 4
She told me all her *f's* had said ;   *The Letters* 25
Thro' troops of unrecording *f's*,   *You might have won* 7
naming those, his *f's*, for whom they were :   *The Brook* 131
'Good,' said his *f*, 'but watch !'   *Aylmer's Field* 275
The man was his, had been his father's, *f*:   ,,   344
his nearer *f* would say 'Screw not the chord   ,,   468
F's, I was bid to speak of such a one   ,,   677
F's, this frail bark of ours,   ,,   715
their guest, their host, their ancient *f*,   ,,   790
'My dearest *f*, Have faith, have faith !'   *Sea Dreams* 156
I found a hard *f* in his loose accounts,   ,,   162
he that wrongs his *f* Wrongs himself   ,,   172
closed by those who mourn a *f* in vain,   *Lucretius* 142
and lady *f's* From neighbour seats :   *Princess, Pro.* 97
They rode ; they betted ; made a hundred *f's*,   ,,   163
Cyril and with Florian, my two *f's*,   ,,   i 52
Went forth again with both my *f's*.   ,,   167
always *f's*, none closer, elm and vine :   ,,   ii 337
'O *f*, we trust that you esteem'd us not   ,,   iii 198
brings our *f's* up from the underworld,   ,,   iv 45
Nor found my *f's* ; but push'd alone on foot   ,,   196
Then came your new *f*: you began to change—   ,,   298
I your old *f* and tried, she new in all ?   ,,   318
'Her,' she said, 'my *f*—Parted from her—   ,,   v 75
—and ours shall see us *f*.   ,,   228
Truest *f* and noblest foe ;   ,,   vi 7
a world Of traitorous *f* and broken system   ,,   195
'We two were *f's*: I go to mine own land   ,,   216
had you got a *f* of your own age,   ,,   251
glittering drops on her sad *f*.   ,,   283
be *f's*, like children, being chid !   ,,   289
Whatever man lies wounded, *f* or foe,   ,,   336
O my *f*, I will not have thee die !   ,,   vii 8
hears his burial talk'd of by his *f's*,   ,,   152
'Look there, a garden !' said my college *f*,   ,, Con. 49
O *f's*, our chief state-oracle is mute: *Ode on Well.* 23
amoighty's a taäkin o' you to 'issén, my *f*,' (repeat)   *N. Farmer, O. S.* 10, 26
Thunder 'Anathema,' *f*, at you ;   *To F. D. Maurice* 8
One writes, that 'Other *f's* remain,'   *In Mem.* vi 1
And unto me no second *f*.   ,,   44
My *f*, the brother of my love ;   ,,   ix 16
saying ; 'Comes he thus, my *f* ?   ,,   xii 13
And flash at once, my *f*, to thee.   ,,   xli 12
Methinks my *f* is richly shrined ;   ,,   lvii 7
'Does my old *f* remember me ?'   ,,   lxiv 28
Since we deserved the name of *f's*,   ,,   lxv 9
Whose jest among his *f's* is free,   ,,   lxvi 1

Fright (s) and died Of *f* in far apartments. — *Princess vi 371*
dead weight trail'd, by a whisper'd *f*, — *Maud I i 14*
F's to my heart; but stay: — *Gareth and L. 90*
call'd him dear protector in her *f*, Nor yet forgot her practice in her *f*, — *Merlin and V. 946*
and the bitter frost and the *f*? — *Rizpah 18*
till 'e'd gotten a *f* at last, — *Village Wife 61*
harass'd by the *f*'s Of my first crew, — *Columbus 67*
she had torn the ring In *f*, — *The Ring 471*
F and foul dissembling, — *Forlorn 32*

Frighted (verb) breed with him, can *f* my faith. — *In Mem. lxxxii 4*

Frighted (*See also* **Half-frighted**) Queen had added Get thee hence,' Fled *f*. — *Guinevere 367*
My *f* Wiclif-preacher whom I crost In flying hither? — *Sir J. Oldcastle 38*
half amazed half *f* all his flock : — *Aylmer's Field 631*
f all free fool from out thy heart; — *Last Tournament 307*
the sight of this So *f* our good friend, — *Lover's Tale iv 383*
I am *f* at life not death.' — *Despair 14*

Frighten'd *See* **Half-frighten'd**

Frightful the bells Lapsed into *f* stillness; — *Lover's Tale iii 30*

Frill door Of his house in a rainbow *f*? — *Maud II ii 17*

Frind (friend) But shure we wor betther *f*'s — *Tomorrow 41*
An' her nabours an' *f*'s 'ud consowl — " *47*
dhry eye thin but was wet for the *f*'s — " *83*

Frindly an' she gev him a *f* nod, — " *58*

Fringe (*See also* **Under-fringe**) Burnt like a *f* of fire. — *Palace of Art 48*
Torn from the *f* of spray. — *D. of F. Women 400*
beard Was tagg'd with icy *f*'s in the moon, — *St. S. Stylites 32*
From *f*'s of the faded eve, — *Move eastward 3*
Upon the skirt and *f* of our fair land, — *Princess v 219*
daisy close Her crimson *f*'s to the shower; — *In Mem. lxxii 12*
f Of that great breaker, sweeping up the strand, — *Com. of Arthur 386*
from the *f* of coppice round them burst — *Balin and Balan 46*
and the narrow *f* Of curving beach— — *Lover's Tale i 38*
we kiss'd the *f* of his beard. — *V. of Maeldune 125*

Fringed (adj. and part.) (*See also* **Gold-fringed, Ray-fringed, Sun-fringed**) hollows of the *f* hills In summer heats, — *Supp. Confessions 153*
A looming bastion *f* with fire. — *In Mem. xv 20*
Pallas flung her *f* ægis. — *Achilles over the T. 4*

Fringed (verb) the knightly growth that *f* his lips. — *M. d'Arthur 220*
the knightly growth that *f* his lips. — *Pass. of Arthur 388*

Frish (fresh) But a *f* gineration had riz, — *Tomorrow 75*

Frith o'er the *f*'s that branch and spread — *In Mem., Con. 115*

Frock Or the *f* and gipsy bonnet — *Maud I xx 19*

Frog When did a *f* coarser croak — *Trans. of Homer 4*

Frolic (adj.) My *f* falcon, with bright eyes, — *Rosalind 2*
in a fit of *f* mirth She strove to span my waist : — *Talking Oak 137*
with a *f* welcome took The thunder and the sunshine, — *Ulysses 46*

Frolic (s) Cyril, howe'er He deal in *f*, — *Princess iv 250*
fury of peoples, and Christless *f* of kings, — *The Dawn 7*

Frolic (verb) come hither and *f* and play; — *Sea-Fairies 18*

Front (adj.) all at once The *f* rank made a sudden halt; — *Lover's Tale iii 29*

Front (s) (*See also* **Minster-front, Palace-front**) More black than ashbuds in the *f* of March.' — *Gardener's D. 28*
but in *f* The gorges, opening wide apart, — *Œnone 11*
In *f* they bound the sheaves. — *Palace of Art 78*
discern The *f* of Sumner-place. — *Talking Oak 248*
Past thro' the solitary room in *f*, — *Enoch Arden 277*
A *f* of timber-crost antiquity, — " *692*
But huge cathedral *f*'s of every age, — *Sea Dreams 218*
some inscription ran along the *f*, — *Princess i 212*
terrace ranged along the Northern *f*, — " *iii 118*
riders *f* to *f*, until they closed In conflict — " *v 490*
Cannon in *f* of them Volley'd and thunder'd; — *Light Brigade 20*
Betwixt the black *f*'s long-withdrawn — *In Mem. cxix 6*
For *f* to *f* in an hour we stood, — *Maud II i 23*
whereof along the *f*, Some blazon'd, — *Gareth and L. 405*
thicker down the *f* With jewels — *Geraint and E. 689*
Kiss'd the white star upon his noble *f*, — " *757*
in *f* of which Six stately virgins, all in white, — *Lover's Tale ii 76*
in *f* of that ravine Which drowsed in gloom, — *Death of Œnone 75*

Front (verb) And the crag that *f*'s the Even, — *Eleänore 40*
And eastward *f*'s the statue, — *Holy Grail 241*
Henceforward rarely could she *f* in hall, — *Guinevere 62*

Front (verb) (*continued*) Shape your heart to *f* the hour, — *Locksley H., Sixty 106*
I will *f* him face to face. — *Happy 19*
Me they *f* With sullen brows. — *Akbar's Dream 51*

Fronted (*See also* **Fair-fronted**) Philip's dwelling *f* on the street, — *Enoch Arden 731*
when first I *f* him, Said, 'Trust him not;' — *Sea Dreams 70*
daily *f* him In some fresh splendour; — *Marr. of Geraint 13*
We *f* there the learning of all Spain, — *Columbus 41*

Frontier And flying reach'd the *f*: — *Princess i 109*
Hard by your father's *f*: — " *148*

Fronting like a star *F* the dawn he moved; — *Œnone 58*

Frontless Suddenly bawls this *f* kitchen-knave, — *Gareth and L. 860*

Frost There is *f* in your breath — *Poet's Mind 17*
the *f* is on the pane: — *May Queen, N. Y's. E. 13*
sparkled keen with *f* against the hilt: — *M. d'Arthur 55*
Rain, wind, *f*, heat, hail, — *St. S. Stylites 16*
With drenching dews, or stiff with crackling *f*. — " *115*
one wide chasm of time and *f* they gave — *Princess, Pro. 93*
Draw toward the long *f* and longest night, — *A Dedication 11*
The *f* is here, And fuel is dear, — *Window, Winter 1*
And *f* is here And has bitten the heel — " *5*
Bite, *f*, bite! (repeat) — " *7, 13*
That grief hath shaken into *f*! — *In Mem. iv 12*
The streets were black with smoke and *f*, — " *lxix 3*
The yule-log sparkled keen with *f*, — " *lxxviii 5*
'My sudden *f* was sudden gain, — " *lxxxi 10*
New leaf, new life—the days of *f* are o'er: — *Last Tournament 278*
sparkled keen with *f* against the hilt: — *Pass. of Arthur 223*
Hard was the *f* in the field, — *First Quarrel 39*
and the bitter *f* and the fright? — *Rizpah 18*
all the heavens flash'd in *f*; — *To E. Fitzgerald 22*
leaf rejoice in the *f* that sears it at night ; — *The Wreck 20*
'No *f* there,' so he said, — " *80*
Sun-flame or sunless *f*, — *Epilogue 66*
His fingers were so stiffen'd by the *f* — *The Ring 239*
When *f* is keen and days are brief— — *To Ulysses 19*

Frost-bead *f-b* melts upon her golden hair; — *Prog. of Spring 10*

Frost-like And tipt with *f-l* spires. — *Palace of Art 52*

Frosty (*See also* **Purple-frosty**) Make thou my spirit pure and clear As are the *f* skies, — *St. Agnes' Eve 10*
For while our cloisters echo'd *f* feet, — *Princess, Pro. 183*
That glitter burnish'd by the *f* dark; — " *v 261*
Made the noise of *f* woodlands, — *Boädicea 75*
The flying cloud, the *f* light: — *In Mem. cvi 2*
Yet in your *f* cells ye feel the fire! — *Balin and Balan 446*
Thaw once of a *f* night I slither'd — *North. Cobbler 19*

Froth Upon the topmost *f* of thought. — *In Mem. lii 4*

Froth'd He *f* his bumpers to the brim; — *D. of the O. Year 19*
is your spleen *f* out, or have ye more? — *Merlin and V. 767*

Frothfly Sweeping the *f* from the fescue — *Aylmer's Field 530*

Frown (s) who may know Whether smile or *f* be fleeter? Whether smile or *f* be sweeter, — *Madeline 12*
F's perfect-sweet along the brow — " *15*
Thy smile and *f* are not aloof From one another, — " *19*
black brows drops down A sudden-curved *f*. (repeat) — " *35, 47*
other *f*'s than those That knit themselves — *Aylmer's Field 723*
He had darken'd into a *f*, — *Maud I xix 62*
Fortune, turn thy wheel with smile or *f*; — *Marr. of Geraint 350*
Met his full *f* timidly firm, and said; — *Geraint and E. 71*

Frown (verb) *F* and we smile, the lords of our own hands; — *Marr. of Geraint 354*
sweet eyes *f*: the lips Seem but a gash. — *Sisters (E. and E.) 106*

Frown'd The seldom-frowning King *f*, — *Lancelot and E. 715*
and you took them tho' you *f*; You *f* and yet you kiss'd them. — *Happy 74*

Frowning (*See also* **Seldom-frowning**) Smiling, *f*, evermore, (repeat) — *Madeline 8, 25*
Florian nodded at him, I *f*; — *Princess iv 160*
Vivien, *f* in true anger, said: — *Merlin and V. 691*
Vivien answer'd *f* wrathfully: — " *704*
Vivien answer'd *f* yet in wrath: — " *768*
With smiling face and *f* heart, — *Lancelot and E. 553*

Froze with surprise *F* my swift speech: — *D. of F. Women 90*
To me you *f*: this was my meed for all. — *Princess iv 302*

Froze (*continued*) how it *f* you from your bride, *Happy* 71
Frozen Till her blood was *f* slowly, *L. of Shalott iv* 30
  Hollow smile and *f* sneer Come not here. *Poet's Mind* 10
  Be fix'd and *f* to permanence: *Two Voices* 237
  My *f* heart began to beat, " 422
  Caught in the *f* palms of Spring. *The Blackbird* 24
  Larger than human on the *f* hills. *M. d'Arthur* 183
  That longs to burst a *f* bud *In Mem. lxxxiii* 15
  Larger than human on the *f* hills. *Pass. of Arthur* 351
  These be no rubies, this is *f* blood, *Last Tournament* 413
  and stood Stiff as a viper *f*; *Merlin and V.* 845
  the placid lip *F* by sweet sleep, *Pelleas and E.* 433
  like a creature *f* to the heart *Death of Œnone* 73
Frugal *f*, savage, arm'd by day and night *Montenegro* 3
Fruit (*See also* **First-fruits**) shoots Of orient green
  giving safe pledge of *f*'s, *Ode to Memory* 18
  Disclosed a *f* of pure Hesperian gold, *Œnone* 66
  Behold this *f*, whose gleaming rind ingrav'n " 72
  Paris held the costly *f* Out at arm's-length, " 135
  cast the golden *f* upon the board, " 226
  enchanted stem, Laden with flower and *f*. *Lotos-Eaters* 29
  ere my flower to *f* Changed, I was ripe for death. *D. of F. Women* 207
  f's and cream Served in the weeping elm; *Gardener's D.* 194
  we stole his *f*, His hens, his eggs; *Walk. to the Mail* 84
  bring me offerings of *f* and flowers: *St. S. Stylites* 128
  This *f* of thine by Love is blest, *Talking Oak* 249
  Where fairer *f* of Love may rest " 251
  flower of knowledge changed to *f* Of wisdom. *Love and Duty* 24
  and *f*'s, and spices, clear of toll, *Golden Year* 45
  cherish that sweet but bitter *f*? *Locksley Hall* 65
  With naked limbs and flowers and *f*, But we nor
  paused for *f* nor flowers. *The Voyage* 55
  Gifts by the children, garden-herbs and *f*, *Enoch Arden* 338
  Divides threefold to show the *f* within. (repeat) *The Brook* 73, 208
  The red *f* of an old idolatry— *Aylmer's Field* 762
  babies roll'd about Like tumbled *f* *Princess, Pro.* 83
  falling in a land Of promise; *f* would follow. " *ii* 140
  To scare the fowl from *f*: " 228
  F, blossom, viand, amber wine, " *iv* 35
  breadth Of Autumn, dropping *f*'s " *vi* 55
  And gathering all the *f*'s of earth *Ode Inter. Exhib.* 41
  Wearing his wisdom lightly, like the *f* *A Dedication* 12
  A life that bears immortal *f* *In Mem. xl* 18
  I'll rather take what *f* may be " *cviii* 13
  Of what in them is flower and *f*; " *Con.* 136
  It is only flowers, they had no *f*'s, *Maud II v* 77
  little pitted speck in garner'd *f*, *Merlin and V.* 394
  sure I think this *f* is hung too high *Lancelot and E.* 774
  your flower Waits to be solid *f* *Last Tournament* 100
  the red *f* Grown on a magic oak-tree " 744
  manners are not idle, but the *f* Of loyal nature, *Guinevere* 335
  said the maid, 'be manners such fair *f*? " 337
  no leaf, no flower, no *f* for me. *Lover's Tale i* 725
  promise of blossom, but never a *f*! *V. of Maeldune* 51
  And we came to the Isle of *F*'s " 55
  in every berry and *f* was the poisonous pleasure " 62
  giddy besides with the *f*'s we had gorged, " 75
  Was flinging *f* to lions; *Tiresias* 67
  earthly flower would be heavenly *f*— *Despair* 35
  She tastes the *f* before the blossom falls, *Ancient Sage* 75
  The kernel of the shrivell'd *f* " 121
  climbing toward her with the golden *f*, *Death of Œnone* 15
  'Mine is the one *f* Alla made for man.' *Akbar's Dream* 40
  heats our earth to yield us grain and *f*, " 105
Fruitage *f* golden-rinded On golden salvers, *Eleänore* 33
  Soft *f*, mighty nuts, and nourishing roots; *Enoch Arden* 555
Fruit-bunches rich *f-b* leaning on each other— *Isabel* 37
Fruited *See* **Heavy-fruited**
Fruitful like the arrow-seeds of the field flower, The
  f wit Cleaving, *The Poet* 20
  F of further thought and deed, *Two Voices* 144
  close to thine in that quick-falling dew Of *f* kisses, *Œnone* 205
  Fast-rooted in the *f* soil. *Lotos-Eaters, C. S.* 38
  I keep smooth plats of *f* ground, *The Blackbird* 3
  When the centuries behind me like a *f* land reposed; *Locksley Hall* 13

Fruitful (*continued*) With *f* cloud and living smoke, *In Mem. xxxix* 3
  The *f* hours of still increase; " *xlvi* 10
  To *f* strifes and rivalries of peace— *Ded. of Idylls* 38
Fruitless Which else were *f* of their due, *In Mem. xlv* 14
  Is shrivell'd in a *f* fire, " *liv* 11
  Who built him fanes of *f* prayer, " *lvi* 12
  'Wherefore grieve Thy brethren with a *f* tear? " *lviii* 10
  glancing from his height On earth a *f* fallow, *Demeter and P.* 118
  Gods Avenge on stony hearts a *f* prayer For pity. *Death of Œnone* 41
Frustration out of long *f* of her care, *Princess vii* 101
Fuel Secret wrath like smother'd *f* Burnt *The Captain* 15
  The frost is here, and *f* is dear, *Window, Winter* 2
  The *f* is all the dearer, " 15
Fuel-smother'd And from it like a *f-s* fire, *Gareth and L.* 684
Fulfil *F*'s him with beatitude. *Supp. Confessions* 62
  God *f*'s himself in many ways, *M. d'Arthur* 241
  discerning to *f* This labour, *Ulysses* 35
  I would but ask you to *f* yourself: *Princess vii* 146
  each *f*'s Defect in each, " 303
  To strive, to fashion, to *f*— *In Mem. cxiii* 7
  F the boundless purpose of their King!' *Com. of Arthur* 475
  God *f*'s himself in many ways, *Pass. of Arthur* 409
Fulfill'd By its own energy *f* itself, *Gardener's D.* 238
  For daily hope *f*, to rise again *Edwin Morris* 38
  My father 'that our compact be *f*: *Princess v* 115
  King was all *f* with gratefulness, *Last Tournament* 593
  delightedly *f* All lovingkindness, *Lover's Tale i* 224
Fulfillest thou *f* thy doom Making him broken gleams, *High. Pantheism* 9
Fulfilling *See* **Still-fulfilling**
Fulfilment to rise again Revolving toward *f*, *Edwin Morris* 39
Full so *f* and deep In thy large eyes, *Eleänore* 85
  and slowly grow To a *f* face, " 92
  So *f*, so deep, so slow, " 95
  Since in his absence *f* of light and joy, *Lover's Tale i* 425
  that strove to rise From my *f* heart. " 712
  It was *f* of old odds an' ends, *First Quarrel* 49
  and the *f* moon stares at the snow. *Rizpah* 4
  'F of compassion and mercy—(repeat) *Rizpah* 62, 63
  My brain is *f* of the crash of wrecks, *The Wreck* 3
  I fun thy pockets as *f* o' my pippins *Church-warden, etc.* 34
  Too *f* for sound and foam, *Crossing the Bar* 6
  And yet, tho' its voice be so clear and *f*, *Poet's Mind* 34
  The warble was low, and *f* and clear; *Dying Swan* 24
  Thy rose-lips and *f* blue eyes *Adeline* 7
  My life is *f* of weary days, *My life is full* 1
  MINE be the strength of spirit, *f* and free, *Mine be the strength* 1
  But my *f* heart, that work'd below, *Two Voices* 44
  Flood with *f* daylight glebe and town? " 87
  They met with two so *f* and bright— *Miller's D.* 86
  While those *f* chestnuts whisper by. " 168
  My eyes are *f* of tears, my heart of love, *Œnone* 31
  her *f* and earnest eye Over her snow-cold breast " 141
  Her slow *f* words sank thro' the silence drear, *D. of F. Women* 121
  He was *f* of joke and jest, *D. of the O. Year* 28
  on one Lay a great water, and the moon was *f*. *M. d'Arthur* 12
  But the *f* day dwelt on her brows, and sunn'd *Gardener's D.* 136
  You know there has not been for these five years So *f* a
  harvest: *Dora* 66
  that when his heart is glad Of the *f* harvest, " 69
  To some *f* music rose and sank the sun, And some
  f music seem'd to move and change *Edwin Morris* 34
  Sneeze out a *f* God-bless-you right and left? " 80
  On the coals I lay, A vessel *f* of sin: *St. S. Stylites* 170
  The *f* south-breeze around thee blow *Talking Oak* 271
  when the first low matin-chirp hath grown *F* quire, *Love and Duty* 99
  amid Her *f* black ringlets downward roll'd, *Day-Dm., Sleep. B.* 12
  barren commonplaces break In *f* and kindly blossom. *Will Water.* 24
  F cold my greeting was and dry; *The Letters* 13
  and made himself *F* sailor; *Enoch Arden* 54
  Out of *f* heart and boundless gratitude " 346
  his *f* tide of youth Broke with a phosphorescence *Aylmer's Field* 115
  with all my heart, With my *f* heart: *Princess i* 127
  and watch A *f* sea glazed with muffled moonlight, " 248
  that *f* voice which circles round the grave, " *ii* 45
  'Alas your Highness breathes *f* East,' " *iii* 231

Full (continued) Not in this frequence can I lend *f* tongue, *Princess iv* 442
and meek Seem'd the *f* lips, „ *vii* 226
The two-cell'd heart beating, with one *f* stroke, „ 307
Not perfect, nay, but *f* of tender wants, „ 319
UPLIFT a thousand voices *f* and sweet, *Ode Inter. Exhib.* 1
Spread thy *f* wings, and waft him o'er. *In Mem. ix* 4
sigh The *f* new life that feeds thy breath „ *lxxxvi* 10
But when the heart is *f* of din, „ *xciv* 13
And if the song were *f* of care, „ *cxxv* 9
underlip, you may call it a little too ripe, too *f*, *Maud I ii* 9
love of a peace that was *f* of wrongs and shames, „ *III vi* 40
Fixing *f* eyes of question on her face, *Com. of Arthur* 312
gathering half the deep And *f* of voices, „ 381
Albeit neither loved with that *f* love *Gareth and L.* 83
your *f* leave to go. „ 134
When waken'd by the wind which with *f* voice „ 176
This railer, that hath mock'd thee in *f* hall— „ 369
The wood is nigh as *f* of thieves as leaves: „ 789
'*F* pardon, but I follow up the quest, „ 886
the stream, *F*, narrow; „ 908
knave that doth thee service as *f* knight „ 1016
so will my knight-knave Miss the *f* flower „ 1297
Met his *f* frown timidly firm, and said; *Geraint and E.* 71
The whole wood-world is one *f* peal of praise. *Balin and Balan* 450
for this *f* love of mine Without the *f* heart *Merlin and V.* 533
that *f* heart of yours Whereof ye prattle, „ 548
He is so *f* of lustihood, he will ride, *Lancelot and E.* 203
then turn'd the tongueless man From the half-face
  to the *f* eye, „ 1262
with *f* affection said, 'Lancelot, my Lancelot, „ 1355
let us meet The morrow morn once more in one *f* field *Holy Grail* 323
That kept the entry, and the moon was *f*. „ 818
My tower is *f* of harlots, like his court, *Last Tournament* 81
free chase and heather-scented air, Pulsing *f* man; „ 692
So then, when both were brought to *f* accord, „ 722
crying with *f* voice 'Traitor, come out, *Guinevere* 105
land was *f* of signs And wonders „ 232
for all the land was *f* of life. „ 259
on one Lay a great water, and the moon was *f*. *Pass. of Arthur* 180
when the *f* city peal'd Thee and thy Prince! *To the Queen ii* 26
and tho' I loiter'd there The *f* day after, *Sisters (E. and E.)* 98
Grew after marriage to *f* height and form? „ 171
Love and Honour join'd to raise the *f* High-tide „ 177
Back to that passionate answer of *f* heart „ 259
golden guess Is morning-star to the *f* round of truth. *Columbus* 44
then full-current thro' *f* man: *De Prof., Two G.* 22
Yield thee *f* thanks for thy *f* courtesy *To Victor Hugo* 13
I can hear Too plainly what *f* tides of onset *Tiresias* 91
that *f* light Of friendship! „ 202
One *f* voice of allegiance, *On Jub. Q. Victoria* 22
would flower into *f* health Among our heath *The Ring* 317
Not less would yield *f* thanks to you *To Ulysses* 33
Whose Faith and Work were bells of *f* accord, *In Mem., W. G. Ward* 2
And borne along by that *f* stream of men, *St. Telemachus* 43
Full-accomplished hers by right of *f-a* Fate; *Palace of Art* 207
Full-arm'd *F-a* upon his charger all day *Pelleas and E.* 216
Full-blown sail'd, *F-b*, before us into rooms *Princess i* 229
Full-brain All the *f-b*, half-brain races, *Locksley H., Sixty* 161
Full-breasted *f-b* swan That, fluting a wild carol *M. d'Arthur* 266
f-b swan That, fluting a wild carol *Pass. of Arthur* 434
Full-busted *f-b* figure-head Stared o'er the ripple *Enoch Arden* 543
Full-cell'd A *f-e* honeycomb of eloquence *Edwin Morris* 26
Full-current then *f-c* thro' full man: *De Prof., Two G.* 22
Fuller More life, and *f*, that I want.' *Two Voices* 399
In the Spring a *f* crimson comes upon the robin's
  breast; *Locksley Hall* 17
A *f* light illumined all, *Day-Dm., Revival* 5
with *f* sound In curves the yellowing river ran, *Sir L. and Q. G.* 14
With *f* profits lead an easier life, *Enoch Arden* 145
and mould The woman to the *f* day.' *Princess iii* 332
So now thy *f* life is in the west, *W. to Marie Alex.* 36
But ring the *f* minstrel in. *In Mem. cvi* 20
For *f* gain of after bliss; „ *cxvii* 4
Till all my blood, a *f* wave, „ *cxxii* 12
they met In twos and threes, or *f* companies, *Marr. of Geraint* 57

Fuller (continued) Her *f* franchise—what would that be
  worth— *The Fleet* 8
Larger and *f*, like the human mind! *Prog. of Spring* 112
When I gits the plaäte *f* o' Soondays *Church-warden, etc.* 40
Fullest his children, ever at its best And *f*; *Lancelot and E.* 337
'Taliessin is our *f* throat of song, *Holy Grail* 300
Full-faced all the *f-f* presence of the Gods *Œnone* 80
F-f above the valley stood the moon; *Lotos-Eaters* 7
glowing *f-f* welcome, she Began to address us, *Princess ii* 183
Full-fair All in a *f-f* manor and a rich, *Gareth and L.* 846
Full-fed a *f-f* river winding slow By herds *Palace of Art* 73
one warm gust, *f-f* with perfume, *Gardener's D.* 113
What dare the *f-f* liars say of me? *Merlin and V.* 692
Full-flowing *f-f* harmony Of thy swan-like stateliness, *Eleänore* 46
f-f river of speech Came down upon my heart. *Œnone* 68
Full-foliaged Rock'd the *f-f* elms, and swung *In Mem. xcv* 58
Full-grown *f-g* O thou, Circled thro' all experiences, *Œnone* 165
suit The *f-g* energies of heaven. *In Mem. xl* 20
Full-handed your Omar drew *F-h* plaudits from our best *To E. Fitzgerald* 38
F-h thunders often have confessed Thy power, *To W. C. Macready* 2
Full-juiced The *f-j* apple, waxing over-mellow, *Lotos-Eaters, C. S.* 33
Full-limb'd those whom God had made *f-l* and tall, *Guinevere* 42
Full-maned the *f-m* horses whirl'd The chariots
  backward, *Achilles over the T.* 24
Fullness (*See also* **Fulness**) But by degrees to
  f wrought, *You ask me, why, etc.* 14
part by part to men reveal'd The *f* of her face— *Of old sat Freedom* 12
Full-orb'd to this present My *f-o* love has waned not. *Lover's Tale i* 734
Full-sail'd How may *f-s* verse express, *Eleänore* 44
and seest me drive Thro' utter dark a *f-s* skiff, *Supp. Confessions* 95
Full-summ'd side by side, *f-s* in all their powers, *Princess vii* 288
Full-summer thro' the field, that shone *F-s*, *Lancelot and E.* 1141
Full-tided at Caerleon the *f-t* Usk, *Geraint and E.* 116
Full-toned swells High over the *f-t* sea: *Sea-Fairies* 15
The nightingale, *f-t* in middle May, *Balin and Balan* 213
Full-tuned break its syllables, to keep My own *f-t*,— *Love and Duty* 40
Full-welling *F-w* fountain-heads of change, *Palace of Art* 166
Fulminated *f* Against the scarlet woman *Sea Dreams* 22
Fulmined She *f* out her scorn of laws Salique *Princess ii* 133
Fulness (*See also* **After-fulness**) Have added *f* to
  the phrase *To Marq. of Dufferin* 11
throng'd my pulses with the *f* of the Spring. *Locksley Hall* 48
The *f* of the pensive mind; *Day-Dm., L'Envoi* 48
Lest of the *f* of my life I leave *Will Water.* 163
the note Had reach'd a thunderous *f*, *Sea Dreams* 214
And weep the *f* from the mind: *In Mem. xx* 6
Fulsome And *f* Pleasure clog him, and drown His heart *Maud I xvi* 4
Affronted with his *f* innocence? *Pelleas and E.* 266
Fulvia You should have clung to *F*'s waist, *D. of F. Women* 259
Fume (s) (*See also* **Incense-fume**) For mockery is
  the *f* of little hearts. *Guinevere* 633
or the *f*'s Of that dark opiate dose you gave me, *Romney's R.* 30
Fume (verb) We fret, we *f*, would shift our skins, *Will Water.* 225
Fuming and near me stood, In *f* sulphur blue and
  green, *Last Tournament* 617
Fun (found) *f* 'um theer a-laäid on 'is faäce *N. Farmer, O. S.* 33
Fur I *f*', when 'er back wur turn'd, *North. Cobbler* 31
Ull be *f*' upo' four short legs *Owd Roä* 16
Then I waäked an' I *f* it was Roäver „ 60
Till I *f* that it warn't not the gaäinist waäy *Church-warden, etc.* 12
I *f* thy pockets as full o' my pippins „ 34
Function plies His *f* of the woodland. *Lucretius* 46
Funeral (adj.) Dark as a *f* scarf from stem to stern, *M. d'Arthur* 194
In sound of *f* or of marriage bells; *Gardener's D.* 36
Dark in its *f* fold. *Ode on Well.* 57
Dark as a *f* scarf from stem to stern, *Pass. of Arthur* 362
tolling of his *f* bell Broke on my Pagan Paradise, *Tiresias* 192
F hearses rolling! *Forlorn* 48
They bore the Cross before you to the chant of *f* hymns. *Happy* 48
And built their shepherd-prince a *f* pile; *Death of Œnone* 63
crying 'Husband!' she leapt upon the *f* pile, „ 105
Find her warrior Stark and dark in his *f* fire. *To Master of B.* 20
Funeral (s) A *f*, with plumes and lights And music, *L. of Shalott ii* 31
the little port Had seldom seen a costlier *f*. *Enoch Arden* 917
Mother weeps At that white *f* of the single life, *Prin. Beatrice* 9

Funeral (s) (*continued*)   toll of *f* in an Angel ear Sounds
   happier   *D. of the Duke of C.* 10
Funereal   at one end of the hall Two great *f* curtains,   *Lover's Tale iv* 214
   And lay on that *f* boat,   *To Marq. of Dufferin* 34
Fur   My father sent ambassadors with *f's*   *Princess i* 42
Furbelow   *See* **Sea-furbelow**
Furious   nature's prideful sparkle in the blood Break
   into *f* flame;   *Geraint and E.* 828
   As after *f* battle turfs the slain On some wild
   down   *Merlin and V.* 657
   they blurt Their *f* formalisms,   *Akbar's Dream* 57
Furiously   *f* Down thro' the bright lawns   *Aylmer's Field* 340
Furl   come hither and *f* your sails,   *Sea-Fairies* 16
   Mariner, mariner, *f* your sails,   „ 21
Furl'd   battle-flags were *f* In the Parliament   *Locksley Hall* 127
   And never sail of ours was *f*,   *The Voyage* 81
Furlough   To yield us farther *f*:'   *Princess iii* 74
Furnace   all the *f* of the light Struck up   *Mariana in the S.* 55
   a heat, As from a seventimes-heated *f*,   *Holy Grail* 843
Furnished   bravely *f* all abroad to fling   *The Poet* 25
Furnitur   O' *f* 'ere i' the 'ouse,   *North. Cobbler* 36
Furr'd   (*See also* **Gay-furr'd**) Tho' smock'd, or *f* and
   purpled,   *Princess iv* 247
Furriner (foreigner)   gawin' to let in *f's* wheät,   *Owd Roä* 45
Furrow   to his mother's calls From the flower'd *f*.   *Supp. Confessions* 160
   sitting well in order smite The sounding *f's*;   *Ulysses* 59
   in the *f* broke the ploughman's head,   *Princess v* 221
   reddening in the *f's* of his chin,   „ *vi* 228
   meteor on, and leaves A shining *f*,   „ *vii* 185
   down in a *f* scathed with flame: *The Victim* 22
   Or in the *f* musing stands;   *In Mem. lxiv* 27
   leaving share in *f* come to see The glories   *Gareth and L.* 243
Furrow-cloven   huddling slant in *f-c* falls   *Princess vii* 207
Furrowing   *f* into light the mounded rack,   *Love and Duty* 100
   Came *f* all the orient into gold.   *Princess iii* 18
   F a giant oak, and javelining With darted spikes   *Merlin and V.* 936
Furrowy   A double hill ran up his *f* forks   *Princess iii* 174
Further   We brook no *f* insult but are gone.'   „ *vi* 342
   at the *f* end Was Ida by the throne,   „ 356
   Not ever to be question'd any more Save on the
   f side;   *Com. of Arthur* 397
   and on the *f* side Arose a silk pavilion,   *Gareth and L.* 909
   For this were shame to do him *f* wrong   „ 954
Furthest   summits slope Beyond the *f* flights of hope,   *Two Voices* 185
   From Camelot in among the faded fields To *f*
   towers;   *Last Tournament* 54
Fury (rage)   (*See also* **Fool-fury**) struck such warbling
   f thro' the words;   *Princess iv* 586
   Had often wrought some *f* on myself,   *Balin and Balan* 62
   'How then? who then? a *f* seized them   *Lancelot and E.* 476
   furies, curses, passionate tears,   *Locksley H., Sixty* 39
   narrower The cage, the more their *f*.   *Akbar's Dream* 51
   remembered what a *f* shook Those pillars   „ 80
   Godless *f* of peoples, and Christless frolic of kings,   *The Dawn* 7
Fury (a deity)   Like to *Furies*, like to Graces,   *Vision of Sin* 41
   numbs the *F's* ringlet-snake, and plucks   *Lucretius* 262
   And Life, a *F* slinging flame.   *In Mem. l* 8
   The household *F* sprinkled with flame   *Maud I xix* 32
   one angel face, And all the *Furies*.   *Sisters (E. and E.)* 159
Furze   (*See also* **Fuzz**) on these dews that drench the *f*,   *In Mem. xi* 6
Furze-cramm'd   *F-c*, and bracken-rooft,   *Last Tournament* 377
Furzy   The *f* prickle fire the dells,   *Two Voices* 71
Fuse   Whose fancy *f's* old and new,   *In Mem. xvi* 18
   They *f* themselves to little spicy baths,   *Prog. of Spring* 33
   power to *f* My myriads into union under one;   *Akbar's Dream* 156
Fused   manhood *f* with female grace   *In Mem. cix* 17
   f together in the tyrannous light—   *Lover's Tale ii* 67
Fusileer   faces of Havelocks good *f's*,   *Def. of Lucknow* 101
Fusillade   better aimed are your flank *f's*—   „ 57
   Hark cannonade, *f*!   „ 95
Fusing   *f* all The skirts of self again,   *In Mem. xlvii* 2
   Of Knowledge *f* class with class,   *Freedom* 17
Fust (first)   then I minded the *f* kiss I gied 'er by
   Thursby thurn;   *North. Cobbler* 45
Futile   O life as *f*, then, as frail!   *In Mem. lvi* 25

Future (adj.)   transfused Thro' *f* time by power of
   thought.   *Love thou thy land* 4
   I think that we Shall never more, at any *f* time,   *M. d'Arthur* 18
   fruit of Love may rest Some happy *f* day.   *Talking Oak* 252
   Some *f* time, if so indeed you will,   *Princess ii* 64
   Perchance upon the *f* man: „ *Con.* 109
   her *f* Lord Was drown'd in passing thro' the ford,   *In Mem. vi* 38
   And leaps into the *f* chance,   „ *cxiv* 7
   I think that we Shall never more, at any *f* time,   *Pass. of Arthur* 186
Future (s)   When I dipt into the *f*,   *Locksley Hall* 15
   For I dipt into the *f*,   „ 119
   this he kept Thro' all his *f*;   *Enoch Arden* 237
   a wind of prophecy Dilating on the *f*;   *Princess ii* 172
   Nemesis Break from a darken'd *f*,   „ *vi* 175
   prescient of whate'er The *F* had in store: *Lover's Tale ii* 133
   And past and *f* mix'd in their being,   *The Ring* 186
   and thence maintain Our darker *f*.   *To one ran down Eng.* 2
   Far as the *F* vaults her skies,   *Mechanophilus* 17
Futurity   the cope Of the half-attain'd *f*,   *Ode to Memory* 33
Fuzz (furze)   Nowt at all but bracken an' *f*,   *N. Farmer, O. S.* 38

G

Gaäinist (nearest)   I fun' that it warn't not the *g*
   waäy to the narra Gaäte,   *Church-warden, etc.* 12
Gaäinsaäy (gainsay)   I weänt *g* it, my lad,   *North. Cobbler* 17
Gaäpin' (gaping)   tha be new to the plaäce—thou'rt *g*—   *Spinster's S's.* 3
Gaäte (gate)   why didn't tha hesp the *g*?   *Village Wife* 124
   an loöok thruf Maddison's *g*!   *Spinster's S's.* 6
   I fun that it warn't not the gaäinist waäy to the
   narra *G*.   *Church-warden, etc.* 12
Gabble   Nothing but idiot *g*!   *Maud II v* 41
Gabbled   She *g*, as she groped in the dead,   *Dead Prophet* 73
   The Baths, the Forum *g* of his death,   *St. Telemachus* 79
Gable   and half A score of *g's*.   *Walk. to the Mail* 14
   overhead Fantastic *g's*, crowding,   *Godiva* 61
Gable-ends   burn'd On the blossom'd *g-e*   *Maud I vi* 9
Gable-wall   held the pear to the *g-w*.   *Mariana* 4
Gabriel   Whose Titan angels, *G*, Abdiel,   *Milton* 5
Gad-fly   sung to, when, this *g-f* brush'd aside,   *Princess v* 414
Gadding   Said the good nuns would check her *g* tongue   *Guinevere* 313
Gaffer   Ran *G*, stumbled Gammer.   *The Goose* 34
Gag   the wholesome boon of gyve and *g*.'   *Gareth and L.* 370
Gagelike   flung defiance down *G* to man,   *Princess v* 178
Gaiety   *G* without eclipse Wearieth me,   *Lilian* 20
Gain (s)   I can but count thee perfect *g*,   *Palace of Art* 198
   But gentle words are always *g*:   *Love thou thy land* 23
   foreheads, vacant of our glorious *g's*,   *Locksley Hall* 175
   his *g's* were dock'd, however small: Small were
   his *g's*, and hard his work;   *Sea Dreams* 7
   His *g* is loss; for he that wrongs his friend   „ 172
   Who, never naming God except for *g*,   „ 188
   Ours the pain, be his the *g*!   *Ode on Well.* 241
   And find in loss a *g* to match?   *In Mem. i* 6
   Or but subserves another's *g*.   „ *liv* 12
   But turns his burthen into *g*.   „ *lxxx* 12
   'My sudden frost was sudden *g*,   „ *lxxxi* 10
   For fuller *g* of after bliss: „ *cxvii* 4
   And lust of *g*, in the spirit of Cain,   *Maud I i* 23
   all for *g* Of glory, and hath added wound   *Lancelot and E.* 566
   allow my pretext, as for *g* Of purer glory.'   „ 586
   that make our griefs our *g's*.   *Sisters (E. and E.)* 231
   The *g* of such large life as match'd   *Ancient Sage* 237
Gain (verb)   And *g* her for my bride.   *Talking Oak* 284
   In hope to *g* upon her flight.   *The Voyage* 60
   man may *g* Letting his own life go.   *Lucretius* 112
   help my prince to *g* His rightful bride,   *Princess iii* 160
   And play the slave to *g* the tyranny,   „ *iv* 132
   He *g* in sweetness and in moral height,   „ *vii* 281
   How *g* in life, as life advances,   *To F. D. Maurice* 39
   g The praise that comes to constancy.'   *In Mem. xxi* 11
   I will walk thro' fire, Mother, to *g* it—   *Gareth and L.* 134
   And glory gain'd, and evermore to *g*.   „ 332

Gain (verb) (*continued*)   I vow'd that could I *g* her, our
fair Queen,   *Marr. of Geraint* 787
she set herself to *g* Him, the most famous man   *Merlin and V.* 165
Woo her and *g* her then: no wavering, boy!   *Sisters (E. and E.)* 39
or if she *g* her earthly-best,   *Locksley H., Sixty* 233
Ere she *g* her Heavenly-best.   271
in the North to *g* Her capital city,   *The Ring* 481
corpse of every man that *g's* a name;   *Romney's R.* 123
As Wisdom hopes to *g*,'   *Politics* 4

Gain'd   'Thou hast not *g* a real height,
but even then she *g* Her bower;   *Two Voices* 91
And *g* a laurel for your brow   *Godiva* 76
G for her own a scanty sustenance,   *You might have won* 3
Philip *g* As Enoch lost;   *Enoch Arden* 259
seaward-bound for health they *g* a coast,   354
We *g* the mother-city thick with towers,   *Sea Dreams* 16
further on we *g* A little street half garden   *Princess* i 112
and *g* The terrace ranged along the Northern front,   ,, iii 117
thus much, nor more I *g*.'   ,, 167
grasping down the boughs I *g* the shore.   ,, iv 189
We cross'd the street and *g* a petty mound   ,, 557
And on they moved and *g* the hall,   ,, vi 352
In such discourse we *g* the garden rails.   ,, Con. 80
He that *g* a hundred fights,   *Ode on Well.* 96
A wretched vote may be *g*.   *Maud* I vi 56
And glory *g*, and evermore to gain.   *Gareth and L.* 332
Took horse, and forded Usk, and *g* the wood;   *Marr. of Geraint* 161
fatal quest Of honour, where no honour can be *g*:   *Geraint and E.* 704
leaving Arthur's court he *g* the beach;   *Merlin and V.* 197
when they *g* the cell wherein he slept,   *Lancelot and E.* 811
Storm at the top, and when we *g* it,   *Holy Grail* 491
she *g* her castle, upsprang the bridge,   *Pelleas and E.* 206
but turning, past and *g* Tintagil,   *Last Tournament* 504
G in the service of His Highness,   *Columbus* 236
Step by step we *g* a freedom   *Locksley H., Sixty* 129
But when she *g* the broader vale,   *Death of Œnone* 91
G their huge Colosseum.   *St. Telemachus* 45

Gaining   Yet oceans daily *g* on the land,   *Golden Year* 29
worship woman as true wife beyond All hopes of *g*,   *Merlin and V.* 24
G a lifelong Glory in battle,   *Batt. of Brunanburh* 7
a glory slowly *g* on the shade,   *Making of Man* 6

Gainsay   *See* **Gaänsaäy**

Galahad (a Knight of the Round Table)   Not even
Lancelot brave, nor *G* clean.   *Merlin and V.* 805
Sir Percivale And pure Sir *G* to uplift the maid;   *Lancelot and E.* 1265
ever moved Among us in white armour, *G*.   *Holy Grail* 135
made a knight Till *G*; and this *G*, when he heard   ,, 139
G, when he heard of Merlin's doom,   ,, 177
G would sit down in Merlin's chair.   ,, 181
and *G* sware the vow, And good Sir Bors,   ,, 199
G on the sudden, and in a voice Shrilling   ,, 288
G, and O *G*, follow me.'   'Ah, *G*, *G*,'   ,, 292
What are ye?' *G's*?—no, nor Percivales' (For thus it
pleased the King to range me close After Sir *G*);   ,, 306
And I myself and *G*, for a strength Was in us   ,, 333
Shouting, 'Sir *G* and Sir Percivale!'   ,, 337
not lost thyself to save thyself As *G*.'   ,, 457
In silver armour suddenly *G* shone Before us,   ,, 458
I, *G*, saw the Grail, The Holy Grail,   ,, 464
G fled along them bridge by bridge,   ,, 504
O brother, saving this Sir *G*,   ,, 561
after I was join'd with *G* Cared not for her,   ,, 611

Galaxy   Hung in the golden *G*.   *L. of Shalott* iii 12

Gale   And merrily, merrily carol the *g's*,   *Sea-Fairies* 23
Sweet *g's*, as from deep gardens, blow   *Fatima* 24
strong *g's* Hold swollen clouds from raining,   *D. of F. Women* 10
last night's *g* had caught, And blown across   *Gardener's D.* 124
Caught the shrill salt, and sheer'd the *g*.   *The Voyage* 12
And to and thro' the counter *g*?   ,, 88
Storm'd in orbs of song, a growing *g*;   *Vision of Sin* 25
Rough-redden'd with a thousand winter *g's*,   *Enoch Arden* 95
drank the *g* That blown about the foliage   *Princess* iii 120
Who changest not in any *g*,   *In Mem.* ii 10
Caught and cuff'd by the *g*:   *Maud* I vi 5
So fierce a *g* made havoc here of late   *Holy Grail* 729

Gale (*continued*)   this *g* Tore my pavilion from the
tenting-pin,   *Holy Grail* 746
ever that evening ended a great *g* blew,   *The Revenge* 114

Galilæe   often mutter low 'Vicisti *G*'; louder again
Spurning a shatter'd fragment of the God,
'Vicisti *G*!'   *St. Telemachus* 15

Galilee   still'd the rolling wave of *G*!   *Aylmer's Field* 709

Galingale   meadow, set with slender *g*;   *Lotos-Eaters* 23

Gall (bitterness)   changed a wholesome heart to *g*.   *L. C. V. de Vere* 44
That was the last drop in the cup of *g*.   *Walk. to the Mail* 69
Unto me my maudlin *g* And my mockeries   *Vision of Sin* 201

Gall (oak-gall)   insects prick Each leaf into a (*g*)   *Talking Oak* 70

Gall (verb)   Began to *g* the knighthood, asking   *Las₁ Tournament* 683

Gallant   My woman-soldier, *g* Kate,   *Kate* 15
the seamen Made a *g* crew, *G* sons of English freemen,   *The Captain* 6
Many a *g* gay domestic Bows before him   *L. of Burleigh* 47
So sang the *g* glorious chronicle,   *Princess*, Pro. 49
To give three *g* gentlemen to death.'   ,, ii 335
He seems a gracious and a *g* Prince,   ,, v 213
I fenced it round with *g* institutes,   ,, 392
A *g* fight, a noble princess—   ,, Con. 19
Who pledgest now thy *g* son;   *In Mem.* vi 10
A passionate ballad *g* and gay,   *Maud* I v 4
THE charge of the *g* three hundred,   *Heavy Brigade* 1
he waved his blade To the *g* three hundred   ,, 10
up the hill, Gallop the *g* three hundred,   ,, 25
'Lost are the *g* three hundred of Scarlett's Brigade!'   ,, 45
O great and *g* Scott,   *Bandit's Death* 1
'*G* Sir Ralph,' said the king.   *The Tourney* 6

Galleon   Four *g's* drew away From the Spanish fleet   *The Revenge* 46
their high-built *g's* came,   ,, 58

Galleried   a minster there, A *g* palace,   *The Ring* 246

Gallery   foremost in thy various *g* Place it,   *Ode to Memory* 84
By garden-wall and *g*,   *L. of Shalott* iv 38
And round the roofs a gilded *g*   *Palace of Art* 29
The light aërial *g*, golden-rail'd,   ,, 47
long-laid *galleries* past a hundred doors   *Princess* vi 375
golden hours, In those long *galleries*,   *The Daisy* 42
made his feet Wings thro' a glimmering *g*,   *Balin and Balan* 404
let his eyes Run thro' the peopled *g*   *Lancelot and E.* 430
Rich *galleries*, lady-laden, weigh'd the necks   *Holy Grail* 346
He glanced and saw the stately *galleries*,   *Last Tournament* 145
Tristram round the *g* made his horse Caracole;   ,, 205
armed feet Thro' the upper from the outer doors   *Guinevere* 413

Gallop   The trumpet, the *g*, the charge,   *Heavy Brigade* 13

Gallopaded   willows two and two By rivers *g*.   *Amphion* 40

Gallop'd-Gallopt   and so *gallop'd* up the knoll.   *Marr. of Geraint* 168
as he *gallop'd* up To join them,   ,, 171
Gallopt the gallant three hundred,   *Heavy Brigade* 25
our men *gallopt* up with a cheer and a shout,   ,, 61

Galloping (*See also* **Heavily-galloping**)   *g* hoofs bare on
the ridge of spears   *Princess* v 489

Gallopt   *See* **Gallop'd**

Gama   His name was *G*; crack'd and small his voice,   ,, i 114
Then *G* turn'd to me: 'We fear, indeed,   ,, v 120
you spake but sense Said *G*.   ,, 207
This *G* swamp'd in lazy tolerance.   ,, 443
can this be he From *G's* dwarfish loins?   ,, 506
And moved beyond his custom, *G* said: ,, vi 229

Gambol   mother he had never known, In *g's*;   *Aylmer's Field* 691
For these your dainty *g's*: wherefore ask;   *Merlin and V.* 309
Nor ever let you *g* in her sight,   *The Ring* 387

Gamboll'd-Gambol'd   when she *gamboll'd* on the greens   *Talking Oak* 77
We *gambol'd*, making vain pretence Of gladness,   *In Mem.* xxx 6
Glanced at the doors or *gambol'd* down the walks;   *Marr. of Geraint* 665
And a hundred *gamboll'd* and pranced on the
wrecks   *V. of Maeldune* 102

Gambolling   Down shower the *g* waterfalls   *Sea-Fairies* 10

Game (thing hunted)   Stoops at all *g* that wing the skies,   *Rosalind* 4
Whither fly ye, what *g* spy ye,   8
touch'd upon the *g*, how scarce it was   *Audley Court* 32
Man is the hunter; woman is his *g*:   *Princess* v 154
He bore but little *g* in hand;   *The Victim* 42
No, there is fatter *g* on the moor,   *Maud* I i 74
Royaller *g* is mine.   *Merlin and V.* 108

Game (pastime) The *g* of forfeits done— *The Epic* 2
dwindled down to some odd *g's* In some odd nooks 8
She remember'd that: A pleasant *g*, *Princess, Pro.* 194
Quoit, tennis, ball—no *g's* ? *iii* 215
At civil revel and pomp and *g*, (repeat) *Ode on Well.* 147, 227
In dance and song and *g* and jest ? *In Mem. xxix* 8
Again our ancient *g's* had place, " *lxxviii* 10
Poor rivals in a losing *g*, " *cii* 19
Be neither song, nor *g*, nor feast; " *cv* 21
moved by an unseen hand at a *g* That pushes *Maud I iv* 26
And play the *g* of the despot kings, " *x* 39
once again the sickening *g*; *Locksley H., Sixty* 127
God must mingle with the *g*: " 271
Romans brawling of their monstrous *g's*; *St. Telemachus* 40
Gamesome 'Then ran she, *g* as the colt, *Talking Oak* 121
Gammer Ran Gaffer, stumbled G. *The Goose* 34
Gamut their shrieks Ran highest up the *g*, *Sea Dreams* 233
Ganymede flush'd G, his rosy thigh Half-buried *Palace of Art* 121
I think he came like G, *Will Water.* 119
'They mounted, G's, To tumble, Vulcans, *Princess iii* 71
Gap from the *g's* and chasms of ruin left *Sea Dreams* 225
fill up the *g* where force might fail *Gareth and L.* 1352
thro' the *g* Glimmer'd the streaming scud: *Holy Grail* 681
thro' the *g* The seven clear stars of Arthur's Table
Round— " 683
new knights to fill the *g* Left by the Holy Quest; *Pelleas and E.* 1
In this *g* between the sandhills, *Locksley H., Sixty* 176
Fought for their lives in the narrow *g* they had
made— *Heavy Brigade* 23
Gape A gulf that ever shuts and *g's*, *In Mem. lxx* 6
too high For any mouth to *g* for save a queen's— *Lancelot and E.* 775
g for flies—we know not whence they come; *Holy Grail* 147
Gaped Lavaine *g* upon him As on a thing miraculous, *Lancelot and E.* 452
tier over tier, Were added mouths that *g*, " 1249
Gaping (*See also* **Gaäpin'**) The passive oxen *g*. *Amphion* 72
fool, Who was *g* and grinning by : *Maud II i* 20
Gap-mouth'd All in a *g-m* circle his good mates *Gareth and L.* 511
Gapp'd their masses are *g* with our grape— *Def. of Lucknow* 42
Gap-tooth'd A gray and *g-t* man as lean as death, *Vision of Sin* 60
Garbaging and Gave to the *g* war-hawk to gorge it, *Batt. of Brunanburh* 109
Garb'd richly, but worn From wasteful living, *Ancient Sage* 4
Garda Lake Gazing at the Lydian laughter of the
G L below *Frater Ave, etc.* 3
Garden (adj.) By *g* porches on the brim, *Arabian Nights* 16
whose root Creeps to the *g* water-pipes beneath, *D. of F. Women* 206
black-hearts ripen dark, All thine, against the
g wall. *Blackbird* 8
There sat we down upon a *g* mound, *Gardener's D.* 214
fountain to his place returns Deep in the *g* lake
withdrawn. *Day-Dm., Sleep P.* 12
Some figure like a wizard pentagram On *g* gravel, *The Brook* 104
all within The sward was trim as any *g* lawn: *Princess, Pro.* 95
found at length The *g* portals. " *iv* 200
To take their leave, about the *g* rails, " *Con.* 38
In such discourse we gain'd the *g* rails, " 80
all by myself in my own dark *g* ground, *Maud I iii* 10
Seem'd her light foot along the *g* wall, " *xviii* 9
And long by the *g* lake I stood, " *xxii* 35
'this *g* rose Deep-hued and many-folded ! *Balin and Balan* 269
And oft they met among the *g* yews, *Lancelot and E.* 645
one morn it chanced He found her in among the
g yews, " 923
Garden (s) (*See also* **Hall-garden, Olive-gardens, Rose-garden**) High-wall'd *g's* green and old; *Arabian Nights* 8
Thence thro' the *g* I was drawn— " 100
When rooted in the *g* of the mind, *Ode to Memory* 26
a *g* bower'd close With plaited alleys " 105
the world Like one great *g* show'd, *The Poet* 34
In the heart of the *g* the merry bird chants. *Poet's Mind* 22
whitest honey in fairy *g's* cull'd— *Eleänore* 26
Sweet gales, as from deep *g's*, blow *Fatima* 24
A spacious *g* full of flowering weeds, *To —— With Pal. of Art* 4
Walking about the *g's* and the halls Of Camelot, *M. d'Arthur* 20
blooms the *g* that I love. *Gardener's D.* 34
between it and the *g* lies A League of grass, " 39

I*

Garden (s) (*continued*) The *g* stretches southward. *Gardener's D.* 115
One after one, thro' that still *g* pass'd; " 201
And cross'd the *g* to the gardener's lodge, *Audley Court* 17
A breeze thro' all the *g* swept, *Day-Dm., Revival* 6
A *g* too with scarce a tree, *Amphion* 3
at the end of all A little *g* blossom. " 104
Parks and order'd *g's* great, *L. of Burleigh* 30
Flourished a little *g* square and wall'd : *Enoch Arden* 734
arranged Her *g*, sow'd her name and kept it
green *Aylmer's Field* 88
Which fann'd the *g's* of that rival rose " 455
Kept to the *g* now, and grove of pines, " 550
that in the *g* snared Picus and Faunus, *Lucretius* 181
A little street half *g* and half house; *Princess i* 214
grace Concluded, and we sought the *g's*: " *ii* 453
Above the *g's* glowing blossom-belts, " *v* 363
'Look there, a *g*!' said my college friend, " *Con.* 49
All round a careless-order'd *g* *To F. D. Maurice* 15
'All among the *g's*, auriculas, anemones, *City Child* 4
So that still *g* of the souls *In Mem. xliii* 10
The gust that round the *g* flew, " *lxxxix* 19
Till from the *g* and the wild " *ci* 17
like the sultan of old in a *g* of spice. *Maud I iv* 42
Maud has a *g* of roses And lilies " *xiv* 1
great Forefathers of the thornless *g*, " *xviii* 27
Come into the *g*, Maud, (repeat) " *xxii* 1, 3
Queen rose of the rosebud *g* of girls, " 53
g by the turrets Of the old manorial hall. " *II iv* 79
But I know where a *g* grows, " *v* 72
And wallow'd in the *g's* of the King. *Com. of Arthur* 25
But this was in the *g* of a king: *Marr. of Geraint* 656
Sir Balin sat Close-bower'd in that *g* *Balin and Balan* 241
a slope of *g*, all Of roses white and red, *Pelleas and E.* 421
Walking about the *g's* and the halls Of Camelot, *Pass. of Arthur* 188
as tho' A man in some still *g* should infuse *Lover's Tale i* 269
the daily want Of Edith in the house, the *g*, *Sisters (E. and E.)* 246
Down we look'd: what a *g*! *V. of Maeldune* 78
Wi' my oän little *g* outside, *Spinster's S's.* 104
Every grim ravine a *g*, *Locksley H., Sixty* 168
I found her not in house Or *g*— *The Ring* 445
from every vale and plain And *g* pass, *To Mary Boyle* 10
Across my *g*! and the thicket stirs, *Prog. of Spring* 53
under the Crosses The dead man's *g*, *Merlin and the G.* 106
like a lonely man In the king's *g*, *Akbar's Dream* 21
I cotch'd tha wonst i' my *g*, *Church-warden, etc.* 33
Garden (verb) I shall never *g* more : *May Queen, N. Y's. E.* 46
Garden-bower Black the *g-b's* and grots *Arabian Nights* 78
To and fro they went Thro' my *g-b*, *The Flower* 6
Gardener The *g* Adam and his wife *L. C. V. de Vere* 51
I and Eustace from the city went To see the G's
Daughter ; *Gardener's D.* 3
'Go and see The G's daughter : " 30
not heard Of Rose, the G's daughter ? " 52
And cross'd the garden to the *g's* lodge, *Audley Court* 17
charge the *g's* now To pick the faded creature *Marr. of Geraint* 670
And made a G putting in a graff, *Merlin and V.* 479
g's hand Picks from the colewort a green caterpillar, *Guinevere* 31
Garden-gate And push'd at Philip's *g-g*. *The Brook* 83
And stood by her *g-g*; *Maud I xiv* 6
looks Upon Maud's own *g-g*: " 16
Garden-glass The *g-g'es* glanced, and momently *Gardener's D.* 117
Garden-herbs Gifts by the children, *g-h* and fruit, *Enoch Arden* 338
Gardening Botanic Treatises, And Works on G *Amphion* 78
Garden-isles meadowy holms And alders, *g-i*; *Edwin Morris* 96
Garden-lawn By grove and *g-l*, and rushing brook, *Holy Grail* 230
Garden-rose outredden All voluptuous *g-r's*. *Ode on Well.* 208
This *g-r* that I found, *Maud I xxi* 3
Garden-square And in the sultry *g-s's*, *The Blackbird* 17
Garden-squirt Half-conscious of the *g-s*, *Amphion* 91
Garden-tools find my *g-t* upon the granary floor: *May Queen, N. Y's. E.* 45
Garden-tree Beneath your sheltering *g-t*, *To E. Fitzgerald* 6
Garden-walks As down the *g-w* I move, *In Mem. cii* 6
Garden-wall By *g-w* and gallery, *L. of Shalott iv* 38
And feeling all along the *g-w*, *Enoch Arden* 773
this side the palace ran the field Flat to the *g-w*: *Princess v* 362

Garden-wall (*continued*) Climb'd to the high top of the *g-w*   *Guinevere* 25

Gareth (a knight of the Round Table) *G*, in a showerful spring Stared at the spate.   *Gareth and L.* 2
'How he went down,' said *G*, 'as a false knight   ,, 5
And *G* went, and hovering round her chair   ,, 33
G answer'd her with kindling eyes, (repeat)   ,, 41, 62
G, 'An ye hold me yet for child,   ,, 99
G answer'd quickly, 'Not an hour,   ,, 132
G cried, 'A hard one, or a hundred,   ,, 149
G was too princely-proud To pass thereby;   ,, 161
Silent awhile was *G*, then replied,   ,, 164
G awhile linger'd.   ,, 172
Then those who went with *G* were amazed,   ,, 197
G answer'd them With laughter,   ,, 208
those with *G* for so long a space Stared at the figures,   ,, 231
they call'd To *G*, 'Lord, the gateway is alive.' And *G* likewise on them fixt his eyes So long,   ,, 235
Then *G*, 'We be tillers of the soil,   ,, 242
G spake Anger'd, 'Old Master,   ,, 279
Whom *G* looking after said, 'My men,   ,, 296
and the sound was good to *G*'s ear.   ,, 312
Then into hall *G* ascending heard A voice,   ,, 317
G saw The shield of Gawain blazon'd rich and bright,   ,, 415
G leaning both hands heavily Down on the shoulders   ,, 439
So *G* all for glory underwent The sooty yoke   ,, 478
G bow'd himself With all obedience to the King,   ,, 487
G was glad. (repeat)   ,, 497, 504
G telling some prodigious tale Of knights,   ,, 508
This, *G* hearing from a squire of Lot   ,, 531
Shame never made girl redder than *G* joy.   ,, 536
G, lightly springing from his knees,   ,, 556
G ask'd, 'Have I not earn'd my cake in baking of it?   ,, 574
with a kindly hand on *G*'s arm Smiled the great King,   ,, 578
Arthur mindful of Sir *G* ask'd,   ,, 624
Sir *G* call'd from where he rose,   ,, 645
on to this Sir *G* strode, and saw without the door   ,, 676
Sir *G* loosed A cloak that dropt from collar-bone   ,, 681
So *G* ere he parted flash'd in arms.   ,, 689
thro' lanes of shouting *G* rode Down the slope street,   ,, 699
So *G* past with joy; but as the cur Pluckt   ,, 701
Mutter'd in scorn of *G* whom he used To harry   ,, 706
To whom Sir *G* drew (And there were none   ,, 743
G to him, 'Master no more! too well I know thee,   ,, 755
G cried again, 'Lead, and I follow,   ,, 759
'Damsel,' Sir *G* answer'd gently,   ,, 772
I shall assay,' said *G* with a smile. That madden'd her,   ,, 783
And *G* following was again beknaved.   ,, 786
G, 'Bound am I to right the wrong'd,   ,, 804
'Lead, and I follow,' *G* cried again,   ,, 807
G loosed the stone From off his neck,   ,, 814
G loosed his bonds and on free feet Set him,   ,, 817
G sharply spake, 'None!   ,, 831
and the Baron set *G* beside her,   ,, 852
seating *G* at another board, Sat down beside him,   ,, 871
G said, 'Full pardon, but I follow up the quest,   ,, 885
Sir *G* spake, 'Lead, and I follow.'   ,, 890
To whom Sir *G* answer'd courteously,   ,, 900
G silent gazed upon the knight,   ,, 933
Said *G*, 'Damsel, whether knave or knight,   ,, 943
G lash'd so fiercely with his brand   ,, 968
Till *G*'s shield was cloven;   ,, 971
G, 'So this damsel ask it of me Good—   ,, 974
G there unlaced his helmet as to slay him,   ,, 978
Sir *G* answer'd, laughingly, 'Parables?   ,, 1007
G's eyes had flying blots Before them   ,, 1031
Whom *G* met midstream?   ,, 1041
Then *G* laid his lance athwart the ford;   ,, 1048
and *G* sent him to the King.   ,, 1051
G, 'Wherefore waits the madman there   ,, 1091
Said *G*, 'Old, and over-bold in brag!   ,, 1107
And *G* overthrew him, lighted, drew,   ,, 1121
G brought him grovelling on his knees,   ,, 1124
Till *G* panted hard, and his great heart,   ,, 1126
so *G* seem'd to strike Vainly,   ,, 1133

Gareth (*continued*) And *G* hearing ever stronglier smote,   *Gareth and L.* 1141
Sir *G*'s brand Clash'd his, and brake it utterly   ,, 1147
G lookt and read—In letters like to those   ,, 1201
star Gleam, on Sir *G*'s turning to him,   ,, 1219
G crying prick'd against the cry;   ,, 1221
Lancelot answer'd, 'Prince, O *G*—   ,, 1237
Then *G*, 'Thou—Lancelot!—thine the hand That threw me?   ,, 1241
'Blessed be thou, Sir *G*! knight art thou   ,, 1258
turning to Lynette he told The tale of *G*,   ,, 1273
Sir *G* drank and ate, and all his life Past into sleep;   ,, 1280
Let *G*, an he will, Change his for mine,   ,, 1299
G, wakening, fiercely clutch'd the shield;   ,, 1304
allured The glance of *G* dreaming on his liege.   ,, 1316
'Lo,' said *G*, 'the foe falls!'   ,, 1317
Said *G* laughing, 'An he fight for this,   ,, 1345
Then *G*, 'Here he rules. I know but one— which Sir *G* graspt, And so, before the two could hinder him,   ,, 1354, 1367
But *G* spake and all indignantly,   ,, 1386
Sir *G*'s head prickled beneath his helm;   ,, 1397
with one stroke Sir *G* split the skull.   ,, 1404
Answer'd Sir *G* graciously to one Not many a moon his younger,   ,, 1414
So large mirth lived and *G* won the quest.   ,, 1426
tale in older times Says that Sir *G* wedded Lyonors,   ,, 1428
Tristram, and Geraint And *G*, a good knight,   *Lancelot and E.* 557

Gargarus topmost *G* Stands up and takes the morning: *Œnone* 10

Garland The *g* of new-wreathed emprise: *Kate* 24
Do make a *g* for the heart: *Miller's D.* 198
knots of flowers, and buds and *g*'s gay,   *May Queen* 11
spears That soon should wear the *g*;   *Aylmer's Field* 112
made *g*'s of the selfsame flower,   *Lover's Tale* i 343
a light Burst from the *g* I had wov'n,   ,, 366
Wreathed round the bier with *g*'s: ,, ii 79
Great *g*'s swung and blossom'd;   ,, iv 191
I, wearing but the *g* of a day,   *To Dante* 6
The bridal *g* falls upon the bier,   *D. of the Duke of C.* 1

Garlandage leaf, and gayest *g* of flowers,   *Balin and Balan* 83

Garlanded Each *g* with her peculiar flower   *Gardener's D.* 202

Garlanding *g* the gnarled boughs With bunch   *Œnone* 101

Garlon (a Knight of the Round Table) *G*, mine heir, Of him demand it,' which this *G* gave With much ado,   *Balin and Balan* 117
more than one of us Cried out on *G*,   ,, 123
Sir *G* too Hath learn'd black magic.   ,, 304
Till when at feast Sir *G* likewise ask'd   ,, 347
Made *G*, hissing; then he sourly smiled.   ,, 355
Then fiercely to Sir *G*, 'Eyes have I That saw to-day   ,, 372
The scorn of *G*, poisoning all his rest,   ,, 383
Sir *G* utter'd mocking-wise;   ,, 389
Then *G*, reeling slowly backward, fell,   ,, 397
This *G* mock'd me, but I heeded not.   ,, 606
And sought for *G* at the castle-gates,   ,, 610

Garment eddying of her *g*'s caught from thee   *Ode to Memory* 31
The woman's *g* hid the woman's heart.'   *Princess* v 305
Fair *g*'s, plain or rich,   *Akbar's Dream* 131

Garner The wrath that *g*'s in my heart;   *In Mem. lxxxii* 14
And *g* all you may!   *Mechanophilus* 32

Garner'd (adj.) time is scarce more brief Than of the *g* Autumn-sheaf.   *Two Voices* 114
Or little pitted speck in *g* fruit,   *Merlin and V.* 394
and bless Their *g* Autumn also,   *Demeter and P.* 147

Garner'd (verb) long ago they had glean'd and *g*   *Lover's Tale* i

Garnet Each like a *g* or a turkis in it;   *Marr. of Geraint* 661

Garnet-headed hear the *g-h* yaffingale Mock them: *Last Tournament* 700

Garnish flowers, except, belike, To *g* meats with?   *Gareth and L.* 1070

Garrick *G* and statelier Kemble,   *To W. C. Macready* 7

Garrison as if hope for the *g* hung but on him;   *Def. of Lucknow* 48
on a sudden the *g* utter a jubilant shout,   98

Garrulity Shame on her own *g* garrulously,   *Guinevere* 312

Garrulous Miriam Lane was good and *g*,   *Enoch Arden* 700
G under a roof of pine: *To F. D. Maurice* 20
With *g* ease and oily courtesies   *Princess* i 164

Gather'd (continued)   Grave faces g in a ring.]   *Day-Dm., Sleep P.* 38
Till they be g up;   *Will Water.* 170
topmost elm-tree g green From draughts   *Sir L. and Q. G.* 8
there again When burr and bine were g;   *Aylmer's Field* 113
G the blossom that rebloom'd,   ,,   142
Easily g either guilt.   *Princess iv* 236
rose A hubbub in the court of half the maids
   G together: ,,   477
the heavy dews G by night and peace,   ,, *v* 244
But such as g colour day by day.   ,, *vii* 118
Abide: thy wealth is g in,   *In Mem. lii* 15
He fought his doubts and g strength,   ,, *xcvi* 13
The maidens g strength and grace   ,, *ciii* 27
He has g the bones for his o'ergrown whelp   *Maud II v* 55
this she g from the people's eyes: *Marr. of Geraint* 61
g trickling dropwise from the cleft,   *Merlin and V.* 274
I stoop'd, I g the wild herbs,   *Lover's Tale i* 342
I have g my baby together—   *Rizpah* 20
But I g my fellows together,   *V. of Maeldune* 2
I would that I were g to my rest,   *Tiresias* 170
Thousands of horsemen had g there   *Heavy Brigade* 14
The vast sun-clusters' g blaze,   *Epilogue* 54

Gathering (adj. and part.)   the mighty moon was g light   *Love and Death* 1
Proserpine in Enna, g flowers: *Edwin Morris* 112
G up from all the lower ground;   *Vision of Sin* 15
And g all the fruits of earth   *Ode Inter. Exhib.* 41
And g freshlier overhead,   *In Mem. xcv* 57
G woodland lilies, Myriads blow together.   *Maud I xii* 7
By shores that darken with the g wolf,   *Aylmer's Field* 767
So much the g darkness charm'd: *Princess, Con.* 107
tho' the g enemy narrow thee,   *Boädicea* 39
g half the deep And full of voices,   *Com. of Arthur* 380
Vivien, g somewhat of his mood,   *Merlin and V.* 842
but g at the base Re-makes itself, and flashes   *Guinevere* 609
And g ruthless gold—   *Columbus* 135
g here and there From each fair plant   *Akbar's Dream* 21

Gathering (s)   A g of the Tory,   *Maud I xx* 33

Gaud   those gilt g's men-children swarm to see.   *To W. C. Macready* 11

Gaudy   Showing a g summer-morn,   *Palace of Art* 62

Gaudy-day   Amends hereafter by some g-d,   *Marr. of Geraint* 818

Gaunt   Lancelot? goodly—ay, but g: *Merlin and V.* 103
G as it were the skeleton of himself, (repeat)   *Lancelot and E.* 764, 816
(The g old Baron with his beetle brow   *Princess ii* 240

Gauntlet   maiden fancies dead In iron g's: ,, *i* 89
added fullness to the phrase Of 'G in the velvet
   glove.'   *To Marq. of Dufferin* 12

Gauntleted   my hand Was g, half slew him;   *Balin and Balan* 57
His passion half had g to death,   ,,   220

Gauntness   Courteous—amends for g—   *Merlin and V.* 104

Gauze   'He dried his wings: like g they grew;   *Two Voices* 13
Purple g's, golden hazes, liquid mazes,   *Vision of Sin* 31
Half-lapt in glowing g and golden brede,   *Princess vi* 134
an Eastern g with seeds of gold—   *Lover's Tale iv* 291

Gave   (See also **Gied, Giv**)   God g her peace; her land reposed;   *To the Queen* 26
And g you on your natal day.   *Margaret* 42
Our thought g answer each to each,   *Sonnet* 10
'She g him mind, the lordliest Proportion,   *Two Voices* 19
sing the foolish song I g you, Alice,   *Miller's D.* 162
thought of that sharp look, mother, I g him yesterday,   *May Queen* 15
flower and fruit, whereof they g To each,   *Lotos-Eaters* 29
my bliss of life, that Nature g,   *D. of F. Women* 210
because the kiss he g me, ere I fell,   ,,   235
He g me a friend, and a true true-love,   *D. of the O. Year* 13
'Hast thou perform'd my mission which I g?   *M. d'Arthur* 67
This, yielding, g into a grassy walk   *Gardener's D.* 111
Kissing the rose she g me o'er and o'er,   ,,   176
G utterance by the yearning of an eye,   *Love and Duty* 62
The trance g way To those caresses,   ,,   65
And g my letters back to me. And g the trinkets
   and the rings,   *The Letters* 20
He g the people of his best: His worst he kept,
   his best he g.   *You might have won* 25
from her baby's forehead clipt A tiny curl, and g it: *Enoch Arden* 236
less Than what she g in buying what she sold: ,,   256
At Annie's door he paused and g his hand,   ,,   447

Gave (continued)   clothes they g him and free passage   *Enoch Arden* 650
Pitying the lonely man, and g him it: ,,   664
the woman g A half-incredulous, half-hysterical cry.   ,,   852
This hair is his: she cut it off and g it,   ,,   894
He g them line: (repeat)   *The Brook* 145, 150
scared with threats of jail and halter g   *Aylmer's Field* 520
the dagger which himself G Edith,   ,,   597
g the verse 'Behold, Your house is left unto you
   desolate!'   ,,   628
G his broad lawns until the set of sun   *Princess, Pro.* 2
they g The park, the crowd, the house;   ,,   93
I said no, Yet being an easy man, g it: ,, *i* 149
we g a costly bribe To guerdon silence,   ,,   203
rooms which g Upon a pillar'd porch,   ,,   229
I g the letter to be sent with dawn;   ,,   245
a glance I g, No more;   ,, *iv* 180
On one knee Kneeling, I g it,   ,,   470
Who g me back my child?'   ,, *v* 105
Let so much out as g us leave to go.   ,,   235
for everything G way before him: ,,   530
Was it for this we g our palace up,   ,, *vi* 244
Refuse her proffer, lastly g his hand.   ,,   347
to them the doors g way Groaning,   ,,   349
pray'd the men, the women: I g assent: ,, *Con.* 7
English Harold g its throne a wife,   *W. to Marie Alex.* 24
and he g the ringers a crown.   *Grandmother* 58
I pluck'd a daisy, I g it you.   *The Daisy* 88
Hexameters no worse than daring Germany g us,   *Trans. of Homer* 5
The Danube to the Severn g   *In Mem. xix* 1
And g all ripeness to the grain,   ,, *lxxxi* 11
Received and g him welcome there;   ,, *lxxxv* 24
With him to whom her hand I g.   ,, *Con.* 70
He fiercely g me the lie,   *Maud II i* 16
By the home that g me birth,   ,, *iv* 7
Merlin took the child, And g him to Sir Anton,   *Com. of Arthur* 222
She g the King his huge cross-hilted sword,   ,,   286
Arthur g him back his territory,   *Gareth and L.* 78
Of whom ye g me to, the Seneschal,   ,,   559
that g upon a range Of level pavement   ,,   666
blue arms, and g a shield Blue also,   ,,   931
and thee the King G me to guard,   ,,   1014
g a shield whereon the Star of Even   ,,   1117
good king g order to let blow His horns   *Marr. of Geraint* 152
g command that all which once was ours   ,,   696
he but g a wrathful groan, Saying,   *Geraint and E.* 398
cousin, slay not him who g you life.'   ,,   783
I rode all-shamed, hating the life He g me,   ,,   853
which this Garlon g With much ado,   *Balin and Balan* 118
best Of ladies living g me this to bear.'   ,,   340
one that hath defamed The cognizance she g me: ,,   485
knew no more, nor g me one poor word;   *Merlin and V.* 277
Use g me Fame at first, and Fame again Increasing
   g me use.   ,,   493
His brother's; which he g to Lancelot,   *Lancelot and E.* 380
Sir Lancelot g A marvellous great shriek   ,,   515
he took, And g, the diamond: ,,   551
he g, And slightly kiss'd the hand to which he g,   ,,   701
I g the diamond: she will render it;   ,,   713
Stript off the case, and g the naked shield;   ,,   979
Then g a languid hand to each, and lay,   ,,   1032
I g No cause, not willingly, for such a love: ,,   1297
G him an isle of marsh whereon to build;   *Holy Grail* 62
to prayer and praise She g herself,   ,,   77
And g herself and all her wealth to me.   ,,   597
in my madness I essay'd the door; It g;   ,,   842
Then g it to his Queen to rear: *Last Tournament* 22
Tristram won, and Lancelot g, the gems,   ,,   190
and Innocence the King G for a prize—   ,,   295
this I g thee, look, Is all as cool and white   ,,   415
he g them charge about the Queen,   *Guinevere* 591
'Hast thou perform'd my mission which I g?   *Pass. of Arthur* 235
So Death g back, and would no further come.   *Lover's Tale i* 115
He that g Her life, to me delightedly fulfill'd   ,,   223
Then playfully she g herself the lie—   ,,   349
'Kiss him,' she said. 'You g me life again.   ,, *iv* 172

Gave (continued) (Meaning the print that you *g* us, *In the Child. Hosp.* 51
chains For him who *g* a new heaven, *Columbus* 20
G glory and more empire to the kings „ 22
g All but free leave for all to work „ 132
G to the garbaging war-hawk to gorge it, *Batt. of Brunanburh* 109
sweet mother land which *g* them birth *Tiresias* 122
He that they *g* me to, mother, *The Wreck* 13
I refused the hand he *g*. *Locksley H., Sixty* 256
and *g* Thy breast to ailing infants *Demeter and P.* 55
g it me, who pass'd it down her own, *The Ring* 270
pardon, O my love, if I ever *g* you pain. *Happy* 68
fumes Of that dark opiate dose you *g* me, *Romney's R.* 31
I sent him back what he *g*,— *Charity* 19

Gaw (go) 'I mun *g* up ageän fur Roä.' '*G* up ageän fur the varmint?' *Owd Roä* 97

Gawain (a knight of the Round Table) *G* and young Modred, her two sons, *Com. of Arthur* 244
G went, and breaking into song Sprang out, „ 320
G, when he came With Modred hither *Gareth and L.* 25
all in fear to find Sir *G*, or Sir Modred, „ 326
The shield of *G* blazon'd rich and bright, „ 416
'I have stagger'd thy strong *G* in a tilt „ 542
rise, O *G*, and ride forth and find the knight. *Lancelot and E.* 537
G, surnamed The Courteous, fair and strong, „ 555
G the while thro' all the region round „ 615
G saw Sir Lancelot's azure lions, „ 662
if *I* dream'd,' said *G*, 'that you love This greatest knight, „ 638
But there the fine *G* will wonder at me, „ 1054
G, who bad a thousand farewells to me, „ 1056
Then came the fine *G* and wonder'd at her, „ 1267
G sware, and louder then the rest.' *Holy Grail* 202
sharply turning, ask'd Of *G*, '*G*, was this Quest for thee?' 'Nay, Lord,' said *G*, 'not for such as I. „ 740
left The hall long silent, till Sir *G*— „ 854
'Hath *G* fail'd in any quest of thine? „ 859
'*G*, and blinder unto holy things „ 870
Three against one: and *G* passing by, *Pelleas and E.* 274
G, looking at the villainy done, Forebore, „ 282
Forth sprang *G*, and loosed him from his bonds, „ 315
G answer'd kindly tho' in scorn, „ 333
and took *G*'s, and said, 'Betray me not, „ 360
'Ay,' said *G*, 'for women be so light.' „ 362
But *G* lifting up his vizor said, '*G* am I, *G* of Arthur's court, „ 370
G, *G* of the Court, Sir *G*— „ 379
straight on thro' open door Rode *G*, „ 383
'Ay,' thought *G*, 'and you be fair enow: „ 388
but a sound Of *G* ever coming, and this lay— „ 396
'Why lingers *G* with his golden news?' „ 411
Bound on her brow, were *G* and Ettarre. „ 435
turn'd herself To *G*: 'Liar, for thou hast not slain „ 490
that *G* fired The hall of Merlin, „ 517
shouting, 'False, And false with *G*!' „ 546
DAGONET, the fool, whom *G* in his mood *Last Tournament* 1
G kill'd In Lancelot's war, the ghost of *G* blown Along a wandering wind, *Pass. of Arthur* 30
Thine, *G*, was the voice— „ 47
Light was *G* in life, and light in death Is *G*, „ 56

Gawin' (going) *g* to let in furriners' wheät, *Owd Roä* 45
I wur *g* that waäy to the bad, „ 71

Gay you were *g* With bridal flowers— *Miller's D.* 164
Or *g*, or grave, or sweet, or stern, *Palace of Art* 91
many songs, But never a one so *g*, *Poet's Song* 14
statue propt against the wall, As *g* as any. *Princess, Pro.* 100
My *g* young hawk, my Rosalind! *Rosalind* 34
and buds and garlands *g*, *May Queen* 11
Or *g* quinquenniads would we reap *Day-Dm., L'Envoi* 23
'And, leg and arm with love-knots *g*, *Talking Oak* 65
With many kinsmen *g*, *Will Water.* 90
Many a gallant *g* domestic Bows before him *L. of Burleigh* 47
I fear'd Lest the *g* navy there should splinter on it, *Sea Dreams* 131
silk pavilion, *g* with gold In streaks and rays, *Gareth and L.* 910
The *g* pavilion and the naked feet, „ 937
Prophet of the *g* time, *The Snowdrop* 6
remembering the *g* playmate rear'd Among them, *Death of Œnone* 59

Gay (continued) one is glad; her note is *g*, *In Mem. xxi* 25
fancies play To find me *g* among the *g*, „ *lxvi* 3
all is *g* with lamps, and loud With sport „ *xcviii* 27
Like things of the season *g*, *Maud I iv* 3
if I cannot be *g* let a passionless peace „ 50
A passionate ballad gallant and *g*, „ *v* 4
Strange, that I felt so *g*, „ *xx* 1
one With whom she has heart to be *g*. „ *xxii* 20
I see her Weeping for some *g* knight in Arthur's hall.' *Marr. of Geraint* 118
And seeing one so *g* in purple silks, „ 284
like a crag was *g* with wilding flowers: „ 319
these to her own faded self And the *g* court, „ 653
Clothed with my gift, and *g* among the *g*.' „ 753
that good mother, making Enid *g* In such apparel „ 757
And all that week week was old Caerleon *g*, „ 837
The three *g* suits of armour which they wore, *Geraint and E.* 95
drew from those dead wolves Their three *g* suits of armour, „ 181
How *g*, how suited to the house of one „ 683
and damsel glitter'd at the feast Variously *g*: *Last Tournament* 225
Thy *g* lent-lilies wave and put them by, *Prog. of Spring* 37
Bountiful, beautiful, apparell'd *g*, „ 62

Gayer But once were *g* than a dawning sky *Death of Œnone* 12
In colours *g* than the morning mist, *Princess ii* 438
My fate or folly, passing *g* youth For one so old, *Merlin and V.* 927
pale blood of the wizard at her touch Took *g* colours, „ 950
Evelyn is *g*, wittier, prettier, *Sisters (E. and E.)* 36

Gayest wealth Of leaf, and *g* garlandage of flowers, *Balin and Balan* 83

Gay-furr'd Her *g-f* cats a painted fantasy, *Princess iii* 186

Gaze (s) Than that earth should stand at *g* *Locksley Hall* 180
her ardent *g* Roves from the living brother's face, *In Mem. xxxii* 6
her hue Changed at his *g*: *Balin and Balan* 279
And were only standing at *g*, *Heavy Brigade* 37
The linnet's bosom blushes at her *g*, *Prog. of Spring* 17

Gaze (verb) Ever retiring thou dost *g* *Ode to Memory* 93
Ev'n while we *g* on it, *Eleänore* 90
g upon My palace with unblinded eyes, *Palace of Art* 41
He *g*'s on the silent dead: *Day-Dm., Arrival* 13
Evermore she seems to *g* *L. of Burleigh* 34
orb That fain would *g* upon him to the last; *Lucretius* 140
climbs a peak to *g* O'er land and main, *Princess vii* 35
I, who *g* with temperate eyes *In Mem. cxii* 2
bear some token of his Queen Whereon to *g*, *Balin and Balan* 189
I cannot brook to *g* upon the dead.' „ 586
Sigh fully, or all-silent *g* upon *Merlin and V.* 182
But who can *g* upon the Sun in heaven? *Lancelot and E.* 123
even while I *g* The crack of earthquake *Pelleas and E.* 464
as one Who sits and *g*'s on a faded fire, *Last Tournament* 157
and we woke To *g* upon each other. *Lover's Tale i* 266
To *g* upon thee till their eyes are dim „ 491
and I *g* at a field in the Past, *By an Evolution.* 17
she used to *g* Down at the Troad; *Death of Œnone* 2
and there *G* at the ruin, often mutter low *St. Telemachus* 14
And *g* on this great miracle, the World, *Akbar's Dream* 122
and is, And is not, what I *g* on— „ 124

Gazed *G* on the Persian girl alone, *Arabian Nights* 134
Two godlike faces *g* below: *Palace of Art* 162
He *g* so long That both his eyes were dazzled, *M. d'Arthur* 58
Averill went and *g* upon his death. *Aylmer's Field* 599
long we *g*, but satiated at length Came to the ruins. *Princess, Pro.* 90
I drew near; I *g*. „ *iii* 183
She *g* awhile and said, 'As these rude bones „ 295
while We *g* upon her came a little stir „ *iv* 373
Clomb to the roofs, and *g* alone for hours „ *vii* 32
place Where first we *g* upon the sky; *In Mem. cii* 2
They *g* on all earth's beauty in their Queen, *Com. of Arthur* 463
Gareth silent *g* upon the knight, *Gareth and L.* 933
on whom the maiden *g*. „ 1281
And kept her off and *g* upon her face, *Marr. of Geraint* 519
King Had *g* upon her blankly and gone by: *Merlin and V.* 161
I never *g* upon it but I dreamt Of some vast charm „ 511
G at the heaving shoulder, and the face Hand-hidden, „ 896
while he *g* wonderingly at her, came *Lancelot and E.* 626

Gazed (continued) while he *g* The beauty of her flesh
abash'd   *Pelleas and E.* 77
she *g* upon the man Of princely bearing,   " 305
Full wonderingly she *g* on Lancelot   " 589
He *g* so long That both his eyes were dazzled   *Pass. of Arthur* 226
three whereat we *g* On that high day,   " 453
for as that other *g*, Shading his eyes   *Lover's Tale i* 305
While I *g* My coronal slowly disentwined itself   " 360
while I *g* My spirit leap'd as with those thrills   " 362
The other, like the sun I *g* upon,   " 507
the stars Did tremble in their stations as I *g*;   " 582
We *g* on it together In mute and glad remembrance,   " *ii* 185
and the light Grew as I *g*,   *Columbus* 77
And we *g* at the wandering wave   *V. of Maeldune* 89
Her heart! I *g* into the mirror,   *The Ring* 369
Gazer greet With lifted hand the *g* in the street.   *Ode on Well.* 22
Gazest When thou *g* at the skies?   *Adeline* 50
Gazing (See also **Seaward-gazing**) *G* on thee for evermore,   *Eleänore* 80
Sometimes with most intensity *G*, I seem to see   " 83
and sense Of Passion *g* upon thee.   " 116
G where the lilies blow Round an island   *L. of Shalott i* 7
In *g* up an Alpine height,   *Two Voices* 362
If *g* on divinity disrobed Thy mortal eyes   *Œnone* 157
eyes grown dim with *g* on the pilot-stars.   *Lotos-Eaters, C. S.* 87
From her isle-altar *g* down,   *Of old sat Freedom* 14
There he sat down *g* on all below;   *Enoch Arden* 723
His *g* in on Annie, his resolve,   " 863
They stood, so rapt, we *g*, came a voice,   *Princess ii* 318
Then murmur'd Florian *g* after her,   " *iii* 97
All open-mouth'd, all *g* to the light,   " *iv* 483
Ida spoke not, *g* on the ground,   " *vi* 227
so fared she *g* there;   " *vii* 41
And *g* on thee, sullen tree,   *In Mem. ii* 13
the friends Of Arthur, *g* on him, tall,   *Com. of Arthur* 278
In scornful stillness *g* as they past;   " 478
that men Were giddy *g* there;   *Gareth and L.* 228
pace At sunrise, *g* over plain and wood;   " 668
And sadly *g* on her bridle-reins,   *Geraint and E.* 494
gone, And left me *g* at a barren board,   *Holy Grail* 893
Pelleas *g* thought, ' Is Guinevere herself so
beautiful?'   *Pelleas and E.* 69
Peace at his heart, and *g* at a star   *Lover's Tale i* 88
To die in *g* on that perfectness   " *ii* 188
g like The Indian on a still-eyed snake,   *Locksley H., Sixty* 32
G for one pensive moment on that founder   *Pro. to Gen. Hamley* 9
And, *g* from this height alone,   *Frater Ave, etc.* 8
G at the Lydian laughter of the Garda Lake
below   *Princess i* 199
Gear We sent mine host to purchase female *g*;   *The Revenge* 5
for my ships are out of *g*,   *N. Farmer, N. S.* 14
Gell (girl) an' soä is scoors o' *g*'s,   *Village Wife* 6
an' 'is *g*'s as thaw they was *g*'s o' mine,   " 18
The *g*'s they counts for nowt,   " 29
An' the *g*'s, they hedn't naw taäils,   " 64
or the *g*'s 'ull goä to the 'Ouse,   " 96
An' I cried along wi' the *g*'s,   " 112
an' 'is *g*'s es belong'd to the land;   *Spinster's S's.* 82
a bouncin' boy an' a *g*.   " 107
g's bobs to ma hoffens es I be abroad i' the laänes,   *Owd Roä* 51
g o' the farm 'at slep wi' tha then   " 69
a-naggin' about the *g* o' the farm,   " 72
the *g* was as howry a trollope   *Gareth and L.* 1203
Gelt left crag-carven o'er the streaming *G*—   *Palace of Art* 188
Gem (s) In hollow'd moons of *g*'s,   *M. d'Arthur* 152
lest the *g*'s Should blind my purpose,   *Princess i* 121
Airing a snowy hand and signet *g*,   " *iv* 480
rainbow robes, and *g*'s and gemlike eyes,   *The Daisy* 7
How like a *g*, beneath, the city Of little Monaco,   *Maud I v* 14
feet like sunny *g*'s on an English green,   *Gareth and L.* 929
All over glanced with dewdrop or with *g*   *Marr. of Geraint* 10
In crimsons and in purples and *g*'s   *Geraint and E.* 294
wont to glance and sparkle like a *g* Of fifty facets;   " 693
so thickly shone the *g*'s.   *Lancelot and E.* 56
he had the *g*'s Pluck'd from the crown,   " 1202
Received at once and laid aside the *g*'s   "

Gem (s) (continued) Tristram won, and Lancelot gave,
the *g*'s,   *Last Tournament* 190
Who left the *g*'s which Innocence the Queen   " 293
lest the *g*'s Should blind my purpose,   *Pass. of Arthur* 320
Which are as *g*'s set in my memory,   *Lover's Tale i* 291
g's Moveable and resettable at will,   " *iv* 198
after he hath shown him *g*'s or gold,   " 246
Swept like a torrent of *g*'s from the sky   *V. of Maeldune* 46
To vex the noon with fiery *g*'s,   *Ancient Sage* 265
Gem (verb) new life that *g*'s the hawthorn line;   *Prog. of Spring* 36
Gemini starry *G* hang like glorious crowns   *Maud III vi* 7
Gem-like a fire-balloon Rose *g-l* up before the dusky
groves   *Princess, Pro.* 75
And rainbow robes, and gems and *g* eyes,   " *iv* 480
Luminous, *g*, ghostlike, deathlike,   *Maud I iii* 8
a meadow *g* chased In the brown wild,   *Geraint and E.* 198
Gemm'd Breaks from a coppice *g* with green and red,   *Marr. of Geraint* 339
Gemmy The *g* bridle glitter'd free,   *L. of Shalott iii* 10
General Upon the *g* decay of faith Right thro' the world,   *The Epic* 18
every face she look'd on justify it) The *g* foe.   *Princess v* 135
should fall Remerging in the *g* Soul,   *In Mem. xlvii* 4
whatsoe'er Our *g* mother meant for me alone,   *Lover's Tale i* 245
Generating See **All-generating**
Generation (See also **Gineration**) And mould a *g*
strong to move   *Princess v* 416
to knit The *g*'s each with each;   *In Mem. xl* 16
jewels Of many *g*'s of his house Sparkled   *Lover's Tale iv* 299
National hatreds of whole *g*'s,   *Vastness* 25
Generous All brave, and many *g*, and some chaste.   *Merlin and V.* 817
Most *g* of all Ultramontanes, Ward,   *In Mem. W. G. Ward* 4
But, having sown some *g* seed,   *Two Voices* 143
everywhere they meet And kindle *g* purpose,   *Tiresias* 128
Genial (See also **Seeming-genial**) With peals of *g*
clamour sent From many a tavern-door,   *Will Water.* 187
so *g* was the hearth: *Enoch Arden* 743
all-generating powers and *g* heat Of Nature,   *Lucretius*
The *g* giant, Arac, roll'd himself   *Princess v* 274
broke A *g* warmth and light once more,   " *vi* 282
For we, the *g* day, the happy crowd,   " Con. 75
A great broad-shoulder'd *g* Englishman,   " 85
partner in the flowery walk Of letters, *g* table-talk,   *In Mem. lxxxiv* 23
And *g* warmth; and o'er the sky The silvery haze   " *xcv* 3
To myriads on the *g* earth,   " *xcix* 14
The *g* hour with mask and mime;   " *cv* 10
Let all my *g* spirits advance To meet   " Con. 77
Fill'd all the *g* courses of his blood   *Geraint and E.* 926
The light and *g* warmth of double day.   *Prin. Beatrice* 22
Genius thou bearest The first-born of thy *g*.   *Ode to Memory* 92
A fairy shield your *G* made And gave you   *Margaret* 41
G of that hour which dost uphold Thy coronal   *Lover's Tale i* 487
Genovese The grave, severe *G* of old.   *The Daisy* 40
Being but a *G*, I am handled worse than had I
been a Moor,   *Columbus* 106
I am but an alien and a *G*.   " 243
Gentle (See also **Stately-gentle**) Lean'd on him,
faithful, *g*, good,   *Two Voices* 416
gently comes the world to those That are cast in *g* mould.   *To J. S.* 4
By *g* words are always gain: *Love thou thy land* 23
A *g* sound, an awful light!   *Sir Galahad* 4
And they speak in *g* murmur,   *L. of Burleigh* 49
And a *g* consort made he, And her *g* mind was such
That she grew a noble lady,   " 73
The *g* shower, the smell of dying leaves,   *Enoch Arden* 611
a languor came Upon him, *g* sickness,   " 824
So that the *g* creature shut from all Her charitable use,   *Aylmer's Field* 565
Softening thro' all the *g* attributes   " 730
came Melissa hitting all we saw with shafts Of *g* satire,   *Princess ii* 469
on my spirits Settled a *g* cloud of melancholy;   " *iv* 570
the yoke, I wish it *G* as freedom '—   " *vi* 206
nor stranger seem'd that hearts So *g*,   " *vii* 67
Sleep, *g* heavens, before the prow; Sleep, *g* winds,
as he sleeps now,   *In Mem. ix* 14
My mother, who was so *g* and good?   *Maud I vi* 67
Of her whose *g* will has changed my fate,   " *xviii* 23
I trust that I did not talk To *g* Maud in our walk   " *xix* 13

Gentle (*continued*) Was it *g* to reprove her For stealing	*Maud I xx* 8
nor meet To fight for *g* damsel, he, who lets His heart be stirr'd with any foolish heat At any *g* damsel's waywardness.	*Gareth and L.* 1177
there fell A horror on him, lest his *g* wife,	*Marr. of Geraint* 29
Am much too *g*, have not used my power:	,, 467
Sank her sweet head upon my *g* breast;	,, 527
That tho' her *g* presence at the lists	,, 795
nor told his *g* wife What ail'd him,	*Geraint and E.* 503
(His *g* charger following him unled)	,, 571
Pray you be *g*, pray you let me be:	,, 708
Dame, to be *g* than ungentle with you;	,, 716
'I will be *g*' he thought 'And passing *g*' caught his hand	*Balin and Balan* 370
Then the *g* Squire 'I hold them happy,	,, 580
I thought that he was *g*, being great:	*Merlin and V.* 871
The *g* wizard cast a shielding arm.	,, 908
Some *g* maiden's gift.	*Lancelot and E.* 605
Death-pale, for lack of *g* maiden's aid.	,, 765
And all the *g* court will welcome me,	,, 1060
To whom the *g* sister made reply,	,, 1073
Know that for this most *g* maiden's death	,, 1291
Unbound as yet, and *g*, as I know.'	,, 1386
That doest right by *g* and by churl,	*Last Tournament* 74
Ah great and *g* lord, Who wast,	*Guinevere* 638
to which her gracious lips Did lend such *g* utterance,	*Lover's Tale i* 457
Then he patted my hand in his *g* way,	*First Quarrel* 67
the crew were *g*, the captain kind;	*The Wreck* 129
Our *g* mother, had *she* lived—	*The Flight* 77
All is gracious, *g*, great and Queenly.	*On Jub. Q. Victoria* 14
and felt a *g* hand Fall on my forehead,	*The Ring* 418
You that would not tread on a worm For your *g* nature ...	*Forlorn* 46
Gentle-hearted The *g-h* wife Sat shuddering	*Sea Dreams* 29
Gentleman bore King Arthur, like a modern *g*	*M. d'Arthur, Ep.* 22
And watch'd by silent *gentlemen*,	*Will Water.* 231
first, a *g* of broken means (His father's fault)	*Princess i* 53
To give three gallant *gentlemen* to death.'	,, ii 335
'You have done well and like a *g*,	,, iv 527
Well have you done and like a *g*.	,, 530
Cooms of a *g* burn:	*N. Farmer, N. S.* 38
G burn! what's *g* burn?	,, 42
The grand old name of *g*,	*In Mem. cxi* 22
O selfless man and stainless *g*,	*Merlin and V.* 792
True *g*, heart, blood and bone,	*Bandit's Death* 2
Gentleness Winning its way with extreme *g*	*Isabel* 23
More soluble is this knot, By *g* than war.	*Princess v* 136
but this firebrand—*g* To such as her!	,, 167
The *g* he seem'd to be,	*In Mem. cxi* 12
sworn to vows Of utter hardihood, utter *g*,	*Gareth and L.* 553
world were one Of utter peace, and love, and *g*!	,, 1289
Yea, God, I pray you of your *g*,	*Geraint and E.* 710
Subdued me somewhat to that *g*,	,, 867
what the King So prizes—overprizes—*g*.	*Balin and Balan* 184
airs of Heaven Should kiss with an unwonted *g*.	*Lover's Tale i* 739
With politic care, with utter *g*,	*Akbar's Dream* 128
Gentler A *g* death shall Falsehood die,	*Clear-headed friend* 16
In *g* days, your arrow-wounded fawn	*In Mem. xxx* 17
We ceased: a *g* feeling crept Upon us:	*Balin and Balan* 208
But golden earnest of a *g* life!'	*Lancelot and E.* 766
Gentler-born The *g-b* maiden, the more bound,	*Lover's Tale i* 738
Gentlest whom the *g* airs of Heaven Should kiss	*De Prof., Two G.* 23
And last in kindly curves, with *g* fall,	*Princess iii* 129
Gentlewoman hammer at this reverend *g*.	*Gareth and L.* 867
Or sit beside a noble *g*.'	*Geraint and E.* 622
There is not one among my *gentlewomen*	,, 682
see ye not my *gentlewomen* here,	,, 686
one among his *gentlewomen* Display'd	*Merlin and V.* 911
and stood, A virtuous and deeply wrong'd,	*Lotos-Eaters, C. S.* 5
Gentlier Music that *g* on the spirit lies,	
Geoffrey (of Monmouth) Of *G*'s book, or him of Malleor's,	*To the Queen ii* 42
Geology Now hawking at *G* and schism;	*The Epic* 16
Astronomy and *G*, terrible Muses!	*Parnassus* 16

Geraint (a Knight of the Round Table) brave *G*, a knight of Arthur's court,	*Marr. of Geraint* 1
so loved *G* To make her beauty vary day by day,	,, 8
Grateful to Prince *G* for service done,	,, 15
Long in their common love rejoiced *G*.	,, 23
Not less *G* believed it;	,, 28
day by day she thought to tell *G*,	,, 65
Prince *G*, Late also, wearing neither hunting-dress	,, 164
G Exclaiming, 'Surely I will learn the name,'	,, 202
Prince *G*, now thinking that he heard	,, 232
came *G*, and underneath Beheld the long street	,, 241
thought *G*, 'I have track'd him to his earth.'	,, 253
Whereat *G* flash'd into sudden spleen:	,, 273
Then rode *G*, a little spleenful yet,	,, 293
Then rode *G* into the castle court,	,, 312
So the sweet voice of Enid moved *G*;	,, 334
So fared it with *G*, who thought and said,	,, 343
thought *G*, 'Here by God's rood is the one maid	,, 367
G, from utter courtesy, forbore.	,, 381
G had longing in him evermore To stoop and kiss	,, 394
But after all had eaten, then *G*,	,, 397
—I am *G* Of Devon—	,, 409
G, a name far-sounded among men For noble deeds?	,, 427
'Well said, true heart,' replied *G*,	,, 474
old And rusty, old and rusty, Prince *G*, Are mine,	,, 478
To whom *G* with eyes all bright replied,	,, 494
And waited there for Yniol and *G*.	,, 538
when *G* Beheld her first in field awaiting him,	,, 539
Increased *G*'s, who heaved his blade aloft,	,, 572
No later than last eve to Prince *G*—	,, 603
She look'd on ere the coming of *G*.	,, 614
G Woke where he slept in the high hall,	,, 754
rejoiced More than *G* to greet her thus attired;	,, 772
So fared it with *G*, (repeat)	*Geraint and E.* 8, 500
Prince *G* Drave the long spear a cubit thro' his breast	,, 85
his lance err'd; but *G*'s, A little in the late encounter	,, 157
G, dismounting, pick'd the lance That pleased him best,	,, 179
G had ruth again on Enid looking pale:	,, 202
G Ate all the mowers' victual unawares,	,, 214
Then said *G*, 'I wish no better fare:	,, 232
Her suitor in old years before *G*, Enter'd,	,, 276
Greeted *G* full face, but stealthily,	,, 279
Then cried *G* for wine and goodly cheer	,, 283
But Enid left alone with Prince *G*,	,, 365
And *G* look'd and was not satisfied.	,, 435
G Waving an angry hand as who should say	,, 443
uttering a dry shriek, Dash'd on *G*,	,, 462
Then like a stormy sunlight smiled *G*,	,, 480
This heard *G*, and grasping at his sword,	,, 725
then *G* upon the horse Mounted, and reach'd a hand,	,, 758
'My lord *G*, I greet you with all love;	,, 785
But while *G* lay healing of his hurt,	,, 931
when *G* was whole again, they past With Arthur	,, 945
tho' *G* could never take again That comfort	,, 949
Enids and *G*'s Of times to be;	,, 965
after Lancelot, Tristram, and *G* And Gareth,	*Lancelot and E.* 556
Germ (*See also* **Baby-germ**) in it is the *g* of all That grows within the woodland.	*Amphion* 7
German No little *G* state are we,	*Third of Feb.* 15
Germander that her clear *g* eye Droopt	*Sea Dreams* 4
Germany worse than daring *G* gave us,	*Trans. of Homer* 5
Get (*See also* **Git**) *g* thee hence—Lest that rough humour	*Gareth and L.* 376
Thou *g* to horse and follow him far away.	,, 584
Flee down the valley before he *g* to horse.	,, 941
with Sir Pelleas as with one Who *g*'s a wound in battle,	*Pelleas and E.* 529
I couldn't *g* back tho' I tried,	*Rizpah* 43
In yon dark city: *g* thee back:	*Ancient Sage* 253
Till Holy St. Pether *g*'s up wid his kays	*Tomorrow* 93
Up, *g* up, and tell him all,	*Forlorn* 55
Up, *g* up, the time is short,	,, 73
I have told you my tale. *G* you gone.	*Charity* 44

Getting See **Gittin'**

Gev (give) yer Honour ye *g* her the top of the mornin', *Tomorrow* 3
an' she *g* him a frindly nod,   " 58

Gewgaw Seeing his *g* castle shine, *Maud I x* 18

Ghastlier And a *g* face than ever has haunted a grave *The Wreck* 8
stared upon By *g* than the Gorgon head, *Death of Œnone* 71

Ghastliest Our dearest faith; our *g* doubt; *In Mem. cxxiv* 2

Ghastly there rain'd a *g* dew From the nations' airy navies *Locksley Hall* 123
They cling together in the *g* sack— *Aylmer's Field* 764
And *g* thro' the drizzling rain *In Mem. vii* 11
For there in the *g* pit long since a body was found, *Maud I i* 5
Walk'd in a wintry wind by a *g* glimmer,   " *iii* 13
The *g* Wraith of one that I know;   " *II i* 32
Trick thyself out in *g* imageries *Gareth and L.* 1390
Lancelot gave A marvellous great shriek and *g* groan, *Lancelot and E.* 516
from the sun there swiftly made at her A *g* something, *Guinevere* 79
He had brought his *g* tools: *In the Child. Hosp.* 69
Flying at top of the roofs in the *g* siege of Lucknow— *Def. of Lucknow* 4
Timur built his *g* tower of eighty thousand human skulls, *Locksley H., Sixty* 82

Ghoäst (ghost) I thowt it wur Charlie's *g* *Village Wife* 82
They was all on 'em fear'd o' the *G* *Owd Roä* 37
the *G* moästlins was nobbut a rat or a mouse.   " 38

Ghost (adj.) So sacred those *G* Lovers hold the gift.' *The Ring* 205
As if—those two *G* lovers—   " 459

Ghost (s) (*See also* **Boggle, Ghoäst**) *g* of passion that no smiles restore— *The form, the form* 11
He thought I was a *g*, mother, *May Queen* 9
we should come like *g's* to trouble joy. *Lotos-Eaters, C. S.* 74
Was haunted with a jolly *g*, that shook *Walk. to the Mail* 36
'Yes, we're flitting,' says the *g*   " 43
Old wishes, *g's* of broken plans, *Will Water.* 29
g of one who bore your name About these meadows, *The Brook* 219
I seem'd to move among a world of *g's* *Princess i* 17
I seem'd to move among a world of *g's*;   " *iv* 561
And doing battle with forgotten *g's*,   " *v* 480
droops the milkwhite peacock like a *g*,   " *vii* 180
And like a *g* she glimmers on to me.   " 181
And in the dark church like a *g* *In Mem. lxvii* 15
O solemn *g*, O crowned soul!   " *lxxxv* 36
Spirit to Spirit, *G* to *G*.   " *xciii* 8
My *G* may feel that thine is near.   " 16
a sudden desire, like a glorious *g*, to glide, *Maud I xiv* 20
A disease, a hard mechanic *g*   " *II ii* 34
some Were pale as at the passing of a *g*, *Com. of Arthur* 263
thou be shadow, here I make thee *g*,' *Balin and Balan* 394
wall That sunders *g's* and shadow-casting men *Merlin and V.* 629
Then like a *g* she lifted up her face, But like a *g* without the power to speak. *Lancelot and E.* 918
Monotonous and hollow like a *G's* *Guinevere* 420
g of Gawain blown Along a wandering wind, *Pass. of Arthur* 31
light in death Is Gawain, for the *g* is as the man;   " 57
And some beheld the faces of old *g's*   " 103
Rather than that gray king, whose name, a *g*, *To the Queen ii* 39
still Haunted us like her *g*; *Sisters (E. and E.)* 247
the *g* of our great Catholic Queen Smiles *Columbus* 187
would scatter the *g's* of the Past, *Despair* 23
my mother's *g* would rise— *The Flight* 51
smiling at the slighter *g*. *Locksley H., Sixty* 9
All the world is *g* to me,   " 253
G of Pindar in you Roll'd an Olympian; *To Prof. Jebb.* 3
Led upward by the God of *g's* and dreams, *Demeter and P.* 5
G in Man, the *G* that once was Man, *The Ring* 35
that half skeleton, like a barren *g*   " 227
Vile, so near the *G* Himself,   " 230
dearer *g* had—wrench'd it away.   " 467
in the night, When the *g's* are fleeting. *Forlorn* 18
rib-grated dungeon of the holy human *g*, *Happy* 31
white fog vanish'd like a *g* Before the day, *Death of Œnone* 67
G of the Brute that is walking and haunting *The Dawn* 23

Ghostlike Luminous, gemlike, *g*, deathlike, *Maud I iii* 8
In either twilight *g-l* to and fro *Lancelot and E.* 849
mist Before her, moving *g* to his doom. *Guinevere* 605

Ghostly morning-breath Of England, blown across her *g* wall: *Enoch Arden* 661
An echo like a *g* woodpecker, *Princess, Pro.* 217
No *g* hauntings like his Highness.   " *ii* 411
for spite of doubts And sudden *g* shadowings   " *iv* 572
Cloud-towers by *g* masons wrought, *In Mem. lxx* 5
while that *g* grace Beam'd on his fancy, *Lancelot and E.* 885
and bid call the *g* man Hither.   " 1099
So when the *g* man had come and gone,   " 1101
Or *g* footfall echoing on the stair. *Guinevere* 507
thro' her dream A *g* murmur floated, *Death of Œnone* 79

Ghoul Some deathsong for the *G's* *Ancient Sage* 17

Giant (adj.) enormous polypi Winnow with *g* arms the slumbering green. *The Kraken* 10
three stanzas that you made About my ' *g* bole;' *Talking Oak* 136
And near the light a *g* woman sat, *Sea Dreams* 98
For tho' the *G* Ages heave the hill And break the shore, *Ode on Well.* 259
g aisles, Rich in model and design; *Ode Inter. Exhib.* 12
The *g* windows' blazon'd fires, *The Daisy* 58
I stood on a *g* deck and mix'd my breath *Maud III vi* 34
Yet God's just wrath shall be wreak'd on a *g* liar;   " 45
thrice that morning Guinevere had climb'd The *g* tower, *Marr. of Geraint* 827
struck, Furrowing a *g* oak, *Merlin and V.* 936
and there My *g* ilex keeping leaf *To Ulysses* 18

Giant (s) a race Of *g's* living, each, a thousand years, *Princess iii* 269
those three stars of the airy *G's* zone,   " *v* 260
genial *g*, Arac, roll'd himself Thrice in the saddle,   " 274
From Arac's arm, as from a *g's* flail,   " 500
The *g* labouring in his youth; *In Mem. cxviii* 2
The *g* answer'd merrily, 'Yea, but one? *Geraint and E.* 128
the King, Who seem'd the phantom of a *G* in it, *Guinevere* 602
weigh'd him down as Ætna does The *G* of Mythology: *Lover's Tale iv* 18
Gnome of the cavern, Griffin and *G*, *Merlin and the G.* 40

Giant-factoried Droopt in the *g-f* city-gloom, *Sea Dreams* 5

Gibber point and jeer, And *g* at the worm, *Romney's R.* 137

Gibbet from the church and not from the *g*— *Rizpah* 84

Gibe With solemn *g* did Eustace banter me. *Gardener's D.* 168
there with *g's* and flickering mockeries *Last Tournament* 186
'Was it muddier than thy *g's*?   " 299

Gibed —him Who *g* and japed—in many a merry tale *Sir J. Oldcastle* 91

Giddiest Ran into its *g* whirl of sound, *Vision of Sin* 29

Giddy or like a girl Valuing the *g* pleasure of the eyes. *M. d'Arthur* 128
that man Were *g* gazing there; *Gareth and L.* 228
or like a girl Valuing the *g* pleasure of the eyes. *Pass. of Arthur* 296
We were *g* besides with the fruits we had gorged, *V. of Maeldune* 75

Gideon those whom *G* school'd with briers. *Buonaparte* 14

Gie (give) An' I says 'I mun *g* tha a kiss,' *North. Cobbler* 3
eärs es 'e'd *g* fur a howry owd book *Village Wife* 45
set oop thy taäil, tha may *g* ma a kiss, *Spinster's S's.* 31
I shall hev to *g* one or tother awaäy.   " 64
Now I'll *g* tha a bit o' my mind *Church-warden, etc.* 21

Gied (gave) toithe were due, an' I *g* it in hond; *N. Farmer, O. S.* 11
an' I *g* our Sally a kick, *North. Cobbler* 36
I seeäd that our Sally went laämed Cos' o' the kick as I *g* 'er,   " 40
I minded the fust kiss I *g* 'er   " 45
I *g* 'er a kiss, an' then anoother.   " 52
upo' coomin' awaäy Sally *g* me a kiss ov 'ersen.   " 56
an' *g* to the tramps goin' by— *Village Wife* 33
'e *g*—I be fear'd fur to tell tha 'ow much—   " 47
it *g* me a scare tother night,   " 81
an' our Nelly she *g* me 'er 'and,   " 111
Till I *g* 'em Hinjian curn,   " 118
Robby I *g* tha a raätin that sattled thy coortin o' me. *Spinster's S's.* 48

Gift (*See also* **Bridal-gift, Chance-gift**) God's great *g* of speech abused *A Dirge* 44
'He owns the fatal *g* of eyes, *Two Voices* 286
Love the *g* is Love the debt. *Miller's D.* 207
'I woo thee not with *g's*. *Œnone* 152
A sinful soul possess'd of many *g's*, *To —— With Pal. of Art* 3
angels rising and descending met With interchange of *g*. *Palace of Art* 144

Gift (continued) we knew your *g* that way At college: *The Epic* 24
The holy Elders with the *g* of myrrh. *M. d'Arthur* 233
Requiring at her hand the greatest *g*, *Gardener's D.* 229
' And yet it was a graceful *g*: *Talking Oak* 233
Let me go : take back thy *g*: *Tithonus* 27
Gods themselves cannot recall their *g's*.' " 49
eagles of her belt, The grim Earl's *g*; *Godiva* 44
g's, when *g's* of mine could please ; *The Letters* 22
G's by the children, garden-herbs *Enoch Arden* 338
shower'd His oriental *g's* on everyone And most on Edith : *Aylmer's Field* 214
Among the *g's* he left her " 217
' A gracious *g* to give a lady, this !' " 240
' Were I to give this *g* of his to one " 242
' Take it,' she added sweetly, ' tho' his *g*; " 246
Nor deeds of *g*, but *g's* of grace he forged, *Sea Dreams* 192
And jewels, *g's*, to fetch her : *Princess* i 43
they saw the king : he took the *g's* " 46
g's of grace, that might express *In Mem. lxxxv* 46
Ah, take the imperfect *g* I bring, " 117
She keeps the *g* of years before, " *xcvii* 25
and saw without the door King Arthur's *g*, *Gareth and L.* 677
branch'd and flower'd with gold, a costly *g* *Marr. of Geraint* 631
' Yea, I know it ; your good *g*, " 688
Your own good *g* !' ' Yea, surely,' said the dame, " 690
I see her now, Clothed with my *g*, and gay among the gay. " 753
Laid from her limbs the costly-broider'd *g*, " 769
your fair child shall wear your costly *g*, " 819
Who knows ? another *g* of the high God, " 821
' I take it as free *g*, then,' said the boy, *Geraint and E.* 222
' These be *g's*, Born with the blood, *Balin and Balan* 174
A seven months' babe had been a truer *g*. *Merlin and V.* 711
broider'd with great pearls, Some gentle maiden's *g*.' *Lancelot and E.* 605
she should ask some goodly *g* of him " 912
price of half a realm, his costly *g*, " 1164
they had been thrice their worth Being your *g*, " 1213
value of all *g's* Must vary as the giver's. " 1214
this life of mine I guard as God's high *g* *Guinevere* 494
holy Elders with the *g* of myrrh. *Pass. of Arthur* 401
my rich *g* is wholly mine to give. *Lover's Tale* iv 350
' Take my free *g*, my cousin, for your wife ; " 363
One golden curl, his golden *g*, before *The Flight* 36
G's from every British zone ; *Open. I. and C. Exhib.* 9
And golden grain, my *g* to helpless man. *Demeter and P.* 111
sacred those Ghost Lovers hold the *g*.' *The Ring* 205
full thanks to you For your rich *g*, *To Ulysses* 34
send A *g* of slenderer value, mine. " 48

Gifted (*See also* **God-gifted**) As some divinely *g* man, *In Mem. lxiv* 2
Gigantesque The sort of mock-heroic *g*, *Princess*, Con. 11
Gigglesby we was shaämed to cross *G* Greeän, *Spinster's S's.* 33
out o' sight o' the winders o' *G* Hinn— " 35
foälk be sa scared at, i' *G* wood. " 24
Gild *g's* the straiten'd forehead of the fool ! *Locksley Hall* 62
grain as sweet As that which *g's* the glebe of England, *To Prof. Jebb* 7
Gilded (adj. and part.) (*See also* **Lichen-gilded**) Kate saith ' the men are *g* flies.' *Kate* 18
And round the roofs a *g* gallery *Palace of Art* 29
Near *g* organ-pipes, her hair Wound with white roses, " 98
The parrot in his *g* wires. *Day-Dm.*, *Sleep*. P. 16
A *g* dragon, also, for the babes. *Enoch Arden* 540
DUST are our frames ; and, *g* dust, our pride *Aylmer's Field* 1
Staring for ever from their *g* walls " 833
steep-up spout whereon the *g* ball Danced like a wisp : *Princess*, Pro. 63
Fly to her, and fall upon her *g* eaves, " iv 94
And slain with laughter roll'd the *g* Squire. " v 22
let his coltish nature break At seasons thro' the *g* pale : *In Mem. cxi* 8
Sweet nature *g* by the gracious gleam Of letters, *Ded. of Idylls* 39
on such a palm As glitters *g* in thy Book of Hours. *Gareth and L.* 46
were birds Of sunny plume in *g* trellis-work; *Marr. of Geraint* 659
I will not fight my way with *g* arms, *Geraint and E.* 21
And call'd herself a *g* summer fly *Merlin and V.* 258
Set every *g* parapet shuddering ; *Lancelot and E.* 299

Gilded (adj. and part.) (continued) from the carven-work behind him crept Two dragons *g*, *Lancelot and E.* 437
the *g* parapets were crown'd With faces, *Pelleas and E.* 165
inflamed the knights At that dishonour done the *g* spur, *Last Tournament* 435
G with broom or shatter'd into spires, *Lover's Tale* i 400
and the *g* snake Had nestled in this bosom-throne of Love, " i 623
A veil, that seemed no more than *g* air, " iv 290
I have broke their cage, no *g* one, I trow— *Sir J. Oldcastle* 3
and once we only saw Your *g* vane, *The Ring* 331
Gilded (verb) Would that have *g* me ? *Columbus* 114
Gilden-peakt pavilions rear'd Above the bushes, *g-p*: *Pelleas and E.* 429
Gildest star that *g* yet this phantom shore? *To Virgil* 26
Gilding Flattery *g* the rift in a throne ; *Vastness* 20
Gileadite The daughter of the warrior *G*, *D. of F. Women* 197
Gillyflowers a rosy sea of *g* About it ; *Aylmer's Field* 159
Gilt (*See also* **Foot-gilt**) as a parrot turns Up thro' *g* wires, a crafty loving eye, *Princess*, Pro. 172
dark old place will be *g* by the touch of a millionaire : *Maud* I i 66
his strong hands gript And dinted the *g* dragons right and left, *Last Tournament* 182
And those *g* gauds men-children swarm to see. *To W. C. Macready* 11
Gilt-head court-Galen poised his *g-h* cane, *Princess* i 19
Gin I'll tell tha. *G*. *North. Cobbler* 7
Thou gits naw *g* fro' the bottle theer, " 10
seeäs stannin' theer, yon big black bottle o' *g*. " 70
summat bewitch'd istead of a quart o' *g* ; " 82
Fur I couldn't 'owd 'ands off *g*, " 84
An' 'e points to the bottle o' *g*, " 90
Gineration (generation) But a frish *g* had riz, *Tomorrow* 75
Gipsy Or the frock and *g* bonnet *Maud* I xx 19
Gird minds did *g* their orbs with beams, *The Poet* 7
Uncared for, *g* the windy grove, *In Mem. ci* 13
Far liefer had I *g* his harness on him, *Marr. of Geraint* 93
many a mystic symbol, *g* the hall : *Holy Grail* 233
Girded *See* **Man-girded**
Girdle (*See also* **Vapour-girdle**) And I would be the *g* *Miller's D.* 175
twist his *g* tight, and pat The girls *Talking Oak* 43
She moving, at her *g* clash The golden keys *To Marq. of Dufferin* 3
Girdled *g* with the gleaming world : *Lotos-Eaters*, C. S. 113
and *g* her with music. *Princess* vii 327
the rebels that *g* us round— *Def. of Lucknow* 22
Girl (*See also* **Baby-girl**, **Gell**, **Market-girl**, **Orphan-girl**)
Gazed on the Persian *g* alone, *Arabian Nights* 134
And the red cloaks of market *g's*, *L. of Shalott* ii 17
the *g's* all kiss'd Beneath the sacred bush *The Epic* 52
like a *g* Valuing the giddy pleasure of the eyes. *M. d'Arthur* 127
' My *g*, I love you well ; *Dora* 42
' Go !—*G*, get you in !' She went— *Edwin Morris* 125
and pat The *g's* upon the cheek, *Talking Oak* 44
This *g*, for whom your heart is sick, " 71
either fixt his heart On that one *g* ; *Enoch Arden* 40
the *g* Seem'd kinder unto Philip than to him ; " 41
I'll be back, my *g*, before you know it.' " 193
as the village *g*, Who sets her pitcher " 206
' Annie, my *g*, cheer up, be comforted, " 218
let me put the boy and *g* to school : " 312
Philip put the boy and *g* to school, " 331
And o'er her second father stoopt a *g*, " 747
the *g* So like her mother, and the boy, my son.' " 790
Where once with Leolin at her side the *g*, *Aylmer's Field* 184
would it be more gracious ' asked the *g* " 241
The *g* might be entangled ere she knew. " 272
g and boy, Sir, know their differences !' " 274
twenty boys and *g's* should marry on it, " 371
found the *g* And flung her down upon a couch of fire, " 573
Born of a village *g*, carpenter's son, " 668
But *g's*, Hetairai, curious in their art, *Lucretius* 52
a group of *g's* In circle waited, *Princess*, Pro. 68
like as many *g's*—Sick for the hollies " 186
lengths of yellow ringlet, like a *g*, " i 3
G's, Knowledge is now no more a fountain " ii 89
G's ?—more like men !' " iii 43
Men ! *g's*, like men ! why, if they had been men " 49

Girl (*continued*) To nurse a blind ideal like a *g*, Methinks
he seems no better than a *g* ; As *g's* were once,
as we ourself have been :   *Princess iii* 217
But children die ; and let me tell you, *g*,   „   253
G after *g* was call'd to trial :   „   *iv* 228
like enough, O *g's*, To unfurl the maiden banner   „   502
and they will beat my *g* Remembering her mother :   „   *v* 88
you spent a stormy time With our strange *g* :   „   122
'Tut, you know them not, the *g's*.   „   151
Let our *g's* flit, Till the storm die !   „   *vi* 337
ill counsel had mislead the *g* To vex true hearts : yet
was she but a *g*—   „   *vii* 241
'So fret not, like an idle *g*,   *In Mem. lii* 13
Like some poor *g* whose heart is set   „   *lx* 3
I play'd with the *g* when a child ;   *Maud I i* 68
'Well if it prove a *g*, the boy (repeat)   „   *vii* 7, 15
And soften as if to a *g*,   „   *x* 16
save from some slight shame one simple *g*.   „   *xviii* 45
Queen rose of the rosebud garden of *g's*,   „   *xxii* 53
Shame never made *g* redder than Gareth joy.   *Gareth and L.* 536
three fair *g's* In gilt and rosy raiment came :   „   926
massacring Man, woman, lad and *g*—   „   1341
Half disarray'd as to her rest, the *g* ;   *Marr. of Geraint* 516
And all in charge of whom ? a *g* :   *Geraint and E.* 125
ye shall share my earldom with me, *g*,   „   626
'*G*, for I see ye scorn my courtesies,   „   671
Sir Lancelot worship no unmarried *g*   *Merlin and V.* 12
beyond All hopes of gaining, than as maiden *g*.   „   24
came the village *g's* And linger'd talking.   *Pelleas and E.* 508
like a *g* Valuing the giddy pleasure of the eyes.   *Pass. of Arthur* 295
thronging fancies come To boys and *g's*   *Lover's Tale i* 555
but Lionel and the *g* Were wedded,   „   *iv* 13
Passionate *g* tho' I was,   *First Quarrel* 15
There was a *g*, a hussy, that workt   „   24
the *g* was the most to blame.   „   26
It's the little *g* with her arms lying out   *In the Child. Hosp.* 58
And so, when I bore him a *g*,   *The Wreck* 33
he the knight for an amorous *g's* romance !   „   44
The *g's* of equal age, but one was fair,   *The Ring* 160
you my *g* Rode on my shoulder here—   „   321
I believing that the *g's* Lean fancy,   „   335
lover's fairy dream, His *g* of *g's* ;   *To Mary Boyle* 44
Girl-graduates sweet *g-g* in their golden hair.   *Princess, Pro.* 142
Girlish Is *g* talk at best ;   *Epilogue* 43
Girt Among the thorns that *g* Thy brow,   *Supp. Confessions* 6
g round With blackness as a solid wall,   *Palace of Art* 273
The land, where *g* with friends or foes   *You ask me, why, etc.* 7
Tho' sitting *g* with doubtful light.   *Love thou thy land* 16
g the region with high cliff and lawn :   *Vision of Sin* 47
Enoch's golden ring had *g* Her finger,   *Enoch Arden* 157
g With song and flame and fragrance,   *Lucretius* 133
G by half the tribes of Britain,   *Boädicea* 5
the King Came *g* with knights.   *Lancelot and E.* 1261
Far off from out an island *g* by foes,   *Achilles over the T.* 8
Girth Alas, I was so broad of *g*,   *Talking Oak* 139
and grown a bulk Of spanless *g*,   *Princess vi* 36
strait *g* of Time Inswathe the fulness of Eternity,   *Lover's Tale i* 482
No stone is fitted in yon marble *g*   *Tiresias* 135
Would my granite *g* were strong   *Helen's Tower* 7
Git (get) *G* ma my aäle, (repeat)   *N. Farmer, O. S.* 4, 68
nobbut a curate, an' weänt niver *g* hissen clear,   „   *N. S.* 27
Squire were at Charlie ageän to *g* 'im to cut off
'is taäil.   *Village Wife* 74
or she weänt *g* a maäte onyhow !   „   104
Robby, *g* down wi'tha, wilt tha ?   *Spinster's S's.* 67
Steevie *g* down.   „   92
An' I says '*G* awaäy, ya beäst,'   *Owd Roä* 62
G oop, if ya're onywaäys good for owt.'   „   77
when I *g's* to the top,   „   83
Too laäte, tha mun *g* tha to bed,   „   117
an' thou'll *g* along, niver fear,   *Church-warden, etc.* 7
I *g's* the plaäte fuller o' Soondays   „   40
if iver tha meäns to *g* 'igher,   „   45
if tha wants to *g* forrards a bit,   „   49
Gittin' (getting) Fur work mun 'a gone to the *g*   *N. Farmer, N. S.* 50

Gittin' (getting) (*continued*) allus afear'd of a man's *g'*
ower fond,   *Spinster's S's.* 27
How be the farm *g* on ? noäways. *G* on i' deeäd !   *Church-warden, etc.* 3
Giv (gave) I niver *g* it a thowt—   *N. Farmer, N. S.* 23
Give (*See also* **Gev, Gie**) Could *g* the warrior kings
of old,   *To the Queen* 4
'Mother, *g* me grace To help me of my weary
load.'   *Mariana in the S.* 29
fill my glass : *g* me one kiss :   *Miller's D.* 17
O would she *g* me vow for vow,   „   119
'O Paris, *G* it to Pallas !'   *Œnone* 170
G us long rest or death, dark death,   *Lotos-Eaters, C. S.* 53
Failing to *g* the bitter of the sweet,   *D. of F. Women* 286
God *g's* us love. Something to love He lends us ;   *To J. S.* 13
What should one *g* to light on such a dream ?'   *Edwin Morris* 58
'*G*? *G* all thou art,' he answer'd,   „   59
like the daughters of the horseleech, '*G*,   *Golden Year* 12
I ask'd thee, '*G* me immortality.'   *Tithonus* 15
wealthy men who care not how they *g*.   „   17
in the rights that name may *g*,   *Day-Dm., L'Envoi* 54
a lily-white doe To *g* his cousin, Lady Clare.   *Lady Clare* 4
'Yet *g* one kiss to your mother dear !   „   49
Little can I *g* my wife.   *L. of Burleigh* 14
And *g* his child a better bringing-up   *Enoch Arden* 87
To *g* his babes a better bringing-up   „   299
—a month—*G* her a month—   „   462
aid me, *g* me strength Not to tell her,   „   785
Take, *g* her this, for it may comfort her :   „   899
'A gracious gift to *g* a lady, this !'   *Aylmer's Field* 240
'Were I to *g* this gift of his to one   „   242
G me my fling, and let me say say.'   „   399
G me your prayers, for he is past   „   751
or a song To *g* us breathing-space.'   *Princess, Pro.* 242
And here I *g* the story and the songs.   „   247
I can *g* you letters to her ;   „   *i* 159
'We *g* you welcome : not without redound   „   *ii* 42
I *g* thee to death My brother !   „   307
g three gallant gentlemen to death.'   „   335
we *g* you, being strange, A license :   „   *iii* 204
If we could *g* them surer, quicker proof—   „   282
g's the manners of your countrywomen ?'   „   *iv* 151
g him your hand : Cleave to your contract :   „   408
And *g's* the battle to his hands.   „   580
G us, then, your mind at large :   „   *v* 123
G's her harsh groom for bridal-gift a scourge ;   „   378
It is not yours, but mine : *g* me the child.'   „   *vi* 141
g her the child ! (repeat)   „   168, 179, 183
G me it : I will *g* it her.'   „   187
what answer should I *g* ?   „   *vii* 6
let her make herself her own To *g* or keep,   „   273
of which I *g* you all The random scheme   „   *Con.* 1
men required that I should *g* throughout   „   10
And yet to *g* the story as it rose,   „   26
G it time To learn its limbs :   „   78
these great Sirs *G* up their parks some dozen times
a year   „   103
he kept us free ; O *g* him welcome,   *Ode on Well.* 92
a weänt niver *g* it to Joänes,   *N. Farmer, O. S.* 59
Who by the Fiend himself his due,   *To F. D. Maurice* 11
one lay-hearth would *g* you welcome   „   11
'We *g* you his life.'   *The Victim* 16
Take you his dearest, *G* us a life.'   „   28
We *g* them the boy'   „   40
'O, Father Odin, We *g* you a life.   „   75
Gods have answer'd ; We *g* them the wife !'   „   79
G her the glory of going on,   *Wages* 5
G her the wages of going on,   „   10
To Sleep I *g* my powers away ;   *In Mem. iv* 1
No joy the blowing season *g's*,   „   *xxxviii* 5
the hoarding sense *G's* out at times   „   *xlvii* 7
And dare we to this fancy *g*,   „   *liii* 5
Hath power to *g* thee as thou wert ?   „   *lxxv* 8
meets the year, and *g's* and takes   „   *cxvi* 1
Some bitter notes my harp would *g*,   „   *cxxv* 2
And I must *g* away the bride ;   „   *Con.* 42

Give (*continued*)   To *g* him the grasp of fellowship ;
  sullen-seeming Death may *g* More life to Love | *Maud I xiii* 16
  squire will *g* A grand political dinner | ,, *xviii* 46
  A learned man Could *g* it a clumsy name. | ,, *xx* 24
  G me thy daughter Guinevere to wife.' | ,, *II ii* 10
  G my one daughter saving to a king, | *Com. of Arthur* 139
  Fear not to *g* this King thine only child, | ,, 143
  G me to right her wrong, and slay the man.' | ,, 413
  let my name Be hidd'n, and *g* me the first quest, | *Gareth and L.* 366
  and so *g*'s the quest to him— | ,, 545
  g him back the shield.' | ,, 864
  Take him to stall, and *g* him corn, | ,, 1344
  Thou shalt *g* back their earldom to thy kin. | *Marr. of Geraint* 371
  Albeit I *g* no reason but my wish, | ,, 585
  Then not to *g* you warning, that seems hard ; | ,, 761
  to *g* him warning, for he rode As if he heard not, | *Geraint and E.* 422
  set his foot upon me, and *g* me life. | ,, 451
  G's him the lie ! There is no being pure, | ,, 850
  But since I will not yield to *g* you power | *Merlin and V.* 51
  But, father, *g* me leave, an if he will, | ,, 373
  if you love, it will be sweet to *g* it ; | *Lancelot and E.* 219
  with mine own hand *g* his diamond to him, | ,, 692
  yea, and you must *g* it— | ,, 760
  G me good fortune, I will strike him dead, | ,, 773
  g at last The price of half a realm, | ,, 1071
  if ye fail, *G* ye the slave mine order | ,, 1163
  G me three days to melt her fancy, | *Pelleas and E.* 270
  'I will flee hence and *g* myself to God '— | ,, 356
  G's birth to a brawling brook, | *Last Tournament* 624
  but you know that you must *g* me back : | *Lover's Tale i* 526
  you shall *g* me back when he returns.' | ,, *iv* 100
  pronounced That my rich gift is wholly mine to *g*. | ,, 112
  would venture to *g* him the nay ? | ,, 350
  he ped me back wid the best he could *g* | *The Wreck* 17
  Yer Honour 'ill *g* me a thrifle to dhrink | *Tomorrow* 42
  Coom *g* hoäver then, weant ye ? | ,, 98
  G your gold to the Hospital, | *Spinster's S's.* 63
  'And if you *g* the ring to any maid, | *On Jub. Q. Victoria* 33
  and *g* place to the beauty that endures, | *The Ring* 200
  'BEAT, little heart—I *g* you this and this ' | *Happy* 36
  For I *g* you this, and I *g* you this ! | *Romney's R.* 1
  a charm no words could *g* ? | ,, 100
  I whisper'd '*g* it to me,' but he would not | *Far—far—away* 16
  and *g* His fealty to the halcyon hour ! | *Bandit's Death* 27
  G me a hand—and you—and you— | *The Wanderer* 11
  Or mine to *g* him meat, | ,, 15
   | *Voice spake, etc.* 8

Given   Achieving calm, to whom was *g* | *Two Voices* 209
  difference, reconcilement, pledges *g*, | *Gardener's D.* 257
  I found him garrulously *g*, | *Talking Oak* 23
  then before thine answer *g* Departest, | *Tithonus* 44
  to me is *g* Such hope, I know not fear ; | *Sir Galahad* 61
  A man had *g* all other bliss, | *Sir G. and Q. G.* 42
  Came, with a month's leave *g* them, | *Sea Dreams* 6
  but *g* to starts and bursts Of revel ; | *Princess i* 54
  the king,' he said, ' Had *g* us letters, | ,, 181
  with mutual pardon ask'd and *g* For stroke and song, | ,, *v* 46
  G back to life, to life indeed, | ,, *vii* 345
  Is *g* in outline and no more. | *In Mem. v* 12
  the shock, so harshly *g*, Confused me | ,, *xvi* 11
  unto thee is *g* A life that bears immortal fruit | ,, *xl* 17
  His who had *g* me life— | *Maud I i* 6
  if she Had *g* her word to a thing so low ? | ,, *xvi* 27
  And *g* false death her hand, | ,, *xviii* 68
  For the prophecy *g* of old And then not understood, | ,, *II v* 42
  'I have *g* him the first quest : | *Gareth and L.* 582
  thou hast *g* me but a kitchen-knave.' | ,, 659
  Canst thou not trust the limbs thy God hath *g*, | ,, 1388
  A creature wholly *g* to brawls and wine, | *Marr. of Geraint* 441
  Woke and bethought her of her promise *g* | ,, 602
  He would not leave her, till her promise *g*— | ,, 605
  g her on the night Before her birthday, | ,, 632
  'And gladly *g* again this happy morn. | ,, 691
  (No reason *g* her) she could cast aside | ,, 807
  Debating his command of silence *g*, | *Geraint and E.* 366
  breaking his command of silence *g*, | ,, 390

Given (*continued*)   sunshine that hath *g* the man A
  growth, | *Balin and Balan* 181
  but neither marry, nor are *g* In marriage, | *Merlin and V.* 15
  He hath *g* us a fair falcon which he train'd ; | ,, 96
  no more thanks than might a goat have *g* | ,, 278
  I fain had *g* them greater wits : | ,, 496
  He promised more than ever king has *g*, | ,, 586
  deem this prize of ours is rashly *g* : | *Lancelot and E.* 541
  'Sweet is true love tho' *g* in vain, | ,, 1007
  a space of land is *g* to the plow. | *Holy Grail* 907
  have the Heavens but *g* thee a fair face, | *Pelleas and E.* 101
  And thou hast *g* thy promise, and I know | ,, 245
  And so, leave *g*, straight on thro' open door | ,, 382
  I to your dead man have *g* my troth, | ,, 389
  Not knowing they were lost as soon as *g*— | *Last Tournament* 42
  And if I do not there is penance *g*— | *Guinevere* 187
  For you have *g* me life and love again, | *Lover's Tale iv* 110
  I would have *g* my life To help his own | *Sir J. Oldcastle* 62
  G thee the keys of the great Ocean-sea ? | *Columbus* 149
  one thing *g* me, to love and to live for, | *The Wreck* 35
  Was to be *g* you—such her dying wish—*G* on
  the morning when you came of age | *The Ring* 76
  Miriam ! have you *g* your ring to her ? | ,, 260
  for *him* who had *g* her the name. | *Charity* 39

Giver   Render thanks to the *G*, (repeat) | *Ode on Well.* 44, 47
  value of all gifts Must vary as the *g*'s. | *Lancelot and E.* 1215
  And were it only for the *g*'s sake, | *Lover's Tale iv* 364

Giving   *g* light To read those laws ; | *Isabel* 18
  g safe pledge of fruits, | *Ode to Memory* 18
  record of the glance That graced the *g*— | *Gardener's D.* 178
  And part it, *g* half to him. | *In Mem. xxv* 12
  G you power upon me thro' this charm, | *Merlin and V.* 514
  In *g* so much beauty to the world, | *Lover's Tale i* 212
  And *g* light to others. | ,, 426
  g him That which of all things is the dearest | ,, *iv* 347
  of a hand *g* bread and wine, | *The Wreck* 114

Glacier   with tears By some cold morning *g* ; | *Princess vii* 116
  And the lilies like *g*'s winded down, | *V. of Maeldune* 42
  set me climbing icy capes And *g*'s, | *To E. Fitzgerald* 26

Glad   (*See also* **Maain-Glad**)   So full of summer
  warmth, so *g*, | *Miller's D.* 14
  when his heart is *g* Of the full harvest, | *Dora* 68
  and we were *g* at heart. | *Audley Court* 89
  I'm *g* I walk'd.   How fresh the meadows look | *Walk. to the Mail* 1
  I was *g* at first To think that in our often-
  ransack'd world | *Sea Dreams* 128
  light is large, and lambs are *g* | *Lucretius* 99
  I am sad and *g* To see you, Florian. | *Princess ii* 306
  Be *g*, because his bones are laid by thine ! | *Ode on Well.* 141
  And *g* to find thyself so fair, | *In Mem. vi* 27
  And one is *g* ; her note is gay, | ,, *xxi* 25
  And *g* at heart from May to May : | ,, *xxii* 8
  I read Of that *g* year which once had been, | ,, *xcv* 22
  'Yea, my kind lord,' said the *g* youth, and went, | *Geraint and E.* 241
  Eat and be *g*, for I account you mine.' | ,, 647
  'How should I be *g* Henceforth in all the world | ,, 648
  Kiss'd the white star upon his noble front, *G* also ; | ,, 758
  Then were I *g* of you as guide and friend : | *Lancelot and E.* 226
  And *g* was I and clomb, but found at top | *Holy Grail* 427
  G that no phantom vext me more, | ,, 538
  so *g* were spirits and men Before the coming | *Guinevere* 269
  'Were they so *g* ? ill prophets were they all, | ,, 272
  Sometimes a troop of damsels *g*, | *L. of Shalott ii* 19
  To-morrow 'ill be the happiest time of all the
  g New-year; (repeat) | *May Queen* 2, 42
  Of all the *g* New-year, mother, | ,, 3
  For I would see the sun rise upon the *g* New-year. | ,, *N. Y's. E.* 2
  Gareth was *g*. (repeat) | *Gareth and L.* 497, 504
  Lancelot, and all as *g* to find thee whole, | ,, 1239
  all *g*, Knightlike, to find his charger yet unlamed, | *Balin and Balan* 427
  so *g* was he. | *Pelleas and E.* 146
  April promise, *g* new-year Of Being, | *Lover's Tale i* 281
  We gazed on it together In mute and *g* remembrance, | ,, *ii* 186
  Let the maim'd in his heart rejoice At this *g*
  Ceremonial, | *On Jub. Q. Victoria* 37

Glad (*continued*)   pierce the *g* and songful air,   *Demeter and P.* 45
   g to seeä tha sa 'arty an' well.   *North. Cobbler* 2
   So *g*? no tear for him, who left you wealth,   *The Ring* 188
   She comes, and Earth is *g* To roll her North   *Prog. of Spring* 48
Gladden   the Shepherd *g*'s in his heart: *Spec. of Iliad* 16
   Come—let us *g* their sad eyes,   *Last Tournament* 222
Gladden'd   a rose that *g* earth and sky,   *Pelleas and E.* 402
Gladder   Put forth and feel a *g* clime.'   *On a Mourner* 15
Glade   (*See also* **Olive-glade**)   With breezes from our
   oaken *g*'s,   *Eleänore* 10
   winding *g*'s high up like ways to Heaven,   *Enoch Arden* 573
   His wonted glebe, or lops the *g*'s;   *In Mem.* ci 22
   thro' many a grassy *g* And valley,   *Marr. of Geraint* 236
   with droopt brow down the long *g*'s he rode;   *Balin and Balan* 311
   Then they reach'd a *g*,   " 460
   drew me thro' the glimmering *g*'s   *Sisters (E. and E.)* 116
Gladed   See **Gloomy-gladed**
Gladiator   *g*'s moving toward their fight,   *St. Telemachus* 54
Gladiatorial   and flung himself between The *g* swords,   " 62
Gladlier   For sure no *g* does the stranded wreck   *Enoch Arden* 828
Gladly   How *g*, were I one of those,   *The Flight* 63
Gladness   a cloudy *g* lighten'd in the eyes of each.   *The Captain* 31
   I grew in *g* till I found My spirits in the golden age.   *To E. L.* 11
   Makes former *g* loom so great?   *In Mem. xxiv* 10
   making vain pretence Of *g*,   " *xxx* 7
   solemn *g* even crown'd The purple brows of Olivet.   " *xxxi* 11
   Borne down by *g* so complete,   " *xxxii* 10
   Neigh'd with all a *g* as they came,   *Geraint and E.* 755
Glaive   See **War-glaive**
Glamour   he had *g* enow In his own blood,   *Gareth and L.* 209
   Gwydion made by *g* out of flowers,   *Marr. of Geraint* 743
   and the harmless *g* of the field;   *Pass. of Arthur* 52
Glance (s)   (*See also* **Half-glance**)   women smile with
   saint-like *g*'s   *Supp. Confessions* 22
   Roof not a *g* so keen as thine: *Clear-headed friend* 7
   Sudden *g*'s, sweet and strange,   *Madeline* 5
   O'erflows thy calmer *g*'s,   " 33
   Every turn and *g* of thine,   *Eleänore* 52
   shaping faithful record of the *g* That graced   *Gardener's D.* 177
   cast back upon him A piteous *g*, and vanish'd.   *Aylmer's Field* 284
   a *g* I gave, No more;   *Princess iv* 180
   one *g* he caught Thro' open doors of Ida   " *v* 342
   striking with her *g* The mother, me, the child;   " *vi* 152
   And sidelong *g*'s at my father's grief,   " *vii* 107
   she fixt A showery *g* upon her aunt,   " *Con.* 33
   and rolling *g*'s lioness-like,   *Boädicea* 71
   In *g* and smile, and clasp and kiss,   *In Mem. lxxxiv* 7
   allured The *g* of Gareth dreaming on his liege.   *Gareth and L.* 1316
   Drew the vague *g* of Vivien, and her Squire;   *Balin and Balan* 464
   That *g* of theirs, but for the street,   *Merlin and V.* 105
   a *g* will serve—the liars!   " 111
   made him at one *g* More bondsman in his heart   *Pelleas and E.* 238
   the *g* That only seems half-loyal to command,—   *Last Tournament* 117
   a single *g* of them Will govern a whole life   *Lover's Tale i* 75
   But cast a parting *g* at me, you saw,   " *iv* 4
   at a *g* And as it were, perforce,   *Tiresias* 55
   when he cast a contemptuous *g*   *The Wreck* 25
   after one quick *g* upon the stars,   *Akbar's Dream* 3
Glance (verb)   Life shoots and *g*'s thro' your veins,   *Rosalind* 12
   In crystal eddies *g* and poise,   *Miller's D.* 52
   rivulet in the flowery dale 'ill merrily *g* and play,   *May Queen* 39
   fall down and *g* From tone to tone,   *D. of F. Women* 166
   I slip, I slide, I gloom, I *g*,   *The Brook* 174
   And here he *g*'s on an eye new-born,   *Lucretius* 137
   how the sun delights To *g* and shift about   " 189
   made them *g* Like those three stars   *Princess v* 259
   And *g* about the approaching sails,   *In Mem. xiii* 18
   Let random influences *g*,   " *xlix* 2
   And every eye but mine will *g* At Maud   *Maud I xx* 36
   Dared not to *g* at her good mother's face,   *Marr. of Geraint* 766
   sideways he let them *g* At Enid,   *Geraint and E.* 246
   stare at open space, nor *g* The one at other,   " 268
   wont to *g* and sparkle like a gem Of fifty facets;   " 294
   To *g* behind me at my former life,   " 863
   speak Of the pure heart, nor seem to *g* at thee?   *Guinevere* 502

Glance (verb) (*continued*)   Not daring yet to *g* at Lionel.   *Lover's Tale iv* 309
   G at the wheeling Orb of change,   *To E. Fitzgerald* 3
   That *g*'s from the bottom of the pool,   *The Ring* 371
   g the tits, and shriek the jays,   *Prog. of Spring* 15
   g's from the sun of our Islâm.   *Akbar's Dream* 79
Glanced   And *g* athwart the glooming flats.   *Mariana* 20
   The damned arrow *g* aside,   *Oriana* 41
   garden-glasses *g*, and momently The twinkling laurel   *Gardener's D.* 117
   She *g* across the plain;   *Talking Oak* 166
   We sat: the Lady *g*:   *Princess ii* 111
   G at the legendary Amazon As emblematic   " 126
   G like a touch of sunshine on the rocks,   " *iii* 357
   I *g* aside, and saw the palace-front   " *v* 508
   I struck out and shouted; the blade *g*,   " 540
   A light of healing, *g* about the couch,   " *vii* 59
   mute she glided forth, Nor *g* behind her,   " 171
   Whereat we *g* from theme to theme,   *In Mem. lxxxix* 33
   shyly *g* Eyes of pure women,   *Gareth and L.* 313
   the hair All over *g* with dewdrop or with gem   " 929
   G at the doors or gambol'd down the walks;   *Marr. of Geraint* 665
   had *g* away From being knighted till he smote the thrall,   *Balin and Balan* 154
   g aside, and paced The long white walk of lilies   " 248
   the King *G* first at him, then her,   *Lancelot and E.* 95
   But Lancelot, when they *g* at Guinevere,   " 270
   maid *G* at, and cried, 'What news from Camelot,   " 620
   yet he *g* not up, nor waved his hand,   " 986
   g and shot Only to holy things   *Holy Grail* 75
   And in he rode, and up I *g*, and saw   " 262
   every moment *g* His silver arms and gloom'd: " 492
   Then *g* askew at those three knights of hers,   *Pelleas and E.* 134
   G down upon her, turn'd and went her way.   " 185
   G from the rosy forehead of the dawn.   " 502
   He *g* and saw the stately galleries,   *Last Tournament* 145
   bluebell, kingcup, poppy *g* About the revels,   " 234
   g at him, thought him cold, High,   *Guinevere* 405
   pale King *g* across the field Of battle: *Pass. of Arthur* 126
   the event *G* back upon them in his after life,   *Lover's Tale iv* 24
   G at the point of law, to pass it by,   " 276
   to love and to live for, *g* at in scorn!   *The Wreck* 35
   She *g* at me, at Muriel, and was mute.   *The Ring* 264
   In passing it *g* upon Hamlet or city,   *Merlin and the G.* 103
   no such light *G* from our Presence   *Akbar's Dream* 113
   a ray red as blood *G* on the strangled face—   *Bandit's Death* 32
Glancing   (*See also* **Dawn-glancing**)   *G* with black-beaded eyes,   *Lilian* 15
   g thence, discuss'd the farm,   *Audley Court* 33
   Philip *g* up Beheld the dead flame   *Enoch Arden* 440
   he saw The mother *g* often toward her babe,   " 754
   The white-faced halls, the *g* rills,   *In Mem., Con.* 113
   Arthur *g* at him, Brought down a momentary brow.   *Gareth and L.* 652
   g like a dragon-fly In summer suit   *Marr. of Geraint* 172
   And *g* all at once as keenly at her   " 773
   and *g* round the waste she fear'd   *Geraint and E.* 50
   g for a minute, till he saw her Pass into it,   " 886
   And *g* on the window, when the gloom Of twilight   *Balin and Balan* 232
   stood with folded hands and downward eyes Of *g* corner,   *Merlin and V.* 70
   slander, *g* here and grazing there;   " 173
   g thro' the hoary boles, he saw,   *Pelleas and E.* 50
   And many a *g* plash and sallowy isle,   *Last Tournament* 422
   g up beheld the holy nuns All round her,   *Guinevere* 666
   I from the altar *g* back upon her,   *Sisters (E. and E.)* 210
   The days and hours are ever *g* by,   *Ancient Sage* 99
   g heavenward on a star so silver-fair,   *Locksley H., Sixty* 191
   g downward on the kindly sphere   *Poets and their B.* 9
   g from his height On earth a fruitless fallow,   *Demeter and P.* 117
   g from the one To the other,   *The Ring* 164
   Whose mantle, every shade of *g* green,   *Prog. of Spring* 53
   and *g* at Elf of the woodland,   *Merlin and the G.* 37
Glare (s)   steady *g* Shrank one sick willow   *Mariana in the S.* 52
   No sun, but a wannish *g* In fold upon fold   *Maud I vi* 2
   in change of *g* and gloom Her eyes and neck   *Merlin and V.* 959
   and thro' a stormy *g*, a heat   *Holy Grail* 842
   Thro' the heat, the drowth, the dust, the *g*,   *Sisters (E. and E.)* 6
   Lured by the *g* and the blare,   *V. of Maeldune* 73

Glare (s) (continued) and aloft the g Flies streaming, — *Achilles over the T.* 11
to the g of a drearier day; — *Despair* 28
in the g of deathless fire ! — *Faith* 8
Glare (verb) G's at one that nods and winks — *Locksley Hall* 136
when the crimson-rolling eye G's ruin, — *Princess* iv 495
But the broad light g's and beats, — *Maud* II iv 89
Would turn, and g at me, and point and jeer, — *Romney's R.* 136
He g's askance at thee as one of those Who mix — *Akbar's Dream* 173
lava-light G's from the lava-lake — *Kapiolani* 14
Glared amazed They g upon the women, — *Princess* vi 361
Under the half-dead sunset g; — *Gareth and L.* 800
G on a huge machicolated tower — *Last Tournament* 424
That was their main test-question—g at me ! — *Sir J. Oldcastle* 155
G on our way toward death, — *Despair* 11
And g at a coming storm. — *Dead Prophet* 24
the glazed eye G at me as in horror. — *The Ring* 451
wrathful sunset g against a cross — *St. Telemachus* 5
G on at the murder'd son, — *Bandit's Death* 33
Glaring In g sand and inlets bright. — *Mariana in the S.* 8
old lion, g with his whelpless eye, — *Princess* vi 99
g, by his own stale devil spurr'd, — *Aylmer's Field* 290
their eyes G, and passionate looks, — *Sea Dreams* 236
Glass (substance) (*See also* **Garden-glass**) fires your
narrow casement g, — *Miller's D.* 243
The g blew in, the fire blew out, — *The Goose* 49
echoing falls Of water, sheets of summer g, — *To E. L.* 2
a fleet of g, That seem'd a fleet of jewels — *Sea Dreams* 122
my poor venture but a fleet of g — 138
Athwart a plane of molten g, — *In Mem.* xv 11
—Others of g as costly— — *Lover's Tale* i 198
and a clatter of hail on the g, — *In the Child. Hosp.* 62
From skies of g A Jacob's ladder falls — *Early Spring* 8
Glass (looking) looking as 'twere in a g, — *A Character* 10
Go, look in any g and say, — *Day-Dm., Moral* 3
O whisper to your g, and say, — *Ep.* 3
having left the g, she turns Once more — *In Mem.* vi 35
Dark in the g of some presageful mood, — *Merlin and V.* 295
As from a g in the sun, — *Lover's Tale* i 371
But whiniver I loöked i' the g — *Spinster's S's.* 20
Glass (drinking) fill my g : give me one kiss: — *Miller's D.* 17
Make prisms in every carven g, — *Day-Dm., Sleep P.* 35
I sit, my empty g reversed, — *Will Water.* 159
It is but yonder empty g That makes me maudlin-moral. — „ 207
g with little Margaret's medicine in it ; — *Sea Dreams* 142
Yours came but from the breaking of a g, — „ 248
Cyril, with whom the bell-mouth'd g had wrought, — *Princess* iv 155
crash'd the g and beat the floor; — *In Mem.* lxxxvii 20
Arrange the board and brim the g ; — „ cvii 16
hev a g o' cowslip wine ! — *Village Wife* 5
sa cowd !—hev another g ! — „ 20
tha mun nobbut hev' one g ot aäle. — *Owd Roä* 20
Glass (spy) get you a seaman's g, Spy out — *Enoch Arden* 215
Borrow'd a g, but all in vain: perhaps She could
not fix the g to suit her eye; — „ 240
Glass (verb) To g herself in dewy eyes — *Move eastward* 7
Glass'd coming wave G in the slippery sand — *Merlin and V.* 293
Glasses (spectacles) Get me my g, Annie: — *Grandmother* 106
wi' 'is g athurt 'is noäse, — *Village Wife* 38
Glassy With a g countenance Did she look to Camelot. — *L. of Shalott* 13
In g bays among their tallest towers.' — *Œnone* 119
On g water drove his cheek in lines; — *Princess* i 116
With a g smile his brutal scorn— — *Maud* I vi 49
Glassy-headed A little g-h hairless man, — *Merlin and V.* 620
Glastonbury that low church he built at G. — *Balin and Balan* 367
Joseph, journeying brought to G, — *Holy Grail* 52
I know That Joseph came of old to G, — „ 60
Holy Cup, That Joseph brought of old to G ? ' — „ 735
Glazed the g eye Glared at me as in horror. — *The Ring* 450
staring eye g o'er with sapless days, — *Love and Duty* 16
think not they are g with wine. — *Locksley Hall* 51
Neither modell'd, g, nor framed : — *Vision of Sin* 188
A full sea g with muffled moonlight, — *Princess* i 248
Gleam (s) g's of mellow light Float by you — *Margaret* 30
Beyond the polar g forlorn, — *Two Voices* 182
That touches me with mystic g's, — „ 380

Gleam (s) (continued) Would love the g's of good
that broke — *Love thou thy land* 89
Dreary g's about the moorland flying over — *Locksley Hall* 4
Thou battenest by the greasy g — *Will Water.* 221
makes a hoary eyebrow for the g Beyond it, — *The Brook* 80
In the green g of the dewy-tassell'd trees : — *Princess* i 94
Making Him broken g's, — *High. Pantheism* 10
A doubtful g of solace lives. — *In Mem.* xxxviii 8
or dives In yonder greening g, — „ cxv 14
nature gilded by the gracious g Of letters, — *Ded. of Idylls* 39
Or sallows in the windy g's of March : — *Merlin and V.* 225
strike it, and awake her with the g ; — *Lancelot and E.* 6
Then flash'd a yellow g across the world, — *Holy Grail* 402
and yellowing leaf And gloom and g, — *Last Tournament* 155
G's of the water-circles as they broke, — *Lover's Tale* i 67
what g on those black ways Where Love could walk — „ 812
that some broken g from our poor earth — *Ded. Poem Prin. Alice* 18
The placid g of sunset after storm ! — *Ancient Sage* 133
'Tho' some have g's or so they say — „ 214
' And idle g's will come and go, — „ 240
And idle g's to thee are light to me. — „ 246
in the sidelong eyes a g of all things ill— — *The Flight* 31
sleeps the g of dying day. — *Locksley H., Sixty* 42
Light the fading g of Even ? — „ 229
the growing glimmer for the g withdrawn. — „ 230
A g from yonder vale, — *Early Spring* 33
still In motion to the distant g, — *Freedom* 14
and a g as of the moon, When first she peers — *Demeter and P.* 13
in the g of a million of suns ? — *Vastness* 4
in the g of those mid-summer dawns, — *The Ring* 183
Look'd in upon me like a g and pass'd, — „ 420
never caught one g of the beauty which endures— — *Happy* 60
I am Merlin Who follow The G. — *Merlin and the G.* 10
The Master whisper'd ' Follow the G.' — „ 34
music Of falling torrents, Flitted the G. — „ 48
Of lowly labour, Slided The G— — „ 61
Arthur the blameless Rested The G. — „ 74
The G, that had waned to a wintry glimmer — „ 83
But clothed with The G. — „ 94
The G flying onward, Wed to the melody, — „ 96
After it, follow it, Follow The G. — „ 131
The cloud was rifted by a purer g — *Akbar's Dream* 78
THE g of household sunshine ends, — *The Wanderer* 1
comes a g of what is higher. — *Faith* 6
Gleam (verb) Saw distant gates of Eden g, — *Two Voices* 212
wherethro' G's that untravell'd world, — *Ulysses* 20
G thro' the Gothic archway in the wall. — *Godiva* 64
Fair g's the snowy altar-cloth, — *Sir Galahad* 33
wisp that g's On Lethe in the eyes of Death. — *In Mem.* xcviii 7
and when he saw the star G, on Sir Gareth's — *Gareth and L.* 1219
this bare dome had not begun to g — *To Mary Boyle* 41
Gleam'd G to the flying moon by fits. — *Miller's D.* 116
now she g Like Fancy made of golden air, — *The Voyage* 65
We parted: sweetly g the stars, — *The Letters* 41
(A bill of sale g thro' the drizzle) — *Enoch Arden* 688
that dawning g a kindlier hope On Enoch — „ 833
dying, g on rocks Roof-pendent, sharp ; — *Balin and Balan* 314
sweetly g her eyes behind her tears — *Merlin and V.* 402
There g a vague suspicion in his eyes : — *Lancelot and E.* 127
G for a moment in her own on earth. — *The Ring* 297
Gleaming A g shape she floated by, — *L. of Shalott* iv 39
A g crag with belts of pines. — *Two Voices* 189
A glowing arm, a g neck, — *Miller's D.* 78
fruit, whose g rind ingrav'n ' For the most fair,' — *Œnone* 72
They saw the g river seaward flow — *Lotos-Eaters* 14
walls Of shadowy granite, in a g pass ; — „ C. S. 4
girdled with the g world : — „ 113
Far-folded mists, and g halls of morn. — *Tithonus* 10
Set in a g river's crescent-curve, — *Princess* i 171
Here half-hid in the g wood, — *Maud* I vi 69
the stars went down across the g pane, — *The Flight* 13
came On three gray heads beneath a g rift. — *Demeter and P.* 83
Glean And g your scatter'd sapience.' — *Princess* ii 259
not now to g, Not now—I hope to do it— — *Sir J. Oldcastle* 11
Gleaned (adj.) Showering thy g wealth into my open breast — *Ode to Memory* 23

Glean'd (verb) long ago they had *g* and garner'd — *Lover's Tale i* 128

Gleaner Homestead and harvest, Reaper and *g*, — *Merlin and the G.* 58

Glebe Flood with full daylight *g* and town? — *Two Voices* 87
Sons of the *g*, with other frowns — *Aylmer's Field* 723
those horn-handed breakers of the *g*, — *Princess ii* 159
the labourer tills His wonted *g*, — *In Mem. ci* 22
That grind the *g* to powder! — *Tiresias* 95
sweet As that which gilds the *g* of England, — *To Prof. Jebb.* 7
lest the naked *g* Should yawn once more — *Demeter and P.* 42

Glee (joy) Love lighted down between them full of *g*, — *Bridesmaid* 6
tyrant's cruel *g* Forces on the freer hour. — *Vision of Sin* 129

Glee (part-music) The merry *g*'s are still; — *All Things will Die* 23
Again the feast, the speech, the *g*, — *In Mem., Con.* 101

Glem Rang by the white mouth of the violent *G*; — *Lancelot and E.* 288

Glen (*See also* **Glin**) And runlets babbling down the *g*. — *Mariana in the S.* 44
The swimming vapour slopes athwart the *g*, — *Œnone* 3
between the piney sides Of this long *g*, — " 94
Among the fragments tumbled from the *g*'s, — " 222
from the darken *g*, 'Saw God divide the night — *D. of F. Women* 224
That watch me from the *g* below. — *Move eastward* 8
And snared the squirrel of the *g*? — *Princess ii* 249
let us hear the purple *g*'s replying: — " iv 11
all the *g*'s are drown'd in azure gloom — " 525
Follow'd up in valley and *g* — *Ode on Well.* 114
Had found a *g*, gray boulder and black tarn. — *Lancelot and E.* 36
they fell and made the *g* abhorr'd: — " 42
Downward thunder in hollow and *g*, — *To Master of B.* 16

Glide would she *g* between your wraths, — *Aylmer's Field* 706
g a sunbeam by the blasted Pine, — *Princess vii* 196
broad water sweetly slowly *g*'s. — *Requiescat* 2
g, Like a beam of the seventh Heaven, — *Maud I xiv* 20
Thy shadow still would *g* from room to room, — *Guinevere* 504
The sisters *g* about me hand in hand, — *Sisters (E. and E.)* 275
and the shadowy warrior *g* Along — *Demeter and P.* 152

Glided *g* thro' all change Of liveliest utterance. — *D. of F. Women* 167
but mute she *g* forth, Nor glanced behind — *Princess vii* 170
Above thee *g* the star. — *Voice and the P.* 8
We *g* winding under ranks Of iris, — *In Mem. ciii* 23
Then *g* out of the joyous wood — *Maud II i* 31
she *g* out Among the heavy breathings — *Geraint and E.* 401
Then rose Elaine and *g* thro' the fields, — *Lancelot and E.* 843
the sweet Grail *G* and past, and close upon it — *Holy Grail* 695
sad eyes fixt on the lost sea-home, as we *g* away, — *The Wreck* 126
Then *g* a vulturous Beldam forth, — *Dead Prophet* 25
he sprang, And *g* lightly down the stairs, — *St. Telemachus* 59

Glidest How surely *g* thou from March to May, — *Prog. of Spring* 109

Gliding *G* with equal crowns two serpents led — *Alexander* 6
past In either twilight ghost-like to and fro *G*, — *Lancelot and E.* 850
Over a wilderness *G*, — *Merlin and the G.* 37
g thro' the branches over-bower'd — *Death of Œnone* 6
The woman, *g* toward the pyre, — *To Master of B.* 18

Glimmer (s) I knew The tearful *g* of the languid dawn — *D. of F. Women* 74
Across a hazy *g* of the west, — *Gardener's D.* 219
the old mysterious *g* steals From thy pure brows, — *Tithonus* 34
Walk'd in a wintry wind by a ghastly *g*, — *Maud I iii* 13
In gloss of satin and *g* of pearls, — " xxii 55
in the light's last *g* Tristram show'd And swung — *Last Tournament* 739
I have had some *g*, at times, — *Despair* 103
Awake! the creeping *g* steals, — *The Flight* 4
light the *g* of the dawn? — *Locksley H., Sixty* 229
eyes may take the growing *g* — " 230
Might find a flickering *g* of relief — *To Mary Boyle* 47
Gleam, that had waned to a wintry *g* On icy fallow — *Merlin and the G.* 83
And slowly brightening Out of the *g*, — " 89

Glimmer (verb) 'A third would *g* on her neck — *Talking Oak* 221
My college friendships *g*. — *Will Water.* 40
G in thy rheumy eyes. — *Vision of Sin* 154
And like a ghost she *g*'s on to me. — *Princess vii* 181
G away to the lonely deep, — *To F. D. Maurice* 28
early light Shall *g* on the dewy decks. — *In Mem. ix* 12
Thy tablet *g*'s to the dawn. — " lxvii 16
on the landward side, by a red rock, *g*'s the Hall; — *Maud I iv* 10
Days that will *g*, I fear, — *The Wreck* 79
She sees the Best that *g*'s thro' the Worst, — *Ancient Sage* 72
light That *g*'s on the marsh and on the grave.' — *The Ring* 341

Glimmer'd Old faces *g* thro' the doors, — *Mariana* 66
And April's crescent *g* cold, — *Miller's D.* 107
Her taper *g* in the lake below: — *Edwin Morris* 135
white kine *g*, and the trees Laid their dark arms (repeat) — *In Mem. xcv* 15, 51
And *g* on his armour in the room. — *Geraint and E.* 386
In Arthur's casement *g* chastely down, — *Merlin and V.* 740
and thro' the gap *G* the streaming scud: — *Holy Grail* 682
And God Hath more than *g* on me. — *Columbus* 144

Glimmer-gowk (owl) sit like a greät *g-g* — *Village Wife* 38

Glimmering (adj. and part.) (*See also* **Green-glimmering**)
the *g* water outfloweth: — *Leonine Eleg.* 1
Vast images in *g* dawn, — *Two Voices* 305
Who paced for ever in a *g* land, — *Palace of Art* 67
Ranges of *g* vaults with iron grates, — *D. of F. Women* 35
cold my wrinkled feet Upon thy *g* thresholds, — *Tithonus* 68
When all the *g* moorland rings — *Sir L. and Q. G.* 35
And on the *g* limit far withdrawn — *Vision of Sin* 223
Naiads oar'd A *g* shoulder under gloom — *To E. L.* 17
Who feels a *g* strangeness in his dream. — *The Brook* 216
half in doze I seem'd To float about a *g* night, — *Princess i* 247
The casement slowly grows a *g* square — " iv 52
By *g* lanes and walls of canvas led — " v 6
Disrobed the *g* statue of Sir Ralph From those rich silks, — " Con. 117
Came *g* thro' the laurels At the quiet evenfall, — *Maud II iv* 77
and made his feet Wings thro' a *g* gallery, — *Balin and Balan* 404
to Almesbury Fled all night long by *g* waste and weald, — *Guinevere* 128
peal Of laughter drew me thro' the *g* glades — *Sisters (E. and E.)* 116
G up the heights beyond me, — *Silent Voices* 9

Glimmering (s) greenish *g*'s thro' the lancets,— — *Aylmer's Field* 622
There was a *g* of God's hand. — *Columbus* 142

Glimpse (s) Like *g*'s of forgotten dreams— — *Two Voices* 381
shout For some blind *g* of freedom — *Love and Duty* 6
A *g* of that dark world where I was born. — *Tithonus* 33
Yet *g*'s of the true. — *Will Water.* 60
The shimmering *g*'s of a stream; — *Princess Con.* 46
And never a *g* of her window pane! — *Window, No Answer* 3
Last year, I caught a *g* of his face, — *Maud I xiii* 27
He never had a *g* of mine untruth, — *Lancelot and E.* 125
Possible—at first *g*, and for a face Gone in a moment— — *Sisters (E. and E.)* 93
Death at the *g* of a finger — *Def. of Lucknow* 23
For larger *g*'s of that more than man — *Tiresias* 21
Green Sussex fading into blue With one gray *g* of sea; — *Pro. to Gen. Hamley* 8
a *g* of a height that is higher. — *By an Evolution.* 20

Glimpse (verb) lift the hidden ore That *g*'s, — *D. of F. Women* 275
Past, Future *g* and fade Thro' some slight spell, — *Early Spring* 31

Glimpsed the herd was driven, Fire *g*; — *Com. of Arthur* 433

Glimpsing And *g* over these, just seen, — *Day-Dm., Sleep. P.* 47

Glin (glen) sthrames runnin' down at the back o' the *g* — *Tomorrow* 24

Glisten (s) oft we saw the *g* Of ice, — *The Daisy* 35

Glisten (verb) O listen, listen, your eyes shall *g* (repeat) — *Sea-Fairies* 35, 37
gracious dews Began to *g* and to fall: — *Princess ii* 317

Glisten'd the torrent ever pour'd And *g*— — *To E. L.* 14
their feet In dewy grasses *g*; — *Gareth and L.* 928
His eyes *g*: she fancied 'Is it for me?' — *Lancelot and E.* 822

Glistening drove The fragrant, *g* deeps, — *Arabian Nights* 14
fill'd With the blue valley and the *g* brooks, — *Lover's Tale i* 331
buds Were *g* to the breezy blue; — *Miller's D.* 61

Glitter flash and *g* Like sunshine on a dancing rill, — *Rosalind* 28
G like a swarm of fire-flies — *Locksley Hall* 10
His mantle *g*'s on the rocks— — *Day-Dm., Arrival* 9
Began to *g* firefly-like in copse — *Princess i* 208
That *g* burnish'd by the frosty dark; — " v 261
on such a palm As *g*'s gilded in thy Book of Hours. — *Gareth and L.* 46
I saw the moonlight *g* on their tears— — *Lover's Tale i* 697

Glitter'd The gemmy bridle *g* free, — *L. of Shalott iii* 10
Large Hesper *g* on her tears, — *Mariana in the S.* 90
The long hall *g* like a bed of flowers. — *Princess ii* 439
the city *g*, Thro' cypress avenues, — *The Daisy* 47
But when it *g* o'er the saddle-bow, — *Gareth and L.* 1119
where it *g* on her pail, The milkmaid left — *Holy Grail* 405
So dame and damsel *g* at the feast — *Last Tournament* 225
brooks *g* on in the light without sound, — *V. of Maeldune* 13

Glitter'd (*continued*)   *g* o'er us a sunbright hand,   *V. of Maldune* 84
Glittering (adj. and part.)   Gold *g* thro' lamplight dim,   *Arabian Nights* 18
Come, blessed brother, come. I know thy *g* face.   *St. S. Stylites* 205
Draw me, thy bride, a *g* star,   *St. Agnes' Eve* 23
'Fresh as the first beam *g* on a sail,   *Princess* iv 44
goes, like *g* bergs of ice,   " 71
fresh young captains flash'd their *g* teeth,   " v 20
The *g* axe was broken in their arms,   " vi 51
shone Thro' *g* drops on her sad friend.   " 283
as the white and *g* star of morn Parts from a bank of snow,   *Marr. of Geraint* 734
Queen who stood All *g* like May sunshine   *Merlin and V.* 88
Her eyes and neck *g* went and came;   " 960
Fled like a *g* rivulet to the tarn: *Lancelot and E.* 52
Whom *g* in enamell'd arms the maid   " 619
yet one *g* foot disturb'd The lucid well;   *Tiresias* 41
The *g* Capitol: *Freedom* 4
Glittering (s)   Blown into *g* by the popular breath,   *Romney's R.* 49
Globe   circles of the *g*'s Of her keen eyes   *The Poet* 43
Thro' the shadow of the *g* we sweep   *Locksley Hall* 183
As thro' the slumber of the *g*   *The Voyage* 23
Thy spirit should fail from off the *g*;   *In Mem.* lxxiv 36
flower, That blows a *g* of after arrowlets,   *Gareth and L.* 1029
We should see the *G* we groan in,   *Locksley H., Sixty* 188
I would the *g* from end to end   *Epilogue* 12
Since our Queen assumed the *g*, the sceptre.   *On Jub. Q. Victoria* 3
MANY a hearth upon our dark *g*   *Vastness* 1
G again, and make Honey Moon.   *The Ring* 15
eyes have known this *g* of ours,   *To Ulysses* 5
hurl'd so high they ranged about the *g*?   *St. Telemachus* 2
Globed   stars that *g* themselves in Heaven,   *Enoch Arden* 597
Globing   *G* Honey Moons Bright as this.   *The Ring* 7
Glode   *G* over earth till the glorious creature   *Batt. of Brunanburh* 29
Gloom (s)   (*See also* City-gloom, Thunder-gloom)   Flinging the *g* of yesternight On the white day;   *Ode to Memory* 9
That over-vaulted grateful *g*,   *Palace of Art* 54
Floods all the deep-blue *g* with beams   *D. of F. Women* 186
A motion toiling in the *g*—   *Love thou thy land* 54
Reading her perfect features in the *g*,   *Gardener's D.* 175
Thy cheek begins to redden thro' the *g*,   *Tithonus* 37
The *g* of ten Decembers.   *Will Water.* 104
glimmering shoulder under *g* Of cavern pillars;   *To E. L.* 17
lying thus inactive, doubt and *g*.   *Enoch Arden* 113
Thicker the drizzle grew, deeper the *g*;   " 679
find a deeper in the narrow *g* By wife and child;   *Aylmer's Field* 840
from utter *g* stood out the breasts,   *Lucretius* 60
Dropt thro' the ambrosial *g*   *Princess* iv 24
Out I sprang from glow to *g*:   " 178
moving thro' the uncertain *g*,   " 216
all the glens are drown'd in azure *g*   " 525
The height, the space, the *g*,   *The Daisy* 59
The *g* that saddens Heaven and Earth,   " 102
and a stifled splendour and *g*.   *High. Pantheism* 10
To touch thy thousand years of *g*:   *In Mem.* ii 12
Thy *g* is kindled at the tips,   " xxxix 11
And passes into *g* again.   " 12
Thro' all its interival *g* In some long trance   " xliii 3
When on the *g* I strive to paint The face   " lxx 2
Recalls, in change of light or *g*,   " lxxxv 74
rollest from the gorgeous *g* Of evening   " lxxxvi 2
And suck'd from out the distant *g*   " xcv 53
But touch'd with no ascetic *g*;   " cix 10
But iron dug from central *g*,   " cxviii 21
And yearn'd to burst the folded *g*,   " cxxii 4
With tender *g* the roof, the wall,   " *Con.* 118
cold face, star-sweet on a *g* profound;   *Maud* I iii 4
And laying his trams in a poison'd *g*   " x 8
Set in the heart of the carven *g*,   " xiv 11
in the fragrant *g* Of foreign churches—   " xix 53
Commingled with the *g* of imminent war,   *Ded. of Idylls* 13
Before a *g* of stubborn-shafted oaks,   *Geraint and E.* 120
thro' the green *g* of the wood they past,   " 195
So bush'd about it is with *g*,   *Balin and Balan* 95
the *g* Of twilight deepens round it,   " 232

Gloom (s) (*continued*)   and in him *g* on *g* Deepen'd: *Balin and Balan* 286
there in *g* cast himself all along, Moaning   " 434
she will call That three-days-long presageful *g*   *Merlin and V.* 320
The tree that shone white-listed thro' the *g*.   " 939
in change of glare and *g* Her eyes and neck   " 959
the sallow-rifted *g*'s Of evening,   *Lancelot and E.* 1002
Came like a driving *g* across my mind.   *Holy Grail* 370
coming out of *g* Was dazzled by the sudden light,   *Pelleas and E.* 104
the *g*, That follows on the turning of the world,   " 548
and yellowing leaf And *g* and gleam,   *Last Tournament* 155
All in a death-dumb autumn-dripping *g*,   " 756
Filling with purple *g* the vacancies   *Lover's Tale* i 2
that shock of *g* had fall'n Unfelt,   " 505
In battle with the *g*'s of my dark will,   " 744
But these, their *g*, the mountains and the Bay,   " iv 16
Drown'd in the *g* and horror of the vault.   " 62
kept it thro' a hundred years of *g*,   " 195
nine long months of antenatal *g*,   *De Prof., Two G.* 8
I closed my heart to the *g*;   *The Wreck* 38
the Godless *g* Of a life without sun,   *Despair* 6
last long stripe of waning crimson *g*,   *Ancient Sage* 221
lost within a growing *g*;   *Locksley H., Sixty* 73
lifts her buried life from *g* to bloom,   *Demeter and P.* 98
g of the evening, Life at a close;   *Vastness* 15
but a murmur of gnats in the *g*,   " 35
in the night, While the *g* is growing.'   *Forlorn* 12
Or does the *g* of Age And suffering   *Romney's R.* 64
the bracken amid the *g* of the heather.   *June Bracken, etc.* 9
front of that ravine Which drowsed in *g*,   *Death of Œnone* 76
the momentary *g*, Made by the noonday blaze   *St. Telemachus* 49
Gloom (verb)   There *g* the dark broad seas.   *Ulysses* 45
I slip, I slide, I *g*, I glance,   *The Brook* 174
That *g*'s his valley, sighs to see the peak   *Balin and Balan* 165
Gloom'd   Would that my *g* fancy were As thine,   *Supp. Confessions* 68
G the low coast and quivering brine   *The Voyage* 42
A black yew *g* the stagnant air,   *The Letters* 2
twilight *g*; and broader-grown the bowers   *Princess* vii 48
mood as that, which lately *g* Your fancy   *Merlin and V.* 325
every moment glanced His silver arms and *g*:   *Holy Grail* 493
never *g* by the curse Of a sin,   *The Wreck* 139
this Earth, a stage so *g* with woe   *The Play* 1
Gloomier   those *g* which forego The darkness   *To the Queen* ii 64
Gloomiest   I have had some glimmer, at times, in my *g* woe,   *Despair* 103
Glooming   (*See also* Dewy-glooming, Green-glooming, Light-glooming)   And glanced athwart the *g* flats.   *Mariana* 20
Or while the balmy *g*, crescent-lit,   *Gardener's D.* 263
we sank From rock to rock upon the *g* quay,   *Audley Court* 84
Or cool'd within the *g* wave;   *In Mem.* lxxxix 45
Sunder the *g* crimson on the marge,   *Gareth and L.* 1365
among the *g* alleys Progress halts on palsied feet,   *Locksley H., Sixty* 219
Gloomy   To anchor by one *g* thought;   *Two Voices* 459
wind made work In which the *g* brewer's soul   *Talking Oak* 55
Sailing along before a *g* cloud   *Sea Dreams* 124
in and out the *g* skirts Of Celidon the forest;   *Lancelot and E.* 291
rolling far along the *g* shores The voice of days   *Pass. of Arthur* 134
Gloomy-gladed   tops of many thousand pines A *g-g* hollow slowly sink   *Gareth and L.* 797
Gloried   I *g* in my knave, Who being still rebuked,   " 1248
Glorify   fountains of the past, To *g* the present;   *Ode to Memory* 3
Glorifying   sparkles on a sty, *G* clown and satyr;   *Princess* v 187
Glorious   But in a city *g*—   *Deserted House* 19
A *g* child, dreaming alone,   *Eleänore* 27
'Whose eyes are dim with *g* tears,   *Two Voices* 151
A *g* Devil, large in heart and brain,   *To —— With Pal. of Art* 5
When I am gather'd to the *g* saints.   *St. S. Stylites* 197
So *g* in his beauty and thy choice,   *Tithonus* 12
vacant of our *g* gains,   *Locksley Hall* 175
So sang the gallant *g* chronicle;   *Princess, Pro.* 49
and albeit their *g* names Were fewer,   " ii 155
who rapt in *g* dreams,   " 442
facets of the *g* mountain flash Above the valleys   *The Islet* 22
the leader in these *g* wars Now to *g* burial slowly borne,   *Ode on Well.* 192
who gaze with temperate eyes On *g* insufficiencies,   *In Mem.* cxii 3
To fool the crowd with *g* lies,   " cxxviii 14

Glorious (*continued*) like a *g* ghost, to glide, Like a beam   *Maud I xiv* 20
  starry Gemini hang like *g* crowns   „   *III vi* 7
  That *g* roundel echoing in our ears,   *Merlin and V.* 426
  —you know Of Arthur's *g* wars.'   *Lancelot and E.* 285
  where the *g* King Had on his cuirass worn our
    Lady's Head,   „   293
  that night the bard Sang Arthur's *g* wars,   *Guinevere* 286
  A *g* company, the flower of men,   „   464
  There came a *g* morning, such a one As dawns   *Lover's Tale i* 299
  G poet who never hast written a line,   *To A. Tennyson* 5
  Havelock's *g* Highlanders answer with conquering
    cheers,   *Def. of Lucknow* 99
  till the *g* creature Sank to his setting.   *Batt. of Brunanburh* 29
  around his head The *g* goddess wreath'd a golden
    cloud,   *Achilles over the T.* 5
  Whose echo shall not tongue thy *g* doom,   *Tiresias* 136
  Thy *g* eyes were dimm'd with pain   *Freedom* 10
  And all her *g* empire, round and round.   *Hands all Round* 24
  Sharers of our *g* past,   *Open. I. and C. Exhib.* 31
  'Hail to the *g* Golden year of her Jubilee !'   *On Jub. Q. Victoria* 64
  g annals of army and fleet,   *Vastness* 7

Glory (**s**)   In marvel whence that *g* came   *Arabian Nights* 94
  God's *g* smote him on the face.'   *Two Voices* 225
  '*G* to God,' she sang, and past afar,   *D. of F. Women* 242
  And the long *glories* of the winter moon.   *M. d'Arthur* 192
  As down dark tides the *g* slides,   *Sir Galahad* 47
  But o'er the dark a *g* spreads,   „   55
  things as they are, But thro' a kind of *g*.   *Will Water.* 72
  Yet he hoped to purchase *g*,   *The Captain* 17
  We lov'd the *glories* of the world,   *The Voyage* 83
  And drops at *G*'s temple-gates,   *You might have won* 34
  glows And *glories* of the broad belt of the world,   *Enoch Arden* 579
  between the less And greater *g* varying   *Aylmer's Field* 73
  Thy *g* fly along the Italian field,   *Lucretius* 71
  redound Of use and *g* to yourselves   *Princess ii* 43
  And the wild cataract leaps in *g*.   „   *iv* 4
  Like a Saint's *g* up in heaven: „   *v* 514
  The path of duty was the way to *g*: (repeat)   *Ode on Well.* 202, 210
  The path of duty be the way to *g*:   „   224
  When can their *g* fade ?   *Light Brigade* 50
  The height, the space, the gloom, the *g* !   *The Daisy* 59
  G of warrior, or of orator, or of song,   *Wages* 1
  G of virtue, to fight, to struggle, to right the wrong—Nay,
    but she aim'd not at *g*, no lover of *g* she: Give her the
    g of going on, and still to be.   „   3
  G about thee, without thee ;   *High. Pantheism* 9
  Thine the liberty, thine the *g*,   *Boädicea* 41
  win A *g* from its being far ;   *In Mem. xxiv* 14
  There comes a *g* on the walls :   „   *lxvii* 4
  The mystic *g* swims away ;   „   9
  He reach'd the *g* of a hand,   „   *lxix* 17
  g of the sum of things Will flash along   „   *lxxxviii* 11
  crown'd with attributes of woe Like *glories*,   „   *cxviii* 19
  dim And dimmer, and a *g* done :   „   *cxxi* 4
  The man of science himself is fonder of *g*,   *Maud I iv* 37
  A *g* I shall not find.   „   *v* 22
  every eye but mine will glance At Maud in all her *g*.   „   *xx* 37
  your true lover may see Your *g* also,   „   48
  g of manhood stand on his ancient height,   „   *III vi* 21
  Whose *g* was, redressing human wrong,   *Ded. of Idylls* 9
  eagle-circles up To the great Sun of *G*,   *Gareth and L.* 22
  her son Beheld his only way to *g*   „   159
  And *g* gain'd, and evermore to gain.   „   332
  Gareth all for *g* underwent The sooty yoke   „   478
  trusts to overthrow, Then wed, with *g*:   „   620
  tilt for lady's love and *g* here,   „   740
  here is *g* enow In having flung the three :   „   1325
  Forgetful of his *g* and his name,   *Marr. of Geraint* 53
  court And all its perilous *glories*:   „   804
  Balan answer'd 'For the sake Of *g* ;   *Balin and Balan* 33
  As fancying that her *g* would be great   *Merlin and V.* 217
  crying 'I have made his *g* mine,'   „   971
  your pretext, O my knight, As all for *g* ;   *Lancelot and E.* 154
  No keener hunter after *g* breathes.   „   156
  need to speak Of Lancelot in his *g* !   „   464

Glory (**s**) (*continued*)   the name Of Lancelot, and a *g*
  one with theirs.   *Lancelot and E.* 478
  wound he spake of, all for gain Of *g*,   „   567
  allow my pretext, as for gain Of purer *g*.'   „   587
  it is my *g* to have loved One peerless,   „   1090
  sons Born to the *g* of thy name and fame,   „   1372
  beheld his fellow's face As in a *g*,   *Holy Grail* 192
  Naked of *g* for His mortal change,   „   448
  spires And gateways in a *g* like one pearl—   „   527
  '*G* and joy and honour to our Lord   „   839
  the heat Of pride and *g* fired her face ;   *Pelleas and E.* 172
  unsunny face To him who won thee *g* !   „   181
  knights Arm'd for a day of *g* before the King.   *Last Tournament* 55
  The *g* of our Round Table is no more.' (repeat)   „   189, 212
  the knights, Glorying in each new *g*,   „   336
  in their stead thy name and *g* cling   *Pass. of Arthur* 53
  And the long *glories* of the winter moon.   „   360
  Quiver'd a flying *g* on her hair,   *Lover's Tale i* 69
  A solid *g* on her bright black hair ;   „   367
  And *g* of broad waters interfused,   „   401
  uphold Thy coronal of *g* like a God,   „   488
  in this *g* I had merged The other,   „   506
  sunset, glows and *glories* of the moon   „   *ii* 110
  for the *g* of the Lord.   *The Revenge* 21
  We have won great *g*, my men !   „   85
  had holden the power and *g* of Spain so cheap   „   106
  Better have sent Our Edith thro' the *glories* of the
    earth,   *Sisters (E. and E.)* 225
  Never with mightier *g* than when we had rear'd   *Def. of Lucknow* 3
  Gave *g* and more empire to the kings   *Columbus* 22
  All *g* to the all-blessed Trinity,   „   61
  All *g* to the mother of our Lord,   „   62
  I saw The *g* of the Lord flash up,   „   82
  To walk within the *g* of the Lord   „   89
  and the *glories* of fairy kings ;   *V. of Maeldune* 90
  Gaining a lifelong *G* in battle,   *Batt. of Brunanburh* 8
  King and Atheling, Each in his *g*,   „   102
  lured by the Hunger of *g*   „   124
  strive Again for *g*, while the golden lyre   *Tiresias* 180
  of her eldest-born, her *g*, her boast,   *Despair* 73
  g and shame dying out for ever in endless time,   „   75
  an' Hiven in its *g* smiled, As the Holy Mother o' *G*
    that smiles   *Tomorrow* 25
  afther her paärints had inter'd *g*,   „   53
  Dead the warrior, dead his *g*,   *Locksley H., Sixty* 30
  how her living *g* lights the hall,   „   181
  stars in heaven Paled, and the *g* grew.   *Pro. to Gen. Hamley* 32
  three hundred whose *g* will never die—   *Heavy Brigade* 10
  G to each and to all, and the charge that they made !
    G to all the three hundred, and all the Brigade !   „   65
  Thou sawest a *g* growing on the night,   *Epit. on Caxton* 2
  Glorying in the *glories* of her people,   *On Jub. Q. Victoria* 26
  once more in varnish'd *g* shine Thy stars   *Prog. of Spring* 38
  plunging down Thro' that disastrous *g*,   *St. Telemachus* 29
  'Thy *g* baffles wisdom.   *Akbar's Dream* 28
  for no Mirage of *g*, but for power to fuse   „   156
  g of Kapiolani be mingled with either on Hawa-i-ee.   *Kapiolani* 5
  Prophet-eyes may catch a *g*   *Making of Man* 6
  Thou wilt strike Thy *g* thro' the day.   *Doubt and Prayer* 14

Glory (**verb**)   how would'st thou *g* in all The splendours   *Ancient Sage* 176
Glory-circled   A center'd, *g-c* memory,   *Lover's Tale i* 446
Glory-crown'd   His own vast shadow *g-c* ;   *In Mem. xcvii* 3
Glorying   upon the bridge of war Sat *g*;   *Spec. of Iliad* 10
  g in their vows and him, his knights Stood round him,   *Com. of Arthur* 458
  stood a moment, ere his horse was brought, *G* ;   *Gareth and L.* 935
  the knights, *G* in each new glory,   *Last Tournament* 336
  A low sea-sunset *g* round her hair   „   508
  g in the blissful years again to be,   *To Virgil* 5
  G between sea and sky,   *Open I. and C. Exhib.* 18
  G in the glories of her people,   *On Jub. Q. Victoria* 26
Gloss   shadow of the flowers Stole all the golden *g*,   *Gardener's D.* 130
  hair In *g* and hue the chestnut, (repeat)   *The Brook* 72, 207
  Let darkness keep her raven *g*:   *In Mem. i* 10
  merge' he said 'in form and *g*   „   *lxxxix* 41
  In *g* of satin and glimmer of pearls,   *Maud I xxii* 5

Glossy   find the stubborn thistle bursting Into *g* purples,   *Ode on Well.* 207
then with a riding whip Leisurely tapping a *g* boot,   *Maud I xiii* 19
and smooth'd The *g* shoulder,   *Lancelot and E.* 348

Glossy-throated   *g-t* grace, Isolt the Queen.   *Last Tournament* 509

Glove   With blots of it about them, ribbon, *g*   *Aylmer's Field* 620
It chanced, her empty *g* upon the tomb   *Princess iv* 596
Come sliding out of her sacred *g*,   *Maud I vi* 85
fit to wear your slipper for a *g*.   *Geraint and E.* 623
added fullness to the phrase Of 'Gauntlet in the velvet *g*.'   *To Marq. of Dufferin* 12

Glow (s)   steady sunset *g* That stays upon thee ?   *Eleänore* 55
sun begins to rise, the heavens are in a *g* ;   *May Queen, Con.* 49
felt my blood Glow with the *g* that slowly crimson'd   *Tithonus* 56
and looks Had yet their native *g* :   *Will Water.* 194
g's And glories of the broad belt of the world,   *Enoch Arden* 578
this kindlier *g* Faded with morning,   *Aylmer's Field* 411
Out I sprang from *g* to gloom :   *Princess iv* 178
With a satin sail of a ruby *g*,   *The Islet* 13
lone and long roar Green-rushing (repeat)   *Voice and the P.* 3, 39
not for thee the *g*, the bloom,   *In Mem. ii* 9
And reach the *g* of southern skies,   ,, *xii* 10
And fix my thoughts on all the *g*   ,, *lxxxiv* 3
earth gone nearer to the *g* Of your soft splendours   *Maud I xviii* 78
sunset, *g*'s and glories of the moon   *Lover's Tale ii* 110
wid all the light an' the *g*,   *Tomorrow* 67
moon was falling greenish thro' a rosy *g*,   *Locksley H., Sixty* 178
groves of olive in the summer *g*,   *Frater Ave, etc.* 3
said with a sudden *g* On her patient face   *Charity* 35

Glow (verb)   vines that *g* Beneath the battled tower.   *D. of F. Women* 219
felt my blood *G* with the glow that slowly crimson'd   *Tithonus* 56
G's forth each softly-shadow'd arm   *Day-Dm., Sleep B.* 13
Between dark stems the forest *g*'s,   *Sir Galahad* 27
over thy dark shoulder *g* Thy silver sister-world,   *Move Eastward* 5
from his ivied nook *G* like a sunbeam :   *Princess, Pro.* 105
now her father's chimney *g*'s In expectation   *In Mem. vi* 29
g In azure orbits heavenly-wise :   ,, *lxxxvii* 37
The wizard lightnings deeply *g*,   ,, *cxxii* 19
G's in the blue of fifty miles away.   *Roses on the T.* 8

Glow'd   His broad clear brow in sunlight *g* ;   *L. of Shalott iii* 28
And on the liquid mirror *g*   *Mariana in the S.* 31
her face *G*, as I look'd at her.   *D. of F. Women* 240
G for a moment as we past.   *The Voyage* 48
before us *g* Fruit, blossom, viand,   *Princess iv* 34
the city Of little Monaco, basking, *g*.   *The Daisy* 8
As he *g* like a ruddy shield   *Maud III vi* 14
his face *G* like the heart of a great fire   *Marr. of Geraint* 559
A holy maid ; tho' never maiden *g*,   *Holy Grail* 7
G intermingling close beneath the sun.   *Lover's Tale i* 436

Glowing   *g* full-faced welcome, she Began   *Princess ii* 183
g round her dewy eyes The circled Iris   ,, *iii* 26
Above the garden's *g* blossom-belts,   ,, *v* 363
Half-lapt in *g* gauze and golden brede,   ,, *vi* 134
she rose *G* all over noble shame;   ,, *vii* 160
She enters, *g* like the moon Of Eden   *In Mem., Con.* 27
and *g* in the broad Deep-dimpled current   *Gareth and L.* 1088
g on him, like a bride's On her new lord,   *Merlin and V.* 616
g in all colours, the live grass,   *Last Tournament* 233
Yet *g* in a heart of ruby—   *Lover's Tale iv* 196
All over *g* with the sun of life,   ,, 381
A *g* arm, a gleaming neck,   *Miller's D.* 78
Between the shadows of the vine-bunches Floated the *g* sunlights,   *Œnone* 182
In *g* health, with boundless wealth,   *L. C. V. de Vere* 61
Love took up the glass of Time, and turn'd it in his *g* hands ;   *Locksley Hall* 31
delicate spark Of *g* and growing light   *Maud I vi* 16
Pass and blush the news Over *g* ships ;   ,, *xvii* 12
above Broaden the *g* isles of vernal blue.   *Prog. of Spring* 60
G with all-colour'd plums   *V. of Maeldune* 60

Glowworm (adj.)   lapt in wreaths of *g* light The mellow breaker   *Princess iv* 435

Glow-worm (s)   And the *g-w* of the grave Glimmer   *Vision of Sin* 153
No bigger than a *g-w* shone the tent   *Princess iv* 25
Now poring on the *g*, now the star,   ,, 211
     ,, *ii* 387

Glutted   *g* all night long breast-deep in corn,

Gnarl'd   Thro' solid opposition crabb'd and *g*.   *Princess iii* 126
All silver-green with *g* bark :   *Mariana* 42
garlanding the *g* boughs With bunch and berry   *Œnone* 101

Gnarr   a thousand wants *G* at the heels   *In Mem. xcviii* 17

Gnash   teeth of Hell flay bare and *g* thee   *Last Tournament* 444

Gnat   (*See also* **Water-gnat**)   chased away the still-recurring *g*,   *Caress'd or Chidden* 7
Not even of a *g* that sings.   *Day-Dm., Sleep P.* 21
I well could wish a cobweb for the *g*,   *Merlin and V.* 370
tiny-trumpeting *g* can break our dream   *Lancelot and E.* 137
but a murmur of *g*'s in the gloom,   *Vastness* 35

Gnaw'd   *g* his under, now his upper lip,   *Geraint and E.* 669
crazed With the grief that *g* at my heart,   *Bandit's Death* 39

Gnawing   lays his foot upon it, *G* and growling :   *Geraint and E.* 563

Gnome   *G* of the cavern, Griffin and Giant,   *Merlin and the G.* 39

Go   (*See also* **Gaw, Goä**)   We are call'd—we must *g*.   *All Things will Die* 20
Nine times *goes* the passing bell :   35
whene'er Earth *goes* to earth, with grief,   *Supp. Confessions* 38
the whirring sail *goes* round, (repeat)   *The Owl i* 4
A weary, weary way I *g*,   *Oriana* 89
Thought seems to come and *g*   *Eleänore* 96
Of that deep grave to which I *g* :   *My life is full* 7
And up and down the people *g*,   *L. of Shalott i* 6
page in crimson clad, *Goes* by to tower'd Camelot ;   ,, *ii* 23
'*G*, vexed Spirit, sleep in trust ;   *Two Voices* 115
' I will *g* forward, sayest thou,   ,, 190
I *g*, weak from suffering here :   ,, 238
Naked I *g*, and void of cheer :   ,, 239
grass Is dry and dewless. Let us *g*.   *Miller's D.* 246
I will rise and *g* Down into Troy,   *Œnone* 261
And let the foolish yeoman *g*.   *L. C. V. de Vere* 72
Little Effie shall *g* with me to-morrow to the green,   *May Queen* 25
The night-winds come and *g*, mother,   ,, 33
and forgive me ere I *g* ;   *May Queen, N. Y's. E.* 34
sweeter far is death than life to me that long to *g*.   *May Queen, Con.* 8
seem'd to *g* right up to Heaven and die   ,, 40
music went that way my soul will have to *g*.   ,, 42
I care not if I *g* to-day.   ,, 43
Slow-dropping veils of thinnest lawn, did *g* ;   *Lotos-Eaters* 11
Old Year, you must not *g* ;   *D. of the O. Year* 15
Old Year, you shall not *g*.   ,, 18
'*G*, take the goose, and wring her throat,   *The Goose* 31
Yet now, I charge thee, quickly *g* again   *M. d'Arthur* 79
' Ah ! my lord Arthur, whither shall I *g* ?   ,, 227
I, the last, *g* forth companionless,   ,, 236
these thou seëst—if indeed I *g*—   ,, 257
But *g* you hence, and never see me more.'   *Dora* 100
I will *g*, And I will have my boy,   ,, 121
I *g* to-night : I come to-morrow morn.   'I *g*, but I return : I would I were The pilot   *Audley Court* 70
let him *g* ; his devil *goes* with him,   *Walk. to the Mail* 27
G' (shrill'd the cotton-spinning chorus) ;   *Edwin Morris* 122
'*G*!—Girl, get you in !'   ,, 124
Power *goes* forth from me.'   *St. S. Stylites* 145
Let me *g* : take back thy gift :   *Tithonus* 27
G to him : it is thy duty :   *Locksley Hall* 52
wind arises, roaring seaward, and I *g*.   ,, 194
G, look in any glass and say,   *Day-Dm., Moral* 3
My breath to heaven like vapour *goes* :   *St. Agnes' Eve* 3
The flashes come and *g* ;   ,, 26
When down the stormy crescent *goes*,   *Sir Galahad* 25
Thro' dreaming towns I *g*,   ,, 50
' Love may come, and love may *g*,   *Edward Gray* 29
How *goes* the time ? 'Tis five o'clock.   *Will Water.* 3
And all the world *g* by them.   ,, 48
But whither would my fancy *g* ?   ,, 145
'Tis gone, and let it *g*.   ,, 180
G, therefore, thou ! thy betters went   ,, 185
Thy latter days increased with pence *G* down among the pots ;   ,, 220
To come and *g*, and come again,   ,, 229
And bless me, mother, ere I *g*.'   *Lady Clare* 56
So she *goes* by him attended,   *L. of Burleigh* 25
O, happy planet, eastward *g* ;   *Move eastward* 4
But thou, *g* by.   *Come not, when, etc.* 6

God (continued) and cried, 'G bless the King, and all his
  fellowship!' *Gareth and L.* 698
my lance Hold, by G's grace, he shall into the mire— „ 723
G wot, so thou wert nobly born, „ 1064
'G wot, I never look'd upon the face, „ 1333
Canst thou not trust the limbs thy G hath given, „ 1388
'Here, by G's grace, is the one voice for me.' *Marr. of Geraint* 344
'Here by G's rood is the one maid for me.' „ 368
Who knows? another gift of the high G, „ 821
I know, G knows, too much of palaces! *Geraint and E.* 236
G's curse, it makes me mad to see you „ 616
flush'd with fight, or hot, G's curse, with anger— „ 661
Yea, G, I pray you of your gentleness, „ 710
Man's word is G in man. *Balin and Balan* 8
and yet—G guide them—young.' *Merlin and V.* 29
by G's rood, I trusted you too much.' „ 376
for love of G and men And noble deeds, „ 412
Her G, her Merlin, the one passionate love „ 955
O G, that I had loved a smaller man! „ 872
G's mercy, what a stroke was there! *Lancelot and E.* 24
but G Broke the strong lance, „ 25
rule the land Hereafter, which G hinder.' „ 66
honours his own word, As if it were his G's?' „ 144
G wot, his shield is blank enough. „ 197
in this heathen war the fire of G Fills him: „ 315
Rapt on his face as if it were a G's. „ 356
No diamonds! for G's love, a little air! „ 505
'Yea, by G's death,' said he, ' ye love him well, „ 679
Not all unhappy, having loved G's best And greatest, „ 1093
I would to G, Seeing the homeless trouble „ 1364
shaped, it seems, By G for thee alone, „ 1367
may G, I pray him, send a sudden Angel „ 1423
'G make thee good as thou art beautiful,' *Holy Grail* 136
named us each by name, Calling 'G speed!' „ 352
seem'd Shoutings of all the sons of G: „ 509
If G would send the vision, well: „ 658
When G made music thro' them, „ 878
Nor the high G a vision, nor that One Who rose again: „ 918
I might have answer'd them Even before high G. *Pelleas and E.* 463
'Fear G: honour the King *Last Tournament* 302
Conceits himself as G that he can make „ 355
woman-worshipper? Yea, G's curse, and I! „ 447
My G, the measure of my hate for Mark „ 537
Pale-blooded, she will yield herself to G.' „ 608
'I will flee hence and give myself to G'— „ 624
May G be with thee, sweet, (repeat) „ 627, 629
My G, the power Was once in vows „ 648
And every follower eyed him as a G; „ 678
those whom G had made full-limb'd and tall, *Guinevere* 42
Would G that thou could'st hide me „ 118
To honour his own word as if his G's, „ 473
I guard as G's high gift from scathe and wrong, „ 494
I forgive thee, as Eternal G Forgives: „ 544
We two may meet before high G, „ 564
hereafter in the heavens Before high G. „ 638
my G, What might I not have made of thy fair world, „ 654
As if some lesser g had made the world, *Pass. of Arthur* 14
Till the High G behold it from beyond, „ 16
My G, thou hast forgotten me in my death: Nay—
  G my Christ—I pass but shall not die.' „ 27
G fulfils himself in many ways, „ 409
knowing G, they lift not hands of prayer „ 420
Bound by gold chains about the feet of G. „ 423
G unknits the riddle of the one, *Lover's Tale i* 181
so much wealth as G had charged her with— „ 213
I said to her, 'A day for G's to stoop,' „ 304
uphold Thy coronal of glory like a G, „ 488
tell him of the bliss he had with G— „ 674
nymph and g ran ever round in gold— „ iv 197
Some cousin of his and hers—O G, so like!' „ 327
G bless you, my own little Nell.' *First Quarrel* 22
I told them my tale, G's own truth— *Rizpah* 34
G 'ill pardon the hell-black raven „ 39
I have been with G in the dark— „ 79
an' the loov o' G fur men, *North. Cobbler* 55

God (continued) 'Fore G I am no coward; *The Revenge* 4
G of battles, was ever a battle like this „ 62
Fall into the hands of G, „ 90
and lodged with Plato's G, *Sisters (E. and E.)* 131
G help the wrinkled children that are Christ's „ 183
My G, I would not live Save that I think „ 228
G help them, our children and wives! *Def. of Lucknow* 8
But G is with me in this wilderness, *Sir J. Oldcastle* 8
G's free air, and hope of better things. „ 10
So much G's cause was fluent in it— „ 17
Had he G's word in Welsh He might be kindlier: „ 22
come, G willing, to outlearn the filthy friar. „ 118
to thee, green boscage, work of G, „ 129
I spread mine arms, G's work, I said, „ 137
'Bury them as G's truer images Are daily buried.' „ 140
Do penance in his heart, G hears him.' „ 143
What profits an ill Priest Between me and my G? „ 145
'No bread, no bread. G's body!' „ 159
Then I, G help me, I So mock'd, „ 162
G pardon all—Me, them, and all the world— „ 168
the fourth Was like the Son of G! „ 176
G willing, I will burn for Him. „ 193
In praise to G who led me thro' the waste. *Columbus* 17
that was clean Against G's word: „ 55
There was a glimmering of G's hand. „ 142
And G Hath more than glimmer'd on me. „ 143
Ah G, the harmless people whom we found „ 181
Who took us for the very G's from Heaven, „ 183
in that flight of ages which are G's „ 202
thunder of G peal'd over us all the day, *V. of Maeldune* 113
Whereon the Spirit of G moves as he will— *De Prof., Two* G 28
dream of a shadow, go—G bless you. *To W. H. Brookfield* 14
and the secret of the G's. My son the G's, despite
  of human prayer, *Tiresias* 8
great G, Arês, burns in anger still „ 11
trembling fathers call'd The G's own son. „ 17
some strange hope to see the nearer G. „ 29
angers of the G's for evil done „ 62
Falling about their shrines before their G's, „ 105
yesternight, To me, the great G Arês, „ 111
stand Firm-based with all her G's. „ 142
and quench The red G's anger, „ 158
flash The faces of the G's— „ 173
those who mix all odour to the G's „ 184
ah G, what a heart was mine to forsake her *The Wreck* 95
'would G, we had never met!' „ 102
but ah G, that night, that night *Despair* 8
Flashing with fires as of G, „ 16
your faith and a G of eternal rage, „ 39
taking the place of the pitying G that should be! „ 42
'Ah G' tho' I felt as I spoke I was taking the name
  in vain—'Ah G' and we turn'd to each other, „ 52
Ah G, should we find Him, perhaps, „ 56
And if I believed in a G, „ 70
but were there a G as you say, „ 101
Of a G behind all—after all—the great G for aught that I
  know; But the G of Love and of Hell together— „ 104
If there be such a G, may the great G „ 106
Or power as of the G's gone blind *Ancient Sage* 80
none but G's could build this house „ 83
To lie, to lie—in G's own house— *The Flight* 52
side by side in G's free light and air, „ 81
meet your paärints agin an' yer Danny O'Roon afore G *Tomorrow* 57
if soä pleäse G, to the hend. *Spinster's S's.* 112
'thank G that I hevn't naw cauf o' my oän.' „ 116
Sons of G, and kings of men *Locksley H., Sixty* 122
'Would to G that we were there'? „ 192
a G must mingle with the game: „ 271
WARRIOR of G, man's friend, and tyrant's foe, *Epit. on Gordon* 1
G the traitor's hope confound! (repeat) *Hands all Round* 10, 22, 34
Pray G our greatness may not fail „ 31
Led upward by the G of ghosts and dreams, *Demeter and P.* 5
when before have G's or men beheld The Life „ 29
Spring from his fallen G, „ 80
we spin the lives of men, And not of G's, „ 86

God (*continued*) he, the *G* of dreams, who heard my cry, | *Demeter and P.* 91
I, Earth-Goddess, cursed the *G's* of Heaven. | „ 102
But younger kindlier *G's* to bear us down, As we bore down the *G's* before us ? *G's*, To quench, not hurl the thunderbolt, | „ 131
G's indeed, To send the noon into the night | „ 134
made themselves as *G's* against the fear Of Death | „ 141
O *G*, I could blaspheme, | *Happy* 15
That *G* would ever slant His bolt from falling | „ 81
trust myself forgiven by the *G* to whom I kneel. | „ 86
Now *G* has made you leper in His loving care | „ 91
In the name Of the everlasting *G*, I will live and die | „ 108
G stay me there, if only for your sake, | *Romney's R.* 34
happy to be chosen Judge of *G's*, | *Death of Œnone* 16
Paris, himself as beauteous as a *G*. | „ 18
Paris, no longer beauteous as a *G*, | „ 25
Before the feud of *G's* had marr'd our peace, | „ 32
Thou knowest, Taught by some *G*, | „ 35
G's Avenge on stony hearts a fruitless prayer | „ 40
Spurning a shatter'd fragment of the *G*, | *St. Telemachus* 16
in his heart he cried 'The call of *G* !' | „ 27
muttering to himself 'The call of *G* ' | „ 42
O *G* in every temple I see people that see thee, | *Akbar's D., Inscrip.* 1
to be reconcil'd ?—No, by the Mother of *G*, | *Bandit's Death* 17
as *G's* own scriptures tell, | *Charity* 3
a woman, *G* bless her, kept me from Hell. | „ 4
Vanish'd shadow-like *G's* and Goddesses, | *Kapiolani* 27
My Father, and my Brother, and my *G* ! | *Doubt and Prayer* 8
Godamoighty (**God Almighty**) *g* an' parson 'ud nobbut le ma aloän, | *N. Farmer, O. S.* 43
Do *g* knaw what a's doing a-taäkin' o' meä ? | „ 45
But *g* a moost taäke meä an' taäke ma now | „ 51
God-bless-you Sneeze out a full *G-b-y* right and left ? | *Edwin Morris* 80
Gript my hand hard, and with *G-b-y* went. | *Sea Dreams* 160
A curse in his *G-b-y*: | „ 164
Goddess (*See also* **Earth-goddess**) if thou canst, O *G*, like ourselves | *Lucretius* 80
presented Maid Or Nymph, or *G*, | *Princess i* 197
Even now the *G* of the Past, | *Lover's Tale i* 16
The glorious *g* wreath'd a golden cloud, | *Achilles over the T.* 5
for the bright-eyed *g* made it burn. | „ 29
O *G'es*, help me up thither ! | *Parnassus* 3
flung the berries, and dared the *G*, | *Kapiolani* 6
believing that Peelè the *G* would wallow | „ 8
climb to the dwelling of Peelè the *G* ! | „ 22
Vanish'd shadow-like Gods and *G'es*, | „ 27
Godfather *G*, come and see your boy ! | *To F. D. Maurice* 2
God-fearing Altho' a grave and staid *G-f* man, | *Enoch Arden* 112
Enoch as a brave *G-f* man Bow'd himself down | „ 185
God-gifted *G-g* organ-voice of England, | *Milton* 3
God-in-man *G-i-m* is one with man-in-God, | *Enoch Arden* 187
Godiva *G*, wife to that grim Earl, | *Godiva* 12
Godless That tumbled in the *G* deep ; | *In Mem. cxxiv* 12
The craft of kindred and the *G* hosts | *Guinevere* 427
three more dark days of the *G* gloom | *Despair* 6
The *G* Jeptha vows his child . . . | *The Flight* 26
G fury of peoples, and Christless frolic of kings, | *The Dawn* 7
God-like (*See also* **Human-Godlike**) *G-l*, grasps the triple forks, | *Of old sat Freedom* 15
But then most *G* being most a man. | *Love and Duty* 31
Together, dwarf'd or *g*, bond or free : | *Princess vii* 260
Her *g* head crown'd with spiritual fire, | *Merlin and V.* 837
Thee the *G*, thee the changeless | *Akbar's D., Hymn* 4
Two *g* faces gazed below ; | *Palace of Art* 162
' O *G-l* isolation which art mine, | „ 197
On God and *G* men we build our trust. | *Ode on Well.* 266
touch of Charity Could lift them nearer *G-l* state | *Lit. Squabbles* 14
Beyond all dreams of *G* womanhood, | *Tiresias* 54
God-speed And left them with *G-s*, | *Gareth and L.* 890
Goest whither *g* thou, tell me where ?' | *Day-Dm., Depart.* 26
And now thou *g* up to mock the King, | *Gareth and L.* 292
thou *g*, he will fight thee first ; | „ 1295

Goin' (**going**) an' gied to the tramps *g* by— | *Village Wife* 33
'Ochone are ye *g'* away ?' '*G*' to cut the Sassenach whate' | *Tomorrow* 13
'An' whin are ye *g'* to lave me ?' | „ 17
Going (*See also* **A-Gawin'**, **Gawin'**, **Goin'**) We heard the steeds to battle *g*, | *Oriana* 15
G before to some far shrine, | *On a Mourner* 17
I am *g* a long way With these thou seëst— | *M. d'Arthur* 256
On a day when they were *g* O'er the lone expanse, | *The Captain* 25
They by parks and lodges *g* | *L. of Burleigh* 17
far end of an avenue, *G* we know not where : | *Enoch Arden* 359
Narrow'd her *g's* out and comings in ; | *Aylmer's Field* 501
And thinner, clearer, farther *g* ! | *Princess iv* 8
Give her the glory of *g* on, | *Wages* 5
Give her the wages of *g* on, | „ 10
And has bitten the heel of the *g* year. | *Window, Winter* 6
The year is *g*, let him go ; | *In Mem. cvi* 7
g to the king, He made this pretext, | *Marr. of Geraint* 32
bent he seem'd on *g* the third day, | „ 604
Bent as he seem'd on *g* this third day, | „ 625
Enid in their *g* had two fears, | *Geraint and E.* 817
Coming and *g*, and he lay as dead | *Merlin and V.* 213
Coming and *g*, and she lay as dead, | „ 644
'*G*? and we shall never see you more. | *Lancelot and E.* 926
but in *g* mingled with dim cries Far in the moonlit | *Pass. of Arthur* 41
I am *g* a long way With these thou seëst— | „ 424
Between the *g* light and growing night ? | *Lover's Tale i* 664
I am *g* to leave you a bit— | *First Quarrel* 80
'*G* ! you're *g* to her—kiss her— | „ 81
Good-night. I am *g*. He calls. | *Rizpah* 86
G? I am old and slighted : | *Columbus* 241
I was not *g* to stab you, | *Bandit's Death* 6
Gold (*adj.*) With that *g* dagger of thy bill | *Blackbird* 11
Bound by *g* chains about the feet of God. | *M. d'Arthur* 255
His face was ruddy, his hair was *g*, | *The Victim* 35
' If we have fish at all Let them be *g* ; | *Marr. of Geraint* 670
true hearts be blazon'd on her tomb In letters *g* and azure !' | *Lancelot and E.* 1345
the cup was *g*, the draught was mud.' | *Last Tournament* 298
Bound by *g* chains about the feet of God. | *Pass. of Arthur* 423
knew not that which pleased it most, The raven ringlet or the *g* ; | *The Ring* 166
bright bird that still is veering there Above his four *g* letters) | „ 333
Gold (*s*) (*See also* **Cloth of Gold**, **Gowd**) laws of marriage character'd in *g* | *Isabel* 16
By Bagdat's shrines of fretted *g*, | *Arabian Nights* 7
G glittering thro' lamplight dim, | „ 18
With royal frame-work of wrought *g* ; | *Ode to Memory* 82
plant in semblance, grew A flower all *g*, | *The Poet* 24
bosoms prest To little harps of *g* ; | *Sea-Fairies* 4
with cymbals, and harps of *g*, | *Dying Swan* 32
With a crown of *g* On a throne ? | *The Merman* 17
I should look like a fountain of *g* | *The Mermaid* 18
Slowly, as from a cloud of *g*, | *Eleänore* 73
Disclosed a fruit of pure Hesperian *g*, | *Œnone* 66
Brow-bound with burning *g*. | *D. of F. Women* 128
Either from lust of *g*, or like a girl | *M. d'Arthur* 127
Three Queens with crowns of *g*— | „ 198
Cursed be the *g* that gilds the straiten'd forehead | *Locksley Hall* 62
Every door is barr'd with *g*, | „ 100
trapt In purple blazon'd with armorial *g*. | *Godiva* 52
Pull off, pull off, the brooch of *g*, | *Lady Clare* 39
Beneath a manelike mass of rolling *g*, | *Aylmer's Field* 68
g that branch'd itself Fine as ice-ferns | „ 221
made pleasant by the baits Of *g* and beauty, | „ 487
heaps of living *g* that daily grow, | „ 655
swore Not by the temple but the *g*, | „ 794
but a gulf of ruin, swallowing *g*, | *Sea Dreams* 79
a long reef of *g*, Or what seem'd *g*: | „ 127
Still so much *g* was left ; | „ 130
Wreck'd on a reef of visionary *g*.' | „ 139
silken ho'od to each, And zoned with *g* ; | *Princess ii* 18
Came furrowing all the orient into *g*. | „ iii 18
Fruit, blossom, viand, amber wine, and *g*. | „ iv 35
gemlike eyes, And *g* and golden heads ; | „ 481

Gold (s) (*continued*) all the *g* That veins the world were
   pack'd
A single band of *g* about her hair,   *Princess iv* 542
Under the cross of *g* That shines over city and
   river,   „ *v* 513
Steel and *g*, and corn and wine,   *Ode on Well.* 49
Whose crying is a cry for *g*:   *Ode Inter. Exhib.* 17
And you with *g* for hair!   *The Daisy* 94
And you my wren with a crown of *g*,   *Window, Spring* 4
gossamers That twinkle into green and *g*:   „ 11
Israel made their gods of *g*,   *In Mem. xi* 8
Ring out the narrowing lust of *g*;   „ *xcvi* 23
the flying *g* of the ruin'd woodlands   „ *cvi* 26
And left his coal all turn'd to *g*   *Maud I i* 12
lost for a little her lust of *g*,   „ *x* 11
egg of mine Was finer *g* than any goose can lay ;   „ *III vi* 39
'*G* ? said I *g*?—ay then, why he, or she,   *Gareth and L.* 43
had the thing I spake of been Mere *g*—   „ 63
howsoe'er at first he proffer'd *g*,   „ 66
and left us neither *g* nor field.'   „ 336
'Whether would ye ? *g* or field ?'   „ *v* 339
thrice the *g* for Uther's use thereof,   „ 340
a cloth of palest *g*, Which down he laid   „ 344
gay with *g* In streaks and rays,   „ 389
There swung an apple of the purest *g*,   „ 910
Affirming that his father left him *g*,   *Marr. of Geraint* 170
a dress All branch'd and flower'd with *g*,   „ 451
strown With *g* and scatter'd coinage,   „ 631
In green and *g*, and plumed with green   *Geraint and E.* 26
A twist of *g* was round her hair,   *Merlin and V.* 89
The snake of *g* slid from her hair,   „ 221
down his robe the dragon writhed in *g*,   „ 888
Sir Lancelot's azure lions, crown'd with *g*,   *Lancelot and E.* 435
both the wings were made of *g*,   „ 663
a crown of *g* About a casque all jewels ;   *Holy Grail* 242
third night hence will bring thee news of *g*.'   „ 410
children sat in white with cups of *g*,   *Pelleas and E.* 357
heard it ring as true as tested *g*.'   *Last Tournament* 142
Either from lust of *g*, or like a girl   „ 284
Three queens with crowns of *g*:   *Pass. of Arthur* 295
Or Cowardice, the child of lust for *g*,   „ 366
rose as it were breath and steam of *g*,   *To the Queen ii* 54
nymph and god ran ever round in *g*—   *Lover's Tale i* 402
G, jewels, arms, whatever it may be.   „ *iv* 197
after he had shown him gems or *g*,   „ 235
an Eastern gauze With seeds of *g*,   „ 246
We brought this iron from our isles of *g*.   „ 292
G ? I had brought your Princes   *Columbus* 3
all The *g* that Solomon's navies carried   „ 105
And gathering ruthless *g*—   „ 113
seas of our discovering over-roll Him and his *g*;   „ 135
When he coin'd into English *g*   „ 140
and the miser would yearn for his *g*,   *The Wreck* 67
make thy *g* thy vassal not thy king,   *Despair* 100
From war with kindly links of *g*,   *Ancient Sage* 259
I hold Mother's love in letter'd *g*,   *Epilogue* 16
Give your *g* to the Hospital,   *Helen's Tower* 4
Mere want of *g*—and still for twenty years   *On Jub. Q. Victoria* 33
g from each laburnum chain Drop to the grass.   *The Ring* 428
Bright in spring, Living ;   *To Mary Boyle* 11
Soberer-hued *G* again.   *The Oak* 5
alchemise old hates into the *g* Of Love,   „ 10
When I make for an Age of *g*,   *Akbar's Dream* 163
   The Dreamer 7

Golden (*See also* **All-golden**) Her subtil, warm, and
   g breath,   *Supp. Confessions* 60
The summer calm of *g* charity,   *Isabel* 8
THOU art not steep'd in *g* languors,   *Madeline* 1
the *g* prime Of good Haroun
   Alraschid. (repeat)   *Arabian Nights* 10, 21, 32, 43, 54, 65,
   76, 87, 98, 109, 120, 131, 142, 153
marble stairs Ran up with *g* balustrade,   *Arabian Nights* 118
THE poet in a *g* clime was born, With *g* stars above ;   *The Poet* 1
sharp clear twang of the *g* chords Runs up the
   ridged sea.   *Sea-Fairies* 38
Two lives bound fast in one with *g* ease ;   *Circumstance* 5

Golden (*continued*) In a *g* curl With a comb of pearl,   *The Mermaid* 6
with fruitage golden-rinded On *g* salvers,   *Eleänore* 34
Grow *g* all about the sky ;   „ 101
Nor *g* largess of thy praise.   *My life is full* 5
branch of stars we see Hung in the *g* Galaxy.   *L. of Shalott iii* 12
the *g* bee Is lily-cradled: *Œnone* 29
And o'er him flow'd a *g* cloud,   „ 105
hair Ambrosial, *g* round her lucid throat And shoulder: „ 178
As she withdrew into the *g* cloud,   „ 191
And cast the *g* fruit upon the board,   „ 226
wherefrom The *g* gorge of dragons spouted forth   *Palace of Art* 23
cloud of incense of all odour steam'd From out a *g* cup.   „ 40
one hand grasp'd The mild bull's *g* horn.   „ 120
the clouds are lightly curl'd Round their *g*
   houses,   *Lotos-Eaters, C. S.* 113
A *g* bill ! the silver tongue,   *The Blackbird* 13
Should fill and choke with *g* sand—   *You ask me, why, etc.* 24
The goose let fall a *g* egg   *The Goose* 11
shadow of the flowers Stole all the *g* gloss,   *Gardener's D.* 130
such a noise of life Swarm'd in the *g* present,   „ 179
lad stretch'd out And babbled for the *g* seal,   *Dora* 135
with *g* yolks Imbedded and injellied ;   *Audley Court* 25
A second flutter'd round her lip Like a *g* butterfly ;   *Talking Oak* 220
Dropt dews upon her *g* head,   „ 227
themselves Move onward, leading up the *g* year.   *Golden Year* 26
And slow and sure comes up the *g* year.   „ 31
Thro' all the season of the *g* year.   „ 36
Roll onward, leading up the *g* year.   „ 41
Enrich the markets of the *g* year.   „ 46
Thro' all the circle of the *g* year ?'   „ 51
,Every moment, lightly shaken, ran itself in *g* sands.   *Locksley Hall* 32
Every door is barr'd with gold, and opens but to *g* keys.   „ 100
mantles from the *g* pegs Droop sleepily: *Day-Dm., Sleep. P.* 19
But dallied with his *g* chain,   *Revival* 31
And, stream'd thro' many a *g* bar,   *Depart.* 15
He lifts me to the *g* doors ;   *St. Agnes' Eve* 25
And raked in *g* barley.   *Will Water.* 128
now she gleam'd Like Fancy made of *g* air,   *The Voyage* 66
Buckled with *g* clasps before ; A light-green tuft
   of plumes she bore Closed in a *g* ring.   *Sir L. and Q. G.* 25
Purple gauzes, *g* hazes, liquid mazes,   *Vision of Sin* 31
I grew in gladness till I found My spirits in the *g* age.   *To E. L.* 12
Then, on a *g* autumn eventide,   *Enoch Arden* 61
first since Enoch's *g* ring had girt Her finger,   „ 157
And sent her sweetly by the *g* isles,   „ 536
the *g* lizard on him paused,   „ 601
many a silvery waterbreak Above the *g* gravel,   *The Brook* 62
Ringing like proven *g* coinage true,   *Aylmer's Field* 182
Had *g* hopes for France and all mankind,   „ 464
dark retinue reverencing death At *g* thresholds ;   „ 843
great Sicilian called Calliope to grace his *g* verse—   *Lucretius* 94
slowly lifts His *g* feet on those empurpled stairs   „ 135
that hour, My *g* work in which I told a truth   „ 260
And sweet girl-graduates in their *g* hair.   *Princess, Pro.* 142
ere the silver sickle of that month Became her *g* shield,   „ *i* 102
read and earn our prize, A *g* brooch :   „ *iii* 301
fight with iron laws, in the end Found *g*:   „ *iv* 76
'O Swallow, flying from the *g* woods,   „ 114
But led by *g* wishes, and a hope   „ 420
gems and gemlike eyes, And gold and *g* heads ;   „ 481
sheathing splendours and the *g* scale Of harness,   „ *v* 41
Creation minted in the *g* moods Of sovereign artists ;   „ 194
When dames and heroines of the *g* year   „ *vi* 64
Half-lapt in glowing gauze and *g* brede,   „ 134
Reels, as the *g* Autumn woodland reels   „ *vii* 357
anthem roll'd Thro' the dome of the *g* cross ;   *Ode on Well.* 61
we hear The tides of Music's *g* sea Setting   „ 252
Mourn'd in this *g* hour of jubilee,   *Ode Inter. Exhib.* 8
And mix the seasons and the *g* hours ;   „ 36
The *g* news along the steppes is blown,   *W. to Marie Alex.* 11
At Florence too what *g* hours,   *The Daisy* 41
And snowy dells in a *g* air.   „ 68
ONCE in a *g* hour I cast to earth a seed.   *The Flower* 1
To rest in a *g* grove, or to bask in a summer sky :   *Wages* 9
Fixt by their cars, waited the *g* dawn.   *Spec. of Iliad* 22

Gone (*continued*) you had *g* to her, She told, perforce; — *Princess iv* 329
found that you had *g*, Ridd'n to the hills, — „ 342
many a pleasant hour with her that's *g*, — „ *vi* 247
We brook no further insult but are *g*.' — „ 342
Blanche had *g*, but left Her child among us, — „ *vii* 56
He is *g* who seem'd so great.—*G*; — *Ode on Well.* 271
AND Willy, my eldest-born, is *g*, — *Grandmother* 1
and Willy, you say, is *g*. — „ 8
I ought to have *g* before him: — „ 14
But all my children have *g* before me, — „ 18
laughing at things that have long *g* by. — „ 92
So Willy has *g*, my beauty, — „ 101
he has but *g* for an hour,—*G* for a minute, my son, — „ 102
work mun 'a *g* to the gittin' whiniver — *N. Farmer, N. S.* 50
there before you are come, and *g*, — *Window, On the Hill* 14
G! *G*, till the end of the year, *G*, and the light
g with her, — „ *Gone* 1
G—flitted away, — „ 4
G, and a cloud in my heart, — „ 6
the grass will grow when I am *g*, — „ *No Answer* 5
when I am there and dead and *g*, — „ 11
Blow then, blow, and when I am *g*, — „ 17
And learns her *g* and far from home; — *In Mem. viii* 4
'How good! how kind! and he is *g*.' — „ *xx* 20
Old sisters of a day *g* by, — „ *xxix* 13
My prospect and horizon. *g*. — „ *xxxviii* 4
She cries, 'A thousand types are *g*: — „ *lvi* 3
Quite in the love of what is *g*, — „ *lxxxv* 114
The violet comes, but we are *g*. — „ *cv* 8
Farewell, we kiss, and they are *g*. — „ *Con.* 92
and slurring the days *g* by, — *Maud I i* 33
So many a million of ages have *g*, — „ *iv* 35
In a moment they were *g*: — „ *ix* 12
lately died, *G* to a blacker pit, — „ *x* 6
Like some of the simple great ones *g* — „ 61
He may stay for a year who has *g* for a week: — „ *xvi* 6
gates of Heaven are closed, and she is *g*. — „ *xviii* 12
our whole earth *g* nearer to the glow — „ 78
Now half to the setting moon are *g*, — „ *xxii* 23
Is it *g*? my pulses beat — „ *II i* 36
It is *g*; and the heavens fall in a gentle rain, — „ 41
paid our tithes in the days that are *g*, — „ *v* 23
We have lost him: he is *g*: — *Ded. of Idylls* 15
So that the realm has *g* to wrack: — *Com. of Arthur* 227
And *g* as soon as seen. — „ 377
Arthur all at once *g* mad replies, — *Gareth and L.* 863
younger brethren have *g* down Before this youth; — „ 1102
a prince whose manhood was all *g*, — *Marr. of Geraint* 59
Reproach you, saying all your force is *g*? — „ 88
with the morning all the court were *g*. — „ 156
when the fourth part of the day was *g*, — *Geraint and E.* 55
For the man's love once *g* never returns. — „ 333
when I am *g* Who used to lay them! — *Balin and Balan* 140
King Had gazed upon her blankly and *g* by: — *Merlin and V.* 161
lists of such a beard as youth *g* out — „ 245
Writ in a language that has long *g* by. — „ 674
Was one year *g*, and on returning found — „ 708
No sooner *g* than suddenly she began: — *Lancelot and E.* 96
take Their pastime now the trustful King is *g*!' — „ 101
g sore wounded, and hath left his prize — „ 530
I mean nothing: so then, get you *g*, — „ 776
on his helm, from which her sleeve had *g*. — „ 982
His very shield was *g*; only the case, — „ 990
when the ghostly man had come and *g*, — „ 1101
the heat is *g* from out my heart, — „ 1116
those that had *g* out upon the Quest, — *Holy Grail* 722
Lost in the quagmire?—lost to me and *g*, — „ 892
g he is To wage grim war against Sir Lancelot — *Guinevere* 192
By couriers *g* before; and on again, — „ 396
listening till those armed steps were *g*, — „ 585
'*G*—my lord! *G* thro' my sin to slay and to be slain! — „ 612
G, my lord the King, My own true lord! — „ 616
'My end draws nigh; 'tis time that I were *g*. — *Pass. of Arthur* 331
and he groan'd, 'The King is *g*.' — „ 443
had *g* Surely, but for a whisper, — *Lover's Tale iv* 19

K

Gone (*continued*) he told me that so many years had
g by, — *First Quarrel* 36
Flesh of my flesh was *g*, — *Rizpah* 51
if my boy be *g* to the fire? — „ 78
half of the short summer night was *g*, — *The Revenge* 65
for a face *G* in a moment—strange. — *Sisters (E. and E.)* 94
Sa 'is taäil wur lost an' 'is boooks wur *g* — *Village Wife* 87
sa o' coorse she be *g* to the bad! — „ 98
(Hath he been here—not found me—*g* again? — *Sir J. Oldcastle* 152
She is *g*—but you will tell the King, — *Columbus* 234
G! He will achieve his greatness. — *Tiresias* 167
the master *g*. *G* into darkness, — „ 201
And *g*—that day of the storm— — *The Wreck* 148
Hence! she is *g*! can I stay? — *Despair* 113
'Lost and *g* and lost and *g*!' — *Ancient Sage* 224
this Hall at last will go—perhaps have *g*, — *The Flight* 27
He's *g* to the States, aroon, — *Tomorrow* 49
dhry eye thin but was wet for the frinds that
was *g*! — „ 83
G the fires of youth, the follies, — *Locksley H., "Sixty* 39
G like fires and floods and earthquakes — „ 40
G the tyrant of my youth, — „ 43
G the comrades of my bivouac, — „ 45
g as all on earth will go. — „ 46
G with whom for forty years my life — „ 47
G our sailor son thy father, — „ 55
G thy tender-natured mother, — „ 57
G for ever! Ever? no— — „ 65
G the cry of 'Forward, Forward,' — „ 73
till ten thousand years have *g*. — „ 78
G at eighty, mine own age, — „ 281
Midnight—and joyless June *g* by, — *Pref. Poem Broth. S.* 9
O THOU so fair in summers *g*, — *Freedom* 1
Child, when thou wert *g*, I envied human wives, — *Demeter and P.* 52
an' screeäd like a Howl *g* wud— — *Owd Roä* 76
So far *g* down, or so far up in life, — *The Ring* 193
Laid on her table overnight, was *g*; — „ 277
g! and *g* in that embrace! — „ 443
but dead so long, *g* up so far, — „ 462
Is memory with your Marian *g* to rest, — *To Mary Boyle* 13
bewail the friend, the wife, For ever *g*. — „ 54

Good (*adj.*) the golden prime Of *g* Haroun
Alraschid. — *Arabian Nights* 11, 22, 33, 44, 55, 66, 77, 88, 99, 110, 121, 132, 143, 154
But *g* things have not kept aloof, — *My life is full* 2
humming of the drowsy pulpit-drone Half God's *g*
sabbath, — *To J. M. K.* 11
'In some *g* cause, not in mine own, — *Two Voices* 148
'Yea!' said the voice, 'thy dream was *g*, — „ 157
Lean'd on him, faithful, gentle, *g*, — „ 416
he set and left behind The *g* old year, the dear
old time, — *May Queen, N. Y's. E.* 6
And that *g* man, the clergyman, has told me
words of peace. — „ *Con.* 12
'The Legend of *G* Women,' long ago Sung — *D. of F. Women* 2
Lest one a custom should corrupt the world. — *M. d'Arthur* 242
'Come With all *g* things, and war shall be no
more.' — „ *Ep.* 28
Who read me rhymes elaborately *g*, — *Edwin Morris* 20
G people, you do ill to kneel to me. — *St. S. Stylites* 133
The *g* old Summers, year by year — *Talking Oak* 39
slow sweet hours that bring us all things *g*, — *Love and Duty* 57
And all *g* things from evil, — „ 59
It is not bad but *g* land, — *Amphion* 6
My *g* blade carves the casques of men, — *Sir Galahad* 1
Like all *g* things on earth! — *Will Water.* 202
I hold it *g*, *g* things should pass: — „ 205
I hold thee dear For this *g* pint of port. — „ 212
We felt the *g* ship shake and reel, — *The Voyage* 15
Wine is *g* for shrivell'd lips, — *Vision of Sin* 79
Virtue!—to be *g* and just— — „ 111
Then her *g* Philip was her all-in-all, — *Enoch Arden* 525
But Miriam Lane was *g* and garrulous, — „ 700
Heard the *g* mother softly whisper 'Bless, — *Aylmer's Field* 187
Till after our *g* parents past away — „ 358

Good (adj.) (*continued*) As *g* need was—thou hast come
   to talk our isle.   *Sir J. Oldcastle* 32

Some cried on Cobham, on the *g* Lord Cobham;   ,,   43

Burnt—*g* Sir Roger Acton, my dear friend!   ,,   79

drawn By this *g* Wiclif mountain down from heaven,   ,,   132

(My *g* friend By this time should be with me.)   ,,   138

I would not spurn *G* counsel of *g* friends,   ,,   146

CHAINS, my *g* lord: in your raised brows I read   *Columbus* 1

Drove me and my *g* brothers home in chains,   ,,   134

O never was time so *g*!   *V. of Maeldune* 87

You needs must have *g* lynx-eyes if I do not escape
   you   *Despair* 114

Steevie be right *g* manners bang thruf   *Spinster's S's.* 66

Hesper, whom the poet call'd the Bringer home of
   all *g* things.   All *g* things   ,,   185

G, this forward, you that preach it,   ,,   216

When our own *g* redcoats sank from sight,   *Heavy Brigade* 42

'e was allus as *g* as gowd.   *Owd Roä* 6

Fur 'e's moor *g* sense na the Parliament man 'at stans
   for us 'ere,   ,,   13

an' I thowt o' the *g* owd times 'at was goan,   ,,   43

An' I says 'I'd be *g* to tha, Bess, if tha'd onywaäys let
   ma be *g*,'   ,,   75

Git oop, if ya're onywaäys *g* for owt.'   And I says 'If I
   beänt noäwaäys—not nowadaäys—*g* fur nowt—   ,,   77

An' Roä was as *g* as the Hangel i' saävin' a son fur me.   ,,   96

the *g* and brave!   He sees me, waves me from him.   *Happy* 18

G, I am never weary painting you.   *Romney's R.* 3

EH? *g* daäy! *g* daäy! thaw it bean't not mooch
   of a daäy,   *Church-warden, etc.* 1

Us, O Just and *G*, Forgive,   *Poland* 11

such strange war with something *g*,   *Two Voices* 302

'Tis only noble to be *g*.   *L. C. V. de Vere* 54

waked with silence, grunted '*G*!'   *M. d'Arthur*, Ep. 4

'*G*! my lady's kinsman! *g*!'   *Aylmer's Field* 198

'*G*: Your oath is broken: we dismiss you: *Princess* iv 599

make us all we would be, great and *g*.'   ,,   599

Were we ourselves but half as *g*, as kind,   ,,   v 201

Good (s) 'She wrought her people lasting *g*,'   *To the Queen* 24

saw thro' life and death, thro' *g* and ill,   *The Poet* 5

'And not to lose the *g* of life—   *Two Voices* 132

'I see the end, and know the *g*.'   ,,   432

or if *G*, *G* only for its beauty, seeing not
   That Beauty, *G*, and Knowledge, are three
   sisters   *To —— With Pal. of Art* 8

Would love the gleams of *g* that broke   *Love thou thy land* 89

What *g* should follow this, if this were done?   *M. d'Arthur* 92

The drowsy hours, dispensers of all *g*,   *Gardener's D.* 185

the *g* and increase of the world. (repeat)   *Edwin Morris* 44, 51, 92

some one say, Then why not ill for *g*?   *Love and Duty* 47

when shall all men's *g* Be each man's rule,   *Golden Year* 47

Subdue them to the useful and the *g*.   *Ulysses* 38

But for some true result of *g*   *Will Water.* 55

He never meant us anything but *g*.   *Enoch Arden* 887

To sell her, those good parents, for her *g*.   *Aylmer's Field* 483

contriving their dear daughter's *g*—   ,,   781

the two contrived their daughter's *g*—   ,,   848

all things work together for the *g* Of those'—   *Sea Dreams* 158

All for the common g of womankind.'   *Princess* ii 209

'All *g* go with thee! take it Sir,'   ,,   vi 207

Whole in himself, a common *g*.   *Ode on Well.* 26

Till each man find his own in all men's *g*,   *Ode Inter. Exhib.* 37

Embrace her as my natural *g*;   *In Mem.* iii 14

And what to me remains of *g*?   ,,   vi 42

Her hands are quicker unto *g*:   ,,   xxxiii 10

Enjoying each the other's *g*:   ,,   xlvii 10

Hold thou the *g*: define it well: ,,   liii 13

g Will be the final goal of ill,   ,,   liv 1

I can but trust that *g* shall fall   ,,   14

I see thee sitting crown'd with *g*,   ,,   lxxxiv 5

lead The closing cycle rich in *g*.   ,,   cv 28

Ring in the common love of *g*.   ,,   cvi 24

High nature amorous of the *g*,   ,,   cix 23

Yet O ye mysteries of *g*,   ,,   cxxviii 8

Behold, I dream a dream of *g*,   ,,   cxxix 11

Good (s) (*continued*) Full to the banks, close on the promised *g*.   *Maud* I xviii 6

Nor let any man think for the public *g*,   ,,   II v 45

It is better to fight for the *g*   ,,   III vi 57

I needs must disobey him for his *g*;   *Geraint and E.* 135

what they long for, *g* in friend or foe,   ,,   876

This *g* is in it, whatsoe'er of ill,   *Lancelot and E.* 1207

as the base man, judging of the *g*,   *Pelleas and E.* 80

None knows it, and my tears have brought me *g*:   *Guinevere* 202

What *g* should follow this, if this were done?   *Pass. of Arthur* 260

fur they weänt niver coom to naw *g*.   *Village Wife* 96

power hath work'd no *g* to aught that lives,   *Tiresias* 77

running after a shadow of *g*;   *Despair* 92

No ill no *g*! such counter-terms, my son,   *Ancient Sage* 250

G, for *G* is *G*, he follow'd,   *Locksley H., Sixty* 60

Truth for truth, and *g* for *g*!   The *G*, the True,
   the Pure, the Just—   ,,   71

preach'd a Gospel, all men's *g*;   ,,   89

Evolution ever climbing after some ideal *g*,   ,,   199

Powers of *G*, the Powers of Ill,   ,,   273

whatsoe'er He wrought of *g* or brave   *Epilogue* 76

That wanders from the public *g*,   *Freedom* 26

Shall we not thro' *g* and ill   *Open I. and C. Exhib.* 33

Goodbye when he came to bid me *g*.   *First Quarrel* 78

I had bid him my last *g*;   *Rizpah* 41

Good Fortune prosperously sail'd The ship '*G F*,'   *Enoch Arden* 528

blown by baffling winds, Like the *G F*,   ,,   629

Goodlier 'A *g* goodly youth and worth a *g* boon!   But
   so thou wilt no *g*, then must Kay,   *Gareth and L.* 450

(And there were none but few *g* than he)   ,,   744

When all the *g* guests are past away,   *Last Tournament* 158

Goodliest The *g* fellowship of famous knights   *M. d'Arthur* 15

he seem'd the *g* man That ever among ladies   *Lancelot and E.* 254

Reputed the best knight and *g* man,   *Guinevere* 382

The *g* fellowship of famous knights   *Pass. of Arthur* 183

Goodly In sooth it was a *g* time,   *Arabian Nights* 20

A *g* place, a *g* time, (repeat)   ,,   31, 53

A *g* time, For it was in the golden prime   ,,   42

When on my *g* charger borne   *Sir Galahad* 49

Nor dealing *g* counsel from a height   *Aylmer's Field* 172

and *g* sheep In haste they drove,   *Spec. of Iliad* 4

her great and *g* arms Stretch'd under all the cornice   *Gareth and L.* 218

Had made his *g* cousin, Tristram, knight,   ,,   394

The *g* knight! What!   ,,   402

'A *g* youth and worth a goodlier boon!   ,,   449

For strong thou art and *g* therewithal,   ,,   878

dreams Of *g* supper in the distant pool,   ,,   1187

'Full merry am I to find my *g* knave   ,,   1291

following with a costrel bore The means of *g*
   welcome,   *Marr. of Geraint* 387

And roam the *g* places that she knew;   ,,   646

Ah, dear, he took me from a *g* house,   ,,   708

Yea, and he brought me to a *g* house;   ,,   713

Men saw the *g* hills of Somerset,   ,,   828

But not to *g* hill or yellow sea   ,,   830

Three horses and three *g* suits of arms,   *Geraint and E.* 124

Then cried Geraint for wine and *g* cheer   ,,   283

Some *g* cognizance of Guinevere,   *Balin and Balan* 195

till his *g* horse, Arising wearily at a fallen oak,   ,,   424

tramples on the *g* shield to show His loathing   ,,   550

and unhooded casting off The *g* falcon free;   *Merlin and V.* 131

for *g* hopes are mine That Lancelot is no more   *Lancelot and E.* 601

she should ask some *g* gift of him For her own self   ,,   912

while I drank the brook, and ate The *g* apples,   *Holy Grail* 388

'Where is that *g* company,' said I,   ,,   432

And then I chanced upon a *g* town   ,,   573

Saving the *g* sword, his prize,   *Pelleas and E.* 359

A *g* brother of the Table Round Swung by
   the neck: *Last Tournament* 431

and felt the *g* hounds Yelp at his heart,   ,,   503

with *g* rhyme and reason for it—   *Sisters (E. and E.)* 92

but the *g* view Was now one blank,   *Death of Œnone* 3

Goodman her small *g* Shrinks in his arm-chair   *Princess* v 453

Goodmorrow *G*—Dark my doom was here,   *Balin and Balan* 623

'Goodnight, true brother here! *g* there!   ,,   628

Speaking a still *g-m* with her eyes.   *Lancelot and E.* 1033

Goodness eye which watches guilt And *g*,   *In Mem. xxvi* 6
Goodnight *G, g*, when I have said *g* for evermore, *May Queen, N. Y's. E.* 41
   G, sweet mother: call me before the day is born.   „ 49
   G! for we shall never bid again Good morrow— *Balin and Balan* 622
   mine again should darken thine, *G*, true brother.'   „ 626
   '*G*, true brother here! goodmorrow there!   „ 628
   the stout Prince bad him a loud *g-n*.   *Geraint and E.* 361
   G-n. I am going. He calls.   *Rizpah* 86
   and soä little Dick, *g-n*.   *Owd Roä* 118
Goods with what she brought Buy *g* and stores— *Enoch Arden* 138
   Bought Annie *g* and stores,   „ 169
   shelf and corner for the *g* and stores.   „ 171
Goodwill *G* to me as well as all— *Supp. Confessions* 27
   Peace and *g*, *g* and peace, Peace and *g*, *In Mem. xxviii* 11
   Bible verse of the Lord's *g w* toward men— *Rizpah* 61
Goose (*See also* **Wild-goose**) He held a *g* upon his arm, *The Goose* 5
   take the *g*, and keep you warm,   „ 7
   She caught the white *g* by the leg, A *g*—   „ 9
   The *g* let fall a golden egg   „ 11
   She dropt the *g*, and caught the pelf,   „ 13
   more the white *g* laid It clack'd and cackled louder.   „ 23
   'Go, take the *g*, and wring her throat,   „ 31
   The *g* flew this way and flew that,   „ 35
   He took the *g* upon his arm,   „ 41
   Quoth she, 'The Devil take the *g*,   „ 55
   He praised his hens, his *geese*, his guinea-hens; *The Brook* 126
   From the long-neck'd *geese* of the world *Maud I iv* 52
   ' Being a *g* and rather tame than wild, *Gareth and L.* 38
   'twere but of the *g* and golden eggs.'   „ 40
   egg of mine Was finer gold than any *g* can lay;   „ 43
   rams and *geese* Troop'd round a Paynim harper *Last Tournament* 321
   swine, goats, asses, *geese* The wiser fools.   „ 325
Gorge (s) (*See also* **Mountain-gorge**) roaring foam
   into the *g* Below us, *If I were loved* 13
   The *g's*, opening wide apart, reveal *Œnone* 12
   craggy ledge High over the blue *g*,   „ 210
   golden *g* of dragons spouted forth A flood *Palace of Art* 23
   Sat often in the seaward-gazing *g*, *Enoch Arden* 589
   Downward from his mountain *g*   „ 636
   Thro' the long *g* to the far light *Ode on Well.* 213
Gorge (verb) Gave to the garbaging war-hawk to
   g it, *Batt. of Brunanburh* 109
Gorged snake-like slimed his victim ere he *g*; *Sea Dreams* 193
   We issued *g* with knowledge, *Princess ii* 388
   Dropt off *g* from a scheme that had left us flaccid *Maud I i* 20
   we stay'd three days, and we *g* and we madden'd, *V. of Maeldune* 67
   giddy besides with the fruits we had *g*,   „ 75
Gorgeous And title-scrolls and *g* heraldries. *Aylmer's Field* 656
   this is he Worthy of our *g* rites, *Ode on Well.* 93
   Starr'd from Jehovah's *g* armouries, *Milton* 6
   That rollest from the *g* gloom Of evening *In Mem. lxxxvi* 2
   Without a mirror, in the *g* gown; *Marr. of Geraint* 739
   Nor meanly, but with *g* obsequies, *Lancelot and E.* 1335
   Mixt with the *g* west the lighthouse shone, *Lover's Tale i* 60
   Raise a stately memorial, Make it regally *g*, *On Jub. Q. Victoria* 45
Gorgon stared upon By ghastlier than the *G* head, *Death. of Œnone* 71
Gorgonised *G* me from head to foot *Maud I xiii* 21
Gorloïs This is the son of *G*, not the King; *Com. of Arthur* 73
   Some calling Arthur born of *G*, Others of Anton?   „ 170
   The prince and warrior *G*, he that held   „ 186
   But she, a stainless wife to *G*,   „ 194
   That *G* and King Uther went to war: And over-
   thrown was *G* and slain.   „ 196
   many hated Uther for the sake Of *G*.   „ 221
   a son of *G* he, Or else the child of Anton,   „ 232
   born the son of *G*, after death,   „ 240
   'Daughter of *G* and Ygerne am I;'   „ 316
   and dark Was *G*, yea and dark was Uther too,   „ 329
   those Who call'd him the false son of *G*: *Guinevere* 288
Gorse blaze of *g*, and the blush Of millions *V. of Maeldune* 43
Gospel The *G*, the Priest's pearl, *Sir J. Oldcastle* 116
   Ah matter, Lord than that thy *G*,   „ 119
   preach'd a *G*, all men's good; *Locksley H., Sixty* 89
Gossamer (adj.) Had seem'd a *g* filament up in air, *Lover's Tale i* 413
Gossamer (s) To trip a tigress with a *g*, *Princess v* 170

Gossamer (s) (*continued*) all the silvery *g's* That twinkle
   into green and gold: *In Mem. xi* 7
Gossip (adj.) A hate of *g* parlance, and of sway, *Isabel* 26
Gossip (s) Fearing the lazy *g* of the port, *Enoch Arden* 335
   By this the lazy *g's* of the port,   „ 472
   The sins of emptiness, *g* and spite *Princess ii* 92
   like a city, with *g*, scandal, and spite; *Maud I iv* 8
   Delight myself with *g* and old wives, *Holy Grail* 553
Gossip (verb) neighbours come and laugh and *g*, *Grandmother* 91
   hear the magpie *g* Garrulous under a roof of pine: *To F. D. Maurice* 19
Gossoon Thin a slip of a *g* call'd, *Tomorrow* 78
Got *G* up betwixt you and the woman there. *Dora* 96
   storming a hill-fort of thieves He *g* it; *Aylmer's Field* 226
   ' Sir Ralph has *g* your colours: *Princess iv* 594
   Now had you *g* a friend of your own age,   „ *vi* 251
   Stook to his taaïl they did, an' 'e 'ant *g* shut on
   'em yet. *N. Farmer, N. S.* 30
   For all have *g* the seed. *The Flower* 20
   At last he *g* his breath and answer'd, *Lancelot and E.* 422
   up the side, sweating with agony, *g*,   „ 494
   So Lancelot *g* her horse, Set her thereon, *Guinevere* 122
   we *g* to the barn, fur the barn wouldn't burn *Owd Roä* 103
   Up she *g*, and wrote him all, *Forlorn* 79
   True we have *g—such* a faithful ally *Riflemen form!* 24
Gothic (adj.) Gleam thro' the *G* archway in the wall. *Godiva* 64
   A *G* ruin and a Grecian house, *Princess, Pro.* 232
Gothic (s) Of finest *G* lighter than a fire,   „ 92
Gotten (*See also* **Well-gotten**) you have *g* the wings of
   love, *Window, Ay* 15
   then 'ed *g* wer leäve, *Owd Roä* 51
   when Moother 'ed *g* to bed,   „ 53
Gourd By heaps of *g's*, and skins of wine, *Vision of Sin* 13
   In us true growth, in her a Jonah's *g*, *Princess iv* 311
Gout *g* and stone, that break Body toward death, *Lucretius* 153
   that I, Rack'd as I am with *g*, *Columbus* 235
Gouty The *g* oak began to move, *Amphion* 20
Govern I have no men to *g* in this wood: *D. of F. Women* 135
   g a whole life from birth to death, *Lover's Tale i* 76
Governance And own the holy *g* of Rome.' *Columbus* 190
Governed ' I *g* men by change, and so I sway'd *D. of F. Women* 130
Governess *See* **Guvness**
Government A land of settled *g*, *You ask me, why, etc.* 9
   And manners, climates, councils, *g's*, *Ulysses* 14
   in arts of *g* Elizabeth and others; *Princess ii* 161
   felt Her low firm voice and tender *g*. *Geraint and E.* 194
Gowd (gold) we wouldn't goä, wi' good *g* o' the Queen, *Village Wife* 49
   booöks mebbe worth their weight i' *g*.'   „ 70
   'e was allus as good as *g*. *Owd Roä* 6
Gown Her cap blew off, her *g* blew up, *The Goose* 51
   She clad herself in a russet *g*, *Lady Clare* 57
   A *g* of grass-green silk she wore, *Sir L. and Q. G.* 24
   they should not wear our rusty *g's*, *Princess, Pro.* 143
   A rosy blonde, and in a college *g*,   „ *ii* 323
   I wore a lilac *g*; *Grandmother* 57
   In which of old I wore the *g*; *In Mem. lxxxvii* 24
   Without a mirror, in the gorgeous *g*; *Marr. of Geraint* 739
   At least put off to please me this poor *g*, *Geraint and E.* 679
   ' In this poor *g* my dear lord found me first,   „ 698
   In this poor *g* I rode with him to court,   „ 700
   In this poor *g* he bad me clothe myself,   „ 702
   And this poor *g* I will not cast aside   „ 705
   taaïl'd in an owd turn *g*, *North. Cobbler* 41
   all the while I wur chaängin' my *g*, *Spinster's S's.* 43
   to my faäce or a teärin' my *g*—   „ 91
   loved by all the younger *g* There at Balliol, *To Master of B.* 2
Gowned One arm aloft—*G* in pure white, *Gardener's D.* 126
Graäce (grace) an' the power ov 'is *G*, *North. Cobbler* 73
   An' saw by the *G* o' the Lord, *Church-warden, etc.* 42
Graäte (grate) red as the Yule-block theer i' the *g*. *Owd Roä* 56
Graäter (greater) They maäkes ma a *g* Laädy nor 'er
   i' the mansion theer, *Spinster's S's.* 110
Grabb'd An' I *g* the munny she maäde, *North. Cobbler* 32
Grace (*See also* **Graäce**) Victoria—since your Royal *g* *To the Queen* 5
   that *g* Would drop from his o'er-brimming love, *Supp. Confessions* 112
   From all things outward you have won A tearful *g*, *Margaret* 12

Grace (*continued*) I watch thy *g*; and in its place My heart   *Eleänore* 127
God in his mercy lend her *g*,   *L. of Shalott* iv 53
Complaining, 'Mother, give me *g*   *Mariana in the S.* 29
'But looking upward, full of *g*, He pray'd,   *Two Voices* 223
and, with a silent *g* Approaching,   *Miller's D.* 159
loveliest in all *g* Of movement,   *Œnone* 75
all *g* Summ'd up and closed in little;—   *Gardener's D.* 12
shelter'd here Whatever maiden *g* The good old
    Summers,   *Talking Oak* 38
So sweet a face, such angel *g*,   *Beggar Maid* 13
But the tender *g* of a day that is dead   *Break, Break, etc.* 15
'Annie, this voyage by the *g* of God   *Enoch Arden* 190
(Claspt hands and that petitionary *g*   *The Brook* 112
Nor deeds of gift, but gifts of *g* he forged,   *Sea Dreams* 192
And so much *g* and power, breathing down   *Princess* ii 38
arts of *g* Sappho and others vied with any man: " 163
At last a solemn *g* Concluded,   " 452
easy *g*, No doubt, for slight delay,   " iv 330
Come, a *g* to me! I am your warrior: " vi 223
who love best have best the *g* to know   *W. to Marie Alex.* 28
and there is *G* to be had;   *Grandmother* 94
The mimic picture's breathing *g*,   *In Mem. lxxviii* 11
With gifts of *g*, that might express   " *lxxxv* 46
with power and *g* And music in the bounds   " *lxxxvii* 33
The maidens gather'd strength and *g*   " *ciii* 27
manhood fused with female *g* In such a sort,   " *cix* 17
Maud in the light of her youth and her *g*,   *Maud I v* 15
Rich in the *g* all women desire,   " x 13
Some peculiar mystic *g* Made her only the child   " *xiii* 39
g that, bright and light as the crest Of a peacock,   " *xvi* 16
May nothing there her maiden *g* affright!   " *xviii* 71
heard that Arthur of his *g* Had made   *Gareth and L.* 393
Treat him with all *g*, Lest he should come to shame   " 468
so my lance Hold, by God's *g*, he shall into the mire—   " 723
I accord it easily as a *g*.'   " 975
and with all *g* Of womanhood and queenhood,   *Marr. of Geraint* 175
'Here, by God's *g*, is the one voice for me.'   " 344
It were but little *g* in any of us,   " 624
I might amend it by the *g* of Heaven,   *Geraint and E.* 53
such a *g* Of tenderest courtesy,   " 861
Both *g* and will to pick the vicious quitch   " 903
with how sweet *g* She greeted my return!   *Balin and Balan* 193
To learn the *g*'s of their Table,   " 238
Name, manhood, and a *g*, but scantly thine,   " 377
into that rude hall Stept with all *g*, and not
    with half disdain Hid under *g*,   *Lancelot and E.* 263
'Do me this *g*, my child, to have my shield   " 382
'A *g* to me,' She answer'd, 'twice to-day.   " 383
The *g* and versatility of the man!   " 472
g's of the court, and songs, Sighs,   " 648
'Stay a little! One golden minute's *g*!   " 684
while that ghostly *g* Beam'd on his fancy,   " 885
'Ye might at least have done her so much *g*,   " 1310
the seven clear stars—O *g* to me   *Holy Grail* 692
mighty reverent at our *g* was he: " 702
glossy-throated *g*, Isolt the Queen.   *Last Tournament* 509
'*G*, Queen, for being loved: she loved me well.   " 602
to yield thee *g* beyond thy peers.'   " 743
beauty, *g* and power, Wrought as a charm   *Guinevere* 143
Who see your tender *g* and stateliness.   " 190
Had yet that *g* of courtesy in him left   " 436
and—not one moment's *g*,   *Lover's Tale i* 659
—so, with that *g* of hers, Slow-moving   " iv 292
praised him to his face with their courtly foreign *g*;   *The Revenge* 99
being damn'd beyond hope of *g*?   *Despair* 109
Art and *G* are less and less: *Locksley H., Sixty* 245
the branching *g* Of leafless elm,   *To Ulysses* 15
they do me too much *g*—for me?   *Romney's R.* 27
Grace (goddess) Like to Furies, like to *G*'s,   *Vision of Sin* 41
Muses and the *G*'s, group'd in threes,   *Princess ii* 27
meet her *G*'s, where they deck'd her   " *vii* 168
Grace (verb) moss or musk, To *g* my city rooms;   *Gardener's D.* 194
Calliope to *g* his golden verse—   *Lucretius* 94
'So ye will *g* me,' answer'd Lancelot,   *Lancelot and E.* 223
Graced the glance That *g* the giving—   *Gardener's D.* 178

Graced (*continued*) ease That *g* the lowliest act in
    doing it.   *Gareth and L.* 490
Graceful (*See also* **All-graceful**) 'And yet it was
    a *g* gift—   *Talking Oak* 233
Divided in a *g* quiet—paused,   *Gardener's D.* 156
What looks so little *g*: 'men'   *Princess iii* 53
Or deep dispute, and *g* jest;   *In Mem. lxxxiv* 24
They sang of what is wise and good And *g*.   " *ciii* 11
The *g* tact, the Christian art;   " *cx* 16
you keep So much of what is *g*:   *Lancelot and E.* 1219
A *g* thought of her Grav'n on my fancy!   *Lover's Tale i* 357
Gracefulness symmetry Of thy floating *g*,   *Eleänore* 50
Graceless Loud laugh'd the *g* Mark.   *Merlin and V.* 62
Gracious Maud could be *g* too, no doubt To a lord,   *Maud I x* 28
G lessons thine And maxims of the mud!   *Merlin and V.* 48
For Lancelot will be *g* to the rat,   " 120
thine is more to me—soft, *g*, kind—   *Last Tournament* 560
thy Mark is kindled on thy lips Most *g*;   " 562
Was *g* to all ladies, and the same In open battle   *Guinevere* 329
All is *g*, gentle, great and Queenly.   *On Jub. Q. Victoria* 14
—well—that were hardly *g*. No!   *Happy* 103
A life that moves to *g* ends   *You might have won* 6
A distant kinship to the *g* blood   *Aylmer's Field* 62
'A *g* gift to give a lady, this!' 'But would it
    be more *g*' ask'd the girl 'Were I to give
    this gift of his to one That is no lady?'
    '*G*? No' said he.   " 240
So *g* was her tact and tenderness: *Princess i* 24
the Lord be *g* to me! A plot, a plot,   " *ii* 191
till the *g* dews Began to glisten and to fall: " 316
those were *g* times.   " *iv* 297
He seems a *g* and a gallant Prince,   " *v* 213
Like creatures native unto *g* act,   " *vii* 27
Not learned, save in *g* household ways,   " 318
Whose hand at home was *g* to the poor: *W. to Marie Alex.* 37
Some *g* memory of my friend;   *In Mem. c* 4
Or Love but play'd with *g* lies,   " *cxxv* 7
Sweet nature gilded by the *g* gleam Of letters,   *Ded. of Idylls* 39
As in the presence of a *g* king.   *Gareth and L.* 316
or what had been those *g* things,   *Geraint and E.* 636
meet The morrow morn once more in one full field
    Of *g* pastime,   *Holy Grail* 324
woman's eyes and innocent, And all her bearing *g*;   " 394
therefore flatter'd him, Being so *g*,   *Pelleas and E.* 120
And all her damsels too were *g* to him,   " 122
So for the last time she was *g* to him.   " 175
Warm with a *g* parting from the Queen,   " 558
this name to which her *g* lips Did lend such gentle
    utterance,   *Lover's Tale i* 456
for the sake Of one recalling *g* times,   *To E. Fitzgerald* 53
Household happiness, *g* children,   *Vastness* 24
She dropt the *g* mask of motherhood,   *The Ring* 384
Watching her large light eyes and *g* looks,   *Prog. of Spring* 19
Gradation Regard *g*, lest the soul Of Discord   *Love thou thy land* 67
Grade Tho' scaling slow from *g* to *g*;   *Two Voices* 174
g's Beyond all *g*'s develop'd?   *Gardener's D.* 156
To leap the *g*'s of life and light,   *In Mem. xli* 11
Gradual Her *g* fingers steal And touch   *Will Water.* 26
while I walk'd with these In Marvel at that *g*
    change,   *Lover's Tale iii* 19
saner lesson might he learn Who reads thy *g*   *Prog. of Spring* 106
Gradually And *g* the powers of the night,   *Princess, Con.* 111
Graduate *See* **Girl-graduates**
Graff made a Gardener putting in a *g*,   *Merlin and V.* 479
Grafted Disrooted, what I am is *g* here.   *Princess ii* 220
my days have been a life-long lie, *G* on half a truth;   *Romney's R.* 42
Grail (*See also* **Holy Grail**) and the *G* Past, and the
    beam decay'd,   *Holy Grail* 121
A crimson *g* within a silver beam;   " 155
Because I had not seen the *G*,   " 196
'Art thou so bold and hast not seen the *G*?'   " 279
I, Galahad, saw the *G*, The Holy Grail,   " 464
Before a burning taper, the sweet *G* Glided and past,   " 694
Could see it, thou hast seen the *G*;'   " 757

Grail *(continued)* And to the Holy Vessel of the *G*.' — *Holy Grail* 840
Grain (corn) four-field system, and the price of *g*; — *Audley Court* 34
  shower the fiery *g* Of freedom broadcast — *Princess* v 421
  A pamphleteer on guano and on *g*, — „ *Con.* 89
  eating hoary *g* and pulse the steeds, — *Spec. of Iliad* 21
  And vacant chaff well meant for *g*. — *In Mem.* vi 4
  grown The *g* by which a man may live? — „ *liii* 8
  And gave all ripeness to the *g*, — „ *lxxxi* 11
  g Storm-strengthen'd on a windy site, — *Gareth and L.* 691
  Smuttier than blasted *g*: — *Last Tournament* 305
  and of the *g* and husk, the grape And ivyberry, — *De Prof., Two G.* 50
  torpid mummy wheat Of Egypt bore a *g* as sweet As that — *To Prof. Jebb.* 6
  thro' olive-yard and vine And golden *g*, — *Demeter and P.* 111
  From buried *g* thro' springing blade, — „ 146
  heats our earth to yield us *g* and fruit, — *Akbar's Dream* 105
Grain (fibre, etc.) Cut Prejudice against the *g*: — *Love thou thy land* 22
  tho' I circle in the *g* Five hundred rings — *Talking Oak* 83
  Nor ever lightning char thy *g*, — „ 277
  the stem Less *g* than touchwood, — *Princess* iv 333
  And twists the *g* with such a roar — „ v 528
  There dwelt an iron nature in the *g*: — „ vi 50
  Too prurient for a proof against the *g* — *Merlin and V.* 487
Grain (particle) like a *g* of conscience made him sour.' — *Vision of Sin* 218
  The city sparkles like a *g* of salt. — *Will* 20
  A little *g* shall not be spilt.' — *In Mem.* lxv 4
  For every *g* of sand that runs, — „ cxvii 9
  Have a *g* of love for me, — *Maud* II ii 53
  When weight is added only *g* by *g*, — *Marr. of Geraint* 526
  Not a *g* of gratitude mine! — *Despair* 62
  in the million-millionth of a *g* — *Ancient Sage* 42
  chains of mountain, *g*'s of sand — *Locksley H., Sixty* 208
Grain (fast dye) one the Master, as a rogue in *g* — *Princess, Pro.* 116
Grained *See* **Hard-grained**
Granary find my garden-tools upon the *g* floor: — *May Queen, N. Y's. E.* 45
  garner'd up Into the *granaries* of memory— — *Lover's Tale* i 129
Grand He look'd so *g* when he was dead. — *The Sisters* 32
  This same *g* year is ever at the doors.' — *Golden Year* 74
  Princess, six feet high, *G*, epic, homicidal; — *Princess, Pro.* 225
  She look'd as *g* as doomsday and as grave: — „ i 187
  true she errs, But in her own *g* way: — „ iii 108
  strange Poet-princess with her *g* Imaginations — „ 273
  Or some *g* fight to kill and make an end: — „ iv 591
  wherein were wrought Two *g* designs; — „ vii 122
  he bore without abuse The *g* old name of gentleman, — *In Mem.* cxi 10
  A *g* political dinner To half the squirelings near; — *Maud* I xx 25
  A *g* political dinner To the men of many acres, — „ 31
Grandchild I wish to see My *g* on my knees — *Dora* 13
Grander And roll'd the floods in *g* space, — *In Mem.* ciii 26
Grandfather I mean your *g*, Annie: — *Grandmother* 23
  Whose old *g* has lately died. — *Maud* I x 5
Grandsire The boy set up betwixt his *g*'s knees, — *Dora* 131
  sorcerer, whom a far-off *g* burnt — *Princess* i 6
  he bestrode the *g*, when he fell, — „ ii 242
  a greatness Got from their *G*'s— — *Batt. of Brunanburh* 16
  Ev'n her *G*'s fifty half forgotten. — *On Jub. Q. Victoria* 41
Grandson To a *g*, first of his noble line, — *Maud* I x 12
  LATE, my *g*! half the morning have I paced — *Locksley H., Sixty* 1
  Here is Locksley Hall, my *g*, — „ 213
  Not the Hall to-night, my *g*! — „ 237
Grange Upon the lonely moated *g*. — *Mariana* 8
  About the lonely moated *g*. — „ 32
  So pass I hostel, hall, and *g*; — *Sir Galahad* 81
  so by tilth and *g*, And vines, — *Princess* i 110
  nail me like a weasel on a *g* For warning: — „ ii 205
  burnt the *g*, nor buss'd the milking-maid, — „ v 222
  That ripple round the lonely *g*; — *In Mem.* xci 12
  No gray old *g*, or lonely fold, — „ c 5
  OLD FITZ, who from your suburb *g*, — *To E. Fitzgerald* 1
  A height, a broken *g*, a grove, — *Ancient Sage* 223
  Rejoicing in the harvest and the *g*. — *Demeter and P.* 127
Granite shadowy *g*, in a gleaming pass; — *Lotos-Eaters, C. S.* 4
  ebb that faintly lipp'd The flat red *g*; — *Audley Court* 13
Grant 'Good soul! suppose I *g* it thee, — *Two Voices* 38

Grant *(continued)* 'But if I *g*, thou mightst defend The thesis — *Two Voices* 337
  didst thou *g* mine asking with a smile, — *Tithonus* 16
  We might be still as happy as God *g*'s — *Enoch Arden* 416
  (Altho' I *g* but little music there) — *Sea Dreams* 253
  You *g* me license; might I use it? — *Princess* iii 235
  I *g* in her some sense of shame, — „ iv 349
  G me your son, to nurse, — „ vi 298
  g my prayer. Help, father, brother, — „ 304
  God *g* I may find it at last! — *Maud* I ii 1
  His face, as I *g*, in spite of spite, — „ xiii 8
  G me some knight to do the battle for me, — *Gareth and L.* 362
  ev'n that thou *g* her none, — „ 368
  g me to serve For meat and drink among thy kitchen-knaves — „ 444
  And pray'd the King would *g* me Lancelot — „ 856
  G me pardon for my thoughts: — *Marr. of Geraint* 816
  if the Queen disdain'd to *g* it! — *Balin and Balan* 191
  'Fairest I *g* her: I have seen; — „ 356
  g me some slight power upon your fate, — *Merlin and V.* 333
  And *g* my re-iterated wish, — „ 353
  O *g* my worship of it Words, as we *g* grief tears. — *Lancelot and E.* 1187
  Only this *G* me, I pray you: — „ 1217
  Queen, if I *g* the jealousy as of love, — „ 1399
Granted Nor yet refused the rose, but *g* it, — *Gardener's D.* 160
  Perfectly beautiful: let it be *g* her: — *Maud* I ii 4
  As fairest, best and purest, *g* me To bear it!' — *Balin and Balan* 350
  What should be *g* which your own gross heart — *Merlin and V.* 916
  But takes it all for *g*: — *Lover's Tale* i 157
  Sanctuary *g* To bandit, thief, assassin— — *Sir J. Oldcastle* 112
Grape (fruit) *(See also* **Father-grape**) But pledge me in the flowing *g*. — *My life is full* 15
  And *g*'s with bunches red as blood; — *Day-Dm., Sleep P.* 44
  Let there be thistles, there are *g*'s; — *Will Water.* 57
  skins of wine, and piles of *g*'s. — *Vision of Sin* 13
  drains The chalice of the *g*'s of God; — *In Mem.* x 16
  bruised the herb and crush'd the *g*, — „ xxxv 23
  shun The foaming *g* of eastern France. — „ *Con.* 80
  when my father dangled the *g*'s, — *Maud* I i 71
  this wine—the *g* from whence it flow'd — *Sisters (E. and E.)* 61
  dangled a hundred fathom of *g*'s, — *V. of Maeldune* 56
  grain and husk, the *g* And ivyberry, choose; — *De Prof., Two G.* 50
  vines with *g*'s Of Eshcol hugeness; — *To E. Fitzgerald* 27
  Are figs of thistles? or *g*'s of thorns? — *Riflemen form!* 10
Grape (shot) their masses are gapp'd with our *g*— — *Def. of Lucknow* 42
  Now double-charge it with *g*! — „ 68
Grape-loaded valleys of *g-l* vines that glow — *D. of F. Women* 219
Grape-thicken'd in a bower *G-t* from the light, — *Eleänore* 36
Grapple And *g*'s with his evil star; — *In Mem.* lxiv 8
Grappling airy navies *g* in the central blue; — *Locksley Hall* 124
Grasp (s) A *g* Having the warmth and muscle — *Aylmer's Field* 179
  To give him the *g* of fellowship; — *Maud* I xiii 16
  of hopeless grief about my heart, — *Lover's Tale* i 126
  I clasp'd her without fear: her weight Shrank in my *g*, — „ ii 203
  Pity for all that aches in the *g* of an idiot power, — *Despair* 43
Grasp (verb) God-like, *g*'s the triple forks, — *Of old sat Freedom* 15
  I will not cease to *g* the hope I hold Of saintdom, — *St. S. Stylites* 5
  his long arms stretch'd as to *g* a flyer: — *Aylmer's Field* 588
  And *g*'s the skirts of happy chance, — *In Mem.* lxiv 6
  To him who *g*'s a golden ball, — „ cxi 3
  Than language *g* the infinite of Love. — *Lover's Tale* i 484
Grasp'd-Graspt one hand *grasp'd* The mild bull's golden horn. — *Palace of Art* 119
  there the world-worn Dante *grasp'd* his song, — „ 135
  And mounted horse and *graspt* a spear, — *Gareth and L.* 691
  long black horn Beside it hanging; which Sir Gareth *graspt*, — „ 1367
  This Balin *graspt*, but while in act to hurl, — *Balin and Balan* 368
  Queen *Graspt* it so hard, that all her hand — *Last Tournament* 411
  her hand *Grasp'd*, made her vail her eyes: — *Guinevere* 663
  I loved her, *graspt* the hand she lov'd, — *Lover's Tale* i 750
  'Woman'—he *graspt* at my arm— — *The Wreck* 120
  tiny fist Had *graspt* a daisy from your Mother's grave— — *The Ring* 323
Graspest Old Yew, which *g* at the stones — *In Mem.* ii 1
  Dark yew, that *g* at the stones — „ xxxix 4

Grasping *g* the pews And oaken finials   *Aylmer's Field* 822
   g down the boughs I gain'd the shore.   *Princess* iv 189
   lo! it was her mother *g* her   *Marr. of Geraint* 676
   This heard Geraint, and *g* at his sword,   *Geraint and E.* 725
   deathly-pale Stood *g* what was nearest,   *Lancelot and E.* 966

Graspt *See* **Grasp'd**

Grass (*See also* **Meadow-grass, Oat-grass, Sparrow-grass,**
   Sword-grass) the dull Saw no divinity in *g*,   *A Character* 8
   And seem'd knee-deep in mountain *g*,   *Mariana in the S.* 42
   Make thy *g* hoar with early rime.   *Two Voices* 66
   You scarce could see the *g* for flowers.   " 453
   the bearded *g* Is dry and dewless.   *Miller's D.* 245
   The grasshopper is silent in the *g*:   *Œnone* 26
   From level meadow-bases of deep *g*   *Palace of Art* 7
   above my head in the long and pleasant *g*.   *May Queen, N. Y's. E.* 32
   petals from blown roses on the *g*,   *Lotos-Eaters, C. S.* 2
   Heap'd over with a mound of *g*,   " 67
   thro' lush green *g'es* burn'd The red anemone.   *D. of F. Women* 71
   A league of *g*, wash'd by a slow broad stream,   *Gardener's D.* 40
   So light upon the *g*:   *Talking Oak* 88
   He lies beside thee on the *g*.   " 239
   All *g* of silky feather grow—   " 269
   Or scatter'd blanching on the *g*.   *Day-Dm., Arrival* 2
   'There I put my face in the *g*—   *Edward Gray* 21
   High-elbow'd grigs that leap in summer *g*.   *The Brook* 54
   the Squire had seen the colt at *g*,   " 139
   Show'd her the fairy footings on the *g*,   *Aylmer's Field* 90
   With neighbours laid along the *g*,   *Lucretius* 214
   babies roll'd about Like tumbled fruit in *g*;   *Princess, Pro.* 83
   Grate her harsh kindred in the *g*:   " iv 125
   Lay like a new-fall'n meteor on the *g*,   " vi 135
   she sat, she pluck'd the *g*, She flung it   " Con. 31
   I may die but the *g* will grow, And the *g* will
   grow when I am gone,   *Window, No Answer* 4
   Spring is here with leaf and *g*:   " 23
   And, since the *g'es* round me wave,   *In Mem.* xxi 2
   I take the *g'es* of the grave,   " 3
   And tuft with a *g* a feudal tower;   " cxxviii 20
   From little cloudlets on the *g*,   " Con. 94
   fall before Her feet on the meadow *g*,   *Maud I* v 26
   A livelier emerald twinkles in the *g*,   " xviii 51
   their feet In dewy *g'es* glisten'd,   *Gareth and L.* 928
   when he found the *g* within his hands He laugh'd;   " 1225
   pluck'd the *g* There growing longest   *Geraint and E.* 256
   Tho' happily down on a bank of *g*,   " 507
   grayly draped With streaming *g*, appear'd,   *Balin and Balan* 333
   'Here are snakes within the *g*;   *Merlin and V.* 33
   lived alone in a great wild on *g*;   " 621
   Went back to his old wild, and lived on *g*,   " 649
   its own voice clings to each blade of *g*,   *Lancelot and E.* 107
   Lay like a rainbow fall'n upon the *g*,   " 431
   eft and snake, In *g* and burdock,   *Holy Grail* 571
   flats, where nothing but coarse *g'es* grew;   " 794
   live *g*, Rose-campion, bluebell, kingcup,   *Last Tournament* 233
   O ay—the winds that bow the *g*!   " 735
   the flowering grove Of *g'es* Lancelot pluck'd   *Guinevere* 34
   Prone by the dashing runnel on the *g*.   *Lover's Tale* ii 101
   an' they sucks the muck fro' the *g*.   *Village Wife* 32
   Who live on milk and meal and *g*;   *To E. Fitzgerald* 13
   And all her golden armour on the *g*,   *Tiresias* 45
   they laid this body they foun' an the *g*   *Tomorrow* 73
   blossom an' spring from the *g*,   " 89
   glory lights the hall, the dune, the *g*!   *Locksley H., Sixty* 181
   Jacob's ladder falls On greening *g*,   *Early Spring* 10
   gold from each laburnum chain Drop to the *g*.   *To Mary Boyle* 11
   delight To roll himself in meadow *g*,   *Romney's R.* 14
   Thy living flower and *g*,   *Doubt and Prayer* 6

Grass-green graves *g-g* beside a gray church-tower,   *Circumstance* 6
   A gown of *g-g* silk she wore,   *Sir L. and Q. G.* 24

Grasshopper the *g* carolleth clearly;   *Leonine Eleg.* 5
   The *g* is silent in the grass: *Œnone* 26

Grassy THE plain was *g*, wild and bare,   *Dying Swan* 1
   gave into a *g* walk Thro' crowded lilac-ambush   *Gardener's D.* 111
   And *g* barrows of the happier dead.   *Tithonus* 71
   By *g* capes with fuller sound In curves   *Sir L. and Q. G.* 14

Grassy (*continued*) I steal by lawns and *g* plots,   *The Brook* 170
   thro' many a *g* glade And valley,   *Marr. of Geraint* 236
   When we had reach'd The *g* platform on some hill,   *Lover's Tale* i 341

Grate (s) (*See also* **Graäte**) glimmering vaults with
   iron *g's*,   *D. of F. Women* 35
   rang the *g* of iron thro' the groove,   *Pelleas and E.* 207

Grate (verb) the harsh shingle should *g* underfoot,   *Enoch Arden* 772
   I *g* on rusty hinges here:'   *Princess* i 86
   G her harsh kindred in the grass: " iv 125

Grated (*See also* **Rib-grated**) faces flat against the
   panes, Sprays *g*,   *Balin and Balan* 345
   Blinkt the white morn, sprays *g*,   " 385
   grew So *g* down and filed away with thought,   *Merlin and V.* 623

Grateful *g* at last for a little thing: *Maud III* vi 3
   G to Prince Geraint for service done,   *Marr. of Geraint* 15
   So *g* is the noise of noble deeds   " 437
   be *g* for the sounding watchword   *Locksley H., Sixty* 198
   And deem me *g*, and farewell!   *The Wanderer* 16
   That over-vaulted *g* gloom,   *Palace of Art* 54
   a *g* people named Enid the Good;   *Geraint and E.* 963
   clouded with the *g* incense-fume   *Tiresias* 183

Gratefullest Hers was the *g* heart I have found   *In the Child. Hosp.* 32

Gratefulness King was all fulfill'd with *g*,   *Last Tournament* 593
   By all the laws of love and *g*,   *Lover's Tale* iv 278

Gratify We would do much to *g* your Prince—   *Princess* v 217

Grating Across the iron *g* of her cell Beat,   *Holy Grail* 81
   Struck from an open *g* overhead High in the wall,   *Lover's Tale* iv 60
   As from the *g* of a sepulchre,   *The Ring* 400

Gratitude Out of full heart and boundless *g*   *Enoch Arden* 346
   This nightmare weight of *g*, I know it;   *Princess* vi 300
   Not a grain of *g* mine!   *Despair* 62
   G—loneliness—desire to keep So skilled   *The Ring* 373

Gratulation and was moving on In *g*,   *Princess* ii 185

Grave (adj.) Or gay, or *g*, or sweet, or stern,   *Palace of Art* 91
   G, florid, stern, as far as eye could see,   *Sea Dreams* 219
   a here lies beneath, *G*, solemn!'   *Princess Pro.* 213
   She look'd as grand as doomsday and as *g*:   " i 187
   In each we sat, we heard The *g* Professor.   " ii 371
   Farewell, Macready; moral, *g*, sublime,   *To W. C. Macready* 12
   And that has made you *g*?   *The Ring* 88
   G mother of majestic works,   *Of old sat Freedom* 13
   Until the *g* churchwarden doff'd,   *The Goose* 19
   G faces gather'd in a ring.   *Day-Dm., Sleep. P.* 38
   Altho' a *g* and staid God-fearing man,   *Enoch Arden* 112
   The *g*, severe Genovese of old.   *The Daisy* 40
   G doubts and answers here proposed,   *In Mem.* xlviii 3

Grave (s) *See also* **Ocean-grave**) when thy *g* Was
   deep,   *Supp. Confessions* 85
   Over its *g* i' the earth so chilly; (repeat)   *A spirit haunts* 10, 22
   the green that folds thy *g*. (repeat)   *A Dirge* 6, 13, 20, 27, 34, 41, 48
   Two *g's* grass-green beside a gray church-tower,   *Circumstance* 6
   the brink Of that deep *g* to which I go: *My life is full* 7
   From winter rains that beat his *g*.   *Two Voices* 261
   A shadow on the *g's* I knew,   " 272
   'From *g* to *g* the shadow crept: " 274
   I shall lie alone, mother, within the moulder-
   ing *g*.   *May Queen, N. Y's. E.* 20
   and upon that *g* of mine,   " 21
   see me till my *g* be growing green: " 43
   His voice was thin, as voices from the *g*;   *Lotos-Eaters* 34
   and ripen toward the *g* In silence;   " C. S. 51
   cord of Love Down to a silent *g*.   *D. of F. Women* 212
   Thou seëst all things, thou wilt see my *g*:   *Tithonus* 73
   Each pluck'd his one foot from the *g*,   *Amphion* 43
   By Ellen's *g*, on the windy hill.   *Edward Gray* 12
   The very *g's* appear'd to smile,   *The Letters* 45
   drop thy foolish tears upon my *g*,   *Come not, when, etc.* 2
   glow-worm of the *g* Glimmer in thy rheumy eyes.   *Vision of Sin* 153
   Till the *g's* begin to move,   " 165
   tho' she mourn'd his absence as his *g*,   *Enoch Arden* 247
   it would vex him even in his *g*,   " 303
   thought to bear it with me to my *g*;   " 896
   shame these mouldy Aylmers in their *g's*:   *Aylmer's Field* 396
   Above them, with his hopes in either *g*.   " 624
   bring Their own gray hairs with sorrow to the *g*—   " 777

Grave (s) (*continued*)   Pity, the violet on the tyrant's *g*.   *Aylmer's Field* 845
  his bones long laid within the *g*,   *Lucretius* 256
  very sides of the *g* itself shall pass,   „ 257
  There above the little *g*, (repeat)   *Princess* ii 12, 13
  that full voice which circles round the *g*,   „ 45
  cram him with the fragments of the *g*,   „ iii 311
  and drank himself into his *g*.   *Grandmother* 6
  Drops in his vast and wandering *g*.   *In Mem.* vi 16
  I take the grasses of the *g*,   „ xxi 3
  yearn'd To hear her weeping by his *g*?   „ xxxi 4
  Or builds the house, or digs the *g*,   „ xxxvi 14
  And darkening the dark *g*'s of men,—   „ xxxix 9
  I wrong the *g* with fears untrue :   „ li 9
  No life may fail beyond the *g*,   „ lv 2
  Unused example from the *g*   „ lxxx 15
  And my prime passion in the *g*:   „ lxxxv 76
  Had fall'n into her father's *g*,   „ lxxxix 48
  fathers bend Above more *g*'s,   „ xcviii 16
  with me, and the *g* Divide us not,   „ cxxii 9
  the *g* That has to-day its sunny side.   „ Con. 71
  To-day the *g* is bright for me,   „ 73
  thing that had made false haste to the *g*—   *Maud* I i 58
  and Orion low in his *g*.   „ iii 14
  Your mother is mute in her *g*   „ iv 58
  Perhaps from a selfish *g*.   „ xvi 23
  into a shallow *g* they are thrust,   „ II v 6
  To have no peace in the *g*, is that not sad ?   „ 16
  Is it kind to have made me a *g* so rough,   „ 97
  Orion's *g* low down in the west,   „ III vi 8
  The cackle of the unborn about the *g*,   *Merlin and V.* 507
  Among the knightly brasses of the *g*'s,   „ 752
  'I shudder, some one steps across my *g*;'   *Guinevere* 57
  that his *g* should be a mystery From all men,   „ 297
  From halfway down the shadow of the *g*,   *To the Queen* ii 6
  to whom I made it o'er his *g* Sacred,   „ 35
  I and the first daisy on his *g*   *Lover's Tale* i 193
  received in a sweet *g* Of eglantines,   „ 528
  That men plant over *g*'s.   „ 538
  the darkness of the *g*, (repeat)   „ 597
  The foul steam of the *g* to thicken by it,   „ 649
  till they fell Half-digging their own *g*'s)   „ ii 47
  over the deep *g*'s of Hope and Fear,   „ 58
  now, will I go down into the *g*,   „ iv 46
  she joined, In and beyond the *g*,   *Sisters (E. and E.)* 272
  From either by the stillness of the *g*—   „ 282
  Break thro' the yews and cypress of thy *g*,   *Ded. Poem Prin. Alice* 12
  we laid him that night in his *g*.   *Def. of Lucknow* 12
  I will have them buried in my *g*.   *Columbus* 201
  some one standing by my *g* will say,   „ 209
  a ghastlier face than ever has haunted a *g*   *The Wreck* 8
  vex you with wretched words, who is best in his *g*?   *Despair* 108
  the world is dark with griefs and *g*'s,   *Ancient Sage* 171
  and weds me to my *g*.   *The Flight* 20
  Fiend would yell, the *g* would yawn,   „ 51
  I seem to see a new-dug *g* up yonder by the yew !   „ 98
  hair was as white as the snow an a *g*.   *Tomorrow* 60
  in wan *g* be the dead boor-tree,   „ 87
  yet he look'd beyond the *g*,   *Locksley H., Sixty* 60
  I repent it o'er his *g*—   „ 255
  cycle-year That dawns behind the *g*.   *Epilogue* 78
  raise a wind To sing thee to thy *g*,   *Freedom* 36
  sowing the nettle on all the laurel'd *g*'s of the Great ;   *Vastness* 22
  graspt a daisy from your Mother's *g*—   *The Ring* 323
  glimmers on the marsh and on the *g*.'   „ 341
  I am fitter for my bed, or for my *g*,   „ 433
  O the night, While the *g* is yawning.   *Forlorn* 60
  I would leap into your *g*.   *Happy* 20
  throbs Thro' earth, and all her *g*'s,   *Romney's R.* 128
  Hush'd as the heart of the *g*,   *Bandit's Death* 26
  I am dressing the *g* of a woman with flowers.   *Charity* 2
  your shadow falls on the *g*.   „ 20
  I am dressing her *g* with flowers.   „ 44
  crimson with battles, and hollow with *g*'s,   *The Dreamer* 12
Gravel   waterbreak Above the golden *g*,   *The Brook* 62
  like a wizard pentagram On garden *g*,   „ 104

Gravel-spread   bed Of silent torrents, *g-s* ;   *The Daisy* 34
Graven   *G* with emblems of the time,   *Arabian Nights* 108
  underneath, A pint-pot neatly *g*.   *Will Water.* 248
  on one side, *G* in the oldest tongue   *Com. of Arthur* 302
  A graceful thought of hers *G* on my fancy !   *Lover's Tale* i 358
  Their names, *G* on memorial columns,   *Tiresias* 124
Graver   No *g* than as when some little cloud   *Enoch Arden* 129
  he turn'd The current of his talk to *g* things   „ 203
  No *g* than a schoolboys' barring out;   *Princess, Con.* 66
  one is somewhat *g* than the other—   *Sisters (E. and E.)* 26
  ·No ! but the paler and the *g*, Edith.   „ 38
  The *g* is the one perhaps for you   „ 40
  COME, when no *g* cares employ,   *To F. D. Maurice* 1
  '*G* cause than yours is mine To curse this hedgerow thief,   *Marr. of Geraint* 308
  Began to break her sports with *g* fits,   *Merlin and V.* 180
Gravest   The *g* citizen seems to lose his head,   *Princess, Con.* 59
Graw (grow)   an' proputty, proputty *g*'s.   *N. Farmer, N. S.* 16
  thou can't *g* this upo' watter !'   *North. Cobbler* 86
Graw'd (grew)   as *g* hall ower the brick ;   *Owd Roä* 26
Gray (Edward)   *See* **Edward Gray**
Gray (adj.)   my hope is *g*, and cold At heart,   *Supp. Confessions* 103
  Come from the woods that belt the *g* hill-side,   *Ode to Memory* 55
  Two graves grass-green beside a *g* church-tower,   *Circumstance* 6
  Four *g* walls, and four *g* towers,   *L. of Shalott* i 15
  I see his *g* eyes twinkle yet At his own jest—*g* eyes lit up   *Miller's D.* 11
  g twilight pour'd On dewy pastures,   *Palace of Art* 85
  wild marsh-marigold shines like fire in swamps and hollows *g*,   *May Queen* 31
  You'll never see me more in the long *g* fields at night;   *May Queen, N. Y's. E.* 26
  range Of waning lime the *g* cathedral towers,   *Gardener's D.* 218
  The set *g* life, and apathetic end.   *Love and Duty* 18
  And this *g* spirit yearning in desire   *Ulysses* 30
  for this *g* shadow, once a man—   *Tithonus* 11
  But I count the *g* barbarian lower than the Christian child.   *Locksley Hall* 174
  my hair Is *g* before I know it.   *Will Water.* 168
  A *g* and gap-tooth'd man as lean as death,   *Vision of Sin* 60
  On thy cold *g* stones, O Sea !   *Break, break, etc.* 2
  high in heaven behind it a *g* down With Danish barrows ;   *Enoch Arden* 6
  His large *g* eyes and weather-beaten face   „ 70
  He, shaking his *g* head pathetically,   „ 714
  See thro' the *g* skirts of a lifting squall   „ 829
  Then Enoch rolling his *g* eyes upon her,   „ 844
  left Their own *g* tower, or plain-faced tabernacle,   *Aylmer's Field* 618
  bring Their own *g* hairs with sorrow to the grave—   „ 777
  a work To assail this *g* preëminence of man !   *Princess* iii 234
  From the flaxen curl to the *g* lock a life   „ iv 426
  and without Found the *g* kings at parle ;   „ v 114
  Look you ! the *g* mare Is ill to live with,   „ 451
  G halls alone among their massive groves ;   „ Con. 43
  O good *g* head which all men knew,   *Ode on Well.* 35
  From Como, when the light was *g*,   *The Daisy* 73
  misty summer And *g* metropolis of the North.   „ 104
  'We shall both be *g*.'   *Window, When* 6
  G nurses, loving nothing new ;   *In Mem.* xxix 14
  The same *g* flats again, and felt The same,   „ lxxxvii 13
  No *g* old grange, or lonely fold,   „ c 5
  A *g* old wolf and a lean.   *Maud* I xiii 28
  Not that *g* old wolf, for he came not back   „ II v 53
  Sleuth-hound thou knowest, and *g*,   *Gareth and L.* 462
  ivy-stems Claspt the *g* walls with hairy-fibred arms,   *Marr. of Geraint* 323
  G swamps and pools, waste places of the hern,   *Geraint and E.* 31
  As the *g* dawn stole o'er the dewy world,   „ 385
  This *g* King Show'd us a shrine wherein   *Balin and Balan* 108
  As that *g* cricket chirpt of at our hearth—   *Merlin and V.* 110
  seem'd a lovely baleful star Veil'd in *g* vapour ;   „ 263
  Had found a glen, *g* boulder and black tarn.   *Lancelot and E.* 36
  Sat on his knee, stroked his *g* face and said,   „ 749
  'May God be with thee, sweet, when old and *g*,   *Last Tournament* 627
  and set me far In the *g* distance,   „ 640

Great (continued) BURY the G Duke With an empire's lamentation, Let us bury the G Duke To the noise — *Ode on Well.* 1

The last *g* Englishman is low.	,, 18
G in council and *g* in war,	,, 30
g World-victor's victor will be seen no more.	,, 42
In that dread sound to the *g* name,	,, 71
Was *g* by land as thou by sea. (repeat)	,, 84, 90
And ever *g* and greater grew,	,, 108
So *g* a soldier taught us there,	,, 131
Attest their *g* commander's claim With honour,	,, 148
reverence and regret To those *g* men who fought,	,, 158
All *g* self-seekers trampling on the right ;	,, 187
Let his *g* example stand Colossal,	,, 220
watching here At this, our *g* solemnity.	,, 244
He is gone who seem'd so *g*.—	,, 271
Sounds of the *g* sea Wander'd about.	*Minnie and Winnie* 7
Like those who cried Diana *g*:	*Lit. Squabbles* 16
Heart, are you *g* enough For a love that never tires ? O heart, are you *g* enough for love ?	*Window, Marr. Morn.* 17
Calm and still light on yon *g* plain	*In Mem.* xi 9
In those *g* offices that suit The full-grown energies	,, xl 19
There must be wisdom with *g* Death :	,, li 11
Upon the *g* world's altar-stairs	,, lv 15
Leaving *g* legacies of thought,	,, lxxxiv 35
The *g* Intelligences fair That range above	,, lxxxv 21
She darkly feels him *g* and wise,	,, xcvii 34
Let her *g* Danube rolling fair Enwind her isles,	,, xcviii 9
one would chant the history Of that *g* race,	,, ciii 35
where we saw A *g* ship lift her shining sides.	,, 40
Brings in *g* logs and let them lie,	,, cvii 17
I would the *g* world grew like thee,	,, cxiv 25
By thee the world's *g* work is heard Beginning,	,, cxxi 10
And the *g* Æon sinks in blood,	,, cxxvii 16
As gentle ; liberal-minded, *g*, Consistent ;	,, Con. 38
She would not do herself this *g* wrong,	*Maud I* x 57
Like some of the simple *g* ones gone For ever	,, 61
yellow vapours choke The *g* city sounding wide ;	,, II iv 64
praying To his own *g* self, as I guess ;	,, v 33
And so there grew *g* tracts of wilderness,	*Com. of Arthur* 10
Of those *g* Lords and Barons of his realm	,, 65
Made lightnings and *g* thunders over him,	,, 108
whatsoever Merlin did In one *g* annal-book,	,, 158
after, the *g* lords Banded, and so brake out in open war.'	,, 236
And simple words of *g* authority,	,, 261
So this *g* brand the king Took,	,, 308
watch'd the *g* sea fall, Wave after wave,	,, 378
And the fringe Of that *g* breaker,	,, 387
From the *g* deep to the *g* deep he goes.'	,, 411
so *g* bards of him will sing Hereafter ;	,, 414
There at the banquet those *g* Lords from Rome,	,, 504
so those *g* lords Drew back in wrath,	,, 513
in twelve *g* battles overcame The heathen hordes,	,, 518
eagle-circles up To the *g* Sun of Glory,	*Gareth and L.* 22
at times the *g* gate shone Only,	,, 194
like the cross her *g* and goodly arms Stretch'd	,, 218
and faith in their *g* King, with pure Affection,	,, 330
But Mark hath tarnish'd the *g* name of king,	,, 426
Lyonors, A lady of high lineage, of *g* lands,	,, 609
Now two *g* entries open'd from the hall,	,, 665
take counsel ; for this lad is *g* And lusty,	,, 730
Till Gareth panted hard, and his *g* heart,	,, 1126
hew'd *g* pieces of his armour off him,	,, 1142
There rides no knight, not Lancelot, his *g* self,	,, 1182
one Of that *g* Order of the Table Round,	*Marr. of Geraint* 3
Thro' that *g* tenderness for Guinevere,	,, 30
watch his mightful hand striking *g* blows	,, 95
by *g* mischance He heard but fragments	,, 112
And here had fall'n a *g* part of a tower,	,, 317
Our hoard is little, but our hearts are *g*. (repeat)	,, 352, 374
For the *g* wave that echoes round the world ;	,, 420
Avenging this *g* insult done the Queen.'	,, 425
his face Glow'd like the heart of a *g* fire at Yule,	,, 559
and still The dew of their *g* labour,	,, 568
' Remember that great insult done the Queen,'	,, 571

Great (continued) fell at last In the *g* battle fighting for the King. — *Marr. of Geraint* 596

And should some *g* court-lady say,	,, 723
As this *g* Prince invaded us, and we,	,, 747
our *g* Queen, In words whose echo lasts,	,, 781
Till the *g* plover's human whistle amazed Her heart,	*Geraint and E.* 49
Saw once a *g* piece of a promontory,	,, 162
I will tell him How *g* a man thou art :	,, 228
While the *g* charger stood, grieved like a man.	,, 535
This work of his is *g* and wonderful	,, 898
A thousand-fold more *g* and wonderful	,, 914
His work was neither *g* nor wonderful,	,, 921
There the *g* Queen once more embraced her friend,	,, 947
They call'd him the *g* Prince and man of men.	,, 961
him who first Brought the *g* faith to Britain	*Balin and Balan* 103
down that range of roses the *g* Queen Came	,, 244
And by the *g* Queen's name, arise and hence.'	,, 482
By the *g* tower—Caerleon upon Usk—	,, 506
I thought the *g* tower would crash down on both—	,, 515
But the *g* Queen herself, fought in her name,	*Merlin and V.* 13
G Nature thro' the flesh herself hath made	,, 50
When Guinevere was crossing the *g* hall	,, 65
Then fell on Merlin a *g* melancholy ;	,, 189
work the charm Upon the *g* Enchanter of the Time,	,, 216
' *G* Master, do ye love me ? ' he was mute.	,, 237
Caught in a *g* old tyrant spider's web,	,, 259
And therefore be as *g* as ye are named,	,, 336
The *g* proof of your love :	,, 354
I heard the *g* Sir Lancelot sing it once,	,, 385
Then the *g* Master merrily answer'd her :	,, 545
Who lived alone in a *g* wild on grass ;	,, 621
I thought that he was gentle, being *g*:	,, 871
he rode to tilt For the *g* diamond in the diamond jousts,	*Lancelot and E.* 31
' Then will ye miss,' he answer'd, ' the *g* deeds Of Lancelot,	,, 81
your *g* name This conquers :	,, 150
With laughter dying down as the *g* knight	,, 179
The *g* and guilty love he bare the Queen,	,, 245
the *g* knight, the darling of the court,	,, 261
By the *g* river in a boatman's hut.	,, 278
' O there, *g* lord, doubtless,' Lavaine said,	,, 281
And seeing me, with a *g* voice he cried,	,, 309
' Save your *g* self, fair lord ; '	,, 320
And after muttering ' The *g* Lancelot,'	,, 421
' Me you call *g*: mine is the firmer seat,	,, 446
Of greatness to know well I am not *g*:	,, 451
Lancelot gave A marvellous *g* shriek and ghastly groan,	,, 516
Came round their *g* Pendragon, saying to him,	,, 528
So *g* a knight as we have seen to-day—	,, 533
knowing he was Lancelot ; his *g* name Conquer'd ;	,, 579
A sleeve of scarlet, broider'd with *g* pearls,	,, 604
flung herself Down on the *g* King's couch,	,, 610
I deem you know full well Where your *g* knight is hidden,	,, 690
Yet the *g* knight in his mid-sickness made	,, 878
Up the *g* river in the boatman's boat.	,, 1038
And there the *g* Sir Lancelot muse at me ;	,, 1055
My knight, the *g* Sir Lancelot of the Lake.'	,, 1373
Or sin seem less, the sinning seeming *g* ?	,, 1418
In our *g* hall there stood a vacant chair,	*Holy Grail* 167
While the *g* banquet lay along the hall,	,, 180
roofs Of our *g* hall are roll'd in thunder-smoke !	,, 220
four *g* zones of sculpture, set betwixt	,, 232
Where twelve *g* windows blazon Arthur's wars,	,, 248
Streams thro' the twelve *g* battles of our King.	,, 250
Knights that in twelve *g* battles splash'd and dyed	,, 311
All the *g* table of our Arthur closed	,, 329
A *g* black swamp and of an evil smell,	,, 499
A thousand piers ran into the *g* Sea.	,, 503
first At once I saw him far on the *g* Sea,	,, 510
With one *g* dwelling in the middle of it ;	,, 574
bound and plunged him into a cell Of *g* piled stones ;	,, 676
a *g* stone slipt and fell, Such as no wind could move :	,, 680
words Of so *g* men as Lancelot and our King	,, 713

Great (*continued*) And in the *g* sea wash away
  my sin.' *Holy Grail* 806
Those two *g* beats rose upright like a man,   " 821
G angels, awful shapes, and wings and eyes.   " 848
And here and there *g* hollies under them; *Pelleas and E.* 27
And she was a *g* lady in her land.   " 98
For she was a *g* lady.   " 123
g tower fill'd with eyes Up to the summit,   " 166
But when she mock'd his vows and the *g* King,   " 252
A *g* and sane and simple race of brutes   " 480
Hath the *g* heart of knighthood in thee fail'd   " 596
cry of a *g* jousts With trumpet-blowings ran *Last Tournament* 51
From the *g* deep to the *g* deep he goes.'   " 133
Sat their *g* umpire, looking o'er the lists.   " 159
G brother, thou nor I have made the world;   " 203
With Arthur's vows on the *g* lake of fire.   " 345
Then at the dry harsh roar of the *g* horn,   " 438
the *g* waters break Whitening for half a league,   " 464
' Flatter me not, for hath not our *g* Queen   " 557
To make one doubt if ever the *g* Queen   " 564
I swore to the *g* King, and am forsworn.   " 661
look'd and saw The *g* Queen's bower was dark,—   " 758
I thank the saints, I am not *g*. *Guinevere* 199
As *g* as those of *g* ones,   " 204
and himself was Knight Of the *g* Table—   " 235
woman in her womanhood as *g* As he was in his manhood,   " 299
The Dragon of the *g* Pendragonship, (repeat)   ", 398, 598
In twelve *g* battles ruining overthrown.   " 432
Far down to that *g* battle in the west,   " 571
Ah *g* and gentle lord, Who wast,   " 638
Now—ere he goes to the *g* Battle ?   " 652
that day when the *g* light of heaven Burn'd *Pass. of Arthur* 90
' Hearest thou this *g* voice that shakes the world,   " 139
on one Lay a *g* water, and the moon was full.   " 180
g brand Made lightnings in the splendour of the moon,   " 304
So *g* a miracle as yonder hilt.   " 324
' From the *g* deep to the *g* deep he goes.'   " 445
Like the last echo born of a *g* cry,   " 459
goal of this *g* world Lies beyond sight: *To the Queen* ii 59
I come, *g* Mistress of the ear and eye: *Lover's Tale* i 22
g pine shook with lonely sounds of joy   " 325
And over all the *g* wood rioting And climbing,   " 403
With that *g* crown of beams about his brows—   " 672
From his *g* hoard of happiness distill'd   " 714
Alone, and in the heart of the *g* forest.   " ii 3
G hills of ruins, and collapsed masses   " 65
g day Peal'd on us with that music which rights all,   " iv 64
By that *g* love they both had borne the dead,   " 181
G garlands swung and blossom'd ;   " 191
at one end of the hall Two *g* funereal curtains,   " 214
while now the *g* San Philip hung above us like a
  cloud *The Revenge* 43
But anon the *g* San Philip,   " 50
We have won *g* glory, my men !   " 85
or ever that evening ended a *g* gale blew,   " 114
could I wed her Loving the other ? do her that
  g wrong ? *Sisters* (E. and E.) 168
the *g* things of Nature and the fair,   " 222
g Tragedian, that had quench'd herself   " 233
Tho' scarce as *g* as Edith's power of love,   " 261
then the *g* 'Laudamus' rose to heaven. *Columbus* 18
g Augustine wrote that none could breathe   " 52
The *g* flame-banner borne by Teneriffe,   " 69
given the *G* Khan's palaces to the Moor,   " 109
Given thee the keys of the *g* Ocean-sea ?   " 149
Only the ghost of our *g* Catholic Queen   " 187
From that *g* deep, before our world begins, *De Prof., Two G.* 27
G Tsernogora ! never since thine own Black ridges *Montenegro* 12
when first the *g* Sun-star of morningtide, *Batt. of Brunanburh* 25
always o'er the *g* Peleion's head Burn'd, *Achilles over the T.* 28
The *g* God, Arès, burns in anger still *Tiresias* 11
statue, rear'd To some *g* citizen,   " 83
g God Arès, whose one bliss Is war,   " 111
stars Send no such light upon the ways of men As
  one *g* deed.   " 162

Great (*continued*) Flowing with easy greatness and
  touching on all things *g*, *The Wreck* 50
first *g* love I had felt for the first and greatest of men ;   " 76
g storm grew with a howl and a hoot of the blast   " 91
after all—the *g* God for aught that I know; *Despair* 104
may the *g* God curse him and bring him to nought !   " 106
Thro' the *g* gray slope of men, *Heavy Brigade* 17
With all the peoples, *g* and small, *Epilogue* 20
' So *g* so noble was he !' *Dead Prophet* 30
' *G* ! for he spoke and the people heard,   " 33
G and noble—O yes—but yet—   " 43
Noble and *g*—O ay—but then,   " 49
Thou third *g* Canning, stand among our best *Epit. on Stratford* 1
To this *g* cause of Freedom, drink, my friends, And
  the *g* name of England, round and round.
  (repeat) *Hands all Round* 11, 35
To this *g* name of England drink, my friends.   " 23
Should this old England fall Which Nelson left so *g*. *The Fleet* 5
All is gracious, gentle, *g* and Queenly. *On Jub. Q. Victoria* 14
Of this *g* Ceremonial And this year of her Jubilee.   " 50
g Earth-Mother, thee, the Power That lifts *Demeter and P.* 97
coming year's *g* good and varied ills, *Prog. of Spring* 93
G the Master, And sweet the Magic, *Merlin and the G.* 15
I stood Before the *g* Madonna-masterpieces *Romney's R.* 86
mixt with the *g* Sphere-music of stars *Parnassus* 8
As some *g* shock may wake a palsied limb, *St. Telemachus* 57
' Forbear In the *g* name of Him who died for men,   " 63
And gaze on this *g* miracle, the World, *Akbar's Dream* 122
O *g* and gallant Scott, *Bandit's Death* 1
By the *g* dead pine—you know it—   " 23
hidden purpose of that Power which alone is *g*, *God and the Univ.* 5
tho' faintly heard Until the *g* Hereafter. *D. of the Duke of C.* 17
O silent faces of the *G* and Wise, *Palace of Art* 195
The name of Britain trebly *g*— *You ask me, why, etc.* 22
Which are indeed the manners of the *g*. *Walk. to the Mail* 66
g and small, Went nutting to the hazels. *Enoch Arden* 63
she perhaps might reap the applause of *G*, *Princess* iii 262
make us all we would be, *g* and good.'   " iv 599
Him who cares not to be *g*, *Ode on Well.* 199
Makes former gladness loom so *g* ? *In Mem. xxiv* 10
Thy kindred with the *g* of old.   " *lxxiv* 8
I care not howsoever *g* he be, *Lancelot and E.* 1069
yet this grief Is added to the griefs the *g* must bear, *Guinevere* 205
bless your haters, said the Greatest of the *g* ; *Locksley H., Sixty* 85
fail Thro' craven fears of being *g*. *Hands all round* 32
sowing the nettle on all the laurel'd graves of the *G* ; *Vastness* 22

Greät Sa like a *g* num-cumpus I blubber'd *North. Cobbler* 14
While 'e sit like a *g* glimmer-gowk *Village Wife* 38
I heärd *g* heäps o' the snaw slushin' down *Owd Roä* 41
Then 'e married a *g* Yerl's darter, *Church-warden, etc.* 20

Greater (*See also* **Graäter**) Art more thro' Love, and
  g than thy years, *Love and Duty* 21
For there are *g* wonders there. *Day-Dm., Depart.* 28
And *g* glory varying to and fro, *Aylmer's Field* 73
And ever great and *g* grew, *Ode on Well.* 108
What know we *g* than the soul ?   " 265
G than I—is that your cry ? *Spiteful Letter* 17
My shame is *g* who remain, *In Mem. cix* 23
from childhood shape His action like the *g* ape,   " *cxx* 11
Behind thee comes the *g* light :   " *cxxi* 12
and evermore As I grew *g* grew with me ; *Com. of Arthur* 352
And, for himself was of the *g* state, *Gareth and L.* 395
Because I fain had given them *g* wits : *Merlin and V.* 496
I should have found in him a *g* heart.   " 873
there lives No *g* leader.' *Lancelot and E.* 317
' And on I rode, and *g* was my thirst. *Holy Grail* 401
The *g* man, the *g* courtesy. *Last Tournament* 633
and draws The *g* to the lesser, *Gardener's D.* 10
why, the *g* their disgrace ! *Aylmer's Field* 384
A *g* than all knowledge, beat her down. *Princess* vii 238
Believed himself a *g* than himself, *Last Tournament* 677

Greatest Requiring at her hand the *g* gift, *Gardener's D.* 229
The *g* sailor since our world began. *Ode on Well.* 86
To thee the *g* soldier comes ;   " 88
For this is England's *g* son,   " 95

Greatest (*continued*)   'that you love This *g* knight, your
pardon !   *Lancelot and E.* 669
what profits me my name Of *g* knight ?   „   1414
Alas for Arthur's *g* knight,   „   1419
'We have heard of thee : thou art our *g* knight,   *Holy Grail* 603
Chancellor, or what is *g* would he be—   *Aylmer's Field* 397
life which all our *g* fain Would follow,   *Lucretius* 78
Our *g* yet with least pretence,   *Ode on Well.* 29
as the *g* only are, In his simplicity   „   33
grieving that their *g* are so small,   *Merlin and V.* 833
to learn this knight were whole, Being our *g* :   *Lancelot and E.* 773
Not all unhappy, having loved God's best And *g*,   „   1094
And calling me the *g* of all knights,   *Holy Grail* 595
My *g* hardly will believe he saw ;   „   896
bless your haters, said the *G* of the great ;   *Locksley H., Sixty* 85

Greatness   *And should your g, and the care*   *To the Queen* 9
Remembering all his *g* in the Past.   *Ode on Well.* 20
if to-night our *g* were struck dead,   *Third of Feb.* 17
I leave thy *g* to be guess'd ;   *In Mem. lxxv* 4
She knows not what his *g* is,   *xcvii* 27
According to his *g* whom she quench'd.   *Merlin and V.* 218
passion of youth Toward *g* in its elder,   *Lancelot and E.* 283
No *g*, save it be some far-off touch Of *g*   „   450
one isle, That knows not her own *g* :   *To the Queen ii* 32
a *g* Got from their Grandsires—   *Batt. of Brunanburh* 15
Gone ! He will achieve his *g*.   *Tiresias* 168
Flowing with easy *g* and touching on all things great,   *The Wreck* 50
Step by step we rose to *g*,   *Locksley H., Sixty* 130
Pray God our *g* may not fail   *Hands all round* 8
increased Her *g* and her self-content.   *To Marq. of Dufferin* 8

Greaves   flamed upon the brazen *g* Of bold Sir
Lancelot.   *L. of Shalott iii* 4
g and cuisses dash'd with drops Of onset ;   *M. d'Arthur* 215
g and cuisses dash'd with drops Of onset ;   *Pass. of Arthur* 383

Grecian   A Gothic ruin and a *G* house,   *Princess, Pro.* 232
Ran down the Persian, *G*, Roman lines   „   *ii* 130
And read a *G* tale re-told, Which, cast in later
G mould,   *To Master of B.* 5

Greeän (green) (adj.)   an' jessmine a-dressin' it *g*,   *Spinster's S's.* 105
Greeän (s)   we was shaämed to cross Gigglesby *G*,   „   33
Greece   fairest and most loving wife in *G*.'   *Œnone* 187
Greed   Blockish irreverence, brainless *g*—   *Columbus* 129
Greedy   Come like a careless and a *g* heir   *Lover's Tale i* 675
Greek (adj.)   my ancient love With the *G* woman.   *Œnone* 261
show'd the house, *G*, set with busts :   *Princess, Pro.* 11
Greek (s)   whilome spakest to the South in *G*   *Sir J. Oldcastle* 29
sphere-music as the *G* Had hardly dream'd of.   *Akbar's Dream* 44
Green (adj.)   *See also* **Dark-green, Grass-green, Greeän,
Light-green, Live-green, Pale-green, Silver-green)**
tears of penitence Which would keep *g*   *Supp. Confessions* 119
Under the hollow-hung ocean *g* !   *The Merman* 38
Are neither *g* nor sappy ;   *Amphion* 90
flourishes *G* in a cuplike hollow of the down.   *Enoch Arden* 9
sow'd her name and kept it *g*   *Aylmer's Field* 88
I trust We are *g* in Heaven's eyes ;   *Holy Grail* 38
heaven appear'd so blue, nor earth so *g*,   „   365
forehead vapour-swathed In meadows ever
g   *Freedom* 8
And see my cedar *g*,   *To Ulysses* 17
High-wall'd gardens *g* and old ;   *Arabian Nights* 8
From the *g* rivage many a fall Of diamond rillets   „   47
Betwixt the *g* brink and the running foam,   *Sea-Fairies* 2
Whither away from the high *g* field,   „   8
Grow *g* beneath the showery *g*,   *My life "is full* 17
And in the middle of the *g* salt sea   *Mine be the strength* 7
in the pits Which some *g* Christmas crams with
weary bones.   *Wan Sculptor* 14
on the casement-edge A long *g* box of mignonette,   *Miller's D.* 83
In this *g* valley, under this *g* hill,   *Œnone* 232
round the cool *g* courts there ran a row Of cloisters,   *Palace of Art* 25
All the valley, mother, 'ill be fresh and *g* still,   *May Queen* 37
Don't let Effie come to see me till my grave
be growing *g* :   *May Queen, N. Y's. E.* 43
and there Grows *g* and broad, and takes no care,   *Lotos-Eaters, C. S.* 28
at the root thro' lush *g* grasses burn'd   *D. of F. Women* 71
'Single I grew, like some *g* plant,   „   205

Green (adj.) (*continued*)   To one *g* wicket in a privet
hedge ;   *Gardener's D.* 110
With one *g* sparkle ever and anon Dipt   *Audley Court* 88
Beyond the fair *g* field and eastern sea.   *Love and Duty* 101
And dewy Northern meadows *g*.   *The Voyage* 36
bathed In the *g* gleam of dewy-tassell'd trees :   *Princess i* 94
' Ye are *g* wood, see ye warp not.   „   *ii* 75
The *g* malignant light of coming storm.   „   *iii* 132
when all the woods are *g* ?   „   *iv* 107
Started a *g* linnet Out of the croft ;   *Minnie and Winnie* 17
Within the *g* the moulder'd tree,   *In Mem. xxvi* 7
Who wears his manhood hale and *g* :   „   *liii* 4
So thro' the *g* gloom of the wood they past,   *Geraint and E.* 195
mist Like that which kept the heart of Eden *g*   „   770
leaves Laid their *g* faces flat against the panes,   *Balin and Balan* 344
Chose the *g* path that show'd the rarer foot,   *Lancelot and E.* 162
g light from the meadows underneath Struck up   „   408
Till all the place whereon she stood was *g* ;   „   1200
And *g* wood-ways, and eyes among the leaves ;   *Pelleas and E.* 139
In fuming sulphur blue and *g*, a fiend—   *Last Tournament* 617
gardener's hand Picks from the colewort a *g*
caterpillar,   *Guinevere* 32
prest together In its *g* sheath,   *Lover's Tale i* 153
G prelude, April promise, glad new-year Of Being,   „   281
Rather to thee, *g* boscage, work of God,   *Sir J. Oldcastle* 129
but the whole *g* Isle was our own,   *V. of Maeldune* 93
Or the young *g* leaf rejoice in the frost   *The Wreck* 20
G Sussex fading into blue   *Pro. to Gen. Hamley* 7
' sitting on *g* sofas contemplate The torment of
the damn'd '   *Akbar's Dream* 48
Green (s)   (*See also* **Chapel-green, Greeän, Gold-green**)
Winnow with giant arms the slumbering *g*.   *The Kraken* 10
and earliest shoots Of orient *g*,   *Ode to Memory* 18
Shot over with purple, and *g*,   *Dying Swan* 20
the *g* that folds thy grave. (repeat)   *A Dirge* 6, 13, 20, 27, 34, 41, 48
In some fair space of sloping *g*'s   *Palace of Art* 106
Effie shall go with me to-morrow to the *g*,   *May Queen* 25
Beneath the hawthorn on the *g*,   *May Queen, N. Y's. E.* 10
branches, fledges with clearest *g*,   *D. of F. Women* 59
The smell of violets, hidden in the *g*,   „   77
like a purple beech among the *g*'s   *Edwin Morris* 84
when she gamboll'd on the *g*'s   *Talking Oak* 77
All creeping plants, a wall of *g*   *Day-Dm., Sleep P.* 45
The topmost elm-tree gather'd *g*   *Sir L. and Q. G.* 8
all the wood stands in a mist of *g*,   *The Brook* 14
pure as lines of *g* that streak the white   *Princess iv* 196
That twinkle into *g* and gold :   *In Mem. xi* 8
This round of *g*, this orb of flame,   „   *xxxiv* 5
And on a simple village *g* ;   „   *lxiv* 4
Thy leaf has perish'd in the *g*,   „   *lxxv* 13
those fall'n leaves which kept their *g*,   „   *xcv* 23
feet like sunny gems on an English *g*,   *Maud I v* 14
damp hill-slopes were quicken'd into *g*,   *Gareth and L.* 184
the live *g* had kindled into flowers,   „   185
Breaks from a coppice gemm'd with *g* and
red,   *Marr. of Geraint* 339
like a shoaling sea the lovely blue Play'd into *g*,   *Geraint and E.* 689
In *g* and gold, and plumed with *g*   *Merlin and V.* 89
And armour'd all in forest *g*,   *Last Tournament* 170
good warhorse left to graze Among the forest *g*'s,   „   491
Modred still in *g*, all ear and eye,   *Guinevere* 24
—its wreaths of dripping *g*—   *Lover's Tale i* 39
recalling fragrance and the *g* Of the dead spring :   „   723
lies Behind the *g* and blue ?   *Ancient Sage* 26
blue of sky and sea, the *g* of earth,   „   41
for a blessin' 'ud come wid the *g* ! '   *Tomorrow* 64
Shallow skin of *g* and azure—   *Locksley H., Sixty* 208
mantle, every shade of glancing *g*,   *Prog. of Spring* 63
earth's *g* stole into heaven's own hue,   *Far—far—away* 2
as summer-new As the *g* of the bracken   *June Bracken, etc.* 9
Green (verb)   *g*'s The swamp, where humm'd the
dropping snipe,   *On a Mourner* 8
Greener   *This laurel g from the brows Of him*   *To the Queen* 7
might have danced The greensward into *g* circles,   *Gardener's D.* 134
Yet the yellow leaf hates the *g* leaf,   *Spiteful Letter* 15

Green-glimmering	G-g toward the summit,	*Lancelot and E.* 483
Green-glooming	g-g twilight of the grove,	*Pelleas and E.* 33
Greening	Her dust is g in your leaf,	*Ancient Sage* 165
	Her mantle, slowly g in the Sun,	*Prog. of Spring* 11
	or dives In yonder g gleam,	*In Mem. cxv* 14
	A Jacob's ladder falls On g grass,	*Early Spring* 10
Greenish	except For g glimmerings thro' the lancets,	*Aylmer's Field* 622
	the moon was falling g thro' a rosy glow,	*Locksley H., Sixty* 178
Green-rushing	G-r from the rosy thrones (repeat)	*Voice and the P.* 4, 40
Green-suited	G-s, but with plumes that mock'd	*Guinevere* 22
Greensward	danced The g into greener circles,	*Gardener's D.* 134
	flit To make the g fresh,	*Talking Oak* 90
Greenwood	Thou liest beneath the g tree,	*Oriana* 95
Greet	to g Troy's wandering prince,	*On a Mourner* 32
	g their fairer sisters of the East.	*Gardener's D.* 188
	To g the sheriff, needless courtesy !	*Edwin Morris* 133
	To meet and g her on her way ;	*Beggar Maid* 6
	'G her with applausive breath,	*Vision of Sin* 135
	To g his hearty welcome heartily ;	*Enoch Arden* 350
	g her, wasting his forgotten heart,	*Aylmer's Field* 689
	ran To g him with a kiss,	*Lucretius* 7
	rose a cry As if to g the king ;	*Princess v* 249
	No more in soldier fashion will he g	*Ode on Well.* 21
	thrice as large as man he bent To g us.	*In Mem ciii* 43
	To meet and g a whiter sun ;	*„ Con.* 78
	Should I fear to g my friend	*Maud II iv* 85
	rejoiced More than Geraint to g her thus attired ;	*Marr. of Geraint* 772
	'My lord Geraint, I g you with all love ;	*Geraint and E.* 785
	the King himself Advanced to g them,	*„* 879
	but how ye g me—fear And fault and doubt—	*Last Tournament* 577
	So sweetly and so modestly she came To g us,	*Lover's Tale iv* 171
	rose from off his throne to g Before	*Columbus* 5
	And g it with a kindly smile ;	*To E. Fitzgerald* 4
	Every morning here we g it,	*Akbar's D., Hymn* 3
Greeted	Maiden, not to be g unbenignly.	*Hendecasyllabics* 21
	G Geraint full face, but stealthily,	*Geraint and E.* 279
	The Lost one Found was g as in Heaven	*Balin and Balan* 81
	and with how sweet grace She g my return !	*„* 194
	Vivien, being g fair, Would fain have wrought	*Merlin and V.* 155
	For silent, tho' he g her, she stood	*Lancelot and E.* 355
	'Have comfort,' whom she g quietly.	*„* 995
	thro' open door Rode Gawain, whom she g	
	courteously.	*Pelleas and E.* 383
	and then on Pelleas, him Who had not g her,	*„* 591
	Passion-pale they met And g.	*Guinevere* 100
	If g by your classic smile,	*To Prof. Jebb* 10
Greeting	Full cold my g was and dry ;	*The Letters* 13
	And gets for g but a wail of pain ;	*Lucretius* 138
	Eternal g's to the dead ;	*In Mem. lvii* 14
	found the g's both of knight and King	*Balin and Balan* 342
	I send a birthday line Of g ;	*To E. Fitzgerald* 46
Grenade	*See* **Hand-grenade**	
Grenville (Sir Richard)	*See* **Richard, Richard Grenville**	
Grew	(*See also* **Graw'd**) G darker from that	
	under-flame :	*Arabian Nights* 91
	mother plant in semblance, g A flower all gold,	*The Poet* 23
	She, as her carol sadder g,	*Mariana in the S.* 13
	'He dried his wings : like gauze they g ;	*Two Voices* 13
	'Single I g, like some green plant,	*D. of F. Women* 205
	G plump and able-bodied ;	*The Goose* 18
	we g The fable of the city where we dwelt.	*Gardener's D.* 5
	hoarded in herself, G, seldom seen ;	*„* 50
	in praise of her G oratory.	*„* 57
	For up the porch there g an Eastern rose,	*„* 123
	Her beauty g ; till Autumn brought an hour For Eustace,	*„* 207
	mound That was unsown, where many poppies g.	*Dora* 73
	wreath of all the flowers That g about,	*„* 83
	Of different ages, like twin-sisters g,	*Edwin Morris* 32
	I g Twice ten long weary weary years	*St. S. Stylites* 89
	And in the chase g wild,	*Talking Oak* 126
	To look as if they g there.	*Amphion* 80
	But such whose father-grape g fat	*Will Water.* 7
	That she g a noble lady,	*L. of Burleigh* 75
	Faint she g, and ever fainter,	*„* 81
	warn'd that madman ere it g too late :	*Vision of Sin* 56

Grew (*continued*)	The voice g faint : there came a further	
	change :	*Vision of Sin* 207
	I g in gladness till I found My spirits	*To E. L.* 11
	third child was sickly-born and g Yet sicklier,	*Enoch Arden* 261
	Philip's rosy face contracting g Careworn and wan ;	*„* 486
	Thicker the drizzle g, deeper the gloom ;	*„* 679
	Heaven in lavish bounty moulded, g.	*Aylmer's Field* 107
	and still G with the growing note,	*Sea Dreams* 213
	g Tired of so much within our little life,	*Lucretius* 225
	lovelier than their names, G side by side ;	*Princess, Pro.* 13
	the brain was like the hand, and g With using ;	*„ ii* 150
	'How g this feud betwixt the right and left.'	*„ iii* 77
	they were still together, g (For so they said themselves)	*„* 88
	I g discouraged, Sir ; but since I knew No rock	*„* 153
	they g Like field-flowers everywhere !	*„* 251
	Sun G broader toward his death and fell,	*„* 364
	Till all men g to rate us at our worth,	*„ iv* 145
	thus a noble scheme G up from seed	*„* 310
	there g Another kind of beauty in detail	*„* 447
	a clamour g As of a new-world Babel,	*„* 486
	That all things g more tragic and more strange ;	*„ vi* 23
	o'er him g Tall as a figure lengthen'd	*„* 160
	And ever great and greater g,	*Ode on Well.* 108
	What slender campanili g	*The Daisy* 13
	it g so tall It wore a crown of light,	*The Flower* 9
	And still g vaster g the shore	*In Mem. ciii* 25
	I would the great world g like thee,	*„ cxiv* 25
	And g to seeming-random forms,	*„ cxviii* 10
	There rolls the deep where g the tree.	*„ cxxiii* 1
	For thee she g, for thee she grows	*„ Con.* 35
	Discussing how their courtship g,	*„* 97
	When it slowly g so thin,	*Maud I xix* 20
	months ran on and rumour of battle g,	*„ III vi* 29
	so there g great tracts of wilderness,	*Com. of Arthur* 10
	they g up to wolf-like men, Worse than the wolves.	*„* 32
	and evermore As I g greater g with me ;	*„* 351
	a slope of land that ever g, Field after field,	*„* 428
	To break him from the intent to which he g,	*Gareth and L.* 140
	under cloud that g To thunder-gloom	*„* 1358
	g Forgetful of his promise to the King,	*Marr. of Geraint* 49
	still she look'd, and still the terror g	*„* 615
	lie still, and yet the sapling g :	*Geraint and E.* 165
	he g Tolerant of what he half disdain'd,	*Merlin and V.* 177
	g So grated down and filed away with thought,	*„* 622
	the dark wood g darker toward the storm	*„* 890
	g between her and the pictured wall.	*Lancelot and E.* 993
	g so cheerful that they deem'd her death	*„* 1131
	then the times G to such evil that the holy cup	*Holy Grail* 57
	sound As from a distance beyond distance g	*„* 112
	till I g One with him, to believe as he believed.	*„* 486
	wholesome flower And poisonous g together,	*„* 776
	flats, where nothing but coarse grasses g ;	*„* 794
	With such a closeness, but apart there g,	*„* 884
	Whereon a hundred stately beeches g,	*Pelleas and E.* 26
	g So witty that ye play'd at ducks and drakes	*Last Tournament* 343
	all this trouble did not pass but g ;	*Guinevere* 84
	And g half-guilty in her thoughts again,	*„* 408
	dolorous day G drearier toward twilight falling,	*Pass. of Arthur* 123
	They g aweary of her fellowship :	*Lover's Tale i* 109
	that my love G with myself—	*„* 165
	sustenance, which, still as thought, g large,	*„* 240
	and g again To utterance of passion.	*„* 546
	Why g we then together in one plot ?	*„ ii* 23
	g at length Prophetical and prescient,	*„* 131
	and each heart G closer to the other,	*„* 187
	a wave like the wave that is raised by an earth-	
	quake g,	*The Revenge* 115
	G after marriage to full height and form ?	*Sisters (E. and E.)* 171
	could it be That trees g downward,	*Columbus* 50
	and the light G as I gazed,	*„* 77
	they prest, as they g, on each other,	*V. of Maeldune* 64
	fixt on mine, till mine g dark For ever,	*Tiresias* 47
	the great storm g with a howl and a hoot	*The Wreck* 91
	stars in heaven Paled, and the glory g.	*Pro. to Gen. Hamley* 32
	souls of men, who g beyond their race,	*Demeter and P.* 140

Grew (continued)   face Of Miriam *g* upon me, till I knew; | *The Ring* 185
   that *g* Blown into glittering by the popular breath, | *Romney's R.* 48
Grewest   Who *g* not alone in power And knowledge, | *In Mem. cxiv* 26
Greys   Brave Inniskillens and *G* | *Heavy Brigade* 33
Gride   *g's* and clangs Its leafless ribs | *In Mem. cvii* 11
Grief   with *g*, not fear, With hopeful *g*, | *Supp. Confessions* 38
   strong Against the *g* of circumstance | " 92
   not weep, nor let your *g* be wild, | *May Queen, N. Y's. E.* 35
   and *g* became A solemn scorn of ills. | *D. of F. Women* 227
   In *g* I am not all unlearn'd; | *To J. S.* 18
   Let *G* be her own mistress still. | " 41
   Words weaker than your *g* would make *G* more. | " 65
   such a distance from his youth in *g*, | *Gardener's D.* 54
   Annie, seated with her *g*, | *Enoch Arden* 280
   if *g's* Like his have worse or better, | " 740
   My *g* and solitude have broken me; | " 857
   I am grieved to learn your *g*— | *Aylmer's Field* 398
   from his height and loneliness of *g* | " 632
   my *g* to find her less than fame, | *Princess i* 73
   tinged with wan from lack of sleep, Or *g*, | " *iii* 26
   Red *g* and mother's hunger in her eye, | " *vi* 146
   Rang ruin, answer'd full of *g* and scorn. | " 333
   sidelong glances at my father's *g*, | " *vii* 107
   Forgive my *g* for one removed, | *In Mem., Pro.* 37
   Let Love clasp *G* lest both be drown'd, | " *i* 9
   That *g* hath shaken into frost! | " *iv* 12
   To put in words the *g* I feel; | " *v* 2
   But that large *g* which these enfold | " 11
   Calm as to suit a calmer *g*, | " *xi* 2
   And hush'd my deepest *g* of all, | " *xix* 10
   The lesser *g's* that may be said, | " *xx* 1
   But there are other *g's* within, | " 11
   And is it that the haze of *g* | " *xxiv* 9
   The voice was not the voice of *g*, | " *lxix* 19
   And by the measure of my *g* I leave | " *lxxv* 3
   A *g*, then changed to something else, | " *lxxvii* 11
   O *g*, can *g* be changed to less? | " *lxxviii* 16
   The *g* my loss in him had wrought, | " *lxxx* 6
   A *g* as deep as life or thought, | " 7
   To this which is our common *g*, | " *lxxxv* 7
   And in my *g* a strength reserved. | " 52
   Or so shall *g* with symbols play | " 95
   And in the midmost heart of *g* | " *lxxxviii* 7
   No more shall wayward *g* abuse | " *cv* 9
   Ring out the *g* that saps the mind, | " *cvi* 9
   'twere possible After long *g* and pain | *Maud II iv* 2
   By reason of the bitterness and *g* | *Com. of Arthur* 209
   overtoil'd By that day's *g* and travel, | *Geraint and E.* 377
   I have *g's* enough: Pray you be gentle, | " 707
   Thy chair, a *g* to all the brethren, | *Balin and Balan* 78
   face Hand-hidden, as for utmost *g* or shame; | *Merlin and V.* 897
   I find with *g*! I might believe you then, | " 922
   Words, as we grant *g* tears. | *Lancelot and E.* 1188
   King himself could hardly speak For *g*, | *Holy Grail* 355
   left alone once more, and cried in *g*, | " 437
   Being so clouded with his *g* and love, | " 656
   And gulf'd his *g's* in inmost sleep; | *Pelleas and E.* 516
   he answer'd not, Or hast thou other *g's*? | " 599
   nor sought, Wrapt in her *g*, for housel | *Guinevere* 149
   sweet lady, the King's *g* For his own self, | " 196
   For if there ever come a *g* to me I cry my cry | " 200
   But even were the *g's* of little ones | " 203
   yet this *g* Is added to the *g's* the great must bear, | " 204
   Grieve with the common *g* of all the realm?' | " 217
   'this is all woman's *g*, That *she* is woman, | " 218
   Grieve with your *g's*, not grieving at your joys, | " 679
   Time and *G* abode too long with Life, | *Lover's Tale i* 107
   Time and *G* did beckon unto Death, | " 110
   The grasp of hopeless *g* about my heart, | " 126
   Because my *g* as yet was newly born | " 613
   I was shut up with *G*; | " 680
   whence without some guilt should such *g* be? | " 795
   Behind the world, that make our *g's* our gains. | *Sisters (E. and E.)* 231
   G for our perishing children, and never a moment
    for *g*, | *Def. of Lucknow* 89

Grief (continued)   chariots backward, knowing *g's*
   at hand; | *Achilles over the T.* 25
   The *g* for ever born from *g's* to be, | *Tiresias* 80
   With present *g*, and made the rhymes, | " 196
   With a *g* that could only be cured, | *Despair* 80
   die for ever, if all his *g's* are in vain, | " 82
   g's by which he once was wrung Were never worth | *Ancient Sage* 127
   O rosetree planted in my *g*, | " 163
   the world is dark with *g's* and graves, | " 171
   You will not leave me thus in *g* | *The Flight* 85
   When all my *g's* were shared with thee, | *Pref. Poem. Broth. S.* 25
   with all its pains, and *g's*, and deaths, | *To Prin. Beatrice* 7
   grieved for man thro' all my *g* for thee,— | *Demeter and P.* 75
   lost in utter *g* I fail'd To send my life | " 109
   the sun, Pale at my *g*, drew down before his time | " 114
   O the *g* when yesterday They bore the Cross | *Happy* 47
   and with *G* Sit face to face, | *To Mary Boyle* 45
   crazed With the *g* that gnaw'd at my heart, | *Bandit's Death* 39
   soften me with *g*! | *Doubt and Prayer* 9
Grieve   heart faints and my whole soul *g's* | *A spirit haunts* 16
   I *g* to see you poor and wanting help; | *Enoch Arden* 406
   With such compelling cause to *g* | *In Mem. xxix* 1
   g Thy brethren with a fruitless tear? | " *lviii* 9
   it is not often I *g*; | *Grandmother* 89
   G with the common grief of all the realm?' | *Guinevere* 217
   G with your griefs, not grieving at your joys, | " 679
Grieved   I am *g* to learn your grief— | *Aylmer's Field* 398
   and she *g* In her strange dream, | *Sea Dreams* 229
   you began to change—I saw it and *g*— | *Princess iv* 398
   be not wroth or *g* At thy new son, | *Marr. of Geraint* 779
   the great charger stood, *g* like a man. | *Geraint and E.* 535
   since I was nurse, had I been so *g* and so vext! | *In the Child. Hosp.* 45
   g for man thro' all my grief for thee,— | *Demeter and P.* 75
Grieving   *g* held his will, and bore it thro'. | *Enoch Arden* 167
   g that their greatest are so small, | *Merlin and V.* 833
   Grieve with your griefs, not *g* at your joys, | *Guinevere* 679
Grievous   He that only rules by terror Doeth *g* wrong. | *The Captain* 2
   Where I will heal me of my *g* wound.' | *M. d'Arthur* 264
   Where I will heal me of my *g* wound.' | *Pass. of Arthur* 432
   after healing of his *g* wound He comes again; | " 450
   All day the men contend in *g* war | *Achilles over the T.* 9
Griffin   On wyvern, lion, dragon, *g*, swan, | *Holy Grail* 350
   Gnome of the cavern, *G* and Giant, | *Merlin and V.* 40
Griffin-guarded   we reached The *g-g* gates. | *Audley Court* 15
Grig   like the dry High-elbow'd *g's* | *The Brook* 54
Grim   Godiva, wife to that *g* Earl, who ruled In Coventry: | *Godiva* 12
   Unclasp'd the wedded eagles of her belt, The *g* Earl's gift: | " 44
   Were their faces *g*. | *The Captain* 54
   'Wrinkled ostler, *g* and thin! | *Vision of Sin* 63
   And with *g* laughter thrust us out at gates. | *Princess iv* 556
   Lifting his *g* head from my wounds. | " *vi* 272
   High on a *g* dead tree before the tower, | *Last Tournament* 430
   g faces came and went Before her, | *Guinevere* 70
   gone is he To wage *g* war against Sir Lancelot | " 193
   Every *g* ravine a garden, every blazing desert
   till'd, | *Locksley H., Sixty* 168
   What hast thou done for me, *g* Old Age, | *By an Evolution.* 9
Grimace   Caught each other with wild *g's*, | *Vision of Sin* 35
Grimed   their foreheads *g* with smoke, and sear'd, | *Holy Grail* 265
Grimly   flickering in a *g* light Dance on the mere. | *Gareth and L.* 826
   G with swords that were sharp from the
   grindstone, | *Batt. of Brunanburh* 41
Grimy   *G* nakedness dragging his trucks | *Maud I x* 7
   And couch'd at night with *g* kitchen-knaves. | *Gareth and L.* 481
Grin   *g's* on a pile of children's bones, | *Maud I i* 46
   chuckle, and *g* at a brother's shame; | " *iv* 29
Grind   A grazing iron collar *g's* my neck; | *St. S. Stylites* 117
   centre-bits *G* on the wakeful ear | *Maud I i* 42
   feet of Tristram *g* The spiring stone that scaled | *Last Tournament* 510
   in these spasms that *g* Bone against bone. | *Columbus* 220
   That *g* the glebe to powder! | *Tiresias* 95
Grinding   I heard the shingle *g* in the surge, | *Holy Grail* 811
Grindstone   swords that were sharp from the *g*, | *Batt. of Brunanburh* 41
Grinning   (See also **Bare-grinning, Deathful-grinning**)
   fool, Who was gaping and *g* by: | *Maud II i* 20

Grinning (*continued*) and tooth'd with *g* savagery.' *Balin and Balan* 197
Grip in the hard *g* of his hand, *Sea Dreams* 163
  An' 'e ligs on 'is back i' the *g*, *N. Farmer, N. S.* 31
Gripe hand in wild delirium, *g* it hard, *Princess vii* 93
Gript *G* my hand hard, and with God-bless-you went. *Sea Dreams* 160
  Each *g* a shoulder, and I stood between; *Holy Grail* 822
  his strong hands *g* And dinted the gilt dragons *Last Tournament* 181
  He *g* it so hard by the throat *Bandit's Death* 28
Grisly haggard father's face and reverend beard Of *g* twine, *Princess vi* 104
  With a *g* wound to be drest he had left the deck, *The Revenge* 66
Gritted and thou shalt cease To pace the *g* floor, *Will Water.* 242
Grizzled a story which in rougher shape Came from a *g* cripple, *Aylmer's Field* 8
  forth a *g* damsel came, *Gareth and L.* 1114
  To me this narrow *g* fork of thine Is cleaner-fashion'd—: *Merlin and V.* 59
Grizzlier Albeit *g* than a bear, to ride And jest with: *Pelleas and E.* 193
Groan (s) exprest By signs or *g*'s or tears; *D. of F. Women* 284
  Down in the south is a flash and a *g*: *Window, Gone* 8
  he but gave a wrathful *g*, Saying, *Geraint and E.* 398
  gave A marvellous great shriek and ghastly *g*, *Lancelot and E.* 516
  'Our mightiest!' answer'd Lancelot, with a *g*; *Holy Grail* 766
  Or Labour, with a *g* and not a voice, *To the Queen ii* 55
  their curses and their *g*'s. *Columbus* 190
  trumpets of victory, *g*'s of defeat; *Vastness* 8
Groan (verb) mother who never has heard us *g*! *Despair* 98
  We should see the Globe we *g* in, *Locksley H., Sixty* 188
  g's to see it, finds no comfort there. *Romney's R.* 45
Groan'd deep brook *g* beneath the mill; *Miller's D.* 113
  as their faces drew together, *g*, *Enoch Arden* 74
  'No trifle,' *g* the husband; *Sea Dreams* 145
  King Leodogran *G* for the Roman legions *Com. of Arthur* 34
  G, and at times would mutter, *Balin and Balan* 173
  g Sir Lancelot in remorseful pain, *Lancelot and E.* 1428
  'Black nest of rats,' he *g*, *Pelleas and E.* 555
  Until he *g* for wrath—so many of those, *Last Tournament* 183
  and he *g*, 'The King is gone.' *Pass. of Arthur* 443
  Found, fear'd me dead, and *g*, *The Flight* 23
  He *g*, he turn'd, and in the mist *Death of Œnone* 49
  while I *g*, From out the sunset pour'd *Akbar's Dream* 191
Groänin' Moother was naggin' an' *g* *Owd Roä* 108
Groaning (*See also* **Groänin'**) turn'd, and *g* said, 'Forgive! *Sea Dreams* 59
  organ almost burst his pipes, *G* for power, *Princess ii* 475
  to them the doors gave way *G*, " *vi* 350
  With hand and rope we haled the *g* sow, *Walk. to the Mail* 91
  Kay near him *g* like a wounded bull— *Gareth and L.* 648
  the fallen man Made answer, *g*, 'Edyrn, *Marr. of Geraint* 576
  g laid The naked sword athwart their naked throats, *Pelleas and E.* 451
  I, *g*, from me flung Her empty phantom: *Lover's Tale, ii* 205
  I heard a *g* overhead, and climb'd " *iv* 136
Grog But if thou wants thy *g*, *North. Cobbler* 8
  But if tha wants ony *g* tha mun goä fur it " 113
Grog-shop *See* **Shebeen**
Groom (a servant) hung with *g*'s and porters on the bridge, *Godiva* 2
  An' they rampaged about wi' their *g*'s, *Village Wife* 36
Groom (bridegroom) (*See also* **Bridegroom**) Gives her harsh *g* for bridal-gift *Princess v* 378
  As drinking health to bride and *g* *In Mem., Con.* 83
Groom'd strongly *g* and straitly curb'd *Geraint and E.* 193
  and now so long By bandits *g*, *Geraint and E.* 193
Groove down the ringing *g*'s of change. *Locksley Hall* 182
  Down rang the grate of iron thro' the *g*, *Pelleas and E.* 207
Grope *g*, And gather dust and chaff, *In Mem. lv* 17
  And grovel and *g* for my son *Rizpah* 8
Groped *g* as blind, and seem'd Always about to fall, *Aylmer's Field* 821
  She gabbled, as she *g* in the dead, *Dead Prophet* 73
Groping feeble twilight of this world *G*, *Geraint and E.* 6
  the girl's Lean fancy, *g* for it, *The Ring* 336
Gross (adj.) In the *g* blackness underneath. *Supp. Confessions* 187
  G darkness of the inner sepulchre *D. of F. Women* 67
  So *g* to express delight, in praise of her *Gardener's D.* 56
  It cannot be but some *g* error lies In this report, *Princess i* 69

Gross (adj.) (*continued*) yet On tiptoe seem'd to touch upon a sphere Too *g* to tread, *Princess vii* 325
  drown His heart in the *g* mud-honey of town, *Maud I xvi* 5
  What should be granted which your own *g* heart *Merlin and V.* 916
  For when had Lancelot utter'd aught so *g* *Last Tournament* 631
  Save that I think this *g* hard-seeming world *Sisters (E. and E.)* 229
  You make our faults too *g*, and thence maintain *To One who ran down Eng.* 1
Gross (s) As flies the lighter thro' the *g*. *In Mem. xli* 4
Grosser with a *g* film made thick These heavy, horny eyes. *St. S. Stylites* 200
  song Might have been worse and sinn'd in *g* lips *Princess iv* 251
  Barbarians, *g* than your native bears— " 537
  draw water, or hew wood, Or *g* tasks; *Gareth and L.* 487
  but *g* grown Than heathen. *Pass. of Arthur* 61
Grossest Love, tho' Love were of the *g*, *Merlin and V.* 461
Grossness the *g* of his nature will have weight *Locksley Hall* 48
Grot The hollow *g* replieth *Claribel* 20
  From many a wondrous *g* and secret cell *The Kraken* 8
  Black the garden-bowers and *g*'s *Arabian Nights* 78
  alleys falling down to twilight *g*'s, *Ode to Memory* 107
  shadow'd *g*'s of arches interlaced, *Palace of Art* 51
Grotesque raillery, or *g*, or false sublime— *Princess iv* 588
Groun' a corp lyin' undher *g*. *Tomorrow* 62
Ground (s) (*See also* **Groun'**, **Mountain-ground**) Till the air And the *g* *Nothing will Die* 28
  And dew is cold upon the *g*, *The Owl i* 2
  All the place is holy *g*; *Poet's Mind* 9
  It would fall to the *g* if you came in. " 23
  And shall fall again to *g*. *Deserted House* 16
  Not that the *g*'s of hope were fix'd, *Two Voices* 227
  from the *g* She raised her piercing orbs, *D. of F. Women* 170
  I keep smooth plats of fruitful *g*, *The Blackbird* 3
  as he near'd His happy home, the *g*. *Gardener's D.* 92
  And mix'd with shadows of the common *g*! " 135
  Dora cast her eyes upon the *g*, *Dora* 89
  perish, falling on the foeman's *g*, *Locksley Hall* 103
  O Lord!—'tis in my neighbour's *g*, *Amphion* 75
  To yonder shining *g*; *St. Agnes' Eve* 14
  vapours weep their burthen to the *g*, *Tithonus* 2
  Release me, and restore me to the *g*; " 72
  perfect fan, Above the teeming *g*, *Sir L. and Q. G.* 18
  Gathering up from all the lower *g*; *Vision of Sin* 15
  And track'd you still on classic *g*, *To E. L.* 10
  All her fair length upon the *g* she lay: *Princess v* 59
  Ida spoke not, gazing on the *g*, " *vi* 227
  To dance with death, to beat the *g*, *In Mem. i* 12
  The chestnut pattering to the *g*: " *xi* 4
  here upon the *g*, No more partaker " *xli* 7
  And hide thy shame beneath the *g*. " *lxxii* 28
  But all is new unhallow'd *g*. " *civ* 12
  flatten'd, and crush'd, and dinted into the *g*: *Maud I i* 7
  all by myself in my own dark garden *g*, " *iii* 10
  O let the solid *g* Not fail beneath my feet " *xi* 1
  Rivulet crossing my *g*, " *xxi* 1
  Laid him that clove it grovelling on the *g*. *Gareth and L.* 972
  Death was cast to *g*, and slowly rose. " 1403
  Two forks are fixt into the meadow *g*, *Marr. of Geraint* 482
  Coursed one another more on open *g* " 522
  And there they fixt the forks into the *g*, " 548
  Then, moving downward to the meadow *g*, *Geraint and E.* 204
  And hurl'd to *g* what knight soever spurr'd *Balin and Balan* 66
  Shot from behind him, run along the *g*, " 323
  Shot from behind me, ran along the *g*; " 374
  Stumbled headlong, and cast him face to *g*. " 426
  I set thee high on vantage *g*, " 534
  Then she, who held her eyes upon the *g*, *Lancelot and E.* 232
  He answer'd with his eyes upon the *g*, " 1352
  made the *g* Reel under us, and all at once, *Lover's Tale ii* 193
  never to say that I laid him in holy *g*. *Rizpah* 58
  and the palace, and death in the *g*! *Def. of Lucknow* 24
  coffinless corpse to be laid in the *g*, " 80
  slowly sinking now into the *g*, *Locksley H., Sixty* 27
  ampler hunting *g*'s beyond the night; " 69
  and you hurl'd them to the *g*. " *Happy* 76

Ground (s) (*continued*)   Christ-like creature that ever stept on
   the g.   *Charity* 32
vaults her skies, From this my vantage g   *Mechanophilus* 18
Ground (verb)   teeth that g As in a dreadful dream,   *Aylmer's Field* 328
For ' g in yonder social mill,   *In Mem. lxxxix* 39
He g his teeth together, sprang with a yell,   *Balin and Balan* 538
Groundflame   g of the crocus breaks the mould   *Prog. of Spring* 1
Ground-plan   'Lo! God's likeness —the g-p-   *Vision of Sin* 187
Ground-swell   a full tide Rose with g-s,   *Sea Dreams* 51
   Roll as a g-s dash'd on the strand,   *W. to Alexandra* 23
Group   A g of Houris bow'd to see   *Palace of Art* 102
   I have shadow'd many a g Of beauties,   *Talking Oak* 61
   a g of girls In circle waited,   *Princess, Pro.* 68
   and in g's they stream'd away.   ,, *Con.* 105
Group'd   Muses and the Graces, g in threes,   ,, *ii* 27
   stood her maidens glimmeringly g   ,, *iv* 190
Grove (*See also* **Sea-Groves**)   lemon g In closest coverture
   upsprung,   *Arabian Nights* 67
From the g's within The wild-bird's   *Poet's Mind* 20
'I, rooted here among the g's   *Talking Oak* 181
Wherever in a lonely g He set up   *Amphion* 21
Hush'd all the g's from fear of wrong :   *Sir L. and Q. G.* 13
Kept to the garden now, and g of pines,   *Aylmer's Field* 550
Thy God is far diffused in noble g's   ,, 653
Rose gem-like up before the dusky g's   *Princess, Pro.* 75
in a poplar g when a light wind wakes   ,, *v* 13
Gray halls alone among their massive g's ;   ,, *Con.* 43
Yet present in his natal g,   *The Daisy* 18
For g's of pine on either hand,   *To F. D. Maurice* 21
To rest in a golden g, or to bask in a summer sky :   *Wages* 9
Burnt and broke the g and altar   *Boädicea* 2
Uncared for, gird the windy g,   *In Mem. ci* 13
In the little g where I sit—   *Maud I iv* 2
A knot, beneath, of snakes, aloft, a g.   *Marr. of Geraint* 325
It seems another voice in other g's ;   *Balin and Balan* 215
With young Lavaine into the poplar g.   *Lancelot and E.* 509
Hid from the wide world's rumour by the g   ,, 522
Touch'd at all points, except the poplar g,   ,, 617
Lavaine across the poplar g Led to the caves :   ,, 804
By g, and garden-lawn, and rushing brook,   *Holy Grail* 230
green-glooming twilight of the g,   *Pelleas and E.* 33
And all talk died, as in a g all song   ,, 607
dark in the golden g Appearing,   *Last Tournament* 379
from the high wall and the flowering g Of grasses   *Guinevere* 33
Rode under g's that look'd a paradise   ,, 389
all the low dark g's, a land of love !   *Lover's Tale i* 332
A height, a broken grange, a g,   *Ancient Sage* 223
thro' all the g's of olive in the summer glow,   *Frater Ave, etc.* 2
palm And orange g of Paraguay,   *To Ulysses* 12
Grovel   Stands at thy gate for thee to g to—   *Aylmer's Field* 652
   g and grope for my son till I find myself   *Rizpah* 8
Grovelike   Once g, each huge arm a tree,   *Aylmer's Field* 510
Grovell'd   unlaced my casque And g on my body,   *Princess vi* 28
   And g with her face against the floor :   *Guinevere* 415
   And while she g at his feet,   ,, 581
Grovelling   Laid him that clove it g on the ground.   *Gareth and L.* 972
   Gareth brought him g on his knees,   ,, 1124
Grow (*See also* **Graw**)   Think my belief would
   stronger g !   *Supp. Confessions* 13
g awry From roots which strike so deep ?   ,, 77
in the rudest wind Never g sere,   *Ode to Memory* 25
g so full and deep In thy large eyes,   *Eleänore* 85
and slowly g To a full face,   ,, 91
G golden all about the sky ;   ,, 101
G green beneath the showery gray,   *My life is full* 17
And on my clay her darnel g ;   ,, 22
How g's the day of human power ?'   *Two Voices* 78
'His sons g up that bear his name,   ,, 256
Some g to honour, some to shame,—   ,, 257
I will g round him in his place, G, live,   *Fatima* 40
a light that g's Larger and clearer,   *Œnone* 108
until endurance g Sinew'd with action,   ,, 164
G's green and broad, and takes no care,   *Lotos-Eaters, C.S.* 28
It g's to guerdon after-days :   *Love thou thy land* 27
She felt her heart g prouder :   *The Goose* 22

Grow (*continued*)   until he g's Of age to help us.'   *Dora* 126
cruel as a schoolboy ere he g's To Pity—   *Walk. to the Mail* 109
that my soul might g to thee,   *St. S. Stylites* 71
Their faces g between me and my book ;   ,, 176
So now 'tis fitted on and g's to me,   ,, 209
Shall g so fair as this.'   *Talking Oak* 244
All grass of silky feather g—   ,, 269
' But we g old. Ah ! when shall all men's good   *Golden Year* 47
The vast Republics that may g,   *Day-Dm., L'Envoi* 15
That g's within the woodland.   *Amphion* 8
g's From England to Van Diemen.   ,, 83
patch of soil To g my own plantation.   ,, 100
I g in worth, and wit, and sense,   *Will Water.* 41
Till, where the street g's straiter,   ,, 142
forget-me-nots That g for happy lovers.   *The Brook* 173
Watching your growth, I seem'd again to g.   *Aylmer's Field* 359
And heaps of living gold that daily g,   ,, 655
as by miracle, g straight and fair—   ,, 676
I saw my father's face G long and troubled   *Princess i* 59
might g To use and power on this Oasis,   ,, *ii* 166
And g for ever and for ever.   ,, *iv* 16
slowly g's a glimmering square,   ,, 52
the child shall g To prize the authentic mother   ,, *v* 432
this shall g A night of Summer from the heat,   ,, *vi* 53
slight-natured, miserable, How shall men g ?   ,, *vii* 266
in the long years liker must they g ;   ,, 279
Purpose in purpose, will in will, they g,   ,, 305
let the sorrowing crowd about it g,   *Ode on Well.* 16
ever weaker g's thro' acted crime,   *Will* 12
I may die but the grass will g, And the grass
   will g when I am gone,   *Window, No Answer* 4
A beam in darkness : let it g.   *In Mem., Pro.* 24
Let knowledge g from more to more,   ,, 25
And g incorporate into thee.   ,, *ii* 16
But as he g's he gathers much,   ,, *xlv* 5
His isolation g's defined.   ,, 12
How blanch'd with darkness must I g !   ,, *lxi* 11
The days that g to something strange,   ,, *lxxi* 11
And year by year the landscape g   ,, *ci* 19
For thee she grew, for thee she g's   ,, *Con.* 35
I should g light-headed, I fear,   *Maud I xix* 100
and ever afresh they g'd to.   ,, *II i* 28
But I know where a garden g's,   ,, *v* 72
change, and g Faint and far-off.   *Balin and Balan* 217
ourselves shall g In use of arms and manhood,   *Lancelot and E.* 63
days will g to weeks, the weeks to months,   *Guinevere* 624
It g's upon me now—the semicircle   *Lover's Tale i* 37
let g The flowers that run poison in their veins.   ,, 346
By firth and lock thy silver sister g,   *Sir J. Oldcastle* 58
But look, the morning g's apace,   *The Flight* 93
Science g's and Beauty dwindles—   *Locksley H., Sixty* 246
where the purple flowers g,   *Frater Ave, etc.* 4
since your name will g with Time,   *To Marq. of Dufferin* 13
Young again you g Out of sight.   *The Ring* 11
the long day of knowledge g's and warms,   *Prog. of Spring* 101
' Father and mother will watch you g '—(repeat)   *Romney's R.* 104, 106
You watch'd not I, she did not g, she died.   ,, 105
there is time for the race to g.   *The Dawn* 20
You, what the cultured surface g's,   *Mechanophilus* 33
Growest   ever thus thou g beautiful In silence,   *Tithonus* 43
   grown In power, and ever g,   *To Dante* 2
Growing (adj. and part.)   (*See also* **A-grawin'**, **Ever-
growing**)   Ere the light on dark was g,   *Oriana* 10
Don't let Effie come to see me till my grave be
   g green :   *May Queen, N. Y's. E.* 43
His face is g sharp and thin.   *D. of the O. Year* 46
g dewy-warm With kisses balmier   *Tithonus* 58
g coarse to sympathise with clay.   *Locksley Hall* 46
gaze On that cottage g nearer,   *L. of Burleigh* 35
May-music g with the g light,   *Gareth and L.* 1080
a promontory, That had a sapling g on it,   *Geraint and E.* 163
grass There g longest by the meadow's edge,   ,, 257
And on the fourth are men with g wings,   *Holy Grail* 237
And g, on her tomb,   *Ancient Sage* 164
Thou sawest a glory g on the night,   *Epit. on Caxton* 2

Growing (adj. or part.) (continued)   in the night, While the
   gloom is g.'   *Forlorn* 12
And ever worse with g time,   *Palace of Art* 270
The warders of the g hour,   *Love thou thy land* 61
harmonies of law The g world assume,   *England and Amer.* 17
Storm'd in orbs of song, a g gale ;   *Vision of Sin* 25
His baby's death, her g poverty,   *Enoch Arden* 705
the dull November day Was g duller twilight,   „ 722
and still Grew with the g note,   *Sea Dreams* 213
who desire you more Than g boys their manhood ;   *Princess iv* 457
roll'd With music in the g breeze of Time,   „ vi 56
From g commerce loose her latest chain,   *Ode Inter. Exhib.* 33
Till g winters lay me low ;   *In Mem. xl* 30
Is shadow'd by the g hour,   „ xlvi 3
Conduct by paths of g powers,   „ lxxxiv 31
G and fading and g (repeat)   *Maud I iii* 7, 9
delicate spark Of glowing and g light   „ vi 16
Still g holier as you near'd the bay,   *Lover's Tale i* 338
Between the going light and g night ?   „ 664
orphan wail came borne in the shriek of a g wind,   *The Wreck* 87
And we turn'd to the g dawn,   *Despair* 22
cry of 'Forward, Forward,' lost within the g gloom ; *Locksley H., Sixty* 13
Aged eyes may take the g glimmer   „ 230
Careless of our g kin,   *Open I. and C. Exhib.* 23

Growing (s)   body slight and round, and like a pear
   In g,   *Walk. to the Mail* 54
Growl   there at their meat would g,   *Com. of Arthur* 30
remembers all, and g's Remembering,   *Gareth and L.* 704
Growl'd   farewell to my sire, who g An answer   *Princess v* 233
so the ruffians g, Fearing to lose,   *Geraint and E.* 563
Growling   g like a dog, when his good bone   „ 559
lays his foot upon it, Gnawing and g :   „ 563
g as before, And cursing their lost time,   „ 575
Grown (See also **Broader-grown, Choicest-grown,
   Full-grown, Half-grown, O'er-grown,
   Slowly-grown, Woman-grown**)   cold, and
   dead, and corpse-like g ?   *Supp. Confessions* 17
That her voice untuneful g,   *The Owl ii* 6
And she is g so dear, so dear,   *Miller's D.* 170
eyes g dim with gazing on the pilot-stars.   *Lotos-Eaters, C. S.* 87
when love is g To ripeness,   *To J. S.* 14
Now am I feeble g ; my end draws nigh ;   *St. S. Stylites* 36
low matin-chirp hath g Full quire,   *Love and Duty* 98
The maiden's jet-black hair has g,   *Day-Dm., Sleep B.* 4
My beard has g into my lap.'   „ *Revival* 22
And wake on science g to more,   „ *L'Envoi* 10
mean Vileness, we are g so proud—   *Aylmer's Field* 756
tho' you have g You scarce have alter'd :   *Princess vi* 305
and g a bulk Of spanless girth,   „ vi 35
soil, left barren, scarce had g The grain   *In Mem. liii* 7
To which thy crescent would have g ;   „ lxxxiv 4
I myself with these have g   „ *Con.* 19
a morbid hate and horror have g   *Maud I vi* 9
g too weak and old To drive the heathen,   *Com. of Arthur* 511
Man am I g, a man's work must I do.   *Gareth and L.* 116
Ten thousand-fold had g, flash'd the fierce shield,   „ 1030
now hath g The vast necessity of heart and life.   *Merlin and V.* 924
g a part of me : but what use in it ?   *Lancelot and E.* 1416
Becomes thee well—art g wild beast thyself.   *Last Tournament* 637
the red fruit G on a magic oak-tree   „ 745
but grosser g Than heathen,   *Pass. of Arthur* 61
To what height The day had g I know not.   *Lover's Tale i* 9
I that was little had g so tall,   *First Quarrel* 27
I had g so handsome and tall—   „ 37
they found I had g so stupid and still   *Rizpah* 49
and g In power, and ever growest,   *To Dante* 1
Have we g at last beyond the passions   *Locksley H., Sixty* 93
For moans will have g sphere-music   *The Dreamer* 29
Growth   Huge sponges of millennial g   *The Kraken* 6
The lavish g's of southern Mexico.   *Mine be the strength* 14
G's of jasmine turn'd Their humid arms   *D. of F. Women* 69
Bear seed of men and g of minds.   *Love thou thy land* 20
Mix'd with the knightly g that fringed his lips.   *M. d'Arthur* 220
Or that Thessalian g,   *Talking Oak* 292
Watching your g, I seem'd again to grow.   *Aylmer's Field* 359

Growth (continued)   bear a double g of those rare souls,   *Princess ii* 180
Is duer unto freedom, force and g Of spirit   „ iv 141
Know you no song, the true g of your soil,   „ 150
In us true g, in her a Jonah's gourd,   „ 311
train To riper g the mind and will :   *In Mem. xlii* 8
How dwarf'd a g of cold and night,   „ lxi 7
For change of place, like g of time,   „ cv 11
And nature g of noble mind ;   „ cxi 16
the sunshine that hath given the man A g,   *Balin and Balan* 182
Mix'd with the knightly g that fringed his lips.   *Pass. of Arthur* 388
Thou didst receive the g of pines   *Lover's Tale i* 11
the g's Of vigorous early days,   „ 132
say rather, was my g, My inward sap,   „ 165
Grudge   he that always bare in bitter g   *Merlin and V.* 6
Grunt   meditative g's of much content,   *Walk. to the Mail* 87
Grunted   waked with silence, g 'Good !'   *M. d'Arthur, Ep.* 4
Grunter   tends her bristled g's in the sludge : '   *Princess v* 27
Guanahani   last the light, the light On G !   *Columbus* 75
Guano   A pamphleteer on g and on grain,   *Princess, Con.* 89
Guard (s)   (See also **Woman-guard**)   Encompass'd by
   his faithful g,   *In Mem. cxxvi* 8
Guard (verb)   g about With triple-mailed trust,   *Supp. Confessions* 65
clear-stemm'd plantans g The outlet,   *Arabian Nights* 23
Upon the cliffs that g my native land,   *Audley Court* 49
enough, Sir ! I can g my own.'   *Aylmer's Field* 276
Brothers, the woman's Angel g's you,   *Princess v* 410
g us, g the eye, the soul Of Europe,   *Ode on Well.* 160
He bad you g the sacred coasts.   „ 172
They knew the precious things they had to g :   *Third of Feb.* 41
And like a beacon g's thee home.   *In Mem. xvii* 12
That g the portals of the house ;   „ xxix 12
So here shall silence g thy fame ;   „ lxxv 17
Yea, too, myself from myself I g,   *Maud I vi* 60
To g thee on the rough ways of the world.'   *Com. of Arthur* 336
For hard by here is one that g's a ford—   *Gareth and L.* 1003
'G it,' and there was none to meddle   „ 1012
the King Gave me to g, and such a dog am I,   „ 1014
one with arms to g his head and yours,   *Geraint and E.* 427
Long since, to g the justice of the King :   „ 934
Or devil or man G thou thine head.'   *Balin and Balan* 553
I shall g it even in death.   *Lancelot and E.* 1115
seeing that the King must g That which he rules,   *Holy Grail* 905
To g thee in the wild hour coming on,   *Guinevere* 446
I g as God's high gift from scathe and wrong,   „ 494
To g and foster her for evermore.   „ 592
value of that jewel, he had to g ?   *Lover's Tale iv* 153
Out yonder.   G the Redan !   *Def. of Lucknow* 36
two repentant Lovers g the ring ; '   *The Ring* 198
Guarded   (See also **Griffin-guarded**)   G the sacred shield
   of Lancelot ;   *Lancelot and E.* 4
Fear not : thou shalt be g till my death.   *Guinevere* 448
You have the ring she g ;   *The Ring* 475
Guardian (adj.)   My g angel will speak out   *In Mem. xliv* 15
Guardian (s)   I to her became Her g and her angel,   *Lover's Tale i* 393
you the lifelong g of the child.   *The Ring* 54
The g of her relics, of her ring.   „ 441
Guarding   G realms and kings from shame ;   *Ode on Well.* 68
Guerdon (s)   Sequel of g could not alter me   *Œnone* 153
What g ?'   Gareth sharply spake,   *Gareth and L.* 830
but take A horse and arms for g ;   *Geraint and E.* 218
' I take it as free gift, then,' said the boy, ' Not g ;   „ 223
hear The legend as in g for your rhyme ?   *Merlin and V.* 554
Our g not alone for what we did,   *Columbus* 33
Nor list for g in the voice of men,   *Ancient Sage* 262
Guerdon (verb)   It grows to g after-days :   *Love thou thy land* 27
we gave a costly bribe To g silence,   *Princess i* 204
Guess (s)   the golden g Is morning-star   *Columbus* 43
the wildest modern g of you and me.   *Locksley H., Sixty* 232
Guess (verb)   cannot g How much their welfare   *Princess iii* 280
The Power in darkness whom we g ;   *In Mem. cxxiv* 4
What art thou then ? I cannot g ;   „ cxxx 5
praying To his own great self, as I g ;   *Maud II v* 33
I might g the chief of those, After the King,   *Lancelot and E.* 183
g at the love of a soul for a soul ?   *Charity* 30
Guess'd   I leave thy greatness to be g ;   *In Mem. lxxv* 4

Guess'd (*continued*) presence might have *g* you one of
those | *Marr. of Geraint* 431
Now *g* a hidden meaning in his arms, | *Lancelot and E.* 17
Guess-work they *g* it, | *Columbus* 43
Guess-work *G-w they* guess'd it, | " 43
No *g-w*! I was certain of my goal; | " 45
Guest Each enter'd like a welcome *g*. | *Two Voices* 411
Head-waiter, honour'd by the *g* Half-mused, | *Will Water.* 73
mellow Death, like some late | " 239
g, their host, their ancient friend, | *Aylmer's Field* 790
Shone, silver-set ; about it lay the *g's*, | *Princess, Pro.* 106
You, likewise, our late *g*, | " v 229
Who is he that cometh, like an honour'd *g*, | *Ode on Well.* 80
father's chimney glows In expectation of a *g* ; | *In Mem.* vi 30
Which brings no more a welcome *g* | " xxix 5
I see myself an honour'd *g*, | " lxxxiv 21
A *g*, or happy sister, sung, | " lxxxix 26
if I Conjecture of a stiller *g*, | " Con. 86
Endures not that her *g* should serve himself.' | *Marr. of Geraint* 379
wine and goodly cheer To feed the sudden *g*, | *Geraint and E.* 284
to thy *g*, Me, me of Arthur's Table. | *Balin and Balan* 379
'Whence comest thou, my *g*, | *Lancelot and E.* 181
one of your own knights, a *g* of ours, | *Holy Grail* 40
all the goodlier *g's* are past away, | *Last Tournament* 158
Was brought before the *g* : and they the *g's*, | *Lover's Tale* iv 204
all The *g's* broke in upon him with meeting hands | " 238
custom steps yet further when the *g* Is loved and honour'd | " 244
This question, so flung down before the *g's*, | " 268
While all the *g's* in mute amazement rose— | " 305
'My *g's*,' said Julian: ' you are honour'd now | " 316
a *g* So bound to me by common love and loss— | " 344
rose up, and with him all his *g's* | " 359
How oft the Cantab supper, host and *g*, | *To W. H. Brookfield* 4
Like would-be *g's* an hour too late, | *Tiresias* 198
therewithin a *g* may make True cheer | *Pro. to Gen. Hamley* 15
Then drink to England, every *g* ; | *Hands all Round* 2
Unfriendly of your parted *g*. | *The Wanderer* 4
Guide (*s*) the silver star, thy *g*, Shines | *Tithonus* 25
'They were dangerous *g's* the feelings— | *Locksley Hall* 95
When each by turns was *g* to each, | *In Mem.* xxiii 13
With you for *g* and master, only you, | *Merlin and V.* 881
Then were I glad of you as *g* and friend : | *Lancelot and E.* 226
far away with good Sir Torre for *g* | " 788
Alla be my *g* ! But come, My noble friend, | *Akbar's Dream* 16
Guide (*verb*) there is a hand that *g's*.' | *Princess, Con.* 79
g Her footsteps, moving side by side | *In Mem.* cxiv 18
I have not made the world, and He that made it will *g*. | *Maud* I iv 48
thou, Sir Prince, Wilt surely *g* me | *Balin and Balan* 478
and clean ! and yet—God *g* them—young.' | *Merlin and V.* 29
and he Will *g* me to that palace, to the doors.' | *Lancelot and E.* 1129
force to *g* us thro' the days I shall not see? | *Locksley H., Sixty* 158
Guided Whose feet are *g* thro' the land, | *In Mem.* lxvi 9
Which not alone had *g* me, | " cxiii 3
Guile pure as he from taint of craven *g*, | *Ode on Well.* 135
A widow with less *g* than many a child. | *Sisters (E. and E.)* 182
Guileless Till ev'n the clear face of the *g* King, | *Guinevere* 85
Guilt When I have purged my *g*.' | *Palace of Art* 296
The *g* of blood is at your door: | *L. C. V. de Vere* 43
To hold his hope thro' shame and *g*, | *Love thou thy land* 82
May wreck itself without the pilot's *g*, | *Aylmer's Field* 716
Easily gather'd either *g*. | *Princess* iv 236
eye which watches *g* And goodness, | *In Mem.* xxvi 5
hasty judger would have call'd her *g*, | *Geraint and E.* 433
subtle beast, Would track her *g* until he found, | *Guinevere* 60
too-fearful *g*, Simpler than any child, | " 370
without some *g* should such grief be ? | *Lover's Tale* i 795
Guiltless Guilty or *g*, to stave off a chance | *Geraint and E.* 353
flushing the *g* air, | *Lucretius* 239
far away the maid in Astolat, Her *g* rival, | *Lancelot and E.* 746
Against the *g* heirs of him from Tyre, | *Tiresias* 12
Being *g*, as an innocent prisoner, | *Lover's Tale* i 787
Guilty (*See also* **Half-guilty**) a little fault Whereof I
was not *g* ; | *Com. of Arthur* 342
be he *g*, by that deathless King Who lived | *Gareth and L.* 382
Touching her *g* love for Lancelot, | *Marr. of Geraint* 25

Guilty (*continued*) To dream she could be *g* of foul
act, | *Marr of Geraint* 120
G or guiltless, to stave off a chance | *Geraint and E.* 353
rooted out the slothful officer Or *g*, | " 939
And full of cowardice and *g* shame, | *Princess* iv 348
like a *g* thing I creep At earliest morning | *In Mem.* vii 7
It is this *g* hand !—— | *Maud* II i 4
Am I *g* of blood ? | " ii 73
The great and *g* love he bare the Queen, | *Lancelot and E.* 245
Guinea jingling of the *g* helps the hurt | *Locksley Hall* 105
Guinea-hens praised his hens, his geese, his *g-h* ; | *The Brook* 126
Guinevere Sir Launcelot and Queen *G* Rode | *Sir L. and Q. G.* 20
G, and in her his one delight. | *Com. of Arthur* 4
G Stood by the castle walls to watch him | " 47
Desiring to be join'd with *G* ; | " 77
Give me thy daughter *G* to wife.' | " 139
Fear not to give this King thine only child, *G* : | " 414
return'd Among the flowers, In May, with *G*. | " 452
Thro' that great tenderness for *G*, | *Marr. of Geraint* 30
G lay late into the morn, Lost in sweet dreams, | " 157
G, not mindful of his face In the King's hall, | " 191
A stately queen whose name was *G*, | " 667
thrice that morning *G* had climb'd The giant tower, | " 826
Some goodly cognizance of *G*, | *Balin and Balan* 195
O me, that such a name as *G's*, | " 489
day When *G* was crossing the great hall | *Merlin and V.* 65
Spake (for she had been sick) to *G*, | *Lancelot and E.* 78
G, The pearl of beauty : | " 113
Lancelot, when they glanced at *G*, | " 270
Sir Lancelot at the palace craved Audience of *G*, | " 1163
And therefore to our Lady *G*, | " 1278
For fair thou art and pure as *G*, | *Pelleas and E.* 44
O my Queen, my *G*, For I will be thine Arthur | " 46
' Is *G* herself so beautiful ? ' | " 70
Said *G*, 'We marvel at thee much, | " 179
' False ! and I held thee pure as *G*.' | " 522
' Am I but false as *G* is pure? | " 524
There with her knights and dames was *G*. | " 588
G had sinn'd against the highest, | *Last Tournament* 570
QUEEN *G* had fled the court, | *Guinevere* 1
When that storm of anger brake From *G*, | " 362
I did not come to curse thee, *G*, | " 533
yet not less, O *G*, For I was ever virgin save for thee, | " 556
Guise and sets before him in rich *g* | *Lover's Tale* iv 247
Gules Langued *g*, and tooth'd with grinning
savagery. | *Balin and Balan* 197
Gulf (*s*) and brought Into the *g's* of sleep. | *D. of F. Women* 52
Sow'd all their mystic *g's* with fleeting stars ; | *Gardener's D.* 262
It may be that the *g's* will wash us down : | *Ulysses* 62
a *g* of ruin, swallowing gold, | *Sea Dreams* 79
Or down the fiery *g* as talk of it, | *Princess* iii 287
Nor shudders at the *g's* beneath, | *In Mem.* xli 15
A *g* that ever shuts and gapes, | " lxx 6
in this stormy *g* have found a pearl | *Maud* I xviii 42
seas of Death and sunless *g's* of Doubt. | *Pref. Son. 19th Cent.* 14
naked glebe Should yawn once more into the *g*, | *Demeter and P.* 43
woods Plunged *g* on *g* thro' all their vales | *Prog. of Spring* 73
Gulf (*verb*) Should *g* him fathom-deep in brine ; | *In Mem.* x 18
Gulf'd And *g* his griefs in inmost sleep ; | *Pelleas and E.* 516
Gulf-stream warm *g-s* of Florida Floats far away | *Mine be the strength* 12
Gulistan any rose of *G* Shall burst her veil · | *Princess* iv 122
Gull laugh'd and scream'd against the *g's*, | *Pelleas and E.* 89
Gull'd break our bound, and *g* Our servants, | *Princess* iv 539
Be not *g* by a despot's plea ! | *Riflemen form !* 9
Gun they waited—Not a *g* was fired. | *The Captain* 40
Each beside his *g*. | " 52
Nor ever lost an English *g* ; | *Ode on Well.* 97
' Charge for the *g's* !' he said : | *Light Brigade* 6
high above us with her yawning tiers of *g's*, | *The Revenge* 41
not arter the birds wi' 'is *g*, | *Village Wife* 41
make way for the *g* ! Now double-charge it | *Def. of Lucknow* 67
Gunner Sabring the *g's* there, | *Light Brigade* 29
Sink me the ship, Master *G*— | *The Revenge* 89
g said ' Ay, ay,' but the seamen made reply: | " 91
Gurgle (*s*) as we sat by the *g* of springs, | *V. of Maeldune* 89

Gurgle (verb) All throats that *g* sweet! *Talking Oak* 266
Gurgling To drench his dark locks in the *g* wave *Princess iv* 187
Gurnion By castle G, where the glorious King *Lancelot and E.* 293
Gush *g'es* from beneath a low-hung cloud. *Ode to Memory* 71
Gush'd between Whose interspaces *g* in *Lover's Tale i* 408
Gushing *g* of the wave Far far away did seem *Lotos-Eaters* 31
Gust one warm *g*, full-fed with perfume, *Gardener's D.* 113
will be chaff For every *g* of chance, *Princess ii* 356
The *g* that round the garden flew, *In Mem. lxxxix* 19
An angry *g* of wind Puff'd out his torch *Merlin and V.* 730
Anon the face, as, when a *g* hath blown, *Last Tournament* 368
Waved with a sudden *g* that sweeping down *Lover's Tale iii* 34
a rougher *g* might tumble a stormier wave, *The Wreck* 131
Gustful a *g* April morn That puff'd the swaying branches *Holy Grail* 14
Gusty She saw the *g* shadow sway. *Mariana* 52
Gutted till he crept from a *g* mine *Maud I x* 9
Guvness (governess) Mun be a *g*, lad, or summut, *N. Farmer, N. S.* 26
Guzzlin' *G* an' soäkin' an' smoäkin' *North. Cobbler* 24
Gwydion *G* made by glamour out of flowers, *Marr. of Geraint* 743
Gynæceum Dwarfs of the *g*, fail so far In high desire, *Princess iii* 279
Gyre Shot up and shrill'd in flickering *g's*, " *vii* 46
mighty *g's* Rapid and vast, of hissing spray *Lover's Tale i* 197
Gyve the wholesome boon of *g* and gag. *Gareth and L.* 370
sight run over Upon his steely *g's*; *Lover's Tale ii* 157

H

H too rough H in Hell and Heaven, *Sea Dreams* 196
Haäche (ache) es be down wi' their *h's* an' their paäins: *Spinster's S's.* 108
Haäcre (acre) Warnt worth nowt a *h*, *N. Farmer, O. S.* 39
wi haäte hoonderd *h* o' Squoire's, " 44
wi' a hoonderd *h* o' sense— *Church-warden, etc.* 22
Haäfe (half) an' mea *h* down wi' my haäy! " 2
Sa I warrants 'e niver said *h* wot 'e thowt, " 18
Wi' *h* o' the chimleys a-twizzen'd an' twined *Owd Roä* 22
Haäf-pot (half-pot) An' a *h-p* o' jam, *Spinster's S's.* 109
Haäte (eight) Meä, wi' *h* hoonderd haäcre o' Squoire's, *N. Farmer, O. S.* 44
Haäte (hate) an' we *h's* boooklarnin' ere. *Village Wife* 24
to be sewer I *h's* 'em, my lass, " 31
a-preächin' *mea* down, they heve, an' I *h's* 'em now, *Church-warden, etc.* 53
Haäted (hated) a-flyin' an' seeädin' tha *h* to see; *Spinster's S's.* 79
Haäy (hay) an' twined like a band o' *h*. *Owd Roä* 22
an' mea haäfe down wi' my *h*! *Church-warden, etc.* 2
Habit (custom) Idle *h* links us yet. *Miller's D.* 212
Or to burst all links of *h*— *Locksley Hall* 157
Drink deep, until the *h's* of the slave, *Princess ii* 91
to us, The fools of *h*, sweeter seems *In Mem. x* 12
Her memory from old *h* of the mind Went slipping *Guinevere* 379
Habit (riding dress) whether The *h*, hat, and feather, *Maud I xx* 18
Hack yea to him Who *h's* his mother's throat— *Sir J. Oldcastle* 114
Hack'd stay the brands That *h* among the flyers, *Com. of Arthur* 121
their arms *H*, and their foreheads grimed with smoke, *Holy Grail* 265
H the battleshield, *Batt. of Brunanburh* 13
Fiercely we *h* at the flyers before us. " 42
Casques were crack'd and hauberks *h* *The Tourney* 7
Hades or the enthroned Persephonè in *H*, *Princess iv* 439
seen the serpent-wanded power Draw downward into *H* *Demeter and P.* 26
A cry that rang thro' *H*, Earth, and Heaven! " 33
break The sunless halls of *H* into Heaven? " 136
shrillings of the Dead When driven to *H*, *Death of Œnone* 22
Haft all the *h* twinkled with diamond sparks, *M. d'Arthur* 56
Struck with a knife's *h* hard against the board, *Geraint and E.* 600
all the *h* twinkled with diamond sparks, *Pass. of Arthur* 224
Haggard And shot from crooked lips a *h* smile. *Princess iv* 364
when she saw The *h* father's face and reverend beard " *vi* 103
An armlet for an arm to which the Queen's Is *h*, *Lancelot and E.* 1227
'What is it?' but that oarsman's *h* face, " 1250
As a vision Unto a *h* prisoner, *Lover's Tale ii* 148
Master scrimps his *h* sempstress of her daily bread, *Locksley H., Sixty* 221
Eve after eve that *h* anchorite Would haunt *St. Telemachus* 12

Hail (s) Where falls not *h*, or rain, or any snow, *M. d'Arthur* 260
Rain, wind, frost, heat, *h*, damp, *St. S. Stylites* 16
with rain or *h*, or fire or snow; *Locksley Hall* 193
And gilds the driving *h*. *Sir Galahad* 56
Sleet of diamond-drift and pearly *h*; *Vision of Sin* 22
Where falls not *h*, or rain, or any snow, *Pass. of Arthur* 428
and a clatter of *h* on the glass, *In the Child. Hosp.* 62
h of Arès crash Along the sounding walls. *Tiresias* 96
Hail (verb) Sets out, and meets a friend who *h's* him, *Walk. to the Mail* 42
city-roar that *h's* Premier or king! *Princess, Con.* 101
And voices *h* it from the brink; *In Mem. cxxi* 14
and all men *h* him for their king.' *Com. of Arthur* 424
ere he came, like one that *h's* a ship, *Geraint and E.* 540
H the fair Ceremonial Of this year of her Jubilee. *On Jub. Q. Victoria* 23
Hear thy myriad laureates *h* thee monarch *Akbar's D., Hymn* 6
Hail (interj.) *H*, hidden to the knees in fern, *Talking Oak* 29
Fair as the Angel that said 'H!' *Aylmer's Field* 681
h once more to the banner of battle unroll'd! *Maud III vi* 42
Prince, Knight, *H*, Knight and Prince, *Gareth and L.* 1271
I will speak. *H*, royal knight, *Balin and Balan* 470
King, Who, when he saw me, rose, and bade me *h*, *Holy Grail* 725
King espied him, saying to him, '*H*, Bors! " 756
H, King! to-morrow thou shalt pass away. *Pass. of Arthur* 34
'*H* to the glorious Golden year of her Jubilee!' *On Jub. Q. Victoria* 64
H ample presence of a Queen, *Prog. of Spring* 61
Hail'd Walter *h* a score of names upon her, *Princess, Pro.* 156
And toward him spurr'd, and *h* him, *Holy Grail* 637
Who never *h* another—was there one? *Lover's Tale i* 798
and there *h* on our houses and halls *Def. of Lucknow* 13
Hair (See also 'Aäir, 'Air) smooth'd his chin and sleek'd his *h*, *A Character* 11
Dressing their *h* with the white sea-flower; *The Merman* 13
Combing her *h* Under the sea, *The Mermaid* 4
With a comb of pearl I would comb my *h*; " 11
I would comb my *h* till my ringlets would fall " 14
With thy floating flaxen *h*; *Adeline* 6
Your *h* is darker, and your eyes Touch'd *Margaret* 49
bright black eyes, her bright black *h*, *Kate* 2
round her neck Floated her *h* *Œnone* 19
his sunny *h* Cluster'd about his temples " 59
From her warm brows and bosom her deep *h* Ambrosial, " 177
her *h* Wound with white roses, slept St. Cecily; *Palace of Art* 98
blessings on his kindly voice and on his silver *h*! *May Queen, Con.* 13
that *h* More black than ashbuds in the front of March.' *Gardener's D.* 27
A single stream of all her soft brown *h* " 128
wound Her looser *h* in braid, " 158
leaf and acorn-ball In wreath about her *h*. *Talking Oak* 288
Catch the wild goat by the *h*, *Locksley Hall* 167
His beard a foot before him, and his *h* A yard behind. *Godiva* 18
The maiden's jet-black *h* has grown, *Day-Dm., Sleep B.* 4
my *h* Is gray before I know it. *Will Water.* 167
With a single rose in her *h*. *Lady Clare* 60
One her dark *h* and lovesome mien. *Beggar Maid* 12
H, and eyes, and limbs, and faces, *Vision of Sin* 39
This *h* is his: she cut it off and gave it, *Enoch Arden* 894
h In gloss and hue the chestnut, (repeat) *The Brook* 71, 206
made The hoar *h* of the Baronet bristle up *Aylmer's Field* 42
His *h* as it were crackling into flames, " 586
not a *h* Ruffled upon the scarfskin, " 659
bring Their own gray *h's* with sorrow to the grave— " 777
Beat breast, tore *h*, cried out upon herself *Lucretius* 277
sweet girl-graduates in their golden *h*. *Princess, Pro.* 142
combing out her long black *h* Damp from the river; " *iv* 276
'You have our son: touch not a *h* of his head: " 407
Robed in the long night of her deep *h*, " 491
And fingering at the *h* about his lip, " *v* 303
and caught his *h*, And so belabour'd him " 340
A single band of gold about her *h*, " 513
His face was ruddy, his *h* was gold, *The Victim* 35
And you with gold for *h*! *Window, Spring* 4
That sittest ranging golden *h*; *In Mem. vi* 26
From youth and babe and hoary *h's*: " *lxix* 10
To reverence and the silver *h* " *lxxxiv* 32

Hair (*continued*) the roots of my *h* were stirred By a shuffled step,   *Maud I i* 13
What if with her sunny *h*,   „ *vi* 23
and thought It is his mother's *h.*   „ *II ii* 70
and follow'd by his flying *h* Ran like a colt,   *Com. of Arthur* 321
dark my mother was in eyes and *h*, And dark in *h* and eyes am I ;   „ 327
Broad brows and fair, a fluent *h* and fine,   *Gareth and L.* 464
the *h* All over glanced with dewdrop or with gem   „ 928
broken wings, torn raiment, and loose *h*,   „ 1208
and drew down from out his night-black *h*   *Balin and Balan* 511
A twist of gold was round her *h* ;   *Merlin and V.* 221
The snake of gold slid from her *h*,   „ 888
And set it in this damsel's golden *h*,   *Lancelot and E.* 205
Her bright *h* blown about the serious face   „ 392
Then shook his *h*, strode off, and buzz'd abroad   „ 722
—all her bright *h* streaming down—   „ 1156
To seize me by the *h* and bear me far,   „ 1425
Clean from her forehead all that wealth of *h*   *Holy Grail* 150
all her shining *h* Was smear'd with earth,   „ 209
black-blue Irish *h* and Irish eyes Had drawn   *Last Tournament* 404
A low sea-sunset glorying round her *h*,   „ 508
His *h*, a sun that ray'd from off a brow   „ 666
all their dewy *h* blown back like flame :   *Guinevere* 284
with her milkwhite arms and shadowy *h*   „ 416
Lest but a *h* of this low head be harm'd.   „ 447
O golden *h*, with which I used to play   „ 547
Quiver'd a flying glory on her *h*,   *Lover's Tale i* 69
A solid glory on her bright black *h* ;   „ 367
her *h* Studded with one rich Provence rose—   „ *iii* 44
thaw niver a *h* wur awry ;   *Village Wife* 84
Harsh red *h*, big voice, big chest,   *In the Child. Hosp.* 4
And his white *h* sank to his heels   *V. of Maeldune* 118
a dreadful light Came from her golden *h*,   *Tiresias* 44
crystal into which I braided Edwin's *h* !   *The Flight* 34
An' yer *h* as black as the night,   *Tomorrow* 32
h was as white as the snow an a grave.   „ 60
And that bright *h* the modern sun,   *Epilogue* 8
'Thy *h* Is golden like thy Mother's,   *The Ring* 103
The frost-bead melts upon her golden *h* ;   *Prog. of Spring* 10
one sleek'd the squalid *h*, One kiss'd   *Death of Œnone* 57

Hair'd   *See* **Dark-hair'd, Fair-hair'd, Golden-hair'd,** **Gray-hair'd, Long-hair'd, White-hair'd**
Hairless   A little glassy-headed *h* man,   *Merlin and V.* 620
Hairm (arm)   An' 'e cotch'd howd hard o' my *h*,   *Owd Roä* 58
wi' my *h* hingin' down to the floor,   „ 65
Hair's-breadth   Not even by one *h-b* of heresy,   *Columbus* 64
Hairshirt   'Fast, *H* and scourge—   *Sir J. Oldcastle* 142
Hairy-fibred   Claspt the gray walls with *h-f* arms,   *Marr. of Geraint* 323
Haithen (heathen)   *h* kings in the flesh for the Jidgemint day,   *Tomorrow* 70
Halcyon (adj.)   and give His fealty to the *h* hour !   *The Wanderer* 12
Halcyon (s)   in her open palm a *h* sits Patient—   *Prog. of Spring* 20
Haldeny (Alderney)   pigs didn't sell at fall, an' wa lost wer *H* cow,   *Church-warden, etc.* 5
Hale (Francis)   *See* **Francis Hale**
Hale   I was strong and *h* of body then ;   *St. S. Stylites* 29
Who wears his manhood *h* and green :   *In Mem. liii* 4
What did he then ? not die : he is here and *h*—   *Lover's Tale iv* 40
Haled   With hand and rope we *h* the groaning sow,   *Walk. to the Mail* 91
The rope that *h* the buckets from the well,   *St. S. Stylites* 64
And fain had *h* him out into the world,   *Aylmer's Field* 467
They *h* us to the Princess where she sat   *Princess iv* 271
h the yellow-ringleted Britoness—   *Boädicea* 55
Haler   and *h* too than I ;   *Guinevere* 685
Half   (*See also* **Haafe**)   *H* shown, are broken and withdrawn.   *Two Voices* 306
a friendship so complete Portioned in *halves* between us,   *Gardener's D.* 5
My words were *h* in earnest, *h* in jest,)   „ 23
H light, *h* shade, She stood,   „ 140
And *h* in love, *h* spite, he woo'd and wed   *Dora* 39
h stands up And bristles ; *h* has fall'n and made a bridge ;   *Walk. to the Mail* 31
I hope my end draws nigh : *h* dead I am,   *St. S. Stylites* 37
love-languid thro' *h* tears would dwell One earnest,   *Love and Duty* 36

Half (*continued*)   *H* is thine and *h* is his : it will be worthy of the two.   *Locksley Hall* 92
shall we pass the bill I mention'd *h* an hour ago ? '   *Day-Dm., Revival* 28
That my youth was *h* divine.   *Vision of Sin* 78
With a score of swarthy faces came.   *Aylmer's Field* 191
his mind *H* buried in some weightier argument,   *Lucretius* 9
H child *h* woman as she was,   *Princess, Pro.* 101
we gain'd A little street *h* garden and *h* house ;   „ *i* 214
then to bed, where *h* in doze I seem'd To float   „ 246
we stroll'd For *h* the day thro' stately theatres   „ *ii* 369
Hers more than *h* the students, all the love.   „ *iii* 39
bearing in my left The weight of all the hopes of *h* the world,   „ *iv* 184
but *h* Without you ; with you, whole ; and of those *halves* You worthiest ;   „ 460
H turning to the broken statue, said,   „ - 593
Lily of the vale ! *h* open'd bell of the woods !   „ *vi* 193
H a league, *h* a league, *H* a league onward,   *Light Brigade* 1
a lie which is *h* a truth is ever the blackest of lies,   *Grandmother* 30
Girt by *h* the tribes of Britain,   *Boädicea* 5
or *h* coquette-like Maiden,   *Hendecasyllabics* 20
I sometimes hold it *h* a sin To put in words   *In Mem. v* 1
like Nature, *h* reveal And *h* conceal the Soul within.   „ 3
A shot, ere *h* thy draught be done,   „ *vi* 11
And part it, giving *h* to him.   „ *xxv* 12
My bosom-friend and *h* of life ;   „ *lix* 3
H jealous of she knows not what,   „ *lx* 7
h exprest And loyal unto kindly laws.   „ *lxxxv* 15
I, the divided *h* of such A friendship as had master'd Time ;   „ 63
And tumbled *h* the mellowing pears !   „ *lxxxix* 20
To count their memories *h* divine ;   „ *xc* 12
Believe me, than in *h* the creeds.   „ *xcvi* 12
These two have striven *h* the day,   „ *cii* 17
Now *h* to the setting moon are gone, And *h* to the rising day ;   *Maud I xxii* 23
H the night I waste in sighs, *H* in dreams I sorrow   „ *II iv* 23
'Thou hast *h* prevail'd against me,'   *Gareth and L.* 30
Or whose'er it was, or *h* the world Had ventured—   „ 64
everyone that owns a tower The Lord for *h* a league.   „ 596
King Arthur's gift, the worth of *h* a town,   „ 677
H fell to right and *h* to left and lay.   „ 1405
Spring after spring, for *h* a hundred years :   *Holy Grail* 19
That have no meaning *h* a league away :   „ 556
With a night's appliances, recall'd   *Lover's Tale iv* 93
But his friend Replied, in *h* a whisper,   „ 336
And the *h* my men are sick.   *The Revenge* 6
For *h* of their fleet to the right and *h* to the left   „ 35
And *h* of the rest of us maim'd for life   „ 77
the great waters break Whitening for *h* a league,   *Last Tournament* 465
Not quite so quickly, no, nor *h* as well.   *Sisters (E. and E.)* 102
For the one *h* slew the other,   *V. of Maeldune* 114
and her tears Are *h* of pleasure, *h* of pain—   *Prin. Beatrice* 11
He married an heiress, an orphan with *h* a shire of estate,—   *Charity* 13

Half-accomplish'd   A spike of *h-a* bells—   *To Ulysses* 24
Half afraid   I myself Am *h* a to wear it.   *The Ring* 472
Half-aghast   Leolin still Retreated *h-a*,   *Aylmer's Field* 330
Half-akin   No longer *h-a* to brute,   *In Mem., Con.* 133
Half-a-league   Yon summit *h-a-l* in air—   *Ancient Sage* 11
Half-allowing   *h-a* smiles for all the world,   *Aylmer's Field* 120
Half-amaze   rabble in *h-a* Stared at him dead,   *St. Telemachus* 9
Half-amazed   Whereat he stared, replying, *h-a*,   *Godiva* 21
seal'd dispatches which the Head Took *h-a*,   *Princess iv* 380
mirth so loud Beyond all use, that, *h-a*, the Queen,   *Last Tournament* 236
that *h-a* I parted from her,   *The Ring* 436
Half-anger'd   *H-a* with my happy lot,   *Miller's D.* 200
Come, I am hunger'd and *h-a*—meat,   *Last Tournament* 719
Half-arisen   came upon him *h-a* from sleep,   *Aylmer's Field* 584
Half-ashamed   Then *h-a* and part-amazed,   *Gareth and L.* 868
Half-asleep   As *h-a* his breath he drew,   *The Sisters* 28
And on me, *h-a*, came back That wholesome heat   *To E. Fitzgerald* 23
Half-assured   their Highnesses Were *h-a*   *Columbus* 60
Half-attain'd   cope Of the *h-a* futurity,   *Ode to Memory* 33

Half-awake *h-a* I heard The parson taking wide and wider sweeps, — *The Epic* 13
h-a he whisper'd, 'Where? O where?' — *Pelleas and E.* 41
Half-awaked sounded as in a dream To ears but *h-a*, — *Last Tournament* 152
Half-awaken'd earliest pipe of *h-a* Birds — *Princess iv* 50
Half-blind sudden light Dazed me *h-b*: — " *v* 12
Half-blinded *H-b* at the coming of a light. — *Com. of Arthur* 266
Half-bold *H-b*, half-frighted, with dilated eyes, — *Geraint and E.* 597
Half-brain All the full-brain, *h-b* races, — *Locksley H., Sixty* 161
Half-bright Star of Even Half-tarnish'd and *h-b*, — *Gareth and L.* 1118
Half-buried *H-b* in the Eagle's down, — *Palace of Art* 122
Half-canonized *H-c* by all that look'd on her, — *Princess i* 23
Half-cheated rathe she rose, *h-c* in the thought — *Lancelot and E.* 340
Half-clench'd hand *h-c* Went faltering sideways — *Merlin and V.* 849
Half-closed dropping low their crimson bells *H-c*, — *Arabian Nights* 63
Half-conscious *H-c* of the garden-squirt, — *Amphion* 91
H-c of their dying clay, — *In Mem. lviii* 7
Half-consent Assumed from thence a *h-c* — *Princess vii* 82
Half-control for man can *h-c* his doom — *Locksley H., Sixty* 277
Half-crazed I, once *h-c* for larger light — *To Ulysses* 29
Half-crown Is it the weight of that *h-c*, — *Will Water.* 155
Half-crush'd *h-c* among the rest A dwarf-like Cato — *Princess vii* 125
Half-cut-down *h-c-d*, a pasty costly-made, — *Audley Court* 23
Half-dead And all things look'd *h-d*, — *Grandmother* 34
H-d to know that I shall die.' — *In Mem. xxxv* 16
Maybe still I am but *h-d*; — *Maud II. v* 99
fire, That lookt *h-d*, brake bright, — *Gareth and L.* 685
Under the *h-d* sunset glared; — " 800
A stump of oak *h-d*, From roots like some black coil — *Last Tournament* 12
dash'd *h-d* on barren sands, was I. — *The Ring* 309
Half-deed shall descend On this *h-d*, and shape it — *Ancient Sage* 89
Half-defended Lo their colony *h-d*! — *Boädicea* 17
Half-despised not look up, or *h-d* the height — *Guinevere* 643
Half-digging they fell *H-d* their own graves) — *Lover's Tale ii* 47
Half-dipt a summer moon *H-d* in cloud: — *Godiva* 46
Half-disdain *h-d* Perch'd on the pouted blossom — *Princess, Pro.* 198
Half-diseased 'And the liver is *h-d*!' — *Dead Prophet* 76
Half-disfame what is Fame in life but *h-d*, — *Merlin and V.* 465
Right well know I that Fame is *h-d*, — " 504
Half-disrooted A tree Was *h-d* from his place — *Princess vi* 186
Half-divine The man I held as *h-d*; — *In Mem. xiv* 10
Half-drain'd a flask Between his knees, *h-d*; — *Day-Dm., Sleep P.* 26
Half-dream Falling asleep in a *h-d*! — *Lotos-Eaters, C. S.* 56
Half-drooping half on her mother propt, *H-d* — *Princess iv* 368
Half-dropt With *h-d* eyelid still, — *Lotos-Eaters, C. S.* 90
Half-embraced And *h-e* the basket cradle-head — *Sea Dreams* 289
Half-English sweet *h-E* Neilgherry air I panted, — *The Brook* 17
Half-entering *H-e* the portals. — *Lover's Tale ii* 123
Half-envious *H-e* of the flattering hand, — *Lancelot and E.* 349
Half-face From the *h-f* to the full eye, — " 1262
Half-fall'n *H-f* across the threshold of the sun, — *D. of F. Women* 63
Half-falling *h-f* from his knees, Half-nestled at his heart, — *Merlin and V.* 904
Half-foresaw She *h-f* that he, the subtle beast, — *Guinevere* 59
Half-forgotten our great deeds, as *h-f* things. — *Lotos-Eaters, C. S.* 78
random rhymes, Ere they be *h-f*; — *Will Water.* 14
Vivien *h-f* of the Queen — *Merlin and V.* 137
Low in the dust of *h-f* kings, — *Lancelot and E.* 1338
Half-frenzied when, *h-f* by the ring, — *The Ring* 213
Half-frighted on the book, *h-f*, Miriam swore. — *Enoch Arden* 843
Half-bold, *h-f*, with dilated eyes, — *Geraint and E.* 597
Half-frighten'd Look'd down, half-pleased, *h-f*, — *Amphion* 54
Half-glance WITH a *h-g* upon the sky — *A Character* 1
Half-grown *H-g* as yet, a child, and vain— — *In Mem. cxiv* 9
Half-guilty grew *h-g* in her thoughts again, — *Guinevere* 408
Half-heard laid his ear beside the doors, And there *h-h*; — *Com. of Arthur* 324
Half-hid Here *h-h* in the gleaming wood, — *Maud I vi* 69
Half-hidden and there, *h-h* by him, stood, — *Holy Grail* 754
Half-historic dealt with knights, Half-legend, *h-h*, — *Princess, Pro.* 30
Half-hour For one *h-h*, and let him talk to me!' — *The Brook* 115
Half-hysterical A half-incredulous, *h-h* cry. — *Enoch Arden* 853
Half-incredulous A *h-i*, half-hysterical cry. — " 853
Half-invisible *H-i* to the view, Wheeling — *Vision of Sin* 36
Half-lapt *H-l* in glowing gauze and golden brede, — *Princess vi* 134

Half-legend dealt with knights, *H-l*, half-historic, — *Princess, Pro.* 30
Half-light In the *h-l*—thro' the dim dawn— — *Gareth and L.* 1384
Half-lost *H-l* in belts of hop and breadths — *Princess, Con.* 45
H-l in the liquid azure bloom — *Maud I iv* 5
Owe you me nothing for a life *h-l*? — *Geraint and E.* 318
Some third-rate isle *h-l* among her seas? — *To the Queen ii* 25
O dear Spirit *h-l* In thine own shadow — *De Prof., Two G.* 39
Half-loyal the glance That only seems *h-l* — *Last Tournament* 118
Half-man He scarce is knight, yea but *h-m*, — *Gareth and L.* 1176
Half-melted moon, *H-m* into thin blue air, — *Lover's Tale i* 421
Half-miracle seem'd *h-m* To those he fought with, — *Lancelot and E.* 497
Half-moulder'd Sweeps suddenly all its *h-m* chords — *Lover's Tale i* 19
Half-muffled answer which, *h-m* in his beard, — *Princess v* 234
Half-mused the guest *H-m*, or reeling ripe, — *Will Water.* 74
Half-naked *H-n* as if caught at once from bed — *Princess iv* 285
Half-nestled half-falling from his knees, *H-n* at his heart, — *Merlin and V.* 905
Half-oblivious (For I was *h-o* of my mask) — *Princess iii* 338
Half-open Thro' *h-o* lattices Coming in the scented breeze, — *Eleänore* 23
Half-opening balmier than *h-o* buds Of April, — *Tithonus* 59
Half-parted *h-p* from a weak and scolding hinge, — *The Brook* 84
Half-pennyworth *See* **Aäpoth.**
Half-pleased Look'd down, *h-p*, half-frighten'd, — *Amphion* 54
Half-possess'd Lilia sang: We thought her *h-p*, — *Princess iv* 585
Half-pot *See* **Haäf-pot.**
Half-right I thought her *h-r* talking of her wrongs; — *Princess v* 285
Half-sardonically I ask'd him *h-s*. — *Edwin Morris* 59
Half-science The sport *h-s*, fill me with a faith, — *Princess, Con.* 76
Half-self my other heart, And almost my *h-s*, — *Princess i* 56
Half-shadow And thought, 'For this *h-s* of a lie — *Gareth and L.* 323
Half-shrouded *h-s* over death In deathless marble. — *Princess v* 74
Half-shut With *h-s* eyes ever to seem Falling — *Lotos-Eaters, C. S.* 55
All unawares before his *h-s* eyes, — *Lover's Tale ii* 153
Half-shy And so it was—half-sly, *h-s*, — *Miller's D.* 133
Half-sick *h-s* at heart, return'd. — *Princess iv* 223
Half-sickening *H-s* of his pension'd afternoon, — *Aylmer's Field* 461
Half-sister Raw Haste, *h-s* to Delay. — *Love thou thy land* 96
Half-sly And so it was—*h-s*, half-shy, — *Miller's D.* 133
Half-spiritual Then fell from that *h-s* height — *To E. Fitzgerald* 19
Half-suffocated till I yell'd again *H-s*, — *Lucretius* 58
H-s in the hoary fell And many winter'd fleece — *Merlin and V.* 840
Half-swallow'd sea-foam sway'd a boat, *H-s* in it, — *Holy Grail* 803
Half-tarnish'd *H-t* and half-bright, — *Gareth and L.* 1118
Half-thinking *h-t* that her lips, Who had devised — *Lancelot and E.* 1287
Half-turn'd fixt On a heart *h-t* to stone. — *Maud I vi* 78
Half-unconscious I saw with *h-u* eye — *The Letters* 15
Half-uncut 'She left the novel *h-u* — *Talking Oak* 117
Half-unwillingly *h-u* Loving his lusty youthhood — *Gareth and L.* 579
Half-views nor take *H-v* of men and things. — *Will Water.* 52
Halfway *h* down the shadow of the grave, — *To the Queen ii* 6
h-w down rare sails, white as white clouds, — *Lover's Tale i* 4
Half-whisper'd drawing nigh *H-w* in his ear, — *Œnone* 186
Half-within Seem'd *h-w* and half-without, — *Miller's D.* 7
Half-without Seem'd half-within and *h-w*, — " 7
Half-world yonder morning on the blind *h-w*; — *Princess vii* 352
Half-wrench'd *H-w* a golden wing; but now— — *Holy Grail* 733
Half-wroth *H-w* he had not ended, but all glad, — *Balin and Balan* 427
Half-yolk hast broken shell, Art yet *h-y*, — " 569
Haling six tall men *h* a seventh along, — *Gareth and L.* 811
Hall (surname) (*See also* **Everard, Everard Hall**) 'Nay, nay,' said *H*, 'Why take the style — *The Epic* 34
HERE ended *H*, and our last light, — *M. d'Arthur, Ep.* 1
Hall (*See also* '**All, Banquet-hall, Council-hall, Sea-hall**) the throne In the midst of the *h*; — *The Mermaid* 22
Round the *h* where I sate, — " 26
Gods Ranged in the *h*'s of Peleus — *Œnone* 81
'No voice,' she shriek'd in that lone *h*, — *Palace of Art* 258
There stands a spectre in your *h*: — *L. C. V. de Vere* 42
You pine among your *h*'s and towers: — " 58
Walking about the gardens and the *h*'s — *M. d'Arthur* 20
how The races went, and who would rent the *h*: — *Audley Court* 31
Far-folded mists, and gleaming *h*'s of morn. — *Tithonus* 10
Dreary gleams about the moorland flying over Locksley *H*; — *Locksley Hall* 4

Hand (part of body) (*continued*)   To Thor and Odin lifted a *h*:   *The Victim* 8

He bore but little game in *h*;	„	42
The King bent low, with *h* on brow,	„	53
and nearer than *h's* and feet.	*High. Pantheism* 12	
I hold you here, root and all, in my *h*,	*Flow. in cran. wall.* 3	
Brandishing in her *h* a dart	*Boädicea* 71	
beat with rapid unanimous *h*,	„	79
Fine little *h's*, fine little feet—	*Window, Letter* 3	
Two little *h's* that meet, (repeat)	*Window, The Answer* 1, 4	
And loving *h's* must part—	„	6
Or reach a *h* thro' time to catch	*In Mem.* i 7	
A hollow form with empty *h's*.'	„ iii 12	
waiting for a *h*, A *h* that can be clasp'd	„ vii 4	
And letters unto trembling *h's*;	„ x 7	
And *h's* so often clasp'd in mine,	„ 19	
where warm *h's* have prest and closed,	„ xiii 7	
Should strike a sudden *h* in mine,	„ xiv 11	
Come then, pure *h's*, and bear the head	„ xviii 9	
Her *h's* are quicker unto good:	„ xxxiii 10	
wrought With human *h's* the creeds of creeds	„ xxxvi 10	
But thou and I have shaken *h's*,	„ xl 29	
I stretch lame *h's* of faith, and grope,	„ lv 17	
And reaps the labour of his *h's*,	„ lxiv 26	
And winds their curls about his *h*:	„ lxvi 12	
He reach'd the glory of a *h*,	„ lxix 17	
A *h* that points, and palled shapes	„ lxx 7	
When the dark *h* struck down thro' time,	„ lxxii 19	
Whate'er thy *h's* are set to do	„ lxxv 19	
Reach out dead *h's* to comfort me.	„ lxxx 16	
Would reach us out the shining *h*,	*In Mem.* lxxxv 43	
How much of act at human *h's*	„ lxxxv 38	
all within was noise Of songs, and clapping *h's*,	„ lxxxvii 19	
Behold their brides in other *h's*;	„ xc 14	
The larger heart, the kindlier *h*;	„ cvi 30	
the child would twine A trustful *h*,	„ cix 19	
A higher *h* must make her mild,	„ cxiv 17	
I take the pressure of thine *h*.	„ cxix 12	
And out of darkness came the *h's*	„ cxxiv 23	
Sweet human *h* and lips and eye;	„ cxxix 6	
With him to whom her *h* I gave.	„ *Con.* 70	
in their *h* Is Nature like an open book;	„ 131	
Pickpockets, each *h* lusting for all that is not its own;	*Maud* I i 22	
or are moved by an unseen *h* at a game	„ iv 26	
Ready in heart and ready in *h*,	„ v 9	
she touch'd my *h* with a smile so sweet,	„ vi 12	
I saw the treasured splendour, her *h*,	„ 84	
She waved to me with her *h*.	„ ix 8	
Ah God, for a man with heart, head, *h*,	„ x 60	
I kiss'd her slender *h*,	„ xii 13	
Sunn'd itself on his breast and his *h's*.	„ xiii 13	
if a *h*, as white As ocean-foam in the moon,	„ xiv 17	
To labour and the mattock-harden'd *h*,	„ xviii 34	
And given false death her *h*,	„ 68	
It is this guilty *h*!—	„ II i 4	
I sorrow For the *h*, the lips, the eyes,	„ iv 27	
And mightier of his *h's* with every blow,	*Com. of Arthur* 110	
But sought to rule for his own self and *h*,	„ 219	
h's Of loyal vassals toiling for their liege.	„ 281	
holy Dubric spread his *h's* and spake,	„ 471	
I could climb and lay my *h* upon it,	*Gareth and L.* 50	
But ever when he reach'd a *h*	„ 52	
And drops of water fell from either *h*;	„ 220	
Toward the sunrise, each with harp in *h*,	„ 261	
Merlin's *h*, the Mage at Arthur's court,	„ 306	
With thine own *h* thou slewest my dear lord,	„ 352	
In either *h* he bore What dazzled all,	„ 386	
ye know we stay'd their *h's* From war	„ 421	
Accursed, who strikes nor lets the *h* be seen !'	„ 435	
Gareth leaning both *h's* heavily Down	„ 439	
a nostril large and fine, and *h's* Large, fair and fine!—	„ 465	
Lying or sitting round him, idle *h's*, Charm'd;	„ 512	
and bow Lowly, to kiss his *h*,	„ 549	
So with a kindly *h* on Gareth's arm	„ 578	
And told him of a cavern hard at *h*,	„ 1189	
h hath fashion'd on the rock The war of Time	„ 1197	

Hand (part of body) (*continued*)   when he found the grass within his *h's* He laugh'd ;   *Gareth and L.* 1225

Lancelot !—thine the *h* That threw me ?	„	1241
O Lancelot, Lancelot'—and she clapt her *h's*—	„	1290
waving to him White *h's*, and courtesy ;	„	1377
Lady Lyonors wrung her *h's* and wept,	„	1395
with her own white *h's* Array'd and deck'd her,	*Marr. of Geraint* 16	
and all flyers from the *h* Of Justice,	„	36
watch his mightful *h* striking great blows	„	95
instinctive *h* Caught at the hilt,	„	209
White from the mason's *h*, (repeat)	„	244, 408
Came forward with the helmet yet in *h*	„	285
Or it may be the labour of his *h's*,	„	341
Frown and we smile, the lords of our own *h's* ;	„	354
And fondling all her *h* in his he said,	„	509
On either shining shoulder laid a *h*,	„	518
and *h* in *h* they moved Down to the meadow	„	536
There came a clapping as of phantom *h's*.	„	566
To seek a second favour at his *h's*.	„	626
and in her *h* A suit of bright apparel,	„	677
Came one with this and laid it in my *h*,	„	699
Help'd by the mother's careful *h* and eye,	„	738
Her by both *h's* he caught, and sweetly said,	„	778
our fair Queen, No *h* but hers, should make	„	788
For by the *h's* of Dubric, the high saint,	„	838
Far liefer by his dear *h* had I die,	*Geraint and E.* 68	
creatures gently born But into bad *h's* fall'n.	„	192
in his *h* Bare victual for the mowers;	„	201
In the mid-warmth of welcome and graspt *h*,	„	280
Geraint Waving an angry. *h* as who should say	„	444
But lift a shining *h* against the sun,	„	473
Nor let her true *h* falter, nor blue eye Moisten,	„	512
after all was done that *h* could do, She rested,	„	517
chafing his pale *h's*, and calling to him.	„	582
chafing his faint *h's*, and calling to him;	„	585
Take my salute,' unknightly with flat *h*,	„	717
reach'd a *h*, and on his foot She set her own and climb'd;	„	759
Put *h* to *h* beneath her husband's heart,	„	767
wrought too long with delegated *h's*,	„	893
set up a stronger race With hearts and *h's*,	„	941
my *h* Was gauntleted, half slew him;	*Balin and Balan* 56	
Lancelot with his *h* among the flowers	„	259
Saint who stands with lily in *h* In yonder shrine.	„	261
' And passing gentle ' caught his *h* away	„	371
Then *h* at ear, and hearkening from what side	„	415
white *h* whose ring'd caress Had wander'd	„	512
The hearts of all this Order in mine *h*—	*Merlin and V.* 56	
damsel bidden rise arose And stood with folded *h's*	„	69
Courteous—amends for gauntness—takes her *h*—	„	104
how *h* lingers in *h*! Let go at last !—	„	106
her left *h* Droop from his mighty shoulder,	„	242
And make a pretty cup of both my *h's*	„	275
And Merlin lock'd his *h* in hers (repeat)	„	290, 470
charm Of woven paces and of waving *h's*, (repeat)	„	330, 968
Merlin loosed his *h* from hers and said,	„	356
It lives dispersedly in many *h's*,	„	457
The wrist is parted from the *h* that waved,	„	551
ringing with their serpent *h's*,	„	578
her *h* half-clench'd Went faltering sideways	„	849
clapt her *h's* Together with a wailing shriek,	„	866
some one put this diamond in her *h*,	*Lancelot and E.* 212	
Half-envious of the flattering *h*,	„	349
So kiss'd her, and Sir Lancelot his own *h*,	„	389
she smote her *h*: wellnigh she swoon'd:	„	625
it will be sweet to have it From your own *h*;	„	694
slightly kiss'd the *h* to which he gave,	„	702
with mine own *h* give his diamond to him,	„	760
His battle-writhen arms and mighty *h's*	„	812
And laid the diamond in his open *h*.	„	827
yet he glanced not up, nor waved his *h*,	„	986
Then gave a languid *h* to each, and lay,	„	1032
lay the letter in my *h* A little ere I die, and close the *h* Upon it.	„	1113
Her father laid the letter in her *h*, And closed the *h* upon it, and she died.	„	1134

Happiness   Spirit of *h* And perfect rest   *Supp. Confessions* 50
all the warmth, the peace, the *h*,   *Enoch Arden* 761
Would shatter all the *h* of the hearth.   „ 770
woman counts her due, Love, children, *h*?'   *Princess iii* 245
What *h* to reign a lonely king,   *Com. of Arthur* 82
From his great hoard of *h* distill'd   *Lover's Tale i* 714
a life More living to some happier *h*,   „ 762
One bloom of youth, health, beauty, *h*,   *Sisters (E. and E.)* 120
tho' the *h* of each in each Were not enough,   „ 220
Household *h*, gracious children,   *Vastness* 24
I am happier in your *h* Than in mine own.   *The Ring* 90
Happt (wrapped)   an' *h* wersens oop as we mowt.   *Owd Roä* 112
Happy   (*See also* '**Appy, Thrice-happy**)   Christians
with *h* countenances—   *Supp. Confessions* 20
that *h* morn When angels spake to men aloud,   „ 24
Thrice *h* state again to be The trustful infant   „ 40
and the *h* blossoming shore?   *Sea-Fairies* 8
Who can light on as *h* a shore All the world o'er,   „ 40
O *h* thou that liest low,   *Oriana* 84
Oh! what a *h* life were mine   *The Merman* 37
O BRIDESMAID, ere the *h* knot was tied,   *Bridesmaid* 1
A *h* bridesmaid makes a *h* bride.'   „ 4
'O *h* bridesmaid, make a *h* bride.' (repeat)   „ 8, 14
'Waiting to strive a *h* strife,   *Two Voices* 130
from a *h* place God's glory smote him on the face.'   „ 224
Have I not found a *h* earth?   *Miller's D.* 25
She wish'd me *h*, but she thought   „ 139
Rest in a *h* place and quiet seats   *Œnone* 131
O *h* tears, and how unlike to these!   O *h* Heaven, how
   canst thou see my face?   O *h* earth, how canst thou
   bear my weight?   „ 235
Pass by the *h* souls, that love to live: „ 240
Lest their shrill *h* laughter come to me   „ 258
h stars above them seem to brighten as they pass;   *May Queen* 34
many a worthier than I, would make him *h* yet.   „ *Con.* 46
h fair with orchard-lawns And bowery hollows   *M. d'Arthur* 262
sweeter than the dream Dream'd by a *h* man,   *Gardener's D.* 72
shook his song together as he near'd His *h* home,   „ 92
Ah, *h* shade—and still went wavering down,   „ 132
A thought would fill my eyes with *h* dew;   „ 197
Made me most *h*, faltering,   „ 235
Might have been *h*: but what lot is pure?   *Walk. to the Mail* 97
do not think yourself alone Of all men *h*.   *Edwin Morris* 78
may rest Some *h* future day.   *Talking Oak* 252
Live *h*; tend thy flowers; be tended by My
   blessing!   *Love and Duty* 87
H days Roll onward, leading up the golden year.   *Golden Year* 40
'Fly, *h h* sails, and bear the Press; Fly *h*
   with the mission of the Cross;   „ 66
Old writers push'd the *h* season back,—   *Ulysses* 63
It may be we shall touch the *H* Isles,   *Tithonus* 70
Of *h* men that have the power to die,   *Locksley Hall* 43
Is it well to wish thee *h*?—   „ 97
Overlive it—lower yet—be *h*!   „ 159
mellow moons and *h* skies,   *Day-Dm., Sleep. P.* 2
Clothes and reclothes the *h* plains,   „ *Depart.* 8
The *h* princess follow'd him.   „ 17
'O eyes long laid in *h* sleep!'   'O *h* sleep, that
   lightly fled!'   'O *h* kiss, that woke thy sleep!'   *L'Envoi* 42
when Adam first Embraced his Eve in *h* hour,   *Amphion* 18
Such *h* intonation,   *Will Water.* 189
With twisted quirks and *h* hits,   *The Voyage* 49
O hundred shores of *h* climes,   *Sir L. and Q. G.* 38
The *h* winds upon her play'd,   *Move eastward* 1
Move eastward, *h* earth, and leave Yon orange
   sunset   „ 4
O, *h* planet, eastward go;   „ 12
And round again to *h* night.   *Enoch Arden* 81
seven *h* years, Seven *h* years of health and com-
   petence,   „ 151
Forward she started with a *h* cry,   „ 416
We might be still as *h* as God grants   „ 502
'he is *h*, he is singing Hosanna in the highest: „ 505
Whereof the *h* people strowing cried   „ 686
In those far-off seven *h* years were born;

Happy (*continued*)   And know that she is *h*.'   *Enoch Arden* 719
sweet forget-me-nots That grow for *h* lovers.   *The Brook* 173
'Too *h*, fresh and fair, Too fresh and fair   „ 217
And you are *h*: let her parents be.'   *Aylmer's Field* 366
sown With *h* faces and with holiday.   *Princess, Pro.* 56
and read My sickness down to *h* dreams?   „ *ii* 253
In looking on the *h* Autumn-fields,   „ *iv* 42
And *h* warriors, and immortal names,   „ *vi* 90
but at the *h* word 'he lives' My father stoop'd,   „ 128
And at the *h* lovers heart in heart—   „ *vii* 108
Fill'd thro' and thro' with Love, a *h* sleep.   „ 172
And find him; by the *h* threshold, he,   „ 200
H he With such a mother!   „ 327
turning saw The *h* valleys, half in light,   *Con.* 41
the *h* crowd, The sport half-science,   „ 75
peacemaker fly To *h* havens under all the sky,   *Ode Inter. Exhib.* 35
Break, *h* land, into earlier flowers!   *W. to Alexandra* 10
The sea-kings' daughter as *h* as fair,   „ 26
But marry me out of hand: we two shall be *h* still.'   *Grandmother* 52
Never jealous—not he: we had many a *h* year;   „ 71
And *h* has been my life; but I would not live it again.   „ 98
But distant colour, *h* hamlet,   *The Daisy* 27
Many and many a *h* year.   *To F. D. Maurice* 48
'The King is *h* In child and wife;   *The Victim* 25
But the Priest was *h*, His victim won: „ 61
And the Priest was *h*,   „ 73
A *h* lover who has come To look on her that loves   *In Mem. viii* 1
The murmur of a *h* Pan: „ *xxiii* 1
Rise, *h* morn, rise, holy morn,   „ *xxx* 29
Her early Heaven, her *h* views;   „ *xxxiii* 6
How fares it with the *h* dead?   „ *xliv* 1
And grasps the skirts of *h* chance,   „ *lxiv* 6
There flutters up a *h* thought,   „ *lxv* 7
sun by sun the *h* days Descend below the golden hills   „ *lxxxiv* 27
A guest, or *h* sister, sung,   „ *lxxxix* 26
Ring, *h* bells, across the snow: „ *cvi* 9
h birds, that change their sky To build and brood;   „ *cxv* 15
For days of *h* commune dead;   „ *cxvi* 14
While thou, dear spirit, *h* star,   „ *cxxvii* 18
O *h* hour, and happier hours Await them.   „ *Con.* 65
O *h* hour, behold the bride With him to whom   „ 69
We wish them store of *h* days.   „ 84
To spangle all the *h* shores By which they rest,   „ 120
In the *h* morning of life and of May,   *Maud I v* 7
Go not, *h* day, (repeat)   „ *xvii* 1, 3
Pass the *h* news, Blush it thro' the West;   „ 15
And you fair stars that crown a *h* day   „ *xviii* 30
It seems that I am *h*, that to me A livelier emerald   „ 50
Beat, *h* stars, timing with things below,   „ 81
The delight of *h* laughter,   „ *II iv* 29
Would the *h* spirit descend,   „ 81
'And gladly given again this *h* morn.   *Marr. of Geraint* 691
But o'er her meek eyes came a *h* mist   *Geraint and E.* 769
Tho' pale, yet *h*, ask'd her not a word,   „ 880
till be crown'd A *h* life with a fair death,   „ 968
'I hold them *h*, so they died for love: *Balin and Balan* 581
What said the *h* sire?   *Merlin and V.* 710
And as it chanced they are *h*, being pure.'   „ 745
But she was *h* enough and shook it off,   *Lancelot and E.* 784
Came on her brother with a *h* face   „ 791
So that would make you *h*: furthermore,   „ 959
As *h* as when we dwelt among the woods,   „ 1036
make me *h*, making them An armlet for the roundest arm   „ 1182
'In *h* time behold our pilot-star!   *Pelleas and E.* 63
'O *h* world,' thought Pelleas, 'all, meseems, Are *h*;   „ 136
Be *h* in thy fair Queen as I in mine.'   *Last Tournament* 204
Crown'd warrant had we for the crowning sin
   That made us *h*:   „ 577
the child of one I honour'd, *h*, dead before thy shame?   *Guinevere* 423
h, fair with orchard-lawns And bowery hollows   *Pass. of Arthur* 430
And he was *h* that he saw it not;   *Lover's Tale i* 192
O day which did enwomb that *h* hour,   „ 485
It was so *h* an hour, so sweet a place,   „ 558
The loved, the lover, the *h* Lionel.   „ 654
Why was I To cross between their *h* star and them?   „ 730

Happy (continued)   Him who loving made The *h* and the unhappy love, — *Lover's Tale i* 753

I was *h* when I was with him, — *First Quarrel* 11

Often I seem'd unhappy, and often as *h* too, — „ 31

He means me I'm sure to be *h* with Willy, — *Rizpah* 76

Here's to your *h* union with my child! — *Sister's (E. and E.)* 68

We left her, *h* each in each, and then, — „ 219

Pour'd in on all those *h* naked isles— — *Columbus* 174

Live, and be *h* in thyself, and serve This mortal race — *De Prof., Two G.* 15

So—your *h* suit was blasted— — *Locksley H., Sixty* 5

H children in a sunbeam sitting on the ribs of wreck. — „ 14

Poet of the *h* Tityrus piping underneath — *To Virgil* 13

the child Is *h*—ev'n in leaving *her*! — *Prin. Beatrice* 12

We planted both together, *h* in our marriage morn? — *Happy* 14

I am *h, h*. Kiss me. — „ 107

Sing like a bird and be *h*, — *Parnassus* 14

'Here again, here, here, here, *h* year! — *The Throstle* 13

Him, *h* to be chosen Judge of Gods, — *Death of Œnone* 16

while we dwelt Together in this valley—*h* then—Too — „ 30

h had I died within thine arms, — „ 30

The morning light of *h* marriage broke — „ 102

O *h* he, and fit to live, On whom a *h* home has power — *The Wanderer* 9

Hapt   *H* in this isle, since Up the East — *Batt. of Brunanburh* 116

Harangue   Lady Psyche will *h* The fresh arrivals — *Princess ii* 95

Harass'd   the thought Haunted and *h* him, — *Enoch Arden* 720

Vext with lawyers and *h* with debt: — *Maud I xix* 722

h by the frights Of my first crew, — *Columbus* 67

Harbour   and clambering on a mast In *h*, — *Enoch Arden* 106

Ev'n in that *h* whence he sail'd before. — „ 666

to seek If any golden *h* be for men — *Pref. Son. 19th Cent.* 13

Desolate offing, sailorless *h's*, — *Vastness* 14

Harbourage   But wilt thou yield this damsel *h*?' — *Gareth and L.* 834

But an this lord will yield us *h*, Well.' — „ 844

Where can I get me *h* for the night? — *Marr. of Geraint* 281

H? truth, good truth, I know not, — „ 290

'O friend, I seek a *h* for the night.' — „ 299

Harbour-bar   Shot o'er the seething *h-b*, — *Sailor Boy* 2

Harbour-buoy   *h-b*, Sole star of phosphorescence — *Audley Court* 86

Harbour-mouth   Yet waft me from the *h-m*, — *You ask me, why, etc.* 25

capes and islands, Many a *h-m*, — *The Captain* 22

painted buoy That tosses at the *h-m*; — *The Voyage* 2

Hard   It seem'd so *h* at first, mother, to leave the blessed sun, And now it seems as *h* to stay, — *May Queen, Con.* 9

The Gods are *h* to reconcile. — *Lotos-Eaters, C. S.* 81

'Tis *h* to settle order once again. — „ 82

How *h* he breathes! over the snow I heard — *D. of the O. Year* 37

A saying, *h* to shape in act; — *Love thou thy land* 49

But vague in vapour, *h* to mark; — „ 62

The blast was *h* and harder. — *The Goose* 50

For how *h* it seem'd to me, When eyes, — *Love and Duty* 35

If the sense is *h* To alien ears, — „ 51

H is my doom and thine: — „ 54

'Your riddle is *h* to read.' — *Lady Clare* 76

H coils of cordage, swarthy fishing-nets, — *Enoch Arden* 17

was it *h* to take The helpless life — „ 556

'Too *h* to bear! why did they take me — „ 781

O *h*, when love and duty clash! — *Princess ii* 293

all those *h* things That Sheba came to ask of Solomon.' — „ 345

'O *h* task,' he cried; 'No fighting shadows here! — „ iii 124

No rock so *h* but that a little wave — „ 154

they will take her, they will make her *h*, — „ v 90

Thus the *h* old King: I took my leave, — „ 467

no tenderness—Too *h*, too cruel: — „ 516

These men are *h* upon us as of old, — „ vi 198

the woman is so *h* Upon the woman. — „ 222

And call her *h* and cold which seem'd a truth: — „ vii 98

you think I am *h* and cold; — *Grandmother* 17

be jealous and *h* and unkind.' — „ 54

I found, tho' crush'd to *h* and dry, — *The Daisy* 97

O little bard, is your lot so *h*, — *Spiteful Letter* 5

H, h, h is it, only not to tumble, — *Hendecasyllabics* 13

'It will be *h*,' they say, 'to find — *In Mem. xx* 7

The words were *h* to understand. — „ lxix 20

'Tis *h* for thee to fathom this; — „ lxxv 90

Hard (continued)   The *h* heir strides about their lands, — *In Mem. xc* 15

how *h* to frame In matter-moulded forms — „ xcv 45

'A *h* one, or a hundred, so I go. — *Gareth and L.* 149

h by here is one will overthrow And slay thee: — „ 896

'Old damsel, old and *h*, Old, — „ 1105

blew A *h* and deadly note upon the horn. — „ 1111

Then not to give you warning, that seems *h*; — *Geraint and E.* 422

How *h* you look and how denyingly! — *Merlin and V.* 338

May this *h* earth cleave to the Nadir hell — „ 349

(Brother, the King was *h* upon his knights) — *Holy Grail* 299

house of ours Where all the brethren are so *h*, — „ 618

H was the frost in the field, — *First Quarrel* 39

I felt that my heart was *h*, — „ 76

So I knew my heart was *h*, — „ 78

But say nothing *h* of my boy, — *Rizpah* 22

you are just as *h* as a stone. — „ 80

they tell me that the world is *h*, and harsh of mind, — *The Flight* 101

But can it be so *h*, so harsh, — *Forlorn* 26

come a witness soon *H* to be confuted, — *Bandit's Death* 28

He gript it so *h* by the throat that the boy — *Supp. Confessions* 116

That God would move And strike the *h, h* rock, — *Two Voices* 118

'*H* task, to pluck resolve,' I cried, — *Dora* 18

he and I Had once *h* words, and parted, — „ 58

and thought *H* things of Dora. — „ 153

for you Will make him *h*, — *Talking Oak* 171

H wood I am, and wrinkled rind, — *Godiva* 37

bade him cry, with sound of trumpet, all The *h* condition; — *Sir Galahad* 6

The *h* brands shiver on the steel, — *Sea Dreams* 8

Small were his gains, and *h* his work; — „ 160

last Gript my hand *h*, and with God-bless-you went. — „ 162

I found a *h* friend in his loose accounts, A loose one in the *h* grip of his hand, — *Third of Feb.* 42

For us, we will not spare the tyrant one *h* word. — *Maud I xiii* 3

That a calamity *h* to be borne? — „ II ii 34

a *h* mechanic ghost That never came from on high — *Marr. of Geraint* 763

Yniol with that *h* message went; — *Lancelot and E.* 460

The *h* earth shake, and a low thunder of arms. — „ 1251

As *h* and still as is the face that men — *Pelleas and E.* 498

over *h* and soft, striking the sod From out the soft, the spark from off the *h*, — „ 512

h his eyes; harder his heart Seem'd; — „ 610

Modred thought, 'The time is *h* at hand.' — *Pass. of Arthur* 166

H on that helm which many a heathen sword — „ 447

clomb The last *h* footstep of that iron crag; — *Sisters (E. and E.)* 240

They found her beating the *h* Protestant doors. — *Sir J. Oldcastle* 20

I find *h* rocks, *h* life, *h* cheer, or none, — „ 66

Vailing a sudden eyelid with his *h* 'Dim Saesneg' — „ 107

Priests Who fear the king's *h* common-sense — *Columbus* 196

harlot draws his clerks Into the suburb—their *h* celibacy, — *Batt. of Brunanburh* 44

These *h* memorials of our truth to Spain — *To Marq. of Dufferin* 45

H was his hand-play, — *Demeter and P.* 107

Beneath a *h* Arabian moon And alien stars. — *Owd Roä* 58

Seem'd nobler than their *h* Eternities. — *The Ring* 292

An' 'e cotch'd howd *h* o' my hairm, — „ 435

she loves her own *h* self, Her firm will, — *St. Telemachus* 40

She clung to me with such a *h* embrace, — *Charity* 10

H Romans brawling of their monstrous games; —

And the *h* blue eyes have it still, —

Hard (heard)   I *h* his Riverence say, — *Tomorrow* 69

tould yer Honour whativer I *h* an' seen, — „ 97

Hard-breathing   cast himself Down on a bench, *h-b*. — *Pelleas and E.* 592

Harden   watch The sandy footprint *h* into stone.' — *Princess iii* 271

Harden'd   (*See also* **Mattock-harden'd, War-harden'd**) only wrapt in *h* skins That fit him like his own; — *Gareth and L.* 1093

His arms are old, he trusts the *h* skin— — „ 1139

But lash'd in vain against the *h* skin, — „ 1143

Harder   The blast was hard and *h*. — *The Goose* 50

H the times were, and the hands of power — *Aylmer's Field* 452

the according hearts of men Seem'd *h* too; — „ 454

Enid answer'd, *h* to be moved Than hardest tyrants — *Geraint and E.* 694

but felt his eyes *H* and drier than a fountain bed — *Pelleas and E.* 507

hard his eyes; *h* his heart Seem'd; — „ 512

But a lie which is part a truth is a *h* matter to fight. — *Grandmother* 32

Tho' carved in *h* stone— — *Epilogue* 59

Hardest   Than *h* tyrants in their day of power, — *Geraint and E.* 695

Hate (verb) (*continued*) he thought—'What, if she *h*
me now?　　　　　　　　　　　　*Last Tournament* 496
thou stridest thro' his halls Who *h's* thee,　　　　" 518
Because he *h's* thee even more than fears;　　　" 533
I should *h* thee more than love.'　　　　　　　" 600
With what a hate the people and the King Must *h* me,' *Guinevere* 158
but who *h's* thee, he that brought The heathen *Pass. of Arthur* 151
I *h* her—an' I *h* you!'　　　　　　　　*First Quarrel* 71
Yet loves and *h's* with mortal hates and loves, *Tiresias* 23
I *h* the black negation of the bier,　　　*Ancient Sage* 204
morning brings the day I *h* and fear;　　　*The Flight* 2
'Kill your enemy, for you *h* him,'　*Locksley H., Sixty* 94
I *h* the rancour of their castes and creeds, *Akbar's Dream* 65
Hated (adj. and part.) this world's curse,—beloved
but *h*—　　　　　　　　　　　　　*Love and Duty* 47
(for Arthur's Knights Were *h* strangers in the hall) *Balin and Balan* 352
with *h* warmth of apprehensiveness.　*Lover's Tale i* 632
Her presence, *h* both of Gods and men.　*Œnone* 229
Thro' madness, *h* by the wise,　　　　*Love and Duty* 7
Hated (verb) (*See also* **Haäted**) I *h* him with the hate of
hell,　　　　　　　　　　　　　　*The Sisters* 22
And death and life she *h* equally,　*Palace of Art* 265
But they *h* his oppression,　　　　　*The Captain* 9
Then they look'd at him they *h*,　　　　　　" 37
H him with a momentary hate.　*Aylmer's Field* 211
Men *h* learned women:　　　　　　*Princess iv* 466
They *h* banter, wish'd for something real, *Con.* 18
many *h* Uther for the sake Of Gorlöis. *Com. of Arthur* 220
And *h* this fair world and all therein,　　　" 344
They *h* her, who took no thought of them, *Geraint and E.* 639
She *h* all the knights, and heard in thought *Merlin and V.* 150
and she *h* all who pledged.　*Lancelot and E.* 744
wail'd and wept, and *h* mine own self, *Holy Grail* 609
'You said that you *h* me, Ellen, *First Quarrel* 79
And we *h* the beautiful Isle,　*V. of Maeldune* 21
And we *h* the Flowering Isle, as we *h* the isle that
was mute,　　　　　　　　　　　　　" 52
Till we *h* the Bounteous Isle　　　　　　" 92
Troubled the track of the host that we *h*, *Batt. of Brunanburh* 40
he learnt that I *h* the ring I wore, *The Wreck* 57
tho' I think I *h* him less,　*Bandit's Death* 17
Hateful *H* is the dark-blue sky, *Lotos-Eaters, C. S.* 39
Your falsehood and yourself are *h* to us: *Princess iv* 545
Horrible, *h*, monstrous, not to be told: *Maud III vi* 41
And this forgetfulness was *h* to her. *Marr. of Geraint* 55
Last night I wasted *h* hours *Fatima* 8
Long, ere the *h* crow shall tread The corners *Will Water.* 235
and when the beauteous *h* isle Return'd upon him, *Enoch Arden* 617
all the *h* fires Of torment,　*Demeter and P.* 151
This house with all its *h* needs no cleaner than the beast, *Happy* 32
in the heart of this most ancient realm A *h* voice be
utter'd,　　　　　　　　　　*Prog. of Spring* 103
Hater What room is left for a *h*? *Spiteful Letter* 14
Love your enemy, bless your *h's*, *Locksley H., Sixty* 85
Hating *H* to wander out on earth, *Supp. Confessions* 57
h to hark The humming of the drowsy pulpit-drone *To J. M. K.* 9
went *H* his own lean heart and miserable. *Aylmer's Field* 526
all-shamed, *h* the life He gave me, *Geraint and E.* 852
Hatred *h* of her weakness, blent with shame. *Princess vii* 30
Shall fears and jealous *h's* flame again? *W. to Marie Alex.* 41
No more of *h* than in Heaven itself, *Balin and Balan* 151
My soul, I felt my *h* for my Mark Quicken *Last Tournament* 519
Love pledge *H* in her bitter draughts, *Lover's Tale i* 776
National *h's* of whole generations, *Vastness* 25
Dark no more with human *h's* *Faith* 8
Hattics (attics) An' Hetty wur weak i' the *h*, *Village Wife* 101
Hauberk shield of Balan prick'd The *h* to the flesh; *Balin and Balan* 560
Casques were crack'd and *h's* hack'd *The Tourney* 7
Haughtier She paused, and added with a *h* smile *Princess iii* 225
Haughtiest Lady Blanche alone Of faded form and *h*
lineaments,　　　　　　　　　　　" ii 448
Imperious, and of *h* lineaments. *Marr. of Geraint* 190
Haughty She, flashing forth a *h* smile, began: *D. of F. Women* 129
My *h* jousts, and took a paramour; *Geraint and E.* 832
but she, *h*, ev'n to him, Lancelot; *Last Tournament* 562

Haughty (*continued*) *H* war-workers who Harried the
Welshman,　　　　　　　*Batt. of Brunanburh* 121
Haunch On his *h'es* rose the steed, *Princess v* 493
Haunt (s) The *h's* of memory echo not. *Two Voices* 369
A *h* of ancient Peace.　　　　*Palace of Art* 88
battenest by the greasy gleam In *h's* of hungry sinners, *Will Water.* 222
A *h* of brawling seamen once, *Enoch Arden* 697
I come from *h's* of coot and hern, *The Brook* 23
A frequent *h* of Edith, *Aylmer's Field* 148
And flood the *h's* of hern and crake; *In Mem. ci* 14
The feeble soul, a *h* of fears,　　　　" cx 3
cells of madness, *h's* of horror and fear, *Maud III vi* 2
in lonely *h's* Would scratch a ragged oval *Gareth and L.* 533
but for those large eyes, the *h's* of scorn, *Pelleas and E.* 75
there In *h's* of jungle-poison'd air *To Marq. of Dufferin* 31
Haunt (verb) A SPIRIT *h's* the year's last hours *A Spirit haunts* 1
than whatever Oread *h* The knolls of Ida, *Œnone* 74
Whose odours *h* my dreams; *Sir Galahad* 68
Will *h* the vacant cup: *Will Water.* 172
Like flies that *h* a wound, or deer, *Aylmer's Field* 571
Gods, who *h* The lucid interspace of world *Lucretius* 104
h About the moulder'd lodges of the Past *Princess iv* 62
They *h* the silence of the breast, *In Mem. xciv* 9
the filmy shapes That *h* the dusk, " xcv 11
Evil *h's* The birth, the bridal; " xcviii 13
'Look, He *h's* me—I cannot breathe— *Pelleas and E.* 597
all that *h's* the waste and wild Mourn, *Pass. of Arthur* 48
those three words would *h* him when a boy, *Far—far—away* 8
anchorite Would *h* the desolated fane, *St. Telemachus* 13
Haunted (adj. and part.) (*See also* **Bandit-haunted, Martin-haunted,
Satan-haunted**) From old well-heads of *h* rills, *Eleänore* 16
Heard by the watcher in a *h* house, *Guinevere* 73
Was *h* with a jolly ghost, that shook The curtains, *Walk. to the Mail* 36
and a hazelwood, By autumn nutters *h*, *Enoch Arden* 7
And *h* by the wrangling daw; *In Mem. c* 12
h by the starry head Of her whose gentle will *Maud I xviii* 22
Haunted (verb) It *h* me, the morning long, *Miller's D.* 69
the thought *H* and harass'd him, *Enoch Arden* 720
still *H* us like her ghost; *Sisters (E. and E.)* 247
ghastlier face than ever has *h* a grave by night, *The Wreck* 57
she that had *h* his pathway still, *Dead Prophet* 61
Haunting (adj. and part.) (*See also* **Roof-haunting**)
phantoms moved Before him *h* him, or he himself
Moved *h* people, *Enoch Arden* 603
a tender Christian hope, *H* a holy text, *Sea Dreams* 42
My *h* sense of hollow shows: *Princess vii* 349
ever *h* round the palm A lusty youth, *Gareth and L.* 47
but shatter'd nerve, Yet *h* Julian, *Lover's Tale iv* 106
This *h* whisper makes me faint, *In Mem. lxxxi* 7
Brute that is walking and *h* us yet, *The Dawn* 23
Haunting (s) No ghostly *h's* like his Highness. *Princess ii* 411
And out of *h's* of my spoken love, " vii 109
Havelock (Gen. Sir Henry) *H* baffled, or beaten, or
butcher'd　　　　　　*Def. of Lucknow* 91
Outram and *H* breaking their way through " 96
H's glorious Highlanders answer with conquering cheers, " 99
Blessing the wholesome white faces of *H's* good fusileers, " 101
Saved by the valour of *H*, " 104
Haven From many an inland town and *h* large, *Œnone* 117
From *h's* hid in fairy bowers, *The Voyage* 54
ships go on To their *h* under the hill; *Break, break, etc.* 10
northward of the narrow port Open'd a larger *h*: *Enoch Arden* 103
Till silent in her oriental *h*. " 537
Where either *h* open'd on the deeps, " 671
To rush abroad all round the little *h*, " 867
That all the houses in the *h* rang. " 911
while I breathed in sight of *h*, he, Poor fellow, *The Brook* 157
peacemaker fly To happy *h's* under all the sky, *Ode Inter. Exhib.* 35
Had built the King his *h's*, *Merlin and V.* 168
You from the *h* Under the sea-cliff, *Merlin and the G.* 2
O young Mariner, Down to the *h*, " 124
Havock-Havoc wrought Such waste and *havock* *Aylmer's Field* 640
Made *havock* among those tender cells, *Lucretius* 22
So fierce a gale made *havoc* here of late *Holy Grail* 729
Haw Nor hoary knoll of ash and *h* *In Mem. c* 9

Hawa-i-ee (one of the Sandwich Islands) and freed the
    people Of *H*!   *Kapiolani* 7
    be mingled with either on *H*.   „ 18
    and drove the demon from *H*.   „ 33

Hawk (s) (*See also* **Sparrow-hawk, War-hawk**) My gay
    young *h*, my Rosalind :   *Rosalind* 34
    The wild *h* stood with the down on his beak,   *Poet's Song* 11
    Lies the *h*'s cast, the mole has made his run,   *Aylmer's Field* 849
    And pastime both of *h* and hound,   *Marr. of Geraint* 711
    Fluttering the *h*'s of this crown-lusting line—   *Sir J. Oldcastle* 57

Hawk (verb) As when a hawker *h*'s his wares.   *The Blackbird* 20
    they ride away—to *h* For waterfowl.   *Merlin and V.* 107

Hawkard (awkward) An' a haxin' ma *h* questions,   *Spinster's S's.* 90

Hawker As when a *h* hawks his wares.   *The Blackbird* 20
    This broad-brimm'd *h* of holy things,   *Maud I x* 41

Hawk-eye Your *h-e*'s are keen and bright,   *Rosalind* 25
    and a cheek of apple-blossom, *H-e*'s ;   *Gareth and L.* 590

Hawking (*See also* **A-hawking**) Now *h* at Geology and
    schism ;   *The Epic* 16

Hawk-mad Speak, if ye be not like the rest, *h-m*,   *Marr. of Geraint* 280

Hawl (awl) poonch'd my 'and wi' the *h*,   *North. Cobbler* 78

Hawmin' (lounging) an' *h* about i' the laänes,   „ 24

Hawthorn (adj.) bury me, my mother, just beneath
    the *h* shade,   *May Queen, N. Y's. E.* 29
    that new life that gems the *h* line;   *Prog. of Spring* 36

Hawthorn (s) Beneath the *h* on the green   *May Queen, N. Y's. E.* 10

Hax'd (asked) An' they hallus paäd what I *h*,   *Village Wife* 115
    When summun 'ed *h* fur a son,   *Owd Roä* 95

Haxin' (asking) An' a *h* ma hawkard questions,   *Spinster's S's.* 90

Hay (*See also* **Haäy**) And rarely smells the new-mown *h*,   *The Owl i* 9
    Stuff his ribs with mouldy *h*.   *Vision of Sin* 66

Haze (*See also* **Sea-haze**) Spread the light *h* along the
    river-shores,   *Gardener's D.* 264
    Purple gauzes, golden *h*'s,   *Vision of Sin* 31
    thro' the dripping *h* The dead weight   *Enoch Arden* 677
    ' This world was once a fluid *h* of light,   *Princess ii* 116
    And is it that the *h* of grief   *In Mem. xxiv* 9
    The silvery *h* of summer drawn;   „ *xcv* 4
    mingled with the *h* And made it thicker;   *Com. of Arthur* 435
    his dream was changed, the *h* Descended,   „ 441
    Far in the moonlit *h* among the hills,   *Pass. of Arthur* 42
    find or feel a way Thro' this blind *h*,   „ 76
    heated *h* to magnify The charm of Edith—   *Sisters (E. and E.)* 129

Haze-hidden to a height, the peak *H-h*,   *Com. of Arthur* 430

Hazel (adj.) about the may-pole and in the *h*
    copse,   *May Queen, N. Y's. E.* 11
    deeply dawning in the dark of *h* eyes—   *Locksley Hall* 28
    but as lissome as a *h* wand;   *The Brook* 70
    I slide by *h* covers;   „ 171

Hazel (s) The thick-set *h* dies;   *Will Water.* 234
    great and small, Went nutting to the *h*'s.   *Enoch Arden* 64
    Down thro' the whitening *h*'s made a plunge   „ 379
    In native *h*'s tassel-hung.'   *In Mem. cii* 12

Hazel-tree on the bridge beneath the *h-t* ?   *May Queen* 14

Hazelwood a *h*, By autumn nutters haunted,   *Enoch Arden* 7

Hazy Across a *h* glimmer of the west,   *Gardener's D.* 219
    Far over the blue tarns and *h* seas,   *Gareth and L.* 499

Head (Edward) *See* **Edward Head**

Head (s) (*See also* **Boat-head, Cradle-head, Death's-head,
    'Ead, Fountain-head, Hatties, Heäd, Lady's-head,
    Lance-head, Mast-head, Shock-head, Well-heads**)
    Madonna-wise on either side her *h*;   *Isabel* 6
    Revered Isabel, the crown and *h*,   „ 10
    Thou wilt never raise thine *h*   *A Dirge* 19
    from *h* to tail Came out clear plates   *Two Voices* 11
    Dominion in the *h* and breast.'   „ 21
    ' The simple senses crown'd his *h* :   „ 277
    Beat time to nothing in my *h*   *Miller's D.* 67
    Upon my lap he laid his *h* :   *The Sisters* 17
    I curl'd and comb'd his comely *h*,   „ 31
    The *h*'s and crowns of kings;   *Palace of Art* 152
    You put strange memories in my *h*.   *L. C. V. de Vere* 26
    With your feet above my *h*   *May Queen, N. Y's. E.* 32
    on his kindly heart and on his silver *h* !   *Con.* 15
    one that from a casement leans his *h*,   *D. of F. Women* 246

Head (s) (*continued*) Her murder'd father's *h*,   *D. of F. Women* 267
    Sleep full of rest from *h* to feet;   *To J. S.* 75
    Where faction seldom gathers *h*,   *You ask me, why, etc.,* 13
    And heap their ashes on the *h* ;   *Love thou thy land* 70
    As *h* and heels upon the floor They flounder'd   *The Goose* 37
    laid his *h* upon her lap,   *M. d'Arthur* 208
    And May with me from *h* to heel.   *Gardener's D.* 81
    She bow'd down her *h*, Remembering the day   *Dora* 105
    Jack, turn the horses' *h*'s and home again.'   *Walk. to the Mail* 46
    my stiff spine can hold my weary *h*,   *St. S. Stylites* 43
    She sank her *h* upon her arm   *Talking Oak* 207
    a sunny fleck, From *h* to ancle fine,   „ 224
    Dropt dews upon her golden *h*,   „ 227
    shook her *h*, And shower'd the rippled ringlets to her knee;   *Godiva* 46
    wide-mouth'd *h*'s upon the spout Had cunning eyes   „ 56
    Were shrivell'd into darkness in his *h*,   „ 70
    This proverb flashes thro' his *h*,   *Day-Dm., Arrival* 15
    You shake your *h*. A random string   *L'Envoi* 1
    All-graceful *h*, so richly curl'd,   „ 38
    power to turn This wheel within my *h*,   *Will Water.* 84
    Live long, ere from thy topmost *h*   „ 233
    Live long, nor feel in *h* or chest   „ 237
    And lay your hand upon my *h*,   *Lady Clare* 55
    Dropt her *h* in the maiden's hand,   „ 63
    To trample round my fallen *h*,   *Come not, when, etc.* 3
    Then raised her *h* with lips comprest,   *The Letters* 19
    I saw within my *h* A gray and gap-tooth'd man   *Vision of Sin* 59
    In her left a human *h*.   „ 138
    Hollow hearts and empty *h*'s !   „ 174
    Then calling down a blessing on his *h*   *Enoch Arden* 327
    over Enoch's early-silvering *h*   „ 622
    He, shaking his gray *h* pathetically,   „ 714
    Held his *h* high, and cared for no man,   „ 848
    ' His *h* is low, and no man cares for him.   „ 850
    As when she laid her *h* beside my own.   „ 881
    those that held their *h*'s above the crowd,   *The Brook* 10
    and holds her *h* to other stars,   „ 195
    A tonsured *h* in middle age forlorn,   „ 200
    Whose eyes from under a pyramidal *h*   *Aylmer's Field* 20
    For heart, I think, help'd *h* :   „ 475
    made Still paler the pale *h* of him,   „ 623
    fork'd Of the near storm, and aiming at his *h*,   „ 727
    The *h*'s of chiefs and princes fall so fast,   „ 763
    his own *h* Began to droop, to fall;   „ 834
    ask'd; but not a word; she shook her *h*.   *Sea Dreams* 116
    Like her, he shook his *h*.   „ 148
    one that arm'd Her own fair *h*,   *Princess, Pro.* 33
    moved the multitude, a thousand *h*'s :   „ 57
    above their *h*'s I saw The feudal warrior lady-clad;   „ 118
    ' Where,' Ask'd Walter, patting Lilia's *h*   „ 125
    o'er his *h* Uranian Venus hung,   „ *i* 243
    such eyes were in her *h*, And so much grace and power,   „ *ii* 37
    some said their *h*'s were less: Some men's were small;   „ 147
    ' everywhere Two *h*'s in council,   „ 173
    axelike edge unturnable, our *H*, The Princess.'   „ 203
    O by the bright *h* of my little niece,   „ 276
    The *H* of all the golden-shafted firm,   „ 405
    the Muses' *h*'s were touch'd Above the darkness   „ *iii* 21
    says the Princess should have been the *H*,   „ 34
    The *h* and heart of all our fair she-world,   „ 163
    He ceasing, came a message from the *H*.   „ 168
    Among her maidens, higher by the *h*,   „ 179
    spoke and turn'd her sumptuous *h* with eyes,   „ *iv* 152
    ' The *H*, the *H*, the Princess, O the *H* !'   „ 176
    underneath The *h* of Holofernes peep'd and saw.   „ 227
    And partly that you were my civil *h*,   „ 306
    seal'd dispatches which the *H* Took half-amazed,   „ 379
    You have our son: touch not a hair of his *h* :   „ 407
    after-beauty makes Such *h* from act to act,   „ 452
    gems and gemlike eyes, And gold and golden *h*'s ;   „ 481
    Not peace she look'd, the *H* :   „ 490
    ' What fear ye, brawlers ? am not I your *H* ?   „ 498
    all one rag, disprinced from *h* to heel.   „ *v* 30
    Like some sweet sculpture draped from *h* to foot,   „ 57
    And at her *h* a follower of the camp,   „ 60

L

Head (verb) Heaven *h's* the count of crimes — *D. of F. Women* 201
  to *h* These rhymings with your name, — *Pro. to Gen. Hamley* 19
Head-blow Some old *h-b* not heeded in his youth — *Gareth and L.* 714
Headed (*See also* **Bare-headed, Brazen-headed, Clear-**
  headed, Glassy-headed, Hoar-headed, Hoary-
  headed, Lean-headed, Light-headed, Many-
  headed, Seven-headed, Sharp-headed, White-
  headed) arrows of his thoughts were *h* And
  wing'd with flame, — *The Poet* 11
  In shining draperies, *h* like a star, — *Princess* ii 109
Head-foremost To drop *h-f* in the jaws — *In Mem. xxxiv* 15
  Not plunge *h* from the mountain there, — *Lover's Tale* iv 41
  all ablaze too plunging in the lake *H-f*— — *The Ring* 252
Head-heavy thus he fell *H-h*, — *Last Tournament* 468
Head-hunter *H-h's* and boats of Dahomey — *The Dawn* 5
Headland Flames, on the windy *h* flare ! — *W. to Alexandra* 16
  He saw them—*h* after *h* flame — *Guinevere* 243
Headless Fly twanging *h* arrows at the hearts, — *Princess* ii 402
Headlong and so hurl'd him *h* o'er the bridge — *Gareth and L.* 1153
  The damsel's *h* error thro' the wood— — ,, 1215
  whose inroad nowhere scales Their *h* passes, — *Montenegro* 5
Headstone About the moss'd *h* : — *Claribel* 12
  And at my *h* whisper low, — *My life is full* 24
Head-waiter O PLUMP *h-w* at The Cock, — *Will Water*. 1
  H-w, honour'd by the guest Half-mused, — ,, 73
  And one became *h-w*. — ,, 144
  H-w of the chop-house here, — ,, 209
Heagle (eagle) An' the *H* 'as hed two heäds — *Owd Roä* 25
Heal (*See also* **All-heal**) I will *h* me of my grievous
  wound. — *M. d'Arthur* 264
  I can *h* him. Power goes forth from me. — *St. S. Stylites* 145
  h me with your pardon ere you go.' — *Princess* iii 65
  To spill his blood and *h* the land : — *The Victim* 44
  a harm no preacher can *h* ; — *Maud* I iv 22
  h the world of all their wickedness ! — *Holy Grail* 94
  and harm'd where she would *h* ; — *Guinevere* 355
  treat their loathsome hurts and *h* mine own ; — ,, 686
  I will *h* me of my grievous wound.' — *Pass. of Arthur* 432
  the hand that would help me, would *h* me— — *The Wreck* 56
  love which once was mine, Help, *h* me. — *Death of Œnone* 46
  ' He, whom thou wouldst not *h* !' — ,, 101
Heal'd To touch my body and be *h*, — *St. S. Stylites* 79
  They say that they are *h*. — ,, 146
  He passes and is *h* and cannot die '— — *Gareth and L.* 503
  he was *h* at once, By faith, of all his ills. — *Holy Grail* 55
  and all the world be *h*.' — ,, 128
  that *h* Thy hurt and heart with unguent and
  caress— — *Last Tournament* 594
  the wound that *would* not be *h*, — *Def. of Lucknow* 84
  he *h* me with sorrow for evermore. — *The Wreck* 58
  blind or deaf, and then Suddenly *h*, — *Ancient Sage* 176
Healing before we came, This craft of *h*. — *Princess* iii 320
  A light of *h*, glanced about the couch, — ,, vii 59
  while Geraint lay *h* of his hurt, — *Geraint and E.* 931
  Lancelot might have seen, The Holy Cup of *h* ; — *Holy Grail* 655
  And after *h* of his grievous wound — *Pass. of Arthur* 450
Health In glowing *h*, with boundless wealth, — *L. C. V. de Vere* 61
  breathing *h* and peace upon her breast : — *Audley Court* 68
  Seven happy years of *h* and competence, — *Enoch Arden* 82
  Now seaward-bound for *h* they gain'd a coast, — *Sea Dreams* 16
  Huge women blowzed with *h*, — *Princess* iv 279
  I that have wasted here *h*, wealth, and time, — ,, 352
  poor men wealth, Than sick men *h*— — ,, 460
  As drinking *h* to bride and groom — *In Mem., Con.* 83
  double *h*, The crowning cup, the three-times-three, — ,, 103
  One bloom of youth, *h*, beauty, — *Sisters (E. and E.)* 120
  Had set the blossom of her *h* again, — ,, 151
  redder than rosiest *h* or than utterest shame, — *V. of Maeldune* 65
  life without sun, without *h*, without hope, — *Despair* 7
  an' I been Dhrinkin' yer *h* — *Tomorrow* 12
  give me a thrifle to dhrink yer *h* in potheen. — ,, 98
  I Had been abroad for my poor *h* — *The Ring* 101
  would flower into full *h* Among our heath — ,, 317
  ' Muriel' *h* Had weaken'd, — ,, 356
  Youth and *H*, and birth and wealth, — *By an Evolution*. 8

Healthful And all about a *h* people stept — *Gareth and L.* 315
  Her countenance with quick and *h* blood— — *Lover's Tale* i 97
Healthfuller Make their neighbourhood *h*, — *On Jub. Q. Victoria* 32
Healthly A *h* frame, a quiet mind.' — *Two Voices* 99
  So *h*, sound, and clear and whole, — *Miller's D.* 15
Heap (s) (*See also* **Heäp**) wealth no more shall rest in
  mounded *h's*, — *Golden Year* 32
  By *h's* of gourds, and skins of wine, — *Vision of Sin* 13
  And *h's* of living gold that daily grow, — *Aylmer's Field* 655
  Each hurling down a *h* of things that rang — *Geraint and E.* 594
  crown'd With my slain self the *h's* of whom I
  slew— — *Balin and Balan* 178
  I saw him, after, stand High on a *h* of slain, — *Lancelot and E.* 307
  horses stumbling as they trode On *h's* of ruin, — *Holy Grail* 717
Heäp (s) *H's* an' *h's* o' boooks, I ha' see'd 'em, — *Village Wife* 71
  An I heärd greät *h's* o' the snaw — *Owd Roä* 41
Heap (verb) And *h* their ashes on the head ; — *Love thou thy land* 70
  coals of fire you *h* upon my head — *Romney's R.* 141
Heaped Of *h* hills that mound the sea, — *Ode to Memory* 98
Heap'd-Heapt *Heap'd* over with a mound of
  grass, — *Lotos-Eaters, C. S.* 67
  Pain *heap'd* ten-hundred-fold to this, — *St. S. Stylites* 23
  heap'd Their firewood, and the winds from off
  the plain — *Spec. of Iliad* 6
  heap'd the whole inherited sin On that huge scapegoat — *Maud* I xiii 41
  Heap'd on her terms of disgrace, — II i 14
  heap'd The pieces of his armour in one place, — *Geraint and E.* 373
  Tho' *heapt* in mounds and ridges all the sea — *Holy Grail* 798
Heaping Still *h* on the fear of ill — *Two Voices* 107
Heapt *See* **Heap'd**
Hear (*See also* **'Ear**) at a burial to *h* The creaking
  cords which wound — *Supp. Confessions* 35
  you may *h* him sob and sigh — *A spirit haunts* 5
  you cannot *h* From the groves within — *Poet's Mind* 19
  never would *h* it : your ears are so dull ; — ,, 35
  I cry aloud : none *h* my cries, — *Oriana* 73
  I *h* the roaring of the sea, — ,, 98
  To *h* the murmur of the strife, — *Margaret* 23
  Come down, come down, and *h* me speak : — ,, 56
  I *h* what I would *h* from thee ; — *Eleänore* 141
  Kate will not *h* of lovers' sighs. — *Kate* 20
  H a song that echoes cheerly — *L. of Shalott* i 30
  H's little of the false or just.' — *Two Voices* 117
  he *h's* His country's war-song thrill his ears : — ,, 152
  ' He will not *h* the north-wind rave, — ,, 259
  ' He seems to *h* a Heavenly Friend, — ,, 295
  Or from the bridge I lean'd to *h* — *Miller's D.* 49
  H me, O Earth, *h* me, O Hills, — *Œnone* 36
  H me, for I will speak, — ,, 39
  unheard *H* all, and see thy Paris judge of Gods.' — ,, 90
  heard me not, Or hearing would not *h* me, — ,, 171
  mother, *h* me yet before I die. (repeat) — *Œnone* 207, 220, 230, 245, 256
  as I *h* Dead sounds at night come from — *Œnone* 248
  H me, O Earth. I will not die alone, — ,, 257
  You seem'd to *h* them climb and fall — *Palace of Art* 70
  king to *h* Of wisdom and of law. — ,, 111
  my soul to *h* her echo'd song Throb thro' — ,, 175
  that *h's* all night The plunging seas — ,, 250
  h the dully sound Of human footsteps — ,, 275
  h's the low Moan of an unknown sea ; — ,, 279
  word That scarce is fit for you to *h* ; — *L. C. V. de Vere* 38
  I shall *h* you when you pass, — *May Queen, N. Y's. E.* 31
  I *h* the bleating of the lamb. — ,, Con. 2
  I did not *h* the dog howl, mother, — ,, 21
  To *h* each other's whisper'd speech ; — *Lotos-Eaters, C. S.* 8
  To *h* the dewy echoes calling From cave to cave — ,, 94
  to *h* and see the far-off sparkling brine, — ,, 98
  Only to *h* were sweet, — ,, 99
  I *h* thee not at all, or hoarse — *The Blackbird* 19
  Ev'n now we *h* with inward strife — *Love thou thy land* 53
  like a horse That *h's* the corn-bin open, — *The Epic* 45
  h The windy clanging of the minster clock ; — *Gardener's D.* 37
  ' *H* how the bushes echo ! — ,, 98
  Yet for the pleasure that I took to *h*, — ,, 228
  blackbird on the pippin hung To *h* him, — *Audley Court* 39

Hear (continued)	
I do not h the bells upon my cap,	Edwin Morris 56
my ears could h Her lightest breath;	" 64
About the windings of the marge to h	" 94
nor heard of her, nor cared to h. (repeat)	" 138
I scarce can h the people hum	St. S. Stylites 38
(And h me with thine ears,)	Talking Oak 82
And h me swear a solemn oath,	" 281
that paused Among her stars to h us;	Love and Duty 74
h These measured words, my work of yestermorn.	Golden Year 20
tremulous eyes that fill with tears To h me?	Tithonus 27
and could h the lips that kiss'd Whispering	" 60
on the moorland did we h the copses ring,	Locksley Hall 35
Thou shalt h the 'Never, never,'	" 83
'O wake for ever, love,' she h's,	Day-Dm., Depart. 11
That lets thee neither h nor see:	" L'Envoi 52
But what is that I h? a sound	Amphion 73
I h a noise of hymns:	Sir Galahad 28
I h a voice but none are there;	" 30
Let him h my song.	The Captain 4
H's him lovingly converse,	L. of Burleigh 26
Before you h my marriage vow.'	The Letters 8
Annie seem'd to h Her own death-scaffold	Enoch Arden 174
H's and not h's, and lets it overflow.	" 209
Nor ever h a kindly voice,	" 582
'Dead,' clamour'd the good woman, 'h him	" 840
left Their own gray tower, or plain-faced tabernacle To h him;	Aylmer's Field 619
you do but h the tide.	Sea Dreams 84
But will you h my dream,	" 203
He, dying lately, left her, as I h,	Princess i 78
To h my father's clamour at our backs	" 105
my very ears were hot To h them:	" 135
h each other speak for noise Of clocks	" 215
'We scarcely thought in our own hall to h	" ii 53
there was one to h And help them?	" 267
H my conditions: promise (otherwise You perish)	" 295
then the Doctors! O to h The Doctors!	" 421
O h me, pardon me.	" iii 31
O hark, O h! how thin and clear,	" iv 7
Blow, let us h the purple glens replying:	" 11
h A trumpet in the distance pealing news	" 80
tell her what they were, and she to h:	" 323
we shall h of it From Lady Psyche.'	" 328
For thus I h; and known at last (my work)	" 347
we h You hold the woman is the better man;	" 409
h me, for I bear, Tho' man, yet human,	" 424
I stood and seem'd to h As in a poplar grove	" v 12
they hate to h me like a wind Wailing	" 98
when I h you prate I almost think	" 152
'Amazed am I to h Your Highness:	" vi 324
h's his burial talk'd of by his friends,	" vii 152
h The tides of Music's golden sea	Ode on Well. 251
Eh!—but he wouldn't h me—	Grandmother 8
Harry and Charlie, I h them too—	" 81
And only h the magpie gossip	To F. D. Maurice 19
That it makes one weary to h.'	The Islet 29
I h the roll of the ages.	Spiteful Letter 8
cannot h The sullen Lethe rolling doom	Lit. Squabbles 10
Speak to Him thou for He h's,	High. Pantheism 11
And the ear of man cannot h,	" 17
But if we could see and h, this Vision—	" 18
Did they h me, would they listen,	Boädicea 8
H Icenian, Catieuchlanian, h (repeat)	Boädicea 10, 34, 47
h it, Spirit of Cassivëlaún! 'H it, Gods! the Gods have heard it,	" 20
Till the victim h within and yearn to hurry	" 58
I h the noise about thy keel;	In Mem. x 1
I h the bell struck in the night:	" 2
And h the ritual of the dead.	" xviii 12
The traveller h's me now and then,	" xxi 5
To h her weeping by his grave?	" xxxi 4
turn mine ears and h The moanings of the homeless sea,	" xxxv 8
And h thy laurel whisper sweet	" xxxvii 7
I h it now, and o'er and o'er,	" lvii 13
I h a wizard music roll,	" lxx 14

Hear (continued)	
I h the sentence that he speaks;	In Mem. lxxx 10
We cannot h each other speak.	" lxxxii 16
hung to h The rapt oration flowing free	" lxxxvii 31
heart and ear were fed To h him,	" lxxxix 23
I h a wind Of memory murmuring the past.	" xcii 7
h The wish too strong for words to name;	" xciii 13
And h the household jar within.	" xciv 16
That h's the latest linnet trill,	" c 10
And sing the songs he loved to h.	" cvii 24
I h a chirp of birds;	" cxix 5
To h the tidings of my friend,	" cxxvi 3
And h at times a sentinel Who moves about	" 9
h A deeper voice across the storm,	" cxxvii 3
I h there where the waters run;	" cxxx 2
A voice as unto him that h's,	" cxxxi 6
Still! I will h you no more,	Maud I v 23
I h the dead at midday moan,	" vi 70
Did I h it half in a doze Long since,	" vii 1
Strange, that I h two men,	" 13
I wish I could h again The chivalrous battle-song	" x 53
The larkspur listens, 'I h, I h;'	" xxii 65
My heart would h her and beat,	" 69
My dust would h her and beat,	" 71
Do I h her sing as of old,	" II iv 44
to h a dead man chatter Is enough to drive one mad.	" v 19
I h A cry from out the dawning of my life,	Com. of Arthur 332
A mother weeping, and I h her say,	" 334
said the King, 'and h ye such a cry?	" 337
To h him speak before he left his life.	" 362
H the child's story.'	Gareth and L. 39
nor sees, nor h's, nor speaks, nor knows.	" 81
H yet once more the story of the child.	" 109
H me—this morn I stood in Arthur's hall,	" 855
Than h thee so missay me and revile.	" 945
H a parable of the knave.	" 1008
stay'd Waiting to h the hounds:	Marr. of Geraint 163
There is good chance that we shall h the hounds:	" 182
They would not h me speak:	" 421
Hath ask'd again, and ever loved to h;	" 436
thro' the crash of the near cataract h's	Geraint and E. 172
soldiers wont to h His voice in battle,	" 174
And h him breathing low and equally.	" 372
What thing soever ye may h, or see,	" 415
I h the violent threats you do not h,	" 420
And ears to h you even in his dreams.'	" 429
Feeding like horses when you h them feed;	" 606
Submit, and h the judgment of the King.' 'He h's the judgment of the King of kings,'	" 799
Damsel and lover? h not what I h.	Balin and Balan 282
swan-mother, sitting, when she h's A strange knee rustle	" 353
Ye scarce can overpraise, will h and know.	Merlin and V. 92
By Heaven that h's I tell you the clean truth,	" 343
will ye h The legend as in guerdon for your rhyme?	" 553
And therefore h my words: go to the jousts:	Lancelot and E. 136
we h it said That men go down before your spear	" 148
as I h It is a fair large diamond,—	" 227
'H, but hold my name Hidden,	" 416
we shall h anon, Needs must we h.'	" 636
'we needs must h anon Of him,	" 756
till the ear Wearies to h it,	" 898
'Speak: that I live to h,' he said, 'is yours.'	" 928
I h of rumours flying thro' your court.	" 1190
'My lord liege Arthur, and all ye that h,	" 1290
To h the manner of thy fight and fall;	Pelleas and E. 347
'Nay, nor will: I see it and h.	Last Tournament 348
I, and Arthur and the angels h,	" 350
lock up my tongue From uttering freely what I freely h?	" 694
h the garnet-headed yaffingale Mock them:	" 700
And miss to h high talk of noble deeds	Guinevere 499
Thro' the thick night I h the trumpet	" 569
I h the steps of Modred in the west,	Pass. of Arthur 59
you may h The moaning of the woman and the child,	Lover's Tale i 519
I heard and trembled, yet I could but h;	" 570
and then I seem'd to h Its murmur, as the drowning seaman h's,	" 634

Hear (*continued*)   Paused in their course to *h* me,   *Lover's Tale* ii 14
I say the bird That will not *h* my call,   „   iv 160
Laud me not Before my time, but *h* me to the close.   „   243
h that cry of my boy that was dead,   *Rizpah* 45
you know that I couldn't but *h*;   „   48
and mercy, the Lord '—let me *h* it again ;   „   62
But I cannot *h* what you say   „   82
Nay—you can *h* it yourself—   „   85
yet she thinks She sees you when she *h*'s.   *Sisters* (*E. and E.*) 193
Not es I cares fur to *h* ony harm,   *Village Wife* 22
I *h*'s as soom o' thy booöks   „   70
you can *h* him—the murderous mole !   *Def. of Lucknow* 26
they came to *h* their preacher.   *Sir J. Oldcastle* 42
Do penance in his heart, God *h*'s him.'   „   143
I shall *h* his voice again—   *Columbus* 159
readier, if the King would *h*, to lead One last crusade   „   238
turn'd upon his heel to *h* My warning   *Tiresias* 72
I can *h* Too plainly what full tides of onset sap   „   90
h, and tho' I speak the truth Believe I speak it,   „   155
the waters—you *h* them call !   *Despair* 47
If thou would'st *h* the Nameless,   *Ancient Sage* 31
She *h*'s the lark within the songless egg,   „   76
And tho' these fathers will not *h*,   *The Flight* 67
and *h* the waters roar,   „   90
h the voices from the field.   *Locksley H., Sixty* 116
Shall I *h* in one dark room a wailing,   „   262
H's he now the Voice that wrong'd him ?   „   269
Moon of married hearts, *H* me, you !   *The Ring* 4
I *h* your Mother's voice in yours.   „   28
I *h* her yet—A sound of anger like a distant storm.   „   118
The storm, you *h* Far-off, is Muriel—   „   138
poor Muriel when you *h* What follows !   „   273
All the world will *h* a voice   *Forlorn* 27
I *h* a charm of song thro' all the land.   *Prog. of Spring* 47
and *h* their words On pathway'd plains ;   „   82
I *h* a death-bed Angel whisper ' Hope.'   *Romney's R.* 148
But I *h* no yelp of the beast,   *By an Evolution.* 19
H my cataract's Downward thunder   *To Master of B.* 15
h The clash of tides that meet in narrow seas.—   *Akbar's Dream* 57
but we *h* Music : our palace is awake,   „   199
H thy myriad laureates hail thee   „ *Hymn* 6

Heard   (*See also* '**Eärd, Far-heard, Half-heard, Hard, Heärd**)   voice of the bird Shall no more be *h*,   *All Things will Die* 25
Waking she *h* the night-fowl crow :   *Mariana* 26
We *h* the steeds to battle going,   *Oriana* 15
She saw me fight, she *h* me call,   „   32
Hast thou *h* the butterflies What they say   *Adeline* 28
Elsinore The war moan along the distant sea,   *Buonaparte* 10
I have *h* that, somewhere in the main,   *If I were loved* 7
She has *h* a whisper say,   *L. of Shalott* ii 3
They *h* her singing her last song,   „   iv 26
H a carol, mournful, holy,   „   28
And *h* her native breezes pass,   *Mariana in the S.* 43
' But *h*, by secret transport led,   *Two Voices* 214
And oft I *h* the tender dove In firry woodlands   *Miller's D.* 41
Sometimes I *h* you sing within ;   „   123
Then first I *h* the voice of her,   *Œnone* 107
Give it to Pallas !' but he *h* me not,   „   170
Indeed I *h* one bitter word That scarce is fit   *L. C. V. de Vere* 37
wild March-morning I *h* the angels call ;   *May Queen, Con.* 25
wild March-morning I *h* them call my soul.   „   28
who made His music *h* below ;   *D. of F. Women* 4
I *h* sounds of insult, shame, and wrong,   „   19
Sudden I *h* a voice that cried,   „   123
I *h* my name Sigh'd forth with life   „   153
h A noise of some one coming thro' the lawn,   „   177
We *h* the lion roaring from his den ;   „   222
I *h* Him, for He spake, and grief became   „   227
Once *h* at dead of night to greet Troy's wandering prince,   *D. of the O. Year* 38
She *h* the torrents meet.   *On a Mourner* 32
half-awake I *h* The parson taking wide and wider sweeps,   *Of old sat Freedom* 4
What is it thou hast seen ? or what hast *h* ?   *The Epic* 13
(repeat)   *M. d'Arthur* 68, 114

Heard (*continued*)   I *h* the ripple washing in the reeds,   *M. d'Arthur* 70
' I *h* the water lapping on the crag,   „   116
Speak out : what is it thou hast *h*, or seen ? '   „   150
He *h* the deep behind him, and a cry Before.   „   184
and indeed The clear church-bells ring   „ *Ep.* 30
Who had not *h* Of Rose, the Gardener's daughter ?   *Gardener's D.* 51
when I *h* her name My heart was like a prophet   „   62
Born out of everything I *h* and saw,   „   66
Nor *h* us come, nor from her tendance turn'd   „   144
all that night I *h* the watchman peal The sliding season :   „   182
all that night I *h* The heavy clocks knolling   „   208
when I *h* his deep ' I will,' Breathed,   *Walk. to the Mail* 47
left *his* wife behind ; for so I *h*.   „   67
I had *h* it was this bill that past,   *Edwin Morris* 109
h with beating heart The Sweet-Gale rustle   „   138
nor *h* of her, nor cared to hear.   *Talking Oak* 25
since I *h* him make reply Is many a weary hour ;   „   98
That oft hast *h* my vows,   *Golden Year* 75
I *h* them blast The steep slate-quarry,   *Tithonus* 62
Like that strange song I *h* Apollo sing,   *Locksley Hall* 110
When I *h* my days before me,   „   123
H the heavens fill with shouting,   *Day-Dm., Sleep B.* 17
She sleeps : her breathings are not *h*   *The Captain* 41
But they *h* the foeman's thunder Roaring   *Vision of Sin* 14
Then methought I *h* a mellow sound,   „   18
they that *h* it sigh'd, Panted hand-in-hand   „   219
At last I *h* a voice upon the slope Cry   *Enoch Arden* 201
Him running on thus hopefully she *h*,   „   205
she *h*, and not *h* him ;   „   582
h The myriad shriek of wheeling ocean-fowl,   „   615
He *h* the pealing of his parish bells ;   „   644
h them talking, his long-bounden tongue Was loosen'd,   „   766
Because things seen are mightier than things *h*,   „   864
As the woman *h*, Fast flow'd the current of her easy tears,   *The Brook* 221
' Have you not *h* ? ' said Katie,   *Aylmer's Field* 43
worse than had he *h* his priest Preach   „   187
H the good mother softly whisper ' Bless,   „   250
And neither loved nor liked the thing he *h*.   „   261
had Sir Aylmer *h*—Nay, but he must—   „   337
till he *h* the ponderous door Close,   *Sea Dreams* 56
thunder from within the cliffs *H* thro' the living roar.   „   136
I woke, I *h* the clash so clearly.   *Lucretius* 5
often when the woman *h* his foot Return   „   26
for thrice I *h* the rain Rushing ;   „   276
She *h* him raging, *h* him fall ;   *Princess* i 185
he *h* her speak ; She scared him ; life !   „   ii 211
' having seen And *h* the Lady Psyche.'   „   331
' Ah—Melissa—you ! You *h* us ?'   „   332
' O pardon me I *h*, I could not help it,   „   370
In each we sat, we *h* The grave Professor.   „   iv 173
like parting hopes I *h* them passing from me :   „   265
behind I *h* the puff'd pursuer ;   „   389
we *h* In the dead hush the papers that she held Rustle :   „   446
I *h* of, after seen The dwarfs of presage :   „   558
saw the lights and *h* The voices murmuring.   „   577
Thy voice is *h* thro' rolling drums,   „   v 7
we *h* The drowsy folds of our great ensign   „   71
She *h*, she moved, She moan'd,   „   265
prated peace, when first I *h* War-music,   „   375
h Of those that iron-cramp'd their women's feet ;   „   vi 19
Seeing I saw not, hearing not I *h* :   „   26
My father *h* and ran In on the lists,   „   39
they *h* A noise of songs they would not understand :   „   150
clamouring on, till Ida *h*, Look'd up,   „   230
' I've *h* that there is iron in the blood,   „   234
you had a heart—I *h* her say it—   „   vii 80
on her foot she hung A moment, and she *h*,   „   190
I *h* her turn the page :   „   335
I have *h* Of your strange doubts :   *Ode on Well.* 65
His captain's-ear has *h* them boom Bellowing victory,   *Third of Feb.* 1
My Lords, we *h* you speak :   *W. to Marie Alex.* 13
Elburz and all the Caucasus have *h* ;   *Sailor Boy* 6
He *h* a fierce mermaiden cry,   *Voice and the P.* 5
All night have I *h* the voice Rave   *Boädicea* 4
Mad and maddening all that *h* her

Heard (*continued*) I *h* 'im a roomlin' by, *Village Wife* 122
but I know that I *h* him say ' All very well— *In the Child. Hosp.* 21
Emmie had *h* him. Softly she call'd from her cot ,, 46
was a phantom cry that I *h* as I tost about, ,, 63
The Lord of the children had *h* her, ,, 72
I *h* his voice between The thunders *Columbus* 145
I *h* his voice, ' Be not cast down. ,, 157
a hundred who *h* it would rush on a thousand
lances *V. of Maeldune* 24
past to the Isle of Witches and *h* their musical cry— ,, 97
and we pray'd as we *h* him pray, ,, 125
oft we two have *h* St. Mary's chimes ! *To W. H. Brookfield* 3
cry of Æakidês Was *h* among the Trojans, *Achilles over the T.* 23
Two voices *h* on earth no more ; *To E. Fitzgerald* 41
Have *h* this footstep fall, *Tiresias* 27
I *h* a voice that said 'Henceforth be blind, ,, 48
who *h* And *h* not, when I spake of famine, ,, 59
are a song *H* in the future ; ,, 125
H from the roofs by night, ,, 140
My hands, when I *h* him coming would drop *The Wreck* 27
I knew not what, when I *h* that voice,— ,, 52
brute mother who never has *h* us groan ! *Despair* 98
That nightingale is *h* ! *Ancient Sage* 20
Powers, that rule Were never *h* or seen.' ,, 30
and *h* his passionate vow, *The Flight* 83
while I *h* the curlews call, *Locksley H., Sixty* 3
only *h* in silence from the silence of a tomb. ,, 74
Because you *h* the lines I read *Pro. to Gen. Hamley* 17
for he spoke and the people *h*, *Dead Prophet* 33
breathing in his sleep, *H* by the land. *Early Spring* 24
thy voice, a music *h* Thro' all the yells and
counter-yells *To Duke of Argyll* 7
And one drear sound I have not *h*, *To Marq. of Dufferin* 40
and *h* The murmurs of their temples chant-
ing me, *Demeter and P.* 71
I *h* one voice from all the three ' We know not, ,, 84
So he, the God of dreams, who *h* my cry, ,, 91
Voices of the day Are *h* across the Voices *The Ring* 40
I *h* the sober rook And carrion crow cry ' Mortgage.' ,, 173
I that *h*, and changed the prayer *Happy* 55
There ! I *h* Our cuckoo call. *To Mary Boyle* 5
My birds would sing, You *h* not. ,, 19
long ravine below, She *h* a wailing cry, *Death of Œnone* 20
shouted, and the shepherds *h* and came. ,, 56
she *h* The shriek of some lost life ,, 89
h an answer ' Wake Thou deedless dreamer, *St Telemachus* 20
And at his ear he *h* a whisper ' Rome ' ,, 26
on to reach Honorius, till he *h* them, ,, 77
I *h* a mocking laugh ' the new Korân ! ' *Akbar's Dream* 183
field without were seen or *h* Fires of Súttee, ,, 195
To have seen thee, and *h* thee, and known. *Bandit's Death* 4
They *h*, they bided their time. ,, 14
and *h* as we crouch'd below, The clatter of arms, ,, 23
when he *h* what an end was mine ? *Charity* 16
tho' faintly *h* Until the great Hereafter. *Death of the Duke of C.* 16
Heärd An' I *h* greät heäps o' the snaw *Owd Roä* 41
Hearer While thus he spoke, his *h's* wept ; *Aylmer's Field* 722
outran The *h* in its fiery course ; *In Mem. cix* 8
and all *h's* were amazed. *Gareth and L.* 655
humbly hopeful, rose Fixt on her *h's*, *Merlin and V.* 87
Hear'st Thou *h* the village hammer clink, *In Mem. cxxi* 15
' *H* thou this great voice that shakes the world, *Pass. of Arthur* 139
Hearing (*part.*) Or *h* would not hear me, *Œnone* 171
How sweet it were, *h* the downward stream, *Lotos-Eaters, C. S.* 54
H the holy organ rolling waves Of sound *D. of F. Women* 191
h his mischance, Came, for he knew the man *Enoch Arden* 120
That shook the heart of Edith *h* him. *Aylmer's Field* 63
Seeing I saw not, *h* not I heard : *Princess vi* 19
h her tumultuous adversaries *Boädicea* 78
This, Gareth *h* from a squire of Lot *Gareth and L.* 531
And Gareth *h* ever strenglier smote, ,, 1141
Not *h* any more his noble voice, *Marr. of Geraint* 98
(Who *h* her own name had stol'n away) ,, 507
red and pale Across the face of Enid *h* her ; ,, 524
crowd, *H* he had a difference with their priests, *Holy Grail* 674

Hearing (*part.*) (*continued*) And *h* ' harlot ' mutter'd
twice or thrice, *Merlin and V.* 843
Hearing (s) Our *h* is not *h*, *Voice and the P.* 35
And in the *h* of the wave. *In Mem. xix* 4
Yet in these ears, till *h* dies, ,, *lvii* 9
Within the *h* of cat or mouse, *Maud II v* 48
But since her mind was bent On *h*, *Pelleas and E.* 115
even into my inmost heart As to my outward *h* : *Lover's Tale i* 429
nor hope for a deathless *h* ! *Parnassus* 14
Hearsay blamed herself for telling *h* tales : *Merlin and V.* 951
Hearse Funeral *h's* rolling ! *Forlorn* 68
Heart (*See also* '**Art, Black-heart, Lion-heart, Woman's-
heart**) When will the *h* be aweary of beating ? *Nothing will Die* 6
The cloud fleets, The *h* beats, ,, 12
Every *h* this May morning in joyance is beating *All Things will Die* 6
The *h* will cease to beat ; ,, 12
cords which wound and eat Into my human *h*, *Supp. Confessions* 37
And loveth so his innocent *h*, ,, 52
What Devil had the *h* to scathe Flowers ,, 83
Albeit, my hope is gray, and cold At *h*, ,, 104
run short pains Thro' his warm *h* ; ,, 162
O spirit and *h* made desolate ! ,, 189
Thro' my very *h* it thrilleth *Lilian* 22
Upon the blanched tablets of her *h* ; *Isabel* 17
Right to the *h* and brain, ,, 22
cords that bind and strain The *h* until it bleeds, *Clear-headed Friend* 5
my bounding *h* entanglest In a golden-netted smile ; *Madeline* 40
My very *h* faints and my whole soul grieves *A spirit haunts* 16
In the *h* of the garden the merry bird chants. *Poet's Mind* 22
Out of the live-green *h* of the dells *Sea-Fairies* 12
My *h* is wasted with my woe, *Oriana* 1
And pierced thy *h*, my love, my bride, ,, 42
Thy *h*, my life, my love, my bride, ,, 44
O breaking *h* that will not break, ,, 64
Up from my *h* unto my eyes, ,, 78
Within thy *h* my arrow lies, ,, 80
Die in their *h's* for the love of me. *The Mermaid* 30
Take the *h* from out my breast. *Adeline* 8
Do beating *h's* of salient springs Keep measure ,, 26
violet woos To his *h* the silver dews ? ,, 32
Encircles all the *h*, and feedeth The senses *Margaret* 16
The burning brain from the true *h*, ,, 39
And the *h's* of purple hills, *Eleänore* 17
My *h* a charmed slumber keeps, ,, 128
Her *h* like a throbbing star. *Kate* 9
And either lived in either's *h* and speech. *Sonnet to —* 14
My hope and *h* is with thee— *To J. M. K.* 1
But spurr'd at *h* with fieriest energy ,, 7
He thought to quell the stubborn *h's* of oak, *Buonaparte* 1
The *h* of Poland hath not ceased To quiver, *Poland* 3
To find my *h* so near the beauteous breast *The form, the form* 7
' O cruel *h*,' she changed her tone, *Mariana in the S.* 69
But my full *h*, that work'd below, *Two Voices* 44
Nor sold his *h* to idle moans, ,, 221
A deeper tale my *h* divines. ,, 269
His *h* forebodes a mystery : ,, 290
My frozen *h* began to beat, ,, 422
From out my sullen *h* a power Broke, ,, 443
And full at *h* of trembling hope, *Miller's D.* 110
Approaching, press'd you *h* to *h*. ,, 160
And her *h* would beat against me, ,, 177
Do make a garland for the *h* : ,, 198
Round my true *h* thine arms entwine ,, 216
still affection of the *h* Became an outward breathing type, ,, 225
My *h*, pierced thro' with fierce delight, *Fatima* 34
My eyes are full of tears, my *h* of love, My *h* is breaking,
and my eyes are dim, *Œnone* 31
My *h* may wander from its deeper woe. ,, 44
all my *h* Went forth to embrace him coming ,, 62
full-flowing river of speech Came down upon my *h*. ,, 69
Thou weighest heavy on the *h* within, ,, 243
Devil, large in *h* and brain, *To ——, With Pal. of Art* 5
hollow shades enclosing *h's* of flame, *Palace of Art* 241
You thought to break a country *h* For pastime, *L. C. V. de Vere* 3
A *h* that doats on truer charms. ,, 14

Heart (*continued*)   You changed a wholesome *h* to gall. *L. C. V. de Vere* 44
Kind *h's* are more than coronets,   ,,   55
Pray Heaven for a human *h*,   ,,   71
They say his *h* is breaking, mother—   *May Queen* 22
O blessings on his kindly *h*   ,, *Con.* 15
music in his ears his beating *h* did make.   *Lotos-Eaters* 36
To lend our *h's* and spirits wholly   ,, *C. S.* 63
Sore task to *h's* worn out by many wars   ,,   86
tho' my *h*, Brimful of those wild tales,   *D. of F. Women* 11
melting the mighty *h's* Of captains and of kings.   ,,   175
the *h* Faints, faded by its heat.   ,,   287
His memory long will live alone In all our *h's*,   *To J. S.* 50
Sleep sweetly, tender *h*, in peace :   ,,   69
And on thy *h* a finger lays,   *On a Mourner* 11
Teach that sick *h* the stronger choice,   ,,   18
wild *h's* the feeble wings That every sophister   *Love thou thy land* 11
Not yet the wise of *h* would cease To hold his hope   81
She felt her *h* grow prouder :   *The Goose* 22
The summer pilot of an empty *h*   *Gardener's D.* 16
So blunt in memory, so old at *h*,   ,,   53
My *h* was like a prophet to my *h*,   ,,   63
we coursed about The subject most at *h*,   223
A woman's *h*, the *h* of her I loved ;   ,,   230
doors that bar The secret bridal chambers of the *h*,   249
h on one wild leap Hung tranced from all pulsation,   259
Make thine *h* ready with thine eyes :   ,,   273
I beheld her ere she knew my *h*,   ,,   276
I have set my *h* upon a match.   *Dora* 14
when his *h* is glad Of the full harvest,   ,,   68
gone to him, But her *h* fail'd her ;   ,,   78
' With all my *h*,' Said Francis.   *Audley Court* 8
And all my *h* turn'd from her,   ,,   54
Dipt by itself, and we were glad at *h*.   ,,   89
I would have hid her needle in my *h*,   *Edwin Morris* 62
heard with beating *h* The Sweet-Gale rustle   ,,   109
Until he plagiarised a *h*,   *Talking Oak* 19
This girl, for whom your *h* is sick,   ,,   71
with throbbing *h* I came To rest beneath thy boughs ?   ,, 155
Streaming eyes and breaking *h's* ?   *Love and Duty* 2
Better the narrow brain, the stony *h*,   ,,   15
Whose foresight preaches peace, my *h* so slow To feel it !   ,, 34
And to the want, that hollow'd all the *h*,   ,,   61
seem to lift a burthen from thy *h* And leave thee freër,   ,, 96
For always roaming with a hungry *h*   *Ulysses* 12
and opposed Free *h's*, free foreheads—   ,,   49
One equal temper of heroic *h's*,   ,,   68
To his great *h* none other than a God !   *Tithonus* 14
And bosom beating with a *h* renew'd.   ,,   36
with what another *h* In days far-off,   ,,   50
lower feelings and a narrower *h* than mine !   *Locksley Hall* 44
hidden from the *h's* disgrace,   ,,   57
tho' my *h* be at the root.   ,,   66
lest thy *h* be put to proof,   ,,   77
hoard of maxims preaching down a daughter's *h*.   ,,   94
Left me with the palsied *h*,   ,,   132
deep *h* of existence beat for ever like a boy's ?   ,,   140
And from a *h* as rough as Esau's hand,   *Godiva* 28
That lie upon her charmed *h*.   *Day-Dm., Sleep. B.* 20
Magic Music in his *h* Beats quick and quicker,   ,, *Arrival* 26
strength of ten, Because my *h* is pure.   *Sir Galahad* 4
But all my *h* is drawn above,   ,,   17
A virgin *h* in work and will.   ,,   24
This weight and size, this *h* and eyes,   ,,   71
' And have you lost your *h* ? ' she said ;   *Edward Gray* 3
Can touch the *h* of Edward Gray.   ,,   8
' To trouble the *h* of Edward Gray.'   ,,   20
And here the *h* of Edward Gray ! '   ,,   28
And there the *h* of Edward Gray ! '   ,,   36
that child's *h* within the man's Begins to move   *Will Water.* 31
I will not cramp my *h*,   ,,   51
But, all his vast *h* sherris-warm'd,   ,,   197
Her *h* within her did not fail :   *Lady Clare* 78
Shame and wrath his *h* confounded,   *The Captain* 61
' If my *h* by signs can tell,   *L. of Burleigh* 2
Thus her *h* rejoices greatly,   ,,   41

Heart (*continued*) Shaped her *h* with woman's meekness   *L. of Burleigh* 71
Which did win my *h* from me ! '   ,,   84
And madly danced our *h's* with joy,   *The Voyage* 3
Across the whirlwind's *h* of peace,   ,,   87
To waste his whole *h* in one kiss   *Sir L. and Q. G.* 44
Pass on, weak *h*, and leave me where I lie :   *Come not, when, etc.* 11
That mock'd the wholesome human *h*,   *The Letters* 10
I spoke with *h*, and heat and force,   ,,   37
Every *h*, when sifted well,   *Vision of Sin* 112
Hollow *h's* and empty heads !   ,,   174
vulture waits To tear his *h* before the crowd !   *You might have won* 36
either fixt his *h* On that one girl ;   *Enoch Arden* 39
Bearing a lifelong hunger in his *h*.   ,,   79
Enoch in his *h* determined all :   ,,   148
But had no *h* to break his purposes To Annie,   ,,   155
Philip's true *h*, which hunger'd for her peace   ,,   272
For where he fixt his *h* he set his hand   ,,   294
He oft denied his *h* his dearest wish,   ,,   336
Out of full *h* and boundless gratitude   ,,   346
Brook'd not the expectant terror of her *h*,   ,,   493
But never merrily beat Annie's *h*.   ,,   513
Then the new mother came about her *h*,   ,,   524
had not his poor *h* Spoken with That,   ,,   618
His *h* foreshadowing all calamity,   ,,   683
While in her *h* she yearn'd incessantly   ,,   866
James Willows, of one name and *h* with her.   *The Brook* 76
there he mellow'd all his *h* with ale,   ,,   155
That shook the *h* of Edith hearing him.   *Aylmer's Field* 63
So these young *h's* not knowing that they loved,   ,,   133
Having the warmth and muscle of the *h*,   ,,   180
And foam'd away his *h* at Averill's ear :   ,,   342
the according *h's* of men Seem'd harder too ;   ,,   453
fragrant in a *h* remembering His former talks   ,,   456
where his worldless *h* had kept it warm,   ,,   471
For *h*, I think, help'd head :   ,,   475
Hating his own lean *h* and miserable.   ,,   526
And bad him with good *h* sustain himself—   ,,   544
down in flood, and dash'd his angry *h*   ,,   633
To greet her, wasting his forgotten *h*,   ,,   689
Long since her *h* had beat remorselessly,   ,,   799
from tender *h's*, And those who sorrow'd   ,,   843
Whose pious talk, when most his *h* was dry,   *Sea Dreams* 186
' I loathe it : he had never kindly *h*,   ,,   200
I had set my *h* on your forgiving him   ,,   269
what *h* had he To die of ? dead ! '   ,,   275
His angel broke his *h*.   ,,   280
bird Makes his *h* voice amid the blaze of flowers :   *Lucretius* 101
What beast has *h* to do it ?   ,,   233
Spout from the maiden fountain in her *h*.   ,,   240
' O noble *h* who, being strait-besieged   *Princess, Pro.* 36
And bites it for true *h* and not for harm,   ,,   174
And still I wore her picture by my *h*,   ,,   *i* 38
my other *h*, And almost my half-self,   ,,   55
with all my *h*, With my full *h* :   ,,   126
think I bear that *h* within my breast,   ,,   *ii* 334
A thousand *h's* lie fallow in these halls,   ,,   400
Fly twanging headless arrows at the *h's*,   ,,   402
And dear is sister Psyche to my *h*,   ,,   418
when your sister came she won the *h* Of Ida ;   ,, *iii* 87
I tried the mother's *h*.   ,,   147
head and *h* of all our fair she-world,   ,,   163
My *h* beat thick with passion and with awe ;   ,,   190
that men may pluck them from our *h's*,   ,,   257
Or in the dark dissolving human *h*,   ,,   312
Rise in the *h*, and gather to the eyes,   ,, *iv* 41
her *h* Would rock the snowy cradle till I died.   ,,   103
cursing Cyril, vext at *h*,   ,,   171
To whom none spake, half-sick at *h*, return'd.   ,,   223
Beaten with some great passion at her *h*,   ,,   388
block and bar Your *h* with system out from mine,   ,,   463
Bursts of great *h* and slips in sensual mire,   ,, *v* 199
The woman's garment hid the woman's *h*.'   ,,   305
Suck'd from the dark *h* of the long hills   ,,   349
living *h's* that crack within the fire   ,,   379
at the *h* Made for all noble motion :   ,,   383

Heart (*continued*) the tender orphan hands Felt at my *h*,   *Princess* v 436
Man with the head and woman with the *h* :   ,,   449
Her noble *h* was molten in her breast ;   ,,   vi 119
Win you the *h's* of women ;   ,,   171
She said You had a *h*—I heard her say it—" Our Ida has a *h* "—just ere she died—   ,,   234
You will not ? well—no *h* have you,   ,,   262
Come to the hollow *h* they slander so !   ,,   288
I cannot keep My *h* an eddy from the brawling hour :   ,,   322
nor stranger seem'd that *h's* So gentle,   ,,   vii 66
And at the happy lovers *h* in *h*—   ,,   108
And all thy *h* lies open unto me.   ,,   183
ill counsel had misled the girl To vex true *h's* :   ,,   242
her great *h* thro' all the faultful Past   ,,   248
two-cell'd *h* beating, with one full stroke,   ,,   307
I waste my *h* in signs : let be.   ,,   359
And a deeper knell in the *h* be knoll'd ;   *Ode on Well.* 59
What long-enduring *h's* could do In that world-earthquake,   ,,   132
On with toil of *h* and knees and hands,   ,,   212
upon whose hand and *h* and brain   ,,   239
Uplifted high in *h* and hope are we,   ,,   254
and change the *h's* of men,   *W. to Marie Alex.* 44
But *h's* that change not,   ,,   46
And in thy *h* the scrawl shall play.'   *Sailor Boy* 12
A devil rises in my *h*,   ,,   23
h to endure for the life of the worm and the fly ?   *Wages* 7
Tear the noble *h* of Britain,   *Boädicea* 12
Till she felt the *h* within her fall and flutter   ,,   81
and the Shepherd gladdens in his *h* :   *Spec. of Iliad* 16
my *h* is there before you are come,   *Window, On the Hill* 14
Gone, and a cloud in my *h*,   ,, *Gone* 6
you bite far into the *h* of the house,   ,, *Winter* 11
You have bitten into the *h* of the earth,   ,,   18
Break—you may break my *h*. Faint *h* never won—   *The Answer* 8
O merry my *h*, you have gotten the wings of love,   *Ay* 15
lighten into my eyes and my *h*, Into my *h* and my blood !   *Marr. Morn.* 15
H, are you great enough (repeat)   ,, 17, 19
And with my *h* I muse and say :   *In Mem.* iv 4
O *h*, how fares it with thee now,   ,,   5
But, for the unquiet *h* and brain,   ,, v 5
but some *h* did break.   ,, vi 8
Doors, where my *h* was used to beat So quickly,   ,, vii 3
O my forsaken *h*, with thee And this poor flower   ,, viii 18
And in my *h*, if calm at all,   ,, xi 15
A void where *h* on *h* reposed ;   ,, xiii 6
I, falling on his faithful *h*,   ,, xviii 14
The darken'd *h* that beat no more ;   ,, xix 2
And melt the waxen *h's* of men.'   ,, xxi 8
And glad at *h* from May to May :   ,, xxii 8
Nor could I weary, *h* or limb,   ,, xxv 9
The *h* that never plighted troth   ,, xxvii 10
To lull with song an aching *h*,   ,, xxxvii 15
I vex my *h* with fancies dim :   ,, xlii 1
the *h* is sick, And all the wheels of Being slow.   ,, l 3
broke the peace Of *h's* that beat from day to day,   ,, lviii 6
Like some poor girl whose *h* is set On one   ,, lx 3
On some unworthy *h* with joy,   ,, lxii 7
Can hang no weight upon my *h*   ,, lxiii 3
You thought my *h* too far diseased ;   ,, lxvi 1
Let this not vex thee, noble *h* !   ,, lxxix 2
The wrath that garners in my *h* ;   ,, lxxxii 14
O *h*, with kindliest motion warm,   ,, lxxxv 34
That marry with the virgin *h*.   ,,   108
My *h*, tho' widow'd, may not rest Quite in the love   ,,   113
in the midmost *h* of grief Thy passion clasps   ,, lxxxviii 7
h and ear were fed To hear him,   ,, lxxxix 22
How pure at *h* and sound in head,   ,, xciv 1
But when the *h* is full of din,   ,,   13
A hunger seized my *h* ; I read Of that glad year   ,, xcv 21
Their *h's* of old have beat in tune,   ,, xcvii 10
He seems to slight her simple *h*.   ,,   20
The pulses of a Titan's *h* ;   ,, ciii 32
The larger *h*, the kindlier hand ;   ,, cvi 30

L*

Heart (*continued*) I will not eat my *h* alone,   *In Mem.* cviii 3
By blood a king, at *h* a clown ;   ,, cxi 4
Doors, where my *h* was used to beat So quickly,   ,, cxix 1
the *h* Stood up and answer'd ' I have felt.'   ,, cxxiv 15
And *h's* are warm'd and faces bloom,   ,, *Con.* 82
closed their gates with a shock on my *h*   *Maud I* i 15
Than the *h* of the citizen hissing in war   ,,   24
May make my *h* as a millstone,   ,,   31
passionate *h* of the poet is whirl'd into folly   ,, iv 39
Ready in *h* and ready in hand,   ,, v 9
Kept itself warm in the *h* of my dreams,   ,, vi 18
On a *h* half-turn'd to stone.   ,,   78
O *h* of stone, are you flesh,   ,,   79
suddenly, sweetly, my *h* beat stronger   ,, viii 8
Sick, sick to the *h* of life, am I.   ,, x 36
Ah God, for a man with *h*, head, hand,   ,,   60
Set in the *h* of the carven gloom,   ,, xiv 11
drown His *h* in the gross mud-honey of town,   ,, xvi 5
Catch not my breath, O clamorous *h*,   ,,   31
shook my *h* to think she comes once more ;   ,, xviii 10
Dear *h*, I feel with thee the drowsy spell.   ,,   72
My own *h's* *h*, my ownest own, farewell ;   ,,   74
Beat with my *h* more blest than *h* can tell,   ,,   82
And that dead man at her *h* and mine :   ,, xix 9
From him who had ceased to share her *h*,   ,,   30
A desire that awoke in the *h* of the child,   ,,   48
To the faults of his *h* and mind,   ,,   68
There is but one With whom she has *h* to be gay.   ,, xxii 20
My *h* would hear her and beat,   ,,   69
It will ring in my *h* and my ears,   ,, II i 35
little *h's* that know not how to forgive :   ,,   44
Shall I nurse in my dark *h*,   ,, ii 55
Courage, poor *h* of stone !   ,, II iii 1
Courage, poor stupid *h* of stone.—   ,,   5
H's with no love for me :   ,, iv 94
And my *h* is a handful of dust,   ,, v 3
surely, some kind *h* will come To bury me,   ,,   102
it is time, O passionate *h*,' said I   ,, III vi 30
' It is time, O passionate *h* and morbid eye,   ,,   32
the *h* of a people beat with one desire ;   ,,   49
flames The blood-red blossom of war with a *h* of fire.   ,,   53
We have proved we have *h's* in a cause,   ,,   55
inheritance Of such a life, a *h*,   *Ded. of Idylls* 33
the spike that split the mother's *h*   *Com. of Arthur* 38
A doubt that ever smoulder'd in the *h's*   ,,   64
And in the *h* of Arthur joy was lord.   ,,   124
when he heard, Leodogran in *h* Debating—   ,,   140
bold in *h* and act and word was he,   ,,   176
there be those who hate him in their *h's*,   ,,   179
Bewildering *h* and eye—   ,,   300
comforted my *h*, And dried my tears,   ,,   349
But brake his very *h* in pining for it,   *Gareth and L.* 57
and tourney-falls, Frights to my *h* ;   ,,   90
Albeit in mine own *h* I knew him King,   ,,   123
felt his young *h* hammering in his ears,   ,,   322
In token of true *h* and feälty.   ,,   399
h of her good horse Was nigh to burst with violence   ,,   762
Gareth panted hard, and his great *h*,   ,,   1126
lets His *h* be stirr'd with any foolish heat   ,,   1178
Sent all his *h* and breath thro' all the horn.   ,,   1369
with true *h* Adored her, as the stateliest   *Marr. of Geraint* 19
Low to her own *h* piteously she said :   ,,   85
Our hoard is little, but our *h's* are great. (repeat)   ,, 352, 374
grateful is the noise of noble deeds To noble *h's*   ,,   438
I seem to suffer nothing *h* or limb,   ,,   472
' Well said, true *h*,' replied Geraint,   ,,   474
Yniol's *h* Danced in his bosom,   ,,   504
Tell her, and prove her *h* toward the Prince.'   ,,   513
their converse in the hall, Proving her *h* :   ,,   521
Glow'd like the *h* of a great fire at Yule,   ,,   559
softly to her own sweet *h* she said :   ,,   618
her *h* All overshadow'd by the foolish dream,   ,,   674
felt that tempest brooding round his *h*,   *Geraint and E.* 11
there he broke the sentence in his *h* Abruptly,   ,,   41
great plover's human whistle amazed Her *h*,   ,,   50

Hearth (*continued*) that gray cricket chirpt of at our h— | *Merlin and V.* 110
Better the King's waste h and aching heart | *Guinevere* 524
And the roof sank in on the h, | *V. of Maeldune* 32
their hoards and their h's and their homes. | *Batt. of Brunanburh* 19
The jungle rooted in his shatter'd h, | *Demeter and P.* 76
MANY a h upon our dark globe sighs | *Vastness* 1
Make all true h's thy home. | *Prog. of Spring* 52
Hearth-flower The little h-f Lilia. | *Princess, Pro.* 166
Heart-hiding H-h smile, and gray persistent eye: | *Guinevere* 64
Hearthstone hissing in war on his own h? | *Maud I i* 24
Heartily they ran To greet his hearty welcome h; | *Enoch Arden* 350
Heartless Insolent, brainless, h! | *Aylmer's Field* 368
Heart-weary H-w and overdone! | *The Dreamer* 18
Hearty (*See also* 'Arty) they ran To greet his h welcome heartily; | *Enoch Arden* 350
Heart-yearning deep h-y's, thy sweet memories | *Last Tournament* 579
Heat (s) (*See also* After-heat, 'Eat, Heät, Hell-heat)
hollows of the fringed hills In summer h's, | *Supp. Confessions* 154
Clear, without h, undying, | *Isabel* 3
Close-latticed to the brooding h, | *Mariana in the S.* 3
But day increased from h to h, | " 39
From h to h the day decreased, | " 78
That h of inward evidence, | *Two Voices* 284
Remembering its ancient h. | " 423
Throbbing thro' all thy h and light, | *Fatima* 4
and the heart Faints, faded by its h. | *D. of F. Women* 288
if in noble h Those men thine arms withstood, | *England and Amer.* 6
Rain, wind, frost, h, hail, damp, | *St. S. Stylites* 16
Then added, all in h: 'What stuff is this! | *Golden Year* 64
I spoke with heart, and h and force, | *The Letters* 37
Or when some h of difference sparkled out, | *Aylmer's Field* 705
all-generating powers and genial h Of Nature, | *Lucretius* 97
With animal h and dire insanity? | " 163
Sun-shaded in the h of dusty fights) | *Princess ii* 241
under arches of the marble bridge Hung, shadow'd from the h: | " 459
while my honest h Were all miscounted | " iv 333
many a bold knight started up in h, | " v 359
What h's of indignation when we heard | " 375
I felt my veins Stretch with fierce h; | " 538
A night of Summer from the h, | " vi 54
Where we withdrew from summer h's and state, | " 245
But yonder, whiff! there comes a sudden h, | " Con. 58
For life outliving h's of youth, | *In Mem. liii* 10
mark The landscape winking thro' the h: | " lxxxix 16
To make a solid core of h; | " cvii 18
not the schoolboy h, The blind hysterics | " cix 15
tread In tracts of fluent h began, | " cxviii 9
true blood spilt had in it a h To dissolve | *Maud I xix* 44
Then Uther in his wrath and h besieged | *Com. of Arthur* 198
His heart be stirr'd with any foolish h | *Gareth and L.* 1178
And after nodded sleepily in the h. | *Geraint and E.* 253
Who, with mild h of holy oratory, | " 866
Took, as in rival h, to holy things; | *Balin and Balan* 100
forget My h's and violences? | " 190
Whom Pellam drove away with holy h. | " 611
Brain-feverous in his h and agony, | *Lancelot and E.* 854
And when the h is gone from out my heart, | " 1116
thro' the casement standing wide for h, | " 1234
And earthly h's that spring and sparkle out | *Holy Grail* 33
And almost burst the barriers in their h, | " 336
and thro' a stormy glare, a h | " 842
the h Of pride and glory fired her face; | *Pelleas and E.* 171
in his h and eagerness Trembled and quiver'd, | " 283
a sudden flush of wrathful h Fired all the pale face | *Guinevere* 356
the white h's of the blinding noons Beat | *Lover's Tale i* 139
Thro' the h, the drowth, the dust, the glare, | *Sisters (E. and E.)* 6
H like the mouth of a hell, | *Def. of Lucknow* 81
none could breathe Within the zone of h; | *Columbus* 53
with thirst in the middle-day h. | *V. of Maeldune* 50
That wholesome h the blood had lost, | *To E. Fitzgerald* 24
the winds were dead for h; | *Tiresias* 34
Of the hellish h of a wretched life | *Despair* 68
Sunn'd with a summer of milder h. | *To Prof. Jebb.* 8

Heat (s) (*continued*) till the h Smote on her brow, | *Death of Œnone* 97
Heät (s) But the h druv hout i' my heyes | *Owd Roä* 84
Heat (verb) the latter fire shall h the deep; | *The Kraken* 13
Let the Sun, Who h's our earth to yield | *Akbar's Dream* 105
Heated (*See also* Seventimes-heated, Wine-heated) high shrine-doors burst thro' with h blasts | *D. of F. Women* 29
came again together on the king With h faces; | *Audley Court* 37
Where sat a company with h eyes, | *Vision of Sin* 7
To chapel; where a h pulpiteer, | *Sea Dreams* 20
and from within Burst thro' the h buds, | *Lover's Tale i* 320
and felt the blast Beat on my h eyelids: | " iii 28
Had made a h haze to magnify The charm of Edith— | *Sisters (E. and E.)* 129
h thro' and thro' with wrath and love, | *Princess iv* 163
And h hot with burning fears, | *In Mem. cxviii* 22
And h the strong warrior in his dreams; | *Marr. of Geraint* 72
H am I? you—you wonder— | *Locksley H., Sixty* 151
Heath (barren country) blackening over h and holt, | *Locksley Hall* 191
Who slowly rode across a wither'd h, | *Vision of Sin* 61
At the Dragon on the h! | " 72
The Priest went out by h and hill; | *The Victim* 29
Arise in open prospect—h and hill, | *Lover's Tale i* 397
Dumb on the winter h he lay. | *Dead Prophet* 13
Lightnings flicker'd along the h; | " 79
Heath (heather) (*See also* Heather) lips in the field above are dabbled with blood-red h, | *Maud I i* 2
And flung myself down on a bank of h, | *Com. of Arthur* 342
all round was open space, And fern and h: | *Pelleas and E.* 29
Among our h and bracken. | *The Ring* 318
Heathen (adj.) from time to time the h host Swarm'd overseas, | *Com. of Arthur* 8
last a h horde, Reddening the sun with smoke | " 36
in twelve great battles overcame The h hordes, | " 519
Red as the rising sun with h blood, | *Lancelot and E.* 308
Yet in this h war the fire of God Fills him: | " 315
Wasted so often by the h hordes, | *Holy Grail* 244
splash'd and dyed The strong White Horse in his own h blood— | " 312
Fool, I came late, the h wars were o'er, | *Last Tournament* 269
Hard on that helm which many a h sword | *Pass. of Arthur* 166
Burn? h men have borne as much as this, | *Sir J. Oldcastle* 185
Christian love among the Churches look'd the twin of h hate. | *Locksley H., Sixty* 86
Heathen (s) (*See also* Haithen) Then he drave The h; | *Com. of Arthur* 59
after, slew the beast, cross-hilted sword, Whereby to drive the h out: | " 287
then or now Utterly smite the h underfoot, | " 423
'Shall Rome or H rule in Arthur's realm? | " 485
To drive the h from your Roman wall, | " 512
Who drave the h hence by sorcery | *Gareth and L.* 204
and fell against the h of the Northern Sea | *Geraint and E.* 969
While all the h lay at Arthur's feet, | *Merlin and V.* 144
till we drive The h, who, some say, | *Lancelot and E.* 65
The h caught and reft him of his tongue. | " 273
sand-shores of Trath Treroit, Where many a h fell; | " 302
The h are upon him, his long lance Broken, | *Last Tournament* 87
The h—but that ever-climbing wave, | " 92
H, the brood by Hengist left; | *Guinevere* 16
For now the H of the Northern Sea, | " 135
And leagued with him the h, | " 155
Godless hosts Of h swarming o'er the Northern Sea; | " 428
To break the h and uphold the Christ, | " 470
Lords of the White Horse, h, and knights, | " 574
but grosser grown Than h, | *Pass. of Arthur* 62
Or thrust the h from the Roman wall, | " 69
shouts of h and the traitor knights, | " 113
Nor any cry of Christian heard thereon, Nor yet of h; | " 129
he that brought The h back among us, | " 152
a shame to speak of them—Among the h— | *Sir J. Oldcastle* 111
Heather find the white h wherever you go, | *Romney's R.* 108
my white h only blooms in heaven | " 110
wild h round me and over me June's high blue, | *June Bracken, etc.* 2
the bracken so bright and the h so brown, | " 3
green of the bracken amid the gloom of the h. | " 9
Heather-scented and h-s air, Pulsing full man; | *Last Tournament* 691

Heaven (*continued*)   peak And pinnacle, and had made it
   spire to *h.*   *Gareth and L.* 309
Rather than—O sweet *h* ! O fie upon him—   ,,   741
Immingled with *H*'s azure waveringly,   ,,   936
'No star of thine, but shot from Arthur's *h*   ,,   1100
'*H* help thee,' sigh'd Lynette.   ,,   1357
And loved her, as he loved the light of *H.* And
   as the light of *H* varies,   *Marr. of Geraint* 5
So aid me *H* when at mine uttermost,   ,,   502
on open ground Beneath a troubled *h,*   ,,   523
Sweet *h,* how much I shall discredit him !   ,,   621
Herself would clothe her like the sun in *H.*   ,,   784
she was ever praying the sweet *h*'s   *Geraint and E.* 44
I might amend it by the grace of *H,*   ,,   53
issuing under open *h*'s beheld A little town   ,,   196
she cried, '*by H,* I will not drink   ,,   664
we love the *H* that chastens us.   ,,   789
The truest eyes that ever answer'd *H,*   ,,   842
Lost one Found was greeted as in *H* With joy   *Balin and Balan* 81
No more of hatred than in *H*   ,,   151
fire of *H* has kill'd the barren cold,   ,,   440
fire of *H* is not the flame of Hell. (repeat)   ,,   443, 447,
                                         451, 455
'The fire of *H* is on the dusty ways.   ,,   448
'The fire of *H* is lord of all things good,   ,,   452
'This fire of *h,* This old sun-worship,   ,,   456
The deathless mother-maidenhood of *H,*   ,,   521
vows like theirs, that high in *h* Love most,   *Merlin and V.* 14
O *H*'s own white Earth-angel,   ,,   80
Was also Bard, and knew the starry *h*'s;   ,,   169
By *H* that hears I tell you the clean truth,   ,,   343
For men at most differ as *H* and earth, But women,
   worst and best, as *H* and Hell.   ,,   814
May yon just *h,* that darkens o'er me,   ,,   931
Scarce had she ceased, when out of *h* a bolt   ,,   934
Vivien, fearing *h* had heard her oath,   ,,   940
But who can gaze upon the Sun in *h* ?   *Lancelot and E.* 123
'*H* hinder,' said the King, 'that such an one,   ,,   532
'I lose it, as we lose the lark in *h,*   ,,   659
And, after *h,* on our dull side of death,   ,,   1382
strength Within us, better offer'd up to *H.*'   *Holy Grail* 36
I trust We are green in *H*'s eyes;   ,,   38
the holy cup Was caught away to *H,*   ,,   58
'My knight, my love, my knight of *h,*   ,,   157
Pray *H,* they be not smitten by the bolt.'   ,,   221
Feasted, and as the stateliest under *h.*   ,,   224
and never yet Had *h* appear'd so blue,   ,,   365
Prick'd with incredible pinnacles into *h.*   ,,   423
the *h*'s Open'd and blazed with thunder   ,,   507
the *h*'s open'd and blazed again Roaring,   ,,   516
Then fell the floods of *h* drowning the deep.   ,,   533
and blest be *H* That brought thee here   ,,   616
Quest and he were in the hands of *H.*   ,,   659
and the stones They pitch up straight to *h:*   ,,   665
heard the hollow-ringing *h*'s sweep Over him   ,,   678
they roll Thro' such a round in *h,*   ,,   686
But *h* had meant it for a sunny one: ,,   706
clouded *h*'s Were shaken with the motion and the sound.   ,,   800
But if indeed there came a sign from *h,*   ,,   873
A rosy dawn kindled in stainless *h*'s,   *Pelleas and E.* 72
Or have the *H*'s but given thee a fair face,   ,,   101
a sacrifice Kindled by fire from *h :*   ,,   146
Till the sweet *h*'s have fill'd it   ,,   510
but when he saw High up in *h* the hall   ,,   553
that young life Being smitten in mid *h*   *Last Tournament* 27
Man was it who marr'd *h*'s image in thee thus?'   ,,   64
We call the harp of Arthur up in *h* ?'   ,,   333
High on all hills, and in the signs of *h.*'   ,,   337
It makes a silent music up in *h,*   ,,   349
sun that ray'd from off a brow Like hillsnow high in *h,*   ,,   667
Dropt down from *h* ? wash'd up from out the deep?   ,,   685
A star in *h,* a star within the mere !   ,,   732
A blot in *h,* the Raven, flying high,   *Guinevere* 133
There came a day as still as *h,*   ,,   292
But help me, *h,* for surely I repent.   ,,   372

Heaven (*continued*)   seem'd the *h*'s upbreaking thro' the
   earth,   *Guinevere* 391
I knew Of no more subtle master under *h*   ,,   478
be his mate hereafter in the *h*'s Before high God.   ,,   637
the great light of *H* Burn'd at his lowest   *Pass. of Arthur* 90
those who falling down Look'd up for *h,*   ,,   112
mightiest of all peoples under *h* ?   *To the Queen* ii 21
trust that *H* Will blow the tempest   ,,   46
From his mid-dome in *H*'s airy halls;   *Lover's Tale* i 66
till earth And *h* pass too, dwelt on my *h,*   ,,   72
Waiting to see some blessed shape in *h,*   ,,   312
and joy In breathing nearer *h;*   ,,   389
To breathe with her as if in *h* itself;   ,,   391
Thy fires from *h* had touch'd it,   ,,   439
Sooner Earth Might go round *H,*   ,,   482
bliss stood round me like the light of *H,*—   ,,   495
Steppeth from *H,* from light to light,   ,,   512
had *H* from all her doors, With all her golden thresholds   ,,   604
whom the gentlest airs of *H* Should kiss   ,,   738
may death Awake them with *h*'s music   ,,   761
Bore her free-faced to the free airs of *H,*   iv 38
wines that, *H* knows when, Had suck'd the fire   ,,   193
Ah *h*'s! Why need I tell you all ?—   ,,   200
Down out o' *h* i' Hell-fire—   *North. Cobbler* 58
melted like a cloud in the silent summer *h;*   *The Revenge* 14
a man's ideal Is high in *H,*   *Sisters (E. and E.)* 131
Cold, but as welcome as free airs of *h*   ,,   197
saved by the blessing of *H* !   *Def. of Lucknow* 104
this good Wiclif mountain down from *h,*   *Sir J. Oldcastle* 132
the great 'Laudamus' rose to *h.*   *Columbus* 18
chains For him who gave a new *h,*   ,,   20
King David call'd the *h*'s a hide,   ,,   47
Who took us for the very Gods from *H,*   ,,   183
Queen of *H* who seest the souls in Hell   ,,   216
high in the *h* above it there flicker'd   *V. of Maeldune* 17
where the *h*'s lean low on the land,   ,,   83
For a wild witch naked as *h*   ,,   100
when a smoke from a city goes to *h*   *Achilles over the T.* 7
from his head the splendour went to *h.*   ,,   14
all the *h*'s flash'd in frost;   *To E. Fitzgerald* 22
more than man Which rolls the *h*'s,   *Tiresias* 22
voice rang out in the thunders of Ocean and *H*   *The Wreck* 88
No soul in the *h* above,   *Despair* 19
higher still, the *h*'s Whereby the cloud   *Ancient Sage* 12
thou sendest thy free soul thro' *h,*   ,,   47
So dark that men cry out against the *H*'s.   ,,   172
earth's dark forehead flings athwart the *h*'s   ,,   200
past into the Nameless, as a cloud Melts into *H.*   ,,   234
The lark has past from earth to *H*   *The Flight* 62
the blessed *H*'s are just,   ,,   67
She bad us love, like souls in *H,*   ,,   88
While the silent *H*'s roll,   *Locksley H., Sixty* 203
sphere of all the boundless *H*'s   ,,   210
the stars in *h* Paled, and the glory grew.   *Pro. to Gen. Hamley* 31
Whole *h*'s within themselves, amaze   *Epilogue* 56
And 'The Curse of the Prophet' in *H.*   *Dead Prophet* 28
Opens a door in *H* ;   *Early Spring* 7
Like some conjectured planet in mid *h*   *To Prin. Beatrice* 20
cry that rang thro' Hades, Earth, and *H* !   *Demeter and P.* 33
I, Earth-Goddess, cursed the Gods of *H.*   ,,   102
break The sunless halls of Hades into *H* ?   ,,   136
MELLOW moon of *h,* Bright in blue,   *The Ring* 1
No sudden *h,* nor sudden hell, for man,   ,,   41
past and future mix'd in *H* and made The rosy twilight   ,,   186
sudden fire from *H* had dash'd him dead,   *Happy* 83
to trace On paler *h*'s the branching grace   *To Ulysses* 15
For his clear *h,* and these few lanes   *To Mary Boyle* 67
H lours, But in the tearful splendour   *Prog. of Spring* 40
all but in *H* Hovers The Gleam.   *Merlin and the G.* 118
This seem'd my lodestar in the *H* of Art,   *Romney's R.* 39
roll The rainbow hues of *h* about it—   ,,   51
my white heather only blooms in *h*   ,,   110
the shout Of His descending peals from *H,*   ,,   127
Human forgiveness touches *h,*   ,,   159
earth's green stole in *h*'s own hue,   *Far—far—away* 2

Helm (helmet) (*continued*) her golden *h* And all her golden armour
on the grass, — *Tiresias* 44
Helm (as of a boat) She took the *h* and he the sail; — *Merlin and V.* 200
but the man that was lash'd to the *h* had gone; — *The Wreck* 110
Whatever statesman hold the *h*. — *Hands all Round* 20
Or should those fail, that hold the *h*, — *Prog. of Spring* 100
Helm (verb) overbears the bark, And him that *h's* it, — *Lancelot and E.* 486
Helmet The *h* and the helmet-feather Burn'd — *L. of Shalott* iii 21
From underneath his *h* flow'd His coal-black curls — " 30
She saw the *h* and the plume, — " 40
out of stricken *h's* sprang the fire. — *Princess* v 495
With Psyche's colour round his *h*, — " 534
And wears a *h* mounted with a skull, — *Gareth and L.* 639
Gareth there unlaced His *h* as to slay him, — " 979
Sat riveting a *h* on his knee, — *Marr. of Geraint* 268
Came forward with the *h* yet in hand — " 285
crack'd the *h* thro', and bit the bone, — " 573
Till his eye darken'd and his *h* wagg'd; — *Geraint and E.* 505
then he bound Her token on his *h*, — *Lancelot and E.* 374
leaving for the cowl The *h* in an abbey far away — *Holy Grail* 6
And once the laces of a *h* crack'd, — *Last Tournament* 164
Tumbling the hollow *h's* of the fallen, — *Pass. of Arthur* 132
spear and *h* tipt With stormy light — *Tiresias* 113
Flicker'd and bicker'd From it to *h*, — *Merlin and the G.* 71
Helmet-feather The helmet and the *h-f* Burn'd — *L. of Shalott* iii 21
Helmet-hidden the face Wellnigh was *h-h*, — *Last Tournament* 456
Helmless I sit within a *h* bark, — *In Mem.* iv 3
Helmsman I leap on board: no *h* steers: — *Sir Galahad* 39
Help (s) without *h* I cannot last till morn. — *M. d'Arthur* 26
I grieve to see you poor and wanting *h*: — *Enoch Arden* 406
a voice Of comfort and an open hand of *h*, — *Aylmer's Field* 174
who promised *h*, and oozed All o'er with honey'd
answer — *Princess* v 241
Because it needed *h* of Love: — *In Mem.* xxv 8
For *h* and shelter to the hermit's cave. — *Gareth and L.* 1209
scaled with *h* a hundred feet Up from the base: — *Balin and Balan* 170
maiden sprang into the hall Crying on *h*: — *Holy Grail* 209
shall I kill myself? What *h* in that? — *Guinevere* 621
without *h* I cannot last till morn. — *Pass. of Arthur* 194
of a Hell without *h*, without end, — *Despair* 26
they maäkes ma a *h* to the poor, — *Church-warden, etc.* 39
Help (verb) (*See also* **'Elp**) grace To *h* me of my
weary load.' — *Mariana in the S.* 30
until he grows Of age to *h* us.' — *Dora* 127
h's the hurt that Honour feels, — *Locksley Hall* 105
h me as when life begun: — " 185
I cannot *h* you as I wish to do Unless— — *Enoch Arden* 407
H me not to break in upon her peace. — " 787
How could I *h* her? 'Would I— — *The Brook* 111
Poor fellow, could he *h* it? — " 158
there was one to hear And *h* them? — *Princess* ii 268
I heard, I could not *h* it, — " 332
oh, Sirs, could I *h* it, but my cheek — " iii 45
(God *h* her) she was wedded to a fool; — " 83
h my prince to gain His rightful bride; — " 160
H, father, brother, *h*; speak to the king: — " vi 305
one That wholly scorn'd to *h* their equal rights — " vii 233
For, saving that, ye *h* to save mankind — *Ode on Well.* 166
How best to *h* the slender store, — *To F. D. Maurice* 37
'God *h* me! save I take my part Of danger — *Sailor Boy* 31
' *H* us from famine And plague and strife! — *The Victim* 9
But *h* thy foolish ones to bear; — *In Mem., Pro.* 31
H thy vain worlds to bear thy light. — " 32
Sent to him, saying ' Arise, and *h* us thou! — *Com. of Arthur* 44
Sweet faces, who will *h* him at his need. — " 279
friends Of Arthur, who should *h* him at his need, — *Gareth and L.* 230
' We sit King, to *h* the wrong'd Thro' all our realm. — " 371
unhappiness Of one who came to *h* thee, — " 1238
' Heaven *h* thee,' sigh'd Lynette. — " 1357
name Slip from my lips if I can *h* it— — *Marr. of Geraint* 446
So this will *h* him of his violences!' — *Balin and Balan* 205
bounden art thou, if from Arthur's hall, To *h* the
weak. — " 473
H, for he follows! take me to thyself! — *Merlin and V.* 82
The sick weak beast seeking to *h* herself — " 498

Help (verb) (*continued*) 'What matter, so I *h* him
back to life?' — *Lancelot and E.* 787
and said, ' Betray me not, but *h*— — *Pelleas and E.* 360
If I, the Queen, May *h* them, loose thy tongue, — " 600
To *h* it from the death that cannot die, — *Guinevere* 66
But *h* me, heaven, for surely I repent. — " 372
friends Of Arthur, who should *h* him at his need?' — *Pass. of Arthur* 456
Sprang up a friendship that may *h* us yet. — *Lover's Tale* iv 144
And *h* us to our joy. — *Sisters (E. and E.)* 224
I should cry to the dear Lord Jesus to *h* me, — *In the Child. Hosp.* 49
given my life To *h* his own from scathe, — *Sir J. Oldcastle* 63
Then I, God *h* me, I So mock'd, — " 162
but Thou wilt *h* us to be. — *De Prof., Human C.* 8
and sail to *h* him in the war; — *Achilles over the T.* 13
hand that would *h* me, would heal me— — *The Wreck* 56
Let be thy wail and *h* thy fellow men, — *Ancient Sage* 258
to *h* his homelier brother men, — *Locksley H., Sixty* 267
O Goddesses, *h* me up thither! — *Parnassus* 3
you will *h* me to overcome it, — " 5
by thy love which once was mine, H, heal me. — *Death of Œnone* 46
Help'd-Helpt and his father *help'd* him not. — *Dora* 51
God, that *help'd* her in her widowhood. — " 113
or *help'd* At lading and unlading the tall barks, — *Enoch Arden* 815
For heart, I think, *help'd* head: — *Aylmer's Field* 475
Came running at the call, and *help'd* us down. — *Princess* i 227
Help'd by the mother's careful hand and eye, — *Marr. of Geraint* 738
Yea, would have *help'd* him to it: — *Geraint and E.* 638
And at Caerleon had he *help'd* his lord, — *Lancelot and E.* 297
some rough use, And *help'd* her from herself.' — " 1307
as would have *help'd* her from her death.' — " 1311
He *helpt* me with death, and he heal'd — *The Wreck* 58
hands of mine Have *helpt* to pass a bucket — *To Mary Boyle* 39
Helper Henceforth thou hast a *h*, me, — *Princess* vii 258
Helpful a *h* harper thou, That harpest downward! — *Last Tournament* 331
Helping *h* back the dislocated Kay To Camelot, — *Gareth and L.* 1213
Her mother silent too, nor *h* her, — *Marr. of Geraint* 768
Helpless his blue eyes All flooded with the *h* wrath of
tears, — *Enoch Arden* 32
The *h* life so wild that it was tame. — " 557
I felt Thy *h* warmth about my barren breast — *Princess* vi 202
And often feeling of the *h* hands, — " vii 111
Than as a little *h* innocent bird, — *Lancelot and E.* 894
Then his *h* heart Leapt, and he cried, — *Pelleas and E.*
to and fro Swaying the *h* hands, — *Pass. of Arthur* 131
till *h* death And silence made him bold— — *Lover's Tale* iv 72
H, taking the place of the pitying God — *Despair* 42
Would echo *h* laughter to your jest! — *To W. H. Brookfield* 5
peasants maim the *h* horse, and drive Innocent
cattle — *Locksley H., Sixty* 95
She tumbled his *h* corpse about. — *Dead Prophet* 65
And golden grain, my gift to *h* man. — *Demeter and P.* 111
Helplessness Enid, in her utter *h*, — *Geraint and E.* 719
Helpmate ' lo mine *h*, one to feel My purpose — *Guinevere* 485
Helpt *See* **Help'd**
Helter-skelter *H-s* runs the age; — *Poets and Critics* 2
Hem (s) in her raiment's *h* was traced in flame — *The Poet* 45
Hem (verb) one but speaks or *h's* or stirs his chair, — *Sonnet To —* 5
Hemlock Diotima, teaching him that died Of *h*; — *Princess* iii 303
the *h*, Brow-high, did strike my forehead — *Lover's Tale* ii 18
Their nectar smack'd of *h* on the lips, — *Demeter and P.* 104
Hen (*See also* **Guinea-hens**) we stole his fruit, His
h's, his eggs; — *Walk. to the Mail* 85
praised his *h's*, his geese, his guinea-hens; — *The Brook* 126
a *h* To her false daughters in the pool; — *Princess* v 328
even in their *h's* and in their eggs— — *Holy Grail* 560
Pluksh!!! the *h's* i' the peäs! — *Village Wife* 124
Hend (end) theer wur a *h* o' the taäil, — " 86
buried togither, an' this wur the *h*. — " 90
if soä please God, to the *h*. — *Spinster's S's.* 112
Hengist Heathen, the brood by *H* left; — *Guinevere* 16
Hennemy (enemy) Theer's thy *h*, man, an' I knaws, — *North. Cobbler* 65
I'll looök my *h* straït i' the faäce, — " 74
Henry (the Third) *H's* fifty years are all in shadow, — *On Jub. Q. Victoria* 39
Hepitaph (epitaph) Nor her wi' the *h* yonder! — *Spinster's S's.* 72
Herald (adj.) The *h* melodies of spring, — *In Mem.* xxxviii 6

Herald (s) The *h* of her triumph, drawing nigh *Œnone* 185
 let her *h*, Reverence, fly Before her *Love thou thy land* 18
 She sent a *h* forth, And bade him cry, *Godiva* 35
 He thrice had sent a *h* to the gates, *Princess* v 332
 And all that morn the *h*'s to and fro, " 369
 The *h* of a higher race, *In Mem.* cxviii 14
Heralded And *h* the distance of this time ! *Lover's Tale* i 562
Heraldry title-scrolls and gorgeous *heraldries*. *Aylmer's Field* 656
 Poor old *H*, poor old History, *Locksley H., Sixty* 249
Herb (*See also* **Garden-herbs**) For the Ox Feeds in the *h*, *Supp. Confessions* 151
 Step deeper yet in *h* and fern, *Talking Oak* 245
 The vilest *h* that runs to seed *Amphion* 95
 bruised as *h* and crush'd the grape, *In Mem.* xxxv 23
 For underfoot the *h* was dry; " xcv 2
 I stoop'd, I gather'd the wild *h*'s, *Lover's Tale* i 342
 whatever *h* or balm May clear the blood from poison, *Death of Œnone* 35
Hercules My *H*, my Roman Antony, *D. of F. Women* 150
 My Eustace might have sat for *H*; *Gardener's D.* 7
Herd (s) By *h*'s upon an endless plain, *Palace of Art* 74
 The *h*, wild hearts and feeble wings *Love thou thy land* 11
 but count not me the *h* ! *Golden Year* 13
 a *h* of boys with clamour bowl'd And stump'd *Princess, Pro.* 81
 and as the leader of the *h* That holds " vi 85
 So thick with lowings of the *h*'s, *In Mem.* xcix 3
 watch her harvest ripen, her *h* increase, *Maud* III vi 25
 the hind fell, the *h* was driven, *Com. of Arthur* 432
 vineyard, hive and horse and *h*; *To Virgil* 10
Herd (verb) I, to *h* with narrow foreheads, *Locksley Hall* 175
Herded thick as *h* ewes, And rainbow robes, *Princess* iv 479
Herdsman Earth Reels, and the *herdsmen* cry; " v 529
Herè *H* comes to-day, Pallas and Aphroditè, *Œnone* 85
 I beheld great *H*'s angry eyes, " 190
 The Samian *H* rises and she speaks *Princess* iii 115
Heresy woman is the better man; A rampant *h*, " iv 411
 the king along with him—All *h*, treason: *Sir J. Oldcastle* 50
 a cross of flesh and blood And holier. That was *h*. " 138
 '*H*.—Penance ? ' ' Fast, Hairshirt and scourge— " 141
 '*H*—Not shriven, not saved ? ' " 143
 '*H*.' (My friend is long in coming.) " 147
 '*H* '—(Hath he been here—not found me— " 151
 Some thought it *h*, but that would not hold. *Columbus* 46
 Not even by one hair's-breadth of *h*, " 64
 Thy elect have no dealings with either *h* or orthodoxy, *Akbar's D., Inscrip.* 7
 H to the heretic, and religion to the orthodox, " 8
 one of those Who mix the wines of *h* *Akbar's Dream* 174
Heretic And burn'd alive as *h*'s ! *Sir J. Oldcastle* 48
 He would be found a *h* to Himself, " 182
 Heresy to the *h*, and religion to the orthodox, *Akbar's D., Inscrip.* 8
Heretical They said with such *h* arrogance *Sir J. Oldcastle* 15
Heritage Will not another take their *h* ? *Aylmer's Field* 786
 Push'd from his chair of regal *h*, *Lover's Tale* i 118
 This *h* of the past; *Freedom* 24
Hermit Knave, my knight, a *h* once was here, *Gareth and L* 1196
 For help and shelter to the *h*'s cave. " 1209
 now for forty years A *h*, who had pray'd, *Lancelot and E.* 403
 Then came the *h* out and bare him in, " 519
 h, skill'd in all The simples and the science " 861
 and thereby A holy *h* in a hermitage, *Holy Grail* 443
 When the *h* made an end, " 457
 there the *h* slaked my burning thirst, " 461
Hermitage thereby A holy hermit in a *h*, " 443
Hermon we shall stand transfigured, like Christ on *H* hill, *Happy* 38
Hern I come from haunts of coot and *h*, *The Brook* 23
 And floods the haunts of *h* and crake; *In Mem.* ci 14
 When the lone *h* forgets his melancholy, *Gareth and L.* 1185
 swamps and pools, waste places of the *h*, *Geraint and E.* 31
 Who lost the *h* we slipt her at, *Lancelot and E.* 657
Hero *h*'es tall Dislodging pinnacle and parapet *D. of F. Women* 25
 Heroic, for a *h* lies beneath, *Princess, Pro.* 212
 Or be yourself your *h* if you will.' " 222
 I answer'd, ' each is *h* in his turn ! " 228
 While horse and *h* fell, *Light Brigade* 44

Hero (*continued*) To greet us, her young *h* in her arms ! *Lover's Tale* iv 171
 as the bravest *h* of song, *V. of Maeldune* 5
 Crept to his North again, Hoar-headed *h* ! *Batt. of Brunanburh* 64
 Never had huger Slaughter of *h*'es " 111
Herod *H*, when the shout was in his ears, *Palace of Art* 219
Heroic (adj.) (*See also* **Mock-heroic, True-heroic**) *H*, for a hero lies beneath, Grave, solemn ! ' *Princess, Pro.* 212
 H if you will, or what you will, " 221
 H seems our Princess as required— " 230
 ' Why take the style of those *h* times ? *The Epic* 35
 One equal temper of *h* hearts, *Ulysses* 68
 So past the strong *h* soul away. *Enoch Arden* 915
 The massive square of his *h* breast, *Marr. of Geraint* 75
 and thou, *H* sailor-soul, *Sir J. Franklin* 2
 golden lyre Is ever sounding in *h* ears *H* hymns, *Tiresias* 181
Heroic (s) In mock *h*'s stranger than our own; *Princess, Con.* 64
Heroine ' Take Lilia, then, for *h*,' " *Pro.* 223
 When dames and *h*'s of the golden year " vi 64
 greatest of women, island *h*, Kapiolani *Kapiolani* 5
Heroism earn from both the praise of *h*, *Sisters (E. and E.)* 251
Heron the *h* rises from his watch beside the mere, *Happy* 3
Herse (horse) Fur 'e smell'd like a *h* a-singein', *Owd Roä* 101
Hesitating Down the long tower-stairs, *h*: *Lancelot and E.* 343
Hesp (hasp) why didn't tha *h* the gaäte ? *Village Wife* 124
Hesper *H* is stayed between the two peaks; *Leonine Eleg.* 11
 False-eyed *H*, unkind, " 16
 Large *H* glitter'd on her tears, *Mariana in the S.* 90
 Sad *H* o'er the buried sun *In Mem.* cxxi 1
 H, whom the poet call'd the Bringer home of all good things. *Locksley H., Sixty* 185
 All good things may move in *H*, perfect peoples, " 186
 H—Venus—were we native to that splendour " 187
Hesperian Disclosed a fruit of pure *H* gold, *Œnone* 66
Hesperus that *H* all things bringeth, *Leonine Eleg.* 13
 ' MERIDIES '—' *H* '—' NOX '—' MORS,' *Gareth and L.* 1204
Hesper-Phosphor Sweet *H-P*, double name *In Mem.* cxxi 17
Hest Yet I thy *h* will all perform at full, *M. d'Arthur* 43
 Yet I thy *h* will all perform at full, *Pass. of Arthur* 211
Hetairai girls, *H*, curious in their art, *Lucretius* 52
Hetty An' *H* wur weak i' the hattics, *Village Wife* 101
Hew my arm was lifted to *h* down A Cavalier *D. of F. Women* 45
 draw water, or *h* wood, Or grosser tasks; *Gareth and L.* 486
Hew'd my race *H* Ammon, hip and thigh, *D. of F. Women* 238
 And *h* great pieces of his armour off him, *Gareth and L.* 1142
 Sympathy *h* out The bosom-sepulchre of Sympathy ? *Lover's Tale* ii 31
 H the lindenwood, Hack'd the battleshield, *Batt. of Brunanburh* 12
 and *h* Like broad oaks with thunder. *The Tourney* 10
Hewing woodman at a bough Wearily *h*. *Balin and Balan* 295
 All that day long labour'd, *h* the pines, *Death of Œnone* 62
Hewn With rugged maxims *h* from life; *Ode on Well.* 184
 the splintering spear, the hard mail *h*, *Pass. of Arthur* 108
Hexameter rise And long roll of the *H*— *Lucretius* 11
 THESE lame *h*'s the strong-wing'd music *Trans. of Homer* 1
 H's no worse than daring Germany gave us, Barbarous experiment, barbarous *h*'s. " 5
Heye (eye) But the heät druv hout i' my *h*'s *Owd Roä* 84
Hiccup man coomin' in wi' a *h* *Spinster's S's.* 98
Hic Jacet by the cold *H J*'s of the dead ! ' *Merlin and V.* 753
Hid (*See also* **Half-hid, 'Id**) For *h* in ringlets day and night, *Miller's D.* 173
 And *h* Excalibur the second time, *M. d'Arthur* 111
 and Dora *h* her face By Mary. *Dora* 156
 h his face From all men, *Walk. to the Mail* 20
 ' I would have *h* her needle in my heart, *Edwin Morris* 62
 Saying, ' I have *h* my feelings, *Locksley Hall* 29
 From havens *h* in fairy bowers, *The Voyage* 54
 Which *h* the Holiest from the people's eyes *Aylmer's Field* 772
 echo like a ghostly woodpecker, *H* in the ruins; *Princess, Pro.* 218
 some *h* and sought In the orange thickets: " ii 459
 The woman's garment *h* the woman's heart.' " v 305
 mumbled it, And *h* her bosom with it; " vi 214
 Woods where we *h* from the wet, *Window, Marr. Morn.* 6
 The moon is *h*; the night is still; *In Mem.* xxviii 2
 The moon is *h*, the night is still; " civ 2

Hid (*continued*)   an Isis *h* by the veil.   *Maud I iv* 43
more exprest Than *h* her, clung about her lissome
   limbs,   *Merlin and V.* 223
and not with half disdain *H* under grace,   *Lancelot and E.* 264
H from the wide world's rumour by the grove   " 522
And *h* Excalibur the second time,   *Pass. of Arthur* 279
and falling *h* the frame.   *Lover's Tale iv* 217
She feels the Sun is *h* but for a night,   *Ancient Sage* 73
Would Earth tho' *h* in cloud   *Happy* 97
left his dagger behind him. I found it. I *h* it away.   *Bandit's Death* 12

Hidalgo   and his *H*'s—shipwrecks, famines,   *Columbus* 225

Hidden   (*See also* **Half-hidden, Haze-hidden, Helmet-
   hidden**)   place with joy *H* in sorrow: *Dying Swan* 23
The smell of violets, *h* in the green,   *D. of F. Women* 77
Gold-mines of thought to lift the *h* ore   " 274
Hail, *h* to the knees in fern,   *Talking Oak* 29
h from the heart's disgrace,   *Locksley Hall* 57
Lay *h* as the music of the moon   *Aylmer's Field* 102
warm-blue breathings of a *h* hearth   " 155
'betwixt these two Division smoulders *h*;   *Princess iii* 79
her face Wellnigh was *h* in the minster gloom;   *Com. of Arthur* 289
let my name Be *h*, and give me the first quest,   *Gareth and L.* 545
Nay, truly we were *h* : this fair lord,   *Balin and Balan* 507
and bottom of the well, Where Truth is *h*.   *Merlin and V.* 48
Now guess'd a *h* meaning in his arms,   *Lancelot and E.* 17
Lancelot saying, 'Hear, but hold my name *H*,   " 417
know full well Where your great knight is *h*,   " 690
echoes in the wall Rang out like hollow woods   *Pelleas and E.* 366
(When first I learnt thee *h* here)   *Guinevere* 539
number'd the bones, I have *h* them all.   *Rizpah* 10
h there from the light of the sun—   *Def. of Lucknow* 63
Mother's diamonds *h* from her there,   *The Ring* 142
And all the winters are *h*.   *The Throstle* 16
A thousand things are *h* still   *Mechanophilus* 23
'Some *h* principle to move,   *Two Voices* 133
'A *h* hope,' the voice replied: " 441
sitting in the deeps Upon the *h* bases of the hills.'   *M. d'Arthur* 106
And draws the veil from *h* worth.   *Day-Dm., Arrival* 4
How dark those *h* eyes must be !'   " 32
See with clear eye some *h* shame   *In Mem. li* 7
distant hills From *h* summits fed with rills   " *ciii* 7
sitting in the deeps Upon the *h* bases of the hills.'   *Pass. of Arthur* 274
that sends the *h* sun Down yon dark sea,   *De Prof., Two G.* 33
Son, in the *h* world of sight, that lives   *Tiresias* 51
Fear not thou the *h* purpose of that Power   *God and the Univ.* 5

Hide   (*See also* **'Ide**)   run to and fro, and *h* and seek,   *The Mermaid* 35
for the tear thou couldst not *h*,   *The Bridesmaid* 11
'I cannot h that some have striven,   *Two Voices* 208
neither *h* the ray From those, not blind,   *Love thou thy land* 14
Where shall I *h* my forehead and my eyes ?   *M. d'Arthur* 228
Oh, *h* thy knotted knees in fern,   *Talking Oak* 93
H me from my deep emotion,   *Locksley Hall* 108
H, *h* them, million-myrtled wilderness,   *Lucretius* 204
And cavern-shadowing laurels, *h* !   " 205
See they sit, they *h* their faces,   *Boädicea* 51
Is there no baseness we would *h* ?   *In Mem. li* 3
And *h* thy shame beneath the ground.   " *lxxii* 28
That evermore she long'd to *h* herself,   *Gareth and L.* 111
will *h* with mantling flowers As if for pity ?'   " 1392
if he die, why earth has earth enough To *h* him.   *Geraint and E.* 555
Well, *h* it, *h* it ; I shall find it out ;   *Merlin and V.* 528
h it therefore ; go unknown : Win !   *Lancelot and E.* 151
therefore would he *h* his name From all men,   " 580
And sharply turn'd about to *h* her face,   " 608
There will I *h* thee, till my life shall end,   *Guinevere* 114
Would God that thou could'st *h* me from myself !   " 118
Where shall I *h* my forehead and my eyes ?   *Pass. of Arthur* 396
Dust to dust—low down—let us *h* !   *Rizpah* 37
H me, Mother ! my Fathers belong'd to the church of old,   *The Wreck* 1
I would *h* from the storm without,   " 9
I will *h* my face, I will tell you all.   " 12
and higher, The cloud that *h*'s it—   *Ancient Sage* 12
Marriage will not *h* it,   *Forlorn* 50

Hideous   Day, mark'd as with some *h* crime,   *In Mem. lxxii* 18

Hideousness   roofs of slated *h* !   *Locksley H., Sixty* 246

Hiding   (*See also* **Heart-hiding**)   To take me to that
   h in the hills.   *Sir J. Oldcastle* 2
Hiding-place   by mine head she knows his *h-p*.'   *Lancelot and E.* 714
High   (*See also* **Breast-high, Brow-high**)   either babbling
   world of *h* and low ;   *Ode on Well.* 182
Peak, That standest *h* above all ?   *Voice and the P.* 10
The Peak is *h* and flush'd   " 29
The Peak is *h*, and the stars are *h*,   " 31
they set him on *h* That all the ships   *Rizpah* 37
She is *h* in the Heaven of Heavens,   *Charity* 42
Some too *h*—no fault of thine—   *Poets and Critics* 12
Whether the *h* field on the bushless Pike,   *Ode to Memory* 96
Heaven flow'd upon the soul in many dreams Of *h* desire.   *The Poet* 32
Whither away from the *h* green field,   *Sea-Fairies* 8
To the pale-green sea-groves straight and *h*,   *The Merman* 19
H things were spoken there, unhanded down ;   *Alexander* 12
live alone unto herself In her *h* palace there.   *Palace of Art* 12
h shrine-doors burst thro' with heated blasts   *D. of F. Women* 29
'The *h* masts flicker'd as they lay afloat ;   " 113
his forehead like a rising sun *H* from the daïs-
   throne—   *M. d'Arthur* 218
Three years I lived upon a pillar, *h* Six cubits,   *St. S. Stylites* 86
this *h* dial, which my sorrow crowns—   " 95
From my *h* nest of penance here proclaim   " 167
H towns on hills were dimly seen,   *The Voyage* 34
That girt the region with *h* cliff and lawn :   *Vision of Sin* 47
trees As *h* as heaven, and every bird that sings :   *Sea Dreams* 102
Both crown'd with stars and *h* among the stars,—   " 241
'And make her some great Princess, six feet *h*,   *Princess, Pro.* 224
Or Nymph, or Goddess, at *h* tide of feast,   " *i* 197
At these *h* words, we conscious of ourselves,   " *ii* 67
fail so far In *h* desire, they know not,   " *iii* 280
They haled us to the Princess where she sat *H* in the
   hall :   " *iv* 272
when a boy, you stoop'd to me From all *h* places,   " 430
From the *h* tree the blossom wavering fell,   " *vi* 80
trust in all things *h* Comes easy to him,   " *vii* 329
Or tower, or *h* hill-convent, seen   *The Daisy* 29
With many a rivulet *h* against the Sun   *The Islet* 21
Calm and deep peace on this *h* wold,   *In Mem. xi* 5
Did ever rise from *h* to higher ;   " *xli* 16
My guardian angel will speak out In that *h* place,   " *xliv* 16
The *h* Muse answer'd : 'Wherefore grieve   " *lviii* 16
And moving up from *h* to higher,   " *lxiv* 13
H nature amorous of the good,   " *cix* 9
up in the *h* Hall-garden I see her pass like a light ;   *Maud I iv* 11
For him did his *h* sun flame,   " 32
Not making his *h* place the lawless perch   *Ded. of Idylls* 22
And even in *h* day the morning star.   *Com. of Arthur* 100
Beheld, so *h* upon the dreary deeps   " 373
To whom arrived, by Dubric the *h* saint,   " 453
In whom *h* God hath breathed a secret thing.   " 501
At times the summit of the *h* city flash'd ;   *Gareth and L.* 192
over all *H* on the top were those three Queens,   " 229
H nose, a nostril large and fine,   " 465
there past into the hall A damsel of *h* lineage,   " 588
Lyonors, A lady of *h* lineage, of great lands,   " 609
rose *H* that the highest-crested helm could ride   " 673
that day a feast had been Held in *h* hall,   " 848
Till *h* above him, circled with her maids,   " 1374
darken'd from the *h* light in his eyes,   *Marr. of Geraint* 100
lords and ladies of the *h* court went In silver tissue   " 662
Geraint Woke where he slept in the *h* hall,   " 755
another gift of the *h* God, Which, maybe,   " 821
giant tower, from whose *h* crest, they say,   " 827
For by the hands of Dubric, the *h* saint,   " 838
Held his head *h*, and thought himself a knight,   *Geraint and E.* 242
For once, when I was up so *h* in pride   " 790
And oft I talk'd with Dubric, the *h* saint,   " 865
but when he mark'd his *h* sweet smile In passing,   *Balin and Balan* 160
'Too *h* this mount of Camelot for me :   " 226
Borne by some *h* Lord-prince of Arthur's hall,   " 466
See now, I set thee *h* on vantage ground,   " 534
And the *h* purpose broken by the worm.   *Merlin and V.* 196
passing one, at the *h* peep of dawn,   " 560

Hignorant (ignorant) ' A *h* village wife as 'ud hev to
  be larn'd her awn plaàce,'   *Village Wife* 106
Hill (surname)   (*See also* **Letty, Letty Hill**) millionaires,
  Here lived the *H*'s—   *Edwin Morris* 11
Hill (*See also* **Chalk-hill, Clover-hill, 'Ill**) Nor the
  wind on the *h*.   *All Things will Die* 26
And hollows of the fringed *h*'s   *Supp. Confessions* 153
ridge Of heaped *h*'s that mound the sea,   *Ode to Memory* 98
Spring Letters cowslips on the *h* ?   *Adeline* 62
And the hearts of purple *h*'s,   *Eleänore* 17
From the bosom of a *h*.   *Kate* 5
flee By town, and tower, and *h*, and cape, and
  isle,   *Mine be the strength* 6
new deluge from a thousand *h*'s   *If I were loved* 12
The willowy *h*'s and fields among,   *L. of Shalott* iv 25
The white chalk-quarry from the *h*   *Miller's D.* 115
Before he mounts the *h*, I know He cometh quickly: *Fatima* 22
a fire Is poured upon the *h*'s,   31
lovelier Than all the valleys of Ionian *h*'s.   *Œnone* 2
Paris, once her playmate on the *h*'s.   ,, 17
the noonday quiet holds the *h*:   ,, 25
Hear me, O Earth, hear me, O *H*'s,   ,, 36
I waited underneath the dawning *h*'s,   ,, 47
In this green valley, under this green *h*,   ,, 232
sounds at night come from the inmost *h*'s,   ,, 249
Or over *h*'s with peaky tops engrail'd,   *Palace of Art* 113
and the crowfoot are over all the *h*,   *May Queen* 38
There's not a flower on all the *h*'s: *May Queen, N. Y's. E.* 13
cock crows from the farm upon the *h*,   ,, 23
His waters from the purple *h*—   *Lotos-Eaters, C. S.* 93
reclined On the *h*'s like Gods together,   110
And thunder on the everlasting *h*'s.   *D. of F. Women* 226
Steps from her airy *h*, and greens The swamp,   *On a Mourner* 8
Had rest by stony *h*'s of Crete.   35
Upon the hidden bases of the *h*'s.'   *M. d'Arthur* 106
Larger than human on the frozen *h*'s.   ,, 183
those that stood upon the *h*'s behind   ,, *Ep.* 25
The cuckoo told his name to all the *h*'s;   *Gardener's D.* 93
till we reach'd The limit of the *h*'s;   *Audley Court* 83
buffet round the *h*'s, from bluff to bluff.   *Golden Year* 77
Rift the *h*'s, and roll the waters,   *Locksley Hall* 186
far across the *h*'s they went In that new world   *Day-Dm., Depart.* 3
Across the *h*'s, and far away   ,, 5
And o'er the *h*'s, and far away Beyond   ,, 29
By Ellen's grave, on the windy *h*.   *Edward Gray* 12
High towns on *h*'s were dimly seen,   *The Voyage* 34
And *h*'s and scarlet-mingled woods Glow'd   ,, 47
go on To their haven under the *h*;   *Break, break, etc.* 10
but as he climb'd the *h*, Just where the prone edge   *Enoch Arden* 66
silent water slipping from the *h*'s,   ,, 633
to the *h*. There he sat down gazing on all below;   ,, 722
By thirty *h*'s I hurry down, '   *The Brook* 27
with her strong feet up the steep *h* Trod out a path: *Sea Dreams* 120
From *h*'s, that look'd across a land of hope,   *Princess* i 169
With whom I sang about the morning *h*'s,   ,, ii 247
still be dear beyond the southern *h*'s;   ,, 265
A double *h* ran up his furrowy forks   ,, iii 174
The river as it narrow'd to the *h*'s.   ,, 196
They faint on *h* or field or river: ,, iv 14
found that you had gone, Ridd'n to the *h*'s,   ,, 343
came As night to him that sitting on a *h*   ,, 574
And Hit the Northern *h*'s.   ,, v 44
Forgotten, rusting on his iron *h*'s,   ,, 146
Suck'd from the dark heart of the long *h*'s   ,, 349
In height and cold, the splendour of the *h*'s?   ,, vii 194
Till o'er the *h*'s her eagles flew   *Ode on Well.* 112
tho' the Giant Ages heave the *h* And break the shore,   ,, 259
and Charlie ploughing the *h*.   *Grandmother* 80
Sown in a wrinkle of the monstrous *h*,   *Will* 19
The Priest went out by heath and *h*;   *The Victim* 29
the stars, the seas, the *h*'s and the plains—   *High. Pantheism* 1
I stand on the slope of the *h*,   *Window, On the Hill* 9
And makes a silence in the *h*'s.   *In Mem.* xix 8
But all the lavish *h*'s would hum   ,, xxiii 11
The Christmas bells from *h* to *h* Answer each other   ,, xxviii 3

Hill (*continued*) sound of streams that swift or slow
  Draw down Æonian *h*'s,   *In Mem.* xxxv 11
whisper sweet About the ledges of the *h*.'   ,, xxxvii 8
Or seal'd within the iron *h*'s?   ,, lvi 20
A distant dearness in the *h*,   ,, lxiv 19
chequer-work of beam and shade Along the *h*'s,   ,, lxxii 16
And *h* and wood and field did print   ,, lxxix 7
Descend below the golden *h*'s With promise   ,, lxxxiv 28
Beyond the bounding *h* to stray,   ,, lxxxix 30
And those fair *h*'s I sail'd below,   ,, xcviii 2
I climb the *h*: from end to end   ,, c 1
Nor quarry trench'd along the *h*   ,, 11
memory fades From all the circle of the *h*'s.   ,, ci 24
distant *h*'s From hidden summits fed with rills   ,, ciii 6
A single church below the *h* Is pealing,   ,, civ 3
The *h*'s are shadows, and they flow From form to form,   ,, cxxiii 5
spread Their sleeping silver thro' the *h*'s;   ,, *Con.* 116
fleet came yonder round by the *h*,   *Maud I* i 49
I am sick of the Hall and the *h*,   ,, 61
Down by the *h* I saw them ride,   ,, ix 1
Plucking the harmless wild-flower on the *h* ?—   ,, *II* i 3
saw The smallest rock far on the faintest *h*,   *Com. of Arthur* 99
Men saw the goodly *h*'s of Somerset,   *Marr. of Geraint* 828
But not to goodly *h* or yellow sea   ,, 830
all night long a cloud clings to the *h*,   *Geraint and E.* 691
Men weed the white horse on the Berkshire *h*'s   ,, 936
he saw Fired from the west, far on a *h*,   *Lancelot and E.* 168
broke The Pagan yet once more on Badon *h*.'   ,, 280
Among the tumbled fragments of the *h*'s.'   ,, 1427
a silver horn from o'er the *h*'s Blown,   *Holy Grail* 109
I rode on and found a mighty *h*,   ,, 421
a lowly vale, Low as the *h* was high,   ,, 441
' There rose a *h* that none but man could climb,   ,, 489
h, or plain, at sea, or flooding ford.   ,, 728
h and wood Went ever streaming by him   *Pelleas and E.* 547
set his name High on all *h*'s,   *Last Tournament* 337
When round him bent the spirits of the *h*'s   *Guinevere* 283
on from *h* to *h*, and every day Beheld at noon   ,, 392
Far in the moonlit haze among the *h*'s,   *Pass. of Arthur* 42
Upon the hidden bases of the *h*'s.'   ,, 274
Larger than human on the frozen *h*'s.   ,, 351
the vacancies Between the tufted *h*'s,   *Lover's Tale* i 3
pines that fledge The *h*'s that watch'd thee,   ,, 12
muse On those dear *h*'s, that never more will meet   ,, 32
Apart, alone together on those *h*'s.   ,, 190
His mountain-altars, his high *h*'s,   ,, 322
reach'd The grassy platform on some *h*,   ,, 341
how native Unto the *h*'s she trod on !   ,, 360
we came To what our people call, ' The *H* of Woe.'   ,, 374
Arise in open prospect—heath and *h*,   ,, 397
' let this be call'd henceforth The *H* of Hope; ' and I
  replied, ' O sister, My will is one with thine; the *H*
  of Hope.'   ,, 462
We trod the shadow of the downward *h*;   ,, 515
Sometimes upon the *h*'s beside the sea   ,, ii 4
Chiefly I sought the cavern and the *h*   ,, 33
Great *h*'s of ruins, and collapsed masses   ,, 65
From out the yellow woods upon the *h*   ,, 80
wander round the bases of the *h*'s,   ,, 121
the woods upon the *h* Waved with a sudden gust   ,, iii 34
cheeks as bright as when she climb'd the *h*.   ,, 47
fain have torrents, lakes, *H*'s,   *Sisters (E. and E.)* 221
To take me to that hiding in the *h*'s.   *Sir J. Oldcastle* 2
spend my one last year among the *h*'s.   *Ancient Sage* 16
the *h*'s are white with rime.   *The Flight* 4
if yonder *h* be level with the flat.   *Locksley H., Sixty* 111
Down the *h*, down the *h*, thousands of Russians,   *Heavy Brigade* 1
up the *h*, up the *h*, up the *h*, Follow'd the Heavy
  Brigade.   ,, 11
and up the *h*, up the *h*, gallopt the gallant three
  hundred,   ,, 24
Up the *h*, up the *h*, up the *h*, out of the field,   ,, 63
domes the red-plow'd *h*'s With loving blue;   *Early Spring* 3
cuckoo cries From out a phantom *h*;   *Pref. Poem Broth. S.* 20
I climb'd the *h* with Hubert yesterday,   *The Ring* 152

Hill (continued)   we shall stand transfigured, like Christ on
Hermon h,   *Happy* 38
Where am I ? snow on all the h's !   *Romney's R.* 12
To wallow in that winter of the h's.   „ 15
I had been among the h's, and brought you down   „ 78
But, while the h's remain, Up h ' Too-slow ' will need the
whip, Down h ' Too-quick,' the chain.   *Politics* 10
Hill-convent   Or tower, or high h-c, seen   *The Daisy* 29
Hill-fort   storming a h-f of thieves He got it ;   *Aylmer's Field* 225
Hillock   Peace Pipe on her pastoral h   *Maud III vi* 24
The mortal h, Would break into blossom ;   *Merlin and the G.* 107
Hill-pass   high h-p'es of stainless snow,   *Dead Prophet* 47
Hill-side (See also 'Ill-Side')   woods that belt the
gray h-s,   *Ode to Memory* 55
The whole h-s was redder than a fox.   *Walk. to the Mail* 3
Hill-slope   damp h-s's were quickened into green,   *Gareth and L.* 184
Hillsnow   a brow Like h high in heaven,   *Last Tournament* 667
Hilt   But with his hand against the h,   *Love thou thy land* 83
sparkled keen with frost against the h :   *M. d' Arthur* 55
But when he saw the wonder of the h,   „ 85
Thou would'st betray me for the precious h ;   „ 126
caught him by the h, and branish'd him (repeat)   „ 145, 160
So great a miracle as yonder h.   „ 156
rich With jewels, elfin Urim, on the h,   *Com. of Arthur* 299
Clash'd his, and brake it utterly to the h.   *Gareth and L.* 1148
Caught at the h, as to abolish him :   *Marr. of Geraint* 210
sparkled keen with frost against the h :   *Pass. of Arthur* 223
But when he saw the wonder of the h,   „ 253
Thou would'st betray me for the precious h ;   „ 294
caught him by the h, and branish'd him (repeat)   „ 313, 328
So great a miracle as yonder h.   „ 324
Hilted   *See* **Golden-Hilted**
Hind   the h fell, the herd was driven, Fire glimpsed ;   *Com. of Arthur* 432
the h To whom a space of land is given to plow.   *Holy Grail* 906
Calling me thy white h, and saying to me   *Last Tournament* 569
Hinder   Came all in haste to h wrong,   *Princess iv* 401
What h's me To take such bloody vengeance   „ 533
And so, before the two could h him,   *Gareth and L.* 1368
rule the land Hereafter, which God h.'   *Lancelot and E.* 66
' Heaven h,' said the King,   „ 532
Hindering (See also **Marriage-hindering**)   Had made the
pretext of a h wound,   „ 582
Hindrance   Divinely thro' all h finds the man   „ 333
Hindustan   Thro' all the warring world of H   *Akbar's Dream* 26
Hinge   The doors upon their h's creak'd ;   *Mariana* 62
So frequent on its h before.   [*Deserted House* 8
Half-parted from a weak and scolding h,   *The Brook* 84
I grate on rusty h's here : '   *Princess i* 86
Hingin' (hanging)   wi' my hairm h down to the floor,   *Owd Roä* 65
Hinjian (Indian)   Till I gied 'em H curn,   *Village Wife* 118
Hinn (Inn)   I started awaäy like a shot, an' down to
the H,   *North. Cobbler* 69
tha mun göa fur it down to the H,   „ 113
out o' sight o' the winders o' Gigglesby H—   *Spinsters S's.* 35
Hint (s)   A little h to solace woe, A h,   *Two Voices* 433
Like h's and echoes of the world   *Day-Dm., Sleep. P.* 7
No h of death in all his frame,   *In Mem. xiv* 18
with shadow'd h confuse A life that leads   „ xxxiii 7
A little flash, a mystic h ;   „ xliv 8
And sowing one ill h from ear to ear,   *Merlin and V.* 143
dark sweet h's of some who prized him   „ 159
Hint (verb)   Ah pity—h it not in human tones,   *Wan Sculptor* 11
Alone might h of my disgrace ;   *Two Voices* 360
laughingly Would h at worse in either.   *Enoch Arden* 481
We whisper, and h, and chuckle,   *Maud I iv* 29
Hinted   matron saw That h love was only wasted bait,   *The Ring* 360
Hip   *See* **Huck**
Hip and Thigh   my race Hew'd Ammon, h a t,   *D. of F. Women* 233
Hire (s)   Money—my h—his money—   *Charity* 19
Hire (verb)   And h thyself to serve for meats   *Gareth and L.* 153
h myself To serve with scullions and with kitchen knaves ;   „ 169
But h us some fair chamber for the night,   *Geraint and E.* 238
Hired   h himself to work within the fields ;   *Dora* 38
Nurse, were you h ?   *Romney's R.* 16
O yes !   I h you for a season there,   „ 20

Hireling   Who had borne my flower on her h heart,   *The Wreck* 143
Hispaniola   Howl'd me from H ;   *Columbus* 118
harmless people whom we found In H's island-Paradise !   „ 182
Hiss   the hot h And bustling whistle of the youth   *Marr. of Geraint* 256
h, snake—I saw him there—Let the fox bark,   *Pelleas and E.* 471
A h as from a wilderness of snakes,   *St. Telemachus* 66
Hiss'd   h each at other's ear What shall not be
wedded her,' he said, Not said, but h it :   *Geraint and E.* 634
He h, ' Let us revenge ourselves,   *Last Tournament* 620
Hissing   Each h in his neighbour's ear ;   *Happy* 63
And dipt in baths of h tears,   *Princess v* 15
h in war on his own hearthstone ?   *In Mem. cxviii* 23
geese of the world that are ever h dispraise   *Maud I i* 24
h spray wind-driven Far thro' the dizzy dark.   „ iv 52
Garlon, h ;   then he sourly smiled.   *Lover's Tale ii* 198
he, h ' I have no sword,' Sprang from the door   *Balin and Balin* 355
roused a snake that h writhed away ;   *Pelleas and E.* 602
Hist   H O H,' he said, ' They seek us :   *Death of Œnone* 88
   Princess iv 218
Historic   *See* **Half-Historic**
History   boyish *histories* Of battle,   *Aylmer's Field* 97
would chant the h Of that great race,   *In Mem. ciii* 34
Now made a pretty h to herself   *Lancelot and E.* 18
old writers Have writ of in *histories*—   *Batt. of Brunanburh* 115
Poor old Heraldry, poor old H,   *Locksley H., Sixty* 249
kindliness Rare in Fable or H,   *On Jub. Q. Victoria* 5
as this poor earth's pale h runs,—   *Vastness* 3
Hit (s)   With twisted quirks and happy h's,   *Will Water.* 189
Hit (verb)   He scarcely h my humour,   *Edwin Morris* 76
And h the Northern hills.   *Princess v* 44
dream can h the mood Of Love on earth ?   *In Mem. xlvii* 11
Some sudden vivid pleasure h him there.   *Lover's Tale iv* 178
An' I h on an old deal-box   *First Quarrel* 48
Has h on this, which you will take My Fitz,   *To E. Fitzgerald* 50
Hither   And on the h side, or so she look'd,   *Princess ii* 107
But on the h side of that loud morn   *Last Tournament* 56
Hitting   aim'd All at one mark, with a h   *Aylmer's Field* 95
h all we saw with shafts Of gentle satire,   *Princess ii* 468
Hive   Audley feast Humm'd like a h all round   *Audley Court* 5
from all the provinces, And fill the h.'   *Princess ii* 98
—Wasps in our good h,   „ iv 535
There the h of Roman liars worship   *Boädicea* 19
h of those wild bees That made such honey   *Holy Grail* 214
vineyard, h and horse and herd ;   *To Virgil* 10
moment's anger of bees in their h ?   *Vastness* 35
Hiven (heaven)   an' H in its glory smiled,   *Tomorrow* 25
An' sorra the bog that's in H   „ 67
An' tell thim in H about Molly Magee   „ 92
Hoälm (Holm)   an' Thurnaby h's to plow !   *N. Farmer, O. S.* 52
Hoam (home)   I walk'd wi' tha all the way h   *Spinster's S's.* 32
Hoar   Make thy grass h with early rime.   *Two Voices* 66
brows in silent hours become Unnaturally h with
rime,   *St. S. Stylites* 166
the lawn as yet Is h with rime,   *To F. D. Maurice* 42
And the willow-branches h and dank,   *Dying Swan* 37
made The h hair of the Baronet bristle up   *Aylmer's Field* 42
descending from the sacred peak Of h
high-templed Faith,   *Pref. Son. 19th Cent.* 10
Hoard (s)   With a little h of maxims preaching   *Locksley Hall* 94
a h of tales that dealt with knights,   *Princess, Pro.* 29
Our h is little, but our hearts are great.
(repeat)   *Marr. of Geraint* 352, 374
From his great h of happiness distill'd   *Lover's Tale i* 714
Struck for their h's and their hearths   *Batt. of Brunanburh* 19
Hoard (verb)   I h it as a sugar-plum for Holmes.'   *The Epic* 43
That h, and sleep, and feed,   *Ulysses* 5
some three suns to store and h myself,   „ 29
To h all savings to the uttermost,   *Enoch Arden* 46
I h in thought The faded rhymes and scraps   *Lover's Tale i* 288
Hoarded   h in herself, Grew, seldom seen :   *Gardener's D.* 9
Hoarding   perhaps the h sense Gives out at times   *In Mem. xliv* 6
Hoarhead   Came on the h woodman at a bough   *Balin and Balan* 294
Hoar-headed   Crept to his North again, H-h
hero !   *Batt. of Brunanburh* 65
Hoarse   I hear thee not at all, or h   *The Blackbird* 19
Hoary   And h to the wind.   *Palace of Art* 80

Hoary (*continued*) O'erflourish'd with the *h* clematis :   *Golden Year* 63
     Set thy *h* fancies free ;   *Vision of Sin* 156
     Still makes a *h* eyebrow for the gleam   *The Brook* 80
     a *h* face Meet for the reverence of the hearth,   *Aylmer's Field* 332
     h Channel Tumbles a billow on chalk and sand ;   *To F. D. Maurice* 23
     Take the *h* Roman head and shatter it,   *Boädicea* 65
     And eating *h* grain and pulse the steeds,   *Spec. of Iliad* 21
     From youth and babe and *h* hairs :   *In Mem. lxix* 10
     Nor *h* knoll of ash and haw   „   *c* 9
     lifted his voice, and call'd A *h* man,   *Com. of Arthur* 145
     Then spake the *h* chamberlain and said,   „   148
     But none spake word except the *h* Earl :   *Marr. of Geraint* 369
     Then suddenly addrest the *h* Earl :   „   402
     Half-suffocated in the *h* fell   *Merlin and V.* 840
     And glancing thro' the *h* boles,   *Pelleas and E.* 50
     From *h* deeps that belt the changeful West,   *Prog. of Spring* 98
     h Sheik, On whom the women shrieking ' Atheist '   *Akbar's Dream* 90
Hoary-headed There musing sat the *h-h* Earl,   *Marr. of Geraint* 295
     Then sigh'd and smiled the *h-h* Earl,   „   307
Hob wi' my oän kettle theere o' the *h*,   *Spinster's S's.* 9
Hob-and-nob Let us *h-a-n* with Death.   *Vision of Sin* 74
     H-a-n with brother Death !   „   194
Hobble *See* **Hopple**
Hoed *See* **Stubb'd**
Hofficer (officer) she walkt awaäy wi' a *h* lad,   *Village Wife* 97
Hog his ploughs, his cows, his *h's*, his dogs ;   *The Brook* 125
     And sleeker shall he shine than any *h*.'   *Gareth and L.* 460
     men brought in whole *h's* and quarter beeves,   *Geraint and E.* 602
Hoggish With colt-like whinny and with *h* whine   *St. S. Stylites* 177
Hold (grasp) shuddering took *h* of all my mind,   *May Queen, Con.* 35
     thrice as sweet As woodbine's fragile *h*,   *Talking Oak* 146
     Nor greatly cared to lose, her *h* on life.   *Aylmer's Field* 568
     And that my *h* on life would break   *In Mem. xxviii* 15
     from my *h* on these Streams virtue—fire—   *Gareth and L.* 1309
     of that token on the shield Relax'd his *h* :   *Balin and Balan* 370
     And sweep me from my *h* upon the world,   *Merlin and V.* 303
     and their law Relax'd its *h* upon us,   *Guinevere* 457
     My inward sap, the *h* I have on earth,   *Lover's Tale i* 166
     Hunger of glory gat *H* of the land.   *Batt. of Brunanburh* 125
     Would loose him from his *h* ;   *Ancient Sage* 118
Hold (stronghold) new-comers in an ancient *h*,   *Edwin Morris* 9
     calmer hours to Memory's darkest *h*,   *Love and Duty* 90
     ev'n the lonest *h* were all as free   *Gareth and L.* 598
     I would track this caitiff to his *h*,   *Marr. of Geraint* 415
     by bandit-haunted *h's*, Gray swamps and pools,   *Geraint and E.* 30
     Right in the gateway of the bandit *h*,   „   774
     broke the bandit *h's* and cleansed the land.   „   944
     Scaped thro' a cavern from a bandit *h*,   *Holy Grail* 207
     And many of those who burnt the *h*,   „   264
     defended the *h* that we held with our lives—   *Def. of Lucknow* 7
Hold (of a ship) And the sick men down in the *h*   *The Revenge* 79
Hold (verb) (*See also* **Howd**, **'Owd**) you that *h* A nobler office upon earth   *To the Queen* 1
     in mild unrest *h's* him beneath in her breast.   *Leonine Eleg.* 12
     To *h* a common scorn of death !   *Supp. Confessions* 34
     We may *h* converse with all forms   *Ode to Memory* 115
     ' Yet how should I for certain *h*,   *Two Voices* 340
     For now the noonday quiet *h's* the hill :   *Œnone* 25
     H swollen clouds from raining,   *D. of F. Women* 11
     To *h* his hope thro' shame and guilt,   *Love thou thy land* 82
     there was no anchor, none, To *h* by.'   *The Epic* 21
     hand On Everard's shoulder, with ' I *h* by him.'   „   22
     Whereof this world's *h's* record.   *M. d'Arthur* 16
     He, by some law that *h's* in love,   *Gardener's D.* 9
     h From thence thro' all the worlds :   „   209
     what it *h's* May not be dwelt on by the common day.   „   270
     I will not cease to grasp the hope I *h*   *St. S. Stylites* 5
     my stiff spine can *h* my weary head,   „   43
     Is that the angel there That *h's* a crown ?   „   204
     I *h* them exquisitely knit,   *Talking Oak* 91
     h passion in a leash, And not leap forth   *Love and Duty* 40
     my purpose *h's* To sail beyond the sunset,   *Ulysses* 59
     Yet *h* me met not for ever in thine East :   *Tithonus* 64
     h thee, when his passion shall have spent   *Locksley Hall* 49
     common sense of most shall *h* a fretful realm in awe,   „   129

Hold (verb) (*continued*) Who *h* their hands to all, and cry   *Will Water.* 45
     I *h* it good, good things shall pass :   „   205
     I *h* thee dear For this good pint of port.   „   211
     Shall *h* their orgies at your tomb.   *You might have won* 12
     Enoch would *h* possession for a week :   *Enoch Arden* 27
     Cast all your cares on God ; that anchor *h's*,   „   222
     But let me *h* my purpose till I die.   „   875
     and *h's* her head to other stars,   *The Brook* 195
     ' O pray God that he *h* up '   *Aylmer's Field* 733
     but he that *h's* The Gods are careless,   *Lucretius* 149
     h Your promise : all, I trust, may yet be well.'   *Princess ii* 360
     substance or the shadow ? will it *h* ?   „   409
     such, my friend, We *h* them slight :   „   *iv* 127
     I *h* These flashes on the surface are not   „   252
     You *h* the woman is the better man ;   „   410
     I *h* That it becomes no man to nurse despair,   „   463
     to-morrow morn We *h* a great convention :   „   511
     yet I *h* her, king, True woman :   *Princess, v* 179
     That *h's* a stately fretwork to the Sun,   „   *vi* 86
     never in your own arms To *h* your own,   „   178
     h against the world this honour of the land.   *Third of Feb.* 48
     For those are few we *h* as dear ;   *To F. D. Maurice* 46
     I *h* you here, root and all, in my hand,   *Flow. in cran. wall* 3
     Take the hoary Roman head and shatter it, *h* it abominable,   *Boädicea* 65
     I sometimes *h* it half a sin   *In Mem. v* 1
     lake That *h's* the shadow of a lark   „   *xvi* 9
     I *h* it true, whate'er befall :   „   *xxvii* 13
     And *h's* it sin and shame to draw   „   *xlviii* 11
     H thou the good : define it well :   „   *liii* 13
     To *h* the costliest love in fee.   „   *lxxix* 4
     So *h* I commerce with the dead ;   „   *lxxxv* 93
     they that *h* apart The promise of the golden hours ?   „   105
     h An hour's communion with the dead.   „   *xciv* 3
     And *h* it solemn to the past.   „   *cv* 16
     High wisdom *h's* my wisdom less,   „   *cxii* 1
     To *h* me from my proper place,   „   *cxvii* 2
     And dream my dream, and *h* it true ;   „   *cxxiii* 10
     Rather than *h* by the law that I made,   *Maud 1 i* 55
     h Awe-stricken breaths at a work divine,   „   *x* 16
     Think I may *h* dominion sweet,   „   *xvi* 12
     Arise, my God, and strike, for we *h* Thee just,   „   *II i* 45
     Whatever the Quaker *h's*, from sin ;   „   *v* 92
     theirs are bestial, *h* them less than man :   *Com. of Arthur* 181
     Hath body enow to *h* his foemen down ? '   „   253
     the good mother *h's* me still a child !   *Gareth and L.* 15
     ' An ye *h* me yet for child,   „   99
     h The King a shadow, and the city real :   „   265
     Return, and meet, and *h* him from our eyes,   „   429
     the mightiest, *h's* her stay'd In her own castle,   „   615
     and so my lance *H*, by God's grace,   „   723
     I *h* He scarce is knight, yea but half-man,   „   1175
     Some *h* that he hath swallow'd infant flesh,   „   1342
     We *h* a tourney here to-morrow morn,   *Marr. of Geraint* 287
     How fast they *h* like colours of a shell   „   681
     I *h* a finger up ; They understand—   *Geraint and E.* 337
     h them outer fiends, Who leap at thee to tear thee ;   *Balin and Balan* 141
     That honour too wherein she *h's* him—   „   180
     ' I *h* them happy, so they died for love :   „   581
     some few—ay, truly—youths that *h*   *Merlin and V.* 21
     Lancelot saying, ' Hear, but *h* my name Hidden,   *Lancelot and E.* 416
     Yet, if he love, and his love *h*,   „   697
     some do *h* our Arthur cannot die,   „   1258
     Not at my years, however it *h* in youth.   „   1296
     Unproven, *h's* himself as Lancelot.   *Holy Grail* 304
     to *h*, *H* her a wealthy bride within thine arms,   „   620
     Or all but *h*, and then—cast her aside,   „   622
     But *h* me for your friend :   *Pelleas and E.* 340
     Some *h* he was a table-knight of thine—   *Last Tournament* 69
     A naked aught—yet swine I *h* thee still,   „   309
     I'll *h* thou hast some touch Of music,   „   313
     There *h* thee with my life against the world.' She answer'd, ' Lancelot, wilt thou *h* me so ?   *Guinevere* 115
     that strong castle where he *h's* the Queen ;   „   194
     I *h* that man the worst of public foes   „   512

Hollow-hung   Under the *h-h* ocean green !   *The Merman* 38
Hollowing (*See also* **Fire-hollowing**)   Or *h* one hand
    against his ear,   *Palace of Art* 109
Hollow-ringing   He heard the *h-r* heavens sweep Over him   *Holy Grail* 678
Hollow-vaulted   look'd to shame The *h-v* dark,   *Arabian Nights* 126
Holly (adj.)   while the *h* boughs Entwine the cold baptismal
    font,   *In Mem. xxix* 9
Holly (s)   Sick for the *hollies* and the yews   *Princess, Pro.* 187
    But this is the time of *hollies.*   *Spiteful Letter* 22
    O *hollies* and ivies and evergreens,   „   23
    weave The *h* round the Christmas hearth ;   *In Mem. xxx* 2
    weave The *h* round the Christmas hearth ;   „   *lxxviii* 2
    let us leave This laurel, let this *h* stand :   „   *cv* 2
    here and there great *hollies* under them ;   *Pelleas and E.* 27
    Black *h*, and white-flower'd wayfaring-tree !   *Sir J. Oldcastle* 130
Holly-hoak   Before a tower of crimson *h-h's*,   *Princess, Con.* 82
Hollyhock   Heavily hangs the *h*, (repeat)   *A spirit haunts* 11, 23
    A summer burial deep in *h's* ;   *Aylmer's Field* 164
Holly-spray   And wearing but a *h-s* for crest,   *Last Tournament* 172
Holm (*See also* **Hoälm**)   soft wind blowing over
    meadowy *h's*   *Edwin Morris* 95
Holmes   The parson *H*, the poet Everard Hall,   *The Epic* 4
    I hoard it as a sugar-plum for *H*.'   „   43
Holofernes   underneath The head of *H* peep'd   *Princess iv* 227
Holp   *h* To lace us up, till, each, in maiden plumes   „   *i* 201
    However much he *h* me at my need,   *Com. of Arthur* 142
    Sir Lancelot *h* To raise the Prince,   *Guinevere* 45
Holpen   had I been *h* half as well By this King Arthur   *Com. of Arthur* 161
    And being lustily *h* by the rest,   *Lancelot and E.* 496
Holt   thro' damp *h's* new-flush'd with may,   *My life is full* 19
    She sent her voice thro' all the *h*   *Talking Oak* 123
    blackening over heath and *h*,   *Locksley Hall* 191
    Of wither'd *h* or tilth or pasturage.   *Enoch Arden* 675
    smells a foul-flesh'd agaric in the *h*,   *Gareth and L.* 747
Holy (*See also* **Holy Ghost, Holy Grail**)   All the place is *h*
    ground ;   *Poet's Mind* 9
    H water will I pour Into every spicy flower   „   12
    Heard a carol, mournful, *h*,   *L. of Shalott iv* 28
    Nor steep our brows in slumber's *h* balm ;   *Lotos-Eaters, C. S.* 21
    Beneath a heaven dark and *h*,   „   91
    h organ rolling waves Of sound on roof   *D. of F. Women* 191
    invade Even with a verse your *h* woe.   *To J. S.* 70
    Sleep, *h* spirit, blessed soul,   „   78
    light that led The *h* Elders with the gift of myrrh.   *M. d'Arthur* 233
    more Than many just and *h* men,   *St. S. Stylites* 131
    ' By *h* rood, a royal beard !   *Day-Dm., Revival* 20
    Then desperately seized the *h* Book,   *Enoch Arden* 495
    Haunting a *h* text, and still to that Returning,   *Sea Dreams* 42
    o'er the rest Arising, did his *h* oily best,   „   195
    ' Storm, and what dreams, ye *h* Gods, what dreams !   *Lucretius* 33
    ' Is this thy vengeance, *h* Venus, thine,   „   67
    And *h* secrets of this microcosm.   *Princess iii* 313
    The *h* Gods, they must be appeased,   *The Victim* 47
    The King was shaken with *h* fear ;   „   57
    lead Thro' prosperous floods his *h* urn.   *In Mem. ix* 8
    Rise, happy morn, rise, *h* morn,   „   *xxx* 29
    That *h* Death ere Arthur died   „   *lxxx* 2
    And He that died in *H* Land   „   *lxxxiv* 42
    And woodlands *h* to the dead ;   „   *xcix* 8
    This broad-brimm'd hawker of *h* things,   *Maud I x* 41
    But speak to her all things *h* and high,   „ *II ii* 78
    But there was heard among the *h* hymns   *Com. of Arthur* 290
    And *h* Dubric spread his hands and spake,   „   471
    Save whom she loveth, or a *h* life.   *Gareth and L.* 622
    Whose *h* hand hath fashion'd on the rock   „   1197
    Who, with mild heat of *h* oratory,   *Geraint and E.* 866
    King Took, as in rival heat, to *h* things ;   *Balin and Balan* 100
    brought By *h* Joseph hither,   „   113
    boss'd With *h* Joseph's legend,   „   363
    King Pellam's *h* spear, Reputed to be red with sinless
    blood,   „   556
    Whom Pellam drove away with *h* heat.   „   611
    saith not *H* Writ the same ? '—   *Merlin and V.* 52
    They bound to *h* vows of chastity !   „   695
    Or else were he, the *h* king, whose hymns   „   765

Holy (*continued*)   Full many a *h* vow and pure resolve.   *Lancelot and E.* 879
    Not knowing he should die a *h* man.   „   1429
    times Grew to such evil that the *h* cup Was caught
    away to Heaven,   *Holy Grail* 57
    But who first saw the *h* thing to-day ? '   „   67
    if ever *h* maid With knees of adoration wore the stone,
    A *h* maid ;   „   70
    glanced and shot Only to *h* things ;   „   76
    Thy *h* nun and thou have seen a sign—   „   295
    thereby A *h* hermit in a hermitage.   „   443
    at the sacring of the mass I saw The *h* elements alone ;   „   463
    This *H* Thing, fail'd from my side,   „   470
    And o'er his head the *H* Vessel hung (repeat)   „ 512, 520
    thence Taking my war-horse from the *h* man,   „   537
    And ev'n the *H* Quest, and all but her ;   „   610
    ' Ridest thou then so hotly on a quest So *h*,'   „   643
    so Lancelot might have seen, The *H* Cup of healing ;   „   655
    Small heart was his after the *H* Quest ;   „   657
    a maid, Who kept our *h* faith among her kin   „   697
    This vision—hast thou seen the *H* Cup,   „   734
    Perhaps, like him of Cana in *H* Writ,   „   762
    Then I spake To one most *h* saint,   „   781
    And to the *H* Vessel of the Grail.'   „   840
    Thy *h* nun and thou have driven men mad,   „   862
    To *h* virgins in their ecstasies,   „   867
    ' Gawain, and blinder unto *h* things   „   870
    To those who went upon the *H* Quest,   „   890
    King Arthur made new knights to fill the gap Left
    by the *H* Quest ;   *Pelleas and E.* 2
    ' Ye, that so dishallow the *h* sleep,   „   446
    sat There in the *h* house at Almesbury Weeping,   *Guinevere* 2
    Then glancing up beheld the *h* nuns All round her,   „   666
    Do each low office of your *h* house ;   „   682
    light that led The *h* Elders with the gift of myrrh.   *Pass. of Arthur* 401
    Each way from verge to verge a *H* Land,   *Lover's Tale i* 337
    I charge you never to say that I laid him in *h* ground.   *Rizpah* 58
    Now reddest with the blood of *h* men,   *Sir J. Oldcastle* 54
    or such crimes As *h* Paul—   „   110
    how I anger'd Arundel asking me To worship *H* Cross !   „   136
    As *h* John had prophesied of me,   *Columbus* 21
    Ferdinand Hath sign'd it and our *H* Catholic queen—   „   30
    All glory to the mother of our Lord, And *H* Church,   „   63
    And free the *H* Sepulchre from thrall.   „   104
    And own the *h* governance of Rome.'   „   190
    And ready—tho' our *H* Catholic Queen,   „   228
    And save the *H* Sepulchre from thrall.   „   240
    the *H* man he assoil'd us, and sadly we sail'd away.   *V. of Maeldune* 126
    As the *H* Mother o' Glory that smiles at her sleepin'
    child—   *Tomorrow* 26
    Till *H* St. Pether gets up wid his kays   „   93
    Near us Edith's *h* shadow, smiling   *Locksley H., Sixty* 54
    My warrior of the *H* Cross and of the conquering sword,   *Happy* 21
    This poor rib-grated dungeon of the *h* human ghost,   „   31
    sway'd the sword that lighten'd back the sun of *h* land,   „   43
    You parted for the *H* War without a word to me,   „   77
    Who reads thy gradual process, *H* Spring.   *Prog. of Spring* 106
    If it be a mosque people murmur the *h* prayer,   *Akbar's D., Inscrip.* 4
Holy Ghost   the warning of the *H G*, I prophesy   *St. S. Stylites* 219
Holy Grail (*See also* **Grail**)   Three angels bear the *h G* :   *Sir Galahad* 42
    Until I find the *h G*.   „   84
    sweet vision of the *H G* Drove me from all vainglories,   *Holy Grail* 31
    To whom the monk : ' The *H G* !—I trust   „   37
    Spake often with her of the *H G*,   „   86
    thought That now the *H G* would come again ;   „   92
    ' Sweet brother, I have seen the *H G* :   „   107
    And down the long beam stole the *H G*, (repeat)   „ 117, 188
    I, Sir Arthur, saw the *H G*, I saw the *H G*   „   290
    I knew That I should light upon the *H G*.   „   367
    if I find the *H G* itself And touch it,   „   438
    saw the Grail, The *H G*, descend upon the shrine :   „   465
    and there Dwelt, and I knew it was the *H G*,   „   531
    I find not there this *H G*,   „   542
    the hope That could I touch or see the *H G*   „   779
    I saw the *H G*, All pall'd in crimson samite,   „   846
Homage   Honour,' she said, ' and *h*, tax and toll,   *Œnone* 116

Homage (*continued*) and render All *h* to his own darling,   *Maud I xx* 49
Lancelot draws From *h* to the best and purest,   *Balin and Balan* 376
knelt In anxious *h*—knelt—what else ?   " 509
bow'd black knees Of *h*, ringing with their serpent
  hands,   *Merlin and V.* 578
bow'd his *h*, bluntly saying, ' Fair damsels,   *Last Tournament* 206

Home (*See also* **Hoam, 'Oäm, Sea-home**) WHEN cats run *h*
  and light is come,   *The Owl I* 1
Come down, come *h*, My Rosalind :   *Rosalind* 33
The *h* of woe without a tear.   *Mariana in the S.* 20
I won his love, I brought him *h*.   *The Sisters* 14
one, an English *h*—gray twilight pour'd   *Palace of Art* 85
For ever and for ever, all in a blessed *h*—   *May Queen, Con.* 57
' Our island *h* Is far beyond the wave ;   *Lotos-Eaters* 44
Then when I left my *h*.'   *D. of F. Women* 120
' at *h* was little left And none abroad :   *The Epic* 19
The lime a summer of murmurous wings.   *Gardener's D.* 48
as he near'd His happy *h*, the ground.   " 92
So *h* we went, and all the livelong way   " 167
So I went, but could not sleep for joy,   " 174
My *h* is none of yours.   *Dora* 45
I will have my boy, and bring him *h* ;   " 122
Brought out a dusky loaf that smelt of *h*,   *Audley Court* 22
And saunter'd *h* beneath a moon,   " 80
sick of *h* went overseas for change.   *Walk. to the Mail* 24
slowly-painful to subdue this *h* Of sin, my flesh,   *St. S. Stylites* 57
And climbing up into my airy *h*,   " 217
' But as for her, she stay'd at *h*,   *Talking Oak* 113
dim fields about the *h*'s Of happy men   *Tithonus* 69
Lay betwixt his *h* and hers ;   *L. of Burleigh* 28
Ancient *h*'s of lord and lady,   " 31
He shall have a cheerful *h* ;   " 38
purchase his own boat, and make a *h* For Annie :   *Enoch Arden* 47
He purchased his own boat, and made a *h* For Annie,   " 58
So all day long till Enoch's last at *h*,   " 172
And make him merry, when I come *h*   " 199
nor loved she to be left Alone at *h*,   " 517
clothes they gave him and free passage *h* ;   " 650
homeward—*h*—what *h*? had he a *h*? His *h*,   " 668
he reach'd the *h* Where Annie lived   " 684
Back toward his solitary *h* again,   " 794
arose the labourers' *h*'s,   *Aylmer's Field* 147
A breaker of the bitter news from *h*,   " 594
his hopes and hates, his *h*'s and fanes,   *Lucretius* 255
Sick for the hollies and the yews of *h*—   *Princess, Pro.* 187
Not for three years to correspond with *h* ;   " *ii* 70
Whose *h* is in the sinews of a man,   " *v* 267
Almost our maids were better at their *h*'s,   " 428
H they brought her warrior dead :   " *vi* 1
From love to love, from *h* to *h* you go,   *W. to Marie Alex.* 8
Whose hand at *h* was gracious to the poor :   " 37
sitting at *h* in my father's farm at eve :   *Grandmother* 90
endure To sit with empty hands at *h*.   *Sailor Boy* 16
this pretty *h*, the *h* where mother dwells ?   *City Child* 2
running on one way to the *h* of my love,   *Window, On the Hill* 8
And learns her gone and far from *h* ;   *In Mem. viii* 4
So draw him *h* to those that mourn   " *ix* 5
And ask a thousand things of *h* ;   " *xiv* 12
And like a beacon guards thee *h*.   " *xvii* 12
Her eyes are *h*'s of silent prayer.   " *xxxii* 1
rise To take her latest leave of *h*,   " *xl* 6
We go, but ere we go from *h*,   " *cii* 9
she went *H* with her maiden posy.   *Maud I xii* 22
I have led her *h*, my love,   " *xviii* 1
And at last, when each came *h*,   " *xix* 61
By the *h* that gave me birth,   " *II iv* 7
we have heard from our wise man at *h* To
  Northward,   *Gareth and L.* 201
So drew him *h* ; but he that fought no more,   " 1049
Prince had found her in her ancient *h* ;   *Marr. of Geraint* 644
Near that old *h*, a pool of golden carp ;   " 648
So the last sight that Enid had of *h*   *Geraint and E.* 24
as a hearth lit in a mountain *h*,   *Balin and Balan* 231
A *h* of bats, in every tower an owl.   " 336
the King, However mild he seems at *h*,   *Lancelot and E.* 311

Home (*continued*) those three knights all set their faces *h*,   *Pelleas and E.* 187
closing round him thro' the journey *h*,   " 202
eyes Had drawn him *h*—what marvel ?   *Last Tournament* 405
That night came Arthur *h*, and while he climb'd,   " 755
boundless *h*'s For ever-broadening England,   *To the Queen ii* 29
(A visible link unto the *h* of my heart),   *Lover's Tale i* 431
within its inmost halls, The *h* of darkness ;   " 524
Solace at least—before he left his *h*.   " *iv* 7
found the dying servant, took him *h*, And fed,   " 263
an' often at *h* in disgrace,   *First Quarrel* 15
To make a good wife for Harry, when Harry came
  h for good.   " 30
And Harry came *h* at last, but he look'd at me   " 35
I have taken them *h*, I have number'd the bones,   *Rizpah* 10
gold that Solomon's navies carried *h*,   *Columbus* 113
for you know The flies at *h*,   " 119
Drove me and my good brothers *h* in chains,   " 134
and their hearths and their *h*'s.   *Batt. of Brunanburh* 19
at *h* if I sought for a kindly caress,   *The Wreck* 31
Having lands at *h* and abroad in a rich West-Indian isle ;   " 46
When he spoke of his tropical *h* in the canes   " 71
sail at last which brings our Edwin *h*.   *The Flight* 92
To mark in many a freeman's *h*   *Freedom* 11
But moving thro' the Mother's *h*,   *To Prin. Beatrice* 17
Go, take thine honours *h* ;   *To W. C. Macready* 6
Hubert brings me *h* With April and the swallow.   *The Ring* 59
far off an old forsaken house, Then *h*,   " 156
then I pass'd *H*, and thro' Venice,   " 192
but—coming *h*—And on your Mother's birthday—   " 247
And send her *h* to you rejoicing.   " 320
hurrying *h*, I found her not in house Or garden—   " 444
But chaining fancy now at *h*   *To Ulysses* 31
Make all true hearths thy *h*.   *Prog. of Spring* 52
And wanders on from *h* to *h* !   *The Wanderer* 9
On whom a happy *h* has power To make   " 10
that which drew from out the boundless deep
  Turns again *h*.   *Crossing the Bar* 8
Home-bred flatters thus Our *h-b* fancies :   *In Mem. x* 11
Home-circle from her own *h-c* of the poor They
  barr'd her :   *Aylmer's Field* 504
Homeless The moanings of the *h* sea,   *In Mem. xxxv* 9
Seeing the *h* trouble in thine eyes,   *Lancelot and E.* 1365
h planet at length will be wheel'd   *Despair* 83
Homelier Strove for sixty widow'd years to help his
  h brother men,   *Locksley H., Sixty* 267
Homely Fills out the *h* quickset-screens,   *On a Mourner* 6
And every *h* secret in their hearts,   *Holy Grail* 552
Ev'n the *h* farm can teach us there is something
  in descent.   *Locksley H., Sixty* 26
beat Thro' all the *h* town from jasper,   *Columbus* 83
Homer But *H*, Plato, Verulam.   *Princess ii* 160
  THESE lame hexameters the strong-wing'd music
  of *H* !   *Trans. of Homer* 1
And so does Earth ; for *H*'s fame,   *Epilogue* 58
golden Iliad vanish, *H* here is *H* there.   *Parnassus* 20
Home-return on our *h-r* the daily want Of Edith   *Sisters (E. and E.)* 245
Homeric faint *H* echoes, nothing-worth,   *The Epic* 39
Homestead the trampled year, The smouldering *h*,   *Princess v* 128
made an English *h* Hell—   *To Mary Boyle* 37
H and harvest, Reaper and gleaner,   *Merlin and the G.* 57
Home-voyage Less lucky her *h-v* :   *Enoch Arden* 541
Homicidal six feet high, Grand, epic, *h* ;   *Princess, Pro.* 225
Homily Distill'd from some worm-canker'd *h* ;   *To J. M. K.* 6
Hond (hand) toithe were due, an' I gied it in *h* ;   *N. Farmer, O. S.* 11
Honest Suddenly *h*, answer'd in amaze,   *Geraint and E.* 410
and I methinks till now Was *h*—   " 486
then do thou, being right *h*, pray That we may meet   " 491
I too would still be *h*.'   " 493
And knowing every *h* face of theirs   *Holy Grail* 550
A square-set man and *h* ; and his eyes,   " 703
at last he said, Lifting his *h* forehead,   *Enoch Arden* 388
Cursed be the sickly forms that err from *h* Nature's
  rule !   *Locksley Hall* 61
h Averill seeing How low his brother's mood   *Aylmer's Field* 403
the woman *h* Work ;   *Sea Dreams* 137

Hoop (*continued*) and roll'd His *h* to pleasure Edith,   *Aylmer's Field* 85
Hoot storm grew with a howl and a *h* of the blast   *The Wreck* 91
Hooved   *See* **White-hooved**
Hop A land of *h's* and poppy-mingled corn,   *Aylmer's Field* 31
    tower Half-lost in belts of *h* and breadths of wheat ;   *Princess*, Con. 45
Hope (s) (*See also* **Oāp**) my *h* is gray, and cold At heart, *Supp. Confessions* 103
    Shall man live thus, in joy and *h*   ,,   169
    without *h* of change, In sleep she seem'd to walk   *Mariana* 29
    Thou leddest by the hand thine infant *H.*   *Ode to Memory* 30
    the breathing spring Of *H* and Youth.   *The Poet* 28
    What *h* or fear or joy is thine ?   *Adeline* 23
    My *h* and heart is with thee—   *To J. M. K.* 1
    Light *H* at Beauty's call would perch and stand, *Caress'd or chidden* 3
    H is other *H* and wanders far,   ,,   10
    'Think you this mould of *h's* and fears   *Two Voices* 28
    raise One *h* that warm'd me in the days   ,,   122
    summits slope Beyond the furthest flights of *h,*   ,,   185
    'Not that the grounds of *h* were fix'd,   ,,   227
    'A hidden *h,*' the voice replied :   ,,   441
    Nature's living motion lent The pulse of *h* to discontent.   ,,   450
    And full at heart of trembling *h,*   *Miller's D.* 110
    With blessings beyond *h* or thought,   ,,   237
    'I was cut off from *h* in that sad place,   *D. of F. Women* 105
    She ceased in tears, fallen from *h* and trust :   ,,   257
    Come *H* and Memory, spouse and bride,   *On a Mourner* 23
    To hold his *h* thro' shame and guilt,   *Love thou thy land* 82
    A crowd of *h's,* That sought to sow themselves *Gardener's D.* 64
    say That my desire, like all strongest *h's,*   ,,   237
    For daily *h* fulfill'd, to rise again   *Edwin Morris* 38
    I will not cease to grasp the *h* I hold   *St. S. Stylites* 5
    and *h* ere death Spreads more and more   ,,   156
    'Twere all as one to fix our *h's* on Heaven   *Golden Year* 57
    Care and Pleasure, *H* and Pain, *Day-Dm., Sleep.* P. 55
    What eyes, like thine, have waken'd *h's,*   ,, *L'Envoi* 45
    to me is given Such *h,* I know not fear ;   *Sir Galahad* 62
    And phantom *h's* assemble ;   *Will Water.* 30
    For I had *h,* by something rare To prove myself   ,,   165
    In *h* to gain upon her flight.   *The Voyage* 60
    Like Heavenly *H* she crown'd the sea,   ,,   70
    'Drink to lofty *h's* that cool—   *Vision of Sin* 147
    April *h's,* the fools of chance ;   ,,   164
    'Youthful *h's,* by scores, to all,   ,,   199
    Cry to the summit, ' Is there any *h* ?'   ,,   220
    It is beyond all *h,* against all chance,   *Enoch Arden* 403
    His *h's* to see his own, And pace the sacred old familiar fields,   ,,   624
    but labour for himself, Work without *h,*   ,,   820
    boat that bears the *h* of life approach   ,,   830
    thro' that dawning gleam'd a kindlier *h* On Enoch   ,,   833
    strong in *h's,* And prodigal of all brain-labour *Aylmer's Field* 446
    Had golden *h's* for France and all mankind,   ,,   464
    saw An end, a *h,* a light breaking upon him.   ,,   480
    Seem'd *h's* returning rose :   ,,   559
    tower'd Above them, with his *h's* in either grave.   ,,   624
    Where she, who kept a tender Christian *h,*   *Sea Dreams* 41
    within As hollow as the *h's* and fears of men ?   *Lucretius* 180
    his *h's* and hates, his homes and fanes,   ,,   255
    hills, that look'd across a land of *h,*   *Princess i* 169
    H, a poising eagle, burns Above the unrisen morrow :'   ,, *iv* 82
    like parting *h's* I heard them passing from me :   ,,   172
    weight of all the *h's* of half the world,   ,,   184
    I bore up in *h* she would be known :   ,,   320
    and a *h* The child of regal compact,   ,,   420
    my *h's* and thine are one :   ,, *vii* 364
    Uplifted high in heart and *h* are we,   *Ode on Well.* 254
    HE rose at dawn and, fired with *h,*   *Sailor Boy* 1
    and darkens and brightens like my *h,* *Window, On the Hill* 18
    As we descended following *H,*   *In Mem. xxii* 11
    The light that shone when *H* was born.   ,, *xxx* 32
    Man dies : nor is there *h* in dust :'   ,, *xxxv* 4
    And *h's* and light regrets that come   ,, *xl* 7
    Beneath all fancied *h's* and fears   ,, *xlix* 13
    And faintly trust the larger *h.*   ,, *lv* 20
    What *h* of answer, or redress ?   ,, *lvi* 27
    With so much *h* for years to come,   ,, *lix* 14

Hope (s) *continued* The pillar of a people's *h,*   *In Mem. lxiv* 15
    What *h* is here for modern rhyme   ,, *lxxvii* 1
    Love, then, had *h* of richer store :   ,, *lxxxi* 5
    Despair of *H,* and earth of thee.   ,, *lxxxiv* 16
    I remain'd, whose *h's* were dim,   ,, *lxxxv* 29
    The mighty *h's* that make us men.   ,,   60
    The *h* of unaccomplish'd years   ,, *xci* 7
    And *h* could never hope too much,   ,, *cxii* 11
    Yet *H* had never lost her youth ;   ,, *cxxv* 5
    Wild Hours that fly with *H* and Fear,   ,, *cxxviii* 9
    why not. I have neither *h* nor trust ;   *Maud I i* 30
    returns the dark With no more *h* of light.   ,, *ix* 16
    brother comes, like a blight On my fresh *h,*   ,, *xix* 103
    a *h* for the world in the coming wars—   ,, *III vi* 11
    in that *h,* dear soul, let trouble have rest,   ,,   12
    his own blood, his princedom, youth and *h's,* *Gareth and L.* 210
    I lived in *h* that sometime you would come *Geraint and E.* 839
    worship woman as true wife beyond All *h's* of gaining,   *Merlin and V.* 24
    goodly *h's* are mine That Lancelot is no more *Lancelot and E.* 601
    'Yea, lord,' she said, ' Thy *h's* are mine,'   ,,   607
    Said good Sir Bors, ' beyond all *h's* of mine,   *Holy Grail* 690
    in the *h* That could I touch or see the Holy Grail   ,,   778
    tho' ye kill my *h,* not yet my love,   *Pelleas and E.* 303
    Leave me that, I charge thee, my last *h.*   *Guinevere* 568
    what *h* ? I think there was a *h,* Except he mock'd me when he spoke of *h* ; His *h* he call'd it ;   ,,   630
    left me *h* That in mine own heart I can live   ,,   635
    O Love, O *H* ! They come, they crowd upon me *Lover's Tale i* 46
    deep vault where the heart of *H* Fell into dust,   ,,   94
    swathe thyself all round *H's* quiet urn For ever ?   ,,   100
    in that hour A *h* flow'd round me,   ,,   449
    which was less than *H,* Because it lack'd the power of perfect *H* ; But which was more and higher than all *H,* Because all other *H* had lower aim ;   ,,   452
    ' let this be call'd henceforth The Hill of *H* ;' and I replied, ' O sister, My will is one with thine ; the Hill of *H.*'   ,,   462
    Her maiden dignities of *H* and Love—   ,,   580
    No wish—no *h.* *H* was not wholly dead.   ,,   584
    Love could walk with banish'd *H* no more ?   ,,   813
    Love's arms were wreath'd about the neck of *H,* And *H*   ,,   815
    Love would die when *H* was gone, And Love mourn'd long, and sorrow'd after *H* ;   ,,   818
    trod The same old paths where Love had walk'd with *H,*   ,,   821
    But over the deep graves of *H* and Fear,   ,, *ii* 58
    Talk of lost *h's* and broken heart !   ,, *iv* 176
    if the *h* of the world were a lie ? *In the Child. Hosp.* 24
    as if *h* for the garrison hung but on him ; *Def. of Lucknow* 48
    faltering *h's* of relief, Havelock baffled,   ,,   90
    God's free air, and *h* of better things. *Sir J. Oldcastle* 10
    drowning *h* Sank all but out of sight,   *Columbus* 156
    h was mine to spread the Catholic Faith,   ,,   230
    Cloud-weaver of phantasmal *h's* and fears, *To Victor Hugo* 2
    some strange *h* to see the nearer God.   *Tiresias* 29
    'We are sinking, and yet there's *h*:   *The Wreck* 121
    life without sun, without health, without *h,*   *Despair* 7
    Bright as with deathless *h*—   ,,   17
    And *H* will have broken her heart,   ,,   92
    being damn'd beyond *h* of grace ?   ,,   109
    market frets or charms The merchant's *h* no more ; *Ancient Sage* 141
    Without their *h* of wings !'   ,,   211
    h I catch at vanishes and youth is turn'd   *The Flight* 16
    H was ever on her mountain, *Locksley H., Sixty* 91
    without the faith, without the *h,*   ,,   137
    yours are *h* and youth, but I Eighty winters leave the dog   ,,   225
    far from here is all the *h* of eighty years.   ,,   254
    As all my *h's* were thine— *Pref. Poem Broth. S.* 26
    God the traitor's *h* confound ! (repeat) *Hands all Round* 10, 22, 34
    Star of the morning, *H* in the sunrise ;   *Vastness* 15
    Yes, for some wild *h* was mine That,   *The Ring* 135
    men have *h's,* which race the restless blood, *Prog. of Spring* 115
    'The miserable have no medicine But only *H* !' *Romney's R.* 150
    Beyond all *h* of warmth, Œnone sat Not moving, *Death of Œnone* 74

Hope (s) (*continued*) blight thy *h* or break thy rest,   *Faith* 2
   Until the great Hereafter. Mourn in *h*!   *Death of the Duke of C.* 17
Hope (verb) trust and *h* till things should cease,   *Supp. Confessions* 31
   Named man, may *h* some truth to find,   *Two Voices* 176
   I *h* my end draws nigh :   *St. S. Stylites* 37
   Could *h* itself return'd ;   *Talking Oak* 12
   I am, To that I *h* to be.   *St. Agnes' Eve* 20
   h with me. Whose shame is that,   *Aylmer's Field* 717
   And hope could never *h* too much,   *In Mem. cxii* 11
   a debt, That I never can *h* to pay ;   *Maud I xix* 88
   And the titmouse *h* to win her   "   *xx* 29
   H more for these than some inheritance   *Ded. of Idylls* 32
   H not to make thyself by idle vows,   *Holy Grail* 871
   and *h* The third night hence will bring thee
     news   *Pelleas and E.* 356
   Australian dying *h*'s he shall return,   *Locksley H., Sixty* 70
   H the best, but hold the Present   "   105
   Bid him farewell for me, and tell him—*H*!   *Romney's R.* 147
   I hear a death-bed Angel whisper '*H*.'   "   148
   H! O yes, I *h*, or fancy that,   "   158
   nor *h* for a deathless hearing !   *Parnassus* 14
   As Wisdom *h*'s to gain,   *Politics* 4
   I *h* to see my Pilot face to face   *Crossing the Bar* 15
Hoped I had *h* that ere this period closed   *St. S. Stylites* 17
   Yet he *h* to purchase glory, *H* to make the name
     Of his vessel great in story,   *The Captain* 17
   she heard, And almost *h* herself ;   *Enoch Arden* 202
   partly that I *h* to win you back,   *Princess iv* 304
   loved and did, And *h*, and suffer'd,   *In Mem., Con.* 135
   They *h* to slay him somewhere on the stream,   *Gareth and L.* 1419
   where I *h* myself to reign as king,   *Lover's Tale i* 591
   cope and crown Of all I *h* and fear'd ?   "   *ii* 28
   Cold words from one I had *h* to warm so far   *Sisters (E. and E.)* 194
   we had *h* for a dawn indeed,   *Despair* 22
   H for a dawn and it came,   "   27
Hopeful Fear-tremulous, but humbly *h*,   *Merlin and V.* 86
   With *h* grief, were passing sweet !   *Supp. Confessions* 39
Hopefuller He, passionately *h*, would go,   *Aylmer's Field* 419
Hopeless hush'd itself at last If *H* of answer :
     "   543
   And sweet as those by *h* fancy feign'd   *Princess iv* 55
   The grasp of *h* grief about my heart,   *Lover's Tale i* 126
   it was all but a *h* case :   *In the Child. Hosp.* 14
   And it was but a *h* case,   "   16
   Came that ' Ave atque Vale ' of the Poet's *h* woe,   *Frater ave, etc.* 5
   In aiming at an all but *h* mark   *The Ring* 346
Hoping *h*, fearing 'is it yet too late ?'   *Guinevere* 691
Hopple (hobble) Tha'd never not *h* thy tongue,   *Church-warden, etc.* 24
Horace half in jest, Old *H* ?   *Epilogue* 46
   you, old popular *H*, you the wise Adviser   *Poets and their B.* 5
Horde thine own land has bow'd to Tartar *h*'s   *W. to Marie Alex.* 23
   There the *h* of Roman robbers mock   *Boädicea* 18
   last a heathen *h*, Reddening the sun   *Com. of Arthur* 36
   overcame The heathen *h*'s, and made a realm   "   519
   Wasted so often by the heathen *h*'s,   *Holy Grail* 244
   clash'd with Pagan *h*'s, and bore them down,   "   479
   In the heart of the Russian *h*'s,   *Heavy Brigade* 50
Horder'd (ordered) To be *h* about, an' waäked,   *Spinster's S's.* 97
Horizon By making all the *h* dark.   *Two Voices* 390
   A length of bright *h* rimm'd the dark.   *Gardener's D.* 181
   With fair *h*'s bound :   *Will Water.* 66
   Ev'n to its last *h*, and of all Who peer'd at him   *Aylmer's Field* 816
   My prospect and *h* gone.   *In Mem. xxxviii* 4
   sometimes on the *h* of the mind Lies folded,   *Lover's Tale i* 49
   To change with her *h*, if true Love Were not   *Sisters (E. and E.)* 226
   The faint *h*'s, all the bounds of earth,   *Far—far—away* 14
Horn (*See also* **Bugle-horn**) wave-worn *h*'s of the echoing
     bank,   *Dying Swan* 39
   one hand grasp'd The mild bull's golden *h*.   *Palace of Art* 120
   Leaning his *h*'s into the neighbour field,   *Gardener's D.* 87
   To where the bay runs up its latest *h*.   *Audley Court* 11
   Betwixt the monstrous *h*'s of elk and deer,   *Princess, Pro.* 23
   The *h*'s of Elfland faintly blowing !   "   *iv* 10
   A little space was left between the *h*'s,   "   207
   blast and bray of the long *h* And serpent-throated
     bugle,   "   *v* 252

Horn (*continued*) like a wild *h* in a land Of echoes,   *Princess v* 486
   Death and Morning on the silver *h*'s,   "   *vii* 204
   affluent Fortune emptied all her *h*.   *Ode on Well.* 197
   outpour'd Their myriad *h*'s of plenty   *Ode Inter. Exhib.* 6
   clangs Its leafless ribs and iron *h*'s Together,   *In Mem. cvii* 12
   A golden foot or a fairy *h*   *Maud II ii* 19
   blew A hard and deadly note upon the *h*.   *Gareth and L.* 1111
   and a long black *h* Beside it hanging ;   "   1366
   Sent all his heart and breath thro' all the *h*.   "   1369
   let blow His *h*'s for hunting on the morrow
     morn.   *Marr. of Geraint* 153
   The noble hart at bay, now the far *h*,   "   233
   fill'd a *h* with wine and held it to her,)   *Geraint and E.* 659
   In these wild woods, the hart with golden *h*'s.   *Merlin and V.* 409
   chased the flashes of his golden *h*'s   "   427
   sent His *h*'s of proclamation out   "   581
   They sit with knife in meat and wine in *h* !   "   694
   Thither he made, and blew the gateway *h*.   *Lancelot and E.* 169
   I heard a sound As of a silver *h* from o'er the hills   *Holy Grail* 109
   O never harp nor *h*, Nor ought we blow with breath,   "   113
   a *h*, inflamed the knights At that dishonour   *Last Tournament* 434
   Till each would clash the shield, and blow the *h*.   "   436
   Then at the dry harsh roar of the great *h*,   "   438
   ' O hunter, and O blower of the *h*, Harper,   "   542
   Made answer, sounding like a distant *h*.   *Guinevere* 249
Hornblende chattering stony names Of shale and *h*,   *Princess iii* 362
Horned (*See also* **White-horned**) things that are forked,
     and *h*,   *The Mermaid* 53
   or fills The *h* valleys all about,   *Supp. Confessions* 152
   shadowing down the *h* flood In ripples,   *In Mem. lxxxvi* 7
Hornet better ha' put my naked hand in a *h*'s nest.   *First Quarrel* 50
Hornet-comb honey from *h-c*'s, And men from
     beasts—   *Last Tournament* 357
Hornfooted tramp of the *h* horse That grind the glebe   *Tiresias* 94
Horn-handed those *h-h* breakers of the glebe,   *Princess ii* 159
Hornless *h* unicorns, Crack'd basilisks,   *Holy Grail* 717
Hornpipes move, And flounder into *h*.   *Amphion* 24
Horny with a grosser film made thick These heavy, *h*
     eyes.   *St. S. Stylites* 201
Horny-nibb'd Left for the *h-n* raven to rend it,   *Batt. of Brunanburh* 108
Horrible And *h* nightmares,   *Palace of Art* 240
   like a blossom'd branch Rapt to the *h* fall :   *Princess iv* 180
   a million *h* bellowing echoes broke   *Maud II i* 24
   H, hateful, monstrous, not to be told ;   " *III vi* 41
   then Went slipping down *h* precipices,   *Geraint and E.* 379
   God 'ill pardon the hell-black raven and *h* fowls of
     the air,   *Rizpah* 39
   Have I crazed myself over their *h* infidel writings ?   *Despair* 87
   it was chain'd, but its *h* yell   *Bandit's Death* 35
Horrid And of the *h* foulness that he wrought,   *Merlin and V.* 41
Horror shot Light *h*'s thro' her pulses :   *Godiva* 59
   hair of the Baronet bristle up With *h*,   *Aylmer's Field* 43
   days Were clipt by *h* from his term of life.   "   603
   ' Can I not fling this *h* off me again,   *Lucretius* 173
   The *h* of the shame among them all :   *Princess v* 95
   Priest in *h* about his altar To Thor and Odin   *The Victim* 7
   ledges drip with a silent *h* of blood,   *Maud I i* 3
   nevermore to brood On a *h* of shatter'd limbs   "   56
   a morbid hate and *h* have grown Of a world   "   *vi* 75
   Felt a *h* over me creep,   "   *xiv* 35
   cells of madness, haunts of *h* and fear,   " *III vi* 2
   spake no word ; Which set the *h* higher :   *Gareth and L.* 1394
   To make a *h* all about the house,   "   1411
   all their foolish fears And *h*'s only proven   "   1425
   fell A *h* on him, lest his gentle wife,   *Marr. of Geraint* 29
   A *h* lived about the tarn,   *Lancelot and E.* 37
   In *h* lest the work by Merlin wrought,   *Holy Grail* 259
   Drown'd in the gloom and *h* of the vault.   *Lover's Tale iv* 62
   H of women in travail among the dying   *Def. of Lucknow* 88
   Life with its anguish, and *h*'s, and errors—   *Despair* 48
   the glazed eye Glared at me as in *h*.   *The Ring* 451
Horror-stricken And Leolin's *h-s* answer, ' I   *Aylmer's Field* 318
   She lied : but *h-s* he,   *Balin and Balan* 525
Horse (*See also* **'Erse, Herse, War-horse**) heavy barges
     trail'd By slow *h*'s ;   *L. of Shalott i* 21

Hospital (*continued*) delicate women who tended the
    h bed,   *Def. of Lucknow* 87
    Sick from the *h* echo them,   100
    Give your gold to the *H*,   *On Jub. Q.'' Victoria* 33
Hospitality   tender ministries Of female hands
    and *h.'*   *Princess vi* 73
    and served With female hands and *h.'*   ,,   96
    broken into Thro' open doors and *h*;   *Marr. of Geraint* 456
    innocent *hospitalities* quench'd in blood,   *Columbus* 176
Host   (**entertainer of guests**)   The *h* and I sat round
    the wassail-bowl,   *The Epic* 5
    Enoch was *h* one day, Philip the next,   *Enoch Arden* 25
    I, their guest, their *h*, their ancient friend,   *Aylmer's Field* 790
    enter'd an old hostel, call'd mine *h* To council,   *Princess i* 173
    We sent mine *h* to purchase female gear,   ,,   199
    'Fair *H* and Earl, I pray you courtesy;   *Marr. of Geraint* 403
    Let *me* lay lance in rest, O noble *h*,   ,,   496
    bad the *h* Call in what men soever   *Geraint and E.* 285
    Call the *h* and bid him bring Charger and palfrey.'   ,,   400
    Till issuing arm'd he found the *h* and cried,   ,,   407
    the *h*, Suddenly honest, answer'd in amaze,   ,,   409
    How oft the Cantab supper, *h* and guest,   *To W. H. Brookfield* 4
Host   (**array of men**)   two *h's* that lay beside the walls,   *Princess vi* 383
    Remember him who led your *h's*;   *Ode on Well.* 171
    Not ours the fault if we have feeble *h's*—   *Third of Feb.* 38
    from time to time the heathen *h* Swarm'd overseas,   *Com. of Arthur* 8
    Arthur's *h* Proclaim'd him Victor,   *Balin and Balan* 89
    craft of kindred and the Godless *h's*   *Guinevere* 427
    They summon me their King to lead mine *h's*   ,,   570
    Who slowly paced among the slumbering *h*,   *Pass. of Arthur* 7
    Then rose the King and moved his *h* by night,   ,,   79
    ever and anon with *h* to *h* Shocks,   ,,   107
    king was on them suddenly with a *h*.   *Sir J. Oldcastle* 41
    Troubled the track of the *h* that we hated,   *Batt. of Brunanburh* 40
    he look'd at the *h* that had halted   *Heavy Brigade* 7
Hostage   And here he keeps me *h* for his son.'   *Princess iv* 405
Hostel   So pass I *h*, hall, and grange;   *Sir Galahad* 81
    enter'd an old *h*, call'd mine host To council,   *Princess i* 173
    riding wearily, Found every *h* full,   *Marr. of Geraint* 255
    And pausing at a *h* in a marsh,   *Lover's Tale iv* 131
    A dismal *h* in a dismal land,   ,,   141
    There is one old *H* left us   *Locksley H.", Sixty* 247
    In this *H*—I remember—I repent it   ,,   255
Hostess   Then stept a buxom *h* forth,   *Princess i* 228
Hot   (*See also* **Fiery-hot, 'Ot, Red-hot**)   my very ears were
    h To hear them: ,,   134
    And heated *h* with burning fears,   *In Mem. cxviii* 22
    h in haste to join Their luckier mates,   *Geraint and E.* 574
    flush'd with fight, or *h*, God's curse, with anger—   ,,   660
    H was the night and silent;   *Pelleas and E.* 395
    snow on all the hills! so *h*, So fever'd!   *Romney's R.* 12
    Returning with *h* cheek and kindled eyes.   *Alexander* 14
    and my *h* lips prest Close,   *Œnone* 203
    Or rosy blossom in *h* ravine,   *The Daisy* 32
    h hiss And bustling whistle of the youth   *Marr. of Geraint* 256
    her hand is *h* With ill desires,   *Last Tournament* 414
    And leave the *h* swamp of voluptuousness   *Ancient Sage* 277
Hot-and-hot   To serve the *h-a-h*;   *Will Water.* 228
Hottentot   And not the Kaffir, *H*, Malay,   *Princess ii* 158
Hotter   her lynx eye To fix and make me *h*,   ,, *iii* 47
Hougoumont   roar of *H* Left mightiest of all peoples   *To the Queen ii.* 20
Hound   (*See also* **Sleuth-hound**)   Francis laid A damask
    napkin wrought with horse and *h*,   *Audley Court* 21
    monstrous males that carve the living *h*,   *Princess iii* 310
    And love in which my *h* has part,   *In Mem. lxiii* 2
    thou knowest, and gray, and all the *h's*,   *Gareth and L.* 462
    stay'd Waiting to hear the *h's*;   *Marr. of Geraint* 163
    There is good chance that we shall hear the *h's*:   ,,   182
    Cavall, King Arthur's *h* of deepest mouth,   ,,   186
    And pastime both of hawk and *h*,   ,,   711
    Who seems no bolder than a beaten *h*;   *Geraint and E.* 61
    weakling, and thrice-beaten *h*:   *Pelleas and E.* 291
    or a traitor proven, or *h* Beaten,   ,,   439
    Like a dry bone cast to some hungry *h*?   *Last Tournament* 196
    heard The *h's* of Mark, and felt the goodly *h's*   ,,   503

Hound (*continued*)   my forefather, with his feet upon
    the *h*.   *Locksley H., Sixty* 28
    I, the finer brute rejoicing in my *h's*,   *By an Evolution.* 7
Hour   (*See also* **Half-hour, Tavern-hour**)   THE winds, as
    at their *h* of birth,   *The winds, etc.* 1
    The cock sung out an *h* ere light: *Mariana* 27
    but most she loathed the *h*   ,,   77
    A SPIRIT haunts the year's last *h's*   *A spirit haunts* 1
    sick man's room when he taketh repose An *h* before death;   ,,   15
    Most delicately *h* by *h* He canvass'd   *A Character* 19
    ere he parted said, 'This *h* is thine: *Love and Death* 9
    So runs the round of life from *h* to *h*.   *Circumstance* 9
    a phantom two *h's* old Of a maiden past away,   *Adeline* 18
    'Were this not well, to bide mine *h*,   *Two Voices* 76
    Who is it that could live an *h*?   ,,   162
    'His face, that two *h's* since hath died;   ,,   242
    So heavenly-toned, that in that *h*   ,,   442
    I wonder'd at the bounteous *h's*,   ,,   451
    But, Alice, what an *h* was that,   *Miller's D.* 57
    And now those vivid *h's* are gone,   ,,   195
    Last night I wasted hateful *h's*   *Fatima* 8
    Is wearied of the rolling *h's*.   *L. C. V. de Vere* 60
    The warders of the growing *h*,   *Love thou thy land* 61
    The lusty bird takes every *h* for dawn: *M. d' Arthur, Ep.* 11
    as tho' it were The *h* just flown,   *Gardener's D.* 83
    ere an *h* had pass'd, We reach'd a meadow   ,,   107
    heavy clocks knolling the drowsy *h's*.   ,,   184
    till Autumn brought an *h* For Eustace,   ,,   207
    this whole *h* your eyes have been intent   ,,   269
    for three *h's* he sobb'd o'er William's child   *Dora* 167
    we met; one *h* I had, no more: *Edwin Morris* 104
    I, whose bald brows in silent *h's* become   *St. S. Stylites* 165
    make reply Is many a weary *h*;   *Talking Oak* 26
    'An *h* had past—and, sitting straight   ,,   109
    slow sweet *h's* that bring us all things good, The slow
    sad *h's* that bring us all things ill,   *Love and Duty* 57
    calmer *h's* to Memory's darkest hold,   ,,   90
    every *h* Must sweat her sixty minutes   *Golden Year* 68
    every *h* is saved From that eternal silence,   *Ulysses* 26
    thy strong *H's* indignant work'd their wills,   *Tithonus* 18
    Made war upon each other for an *h*,   *Godiva* 34
    A pleasant *h* has passed away   *Day-Dm., Pro.* 2
    shall we pass the bill I mention'd half an *h* ago?'   ,, *Revival* 28
    The Poet-forms of stronger *h's*,   ,, *L'Envoi* 14
    Embraced his Eve in happy *h*,   ,,   42
    Still creeping with the creeping *h's*   *St. Agnes' Eve* 7
    To-day I sat for an *h* and wept,   *Edward Gray* 11
    Thro' many an *h* of summer suns,   *Will Water.* 33
    But for my pleasant *h*, 'tis gone;   ,,   179
    H's, when the Poet's words and looks   ,,   193
    Let us have a quiet *h*,   *Vision of Sin* 73
    tyrant's cruel glee Forces on the freer *h*.   ,,   130
    An *h* behind; but as he climb'd the hill,   *Enoch Arden* 69
    Had his dark *h* unseen, and rose and past   ,,   78
    To find the precious morning *h's* were lost.   ,,   302
    remember'd one dark *h* Here in this mood,   ,,   385
    That was your *h* of weakness. I was wrong,   ,,   449
    'O would I take her father for one *h*,   *The Brook* 114
    He wasted *h's* with Averill;   *Aylmer's Field* 109
    but so they wander'd, *h* by *h* Gathered the blossom   ,,   141
    Fairer his talk, a tongue that ruled the *h*,   ,,   194
    Lightning of the *h*, the pun,   ,,   441
    Some niggard fraction of an *h*,   ,,   450
    Thro' weary and yet ever wearier *h's*,   ,,   828
    but later by an *h* Here than ourselves,   *Sea Dreams* 263
    crowds that in an *h* Of civic tumult jam the doors,   *Lucretius* 168
    that *h* perhaps Is not so far when momentary man   ,,   252
    till that *h*, My golden work in which I told a truth   ,,   259
    And with that woman closeted for *h's*!'   *Princess iii* 56
    Yet let us breathe for one *h* more in Heaven'   ,,   69
    Its range of duties to the appointed *h*.   ,,   177
    Such head from act to act, from *h* to *h*,   ,, *iv* 452
    O would I had his sceptre for one *h*!   ,,   538
    I took it for an *h* to mine own bed This morning: ,, *v* 434
    Sole comfort of my dark *h*,   ,, *vi* 194

Hour (*continued*) many a pleasant *h* with her that's gone, *Princess vi* 247
With one that cannot keep her mind an *h* : „ 287
My heart an eddy from the brawling *h* : „ 322
Clomb to the roofs, and gazed alone for *h's* „ *vii* 32
To wile the length from languorous *h's*, „ 63
Melts mist-like into this bright *h*, „ 355
Who never sold the truth to serve the *h*, *Ode on Well.* 179
Mourn'd in this golden *h* of jubilee, *Ode Inter. Exhib.* 8
mix the seasons and the golden *h's* ; „ 36
he has but gone for an *h*,— *Grandmother* 102
O LOVE, what *h's* were thine and mine, *The Daisy* 1
At Florence too what golden *h's*, „ 41
ONCE in a golden *h* I cast to earth *The Flower* 1
Her quiet dream of life this *h* may cease. *Requiescat* 6
that the victor *H's* should scorn The long result of love, *In Mem. i* 13
wrought At last *h* to please him well ; „ *vi* 18
learn That I have been an *h* away. „ *xii* 20
an *h* For private sorrow's barren song, „ *xxi* 13
But for one *h*, O Love, I strive „ *xxxv* 6
To thee too comes the golden *h* When „ *xxxix* 6
Could we forget the widow'd *h* „ *xl* 1
Unconscious of the sliding *h*, „ *xliii* 5
Is shadow'd by the growing *h*, „ *xlvi* 3
The fruitful *h's* of still increase ; „ 10
Ye watch, like God, the rolling *h's* „ *li* 14
Who usherest in the dolorous *h* „ *lxxii* 9
But that remorseless iron *h* „ *lxxxiv* 14
And all the train of bounteous *h's* „ 30
The promise of the golden *h's* ? „ *lxxxv* 106
And buzzings of the honied *h's*. „ *lxxxix* 52
An *h's* communion with the dead. „ *xciv* 4
Thy feet have stray'd in after *h's* „ *cii* 14
That wakens at this *h* of rest „ *civ* 6
No more shall wayward grief abuse The genial *h* „ *cv* 10
and join'd Each office of the social *h* „ *cxi* 14
In watching thee from *h* to *h*, „ *cxii* 12
O days and *h's*, your work is this „ *cxvii* 1
Which every *h* his couriers bring. „ *cxxvi* 4
Wild *H's* that fly with Hope and Fear, „ *cxxviii* 9
O happy *h*, and happier *h's* Await them. „ *Con.* 65
O happy *h*, behold the bride With him „ 69
cannot be kind to each other here for an *h* ; *Maud I iv* 28
Thro' the livelong *h's* of the dark „ *vi* 17
Did I dream it an *h* ago, „ *vii* 3
twelve sweet *h's* that past in bridal white, „ *xviii* 65
For front to front in an *h* we stood, „ *II i* 23
For one short *h* to see The souls we loved,' „ *iv* 14
holden far apart Until his *h* should come ; *Com. of Arthur* 215
when Merlin (for his *h* had come) Brought Arthur „ 228
those first days had golden *h's* for me, „ 357
As glitters gilded in thy Book of *H's*. *Gareth and L.* 46
' Not an *h*, So that ye yield me— „ 132
till an *h*, When waken'd by the wind „ 175
' I fly no more : I allow thee for an *h*. „ 892
Allow me for mine *h*, and thou wilt find My fortunes „ 902
that *h* When the lone hern forgets his melancholy, „ 1184
I will eat With all the passion of a twelve *h's'* fast.' *Marr. of Geraint* 306
How many among us at this very *h* Do forge *Geraint and E.* 2
O pardon me ! the madness of that *h*, „ 346
So for long *h's* sat Enid by her lord, „ 580
And now their *h* has come : and Enid said : „ 697
in that perilous *h* Put hand to hand „ 766
Was half a bandit in my lawless *h*, „ 795
but this *h* We ride a-hawking with Sir Lancelot. *Merlin and V.* 94
you which ruin'd man Thro' woman the first *h* ; „ 363
lay the reckling, one But one *h* old ! „ 710
To crop his own sweet rose before the *h* ? ' „ 725
And not the one dark *h* which brings remorse, „ 763
Joust for it, and win, and bring it in an *h*, *Lancelot and E.* 204
In darkness thro' innumerable *h's* *Holy Grail* 677
But never let me bide one *h* at peace. *Pelleas and E.* 387
and say his *h* is come, The heathen are upon him, *Last Tournament* 86
as when an *h* of cold Falls on the mountain „ 227
the warm *h* returns With veer of wind, „ 230
spake not any word, But bode his *h*, „ 386

Hour (*continued*) And so returns belike within an *h*. *Last Tournament* 531
To see thee—yearnings ?—ay ! for, *h* by *h*, „ 583
O ay—the wholesome madness of an *h*— „ 675
ptarmigan that whitens ere this *h* Woos his own end ; „ 697
Many a time for *h's*, Beside the placid breathings *Guinevere* 68
It was their last *h*, A madness of farewells. „ 102
' Late ! so late ! What *h*, I wonder, now ? ' „ 161
an *h* or maybe twain After the sunset, „ 237
To guard thee in the wild *h* coming on, „ 446
And well for thee, saying in my dark *h*, *Pass. of Arthur* 159
wealthier—wealthier—*h* by *h* ! *To the Queen ii* 23
And wordy trucklings to the transient *h*, „ 51
On the same morning, almost the same *h*, *Lover's Tale i* 198
that little *h* was bound Shut in from Time, „ 437
and in that *h* A hope flow'd round me, „ 448
Else had the life of that delighted *h* „ 471
O day which did enwomb that happy *h*, „ 485
Genius of that *h* which dost uphold „ 487
Thy name is ever worshipp'd among *h's* ! „ 493
It was so happy an *h*, so sweet a place, „ 558
So died that *h*, and fell into the abysm „ 796
So that *h* died Like odour rapt into the winged wind „ 800
All thro' the livelong *h's* of utter dark, „ 810
Well he had One golden *h*— „ *iv* 6
Would you had seen him in that *h* of his ! „ 8
I may not stay, No, not an *h* ; „ 116
after this, An *h* or two, Camilla's travail came Upon her, „ 127
Travelling that land, and meant to rest an *h* ; „ 133
To come and revel for one *h* with him „ 182
(I told you that he had his golden *h*), „ 206
Down to this last strange *h* in his own hall ; „ 358
I'll come for an *h* to-morrow, *First Quarrel* 46
I have only an *h* of life. *Rizpah* 22
I spent What seem'd my crowning *h*, *Sisters (E. and E.)* 124
talk to 'em *h's* after *h's* ! *In the Child. Hosp.* 34
And the doctor came at his *h*, „ 68
when the wild *h* and the wine Had set the wits aflame. *Sir J. Oldcastle* 94
I have not broken bread for fifty *h's*. „ 199
Once in an *h* they cried, *V. of Maeldune* 29
nor, in *h's* Of civil outbreak, *Tiresias* 67
Like would-be guests an *h* too late, „ 198
Remembering all the golden *h's* Now silent, „ 210
Why should we bear with an *h* of torture, *Despair* 81
What rulers but the Days and *H's* *Ancient Sage* 95
The days and *h's* are ever glancing by, „ 99
But with the Nameless is nor Day nor *H* ; „ 102
hands point five—O me—it strikes the *h*— *The Flight* 94
a hiccup at ony *h* o' the night ! *Spinster's S's.* 98
Shape your heart to front the *h*, but dream not that the *h* will last. *Locksley H., Sixty* 106
On this day and at this *h*, „ 175
Insects of an *h*, that hourly work their brother insect wrong, „ 202
the first dark *h* of his last sleep alone. „ 238
Expecting all things in an *h*— *Freedom* 39
breaks into the crocus-purple *h* That saw thee vanish. *Demeter and P.* 50
The man, that only lives and loves an *h*, „ 106
waäit till tha 'ears it be strikin' the *h*, *Owd Roä* 18
after *h's* of search and doubt and threats, *The Ring* 278
still drawn downward for an *h*, „ 477
And *h* by *h* unfolding woodbine leaves *Prog. of Spring* 7
Beyond the darker *h* to see the bright, „ 88
and make her festal *h* Dark with the blood *St. Telemachus* 79
' wasting the sweet summer *h's* ' ? *Charity* 1
I was close on that *h* of dishonour, „ 28
give His fealty to the halcyon *h* ! *The Wanderer* 12
WHEN the dumb *H*, clothed in black, *Silent Voices* 1

Houri A group of *H's* bow'd to see The dying Islamite, *Palace of Art* 102
Hourly Daily and *h*, more and more. *Eleänore* 71
And *h* visitation of the blood, *Lover's Tale i* 206
Hourly-mellowing summer's *h-m* change May breathe, *In Mem. xci* 9
House (s) (*See also* **Ale-house, Chop-house, City-house, 'Ouse, Pleasure-house**) All day within the dreamy *h*, *Mariana* 61
and vacancy Of the dark deserted *h*. *Deserted House* 12

M

House (s) (*continued*)   The *h* was builded of the earth,   *Deserted House* 15
The first *h* by the water-side,   *L. of Shalott iv* 34
Dead-pale between the *h's* high,   „ 40
The *h* thro' all the level shines,   *Mariana in the S.* 2
On to God's *h* the people prest :   *Two Voices* 409
To move about the *h* with joy,   *Miller's D.* 95
In this great *h* so royal-rich,   *Palace of Art* 191
I saw you sitting in the *h*,   *May Queen, Con.* 30
lightly curl'd Round their golden *h's*,   *Lotos-Eaters, C. S.* 113
And fill'd the *h* with clamour.   *The Goose* 36
nightmare on his bed When all the *h* is mute.   *M. d'Arthur* 178
' this wonder keeps the *h*.'   He nodded,   *Gardener's D.* 119
So rapt, we near'd the *h* ;   „ 142
He had been always with her in the *h*,   *Dora* 7
he left his father's *h*, And hired himself to work   „ 37
Then Dora went to Mary's *h*,   „ 110
Then thou and I will live within one *h*,   „ 125
So those four abode Within one *h* together ;   „ 170
Whose *h* is that I see ?   *Walk. to the Mail* 11
but his *h*, for so they say, Was haunted   „ 35
So in mine earthly *h* I am,   *St. Agnes' Eve* 19
For I am of a numerous *h*,   *Will Water.* 89
' Let us see these handsome *h's*   *L. of Burleigh* 23
She is of an ancient *h* ;   *Vision of Sin* 140
Three children of three *h's*,   *Enoch Arden* 11
the children play'd at keeping *h*.   „ 24
' This is my *h* and this my little wife.'   „ 28
So might she keep the *h* while he was gone.   „ 140
Lords of his *h* and of his mill were they ;   „ 351
' You have been as God's good angel in our *h*.   „ 423
The babes, their babble, Annie, the small *h*,   „ 606
With daily-dwindling profits held the *h* ;   „ 696
So broken—all the story of his *h*.   „ 704
Far-blazing from the rear of Philip's *h*,   „ 727
The latest *h* to landward.   „ 732
But kept the *h*, his chair, and last his bed.   „ 826
That all the *h's* in the haven rang.   „ 911
like a storm he came, And shook the *h*,   *Aylmer's Field* 216
the thunders of the *h* Had fallen first,   „ 278
beheld the Powers of the *H* On either side the hearth,   „ 287
The last remaining pillar of their *h*,   „ 295
Forbad her first the *h* of Averill,   „ 502
to spy The weakness of a people or a *h*,   „ 570
Your *h* is left unto you desolate !' (repeat)   „ 629, 797
' My *h* is left unto me desolate.'   „ 721
' Our *h* is left unto us desolate ' ?   „ 737
The deathless ruler of thy dying *h*   „ 661
Who entering fill'd the *h* with sudden light.   „ 682
when he felt the silence of his *h* About him,   „ 830
Walter show'd the *h*, Greek, set with busts :   *Princess, Pro.* 10
they gave The park, the crowd, the *h* ;   „ 94
A Gothic ruin and a Grecian *h*,   „ 232
There lived an ancient legend in our *h*.   „ *i* 5
An old and strange affection of the *h*.   „ 13
He cared not for the affection of the *h* ;   „ 26
A little street half garden and half *h* ;   „ 214
wish'd to marry ; they could rule a *h* ;   „ *ii* 465
came Upon me, the weird vision of our *h* :   „ *iii* 184
Still in his coffin the Prince   *G. of Swainston* 10
this pretty *h*, this city-house of ours ?   *City Child* 7
And bread from out the *h's* brought,   *Spec. of Iliad* 6
you bite far into the heart of the *h*,   *Window, Winter* 11
Dark *h*, by which once more I stand   *In Mem. vii* 1
Are but as servants in a *h*   „ *xx* 3
That guard the portals of the *h* ;   „ *xxix* 12
And home to Mary's *h* return'd,   „ *xxxi* 2
From every *h* the neighbours met,   „ 9
Should murmur from the narrow *h*,   „ *xxxv* 2
Or builds the *h*, or digs the grave,   „ *xxxvi* 14
In that dark *h* where she was born.   „ *lx* 12
link thy life with one Of mine own *h*,   „ *lxxxiv* 12
And in the *h* light after light Went out,   „ *xcv* 19
She knows but matters of the *h*,   „ *xcvii* 31
he told me that he loved A daughter of our *h* ;   „ *Con.* 7
Living alone in an empty *h*,   *Maud I. vi* 68

House (s) (*continued*)   all round the *h* I beheld The death-
white curtain   *Maud I xiv* 33
sprinkled with blood By which our *h's* are torn :   „ *xix* 33
Wrought for his *h* an irredeemable woe ;   „ *II i* 22
stand at the diamond door Of his *h* in a rainbow frill ?   „ *ii* 17
shouted at once from the top of the *h* ;   „ *v* 50
To make a horror all about the *h*,   *Gareth and L.* 1411
Lady Lyonors and her *h*, with dance And revel   „ 1422
slender entertainment of a *h* Once rich,   *Marr. of Geraint* 301
Rest ! the good *h*, tho' ruin'd,   „ 378
reverencing the custom of the *h* Geraint,   „ 380
Before my Enid's birthday, sack'd my *h* ;   „ 458
when Edyrn sack'd their *h*, And scatter'd all they had   „ 634
He found the sack and plunder of our *h* All scatter'd
thro' the *h's* of the town ;   „ 694
Ah, dear, he took me from a goodly *h*,   „ 708
Yea, and he brought me to a goodly *h* ;   „ 713
Call for the woman of the *h*,'   *Geraint and E.* 263
Among the heavy breathings of the *h*,   „ 402
how suited to the *h* of one Who loves that beauty   „ 683
mother of the *h* There was not :   *Lancelot and E.* 177
warn'd me of their fierce design Against my *h*,   „ 275
shuddering, ' Hark the Phantom of the *h*   „ 1022
this discomfort he hath done the *h*.'   „ 1072
There sat the lifelong creature of the *h*,   „ 1143
saw One of her *h*, and sent him to the Queen   „ 1168
and fair the *h* whereby she sat,   *Holy Grail* 392
h Became no better than a broken shed,   „ 397
brought thee here to this poor *h* of ours   „ 617
and out again, But sit within the *h*.   „ 715
But always in the quiet *h* I heard,   „ 832
sat There in the holy *h* at Almesbury   *Guinevere* 2
Heard by the watcher in a haunted *h*,   „ 73
Whom he knows false, abide and rule the *h* :   „ 515
Do each low office of your holy *h* ;   „ 682
Modred, unharm'd, the traitor of thine *h*.'   *Pass. of Arthur* 153
spake the King : ' My *h* hath been my doom.   „ 154
But call not thou this traitor of my *h*   „ 155
My *h* are rather they who sware my vows,   „ 157
nightmare on his bed When all the *h* is mute.   „ 346
But thou didst sit alone in the inner *h*,   *Lover's Tale i* 112
Still larger moulding all the *h* of thought,   „ 241
O blossom'd portal of the lonely *h*,   „ 280
Back to his mother's *h* among the pines.   „ *iv* 15
to the mother's *h* where she was born.   „ 91
But all their *h* was old and loved them both, And
all the *h* had known the loves of both ;   „ 122
such a *h* as his, And his was old,   „ 202
jewels Of many generations of his *h* Sparkled and flash'd,   „ 299
my *h* an' my man were my pride,   *First Quarrel* 41
So I set to righting the *h*,   „ 47
our *h* has held Three hundred years—   *Sisters (E. and E.)* 52
thick of question and reply I fled the *h*,   „ 158
want Of Edith in the *h*, the garden,   „ 246
there hail'd on our *h's* and halls   *Def. of Lucknow* 13
none but Gods could build this *h* of ours,   *Ancient Sage* 83
To lie, to lie—in God's own *h*,   *The Flight* 52
A door was open'd in the *h*—   „ 69
To both our *H's*, may they see Beyond   *Hands all Round* 27
Deck your *h's*, illuminate All your towns   *On Jub. Q. Victoria* 18
Theere, when the 'ouse wur a *h*,   *Owd Roä* 29
the *h* is afire,' she said.   „ 68
We saw far off an old forsaken *h*,   *The Ring* 155
being waked By noises in the *h*—   „ 417
I found her not in *h* Or garden—   „ 444
O the night, While the *h* is sleeping.   *Forlorn* 42
This *h* with all its hateful needs   *Happy* 32
This worn-out Reason dying in her *h*   *Romney's R.* 145
Lord let the *h* of a brute   *By an Evolution.* 1
House (verb)   That *h* the cold crown'd snake !   *Œnone* 37
H in the shade of comfortable roofs,   *St. S. Stylites* 107
Housed   the children, *h* In her foul den,   *Com. of Arthur* 29
those black foldings, that which *h* therein.   *Gareth and L.* 1380
Scarce *h* within the circle of this Earth,   *Lover's Tale i* 479
Household (adj.)   *h* shelter crave From winter rains   *Two Voices* 260

Household (adj.) (continued)   For surely now our *h* hearths are cold :   *Lotos-Eaters, C. S.* 72
Virtue, like a *h* god Promising empire ;   *On a Mourner* 30
Meet adoration to my *h* gods,   *Ulysses* 42
farmer vext packs up his beds and chairs, And all his *h* stuff ;   *Walk. to the Mail* 40
While yet she went about her *h* ways,   *Enoch Arden* 453
Their slender *h* fortunes (for the man   *Sea Dreams* 9
common vein of memory Sweet *h* talk,   *Princess* ii 315
and the *h* flower Torn from the lintel—   „ v 128
As daily vexes *h* peace,   *In Mem.* xxix 2
Moving about the *h* ways,   „ lx 11
And hear the *h* jar within.   „ xciv 16
From *h* fountains never dry ;   „ cix 2
The *h* Fury sprinkled with blood   *Maud* I xix 32
Beyond all titles, and a *h* name,   *Ded. of Idylls* 42
And like a *h* Spirit at the walls Beat,   *Geraint and E.* 403
And trustful courtesies of *h* life,   *Guinevere* 86
Red in thy birth, redder with *h* war,   *Sir J. Oldcastle* 53
Which from her *h* orbit draws the child   *Prin. Beatrice* 7
H happiness, gracious children,   *Vastness* 24
And lured me from the *h* fire on earth.   *Romney's R.* 40
THE gleam of *h* sunshine ends,   *The Wanderer* 1
Household (s)   Her *h* fled the danger,   *The Goose* 54
And lift the *h* out of poverty ;   *Enoch Arden* 485
example follow'd, Sir, In Arthur's *h* ?'—   *Merlin and V.* 20
Leaving her *h* and good father,   *Lancelot and E.* 14
Housel   nor sought, Wrapt in her grief, for *h*   *Guinevere* 149
Houseless   The *h* ocean's heaving field,   *The Voyage* 30
Housemaid   His daughter and his *h* were the boys :   *Princess* i 190
Hove   Then saw they how there *h* a dusky barge,   *M. d'Arthur* 193
Then saw they how there *h* a dusky barge,   *Pass. of Arthur* 361
Hovell'd   the poor are *h* and hustled together,   *Maud* I i 34
Hover   (See also **Wind-hover**)   all his life the charm did talk About his path, and *h* near   *Day-Dm., Arrival* 22
Wings flutter, voices *h* clear :   *Sir Galahad* 78
They come and sit by my chair, they *h* about my bed—   *Grandmother* 83
And the bird of prey will *h*,   *Maud* I xx 28
Hover'd   wherefore *h* round Lancelot, but when he mark'd   *Balin and Balan* 159
That *h* between war and wantonness,   *To the Queen* ii 44
Hovering   *h* o'er the dolorous strait To the other shore,   *In Mem.* lxxxiv 39
and *h* round her chair Ask'd, 'Mother,   *Gareth and L.* 33
breath Of her sweet tendance *h* over him,   *Geraint and E.* 926
Whenever in her *h* to and fro The lily maid   *Lancelot and E.* 326
A vision *h* on a sea of fire,   *Pelleas and E.* 52
Her spirit *h* by the church,   *The Ring* 478
Hoveringly   *h* a sword Now over and now under,   *Lucretius* 61
How   setting the *how much* before the *h*,   *Golden Year* 11
Howard   (See also **Thomas Howard**)   I should count myself the coward if I left them, my Lord *H*,   *The Revenge* 11
Lord *H* past away with five ships of war   „ 13
Howd (hold)   whoä's to *h* the lond ater meä   *N. Farmer, O. S.* 58
'e could *h* 'is oan,   *Owd Roä* 7
An' 'e cotch'd *h* hard o' my hairm,   „ 58
till 'e feeäld 'e could *h* 'is oän,   *Church-warden, etc.* 19
Howd (old)   hes now be a-grawin' sa *h*,   *Village Wife* 107
Howdin' (holding)   Thy Moother was *h* the lether,   *Owd Roä* 85
Howl (verb)   I did not hear the dog *h*, mother,   *May Queen, Con.* 21
h in tune With nothing but the Devil !'   *Sea Dreams* 260
Crack them now for yourself, and *h*,   *Maud* II v 56
H as he may.   But hold me for your friend :   *Pelleas and E.* 340
Howl (s)   rose the *h* of all the cassock'd wolves,   *Sir J. Oldcastle* 158
the great storm grew with a *h* and a hoot   *The Wreck* 91
Howl (owl)   an' screeäd like a *H* gone wud—   *Owd Roä* 76
Howlaby Beck   But I minds when i' *H B* won daäy   *Church-warden, etc.* 27
Howlaby Daäle   when we was i' *H D.*   „
I wants to tell tha o' Roä when we lived i' *H D.*   19
Howl'd   She *h* aloud, ' I am on fire within.   *Palace of Art* 285
In blood-red armour sallying, *h* to the King,   *Last Tournament* 443
whereat He shrank and *h*, and from his brow   *Lover's Tale* ii 92
H me from Hispaniola ;   *Columbus* 118
Howlest   And *h*, issuing out of night,   *In Mem.* lxxii 2
Howling   The wind is *h* in turret and tree.   *The Sisters* 9

Howling (continued)   on her threshold lie *H* in outer darkness.   *To——, With Pal. of Art* 16
The *h*'s from forgotten fields ;   *In Mem.* xli 16
heard them pass like wolves *H* ;   *Balin and Balan* 408
The brute world *h* forced them into bonds,   *Merlin and V.* 744
When the wolves are *h*.   *Forlorn* 72
How much   setting the *h m* before the *how*,   *Golden Year* 11
Howry (dirty)   the gell was as *h* a trollope   *Owd Roä* 72
I eärs es 'e'd gie fur a *h* owd book   *Village Wife* 45
Hubbub   A sudden *h* shook the hall,   *Day-Dm., Revival* 7
A *h* in the court of half the maids   *Princess* iv 476
for those That stir this *h*—you and you—   „ 509
clamour of liars belied in the *h* of lies ;   *Maud* I iv 51
Thro' the *h* of the market I steal,   „ II iv 68
Ask'd yet once more what meant the *h* here ?   *Marr. of Geraint* 264
search and doubt and threats, And *h*,   *The Ring* 279
Hubert   The prophet of his own, my *H*—   „ 23
' Air and Words,' Said *H*,   „ 25
H brings me home With April and of swallow.   „ 59
What need to wish when *H* weds in you The heart of Love, and you the soul of Truth In *H* ?   „ 61
I climb'd the hill with *H* yesterday,   „ 152
Huck (hip)   I slither'd and hurted my *h*,   *North. Cobbler* 19
Huckster   This *h* put down war !   *Maud* I x 44
Huddled   The cattle *h* on the lea ;   *In Mem.* xv 6
h here and there on mound and knoll,   *Geraint and E.* 803
An' we cuddled an' *h* togither,   *Owd Roä* 112
Huddling   *h* slant in furrow-cloven falls   *Princess* vii 207
Hue (verb)   blue heaven which *h*'s and paves The other ?   *Supp. Confessions* 134
Hue (s)   *H*'s of the silken sheeny woof   *Madeline* 22
Touch'd with a somewhat darker *h*,   *Margaret* 50
And your cheek, whose brilliant *h*   *Rosalind* 39
shapes and *h*'s that please me well !   *Palace of Art* 194
cannot fail but work in *h*'s to dim The Titianic Flora.   *Gardener's D.* 170
By Cupid-boys of blooming *h*—   *Day-Dm., Ep.* 10
Moved with violence, changed in *h*,   *Vision of Sin* 34
we know the *h* Of that cap upon her brows.   „ 141
hair In gloss and *h* the chestnut, (repeat)   *The Brook* 72, 207
a but less vivid *h* Than of that islet   *Aylmer's Field* 64
Academic silks, in *h* The lilac,   *Princess* ii 16
the other distance and the *h*'s Of promise ;   „ iv 86
thoughts that changed from *h* to *h*,   „ 210
And as the fiery Sirius alters *h*,   „ v 262
o'er her forehead past A shadow, and her *h* changed,   „ vi 107
And shapes and *h*'s of Art divine !   *Ode Inter. Exhib.* 22
bays, the peacock's neck in *h* ;   *The Daisy* 14
h's are faint And mix with hollow masks   *In Mem.* lxx 3
The distance takes a lovelier *h*,   „ cxv 6
and all Lent-lily in *h*, Save that the dome was purple,   *Gareth and L.* 911
Sculptured, and deckt in slowly-waning *h*'s.   „ 1195
A tribe of women, dress'd in many *h*'s,   *Geraint and E.* 598
her *h* Changed at his gaze :   *Balin and Balan* 278
Embathing all with wild and woful *h*'s,   *Lover's Tale* ii 64
And earth as fair in *h* !   *Ancient Sage* 24
with the living *h*'s of Art.   *Locksley H., Sixty* 140
may roll The rainbow *h*'s of heaven about it—   *Romney's R.* 51
heaven's own *h*, Far—far—away ?   *Far—far—away* 2
Hued   (See also **Crimson-hued, Deep-hued, Rose-hued, Soberer-hued**)   ' whose flower, *H* with the scarlet of a fierce sunrise,   *Lover's Tale* i 353
Hueless   In the *h* mosses under the sea   *The Mermaid* 49
In fold upon fold of *h* cloud,   *Maud* I vi 3
Nor settles into *h* gray,   *To Marq. of Dufferin* 50
Huge   above him swell *H* sponges of millennial growth   *The Kraken* 6
lie Battening upon *h* seaworms in his sleep,   „ 12
A *h* crag-platform, smooth as burnish'd brass   *Palace of Art* 5
whisper of *h* trees that branch'd And blossom'd   *Enoch Arden* 585
Once grovelike, each *h* arm a tree,   *Aylmer's Field* 510
Now striking on *h* stumbling-blocks of scorn   „ 538
But *h* cathedral fronts of every age,   *Sea Dreams* 218
H Ammonites, and the first bones of Time ;   *Princess, Pro.* 15
H women blowzed with health, and wind,   „ iv 279
The *h* bush-bearded Barons heaved and blew,   „ v 21

Huge (continued)   rode we with the old king across
the lawns Beneath *h* trees,   *Princess v* 237
A raiser of *h* melons and of pine,   „ *Con.* 87
On that *h* scapegoat of the race,   *Maud I xiii* 42
She gave the King his *h* cross-hilted sword,   *Com. of Arthur* 286
A *h* man-beast of boundless savagery.   *Gareth and L.* 637
H on a *h* red horse, and all in mail   „ 1026
A *h* pavilion like a mountain peak   „ 1364
The *h* pavilion slowly yielded up,   „ 1379
At this he hurl'd his *h* limbs out of bed,   *Marr. of Geraint* 124
h Earl Doorm, Broad-faced with under-fringe of
russet beard,   *Geraint and E.* 536
return'd The *h* Earl Doorm with plunder to the hall.   „ 592
Here the *h* Earl cried out upon her talk,   „ 651
told How the *h* Earl lay slain within his hall.   „ 806
canst endure To mouth so *h* a foulness—   *Balin and Balan* 379
Before an oak, so hollow, *h* and old   *Merlin and V.* 3
other was the song that once I heard By this *h* oak,   „ 406
seem'd to me the Lord of all the world, Being so *h.*   *Holy Grail* 415
O towers so strong, *H*, solid,   *Pelleas and E.* 464
Glared on a *h* machicolated tower   *Last Tournament* 424
(*H* blocks, which some old trembling of the world   *Lover's Tale ii* 45
With his *h* sea-castles heaving upon the weather
bow.   *The Revenge* 24
For a *h* sea smote every soul from the decks   *The Wreck* 109
Earth so *h*, and yet so bounded—   *Locksley H., Sixty* 207
and flamed On one *h* slope beyond,   *St Telemachus* 8
Gain'd their *h* Colosseum.   „ 45
Huger   drumming thunder of the *h* fall At distance,   *Geraint and E.* 173
Well—can I wish her any *h* wrong   *Last Tournament* 596
their fears Are morning shadows *h* than the shapes   *To the Queen ii* 63
Taller than all the Muses, and *h* than all the mountain?   *Parnassus* 10
Hugest   Nor all Calamity's *h* waves confound,   *Will* 5
place which now Is this world's *h*,   *Lancelot and E.* 76
apples, the *h* that ever were seen,   *V. of Maeldune* 91
Hugg'd   And *h* and never *h* it close enough,   *Princess vi* 212
clung to him and *h* him close;   *Merlin and V.* 945
wrought upon his mood and *h* him close.   „ 948
Hugger-mugger (untidy)   *H-m* they lived, but they
wasn't that easy to please,   *Village Wife* 117
Hugh   'this,' he said, ' was *H's* at Agincourt;   *Princess, Pro.* 25
Hugly (ugly)   But I niver wur downright *h*,   *Spinster's S's.* 16
An' a-callin' ma '*h*' mayhap to my faäce   „ 91
Hull   *h* Look'd one black dot against the verge of dawn,   *M. d'Arthur* 270
Than if my brainpan were an empty *h*,   *Princess ii* 398
h Look'd one black dot against the verge of dawn,   *Pass. of Arthur* 438
mark'd the black *h* moving yet, and cried,   „ 448
Till it smote on their *h's* and their sails   *The Revenge* 116
the low dark *h* dipt under the smiling main,   *The Wreck* 127
Hum (s)   With the *h* of swarming bees   *Eleänore* 29
Hum (verb)   scarce can hear the people *h* About the
column's base,   *St. S. Stylites* 38
And here by thee will *h* the bee,   *A Farewell* 11
all the lavish hills would *h* The murmur of a happy
Pan: *In Mem. xxiii* 11
by and by began to *h* An air the nuns   *Guinevere* 162
Human   Is not my *h* pride brought low?   *Supp. Confessions* 14
cords that wound and eat Into my *h* heart,   „ 37
brook the rod And chastisement of *h* pride;   „ 108
cuts atwain The knots that tangle *h* creeds,   *Clear-headed friend* 3
hour by hour He canvass'd *h* mysteries,   *A Character* 20
But more *h* in your moods,   *Margaret* 47
Far off from *h* neighbourhood,   *Eleänore* 6
Ah pity—hint it not in *h* tones,   *Wan Sculptor* 11
How grows the day of *h* power?'   *Two Voices* 78
While still I yearn'd for *h* praise.   „ 123
Free space for every *h* doubt,   „ 137
That I first was in *h* mould?   „ 342
No life that breathes with *h* breath   „ 395
With cycles of the *h* tale Of this wide world,   *Palace of Art* 146
hear the dully sound Of *h* footsteps fall.   „ 276
Pray Heaven for a *h* heart,   *L. C. V. de Vere* 71
To mingle with the *h* race,   *Of old sat Freedom* 10
h things returning on themselves Move onward,   *Golden Year* 25
Beyond the utmost bound of *h* thought.   *Ulysses* 32

Human (continued)   I dipt into the future far as *h*
eye could see; (repeat)   *Locksley Hall* 15, 119
song That mock'd the wholesome *h* heart,   *The Letters* 10
In her left a *h* head.   *Vision of Sin* 138
Cared not to look on any *h* face,   *Enoch Arden* 282
No want was there of *h* sustenance,   „ 554
He could not see, the kindly *h* face,   „ 581
Brown, looking hardly *h*, strangely clad,   „ 638
Nor sound of *h* sorrow mounts to mar   *Lucretius* 109
Or in the dark dissolving *h* heart,   *Princess iii* 312
Tho' man, yet *h*, whatsoe'er your wrongs,   „ *iv* 425
Then springs the crowning race of *h* kind.   „ *vii* 295
The proof and echo of all *h* fame,   *Ode on Well.* 145
Till in all lands and thro' all *h* story   „ 223
What would you have of us?   *H* life?   *The Victim* 12
Thou seemest *h* and divine,   *In Mem., Pro.* 13
It never look'd to *h* eyes Since our first Sun   „ *xxiv* 7
wrought With *h* hands the creed of creeds   „ *xxxvi* 10
And render *h* love his dues;   „ *xxxvii* 16
To point the term of *h* strife,   „ *l* 14
Nor *h* frailty do me wrong.   „ *lii* 3
sweetest soul That ever look'd with *h* eyes.   „ *lvii* 12
The perfect flower of *h* time;   „ *lxi* 12
What fame is left for *h* deeds In endless age?   „ *lxxiii* 11
But somewhere, out of *h* view,   „ *lxxv* 18
I know transplanted *h* worth Will bloom   „ *lxxxii* 11
How much of act at *h* hands The sense of *h* will   „ *lxxxv* 38
But in dear words of *h* speech   „ 83
there swims The reflex of a *h* face.   „ *cviii* 12
take what fruit may be Of sorrow under *h* skies: „ 14
Nor dream of *h* love and truth,   „ *cxviii* 3
That sees the course of *h* things.   „ *cxxviii* 4
Known and unknown; *h*, divine; Sweet *h* hand and
lips and eye;   „ *cxxix* 5
Whose glory was, redressing *h* wrong;   *Ded. of Idylls* 9
lent her fierce teat To *h* sucklings;   *Com. of Arthur* 29
Till the great plover's *h* whistle amazed   *Geraint and E.* 49
They ride abroad redressing *h* wrongs!   *Merlin and V.* 693
With such a fervent flame of *h* love,   *Holy Grail* 74
And leaving *h* wrongs to right themselves,   „ 898
Beast too, as lacking *h* wit—disgraced,   *Pelleas and E.* 476
To ride abroad redressing *h* wrongs,   *Guinevere* 471
Thou art the highest and most *h* too,   „ 649
Dark with the smoke of *h* sacrifice,   *Sir J. Oldcastle* 84
Cried from the topmost summit with *h* voices and
words;   *V. of Maeldune* 28
French of the French, and Lord of *h* tears;   *To Victor Hugo* 3
My son, the Gods, despite of *h* prayer, Are slower to
forgive than *h* kings.   *Tiresias* 9
whose one bliss Is war, and *h* sacrifice—   „ 112
In height and prowess more than *h*,   „ 179
we broke away from the Christ, our *h* brother   *Despair* 25
and the *h* heart, and the Age.   „ 40
Set the sphere of all the boundless Heavens within
the *h* eye, Sent the shadow of Himself, the
boundless, thro' the *h* soul,   *Locksley H., Sixty* 210
Would she find her *h* offspring this ideal man at rest?   „ 234
Forward, till you see the highest *H* Nature is
divine.   „ 276
As a lord of the *H* soul,   *Dead Prophet* 54
at the doubtful doom of *h* kind;   *To Virgil* 24
sunder'd once from all the *h* race,   „ 36
too fierce and fast This order of Her *H* Star,   *Freedom* 23
Two Suns of Love make day of *h* life,   *Prin. Beatrice* 1
You see your Art still shrined in *h* shelves,   *Poets and their B.* 11
I envied *h* wives, and nested birds,   *Demeter and P.* 53
This poor rib-grated dungeon of the holy *h* ghost,   *Happy* 31
As dead from all the *h* race as if beneath the mould;   „ 95
Larger and fuller, like the *h* mind!   *Prog. of Spring* 112
On *h* faces, And all around me,   *Merlin and the G.* 20
H forgiveness touches heaven, and thence—   *Romney's R.* 159
Hold the sceptre, *h* Soul,   *By an Evolution.* 16
The dust send up a steam of *h* blood,   *St. Telemachus* 53
Every morning is thy birthday gladdening *h* hearts
and eyes.   *Akbar's D., Hymn* 2

Human (*continued*)   Head-hunters and boats of Dahomey
   that float upon *h* blood !   *The Dawn* 5
Neither mourn if *h* creeds be lower   *Faith* 5
Dark no more with *h* hatreds in the glare   „ 8
'Spirit, nearing yon dark portal at the limit of
   thy *h* state,   *God and the Univ.* 4
Larger than *h* on the frozen hills.   *M. d'Arthur* 183
Larger than *h* on the frozen hills.   *Pass. of Arthur* 351
Human-amorous   Her Deity false in *h-a* tears,   *Lucretius* 90
Human-godlike   Thine eyes Again were *h-g*,   *Demeter and P.* 19
Human-hearted   The *h-h* man I loved,   *In Mem. xiii* 11
Humanity   amaze Our brief *humanities*;   *Epilogue* 57
  for the rights of an equal *h*,   *Beautiful City* 2
Human-kind   springs the crowning race of *h-k.*   *Princess vii* 295
Humbling   now desired the *h* of their best,   *Geraint and E.* 637
Humid   Their *h* arms festooning tree to tree,   *D. of F. Women* 70
Humiliated   The woman should have borne, *h*,   *Aylmer's Field* 356
  me they lash'd and *h*, (repeat)   *Boädicea* 45, 67
Humility   late he learned *h* Perforce,   *Buonaparte* 13
  she had fail'd In sweet *h*; had fail'd in all;   *Princess vii* 229
  memories all too free For such a *wise h*   *Ode on Well.* 249
  'O son, thou hast not true *h*,   *Holy Grail* 445
Humm'd   swamp, where *h* the dropping snipe,   *On a Mourner* 9
  Audley feast *H* like a hive   *Audley Court* 5
  Roundhead rode, And *h* a surly hymn.   *Talking Oak* 300
  I turn'd and *h* a bitter song   *The Letters* 9
  Her father's latest word *h* in her ear,   *Lancelot and E.* 780
Hummeth   At noon the wild bee *h*   *Claribel* 11
Humming   (*See also* **Huzzin'**)   hating to hark The *h* of the
   drowsy pulpit-drone   *To J. M. K.* 10
  But while I past he was *h* an air,   *Maud I xiii* 11
  smooth'd The glossy shoulder, *h* to himself.   *Lancelot and E.* 348
  News from the *h* city comes to it   *Gardener's D.* 35
  With summer spice the *h* air ;   *In Mem. ci* 8
Humour   And *h* of the golden prime   *Arabian Nights* 120
  According to my *h* ebb and flow.   *D. of F. Women* 134
  He scarcely hit my *h*, and I said :   *Edwin Morris* 76
  According as his *h's* lead,   *Day-Dm., Moral* 11
  Lest that rough *h* of the kings of old Return   *Gareth and L.* 377
Humorous   he sigh'd Then with another *h* ruth   *Geraint and E.* 250
Humorous-melancholy   You man of *h-m* mark,   *To W. H. Brookfield* 9
Humpback'd   There by the willow ;   *Walk. to the Mail* 31
Hunchback   And all but a *h* too ;   *The Wreck* 43
Hunch'd   *H* as he was, and like an old dwarf-elm   *Pelleas and E.* 543
  But, if a man were halt or *h*,   *Guinevere* 41
Hundred (adj.)   (*See also* **Hoonderd, Nineteen-hundred**) In
   yonder *h* million spheres ? '   *Two Voices* 30
  I knit a *h* others new :   „ 234
  A *h* winters snow'd upon his breast,   *Palace of Art* 139
  The daughter of a *h* Earls,   *L. C. V. de Vere* 7
  Is worth a *h* coats-of-arms.   „ 16
  He shines upon a *h* fields, and all of them I know.   *May Queen, Con.* 50
  At this a *h* bells began to peal,   *M. d'Arthur, Ep.* 29
  Were worth a *h* kisses press'd on lips   *Gardener's D.* 151
  Bow down one thousand and two *h* times,   *St. S. Stylites* 111
  I circle in the grain Five *h* rings of years—   *Talking Oak* 84
  when a *h* times In that last kiss,   *Love and Duty* 66
  Was clash'd and hammer'd from a *h* towers,   *Godiva* 75
  Till all the *h* summers pass,   *Day-Dm., Sleep. P.* 33
  When will the *h* summers die,   „ 49
  'I'd sleep another *h* years,   „ *Depart.* 9
  'A *h* summers ! can it be ?   „ 25
  And every *h* years to rise And learn the world,   *L'Envoi* 7
  O *h* shores of happy climes,   *The Voyage* 49
  Here on this beach a *h* years ago,   *Enoch Arden* 10
  And half a *h* bridges.   *The Brook* 30
  Hung with a *h* shields, the family tree   *Aylmer's Field* 15
  To turn and ponder those three *h* scrolls   *Lucretius* 12
  they betted ; made a *h* friends,   *Princess, Pro.* 163
  That he would send a *h* thousand men,   „ *i* 64
  we mixt with those Six *h* maidens clad in purest white,   „ *ii* 472
  Shall strip a *h* hollows bare of Spring,   „ *vi* 65
  and led A *h* maids in train across the Park.   „ 76
  And follow'd up by a *h* airy does,   „ 87
  thro' The long-laid galleries past a *h* doors   „ 375

Hundred (adj.) (*continued*)   He that gain'd a *h* fights,   *Ode on Well.* 96
  in a *h* years it 'll all be the same,   *Grandmother* 47
  A mount of marble, a *h* spires !   *The Daisy* 60
  Ay is life for a *h* years,   *Window, No Answer* 9
  A *h* spirits whisper ' Peace.'   *In Mem. lxxxvi* 16
  War with a thousand battles, and shaking a *h* thrones.   *Maud I i* 48
  A *h* voices cried, ' Away with him !   *Com. of Arthur* 231
  And *h* winters are but as the hands   „ 281
  And I can topple over a *h* such.   *Gareth and L.* 651
  Came riding with a *h* lances up ;   *Geraint and E.* 539
  Hath hardly scaled with help a *h* feet   *Balin and Balan* 170
  The *h* under-kingdoms that he sway'd   *Merlin and V.* 582
  province with a *h* miles of coast, (repeat)   „ 588, 647
  Spring after spring, for half a *h* years :   *Holy Grail* 19
  A man wellnigh a *h* winters old,   „ 85
  And each of these a *h* winters old,   „ 88
  Scarr'd with a *h* wintry water-courses—   „ 490
  Yea, rotten with a *h* years of death,   „ 496
  Whereon a *h* stately beeches grew,   *Pelleas and E.* 26
  A *h* goodly ones—the Red Knight, he—   *Last Tournament* 170
  whereon There tript a *h* tiny silver deer,   „ 171
  but Arthur with a *h* spears Rode far,   „ 420
  and a *h* meres About it,   „ 481
  (As I have seen them many a *h* times)   *Lover's Tale ii* 145
  And kept it thro' a *h* years of gloom,   „ *iv* 195
  He had only a *h* seamen to work the ship   *The Revenge* 22
  With her *h* fighters on deck,   „ 34
  mountain-like San Philip that, of fifteen *h* tons,   „ 40
  which our house has held Three *h* years—   *Sisters (E. and E.)* 53
  dangled a *h* fathom of grapes,   *V. of Maeldune* 56
  KING, that hast reign'd six *h* years,   *To Dante* 1
  Thou seest the Nameless of the *h* names.   *Ancient Sage* 49
  beyond A *h* ever-rising mountain lines,   „ 282
  swarm Of Turkish Islam for five *h* years,   *Montenegro* 11
  Those three *h* millions under one Imperial
   sceptre now,   *Locksley H., Sixty* 117
  through twice a *h* years, on thee.   *To W. C. Macready* 14
  Who meant to sleep her *h* summers out   *The Ring* 66
  And more than half a *h* years ago,   *To Mary Boyle* 27
  Following a *h* sunsets, and the sphere   *St. Telemachus* 31
  men of a *h* thousand, a million summers away ?   *The Dawn* 25
Hundred (s)   (*See also* **'Oonderd, Six hundred, Three
   hundred**)   Seeing forty of our poor *h* were slain,   *The Revenge* 76
  from fight Before their dauntless *h's*,   *Montenegro* 7
Hundred-fold   his love came back a *h-f*;   *Dora* 166
Hundredth   *See* **Four-hundredth**
Hundred-throated   As 'twere a *h-t* nightingale,   *Vision of Sin* 27
Hung   (*See also* **Hollow-hung, Low-hung, Tassel-hung**) As
   thunder-clouds that, *h* on high,   *Eleänore* 98
  H in the golden Galaxy.   *L. of Shalott iii* 12
  A mighty silver bugle *h*,   „ 16
  chestnuts near, that *h* In masses thick with milky cones.   *Miller's D.* 55
  some were *h* with arras green and blue,   *Palace of Art* 61
  choice paintings of wise men I *h* The royal dais round.   „ 131
  H tranced from all pulsation,   *Gardener's D.* 260
  golden seal, that *h* From Allan's watch,   *Dora* 135
  blackbird on the pippin *h* To hear him,   *Audley Court* 38
  stars that *h* Love-charm'd to listen :   *Love and Duty* 74
  with a mute observance *h*.   *Locksley Hall* 22
  I *h* with grooms and porters on the bridge,   *Godiva* 2
  h upon him, play'd with him And call'd him   *Enoch Arden* 353
  for Enoch *h* A moment on her words,   „ 872
  he stood firm ; and so the matter *h* ; (repeat)   *The Brook* 144, 148
  capacious hall, *H* with a hundred shields,   *Aylmer's Field* 15
  h With wings of brooding shelter o'er her peace,   „ 138
  His own forefathers' arms and armour *h*.   *Princess, Pro.* 24
  Thro' the wild woods that *h* about the town ;   „ *i* 91
  And o'er his head Uranian Venus *h*,   „ 243
  Or under arches of the marble bridge *H*,   „ *ii* 459
  Which melted Florian's fancy as she *h*,   „ *iv* 370
  But on my shoulder *h* their heavy hands,   „ 553
  sword to sword, and horse to horse we *h*,   „ *v* 539
  H round the sick : the maidens came,   „ *vii* 22
  on her foot she *h* A moment, and she heard,   „ 79
  Love, like an Alpine harebell *h* with tears   „ 115

Hung (continued) Once the weight and fate of Europe h.   *Ode on Well.* 240
and Jenny h on his arm.   *Grandmother* 42
H in the shadow of a heaven ?   *In Mem. xvi* 10
h to hear The rapt oration flowing free   ,, *lxxxvii* 31
On thee the loyal-hearted h,   ,, *cx* 5
H over her dying bed—   *Maud I xix* 36
And down from one a sword was h,   *Gareth and L.* 221
he loosed a mighty purse, H at his belt,   *Geraint and E.* 23
Enid had no heart To wake him, but h o'er him,   ,, 370
And h his head, and halted in reply,   ,, 811
high on a branch H it, and turn'd aside   *Balin and Balan* 433
drawing down the dim disastrous brow That o'er him h,   ,, 598
a troop of carrion crows H like a cloud   *Merlin and V.* 599
She paused, she turn'd away, she h her head,   ,, 887
sure I think this fruit is h too high   *Lancelot and E.* 774
o'er her h The silken case with braided blazonings,   ,, 1148
o'er his head the Holy Vessel h (repeat)   *Holy Grail* 512, 520
down a streetway h with folds of pure White samite,   *Last Tournament* 140
the sloping seas H in mid-heaven,   *Lover's Tale i* 4
day H From his mid-dome in Heaven's airy halls ;   ,, 65
H round with ragged rims and burning folds,—   ,, *ii* 63
H round with paintings of the sea,   ,, 168
Took the edges of the pall, and blew it far Until it h,   ,, *iii* 36
the great San Philip h above us like a cloud   *The Revenge* 43
as if hope for the garrison h but on him ;   *Def. of Lucknow* 48
I have h them by my bed,   *Columbus* 200
the long convolvulus h ;   *V. of Maeldune* 40
The sun h over the gates of Night,   *Dead Prophet* 23
The shadow of a crown, that o'er him h,   *D. of the Duke of C.* 2
Hungary shall I shriek if a H fail ?   *Maud I iv* 46
Hunger (s) In h's and in thirsts, fevers and cold,   *St. S. Stylites* 12
Bearing a lifelong h in his heart.   *Enoch Arden* 79
Philip with eyes Full of that lifelong h,   ,, 464
Red grief and mother's h in her eye,   *Princess vi* 146
And in her h mouth'd and mumbled it,   ,, 213
A h seized my heart ; I read   *In Mem. xcv* 21
Some dead of h, some beneath the scourge,   *Columbus* 177
for H hath the Evil eye—   *Ancient Sage* 264
Crime and h cast our maidens   *Locksley H., Sixty* 220
Hunger (verb) Long for my life, or h for my death,   *Geraint and E.* 81
Hunger'd true heart, which h for her peace   *Enoch Arden* 272
Come, I am h and half-anger'd—   *Last Tournament* 719
Hungering staring wide And h for the gilt   *Lover's Tale iv* 313
Hungerworn how weak and h I seem—leaning on these ?   *Gareth and L.* 443
Hungry For always roaming with a h heart   *Ulysses* 12
Slowly comes a h people, as a lion creeping nigher,   *Locksley Hall* 135
greasy gleam In haunts of h sinners,   *Will Water.* 222
every captain waits H for honour,   *Princess v* 314
Like a dry bone cast to some h hound ?   *Last Tournament* 196
Hunt (s) Forgetful of the falcon and the h,   *Marr. of Geraint* 51
petition'd for his leave To see the h,   ,, 155
her love For Lancelot, and forgetful of the h ;   ,, 159
I but come like you to see the h,   ,, 179
And while they listen'd for the distant h,   ,, 184
A little vext at losing of the h,   ,, 234
Hunt (verb) Do h me, day and night.'   *D. of F. Women* 256
Like a dog, he h's in dreams,   *Locksley Hall* 79
' They h old trails,' said Cyril   *Princess ii* 390
We h them for the beauty of their skins ;   ,, *v* 156
who will h for me This demon of the woods ?   *Balin and Balan* 136
not Arthur's use To h by moonlight ; '   *Holy Grail* 111
To h the tiger of oppression out From office ;   *Akbar's Dream* 158
Hunted (adj.) As hunters round a h creature draw   *Aylmer's Field* 499
Hunted (verb) The swallow stopt as he h the fly,   *Poet's Song* 9
Hunter (huntsman) (*See also* **Head-Hunter**) with puff'd
cheek the belted h blew   *Palace of Art* 63
As h's round a hunted creature draw   *Aylmer's Field* 499
Nor her that o'er her wounded h wept   *Lucretius* 89
the h rued His rash intrusion, manlike,   *Princess iv* 203
Man is the h ; woman is his game :   ,, *v* 154
made Broad pathways for the h and the knight   *Com. of Arthur* 61
No keener h after glory breathes   *Lancelot and E.* 156
' O h, and O blower of the horn, Harper,   *Last Tournament* 542
' Ah then, false h and false harper,   ,, 567
and h's race The shadowy lion,   *Tiresias* 177

Hunter (horse) And rode his h down.   *Talking Oak* 104
Hunting (*See also* **'Untin', Wife-hunting**) The King was h
in the wild ;   *The Victim* 30
gave order to let blow His horns for h   *Marr. of Geraint* 153
he went To-day for three days' h—   *Last Tournament* 530
Hunting-dress wearing neither h-d Nor weapon,   *Marr. of Geraint* 165
Hunting-morn the third day from the h-m   ,, 597
Hunting-tide Rang out like hollow woods at h-t.   *Pelleas and E.* 367
Hup-on-end (up-on-end) An' I slep i' my chair h-o-e,   *Owd Roä* 54
Hupside (upside) an' the 'ole 'ouse h down.   *North Cobbler* 43
Hurl h their lances in the sun ;   *Locksley Hall* 170
Balin graspt, but while in act to h,   *Balin and Balan* 368
Mark was half in heart to h his cup   *Merlin and V.* 30
when he stopt we long'd to h together,   ,, 420
Twice do we h them to earth   *Def. of Lucknow* 58
Gods, To quench, not h the thunderbolt,   *Demeter and P.* 133
Hurl'd the bolts are h Far below them   *Lotos-Eaters, C. S.* 111
And h the pan and kettle.   *The Goose* 28
H as a stone from out a catapult   *Gareth and L.* 965
They madly h together on the bridge ;   ,, 1120
h him headlong o'er the bridge Down to the river,   ,, 1153
At this he h his huge limbs out of bed,   *Marr. of Geraint* 124
Hung at his belt, and h it toward the squire.   *Geraint and E.* 23
h to ground what knight soever spurr'd Against us,   *Balin and Balan* 66
h it from him Among the forest weeds,   ,, 541
he h into it Against the stronger ;   *Lancelot and E.* 462
H back again so often in empty foam,   *Last Tournament* 93
h The tables over and the wines,   ,, 474
Leapt on him, and h him headlong,   *Guinevere* 108
you h them to the ground.   *Happy* 76
Been h so high they ranged about the globe ?   *St. Telemachus* 2
when she h a plaäte at the cat   *Church-warden, etc.* 25
Noble the Saxon who h at his Idol   *Kapiolani* 4
Hurling Each h down a heap of things that rang   *Geraint and E.* 594
Hurrah we roar'd a h, and so The little Revenge   *The Revenge* 32
Hurricane like the smoke in a h whirl'd.   *Boädicea* 59
The h of the latitude on him fell,   *Columbus* 138
Crash'd like a h, Broke thro' the mass   *Heavy Brigade* 28
Hurried Edith's eager fancy h with him   *Aylmer's Field* 208
Hurry (s) (*See also* **Urry**) all three in h and fear Ran
to her,   *Lancelot and E.* 1024
Hurry (verb) By thirty hills I h down,   *The Brook* 27
and yearn to h precipitously   *Boädicea* 58
Hurrying Myriads of rivulets h thro' the lawn,   *Princess vii* 220
Driving, h, marrying, burying,   *Maud II v* 12
Another h past, a man-at-arms,   *Geraint and E.* 526
Then, h home, I found her not in house   *The Ring* 444
Hurt (s) helps the h that Honour feels,   *Locksley Hall* 105
swathed the h that drain'd her dear lord's life.   *Geraint and E.* 516
Then, fearing for his h and loss of blood,   ,, 777
came The King's own leech to look into his h ;   ,, 923
But while Geraint lay healing of his h,   ,, 931
tho' he call'd his wound a little h   *Lancelot and E.* 852
when Sir Lancelot's deadly h was whole,   ,, 904
Like a king's heir, till all his h's be whole.   *Last Tournament* 91
heal'd Thy h and heart with unguent and caress—   ,, 595
treat their loathsome h's and heal mine own ;   *Guinevere* 686
Hurt (verb and part.) Love is h with jar and fret.   *Miller's D.* 209
H in that night of sudden ruin and wreck,   *Enoch Arden* 564
There by a keeper shot at, slightly h,   *Aylmer's Field* 548
almost all that is, hurting the h—   ,, 572
With their own blows they h themselves,   *Princess vi* 49
I trust that there is no one h to death,   ,, 242
H in his first tilt was my son, Sir Torre.   *Lancelot and E.* 196
' But parted from the jousts H in the side,'   ,, 623
h Whom she would soothe, and harm'd   *Guinevere* 354
Hurted I slither'd and h my huck,   *North. Cobbler* 19
Hurting almost all that is, h the hurt—   *Aylmer's Field* 572
Husban' at yer wake like h an' wife.   *Tomorrow* 82
Husband (*See also* **Husban'**) As the h is, the wife is :   *Locksley Hall* 47
of what he wish'd, Enoch, your h :   *Enoch Arden* 292
Has she no fear that her first h lives ?   ,, 806
only near'd Her h inch by inch,   *Aylmer's Field* 807
' No trifle,' groan'd the h ;   *Sea Dreams* 145
The field was pleasant in my h's eye.'   *Gareth and L.* 342

Ill (s) (continued) Then why not *i* for good? — Love and Duty 27
good Will be the final goal of *i*, — In Mem. liv 2
Who loved, who suffer'd countless *i's*, — „ lvi 17
honey of poison-flowers and all the measureless *i*. — Maud I iv 56
For years, a measureless *i*, For years, — „ II ii 49
Better to fight for the good than to rail at the *i*; — „ III vi 57
There most in those who most have done them *i*. — Geraint and E. 877
This good is in it, whatsoe'er of *i*, — Lancelot and E. 1207
he was heal'd at once, By faith, of all his *i's*. — Holy Grail 56
And *i's* and aches, and teethings, — „ 554
so worship him That *i* to him is *i* to them; — „ 652
No *i* no good! such counter-terms, — Ancient Sage 250
I meet my fate, whatever *i's* betide! — The Flight 95
Powers of Good, the Powers of *I*, — Locksley H., Sixty 273
Shall we not thro' good and *i* — Open I. and C. Exhib. 33
year's great good and varied *i's*, — Prog. of Spring 93
'Ill (hill) Wrigglesby beck cooms out by the *'i*! — N. Farmer, N. S. 53
Ill-content Dwelt with eternal summer, *i-c*. — Enoch Arden 562
I, Earth-Goddess, am but *i-c* — Demeter and P. 128
Ill-done It was *i-d* to part you, Sisters fair; — Lover's Tale i 814
Ill-fated *I-f* that I am, what lot is mine — Love and Duty 33
i-f as they were, A bitterness to me! — Last Tournament 40
Illigant (elegant) An' sorra the Queen wid her sceptre in sich an *i* han', — Tomorrow 35
Illimitable lordly music flowing from The *i* years. — Ode to Memory 42
Ruining along the *i* inane, — Lucretius 40
light and shadow *i*, — Boädicea 42
till o'er the *i* reed, And many a glancing plash — Last Tournament 421
Illiterate not *i*; nor of those Who dabbling — The Brook 92
Ill-omen'd Remembering his *i-o* song, — Princess vi 159
'Ill-side (hill-side) What's the 'eät of this little *'i-s* — North. Cobbler 6
Ill-suited such a feast, *i-s* as it seem'd To such a time, — Lover's Tale iv 207
Illuminate *i* All your towns for a festival, — On Jub. Q. Victoria 18
Illumined (*See also* **Long-illumined**) from the *i* hall Long lanes of splendour — Princess iv 477
Illumined (verb) A fuller light *i* all, — Day-Dm., Revival 5
Illumineth I saw, wherever light *i*, — D. of F. Women 14
Ill-usage Or sicken with *i-u*, — Princess v 86
Ill-used Chanted from an *i-u* race of men — Lotos-Eaters, C. S. 120
Francis, muttering, like a man *i-u*, — M. d'Arthur, Ep. 12
Illusion 'Confusion, and *i*, and relation, — Gareth and L. 287
The phantom walls of this *i* fade, — Ancient Sage 181
Illyrian *I* woodlands, echoing falls Of water, — To E. L. 1
Image An *i* with profulgent brows, — Supp. Confessions 145
An *i* seem'd to pass the door, (repeat) — Mariana in the S. 65, 74
Vast *i's* in glimmering dawn, — Two Voices 305
Which was an *i* of the mighty world; — M. d'Arthur 235
Would play with flying forms and *i's*, — Gardener's D. 60
I fixt My wistful eyes on two fair *i's*, — Sea Dreams 240
An *i* comforting the mind, — In Mem. lxxxv 51
To one pure *i* of regret. — „ cii 24
Your mother is mute in her grave as her *i* in marble above; — Maud I iv 58
finding there unconsciously Some *i* of himself— — Ded. of Idylls 3
Full often the bright *i* of one face, — Lancelot and E. 882
'Let her tomb Be costly, and her *i* thereupon, — „ 1340
Stamp'd with the *i* of the King; — Holy Grail 27
Man was it who marr'd heaven's *i* in thee thus?' — Last Tournament 27
Which was an *i* of the mighty world, — Pass. of Arthur 403
Thine *i*, like a charm of light and strength — Lover's Tale i 91
for tho' mine *i*, The subject of thy power, — „ 781
I could stamp my *i* on her heart! — Sisters (E. and E.) 195
'*I's*?' 'Bury them as God's truer *i's* — Sir J. Oldcastle 139
each like a golden *i* was pollen'd from — V. of Maeldune 49
Imagery Trick thyself out in ghastly *imageries* — Gareth and L. 1390
Imagination Poet-princess with her grand *I's* — Princess iii 274
I's calm and fair, — In Mem. xciv 10
The strong *i* roll A sphere of stars — „ cxxii 6
Imaginative Likewise the *i* woe, — „ lxxxv 53
Imagined *I* more than seen, the skirts of France. — Princess, Con. 48
Imagining Nor feed with crude *i's* — Love thou thy land 10
Imbecile the man became *I*; his one word was 'desolate,' — Aylmer's Field 836
Imbedded with golden yolks *I* and injellied; — Audley Court 26
Imbibing O to watch the thirsty plants *I*! — Princess ii 423

M*

Imbower (*See also* **Embower**) silent isle *i's* The Lady of Shalott. — L. of Shalott i 17
Imbower'd *I* vaults of pillar'd palm, — Arabian Nights 39
Imbrashin' (embracing) *I* an' kissin' aich other— — Tomorrow 90
Imitate *I's* God, and turns her face To every land — On a Mourner 2
Imitative vague desire That spurs an *i* will. — In Mem. cx 20
Immantled *I* in ambrosial dark, — „ lxxxix 14
Immeasurable Toiling in *i* sand, — Will 16
As one who feels the *i* world, — Dedication 7
the *i* heavens Break open to their highest, — Spec. of Iliad 14
I Reality! Infinite Personality! — De Prof., Human C. 3
backward, forward, in the *i* sea, — Locksley H., Sixty 193
Immemorial Bound in an *i* intimacy, — Aylmer's Field 39
but an *i* intimacy, Wander'd at will, — „ 136
The moan of doves in *i* elms, — Princess vii 221
Immerging *i*, each, his urn In his own well, — Tiresias 88
Immersed *I* in rich foreshadowings of the world, — Princess vii 312
But when the Queen *i* in such a trance, — Guinevere 401
Imminent Commingled with the gloom of *i* war, — Ded. of Idylls 13
Immodesty Accuse her of the least *i*: — Geraint and E. 111
Immolation than by single act Of *i*, — Princess iii 285
Immortal on my face The star-like sorrows of *i* eyes, — D. of F. Women 91
Thy brothers and *i* souls. — Love thou thy land 8
To dwell in presence of *i* youth, I age beside *i* youth, — Tithonus 21
and plucks The mortal soul from out *i* hell, — Lucretius 263
And happy warriors, and *i* names, — Princess vi 93
STRONG Son of God, *i* Love, — In Mem., Pro. 1
A life that bears *i* fruit In those great offices — xl 18
Or am I made *i*, or my love Mortal once more?' — Lover's Tale iv 79
Hell? if the souls of men were *i*, — Despair 99
Thou canst not prove thou art *i*, — Ancient Sage 62
Immortality feel their *i* Die in their hearts — The Mermaid 29
Me only cruel *i* Consumes: — Tithonus 5
I ask'd thee, 'Give me *i*.' — „ 15
length of days, and *i* Of thought, — Lover's Tale i 105
Impaled the King *i* him for his piracy; — Merlin and V. 569
Impart *i* The life that almost dies in me; — In Mem. xviii 15
Impassion'd *I* logic, which outran The hearer — „ cix 7
Impearled *See* **Dew-impearled**
Imperfect Ah, take the *i* gift I bring, — „ lxxxv 117
accept this old *i* tale, New-old, — To the Queen ii 36
Imperial Serene! *i* Eleänore! (repeat) — Eleänore 81, 121
come and go In thy large eyes, *i* Eleänore. — „ 97
And in the *i* presence found the king. — Princess i 143
blazon'd lions o'er the *i* tent Whispers of war. — „ v 9
Has given our Prince his own *i* Flower, — W. to Marie Alex. 4
I halls, or open plain; — In Mem. xcviii 29
and thine *I* mother smile again, — Ded. Poem Prin. Alice 13
Those three hundred millions under one *I* sceptre now, — Locksley H., Sixty 117
rhythm sound for ever of *I* Rome— — To Virgil 32
'Sons, be welded each and all, Into one *i* whole, — Open. I. and C. Exhib. 37
Some *I* Institute, Rich in symbol, — On Jub. Q. Victoria 46
Child, those *i*, disimpassion'd eyes — Demeter and P. 23
and in her soft *i* way And saying gently: — The Ring 267
Imperial-moulded O *i-m* form, And beauty — Guinevere 548
Imperious *I*, and of haughtiest lineaments. — Marr. of Geraint 190
Implied that vague fear *i* in death; — In Mem. xli 14
Imply That to begin *implies* to end; — Two Voices 339
Impolitic As ignorant and *i* as a beast— — Columbus 128
Impossible Things in an Aylmer deem'd *i*, — Aylmer's Field 305
Such a match as this! *I*, prodigious!' — „ 315
And swearing men to vows *i*, — Lancelot and E. 130
Follows; but him I proved *i*; — Lucretius 193
Impotence In *i* of fancied power. — A Character 24
Impotent *i* To win her back before I die— — Romney's R. 117
Impressions took Full easily all *i* from below, — Guinevere 642
Imprison'd Which to the *i* spirit of the child, — Lover's Tale i 204
Imprisoning pillar'd palm, *I* sweets, — Arabian Nights 40
Impulse With the selfsame *i* wherewith he was thrown — Mine be the strength 3
'An inner *i* rent the veil Of his old husk: — Two Voices 10
Impute *i* a crime Are pronest to it, and *i* — Merlin and V. 825
Imputing Polluting, and *i* her whole self, — „ 803
Inactive lying thus *i*, doubt and gloom. — Enoch Arden 113

Inane   Ruining along the illimitable *i*,   *Lucretius* 40
Inarticulate   idiotlike it seem'd, With *i* rage,   *Enoch Arden* 640
Inaudible   Alway the *i* invisible thought,   *Lover's Tale ii* 102
Incense (s)   Like two streams of *i* free   *Eleänore* 58
   A cloud of *i* of all odour steam'd   *Palace of Art* 39
   And that sweet *i* rise?' For that sweet *i* rose and never fail'd,   "   44
   a mist Of *i* curl'd about her, and her face   *Com. of Arthur* 288
   Roll'd *i*, and there past along the hymns   "   464
   Absorbing all the *i* of sweet thoughts   *Lover's Tale i* 469
Incense (verb)   fear'd To *i* the Head once more;   *Princess vii* 77
Incense-fume   clouded with the grateful *i-f*   *Tiresias* 183
Incest   crowded couch of *i* in the warrens of the poor.   *Locksley H., Sixty* 224
Inch   Why *i* by *i* to darkness crawl?   *Two Voices* 200
   only near'd Her husband *i* by *i*,   *Aylmer's Field* 807
   strain to make an *i* of room For their sweet selves   *Lit. Squabbles* 9
   in the pause she crept an *i* Nearer,   *Guinevere* 527
Incited   each *i* each to noble deeds.   *Merlin and V.* 414
Incline   over rainy mist *i*'s A gleaming crag   *Two Voices* 188
   Till all thy life one way *i* With one wide Will   *On a Mourner* 19
Incompetent   must I be *I* of memory: *Two Voices* 375
Incomplete   WHILE man and woman are still *i*,   *On one who effec. E. M.* 1
Inconsiderate   And like an *i* boy,   *In Mem. cxxii* 14
Incorporate   And grow *i* into thee.   "   *ii* 16
   The *i* blaze of sun and sea.   *Lover's Tale i* 409
Incorruptible   have bought A mansion *i*.   *Deserted H.* 21
Increase (s)   for the good and *i* of the world. (repeat)   *Edwin Morris* 44, 51, 92
   The fruitful hours of still *i*;   *In Mem. xlvi* 10
Increase (verb)   While the stars burn, the moons *i*,   *To J. S.* 71
   watch her harvest ripen, her herd *i*,   *Maud III vi* 25
Increased   lest brute Power be *i*,   *Poland* 6
   But day *i* from heat to heat,   *Mariana in the S.* 39
   light *i* With freshness in the dawning east.   *Two Voices* 404
   and with each The year *i*.   *Gardener's D.* 199
   Thy latter days *i* with pence   *Will Water.* 219
   His beauty still with his years *i*,   *The Victim* 34
   For them the light of life *i*,   *In Mem., Con.* 74
   i, Upon a pastoral slope as fair,   *Maud I xviii* 18
   I Geraint's, who heaved his blade aloft,   *Marr. of Geraint* 572
   that ruling has *i* Her greatness and her self-content.   *To Marq. of Dufferin* 7
Increasing   Which with *i* might doth forward flee   *Mine be the strength* 5
   I doubt not thro' the ages one *i* purpose runs,   *Locksley Hall* 137
   and Fame again *I* gave me use.   *Merlin and V.* 494
Incredible   spires Prick'd with *i* pinnacles into heaven.   *Holy Grail* 423
Incredulous   *See* Half-incredulous
In-crescent   Between the *i-c* and de-crescent moon,   *Gareth and L.* 529
Ind   sways the floods and lands From *I* to *I*,   *Buonaparte* 4
Indecent   *See* Ondecent
Indeed   soldier of the Cross? it is he and he *i*!   *Happy* 12
   Life, which is Life *i*.   *Prog. of Spring* 117
India   all the sultry palms of *I* known,   *W. to Marie Alex.* 14
   Where some refulgent sunset of *I*   *Milton* 13
   upon the topmost roof our banner in *I* blew.   *Def. of Lucknow* 72
   For he—your *I* was his Fate,   *To Marq. of Dufferin* 21
   Queen, and Empress of *I*,   *On Jub. Q. Victoria* 6
Indian (*See also* Hinjian, West-Indian)   *I* reeds blown from his silver tongue,   *The Poet* 13
   The throne of *I* Cama slowly sail'd   *Palace of Art* 115
   Fire-hollowing this in *I* fashion,   *Enoch Arden* 569
   My lady's *I* kinsman unannounced   *Aylmer's Field* 190
   My lady's *I* kinsman rushing in,   "   593
   less from *I* craft Than beelike instinct hiveward,   *Princess iv* 198
   yet the morn Breaks hither over *I* seas,   *In Mem. xxvi* 14
   gazing like The *I* on a still-eyed snake,   *Lover's Tale ii* 189
   Praise to our *I* brothers,   *Def. of Lucknow* 7
   not That *I* isle, but our most ancient East   *Columbus* 80
   I warriors dream of ampler hunting grounds   *Locksley H., Sixty* 69
   To England under *I* skies,   *Hands all Round* 17
   I, Australasian, African,   *On Jub. Q. Victoria* 60
   Will my *I* brother come?   *Romney's R.* 143
   wail of baby-wife, Or *I* widow?   *Akbar's Dream* 197
Indies   Of the Ocean—of the *I*—Admirals we—   *Columbus* 31

Indies (*continued*)   Rome's Vicar in our *I*?   *Columbus* 195
Indifference   Attain the wise *i* of the wise;   *A Dedication* 8
   And Love the *i* to be,   *In Mem. xxvi* 12
Indignant   But thy strong Hours *i* work'd their wills,   *Tithonus* 18
   On either side the hearth, *i*;   *Aylmer's Field* 288
   and she returned *I* to the Queen; (repeat)   *Marr. of Geraint* 202, 414
Indignantly   Gareth spake and all *i*,   *Gareth and L.* 1386
   And yet he answer'd half *i*:   *Merlin and V.* 404
Indignation   What heats of *i* when we heard   *Princess v* 375
   her white neck Was rosed with *i*:   "   *vi* 344
Indistinct   muffled booming *i* Of the confused floods,   *Lover's Tale i* 637
   masses Of thundershaken columns *i*,   "   *ii* 66
Individual (adj.)   And *i* freedom mute;   *You ask me why, etc.* 20
   Matures the *i* form.   *Love thou thy land* 40
   There—closing like an *i* life—   *Love and Duty* 79
Individual (s)   And the *i* withers,   *Locksley Hall* 142
Individuality   Distinct in *individualities*,   *Princess vii* 291
Indolent   O YOU chorus of *i* reviewers, Irresponsible, *i* reviewers,   *Hendecasyllabics* 1
   Waking laughter in *i* reviewers.   "   8
   All that chorus of *i* reviewers.   "   12
   believe me Too presumptuous, *i* reviewers.   "   16
Indoor   an' a trouble an' plague wi' *i*.   *Spinster's S's.* 10
Indrawing   Like some old wreck on some *i* sea,   *St. Telemachus* 44
Induce   persecute Opinion, and *i* a time   *You ask me why, etc.* 18
Indue   His eyes To *i* his lustre;   *Lover's Tale i* 424
   my love should ne'er *i* the front And mask of Hate,   "   774
Ineffable   Toil and I weariness,   *Def. of Lucknow* 90
   Beyond all dreams of Godlike womanhood, *I* beauty,   *Tiresias* 55
Inexorable   No saint—*i*—no tenderness—   *Princess v* 515
   fall the battle-axe, unexhausted, *i*.   *Boädicea* 55
Infancy   In the silken sail of *i*,   *Arabian Nights* 2
   O'er the deep mind of dauntless *i*.   *Ode to Memory* 36
   With those old faces of our *i*   *Lotos-Eaters, C. S.* 66
   To ailing wife or wailing *i*   *Aylmer's Field* 177
   flaxen ringlets of our *infancies* Wander'd,   *Lover's Tale i* 234
   As was our childhood, so our *i*,   "   249
Infant (adj.)   Or an *i* civilisation be ruled with rod or with knout?   *Maud I iv* 47
   Some hold that he hath swallow'd *i* flesh,   *Gareth and L.* 1342
   You claspt our *i* daughter, heart to heart.   *Romney's R.* 77
Infant (s)   The trustful *i* on the knee!   *Supp. Confessions* 41
   Which mixing with the *i*'s blood.   "   61
   clear Delight, the *i*'s dawning year.   "   67
   Thou leddest by the hand thine *i* Hope.   *Ode to Memory* 30
   And laid the feeble *i* in his arms;   *Enoch Arden* 152
   more than *i*'s in their sleep.   *Princess vii* 54
   Shall we deal with it as an *i*?   *Boädicea* 33
   An *i* crying in the night: An *i* crying for the light: *In Mem. liv* 18
   shaping an *i* ripe for his birth,   *Maud I iv* 34
   gave Thy breast to ailing *i*'s in the night,   *Demeter and P.* 56
Infidel (adj.)   Have I crazed myself over their horrible *i* writings?   *Despair* 87
Infidel (s)   that large *i* Your Omar;   *To E. Fitzgerald* 9
   I loathe the very name of *i*.   *Akbar's Dream* 70
Infinite (*See also* Finite-infinite)   Because the scale is *i*.   *Two Voices* 93
   and serve that *I* Within us, as without,   *Akbar's Dream* 145
   'Mid onward-sloping motions *i*,   *Palace of Art* 247
   and *i* torment of flies,   *Def. of Lucknow* 82
   And shatter'd phantom of that *i* One,   *De Prof., Two G.* 47
   I Ideality! Immeasurable Reality! *I* Personality!   "   *Human C.* 2
   I should call on that *I* Love that has served us so well?   *Despair* 95
   I cruelty rather that made everlasting Hell,
Infinity   Like emblems of *i*, The trenched   *Ode to Memory* 103
In flagrante   Caught *i f*—what's the Latin word?—   *Walk. to the Mail* 34
Inflame   twelve-divided concubine To *i* the tribes: *Aylmer's Field* 760
Inflamed   like a rising moon, *I* with wrath: *Princess i* 60
   a horn, *i* the knights At that dishonour   *Last Tournament* 434
Inflate   *I* themselves with some insane delight,   *Merlin and V.* 834
Influence   self-same *i* Controlleth all the soul   *Eleänore* 114
   'Who forged that other *i*,   *Two Voices* 283
   To the *i* of mild-minded melancholy;   *Lotos-Eaters, C. S.* 64
   and use Her *i* on the mind,   *Will Water.* 12
   sacred from the blight Of ancient *i* and scorn.   *Princess ii* 169
   Twice as magnetic to sweet *i*'s Of earth   "   *v* 191

Influence (*continued*)   By many a varying *i* and so long.   *Princess* vi 267
  A kindlier *i* reign'd ;   „ vii 20
  Or in their silent *i* as they sat,   „ Con. 15
  Mourn for the man of amplest *i*,   *Ode on Well.* 27
  Let random *i*'s glance,   *In Mem.* xlix 2
Influence-rich *i-r* to soothe and save,   „ lxxx 14
Infold *See* **Self-infold**
Inform beauty doth *i* Stillness with love,   *Day-Dm., Sleep* B. 15
  early risen she goes to *i* The Princess :   *Princess* iii 62
Inform'd *I* the pillar'd Parthenon,   *Freedom* 3
Infuse Desire in me to *i* my tale of love   *Princess* v 240
  Should *i* Rich atar in the bosom of the rose,   *Lover's Tale* i 269
Ingrav'n (*See also* **Engraven**) rind *i* 'For the most fair,'   *Œnone* 72
Ingress for your *i* here Upon the skirt   *Princess* v 218
Ingroove be free To *i* itself with that which flies,   *Love thou thy land* 46
Inhabitant liker to the *i* Of some clear planet   *Princess* ii 35
Inherit Our sons *i* us : our looks are strange :   *Lotos-Eaters*, C. S. 73
  'The meek shall *i* the earth'   *The Dreamer* 2
Inheritance some *i* Of such a life, a heart,   *Ded. of Idylls* 32
  And standeth seized of that *i*   *Gareth and L.* 359
  But lately come to his *i*,   *Pelleas and E.* 18
Inherited (*adj.*)   heap'd the whole *i* sin On that huge scapegoat   *Maud* I xiii 41
  But if sin be sin, not *i* fate,   *The Wreck* 85
Inherited (*verb*)   And he that next *i* the tale   *Princess* iv 592
Injellied golden yolks Imbedded and *i*;   *Audley Court* 26
Injured *See* **Seeming-injured**
Injuries life-long *i* burning unavenged,   *Geraint and E.* 696
Inky Draw the vast eyelid of an *i* cloud,   *Merlin and V.* 634
Inlaid Distinct with vivid stars *i*,   *Arabian Nights* 90
Inland And ripples on an *i* mere ?   *Supp. Confessions* 131
  Crimsons over an *i* mere,   *Eleänore* 42
  From many an *i* town and haven large,   *Œnone* 117
  thro' mountain clefts the dale Was seen far *i*,   *Lotos-Eaters* 21
Inlay deep *i* Of braided blooms unmown,   *Arabian Nights* 28
Inlet In glaring sand and *i*'s bright.   *Mariana in the S.* 8
Inmingled *I* with Heaven's azure waveringly,   *Gareth and L.* 936
Inmost Upon the mooned domes aloof In *i* Bagdat,   *Arabian Nights* 128
  As tho' a star, in *i* heaven set,   *Eleänore* 89
  Dead sounds at night come from the *i* hills,   *Œnone* 249
  'And even into my *i* ring A pleasure   *Talking Oak* 173
  Then fled she to her *i* bower,   *Godiva* 42
  clamour thicken'd, mixt with *i* terms   *Princess* ii 446
  Came in long breezes rapt from *i* south And blown to *i* north ;   „ iv 431
  As some rare little rose, a piece of *i* Horticultural art,   *Hendecasyllabics* 19
  wordy snares to track Suggestion to her *i* cell.   *In Mem.* xcv 32
  And gulf'd his griefs in *i* sleep;   *Pelleas and E.* 516
  Not ev'n in *i* thought to think again   *Guinevere* 374
  like a little star Were drunk into the *i* blue,   *Lover's Tale* i 309
  Spoke loudly even into my *i* heart   „ 428
  streams Running far on within its *i* halls,   „ 523
  For all the secret of her *i* heart,   „ 588
  tight chain within my *i* frame Was riven in twain :   „ 595
  Woman to her *i* heart, and woman to her tender feet,   *Locksley H., Sixty* 50
Inn (*See also* **Hinn**) And lighted at a ruin'd *i*, and said :   *Vision of Sin* 62
  tha mun goä fur it down to the *i*.   *North. Cobbler* 8
  like old-world *i*'s that take Some warrior   *Pro. to Gen. Hamley* 13
Inner with shows of flaunting vines Unto mine *i* eye,   *Ode to Memory* 49
  With an *i* voice the river ran,   *Dying Swan* 5
  Springing alone With a shrill *i* sound,   *Mermaid* 20
  All the *i*, all the outer world of pain   *If I were loved* 5
  'An *i* impulse rent the veil Of his old husk :   *Two Voices* 10
  river seaward flow From the *i* land :   *Lotos-Eaters* 14
  Nor harken what the *i* spirit sings,   „ C. S. 22
  Gross darkness of the *i* sepulchre Is not so deadly still   *D. of F. Women* 67
  green that streak the white Of the first snowdrop's *i* leaves ;   *Princess* v 197
  when sundown skirts the moor An *i* trouble I behold,   *In Mem.* xli 18
  That stir the spirit's *i* deeps,   „ xlii 10
  No *i* vileness that we dread ?   „ li 4
  His *i* day can never die,   „ lxvi 15

Inner (*continued*)   Made dull his *i*, keen his outer eye   *Last Tournament* 366
  But thou didst sit alone in the *i* house,   *Lover's Tale* i 112
  vessel, as with *i* life, Began to heave   „ ii 191
Innermost Flash'd thro' my eyes into my *i* brain,   „ 95
  Death in our *i* chamber,   *Def. of Lucknow* 15
Inniskillens Brave *I* and Greys   *Heavy Brigade* 33
Innocence Affronted with his fulsome *i* ?   *Pelleas and E.* 266
  'Take thou the jewels of this dead *i*,   *Last Tournament* 31
  Our one white day of *I* hath past,   „ 218
  small damosels white as *I*, In honour of poor *I*   „ 291
  left the gems with *I* the Queen Lent to the King, and *I*   „ 293
  Which lives with blindness, or plain *i* Of nature,   *Sisters* (E. and E.) 249
  I seethed in her mother's milk,   *Vastness* 9
Innocency O yield me shelter for mine *i*   *Merlin and V.* 83
Innocent (*adj.*)   And loveth so his *i* heart,   *Supp. Confessions* 52
  The little *i* soul flitted away.   *Enoch Arden* 270
  nightly wirer of their *i* hare Falter   *Aylmer's Field* 490
  for her fresh and *i* eyes Had such a star   „ 691
  and reach its fatling *i* arms And lazy lingering fingers.   *Princess* vi 138
  Then as a little helpless *i* bird,   *Lancelot and E.* 894
  And kind the woman's eyes and *i*,   *Holy Grail* 393
  'Will the child kill me with her *i* talk ? '   *Guinevere* 214
  Why should *she* weep ? O *i* of spirit—   *Lover's Tale* i 737
  Being guiltless, as an *i* prisoner,   „ 787
  Their *i* hospitalities quench'd in blood,   *Columbus* 176
  a heedless and *i* bride—   *The Wreck* 13
  and drive *I* cattle under thatch,   *Locksley H., Sixty* 96
  I maidens, Garrulous children,   *Merlin and the G.* 55
Innocent (s)   Themselves had wrought on many an *i*.   *Geraint and E.* 178
Innocent-arch So *i-a*, so cunning-simple,   *Lilian* 13
Innumerable (*See also* **Numerable-innumerable**) In copse and fern Twinkled the *i* ear and tail.   *The Brook* 134
  And sated with the *i* rose,   *Princess* iii 122
  And murmuring of *i* bees.'   „ vii 222
  bark and blacken *i*,   *Boädicea* 13
  I, pitiless, passionless eyes,   *Maud* I xviii 38
  Thro' knots and loops and folds *i*   *Lancelot and E.* 439
  lying bounden there In darkness thro' *i* hours   *Holy Grail* 677
  are these but symbols of man,   *Locksley H., Sixty* 195
Innumerous A lisping of the *i* leaf and dies,   *Princess* v 14
Inosculated (For so they said themselves) *i* ;   „ iii 89
Inquire Who scarcely darest to *i*,   *In Mem.* iv 7
Inquisition To these *I* dogs and the devildoms of Spain.'   *The Revenge* 12
Inrunning (*See also* **Deep-inrunning**) And at the *i* of a little brook Sat by the river   *Lancelot and E.* 1388
Insane Inflate themselves with some *i* delight,   *Merlin and V.* 834
Insanity With animal heat and dire *i* ?   *Lucretius* 163
  Roll'd again back on itself in the tides of a civic *i* !   *Beautiful City* 4
Inscription And some *i* ran along the front,   *Princess* i 212
  How saw you not the *i* on the gate,   „ ii 194
  'for that *i* there, I think no more of deadly lurks   „ 225
  I urged the fierce *i* on the gate,   „ iii 141
Insect *i*'s prick Each leaf into a gall)   *Talking Oak* 69
  The lightning flash of *i* and of bird,   *Enoch Arden* 575
  Or eagle's wing, or *i*'s eye ;   *In Mem.* cxxiv 6
  I's of an hour, that hourly work their brother *i* wrong,   *Locksley H., Sixty* 202
Insipid *I* as the Queen upon a card ;   *Aylmer's Field* 28
Insolence blustering I know not what Of *i*   *Princess* v 397
  Smelling of musk and of *i*,   *Maud* I vi 45
Insolent *I*, brainless, heartless !   *Aylmer's Field* 368
  '*I* scullion : *I* of thee ?   *Gareth and L.* 976
Inspiration Ancient founts of *i* well   *Locksley Hall* 188
Instance That wilderness of single *i*'s,   *Aylmer's Field* 437
  But Vivien, deeming Merlin overborne By *i*,   *Merlin and V.* 801
Instant *I* were his words.   *Gareth and L.* 1353
  Abash'd Lavaine, whose *i* reverence,   *Lancelot and E.* 418
Instep brandish'd plume Brushing his *i*,   *Geraint and E.* 360
Instinct of the moral *i* would she prate   *Palace of Art* 205
  And that mysterious *i* wholly died.   *Enoch Arden* 526
  less from Indian craft Than beelike *i*   *Princess* iv 199
  a dearer being, all dipt In Angel *i*'s,   „ vii 321

Instinctive his quick *i* hand Caught at the hilt, — *Marr. of Geraint* 209
Institute their *I* Of which he was the patron. — *Princess, Pro.* 5
  The patient leaders of their *I* Taught them — " 58
  I fenced it round with gallant *i*'s, — " v 392
  Some Imperial *I*, Rich in symbol, — *On Jub. Q. Victoria* 46
Insufficiencies temperate eyes On glorious *i*, — *In Mem. cxii* 3
Insult I heard sounds of *i*, shame, and wrong, — *D. of F. Women* 19
  We brook no further *i* but are gone.' — *Princess vi* 342
  ' I will avenge this great *i*, noble Queen, — *Marr. of Geraint* 215
  Avenging this great *i* done the Queen.' — " 425
  ' Remember that great *i* done the Queen,' — " 571
  Crave pardon for that *i* done the Queen, — " 583
  your wretched dress, A wretched *i* on you, — *Geraint and E.* 328
  Oaths, *i*, filth, and monstrous blasphemies, — *Pass. of Arthur* 114
Inswathe *I* the fulness of Eternity, — *Lover's Tale i* 483
Inswathed *I* sometimes in wandering mist, — *St. S. Stylites* 75
Intellect thorough-edged *i* to part Error from crime; — *Isabel* 14
  Thy kingly *i* shall feed, — *Clear-headed friend* 20
  All-subtilising *i*: — *In Mem. lxxxv* 48
  Or ev'n for *i* to reach Thro' memory — " xcv 47
  Seraphic *i* and force To seize and throw — " cix 5
  For can I doubt, who knew thee keen In *i*, — " cxiii 6
Intellectual *i* throne. — *Palace of Art* 216
  bow'd myself down as a slave to his *i* throne. — *The Wreck* 66
Intelligence The great *I*'s fair That range — *In Mem. lxxxv* 21
Intelligible From over-fineness not *i* — *Merlin and V.* 796
Intend (*See also* **Intind**) The thesis which thy words *i*— — *Two Voices* 338
   — " 40
Intense ' Or will one beam be less *i*, — *Maud II ii* 59
  when fraught With a passion so *i* — *Eleänore* 82
Intensity Sometimes, with most *i* Gazing, — *Gardener's D.* 269
Intent (*adj.*) have been *i* On that veil'd picture— — *Princess ii* 442
  I kept mine own *I* on her, — *Gardener's D.* 146
Intent (*s*) almost ere I knew mine own *i*, — *Maud I vi* 41
  eye seem'd full Of a kind *i* to me, — *The Ring* 345
  But after ten slow weeks her fix'd *i*, — *Owd Roä* 61
  fur I noäwaäys knaw'd 'is *i*; —
Interchange angels rising and descending met With *i* of gift. — *Palace of Art* 144
  And frequent *i* of foul and fair, — *Enoch Arden* 533
Interest To close the *i*'s of all. — *Love thou thy land* 36
  From all a closer *i* flourish'd up, — *Princess vii* 113
  catch The far-off *i* of tears; — *In Mem. i* 8
Interfused And glory of broad waters *i*, — *Lover's Tale i* 401
Interlaced shadow'd grots of arches *i*, — *Palace of Art* 51
Interlock'd My lady with her fingers *i*, — *Aylmer's Field* 199
Intermitted tenfold dearer by the power Of *i* usage; — *Marr. of Geraint* 811
Interpret True love *i*'s—right alone. — *Miller's D.* 188
  with such a stupid heart To *i* ear and eye, — *Lancelot and E.* 942
Interpretation a tongue To blare its own *i*— — " 943
Interpreter *I* between the Gods and men, — *Princess vii* 322
  How, in the mouths of base *i*'s, — *Merlin and V.* 795
Interpreting she broke out *i* my thoughts: — *Princess iii* 275
Interspace flowing rapidly between Their *i*'s, — *Arabian Nights* 84
  The lucid *i* of world and world, — *Lucretius* 105
  between Whose *i*'s gush'd in blinding bursts — *Lover's Tale i* 408
Intertwisted A lodge of *i* beechen-boughs — *Last Tournament* 376
Interval fill'd with light The *i* of sound. — *D. of F. Women* 172
  Miriam watch'd and dozed at *i*'s, — *Enoch Arden* 909
  streak'd or starr'd at *i*'s With falling brook — *Lover's Tale i* 404
  sick with love, Fainted at *i*'s, — " 546
  thence at *i*'s A low bell tolling. — " ii 82
Intervital spirit's folded them Thro' all its *i* gloom — *In Mem. xliii* 3
Intimacy Bound in an immemorial *i*, — *Aylmer's Field* 39
  Bound, but an immemorial *i*, — " 136
Intind (intend) an' she didn't *i* to desave, — *Tomorrow* 59
Intolerable became Anguish *i*. — *Lover's Tale ii* 138
Intolerant The menacing poison of *i* priests, — *Akbar's Dream* 165
Intonation a tuneful tongue, Such happy *i*, — *Amphion* 18
Intone Delicate-handed priest *i*. — *Maud I viii* 11
Intricate wanderings Of this most *i* Universe — *A Character* 3
Intrusion hunter rued His rash *i*, manlike, — *Princess iv* 204
Intuitive *i* decision of a bright And thorough-edged intellect — *Isabel* 13
Inutterable Kill'd with *i* unkindliness.' — *Merlin and V.* 886
Invade *i* Even with a verse your holy woe. — *To J. S.* 7
Invaded ' Our land *i*, 'sdeath! — *Princess v* 276

Invaded (*continued*) for whose love the Roman Cæsar first *I* Britain, But we beat him back, As this great Prince *i* us, — *Marr. of Geraint* 746
  Was mine a mood To be *i* rudely, — *Lover's Tale i* 678
Invalid *i*, since my will Seal'd not the bond— — *Princess v* 398
Invective a tide of fierce *I* seem'd to wait — " iv 472
Invent the years *i*; Each month is various — *Two Voices* 73
  But when did woman ever yet *i*?' — *Princess ii* 391
Invented Was this fair charm *i* by yourself? — *Merlin and V.* 540
Inventor O MIGHTY-MOUTH'D *i* of harmonies, — *Milton* 1
Inverted he heard his priest Preach an *i* scripture, — *Aylmer's Field* 44
Invested Slipt round, and in the dark *i* you, — *Princess iv* 404
Inveterately Time Were nothing, so *i*, — *Gareth and L.* 227
Invidious Who breaks his birth's *i* bar, — *In Mem. lxiv* 5
Inviolable a doubtful lord To bind them by *i* vows, — *Last Tournament* 688
Inviolate *And compass'd by the i sea.'* — *To the Queen* 36
  Nor ever drank the *i* spring — *In Mem. xc* 2
Invisible And praise the *i* universal Lord, — *Ode Inter. Exhib.* 3
  Alway the inaudible *i* thought, — *Lover's Tale ii* 102
  I but deathless, waiting still The edict — " 160
Invited For I am not *i*, But, with the Sultan's pardon, — *Maud I xx* 38
Invoke That which we dare *i* to bless; — *In Mem. cxxiv* 1
Involuntary from my breast the *i* sigh Brake, — *Princess iii* 191
Involve My love *i*'s the love before; — *In Mem. cxxx* 9
Involved (*See also* **Self-involved**) but in you I found My boyish dream *i* — *Princess iv* 450
  Assumed from thence a half-consent *i* In stillness, — " vii 82
  To the other shore, *i* in thee, — *In Mem. lxxxiv* 40
  My mind *i* yourself the nearest thing — *Merlin and V.* 300
Involving worlds before the man *I* ours— — *Epilogue* 26
Inward from the outward to the *i* brought, — *Eleänore* 4
  More *i* than at night or morn, — *Mariana in the S.* 58
  a knight would pass Outward, or *i* to the hall: — *Gareth and L.* 311
  portal of King Pellam's chapel wide And *i* to the wall; — *Balin and Balan* 406
  the rest Were crumpled *i*'s. Dead !— — *The Ring* 454
  With an ancient melody Of an *i* agony, — *Claribel* 7
  That heat of *i* evidence, — *Two Voices* 284
  ' Weep, weeping dulls the *i* pain.' — *To J. S.* 40
  Ev'n now we hear with *i* strife — *Love thou thy land* 53
  Again in deeper *i* whispers ' lost !' — *Enoch Arden* 716
  With *i* yelp and restless forefoot plies — *Lucretius* 45
  My *i* sap, the hold I have on earth, — *Lover's Tale i* 166
  address'd More to the *i* than the outward ear, — " 721
  Dead of some *i* agony—is it so? — *To W. H. Brookfield* 10
Inwoven dusky strand of Death *i* here — *Maud I xviii* 60
Inwrapt *I* tenfold in slothful shame, — *Palace of Art* 262
Inwreathe *i* (How lovelier, nobler then !) — *Lover's Tale i* 458
Inwrought diaper'd With *i* flowers, — *Arabian Nights* 149
Ionian Than all the valleys of *I* hills. — *Œnone* 2
  And there the *I* father of the rest; — *Palace of Art* 137
Io t'amo ' *I t*'—and these diamonds— — *The Ring* 70
  This very ring *I t*? — " 134
  sent This ring ' *I t*' to his best beloved, — " 210
  and cried ' I see him, *I t, I t*.' — " 223
  call thro' this ' *I t*' to the heart Of Miriam ; — " 234
  ' *I t*, all is well then.' Muriel fled. — " 271
  You love me still ' *I t*.' — " 291
  No! ' *I t, I t*'! flung herself Against my heart, — " 397
  even that ' *I t*,' those three sweet Italian words, — " 406
Irân Alla call'd In old *I* the Sun of Love? — *Akbar's Dream* 87
  A voice from old *I*! Nay, but I know it— — " 89
Ire The plaintive cry jarr'd on her *i*; — *Princess iv* 393
Ireland Sailing from *I*.' — *Last Tournament* 555
Iris (prismatic colours) *i* changes on the burnish'd dove; — *Locksley Hall* 19
  The circled *I* of a night of tears; — *Princess iii* 27
Iris (flag-flower) glided winding under ranks Of *i*, — *In Mem. ciii* 24
Iris (messenger of the Gods) But light-foot *I* brought it yester-eve, — *Œnone* 83
  So saying, light-foot *I* pass'd away. — *Achilles over the T.* 1
Irish The black-blue *I* hair and *I* eyes Had drawn — *Last Tournament* 404
Irish Bog aisier work av they lived be an *I b.* — *Tomorrow* 72
Iron (*adj.*) One show'd an *i* coast and angry waves. — *Palace of Art* 69
  Ranges of glimmering vaults with *i* grates, — *D. of F. Women* 35
  Which men call'd Aulis in those *i* years: — " 106

Iron (adj.) *(continued)* A grazing *i* collar grinds my
  neck;   *St. S. Stylites* 117
I jointed, supple-sinew'd, they shall dive,   *Locksley Hall* 169
Paled at a sudden twitch of his *i* mouth;   *Aylmer's Field* 732
crush her pretty maiden fancies dead In *i* gauntlets: *Princess* i 89
Binds me to speak, and O that *i* will,   ,,   ii 202
Nor would I fight with *i* laws,   ,,   iv 75
Forgotten, rusting on his *i* hills,   ,,   v 146
he clash'd His *i* palms together with a cry;   ,,   354
There dwelt an *i* nature in the grain: ,,   vi 50
Her *i* will was broken in her mind;   ,,   118
in the Vestal entry shriek'd The virgin marble under
  i heels;   ,,   351
and saw Thee woman thro' the crust of *i* moods   ,,   vii 342
O *i* nerve to true occasion true,   *Ode on Well.* 37
Till one that sought but Duty's *i* crown   ,,   122
Their ever-loyal *i* leader's fame,   ,,   229
Or seal'd within the *i* hills?   *In Mem.* lvi 20
But that remorseless *i* hour Made cypress   ,,   lxxxiv 14
An *i* welcome when they rise: ,,   xc 8
and clangs Its leafless ribs and *i* horns   ,,   cvii 12
That makes you tyrants in your *i* skies,   *Maud* I xviii 37
That an *i* tyranny now should bend or cease,   ,,   III vi 20
Across the *i* grating of her cell Beat,   *Holy Grail* 81
The last hard footstep of that *i* crag;   *Pass. of Arthur* 447
butted with the shuddering War-thunder of *i* rams;   *Tiresias* 100
Brass mouths and *i* lungs!   *Freedom* 40
And I clash with an *i* Truth,   *The Dreamer* 6
Iron (s) clad in *i* burst the ranks of war,   *Princess* iv 504
This red-hot *i* to be shaped with blows.   ,,   v 209
'I've heard that there is *i* in the blood,   ,,   vi 230
But *i* dug from central gloom,   *In Mem.* cxviii 21
fight my way with gilded arms, All shall be *i*;'   *Geraint and E.* 22
That laughs at *i*—as our warriors did—   *Merlin and V.* 429
drew The rustiest *i* of old fighters' hearts;   ,,   574
We brought this *i* from our isles of gold.   *Columbus* 3
Iron-clanging an *i-c* anvil bang'd With hammers;   *Princess* v 504
Iron-clashing such a stern and *i-c* close,   *Merlin and V.* 419
Iron-cramp'd those that *i-c* their women's feet;   *Princess* v 376
Iron-hearted *i-h* victors they.   *Locksley H., Sixty* 80
Iron-stay'd *i-s* In damp and dismal dungeons   *Lover's Tale* ii 148
Iron-worded wall about thy cause With *i-w* proof,   *To J. M. K.* 9
Irony call her sweet, as if in *i*,   *Princess* vii 97
Irredeemable Wrought for his house an *i* woe;   *Maud* II i 22
Irrepressible cloud of thought Keen, *i*.   *Lover's Tale* ii 165
Irresponsible *I*, indolent reviewers,   *Hendecasyllabics* 2
Irreverence Blockish, brainless greed—   *Columbus* 129
Irreverent you have miss'd the *i* doom   *You might have won* 9
A reckless and *i* knight was he,   *Holy Grail* 856
Irritable being vicious, old and *i*,   *Marr. of Geraint* 194
Is For was, and *i*, and will be, are but *i*;   *Princess* iii 324
Isabel Revered *I*, the crown and head,   *Isabel* 10
Crown'd *I*, thro' all her placid life,   ,,   27
Iscariot Pontius and *I* by my side   *St. S. Stylites* 168
Isis an *I* hid by the veil.   *Maud* I iv 43
Islam beating back the swarms Of Turkish *I*   *Montenegro* 11
Islám Polytheism and *I* feel after thee.   *Akbar's D., Inscrip.* 2
gleam Than glances from the sun of our *I*.   *Akbar's Dream* 79
Myself am such in our *I*,   ,,   155
Islamite Houris bow'd to see The dying *I*,   *Palace of Art* 103
Island (adj.) 'Our *i* home Is far beyond the wave;   *Lotos-Eaters* 44
Or else the *i* princes over-bold   ,,   C. S. 75
bind with bands That *i* queen who sways   *Buonaparte* 3
Not once or twice in our rough *i* story,   *Ode on Well.* 201
Revenge herself went down by the *i* crags   *The Revenge* 118
made your fathers great In our ancient *i*
  State,   *Open. I. and C. Exhib.* 16
greatest of women, *i* heroine, Kapiolani   *Kapiolani* 5
Island (s) on the land Over the *i*'s free;   *Sea-Fairies* 26
Round an *i* there below, The *i* of Shalott.   *L. of Shalott* i 8
By the *i* in the river Flowing down to Camelot.   ,,   13
Boat, *i*, ruins of a castle,   *Edwin Morris* 6
On from *i* unto *i* at the gateways of the day.   *Locksley Hall* 158
So they past by capes and *i*'s,   *The Captain* 21
The blaze upon his *i* overhead;   *Enoch Arden* 595

Island (s) *(continued)* Thine *i* loves thee well,   *Ode on Well.* 85
For out of the waste *i*'s had he come,   *Pelleas and E.* 86
Drew to this *i*: Doom'd to the death.   *Batt. of Brunanburh* 50
Far off from out an *i* girt by foes,   *Achilles over the T.* 8
follow Edwin to those isles, those *i*'s of the Blest!   *The Flight* 42
I, from out the Northern *I* sunder'd once   *To Virgil* 35
shake with her thunders and shatter her *i*,   *Kapiolani* 10
'Woe to this *i* if ever a woman (repeat)   ,,   20, 22
Island-crag Set in a cataract on an *i-c*,   *Princess* v 347
Island-myriads Her *i-m* fed from alien lands—   *The Fleet* 12
Island-Paradise In Hispaniola's *i-P*!   *Columbus* 182
Island-sides Far-fleeted by the purple *i-s*,   *Princess* vii 166
Island-story once or twice in our rough *i-s*,   *Ode on Well.* 201
Not once or twice in our fair *i-s*,   ,,   209
Island-valley To the *i-v* of Avilion;   *M. d'Arthur* 259
To the *i-v* of Avilion;   *Pass. of Arthur* 427
Isle (s) *(See also* **Bounteous Isle, Eden-isle, Garden-isles,**
  South - sea - isle, World-isle) flee By town, and
  tower, and hill, and cape, and *i*,   *Mine be the strength* 6
the silent *i* imbowers The Lady of Shalott.   *L. of Shalott* i 17
Is there confusion in the little *i*?   *Lotos-Eaters, C. S.* 79
where the moving *i*'s of winter shock By night,   *M. d'Arthur* 140
mellow brickwork on an *i* of bowers.   *Edwin Morris* 12
The rentroll Cupid of our rainy *i*'s.   ,,   103
To whom I leave the sceptre and the *i*—   *Ulysses* 34
It may be we shall touch the Happy *I*'s,   ,,   63
Summer *i*'s of Eden lying in dark-purple   *Locksley Hall* 164
breaker sweep The nutmeg rocks and *i*'s of clove.   *The Voyage* 40
Blue *i*'s of heaven laugh'd between,   *Sir L. and Q. G.* 6
over lake and lawn, and *i*'s and capes—   *Vision of Sin* 11
And sent her sweetly by the golden *i*'s,   *Enoch Arden* 536
stranding on an *i* at morn Rich,   ,,   552
Far in a darker *i* beyond the line;   ,,   605
beauteous hateful *i* Return'd upon him,   ,,   617
Stay'd by this *i*, not knowing where she lay: ,,   630
Across a break on the mist-wreathen *i*   ,,   632
Thou That didst uphold me on my lonely *i*,   ,,   783
and battle-clubs From the *i*'s of palm: *Princess, Pro.* 22
As yet we find in barbarous *i*'s,   ,,   ii 122
over them the tremulous *i*'s of light Slided,   ,,   vi 81
O saviour of the silver-coasted *i*,   *Ode on Well.* 136
Maoris and that *I* of Continent,   *W. to Marie Alex.* 18
(Take it and come) to the *I* of Wight;   *To F. D. Maurice* 12
For in all that exquisite *i*, my dear,   *The Islet* 26
She desires no *i*'s of the blest,   *Wages* 8
'Fear not, *i* of blowing woodland, *i* of silvery parapets!   *Boädicea* 38
Streams o'er a rich ambrosial ocean *i*,   *Milton* 11
Is dash'd with wandering *i*'s of night.   *In Mem. xxiv* 4
Danube rolling fair Enwind her *i*'s,   ,,   xcviii 10
over all whose realms to their last *i*,   *Ded. of Idylls* 12
a petty king ere Arthur came Ruled in this *i*,   *Com. of Arthur* 6
'He passes to the *I* Avilion,   *Gareth and L.* 502
Heard by the lander in a lonely *i*,   *Marr. of Geraint* 330
Whose bark had plunder'd twenty nameless *i*'s;   *Merlin and V.* 559
Lords of waste marches, kings of desolate *i*'s,   *Lancelot and E.* 527
Gave him an *i* of marsh whereon to build;   *Holy Grail* 62
And this new knight, Sir Pelleas of the *i*'s—   *Pelleas and E.* 17
And lord of many a barren *i* was he—   ,,   19
Scarce any but the women of his *i*'s,   ,,   88
many a glancing plash and sallowy *i*,   *Last Tournament* 422
Farewell! there is an *i* of rest for thee.   *Pass. of Arthur* 35
where the moving *i*'s of winter shock By night,   ,,   308
third-rate *i* half-lost among her seas?   *To the Queen* ii 25
throne In our vast Orient, and one *i*, one *i*,   ,,   31
All day I watch'd the floating *i*'s of shade,   *Lover's Tale* ii 5
But work was scant in the *I*,   *First Quarrel* 43
thou hast come to talk our *i*.   *Sir J. Oldcastle* 32
not That Indian *i*, but our most ancient East   *Columbus* 80
Pour'd in on all those happy naked *i*'s—   ,,   173
He lived on an *i* in the ocean—   *V. of Maeldune* 7
And we came to the *i* in the ocean,   ,,   9
And we came to the Silent *I*   ,,   11
And we hated the beautiful *I*,   ,,   21
And we came to the *I* of Shouting,   ,,   27
And we came to the *I* of Flowers :   ,,   37

Isle (s) (*continued*) And we hated the Flowering I, as
  we hated the *i* that was mute,   *V. of Maeldune* 52
And we came to the *I* of Fruits :   „   55
And we came to the *I* of Fire :   „   71
For the whole *i* shudder'd and shook like a man   „   74
  and we past Over that undersea *i*,   „   77
but the whole green *I* was our own,   „   93
And we past to the *I* of Witches   „   97
And we came in an evil time to the *I* of the Double Towers, „   105
And we came to the *I* of a Saint   „   115
He had lived ever since on the *I*   „   116
Go back to the *I* of Finn   „   124
we came to the *I* we were blown from,   „   127
I landed again, with a tithe of my men, on the *I* of Finn. „   130
Hapt in this *i*, since Up from the East   *Batt. of Brunanburh* 116
and abroad in a rich West-Indian *i* ;   *The Wreck* 46
The broad white brow of the *I*—   „   135
follow Edwin to those *i*'s, those islands of the Blest !   *The Flight* 42
ocean softly washing all her warless *I*'s.   *Locksley H., Sixty* 170
His *i*, the mightiest Ocean-power on earth, Our own
  fair *i*, the lord of every sea—   *The Fleet* 6
From *i* and cape and continent,   *Open I. and C. Exhib.* 4
Blossom again on a colder *i*.   *To Prof. Jebb* 12
Broaden the glowing *i*'s of vernal blue.   *Prog. of Spring* 60
Isle (verb) And *i*'s a light in the offing :   *Enoch Arden* 131
Isle-altar From her *i-a* gazing down,   *Of old sat Freedom* 14
Isled And, *i* in sudden seas of light,   *Fatima* 33
Thank Him who *i* us here,   *Ode on Well.* 154
Lion and stoat have *i* together,   *Gareth and L.* 893
Isle-nurtured *i-n* eyes Waged such unwilling   *Merlin and V.* 570
Isle-side whole *i-s* flashing down from the peak   *V. of Maeldune* 45
Islet (*See also* **Ocean-islet**) The peaky *i* shifted shapes,   *The Voyage* 33
that *i* in the chestnut-bloom Flamed in his cheek ;   *Aylmer's Field* 65
A mountain *i* pointed and peak'd ;   *The Islet* 15
Betwixt the cressy *i*'s white in flower;   *Geraint and E.* 475
Isolated came a broad And solid beam of *i* light,   *Lover's Tale ii* 173
Isolation 'O God-like *i* which art mine,   *Palace of Art* 197
he work'd among the rest and shook His *i* from
  him.   *Enoch Arden* 652
remain Orb'd in your *i* : he is dead,   *Princess vi* 169
His *i* grows defined.   *In Mem. xlv* 12
Isolt *I* the White—Sir Tristram of the Woods—   *Last Tournament* 177
thou playest that air with Queen *I*,   „   263
Before him fled the face of Queen *I*   „   363
Built for a summer day with Queen *I*   „   378
I, the daughter of the King ? ' *I* Of the white hands'   „   397
I of Britain and his bride,   „   408
And glossy-throated grace, *I* the Queen.   „   509
Softly laugh'd *I* ; 'Flatter me not,   „   556
To whom *I*, ' Ah then, false hunter and false harper,   „   566
And, saddening on the sudden, spake *I*,   „   581
I of Britain dash'd Before *I* of Brittany   „   588
I ?—I fought his battles, for *I* !   „   604
I ! The name was ruler of the dark—*I* ?   „   605
I answer'd ' Yea, and why not I ?   „   609
Then came the sin of Tristram and *I* ;   *Guinevere* 488
Israel Wrestled with wandering *I*,   *Clear-headed friend* 26
' The torrent brooks of hallow'd *I*   *D. of F. Women* 181
' The balmy moon of blessed *I*   „   185
I made their gods of gold,   *In Mem. xcvi* 23
Issa Ben Mariam *I B M*, his own prophet,   *Akbar's Dream* 75
Issue (s) Whereof I catch the *i*, as I hear   *Œnone* 248
Fame for spouse and your great deeds For *i*,   *Princess iii* 243
streams that float us each and all To the *i*,   „   *iv* 71
reasons why she should Bide by this *i* :   „   *v* 326
Her words had *i* other than she will'd.   *Merlin and V.* 806
noble *i*, sons Born to the glory of thy name   *Lancelot and E.* 1371
Issue (verb) To those that seek them *i* forth ;   *Day-Dm., Arrival* 2
Victor from vanquish'd *i*'s at the last,   *Gareth and L.* 1262
Issued ridge Of breaker *i* from the belt,   *Sea Dreams* 212
i in a court Compact of lucid marbles,   *Princess ii* 23
We *i* gorged with knowledge,   „   388
i in the sun, that now Leapt from the dewy shoulders „   *v* 42
Whence he *i* forth anew,   *Ode on Well.* 107
out from this *I* the bright face of a blooming boy   *Gareth and L.* 1408

Issued (*continued*) As last they *i* from the world of
  wood,   *Marr. of Geraint* 238
Whereout the Demon *i* up from Hell.   *Balin and Balan* 317
Vext at a rumour *i* from herself   *Merlin and V.* 153
from the city gates *I* Sir Lancelot riding   *Pelleas and E.* 557
Issuing And, *i* shorn and sleek,   *Talking Oak* 42
lightly *i* thro', I would have paid her   „   194
the voice Of Ida sounded, *i* ordinance :   *Princess vi* 373
And howlest, *i* out of night,   *In Mem. lxxii* 2
Geraint, who *i* forth That morning,   *Geraint and E.* 8
i under open heavens beheld A little town   „   196
i arm'd he found the host and cried,   „   407
And *i* found the Lord of Astolat   *Lancelot and E.* 173
loud stream, Forth *i* from his portals   *Lover's Tale i* 430
Issus Satrap bled At *I* by the Syrian gates,   *Alexander* 3
Italian Thy glory fly along the *I* field,   *Lucretius* 71
Fair ship, that from the *I* shore   *In Mem. ix* 1
On a sudden after two *I* years   *Sisters (E. and E.)* 150
All in white *I* marble,   *Locksley H., Sixty* 35
those three sweet *I* words, became a weariness.   *The Ring* 407
Italy *I* to the East And he for *I*—   *The Brook* 407
And now it tells of *I*.   *The Daisy* 90
Florence now the crown of *I*,   *To Dante* 4
Iteration came Her sicklier *i*. Last he said,   *Aylmer's Field* 299
Ithacensian Like the *I* suitors in old time,   *Princess iv* 118
Ivery (every) ye set me heart batin' to music wid *i* word !   *Tomorrow* 34
Ivied Many a night from yonder *i* casement,   *Locksley Hall* 7
warrior from his *i* nook Glow like a sunbeam :   *Princess, Pro.* 104
It look'd a tower of *i* masonwork,   *Merlin and V.* 4
Ivin' (ivy) An' they niver 'ed seed sich *i*   *Owd Roä* 26
Sa I sticks like the *i* as long as I lives   *Church-warden, etc.* 15
Ivory (adj.) She took the little *i* chest,   *The Letters* 17
Ivory (s) Laborious orient *i* sphere in sphere,   *Princess, Pro.* 20
Ivory-beak'd In a shallop of crystal *i-b*,   *The Islet* 12
Ivry (every) I've 'ed my point o' aäle *i* noight sin' I
  beän 'ere.   *N. Farmer, O. S.* 7
An' I've 'ed my quart *i* market-night for foorty year.   „   8
an' sweär'd as I'd breäk *i* stick   *North." Cobbler* 35
An' *i* darter o' Squire's hed her awn ridin-erse   *Village Wife* 35
Ivy (*See also* **Ivin'**) overhead the wandering *i* and vine,   *Œnone* 248
And thro' the moss the *ivies* creep,   *Lotos-Eaters, C. S.* 9
Thorns, *ivies*, woodbine, mistletoes,   *Day-Dm., Sleep. P.* 43
There is Darnley bridge, It has more *i* ;   *The Brook* 37
O hollies and *ivies* and evergreens,   *Spiteful Letter* 23
and wings Moved in her *i*,   *Marr. of Geraint* 599
Betwixt the close-set *ivies* came   *Lover's Tale ii* 172
Ivyberry husk, the grape And *i*, choose ;   *De Prof., Two G.* 51
Ivy-clad In Autumn, parcel *i-c* ;   *Aylmer's Field* 154
Ivy-claspt High-arch'd and *i-c*, Of finest Gothic   *Princess, Pro.* 91
Ivy-matted Whose *i-m* mouth she used to gaze   *Death of Œnone* 2
Ivy-net Now on some twisted *i-n*,   *Sir L. and Q. G.* 28
Ivy-screen Tearing the bright leaves of the *i-s*,   *Lover's Tale ii* 40
Ivy-stems monstrous *i-s* Claspt the gray walls   *Marr. of Geraint* 322
Ivytods The battlement overtopt with *i*,   *Balin and Balan* 335
Ivy-tress Until the plaited *i-t* had wound Round   *Lover's Tale i* 618
Ivy-wreath briony-vine and *i-w* Ran forward   *Amphion* 29
I will I heard his deep ' *I w*,' Breathed,   *Gardener's D.* 208
Her sweet ' *I w* ' has made you one.   *In Mem., Con.* 56
Before the first ' *I w* ' was utter'd,   *Sisters (E. and E.)* 211
Ixionian stays the rolling *I* wheel,   *Lucretius* 261
Ixion-like Embracing cloud, *I-l* ;   *Two Voices* 195

J

Jacet by the cold Hic *J*'s of the dead !'   *Merlin and V.* 753
Jacinth-work and *j-w* Of subtlest jewellery.   *M. d'Arthur* 57
and *j-w* Of subtlest jewellery.   *Pass. of Arthur* 225
Jack *J*, turn the horses' heads and home   *Walk. to the Mail* 46
J on his ale-house bench has as many lies as a Czar ;   *Maud I iv* 9
Jackass A *j* heehaws from the rick,   *Amphion* 71
Jackman An' my oän fine *J* i' purple   *Spinster's S's.* 106
Jacobinism after massacre, *J* and Jacquerie,   *Locksley H., Sixty* 157

Jacquerie after massacre, Jacobinism and *J*,   *Locksley H., Sixty* 157
Jacynth chrysoprase, *J*, and amethyst—   *Columbus* 86
Jael a cymbal'd Miriam and a *J*,   *Princess v* 511
Jail scared with threats of *j* and halter   *Aylmer's Field* 520
Jailer And the *j* forced me away. (repeat)   *Rizpah* 41, 44
Jailing And tame thy *j* princess to thine hand.   *Pelleas and E.* 344
Jam (s) An' a haäf-pot o' *j*, or a mossel o' meät   *Spinster's S's.* 109
Jam (verb) *j* the doors, and bear The keepers   *Lucretius* 169
James (*See also* **James Willows, Willows**) Old *J* was with
   me : we that day had been Up Snowdon ;   *Golden Year* 3
in mimic cadence answer'd *J*—' Ah, folly !   ” 53
J,—you know him,—old, but full Of force   ” 60
She and *J* had quarrell'd. Why ?   *The Brook* 96
she said, no cause ; *J* had no cause : but when I prest
   the cause, I learnt that *J* had flickering jealousies
   which anger'd her. Who anger'd *J* ? I said.   ” 98
till I ask'd If *J* were coming. ' Coming every day,'   ” 106
J departed vext with him and her.'   ” 110
I saw where *J* Made toward us,   ” 116
My brother *J* is in the harvest-field :   ” 227
James (II.) We flung the burthen of the second *J*.   *Third of Feb.* 28
James Willows (*See also* **James, Willows**) *J W*, of one
   name and heart with her.   *The Brook* 76
Jane And what do I care for *J*,   *Grandmother* 51
Jangled again the bells *J* and clang'd :   *Lover's Tale iii* 53
daws flew out of the Towers and *j* and wrangled in
   vain,   *V. of Maeldune* 109
Jangling *j*, the casque Fell, and he started up   *Geraint and E.* 388
In clanging cadence *j* peal on peal—   *Lover's Tale iii* 22
January (adj.) Fine as ice-ferns on *J* panes   *Aylmer's Field* 222
January (s) woodlands, when they shiver in *J*,   *Boädicea* 75
Japan From Corrientes to *J*   *To Ulysses* 4
Japed —him Who gibed and *j*—in many a merry tale   *Sir J. Oldcastle* 91
Jaques Our kindlier, trustier *J*, past away !   *To W. H. Brookfield* 11
Jar (s) Love is hurt with *j* and fret.   *Miller's D.* 209
And hear the household *j* within.   *In Mem. xciv* 16
Jar (verb) no mortal motion *j*'s The blackness   *On a Mourner* 26
shriek of hate would *j* all the hymns of heaven :   *Sea Dreams* 259
May *j* thy golden dream Of Knowledge   *Freedom* 16
Jarr'd something *j* ; Whether he spoke too largely ;   *Edwin Morris* 72
The plaintive cry *j* on her ire ;   *Princess iv* 393
He laugh'd ; the laughter *j* upon Lynette :   *Gareth and L.* 1226
Love and Honour *j* Tho' Love and Honour   *Sisters (E. and E.)* 176
Jarring Who touch'd a *j* lyre at first,   *In Mem. xcvi* 7
For those that are crush'd in the clash of *j* claims,   *Maud III vi* 44
relic of Javelins over The *j* breaker,   *Batt. of Brunanburh* 97
Jasmine (*See also* **Jessamine, Jessmine**) Growths of *j*
   turn'd Their humid arms   *D. of F. Women* 69
close-set robe of *j* sown with stars :   *Aylmer's Field* 158
In meshes of the *j* and the rose :   *Princess i* 219
Jasmine-leaves dawn Upon me thro' the *j-l.*   *Margaret* 68
Jasper In the branching *j*'s under the sea ;   *The Mermaid* 47
j, sapphire, Chalcedony, emerald,   *Columbus* 83
Jaundice That veil'd the world with *j*,   *Walk. to the Mail* 20
Jaundiced and left me with thy eye ;   *Locksley Hall* 132
Javelin lay many a man Marr'd by the *j*,   *Batt. of Brunanburh* 32
rush of the *j*'s, The crash of the charges,   ” 88
Blood-redden'd relic of *J*'s over The jarring breaker,   ” 96
Javelining *j* With darted spikes and splinters   *Merlin and V.* 936
Jaw The *j* is falling, The red cheek paling,   *All Things will Die* 30
Into the *j*'s of Death,   *Light Brigade* 24
Came thro' the *j*'s of Death,   ” 46
in the *j*'s Of vacant darkness   *In Mem. xxxiv* 15
down-hung The *j*'s of Death :   *Lover's Tale ii* 205
Jay Ring sudden scritches of the *j*,   *My life is full* 20
glance the tits, and shriek the *j*'s,   *Prog. of Spring* 15
Jealous (*See also* **Over-jealous**) be *j* and hard and unkind.'   *Grandmother* 54
Never *j*—not he : we had many a happy year ;   ” 71
Half *j* of she knows not what,   *In Mem. lx* 7
O to what end, except a *j* one, And one to make me
   j if I love,   *Merlin and V.* 538
What wonder, being *j*, that he sent His horns   ” 580
And made her good man *j* with good cause.   ” 605
I was *j*, anger'd, vain,   *Happy* 66
I meant to make *you j*. Are you *j* of me now ?   ” 67

Jealous (*continued*) But yet your mother's *j* temperament—   *Princess ii* 338
'tis my mother, Too *j*,   ” *iii* 80
Shall fears and *j* hatreds flame again ?   *W. to Marie Alex.* 41
Sick, am I sick of a *j* dread ?   *Maud I x* 1
Not rather dead love's harsh heir, *j* pride ?   *Lancelot and E.* 1398
Jealousy (*See also* **Semi-jealousy**) James had flickering
   jealousies   *The Brook* 99
Down with ambition, avarice, pride, *J*, down !   *Maud I x* 48
all narrow *jealousies* Are silent ;   *Ded. of Idylls* 16
No more of *j* than in Paradise.'   *Balin and Balan* 152
A sudden spurt of woman's *j*,—   *Merlin and V.* 524
And as to woman's *j*, O why not ?   ” 537
Forgive me ; mine was *j* in love.'   *Lancelot and E.* 1351
' *J* in love ?' Not rather dead love's harsh heir,   ” 1397
Queen, if I grant the *j* as of love,   ” 1399
youthful *j* is a liar.   *Locksley H., Sixty* 240
Jeer Began to scoff and *j* and babble of him   *Marr. of Geraint* 58
point and *j*, And gibber at the worm,   *Romney's R.* 136
Jehovah Starr'd from *J*'s gorgeous armouries,   *Milton* 6
Jenneting To fret the summer *j*.   *The Blackbird* 12
Jenny *J*, my cousin, had come to the place, and I knew
   right well That *J* had tript in her time :   *Grandmother* 25
J, to slander me, who knew what *J* had been !   ” 35
and *J* hung on his arm.   ” 42
J, the viper, made me a mocking curtsey   ” 46
Jephtha Pale as the *J*'s daughter,   *Aylmer's Field* 280
The Godless *J* vows his child . . .   *The Flight* 99
Jeroosilim (Jerusalem) May all the flowers o' *J*   *Tomorrow* 89
Jersey I ha' six weeks' work in *J*   *First Quarrel* 88
Jerusalem (*See also* **Jeroosilim**) but our most ancient East
   Moriah with *J* ;   *Columbus* 81
Jess Diet and seedling, *j'es*, leash and lure.   *Merlin and V.* 125
Jessamine (*See also* **Jasmine, Jessmine**) All night has
   the casement *j* stirr'd   *Maud I xxii* 15
Jessmine (*See also* **Jasmine, Jessamine**) door-porch wi'
   the woodbine an' *j*   *Spinster's S's.* 105
Jest (s) eyes twinkle yet At his own *j*—   *Miller's D.* 12
He was full of joke and *j*,   *D. of the O. Year* 28
My words were half in earnest, half in *j*,)   *Gardener's D.* 23
I am not all as wrong As a bitter *j* is dear.   *Vision of Sin* 198
The *j*'s, that flash'd about the pleader's room,   *Aylmer's Field* 440
Dabbling a shameless hand with shameful *j*,   *Princess iii* 314
The *j* and earnest working side by side,   ” *iv* 563
beneath his vaulted palm A whisper'd *j*   ” *v* 32
and ere the windy *j* Had labour'd down   ” 272
In dance and song and game and *j* ?   *In Mem. xxix* 8
Whose *j* among his friends is free,   ” *lxvi* 10
Or deep dispute, and graceful *j* ;   ” *lxxxiv* 24
Merlin in our time Hath spoken also, not in *j*,   *Com. of Arthur* 420
We will not touch upon him ev'n in *j*.'   *Marr. of Geraint* 311
some light *j* among them rose With laughter dying   *Lancelot and E.* 178
vext he could not go : A *j*, no more !   ” 211
(But all was *j* and joke among ourselves) Then must
   she keep it safelier. All was *j*.   ” 217
moved to merriment at a passing *j*.   *Sisters (E. and E.)* 121
he was one of those who would break their *j*'s
   on the dead,   *In the Child. Hosp.* 8
Would echo helpless laughter to your *j* !   *To W. H. Brookfield* 5
As he did half in *j*, Old Horace ?   *Epilogue* 45
shameless laughter, Pagan oath, and *j*,   *St. Telemachus* 39
Jest (verb) ' You *j* : ill jesting with edge-tools !   *Princess ii* 201
grizzlier than a bear, to ride And *j* with :   *Pelleas and E.* 194
Who *j* and laugh so easily and so well.   *Sisters (E. and E.)* 41
Jested while he *j* thus, A thought flash'd   *Princess i* 194
Drank till he *j* with all ease,   *Geraint and E.* 290
Have *j* also, but for Julian's eyes,   *Lover's Tale iv* 223
Jesting ' You jest : ill *j* with edge-tools !   *Princess ii* 201
Jesus (*See also* **Christ, Christ Jesus, Lord Jesus**) O *J*, if
   thou wilt not save my soul,   *St. S. Stylites* 46
Jet (s) (*See also* **Fountain-jets**) From those four *j*'s four
   currents in one swell   *Palace of Art* 33
The fountain pulses high in sunnier *j*'s,   *Prog. of Spring* 54
Jet (verb) *J* upward thro' the mid-day blossom.   *Demeter and P.* 47
Jet-black Leading a *j-b* goat white-horn'd,   *Œnone* 51
The maiden's *j-b* hair has grown,   *Day-Dm., Sleep. B.* 4

Joust (verb) For pastime ; yea, he said it : *j* can I.   *Gareth and L. 543*
For here be mighty men to *j* with,   „   880
since I go to *j* as one unknown At Camelot   *Lancelot and E. 190*
he will ride, *J* for it, and win,   „   204
That he might *j* unknown of all,   „   583
Jovial He must have been a *j* king.   *Day-Dm., Sleep. P. 40*
Jowl Cheek by *j*, and knee by knee :   *Vision of Sin 84*
Joy The *j* I had in my freewill All cold,   *Supp. Confessions 16*
Scarce outward signs of *j* arise,   „   49
Shall man live thus, in *j*   „   169
wild swan's death-hymn took the soul Of that waste place with *j*   *Dying Swan 22*
What hope or fear or *j* is thine ?   *Adeline 23*
all day long you sit between *j* and woe,   *Margaret 64*
Because you are the soul of *j*,   *Rosalind 20*
' Twere *j*, not fear, claspt hand-in-hand   *If I were loved 9*
The *j* that mixes man with Heaven :   *Two Voices 210*
To move about the house with *j*,   *Miller's D. 95*
' There is no *j* but calm ! '   *Lotos-Eaters, C. S. 23*
we should come like ghosts to trouble *j*.   „   74
emptied of all *j*, Leaving the dance and song,   *D. of F. Women 215*
Such *j* as you have seen with us,   *D. of the O. Year 17*
But Thou rejoice with liberal *j*,   *England and Amer. 11*
lark could scarce get out his notes for *j*,   *Gardener's D. 90*
So home I went, but could not sleep for *j*,   „   174
perfect *J*, perplex'd for utterance,   „   255
I look'd at him with *j* :   *Talking Oak 106*
reaps not harvest of his youthful *j*'s,   *Locksley Hall 139*
I muse on *j* that will not cease,   *Sir Galahad 65*
A private life was all his *j*,   *Will Water. 129*
And madly danced our hearts with *j*,   *The Voyage 3*
LIKE souls that balance *j* and pain,   *Sir L. and Q. G. 1*
O *j* to the people and *j* to the throne,   *W. to Alexandra 29*
Making the little one leap for *j*.   *To F. D. Maurice 4*
The Priest beheld him, And cried with *j*,   *The Victim 38*
They bring me sorrow touch'd with *j*,   *In Mem. xxviii 19*
And doubtful *j*'s the father move,   „   xl 9
On some unworthy heart with *j*,   „   lxii 7
Thy passion clasps a secret *j* :   „   lxxxviii 8
O *j* to him in this retreat,   „   lxxxix 13
As in the former flash of *j*,   „   cxxii 15
tells The *j* To every wandering breeze ;   „   Con. 62
And, tho' in silence, wishing *j*.   „   88
the ringing *j* of the Hall,   *Maud I i 70*
With a *j* in which I cannot rejoice,   „   v 21
That she warbled alone in her *j* !   „   x 55
in the heart of Arthur *j* was lord.   *Com. of Arthur 124*
Stood round him, and rejoicing in his *j*.   „   459
Shame never made girl redder than Gareth *j*.   *Gareth and L. 536*
So Gareth past with *j* ; but as the cur Pluckt   „   701
Not beat him back, but welcomed him with *j*.   *Marr. of Geraint 748*
Lost one Found was greeted as in Heaven With *j*   *Balin and Balan 82*
Lady, my liege, in whom I have my *j*,   *Lancelot and E. 1180*
I pray you : have your *j*'s apart.   „   1217
thou in whom I have Most *j* and most affiance,   „   1357
Redder than any rose, a *j* to me,   *Holy Grail 521*
And each made *j* of either ; then he ask'd,   „   638
' Glory and *j* and honour to our Lord   „   839
' I had forgotten all in my strong *j* To see thee—   *Last Tournament 582*
Himself beheld three spirits mad with *j*   *Guinevere 252*
feel My purpose and rejoicing in my *j*.'   „   486
not grieving at my *j*'s, But not rejoicing ;   „   679
London roll'd one tide of *j* thro' all Her trebled millions,   *To the Queen ii 8*
great pine shook with lonely sounds of *j*   *Lover's Tale i 325*
to both there came The *j* of life in steepness overcome,   „   386
and *j* In breathing nearer heaven ; and *j* to me,   „   388
more than *j* that I to her became Her guardian   „   392
Since in his absence full of light and *j*,   „   425
All *j*, to whom my agony was a *j*.   „   656
from commonplace, And help us to our *j*.   *Sisters (E. and E.) 224*
Little guess what *j* can be got from a cowslip   *In the Child. Hosp. 36*
within The city comes a murmur void of *j*,   *Tiresias 101*
when I held it aloft in my *j*,   *The Wreck 33*
is it well to wish you *j* ?   *Locksley H., Sixty 216*

Joy (continued) Wish me *j* !   *The Ring 60*
this life of mingled pains And *j*'s to me,   *To Mary Boyle 50*
world-whisper, mystic pain or *j*,   *Far—far—away 7*
Joyance this May morning in *j* is beating Full merrily ;   *All Things will Die 6*
To keep them in all *j* : more than this I could not ;   *Lancelot and E. 1324*
Joyful led *J* to that palm-planted fountain-fed   *Alexander 7*
to have been *J* and free from blame.   *D. of F. Women 80*
J came his speech :   *The Captain 30*
Took *j* note of all things *j*,   *Aylmer's Field 67*
a shout More *j* than the city-roar that hails   *Princess, Con. 101*
WHEN the breeze of a *j* dawn blew free   *Arabian Nights 1*
CLEAR-HEADED friend, whose *j* scorn,   *Clear-headed friend 1*
' I sung the *j* Pæan clear,   *Two Voices 127*
by my life, These birds have *j* thoughts.   *Gardener's D. 99*
A fairy Prince, with *j* eyes,   *Day-Dm., Arrival 7*
The streets were fill'd with *j* sound,   *In Mem. xxxi 10*
Mute symbols of a *j* morn,   „   Con. 58
With a *j* spirit I Sir Richard Grenville die ! '   *The Revenge 103*
Joyfully You then *j*, all of you,   *On Jub. Q. Victoria 15*
Joying *J* to feel herself alive,   *Palace of Art 178*
Joyless Touch thy dull goal of *j* gray,   *In Mem. lxxii 27*
cuckoo of a *j* June Is calling out of doors :   *Pref. Poem Broth. S. 3*
Midnight—and *j* June gone by,   „   9
Till the *j* birthday came of a boy born happily dead.   „   *Charity 34*
Joyous She seem'd a part of *j* Spring :   *Sir L. and Q. G. 23*
A *j* to dilate, as toward the light.   *Aylmer's Field 77*
Then glided out of the *j* wood   *Maud II i 31*
Jubilant But anon her awful *j* voice,   *Dying Swan 28*
While all the younger ones with *j* cries   *Enoch Arden 377*
Heaven flash'd a sudden *j* ray,   *Ode on Well. 129*
Roll and rejoice, *j* voice,   *W. to Alexandra 22*
All on a sudden the garrison utter a *j* shout,   *Def. of Lucknow 98*
a *j* challenge to Time and to Fate ;   *Vastness 21*
Before her skims the *j* woodpecker,   *Prog. of Spring 16*
You should be *j* that you flourish'd here   *Poets and their B. 12*
Jubilee With pleasure and love and *j* :   *Sea-Fairies 36*
Mourn'd in this golden hour of *j*,   *Ode Inter. Exhib. 8*
Utter your *j*, steeple and spire !   *W. to Alexandra 17*
Crowning year of her *J*.   *On Jub. Q. Victoria 11*
Ceremonial Of this year of her *J*.   „   24
And this year of her *J*. (repeat)   „   38, 51
' Hail to the glorious Golden year of her *J* ! '   „   65
darkness Dawns into the *J* of the Ages.   „   71
Judah Not least art thou, thou little Bethlehem In *J*,   *Sir J. Oldcastle 25*
Judge (s) Himself the *j* and jury,   *Sea Dreams 175*
God, not man, is the *J* of us all   *Grandmother 95*
Modred for want of worthier was the *j*.   *Gareth and L. 28*
I came into court to the *J* and the lawyers.   *Rizpah 33*
Him, happy to be chosen *J* of Gods,   *Death of Œnone 16*
Judge (verb) and see thy Paris *j* of Gods.'   *Œnone 90*
J thou me by what I am,   „   154
Thy mortal eyes are frail to *j* of fair,   „   158
' Let the Princess *j* Of that '   *Princess ii 234*
pray'd me not to *j* their cause from her   „   vii 235
bring him here, that I may *j* the right,   *Gareth and L. 380*
And *j* all nature from her feet of clay,   *Merlin and V. 835*
If one may *j* the living by the dead,   *Lancelot and E. 1368*
To *j* between my slander'd self and me—   *Columbus 125*
Judged now the Priest has *j* for me.   *The Victim 56*
Judger hasty *j* would have call'd her guilt,   *Geraint and E. 433*
Judging he should come to shame thy *j* of him.'   *Gareth and L. 469*
as the base man, *j* of the good,   *Pelleas and E. 80*
Judgment my own weakness fools My *j*,   *Supp. Confessions 137*
pick'd offenders from the mass For *j*.   *Princess i 30*
You shame your mother's *j* too.   „   vi 261
He would not make his *j* blind,   *In Mem. xcvi 14*
And shalt abide her *j* on it ;   *Marr. of Geraint 584*
Submit, and hear the *j* of the King.' ' He hears the *j* of the King of kings,'   *Geraint and E. 799*
naked Ignorance Delivers brawling *j*'s,   *Merlin and V. 665*
Rash were my *j* then, who deem this maid   *Lancelot and E. 239*
and hollow like a Ghost's Denouncing *j*,   *Guinevere 421*

K

Kay (a Knight of the Round Table) (*continued*) Knowest
thou not me? thy master? I am K. *Gareth and L.* 753
'Have at thee then,' said K: they shock'd, and K
  Fell shoulder-slipt,   „ 758
helping back the dislocated K To Camelot,   „ 1213
Arthur turn'd to K the seneschal, *Last Tournament* 89
Kays (keys) Till Holy St Pether gets up wid his k an'
  opens the gate!   *Tomorrow* 93
Keäper (keeper) K's it wur; fo' they fun 'um
  theer   *N. Farmer, O. S.* 33
Keeäp (keep) an' I k's 'im cleän an' bright, *North. Cobbler* 97
I says to tha ' k 'em, an' welcome ' *Church-warden, etc.* 36
an' k's thysen to thysen.   „ 48
Keeäper (keeper) An' k 'e seed ya an roon'd,   „ 28
Keel round about the k with faces pale, *Lotos-Eaters* 25
Sweet-Gale rustle round the shelving k; *Edwin Morris* 110
The broad seas swell'd to meet the k, *The Voyage* 13
no ruder air perplex Thy sliding k, *In Mem. ix* 10
I hear the noise about thy k;   „ x 1
ship sail K upward, and mast downward, *Gareth and L.* 254
Light-green with its own shadow, k to k. *Lover's Tale i* 43
Keen hawk-eyes are k and bright, K with triumph, *Rosalind* 25
Made dull his inner, k his outer eye *Last Tournament* 366
cloud of thought K, irrepressible. *Lover's Tale ii* 165
then so k to seek The meanings ambush'd *Tiresias* 4
I am not k of sight,   *The Ring* 258
Roof not a glance so k as thine: *Clear-headed friend* 7
Those spirit-thrilling eyes so k and beautiful *Ode to Memory* 39
about the circles of the globes Of her k eyes. *The Poet* 44
And sparkled k with frost against the hilt: *M. d'Arthur* 55
Thro' all yon starlight k, *St. Agnes' Eve* 22
His own, tho' k and bold and soldierly *Aylmer's Field* 192
Did he shriek ' Yes love, yes, Edith,   „ 582
Pierces the k seraphic flame From orb to orb, *In Mem. xxx* 27
The yule-clog sparkled k with frost,   „ *lxxviii* 5
And k thro' wordy snares to track   „ *xcv* 31
can I doubt, who knew thee k In intellect,   „ *cxiii* 5
And sparkled k with frost against the hilt: *Pass. of Arthur* 223
When frost is k and days are brief— *To Ulysses* 19
Keener No k hunter after glory breathes. *Lancelot and E.* 156
The memory's vision hath a k edge. *Lover's Tale i* 36
Keenest Still with their fires Love tipt his k darts; *D. of F. Women* 173
Keenin' (crying) Him an' his childer wor k *Tomorrow* 86
Keenlier That k in sweet April wakes, *In Mem. cxvi* 2
Keenly glancing all at once as k at her *Marr. of Geraint* 773
Keep (s) there is the k; He shall not cross us *Geraint and E.* 341
Keep (verb) (*See also* **Keeäp**) tears of penitence Which
  would k green   *Supp. Confessions* 119
So k where you are: you are foul with sin; *Poet's Mind* 36
hearts of salient springs K measure with thine own? *Adeline* 27
K's real sorrow far away. *Margaret* 44
Too long you k the upper skies; *Rosalind* 35
We must bind And k you fast,   „ 43
heart a charmed slumber k's, *Eleänore* 128
K's his blue waters fresh for many a mile. *Mine be the strength* 8
Nor any train of reason k: *Two Voices* 50
Let us swear an oath, and k it *Lotos-Eaters, C. S.* 108
I k smooth plats of fruitful ground, *The Blackbird* 3
K dry their light from tears; *Of old sat Freedom* 20
' Here, take the goose, and k you warm, *The Goose* 7
' So k you cold, or k you warm,   „ 43
k a thing, its use will come. *The Epic* 42
' Eustace,' I said, ' this wonder k's the house.' *Gardener's D.* 119
Could k me from that Eden where she dwelt.   „ 191
k's us all in order more or less— *Walk. to the Mail* 23
that trims us up, And k's us tight; *Edwin Morris* 47
and try If yet he k's the power. *Talking Oak* 28
to k My own full-tuned,— *Love and Duty* 39
but that all Should k within, door shut, *Godiva* 41
His state the king reposing k's. *Day-Dm., Sleep. P.* 39
So k I fair thro' faith and prayer *Sir Galahad* 23
To k the best man under the sun *Lady Clare* 31
' But k the secret for your life,   „ 34
' But k the secret all ye can.'   „ 42
While we k a little breath ! *Vision of Sin* 192

Keep (verb) (*continued*) betray the trust: K nothing
  sacred: *You might have won* 19
So might she k the house while he was gone. *Enoch Arden* 140
K a clean hearth and a clear fire for me,   „ 192
till I come again K everything shipshape,   „ 220
Not k it noble, make it nobler ? *Aylmer's Field* 386
k him from the lust of blood That makes *Lucretius* 83
we k a chronicle With all about him '— *Princess, Pro.* 27
That love to k us children !   „ 133
k your hoods about the face ;   „ *ii* 358
surely, if your Highness k Your purport,   „ *iii* 211
I broke the letter of it to k the sense.   „ *iv* 338
And here he k's me hostage for his son.'   „ 405
We did but k your surety for our son,   „ *v* 25
For now will cruel Ida k her back ;   „ 84
she would not k Her compact.'   „ 323
O if, I say, you k One pulse that beats true woman,   „ *vi* 179
With one that cannot k her mind an hour :   „ 287
What use to k them here—now ?   „ 304
I cannot k My heart an eddy from the brawling hour :   „ 321
willing she should k Court-favour :   „ *vii* 57
seem to k her up but drag her down—   „ 270
make herself her own To give or k,   „ 273
k's his wing'd affections clipt with crime :   „ 316
God bless the narrow sea which k's her off, *Con.* 51
And k's our Britain, whole within herself,   „ 52
k it ours, O God, from brute control ; *Ode on Well.* 159
k our noble England whole,   „ 161
k the soldier firm, the statesman pure :   „ 222
thank God that I k my eyes. *Grandmother* 106
Let darkness k her raven gloss : *In Mem. i* 10
Who k's the keys of all the creeds,   „ *xxiii* 5
How dare we k our Christmas-eve ;   „ *xxix* 4
I strive To k so sweet a thing alive : '   „ *xxxv* 7
' What k's a spirit wholly true   „ *lii* 9
She k's the gift of years before,   „ *xcvii* 25
For who would k an ancient form   „ *cv* 19
We k the day. With festal cheer,   „ *cvii* 21
force, that k's A thousand pulses dancing,   „ *cxxv* 15
tho' as yet I k Within his court on earth,   „ *cxxvi* 6
I k but a man and a maid, *Maud I iv* 19
I would not marvel at either, but k a temperate brain ;   „ 40
Should Nature k me alive,   „ *vi* 32
Her brother, from whom I k aloof,   „ 46
K watch and ward, (repeat)   „ 58
How can ye k me tether'd to you— *Gareth and L.* 115
yet the which No man can k ;   „ 272
my knighthood k the vows they swore,   „ 602
And k's me in this ruinous castle here, *Marr. of Geraint* 462
k's the wear and polish of the wave.   „ 40
dress her beautifully and k her true '— *Geraint and E.* 40
not to speak to me, And thus ye k it !   „ 79
To k them in the wild ways of the wood,   „ 187
k a touch of sweet civility Here in the heart   „ 312
And if it were so do not k it back :   „ 316
To k him bright and clean as heretofore,   „ 937
Eats scarce enow to k his pulse abeat ; *Balin and Balan* 105
We could not k him silent, out he flash'd, *Merlin and V.* 416
To k me all to your own self,—   „ 523
I needed then no charm to k them mine But youth   „ 547
the Queen Might k her all his own :   „ 585
meaning by it To k the list low and pretenders back,   „ 592
For k it like a puzzle chest in chest,   „ 654
But k that oath ye sware, ye might, perchance,   „ 688
Then must she k it safelier. All was jest. *Lancelot and E.* 218
you k So much of what is graceful ;   „ 1218
To k them in all joyance ;   „ 1324
K him back Among yourselves. *Pelleas and E.* 190
take him to you, k him off,   „ 194
And if thou k me in thy donjon here,   „ 480
Vows ! did you k the vow you made to Mark *Last Tournament* 655
house, That k's the rust of murder on the walls— *Guinevere* 74
Not only to k down the base in man,   „ 480
A strain to shame us ' k you to yourselves ; *To the Queen ii* 15
K thou thy name of ' Lover's Bay.' *Lover's Tale i* 15

Keep (verb) *(continued)* yet in him *k*'s A draught of that
   sweet fountain   *Lover's Tale i* 140
It seem'd to *k* its sweetness to itself,   ,,   154
Are fashion'd by the channel which they *k*),   ,,   567
And *k* yourself, none knowing, to yourself ;   ,,   *iv* 114
Sally she wesh'd foälks' cloäths to *k* the wolf fro'
   the door,   *North. Cobbler* 29
K the revolver in hand !   *Def. of Lucknow* 26
The love that *k*'s this heart alive   *The Flight* 35
Could *k* their haithen kings in the flesh   *Tomorrow* 70
To *k* our English Empire whole !   *Hands all Round* 14
I bad her *k*, Like a seal'd book,   *The Ring* 122
desire to *k* So skilled a nurse about you always—   ,,   373
How bright you *k* your marriage-ring !   *Romney's R.* 59
Keeper *(See also* **Keäper, Keeäper**) There by a *k* shot at,
   slightly hurt,   *Aylmer's Field* 548
escaped His *k*'s, and the silence which he felt,   ,,   839
jam the doors, and bear The *k*'s down,   *Lucretius* 170
the *k* was one, so full of pride,   *Maud II v* 79
not with such a craziness as needs A cell and *k*),   *Lover's Tale iv* 164
Keeping the children play'd at *k* house.   *Enoch Arden* 24
did Enid, *k* watch, behold In the first shallow   *Geraint and E.* 118
' It is not worth the *k* : let it go :   *Merlin and V.* 396
to have my shield In *k* till I come.'   *Lancelot and E.* 383
I said ' You were *k* with her,   *First Quarrel* 64
My giant ilex *k* leaf When frost is keen   *To Ulysses* 18
Kelt *(See also* **Celt**) Slav, Teuton, *K*, I count them all   *Epilogue* 18
Kem (came) An' the sun *k* out of a cloud   *Tomorrow* 37
Kemble Garrick and statelier *K*, and the rest   *To W. C. Macready* 7
Ken to sea, as far as eye could *k*,—   *Lover's Tale i* 336
Kendal I am all but sure I have—in *K* church—   *Romney's R.* 19
Kent lands in *K* and messuages in York,   *Edwin Morris* 127
On capes of Afric as on cliffs of *K*,   *W. to Marie Alex.* 17
Kep (kept) ' Siver, I *k* 'um, I *k* 'um, my lass,   *N. Farmer, O. S.* 23
fur to kick our Sally as *k* the wolf fro' the door,   *North. Cobbler* 59
I 'a *k* thruf thick an' thin   *Spinster's S's.* 12
boäth on us *k* out o' sight o' the winders   ,,   35
fur, Steevie, tha *k*' it sa neät   ,,   77
An' 'e *k* his heäd hoop like a king,   *Owd Roä* 9
Sa I *k* i' my chair, fur I thowt she was nobbut a-rilin'   ,,   74
k a-callin' o' Roä till 'e waggled 'is taäil fur a bit, But
   the cocks *k* a-crawin' an' crawin'   ,,   105
I *k*' mysen meeäk as a lamb,   *Churchwarden, etc.* 41
Kept *(See also* **Kep**) Which *k* her throne unshaken still,   *To the Queen* 34
But good things have not *k* aloof,   *My life is full* 2
K watch, waiting decision,   *Œnone* 143
this *k*, Stored in some treasure-house   *M. d'Arthur* 100
on the leads we *k* her till she pigg'd.   *Walk. to the Mail* 92
But that his heavy rider *k* him down.   *Vision of Sin* 4
His worst he *k*, his best he gave.   *You might have won* 26
this he *k* Thro' all his future ;   *Enoch Arden* 236
Smote him, as having *k* aloof so long.   ,,   274
but he was gone Who *k* it ;   ,,   695
put her little ones to school, And *k* them in it,   ,,   707
K him a living soul.   ,,   804
But *k* the house, his chair, and last his bed.   ,,   826
His gazing in on Annie, his resolve, And how he *k* it.   ,,   864
sow'd her name and *k* it green In living letters,   *Aylmer's Field* 88
where his worldless heart had *k* it warm,   ,,   471
yet her cheek *K* colour : wondrous !   ,,   506
K to the garden now, and grove of pines,   ,,   550
she, who *k* a tender Christian hope,   *Sea Dreams* 41
(I *k* the book and had my finger in it)   *Princess, Pro.* 53
I *k* mine own Intent on her,   ,,   *ii* 441
She *k* her state, and left the drunken king   ,,   *iii* 229
then, climbing, Cyril *k* With Psyche,   ,,   354
Saw that they *k* apart, no mischief done ;   ,,   *iv* 340
why *k* ye not your faith ? O base and bad !   ,,   *v* 77
Part sat like rocks : part reel'd but *k* their seats :   ,,   496
His foes were thine ; he *k* us free ;   *Ode on Well.* 91
great men who fought, and *k* it ours.   ,,   158
Like ballad-burthen music, *k*,   *The Daisy* 77
My blood an even tenor *k*,   *In Mem. lxxxv* 17
In those fall'n leaves which *k* their green,   ,,   *xcv* 23
K itself warm in the heart of my dreams,   *Maud I vi* 18

Kept *(continued)* and *k* and coax'd and whistled to—   *Gareth and L.* 14
Wherein she *k* them folded reverently   *Marr. of Geraint* 137
And *k* her off and gazed upon her face,   ,,   519
But *k* it for a sweet surprise at morn.   ,,   703
But Enid ever *k* the faded silk,   ,,   841
Because she *k* the letter of his word,   *Geraint and E.* 455
Like that which *k* the heart of Eden green   ,,   770
But *k* myself aloof till I was changed ;   ,,   872
And there he *k* the justice of the King   ,,   956
Some lost, some stolen, some as relics *k*.   *Merlin and V.* 453
since he *k* his mind on one sole aim,   ,,   626
Some cause had *k* him sunder'd from his wife :   ,,   715
and took the shield, There *k* it,   *Lancelot and E.* 398
friend Might have well *k* his secret.   ,,   593
k The one-day-seen Sir Lancelot in her heart,   ,,   746
And faith unfaithful *k* him falsely true.   ,,   877
There two stood arm'd, and *k* the door ;   ,,   1247
a maid, Who *k* our holy faith among her kin   *Holy Grail* 697
Arthur *k* his best until the last ;   ,,   763
a lion on each side That *k* the entry,   ,,   818
Sir Pelleas *k* the field With honour :   *Pelleas and E.* 168
still he *k* his watch beneath the wall.   ..   223
Wide open were the gates, And no watch *k* ;   ,,   415
this *k*, Stored in some treasure-house   *Pass. of Arthur* 268
But still I *k* my eyes upon the sky.   *Lover's Tale i* 572
And *k* it thro' a hundred years of gloom,   ,,   *iv* 195
' Bygones ! you *k* yours hush'd,' I said,   *First Quarrel* 68
They *k* their faith, their freedom,   *Montenegro* 2
saw the death, but *k* the deck,   *Locksley H., Sixty* 63
and Ætna *k* her winter snow.   *Demeter and P.* 115
you—you loved me, *k* your word.   *The Ring* 290
k their watch upon the ring and you.   ,,   300
I *k* it as a sacred amulet About me,—   ,,   442
a woman, God bless her, *k* me from Hell.   *Charity* 4
Kerchief about them, ribbon, glove Or *k* ;   *Aylmer's Field* 621
Kernel trash ' he said, ' but with a *k* in it.   *Princess ii* 395
The *k* of the shrivell'd fruit   *Ancient Sage* 121
Kestrel Kite and *k*, wolf and wolfkin,   *Boädicea* 15
Kettle *(See also* **Kittle**) And hurl'd the pan and *k*.   *The Goose* 28
wi' my oän *k* theere o' the hob,   *Spinster's S's.* 9
Kex tho' the rough *k* break The starr'd mosaic,   *Princess iv* 77
Key *(See also* **Kays**) and opens but to golden *k*'s.   *Locksley Hall* 100
With half a sigh she turn'd the *k*,   *The Letters* 18
Who keeps the *k*'s of all the creeds,   *In Mem. xxiii* 1
That Shadow waiting with the *k*'s,   ,,   *xxvi* 15
And lives to clutch the golden *k*'s,   ,,   *lxiv* 2
Cries of the partridge, like a rusty *k* Turn'd in
   a lock,   *Lover's Tale ii* 115
' Authority of the Church, Power of the *k*'s ! '—   *Sir J. Oldcastle* 162
Given thee the *K* of the great Ocean-sea ?   *Columbus* 149
and since The *k* to that weird casket,   *Ancient Sage* 254
The golden *k*'s of East and West.   *To Marq. of Dufferin* 4
I felt for what I could not find, the *k*,   *The Ring* 440
Keys (of a piano) Turn'd as he sat, and struck the *k*   *The Islet* 7
and by their clash, And prelude on the *k*,   *Sisters (E. and E.)* 2
would drop from the chords or the *k*,   *The Wreck* 27
Keystone For barefoot on the *k*,   *Gareth and L.* 214
Khan given the Great *K*'s palaces to the Moor,   *Columbus* 109
Kick all women *k* against their Lords   *Princess iv* 412
an' I gied our Sally a *k*,   *North. Cobbler* 36
I seeäd that our Sally went laämed Cos' o' the *k* as
   I gied 'er,   ,,   40
Heer wur a fall fro' a kiss to a *k*   ,,   57
fur to *k* our Sally as kep the wolf fro' the door,   ,,   59
mob's million feet Will *k* you from your place,   *The Fleet* 19
I fetcht 'im a *k* an' 'e went.   *Owd Roä* 62
Kick'd *K*, he returns : do ye not hate him,   *Pelleas and E.* 264
An' I thowt 'at I *k* 'im ageän, but I *k* thy Moother
   istead.   *Owd Roä* 67
Kid Seethed like the *k* in its own mother's milk !   *Merlin and V.* 869
Kilaueä wallow in fiery riot and revel On *K*,   *Kapiolani* 9
Kill eyes, That care not whom they *k*,   *Rosalind* 37
why should you *k* yourself And make them orphans   *Enoch Arden* 394
monsters only made to *k* Time by the fire in
   winter.'   *Princess, Pro.* 204

Kill (*continued*) ' *K* him now, The tyrant ! *k* him   *Princess, Pro.* 206
K us with pity, break us with ourselves—   "   iii 258
some grand fight to *k* and make an end :   "   iv 591
tenderness, not yours, that could not *k*,   "   vi 186
that Which *k's* me with myself, and drags   "   307
Mammonite mother *k's* her babe for a burial fee,   *Maud I i* 45
the churchmen fain would *k* their church,   " *II v* 28
K the foul thief, and wreak me for my son.'   *Gareth and L.* 363
I speak, and tho' he *k* me for it,   *Geraint and E.* 137
shivers, ere he springs and *k's*.   *Pelleas and E.* 286
tho' ye *k* my hope, not yet my love,   " 303
Christ *k* me then But I will slice him   " 337
' Will the child *k* me with her innocent talk ? '   *Guinevere* 214
' Will the child *k* me with her foolish prate ? '   " 225
shall I *k* myself ? What help in that ? I cannot *k* my
sin, If soul be soul ; nor can I *k* my shame ;   " 620
K or be kill'd, live or die,   *Def. of Lucknow* 41
k Their babies at the breast for hate of Spain—   *Columbus* 179
' *K* you enemy, for you hate him,'   *Locksley H., Sixty* 94
Mother, dare you *k* your child ?   *Forlorn* 37

Kill'd I have *k* my son. I have *k* him—   *Dora* 159
Till, *k* with some luxurious agony,   *Vision of Sin* 43
latest fox—where started—*k* In such a bottom :   *Aylmer's Field* 253
This truthful change in thee has *k* it.   *Princess vii* 350
bees are still'd, and the flies are *k*,   *Window, Winter* 10
Or *k* in falling from his horse.   *In Mem. vi* 40
As the churches have *k* their Christ.   *Maud II v* 29
I should not less have *k* him.   *Geraint and E.* 845
fire of Heaven has *k* the barren cold,   *Balin and Balan* 440
K with a word worse than a life of blows !   *Merlin and V.* 870
K with unutterable unkindliness.'   " 886
And here a thrust that might have *k*,   *Lancelot and E.* 25
K in a tilt, come next, five summers back,   *Guinevere* 321
Gawain *k* In Lancelot's war,   *Pass. of Arthur* 30
they *k* him, they *k* him for robbing the mail.   *Rizpah* 34
lawyer who *k* him and hang'd him there.   " 40
Kill or be *k*, live or die,   *Def. of Lucknow* 41
Those that in barbarian burials *k* the slave,   *Locksley H., Sixty* 67
tiger madness muzzled, every serpent passion *k*,   " 167
My quick tears *k* the flower,   *Demeter and P.* 108
' She has *k* him, has *k* him, has *k* him '   *Bandit's Death* 36

Killest O thou that *k*, hads't thou known,   *Aylmer's Field* 738

Killing and, half *k* him With kisses,   *Lover's Tale iv* 377

Kin lift His axe to slay my *k*.   *Talking Oak* 236
I am well-to-do—no *k*, no care,   *Enoch Arden* 418
shafts Of gentle satire, *k* to charity,   *Princess ii* 469
If easy patrons of their *k*   *Third of Feb.* 39
but felt him mine, Of closest *k* to me :   *Gareth and L.* 127
Thou that art her *k*, Go likewise ;   " 378
Thou shalt give back their earldom to thy *k*.   *Marr. of Geraint* 585
in the field were Lancelot's kith and *k*,   *Lancelot and E.* 466
drave his kith and *k*, And all the Table Round   " 498
little cause for laughter : his own *k*—   " 597
His kith and *k*, not knowing, set upon him ;   " 599
Past up the still rich city to his *k*,   " 802
Far up the dim rich city to her *k* ;   " 845
Lancelot's kith and *k* so worship him   *Holy Grail* 651
kept our holy faith among her *k* In secret,   " 697
and all his kith and *k* Clave to him,   *Guinevere* 439
call My sister's son—no *k* of mine,   " 573
laid her in the vault of her own *k*.   *Lover's Tale iv* 39
There was a farmer in Dorset of Harry's *k*,   *First Quarrel* 17
are *they* his mother ? are *you* of his *k* ?   *Rizpah* 70
noä, not fur Sally's oän *k*.   *North. Cobbler* 114
and vaulted our kith and our *k*,   *V. of Maeldune* 47
serve This mortal race thy *k* so well,   *De Prof., Two G.* 16
Amy's *k* and mine are left to me.   *Locksley H., Sixty* 56

Kind (*adj.*) a nature never *k* !   *Walk. to the Mail* 62
K nature is the best :   " 64
' Her kisses were so close and *k*,   *Talking Oak* 169
love her, as I knew her, *k* ?   *Locksley Hall* 70
But may she still be *k*,   *Will Water.* 10
Whom all men are *k* and hospitable :   *Princess i* 71
we ourselves but half as good, as *k*,   " v 201
Is it *k* ? Speak to her I say :   " vi 248

Kind (*adj.*) (*continued*) *K*, like a man, was he ; like a
man,   *Grandmother* 70
Stiles where we stay'd to be *k*,   *Window, Marr. Morn.* 7
So *k* an office hath been done,   *In Mem. xvii* 17
' How good ! how *k* ! and he is gone.'   " xx 20
He looks so cold : she thinks him *k*.   " xcvii 24
we cannot be *k* to each other here for an hour ;   *Maud I iv* 28
Nor her, who is neither courtly nor *k*,   " v 27
her eye seem'd full Of a *k* intent to me,   " vi 41
Now I thought she was *k*   " xiv 26
And says he is rough but *k*,   " xix 70
K ? but the deathbed desire Spurn'd by this heir   " 77
Rough but *k* ? yet I know He had plotted against me   " 79
K to Maud ? that were not amiss.   " 82
Well, rough but *k* ; why let it be so :   " 83
Not beautiful now, not even *k* ;   " II v 66
Is it *k* to have made me a grave so rough,   " 97
surely, some *k* heart will come To bury me,   " 102
such a silence is more wise than *k*.'   *Merlin and V.* 289
And *k* the woman's eyes and innocent,   *Holy Grail* 393
thine is more to me—soft, gracious, *k*—   *Last Tournament* 560
May those *k* eyes for ever dwell !   *Miller's D.* 220
K hearts are more than coronets,   *L. C. V. de Vere* 55
And say to Robin a *k* word,   *May Queen, Con.* 45
But though we love *k* Peace so well,   *Third of Feb.* 9
' Yea, my *k* lord,' said the glad youth,   *Geraint and E.* 241
' Would some of your *k* people take him up,   " 543
Manners so *k*, yet stately, such a grace   " 861
but his voice and his face were not *k*,   *In the Child. Hosp.* 15
the crew were gentle, the captain *k* ;   *The Wreck* 129
yer Honour's the thrue ould blood that always manes
to be *k*,   *Tomorrow* 5
Than ha' spoken as *k* as you did,   *First Quarrel* 73
he was always *k* to me.   " 90
for it's *k* of you, Madam, to sit by an old dying
wife.   *Rizpah* 21
I think that you mean to be *k*,   " 81
so harsh, as those that should be *k* ?   *The Flight* 102
you look so *k* That you will not deny   *Romney's R.* 21
I count you *k*, I hold you true ;   *The Wanderer* 13

Kind (s) (*See also* **Human-kind**) Yet is there plenty
of the *k*.'   *Two Voices* 33
She had the passions of her *k*,   *L. C. V. de Vere* 35
Would serve his *k* in deed and word,   *Love thou thy land* 86
all *k's* of thought, That verged upon them,   *Gardener's D.* 70
ever cared to better his own *k*,   *Sea Dreams* 201
Beastlier than any phantom of his *k*   *Lucretius* 196
Lucius Junius Brutus of my *k* ?   *Princess ii* 284
According to the coarseness of their *k*,   " iv 346
there grew Another *k* of beauty in detail   " 448
in a pleasant *k* of a dream.   *Grandmother* 82
Has made me kindly with my *k*,   *In Mem. lxvi* 7
But thou and I are one in *k*,   " lxxix 5
What *k* of life is that I lead ;   " lxxxv 8
I will not shut me from my *k*,   " cviii 1
and that of a *k* The viler, as underhand,   *Maud I i* 27
I am one with my *k*,   " III vi 58
think what *k* of bird it is That sings   *Marr. of Geraint* 331
Came purer pleasure unto mortal *k*   *Geraint and E.* 765
and to hate his *k* With such a hate,   *Balin and Balan* 127
But kindly man moving among his *k* :   *Lancelot and E.* 265
Being mirthful he, but in a stately *k*—   " 322
in me lived a sin, So strange, of such a *k*,   *Holy Grail* 773
Seem'd my reproach ? He is not of my *k*.   *Pelleas and E.* 311
Experience, in her *k* Hath foul'd me—   *Last Tournament* 317
chain that bound me to my *k*.   *Locksley H., Sixty* 52
sadness at the doubtful doom of human *k* ;   *To Virgil* 24
till Self died out in the love of his *k* ;   *Vastness* 28
Some half remorseful *k* of pity too—   *The Ring* 375

Kinder girl Seem'd *k* unto Philip than to him ;   *Enoch Arden* 42
The night to me was *k* than the day ;   *Lover's Tale i* 611

Kindle The dim curls *k* into sunny rings ;   *Tithonus* 54
For an your fire be low ye *k* mine !   *Gareth and L.* 711
leaves i' the middle to *k* the fire ;   *Village Wife* 72
they meet And *k* generous purpose,   *Tiresias* 128

Kindled (adj. and part)   (*See also* **All-kindled, Rosy-kindled**)   Returning with hot cheek and *k* eyes.   *Alexander* 14
She spake With *k* eyes :   *Princess iii* 334
Thy gloom is *k* at the tips,   *In Mem. xxxix* 11
And the live green had *k* into flowers,   *Gareth and L.* 185
hear His voice in battle, and be *k* by it,   *Geraint and E.* 175
her bloom A rosy dawn *k* in stainless heavens,   *Pelleas and E.* 72
a sacrifice *K* by fire from heaven :   " 146
but *k* from within As 'twere with dawn.   *Lover's Tale i* 73
Mark is *k* on thy lips Most gracious ;   *Last Tournament* 561
And, who, when his anger was *k*,   *The Wreck* 17
Kindled (verb)   When wine and free companions *k* him,   *Geraint and E.* 293
And *k* all the plain and all the wold.   *Balin and Balan* 441
k the pyre, and all Stood round it,   *Death of Œnone* 65
Kindlier   since man's first fall, Did *k* unto man,   *Lancelot and E.* 860
He might be *k* : happily come the day !   *Sir J. Oldcastle* 23
For thro' that dawning gleam'd a *k* hope   *Enoch Arden* 833
but *k* than themselves To ailing wife   *Aylmer's Field* 176
After an angry dream this *k* glow   " 411
A *k* influence reign'd ;   *Princess vii* 20
And out of memories of her *k* days,   " 106
And each reflects a *k* day ;   *In Mem. c* 18
The larger heart, the *k* hand ;   " *cvi* 30
And yielding to his *k* moods,   *Merlin and V.* 174
With all the *k* colours of the field.'   *Last Tournament* 224
Our *k*, trustier Jaques, past away !   *To W. H. Brookfield* 11
and burn the *k* brutes alive.   *Locksley H., Sixty* 96
Something *k*, higher, holier—   " 160
But younger *k* Gods to bear us down,   *Demeter and P.* 131
Kindliest   O heart, with *k* motion warm,   *In Mem. lxxxv* 34
The truest, *k*, noblest-hearted wife   *Romney's R.* 35
Kindliness   She beloved for a *k* Rare in Fable   *On Jub. Q. Victoria* 4
Kindling   And Gareth answer'd her with *k* eyes, (repeat)   *Gareth and L.* 41, 62
A head with *k* eyes above the throng,   " 646
Kindly   O blessings on his *k* voice and on his silver hair !   *May Queen, Con.* 13
O blessings on his *k* heart and on his silver head !   " 15
But you can talk ! yours is a *k* vein :   *Edwin Morris* 81
break In full and *k* blossom.   *Will Water.* 24
To vary from the *k* race of men,   *Tithonus* 29
And the *k* earth shall slumber,   *Locksley Hall* 130
Proudly turns he round and *k*,   *L. of Burleigh* 55
And dwelt a moment on his *k* face,   *Enoch Arden* 326
He could not see, the *k* human face, Nor ever hear a *k* voice,   " 581
officers and men Levied a *k* tax upon themselves,   " 663
Never one *k* smile, one *k* word :   *Aylmer's Field* 564
'Nay,' said the *k* wife to comfort him,   *Sea Dreams* 140
'I loathe it : he had never *k* heart,   " 200
A word, but one, one little *k* word,   *Princess vi* 258
Has made me *k* with my kind,   *In Mem. lxvi* 7
half exprest And loyal unto *k* laws.   " *lxxv* 16
To pledge them with a *k* tear,   " *xc* 10
How modest, *k*, all-accomplish'd, wise,   *Ded. of Idylls* 18
So with a *k* hand on Gareth's arm   *Gareth and L.* 578
Here ceased the *k* mother out of breath ;   *Marr. of Geraint* 732
And all the *k* warmth of Arthur's hall   *Balin and Balan* 236
But *k* man moving among his kind :   *Lancelot and E.* 265
There the good mother's *k* ministering,   *Lover's Tale iv* 92
bear the sword Of Justice—what ! the kingly *k* boy ;   *Sir J. Oldcastle* 88
Their *k* native princes slain or slaved,   *Columbus* 174
I sorrow for that *k* child of Spain   " 212
Thanks to the *k* dark faces who fought with us,   *Def. of Lucknow* 70
And last in *k* curves, with gentlest fall,   *De Prof., Two G.* 23
And greet it with a *k* smile :   *To E. Fitzgerald* 4
And at home if I sought for a *k* caress,   *The Wreck* 31
K landlord, boon companion—   *Locksley H., Sixty* 240
From war with *k* links of gold,   *Epilogue* 16
If, glancing downward on the *k* sphere   *Poets and their B.* 9
smiled, and making with a *k* pinch   *The Ring* 314
Nor ever cheer'd you with a *k* smile,   " 388
Kindly-hearted   So spake the *k-h* Earl,   *Marr. of Geraint* 514
Kindness   *I could trust Your* k.   *To the Queen* 20
looking ancient *k* on thy pain.   *Locksley Hall* 85
I think your *k* breaks me down;   *Enoch Arden* 318

Kindness (*continued*)   money can be repaid ; Not *k* such as yours.'   *Enoch Arden* 321
Soul-stricken at their *k* to him,   *Aylmer's Field* 525
summer of his faded love, Or ordeal by *k* ;   " 561
more in *k* than in love,   *Merlin and V.* 907
your brother's love, And your good father's *k*.'   *Lancelot and E.* 945
he wrote ' Their *k*,' and he wrote no more ;   *To Marq. of Dufferin* 36
Kindred (adj.)   But branches current yet in *k* veins.'   *Princess ii* 245
To black and brown on *k* brows.   *In Mem. lxxix* 16
To-day they count as *k* souls ;   " *xcix* 19
But each has pleased a *k* eye,   " *c* 17
Kindred (s)   Grate her harsh *k* in the grass :   *Princess iv* 125
Thy *k* with the great of old.   *In Mem. lxxiv* 11
craft of *k* and the Godless hosts Of heathen   *Guinevere* 427
Kine   Sadly the far *k* loweth :   *Leonine Eleg.* 9
fields between Are dewy-fresh, browsed by deep-udder'd *k*,   *Gardener's D.* 46
white *k* glimmer'd, and the trees (repeat)   *In Mem. xcv* 15, 51
King   (*See also* **Sea-king, Warrior-king**)   Could give the warrior *k*'s of old,   *To the Queen* 4
K's have no such couch as thine,   *A Dirge* 40
But the *k* of them all would carry me,   *The Mermaid* 45
' Reign thou apart, a quiet *k*,   *Palace of Art* 14
stay'd the Ausonian *k* to hear Of wisdom and of law.   " 111
The heads and crowns of *k*'s ;   " 152
black-bearded *k*'s with wolfish eyes,   *D. of F. Women* 111
the mighty hearts Of captains and of *k*'s.   " 176
kneeling, with one arm about her *k*,   " 270
took it, and have worn it, like a *k* :   *M. d'Arthur* 33
' It is not meet, Sir *K*, to leave thee thus,   " 40
So strode he back slow to the wounded *K*. (repeat)   " 65, 112
if a *k* demand An act unprofitable,   " 95
K is sick, and knows not what he does.   " 97
Stored in some treasure-house of mighty *k*'s,   " 101
Authority forgets a dying *k*,   " 121
And lightly went the other to the *K*.   " 147
So sigh'd the *K*, Muttering and murmuring   " 178
three Queens Put forth their hands, and took the *K*,   " 206
So like a shatter'd column lay the *K* ;   " 221
charged Before the eyes of ladies and of *k*'s.   " 225
And came again together on the *k*   *Audley Court* 36
There came a mystic token from the *k*   *Edwin Morris* 132
Ir little profits that an idle *k*,   *Ulysses* 1
Than those old portraits of old *k*'s,   [*Day-Dm., Sleep. P.* 23
His state the *k* reposing keeps. He must have been a jovial *k*.   " 39
And last with these the *k* awoke,   *Revival* 17
' Pardy,' return'd the *k*, ' but still My joints   " 25
In robe and crown the *k* stept down,   *Beggar Maid* 5
' Death is *k*, and Vivat Rex !   *Vision of Sin* 179
No blazon'd statesman he, nor *k*.   *You might have won* 24
Like that long-buried body of the *k*,   *Aylmer's Field* 3
Sprang from the midriff of a prostrate *k*—   " 16
the voice that calls Doom upon *k*'s,   " 742
broke The statues, *k* or saint, or founder fell ;   *Sea Dreams* 224
K of the East altho' he seem,   *Lucretius* 133
Whose death-blow struck the dateless doom of *k*'s,   " 236
counts and *k*'s Who laid about them at their wills   *Princess, Pro.* 30
being strait-besieged By this wild *k*   " 37
my good father thought a *k* a *k* ;   " *i* 25
they saw the *k* ; he took the gifts ;   " 46
Tore the *k*'s letter, snow'd it down,   " 61
In this report, this answer of a *k*,   " 70
' No ! ' Roar'd the rough *k*, ' you shall not ;   " 87
And in the imperial palace found the *k*.   " 113
without a star, Not like a *k* :   " 118
Thus the *k* ; And I, tho' nettled   " 162
show'd the late-writ letters of the *k*.   " 175
' If the *k*,' he said, ' Had given us letters,   " 180
The *k* would bear him out : '   " 182
when the *k* Kiss'd her pale cheek,   " *ii* 263
' Our *k* expects—was there no precontract ?   " *iii* 207
kept her state, and left the drunken *k*   " 229
the tumult and the *k*'s Were shadows ;   " *iv* 564
old *k*'s Began to wag their baldness   " *v* 18

Kinsman (continued)   His *k* travelling on his own affair   *Merlin and V*. 717
but then A *k*, dying, summon'd me to Rome—   *The Ring* 178
him, who left you wealth, Your *k* ?   "   189
Kirtle   blood Was sprinkled on your *k*,   *Princess ii* 274
Kiss (s)   (*See also* **Bride-kiss**)   kiss sweet *k'es*, and
   speak sweet words :   *Sea-Fairies* 34
Yet fill my glass : give me one *k* :   *Miller's D*. 17
The *k*, The woven arms, seem but to be Weak symbols   "   231
once he drew With one long *k* my whole soul   *Fatima* 20
that quick-falling dew Of fruitful *k'es*,   *Œnone* 205
Seal'd it with *k'es* ? water'd it with tears ?   "   234
the wild *k*, when fresh from war's alarms,   *D. of F. Women* 149
Because the *k* he gave me, ere I fell,   "   235
worth a hundred *k'es* press'd on lips   *Gardener's D*. 151
k'es, where the heart on one wild leap   "   259
' Her *k'es* were so close and kind,   *Talking Oak* 169
I would have paid her *k* for *k*,   "   195
that last *k*, which never was the last,   *Love and Duty* 67
k'es balmier than half-opening buds Of April,   *Tithonus* 59
His own are pouted to a *k* :   *Day-Dm., Sleep. P*. 31
A TOUCH, a *k* ! the charm was snapt.   "   *Revival* 1
O love, for such another *k* ; '   "   *Depart*. 10
' O happy *k*, that woke thy sleep ! '   ' O love,
   thy *k* would wake the dead ! '   "   19
evermore a costly *k* The prelude to some
   brighter world.   "   *L' Envoi* 39
A sleep by *k'es* undissolved,   "   51
I never felt the *k* of love,   *Sir Galahad* 19
' Yet give one *k* to your mother dear !   *Lady Clare* 49
' Yet here's a *k* for my mother dear,   "   53
To waste his whole heart in one *k*   *Sir L. and Q. G*. 44
Many a sad *k* by day by night renew'd   *Enoch Arden* 161
Never : no father's *k* for me—   "   790
that one *k* Was Leolin's one strong rival   *Aylmer's Field* 556
and ran To greet him with a *k*,   *Lucretius* 7
little maid, That ever crow'd for *k'es*.'   *Princess ii* 280
' Dear as remember'd *k'es* after death,   "   *iv* 54
her mother, shore the tress With *k'es*,   "   *vi* 114
In glance and smile, and clasp and *k*,   *In Mem. lxxxiv* 7
And every *k* of toothed wheels,   "   *cxvii* 11
She took the *k* sedately.   *Maud I xii* 14
made my Maud by that long loving *k*,   "   *xviii* 58
embraces Mixt with *k'es* sweeter sweeter   "   *II iv* 9
had been A clinging *k*—   *Merlin and V*. 106
I am silent then, And ask no *k* : '   "   254
Win ! by this *k* you will :   *Lancelot and E*. 152
Yet rosy-kindled with her brother's *k*—   "   393
we twain Had never kiss'd a *k*, or vow'd a vow.   *Holy Grail* 584
Constraining it with *k'es* close and warm,   *Lover's Tale i* 468
answering lisp'd To *k'es* of the wind,   "   545
Love drew in her breath In that close *k*,   "   817
and, half killing him With *k'es*,   "   *iv* 378
then I minded the fust *k* I gied 'er   *North. Cobbler* 45
An' I says ' I mun gie tha a *k*,'   "   51
I gied 'er a *k*, an' then anoother,   "   52
Sally gied me a *k* ov 'ersen.   "   56
Heer wur a fall fro' a *k* to a kick   "   57
fatal *k*, Born of true life and love,   *Ded. Poem Prin. Alice* 2
k fell chill as a flake of snow on the cheek ;   *The Wreck* 32
Never a *k* so sad, no, not since the coming of man !   *Despair* 60
sowl dead for a *k* of ye, Molly Magee.   *Tomorrow* 40
tha may gie ma a *k*,   *Spinster's S's*. 31
Before a *k* should wake her.   *The Ring* 67
then with my latest *k* Upon them,   "   298
That trembles not to *k'es* of the bee :   *Prog. of Spring* 4
I blind your pretty blue eyes with a *k* !   *Romney's R*. 101
Too early blinded by the *k* of death—   "   103
his *k'es* were red with his crime,   *Bandit's Death* 13
Kiss (verb)   When I would *k* thy hand,   *Madeline* 31
If my lips should dare to *k* Thy taper fingers   "   43
k sweet kisses, and speak sweet words :   *Sea-Fairies* 34
I would *k* them often under the sea, And *k* them again
   till they kiss'd me (repeat)   *The Merman* 15, 34
And *k* away the bitter words From off your rosy
   mouth.   *Rosalind* 50

Kiss (verb) (continued)   You'll *k* me, my own mother,   *May Queen, N. Y.'s E*. 34
I have been to blame.   *K* me, my children.'   *Dora* 162
O *k* him once for me.   *Talking Oak* 240
' O *k* him twice and thrice for me, That have no lips
   to *k*,   "   241
I *k* it twice, I *k* it thrice,   "   253
Go to him : it is thy duty : *k* him :   *Locksley Hall* 52
He stoops—to *k* her—on his knee.   *Day-Dm., Arrival* 30
That I might *k* those eyes awake !   "   *L' Envoi* 28
I *k* the lips I once have kiss'd ;   *Will Water*. 37
I cry to thee To *k* thy Mavors,   *Lucretius* 82
And *k* again with tears !   *Princess ii* 9
He reddens what he *k'es* :   "   *v* 165
k her ; take her hand, she weeps :   "   *vi* 225
K and be friends, like children being chid !   "   289
Stoop down and seem to *k* me ere I die.'   "   *vii* 150
as good to cuddle an' *k* as a lass as 'ant nowt ?   *N. Farmer, N. S.* 24
Trail and twine and clasp and *k*, *K*, *k* ;   *Window, At the Wind*. 4
Drop me a flower, a flower, to *k*, *K*, *k*—   "   11
Farewell, we *k*, and they are gone.   *In Mem., Con*. 92
flush, and bow Lowly, to *k* his hand,   *Gareth and L*. 549
To stoop and *k* the tender little thumb,   *Marr. of Geraint* 395
' Rise, my sweet King, and *k* me on the lips,   *Balin and Balan* 516
tread me down And I will *k* you for it ; '   *Merlin and V*. 229
pearls Ran down the silken thread to *k* each other   "   455
we *k* the child That does the task assign'd,   *Lancelot and E*. 828
he bow'd to *k* the jewell'd throat,   *Last Tournament* 751
let us in, tho' late, to *k* his feet !   *Guinevere* 178
airs of Heaven Should *k* with an unwonted
   gentleness.   *Lover's Tale i* 739
And *k* her on the lips.   She is his no more :   "   *iv* 48
and I go down To *k* the dead.'   "   50
' *K* him,' she said.   ' You gave me life again.   "   172
K him, and then Forgive him,   "   174
an' *k* you before I go.'   *First Quarrel* 46
Didn't you *k* me an' promise ?   "   53
—you'll *k* me before I go ? '   "   80
k her—if you will,' I said—   "   81
You wouldn't *k* me, my lass,   "   86
and he call'd to me ' *K* me ! '   *The Wreck* 104
I stoopt To take and *k* the ring.   *The Ring* 132
nurse is waiting.   *K* me child and go.   "   489
when I let him *k* my brow ;   *Happy* 65
I am happy, happy.   *K* me.   "   107
Kiss'd   dew-impearl'd winds of dawn have *k*,   *Ode to Memory* 14
And kiss them again till they *k* me (repeat)   *The Merman* 16, 35
I would not be *k* by all who would list,   *The Mermaid* 41
And if you *k* her feet a thousand years,   *The form, the form* 13
' His little daughter, whose sweet face He *k*,   *Two Voices* 254
I *k* away before they fell.   *Miller's D*. 152
I *k* his eyelids into rest ;   *The Sisters* 19
girls all *k* Beneath the sacred bush   *The Epic* 2
So the women *k* Each other,   *Dora* 128
clung about The old man's neck, and *k* him many times.   "   164
She turn'd, we closed, we *k*, swore faith,   *Edwin Morris* 114
And found, and *k* the name she found,   *Talking Oak* 159
She *k* me once again.   "   168
could hear the lips that *k* Whispering   *Tithonus* 60
I kiss the lips I once have *k* ;   *Will Water*. 37
He turn'd and *k* her where she stood :   *Lady Clare* 82
And *k* his wonder-stricken little ones ;   *Enoch Arden* 229
and *k* him in his cot.   "   430
as they *k* each other In darkness,   *Aylmer's Field* 555
She look'd so sweet, he *k* her tenderly   *Lucretius* 280
Clasp'd, *k* him, wail'd : he answer'd,   *Princess ii* 5
And *k* again with tears.   "   14
when the king *K* her pale cheek,   "   264
With that she *k* His forehead,   "   311
I *k* it and I read.   ' O brother,   "   *v* 373
here she *k* it : then—' All good go with thee !   "   *vi* 206
I *k* her slender hand,   *Maud I xii* 13
Whom first she *k* on either cheek,   *Marr. of Geraint* 517
claspt and *k* her, and they rode away.   "   825
K the white star upon his noble front,   *Geraint and E*. 757

Kiss'd (*continued*)   he turn'd his face And *k* her climbing,   *Geraint and E.* 761

And *k* her with all pureness, brother-like,   " 884

brow That o'er him hung, he *k* it, moan'd, and spake;   *Balin and Balan* 598

lay she all her length and *k* his feet,   *Merlin and V.* 219

she *k* them, crying, 'Trample me, Dear feet,   " 226

k her, and Sir Lancelot his own hand,   *Lancelot and E.* 389

k the hand to which he gave, The diamond,   " 702

does the task assign'd, he *k* her face.   " 829

And *k* her quiet brows, and saying to her   " 1150

he wellnigh *k* her feet For loyal awe,   " 1172

She *k* me saying, 'Thou art fair, my child,   " 1409

we twain Had never *k* a kiss, or vow'd a vow.   *Holy Grail* 584

Embraced me, and so *k* me the first time,   " 596

There *k*, and parted weeping :   *Guinevere* 125

And Hope *k* Love, and Love drew in her breath   *Lover's Tale* i 125

And *k* her more than once,   " iv 72

' I had sooner be cursed than *k* !'—   *First Quarrel* 83

I *k* my boy in the prison,   *Rizpah* 23

I *k* 'em, I buried 'em all—   " 55

Cold were his brows when we *k* him—   *Def. of Lucknow* 12

And we *k* the fringe of his beard   *V. of Maeldune* 125

And the Motherless Mother *k* it,   *The Wreck* 62

'The heart, the heart ! ' I *k* him,   " 105

we *k*, we embraced, she and I,   *Despair* 53

took and *k* me, and again He *k* me ;   *The Flight* 23

I remember how you *k* the miniature   *Locksley H., Sixty* 12

dreamer stoopt and *k* her marble brow.   " 38

A ring too which you *k*, and I, she said,   *The Ring* 114

You frown'd and yet you *k* them.   *Happy* 75

One *k* his hand, another closed his eyes,   *Death of Œnone* 58

I wept, and I *k* her hands,   *Charity* 38

Kissin'   Imbrashin' an' *k* aich other—   *Tomorrow* 90

Kissing   (*See also* **Kissin'**) *K* the rose she gave me o'er and o'er,   *Gardener's D.* 176

K his vows upon it like a knight.   *Aylmer's Field* 472

And satisfy my soul with *k* her :   *Princess* v 103

our baby lips, *K* one bosom,   *Lover's Tale* i 238

K the war-harden'd hand of the Highlander   *Def. of Lucknow* 102

Kitchen (adj.)   The *k* brewis that was ever supt   *Gareth and L.* 781

Kitchen (s)   out of *k* came The thralls in throng,   " 694

Thou smellest all of *k* as before.'   " 771

Nay—for thou smellest of the *k* still.   " 843

The savour of thy *k* came upon me   " 993

because their hall must also serve For *k*,   *Marr. of Geraint* 391

in the Divil's *k* below.   *Tomorrow* 68

Kitchendom   lent me thee, the flower of *k*,   *Gareth and L.* 1071

Kitchen-grease   thou smellest all of *k-g*.   " 751

Kitchen-knave   Among the scullions and the *k-k's*,   " 154

To serve with scullions and with *k-k's* ;   " 170

among thy *k-k's* A twelvemonth and a day,   " 445

And couch'd at night with grimy *k-k's*.   " 481

'Yea, King, thou knowest thy *k-k* am I,   " 649

And thou hast given me but a *k-k*.'   " 659

beside The field of tourney, murmuring ' *k-k*.'   " 664

Nor shamed to bawl himself a *k-k*.   " 717

O fie upon him—His *k-k*.'   " 742

'Sir *K-k*, I have miss'd the only way   " 787

And in a sort, being Arthur's *k-k*!—   " 838

bawls this frontless *k-k*, 'The quest is mine ; thy *k-k* am I,   " 860

'Friend, whether thou be *k-k*, or not,   " 873

thy much folly hath sent thee here His *k-k* :   " 920

' A *k-k*, and sent in scorn of me :   " 952

The damsel crying, 'Well-stricken, *k-k* ! '   " 970

and say His *k-k* hath sent thee.   " 985

When I was *k-k* among the rest Fierce was the hearth,   " 1009

' Here is a *k-k* from Arthur's hall   " 1036

Thou art the kingliest of all *k-k's*.   " 1158

And tumbled back into the *k-k*,   " 1228

Kitchen-vassalage   Low down thro' villain *k-v*,   " 160

Gareth all for glory underwent The sooty yoke of *k-v* ;   " 479

Kite (bird)   *K* and kestrel, wolf and wolfkin,   *Boädicea* 15

Kite (toy)   Had tost his ball and flown his *k*,   *Aylmer's Field* 84

Kite (toy) (*continued*)   Flung ball, flew *k*, and raced the purple fly,   *Princess* ii 248

coostom flitted awaäy like a *k* wi' a brokken string.   *North. Cobbler* 28

Kith   in the field were Lancelot's *k* and kin,   *Lancelot and E.* 466

drave his *k* and kin, And all the Table Round   " 498

His *k* and kin, not knowing, set upon him ;   " 599

Lancelot's *k* and kin so worship him   *Holy Grail* 651

and all his *k* and kin Clave to him,   *Guinevere* 439

and vaunted our *k* and our kin,   *V. of Maeldune* 47

Kitten   laugh As those that watch a *k* ;   *Merlin and V.* 177

Kittenlike   *K* he roll'd And paw'd about her sandal.   *Princess* iii 181

Kittle (kettle)   ater meä mayhap wi' 'is *k* o' steäm   *N. Farmer, O. S.* 61

Knave   (*See also* **Kitchen-knave**)   neither *k* nor clown Shall hold their orgies   *You might have won* 11

My Shakespeare's curse on clown and *k*   " 27

K's are men, That lute and flute fantastic tenderness,   *Princess* iv 128

The King hath past his time—My scullion *k* !   *Gareth and L.* 710

Begone ! my *k* !—belike and like enow   " 713

Well—I will after my loud *k*,   " 720

overfine To mar stout *k's* with foolish courtesies : '   " 733

But, *k*, anon thou shalt be met with, *k*,   " 779

Setting this *k*, Lord Baron, at my side.   " 854

Lion and stoat have isled together, *k*, In time of flood.   " 893

slay thee unarm'd ; he is not knight but *k*.'   " 922

Thou art not knight but *k*.' Said Gareth, 'Damsel, whether *k* or knight,   " 942

Come, therefore, leave thy lady lightly, *k*. Avoid : for it beseemeth not a *k* To ride with such a lady.'   " 957

K, when I watch'd thee striking on the bridge   " 992

thou art not knight but *k*.'   " 1006

' Parables ? Hear a parable of the *k*.   " 1008

knight or *k*—The *k* that doth these service   " 1015

' Ay, Sir *K* ! Ay, *k*, because thou strikest as a knight, Being but *k*, I hate thee all the more.'   " 1019

being but *k*, I throw thine enemies.'   " 1023

this strong fool whom thou, Sir *K*,   " 1058

O *k*, as noble as any of all the knights—   " 1136

I heard thee call thyself a *k*,—   " 1163

but, being *k*, Hast mazed my wit :   " 1169

' Sir *K*, my knight, a hermit once was here,   " 1196

I gloried in my *k*, Who being still rebuked,   " 1248

Knight, *k*, prince and fool, I hate thee and for ever.'   " 1255

find my goodly *k* Is knight and noble.   " 1291

teeming with liars, and madmen, and *k's*,   *The Dreamer* 9

Knave-knight   ' Well done, *k-k*, well stricken,   *Gareth and L.* 1135

Knaw (know)   Doctors, they *k's* nowt,   *N. Farmer, O. S.* 5

Thaw a *k's* I hallus voäted wi' Squoire   " 15

Bessy Marris's barne ! thaw *k's* she laäid it to meä.   " 21

Do godamoighty *k* what a doing   " 45

Fur they *k's* what I beän to Squoire   " 55

a *k's* naw moor nor a floy ;   " 67

Dosn't thou *k* that a man mun be eäther   *N. S.* 6

I *k's* what maäkes tha sa mad.   " 17

it's them as niver *k's* wheer a meäls to be 'ad.   " 47

I *k's*, as *k's* tha sa well,   *North. Cobbler* 65

Doesn't tha *k* 'er—sa pratty,   " 108

tha dosn *k* what that be ? But I *k's* the law, I does,   *Village Wife* 15

Not es I cares to hear ony harm, but I likes to *k*.   " 22

thou *k's* thebbe naither 'ere nor theer.   " 28

an' booöks, as thou *k's*, beänt nowt.   " 52

I *k's* that mooch o' sheä,   " 108

a cat may looök at a king thou *k's*   *Spinster's S's.* 34

an' I *k's* it be all fur the best.   " 52

an' one o' ye deäd ye *k's* !   " 62

I *k's* I 'ed led tha a quieter life   *Owd Roä* 17

but I *k's* they runs upo' four,—   *Church-warden, etc.* 6

An' it beäts ma to *k* wot she died on,   " 29

ya tell'd 'im to *k* his awn plaäce   " 116

Knaw'd (knew)   An' I niver *k* whot a meän'd   *N. Farmer, O. S.* 19

I *k* a Quaäker feller as often 'as towd ma this :   *N. S.* 19

Fur I *k* naw moor what I did   *North. Cobbler* 38

sa I *k* es 'e 'd coom to be poor ;   *Village Wife* 46

An' 'e niver *k* nowt but booöks,   " 52

An' they *k* what butter wur, an' they *k* what a hegg wur an' all ;   " 116

Knaw'd (**knew**) (*continued*) ye *k* it wur pleasant to 'ear,   *Spinster's S's.* 21
Roä was the dog as *k* when an' wheere   *Owd Roä* 8
fur I noäwaäys *k* 'is intent ;   „ 61
Knee   The trustful infant on the *k* !   *Supp. Confessions* 41
when with brows Propt on thy *k's*,   „ 70
Low on her *k's* herself she cast,   *Mariana in the S.* 27
He sat upon the *k's* of men In days that never come again.   *Two Voices* 323
took with care, and kneeling on one *k*,   *M. d'Arthur* 173
I would wish to see My grandchild on my *k's* before I die :   *Dora* 13
The boy set up betwixt his grandsire's *k's*,   „ 131
with his boy Betwixt his *k's*, his wife upon the tilt,   *Walk. to the Mail* 41
Hail, hidden to the *k's* in fern,   *Talking Oak* 29
Oh, hide thy knotted *k's* in fern,   „ 93
O muffle round thy *k's* with fern,   „ 149
she wander'd round and round These knotted *k's* of mine,   „ 158
shower'd the rippled ringlets to her *k* ;   *Godiva* 47
a flask Between his *k's*, half-drain'd ;   *Day-Dm., Sleep P.* 26
He stoops—to kiss her—on his *k*.   „ 30
My *k's* are bow'd in crypt and shrine :   *Sir Galahad* 18
Cheek by jowl, and *k* by *k*:   *Vision of Sin* 84
God bless him, he shall sit upon my *k's*   *Enoch Arden* 197
Stout, rosy, with his babe across his *k's*;   „ 746
Hers, yet not his, upon the father's *k*,   „ 760
knelt, but that his *k's* Were feeble,   „ 778
And rotatory thumbs on silken *k's*,   *Aylmer's Field* 200
And scoundrel in the supple-sliding *k*.'   *Sea Dreams* 168
And rosy *k's* and supple roundedness,   *Lucretius* 190
held her round the *k's* against his waist,   *Princess ii* 363
That lent my *k* desire to kneel,   „ iii 193
On one *k* Kneeling, I gave it,   „ iv 469
He sees his brood about thy *k*;   „ 582
Set his child upon her *k*—   „ vi 14
Knelt on one *k*,—the child on one,—   „ 91
Trail'd himself up on one *k*:   „ 155
On with toil of heart and *k's* and hands,   *Ode on Well.* 212
one about whose patriarchal *k* Late the little children clung :   „ 236
He stay'd his arms upon his *k*:   *The Victim* 54
Who takes the children on his *k*,   *In Mem. lxvi* 11
At one dear *k* we proffer'd vows,   „ lxxix 13
boys of thine Had babbled ' Uncle' on my *k*;   „ lxxxiv 13
For I that danced her on my *k*,   „ *Con.* 45
I leap from Satan's foot to Peter's *k*—   *Gareth and L.* 538
Gareth, lightly springing from his *k's*,   „ 556
Gareth brought him grovelling on his *k's*,   „ 1124
Sat riveting a helmet on his *k*,   *Marr. of Geraint* 268
on her *k's*, Who knows ? another gift of the high God,   „ 820
A strange *k* rustle thro' her secret reeds,   *Balin and Balan* 354
Writhed toward him, slided up his *k* and sat,   *Merlin and V.* 239
Across her neck and bosom to her *k*,   „ 257
bow'd black *k's* Of homage,   „ 577
she sat, half-falling from his *k's*, Half-nestled   „ 904
Sat on his *k*, stroked his gray face   *Lancelot and E.* 749
holy maid With *k's* of adoration wore the stone,   *Holy Grail* 71
With supplication both of *k's* and tongue :   „ 602
Full sharply smote his *k's*, and smiled,   *Guinevere* 47
took with care, and kneeling on one *k*,   *Pass. of Arthur* 341
an' sattled 'ersen o' my *k*,   *North. Cobbler* 79
My father with a child on either *k*,   *Sisters (E. and E.)* 54
dog that had loved him and fawn'd at his *k*—   *In the Child. Hosp.* 9
dear Lord Jesus with children about his *k's*.)   „ 52
To thee, dead wood, I bow not head nor *k's*.   *Sir J. Oldcastle* 128
plant on shoulder, hand and *k*,   *To E. Fitzgerald* 9
k was prest Against the margin flowers;   *Tiresias* 42
Is feebler than his *k's*;   *Ancient Sage* 135
wid her stick, she was lamed iv a *k*,   *Tomorrow* 71
Rob, coom oop 'ere o' my *k*.   *Spinster's S's.* 11
let Steevie coom oop o' my *k*.   „ 67
swept The dust of earth from her *k*.   *Dead Prophet* 32
Nor ever cared to set you on her *k*,   *The Ring* 386
Knee-deep   seem'd *k-d* in mountain grass,   *Mariana in the S.* 42
FULL *k-d* lies the winter snow,   *D. of the O. Year* 1
Kneel   Good people, you do ill to *k* to me.   *St. S. Stylites* 133

Kneel (*continued*) in your looking you may *k* to God.   *St. S. Stylites* 141
That lent my knee desire to *k*,   *Princess iii* 193
' Why *k* ye there ? What evil have ye wrought ?   *Merlin and V.* 67
Will ye not lie ? not swear, as there ye *k*,   *Last Tournament* 646
Shall I take *him* ? I *k* with *him* ?   *The Flight* 49
Who saw you *k* beside your bier,   *Happy* 54
trust myself forgiven by the God to whom I *k*.   „ 86
I am a trouble to you, Could *k* for your forgiveness.   *Romney's R.* 26
below the dome of azure *K* adoring Him the Timeless   *Akbar's D., Hymn* 8
Kneel'd   A red-cross knight for ever *k*   *L. of Shalott iii* 6
What dame or damsel have ye *k* to last ?   *Last Tournament* 550
Kneeler   I loved you like this *k*,   *Princess iv* 296
Kneeling   Who *k*, with one arm about her king,   *D. of F. Women* 270
took with care, and *k* on one knee,   *M. d'Arthur* 173
On one knee *K*, I gave it,   *Princess iv* 470
Or where the *k* hamlet drains The chalice   *In Mem. x* 15
when they rose, knighted from *k*, some Were pale   *Com. of Arthur* 263
And offer'd you it *k* :   *Merlin and V.* 276
Lancelot *k* utter'd, ' Queen, Lady, my liege,   *Lancelot and E.* 1179
took with care, and *k* on one knee,   *Pass. of Arthur* 341
And *k* there Down in the dreadful dust   *Lover's Tale iv* 66
Knell   every hoof a *k* to my desires,   *Princess iv* 174
a deeper *k* in the heart be knoll'd ;   *Ode on Well.* 59
the silver *k* Of twelve sweet hours that past   *Maud I xviii* 64
that low *k* tolling his lady dead—   *Lover's Tale iv* 33
Knelt   Bow myself down, where thou hast *k*,   *Supp. Confessions* 80
I blest him, as he *k* beside my bed.   *May Queen, Con.* 16
he would have *k*, but that his knees Were feeble,   *Enoch Arden* 778
shaken with her sobs, Melissa *k* ;   *Princess iv* 290
Florian *k*, and ' Come' he whisper'd to her,   „ v 63
K on one knee,—the child on one,—   „ vi 91
he laid before the throne, and *k*, Delivering,   *Gareth and L.* 390
had you cried, or *k*, or pray'd to me,   *Geraint and E.* 844
k In amorous homage—*k*—what else ?   *Balin and Balan* 508
K, and drew from out his night-black hair   „ 511
Cast herself down, *k* to the Queen,   *Merlin and V.* 66
camels *k* Unbidden, and the brutes of mountain back   „ 575
she *k* lowly by the corners of his bed,   *Lancelot and E.* 825
and enter'd, and we *k* in prayer.   *Holy Grail* 460
and spake To Tristram, as he *k* before her,   *Last Tournament* 541
And *k*, and lifted hand and heart and voice   *Columbus* 16
We have *k* in your know-all chapel   *Despair* 94
where of old we *k* in prayer,   *Locksley H., Sixty* 33
She *k*— ' We worship him'—all but wept—   *Dead Prophet* 29
The topmost—a chest there, by which you *k*—   *The Ring* 112
Knew   (*See also* **Knaw'd**) Who *k the seasons when to take Occasion*   *To the Queen* 30
that *k* The beauty and repose of faith,   *Supp Confessions* 74
tho' I *k* not in what time or place,   *Sonnet To* —— 12
prest thy hand, and *k* the press return'd,   *The Bridesmaid* 12
Dreaming, she *k* it was a dream :   *Mariana in the S.* 49
The place he *k* forgetteth him.'   *Two Voices* 264
A shadow on the graves I *k*,   „ 272
And who that *k* him could forget   *Miller's D.* 3
I *k* your taper far away,   „ 109
I *k* you could not look but well ;   „ 150
Dear eyes, since first I *k* them well.   „ 222
I *k* the flowers, I *k* the leaves, I *k* Touch'd ; and I *k* no more."   *D. of F. Women* 73
  „ 116
When she made pause I *k* not for delight ;   „ 169
her who *k* that Love can vanquish Death,   „ 269
I *k* your brother : his mute dust I honour   *To J. S.* 29
I *k* an old wife lean and poor,   *The Goose* 1
' we *k* your gift that way At college :   *The Epic* 24
And almost ere I *k* mine own intent,   *Gardener's D.* 146
Requiring, tho' I *k* it was mine own,   „ 227
I beheld her ere she *k* my heart,   „ 276
You *k* my word was law, and yet you dared   *Dora* 98
from his father's vats, Prime, which I *k*;   *Audley Court* 28
I set the words, and added names I *k*.   „ 61
built When men *k* how to build,   *Edwin Morris* 7
he that *k* the names, Long learned names   „ 16
since I *k* the right And did it ;   *Love and Duty* 29
And see the great Achilles, whom we *k*,   *Ulysses* 64

Knew (*continued*) Whispering I *k* not what of wild and sweet, *Tithonus* 61
and love her, as I *k* her, kind ? *Locksley Hall* 70
Mother-Age (for mine I *k* not) help me　　　　　　　" 185
And she, that *k* not, pass'd: *Godiva* 73
We *k* the merry world was round, *The Voyage* 7
she loved Enoch; tho' she *k* it not, *Enoch Arden* 43
for he *k* the man and valued him,　　　　　　　" 121
He *k* her, as a horseman knows his horse—　　" 136
he had loved her longer than she *k*,　　　　　　" 455
she *k* that she was bound—　　　　　　　　　" 462
simple folk that *k* not their own minds,　　　　" 478
fall beside her path, She *k* not whence ; a whisper on her
　　ear, She *k* not what;　　　　　　　　　" 515
Philip thought he *k*: Such doubts and fears　　" 520
tho' he *k* not wherefore, started up Shuddering,　" 616
and making signs They *k* not what:　　　　　" 641
Seeking a tavern which of old he *k*,　　　　　" 691
' Know him ? ' she said ' I *k* him far away.　　" 846
see me dead, Who hardly *k* me living,　　　　" 889
He *k* the man : the colt would fetch its price ; *The Brook* 149
Sir, if you *k* her in her English days,　　　　" 224
one they *k*—Raw from the nursery— *Aylmer's Field* 263
The girl might be entangled ere she *k*.　　　　" 272
but he had powers, he *k* it:　　　　　　　　" 393
Nor *k* he wherefore he had made the cry ;　　" 589
And all but those who *k* the living God—　　　" 637
Was always with her, whom you also *k*.　　　" 711
Poor souls, and *k* not what they did, *Sea Dreams* 72
I lost it, *k* him less ;　　　　　　　　　　" 230
In her strange dream, she *k* not why,　　　　" 270
I had set my heart on your forgiving him Before you *k*. *Lucretius* 43
that was mine, my dream, I *k* it—　　　　　" —
' I *k* you at the first: tho' you have grown *Princess ii* 305
I never *k* my father, but she says　　　　　　" *iii* 82
Melissa, knowing, saying not she *k*:　　　　　" 148
since I *k* No rock so hard but that a little wave　" 153
I stammer'd that I *k* him—could have wish'd　　" 206
laugh'd with alien lips, And *k* not what they meant ; " *iv* 120
She, question'd if she *k* us men,　　　　　　" 231
And then, demanded if her mother *k*,　　　　" 233
Then came these wolves ; *they k* her :　　　" *iv* 321
We *k* not your ungracious laws,　　　　　　" 399
nor *k* There dwelt an iron nature in the grain :　" *vi* 49
she nor cared Nor *k* it, clamouring on,　　　" 150
I had been wedded wife, I *k* mankind,　　　" 327
Nor *k* what eye was on me, nor the hand That nursed me, " *vii* 53
call her Ida, tho' I *k* her not,　　　　　　　" 96
I saw the forms : I *k* not where I was :　　　" 133
But if you be that Ida whom I *k*,　　　　　" 147
she *k* it, she had fail'd In sweet humility ;　　" 228
O good gray head which all men *k*, *Ode on Well.* 35
He *k* their voices of old.　　　　　　　　　" 63
They *k* the precious things they had to guard : *Third of Feb.* 41
the soldier *k* Some one had blunder'd : *Light Brigade* 11
I *k* right well That Jenny had tript in her time : I *k*,
　　but I would not tell. *Grandmother* 25
who *k* what Jenny has been !　　　　　　　" 35
I started, and spoke I scarce *k* how ;　　　　" 43
I *k* them all as babies,　　　　　　　　　" 88
Nor *k* we well what pleased us most, *The Daisy* 25
Ye never *k* the sacred dust : *In Mem. xxi* 22
That never *k* the summer woods :　　　　　" *xxvii* 4
I know not : one indeed I *k*　　　　　　　" *xcvi* 5
fool Was soften'd, and he *k* not why ;　　　" *cx* 12
can I doubt, who *k* thee keen In intellect,　　" *cxiii* 5
K that the death-white curtain meant *Maud I xiv* 37
O, if she *k* it, To know her beauty　　　　　" *xvi* 18
He *k* not whither he should turn for aid. *Com. of Arthur* 40
Are like to those of Uther whom we *k*.　　　" 72
A red-faced bride who *k* herself so vile, *Gareth and L.* 109
Albeit in mine own heart I *k* him King, 　　" 123
I that *k* him fierce and turbulent Refused her *Marr. of Geraint* 447
And roam the goodly places that she *k*;　　" 646
she *k* That all was bright ;　　　　　　　" 657
Then suddenly she *k* it and rejoiced,　　　　" 687

Knew (*continued*) Enid, all abash'd she knew not
　　why, *Marr. of Geraint* 765
And *k* her sitting sad and solitary. *Geraint and E.* 282
Except he surely *k* my lord was dead.'　　　" 721
And since I *k* this Earl, when I myself Was half　" 794
Because I *k* my deeds were known, I found,　" 858
lightly so return'd, and no man *k*. *Balin and Balan* 42
I *k* thee wrong'd. I brake upon thy rest,　　" 499
Why had ye not the shield I ?　　　　　　　" 601
Merlin, who *k* the range of all their arts, *Merlin and V.* 167
Was also Bard, and *k* the starry heavens ;　" 169
then you drank And *k* no more,　　　　　" 277
I felt as tho' you *k* this cursed charm,　　　" 435
And either slept, nor *k* of other there ;　　　" 738
she that *k* not ev'n his name ? *Lancelot and E.* 29
Sir Lancelot *k* there lived a knight Not far from Camelot, " 401
sally forth In quest of whom he *k* not,　　　" 561
when the King demanded how she *k*,　　　　" 575
' He won.' ' I *k* it,' she said.　　　　　　" 622
they talk'd, Meseem'd, of what they *k* not ;　" 675
k ye what all others know, And whom he loves.'　" 680
there told the King What the King *k*,　　　" 707
she *k* right well What the rough sickness meant, but what
　　this meant She *k* not,　　　　　　　" 887
And Lancelot *k* the little clinking sound ;　　" 983
Lancelot *k* that she was looking at him.　　" 985
I *k* For one of those who eat in Arthur's hall ; *Holy Grail* 23
I *k* That I should light upon the Holy Grail.　" 366
and fell down Before it, and I *k* not why,　　" 407
I *k* the veil had been withdrawn.　　　　　" 522
and I *k* it was the Holy Grail,　　　　　　" 531
As well as ever shepherd *k* his sheep,　　　" 551
' So spake the King : I *k* not all he meant.'　" 920
there were those who *k* him near the King, *Pelleas and E.* 15
and he *k* himself Loved of the King :　　　" 153
Some rough old knight who *k* the wordly way,　" 192
Awaking *k* the sword, and turn'd herself To Gawain : " 489
He *k* not whence or wherefore,　　　　　　" 504
made his beast that better *k* it, swerve　　　" 551
Watch'd her lord pass, and *k* not that she sigh'd. *Last Tournament* 130
Lancelot *k*, had held sometime with pain　　" 178
Who *k* thee swine enow before I came,　　　" 304
He ended : Arthur *k* the voice ;　　　　　" 455
and *k* that thou wert nigh.'　　　　　　　" 520
he *k* the Prince tho' marr'd with dust, *Guinevere* 36
no man *k* from whence he came ;　　　　　" 289
indeed I *k* Of no more subtle master　　　　" 477
merry linnet *k* me, The squirrel *k* me, *Lover's Tale ii* 15
And partly made them—tho' he *k* it not.　　" *iv* 25
He *k* the meaning of the whisper now, Thought that
　　he *k* it.　　　　　　　　　　　　" 43
Stung by his loss had vanish'd, none *k* where.　" 102
I *k* Some sudden vivid pleasure hit him　　　" 177
I *k* a man, not many years ago ;　　　　　" 255
I *k* another, not so long ago,　　　　　　" 262
She never had a sister. I *k* none.　　　　" 326
So I *k* my heart was hard, *First Quarrel* 78
He was devil for aught they *k*, *The Revenge* 108
Evelyn *k* not of my former suit, *Sisters (E. and E.)* 205
She died and she was buried ere we *k*.　　　" 241
or butcher'd for all that we *k*— *Def. of Lucknow* 91
I would I *k* their speech ; *Sir J. Oldcastle* 11
Thou art so well disguised, I *k* thee not.　　" 198
I *k* we should fall on each other, *V. of Maeldune* 104
As if they *k* your diet spares *To E. Fitzgerald* 10
I *k* the twain Would each waste each, *Tiresias* 68
these eyes will find The men I *k*,　　　　　" 176
I *k* not what, when I heard that voice,— *The Wreck* 52
the days went by, but I *k* no more—　　　" 111
O Mother, was not the face that I *k*.　　　" 116
I *k* that hand too well—　　　　　　　　" 145
we *k* that their light was a lie— *Despair* 16
Nature who *k* not that which she bore !　　　" 34
Who *k* no books and no philosophies, *Ancient Sage* 218
she *k* this father well ; *The Flight* 87

N

Know (*continued*) I *k* not: but we sitting, as I said,   *M. d'Arthur, Ep.* 9
K you not Such touches are but embassies of love,   *Gardener's D.* 17
nor did they *k* Who sent it;   *Dora* 53
You *k* there has not been for these five years   „ 65
may he never *k* The troubles I have gone thro' ! '   „ 149
shovell'd up into some bloody trench Where no one *k's*   *Audley Court* 43
Nay, who *k's* ? he's here and there.   *Walk. to the Mail* 26
What *k* we of the secret of a man ?   „ 104
Heaven *k's*—as much within;   *Edwin Morris* 82
scarce can recognise the fields I *k*;   *St. S. Stylites* 40
I *k* not well, For that the evil ones come here,   „ 97
I think you *k* I have some power with Heaven   „ 143
I *k* thy glittering face.   „ 205
yesterday, you *k*, the fair Was holden at the town;   *Talking Oak* 101
James,—you *k* him,—old, but full Of force   *Golden Year* 60
but well I *k* That unto him who works,   „ 72
That hoard, and sleep, and feed, and *k* not me.   *Ulysses* 5
but I *k* my words are wild,   *Locksley Hall* 173
Such hope, I *k* not fear;   *Sir Galahad* 62
my hair Is gray before I *k* it.   *Will Water.* 168
We *k* not what we *k*.   „ 178
I will *k* If there be any faith in man.'   *Lady Clare* 43
We *k* the merry world is round,   *The Voyage* 95
Well I *k*, when I am gone,   *Vision of Sin* 109
For they *k* not what they mean.   „ 126
we *k* the hue Of that cap upon her brows.   „ 141
Madam—if I *k* your sex,   „ 181
The many-headed beast should *k*.'   *You might have won* 20
knew her, as a horseman *k's* his horse—   *Enoch Arden* 136
I'll be back, my girl, before you *k* it.'   „ 193
And yet for all your wisdom well I *k*   „ 211
If he could *k* his babes were running wild   „ 304
end of an avenue, Going we *k* not where: „ 359
I *k* not why—Their voices make me feel so solitary.'   „ 396
I *k* not when it first came there, I *k* that it will out at last.   „ 401
Perhaps you *k* what I would have you *k*—   „ 409
I have loved you longer than you *k*.'   „ 421
If question'd, aught of what he cared to *k*.   „ 654
look on her sweet face again And *k* that she is happy.'   „ 719
Not to tell her, never to let her *k*. (repeat)   „ 786, 798
must I not speak to these ? They *k* me not.   „ 789
' After the Lord has call'd me she shall *k*,   „ 810
' Did you *k* Enoch Arden of this town ?' ' *K* him ?' she said ' I knew him far away.   „ 845
Nevertheless, *k* you that I am he Who married—   „ 858
glory varying to and fro, We *k* not wherefore;   *Aylmer's Field* 74
other, save for Leolin's—Who *k's* ?   „ 141
I *k* not, for he spoke not, only shower'd   „ 213
I *k* not whence at first, Nor of what race,   „ 223
did Sir Aylmer *k* That great pock-pitten fellow   „ 255
' The girl and boy, Sir, *k* their differences !'   „ 274
indeed you *k* That you meant nothing.   „ 313
I *k* her: the worst thought she has Is whiter   „ 362
Nor let them *k* themselves betray'd;   „ 524
when I came To *k* him more, I lost it,   *Sea Dreams* 72
—nor *k's* he what he sees;   *Lucretius* 132
O ye Gods, I *k* you careless,   „ 208
Howbeit I *k* thou surely must be mine   „ 270
none of all our blood should *k* The shadow from the substance,   *Princess i* 8
Myself too had weird seizures, Heaven *k's* what: „ 14
she, you *k*, Who wedded with a nobleman   „ 76
they that *k* such things—I sought but peace;   „ 144
and more We *k* not,—only this: „ 152
O we fell out I *k* not why,   *ii* 4
let us *k* The Princess Ida waited—   „ 20
She answer'd, ' then ye *k* the Prince ?'   „ 49
I *k* the substance when I see it.   „ 413
fly, while yet you may ! My mother *k's*:   *iii* 29
' Why—these—*are*—men :' I shudder'd: ' and you *k* it.'   „ 58
And she *k's* too, And she conceals it.'   „ 59
She calls her plagiarist; I *k* not what: „ 94
At no man's beck, but *k* ourself and thee,   „ 227

Know (*continued*) I *k* the Prince, I prize his truth: *Princess iii* 232
fail so far In high desire, they *k* not,   „ 280
yet we *k* Knowledge is knowledge,   „ 315
' Tears, idle tears, I *k* not what they mean,   *iv* 39
' *K* you no song of your own land,'   „ 84
K you no song, the true growth of your soil,   „ 150
I—you *k* it—I will not boast: „ 353
We did not *k* the real light,   „ 357
I *k* Your faces there in the crowd—   „ 509
' Tut, you *k* them not, the girls.   *v* 151
something may be done—I *k* not what—   „ 228
who *k's* ? we four may build some plan   „ 230
—I myself, What *k* I of these things ?   „ 284
blustering I *k* not what Of insolence and love,   „ 396
and whereas I *k* Your prowess, Arac,   „ 403
name is yoked with children's, *k* herself;   „ 418
And right ascension, Heaven *k's* what;   *vi* 257
This nightmare weight of gratitude, I *k* it;   „ 300
that *k* The woman's cause is man's: *vii* 258
' Alone,' I said, ' from earlier than I *k*,   „ 311
dark gates across the wild That no man *k's*.   „ 363
What *k* we greater than the soul ?   *Ode on Well.* 265
who love best have best the grace to *k*   *W. to Marie Alex.* 28
I *k* for a truth, there's none of them left   *Grandmother* 85
To a sweet little Eden on earth that I *k*,   *The Islet* 14
Well—if it be so, so it is, you *k*;   *Spiteful Letter* 19
I should *k* what God and man is.   *Flow. in cran. wall* 6
Flown to the east or the west, flitted I *k* not where !   *Window, Gone* 1
Somebody *k's* that she'll say ay ! (repeat)   „ *Letter* 8, 15
Thou madest man, he *k's* not why,   *In Mem., Pro.* 10
Our wills are ours, we *k* not how;   „ 15
We have but faith: we cannot *k*;   „ 21
Ye *k* no more than I who wrought   *vi* 17
And beckoning unto those they *k*;   *xvi* 7
But *k's* no more of transient form   „ 7
I *k* that this was Life,—   *xxv* 1
Half-dead to *k* that I shall die.'   *xxxv* 16
My paths are in the fields I *k*,   *xl* 31
When one that loves but *k's* not, reaps A truth from one that loves and *k's*?   *xlii* 11
(he *k's* not whence) A little flash,   *xliv* 7
I shall *k* him when we meet: *xlvii* 8
Behold, we *k* not anything;   *liv* 9
spirit does but mean the breath I *k* no more.'   *lvi* 8
howsoe'er I *k* thee, some Could hardly tell   *lix* 15
Half jealous of she *k's* not what,   *lx* 7
I *k* that in thy place of rest   *lxvii* 2
And then I *k* the mist is drawn   „ 13
Death's twin-brother, *k's* not Death,   *lxviii* 2
Which makes me sad I *k* not why   „ 11
I strive to paint The face I *k*;   *lxx* 3
How *k* I what had need of thee,   *lxxiii* 3
and *k* Thy likeness to the wise below,   *lxxiv* 6
I *k* thee of what force thou art   *lxxix* 3
I *k* transplanted human worth Will bloom to profit,   *lxxxii* 1
Yet none could better *k* than I,   *lxxxv* 37
wear the form by which I *k* Thy spirit   *xci* 5
tell me, doubt is Devil-born. I *k* not: *xcvi* 5
She *k's* not what his greatness is,   *xcvii* 27
She *k's* but matters of the house, And he, he *k's* a thousand things.   „ 31
They *k* me not, but mourn with me.   *xcix* 20
That these are not the bells I *k*.   *civ* 8
Let her *k* her place;   *cxiv* 15
But, crying, *k's* his father near;   *cxxiv* 20
Did he fling himself down ? who *k's* ?   *Maud I i* 9
who *k's* ? we are ashes and dust.   „ 32
I have heard, I *k* not whence,   „ 67
the fiend best *k's* whether woman or man be the worse   „ 75
I *k* it, and smile a hard-set smile,   *iv* 20
Who *k's* the ways of the world,   „ 44
Did I hear in half a doze Long since, I *k* not where ?   *vii* 19
I *k* the way she went Home with her maiden posy,   *xii* 21
And she *k's* it not: O, if she knew it,   *xvi* 18
To *k* her beauty might half undo it.   „ 19

Knowledge (*See also* **Self-knowledge**) In midst of *k*,

dream'd not yet.	*Two Voices* 90
'That men with *k* merely play'd,	„ 172
In *k* of their own supremacy.'	*Œnone* 133
And *K* for its beauty;	*To ——, With Pal. of Art* 8
Beauty, Good, and *K*, are three sisters	„ 10
the *k* of his art Held me above the subject,	*D. of F. Women* 9
And me this *k* bolder made,	*To J. S.* 5
Make *k* circle with the winds;	*Love thou thy land* 17
Certain, if *k* bring the sword, That *k* takes the sword away—	„ 87
flower of *k* changed to fruit Of wisdom.	*Love and Duty* 24
yearning in desire To follow *k* like a sinking star,	*Ulysses* 31
K comes, but wisdom lingers, (repeat)	*Locksley Hall* 141, 143
And newer *k*, drawing nigh,	*Day-Dm., Sleep P.* 51
Like Virtue firm, like *K* fair,	*The Voyage* 68
Without the captain's *k*: hope with me.	*Aylmer's Field* 717
k, so my daughter held, Was all in all:	*Princess i* 135
As arguing love of *k* and of power;	„ *ii* 57
K is now no more a fountain seal'd:	„ 90
We issued gorged with *k*, and I spoke:	„ 388
yet we know *K* is *k*, and this matter hangs:	„ *iii* 316
each Disclaim'd all *k* of us:	„ *iv* 229
K in our own land make her free,	„ *v* 419
sought far less for truth than power In *k*:	„ *vii* 237
A greater than all *k*, beat her down.	„ 238
For *k* is of things we see;	*In Mem., Pro.* 22
Let *k* grow from more to more,	„ 25
power to think And all my *k* of myself;	„ *xvi* 16
All *k* that the sons of flesh Shall gather	„ *lxxxv* 27
Who loves not *K*? Who shall rail Against her beauty?	„ *cxiv* 1
grewest not alone in power And *k*,	„ 27
eye to eye, shall look On *k*;	„ *Con.* 130
behold, Without *k*, without pity,	*Maud II iv* 53
This is my sum of *k*—that my love Grew with myself—	*Lover's Tale i* 164
For *K* is the swallow on the lake	*Ancient Sage* 37
Of *K* fusing class with class,	*Freedom* 17
Without his *k*, from him flits to warn	*Demeter and P.* 89
likeness of thyself Without thy *k*,	„ 93
And utter *k* is but utter love—	*The Ring* 43
While the long day of *k* grows and warms,	*Prog. of Spring* 101

Known (*See also* **Long-known, Well-known**) Or is she *k*

in all the land,	*L. of Shalott i* 26
To perish, wept for, honour'd, *k*,	*Two Voices* 149
In aftertime, this also shall be *k*:	*M. d'Arthur* 35
Like one that never can be wholly *k*,	*Gardener's D.* 206
Much have I seen and *k*;	*Ulysses* 13
having *k* me—to decline On a range of lower feelings	*Locksley Hall* 43
'No more of love; your sex is *k*:	*The Letters* 29
Not only to the market-cross were *k*,	*Enoch Arden* 96
Have we not *k* each other all our lives? (repeat)	„ 306, 420
k Far in a darker isle beyond the line;	„ 604
He must have *k*, himself had *k*:	*Aylmer's Field* 346
He had a man, a quintessence of man,	„ 388
learn a language *k* but smatteringly	„ 433
many too had *k* Edith among the hamlets round,	„ 614
As with the mother he had never *k*,	„ 690
O thou that killest, hadst thou *k*,	„ 738
And whatsoever can be taught and *k*;	*Princess ii* 385
falling on my face was caught and *k*.	„ *iv* 270
I bore up in hope she would be *k*:	„ 320
public use required she should be *k*;	„ 336
and *k* at last (my work) And full of cowardice.	„ 347
when *k*, there grew Another kind of beauty	„ 447
'O brother, you have *k* the pangs we felt,	„ 374
And all the sultry palms of India *k*,	*W. to Marie Alex.* 14
Two dead men have I *k* In courtesy like to thee:	*G. of Swainston* 11
Who makes by force his merit *k*	*In Mem. lxiv* 9
And which, tho' veil'd, was *k* to me,	„ *ciii* 13
And that dear voice, I once have *k*,	„ *cxvi* 11
K and unknown; human, divine;	„ *cxxix* 5
She is singing an air that is *k* to me,	*Maud I v* 3
Everything came to be *k*.	„ *II v* 51

Known (*continued*) And there be made *k* to the stately

Queen,	*Marr. of Geraint* 607
Because I knew my deeds were *k*, I found,	*Geraint and E.* 858
Not willing to be *k*, He left the barren-beaten thoroughfare,	*Lancelot and E.* 160
K as they are, to me they are unknown.'	„ 186
'*K* am I, and of Arthur's hall, and *k*,	„ 188
Robed in red samite, easily to be *k*,	„ 433
love In women, whomsoever I have *k*.	„ 1294
make men worse by making my sin *k*?	„ 1417
never have I *k* the world without,	*Holy Grail* 20
'O brother, had you *k* our mighty hall,	„ 225
'And, brother, had you *k* our hall within,	„ 246
O brother, had you *k* our Camelot,	„ 339
But her thou hast not *k*:	„ 454
he had *k* Scarce any but the women of his isles,	*Pelleas and E.* 87
trampled out his face from being *k*,	*Last Tournament* 470
wish her any huger wrong Than having *k* thee?	„ 597
It surely was my profit had I *k*:	*Guinevere* 658
In aftertime, this also shall be *k*:	*Pass. of Arthur* 203
Never yet Before or after have I *k* the spring	*Lover's Tale i* 314
I died then, I had not *k* the death;	„ 496
love Shall ripen to a proverb, unto all *K*,	„ 759
Not know? with such a secret to be *k*.	„ *iv* 121
all the house had *k* the loves of both;	„ 123
Had I not *k* where Love, at first a fear,	*Sisters (E. and E.)* 170
that hast never *k* the embrace of love,	*Tiresias* 164
But the face I had *k*, O Mother,	*The Wreck* 116
That which knows, And is not *k*, but felt	*Ancient Sage* 86
gain'd a freedom *k* to Europe, *k* to all ;	*Locksley H., Sixty* 129
and flows that can be *k* to you or me.	„ 194
k By those who love thee best.	*Pref. Poem Broth. S.* 7
Makes the might of Britain *k*;	*Open. I. and C. Exhib.* 19
one other whom you have not *k*.	*The Ring* 55
Whose eyes have *k* this globe of ours,	*To Ulysses* 2
Had I but *k* you as I know you now—	*Romney's R.* 90
On those two *k* peaks they stand	*Parnassus* 11
To have seen thee, and heard thee, and *k*.	*Bandit's Death* 4
thousand things are hidden still, And not a hundred *k*.	*Mechanophilus* 24

Know-nothing We had read their *k-n* books   *Despair* 55
For their knowing and *k-n* books   „ 93

Knuckled boy That *k* at the taw :   *Will Water.* 132

Korân I stagger at the *K* and the sword.   *Akbar's Dream* 71

'hast *thou* brought us down a new *K* From heaven ?   „ 116
I heard a mocking laugh 'the new *K* !'   „ 183

Kraken uninvaded sleep The *K* sleepeth :   *The Kraken* 4

Kypris Ay, and this *K* also—did I take That popular name   *Lucretius* 95

L

Laädy (lady) yon *l* a-steppin' along the streeät,   *North. Cobbler* 107
But owd Squire*'s l* es long es she lived   *Village Wife* 53
They maäkes ma a graäter *L*   *Spinster's S's.* 110

Laäid (laid) tha knaws she *l* it to meä.   *N. Farmer, O. S.* 21
Wi' lots o' munny *l* by,   „ *N. S.* 22
Could'n I luvv thy muther by cause o' 'er munny *l* by?   „ 35
an' thy *l* big heggs es tha seeas,   *Village Wife* 118

Laäme (lame) An' Lucy wur *l* o' one leg,   „ 99

Laämed (lamed) I seeäd that our Sally went *l*   *North. Cobbler* 39

Laäne (lane) an' hawmin' about i' the *l*'s,   „ 24
Goä to the *l* at the back,   *Spinster's S's.* 6
by the brokken shed i' the *l* at the back,   „ 37
es I be abroad i' the *l*'s   „ 107

Laäte (late) fur he coom'd last night sa *l*—   *Village Wife* 123
What maäkes 'er sa *l*?   *Spinster's S's.* 5
what ha maäde our Molly sa *l*?   „ 113
I says to him 'Squire, ya're *l*,'   *Owd Roä* 55
Too *l*—but it's all ower now—   „ 116
Too *l*—tha mun git tha to bed,   „ 117

Laäy (lay) says Parson, and *l*'s down 'is 'at,   *North. Cobbler* 89

Laäzy (lazy) Them or thir feythers, tha sees, mun
'a beän a *l* lot, — *N. Farmer, N. S.* 49
Laborious *L* orient ivory sphere in sphere, — *Princess, Pro.* 20
And, lo! the long *l* miles Of Palace; — *Ode Inter. Exhib.* 11
L for her people and her poor— — *Ded. of Idylls* 35
You, the hardy, *l*, Patient children of Albion, — *On Jub. Q. Victoria* 58
Labour (s) (*See also* **Brain-labour**) gaze On the prime
l of thine early days: — *Ode to Memory* 94
So were thy *l* little-worth. — *Two Voices* 171
A *l* working to an end. — " 297
why Should life all *l* be? Let us alone. — *Lotos-Eaters, C. S.* 42
Long *l* unto aged breath, — " 85
the shore Than *l* in the deep mid-ocean, — " 127
And rested from her *l's*. — *The Goose* 16
discerning to fulfil This *l*, — *Ulysses* 36
Confused the chemic *l* of the blood, — *Lucretius* 20
A present, a great *l* of the loom; — *Princess i* 44
A blessing on her *l's* for the world. — " *ii* 479
health, and wind, and rain, And *l*. — " *iv* 280
That all her *l* was but as a block — " *vii* 230
Science, Art, and *L* have outpour'd — *Ode Inter. Exhib.* 5
And reaps the *l* of his hands, — *In Mem. lxiv* 26
thy prosperous *l* fills The lips of men — " *lxxxiv* 25
band Of youthful friends, on mind and art, And *l*, — " *lxxxvii* 23
To *l* and the mattock-harden'd hand, — *Maud I xviii* 34
Or it may be the *l* of his hands, — *Marr. of Geraint* 341
dew of their great *l*, and the blood Of their strong
bodies, — " 568
Her own poor work, her empty *l*, left. — *Lancelot and E.* 991
Or *L*, with a groan and not a voice, — *To the Queen ii* 55
the *l* of fifty that had to be done by five, — *Def. of Lucknow* 77
And rough-ruddy faces Of lowly *l*, — *Merlin and the G.* 60
Labour (verb) No memory *l's* longer from the deep
Gold-mines — *D. of F. Women* 273
Yet since he did but *l* for himself, — *Enoch Arden* 819
would go, *L* for his own Edith, — *Aylmer's Field* 420
and *l* him Beyond his comrade of the hearth, — *Gareth and L.* 484
'Friend, he that *l's* for the sparrow-hawk — *Marr. of Geraint* 271
As one that *l's* with an evil dream, — *Merlin and V.* 101
Labour'd (adj. and part) Or *l* mine undrainable of ore. — *Œnone* 115
Had *l* down within his ample lungs, — *Princess v* 273
vast designs Of his *l* rampart-lines, — *Ode on Well.* 105
A hermit, who had pray'd, *l* and pray'd, — *Lancelot and E.* 403
Had *l* in lifting them out of slime, — *Dead Prophet* 11
Labour'd (verb) *l* thro' His brief prayer-prelude, — *Aylmer's Field* 627
The bosom with long sighs *l*; — *Princess vii* 225
L with him, for he seem'd as one That all in later, — *Gareth and L.* 1128
All that day long *l*, hewing the pines, — *Death of Œnone* 62
Labourer woo'd and wed A *l's* daughter, — *Dora* 40
By sallowy rims, arose the *l's* homes, — *Aylmer's Field* 429
year by year the *l* tills His wonted glebe, — *In Mem. ci* 21
Labouring And onward drags a *l* breast, — " *xv* 18
The giant *l* in his youth; — " *cxviii* 2
The lusty mowers *l* dinnerless, — *Geraint and E.* 251
Arthur came, and *l* up the pass, — *Lancelot and E.* 47
ever *l* had scoop'd himself In the white rock — " 404
Labourless till the *l* day dipt under the West; — *V. of Maeldune* 86
Laburnum (adj.) all the gold from each *l* chain Drop
to the grass. — *To Mary Boyle* 11
Laburnum (s) *L's*, dropping-wells of fire. — *In Mem. lxxxiii* 12
Labyrinth Charm'd him thro' every *l* — *Aylmer's Field* 479
He thrids the *l* of the mind, — *In Mem. xcvii* 21
Labyrinthine following out A league of *l* darkness, — *Demeter and P.* 82
Lace (fabric) The shadow of some piece of pointed *l*, — *Lancelot and E.*1174
books, the miniature, the *l* are hers, — *The Ring* 288
Dresses and *l's* and jewels and never a ring — *Charity* 6
Lace (a cord) burst The *l's* toward her babe; — *Princess vi* 149
And once the *l's* of a helmet crack'd, — *Last Tournament* 164
Lace (verb) holp To *l* us up, till, each, — *Princess i* 202
Laced *See* **Strait-laced**
Lack (s) tinged with wan from *l* of sleep, — *Princess iii* 25
Death-pale, for *l* of gentle maiden's aid. — *Lancelot and E.* 765
'Belike for *l* of wiser company — *Last Tournament* 245
Lack (verb) We *l* not rhymes and reasons, — *Will Water.* 62
We *l* thee by the hearth.' — *Gareth and L.* 754

Lack'd-lackt I have not *lack'd* thy mild reproof, — *My life is full* 4
for, were Sir Lancelot *lackt*, at least — *Gareth and L.* 738
Because it *lack'd* the power of perfect Hope; — *Lover's Tale i* 453
angers of the Gods for evil done And expiation *lack'd* — *Tiresias* 63
Lackest Asks what thou *l*, thought resign'd, — *Two Voices* 98
Lacking given thee a fair face, *L* a tongue?' — *Pelleas and E.* 102
Beast too, as *l* human wit—disgraced, — " 476
Lack-lustre And a *l-l* dead-blue eye, — *A Character* 17
Lackt *See* **Lack'd**
Lactantius Some cited old *L*: — *Columbus* 49
Lad (*See also* **Shepherd-lad**) There's many a bolder *l* 'ill
woo me — *May Queen* 23
the shepherd *l's* on every side 'ill come — " 27
the *l* stretch'd out And babbled for the golden seal, — *Dora* 134
O well for the sailor *l*, That he sings in his boat — *Break, break, etc.* 7
Enoch Arden, a rough sailor's *l* — *Enoch Arden* 14
'Poor *l*, he died at Florence, — *The Brook* 35
Leolin's emissary, A crippled *l*, — *Aylmer's Field* 519
long-limb'd *l* that had a Psyche too; — *Princess ii* 406
Himself would tilt it out along the *l's*: — " *v* 355
Warn't I craäzed fur the lasses mysén when
wur a *l*? — *N. Farmer, N. S.* 18
Mun be a guvness, *l*, or summut, and addle
her bread: — " 26
Breäk me a bit o' the esh for his 'eäd, *l*, — " 53
fair and fine!—Some young *l's* mystery— — *Gareth and L.* 466
an the *l* were noble, he had ask'd For horse and armour: — " 473
Ate with young *l's* his portion by the door, — " 480
take counsel; for this *l* is great And lusty, — " 730
massacring Man, woman, *l* and girl— — " 1341
This *l*, whose lightest word Is mere white truth — *Balin and Balan* 517
had need Of a good stout *l* at his farm — *First Quarrel* 18
poor *l*, an' we parted in tears. — " 20
For he thought—there were other *l's*— — " 38
you haven't done it, my *l*, — " 53
I weänt gaäinsaäy it, my *l*, — *North. Cobbler* 17
not hafe ov a man, my *l*— — " 21
Proud on 'im, like, my *l*, an' I keeäps — " 97
But I moänt, my *l*, and I weänt, — " 102
'*L*, thou mun cut off thy taäil, — *Village Wife* 64
she walkt awaäy wi' a hofficer *l*, — " 97
l will need little more of your care.' — *In the Child." Hosp.* 17
Steevie, my *l*, thou 'ed very nigh been — *Spinster's S's.* 68
But I cleän forgot tha, my *l*, — *Owd Roä* 53
wheere thou was a-liggin, my *l*, — " 87
But sich an obstropulous *l*— — *Churchwarden, etc.* 23
an' 'e beal'd to ya ' *L* coom hout ' — " 28
fur thou was the Parson's *l*. — " 36
Ladder (*See also* **Lether**) lean a *l* on the shaft, — *St. S. Stylites* 216
hurl them to earth from the *l's* — *Def. of Lucknow* 58
shifting *l's* of shadow and light, — *Dead Prophet* 21
A Jacob's *l* falls On greening grass, — *Early Spring* 9
Ladder-of-heaven the *l-o-h* that hangs on a star. — *By an Evolution.* 12
Laddie *See* **Soldier-laddie**
Laden (*See also* **Barge-laden, Lady-laden**) enchanted
stem, *L* with flower and fruit, — *Lotos-Eaters* 29
Knowledge comes, but wisdom lingers, and he bears
a *l* breast, — *Locksley Hall* 143
came the children *l* with their spoil; — *Enoch Arden* 445
Two sets of three *l* with jingling arms, — *Geraint and E.* 188
Boughs on each side, *l* with wholesome shade, — *Lover's Tale i* 230
soft winds, *L* with thistledown and seeds — " *ii* 542
Lading *l* and unlading the tall barks, — *Enoch Arden* 816
The *l* of a single pain, — *In Mem. xxv* 11
Lady (adj.) and *l* friends From neighbour seats: — *Princess, Pro.* 97
In mine own *l* palms I cull'd the spring — *Merlin and V.* 273
Lady (s) (*See also* **Court-lady, Laädy, Liege-lady**) The
sweetest *l* of the time, — *Arabian Nights* 141
Rise from the feast of sorrow, *l*, — *Margaret* 62
In dreaming of my *l's* eyes. — *Kate* 28
knight for ever kneel'd To a *l* in his shield, — *L. of Shalott iii* 7
Before Our *L* murmur'd she; — *Mariana in the S.* 28
bore a *l* from a leaguer'd town; — *D. of F. Women* 47
At length I saw a *l* within call, — " 85
'No marvel, sovereign *l*: in fair field — " 97

Laid (*continued*) faced the spectres of the mind And

l them :	*In Mem. xcvi 16*
l On the hasp of the window,	*Maud I xiv 18*
He *l* a cruel snare in a pit	„ *II v 84*
Bleys *L* magic by, and sat him down,	*Com. of Arthur 156*
Modred *l* his ear beside the doors,	„ 323
Eagle, *l* Almost beyond eye-reach,	*Gareth and L. 44*
Which down he *l* before the throne, and knelt,	„ 390
one stroke *L* him that clove it grovelling	„ 972
Gareth *l* his lance athwart the ford,	„ 1048
Far better were I *l* in the dark earth,	*Marr. of Geraint 97*
With sprigs of summer *l* between the folds,	„ 138
and everywhere Was hammer *l* to hoof,	„ 256
crost the trencher as she *l* it down :	„ 396
On either shining shoulder *l* a hand,	„ 518
bright apparel, which she *l* Flat on the couch,	„ 678
Came one with this and *l* it in my hand,	„ 699
L from her limbs the costly-broider'd gift,	„ 769
one command I *l* upon you, not to speak to me,	*Geraint and E. 78*
raised and *l* him on a litter-bier,	„ 566
l him on it All in the hollow of his shield,	„ 568
l his lance In rest, and made as if to fall	„ 775
And all the penance the Queen *l* upon me	„ 854
leaves *L* their green faces flat against the panes,	*Balin and Balan 344*
And *l* the diamond in his open hand.	*Lancelot and E. 827*
Her father *l* the letter in her hand,	„ 1134
on the black decks *l* her in her bed,	„ 1147
Received at once and *l* aside the gems	„ 1202
when the knights had *l* her comely head	„ 1337
made him hers, and *l* her mind On him,	*Holy Grail 164*
against the chapel door *L* lance, and enter'd,	„ 460
groaning *l* The naked sword athwart their naked throats,	*Pelleas and E. 451*
he *l* His brows upon the drifted leaf	*Last Tournament 405*
and *l* her hands about his feet.	*Guinevere 528*
L widow'd of the power in his eye	*Pass. of Arthur 290*
l his head upon her lap, And loosed the shatter'd casque,	„ 376
l it in a sepulchre of rock Never to rise again.	*Lover's Tale i 683*
graspt the hand she lov'd, And *l* it in her own,	„ 751
winds *L* the long night in silver streaks and bars,	„ *ii 112*
And *l* her in the vault of her own kin.	„ *iv 39*
never to say that I *l* him in holy ground.	*Rizpah 58*
we *l* them on the ballast down below ;	*The Revenge 18*
Where they *l* him by the mast,	„ 98
this ward where the younger children are *l* :	*In the Child. Hosp. 27*
corpse to be *l* in the ground,	*Def. of Lucknow 12*
And she *l* her hand in my own—	„ 80
Or if lip were *l* to lip on the pillows	*Despair 49*
an' *l* himself undher yer feet,	*The Flight 48*
they *l* this body they foun' an the grass	*Tomorrow 38*
Whin we *l* yez, aich by aich,	„ 73
Who *l* thee at Eleusis, dazed and dumb	„ 82
L on her table overnight, was gone ;	*Demeter and P. 6*
forgotten by old Time, *L* on the shelf—	*The Ring 277*
	To Mary Boyle 24

Lain There hath he *l* for ages and will lie

fed on the roses and *l* in the lilies of life.	*The Kraken 11*
Had I *l* for a century dead ;	*Maud I iv 60*
For after I had *l* so many nights,	„ *xxii 72*
Hath *l* for years at rest—and renegades,	*Holy Grail 569*
I had *l* as dead, Mute, blind and motionless	*Last Tournament 94*
Would I had *l* Until the plaited ivy-tress	*Lover's Tale i 606*
and had *l* three days without a pulse :	„ 617
dark body which had *l* Of old in her embrace,	„ *iv 34*
	Death of Œnone 93

Lake (*See also* **Lava-lake**) canal Is rounded to as clear a *l*.

counterchanged The level *l* with diamond-plots	*Arabian Nights 46*
an arm Rose up from out the bosom of the *l*,	„ 85
Came on the shining levels of the *l*.	*M. d'Arthur 30*
Wrought by the lonely maiden of the *L*.	„ 51
on a sudden, lo ! the level *l*,	„ 104
O ME, my pleasant rambles by the *l*, (repeat)	„ 191
By ripply shallows of the lisping *l*,	*Edwin Morris 1, 13*
The friendly mist of morn Clung to the *l*.	„ 98
	„ 108

Lake (*continued*) Her taper glimmer'd in the *l* below :

She moves among my visions of the *l*,	*Edwin Morris 135*
then we crost Between the *l*'s,	„ 144
Deep in the garden *l* withdrawn.	*Golden Year 6*
Dreams over *l* and lawn, and isles and capes—	*Day-Dm., Sleep. P. 12*
round the *l* A little clock-work steamer	*Vision of Sin 11*
The long light shakes across the *l*'s,	*Princess, Pro. 70*
quenching *l* by *l* and tarn by tarn	„ *iv 3*
And slips into the bosom of the *l* :	„ *vii 40*
Had blown the *l* beyond his limit,	„ 187
One tall Agavè above the *l*.	*The Daisy 71*
some dead *l* That holds the shadow of a lark	„ 84
And long by the garden *l* I stood,	*In Mem. xvi 16*
From the *l* to the meadow and on to the wood,	*Maud I xxii 35*
The white lake-blossom fell into the *l*	„ 37
sword That rose from out the bosom of the *l*,	„ 47
like an ever-fleeting wave, The Lady of the *L* stood :	*Com. of Arthur 296*
Bala *l* Fills all the sacred Dee.	*Gareth and L. 216*
the *l* whiten'd and the pinewood roar'd,	*Geraint and E. 929*
you ride with Lancelot of the *L*,'	*Merlin and V. 637*
Than you believe me, Lancelot of the *L*.	*Lancelot and E. 417*
' Most noble lord, Sir Lancelot of the *L*,	„ 1205
My knight, the great Sir Lancelot of the *L*.'	„ 1272
Lancelot, whom the Lady of the *L* Caught	„ 1373
Arthur's vows on the great *l* of fire.	„ 1404
an arm Rose up from out the bosom of the *l*,	*Last Tournament 345*
Came on the shining levels of the *l*.	*Pass. of Arthur 198*
Wrought by the lonely maiden of the *L*.	„ 219
And on a sudden, lo ! the level *l*,	„ 272
Lower down Spreads out a little *l*,	„ 359
ran over The rippling levels of the *l*,	*Lover's Tale i 534*
one lightning-fork Flash'd out the *l* ;	„ *iii 4*
thunder-sketch Of *l* and mountain conquers all the day.	*Sisters (E. and E.) 97*
must fain have torrents, *l*'s, Hills,	„ 100
Knowledge is the swallow on the *l*	„ 221
Gazing at the Lydian laughter of the Garda *L* below	*Ancient Sage 37*
And all ablaze too in the *l* below !	*Frater Ave, etc. 8*
all ablaze too plunging in the *l* Head-foremost—	*The Ring 84*
A light shot upward on them from the *l*.	„ 251
The mist of autumn gather from your *l*,	„ 256
Your wonder of the boiling *l* ;	„ 329
With your own shadow in the placid *l*,	*To Ulysses 40*
	Romney's R. 76

Lake-blossom The white *l-b* fell into the lake — *Maud I xxii 47*

Lakelet brook that feeds this *l* murmur'd ' debt,' — *The Ring 171*

Lamb ' Bring this *l* back into Thy fold,

in the flocks The *l* rejoiceth in the year,	*Supp. Confessions 105*
live thus, in joy and hope As a young *l*,	„ 156
Nor bird would sing, nor *l* would bleat,	„ 169
in the fields all round I hear the bleating of the *l*.	*Mariana in the S. 37*
sweeter is the young *l*'s voice to me	*May Queen, Con. 2*
very whitest *l* in all my fold Loves you :	„ 6
and light is large, and *l*'s are glad	*Aylmer's Field 361*
this lost *l* (she pointed to the child)	*Lucretius 99*
at once the lost *l* at her feet Sent out	*Princess iv 361*
saintly youth, the spotless *l* of Christ,	„ 391
bleat of a *l* in the storm and the darkness	*Merlin and V. 749*
The shepherd brings his adder-bitten *l*,	*In the Child. Hosp. 64*
I kep' mysen meeàk as a *l*,	*Death of Œnone 38*
	Church-warden, etc. 41

Lamb (**Christ**) So shows my soul before the *L*,

I am written in the *L*'s own Book of Life	*St. Agnes' Eve 17*
	Columbus 88

Lame (*See also* **Laäme**) abidest *l* and poor,

Now mate is blind and captain *l*,	*Two Voices 197*
But, blind or *l* or sick or sound,	*The Voyage 91*
THESE *l* hexameters the strong-wing'd music of Homer !	„ 93
I wander, often falling *l*,	*Trans. of Homer 1*
I stretch *l* hands of faith, and grope,	*In Mem. xxiii 6*
Myself would work eye dim, and finger *l*,	„ *lv 17*
' why ? said he, ' for why should I go *l* ?'	*Marr. of Geraint 628*
and half of the cattle went *l*,	*Sisters (E. and E.) 59*
leave the dog too *l* to follow with the cry,	*V. of Maeldune 31*
L and old, and past his time,	*Locksley H., Sixty 226*
L, crooked, reeling, livid, thro' the mist Rose,	„ 227
	Death of Œnone 27

Lame-born as a boy *l-b* beneath a height, — *Balin and Balan 164*

N*

Land (*continued*) And o'er a weary sultry *l*,   *Will* 17
'The Gods are moved against the *l*.'   *The Victim* 6
To spill his blood and heal the *l*:   ,, 44
The *l* is sick, the people diseased,   ,, 45
Thine the *l*'s of lasting summer,   *Boädicea* 43
Ran the *l* with Roman slaughter,   ,, 84
And travell'd men from foreign *l*'s;   *In Mem. x* 6
That thou hadst touch'd the *l* to-day,   ,, *xiv* 2
The violet of his native *l*.   ,, *xviii* 4
Thro' *l*'s where not a leaf was dumb;   ,, *xxiii* 10
We heard them sweep the winter *l*;   ,, *xxx* 10
And thine in undiscover'd *l*'s.   ,, *xl* 32
Whose feet are guided thro' the *l*,   ,, *lxvi* 9
And He that died in Holy *L*   ,, *lxxxiv* 42
And all the framework of the *l*;   ,,*lxxxvii*24
The hard heir strides about their *l*'s,   ,, *xc* 15
That stays him from the native *l*   ,, *xciii* 3
In *l*'s where not a memory strays,   ,, *civ* 10
We live within the stranger's *l*,   ,, *cv* 3
Ring out the darkness of the *l*,   ,, *cvi* 31
that live their lives From *l* to *l* ;   ,, *cxv* 17
They melt like mist, the solid *l*'s,   ,, *cxxiii* 7
better war! loud war by *l* and by sea,   *Maud I i* 47
sapphire-spangled marriage ring of the *l* ?   ,, *iv* 6
To the death, for their native *l*.   ,, *v* 11
riding at set of day Over the dark moor *l*,   ,, *ix* 6
One still strong man in a blatant *l*,   ,, *x* 63
I past him, I was crossing his *l*'s ;   ,, *xiii* 6
From underneath in the darkening *l*—   ,, *II i* 6
High over the shadowy *l*.   ,, 40
Flying along the *l* and the main—   ,, *ii* 38
a *l* that has lost for a little her lust   ,, *III vi* 39
I have felt with my native *l*,   ,, 58
Dear to thy *l* and ours, a Prince indeed,   *Ded. of Idylls* 41
waging war Each upon other, wasted all the *l* ;   *Com. of Arthur* 7
And thus the *l* of Cameliard was waste,   ,, 20
Shall I not lift her from this *l* of beasts Up to my throne,   ,, 80
power on this dark *l* to lighten it,   ,, 93
a slope of *l* that ever grew, Field after field,   ,, 428
and all the *l* from roof and rick,   ,, 433
name of evil savour in the *l*, The Cornish king.   *Gareth and L.* 385
lady of high lineage, of great *l*'s,   ,, 609
and they past to their own *l* ;   *Marr. of Geraint* 45
and we smile, the lords of many *l*'s ;   ,, 353
I know not, but he past to the wild *l*.   ,, 443
a dreadful loss Falls in a far *l*   *Geraint and E.* 497
In a hollow *l*, From which old fires have broken,   ,, 821
pray'd me for my leave To move to your own *l*,   ,, 889
I will weed this *l* before I go.   ,, 907
broke the bandit holds and cleansed the *l*.   ,, 944
and they past to their own *l*.   ,, 955
And brought report of azure *l*'s and fair,   *Balin and Balan* 168
a silver shadow slipt away Thro' the dim *l* ; and   *Merlin and V.* 424
    all day long we rode Thro' the dim *l*
two fair babes, and went to distant *l*'s ;   ,, 707
Moaning and calling out of other *l*'s,   ,, 962
The heathen, who, some say, shall rule the *l*   *Lancelot and E.* 65
and Prince and Lord am I In mine own *l*,   ,, 917
Endow you with broad *l* and territory   ,, 957
Estate them with large *l* and territory   ,, 1322
This, from the blessed *l* of Aromat,   *Holy Grail* 48
and higher than any in all the *l*'s !   ,, 247
in a *l* of sand and thorns, (repeat)   ,, 376, 390
wearying in a *l* of sand and thorns.   ,, 420
his *l* and wealth and state were hers.   ,, 587
thou shalt be as Arthur in our *l*.'   ,, 606
the hind To whom a space of *l* is given to plow.   ,, 907
And she was a great lady in her *l*.   *Pelleas and E.* 98
served with choice from air, *l*, stream, and sea,   ,, 149
So those three days, aimless about the *l*,   ,, 391
l Was freed, and the Queen false,   *Last Tournament* 338
Tintagil, half in sea, and high on *l*,   ,, 505
Clung to the dead earth, and the *l* was still.   *Guinevere* 8
And blackening, swallow'd all the *l*,   ,, 82
'O Lancelot, get thee hence to thine own *l*,   ,, 88

Land (*continued*) Back to his *l* ; but she to Almesbury Fled   *Guinevere* 127
Began to slay the folk, and spoil the *l*.'   ,, 137
the *l* was full of signs And wonders   ,, 232
sent a deep sea-voice thro' all the *l*,   ,, 247
for all the *l* was full of life.   ,, 259
Have everywhere about this *l* of Christ   ,, 431
Clave to him, and abode in his own *l*.   ,, 440
A *l* of old upheaven from the abyss   *Pass. of Arthur* 82
That stood on a dark strait of barren *l*:   ,, 178
All night in a waste *l*, where no one comes,   ,, 370
And loyal to thy *l*, as this to thee—   *To the Queen ii* 2
The voice of Britain, or a sinking *l*,   ,, 24
Betwixt the native *l* of Love and me,   *Lover's Tale i* 25
And all the low dark groves, a *l* of love! A *l* of
    promise, a *l* of memory, A *l* of promise flowing
    with the milk And honey   ,, 332
Each way from verge to verge a Holy *L*,   ,, 337
Was not the *l* as free thro' all her ways   ,, 662
when their faces are forgot in the *l*—   ,, 759
Borne into alien *l*'s and far away.   ,, 802
whole *l* weigh'd him down as Ætna does The Giant
    of Mythology : he would go, Would leave the *l*
    for ever,   *iv* 17
(for in Julian's *l* They never nail a dumb head   ,, 36
So bore her thro' the solitary *l*   ,, 90
And all the *l* was waste and solitary :   ,, 125
Heir of his face and *l*, to Lionel.   ,, 129
myself was then Travelling that *l*,   ,, 133
A dismal hostel in a dismal *l*,   ,, 141
Before he left the *l* for evermore ;   ,, 183
Scatteringly about that lonely *l* of his,   ,, 185
self-exile from a *l* He never would revisit,   ,, 209
question'd if she came From foreign *l*'s,   ,, 331
I leave this *l* for ever.'   ,, 368
He past for ever from his native *l*;   ,, 387
wailing, wailing, the wind over *l*-and sea—   *Rizpah* 1
'Cast awaäy on a disolut *l* wi' a vartical soon !'   *North. Cobbler* 3
sick men from the *l* Very carefully and slow,   *The Revenge* 15
When he leaps from the water to the *l*.   ,, 55
When a wind from the *l*'s they had ruin'd   ,, 112
all the broad *l*'s in your view   *Sisters (E. and E.)* 51
an niver lookt arter the *l*—   *Village Wife* 25
Fur we puts the muck o' the *l*   ,, 32
For 'e warn't not burn to the *l*,   ,, 44
An' 'e digg'd up a loomp i' the *l*   ,, 48
an' 'is gells es belong'd to the *l*   ,, 112
Fresh from the surgery-schools of France and of
    other *l*'s—   *In the Child. Hosp.* 3
from the beach and rioted over the *l*,   *V. of Maeldune* 58
Isle, where the heavens lean low on the *l*,   ,, 83
Hunger of glory gat Hold of the *l*.   *Batt. of Brunanburh* 124
in my wanderings all the *l*'s that lie   *Tiresias* 122
For that sweet mother *l* which gave them birth   ,, 122
Having *l*'s at home and abroad   *The Wreck* 46
warm winds had gently breathed us away from the *l*—   ,, 63
Rich was the rose of sunset there, as we drew to the *l*;   ,, 136
and dogg'd us, and drew me to *l* ?   *Despair* 2
fatal neck Of *l* running out into rock—   ,, 10
all that suffers on *l* or in air or the deep,   ,, 45
I am left alone on the *l*,   ,, 63
down the rocks he went, how loth to quit the *l* !   *The Flight* 38
without a friend, and in a distant *l*.   ,, 100
pools of salt, and plots of *l*—   *Locksley H., Sixty* 207
And shine the level *l*'s,   *Early Spring* 15
Heard by the *l*.   ,, 24
Dominant over sea and *l*.   *Helen's Tower* 2
True leaders of the *l*'s desire !   *Hands all Round* 26
On you will come the curse of all the *l*,   *The Fleet* 3
island-myriads fed from alien *l*'s—   ,, 12
And splendours of the morning *l*,   *Open I. and C. Exhib.* 8
Falls on the threshold of her native *l*,   *Demeter and P.* 3
of their flight To summer *l*'s !   *The Ring* 87
sword that lighten'd back the sun of Holy *l*,   *Happy* 43
your tale of *l*'s I know not,   *To Ulysses* 34
paced his *l* In fear of worse,   *To Mary Boyle* 29

Land (*continued*) I hear a charm of song thro' all
  the *l*.   *Prog. of Spring* 47
  basking in the sultry plains About a *l* of canes;   " 78
  so to the *l*'s Last limit I came—   *Merlin and the G.* 109
Landaulet An open *l* Whirl'd by, which,   *Sisters (E. and E.)* 85
  phantom of the whirling *l* For ever past me by: " 114
Landbird at length The *l*, and the branch   *Columbus* 73
Landed moving up the coast they *l* him,   *Enoch Arden* 665
  we came to the Isle of Shouting, we *l*,   *V. of Maeldune* 27
  When I *l* again, with a tithe of my men,   " 130
  So they row'd, and there we *l*—   *Frater Ave, etc.* 2
Lander Heard by the *l* in a lonely isle,   *Marr. of Geraint* 330
Landing sent a crew that *l* burst away   *Enoch Arden* 634
Landing-place Some *l-p*, to clasp and say, 'Farewell!'   *In Mem. xlvii* 15
Landlike cloud That *l* slept along the deep.   *ciii* 56
Landlord Kindly *l*, boon companion—   *Locksley H., Sixty* 240
Landmark Nor *l* breathes of other days,   *In Mem. civ* 11
  Will see me by the *l* far away,   *Demeter and P.* 124
Landscape Nor these alone, but every *l* fair,   *Palace of Art* 89
  And her the Lord of all the *l* round   *Aylmer's Field* 815
  The eternal *l* of the past;   *In Mem. xlvi* 8
  The *l* winking thro' the heat: " *lxxxix* 16
  from end to end Of all the *l* underneath,   " *c* 2
  l grow Familiar to the stranger's child;   " *ci* 19
  Framing the mighty *l* to the west,   *Lover's Tale i* 406
  a *l* which your eyes Have many a time ranged over   *The Ring* 150
Landscape-lover *L-l*, lord of language   *To Virgil* 5
Landscape-painter He is but a *l-p*,   *L. of Burleigh* 7
  that he Were once more than *l-p*,   " 83
Landskip man and woman, town And *l*,   *Princess iv* 446
  The light retreated, The *l* darken'd,   *Merlin and the G.* 31
  Blurr'd like a *l* in a ruffled pool,—   *Romney's R.* 114
Landslip Like some great *l*, tree by tree,   *Amphion* 51
Landward Or often journeying *l*;   *Enoch Arden* 92
  The latest house to *l*;   " 732
  I found Only the *l* exit of the cave,   *Sea Dreams* 96
  And here on the *l* side, by a red rock, glimmers
  the Hall;   *Maud I iv* 10
Lane (Miriam) *See* **Miriam, Miriam Lane**
Lane (*See also* **By-lane, Laäne, Ocean-lane, Sea-lane**)
  The *l*'s, you know, were white with may,   *Miller's D.* 130
  like a *l* of beams athwart the sea,   *Golden Year* 50
  in the leafy *l*'s behind the down,   *Enoch Arden* 97
  climbing street, the mill, the leafy *l*'s,   " 607
  He led me thro' the short sweet-smelling *l*'s   *The Brook* 122
  Long *l*'s of splendour slanted   *Princess iv* 478
  By glimmering *l*'s and walls of canvas   " *v* 6
  A light-blue *l* of early dawn,   *In Mem. cxix* 7
  Fled down the *l* of access to the King,   *Gareth and L.* 661
  thro' *l*'s of shouting Gareth rode Down the slope street,   " 699
  Where under one long *l* of cloudless air   *Balin and Balan* 461
  up that *l* of flight into the setting sun.   *The Flight* 40
  few *l*'s of elm And whispering oak.   *To Mary Boyle* 67
Language (*See also* **Love-language**) In the *l* where-
  with Spring Letters cowslips   *Adeline* 61
  Such as no *l* may declare.'   *Two Voices* 384
  To learn a *l* known but smatteringly   *Aylmer's Field* 433
  Your *l* proves you still the child.   *Princess ii* 374
  whose *l* rife With rugged maxims hewn from life;   *Ode on Well.* 183
  A use in measured *l* lies;   *In Mem. v* 6
  And with no *l* but a cry.   " *liv* 20
  Writ in a *l* that has long gone by.   *Merlin and V.* 674
  Than *l* grasp the infinite of Love.   *Lover's Tale i* 484
  The music that robes it in *l*   *The Wreck* 24
  thro' that mirage of overheated *l*   *Locksley H., Sixty* 113
  lord of *l* more than he that sang the Works   *To Virgil* 5
  in every *l* I hear spoken, people praise thee.   *Akbar's D., Inscrip.* 1
Langued *L* gules, and tooth'd with grinning savagery.'   *Balin and Balan* 197
Languid (*See also* **Love-languid**) His bow-string
  slacken'd, *l* Love,   *Eleänore* 117
  a *l* fire creeps Thro' my veins   " 130
  The *l* light of your proud eyes   *L. C. V. de Vere* 59
  All round the coast the *l* air did swoon,   *Lotos-Eaters* 5
  tearful glimmer of the *l* dawn On those long,   *D. of F. Women* 74
  O'er both his shoulders drew the *l* hands,   *M. d'Arthur* 174

Languid (*continued*) That, stirr'd with *l* pulses of the oar,   *Gardener's D.* 41
  Suffused them, sitting, lying, *l* shapes,   *Vision of Sin* 12
  and due To *l* limbs and sickness;   *Princess vi* 377
  And myself so *l* and base.   *Maud I v* 18
  Struck me before the *l* fool,   " *II i* 19
  Pipe on her pastoral hillock a *l* note,   " *III vi* 24
  Then gave a *l* hand to each, and lay,   *Lancelot and E.* 1032
  O'er both his shoulders drew the *l* hands,   *Pass. of Arthur* 342
  my blood Crept like marsh drains thro' all my *l*
  limbs;   *Lover's Tale ii* 53
Languish And so would *l* evermore,   *Eleänore* 120
  And *l* for the purple seas.   *You ask me, why, etc.* 4
  thought of which my whole soul *l*'es And faints,   *Lover's Tale i* 267
Languor THOU art not steep'd in golden *l*'s,   *Madeline* 1
  The *l*'s of thy love-deep eyes   *Eleänore* 76
  a *l* came Upon him, gentle sickness,   *Enoch Arden* 823
  thro' her limbs a drooping *l* wept: *Princess vi* 268
  all for *l* and self-pity ran Mine down my face,   " *vii* 139
  and out of *l* leapt a cry;   " 155
Languorous To wile the length from *l* hours,   " *vii* 63
  half plagued by Lancelot's *l* mood,   *Last Tournament* 194
Lank 'Slip-shod waiter, *l* and sour,   *Vision of Sin* 71
Lantern Swung round the lighted *l* of the hall;   *Guinevere* 262
Lap (knees, etc.) Upon my *l* he laid his head: *The Sisters* 17
  Those in whose *l*'s our limbs are nursed,   *To J. S.* 10
  And fairest, laid his head upon her *l*,   *M. d'Arthur* 208
  My beard has grown into my *l*.'   *Day-Dm., Revival* 22
  Too ragged to be fondled on her *l*,   *Aylmer's Field* 686
  creature laid his muzzle on your *l*,   *Princess ii* 272
  Leapt from her session on his *l*,   *Merlin and V.* 844
  And fairest, laid his head upon her *l*,   *Pass. of Arthur* 376
  one soft *l* Pillow'd us both: *Lover's Tale i* 235
  sat each on the *l* of the breeze;   *V. of Maeldune* 38
Lap (drink) Till Robby an' Steevie 'es 'ed their *l*   *Spinster's S's.* 121
Lap (verb) Lest we should *l* him up in cloth of lead,   *Gareth and L.* 430
Lapidoth Like that great dame of *L*   *Princess vi* 32
Lapping And the wild water *l* on the crag.'   *M. d'Arthur* 71
  I heard the water *l* on the crag,   " 116
  And the wild water *l* on the crag.'   *Pass. of Arthur* 239
  I heard the water *l* on the crag,   " 284
Lapse (s) No *l* of moons can canker Love,   *In. Mem. xxvi* 3
  But from my farthest *l*, my latest ebb,   *Lover's Tale i* 90
Lapse (verb) or seem To *l* far back in some confused
  dream   *Sonnet To ——* 3
  kingdoms overset, Or *l* from hand to hand,   *Talking Oak* 258
Lapsed 'But, if I *l* from nobler place,   *Two Voices* 358
  But *l* into so long a pause again   *Aylmer's Field* 630
  the bells *L* into frightful stillness;   *Lover's Tale iii* 30
Lapsing *See* **Down-lapsing**
Lapt (*See also* **Close-lapt, Half-lapt**) earth shall slumber,
  l in universal law.   *Locksley Hall* 130
  l In the arms of leisure,   *Princess iv* 435
  l in wreaths of glowworm light The mellow breaker   *Locksley Hall* 18
Lapwing (*See also* **Pewit**) *l* gets himself another crest;   *Princess iv* 129
Lar lay at wine with *L* and Lucumo   *Lotos-Eaters, C. S.* 106
Larboard Roll'd to starboard, roll'd to *l*,   *The Revenge* 48
  two upon the *l* and two upon the starboard   *In. Mem. xci* 7
Larch When rosy plumelets tuft the *l*,   *In. Mem. xci* 7
  There amid perky *l*'es and pine,   *Maud I. x* 20
Lard *See* **Saäme**
Larded Old boxes, *l* with the steam   *Will Water.* 223
  See thou have not *L* thy last,   *Gareth and L.* 1084
Larder And a whirlwind clear'd the *l*:   *The Goose* 52
Larding these be for the spit, *L* and basting.   *Gareth and L.* 1082
Large brazen urn In order, eastern flowers *l*,   *Arabian Nights* 61
  L dowries doth the raptured eye   *Ode to Memory* 72
  With his *l* calm eyes for the love of me.   *The Mermaid* 27
  grow so full and deep In thy *l* eyes,   *Eleänore* 86
  Thought seems to come and go In thy *l* eyes,   " 97
  L Hesper glitter'd on her tears,   *Mariana in the S.* 90
  From many an inland town and haven *l*,   *Œnone* 117
  A glorious Devil, *l* in heart and brain,   *To ——, With Pal. of Art* 5
  Lit with a low *l* moon.   *Palace of Art* 68
  We saw the *l* white stars rise one by one,   *D. of F. Women* 223

Large (*continued*) And all about the *l* lime feathers low, *Gardener's D.* 47
L range of prospect had the mother sow, *Walk. to the Mail* 93
Wait: my faith is *l* in Time, *Love and Duty* 25
Yearning for the *l* excitement that the coming years would yield, *Locksley Hall* 111
His *l* gray eyes and weather-beaten face *Enoch Arden* 70
Drank the *l* air, and saw, but scarce believed *Sea Dreams* 34
and light is *l*, and lambs are glad *Lucretius* 99
The *l* blows rain'd, as here and everywhere He rode *Princess v* 501
But that *l* grief which these enfold *In. Mem. v* 11
A lord of *l* experience, train To riper growth ,, *xlii* 7
O Love, thy province were not *l*, ,, *xlvi* 13
Nor dare she trust a *l* lay, ,, *xlviii* 13
self-infolds the *l* results Of force that would have forged a name. ,, *lxxiii* 15
Be *l* and lucid round thy brow. ,, *xci* 8
breeze began to tremble o'er The *l* leaves of the sycamore, ,, *xcv* 55
But thrice as *l* as man he bent To greet us. ,, *ciii* 42
L elements in order brought, ,, *cxii* 13
With *l*, divine, and comfortable words, *Com. of Arthur* 268
Would yield him this *l* honour all the more; *Gareth and L.* 397
High nose, a nostril *l* and fine, and hands *L*, fair and fine!— , 465
So *l* mirth lived and Gareth won the quest. ,, 1426
Bribed with *l* promises the men who served *Marr. of Geraint* 453
Then Lancelot lifted his *l* eyes; *Balin and Balan* 277
as I hear It is a fair *l* diamond,— *Lancelot and E.* 228
'A fair *l* diamond,' added plain Sir Torre, ,, 230
So fine a fear in our *l* Lancelot Must needs have moved my laughter: ,, 595
his *l* black eyes Yet larger thro' his leanness, ,, 834
Estate them with *l* land and territory ,, 1322
For her violet eyes look'd, and her bloom A rosy dawn *Pelleas and E.* 71
And but for those *l* eyes, the haunts of scorn, ,, 75
a moon With promise of *l* light on woods and ways. ,, 394
And therefore is my love so *l* for thee, *Last Tournament* 702
that *l* infidel Your Omar; *To E. Fitzgerald* 36
The gain of such *l* life as match'd with ours *Ancient Sage* 237
that *l* phrase of yours ' A Star among the stars.' *Epilogue* 41
Watching her *l* light eyes and gracious looks, *Prog. of Spring* 19
She spoke at *l* of many things, *Miller's D.* 155
Large-brow'd Plato the wise, and *l-b* Verulam, *Palace of Art* 163
Large-moulded that *l-m* man, His visage all agrin *Princess v* 520
Larger like a light that grows *L* and clearer, *Œnone* 109
L than human on the frozen hills. *M. d'Arthur* 183
with a *l* faith appeal'd Than Papist unto Saint. *Talking Oak* 15
L constellations burning, *Locksley Hall* 159
Cock was of a *l* egg Than modern poultry drop, *Will Water.* 121
Ten miles to northward of the narrow port Open'd a *l* haven: *Enoch Arden* 103
Become the master of a *l* craft, ,, 144
then I saw one lovely star *L* and *l*. *Sea Dreams* 94
No *l* feast than under plane or pine *Lucretius* 213
Nor lose the childlike in the *l* mind; *Princess vii* 284
rolling hours With *l* other eyes that ours, *In. Mem. li* 15
And faintly trust the *l* hope. ,, *lv* 20
The *l* heart, the kindlier hand; ,, *cvi* 30
Whereof one seem'd far *l* than her lord, *Geraint and E.* 122
But work as vassal to the *l* love, *Merlin and V.* 491
The text no *l* than the limbs of fleas; ,, 672
Yet *l* thro' his leanness, dwelt upon her, *Lancelot and E.* 835
l than themselves In their own darkness, *Pelleas and E.* 457
Mine is the *l* need, who am not meek, *Last Tournament* 610
For *l* glimpses of that more than man *Tiresias* 21
But days of a *l* light than I ever again shall know— *The Wreck* 78
Charm us, Orator, till the Lion look no *l* than the Cat, Till the Cat thro' that mirage of overheated language loom *L* than the Lion,— *Locksley H., Sixty* 112
Stronger ever born of weaker, lustier body, *l* mind? ,, 164
Has enter'd on the *l* woman-world Of wives *The Ring* 486
I, once half-crazed for *l* light *To Ulysses* 29

Larger (*continued*) *L* and fuller, like the human mind! *Prog. of Spring* 112
But find their limits by that *l* light, *Akbar's Dream* 99
Larger-limb'd and one Is *l-l* than you are, *Geraint and E.* 144
And every man were *l-l* than I, ,, 148
Largess Nor golden *l* of thy praise. *My life is full* 5
With shower'd *l* of delight In dance and song *In. Mem. xxix* 7
Largest Await the last and *l* sense to make *Ancient Sage* 180
Lariano The *L* crept To that fair port *The Daisy* 78
Lari Maxume Virgilian rustic measure Of *L M*, ,, 76
Lark The quick *l's* closest-caroll'd strains, *Rosalind* 10
The *l* could scarce get out his notes *Gardener's D.* 90
quail and pigeon, *l* and leveret lay, *Audley Court* 24
livelier than a *l* She sent her voice *Talking Oak* 122
His spirit flutters like a *l*, *Day-Dm., Arrival* 29
And the *l* drop down at his feet. *Poet's Song* 8
morn by morn the *l* Shot up and shrill'd *Princess vii* 45
merry in heaven, O *l's*, and far away, *Window, Ay* 3
That holds the shadow of a *l* *In Mem. xvi* 9
But ere the *l* hath left the lea ,, *lxviii* 13
The *l* becomes a sightless song. ,, *cxv* 8
Then would he whistle rapid as any *l*, *Gareth and L.* 505
' What knowest thou of birds, *l*, mavis, merle, ,, 1078
lose it, as we lose the *l* in heaven, *Lancelot and E.* 659
Clear as a *l*, high o'er me as a *l*, *Holy Grail* 833
carol of clear-throated *l's* Fill'd all the March of life!— *Lover's Tale i* 283
the morning song of the *l*, *First Quarrel* 33
Theer wur a *l* a-singin' 'is best *North. Cobbler* 46
heaven above it there flicker'd a songless *l*, *V. of Maeldune* 17
hears the *l* within the songless egg, *Ancient Sage* 76
The *l* has past from earth to Heaven *The Flight* 62
Molly Magee kem flyin' acrass me, as light as a *l*, *Tomorrow* 21
An' the *l* fly out o' their flowers ,, 91
Up leaps the *l*, gone wild to welcome *Prog. of Spring* 14
Larkspur The *l* listens, ' I hear, I hear; ' *Maud I xxii* 65
Larn (learn) I reckons I 'annot sa mooch to *l*. *N. Farmer, O. S.* 13
Larn'd (learned) *L* a ma' beä. ,, 13
hignorant village wife as 'ud hev to be *l* her awn plaäce,' *Village Wife* 106
Lash (eyelash) and *l'es* like to rays Of darkness, *Arabian Nights* 136
Lash (whip) Doom'd them to the *l*. *The Captain* 12
Lash (verb) My men shall *l* you from them like a dog; *Aylmer's Field* 325
like a pedant's wand To *l* offence, *Princess i* 28
war's avenging rod Shall *l* all Europe into blood; *To F. D. Maurice* 34
L the maiden into swooning, *Boädicea* 67
l with storm the streaming pane? *In Mem. lxxii* 4
l the treasons of the Table Round.' *Pelleas and E.* 566
The breakers *l* the shores; *Pref. Poem Broth. S.* 2
Lash'd me they *l* and humiliated, (repeat) *Boädicea* 49, 67
L at the wizard as he spake the word, *Com. of Arthur* 388
Gareth *l* so fiercely with his brand *Gareth and L.* 968
But *l* in vain against the harden'd skin, ,, 1143
dishorsed and drawing, *l* at each So often *Marr. of Geraint* 563
And *l* it at the base with slanting stroke, *Merlin and V.* 635
but the man that was *l* to the helm had gone; *The Wreck* 110
Lass ' Siver, I kep 'um, I kep 'um, my *l*, *N. Farmer, O. S.* 23
D'ya moind the waäste, my *l*? ,, 29
Doctor's a 'toättler, *l*, ,, 66
thou's sweet upo' parson's *l*— ,, *N. S.* 11
Warn't I craäzed fur the *l'es* mysén when I wur a lad? ,, 18
as good to cuddle an' kiss as a *l* as 'ant nowt? ,, 24
Parson's *l* 'ant nowt, an she weänt ,, 25
thou can luvv thy *l* an' 'er munny too, ,, 33
thy muther says thou wants to marry the *l*, ,, 37
' What can it matter, my *l*, *First Quarrel* 59
' Wait a little, my *l*, (repeat) ,, 74, 91
You wouldn't kiss me, my *l*, ,, 86
' My *l*, when I cooms to die, *North. Cobbler* 103
' OUSE-KEEPER sent tha my *l*, *Village Wife* 1
Fur 'staäte be i' taäle, my *l*: ,, 15
can tha tell ony harm on 'im *l*?— ,, 19
to be sewer I haätes 'em, my *l*, ,, 31
I laugh'd when the *l'es* 'ud talk o' their Missis's waäys, An' the Missisis talk'd o' the *l'es*.— ,, 57

Last (verb) *(continued)* without help I cannot *l* till morn. *Pass. of Arthur* 194
 Obedient to her second master now; Which will
  not *l*. *Lover's Tale iv* 344
 A crown the Singer hopes may *l*, *Epilogue* 38
 a name may *l* for a thousand years, *Dead Prophet* 59
 As either love, to *l* as long! *Helen's Tower* 8
 'Light—more Light—while Time shall *l*!' *Epit. on Caxton* 1
 Vows that will *l* to the last deathruckle, *Vastness* 26
 world and all within it Will only *l* a minute!' *Voice spake, etc.* 4
 but, *l*, Allowing it, the Prince and Enid
  rode, *Marr. of Geraint* 42
 L in a roky hollow, belling, heard *Last Tournament* 502
 L, as by some one deathbed often wail *Pass. of Arthur* 118
 L we came To what our people call *Lover's Tale i* 373
 and *l*, Framing the mighty landscape to the west, " 405
 And *l* on the forehead Of Arthur the blameless *Merlin and the G.* 72
Laste (least) yer *l* little whishper was sweet as the lilt
 of a bird! *Tomorrow* 33
Lasted Long as the daylight *L*, *Batt. of Brunanburh* 39
Lasting 'She wrought her people *l* good; *To the Queen* 24
 Thine the lands of *l* summer, *Boädicea* 43
Latangor King Brandagoras of *L*, *Com. of Arthur* 114
Latch (*See also* **Sneck**) Unlifted was the clinking *l*; *Mariana* 6
 When merry milkmaids click the *l*, *The Owl i* 8
 The door was off the *l*: they peep'd *Dora* 130
 Her hand dwelt lingeringly on the *l*, *Enoch Arden* 519
Late (*See also* **Laäte**) *l* he learned humility Perforce, *Buonaparte* 13
 I fear it is too *l*, and I shall die.' *M. d'Arthur* 180
 'But I was born too *l*: *Golden Year* 15
 not too *l* to seek a newer world. *Ulysses* 57
 And he for Italy—too *l*—too *l*: *The Brook* 2
 Too ripe, too *l*! they come too *l* for use. *Sea Dreams* 67
 Or soon or *l*, yet out of season, *Lucretius* 271
 'They seek us: out so *l* is out of rules. *Princess iv* 219
 You, likewise, our *l* guests, if so you will, " *v* 229
 They rise, but linger; it is *l*; *In Mem., Con.* 91
 the white rose weeps, 'She is *l*;' *Maud I xxii* 64
 And now of *l* I see him less and less, *Com. of Arthur* 356
 for Prince Geraint, *L* also, *Marr. of Geraint* 165
 '*L*, *l*, Sir Prince,' she said, " 177
 so *l* That I but come like you to see the hunt, " 178
 And came at last, tho' *l*, to Astolat: *Lancelot and E.* 618
 So fierce a gale made havoc here of *l* *Holy Grail* 729
 in herself she moaned 'Too *l*, too *l*!' *Guinevere* 131
 '*L*! so *l*! What hour, I wonder, now?' " 160
 air the nuns had taught her; '*L*, so *l*!' " 163
 L, *l*, so *l*! and dark the night and chill! *L*, *l*, so *l*!
  but we can enter still. 168
 Too *l*, too *l*! ye cannot enter now. (repeat) *Guinevere* 170," 173, 176
 'No light: so *l*! and dark and chill the night! *Guinevere* 174
 O let us in, tho' *l*, to kiss his feet! No, no, too *l*! ye
  cannot enter now.' " 178
 Will tell the King I love him tho' so *l*? " 651
 Still hoping, fearing 'is it yet too *l*?' " 691
 I fear it is too *l*, and I shall die.' *Pass. of Arthur* 348
 'you have not been here of *l*. *Sisters (E. and E.)* 186
 Like would-be guests an hour too *l*, *Tiresias* 198
 As if the *l* and early were but one— *Ancient Sage* 222
 some of *l* would raise a wind To sing thee to thy
  grave, *Freedom* 35
 But then too *l*, too *l*. *The Fleet* 20
 Whole weeks and months, and early and *l*, *The Sisters* 10
 Now, tho' my lamp was lighted *l*, there's One will
  let me in: *May Queen, Con.* 18
 Till mellow Death, like some *l* guest, *Will Water.* 239
 The *l* and early roses from his wall, *Enoch Arden* 339
 all of an evening *l* I climb'd to the top of the garth, *Grandmother* 37
 L, my grandson! half the morning have I paced
  these sandy tracts, *Locksley H., Sixty* 1
 Warless? war will die out *l* then. Will it ever? *l*
  or soon? " 173
 Not to-night in Locksley Hall—to-morrow—you,
  you come so *l*. " 214
 But while my life's *l* eve endures, *To Marq. of Dufferin* 49
 she that came to part them all too *l*, *The Ring* 216

Late-left *L-l* an orphan of the squire, *Miller's D.* 34
Late-lost A *l-l* form that sleep reveals, *In Mem. xiii* 2
Later A *l* but a loftier Annie Lee, *Enoch Arden* 748
 But that was *l*, boyish histories Of battle, *Aylmer's Field* 97
 One of our town, but *l* by an hour *Sea Dreams* 263
 Warring on a *l* day, *Ode on Well.* 102
 For it hangs one moment *l*. *Spiteful Letter* 16
 The primrose of the *l* year, *In Mem. lxxxv* 119
 for he seem'd as one That all in *l*, *Gareth and L.* 1129
 by great mischance He heard but fragments of her
  l words, *Marr. of Geraint* 113
 'Late, late, Sir Prince,' she said,' *l* than we! " 177
 This *l* light of Love have risen in vain, *Prin. Beatrice* 16
 Which, cast in *l* Grecian mould, *To Master of B.* 6
Later-rising and one The *l-r* Sun of spousal Love, *Prin. Beatrice* 6
Late-shown thought Of all my *l-s* prowess *Holy Grail* 362
Latest *As noble till the* l *day!* *To the Queen* 22
 To where the bay runs up its *l* horn. *Audley Court* 11
 my *l* rival brings thee rest. *Locksley Hall* 89
 Not only we, the *l* seed of Time, *Godiva* 5
 Ev'n as she dwelt upon his *l* words, *Enoch Arden* 454
 The *l* house to landward; but behind, " 732
 my *l* breath Was spent in blessing her " 883
 Then of the *l* fox—where started— *Aylmer's Field* 253
 Was it the first beam of my *l* day? *Lucretius* 59
 From growing commerce loose her *l* chain, *Ode Inter. Exhib.* 33
 charms Her secret from the *l* moon?' *In Mem. xxi* 20
 To take her *l* leave of home, " *xl* 6
 To where he breathed his *l* breath, " *xcviii* 5
 That hears the *l* linnet trill, " *c* 10
 Her father's *l* word humm'd in her ear, *Lancelot and E.* 780
 But from my farthest lapse, my *l* ebb, *Lover's Tale i* 90
 There, there, my *l* vision—then the event! *iii* 59
 Days that will glimmer, I fear, thro' life to my *l*
  breath; *The Wreck* 79
 Here we met, our *l* meeting—Amy—sixty years
  ago— *Locksley H., Sixty* 177
 Then I leave thee Lord and Master, *l* Lord of
  Locksley Hall. 282
 And sacred is the *l* word; *To Marq. of Dufferin* 37
 Miriam, breaks her *l* earthly link With me to-day. *The Ring* 47
 then with my *l* kiss Upon them, " 298
 Till earth has roll'd her *l* year— *To Ulysses* 28
Latest-born Nursing the sickly babe, her *l-b*. *Enoch Arden* 150
Latest-left For thou, the *l-l* of all my knights *M. d'Arthur* 124
 For thou, the *l-l* of all my knights, *Pass. of Arthur* 292
Late-writ show'd the *l-w* letters of the king. *Princess i* 175
Latin (adj.) in flagrante—what's the *L* word?— *Walk. to the Mail* 34
 As in the *L* song I learnt at school, *Edwin Morris* 79
 But as a *L* Bible to the crowd; *Sir J. Oldcastle* 31
 And then in Latin to the *L* crowd, " 31
Latin (s) And then in *L* to the Latin crowd, " 31
 speaking clearly in thy native tongue—No *L*— " 134
Latitude hurricane of the *l* on him fell, *Columbus* 138
Latter Until the *l* fire shall heat the deep; *The Kraken* 13
 thou wilt be A *l* Luther, and a soldier-priest *To J. M. K.* 2
 But in these *l* springs I saw *Talking Oak* 75
 Thy *l* days increased with pence Go down among
  the pots: *Will Water.* 219
 And men the flies of *l* spring, *In Mem. l* 10
 (For then was *l* April) and return'd *Com. of Arthur* 451
Lattice (adj.) here and there on *l* edges Lay Or book
  or lute; *Princess ii* 29
Lattice (s) Thro' half-open *l*'s Coming in the scented breeze, *Eleänore* 23
 As by the *l* you reclined, *Day-Dm., Pro.* 5
 if I could follow, and light Upon her *l*, *Princess iv* 100
 thro' a *l* on the soul Looks thy fair face *In Mem. lxx* 15
Lattice-blind Backward the *l-b* she flung, *Mariana in the S.* 87
Latticed (*See also* **Close-latticed**) From the long
  alley's *l* shade Emerged, *Arabian Nights* 112
Laud *L* me not Before my time, *Lover's Tale iv* 242
 I cannot *l* this life, it looks so dark; *To W. H. Brookfield* 12
Laudamus then the great '*L*' rose to heaven. *Columbus* 18
Laugh (s) Thereto she pointed with a *l*, *D. of F. Women* 159
 He laugh'd a *l* of merry scorn: *Lady Clare* 81

Laugh (s) *(continued)* a *l* Ringing like proven golden
    coinage true,   *Aylmer's Field* 181
  a light *l* Broke from Lynette,   *Gareth and L.* 836
  answer'd with a low and chuckling *l*:   *Merlin and V.* 780
  She broke into a little scornful *l*:   *Lancelot and E.* 120
  I heard a mocking *l* ' the new Korân !'   *Akbar's Dream* 183
Laugh (verb) We did so *l* and cry with you,   *D. of the O. Year* 25
  Baby lips will *l* me down: *Locksley Hall* 89
  Spy out my face, and *l* at all your fears.'   *Enoch Arden* 216
  a tale To *l* at—more to *l* at in myself—   *Lucretius* 183
  she *l*'s at you and man: *Princess v* 116
  the neighbours come and *l* and gossip,   *Grandmother* 91
  Why *l* ye ? that ye blew your boast   *Gareth and L.* 1229
  we maidens often *l* When sick at heart,   *Balin and Balan* 497
  l As those that watch a kitten;   *Merlin and V.* 176
  vanish'd by the fairy well That *l*'s at iron—   "   429
  and cry, ' *L*, little well !'   "   431
  l's Saying, his knights are better men   *Lancelot and E.* 313
  The wide world *l*'s at it.   *Last Tournament* 695
  Ye would but *l*, If I should tell you   *Lover's Tale i* 287
  L, for the name at the head of my verse   *To A. Tennyson* 6
  Who jest and *l* so easily and so well.   *Sisters (E. and E.)* 41
  For all that *l*, and all that weep   *Ancient Sage* 187
  to *l* at love in death !   *The Ring* 231
  l's upon thy field as well as mine,   *Akbar's Dream* 106
Laughable They would not make them *l* in all eyes,   *Geraint and E.* 326
Laugh'd over his left shoulder *l* at thee,   *The Bridesmaid* 7
  The still voice *l*. ' I talk,' said he,   *Two Voices* 385
  She spoke and *l*: I shut my sight for fear: *Œnone* 184
  He *l*, and I, tho' sleepy,   *The Epic* 44
  Lightly he *l*, as one that read my thought,   *Gardener's D.* 106
  With heated faces; till he *l* aloud;   *Audley Court* 37
  And I and Edwin *l*;   *Edwin Morris* 93
  About me leap'd and *l* The modish Cupid   *Talking Oak* 66
  l, and swore by Peter and by Paul;   *Godiva* 24
  He *l* a laugh of merry scorn: *Lady Clare* 81
  Blue isles of heaven *l* between,   *Sir L. and Q. G.* 6
  He *l*, and yielded readily to their wish,   *Enoch Arden* 477
  And others *l* at her and Philip too,   "   477
  Caught at and ever miss'd it, and they *l*;   "   752
  Katie *l*, and laughing blush'd, till he *L* also,   *The Brook* 214
  easily forgives it as his own, He *l*;   *Aylmer's Field* 402
  Petulant she spoke, and at herself she *l*;   *Princess, Pro.* 153
  something so mock-solemn, that I *l* And Lilia woke   "   215
  Push'd her flat hand against his face and *l*;   " *ii* 366
  eye To fix and make me hotter, till she *l*;   " *iii* 47
  Stared with great eyes, and *l* with alien lips,   " *iv* 119
  The little seed they *l* at in the dark,   " *vi* 34
  This brother had *l* her down,   *Maud I xix* 60
  He *l* upon his warrior whom he loved   *Com. of Arthur* 125
  He *l* as is his wont, and answer'd me   "   401
  With all good cheer He spake and *l*,   *Gareth and L.* 302
  He *l*; he sprang.   "   537
  when he found the grass within his hands He *l*;   "   1226
  Arthur *l* upon him.   *Balin and Balan* 16
  Thereat she suddenly *l* and shrill,   "   493
  Loud *l* the graceless Mark.   *Merlin and V.* 62
  l the father saying, ' Fie, Sir Churl,   *Lancelot and E.* 200
  and in her heart she *l*,   "   808
  wives, that *l* and scream'd against the gulls,   *Pelleas and E.* 89
  ' Ay, that will I,' she answer'd, and she *l*,   "   132
  Till all her ladies *l* along with her.   "   135
  L, and unbound, and thrust him from the gate.   "   260
  And her knights *L* not, but thrust him bounden out of door.   "   314
  under her black brows a swarthy one *L* shrilly,   *Last Tournament* 217
  Softly *l* Isolt; ' Flatter me not,   "   556
  When Sir Lancelot told This matter to the Queen, at
    first she *l* Lightly,   *Guinevere* 54
  Then *l* again, but faintlier,   "   58
  bones that had *l* and had cried—   *Rizpah* 53
  Sir Richard spoke and he *l*,   *The Revenge* 32
  soldiers look'd down from their decks and *l*,   "   37
  'ow I *l* when the lasses 'ud talk   *Village Wife* 57
  sold This ring to me, then *l* ' the ring is weird.'   *The Ring* 195
  fleshless world of spirits, *l*: A hollow laughter !   "   228

Laugh'd *(continued)* *l* a little and found her two—
     The Ring 337
  and it *l* like a dawn in May.   *Bandit's Death* 20
Laughing *L* all she can;   *Lilian* 5
  L and clapping their hands between,   *The Merman* 29
  Francis, *l*, clapt his hand On Everard's shoulder,   *The Epic* 21
  Juliet answer'd *l*, ' Go and see The Gardener's daughter: *Gardener's D.* 29
  Katie laugh'd, and *l* blush'd;   *The Brook* 214
  Then *l* ' what, if these weird seizures   *Princess i* 82
  l at things that have long gone by.   *Grandmother* 92
  Gareth *l*, ' An' he fight for this,   *Gareth and L.* 1345
  He answer'd *l*, ' Nay, not like to me.   *Merlin and V.* 618
  Whereat Lavaine said, *l*, ' Lily maid,   *Lancelot and E.* 385
  And parted, *l* in his courtly heart.   "   1176
  And *l* back the light,   *Ancient Sage* 168
  Then Tristram *l* caught the harp,   *Last Tournament* 730
  l sober fact to scorn,   *Locksley H., Sixty* 109
  whom the *l* shepherd bound with flowers ;   *To Virgil* 15
Laughingly till they kiss'd me *L*, *l*;   *The Merman* 17, 36
Laughing-stock drunkard's football, *l-s*'s of Time,   *Princess iv* 517
Laughter Till the lightning *l*'s dimple   *Lilian* 16
  crimson-threaded lips Silver-treble *l* trilleth: "   24
  whose joyful scorn, Edged with sharp *l*,   *Clear-headed friend* 2
  Her rapid *l*'s wild and shrill, As *l*'s of the woodpecker   *Kate* 3
  With her *l* or her sighs,   *Miller's D.* 184
  Lest their shrill happy *l* come to me   *Œnone* 258
  from out that mood *L* at her self-scorn.   *Palace of Art* 232
  light Of *l* dimpled in his swarthy cheek ;   *Edwin Morris* 61
  Marrow of mirth and *l*;   *Will Water.* 214
  Save, as his Annie's, were a *l* to him.   *Enoch Arden* 184
  And *l* to their lords: *Aylmer's Field* 498
  Will there be children's *l* in their hall   "   787
  Dislink'd with shrieks and *l*:   *Princess, Pro.* 70
  a sight to shake The midriff of despair with *l*,   " *i* 201
  and back again With *l*:   " *ii* 462
  And secret *l* tickled all my soul.   " *iv* 267
  with grim *l* thrust us out at gates.   "   556
  slain with *l* roll'd the gilded Squire.   " *v* 22
  spied his mother and began A blind and babbling *l*,   " *vi* 137
  Waking *l* in indolent reviewers.   *Hendecasyllabics* 8
  The delight of happy *l*,   *Maud II iv* 29
  Gareth answer'd them With *l*,   *Gareth and L.* 209
  He laugh'd; the *l* jarr'd upon Lynette: "   1226
  And crown'd with fleshless *l*—   "   1383
  he moved the Prince To *l* and his comrades to
    applause.   *Geraint and E.* 296
  It made the *l* of an afternoon   *Merlin and V.* 163
  some light jest among them rose With *l*   *Lancelot and E.* 179
  Must needs have moved my *l*: now remains But
    little cause for *l*:   "   596
  And *l* at the limit of the wood,   *Pelleas and E.* 49
  Is all the *l* gone dead out of thee?—   *Last Tournament* 300
  With shrieks and ringing *l* on the sand   *Lover's Tale iii* 32
  Crazy with *l* and babble and earth's new wine,   *To A. Tennyson* 2
  one quick peal Of *l* drew me thro' the glimmering
    glades   *Sisters (E. and E.)* 116
  Breaking with *l* from the dark ;   *De Prof., Two G.* 18
  echo helpless *l* to your jest !   *To W. H. Brookfield* 5
  moving on With easy *l* find the gate   *Tiresias* 200
  As *l* over wine, And vain the *l* as the tears,   *Ancient Sage* 184
  ' L, wine and *l* friends !   "   195
  Gazing at the Lydian *l* of the Garda Lake   *Frater Ave, etc.* 8
  fleshless world of spirits, laugh'd: A hollow *l* !   *The Ring* 229
  There is *l* down in Hell   *Forlorn* 15
  there past a crowd With shameless *l*,   *St. Telemachus* 39
Laughter-stirr'd his deep eye *l-s* With merriment   *Arabian Nights* 150
Launcelot Sir *L* and Queen Guinevere Rode   *Sir L. and Q. G.* 20
Launch *L* your vessel, And crowd your canvas,   *Merlin and the G.* 126
Laureate Hear thy myriad *l*'s hail thee monarch   *Akbar's D., Hymn* 6
Laurel There in a silent shade of *l* brown   *Alexander* 9
  The peacock in his *l* bower,   *Day-Dm., Sleep. P.* 15
  This l greener from the brows   *To the Queen* 7
  The twinkling *l* scatter'd silver lights.   *Gardener's D.* 118
  she comes and dips Her *l* in the wine,   *Will Water.* 18
  gain'd a *l* for your brow Of sounder leaf   *You might have won* 3
  And cavern-shadowing *l*'s, hide !   *Lucretius* 205

Lawless (adj.) (continued) Thou loather of the *l* crown As of

the *l* crowd ;   *Freedom* 31
Lawless (s) Nothing of the *l*, of the Despot,   *On Jub. Q. Victoria* 12
Lawn (grassy level) (*See also* **Garden-lawn, Orchard-lawns, Terrace-lawn**) And many a shadow-chequer'd *l*   *Arabian Nights* 102
It springs on a level of bowery *l*,   *Poet's Mind* 31
Or only look across the *l*,   *Margaret* 65
The *l*'s and meadow-ledges midway down   *Œnone* 6
Aloft the mountain *l* was dewy-dark,   ,, 48
In each a squared *l*,   *Palace of Art* 22
Leading from *l* to *l*.   *D. of F. Women* 76
A noise of some one coming thro' the *l*,   ,, 178
broad sunshine laves The *l* by some cathedral,   ,, 190
the range of *l* and park :   *The Blackbird* 6
Flow, softly flow, by *l* and lea,   *A Farewell* 5
Dreams over lake and *l*,   *Vision of Sin* 11
girt the region with high cliff and *l* :   ,, 47
l's And winding glades high up like ways to Heaven,   *Enoch Arden* 572
I steal by *l*'s and grassy plots,   *The Brook* 170
thro' the bright *l*'s to his brother's ran,   *Aylmer's Field* 341
princely halls, and farms, and flowing *l*'s,   ,, 654
Gave his broad *l*'s until the set of sun   *Princess, Pro.* 2
The sward was trim as any garden *l* :   ,, 95
others lay about the *l*'s, Of the older sort,   ,, ii 462
fields Are lovely, lovelier not the Elysian *l*'s,   ,, iii 342
rosy heights came out above the *l*'s.   ,, 365
rode we with the old king across the *l*'s   ,, v 236
Myriads of rivulets hurrying thro' the *l*,   ,, vii 220
the *l* as yet Is hoar with rime, or spongy-wet ;   *To F. D. Maurice* 41
voice and the Peak Far over summit and *l*,   *Voice and the P.* 2
counterchange the floor Of this flat *l*   *In Mem. lxxxix* 2
lay and read The Tuscan poets on the *l* :   ,, 24
By night we linger'd on the *l*,   ,, xcv 1
Now dance the lights on *l* and lea,   ,, cxv 9
And lilies fair on a *l* ;   *Maud I xiv* 2
But the rivulet on from the *l*   ,, 29
saw deep *l*'s, and then a brook,   *Holy Grail* 380
apples by the brook Fallen, and on the *l*'s.   ,, 385
So on for all that day from *l* to *l*   *Last Tournament* 373
the dews, the fern, the founts, the *l*'s ;   ,, 727
dimly-glimmering *l*'s Of that Elysium,   *Demeter and P.* 150
Lawn (linen) Slow-dropping veils of thinnest *l*,   *Lotos-Eaters* 11
broad earth-sweeping pall of whitest *l*,   *Lover's Tale ii* 78
Lawrence (Sir Henry) our *L* the best of the brave :   *Def. of Lucknow* 11
Lawrence Aylmer (*See also* **Aylmer**) So *L A*, seated on a stile In the long hedge,   *The Brook* 197
Lawyer was a God, and is a *l*'s clerk,   *Edwin Morris* 102
Vext with *l*'s and harass'd with debt :   *Maud I xix* 22
I came into court to the Judge and the *l*'s.   *Rizpah* 33
But not the black heart of the *l* who kill'd him   ,, 40
I stole them all from the *l*'s—   ,, 52
For the *l* is born but to murder—   ,, 64
I knaws the law, I does, for the *l* ha towd it me.   *Village Wife* 16
the *l* he towd it me That 'is taäil were soä tied up   ,, 29
Lay (s) woke her with a *l* from fairy land.   *Caress'd or chidden* 8
So, Lady Flora, take my *l*,   *Day-Dm., Moral* 1
So, Lady Flora, take my *l*,   ,, *Ep.* 1
In *l*'s that will outlast thy Deity ?   *Lucretius* 72
If these brief *l*'s, of Sorrow born,   *In Mem. xlviii* 1
Nor dare she trust a larger *l*,   ,, 13
And lo, thy deepest *l*'s are dumb   ,, *lxxvi* 7
Demand not thou a marriage *l* ;   ,, *Con.* 2
Has link'd our names together in his *l*,   *Lancelot and E.* 112
this *l*—Which Pelleas had heard sung before the Queen,   *Pelleas and E.* 396
many a mystic *l* of life and death   *Guinevere* 281
Adviser of the nine-years-ponder'd *l*,   *Poets and their B.* 6
Lay (verb) (*See also* **Laäy**) thick-moted sunbeam *l* Athwart the chambers,   *Mariana* 78
An open scroll, Before him *l* :   *The Poet* 9
They should have stabb'd me where I *l*, (repeat)   *Oriana* 55, 60
She loosed the chain, and down she *l* ;   *L. of Shalott* 16
and *l* Upon the freshly-flower'd slope.   *Miller's D.* 111
To win his love I *l* in wait :   *The Sisters* 11

Lay (verb) (continued) *L*, dozing in the vale of Avalon,   *Palace of Art* 107
L there exiled from eternal God,   ,, 263
you may *l* me low i' the mould and think no more of me.   *May Queen, N. Y's. E.* 4
high masts flicker'd as they *l* afloat ;   *D. of F. Women* 113
And on thy heart a finger *l*'s,   *On a Mourner* 11
On one side *l* the Ocean, and on one *L* a great water,   *M. d'Arthur* 11
Where *l* the mighty bones of ancient men,   ,, 47
So like a shatter'd column *l* the King,   ,, 221
Where quail and pigeon, lark and leveret *l*,   *Audley Court* 24
L great with pig, wallowing in sun and mud.   *Walk. to the Mail* 88
I *l* Pent in a roofless close of ragged stones ;   *St. S. Stylites* 73
this is none of mine ; *L* it not to me.   ,, 124
On the coals I *l*, A vessel full of sin :   ,, 169
And at my feet she *l*.   *Talking Oak* 208
but a moment *l* Where fairer fruit of Love   ,, 250
I *l*, Mouth, forehead, eyelids,   *Tithonus* 57
The dewy sister-eyelids *l*.   *Day-Dm., Pro.* 4
On the mossy stone, as I *l*,   *Edward Gray* 26
And *l*'s it thrice upon my lips,   *Will Water.* 19
And *l* your hand upon my head,   *Lady Clare* 55
Leapt up from where she *l*,   ,, 62
In their blood, as they *l* dying,   *The Captain* 55
L betwixt his home and hers ;   *L. of Burleigh* 28
And while he *l* recovering there,   *Enoch Arden* 108
Enoch *l* long-pondering on his plans ;   ,, 133
L lingering out a five-years' death-in-life.   ,, 565
Stay'd by this isle, not knowing where she *l* :   ,, 630
fail'd a little, And he *l* tranced ;   ,, 793
L hidden as the music of the moon   *Aylmer's Field* 102
L deeper than to wear it as his ring—   ,, 122
silenced by that silence *l* the wife,   *Sea Dreams* 46
I *l*,' said he, ' And mused upon it,   ,, 107
right across its track there *l*,   ,, 126
belt, it seem'd, of luminous vapour, *l*,   ,, 209
l's hast and filthy hands upon my will,   *Lucretius* 219
on the pavement *l* Carved stones of the Abbey-ruin   *Princess, Pro.* 13
about it *l* the guests, And there we join'd them :   ,, 106
patting Lilia's head (she *l* Beside him)   ,, 125
there on lattice edges *l* Or book or lute ;   ,, ii 29
spoke of those That *l* at wine with Lar and Lucumo ;   ,, 129
others *l* about the lawns,   ,, 462
court that *l* three parts In shadow,   ,, iii 20
L out the viands.'   ,, 347
And *l* me on her bosom, and her heart   ,, iv 103
on the purple footcloth, *l* The lily-shining child ;   ,, 286
glove upon the tomb *L* by her like a model   ,, 597
All her fair length upon the ground she *l* :   ,, v 59
And *l* my little blossom at my feet,   ,, 100
As in some mystic middle state I *l*,   ,, vi 18
l's on every side A thousand arms and rushes   ,, 36
To where her wounded brethren *l* ;   ,, 90
L like a new-fall'n meteor on the grass,   ,, 135
but he that *l* Beside us, Cyril,   ,, 153
or if you scorn to *l* it, Yourself,   ,, 183
those two hosts that *l* beside the walls,   ,, 383
L silent in the muffled cage of life :   ,, vii 47
l Quite sunder'd from the moving Universe,   ,, 51
I *l* still, and with me oft she sat :   ,, 91
I could no more, but *l* like one in trance,   ,, 151
while with shut eyes I *l* Listening ;   ,, 223
L thy sweet hands in mine and trust in me.'   ,, 366
Where shall we *l* the man whom we deplore ?   *Ode on Well.* 8
L your earthly fancies down,   ,, 279
There *l* the sweet little body   *Grandmother* 62
Sun-smitten Alps before me *l*.   *The Daisy* 62
in his coffin the Prince of courtesy *l*.   *G. of Swainston* 10
And dead men *l* all over the way,   *The Victim* 21
there at tables of ebony *l*,   *Boädicea* 61
Till growing winters *l* me low ;   *In Mem. xl* 30
That *l* their eggs, and sting and sing   ,, *l* 11
l and read The Tuscan poets on the lawn.   ,, *lxxxix* 23
little shallop *l* At anchor in the flood below ;   ,, *ciii* 19
l Sick once, with a fear of worse,   *Maud I xix* 72
Was it he *l* there with a fading eye ?   ,, *II i* 29

Lay (verb) (*continued*)   When he *l* dying there,   *Maud II ii* 67
Then to strike him and him *l* low,   " *v* 90
Shrunk like a fairy changeling *l* the mage;   *Com. of Arthur* 363
I could climb and *l* my hand upon it,   *Gareth and L.* 50
l him low and slay him not, But bring him here,   " 379
fortunes all as fair as hers who *l* Among the ashes   " 903
Half fell to right and half to left and *l*.   " 1405
his princedom *l* Close on the borders   *Marr. of Geraint* 33
Guinevere *l* late into the morn,   " 157
L's claim to for the lady at his side,   " 487
Let *me l* lance in rest, O noble host,   " 496
but *l* Contemplating her own unworthiness;   " 532
l With her fair head in the dim-yellow light,   " 599
And tho' she *l* dark in the pool,   " 657
Enid listen'd brightening as she *l*;   " 733
down his enemy roll'd, And there *l* still;   *Geraint and E.* 161
So *l* the man transfixt.   " 166
fears To lose his bone, and *l*'s his foot upon it,   " 562
And cast him and the bier in which he *l*   " 572
yet *l* still, and feign'd himself as dead,   " 588
(It *l* beside him in the hollow shield),   " 726
And here I *l* this penance on myself,   " 739
the huge Earl *l* slain within his hall.   " 806
But while Geraint *l* healing of his hurt,   " 931
when I am gone Who used to *l* them!   *Balin and Balan* 141
thou couldst *l* the Devil of these woods If arm of flesh could *l* him.'   " 298
To *l* that devil would *l* the Devil in me.'   " 301
Crawl'd slowly with slow moans to where he *l*,   " 592
At Merlin's feet the wily Vivien *l*.   *Merlin and V.* 5
While all the heathen *l* at Arthur's feet,   " 144
and he *l* as dead And lost to life   " 213
l she all her length and kiss'd his feet,   " 219
l Foot-gilt with all the blossom-dust   " 281
that I *l* And felt them slowly ebbing,   " 436
she *l* as dead, And lost all use of life;   " 644
there *l* the reckling, one But one hour old!   " 709
And in the hollow oak he *l* as dead,   " 969
l till all their bones were bleach'd,   *Lancelot and E.* 43
L like a rainbow fall'n upon the grass,   " 431
brought his horse to Lancelot where he *l*.   " 493
And ever-tremulous aspen-trees, he *l*.   " 524
arms and mighty hands *L* naked on the wolfskin,   " 813
l, Speaking a still good-morrow with her eyes.   " 1032
l the letter in my hand A little ere I die,   " 1113
In all I have of rich, and *l* me on it.   " 1120
Pall'd all its length in blackest samite, *l*.   " 1142
But fast asleep, and *l* as tho' she smiled.   " 1161
past the barge Whereon the lily maid of Astolat *L* smiling, " 1243
from his face who near To hers which *l* so silent,   " 1286
great banquet *l* along the hall.   *Holy Grail* 180
power To *l* the sudden heads of violence flat,   " 310
as he *l* At random looking over the brown earth   *Pelleas and E.* 31
Froz'n by sweet sleep, four of her damsels *l*:   " 433
she *l*, The circlet of the tourney round her brows,   " 453
so *l* Till shaken by a dream,   " 516
like a subtle beast *L* couchant with his eyes   *Guinevere* 11
I made them *l* their hands in mine and swear   " 467
On one side *l* the Ocean, and on one *L* a great water,   *Pass. of Arthur* 179
Where *l* the mighty bones of ancient men,   " 215
So like a shatter'd column *l* the King;   " 389
a common light of eyes Was on us as we *l*:   *Lover's Tale i* 237
maiden empire of her mind, *L* like a map before me,   " 590
Mute, blind and motionless as them I *l*;   " 607
and two upon the starboard *l*,   *The Revenge* 48
Spanish fleet with broken sides *l* round us all in a ring;   " 71
And the lion there *l* dying,   " 96
I *l* at leisure, watching overhead   *Sisters (E. and E.)* 83
she *l* with a flower in one hand   *In the Child. Hosp.* 39
I *l* At thy pale feet this ballad   *Ded. Poem Prin. Alice* 19
To *l* me in some shrine of this old Spain,   *Columbus* 207
melon *l* like a little sun on the tawny sand,   *V. of Maeldune* 57
There *l* many a man Marr'd by the javelin,   *Batt. of Brunanburh* 31
and lifts, and *l*'s the deep,   *Tiresias* 22

Lay (verb) (*continued*)   five-fold thy term Of years, I *l*;   *Tiresias* 33
l like the dead by the dead   *The Wreck* 112
and there in the boat I *l*   " 125
l thine uphill shoulder to the wheel,   *Ancient Sage* 279
all night so calm you *l*,   *The Flight* 9
Dumb on the winter heath he *l*.   *Dead Prophet* 13
And *l* on that funereal boat,   *To Marq. of Dufferin* 34
The fatal ring *l* near her;   *The Ring* 450
Who yearn to *l* my loving head upon your leprous breast.   *Happy* 26
L your Plato for one minute down,   *To Master of B.* 4
when shall we *l* The Ghost of the Brute   *The Dawn* 22
Layer   spread his dark-green *l*'s of shade.   *Gardener's D.* 116
Layest   O moon, that *l* all to sleep again,   *Gareth and L.* 1061
Lay-hearth   one *l-h* would give you welcome   *To F. D. Maurice* 11
Laying   *l* down an unctuous lease Of life,   *Will Water.* 243
Autumn *l* here and there A fiery finger   *In Mem. xcix* 1
l his trams in a poison'd gloom Wrought,   *Maud I x* 8
it fell Like flaws in summer *l* lusty corn: *Marr. of Geraint* 764
l there thy golden head,   *Guinevere* 535
And him the last; and *l* flowers,   *Tiresias* 212
Lay-men   *l-m*, lay-women, who will come,   *Sir J. Oldcastle* 117
Lay-women   lay-men, *l-w*, who will come,   " 117
Lazar   And him, the *l*, in his rags: *In Mem. cxxvii* 10
Shaking his hands, as from a *l*'s rags   *Pelleas and E.* 317
Lazarus   When *L* left his charnel-cave,   *In Mem. xxxi* 1
sanguine *L* felt a vacant hand Fill with *his* purse.   *To Mary Boyle* 31
Laziness   I thought *L*, vague love-longings,   *Sisters (E. and E.)* 128
Lazy (*See also* **Laäzy**)   In *l* mood I watch'd the little circles die;   *Miller's D.* 73
Waves all its *l* lilies, and creeps on,   *Gardener's D.* 42
Fearing the *l* gossip of the port,   *Enoch Arden* 335
By this the *l* gossips of the port,   " 472
evermore His fancy fled before the *l* wind Returning,   " 657
Sir Aylmer half forgot his *l* smile   *Aylmer's Field* 197
Slipt o'er those *l* limits down the wind   " 495
This Gama swamp'd in *l* tolerance.   *Princess v* 443
reach its fatling innocent arms And *l* lingering fingers.   " *vi* 139
And *l* lengths on boundless shores;   *In Mem. lxx* 12
From a little *l* lover Who but claims her as his due?   *Maud I xx* 10
Lazying   *l* out a life Of self-suppression,   *St. Telemachus* 21
Lazy-plunging   low dune, and *l-p* sea.   *Last Tournament* 484
Lea   From wandering over the *l*:   *Sea-Fairies* 11
Playing mad pranks along the healthy *l*'s;   *Circumstance* 2
The sunlight driving down the *l*,   *Rosalind* 13
From his loud fount upon the echoing *l*:—   *Mine be the strength* 4
tufted plover pipe along the fallow *l*,   *May Queen, N. Y's. E.* 18
flourish high, with leafy towers, And overlook the *l*,   *Talking Oak* 198
For never yet was oak on *l* Shall grow so fair as this.'   " 243
Flow, softly flow, by lawn and *l*,   *A Farewell* 5
From him that on the mountain *l*   *To E. L.* 21
And blight and famine on all the *l*:   *The Victim* 46
The cattle huddled on the *l*;   *In Mem. xv* 6
Who ploughs with pain his native *l*   " *lxiv* 25
But ere the lark hath left the *l*   " *lxviii* 13
Now dance the lights on lawn and *l*,   " *cxv* 9
As the pimpernel dozed on the *l*;   *Maud I xxii* 48
rain, and sun! a rainbow on the *l*!   *Com. of Arthur* 406
Lead (s)   on the *l*'s we kept her till she pigg'd.   *Walk. to the Mail* 92
The tempest crackles on the *l*'s,   *Sir Galahad* 53
A clog of *l* was round my feet,   *The Letters* 5
Lest we should lap him up in cloth of *l*,   *Gareth and L.* 430
Lead (verb)   O! hither *l* thy feet!   *Ode to Memory* 64
These three alone *l* life to sovereign power.   *Œnone* 145
take Example, pattern: *l* them to thy light.   *St. S. Stylites* 224
l's the clanging rookery home.   *Locksley Hall* 68
According as his humours *l*,   *Day-Dm., Moral* 11
creeping hours That *l* me to my Lord: *St. Agnes' Eve* 8
L's her to the village altar,   *L. of Burleigh* 15
Take my brute, and *l* him in,   *Vision of Sin* 65
With fuller profits *l* an easier life,   *Enoch Arden* 145
The babe shall *l* the lion.   *Aylmer's Field* 648
To *l* an errant passion home again.   *Lucretius* 17
meant Surely to *l* my Memmius in a train   " 119
we still may *l* The new light up,   *Princess ii* 347
L out the pageant: sad and slow,   *Ode on Well.* 13

Lead (verb) (*continued*) *l* Thro' prosperous floods his holy
 urn.   *In Mem.* ix 7
Or on to where the pathway *l*'s;   „   *xxiii* 8
A life that *l*'s melodious days.   „   *xxxiii* 8
What kind of life is that I *l*;   „   *lxxxv* 8
and *l* The closing cycle rich in good.   „   *cv* 27
It *l*'s me forth at evening,   *Maud* II iv 17
way to glory *l* Low down thro' villain kitchen-
 vassalage,   *Gareth and L.* 159
L, and I follow.' (repeat)   *Gareth and L.* 746, 760, 807,
                                           891, 990, 1053, 1155
'Follow, I *l*!' so down among the pines He plunged; *Gareth and L.* 808
'I *l* no longer; ride thou at my side;   „   1157
Thro' which he bad her *l* him on,   *Geraint and E.* 29
Go likewise: shall I *l* you to the King?' 'L then,'
 she said; and thro' the woods they went.   *Pelleas and E.* 107
to *l* her to his lord Arthur,   *Guinevere* 383
To *l* sweet lives in purest chastity,   „   474
They summon me their King to *l* mine hosts   „   570
that way my wish *l*'s me evermore Still to believe it— *Lover's Tale* i 274
Yes. *L* on them. *Up* the mountain?   *Sir J. Oldcastle* 203
be consecrate to *l* A new crusade against the Saracen, *Columbus* 102
I *l* thee by the hand, Fear not.'   „   158
to *l* One last crusade against the Saracen,   „   238
short, or long, as Pleasure *l*'s, or Pain;   *Ancient Sage* 101
two that love thee, *l* a summer life,   *To Prin. Beatrice* 18
Hand of Light will *l* her people,   *On Jub. Q. Victoria* 68
Leaden-colour'd the low moan of *l-c* seas.   *Enoch Arden* 612
Leader patient *l*'s of their Institute   *Princess,* Pro. 58
The *l* wildswan in among the stars   „   iv 434
as the *l* of the herd That holds a stately fretwork „   vi 85
Mourning when their *l*'s fall,   *Ode on Well.* 5
Lo, the *l* in these glorious wars   „   192
Their ever-loyal iron *l*'s fame,   „   229
For a man and *l* of men.   *Maud* I x 59
there lives No greater *l*.'   *Lancelot and E.* 317
But ye, that follow but the *l*'s bell'   *Holy Grail* 298
Ready! take aim at their *l*'s—   *Def. of Lucknow* 42
Then the Norse *l*, Dire was his need of it,   *Batt. of Brunanburh* 56
True *l*'s of the land's desire!   *Hands all Round* 26
Leading *L* a jet-black goat white-horn'd,   *Œnone* 51
L from lawn to lawn.   *D. of F. Women* 76
onward, *l* up the golden year. (repeat)   *Golden Year* 26, 41
L on from hall to hall.   *L. of Burleigh* 52
children *l* evermore Low miserable lives   *Enoch Arden* 115
But sorrow seize me if ever that light be my *l* star! *Maud* I iv 12
And *l* all his knighthood threw the kings   *Com. of Arthur* 111
Enid *l* down the tracks Thro' which he bad her lead *Geraint and E.* 28
up the rocky pathway disappear'd, *L* the horse,   „   244
Arthur *l*, slowly went The marshall'd Order   *Lancelot and E.* 1331
The *l* of his younger knights to me.   *Last Tournament* 110
Ever, ever, and for ever was the *l* light of man. *Locksley H., Sixty* 66
Thro' which I follow'd line by line Your *l* hand, *To Ulysses* 46
Leading-strings be sweet, to sin in *l-s*,   *Last Tournament* 574
all the rest are as yet but in *l-s*.   *The Dawn* 10
Lead-like those *l-l* tons of sin,   *St. S. Stylites* 25
Leaf (*See also* **Jasmine-leaves, Rose-leaf**) Flush'd all
 the leaves with rich gold-green,   *Arabian Nights* 82
moist rich smell of the rotting *leaves*,   *A spirit haunts* 17
The sun came dazzling thro' the *leaves*,   *L. of Shalott* iii 3
The *leaves* upon her falling light—   „   iv 21
'The memory of the wither'd *l*   *Two Voices* 112
I whirl like *leaves* in roaring wind.   *Fatima* 7
blossom on the blackthorn, the *l* upon the tree. *May Queen, N. Y's. E.* 8
folded *l* is woo'd from out the bud   *Lotos-Eaters, C. S.* 26
I knew the flowers, I knew the *leaves*,   *D. of F. Women* 73
Shall sing for want, ere *leaves* are new,   *The Blackbird* 23
And, sitting muffled in dark *leaves*,   *Gardener's D.* 37
In whispers, like the whispers of the *leaves*   „   253
dimly rain'd about the *l* Twilights of airy silver, *Audley Court* 81
else may insects prick Each *l* into a gall)   *Talking Oak* 70
'I swear, by *l*, and wind, and rain,   „   81
When that, which breathes within the *l*,   „   187
Thro' all the summer of my *leaves*   „   211
Thy *l* shall never fail, nor yet Thine acorn   „   259

Leaf (*continued*) shall wear Alternate *l* and acorn-ball *Talking Oak* 287
Here rests the sap within the *l*,   *Day-Dm., Sleep* P. 3
As dash'd about the drunken *leaves*   *Amphion* 55
And the *l* is stamp'd in clay.   *Vision of Sin* 82
Of sounder *l* than I can claim;   *You might have won* 4
and thatch'd with *leaves* of palm, a hut,   *Enoch Arden* 559
gentle shower, the smell of dying *leaves*,   „   611
dead weight of the dead *l* bore it down: „   678
touch'd On such a time as goes before the *l*,   *The Brook* 13
A lisping of the innumerous *l* and dies,   *Princess* v 14
Of the first snowdrop's inner *leaves*;   „   197
leaves were wet with women's tears: „   vi 39
This faded *l*, our names are as brief;   *Spiteful Letter* 13
Yet the yellow *l* hates the greener *l*,   „   15
Brief, brief is a summer *l*,   „   21
Like the *l* in a roaring whirlwind,   *Boädicea* 59
Spring is here with *l* and grass;   *Window, No Answer* 23
And only thro' the faded *l* The chestnut   *In Mem.* xi 3
These *leaves* that redden to the fall;   „   14
The last red *l* is whirl'd away,   „   xv 3
Thro' lands where not a *l* was dumb;   „   xxiii 10
In many a figured *l* enrolls The total world   „   xliii 11
That seem'd to touch it into *l*:   „   lxix 18
Thy *l* has perish'd in the green,   „   lxxv 13
Thy spirits in the darkening *l*,   „   lxxxviii 6
In those fall'n *leaves* which kept their green,   „   xcv 23
The large *leaves* of the sycamore,   „   55
park and suburb under brown Of lustier *leaves*;   „   xcviii 25
A fiery finger on the *leaves*;   „   xcix 12
The time admits not flowers or *leaves*   „   cvii 6
The dead *l* trembles to the bells.   *Con.* 64
When the shiver of dancing *leaves* is thrown   *Maud* I vi 73
like a sudden wind Among dead *leaves*,   *Gareth and L.* 515
wood is nigh as full of thieves as *leaves*:   „   789
For as a *l* in mid-November is To what   *Marr. of Geraint* 611
as the worm draws in the wither'd *l*   *Geraint and E.* 633
wealth Of *l*, and gayest garlandage of flowers,   *Balin and Balan* 83
leaves Laid their green faces flat   „   343
dim thro' *leaves* Blinkt the white morn,   „   384
The new *l* ever pushes off the old.   „   442
glittering like May sunshine on May *leaves*   *Merlin and V.* 88
left hand Droop from his mighty shoulder, as a *l*, „   1199
Must our true man change like a *l* at last?   *Lancelot and E.* 686
L after *l*, and tore, and cast them off,   „   1199
green wood-ways, and eyes among the *leaves*;   *Pelleas and E.* 139
as a hand that pushes thro' the *l*   „   436
Danced like a wither'd *l* before the hall. (repeat) *Last Tournament* 4, 242
and yellowing *l* And gloom and gleam,   „   154
l is dead, the yearning past away: New *l*,   „   277
laid His brows upon the drifted *l* and dream'd.   „   406
And rode beneath an ever-showering *l*,   „   492
And pale and fibrous as a wither'd *l*,   *Lover's Tale* i 422
No bud, no *l*, no flower, no fruit   „   725
Tearing the bright *leaves* of the ivy-screen,   „   ii 40
All crisped sounds of wave and *l* and wind,   „   106
lasses 'ed teärd out *leaves* i' the middle   *Village Wife* 72
without *l* or a thorn from the bush   *V. of Maeldune* 44
Or the young green *l* rejoice in the frost   *The Wreck* 20
Her dust is greening in your *l*,   *Ancient Sage* 165
and from each The light *l* falling fast,   *Pro. to Gen. Hamley* 2
l fell, and the sun, Pale at my grief,   *Demeter and P.* 113
and there My giant ilex keeping *l*   *To Ulysses* 35
by hour unfolding woodbine *leaves*   *Prog. of Spring* 7
leaves possess the season in their turn,   „   107
Light again, *l* again, life again, love again,'   *The Throstle* 3
All his *leaves* Fall'n at length,   *The Oak* 11
Vary like the *leaves* and flowers,   *Poets and Critics* 4
Leafless (*See also* **Seeming-leafless**) What?—that the
 bush were *l*?   *Lucretius* 206
wood which grides and clangs Its *l* ribs and iron horns *In Mem.* cvii 12
the branching grace Of *l* elm, or naked lime,   *To Ulysses* 16
Leaflet with hardly a *l* between,   *V. of Maeldune* 64
Leafy its walls And chimneys muffled in the *l* vine. *Audley Court* 19
O flourish high, with *l* towers,   *Talking Oak* 197
But in the *l* lanes behind the down,   *Enoch Arden* 97

Leafy (*continued*)   The climbing street, the mill, the *l*
   lanes,
Till they were swallow'd in the *l* bowers,   *Lover's Tale iii 57*
     Enoch Arden 607

League (s)   (*See also* **Half-a-league**)   For *l's* no other
   tree did mark The level waste,   *Mariana 43*
Flung *l's* of roaring foam into the gorge   *If I were loved 13*
A *l* of grass, wash'd by a slow broad stream,   *Gardener's D. 40*
l's along that breaker-beaten coast   *Enoch Arden 51*
Many a long *l* back to the North.   *Princess i 168*
heave and thump A *l* of street in summer solstice   " *iii 128*
we rode a *l* beyond, And, o'er a bridge of pinewood   " *334*
HALF a *l*, half a *l*, onward,   *Light Brigade 1*
On *l's* of odour streaming far,   *In Mem. lxxxvi 14*
At the shouts, the *l's* of lights,   *Maud II iv 21*
everyone that owns a tower The Lord for half a *l*.   *Gareth and L. 596*
A *l* beyond the wood, All in a full-fair manor   " *845*
A *l* of mountain full of golden mines,   *Merlin and V. 587*
King Made proffer of the *l* of golden mines,   " *646*
That have no meaning half a *l* away: *Holy Grail 556*
great waters break Whitening for half a *l*,   *Last Tournament 465*
And ever push'd Sir Modred, *l* by *l*,   *Pass. of Arthur 80*
and loud *l's* of man And welcome !   *To the Queen ii 9*
following out A *l* of labyrinthine darkness,   *Demeter and P. 82*
League (verb)   who *l's* With Lords of the White Horse,   *Guinevere 573*
Leagued   And *l* him with the heathen,   " *155*
l again Their lot with ours to rove the world   *Pref. Son. 19th Cent. 10*
League-long   *l-l* roller thundering on the reef,   *Enoch Arden 584*
Thro' many a *l-l* bower he rode.   *Last Tournament 374*
You saw the *l-l* rampart-fire Flare from Tel-el-
   Kebir   *Pro. to Gen. Hamley 27*
Leaguer   for hours On that disastrous *l*,   *Princess vii 33*
Leaguer'd   That bore a lady from a *l* town;   *D. of F. Women 47*
Leaky   or prove The Danaïd of a *l* vase,   *Princess ii 340*
Leal   fain Have all men true and *l*,   *Merlin and V. 794*
I will be *l* to thee and work thy work,   *Pelleas and E. 343*
Lean (adj.)   I KNEW an old wife *l* and poor,   *The Goose 1*
And in my weak, *l* arms I lift the cross,   *St. S. Stylites 118*
A gray and gap-tooth'd man as *l* as death,   *Vision of Sin 60*
Remains the *l* P. W. on his tomb: *The Brook 193*
All over with the fat affectionate smile That makes
   the widow *l*.   *Sea Dreams 156*
went Hating his own *l* heart and miserable.   *Aylmer's Field 526*
Down from the *l* and wrinkled precipices,   *Princess iv 22*
But still her lists were swell'd and mine were *l*;   " *319*
A gray old wolf and a *l*.   *Maud I xiii 28*
So *l* his eyes were monstrous;   *Merlin and V. 624*
And a *l* Order—scarce return'd a tithe—   *Holy Grail 894*
Her dear, long, *l*, little arms lying out   *In the Child. Hosp. 70*
And tho', in this *l* age forlorn,   *Epilogue 71*
Opulent Avarice, *l* as Poverty;   *Vastness 20*
till I believing that the girl's *L* fancy,   *The Ring 336*
Lean (verb)   *l* out from the hollow sphere of the sea,   *The Mermaid 54*
And a rose-bush *l's* upon,   *Adeline 14*
Enormous elm-tree-boles did stoop and *l*   *D. of F. Women 57*
that from a casement *l's* his head,   " *246*
'Tis strange that those we *l* on most,   *To J. S. 9*
and *l* a ladder on the shaft,   *St. S. Stylites 216*
' On that which *l's* to you.   *Princess iii 232*
but *l* me down, Sir Dagonet,   *Last Tournament 272*
And so thou *l* on our fair father Christ,   *Guinevere 562*
He *l's* on Antichrist;   *Sir J. Oldcastle 74*
let me *l* my head upon your breast.   *Romney's R. 154*
Lean'd-Leant   And *lean'd* upon the balcony.   *Mariana in the S. 88*
prudent partner of his blood *Lean'd* on him,   *Two Voices 416*
Or from the bridge I *lean'd* to hear   *Miller's D. 49*
o'er him flow'd a golden cloud, and *lean'd* Upon him,   *Œnone 105*
And on her lover's arm she *leant*,   *Day-Dm., Depart. 1*
He *lean'd* not on his fathers but himself.   *Aylmer's Field 56*
Once she *lean'd* on me, Descending;   *Princess iv 26*
What reed was that on which I *leant*?   *In Mem. lxxxiv 45*
Push'd thro' an open casement down, *lean'd* on it,   *Balin and Balan 413*
Sir Lancelot *leant*, in half disdain At love,   *Lancelot and E. 1238*
all whereon I *lean'd* in wife and friend   *Pass. of Arthur 24*
As I *lean'd* away from his arms—   *The Wreck 102*
and we *lean'd* to the darker side—   *Despair 55*

Lean'd-Leant (*continued*)   She *lean'd* to from her Spiritual
   sphere,   *The Ring 484*
Leaneth   Thou art light, To which my spirit *l*   *Lover's Tale i 104*
Lean-headed   *L-h* Eagles yelp alone,   *Princess vii 211*
Leaning   (*See also* **A-leanin'**)   *L* upon the ridged sea,   *The Winds, etc. 1*
A *l* and upbearing parasite,   *Isabel 34*
rich fruit-bunches *l* on each other—   " *37*
L his cheek upon his hand,   *Eleänore 118*
And you were *l* from the ledge   *Miller's D. 84*
She, *l* on a fragrant twined with vine,   *Œnone 20*
Upon her pearly shoulder *l* cold,   " *140*
Robin *l* on the bridge beneath the hazel-tree ?   *May Queen 14*
L his horns into the neighbour field,   *Gardener's D. 87*
And *l* there on those balusters,   *Princess iii 119*
There *l* deep in broider'd down we sank   " *iv 32*
Gareth *l* both hands heavily   *Gareth and L. 439*
and hungerworn I seem—*l* on these ?   " *444*
eyes all bright replied, *L* a little toward him,   *Marr. of Geraint 495*
And speaking not, but *l* over him,   *Merlin and V. 477*
when I was *l* out Above the river—   *Last Tournament 43*
L its roses on my faded eyes.   *Lover's Tale i 621*
The slant seas *l* on the mangrove copse.   *Prog. of Spring 76*
Leanness   black eyes, Yet larger thro' his *l*,   *Lancelot and E. 835*
Leant   *See* **Lean'd**
Leap (s)   heart on one wild *l* Hung tranced from all
   pulsation,   *Gardener's D. 259*
this a bridge of single arc Took at a *l*;   *Gareth and L. 909*
and stirs the pulse With devil's *l's*,   *Guinevere 522*
And leave the name of Lover's *L*:   *Lover's Tale iv 42*
Leap (verb)   Where he was wont to *l* and climb,   *Supp. Confessions 165*
In the middle *l's* a fountain   *Poet's Mind 24*
like a wave I would *l* From the diamond-ledges   *The Mermaid 39*
And not *l* forth and fall about thy neck,   *Love and Duty 41*
his spirit *l's* within him to be gone   *Locksley Hall 115*
and *l* the rainbows of the brooks,   " *171*
Be still the first to *l* to light   *Day-Dm., L'Envoi 27*
I *l* on board: no helmsman steers: *Sir Galahad 39*
High-elbow'd grigs that *l* in summer grass.   *The Brook 54*
To *l* the rotten pales of prejudice,   *Princess ii 142*
And the wild cataract *l's* in glory.   " *iv 4*
l's in Among the women, snares them by the score   " *v 162*
Whatever record *l* to light He never shall be shamed.   *Ode on Well. 190*
Making the little one *l* for joy.   *To F. D. Maurice 4*
To *l* the grades of life and light,   *In Mem. xli 11*
But at his footstep *l's* no more,   " *lxxxv 112*
And *l's* into the future chance,   " *cxiv 7*
snubnosed rogue would *l* from his counter and till,   *Maud I i 51*
the red man's babe *L*, beyond the sea.   " *xvii 20*
many a darkness into the light shall *l*,   " *III vi 46*
I *l* from Satan's foot to Peter's knee—   *Gareth and L. 538*
Who *l* at thee to tear thee;   *Balin and Balan 142*
who had ever Made my heart *l*;   *Holy Grail 842*
how her choice did *l* forth from his eyes !   *Lover's Tale i 657*
When he *l's* from the water to the land.   *The Revenge 55*
if the tigers *l* into the fold unawares—   *Def. of Lucknow 51*
I would *l* into your grave.   *Happy 20*
Up *l's* the lark, gone wild to welcome   *Prog. of Spring 14*
Leap'd-Leapt   Then *leapt* a trout. In lazy mood   *Miller's D. 73*
My mailed Bacchus *leapt* into my arms,   *D. of F. Women 151*
My words *leapt* forth: 'Heaven heads the count
   of crimes   " *201*
About me *leap'd* and laugh'd The modish Cupid   *Talking Oak 66*
And sixty feet the fountain *leapt*.   *Day-Dm., Revival 8*
doe Lord Ronald had brought *Leapt* up from where
   she lay,   *Lady Clare 62*
no one cared for, *leapt* To greet her,   *Aylmer's Field 688*
Two Proctors *leapt* upon us, crying, 'Names:'   *Princess iv 259*
Leapt from the dewy shoulders of the Earth,   " *v 43*
And into fiery splinters *leapt* the lance,   " *494*
o'er the statues *leapt* from head to head,   " *vi 155*
out of languor *leapt* a cry; *Leapt* fiery Passion   " *vii 155*
Thought *leapt* out to wed with Thought   *In Mem. xxiii 15*
Ran like a colt, and *leapt* at all he saw: *Com. of Arthur 322*
Leapt in a semicircle, and lit on earth;   *Balin and Balan 414*
his evil spirit upon him *leapt*,   " *537*

Leap'd-Leapt (*continued*)   Then *leapt* her palfrey o'er
    the fallen oak,   *Balin and Balan* 587
Leapt from her session on his lap,   *Merlin and V.* 844
the harlot *leapt* Adown the forest,   „ 972
Leapt on his horse, and carolling as he went   *Lancelot and E.* 704
from the boat I *leapt*, and up the stairs.   *Holy Grail* 819
his helpless heart *Leapt*, and he cried,   *Pelleas and E.* 131
shouted and *leapt* down upon the fall'n ;   *Last Tournament* 469
Leapt on him, and hurl'd him headlong,   *Guinevere* 108
Leapt like a passing thought across her eyes ;   *Lover's Tale i* 70
My spirit *leap'd* as with those thrills of bliss   „ 363
Leapt lightly clad in bridal white—   „ *iii* 44
One has *leapt* up on the breach,   *Def. of Lucknow* 64
There were some *leap'd* into the fire;   *V. of Maeldune* 76
she *leapt* upon the funeral pile.   *Death of Œnone* 105
Leaping   So, *l* lightly from the boat,   *Arabian Nights* 92
The *l* stream, the very wind,   *Rosalind* 14
O follow, *l* blood,   *Early Spring* 25
Then *l* out upon them unseen   *The Merman* 33
And, *l* down the ridges lightly,   *M. d'Arthur* 134
Pelleas, *l* up, Ran thro' the doors   *Pelleas and E.* 538
walls of my cell were dyed With rosy colours *l* on
    the wall ;   *Holy Grail* 120
And, *l* down the ridges lightly,   *Pass. of Arthur* 302
Leapt   *See* **Leap'd**
Learn   (*See also* **Larn**)   Will *l* new things when I am not.'   *Two Voices* 63
l at full How passion rose thro' circumstantial   *Gardener's D.* 239
he will *l* to slight His father's memory ;   *Dora* 153
A thousand thanks for what I *l*   *Talking Oak* 203
Drug thy memories, lest thou *l* it,   *Locksley Hall* 77
And *l* the world, and sleep again ;   *Day-Dm., L'Envoi* 8
For since I came to live and *l*,   *Will Water.* 81
Then may she *l* I lov'd her to the last.'   *Enoch Arden* 835
sent the bailliff to the farm To *l* the price,   *The Brook* 142
I am grieved to *l* your grief   *Aylmer's Field* 398
and as we task ourselves To *l* a language   „ 433
l A man is likewise counsel for himself,   *Sea Dreams* 181
Here might they *l* whatever men were taught: *Princess ii* 146
women were too barbarous, would not *l* ;   „ 298
Who *l's* the one ΠΟΥ ΣΤΟ whence after-hands   „ *iii* 263
l With whom they deal,   „ *iv* 512
To *l* if Ida yet would cede our claim,   „ *v* 333
To give or keep, to live and *l* and be All that   „ *vii* 273
Give it time To *l* its limbs :   „ *Con.* 79
and *l's* to deaden Love of self,   *Ode on Well.* 204
And *l's* her gone and far from home ;   *In Mem. viii* 4
and *l* That I have been an hour away.   „ *xii* 19
And *l's* the use of ' I ' and ' me,'   „ *xlv* 6
Had man to *l* himself anew   „ 15
desire or admire, if a man could *l* it,   *Maud I iv* 41
after-years Will *l* the secret of our Arthur's birth.'   *Com. of Arthur* 159
and *l* Whether he know me for his master   *Gareth and L.* 720
' If Enid errs, let Enid *l* her fault.'   *Marr. of Geraint* 132
' Surely I will *l* the name,'   „ 203
by the bird's song ye may *l* the nest,'   „ 359
I will break his pride and *l* his name,   „ 424
But coming back he *l's* it,   *Geraint and E.* 498
As children *l*, be thou Wiser for falling !   *Balin and Balan* 75
and came To *l* black magic,   „ 127
To *l* what Arthur meant by courtesy,   „ 158
To *l* the graces of their Table,   „ 238
suffer from the things before me, know, L nothing ;   „ 285
make me wish still more to *l* this charm   *Merlin and V.* 329
Who have to *l* themselves and all the world,   „ 365
we needs must *l* Which is our mightiest,   *Lancelot and E.* 62
l If his old prowess were in aught decay'd ; And
    added, ' Our true Arthur, when he *l's*,   „ 583
Whence you might *l* his name ?   „ 654
So ye will *l* the courtesies of the court,   „ 699
fain were I to *l* this knight were whole,   „ 772
bode among them yet a little space Till he should *l* it ;   „ 922
Till overborne by one, he *l's*—   *Holy Grail* 305
thou remaining here wilt *l* the event ;   *Guinevere* 577
Must *l* to use the tongues of all the world.   *Sir J. Oldcastle* 34
He might have come to *l* Our Wiclif's learning: „ 64

Learn (*continued*)   haply *l* the Nameless hath a voice,   *Ancient Sage* 34
simpler, saner lesson might he *l*   *Prog. of Spring* 105
Before I *l* that Love, which is,   *Doubt and Prayer* 7
Learnable   not *l*, divine, Beyond *my* reach.   *Balin and Balan* 175
Learned (**adj.**)   Long *l* names of agaric, moss and fern,   *Edwin Morris* 17
Men hated *l* women :   *Princess i* 466
Not *l*, save in gracious household ways,   „ *vii* 318
a *l* man Could give it a clumsy name.   *Maud II ii* 9
Learned (**s**)   The *L* all his lore :   *Ancient Sage* 139
Learned-Learnt (*verb*)   (*See also* **Larn'd**)   late he *learned*
    humility Perforce,   *Buonaparte* 13
all at once a pleasant truth I *learn'd*,   *The Bridesmaid* 9
As in the Latin song I *learnt* at school,   *Edwin Morris* 79
a saying *learnt*, In days far-off,   *Tithonus* 47
I *learnt* that James had flickering jealousies   *The Brook* 99
' have you *learnt* No more from Psyche's lecture,   *Princess ii* 392
And *learnt*?   I *learnt* more from her in a flash,   „ 397
since we *learnt* our meaning here,   „ *iii* 222
learnt, For many weary moons before we came,   „ 318
We knew not your ungracious laws, which *learnt*,   „ *iv* 399
but when she *learnt* his face, Remembering   „ *vi* 158
Much had she *learnt* in little time.   „ *vii* 240
One lesson from one book we *learn'd*,   *In Mem. lxxix* 14
when they *learnt* that I must go They wept   „ *ciii* 17
shall have *learn'd* to lisp you thanks.   *Marr. of Geraint* 822
ere he *learnt* it, ' Take Five horses and their
    armours ; '   *Geraint and E.* 408
Sir Garlon too Hath *learn'd* black magic,   *Balin and Balan* 305
And *learnt* their elemental secrets,   *Merlin and V.* 632
' He *learnt* and warn'd me of their fierce design   *Lancelot and E.* 274
' Sire, my liege, so much I *learnt* ;   „ 708
Lied, say ye ?   Nay, but *learnt*,   *Last Tournament* 656
(When first I *learnt* thee hidden here)   *Guinevere* 539
and *learn'd* To lisp in tune together ;   *Lover's Tale i* 257
Because she *learnt* them with me ;   „ 292
Had I not *learnt* my loss before he came ?   *Lover's Tale i* 665
I *learnt* the drearier story of his life ;   „ *iv* 147
I *learnt* it first.   I had to speak.   *Sisters (E. and E.)* 242
he *learnt* that I hated the ring I wore,   *The Wreck* 57
I scarce have *learnt* the title of your book,   *The Ring* 126
and woke me And *learn'd* me Magic !   *Merlin and the G.* 14
when I *learn'd* my fate.   *Charity* 14
when I *learnt* it at last, I shriek'd,   „ 37
Learning (**part.**)   *l* this, the bridegroom will relent.   *Guinevere* 172
l it (They told me somewhat rashly as I think)   *Lover's Tale i* 97
Learning (**s**)   what was *l* unto them ?   *Princess ii* 464
wearing all that weight Of *l* lightly   *In Mem., Con.* 40
He might have come to learn Our Wiclif's *l*:   *Sir J. Oldcastle* 65
We fronted there the *l* of all Spain,   *Columbus* 41
Learnt   *See* **Learn'd**
Lease   laying down an unctuous *l* Of life,   *Will Water.* 243
brooding on his briefer *l* of life,   *Locksley H., Sixty* 23
Leash   hold passion in a *l*,   *Love and Duty* 40
Diet and seeling, jesses, *l* and lure.   *Merlin and V.* 125
Least   (*See also* **Laste**)   And trampled under by the last
    l Of men ?   *Poland* 3
her *l* remark was worth The experience of the wise.   *Edwin Morris* 65
Nor ever falls the *l* white star of snow,   *Lucretius* 107
In whose *l* act abides the nameless charm   *Princess v* 70
Our greatest yet with *l* pretence,   *Ode on Well.* 29
I seem to meet their *l* desire,   *In Mem. lxxxiv* 17
Or the *l* little delicate aquiline curve in a sensitive
    nose, From which I escaped heart-free, with the
    l little touch of spleen.   *Maud I ii* 10
to her own bright face Accuse her of the *l*
    immodesty :   *Geraint and E.* 111
Love-loyal to the *l* wish of the Queen   *Lancelot and E.* 89
Love-loyal to the *l* wish of the Queen,   *Guinevere* 126
my strongest wish Falls flat before your *l* unwillingness.   *Romney's R.* 72
Myself not *l*, but honour'd of them   *Ulysses* 15
Some men's were small ; not they the *l* of men ;   *Princess ii* 148
feel, at *l*, that silence here were sin,   *Third of Feb.* 37
' Thou pratest here where thou art *l* ;   *In Mem. xxxvii* 2
I saw the *l* of little stars Down on the waste,   *Holy Grail* 524
made our mightiest madder than our *l*.   „ 863

Leather   *See* **Saddle-leather**

Leave-Leäve (holiday)   with a month's *leave* given them,   *Sea Dreams* 6
   then 'ed gotten wer *leäve*,   *Owd Roä* 51

Leave (permission)   so much out as gave us *l* to go.   *Princess* v 235
   I'll have *l* at times to play   *In Mem. lix* 11
   to gain it—your full *l* to go.   *Gareth and L.* 134
   Sir Kay nodded him *l* to go,   „   520
   Queen petition'd for his *l* To see the hunt,   *Marr. of Geraint* 154
   'Thy *l*! Let *me* lay lance in rest,   „   495
   'Have I *l* to speak?'   *Geraint and E.* 140
   'Your *l*, my lord, to cross the room,   „   298
   free *l*,' he said;   'Get her to speak: „   300
   my *l* To move to your own land,   „   888
   But, father, give me *l*, an if he will,   *Lancelot and E.* 219
   But left him *l* to stammer,' Is it indeed?   „   420
   And so, *l* given, straight on thro' open door   *Pelleas and E.* 382
   dare without your *l* to head These rhymings   *Pro. to Gen. Hamley* 19
   saying gently: 'Muriel, by your *l*,'   *The Ring* 268

Leave (farewell)—took my *l*, for it was nearly noon: *Princess* v 468
   crowd were swarming now, To take their *l*,   „ *Con.* 38
   To take her latest *l* of home,   *In Mem. xl* 6
   And thou shalt take a nobler *l*.'   „ *lviii* 12
   But how to take last *l* of all I loved?   *Guinevere* 546
   you still delay to take Your *l* of Town,   *To Mary Boyle* 2

Leave (verb)   (*See also* **Lave, Leäve**)   And *l* us rulers
   of your blood   *To the Queen* 21
   hard at first, mother, to *l* the blessed sun,   *May Queen, Con.* 9
   Which wilt not *l* the myrrh-bush on the height;   *Lotos-Eaters, C. S.* 58
   'It is not meet, Sir King, to *l* thee thus,   *M. d'Arthur* 40
   it seem'd Better to *l* Excalibur conceal'd   „   62
   '*L*,' she cried 'O *l* me!' 'Never,   *Edwin Morris* 116
   I will *l* my relics in your land,   *St. S. Stylites* 194
   But *l* thou mine to me.   *Talking Oak* 200
   And *l* thee freër, till thou wake refresh'd   *Love and Duty* 97
   To whom I *l* the sceptre and the isle—   *Ulysses* 34
   COMRADES, *l* me here a little,   *Locksley Hall* 1
   L me here, and when you want me,   „   2
   Eager-hearted as boy when first he *l's* his father's field,   „   112
   I *l* the plain, I climb the height;   *Sir Galahad* 57
   I *l* an empty flask.   *Will Water.* 164
   And they *l* her father's roof.   *L. of Burleigh* 12
   and *l* Yon orange sunset waning slow: *Move eastward* 1
   Pass on, weak heart, and *l* me where I lie: *Come not, when, etc.* 11
   Nor *l* his music as of old,   *You might have won* 14
   go this weary way, And *l* you lonely?   *Enoch Arden* 297
   five years' death-in-life. They could not *l* him.   „   566
   One who cried, '*L* all and follow me.'   *Aylmer's Field* 664
   L us you may go: *Princess* ii 94
   '*L* me to deal with that.'   „ iii 149
   Ill mother that I was to *l* her there,   „ v 93
   meteor on, and *l's* A shining furrow,   „ vii 184
   l The monstrous ledges there to slope,   „   211
   Will *l* her space to burgeon out of all   „   271
   And in the vast cathedral *l* him   *Ode on Well.* 280
   They *l* the heights and are troubled,   *Voice and the P.* 15
   l it gorily quivering?   *Boädicea* 12
   Thou wilt not *l* us in the dust: *In Mem., Pro.* 9
   I *l* this mortal ark behind,   „ xii 6
   And *l* the cliffs, and haste away   „   8
   L thou thy sister when she prays,   „ xxxiii 5
   But half my life I *l* behind: „ lvii 6
   And what I see I *l* unsaid,   „ lxxiv 10
   I *l* thy praises unexpress'd   „ lxxv 1
   I *l* thy greatness to be guess'd;   „   4
   You *l* us: you will see the Rhine,   „ xcviii 1
   We *l* the well-beloved place   „ cii 1
   To *l* the pleasant fields and farms;   „   22
   And wilt thou *l* us now behind?'   „ ciii 48
   To-night ungather'd let us *l* This laurel,   „ cv 1
   They *l* the porch, they pass the grave   „ *Con.* 71
   your sweetness hardly *l's* me a choice   *Maud I* v 24
   When will the dancers *l* her alone?   „ xxii 21
   past and *l's* The Crown a lonely splendour.   *Ded. of Idylls* 48
   wilt thou *l* Thine easeful biding here,   *Gareth and L.* 127
   and *l* my man to me.'   „   477

Leave (verb) (*continued*)   I *l* not till I finish this fair
   quest,   *Gareth and L.* 774
   Come, therefore, *l* thy lady lightly, knave.   „   957
   and *l's* me fool'd and trick'd,   „   1251
   not *l* her, till her promise given—   *Marr. of Geraint* 605
   L me to-night: I am weary to the death.'   *Geraint and E.* 358
   bounding forward '*L* them to the wolves.'   *Balin and Balan* 588
   he rose To *l* the hall, and, Vivien following   *Merlin and V.* 32
   To *l* an equal baseness;   „   830
   ere I *l* thee let me swear once more   „   929
   made him *l* The banquet,   *Lancelot and E.* 561
   let me *l* My quest with you;   „   690
   Before ye *l* him for this Quest,   *Holy Grail* 325
   l The leading of his younger knights to me.   *Last Tournament* 109
   an arrow from the bush Should *l* me all alone   „   536
   And of this remnant will I *l* a part,   *Guinevere* 444
   Yet must I *l* thee, woman, to thy shame.   „   511
   L me that, I charge thee, my last hope.   „   567
   'It is not meet, Sir King, to *l* thee thus,   *Pass. of Arthur* 208
   it seem'd Better to *l* Excalibur conceal'd   „   230
   lake, that, flooding, *l's* Low banks of yellow
   sand;   *Lover's Tale i* 534
   HE flies the event: he *l's* the event to me: „ iv 1
   Would *l* the land for ever,   „   19
   And *l* the name of Lover's Leap?   „   42
   And *l* him in the public way to die.   „   261
   I *l* this land for ever.'   „   368
   I am going to *l* you a bit—   *First Quarrel* 80
   go, go, you may *l* me alone—   *Rizpah* 79
   highway running by it *l's* a breadth Of sward   *Sisters (E. and E.)* 80
   you *l* 'em outside on the bed—   *In the Child. Hosp.* 56
   Or in that vaster Spain I *l* to Spain.   *Columbus* 208
   And *l* him, blind of heart and eyes,   *Ancient Sage* 113
   And *l* the hot swamp of voluptuousness   „   277
   blackthorn-blossom fades and falls and *l's* the
   bitter sloe,   *The Flight* 15
   You will not *l* me thus in grief   „   85
   if dynamite and revolver *l* you courage   *Locksley H., Sixty* 107
   Eighty winters *l* the dog too lame   „   226
   L the Master in the first dark hour   „   238
   Then I *l* thee Lord and Master,   „   282
   Birds and brides must *l* the nest.   *The Ring* 89
   Queen, who *l's* Some colder province in the North   „   480
   shadow *l* the Substance in the brooding light of noon?   *Happy* 99
   now arching *l's* her bare To breaths of balmier
   air;   *Prog. of Spring* 12
   l's me harlot-like, Who love her still,   *Romney's R.* 116
   May *l* the windows blinded,   „   146

Leäve (verb)   if thou marries a good un I'll *l* the
   land to thee.   *N. Farmer, N. S.* 56
   if thou marries a bad 'un, I'll *l* the land to Dick.—   „   58
   Let's them inter 'eaven easy es *l's*   *Village Wife* 94

Leäved (left)   but 'e *l* it to Charlie's son,   „   42
   they *l* their nasty sins i' *my* pond,   *Churchwarden, etc.* 54

Leaved   *See* **Long-leaved, Thick-leaved**

Leaven (s)   the old *l* leaven'd all: *Princess* v 386

Leaven (verb)   But now to *l* play with profit,   „ iv 149
   Of Love to *l* all the mass,   *Freedom* 19

Leaven'd   the old leaven *l* all: *Princess* v 386
   then as Arthur in the highest *L* the world,   *Merlin and V.* 141
   but all was joust and play, *L* his hall.   „   146

Leave-taking   Low at *l-t*, with his brandish'd plume   *Geraint and E.* 359

Leaving   (*See also* **Lavin'**)   *L* door and windows wide: *Deserted House* 3
   l my ancient love With the Greek woman.   *Œnone* 260
   L the dance and song, '*L* the olive-gardens far
   below, *L* the promise of my bridal bower,   *D. of F. Women* 216
   L great legacies of thought,   *In Mem. lxxxiv* 35
   And, *l* these, to pass away,   „ c 19
   l night forlorn.   „ cvii 4
   who camest to thy goal So early, *l* me behind,   „ cxiv 24
   Who *l* share in furrow come to see The glories   *Gareth and L.* 243
   ramp and roar at *l* of your lord!—   „   1307
   never *l* her, and grew Forgetful of his promise   *Marr. of Geraint* 49
   so *l* him, Now with slack rein and careless   *Balin and Balan* 308
   So *l* Arthur's court he gain'd the beach;   *Merlin and V.* 197

Leaving (*continued*)   *L* her household and good father,   *Lancelot and E.* 14
l for the cowl The helmet in an abbey   *Holy Grail* 5
l the pale nun, I spake of this To all men ;   „ 129
And *l* human wrongs to right themselves,   „ 898
her anger, *l* Pelleas, burn'd Full on her knights   *Pelleas and E.* 289
Thieves, bandits, *l's* of confusion,   *Last Tournament* 95
now *l* to the skill Of others their old craft   *Pref. Son. 19th Cent.* 2
L his son too Lost in the carnage,   *Batt. of Brunanburh* 72
the child Is happy—ev'n in *l* her !   *To Prin. Beatrice* 12
Leavy   Moving in the *l* beech.   *Margaret* 61
Lebanon   O, art thou sighing for *L*   *Maud I xviii* 15
Sighing for *L*, Dark cedar,   „ 17
Lebanonian   in halls Of *L* cedar :   *Princess ii* 352
Lecher   The *l* would cleave to his lusts,   *Despair* 100
Lecture (adj.)   On the *l* slate The circle rounded   *Princess ii* 371
Lecture (s)   A classic *l*, rich in sentiment,   „ 374
' have you learnt No more from Psyche's *l*,   „ 393
Led   (*See also* **Moon-led**)   And like a bride of old In triumph *l*,   *Ode to Memory* 76
Gliding with equal crowns two serpents *l*   *Alexander* 6
' But heard, by secret transport *l*,   *Two Voices* 214
light that *l* The holy Elders with the gift of myrrh.   *M. d'Arthur* 232
Fancy, *l* by Love, Would play with flying forms   *Gardener's D.* 59
still we follow'd where she *l*, (repeat)   *The Voyage* 59, 90
took him by the curls, and *l* him in,   *Vision of Sin* 6
l the way To where the rivulets of sweet water ran ;   *Enoch Arden* 641
l me thro' the short sweet-smelling lanes   *The Brook* 122
Thro' which a few, by wit or fortune *l*,   *Aylmer's Field* 438
I *l* you then to all the Castalies ;   *Princess iv* 294
But *l* by golden wishes,   „ 420
l Threading the soldier-city,   „ v 6
l A hundred maids in train across the Park.   „ vi 75
Remember him who *l* your hosts,   *Ode on Well.* 171
Love has *l* thee to the stranger land,   *W. to Marie Alex.* 31
Which *l* by tracts that pleased us well,   *In Mem. xxii* 2
And *l* him thro' the blissful climes,   „ lxxxv 25
They wept and wail'd, but *l* the way   „ ciii 18
I have *l* her home, my love,   *Maud I xviii* 1
' Lead and I follow.' Quietly she *l*.   *Gareth and L.* 1053
L from the territory of false Limours   *Geraint and E.* 437
answering not one word, she *l* the way.   „ 495
across the poplar grove *L* to the caves :   *Lancelot and E.* 805
like a flying star *L* on the gray-hair'd wisdom   *Holy Grail* 453
But when they *l* me into hall, behold,   „ 577
loosed his horse, and *l* him to the light.   *Pelleas and E.* 61
l her forth, and far ahead Of his and her retinue   *Guinevere* 384
light that *l* The holy Elders with the gift of myrrh.   *Pass. of Arthur* 400
l on with light In trances and in visions :   *Lover's Tale i* 77
I was *l* mute Into her temple like a sacrifice ;   „ 684
Then those who *l* the van, and those in rear,   „ iii 24
whirling rout *L* by those two rush'd into dance,   „ 55
L his dear lady to a chair of state.   „ iv 321
am *l* by the creak of the chain,   *Rizpah* 7
far liever *l* my friend Back to the pure   *Sir J. Oldcastle* 70
In praise of God who *l* me thro' the waste.   *Columbus* 17
I know that he has *l* me all my life,   „ 160
sometimes wish I had never *l* the way.   „ 186
L backward to the tyranny of one ?   *Tiresias* 76
I knaws I 'ed *l* tha a quieter life   *Spinster's S's.* 71
Ages after, while in Asia, he that *l* the wild Moguls,   *Locksley H., Sixty* 81
half-brain races, *l* by Justice, Love, and Truth ;   „ 161
know them, follow him who *l* the way,   „ 266
L upward by the God of ghosts and dreams,   *Demeter and P.* 5
L me at length To the city and palace   *Merlin and the G.* 64
Till, *l* by dream and vague desire,   *To Master of B.* 17
And the Vision that *l* me of old,   *The Dreamer* 5
Leddest   *l* by the hand thine infant Hope.   *Ode to Memory* 30
Ledge   (*See also* **Diamond-ledge, Meadow-ledges**) And you were leaning from the *l*   *Miller's D.* 84
tall dark pines, that plumed the craggy *l*   *Œnone* 209
Of *l* or shelf The rock rose clear,   *Palace of Art* 9
from the craggy *l* The poppy hangs in sleep.   *Lotos-Eaters, C. S.* 11
leave The monstrous *l's* there to slope,   *Princess vii* 212
About the *l's* of the hill.'   *In Mem. xxxvii* 8

Ledge (*continued*)   red-ribb'd *l's* drip with a silent horror of blood,   *Maud I i* 3
Athwart the *l's* of rock,   „ *II ii* 28
on the window *l*, Close underneath his eyes,   *Lancelot and E.* 1239
And a hundred splash'd from the *l's*,   *V. of Maeldune* 103
Ledger   When only the *l* lives,   *Maud I i* 35
Lee (Annie)   *See* **Annie, Annie Lee**
Leech (blood-sucker)   swarm'd His literary *l'es*.   *Will Water.* 200
Leech (physician)   King's own *l* to look into his hurt ;   *Geraint and E.* 923
King will send thee his own *l*—   *Balin and Balan* 275
l forsake the dying bed for terror of his life ?   *Happy* 98
Leering   *L* at his neighbour's wife.   *Vision of Sin* 118
Lees   I will drink Life to the *l* :   *Ulysses* 7
Dregs of life, and *l* of man :   *Vision of Sin* 205
Left (adj.)   And over his *l* shoulder laugh'd at thee,   *Bridesmaid* 7
And on the *l* hand of the hearth he saw   *Enoch Arden* 753
letting her *l* hand Droop from his mighty shoulder,   *Merlin and V.* 242
from whose *l* hand floweth The Shadow of Death,   *Lover's Tale i* 498
And he call'd ' *L* wheel into line ! '   *Heavy Brigade* 6
Left (s)   In her *l* a human head.   *Vision of Sin* 138
left but narrow breadth to *l* and right   *Enoch Arden* 674
And she the *l*, or not, or seldom used ;   *Princess iii* 38
' How grew this feud betwixt the right and *l*.'   „ 77
Oaring one arm, and bearing in my *l*   „ *iv* 183
here and there to *l* and right Struck,   *Holy Grail* 494
To right ? to *l* ? straight forward ?   *Pelleas and E.* 67
Left (verb)   (*See also* **Leaved**)   And what is *l* to me, but Thou,   *Supp. Confessions* 18
With silver anchor *l* afloat,   *Arabian Nights* 93
She *l* the web, she *l* the loom,   *L. of Shalott iii* 37
Beneath a willow *l* afloat,   „ *iv* 7
Is this the end to be *l* alone,   *Mariana in the S.* 71
And day and night I am *l* alone   „ 83
And *l* a want unknown before ;   *Miller's D.* 228
And I was *l* alone within the bower ;   *Œnone* 192
lock'd in with bars of sand, *L* on the shore ;   *Palace of Art* 250
he set and *l* behind The good old year,   *May Queen, N. Y's. E.* 5
Then when I *l* my home.'   *D. of F. Women* 120
What else was *l* ? look here ! '   „ 156
flow Of music *l* the lips of her that died   „ 195
She lock'd her lips : she *l* me where I stood :   „ 241
Falls off, and love is *l* alone.   *To J. S.* 16
' at home was little *l*, And none abroad :   *The Epic* 19
moved away, and *l* me, statue-like,   *Gardener's D.* 161
l his father's house, And hired himself to work   *Dora* 37
He spied her, and he *l* his men at work,   „ 86
We *l* the dying ebb that faintly lipp'd   *Audley Court* 12
He *l* his wife behind ; for so I heard.   *Walk. to the Mail* 47
He *l* her, yes. I met my lady once :   „ 48
till she was *l* alone Upon her tower,   „ 98
and now we *l* The clerk behind us,   *Edwin Morris* 96
So *l* the place, *l* Edwin, nor have seen Him since,   „ 137
Yet this way was *l*, And by this way   *St. S. Stylites* 178
Her father *l* his good arm-chair,   *Talking Oak* 103
' She *l* the novel half-uncut Upon the rosewood shelf ; She *l* the new piano shut :   „ 117
tho' they could not end me, *l* me maim'd   *Tithonus* 20
my passion sweeping thro' me *l* me dry, *L* me with the palsied heart, and *l* me with the jaundiced eye ;   *Locksley Hall* 131
I was *l* a trampled orphan,   „ 156
So *l* alone, the passions of her mind.   *Godiva* 32
My father *l* a park to me,   *Amphion* 1
He *l* a small plantation ;   „ 20
WE *l* behind the painted buoy   *The Voyage* 1
LONG lines of cliff breaking have *l* a chasm ;   *Enoch Arden* 1
daily *l* The little footprint daily wash'd away.   „ 21
(Since Enoch *l* he had not look'd upon her),   „ 273
ten years Since Enoch *l* his hearth   „ v 360
he who *l* you ten long years ago Should still be living ;   „ 404
nor loved she to be *l* Alone at home,   „ 516
l but narrow breadth to left and right   „ 674
Among the gifts he *l* her (possibly He flow'd   *Aylmer's Field* 217
And *l* the living scandal that shall die—   „ 444
Then *l* alone he pluck'd her dagger forth   „ 470

Left (verb) (*continued*)   *l* Their own gray tower, or plain-faced tabernacle,   *Aylmer's Field* 617

Your house is *l* unto you desolate ! ' (repeat)   „ 629, 797

Eight that were *l* to make a purer world—   „ 638

' My house is *l* unto me desolate.'   „ 721

' Our house is *l* unto us desolate ' ?   „ 737

Have not our love and reverence *l* them bare ?   „ 785

or one stone *L* on another,   „ 789

And *l* their memories a world's curse—   „ 796

Still so much gold was *l* ;   *Sea Dreams* 130

from the gaps and chasms of ruin *l*   „ 225

L him one hand, and reaching thro' the night   „ 287

scrolls *L* by the Teacher, whom he held divine.   *Lucretius* 13

The fire that *l* a roofless Ilion.   „ 65

if I go *my* work is *l* Unfinish'd—*if* I go.   „ 103

to take Only such cups as *l* us friendly-warm,   „ 215

He, dying lately, *l* her, as I hear,   *Princess i* 78

last not least, she who had *l* her place,   „ *ii* 165

(what other way was *l*) I came.'   „ 217

chapel bells Call'd us : we *l* the walks ;   „ 471

l the drunken king To brawl at Shushan   „ *iii* 229

(For since her horse was lost I *l* her mine)   „ *iv* 197

With many thousand matters *l* to do,   „ 458

what was *l* of faded woman-slough   „ *v* 40

We *l* her by the woman,   „ 113

which she *l* : She shall not have it back :   „ 431

Pharos from his base Had *l* us rock.   „ *vi* 340

l me in it ; And others otherwise they laid ;   „ 377

but some were *l* of those Held sagest,   „ 381

Blanche had gone, but *l* Her child among us,   „ *vii* 56

And *l* her woman, lovelier in her mood   „ 162

her labour was but as a block *L* in the quarry ;   „ 231

might be *l* some record of the things we said.   *Third of Feb.* 18

Have *l* the last free race with naked coasts !   „ 40

All that was *l* of them, *L* of six hundred.   *Light Brigade* 48

my Annie who *l* me at two,   *Grandmother* 77

there's none of them *l* alive ;   „ 85

There is but a trifle *l* you,   „ 107

Nobbut a bit on it's *l*,   *N. Farmer, O. S.* 41

What room is *l* for a hater ?   *Spiteful Letter* 14

if *l* to pass His autumn into seeming-leafless days—   *A Dedication* 9

light gone with her, and *l* me in shadow here !   *Window, Gone* 3

And, having *l* the glass, she turns   *In Mem. vi* 35

When Lazarus *l* his charnel-cave,   „ *xxxi* 1

soil, *l* barren, scarce had grown The grain   „ *liii* 7

But ere the lark hath *l* the lea I wake,   „ *lxviii* 13

What fame is *l* for human deeds In endless age ?   „ *lxxiii* 11

As in the winters *l* behind,   „ *lxxviii* 9

I felt and feel, tho' *l* alone,   „ *lxxxv* 42

Which *l* my after-morn content.   „ *ciii* 4

Our father's dust is *l* alone   „ *cv* 5

a scheme that had *l* us flaccid and drain'd.   *Maud I i* 20

l his coal all turn'd into gold To a grandson,   „ *x* 11

And *l* the daisies rosy.   „ *xii* 24

This lump of earth has *l* his estate   „ *xvi* 1

For who was *l* to watch her but I ?   „ *xix* 10

That, if *l* uncancell'd, had been so sweet :   „ 46

That he *l* his wine and horses and play,   „ 74

From the meadow your walks have *l* so sweet   „ *xxii* 39

That thou art *l* for ever alone :   „ *II iii* 4

L her and fled, and Uther enter'd in,   *Com. of Arthur* 201

And ere it *l* their faces,   „ 272

To hear him speak before he *l* his life.   „ 362

the two *L* the still King, and passing forth to breathe,   „ 369

but when they *l* the shrine Great Lords from Rome   „ 476

and *l* us neither gold nor field.'   *Gareth and L.* 339

thou that slewest the sire hast *l* the son.   „ 360

war among themselves, but *l* them kings ;   „ 422

many a viand *l*, And many a costly cate,   „ 848

l The damsel by the peacock in his pride,   „ 869

And *l* them with God-speed,   „ 890

l crag-carven o'er the streaming Gelt—   „ 1203

Affirming that his father *l* him gold,   *Marr. of Geraint* 451

And *l* her maiden couch, and robed herself,   „ 737

When late *l* Caerleon, our great Queen,   „ 781

Left (verb) (*continued*)   Than when I *l* your mowers dinnerless.   *Geraint and E.* 234

Leading the horse, and they were *l* alone.   „ 244

Enid *l* alone with Prince Geraint,   „ 365

Nor *l* untold the craft herself had used ;   „ 393

and so *l* him stunn'd or dead,   „ 464

There is not *l* the twinkle of a fin   „ 474

And *l* him lying in the public way ;   „ 478

Not a hoof *l* : and I methinks till now   „ 485

But *l* two brawny spearmen, who advanced,   „ 558

and the two Were *l* alone together,   „ 734

That trouble which has *l* me thrice your own :   „ 737

whom Uther *l* in charge Long since,   „ 933

when we *l*, in those deep woods we found   *Balin and Balan* 120

an enemy that has *l* Leath in the living waters,   *Merlin and V.* 147

lists of such a beard as youth gone out Had *l* in ashes :   „ 246

Whose kinsman *l* him watcher o'er his wife   „ 706

l Not even Lancelot brave, nor Galahad clean.   „ 804

And ending in a ruin—nothing *l*,   „ 883

Had *l* the ravaged woodland yet once more To peace ;   „ 963

He *l* it with her, when he rode to tilt   *Lancelot and E.* 30

He *l* the barren-beaten thoroughfare,   „ 161

But *l* her all the paler,   „ 378

But *l* him leave to stammer ' Is it indeed ? '   „ 420

If any man that day were *l* afield,   „ 459

and hath *l* his prize Untaken,   „ 530

Here was the knight, and here he *l* a shield ;   „ 634

Why ask you not to see the shield he *l*,   „ 653

As yon proud Prince who *l* the quest to me.   „ 762

and being in his moods *L* them,   „ 800

Her own poor work, her empty labour, *l*.   „ 991

But when they *l* her to herself again,   „ 998

Come, for you *l* me taking no farewell,   „ 1274

I *l* her and I bad her no farewell.   „ 1304

Fell into dust, and I was *l* alone, (repeat)   *Holy Grail* 389, 400, 419

plowman *l* his plowing, and fell down Before it ;   „ 404

milkmaid *l* her milking, and fell down Before it,   „ 406

Was *l* alone once more, and cried in grief,   „ 437

a remnant that were *l* Paynim amid their circles,   „ 663

shattered talbots, which had *l* the stones Raw,   „ 719

Lancelot *l* The hall long silent,   „ 853

And *l* me gazing at a barren board,   „ 893

new knights to fill the gap *L* by the Holy Quest ;   *Pelleas and E.* 2

And he was *l* alone in open field.   „ 208

There *l* it, and them sleeping ;   „ 453

so *l* him bruised And batter'd, and fled on,   „ 546

Who *l* the gems which Innocence the Queen   *Last Tournament* 293

Which *l* thee less than fool,   „ 308

After she *l* him lonely here ?   „ 395

But *l* her all as easily, and return'd.   „ 403

warhorse *l* to graze Among the forest greens,   „ 490

' my man Hath *l* me or is dead ; '   „ 495

her too hast thou *l* To pine and waste   „ 597

Heathen, the brood by Hengist *l* ;   *Guinevere* 16

Modred whom he *l* in charge of all,   „ 195

come next, five summers back, And *l* me ;   „ 322

Then that other *l* alone Sigh'd,   „ 367

Had yet that grace of courtesy in him *l*   „ 436

For when the Roman *l* us, and their law   „ 456

For which of us, who might be *l*, could speak   „ 501

l me hope That in mine own heart I can live down sin   „ 635

roar of Hougoumont *L* mightiest of all peoples   *To the Queen ii* 21

L her own life with it ;   *Lover's Tale i* 215

To know her father *l* us just before   „ 293

Before he *l* the land for evermore ;   „ *iv* 183

Lest there be none *l* here to bring her back :   „ 367

One had deceived her an' *l* her alone   *First Quarrel* 25

nay—what was there *l* to fall ?   *Rizpah* 9

but bone of my bone was *l*—   „ 51

an' if Sally be *l* aloän,   *North. Cobbler* 105

should count myself the coward if I *l* them,   *The Revenge* 11

blest him in their pain, that they were not *l* to Spain,   „ 20

be little of us *l* by the time this sun be set.'   „ 28

within her womb that had *l* her ill content ;   „ 51

wound to be drest he had *l* the deck,   „ 66

Left (verb) (*continued*) THEY have *l* the doors ajar ; *Sisters (E. and E.)* 1
l me this, Which yet retains a memory of its youth,   ,, 65
We *l* her, happy each in each,   ,, 219
' Bread—Bread *l* after the blessing ? '   *Sir J. Oldcastle* 154
brought your Princes gold enough If *l* alone !   *Columbus* 106
And we *l* the dead to the birds   *V. of Maeldune* 36
And we *l* but a naked rock,   ,, 54
Many a carcase they *l* to be carrion,   *Batt. of Brunanburh* 105
L for the white-tail'd eagle to tear it, and *L* for
   the horny-ribb'd raven to rend it,   ,, 107
when I *l* my darling alone.'   *The Wreck* 97
the one man *l* on the wreck—   ,, 119
fossil skull that is *l* in the rocks   *Despair* 37
He *l* us weeping in the woods,   *The Flight* 37
That other *l* us to ourselves ;   ,, 78
but 'a *l* me the work to do,   *Spinster's S's.* 55
I was *l* within the shadow sitting on the wreck   *Locksley H., Sixty* 16
Amy's kin and mine are *l* to me.   ,, 56
Gone thy tender-natured mother, wearying to be
  l alone,   ,, 57
But ere he *l* your fatal shore,   *To Marq. of Dufferin* 33
For Naples which we only *l* in May ?   *The Ring* 58
l to me, A ring too which you kiss'd,   ,, 113
He *l* me wealth—and while I journey'd hence,   ,, 179
no tear for him, who *l* you wealth,   ,, 188
I took, I *l* you there ;   ,, 347
oftener *l* That angling to the mother.   ,, 355
With earth is broken, and has *l* her free,   ,, 476
if *I* had been the leper would you have *l* the wife ?   *Happy* 100
For ere she *l* us, when we met,   *To Mary Boyle* 15
' Why *l* you wife and children ?   *Romney's R.* 129
had *l* His aged eyes, he raised them,   *St. Telemachus* 50
one day He had *l* his dagger behind him.   *Bandit's Death* 12
She has *l* me enough to live on.   *Charity* 40
Left *See also* **Late-left, Latest-left.**
Leg She caught the white goose by the *l*,   *The Goose* 9
My right *l* chain'd into the crag,   *St. S. Stylites* 73
' And, *l* and arm with love-knots gay,   *Talking Oak* 65
And *l's* of trees were limber,   *Amphion* 14
Stept forward on a firmer *l*,   *Will Water.* 123
Callest thou that thing a *l* ?   *Vision of Sin* 89
and white, and strong on his *l's*,   *Grandmother* 2
' Here's a *l* for a babe of a week ! '   ,, 11
Strong of his hands, and strong on his *l's*,   ,, 13
DOSN'T thou 'ear my 'erse's *l's*,   *N. Farmer, N. S.* 2
moor sense i' one o' 'is *l's* nor in all thy braaïns.   ,, 4
Lets down his other *l*, and stretching,   *Gareth and L.* 1186
craven shifts, and long crane *l's* of Mark,   *Last Tournament* 729
An' Lucy wur laäme o' one *l*,   *Village Wife* 99
wi'out ony harm i' the *l's*,   ,, 101
Ull be fun' opo' four short *l's*   *Owd Roä* 16
Legacy Leaving great *legacies* of thought,   *In Mem. lxxxiv* 35
Some *l* of a fallen race Alone might hint   *Two Voices* 359
Legend (*See also* **Half-legend**) Nor these alone : but
  every *l* fair   *Palace of Art* 125
' The *L* of Good Women,' long ago Sung   *D. of F. Women* 2
I shaped The city's ancient l into this :—   *Godiva* 4
The reflex of a *l* past,   *Day-Dm., Pro.* 11
The violet of a *l* blow   *Will Water.* 147
There lived an ancient *l* in our house.   *Princess i* 5
I almost think That idiot *l* credible.   ,, *v* 153
And fading *l* of the past ;   *In Mem. lxii* 4
boss'd With holy Joseph's *l*,   *Balin and Balan* 363
The *l* as in guerdon for your rhyme ?   *Merlin and V.* 554
A *l* handed down thro' five or six,   *Holy Grail* 87
Moreover, that weird *l* of his birth,   *Last Tournament* 669
So may this *l* for awhile,   *To Prof. Jebb* 9
And then he told their *l* :   *The Ring* 206
L or true ? so tender should be true !   ,, 224
Legendary Glanced at the *l* Amazon   *Princess ii* 126
Legion King Leodogran Groan'd for the Roman *l's*   *Com. of Arthur* 33
And all his *l's* crying Christ and him,   *Lancelot and E.* 305
follow'd up by her vassal *l* of fools ;   *Vastness* 12
Legionary those Neronian *legionaries* Burnt and broke   *Boädicea* 1
Perish'd many a maid and matron, many a valorous *l*,   ,, 85

Leisure And in the fallow *l* of my life   *Audley Court* 77
lapt In the arms of *l*,   *Princess ii* 168
Mine eyes have *l* for their tears ;   *In Mem. xiii* 16
Leman wert lying in thy new *l's* arms.'   *Last Tournament* 625
Lemon *l* grove In closest coverture upsprung,   *Arabian Nights* 67
Lend God in his mercy *l* her grace,   *L. of Shalott iv* 53
To *l* our hearts and spirits wholly   *Lotos-Eaters, C. S.* 63
Something to love He *l's* us ;   *To J. S.* 14
Or *l* an ear to Plato where he says,   *Lucretius* 147
in this frequence can I *l* full tongue,   *Princess iv* 442
wi' noän to *l* 'im a shuvv,   *N. Farmer, N. S.* 31
That Nature *l's* such evil dreams ?   *In Mem. lv* 6
To *l* thee horse and shield :   *Gareth and L.* 1324
I pray you *l* me one, if such you have, Blank,   *Lancelot and E.* 193
so did Pelleas *l* All the young beauty of his own soul   *Pelleas and E.* 82
L me thine horse and arms,   ,, 345
her gracious lips Did *l* such gentle utterance,   *Lover's Tale i* 457
Nor *l* an ear to random cries,   *Politics* 7
Length (*See also* **Arm's-length**) All its allotted
  l of days,   *Lotos-Eaters, C. S.* 35
l of bright horizon rimm'd the dark.   *Gardener's D.* 181
to such *l* of years should come   *Locksley Hall* 67
Cut off the *l* of highway on before,   *Enoch Arden* 673
Dangled a *l* of ribbon and a ring To tempt   ,, 750
With *l's* of yellow ringlet, like a girl,   *Princess i* 3
boss'd with *l's* Of classic frieze,   ,, *ii* 24
All her fair *l* upon the ground she lay :   ,, *v* 59
To wile the *l* from languorous hours,   ,, *vii* 63
And lazy *l's* on boundless shores ;   *In Mem. lxx* 12
till at *l* Sir Gareth's brand Clash'd his,   *Gareth and L.* 1147
Down by the *l* of lance and arm beyond   *Geraint and E.* 463
and seem'd at *l* in peace.   *Balin and Balan* 239
At *l*, and dim thro' leaves Blinkt the white morn,   ,, 384
lay she all her *l* and kiss'd his feet,   *Merlin and V.* 219
Pall'd all its *l* in blackest samite,   *Lancelot and E.* 1142
wilt at *l* Yield me thy love and know me   *Pelleas and E* 248
At *l* A lodge of intertwisted beechen-boughs   *Last Tournament* 375
At *l* Descending from the point and standing   *Lover's Tale i* 410
grew at *l* Prophetical and prescient   ,, *ii* 131
at *l* When some were doubtful how the law   ,, *iv* 269
But at *l* we began to be weary,   *V. of Maeldune* 91
All the millions one at *l*   *Locksley H., Sixty* 193
Led me at *l* To the city and palace Of Arthur   *Merlin and the G.* 64
brought you down A *l* of staghorn-moss,   *Romney's R.* 79
All his leaves Fall'n at *l*,   *The Oak* 13
at *l* he touch'd his goal, The Christian city.   *St. Telemachus* 34
Lengthen'd Tall as a figure *l* on the sand   *Princess vi* 161
With a *l* loud halloo,   *The Owl* 13
Lent (fast) If it may be, fast Whole *L's*,   *St. S. Stylites* 182
Lent (verb) Who *l* you, love, your mortal dower   *Margaret* 5
motion *l* The pulse of hope to discontent.   *Two Voices* 449
That *l* broad verge to distant lands,   *Palace of Art* 30
That *l* my knee desire to kneel,   *Princess iii* 193
once or twice she *l* her hand,   ,, *iv* 27
I, that have *l* my life to build up yours,   ,, 351
Still in the little book you *l* me,   *The Daisy* 99
And, crown'd with all the season *l*,   *In Mem. xxii* 6
A willing ear We *l* him.   ,, *lxxvii* 31
l her fierce teat To human sucklings ;   *Com. of Arthur* 28
hath not our good King Who *l* me thee,   *Gareth and L.* 1071
Clung to the shield that Lancelot *l* him,   ,, 1320
Pelleas *l* his horse and all his arms,   *Pelleas and E.* 358
which Innocence the Queen *L* to the King,   *Last Tournament* 294
l The sceptres of her West, her East,   *To Marq. of Dufferin* 5
Lenten That *L* fare makes *L* thought,   *To E. Fitzgerald* 31
Lent-lily and all *L-l* in hue,   *Gareth and L.* 911
Thy gay *lent-lilies* wave and put them by,   *Prog. of Spring* 37
Leodogran *L*, the King of Cameliard,   *Com. of Arthur* 1
King *L* Groan'd for the Roman legions   ,, 33
His new-made knights, to King *L*,   ,, 137
L in heart Debating—' How should I that am a king,   ,, 140
To whom the King *L* replied,   ,, 160
Thereat *L* rejoiced, but thought   ,, 310
She spake and King *L* rejoiced,   ,, 425
L awoke, and sent Ulfius, and Brastias and Bedivere,   ,, 444

Letty Hill (*See also* **Hill, Letty**) Tho' if, in dancing
after *L H*,   *Edwin Morris* 55
Level (adj.) counterchanged The *l* lake with diamond-
plots   *Arabian Nights* 85
For leagues no other tree did mark The *l* waste,   *Mariana* 44
Or opening upon *l* plots Of crowned lilies,   *Ode to Memory* 108
They past into the *l* flood,   *Miller's D.* 75
From *l* meadow-bases of deep grass   *Palace of Art* 7
Crisp foam-flakes scud along the *l* sand,   *D. of F. Women* 39
And on a sudden, lo ! the *l* lake,   *M. d'Arthur* 191
But when we planted *l* feet, and dipt   *Princess iv* 30
As waits a river *l* with the dam Ready to burst   " 473
And on by many a *l* mead,   *In Mem. ciii* 21
range Of *l* pavement where the King would pace   *Gareth and L.* 667
And on a sudden, lo ! the *l* lake,   *Pass. of Arthur* 359
And shine the *l* lands,   *Early Spring* 15
Level (s) Ridged the smooth *l*,   *Arabian Nights* 35
It springs on a *l* of bowery lawn,   *Poet's Mind* 31
The house thro' all the *l* shines,   *Mariana in the S.* 2
Came on the shining *l's* of the lake.   *M. d'Arthur* 51
thou shalt lower to his *l* day by day,   *Locksley Hall* 45
came On flowery *l's* underneath the crag,   *Princess iii* 336
waterily starts and slides Upon the *l*   " *iv* 256
Came on the shining *l's* of the lake.   *Pass. of Arthur* 219
The rippling *l's* of the lake,   *Lover's Tale iii* 4
O yes, if yonder hill be *l* with the flat.   *Locksley H., Sixty* 111
Down from the mountain And over the *l*,   *Merlin and the G.* 50
climb'd from the dens in the *l* below,   *The Dawn* 17
Level (verb) Not to feel lowest makes them *l* all ;   *Merlin and V.* 828
Lever A *l* to uplift the earth   *In Mem. cxiii* 15
Leveret quail and pigeon, lark and *l* lay,   *Audley Court* 24
Levied *L* a kindly tax upon themselves,   *Enoch Arden* 663
Levin-brand Then flash'd a *l-b*,   *Last Tournament* 616
Lewd when was Lancelot wanderingly *l* ?   *Holy Grail* 148
Lewdness *l*, narrowing envy, monkey-spite,   *Lucretius* 211
Lewes Were those your sires who fought at *L* ?   *Third of Feb.* 33
Liana And cliffs all robed in *l's*   *The Wreck* 73
Liar (*See also* **Hustings-liar, Loiar**) I raged against
the public *l* ;   *The Letters* 26
Let the canting *l* pack !   *Vision of Sin* 108
and slandering me, the base little *l* !   *Grandmother* 27
There the hive of Roman *l's*   *Boädicea* 19
And rave at the lie and the *l*,   *Maud I i* 60
clamour of *l's* belied in the hubbub of lies ;   " *iv* 51
Spurn'd by this heir of the *l*—   " *xix* 78
wrath shall be wreak'd on a giant *l* ;   " *III vi* 45
one said ' Eat in peace ! a *l* is he,   *Balin and Balan* 607
a glance will serve—the *l's* ?   *Merlin and V.* 111
' What dare the full-fed *l's* say of me ?   " 692
the King Hath made us fools and *l's*.   *Pelleas and E.* 479
' *L*, for thou hast not slain This Pelleas !   " 490
' Tell thou the King and all his *l's*,   *Last Tournament* 77
youthful jealousy is a *l*.   *Locksley H., Sixty* 240
teeming with *l's*, and madmen, and knaves,   *The Dreamer* 9
Libation No vain *l* to the Muse,   *Will Water.* 9
Liberal But Thou rejoice with *l* joy,   *England and Amer.* 11
And *l* applications lie In Art like Nature,   *Day-Dm., Moral* 13
Two in the *l* offices of life,   *Princess ii* 175
but come, We will be *l*, since our rights are won.   " *vi* 68
shook to all the *l* air The dust and din   *In Mem. lxxxix* 7
Liberal-minded *l-m*, great, Consistent ;   " *Con.* 38
Libera me, Domine ' *L m, D* !' you sang the Psalm,   *Happy* 49
Libera nos, Domine ' *L n, D* '—you knew not one was there   " 53
Liberty ' He that roars for *l* Faster binds   *Vision of Sin* 127
She bore the blade of *L*.   *The Voyage* 72
Close at the boundary of the *liberties* ;   *Princess i* 172
And boldly ventured on the *liberties*.   " 205
Not for three years to cross the *liberties* ;   " *ii* 71
To compass our dead sisters' *liberties*.'   " *iii* 288
Thine the *l*, thine the glory,   *Boädicea* 41
Me the wife of rich Prasútagus, me the lover of *l*,   " 48
Libyan ' We drank the *L* Sun to sleep,   *D. of F. Women* 145
License give you, being strange, A *l* :   *Princess iii* 205
You grant me *l* ; might I use it ?   " 235
takes His *l* in the field of time,   *In Mem. xxvii* 6

Licensed Should *l* boldness gather force,   *In Mem. cxiii* 13
Lichen I scraped the *l* from it :   *The Brook* 193
And a morbid eating *l* fixt On a heart   *Maud I vi* 77
Root-bitten by white *l*,   *Gareth and L.* 454
Lichen-bearded the hall Of Pellam, *l-b*,   *Balin and Balan* 332
Lichen'd *l* into colour with the crags :   *Lancelot and E.* 44
Lichen-gilded With turrets *l-g* like a rock :   *Edwin Morris* 8
Lidded *See* **Argent-lidded**
Lidless A *l* watcher of the public weal,   *Princess iv* 325
Lie (s) Can do away that ancient *l* ;   *Clear-headed friend* 15
' Wilt thou make everything a *l*,   *Two Voices* 203
Perplexing me with *l's* ;   *St. S. Stylites* 102
Cursed be the social *l's*   *Locksley Hall* 60
neither capable of *l's*, Nor asking overmuch   *Enoch Arden* 251
dare not ev'n by silence sanction *l's*.   *Third of Feb.* 10
a *l* which is half a truth is ever the blackest of *l's*,
That a *l* which is all a *l* may be met and fought
with outright, But a *l* which is part a truth is a
harder   *Grandmother* 30
Or Love but play'd with gracious *l's*,   *In Mem. cxxv* 7
To fool the crowd with glorious *l's*,   " *cxxviii* 14
and a wretched swindler's *l* ?   *Maud I i* 56
And rave at the *l* and the liar,   " 60
Jack on his ale-house bench has as many *l's* as a Czar ;   " *iv* 9
clamour of liars belied in the hubbub of *l's* ;   " *vi* 55
In another month to his brazen *l's*,   " *II i* 16
He fiercely gave me the *l*,   *Gareth and L.* 293
Who cannot brook the shadow of any *l*.'   " 297
Our one white *l* sits like a little ghost   " 323
' For this half-shadow of a *l* The trustful King
Gives him the *l* !   *Merlin and V.* 51
cloaks the scar of some repulse with *l's* ;   " 818
I should suck *L's* like sweet wines :   *Last Tournament* 645
Then playfully she gave herself the *l*—   *Lover's Tale i* 349
and he never has told me a *l*.   *Rizpah* 24
if the hope of the world were a *l* ?   *In the Child. Hosp.* 24
we knew that their light was a *l*—   *Despair* 16
To lie, to lie—in God's own house—the blackest of all *lies* !   *The Flight* 52
madness ? written, spoken *l's* ?   *Locksley H., Sixty* 108
L's upon this side, *l's* upon that side,   *Vastness* 5
voices drowning his own in a popular torrent of *l's* upon *l's* ;   " 6
Do not die with a *l* in your mouth,   *Forlorn* 57
A *l* by which he thought he could subdue   *Happy* 64
To you my days have been a life-long *l*,   *Romney's R.* 41
more Than all the myriad *l's*,   " 122
I may claim it without a *l*.   *Bandit's Death* 7
Lie (verb) (*See also* **Lig**) In the dark we must *l*.   *All Things will Die* 22
There hath he lain for ages and will *l*   *The Kraken* 11
Within thy heart my arrow *l's*,   *Oriana* 80
dead lineaments that near thee *l* ?   *Wan Sculptor* 2
On either side the river *l*   *L. of Shalott i* 1
Come from the wells where he did *l*.   *Two Voices* 9
to *l* Beside the mill-wheel in the stream,   *Miller's D.* 166
I would *l* so light, so light,   " 185
There *l's* a vale in Ida,   *Œnone* 1
on her threshold *l* Howling in outer
darkness.   *To ——, With Pal. of Art* 15
God, before whom ever *l* bare The abysmal
deeps   *Palace of Art* 222
But I shall *l* alone, mother,   *May Queen, N. Y's. E.* 20
All night I *l* awake,   " 50
To *l* within the Light of God, as I *l*   " *Con.* 59
Music that gentlier on the spirit *l's*,   *Lotos-Eaters, C. S.* 5
For they *l* beside their nectar,   " 111
Full knee-deep *l's* the winter snow,   *D. of the O. Year* 1
For the old year *l's* a-dying,   " 5
L still, dry dust, secure of change.   *To J. S.* 76
Nature, so far as in her *l*,   *On a Mourner* 1
but it *l's* Deep-meadow'd, happy fair   *M. d'Arthur* 261
between it and the garden *l's* A league of grass,   *Gardener's D.* 39
Beyond the lodge the city *l's*,   *Talking Oak* 5
He *l's* beside thee on the grass.   " 239
Peace *L* like a shaft of light   *Golden Year* 49
' Ah folly ! for it *l's* so far away,   " 54
There *l's* the port : the vessel puffs   *Ulysses* 44

Life (continued) Godless gloom Of a *l* without sun, — *Despair* 7
I am frighted at *l* not death.' — „ 14
L with its anguish, and horrors, — „ 48
and you saved me, a valueless *l*. — „ 61
Of the hellish heat of a wretched *l* — „ 68
whether this earth-narrow *l* Be yet but yolk, — *Ancient Sage* 129
gain of such large *l* as match'd with ours — „ 237
lose thy *l* by usage of thy sting ; — „ 270
daughter yield her *l*, heart, soul to one— — *The Flight* 28
And all my *l* was darken'd, — „ 39
where summer never dies, with Love, the Sun of *l* ! — „ 44
an the face of the thraithur agin in *l* ! — *Tomorrow* 50
ye would start back agin into *l*, — „ 81
I knaws i 'ed led tha a quieter *l* — *Spinster's S's.* 71
In my *l* there was a picture, — *Locksley H., Sixty* 15
brooding on his briefer lease of *l*, — „ 23
my *l* in golden sequence ran, — „ 47
the sacred passion of the second *l*. — „ 68
Fought for their *lives* in the narrow gap — *Heavy Brigade* 23
The light of days when *l* begun, — *Pref. Poem Broth. S.* 23
With stronger *l* from day to day ; — *Hands all Round* 6
Two Suns of Love make day of human *l*, — *To Prin. Beatrice* 1
Mother weeps At that white funeral of the single *l*, — „ 9
two that love thee, lead a summer *l*, — „ 18
One *l*, one flag, one fleet, one Throne !' — *Open. I. and C. Exhib.* 39
flame of *l* went wavering down — *To Marq. of Dufferin* 32
while my *l*'s late eve endures, — „ 49
The *L* that had descended re-arise, — *Demeter and P.* 30
we spin the *lives* of men, And not of Gods, — „ 85
Power That lifts her buried *l* from gloom to bloom, — „ 98
I fail'd To send my *l* thro' olive-yard — „ 110
Shalt ever send thy *l* along with mine — „ 145
gloom of the evening, *L* at a close ; — *Vastness* 15
in the misery of my married *l*, — *The Ring* 136
So far gone down, or so far up in *l*, — „ 193
Made every moment of her after *l* — „ 220
And there the light of other *l*, — „ 295
Saved when your *l* was wreck'd ! — „ 305
That now their ever-rising *l* has dwarf'd — „ 463
silent brow when *l* had ceased to beat. — *Happy* 52
snap the bond that link'd us *l* to *l*, — „ 61
leech forsake the dying bed for terror of his *l* ? — „ 98
this *l* of mingled pains And joys to me, — *To Mary Boyle* 49
long walk thro' desert *l* Without the one. — „ 55
new *l* that gems the hawthorn line ; — *Prog. of Spring* 36
his fresh *l* may close as it began, — „ 89
L, which is *L* indeed. — „ 117
As he stands on the heights of his *l* — *By an Evolution* 20
A whisper from his dawn of *l* ? — *Far—far—away* 10
Light again, leaf again, *l* again, love again,' — *The Throstle* 3
LIVE thy *L*, Young and old, — *The Oak* 1
My *l* and death are in thy hand. — *Death of Œnone* 40
Let me owe my *l* to thee. — „ 42
she heard The shriek of some lost *l* — „ 90
lazying out a *l* Of self-suppression, — *St. Telemachus* 21
Reason in the dusky cave of *L*, — *Akbar's Dream* 121
on this bank in *some* way live the *l* Beyond the bridge, — „ 144
To make him trust his *l*, — *The Wanderer* 11
The face of Death is toward the Sun of *L*, — *D. of the Duke of C.* 12
Lifeblood New *l* warm the bosom, — *Will Water.* 22
Life-bubbling who sliced a red *l-b* way — *Gareth and L.* 509
Lifeless I have cursed him even to *l* things) — *Maud I xix* 15
Lifelong rose and past Bearing a *l* hunger in his heart. — *Enoch Arden* 79
Then Philip with his eyes Full of that *l* hunger, — „ 464
A *l* tract of time reveal'd ; — *In Mem. xlvi* 9
Do forge a *l-l* trouble of ourselves, — *Geraint and E.* 3
With *l-l* injuries burning unavenged, — „ 696
There sat the *l* creature of the house, — *Lancelot and E.* 1143
Gaining a *l* Glory in battle, — *Batt. of Brunanburh* 7
And you the *l* guardian of the child. — *The Ring* 54
To you my days have been a *l-l* lie, — *Romney's R.* 41
Lifetime Ere half the *l* of an oak. — *In Mem. lxxvi* 12
Lift Many an arch high up did *l*, — *Palace of Art* 142
to *l* the hidden ore That glimpses, — *D. of F. Women* 274
L up thy rocky face, — *England and Amer.* 12

Lift (continued) knowing God, they *l* not hands of prayer — *M. d'Arthur* 252
in my weak, lean arms I *l* the cross, — *St. S. Stylites* 118
when I see the woodman *l* His axe to slay my kin. — *Talking Oak* 235
seem to *l* a burthen from thy heart — *Love and Duty* 96
He *l*'s me to the golden doors ; — *St. Agnes' Eve* 25
And *l* the household out of poverty ; — *Enoch Arden* 485
slowly *l*'s His golden feet on those empurpled stairs — *Lucretius* 134
l your natures up : Embrace our aims : — *Princess ii* 88
To *l* the woman's fall'n divinity — „ *iii* 223
fair philosophies That *l* the fancy ; — „ 341
'*L* up your head, sweet sister : — „ *v* 64
l thine eyes ; my doubts are dead, — „ *vii* 348
Could *l* them nearer God-like state — *Lit. Squabbles* 14
L as thou may'st thy burthen'd brows — *In Mem. lxxii* 21
And seem to *l* the form, and glow — „ *lxxxvii* 37
A great ship *l* her shining sides. — „ *ciii* 40
That we may *l* from out of dust — „ *cxxxi* 5
Shall I not *l* her from this land of beasts — *Com. of Arthur* 80
' Blow trumpet ! he will *l* us from the dust. — „ 491
Nor did she *l* an eye nor speak a word, — *Marr. of Geraint* 528
But *l* a shining hand against the sun, — *Geraint and E.* 473
Without the will to *l* their eyes, — *Merlin and V.* 836
Not *l* a hand—not, tho' he found me thus ! — *Last Tournament* 528
He spared to *l* his hand against the King — *Guinevere* 437
knowing God, they *l* not hands of prayer — *Pass. of Arthur* 252
To *l* us as it were from commonplace, — *Sisters (E. and E.)* 223
but 'e niver not *l* oop 'is 'eäd : — *Village Wife* 88
and *l*'s, and lays the deep, — *Tiresias* 22
Power That *l*'s her buried life — *Demeter and P.* 98
To thoughts that *l* the soul of men, — *To Master of B.* 14
I can but *l* the torch Of Reason — *Akbar's Dream* 120
Lifted (adj. and part.) And once my arm was *l* to hew down — *D. of F. Women* 45
So *l* up in spirit he moved away. — *Enoch Arden* 330
from her *l* hand Dangled a length of ribbon — „ 749
under his own lintel stood Storming with *l* hands, — *Aylmer's Field* 332
her arm *l*, eyes on fire— — *Princess, Pro.* 41
With *l* hand the gazer in the street. — *Ode on Well.* 22
till the cloud that settles round his birth Hath *l* but a little. — *Gareth and L.* 131
Which our high Lancelot hath so *l* up, — *Balin and Balan* 490
But when my name was *l* up, the storm Brake — *Merlin and V.* 502
' And I was *l* up in heart, and thought — *Holy Grail* 361
Till he, being *l* up beyond himself, — *Last Tournament* 679
and morn Has *l* the dark eyelash of the Night — *Akbar's Dream* 201
Lifted (verb) A limb was broken when they *l* him ; — *Enoch Arden* 107
l up A weight of emblem, — *Princess iv* 201
At which she *l* up her voice and cried. — „ *v* 81
Then us they *l* up, dead weights, — „ *vi* 348
To Thor and Odin *l* a hand : — *The Victim* 8
And once, but once, she *l* her eyes, — *Maud I viii* 5
l his voice, and call'd A hoary man, — *Com. of Arthur* 144
she *l* either arm, ' Fie on thee, King ! — *Gareth and L.* 657
How the villain *l* up his voice, — „ 716
L an arm, and softly whisper'd, — „ 1361
Crost and came near, *l* adoring eyes, — *Geraint and E.* 304
At which her palfrey whinnying *l* heel, — „ 533
gravely smiling, *l* her from horse, — „ 883
Then Lancelot *l* his large eyes ; — *Balin and Balan* 277
and *he l* faint eyes ; he felt One near him ; — „ 594
and they *l* up Their eager faces, — *Merlin and V.* 132
when she *l* up A face of sad appeal, — „ 233
And the Queen *L* her eyes, — *Lancelot and E.* 84
L her eyes, and read his lineaments. — „ 244
And noblest, when she *l* up her eyes. — „ 256
she *l* up her eyes And loved him, — „ 259
And *l* her fair face and moved away : — „ 682
Then like a ghost she *l* up her face, — „ 918
and *l* up his eyes And saw the barge — „ 1390
Pelleas *l* up an eye so fierce She quail'd ; — *Pelleas and E.* 601
Working a tapestry, *l* up her head, — *Last Tournament* 129
l up a face All over glowing with the sun — *Lover's Tale iv* 380
and *l* hand and heart and voice In praise to God — *Columbus* 16
she *l* her head— — *Tomorrow* 79
Then I *l* up my eyes, — *Happy* 82

Light (s) (continued) The maiden standing in the
dewy l. *Lancelot and E.* 352
The green l from the meadows underneath " 408
O damsel, in the l of your blue eyes ; " 660
the blood-red l of dawn Flared on her face, " 1025
I heard the sound, I saw the l, *Holy Grail* 280
all her form shone forth with sudden l " 450
A l was in the crannies, " 838
This l that strikes his eyeball is not l, " 913
loosed his horse, and led him to the l. *Pelleas and E.* 61
Was dazzled by the sudden l, " 105
a moon With promise of large l on woods " 394
And spied not any l in hall or bower, " 419
golden beard that clothed his lips with l— *Last Tournament* 668
Then in the l's last glimmer Tristram show'd " 739
one low l betwixt them burn'd *Guinevere* 4
' No l had we : for that we do repent ; " 171
' No l : so late ! and dark and chill the night ! O let
us in, that we may find the l ! " 174
in the l the white mermaiden swam, " 245
What knowest thou of the world, and all its l's And
shadows, " 343
thou reseated in thy place of l, " 525
near him the sad nuns with each a l Stood, " 590
Wet with the mists and smitten by the l's, " 597
That pure severity of perfect l— " 646
O l upon the wind, *Pass. of Arthur* 46
great l of heaven Burn'd at his lowest " 90
cryings for the l, Moans of the dying, " 116
the l that led The holy Elders with the gift of myrrh. " 400
when, clothed with living l, They stood before his throne " 454
From less to less and vanish into l. " 468
For when the outer l's are darken'd thus, *Lover's Tale* i 35
led on with l In trances and in visions : " 77
image, like a charm of l and strength " 91
Thou art l, To which my spirit leaneth " 103
Looking on her that brought him to the l : " 160
From the same clay came into l at once. " 194
a common l of eyes Was on us as we lay : " 236
till the morning l Sloped thro' the pines, " 263
Pour with such sudden deluges of l " 315
Methought a l Burst from the garland I had wov'n, " 365
A l methought broke from her dark, " 368
mystic l flash'd ev'n from her white robe " 370
a tissue of l Unparallel'd. " 419
Since in his absence full of l and joy, And giving l to
others. " 425
dwelling on the l and depth of thine, " 492
bliss stood round me like the l of Heaven,— " 495
whose right hand the l Of Life issueth, " 497
Steppeth from Heaven to Heaven, from l to l, " 512
We past from l to dark. " 516
eyes too weak to look upon the l ; " 614
The white l of the weary moon above, " 640
Between the going l and growing night ? " 664
Robed in those robes of l I must not wear, " 671
hold out the l's of cheerfulness ; " 807
Showers slanting l upon the dolorous wave. " 811
what l, what gleam on those black ways " 812
fused together in the tyrannous l— " ii 67
bliss, which broke in l Like morning " 143
Now the l Which was their life, " 163
And solid beam of isolated l, " 173
l Of smiling welcome round her lips— " iii 45
And, making there a sudden l, " iv 53
The l was but a flash, and went again. " 55
Wonder'd at some strange l in Julian's eyes " 205
him nor l's nor feast Dazed or amazed, " 310
an' puts 'im back i' the l. *North. Cobbler* 98
O diviner l, *Sisters (E. and E.)* 16
Break, diviner l ! " 23
dress thy deeds in l, Ascends to thee ; *Ded. Poem Prin. Alice* 9
hidden there from the l of the sun— *Def. of Lucknow* 63
Before thy l, and cry continually— *Sir J. Oldcastle* 85
Her love of l quenching her fear of pain— " 190

Light (s) (continued) last the l, the l On Guanahani ! *Columbus* 74
and the l Grew as I gazed, " 76
Sunless and moonless, utter l— " 90
Set thee in l till time shall be no more ? " 150
brooks glitter'd on in the l without sound, *V. of Maeldune* 13
we were lured by the l from afar, " 71
Waste dawn of multitudinous-eddying l— *De Prof., Two G.* 4
—her dark orb Touch'd with earth's l— " 10
that one l no man can look upon, " 37
the lost l of those dawn-golden times, *To W. H. Brookfield* 7
O YOU that were eyes and l to the King *To Prin. F. of H.* 1
dreadful l Came from her golden hair, *Tiresias* 43
spear and helmet tipt With stormy l " 114
Send no such l upon the ways of men " 161
Gone into darkness, that full l Of friendship ! " 202
and awake to a livid l, *The Wreck* 7
in the l of a dowerless smile, " 45
days of a larger l than I ever again shall know— " 78
we knew that their l was a lie— *Despair* 16
When the l of a Sun that was coming " 23
baby-girl, that had never look'd on the l : " 71
And, darkening in the l, *Ancient Sage* 151
And laughing back the l, " 168
doors of Night may be the gates of L ; " 174
Some say, the L was father of the Night, And some,
the Night was father of the L, " 247
up that lane of l into the setting sun. *The Flight* 40
side by side in God's free l and air, " 81
wid all the l an' the glow, *Tomorrow* 67
when Molly 'd put out the l, *Spinster's S's.* 97
for ever was the leading l of man. *Locksley H., Sixty* 66
France had shown a l to all men, " 89
shriek'd and slaked the l with blood. " 90
in that point of peaceful l ? " 190
were half as eager for the l. " 228
L the fading gleam of Even ? l the glimmer of the
dawn ? " 229
Follow L, and do the Right— " 277
Whirling their sabres in circles of l ! *Heavy Brigade* 34
L among the vanish'd ages ; *To Virgil* 25
shifting ladders of shadow and l, *Dead Prophet* 21
The l of days when life begun, *Pref. Poem Broth. S.* 23
THY prayer was ' L—more L— *Epit. on Caxton* 1
shadows which that l would cast, Till shadows vanish
in the L of L. " 3
This later l of Love have risen in rain, *To Prin. Beatrice* 16
l and genial warmth of double day. " 22
Trust the Hand of L will lead her people, *On Jub. Q. Victoria* 68
And the L is Victor, " 70
And all the Shadow die into the L, *Demeter and P.* 138
I'll coom an' I'll squench the l, *Owd Roä* 117
stings him back to the curse of the l ; *Vastness* 18
A l shot upward on them from the lake. *The Ring* 256
And there the l of other life, " 295
saw Your gilded vane, a l above the mist '— " 331
' and the l,' She said, ' was like that l '— " 333
l That glimmers on the marsh and on the grave.' " 340
one betwixt the dark and l had seen Her, " 414
soul in soul and l in l, *Happy* 39
in the brooding l of noon ? " 99
I, once half-crazed for larger l *To Ulysses* 29
Her l makes rainbows in my closing eyes, *Prog. of Spring* 46
still-fulfilling promise of a l " 90
l retreated, The landskip darken'd, *Merlin and the G.* 30
Could make pure l live on the canvas ? *Romney's R.* 10
Reflected, sends a l on the forgiven. " 161
L again, leaf again, life again, love again,' *The Throstle* 3
star of eve was drawing l From the dead sun, *Death of Œnone* 64
What l was there ? " 84
The morning l of happy marriage broke " 102
' L of the nations ' ask'd his Chronicler Of Akbar *Akbar's Dream* 1
There is l in all, And l, " 45
But find their limits by that larger l, " 99
By deeds a l to men ? " 111
But no such l Glanced from our Presence " 112

Light (s) (*continued*) arrowing *l* from clime to clime, *Akbar's Dream, Hymn* 5
  ' I am losing the *l* of my Youth *The Dreamer* 4
Light (come upon, etc.) Who can *l* on as happy a shore *Sea-Fairies* 40
  You could not *l* upon a sweeter thing : *Walk. to the Mail* 52
  What should you give to *l* on such a dream ? ' *Edwin Morris* 58
  He trusts to *l* on something fair ; *Day-Dm., Arrival* 20
  L on a broken word to thank him with. *Enoch Arden* 347
  if I could follow, and *l* Upon her lattice, *Princess* iv 99
  Britain *l* upon auguries happier ? *Boädicea* 45
  may you *l* on all things that you love, *Marr. of Geraint* 226
  but if ye know Where I can *l* on arms, *„* 422
  I should *l* upon the Holy Grail *Holy Grail* 367
  tha'll *l* of a livin' somewheers i' the Wowd *Church-warden, etc.* 47
  we shall *l* upon some lonely shore, *The Flight* 89
Light (kindle) *l* The light that shone when Hope was born. *In Mem. xxx* 31
Light (to illuminate) They *l* his little life away ; *Supp. Confessions* 46
  I let a sunbeam slip, To *l* her shaded eye ; *Talking Oak* 218
  God within him *l* his face, *In Mem. lxxxvii* 36
  L's with herself, when alone She sits *Maud I xiv* 12
  and *l's* the old church-tower, And *l's* the clock ! *The Flight* 93
'Light (to alight) Who '*l's* and rings the gateway bell, *In Mem. viii* 3
  That float thro' Heaven, and cannot *l* ? *Day-Dm., Ep.* 8
Light-blue Sweet-hearted, you, whose *l-b* eyes *In Mem. xcvi* 2
  A *l-b* lane of early dawn, *cxix* 7
Light Brigade Forward, the *L B* ! (repeat) *Light Brigade* 5, 9
  Honour the *L B,* *„* 54
Lighted (adj.) (*See also* **Evening-lighted, Never-**
  lighted, Silent-lighted, Still-lighted) And
  in the *l* palace near *L. of Shalott* iv 47
  Swung round the *l* lantern of the hall ; *Guinevere* 262
Lighted (kindled) tho' my lamp was *l* late, *May Queen, Con.* 18
Lighted (shone) from it *l* an all-shining flame. *Achilles over the T.* 6
Lighted (illuminated) *l* from below By the red race of
  fiery Phlegethon ; *Demeter and P.* 27
  And *l* from above him by the Sun ? *„* 31
Lighted (alighted) Love *l* down between them *The Bridesmaid* 6
  And *l* at a ruin'd inn, *Vision of Sin* 62
  Gareth overthrew him, *l*, drew, *Gareth and L.* 1121
  Molly belike may 'a *l* to-night upo' one. *Spinster's S's.* 7
  following *l* on him there, And shouted, *Death of Œnone* 55
Lighted on those of old That *l o* Queen Esther, *Marr. of Geraint* 731
  till she had *l o* his wound, *Geraint and E.* 513
  I *l o* the maid, Whose sleeve he wore ; *Lancelot and E.* 710
  mutter'd, ' I have *l o* a fool, *Pelleas and E.* 113
  and the great King, *L o* words : *„* 253
Lighten (illuminate) Have power on this dark land
  to *l* it, *Com. of Arthur* 93
Lighten (to flash) *L's* from her own central Hell— *Aylmer's Field* 761
  now she *l's* scorn At him that mars her plan, *Princess* v 131
  You flash and *l* afar, *Window, Marr. Morn.* 10
  O, *l* into my eyes and my heart, *„* 15
  l thro' The secular abyss to come, *In Mem. lxxvi* 5
  What *l's* in the lucid east *„* cv 24
  The brute earth *l's* to the sky, *„* cxxvii 15
  Flash upon flash they *l* thro' me— *Lover's Tale i* 51
Lighten (to make lighter) One burthen and she would
  not *l* it ? *Aylmer's Field* 703
  To *l* this great clog of thanks, *Princess* vi 126
Lighten'd (flashed) The random sunshine *l* ! *Amphion* 56
  a cloudy gladness *l* In the eyes of each. *The Captain* 31
  stars all night above the brim Of waters *l* into view ; *The Voyage* 26
  silver rays, that *l* as he breathed ; *Lancelot and E.* 296
  sword that *l* back the sun of Holy land, *Happy* 43
Lighten'd (made lighter) but a dream, yet it *l* my despair *Maud III vi* 18
Lightening Came *l* downward, and so spilt itself *Pelleas and E.* 426
Lighter (adj.) touch him with thy *l* thought. *Locksley Hall* 99
  Of finest Gothic *l* than a fire, *Princess, Pro.* 92
  My *l* moods are like to these, *In Mem. xx* 9
  The *l* by the loss of his weight ; *Maud I xvi* 2
Lighter (s) As flies the *l* thro' the gross. *In Mem. xli* 4
Lighter-footed And *l-f* than the fox. *Day-Dm., Arrival* 8
Lightest my ears could hear Her *l* breath ; *Edwin Morris* 65
  Of *l* echo, then a loftier form Than female, *Princess* iv 215
  The *l* wave of thought shall lisp, *In Mem. xlix* 5
  This lad, whose *l* word Is mere white truth *Balin and Balan* 517

Lightest (*continued*) whose *l* whisper moved him more *Pelleas and E.* 155
Light-foot *l-f* Iris brought it yester-eve, *Œnone* 83
  So saying, *l-f* Iris pass'd away. *Achilles over the T.* 1
Light-glooming *L-g* over eyes divine, *Madeline* 16
Light-green A *l-g* tuft of plumes she bore *Sir L. and Q. G.* 26
  L-g with its own shadow, keel to keel, *Lover's Tale i* 43
Light-headed I should grow *l-h*, I fear, *Maud I xix* 100
  ' O my child, ye seem *L-h*, *Lancelot and E.* 1063
Lighthouse with the gorgeous west the *l* shone, *Lover's Tale i* 60
  that night When the rolling eyes of the *l* *Despair* 9
Lighting *l* upon days like these ? *Locksley Hall* 99
Lightning (adj.) Till the *l* laughters dimple *Lilian* 16
  Those writhed limbs of *l* speed ; *Clear-headed friend* 23
  The *l* flash atween the rains, *Rosalind* 12
  The *l* flash of insect and of bird, *Enoch Arden* 574
Lightning (s) (*See also* **Cross-lightnings, Sheet-lightnings**)
  as the *l* to the thunder Which follows it, *The Poet* 50
  In the middle leaps a fountain Like sheet *l*, *Poet's Mind* 25
  wilt shoot into the dark Arrows of *l's.* *To J. M. K.* 14
  With thunders, and with *l's,* *Buonaparte* 6
  With summer *l's* of a soul *Miller's D.* 13
  great brand Made *l's* in the splendour of the moon, *M. d'Arthur* 137
  Nor ever *l* char thy grain, *Talking Oak* 277
  flash thy *l's*, weigh the Sun. *Locksley Hall* 186
  L of the hour, the pun, *Aylmer's Field* 441
  The wizard *l's* deeply glow, *In Mem. cxxii* 19
  That like a silent *l* under the stars *Maud III* vi 9
  Made *l's* and great thunders over him, *Com. of Arthur* 108
  And *l's* play'd about it in the storm, *Gareth and L.* 68
  so quick and thick The *l's* here and there *Holy Grail* 494
  Makes wicked *l's* of her eyes, *Guinevere* 520
  great brand Made *l's* in the splendour of the
  moon, *Pass. of Arthur* 305
  Thunderless *l's* striking under sea *To the Queen ii* 12
  tears, that shot the sunset in *l's* round me ; *Lover's Tale i* 443
  L's flicker'd along the heath ; *Dead Prophet* 79
  L may shrivel the laurel of Cæsar, *Parnassus* 4
  evergreen laurel is blasted by more than *l* ! *„* 12
Lightning-fork one *l-f* Flash'd out the lake ; *Sisters (E. and E.)* 96
Light-of-love he whom men call *l-o-l* ? ' *Pelleas and E.* 361
Lightsome Self-balanced on a *l* wing : *In Mem. lxv* 8
Light-wing'd *l-w* spirit of his youth return'd *Balin and Balan* 21
Like (adj., adv., s.) Her heart is *l* a throbbing star. *Kate* 9
  L men, *l* manners : *l* breeds *l*, they say : *Walk. to the Mail* 63
  L to Furies, *l* to Graces, *Vision of Sin* 41
  Am I so *l* her ? so they said on board. *The Brook* 223
  and *l* a gentleman, And *l* a prince : *Princess* iv 527
  Not *l* to *l*, but *l* in difference. *„* vii 278
  L the leaf in a roaring whirlwind, *l* *Boädicea* 59
  For words, *l* Nature, half reveal And half conceal *In Mem.* v 3
  l a stoic, or *l* A wise epicurean, *Maud I iv* 20
  There is none *l* her, none. (repeat) *Maud I. xviii* 2, 13
  Not thou, but *l* to thee : *„* II iv 12
  Tell me, was he *l* to thee ? ' *Merlin and V.* 613
  But up *l* fire he started : *Gareth and L.* 1123
  but one *l* him.' ' Why that *l* was he.' *Lancelot and E.* 574
  Not *l* him, ' Not *l* my Lancelot '— *Guinevere* 406
  And *l* the all-enduring camel, *Lover's Tale i* 136
  Made all our tastes and fancies *l*, *„* 242
  L to a low-hung and a fiery sky *„* ii 61
  And heard him muttering, ' So *l*, so *l* *„* iv 325
  cousin of his and hers—O God, so *l* ! ' *„* 327
  says, ' Good ! very *l* ! not altogether he.' *Sisters (E. and E.)* 136
  What be the next un *l* ? can tha tell *Village Wife* 19
  Those three ! the fourth Was *l* the Son of God ! *Sir J. Oldcastle* 176
  those two *l's* might meet and touch. *Two Voices* 357
  life ! he never saw the *l* ; *Princess* i 186
  To prick us on to combat ' *L* to *l* ! *„* v 304
  Pass, and mingle with your *l's*. *„* vi 341
  There was not his *l* that year in twenty parishes *Grandmother* 12
  Not violating the bond of *l* to *l*. *Lancelot and E.* 241
  I never saw his *l* ; there lives No greater leader.' *„* 316
  Camelot seen the *l*, since Arthur came ; *Holy Grail* 332
  love will go by contrast, as by *l's*. *Sisters (E. and E.)* 42
Like (verb) How *l* you this old satire ? ' *Sea Dreams* 198

Like (verb) (*continued*) we *l* them well: But children die;   *Princess iii* 252
   I *l* her none the less for rating at her!   " *v* 461
   Not es I cares fur to hear ony harm, but I *l*'s to knaw.   *Village Wife* 22

Like *See also* **Artist-like, Beastlike, Bell-like, Brother-like, Catlike, Chasm-like, Childlike, Christ-like, Cleopatra-like, Colt-like, Coquette-like, Deathlike, Dreamlike, Dryad-like, Dwarf-like, Eagle-like, Echo-like, Fatherlike, Firefly-like, Fool-like, Frost-like, Gem-like, Ghostlike, God-like, Grovelike, Harlot-like, Idiotlike, Ixion-like, King-like, Knightlike, Lancelot-like, Landlike, Lead-like, Lilylike, Lioness-like, Lionlike, Loike, Magnet-like, Maidenlike, Manlike, Mist-like, Moonlike, Mountain-like, Nestlike, Oration-like, Poet-like, Princelike, Saint-like, Shadow-like, Snowlike, Soldierlike, Star-like, Statue-like, Sun-like, Swanlike, Tusklike, Unking-like, Unknightlike, Wizard-like, Womanlike**

Liked more he look'd at her The less he *l* her;   *Dora* 35
   neither loved nor *l* the thing he heard.   *Aylmer's Field* 250
   she *l* it more Than magic music,   *Princess, Pro.* 194
   Nor tho' she *l* him, yielded she,   " *vii* 76
   But I *l* a bigger feller to fight   *North. Cobbler* 100
   I *l* the owd Squire an' 'is gells   *Village Wife* 6
   I *l* 'er the fust on 'em all,   " 9
Likelihood Needs must be lesser *l*,   *Lancelot and E.* 367
Likely ' O ay,' said Vivien, ' that were *l* too.   *Merlin and V.* 746
Liken'd he that tells the tale *L* them,   *Last Tournament* 227
Likeness ' Lo! God's *l*—the ground-plan—   *Vision of Sin* 187
   darkening thine own To thine own *l*;   *Aylmer's Field* 674
   Found a still place, and pluck'd her *l* out;   *Princess i* 92
   A *l*, hardly seen before, Comes out—   *In Mem. lxxiv* 3
   Thy *l* to the wise below,   " 7
   If any vision should reveal Thy *l*,   " *xcii* 2
   A momentary *l* of the King: *Com. of Arthur* 271
   That shadow of a *l* to the king   *Demeter and P.* 16
   Last as the *l* of a dying man,   " 88
   the *l* of thyself Without thy knowledge,   " 92
   groping for it, could not find One *l*,   *The Ring* 337
Liker light shall spread, and man be *l* man   *Golden Year* 35
   The Princess; *l* to the inhabitant Of some clear planet   *Princess ii* 35
   Yet in the long years *l* must they grow;   " *vii* 279
Likest seeing men, in power Only, are *l* gods,   *Œnone* 130
   The *l* God within the soul?   *In Mem. lv* 4
Lilac (adj.) So Willy and I were wedded: I wore a *l* gown;   *Grandmother* 57
Lilac (s) And makes the purple *l* ripe,   *On a Mourner* 7
   Academic silks, in hue The *l*,   *Princess ii* 17
Lilac-ambush Thro' crowded *l-a* trimly pruned;   *Gardener's D.* 112
Lilia And sister *L* with the rest.'   *Princess. Pro.* 52
   And *L* with the rest, and lady friends   " 97
   L, wild with sport, Half child half woman   " 100
   ' Where,' Ask'd Walter, patting *L*'s head   " 125
   Quick answer'd *L* ' There are thousands now   " 127
   If there were many *L*'s in the brood,   " 146
   The little hearth-flower *L*.   " 166
   and not for harm, So he with *L*'s.   " 175
   As many little trifling *L*'s—   " 188
   Said *L*; ' Why not now?' the maiden Aunt.   " 208
   L woke with sudden-shrilling mirth   " 216
   ' Take *L* then, for heroine,' clamour'd he,   " 223
   So *L* sang: we thought her half-possess'd,   " *iv* 585
   With which we banter'd little *L* first: " *Con.* 12
   L pleased me, for she took no part In our dispute: " 29
   L, rising quietly, Disrobed the glimmering statue   " 116
Lilian (*See also* **May Lilian**) AIRY, fairy *L*, Flitting, fairy *L*,   *Lilian* 1
   Cruel little *L*.   " 7
Lilied The streams through many a *l* row   *The winds, etc.* 5
Lilt whisper was sweet as the *l* of a bird!   *Tomorrow* 33
Lilted scraps of thundrous Epic *l* out   *Princess ii* 375
Lilting I was *l* a song to the babe,   *Bandit's Death* 20
Lily (adj.) holding out her *l* arms Took both his hands,   *Princess ii* 303
Lily (s) (*See also* **Gold-lily, Lent-lily, Tiger-lily, Water-lily**) to brush the dew From thine own *l*,   *Supp. Confessions* 85

Lily (s) (*continued*) Or opening upon level plots Of crowned *lilies*,   *Ode to Memory* 109
   Like a *l* which the sun Looks thro'   *Adeline* 12
   breath Of the *lilies* at sunrise?   " 37
   Gazing where the *lilies* blow   *L. of Shalott i* 7
   amaracus, and asphodel, Lotos and *lilies*:   *Œnone* 98
   Waves all its lazy *lilies*,   *Gardener's D.* 42
   Pure *lilies* of eternal peace,   *Sir Galahad* 67
   IT was the time when *lilies* blow,   *Lady Clare* 1
   The silver *l* heaved and fell;   *To E. L.* 19
   steamer paddling plied And shook the *lilies*:   *Princess, Pro.* 72
   than wear Those *lilies*, better blush   " *iii* 68
   violet varies from the *l* as far As oak from elm: " *v* 182
   ' Pretty bud! *L* of the vale!   " *vi* 193
   Now folds the *l* all her sweetness up,   " *vii* 186
   Roses and *lilies* and Canterbury-bells.'   *City Child* 5
   and flung The *lilies* to and fro,   *In Mem. xcv* 60
   fed on the roses and lain in the *lilies* of life.   *Maud I iv* 60
   Gathering woodland *lilies*,   " *xii* 7
   Maud is here, here, here In among the *lilies*.   " 12
   And *lilies* fair on a lawn;   " *xiv* 2
   Bright English *l*, breathing a prayer To be friends,   " *xix* 55
   I said to the *l*, ' There is but one   " *xxii* 19
   The *lilies* and roses were all awake,   " 51
   Queen *l* and rose in one;   " 56
   And the *l* whispers, ' I wait.'   " 66
   All made up of the *l* and rose That blow   " *II v* 74
   Have I beheld a *l* like yourself.   *Geraint and E.* 620
   A walk of *lilies* crost it to the bower: *Balin and Balan* 243
   white walk of *lilies* toward the bower.   " 249
   Saint who stands with *l* in hand In yonder shrine.   " 261
   Flow'd from the spiritual *l* that she held.   " 264
   Set in her hand a *l*, o'er her hung The silken case   *Lancelot and E* 1148
   In her right hand the *l*, in her left The letter—   " 1155
   Be carven, and her *l* in her hand.   " 1342
   Farewell too—now at last—Farewell, fair *l*.   " 1397
   spire of the mountain was *lilies* in lieu of snow, And the *lilies* like glaciers winded down,   *V. of Maeldune* 41
   And we wallow'd in beds of *lilies*,   " 48
   Had set the *l* and rose By all my ways   *Ancient Sage* 156
   My *l* of truth and trust—   " 160
   They made her *l* and rose in one,   " 161
   O slender *l* waving there,   " 167
Lily-avenue A *l-a* climbing to the doors;   *Aylmer's Field* 162
Lily-cradled the golden bee Is *l-c*:   *Œnone* 30
Lily-handed No little *l-h* Baronet he,   *Princess, Con.* 84
Lilylike The *l* Melissa droop'd her brows;   " *iv* 161
Lily maid Elaine, the *l m* of Astolat,   *Lancelot and E.* 2
   How came the *l m* by that good shield of Lancelot,   " 28
   close behind them stept the *l m* Elaine,   " 176
   l m Elaine, Won by the mellow voice   " 242
   Low to her own heart said the *l m*,   " 319
   The *l m* had striven to make him cheer,   " 327
   ' *L m*, For fear our people call you *l m* In earnest,   " 385
   Lancelot and the *l m* Smiled at each other,   " 738
   Then spake the *l m* of Astolat—   " 1085
   barge Whereon the *l m* of Astolat Lay smiling,   " 1242
Lily-shining lay The *l-s* child;   *Princess iv* 287
Lily-white Lord Ronald brought a *l-w* doe   *Lady Clare* 3
   The *l-w* doe Lord Ronald had brought   " 61
Limb The strong *l*'s failing;   *All Things will Die* 32
   profulgent brows, And perfect *l*'s,   *Supp. Confessions* 146
   Those writhed *l*'s of lightning speed;   *Clear-headed friend* 23
   her clear and bared *l*'s O'erthwarted   *Œnone* 138
   Resting weary *l*'s at last on beds of asphodel.   *Lotos-Eaters, C. S.* 125
   Those in whose lap our *l*'s are nursed,   *To J. S.* 10
   Denying not these weather-beaten *l*'s   *St. S. Stylites* 19
   Till all my *l*'s drop piecemeal from the stone,   " 44
   coverlid Unto her *l*'s itself doth mould   *Day-Dm., Sleep. B.* 10
   With naked *l*'s and flowers and fruit,   *The Voyage* 55
   Hair, and eyes, and *l*'s, and faces,   *Vision of Sin* 39
   A *l* was broken when they lifted him;   *Enoch Arden* 107
   Enoch took, and handled all his *l*'s,   " 153
   Till the little *l*'s are stronger.   *Sea Dreams* 306

Limb (continued)   Down thro' her *l*'s a drooping languor
wept :

and due To languid *l*'s and sickness ;	*Princess vi* 268
Give it time To learn its *l*'s :	,, 377
this weight of body and *l*,	,, *Con.* 79
Nor could I weary, heart or *l*,	*High. Pantheism* 5
And watch'd them, wax'd in every *l* ;	*In Mem. xxv* 9
brood On a horror of shatter'd *l*'s	,, *ciii* 30
Dark cedar, tho' thy *l*'s have here increased,	*Maud I i* 56
find nor face nor bearing, *l*'s nor voice,	,, *xviii* 18
nor pang Of wrench'd or broken *l*—	*Com. of Arthur* 71
and risk thine all, Life, *l*'s,	*Gareth and L.* 88
Brute bulk of *l*, or boundless savagery	,, 129
not trust the *l*'s thy God hath given,	,, 1330
At this he hurl'd his huge *l*'s out of bed,	,, 1388
I seem to suffer nothing heart or *l*,	*Marr. of Geraint* 124
Laid from her *l*'s the costly-broider'd gift,	,, 472
strongly striking out her *l*'s awoke ;	,, 769
free to stretch his *l*'s in lawful fight,	*Geraint and E.* 380
clung about her lissome *l*, In colour	,, 754
The text no larger than the *l*'s of fleas ;	*Merlin and V.* 223
Spake thro' the *l*'s and in the voice—	,, 672
round her *l*'s, mature in womanhood ;	*Holy Grail* 23
but so weary were his *l*'s,	*Pelleas and E.* 73
his unbroken *l*'s from the dark field,	,, 513
Strength of heart And might of *l*,	,, 585
The weight as if of age upon my *l*'s,	*Last Tournament* 198
ivy-tress had wound Round my worn *l*'s,	*Lover's Tale i* 125
blood Crept like marsh drains thro' all my languid *l*'s,	,, 619
' body and soul And life and *l*'s,	,, *ii* 53
happier using the knife than in trying to save the *l*,	,, *iv* 283
we were English in heart and in *l*,	*In the Child. Hosp.* 6
Lobbing away of the *l* by the pitiful-pitiless knife,—	*Def. of Lucknow* 46
a babe in lineament and *l* Perfect,	,, 85
I touch'd my *l*'s, the *l*'s Were strange	*De Prof., Two G.* 11
Death will freeze the supplest *l*'s—	*Ancient Sage* 234
great shock may wake a palsied *l*,	*Happy* 46
moved but by the living *l*,	*St. Telemachus* 57
	Akbar's Dream 133

Limbed *See* **Broad-limbed, Full-limbed, large-limbed, Long-limb'd, Snow-limbed**

Limber And legs of trees were *l*,	*Amphion* 14
Lime (tree) arching *l*'s are tall and shady,	*Margaret* 59
Not thrice your branching *l*'s have blown	*L. C. V. de Vere* 27
beech and *l* Put forth and feel a gladder clime.'	*On a Mourner* 14
all about the large *l* feathers low, The *l*	*Gardener's D.* 47
and over many a range Of waning *l*	,, 218
bard has honour'd beech or *l*,	*Talking Oak* 291
overhead The broad ambrosial aisles of lofty *l*	*Princess, Pro.* 87
Up that long walk of *l*'s I past	*In Mem. lxxxvii* 15
million emeralds break from the ruby-budded *l*	*Maud I iv* 1
Of leafless elm, or naked *l*,	*To Ulysses* 16
Lime (earth) To feed thy bones with *l*,	*Two Voices* 326
As dying Nature's earth and *l* ;	*In Mem. cxviii* 4
I am mortal stone and *l*.	*Helen's Tower* 6
Lime (verb) That every sophister can *l*.	*Love thou thy land* 12
Limed True—we had *l* ourselves With open eyes,	*Princess iii* 142
Limit till we reach'd The *l* of the hills ;	*Audley Court* 83
Here at the quiet *l* of the world,	*Tithonus* 7
on the glimmering *l* far withdrawn	*Vision of Sin* 223
and ran Ev'n to the *l* of the land,	*Enoch Arden* 578
Twofooted at the *l* of his chain,	*Aylmer's Field* 127
Slipt o'er those lazy *l*'s down the wind	,, 495
love-whispers may not breathe Within this vestal *l*,	*Princess ii* 222
storm and blast Had blown the lake beyond his *l*,	*The Daisy* 71
The *l* of his narrower fate,	*In Mem. lxiv* 21
No *l* to his distress ;	*Maud II v* 31
And in what *l*'s, and how tenderly ;	*Ded. of Idylls* 20
utter purity Beyond the *l* of their bond,	*Merlin and V.* 27
there ye fixt Your *l*, oft returning with the tide.	*Lancelot and E.* 1041
And laughter at the *l* of the wood,	*Pelleas and E.* 49
As from beyond the *l* of the world,	*Pass. of Arthur* 458
O'erbore the *l*'s of my brain :	*Lover's Tale i* 689

Limit (continued) Spain should oust The Moslem from her *l*,	*Columbus* 97
mortal *l* of the Self was loosed,	*Ancient Sage* 232
to know The *l*'s of resistance,	*To Duke of Argyll* 2
so to the land's Last *l* I came—	*Merlin and the G.* 110
find their *l*'s by that larger light,	*Akbar's Dream* 99
at the *l* of thy human state,	*God and the Univ.* 4
Limitless suns of the *l* Universe sparkled and shone in the sky,	*Despair* 15
Limn'd Sun himself has *l* the face for me.	*Sisters (E. and E.)* 101
Limours suitors as this maiden ; first *L*.	*Marr. of Geraint* 440
Enter'd, the wild lord of the place, *L*.	*Geraint and E.* 277
Earl *L* Drank till he jested with all ease,	,, 289
when the Prince was merry, ask'd *L*,	,, 297
Then rose *L*, and looking at his feet,	,, 302
told him all that Earl *L* had said,	,, 391
Led from the territory of false *L*	,, 437
moment after, wild *L*, Borne on a black horse,	,, 457
In combat with the follower of *L*,	,, 501
Limpet And on thy ribs the *l* sticks,	*Sailor Boy* 11
Limpin' Molly kem *l* up wid her stick,	*Tomorrow* 77
Linden (adj.) firefly-like in copse And *l* alley :	*Princess i* 209
on the sward, and up the *l* walks,	,, *iv* 209
Linden (s) The *l* broke her ranks and rent	*Amphion* 33
Lindenwood Hew'd the *l*, Hack'd the battleshield,	*Batt. of Brunanburh* 12
Line (s) (*See also* **Lion-line, Sea-line**) What time the foeman's *l* is broke,	*Two Voices* 155
Beyond, a *l* of heights, and higher	*Palace of Art* 82
tender curving *l*'s of creamy spray ;	*Lotos-Eaters, C. S.* 62
We past long *l*'s of Northern capes	*The Voyage* 35
LONG *l*'s of cliff breaking have left a chasm ;	*Enoch Arden* 1
known Far in a darker isle beyond the *l* ;	,, 605
He gave them *l* : (repeat)	*The Brook* 145, 181
Love, let me quote these *l*'s,	*Sea Dreams* 181
those *l*'s of cliffs were cliffs no more,	,, 217
On glassy water drove his cheek in *l*'s ;	*Princess i* 116
the Persian, Grecian, Roman *l*'s Of empire,	,, *ii* 130
' The fifth in *l* from that old Florian,	,, 238
l's of green that streak the white	,, *v* 196
ride with us to our *l*'s, And speak with Arac :	,, 225
long *l* of the approaching rookery swerve	,, *Con.* 97
Right thro' the *l* they broke ;	*Light Brigade* 19
Sunny tokens of the *L*,	*Ode Inter. Exhib.* 19
And never a *l* from my lady yet !	*Window, No Answer* 15
My blessing, like a *l* of light,	*In Mem. xvii* 10
So word by word, and *l* by *l*,	,, *xcv* 33
a grandson, first of his noble *l*,	*Maud I x* 12
face is practised when I spell the *l*'s,	*Merlin and V.* 367
Yet is there one true *l*, the pearl of pearls :	,, 459
Which is the second in a *l* of stars	,, 509
High with the last *l* scaled her voice,	*Lancelot and E.* 1019
with wandering *l*'s of mount and mere,	*Holy Grail* 252
Breast-high in that bright *l* of bracken stood :	*Pelleas and E.* 56
Glorious poet who never hast written a *l*,	*To A. Tennyson* 5
to the 'eat o' the *l* ?	*North. Cobbler* 6
We are six ships of the *l* ;	*The Revenge* 7
Clean from our *l*'s of defence	*Def. of Lucknow* 62
Fluttering the hawks of this crown-lusting *l*—	*Sir J. Oldcastle* 57
I send a birthday *l* Of greeting ;	*To E. Fitzgerald* 45
A hundred ever-rising mountain *l*'s,	*Ancient Sage* 282
Because you heard the *l*'s I read	*Pro. to Gen. Hamley* 17
call'd ' Left wheel into *l* ! '	*Heavy Brigade* 6
Virgil who would write ten *l*'s,	*Poets and their B.* 2
To you that bask below the *L*,	*To Ulysses* 45
follow'd *l* by *l* Your leading hand,	*To Mary Boyle* 40
bucket from the well Along the *l*,	*Prog. of Spring* 36
new life that gems the hawthorn *l* ;	*In Mem. lxxvii* 6
Line (verb) May bind a book, may *l* a box,	*In Mem. lxxvii* 6
Lineage past into the hall A damsel of high *l*,	*Gereth and L.* 588
A lady of high *l*, of great lands,	,, 609
I spring from loftier *l* than thine own.'	,, 961
Lineament Every *l* divine,	*Eleänore* 53
to take the cast Of those dead *l*'s	*Wan Sculptor* 2
Of faded form and haughtiest *l*'s,	*Princess ii* 448
writhing barbarous *l*'s,	*Boädicea* 74

Lineament (*continued*) Imperious, and of haughtiest *l's*.	*Marr. of Geraint* 190
Lifted her eyes, and read his *l's*.	*Lancelot and E.* 244
a babe in *l* and limb Perfect,	*De Prof., Two G.* 11
Lined *l* And rippled like an ever-fleeting wave,	*Gareth and L.* 214
And hollow *l* and wooded to the lips,	*Lover's Tale i* 398
Linen Fares richly, in fine *l*,	*Aylmer's Field* 659
Linger Knowledge comes, but wisdom *l's*, and I *l* on the shore,	*Locksley Hall* 141
Knowledge comes, but wisdom *l's*,	" 143
I *l* by my shingly bars ;	*The Brook* 180
To *l* here with one that loved us.'	*Princess iii* 339
And *l* weeping on the marge,	*In Mem. xii* 12
They rise, but *l* ; it is late ;	" *Con.* 91
brother *l's* late With a roystering company)	*Maud I xiv* 14
rose-garden, And mean to *l* in it	" *xx* 42
L with vacillating obedience;	*Gareth and L.* 13
I hate that he should *l* here ;	*Marr. of Geraint* 91
how hand *l's* in hand ! Let go at last !	*Merlin and V.* 106
' Why *l's* Gawain with his golden news ? '	*Pelleas and E.* 411
and *l* there To silver all the valleys	*Tiresias* 31
may *l*, till she sees Her maiden coming	*The Ring* 479
l, till her own, the babe She lean'd	" 483
Linger'd charmed sunset *l* low adown	*Lotos-Eaters* 19
altho' I *l* there Till every daisy slept,	*Gardener's D.* 164
but ever at a breath She *l*,	*Godiva* 45
Long o'er his bent brows *l* Averill,	*Aylmer's Field* 625
I *l* ; all within was noise Of songs,	*In Mem. lxxxvii* 18
By night we *l* on the lawn,	" *xcv* 1
For while he *l* there,	*Com. of Arthur* 63
Gareth awhile *l*.	*Gareth and L.* 172
L that other, staring after him ;	*Lancelot and E.* 721
L Ettarre : and seeing Pelleas droop,	*Pelleas and E.* 178
came the village girls And *l* talking,	" 509
well I could have *l* in that porch,	*Lover's Tale i* 186
As if perpetual sunset *l* there,	*The Ring* 83
preacher's *l* o'er his dying words,	*St. Telemachus* 75
Lingereth ' Why *l* she to clothe her heart	*Princess iv* 105
Lingering After a *l*,—ere she was aware,—	*Enoch Arden* 268
l out a five-years' death-in-life.	" 565
L about the thymy promontories,	*Sea Dreams* 38
and reach its fatling innocent arms And lazy *l* fingers.	*Princess vi* 139
by the field of tourney *l* yet	*Gareth and L.* 736
Lingeringly So *l* long, that half-amazed	*The Ring* 436
Link (s) Or to burst all *l's* of habit—	*Locksley Hall* 157
maids, That have no *l's* with men.	*Princess vi* 292
A *l* among the days, to knit The generations	*In Mem. xl* 15
lost the *l's* that bound Thy changes ;	" *xli* 6
closer I Betwixt us and the crowning race	" *Con.* 127
all in loops and *l's* among the dales	*Lancelot and E.* 166
(A visible *l* unto the home of my heart),	*Lover's Tale i* 431
seem'd as tho' a *l* Of some tight chain	" 594
From war with kindly *l's* of gold,	*Epilogue* 16
breaks her latest earthy *l* With me to-day.	*The Ring* 47
is making a new *l* Breaking an old one ?	" 50
that poor *l* With earth is broken,	" 475
And that was a *l* between us ;	*Bandit's Death* 16
We return'd to his cave—the *l* was broken—	" 29
Link (verb) Idle habit *l's* us yet.	*Miller's D.* 212
To which she *l's* a truth divine !	*In Mem. xxxiii* 12
thou should'st *l* thy life with one	" *lxxxiv* 11
Seems but a cobweb filament to *l* The yawning	*Lover's Tale i* 376
Link'd-Linkt *Link'd* month to month with such a chain	*Two Voices* 167
vapour touch'd the palace gate, And *link'd* again.	*Vision of Sin* 59
Which else had *link'd* their race with times to come—	*Aylmer's Field* 779
As *link'd* with thine in love and fate,	*In Mem. lxxxiv* 38
He *linkt* a dead man there to a spectral bride ;	*Maud II v* 80
love that *linkt* the King And Lancelot—	*Gareth and L.* 492
force in her *Link'd* with such love for me,	*Marr. of Geraint* 806
Has *link'd* our names together in his lay,	*Lancelot and E.* 112
built a way, where, *link'd* with many a bridge,	*Holy Grail* 502
broke Flying, and *link'd* again.	*Guinevere* 258
She that *link'd* again the broken chain	*Locksley H., Sixty* 52

O*

Link'd-Linkt (*continued*) snap the bond that *link'd* us life to life,	*Happy* 61
starved the wild beast that was *linkt* with thee	*By an Evolution.* 11
Linking and *l* tree to tree,	*Death of Œnone* 11
Linkt *See* **Link'd**	
Lin-lan-lone mellow *l-l-l* of evening bells	*Far—far—away* 5
Linnet (*See also* **Lintwhite**) Sometimes the *l* piped his song :	*Sir L. and Q. G.* 10
Like *l's* in the pauses of the wind :	*Princess, Pro.* 246
Started a green *l* Out of the croft ;	*Minnie and Winnie* 17
O merry the *l* and dove,	*Window, A* y 13
And pipe but as the *l's* sing :	*In Mem. xxi* 24
The *l* born within the cage,	" *xxvii* 3
That hears the latest *l* trill,	" *c* 10
' What knowest thou of birds, lark, mavis, merle, *L* ?	*Gareth and L.* 1079
three gray *l's* wrangle for the seed :	*Guinevere* 255
merry *l* knew me, The squirrel knew me,	*Lover's Tale i* 15
The *l's* bosom blushes at her gaze,	*Prog. of Spring* 17
Lintel and under his own *l* stood Storming the household flower Torn from the *l*—	*Aylmer's Field* 331
	Princess v 129
Lintwhite (*See also* **Linnet**) Her song the *l* swelleth,	*Claribel* 15
Lion (adj.) Folded her *l* paws, and look'd to Thebes.	*Tiresias* 149
Lion (s) (*See also* **Shield-lion**) The *l* on your old stone gates	*L. C. V. de Vere* 23
We heard the *l* roaring from his den :	*D. of F. Women* 222
comes a hungry people, as a *l*	*Locksley Hall* 135
The babe shall lead the *l*.	*Aylmer's Field* 648
and in her *l's* mood Tore open,	*Princess iv* 380
blazon'd *l's* o'er the imperial tent	" *v* 9
old *l*, glaring with his whelpless eye,	" *vi* 99
your long locks play the *L's* mane !	" 164
Porch-pillars on the *l* resting,	*The Daisy* 55
To have her *l* roll in a silken net	*Maud I vi* 29
A *l* ramps at the top,	" *xiv* 7
glow'd like a ruddy shield on the *L's* breast.	" *III vi* 14
Cover the *l's* on thy shield,	*Gareth and L.* 585
L and stoat have isled together,	" 893
' Ramp ye lance-splintering *l's*,	" 1305
prize The living dog have the dead *l* :	*Balin and Balan* 585
Gawain saw Sir Lancelot's azure *l's*,	*Lancelot and E.* 663
On wyvern, *l*, dragon, griffin, swan,	*Holy Grail* 350
For now there is a *l* in the way.'	" 645
none Stood near it but a *l* on each side	" 817
And the *l* there lay dying,	*The Revenge* 96
Was flinging fruit to *l's* ;	*Tiresias* 67
and hunters race The shadowy *l*,	" 178
till the *L* look no larger than the Cat, Till the Cat thro' that mirage of overheated language loom Larger than the *L*,—	*Locksley H., Sixty* 112
peasant cow shall butt the ' *L* passant '	" 248
trailing a dead *l* away, One, a dead man.	*St. Telemachus* 47
Lionel The friend, the neighbour, *L*, the beloved, The loved, the lover, the happy *L*, The low-voiced, tender-spirited *L*,	*Lover's Tale i* 653
L, the happy, and her, and her, his bride !	" 755
very face and form of *L* Flash'd	" *ii* 94
but *L* and the girl Were wedded,	" *iv* 13
bid him come : ' but *L* was away—	" 101
Heir of his face and land, to *L*.	" 129
And, tho' he loved and honour'd *L*,	" 148
And sent at once to *L*, praying him	" 180
to *L's* loss and his And that resolved self-exile	" 208
To one who had not spoken, *L*.	" 272
Not daring yet to glance at *L*.	" 309
I, by *L* sitting, saw his face Fire,	" 322
all but he, *L*, who fain had risen,	" 361
He slowly brought them both to *L*.	" 371
L, when at last he freed himself From wife and child,	" 379
Lioness *L* That with your long locks play	*Princess vi* 163
Yea, the cubb'd *l* ;	*Demeter and P.* 54
Lioness-like and rolling glances *l-l*,	*Boädicea* 71
Lion-guarded Here is Locksley Hall, my grandson, here the *l-g* gate.	*Locksley H., Sixty* 213
Lion-heart The *l-h*, Plantagenet,	*Margaret* 34
Lionlike rushing outward *l* Leapt on him,	*Guinevere* 107

List (strip, division)   a comb of pearl to part The *l's* of
   such a beard   *Merlin and V.* 245
List (to hear)   To *l* a foot-fall, ere he saw   *Palace of Art* 110
Listed   *See* **White-listed**
Listen   (*See also* **Listhen**)   O *l, l*, your eyes shall glisten
   (repeat)   *Sea-Fairies* 35, 37
   Whither away ? *l* and stay :   "   42
   stars that hung Love-charm'd to *l* :   *Love and Duty* 75
   But if you care indeed to *l*, hear   *Golden Year* 20
   Whisper'd '*L* to my despair :   *Edward Gray* 22
   '*L*, Annie, How merry they are down yonder   *Enoch Arden* 388
   Sit, *l*.'   Then he told her of his voyage,   "   861
   Call'd all her vital spirits into each ear To *l* :   *Aylmer's Field* 202
   l ! here is proof that you were miss'd :   *Princess, Pro.* 177
   I fear you'll *l* to tales,   *Grandmother* 54
   Did they hear me, would they *l*,   *Boädicea* 8
   They can but *l* at the gates,   *In Mem. xciv* 15
   The larkspur *l's*, ' I hear, I hear ; '   *Maud I xxii* 65
   I know that he lies and *l's* mute   *II v* 60
   That *l's* near a torrent mountain-brook,   *Geraint and E.* 171
   But *l* to me, and by me be ruled,   "   624
   And it shall answer for me. *L* to it.   *Merlin and V.* 386
   while the King Would *l* smiling.   *Lancelot and E.* 116
   but *l* to me, If I must find you wit :   "   147
   Would I for her coming and regret   "   866
   To vex an ear too sad to *l* to me,   *Guinevere* 315
   To speak no slander, no, nor *l* to it,   "   472
   L's the muffled booming indistinct   *Lover's Tale i* 637
   l how the birds Begin to warble   *The Flight* 60
   ' If he ? yes, he . . . lurks, *l's*,   "   71
   Your song—Sit, *l* !   *Romney's R.* 92
   L ! we three were alone in the dell   *Bandit's Death* 19
Listen'd   my hands upheld In thine, I *l* to thy vows,   *Supp. Confessions* 71
   I look'd And *l*, the full-flowing river of speech   *Œnone* 68
   thought that it was fancy, and I *l* in my bed,   *May Queen, Con.* 33
   from them clash'd The bells ; we *l* ;   *Gardener's D.* 221
   The deep air *l* round her as she rode,   *Godiva* 54
   Amazed and melted all who *l* to it ;   *Enoch Arden* 649
   While I *l*, came On a sudden the weird seizure   *Princess iv* 559
   Who spake no slander, no, nor *l* to it ;   *Ded. of Idylls* 10
   And while they *l* for the distant hunt,   *Marr. of Geraint* 184
   Enid *l* brightening as she lay ;   "   733
   I *l*, And her words stole with most prevailing
    sweetness   *Lover's Tale i* 552
   that I niver not *l* to noän !   *Spinster's S's.* 8
Listener   not to die a *l*, I arose,   *The Brook* 163
   but every roof Sent out a *l* :   *Aylmer's Field* 614
Listenest   Thou *l* to the closing door,   *In Mem. cxxi* 7
Listening (adj. and part.)   *L* the lordly music flowing   *Ode to Memory* 41
   For at eventide, I earnestly,   *A spirit haunts* 4
   L, whispers ' 'Tis the fairy Lady of Shalott.'   *L. of Shalott i* 35
   slow dilation roll'd Dry flame, she *l* ;   *Princess vi* 190
   with shut eyes I lay *L* ; then look'd.   *vii* 224
   L now to the tide in its broad-flung   *Maud I iii* 11
   And seen her sadden *l*—vext his heart,   *Pelleas and E.* 398
   She sat Stiff-stricken, *l* ;   *Guinevere* 412
   l till those armed steps were gone,   "   585
   but in all the *l* eyes Of those tall knights,   *Gareth and L.* 327
   The *l* rogue hath caught the manner of it.   "   778
   I came on him once at a ball, the heart of a *l* crowd—   *The Wreck* 47
   Sounding for ever and ever thro' Earth and her *l*
    nations,   *Parnassus* 7
Listening (s)   lonely *l's* to my mutter'd dream,   *Princess vii* 110
Listhen (listen)   'ud *l* to naither at all, at all.   *Tomorrow* 46
Listless   To be the long and *l* boy   *Miller's D.* 33
   L in all despondence,—read ;   *Aylmer's Field* 534
   And into many a *l* annulet,   *Geraint and E.* 258
Lists   Shot thro' the *l* at Camelot,   *M. d'Arthur* 224
   They reel, they roll in clanging *l*,   *Sir Galahad* 9
   All that long morn the *l* were hammer'd up,   *Princess v* 368
   woke it was the point of noon, The *l* were ready.   "   483
   He rode the mellay, lord of the ringing *l*,   "   502
   father heard and ran In on the *l*,   *vi* 27
   Thro' open field into the *l* they wound Timorously ;   "   84
   and settling circled all the *l*.   *Marr. of Geraint* 547

Lists (*continued*)   tho' her gentle presence at the *l*   *Marr. of Geraint* 795
   hope that sometime you would come To these
    my *l* with him   *Geraint and E.* 840
   Lancelot, and his prowess in the *l*,   *Lancelot and E.* 82
   Favour of any lady in the *l*. (repeat)   "   364, 474
   when they reach'd the *l* By Camelot in the meadow,   "   428
   They that assail'd, and they that held the *l*,   "   455
   the Table Round that held the *l*, (repeat)   "   467, 499
   on that day when Lancelot fled the *l*,   "   525
   Of all my late-shown prowess in the *l*,   *Holy Grail* 362
   ' Queen of Beauty,' in the *l* Cried—   *Pelleas and E.* 116
   withheld His older and his mightier from the *l*,   "   160
   with cups of gold, Moved to the *l*,   *Last Tournament* 143
   Sat their great umpire, looking o'er the *l*.   "   159
   Shot thro' the *l* at Camelot,   *Pass. of Arthur* 392
Lit (came upon, etc.)   bore Them earthward till they *l* ;   *The Poet* 18
   On the tree-tops a crested peacock *l*,   *Œnone* 104
   And here we *l* on Aunt Elizabeth,   *Princess, Pro.* 96
   And wheel'd or *l* the filmy shapes   *In Mem. xcv* 10
   Leapt in a semicircle, and *l* on earth ;   *Balin and Balan* 414
Lit (kindled, etc.)   *l* your eyes with tearful power,   *Margaret* 3
   from her wooden walls,—*l* by sure hands,—   *Buonaparte* 5
   gray eyes *l* up With summer lightnings   *Miller's D.* 12
   L up a torrent-bow.   *Palace of Art* 36
   L with a low large moon.   "   68
   L light in wreaths and anadems,   "   186
   and *l* Lamps which out-burn'd Canopus.   *D. of F. Women* 145
   She *l* the spark within my throat,   *Will Water.* 109
   Thus, as a hearth *l* in a mountain home,   *Balin and Balan* 231
   Her smile *l* up the rainbow on my tears,   *Lover's Tale i* 254
   itself *l* up There on the depth of an unfathom'd woe   "   745
   After their marriage *l* the lover's Bay,   "   *iv* 28
   an' just as candles was *l*,   *North. Cobbler* 87
   this shore *l* by the suns and moons   *De Prof., Two G.* 38
Lit   *See also* **Crescent-lit, Dew-lit, Dim-lit, Fame-lit,**
   Lamp-lit, Moon-lit
Litany   solemn psalms, and silver *litanies*,   *Princess ii* 477
Literary   swarm'd His *l* leeches.   *Will Water.* 200
Lithe   bent or broke The *l* reluctant boughs   *Enoch Arden* 381
   and made her *l* arm round his neck Tighten,   *Merlin and V.* 614
Litter-bier   Yet raised and laid him on a *l-b*,   *Geraint and E.* 566
Little   They light his *l* life alway ;   *Supp. Confessions* 46
   Had I So *l* love for thee ?   "   88
   Cruel *l* Lilian.   *Lilian* 7
   Like *l* clouds sun-fringed, are thine,   *Madeline* 17
   and bosoms prest To *l* harps of gold ;   *Sea-Fairies* 4
   Or when *l* airs arise,   *Adeline* 33
   L breezes dusk and shiver   *L. of Shalott i* 11
   And *l* other care hath she,   *ii* 8
   ' His *l* daughter, whose sweet face He kiss'd,   *Two Voices* 253
   ' Before the *l* ducts began To feed thy bones with lime,   "   325
   The *l* maiden walk'd demure,   "   419
   A *l* whisper silver-clear,   "   428
   A *l* hint to solace woe,   "   433
   You would, and would not, *l* one !   *Miller's D.* 134
   but she thought I might have look'd a *l* higher ;   "   140
   A thousand *l* shafts of flame Were shiver'd   *Fatima* 17
   And in a *l* while our lips are dumb.   *Lotos-Eaters, C. S.* 44
   Like a tale of *l* meaning tho' the words are strong ;   "   119
   Storing yearly *l* dues of wheat, and wine and oil ;   "   122
   Each *l* sound and sight.   *D. of F. Women* 277
   for this star Rose with you thro' a *l* arc   *To L.* 26
   A *l* thing may harm a wounded man.   *M. d'Arthur* 42
   And in the compass of three *l* words,   *Gardener's D.* 232
   And made a *l* wreath of all the flowers That grew about,   *Dora* 82
   To save her *l* finger from a scratch   *Edwin Morris* 63
   yet long ago I have pardon'd *l* Letty ;   "   140
   Or in the night, after a *l* sleep, I wake :   *St. S. Stylites* 113
   'Tis *l* more : the day was warm ;   *Talking Oak* 205
   and drew My *l* oakling from the cup,   "   231
   Life piled on life Were all too *l*,   *Ulysses* 25
   Comrades, leave me here a *l*,   *Locksley Hall* 1
   With a *l* hoard of maxims preaching down a daughter's
    heart.   "   94
   ' You would not let your *l* finger ache For such as *these* ? '—   *Godiva* 22

Little (*continued*)   The *l* wide-mouth'd heads upon the spout   *Godiva* 56
Boring a *l* auger-hole in fear, Peep'd—   ,, 68
and shows At distance like a *l* wood ;   *Day-Dm., Sleep. P.* 42
from the valleys underneath Came *l* copses climbing.   *Amphion* 32
Nor yet the fear of *l* books Had made him talk for show ;   *Will Water.* 195
She took the *l* ivory chest,   *The Letters* 17
While we keep a *l* breath !   *Vision of Sin* 192
A *l* grain of conscience made him sour.'   ,, 218
The *l* life of bank and brier,   *You might have won* 30
Annie Lee, The prettiest *l* damsel in the port,   *Enoch Arden* 12
daily left The *l* footprint daily wash'd away.   ,, 22
' This is my house and this my *l* wife,'   ,, 28
at this The *l* wife would weep for company,   ,, 34
And say she would be *l* wife to both.   ,, 36
No graver than as when some *l* cloud   ,, 129
set his hand To fit their *l* streetward sitting-room   ,, 170
This pretty, puny, weakly *l* one,—   ,, 195
And kiss'd his wonder-stricken *l* ones ;   ,, 229
The *l* innocent soul flitted away.   ,, 270
' I may see her now, May be some *l* comfort ; '   ,, 276
Fresh from the burial of her *l* one,   ,, 281
And past into the *l* garth beyond.   ,, 329
How Philip put her *l* ones to school,   ,, 706
Flourish'd a *l* garden square and wall'd :   ,, 734
Uphold me, Father, in my loneliness A *l* longer !   ,, 785
To rush abroad all round the *l* haven,   ,, 867
the *l* port Had seldom seen a costlier funeral.   ,, 916
By twenty thorps, a *l* town,   *The Brook* 29
The *l* dells of cowslip, fairy palms,   *Aylmer's Field* 91
Has often toil'd to clothe your *l* ones ;   ,, 699
(for the man Had risk'd his *l*) like the *l* thrift,   *Sea Dreams* 10
And musing on the *l* lives of men,   ,, 48
A sort of absolution in the sound To hate a *l* longer !   ,, 62
broke The glass with *l* Margaret's medicine in it ;   ,, 142
(Altho' I grant but *l* music there)   ,, 253
Sleep, *l* birdie, sleep ! will she not sleep Without her " *l* birdie " ?   ,, 282
What does *l* birdie say In her nest at peep of day ?   ,, 293
Let me fly, says *l* birdie,   ,, 295
Birdie, rest a *l* longer, Till the *l* wings are stronger.   ,, 297
So she rests a *l* longer, Then she flies away.   ,, 299
What does *l* baby say, In her bed at peep of day ?   ,, 301
Baby says, like *l* birdie, Let me rise and fly away.   ,, 303
Baby, sleep a *l* longer, Till the *l* limbs are stronger.   ,, 305
If she sleeps a *l* longer, Baby too shall fly away.   ,, 307
Tired of so much within our *l* life, Or of so *l* in our *l* life—   *Lucretius* 226
Poor *l* life that toddles half an hour   ,, 228
round the lake A *l* clock-work steamer paddling plied   *Princess, Pro.* 71
A rosebud set with *l* wilful thorns,   ,, 154
The *l* hearth-flower Lilia.   ,, 166
As many *l* trifling Lilias—play'd Charades   ,, 188
(A *l* sense of wrong had touch'd her face With colour)   ,, 219
A *l* dry old man, without a star,   ,, *i* 117
A *l* street half garden and half house ;   ,, 214
There above the *l* grave, O there above the *l* grave,   ,, *ii* 12
O by the bright head of my *l* niece,   ,, 276
' The mother of the sweetest *l* maid,   ,, 279
While my *l* one, while my pretty one, sleeps.   ,, *iii* 8
Sleep, my *l* one, sleep, my pretty one, sleep.   ,, 16
What looks so *l* graceful ' men '   ,, 53
Many a *l* hand Glanced like a touch of sunshine on the rocks,   ,, 356
A *l* space was left between the horns,   ,, *iv* 207
Upon the level in *l* puffs of wind,   ,, 256
while We gazed upon her came a *l* stir About the doors,   ,, 373
A *l* shy at first, but by and by We twain,   ,, *v* 45
The child is hers—for every *l* fault,   ,, 87
And lay my *l* blossom at my feet,   ,, 100
indeed I think Our chiefest comfort is the *l* child   ,, 430
And on the *l* clause ' take not his life : '   ,, 470
The *l* seed they laugh'd at in the dark,   ,, *vi* 34
while Psyche ever stole A *l* nearer,   ,, 133

Little (*continued*)   and now A word, but one, one *l* kindly word,   *Princess vi* 258
Her head a *l* bent ; and on her mouth A doubtful smile   ,, 269
bird, That early woke to feed her *l* ones,   ,, *vii* 252
With which we banter'd *l* Lilia first :   ,, *Con.* 12
Then rose a *l* feud betwixt the two,   ,, 23
The *l* boys begin to shoot and stab,   ,, 61
and look'd No *l* lily-handed Baronet he,   ,, 84
Last *l* Lilia, rising quietly,   ,, 116
For one about whose patriarchal knee Late the *l* children clung :   *Ode on Well.* 237
No *l* German state are we,   *Third of Feb.* 15
AND Willy, my eldest-born, is gone, you say, *l* Annie ?   *Grandmother* 1
And she to be coming and slandering me, the base *l* liar !   ,, 27
Shadow and shine is life, *l* Annie, flower and thorn.   ,, 60
There lay the sweet *l* body that never had drawn a breath :   ,, 62
I had not wept, *l* Annie, not since I had been a wife ;   ,, 63
His dear *l* face was troubled, as if with anger or pain :   ,, 65
I look'd at the still *l* body—his trouble had all been in vain.   ,, 66
Patter she goes, my own *l* Annie, an Annie like you :   ,, 78
And in this Book, *l* Annie, the message is one of Peace.   ,, 96
the city Of *l* Monaco, basking, glow'd.   *The Daisy* 8
Still in the *l* book you lent me,   ,, 99
Making the *l* one leap for joy.   *To F. D. Maurice* 4
Read my *l* fable : He that runs may read.   *The Flower* 17
For a score of sweet *l* summers or so ? '   *The Islet* 2
The sweet *l* wife of the singer said.   ,, 3
To a sweet *l* Eden on earth that I know,   ,, 14
DAINTY *l* maiden, whither would you wander ? (repeat)   *City Child* 1, 6
' Far and far away,' said the dainty *l* maiden, (repeat)   ,, 3, 8
Sleep, *l* ladies ! And they slept well.   *Minnie and Winnie* 5
Sleep, *l* ladies ! Wake not soon !   ,, 9
Wake, *l* ladies, The sun is aloft !   ,, 19
O *l* bard, is your lot so hard,   *Spiteful Letter* 5
And do their *l* best to bite   *Lit. Squabbles* 6
He bore but *l* game in hand ;   *Victim* 42
I hold you here, root and all, in my hand,   *L* flower—   *Flow. in cran. wall* 4
dash the brains of the *l* one out,   *Boädicea* 68
As some rare *l* rose, a piece of inmost Horticultural art,   *Hendecasyllabics* 19
O lights, are you flying over her sweet *l* face ?   *Window, On the Hill* 13
Go, *l* letter, apace, apace,   *The Letter* 11
Two *l* hands that meet, (repeat)   *Answer* 1, 4
Look how they tumble the blossom, the mad *l* tits !   *Ay* 9
Our *l* systems have their day ;   *In Mem., Pro.* 17
the clock Beats out the *l* lives of men.   ,, *ii* 8
'Tis *l* ; but it looks in truth As if the quiet bones   ,, *xviii* 5
For now her *l* ones have ranged ;   ,, *xxi* 26
or to use A *l* patience ere I die ;   ,, *xxxiv* 12
And owning but a *l* art To lull with song an aching heart,   ,, *xxxviii* 14
A *l* flash, a mystic hint ;   ,, *xliv* 8
Abide a *l* longer here,   ,, *lviii* 11
The *l* village looks forlorn ;   ,, *lx* 8
When he was *l* more than boy,   ,, *lxii* 6
A *l* grain shall not be spilt.'   ,, *lxv* 4
breeze of song To stir a *l* dust of praise.   ,, *lxxv* 12
The *l* speedwell's darling blue,   ,, *lxxxiii* 6
Whose life, whose thoughts were *l* worth,   ,, *lxxxv* 30
but led the way To where a *l* shallop lay   ,, *ciii* 19
A *l* spare the night I loved,   ,, *cv* 15
A *l* while from his embrace,   ,, *cxvii* 3
From *l* cloudlets on the grass,   ,, *Con.* 94
I HATE the dreadful hollow behind the *l* wood,   *Maud I i* 1
Or the least *l* delicate aquiline curve in a sensitive nose, From which I escaped heart-free, with the least *l* touch of spleen.   ,, *ii* 10
In the *l* grove where I sit—ah,   ,, *iv* 2
whole *l* wood where I sit is a world of plunder and prey.   ,, 24
However we brave it out, we men are a *l* breed.   ,, 30
Because their natures are *l*, and, whether he heed it or not,   ,, 53

Live (verb) (*continued*)   in mine own heart I can *l* down
sin | *Guinevere* 636
and still I *l* Who love thee ; | *Pass. of Arthur* 150
Not tho' I *l* three lives of mortal men, | " 323
In that I I *l* love ; because I love I *l* : | *Lover's Tale* i 178
blight *L*'s in the dewy touch of pity | " 695
mask of Hate, who *l*'s on others' moans. | " 775
the Saviour *l*'s but to bless. | *Rizpah* 64
l to fight again and to strike another blow.' | *The Revenge* 95
My God, I would not *l* Save that I think | *Sisters (E. and E.)* 228
necessity for talk Which *l*'s with blindness, | " 249
she'll never *l* thro' it, I fear.' | *In the Child. Hosp.* 42
' He says I shall never *l* thro' it, | " 47
that, which lived True life, *l* on— | *Ded. Poem Prin. Alice* 2
Kill or be kill'd, *l* or die, | *Def. of Lucknow* 41
For I must *l* to testify by fire. | *Sir J. Oldcastle* 206
L, and be happy in thyself, | *De Prof., Two G.* 15
channel where thy motion *l*'s Be prosperously shaped, | " 19
L thou ! and of the grain and husk, | " 50
Who *l* on milk and meal and grass ; | *To E. Fitzgerald* 13
that *l*'s Behind this darkness, | *Tiresias* 51
work'd no good to aught that *l*'s, | " 77
one thing given me, to love and to *l* for, | *The Wreck* 35
Why should I *l* ? | *Despair* 69
Let it *l* then—ay, till when ? | *Epilogue* 63
May freedom's oak for ever *l* | *Hands all Round* 5
man, that only *l*'s and loves an hour, | *Demeter and P.* 106
which *l*'s Beyond our burial and our buried eyes, | *The Ring* 295
You will *l* till *that* is born, | *Forlorn* 63
leper's hut, where *l*'s the living-dead. | *Happy* 4
would he *l* and die alone ? | " 5
then I am dead, who only *l* for you. | " 96
I will *l* and die with you. | " 108
Could make pure light *l* on the canvas ? | *Romney's R.* 10
can Music make you *l* Far—far—away ? | *Far—far—away* 17
L thy Life, Young and old, | *The Oak* 1
l the life Beyond the bridge, | *Akbar's Dream* 144
I sticks like the ivin as long as I *l*'s | *Church-warden, etc.* 15
She has left me enough to *l* on. | *Charity* 40
O happy he, and fit to *l*, | *The Wanderer* 9

Lived   *l* in either's heart and speech. | *Sonnet To ——* 14
Have *l* and loved alone so long, | *Miller's D.* 38
If I had *l*—I cannot tell— | *May Queen, Con.* 47
You *l* with us so steadily, | *D. of the O. Year* 8
I have *l* my life, and that which I have done | *M. d'Arthur* 244
nor less among us *l* Her fame from lip to lip. | *Gardener's D.* 50
Dora *l* unmarried till her death. | *Dora* 172
The farmer's son, who *l* across the bay, | *Audley Court* 75
There *l* a flayflint near ; | *Walk. to the Mail* 84
Here I the Hills— | *Edwin Morris* 11
while I *l* In the white convent down the valley | *St. S. Stylites* 61
I *l* up there on yonder mountain side. | " 72
Three years I *l* upon a pillar, | " 86
Farewell, like endless welcome, *l* and died. | *Love and Duty* 68
They said he *l* shut up within himself, | *Golden Year* 9
O had I *l* when song was great | *Amphion* 9
And *l* a life of silent melancholy. | *Enoch Arden* 260
fell Sun-stricken, and that other *l* alone. | " 570
Where Annie and loved him, | " 685
O had he *l* ! In our schoolbooks we say, | *The Brook* 9
I *l* for years a stunted sunless life ; | *Aylmer's Field* 357
In other scandals that have *l* and died, | " 443
I thought I *l* securely as yourselves— | *Lucretius* 210
There *l* an ancient legend in our house. | *Princess* i 5
L thro' her to the tips of her long hands, | " ii 40
bones of some vast bulk that *l* and roar'd | " iii 294
You prized my counsel, *l* upon my lips : | " iv 293
l in all fair lights, | " 430
equal baseness *l* in sleeker times | " v 385
and *l* but for mine own. | " 389
My dream had never died or *l* again. | " vi 17
Sweet order *l* again with other laws : | " vii 19
as dearer thou for faults *L* over : | " 348
the sooner, for he *l* far away. | *Grandmother* 16
Aurelius *l* and fought and died, | *Com. of Arthur* 13

Lived (*continued*)   King Who *l* and died for men, | *Gareth and L.* 383
So large mirth *l* and Gareth won the quest. | " 1426
Tho' yet there *l* no proof, | *Marr. of Geraint* 26
so there *l* some colour in your cheek, | *Geraint and E.* 621
l thro' her, who in that perilous hour | " 766
l in hope that sometime you would come | " 839
I have not *l* my life delightsomely : | *Balin and Balan* 60
There *l* a king in the most Eastern East, | *Merlin and V.* 555
And *l* there neither dame nor damsel | " 606
Who *l* alone in a great wild on grass ; | " 621
back to his old wild, and *l* on grass, | " 649
One child they had : it *l* with her ; she died : | " 716
And saved him : so she *l* in fantasy. | *Lancelot and E.* 27
A horror *l* about the tarn, | " 37
all night long his face before her *l*, | " 331
the face before her *l*, Dark-splendid, | " 337
There kept it, and so *l* in fantasy. | " 398
Sir Lancelot knew there *l* a knight | " 401
Struck up and *l* along the milky roofs ; | " 409
in me *l* a sin So strange, of such a kind, | *Holy Grail* 772
She *l* a moon in that low lodge with him : | *Last Tournament* 381
an Abbess, *l* For three brief years, | *Guinevere* 696
I have *l* my life, and that which I have done | *Pass. of Arthur* 412
So that, in that I *have* *l*, do I live, | *Lover's Tale* i 120
how should I have *l* and not have loved ? | " 170
we *l* together, Apart, alone together on those hills. | " 189
But many weary moons I *l* alone— | " ii 2
l Scatteringly about that lonely land | " iv 184
Affirming that as long as either *l*, | " 277
Ah—you, that have *l* so soft, | *Rizpah* 17
he *l* with a lot of wild mates, | " 29
Squire's laädy es long es she *l* | *Village Wife* 53
long es she *l* I niver held none of 'er darters 'ere ; | " 54
Hugger-mugger they *l*, but they wasn't | " 117
which *l* True life, live on— | *Ded. Poem Prin. Alice* 1
He *l* on an isle in the ocean— | *V. of Maeldune* 7
He had *l* ever since on the Isle | " 116
I had *l* a wild-flower life, | *The Wreck* 37
Our gentle mother, had *she l*— | *The Flight* 77
aisier work av they *l* be an Irish bog. | *Tomorrow* 72
But I couldn't 'a *l* wi' a man | *Spinster's S's.* 52
that you have not *l* in vain. | *Locksley H., Sixty* 242
An' 'e sarved me sa well when 'e *l*, | *Owd Roä* 11
when we *l* i' Howlaby Daäle, | " 19
He that has *l* for the lust of the minute, | *Vastness* 27
l With Muriel's mother on the down, | *The Ring* 147
Live-green   Out of the *l-g* heart of the dells | *Sea-Fairies* 12
Livelier   And *l* than a lark She sent her voice | *Talking Oak* 122
In the Spring a *l* iris changes on the burnish'd dove ; | *Locksley Hall* 19
then we crost To a *l* land ; | *Princess* i 110
Then Florian, but no *l* than the dame | " ii 112
Nor less it pleased in *l* moods, | *In Mem.* lxxxix 29
No *l* than the wisp that gleams On Lethe | " xcviii 7
Be quicken'd with a *l* breath, | " cxxii 13
that to me A *l* emerald twinkles in the grass, | *Maud* I xviii 51
Liveliest   glided thro' all change Of *l* utterance. | *D. of F. Women* 168
Livelong   Pour round mine ears the *l* bleat | *Ode to Memory* 65
Past Yabbok brook the *l* night, | *Clear-headed friend* 27
Thro' which the *l* day my soul did pass, | *Palace of Art* 55
There will not be a drop of rain the whole of the *l* day, | *May Queen* 35
all the *l* way With solemn gibe did Eustace | *Gardener's D.* 167
break the *l* summer day With banquet | *In Mem.* lxxxix 31
light Thro' the *l* hours of the dark | *Maud* I vi 17
All thro' the *l* hours of utter dark, | *Lover's Tale* i 810
Lively   Rapt in sweet talk or *l*, all on love | *Guinevere* 386
Liver (one who lives)   Truth-speaking, brave, good *l*'s, | *Gareth and L.* 424
Liver (organ of the body)   pierces the *l* and blackens the blood ; | *The Islet* 35
red ' Blood-eagle ' of *l* and heart ; | *Dead Prophet* 71
' And the *l* is half-diseased ! ' | " 76
Liveried   dashing runnel in the spring Had *l* | *Lover's Tale* ii 50
Livest   by what name *L* between the lips ? | *Lancelot and E.* 182
Thou *l* in all hearts, | *Epit. on Gordon* 3
Livid   *L* he pluck'd it forth, | *Aylmer's Field* 627
Many a *l* one, many a sallow-skin— | *Batt. of Brunanburh* 106
I am roused by the wail of a child, and awake to a *l* light, | *The Wreck* 7

Livid (*continued*) crooked, reeling, *l*, thro' the mist Rose, *Death of Œnone* 27
Livid-flickering dazzled by the *l-f* fork, *Merlin and V.* 941
Livin' (benefice) I reckons tha'll light of a *l* *Church-warden, etc.* 47
Living (*See also* **Ever-living**) *L*, but that he shall live on? *Supp. Confessions* 171
The *l* airs of middle night Died round the bulbul *Arabian Nights* 69
A *l* flash of light he flew.' *Two Voices* 15
Nature's *l* motion lent The pulse of hope ,, 449
L together under the same roof, *To ——, With Pal. of Art* 12
each a perfect whole From *l* Nature, *Palace of Art* 59
his mute dust I honour and his *l* worth : *To J. S.* 30
And feeding high, and *l* soft, *The Goose* 17
Cursed be the social lies that warp us from the *l* truth ! *Locksley Hall* 60
Pure spaces clothed in *l* beams, *Sir Galahad* 66
That he who left you ten long years ago Should still be *l* : *Enoch Arden* 405
evermore Prayer from a *l* source within the will, ,, 801
Like fountains of sweet water in the sea, Kept him a *l* soul. ,, 804
Who hardly knew me *l*, let them come, ,, 889
But Leolin, his brother, *l* oft With Averill, *Aylmer's Field* 57
sow'd her name and kept it green In *l* letters, ,, 89
And left the *l* scandal that die— ,, 444
As if the *l* passion symbol'd there Were *l* nerves to feel the rent ; ,, 535
And all but those who knew the *l* God— ,, 637
And heaps of *l* gold that daily grow, ,, 655
Not past the *l* fount of pity in Heaven. ,, 752
Dead claps of thunder from within the cliffs Heard thro' the *l* roar. *Sea Dreams* 56
(the same as that *L* within the belt) ,, 216
Or Heliconian honey in *l* words, *Lucretius* 224
a race Of giants *l*, each, a thousand years, *Princess iii* 269
Those monstrous males that carve the *l* hound, ,, 310
but *l* wills, and sphered Whole in ourselves ,, *iv* 147
Of *l* hearts that crack within the fire ,, *v* 379
I believed that in the *l* world My spirit closed ,, *vii* 157
Thy *l* voice to me was as the voice of the dead, *V. of Cauteretz* 8
voice of the dead was a *l* voice to me. ,, 10
Roves from the *l* brother's face, *In Mem. xxxii* 7
With fruitful cloud and *l* smoke, ,, *xxxix* 3
The wish, that of the *l* whole No life may fail ,, *lv* 1
Which sicken'd every *l* bloom, ,, *lxxii* 7
That warms another *l* breast. ,, *lxxxv* 116
The *l* soul was flash'd on mine, ,, *xcv* 36
And drown'd in yonder *l* blue The lark becomes ,, *cxv* 7
O *l* will that shalt endure ,, *cxxxi* 1
And the most *l* words of life Breathed in her ear. ,, *Con.* 52
L alone in an empty house, *Maud I vi* 68
Void of the little *l* will That made it stir ,, *II ii* 14
Blow thro' the *l* world—' Let the King reign.' *Com. of Arthur* 484
thou art but swollen with cold snows And mine is *l* blood : *Gareth and L.* 10
gown I will not cast aside Until himself arise a *l* man, *Geraint and E.* 706
' For the fairest and the best Of ladies *l* gave me *Balin and Balan* 340
' I better prize The *l* dog than the dead lion : ,, 585
Death in the *l* waters, and withdrawn, *Merlin and V.* 148
who was yet a *l* soul. *Lancelot and E.* 253
She still took note that when the *l* smile Died ,, 323
' I never yet have done so much For any maiden *l*,' ,, 376
Become a *l* creature clad with wings ? *Holy Grail* 519
since the *l* words Of so great men as Lancelot and our King ,, 712
fern without Burnt as a *l* fire of emeralds, *Pelleas and E.* 35
Makers of nets, and *l* from the sea. ,, 90
more Than any have sung thee *l*, ,, 351
Again with *l* waters in the change Of seasons : ,, 511
No, nor by *l* can I live it down. *Guinevere* 623
On that high day, when, clothed with *l* light, *Pass. of Arthur* 454
thro' thy *l* love For one to whom I made it *To the Queen ii* 34
Scarce *l* in the Æolian harmony, *Lover's Tale i* 477
More *l* to some happier happiness, ,, 762

Living (*continued*) if Affection *L* slew Love, *Lover's Tale ii* 31
And all the fragments of the *l* rock ,, *ii* 44
told the *l* daughter with what love Edith *Sisters (E. and E.)* 253
And mangle the *l* dog that had loved him *In the Child. Hosp.* 9
DEAD PRINCESS, *l* Power, if that, which lived *Ded. Poem Prin. Alice* 1
Rather to thee, thou *l* water, *Sir J. Oldcastle* 131
That miss'd his *l* welcome, seem *Tiresias* 197
Wander'd back to *l* boyhood while I heard the curlews call, *Locksley H., Sixty* 3
Paint the mortal shame of nature with the *l* hues of Art. ,, 140
Dead, but how her *l* glory lights the hall, ,, 181
woods with *l* airs How softly fann'd, *Early Spring* 19
To share his *l* death with him, *Happy* 8
A beauty came upon your face, not that of *l* men, ,, 51
worm, who, *l*, made The wife of wives a widow-bride, *Romney's R.* 137
Bright in spring, *L* gold ; *The Oak* 5
FAREWELL, whose *l* like I shall not find, *In Mem. W. G. Ward* 1
Look how the *l* pulse of Alla beats Thro' all His world. *Akbar's Dream* 41
moved but by the *l* limb, ,, 133
And is a *l* form ? *Mechanophilus* 16
Draw from my death Thy *l* flower and grass, *Doubt and Prayer* 6
earn'd a scanty *l* for himself : *Enoch Arden* 818
war stood Silenced, the *l* quiet as the dead, *Com. of Arthur* 123
If one may judge the *l* by the dead, *Lancelot and E.* 1368
molten Into adulterous *l*, *Sir J. Oldcastle* 109
were worth Our *l* out ? *Tiresias* 209
but worn From wasteful *l*, follow'd— *Ancient Sage* 5
attic holds the *l* and the dead. *Locksley H., Sixty* 222
Living-dead where lives the *l-d*. *Happy* 4
Living-place river runs in three loops about her *l-p* ; *Gareth and L.* 612
Lizard *l*, with his shadow on the stone, *Œnone* 27
the golden *l* on him paused, *Enoch Arden* 601
Lizard-point fairest-spoken tree From here to *L-p*. *Talking Oak* 264
Llanberis And found him in *L* : *Golden Year* 5
Llanberris I came on lake *L* in the dark, *Sisters (E. and E.)* 95
Load grace To help me of my weary *l*.' *Mariana in the S.* 30
Loaded *See* **Grape-loaded**
Loaf a dusky *l* that smelt of home, *Audley Court* 22
Loan arms On *l*, or else for pledge ; *Marr. of Geraint* 220
Loath (*See also* **Loth**) be *loath* To part them, or part from them : *Sisters (E. and E.)* 49
Loathe ' To breathe and *loathe*, to live and sigh, *Two Voices* 104
I *loathe* it : he had never kindly heart, *Sea Dreams* 200
and she *Loathes* him as well : *Lucretius* 200
And I *loathe* the squares and streets, *Maud II iv* 92
and *loathe* to ask thee aught. *Gareth and L.* 356
flyers from the hand Of Justice, and whatever *loathes* a law : *Marr. of Geraint* 37
came to *loathe* His crime of traitor, ,, 593
loathe, fear—but honour me the more.' *Merlin and V.* 122
whom ye *loathe*, him will I make you love.' *Pelleas and E.* 390
I *loathe* her, as I loved her to my shame. ,, 483
on thine polluted, cries ' I *loathe* thee : ' *Guinevere* 556
for I *loathe* The seed of Cadmus— *Tiresias* 116
waken every morning to that face I *loathe* to see : *The Flight* 8
To love him most, whom most I *loathe*, ,, 50
I *loathe* the very name of infidel. *Akbar's Dream* 77
Loathed but most she *l* the hour *Mariana* 77
And *l* to see them overtax'd ; *Godiva* 9
His power to shape : he *l* himself ; *Lucretius* 23
l the bright dishonour of his love, *Com. of Arthur* 194
I that, *l*, have come to love him. *Locksley H., Sixty* 280
When Dives *l* the times, *To Mary Boyle* 29
Loather Thou *l* of the lawless crown *Freedom* 31
Loathing Deep dread and *l* of her solitude *Palace of Art* 229
and fain, For hate and *l*, *Balin and Balan* 388
to show His *l* of our Order and the Queen. ,, 551
Merlin to his own heart, *l*, said ; *Merlin and V.* 790
L to put it from herself for ever, *Lover's Tale i* 214
Loathly ' Overquick art thou To catch a *l* plume fall'n from the wing *Merlin and V.* 727
Loathsome What is *l* to the young Savours well to thee and me. *Vision of Sin* 157

Loathsome (*continued*) till the *l* opposite Of all my heart

had destined did obtain, *Guinevere* 490

And treat their *l* hurts and heal mine own ; " 686

and stood Stiff as a viper frozen ; *l* sight, *Merlin and V.* 845

How could I bear with the sights and the *l*

smells of disease *In the Child. Hosp.* 25

Lobby whined in *lobbies*, tapt at doors, *Walk. to the Mail* 37

Loch By firth and *l* thy silver sister grow, *Sir J. Oldcastle* 58

Lock (fastening) Break *l* and seal : *You might have won* 18

Melissa, with her hand upon the *l*, *Princess ii* 322

Cries of the partridge like a rusty key Turn'd

in a *l*, *Lover's Tale ii* 116

Lock (of tresses) *l's* not wide-dispread, *Isabel* 5

Stays on her floating *l's* the lovely freight *Ode to Memory* 16

holding them back by their flowing *l's* *The Merman* 14

I would fling on each side my low-flowing *l's*, *The Mermaid* 32

While his *l's* a-drooping twined *Adeline* 57

When the *l's* are crisp and curl'd ; *Vision of Sin* 200

To drench his dark *l's* in the gurgling wave *Princess iv* 187

From the flaxen curl to the gray *l* " 426

with your long *l's* play the Lion's mane ! " vi 164

May serve to curl a maiden's *l's*, *In Mem. lxxvii* 7

Smoothing their *l's*, as golden as his own *Sisters (E. and E.)* 56

Lock (verb) *l* up my tongue From uttering freely *Last Tournament* 693

Lock'd salt pool, *l* in with bars of sand, *Palace of Art* 249

She *l* her lips : she left me where I stood : *D. of F. Women* 241

She might have *l* her hands. *Talking Oak* 144

slept the sleep With Balin, either *l* in either's

arm. *Balin and Balan* 632

And Merlin *l* his hand in hers (repeat) *Merlin and V.* 290, 470

a puzzle chest in chest, With each chest *l* " 655

Locket pluck from this true breast the *l* that I wear, *The Flight* 33

Locksley Dreary gleams about the moorland flying over

L Hall ; *Locksley Hall* 4

L Hall, that in the distance overlooks the sandy tracts, " 5

a long farewell to *L* Hall ! " 189

Let it fall on *L* Hall, with rain or hail, " 193

I myself so close on death, and death itself in *L*

Hall. *Locksley H., Sixty* 4

Close beneath the casement crimson with the

shield of *L*— " 34

In this gap between the sandhills, whence you see

the *L* tower, " 176

Here is *L* Hall, my grandson, here the lion-guarded

gate. Not to-night in *L* Hall—to-morrow— " 213

one old Hostel left us where they swing the *L* shield, " 247

Then I leave thee Lord and Master, latest Lord

of *L* Hall. " 282

Lodestar seem'd my *l* in the Heaven of Art, *Romney's R.* 39

Lodge (s) cross'd the garden to the gardener's *l*, *Audley Court* 17

Beyond the *l* the city lies, *Talking Oak* 5

They by parks and *l's* going *L. of Burleigh* 17

beyond her *l's*, where the brook Vocal, *Aylmer's Field* 145

haunt About the moulder'd *l's* of the Past *Princess iv* 63

A *l* of intertwisted beechen-boughs *Last Tournament* 376

She lived a moon in that low *l* with him : " 381

that desert *l* to Tristram lookt So sweet, " 387

that low *l* return'd, Mid-forest, " 488

Some *l* within the waste sea-dunes, *The Flight* 90

Lodge (verb) *L* with me all year ! *Prog. of Spring* 26

Lodged Vivien, into Camelot stealing, *l* Low in the city, *Merlin and V.* 63

A priory not far off, there *l*, *Pelleas and E.* 214

and *l* with Plato's God, *Sisters (E. and E.)* 131

Lodging let him into *l* and disarm'd. *Lancelot and E.* 171

ere they past to *l*, she, Taking his hand, *Pelleas and E.* 125

Lodi At *L*, rain, Piacenza, rain. *The Daisy* 52

Loft in a *l*, with none to wait on him, *Lover's Tale iv* 138

Loftier A later but a *l* Annie Lee, *Enoch Arden* 748

then a *l* form Than female, *Princess iv* 215

I spring from *l* lineage than thine own.' *Gareth and L.* 961

A temple, neither Pagod, Mosque, nor Church,

But *l*, simpler, *Akbar's Dream* 179

Loftiest A wild witch naked as heaven stood on each

of the *l* capes, *V. of Maeldune* 100

Lofty ' Drink to *l* hopes that cool— *Vision of Sin* 147

Lofty (*continued*) broad ambrosial aisles of *l* lime Made

noise with bees *Princess, Pro.* 87

Ilion's *l* temples robed in fire, *To Virgil* 2

Log (*See also* **Yule-log**) drove his heel into the

smoulder'd *l*, *M. d'Arthur, Ep.* 14

Bring in great *l's* and let them lie, *In Mem. cvii* 17

Lies like a *l*, and all but smoulder'd out ! *Gareth and L.* 75

Dagonet stood Quiet as any water-sodden *l* *Last Tournament* 253

Logic Severer in the *l* of a life ? *Princess v* 190

Impassion'd *l*, which outran *In Mem. cix* 7

Loiar (liar) I weänt saäy men be *l's*, *N. Farmer, O. S.* 27

Loife (life) thaw *l* they says is sweet, " 63

Loike (like) Moäst *l* a butter-bump, " 31

Loins For many weeks about my *l* I wore *St. S. Stylites* 63

can this be he From Gama's dwarfish *l* ? *Princess v* 506

Loiter from pine to pine, And *l's*, slowly drawn. *Œnone* 5

I *l* round my cresses ; *The Brook* 181

With weary steps I *l* on, *In Mem. xxxviii* 1

The foot that *l's*, bidden go,— *Last Tournament* 117

Would often *l* in her balmy blue, *Lover's Tale i* 62

Loiter'd And *l* in the master's field, *In Mem. xxxvii* 23

and tho' I *l* there The full day after, *Sisters (E. and E.)* 97

Lombard But when we crost the *L* plain *The Daisy* 49

look'd the *L* piles ; " 54

You see yon *L* poplar on the plain. *Sisters (E. and E.)* 79

Lond (land) as I 'a done boy the *l*. (repeat) *N. Farmer, O. S.* 12, 24

an' *l* o' my oän. " 44

whoä's to howd the *l* ater meä " 58

London (adj.) For in the dust and drouth of *L* life *Edwin Morris* 143

When, in our younger *L* days, *To E. Fitzgerald* 54

London (s) (*See also* **Lunnon**) Sees in heaven the

light of *L* flaring *Locksley Hall* 114

Here, in streaming *L's* central roar. *Ode on Well.* 9

L, Verulam, Cámulodúne. *Boädicea* 86

Your father is ever in *L*, *Maud I iv* 59

And *L* roll'd one tide of joy *To the Queen ii* 8

Roaring *L*, raving Paris, *Locksley H., Sixty* 190

And *L* and Paris and all the rest *The Dawn* 10

Lone At eve the beetle boometh Athwart the thicket *l* : *Claribel* 10

never more Shall *l* Œnone see the morning mist *Œnone* 216

' No voice,' she shriek'd in that *l* hall, *Palace of Art* 258

Thro' every hollow cave and alley *l* *Lotos-Eaters, C. S.* 103

On a day when they were going O'er the *l* expanse, *The Captain* 26

The bird that pipes his *l* desire *You might have won* 31

The *l* glow and long roar (repeat) *Voice and the P.* 3, 39

Her life is *l*, he sits apart, *In Mem. xcvii* 1

When the *l* hern forgets his melancholy, *Gareth and L.* 1185

' Enid, the pilot star of my *l* life, *Geraint and E.* 306

' And even in this *l* wood, Sweet lord, *Balin and Balan* 528

Perchance in *l* Tintagil far from all *Last Tournament* 392

Till one *l* woman, weeping near a cross, " 493

And those *l* rites I have not seen, *To Marq. of Dufferin* 39

Lonelier *l*, darker, earthlier for my loss. *Aylmer's Field* 750

Loneliest but the *l* in a lonely sea. *Enoch Arden* 553

The *l* ways are safe from shore to shore. *Last Tournament* 102

Loneliness Uphold me, Father, in my *l* *Enoch Arden* 784

from his height and *l* of grief Bore down in flood, *Aylmer's Field* 632

Me rather all that bowery *l*, *Milton* 9

' Hast thou no pity upon my *l* ? *Gareth and L.* 73

Gratitude—*l*—desire to keep So skilled a nurse *The Ring* 373

Lonely ancient thatch Upon the *l* moated grange. *Mariana* 8

winds woke the gray-eyed morn About the *l* moated grange. " 32

Those *l* lights that still remain, *Two Voices* 83

Wrought by the *l* maiden of the Lake. *M. d'Arthur* 104

Wherever in a *l* grove He set up his forlorn pipes, *Amphion* 21

Sometimes on *l* mountain-meres I find a magic bark ; *Sir Galahad* 37

l seabird crosses With one waft of the wing. *The Captain* 71

Close to the sun in *l* lands, *The Eagle* 2

And he sat him down in a *l* place, *Poet's Song* 5

And peacock-yewtree of the *l* Hall, *Enoch Arden* 99

And leave you *l* ? not to see the world— " 297

but the loneliest in a *l* sea. " 553

The peacock-yewtree and the *l* Hall, " 608

when his *l* doom Came suddenly to an end. " 626

Pitying the *l* man, and gave him it : " 664

Lonely (*continued*) Thou That didst uphold me on my *l*
isle, — *Enoch Arden* 783
His wreck, his *l* life, his coming back, — „ 862
And *l* listenings to my mutter'd dream, — *Princess* vii 110
zones of light and shadow Glimmer away to the
l deep, — *To F. D. Maurice* 28
And a storm never wakes on the *l* sea, — *The Islet* 33
To breathe thee over *l* seas. — *In Mem.* xvii 4
That beats within a *l* place, — „ lxxxv 110
I find not yet one *l* thought That cries — „ xc 23
That ripple round the *l* grange ; — „ xci 12
No gray old grange, or *l* fold, — „ c 5
I have climb'd nearer out of *l* Hell. — *Maud* I xviii 80
(For often in *l* wanderings I have cursed him — „ xix 14
has past and leaves The Crown a *l* splendour. — *Ded. of Idylls* 49
What happiness to reign a *l* king, — *Com. of Arthur* 82
in *l* haunts Would scratch a ragged oval on the
sand, — *Gareth and L.* 533
Whom he loves most, *l* and miserable. — *Marr. of Geraint* 123
Heard by the lander in a *l* isle, — „ 330
good damsel there who sits apart, And seems so *l* ?' — *Geraint and E.* 300
That Lancelot is no more a *l* heart. — *Lancelot and E.* 602
Who might have brought thee, now a *l* man — „ 1370
built with wattles from the marsh A little *l* church — *Holy Grail* 64
Here one black, mute midsummer night I sat, *L*, — *Last Tournament* 613
All down the *l* coast of Lyonnesse, — *Guinevere* 240
To sit once more within his *l* hall, — „ 497
As of some *l* city sack'd by night, — *Pass. of Arthur* 43
Wrought by the *l* maiden of the Lake. — „ 272
O blossom'd portal of the *l* house, — *Lover's Tale* i 280
great pine shook with *l* sounds of joy — „ 325
And thus our *l* lover rode away, — „ iv 130
who lived Scatteringly about that *l* land of his, — „ 185
But I was the *l* slave of an often-wandering mind ; — *The Wreck* 130
O we poor orphans of nothing—alone on that *l* shore— — *Despair* 33
and we shall light upon some *l* shore, — *The Flight* 89
World-isles in *l* skies, — *Epilogue* 55
charm of all the Muses often flowering in a *l* word ; — *To Virgil* 12
seated in the dusk Of even, by the *l* threshing-floor, — *Demeter and P.* 126
The *l* maiden-Princess of the wood, — *The Ring* 65
Her *l* maiden-Princess, crown'd with flowers, — „ 485
you, that now are *l*, and with Grief Sit face to face, — *To Mary Boyle* 45
I seem no longer like a *l* man In the king's garden, — *Akbar's Dream* 20

Lonest Till ev'n the *l* hold were all as free — *Gareth and L.* 598
Sir Bors Rode to the *l* tract of all the realm, — *Holy Grail* 661

Long (*adj. and adv.*) (*See also* **Life-long**) From the *l*
alley's latticed shade Emerged, — *Arabian Nights* 112
L alleys falling down to twilight grots, — *Ode to Memory* 107
Now is done thy *l* day's work ; — *A Dirge* 1
And *l* purples of the dale. — „ 31
When the *l* dun wolds are ribb'd with snow, — *Oriana* 5
How *l*, O God, shall men be ridden down, — *Poland* 1
How *l* this icy-hearted Muscovite Oppress the region ?' — „ 10
L fields of barley and of rye, — *L. of Shalott* i 2
Still moving after truth *l* sought, — *Two Voices* 62
But *l* disquiet merged in rest. — „ 249
To be the *l* and listless boy Late-left an orphan — *Miller's D.* 33
Like those *l* mosses in the stream. — „ 48
on the casement-edge A *l* green box of mignonette, — „ 83
l shadow of the chair Flitted across into the night, — „ 126
burning drouth Of that *l* desert to the south. — *Fatima* 14
once he drew Mine own *l* kiss my whole soul thro' My lips, — „ 20
roars The *l* brook falling thro' the clov'n ravine — *Œnone* 8
between the piney sides Of this *l* glen. — „ 94
higher All barr'd with *l* white cloud the scornful
crags, — *Palace of Art* 83
Smile at the claims of *l* descent. — *L. C. V. de Vere* 52
You'll never see me more in the *l* gray fields
at night ; — *May Queen, N. Y's. E.* 26
With your feet above my head in the *l* and
pleasant grass. — „ 32
Give us *l* rest or death, dark death, — *Lotos-Eaters, C. S.* 53
L labour unto aged breath, — „ 85
To watch the *l* bright river drawing slowly — „ 92
glimmer of the languid dawn On those *l*, rank, — *D. of F. Women* 75

Long (*adj. and adv.*) (*continued*) So *l* as you have been
with us, — *D. of the O. Year* 16
Brightening the skirts of a *l* cloud, — *M. d'Arthur* 54
And the *l* ripple washing in the reeds.' — „ 117
And the *l* glories of the winter moon. — „ 192
I am going a *l* way With things thou seëst— — „ 256
whispering rain Night slid down one *l* stream — *Gardener's D.* 267
L learned names of agaric, moss and fern, — *Edwin Morris* 17
Twice two *l* weary weary years to this, — *St. S. Stylites* 90
Or else I dream—and for so *l* a time, — „ 93
thou hast suffer'd *l* For ages and for ages !' — „ 99
I have some power with Heaven From my *l* penance : — „ 144
The *l* mechanic pacings to and fro, — *Love and Duty* 17
The *l* day wanes : — *Ulysses* 55
With the fairy tales of science, and the *l* result
of Time ; — *Locksley Hall* 12
' Dost thou love me, cousin ?' weeping, ' I have loved
thee *l*.' — „ 30
a *l* farewell to Locksley Hall ! — „ 189
The poplars, in *l* order due, — *Amphion* 37
We past *l* lines of Northern capes — *The Voyage* 35
Where those *l* swells of breaker sweep — „ 39
' Thou art mazed, the night is *l*, — *Vision of Sin* 195
The *l* divine Peneïan pass, — *To E. L.* 3
L lines of cliff breaking have left a chasm ; — *Enoch Arden* 1
higher A *l* street climbs to one tall-tower'd mill ; — „ 5
That he who left you ten *l* years ago — „ 404
Then after a *l* tumble about the Cape — „ 532
then winds variable, Then baffling, a *l* course of them ; — „ 546
lustre of the *l* convolvuluses That coil'd around — „ 576
And dull the voyage was with *l* delays, — „ 655
Then down the *l* street having slowly stolen, — „ 682
his *l* wooing her, Her slow consent, and marriage, — „ 707
All down the *l* and narrow street he went — „ 795
And there he told a *l* long-winded tale — *The Brook* 138
Katie walks By the *l* wash of Australasian seas — „ 194
seated on a stile In the *l* hedge, — „ 198
L since, a bygone Rector of the place, — *Aylmer's Field* 1
crashing with *l* echoes thro' the land, — „ 338
And his *l* arms stretch'd as to grasp a flyer : — „ 588
But lapsed into so *l* a pause again — „ 630
Ran in and out the *l* sea-framing caves, — *Sea Dreams* 33
a *l* reef of gold, Or what seem'd gold : — „ 127
He dodged me with a *l* and loose account. — „ 149
rise And *l* roll of the Hexameter— — *Lucretius* 11
And blasting the *l* quiet of my breast — „ 162
And our *l* walks were stript as bare as brooms, — *Princess, Pro.* 184
and with *l* arms and hands Reach'd out, — „ i 28
Grow *l* and troubled like a rising moon, — „ 59
there did a compact pass *L* summers back, — „ 124
We rode Many a *l* league back to the North. — „ 168
He with a *l* low sibilation, stared As blank as death — „ 176
every turn Lived thro' her to the tips of her *l* hands, — „ ii 40
And glutted all night *l* breast-deep in corn, — „ 387
The *l* hall glitter'd like a bed of flowers, — „ 439
A *l* melodious thunder to the sound Of solemn
psalms, — „ 476
' O *l* ago,' she said, ' betwixt these two — „ iii 78
so Went forth in *l* retinue following up — „ 195
The *l* light shakes across the lakes, — „ iv 3
' O tell her, brief is life but love is *l*, — „ 111
combing out her *l* black hair Damp from the river ; — „ 276
Came in *l* breezes rapt from inmost south — „ 431
L lanes of splendour slanted o'er a press — „ 478
rising up Robed in the *l* night of her deep hair, — „ 491
l fantastic night With all its doings — „ 565
blast and bray of the *l* horn And serpent-throated bugle, — „ v 252
Suck'd from the dark heart of the *l* hills roll — „ 349
All that *l* morn the lists were hammer'd up, — „ 368
Lioness That with your *l* locks play the Lion's mane ! — „ vi 164
Till out of *l* frustration of her care, — „ vii 101
The bosom with *l* sighs labour'd ; — „ 225
Yet in the *l* years liker must they grow ; — „ 279
made The *l* line of the approaching rookery swerve — „ Con. 97
Let the *l l* procession go, — *Ode on Well.* 15

Long (adj. and adv.) (*continued*) The *l* self-sacrifice of life
is o'er. *Ode on Well.* 14
Thro' the *l* gorge to the far light has won 213
lo ! the *l* laborious miles Of Palace ; *Ode Inter.* "*Exhib.* 11
WHEER 'asta beän saw *l* and meä liggin' 'ere aloän ? *N. Farmer, O. S.* 1
In those *l* galleries, were ours ; *The Daisy* 42
The lone glow and *l* roar (repeat) *Voice and the P.* 3, 39
Draw toward the *l* frost and longest night, *A Dedication* 11
' Ah, the *l* delay.' *Window, When* 10
Than that the victor Hours should scorn The *l* result
of love, *In Mem.* i 14
once more I stand Here in the *l* unlovely street, „ vii 2
As parting with a *l* embrace She enters other realms
of love ; „ xl 11
In some *l* trace should slumber on ; „ xliii 4
And in the *l* harmonious years „ xliv 9
But with *l* use her tears are dry. „ lxxviii 20
and last Up that *l* walk of limes I past „ lxxxvii 15
' We served thee here,' they said, ' so *l*, „ ciii 47
L sleeps the summer in the seed ; „ cv 26
Now fades the last *l* streak of snow, „ cxv 1
Now rings the woodland loud and *l*, „ 5
There where the *l* street roars, „ cxxiii 3
O true and tried, so well and *l*, „ *Con.* 1
Or the voice of the *l* sea-wave as it swell'd *Maud* I xiv 31
In the *l* breeze that streams to thy delicious East, „ xviii 16
Here will I lie, while these *l* branches sway, „ 29
Maud made my Maud by that *l* loving kiss, „ 58
swell Of the *l* waves that roll in yonder bay ? „ 63
One *l* milk-bloom on the tree ; „ xxii 46
And as *l*, O God, as she Have a grain of love for me, II *l* 52
After *l* grief and pain To find the arms „ iv 2
We stood tranced in *l* embraces Mixt with kisses „ 8
Dead, *l* dead, *L* dead ! „ v 1
My life has crept so *l* on a broken wing III vi 1
Blow trumpet, for the *l* night hath roll'd away ! *Com. of Arthur* 483
Then those with Gareth for so *l* a space *Gareth and L.* 231
seems Wellnigh as *l* as thou art statured tall ! „ 282
For, midway down the side of that *l* hall A stately pile,— „ 404
Down the *l* avenues of a boundless wood, „ 785
Then after one *l* slope was mounted, saw, „ 795
Then to the shores of one of those *l* loops „ 905
and a *l* black horn Beside it hanging ; „ 1366
Prince Three times had blown—after *l* hush— „ 1378
Beheld the *l* street of a little town In a *l* valley, *Marr. of Geraint* 242
And down the *l* street riding wearily, „ 254
Geraint Drave the *l* spear a cubit thro' his breast *Geraint and E.* 86
slide From the *l* shore-cliff's windy walls to the beach, „ 164
made The *l* way smoke beneath him in his fear ; „ 532
So for *l* hours sat Enid by her lord, „ 580
paced The *l* white walk of lilies toward the bower. *Balin and Balan* 249
Now with droopt brow down the *l* glades he rode ; „ 311
Where under one *l* lane of cloudless air „ 461
blind wave feeling round his *l* sea-hall In silence : *Merlin and V.* 232
l sleepless nights Of my *l* life have made it easy to me. „ 679
A *l*, *l* weeping, not consolable. „ 856
she stole Down the *l* tower-stairs, hesitating : *Lancelot and E.* 343
Far o'er the *l* backs of the bushless downs, „ 400
Rode o'er the *l* backs of the bushless downs To
Camelot, „ 789
And after my *l* voyage I shall rest ! ' „ 1061
And down the *l* beam stole the Holy Grail,
(repeat) *Holy Grail* 117, 188
out of this she plaited broad and *l* A strong
sword-belt, „ 152
where the *l* Rich galleries, lady-laden, „ 345
Then a *l* silence came upon the hall, *Pelleas and E.* 609
his *l* lance Broken, and his Excalibur a straw.' *Last Tournament* 87
Sir Dagonet, one of thy *l* asses' ears, „ 273
run itself All out like a *l* life to a sour end— „ 288
The *l* low dune, and lazy-plunging sea. „ 484
And craven shifts, and *l* crane legs of Mark— „ 729
l wave broke All down the thundering shores of Bude
and Bos, *Guinevere* 290
Thro' the *l* gallery from the outer doors „ 413

Long (adj. and adv.) (*continued*) down the *l* wind the
dream Shrill'd ; *Pass. of Arthur* 40
l mountains ended in a coast Of ever-shifting sand, „ 85
Brightening the skirts of a *l* cloud, „ 222
And the *l* ripple washing in the reeds.' „ 285
And the *l* glories of the winter moon. „ 360
I am going a *l* way With these thou seëst— „ 424
Down that *l* water opening on the deep „ 466
L time entrancement held me. *Lover's Tale* i 626
her *l* ringlets moved, Drooping and beaten by the
breeze, „ 699
winds Laid the *l* night in silver streaks and bars, „ ii 112
A *l* loud clash of rapid marriage-bells. „ iii 23
I knew another, not so *l* ago, „ iv 262
Who let her in ? how *l* has she been ? *Rizpah* 13
Revenge ran on thro' the *l* sea-lane between. *The Revenge* 36
Fur Molly the *l* un she walkt awaäy wi' a hofficer
lad, *Village Wife* 97
Her dear, *l*, lean, little arms lying out on the
counterpane ; *In the Child. Hosp.* 70
but how *l*, O Lord, how *l* ! *Sir J. Oldcastle* 124
Eighteen *l* years of waste, seven in your Spain, *Columbus* 36
l waterfalls Pour'd in a thunderless plunge *V. of Maeldune* 13
starr'd with a myriad blossom the *l* convolvulus hung ; „ 40
And nine *l* months of antenatal gloom, *De Prof., Two G.* 8
once for ten *l* weeks I tried Your table of
Pythagoras, *To E. Fitzgerald* 14
Ten *l* sweet summer days upon deck, *The Wreck* 64
Ten *l* days of summer and sin— „ 77
' Ten *l* sweet summer days ' of fever, „ 147
The last *l* stripe of waning crimson gloom, *Ancient Sage* 221
all the summer *l* we roam'd in these wild woods *The Flight* 79
now thy *l* day's work hath ceased, *Epit. on Stratford* 2
I seed the beck coomin' down like a *l* black snaäke i'
the snaw, *Owd Roä* 40
Had been abroad for my poor health so *l* *The Ring* 101
—and there she paused, And *l* ; „ 335
L before the dawning. *Forlorn* 54
—the crash was *l* and loud— *Happy* 80
Not *l* to wait— *To Mary Boyle* 58
While the *l* day of knowledge grows and warms, *Prog. of Spring* 101
Anon from out the *l* ravine below, *Death of Œnone* 19
By the *l* torrent's ever-deepen'd roar, „ 85
Sa I sticks like the ivin as *l* as I lives to the
owd chuch now, *Churchwarden, etc.* 15

Long (verb) I *l* to see a flower so before *May Queen, N. Y's. E.* 16
sweeter far is death than life to me that *l* to go. „ *Con.* 8
that's all, and *l* for rest ; *Grandmother* 99
I *l* to prove No lapse of moons *In Mem.* xxvi 2
That *l*'s to burst a frozen bud „ lxxxiii 15
I *l* to creep Into some still cavern deep, *Maud* II iv 95
a sense might make her *l* for court *Marr. of Geraint* 803
L for my life, or hunger for my death, *Geraint and E.* 81
credulous Of what they *l* for, „ 876
l To have thee back in lusty life again, *Pelleas and E.* 351

Long-arm'd To meet the *l-a* vines with grapes *To E. Fitzgerald* 27
Long-bearded Stept the long-hair'd *l-b* solitary, *Enoch Arden* 637
From out thereunder came an ancient man, *L-b*, *Gareth and L.* 241
Long-betroth'd Lovers *l-b* were they : *Lady Clare* 6
Long-bounden his *l-b* tongue Was loosen'd, *Enoch Arden* 644
Long-buried Like that *l-b* body of the king, *Aylmer's Field* 3
Long-closeted *L-c* with her the yestermorn, *Princess* iv 322
Long'd Has ever truly *l* for death. *Two Voices* 396
Annie's children *l* To go with others, *Enoch Arden* 362
And swore he *l* at college, only *l*, *Princess, Pro.* 158
bird of passage flying south but *l* To follow : „ iii 210
I *l* so heartily then and there *Maud* I xiii 15
That evermore she *l* to hide herself, *Gareth and L.* 111
That when he stopt we *l* to hurl together, *Merlin and V.* 420
I never heard his voice But *l* to break away. *Pelleas and E.* 256
Had whatsoever meat he *l* for served *Guinevere* 265
away she sail'd with her loss and *l* for her own ; *The Revenge* 111
till we *l* for eternal sleep. *Despair* 46
Long-enduring Mourn for the man of *l-e* blood, *Ode on Well.* 24
What *l-e* hearts could do In that world-earthquake, „ 132

Longer   the *l* night is near :   *Vision of Sin* 196
   That he had loved her *l* than she knew,   *Enoch Arden* 455
   So she rests a little *l*,   *Sea Dreams* 299
   If she sleeps a little *l*,   „ 307
   ripen'd earlier, and her life Was *l* ;   *Princess* ii 155
   I last but a moment *l*.   *Spiteful Letter* 12
   until I heard no *l* The snowy-banded, dilettante,   *Maud I* viii 9
   ' I lead no *l* ; ride thou at my side ;   *Gareth and L.* 1157
   but in scarce *l* time Than at Caerleon the full-tided Usk,   *Geraint and E.* 115
   Clung closer to us for a *l* term Than any friend   *Columbus* 197
   Then a little *l* . . .   *Forlorn* 64
   Fell on a shadow, No *l* a shadow,   *Merlin and the G.* 93
   And can no *l*, But die rejoicing,   „ 111
   Paris, no *l* beauteous as a God,   *Death of Œnone* 25
   an old fane No *l* sacred to the Sun,   *St. Telemachus* 7
   DOUBT no *l* that the Highest is the wisest   *Faith* 1
Longest   growing *l* by the meadow's edge,   *Geraint and E.* 257
   The *l* lance his eyes had either seen,   *Balin and Balan* 411
   Draw toward the long frost and *l* night,   *A Dedication* 11
Long-forgotten   Sung by a *l-f* mind.   *In Mem.* lxxvii 12
Long-hair'd   *l-h* page in crimson clad,   *L. of Shalott* ii 22
   Stept the *l-h* long-bearded solitary,   *Enoch Arden* 637
Long-illumined   when the *l-i* cities flame,   *Ode on Well.* 228
Longing (part.)   ever *l* to explain,   *The Brook* 107
Longing (s)   (*See also* **Love-longing**)   Geraint had *l* in him evermore   *Marr. of Geraint* 394
   And Enid fell in *l* for a dress   „ 630
   my heart Went after her with *l* :   *Holy Grail* 583
   her *l* and her will Was toward me as of old ;   „ 590
   Love and *L* dress thy deeds in light,   *Ded. Poem Prin. Alice* 9
Long-known   the view *L-k* and loved by me,   *Pro. to Gen. Hamley* 6
Long-laid   *l-l* galleries past a hundred doors   *Princess* vi 375
Long-lanced   The *l-l* battle let their horses run.   *Com. of Arthur* 104
Long-leaved   in the stream the *l-l* flowers weep,   *Lotos-Eaters, C. S.* 10
Long-limb'd   *l-l* lad that had a Psyche too !   *Princess* ii 406
Long-neck'd   From the *l-n* geese of the world   *Maud I* iv 52
Long-pent   all the *l-p* stream of life   *Day-Dm., Revival* 15
Long-pondering   Enoch lay *l-p* on his plans ;   *Enoch Arden* 133
Long-promised   I go On that *l-p* visit to the North.   *Sisters (E. and E.)* 188
Long-sounding   Full of *l-s* corridors it was,   *Palace of Art* 53
Long-sufferance   Trying his truth and his *l-s*,   *Enoch Arden* 470
Long-suffering   I that thought myself *l-s*,   *Aylmer's Field* 753
   ' Full of compassion and mercy—*l-'s*.'   *Rizpah* 63
   Suffering—O *l-s*—yes,   „ 67
Long-sweeping   those *l-s* beechen boughs Of our New Forest.   *Sisters (E. and E.)* 112
Long-tail'd   Like *l-t* birds of Paradise,   *Day-Dm., Ep.* 7
Long-tormented   Thro' the *l-t* air   *Ode on Well.* 128
Long-vaulted   Far over heads in that *l-v* hall   *Gareth and L.* 319
Long-winded   her father came across With some *l-w* tale,   *The Brook* 109
   And there he told a long *l-w* tale   „ 138
Long-wish'd-for   Calming itself to the *l-w-f* end,   *Maud I* xviii 5
Long-withdrawn   Betwixt the black fronts *l-w*   *In Mem.* cxix 6
Look (s)   Wherefore those dim *l's* of thine,   *Adeline* 9
   Hence that *l* and smile of thine,   „ 63
   He thought of that sharp *l*, mother,   *May Queen* 15
   sons inherit us : our *l's* are strange :   *Lotos-Eaters, C. S.* 73
   with sick and scornful *l's* averse,   *D. of F. Women* 101
   How sweet are *l's* that ladies bend   *Sir Galahad* 13
   Hours, when the Poet's words and *l's*   *Will Water.* 193
   their eyes Glaring, and passionate *l's*,   *Sea Dreams* 236
   A liquid *l* on Ida, full of prayer,   *Princess* iv 369
   This *l* of quiet flatters thus   *In Mem.* x 10
   Treasuring the *l* it cannot find,   „ xviii 19
   And look thy *l*, and go thy way,   „ xlix 9
   The voice was low, the *l* was bright ;   „ lxix 15
   they meet thy *l* And brighten like the star   „ Con. 30
   her *l* Bright for all others,   *Pelleas and E.* 176
   large light eyes and her gracious *l's*,   *Prog. of Spring* 19
Look (verb)   (*See also* **Loŏk**)   Shall we not *l* into the laws Of life and death,   *Supp. Confessions* 172
   She could not *l* on the sweet heaven,   *Mariana* 15
   How could I *l* upon the day ?   *Oriana* 59
   I should *l* like a fountain of gold   *The Mermaid* 18

Look (verb) (*continued*)   *l* in at the gate With his large calm eyes   *The Mermaid* 26
   the sun *L's* thro' in his sad decline,   *Adeline* 13
   Or only *l* across the lawn, *L* out below your bower-eaves, *L* down, and let your blue eyes dawn   *Margaret* 65
   curse is on her if she stay To *l* down to Camelot.   *L. of Shalott* ii 5
   With a glassy countenance Did she *l* to Camelot.   „ iv 14
   To *l* at her with slight, and say   *Mariana in the S.* 66
   To *l* into her eyes and say,   „ 75
   L up thro' night : the world is wide.   *Two Voices* 24
   L up, the fold is on her brow.   „ 192
   L's down upon the village spire :   *Miller's D.* 36
   I knew you could not *l* but well ;   „ 150
   L thro' mine eyes with thine.   „ 215
   L thro' my very soul with thine !   „ 218
   l, the sunset, south and north,   „ 241
   I shall *l* upon your face ;   *May Queen, N. Y's. E.* 38
   O *l* ! the sun begins to rise,   „ Con. 49
   ' Come here, That I may *l* on thee.'   *D. of F. Women* 124
   What else was left ? *l* here ! '   „ 156
   ' Turn and *l* on me :   „ 250
   He cried, ' *L* ! *l* ! '   Before he ceased I turn'd,   *Gardener's D.* 121
   therefore *l* to Dora ; she is well To *l* to ;   *Dora* 15
   L to it ; Consider, William :   „ 228
   for you may *l* on me, And in your looking dipt and rose, And turn'd to *l* at her.   *St. S. Stylites* 140
   Talking Oak 132
   L further thro' the chace,   „ 246
   O might it come like one that *l's* content,   *Love and Duty* 93
   Did I *l* on great Orion sloping slowly to the West.   *Locksley Hall* 8
   whom to *l* at was to love.   „ 72
   Underneath the light he *l's* at,   „ 116
   No eye *l* down, she passing ;   *Godiva* 40
   Nor *l* with that too-earnest eye—   *Day-Dm., Pro.* 18
   Go, *l* in any glass and say,   *Moral* 3
   I *l* at all things as they are,   *Will Water.* 71
   And he came to *l* upon her,   *L. of Burleigh* 93
   As *l's* a father on the things Of his dead son,   *The Letters* 23
   ' O ! we two as well can *l* Whited thought   *Vision of Sin* 115
   know I That I shall *l* upon your face no more.'   *Enoch Arden* 212
   ' Well then,' said Enoch, ' I shall *l* on yours.   „ 219
   L to the babes, and till I come again   „ 282
   Cared not to *l* on any human face   „ 315
   ' I cannot *l* you in the face I seem so foolish   „ 461
   So much to *l* to—such a change—   „ 718
   ' If I might *l* on her sweet face again   *Aylmer's Field* 2
   our pride *L's* only for a moment whole   *Princess* i 154
   l upon her As on a kind of paragon ;   „ ii 75
   L, our hall ! Our statues !—   „ 86
   since to *l* on noble forms Makes noble   „ 268
   l ! for such are these and I.'   „ iii 256
   blessing those that *l* on them.   „ iv 529
   you *l* well too in your woman's dress :   „ 547
   Begone : we will not *l* upon you more.   „ v 32
   ' *L*, He has been among his shadows.'   „ 66
   l up : be comforted :   „ vii 351
   L up, and let thy nature strike on mine,   „ Con. 49
   ' *L* there, a garden ! ' said my college friend,   *Grandmother* 2
   strong on his legs, he *l's* like a man.   „ 17
   Why do you *l* at me, Annie ?   *In Mem.* viii 2
   To *l* on her that loves him well,   „ xl 2
   And *l* on Spirits breathed away,   „ xlix 9
   And *l* thy look, and go thy way,   „ li 12
   The dead shall *l* me thro' and thro'.   „ lxiv 5
   Dost thou *l* back on what hath been,   „ lxx 16
   L's thy fair face and makes it still.   „ cxxv 6
   She did but *l* thro' dimmer eyes ;   „ Con. 129
   eye to eye, shall *l* On knowledge ;   *Maud I* x 22
   (*L* at it) pricking a cockney ear.   „ xii 29
   L, a horse at the door,   „ xiv 15
   l's Upon Maud's own garden-gate :   „ xvi 11
   That I dare to *l* her way ;   *Com. of Arthur* 70
   we *l* at him, And find nor face nor bearing,   *Gareth and L.* 281
   beard That *l's* as white as utter truth,   „ 434
   Kay the seneschal *L* to thy wants,   „ 583
   L therefore when he calls for this in hall,

Look (verb) (continued) *l* who comes behind,'

(repeat)	*Gareth and L.* 752, 1210
Shalt not once dare to *l* him in the face.'	„ 782
and *l* thou to thyself :	„ 920
L on it, child, and tell me if ye know it.'	*Marr. of Geraint* 684
And once again she rose to *l* at it,	*Geraint and E.* 387
Eat ! *L* yourself. Good luck had your good man,	„ 617
Until my lord arise and *l* upon me ? '	„ 650
I will not *l* at wine until I die.'	„ 667
came The King's own leech to *l* into his hurt ;	„ 923
L to the cave.'	*Balin and Balan* 306
these be fancies of the churl, *L* to thy woodcraft,'	„ 308
Squire had loosed them, ' Goodly !—*l* !	„ 576
How hard you *l* and how denyingly !	*Merlin and V.* 338
A square of text that *l's* a little blot,	„ 671
For *l* upon his face !—but if he sinn'd,	„ 761
A sight ye love to *l* on.'	*Lancelot and E.* 83
wherefore would ye *l* On this proud fellow again,	„ 1064
and she, *L* how she sleeps—	„ 1255
' See ! *l* at mine ! but wilt thou fight	*Pelleas and E.* 127
' *L*, He haunts me—I cannot breathe—	„ 226
ye *l* amazed, Not knowing they were lost	*Last Tournament* 41
cried the Breton, ' *L*, her hand is red !	„ 412
this I gave thee, *l*, Is all as cool and white	„ 415
Art thou King ?—*L* to thy life !'	„ 454
not *l* up, or half-despised the height	*Guinevere* 643
face of old ghosts *L* in upon the battle ;	*Pass. of Arthur* 104
l at them, You lose yourself in utter ignorance ;	*Lover's Tale i* 78
Of eyes too weak to *l* upon the light ;	„ 614
And could I *l* upon her tearful eyes ?	„ 735
would not *l* at her—No not for months :	„ *iv* 26
an' *l's* so wan an' so white :	*First Quarrel* 2
I had but to *l* in his face.	„ 16
he was fear'd to *l* at me now.	„ 38
L at the cloäths on 'er back,	*North. Cobbler* 109
For *l* you here—the shadows are too deep,	*Sisters (E. and E.)* 103
l's at it, and says, ' Good ! very like !	„ 135
that one light no man can *l* upon,	*De Prof., Two G.* 37
I cannot laud this life, it *l's* so dark :	*To W. H. Brookfield* 12
l yonder,' he cried, ' a sail '	*The Wreck* 121
I shall *l* on the child again.	„ 124
whence, if thou *L* higher,	*Ancient Sage* 281
But *l*, the morning grows apace,	*The Flight* 93
till the Lion *l* no larger than the Cat,	*Locksley H., Sixty* 112
O heart, *l* down and up Serene,	*Early Spring* 27
from thine own To that which *l's* like rest,	*Pref. Poem Broth. S.* 6
Why do you *l* so gravely at the tower ?	*The Ring* 80
but you *l* so kind That you will	*Romney's R.* 21
L, the sun has risen To flame along another dreary day.	„ 57
L, in their deep double shadow	*Parnassus* 13
morning that *l's* so bright from afar !	*By an Evolution.* 10
L, he stands, Trunk and bough,	*The Oak* 13
L how the living pulse of Alla beats	*Akbar's Dream* 41
L to your butts, and take good aims !	*Riflemen form !* 16

Look'd-Lookt (*See also* Looök'd-Looökt) broken sheds

look'd sad and strange :	*Mariana* 5
look'd to shame The hollow-vaulted dark,	*Arabian Nights* 125
Hast thou *look'd* upon the breath Of the lilies	*Adeline* 36
when first I *look'd* upon your face,	*Sonnet To ——* 9
She *look'd* down to Camelot.	*L. of Shalott iii* 41
I might have *look'd* a little higher ;	*Miller's D.* 140
And turning *look'd* upon your face,	„ 157
I *look'd* athwart the burning drouth	*Fatima* 13
I *look'd* And listen'd, the full-flowing river	*Œnone* 63
when I *look'd*, Paris had raised his arm,	„ 189
He *look'd* so grand when he was dead.	*The Sisters* 32
slept St. Cecily ; An angel *look'd* at her.	*Palace of Art* 100
her face Glow'd, as I *look'd* at her.	*D. of F. Women* 240
I have not *look'd* upon you nigh,	*To J. S.* 33
when I *look'd* again, behold an arm,	*M. d'Arthur* 158
this is also true, that, long before I *look'd* upon her,	*Gardener's D.* 62
She *look'd* : but all Suffused with blushes—	„ 153
He often *look'd* at them, And often thought,	*Dora* 3
more he *look'd* at her The less he liked her ;	„ 34

Look'd-Lookt (*continued*)   Mary sat And *look'd* with tears upon

her boy,	*Dora* 57
I *look'd* at him with joy :	*Talking Oak* 106
She *look'd* with discontent.	„ 116
Look'd down, half-pleased, half-frighten'd,	*Amphion* 54
She *look'd* into Lord Ronald's eyes,	*Lady Clare* 79
Then they *look'd* at him they hated,	*The Captain* 37
And he *look'd* at her and said,	*L. of Burleigh* 94
She *look'd* so lovely, as she sway'd	*Sir L. and Q. G.* 40
things Of his dead son, I *look'd* on these.	*The Letters* 24
then I *look'd* up toward a mountain-tract,	*Vision of Sin* 46
And all men *look'd* upon him favourably :	*Enoch Arden* 56
Philip *look'd*, And in their eyes and faces	„ 72
(Since Enoch left he had not *look'd* upon her),	„ 273
silent, tho' he often *look'd* his wish ;	„ 482
he *look'd* up. There stood a maiden near,	*The Brook* 204
and here he *look'd* so self-perplext,	„ 213
What *look'd* a flight of fairy arrows	*Aylmer's Field* 94
One *look'd* all rosetree, and another wore	„ 157
And after *look'd* into yourself,	„ 312
Half-canonized by all that *look'd* on her,	*Princess i* 23
hills, that *look'd* across a land of hope,	„ 169
And every face she *look'd* on justify it)	„ *v* 134
then once more she *look'd* at my pale face :	„ *vi* 115
Look'd up, and rising slowly from me,	„ 151
down she *look'd* At the arm'd man sideways,	„ 156
with shut eyes I lay Listening ; then *look'd*.	„ *vii* 224
Who *look'd* all native to her place,	„ 323
and *look'd* the thing that he meant ;	*Grandmother* 45
I *look'd* at the still little body—	„ 66
look'd the Lombard piles ;	*The Daisy* 54
And *look'd* at by the silent stars :	*Lit. Squabbles* 4
That ever *look'd* with human eyes.	*In Mem. lvii* 12
He *look'd* upon my crown and smiled :	„ *lxix* 16
I *look'd* on these and thought of thee	„ *xcvii* 6
and the mine eyes Have *look'd* on : if they *look'd* in vain,	„ *cix* 22
And how she *look'd*, and what he said,	„ *Con.* 99
The sun *look'd* out with a smile	*Maud I ix* 3
I *look'd*, and round, all round the house	„ *xiv* 33
To have *look'd*, tho' but in a dream, upon eyes	„ *III vi* 16
and *look'd* no more—But felt his young heart	*Gareth and L.* 321
fire, That *lookt* half-dead, brake bright,	„ 685
lord Now *look'd* at one and now at other,	„ 869
and Gareth *lookt* and read—In letters	„ 1201
' God wot, I never *look'd* upon the face,	„ 1333
He *look'd* and saw that all was ruinous.	*Marr. of Geraint* 315
dress that now she *look'd* on to the dress She *look'd* on ere the coming of Geraint.	„ 613
still she *look'd*, and still the terror grew	„ 615
Enid *look'd*, but all confused at first,	„ 685
not to goodly hill or yellow sea *Look'd* the fair Queen,	„ 831
They rode so slowly and they *look'd* so pale,	*Geraint and E.* 35
he turn'd and *look'd* as keenly at her	„ 430
And Geraint *look'd* and was not satisfied.	„ 435
Once she *look'd* back, and when she saw him ride	„ 441
By having *look'd* too much thro' alien eyes,	„ 892
have ye *look'd* At Edyrn ? have ye seen how nobly changed ?	„ 896
He *look'd* and found them wanting ;	„ 935
It *look'd* a tower of ivied masonwork,	*Merlin and V.* 4
when I *look'd*, and saw you following still,	„ 299
Merlin *look'd* and half believed her true,	„ 400
Won by the mellow voice before she *look'd*,	*Lancelot and E.* 243
He *look'd*, and more amazed Than if seven men	„ 350
Lancelot *look'd* and was perplext in mind,	„ 838
wherein she deem'd she *look'd* her best,	„ 907
and *look'd* Down on his helm.	„ 981
whence the King *Look'd* up, calling aloud,	*Holy Grail* 219
large her violet eyes *look'd*, and her bloom A rosy dawn	*Pelleas and E.* 71
turn'd the lady round And *look'd* upon her people ;	„ 92
Pelleas *look'd* Noble among the noble,	„ 151
The Queen *Look'd* hard upon her lover,	„ 605

Look'd-Lookt (continued) He look'd but once, and vail'd his eyes — *Last Tournament* 150
that desert lodge to Tristram lookt So sweet, — " 387
look'd and saw The great Queen's bower was dark,— " 757
Which when she heard, the Queen look'd up, — *Guinevere* 164
the pale Queen look'd up and answer'd her, — " 327
she look'd and saw The novice, weeping, — " 663
of those who falling down Look'd up for heaven, — *Pass. of Arthur* 112
But when I look'd again, behold an arm, — " 326
A stately mountain nymph she look'd ! — *Lover's Tale i* 359
bridge is there, that, look'd at from beneath Seems — " 375
looking down On all that had look'd down on us ; — " 388
Look'd forth the summit and the pinnacles — " ii 81
All that look'd on her had pronounced her dead. — " iv 35
look'd No less than one divine apology. — " 168
look'd, as he is like to prove, — " 314
but he look'd at me sidelong and shy, — *First Quarrel* 35
the Lord has look'd into my care, — *Rizpah* 75
soldiers look'd down from their decks and laugh'd, — *The Revenge* 37
an niver lookt arter the land— — *Village Wife* 25
can well believe, for he look'd so coarse and so red, — *In the Child. Hosp.* 7
Each of them look'd like a king, — *V. of Maeldune* 3
Down we look'd : what a garden ! — " 78
Folded her lion paws, and look'd to Thebes. — *Tiresias* 149
He look'd at it coldly, and said — *The Wreck* 34
and I look'd at him, first, askance, With pity— — " 43
baby-girl, that had never look'd on the light : — *Despair* 71
yet he look'd beyond the grave, — *Locksley H., Sixty* 60
look'd the twin of heathen hate. — " 86
You came, and look'd and loved the view — *Pro. to Gen. Hamley* 5
Then he look'd at the host that had halted — *Heavy Brigade* 7
and a sudden face Look'd in upon me — *The Ring* 420
When I look'd at the bracken so bright — *June Bracken, etc.* 3

Looketh moon cometh, And l down alone. — *Claribel* 14

Looking She, l thro' and thro' me — *Lilian* 10
But, l fixedly the while, — *Madeline* 39
Then l as 'twere in a glass, — *A Character* 10
All l up for the love of me. — *The Mermaid* 51
All l down for the love of me. — " 55
As a Naiad in a well, L at the set of day, — *Adeline* 17
Sang l thro' his prison bars ? — *Margaret* 35
' But l upward, full of grace, — *Two Voices* 223
Grow, live, die l on his face, — *Fatima* 41
l over wasted lands, — *Lotos-Eaters, C. S.* 114
And l wistfully with wide blue eyes — *M. d'Arthur* 169
And in your l you may kneel to God. — *St. S. Stylites* 141
l ancient kindness on thy pain. — *Locksley Hall* 85
Brown, l hardly human, — *Enoch Arden* 638
Then l at her ; ' Too happy, fresh and fair, — *The Brook* 217
In l on the happy Autumn-fields, — *Princess iv* 42
stood The placid marble Muses, l peace. — " 489
And l back to whence I came, — *In Mem. xxiii* 7
Sat silent, l each at each. — " xxx 12
Lest life should fail in l back. — " xlvi 4
Now l to some settled end, — " lxxxv 97
And l to the South, and fed With honey'd rain — *Maud I xviii* 20
L, thinking of all I have lost ; — " II ii 46
Arthur, l downward as he past, — *Com. of Arthur* 55
slowly spake the mother l at him, — *Gareth and L.* 151
Gareth l after said, ' My men, — " 296
Not turning round, nor l at him, — *Marr. of Geraint* 270
And l round he saw not Enid there, — " 506
Then rose Limours, and l at his feet, — *Geraint and E.* 302
then he spoke and said, Not l at her, — *Merlin and V.* 247
' I once was l for a magic weed, — " 471
l at her, Full courtly, yet not falsely, — *Lancelot and E.* 235
Lancelot knew that she was l at him. — " 985
l often from his face who read — " 1285
l up, Behold, the enchanted towers of Carbonek, — *Holy Grail* 812
as he lay At random l over the brown earth — *Pelleas and E.* 32
So that his eyes were dazzled l at it. — " 36
Gawain, l at the villainy done, — " 282
Sat their grea umpire, l o'er the lists. — *Last Tournament* 159

Looking (continued) Here l down on thine polluted, — *Guinevere* 555
And l wistfully with wide blue eyes — *Pass. of Arthur* 337
L on that brought him to the light : — *Lover's Tale i* 160
We often paused, and, l back, — " 329
l down On all that had look'd down on us ; — " 387
l round upon his tearful friends, — " 792
And l as much lovelier as herself — " iv 287
in the chapel there l over the sand ? — *Despair* 1
your know-all chapel too l over the sand. — " 94
l still as if she smiled, — *Locksley H., Sixty* 35
l upward to the practised hustings-liar ; — " 123
but wool's l oop ony how. — *Church-warden, etc.* 6
With farther l's on. — *Miller's D.* 231

Lookt *See* Look'd

Loom (s) She left the web, she left the l, — *L. of Shalott iii* 37
A present, a great labour of the l ; — *Princess i* 44
rent The wonder of the l thro' warp and woof — " 62
L and wheel and enginery, — *Ode Inter. Exhib.* 15
Display'd a splendid silk of foreign l, — *Geraint and E.* 687
Thy presence in the silk of sumptuous l's ; — *Ancient Sage* 266
Loom (verb) smoke go up thro' which I l to her — *Princess v* 130
Makes former gladness l so great ? — *In Mem. xxiv* 10
overheated language l Larger than the Lion,— — *Locksley H., Sixty* 113
Looming To sail with Arthur under l shores, — *M. d'Arthur, Ep.* 17
A l bastion fringed with fire. — *In Mem. xv* 20
a phantom king, Now l, and now lost ; — *Com. of Arthur* 431
Loomp (lump) the poor in a l is bad. — *N. Farmer, N. S.* 48
An' 'e digg'd up a l i' the land — *Village Wife* 48
Loon Dish-washer and broach-turner, l ! — *Gareth and L.* 770
Loök (look) Dubbut l at the waäste : — *N. Farmer, O. S.* 37
an' fuzz, an' l at it now— — " 38
L 'ow quoloty smoiles — " 53
L thou theer wheer Wrigglesby beck cooms out — " N. S. 53
I'll my hennemy strait i' the faäce, — *North. Cobbler* 74
an' let ma l at 'im then, — " 75
Fur a cat may l at a king — *Spinster's S's.* 6
Loök'd-Loökt (look'd-lookt) I loök'd cock-eyed at my noäse — *North. Cobbler* 26
an' Sally loökt up an' she said, — " 62
But 'e niver loökt ower a bill, — *Village Wife* 51
ghoäst i' the derk, fur it loökt sa white. — " 82
But whiniver I loöked i' the glass — *Spinster's S's.* 20
An' I loökt out wonst at the night, — *Owd Roä* 39
Loop (*See also* River-loop) a river Runs in three l's about her living-place ; — *Gareth and L.* 612
Then to the shore of one of those long l's — " 905
all in l's and links among the dales — *Lancelot and E.* 166
Thro' knots and l's and folds innumerable — " 439
Loophole death from the l's around, — *Def. of Lucknow* 79
Looping great funereal curtains, l down, — *Lover's Tale iv* 214
Loose (adj.) He dodged me with a long and l account. — *Sea Dreams* 149
I found a hard friend in his l accounts, A l one — " 162
torn raiment and l hair, — *Gareth and L.* 1208
one night I cooms 'oäm like a bull gotten l at a faäir, — *North. Cobbler* 33
Loose (verb) that she would l The people : — *Godiva* 37
Let me l thy tongue with wine : — *Vision of Sin* 88
' Fear not thou to l thy tongue ; — " 155
when they ran To l him at the stables, — *Aylmer's Field* 126
l A flying charm of blushes o'er this cheek, — *Princess ii* 429
growing commerce l her latest chain, — *Ode Inter. Exhib.* 33
—dismount and l their casques — *Balin and Balan* 573
l thy tongue, and let me know.' — *Pelleas and E.* 600
l the bond, and go.' — *To the Queen ii* 17
Would l him from his hold ; — *Ancient Sage* 118
Shall we hold them ? shall we l them ? — *Locksley H., Sixty* 118
Loosed She l the chain, and down she lay ; — *L. of Shalott iv* 16
And l the shatter'd casque, — *M. d'Arthur* 209
l their sweating horses from the yoke, — *Spec. of Iliad* 2
and l him from his vow. — *Gareth and L.* 530
Sir Gareth l A cloak that dropt — " 681
Gareth l the stone From off his neck, — " 814
l his bonds and on free feet Set him, — " 817
he l a mighty purse, Hung at his belt, — *Geraint and E.* 22

Lordly (*continued*) I BUILT my soul a *l* pleasure-house,   *Palace of Art* 1
They by parks and lodges going See the *l* castles
   stand :   *L. of Burleigh* 18
The lovely, *l* creature floated on   *Princess* vi 89
down from this a *l* stairway sloped   *Gareth and L.* 669
They past on, The *l* Phantasms !   *Lover's Tale* ii 99
Lord-manufacturer You, the *L-m*,   *On Jub. Q. Victoria* 57
Lord of Astolat) (*See also* **Astolat**) And issuing
   found the *L o A*   *Lancelot and E.* 173
then the *L o A* : ' Whence comest thou,   " 180
said the *L o A*, ' Here is Torre's :   " 195
came The *L o A* out, to whom the Prince   " 627
To whom the *L o A* ' Bide with us,   " 632
Lord of Burleigh *L o B*, fair and free,   *L. of Burleigh* 58
Deeply mourn'd the *L o B*,   " 91
Lord-prince high *l-p* of Arthur's hall,   *Balin and Balan* 466
Lord-territorial You, the *L-t*,   *On Jub. Q. Victoria* 56
Lore (*See also* **Love-lore**) As wild as aught of
   fairy *l* ;   *Day-Dm., L'Envoi* 12
The Learned all his *l* ;   *Ancient Sage* 139
Lose I *l* my colour, I *l* my breath,   *Eleänore* 137
And not to *l* the good of life—   *Two Voices* 132
Oft *l* whole years of darker mind.   " 372
Nor greatly cared to *l*, her hold on life.   *Aylmer's Field* 568
they must *l* the child, assume The woman :   *Princess* i 137
Dwell with these, and *l* Convention,   " ii 85
I *l* My honour, these their lives.'   " 341
To our point : not war : Lest I *l* all.'   " v 205
she fear'd that I should *l* my mind,   " vii 99
Nor *l* the wrestling thews that throw the world ;   " 282
Nor *l* the childlike in the larger mind ;   " 284
The gravest citizen seems to *l* his head,   " Con. 59
I too, talk, and *l* the touch I talk of.   *Lit. Squabbles* 17
Nor *l* their mortal sympathy,   *In Mem. xxx* 23
We *l* ourselves in light.'   " xlvii 16
I shall not *l* thee tho' I die.   " cxxx 16
and he fears To *l* his bone, and lays his foot
   upon it,   *Geraint and E.* 562
Fearing to *l*, and all for a dead man,   " 564
And *l* the quest he sent you on,   *Lancelot and E.* 655
' I *l* it, as we *l* the lark in heaven,   " 659
Sweet father, will you let me *l* my wits ? '   " 752
not *l* your wits for dear Lavaine.   " 755
Pleasure to have it, none ; to *l* it, pain :   " 1415
' No man could sit but he should *l* himself : '   *Holy Grail* 174
' If I *l* myself, I save myself ! '   " 178
' I will embark and I will *l* myself,   " 805
Not greatly care to *l* ;   *Guinevere* 495
You *l* yourself in utter ignorance ;   *Lover's Tale* i 79
And *l* thy life by usage of thy sting ;   *Ancient Sage* 270
say ' that those who *l* can find.'   *The Ring* 282
All is well If I *l* it and myself   *Happy* 58
They *l* themselves and die   *Prog. of Spring* 35
And yet The world would *l*,   *Romney's R.* 68
Losing *L* his fire and active might   *Eleänore* 104
L her carol I stood pensively,   *D. of F. Women* 245
Nor mine the fault, if *l* both of these   *Aylmer's Field* 719
odes About this *l* of the child ;   *Princess* i 141
Poor rivals in a *l* game,   *In Mem. cii* 19
A little vext at *l* of the hunt,   *Marr. of Geraint* 234
' I am *l* the light of my Youth   *The Dreamer* 4
Loss Although the *l* had brought us pain, That *l*   *Miller's D.* 229
Your *l* is rarer ; for this star Rose   *To J. S.* 25
And but for daily *l* of one she loved   *Walk. to the Mail* 94
l of all But Enoch and two others.   *Enoch Arden* 549
Am lonelier, darker, earthlier for my *l*.   *Aylmer's Field* 750
His gain is *l* ; for he that wrongs his friend   *Sea Dreams* 172
And the volleying cannon thunder his *l* ;   *Ode on Well.* 62
And find in *l* a gain to match ?   *In Mem. i* 6
Ah, sweeter to be drunk with *l*,   " 11
' Thou shalt not be the fool of *l*.'   " iv 16
' *L* is common to the race '—   " vi 2
That *l* common would not make   " 5
Which weep a *l* for ever new,   " xiii 5
Thy spirit ere our fatal *l*   " xli 6

Loss (*continued*) His night of *l* is always there.   *In Mem. lxvi* 16
To breathe my *l* is more than fame,   " lxxvii 15
The grief my *l* in him had wrought,   " lxxx 6
The lighter by the *l* of his weight ;   *Maud I xvi* 2
By the *l* of that dead weight,   " xix 99
shadow of His *l* drew like eclipse,   *Ded. of Idylls* 14
Than that my lord should suffer *l* or shame.'   *Geraint and E.* 69
Enid, the *l* of whom hath turn'd me wild—   " 308
as a man to whom a dreadful *l* Falls in a far land   " 496
l So pains him that he sickens nigh to death ;   " 498
Then, fearing for his hurt and *l* of blood,   " 777
I rather dread the *l* of use than fame ;   *Merlin and V.* 519
With *l* of half his people arrow-slain ;   " 565
dame nor damsel then Wroth at a lover's *l* ?   " 607
Had I not learnt my *l* before he came ?   *Lover's Tale* i 665
Stung by his *l* had vanish'd, none knew where.   " iv 102
ill-suited as it seem'd To such a time, to Lionel's *l*   " 208
—his *l* Weigh'd on him yet—   " 274
guest So bound to me by common love and *l*—   " 345
away she sail'd with her *l* and long'd for her own ;   *The Revenge* 111
lost to the *l* that was mine,   *The Wreck* 113
and thro' *l* of Self The gain of such large life   *Ancient Sage* 236
Moaning your *l*es, O Earth,   *The Dreamer* 17
Thrones are clouded by your *l*,   *D. of the Duke of C.* 6

Lost (*See also* **Half-lost, Late-lost**) That these have
   never *l* their light.   *Miller's D.* 88
Her cheek had *l* the rose,   *Œnone* 18
one silvery cloud Had *l* his way   " 93
L to her place and name ;   *Palace of Art* 264
Stream'd onward, *l* their edges,   *D. of F. Women* 50
Fall into shadow, soonest *l* :   *To J. S.* 11
thus be *l* for ever from the earth,   *M. d'Arthur* 90
much honour and much fame were *l*.'   " 109
l the sense that handles daily life—   *Walk. to the Mail* 22
have you *l* your heart ? ' she said ;   *Edward Gray* 3
And now we *l* her, now she gleam'd   *The Voyage* 65
the precious morning hours were *l*.   *Enoch Arden* 302
Philip gain'd As Enoch *l* ;   " 355
' The ship was *l*,' he said ' the ship was *l* !   " 393
Enoch, poor man, was cast away and *l*.'   " 713
Repeated muttering ' cast away and *l* ; ' Again in
   deeper inward whispers ' *l* ! '   " 715
slowly *l* Nor greatly cared to lose,   *Aylmer's Field* 567
Softening thro' all the gentle attributes Of his
   l child,   " 731
I came To know him more, I *l* it,   *Sea Dreams* 72
But now when all was *l* or seem'd as *l*—   *Princess, Pro.* 39
They *l* their weeks ; they vext the souls of deans ;   " 162
a pillar'd porch, the bases *l* In laurel :   " i 230
the child We *l* in other years,   " ii 11
some ages had been *l* ;   " 153
an erring pearl *L* in her bosom :   " iv 61
Wiser to weep a true occasion *l* :   " 68
(For since her horse was *l* I left her mine)   " 197
For this *l* lamb (she pointed to the child)   " 361
at once the *l* lamb at her feet Sent out a bitter
   bleating   " 391
' Be comforted : have I not *l* her too,   " v 69
our side was vanquish'd and my cause For ever *l*,   " vi 25
slip Into my bosom and be *l* in me.'   " vii 189
Nor ever *l* an English gun ;   *Ode on Well.* 97
flying to by be *l* on an endless sea—   *Wages* 2
' Behold the man that loved and *l*,   *In Mem. i* 15
Something it is which thou hast *l*,   " iv 9
With my *l* Arthur's loved remains,   " ix 3
'Tis better to have loved and *l*   " xxvii 15
l the links that bound Thy changes ;   " xli 6
So then were nothing *l* to man :   " xliii 9
' Love's too precious to be *l*,   " lxv 3
And like to him whose sight is *l* ;   " lxvi 8
That Nature's ancient power was *l* :   " lxix 2
The quiet sense of something *l*.   " lxxviii 8
'Tis better to have loved and *l*,   " lxxxv 5
No visual shade of some one *l*,   " xciii 5
Day, when I *l* the flower of men ;   " xcix 4

Lost (*continued*) With thy *l* friend among the bowers,   *In Mem. cii* 15
Hope had never *l* her youth ;   " *cxxv* 5
Dear friend, far off, my *l* desire,   " *cxxix* 1
l in trouble and moving round Here   *Maud I xxi* 5
Looking, thinking of all I have *l* ;   " *II ii* 46
Of a land that has *l* for a little her lust of gold,   " *III vi* 39
We have *l* him : he is gone :   *Ded. of Idylls* 15
a night In which the bounds of heaven and earth were *l*—   *Com. of Arthur* 372
a phantom king, Now looming, and now *l* ;   " 431
l in blowing trees and tops of towers ;   *Gareth and L.* 670
L in sweet dreams, and dreaming of her love   *Marr. of Geraint* 158
enter'd, and were *l* behind the walls.   " 252
So sadly *l* on that unhappy night ;   " 689
Yourself shall see my vigour is not *l*.'   *Geraint and E.* 82
scour'd into the coppices and was *l*,   " 534
And cursing their *l* time, and the dead man,   " 576
your charger is without, My palfrey *l*.'   " 750
held and *l* with Lot In that first war,   *Balin and Balan* 1
The *L* one Found was greeted as in Heaven   " 81
l itself in darkness, till she cried—   " 514
l to life and use and name and fame. (repeat)   *Merlin and V.* 214, 970
and there We *l* him :   " 433
Some *l*, some stolen, some as relics kept.   " 453
lay as dead, And *l* all use of life :   " 645
fought together ; but their names were *l* ;   *Lancelot and E.* 40
Else had he not *l* me : but listen to me,   " 147
Full often *l* in fancy, *l* his way ;   " 164
waste downs whereon I *l* myself,   " 225
new design wherein they *l* themselves,   " 441
Who *l* the hern we slipt her at,   " 657
had you not *l* your own.   " 1213
Merlin sat In his own chair, and so was *l* ;   *Holy Grail* 176
while ye follow wandering fires *L* in the quagmire !   " 320
hast not I thyself to save thyself As Galahad.'   " 456
wandering fires *L* in the quagmire ?—*l* to me and gone,   " 892
and one that, Because the way was *l*.   *Pelleas and E.* 59
at Caerleon, but have *l* our way :   " 66
L in a doubt, Pelleas wandering Waited,   " 392
Among the roses, and was *l* again.   " 427
she cried, ' Plunge and be *l*—   *Last Tournament* 40
Not knowing they were *l* as soon as given—   " 42
Thy lord has wholly *l* his love for thee.   *Guinevere* 509
city sack'd by night, When all is *l*,   *Pass. of Arthur* 44
thus be *l* for ever from the earth,   " 258
much honour and much fame were *l*.'   " 277
my *l* love Symbol'd in storm.   *Lover's Tale ii* 184
Talk of *l* hopes and broken heart !   " *iv* 176
tho' she seem so like the one you *l*,   " 365
And if *he* be *l*—but to save *my* soul,   *Rizpah* 77
seen And *l* and found again,   *Sisters (E. and E.)* 147
or desire that her *l* child Should earn   " 250
fur 'e *l* 'is taäil i' the beck.   *Village Wife* 86
Sa 'is taäil wur I an' 'is booöks wur gone   " 87
We have *l* her who loved her so much—   *In the Child. Hosp.* 29
Him, the *l* light of those dawn-golden times,   *To W. H. Brookfield* 7
Leaving his son too *L* in the carnage,   *Batt. of Brunanburh* 73
wholesome heat the blood had *l*,   *To E. Fitzgerald* 24
To be *l* evermore in the main.   *The Revenge* 119
and there *L*, head and heart,   *The Wreck* 30
L myself—lay like the dead   " 112
l to the loss that was mine,   " 113
With sad eyes fixt on the *l* sea-home,   " 126
And now is *l* in cloud ;   *Ancient Sage* 143
' *L* and gone and *l* and gone !'   " 224
What had he loved, what had he *l*,   " 227
wor keenin' as if he had *l* thim all.   *Tomorrow* 86
Leonard early *l* at sea ;   *Locksley H., Sixty* 55
l within a growing gloom ; *L*, or only heard in silence   73
' *L* are the gallant three hundred   *Heavy Brigade* 45
' *L* one and all ' were the words Mutter'd   " 46
all is *l* In what they prophesy,   *Epilogue* 64
Might break thro' clouded memories once again On thy *l* self.   *Demeter and P.* 11
l in the gloom of doubts that darken the schools ;   *Vastness* 11

Lost (*continued*) Swallow'd in Vastness, *l* in Silence,   *Vastness* 34
l the moment of their past on earth,   *The Ring* 464
have you *l* him, is he fled ?   *Happy* 2
and *l* Salvation for a sketch.   *Romney's R.* 138
she heard The shriek of some *l* life among the pines,   *Death of Œnone* 90
Who all but *l* himself in Alla,   *Akbar's Dream* 93
an' wa *l* wer Haldeny cow,   *Church-warden, etc.* 5
And less will be *l* than won,   *The Dreamer* 22

Lot ' I might forget my weaker *l* ;   *Two Voices* 367
Half-anger'd with my happy *l*,   *Miller's D.* 200
been happy : but what *l* is pure ?   *Walk. to the Mail* 97
Ill-fated that I am, what *l* is mine   *Love and Duty* 33
Would quarrel with our *l* ;   *Will Water.* 226
I stubb'd 'um oop wi' the *l*,   *N. Farmer, O. S.* 32
Warnt worth nowt a haäcre, an' now theer's *l*'s o' feeäd,   " 39
Wi' *l*'s o' munny laäid by,   " *N. S.* 22
coom'd to the parish wi' *l*'s o' Varsity debt,   " 29
Them or thir feythers, tha sees, mun 'a beän a laäzy *l*,   " 49
O little bard, is your *l* so hard,   *Spiteful Letter* 5
hate me not, but abide your *l*,   " 11
She finds the baseness of her *l*,   *In Mem. lx* 6
To chances where our *l*'s were cast   " *xcii* 5
maidens with one mind Bewail'd their *l* ;   " *ciii* 46
let a passionless peace be my *l*,   *Maud I iv* 50
he lived with a *l* of wild mates,   *Rizpah* 29
Their *l* with ours to rove the world   *Pref. Son. 19th Cent.* 11
drew perchance a happier *l* Than ours,   *Epilogue* 50
I would it had been my *l* To have seen thee,   *Bandit's Death* 3
fur a *l* on 'em coom'd ta-year—   *Church-warden, etc.* 13

Lot (**King of Orkney**) Morganore And *L* of Orkney.   *Com. of Arthur* 116
L's wife, the Queen of Orkney, Bellicent, (repeat)   190, 245
last tall son of *L* and Bellicent,   *Gareth and L.* 1
where thy father *L* beside the hearth   " 74
Till falling into *L*'s forgetfulness   " 96
L and many another rose and fought   " 354
Gareth hearing from a squire of *L*   " 531
son Of old King *L* and good Queen Bellicent,   " 1231
held and lost with *L* In that first war,   *Balin and Balan* 1
Sir Modred's brother, and the child of *L*,   *Lancelot and E.* 558

Lot (**nephew of Abraham**) see how you stand Stiff as *L*'s wife,   *Princess vi* 241

Loth (*See also* **Loath**) were much *l* to breed Dispute betwixt myself and mine :   " *i* 156
but she still were *l*, She still were *l* to yield herself   " *vii* 231
And now full *l* am I to break thy dream,   *Balin and Balan* 500
how *l* to quit the land !   *The Flight* 38

Lotos-Lotus asphodel, *Lotos* and lilies :   *Œnone* 98
Eating the *Lotos* day by day,   *Lotos-Eaters, C. S.* 60
The *Lotos* blooms below the barren peak :   " 100
The *Lotos* blows by every winding creek :   " 101
Cry to the *lotus* ' No flower thou ' ?   *Akbar's Dream* 37

Lotos-dust the yellow *L-d* is blown.   *Lotos-Eaters, C. S.* 104

Lotos-eaters mild-eyed melancholy *L-e* came.   *Lotos-Eaters* 27

Lotos-land In the hollow *L-l* to live   " *C. S.* 109

Lotus *See* **Lotos**

Loud With a lengthen'd *l* halloo,   *The Owl ii* 13
L, *l* rung out the bugle's brays,   *Oriana* 48
From his *l* fount upon the echoing lea :—   *Mine be the strength* 4
Between the *l* stream and the trembling stars.   *Œnone* 219
If you do not call me *l* when the day begins to break :   *May Queen* 10
Whereof my fame is *l* amongst mankind,   *St. S. Stylites* 81
And chanted a melody *l* and sweet,   *Poet's Song* 6
while the rest were *l* in merrymaking,   *Enoch Arden* 77
There came so *l* a calling of the sea,   " 910
he spread his arms abroad Crying with a *l* voice ' A sail ! a sail !   " 913
On that *l* sabbath shook the spoiler down ;   *Ode on Well.* 123
and we refrain From talk of battles *l* and vain,   " 247
For him nor moves the world's random mock,   *Will* 4
Winds are *l* and you are dumb,   *Window, No Answer* 19
Winds are *l* and winds will pass !   " 22
That makes the barren branches *l* ;   *In Mem. xv* 13

Love (s) (*continued*) L is and was my King and Lord,   *In Mem.* cxxvi 5
The *l* that rose on stronger wings,   „   cxxviii 1
My *l* involves the *l* before ;   „   cxxx 9
My *l* is vaster passion now ;   „   10
And yet is *l* not less, but more ;   Con. 12
Regret is dead, but *l* is more   „   17
there was *l* in the passionate shriek, L for the
   silent thing that had made false haste   *Maud* I i 57
I flee from the cruel madness of *l*,   „   iv 55
I fear, the new strong wine of *l*,   „   vi 82
I have led her home, my *l*,   „   xviii 1
Death may give More life to L than is or ever was   „   47
L, like men in drinking-songs,   „   55
With dear *L's* tie, makes *L* himself more dear.'   „   61
now by this my *l* has closed her sight   „   67
And the planet of *L* is on high,   „   xxii 8
Have a grain of *l* for me,   „   II ii 53
Let me and my passionate *l* go by,   „   77
Me and my harmful *l* go by ;   „   80
To find the arms of my true *l* Round me   „   iv 3
Hearts with no *l* for me :   „   94
l of a peace that was full of wrongs and shames,   „   III vi 40
May all *l*, His *l*, unseen but felt,   *Ded. of Idylls* 50
The *l* of all Thy sons encompass Thee, The *l* of all
   Thy daughters cherish Thee, The *l* of all Thy
   people comfort Thee, Till God's *l* set Thee at his
   side again !   „   52, 53, 54
Sware on the field of death a deathless *l*.   *Com. of Arthur* 132
Uther cast upon her eyes of *l* :   „   193
loathed the bright dishonour of his *l*,   „   195
Sware at the shrine of Christ a deathless *l* :   „   466
I charge thee by my *l*,'   *Gareth and L.* 55
' True *l*, sweet son, had risk'd himself   „   60
l I feel for thee, nor worthy such a *l* :   „   83
thy *l* to me, Thy Mother,—I demand.'   „   146
l be blamed for it, not she, nor I :   „   299
Eyes of pure women, wholesome stars of *l* ;   „   314
Peace to thee, woman, with thy *l's* and hates !   „   373
one would praise the *l* that linkt the King   „   492
And, loving, utter faithfulness in *l*,   „   554
And as for *l*, God wot, I love not yet,   „   561
Who tilt for lady's *l* and glory here,   „   740
Smile sweetly, thou ! my *l* hath smiled on me.'   „   1001
twice my *l* hath smiled on me.' (repeat)   „   1062, 1077
What knowest thou of lovesong or of *l* ?   „   1063
A foolish *l* for flowers ?   „   1072
thrice my *l* hath smiled on me.'   „   1161
Of utter peace, and *l*, and gentleness !   „   1289
Long in their common *l* rejoiced Geraint.   *Marr. of Geraint* 23
Touching her guilty *l* for Lancelot,   „   25
dwelling on his boundless *l*,   „   63
and dreaming of her *l* For Lancelot,   „   158
l or fear, or seeking favour of us,   „   700
for whose *l* the Roman Cæsar first Invaded Britain,   „   745
' Earl, entreat her by my *l*,   „   760
force in her Link'd with such *l* for me,   „   806
Enid, my early and my only *l*,   *Geraint and E.* 307
For the man's *l* once gone never returns.   „   333
lord Geraint, I greet you with all *l* ;   „   785
love you, Prince, with something of the *l*   „   788
With deeper and with ever deeper *l*,   „   928
bearing in their common bond of *l*,   *Balin and Balan* 150
sought to win my *l* Thro' evil ways :   „   474
And yet hast often pleaded for my *l*—   „   571
' I hold them happy, so they died for *l* :   „   581
L, if *L* be perfect, casts out fear,   *Merlin and V.* 40
flatter his own wish in age for *l*,   „   185
Death in all life and lying in all *l*,   „   194
As if in deepest reverence and in *l*.   „   220
wise in *l* Love most, say least,'   „   247
ask'd again : for see you not, dear *l*,   „   324
The great proof of your *l* :   „   354
' In *L*, if *L* be *L*, if *L* be ours,   „   387
for *l* of God and men And noble deeds,   „   412
L, tho' *L* were of the grossest, carves   „   461

Love (s) (*continued*)   rest : and *L* Should have some rest
   and pleasure   *Merlin and V.* 484
But work as vassal to the larger *l*, That dwarfs the
   petty *l* of one to one.   „   491
this full *l* of mine Without the full heart back   „   533
Full many a *l* in loving youth was mine ;   „   546
charm to keep them mine But youth and *l* ;   „   548
How from the rosy lips of life and *l*,   „   846
(For in a wink the false *l* turns to hate)   „   852
O vainly lavish'd *l* !   „   859
for what shame in *l*, So *l* be true,   „   861
more in kindness than in *l*,   „   907
' There must be now no passages of *l*   „   913
Merlin, the one passionate *l* Of her whole life ;   „   955
my *l* is more Than many diamonds,'   *Lancelot and E.* 87
great and guilty *l* he bare the Queen,   „   245
In battle with the *l* he bare his lord,   „   246
loved him, with that *l* which was her doom.   „   260
' *L*, are you yet so sick ? '   „   571
And I, when often they have talk'd of *l*,   „   673
I know not if I know what true *l* is,   „   676
cross our mighty Lancelot in his *l's* !   „   688
Yet, if he love, and his *l* hold,   „   697
About the maid of Astolat, and her *l*.   „   723
woman's *l*, Save one, he not regarded,   „   840
but her deep *l* Upbore her ;   „   860
loved her with all *l* except the *l* Of man and woman   „   868
shackles of an old *l* straiten'd him,   „   875
' Your *l*,' she said, ' your *l*—to be your wife.'   „   933
ill then should I quit your brother's *l*,   „   944
This is not *l* : but *l's* first flash in youth,   „   949
she by tact of *l* was well aware That Lancelot   „   984
her song, ' The Song of *L* and Death,'   „   1005
' Sweet is true *l* tho' given in vain,   „   1007
' *L*, art thou sweet ? then bitter death must be :
   L, thou art bitter ; sweet is death to me. O *L*,
   if death be sweeter, let me die.   „   1010
' Sweet *l*, that seems not made to fade away,   „   1013
' I fain would follow *l*, if that could be ;   „   1016
there the King will know me and my *l*,   „   1058
she returns his *l* in open shame ;   „   1083
And greatest, tho' my *l* had no return :   „   1094
take the little bed on which I died For Lancelot's *l*,   „   1118
in half disdain At *l*, life, all things,   „   1239
I loved you, and my *l* had no return, And therefore
   my true *l* has been my death.   „   1276
loved me with a *l* beyond all *l* In women,   „   1293
No cause, not willingly, for such a *l* :   „   1298
I told her that her *l* Was but the flash of youth,   „   1317
Forgive me ; mine was jealousy in *l*.'   „   1351
' That is *l's* curse ; pass on, my Queen,   „   1353
if what is worthy *l* Could bind him, but free *l* will
   not be bound.'   „   1378
' Free *l*, so bound, were freëst,' said the King.   „   1380
' Let *l* be free ; free *l* is for the best :   „   1381
What should be best, if not so pure a *l*   „   1383
with a *l* Far tenderer than my Queen's.   „   1394
' Jealousy in *l* ? ' Not rather dead *l's* harsh heir,   „   1397
Queen, if I grant the jealousy as of *l*,   „   1399
Speak, as it waxes, of a *l* that wanes ?   „   1401
A way by *l* that waken'd *l* within,   *Holy Grail* 11
With such a fervent flame of human *l*,   „   74
' My knight, my *l*, my knight of heaven, O thou,
   my *l*, whose *l* is one with mine,   „   157
To find thine own first *l* once more—   „   620
Being so clouded with his grief and *l*,   „   656
That Pelleas might obtain his lady's *l*,   *Pelleas and E.* 161
wilt at length Yield me thy *l* and know me   „   249
I had liefer ye were worthy of my *l*,   „   301
tho' ye kill my hope, not yet my *l*,   „   303
this man loves, If *l* there be :   „   308
Dishonour'd all for trial of true *l*—L ?—we be all alike :   „   477
thro' her *l* her life Wasted and pined,   „   495
Sole Queen of Beauty and of *l*,   *Last Tournament* 208
' Free *l*—free field—we love (repeat)   „   275, 281

Love (s) (*continued*) self-suppression, not of selfless *l*.'   *St. Telemachus* 22
if it be a Christian Church, people ring the bell
   from *l* to Thee.   *Akbar's D., Inscrip.* 4
The Alif of Thine alphabet of *L*.'   *Akbar's Dream* 31
' Alla ' says their sacred book, ' is *L*,'   ,,   73
Alla call'd In old Irân the Sun of *L* ? and *L* The net
   of truth ? '   ,,   87
in the *l* of Truth, The truth of *L*.   ,,   101
Express him also by their warmth of *l*   ,,   109
alchemise old hates into the gold Of *L*,   ,,   164
a well of *l* My heart is for my son,   ,,   170
L and Justice came and dwelt therein ; (repeat) ,, 181, 194
guess at the *l* of a soul for a soul ?   *Charity* 30
Before I learn that *L*, which is,   *Doubt and Prayer* 7
For if this earth be ruled by Perfect *L*,   *D. of the Duke of C.* 8
Sleep, Ellen Aubrey, *l*, and dream of me.'   *Audley Court* 73
Love (verb) (*See also* **Loov, Loove, Luvv**) When I ask her if she
   l me,   *Lilian* 3
She'll not tell me if she *l* me,   ,,   6
brook that *l's* To purl o'er matted cress   *Ode to Memory* 58
thou dearly *l* thy first essay,   ,,   83
' Who is it *l's* me ? who *l's* not me ? '   *The Mermaid* 13
You *l*, remaining peacefully,   *Margaret* 22
And clip your wings, and make you *l* :   *Rosalind* 45
Kate *l's* well the bold and fierce ;   *Kate* 29
For ah ! the slight coquette, she cannot *l*,   *The form, the form* 12
To live forgotten, and *l* forlorn. (repeat)*Mariana in the S.* 12, 24, 84, 96
' Do men *l* thee ? Art thou so bound To men, *Two Voices* 109
' Yet must I *l* her for your sake ;   *Miller's D.* 142
That loss but made us *l* the more,   ,,   230
I shall *l* thee well and cleave to thee,   *Œnone* 160
Pass by the happy souls, that *l* to live :   ,,   240
That did *l* Beauty only, (Beauty seen In all
   varieties   *To ——, With Pal. of Art* 6
You sought to prove how I could *l*,   *L. C. V. de Vere* 21
Those we *l* first are taken first.   *To J. S.* 12
Something to *l* He lends us ;   ,,   13
But lives and *l's* in every place ;   *On a Mourner* 5
L thou thy land, with love far-brought *Love thou thy land* 1
Would *l* the gleams of good that broke   ,,   89
blooms the garden that I *l*.   *Gardener's D.* 34
And told me I should *l*.   ,,   64
' My girl, I *l* you well ;   *Dora* 42
I come For Dora : take her back ; she *l's* you well. ,,   143
' Oh ! who would *l* ? I woo'd a woman once, *Audley Court* 52
Old oak, I *l* thee well ;   *Talking Oak* 202
God *l* us, as if the seedsman,   *Golden Year* 70
and the wild team Which *l* thee,   *Tithonus* 40
Saying, ' Dost thou *l* me, cousin ? '   *Locksley Hall* 30
and *l* her, as I knew her, kind ?   ,,   70
whom to look at was to *l*.   ,,   72
and *l* her for the love she bore ?   ,,   73
I will *l* no more, no more,   *Edward Gray* 31
' He does not *l* me for my birth,   *Lady Clare* 9
He *l's* me for my own true worth,   ,,   11
' There is none I *l* like thee.'   *L. of Burleigh* 6
And I *l* thee more than life.'   ,,   16
Says to her that *l's* him well,   ,,   22
O but she will *l* him truly !   ,,   37
Fish are we that *l* the mud,   *Vision of Sin* 101
' No, I *l* not what is new ;   ,,   139
I *l* him all the better for it—   *Enoch Arden* 196
I do think They *l* me as a father : I am sure that I *l*
   them as if they were mine own ;   ,,   412
Can one *l* twice ? can you be ever loved   ,,   426
the days That most she *l's* to talk of,   *The Brook* 226
and he said ' Why then I *l* it :'   *Aylmer's Field* 249
whitest lamb in all my fold *L's* you :   ,,   362
because I *l* their child They hate me :   ,,   423
you then, That *l* to keep us children ! *Princess, Pro.* 133
Her brethren, tho' they *l* her,   ,,   i 154
When we fall out with those we *l*   ,,   ii 8
' Albeit so mask'd, Madam, the truth ;   ,,   213
If I could *l*, why this were she :   ,,   iii 99
she cried, ' you *l* The metaphysics !   ,,   299

Love (verb) (*continued*) That sinks with all we *l* below
   the verge ;   *Princess iv* 47
and to shame That which he says he *l's* :   ,,   249
That *l* their voices more than duty,   ,,   512
and yet they say that still You *l* her.   ,,   v 123
shards with catapults, She would not *l* ;—   ,,   139
Not ever would she *l* ; but brooding   ,,   141
They *l* us for it, and we ride them down.   ,,   157
one *l's* the soldier, one The silken priest   ,,   183
she can be sweet to those she *l's*,   ,,   289
You *l* nor her, nor me, nor any ;   ,,   vi 260
And trust, not *l*, you less.   ,,   296
I *l* not hollow cheek or faded eye :   ,,   vii 7
But like each other ev'n as those who *l*.   ,,   292
It seems you *l* to cheat yourself with words :   ,,   334
Never, Prince ; You cannot *l* me.'   ,,   338
to life indeed, thro' thee, Indeed I *l* :   ,,   346
I *l* thee : come, Yield thyself up :   ,,   363
Thine island *l's* thee well,   *Ode on Well.* 85
We *l* not this French God, the child of Hell, *Third of Feb.* 7
But though we *l* kind Peace so well,   ,,   9
But some *l* England and her honour yet.   ,,   46
Come to us, *l* us and make us your own : *W. to Alexandra* 30
who *l* best have best the grace to know *W. to Marie Alex.* 28
You cannot *l* me at all, if you *l* not   *Grandmother* 48
' Sweetheart, I *l* you so well that your good name   ,,   50
To *l* once and for ever.   *Window, Spring* 8
L me now, you'll *l* me then :   ,, *No Answer* 27
Love can *L* but once a life.   ,,   28
To look on her that *l's* him well,   *In Mem. viii* 2
Come quick, thou bringest all I *l*.   ,,   xvii 8
And come, whatever *l's* to weep,   ,,   xviii 11
He *l's* to make parade of pain,   ,,   xxi 10
But in the songs I *l* to sing   ,,   xxxviii 7
When one that *l's* but knows not, reaps A truth
   from one that *l's* and knows ?   ,,   xlii 11
I cannot *l* thee as I ought,   ,,   lii 1
My spirit loved and *l's* him yet,   ,,   lx 2
How should he *l* a thing so low ? '   ,,   16
I loved thee, Spirit, and, *l*, nor can The soul of
   Shakespeare *l* thee more.   ,,   lxi 11
' More years had made me *l* thee more.   ,,   lxxxi 8
Discuss'd the books to *l* or hate,   ,, lxxxix 34
Are earnest that he *l's* her yet,   ,, xcvii 15
He *l's* her yet, she will not weep,   ,,   18
For that, for all, she *l's* him more.   ,,   28
' I cannot understand : I *l*.'   ,,   36
shape of him I loved, and *l* For ever :   ,,   ciii 14
Who *l's* not Knowledge ?   ,,   cxiv 1
I do not therefore *l* thee less :   ,,   cxxx 8
I seem to *l* thee more and more.   ,,   12
be born and think, And act and *l*,   *Con.* 127
That God, which ever lives and *l's*,   ,,   141
I am quite sure That there is one to *l* me ; *Maud I xi* 11
Should I *l* her so well if she (repeat)   ,, xvi 26, 28
I see she cannot but I *l* him,   ,,   xix 69
Beginning to faint in the light that she *l's*   ,,   xxii 9
To faint in the light of the sun she *l's*,   ,,   11
But she, she would *l* me still ;   ,,   II ii 51
wheedle a world that *l's* him not,   ,,   v 39
we will work thy will Who *l* thee.' *Com. of Arthur* 260
chance what will, I *l* thee to the death ! '   ,,   468
' King and my lord, I *l* thee to the death ! '   ,,   470
' Reign ye, and live and *l*,   ,,   472
Sweet mother, do ye *l* the child ? ' *Gareth and L.* 35
' Then, mother, an' ye *l* the child,'   ,,   37
The woman *l's* her lord.   ,,   372
God wot, I *l* not yet, But *l* I shall,   ,,   561
and whom they could but *l*,   ,,   696
I accept thee aught the more Or *l* thee better,   ,,   767
I cannot *l* my lord and not his name. *Marr. of Geraint* 92
in the sweet face of her Whom he *l's* most,   ,,   123
may you light on all things that you *l*, And live to
   wed with her whom first you *l* :   ,,   226
wheel and thee we neither *l* nor hate. (repeat)   ,, 349, 358

Love (verb) (*continued*) For truly there are those who

l me yet;	*Marr. of Geraint* 461
Except the lady he *l*'s best be there.	„ 481
I would the two Should *l* each other :	„ 792
he *l*'s to know When men of mark are in his territory :	*Geraint and E.* 228
doth he *l* you as of old ?	„ 323
men may bicker with the things they *l*,	„ 325
that this man *l*'s you no more.	„ 329
But here is one who *l*'s you as of old ;	„ 334
' Earl, if you *l* me as in former years,	„ 355
village boys Who *l* to vex him eating,	„ 561
I *l* that beauty should go beautifully :	„ 681
I never loved, can never *l* but him :	„ 709
Who *l* you, Prince, with something of the love Wherewith we *l* the Heaven that chastens us.	„ 788
A year ago—nay, then I *l* thee not—	*Balin and Balan* 504
vows like theirs, that high in heaven *L* most,	*Merlin and V.* 15
' O Merlin, do ye *l* me ? ' (repeat)	„ 235, 236
' Great Master, do ye *l* me ?	„ 237
' Who are wise in love *L* most, say least,'	„ 248
Master, do ye *l* my tender rhyme ? '	„ 399
methinks you think you *l* me well ; For me, I *l* you somewhat ; rest :	„ 483
' Man dreams of Fame while woman wakes to *l*.'	„ 460
proof against the grain Of him ye say ye *l* :	„ 488
However well ye think ye *l* me now	„ 516
try this charm on whom ye say ye *l*.'	„ 525
My daily wonder is, I *l* at all.	„ 536
And one to make me jealous if I *l*,	„ 539
must be to *l* thee still.	„ 928
' O Merlin, tho' you do not *l* me, save, Yet save me ! '	„ 944
A sight ye *l* to look on.'	*Lancelot and E.* 83
who *l*'s me must have a touch of earth ;	„ 133
He *l*'s it in his knights more than himself :	„ 157
Ill news, my Queen, for all who *l* him,	„ 598
' that you *l* This greatest knight,	„ 668
But if I know, then, if I *l* not him, I know there is none other I can *l*.'	„ 677
' Yea, by God's death,' said he, ' ye *l* him well,	„ 679
knew ye what all others know, And whom he *l*'s.'	„ 681
For if you *l*, it will be sweet to give it ; And if he *l*, it will be sweet to have it	„ 692
whether he *l* or not, A diamond is a diamond.	„ 694
Yet, if he *l*, and his love hold,	„ 697
Whose sleeve he wore ; she *l*'s him ;	„ 711
' The maid of Astolat *l*'s Sir Lancelot, Sir Lancelot *l*'s the maid of Astolat.'	„ 725
But did not *l* the colour ;	„ 840
love Of man and woman when they *l* their best,	„ 869
He will not *l* me : how then ?	„ 893
' I have gone mad. I *l* you :	„ 930
Sir Lancelot's fault Not to *l* me, than it is mine to *l* Him	„ 1076
He *l*'s the Queen, and in an open shame :	„ 1082
Yet to be loved makes not to *l* again :	„ 1295
All that belongs to knighthood, and I *l*.'	*Pelleas and E.* 9
I *l* thee, tho' I know thee not.	„ 43
win me this fine circlet, Pelleas, That I may *l* thee ? '	„ 129
on the morrow knighted, sware To *l* one only.	„ 141
' To those who *l* them, trials of our faith.	„ 210
and if ye *l* me not, I cannot bear to dream	„ 299
this man *l*'s, If love there be :	„ 307
He could not *l* me, did he know me well.	„ 312
' Avaunt,' they cried, ' our lady *l*'s thee not.'	„ 369
That whom ye loathe, him will I make you *l*.'	„ 390
He dies who *l*'s it,—if the worm be there.'	„ 409
What faith have these in whom they sware to *l* ?	*Last Tournament* 188
' Free love—free field—we *l* (repeat)	„ 275, 281
What, if she *l* me still ?	„ 497
He find thy favour changed and *l* thee not '—	„ 500
I should hate thee more than *l*.'	„ 600
Did I *l* her ? the name at least I loved.	„ 603
I say, Swear to me thou wilt *l* me ev'n when old,	„ 652
my soul, we *l* but while we may ;	„ 701

Love (verb) (*continued*) ' We *l* but while we may.' Well then,

	Last Tournament 712
and I will *l* thee to the death,	„ 720
' O Lancelot, if thou *l* me get thee hence.'	*Guinevere* 95
True men who *l* me still, for whom I live,	„ 445
To *l* one maiden only, cleave to her,	„ 475
tho' thou wouldst not *l* thy lord,	„ 508
that my doom is, I *l* thee still.	„ 559
Let no man dream but that I *l* thee	„ 560
tell the King I *l* him tho' so late ?	„ 651
I must not scorn myself : he *l*'s me still.	„ 673
Let no one dream but that he *l*'s me still.	„ 674
thy life is whole, and still I live Who *l* thee ;	*Pass. of Arthur* 151
sons, who *l* Our ocean-empire	*To the Queen ii* 28
draught of that sweet fountain that he *l*'s,	*Lover's Tale i* 141
Ye ask me, friends, When I began to *l*.	„ 145
So know I not when I began to *l*.	„ 163
In that I live I *l* ; because I *l* I live :	„ 178
Than the gray cuckoo *l*'s his name,	„ 257
I found, they two did *l* each other,	„ 728
Did I *l* her ? Ye know that I did *l* her ;	„ 732
Did I *l* her, And could I look upon her	„ 735
Let them so *l* that men and boys may say, ' Lo ! how they *l* each other ! '	„ 756
Deem that I *l* thee but as brothers do, So shalt thou *l* me still as sisters do ;	„ 767
had there been none else To *l* as lovers,	„ 771
I will be alone with all I *l*,	*iv* 47
solemn offering of you To him you *l*.'	„ 119
I'll never *l* any but you, (repeat)	*First Quarrel* 22, 32, 33, 34
I loved Edith, made Edith *l* me.	*Sisters (E. and E.)* 139
I know not which of these I *l* the best.	„ 283
But *you* I *l* Edith ; and her own true eyes	„ 284
I think *I* likewise *l* your Edith most.	„ 293
Better to fall by the hands that they *l*,	*Def. of Lucknow* 53
Ay, for they *l* me !	*Sir J. Oldcastle* 44
Who dost not *l* our England—	*To Victor Hugo* 9
Yet *l*'s and hates with mortal hates and loves,	*Tiresias* 23
thou art wise enough, Tho' young, to *l* thy wiser,	„ 154
one thing given me, to *l* and to live for,	*The Wreck* 35
Stephen, I *l* you, I *l* you, and yet '—	„ 101
The wife, the sons, who *l* him best	*Ancient Sage* 125
I swear and swear forsworn To *l* him most,	*The Flight* 50
They *l* their mates, to whom they sing ;	„ 65
She bad us *l*, like souls in Heaven,	„ 88
every heart that *l*'s with truth is equal to endure.	„ 104
L your enemy, bless your haters,	*Locksley H., Sixty* 85
I that loathed, have come to *l* him.	„ 280
who *l*'s War for War's own sake Is fool,	*Epilogue* 30
only to be known By those who *l* thee best.	*Pref. Poem Broth. S.* 8
Who *l*'s his native country best.	*Hands all Round* 4
To Canada whom we *l* and prize,	„ 19
between The two that I *l* thee,	*To Prin. Beatrice* 18
Your rule has made the people *l* Their ruler.	*To Marg. of Dufferin* 9
man, that only lives and *l*'s an hour,	*Demeter and P.* 106
Till thy dark lord accept and *l* the Sun,	„ 137
for I loved him, and *l* him for ever :	*Vastness* 36
And bind the maid to *l* you by the ring ;	*The Ring* 202
flaunted it Before that other whom I loved and *l*.	„ 244
Miriam, if you *l* me take the ring ! '	„ 263
if you cannot *l* me, let it be.'	„ 265
You *l* me still ' Io t'amo.'—Muriel—no—She cannot *l* ; she *l*'s her own hard self,	„ 291
Why had I made her *l* me thro' the ring,	„ 391
' That weak and watery nature *l* you ?	„ 396
but now I *l* you most ;	*Happy* 29
whisper'd me ' your Ulric *l*'s '	„ 62
Who *l* the winter woods,	*To Ulysses* 14
Who *l* her still, and whimper,	*Romney's R.* 117
I *l* you more than when we married.	„ 157
cried ' *L* one another little ones '	*Akbar's Dream* 76
L me ? O yes, no doubt—how long—	*Charity* 5
and *l*'s the world from end to end,	*The Wanderer* 7

Loveable ELAINE the fair, Elaine the *l*, *Lancelot and E.* 1

Love-charm'd stars that hung *L-c* to listen : *Love and Duty* 75

Loved (*See also* **Loov'd, Luvv'd, Well-loved, Yet-loved**) Ev'n

in her sight he *l* so well ?	*Margaret* 40
If I were *l*, as I desire to be,	*If I were loved* 1
—if I were *l* by thee ?	„ 4
I *l* thee for the tear thou couldst not hide,	*The Bridesmaid* 11
Have lived and *l* alone so long,	*Miller's D.* 38
I *l*, and love dispell'd the fear	„ 89
I *l* the brimming wave that swam Thro' quiet meadows	„ 97
I *l* you better for your fears,	„ 149
But I his beauty passing well.	*The Sisters* 23
silver tongue, Cold February *l*, is dry :	*The Blackbird* 14
a sleep They sleep—the men I *l*.	*M. d'Arthur* 17
we *l* the man, and prized his work ;	*Ep.* 8
woman's heart, the heart of her I *l* ;	*Gardener's D.* 230
on the cheeks, Like one that *l* him :	*Dora* 134
I have kill'd him—but I *l* him—	„ 160
l At first like dove and dove were cat and dog	*Walk. to the Mail* 57
but for daily loss of one she *l*	„ 94
and Duty *l* of Love—	*Love and Duty* 46
both with those That *l* me, and alone ;	*Ulysses* 9
weeping, ' I have *l* thee long.'	*Locksley Hall* 30
I had *l* thee more than ever wife was *l*.	„ 64
No—she never *l* me truly :	„ 74
to have *l* so slight a thing.	„ 148
l the people well, And loathed to see them overtax'd ;	*Godiva* 8
therefore, as they *l* her well,	„ 38
' Ellen Adair she *l* me well,	*Edward Gray* 9
And the people *l* her much.	*L. of Burleigh* 76
We *l* the glories of the world,	*The Voyage* 83
And you, whom once I *l* so well,	*The Letters* 35
But Philip *l* in silence ;	*Enoch Arden* 41
But she *l* Enoch ; tho' she knew it not,	„ 43
And her, he *l*, a beggar :	„ 117
To sell the boat—and yet he *l* her well—	„ 134
I have *l* you longer than you know.'	„ 421
can you be ever *l* As Enoch was ?	„ 426
to be *l* A little after Enoch.'	„ 428
he had *l* longer than she knew,	„ 455
nor *l* she to be left Alone at home,	„ 516
home Where Annie lived and *l* him,	„ 685
Then may she learn I *l* her to the last.'	„ 835
yet the brook he *l*, For which,	*The Brook* 15
fancies of the boy, To me that *l* him ;	„ 20
he *l* As heiress and not heir regretfully ?	*Aylmer's Field* 23
young hearts not knowing that they *l*,	„ 133
He but less *l* than Edith, of her poor :	„ 167
He, *l* for her and for himself.	„ 179
neither *l* nor liked the thing he heard.	„ 250
for I have *l* you more as son Than brother,	„ 351
The life of all—who madly *l*—and he,	„ 389
They *l* me, and because I love their child	„ 423
Him too you *l*, for he was worthy love.	„ 712
woman half turn'd round from him she *l*,	*Sea Dreams* 286
tho' he *l* her none the less,	*Lucretius* 4
the mind, except it *l* them, clasp These idols	„ 164
l to live alone Among her women,	*Princess i* 49
eyes that ever *l* to meet Star-sisters	„ ii 427
' To linger here with one that *l* us.'	„ iii 339
I *l* her. Peace be with her.	„ iv 136
I *l* you like this kneeler,	„ 296
he That *l* me closer than his own right eye,	„ v 531
Call'd him worthy to be *l*,	„ vi 6
if you *l* The breast that fed or arm that dandled you,	„ 180
Dear traitor, too much *l*, why ?—why ?—	„ 293
I *l* the woman : he, that doth not,	„ vii 313
there was one thro' whom I *l* her,	„ 317
Ere seen I *l*, and I thee seen,	„ 341
We *l* the hall, tho' white and cold,	*The Daisy* 37
I walk'd with one I *l* two and thirty years ago.	*V. of Cauteretz* 4
Two dead men have I *l* With a love	*G. of Swainston* 13
Three dead men have I *l* and thou art last of the three.	„ 15
I find him worthier to be *l*.	*In Mem., Pro.* 40
' Behold the man that *l* and lost,	„ i 15
With my lost Arthur's *l* remains,	„ ix 3
The human-hearted man I *l*,	„ xiii 11

Loved (*continued*)

I *l* the weight I had to bear,	*In Mem.* xxv 7
'Tis better to have *l* and lost Than never to have *l* at all.	„ xxvii 15
As when he *l* me here in Time,	„ xliii 14
Who *l*, who suffer'd countless ills,	„ lvi 17
My spirit *l* and loves him yet,	„ lx 2
I *l* thee, Spirit, and love,	„ lxi 11
'Tis better to have *l* and lost, Than never to have *l* at all—	„ lxxxv 3
That *l* to handle spiritual strife,	„ 54
He *l* to rail against it still,	„ lxxxix 38
The shape of him I *l*, and love For ever :	„ ciii 14
The man we *l* was there on deck,	„ 41
A little spare the night I *l*,	„ cv 15
And sing the songs he *l* to hear.	„ cvii 24
And *l* them more, that they were thine,	„ cx 15
O *l* the most, when most I feel	„ cxxix 3
L deeplier, darklier understood ;	„ 10
Until we close with all we *l*,	„ cxxxi 11
told me that he *l* A daughter of our house ;	„ Con. 6
For all we thought and *l* and did,	„ 134
To speak of the mother she *l*	*Maud I* xix 27
one short hour to see The souls we *l*,	„ *II* iv 15
l one only and who clave to her—'	*Ded. of Idylls* 11
He laugh'd upon his warrior whom he *l* And honour'd most.	*Com. of Arthur* 125
Stern too at times, and then I *l* him not, But sweet again, and then I *l* him well.	„ 354
Arthur charged his warrior, whom he *l* And honour'd most,	„ 447
One, that had *l* him from his childhood,	*Gareth and L.* 53
l with that full love I feel for thee,	„ 83
Kay the seneschal, who *l* him not,	„ 483
And *l* her, as he *l* the light of Heaven.	*Marr. of Geraint* 5
so *l* Geraint To make her beauty vary	„ 8
and *l* her in a state Of broken fortunes,	„ 12
L her, and often with her own white hands	„ 16
And Enid *l* the Queen, and with true heart	„ 19
tho' he *l* and reverenced her too much	„ 119
that dress, and how he *l* her in it, (repeat)	„ 141, 843
Hath ask'd again, and ever *l* to hear ;	„ 436
Might well have served for proof that I was *l*,	„ 796
Perhaps because he *l* her passionately,	*Geraint and E.* 10
The being he *l* best in all the world,	„ 103
Not while they *l* them ;	„ 327
Enid never *l* a man but him,	„ 363
Except the passage that he *l* her not ;	„ 392
And *l* me serving in my father's hall :	„ 699
I never *l*, can never love but him :	„ 709
To these my lists with him whom best you *l* ;	„ 840
with your own true eyes Beheld the man you *l*	„ 847
her ladies *l* to call Enid the Fair,	„ 962
I *l* thee first, That warps the wit.'	*Merlin and V.* 60
O God, that I had *l* a smaller man !	„ 872
Who *l* to make men darker than they are,	„ 876
My Queen, that summer, when ye *l* me first.	*Lancelot and E.* 104
she lifted up her eyes And *l* him,	„ 260
darling of the court, *L* of the loveliest,	„ 262
l her with all love except the love	„ 868
' If I be *l*, these are my festal robes,	„ 909
' I never *l* him : an I meet with him,	„ 1068
it is my glory to have *l* One peerless,	„ 1090
having *l* God's best And greatest,	„ 1093
I *l* you, and my love had no return,	„ 1276
l me with a love beyond all love In women,	„ 1293
Yet to be *l* makes not to love again ;	„ 1295
And I thy courtesies and thee, a man Made to be *l*;	„ 1363
Thou couldst have *l* this maiden,	„ 1366
to be *l*, if what is worthy love Could bind him,	„ 1378
Ye *l* me, damsel, surely with a love	„ 1394
l him much beyond the rest, And honour'd him,	*Holy Grail* 9
And since he *l* all maidens,	*Pelleas and E.* 40
for he dream'd His lady *l* him, and he knew himself *L* of the King :	„ 153

P

Loved (continued) Then rang the shout his lady *l* : — *Pelleas and E.* 171
I *l* you and I deem'd you beautiful, — „ 297
Than to be *l* again of you—farewell ; — „ 302
yet him I *l* not. Why ? I deem'd him fool ? — „ 308
For why should I have *l* her to my shame ? I
  loathe her, as I *l* her to my shame. — „ 482
I never *l* her, I but lusted for her— — „ 484
l it tenderly, And named it Nestling ; — *Last Tournament* 24
And I *l* him well, until himself had thought He *l*
  her also, — „ 401
' Grace, Queen, for being *l* : she *l* me well. — „ 602
Did I love her ? the name at least I *l*. — „ 603
Her to be *l* no more ? — „ 641
I *l* This knightliest of all knights,
  how to take last leave of all I *l* ? — *Guinevere* 546
Had I but *l* thy highest creatures here ? It was
  my duty to have *l* the highest : — „ 656
We needs must *l* the highest when we see it, — „ 660
knights Once thine, whom thou hast *l*, — *Pass. of Arthur* 61
And they my knights, who *l* me once, — „ 73
Such a sleep They sleep—the men I *l*. — „ 185
how should I have lived and not have *l* ? — *Lover's Tale* i 170
we *l* The sound of one-another's voices — „ 255
Next to her presence whom I *l* so well, — „ 427
Parting my own mountains was received, — „ 433
Even the feet of her I *l*, I fell, — „ 600
The *l*, the lover, the happy Lionel, — „ 654
for I *l* her, lost my love in Love ; I, for I *l* her,
  graspt the hand she *l*, — „ 749
dream but how I could have *l* thee, had there been
  none else To love as lovers, *l* again by thee. — „ 770
How I had *l* her from the first ; — „ ii 91
my spirit Was of so wide a compass it took in All
  I had *l*, — „ 136
the settled countenance Of her I *l*, — „ iii 40
all their house was old and I *l* them both, — „ iv 122
And, tho' he *l* and honour'd Lionel, — „ 148
when the guest Is *l* and honour'd to the uttermost. — „ 245
one who I His master more than all on earth — „ 256
I *l* him better than play ; — *First Quarrel* 12
an' I *l* him better than all. — „ 14
an' I never *l* any but you ; — „ 86
mother and her sister *l* More passionately still. — *Sisters (E. and E.)* 44
Only, believing I *l* Edith, — „ 138
Had I not dream'd I *l* her yestermorn ? — „ 169
she That *L* me—our true Edith— — „ 235
In and beyond the grave, that one she *l*. — „ 272
dog that had *l* him and fawn'd at his knee— — *In the Child. Hosp.* 9
We have lost her who *l* her so much— — „ 29
Voice of the dead whom we *l*, — *Def. of Lucknow* 1
freedom, or the sake of those they *l*, — *Sir J. Oldcastle* 186
Old Brooks, who *l* so well to mouth my rhymes, — *To W. H. Brookfield* 2
those dawn-golden times, Who *l* you well ! — „ 8
a man men fear is a man to be *l* by the women
  they say. And I could have *l* him too, — *The Wreck* 18
Seer Whom one that *l*, and honour'd him, — *Ancient Sage* 3
What had he *l*, what had he lost, — „ 227
I *l* him then ; he *was* my father then. — *The Flight* 24
My Edwin *l* to call us then — „ 80
I *l* ye meself wid a heart and a half, — *Tomorrow* 39
Amy *l* me, Amy fail'd me, — *Locksley H., Sixty* 19
All I *l* are vanish'd voices, — „ 252
a wailing, ' I have *l* thee well.' — „ 262
You came, and look'd and *l* the view Long-known
  and *l* by me, — *Pro. to Gen. Hamley* 5
I that *l* thee since my day began, — *To Virgil* 38
cried ' Where is my *l* one ? — *Demeter and P.* 60
for I *l* him, and love him for ever : — *Vastness* 36
He *l* my name not me ; — *The Ring* 191
flaunted it Before that other whom I *l* and love. — „ 244
Miriam *l* me from the first, — „ 274
you—you *l* me, kept your word. — „ 290
all her talk was of the babe she *l* ; — „ 353
I *l* you first when young and fair, — *Happy* 29
The king who *l* me, And cannot die ; — *Merlin and the G.* 79

Loved (continued) *l* by all the younger gown There at
  Balliol, — *To Master of B.* 2
and he *l* to dandle the child, — *Bandit's Death* 15
He was *l* at least by his dog : — „ 35
Love-deep languors of thy *l-d* eyes — *Eleänore* 76
Love-drunken who was he with such *l-d* eyes — *The Ring* 21
Love-knots leg and arm with *l-k* gay, — *Talking Oak* 65
Love-language heard The low *l-l* of the bird — *In Mem.* cii 11
Love-languid eyes, *l-l* thro' half tears — *Love and Duty* 36
Loveless Sweet death, that seems to make us *l* clay, — *Lancelot and E.* 1014
Lovelier Than all the valleys of Ionian hills. — *Œnone* 11
As *l* than whatever Oread haunt The knolls of Ida, — „ 74
What *l* of his own had he than her, — *Aylmer's Field* 22
Flowers of all heavens, and *l* than their names, — *Princess, Pro.* 2
these fields Are lovely, *l* not the Elysian lawns, — „ iii 342
And left her woman, *l* in her mood — „ vii 162
The distance takes a *l* hue, — *In Mem.* cxv 6
A *l* life, a more unstain'd, than his ! — *Ded. of Idylls* 30
' Far *l* in our Lancelot had it been, — *Lancelot and E.* 589
l than when first Her light feet fell — *Last Tournament* 553
might inwreathe (How *l*, nobler then !) — *Lover's Tale* i 459
Far *l* than its cradle ; — „ 530
l as herself Is *l* than all others— — „ iv 287
Loveliest true To what is *l* upon earth.' — *Mariana in the S.* 64
l in all grace Of movement, — *Œnone* 75
Their feet in flowers, her *l* : — *Princess* vi 78
Array'd and deck'd her, as the *l*, — *Marr. of Geraint* 17
And *l* of all women upon earth. — „ 21
darling of the court, Loved of the *l*, — *Lancelot and E.* 262
Most *l*, earthly-heavenliest harmony ? — *Lover's Tale* i 279
Turning my way, the *l* face on earth. — *Sisters (E. and E.)* 87
Loveliness Her *l* with shame and with surprise — *D. of F. Women* 89
A miniature of *l*, all grace Summ'd up — *Gardener's D.* 12
In *l* of perfect deeds, — *In Mem.* xxxvi 11
so pure a love Clothed in so pure a *l* ? — *Lancelot and E.* 1384
Queen Paramount of love And *l*— — *Last Tournament* 553
Love-longing I thought Laziness, vague *l-l's*, — *Sisters (E. and E.)* 128
Love-lore Thou art perfect in *l-l*. (repeat) — *Madeline* 9, 26
Lovelorn With melodious airs *l*, — *Adeline* 55
Love-loyal *L-l* to the least wish of the Queen, — *Lancelot and E.* 89
L-l to the least wish of the Queen, — *Guinevere* 126
Lovely (*See also* **Lowly-lovely**) A *l* time, For it was
  in the golden prime — *Arabian Nights* 86
Stays on her floating locks the *l* freight — *Ode to Memory* 16
He said, ' She has a *l* face. — *L. of Shalott* iv 52
And whisper *l* words, and use Her influence — *Will Water.* 11
She look'd so *l*, as she sway'd The rein — *Sir L. and Q. G.* 40
' Look what a *l* piece of workmanship ! ' — *Aylmer's Field* 237
then I saw one *l* star Larger and larger. — *Sea Dreams* 93
these fields Are *l*, lovelier not the Elysian lawns, — *Princess* iii 342
The *l*, lordly creature floated on — „ vi 89
Be sometimes *l* like a bride, — *In Mem.* lix 6
See what a *l* shell, Small and pure as a pearl, — *Maud* II ii 1
Where like a shoaling sea the *l* blue — *Geraint and E.* 688
But rather seem'd a *l* baleful star Veil'd — *Merlin and V.* 262
and that clear-featured face Was *l*, — *Lancelot and E.* 1160
Love-offering last *L-o* and peace-offering — *Last Tournament* 748
Love-poem and this A mere *l-p* ! — *Princess* iv 126
Lover (*See also* **Landscape-lover, Truth-lover**) Two *l's*
  whispering by an orchard wall — *Circumstance* 4
Came two young *l's* lately wed ; — *L. of Shalott* ii 34
my *l*, with whom I rode sublime On Fortune's
  neck : — *D. of F. Women* 141
And on her *l's* arm she leant, — *Day-Dm., Depart.* 1
L's long-betroth'd were they : — *Lady Clare* 6
But he clasp'd her like a *l*, — *L. of Burleigh* 67
He like a *l* down thro' all his blood — *Enoch Arden* 659
That grow for happy *l's*. — *The Brook* 173
Yet once by night again the *l's* met, — *Aylmer's Field* 413
l heeded not, But passionately restless — „ 545
And at the happy *l's* heart in heart— — *Princess* vii 108
As thou with thy young *l* hand in hand — *W. to Marie Alex.* 34
she aim'd not at glory, no *l* of glory she : — *Wages* 4
me the *l* of liberty, — *Boädicea* 48
A jewel, a jewel dear to a *l's* eye ! — *Window, On the Hill* 1

Lover (*continued*) A happy *l* who has come To look on her *In Mem.* viii 1
From a little lazy *l* Who but claims *Maud I xx* 10
Come out to your own true *l*, That your true *l* may
see Your glory also, „ 46
For, call it *l's* quarrels, yet I know *Geraint and E.* 324
one true *l* whom you ever own'd, „ 344
shall we strip him there Your *l* ? „ 489
' The little rift within the *l's* lute *Merlin and V.* 393
neither dame nor damsel then Wroth at a *l's* loss ? „ 607
chant thy praise As prowest knight and truest *l*, *Pelleas and E.* 350
as the one true knight on earth, And only *l* ; „ 495
The Queen Look'd hard upon her *l*, „ 605
How darest thou, if *l*, push me *Last Tournament* 638
The loved, the *l*, the happy Lionel, *Lover's Tale i* 654
The blissful *l*, too, From his great hoard „ 713
had there been none else To love as *l's*, „ 771
And leave the name of *L's* Leap : „ iv 42
And thus our lonely *l* rode away, „ 130
I with our *l* to his native Bay. „ 155
What was it ? for our *l* seldom spoke, „ 225
The *l* answer'd, ' There is more than one „ 241
For man is a *l* of Truth, *Dead Prophet* 44
souls Of two repentant *L's* guard the ring ; ' *The Ring* 198
sacred those Ghost *L's* hold the gift.' „ 205
Two *l's* parted by a scurrilous tale „ 208
as the bygone *l* thro' this ring Had sent his cry „ 232
on that day Two *l's* parted „ 427
As if—those two Ghost *l's*— „ 459
L's yet— *Miriam.* Yes, yes ! „ 460
you were than a *l's* fairy dream, *To Mary Boyle* 43
For Ralph was Edith's *l*, *The Tourney* 2
Lover's Bay Keep thou thy name of ' *L B.* ' *Lover's Tale i* 15
Love-sighs passion seeks Pleasance in *l-s*, *Lilian* 9
Lovesome One her dark hair and *l* mien. *Beggar Maid* 12
Love-song A *l-s* I had somewhere read, *Miller's D.* 65
What knowest thou of *l* or of love ? *Gareth and L.* 1063
Lovest *L* thou the doleful wind *Adeline* 49
I think thou *l* me well.' *L. of Burleigh* 4
Lovetale The wind Told a *l* beside us, *Lover's Tale i* 543
Loveth And *l* so his innocent heart, *Supp. Confessions* 52
She *l* her own anguish deep *To J. S.* 42
she will not wed Save whom she *l*, *Gareth and L.* 622
Love-whispers Affianced, Sir ? *l-w* may not breathe *Princess ii* 221
Loving (*See also* **A-loving, England-loving, Loovin'**) ' I
promise thee The fairest and most *l* wife in Greece,' *Œnone* 187
Most *l* is she ? „ 201
When thy nerves could understand What there is
in *l* tears, *Vision of Sin* 161
Blessing her, praying for her, *l* her ; *Enoch Arden* 879
l her As when she laid her head beside my own. „ 880
For she—so lowly-lovely and so *l*. *Aylmer's Field* 168
Up thro' gilt wires a crafty *l* eye, *Princess, Pro.* 172
And *l* hands must part— *Window, Answer* 6
Gray nurses, *l* nothing new ; *In Mem.* xxix 14
Two spirits of a diverse love Contend for *l* masterdom. „ cii 8
Maud made my Maud by that long *l* kiss, *Maud I xviii* 58
And, I, utter faithfulness in love, *Gareth and L.* 554
L his lusty youthhood yielded to him. „ 580
l the battle as well As he that rides him.' „ 1301
(As sons of kings *l* in pupilage *Merlin and V.* 517
For Arthur, *l* his young knight, *Pelleas and E.* 159
Dust, as he said, that once was *l* hearts, *Lover's Tale iv* 68
nay, but could I wed her *L* the other ? *Sisters (E. and E.)* 168
Who yearn to lay my *l* head upon your leprous breast. *Happy* 26
Now God has made you leper in His *l* care for both, „ 91
domes the red-plow'd hills With *l* blue ; *Early Spring* 4
Lovingkindness delightedly fulfill'd All *l'es*, *Lover's Tale i* 225
Low (adj. and adv.) Is not my human pride brought *l* ? *Supp. Confessions* 14
stooping Unto the death, not sunk ! „ 97
Breathed *l* around the rolling earth *The winds, etc.* 3
an accent very *l* In blandishment, *Isabel* 19
And ever when the moon was *l*, *Mariana* 49
But when the moon was very *l*, „ 53
The *l* and bloomed foliage, *Arabian Nights* 13
oh, haste, Visit my *l* desire ! *Ode to Memory* 4

Low (adj. and adv.) (*continued*) at first to the ear The
warble was *l*, *Dying Swan* 24
L thunder and light in the magic night— *The Merman* 23
my ringlets would fall *L* adown, *l* adown, From
under my starry sea-bud crown *L* adown *The Mermaid* 15
And at my headstone whisper *l*, *My life is full* 24
Heavily the *l* sky raining Over tower'd Camelot ; *L. of Shalott iv* 4
L on her knees herself she cast, *Mariana in the S.* 27
Oh your sweet eyes, your *l* replies : *L. C. V. de Vere* 29
Lit with a *l* large moon. *Palace of Art* 68
Her *l* preamble all alone, „ 174
hears the *l* Moan of an unknown sea ; „ 279
Then *l* and sweet I whistled thrice ; *Edwin Morris* 113
Then when the first *l* matin-chirp hath grown *Love and Duty* 98
L thunders bring the mellow rain, *Talking Oak* 279
And all the *l* wind hardly breathed for fear. *Godiva* 55
And one *l* churl, compact of thankless earth, „ 66
Gloom'd the *l* coast and quivering brine *The Voyage* 42
L breezes fann'd the belfry bars, *The Letters* 43
Ever brightening With a *l* melodious thunder ; *Poet's Mind* 27
L voluptuous music winding trembled, *Vision of Sin* 17
Swung themselves, and in *l* tones replied ; „ 20
children leading evermore *L* miserable lives of
hand-to-mouth, *Enoch Arden* 116
And the *l* moan of leaden-colour'd seas. „ 612
' His head is *l*, and no man cares for him. „ 850
On a sudden a *l* breath Of tender air *The Brook* 201
Somewhere beneath his own *l* range of roofs, *Aylmer's Field* 47
call'd away By one *l* voice to one dear neighbourhood, „ 60
on *l* knolls That dimpling died into each other, „ 148
Averill seeing How *l* his brother's mood had fallen, „ 405
Last, some *l* fever ranging round to spy „ 569
Which from the *l* light of mortality „ 641
thro' the smoke The blight of *l* desires— „ 673
L was her voice, but won mysterious way „ 695
ever in it a *l* musical note Swell'd up and died ; *Sea Dreams* 210
He with a long *l* sibilation, stared As blank *Princess i* 176
Some to a *l* song oar'd a shallop by, „ ii 457
Sweet and *l*, sweet and *l*, „ iii 1
L, *l*, breathe and blow, „ 3
everywhere *L* voices with the ministering hand „ vii 21
There to herself, all in *l* tones, she read. „ 175
The last great Englishman is *l*. *Ode on Well.* 18
Thro' either babbling world of high and *l* ; „ 182
Light, so *l* upon earth, *Window, Marr. Morn* 1
Light, so *l* in the vale You flash and lighten afar, „ 9
' What is it makes me beat so *l* ? ' *In Mem. iv* 8
Till growing winters lay me *l* ; „ xl 30
Be near me when my light is *l*, „ l 1
on the *l* dark verge of life The twilight of eternal day. „ 15
How should he love a thing so *l* ? ' „ lx 16
Whose life in *l* estate began „ lxiv 3
The voice was *l*, the look was bright ; „ lxix 15
and break The *l* beginnings of content. „ lxxxiv 48
Or *l* morass and whispering reed, „ c 6
and heard The *l* love-language of the bird „ cii 11
shining daffodil dead, and Orion *l* in his grave. *Maud I iii* 14
Had given her word to a thing so *l* ? „ xvi 27
More life to Love than is or ever was In our *l* world, „ xviii 48
L on the sand and loud on the stone „ xxii 25
The delight of *l* replies. „ II iv 30
Then to strike him and bay him *l*, „ v 90
Over Orion's grave *l* down in the west, „ III vi 8
Then the King in *l* deep tones, *Com. of Arthur* 260
Go likewise ; lay him *l* and slay him not, *Gareth and L.* 379
As Mark would sully the *l* state of churl : „ 427
For an your fire be *l* ye kindle mine ! „ 711
I have not fall'n so *l* as some would wish. *Marr. of Geraint* 129
Made a *l* splendour in the world, „ 598
felt Her *l* firm voice and tender government. *Geraint and E.* 194
L at leave-taking, with his brandish'd plume „ 359
But answer'd in *l* voice, her meek head yet Drooping, „ 640
Faint in the *l* dark hall of banquet : *Balin and Balan* 343
walls Of that *l* church he built at Glastonbury. „ 367
Beneath a *l* door dipt, and made his feet „ 403

Low (adj. and adv.) (*continued*)   Crawl'd slowly with *l*
    moans to where he lay,   *Balin and Balan* 592
She answer'd with a *l* and chuckling laugh :   *Merlin and V.* 780
we scarce can sink as *l* :   ,,   813
or *l* desire Not to feel lowest makes them level all ;   ,,   827
But into some *l* cave to crawl, and there,   ,,   884
The *l* sun makes the colour : I am yours,   *Lancelot and E.* 134
The hard earth shake, and a *l* thunder of arms.   ,,   460
Then came her father, saying in *l* tones,   ,,   994
If this be high, what is it to be *l* ? '   ,,   1084
But spake with such a sadness and so *l*   *Holy Grail* 42
L as the hill was high, and where the vale Was lowest,   ,,   441
then one *l* roll Of Autumn thunder,   *Last Tournament* 152
She lived a moon in that *l* lodge with him :   ,,   381
out beyond them flush'd The long *l* dune,   ,,   484
that *l* lodge return'd, Mid-forest,   ,,   488
A *l* sea-sunset glorying round her hair   ,,   508
one *l* light betwixt them burn'd   *Guinevere* 4
' Liest thou here so *l*, the child of one I honour'd,   ,,   422
Lest but a hair of this *l* head be harm'd.   ,,   447
Do each *l* office of your holy house ;   ,,   682
And all the *l* dark groves, a land of love !   *Lover's Tale i* 332
lake, that, flooding, leaves *l* banks of yellow sand ;   ,,   535
Held converse sweet and *l—l* converse sweet,   ,,   541
At first her voice was very sweet and *l*,   ,,   563
for the sound Of that dear voice so musically *l*,   ,,   708
Unfrequent, *l*, as tho' it told its pulses ;   ,,   ii 55
thence at intervals A *l* bell tolling.   ,,   83
For that *l* knell tolling his lady dead—   ,,   iv 33
l down in a rainbow deep Silent palaces,   *V. of Maeldune* 79
And his voice was *l* as from other worlds,   ,,   117
By the *l* foot-lights of the world—   *The Wreck* 40
L warm winds had gently breathed us away from the
    land—   ,,   63
I sigh'd, as the *l* dark hull dipt under the smiling main,   ,,   127
' Is it *he* then brought so *l* ? '   *Dead Prophet* 6
And behind him, *l* in the West,   ,,   20
You speak so *l*, what is it ?   *The Ring* 49
A footstep, as *l* throbbing in the walls,   ,,   409
And these *l* bushes dipt their twigs in foam,   *Prog. of Spring* 51
Where I sank with the body at times in the sloughs
    of a *l* desire,   *By an Evolution.* 18
Sing thou *l* or loud or sweet,   *Poets and Critics* 6
Some too *l* would have thee shine,   ,,   11

Low (s)   In summer heats, with placid *l*'s
    Unfearing,   *Supp. Confessions* 154
From the dark fen the oxen's *l*   *Mariana* 28

Low (verb)   and the bull couldn't *l*,   *V. of Maeldune* 18

Low-brow'd   or safely moor'd Beneath a *l-b* cavern,   *Lover's Tale i* 55

Low-built   appear'd, *l-b* but strong ;   *Balin and Balan* 333

Low-couch'd   Indian on a still-eyed snake, *l-c*   *Lover's Tale ii* 189

Low-cowering   *L-c* shall the Sophist sit ;   *Clear-headed friend* 10

Low-drooping   *L-d* till he well-nigh kiss'd her feet   *Lancelot and E.* 1172

Low-dropt   murmur at the *l-d* eaves of sleep,   *Lover's Tale ii* 122

Lower   She breathed in sleep a *l* moan,   *Mariana in the S.* 45
Calling thyself a little *l* ' Than angels.   *Two Voices* 198
' Or if thro' *l* lives I came—   ,,   364
And *l* voices saint me from above.   *St. S. Stylites* 154
On a range of *l* feelings and a narrower heart   *Locksley Hall* 44
But I count the gray barbarian *l* than the Christian
    child.   ,,   174
Like a beast with *l* pleasures, like a beast with *l*
    pains ?   ,,   176
Gathering up from all the *l* ground ;   *Vision of Sin* 15
And slowly quickening into *l* forms ;   ,,   210
We ranging down this *l* track,   *In Mem. xlvi* 1
No *l* life that earth's embrace May breed with him,   ,, *lxxxii* 3
when most I feel There is a *l* and a higher ;   ,, *cxxix* 4
And, moved thro' life of *l* phase,   ,, *Con.* 125
Tells of a manhood ever less and *l* ?   *Last Tournament* 121
Because all other Hope had *l* aim ;   *Lover's Tale i* 455
my lord is *l* than his oxen or his swine.   *Locksley H., Sixty* 126
youth and age are scholars yet but in the *l* school,   ,,   243
altogether can escape From the *l* world within him,   *Making of Man* 2
Neither mourn if human creeds be *l*   *Faith* 5

Lower (*continued*)   So the Higher wields the *L*, while
    the *L* is the Higher.   *Locksley H., Sixty* 124

Lower (verb)   shalt *l* to his level day by day,   *Locksley Hall* 45
Fortune, turn thy wheel and *l* the proud ;   *Marr. of Geraint* 347

Lower'd   *L* softly with a threefold cord of love   *D. of F. Women* 211
he spake to these his helm was *l*,   *Guinevere* 593
They *l* me down the side,   *The Wreck* 125
(deferentially With nearing chair and *l* accent)   *Aylmer's Field* 267

Lowest   from a height That makes the *l* hate it,   ,,   173
Nor ever *l* roll of thunder moans,   *Lucretius* 108
barbarous isles, and here Among the *l*.'   *Princess ii* 123
so Vivien in the *l*, Arriving at a time   *Merlin and V.* 141
low desire Not to feel *l* makes them level all ;   ,,   828
And in the *l* beasts are slaying men,   *Holy Grail* 234
where the vale Was *l*, found a chapel,   ,,   442
I could hardly sin against the *l*.'   *Last Tournament* 572
Sorrowing with the sorrows of the *l* !   *On Jub. Q. Victoria* 27
Is brother of the Dark one in the *l*,   *Demeter and P.* 95

Low-flowing   fling on each side my *l-f* locks,   *The Mermaid* 32
L-F breezes are roaming the broad valley   *Leonine Eleg.* 7

Low-folded   breathless burthen of *l-f* heavens   *Aylmer's Field* 612

Low-hung   gushes from beneath a *l-h* cloud.   *Ode to Memory* 71
Like to a *l-h* and a fiery sky   *Lover's Tale ii* 61

Lowing (part.)   And *l* to his fellows.   *Gardener's D.* 88

Lowing (s)   So thick with *l*'s of the herds,   *In Mem. xcix* 3

Lowland   Toward the *l* ways behind me,   *Silent Voices* 5

Lowlier   We taught him *l* moods, when Elsinore   *Buonaparte* 9

Low-lieth   WHERE Claribel *l-l* (repeat)   *Claribel* 1, 8, 21

Lowlihead   perfect wifehood and pure *l*.   *Isabel* 12

Lowliness   sure of Heaven If *l* could save her.   *Maud I xii* 20

Lowly (adj.)   Or even a *l* cottage whence we see   *Ode to Memory* 100
When truth embodied in a tale Shall enter in
    at *l* doors.   *In Mem. xxxvi* 8
or rest On Enid at her *l* handmaid-work,   *Marr. of Geraint* 400
' And thence I dropt into a *l* vale,   *Holy Grail* 440
For *l* minds were madden'd to the height   *To Mary Boyle* 33
Within the bloodless heart of *l* flowers   *Prog. of Spring* 84
And rough-ruddy faces Of *l* labour.   *Merlin and the G.* 60

Lowly (s)   All the *l*, the destitute,   *On Jub. Q. Victoria* 31

Lowly-lovely   she—so *l-l* and so loving,   *Aylmer's Field* 168

Lowly-sweet   Edith, yet so *l-s*,   *Locksley H., Sixty* 49

Lowness   The *l* of the present state,   *In Mem. xxiv* 11

Low-spoken   *L-s*, and of so few words,   *Geraint and E.* 395

Low-throned   *L-t* Hesper is stayed between the two
    peaks ;   *Leonine Eleg.* 11

Low-tinkled   *L-t* with a bell-like flow   *The winds, etc.* 7

Low-toned   So she *l-t* ; while with shut eyes I lay   *Princess vii* 223

Low-tongued   Doth the *l-t* Orient Wander   *Adeline* 51

Low-voiced   The *l-v*, tender-spirited Lionel,   *Lover's Tale i* 655

Low-wheel'd   Within the *l-w* chaise,   *Talking Oak* 110

Loyal   (*See also* **Ever-loyal, Half-loyal, Love-loyal,**
    Mock-loyal)   She hath no *l* knight and true,   *L. of Shalott ii* 25
' The slight she-slips of *l* blood,   *Talking Oak* 169
Queenly responsive when the *l* hand   *Aylmer's Field* 169
The *l* warmth of Florian is not cold,   *Princess ii* 244
The *l* pines of Canada murmur thee,   *W. to Marie Alex.* 19
Our *l* passion for our temperate kings ;   *Ode on Well.* 165
And *l* unto kindly laws.   *In Mem. lxxxv* 16
With a *l* people shouting a battle cry,   *Maud III vi* 22
Hath ever like a *l* sister cleaved To Arthur,—   *Com. of Arthur* 191
Of *l* vassals toiling for their liege.   ,,   282
Art thou so little *l* to thy Queen,   *Balin and Balan* 251
' Fain would I still be *l* to the Queen.'   ,,   254
So *l* scarce is *l* to thyself,   ,,   256
But have ye no one word of *l* praise For Arthur,   *Merlin and V.* 778
But now my *l* worship is allow'd Of all men :   *Lancelot and E.* 110
Nor often *l* to his word, and now Wroth   ,,   559
' Prince, O *l* nephew of our noble King,   ,,   652
L, the dumb old servitor, on deck,   ,,   1144
Low-drooping till he wellnigh kiss'd her feet For
    l awe,   ,,   1173
To *l* hearts the value of all gifts Must vary   ,,   1214
' Hail, Bors ! if every *l* man and true Could see it,   *Holy Grail* 756
For *l* to the uttermost am I.'   *Pelleas and E.* 212
but the fruit Of *l* nature, and of noble mind.'   *Guinevere* 336

Loyal (*continued*) O *L* to the royal in thyself, And *l* to
  thy land,   *To the Queen ii* 1
  So *l* is too costly ! friends—   " 16
  The *l* to their crown Are *l* to their own own far sons,   " 27
  That I am *l* to him till the death,   *Columbus* 227
  she was always *l* and sweet—   *Despair* 49
  To all the *l* hearts who long To keep   *Hands all Round* 13
  multitude. *L*, each, to the heart of it,   *On Jub. Q. Victoria* 21
  where the *l* bells Clash welcome—   *The Ring* 482
  How *l* in the following of thy Lord !   *In Mem. W. G. Ward* 6
Loyal-hearted On thee the *l-h* hung,   *In Mem. cx* 5
Lubber Then, narrow court and *l* King, farewell !   *Merlin and V.* 119
Lucid golden round her *l* throat And shoulder :   *Œnone* 178
  The *l* outline forming round thee ;   *Tithonus* 53
  Gods, who haunt The *l* interspace of world and world,   *Lucretius* 105
  issued in a court Compact of *l* marbles,   *Princess ii* 24
  the mist is drawn A *l* veil from coast to coast,   *In Mem. lxvii* 14
  Be large and *l* round thy brow.   " *xci* 8
  What lightens in the *l* east Of rising worlds   " *cv* 24
  The *l* chambers of the morning star,   *Lover's Tale i* 28
  yet one glittering foot disturb'd The *l* well ;   *Tiresias* 42
Lucilia *L*, wedded to Lucretius, found   *Lucretius* 1
Lucius Junius Brutus The *L J B* of my kind ?   *Princess ii* 284
Luck good *l* Shall fling her old shoe after.   *Will Water.* 178
  Good *l* had your good man,   *Geraint and E.* 617
  but rosier *l* will go With these rich jewels,   *Last Tournament* 45
Luckier so prosper'd that at last A *l* or a bolder fisherman,   *Enoch Arden* 27
  hot in haste to join Their *l* mates,   *Geraint and E.* 575
Lucknow in the ghastly siege of *L*—   *Def. of Lucknow* 4
Lucky Less *l* her home-voyage :   *Enoch Arden* 541
  For *l* rhymes to him were scrip and share,   *The Brook* 4
Lucretius LUCILIA, wedded to *L*, found   *Lucretius* 1
Lucumo lay at wine with Lar and *L* ;   *Princess ii* 129
Lucy An' *L* wur laäme o' one leg,   *Village Wife* 99
  Straänge an' unheppen Miss *L* !   " 100
Lull (while warm airs *l* us, blowing lowly)   *Lotos-Eaters, C. S.* 89
  Perchance, to *l* the throbs of pain,   *The Daisy* 105
  To *l* with song an aching heart,   *In Mem. xxxvii* 15
  I *l* a fancy trouble-tost   " *lxv* 2
Lullabies These mortal *l* of pain May bind a book,   " *lxxvii* 5
Lull'd THY tuwhits are *l*, I wot,   *The Owl ii* 1
  hum of swarming bees Into dreamful slumber *l*.   *Eleänore* 30
  L echoes of laborious day Come to you,   *Margaret* 29
  And *l* them in my own.   *Talking Oak* 145
  A fall of water *l* the noon asleep.   *Romney's R.* 83
Lulling *L* the brine against the Coptic sands.   *Buonaparte* 8
  l random squabbles when they rise,   *Holy Grail* 557
Lumber the waste and *l* of the shore,   *Enoch Arden* 16
Luminous his stedfast shade Sleeps on his *l* ring.'   *Palace of Art* 16
  A belt, it seem'd, of *l* vapour, lay,   *Sea Dreams* 209
  meek Seem'd the full lips, and mild the *l* eyes,   *Princess vii* 226
  L, gemlike, ghostlike, deathlike,   *Maud I iii* 8
  Holy Grail All over cover'd with a *l* cloud,   *Holy Grail* 189
  Holy Vessel hung Clothed in white samite or a *l* cloud.   " 513
Lump (*See also* **Loomp**) This *l* of earth has left his estate   *Maud I xvi* 1
Lungs labour'd down within his ample *l*,   *Princess v* 273
  writhings, anguish, labouring of the *l*   *Pass. of Arthur* 115
  Brass mouths and iron *l* !   *Freedom* 40
  You that lie with wasted *l*   *Forlorn* 21
Lunnon (**London**) Squoire's i' *L*, an'
  summun   *N. Farmer, O. S.* 57
Lurdane droned her *l* knights Slumbering,   *Pelleas and E.* 430
Lure (s) Diet and seeling, jesses, leash, and *l*.   *Merlin and V.* 125
  follow, leaping blood, The season's *l* !   *Early Spring* 26
Lure (verb) splendour fail'd To *l* those eyes   *St. Telemachus* 36
Lured When we have *l* you from above,   *Rosalind* 46
  him they *l* Into their net made pleasant   *Aylmer's Field* 485
  one unctuous mouth which *l* him,   *Sea Dreams* 14
  L by the crimes and frailties of the court,   *Guinevere* 136
  Which often *l* her from herself ;   " 152
  we were *l* by the light from afar,   *V. of Maeldune* 71
  L by the glare and the blare,   " 73
  Earls that were *l* by the Hunger of glory   *Batt. of Brunanburh* 123
  Eyes that *l* a doting boyhood   *Locksley H., Sixty* 10
  My beauty *l* that falcon from his eyry   *Happy* 59

Lured (*continued*) WHAT sight so *l* him thro 'the fields   *Far—far—away* 1
  l me from the household fire on earth.   *Romney's R.* 40
Lurid Wrapt in drifts of *l* smoke   *Maud II iv* 66
  when now Bathed in that *l* crimson—   *St. Telemachus* 18
  His face deform'd by *l* blotch and blain—   *Death of Œnone* 72
Lurk I think no more of deadly *l*'s therein,   *Princess ii* 226
  such as *l*'s In some wild Poet,   *In Mem. xxxiv* 6
  ' There *l* three villains yonder in the wood,   *Geraint and E.* 142
  If he ? yes, he . . . *l*'s, listens,   *The Flight* 71
Lurking Balan *l* there (His quest was
  unaccomplish'd)   *Balin and Balan* 546
  Vivien, *l*, heard. She told Sir Modred.   *Guinevere* 98
Luscious Nor roll thy viands on a *l* tongue.   *Ancient Sage* 267
Lush at the root thro' *l* green grasses burn'd   *D. of F. Women* 71
Lusitanian father-grape grew fat On *L* summers.   *Will Water.* 8
Lust Either from *l* of gold, or like a girl   *M. d'Arthur* 127
  Crown thyself, worm, and worship thine own *l*'s !—   *Aylmer's Field* 650
  and keep him from the *l* of blood   *Lucretius* 83
  And twisted shapes of *l*, unspeakable,   " 157
  For *l* or lusty blood or provender :   " 198
  in his *l* and voluptuousness,   *Boädicea* 66
  Ring out the narrowing *l* of gold ;   *In Mem. cvi* 26
  And *l* of gain, in the spirit of Cain,   *Maud I. i* 23
  feeble vassals of wine and anger and *l*,   " *II i* 43
  land that has lost for a little her *l* of gold,   " *III vi* 39
  live the strength and die the *l* !   *Com. of Arthur* 492
  own no *l* because they have no law !   *Pelleas and E.* 481
  Either from *l* of gold, or like a girl   *Pass. of Arthur* 295
  thro' which the *l*, Villany, violence,   *Columbus* 171
  The lecher would cleave to his *l*'s,   *Despair* 100
  craft and madness, *l* and spite,   *Locksley H., Sixty* 189
  He that has lived for the *l* of the minute,   *Vastness* 27
  wallow in this old *l* Of Paganism,   *St. Telemachus* 78
Lusted I never loved her, I but *l* for her—   *Pelleas and E.* 484
  ghastliest That ever I *l* for a body,   *Lover's Tale i* 648
Lustful A *l* King, who sought to win my love   *Balin and Balan* 474
Lustier By park and suburb under brown Of *l* leaves ;   *In Mem. xcviii* 25
  Until they find a *l* than themselves. '   *Balin and Balan* 19
  Stronger ever born of weaker, *l* body, larger
  mind ?   *Locksley H., Sixty* 164
Lustihood He is so full of *l*, he will ride,   *Lancelot and E.* 203
Lusting *l* for all that is not its own ;   *Maud I i* 22
Lustre (*See also* **Lace-lustre**) Soft *l* bathes the range
  of urns   *Day-Dm., Sleep. P.* 9
  The *l* of the long convolvuluses   *Enoch Arden* 576
  His eyes To indue his *l* ;   *Lover's Tale i* 424
Lustreless one was patch'd and blurr'd and *l*   *Marr. of Geraint* 649
Lustrous and the light and *l* curls—   *M. d'Arthur* 216
  And all about him roll'd his *l* eyes ;   *Love and Death* 3
  Slides the bird o'er *l* woodland,   *Locksley Hall* 162
  and the light and *l* curls—   *Pass. of Arthur* 384
Lusty The *l* bird takes every hour for dawn :   *M. d'Arthur, Ep.* 11
  And here and there a *l* trout,   *The Brook* 57
  For lust or *l* blood or provender :   *Lucretius* 198
  A *l* brace Of twins may weed her of her folly.   *Princess v* 463
  Fair empires branching, both, in *l* life !—   *W. to Marie Alex.* 21
  A *l* youth, but poor, who often saw   *Gareth and L.* 48
  Loving his *l* youthhood yielded to him.   " 580
  for this lad is great And *l*,   " 731
  it fell Like flaws in summer laying *l* corn :   *Marr. of Geraint* 764
  The *l* mowers labouring dinnerless,   *Geraint and E.* 251
  His *l* spearmen follow'd him with noise :   " 593
  Strike down the *l* and long practised knight,   *Lancelot and E.* 1361
  till she long To have thee back in *l* life again,   *Pelleas and E.* 352
  I might have stricken a *l* stroke for him,   *Sir J. Oldcastle* 69
Lute (s) on lattice edges lay Or book or *l* ;   *Princess ii* 30
  ' It is the little rift within the *l*,   *Merlin and V.* 390
  ' The little rift within the lover's *l*   " 393
Lute (verb) That *l* and flute fantastic tenderness,   *Princess iv* 129
Luther thou wilt be A latter *L*,   *To J. M. K.* 2
Lutterworth Nor thou in Britain, little *L*,   *Sir J. Oldcastle* 26
Luvv (**love**) (s) Noä—thou'll marry for *l*—   *N. Farmer, N. S.* 12
  fur, Sammy, 'e married fur *l*.   " 32
  L ? what's *l* ? thou can luvv thy lass an' 'er munny
  too,   " 33

Made (*continued*) 'More years had *m* me love thee more. *In Mem. lxxxi* 8
I *m* a picture in the brain,	,, *lxxx* 9
And tracts of calm from tempest *m*,	,, *cxii* 14
In that which *m* the world so fair.	,, *cxvi* 8
flood Of onward time shall yet be *m*,	,, *cxxviii* 6
Her sweet ' I will ' has *m* you one.	,, *Con.* 56
Rather than hold by the law that I *m*,	*Maud I i* 55
I have not *m* the world, and He that *m* it	,, *iv* 48
She *m* me divine amends For a courtesy	,, *vi* 13
M her only the child of her mother,	,, *xiii* 40
There were but a step to be.	,, *xiv* 22
And *m* my life a perfumed altar-flame ;	,, *xviii* 24
Maud *m* my Maud by that long loving kiss,	,, 58
M so fairily well With delicate spire and whorl,	,, *II ii* 5
living will That *m* it stir on the shore.	,, 15
All *m* up of the lily and rose That blow by night,	,, *v* 74
star Which shone so close beside Thee that ye *m* One light together,	*Ded. of Idylls* 47
and *m* a realm, and reign'd. (repeat)	*Com. of Arthur* 19, 519
m Broad pathways for the hunter and the knight	,, 60
M head against him, crying,	,, 68
M lightnings and great thunders over him,	,, 108
the King *M* feast for, saying,	,, 247
the Queen *m* answer, ' What know I ?	,, 326
mingled with the haze And *m* it thicker ;	,, 436
crush'd The Idolators, and *m* the people free ?	*Gareth and L.* 137
The birds *m* Melody on branch,	,, 183
that old Seer *m* answer playing on him	,, 252
and had *m* it spire to heaven.	,, 309
m his goodly cousin, Tristram, knight,	,, 394
Repentant of the word she *m* him swear,	,, 527
Shame never *m* girl redder than Gareth joy.	,, 536
and *m* him flush, and bow Lowly,	,, 548
M thee my knight ? my knights are sworn	,, 552
' Thou hast *m* us lords, and canst not put us down ! '	,, 1132
Always he *m* his mouthpiece of a page	,, 1337
rode In converse till she *m* her palfrey halt,	,, 1360
What madness *m* thee challenge the chief knight	,, 1416
dance And revel and song, *m* merry over Death,	,, 1423
wherefore going to the King, He *m* this pretext,	*Marr. of Geraint* 33
Was ever man so grandly *m* as he ?	,, 81
the strong passion in her *m* her weep	,, 110
M answer sharply that she should not know.	,, 196
M sharply to the dwarf, and ask'd it of him,	,, 204
And *m* him like a man abroad at morn	,, 335
M a low splendour in the world,	,, 598
M her cheek burn and either eyelid fall,	,, 775
Which *m* him look so cloudy and so cold ;	*Geraint and E.* 48
and suffering thus he *m* Minutes an age :	,, 114
And *m* it of two colours ;	,, 292
Him that *m* me The one true lover whom you ever own'd,	,, 343
M her cheek burn and either eyelid fall.	,, 434
It wellnigh *m* her cheerful ;	,, 443
m The long way smoke beneath him in his fear ;	,, 531
M but a single bound, and with a sweep of it	,, 727
and *m* as if to fall upon him.	,, 776
I, therefore, *m* him of our Table Round,	,, 908
m Those banners of twelve battles overhead Stir,	*Balin and Balan* 87
and the Queen, and all the world *M* music,	,, 211
m that mouth of night Whereout the Demon	,, 316
M Garlon, hissing ; then he sourly smiled.	,, 355
m his feet Wings thro' a glimmering gallery,	,, 403
m him quickly dive Beneath the boughs,	,, 422
Nature through the flesh herself hath *m*	*Merlin and V.* 50
It *m* the laughter of an afternoon	,, 163
M with her right a comb of pearl to part The lists	,, 244
And *m* a pretty cup of both my hands	,, 275
M answer, either eyelid wet with tears :	,, 379
And *m* a Gardener putting in a graff,	,, 479
but afterwards He *m* a stalwart knight.	,, 482
Then *m* her Queen : but those isle-nurtured eyes	,, 570
lady never *m* *unwilling* war With those fine eyes :	,, 603
And *m* her good man jealous with good cause.	,, 605
and *m* her lithe arm round his neck Tignten,	,, 614

Made (*continued*) King *M* proffer of the league of golden mines,	*Merlin and V.* 646
sleepless nights Of my long life have *m* it easy	,, 680
That wreathen round it *m* it seem his own :	,, 735
And wearied out *m* for the couch and slept,	,, 736
and *m* A snowy penthouse for his hollow eyes,	,, 807
crying ' I have *m* his glory mine,'	,, 971
Now *m* a pretty history to herself	*Lancelot and E.* 18
every scratch a lance had *m* upon it,	,, 20
down they fell and *m* the glen abhorr'd :	,, 42
Thither he *m*, and blew the gateway horn.	,, 169
m a sudden step to the gate, and there—	,, 391
backward by the wind they *m* In moving,	,, 480
' Sweet love, that seems not *m* to fade away,	,, 1013
He makes no friend who never *m* a foe.	,, 1089
and *m* him hers, and laid her mind On him,	*Holy Grail* 164
wild bees That *m* such honey in his realm.	,, 215
mould Of Arthur, *m* by Merlin, with a crown,	,, 239
crown And both the wings are *m* of gold,	,, 242
A sign to maim this Order which I *m*.	,, 297
since your vows are sacred, being *m* :	,, 314
Rejoicing in that Order which he *m*.'	,, 327
Lord of all things *m* Himself Naked of glory	,, 447
When the hermit *m* an end,	,, 457
past thro' Pagan realms, and *m* them mine,	,, 478
Thither I *m*, and there was I disarm'd	,, 575
that one only, who had ever *M* my heart leap ;	,, 580
And each *m* joy of either ;	,, 638
So fierce a gale *m* havoc here of late	,, 729
Who *m* me sure the Quest was not for me ;	,, 743
m our mightier madder than our least.	,, 863
When God *m* music thro' them,	,, 878
KING ARTHUR *m* new knights to fill the gap	*Pelleas and E.* 1
and Arthur *m* him knight.	,, 16
Then Arthur *m* vast banquets,	,, 147
So *m* his moan ; and, darkness falling,	,, 213
sight Of her rich beauty *m* him at one glance	,, 238
whom late our Arthur *m* Knight of his table ;	,, 319
only the King Hath *m* us fools and liars.	,, 479
sword That *m* it plunges thro' the wound again,	,, 530
And Percivale *m* answer not a word.	,, 534
he twitch'd the reins, And *m* his beast	,, 551
Had *m* mock-knight of Arthur's Table Round,	*Last Tournament* 2
M answer, ' Ay, but wherefore toss me this	,, 195
Great brother, thou nor I have *m* the world ;	,, 203
Tristram round the gallery *m* his horse Caracole ;	,, 205
M answer, ' I had liefer twenty years	,, 257
I *m* it in the woods, And heard it ring as true	,, 283
did ye mark that fountain yesterday *M* to run wine ?—	,, 287
but when the King Had *m* thee fool,	,, 306
M dull his inner, keen his outer eye	,, 366
up thro' Alioth and Alcor, *M* all above it,	,, 481
the crowning sin That *m* us happy :	,, 577
The King prevailing *m* his realm :—	,, 651
did you keep the vow you *m* to Mark	,, 655
And so the realm was *m* ; but then their vows—	,, 681
M such excuses as he might,	*Guinevere* 38
And from the sun there swiftly *m* at her	,, 78
To which a mournful answer *m* the Queen :	,, 341
sins that *m* the past so pleasant to us :	,, 375
m her face a darkness from the King :	,, 417
He spared to lift his hand against the King Who *m* him knight :	,, 438
Thou hast not *m* my life so sweet to me,	,, 451
I *m* them lay their hands in mine and swear	,, 467
I am not *m* of so slight elements.	,, 510
Enwound him fold by fold, and *m* him gray And grayer,	,, 603
What might I not have *m* of thy fair world,	,, 655
First *m* and latest left of all the knights,	*Pass. of Arthur* 2
As if some lesser god had *m* the world,	,, 14
uttering this the King *M* at the man :	,, 165
I perish by this people which I *m*,—	,, 190
great brand *M* lightnings in the splendour of the moon,	,, 305
here the faith That *m* us rulers ?	*To the Queen ii* 19

Made (*continued*) to whom I *m* it o'er his grave Sacred, *To the Queen ii* 35
attracted, won, Married, *m* one with, *Lover's Tale i* 134
M all our tastes and fancies like, " 242
m garlands of the selfsame flower, " 343
had *m* The red rose there a pale one— " 695
m The happy and the unhappy love, " 752
one other, worth the life That *m* it sensible— " 800
M strange division of its suffering " *ii* 128
m the ground Reel under us, " 193
The front rank *m* a sudden halt ; " *iii* 29
And partly *m* them—tho' he knew it not. " *iv* 25
till helpless death And silence *m* him bold— " 73
Or am I *m* immortal, or my love Mortal once more ? ' " 79
things familiar to her youth Had *m* a silent answer : " 96
sudden wail his lady *m* Dwelt in his fancy : " 149
And Julian *m* a solemn feast : " 187
Then Julian *m* a secret sign to me " 284
answer'd not a word, Which *m* the amazement more, " 334
he *m* me the cowslip ball, *First Quarrel* 13
you were only *m* for the day. *Rizpah* 19
The King should have *m* him a soldier, " 28
seamen *m* mock at the mad little craft *The Revenge* 38
gunner said ' Ay, ay,' but the seamen *m* reply : " 91
Had *m* a heated haze to magnify The charm of
Edith— *Sisters* (*E. and E.*) 129
he had seen it and *m* up his mind, *In the Child. Hosp.* 16
m West East, and sail'd the Dragon's mouth, *Columbus* 25
vow I *m* When Spain was waging war against the Moor— " 92
m by me, may seek to unbury me, " 206
Who *m* thee unconceivably Thyself *De Prof., Two G.* 48
for the bright-eyed goddess *m* it burn. *Achilles over the T.* 29
but *m* me yearn For larger glimpses *Tiresias* 20
The noonday crag *m* the hand burn ; " 35
With present grief, and *m* the rhymes, " 196
I took it, he *m* it a cage, *The Wreck* 83
M us, foreknew us, foredoom'd us, *Despair* 97
' The years that *m* the stripling wise *Ancient Sage* 111
They *m* her lily and rose in one, " 161
Only That which *m* us, meant us to be mightier *Locksley H., Sixty* 209
Fought for their lives in the narrow gap they
had *m*— *Heavy Brigade* 23
Glory to each and to all, and the charge that they *m* ! " 65
Which has *m* your fathers great *Open. I. and C. Exhib.* 15
Who *m* a nation purer through their art. *To W. C. Macready* 8
Your rule has *m* the people love Their ruler. *To Marq. of Dufferin* 9
have I *m* the name A golden portal to my rhyme : " 15
m themselves as Gods against the fear *Demeter and P.* 141
They *m* a thousand honey moons of one ? *The Ring* 22
And that has *m* you grave ? " 88
and *m* The rosy twilight of a perfect day. " 186
M every moment of her after life A virgin victim " 220
Why had I *m* her love me thro' the ring, " 391
But still she *m* her outcry for the ring ; " 403
m him leper to compass him with scorn— *Happy* 16
I *m* one barren effort to break it at the last. " 72
Now God has *m* you leper in His loving care " 91
m an English homestead Hell— *To Mary Boyle* 37
I might have *m* you once, *Romney's R.* 89
m The wife of wives a widow-bride, " 137
M by the noonday blaze without, *St. Telemachus* 50
' Mine is the one fruit Alla *m* for man.' *Akbar's Dream* 40
Adoring That who *m*, and makes, " 123
Alphabet-of-heaven-in-man *M* vocal— " 137
Man as yet is being *m*, *Making of Man* 3
' It is finish'd. Man is *m*.' " 8
Madeline Ever varying *M*. (repeat) *Madeline* 3, 18, 27
Madest Who *m* him thy chosen, *Tithonus* 13
Thou *m* Life in man and brute ; Thou *m* Death ; *In Mem., Pro.* 6
Thou *m* man, he knows not why, " 10
Madhouse I would not be mock'd in a *m* ! *Despair* 79
Madly That you should carol so *m* ? *The Throstle* 8
Madman *M* !—to chain with chains, *Buonaparte* 2
warn'd that *m* ere it grew too late : *Vision of Sin* 56
he struck me, *m*, over the face, *Maud II i* 18
' Wherefore waits the *m* there Naked *Gareth and L.* 1091

Madman (*continued*) And like a *m* brought her to the
court, *Marr. of Geraint* 725
A *m* to vex you with wretched words, *Despair* 108
teeming with liars, and *madmen*, and knaves, *The Dreamer* 9
Madness Then in *m* and in bliss, *Madeline* 42
From cells of *m* unconfined, *Two Voices* 371
Thro' *m*, hated by the wise, *Love and Duty* 7
Mingle *m*, mingle scorn ! *Vision of Sin* 204
Vext with unworthy *m*, and deform'd. *Aylmer's Field* 335
Is this a time to madden *m* then ? " 769
No *m* of ambition, avarice, none : *Lucretius* 212
The accomplice of your *m* unforgiven, *Princess vi* 276
kinsman thou to death and trance And *m*, *In Mem. lxxi* 2
the vitriol *m* flushes up in the ruffian's head, *Maud I i* 37
I flee from the cruel *m* of love, " *iv* 55
Perhaps from *m*, perhaps from crime, " *xvi* 22
And do accept my *m*, and would die " *xviii* 44
Thro' cells of *m*, haunts of horror and fear, " *III vi* 2
What *m* made thee challenge the chief knight *Gareth and L.* 1416
O pardon me ! the *m* of that hour, *Geraint and E.* 346
And after *m* acted question ask'd : " 813
break Into some *m* ev'n before the Queen ? ' *Balin and Balan* 230
My *m* all thy life has been thy doom, " 619
' This *m* has come on us for our sins.' *Holy Grail* 357
former *m*, once the talk And scandal of our table, " 649
A dying fire of *m* in his eyes— " 768
My *m* came upon me as of old, " 787
And in my *m* to myself I said, " 804
Then in my *m* I essay'd the door ; " 841
And but for all my *m* and my sin, " 849
And all the sacred *m* of the bard, " 877
—the wholesome *m* of an hour— *Last Tournament* 675
It was their last hour, A *m* of farewells. *Guinevere* 103
curb The *m* of our cities and their kings. *Tiresias* 71
My father's *m* makes me mad— *The Flight* 59
age so cramm'd with menace ? *m* ? written,
spoken lies ? *Locksley H., Sixty* 108
After *m*, after massacre, Jacobinism and Jacquerie, " 157
Every tiger *m* muzzled, every serpent passion kill'd, " 167
dream of wars and carnage, craft and *m*, lust and spite, " 189
Cast the poison from your bosom, oust the *m* from
your brain. " 241
The theft were death or *m* to the thief, *The Ring* 204
And eased her heart of *m*. . . . *Forlorn* 82
Madonna ' *M*, sad is night and morn,' *Mariana in the S.* 22
Madonna-masterpieces *M-m* Of ancient Art in Paris, *Romney's R.* 86
Madonna-wise *M-w* on either side her head, *Isabel* 6
Maeldune ' O *M*, let be this purpose of thine ! *V. of Maeldune* 119
Magazine O blatant *M's*, regard me rather— *Hendecasyllabics* 17
Mage ' And there I saw *m* Merlin, *Com. of Arthur* 280
like a fairy changeling lay the *m* ; " 363
Merlin's hand, the *M* at Arthur's court, *Gareth and L.* 306
Magee (Molly) *See* **Molly, Molly Magee**
Maggot tickle the *m* born in an empty head, *Maud II v* 38
' O worms and *m's* to-day *Ancient Sage* 210
Magic (adj.) Low thunder and light in the *m* night— *The Merman* 23
A *m* web with colours gay. *L. of Shalott ii* 2
To weave the mirror's *m* sights, " 29
Saw the heavens fill with commerce, argosies of
m sails, *Locksley Hall* 121
The *M* Music in his heart Beats quick and
quicker, *Day-Dm., Arrival* 26
on lonely mountain-meres I find a *m* bark ; *Sir Galahad* 38
drank The *m* cup that fill'd itself anew. *Aylmer's Field* 143
she liked it more Than *m* music, forfeits, *Princess, Pro.* 195
all the *m* light Dies off at once *In Mem. viii* 5
wise man that ever served King Uther thro' his
m art *Com. of Arthur* 152
' I once was looking for a *m* weed, *Merlin and V.* 471
red fruit Grown on a *m* oak-tree in mid-heaven, *Last Tournament* 745
forms which ever stood Within the *m* cirque of
memory, *Lover's Tale ii* 159
Magic (s) Is there some *m* in the place ? *Will Water.* 79
Bleys, Who taught him *m* ; *Com. of Arthur* 154
Bleys Laid *m* by, and sat him down, " 156

P*

Maiden (adj.) (continued)   nor yet to the wife—to her m
   name !   *The Wreck* 144
Set the m fancies wallowing in the troughs of
   Zolaism,—   *Locksley H., Sixty* 145
Her m daughter's marriage ;   *Prin. Beatrice* 10
But ere thy m birk be wholly clad,   *Prog. of Spring* 50
Maiden (s)   phantom two hours old Of a m past away,   *Adeline* 19
The little m walk'd demure,   *Two Voices* 419
A simple m in her flower   *L. C. V. de Vere* 15
of the warrior Gileadite, A m pure ;   *D. of F. Women* 198
' Would I had been some m coarse and poor !   "   253
Wrought by the lonely m of the Lake.   *M. d'Arthur* 104
whose touch may press The m's tender palm.   *Talking Oak* 180
The m's jet-black hair has grown,   *Day-Dm., Sleep. B.* 4
Nor m's hand in mine.   *Sir Galahad* 20
Dropt her head in the m's hand,   *Lady Clare* 63
M, I have watch'd thee daily,   *L. of Burleigh* 3
And a village m she.   "   8
A m of our century, yet most meek ;   *The Brook* 68
There stood a m near, Waiting to pass.   "   204
more and more, the m woman-grown,   *Aylmer's Field* 108
All wild to found an University For m's,   *Princess i* 151
Six hundred m's clad in purest white,   "   ii 472
' O marvellously modest m, you !   "   iii 48
' An open-hearted m, true and pure.   "   98
Among her m's, higher by the head,   "   179
Her college and her m's, empty masks,   "   187
There stood her m's glimmeringly group'd   "   iv 190
All her m's, watching, said,   "   vi 3
Stole a m from her place,   "   9
many a m passing home Till happier times ;   "   380
m's came, they talk'd, They sang,   "   vii 22
m, whither would you wander ? (repeat)   *City Child* 1, 6
far away,' said the dainty little m, (repeat)   "   3, 8
Lash the m into swooning,   *Boädicea* 67
or half coquette-like M,   *Hendecasyllabics* 21
As on a m in the day When first she wears   *In Mem. xl* 3
May serve to curl a m's locks,   "   lxxvii 7
I dwelt within a hall, And m's with me :   "   ciii 6
The m's gather'd strength and grace   "   27
m's with one mind Bewail'd their lot ;   "   45
m's of the place, That pelt us in the porch   "   Con. 67
Go not, happy day, Till the m yields.   *Maud I xvii* 4
Or whether it be the m's fantasy,   *Gareth and L.* 874
Whereat the m, petulant, ' Lancelot,   "   1246
on whom the m gazed.   "   1281
set the horror higher : a m swoon'd ;   "   1394
But rose at last, a single m with her, Took horse, *Marr. of Geraint* 160
sent Her m to demand it of the dwarf ;   "   193
Done in your m's person to yourself :   "   216
Sent her own m to demand the name,   "   411
never yet had woman such a pair Of suitors as this m ;   "   440
' Mother, a m is a tender thing,   "   510
Let never m think, however fair,   "   721
the m rose, And left her maiden couch.   "   736
call'd her like that m in the tale,   "   742
we m's often laugh When sick at heart,   *Balin and Balan* 497
shelter for mine innocency Among thy m's !'   *Merlin and V.* 84
m dreamt That some one put this diamond   *Lancelot and E.* 211
And yield it to this m, if you will.'   "   229
saw The m standing in the dewy light.   "   352
never yet have done so much For any m living,'   "   376
broider'd with great pearls, Some gentle m's gift.'   "   605
for lack of gentle m's aid.   The gentler-born the m,   "   765
m, while that ghostly grace Beam'd on his fancy,   "   885
So in her tower alone the m sat :   "   989
' Is this Elaine ? ' till back the m fell,   "   1031
Know that for this most gentle m's death   "   1291
to see The m buried, not as one unknown,   "   1334
Thou could'st have loved this m,   "   1366
A holy maid ; tho' never m glow'd,   *Holy Grail* 72
' O Father !' ask'd the m,   "   95
•sweet m, shore away Clean from her forehead   "   149
I, m, round thee, m, bind my belt.   "   159
An outraged m sprang into the hall   ,.   208

Maiden (s) (continued)   By m's each as fair as any flower :   *Holy Grail* 576
she a slender m, all my heart Went after her   "   582
And merry m's in it ;   "   746
blew my merry m's all about With all discomfort ;   "   748
And since he loved all m's,   *Pelleas and E.* 40
' O m, if indeed ye list to sing,   *Guinevere* 165
' Such as thou art be never m more   "   358
aghast the m rose, White as her veil,   "   362
love one m only, cleave to her,   "   475
Meek m's, from the voices crying " shame."   "   672
Wrought by the lonely m of the Lake.   *Pass. of Arthur* 272
m's, wives, And mothers with their babblers   *Tiresias* 102
Crime and hunger cast our m's by the thousand
   on the street.   *Locksley H., Sixty* 220
Love for the m, crown'd with marriage,   *Vastness* 23
Her m coming like a Queen,   *The Ring* 480
Innocent m's, Garrulous children,   *Merlin and the G.* 55
Maiden-cheek   Engirt with many a florid m-c,   *Princess iii* 350
Maidenhood   (*See also* **Mother-maidenhood**)   To her,
   perpetual m,   *In Mem. vi* 43
Would mar their charm of stainless m.'   *Balin and Balan* 268
To get me shelter for my m.   "   480
But that was in her earlier m,   *Holy Grail* 73
Maidenlike   m as far As I could ape their treble,   *Princess iv* 91
Maiden-meek   m-m I pray'd Concealment :   "   iii 134
Maid-mother   Or the m-m by a crucifix,   *Palace of Art* 93
Maiden-Princess   lonely m-P of the wood,   *The Ring* 65
Her lonely m-P, crown'd with flowers,   "   485
Maid of Astolat   (*See also* **Astolat**)   Elaine, the lily
   m o A,   *Lancelot and E.* 2
About the m o A, and her love.   "   723
' The m o A loves Sir Lancelot, Sir Lancelot loves
   the m o A.'   "   725
Then spake the lily m o A :   "   1085
past the barge Whereon the lily m o A Lay smiling,   "   1242
I, sometime call'd the m o A,   "   1273
Maid-of-honour   The m-o-h blooming fair ;   *Day-Dm., Sleep. P.* 28
Poor soul ! I had a m o h once ;   *Princess iv* 133
Mail (armour)   from head to tail Came out clear plates
   of sapphire m.   *Two Voices* 12
And, ringing, springs from brand and m ;   *Sir Galahad* 54
and all in m Burnish'd to blinding,   *Gareth and L.* 1026
till he felt, despite his m, Strangled,   "   1151
splintering spear, the hard m hewn,   *Pass. of Arthur* 108
Mail (coach)   The m ?   At one o'clock.   *Walk. to the Mail* 8
I fear That we shall miss the m,   "   112
They swore he dare not rob the m,   *Rizpah* 30
they kill'd him for robbing the m.   "   34
Mailed   (*See also* **Hard-mailed**, **Triple-mailèd**)   My m
   Bacchus leapt into my arms,   *D. of F. Women* 151
with each light air On our m heads :   *Princess v* 245
Breaking their m fleets and armed towers,   *Ode Inter. Exhib.* 39
Drove his m heel athwart the royal crown,   *Balin and Balan* 540
Maim   A sign to m this Order, which I made.   *Holy Grail* 297
Maim'd (adj. and part.)   left me m To dwell in presence of
   immortal youth,   *Tithonus* 20
Speak ! is there any of you halt or m ?   *St. S. Stylites* 142
that there Lie bruised and m,   *Princess vi* 72
and all the good knights m,   "   241
I see them m, Mangled !   *Gareth and L.* 1326
with blunt stump Pitch-blacken'd sawing the air,
   said the m churl,   *Last Tournament* 67
And half of the rest of us m for life   *The Revenge* 77
What life, so m by night, were worth Our living out ?   *Tiresias* 208
Maim'd (s)   And cured some halt and m ;   *St. S. Stylites* 137
Let the m in his heart rejoice   *On Jub. Q. Victoria* 36
Maim'd (verb)   and him they caught and m ;   *Lancelot and E.* 275
M me and maul'd, and would outright have slain,   *Last Tournament* 75
Main (adj.)   (*See also* **Maäin-glad**)   till Arthur by m might,   *Com. of Arthur* 109
And out by this m doorway past the King.   *Gareth and L.* 671
And bare her by m violence to the board,   *Geraint and E.* 654
(With one m purpose ever at my heart),   "   831
but for my m purpose in these jousts,   "   837
Could call him the m cause of all their crime ;   *Merlin and V.* 788
That was their m test-question—   *Sir J. Oldcastle* 155

Main (adj.) (*continued*) Fonseca my *m* enemy at their
    court, *Columbus* 126
Main (s) heard that, somewhere in the *m*, *If I were loved* 7
    Just breaking over land and *m* ? *Two Voices* 84
    On open *m* or winding shore ! *The Voyage* 6
    And mighty courteous in the *m*— *Aylmer's Field* 121
    spire of land that stands apart Cleft from the *m*, *Princess* iv 282
    Let the great river take me to the *m* : ,, vii 13
    climbs a peak to gaze O'er land and *m*, ,, 36
    Blown from over every *m*, *Ode Inter. Exhib.* 26
    To mingle with the bounding *m* : *In Mem.* xi 12
    I am sick of the moor and the *m*. *Maud I* i 61
    Flying along the land and the *m*— ,, II ii 38
    out to open *m* Glow'd intermingling close beneath
    the sun. *Lover's Tale* i 435
    To be lost evermore in the *m*. *The Revenge* 119
    hull dipt under the smiling *m*, *The Wreck* 127
    sea-current would sweep us out to the *m*. *Despair* 51
    O will she, moonlike, sway the *m*, *Mechanophilus* 13
Main-current Watch what *m-c's* draw the years : *Love thou thy land* 21
Main-miracle But this *m-m*, that thou art thou, *De Prof., Two G.* 55
Maintain thy heart a fortress to *m* The day *To Duke of Argyll* 5
    and thence *m* Our darker future. *To one who ran down Eng.* 1
Maintained should at least by me be *m* : *Maud I* i 18
Maintaining *M* that with equal husbandry *Princess* i 130
Maintenance all That appertains to noble *m*. *Marr. of Geraint* 712
Maize hand in hand with Plenty in the *m*, *Princess* vii 201
    Of olive, aloe, and *m* and vine. *The Daisy* 4
Majestic Grave mother of *m* works, *Of old sat Freedom* 13
    Sees a mansion more *m* Than all those *L. of Burleigh* 45
    Who scarce can tune his high *m* sense *Lover's Tale* i 475
    Thou *m* in thy sadness at the doubtful doom of human
    kind ; *To Virgil* 23
    But scarce of such *m* mien *Freedom* 6
Majesty New *Majesties* of mighty states— *Love thou thy land* 60
    Nothing to mar the sober *majesties* *Lucretius* 217
    and so unmoved a *m* She might have seem'd her
    statue, *Lancelot and E.* 1170
Make (*See also* **Maäke, May, Re-make**) *yield you*
    time To m *demand of modern rhyme* *To the Queen* 11
    and m *The bounds of freedom wider* ,, 31
    Shall *m* the winds blow Round and round, *Nothing will Die* 23
    Whose chillness would *m* visible *Supp. Confessions* 59
    Rain *m's* music in the tree *A Dirge* 26
    M's thy memory confused ? ,, 45
    the wave would *m* music above us afar— *The Merman* 22
    M a carcanet of rays, *Adeline* 59
    clip your wings, and *m* you love : *Rosalind* 45
    happy bridesmaid *m's* a happy bride.' *The Bridesmaid* 4
    happy bridesmaid, *m* a happy bride.' (repeat) ,, 8, 14
    ' What drug can *m* A wither'd palsy cease to shake ? ' *Two Voices* 56
    M thy grass hoar with early rime. ,, 66
    ' Or *m* that morn, from his cold crown ,, 85
    ' Wilt thou *m* everything a lie, ,, 203
    Not *m* him sure that he should cease ? ,, 282
    ' I cannot *m* this matter plain, ,, 343
    Far thought with music that it *m's* : ,, 438
    His memory scarce can *m* me sad. *Miller's D.* 16
    And *m's* me talk too much in age. ,, 194
    Do *m* a garland for the heart : ,, 198
    ' *M* me a cottage in the vale,' *Palace of Art* 291
    To *m* him trust his modest worth, *L. C. V. de Vere* 46
    many a worthier than I, would *m* him happy yet. *May Queen, Con.* 46
    what is life, that we should moan ? why *m* we
    such ado ? ,, 56
    music in his ears his beating heart did *m*. *Lotos-Eaters* 36
    And *m* perpetual moan, ,, C. S. 17
    That *m's* my only woe. *D. of F. Women* 136
    Words weaker than your grief would *m* Grief more. *To J. S.* 65
    And *m's* the purple lilac ripe, *On a Mourner* 7
    Power should *m* from land to land *You ask me, why, etc.* 21
    M bright our days and light our dreams, *Of old sat Freedom* 22
    She stood, a sight to *m* an old man young. *Gardener's D.* 141
    M thine heart ready with thine eyes : ,, 273
    ' I'll *m* them man and wife.' *Dora* 4

Make (*continued*) To *m* him pleasing in her uncle's eye. *Dora* 84
    let me have my boy, for you Will *m* him hard, ,, 153
    To *m* me an example of mankind, *St. S. Stylites* 188
    The love, that *m's* me thrice a man, *Talking Oak* 11
    But since I heard him *m* reply ,, 25
    To *m* the necklace shine ; ,, 222
    mellow rain, That *m's* thee broad and deep ! ,, 280
    words That *m* a man feel strong in speaking
    truth ; *Love and Duty* 70
    How dull it is to pause, to *m* an end, *Ulysses* 22
    by slow prudence to *m* mild A rugged people, ,, 36
    Can thy love, Thy beauty, *m* amends, *Tithonus* 24
    And *m* me tremble lest a saying learnt, ,, 47
    M me feel the wild pulsation *Locksley Hall* 109
    M prisms in every carven glass, *Day-Dm., Sleep. P.* 35
    And *m* her dance attendance ; *Amphion* 62
    M Thou thy spirit pure and clear *St. Agnes' Eve* 9
    Heavenly Bridegroom waits, To *m* me pure of sin. ,, 32
    To *m* me write my random rhymes, *Will Water.* 13
    Until the charm have power to *m* New lifeblood ,, 21
    To *m* my blood run quicker, ,, 110
    How out of place she *m's* The violet of a legend blow ,, 146
    empty glass That *m's* me maudlin-moral. ,, 208
    Hoped to *m* the name Of his vessel great in story, *The Captain* 18
    ' I can *m* no marriage present : *L. of Burleigh* 13
    Love will *m* our cottage pleasant, ,, 15
    All he shows her *m's* him dearer ,, 33
    I follow till I *m* thee mine.' *The Voyage* 64
    sweetest meal she *m's* On the first-born *Vision of Sin* 145
    Who *m* it seem more sweet to be *You might have won* 29
    purchase his own boat, and *m* a home For Annie : *Enoch Arden* 47
    m him merry, when I come home again. ,, 199
    kill yourself And *m* them orphans quite ? ' ,, 395
    Their voices m me feel so solitary.' ,, 397
    To *m* the boatmen fishing-nets, ,, 815
    himself could *m* The thing that is not as the thing *The Brook* 7
    I *m* a sudden sally, ,, 24
    Still *m's* a hoary eyebrow for the gleam ,, 80
    I *m* the netted sunbeam dance ,, 176
    Roaring to a third : *Aylmer's Field* 128
    counsel from a height That *m's* the lowest hate it, ,, 173
    for your fortunes are to *m*. I swear you shall not
    m them out of mine. ,, 300
    every star in heaven Can *m* it fair : *Sea Dreams* 84
    A trifle *m's* a dream, a trifle breaks.' ,, 144
    fat affectionate smile That *m's* the widow lean. ,, 156
    —it *m's* me sick to quote him— ,, 159
    Went both to *m* your dream : ,, 254
    m our passions far too like The discords ,, 257
    m Another and another frame of things *Lucretius* 41
    my rich procemion *m's* Thy glory fly ,, 70
    blood That *m's* a steaming slaughter-house of Rome. ,, 84
    bird *M's* his heart voice amid the blaze of flowers : ,, 101
    To *m* a truth less harsh, ,, 225
    I would *m* it death For any male thing *Princess, Pro.* 151
    And sweet as English air could *m* her, ,, 155
    ' And *m* her some great Princess, ,, 224
    doubt that we might *m* it worth his while. ,, i 184
    her lynx eye To fix and *m* me hotter, ,, iii 47
    your pains May only *m* that footprint ,, 239
    and *m* One act a phantom of succession : ,, 328
    pipe and woo her, and *m* her mine, ,, iv 115
    Would *m* all women kick against their Lords ,, 412
    ' And *m* us all we should be, great and good.' ,, 599
    will take her, they will *m* her hard, ,, v 90
    Knowledge in our own land *m* free, ,, 419
    The mother *m's* us most—and in my dream ,, 507
    let me my dream All that I would. ,, 519
    let her *m* herself her own To give or keep, ,, vii 272
    —why Not *m* her true-heroic— ,, Con. 20
    break the shore, and evermore *M* and break, *Ode on Well.* 261
    And you, my Lords, you *m* the people muse *Third of Feb.* 31
    Come to us, love us and *m* us your own : *W. to Alexandra* 30
    Annie, will never *m* oneself clean. *Grandmother* 36
    it *m's* me angry now. ,, 44

Make (*continued*) My father's madness *m's* me mad— *The Flight* 59
You only know the love that *m's* the world a world to me ! ,, 76
therewithin a guest may *m* True cheer *Pro. to Gen. Hamley* 15
must fight To *m* true peace his own, *Epilogue* 27
The falling drop will *m* his name ,, 60
Heavenly Power *M's* all things new, (repeat) *Early Spring* 2, 44
and thy will, a power to *m* *To Duke of Argyll* 9
Two Suns of Love *m* day of human life, *To Prin. Beatrice* 1
M's the might of Britain known ; *Open. I. and C. Exhib.* 19
M their neighbourhood healthfuller, *On Jub. Q. Victoria* 32
M it regally gorgeous, ,, 45
do ye *m* your moaning for my child ? ' *Demeter and P.* 65
Globe again, and *m* Honey Moon. *The Ring* 15
she *m's* Her heart a mirror that reflects ,, 365
And I meant to *m you* jealous. *Happy* 67
faults your Poet *m's* Or many or few, *To Mary Boyle* 61
Her light *m's* rainbows in my closing eyes, *Prog. of Spring* 46
M all true hearths thy home. ,, 52
Could *m* pure light live on the canvas ? *Romney's R.* 10
plead for my own fame with me To *m* it dearer. ,, 56
but *m* it as clean as you can, *By an Evolution.* 3
can Music *m* you live Far—far—away ? *Far—far—away* 17
You *m* our faults too gross, *To one who ran down Eng.* 1
m her festal hour Dark with the blood *St. Telemachus* 79
Adoring That who made, and *m's*, *Akbar's Dream* 123
M but one music, harmonising ' Pray.' ,, 151
gold Of Love, and *m* it current ; ,, 164
I could *m* Sleep Death, if I would— *Bandit's Death* 32
when he promised to *m* me his bride, *Charity* 11
When I *m* for an Age of gold, *The Dreamer* 7
Or *m's* a friend where'er he come, *The Wanderer* 6
To *m* him trust his life, ,, 11
when the man will *m* the Maker ,, *Faith* 7
Make-believes *m-b* For Edith and himself : *Aylmer's Field* 95
Maker (the Creator) For the drift of the *M* is dark, *Maud I iv* 43
thou dost His will. The *M's*, *Gareth and L.* 11
voices blend in choric Hallelujah to the *M* *Making of Man* 8
when the man will make the *M* *Faith* 7
Maker (*See also* **Marriage-maker, Shadow-maker**) *M's* of nets, and living from the sea. *Pelleas and E.* 90
Makest ' Thou *m* thine appeal to me : *In Mem. lvi* 5
And *m* merry when overthrown. *Gareth and L.* 1270
Thou *m* broken music with thy bride, *Last Tournament* 264
Making (*See also* **Maakin', Merrymaking**) *M* earth wonder, *The Poet* 52
By *m* all the horizon dark, *Two Voices* 390
In firry woodlands *m* moan ; *Miller's D.* 42
M sweet close of his delicious toils— *Palace of Art* 185
M for one sure goal. ,, 248
Thro' many agents *m* strong, *Love thou thy land* 39
The younger people *m* holiday, *Enoch Arden* 62
and *m* signs They knew not what : ,, 640
gulf of ruin, swallowing gold, Not *m*. *Sea Dreams* 80
M the little one leap for joy. *To F. D. Maurice* 4
M Him broken gleams, and a stifled splendour *High. Pantheism* 10
m vain pretence Of gladness, *In Mem. xxx* 6
m his high place the lawless perch *Ded. of Idylls* 22
m slide apart Their dusk wing-cases, *Gareth and L.* 686
good mother *m* Enid gay In such apparel *Marr. of Geraint* 757
comrades *m* slowlier at the Prince, *Geraint and E.* 167
score with pointed lances, *m* at him— *Balin and Balan* 401
M a roan horse caper and curvet *Lancelot and E.* 792
M a treacherous quiet in her heart, ,, 883
m them An armlet for the roundest arm ,, 1182
make men worse by *m* my sin known ? ,, 1417
m all the night a steam of fire. *Guinevere* 599
And, *m* there a sudden light, *Lover's Tale iv* 53
M fresh and fair All the bowers *Sisters (E. and E.)* 9
is *m* a new link Breaking an old one ? *The Ring* 50
,, 314
m with a kindly pinch Each poor pale cheek *Akbar's Dream* 29
tracks Of science *m* toward Thy Perfectness *M. d'Arthur* 203
Or hath come, since the *m* of the world. *Maud I iv* 35
ages have gone to the *m* of man : ,, *III vi* 47
the sudden *m* of splendid names, *Pass. of Arthur* 371
Or hath come, since the *m* of the world.

Malarian A flat *m* world of reed and rush ! *Lover's Tale iv* 142
Malay not the Kaffir, Hottentot, *M*, *Princess ii* 158
Malayan Ran a *M* amuck against the times, *Aylmer's Field* 463
The cursed *M* crease, *Princess, Pro.* 21
Male (*adj.*) make it death For any *m* thing but to peep at us.' ,, 152
I dare All these *m* thunderbolts : ,, *iv* 500
Thaw this *m* nature to some touch of that ,, *vi* 306
all *m* minds perforce Sway'd to her ,, *vii* 325
Which types all Nature's *m* and female plan, *On One who affec. E. M.* 3
Male (*s*) (*See also* **Maäle**) maids should ape Those monstrous *m's* *Princess iii* 310
Malice crime of sense became The crime of *m*, *Vision of Sin* 216
My *m* is no deeper than a moat, *Geraint and E.* 340
In one, their *m* on the placid lip *Pelleas and E.* 432
phrase that masks his *m* now— *The Flight* 30
Malignant The green *m* light of coming storm. *Princess ii* 132
my honest heat Were all miscounted as *m* haste ,, *iv* 334
Malison I have no sorcerer's *m* on me, ,, *ii* 410
Malkin (*See also* **Mawkin**) the swineherd's *m* in the mast ? *Last Tournament* 632
Malleor Of Geoffrey's book, or him of *M's*, *To the Queen II* 42
Mallow set With willow-weed and *m*. *The Brook* 46
Mammon This filthy marriage-hindering *M* *Aylmer's Field* 374
Mammonite When a *M* mother kills her babe *Maud I* 45
Mammoth old-world *m* bulk'd in ice, *Princess v* 148
Man (*See also* **Countryman, Half-man, Lay-men, Men-at-arms, Men-children, Men-tommies, Methody-man, Serving-man, Watchman, Welshman, Woman-man, Woodman, Workman**)
As all *men* know, Long ago, *All Things will Die* 39
Men say that Thou Didst die for me, *Supp. Confessions* 2
Men pass me by ; ,, 19
When Angels spake to *men* aloud, ,, 25
where *m* Hath moor'd and rested ? ,, 124
It is *m's* privilege to doubt, ,, 142
Shall *m* live thus, in joy and hope ,, 169
Then once by *m* and angels to be seen, *The Kraken* 14
As a sick *m's* room when he taketh repose *A spirit haunts* 14
riving the spirit of *m*, Making earth wonder, *The Poet* 51
Kate saith ' the *men* are gilded flies.' *Kate* 18
How long, O God, shall *men* be ridden down, And trampled under by the last and least Of men ? *Poland* 1
And in the sixth she moulded *m*. *Two Voices* 18
' And *men*, thro' novel spheres of thought ,, 61
' He dared not tarry,' *men* will say, ,, 101
heaping on the fear of ill The fear of *men*, ,, 108
' Do *men* love thee ? Art thou so bound To *men*, ,, 109
That *men* with knowledge merely play'd, ,, 172
this dreamer, deaf and blind, Named *m*, ,, 176
The joy that mixes *m* with Heaven : ,, 210
' Why, if *m* rot in dreamless ease, ,, 280
He sat upon the knees of *men* ,, 323
till thou wert also *m* : ,, 327
in trances, *men* Forget the dream that happens then, ,, 352
' And *men*, whose reason long was blind, ,, 370
And with the certain step of *m*. *Miller's D.* 96
men, in power Only, are likest gods, *Œnone* 129
hated both of Gods and *men*. ,, 229
Rings ever in her ears of armed *men*. ,, 265
friends to *m*, Living together under the same roof, *To ——, With Pal. of Art* 11
tears Of angels to the perfect shape of *m*. ,, 19
choice paintings of wise *men* I hung *Palace of Art* 131
once more like some sick *m* declined, ,, 155
' I take possession of *m's* mind and deed. ,, 209
that good *m*, the clergyman, has told me words of peace. *May Queen, Con.* 12
from an ill-used race of *men* that cleave the soil, *Lotos-Eaters, C. S.* 120
Squadrons and squares of *men* in brazen plates, *D. of F. Women* 33
men call'd Aulis in those iron years : ,, 106
' I govern'd *men* by change, and so I sway'd All moods. ,, 130
'Tis long since I have seen a *m*. ,, 131
I have no *men* to govern in this wood : ,, 135
' The *m*, my lover, with whom I rode sublime ,, 141
I am that Rosamond, whom *men* call fair, ,, 251

Man (*continued*) our true *m* change like a leaf at last ?   *Lancelot and E.* 686

since *m's* first fall, Did kindlier unto *m*,	,,	859
the sick *m* forgot her simple blush,	,,	864
love Of *m* and woman when they love their best,	,,	869
Another world for the sick *m* ;	,,	874
no *m* there will dare to mock at me ;	,,	1053
it is mine to love Him of all *men*	,,	1077
never yet Was noble *m* but made ignoble talk.	,,	1088
and bid call the ghostly *m* Hither,	,,	1099
when the ghostly *m* had come and gone,	,,	1101
therefore let our dumb old *m* alone Go with me,	,,	1127
Our bond, as not the bond of *m* and wife,	,,	1191
Our bond is not the bond of *m* and wife.	,,	1206
hard and still as is the face that *men* Shape to their fancy's eye	,,	1251
then turn'd the tongueless *m* From the half-face	,,	1261
a *m* Made to be loved ;	,,	1363
now a lonely *m* Wifeless and heirless,	,,	1370
To make *men* worse by making my sin known ?	,,	1417
Arthur's greatest knight, a *m* Not after Arthur's heart !	,,	1419
Not knowing he should die a holy *m*.	,,	1429
m Could touch or see it, he was heal'd at once,	*Holy Grail*	54
A *m* wellnigh a hundred winters old,	,,	85
all *men's* hearts became Clean for a season,	,,	90
pale nun, I spake of this To all *men* ;	,,	130
letters in a tongue no *m* could read.	,,	171
' No *m* could sit but he should lose himself : '	,,	174
staring each at other like dumb *men* Stood,	,,	193
And in the lowest beasts are slaying *men*, And in the second *men* are slaying beasts, And on the third are warriors, perfect *men*, And on the fourth are *men* with growing wings,	,,	234
' but *men* With strength and will to right the wrong'd,	,,	308
men and boys astride On wyvern, lion,	,,	349
Thou mightiest and thou purest among *men* !'	,,	426
but found at top No *m*, nor any voice.	,,	428
I saw That had once dwelt there ;	,,	430
I found Only one *m* of an exceeding age.	,,	431
rose a hill that none but *m* could climb,	,,	489
Part black, part whiten'd with the bones of *men*,	,,	500
Taking my war-horse from the holy *m*,	,,	537
Rejoice, small *m*, in this small world of mine,	,,	559
phantoms in your quest, No *m*, no woman ?'	,,	563
' All *men*, to one so bound by such a vow,	,,	565
Then said the monk, ' Poor *men*, when yule is cold,	,,	613
and their wise *men* Were strong in that old magic	,,	665
A square-set *m* and honest ;	,,	703
words Of so great *men* as Lancelot and our King	,,	713
Therefore I commuued with a saintly *m*,	,,	742
if ever loyal *m* and true Could see it,	,,	756
There was I beaten down by little *men*,	,,	789
great beasts rose upright like a *m*,	,,	821
nun and thou have driven *men* mad,	,,	862
all of true and noble in knight and *m*	,,	882
For as the base *m*, judging of the good,	*Pelleas and E.*	80
as he came away, The *men* who met him	,,	142
No *men* to strike ? Fall on him all at once,	,,	268
she gazed upon the *m* Of princely bearing,	,,	305
this *m* loves, If love there be :	,,	307
Art thou not he whom *men* call light-of-love ?'	,,	361
I to your dead *m* have given my troth,	,,	389
' Why then let *men* couple at once with wolves.	,,	536
M was it who marr'd heaven's image in thee thus ?'	*Last Tournament*	64
honey from hornet-combs, And *men* from beasts—	,,	358
as from *men* secure Amid their marshes,	,,	426
Men, women, on their sodden faces,	,,	474
' my *m* Hath left me or is dead ;'	,,	494
I—misyoked with such a want of *m*—	,,	571
my Mark's, by whom all *men* Are noble,	,,	599
The greater *m*, the greater courtesy.	,,	633
The *m* of *men*, our King—My God, the power Was once in vows when *men* believed the King !	,,	648
' *M*, is he *m* at all ?' methought,	,,	663

Man (*continued*) he seem'd to me no *m*, But Michaël trampling Satan ;   *Last Tournament* 672

heather-scented air, Pulsing full *m* ;	,,	692
reverencing king's blood in a bad *m*,	*Guinevere*	37
But, if a *m* were halt or hunch'd,	,,	41
such a feast As never *m* had dream'd ;	,,	264
so glad were spirits and *men* Before the coming	,,	269
prophets were they all, Spirits and *men* :	,,	273
the King As wellnigh more than *m*,	,,	287
For there was no *m* knew from whence he came ;	,,	289
a mystery From all *men*, like his birth ;	,,	298
Were the most nobly-manner'd *men* of all ;	,,	334
Reputed the best knight and goodliest,	,,	382
True *men* who love me still, for whom I live,	,,	445
glorious company, the flower of *men*,	,,	464
Not only to keep down the base in *m*,	,,	480
love of truth, and all that makes a *m*.	,,	483
I hold that *m* the worst of public foes	,,	512
She like a new disease, unknown to *men*,	,,	518
Worst of the worst were that *m* he that reigns !	,,	523
no *m* dream but that I love thee still.	,,	560
strike against the *m* they call My sister's son—	,,	572
when the *m* was no more than a voice	*Pass. of Arthur*	3
in His ways with *men* I find Him not.	,,	11
that these eyes of *men* are dense and dim,	,,	19
for the ghost is as the *m* ;	,,	57
but no *m* was moving there ;	,,	127
uttering this the King Made at the *m* :	,,	165
Until King Arthur's Table, *m* by *m*,	,,	172
They sleep—the *men* I loved.	,,	185
A little thing may harm a wounded *m* ;	,,	210
Where lay the mighty bones of ancient *men*, Old knights,	,,	215
This is a shameful thing for *men* to lie.	,,	246
might have pleased the eyes of many *men*.	,,	259
some old *m* speak in the aftertime To all the people,	,,	275
for a *m* may fail in duty twice,	,,	297
I live three lives of mortal *men*,	,,	323
Among new *men*, strange faces,	,,	406
are *men* better than sheep or goats	,,	418
and loud leagues of *m* And welcome !	*To the Queen* ii 9
Ideal manhood closed in real *m*,	,,	38
Or as *men* know not when they fall asleep	*Lover's Tale* i 161
as tho' A *m* in some still garden	,,	269
we found The dead *m* cast upon the shore ?	,,	295
she answered, ' Ay, And *men* to soar : '	,,	305
A woful *m* (for so the story went)	,,	379
That *men* plant over graves.	,,	538
like a vain rich *m*, That, having always prosper'd	,,	715
Let them so love that *men* and boys may say,	,,	756
Beneath the shadow of the curse of *m*,	,,	790
the *m* who stood with me Stept gaily forward,	,,	iii 50
the dreadful dust that once was *m*,	,,	iv 67
dead *men's* dust and beating hearts.	,,	140
when a *m* Will honour those who feast with him,	,,	231
I knew a *m*, not many years ago ;	,,	255
Dazed or amazed, nor eyes of *men* ;	,,	311
but after my *m* was dead ;	*First Quarrel*	6
The *men* would say of the maids,	,,	28
my house an' my *m* were my pride,	,,	41
been as true to you as ever a *m* to his wife ;	,,	60
The *m* isn't like the woman,	,,	63
Harry, my *m*, you had better ha' beaten me	,,	72
Bible verse of the Lord's good will toward *men*—	*Rizpah*	61
and the sea that 'ill moan like a *m* ?	,,	72
not hafe ov a *m*, my lad—	*North. Cobbler*	21
an' the loov of God fur *men*,	,,	55
thou'rt like the rest o' the *men*,	,,	63
Theer's thy hennemy, *m*,	,,	65
And the half my *men* are sick.	*The Revenge*	6
I've ninety *men* and more that are lying	,,	10
bore in hand all his sick *men* from the land	,,	15
Men of Bideford in Devon,	,,	17
' We be all good English *men*.	,,	29

Man 452 Man

Man (*continued*)   sick *men* down in the hold were most
  of them stark and cold,   *The Revenge* 79
We have won great glory, my *men* !   „ 85
stately Spanish *men* to their flagship bore him then,   „ 97
fought for Queen and Faith like a valiant *m* and true ;   „ 101
only done my duty as a *m* is bound to do :   „ 102
Was he devil or *m* ?   He was devil for aught   „ 108
a *m's* ideal Is high in Heaven,   *Sisters* (*E. and E.*) 130
In some such fashion as a *m* may be   „ 133
Selfish, strange !   What dwarfs are *men* !   „ 199
an' was 'untin' arter the *men*,   *Village Wife* 36
every *m* die at his post !' (repeat)   *Def. of Lucknow* 10, 13, 52
Handful of *men* as we were,   „ 46
Men will forget what we suffer and not what we do.   „ 73
to call *men* traitors May make *men* traitors.   *Sir J. Oldcastle* 50
reddest with the blood of holy *men*,   „ 54
nay, let a *m* repent, Do penance in his heart,   „ 142
poor *m's* money gone to fat the friar.   „ 150
heathen *men* have borne as much as this,   *Columbus* 50
men Walk'd like the fly on ceilings ?   „ 152
thou hast done so well for *men*, that *men*   „ 152
the *men* that were mighty of tongue   *V. of Maeldune* 23
the *men* dropt dead in the valleys   „ 31
shook like a *m* in a mortal affright ;   „ 74
it open'd and dropt at the side of each *m*,   „ 85
And the Holy *m* he assoil'd us,   „ 126
The *m* that had slain my father.   „ 128
landed again, with a tithe of my *men*,   „ 130
and prophet of the perfect *m* ;   *De Prof., Two G.* 12
that *men* May bless thee as we bless thee,   „ 16
then full-current thro' full *m* :   „ 22
' Let us make *m* ' and that which should be *m*, From
  that one light no *m* can look upon,   „ 36
seek If any golden harbour be for *men*   *Pref. Son. 19th Cent.* 13
You *m* of humorous-melancholy mark,   *To W. H. Brookfield* 9
England, France, all *m* to be Will make one people
  ere *m's* race be run :   *To Victor Hugo* 10
lay many a *m* Marr'd by the javelin,   *Batt. of Brunanburh* 31
Men of the Northland Shot over shield.   „ 33
All day the *men* contend in grievous war   *Achilles over the T.* 9
airy-light To float above the ways of *men*,   *To E. Fitzgerald* 18
What omens may foreshadow fate to *m* And woman,   *Tiresias* 7
more than *m* Which rolls the heavens,   „ 21
moves unseen among the ways of *men*,   „ 24
speak the truth that no *m* may believe.'   „ 50
While *men* shall move the lips :   „ 133
light upon the ways of *men* As one great deed.   „ 161
wise *m's* word, Here trampled by the populace   „ 173
these eyes will find The *men* I knew,   „ 176
princelier looking *m* never stept thro' a Prince's hall.   *The Wreck* 16
And a *m men* fear is a *m* to be loved   „ 18
and *men* at the helm of state—   „ 49
he, poor *m*, when he learnt that I hated the ring   „ 57
felt for the first and greatest of *men* ;   „ 76
all but the *m* that was lash'd to the helm had gone ;   „ 110
the one *m* left on the wreck—   „ 110
kiss so sad, no, not since the coming of *m* !   *Despair* 60
You have parted the *m* from the wife.   „ 62
If every *m* die for ever,   „ 82
if the souls of *men* were immortal, as *men* have been told,   „ 99
till that old *m* before A cavern   *Ancient Sage* 6
m to-day is fancy's fool As *m* hath ever been.   „ 27
never spake with *m*, And never named the Name '—   „ 55
beyond All work of *m*, yet, like the work of *m*,   „ 85
The last and least of *men* ;   „ 114
For *m* has overlived his day   „ 150
So dark that *men* cry out against the Heavens,   „ 172
Who knows but that the darkness is in *m* ?   „ 173
Word Of that world-prophet in the heart of *m*.   „ 213
But in the hand of what is more than *m*, Or in *m's*
  hand when *m* is more than *m*, Let be thy wail
  and help thy fellow *men*,   „ 256
Nor list for guerdon in the voice of *men*,   „ 262
tould her to come away from the *m*,   *Tomorrow* 20
an' a dhrame of a married *m*, death alive,   „ 51

Man (*continued*)   An' where 'ud the poor *m*, thin,   *Tomorrow* 65
bogs whin they swallies the *m* intire !   „ 66
Thou sees that i' spite o' the *men*   *Spinster's S's.* 11
allus afear'd of a *m's* gittin' ower fond,   „ 27
That a *m* be a durty thing an' a trouble   „ 50
But I couldn't 'a lived wi' a *m*   „ 52
By a *m* coomin' in wi' a hiccup   „ 98
'es hallus to hax of a *m* how much to spare   „ 111
she with all the breadth of *m*,   *Locksley H., Sixty* 48
for ever was the leading light of *m*.   „ 66
alms of Blessing *m* had coin'd himself a curse :   „ 87
France had shown a light to all *men*, preach'd a
  Gospel, all *men's* good ;   „ 89
still, ' your enemy ' was a *m*.   „ 94
Are we devils ? are we *men* ?   „ 99
Sons of God, and kings of *men*   „ 122
to lower the rising race of *men* ;   „ 147
no *m* halt, or deaf or blind ;   „ 163
who can fancy warless *men* ?   „ 172
are these but symbols of innumerable *m*, M or
  Mind that sees a shadow   „ 195
What are *men* that He should heed us ?   „ 201
before her highest, *m*, was born,   „ 205
offspring this ideal *m* at rest ?   „ 234
Nor is he the wisest *m*, who never proved   „ 244
to help his homelier brother *men*,   „ 267
—for *m* can half-control his doom   „ 277
you and all your *men* Were soldiers   *Pro. to Gen. Hamley* 24
Thro' the great gray slope of *men*,   *Heavy Brigade* 17
our *men* gallopt up with a cheer and a shout,   „ 61
In worlds before the *m* Involving ours—   *Epilogue* 25
now we see, The *m* in Space and Time,   „ 49
what they prophesy, our wise *men*,   „ 65
all in vain As far as *m* can see, except The *m* himself
  remain ;   „ 69
That *m* can have no after-morn,   „ 73
The *m* remains, and whatsoe'er He wrought   „ 75
measure ever moulded by the lips of *m*.   *To Virgil* 40
touch'd on the whole sad planet of *m*,   *Dead Prophet* 39
For *m* is a lover of Truth,   „ 44
Was he noblier-fashion'd than other *men* ?   „ 51
WARRIOR of God, *m's* friend,   *Epit. on Gordon* 1
for all *men* know This earth has never borne a
  nobler *m*.   „ 3
That *m's* the best Cosmopolite   *Hands all Round* 3
That *m's* the true Conservative   „ 7
Men loud against all forms of power—   *Freedom* 37
When all *men* starve, the wild mob's million feet   *The Fleet* 18
Men that in a narrower day—   *Open. I. and C. Exhib.* 25
when before have Gods or *men* beheld   *Demeter and P.* 29
fled by many a waste, forlorn of *m*, And grieved for
  m thro' all my grief for thee,—   „ 74
we spin the lives of *men*, And not of Gods,   „ 85
Last as the likeness of a dying *m*,   „ 88
m, that only lives and loves an hour,   „ 106
vine And golden grain, my gift to helpless *m*.   „ 111
the praise And prayer of *men*,   „ 120
souls of *men*, who grew beyond their race,   „ 140
thou that hast from *men*, As Queen of Death,   „ 142
nor I iver owäd mottal *m*.   *Owd Roä* 4
moor good sense na the Parliament *m* 'at stans fur
  us 'ere,   „ 13
men ater supper 'ed sung their songs   „ 35
Howiver was I fur to find my rent an' to paäy my *men* ?   „ 47
Ghost in *M*, the Ghost that once was *M*, But cannot
  wholly free itself from *M*,   *The Ring* 35
No sudden heaven, nor sudden hell, for *m*,   „ 41
I had seen the *m* but once ;   „ 190
till the *m* repenting sent This ring   „ 209
bad the *m* engrave ' From Walter ' on the ring,   „ 235
as a *m* Who sees his face in water,   „ 369
so fickle are *men*—the best !   „ 392
beauty came upon your face, not that of living *men*,   *Happy* 51
If *m* and wife be but one flesh,   „ 94
ULYSSES, much-experienced *m*,   *To Ulysses* 1

Man (*continued*) Her tribes of *men*, and trees, and flowers, *To Ulysses* 3
Where *m*, nor only Nature smiles ;   „ 39
That I might mix with *men*, and hear their words   *Prog. of Spring* 82
I too would teach the *m*   „ 87
dwellings of the kings of *men* ;   „ 99
men have hopes, which race the restless blood,   „ 115
under the Crosses The dead *m's* garden,   *Merlin and the G.* 106
blacken round The copse of every *m*   *Romney's R.* 123
Should I know the *m* ?   „ 144
And the *m* said ' Am I your debtor ? '   *By an Evolution.* 2
M is quiet at last As he stands on the heights   „ 19
WHILE *m* and woman are still incomplete, I prize
    that soul where *m* and woman meet,   *On one who affec. E. M.* 1
thoughts that lift the soul of *men*,   *To Master of B.* 14
M is but the slave of Fate.   *Death of Œnone* 44
and forgetful of the *m*,   „ 60
But every *m* was mute for reverence.   „ 96
The *m*, whose pious hand had built the cross, A *m*
    who never changed a word with *men*,   *St. Telemachus* 9
borne along by that full stream of *men*,   „ 43
trailing a dead lion away, One, a dead *m*.   „ 48
Christian faces watch *M* murder *m*.   „ 56
barrier that divided beast from *m* Slipt,   „ 60
In the great name of Him who died for *men*,   „ 63
Dark with the blood of *m* who murder'd *m*.   „ 80
only conquers *men* to conquer peace,   *Akbar's Dream* 15
I seem no longer like a lonely *m*   „ 20
knows Himself, *men* nor themselves nor Him,   „ 32
' Mine is the one fruit Alla made for *m*.'   „ 40
men may taste Swine-flesh, drink wine ;   „ 53
I let *men* worship as they will,   „ 66
By deeds a light to *men* ?   „ 111
Ritual, varying with the tribes of *men*.   „ 125
and *men*, below the dome of azure Kneel   „ *Hymn* 7
and voices, and *men* passing to and fro.   *Bandit's Death* 24
And a *m* ruin'd mine,   *Charity* 7
Would the he have a touch of remorse   „ 17
M, can you even guess at the love of a soul for a soul ?   „ 30
M with his brotherless dinner on *m*   *The Dawn* 3
Men, with a heart and a soul,   „ 18
We are far from the noon of *m*,   „ 20
The *men* of a hundred thousand,   „ 25
M as yet is being made,   *Making of Man* 3
' It is finish'd. *M* is made.'   „ 8
That no *m* would believe.   *Mechanophilus* 28
To a just *m* and a wise—   *Voice spake, etc.* 2
when the *m* will make the Maker   *Faith* 7
Manage Hadn't a head to *m*,   *Grandmother* 6
    How best to *m* horse, lance, sword and shield,   *Gareth and L.* 1351
Managed I 'a *m* for Squoire coom Michaelmas   *N. Farmer, O. S.* 48
Man-at-arms Another hurrying past, a *m-a-a*,   *Geraint and E.* 526
Man-beast *m-b* of boundless savagery.   *Gareth and L.* 637
Man-breasted strong *m-b* things stood from the sea, *Guinevere* 246
Manchester throats of *M* may bawl,   *Third of Feb.* 43
Manchet And in her veil enfolded, *m* bread.   *Marr. of Geraint* 389
Mander (**manner**) noä *m* o' use to be callin' 'im Roä, *Owd Roä* 1
Mane shake the darkness from their loosen'd *m's*,   *Tithonus* 41
    To break my chain, to shake my *m* :   *Princess ii* 424
    with your long locks play the Lion's *m* !   *vi* 164
    With sudden-flaring *m's* Those two great beasts *Holy Grail* 820
Maned *See* **Full-maned, Midnight-maned**
Manelike Beneath a *m* mass of rolling gold,   *Aylmer's Field* 68
Manes (**mean**) An' yer Honour's the thrue ould blood
    that always *m* to be kind,   *Tomorrow* 5
Manful Between your peoples truth and *m* peace, *W. to Marie Alex.* 49
    Right thro' his *m* breast darted the pang   *Marr. of Geraint* 121
    Nor know I whether I be very base Or very *m*,   „ 469
Manfulness he, from his exceeding *m*   „ 211
Man-girdled Than thus *m-g* here :   *Princess v* 429
Mangle And *m* the living dog that had loved him *In the Child. Hosp.* 9
Mangle (**mangold**) Goan into *m's* an' tonups,   *Owd Roä* 28
Mangled *M*, and flatten'd, and crush'd,   *Maud I i* 7
    I see thee maim'd, *M* :   *Gareth and L.* 1327
    M to morsels, A youngster in war !   *Batt. of Brunanburh* 74
Mango The *m* spurn the melon at his foot ?   *Akbar's Dream* 39

Mangold *See* **Mangle**
Mangrove The slant seas leaning on the *m* copse,   *Prog. of Spring* 76
Manhood Nature's evil star Drive men in *m*,   *Love thou thy land* 74
    The darling of my *m*, and, alas !   *Gardener's D.* 278
    who desire you more Than growing boys their *m* ;   *Princess iv* 457
    Accomplish thou my *m* and thyself ;   „ *vii* 365
    Some civic *m* firm against the crowd—   „ *Con.* 57
    The highest, holiest *m*, thou :   *In Mem., Pro.* 14
    Tho' truths in *m* darkly join,   „ *xxxvi* 1
    Who wears his *m* hale and green :   „ *liii* 4
    m fused with female grace In such a sort,   „ *cix* 17
    glory of *m* stand on his ancient height,   *Maud III vi* 21
    So make thy *m* mightier day by day ;   *Gareth and L.* 92
    I felt Thy *m* thro' that wearied lance of thine.   „ 1266
    a prince whose *m* was all gone,   *Marr. of Geraint* 59
    when it weds with *m*, makes a man.   *Geraint and E.* 868
    Thy too fierce *m* would not let thee lie.   *Balin and Balan* 74
    To learn what Arthur meant by courtesy, *M*, and
        knighthood ;   „ 159
    Name, *m*, and a grace, but scantly thine,   „ 377
    Vivien, save ye fear The monkish *m*,   *Merlin and V.* 35
    The pretty, popular name such *m* earns,   „ 787
    ourselves shall grow In use of arms and *m*,   *Lancelot and E.* 64
    Friends, thro' your *m* and your fëalty,—   *Last Tournament* 97
    Tells of a *m* ever less and lower ?   „ 121
    Who fain had clipt free *m* from the world—   „ 446
    as great As he was in his *m*,   *Guinevere* 300
    Ideal *m* closed in real man,   *To the Queen ii* 38
    Yet you in your mid *m*—   *Happy* 47
Maniac Time, a *m* scattering dust,   *In Mem. l* 7
Manifold With a music strange and *m*,   *Dying Swan* 29
    But *m* entreaties, many a tear,   *Enoch Arden* 160
    Thro' *m* effect of simple powers—   *Prog. of Spring* 86
    Sent notes of preparation *m*,   *Lover's Tale i* 207
Man-in-God God-in-man is one with *m-i-G*,   *Enoch Arden* 187
Mankind like Gods together, careless of *m*.   *Lotos-Eaters, C. S.* 110
    ALTHO' I be the basest of *m*,   *St. S. Stylites* 1
    Whereof my fame is loud amongst *m*,   „ 81
    To make me an example to *m*,   „ 188
    in the thoughts that shake *m*.   *Locksley Hall* 166
    Had golden hopes for France and all *m*,   *Aylmer's Field* 464
    Let them not lie in the tents with coarse *m*,   *Princess vi* 69
    I had been wedded wife, I knew,   „ 327
    For, saving that, ye help to save *m*   *Ode on Well.* 166
    But while the races of *m* endure,   „ 219
    Peace and goodwill, to all *m*.   *In Mem. xxviii* 12
    This bitter seed among *m* ;   „ *xc* 4
    Ring in redress to all *m*.   „ *cvi* 12
    For each is at war with *m*.   *Maud I x* 52
    Being but ample means to serve *m*,   *Merlin and V.* 489
    so might there be Two Adams, two *m's*,   *Columbus* 54
    My friend, the most unworldly of *m*,   *In Mem., W. G. Ward* 3
Manless when earth is *m* and forlorn,   *Locksley H., Sixty* 206
Manlike *m* end myself ?—our privilege—   *Lucretius* 232
    open-work in which the hunter rued His rash
        intrusion, *m*,   *Princess iv* 204
Manly Is this the *m* strain of Runnymede ?   *Third of Feb.* 34
Man-minded When his *m-m* offset rose   *Talking Oak* 51
Man-mode in all *M-m's* of worship ;   *Akbar's Dream* 47
Manna As *m* on my wilderness   *Supp. Confessions* 114
Mann'd *m* the Revenge with a swarthier alien crew, *The Revenge* 110
Manner (*See also* **Mander**) listening rogue hath caught
    the *m* of it.   *Gareth and L.* 778
    I fain would know what *m* of men they be.'   *Balin and Balan* 574
    His tenderness of *m*, and chaste awe,   *Pelleas and E.* 110
    Restrain'd him with all *m* of device,   „ 204
    To hear the *m* of thy fight and fall ;   „ 347
    A *m* somewhat fall'n from reverence—   *Last Tournament* 119
Manner'd *See* **Nobly-manner'd**
Manners Her *m* had not that repose   *L. C. V. de Vere* 39
    Like men, like *m*: like breeds like, they say : Kind
        nature is the best : those *m* next   *Walk. to the Mail* 63
    What are indeed the *m* of the great.   „ 66
    cities of men And *m*, climates, councils,   *Ulysses* 14
    That gives the *m* of your countrywomen ?   *Princess iv* 151

Margin (s) (*continued*) Comes a vapour from the *m*, *Locksley Hall* 191
every *m* scribbled, crost, and cramm'd *Merlin and V.* 677
And bear me to the *m* ; *Pass. of Arthur* 333
ere it vanishes Over the *m*, *Merlin and the G.* 129
Mariam *See* **Issa Ben Mariam**
Marian Is memory with your *M* gone to rest, *To Mary Boyle* 13
Marie (*See also* **Alexandrovna, Marie Alexandrovna**)
Here also *M*, shall thy name be blest, *W. to Marie Alex.* 39
Marie Alexandrovna (*See also* **Alexandrovna, Marie**)
From mother unto mother, stately bride, *M A* ! ,, 10
loyal pines of Canada murmur thee, *M A*, ,, 20
Love by right divine is deathless king, *M A* ! ,, 30
Here also, Marie, shall thy name be blest, *M A* ! ,, 40
Marigold *See* **Marsh-marigold**
Mariner Slow sail'd the weary *m*'s and saw, *Sea Fairies* 1
M, *m*, furl your sails, ,, 21
listen and stay : *m*, *m*, fly no more. ,, 42
Oh rest ye, brother *m*'s, *Lotos-Eaters, C. S.* 128
My *m*'s, Souls that have toil'd, *Ulysses* 45
O young *M*, Down to the haven, *Merlin and the G.* 123
Marish thro' the *m* green and still *Dying Swan* 18
Marish-flowers the silvery *m-f* that throng ,, 40
Marish-mosses The cluster'd *m-m* crept. *Mariana* 40
Marish-pipe With moss and braided *m-p*, *On a Mourner* 10
Mark (coin) A thousand *m*'s are set upon my head. *Sir J. Oldcastle* 195
Mark (s) (*See also* **Merk**) thou,' said I, ' hast missed thy *m*, *Two Voices* 388
he thought himself A *m* for all, *Walk. to the Mail* 73
arrows aim'd All at one *m*, all hitting : *Aylmer's Field* 95
push beyond her *m*, and be Procuress *In Mem. liii* 15
No single tear, no *m* of pain : ,, *lxxviii* 14
master-bowman, he, Would cleave the *m*. ,, *lxxxvii* 30
loves to know When men of *m* are in his territory : *Geraint and E.* 229
meant to stamp him with her master's *m* ; *Merlin and V.* 759
Yon man of humorous-melancholy *m*, *To W. H. Brookfield* 9
an' the *m* o' 'is 'eäd o' the chairs ! *Spinster's S's.* 100
In aiming at an all but hopeless *m* *The Ring* 346
A red *m* ran All round one finger ,, 452
And set a crueller *m* than Cain's on him, *Happy* 18
Mark (Christian Name) came in hall the messenger of *M*, *Gareth and L.* 384
shall the shield of *M* stand among these ? ' ,, 403
M hath tarnish'd the great name of king, ,, 426
M would sully the low state of churl : ,, 427
dumb'd by one from out the hall of *M* *Balin and Balan* 437
M The Cornish King, had heard a wandering voice, *Merlin and V.* 7
(She sat beside the banquet nearest *M*), ,, 18
M was half in heart to hurl his cup ,, 30
Loud laugh'd the graceless *M*. ,, 62
Poor wretch—no friend !—and now by *M* the King ,, 75
Nay—we believe all evil of thy *M*— ,, 93
M her lord had past, the Cornish King, *Last Tournament* 382
heard The hounds of *M*, and felt the goodly hounds ,, 503
Crying aloud, ' Not *M*—not *M*, my soul ! ,, 514
Catlike thro' his own castle steals my *M*, ,, 516
my hatred for my *M* Quicken within me, ,, 519
Let be thy *M*, seeing he is not thine.' ,, 522
bitten, blinded, marr'd me somehow—*M* ? ,, 526
M's way, my soul !—but eat not thou with *M*, ,, 532
Should leave me all alone with *M* and hell. My God, the measure of my hate for *M* ,, 536
M is kindled on thy lips Most gracious ; ,, 561
my *M*'s, by whom all men Are noble, ,, 599
M's way to steal behind one in the dark—For there was *M* : ,, 618
Broken with *M* and hate and solitude, ,, 643
' Vows ! did you keep the vow you made to *M* ,, 655
craven shifts, and long crane legs of *M*— ,, 729
' *M*'s way,' said *M*, and clove him thro' the brain. ,, 754
Mark (verb) no other tree did *m* The level waste, *Mariana* 43
I will stand and *m*. *To J. M. K.* 14
But vague in vapour, hard to *m* ; *Love thou thy land* 62
m me and understand, While I have power to speak. *Enoch Arden* 876
m me ! for your fortunes are to make. *Aylmer's Field* 300
and *m* The landscape winking thro' the heat : *In Mem. lxxxix* 15
Hither, boy—and *m* me well. *Balin and Balan* 502

Mark (verb) (*continued*) Friend, did ye *m* that fountain yesterday *Last Tournament* 286
for some are scared, who *m*, Or wisely or unwisely, *To the Queen ii* 48
M him—he falls ! then another, *Def. of Lucknow* 65
To *m* in many a freeman's home *Freedom* 11
I may *m* The coming year's great good *Prog. of Spring* 92
Mark Antony Prythee, friend, Where is *M A* ? *D. of F. Women* 140
Mark'd wave Returning, while none *m* it, *Sea Dreams* 234
They *m* it with the red cross to the fall, *Princess vi* 41
Day, *m* as with some hideous crime, *In Mem. lxxii* 18
saw him not, or *m* not, if she saw, *Com. of Arthur* 53
for he *m* Kay near him groaning like a wounded bull— *Gareth and L.* 647
and all that *m* him were aghast. ,, 1399
saw me not, or *m* not if you saw ; *Geraint and E.* 870
he *m* his high sweet smile In passing, *Balin and Balan* 160
So *m* not on his right a cavern-chasm ,, 312
He *m* not this, but blind and deaf ,, 318
he *m* The portal of King Pellam's chapel ,, 404
Vivien follow'd, but he *m* her not. *Merlin and V.* 199
Had marr'd his face, and *m* it ere his time. *Lancelot and E.* 247
Who *m* Sir Lancelot where he moved apart, ,, 1349
I *m* Him in the flowering of His fields, *Pass. of Arthur* 10
Thence *m* the black hull moving yet, ,, 448
Market (adj.) The *m* boat is on the stream, *In Mem. cxxi* 13
Market (s) (*See also* **Woman-markets**) Enrich the *m*'s of the golden year. *Golden Year* 46
Every gate is throng'd with suitors, all the *m*'s overflow. *Locksley Hall* 101
and bought Quaint monsters for the *m* *Enoch Arden* 539
Stumbling across the *m* to his death, *Aylmer's Field* 820
Thro' the hubbub of the *m* I steal, *Maud II iv* 68
The changing *m* frets or charms *Ancient Sage* 140
Pillory Wisdom in your *m*'s, *Locksley H., Sixty* 134
Market-cross Not only to the *m-c* were known, *Enoch Arden* 96
Chafferings and chatterings at the *m-c*, *Holy Grail* 558
Market-girl the red cloaks of *m-g*'s, *L. of Shalott ii* 17
Market-noight (night) 'ed my quart ivry *m-n* *N. Farmer, O. S.* 8
Market-place Spiritual in Nature's *m-p*— *Akbar's Dream* 135
Marking *m* how the knighthood mock thee, *Last Tournament* 301
Marksmen their *m* were told of our best, *Def. of Lucknow* 19
Marr'd beat me down and *m* and wasted me, *Tithonus* 19
what follows ! war ; Your own work *m* : *Princess ii* 230
Brake on us at our books, and *m* our peace, ,, *v* 395
Had *m* his face, and mark'd it ere his time. *Lancelot and E.* 247
M as he was, he seem'd the goodliest man ,, 254
However *m*, of more than twice her years, ,, 257
M her friend's aim with pale tranquillity. ,, 733
I cannot brook to see your beauty *m* *Pelleas and E.* 298
M tho' it be with spite and mockery now, ,, 327
vext his heart, And *m* his rest— ,, 399
Man was it who *m* heaven's image in thee thus ? ' *Last Tournament* 64
Scratch'd, bitten, blinded, *m* me somehow— ,, 526
he knew the Prince tho' *m* with dust, *Guinevere* 36
lay many a man *M* by the javelin, *Batt. of Brunanburh* 32
My beauty *m* by you ? by you ! *Happy* 57
Before the feud of Gods had *m* our peace, *Death of Œnone* 32
Marriage (adj.) In sound of funeral or of *m* bells ; *Gardener's D.* 36
And when my *m* morn may fall, *Talking Oak* 285
' I can make no *m* present : *L. of Burleigh* 13
Heaven and earth shall meet Before you hear my *m* vow.' *The Letters* 8
There comes a sound of *m* bells. ,, 48
Demand not thou a *m* lay : In that it is thy *m* day *In Mem., Con.* 2
silent sapphire-spangled *m* ring of the land ? *Maud I iv* 6
Now over, now beneath her *m* ring, *Gareth and E.* 259
We planted both together, happy in our *m* morn, *Happy* 14
that you, that I, would slight our *m* oath : ,, 89
Marriage (s) (*See also* **Border-marriage**) laws of *m* character'd in gold *Isabel* 16
The queen of *m*, a most perfect wife. ,, 28
I have wish'd this *m*, night and day, *Dora* 21
Her slow consent, and *m*, *Enoch Arden* 708
There was an Aylmer-Averill *m* once. *Aylmer's Field* 49

Marriage (s) (*continued*, *m's* are made in Heaven.' *Aylmer's Field* 188
naked *m's* Flash from the bridge, ” 765
in true *m* lies Nor equal, nor unequal : *Princess* vii 302
neither marry, nor are given In *m*, *Merlin and V.* 16
And *m* with a princess of that realm, *Last Tournament* 176
Thy *m* and mine own, that I should suck ” 391
eleventh moon After their *m* lit the lover's Bay, ” 644
Once more—a happier *m* than my own ! *Lover's Tale* iv 28
Grew after *m* to full height and form? Yet *Sisters (E. and E.)* 78
after *m*, that mock-sister there— ” 171
that had sunn'd The morning of our *m*, ” 244
counsel me ; this *m* must not be. *The Flight* 75
Her maiden daughter's *m* ; *To Prin. Beatrice* 10
Love for the maiden, crown'd with *m*, *Vastness* 23
Had ask'd us to their *m*, and to share *The Ring* 430
M will conceal it . . . *Forlorn* 10
Shame and *m*, Shame and *m*, ” 31
M will not hide it, ” 50
Death and *m*, Death and *m*! ” 67
The morning light of happy *m* broke *Death of Œnone* 102
Marriageable prince his heir, when tall and *m*, *Gareth and L.* 102
Marriage-banquet and to share Their *m.-b.* *The Ring* 431
Marriage-bell (*See also* **Marriage** (adj.)) Four merry bells,
four merry *m-b's* *Lover's Tale* iii 21
A long loud crash of rapid *m-b's.* ” 23
the bells, Those *m-b's*, echoing in ear and heart— ” iv 3
Whether they *were* his lady's *m-b's*, ” 11
Sounds happier than the merriest *m-b.* *D. of the Duke of C.* 11
Marriage-day on the dark night of our *m-d* The
great Tragedian, *Sisters (E. and E.)* 232
Marriage-hindering filthy *m-h* Mammon made The
harlot *Aylmer's Field* 374
Marriage-maker For the maids and *m-m's*, *Maud I xx* 35
Marriage-morn And move me to my *m-m*, *Move eastward* 11
but on her *m-m* This birthday, *The Ring* 275
Marriage-pillow To thy widow'd *m-p's*, *Locksley Hall* 82
Marriage-ring (*See also* **Marriage** (adj.)) That ever wore a
Christian *m-r.* *Romney's R.* 36
How bright you keep your *m-r* ! ” 59
Married I *m* late, but I would wish to see *Dora* 12
Who *m*, who was like to be, *Audley Court* 31
' And are you *m* yet, Edward Gray ? ' *Edward Gray* 4
Nevertheless, know you that I am he Who *m*— *Enoch Arden* 859
I *m* her who *m* Philip Ray. ” 860
fur, Sammy, 'e *m* fur luvv. *N. Farmer, N. S.* 32
the King That morn was *m*, *Com. of Arthur* 456
Had *m* Enid, Yniol's only child, *Marr. of Geraint* 4
attracted, won, *M*, made one with, *Lover's Tale* i 134
Harry and I were *m*: *First Quarrel* 5
we were *m* o' Christmas day, *M* among the red
berries, ” 39
kept yours hush'd,' I said, ' when you *m* me ! ” ·68
Meä and thy sister was *m*, *North. Cobbler* 11
Indissolubly *m* like our love ; *De Prof., Two G.* 14
an' he's *m* another wife, *Tomorow* 49
But if I 'ed *m* tha, Robby, *Spinster's S's.* 54
Hed I *m* the Tommies—O Lord, ” 95
and the charm of *m* brows.' *Œnone* 76
Two partners of a *m* life— *In Mem.* xcvii 5
Moon of *m* hearts, Hear me, you ! *The Ring* 3
came of age Or on the day you *m*. ” 78
That, in the misery of my *m* life, ” 136
Then I and she were *m* for a year, ” 283
well, you know I *m* Muriel Erne. ” 376
hovering by the church, where she Was *m* too, ” 479
sang the *m* 'nos' for the solitary ' me.' *Happy* 56
I love you more than when we *m*. *Romney's R.* 157
Then 'e *m* a greät Yerl's darter, *Church-warden, etc.* 20
He *m* an heiress, an orphan *Charity* 13
I had cursed the woman he *m*, ” 24
Marris (Bessy) *See* **Bessy Marris.**
Marrow *M* of mirth and laughter; *Will Water.* 214
Fool to the midmost *m* of his bones, *Pelleas and E.* 258
He withers *m* and mind ; *Ancient Sage* 120

Marry Woo me, and win me, and *m* me, *The Mermaid* 46
' I cannot *m* Dora ; by my life, I will not *m* Dora.' *Dora* 23
where the waters *m*—crost, *The Brook* 81
' he that *marries* her *marries* her name ' *Aylmer's Field* 25
twenty boys and girls should *m* on it, ” 371
learning unto them? They wish'd to *m* ; *Princess* ii 465
But *m* me out of hand : *Grandmother* 52
' *M* you, Willy ! ' said I, ” 53
Thou'll not *m* for munny— *N. Farmer, N. S.* 11
Noä—thou'll *m* for luvv— ” 12
' Doänt thou *m* for munny, ” 20
thy muther says thou wants to *m* the lass, ” 37
if thou *marries* a good un I'll leäve the land to thee. ” 56
But if thou *marries* a bad un, I'll leäve the land to Dick.— ” 58
Ask her to *m* me by and by ? *Window, Letter* 6
That *m* with the virgin heart. *In Mem.* lxxxv 108
but neither *m*, nor are given In marriage, *Merlin and V.* 15
and yet one Should *m*, or all the broad lands *Sister's (E. and E.)* 51
Tha thowt tha would *m* ma, did tha ? *Spinster's S's.* 74
when she comes of age, or when She *marries* ; *The Ring* 290
Marrying could not ever rue his *m* me— *Dora* 146
Driving, hurrying, *m*, burying, *Maud II v* 12
Mars pointed to *M* As he glow'd like a ruddy shield ” *III vi* 13
native to that splendour or in *M*, *Locksley H., Sixty* 187
Marsh (adj.) my blood Crept like *m* drains thro' all my
languid limbs ; *Lover's Tale* ii 53
Marsh (s) wide and wild the waste enormous *m*, *Ode to Memory* 101
Gave him an isle of *m* whereon to build ; And there
he built with wattles from the *m* *Holy Grail* 62
and sliding down the blacken'd *m* Blood-red, ” 473
The wide-wing'd sunset of the misty *m* *Last Tournament* 423
as from men secure Amid their *m'es*, ” 427
That sent the face of all the *m* aloft ” 439
And pausing at a hostel in a *m*, *Lover's Tale* iv 131
light That glimmers on the *m* and on the grave.' *The Ring* 341
steaming *m'es* of the scarlet cranes, *Prog. of Spring* 75
Marshall'd slowly went The *m* Order of their Table
Round, *Lancelot and E.* 1332
Marsh-diver *m-d's*, rather, maid, Shall croak *Princess* iv 123
Marsh-marigold the wild *m-m* shines like fire *May Queen* 31
Mart labour, and the changing *m*, *In Mem.* lxxxvii 23
Marthyr (Martyr) Wid his blessed *M's* an' Saints ; ' *Tomorrow* 58
an' Saints an' *M's* galore, ” 95
Martial Which men delight in, *m* exercise ? *Princess* iii 216
merrily-blowing shrill'd the *m* fife ; ” v 251
And let the mournful *m* music blow ; *Ode on Well.* 11
A *m* song like a trumpet's call ! *Maud I v* 5
Martin Roof-haunting *m's* warm their eggs : *Day-Dm., Sleep P.* 11
The fire shot up, the *m* flew, *Revival* 11
A *M's* summer of his faded love, *Aylmer's Field* 560
plaster'd like a *m's* nest To these old walls— *Holy Grail* 548
Martin-haunted almost to the *m-h* eaves *Aylmer's Field* 163
Martyr (*See also* **Marthyr**) did not all thy *m's* die one
death ? *St. S. Stylites* 50
Charity setting the *m* aflame ; *Vastness* 9
Martyrdom arks with priceless bones of *m*, *Balin and Balan* 110
Martyr-flames *m-f*, nor trenchant swords Can do *Clear-headed friend* 1
Marvel (s) In *m* whence that glory came Upon me, *Arabian Nights* 94
The *m* of the everlasting will, *The Poet* 7
' No *m*, sovereign lady; *D. of F. Women* 97
The *m* dies, and leaves me fool'd and trick'd, *Gareth and L.* 1251
and all Had *m* what the maid might be, *Lancelot and E.* 728
Some little of this *m* he too saw, *Holy Grail* 216
With miracles and *m's* like to these, ” 543
Had drawn him home—what *m* ? *Last Tournament* 405
(what *m*—she could see) ” 547
What *m* my Camilla told me all ? (repeat) *Lover's Tale* i 557, 579
In *m* at that gradual change, ” iii 9
m among us that one should be left alive, *Def. of Lucknow* 78
The *m* of that fair new nature— *Columbus* 79
Half the *m's* of my morning, *Locksley H., Sixty* 75
Marvel (verb) ' I *m* if my still delight *Palace of Art* 190
And *m* what possess'd my brain ; *In Mem.* xiv 16
I would not *m* at either, *Maud I iv* 40
mazed my wit : I *m* what thou art, *Gareth and L.* 1170

Master (s) (*continued*) M whisper'd 'Follow the
Gleam.' — *Merlin and the G.* 33
    My curse upon the *M's* apothegm, — *Romney's R.* 37
    or am I conscious, more Than other *M's*, — " 63
    DEAR *M* in our classic town, — *To Master of B.* 1
    proclaimed His *M* as ' the Sun of Righteousness,' — *Akbar's Dream* 83
Master (*verb*) *m's* Time indeed, and is Eternal, — *In Mem. lxxxv* 65
    break it, when his passion *m's* him. — *Geraint and E.* 43
Master-bowman the *m-b*, he, Would cleave the mark. — *In Mem. lxxxvii* 29
Master-chord the *m-c* Of all I felt and feel. — *Will Water.* 27
Masterdom Contend for loving m. — *In Mem. cii* 8
Master'd Not *m* by some modern term ; — *Love thou thy land* 30
    call them masterpieces : They *m* me. — *Princess i* 146
    Or *m* by the sense of sport, — " *iv* 156
    dream involved and dazzled down And *m*, — " 451
    such A friendship as had *m* Time ; — *In Mem. lxxxv* 64
    Theere ! I ha' *m* them ! — *Spinster's S's.* 95
Mastering M the lawless science of our law, — *Aylmer's Field* 435
Master-passion Brooded one *m-p* evermore, — *Lover's Tale ii* 60
Masterpiece (*See also* **Madonna-masterpieces**) You
scarce can fail to match his *m*.' — *Gardener's D.* 31
    No critic I—would call them *m's* : — *Princess i* 145
Mastery So there were any trial of *m*, — *Gareth and L.* 517
    Paynim bard Had such a *m* of his mystery — *Last Tournament* 327
Mast-head like the mystic fire on a *m-h*, — *Princess iv* 274
Mastodon nature brings not back the *M*, — *The Epic* 36
Mast-throng'd *M-t* beneath her shadowing citadel — *Œnone* 118
Mat an' tother Tom 'ere o' the *m*. — *Spinster's S's.* 94
Match (an equal) ' but thou shalt meet thy *m*.' — *Gareth and L.* 1024
    lighted on Queen Esther, has her *m*.' — *Marr. of Geraint* 731
Match (marriage contract) I have set my heart upon a *m*. — *Dora* 14
    Such a *m* as this ! Impossible, — *Aylmer's Field* 314
    wealth enough was theirs For twenty *m'es*. — " 370
Match (*verb*) scarce can fail to *m* his masterpiece.' — *Gardener's D.* 31
    Will you *m* My Juliet ? — " 171
    May *m* his pains with mine ; — *St. S. Stylites* 139
    And find in loss a gain to *m* ? — *In Mem. i* 6
Match'd M with an aged wife, — *Ulysses* 3
    all thy passions, *m* with mine, — *Locksley Hall* 151
    Were mellow music *m* with him. — *In Mem. lvi* 24
    But either's force was *m* till Yniol's cry, — *Marr. of Geraint* 570
    m with the pains Of the hellish heat — *Despair* 67
    life as *m* with ours Were Sun to spark— — *Ancient Sage* 237
Mate (partner) (*See also* **Co-mate, Maäte**) Whence shall she
take a fitting *m*? — *Kate* 13
    She cannot find a fitting *m*. — " 31
    Your pride is yet no *m* for mine, — *L. C. V. de Vere* 11
    as years Went forward, Mary took another *m* ; — *Dora* 171
    Feeling from her *m* the Deed. — *The Brook* 95
    Raw from the prime, and crushing down his *m* ; — *Princess ii* 121
    That I shall be thy *m* no more, — *In Mem. xli* 20
    With one that was his earliest *m* ; — " *lxiv* 24
    his good *m's* Lying or sitting round him, — *Gareth and L.* 511
    A woman weeping for her murder'd *m* — *Geraint and E.* 522
    hot in haste to join Their luckier *m's*, — " 575
    ' Yet weep not thou, lest, if thy *m* return, — *Last Tournament* 499
    be his *m* hereafter in the heavens — *Guinevere* 637
    Amid thy melancholy *m's* far-seen, — *Lover's Tale i* 489
    he lived with a lot of wild *m's*, — *Rizpah* 29
    They love their *m's*, to whom they sing ; — *The Flight* 65
    likeness to the king Of shadows, thy dark *m*. — *Demeter and P.* 17
    Is he sick your *m* like mine ? — *Happy* 2
Mate (of a ship) Now *m* is blind and captain lame, — *The Voyage* 91
    For since the *m* had seen at early dawn — *Enoch Arden* 631
Mated thou art *m* with a clown, — *Locksley Hall* 47
    M with a squalid savage— — " 177
    ere I *m* with my shambling king, — *Last Tournament* 544
Material could she climb Beyond her own *m* prime ? — *Two Voices* 378
Matin By some wild skylark's *m* song. — *Miller's D.* 40
    And if the *m* songs, that woke The darkness — *In Mem. lxxvi* 9
    ' Here thy boyhood sung Long since its *m* song, — " *cii* 10
Matin-chirp low *m-c* hath grown Full quire, — *Love and Duty* 98
Matins I know At *m* and at evensong, — *Supp. Confessions* 99
Matin-song (*See also* **Matin**) when the first *m-s* hath
waken'd loud — *Ode to Memory* 68

Matin-song (*continued*) And sang aloud the *m-s* of
life. — *Lover's Tale i* 232
Matron Perish'd many a maid and *m*, — *Boädicea* 85
    the *m* saw That hinted love was only wasted bait, — *The Ring* 359
Matted *See also* **Close-matted, Ivy-matted** To purl o'er
m cress and ribbed sand, — *Ode to Memory* 59
Matter (s) No *m* what the sketch might be ; — " 95
    A *m* to be wept with tears of blood ! — *Poland* 14
    ' I cannot make this *m* plain, — *Two Voices* 343
    dealing but with time, And he with *m*, — " 377
    A goose—'twas no great *m*. — *The Goose* 10
    we sat and eat And talk'd old *m's* over ; — *Audley Court* 29
    and so the *m* hung ; (repeat) — *The Brook* 144, 148
    Bound on a *m* he of life and death : — *Sea Dreams* 151
    Thro' her this *m* might be sifted clean.' — *Princess i* 151
    Knowledge is knowledge, and this *m* hangs : — " *iii* 316
    With many thousand *m's* left to do, — " *iv* 458
    lie which is part a truth is a harder *m* to fight. — *Grandmother* 32
    Till you should turn to dearer *m's*, — *To F. D. Maurice* 35
    Is *m* for a flying smile. — *In Mem. lxii* 12
    Tho' rapt in *m's* dark and deep — " *xcvii* 19
    She knows but *m's* of the house, — " 31
    What *m* if I go mad, — *Maud I xi* 6
    Is that a *m* to make me fret ? — " *xiii* 2
    but my belief In all this *m*— — *Com. of Arthur* 184
    ' I have quite foregone All *m's* of this world : — *Balin and Balan* 117
    Sick ? or for any *m* anger'd at me ?' — " 276
    what was once to me Mere *m* of the fancy, — *Merlin and V.* 342
    ' What *m*, so I help him back to life ?' — *Lancelot and E.* 787
    and if he fly us, Small *m* ! let him.' — *Pelleas and E.* 200
    Sir Lancelot told This *m* to the Queen, — *Guinevere* 54
    What *m* ? there are others in the wood. — *Lover's Tale iv* 162
Matter (verb) What can it *m*, Margaret, — *Margaret* 32
    then What *m's* Science unto men, — *In Mem. cxx* 7
    ' What can it *m*, my lass, — *First Quarrel* 59
    We die ? does it *m* when ? — *The Revenge* 88
    Does it *m* so much what I felt ? — *Despair* 4
    Does it *m* how many they saved ? — " 12
    Does it *m* so much whether crown'd — " 76
    That *m's* not : let come what will ; — *The Flight* 103
    this fine Artist' ! Fool, What *m's* ? — *Romney's R.* 125
    would it *m* so much if I came on the street ? — *Charity* 8
Matter-moulded In *m-m* forms of speech, — *In Mem. xcv* 46
Matting conscious of ourselves, Perused the *m* ; — *Princess ii* 68
Mattock-harden'd labour and the *m-h* hand, — *Maud I xviii* 34
Mature (adj.) For now is love *m* in ear.' — *In Mem. lxxxi* 4
    And round her limbs, *m* in womanhood ; — *Pelleas and E.* 73
Mature (verb) *M's* the individual form. — *Love thou thy land* 40
Mat-work made a silken *m-w* for her feet ; — *Holy Grail* 151
Maud of the singular beauty of *M* ; — *Maud I i* 67
    M with her venturous climbings and tumbles — " 69
    M the delight of the village, — " 70
    M with her sweet purse-mouth — " 71
    M the beloved of my mother, — " 72
    It will never be broken by *M*, — " *ii* 2
    Ah *M*, you milkwhite fawn, — " *iv* 57
    M with her exquisite face, — " *v* 12
    M in the light of her youth and her grace, — " 15
    Whom but *M* should I meet? (repeat) — " *vi* 7, 11
    If *M* were all that she seem'd, (repeat) — " 36, 92
    M could be gracious too, no doubt To a lord, — " *x* 28
    M, M, M, M, They were crying and calling. — " *xii* 3
    Where was *M*? in our wood. — " 5
    M is here, here, here In among the lilies. — " 11
    M is not seventeen, But she is tall and stately. — " 15
    O *M* were sure of heaven If lowliness could save her. — " 19
    Where is *M, M, M*? — " 27
    M is as true as *M* is sweet : — " *xiii* 32
    M to him is nothing akin : — " 38
    M has a garden of roses And lilies — " *xiv* 1
    M's own little oak-room (Which *M*, like a precious stone — " 9
    looks Upon *M's* own garden-gate : — " 16
    Make answer, *M* my bliss, — " *xviii* 57
    M made my *M* by that long loving kiss, — " 58
    I trust that I did not talk To gentle *M* in our walk — " *xix* 13

Meadow-crake   the *m-c* Grate her harsh kindred   *Princess iv* 124
Meadow'd   *See* Deep-meadow'd
Meadow-grass   (*See also* Meadow (adj.))   come and go,
   mother, upon the *m-g*,   *May Queen* 33
   Across the silent seeded *m-g*   *Pelleas and E.* 561
Meadow-ledges   *m-l* midway down Hang rich in flowers,   *Œnone* 6
Meadow-sweet   waist-deep in *m-s.*   *The Brook* 118
Meadow-trenches   by the *m-t* blow the faint sweet
   cuckoo-flowers;   *May Queen* 30
Meadowy   soft wind blowing over *m* holms And alders,   *Edwin Morris* 95
   Drew in the dewy *m* morning-breath Of England,   *Enoch Arden* 660
   rivulet that swerves To left and right thro' *m* curves,   *In Mem. c* 15
Meagre   Her pendent hands, and narrow *m* face   *Aylmer's Field* 813
   I was changed to wan And *m,*   *Holy Grail* 572
Meal (ground corn)   Made misty with the floating *m.*   *Miller's D.* 104
   With some pretext of fineness in the *m*   *Enoch Arden* 341
   Who live on milk and *m* and grass;   *To E. Fitzgerald* 13
Meal (repast)   (*See also* Meäl)   sweetest *m* she makes
   On the first-born   *Vision of Sin* 145
   scarce a coin to buy a *m* withal,   *Columbus* 169
Meäl (repast)   an' taäkes their regular *m's.*   *N. Farmer, N. S.* 46
   it's them as niver knaws wheer a *m's* to be 'ad.   " 47
Meal-sacks   The *m-s* on the whiten'd floor,   *Miller's D.* 101
Mealy-mouth'd   nursed by *m-m* philanthropies,   *The Brook* 94
Mean (adj.)   weep for a time so sordid and *m,*   *Maud I v* 17
   since the proud man often is the *m,*   *Marr. of Geraint* 449
   thought it never yet had look'd so *m.*   " 610
   M knights, to whom the moving of my sword   *Holy Grail* 790
   that would sound so *m* That all the dead,   *Romney's R.* 131
Mean (s)   debtless competence, golden *m;*   *Vastness* 24
Mean (verb)   (*See also* Manes, Meän Meäns)   another which
   you had, I *m* of verse   *The Epic* 26
   For they know not what they *m.*   *Vision of Sin* 126
   and *m* Vileness, we are grown so proud—   *Aylmer's Field* 755
   Whether I *m* this day to end myself,   *Lucretius* 146
   'Tears, idle tears, I know not what they *m,*   *Princess iv* 39
   I *m* your grandfather, Annie;   *Grandmother* 23
   my noätions, Sammy, wheerby I *m's* to stick;   *N. Farmer, N. S.* 57
   The spirit does but *m* the breath: *In Mem. lvi* 7
   her own rose-garden, And to linger in it   *Maud I xx* 42
   'What *m's* the tumult in the town?'   *Marr. of Geraint* 259
   They understand: nay; I do not *m* blood: *Geraint and E.* 338
   were all as tame, I *m,* as noble,   *Merlin and V.* 608
   the good king *m's* to blind himself,   " 783
   I do not *m* the force alone—   *Lancelot and E.* 471
   Nay, I *m* nothing: so then, get you gone,   " 776
   What might she *m* by that?   " 834
   He *m's* me I'm sure to be happy   *Rizpah* 76
   I think that you *m* to be kind,   " 81
   show In some fifth Act what this wild Drama *m's.*   *The Play* 4
   only the Devil can tell what he *m's.*   *Riflemen form!* 25
Meän (verb)   she didn't not solidly *m* I wur gawin'   *Owd Roä* 71
Meän'd (meant)   An' I niver knaw'd whot a *m*   *N. Farmer, O. S.* 19
   an' I *m* to 'a stubb'd it at fall, Done it ta-year I *m,*   " 41
Meanest (adj.)   Better to me the *m* weed That blows upon its
   mountain,   *Amphion* 93
   'Thro' slander, *m* spawn of Hell—   *The Letters* 33
   put on thy worst and *m* dress And ride with me.'   *Marr. of Geraint* 130
   Put on your worst and *m* dress,'   " 848
Meanest (s)   *m* having power upon the highest,   *Merlin and V.* 195
Meaning (part.)   life He gave me, *m* to be rid of it.   *Geraint and E.* 853
   m by it To keep the tists low and pretenders back,   *Merlin and V.* 591
   (*M* the print that you gave us,   *In the Child. Hosp.* 51
Meaning (s)   So was their *m* to her words.   *The Poet* 53
   Like a tale of little *m* tho' the words   *Lotos-Eaters, C. S.* 119
   O take the *m,* Lord: *St. S. Stylites* 21
   A *m* suited to his mind.   *Day-Dm., Moral* 12
   To search a *m* for the song,   " *L'Envoi* 35
   And, if you find a *m* there,   " *Ep.* 2
   Nor the *m* can divine,   *L. of Burleigh* 54
   That was nothing to her: No *m* there: *Enoch Arden* 499
   Being other—since we learnt our *m* here,   *Princess iii* 222
   there's a downright honest *m* in her;   " *v* 280
   Her secret *m* in her deeds,   *In Mem. lv* 10
   I will not ask your *m* in it: *Geraint and E.* 743

Meaning (s) (*continued*)   this, indeed, her voice And *m,*   *To the Queen ii* 20
   Now guess'd a hidden *m* in his arms,   *Lancelot and E.* 17
   He thinking that he read her *m* there,   " 86
   That have no *m* half a league away: *Holy Grail* 556
   while they rode, the *m* in his eyes,   *Pelleas and E.* 109
   Her words did of their *m* borrow sound,   *Lover's Tale i* 568
   until The *m* of the letters shot into My brain;   " *ii* 8
   He knew the *m* of the whisper now,   " *iv* 43
   to seek The *m's* ambush'd   *Tiresias* 5
Meaningless   drown'd in the deeps of a *m* Past?   *Vastness* 34
Meanness   sense Of *m* in her unresisting life.   *Aylmer's Field* 801
Means   Or m to pay the voice who best could tell   *Enoch Arden* 266
   The first, a gentleman of broken *m*   *Princess i* 53
   spirit of murder works in the very *m* of life,   *Maud I i* 40
   following with a costrel bore The *m* of goodly
   welcome,   *Marr. of Geraint* 387
   Because my *m* were somewhat broken into   " 455
   Being but ampler *m* to serve mankind,   *Merlin and V.* 489
   should strike upon a sudden *m* To dig,   " 659
Meäns   *m's* fur to maäke 'is owd aäge   *Owd Roä* 3
   if iver tha *m's* to git 'igher,   *Church-warden, etc.* 45
Meant   (*See also* Meän'd)   We met, but only *m* to part.   *The Letters* 12
   He never *m* us anything but good.   *Enoch Arden* 887
   you find That you *m* nothing—us indeed you
   know That you *m* nothing.   *Aylmer's Field* 313
   I should find he *m* me well;   *Sea Dreams* 153
   he *m,* he said he *m,* Perhaps he *m,* or partly *m,*
   you well.'   " 178
   'Ay, but I *m* not thee; I *m* not her,   *Lucretius* 85
   and *m* Surely to lead my Memmius in a train   " 118
   M? I *m*? I have fogotten what I *m*:   " 121
   That she but *m* to win him back,   " 279
   alien lips, And knew not what they *m*;   *Princess iv* 120
   And vacant chaff well *m* for grain.   *In Mem. vi* 4
   She *m* to weave me a snare Of some coquettish deceit,   *Maud I vi* 25
   Knew that the death-white curtain *m* but sleep,   " *xiv* 37
   Ask'd yet once more what *m* was the hubbub here?   *Marr. of Geraint* 264
   To learn what Arthur *m* by courtesy;   *Balin and Balan* 158
   m to eat her up in that wild wood   *Merlin and V.* 260
   m to stamp him with her master's mark;   " 759
   m once more perchance to tourney in it.   *Lancelot and E.* 810
   rough sickness *m,* but what this *m*   " 888
   (He *m* to break the passion in her)   " 1079
   But when I thought he *m* To crush me,   *Holy Grail* 415
   But heaven had *m* it for a sunny one: " 706
   spake the King: I knew not all he *m.*   " 920
   'The simple, fearful child *M* nothing,   *Guinevere* 370
   Our general mother *m* for me alone,   *Lover's Tale i* 245
   and *m* to rest an hour;   " *iv* 133
   I didn't know well what I *m,*   *First Quarrel* 83
   If a curse *m* ought, I would curse   *Despair* 64
   m us to be mightier by and by,   *Locksley H., Sixty* 209
   Those gray heads, What *m* they   *Demeter and P.* 130
   Muriel claim'd and open'd what I *m* For Miriam,   *The Ring* 242
   And I *m* to make *you* jealous.   *Happy* 67
   you knew that he *m* to betray me—   *Charity* 12
Measure (s)   (*See also* Slow-measure)   hearts of salient
   springs Keep *m*   *Adeline* 27
   I crouch'd on one that rose Twenty by *m*;   *St. S. Stylites* 89
   fresh to men, And wanton without *m*;   *Amphion* 58
   Tread a *m* on the stones,   *Vision of Sin* 180
   As meted by his *m* of himself,   *Aylmer's Field* 316
   The highest is the *m* of the man,   *Princess ii* 157
   rich Virgilian rustic *m* Of Lari Maxume,   *The Daisy* 75
   draw The deepest *m* from the chords: *In Mem. xlviii* 12
   by the *m* of my grief I leave thy greatness   " *lxxv* 3
   God, the *m* of my hate for Mark Is as the *m*   *Last Tournament* 537
   how should Earthly *m* mete The Heavenly-
   unmeasured   *Lover's Tale i* 473
   Wielder of the stateliest *m* ever moulded   *To Virgil* 39
Measure (verb)   *m* time by yon slow light,   *St. S. Stylites* 94
   in the flame that *m's* Time!   *Akbar's D., Hymn* 8
Measured   How many *m* words adore The full-flowing
   harmony   *Eleänore* 45
   With *m* footfall firm and mild,   *Two Voices* 413

Measured (*continued*) An echo from a *m* strain, *Miller's D.* 66
hear These *m* words, my work of yestermorn. *Golden Year* 21
A use in *m* language lies ; *In Mem.* v 6
The *m* pulse of racing oars Among the willows ; „ *lxxxvii* 10
Run out your *m* arcs, and lead The closing cycle „ *cv* 27
three paces *m* from the mound, *Princess* v 1
Measureless honey of poison-flowers and all the *m* ill. *Maud* I iv 56
For years, a *m* ill, „ *II ii* 49
Measuring Æonian music *m* out The steps *In Mem. xcv* 41
Oft in mid-banquet *m* with his eyes *Pelleas and E.* 150
Meat (*See also* **Meät**) Yea ev'n of wretched *m* and drink, *Maud* I xv 8
In her foul den, there at their *m* would growl, *Com. of Arthur* 30
King Made feast for, saying, as they sat at *m*, „ 247
hire thyself to serve for *m's* and drinks *Gareth and L.* 153
grant me to serve For *m* and drink „ 445
Kay, The master of the *m's* and drinks, „ 451
No mellow master of the *m's* and drinks ! „ 560
mighty thro' thy *m's* and drinks (repeat) „ 650, 862
except, belike, To garnish *m's* with ? „ 1070
Where bread and baken *m's* and good red wine „ 1190
Sir Lancelot, is hard by, with *m's* and drinks „ 1276
sit with knife in *m* and wine in horn ! *Merlin and V.* 694
with *m's* and vintage of their best *Lancelot and E.* 266
where the *m's* became As wormwood, „ 743
m, Wine, wine,—and I will love thee *Last Tournament* 719
had comforted the blood With *m's* and wines, „ 725
Had whatsoever *m* he long'd for served *Guinevere* 265
our lover seldom spoke, Scarce touch'd the *m's* ; *Lover's Tale* iv 226
Or mine to give him, *Voice spake, etc.* 8
Meät or a mossel o' *m* when it beänt too dear, *Spinster's S's.* 109
Mechanic (adj.) The long *m* pacings to and fro, *Love and Duty* 17
The sad *m* exercise, *In Mem.* v 7
A disease, a hard *m* ghost That never came from on high, *Maud* II ii 34
Mechanic (s) see the raw *m's* bloody thumbs *Walk. to the Mail* 75
Meddle and there was none to *m* with it. *Gareth and L.* 1012
Meddling Some *m* rogue has tamper'd with him— *Lancelot and E.* 128
Medicine glass with little Margaret's *m* in it ; *Sea Dreams* 142
blush and smile, a *m* in themselves *Princess* vii 62
' The miserable have no *m* But only Hope ! ' *Romney's R.* 149
Meditated while I *m* A wind arose and rush'd *Princess* i 96
Meditating long and bitterly *m*, *Boädicea* 35
Meditation In a silent *m*, *Eleänore* 105
Meditative With *m* grunts of much content, *Walk. to the Mail* 87
Mediterranean About the soft *M* shores, *Sir J. Oldcastle* 30
Medley This *were* a *m* ! we should have him *Princess, Pro.* 237
Meeäk (meek) I kep' mysen *m* as a lamb, *Church-warden, etc.* 41
Meeätin' (meeting) An' when we coom'd into *M*, *North. Cobbler* 53
Meed claiming each This *m* of fairest. *Œnone* 87
The *m* of saints, the white robe and the palm. *St. S. Stylites* 20
this was my *m* for all. *Princess* iv 302
Meek (adj.) (*See also* **Maiden-meek, Meeäk, Mock-meek**)
With lips depress'd as he were *m*, *A Character* 25
' His lips are very mild and *m* : *Two Voices* 250
And Dora promised, being *m*. *Dora* 46
maiden of our century, yet most *m* ; *The Brook* 68
Him, to her *m* and modest bosom prest In agony, *Aylmer's Field* 416
thought myself long-suffering, *m*, „ 753
m Seem'd the full lips, and mild the luminous eyes, *Princess* vii 225
why come you so cruelly *m*, *Maud* I iii 1
Tut : he was tame and *m* enow with me, *Gareth and L.* 718
and *m* withal As any of Arthur's best, „ 1168
O pale, pale face so sweet and *m*, *Oriana* 66
O somewhere, *m*, unconscious dove, *In Mem.* vi 25
But answer'd in low voice, her *m* head yet Drooping, *Geraint and E.* 640
But o'er her *m* eyes came a happy mist „ 769
Yet not so misty were her *m* blue eyes, „ 772
And there, poor cousin, with your *m* blue eyes, „ 841
Ye know right well, how *m* soe'er he seem, *Lancelot and E.* 155
but the *m* maid Sweetly forbore him ever, „ 855
So Arthur bad the *m* Sir Percivale „ 1264
M maidens, from the voices crying " shame." *Guinevere* 672
an' 'e says to 'im, *m* as a mouse, *Village Wife* 63
our darling, our *m* little maid *In the Child. Hosp.* 28
Except his own *m* daughter yield her life, *The Flight* 28
but set no *m* ones in their place ; *Locksley H., Sixty* 133

Meek (adj.) (*continued*) patient, and prayerful, *m*, Pale-blooded, *Last Tournament* 607
who am not *m*, Pale-blooded, prayerful. „ 610
Meek (s) ' The *m* shall inherit the earth ' *The Dreamer* 2
The Reign of the *M* upon earth, „ 25
Meeker *M* than any child to a rough nurse, *Lancelot and E.* 857
Some *m* pupil you must find, *L. C. V. de Vere* 18
Meekness Shaped her heart with woman's *m* *L. of Burleigh* 71
Meet (adj.) *M* is it changes should control Our being, *Love thou thy land* 41
' It is not *m*, Sir King, to leave thee thus, *M. d'Arthur* 40
scarce *m* For troops of devils, *St. S. Stylites* 3
I am whole, and clean, and *m* for Heaven. „ 213
pay *M* adoration to my household gods, *Ulysses* 42
should pause, as is most *m* for all ? *Tithonus* 31
M for the reverence of the hearth, *Aylmer's Field* 333
surely rest is *m* : ' They rest,' we said, *In Mem. xxx* 18
Becoming as is *m* and fit A link among the days, „ *xl* 14
nor *m* To fight for gentle damsel, *Gareth and L.* 1176
fare is coarse, And only *m* for mowers ; ' *Geraint and E.* 209
M is it the good King be not deceived. *Balin and Balan* 533
' It is not *m*, Sir King, to leave thee thus, *Pass. of Arthur* 207
Meet (verb) That clothe the wold and the sky ; *L. of Shalott* i 3
For those two likes might *m* and touch. *Two Voices* 357
I could *m* with her The Abominable, *Œnone* 223
blessings on his whole life long, until he *m* me there ! *May Queen, Con.* 14
token when the night and morning *m* : „ 22
Counts nothing that she *m's* with base, *On a Mourner* 4
She heard the torrents *m*. *Of old sat Freedom* 4
In whom should *m* the offices of all, *M. d'Arthur* 125
Sets out, and *m's* a friend who hails him, *Walk. to the Mail* 42
robed and crown'd, To *m* her lord, *Godiva* 78
airs of heaven That often *m* me here. *Sir Galahad* 64
sometimes two would *m* in one, *Will Water.* 95
broad seas swell'd to *m* the keel, *The Voyage* 13
To *m* and greet her on her way ; *Beggar Maid* 6
' Cold altar, Heaven and earth shall *m* *The Letters* 7
year Roll'd itself round again to *m* the day When Enoch *Enoch Arden* 822
Stands Philip's farm where brook and river *m*. *The Brook* 38
Katie never ran : she moved To *m* me, „ 88
Abase those eyes that ever loved to *m* Star-sisters *Princess* ii 427
Not yet endured to *m* her opening eyes, „ iv 195
I fear'd To *m* a cold ' We thank you, „ 328
The next, like fire he *m's* the foe, „ 583
to *m* us lightly pranced Three captains out ; „ v 254
then he drew Her robe to *m* his lips, „ vi 156
turn'd half-round to Psyche as she sprang To *m* it, „ 210
To *m* her Graces, where they deck'd her „ vii 168
Who lets once more in peace the nations *m*, *Ode Inter. Exhib.* 4
To *m* the sun and sunny waters, *The Daisy* 11
In middle ocean *m's* the surging shock, *Will* 8
and Spirit with Spirit can *m*— *High. Pantheism* 11
Two little hands that *m*, (repeat) *Window, The Answer* 1, 4
In which we two were wont to *m*, *In Mem.* viii 10
I shall know him when we *m* : „ xlvii 8
And envying all that *m* him there. „ lx 8
I seem to *m* their least desire, „ lxxxiv 17
O let me where the passions *m*, „ lxxxviii 4
And *m's* the year, and gives and takes „ cxvi 3
And unto meeting when we *m*, „ cxvii 7
they *m* thy look And brighten like the star „ Con. 30
advance To *m* and greet a whiter sun ; „ 78
Whom but Maud should I *m* ? (repeat) *Maud* I vi 7, 11
She remembers it now we *m*. „ 88
To the woody hollows in which we *m* „ xxii 43
When I was wont to *m* her In the silent woody places „ II iv 5
In a moment we shall *m* ; „ 39
And the faces that one *m's*, „ 93
Return, and *m*, and hold him from our eyes, *Gareth and L.* 429
' but thou shalt *m* thy match.' „ 1024
one might *m* a mightier than himself ; „ 1350
pray That we may *m* the horsemen of Earl Doorm, *Geraint and E.* 492
shadow from the counter door Sir Lancelot as to *m* her, *Balin and Balan* 247

Meet (verb) (*continued*) *m's* And dallies with him in
  the Mouth of Hell.' | *Balin and Balan* 614
Moving to *m* him in the castle court ; | *Lancelot and E.* 175
strike spur, suddenly move, *M* in the midst, | „ 457
we two May *m* at court hereafter : | „ 698
' I never loved him : an I *m* with him, | „ 1068
I go in state to court, to *m* the Queen. | „ 1124
flash'd, as it were, Diamonds to *m* them, | „ 1237
let us *m* The morrow morn once more | *Holy Grail* 322
she rose Opening her arms to *m* me, | „ 395
I will be thine Arthur when we *m*.' | *Pelleas and E.* 47
if thou tarry we shall *m* again, And if we *m* again,
  some evil chance | *Guinevere* 89
to *m* And part for ever. | „ 97
that I march to *m* my doom. | „ 450
We two may *m* before high God, | „ 564
and *m* myself Death, or I know not what mysterious
  doom. | „ 575
In whom should *m* the offices of all, | *Pass. of Arthur* 293
never more will *m* The sight that throbs | *Lover's Tale i* 32
But I cannot *m* them here, | *The Revenge* 5
My friend should *m* me somewhere | *Sir J. Oldcastle* 1
My friend should *m* me here. Here is the copse, | „ 126
The city deck'd herself To *m* me, | *Columbus* 10
roll'd To *m* me long-arm'd vines with grapes | *To E. Fitzgerald* 27
they *m* And kindle generous purpose, | *Tiresias* 127
their songs, that *m* The morning with such music, | *The Flight* 65
I bide no more, I *m* my fate, | „ 95
' An' whin will ye *m* me agin ? ' | *Tomorrow* 15
I'll *m* you agin tomorra,' says he, | „ 16
shure thin ye'll *m* me tomorra ? ' | „ 18
an' shure he'll *m* me agin. | „ 52
That ye'll *m* your paärints agin | „ 57
' He said he would *m* me tomorra ! ' | „ 80
one of those I fain would *m* again, | *Pro. to Gen. Hamley* 22
and I may *m* him soon ; | *To Marq. of Dufferin* 48
She always came to *m* me carrying you, | *The Ring* 352
She came no more to *m* me, | „ 385
A clamorous cuckoo stoops to *m* her hand ; | *Prog. of Spring* 45
that soul where man and woman *m*, | *On one who effec. E. M.* 2
hear The clash of tides that *m* in narrow
  seas.— | *Akbar's Dream* 58
Ready, be ready to *m* the storm ! (repeat) | *Riflemen form !* 13, 27
All at all points thou canst not *m*, | *Poets and Critics* 7

Meeting (part.) Two strangers *m* at a festival ; | *Circumstance* 3
A stranger *m* them had surely thought | *Geraint and E.* 34
guests broke in upon him with *m* hands | *Lover's Tale iv* 238

Meeting (s) (*See also* **Meeätin'**) might I tell of *m's*, of
  farewells— | *Gardener's D.* 251
A perilous *m* under the tall pines | *Aylmer's Field* 414
And oft at Bible *m's*, o'er the rest Arising, | *Sea Dreams* 194
A *m* somewhere, love with love, | *In Mem. lxxxv* 99
Their *m's* made December June | „ *xcvii* 11
And unto me when we meet, | „ *cxvii* 7
For the *m* of the morrow, | *Maud II iv* 28
Have I mislearnt our place of *m* ?) | *Sir J. Oldcastle* 153
Here we met, our latest *m*— | *Locksley H., Sixty* 177

Meg tavern-catch Of Moll and *M*, | *Princess iv* 158

Melancholy (adj.) (*See also* **Humorous-melancholy**)
Her *m* eyes divine, | *Mariana in the S.* 19
The mild-eyed *m* Lotos-eaters came. | *Lotos-Eaters* 27
I used to walk This Terrace—morbid, *m* ; | *The Ring* 168

Melancholy (s) Your *m* sweet and frail | *Margaret* 7
To the influence of mild-minded *m* ; | *Lotos-Eaters, C. S.* 64
And lived a life of silent *m*. | *Enoch Arden* 260
Settled a gentle cloud of *m* ; | *Princess iv* 570
To beguile her *m* ; | *Maud I xx* 3
that hour When the lone hern forgets his *m*, | *Gareth and L.* 1185
Then fell on Merlin a great *m* ; | *Merlin and V.* 189
For these have broken up my *m*.' | „ 267
across him came a cloud Of *m* severe, | *Lancelot and E.* 325

Melissa *M*, with her hand upon the lock, | *Princess ii* 322
' Ah—*M*—you ! You heard us ? ' and *M*, | „ 330
' Ah, fear me not ' Replied *M* ; | „ 343
came *M* hitting all we saw with shafts | „ 468

Melissa (*continued*) approach'd *M*, tinged with wan from
  lack of sleep, | *Princess iii* 25
' What pardon, sweet *M*, for a blush ? ' | „ 66
M shook her doubtful curls, | „ 75
Shame might befall *M*, knowing, | „ 148
Cyril kept With Psyche, with *M* Florian, | „ 355
The lilylike *M* droop'd her brows ; | „ *iv* 161
M clamour'd ' Flee the death ;' | „ 166
last of all, *M* : trust me, Sir, I pitied her. | „ 230
white shoulder shaken with her sobs, *M* knelt ; | „ 290
Rise ! ' and stoop'd to updrag *M* : | „ 367
with her oft, *M* came ; for Blanche had gone, | „ *vii* 56

Mellay here and everywhere He rode the *m*, | „ *v* 502

Meller (**mellow**) Fine an' *m* 'e mun be by this, | *North. Cobbler* 101

Mellow (adj.) (*See also* **Meller, Over-mellow**) With *m*
  preludes, ' We are free.' | *The winds, etc.* 4
gleams of *m* light Float by you on the verge of night. | *Margaret* 30
The *m* ouzel fluted in the elm ; | *Gardener's D.* 94
a Tudor-chimnied bulk Of *m* brickwork on an isle of
  bowers. | *Edwin Morris* 12
Low thunders bring the *m* rain, | *Talking Oak* 279
Many a night I saw the Pleiads, rising thro' the
  m shade, | *Locksley Hall* 9
m moons and happy skies, | „ 159
Till *m* Death, like some late quest, | *Will Water.* 239
Then methought I heard a *m* sound, | *Vision of Sin* 14
And *m* metres more than cent for cent ; | *The Brook* 5
lapt in wreaths of glowworm light The *m* breaker
  murmur'd Ida. | *Princess iv* 436
Were *m* music match'd with him. | *In Mem. lvi* 24
No *m* master of the meats and drinks ! | *Gareth and L.* 560
Won by the *m* voice before she look'd, | *Lancelot and E.* 244
Here too, all hush'd below the *m* moon, | *Pelleas and E.* 424
I heard that voice,—as *m* and deep | *The Wreck* 52
M moon of heaven, Bright in blue, | *The Ring* 1
The *m* lin-lan-lone of evening bells | *Far—far—away* 5

Mellow (verb) but as his brain Began to *m*, | *Princess i* 180

Mellow-deep Drawn from each other *m-d* ; | *Eleänore* 67

Mellow'd (adj.) The *m* reflex of a winter moon ; | *Isabel* 29
then perhaps The *m* murmur of the people's
  praise | *Ded. Poem Prin. Alice* 7

Mellow'd (verb) And there he *m* all his heart with ale, | *The Brook* 155

Mellower All day the wind breathes low with *m*
  tone : | *Lotos-Eaters, C. S.* 102
There cannot come a *m* change, | *In Mem. lxxxi* 3

Mellowing (*See also* **Hourly-mellowing, Slowly-mellowing**)
into mournful twilight *m*, dwelt Full on the child ; | *Princess vi* 191
And tumbled half the mars ! | *Im Mem. lxxxix* 20

Mellowness Touch'd by thy spirit's *m*, | *Eleänore* 103

Melodious Ever brightening With a low *m* thunder ; | *Poet's Mind* 27
lowly bent With *m* airs lovelorn, | *Adeline* 55
whose sweet breath Preluded those *m* bursts | *D. of F. Women* 6
rolling thro' the court A long *m* thunder | *Princess ii* 476
shadow'd hint confuse A life that leads *m* days. | *In Mem. xxxiii* 8
like a golden mist Charm'd amid eddies of *m* airs, | *Lover's Tale i* 450

Melodist mystic *m* Who all but lost himself | *Akbar's Dream* 92

Melody ancient *m* Of an inward agony, | *Claribel* 6
Filling with light And vagrant *melodies* | *The Poet* 17
They were modulated so To an unheard *m*, | *Eleänore* 64
from Memnon, drew Rivers of *melodies*. | *Palace of Art* 172
Plenty corrupts the *m* That made thee famous | *The Blackbird* 15
Wheeling with precipitate paces To the *m*, | *Vision of Sin* 38
nerve-dissolving *m* Flutter'd headlong | „ 44
And chanted a *m* loud and sweet, | *Poet's Song* 6
The herald *melodies* of spring, | *In Mem. xxxviii* 6
M on branch, and *m* in mid air. | *Gareth and L.* 183
And talk and minstrel *m* entertain'd. | *Lancelot and E.* 267
half-moulder'd chords To some old *m*, | *Lover's Tale i* 20
It makes a constant bubbling *m* That drowns | „ 532
Moving to *m*, Floated The Gleam. | *Merlin and the G.* 22
Blind to the magic, And deaf to the *m*, | „ 27
landskip darken'd, The *m* deaden'd, | „ 32
Then to the *m*, Over a wilderness Gliding, | „ 35
Then, with a *m* Stronger and statelier, | „ 62
slowly moving again to a *m* Yearningly tender, | „ 90

Melody (*continued*) Gleam flying onward, Wed to the *m*,	*Merlin and the G.* 97
All her *melodies*, All her harmonies	*To Master of B.* 11
Melon A raiser of huge *m's* and of pine,	*Princess*, Con. 87
m lay like a little sun on the tawny sand,	*V. of Maeldune* 57
The mango spurn the *m* at his foot ?	*Akbar's Dream* 39
Melpomene And my *M* replies,	*In Mem.* xxxvii 9
Melt To the earth—until the ice would *m*	*Supp. Confessions* 81
I wish the snow would *m*	*May Queen, N. Y's. E.* 15
And from it *m* the dews of Paradise	*St. S. Stylites* 210
light shall slowly *m* In many streams	*Golden Year* 33
I will *m* this marble into wax	*Princess* iii 73
' embrace me, come, Quick while I *m* ;	,, vi 286
M's mist-like into this bright hour,	,, vii 355
M into stars for the land's desire !	*W. to Alexandra* 21
And *m* the waxen hearts of men.'	*In Mem.* xxi 8
They *m* like mist, the solid lands,	,, cxxiii 7
A warmth within the breast would *m*	,, cxxiv 13
A purer sapphire *m's* into the sea.	*Maud I* xviii 52
Give me three days to *m* her fancy,	*Pelleas and E.* 356
And *m's* within her hand—her hand is hot	*Last Tournament* 414
as a cloud *M's* into Heaven.	*Ancient Sage* 234
frost-bead *m's* upon her golden hair ;	*Prog. of Spring* 10
Melted (*See also* **Half-melted**) rites and forms before his burning eyes *M* like snow.	*The Poet* 40
The twilight *m* into morn.	*Day-Dm., Depart.* 16
Amazed and *m* all who listen'd to it :	*Enoch Arden* 649
Which in Florian's fancy as she hung,	*Princess* iv 370
all his force Is *m* into mere effeminacy ?	*Marr. of Geraint* 107
Till he *m* like a cloud in the silent summer heaven ;	*The Revenge* 14
Sank from their thrones, and *m* into tears.	*Columbus* 15
Melteth *m* in the source Of these sad tears,	*Lover's Tale* i 783
Melting *m* the mighty hearts Of captains	*D. of F. Women* 175
Member (**M.P.**) (*See also* **County Member**) The Tory *m's* elder son,	*Princess*, Con. 50
Memmian Beyond the *M* naphtha-pits,	*Alexander* 4
Memmius Surely to lead my *M* in a train	*Lucretius* 119
Memnon from *M*, drew Rivers of melodies.	*Palace of Art* 171
M smitten with the morning Sun.'	*Princess* iii 116
Memorial (adj.) I seem'd to move in old *m* tilts,	,, v 479
Their names, Graven on *m* columns,	*Tiresias* 124
Memorial (s) I stored it full of rich *m* :	*Princess* v 391
My sole *m* Of Edith—no, the other,—	*Sisters (E. and E.)* 107
These hard *m's* of our truth to Spain	*Columbus* 196
Raise a stately *m*,	*On Jub. Q. Victoria* 44
Memory Thou dewy dawn of *m*. (repeat)	*Ode to Memory* 7, 45, 124
Unto mine inner eye, Divinest *M* !	,, 50
Well hast thou done, great artist *M*,	,, 80
Makes thy *m* confused :	*A Dirge* 45
In painting some dead friend from *m* ?	*Wan Sculptor* 4
' The *m* of the wither'd leaf	*Two Voices* 112
Because my *m* is so cold,	,, 341
The haunts of *m* echo not.	,, 369
must I be Incompetent of *m* : ' For *m* dealing but with time,	,, 375
His *m* scarce can make me sad.	*Miller's D.* 16
foundation-stones were laid Since my first *m* ? '	*Palace of Art* 236
put strange *memories* in my head.	*L. C. V. de Vere* 26
To muse and brood and live again in *m*,	*Lotos-Eaters, C. S.* 65
Dear is the *m* of our wedded lives,	,, 69
No *m* labours longer from the deep	*D. of F. Women* 273
His *m* long will live alone In all our hearts,	*To J. S.* 49
M standing near Cast down her eyes,	,, 53
Come Hope and *M*, spouse and bride,	*On a Mourner* 23
Sir Bedivere Revolving many *memories*,	*M. d'Arthur* 270
So blunt in *m*, so old at heart,	*Gardener's D.* 53
And sure this orbit of the *m* folds	,, 74
while I mused came *M* with sad eyes,	,, 243
Now the most blessed *m* of mine age.	,, 279
he will learn to slight His father's *m* ;	*Dora* 154
For calmer hours to *M's* darkest hold,	*Love and Duty* 90
Drug thy *memories*, lest thou learn it,	*Locksley Hall* 77
a thousand *memories* roll upon him,	*Enoch Arden* 724
Old, and a mine of *memories*—	*Aylmer's Field* 10
left their *memories* a world's curse—	,, 796

Memory (*continued*) From out a common vein of *m* Sweet household talk,	*Princess* ii 314
Rose from the distance on her *m*,	,, vi 112
And out of *memories* of her kindlier days,	,, vii 106
brawling *memories* all too free	*Ode on Well.* 248
From whence clear *m* may begin,	*In Mem.* xlv 10
To count their *memories* half divine ;	,, xc 12
I hear a wind Of *m* murmuring the past.	,, xcii 8
The *m* like a cloudless air,	,, xciv 11
Or ev'n for intellect to reach Thro' *m*	,, xcv 48
Memories of bridal, or of birth,	,, xcix 15
Some gracious *m* of my friend ;	,, c 4
year by year our *m* fades From all the circle of the hills.	,, ci 23
In lands where not a *m* strays,	,, civ 10
To whom a thousand *memories* call,	,, cxi 10
My drooping *m* will not shun The foaming grape	,, Con. 79
Mix not *m* with doubt,	*Maud II* iv 57
THESE to His *M*—since he held them dear,	*Ded. of Idylls* 1
m of that cognizance on shield Weighted	*Balin and Balan* 224
m of that token on the shield Relax'd his hold :	,, 369
No *m* in me lives ;	*Holy Grail* 535
Vext her with plaintive *memories* of the child :	*Last Tournament* 29
Then ran across her *m* the strange rhyme	,, 131
sweet *memories* Of Tristram in that year he was away.'	,, 579
O sweeter than all *memories* of thee,	,, 585
pine and waste in those sweet *memories*.	,, 598
Nor let me shame my father's *m*,	*Guinevere* 318
Her *m* from old habit of the mind Went slipping back	,, 379
Sir Bedivere Revolving many *memories*,	*Pass. of Arthur* 438
The *m's* vision hath a keener edge.	*Lover's Tale* i 36
garner'd up Into the granaries of *m*—	,, 129
Doth question'd *m* answer not,	,, 277
Which are as gems set in my *m*,	,, 291
A land of promise, a land of *m*,	,, 333
milk And honey of delicious *memories* !	,, 335
my name has been A hallow'd *m* like the names of old, A center'd, glory-circled *m*,	,, 445
Ye cannot shape Fancy so fair as is this *m*.	,, 548
At last she sought out *M*, and they trod	,, 820
And *M* fed the soul of Love with tears.	,, 822
Within the magic cirque of *m*,	,, ii 159
Which yet retains a *m* of its youth,	*Sisters (E. and E.)* 66
Unvenerable will thy *m* be While men	*Tiresias* 132
My *memories* of his briefer day	*To Marq. of Dufferin* 15
break thro' clouded *memories* once again	*Demeter and P.* 10
A virgin victim to his *m*,	*The Ring* 221
Or is it some half *m* of a dream ?	,, 422
Is *m* with your Marian gone to rest,	*To Mary Boyle* 13
Menace When was age so cramm'd with *m* ?	*Locksley H., Sixty* 108
Menacing beat back The *m* poison of intolerant priests,	*Akbar's Dream* 165
Men-at-arms *m-a-a*, A score with pointed lances,	*Balin and Balan* 400
Men-children gauds *m-c* swarm to see.	*To W. C. Macready* 11
Mend (*See also* **Clump**) How *m* the dwellings, of the poor ;	*To F. D. Maurice* 38
Mended (adj.) Our *m* fortunes and a Prince's bride :	*Marr. of Geraint* 718
Mended (verb) Robins—a niver *m* a fence :	*N. Farmer, O. S.* 50
Mene Wrote ' *M*, *m*,' and divided quite	*Palace of Art* 227
Menial bad his *m's* bear him from the door,	*Lover's Tale* iv 260
Menœceus *M*, thou hast eyes, and I can hear	*Tiresias* 90
Mental Wanting the *m* range ;	*Merlin and V.* 827
Mention seal'd book, all *m* of the ring,	*The Ring* 123
Mention'd bill I *m* half an hour ago ? '	*Day-Dm., Revival* 28
when the day, that Enoch *m*, came,	*Enoch Arden* 239
Men-tommies Ye be wuss nor the *m-t*,	*Spinster's S's.* 93
Merchant As tho' they brought but *m's* bales,	*In Mem.* xiii 19
market frets or charms The *m's* hope no more ;	*Ancient Sage* 141
Merchantman served a year On board a *m*,	*Enoch Arden* 53
Mercian Mighty the *M*, Hard was his hand-play,	*Batt. of Brunanburh* 43
Merciful were any bounteous, *m*,	*Gareth and L.* 423
Merciless big voice, big chest, big *m* hands !	*In the Child. Hosp.* 4
Mercury as it were with *M's* ankle-wing,	*Lucretius* 201
M On such a morning would have flung himself	*Lover's Tale* i 300

Mercy (*See also* **Marcy**) O God ! my God ! have
     m now.   *Supp. Confessions* 1
     God in his *m* lend her grace.   *L. of Shalott* iv 53
     He taught me all the *m*,   *May Queen, Con.* 17
     Have *m*, Lord, and take away my sin.   *St. S. Stylites* 8
     Have *m*, *m* : take away my sin.   „   45
     Have *m*, *m* ! cover all my sin.   „   84
     O *m*, *m* ! wash away my sin.   „   120
     And ah God's *m*, what a stroke was there !   *Lancelot and E.* 24
     His *m* choked me.   *Guinevere* 616
     ' Full of compassion and *m*, (repeat)   *Rizpah* 62, 63

Mere (adj.) M chaff and draff, much better burnt.'   *The Epic* 40
     and this A *m* love-poem !   *Princess* iv 126
     M fellowship of sluggish moods,   *In Mem. xxxv* 21
     had the thing I spake of been *M* gold—   *Gareth and L.* 66
     Full cowardly, or by *m* unhappiness,   „   768
     Hast overthrown thro' *m* unhappiness),   „   1059
     I know not, all thro' *m* unhappiness—   „   1234
     O Gareth—thro' the *m* unhappiness   „   1237
     And molten down in *m* uxoriousness.   *Marr. of Geraint* 60
     Is melted into *m* effeminacy ?   „   107
     whose lightest word Is *m* white truth   *Balin and Balan* 518
     a *m* child Might use it to the harm of anyone,   *Merlin and V.* 684
     what was once to me *M* matter of the fancy,   „   924
     What I by *m* mischance have brought, my
         shield.   *Lancelot and E.* 189
     M want of gold—   *The Ring* 428

Mere (s) (*See also* **Mountain-mere**) curls And
     ripples of an inland *m* ?   *Supp. Confessions* 131
     Crimsons over an inland *m*,   *Eleänore* 42
     When *m's* begin to uncongeal,   *Two Voices* 407
     And fling him far into the middle *m* :   *M. d'Arthur* 37
     Or voice, or else a motion of the *m*.   „   77
     and paced beside the *m*,   „   83
     and drew him under in the *m*. (repeat)   „ 146,161
     And on the *m* the wailing died away.   „   272
     in the deeps whereof a *m*, Round as the red eye   *Gareth and L.* 798
     ' They have bound my lord to cast him in the *m*.'   „   803
     and there, blackshadow'd nigh the *m*,   „   809
     then in the *m* beside Tumbled it ; oilily bubbled up
         the *m*.   „   815
     flickering in a grimly light Dance on the *m*.   „   827
     in her arms She bare me, pacing on the
         dusky *m*.   *Lancelot and E.* 1411
     And fling me deep in that forgotten *m*,   „   1426
     Wealthy with wandering lines of mount and *m*,   *Holy Grail* 252
     and in the sleepy *m* below Blood-red.   „   475
     hundred *m's* About it, as the water Moab saw   *Last Tournament* 481
     star in heaven, a star within the *m* !   „   732
     O ay—the winds that move the *m*,   „   738
     And fling him far into the middle *m* :   *Pass. of Arthur* 205
     Or voice, or else a motion of the *m*.   „   245
     and paced beside the *m*,   „   251
     and drew him under in the *m*. (repeat)   „ 314, 329
     And on the *m* the wailing died away.   „   440
     heron rises from his watch beside the *m*,   *Happy* 3

Merely Nor in a *m* selfish cause—   *Two Voices* 147
Merge *m'* he said ' in form and gloss   *In Mem. lxxxix* 41
Merged But long disquiet in *m* rest.   *Two Voices* 249
     fulfill'd itself, *M* in completion ?   *Gardener's D.* 239
     in this glory I had *m* The other,   *Lover's Tale* i 506
Merides ' Phosphorus,' then ' *M* '—' Hesperus '—   *Gareth and L.* 1204
Merit (s) For *m* lives from man to man,   *In Mem., Pro.* 35
     Who makes by force his *m* known   „ *lxiv* 9
     That were a public *m*, far,   *Maud II* v 91
     You found some *m* in my rhymes,   *To E. Fitzgerald* 55
Merit (verb) is it I can have done to *m* this ?   *St. S. Stylites* 134
     may *m* well Your term of overstrain'd.   *Merlin and V.* 534
Merk (mark) fur the *m's* o' thy shou'der yit ;   *Owd Roä* 90
Merle (*See also* **Blackbird**) lark, mavis, *m*, Linnet ?   *Gareth and L.* 1078
Merlin *M* sware that I should come again   *M. d'Arthur* 23
     and one Is *M*, the wise man   *Com. of Arthur* 151
     one Is *M's* master (so they call him) Bleys,   „   153
     wrote All things and whatsoever *M* did   „   157
     Deliver'd at a secret postern-gate To *M*,   „   214

Merlin (*continued*) Wherefore *M* took the child,
     And gave him to Sir Anton,   *Com. of Arthur* 221
     when *M* (for his hour had come) Brought Arthur   „   228
     Yet *M* thro' his craft,   „   234
     ' And there I saw mage *M*   „   280
     old *M* counsell'd him, ' Take thou and strike !   „   306
     Or brought by *M*, who, they say,   „   347
     For Bleys, our *M's* master, as they say,   „   360
     And *M* ever served about the King,   „   365
     and rode to *M's* feet, Who stoopt and caught   „   384
     I met *M*, and ask'd him if these things were truth—   „   398
     ' So *M* riddling anger'd me ;   „   412
     and *M* in our time Hath spoken also,   „   419
     drave the heathen hence by sorcery And *M's*
         glamour.'   *Gareth and L.* 205
     To plunge old *M* in the Arabian sea ;   „   211
     Which *M's* hand, the Mage at Arthur's court,   „   306
     At *M's* feet the wily Vivien lay.   *Merlin and V.* 5
     M, who knew the range of all their arts,   „   167
     Then fell on *M* a great melancholy ;   „   189
     And then she follow'd *M* all the way,   „   203
     For *M* once had told her of a charm,   „   205
     ' O *M*, do ye love me ? ' (repeat)   „ 235, 236
     M lock'd his hand in hers and said, (repeat)   „ 290, 470
     O, *M*, teach it me.   „   331
     O *M*, may this earth, if ever I,   „   345
     M loosed his hand from hers and said,   „   356
     M lok'd and half believed her true,   „   400
     Then answer'd *M* careless of her words :   „   700
     Then answer'd *M*, ' Nay, I know the tale.   „   713
     M answer'd, ' Overquick art thou To catch   „   726
     M answer'd careless of her charge,   „   754
     M to his own heart, loathing, said :   „   790
     Vivien, deeming *M* overborne By instance,   „   800
     ' O *M*, tho' you do not love me, save,   „   944
     her *M*, the one passionate love Of her whole life ;   „   955
     M, overtalk'd and overworn, Had yielded,   „   965
     Fashion'd by *M* ere he past away,   *Holy Grail* 168
     M call'd it ' The Siege perilous,'   „   172
     M sat In his own chair, and so was lost ;   „   175
     Galahad, when he heard of *M's* doom, Cried,   „   177
     Galahad would sit down in *M's* chair.   „   181
     Which *M* built for Arthur long ago !   „   226
     Climbs to the mighty hall that *M* built.   „   231
     mould Of Arthur, made by *M*, with a crown,   „   239
     In horror lest the work by *M* wrought,   „   259
     And from the statue *M* moulded for us   „   732
     that Gawain fired The hall of *M*,   *Pelleas and E.* 518
     saw High up in heaven the hall that *M* built,   „   553
     ran across her memory the strange rhyme Of
         bygone *M*,   *Last Tournament* 132
     M's mystic babble about his end Amazed me ;   „   670
     M sware that I should come again   *Pass. of Arthur* 191
     I am *M*, And I am dying, I am *M* Who follow
         The Gleam.   *Merlin and the G.* 7

Mermaid With the *m's* in and out of the rocks,   *The Mermaid* 12
     Who would be A *m* fair,   *The Mermaid* 1
     I would be a *m* fair ;   „   9
Mermaiden He heard a fierce *m* cry,   *Sailor Boy* 2
     And in the light the white *m* swam,   *Guinevere* 245
Merman Who would be A *m* bold,   *The Merman* 2
     I would be a *m* bold,   „   8
     And all the *mermen* under the sea   *The Mermaid* 28
     and play With the *mermen* in and out of the rocks ;   „   34
     bold merry *mermen* under the sea,   „   42
Merrier The *m*, prettier, wittier, as they talk,   *Sisters (E. and E.)* 286
Merriest Of all the glad New-year, mother, the
     maddest *m* day ;   *May Queen* 3
     To-morrow 'ill be of all the year the maddest *m* day,   „   43
     Sounds happier than the *m* marriage-bell.   *D. of the Duke of C.* 11
Merrily Chasing each other *m*.   *The Merman* 20
     All night, *m*, *m* ; (repeat)   „ 27, 30
     We would live *m*, *m*.   „   40
Merrily-blowing *m-b* shrill'd the martial fife ;   *Princess* v 251
Merriment With *m* of kingly pride,   *Arabian Nights* 151

Merriment (*continued*)   And moved to *m* at a passing
    jest.   *Sisters E. and E.* 121
Merry   The *m* glees are still ;   *All Things will Die* 23
   Ye *m* souls, farewell.   "   36
   When *m* milkmaids click the latch,   *The Owl* i 8
   In the heart of the garden the *m* bird chants.   *Poet's Mind* 22
   For *m* brides are we :   *Sea-Fairies* 33
   Of the bold *m* mermen under the sea ;   *The Mermaid* 42
   How the *m* bluebell rings   *Adeline* 34
   A *m* boy in sun and shade ? ' A *m* boy they call'd
     him then,   *Two Voices* 321
   I said, ' O Soul, make *m* and carouse,   *Palace of Art* 3
   Last May we made a crown of flowers : we
     had a *m* day ;   *May Queen, N. Y's. E.* 9
   But all his *m* quips are o'er.   *D. of the O. Year* 29
   Hark, my *m* comrades call me,   *Locksley Hall* 145
   And many a *m* wind was borne,   *Day-Dm., Depart.* 14
   He laugh'd a laugh of *m* scorn :   *Lady Clare* 81
   We knew the *m* world was round,   *The Voyage* 7
   We know the *m* world is round,   "   95
   And make him *m*, when I come home again.   *Enoch Arden* 199
   How *m* they are down yonder in the wood.   "   389
   Clash, ye bells, in the *m* March air !   *W. to Alexandra* 18
   Be *m*, all birds, to-day, Be *m* on earth as you never
     were *m* before, Be *m* in heaven, O larks, and far
     away, And *m* for ever and ever, and one day
     more.   *Window, Ay* 1
   O *m* the linnet and dove,   "   13
   O *m* my heart, you have gotten the wings of love,   "   15
   The *m* bells of Yule.   *In Mem. xxviii* 20
   A *m* song we sang with him Last year :   "   *xxx* 15
   Many a *m* face Salutes them—   "   *Con.* 66
   Go in and out as if at *m* play,   *Maud I xviii* 31
   I fear, Fantastically *m* ;   "   *xix* 101
   ' Full *m* am I to find my goodly knave   *Gareth and L.* 1291
   And we will make us as we may.   *Marr. of Geraint* 373
   Then, when the Prince was *m*, ask'd Limours,   *Geraint and E.* 297
   And *m* maidens in it ;   *Holy Grail* 746
   And blew my *m* maidens all about   "   748
   should ye try him with a *m* one To find his mettle,   *Pelleas and E.* 198
   Open gates, And I will make you *m*.'   "   374
   Down in the cellars *m* bloated things   *Guinevere* 267
   m linnet knew me, The squirrel knew me,   *Lover's Tale ii* 15
   Four *m* bells, four *m* marriage-bells,   "   *iii* 21
   Married among the red berries, an' all as *m* as May—   *First Quarrel* 40
   Lest the false faith make *m* over them !   *Sir J. Oldcastle* 82
   in many a *m* tale That shook our sides—   "   91
Merrymaking   our friends are all forsaking The wine
     and the *m*.   *All Things will Die* 19
   no more of mirth Is here or *m-m* sound.   *Deserted House* 14
   while the rest were loud in *m-m*,   *Enoch Arden* 77
Mersey   New-comers from the *M*,   *Edwin Morris* 10
Meseems   ' *M*, that here is much discourtesy,   *Gareth and L.* 853
   Is all as good, *m*, as any knight   "   1017
   My quest, *m*, is here.   *Balin and Balan* 552
Mesh   In *m*'s of the jasmine and the rose :   *Princess i* 219
Message   with His *m* ringing in thine ears,   *Aylmer's Field* 666
   They flash'd a saucy *m* to and fro   *Princess, Pro.* 78
   I brought a *m* here from Lady Blanche.'   "   *ii* 319
   He ceasing, came a *m* from the Head.   "   *iii* 168
   With *m* and defiance, went and came ;   "   *v* 370
   in this Book, little Annie, the *m* is one of Peace.   *Grandmother* 96
   Some dolorous *m* knit below   *In Mem. xii* 3
   Till on mine ear this *m* falls,   "   *lxxv* 18
   Yniol with that hard *m* went ;   *Marr. of Geraint* 763
   Save that he sware me to a *m*, saying,   *Last Tournament* 76
   And waited for her *m*, piece by piece   *Lover's Tale iv* 146
Messenger   Then came in hall the *m* of Mark,   *Gareth and L.* 384
Messuage   lands in Kent and *m*'s in York,   *Edwin Morris* 127
Met   (*See also* **Chance-met**) ' *And statesmen at her*
     council m   *To the Queen* 29
   talking to himself, first *m* his sight :   *Love and Death* 6
   Methought that I had often *m* with you,   *Sonnet To* —— 13
   They *m* with two so full and bright—   *Miller's D.* 86
   And angels rising and descending *m*   *Palace of Art* 143

Met (*continued*)   When thus he *m* his mother's view,   *L. C. V. de Vere* 34
   or as once we *m* Unheedful,   *Gardener's D.* 265
   I *m* my lady once :   *Walk. to the Mail* 48
   those moments when we *m*, The crown of all, we
     m to part no more.'   *Edwin Morris* 69
   we *m* ; one hour I had, no more :   "   104
   I am a part of all that I have *m* ;   *Ulysses* 18
   M me walking on yonder way,   *Edward Gray* 2
   then we *m* in wrath and wrong, We *m*, but only
     meant to part.   *The Letters* 11
   He *m* the bailiff at the Golden Fleece,   *The Brook* 146
   Yet once by night again the lovers *m*,   *Aylmer's Field* 413
   I *m* him suddenly in the street,   *Sea Dreams* 146
   Here Cyril *m* us. A little shy at first,   *Princess v* 44
   a lie which is all a lie may be *m* and fought with
     outright,   *Grandmother* 31
   Meadows in which we *m* !   *Window, Marr. Morn.* 8
   And ever *m* him on his way   *In Mem. vi* 22
   And all we *m* was fair and good,   "   *xxiii* 17
   If all was good and fair we *m*,   "   *xxiv* 5
   From every house the neighbours *m*,   "   *xxxi* 9
   I *m* with scoffs, I *m* with scorns   "   *lxix* 9
   For other friends that once I *m* ;   "   *lxxxv* 58
   Where God and Nature met in light ;   "   *cxi* 20
   Unpalsied when he *m* with Death,   "   *cxviii* 2
   I *m* her to-day with her brother,   *Maud I iv* 14
   To entangle me when we *m*,   "   *vi* 28
   blush'd To find they were *m* by my own ;   "   *viii* 7
   Alas for her that *m* me,   "   *II iv* 75
   I *m* Merlin, and ask'd him if these things   *Com. of Arthur* 397
   knave, anon thou shalt be *m* with, knave,   *Gareth and L.* 779
   Whom Gareth *m* midstream : no room was there   "   1041
   Gareth overthrew him, lighted, drew, There *m* him
     drawn,   "   1122
   when they *m* In twos and threes,   *Marr. of Geraint* 56
   then descending *m* them at the gates,   "   833
   M his full frown timidly firm,   *Geraint and E.* 71
   m The scorner in the castle court,   *Balin and Balan* 386
   Had *m* her, Vivien, being greeted fair,   *Merlin and V.* 155
   would often when they *m* Sigh fully,   "   181
   here we *m*, some ten or twelve of us,   "   407
   two brothers, one a king, had *m* And fought   *Lancelot and E* 39
   And oft they *m* among the garden yews,   "   645
   They *m*, and Lancelot kneeling utter'd,   "   1179
   He raised his head, their eyes *m* and hers fell,   "   1312
   M foreheads all along the street   *Holy Grail* 344
   ' And then, with small adventure *m*,   "   660
   And steps that *m* the breaker !   "   816
   The men who *m* him rounded on their heels   *Pelleas and E.* 142
   he *m* A cripple, one that held a hand for alms—   "   541
   Flush'd, started, *m* him at the doors,   *Last Tournament* 512
   But harken ! have ye met him ?   "   529
   And still they *m* and *m*. Again she said,   *Guinevere* 94
   Passion-pale they *m* And greeted.   "   99
   We turn'd ; our eyes *m* : hers were bright,   *Lover's Tale i* 441
   Parted a little ere they *m* the floor,   "   *iv* 215
   their breath *m* us out on the seas,   *V. of Maeldune* 37
   ' would God, we had never *m* ! '   *The Wreck* 102
   Here we *m*, our latest meeting—   *Locksley H., Sixty* 177
   Like a clown—by chance he *m* me—   "   256
   century's three strong eights have *m*   *To Ulysses* 7
   For ere she left us, when we *m*,   *To Mary Boyle* 15
   Have I not *m* you somewhere long ago ?   *Romney's R.* 18
   when I *m* you first—when *he* brought you !—   *Charity* 9
Metal   Bright *m* all without alloy.   *Rosalind* 21
Metaphysics   she cried, ' you love The *m* !   *Princess iii* 300
Mete   And *m* the bounds of hate and love—   *Two Voices* 135
   I *m* and dole Unequal laws unto a savage race,   *Ulysses* 3
Meted   As *m* by his measure of himself,   *Aylmer's Field* 316
Meteor   Some bearded *m*, trailing light,   *L. of Shalott iii* 26
   The *m* of a splendid season, she   *Aylmer's Field* 205
   like a new-fall'n *m* on the grass,   *Princess vi* 135
   Now slides the silent *m* on,   "   *vii* 184
   While thou, a *m* of the sepulchre,   *Lover's Tale i* 99
Meteorite   and your fiery clash of *m*'s ?   *God and the Univ.* 3

Q

Methinks *m* Some ruth is mine for thee.   *Gareth and L.* 894
m There rides no knight, not Lancelot,   " 1181
Method *M's* of transplanting trees   *Amphion* 79
Methody-man 'Thou'rt but a *M-m*,' says Parson,   *North. Cobbler* 89
Methought yet *m* I saw the Holy Grail   *Holy Grail* 846
m The cloud was rifted by a purer gleam   *Akbar's Dream* 77
Metre mellow *m's* more than cent for cent;   *The Brook* 5
All composed in a *m* of Catullus,   *Hendecasyllabics* 4
So fantastical is the dainty *m.*   " 14
Metrification Thro' this *m* of Catullus,   " 10
Metropolis And gray *m* of the North.   *The Daisy* 104
Above some fair *m*, earth-shock'd,—   *Lover's Tale ii* 62
Mettle It stirr'd the old wife's *m*:   *The Goose* 26
try him with a merry one To find his *m*, good: *Pelleas and E.* 199
Mew (sea-gull) Here it is only the *m* that wails;   *Sea-Fairies* 19
and wail'd about with *m's.*   *Princess iv* 282
Mew (cry of a cat) *M* ! *m* !—Bess wi' the milk !   *Spinster's S's.* 113
Mewin (mewing) what art'a *m* at, Steevie?   " 41
Mexico lavish growths of southern *M.*   *Mine be thy strength* 14
Michaël But *M* trampling Satan,   *Last Tournament* 673
Michael Angelo The bar of *M A.*   *In Mem. lxxxvii* 40
Michaelmas for Squoire coom *M* thutty year.   *N. Farmer, O. S.* 48
Microcosm holy secrets of this *m.*   *Princess iii* 313
Mid birds made Melody on branch, and melody in *m* air.   *Gareth and L.* 183
In the *m* might and flourish of his May,   *Lancelot and E.* 554
and started thro' *m* air Bearing an eagle's nest: *Last Tournament* 14
life Being smitten in *m* heaven with mortal cold   " 27
as a stream that spouting from a cliff Fails in *m* air,   *Guinevere* 609
Like some conjectured planet in *m* heaven   *Prin. Beatrice* 20
and like May-blossoms in *m* autumn—   *The Ring* 255
Yet you in your *m* manhood—   *Happy* 47
Mid-banquet in *m-b* measuring with his eyes   *Pelleas and E.* 150
Mid-channel in the gurgling wave *M-c.*   *Princess iv* 188
Mid-day Jet upward thro' the *m-d* blossom.   *Demeter and P.* 47
Midder (meadow) an' the *m's* as white,   *Owd Roä* 31
Middle (adj.) The living airs of night Died round   *Arabian Nights* 69
Shrill music reach'd them on the *m* sea.   *Sea-Fairies* 6
And fling him far into the *m* mere :   *M. d'Arthur* 37
But Enoch shunn'd the *m* walk and stole Up by the wall,   *Enoch Arden* 738
but in the *m* aisle Reel'd,   *Aylmer's Field* 818
As in some mystic *m* state I lay ;   *Princess vi* 89
In *m* ocean meets the surging shock,   *Will* 8
The nightingale, full-toned in *m* May,   *Balin and Balan* 213
As the poach'd filth that floods the *m* street,   *Merlin and V.* 798
all in *m* street the Queen Who rode by Lancelot,   *Holy Grail* 355
And fling him far into the *m* mere—   *Pass. of Arthur* 205
Who toils across the *m* moonlit nights,   *Lover's Tale i* 138
with such sudden deluges of light Into the *m* summer;   " 316
All the west And ev'n unto the *m* south was ribb'd   " 415
And slowly pacing to the *m* hall,   " *iv* 306
For the Spring and the *m* Summer sat   *V. of Maeldune* 38
Middle (s) It was the *m* of the day.   *Dying Swan* 8
And in the *m* of the green salt sea   *Mine be the strength* 7
one great dwelling in the *m* of it;   *Holy Grail* 574
All in the *m* of the rising moon   " 636
Middle-day each was as dry as a cricket, with thirst in the *m-d* heat.   *V. of Maeldune* 50
Mid-dome day hung From his *m-d* in Heaven's   *Lover's Tale i* 66
Mid-forest that low lodge return'd, *M-f,*   *Last Tournament* 489
black brooks Of the *m* heard me—   *Lover's Tale ii* 12
Mid-heaven Grown on a magic oak-tree in *m-h,*   *Last Tournament* 745
the sloping seas Hung in *m-h,*   *Lover's Tale i* 4
Midmost (adj.) in the *m* heart of grief Thy passion clasps a secret joy;   *In Mem. lxxxviii* 7
for save he be Fool to the *m* marrow of his bones,   *Pelleas and E.* 258
Midmost (s) the *m* and the highest Was Arac :   *Princess v* 256
And at the *m* charging, Prince Geraint   *Geraint and E.* 85
Midnight At *m* the moon cometh,   *Claribel* 13
Ask the sea At *m*,   *Supp. Confessions* 126
At *m* the cock was crowing,   *Oriana* 12
When *m* bells cease ringing suddenly,   *D. of F. Women* 247
rode till *m* when the college lights   *Princess i* 207
sitting on a hill Sees the midsummer, *m*,   " *iv* 575

Midnight (continued) but rode Ere *m* to her walls,   *Pelleas and E.* 413
As rain of the midsummer *m* soft,   *Lover's Tale i* 722
burnt at *m*, found at morn,   *Locksley H., Sixty* 97
M—in no midsummer tune The breakers   *Pref. Poem Broth. S.* 1
M—and joyless June gone by,   " 9
And thro' this *m* breaks the sun   " 21
forth again Among the wail of *m* winds,   *Demeter and P.* 59
On a *m* in midwinter when all but the winds   *The Dreamer* 1
Midnight-maned their arch'd necks, *m-m,*   *Demeter and P.* 46
Midnoon It was the deep *m*:   *Œnone* 92
Mid-November For as a leaf in *m-N* is   *Marr. of Geraint* 611
Mid-ocean Than labour in the deep *m-o*,   *Lotos-Eaters, C. S.* 173
whatever tempest mars *M-o*, spare thee,   *In Mem. xvii* 14
one A vessel in *m-o*, her heaved prow Clambering,   *Lover's Tale ii* 169
Mid-October To what it was in *m-O*,   *Marr. of Geraint* 612
Midriff Sprang from the *m* of a prostrate king—   *Aylmer's Field* 16
shake The *m* of despair with laughter,   *Princess i* 201
Mid-sickness great knight in this *m-s* made   *Lancelot and E.* 878
Midst Over the throne In the *m* of the hall;   *The Mermaid* 22
And every marge enclosing in the *m*   *Merlin and V.* 670
Midstream Whom Gareth met *m*:   *Gareth and L.* 1041
Midsummer sitting on a hill Sees the *m*, midnight,   *Princess iv* 575
As rain of the *m* midnight soft,   *Lover's Tale i* 722
in the gleam of those *m-s* dawns,   *The Ring* 183
as when an hour of cold Falls on the mountain in *m* snows,   *Last Tournament* 228
Here one, black, mute *m* night I sat, Lonely,   " 612
MIDNIGHT—in no *m* tune The breakers lash the shores;   *Pref. Poem. Broth. S.* 1
Mid-thigh-deep *m-t-d* in bulrushes and reed,   *Gareth and L.* 810
Mid-warmth In the *m-w* of welcome and graspt   *Geraint and E.* 280
Midway *m* down the side of that long hall   *Gareth and L.* 404
Midwinter (adj.) And on this white *m* day—   *To Master of B.* 9
Midwinter (s) On a midnight in *m* when all but the winds   *The Dreamer* 1
Mien One her dark hair and lovesome *m.*   *Beggar Maid* 12
then Kay, a man of *m* Wan-sallow   *Gareth and L.* 452
But scarce of such majestic *m*   *Freedom* 6
Might (*See also* **Mowt**) Losing his fire and active *m*   *Eleänore* 104
with increasing *m* doth forward flee   *Mine be the strength* 5
O LOVE, Love, Love ! O withering *m* !   *Fatima* 1
Deliver not the tasks of *m* To weakness,   *Love thou thy land* 13
smote on all the chords with *m*;   *Locksley Hall* 33
Toward that great year of equal *m's* and rights,   *Princess iv* 74
That I could wing my will with *m*   *In Mem. xli* 10
with *m* To scale the heaven's highest height,   " *cviii* 6
Her likewise would I worship an I *m.*   *Balin and Balan* 185
m, Name, manhood, and a grace, but scantly thine,   " 376
In the mid *m* and flourish of his May,   *Lancelot and E.* 554
His neighbour's make and *m* :   *Pelleas and E.* 151
Strength of heart And *m* of limb,   *Last Tournament* 198
Mightful And watch his *m* hand striking great blows   *Marr. of Geraint* 95
Mightier Because things seen are *m* than things heard,   *Enoch Arden* 766
And *m* of his hands with every blow,   *Com. of Arthur* 110
Wave after wave, each *m* than the last,   " 379
Blow, for our Sun is *m* day by day !   " 498
So make thy manhood *m* day by day ;   *Gareth and L.* 92
we be *m* men than all In Arthur's court ;   *Balin and Balan* 33
Did *m* deeds than elsewise he had done,   *Last Tournament* 680
One twofold *m* than the other was,   *Lover's Tale i* 211
Never with *m* glory than when we had rear'd thee on high   *Def. of Lucknow* 3
Has breathed a race of *m* mountaineers.   *Montenegro* 14
Only That which made us, meant us to be *m* by and by,   *Locksley H., Sixty* 209
When one might meet a *m* than himself ;   *Gareth and L.* 1350
withheld His older and his *m* from the lists,   *Pelleas and E.* 160
Mightiest But Arthur *m* on the battle-field—   *Gareth and L.* 496
and a fourth And of that four the *m*,   " 615
Then others, following these my *m* knights,   *Guinevere* 489
Spain then the *m*, wealthiest realm on earth,   *Columbus* 205
His isle, the *m* Ocean-power on earth,   *The Fleet* 6
we needs must learn Which is our *m*,   *Lancelot and E.* 63
Thou *m* and thou purest among men ! '   *Holy Grail* 426

Mightiest (*continued*) ' my friend, Our *m*, hath this
  Quest avail'd for thee ? ' ' Our *m* ! ' answer'd
  Lancelot, with a groan ;   *Holy Grail* 765
  Yea, made our *m* madder than our least.   ,, 863
  my right arm The *m* of my knights,   *Guinevere* 430
Mighty   As when a *m* people rejoice With shawms,   *Dying Swan* 31
  WHAT time the *m* moon was gathering light   *Love and Death* 1
  A *m* silver bugle hung,   *L. of Shalott iii* 16
  row Of cloisters, branch'd like *m* woods,   *Palace of Art* 26
  melting the *m* hearts Of captains and of kings.   *D. of F. Women* 175
  fragments of her *m* voice Came rolling on the
    wind.   *Of old sat Freedom* 7
  New Majesties of *m* States—   *Love thou thy land* 60
  Where lay the *m* bones of ancient men,   *M. d'Arthur* 47
  Stored in some treasure-house of *m* kings,   ,, 101
  Which was an image of the *m* world ;   ,, 235
  Let this avail, just, dreadful, O God,   *St. S. Stylites* 9
  For the *m* wind arises, roaring seaward, and I go.   *Locksley Hall* 194
  To sleep thro' terms of *m* wars,   *Day-Dm., L'Envoi* 9
  The tavern-hours of *m* wits,   *Will Water.* 191
  and floods Of *m* mouth, we scudded fast,   *The Voyage* 46
  Soft fruitage, *m* nuts, and nourishing roots ;   *Enoch Arden* 555
  And *m* courteous in the main—   *Aylmer's Field* 121
  Which things appear the work of— *m* Gods.   *Lucretius* 102
  I wish I were Some *m* poetess,   *Princess, Pro.* 132
  Then those eight *m* daughters of the plough   ,, *iv* 550
  To the noise of the mourning of a *m* nation,   *Ode on Well.* 4
  M Seaman, this is he Was great by land   ,, 83
  M Seaman, tender and true,   ,, 134
  thou shalt be the *m* one yet !   *Boädicea* 40
  When in Love would cleave in twain   *In Mem. xxv* 10
  To mould a *m* state's decrees,   ,, *lxiv* 11
  The *m* hopes that make us men.   ,, *lxxxv* 60
  I seem as nothing in the *m* world,   *Com. of Arthur* 87
  Seeing the *m* swarm about their walls,   ,, 200
  ' Blow, for our Sun is *n* in his May !   ,, 497
  And all these four be fools, but *m* men,   *Gareth and L.* 643
  And *m* thro' thy meats and drinks am I, (repeat) ,, 650, 862
  For here be *m* men to joust with,   ,, 880
  four strokes they struck With sword, and these were *m* ;   ,, 1043
  he loosed a *m* purse, Hung at his belt,   *Geraint and E.* 22
  But like a *m* patron, satisfied   ,, 644
  letting her left hand Droop from his *m* shoulder,   *Merlin and V.* 243
  To cross our *m* Lancelot in his loves !   *Lancelot and E.* 688
  His battle-writhen arms and hands   ,, 812
  ' O brother, had you known our *m* hall,   *Holy Grail* 225
  Climbs to the *m* hall that Merlin built.   ,, 231
  ' And I rode on and found a *m* hill,   ,, 421
  Where lay the *m* bones of ancient men,   *Pass. of Arthur* 215
  Stored in some treasure-house of *m* kings,   ,, 269
  Framing the *m* landscape to the west,   *Lover's Tale i* 418
  shower'd down Rays of a *m* circle,   ,, 418
  m gyres Rapid and vast, of hissing spray wind-driven   ,, *ii* 197
  And bearing high in arms the *m* babe,   ,, *iv* 295
  And the men that were *m* of tongue   *V. of Maeldune* 23
  M the Mercian, Hard was his hand-play,   *Batt. of Brunanburh* 43
  Thrice from the dyke he sent his *m* shout,   *Achilles over the T.* 30
  as mellow and deep As a psalm by a *m* master   *The Wreck* 53
  We founded many a *m* state,   *Hands all Round* 30
  M the Wizard Who found me at sunrise   *Merlin and the G.* 11
  Bards, that the *m* Muses have raised   *Parnassus* 2
  You, the *m*, the Fortunate,   *On Jub. Q. Victoria* 55
  For thro' the Magic Of Him the *M*,   *Merlin and the G.* 114
Mighty-mouth'd   O *m-m* inventor of harmonies,   *Milton* 1
Mignonette   A long green box of *m*,   *Miller's D.* 83
  parlour-window and the box of *m*.   *May Queen, N. Y's. E.* 48
  But miss'd the *m* of Vivian-place,   *Princess, Pro.* 165
Milan   O *M*, O the chanting quires,   *The Daisy* 57
Mild   Throbbing in *m* unrest holds him beneath   *Leonine Eleg.* 12
  beheld Thy *m* deep eyes upraised,   *Supp. Confessions* 74
  I have not lack'd thy *m* reproof,   *My life is full* 4
  ' His lips are very *m* and meek :   *Two Voices* 250
  With measured footfall firm and *m*,   ,, 413
  She with a subtle smile in her *m* eyes,   *Œnone* 184
  one hand grasp'd The *m* bull's golden horn.   *Palace of Art* 120

Mild (*continued*) Beside him Shakespeare bland and *m* ;   *Palace of Art* 134
  by slow prudence to make *m* A rugged people,   *Ulysses* 36
  My mother was as *m* as any saint,   *Princess i* 22
  meek Seem'd the full lips, and *m* the luminous eyes,   *vii* 226
  The stern were *m* when thou wert by,   *In Mem. cx* 9
  A higher hand must make her *m*,   ,, *cxiv* 17
  With difficulty in *m* obedience Driving them on :   *Geraint and E.* 104
  Fearing the *m* face of the blameless King,   ,, 812
  Who, with *m* heat of holy oratory,   ,, 866
  However *m* he seems at home, nor cares   *Lancelot and E.* 311
Milder   *M* than any mother to a sick child,   ,, 858
  with flame *M* and purer.   *Lover's Tale i* 323
  Sunn'd with a summer of *m* heat.   *To Prof. Jebb* 8
Mildew'd   Who had *m* in their thousands,   *Aylmer's Field* 383
Mild-eyed   The *m-e* melancholy Lotos-eaters   *Lotos-Eaters* 27
Mild-minded   the influence of *m-m* melancholy ;   *Lotos-Eaters, C. S.* 64
Mile   A *m* beneath the cedar-wood.   *Eleänore* 8
  Keeps his blue waters fresh for many a *m*.   *Mine be the strength* 8
  Ten *m's* to northward of the narrow port   *Enoch Arden* 102
  the long laborious *m's* Of Palace ;   *Ode Inter. Exhib.* 11
  Flash for a million *m's*.   *Window, Marr. Morn.* 24
  I was walking a *m*, More than a *m*   *Maud I ix* 1
  A *m* beneath the forest,   *Balin and Balan* 12
  race thro' many a *m* Of dense and open,   ,, 423
  province with a hundred *m's* of coast, (repeat)   *Merlin and V.* 588, 647
  But for a *m* all round was open space,   *Pelleas and E.* 28
  flash a million *m's* a day.   *Locksley H., Sixty* 204
  Glows in the blue of fifty *m's* away.   *Roses on the T.* 8
Milk   (*See also* **Wolf's-milk**)   I fed you with the *m* of
    every Muse ;   *Princess iv* 295
  The *m* that bubbled in the pail,   *In Mem. lxxxix* 51
  clean as blood of babes, as white as *m* :   *Merlin and V.* 344
  Seethed like the kid in its own mother's *m* !   ,, 869
  m From burning spurge, honey from hornet-combs,   *Last Tournament* 356
  land of promise flowing with the *m* And honey   *Lover's Tale i* 334
  Hafe a pint o' *m* runs out   *Village Wife* 4
  the babe Will suck in with his *m* hereafter—   *Columbus* 38
  Who live on *m* and meal and grass ;   *To E. Fitzgerald* 13
  M for my sweet-arts, Bess !   *Spinster's S's.* 1
  thou'd not 'a been worth thy *m*,   ,, 54
  Mew ! mew !—Bess wi' the *m* !   ,, 113
  Innocence seethed in her mother's *m*,   *Vastness* 9
  nurse my children on the *m* of Truth,   *Akbar's Dream* 162
Milk-bloom   One long *m-b* on the tree ;   *Maud I xxii* 46
Milkier   And *m* every milky sail   *In Mem. cxv* 11
Milking   The milkmaid left her *m*, and fell   *Holy Grail* 406
Milking-maid   burnt the grange, nor buss'd the *m-m*,   *Princess v* 222
Milkmaid   When merry *m's* click the latch,   *The Owl i* 8
  The *m* left her milking, and fell down   *Holy Grail* 406
Milk-white   opening out his *m-w* palm Disclosed a fruit   *Œnone* 65
  Now droops the *m* peacock like a ghost,   *Princess vii* 165
  Ah Maud, you *m* fawn, you are all unmeet for a wife.   *Maud I iv* 57
  There with her *m* arms and shadowy hair   *Guinevere* 416
Milky   like morning doves That sun their *m* bosoms   *Princess i* 103
  The soft and *m* rabble of womankind,   ,, *vi* 309
  if below the *m* steep Some ship of battle   *To F. D. Maurice* 25
  And milkier every *m* sail On winding stream   *In Mem. cxv* 11
  Struck up and lived along the *m* roofs :   *Lancelot and E.* 409
  either *m* arm Red-rent with hooks of bramble,   *Holy Grail* 210
  Old *m* fables of the wolf and sheep,   *Pelleas and E.* 196
Milky-bell'd   A *m-b* amaryllis blew.   *The Daisy* 16
Milky-way   this, a *m-w* on earth,   *Aylmer's Field* 160
Milky-white   Taller than all his fellows, *m-w*,   *Marr. of Geraint* 150
Mill   Thro' quiet meadows round the *m*,   *Miller's D.* 98
  The deep brook groan'd beneath the *m* ;   ,, 113
  To yon old *m* across the wolds ;   ,, 240
  long street climbs to one tall-tower'd *m* ;   *Enoch Arden* 5
  narrow street that clamber'd toward the *m*.   ,, 60
  flour From his tall *m* that whistled on the waste.   ,, 343
  Lords of his house and of his *m* were they ;   ,, 351
  Blanch'd with his *m*, they found ;   ,, 367
  climbing street, the *m*, the leafy lanes,   ,, 607
  an' I runs oop to the *m* ;   *N. Farmer, N. S.* 54
  ' ground in yonder social *m* We rub each other's
    angles down,   *In Mem. lxxxix* 39

Mind (s) (*continued*) those maidens with one *m* Bewail'd

their lot ;	*In Mem. ciii* 45
Ring out the grief that saps the *m*,	,, *cvi* 9
And native growth of noble *m* ;	,, *cxi* 16
For she is earthly of the *m*,	,, *cxiv* 21
these are the days of advance, the works of the	
men of *m*,	*Maud I i* 25
Be still, for you only trouble the *m*	,, *v* 20
cut off from the *m* The bitter springs of anger	
and fear ;	,, *x* 48
The fancy flatter'd my *m*,	,, *xiv* 23
So dark a *m* within me dwells,	,, *xv* 1
To the faults of his heart and *m*,	,, *xix* 68
Strange, that the, *m*, when fraught With a passion	,, *II ii* 58
for she never speaks her *m*,	,, *v* 67
awaked, as it seems, to the better *m* ;	,, *III vi* 56
inheritance Of such a life, a heart, a *m* as thine,	*Ded. of Idylls* 33
but all brave, all of one *m* with him ;	*Com. of Arthur* 255
in my *m* I hear A cry from out the dawning	,, 332
Ranging and ringing thro' the *m*'s of men,	,, 416
Across her *m*, and bowing over him,	*Marr. of Geraint* 84
And ever in her *m* she cast about	*Geraint and E.* 46
of one *m* and all right-honest friends !	,, 484
with her *m* all full of what had chanced,	,, 778
My *m* involved yourself the nearest thing	*Merlin and V.* 300
since he kept his *m* on one sole aim,	,, 626
densest condensation, hard To *m* and eye ;	,, 679
To sleek her ruffled peace of *m*,	,, 899
The shape and colour of a *m* and life,	*Lancelot and E.* 335
he turn'd Her counsel up and down within his *m*,	,, 369
Lancelot look'd and was perplext in *m*,	,, 838
So cannot speak my *m*. An end to this !	,, 1222
made him hers, and laid her *m* On him,	*Holy Grail* 164
Came like a driving gloom across my *m*.	,, 370
since her *m* was bent On hearing,	*Pelleas and E.* 114
Went wandering somewhere darkling in his *m*.	*Last Tournament* 457
loyal nature, and of noble *m*.'	*Guinevere* 336
Her memory from old habit of the *m*	,, 379
With whom he dwelt, new faces, other *m*'s.	*Pass. of Arthur* 5
dividing the swift *m*, In act to throw :	,, 228
Among new men, strange faces, other *m*'s.'	,, 406
(For all my *m* is clouded with a doubt)—	,, 426
Like to a quiet *m* in the loud world,	*Lover's Tale i* 7
sometimes on the horizon of the *m* Lies folded,	,, 49
daylight of your *m*'s But cloud and smoke,	,, 296
And all the maiden empire of her *m*,	,, 589
She deem'd I wore a brother's *m* :	,, 741
whether the *m*, With some revenge—	,, *ii* 126
born Not from believing *m*, but shatter'd nerve,	,, *iv* 105
This love is of the brain, the *m*, the soul :	,, 156
But arter I chäinged my *m*,	*North. Cobbler* 105
he had seen it and made up his *m*,	*In the Child. Hosp.* 16
his *m*, So quick, so capable in soldiership,	*Sir J. Oldcastle* 74
When he clothed a naked *m* with the wisdom	*The Wreck* 130
I was the lonely slave of an often-wandering *m* ;	,, 130
the blasphemy to *my m* lies all in the way	*Despair* 112
' What Power ? ' aught akin to M, The *m*	*Ancient Sage* 78
thin *m*'s, who creep from thought to thought,	,, 103
He withers marrow and *m* ;	,, 120
the world is hard, and harsh of *m*,	*The Flight* 101
for Molly was out of her *m*.	*Tomorrow* 6
nurse of ailing body and *m*,	*Locksley H., Sixty* 51
kings of men in utter nobleness of *m*,	,, 122
lustier body, larger *m* ?	,, 164
Man or M that sees a shadow of the planner or the plan ?	,, 196
Universal Nature moved by Universal *M* ;	*To Virgil* 22
How long thine ever-growing *m*	*Freedom* 33
died in the doing it, flesh without *m* ;	*Vastness* 27
When the *m* is failing !	*Forlorn* 36
For lowly *m*'s were madden'd to the height	*To Mary Boyle* 33
Larger and fuller, like the human *m* !	*Prog. of Spring* 112
of the *m* Mine ; worse, cold, calculated.	*Romney's R.* 151
How subtle at tierce and quart of *m* with *m*,	*In Mem. W. G. Ward* 5
Now I'll gie tha a bit o' my *m*	*Church-warden, etc.* 21
M's on this round earth of ours	*Poets and Critics* 3

Mind (verb) (*See also* **Moind**)   I *m* him coming down

the street ;	*Enoch Arden* 847
m us of the time When we made bricks in Egypt.	*Princess iv* 127
To *m* me of the secret vow I made	*Columbus* 92
fur I *m* tha sa well,	*Church-warden, etc.* 23
But I *m* when i' Howlaby beck won daäy	,, 27

Minded   *See* **Cheerful-minded, Liberal-minded, Man-minded, Mild-minded, Myriad-minded**

Mindful   Guinevere, not *m* of his face   *Marr. of Geraint* 191

And *m* of her small and cruel hand,	*Pelleas and E.* 201

Mindless   One truth will damn me with the *m* mob,   *Romney's R.* 120

Mind-mist   yourself the nearest thing In that *m-m* :   *Merlin and V.* 301

Mine   (*See also* **Gold-mine**)   Or labour'd *m* undrainable

of ore.	*Œnone* 115
Old, and a *m* of memories—	*Aylmer's Field* 10
To buy strange shares in some Peruvian *m*.	*Sea Dreams* 15
there is no such *m*, None ; but a gulf of ruin,	,, 78
she said, ' by working in the *m*'s : '	,, 114
Secrets of the sullen *m*,	*Ode Inter. Exhib.* 16
till he crept from a gutted *m*	*Maud I x* 9
A league of mountain full of golden *m*'s,	*Merlin and V.* 587
Made proffer of the league of golden *m*'s,	,, 646
M ? yes, a *m* ! Countermine !	*Def. of Lucknow* 25
but the foe sprung his *m* many times,	,, 31
in a moment two *m*'s by the enemy sprung	,, 54
Ever the *m* and assault, our sallies,	,, 75
All but free leave for all to work the *m*'s,	*Columbus* 133
Mount and *m*, and primal wood ;	*Open. I. and C. Exhib.* 6

Mingle   Thought and motion *m*, M ever.

To *m* with the human race,	*Eleänore* 60
And star-like *m*'s with the stars.	*Of old sat Freedom* 10
M madness, *m* scorn !	*Sir Galahad* 48
Pass, and *m* with your likes.	*Vision of Sin* 204
To *m* with the bounding main :	*Princess vi* 341
And *m*'s all without a plan ?	*In Mem. xi* 12
And *m* all the world with thee.	,, *xvi* 20
and *m* with our folk ;	,, *cxxix* 12
wherefore shouldst thou care to *m* with it,	*Holy Grail* 549
m with your rites ; Pray and be pray'd for ;	*Last Tournament* 105
soul twines and *m*'s with the growths	*Guinevere* 680
God must *m* with the game :	*Lover's Tale i* 132
let the stormy moment fly and *m* with the Past.	*Locksley H., Sixty* 271
I would not *m* with their feasts ;	,, 279
	Demeter and P. 103

Mingled   (*See also* **Poppy-mingled, Scarlet-mingled**)

Ceasing not, *m*, unrepress'd,	*Arabian Nights* 74
Desiring what is *m* with past years,	*D. of F. Women* 282
a Rose In roses, *m* with her fragrant toil,	*Gardener's D.* 143
And ever as he *m* With the crew,	*Enoch Arden* 643
this, at times, she *m* with his drink,	*Lucretius* 18
Will rank you nobly, *m* up with me.	*Princess ii* 46
The sole men to be *m* with our cause,	,, *v* 411
m with the haze And made it thicker ;	*Com. of Arthur* 434
And *m* with the spearmen :	*Geraint and E.* 599
bank Of maiden snow *m* with sparks of fire.	*Last Tournament* 149
m with dim cries Far in the moonlit haze	*Pass. of Arthur* 41
m with the famous kings of old,	*Tiresias* 171
will the glory of Kapiolani be	*Kapiolani* 18
this life of *m* pains And joys to me,	*To Mary Boyle* 49

Miniature   A *m* of loveliness,   *Gardener's D.* 12

I remember how you kiss'd the *m*	*Locksley H., Sixty* 12
' The books, the *m*, the lace are hers,	*The Ring* 288

Minion   A downward crescent of her *m* mouth,   *Aylmer's Field* 533

Minion-knight   had overthrown Her *m-k*'s,   *Pelleas and E.* 235

Minister   Who may *m* to thee ?   Summer herself should *m*   *Eleänore* 31

Ministering   Friday fare was Enoch's *m*.   *Enoch Arden* 100

There the good mother's kindly *m*,	*Lover's Tale iv* 92
everywhere Low voices with the *m* hand	*Princess vii* 21

Ministration   for the power of *m* in her,   *Guinevere* 694

Ministries   tender *m* Of female hands and hospitality.'   *Princess vi* 72

Minneth   from Aroer On Arnon unto M.'   *D. of F. Women* 239

Minnie   M and Winnie Slept in a shell.   *Minnie and Winnie* 1

Minnow   And see the *m*'s everywhere   *Miller's D.* 51

Minster (adj.)   windy clanging of the *m* clock ;   *Gardener's D.* 38

south-breeze around thee blow The sound of	
m bells.	*Talking Oak* 272

Minster (adj.) (continued)   face Wellnigh was hidden
   in the m gloom ;   *Com. of Arthur* 289
Minster (s)   whose hymns Are chanted in the m,   *Merlin and V.* 766
   trees like the towers of a m,   *The Wreck* 74
   Here silent in our M of the West   *Epit. on Stratford* 3
   mountain stay'd me here, a m there,   *The Ring* 245
Minster-front   on one of those dark m-f's—   *Sea Dreams* 243
Minster-tower   bridge Crown'd with the m-t's.   *Gardener's D.* 44
Minstrel (adj.)   And talk and melody entertain'd.   *Lancelot and E.* 267
Minstrel (s)   the m sings Before them of the ten years'
   war   *Lotos-Eaters, C. S.* 76
   But ring the fuller m in.   *In Mem.* cvi 20
   A m of Caerleon by strong storm Blown into shelter   *Merlin and V.* 9
   And every m sings it differently ;   " 458
Mint   he has a m of reasons : ask.   *The Epic* 33
   As moulded like in Nature's m ;   *In Mem.* lxxix 6
   cleän Es a shillin' fresh fro' the m   *Spinster's S's.* 76
Minted   Creation m in the golden moods   *Princess* v 194
Minuet   thro' the stately m of those days :   *Aylmer's Field* 207
Minute (adj.)   How exquisitely m !   *Maud* II ii 7
Minute (s)   sweat her sixty m's to the death,   *Golden Year* 69
   The m's fledged with music : '   *Princess* iv 37
   came a m's pause, and Walter said,   " *Con.* 4
   Gone for a m, my son, from this room into the next ;
   I, too, shall go in a m.   *Grandmother* 103
   For a m, but for a m,   *Maud* I xx 45
   and suffering thus he made M's an age :   *Geraint and E.* 115
   glancing for a m, till he saw her Pass into it,   " 886
   Balin the stillness of a m broke   *Balin and Balan* 51
   ' Stay a little ! One golden m's grace ! '   *Lancelot and E.* 684
   An' Dan stood there for a m,   *Tomorrow* 22
   He that has lived for the lust of the m,   *Vastness* 27
   Lay your Plato for one m down,   *To Master of B.* 4
   Will only last a m ?   *Voice spake, etc.* 4
   Were nothing the next m ?   " 10
Miracle   (*See also* **Half-miracle, Main-miracle**)   So
   great a m as yonder hilt.   *M. d'Arthur* 156
   A certain m of symmetry,   *Gardener's D.* 11
   they say then that I work'd m's,   *St. S. Stylites* 80
   It may be I have wrought some m's,   " 136
   Can I work m's and not be saved ?   " 150
   Should, as by m, grow straight and fair—   *Aylmer's Field* 676
   ' O m of women,' said the book,   *Princess, Pro.* 35
   O m of noble womanhood ! '   " 48
   A m of design !   *Maud* II ii 8
   wonders ye have done ; M's ye cannot :   *Gareth and L.* 1325
   Mute of this m, far as I have read.   *Holy Grail* 66
   ' Then came a year of m :   " 166
   With m's and marvels like to these,   " 543
   hollow-ringing heavens sweep Over him till by m—   " 679
   With signs and m's and wonders,   *Guinevere* 222
   And simple m's of thy nunnery ? '   " 230
   Till he by m was approven King :   " 296
   So great a m as yonder hilt.   *Pass. of Arthur* 324
   a very m Of fellow-feeling and communion.   *Lover's Tale* i 250
   Heirlooms, and ancient m's of Art,   " iv 192
   That was a m to convert the king.   *Sir J. Oldcastle* 178
   this Caiaphas-Arundel What m could turn ?   " 180
   art *thou* the Prophet ? canst *thou* work M's ?   *Akbar's Dream* 118
   M's ! no, not I Nor he, nor any.   " 119
   And gaze on this great m, the World,   " 122
Miraculous   gaped upon him As on a thing m,   *Lancelot and E.* 453
   These have told us all their anger in m utterances,   *Boädicea* 23
Mirage   And a moist m in desert eyes,   *Maud* I vi 53
   finds the fountain where they wail'd ' M ' !   *Ancient Sage* 77
   thro' that m of overheated language   *Locksley H., Sixty* 113
   for no M of glory, but for power to fuse   *Akbar's Dream* 156
Mire   great heart and slips in sensual m,   *Princess* v 199
   by God's grace, he shall into the m—   *Gareth and L.* 723
   sank his head in m, and slimed themselves :   *Last Tournament* 471
   But curb the beast would cast thee in the m,   *Ancient Sage* 276
   from wallowing in the m of earth,   *Akbar's Dream* 141
Miriam   (*See also* **Miriam Erne, Miriam Lane**)   ' This
   miller's wife ' He said to M   *Enoch Arden* 805
   And on the book, half-frighted, M swore.   " 843

Miriam (continued)   M watch'd and dozed at intervals,   *Enoch Arden* 909
   Between a cymbal'd M and a Jael,   *Princess* v 511
   My M, breaks her latest earthly link   *The Ring* 47
   Your ' M breaks '—is making a new link   " 50
   Well, One way for M.   Miriam.   M am I not ?   " 73
   M your Mother might appear to me.   " 137
   M sketch'd and Muriel threw the fly ;   " 159
   and the face Of M grew upon me,   " 185
   this ' Io t'amo ' to the heart Of M ;   " 235
   he scrawl'd A ' M ' that might seem a ' Muriel ' ;   " 241
   Muriel claim'd and open'd what I meant For M,   " 242
   Muriel and M, each in white,   " 254
   M ! have you given your ring to her ?   " 260
   O M ! ' M redden'd, Muriel clench'd The hand that
   wore it,   " 261
   ' O M, if you love me take the ring ! '   " 263
   M loved me from the first, Not thro' the ring ;   " 274
   My M nodded with a pitying smile,   " 281
   And you my M born within the year ; And she my
   M dead within the year.   " 285
   Promise me, M not Muriel—she shall have the ring.'   " 294
   M, I am not surely one of those   " 343
   ' Muriel's health Had weaken'd, nursing little M.   " 357
   I told her ' sent To M,'   " 363
   M, on that day Two lovers parted by no scurrilous
   tale—   " 426
Miriam Erne   (*See also* **Miriam**)   M E And Muriel Erne—   " 146
Miriam Lane   (*See also* **Miriam**)   his widow M L, With
   daily-dwindling profits   *Enoch Arden* 695
   But M L was good and garrulous,   " 700
   Then he, tho' M L had told him all,   " 765
   He call'd aloud for M L and said   " 836
   M L Made such a voluble answer promising all,   " 902
Miring   harpies m every dish,   *Lucretius* 159
Mirror   (*See also* **Ocean-Mirror**)   Opposed m's each
   reflecting each—   *Sonnet to ——* 11
   And moving thro' a m clear That hangs   *L. of Shalott* ii 10
   sometimes thro' the m blue The knights came   " 24
   To weave the m's magic sights,   " 29
   He flash'd into the crystal m,   " iii 34
   The m crack'd from side to side ;   " 43
   on the liquid m glow'd The clear perfection   *Mariana in the S.* 31
   Without a m, in the gorgeous gown,   *Marr. of Geraint* 739
   realities Of which they were the m's.   *Lover's Tale* ii 163
   she makes Her heart a m that reflects   *The Ring* 366
   I gazed into the m, as a man Who sees his face   " 369
Mirror'd   a favourable speed Ruffle thy m mast,   *In Mem.* ix 7
Mirth   Come away : no more of m Is here   *Deserted House* 13
   Singing and murmuring in her feastful m,   *Palace of Art* 177
   not the less held she her solemn m,   " 215
   in a fit of frolic m She strove to span   *Talking Oak* 137
   Marrow of m and laughter ;   *Will Water.* 214
   I laugh'd And Lilia woke with sudden-shrilling m   *Princess, Pro.* 216
   clamouring etiquette to death, Unmeasured m ;   " v 18
   So large m lived and Gareth won the quest.   *Gareth and L.* 1426
   and with m so loud Beyond all use,   *Last Tournament* 235
Mirthful   m he, but in a stately kind—   *Lancelot and E.* 322
   And m sayings, children of the place,   *Holy Grail* 555
Misadventure   whom I rode, Hath suffer'd m,   *Balin and Balan* 476
Miscellany   Not like the piebald m, man,   *Princess* v 198
Mischance   Seeing all his own m—   *L. of Shalott* iv 12
   by m he slipt and fell : A limb was broken   *Enoch Arden* 106
   hearing his m, Came, for he knew the man   " 120
   So now that shadow of m appear'd No graver   " 128
   touch of all m but came As night to him   *Princess* iv 573
   by great m He heard but fragments of her later
   words,   *Marr. of Geraint* 112
   What I by mere m have brought, my shield.   *Lancelot and E.* 189
Mischief   they kept apart, no m done ;   *Princess* iv 340
Miscounted   Were all m as malignant haste   " 334
Miser   and the m would yearn for his gold,   *Despair* 100
Miserable   ' Ah, m and unkind, untrue,   *M. d'Arthur* 119
   Hating his own lean heart and m.   *Aylmer's Field* 526
   More m than she that has a son And sees him err :   *Princess* iii 260
   If she be small, slight-natured, m,   " vii 265

Miserable (*continued*) hide their faces, *m* in ignominy !   *Boädicea* 51
   her Whom he loves most, lonely and *m*.   *Marr. of Geraint* 123
   ' Ah, *m* and unkind, untrue,   *Pass. of Arthur* 287
   ' The *m* have no medicine But only Hope ! '   *Romney's R.* 149
   Not with blinded eyesight poring over *m* books—   *Locksley Hall* 172
   Low *m* lives of hand-to-mouth,   *Enoch Arden* 116
   O PURBLIND race of *m* men,   *Geraint and E.* 1

Misery Oh ! *m* ! Hark ! death is calling While
   I speak   *All Things will Die* 27
   In this extremest *m* Of ignorance,   *Supp. Confessions* 8
   ' Thou are so full of *m*,   *Two Voices* 2
   ' Thou art so steep'd in *m*,   "   47
   step beyond Our village *miseries*,   *Ancient Sage* 207
   in the *m* of my married life,   *The Ring* 136

Misfaith turn of anger born Of your *m* ;   *Merlin and V.* 532

Misfeaturing strange *m* mask that I saw so amazed
   me,   *The Wreck* 117

Mislearnt Have I *m* our place of meeting ?)   *Sir J. Oldcastle* 153

Misled ill counsel had *m* the girl   *Princess vii* 241

Mismated Not all *m* with a yawning clown,   *Geraint and E.* 426

Miss (s) The wither'd *M's* ! how they prose   *Amphion* 81

Miss (verb) Who *m* the brother of your youth ?   *To J. S.* 59
   I fear That we shall *m* the mail :   *Walk. to the Mail* 112
   yet may live in vain, and *m*, Meanwhile,   *Princess iii* 243
   Why should they *m* their yearly due   *In Mem. xxix* 15
   ye *m*,' he answer'd, ' the great deeds Of
   Lancelot,   *Lancelot and E.* 81
   And *m* the wonted number of my knights, And *m* to
   hear high talk of noble deeds   *Guinevere* 498

Missaid rebuked, reviled, *M* thee ;   *Gareth and L.* 1165

Missay hear thee so *m* me and revile.   "   945

Miss'd thou,' said I, ' hast *m* thy mark,   *Two Voices* 388
   And you have *m* the irreverent doom   *You might have won* 9
   Caught at and ever *m* it,   *Enoch Arden* 752
   But *m* the mignonette of Vivian-place,   *Princess, Pro.* 165
   O yes, you *m* us much.   "   169
   ' Come, listen ! here is proof that you were *m* :   "   177
   For blind with rage she *m* the plank,   " *iv* 177
   Till even those that *m* her most   *In Mem. xl* 27
   The head hath *m* an earthly wreath :   " *lxxiii* 6
   I have *m* the only way (repeat)   *Gareth and L.* 787, 792
   m, and brought Her own claw back,   *Merlin and V.* 499
   That *m* his living welcome,   *Tiresias* 197
   he *m* The wonted steam of sacrifice,   *Demeter and P.* 118

Misshaping Is our *m* vision of the Powers   *Sisters* (*E. and E.*) 230

Missile whelm'd with *m's* of the wall,   *Princess, Pro.* 45

Missing One flash, that, *m* all things else,   *Merlin and V.* 932

Mission ' Hast thou perform'd my *m* which I gave ?   *M. d'Arthur* 67
   Fly happy with the *m* of the Cross ;   *Golden Year* 43
   Her lavish *m* richly wrought,   *In Mem. lxxxiv* 34
   A soul on highest *m* sent,   " *cxiii* 10
   If this were all your *m* here,   " *cxxviii* 12
   On a blushing *m* to me,   *Maud I xxi* 11
   Rode on a *m* to the bandit Earl ;   *Geraint and E.* 527
   ' Hast thou perform'd my *m* which I gave ?   *Pass. of Arthur* 235
   My *m* be accomplish'd ! '   *Akbar's Dream* 199

Missis An' once I said to the *M*,   *North. Cobbler* 103
   the lasses 'ud talk o' their *M's* waäys, An' the *M'is*
   talk'd o' the lasses.—   *Village Wife* 57
   As I says to my to-daay,   *Church-warden, etc.* 25

Missive let our *m* thro', And you shall have her answer   *Princess v* 326

Mist (*See also* **Mind-mist, Morning-mist**) thou camest
   with the morning *m*, (repeat)   *Ode to Memory* 12, 21
         "   38
   she deem'd no *m* of earth could dull   *Two Voices* 188
   As over rainy *m* inclines A gleaming crag   *Œnone* 216
   Œnone see the morning *m* Sweep thro' them ;   *You ask me, why, etc.* 3
   Whose spirits falter in the *m*,   *Edwin Morris* 107
   The friendly *m* of morn Clung to the lake.   *St. S. Stylites* 75
   Inswathed sometimes in wandering *m*,   *Love and Duty* 43
   Rain out the heavy *m* of tears.   *Tithonus* 10
   Far-folded *m's*, and gleaming halls   "   63
   While Ilion like a *m* rose into towers.   *Will Water.* 39
   And softly, thro' a vinous *m*,   "
   When all the wood stands in a *m* of green,   *The Brook* 14
   In colours gayer than the morning *m*,   *Princess ii* 438

Mist (*continued*) two and thirty years were a *m* that
   rolls away ;   *V. of Cauteretz* 6
   The *m* and the rain, the *m* and the rain !   *Window, No Answer* 1
   Answer each other in the *m*.   *In Mem. xxviii* 4
   And then I know the *m* is drawn   " *lxvii* 13
   Is pealing, folded in the *m*.   " *civ* 4
   They melt like *m*, the solid lands,   " *cxxiii* 7
   turrets half-way down Prick'd thro' the *m* ;   *Gareth and L.* 194
   (Your city moved so weirdly in the *m*)   "   245
   o'er her meek eyes came a happy *m*   *Geraint and E.* 769
   An ever-moaning battle in the *m*,   *Merlin and V.* 192
   Or in the noon of *m* and driving rain,   "   636
   clave Like its own *m's* to all the mountain side :   *Lancelot and E.* 38
   light betwixt them burn'd Blurr'd by the creeping *m*,   *Guinevere* 5
   white *m*, like a face-cloth to the face,   "   7
   she saw, Wet with the *m's* and smitten by the lights,   "   597
   till himself became as *m* Before her,   "   604
   A deathwhite *m* slept over sand and sea :   *Pass. of Arthur* 95
   friend and foe were shadows in the *m*,   "   100
   and in the *m* Was many a noble deed,   "   104
   Look'd up for heaven, and only saw the *m* ;   "   112
   labourings of the lungs In that close *m*,   "   116
   blew The *m* aside, and with that wind the tide Rose,   "   125
   And whiter than the *m* that all day long   "   137
   like a golden *m* Charm'd amid eddies   *Lover's Tale i* 449
   As moonlight wandering thro' a *m* :   " *ii* 52
   That flings a *m* behind it in the sun—   " *iv* 294
   in the *m* and the wind and the shower   *Rizpah* 68
   Thro' the blotting *m*, the blinding showers,   *Sisters* (*E. and E.*) 18
   The *m* of autumn gather from your lake,   *The Ring* 329
   saw Your gilded vane, a light above the *m* '—   "   331
   dead cords that ran Dark thro' the *m*,   *Death of Œnone* 11
   crooked, reeling, livid, thro' the *m* Rose,   "   27
   and in the *m* at once Became a shadow,   "   49
   till the mortal morning *m's* of earth Fade   *Akbar's Dream* 96

Mist-blotted a great *m-b* light Flared on him,   *Enoch Arden* 680

Mistletoe Thorns, ivies, woodbine, *m's*,   *Day-Dm., Sleep. P.* 43

Mist-like Melts *m-l* into this bright hour,   *Princess vii* 355

Mistress (*See also* **Missis**) Let Grief be her own *m* still.   *To J. S.* 41
   Beauty such a *m* of the world.   *Gardener's D.* 58
   While Annie still was *m* ;   *Enoch Arden* 26
   No casual *m*, but a wife,   *In Mem. lix* 2
   The slowly-fading *m* of the world,   *Com. of Arthur* 505
   I come, great *M* of the ear and eye :   *Lover's Tale i* 22

Mistrust never shadow of *m* can cross Between us.   *Marr. of Geraint* 815
   shadow of *m* should never cross Betwixt them,   *Geraint and E.* 248

Mistrusted Saving that you *m* our good King   *Gareth and L.* 1172

Mistrustful same *m* mood That makes you seem less
   noble   *Merlin and V.* 321

Mist-wreathen Across a break on the *m-w* isle   *Enoch Arden* 632

Misty (*See also* **Silver-misty**) very air about the door
   Made *m* with the floating meal.   *Miller's D.* 104
   Across the mountain stream'd below In *m* folds,   *Palace of Art* 35
   From *m* men of letters ;   *Will Water.* 190
   the *m* summer And gray metropolis of the North.   *The Daisy* 103
   He finds on *m* mountain-ground His own vast
   shadow   *In Mem. xcvii* 2
   Wrapt in drifts of lurid smoke On the *m* river-tide.   *Maud II iv* 67
   Yet not so *m* were her meek blue eyes   *Geraint and E.* 772
   I cared not for it : a single *m* star,   *Merlin and V.* 508
   All in a *m* moonshine, unawares   *Lancelot and E.* 48
   The wide-wing'd sunset of the *m* marsh   *Last Tournament* 423

Misused cancell'd a sense *m* :   *Godiva* 72

Misyoked I—*m* with such a want of man—   *Last Tournament* 571

Mitred while this *m* Arundel Dooms our unlicensed
   preacher   *Sir J. Oldcastle* 104
      "   106

Mitre-sanction'd *m-s* harlot draws his clerks   *Two Voices* 210

Mix joy that *m'es* man with Heaven :   *Love thou thy land* 56
   Yearning to *m* himself with Life.   *Tithonus* 65
   can my nature longer *m* with thine ?   *Locksley Hall* 98
   I myself must *m* with action,   *Will Water.* 201
   So *m* for ever with the past,   *Princess ii* 251
   m the foaming draught Of fever,   "   360
   Speak little ; *m* not with the rest ;   " *iii* 113
   Hebes are they to hand ambrosia, *m* The nectar ;

Mix (*continued*)　while the fires of Hell *M* with his hearth :　*Princess v* 455
　think that you might *m* his draught with death,　" *vi* 277
　And *m* the seasons and the golden hours ;　*Ode Inter. Exhib.* 36
　' The sands and yeasty surges *m*　*Sailor Boy* 9
　And *m* with hollow masks of night ;　*In Mem. lxx* 4
　O tell me where the senses *m*,　" *lxxxviii* 3
　They *m* in one another's arms,　" *cii* 23
　May she *m* With men and prosper !　" *cxiv* 2
　M not memory with doubt,　*Maud II iv* 57
　Of those who *m* all odour to the Gods　*Tiresias* 184
　To *m* with the plow'd ;　*Ancient Sage* 145
　senses break away To *m* with ancient Night.'　" 153
　Will *m* with love for you and yours.　*To Marq. of Dufferin* 52
　That I might *m* with men, and hear their words　*Prog. of Spring* 82
　one of those Who *m* the wines of heresy　*Akbar's Dream* 174
　M me this Zone with that !　*Mechanophilus* 8
Mix'd-Mixt　The elements were kindlier *mix'd*.'　*Two Voices* 228
　She *mix'd* her ancient blood with shame.　*The Sisters* 8
　Mix'd with the knightly growth that fringed his
　　lips.　*M. d'Arthur* 220
　mix'd with shadows of the common ground !　*Gardener's D.* 135
　A welcome *mix'd* with sighs.　*Talking Oak* 212
　lights of sunset and of sunrise *mix'd*　*Love and Duty* 72
　In mosses *mixt* with violet　*Sir L. and Q. G.* 30
　Mix'd with cunning sparks of hell.　*Vision of Sin* 114
　rain of heaven, *mixt* Upon their faces,　*Aylmer's Field* 429
　on those cliffs Broke, *mixt* with awful light　*Sea Dreams* 215
　on the crowd Broke, *mixt* with awful light,　" 235
　cry Which *mixt* with little Margaret's,　" 246
　And *mixt* with these, a lady,　*Lucretius* 56
　mixt with inmost terms Of art and science :　*Princess, Pro.* 32
　we *mixt* with those Six hundred maidens　" *ii* 446
　our dreams ; he *mixt* with them :　" *iii* 220
　Part stumbled *mixt* with floundering horses.　" *v* 498
　like night and evening *mixt* Their dark and gray,　" *vi* 131
　And *mixt*, as life is *mixt* with pain,　*Ode Inter. Exhib.* 27
　Mixt with myrtle and clad with vine,　*The Islet* 19
　No—*mixt* with all this mystic frame,　*In Mem. lxxviii* 18
　He *mixt* in all our simple sports ;　" *lxxxix* 10
　Mixt their dim lights, like life and death,　" *xcv* 63
　Tho' *mix'd* with God and Nature thou,　" *cxxx* 11
　a world in which I have hardly *mixt*,　*Maud I vi* 76
　Mixt with kisses sweeter sweeter　" *II iv* 9
　mix'd my breath With a loyal people shouting　" *III vi* 34
　wildly fly, *Mixt* with the flyers.　*Geraint and E.* 483
　she *mixt* Her fancies with the sallow-rifted glooms　*Lancelot and E.* 1001
　brambles *mixt* And overgrowing them,　*Pelleas and E.* 422
　Nor with them *mix'd*, nor told her name,　*Guinevere* 148
　Mix'd with the knightly growth that fringed his
　　lips.　*Pass. of Arthur* 388
　Mixt with the gorgeous west the lighthouse shone,　*Lover's Tale i* 60
　and these *Mixt* with her own, because the fierce beast　*Tiresias* 151
　And *mixt* the dream of classic times　" 194
　past and future *mix'd* in Heaven　*The Ring* 186
　Black with bridal favours *mixt* !　*Forlorn* 69
　mixt with the great Sphere-music of stars　*Parnassus* 8
　mixt herself with *him* and past in fire.　*Death of Œnone* 106
Mixen　cast it on the *m* that it die.'　*Marr. of Geraint* 672
Mixing　Ice with the warm blood *m* ;　*All Things will Die* 33
　Which *m* with the infant's blood,　*Supp. Confessions* 61
　He *m* with his proper sphere,　*In Mem. lx* 5
Mixt　*See* **Mix'd**
Mizpeh　she went along From *M's* tower'd gate　*D. of F. Women* 199
Mnemosyne　That claspt the feet of a *M*,　*Princess iv* 269
Moab　water *M* saw Come round by the East,　*Last Tournament* 482
Moan (s)　(*See also* **Moän**)　Heard the war *m* along the
　distant sea,　*Buonaparte* 10
　But ' Ave Mary,' made she *m*,　*Mariana in the S.* 9
　And ' Ave Mary,' was her *m*,　" 21
　' Is this the form,' she made her *m*,　" 33
　She breathed in sleep a lower *m*,　" 45
　She whisper'd, with a stifled *m*　" 57
　' The day to night,' she made her *m*,　" 81
　And weeping then she made her *m*,　" 93

Moan (s) (*continued*)　Nor sold his heart to idle *m's*,　*Two Voices* 221
　In firry woodlands making *m* ;　*Miller's D.* 42
　hears the low *M* of an unknown sea ;　*Palace of Art* 280
　And make perpetual *m*,　*Lotos-Eaters, C. S.* 17
　And the low *m* of leaden-colour'd seas.　*Enoch Arden* 612
　The *m* of doves in immemorial elms,　*Princess vii* 221
　m of an enemy massacred,　*Boädicea* 25
　Is that enchanted *m* only the swell　*Maud I xviii* 62
　Crawl'd slowly with low *m's* to where he lay,　*Balin and Balan* 592
　And to all other ladies, I make *m* :　*Lancelot and E.* 1279
　So made his *m*, and, darkness falling,　*Pelleas and E.* 213
　M's of the dying, and voices of the dead.　*Pass. of Arthur* 117
　But when that *m* had past for evermore,　441
　mask of Hate, who lives on others' *m's*.　*Lover's Tale i* 775
　From under rose a muffled *m* of floods ;　*Prog. of Spring* 77
　and the *m* of my waves I whirl,　*The Dreamer* 13
　For *m's* will have grown sphere-music　29
Moän (s)　I 'eärd 'er a maäkin' 'er *m*,　*Spinster's S's.* 15
Moan (verb)　what is life, that we should *m* ?　*May Queen, Con.* 56
　the deep *M's* round with many voices.　*Ulysses* 56
　Nor ever lowest roll of thunder *m's*,　*Lucretius* 108
　or bits of roasting ox *M* round the spit—　" 132
　' Not such as *m's* about the retrospect,　*Princess iv* 85
　And *m* and sink to their rest.　*Voice and the P.* 16
　I hear the dead at midday *m*,　*Maud I vi* 70
　heard the Spirits of the waste and weald *M* as she
　　fled, or thought she heard them *m* :　*Guinevere* 130
　and the sea that 'ill *m* like a man ?　*Rizpah* 72
　water began to heave and the weather to *m*,　*The Revenge* 113
　ask'd the waves that *m* about the world　*Demeter and P.* 64
　' We know not, and we know not why we *m*.'　" 67
　M to myself ' one plunge—　*Charity* 16
Moan'd　the passion in her *m* reply　*Enoch Arden* 286
　She heard, she moved, She *m*,　*Princess v* 72
　And ever and aye the Priesthood *m*,　*The Victim* 23
　Weighted it down, but in himself he *m* :　*Balin and Balan* 225
　he kiss'd it, *m* and spake :　" 598
　All that had chanced, and Balan *m* again.　" 604
　and madden'd with himself and *m* :　*Pelleas and E.* 460
　And in herself she *m* ' Too late, too late ! '　*Guinevere* 131
　' O, you warm heart,' he *m*,　*Lover's Tale iv* 76
　' O Stephen,' I *m*, ' I am coming to thee　*The Wreck* 132
　m, I am fitter for my bed, or for my grave,　*The Ring* 432
　and *m* ' Œnone, *my* Œnone,　*Death of Œnone* 28
Moaneth　Wherefore he *m* thus,　*Supp. Confessions* 132
Moänin'　an' *m* an' naggin' agëän ;　*Owd Roä* 108
Moaning (adj. and part.)　(*See also* **Ever-moaning, Moänin'**)　Nor, *m*, household shelter crave　*Two Voices* 260
　And circle in the air :　*In Mem. xii* 15
　Uther died himself, *M* and wailing for an heir　*Com. of Arthur* 207
　Uther in Tintagil past away *M* and wailing for an
　　heir,　368
　M ' My violences, my violences ! '　*Balin and Balan* 435
　M and calling out of other lands,　*Merlin and V.* 962
　The phantom circle of a *m* sea.　*Pass. of Arthur* 87
　stones Strewn in the entry of the *m* cave ;　*Lover's Tale iii* 2
　But I could wish yon *m* sea would rise　*The Flight* 11
　I found myself *m* again　*The Wreck* 134
　Are there thunders *m* in the distance ?　*On Jub. Q. Victoria* 66
　M your losses, O Earth,　*The Dreamer* 7
Moaning (s)　Yes, as your *m's* witness,　*Aylmer's Field* 749
　The *m's* of the homeless sea,　*In Mem. xxxv* 9
　glooms Of evening, and the *m's* of the wind.　*Lancelot and E.* 1003
　Heard in his tent the *m's* of the King :　*Pass. of Arthur* 8
　The *m* of the woman and the child,　*Lover's Tale i* 520
　The *m's* in the forest, the loud brook,　" *ii* 114
　do ye make your *m* for my child ? '　*Demeter and P.* 65
　And may there be no *m* of the bar,　*Crossing the Bar* 3
Moat　My malice is no deeper than a *m*,　*Geraint and E.* 340
Moated　Upon the lonely *m* grange.　*Mariana* 8
　About the lonely *m* grange.　32
Mob (s)　Confused by brainless *m's*　*Ode on Well.* 153
　m's million feet Will kick you from your place,　*The Fleet* 18
　One truth will damn me with the mindless *m*,　*Romney's R.* 120
Mob (verb)　From my fixt height to *m* me up　*Princess vi* 308

Mock (adj.)   Autumn's *m* sunshine of the faded woods   *Aylmer's Field* 610
down rolls the world In *m* heroics stranger than our
own ;   *Princess, Con.* 64
Mock (s)   nor moves the loud world's random *m*,   *Will* 4
seamen made *m* at the mad little craft   *The Revenge* 38
Mock (verb)   I would *m* thy chaunt anew ;   *The Owl* ii 8
' *M* me not ! *m* me not ! love, let us go.'   *The Islet* 30
m at a barbarous adversary.   *Boädicea* 18
We *m* thee when we do not fear :   *In Mem., Pro.* 30
And *m* their foster-mother on four feet,   *Com. of Arthur* 31
I *m* thee not but as thou mockest me,   *Gareth and L.* 289
And now thou goest up to *m* the King,   " 292
' Is this thy courtesy—to *m* me, ha ?   *Balin and Balan* 495
And no man there will dare to *m* at me ;   *Lancelot and E.* 1053
marking how the knighthood *m* thee, fool—   *Last Tournament* 301
hear the garnet-headed yaffingale *M* them :   " 701
he never *m*'s, For mockery is the fume   *Guinevere* 632
Mock-disease   old hysterical *m-d* should die.'   *Maud* III vi 33
Mock'd   That *m* the wholesome human heart,   *The Letters* 13
That *m* him with returning calm,   *Lucretius* 25
This railer, that hath *m* thee in full hall—   *Gareth and L.* 369
first they *m*, but, after, reverenced him.   " 507
Garlon *m* me, but I heeded not.   *Balin and Balan* 606
he smote his thigh, and *m* : ' Right was the
King !   *Lancelot and E.* 664
But when she *m* his vows and the great King,   *Pelleas and E.* 252
but with plumes that *m* the may,   *Guinevere* 22
Except he *m* me when he spake of hope ;   " 631
I So *m*, so spurn'd, so baited two whole days—   *Sir J. Oldcastle* 163
I would not be *m* in a madhouse !   *Despair* 79
Mocker   Betwixt the *m*'s and the realists :   *Princess, Con.* 24
the *m* ending here Turn'd to the right,   *Gareth and L.* 294
Mockery   And my *mockeries* of the world.   *Vision of Sin* 202
A *m* to the yeomen over ale,   *Aylmer's Field* 497
I seem A *m* to my own self.   *Princess* vii 337
not wholly brain, Magnetic *mockeries*,   *In Mem.* cxx 3
Marr'd tho' it be with spite and *m* now,   *Pelleas and E.* 327
But these in earnest those in *m* call'd   *Last Tournament* 135
there with gibes and flickering *mockeries*   " 186
The *m* of my people, and their bane.'   *Guinevere* 526
For *m* is the fume of little hearts.   " 633
Mockest   Why *m* thou the stranger   *Gareth and L.* 283
but as thou *m* me, And all that see thee,   " 289
Mock-heroic   The sort of *m-h* gigantesque,   *Princess, Con.* 11
Mock-honour   Did her *m-h* as the fairest fair,   *Geraint and E.* 833
Mock-Hymen   *M-H* were laid up like winter bats,   *Princess* iv 144
Mocking   made me a *m* curtsey and went.   *Grandmother* 46
almost Arthur's words—A *m* fire :   *Holy Grail* 670
Now *m* at the much ungainliness,   *Last Tournament* 728
O the formal *m* bow,   *The Flight* 27
I heard a *m* laugh ' the new Korân ! '   *Akbar's Dream* 183
Mocking-wise   Sir Garlon utter'd *m-w* ;   *Balin and Balan* 389
Mock-knight   Had made *m-k* of Arthur's Table
Round,   *Last Tournament* 2
Mock-love   same *m-l*, and this Mock-Hymen   *Princess* iv 143
Mock-loyal   With reverent eyes *m-l*,   *Merlin and V.* 54
Mock-meek   That *m-m* mouth of utter Antichrist,   *Sir J. Oldcastle* 170
Mock-sister   after marriage, that *m-s* there—   *Sisters (E. and E.)* 172
Mock-solemn   something so *m-s*, that I laugh'd   *Princess, Pro.* 215
Mode   (See also **Man-mode**)   Odalisques, or oracles of *m*,   *Princess* ii 77
Ring in the nobler *m*'s of life,   *In Mem.* cvi 15
Model (adj.)   ' This *m* husband, this fine Artist ' !   *Romney's R.* 124
Model (s)   why should any man Remodel *m*'s ?   *The Epic* 38
A dozen angry *m*'s jetted steam :   *Princess, Pro.* 73
glove upon the tomb Lay by her like a *m* of her hand.   " iv 597
This mother is your *m*.   " vii 335
the giant aisles, Rich in *m* and design ;   *Ode Inter. Exhib.* 13
To serve as *m* for the mighty world,   *Guinevere* 465
Accomplish that blind *m* in the seed,   *Prog. of Spring* 114
Modell'd   Is but *m* on a skull.   *Vision of Sin* 178
Neither *m*, glazed, nor framed :   " 188
Moderate   statesman-warrior, *m*, resolute,   *Ode on Well.* 25
Modern   To make demand of *m* rhyme   *To the Queen* 11
Not master'd by some *m* term ;   *Love thou thy land* 30
Perhaps some *m* touches here and there   *M. d'Arthur, Ep.* 6

Modern (continued)   King Arthur, like a *m* gentleman
Of stateliest port ;   *M. d'Arthur, Ep.* 22
Or something of a wayward *m* mind Dissecting
passion.   *Edwin Morris* 87
The *m* Muses reading.   *Amphion* 76
Cock was of a larger egg Than *m* poultry drop,   *Will Water.* 122
What hope is here for *m* rhyme To him,   *In Mem.* lxxvii 1
Full-handed plaudits from our best In *m* letters,   *To E. Fitzgerald* 39
your *m* amourist is of easier, earthlier make.   *Locksley H., Sixty* 18
Something other than the wildest *m* guess of you
and me.   " 232
And that bright hair the *m* sun,   *Epilogue* 8
Modest   To make him trust his *m* worth,   *L. C. V. de Vere* 46
like a pear In growing, *m* eyes, a hand.   *Walk. to the Mail* 54
Him, to her meek and *m* bosom prest   *Aylmer's Field* 416
' O marvellously *m* maiden, you !   *Princess* iii 48
How *m*, kindly, all-accomplish'd, wise,   *Ded. of Idylls* 18
Modish   The *m* Cupid of the day,   *Talking Oak* 67
Modred (**A knight of the Round Table**)   Gawain and
young *M*, her two sons,   *Com. of Arthur* 244
M laid his ears beside the doors,   " 323
came With *M* hither in the summertime,   *Gareth and L.* 26
M for want of worthier was the judge.   " 28
M biting his thin lips was mute,   " 31
all in fear to find Sir Gawain or Sir *M*,   " 326
And *M*'s blank as death ;   " 417
Sir *M*'s brother, and the child of Lot,   *Lancelot and E.* 558
M thought, ' The time is hard at hand.'   *Pelleas and E.* 610
show'd him, like a vermin in its hole, *M*, a
narrow face :   *Last Tournament* 166
her cause of flight Sir *M* ;   *Guinevere* 10
M still in green, all ear and eye.   " 24
laugh'd Lightly, to think of *M*'s dusty fall, Then
shudder'd,   " 55
M's narrow foxy face, Heart-hiding smile,   " 63
M brought His creatures to the basement   " 103
that Sir *M* had usurp'd the realm,   " 154
And *M* whom he left in charge of all,   " 195
And many more when *M* raised revolt,   " 441
clave To *M*, and a remnant stays with me.   " 443
I hear the steps of *M* in the west,   *Pass. of Arthur* 59
And ever push'd Sir *M*, league by league,   " 80
yonder stands, *M*, unharm'd, the traitor of
thine house.'   " 153
then *M* smote his liege Hard on that helm   " 165
Modulate   *M* me, Soul of mincing mimicry !   *Princess* ii 425
Modulated   They were *m* so To an unheard melody,   *Eleänore* 63
Mogul   he that led the world *M*'s,   *Locksley H., Sixty* 81
Moind (**mind**)   D'ya *m* the waäste, my lass ?   *N. Farmer, O. S.* 29
Moist   And *m* and dry, devising long,   *Love thou thy land* 38
At the *m* rich smell of the rotting leaves,   *A spirit haunts* 17
And a *m* mirage in desert eyes,   *Maud* I vi 53
or the fancy of it, Made his eye *m* ; but Enid
fear'd his eyes, *M* as they were,   *Geraint and E.* 350
and *m* or dry, Full-arm'd upon his charger   *Pelleas and E.* 215
Moisten   her true hand falter, nor blue eye *M*,   *Geraint and E.* 513
Moisture   blew Coolness and *m* and all smells   *Lover's Tale* iii 5
Mole (**animal**)   The four-handed *m* shall scrape,   *My life is full* 12
the *m* has made his run,   *Aylmer's Field* 849
you can hear him—the murderous *m* !   *Def. of Lucknow* 26
Mole (**on the skin**)   Were it but for a wart or a *m* ? '   *Dead Prophet* 56
Moll   tavern-catch Of *M* and Meg,   *Princess* iv 158
Molly   (See also **Molly Magee**)   *M* the long un she walkt
awaäy wi' a hofficer lad,   *Village Wife* 97
for *M* was out of her mind.   *Tomorrow* 6
' *M* asthore, I'll meet you agin tomorra,'   " 15
Thin *M*'s ould mother, yer Honour,   " 19
But *M*, begorrah, 'ud listhen to naither at all,   " 46
But *M* says ' I'd his hand-promise,   " 52
' *M*, you're manin',' he says, me dear,   " 56
But *M* kem limpin' up wid her stick,   " 77
Och, *M*, we thought, machree,   " 81
When *M* cooms in fro' the far-end close   *Spinster's S's.* 2
M belike may 'a lighted to-night upo' one.   " 7
An' *M* and me was agreed,   " 49

Q*

Monstrous (*continued*)   *m* blasphemies, Sweat, writhings, anguish,   *Pass. of Arthur* 114

Hard Romans brawling of their *m* games ;   *St. Telemachus* 40

Monte Rosa   how phantom-fair, Was *M R*,   *The Daisy* 66

Montfort (Edith)   *See* **Edith, Edith Montfort**

Month (*See also* **Seven-months'**)   Each *m* is various to present The world   *Two Voices* 74

Link'd *m* to *m* with such a chain Of knitted purport,   ,, 167

Whole weeks and *m's*, and early and late,   *The Sisters* 10

Earn well the thrifty *m's*,   *Love thou thy land* 95

Consider, William : take a *m* to think,   *Dora* 29

before The *m* was out he left his father's house,   ,, 37

Above the river, and, but a *m* ago,   *Walk. to the Mail* 2

in one *m* They wedded her to sixty thousand pounds,   *Edwin Morris* 125

and oft I fall, Maybe for *m's*,   *St. S. Stylites* 103

I must work thro' *m's* of toil,   *Amphion* 97

Each *m*, a birth-day coming on,   *Will Water.* 93

Came floating on for many a *m* and year,   *Vision of Sin* 54

a *m*—Give her a *m*—she knew that she was bound— A *m*—   *Enoch Arden* 461

So *m* by *m* the noise about their doors,   *Aylmer's Field* 488

face to face With twenty *m's* of silence,   ,, 567

In one *m*; Thro' weary and yet ever wearier hours,   ,, 827

Came, with a *m's* leave given them,   *Sea Dreams* 6

ere the silver sickle of that *m*   *Princess i* 101

' A *m* hence, a *m* hence.   *Window, When* 7

The all-assuming *m's* and years   *In Mem. lxxxv* 67

And tho' the *m's*, revolving near,   ,, *xcii* 11

As nine *m's* go to the shaping an infant   *Maud I iv* 34

In another *m* to his brazen lies,   ,, *vi* 55

as *m's* ran on and rumour of battle grew,   ,, *III vi* 29

So for a *m* he wrought among the thralls ;   *Gareth and L.* 525

weeks to *m's*, The *m's* will add themselves   *Guinevere* 624

would not look at her—No not for *m's* ;   *Lover's Tale iv* 27

nine long *m's* of antenatal gloom,   *De Prof., Two G.* 8

last *m* they wor diggin' the bog,   *Tomorrow* 61

Altho' the *m's* have scarce begun,   *To Ulysses* 22

Monument   A *m* of childhood and of love ;   *Lover's Tale ii* 183

Mood   Were fixed shadows of thy fixed *m*,   *Isabel* 9

But more human in your *m's*,   *Margaret* 47

We taught him lowlier *m's*,   *Buonaparte* 9

In lazy *m* I watch'd the little circles die ;   *Miller's D.* 73

fit for every *m* And change of my still soul.   *Palace of Art* 59

As fit for every *m* of mind,   ,, 90

from which *m* was born Scorn of herself ; again, from out that *m* Laughter at her self-scorn.   ,, 230

' I govern'd men by change, and so I sway'd All *m's*.   *D. of F. Women* 131

but betwixt this *m* and that,   *Gardener's D.* 155

I went thro' many wayward *m's*   *Day-Dm., Pro.* 6

She changes with that *m* or this,   *Will Water.* 107

cruel Seem'd the Captain's *m*.   *The Captain* 14

But subject to the season or the *m*,   *Aylmer's Field* 71

How low his brother's *m* had fallen,   ,, 404

and in her lion's *m* Tore open,   *Princess iv* 380

Creation minted in the golden *m's* Of sovereign artists ;   ,, *v* 194

And left her woman, lovelier in her *m*   ,, *vii* 162

saw Thee woman thro' the crust of iron *m's*   ,, 342

My lighter *m's* are like to these,   *In Mem. xx* 9

I envy it in any *m's* The captive void   ,, *xxvii* 1

Mere fellowship of sluggish *m's*,   ,, *xxxv* 21

What vaster dream can hit the *m* Of Love on earth ?   ,, *xlvii* 11

She takes, when harsher *m's* remit,   ,, *xlviii* 6

And put thy harsher *m's* aside,   ,, *lix* 7

Nor less it pleased in livelier *m's*,   ,, *lxxxix* 29

am I raging alone as my father raged in his *m* ?   *Maud I i* 53

My *m* is changed, for it fell at a time of year   ,, *III vi* 4

coming up quite close, and in his *m*   *Geraint and E.* 714

Let not thy *m's* prevail, when I am gone   *Balin and Balan* 140

So when his *m's* were darken'd,   ,, 235

fain have wrought upon his cloudy *m*   *Merlin and V.* 156

And yielding to his kindlier *m's*,   ,, 174

Dark in the glass of some presageful *m*,   ,, 295

Mood (*continued*)   fled from Arthur's court To break the *m*.   *Merlin and V.* 298

Not half so strange as that dark *m* of yours.   ,, 314

same mistrustful *m* That makes you seem less noble   ,, 321

such a *m* as that, which lately gloom'd   ,, 325

As high as woman in her selfless *m*.   ,, 443

or a *m* Of overstrain'd affection,   ,, 521

Vivien, gathering somewhat of his *m*,   ,, 842

wrought upon his *m* and hugg'd him close.   ,, 948

but in him His *m* was often like a fiend,   *Lancelot and E.* 251

Arthur to the banquet, dark in *m*, Past,   ,, 564

turn'd Sir Torre, being in his *m's* Left them,   ,, 799

Gawain in his *m* Had made mock-knight   *Last Tournament* 1

Tristram, half plagued by Lancelot's languorous *m*,   ,, 194

Was mine a *m* To be invaded rudely,   *Lover's Tale i* 677

At times too shrilling in her angrier *m's*,   *The Ring* 395

your opiate then Bred this black *m* ?   *Romney's R.* 62

each philosophy And *m* of faith   *Akbar's Dream* 56

m's of tiger, or of ape ?   *Making of Man* 2

Moon (*See also* **Crescent-moon, Honeymoon**)   At midnight the *m* cometh,   *Claribel* 13

The mellow'd reflex of a winter *m* ;   *Isabel* 29

And ever when the *m* was low,   *Mariana* 49

But when the *m* was very low,   ,, 53

WHAT time the mighty *m* was gathering light   *Love and Death* 1

There would be neither *m* nor star ;   *The Merman* 21

Neither *m* nor star.   ,, 24

Which the *m* about her spreadeth,   *Margaret* 20

Breathes low between the sunset and the *m* ;   *Eleänore* 124

And by the *m* the reaper weary,   *L. of Shalott i* 33

Or when the *m* was overhead,   ,, *ii* 33

' For every worm beneath the *m*   *Two Voices* 178

Gleam'd to the flying *m* by fits.   *Miller's D.* 116

Faints like a dazzled morning *m*.   *Fatima* 12

Lit with a low large *m*.   *Palace of Art* 68

In hollow'd *m's* of gems,   ,, 188

It was when the *m* was setting,   *May Queen, Con.* 26

Full-faced above the valley stood the *m* ;   *Lotos-Eaters* 7

Between the sun and *m* upon the shore ;   ,, 38

and in the *m* Nightly dew-fed ;   ,, *C. S.* 29

Once, like the *m*, I made The ever-shifting currents   *D. of F. Women* 132

Far-heard beneath the *m*.   ,, 184

balmy *m* of blessed Israel Floods all the deep-blue gloom   ,, 185

the next *m* was roll'd into the sky,   ,, 229

While the stars burn, the *m's* increase,   *To J. S.* 71

Lay a great water, and the *m* was full.   *M. d'Arthur* 12

And in the *m* athwart the place of tombs,   ,, 46

the winter *m* Brightening the skirts of a long cloud,   ,, 53

great brand Made lightnings in the splendour of the *m*,   ,, 137

And the long glories of the winter *m*.   ,, 192

colourless, and like the wither'd *m*   ,, 213

for some three careless *m's*,   *Gardener's D.* 15

rose And saunter'd home beneath a *m*, that, just In crescent,   *Audley Court* 80

But thirty *m's*, one honeymoon to that,   *Edwin Morris* 29

my beard Was tagg'd with icy fringes in the *m*,   *St. S. Stylites* 32

Sun will run his orbit, and the *M* Her circle.   *Love and Duty* 22

long day wanes : the slow *m* climbs :   *Ulysses* 55

mellow *m's* and happy skies,   *Locksley Hall* 159

stand at gaze like Joshua's *m* in Ajalon !   ,, 180

like a summer *m* Half-dipt in cloud :   *Godiva* 45

the snows Are sparkling to the *m* :   *St. Agnes' Eve* 2

Far ran the naked *m* across The houseless ocean's   *The Voyage* 29

A thousand *m's* will quiver ;   *A Farewell* 14

As shines the *m* in clouded skies,   *Beggar Maid* 9

beneath a clouded *m* He like a lover   *Enoch Arden* 658

I murmur under *m* and stars In brambly wildernesses ;   *The Brook* 178

music of the *m* Sleeps in the plain eggs   *Aylmer's Field* 102

Beneath a pale and unimpassion'd *m*,   ,, 334

father's face Grow long and troubled like a rising *m*,   *Princess i* 59

Come from the dying *m*, and blow,   ,, *iii* 6

out of the west Under the silver *m* :   ,, 15

with the sun and *m* renew their light For ever,   ,, 255

Moon (*continued*) For many weary *m*'s before we came, *Princess iii* 319
And brief the *m* of beauty in the South. ,, iv 113
I babbled for you, as babies for the *m*, ,, 428
A maiden *m* that sparkles on a sty, ,, v 186
like a clouded *m* In a still water : ,, vi 270
Now set a wrathful Dian's *m* on flame, ,, 368
Ask me no more : the *m* may draw the sea ; ,, vii 1
our God Himself is *m* and sun. *Ode on Well.* 217
The *m* have a rick on fire was rising *Grandmother* 39
Echo on echo Dies to the *m*. *Minnie and Winnie* 12
THE sun, the *m*, the stars, *High. Pantheism* 1
when in heaven the stars about the *m* *Spec. of Iliad* 11
Sun comes, *m* comes, Time slips away. Sun sets,
m sets, Love, fix a day. *Window, When* 1
charms Her secret from the latest *m* ? ' *In Mem. xxi* 20
No lapse of *m*'s can canker Love, ,, xxvi 3
The *m* is hid ; the night is still ; ,, xxviii 2
Or when a thousand honey *m*'s shall wane ,, lxxvii 8
Or sadness in the summer *m*'s ? ,, lxxxiii 8
flung A ballad to the brightening *m* : ,, lxxxix 28
The sailing *m* in creek and cove ; ,, ci 16
The *m* is hid, the night is still ; ,, civ 2
glowing like the *m* Of Eden on its bridal bower : ,, *Con.* 27
And rise, O *m*, from yonder down, ,, 109
hand, as white As ocean-foam in the *m*, *Maud I xiv* 18
And a hush with the setting *m*. ,, xxii 18
Now half to the setting *m* are gone, ,, 23
Not many *m*'s, King Uther died himself, *Com. of Arthur* 206
Between the in-crescent and de-crescent *m*, *Gareth and L.* 529
O *m*, that layest all to sleep again, ,, 1061
Answer'd Sir Gareth graciously to one Not many
a *m* his younger, ,, 1415
by night With *m* and trembling stars, *Marr. of Geraint* 8
but three brief *m*'s had glanced away *Balin and Balan* 154
Those twelve sweet *m*'s confused his fatherhood.' *Merlin and V.* 712
All in the middle of the rising *m* : *Holy Grail* 636
And with me drove the *m* and all the stars ; ,, 809
That kept the entry, and the *m* was full. ,, 818
the rounded *m* Thro' the tall oriel on the rolling sea. ,, 830
until the third night brought a *m* *Pelleas and E.* 393
Here too, all hush'd below the mellow *m*, ,, 424
their own darkness, throng'd into the *m*. ,, 458
She lived a *m* in that low lodge with him : *Last Tournament* 381
Far over sands marbled with *m* and cloud, ,, 466
Beneath a *m* unseen albeit at full, *Guinevere* 6
on one Lay a great water, and the *m* was full, *Pass of Arthur* 180
in the *m* athwart the place of tombs, ,, 214
winter *m*, Brightening the skirts of a long cloud, ,, 221
great brand Made lightnings in the splendour of the *m*, ,, 305
And the long glories of the winter *m*. ,, 360
face was white And colourless, and like the wither'd *m* ,, 381
the *m*, Half-melted into thin blue air, *Lover's Tale i* 420
came in The white light of the weary *m* above, ,, 640
But many weary *m*'s I lived alone— ,, ii 2
glows and glories of the *m* Below black firs, ,, 110
eleventh *m* After their marriage lit the lover's Bay, ,, iv 27
m Struck from an open grating overhead ,, 59
and the full *m* stares at the snow. *Rizpah* 4
Willy—the *m*'s in a cloud— ,, 86
With this last *m*, this crescent— *De Prof., Two G.* 9
ninth *m*, that sends the hidden sun Down yon
dark sea, ,, 33
Drew to this shore lit by the suns and *m*'s ,, 38
this roaring *m* of daffodil And crocus, *Pref. Son., 19th Cent.* 7
Rejoicing that the sun, the *m*, the stars *Tiresias* 160
and crows to the sun and the *m*, *Despair* 91
Till the Sun and the *M* of our science ,, 91
there was but a slip of a *m*, *Tomorrow* 9
wid his song to the Sun an' the *M*, ,, 91
dead as yon dead world the *m* ? *Locksley H., Sixty* 174
m was falling greenish thro' a rosy glow, ,, 178
Beneath a hard Arabian *M* And alien stars. *To Marq. of Dufferin* 45
gleam as of the *m*, When first she peers along *Demeter and P.* 13
dwell For nine white *m*'s of each whole year ,, 120
To send the *m* into the night and break ,, 135

Moon (*continued*) MELLOW *m* of heaven, Bright in blue, *M* of
married hearts, Hear me, you ! *The Ring* 1
Globing Honey *M*'s Bright as this. ,, 7
M, you fade at times From the night. ,, 9
Globe again, and make Honey *M*. ,, 16
Shall not *my* love last, *M*, with you, ,, 18
They made a thousand honey *m*'s of one ? ,, 22
And while the *m* was setting. *Forlorn* 84
not be follow'd by the *M* ? *Happy* 97
Mooned Upon the *m* domes aloof In inmost Bagdat, *Arabian Nights* 127
Mooney (**money**) Parson as hesn't the call, nor the *m*, *Village Wife* 91
Moon-faced Maud the beloved of my mother, the *m-f*
darling of all,— *Maud I i* 72
Moon-led Their *m-l* waters white. *Palace of Art* 252
Moonless Storm, such as drove her under *m* heavens *Enoch Arden* 547
Grind on the wakeful ear in the hush of the *m* nights, *Maud I i* 42
A *m* night with storm— *Sisters (E. and E.)* 96
Sunless and *m*, utter light—but no ! *Columbus* 90
Moonlight By star-shine and by *m*, *Oriana* 24
Like *m* on a falling shower ? *Margaret* 4
Are as *m* unto sunlight, *Locksley Hall* 152
A full sea glazed with muffled *m*, *Princess i* 248
A cypress in the *m* shake, *The Daisy* 82
m touching o'er a terrace One tall Agavè ,, 83
When on my bed the *m* falls, *In Mem. lxvii* 1
From off my bed the *m* dies ; ,, 10
' It is not Arthur's use To hunt by *m* ; ' *Holy Grail* 111
There in the shuddering *m* brought its face *Lover's Tale i* 650
I saw the *m* glitter on their tears— ,, 697
As *m* wandering thro' a mist : ,, ii 52
His lady with the *m* on her face ; ,, iv 57
Yet the *m* is the sunlight, *Locksley H., Sixty* 182
Not of the *m*, Not of the starlight ! *Merlin and the G.* 121
Moonlike glooms of my dark will, *M* emerged, *Lover's Tale i* 745
O will she, *m*, sway the main, *Mechanophilus* 3
Moon-lit The sloping of the *m-l* sward *Arabian Nights* 27
With narrow *m-l* slips of silver cloud, *Œnone* 218
Far in the *m* haze among the hills, *Pass. of Arthur* 42
Who toils across the middle *m* nights, *Lover's Tale i* 138
Moon-rise little before *m-r* hears the low Moan *Palace of Art* 279
Moonshine eyes all wet, in the sweet *m* : *Grandmother* 49
labouring up the pass, All in a misty *m*, *Lancelot and E.* 48
Moony The *m* vapour rolling round the King, *Guinevere* 601
Moor (**adj.**) Over the dark *m* land, *Maud I ix* 6
Moor (**land**) From far and near, on mead and *m*, *In Mem. xxviii* 6
Yet oft when sundown skirts the *m* ,, xli 17
I am sick of the *m* and the main. *Maud I i* 61
No, there is fatter game on the *m* ; ,, 74
I bow'd to his lady-sister as she rode by on the *m* ; ,, iv 15
Betwixt the cloud and the *m* ,, ix 4
And over the sullen-purple *m* (Look at it) ,, x 21
Go back, my lord, across the *m*, ,, xii 31
ye meanwhile far over *m* and fell ,, xviii 76
When I bow'd to her on the *m*. ,, xix 66
I will wander till I die about the barren *m*'s. *The Flight* 56
Is that the leper's hut on the solitary *m*, *Happy* 9
Moor (**more**) Says that I moänt 'a naw *m* aäle : *N. Farmer, O. S.* 3
Moor (**race of people**) When Spain was waging war against
the *M*—I strove myself with Spain against the *M*. *Columbus* 93
I am handled worse than had I been a *M*, ,, 107
given the Great Khan's palaces to the *M*, Or clutch'd the
sacred crown of Prester John, And cast it to the *M* : ,, 109
Moor'd where man Hath *m* and rested ? *Supp. Confessions* 124
Were borne about the bay or safely *m* *Lover's Tale i* 54
Moorland (*See also* **Moor** (**adj.**)) Dreary gleams about the *m* *Locksley Hall* 4
Many a morning on the *m* ,, 35
O the dreary, dreary *m* ! ,, 40
glimmering *m* rings With jingling bridle-reins. *Sir L. and Q. G.* 35
wastest *m* of our realm shall be Safe, *Gareth and L.* 603
Mooted ne'er been *m*, but as frankly theirs *Princess v* 203
Moother (**mother**) *M* 'ed tell'd ma to bring tha down, *Owd Roä* 50
when *M* 'ed gotten to bed, ,, 55
I kick'd 'im ageän, but I kick'd thy *M* instead. ,, 67
M 'ed beän a-naggin' about the gell o' the farm, ,, 69
But *M* was free of 'er tongue, ,, 73

Moother (mother) (*continued*) Thy *M* was howdin' the
    lether,   *Owd Roä* 85
M was naggin' an' groänin' an' moänin'   „   108
M 'ed beän sa soäk'd wi' the thaw   „   113
Moral (adj.) (*See also* **Maudlin-moral**) Then of the
    m instinct would she prate   *Palace of Art* 205
' Last of the train, a *m* leper, I,   *Princess* iv 222
He gain in sweetness and in *m* height,   „   vii 281
' A *m* child without the craft to rule,   *Lancelot and E.* 146
Farewell, Macready ; *m*, grave, sublime ;   *To W. C. Macready* 12
Moral (s) And if you find no *m* there,   *Day-Dm., Moral* 2
    What *m* is in being fair.   „   4
is there any *m* shut Within the bosom   „   7
You'd have *my m* from the song,   „ *L' Envoi* 31
Are clasp'd the *m* of thy life,   „   55
The *m's*, something of the frame,   *Princess* ii 382
Morass Or low *m* and whispering reed,   *In Mem.* c 6
Morbid Vex'd with a *m* devil in his blood   *Walk. to the Mail* 19
Till a *m* hate and horror have grown   *Maud* I vi 7
And a *m* eating lichen fixt On a heart   „   77
' It is time, O passionate heart and *m* eye,   „ *III* vi 32
I used to walk This Terrace—*m*, melancholy ;   *The Ring* 168
More *See* **Moor**
Moreland (Emma) *See* **Emma Moreland**
Morganore *M*, And Lot of Orkney.   *Com. of Arthur* 115
Moriah the dead Went wandering o'er *M*—   *Holy Grail* 50
    our most ancient East *M* with Jerusalem ;   *Columbus* 81
Morion shone Their *m's*, wash'd with morning,   *Princess* v 264
Morn (*See also* **After-morn, Christmas-morn, Hunting-morn, Marriage-morn, Murn, Summer-morn, Yestermorn**) For even and *m* Ever will be
    Thro' eternity.   *Nothing will Die* 33
For even and *m* Ye will never see Thro'
    eternity.   *All Things will Die* 44
she bow'd Above Thee, on that happy *m*   *Supp. Confessions* 24
' Yet,' said I, in my *m* of youth,   „   139
Either at *m* or eventide.   *Mariana* 16
Till cold winds woke the gray-eyed *m*   „   31
Ray-fringed eyelids of the *m*   *Clear-headed friend* 6
amber *m* Forth gushes from beneath a low-hung
    cloud.   *Ode to Memory* 70
Wander from the side of the *m*,   *Adeline* 52
Thou wert born, on a summer *m*   *Eleänore* 7
And ' Ave Mary,' night and *m*,   *Mariana in the S.* 10
' Madonna, sad is night and *m*,'   „   22
' That won his praises night and *m* ? '   „   34
And murmuring, as at night and *m*,   „   46
More inward than at night or *m*,   „   58
' The day to night, the night to *m*,   „   82
' The night comes on that knows not *m*,   „   94
' Or make that *m*, from his cold crown   *Two Voices* 85
Or in the gateways of the *m*.   „   183
' Behold, it is the Sabbath *m*.'   „   402
Each *m* my sleep was broken thro'   *Miller's D.* 39
in the dark *m* The panther's roar came muffled,   *Œnone* 213
from her lips, as *m* from Memnon, drew Rivers   *Palace of Art* 171
All night I lie awake, but I fall asleep at *m* ;   *May Queen, N. Y's. E.* 50
The dim red *m* had died,   *D. of F. Women* 61
M broaden'd on the borders of the dark,   „   265
From out the borders of the *m*,   *On a Mourner* 24
without help I cannot last till *m*.   *M. d'Arthur* 26
Shot like a streamer of the northern *m*,   „   139
dark East, Unseen, is brightening to his bridal *m*.   *Gardener's D.* 73
hour just flown, that *m* with all its sound,   „   83
I come to-morrow *m*. I go,   *Audley Court* 70
friendly mist of *m* Clung to the lake.   *Edwin Morris* 107
And when my marriage *m* may fall,   *Talking Oak* 285
Far-folded mists, and gleaming halls of *m*.   *Tithonus* 10
Thou wilt renew thy beauty *m* by *m* ;   „   74
leave me here a little, while as yet 'tis early *m* :   *Locksley Hall* 1
The twilight melted into *m*.   *Day-Dm., Depart.* 16
The cock crows ere the Christmas *m*,   *Sir Galahad* 51
They two will wed the morrow *m* :   *Lady Clare* 7
We two will wed to-morrow *m*,   „   87
And perplex'd her, night and *m*,   *L. of Burleigh* 78

Morn (*continued*) Nor anchor dropt at eve or *m* ;   *The Voyage* 82
Have a rouse before the *m* : (repeat)   *Vision of Sin* 96, 120
Ascending tired, heavily slept till *m*.   *Enoch Arden* 181
drifted, stranding on an isle at *m* Rich,   „   552
m That mock'd him with returning calm,   *Lucretius* 24
' That on her bridal *m* before she past   *Princess* ii 262
M in the white wake of the morning star   „   iii 17
To tumble, Vulcans, on the second *m*.'   „   72
to-morrow *m* We hold a great convention :   „   iv 510
so here upon the flat All that long *m*   „   v 368
all that *m* the heralds to and fro,   „   369
Between the Northern and the Southern *m*.'   „   423
m by *m* the lark Shot up and shrill'd   „   vii 45
this Is *m* to more, and all the rich to-come Reels,   „   356
Fair-hair'd and redder than a windy *m* ;   „ *Con.* 91
I shall see him another *m* :   *Grandmother* 67
Calm in the *m* without a sound,   *In Mem.* xi 1
ere yet the *m* Breaks hither over Indian seas,   „ xxvi 13
Rise, happy *m*, rise, holy *m*,   „ xxx 29
Reveillée to the breaking *m*.   „ lxviii 8
With promise of a *m* as fair ;   „ lxxxiv 29
Mute symbols of a joyful *m*,   „ *Con.* 58
the King That *m* was married,   *Com. of Arthur* 456
Far off they saw the silver-misty *m*   *Gareth and L.* 189
Hear me—this *m* I stood in Arthur's hall,   „   855
next *m*, the lord whose life he saved Had,   „   888
At last, it chanced that on a summer *m*   *Marr. of Geraint* 69
blow His horns for hunting on the morrow *m*.   „   153
But Guinevere lay late into the *m*,   „   157
We hold a tourney here to-morrow *m*,   „   287
made him like a man abroad at *m*   „   335
' And gladly given again this happy *m*.   „   691
kept it for a sweet surprise at *m*.   „   703
as the white and glittering star of *m*   „   734
like a shoal Of darting fish, that on a summer *m*   *Geraint and E.* 469
Blinkt the white *m*, sprays grated,   *Balin and Balan* 385
There *m* by *m*, arraying her sweet self   *Lancelot and E.* 906
eve and *m* She kiss'd me saying,   „   1408
gustful April *m* That puff'd the swaying branches   *Holy Grail* 14
let us meet The morrow *m* once more in one full field   „   323
till one fair *m*, I walking to and fro   „   591
But on the hither side of that loud *m*   *Last Tournament* 56
And little Dagonet on the morrow *m*,   „   240
it chanced one *m* when all the court,   *Guinevere* 21
Till in the cold wind that foreruns the *m*,   „   132
without help I cannot last till *m*.   *Pass. of Arthur* 194
Shot like a streamer of the northern *m*,   „   307
this March *m* that sees Thy Soldier-
    brother's   *Ded. Poem Prin. Alice* 10
we sail'd on a Friday *m*—   *V. of Maeldune* 7
The night was calm, the *m* is calm,   *The Flight* 10
and now the *m* appears,   „   18
burnt at midnight, found at *m*,   *Locksley H., Sixty* 97
planted both together, happy in our marriage *m* ?   *Happy* 14
my fair meadow zoned with airy *m* ;   *Prog. of Spring* 69
m Has lifted the dark eyelash of the Night   *Akbar's Dream* 200
Mornin' yer Honour ye gev her the top of the *m*,   *Tomorrow* 3
whin are ye goin' to lave me ? ' ' O' Monday *m* '
    says he,   „   17
But airth was at pace nixt *m*,   „   25
Morning (adj.) Whilome thou camest with the *m*
    mist, (repeat)   *Ode to Memory* 12, 21
never more Shall lone Œnone see the *m* mist   *Œnone* 216
long ago Sung by the *m* star of song,   *D. of F. Women* 3
The maiden splendours of the *m* star   „   55
And fluted to the *m* sea.   *To E. L.* 24
To find the precious *m* hours were lost.   *Enoch Arden* 302
when the *m* flush Of passion and the first embrace   *Lucretius* 2
like *m* doves That sun their milky bosoms   *Princess* ii 102
With whom I sang about the *m* hills,   „   247
In crystal currents of clear *m* seas,   „   328
In colours gayer than the *m* mist,   „   438
Morn in the white wake of the *m* star   „ iii 17
A Memnon smitten with the *m* Sun.'   „   116
Alpine harebell hung with tears By some cold *m* glacier ;   „ vii 116

Morning (adj.) (continued)   And whistled to the m star.   *Sailor Boy* 4
And you are his m star.   *Window, Marr. Morn.* 12
Thro' clouds that drench the m star,   *In Mem. lxxii* 22
The sweep of scythe in m dew,   ,, *lxxix* 18
Who stay to share the m feast,   ,, *Con.* 75
And even in high day the m star.   *Com. of Arthur* 100
thereon the m star, And Gareth silent gazed   *Gareth and L.* 932
And then she sang, ' O m star '   ,, 996
' O m star that smilest in the blue, O star, my m
   dream hath proven true,   ,, 999
' O birds, that warble to the m sky,   ,, 1075
But that same strength which threw the M Star   ,, 1108
and the m star Reel'd in the smoke,   *Pelleas and E.* 518
their fears Are m shadows huger than the shapes   *To the Queen ii* 63
The lucid chambers of the m star,   *Lover's Tale i* 28
A m air, sweet after rain, ran over   ,, *iii* 3
the m song of the lark,   *First Quarrel* 33
lark has past from earth to Heaven upon the m
   breeze !   *The Flight* 62
And splendours of the m land,   *Open. I. and C. Exhib.* 8
till the mortal m mists of earth Fade   *Akbar's Dream* 96
The m light of happy marriage broke   *Death of Œnone* 102

Morning (s)   (*See also* **March-morning, Mornin' Murnin'**)
Every heart this May m in joyance is beating   *All Things will Die* 6
Thou comest m or even ; she cometh not m or even.   *Leonine Eleg.* 15
' Still sees the sacred m spread   *Two Voices* 80
In her still place the m wept :   ,, 275
It haunted me, the m long,   *Miller's D.* 69
you had set, That m, on the casement-edge   ,, 82
Gargarus Stands up and takes the m :   *Œnone* 11
Far up the solitary m smote The streaks   ,, 55
In the early early m the summer sun   *May Queen, N. Y's. E.* 22
How sadly, I remember, rose the m of the year !   ,, *Con.* 3
came a sweeter token when the night and m meet :   ,, 22
It is a stormy m.'   *The Goose* 44
every m brought a noble chance,   *M. d'Arthur* 230
THIS m is the m of the day,   *Gardener's D.* 1
The northern m o'er thee shoot,   *Talking Oak* 275
m driv'n her plow of pearl Far furrowing   *Love and Duty* 99
Many a m on the moorland   *Locksley Hall* 35
And in the m of the times.   *Day-Dm., L' Envoi* 20
I saw that every m, far withdrawn   *Vision of Sin* 48
Enoch faced this m of farewell Brightly   *Enoch Arden* 182
in those uttermost Parts of the m ?   ,, 224
that same m officers and men Levied a kindly tax   ,, 662
this kindlier glow Faded with m,   *Aylmer's Field* 412
eyes Had such a star of m in their blue,   ,, 692
And me that m Walter show'd the house,   *Princess, Pro.* 10
That m in the presence room I stood   ,, *i* 51
shone Their morions, wash'd with m,   ,, *v* 264
I took it for an hour in mine own bed This m :   ,, 435
I mused on that wild m in the woods,   ,, 471
Death and M on the silver horns,   ,, *vii* 204
Like yonder m on the blind half-world ;   ,, 352
the winds are up in the m ? (repeat)   *Window, On the Hill* 5, 10, 15, 20
For this is the golden m of love,   ,, *Marr. Morn.* 11
With m wakes the will, and cries,   *In Mem. iv* 15
Never m wore To evening, but some heart   ,, *vi* 7
I creep At earliest m to the door.   ,, *vii* 8
Singing alone in the m of life, In the happy m of life and
   of May,   *Maud I v* 6
M arises stormy and pale,   ,, *vi* 1
Till at last when the m came In a cloud,   ,, 20
O when did a m shine So rich in atonement   ,, *xix* 5
For a breeze of m moves,   ,, *xxii* 7
'Tis a m pure and sweet, (repeat)   *Maud II iv* 31, 35
So with the m all the court were gone.   *Marr. of Geraint* 156
To ride with him this m to the court,   ,, 606
And now this m when he said to her,   ,, 847
Geraint, who issuing forth That m,   *Geraint and E.* 9
Their course of booty from the m's raid,   ,, 565
Then chanced, one m, that Sir Balin sat   *Balin and Balan* 240
Came with slow steps, the m on her face ;   ,, 245
And all this m when I fondled you :   *Merlin and V.* 286
she placed where m's earliest ray Might strike it,   *Lancelot and E.* 5

Morning (s) (continued) o'er and o'er For all an April m,   *Lancelot and E.* 897
ten slow m's past, and on the eleventh   ,, 1133
blush'd and brake the m of the jousts,   *Pelleas and E.* 157
but rose With m every day, and, moist or dry,   ,, 215
But when the m of a tournament,   *Last Tournament* 134
every m brought a noble chance,   *Pass. of Arthur* 398
On the same m, almost the same hour,   *Lover's Tale i* 198
There came a glorious m, such a one   ,, 299
Mercury On such a m would have flung   ,, 301
broke in light Like m from her eyes—   ,, *ii* 144
One m when the upblown billow ran Shoreward   ,, 178
One bright May m in a world of song,   *Sisters (E. and E.)* 82
had sunn'd The m of our marriage,   ,, 244
Then in the gray of the m it seem'd   *In the Child. Hosp.* 67
on another wild m another wild earthquake   *Def. of Lucknow* 45
I saw your face that m in the crowd,   *Columbus* 7
one m a bird with a warble   *The Wreck* 81
the m brings the day I hate and fear ;   *The Flight* 2
waken every m to that face I loathe to see :   ,, 8
their songs, that meet The m with such music,   ,, 66
But look, the m grows apace,   ,, 93
half the m have I paced these sandy tracts,   *Locksley H., Sixty* 1
Half the marvels of my m,   ,, 75
Star of the m, Hope in the sunrise ;   *Vastness* 15
Given on the m when you came of age   *The Ring* 77
Why not bask amid the senses while the sun of
   m shines,   *By an Evolution.* 6
Would I had past in the m that looks so bright   ,, 10
m of my reign Was redden'd by that cloud   *Akbar's Dream* 82
Every m is thy birthday   ,, *Hymn* 2
Every m here we greet it,   ,, 3

Morning-breath   dewy meadowy m-b Of England,   *Enoch Arden* 660
Morning-mist   thro' the sunless winter m-m In silence   *Death of Œnone* 8
Morning-star   (*See also* **Morning** (adj.))   Sung by the m s
   of song,   *D. of F. Women* 3
maiden splendours of the m s Shook   ,, 55
Toward the m-s.   ,, 244
And whistled to the m s.   *Sailor Boy* 4
M-S, and Noon-Sun, and Evening-Star,   *Gareth and L.* 634
' Nay, nay,' she said, ' Sir M-S.   ,, 918
And servants of the M-S, approach,   ,, 924
golden guess Is m-s to the full round of truth.   *Columbus* 44
Morningtide   great Sun-star of m,   *Batt. of Brunanburh* 26
Morris (**Edwin**)   *See* **Edwin, Edwin Morris**
Morrison (**Mary**)   *See* **Mary, Mary Morrison**
Morrow (adj.)   (*See also* **To-morrow**)   They two will wed the
   m morn :   *Lady Clare* 7
blow His horns for hunting on the m morn.   *Marr. of Geraint* 153
let us meet The m morn once more in one full field   *Holy Grail* 323
And little Dagonet on the m morn,   *Last Tournament* 240
Morrow (s)   (*See also* **Goodmorrow, Tomorra, To-morrow**)
when the m came, she rose and took The child   *Dora* 80
till the m, when he spoke.   *Enoch Arden* 156
a poising eagle, burns Above the unrisen m : '   *Princess iv* 83
For the meeting of the m,   *Maud II iv* 28
As pass without good m to thy Queen ? '   *Balin and Balan* 252
Then being on the m knighted, sware   *Pelleas and E.* 8
and expectancy of worse Upon the m,   *Lover's Tale ii* 152
Mors   ' MERIDIES '—' HESPERUS '—' NOX '—' M,'   *Gareth and L.* 1205
Morsel   (*See also* **Mossel**)   Mangled to m's, A youngster
   in war !   *Batt. of Brunanburh* 74
Mortal (adj.)   (*See also* **Mortial, Mottal**)   your m dower Of
   pensive thought   *Margaret* 5
' Then dying of a m stroke,   *Two Voices* 154
Who sought'st to wreck my m ark,   ,, 389
Thy m eyes are frail to judge of fair,—   *Œnone* 158
And when no m motion jars The blackness   *On a Mourner* 26
Not tho' I live three lives of men,   *M. d'Arthur* 155
made blank of crimeful record all My m archives.   *St. S. Stylites* 159
tho' my m summers to such length of years   *Locksley Hall* 67
My spirit beats her m bars,   *Sir Galahad* 46
This m armour that I wear,   ,, 70
plucks The m soul from out immortal hell,   *Lucretius* 263
Her stature more than m in the burst Of sunrise,   *Princess, Pro.* 40
The fading politics of m Rome,   ,, *ii* 286

Mother (**s**) (*continued*) but when the boy beheld His *m*,   *Dora* 138
     Christ, the Virgin *M*, and the saints ;   *St. S. Stylites* 112
     Her *m* trundled to the gate Behind the dappled
       grays.   *Talking Oak* 111
     press me from the *m's* breast.   *Locksley Hall* 90
     m's brought Their children, clamouring,   *Godiva* 14
     Against her father's and *m's* will :   *Edward Gray* 10
     O *m*,' she said, ' if this be true,   *Lady Clare* 30
     ' Yet give one kiss to your *m* dear !   ,, 49
     ' O *m, m, m*,' she said,   ,, 51
     ' Yet here's a kiss for my *m* dear, My *m* dear, if this be so,   ,, 53
     And bless me, *m*, ere I go.'   ,, 56
     Every *m's* son—Down they dropt—   *The Captain* 50
     m cared for it With all a *m's* care :   *Enoch Arden* 262
     Then the new *m* came about her heart,   ,, 524
     saw The *m* glancing often toward her babe,   ,, 754
     the girl So like her *m*,   ,, 791
     Annie, whom I saw So like her *m*,   ,, 883
     from the plaintive *m's* teat he took   *The Brook* 129
     My *m*, as it seems you did,   ,, 225
     Heard the good *m* softly whisper ' Bless,   *Aylmer's Field* 187
     nature crost Was *m* of the foul adulteries   ,, 376
     The *m* flow'd in shallower acrimonies :   ,, 563
     Yet the sad *m*, for the second death   ,, 604
     As with the *m* he had never known,   ,, 690
     The childless *m* went to seek her child ;   ,, 829
     wail'd and woke The *m*, and the father suddenly
       cried,   *Sea Dreams* 58
     The Virgin *M* standing with her child   ,, 242
     the child Clung to the *m*, and sent out a cry   ,, 245
     M, let me fly away.   ,, 296
     lambs are glad Nosing the *m's* udder,   *Lucretius* 100
     For so, my *m* said, the story ran.   *Princess i* 11
     My *m* pitying made a thousand prayers ;   ,, 21
     My *m* was as mild as any saint,   ,, 22
     ' The *m* of the sweetest little maid,   ,, *ii* 279
     why should I not play The Spartan *M* with emotion,   ,, 283
     Our *m*, is she well ?'   ,, 310
     clad her like an April daffodilly (Her *m's* colour)   ,, 325
     But yet your *m's* jealous temperament—   ,, 338
     Rest, rest, on *m's* breast,   ,, *iii* 11
     ' O fly, while yet you may !   My *m* knows : '   ,, 29
     My *m*, 'tis her wont from night to night   ,, 32
     (for still My *m* went revolving on the word)   ,, 54
     So my *m* clutch'd The truth at once,   ,, 60
     'tis my *m*, Too jealous, often fretful as the wind   ,, 79
     my *m* still Affirms your Psyche thieved her theories,   ,, 91
     I tried the *m's* heart.   ,, 111
     And then, demanded if her *m* knew,   ,, *iv* 233
     and you me Your second *m* :   ,, 297
     she, half on her *m* propt, Half-drooping from her,   ,, 367
     dismiss'd in shame to live No wiser than their *m's*,   ,, 514
     they will beat my girl Remembering her *m* :   ,, *v* 89
     Ill *m* that I was to leave her there,   ,, 93
     I won Your *m*, a good *m*, a good wife,   ,, 166
     and she of whom you speak, My *m*,   ,, 193
     M's—that, all prophetic pity,   ,, 381
     and what *m's* blood You draw from, fight ;   ,, 404
     risk'd it for your own ; His *m* lives :   ,, 408
     chiefest comfort is the little child Of one unworthy *m* ;   ,, 431
     prize the authentic *m* of her mind.   ,, 433
     The *m* makes us most—   ,, 507
     good Queen, her *m*, shore the tress With kisses,   ,, *vi* 113
     spied its *m* and began A blind and babbling laughter,   ,, 136
     So stood the unhappy *m* open-mouth'd,   ,, 143
     Red grief and *m's* hunger in her eye,   ,, 146
     half The sacred *m's* bosom, panting,   ,, 148
     striking with her glance, The *m*, me, the child ;   ,, 153
     thy *m* prove As true to thee as false,   ,, 203
     Not from your *m*, now a saint with saints.   ,, 233
     You shame your *m's* judgment too.   ,, 261
     Not only he, but by my *m's* soul,   ,, 335
     Happy he With such a *m* !   ,, *vii* 328
     This *m* is your model.   ,, 335
     From *m* unto *m*, stately bride,   *W. to Marie Alex.* 9

Mother (**s**) (*continued*) ' My *m* clings about my neck,   *Sailor Boy* 17
     this pretty home, the home where *m* dwells ?   *City Child* 2
     They found the *m* sitting still ;   *The Victim* 31
     The *m* said, ' They have taken the child   ,, 43
     Chop the breasts from off the *m*,   *Boädicea* 68
     O *m*, praying God will save Thy sailor,—   *In Mem. vi* 13
     Dear as the *m* to the son,   ,, *ix* 19
     And tears are on the *m's* face,   ,, *xl* 10
     That feed the *m's* of the flock ;   ,, *c* 16
     The shrill-edged shriek of a *m*   *Maud I i* 16
     a Mammonite *m* kills her babe for a burial fee,   ,, 45
     Maud the beloved of my *m*,   ,, 72
     Your *m* is mute in her grave as her image in marble
       above ;   ,, *iv* 58
     My *m*, who was so gentle and good ?   ,, *vi* 67
     Her *m* has been a thing complete,   ,, *xiii* 35
     Made her only the child of her *m*,   ,, 40
     Darken'd watching a *m* decline   ,, *xix* 8
     I did not speak Of my *m's* faded cheek   ,, 19
     Maud was moved To speak of the *m* she loved   ,, 27
     and thought It is his *m's* hair.   ,, *II ii* 70
     spike that split the *m's* heart Spitting the child,   *Com. of Arthur* 38
     the bitterness and grief That vext his *m*,   ,, 211
     For dark my *m* was in eyes and hair,   ,, 327
     A *m* weeping, and I hear her say,   ,, 334
     in my good *m's* hall Linger with vacillating
       obedience,   *Gareth and L.* 12
     Since the good *m* holds me still a child !   ,, 15
     Good *m* is bad *m* unto me !   ,, 16
     ' *M*, tho' ye count me still the child, Sweet *m*, do ye
       love the child ? '   ,, 34
     ' Then, *m*, an ye love the child,'   ,, 37
     good *m*, but this egg of mine Was finer gold   ,, 42
     so the boy, Sweet *m*, neither clomb,   ,, 56
     m said, ' True love, sweet son, had risk'd himself   ,, 59
     m, there was once a King, like ours.   ,, 101
     M, How can ye keep me tether'd to you—   ,, 114
     To whom the *m* said, ' Sweet son,   ,, 120
     I will walk thro' fire, *M*, to gain it—   ,, 134
     obedience and thy love to me, Thy *m*,—I demand.'   ,, 147
     slowly spake the *m* looking at him,   ,, 151
     And since thou art my *m*, must obey.   ,, 167
     The *m's* eye Full of the wistful fear   ,, 172
     Before the wakeful *m* heard him, went.   ,, 180
     ' Son, the good *m* let me know thee here,   ,, 550
     Seem I not as tender to him As any *m* ?   ,, 1284
     ' *M*, a maiden is a tender thing,   *Marr. of Geraint* 510
     arose, and raised Her *m* too,   ,, 536
     a costly gift Of her good *m*,   ,, 632
     For while the *m* show'd it, and the two   ,, 636
     it was her *m* grasping her To get her well awake ;   ,, 676
     Here ceased the kindly *m* out of breath ;   ,, 732
     Help'd by the *m's* careful hand and eye,   ,, 738
     Yniol made report Of that good *m* making Enid gay   ,, 757
     Dared not to glance at her good *m's* face,   ,, 766
     Her *m* silent too, nor helping her,   ,, 768
     Then seeing cloud upon the *m's* brow,   ,, 777
     ' O my new *m*, be not wroth or grieved   ,, 779
     He spoke : the *m* smiled, but half in tears,   ,, 823
     Pure as our own true *M* is our Queen.'   *Balin and Balan* 617
     My *m* on his corpse in open field ; (repeat)   *Merlin and V.* 43, 73
     Seethed like the kid in its own *m's* milk !   ,, 869
     m of the house There was not :   *Lancelot and E.* 177
     Wish'd it had been my *m*, for they talk'd,   ,, 674
     Milder than any *m* to a sick child,   ,, 858
     Nay, by the *m* of our Lord himself,   ,, 1230
     Lady of the Lake Caught from his *m's* arms—   ,, 1405
     The highest virtue, *m* of them all ;   *Holy Grail* 446
     Such as the wholesome *m's* tell their boys.   *Pelleas and E.* 197
     sister of my *m*—she that bore Camilla   *Lover's Tale i* 202
     My *m's* sister, *m* of my love,   ,, 209
     whatsoe'er Our general *m* meant for me alone, Our
       mutual *m* dealt to both of us :   ,, 245
     Why were our *m's'* branches of one stem ?   ,, *ii* 25
     Back to his *m's* house among the pines.   ,, *iv* 15

Mother (s) (*continued*)   All softly as his *m* broke it to

him—	*Lover's Tale iv*	31
Back to the *m's* house where she was born.	,,	91
Then the good *m's* kindly ministering,	,,	92
You'll make her its second *m* !	*First Quarrel*	71
' O *m*, come out to me.'	*Rizpah*	2
' O *m* !' I heard him cry.	,,	42
' *M*, O *m* !'—he call'd in the dark	,,	47
How do they know it ? are *they* his *m* ?	,,	70
their *m* and her sister loved More passionately		
still.	*Sisters (E. and E.)*	44
The *m* fell about the daughter's neck,	,,	154
Edith wrote : ' My *m* bids me ask '	,,	181
I told your wayside story to my *m*	,,	189
' Pray come and see my *m*.	,,	191
' Pray come and see my *m*, and farewell.'	,,	196
the simple *m* work'd upon By Edith	,,	206
The *m* broke her promise to the dead,	,,	252
m's garrulous wail For ever woke the unhappy		
Past	,,	262
Miss Annie were was stuck oop, like 'er *m* afoor—	*Village Wife*	59
And thine Imperial *m* smile again,	*Ded. Poem Prin. Alice*	13
yea to him Who hacks his *m's* throat—denied to him,		
Who finds the Saviour in his mother tongue.	*Sir J. Oldcastle*	114
All glory to the *m* of our Lord,	*Columbus*	62
dear *m's*, crazing Nature, kill Their babies	,,	179
—honouring his wise *m's* word—	*Achilles over the T.*	16
maidens, wives, And *m's* with their babblers	*Tiresias*	103
HIDE me, *M* ! my Fathers belong'd to the church	*The Wreck*	1
I was the tempter, *M*,	,,	11
He that they gave me to, *M*,	,,	13
M, I have not—however their tongues may have		
babbled	,,	41
for *M*, the voice was the voice of the soul ;	,,	54
but it coo'd to the *M* and smiled.	,,	60
And the Motherless *M* kiss'd it,	,,	62
M, one morning a bird with a warble	,,	81
' The heart ! not a *m's* heart,	,,	97
cloud of the *m's* shame will enfold her	,,	100
M, the ship stagger'd under a thunderous shock,	,,	107
the face I had known, O *M*, was not the face	,,	116
O *M*, she came to me there.	,,	148
Struck hard at the tender heart of the *m*,	*Despair*	74
Better our dead brute *m* who never	,,	98
grave would yawn, my *m's* ghost would rise—	*The Flight*	51
Our gentle *m*, had *she* lived—	,,	77
Our dying *m* in our hands	,,	87
Thin Molly's ould *m*, yer Honour,	*Tomorrow*	19
As the Holy *M* o' Glory that smiles	,,	26
To be there wid the Blessed *M*,	,,	95
—father, *m*,—be content,	*Locksley H., Sixty*	25
dead the *m*, dead the child.	,,	36
Gone thy tender-natured *m*,	,,	57
Clinging to the silent *m* !	,,	99
Sun of dawn That brightens thro' the *M's* tender		
eyes,	*To Prin. Beatrice*	4
M weeps At that white funeral of the single life,	,,	8
But moving thro' the *M's* home,	,,	17
The *m* featured in the son ;	*Open. I. and C. Exhib.*	12
Drove from out the *m's* nest That young eagle	,,	27
' *M* !' and I was folded in thine arms.	*Demeter and P.*	22
disimpassion'd eyes Awed even me at first, thy *m*—	,,	24
So mighty was the *m's* childless cry,	,,	32
And set the *m* waking in amaze	,,	57
chanting me, Me, me, the desolate *M* !	,,	73
Because I hear your *M's* voice in yours.	*The Ring*	28
ring bequeath'd you by your *m*, child,	,,	75
My *M's* nurse and mine.	,,	97
I ask'd About my *M*, and she said, Thy hair Is golden		
like thy *M's*, not so fine.	,,	103
Of my dear *M* on your bracket here—	,,	110
and I, she said, I babbled, *M*, *M*—	,,	115
Miriam your *M* might appear to me.	,,	137
Vext, that you thought my *M* came to me ? Or at		
my crying ' *M* ? ' or to find My *M's* diamonds hidden	,,	140

Mother (s) (*continued*)   Your *M* and step-mother—

	The Ring	146
lived With Muriel's *m* on the down,	,,	148
And on your *M's* birthday—	,,	248
poor *M* ! And you, poor desolate Father,	,,	302
Muriel's *m* sent, And sure am I,	,,	311
Had graspt a daisy from your *M's* grave—	,,	323
You scorn my *M's* warning,	,,	326
For Muriel nursed you with a *m's* care ;	,,	349
but oftener left That angling to the *m*.	,,	356
And the face, The hand,—my *M*.	,,	425
larger woman-world Of wives and *m's*.	,,	487
M, dare you kill your child ?	*Forlorn*	37
I see the picture yet, *M* and child.	*Romney's R.*	81
' Father and *M* will watch you grow '—(repeat)	,,	104, 106
fair *m's* they Dying in childbirth of dead sons.	*Akbar's Dream*	11
to be reconciled ?—No, by the *M* of God,	*Bandit's Death*	17
Mother-age O thou wondrous *M-A* !	*Locksley Hall*	108
M- A (for mine I knew not)	,,	185
Mother-city gain'd the *m-c* thick with towers,	*Princess i*	112
Motherhood heart of *m* Within me shudder,	*Demeter and P.*	41
She dropt the gracious mask of *m*,	*The Ring*	384
Motherless She was *m* And I without a father.	*Lover's Tale i*	218
M evermore of an ever-vanishing race,	*Despair*	84
The *m* bleat of a lamb in the storm	*In the Child. Hosp.*	64
And the *M* Mother kiss'd it,	*The Wreck*	62
Mother-maidenhood deathless *m-m* of Heaven,	*Balin and Balan*	521
Motion A *m* from the river won Ridged the smooth		
level,	*Arabian Nights*	34
Thought and *m* mingle, Mingle ever. *M's* flow To one		
another,	*Eleänore*	60
With *m's* of the outer sea :	,,	113
' We find no *m* in the dead.'	*Two Voices*	279
With *m's*, checks, and counterchecks.	,,	300
Nature's living *m* lent The pulse of hope	,,	449
I had no *m* of my own.	*Miller's D.*	44
all those names, that in their *m* were	*Palace of Art*	165
'Mid onward-sloping *m's* infinite	,,	247
We have had enough of action, and of *m* we,	*Lotos-Eaters, C. S.*	105
There was no *m* in the dumb dead air,	*D. of F. Women*	65
Because with sudden *m* from the ground	,,	170
when no mortal *m* jars The blackness	*On a Mourner*	26
A *m* toiling in the gloom—	*Love thou thy land*	54
Or voice, or else a *m* of the mere.	*M. d'Arthur*	77
Like those blind *m's* of the Spring,	*Talking Oak*	175
And her eyes on all my *m's*	*Locksley Hall*	22
Nature made them blinder *m's*	,,	150
No shadow past, nor *m* :	*Enoch Arden*	710
his passions all in flood And masters of his *m*,	*Aylmer's Field*	340
I thought the *m* of the boundless deep	*Sea Dreams*	91
The *m* of the great deep bore me on,	,,	111
And then the *m* of the current ceased,	,,	117
Read rascal in the *m's* of his back,	,,	167
faces toward us and address'd Their *m* :	*Princess iv*	552
about his *m* clung The shadow of his sister,	,,	v 257
the heart Made for all noble *m* :	,,	384
All in quantity, careful of my *m*,	*Hendecasyllabics*	5
That all thy *m's* gently pass	*In Mem. xv*	10
Whose muffled *m's* blindly drown	,, *xlix*	15
As, unto vaster *m's* bound,	,, *lxiii*	10
O heart, with kindliest *m* warm,	,, *lxxxv*	34
No dance, no *m*, save alone What lightens	,, *cv*	23
In all her *m* one with law ;	,, *cxxii*	8
having the nerves of *m* as well as the nerves of pain,	*Maud I i*	63
In counter *m* to the clouds,	*Gareth and L.*	1315
put his horse in *m* toward the knight,	*Marr. of Geraint*	206
But at the flash and *m* of the man	*Geraint and E.*	467
So, scared but at the *m* of the man,	,,	476
heavens Were shaken with the *m* and the sound.	*Holy Grail*	801
Or voice, or else a *m* of the mere.	*Pass. of Arthur*	245
or set apart Their *m's* and their brightness	*Lover's Tale i*	174
And saw the *m* of all other things ;	,,	574
m's of my heart seem'd far within me,	,, *ii* 54
soul, life And breath and *m*, past and flow'd away	,,	195
The feebler *m* underneath his hand.	,, *iv* 83
fated channel where thy *m* lives	*De Prof., Two G.*	19

Motion (*continued*)　the boundless *m* of the deep.　*Ancient Sage* 194
　still In *m* to the distant gleam,　*Freedom* 14
Motionless　Enoch slumber'd *m* and pale,　*Enoch Arden* 908
　Mute, blind and *m* as then I lay ;　*Lover's Tale i* 607
Mottal (*mortal*)　I owäs owd Roäver moor nor I iver owäd
　m man.　*Owd Roä* 4
Motto　Blazon your *m'es* of blessing　*W. to Alexandra* 12
　this for *m*, ' Rather use than fame.'　*Merlin and V.* 480
Mould (**earth**)　you may lay me low i' the *m*　*May Queen, N. Y's. E.* 4
　And render him to the *m*.　*Ode on Well.* 48
　and flung the *m* upon your feet,　*Happy* 50
　dead from all the human race as if beneath the *m* ;　" 95
　groundflame of the crocus breaks the *m*,　*Prog. of Spring* 1
　Six foot deep of burial *m* Will dull their comments !　*Romney's R.* 125
Mould (**form**)　' Think you this *m* of hopes and fears　*Two Voices* 28
　That I was first in human *m* ?　" 342
　(Beauty seen In all varieties of *m* and
　　mind)　*To ——, With Pal. of Art* 7
　those That are cast in gentle *m*.　*To J. S.* 4
　lovelier in her mood Than in her *m* that other,　*Princess vii* 163
　Those niched shapes of noble *m*,　*The Daisy* 38
　over all one statue in the *m* Of Arthur,　*Holy Grail* 238
　Which, cast in later Grecian *m*,　*To Master of B.* 6
Mould (**verb**)　Unto her limbs itself doth *m*　*Day-Dm., Sleep. B.* 10
　and *m* The woman to the fuller day.'　*Princess iii* 331
　And *m* a generation strong to move　" *v* 416
　To *m* a mighty state's decrees,　*In Mem. lxiv* 30
　wrought To *m* the dream ;　*To E. Fitzgerald* 30
　and the strength To *m* it into action　*Tiresias* 129
　Will *m* him thro' the cycle-year That dawns　*Epilogue* 77
　M them for all his people.　*Akbar's Dream* 129
Moulded　(*See also* **Imperial-moulded, Large-moulded, Master-
　moulded, Well-moulded**)　*M* thy baby thought.　*Eleänore* 5
　And in the sixth she *m* man.　*Two Voices* 18
　M by God, and temper'd with the
　　tears　*To ——, With Pal. of Art* 18
　Heaven in lavish bounty *m*,　*Aylmer's Field* 107
　As *m* like in Nature's mint ;　*In Mem. lxxix* 6
　And *m* in colossal calm.　" *Con.* 16
　Be *m* by your wishes for her weal ;　*Marr. of Geraint* 799
　from the statue Merlin *m* for us　*Holy Grail* 732
　M the audible and visible ;　*Lover's Tale ii* 105
　the heavens Whereby the cloud was *m*,　*Ancient Sage* 13
　stateliest measure ever *m* by the lips of man.　*To Virgil* 40
Moulder　cannons *m* on the seaward wall ;　*Ode on Well.* 173
　That rotting inward slowly *m's* all.　*Merlin and V.* 395
　Their heads should *m* on the city gates.　" 594
　but here too much We *m*—　*Holy Grail* 39
Moulder'd　(*See also* **Half-moulder'd**)　I see the *m*
　　Abbey-walls,　*Talking Oak* 3
　Shall it not be scorn to me to harp on such a *m*
　　string ?　*Locksley Hall* 147
　red roofs about a narrow wharf In cluster ; then a *m*
　　church ;　*Enoch Arden* 4
　never man, I think, So *m* in a sinecure as he :　*Princess, Pro.* 182
　About the *m* lodges of the Past　" *iv* 63
　A *m* citadel on the coast,　*The Daisy* 28
　hath power to see Within the green the *m* tree,　*In Mem. xxvi* 7
　I heard a groaning overhead, and climb'd The *m*
　　stairs　*Lover's Tale iv* 137
　And a tree with a *m* nest On its barkless bones,　*Dead Prophet* 18
　Who lops the *m* branch away.　*Hands all Round* 8
　Found in a chink of that old *m* floor !'　*The Ring* 280
　what a fury shook Those pillars of a *m* faith,　*Akbar's Dream* 81
Mouldering　mouse Behind the *m* wainscot shriek'd,　*Mariana* 64
　Earthward he boweth the heavy stalks Of the *m*
　　flowers :　*A spirit haunts* 8
　But I shall lie alone, mother, within the *m*
　　grave.　*May Queen, N. Y's. E.* 20
　Yet how often I and Amy in the *m* aisle have
　　stood,　*Locksley H., Sixty* 31
　From that casement where the trailer mantles all
　　the *m* bricks,　" 257
　m with the dull earth's *m* sod,　*Palace of Art* 261
　sunlit ocean tosses O'er them *m*,　*The Captain* 70

Mouldering (*continued*)　Before the *m* of a yew ;　*In Mem. lxxvi* 8
　Still larger *m* all the house of thought,　*Lover's Tale i* 241
Moulding　reach thro' nature, *m* men.　*In Mem. cxxiv* 24
Mouldy　To shame these *m* Aylmers in their graves :　*Aylmer's Field* 396
　Stuff his ribs with *m* hay.　*Vision of Sin* 66
　' Trooping from their *m* dens The chap-fallen circle
　　spreads :　" 171
Moult　Some birds are sick and sullen when they *m*.　*Sisters (E. and E.)* 73
Mound (**s**)　A realm of pleasance, many a *m*,　*Arabian Nights* 101
　Heap'd over with a *m* of grass,　*Lotos-Eaters, C. S.* 67
　There sat we down upon a garden *m*,　*Gardener's D.* 214
　and sat upon a *m* That was unsown,　*Dora* 72
　took The child once more, and sat upon the *m* ;　" 81
　and gain'd a petty *m* Beyond it,　*Princess iv* 557
　scarce three paces measured from the *m*,　" *v* 1
　huddled here and there on *m* and knoll,　*Geraint and E.* 803
　whelm all this beneath as vast a *m*　*Merlin and V.* 656
　Tho' heapt in *m's* and ridges all the sea　*Holy Grail* 798
　Near him a *m* of even-sloping side,　*Pelleas and E.* 25
Mound (**verb**)　heaped hills that *m* the sea,　*Ode to Memory* 98
Mounded　Far furrowing into light the *m* rack,　*Love and Duty* 100
　When wealth no more shall rest in *m* heaps,　*Golden Year* 32
Mount (**s**)　A *m* of marble, a hundred spires !　*The Daisy* 60
　Rolling her smoke about the Royal *m*,　*Gareth and L.* 190
　Right o'er a *m* of newly-fallen stones,　*Marr. of Geraint* 552
　' Too high this *m* of Camelot for me :　*Balin and Balan* 226
　on the *m* Of Badon I myself beheld the King　*Lancelot and E.* 302
　For all the sacred *m* of Camelot,　*Holy Grail* 227
　Wealthy with wandering lines of *m* and mere,　" 252
　Strike on the *M* of Vision !　*Ancient Sage* 285
　M and mine, and primal wood ;　*Open. I. and C. Exhib.* 6
Mount (**verb**)　Before he *m's* the hill, I know　*Fatima* 22
　Nor sound of human sorrow *m's* to mar　*Lucretius* 109
　As *m's* the heavenward altar-fire,　*In Mem. xli* 3
　never *m* As high as woman in her selfless mood.　*Merlin and V.* 442
　What did the wanton say ? ' Not *m* as high ;'　" 813
Mountain (**adj.**)　why he Slumbers not like a *m*
　　tarn ?　*Supp. Confessions* 129
　And seem'd knee-deep in *m* grass,　*Mariana in the S.* 42
　O *m* brooks, I am the daughter of a River-God,　*Œnone* 37
　Aloft the *m* lawn was dewy-dark, And dewy dark aloft
　　the *m* pine :　" 48
　Ah me, my *m* shepherd, that my arms　" 202
　thro' *m* clefts the dale Was seen far inland,　*Lotos-Eaters* 20
　I lived up there on yonder *m* side.　*St. S. Stylites* 72
　He watches from his *m* walls,　*The Eagle* 5
　Like torrents from a *m* source We rush'd　*The Letters* 39
　From him that on the *m* lea　*To E. L.* 21
　Downward from his *m* gorge Stept the long-hair'd
　　long-bearded solitary,　*Enoch Arden* 636
　Turbia show'd In ruin, by the *m* road ;　*The Daisy* 6
　Now watching high on *m* cornice,　" 19
　oft we saw the glisten Of ice, far up on a *m* head.　" 36
　A *m* islet pointed and peak'd ;　*The Islet* 15
　The fortress, and the *m* ridge,　*In Mem. lxxi* 14
　And catch at every *m* head,　" *Con.* 114
　A huge pavilion like a *m* peak　*Gareth and L.* 1364
　Thus, as a hearth lit in a *m* home,　*Balin and Balan* 231
　brutes of *m* back That carry kings in castles,　*Merlin and V.* 576
　Like its own mists to all the *m* side :　*Lancelot and E.* 38
　and on the naked *m* top Blood-red,　*Holy Grail* 474
　all the purple slopes of *m* flowers Pass under
　　white,　*Last Tournament* 229
　Streams like a cloud, man-shaped, from *m* peak,　*To the Queen ii* 40
　A *m* nest—the pleasure-boat that rock'd,　*Lover's Tale i* 42
　As *m* streams Our bloods ran free :　" 326
　A stately *m* nymph she look'd !　" 359
　On the other side Is scoop'd a cavern and a *m* hall,　" 517
　waterfalls Pour'd in a thunderless plunge to the
　　base of the *m* walls,　*V. of Maeldune* 14
　beyond A hundred ever-rising *m* lines,　*Ancient Sage* 282
　And we will feed her with our *m* air,　*The Ring* 319
Mountain (**s**)　From the brain of the purple *m*　*Poet's Mind* 29
　And the *m* draws it from Heaven above,　" 32
　Apart upon a *m*, tho' the surge　*If I were loved* 11

Mountain (s) (*continued*)   Across the *m* stream'd below In misty folds — *Palace of Art* 34
THE wind, that beats the *m*, — *To J. S.* 1
roll'd Among the *m*'s by the winter sea ; — *M. d'Arthur* 2
curves of *m*, bridge, Boat, island, — *Edwin Morris* 5
The *m* stirr'd its bushy crown, — *Amphion* 25
meanest weed That blows upon its *m*, — " 94
The *m* wooded to the peak, — *Enoch Arden* 572
A *m*, like a wall of burs and thorns ; — *Sea Dreams* 119
The *m* there has cast his cloudy slough, Now towering o'er him in serenest air, A *m* o'er a *m*,— — *Lucretius* 177
The *m* quickens into Nymph and Faun, — " 187
With fold to fold, of *m* or of cape ; — *Princess* vii 3
The facets of the glorious *m* flash — *The Islet* 22
storm Brake on the *m* and I cared not — *Merlin and V.* 503
A league of *m* full of golden mines, — " 587
And the cairn'd *m* was a shadow, — " 638
So long, that *m*'s have arisen since — " 675
they would pare the *m* to the plain, — " 829
Falls on the *m* in midsummer snows, — *Last Tournament* 228
m's ended in a coast Of ever-shifting sand, — *Pass. of Arthur* 85
roll'd Among the *m*'s by the winter sea ; — " 171
with balanced wings To some tall *m* : — *Lover's Tale i* 303
clefts and openings in the *m*'s fill'd — " 330
fell about My footsteps on the *m*'s. — " 372
Beyond the nearest *m*'s bosky brows, — " 396
sea Parting my own loved *m*'s was received, — " 433
trembling of the world Had loosen'd from the *m*, — " ii 46
The *m*, the three cypresses, the cave, — " 109
But these, their gloom, the *m*'s and the Bay, — " iv 16
Not plunge headforemost from the *m* there, — " 41
thunder-sketch Of lake and *m* conquers all the day. — *Sisters (E. and E.)* 99
drawn By this good Wiclif *m* down from heaven, — *Sir J. Oldcastle* 132
Up the *m* ? Is it far ? Not far. — " 203
And came upon the *M* of the World, — *Columbus* 26
And the topmost spire of the *m* — *V. of Maeldune* 41
the *m* arose like a jewell'd throne — " 59
And the peak of the *m* was apples, — " 63
Hope was ever on her *m*, — *Locksley H., Sixty* 91
chains of *m*'s, grains of sand — " 208
Set the *m* aflame to-night, — *On Jub. Q. Victoria* 16
A *m* stay'd me here, a minster there, — *The Ring* 245
For on a tropic *m* was I born, — *Prog. of Spring* 67
In early summers, Over the *m*, — *Merlin and the G.* 19
And wraiths of the *m*, — " 43
Down from the *m* And over the level, — " 49
Muses have raised to the heights of the *m*, — *Parnassus* 2
Steep is the *m*, but you, you will help — " 5
and huger than all the *m* ? — " 10
ere the *m* rolls into the plain, — *Death of Œnone* 51
dragg'd me up there to his cave in the *m*, — *Bandit's Death* 11
Clomb the *m*, and flung the berries, — *Kapiolani* 6
vapour in daylight Over the *m* Floats, — " 17
as Kapiolani ascended her *m*, — " 28
Strow yonder *m* flat, — *Mechanophilus* 6
Quail not at the fiery *m*, — *Faith* 3
Mountain-altars   His *m-a*, his high hills, — *Lover's Tale i* 322
Mountain-brook   listens near a torrent *m-b*, — *Geraint and E.* 171
Mountain-cleft   came from out a sacred *m-c* — *Gareth and L.* 260
Mountain-cones   A purple range of *m-c*, — *Lover's Tale i* 407
Mountain-eaves   And shepherds from the *m-e* — *Amphion* 53
Mountaineer   breathed a race of mightier *m*'s. — *Montenegro* 14
Mountain-gorge   in a seaward-gazing *m-g* — *Enoch Arden* 558
Mountain-ground   He finds on misty *m-g* — *In Mem. xcvii* 2
Mountain-like   till delay'd By their *m-l* San Philip that, — *The Revenge* 40
Mountain-mere   Sometimes on lonely *m-m*'s — *Sir Galahad* 37
Mountain-range   uprose the mystic *m-r* : — *Vision of Sin* 208
Mountain-shade   the *m-s* Sloped downward — *Œnone* 21
Mountain-side   I lived up there on yonder *m s.* — *St. S. Stylites* 72
Struck out the streaming *m-s*, — *Lucretius* 29
Like its own mists to all the *m s* : — *Lancelot and E.* 38
star-crowns of his palms on the deep-wooded *m-s*, — *The Wreck* 72
Mountain-top   three *m-t*'s, Three silent pinnacles — *Lotos-Eaters* 15

Mountain-top (*continued*)   Had chanted on the smoky *m-t*'s, — *Guinevere* 282
Mountain-tract   then I look'd up toward a *m-t*, — *Vision of Sin* 46
Mountain-wall   (*See also* **Mountain (adj.)**)   thro' the *m-w*'s A rolling organ-harmony — *Sir Galahad* 74
He watches from his *m w*'s, — *The Eagle* 5
o'er the *m-w*'s Young angels pass. — *Early Spring* 11
Mounted (**adj. and part.**)   (*See also* **Highest-mounted**)   Thou from a throne *M* in heaven wilt shoot into the dark Arrows of lightnings. — *To J. M. K.* 13
Where this old mansion *m* high Looks down — *Miller's D.* 35
what you will—Has *m* yonder ; — *Lucretius* 127
And rarely pipes the *m* thrush ; — *In Mem. xci* 2
And wears a helmet *m* with a skull, — *Gareth and L.* 639
Then after one long slope was *m*, saw, — " 795
And he that bore The star, when *m*, cried — " 951
Mounted (**verb**)   And, while day sank or *m* higher, — *Palace of Art* 46
m our good steeds, And boldly ventured — *Princess i* 204
' They, *m*, Ganymedes, To tumble, Vulcans, — " iii 71
And *m* horse and graspt a spear, — *Gareth and L.* 691
M in arms, threw up their caps and cried, — " 697
Then *m*, on thro' silent faces rode — " 734
Geraint upon the horse *M*, and reach'd a hand, — *Geraint and E.* 759
found His charger, *m* on him and away. — *Balin and Balan* 418
Set her thereon, and on his own, — *Guinevere* 123
We *m* slowly ; yet to both there came — *Lover's Tale i* 385
Mounting   (*See also* **A-mountin'**)   Their common shout in chorus, *m*, — *Balin and Balan* 87
forth he past, and *m* on his horse — *Pelleas and E.* 456
m these He past for ever from his native land ; — *Lover's Tale iv* 386
' This *m* wave will roll us shoreward soon.' — *Lotos-Eaters* 2
Mount of Blessing   And climb the *M o B*, — *Ancient Sage* 280
Mourn   Over the pools in the burn water-gnats murmur and *m*. — *Leonine Eleg.* 8
' Where I may *m* and pray. — *Palace of Art* 292
did seem to *m* and rave On alien shores ; — *Lotos-Eaters* 32
and to clamour, *m* and sob, — *St. S. Stylites* 6
closed by those who *m* a friend in vain, — *Lucretius* 142
m half-shrouded over death In deathless marble. — *Princess v* 74
M, for to us he seems the last, — *Ode on Well.* 19
M for the man of long-enduring blood, — " 24
M for the man of amplest influence, — " 27
So draw him home to those that *m* In vain ; — *In Mem. ix* 5
crime To *m* for any overmuch ; — " lxxxv 62
They know me not, but *m* with me. — " xcix 20
all that haunts the waste and wild *M*, — *Pass. of Arthur* 49
silver year should cease to *m* and sigh— — *To Mary Boyle* 57
Neither *m* if human creeds be lower — *Faith* 3
M ! That a world-wide Empire *m*'s — *D. of the Duke of C.* 5
Until the great Hereafter.   *M* in hope ! — " 17
Mourn'd   Deeply *m* the Lord of Burleigh, — *L. of Burleigh* 91
she *m* his absence as his grave, — *Enoch Arden* 247
And all the men *m* at his side : — *Princess iii* 353
M in this golden hour of jubilee, — *Ode Inter. Exhib.* 8
Love *m* long, and sorrow'd after Hope ; — *Lover's Tale i* 819
truthless violence *m* by the Wise, — *Vastness* 5
Mournful   Heard a carol, *m*, holy, — *L. of Shalott iv* 28
M Œnone, wandering forlorn Of Paris, — *Œnone* 16
as *m* light That broods above the fallen sun, — *To J. S.* 50
And, into *m* twilight mellowing, — *Princess vi* 191
Then Violet, she that sang the *m* song, — " 318
And let the *m* martial music blow ; — *Ode on Well.* 17
Ring out, ring out my *m* rhymes ; — *In Mem. cvi* 19
To which a *m* answer made the Queen : — *Guinevere* 341
Mourning (**part.**)   I went *m*, ' No fair Hebrew boy — *D. of F. Women* 213
M when their leaders fall, — *Ode on Well.* 5
And ever *m* over the feud, — *Maud I xix* 31
Mourning (**s**)   in *m* these, and those With blots of it — *Aylmer's Field* 619
To the noise of the *m* of a mighty nation, — *Ode on Well.* 4
Mouse   *m* Behind the mouldering wainscot shriek'd, — *Mariana* 63
the thin weasel there Follows the *m* ; — *Aylmer's Field* 853
knaw that a man mun be eäther a man or a *m* ? — *N. Farmer, N. S.* 6
the shrieking rush of the wainscot *m*, — *Maud I vi* 71
Within the hearing of cat or *m*, — " II v 48
an' 'e says to 'im, meek as a *m*, — *Village Wife* 63

Mouse (*continued*)   Thou'd niver 'a cotch'd ony *mice*   *Spinster's S's.* 55
thou be es 'ansom a tabby es iver patted a *m.*   „   70
Ghoäst moästlins was nobbut a rat or a *m.*   *Owd Roä* 38

Mouth (s)   (*See also* **Cavern-mouth, Harbour-mouth, Purse-**
     mouth)   bitter words From off your rosy *m.*   *Rosalind* 51
smite him on the cheek, And on the *m,*   *Two Voices* 252
I crush'd them on my breast, my *m;*   *Fatima* 12
common *m,* So gross to express delight,   *Gardener's D.* 55
M, forehead, eyelids, growing dewy-warm   *Tithonus* 58
steaming flats, and floods Of mighty *m,*   *The Voyage* 46
A downward crescent of her minion *m,*   *Aylmer's Field* 533
Paled at a sudden twitch of his iron *m;*   „   732
that one unctuous *m* which lured him,   *Sea Dreams* 14
And often told a tale from *m* to *m*   *Princess,* Pro. 191
Walter warp'd his *m* at this To something   „   214
a twitch of pain Tortured her *m,*   „ *vi* 106
on her *m* A doubtful smile dwelt   „   269
Into the *m* of Hell Rode the six hundred.   *Light Brigade* 25
Back from the *m* of Hell,   „   47
A rabbit *m* that is ever agape—   *Maud I x* 31
And a rose her *m* (repeat)   „ *xvii* 8, 28
deathful-grinning *m's* of the fortress,   „ *III vi* 52
King Arthur's hound of deepest *m,*   *Marr. of Geraint* 186
made that *m* of night Whereout the Demon   *Balin and Balan* 316
meets And dallies with him in the *M* of Hell.'   „   615
How, in the *m's* of base interpreters,   *Merlin and V.* 795
Rang by the white *m* of the violent Glem   *Lancelot and E.* 288
too high For any *m* to gape for save a queen's—   „   775
Were added *m's* that gaped, and eyes that ask'd   „   1249
An' I wur down i' tha *m,*   *North. Cobbler* 77
as big i' the as a cow,   *Village Wife* 103
Heat like the *m* of a hell,   *Def. of Lucknow* 81
That mock-meek *m* of utter Antichrist,   *Sir J. Oldcastle* 170
and sail'd the Dragon's *m,*   *Columbus* 25
Brass *m's* and iron lungs !   *Freedom* 40
wi' my bairn i' 'is m to the winder   *Owd Roä* 92
Do not die with a lie in your *m,*   *Forlorn* 57
Whose ivy-matted *m* she used to gaze   *Death of Œnone* 2

Mouth (verb)   How she *m's* behind my back.   *Vision of Sin* 110
endure To *m* so huge a foulness—   *Balin and Balan* 379
actor *m* his last upon the stage.   *Locksley H., Sixty* 152

Mouth'd   (*See also* **Bell-mouthed, Gap-mouth'd, Mealy-**
     mouth'd, Mighty-mouthed, Open-mouth'd, Wide-
     mouthed) in her hunger *m* and mumbled it,   *Princess vi* 213

Mouthing   *m* out his hollow oes and aes,   *The Epic* 50
While scandal is *m* a bloodless name   *The Dawn* 12

Mouthpiece   he made his *m* of a page Who came and
     went,   *Gareth and L.* 1337
I come the *m* of our King to Doorm   *Geraint and E.* 796

Move   pray—that God would *m* And strike   *Supp. Confessions* 115
You *m* not in such solitudes,   *Margaret* 45
Or sometimes they swell and *m,*   *Eleänore* 111
phantom of a wish that once could *m,*   *The form, the form* 10
trailing light, *M's* over still Shalott.   *L. of Shalott iii* 27
' Some hidden principle to *m,*   *Two Voices* 133
To *m* about the house with joy,   *Miller's D.* 95
And there I *m* no longer now,   *May Queen,* Con. 51
these did *m* Me from my bliss of life,   *D. of F. Women* 209
He lieth still : he doth not *m :*   *D. of the O. Year* 10
some full music seem'd to *m* and change   *Edwin Morris* 35
She *m's* among my visions of the lake,   „   144
wake and sleep, but all things *m;*   *Golden Year* 22
M onward, leading up the golden year.   „   26
For ever and for ever when I *m.*   *Ulysses* 21
sweetly did she speak and *m :*   *Locksley Hall* 71
Science *m's,* but slowly slowly,   „   134
And *m's* not on the rounded curl.   *Day-Dm., Sleep. B.* 8
The gouty oak began to *m,*   *Amphion* 23
I could not *m* a thistle ;   „   66
Me mightier transports *m* and thrill ;   *Sir Galahad* 22
Then *m* the trees, the copses nod,   „   77
Begins to *m* and tremble.   *Will Water.* 32
And wheresoe'er thou *m,* good luck   „   215
But thou wilt never *m* from hence,   „   217
M eastward, happy earth,   *Move eastward* 1

Move (*continued*)   And *m* me to my marriage-morn,   *Move Eastward* 11
Till the graves begin to *m,*   *Vision of Sin* 165
A life that *m's* to gracious ends   *You might have won* 6
I *m* the sweet forget-me-nots That grow   *The Brook* 172
bough That moving *m's* the nest and nestling,   *Sea Dreams* 291
never creeps a cloud, or *m's* a wind,   *Lucretius* 106
But *m* as rich as Emperer-moths,   *Princess,* Pro. 144
I seem'd to *m* among a world of ghosts,   „ *i* 17
Who *m's* about the Princess ;   „   76
whene'er she *m's* The Samian Herè rises   „ *iii* 114
enter'd ; found her there At point to *m,*   „   131
we *m,* my friend, At no man's beck,   „   226
whence after-hands May *m* the world,   „   264
lightlier *m* The minutes fledged with music :'   „ *iv* 36
I seem'd to *m* among a world of ghosts ;   „   561
And mould a generation strong to *m*   „ *v* 416
I seem'd to *m* in old memorial tilts,   „   479
fangs Shall *m* the stony bases of the world.   „ *vi* 58
cannot speak, nor *m,* nor make one sign,   „ *vii* 153
But cease to *m* so near the Heavens,   „   195
m's with him to one goal,   „   263
If love of country *m* thee there   *Ode on Well.* 140
The dark crowd *m's,* and there are sobs   „   268
For him nor *m's* the loud world's random mock,   *Will* 4
And *m's* his doubtful arms, and feels   *In Mem. xiii* 3
For I in spirit saw thee *m*   „ *xvii* 5
But this it was that made me *m*   „ *xxv* 5
And doubtful joys the father *m,*   „ *xl* 9
Should *m* his rounds, and fusing all   „ *xlvii* 2
' Thou canst not *m* me from thy side,   „ *lii* 7
My centred passion cannot *m.*   „ *lix* 9
And *m* thee on to noble ends.   „ *lxv* 12
Her faith is fixt and cannot *m,*   „ *xcvii* 33
As down the garden-walks I *m,*   „ *cii* 6
m his course, and show That life is not an idle ore,   „ *cxviii* 19
M upward, working out the beast,   „   27
a sentinel Who *m's* about from place to place,   „ *cxxvi* 10
To which the whole creation *m's.*   „ *Con.* 144
Do we *m* ourselves, or are moved   *Maud I iv* 26
But to *m* to the meadow and fall before   „ *v* 25
For a breeze of morning *m's,*   „ *xxii* 7
But only *m's* with the moving eye,   „ *II ii* 37
Pass and cease to *m* about !   „ *iv* 59
Began to *m,* seethe, twine and curl :   *Gareth and L.* 234
that ev'n to him they seem'd to *m.*   „   237
M's him to think what kind of bird it is   *Marr. of Geraint* 331
pushing could *m* The chair of Idris.   „   542
When first I parted from thee, *m's* me yet.'   *Geraint and E.* 347
my leave To *m* to your own land,   „   889
walk with me, and *m* To music with thine Order   *Balin and Balan* 76
How far beyond him Lancelot seem'd to *m,*   „   172
he felt his being *m* In music with his Order,   „   211
you cannot *m* To these fair jousts ? '   *Lancelot and E.* 79
strike spur, suddenly *m,* Meet in the midst,   „   456
dream Of dragging down his enemy made them *m.*   „   814
the rough Torre began to heave and *m,*   „   1066
In which as Arthur's Queen I *m* and rule :   „   1221
Such as no mind could *m :*   *Holy Grail* 681
M with me toward their quelling,   *Last Tournament* 101
O ay—the winds that *m* the mere.'   „   738
in this battle in the west Whereto we *m,*   *Pass. of Arthur* 67
wastes the narrow realm whereon we *m,*   „   140
M with me to the event.   *Lover's Tale i* 298
The boat was beginning to *m,*   *First Quarrel* 21
You *m* about the Court, I pray you tell   *Columbus* 222
Whereon the Spirit of God *m's* as he will—   *De Prof., Two G.* 28
And *m's* unseen among the ways of men.   *Tiresias* 24
While men shall *m* the lips :   „   133
boundless deep That *m's,* and all is gone.'   *Ancient Sage* 190
All good things may *m* in Hesper,   *Locksley H., Sixty* 186
M among your people, know them,   „   266
draws the child To *m* in other spheres.   *To Prin. Beatrice* 8
Thy power, well-used to *m* the public breast.   *To W. C. Macready* 3
WE *m,* the wheel must always *m,*   *Politics* 1
And if we *m* to such a goal As Wisdom   „   3

Move (*continued*) Will you *m* a little that way ? *Charity* 20
Moveable some with gems *M* and resettable at will, *Lover's Tale* iv 199
Moved *M* from beneath with doubt and fear. *Supp. Confessions* 138
At last you rose and *m* the light, *Miller's D.* 125
Your ripe lips *m* not, but your cheek Flush'd „ 131
Fronting the dawn he *m* ; *Œnone* 58
Floated the glowing sunlights, as she *m.* „ 182
bells that swung, *M* of themselves, *Palace of Art* 130
Its office, *m* with sympathy. *Love thou thy land* 48
barge with oar and sail *M* from the brink, *M. d'Arthur* 266
And *m* away, and left me, statue-like, *Gardener's D.* 161
she *m*, Like Proserpine in Enna, *Edwin Morris* 111
strength which in old days *M* earth and heaven ; *Ulysses* 67
You *m* her at your pleasure. *Amphion* 60
She faintly smiled, she hardly *m* ; *The Letters* 14
M with violence, changed in hue, *Vision of Sin* 34
So lifted up in spirit he *m* away. *Enoch Arden* 330
A phantom made of many phantoms *m* Before him
  haunting him, or he himself *M* haunting people, „ 602
Katie never ran : she *m* To meet me, *The Brook* 87
There *m* the multitude a thousand heads : *Princess, Pro.* 57
for still we *m* Together, „ i 56
so To the open window *m*, „ iv 492
Set into sunrise ; then we *m* away. „ 576
She heard, she *m*, She moan'd, „ v 72
Yet she neither spoke nor *m.* „ vi 8
Yet she neither *m* nor wept. „ 12
whether *m* by this, or was it chance, „ 97
And *m* beyond his custom, Gama said : „ 229
So said the small king *m* beyond his wont. „ 265
on they *m* and gain'd the hall, and there Rested : „ 352
And in their own clear element, they *m.* „ vii 28
I *m* : I sigh'd : a touch Came round my wrist, „ 137
She *m*, and at her feet the volume fell. „ 254
Sway'd to her from their orbits as they *m*, „ 326
I *m* as in a strange diagonal, „ *Con.* 27
' The Gods are *m* against the land.' *The Victim* 6
The Wye is hush'd nor *m* along, *In Mem.* xix 9
M in the chambers of the blood ; „ xxiii 20
We saw not, when we *m* therein ? „ xxiv 16
and *m* Upon the topmost froth of thought. „ lii 3
Had *m* me kindly from his side, „ lxxx 3
And, *m* thro' life of lower phase, „ *Con.* 125
m by an unseen hand at a game That pushes *Maud* I iv 26
Maud was *m* To speak of the mother she loved „ xix 26
and we see him as he *m*, *Ded. of Idylls* 17
(Your city *m* so weirdly in the mist) *Gareth and L.* 245
So the sweet voice of Enid *m* Geraint ; *Marr. of Geraint* 334
M the fair Enid, all in faded silk, „ 366
they *m* Down to the meadow where the jousts „ 536
and wings *M* in her ivy, „ 599
thus he *m* the Prince To laughter *Geraint and E.* 295
harder to be *m* Than hardest tyrants „ 694
Was so much the more, and shriek'd again, „ 782
They said a light came from her when she *m* : *Merlin and V.* 567
Thus they *m* away : she stay'd a minute, *Lancelot and E.* 390
Must needs have *m* my laughter ? „ 596
And *m* about her palace, proud and pale. „ 614
And lifted her fair face and *m* away : „ 682
Who had devised the letter, *m* again. „ 1288
mark'd Sir Lancelot where he *m* apart, „ 1349
m Among us in white armour, Galahad. *Holy Grail* 134
on me *m* In golden armour with a crown of gold „ 409
when I *m* of old A slender page about her father's
  hall, „ 580
whose lightest whisper *m* him more *Pelleas and E.* 155
for nothing *m* but his own self, „ 417
with cups of gold, *M* to the lists, *Last Tournament* 143
might have *m* slow-measure to my tune, „ 282
ending, he *m* toward her, and she said, „ 704
which had noblest, while you *m* Among them, *Guinevere* 325
rose the King and *m* his host by night, *Pass. of Arthur* 79
barge with oar and sail *M* from the brink, „ 434
Thereat once more he *m* about, „ 462
M from the cloud of unforgotten things, *Lover's Tale* i 48

Moved (*continued*) By that name I *m* upon her breath ; *Lover's Tale* i 560
rain Fell on my face, and her long ringlets *m*, „ 699
M with one spirit round about the bay, „ iii 17
He *m* thro' all of it majestically— „ iv 9
they are mine—not theirs—they had *m* in my side. *Rizpah* 54
And *m* to merriment at a passing jest. *Sisters* (*E. and E.*) 121
it often *m* me to tears, *In the Child. Hosp.* 31
an earthquake always *m* in the hollows *V. of Maeldune* 107
Whatever *m* in that full sheet Let down to Peter *To E. Fitzgerald* 11
Universal Nature *m* by Universal Mind ; *To Virgil* 22
m but by the living limb, *Akbar's Dream* 133
Movement in its onward current it absorbs With swifter *m* *Isabel* 32
loveliest in all grace Of *m*, *Œnone* 76
without light Or power of *m*, *Palace of Art* 246
Movest Nor canst thou prove the world thou *m* in, *Ancient Sage* 58
Moving (*See also* **Slow-moving**) *M* thro' a fleecy night. *Margaret* 21
M in the leavy beech. „ 61
m thro' a mirror clear That hangs before her *L. of Shalott* ii 10
Still *m* after truth long sought, *Two Voices* 62
lift the hidden ore That glimpses, *m* up, *D. of F. Women* 275
Seen where the *m* isles of winter shock By night, *M. d'Arthur* 140
m toward the stillness of his rest. *Locksley Hall* 144
Then *m* homeward came on Annie pale, *Enoch Arden* 149
The *m* whisper of huge trees that branch'd „ 585
Then *m* up the coast they landed him, „ 665
in *m* on I found Only the landward exit of the cave, *Sea Dreams* 95
bough That *m* moves the nest and nestling, „ 291
and was *m* on In gratulation, *Princess* ii 184
m thro' the uncertain gloom, „ iv 216
isles of light Slided, they *m* under shade : „ vi 82
lay Quite sunder'd from the *m* Universe, „ vii 52
M about the household ways, *In Mem.* lx 11
And *m* up from high to higher, „ lxiv 13
Eternal process *m* on, „ lxxxii 5
m side by side With wisdom, „ cxiv 19
And see'st the *m* of the team. „ cxxi 16
lost in trouble and *m* round Here at the head *Maud* I xxi 5
But only moves with the *m* eye, „ II ii 37
sang the knighthood, *m* to their hall. *Com. of Arthur* 503
Who, *m*, cast the coverlet aside, *Marr. of Geraint* 73
And *m* toward a cedar cabinet, „ 136
I saw you *m* by me on the bridge, „ 429
So *m* without answer to her rest She found no rest, „ 530
Then, *m* downward to the meadow ground, *Geraint and E.* 204
He *m* up with pliant courtliness, „ 278
He *m* homeward babbled to his men, „ 362
m back she held Her finger up, „ 452
And *m* out they found the stately horse, „ 752
And Edyrn *m* frankly forward spake : „ 784
m everywhere Clear'd the dark places „ 942
M to meet him in the castle court ; *Lancelot and E.* 175
But kindly man *m* among his kind : „ 265
plumes driv'n backward by the wind they made In *m*, „ 481
saw the barge that brought her *m* down, „ 1391
thought he meant To crush me, *m* on me, *Holy Grail* 416
but *m* with me night and day, „ 471
Mean knights, to whom the *m* of my sword „ 790
and far ahead Of his and her retinue *m*, *Guinevere* 385
And *m* thro' the past unconsciously, „ 402
m ghostlike to his doom. „ 605
but no man was *m* there ; *Pass. of Arthur* 127
Seen where the *m* isles of winter shock By night, „ 308
Thence mark'd the black hull *m* yet, „ 448
down the highway *m* on With easy laughter *Tiresias* 199
But *m* thro' the Mother's home, *To Prin. Beatrice* 17
She *m*, at her girdle clash The golden keys *To Marq. of Dufferin* 3
Are there spectres *m* in the darkness ? *On Jub. Q. Victoria* 67
And *m* each to music, soul in soul *Happy* 39
M to melody, Floated The Gleam. *Merlin and the G.* 22
slowly *m* again to a melody Yearningly tender, „ 90
Œnone sat Not *m*, till in front of that ravine *Death of Œnone* 75
Then *m* quickly forward till the heat „ 97
The gladiators *m* toward their fight, *St. Telemachus* 54
m easily Thro' after-ages in the love of Truth, *Akbar's Dream* 100
But such a tide as *m* seems asleep, *Crossing the Bar* 5

Mower and *m's* mowing in it : — *Geraint and E.* 199
in his hand Bare victual for the *m's* : — „ 202
fare is coarse, And only meet for *m's* ; ' — „ 209
Ate all the *m's'* victual unawares, — „ 215
Fresh victual for these *m's* of our Earl ; — „ 225
serve thee costlier than with *m's'* fare.' — „ 231
Than when I left your *m's* dinnerless. — „ 234
The lusty *m's* labouring dinnerless, — „ 251
Mowing and mowers *m* in it : — „ 199
Mown *See* **New-mown**
Mowt (might) *M* a beän, mayhap, for she wur a
bad un, — *N. Farmer, O. S.* 22
or I *m* 'a liked tha as well. — *Spinster's S's.* 43
Much After *m* wailing, hush'd itself at last — *Aylmer's Field* 542
Still so *m* gold was left ; — *Sea Dreams* 130
touch'd on Mahomet With *m* contempt, — *Princess ii* 135
m profit ! Not one word ; No ! — „ *vi* 239
For himself has done *m* better. — *Spiteful Letter* 4
thy *m* folly hath sent thee here His kitchen-knave : — *Gareth and L.* 919
Much-beloved And he the *m-b* again, — *In Mem. xlii* 6
Much-experienced ULYSSES, *m-e* man, — *To Ulysses* 1
Muck slaäpe down i' the squad an' the *m* : — *North. Cobbler* 20
Fur we puts the *m* o' the land an' they sucks the *m*
fro' the grass. — *Village Wife* 32
Mucky an' their *m* bibs, an' the clats an' the clouts, — *Spinster's S's.* 87
Mud (*See also* **Squad**) Lay great with pig, wallowing
in sun and *m.* — *Walk. to the Mail.* 88
Fish are we that love the *m,* — *Vision of Sin* 101
Gracious lessons thine And maxims of the *m* ! — *Merlin and V.* 49
Swine in the *m,* that cannot see for slime, — *Holy Grail* 771
the cup was gold, the draught was *m.*' — *Last Tournament* 298
an' the *m* o' 'is boots o' the stairs, — *Spinster's S's.* 99
Reversion ever dragging Evolution in the *m.* — *Locksley H., Sixty* 200
Muddier ' Was it *m* than thy gibes ? — *Last Tournament* 299
Muddle lond ater meä thot *m's* ma quoit ; — *N. Farmer, O. S.* 58
Muddy clear stream flowing with a *m* one, — *Isabel* 30
Mud-honey His heart in the gross *m-h* of town, — *Maud I xvi* 5
Muffle O *m* round thy knees with fern, — *Talking Oak* 149
Muffled (*See also* **Half-muffled**) The panther's roar came *m,* — *Gardener's D.* 37
And, sitting in dark leaves, — *Gardener's D.* 37
And chimneys *m* in the leafy vine. — *Audley Court* 19
watch A full sea glazed with *m* moonlight, — *Princess i* 248
but we three Sat *m* like the Fates ; — „ *ii* 467
but I Lay silent in the *m* cage of life : — „ *vii* 47
Now, to the roll of *m* drums, — *Ode on Well.* 87
And standing, *m* round with woe, — *In Mem. xiv* 5
Whose *m* motions blindly drown The bases of my life
in tears. — „ *xlix* 15
Whereon were hollow tramplings up and down And
m voices heard, — *Gareth and L.* 1373
Not *m* round with selfish reticence. — *Merlin and V.* 337
Listens the *m* booming indistinct Of the confused
floods, — *Lover's Tale i* 637
From under rose a *m* moan of floods ; — *Prog. of Spring* 70
Muffling And *m* up her comely head, — *Death of Œnone* 104
Muggins An' *M* 'e preäch'd o' Hell-fire — *North. Cobbler* 55
Mulberry-faced made The *m-f* Dictator's orgies worse — *Lucretius* 54
Mule Her cream-white *m* his pastern set : — *Sir L. and Q. G.* 31
Multiplied Thus truth was *m* on truth, — *The Poet* 33
Thrice *m* by superhuman pangs, — *St. S. Stylites* 11
Multitude and so press in, perforce Of *m,* — *Lucretius* 168
There moved the *m,* a thousand heads : — *Princess, Pro.* 57
To cast wise words among the *m* — *Tiresias* 66
And in each let a *m* Loyal, — *On Jub. Q. Victoria* 20
Multitudinous Phantom wail of women and children, *m*
agonies. — *Boädicea* 26
Ran the land with Roman slaughter, *m* agonies. — „ 84
still'd Thro' all its folds the *m* beast, — *Tiresias* 15
Multitudinous-eddying Waste down of *m-e* light— — *De Prof., Two G.* 4
Mumble priest, who *m* worship in your quire— — *Balin and Balan* 444
Mumbled in her hunger mouth'd and *m* it, — *Princess vi* 213
m that white hand whose ring'd caress — *Balin and Balan* 512
' She too might speak to-day,' she *m.* — *The Ring* 125
Mumbling Muttering and *m,* idiotlike, — *Enoch Arden* 639
Mummy That here the torpid *m* wheat Of Egypt — *To Prof. Jebb* 5

Munney (money) An' the *m* they maäde by the war, — *Owd Roä* 44
Munny (money) Thou'll not marry for *m*— — *N. Farmer, N. S.* 11
soä is scoors o' gells, Them as 'as *m* an' all— — „ 15
' Doänt thou marry for *m,* but goä wheer *m* is ! ' — „ 20
An' I went wheer *m* war : an' thy muther coom
to 'and, Wi' lots o' *m* laaïd by, — „ 21
thou can luvv thy lass an' 'er *m* too. — „ 33
Could'n I luvv thy muther by cause o' 'er *m* laaïd by ? — „ 35
Tis'n them as 'as *m* as breäks into 'ouses an' steäls, — „ 45
work mun 'a gone to the gittin' whiniver *m* was got. — „ 50
Feyther 'ad ammost nowt ; leästways 'is *m* was 'id. — „ 51
I grabb'd the *m* she maäde, — *North. Cobbler* 32
Murder (*See also* **Wife-murder**) spirit of *m* works in
the very means of life, — *Maud I i* 40
That keeps the rust of *m* on the walls— — *Guinevere* 74
Her love did *m* mine ? What then ? — *Lover's Tale i* 740
For the lawyer is born but to *m*— — *Rizpah* 64
how long shall the *m* last ? — *V. of Maeldune* 123
dying worm in a world, all massacre, *m,* and wrong. — *Despair* 32
M would not veil your sin, — *Forlorn* 49
Murder'd (*See also* **Ever-murder'd**) A woman weeping
for her *m* mate — *Geraint and E.* 522
Self-starved, they say—nay, *m,* doubtless dead. — *Sir J. Oldcastle* 60
Glared on at the *m* son, and the murderous father
at rest, . . . — *Bandit's Death* 33
Murderer prov'n themselves Poisoners, *m's.* — *Sir J. Oldcastle* 168
Murderous Or pinch a *m* dust into her drink, — *Merlin and V.* 610
you can hear him—the *m* mole ! — *Def. of Lucknow* 26
and the *m* father at rest, . . . — *Bandit's Death* 33
Muriel (*See also* **Muriel Erne**) Far-off, is *M*—your
stepmother's voice. — *The Ring* 139
lived With *M's* mother on the down, — „ 148
Miriam sketch'd and *M* threw the fly ; — „ 159
The form of *M* faded, and the face Of Miriam — „ 184
A ' Miriam ' that might seem a ' *M* ' ; — „ 241
M claim'd and open'd what I meant For Miriam, — „ 242
M and Miriam, each in white, — „ 254
But coming nearer—*M* had the ring— — „ 259
M clench'd The hand that wore it, — „ 261
She glanced at me, at *M,* and was mute. — „ 264
Then—*M* standing ever statue-like— — „ 266
And saying gently : ' *M,* by your leave,' — „ 268
M fled. Poor *M* ! Ay, poor *M* — „ 271
M enter'd with it, ' See !—Found in a chink — „ 279
M—no—She cannot love ; she loves her own hard self, — „ 291
Promise me, Miriam not *M*—she shall have the ring.' — „ 294
M's mother sent, And sure am I, by *M,* — „ 311
By the lych-gate was *M.* — „ 324
For *M* nursed you with a mother's care ; — „ 349
' *M's* health Had weaken'd, nursing little Miriam. — „ 356
' I take thee *M* for my wedded wife '— — „ 377
M, paler then Than ever you were in your cradle, — „ 431
Among them *M* lying on her face—I raised her, call'd
her ' *M, M* wake ! ' — „ 448
Muriel Erne (*See also* **Muriel**) Miriam Erne And *M E*— — „ 147
well, you know I married *M E.* — „ 376
Murmur (s) Overblown with *m's* harsh, — *Ode to Memory* 99
And no *m* at the door, — *Deserted House* 7
To hear the *m* of the strife, — *Margaret* 23
The *m* of the fountain-head— — *Two Voices* 216
A *m* ' Be of better cheer.' — „ 429
There comes no *m* of reply. — *Palace of Art* 286
And *m's* of a deeper voice, — *On a Mourner* 16
This *m* broke the stillness of that air — *Gardener's D.* 147
Not whisper, any *m* of complaint. — *St. S. Stylites* 22
The *m's* of the drum and fife. — *Talking Oak* 215
Faint *m's* from the meadows come, — *Day-Dm., Sleep. P.* 6
Made a *m* in the land. — *L. of Burleigh* 20
And they speak in gentle *m,* — „ 49
But finding neither light nor *m* there — *Enoch Arden* 687
Came *m's* of her beauty from the South, — *Princess i* 36
By this a *m* ran Thro' all the camp — „ *v* 110
a *m* heard aërially, — *Boädicea* 24
And *m's* from the dying sun : — *In Mem. iii* 8
And dull'd the *m* on thy lip, — „ *xxii* 16

Murmur (s) (*continued*)   lavish hills would hum The *m* of
a happy Pan :   *In Mem. xxiii* 12
A single *m* in the breast,   „ *civ* 7
cackle of your bourg The *m* of the world !   *Marr. of Geraint* 277
They take the rustic *m* of their bourg   „ 419
m's ' Lo, thou likewise shalt be King.'   *Lancelot and E.* 55
and then I seem'd to hear Its *m*,   *Lover's Tale i* 635
mellow'd *m* of the people's praise   *Ded. Poem Prin. Alice* 7
but never a *m*, a breath—   *V. of Maeldune* 19
from within The city comes a *m* void of joy,   *Tiresias* 101
a flower Had *m's* ' Lost and gone   *Ancient Sage* 224
but a *m* of gnats in the gloom,   *Vastness* 35
thro' her dream A ghostly *m* floated,   *Death of Œnone* 79
Murmur (verb)   in the burn water-gnats *m* and mourn.   *Leonine Eleg.* 8
At heart, thou wouldest *m* still—   *Supp. Confessions* 104
And the nations do but *m*,   *Locksley Hall* 106
I *m* under moon and stars In brambly wildernesses ;   *The Brook* 178
The dove may *m* of the dove,   *Princess iii* 105
loyal pines of Canada *m* thee,   *W. to Marie Alex.* 19
Should *m* from the narrow house,   *In Mem. xxxv.* 2
the crowd Will *m*, ' Lo the shameless ones,   *Lancelot and E.* 100
And *m* at the low-dropt eaves of sleep,   *Lover's Tale ii* 122
and *m* down Truth in the distance—   *Columbus* 102
will *m* thee To thine own Thebes,   *Tiresias* 140
clasp the hands and *m*, ' Would to God   *Locksley H., Sixty* 192
If it be a mosque people *m* the holy prayer,   *Akbar's D., Inscrip.* 4
Murmur'd   Before Our Lady *m* she ;   *Mariana in the S.* 28
low voice, full of care, *M* beside me :   *D. of F. Women* 250
m Arthur, ' Place me in the barge,'   *M. d'Arthur* 204
And sweetly *m* thine.   *Talking Oak* 160
m ' Oh, that he Were once more that landscape-
painter,   *L. of Burleigh* 82
But each man *m*, ' O my Queen,   *The Voyage* 63
And double death were widely *m*,   *Aylmer's Field* 617
For all the sloping pasture *m*,   *Princess, Pro.* 55
and *m* that their May Was passing :   „ *ii* 463
Then *m* Florian gazing after her,   „ *ii* 97
The mellow breaker *m* Ida.   „ *iv* 436
' I *m*, as I came along,   *In Mem. xxxvii* 21
She past ; and Vivien *m* after ' Go !   *Merlin and V.* 98
She *m*, ' Vain, in vain : it cannot be.   *Lancelot and E.* 892
m Arthur, ' Place me in the barge.'   *Pass. of Arthur* 372
when the bridegroom *m*, ' With this ring,'   *The Ring* 438
Murmurest   Who *m* in the foliaged eaves   *In Mem. xcix* 9
Then Kay, ' What *m* thou of mystery ?   *Gareth and L.* 470
Murmuring   And *m*, as at night and morn,   *Mariana in the S.* 46
Singing and *m* in her feastful mirth,   *Palace of Art* 177
Muttering and *m* at his ear ' Quick,   *M. d'Arthur* 179
we saw the lights and heard The voices *m*.   *Princess iv* 559
And *m* of innumerable bees.'   „ *vii* 222
The brooks of Eden mazily *m*,   *Milton* 10
a wind Of memory *m* the past.   *In Mem. xcii* 8
field of tourney, *m* ' kitchen-knave.'   *Gareth and L.* 664
one *M*, ' All courtesy is dead,'   *Last Tournament* 211
M a light song I had heard thee sing,   „ 614
A *m* whisper thro' the nunnery ran,   *Guinevere* 410
Muttering and *m* at his ear, ' Quick,   *Pass. of Arthur* 347
Murmurous   lime a summer home of *m* wings.   *Gardener's D.* 48
Murn (morn)   lark a-singin' 'is best of a Sunday at *m*,   *North. Cobbler* 46
Murnin' (morning)   An' when I waäk'd i' the *m*   „ 39
D'ya mind the *m* when we was a-walkin'
togither,   *Spinster's S's.* 23
Muscle   Having the warmth and *m* of the heart,   *Aylmer's Field* 180
arms on which the standing *m* sloped,   *Marr. of Geraint* 76
Muscovite   How long this icy-hearted *M*   *Poland* 10
Muscular   So he spread, so broad of breast.   *Gardener's D.* 8
Muse (s)   The modern *M's* reading.   *Amphion* 76
No vain libation to the *M*,   *Will Water.* 9
The *M*, the jolly *M*, it is !   „ 105
hard-grain'd *M's* of the cube and square   *Princess, Pro.* 180
M's and the Graces, group'd in threes,   „ *ii* 27
And every *M* tumbled a science in.   „ 399
the *M's'* heads were touch'd Above the darkness   „ *iii* 21
So they blaspheme the *m* !   „ *iv* 137
I fed you with the milk of every *M*   „ 295

Muse (s) (*continued*)   above them stood The placid marble
M's, looking peace.   *Princess iv* 489
O civic *m*, to such a name,   *Ode on Well.* 75
sound ever heard, ye *M's*, in England ?   *Trans. of Homer* 3
' For I am but an earthly *M*,   *In Mem. xxxvii* 13
high *M* answer'd : ' Wherefore grieve Thy brethren   „ *lviii* 9
A life that all the *M's* deck'd With gifts of grace,   „ *lxxxv* 45
That saw thro' all the *M's* walk,   „ *cix* 4
charm of all the *M's* often flowering   *To Virgil* 11
the *M's* cried with a stormy cry   *Dead Prophet* 2
M's have raised to the heights of the mountain,   *Parnassus* 2
Taller than all the *M's*,   „ 10
Astronomy and Geology, terrible *M's* !   „ 16
Muse (verb)   *m*, as in a trance,   *Eleänore* 75
While I *m* upon thy face ;   „ 129
with downcast eyes we *m* and brood,   *Sonnet To —* 1
To *m* and brood and live again in memory,   *Lotos-Eaters, C. S.* 65
I *m* on joy that will not cease,   *Sir Galahad* 65
my Lords, you make the people *m*   *Third of Feb.* 31
And with my heart I *m* and say :   *In Mem. iv* 4
face shine Upon me, while I *m* alone ;   „ *cxvi* 10
And there the great Sir Lancelot *m* at me ;   *Lancelot and E.* 1055
O my Queen, I *m* Why ye not wear on arm,   *Last Tournament* 35
and *m* On those dear hills,   *Lover's Tale i* 31
Mused   (*See also* **Half-mused**)   while they *m* Whispering
to each other half in fear,   *Sea-Fairies* 4
But Lancelot *m* a little space ;   *L. of Shalott iv* 51
But while I *m* came Memory with sad eyes,   *Gardener's D.* 243
while I *m*, Love with knit brows went by,   „ 245
M, and was mute.   *The Brook* 201
And *m* upon it, drifting up the stream   *Sea Dreams* 108
I *m* on that wild morning in the woods,   *Princess v* 471
Who *m* on all I had to tell,   *In Mem. vi* 19
is it pride, and *m* and sigh'd ' No surely,   *Maud I viii* 12
the King *M* for a little on his plea,   *Marr. of Geraint* 42
She *m* a little, and then clapt her hands   *Merlin and V.* 866
Crept to her father, while he *m* alone,   *Lancelot and E.* 748
Lancelot later came and *m* at her,   „ 1268
while I *m* nor yet endured to take So rich a prize,   *Lover's Tale iii* 49
Museth   *m* where broad sunshine laves The lawn   *D. of F. Women* 189
Music   (*See also* **Bridal-music, May-music, Sphere-music,
Thunder-music, War-music**)   *Then—while a sweeter*
m wakes,   *To the Queen* 13
m flowing from The illimitable years.   *Ode to Memory* 41
led, With *m* and sweet showers Of festal flowers,   „ 77
Shrill *m* reach'd them on the middle sea.   *Sea-Fairies* 6
With a *m* strange and manifold,   *Dying Swan* 29
Rain makes *m* in the tree   *A Dirge* 26
the wave would make *m* above us afar—   *The Merman* 22
A funeral, with plumes, and lights And *m*,   *L. of Shalott ii* 32
overtakes Far thought with *m* that it makes :   *Two Voices* 438
Rose slowly to a *m* slowly breathed,   *Œnone* 41
up the valley came a swell of *m* on the wind.   *May Queen, Con.* 32
up the valley came again the *m* on the wind.   „ 36
The blessed *m* went that way my soul   „ 42
m in his ears his beating heart did make.   *Lotos-Eaters* 36
THERE is sweet *m* here that softer falls   „ *C. S.* 1
M that gentlier on the spirit lies,   „ 5
M that brings sweet sleep down from the blissful skies.   „ 7
they find a *m* centred in a doleful song   „ 117
who made His *m* heard below ;   *D. of F. Women* 4
that flow Of *m* left the lips of her that died   „ 195
Deep-chested *m*, and to this result.   *The Epic* 51
To some full *m* rose and sank the sun,   *Edwin Morris* 34
full *m* seem'd to move and change   „ 35
I scarce have other *m* : yet say on.   „ 57
The *m* from the town—
pass'd in *m* out of sight.   *Talking Oak* 214
The Magic *M* in his heart Beats quick   *Locksley Hall* 34
Low voluptuous *m* winding trembled,   *Day-Dm., Arrival* 26
Then the *m* touch'd the gates and died ;   *Vision of Sin* 17
Nor leave his *m* as of old,   „ 23
Lay hidden as the *m* of the moon Sleeps   *You might have won* 14
and coming fitfully Like broken *m*,   *Aylmer's Field* 102
Broke into nature's *m* when they saw her.   „ 477
     „ 694

N

Naäil (nail) toäner 'ed shot 'um as deäd as a n.   *N. Farmer, O. S.* 35
Naäkt (naked) An' ya stood oop n i' the beck,   *Church-warden, etc.* 29
Naäme (name) ' Stan' 'im theer i' the n o' the Lord   *North. Cobbler* 73
    coom'd like a Hangel o' marcy as soon as 'e 'eärd 'is n,   *Owd Roä* 93
Naämed (named) we n her ' Dot an' gaw one! '   *Village Wife* 100
Nabour (neighbour) An' her n's an frinds 'ud consowl and condowl wid her,   *Tomorrow* 47
Nadir hard earth cleave to the N hell   *Merlin and V.* 349
Nager (nigger) Thim ould blind n's in Agypt,   *Tomorrow* 69
Naggin' Moother was n an' groänin' an' moänin' an' n ageän ;   *Owd Roä* 108
Nagging *See* **A-naggin', Naggin'**
Naiad but the N Throbbing in mild unrest   *Leonine Eleg.* 11
    faintly smilest still, As a N in a well,   *Adeline* 16
    and N's oar'd A glimmering shoulder   *To E. L.* 16
Nail (s) (*See also* **Finger-nail, Naäil**) The rusted n's fell from the knots   *Mariana* 3
    seem'd All-perfect, finish'd to the finger n.   *Edwin Morris* 22
    children cast their pins and n's,   *Merlin and V.* 430
Nail (verb) n me like a weasel on a grange   *Princess ii* 205
    They never n a dumb head up in elm),   *Lover's Tale iv* 37
Nail'd (adj.) Then with their n prows Parted the Norsemen,   *Batt. of Brunanburh* 93
Nail'd (verb) He that has n all flesh to the Cross,   *Vastness* 28
Naked (*See also* **Half-naked, Naäkt, Nigh-naked**) N I go, and void of cheer :   *Two Voices* 239
    As n essence, must I be Incompetent of memory :   " 374
    All n in a sultry sky,   *Fatima* 37
    N they came to that smooth-swarded bower,   *Œnone* 95
    ' Ride too n thro' the town,   *Godiva* 29
    Far too n to be shamed !   *Vision of Sin* 190
    I rate your chance Almost at n nothing.'   *Princess i* 161
    N, a double light in air and wave,   " *vii* 167
    mighty hands Lay n on the wolfskin,   *Lancelot and E.* 813
    Far ran the n moon across The houseless ocean's   *The Voyage* 29
    With n limbs and flowers and fruit,   " 55
    n marriages Flash from the bridge,   *Aylmer's Field* 765
    Have left the last free race with n coasts !   *Third of Feb.* 40
    down the wave and in the flame was borne A n babe,   *Com. of Arthur* 384
    The shining dragon and the n child   " 399
    And truth or clothed or n let it be.   " 408
    A n babe, of whom the Prophet spake,   *Gareth and L.* 501
    The gay pavilion and the n feet,   " 937
    rose-red from the west, and all N it seem'd,   " 1088
    ' Wherefore waits the madman there N in open dayshine ? '   " 1092
    ' Not n, only wrapt in harden'd skins   " 1093
    weep True tears upon his broad and n breast,   *Marr. of Geraint* 111
    And bore him to the n hall of Doorm,   *Geraint and E.* 570
    There in the n hall, propping his head,   " 581
    And ate with tumult in the n hall,   " 605
    I smote upon the n skull A thrall of thine   *Balin and Balan* 55
    say That out of n knightlike purity   *Merlin and V.* 11
    But that where blind and n Ignorance   " 664
    Stript off the case, and read the n shield,   *Lancelot and E.* 16
    battle-writhen arms and mighty hands Lay n on the wolfskin,   " 813
    Stript off the case, and gave the n shield ;   " 979
    Himself N of glory for His mortal change,   *Holy Grail* 448
    and on the n mountain top Blood-red,   " 474
    then I came All in my folly to the n shore,   " 793
    laid The n sword athwart their n throats,   *Pelleas and E.* 452
    A n aught—yet swine I hold thee still,   *Last Tournament* 309
    then They found a n child upon the sands   *Guinevere* 293
    Above the n poisons of his heart In his old age.'   *Lover's Tale i* 356
    pour'd Into the shadowing pencil's n forms   " *ii* 180
    I had better ha' put my n hand in a hornets' nest.   *First Quarrel* 50
    Pour'd in on all those happy n isles—   *Columbus* 173

Naked (*continued*) And we left but a n rock,   *V. of Maeldune* 54
    For a wild witch n as heaven stood   " 100
    One n peak—the sister of the sun   *Tiresias* 30
    When he clothed a n mind with the wisdom   *The Wreck* 65
    lest the n glebe Should yawn once more   *Demeter and P.* 42
    The scorpion crawling over n skulls ;—   " 78
    Of leafless elm, or n lime,   *To Ulysses* 16
    Trunk and bough, N strength.   *The Oak* 15
    gliding thro' the branches over-bower'd The n Three,   *Death of Œnone* 7
    same who first had found Paris, a n babe,   " 54
    I stood there, n, amazed   *Despair* 77
    forward—n—let them stare.   *Locksley H., Sixty* 142
Nakedness we shall see The n and vacancy   *Deserted House* 11
    These prodigies of myriad n'es,   *Lucretius* 156
    Grimy n dragging his trucks And laying   *Maud I x* 7
    Is mere white truth in simple n,   *Balin and Balan* 518
    roll'd his n everyway That all the crowd   *Dead Prophet* 15
Name (s) (*See also* **Naäme**) WISDOM, a n to shake All evil dreams of power—a sacred n.   *The Poet* 46
    From thy rose-red lips MY n Floweth ;   *Eleänore* 133
    Yet tell my n again to me,   " 142
    round the prow they read her n,   *L. of Shalott iv* 44
    how thy n may sound Will vex thee lying underground ?   *Two Voices* 110
    ' His sons grow up that bear his n,   " 256
    He names the n Eternity.   " 291
    Last night, when some one spoke his n,   *Fatima* 1
    all those n's, that in their motion were   *Palace of Art* 165
    Lost to her place and n ;   " 264
    I know you proud to bear your n,   *L. C. V. de Vere* 10
    ' I had great beauty : ask thou not my n :   *D. of F. Women* 93
    when I heard my n Sigh'd forth with life   " 153
    my crown about my brows, A n for ever !—   " 163
    The n of Britain trebly great—   *You ask me, why, etc.* 22
    ' Thou hast betray'd thy nature and thy n,   *M. d'Arthur* 73
    call'd him by his n, complaining loud,   " 210
    when I heard her n My heart was like a prophet   *Gardener's D.* 62
    The cuckoo told his n to all the hills ;   " 93
    if I carved my n Upon the cliffs that guard   *Audley Court* 48
    set the words, and added n's I knew.   " 61
    he that knew the n's, Long learned n's   *Edwin Morris* 16
    I spoke her n alone.   " 68
    n's Are register'd and calendar'd for saints.   *St. S. Stylites* 131
    thou, whereon I carved her n, (repeat)   *Talking Oak* 33, 97
    tell me, did she read her n,   " 153
    found, and kiss'd the n she found,   " 159
    I am become a n ;   *Ulysses* 11
    And built herself an everlasting n.   *Godiva* 79
    n of wife, And in the rights that n may give,   *Day-Dm., L'Envoi* 53
    Hoped to make the n Of his vessel great in story,   *The Captain* 18
    in whom he had reliance For his noble n,   " 58
    What care I for any n ?   *Vision of Sin* 85
    ' N and fame ! to fly sublime Thro' the courts,   " 103
    You might have won the Poet's n,   *You might have won* 1
    but that n has twice been changed—   *Enoch Arden* 859
    James Willows, of one n and heart with her.   *The Brook* 76
    ' Willows.' ' No ! ' ' That is my n.'   " 212
    ghost of one who bore your n About these meadows,   " 219
    ' he that marries her marries her n '   *Aylmer's Field* 25
    almost all the village had one n;   " 35
    sow'd her n and kept it green In living letters,   " 88
    The one transmitter of their ancient n,   " 296
    N, too, n ! Their ancient n !   " 377
    Fall back upon a n ! rest, rot in that !   " 385
    make a n, N, fortune too :   " 394
    And crying upon the n of Leolin,   " 576
    that moment, when she named his n,   " 581
    So never took that useful n in vain,   *Sea Dreams* 189
    did I take That popular n of thine to shadow forth   *Lucretius* 96
    bears one n with her Whose death-blow struck   " 235
    and lovelier than their n's,   *Princess, Pro.* 12
    Walter hail'd a score of n's upon her,   " 156
    His n was Gama ; crack'd and small his voice,   " *i* 114
    albeit their glorious n's Were fewer,   " *ii* 155

Name (s) (*continued*)   great *n* flow on with broadening time For ever.'   *Princess* iii 164
chattering stony *n's* Of shale and hornblende,   ,,   361
Proctor's leapt upon us, crying ' *N's:*'   ,,   iv 259
Swear by St. something—I forget her *n*—   ,,   v 293
Whose *n* is yoked with children's,   ,,   418
happy warrior's, and immortal *n's*,   ,,   vi 93
She needs must wed him for her own good *n*;   ,,   vii 74
In that dread sound to the great *n*,   *Ode on Well.* 71
O civic muse, to such a *n*, To such a *n* for ages long, To such a *n*,   ,,   75
Eternal honour to his *n*. (repeat)   ,, 150, 231
at thy *n* the Tartar tents are stirr'd;   *W to Marie Alex.* 12
Thy *n* was blest within the narrow door;   ,,   38
Here also, Marie, shall thy *n* be blest,   ,,   39
You cannot love me at all, if you love not my good *n*.'   *Grandmother* 48
I love you so well that your good *n* is mine.   ,,   50
My *n* in song has done him much wrong,   *Spiteful Letter* 3
This faded leaf, our *n's* are as brief;   ,,   13
Milton, a *n* to resound for ages;   *Milton* 4
quiet bones were blest Among familiar *n's* to rest   *In Mem.* xxxvi 3
We yield all blessing to the *n*   ,,   xxxvi 3
Could hardly tell what *n* were thine.   ,,   lix 16
Since we deserved the *n* of friends,   ,,   lxv 9
Along the letters of thy *n*,   ,,   lxvii 7
force that would have forged a *n*.   ,,   lxxiii 16
Another *n* was on the door: ,,   lxxxvii 17
The grand old *n* of gentleman,   ,,   cxi 22
Sweet Hesper-Phosphor, double *n*   ,,   cxxi 17
sign your *n's*, which shall be read,   *Con.* 57
The *n's* are signed, and overhead Begins the clash   ,,   60
And my own sad *n* in corners cried,   *Maud* I vi 72
a learned man Could give it a clumsy *n*.   ,,   II ii 10
the sudden making of splendid *n's*,   ,,   III vi 47
a household, n, Hereafter, thro' all times,   *Ded. of Idylls* 42
Nor shalt thou tell thy *n* to anyone.   *Gareth and L.* 156
Not tell my *n* to any—no, not the King.'   ,,   171
A *n* of evil savour in the land,   ,,   385
without a sign Saving the *n* beneath;   ,,   415
Mark hath tarnish'd the great *n* of king,   ,,   426
A twelvemonth and a day, nor seek my *n*.   ,,   446
let my *n* Be hidd'n, and give me the first quest,   ,,   544
Let be my *n* until I make my *n*!   ,,   576
What is thy *n*? thy need?' 'My *n*?' she said—   ,,   605
'Lynette my *n*;   ,,
Forgetful of his glory and his *n*,   *Marr. of Geraint* 53
I cannot love my lord and not his *n*.   ,,   92
desired his *n*, and sent Her maiden to demand it of the dwarf;   ,,   192
'Surely I will learn the *n*,'   ,,   203
His *n*? but no, good faith, I will not have it: ,,   405
Sent her own maiden to demand the *n*,   ,,   411
I will break his pride and learn his *n*,   ,,   424
Geraint, a *n* far-sounded among men   ,,   427
I will not let his *n* Slip from my lips   ,,   445
earn'd himself the *n* of sparrow-hawk.   ,,   492
her *n* will yet remain Untarnish'd as before;   ,,   500
(Who hearing her own *n* had stol'n away)   ,,   507
'Thy *n*!' To whom the fallen man Made answer,   ,,   575
A stately queen whose *n* was Guinevere,   ,,   667
the Queen's fair *n* was breathed upon,   *Geraint and E.* 951
Arthur seeing ask'd 'Tell me your *n's*;   *Balin and Balan* 50
Saying ' An unmelodious *n* to thee,   ,,   52
realm Hath prosper'd in the *n* of Christ,   ,,   99
a *n* that branches o'er the rest,   ,,   182
might, *N*, manhood, and a grace,   ,,   377
by the great Queen's *n*, arise and hence.'   ,,   482
O me, that such a *n* as Guinevere's,   ,,   489
And thus foam'd over at a rival *n*:   ,,   567
fought in her *n*, Sware by her—   *Merlin and V.* 13
Their lavish comment when her *n* was named.   ,,   151
lost to life and use and *n* and fame. (repeat)   ,, 214, 970
My use and *n* and fame.   ,,   304
Upon my life and use and *n* and fame,   ,,   374
felt them slowly ebbing, *n* and fame.'   ,,   437

Name (s) (*continued*)   My *n*, once mine, now thine,   *Merlin and V.* 446
But when my *n* was lifted up,   ,,   502
whose whole prey Is man's good *n*:   ,,   729
The pretty, popular *n* such manhood earns,   ,,   787
Rage like a fire among the noblest *n's*,   ,,   802
Some stain or blemish in a *n* of note,   ,,   832
she that knew not ev'n his *n*?   *Lancelot and E.* 29
and by that *n* Had named them,   ,,   32
fought together; but their *n's* were lost;   ,,   40
Has link'd our *n's* together in his lay,   ,,   112
your great *n*, This conquers: ,,   150
and by what *n* Livest between the lips?   ,,   181
Elaine, and heard her *n* so tost about,   ,,   233
'Fair lord, whose *n* I know not—   ,,   360
'Hear, but hold my *n* Hidden,   ,,   416
fiery family passion for the *n* Of Lancelot,   ,,   477
his great *n* Conquer'd; and therefore would he hide his *n*   ,,   579
Whence you might learn his *n*?   ,,   654
How know ye my lord's *n* is Lancelot?'   ,,   797
To win his honour and to make his *n*,   ,,   1362
sons Born to the glory of thy *n* and fame,   ,,   1372
Why did the King dwell on my *n* to me?   ,,   1402
Mine own *n* shames me,   ,,   1403
profits me my *n* Of greatest knight?   ,,   1413
named us each by *n*, Calling 'God speed!'   *Holy Grail* 351
the knights, So many and famous *n's*;   ,,   364
after trumpet blown, her *n* And title,   *Pelleas and E.* 115
Full on her knights in many an evil *n*   ,,   290
'And oft in dying cried upon our *n*.'   ,,   385
Lancelot, saying, ' What *n* hast thou That ridest   ,,   563
' No *n*, no *n*,' he shouted, ' a scourge am I   ,,   565
but thy *n*?' ' I have many *n's*,' he cried: ,,   567
And when I call'd upon thy *n*   *Last Tournament* 73
set his *n* High on all hills,   ,,   336
a *n*? Was it the *n* of one in Brittany,   ,,   395
the sweet *n* Allured him first,   ,,   398
n Went wandering somewhere darkling in his mind.   ,,   456
Of one—his *n* is out of me—the prize,   ,,   546
Did I love her? the *n* at least I loved.   ,,   603
The *n* was ruler of the dark—Isolt?   ,,   606
And once or twice I spake thy *n* aloud.   ,,   615
hers Would be for evermore a *n* of scorn.   *Guinevere* 61
and yield me sanctuary, nor ask Her *n*   ,,   142
Nor with them mix'd, nor told her *n*,   ,,   148
And drawing foul ensample from fair *n's*,   ,,   490
And mine will ever be a *n* of scorn.   ,,   627
in their stead thy *n* and glory cling   *Pass. of Arthur* 53
'Thou hast betrayed thy nature and thy *n*,   ,,   241
call'd him by his *n*, complaining loud,   ,,   378
Rather than that gray king, whose *n*, a ghost,   *To the Queen*, ii 39
Keep thou thy *n* of 'Lover's Bay.'   *Lover's Tale* i 15
more Than the gray cuckoo loves his *n*,   ,,   257
and my *n* was borne Upon her breath;   ,,   443
Henceforth my *n* has been A hallow'd memory like the *n's* of old,   ,,   444
this *n* to which her gracious lips Did lend such gentle utterance, this one *n*, In such obscure hereafter,   ,,   456
Nevertheless, we did not change the *n*.   ,,   464
Thy *n* is ever worshipp'd among hours!   ,,   493
And by that *n* I moved upon her breath; Dear *n*, which had too much of nearness in it   ,,   560
Him who should own that *n*?   ,,   643
If so be that the echo of that *n*   ,,   644
upon the sands Insensibly I drew her *n*,   ,,   ii 7
And leave the *n* of Lover's Leap: ,,   iv 42
Forgive him, if his *n* be Julian too.'   ,,   175
GOLDEN-HAIR'D Ally whose *n* is one with mine,   *To A. Tennyson*, 1
the *n* at the head of my verse is thine.   ,,   6
May'st thou never be wrong'd by the *n* that is mine!   ,,   7
we had always borne a good *n*—   *Rizpath* 35
Yet must you change your *n*:   *Sisters (E. and E.)* 69
An old and worthy *n*!   ,,   74
care not for a *n*—no fault of mine.   ,,   77
city deck'd herself To meet me, roar'd my *n*;   *Columbus* 10

Name (s) (*continued*) I changed the *n*; San Salvador I call'd it; *Columbus* 75
HALLOWED be Thy *n*—Halleluiah! (repeat) *De Prof., Human C.* 1, 5, 9
n's who dare For that sweet mother land *Tiresias* 121
Their *n*'s, Graven on memorial columns,   "   123
ring thy *n* To every hoof that clangs it,   "   137
I have sullied a noble *n*, *The Wreck* 5
—to her maiden *n*!   "   144
felt as I spoke I was taking the *n* in vain— *Despair* 52
seest the Nameless of the hundred *n*'s. *Ancient Sage* 49
And never named the *N*'—   "   56
Not even his own *n*.   "   149
an age of noblest English *n*'s, *Locksley H. Sixty* 83
and dying while they shout her *n*.   "   128
leave to head These rhymings with your *n*, *Pro. to Gen. Hamley* 20
will you set your *n* A star among the stars. *Epilogue* 1
falling drop will make his *n* As mortal   "   60
till his Word Had won him a noble *n*. *Dead Prophet* 36
a *n* may last for a thousand years,   "   59
great *n* of England, round and round. (repeat) *Hands all Round* 12, 36
To this great *n* of England drink, my friends,   "   23
But since your *n* will grow with Time, *To Marq. of Dufferin* 13
have I made the *n* A golden portal to my rhyme :   "   15
and recks not to ruin a realm in her *n*. *Vastness* 10
He loved my *n* not me; *The Ring* 191
wrote *N*, Surname, all as clear as noon,   "   237
Earth and Hell will brand your *n*, *Forlorn* 51
In the *n* Of the everlasting God, *Happy* 107
A *n* that earth will not forget *To Ulysses* 27
corpse of every man that gains a *n*; *Romney's R.* 123
all Stood round it, hush'd, or calling on his *n*. *Death of Œnone* 66
In the great *n* of Him who died for men, *St. Telemachus* 63
I loathe the very *n* of infidel. *Akbar's Dream* 70
her *n*? what was it? I asked her. *Charity* 35
for *him* who had given her the *n*.   "   39
Priests in the *n* of the Lord *The Dawn* 4
scandal is mouthing a bloodless *n*   "   12
Form in Freedom's *n* and the Queen's! *Riflemen form!* 23
his truer *n* Is 'Onward,' *D. of the Duke of C.* 13
Name (verb) He *n*'s the name Eternity. *Two Voices* 291
That *n* the under-lying dead, *In Mem. ii* 2
The wish too strong for words to *n*; *xciii* 14
The Sultan, as we *n* him,— *Maud I xx* 4
Let him *n* it who can,   " *II ii* 11
He *n*'s himself the Night and oftener Death, *Gareth and L.* 638
' Peradventure he, you *n*, May know my shield.   "   1298
since you *n* yourself the summer fly, *Merlin and V.* 369
break faith with one I may not *n*? *Lancelot and E.* 685
she spake on, for I did *n* no wish, (repeat) *Lover's Tale i* 578, 583
those about us whom we neither see nor *n*, *Locksley H., Sixty* 272
Named (*See also* **Naämed**) dreamer, deaf and blind, *N* man, *Two Voices* 176
ship I sail in passes here (He *n* the day) *Enoch Arden* 215
that moment, when she *n* his name, *Aylmer's Field* 581
would bawl for civil rights, No woman *n*: *Princess v* 388
Truth-teller was our England's Alfred *n*; *Ode on Well.* 188
under every shield a knight was *n*: *Gareth and L.* 409
follows, being *n*, His owner, but remembers all,   "   703
That *n* himself the Star of Evening,   "   1090
a grateful people *n* Enid the Good; *Geraint and E.* 963
lavish comment when her name was *n*. *Merlin and V.* 151
therefore be as great as you are *n*,   "   336
n them, since a diamond was the prize. *Lancelot and E.* 33
n us each by name, Calling 'God speed!' *Holy Grail* 351
Thro' such a round in heaven, we *n* the stars,   "   686
loved it tenderly, And *n* it Nestling; *Last Tournament* 25
this I *n* from her own self, Evelyn; *Sisters (E. and E.)* 270
And never *n* the Name'— *Ancient Sage* 56
Drew to the valley *N* of the shadow, *Merlin and the G.* 87
Nameless (adj.) In whose least act abides the *n* charm *Princess v* 70
But spoke not, rapt in *n* reverie.   " *Con.* 108
Such clouds of *n* trouble cross All night *In Mem. iv* 13
Your father has wealth well-gotten, and I am *n* and poor. *Maud I iv* 18

Nameless (adj.) (*continued*) Sick of a *n* fear, *Maud II ii* 44
Whose bark had plunder'd twenty *n* isles; *Merlin and V.* 559
Blazed the last diamond of the *n* king. *Lancelot and E.* 444
The *n* Power, or Powers, that rule *Ancient Sage* 29
Nameless (s) If thou would'st hear the *N*,   "   31
thou May'st haply learn the *N* hath a voice,   "   34
Or even than the *N* is to me.   "   46
Thou seest the *N* of the hundred names. And if the *N* should withdraw from all   "   49
The *N* never came Among us,   "   54
Thou canst not prove the *N*, O my son,   "   57
But with the *N* is nor Day nor Hour;   "   102
past into the *N*, as a cloud Melts into Heaven.   "   233
A cloud between the *N* and thyself,   "   278
Namesake Her daintier *n* down in Brittany— *Last Tournament* 265
And she, my *n* of the hands,   "   594
Naming *n* each, And *n* those, his friends, *The Brook* 130
Who, never *n* God except for gain, *Sea Dreams* 188
Nap 'Twas but an after-dinner's *n*. *Day-Dm., Revival* 24
Nape the very *n* of her white neck Was rosed *Princess vi* 343
and the skull Brake from the *n*, *Lancelot and E.* 50
Naphtha-pits Beyond the Memmian *n-p*, *Alexander* 4
Napkin *n* wrought with horse and hound, *Audley Court* 1
like the common breed That with the *n* dally; *Will Water.* 118
Naples quite worn out, Travelling to *N*. *The Brook* 36
For *N* which we only left in May? *The Ring* 58
Narcotics Like dull *n*'s, numbing pain. *In Mem. v* 8
Narded *N* and swathed and balm'd it *Lover's Tale i* 682
Narra (narrow) I fun that it warn't not the gaäinist waäy to the *n* Gaäte. *Church-warden, etc.* 12
Narrow (adj.) (*See also* **Earth-narrow, Narra**) Oh! *n*, *n* was the space, *Oriana* 46
Drawing into his *n* earthen urn, *Ode to Memory* 61
And fires your *n* casement glass, *Miller's D.* 243
Were shiver'd in my *n* frame. *Fatima* 18
With *n* moon-lit slips of silver cloud, *Œnone* 218
Better the *n* brain, the stony heart, *Love and Duty* 15
Humm'd like a hive all round the *n* quay, *Audley Court* 5
I, to herd with *n* foreheads, *Locksley Hall* 175
red roofs about a *n* wharf In cluster; *Enoch Arden* 7
A *n* cave ran in beneath the cliff: "   23
halfway up The *n* street that clamber'd   "   60
Ten miles to northward of the *n* port   "   102
and his careful hand,—The space was *n*,—   "   177
And left but *n* breadth to left and right   "   674
Down to the pool and *n* wharf he went,   "   690
All down the long and *n* street he went   "   795
Doubtless our *n* world must canvass it: *Aylmer's Field* 774
n meagre face Seam'd with the shallow cares   "   813
To find a deeper in the *n* gloom   "   840
God bless the *n* sea which keeps her off, *Princess, Con.* 51
God bless the *n* seas!   "   70
Thy name was blest within the *n* door; *W. to Marie Alex.* 38
Till, in a *n* street and dim, *The Daisy* 22
Should murmur from the *n* house, *In Mem. xxxv* 2
She sighs amid her *n* days,   " *lx* 10
And Spring that swells the *n* brooks,   " *lxxxv* 70
all *n* jealousies Are silent; *Ded. of Idylls* 16
the stream Full, *n*; *Gareth and L.* 908
Anon they past a *n* comb wherein   "   1193
To me this *n* grizzled fork of thine *Merlin and V.* 59
Then, *n* court and lubber King, farewell!   "   119
In mine own realm beyond the *n* seas, *Lancelot and E.* 1323
like a vermin in its hole, Modred, a *n* face: *Last Tournament* 166
Or elsewhere, Modred's *n* foxy face, *Guinevere* 63
And wastes the *n* realm wherein we move, *Pass. of Arthur* 140
and the *n* fringe Of curving beach— *Lover's Tale i* 38
floods with redundant life Her *n* portals.   "   85
o'erstept The slippery footing of his *n* wit,   "   102
Small pity for those that have ranged from the *n* warmth of your fold, *Despair* 38
Fought for their lives in the *n* gap they had made— *Heavy Brigade* 23
The clash of tides that meet in *n* seas.— *Akbar's Dream* 58
Narrow (verb) tho' the gathering enemy *n* thee, *Boädicea* 39

Nature (continued)   Like simple noble *n's*, credulous · · · · · · · · · · · · · *Geraint and E* 875
N thro' the flesh herself hath made · · · · · *Merlin and V.* 50
the charm Of *n* in her overbore their own : · · · · ” 596
judge all *n* from her feet of clay, · · · · · · ” 835
tenderness Of manners and of *n*: and she thought
 That all was *n*, all, perchance for her. · · · *Lancelot and E.* 329
some discourtesy Against my *n*: · · · · · · · ” 1303
baseness in him by default Of will and *n*, · · · *Pelleas and E.* 82
not idle, but the fruit Of loyal *n*, · · · · · · *Guinevere* 336
‘ Thou hast betray'd thy *n* and thy name, · · · *Pass. of Arthur* 241
‘ Nothing in *n* is unbeautiful ; · · · · · · · *Lover's Tale i* 350
the great things of *N* and the fair, · · · · · *Sisters (E. and E.)* 222
lives with blindness, or plain innocence Of *n*, · · · ” 250
The marvel of that fair new *n*— · · · · · · · *Columbus* 79
dear mothers, crazing *N*, kill Their babies · · · ” 179
magnet of Art to the which my *n* was drawn, · · · *The Wreck* 22
Born of the brainless *N* who knew not · · · · · *Despair* 34
Tumble *N* heel o'er head, · · · · · · *Locksley H., Sixty* 135
Paint the mortal shame of *n* · · · · · · · · · ” 140
see the highest Human *N* is divine. · · · · · · ” 276
seëst Universal *N* moved by Universal Mind ; · · · *To Virgil* 22
Who yet, like *N*, wouldst not mar By changes · · · *Freedom* 21
‘ That weak and watery *n* love you ? · · · · · · *The Ring* 396
For your gentle *n* . . . · · · · · · · · · · *Forlorn* 46
My *n* was too proud. · · · · · · · · · · · · *Happy* 78
Where man, nor only *N* smiles ; · · · · · · · *To Ulysses* 39
whether, since our *n* cannot rest, · · · · · *Prog. of Spring* 96
Which types all *N's* male and female plan, · · · *On one who effec. E. M.* 3
The Spiritual in *N's* market-place— · · · · · · *Akbar's Dream* 135
from the terrors of *N* a people have fashion'd · · · *Kapiolani* 1
Let not all that saddens *N* · · · · · · · · · *Faith* 2

Natured   *See* **Best-natured, Noble-natured, Tender-natured**

Nave   bore along the *n* Her pendent hands, · · · *Aylmer's Field* 812
Navy   From the nations' airy *navies* · · · · · *Locksley Hall* 124
gay *n* there should splinter on it, · · · · · · *Sea Dreams* 131
sea plunged and fell on the shot-shatter'd *n* of
 Spain, · · · · · · · · · · · · · · · · · *The Revenge* 117
gold that Solomon's *navies* carried home, · · · · *Columbus* 113
Near   now I think my time is *n*.   I trust it is. · · *May Queen, Con.* 41
Ride on ! the prize is *n*.' · · · · · · · · · *Sir Galahad* 80
I could not weep—my own time seem'd so *n*. · · · *Grandmother* 72
Yet both are *n*, and both are dear, · · · · · · *The Victim* 59
DEAR, *n* and true—no truer Time · · · · · · · *A Dedication* 1
He seems so *n* and yet so far, · · · · · · · *In Mem. xcvii* 23
But now set out : the moon is *n*, · · · · · · · ” *Con.* 41
red rose cries, ‘ She is *n*, she is *n* ;' · · · · *Maud I xxii* 63
Wounded and wearied needs must he be *n*. · · · *Lancelot and E.* 538
And one was far apart, and one was *n*: · · · · *Last Tournament* 734
I was *n* my time wi' the boy, · · · · · · · · *First Quarrel* 82
Vile, so *n* the ghost Himself, · · · · · · · · *The Ring* 230
noises in the house—and no one *n*— · · · · · · ” 417
The fatal ring lay *n* her ; · · · · · · · · · ” 450
I knew that you were *n* me · · · · · · · · · *Happy* 65
but fork'd Of the *n* storm, · · · · · · · · · *Aylmer's Field* 727
Near'd   as he *n* His happy home, the ground. · · · *Gardener's D.* 91
So rapt, we *n* the house ; · · · · · · · · · · ” 142
went she Norward, Till she *n* the foe. · · · · · *The Captain* 36
only *n* Her husband inch by inch, · · · · · · *Aylmer's Field* 806
n, Touch'd, clink'd, and clash'd, and vanish'd, · · · *Sea Dreams* 134
Still growing holier as you *n* the bay, · · · · *Lover's Tale i* 338
Nearer   Nor art thou *n* to the light, · · · · · *Two Voices* 92
Could lift them *n* God-like state · · · · · · *Lit. Squabbles* 14
and *n* than hands and feet. · · · · · · · · *High. Pantheism* 12
tho' he make you evermore Dearer and *n*, · · · *A Dedication* 3
coming *n* and *n* again than before— · · · · · *Def. of Lucknow* 28
and find *N* and ever *n* Him, · · · · · · · *De Prof., Two G.* 53
coming *n*—Muriel had the ring— · · · · · · · *The Ring* 259
No *n* ? do you scorn me when you tell me, · · · · *Happy* 23
May I come a little *n*, I that heard, · · · · · · ” 55
—a little *n* still—He hiss'd, · · · · · · · · ” 62
A little *n* ?   Yes.   I shall hardly be content · · · ” 87
A little *n* yet ! · · · · · · · · · · · · · ” 104
his *n* friend would say, ‘ Screw not the chord · · · *Aylmer's Field* 468
My spring is all the *n*, · · · · · · · · · *Window, Winter* 17

Nearer (continued)   bubbling melody That drowns
 the *n* echoes. · · · · · · · · · · · · · *Lover's Tale i* 533
Nearest   (*See also* **Gaäinist**)   Were it our *n*, Were it our
 dearest, · · · · · · · · · · · · · · · *The Victim* 13
Which was his *n* ?   Who was his dearest ? · · · ” 76
While I, thy *n*, sat apart, · · · · · · · · · *In Mem. cx* 13
the King Spake to me, being *n*, ‘ Percivale,' · · · *Holy Grail* 268
My mind involved yourself the *n* thing · · · · *Merlin and V.* 300
Beyond the *n* mountain's bosky brows, · · · · *Lover's Tale i* 396
Nearing   And I am *n* seventy-four, · · · · *To E. Fitzgerald* 43
That he was *n* his own hundred, · · · · · · · *The Ring* 194
‘ Spirit, *n* yon dark portal at the limit · · · *God and the Univ.* 4
With *n* chair and lower'd accent) · · · · · · *Aylmer's Field* 267
Nearness   touch'd her thro' that *n* of the first, · · · ” 605
Desire of *n* doubly sweet ; · · · · · · · · *In Mem. cxvii* 6
name, which had too much of *n* in it · · · · *Lover's Tale i* 561
same *n* Were father to this distance, · · · · · ” *ii* 28
Brother-in-law—the fiery *n* of it— · · · · · *Sisters (E. and E.)* 173
Neat   (*See also* **Neät**)   a home For Annie, *n* and nestlike, · · · *Enoch Arden* 59
order'd all Almost as *n* and close · · · · · · ” 178
Neät   Sally sa pratty an' *n* an' sweeät, · · · *North. Cobbler* 43
sa pratty, an' feät, an' *n*, an' sweeät ? · · · · ” 108
fur, Steevie, tha' kep' it sa *n* · · · · · · · *Spinster's S's.* 77
Neater   Be the *n* and completer ; · · · · · · *Maud I xx* 20
Neat-herds   while his *n-h* were abroad ; · · · *Lucretius* 88
Nebulous   ‘ There sinks the *n* star we call the Sun, · · · *Princess iv* 19
Necessity   seem'd So justified by that *n*, · · · *Geraint and E.* 396
The vast *n* of heart and life. · · · · · · · *Merlin and V.* 925
Whom weakness or *n* have cramp'd · · · · · · *Tiresias* 87
Neck   fingers play About his mother's *n*, · · · *Supp. Confessions* 43
locks a-drooping twined Round thy *n* in subtle ring · · · *Adeline* 58
A glowing arm, a gleaming *n*, · · · · · · · *Miller's D.* 78
I'd touch her *n* so warm and white. · · · · · ” 174
round her *n* Floated her hair or seem'd to float · · · *Œnone* 18
I rode sublime On Fortune's *n*: · · · · · · *D. of F. Women* 142
Then they clung about The old man's *n*, · · · · *Dora* 164
A grazing iron collar grinds my *n*, · · · · · *St. S. Stylites* 117
‘ A third would glimmer on her *n* · · · · · · *Talking Oak* 221
And not leap forth and fall about thy *n*, · · · *Love and Duty* 41
Disyoke their *n's* from custom, · · · · · · · *Princess ii* 143
Drew from my *n* the painting and the tress, · · · ” *vi* 110
See, your foot is on our *n's*, · · · · · · · · ” 166
nape of her white *n* Was rosed with indignation : · · · ” 343
grew By bays, the peacock's *n* in hue ; · · · · *The Daisy* 14
‘ My mother clings about my *n*, · · · · · · · *Sailor Boy* 1
And fell in silence on his *n*: · · · · · · · *In Mem. ciii* 44
‘ Climb not lest thou break thy *n*, I charge thee by
 my love,' and so the boy, Sweet mother, neither
 clomb, nor break his *n*, · · · · · · · · · *Gareth and L.* 54
A stone about his *n* to drown him in it. · · · · ” 812
Gareth loosed the stone From off his *n*, · · · · ” 815
Drown him, and with a stone about his *n* ; · · · ” 823
with a sweep of it Shore thro' the swarthy *n*, · · · *Geraint and E.* 728
Sir Balan drew the shield from off his *n*, · · · *Balin and Balan* 429
curved an arm about his *n*, Clung like a snake ; · · · *Merlin and V.* 241
mantle of his beard Across her *n*, · · · · · · ” 257
to kiss each other On her white *n*— · · · · · ” 456
made her lithe arm round his *n* Tighten, · · · ” 614
Her eyes and *n* glittering went and came ; · · · ” 960
a *n* to which the swan's Is tawnier · · · · · *Lancelot and E.* 1184
a necklace for a *n* O as much fairer— · · · · ” 1227
n's Of dragons clinging to the crazy walls, · · · *Holy Grail* 346
raised a bugle hanging from his *n*, · · · · · *Pelleas and E.* 364
This ruby necklace thrice around her *n*, · · · *Last Tournament* 19
I muse Why ye not wear on arm, or *n*, or zone · · · ” 36
ye fling those rubies round my *n* · · · · · · ” 312
Queen Isolt With ruby-circled *n*, · · · · · · ” 364
brother of the Table Round Swung by the *n*: · · · ” 432
flinging round her *n*, Claspt it, · · · · · · ” 749
felt the King's breath wander o'er her *n*, · · · *Guinevere* 582
Bent o'er me, and my *n* his arm upstay'd. · · · *Lover's Tale i* 690
floated on and parted round her *n*, · · · · · ” 704
Love's arms were wreath'd about the *n* of Hope, · · · ” 815
He softly put his arm about her *n* · · · · · · ” *iv* 71
The mother fell about the daughter's *n*, · · · *Sisters (E. and E.)* 154

Neck (*continued*)   an' Charlie 'e brok 'is *n*,   *Village Wife* 85
    on the fatal *n* Of land running out into rock—   *Despair* 9
    Amy's arms about my *n*—   *Locksley H., Sixty* 13
    she that clasp'd my *n* had flown;   „ 15
    their arch'd *n's*, midnight-maned,   *Demeter and P.* 46
    I feeäld it drip o' my *n*.   *Owd Roä* 42
    as if 'e'd 'a brokken 'is *n*,   „ 63
Neck-an-crop   I coom'd *n-a-c* soomtimes   *North. Cobbler* 20
Neck'd   *See* **Long-neck'd**
Necklace (*See also* **Pearl-necklace**)   And I would be the *n*,   *Miller's D.* 181
    To make the *n* shine;   *Talking Oak* 222
    And fling the diamond *n* by.'   *Lady Clare* 40
    Or *n* for a neck to which the swan's   *Lancelot and E.* 1184
    or a *n* for a neck O as much fairer—   „ 1227
    This ruby *n* thrice around her neck,   *Last Tournament* 19
    diamond *n* dearer than the golden ring,   *Locksley H., Sixty* 21
Nectar   For they lie beside their *n*,   *Lotos-Eaters, C. S.* 111
    Hebes are they to hand ambrosia, mix The *n*;   *Princess iii* 114
    n smack'd of hemlock on the lips,   *Demeter and P.* 104
Need (s)   wasted Truth in her utmost *n*.   *Clear-headed friend* 19
    Our dusted velvets have much *n* of thee :   *To J. M. K.* 4
    And if some dreadful *n* should rise   *Love thou thy land* 91
    vows, where there was never *n* of vows,   *Gardener's D.* 258
    As I might slay this child, if good *n* were,   *Princess ii* 287
    How know I what had *n* of thee,   *In Mem. lxxiii* 3
    What is thy name ? thy *n* ?'   *Gareth and L.* 605
    my *n*, a knight To combat for my sister,   „ 607
    cruel *n* Constrain'd us,   *Marr. of Geraint* 715
    All to be there against a sudden *n* ;   *Geraint and E.* 375
    Mine is the larger *n*, who am not meek,   *Last Tournament* 610
    friends Of Arthur, who should help him at his *n* ?'   *Pass. of Arthur* 456
    had *n* Of a good stout lad at his farm;   *First Quarrel* 17
    no *n* to make such a stir.'   „ 63
    ' All the more, *n*,' I told him,   *In the Child. Hosp.* 18
    As good *n* was—thou hast come to talk   *Sir J. Oldcastle* 32
    false at last In our most *n*, appall'd them,   *Columbus* 71
    Bread enough for his *n* till the labourless day   *V. of Maeldune* 86
    Then the Norse leader, Dire was his *n* of it,   *Batt. of Brunanburh* 56
    What *n* to wish when Hubert weds in you   *The Ring* 61
    house with all its hateful *n's*   *Happy* 32
Need (verb)   all Life *n's* for life is possible   *Love and Duty* 86
    ' Wild natures *n* wise curbs.   *Princess v* 173
    whence they *n* More breadth of culture :   „ 187
    Whether I *n* have fled ?   *Maud II ii* 72
    I *n* not tell thee foolish words,—   *Holy Grail* 855
    He *n's* no aid who doth his lady's will.'   *Pelleas and E.* 281
    I *n* Him now.   *Last Tournament* 630
    such a craziness as *n's* A cell and keeper),   *Lover's Tale iv* 164
    Ah heavens ! Why *n* I tell you all ?—   „ 201
    ' The lad will *n* little more of your care.'   *In the Child. Hosp.* 17
    You *n* not wave me from you.   *Happy* 20
    music here be mortal *n* the singer greatly care ?   *Parnassus* 18
    Up hill ' Too-slow' will *n* the whip,   *Politics* 11
    I *n* no wages of shame.   *Charity* 40
Needed   With all that seamen *n* or their wives—   *Enoch Arden* 139
    yea twice or thrice—As oft as *n*—   „ 143
    Or thro' the want of what it *n* most,   „ 265
    voice who best could tell What most it *n*—   „ 267
    Because it *n* help of Love :   *In Mem. xxv* 8
    I *n* then no charm to keep them mine   *Merlin and V.* 547
Needful   And bought them *n* books, and everyway,   *Enoch Arden* 332
    My *n* seeming harshness, pardon it.   *Princess iii* 309
    Are but the *n* preludes of the truth :   „ *Con.* 74
    thou knowest I hold that forms Are *n* :   *Akbar's Dream* 127
Needing   (His father lying sick and *n* him)   *Enoch Arden* 65
Needle   ' I would have hid her *n* in my heart,   *Edwin Morris* 62
    Man for the sword and for the *n* she :   *Princess v* 448
    Are sharpen'd to a *n's* end ;   *In Mem. lxxvi* 4
    Be *n* to the magnet of your word,   *To Mary Boyle* 7
Needless   To greet the sheriff, *n* courtesy !   *Edwin Morris* 133
Needs (adv.)   he *n* Must wed that other, whom no man
    desired,   *Gareth and L.* 108
    one with me in all, he *n* must know.'   „ 566
    I *n* must disobey him for his good ;   *Geraint and E.* 135
    You *n* must work my work.   *Merlin and V.* 505

Needy   Let the *n* be banqueted,   *On Jub. Q. Victoria* 35
Negation   I hate the black *n* of the bier,   *Ancient Sage* 204
Neglect   If men *n* your pages ?   *Spiteful Letter* 6
Neglected   That all *n* places of the field   *Aylmer's Field* 693
    For thanks it seems till now *n*,   *Merlin and V.* 308
Neighbour (adj.)   from all *n* crowns Alliance and
    allegiance,   *Œnone* 124
    Leaning his horns into the *n* field,   *Gardener's D.* 87
    and lady friends From *n* seats :   *Princess, Pro.* 98
    But if my *n* whistle answers him—   *Lover's Tale iv* 161
Neighbour (s)   (*See also* **Nabour**)   While all the *n's* shoot
    thee round,   *The Blackbird* 2
    And ran to tell her *n's*;   *The Goose* 14
    Yet say the *n's* when they call,   *Amphion* 5
    O Lord !—'tis in my *n's* ground,   „ 75
    Leering at his *n's* wife.   *Vision of Sin* 118
    The next day came a *n*.   *Aylmer's Field* 251
    With *n's* laid along the grass,   *Lucretius* 214
    Each hissing in his *n's* ear;   *Princess v* 15
    the *n's* come and laugh and gossip,   *Grandmother* 91
    From every house the *n's* met,   *In Mem. xxxi* 9
    The foolish *n's* come and go,   „ *lx* 13
    measuring with his eyes His *n's* make and might: *Pelleas and E.* 151
    friend, the *n*, Lionel, the beloved,   *Lover's Tale i* 653
    if perchance the *n's* round May see,   *Achilles over the T.* 12
Neighbourhood   Far off from human *n*,   *Eleänore* 6
    As from some blissful *n*,   *Two Voices* 430
    By one low voice to one dear *n*,   *Aylmer's Field* 60
    Make their *n* healthfuller,   *On Jub. Q. Victoria* 32
Neighbouring   half The *n* borough with their Institute   *Princess, Pro.* 5
    betroth'd To one, a *n* Princess :   „ *i* 33
Neigh'd   Lancelot's charger fiercely *n*,   *Gareth and L.* 1400
    N with all gladness as they came,   *Geraint and E.* 755
    the warhorse *n* As at a friend's voice,   *Guinevere* 530
Neighing   strong *n's* of the wild white Horse   *Lancelot and E.* 298
Neilgherry   the sweet half-English *N* air   *The Brook* 17
Nell   God bless you, my own little *N*.   *First Quarrel* 22
Nelly   ' Our *N's* the flower of 'em all.'   „ 28
    But *N*, the last of the cletch,   *Village Wife* 9
    N wur up fro' the craädle as big i' the mouth   „ 103
    an' our *N* she gied me 'er 'and,   „ 111
Nelson   old England fall Which *N* left so great.   *The Fleet* 5
Nemesis   great *N* Break from a darken'd future,   *Princess vi* 174
Nephew   sparrow-hawk, My curse, my *n*—   *Marr. of Geraint* 445
    if the sparrow-hawk, this *n*, fight   „ 475
    And tilts with my good *n* thereupon,   „ 488
    Then Yniol's *n*, after trumpet blown,   „ 551
    O loyal *n* of our noble King,   *Lancelot and E.* 652
Neronian   those *N* legionaries   *Boädicea* 1
Nerve (s)   'Tis life, whereof our *n's* are scant,   *Two Voices* 397
    His *n's* were wrong. What ails us,   *Walk. to the Mail* 105
    like those, who clench their *n's* to rush   *Love and Duty* 77
    My *n's* have dealt with stiffer.   *Will Water.* 78
    When thy *n's* could understand   *Vision of Sin* 160
    Were living *n's* to feel the rent ;   *Aylmer's Field* 536
    O iron *n* to true occasion true,   *Ode on Well.* 37
    A weight of *n's* without a mind,   *In Mem. xii* 7
    blood creeps, and the *n's* prick And tingle ;   „ *l* 2
    Where all the *n* of sense is numb;   „ *xciii* 7
    O, having the *n's* of motion as well as the *n's*   *Maud I i* 63
    believing mind, but shatter'd *n*,   *Lover's Tale iv* 105
Nerve (verb)   ' The song that *n's* a nation's heart,   *Epilogue* 81
Nerve-dissolving   The *n-d* melody   *Vision of Sin* 44
Nest   From my high *n* of penance here proclaim   *St. S. Stylites* 167
    huts At random scatter'd, each a *n* in bloom.   *Aylmer's Field* 150
    bough That moving moves the *n* and nestling,   *Sea Dreams* 291
    birdie say In her *n* at peep of day ?   „ 294
    However deep you might embower the *n*,   *Princess, Pro.* 147
    Father will come to his babe in the *n*,   „ *iii* 13
    in the North long since my *n* is made.   „ *iv* 110
    built the *n* ' she said, ' To hatch the cuckoo.   „ 365
    We seem a *n* of traitors—   „ *v* 426
    And all in a *n* together.   *Window, Spring* 16
    there were cries and clashings in the *n*,   *Gareth and L.* 70
    by the bird's song ye may learn the *n*,'   *Marr. of Geraint* 359

Nest (continued) we will live like two birds in one n,   *Geraint and E.* 627
   And yellow-throated nestling in the n.   *Lancelot and E.* 12
   almost plaster'd like a martin's n   *Holy Grail* 548
   find a n and feels a snake, he drew: *Pelleas and E.* 437
   ' Black n of rats,' he groan'd,   " 555
   started thro' mid air Bearing an eagle's n: *Last Tournament* 15
   Sir Lancelot from the perilous n,   " 18
   A mountain n—the pleasure-boat that rock'd,   *Lover's Tale i* 42
   better ha' put my naked hand in a hornets' n.   *First Quarrel* 50
   And a tree with a moulder'd n   *Dead Prophet* 18
   Drove from out the mother's n   *Open. I. and C. Exhib.* 27
   Birds and brides must leave the n.   *The Ring* 89
   song again, n again, young again,'   *The Throstle* 9

Nested (adj.) (*See also* **Half-nested**) I envied human
   wives, and n birds,   *Demeter and P.* 53
Nested (verb) Wherein we n sleeping or awake,   *Lover's Tale i* 231
Nestled and the gilded snake Had n   " 624
Nestlike a home For Annie, neat and n,   *Enoch Arden* 59
Nestling bough That moving moves the nest and n,   *Sea Dreams* 291
   And yellow-throated n in the nest.   *Lancelot and E.* 12
   loved it tenderly, And named it N;   *Last Tournament* 25
   ' Peace to thine eagle-borne Dead n,   " 34

Net (s) (*See also* **Ivy-net, Fishing-nets**) Love that hath us
   in the n,   *Miller's D.* 203
   n made pleasant by the baits Of gold   *Aylmer's Field* 486
   To catch a dragon in a cherry n,   *Princess v* 169
   To have her lion roll in a silken n   *Maud I vi* 29
   Makers of n's, and living from the sea.   *Pelleas and E.* 90
   and Love The n of truth?'   *Akbar's Dream* 88
Net (verb) fibres n the dreamless head,   *In Mem. ii* 3
Netted (*See also* **Golden-netted**) I make the n sunbeam
   dance   *The Brook* 176
Nettle round and round In dung and n's!   *Pelleas and E.* 471
   sowing the n on all the laurel'd graves   *Vastness* 22
Nettled tho' n that he seem'd to slur   *Princess i* 163
Never Thou shalt hear the ' N, n,'   *Locksley Hall* 83
Never-changing In changing, chime with n-c Law.   *To Duke of Argyll* 11
   And over all, the n-c One   *Akbar's Dream* 147
Never-ended Here in the n-e afternoon,   *Last Tournament* 584
Never-lighted Beside the n-l fire.   *In Mem. lxxxiv* 20

New (*See also* **Fiery-new, Spick-span-new**) Kate hath a spirit
   ever strung like a n bow,   *Kate* 11
   Transgress his ample bound to some n crown:—   *Poland* 8
   tho' the surge Of some n deluge from a thousand
   hills   *If I were loved* 12
   Will learn n things when I am not.'   *Two Voices* 63
   I knit a hundred others n: " 234
   With this old soul in organs n?   " 393
   ' I have found A n land, but I die.'   *Palace of Art* 284
   N from its silken sheath   *D. of F. Women* 60
   Sweet as n buds in Spring.   " 272
   Shall sing for want, ere leaves are n,   *The Blackbird* 23
   There's a n foot on the floor, my friend, And a n
   face at the door, my friend, A n face at the
   door.   *D. of the O. Year* 52
   Nothing comes to thee n or strange.   *To J. S.* 74
   N Majesties of mighty States—   *Love thou thy land* 60
   He thought that nothing n was said,   *The Epic* 30
   Among n men, strange faces, other minds.'   *M. d'Arthur* 238
   each in passing touch'd with some n grace   *Gardener's D.* 204
   N things and old, himself and her, she sour'd   *Walk. to the Mail* 61
   I breathed In some n planet: *Edwin Morris* 115
   She left the n piano shut: *Talking Oak* 119
   fair n forms, That float about the threshold of an age,   *Golden Year* 15
   something more, A bringer of n things;   *Ulysses* 28
   In that n world which is the old: *Day-Dm., Depart.* 4
   Thro' sunny decades n and strange,   *L'Envoi* 22
   If old things, there are n;   *Will Water.* 58
   N stars all night above the brim Of waters   *Voyage* 25
   ' No, I love not what is n;   *Vision of Sin* 139
   And the n warmth of life's ascending sun   *Enoch Arden* 38
   Then her n child was as herself renew'd, Then the n
   mother came about her heart,   " 523
   ' that we still may lead The n light up,   *Princess ii* 348
   those were gracious times. Then came your n friend: " *iv* 298

New (continued) I your old friend and tried, she n in all?   *Princess iv* 318
   n day comes, the light Dearer for night,   " *vii* 346
   Gray nurses, loving nothing n;   *In Mem. xxix* 14
   Shall count n things as dear as old: " *xl* 28
   The baby n to earth and sky,   " *xlv* 1
   The full n life that feeds thy breath   " *lxxxvi* 10
   But all is n unhallow'd ground.   " *civ* 12
   With old results that look like n: " *cxxviii* 11
   But, I fear, the n strong wine of love,   *Maud I vi* 82
   N as his title, built last year,   " *x* 19
   And that same night, the night of the n year,   *Com. of Arthur* 209
   N things and old co-twisted, as if Time Were
   nothing,   *Gareth and L.* 226
   the n knight Had fear he might be shamed;   " 1043
   n sun Beat thro' the blindless casement of the
   room,   *Marr. of Geraint* 70
   Ride into that n fortress by your town,   " 407
   Built that n fort to overawe my friends,   " 460
   She is not fairer in n clothes than old.   " 722
   ' O my n mother, be not wroth or grieved At thy
   n son,   " 779
   A splendour dear to women, n to her, And therefore
   dearer; or if not so n,   " 808
   The n leaf ever pushes off the old.   *Balin and Balan* 442
   like a bride's On her n lord, her own,   *Merlin and V.* 617
   But once in life was fluster'd with n wine,   " 756
   Meanwhile the n companions past away   *Lancelot and E.* 399
   till they found The n design wherein they lost
   themselves,   " 441
   Not for me! For her! for your n fancy.   " 1216
   KING ARTHUR made n knights to fill the gap   *Pelleas and E.* 1
   And this n knight, Sir Pelleas of the isles—   " 17
   N leaf, n life—the days of frost are o'er: N life, n
   love, to suit the newer day: N loves are sweet
   as those that went before: *Last Tournament* 278
   the knights, Glorying in each n glory,   " 336
   And thou wert lying in thy n leman's arms.'   " 625
   She like a n disease, unknown to men,   *Guinevere* 518
   to those With whom he dwelt, n faces, other minds.   *Pass. of Arthur* 5
   wife and child with wail Pass to n lords;   " 45
   Among n men, strange faces, other minds.'   " 406
   And the n sun rose bringing the n year.   " 469
   rather seem'd For some n death than for a life
   renew'd;   *Lover's Tale iv* 374
   Crazy with laughter and babble and earth's n
   wine,   *To A. Tennyson* 2
   those long-sweeping beechen boughs Of our N
   Forest.   *Sisters (E. and E.)* 113
   fur N Squire coom'd last night.   *Village Wife* 1
   Sa n Squire's coom'd wi' 'is taäil in 'is 'and, (repeat)   " 14, 121
   an' dizen'd out, an' a-buyin' n cloäthes,   " 37
   chains For him who gave a n heaven, a n earth,   *Columbus* 20
   The marvel of that fair n nature—   " 79
   Whatever wealth I bought from that n world   " 101
   be consecrate to lead A n crusade against the Saracen,   " 103
   For these are the n dark ages, you see,   *Despair* 88
   Eh! tha be n to the plaäce—   *Spinster's S's.* 3
   Dead the n astronomy calls her. . . .   *Locksley H., Sixty* 175
   And some n Spirit o'erbear the old,   *Epilogue* 14
   ONCE more the Heavenly Power Makes all things n,   *Early Spring* 2
   For now the Heavenly Power Makes all things n,   " 44
   N England of the Southern Pole?   *Hands all Round* 14
   For ten thousand years Old and n?   *The Ring* 20
   —is making a n link Breaking an old one?   " 50
   On that n life that gems the hawthorn line;   *Prog. of Spring* 36
   And n developments, whatever spark   " 94
   Sing the n year in under the blue.   *The Throstle* 5
   ' N, n, n, n! Is it then so n   " 7
   ' hast thou brought us down a n Korân From
   heaven?   *Akbar's Dream* 116
   I heard a mocking laugh ' the n Korân!'   " 183
   The wonders were so wildly n,   *Mechanophilus* 27
   If N and Old, disastrous feud,   *Love thou thy land* 77
   'The old order changeth, yielding place to n,   *M. d'Arthur* 240
   Whose fancy fuses old and n,   *In Mem. xvi* 18

R

Noble (adj.) (*continued*)   We have proved we have hearts in
  a cause, we are *n* still,   *Maud III vi* 55
Thou *n* Father of her Kings to be,   *Ded. of Idylls* 34
But thou art closer to this *n* prince,   *Com. of Arthur* 314
When some good knight had done one *n* deed,   *Gareth and L.* 411
Tut, an the lad were *n*,   ,, 473
All kind of service with a *n* ease   ,, 489
'Lynette my name ; *n*; my need, a knight   ,, 607
Sweet lord, how like a *n* knight he talks !   ,, 777
Or sit beside a *n* gentlewoman.'   ,, 867
O knave, as *n* as any of all the knights—   ,, 1136
Missaid thee : *n* I am ; and thought the King   ,, 1165
Then turn'd the *n* damsel smiling at him,   ,, 1188
'Nay, *n* damsel, but that I, the son   ,, 1230
merry am I to find my goodly knave Is knight and *n*.   ,, 1292
O *n* Lancelot, from my hold on these Streams virtue—   ,, 1309
'O *n* breast and all-puissant arms,   *Marr. of Geraint* 86
Not hearing any more his *n* voice,   ,, 98
'Yea, *n* Queen,' he answer'd,   ,, 178
now thinking that he heard The *n* hart at bay,   ,, 233
Geraint, a name far-sounded among men For *n* deeds ?   ,, 428
So grateful is the noise of *n* deeds To *n* hearts   ,, 437
Let *me* lay lance in rest, O *n* host,   ,, 496
'This *n* prince who won our earldom back,   ,, 619
all That appertains to *n* maintenance.   ,, 712
See ye take the charger too, A *n* one.'   *Geraint and E.* 556
she Kiss'd the white star upon his *n* front,   ,, 757
Such fine reserve and *n* reticence,   ,, 860
Like simple *n* natures, credulous   ,, 875
Our *n* King will send thee his own leech—   *Balin and Balan* 275
Not, doubtless, all unearn'd by *n* deeds.   ,, 471
Our *n* Arthur, him Ye scarce can overpraise,   *Merlin and V.* 91
'She is too *n*' he said ' to check at pies,   ,, 126
That makes you seem less *n* than yourself,   ,, 322
for love of God and men And *n* deeds, the flower of all
  the world. And each incited each to *n* deeds.   ,, 413
such a *n* song was that.   ,, 433
were all as tame, I mean, as *n*, as their Queen   ,, 608
Is that an answer for a *n* knight ?   *Lancelot and E.* 201
shame me not Before this *n* knight,'   ,, 208
To ride to Camelot with this *n* knight :   ,, 220
full Of *n* things, and held her from her sleep.   ,, 339
'Fair lord, whose name I know not—*n* it is,   ,, 360
Needs must be lesser likelihood, *n* lord,   ,, 367
And ride no more at random, *n* Prince !   ,, 633
O loyal nephew of our *n* King,   ,, 652
to be sweet and serviceable To *n* knights in sickness,   ,, 768
'Nay, *n* maid,' he answer'd, ' ten times nay !   ,, 948
Was *n* man but made ignoble talk.   ,, 1088
'Most *n* lord, Sir Lancelot of the Lake,   ,, 1272
Wifeless and heirless, *n* issue, sons Born   ,, 1371
This chance of *n* deeds will come and go
  Unchallenged,   *Holy Grail* 318
So strange, of such a kind, that all of pure *N*,   ,, 774
All of true and *n* in knight and man   ,, 882
and Pelleas look'd *N* among the *n*,   *Pelleas and E.* 152
fire of honour and all *n* deeds Flash'd,   ,, 278
O *n* vows ! O great and sane and simple race   ,, 479
By *n* deeds at one with *n* vows,   *Last Tournament* 123
by whom all men Are *n*,   ,, 600
'O pray you, *n* lady, weep no more ;   *Guinevere* 184
Full many a *n* war-song had he sung,   ,, 278
'Sir Lancelot, as became a *n* knight,   ,, 328
fruit Of loyal nature, and of *n* mind.'   ,, 336
Less *n*, being, as all rumour runs,   ,, 339
If ever Lancelot, that most *n* knight, Were for one
  hour less in than himself,   ,, 345
Sir Lancelot's, were as *n* as the King's,   ,, 351
And worship her by years of *n* deeds,   ,, 476
And miss to hear high talk of *n* deeds   ,, 499
and in the mist Was many a *n* deed,   *Pass. of Arthur* 105
as beseem'd Thy fëalty, nor like a *n* knight :   ,, 243
When every morning brought a *n* chance, And
  every chance brought out a *n* knight.   ,, 398
And bearing on one arm the *n* babe,   *Lover's Tale iv* 370

Noble (adj.) (*continued*)   and was *n* in birth as in
  worth,   *V. of Maeldune* 3
I have sullied a *n* name,   *The Wreck* 5
to crown with song The warrior's *n* deed—   *Epilogue* 37
' So great so *n* was he !'   *Dead Prophet* 30
till his Word Had won him a *n* name. *N* ! he sung,   ,, 36
Great and *n*—O yes—but yet—   ,, 43
N and great—O ay—but then,   ,, 49
To all our *n* sons, the strong New England   *Hands all Round* 15
Where in Ulric dwells forlorn,   *Happy* 10
But come, My *n* friend, my faithful counsellor,   *Akbar's Dream* 18
N the Saxon who hurl'd at his Idol   *Kapiolani* 4
Noble (s)   Where the wealthy *n*'s dwell.'   *L. of Burleigh* 24
The *n* and the convict of Castile,   *Columbus* 117
Nobleman   she, you know, Who wedded with a *n* from
  thence :   *Princess i* 77
Noble-natured   the boy Is *n-n*.   *Gareth and L.* 468
Nobleness   With such a vantage-ground for *n* !   *Aylmer's Field* 387
And much I praised her *n*,   *Princess, Pro.* 124
That you trust me in your own *n*,   *Lancelot and E.* 1195
Some root of knighthood and pure *n* ;   *Holy Grail* 886
the wines being of such *n*—   *Lover's Tale iv* 222
kings of men in utter *n* of mind,   *Locksley H., Sixty* 122
Nobler   am I not the *n* thro' thy love ?   *Love and Duty* 19
Not *keep* it noble, make it *n* ?   *Aylmer's Field* 386
Balmier and *n* from her bath of storm,   *Lucretius* 175
And since the *n* pleasure seems to fade.   ,, 230
as to slay One *n* than thyself.'   *Gareth and L.* 981
A something—was it *n* than myself ?—   *Pelleas and E.* 310
might inwreathe (How lovelier, *n* then !)   *Lover's Tale i* 459
Seem'd *n* than their hard Eternities.   *Demeter and P.* 107
O you that hold A *n* office upon earth   *To the Queen* 2
A *n* yearning never broke her rest   *The form, the form* 2
' But, if I lapsed from *n* place,   *Two Voices* 358
As emblematic of a *n* age ;   *Princess ii* 127
Tho' all men else their *n* dreams forget,   *Ode on Well.* 152
There must be other *n* work to do   ,, 256
And thou shalt take a *n* leave.'   *In Mem. lviii* 12
He past ; a soul of *n* tone :   *In Mem. lx* 1
Ring in the modes of life,   ,, *cvi* 15
Are breathers of an ampler day For ever *n* ends.   ,, *cxviii* 7
The fair beginners of a *n* time,   *Com. of Arthur* 457
how can Enid find A *n* friend ?   *Marr. of Geraint* 793
in my heart of hearts I did acknowledge *n*.   *Lancelot and E.* 1211
This earth has never borne a *n* man.   *Epit. on Gordon* 4
thro' all the *n* hearts In that vast Oval   *St. Telemachus* 72
Noblest   Truest friend and *n* foe ;   *Princess vi* 7
The *n* answer unto such Is perfect stillness   *Lit. Squabbles* 19
but he, Our *n* brother, and our truest man,   *Gareth and L.* 565
let Lancelot know, Thy *n* and thy truest !'   ,, 568
let her tongue Rage like a fire among the *n* names,   *Merlin and V.* 802
goodliest man That ever among ladies ate in hall,
  And *n*,   *Lancelot and E.* 256
one Of *n* manners, tho' himself would say Sir
  Lancelot had the noblest ;   *Guinevere* 319
But pray you, which had *n*, while you moved   ,, 325
here in Edward's time, an age of *n* English names,   *Locksley H., Sixty* 83
All that is *n*, all that is basest,   *Vastness* 32
One of our *n*, our most valorous,   *Geraint and E.* 910
noble it is, I well believe, the *n*—   *Lancelot and E.* 361
knight of Arthur's *n* dealt in scorn ;   *Guinevere* 40
would say Sir Lancelot had the *n* ;   ,, 320
Noblest-hearted   truest, kindliest, *n-h* wife   *Romney's R.* 35
Noblier-fashion'd   Was he *n-f* than other men ?   *Dead Prophet* 51
Nobly   have ye seen how *n* changed ?   *Geraint and E.* 897
Nobly-manner'd   Were the most *n-m* men of all ;   *Guinevere* 334
Nod (s)   And flooded at our *n*.   *D. of F. Women* 144
With frequent smile and *n* departing   *Marr. of Geraint* 515
an' she gev him a frindly *n*,   *Tomorrow* 58
Nod (verb)   Glares at one that *n*'s and winks   *Locksley Hall* 136
Then moves the trees, the copses *n*,   *Sir Galahad* 77
Nodded   The parson smirk'd and *n*.   *The Goose* 20
He *n*, but a moment afterwards He cried,   *Gardener's D.* 120
And Walter *n* at me ; ' He began,   *Princess, Pro.* 200
Florian *n* at him, I frowning ;   ,, *iv* 159

November (*See also* **Mid-November**) *N* dawns and dewy-glooming downs, — *Enoch Arden* 610
N day Was growing duller twilight, — " 721
Novice none with her save a little maid, A *n* : — *Guinevere* 4
sang the *n*, while full passionately, — " 180
said the little *n* prattling to her, — " 183
To whom the little *n* garrulously, — " 231
To whom the *n* garrulously again — " 276
the *n* crying, with clasp'd hands, — " 311
said the little *n*, 'I pray for both ; — " 349
and saw The *n*, weeping, suppliant, — " 664
Now 'Thens' and 'Whens' the Eternal *N* : — *Ancient Sage* 104
Now-recover'd brought From Solomon's *n-r* Ophir — *Columbus* 112
Nowt (nothing) Noorse? thourt *n* o' a noorse : — *N. Farmer, O. S.* 2
Doctors, they knaws *n*, fur a says what's nawways true : — " 5
N at all but bracken an' fuzz, — " 38
Warn't worth *n* a haäcre. — " 39
Parson's lass 'ant *n*, an' she weänt 'a *n* when 'e's deäd, — " *N. S.* 25
an ass as near as mays *n*— — " 39
Feyther 'ad ammost *n* ; — " 51
I 'a *n* but Adam's wine : — *North. Cobbler* 5
The gells they counts fur *n*, — *Village Wife* 18
knaw'd *n* but boooks, an' boooks, as thou knaws, beänt. — " 52
niver done *n* to be shaämed on, — *Owd Roä* 10
not nowadaäys—good fur *n*— — " 78
Yit I beänt sich a *N* of all *N's* — " 79
They says 'at he coom'd fra *n*— — *Church-warden, etc.* 17
Nox 'MERIDIES'—'HESPERUS'—'*N*'—'MORS,' — *Gareth and L.* 1205
Nudd answer, groaning, 'Edyrn, son of *N* ! — *Marr. of Geraint* 576
'Then, Edyrn, son of *N*,' replied — " 579
Beholding it was Edyrn son of *N*, — *Geraint and E.* 781
Null icily regular, splendidly *n*, — *Maud I ii* 6
Numb (adj.) Where all the nerve of sense is *n* ; — *In Mem. xciii* 7
Numb (verb) And *n's* the Fury's ringlet-snake, — *Lucretius* 262
Number (s) And o'er the *n* of thy years. — *In Mem. lxvii* 8
And miss the wonted *n* of my knights, — *Guinevere* 498
numberless *n's*, Shipmen and Scotsmen. — *Batt. of Brunanburh* 54
Number (verb) Whose troubles *n* with his days : — *Two Voices* 330
That *n's* forty cubits from the soil. — *St. S. Stylites* 91
Could *n* five from ten. — *Talking Oak* 80
Love and I do *n* equal years, — *Lover's Tale i* 195
Number'd *n* o'er Some thrice three years : — *In Mem. Con.* 9
I have *n* the bones, — *Rizpah* 10
Numberest tho' thou *n* with the followers — *Aylmer's Field* 663
Numberless *n* numbers, Shipmen and Scotsmen. — *Batt. of Brunanburh* 54
Numbing Like dull narcotics, *n* pain. — *In Mem. v* 8
Num-cumpus So like a greät *n-c* I blubber'd — *North. Cobbler* 61
Numerable-innumerable Among the *n-i* Sun, — *De Prof., Two G.* 44
Numerous For I am of a *n* house, — *Will Water.* 89
Nun monk and *n*, ye scorn the world's desire, — *Balin and Balan* 445
'A woman,' answer'd Percivale, 'a *n*, — *Holy Grail* 68
N as she was, the scandal of the Court, — " 78
leaving the pale *n*, I spake of this To all men ; — " 129
saw it, as the *n* My sister saw it ; — " 198
Thy holy *n* and thou have seen a sign— — " 295
Thy holy *n* and thou have driven men mad, — " 862
she spake There to the *n's*, and said, — *Guinevere* 139
many a week, unknown, among the *n's* ; — " 147
hum An air the *n's* had taught her ; — " 163
Our simple-seeming Abbess and her *n's*, — " 309
the good *n's* would check her gadding tongue — " 313
near him the sad *n's* with each a light Stood, — " 590
Then glancing up beheld the holy *n's* — " 666
Wear black and white, and be a *n* like you, — " 677
Nunnery (adj.) 'O little maid, shut in by *n* walls, — " 227
Nunnery (s) monkeries And *nunneries*, — *Sir J. Oldcastle* 94
And simple miracles of thy *n* ?' — *Guinevere*
A murmuring whisper thro' the *n* ran, — " 410
Nunnery-walls (*See also* **Nunnery (adj.)**) 'O closed about by narrowing *n-w*, — " 342
O shut me round with narrowing *n-w*, — " 671
Nuptial But rich as for the *n's* of a king. — *Lover's Tale iv* 212
Nurse (s) (*See also* **Noorse**) In there came old Alice the *n*, — *Lady Clare* 13

Nurse (s) (*continued*) said Alice the *n*, (repeat) — *Lady Clare* 17, 23, 33, 41, 45
'Are ye out of your mind, my *n*, my *n*?' — *Lady Clare* 21
And told him all her *n's* tale. — " 80
Leolin's first *n* was, five years after, hers : — *Aylmer's Field* 79
my *n* would tell me of you ; — *Princess iv* 427
Rose a *n* of ninety years, — " *vi* 13
Let them not lie in the tents with coarse mankind, Ill *n's* ; — " 70
Gray *n's*, loving nothing new ; — *In Mem. xxix* 14
That watch'd her on her *n's* arm, — " *Con.* 46
And tended her like a *n*. — *Maud I xix* 76
Meeker than any child to a rough *n*, — *Lancelot and E.* 857
dirty *n*, Experience, in her kind Hath foul'd me— — *Last Tournament* 317
N, I must do it to-morrow ; — *In the Child. Hosp.* 42
Never since I was *n*, had I been so grieved — " 45
That day my *n* had brought me the child. — *The Wreck* 59
I wrote to the *n* Who had borne my flower on her hireling heart ; and an answer came Not from the *n*— — " 142
n of ailing body and mind, — *Locksley H., Sixty* 51
Your *n* is here ! Miriam. My Mother's *n* — *The Ring* 96
woman came And caught me from my *n*. — " 118
Poor *n* ! I bad her keep, — " 121
third September birthday with your *n*, — " 130
desire to keep So skilled a *n* about you always— — " 374
I cried for *n*, and felt a gentle hand — " 418
Your *n* is waiting. Kiss me child and go. — " 489
N, were you hired ? — *Romney's R.* 16
caught when a *n* in a hospital ward. — *Charity* 41
Nurse (verb) To *n* a blind ideal like a girl, — *Princess iii* 217
it becomes no man to *n* despair, — " *iv* 464
Grant me your son, to *n*, — " *vi* 298
Shall I *n* in my dark heart, — *Maud II ii* 55
You'll have her to *n* my child, — *First Quarrel* 70
To *n* my children on the milk of Truth, — *Akbar's Dream* 162
Nursed Thou wert not *n* by the waterfall — *Ode to Memory* 51
wert *n* in some delicious land Of lavish lights, — *Eleänore* 11
Those in whose laps our limbs are *n*, — *To J. S.* 10
And *n* by mealy-mouth'd philanthropies, — *The Brook* 94
The wrath I *n* against the world : — *Princess v* 437
And *n* by those for whom you fought, — " *vi* 95
nor the hand That *n* me, — " *vii* 54
she had *n* me there from week to week : — " 239
n at ease and brought to understand — *Maud I xviii* 35
and his wife *N* the young prince, — *Com. of Arthur* 224
we were *n* in the drear night-fold — *Despair* 21
Muriel *n* you with a mother's care ; — *The Ring* 349
She watch'd me, she *n* me, she fed me, — *Charity* 33
Nurseling This *n* of another sky — *The Daisy* 98
Nursery one they knew—Raw from the *n*— — *Aylmer's Field* 264
In our young *n* still unknown, — *Princess iv* 332
Gray relics of the *nurseries* of the world, — *Lover's Tale i* 290
Nursing 'Muriel's health Had weaken'd, *n* little Miriam. — *The Ring* 357
Annie pale, *N* the sickly babe, — *Enoch Arden* 150
N a child, and turning to the warmth — *Aylmer's Field* 185
Nurtured *See* **Isle-nurtured**
Nut if the *n's'* he said 'be ripe again : — *Enoch Arden* 459
mighty *n's*, and nourishing roots ; — " 555
As fancies like the vermin in a *n* — *Princess vi* 263
Nutmeg The *n* rocks and isles of clove. — *The Voyage* 40
Nutter hazlewood, By autumn *n's* haunted, — *Enoch Arden* 8
Nutting great and small, Went *n* to the hazels. — " 64
long'd To go with others, *n* to the wood, — " 363
Nymph (*See also* **Wood-nymph**) mountain quickens into *N* and Faun ; — *Lucretius* 187
presented Maid Or *N*, or Goddess, — *Princess i* 197
how like a *n*, A stately mountain *n* she look'd ! — *Lover's Tale i* 358
Where *n* and god ran ever round in gold— — " *iv* 197

O

O mouthing out his hollow *oes* and aes, — *The Epic* 50
Oak (*See also* **Baby-oak, Brother-oak**) HE thought to quell the stubborn hearts of *o*, — *Buonaparte* 1

Oak (*continued*) I turn to yonder *o*. — *Talking Oak* 8
To yonder *o* within the field I spoke — „ 13
Broad *O* of Sumner-chace, — „ 30
Old *o*, I love thee well; — „ 202
For never yet was *o* on lea — „ 243
The gouty *o* began to move, — *Amphion* 23
Parks with *o* and chestnut shady, — *L. of Burleigh* 29
What amulet drew her down to that old *o*, — *Aylmer's Field* 507
violet varies from the lily as far As *o* from elm: — *Princess v* 183
when the winds of winter tear an *o* — *Boädicea* 77
Ere half the lifetime of an *o*. — *In Mem. lxxvi* 12
Before a gloom of stubborn-shafted *o*'s, — *Geraint and E.* 120
Arising wearily at a fallen *o*, — *Balin and Balan* 425
Then leapt her palfrey o'er the fallen *o*, — „ 587
Before an *o*, so hollow, huge and old — *Merlin and V.* 3
song that once I heard By this huge *o*, — „ 406
Call'd her to shelter in the hollow *o*, — „ 894
struck, Furrowing a giant *o*, — „ 936
And in the hollow *o* he lay as dead, — „ 969
A stump of half-dead, — *Last Tournament* 12
May freedom's *o* for ever live — *Hands all Round* 5
few lanes of elm And whispering *o*. — *To Mary Boyle* 68
Young and old, Like yon *o*, — *The Oak* 3
hew'd Like broad *o*'s with thunder. — *The Tourney* 11
Oaken With breezes from our *o* glades, — *Eleänore* 10
And like an *o* stock in winter woods, — *Golden Year* 62
And *o* finials till he touch'd the door; — *Aylmer's Field* 823
The three decker's *o* spine — *Maud II ii* 27
he lay Down on an *o* settle in the hall, — *Geraint and E.* 573
Oakling drew My little *o* from the cup, — *Talking Oak* 231
Oak-room Maud's own little *o-r* — *Maud I xiv* 9
Oak-tree But the solemn *o-t* sigheth, — *Claribel* 4
An *o-t* smoulder'd there. — *Gareth and L.* 402
red fruit Grown on a magic *o-t* in mid-heaven, — *Last Tournament* 745
'Oäm (**home**) one night I cooms '*o* like a bull — *North. Cobbler* 33
'e were that outdacious at '*o*, — *Village Wife* 75
boäth slinkt '*o* by the brokken shed — *Spinster's S's.* 37
Oän (**own**) wi' the Divil's *o* teäm. — *N. Farmer, O. S.* 62
an' 'e's the Divil's *o* sen.' — *North. Cobbler* 76
An' Squire, his *o* very sen, — „ 91
noa, not fur Sally's *o* kin. — „ 114
So I sits i' my *o* armchair wi' my *o* kettle — *Spinster's S's.* 9
fro' my *o* two 'oonderd a-year. — „ 58
'ere i' my *o* blue chaumber to me. — „ 80
'ud 'a let me 'a hed my *o* waäy, — „ 101
An' I sits i' my *o* little parlour, an' sarved by my *o*
little lass, Wi' my *o* little garden outside, an' my
o bed o' sparrow-grass, An' my *o* door-poorch wi'
the woodbine — „ 103
'thank God that I hevn't naw cauf o' my *o*.' — „ 117
An' I'd voät fur 'im, my *o* sen, — *Owd Roä* 14
Oäp (**hope**) An' I '*o*'s es 'e beänt boooklarn'd : — *Village Wife* 23
es I '*o*'s es thou'll 'elp me a bit, — „ 65
sewer an' sartin '*o* o' the tother side; — „ 92
Oar weary seem'd the sea, weary the *o*, — *Lotos-Eaters* 41
wind and wave and *o*; — „ *C. S.* 127
barge with *o* and sail Moved from the brink, — *M. d'Arthur* 265
stirr'd with languid pulses of the *o*, — *Gardener's D.* 41
The measured pulse of racing *o*'s — *In Mem. lxxxvii* 10
barge with *o* and sail Moved from the brink, — *Pass. of Arthur* 433
Oar'd Naiads *o* A glimmering shoulder — *To E. L.* 16
Some to a low song *o* a shallop by, — *Princess ii* 457
the dead, *O* by the dumb, went upward — *Lancelot and E.* 1154
Oaring *O* one arm, and bearing in my left — *Princess iv* 183
Oarless unlaborious earth and *o* sea; — *To Virgil* 20
Oarsman *o*'s haggard face, As hard and still — *Lancelot and E.* 1250
Oasis fountain-fed Ammonian *O* in the waste. — *Alexander* 8
My one *O* in the dust and drouth Of city life ! — *Edwin Morris* 3
they might grow To use and power on this *O*, — *Princess i* 167
Oat (*See also* **Whoats**) had the wild *o* not been
sown, — *In Mem. liii* 6
Oat-grass On the *o-g* and the sword-grass, — *May Queen, N. Y's. E.* 28
Oath Let us swear an *o*, and keep it — *Lotos-Eaters, C. S.* 108
Heaven heads the count of crimes With that
wild *o*.' — *D. of F. Women* 202

R*

Oath (*continued*) And hear me swear a solemn *o*, — *Talking Oak* 281
Cophetua sware a royal *o*: — *Beggar Maid* 15
since my *o* was ta'en for public use, — *Princess iv* 337
Your *o* is broken: we dismiss you: — „ 360
But keep that *o* ye sware, — *Merlin and V.* 688
Vivien, fearing heaven had heard her *o*, — „ 940
O's, insult, filth, and monstrous blasphemies, — *Pass. of Arthur* 114
that you, that I, would slight our marriage *o*: — *Happy* 89
laughter, Pagan *o*, and jest, — *St. Telemachus* 39
Obaäy (**obey**) To loove an' *o* the Tommies ! — *Spinster's S's.* 96
Obedience Seeing *o* is the bond of rule. — *M. d'Arthur* 94
Linger with vacillating *o*, — *Gareth and L.* 13
Of thine *o* and thy love to me, — „ 146
bow'd himself With all *o* to the King, — „ 488
And uttermost *o* to the King.' — „ 555
For uttermost *o* to make demand — „ 558
In uttermost *o* to the King. — „ 833
But silently, in all *o*, — *Marr. of Geraint* 767
With difficulty in mild *o* Driving them on: — *Geraint and E.* 104
O is the courtesy due to kings.' — *Lancelot and E.* 718
Seeing *o* is the bond of rule. — *Pass of Arthur* 262
bankrupt of all claim On your *o*, — *Romney's R.* 71
Obedient most valorous, Sanest and most *o*: — *Geraint and E.* 911
O to her second master now; — *Lover's Tale iv* 343
Obeisance curtseying her *o*, let us know — *Princess ii* 20
Obelisk *o*'s Graven with emblems of the time, — *Arabian Nights* 107
Obey (*See also* **Obaäy**) A courage to endure and to *o*; — *Isabel* 25
'Will be *o* when one commands ? — *Two Voices* 244
well to *o* then, if a king demand An act un-
profitable, — *M. d'Arthur* 95
Man to command and woman to *o*; — *Princess v* 450
And since thou art my mother, must *o*. — *Gareth and L.* 167
'I charge thee, ask not, but *o*.' — *Marr. of Geraint.* 133
How should I dare *o* him to his harm? — *Geraint and E.* 136
I swear it would not ruffle me so much As you
that not *o* me. — „ 151
that ye speak not but *o*.' — „ 417
I know Your wish, and would *o*; — „ 419
Almost beyond me: yet I would *o*.' — „ 423
Rise therefore ; robe yourself in this : *o*.' — „ 685
Who knowing nothing knows but to *o*, — *Guinevere* 186
well to *o* then, if a king demand An act un-
profitable, — *Pass. of Arthur* 263
race to command, to *o*, to endure, — *Def. of Lucknow* 47
Who shaped the forms, *o* them, — *Akbar's Dream* 143
Obey'd 'I have *o* my uncle until now, — *Dora* 59
and they wheel'd and *o*. — *Heavy Brigade* 6
Object beyond his *o* Love can last: His *o* lives: — *Wan Sculptor* 5
burn'd upon its *o* thro' such tears — *Love and Duty* 63
Oblique 'If straight thy track, or if *o*, — *Two Voices* 193
Oblivion With all forgiveness, all *o*, — *Princess vi* 295
Oblivious *See* **Half-oblivious**
Obscure In some *o* hereafter, might inwreathe — *Lover's Tale i* 458
Obscurity I faint in this *o*, (repeat) — *Ode to Memory* 6, 44, 123
Obsequies Nor meanly, but with gorgeous *o*, — *Lancelot and E.* 1335
Observance with a mute *o* hung. — *Locksley Hall* 22
He compass'd her with sweet *o*'s — *Marr. of Geraint* 48
To compass her with sweet *o*'s, — *Geraint and E.* 39
Obstinacy At which the warrior in his *o*, — „ 454
Obstinate *See* **Stunt**
Obstreperous *See* **Obstropulous**
Obstropulous (**obstreperous**) But sich an *o* lad— — *Church-warden, etc.* 23
Obtain Pelleas might *o* his lady's love, — *Pelleas and E.* 161
all my heart had destined did *o*, — *Guinevere* 492
Obtain'd second suit *o* At first with Psyche. — *Princess vii* 71
Occasion *seasons* when to take O *by the hand*, — *To the Queen* 31
written as she found Or made *o*, — *Aylmer's Field* 478
Wiser to weep a true *o* lost, — *Princess iv* 68
O iron nerve to true *o* true, — *Ode on Well.* 37
Elusion, and *o*, and evasion' ? — *Gareth and L.* 288
A little at the vile *o*, rode, — *Marr. of Geraint* 235
The vast *o* of our stronger life— — *Columbus* 35
Ocean (*See also* **Mid-ocean**) Under the hollow-hung
o green ! — *The Merman* 38
On one side lay the *O*, — *M. d'Arthur* 11

Ocean (continued) Yet o's daily gaining on the land, — *Golden Year* 29
    There the sunlit o tosses — *The Captain* 69
    The houseless o's heaving field, — *The Voyage* 30
    The hollower-bellowing o, — *Enoch Arden* 598
    Now pacing mute by o's rim; — *The Daisy* 21
    Or olive-hoary cape in o; — " 31
    In middle o meets the surging shock, — *Will.* 8
    Cataract brooks to the o run, — *The Islet* 17
    Thine the myriad-rolling o, — *Boädicea* 42
    Charm, as a wanderer out in o, — *Milton* 12
    Streams o'er a rich ambrosial o isle, — " 14
    By which they rest, and o sounds, — *In Mem., Con.* 121
    As on a dull day in an O cave — *Merlin and V.* 231
    On one side lay the O, — *Pass. of Arthur* 179
    as o on every side Plunges and heaves — *Def. of Lucknow* 38
    Chains for the Admiral of the O! — *Columbus* 19
    Chains! we are Admirals of the O, — " 28
    Of the O—of the Indies—Admirals we— — " 31
    He lived on an isle in the o— — *V. of Maeldune* 7
    And we came to the isle in the o, — " 9
    silent o always broke on a silent shore, — " 12
    voice rang out in the thunders of O and Heaven — *The Wreck* 88
    Universal o softly washing all her warless Isles. — *Locksley H., Sixty* 170
    There on the border Of boundless O, — *Merlin and the G.* 117
    Dash back that o with a pier, — *Mechanophilus* 5
Ocean-empire who love Our o-e with her boundless homes — *To the Queen ii* 29
Ocean-foam as white As o-f in the moon, — *Maud I xiv* 18
Ocean-fowl myriad shriek of wheeling o-f, — *Enoch Arden* 583
Ocean-grave ' I am coming to thee in thine O-g.' — *The Wreck* 132
Ocean-islet about their o-i's flash The faces — *Tiresias* 172
Ocean-lane Fall from his O-l of fire, — *The Voyage* 19
Ocean-mirror O'er o-m's rounded large, — *In Mem. xii* 9
Ocean-plain Sailest the placid o-p's — " ix 2
Ocean-power the mightiest O-p on earth, — *The Fleet* 6
Ocean-ridge hollow o-r's roaring into cataracts. — *Locksley Hall* 6
Ocean-roll Tho' thine o-r of rhythm sound — *To Virgil* 31
Ocean-sea Given thee the keys of the great O-s? — *Columbus* 149
Ocean-smelling ocean-spoil In o-s osier, — *Enoch Arden* 94
Ocean-sounding o-s welcome to one knight, — *Last Tournament* 168
Ocean-spoil o-s In ocean-smelling osier, — *Enoch Arden* 94
Ochone but we hard it cryin' 'O!' — *Tomorrow* 84
O'clock 'Tis nearly twelve o. — *D. of the O. Year* 41
    The mail? At one o. — *Walk. to the Mail* 8
    How goes the time? 'Tis five o. — *Will Water.* 3
October *See* **Mid-October**
Odalisque Sleek O's, or oracles of mode, — *Princess ii* 77
Odd (adj.) From some o corner of the brain, — *Miller's D.* 68
    or dwindled down to some o games In some o nooks like this; — *The Epic* 8
Odd (s) And strength against all o's, — *Balin and Balan* 183
    It was full of old o's an' ends, — *First Quarrel* 49
Ode then, Sir, awful o's she wrote, — *Princess i* 138
    o's About this losing of the child; — " 140
    quoted o's, and jewels five-words-long — " ii 377
Odin To Thor and O lifted a hand: — *The Victim* 8
    'O, Father O, We give you a life. — " 74
Odorous wasting o sighs All night long — *Adeline* 43
    the amorous, o wind Breathes low — *Eleänore* 123
    Whisper in o heights of even. — *Milton* 16
Odour fed the time With o — *Arabian Nights* 65
    A cloud of incense of all o steam'd — *Palace of Art* 39
    Distilling o's on me as they went — *Gardener's D.* 187
    Whose o's haunt my dreams; — *Sir Galahad* 68
    On leagues of o streaming far, — *In Mem. lxxxvi* 14
    Saying in o and colour, 'Ah, be Among the roses — *Maud I xxi* 12
    And flowing o of the spacious air, — *Lover's Tale i* 478
    that hour died Like o rapt into the winged wind — " 801
    those who mix all o to the Gods — *Tiresias* 184
Œnone Mournful Œ, wandering forlorn — *Œnone* 16
    'My own Œ, Beautiful-brow'd Œ, — " 70
    never more Shall lone Œ see the morning mist — " 216
    Œ sat within the cave from out — *Death of Œnone* 1
    downward thunder of the brook Sounded 'Œ'; — " 24
    and moan'd ' Œ, my Œ, — " 29

Œnone (continued) Œ, by thy love which once was mine, — *Death of Œnone* 45
    Œ sat Not moving, — " 74
    ghostly murmur floated, 'Come to me, Œ! — " 80
    I can wrong thee now no more, Œ, my Œ,' — " 81
O'er-brimming Would drop from his o-b love, — *Supp. Confessions* 113
O'er-driven Yet pity for a horse o-d, — *In Mem. lxiii* 1
O'erflourish'd O with the hoary clematis: — *Golden Year* 63
O'erflow O's thy calmer glances, — *Madeline* 33
O'er-grown Till that o-g Barbarian in the East — *Poland* 7
    He has gather'd the bones for his o-g whelp to crack; — *Maud II v* 55
O'erlook'st O the tumult from afar, — *In Mem. cxxvii* 19
O'ershadow His love, unseen but felt, o Thee, — *Ded. of Idylls* 51
O'erstept hath o The slippery footing — *Lover's Tale i* 101
O'erthwarted O with the brazen-headed spear — *Œnone* 139
Offal Stench of old o decaying, — *Def. of Lucknow* 82
    pelt your o at her face. — *Locksley H., Sixty* 134
Offence To save the o of charitable, — *Enoch Arden* 342
    like a pedant's wand To lash o, — *Princess i* 28
    without o, Has link'd our names together — *Lancelot and E.* 111
    an' tha weant be taakin' o, — *Church-warden, etc.* 21
Offend Your finer female sense o's. — *Day-Dm., L'Envoi* 2
Offender pick'd o's from the mass For judgment. — *Princess i* 29
Offer (s) I trample on your o's and on you: — " iv 546
Offer (verb) I o boldly: we will seat you highest: — " iii 159
    I would o this book to you, — *June Bracken, etc.* 4
Offer'd then and there had o something more, — *The Brook* 147
    Not ev'n a rose, were o to thee? — *Lucretius* 89
    cup of both my hands And o you it kneeling: — *Merlin and V.* 276
    better o up to Heaven.' — *Holy Grail* 36
Offering (*See also* **Love-offering, Peace-offering**) bring me o's of fruit and flowers: — *St. S. Stylites* 128
    dress the victim to the o up. — *Princess iv* 130
    I will make a solemn o of you — *Lover's Tale iv* 118
Office O you that hold A nobler o upon earth — *To the Queen* 2
    a joint of state, that plies Its o, — *Love thou thy land* 48
    In whom should meet the o's of all, — *M. d'Arthur* 125
    decent not to fail In o's of tenderness, — *Ulysses* 41
    Two in the liberal o's of life, — *Princess ii* 175
    With books, with flowers, with Angel o's, — " vii 26
    So kind an o hath been done, — *In Mem. xvii* 17
    Her o there to rear, to teach, — " xl 13
    In those great o's that suit The full-grown energies — " 19
    join'd Each o of the social hour To noble manners, — " cxi 14
    If all your o had to do With old results — " cxxviii 10
    touch of their o might have sufficed, — *Maud II v* 27
    Do each low o of your holy house; — *Guinevere* 682
    In whom should meet the o's of all, — *Pass. of Arthur* 293
    all o's Of watchful care and trembling tenderness. — *Lover's Tale i* 225
    joins us once again, to his either o true: — *Happy* 106
    hunt the tiger of oppression out From o; — *Akbar's Dream* 159
Officer (*See also* **Hofficer**) o's and men Levied a kindly tax — *Enoch Arden* 662
    an o Rose up, and read the statutes, — *Princess ii* 68
    He rooted out the slothful o — *Geraint and E.* 938
Officious *See* **Too-officious**
Offing And isles a light in the o: — *Enoch Arden* 131
    Desolate o, sailorless harbours, — *Vastness* 14
Offset man-minded o rose To chase the deer — *Talking Oak* 51
Offspring with their o, born-unborn, — *Locksley H., Sixty* 98
    Would she find her human o — " 234
Often-ransack'd To think that in our o-r world — *Sea Dreams* 129
Often-wandering I was the lonely slave of an o-w mind; — *The Wreck* 130
Ogress 'petty O,' and 'ungrateful Puss,' — *Princess, Pro.* 157
Oil realms of upland, prodigal in o, — *Palace of Art* 79
    pure quintessences of precious o's — " 187
    little dues of wheat, and wine and o; — *Lotos-Eaters, C. S.* 122
    Or burn'd in fire, or boil'd in o, — *St. S. Stylites* 52
    Like calming o on all their stony creeds, — *Akbar's Dream* 160
Oil'd (*See also* **Well-oiled**) That o and curl'd Assyrian Bull — *Maud I vi* 44
Oilily o bubbled up the mere. — *Gareth and L.* 816
Oily lower down The bay was o calm; — *Audley Court* 86
    o'er the rest Arising, did his holy o best, — *Sea Dreams* 195
    and o courtesies Our formal compact, — *Princess i* 164

One (*continued*)   Why were we *o* in all things, save in that Where to have been *o* had been the cope and crown   *Lover's Tale ii* 26
O with Britain, heart and soul!   *Open. I. and C. Exhib.* 38
One-day-seen   The *o-d-s* Sir Lancelot in her heart,   *Lancelot and E.* 747
One-sided   'O dull, *o-s* voice,' said I,   *Two Voices* 202
Only (*adj.*)   His *o* child, his Edith, whom he loved   *Aylmer's Field* 23
'We have his dearest, His *o* son!'   *The Victim* 64
Fear not to give this King thine *o* child,   *Com. of Arthur* 413
when her son Beheld his *o* way to glory   *Gareth and L.* 159
I have miss'd the *o* way (repeat)   " 787, 792
Had married Enid, Yniol's *o* child,   *Marr. of Geraint* 4
Onset   greaves and cuisses dash'd with drops Of *o* ;   *M. d'Arthur* 216
A day of *o*'s of despair!   *Ode on Well.* 124
Rings to the roar of an angel *o*—   *Milton* 8
and so they crash'd In *o*,   *Balin and Balan* 556
greaves and cuisses dash'd with drops Of *o*;   *Pass. of Arthur* 384
Onslaught   make an *o* single on a realm   *Geraint and E.* 917
Onward (*adj. and adv.*)   Still *o* ; and the clear canal Is rounded   *Arabian Nights* 45
Till in its *o* current it absorbs   *Isabel* 31
fiery-hot to burst All barriers in her *o* race For power.   *In Mem.* cxiv 14
vast eddies in the flood Of *o* time   " cxxviii 6
A moment, ere the *o* whirlwind shatter it,   *Lover's Tale i* 451
But in the *o* current of her speech,   " 565
Onward (*adj.*)   his truer name Is '*O*,'   *D. of the Duke of C.* 14
Onward-sloping   'Mid *o-s* motions infinite   *Palace of Art* 247
'Oonderd (**hundred**)   an' thin my two '*o* a-year   *Spinster's S's.* 12
wellnigh purr'd ma awaäy fro' my oän two '*o* a-year.   " 58
Oorali   Drench'd with the hellish *o*—   *In the Child. Hosp.* 10
Ooze (*s*)   For I was drench'd with *o*,   *Princess v* 28
Ooze (*verb*)   bloat himself, and All over   *Sea Dreams* 154
Oozed   *o* All o'er with honey'd answer   *Princess v* 241
Opal   gayer colours, like an *o* warm'd.   *Merlin and V.* 950
Open (*adj.*)   The costly doors flung *o* wide,   *Arabian Nights* 17
Showering thy gleaned wealth into my *o* breast   *Ode to Memory* 23
An *o* scroll, Before him lay :   *The Poet* 8
Wide, wild, and *o* to the air,   *Dying Swan* 1
Thro' the *o* gates of the city afar,   " 34
Her *o* eyes desire the truth.   *Of old sat Freedom* 17
More softly round the *o* wold,   *To J. S.* 2
On *o* main or winding shore !   *The Voyage* 6
Were *o* to each other ;   *Aylmer's Field* 40
voice Of comfort and an *o* hand of help,   " 174
Follows the mouse, and all is *o* field.   " 853
we had limed ourselves With *o* eyes,   *Princess iii* 143
and in her lion's mood Tore *o*,   " iv 381
so To the *o* window moved,   " 492
one glance he caught Thro' *o* doors of Ida   " v 343
Thro' *o* field into the lists they wound   " vi 84
And all thy heart lies *o* unto me.   " vii 183
He, on whom from both her *o* hands   *Ode on Well.* 195
immeasurable heavens Break *o* to their highest,   *Spec. of Iliad* 15
But *o* converse is there none,   *In Mem.* xx 17
Imperial halls, or *o* plain ;   " xcviii 29
in their hand Is Nature like an *o* book ;   " Con. 132
lords Banded, and so brake out in *o* war.'   *Com. of Arthur* 237
'Wherefore waits the madman there Naked in *o* dayshine ?'   *Gareth and L.* 1092
rang Clear thro' the *o* casement of the hall,   *Marr. of Geraint* 328
Thro' *o* doors and hospitality ;   " 456
Coursed one another more on *o* ground   " 522
And issuing under *o* heavens beheld   *Geraint and E.* 196
Painted, who stare at *o* space, nor glance   " 268
I smote upon the naked skull A thrall of thine in *o* hall,   *Balin and Balan* 56
under *o* blue Came on the hoarhead woodman   " 293
Push'd thro' an *o* casement down,   " 413
My mother on his corpse in *o* field ; (repeat)   *Merlin and V.* 43, 73
And laid the diamond in his *o* hand.   *Lancelot and E.* 827
He loves the Queen, and in an *o* shame : And she returns his love in *o* shame ;   " 1082
But for a mile all round was *o* space,   *Pelleas and E.* 28
And he was left alone in *o* field.   " 208
straight on thro' *o* door Rode Gawain,   " 382

Open (*adj.*) (*continued*)   Wide *o* were the gates, And no watch kept ;   *Pelleas and E.* 414
'Nay, fool,' said Tristram, 'not in *o* day.'   *Last Tournament* 347
huge machicolated tower That stood with *o* doors,   " 425
but sprang Thro' *o* doors, and swording right and left   " 473
In *o* battle or the tilting-field (repeat)   *Guinevere* 330, 332
o flower tell What sort of bud it was,   *Lover's Tale i* 151
Arise in *o* prospect—heath and hill,   " 397
Forthgazing on the waste and *o* sea,   " ii 177
moon Struck from an *o* grating overhead   " iv 60
An *o* landaulet Whirl'd by, which, after it had past me,   *Sisters (E. and E.)* 85
Rip your brothers' vices *o*,   *Locksley H., Sixty* 141
We often walk In *o* sun,   *The Ring* 328
There, the chest was *o*—all The sacred relics   " 446
The door is *o*. He ! is he standing at the door,   *Happy* 11
And in her *o* palm a halcyon sits Patient—   *Prog. of Spring* 20
Wait till Death has flung them *o*,   *Faith* 7
Open   race thro' many a mile Of dense and *o*,   *Balin and Balan* 424
Open (*verb*)   Heaven *o*'s inward, chasms yawn,   *Two Voices* 304
like a horse That hears the corn-bin *o*,   *The Epic* 45
and *o*'s but to golden keys.   *Locksley Hall* 100
o to me, And lay my little blossom at my feet,   *Princess v* 99
'O dewy flowers that *o* to the sun,   *Gareth and L.* 1066
The wayside blossoms *o* to the blaze.   *Balin and Balan* 444
To dig, pick, *o*, find and read the charm :   *Merlin and V.* 660
O gates, And I will make you merry.'   *Pelleas and E.* 373
The golden gates would *o* at a word.   *Sisters (E. and E.)* 145
He would *o* the books that I prized,   *The Wreck* 21
Till Holy St. Pether gets up wid his kays an' *o*'s the gate!   *Tomorrow* 93
O's a door in Heaven ;   *Early Spring* 7
Open-door'd   Once rich, now poor, but ever *o-d*.'   *Marr. of Geraint* 302
always *o-d* To every breath from heaven,   *Akbar's Dream* 179
Open'd (*adj.*)   Lily of the vale ! half *o* bell of the woods !   *Princess vi* 193
Open'd (*verb*)   Thy dark eyes on me,   *Eleänore* 1
northward of the narrow port O a larger haven :   *Enoch Arden* 103
Where either haven *o* on the deeps,   " 671
With one small gate that *o* on the waste,   " 733
Crept to the gate, and *o* it,   " 775
counter door to that Which Leolin *o*,   *Aylmer's Field* 283
Books (see Daniel seven and ten) Were *o*,   *Sea Dreams* 153
gate shone Only, that *o* on the field below :   *Gareth and L.* 195
Now two great entries *o* from the hall,   " 665
But yesterday you never *o* lip,   *Merlin and V.* 271
O his arms to embrace me as he came,   *Holy Grail* 417
all the heavens *O* and blazed with thunder   " 508
the heavens *o* and blazed again Roaring,   " 516
Sat by the walls, and no one *o* to him.   *Pelleas and E.* 217
o on the pines with doors of glass,   *Lover's Tale i* 41
door for scoundrel scum I *o* to the West,   *Columbus* 171
it *o* and dropt at the side of each man,   *V. of Maeldune* 85
I shook as I *o* the letter—   *The Wreck* 145
A door was *o* in the house—   *The Flight* 69
Muriel claim'd and *o* what I meant For Miriam,   *The Ring* 242
And bolted doors out of themselves :   " 413
Opener   nor the silent O of the Gate.'   *God and the Univ.* 6
Open-hearted   'An *o-h* maiden, true and pure.   *Princess iii* 98
Opening (*adj. and part.*)   (*See also* **Half-opening**)   *o* upon level plots Of crowned lilies,   *Ode to Memory* 108
in front The gorges, *o* wide apart,   *Œnone* 12
and *o* out his milk-white palm   " 65
The cloudy porch oft *o* on the Sun ?   *Love and Duty* 9
struck it thrice, and, no one *o*, Enter'd ;   *Enoch Arden* 279
o this I read Of old Sir Ralph a page or two   *Princess, Pro.* 120
Not yet endured to meet her *o* eyes,   " iv 195
and she rose *O* her arms to meet me,   *Holy Grail* 395
in a moment when they blazed again *O*,   " 524
long water *o* on the deep Somewhere   *Pass. of Arthur* 466
in the end, *O* on darkness,   *Lover's Tale ii* 125
an ever *o* height, An ever lessening earth—   *The Ring* 45
Opening (*s*)   About the *o* of the flower,   *Two Voices* 161
we saw The clefts and *o*'s in the mountains   *Lover's Tale i* 330
Open-mouth'd   All *o-m*, all gazing to the light,   *Princess iv* 483
So stood the unhappy mother *o-m*,   " vi 143

Oriana My heart is wasted with
  my woe, O. (repeat)   *Oriana* 2, 4, 7, 9, 11, 13, 16, 18, 20, 22, 25,
                           27, 29, 31, 34, 36, 38, 40, 43, 45, 47,
                           49, 52, 54, 56, 58, 61, 63, 65, 67, 70,
                           72, 74, 76, 79, 81, 83, 85, 88, 90, 92,
                           94, 97, 99
Oriel She sat betwixt the shining *O's*,   *Palace of Art* 159
  thro' the topmost *O's'* coloured flame   ,, 161
  The beams, that thro' the *O* shine,   *Day-Dm., Sleep.* P. 34
  All in an *o* on the summer side,   *Lancelot and E.* 1177
  moon Thro' the tall *o* on the rolling sea.   *Holy Grail* 831
Oriel-embowering Brake from the vast *o-e* vine   *Lancelot and E.* 1198
Orient (adj.) (*See also* **Re-orient**) Tall *o* shrubs, and
  obelisks   *Arabian Nights* 107
  but robed in soften'd light Of *o* state.   *Ode to Memory* 11
  and earliest shoots Of *o* green,   ,, 18
  Sunn'd by those *o* skies;   *The Poet* 42
  Laborious *o* ivory sphere in sphere,   *Princess, Pro.* 20
  To where in yonder *o* star   *In Mem.* lxxxvi 15
Orient (s) Doth the low-tongued *O* Wander from the side
  of the morn,   *Adeline* 51
  Deep in yonder shining *O*,   *Locksley Hall* 154
  Came furrowing all the *o* into gold.   *Princess* iii 18
  and her throne In our vast *O*,   *To the Queen* ii 31
  There is a custom in the *O*, friends—   *Lover's Tale* iv 230
Oriental Till silent in her *o* haven.   *Enoch Arden* 537
  flattering thy childish thought The *o* fairy brought,   *Eleänore* 14
  shower'd His *o* gifts on everyone And most on
  Edith :   *Aylmer's Field* 214
  Your *O* Eden-isles,   *To Ulysses* 38
Orion great *O* sloping slowly to the West.   *Locksley Hall* 8
  shining daffodil dead, and *O* low in his grave.   *Maud* I iii 14
  Over *O's* grave low down in the west,   ,, III vi 8
Orkney Morganore, And Lot of *O*.   *Com. of Arthur* 116
  Lot's wife, the Queen of *O*, (repeat)   ,, 190, 245
Ornament Found lying with his urns and *o's*,   *Aylmer's Field* 4
  And darkling felt the sculptured *o*   *Merlin and V.* 734
  In hanging robe or vacant *o*,   *Guinevere* 506
  read Some wonder at our chamber *o's*.   *Columbus* 2
  Institute, Rich in symbol, in *o*,   *On Jub. Q. Victoria* 47
Orphan (adj.) His wife, an unknown artist's *o*
  child—   *Sea Dreams* 2
  Made *o* by a winter shipwreck,   *Enoch Arden* 15
  there the tender *o* hands Felt at my heart,   *Princess* v 435
  'None wrought, but suffer'd much, an *o* maid !   *Merlin and V.* 71
  When her *o* wail came borne in the shriek   *The Wreck* 87
Orphan (s) Late-left an *o* of the squire,   *Miller's D.* 34
  And for this *o*, I am come to you :   *Dora* 64
  I was left a trampled *o*,   *Locksley Hall* 156
  kill yourself And make them *o's* quite ? '   *Enoch Arden* 395
  Here is the cot of our *o*,   *In the Child. Hosp.* 28
  O we poor *o's* of nothing—   *Despair* 33
  an *o* with half a shire of estate,—   *Charity* 13
Orphan-boy Oh ! teach the *o-b* to read,   *L. C. V. de Vere* 69
Orphan'd So were we born, so *o*.   *Lover's Tale* i 218
Orphan-girl Or teach the *o-g* to sew,   *L. C. V. de Vere* 70
O'Roon (Danny) *See* **Danny, Danny O'Roon**
Orthodox Our *o* coroner doubtless will find it a
  felo-de-se,   *Despair* 115
  Heresy to the heretic, and religion to the *o*,   *Akbar's D., Inscrip.* 8
Orthodoxy Thy elect have no dealings with either
  heresy or *o*;   ,, 7
O'Shea (Shamus) *See* **Shamus, Shamus O'Shea**
Osier ocean-spoil In ocean-smelling *o*,   *Enoch Arden* 94
Ostler 'Wrinkled *o*, grim and thin !   *Vision of Sin* 63
Ostleress A plump-arm'd *O* and a stable wench   *Princess* i 226
'Ot (hot) 'Summat to drink—sa' *o* ?'   *North. Cobbler* 5
Other (*See also* **Tother**) And little *o* care hath she,   *L. of Shalott* ii 8
  There is no *o* thing express'd   *Two Voices* 248
  'Who forged that *o* influence,   ,, 283
  He hath no *o* life above.   *D. of the O. Year* 12
  Among new men, strange faces, *o* minds.'   *M. d'Arthur* 238
  and with what *o* eyes I used to watch—   *Tithonus* 51
  'Some *o* race of Averills'—prov'n or no,   *Aylmer's Field* 54
  became in *o* fields A mockery to the yeomen   ,, 496

Other (*continued*) *o* frowns than those That knit
  themselves   *Aylmer's Field* 723
  last, my *o* heart, And almost my half-self,   *Princess* i 55
  And thus (what *o* way was left) I came.'   ,, ii 217
  Sweet order lived again with *o* laws :   ,, vii 19
  On the *o* side Hortensia spoke against the tax ;   ,, 126
  Follow'd by the brave of *o* lands,   *Ode on Well.* 194
  One writes, that ' *O* friends remain,'   *In Mem.* vi 1
  But there are *o* griefs within,   ,, xx 11
  Nor *o* thought her mind admits   ,, xxxii 2
  She enters *o* realms of love ;   ,, xl 12
  With larger *o* eyes than ours,   ,, li 15
  the while His *o* passion wholly dies,   ,, lxii 10
  To the *o* shore, involved in thee,   ,, lxxxiv 40
  O sacred essence, *o* form,   ,, lxxxv 35
  For *o* friends that once I met ;   ,, 58
  Behold their brides in *o* hands ;   ,, xc 14
  Nor landmark breathes of *o* days,   ,, civ 11
  And silent under *o* snows :   ,, cv 6
  But I was *born* to *o* things.   ,, cxx 12
  Had one fair daughter, and none *o* child ;   *Com. of Arthur* 2
  Lets down his *o* leg, and stretching,   *Gareth and L.* 1186
  Three *o* horsemen waiting, wholly arm'd,   *Geraint and E.* 121
  It seems another voice in *o* groves ;   *Balin and Balan* 215
  And when we halted at that *o* well,   *Merlin and V.* 280
  Why will ye never ask some *o* boon ?   ,, 375
  That *o* fame, To one at least,   ,, 505
  Moaning and calling out of *o* lands,   ,, 962
  She might have made this and that *o* world   *Lancelot and E.* 873
  A mocking fire : ' what *o* fire than he,   *Holy Grail* 670
  ' Or hast thou *o* griefs ?   *Pelleas and E.* 599
  Among new men, strange faces, *o* minds.'   *Pass. of Arthur* 406
  And, like all *o* friends i' the world,   *Lover's Tale* i 108
  fall asleep Into delicious dreams, our *o* life,   ,, 162
  On the *o* side Is scoop'd a cavern   ,, 516
  And saw the motion of all *o* things ;   ,, 574
  had never seen it once. His *o* father you !   ,, iv 174
  For he thought—there were *o* lads—   *First Quarrel* 38
  Fresh from the surgery-schools of France and
  of *o* lands—   *In the Child. Hosp.* 3
  For every *o* cause is less than mine.   *Sir J. Oldcastle* 188
  And his voice was low as from *o* worlds,   *V. of Maeldune* 117
  Was he noblier-fashion'd than *o* men ?   *Dead Prophet* 51
  And there the light of *o* life, which lives   *The Ring* 295
  O songs for *o* worlds !   *Parnassus* 19
Ottoman Emperor, *O*, which shall win :   *To F. D. Maurice* 32
Ought Sweet is it to have done the thing one *o*,   *Princess* v 67
  I cannot love thee as I *o*,   *In Mem.* lii 1
Ould (old) yer Honour's the thrue *o* blood   *Tomorrow* 5
  Thin Molly's *o* mother, yer Honour,   ,, 19
  best he could give at *o* Donovan's wake—   ,, 42
  Thim *o* blind nagers in Agypt,   ,, 69
  Danny O'Roon wid his *o* woman, Molly Magee.   ,, 88
'Ouse (house) theer's a craw to pluck wi' tha, Sam :
  yon's parson's *o*—   *N. Farmer, N. S.* 5
  Tis'n them as 'as munny as breäks into *'o's* an'
  steäls,   ,, 45
  sweär'd as I'd breäk ivry stick O' furnitur 'ere i'
  the *'o*,   *North. Cobbler* 36
  an' the *'ole 'o* hupside down.   ,, 42
  'When theer's naw 'eäd to a *'O*   *Village Wife* 17
  or the gells 'ull goä to the *'O*,   ,, 64
  'e wur burn an' bred i' the *'o*,   *Spinster's S's.* 69
  An' the stink o' *'is* pipe i' the *'o*,   ,, 100
  a roäbin' the *'o* like a Queeän,   ,, 106
  Straänge an' owd-farran'd the *'o*,   *Owd Roä* 21
  An' theere i' the *'o* one night—   ,, 27
  Theere, when the *'o* wur a house,   ,, 29
  an' dussn't not sleeäp i' the *'o*,   ,, 37
'Ouse-keeper (housekeeper) *'O-k* sent tha my lass,   *Village Wife* 1
Oust *o* the madness from your brain.   *Locksley H., Sixty* 241
Ousted From mine own earldom foully *o* me ;   *Marr. of Geraint* 459
Outbreak nor, in hours Of civil *o*,   *Tiresias* 68
Outburn'd lit Lamps which *o* Canopus.   *D. of F. Women* 146
Outbuzz'd *o* me so That even our prudent king,   *Columbus* 121

Overthrew (*continued*) *o* So many knights that all the
   people cried,   *Holy Grail* 334
Pelleas *o* them as they dash'd Against him   *Pelleas and E.* 221
   down they went, And Pelleas *o* them   „ 230
   by those he *o* Be bounden straight,   „ 235
Pelleas *o* them, one to three;   „ 287
Overthrow (s)   quick! by *o* Of these or those,   *Princess v* 316
Overthrow (verb)   Lancelot whom he trusts to *o*,   *Gareth and L.* 620
   hard by here is one will *o* And slay thee: „ 896
   I know That I shall *o* him.'   „ 949
   o My proud self, and my purpose three years old,   *Geraint and E.* 848
   Whether me likewise ye can *o*.'   *Balin and Balan* 40
Overthrower   And *o* from being overthrown.   *Gareth and L.* 1263
Overthrowing (part.)   challenging And *o* every knight   *Balin and Balan* 13
Overthrowing (s)   With *o's*, and with cries,   *In Mem. cxiii* 19
   By *o* me you threw me higher.   *Geraint and E.* 792
Overthrown   And like a warrior *o*;   *Two Voices* 150
   And *o* was Gorloïs and slain.   *Com. of Arthur* 197
   Thou hast *o* and slain thy master—   *Gareth and L.* 769
   Or some device, hast foully *o*),   „ 998
   Hath *o* thy brother, and hath his arms.'   „ 1037
   Hast *o* thro' mere unhappiness),   „ 1059
   'Shamed and *o*, And tumbled back   „ 1227
   To call him shamed, who is but *o*?   „ 1260
   And overthrower from being *o*.   „ 1263
   And makest merry when *o*.   „ 1270
   I have never yet been *o*, And thou hast *o* me,   *Marr. of Geraint* 588
   Or I or he have easily *o*.'   *Balin and Balan* 36
   strong hand, which had *o* Her minion-knights,   *Pelleas and E.* 234
   'And thou hast *o* him?' 'Ay, my Queen.'   „ 594
   In twelve great battles ruining *o*.   *Guinevere* 432
Overtoil'd   *o* By that day's grief and travel,   *Geraint and E.* 376
Overtopt   The battlement *o* with ivytods,   *Balin and Balan* 335
Over-tragic   Deem this *o-t* drama's closing curtain is
   the pall!   *Locksley H., Sixty* 62
Overtrailed   Half *o* with a wanton weed,   *Lover's Tale i* 525
Overtrue   'O ay,' said Vivien, '*o* a tale.   *Merlin and V.* 720
Overtrust   wink no more in slothful *o*.   *Ode on Well.* 170
Overturn   Behold me *o* and trample on him.   *Geraint and E.* 843
Overturn'd (*See also* **Skelpt**)   schemed and wrought
   Until I *o* him;   „ 830
Over-vaulted   That *o-v* grateful gloom,   *Palace of Art* 54
Overwhelm'd   shook And almost *o* her,   *Enoch Arden* 530
Over-wise   has written: she never was *o-w*, (repeat)   *Grandmother* 3, 105
Overworn   But all he was is *o*.'   *In Mem. i* 16
   Merlin, overtalk'd and *o*, Had yielded,   *Merlin and V.* 965
Overwrought   that his brain is *o*:   *Locksley Hall* 53
   being so *o*, Suddenly strike on a sharper sense   *Maud II ii* 62
Owä (owe)   Fur I *o's* owd Roäver moor   *Owd Roä* 4
Owäd (owed)   nor I iver *o* mottal man.   „ 4
Owd (old)   A mowt 'a taäen *o* Joänes,   *N. Farmer, O. S.* 49
   Doctor's a 'toättler, lass, an' a's hallus i' the *o*
   taäle;   „ 66
   I could fettle and clump *o* booöts   *North. Cobbler* 13
   wheer Sally's a stockin' wur 'id,   „ 31
   an' draggle taäil'd in an *o* turn gown,   „ 41
   I liked the *o* Squire an' 'is gells   *Village Wife* 6
   new Squire's coom'd wi' 'is taäil in 'is 'and, an' *o*
   Squire's gone. (repeat)   „ 14, 121
   'e'd gie fur a howry *o* book thutty pound an' moor,   „ 45
   An' 'e'd wrote an *o* book, his awn sen,   „ 46
   fur an *o* scratted stoän,   „ 47
   An' 'e bowt *o* money, es wouldn't goä,   „ 49
   But *o* Squire's laädy es long es she lived   „ 53
   moäst on 'is *o* big booöks fetch'd nigh to nowt at the saäle,   „ 73
   Siver the mou'ds rattled down upo' poor *o* Squire i'
   the wood,   „ 95
   I didn't not taäke it kindly ov *o* Miss Annie   „ 109
   I meäns fur to maäke 'is *o* aäge as 'appy as iver I can,   *Owd Roä* 3
   I owäs *o* Roäver moor nor I iver owäd mottal man.   „ 4
   afoor thou was gotten too *o*,   „ 5
   an' I thowt o' the good *o* times 'at was goan,   „ 43
   an' clemm'd *o* Roä by the 'eäd,   „ 99
   Sa I sticks like the ivin as long as I lives to the *o*
   chuch now,   *Church-warden, etc.* 15

'Owd (hold)   Fur I couldn't 'o 'ands off gin,   *North. Cobbler* 84
   pockets as full o' my pippins as iver they'd 'o,   *Church-warden, etc.* 34
Owd-farran'd (old-fashioned)   Straänge an' *o-f* the 'ouse,   *Owd Roä* 21
Owe (*See also* **Owä**)   we *o* you bitter thanks: *Princess iv* 531
   I feel I shall *o* you a debt,   *Maud I xix* 87
   forget That I *o* this debt to you   „ 90
   O you me nothing for a life half-lost?   *Geraint and E.* 318
   ask your boon, for boon I *o* you thrice,   *Merlin and V.* 306
   To you and yours, and still would *o*.   *To Marq. of Dufferin* 20
   Let me *o* my life to thee.   *Death of Œnone* 42
Owed (*See also* **Owäd**)   Whole in ourselves and *o* to none.   *Princess iv* 148
   how dear a debt We *o* you, and are owing
   yet   *To Marq. of Dufferin* 19
Owing   and are *o* yet To you and yours,   „ 19
Owl (*See also* **Eagle-owl, Glimmer-gowk, Howl**)   The
   white *o* in the belfry sits. (repeat)   *The Owl i* 7, 14
   I drown'd the whoopings of the *o*   *St. S. Stylites* 33
   bats wheel'd, and *o's* whoop'd,   *Princess, Con.* 110
   An *o* whoopt: 'Hark the victor pealing there!'   *Gareth and L.* 1318
   A home of bats, in every tower an *o*.   *Balin and Balan* 336
   the *o's* Wailing had power upon her,   *Lancelot and E.* 1000
   thrice as blind as any noonday *o*,   *Holy Grail* 866
   and the *o's* are whooping at noon,   *Despair* 89
   The night, When the *o's* are wailing!   *Forlorn* 30
Owlby   He'll niver swap *O* an' Scratby   *Church-warden, etc.* 44
Owlet   shrilly the *o* halloos;   *Leonine Eleg.* 6
Owl-whoop   *o-w* and dorhawk-whirr Awoke me not,   *Lover's Tale ii* 116
Own (adj.)   (*See also* **Oän**)   to brush the dew From
   thine *o* lily,   *Supp. Confessions* 85
   till his *o* blood flows About his hoof.   „ 155
   I see his gray eyes twinkle yet At his *o* jest—   *Miller's D.* 12
   My *o* sweet Alice, we must die.   „ 18
   You'll kiss me, my *o* mother, and forgive me
   ere I go;   *May Queen, N. Y's. E.* 34
   Once thro' mine *o* doors Death did pass;   *To J. S.* 19
   And tho' mine *o* eyes fill with dew,   „ 37
   She loveth her *o* anguish deep   „ 42
   So spake he, clouded with his *o* conceit,   *M. d'Arthur* 110
   His *o* thought drove him, like a goad.   „ 185
   It may be, for her *o* dear sake but this,   *Edwin Morris* 141
   But in these latter springs I saw Your *o* Olivia blow,   *Talking Oak* 76
   This is my son, mine *o* Telemachus,   *Ulysses* 33
   Upon my proper patch of soil To grow my *o* plantation.   *Amphion* 100
   He loves me for my *o* true worth,   *Lady Clare* 11
   I buried her like my *o* sweet child,   „ 27
   He not for his *o* self caring but her,   *Enoch Arden* 165
   while Annie seem'd to hear Her *o* death-scaffold rising,   „ 175
   'Take your *o* time, Annie, take your *o* time.'   „ 466
   Her *o* son Was silent, tho' he often look'd his wish;   „ 481
   And his *o* children tall and beautiful,   „ 762
   And following our *o* shadows thrice as long   *The Brook* 166
   bearing hardly more Than his *o* shadow in a sickly
   sun.   *Aylmer's Field* 30
   Somewhere beneath his *o* low range of roofs,   „ 47
   Him, glaring, by his *o* stale devil spurr'd,   „ 290
   under his *o* lintel stood Storming with lifted hands,   „ 331
   would go, Labour for his *o* Edith, and return   „ 420
   Burst his *o* wyvern on the seal, and read   „ 516
   went Hating his *o* lean heart and miserable   „ 526
   Now chafing at his *o* great self defied,   „ 537
   left Their *o* gray tower, or plain-faced tabernacle,   „ 618
   And worship their *o* darkness in the Highest?   „ 643
   Crown thyself, worm, and worship thine *o* lusts!—   „ 650
   darkening thine own To thine *o* likeness;   „ 674
   Is not our *o* child on the narrow way,   „ 743
   earth Lightens from her *o* central Hell—   „ 761
   Who, thro' their *o* desire accomplish'd, bring Their *o*
   gray hairs with sorrow to the grave—   „ 776
   but sat Ignorant, devising their *o* daughter's death!   „ 783
   and made Their *o* traditions God, and slew the Lord,   „ 795
   Then her *o* people bore along the nave Her pendent
   hands,   „ 812
   Fought with what seem'd my *o* uncharity;   *Sea Dreams* 73
   Nor ever cared to better his *o* kind,   „ 201
   His *o* forefathers' arms and armour hung.   *Princess, Pro.* 24

Own (adj.) (*continued*)   a lady, one that arm'd Her *o* fair head,   *Princess Pro.* 33

'We scarcely thought in our *o* hall to hear   "   ii 53

what follows? war; Your *o* work marr'd: "   230

true she errs, But in her *o* grand way: "   iii 108

That we might see our *o* work out,   "   270

'Know you no song of your *o* land,' she said,   "   iv 84

What time I watch'd the swallow winging south From mine *o* land,   "   90

And partly conscious of my *o* deserts,   "   305

You stood in your *o* light and darken'd mine.   "   314

Our *o* detention, why, the causes weigh'd,   "   v 215

Or by denial flush her babbling wells With her *o* people's life: "   335

And Knowledge in our *o* land make her free,   "   419

he That loved me closer than his *o* right eye,   "   531

With their *o* blows they hurt themselves,   "   vi 49

all dabbled with the blood Of his *o* son,   "   105

O let me have him with my brethren here In our *o* palace,   "   124

never in your *o* arms To hold your own,   "   177

I go to mine *o* land For ever: "   216

Now had you got a friend of your *o* age,   "   251

to wait upon him, Like mine *o* brother.   "   299

And in their *o* clear element, they moved.   "   vii 28

She needs must wed him for her *o* good name;   "   74

'Dear, but let us type them now In our *o* lives,   "   300

I seem A mockery to my *o* self.   "   337

Has given our Prince his *o* imperial Flower,   *W. to Marie Alex.* 4

Yet thine *o* land has bow'd to Tartar hordes   "   23

And he died, and I could not weep—my *o* time seem'd so near.   *Grandmother* 72

Patter she goes, my *o* little Annie, an Annie like you: "   78

My *o* dim life should teach me this,   *In Mem. xxxiv* 1

When thou should'st link thy life with one Of mine *o* house,   "   lxxxiv 12

His *o* vast shadow glory-crown'd;   "   xcvii 3

But mine *o* phantom chanting hymns?   "   cviii 10

heart of the citizen hissing in war on his *o* hearthstone?   *Maud I i* 24

But arose, and all by myself in my *o* dark garden ground,   "   iii 10

finer politic sense To mask, tho' but in his *o* behoof,   "   vi 48

How prettily for his *o* sweet sake   "   51

For often a man's *o* angry pride Is cap and bells for a fool.   "   62

And my *o* sad name in corners cried,   "   72

Down too, down at your *o* fireside.   "   x 50

Maud's *o* little oak-room   "   xiv 9

looks Upon Maud's *o* garden-gate: "   16

Running down to my *o* dark wood;   "   30

My *o* heart's heart, my ownest own, farewell;   "   xviii 74

For I know her *o* rose-garden,   "   xx 41

Come out to your *o* true lover,   "   46

and render All homage to his *o* darling,   "   49

My *o* dove with the tender eye?   "   II iv 46

praying To his *o* great self, as I guess;   "   v 33

Her *o* brood lost or dead, lent her fierce teat   *Com. of Arthur* 28

nor make myself in mine *o* realm Victor and lord.   "   89

for each But sought to rule for his *o* self and hand,   "   219

Bound them by so strait vows to his *o* self,   "   262

But thou art closer to this noble prince, Being his *o* dear sister;'   "   315

Albeit in mine *o* heart I knew him King,   *Gareth and L.* 123

Her *o* true Gareth was too princely-proud   "   161

swearing he had glamour enow In his *o* blood,   "   210

'Old Master, reverence thine *o* beard That looks as white   "   280

With thine *o* hand thou slewest my dear lord,   "   352

see thou to it That thine *o* fineness, Lancelot,   "   476

holds her stay'd In her *o* castle,   "   616

often with her *o* white hands Array'd and deck'd her, as the loveliest, Next after her *o* self,   *Marr. of Geraint* 16

and they past to their *o* land.   "   45

Low of her *o* heart piteously she said: "   85

Frown and we smile, the lords of our *o* hands;   "   354

then have I sworn From his *o* lips to have it—   "   409

Queen Sent her *o* maiden to demand the name,   "   411

Raised my *o* town against me in the night   "   457

Own (adj.) (*continued*)   From mine *o* earldom foully ousted me;   *Marr. of Geraint* 459

(Who hearing her *o* name had stol'n away)   "   507

but lay Contemplating her *o* unworthiness;   "   533

And softly to her *o* sweet heart she said: "   618

made comparison Of that and these to her *o* faded self   "   652

So sadly lost on that unhappy night; Your *o* good gift!'   "   690

Or whether some false sense in her *o* self   "   800

child shall wear your costly gift Beside your *o* warm hearth,   "   820

to her *o* bright face Accuse her of the least immodesty: *Geraint and E.* 110

That she *could* speak whom his *o* ear had heard   "   113

I call mine *o* self wild, But keep a touch of sweet civility   "   311

At this the tender sound of his *o* voice   "   348

And their *o* Earl, and their *o* souls, and her.   "   577

And found his *o* dear bride propping his head,   "   584

And said to his *o* heart, 'She weeps for me:'   "   587

And say to his *o* heart, 'She weeps for me.'   "   590

Not, tho' mine *o* ears heard you yestermorn—   "   740

in the King's *o* ear Speak what has chanced;   "   808

with your *o* true eyes Beheld the man you loved   "   846

ye pray'd me for my leave To move to your *o* land,   "   889

came The King's *o* leech to look into his hurt;   "   923

and they past to their *o* land.   "   955

ask'd To bear her *o* crown-royal upon shield,   *Balin and Balan* 200

Our noble King will send thee his *o* leech—   "   274

Who, sitting in thine *o* hall, canst endure   "   378

Had wander'd from her *o* King's golden head,   "   513

Pure as our *o* true Mother is our Queen.'   "   617

Be thine the balm of pity, O Heaven's *o* white Earth-angel,   *Merlin and V.* 80

at times Would flatter his *o* wish in age for love,   "   185

In mine *o* lady palms I cull'd the spring   "   273

brought Her *o* claw back, and wounded her *o* heart.   "   500

His kinsman travelling on his *o* affair   "   717

To crop his *o* sweet rose before the hour?   "   725

Then Merlin to his *o* heart, loathing, said: "   790

Who wouldst against thine *o* eye-witness fain   "   793

Seethed like the kid in its *o* mother's milk!   "   869

What should be granted which your *o* gross heart   "   916

All the devices blazon'd on the shield In their *o* tinct,   *Lancelot and E.*

clave Like its *o* mists to all the mountain side: "   38

When its *o* voice clings to each blade of grass,   "   107

I Before a King who honours his *o* word,   "   144

For if his *o* knight cast him down, he laughs   "   313

Low for her *o* heart said the lily maid,   "   319

So kiss'd her, and Sir Lancelot his *o* hand,   "   389

Dearer to true young hearts than their *o* praise,   "   419

and a spear Prick'd sharply his *o* cuirass,   "   489

his *o* kin—Ill news, my Queen,   "   597

it will be sweet to have it From your *o* hand;   "   694

And with mine *o* hand give his diamond to him,   "   760

His *o* far blood, which dwelt at Camelot;   "   803

she should ask some goodly gift of him For her *o* self or hers;   "   913

and Prince and Lord am I In mine *o* land,   "   917

and such a tongue To blare its *o* interpretation—   "   943

Most common: yea, I know it of mine *o* self: And you yourself will smile at your *o* self Hereafter,   "   950

only the case, Her *o* poor work, her empty labour, left.   "   991

There surely I shall speak for mine *o* self,   "   1125

these, as I trust That you trust me in your *o* nobleness,   "   1195

In mine *o* realm beyond the narrow seas,   "   1323

Mine *o* name shames me, seeming a reproach,   "   1403

Yet one of your *o* knights, a guest of ours,   *Holy Grail* 40

And once by misadvertence Merlin sat In his *o* chair,   "   176

dyed The strong White Horse in his *o* heathen blood—   "   312

But wail'd and wept, and hated mine *o* self,   "   609

but O the pity To find thine *o* first love once more—   "   620

Where saving his *o* sisters he had known   *Pelleas and E.* 87

'For pity of thine *o* self, Peace, Lady, peace: "   253

And heard but his *o* steps, and his *o* heart Beating, for nothing moved but his *o* self, And his *o* shadow.   "   416

Own (adj.) (continued) towers that, larger than them-
selves In their *o* darkness,   *Pelleas and E.* 458
And whatsoever his *o* knights have sworn   *Last Tournament* 79
Nor heard the King for their *o* cries,   „   472
Catlike thro' his *o* castle steals my Mark,   „   516
ptarmigan that whitens ere his hour Woos his *o* end;   „   698
and cast thee back Thine *o* small saw,   „   712
'O Lancelot, get thee hence to thine *o* land,   *Guinevere* 88
the King's grief For his *o* self, and his *o* Queen,   „   197
Then to her *o* sad heart mutter'd the Queen,   „   213
Shame on her *o* garrulity garrulously,   „   312
In open battle or the tilting-field Forbore his *o* advantage,
   and the King In open battle or the tilting-field Forbore
   his *o* advantage,   „   331
fearful child Meant nothing, but my *o* too-fearful guilt,   „   370
kith and kin Clave to him, and abode in his *o* land.   „   440
To honour his *o* word as if his God's,   „   473
do thou for thine *o* soul the rest.   „   545
and mine *o* flesh, Here looking down on thine polluted,   „   555
Gone, my lord the King, My *o* true lord!   „   617
That in mine *o* heart I can live down sin   „   636
So spake he, clouded with his *o* conceit,   *Pass. of Arthur* 278
His *o* thought drove him like a goad.   „   353
The loyal to their crown Are loyal to their *o* far
   sons,   *To the Queen ii* 28
That knows not her *o* greatness: „   32
ruling that which knows To its *o* harm: „   59
In thine *o* essence, and delight thyself   *Lover's Tale i* 13
pleasure-boat that rock'd, Light-green with its *o*
   shadow,   „   43
Loathing to put it from herself for ever, Left her
   o life with it;   „   215
Till, drunk with its *o* wine, and over-full Of sweetness,
   and in smelling of itself, It fall on its *o* thorns—   „   271
Parting my *o* loved mountains was received,   „   433
Yet bearing round about him his *o* day,   „   510
As from a dismal dream of my *o* death,   „   748
till they fell Half-digging their *o* graves)   „ *ii* 47
And laid her in the vault of her *o* kin.   „ *iv* 39
as her *o* reproof At some precipitance in her burial.   „   106
Then, when her *o* true spirit had return'd,   „   108
And crossing her *o* picture as she came,   „   286
thence Down to this last strange hour in his *o* hall;   „   358
When Harry an' I were children, he call'd me his *o*
   little wife;   *First Quarrel* 10
God bless you, my *o* little Nell.'   „   22
When I cannot see my *o* hand, but am led by the creak
   of the chain,   *Rizpah* 7
I told mine *o* tale, God's *o* truth—   „   34
if true Love Were not his *o* imperial all-in-all.   *Sisters (E. and E.)* 227
A second—this I named from her *o* self, Evelyn;   „   270
mellow'd murmur of the people's praise From
   thine *o* State,   *Ded. Poem Prin. Alice* 8
Yet art thou thine *o* witness that thou bringest
   Not peace,   *Sir J. Oldcastle* 35
I am written in the Lamb's *o* Book of Life   *Columbus* 88
Tho' quartering your *o* royal arms of Spain,   „   115
Some over-labour'd, some by their *o* hands,—   „   178
in that flight of ages which are God's *O* voice to justify
   the dead—   „   203
O dear Spirit half-lost In thine *o* shadow   *De Prof., Two G.* 40
With power on thine *o* act and on the world.   „   56
never since thine *o* Black ridges drew the cloud   *Montenegro* 12
Went to his own in his *o* West-Saxon-land,   *Batt. of Brunanburh* 103
All day the men contend in grievous war From
   their *o* city,   *Achilles over the T.* 10
which our trembling fathers call'd The God's *o* son.   *Tiresias* 17
immerging, each, his urn In his *o* well,   „   89
yet if one of these By his *o* hand—   „   118
will murmur thee To thine *o* Thebes,   „   141
let thine *o* hand strike Thy youthful pulses into rest   „   156
And pity for our *o* selves on an earth that bore not a
   flower;   *Despair* 44
And pity for our *o* selves till we long'd for eternal sleep.   „   46
wilt dive Into the Temple-cave of thine *o* self,   *Ancient Sage* 32

Own (adj.) (continued) Except his *o* meek daughter yield her
   life,   *The Flight* 28
To lie, to lie—in God's *o* house—the blackest of all lies!   „   52
Arise, my *o* true sister, come forth! the world is wide.   „   96
'Ud 'a shot his *o* sowl dead for a kiss of ye, Molly Magee.   *Tomorrow* 40
Yer Honour's *o* agint, he says to me wanst,   „   63
Demos end in working its *o* doom.   *Locksley H., Sixty* 114
strip your *o* foul passions bare;   „   141
Gone at eighty, mine *o* age,   „   281
When our *o* good redcoats sank from sight,   *Heavy Brigade* 42
And who loves War for War's *o* sake Is fool,   *Epilogue* 30
Our *o* fair isle, the lord of every sea—   *The Fleet* 7
What is it all, if we all of us end but in being our *o* corpse-
   coffins at last,   *Vastness* 33
That was nearing his *o* hundred,   *The Ring* 194
She cannot love; she loves her *o* hard self,   „   292
Till from her *o* hand she had torn the ring   „   470
forgotten mine *o* rhyme By mine old self,   *To Mary Boyle* 21
or came of your *o* will To wait on one so broken,   *Romney's R.* 16
Her sad eyes plead for my *o* fame with me   „   55
With your *o* shadow in the placid lake,   „   76
As where earth's green stole into heaven's *o* hue,   *Far—far—away* 2
For a woman ruin'd the world, as God's *o* scriptures tell,   *Charity* 3
every dawn Struck from him his *o* shadow on to
   Rome.   *St. Telemachus* 33
Issa Ben Mariam, his *o* prophet, cried   *Akbar's Dream* 75
Own (s) darkening thine *o* To thine own likeness;   *Aylmer's Field* 673
never in your own arms To hold your *o*,   *Princess vi* 178
My own heart's heart, my ownest *o*, farewell;   *Maud I xviii* 74
at which his *o* began To pulse with such a
   vehemence   *Lover's Tale iv* 81
Went to his *o* in his own West-Saxon-land,   *Batt. of Brunanburh* 103
and will be his, his *o* and only *o*,   *Happy* 7
Own (verb) better than to *o* A crown, a sceptre,   *Ode to Memory* 120
'He *o's* the fatal gift of eyes,   *Two Voices* 286
o one port of sense not flint to prayer,   *Princess vi* 182
everyone that *o's* a tower The Lord for half a
   league.   *Gareth and L.* 595
That *o* no lust because they have no law!   *Pelleas and E.* 481
The Christians *o* a Spiritual Head;   *Akbar's Dream* 153
Own'd one of my co-mates *O* a rough dog,   *Gareth and L.* 1011
The one true lover whom you ever *o*,   *Geraint and E.* 344
yourself have *o* ye did me wrong.   *Merlin and V.* 316
nor tasted flesh, Nor *o* a sensual wish,   „   628
while they brake them, *o* me King.   *Pass. of Arthur* 158
Owner follows, being named, His *o*,   *Gareth and L.* 704
Ownest My own heart's heart, my *o*, own,   *Maud I xviii* 74
Owning *o* but a little more Than beasts,   *Two Voices* 196
earthly Muse, And *o* but a little art   *In Mem. xxxvii* 14
Ox For the *O* Feeds in the herb,   *Supp. Confessions* 150
From the dark fen the *oxen's* low Came   *Mariana* 28
The passive *oxen* gaping.   *Amphion* 72
Reel'd, as a footsore *o* in crowded ways   *Aylmer's Field* 819
roasting *o* Moan round the spit—   *Lucretius* 131
oxen from the city, and goodly sheep   *Spec. of Iliad* 4
my lord is lower than his *oxen* or his swine.   *Locksley H., Sixty* 126
May seem the black *o* of the distant plain.   *To one ran down Eng.* 4
Oxlip As cowslip unto *o* is,   *Talking Oak* 107

P

Paäid (paid) eäsy es leäves their debts to be *p*.   *Village Wife* 94
An' they hallus *p* what I hax'd,   „   115
Paäil (pail) wi' her *p's* fro' the cow.   *Spinster's S's.* 2
ye shant hev a drop fro' the *p*.   „   65
Paäin (pain) Sam, thou's an ass for thy *p's*:   *N. Farmer, N. S.* 3
an arn'd naw thanks fur 'er *p's*.   *Village Wife* 12
es be down wi' their haäches an' their *p's*:   *Spinster's S's.* 108
Paärint (parent) afther her *p's* had inter'd glory,   *Tomorrow* 53
That ye'll meet your *p's* agin   „   57
Paäy (pay) find my rent an' to *p* my men?   *Owd Roä* 47
'can ya *p* me the rent to-night?'   „   57

Pain (s) (*continued*) The lading of a single *p*,   *In Mem. xxv* 11
This year I slept and woke with *p*,   ,, *xxviii* 13
I would set their *p's* at ease.   ,, *lxiii* 8
Who ploughs with *p* his native lea   ,, *lxiv* 25
These mortal lullabies of *p*   ,, *lxxvii* 5
No single tear, no mark of *p*:   ,, *lxxviii* 14
Some painless sympathy with *p*?'   ,, *lxxxv* 88
nerves of motion as well as the nerves of *p*,   *Maud I i* 63
possible After long grief and *p* To find the arms   ,, *II iv* 2
Pass, thou deathlike type of *p*   ,, 58
And my bones are shaken with *p*,   ,, v 5
Sun, that wakenest all to bliss or *p*,   *Gareth and L.* 1060
all my *p's*, poor man, for all my *p's*,   *Marr. of Geraint* 116
p she had To keep them in the wild ways   *Geraint and E.* 186
sharpness of that *p* about her heart: ,, 190
and down he sank For the pure *p*,   *Lancelot and E.* 518
sweet is death who puts an end to *p*:   ,, 1008
Pleasure to have it, none; to lose it, *p* ;   ,, 1415
So groan'd Sir Lancelot in remorseful *p*,   ,, 1428
I climb'd a thousand steps With *p* :   *Holy Grail* 836
I know That all these *p's* are trials of my faith,   *Pelleas and E.* 246
had held sometime with *p* His own against him,   *Last Tournament* 178
and in her bosom *p* was lord.   ,, 239
in the heart of Arthur *p* was lord.   ,, 486
rose, Slowly, with *p*, reclining on his arm,   *Pass. of Arthur* 336
now first heard with any sense of *p*,   *Lover's Tale i* 709
suffering view'd had been Extremest *p*;   ,, *ii* 130
My heart was cloven with *p*;   ,, 200
And they blest him in their *p*,   *The Revenge* 20
Patient of *p* tho' as quick as a sensitive plant   *In the Child. Hosp.* 30
Her love of light quenching her fear of *p*—   *Sir J. Oldcastle* 190
I am rack'd with *p's*.   *Columbus* 199
and wrench'd with *p's* Gain'd in the service   ,, 235
p Of this divisible-indivisible world   *De Prof., Two G.* 42
I had now—with *him*—been out of my *p*.'   *The Wreck* 128
match'd with the *p's* Of the hellish heat   *Despair* 67
hour of torture, a moment of *p*,   ,, 81
short, or long, as Pleasure leads, or *P* ;   *Ancient Sage* 101
The plowman passes, bent with *p*,   ,, 144
whose *p's* are hardly less than ours !   *Locksley H., Sixty* 102
or *p* in every peopled sphere ?   ,, 197
Thy glorious eyes were dimm'd with *p*   *Freedom* 10
with all its *p's*, and griefs, and deaths,   *To Prin. Beatrice* 2
her tears Are half of pleasure, half of *p*—   ,, 11
P, that has crawl'd from the corpse of Pleasure,   *Vastness* 17
pardon, O my love, if I ever gave you *p*.   *Happy* 68
life of mingled *p's* And joys to me,   *To Mary Boyle* 49
world-whisper, mystic *p* or joy,   *Far—far—away* 7

Pain (verb) (*See also* **Paäin**) *p's* him that he sickens
nigh to death;   *Geraint and E.* 499

Pain'd *P*, and, as bearing in myself the shame   *Aylmer's Field* 355
Her crampt-up sorrow *p* her,   ,, 800

Painful (*See also* **Slowly-painful**) Full oft the riddle of
the *p* earth   *Palace of Art* 213
Completion in a *p* school;   *Love thou thy land* 58
Till out of *p* phases wrought   *In Mem. lxv* 6

Painless Some *p* sympathy with pain?'   ,, *lxxxv* 88

Paint 'When will *you* *p* like this?'   *Gardener's D.* 22
And *p* the gates of Hell with Paradise,   *Princess iv* 131
I strive to *p* The face I know;   *In Mem. lxx* 2
And every dew-drop *p's* a bow,   ,, *cxxii* 18
harlots *p* their talk as well as face   *Merlin and V.* 821
Behind it, and so *p's* him that his face,   *Lancelot and E.* 334
P the mortal shame of nature   *Locksley H., Sixty* 140

Painted (adj.) (*See also* **Point-painted**) WE left behind
the *p* buoy   *The Voyage* 1
those fixt eyes of *p* ancestors Staring for ever   *Aylmer's Field* 832
Her gay-furr'd cats a *p* fantasy,   *Princess iii* 186
silent light Slept on the *p* walls,   ,, *vii* 121
So like a *p* battle the war stood Silenced,   *Com. of Arthur* 122
Or two wild men supporters of a shield, *P*,   *Geraint and E.* 268
when all at once That *p* vessel, as with inner life,
Began to heave upon that *p* sea,   *Lover's Tale ii* 191

Painted (verb) Eustace *p* her, And said to me,   *Gardener's D.* 20
a couple, fair As ever painter *p*,   *Aylmer's Field* 106

Painter (*See also* **Landscape-painter**) sorrowest thou,
pale *P*, for the past,   *Wan Sculptor* 3
a couple, fair As ever *p* painted,   *Aylmer's Field* 106
Musician, *p*, sculptor, critic,   *Princess ii* 178
As when a *p*, poring on a face,   *Lancelot and E.* 332
'Take comfort you have won the *P's* fame,'   *Romney's R.* 43
Wrong there ! The *p's* fame ?   ,, 48

Painting (part) *p* some dead friend from memory ?   *Wan Sculptor* 4
And then was *p* on it fancied arms,   *Merlin and V.* 474
Good, I am never weary *p* you.   *Romney's R.* 3

Painting (s) with choice *p's* of wise men I hung   *Palace of Art* 131
Drew from my neck the *p* and the tress,   *Princess vi* 110
p on the wall Or shield of knight;   *Holy Grail* 829
Hung round with *p's* of the sea,   *Lover's Tale ii* 168
In the hall there hangs a *p*—   *Locksley H., Sixty* 13

Pair we went along, A pensive *p*,   *Miller's D.* 164
saw the *p*, Enoch and Annie, sitting   *Enoch Arden* 68
welded in one love Than *p's* of wedlock;   *Princess vi* 254
His craven *p* Of comrades making slowlier   *Geraint and E.* 166
like that false *p* who turn'd Flying,   ,, 176
With a low whinny toward the *p* :   ,, 756

Palace (adj.) 'Yet pull not down my *p* towers,   *Palace of Art* 293
High up, the topmost *p* spire.   *Day-Dm., Sleep P.* 48
In *p* chambers far apart.   ,, *Sleep B.* 18
When that cold vapour touch'd the *p* gate,   *Vision of Sin* 58
clocks Throbb'd thunder thro' the *p* floors,   *Princess vii* 104
Nor waves the cypress in the *p* walk;   ,, 177
sound ran Thro' *p* and cottage door,   *Dead Prophet* 38

Palace (s) (*See also* **Summer-palace**) And in the lighted
p near   *L. of Shalott iv* 47
unto herself In her high *p* there.   *Palace of Art* 12
gaze upon My *p* with unblinded eyes,   ,, 42
Full of great rooms and small the *p* stood,   ,, 57
in dark corners of her *p* stood Uncertain shapes;   ,, 237
forms that pass'd at windows and on roofs Of
marble *p's*,   *D. of F. Women* 24
The *p* bang'd, and buzz'd and clackt,   *Day-Dm., Revival* 14
And from the *p* came a child of sin,   *Vision of Sin* 5
Which rolling o'er the *p's* of the proud,   *Aylmer's Field* 636
And in the imperial *p* found the king.   *Princess i* 113
I promise you Some *p* in our land,   ,, *iii* 162
took this *p* ; but even from the first   ,, *iv* 313
we this night should pluck your *p* down ;   ,, 414
who goes?' 'Two from the *p*' I.   ,, *v* 3
All on this side the *p* ran the field   ,, 361
high upon the *p* Ida stood With Psyche's babe   ,, *vi* 30
with my brethren here In our own *p* :   ,, 124
Was it for this we gave our *p* up,   ,, 244
the long laborious miles Of *P* ;   *Ode Inter. Exhib.* 12
Or *p*, how the city glitter'd,   *The Daisy* 47
Fairily-delicate *p's* shine Mixt with myrtle   *The Islet* 18
Lo the *p's* and the temple,   *Boädicea* 53
Burst the gates, and burn the *p's*,   ,,
Camelot, a city of shadowy *p's* And stately,   *Gareth and L.* 303
And he will have thee to his *p* here,   *Geraint and E.* 230
And into no Earl's *p* will I go.   ,, 235
I know, God knows, too much of *p's* !   ,, 236
hundred miles of coast, A *p* and a princess,   *Merlin and V.* 589
hundred miles of coast, The *p* and the princess,   ,, 648
many corridor'd complexities Of Arthur's *p*:   ,, 733
moved about her *p*, proud and pale.   *Lancelot and E.* 614
Until he found the *p* of the King.   ,, 1044
Until I find the *p* of the King.   ,, 1051
he Will guide me to that *p*, to the doors.'   ,, 1129
Sir Lancelot at the *p* craved Audience of Guinevere,   ,, 1162
of Arthur's *p* toward the stream,   ,, 1178
And all the broken *p's* of the Past,   *Lover's Tale ii* 59
Death from the heights of the mosque and the *p*,   *Def. of Lucknow* 24
given the Great Khan's *p's* to the Moor,   *Columbus* 109
down in a rainbow deep Silent *p's*,   *V. of Maeldune* 80
Thro' many a *p*, many a cot,   *Demeter and P.* 55
A galleried *p*, or a battlefield,   *The Ring* 246
To the city and *p* Of Arthur the king;   *Merlin and the G.* 65
our *p* is awake, and morn Has lifted   *Akbar's Dream* 200

Palace-doorway On to the *p-d* sliding, paused.   *Lancelot and E.* 1246

Palace-front *p-f* Alive with flattering scarfs   *Princess v* 508
Palace-gate (*See also* **Palace** (adj.)) youth came riding
   toward a *p-g,*   *Vision of Sin* 2
Palace-walls *Where all about your* p-w   *To the Queen* 15
   Fleeting betwixt her column'd *p-w,*   *St. Telemachus* 37
Palate Whither beneath the *p,*   *D. of F. Women* 287
Pale (adj.) (*See also* **Dead-pale, Deathly-pale, Death-pale,**
   Passion-pale) Then her cheek was *p* and thinner   *Locksley Hall* 21
P he turn'd and red,   *The Captain* 62
P again as death did prove: *L. of Burleigh* 66
Then moving homeward came on Annie *p,*   *Enoch Arden* 149
Enoch slumber'd motionless and *p,*   ,, 908
P, for on her the thunders of the house   *Aylmer's Field* 278
P as the Jephtha's daughter,   ,, 280
Beneath a *p* and unimpassion'd moon,   ,, 334
how *p* she had look'd Darling, to-night !   ,, 379
made Still paler the *p* head of him,   ,, 623
seem'd he saw no *p* sheet-lightnings from afar,   ,, 726
when the king Kiss'd her *p* cheek,   *Princess ii* 264
' *P* one, blush again :   ,, iii 67
some red, some *p,* All open-mouth'd,   ,, iv 482
raised the cloak from brows as *p* and smooth   ,, v 73
Dishelm'd and mute, and motionlessly *p,*   ,, vi 101
And then once more she look'd at my *p* face :   ,, 115
P was the perfect face ;   ,, vii 224
Come ; let us go : your cheeks are *p* ;   *In Mem. lvii* 5
P with the golden beam of an eyelash dead on the
   cheek, Passionless, *p,*   *Maud I iii* 3
ever as *p* as before Growing and fading   ,, 6
Morning arises stormy and *p,*   ,, vi 1
some Were *p* as at the passing of a ghost,   *Com. of Arthur* 264
red and the *p* Across the face of Enid hearing her ;   *Marr. of Geraint* 523
when the *p* and bloodless east began To quicken   ,, 534
They rode so slowly and they look'd so *p,*   *Geraint and E.* 35
Had ruth again on Enid looking *p* :   ,, 203
Femininely fair and dissolutely *p.*   ,, 275
and at his side all *p* Dismounting,   ,, 510
And chafing his *p* hands, and calling to him.   ,, 582
I never yet beheld a thing so *p.*   ,, 615
and beholding her Tho' *p,* yet happy,   ,, 880
break her sports with graver fits, Turn red or *p,*   *Merlin and V.* 181
The *p* blood of the wizard at her touch Took gayer
   colours,   ,, 949
moved about her palace, proud and *p.*   *Lancelot and E.* 614
Marr'd her friend's aim with *p* tranquillity.   ,, 733
how *p* ! what are they ? flesh and blood ?   ,, 1256
Brake into hall together, worn and *p.*   *Pelleas and E.* 587
When, *p* as yet, and fever-worn,   *To the Queen ii* 4
sun, *P* at my grief, drew down before his time   *Deneter and P.* 114
are faint And *p* in Alla's eyes,   *Akbar's Dream* 11
Bramble roses, faint and *p,*   *A Dirge* 30
O *p,* *p* face so sweet and meek,   *Oriana* 66
O SWEET *p* Margaret, O rare *p* Margaret, (repeat)   *Margaret* 1, 54
Of pensive thought and aspect *p,*   ,, 6
O sorrowest thou, *p* Painter, for the past,   *Wan Sculptor* 3
The *p* yellow woods were waning,   *L. of Shalott iv* 2
And round about the keel with faces *p,* Dark faces
   p against that rosy flame,   *Lotos Eaters* 25
To whom replied King Arthur, faint and *p* :   *M. d'Arthur* 72
At this *p* taper's earthly spark,   *St. Agnes' Eve* 4
Panted hand-in-hand with faces *p,*   *Vision of Sin* 19
' Then leaving the *p* nun, I spake of this   *Holy Grail* 129
And *p* he turn'd, and reel'd, and would have fall'n,   *Guinevere* 304
Then the *p* Queen look'd up and answer'd her,   ,, 327
wrathful heat Fired all the *p* face of the Queen,   ,, 357
Rose the *p* Queen, and in her anguish found   ,, 586
the *p* King glanced across the field Of battle :   *Pass. of Arthur* 126
To whom replied King Arthur, faint and *p* :   ,, 240
its wreaths of dripping green—Its *p* pink shells—   *Lover's Tale i* 40
And *p* and fibrous as a wither'd leaf,   ,, 422
dewy touch of pity had made The red rose there a *p* one—   ,, 696
The bridesmaid *p,* statuelike, passionless—   *Sisters (E. and E.)* 212
I lay At thy *p* feet this ballad of the deeds   *Ded. Poem Prin. Alice* 20
Then his *p* face twitch'd ; ' O Stephen,   *The Wreck* 101
I have scared you *p* with my scandalous talk,   *Despair* 111

Pale (adj.) (*continued*) as this poor earth's *p* history runs,—   *Vastness* 3
Each poor *p* cheek a momentary rose—   *The Ring* 315
Pale (s) By bridge and ford, by park and *p,*   *Sir Galahad* 82
To leap the rotten *p's* of prejudice,   *Princess ii* 142
break At seasons thro' the gilded *p* :   *In Mem. cxi* 8
Nor ever stray'd beyond the *p* :   *Holy Grail* 21
Pale-blooded patient, and prayerful, meek, P-b,   *Last Tournament* 608
who am not meek, P-b, prayerful.   ,, 611
Paled *P* at a sudden twitch of his iron mouth ;   *Aylmer's Field* 732
stars in heaven *P,* and the glory grew.   *Pro. to Gen. Hamley* 32
Pale-green *p-g* sea-groves straight and high,   *The Merman* 19
Paleness a *p,* an hour's defect of the rose,   *Maud I ii* 8
Paler made Still *p* the pale head of him,   *Aylmer's Field* 623
Or made her *p* with a poison'd rose ?   *Merlin and V.* 611
But left her all the *p,* when Lavaine   *Lancelot and E.* 378
but the child Is *p* than before.   *The Ring* 327
Muriel, *p* then Than ever you were in your cradle,   ,, 431
No ! but the *p* and the graver, Edith.   *Sisters (E. and E.)* 38
to trace On *p* heaven's the branching grace   *To Ulysses* 15
Palest Between two showers, a cloth of *p* gold,   *Gareth and L.* 389
Palfrey there she found her *p* trapt   *Godiva* 54
her *p's* footfall shot Light horrors   ,, 58
In converse till she made her *p* halt,   *Gareth and L.* 1360
and cried, ' My charger and her *p* ;'   *Marr. of Geraint* 126
Call the host and bid him bring Charger and *p.*'   *Geraint and E.* 401
has your *p* heart enough To bear his armour ?   ,, 489
At which her *p* whinnying lifted heel,   ,, 533
your charger is without, My *p* lost.'   ,, 750
Then leapt her *p* o'er the fallen oak,   *Balin and Balan* 587
Palisade our walls and our poor *p's.*   *Def. of Lucknow* 55
Pall (s) pass the gate Save under *p* with bearers.   *Aylmer's Field* 827
Warriors carry the warrior's *p,*   *Ode on Well.* 6
This truth came borne with bier and *p,*   *In Mem. lxxxv* 1
upbare A broad earth-sweeping *p* of whitest lawn,   *Lover's Tale ii* 78
Took the edges of the *p,* and blew it far   ,, iii 35
and forget The darkness of the *p.*'   *Ancient Sage* 198
drama's closing curtain is the *p* !   *Locksley H., Sixty* 62
and I and you will bear the *p* ;   ,, 281
Pall (verb) Pain rises up, old pleasures *p.*   *Two Voices* 164
Pallas (*See also* **Pallas Athene**) when they wish to charm
   P and Juno sitting by :   *A Character* 15
Here comes to-day, *P* and Aphrodite,   *Œnone* 86
P where she stood, Somewhat apart,   ,, 137
' O Paris, Give it to *P* !'   ,, 170
There stood a bust of *P* for a sign,   *Princess i* 222
Now fired an angry *P* on the helm,   ,, i 367
some wild *P* from the brain Of Demons ?   *In Mem. cxiv* 12
P flung Her fringed ægis,   *Achilles over the T.* 3
and *P* far away Call'd ;   ,, 17
blunt the curse Of *P,* hear,   *Tiresias* 155
Pallas Athene saw *P A* climbing from the bath   ,, 40
Palled (adj.) *p* shapes In shadowy thoroughfares of
   thought ;   *In Mem. lxx* 7
Pall'd (draped) *P* all its length in blackest samite,   *Lancelot and E.* 1142
All *p* in crimson samite,   *Holy Grail* 847
Pall'd (stale) well I know it—*p*—For I know men :   *Geraint and E.* 331
Pallid On her *p* cheek and forehead came a colour   *Locksley Hall* 25
Palling grew To thunder-gloom *p* all stars,   *Gareth and L.* 1359
Palm (of the hand) Fold thy *p's* across thy breast,   *A Dirge* 2
' His *p's* are folded on his breast :   *Two Voices* 247
opening out his milk-white *p* Disclosed   *Œnone* 65
Caught in the frozen *p's* of Spring.   *The Blackbird* 24
he smote His *p's* together, and he cried   *M. d'Arthur* 87
may press The maiden's tender *p.*   *Talking Oak* 180
Between his *p's* a moment up and down—   *Aylmer's Field* 259
Bow'd on her *p's* and folded up from wrong,   *Princess iv* 288
some one sent beneath his vaulted *p* A whisper'd jest   ,, v 31
he clash'd His iron *p's* together with a cry ;   ,, 354
nor more Sweet Ida : *p* to *p* she sat :   ,, vii 135
What time his tender *p* is prest   *In Mem. xlv* 2
In mine own lady *p's* I cull'd the spring   *Merlin and V.* 273
clench'd her fingers till they bit the *p,*   *Lancelot and E.* 611
he smote His *p's* together, and he cried   *Pass. of Arthur* 255
The rough brier tore my bleeding *p's* ;   *Lover's Tale ii* 18
Screams of a babe in the red-hot *p's* of a Moloch of Tyre,   *The Dawn* 2

Palm (of the hand) (*continued*) in her open *p*
  halcyon sits Patient— *Prog. of Spring* 20
Palm (sallow-bloom) In colour like the satin-shining *p* *Merlin and V.* 224
Palm (tree) (*See also* **Coco-palm**) Imbower'd vaults of
  pillar'd *p*, *Arabian Nights* 39
  the solemn *p*'s were ranged Above, „ 79
  And many a tract of *p* and rice, *Palace of Art* 114
  and the yellow down Border'd with *p*, *Lotos-Eaters* 22
  The *p*'s and temples of the South. *You ask me, why, etc.* 28
  the white robe and the *p*. *St. S. Stylites* 20
  Breadths of tropic shade and *p*'s *Locksley Hall* 160
  these be *p*'s Whereof the happy people *Enoch Arden* 504
  built, and thatch'd with leaves of *p*, a hut, „ 559
  Among the *p*'s and ferns and precipices; „ 593
  little dells of cowslip, fairy *p*'s, *Aylmer's Field* 91
  battle-clubs From the isles of *p*: *Princess, Pro.* 22
  To brawl at Shushan underneath the *p*'s.' „ iii 230
  all the sultry *p*'s of India known, *W. to Marie Alex.* 14
  In lands of *p* and southern pine; In lands of *p*, of
  orange-blossom, *The Daisy* 2
  Not the clipt *p* of which they boast; „ 26
  Above the valleys of *p* and pine.' *The Islet* 23
  Betwixt the *p*'s of paradise. *In Mem., Con.* 32
  a *p* As glitters gilded in thy Book of Hours. *Gareth and L.* 45
  was ever haunting round the *p* A lusty youth, „ 47
  from the diamond fountain by the *p*'s, *Lover's Tale i* 137
  not those alien *p*'s, *Columbus* 78
  the high star-crowns of his *p*'s *The Wreck* 72
  by the *p* And orange grove of Paraguay, *To Ulysses* 11
  Your cane, your *p*, tree-fern, bamboo, „ 36
  p Call to the cypress 'I alone am fair'? *Akbar's Dream* 37
Palm-planted *p-p* fountain-fed Ammonian Oasis *Alexander* 7
Palm-tree 'Under the *p-t*.' That was nothing to her: *Enoch Arden* 498
  Under a *p-t*, over him the Sun: „ 501
Palmwood crimson-hued the stately *p*'s *Milton* 15
Palmy Sailing under *p* highlands *The Captain* 23
  Fairer than Rachel by the *p* well, *Aylmer's Field* 679
Palmyrene with the *P* That fought Aurelian, *Princess ii* 83
Palpitated tempestuous treble throbb'd and *p*; *Vision of Sin* 28
  P, her hand shook, and we heard In the dead hush *Princess iv* 389
Palpitation blissful *p*'s in the blood, „ 28
Palsied Left me with the *p* heart, *Locksley Hall* 132
  among the glooming alleys Progress halts on *p* feet, *Locksley H., Sixty* 219
  As some great shock may wake a *p* limb, *St. Telemachus* 57
Palsy A wither'd *p* cease to shake?' *Two Voices* 57
  Cured lameness, *palsies*, cancers. *St. S. Stylites* 82
  wife or wailing infancy Or old bedridden *p*,— *Aylmer's Field* 178
  p, death-in-life, And wretched age— *Lucretius* 154
  The *p* wags his head; *Ancient Sage* 124
Palter to dodge and *p* with a public crime? *Third of Feb.* 24
Palter'd Nor *p* with Eternal God for power; *Ode on Well.* 180
Pamper But *p* not a hasty time, *Love thou thy land* 9
  And *p* him with papmeat, if ye will, *Pelleas and E.* 195
Pamphleteer A *p* on guano and on grain, *Princess, Con.* 89
Pan (a god) The murmur of a happy *P*: *In Mem. xxiii* 12
Pan (a vessel) And hurl'd the *p* and kettle. *The Goose* 28
Pane (*See also* **Window-pane**) The blue fly sung in the *p*; *Mariana* 63
  the frost is on the *p*: *May Queen, N. Y.'s. E.* 13
  I peer'd athwart the chancel *p* *The Letters* 3
  Fine as ice-ferns on January *p*'s *Aylmer's Field* 222
  Oh is it the brook, or a pool, or her window *p*, *Window, On the Hill* 4
  And never a glimpse of her window *p*! *No Answer* 3
  And lash with storm the streaming *p*? *In Mem. lxxii* 4
  The prophet blazon'd on the *p*'s; „ lxxxvii 8
  Laid their green faces flat against the *p*'s, *Balin and Balan* 344
  thro' the pines, upon the dewy *p* Falling, *Lover's Tale i* 264
  stars went down across the gleaming *p*, *The Flight* 13
  small black fly upon the *p* *To one who ran down Eng.* 3
Pang Struck thro' with *p*'s of hell. *Palace of Art* 220
  Thrice multiplied by superhuman *p*'s, *St. S. Stylites* 11
  I felt a *p* within *Talking Oak* 234
  Whence follows many a vacant *p*; *Princess ii* 403
  brother, you have known the *p*'s we felt, „ v 374
  rack'd with *p*'s that conquer trust; *In Mem. l* 6
  To *p*'s of nature, sins of will, „ liv 3

Pang (*continued*) nor *p* Of wrench'd or broken limb— *Gareth and L.* 87
  Right thro' his manful breast darted the *p* *Marr. of Geraint* 121
  The *p*—which while I weigh'd thy heart *Guinevere* 540
Panic and a boundless *p* shook the foe. *Achilles over the T.* 18
Panic-stricken *p-s*, like a shoal Of darting fish, *Geraint and E.* 468
Pansy eyes Darker than darkest *pansies*, *Gardener's D.* 27
Pant life, not death, for which we *p*; *Two Voices* 398
Panted as he walk'd, King Arthur *p* hard, *M. d'Arthur* 176
  P hand-in-hand with faces pale, *Vision of Sin* 19
  sweet half-English Neilgherry air I *p*, *The Brook* 18
  P from weary sides ' King, you are free! *Princess v* 24
  Gareth *p* hard, and his great heart, *Gareth and L.* 1126
  as he walk'd, King Arthur *p* hard, *Pass. of Arthur* 344
Panther A *p* roar came muffled, *Œnone* 214
  A *p* sprang across her path, *Death of Œnone* 89
Panting *p*, burst The laces toward her babe; *Princess vi* 148
Pantomime Nor flicker down to brainless *p*, *To W. C. Macready* 10
Pap their bottles o' *p*, an' their mucky bibs, *Spinster's S's.* 87
Papal Prick'd by the *P* spur, we rear'd, *Third of Feb.* 27
Paper There at a board by tome and *p* sat, *Princess ii* 32
  heard In the dead hush the *p*'s that she held Rustle: „ iv 390
  sack'd My dwelling, seized upon my *p*'s, *Columbus* 130
  a scrap, clipt out of the 'deaths' in a *p*, fell. *The Wreck* 146
Paphian new-bathed in *P* wells, *Œnone* 175
Papist Than *P* unto Saint. *Talking Oak* 16
Papmeat And pamper him with *p*, if ye will, *Pelleas and E.* 195
Parable second brother in their fool's *p*— *Gareth and L.* 1004
  P's? Hear a *p* of the knave. „ 1008
Parachute And dropt a fairy *p* and past: *Princess, Pro.* 76
Parade He loves to make *p* of pain, *In Mem. xxi* 10
Paradise (*See also* **Island-Paradise**) Love paced the
  thymy plots of *P*, *Love and Death* 2
  Or thronging all one porch of *P* *Palace of Art* 101
  And from it melt the dews of *P*, *St. S. Stylites* 210
  palms in cluster, knots of *P*. *Locksley Hall* 160
  Like long-tail'd birds of *P* *Day-Dm., Ep.* 7
  And paint the gates of Hell with *P*, *Princess iv* 131
  dipt In Angel instincts, breathing *P*, „ vii 321
  many-blossoming *P*'s, *Boädicea* 43
  This earth had been the *P* *In Mem. xxiv* 6
  shook Betwixt the palms of *p*. „ Con. 32
  And the valleys of *P*. *Maud I xxii* 44
  since high in *P* O'er the four rivers *Geraint and E.* 763
  No more of jealousy than in *P*.' *Balin and Balan* 152
  Now talking of their woodland *p*, *Last Tournament* 726
  groves that look'd a *p* Of blossom, *Guinevere* 389
  I stood upon the stairs of *P*. *Sisters (E. and E.)* 144
  And saw the rivers roll from *P*! *Columbus* 27
  O bliss, what a *P* there! *V. of Maeldune* 78
  and the *P* trembled away. „ 82
  Broken on my Pagan *P*, *Tiresias* 193
  ' *P* there!' so he said, but I seem'd in *P* then *The Wreck* 75
  In earth's recurring *P*. *Helen's Tower* 12
  A silken cord let down from *P*, *Akbar's Dream* 139
Paragon look upon her As on a kind of *p*; *Princess i* 155
Paraguay palm And orange grove of *P*, *To Ulysses* 12
Paramount Tristram, 'Last to my Queen *P*, Here
  now to my Queen *P* *Last Tournament* 551
Paramour My haughty jousts, and took a *p*; *Geraint and E.* 832
  Slain was the brother of my *p* *Last Tournament* 448
Parapet heroes tall Dislodging pinnacle and *p* *D. of F. Women* 26
  isle of silvery *p*'s! *Boädicea* 38
  Set every gilded *p* shuddering; *Lancelot and E.* 299
  gilded *p*'s were crown'd With faces, *Pelleas and E.* 165
Parasite A leaning and upbearing, *Isabel* 34
Parasitic Will clear away the *p* forms *Princess vii* 269
Parcel Portions and *p*'s of the dreadful Past. *Lotos-Eaters, C. S.* 47
Parcel-bearded *p-b* with the traveller's-joy In Autumn, *Aylmer's Field* 153
Parcell'd the broad woodland *p* into farms; „ 847
Parch'd *p* and wither'd, deaf and blind, *Fatima* 6
  p with dust; Or, clotted into points *M. d'Arthur* 218
  p with dust; Or, clotted into points *Pass. of Arthur* 386
Pard a wild and wanton *p*, Eyed like the evening star, *Œnone* 199
Pardon (s) heal me with your *p* ere you go.' *Princess iii* 65
  'What *p*, sweet Melissa, for a blush?' „ 66

Pardon (s) (*continued*) and sinn'd in grosser lips Beyond all p— | *Princess iv* 252
with mutual p ask'd and given For stroke | „ *v* 46
I crave your p, O my friend; | *In Mem. lxxxv* 100
with the Sultan's p, I am all as well delighted, | *Maud I xx* 39
Thy p; I but speak for thine avail, | *Gareth and L.* 883
'Full p, but I follow up the quest, | „ 886
crave His p for thy breaking of his laws. | „ 986
and now thy p, friend, | „ 1166
Crave p for that insult done the Queen, | *Marr. of Geraint* 583
Grant me p for my thoughts? | „ 816
Your p, child. Your pretty sports have brighten'd | *Merlin and V.* 304
your p! lo, ye know it! Speak therefore: | *Lancelot and E.* 669
dazzled by the sudden light, and crave P: | *Pelleas and E.* 106
Madam, I beg your p! | *Rizpah* 81
Nay, your p, cry your 'forward,' | *Locksley H., Sixty* 225
Your p, O my love, if I ever gave you pain. | *Happy* 68

Pardon (verb) ' Pray stay a little: p me; | *The Brook* 210
I cared not for it. O p me, | *Aylmer's Field* 244
and I (P me saying it) were much loth to breed | *Princess i* 156
My needful seeming harshness, p it. | „ *ii* 309
'O p me I heard, I could not help it, | „ 331
Yet mine in part. O hear me, p me, | „ *iii* 31
P, I am shamed That I must needs repeat | „ 51
We p it; and for your ingress here | „ *v* 218
'P me, O stranger knight; | *Marr. of Geraint* 286
O p me! the madness of that hour, | *Geraint and E.* 346
Again she sigh'd 'P, sweet lord!' | *Balin and Balan* 497
sin in words Perchance we both can p: | *Lancelot and E.* 1189
God 'ill p the hell-black raven | *Rizpah* 39
God p all—Me, them, and all the world— | *Sir J. Oldcastle* 168
and yet P—too harsh, unjust. | *Columbus* 199

Pardonable 'Rough, sudden, And p, | *Gareth and L.* 654
Pardon'd I have p little Letty; | *Edwin Morris* 140
Pardoner at P's, Summoners, Friars, | *Sir J. Oldcastle* 92
Pare would p the mountain to the plain, | *Merlin and V.* 829
Parent (*See also* Päärint) and their p's underground) | *Aylmer's Field* 83
Till after our good p's past away | „ 358
And you are happy: let her p's be.' | „ 366
sell her, those good p's, for her good. | „ 483
The p's' harshness and the hapless loves | „ 616
do not doubt Being a watchful p, | *Sisters (E. and E.)* 31

Paris (city of) Roaring London, raving P, | *Locksley H., Sixty* 190
Madonna-masterpieces Of ancient Art in P, or in Rome. | *Romney's R.* 87
And London and P and all the rest | *The Dawn* 10

Paris (son of Priam) Œnone, wandering forlorn Of P, | *Œnone* 17
Beautiful P, evil-hearted P, | „ 50
Hear all, and see thy P judge of Gods.' | „ 90
She to P made Proffer of royal power, | „ 110
From me, Heaven's Queen, P, to thee king-born, | „ 127
P held the costly fruit Out at arm's-length, | „ 135
And P ponder'd, and I cried, 'O P, Give it to Pallas!' | „ 169
when I look'd, P had raised his arm, | „ 189
P, himself as beauteous as a God. | *Death of Œnone* 18
on a sudden he, P, no longer beauteous as a God, | „ 25
who first had found P, a naked babe, | „ 54

Parish (adj.) He heard the pealing of his p bells; | *Enoch Arden* 615
To him that fluster'd his poor p wits | *Aylmer's Field* 521

Parish (s) like that year in twenty p'es round. | *Grandmother* 12
'e coom'd to the p wi' lots o' Varsity debt, | *N. Farmer, N. S.* 29
An' all o' the wust i' the p— | *Village Wife* 34
an' nöne of the p knew. | *Tomorrow* 76
Haäfe of the p runn'd oop | *Owd Roä* 115
I beän chuch-warden i' the p fur fifteen year. | *Church-warden, etc.* 8

Parish-clerks Friars, bellringers, P-c— | *Sir J. Oldcastle* 160
Park the range of lawn and p: | *The Blackbird* 6
The wild wind rang from p and plain, | *The Goose* 45
voice thro' all the holt Before her, and the p. | *Talking Oak* 124
Mr father left a p to me, | *Amphion* 1
By bridge and ford, by p and pale, | *Sir Galahad* 82
They by p's and lodges going | *L. of Burleigh* 17
P's with oak and chestnut shady, | „ 29
P's and order'd gardens great, | „ 30
lay Carved stones of the Abbey-ruin in the p, | *Princess, Pro.* 14
Down thro' the p: strange was the sight | „ 54

Park (*continued*) they gave The p, the crowd, the house; | *Princess, Pro.* 94
A hundred maids in train across the P. | „ *vi* 76
Give up their p's some dozen times a year | „ *Con.* 103
tides of chariots flow By p and suburb | *In Mem. xcviii* 24
To range the woods, to roam the p, | „ *Con.* 96
from the deluged p The cuckoo of a worse July | *Pref. Poem Broth. S.* 10

Parlance A hate of gossip p, | *Isabel* 26
Parle (s) Found the gray kings at p: | *Princess v* 114
Parle (verb) wakeful portress, and didst p with Death,— | *Lover's Tale i* 113
Parliament moor good sense na the p man 'at stans fur us 'ere, | *Owd Roä* 13
Parliament (s) furl'd In the P of man, | *Locksley Hall* 128
A potent voice of P, | *In Mem. cxiii* 11
Parlour I sits i' my oän little p, | *Spinster's S's.* 103
Parlour-window rosebush that I set About the p-w | *May Queen, N. Y's. E.* 48
Parma Of rain at Reggio, rain at P; | *The Daisy* 51
Parnassus On thy P set thy feet, | *In Mem. xxxvii* 6
Parrot Whistle back the p's call, | *Locksley Hall* 171
The p in his gilded wires. | *Day-Dm., Sleep. P.* 16
The p scream'd, the peacock squall'd, | „ *Revival* 12
p turns Up thro' gilt wires a crafty loving eye, | *Princess, Pro.* 171
Parsee Buddhist, Christian, and P, | *Akbar's Dream* 25
Parson The p smirk'd and nodded, | *The Goose* 20
The p Holmes, the poet Everard Hall, | *The Epic* 2
The p taking wide and wider sweeps, | „ 14
At which the P, sent to sleep with sound, | *M. d'Arthur, Ep.* 3
'P,' said I, you pitch the pipe too low: | *Edwin Morris* 52
the p made it his text that week, | *Grandmother* 29
P's a beän loikewoise, | *N. Farmer, O. S.* 9
But P a cooms an' a goäs, | „ 25
p 'ud nobbut let ma aloän, | „ 43
yon's p's 'ouse—Doesn't thou knaw | „ *N. S.* 5
thou's sweet upo' p's lass— | „ 11
P's lass 'ant nowt, | „ 25
'Thou'rt but a Methody-man,' says P, | *North. Cobbler* 89
An' P as hesn't the call, nor the mooney, | *Village Wife* 91
An' soä they've maäde tha a p, | *Church-warden, etc.* 7
ther mun be p's an' all, | „ 36
fur thou was the P's lad. | „ 37
An' P 'e 'ears on it all, | „ 43
But P 'e *will* speäk out, | „ 43

Part (adv.) a lie which is p a truth | *Grandmother* 32
spoke in words p heard, in whispers p, | *Merlin and V.* 839
P black, p whiten'd with the bones of men, | *Holy Grail* 500

Part (s) they had their p Of sorrow; | *Miller's D.* 223
seems a p of those fresh days to me; | *Edwin Morris* 142
Love himself took p against himself | *Love and Duty* 45
I am a p of all that I have met; | *Ulysses* 18
fitted to thy petty p's, | *Locksley Hall* 93
She seem'd a p of joyous Spring: | *Sir L. and Q. G.* 23
I will tell him tales of foreign p's, | *Enoch Arden* 198
in those uttermost P's of the morning? | „ 224
And been himself a p of what he told. | *Aylmer's Field* 12
a p Falling had let appear the brand of John— | „ 508
p were drown'd within the whirling brook: | *Princess, Pro.* 47
As p's, can see but p's, now this, now that, | „ *iii* 327
p made long since, and p Now while I sang, | „ *iv* 90
P sat like rocks: p reel'd but kept their seats: | „ *v* 496
P roll'd on the earth and rose again and drew: | „ 497
P stumbled mixt with floundering horses. | „ 498
for she took no p In our dispute: | „ *Con.* 29
'God help me! save I take my p Of danger | *Sailor Boy* 21
And love in which my hound has p, | *In Mem. lxiii* 2
A p of mine may live in thee | „ *lxv* 11
Can take no p away from this: | „ *lxxxv* 68
A p of stillness, yearns to speak: | „ 78
The freezing reason's colder p, | „ *cxxiv* 14
when the fourth p of the day was gone, | *Geraint and E.* 55
'Him, or the viler devil who plays his p, | *Balin and Balan* 300
Now grown a p of me: | *Lancelot and E.* 1416
of this remnant will I leave a p, | *Guinevere* 444
is also past—p. And all is past, | „ 542
low converse sweet, In which our voices bore least p. | *Lover's Tale i* 542
I seem'd the only p of Time stood still; | „ 573
but were a p of sleep, | „ *ii* 117

Pass (verb) (*continued*) there did a compact *p* Long summers

back,	*Princess* i 123
and *p* With all fair theories only made to gild	,, ii 232
he said, '*p* on; His Highness wakes:'	,, v 4
she will *p* me by in after-life	,, 91
P, and mingle with your likes.	,, vi 341
Her peaceful being slowly *p'es* by	*Requiescat* 7
the voice, the peak, the star *P*,	*Voice and the P.* 28
if left to *p* His autumn into seeming-leafless days—	*A Dedication* 9
Winds are loud and winds will *p*!	*Window, No Answer* 22
That all thy motions gently *p*	*In Mem.* xv 10
The salt sea-water *p'es* by,	,, xix 6
And *p'es* into gloom again.	,, xxxix 12
I shall *p*; my work will fail.	,, lvii 8
We *p*: the path that each man trod	,, lxxiii 9
That these things *p*, and I shall prove	,, lxxxv 98
And, leaving these, to *p* away,	,, c 19
in the drifts that *p* To darken on the rolling brine	,, cvii 13
They leave the porch, they *p* the grave	*Con.* 71
But sweeps away as out we *p*	,, 95
And *p* the silent-lighted town,	,, 112
I see her *p* like a light;	*Maud* I iv 11
P and blush the news Over glowing ships;	,, xvii 11
P the happy news, Blush it thro' the West;	,, 15
And trying to *p* to the sea,	,, xxi 7
P, thou deathlike type of pain,	,, II iv 58
P and cease to move about!	,, 59
Guinevere Stood by the castle walls to watch him *p*;	*Com. of Arthur* 48
and sign'd To those two sons to *p*,	,, 319
he will not die, But *p*, again to come;	,, 422
Gareth was so princely-proud To *p* thereby;	*Gareth and L.* 162
so thou *p* Beneath this archway,	,, 267
P not beneath this gateway,	,, 273
a knight would *p* Outward, or inward to the hall:	,, 310
'He *p'es* to the Isle Avilion,	,, 502
He *p'es* and is heal'd and cannot die'—	,, 503
jewell'd harness, ere they *p* and fly.	,, 688
For whom we let thee *p*.'	,, 917
And quickly *p* to Arthur's hall,	,, 984
Else yon black felon had not let me *p*,	,, 1293
like a phantom *p* Chilling the night:	,, 1335
until! we *p* and reach That other,	*Geraint and E.* 6
Wait here, and when he *p'es* fall upon him.'	,, 129
they will fall upon you while ye *p*.'	,, 145
glancing for a minute, till he saw her *P* into it,	,, 887
Wilt thou undertake them as we *p*,	*Balin and Balan* 14
As *p* without good morrow to thy Queen?'	,, 252
'Yea so' she said, 'but so to *p* me by—	,, 255
and *p* And vanish in the woods;	,, 326
heard them *p* like wolves Howling;	,, 407
He must not *p* uncared for.	*Lancelot and E.* 536
Only ye would not *p* beyond the cape	,, 1039
I cried because ye would not *p* Beyond it,	,, 1042
that I may *p* at last Beyond the poplar	,, 1049
so let me *p*, My father, howsoe'er I seem to you,	,, 1091
But that he *p'es* into Fairyland.'	,, 1259
'That is love's curse; *p* on, my Queen, forgiven.'	,, 1353
Who *p'es* thro' the vision of the night—	,, 1406
'Then on a summer night it came to *p*,	*Holy Grail* 179
cries of all my realm *P* thro' this hall—	,, 316
the street of those Who watch'd us *p*;	,, 345
go forth and *p* Down to the little thorpe	,, 546
P not from door to door and out again,	,, 714
resolve To *p* away into the quiet life,	,, 738
Cares but to *p* into the silent life.	,, 899
And *p* and care no more.	*Pelleas and E.* 77
like a poisonous wind I *p* to blast	,, 569
'First over me,' said Lancelot, 'shalt thou *p*.'	,, 571
Watch'd her lord *p*, and knew not that she sigh'd.	*Last Tournament* 130
purple slopes of mountain flowers *P* under white,	,, 230
one will ever shine and one will *p*.	,, 737
all this trouble did not *p* but grew	*Guinevere* 84
I waged His wars, and now I *p* and die.	*Pass. of Arthur* 12
God my Christ—I *p* but shall not die.'	,, 28

Pass (verb) (*continued*) King! To-morrow tnou shalt *p*

away.	*Pass. of Arthur* 34
wife and child with wail *P* to new lords;	,, 45
'O me, my King, let *p* whatever will,	,, 51
but as yet thou shalt not *p*.	,, 55
one last act of knighthood shalt thou see Yet, ere I *p*.'	,, 164
'He *p'es* to be King among the dead,	,, 449
Somewhere far off, *p* on and on,	,, 467
To *p* my hand across my brows,	*Lover's Tale* i 31
And mine with one that will not *p*, till earth And heaven *p* too,	,, 71
P we then A term of eighteen years.	,, 286
So that they *p* not to the shrine of sound	,, 470
Which *p* with that which breathes them?	,, 481
'It was my wish,' he said, 'to *p*, to sleep,	,, iv 63
Glanced at the point of law, to *p* it by,	,, 276
Three hundred years—will *p* collaterally:	*Sisters (E. and E.)* 53
but I thought that it never would *p*.	*In the Child. Hosp.* 61
with his hard 'Dim Saesneg' *p'es*,	*Sir J. Oldcastle* 21
and life *P* in the fire of Babylon!	,, 124
The plowman *p'es*, bent with pain,	*Ancient Sage* 144
but *p* From sight and night to lose themselves and the sun himself will *p*.	*Locksley H., Sixty* 182
Many an Æon too may *p*	,, 206
Earth *p'es*, all is lost In what they prophesy,	*Epilogue* 64
kings and realms that *p* to rise no more;	*To Virgil* 28
o'er the mountain-walls Young angels *p*.	*Early Spring* 12
Till the thunders *p*, the spectres vanish.	*On Jub. Q. Victoria* 69
Your plague but *p'es* by the touch.	*Happy* 104
helpt to *p* a bucket from the well	*To Mary Boyle* 39
p on! the sight confuses—	*Parnassus* 15
æon after æon *p* and touch him into shape?	*Making of Man* 4
Some will *p* and some will pause.	*Poets and Critics* 8
From sin thro' sorrow into Thee we *p*	*Doubt and Prayer* 3

Passage clothes they gave him and free *p* home;

Except the *p* that he loved her not;	*Enoch Arden* 650
There must be now no *p'es* of love	*Geraint and E.* 392
That has but one plain *p* of few notes,	*Merlin and V.* 913
Will sing the simple *p* o'er and o'er	*Lancelot and E.* 895
	,, 896

Passant cow shall butt the 'Lion *p*' *Locksley H., Sixty* 248

Pass'd *See* **Past**

Passenger Should see thy *p's* in rank *In Mem.* xiv 6

Passest thou *p* any wood Close vizor, *Last Tournament* 534

Passeth shadow *p* when the tree shall fall, *Love and Death* 14

Love *p* not the threshold of cold Hate, *Lover's Tale* i 778

Passin' when they seeäs ma a *p* boy, *N. Farmer, O. S.* 53

Passing (*See also* **Passin'**) *P* the place where each

must rest,	*Two Voices* 410
each in *p* touch'd with some new grace	*Gardener's D.* 204
In *p*, with a grosser film made thick	*St. S. Stylites* 200
No eye look down, she *p*;	*Godiva* 40
She *p* thro' the summer world again,	*Enoch Arden* 534
Not sowing hedgerow texts and *p* by,	*Aylmer's Field* 171
as not *p* thro' the fire Bodies, but souls—	,, 671
and murmur'd that their May Was *p*:	*Princess* ii 464
like parting hopes I heard them *p*	,, iv 173
many a maiden *p* home Till happier times;	,, vi 380
Nine times goes the *p* bell:	*All Things will Die* 35
P with the weather,	*Window, Spring* 6
Was drown'd in *p* thro' the ford,	*In Mem.* vi 39
p, turn the page that tells A grief,	,, lxxvii 10
Nor feed with sighs a *p* wind;	,, cviii 4
The shade of *p* thought, the wealth Of words	,, Con. 102
With never an end to the stream of *p* feet,	*Maud* II v 11
Arthur, *p* thence to battle, felt Travail,	*Com. of Arthur* 75
and *p* forth to breathe,	,, 369
'And *p* gentle' caught his hand away	*Balin and Balan* 371
That makes me *p* wrathful;	*Merlin and V.* 341
And *p* one, at the high peep of dawn,	,, 560
I fear My fate or folly, *p* gayer youth For one so old,	,, 927
sigh'd in *p* 'Lancelot, Forgive me;	*Lancelot and E.* 1350
Three against one: and Gawain *p* by,	*Pelleas and E.* 274
He saw her, for Sir Lancelot *p* by	*Guinevere* 30
Leapt like a *p* thought across her eyes;	*Lover's Tale* i 70
that *p* lightly Adown a natural stair	,, 526

Passing (*continued*) ships of the world could stare at him,
 p by. — *Rizpah* 83
And moved to merriment at a *p* jest. — *Sisters (E. and E.)* 121
Art *p* on thine happier voyage now — *Sir J. Franklin* 3
But make the *p* shadow serve thy will. — *Ancient Sage* 110
and *p* now into the night; — *Locksley H., Sixty* 227
poor old Poetry, *p* hence, — " 249
p thro' at once from state to state, — *Demeter and P.* 7
clatter of arms, and voices, and men *p* to and fro. — *Bandit's Death* 24
p souls thro' fire to the fire, — *The Dawn* 4
The *p* of the sweetest soul — *In Mem. lvii* 11
some Were pale as at the *p* of a ghost, — *Com. of Arthur* 264
And o'er it are three *p*'s, and three knights Defend
 ·the *p*'s, — *Gareth and L.* 613
he mark'd his high sweet smile In *p*, — *Balin and Balan* 161
In *p* it glanced upon Hamlet or city, — *Merlin and the G.* 103
Passion (*See also* **Master-passion**) When my *p* seeks
 Pleasance — *Lilian* 8
By veering *p* fann'd, — *Madeline* 29
And those whom *p* hath not blinded, — *Ode to Memory* 117
In thee all *p* becomes passionless, — *Eleänore* 102
the soul and sense Of *P* gazing upon thee. — " 116
A ghost of *p* that no smiles restore— — *The form, the form* 11
Wilt thou find *p*, pain or pride ? — *Two Voices* 243
She had the *p*'s of her kind. — *L. C. V. de Vere* 35
lyre of widest range Struck by all *p*, — *D. of F. Women* 166
How *p* rose thro' circumstantial grades — *Gardener's D.* 240
I ask'd him of his early life, And his first *p* ; — *Edwin Morris* 24
something of a wayward modern mind Dissecting *p*. — " 88
For when my *p* first began, — *Talking Oak* 9
hold *p* in a leash, And not leap forth — *Love and Duty* 40
In one blind cry of *p* and of pain, — " 80
p shall have spent its novel force, — *Locksley Hall* 49
I triumph'd ere my *p* sweeping thro' me — " 131
my foolish *p* were a target for their scorn : — " 146
and all thy *p*'s, match'd with mine, — " 151
There the *p*'s cramp'd no longer — " 167
p's of her mind. As winds from all the compass — *Godiva* 32
He spoke ; the *p* in her moan'd reply — *Enoch Arden* 286
where a *p* yet unborn perhaps Lay hidden — *Aylmer's Field* 101
his *p*'s all in flood And masters of his motion, — " 339
living *p* symbol'd there Were living nerves — " 535
make our *p*'s far too like The discords — *Sea Dreams* 257
flush Of *p* and the first embrace had died — *Lucretius* 3
To lead an errant *p* home again. — " 17
My heart beat thick with *p* and with awe ; — *Princess iii* 190
How much their welfare is a *p* to us. — " 281
She ended with such *p* that the tear, — " *iv* 59
rhythm have dash'd The *p* of the prophetess ; — " 140
Beaten with some great *p* at her heart, — " 388
Leapt fiery *P* from the brinks of death ; — " *vii* 156
loyal *p* for our temperate kings ; — *Ode on Well.* 165
sang Of a *p* that lasts but a day ; — *G. of Swainston* 9
My centred *p* cannot move, — *In Mem lix* 9
His other *p* wholly dies, — " *lxii* 10
my *p* hath not swerved To works of weakness, — " *lxxxv* 49
And my prime *p* in the grave : — " 76
O tell me where the *p*'s meet, — " *lxxxviii* 4
Thy *p* clasps a secret joy : — " 8
And *p* pure in snowy bloom Thro' all the years — " *cix* 11
My love is vaster *p* now ; — " *cxxx* 10
Put down the *p*'s that make earth Hell ! — *Maud I x* 46
mind, when fraught With a *p* so intense — " *II ii* 59
the strong *p* in her made her weep — *Marr. of Geraint* 110
all the *p* of a twelve hours' fast.' — " 306
So burnt he was with *p*, crying out, — " 560
break it, when his *p* masters him. — *Geraint and E.* 43
With more exceeding *p* than of old : — " 335
And all in *p* uttering a dry shriek, — " 461
His *p* half had gauntleted to death, — *Balin and Balan* 220
I, that flattering my true *p*, saw The knights, — *Merlin and V.* 874
Till now the storm, its burst of *p* spent, — " 961
sweet and sudden *p* of youth Toward greatness, — *Lancelot and E.* 282
A fiery family *p* for the name Of Lancelot, — " 477
Crush'd the wild *p* out against the floor — " 742

Passion (*continued*) To blunt or break her *p*.' — *Lancelot and E.* 974
(He meant to break the *p* in her) — " 1079
To break her *p*, some discourtesy — " 1302
My brother ? was it earthly *p* crost ? ' — *Holy Grail* 29
' Nay,' said the knight ; ' for no such *p* mine. — " 30
sent the deathless *p* in her eyes Thro' him, — " 163
Than is the maiden *p* for a maid, — *Guinevere* 479
and grew again To utterance of *p*. — *Lover's Tale i* 547
As I of mine, and my first *p*. — *Sisters (E. and E.)* 67
I spoke it—told her of my *p*, — " 146
For the *p* of battle was in us, — *V. of Maeldune* 96
Till the *p* of battle was on us, — " 111
my boy-phrase ' The *P* of the Past.' — *Ancient Sage* 219
the sacred *p* of the second life. — *Locksley H., Sixty* 68
at last beyond the *p* of the primal clan ? — " 93
strip your own foul *p*'s bare ; — " 141
every serpent *p* kill'd, — " 167
Passionate and show'd their eyes Glaring, and *p* looks, — *Sea Dreams* 236
P tears Follow'd : — *Princess vi* 311
there was *love* in the *p* shriek, — *Maud I i* 57
p heart of the poet is whirl'd into folly and vice. — " *iv* 39
A *p* ballad gallant and gay, — " *v* 4
there rises ever a *p* cry From underneath — " *II i* 5
And there rang on a sudden a *p* cry, — " 33
Let me and my *p* love go by, — " *ii* 77
But there rings on a sudden a *p* cry, — " *iv* 47
' It is time, it is time, O *p* heart,' — " *III vi* 30
' It is time, O *p* heart and morbid eye, — " 32
So *p* for an utter purity Beyond the limit of their bond, — *Merlin and V.* 26
Her God, her Merlin, the one *p* love — " 955
That *p* perfection, my good lord— — *Lancelot and E.* 122
Went on in *p* utterance : — *Guinevere* 611
The *p* moment would not suffer that— — *Lover's Tale iv* 356
P girl tho' I was, an' often at home in disgrace, — *First Quarrel* 15
Back to that *p* answer of full heart — *Sisters (E and E.)* 259
tone so rough that I broke into *p* tears, — *The Wreck* 122
and heard his *p* vow, — *The Flight* 83
the follies, furies, curses, *p* tears, — *Locksley H., Sixty* 39
You wrong me, *p* little friend. — *Epilogue* 10
O you with your *p* shriek for the rights — *Beautiful City* 2
Passionately Then suddenly and *p* she spoke : — *Lancelot and E.* 929
while full *p*, Her head upon her hands, — *Guinevere* 180
Passion-flower He is claspt by a *p-f*. — *Maud I xiv* 8
splendid tear From the *p-f* at the gate. — " *xxii* 60
And the red *p-f* to the cliffs, — *V. of Maeldune* 39
Passionless In thee all passion becomes *p*, — *Eleänore* 102
P bride, divine Tranquillity, — *Lucretius* 266
P, pale, cold face, star-sweet — *Maud I iii* 4
Where if I cannot be gay let a *p* peace be my lot, — " *iv* 50
Innumerable, pitiless, *p* eyes, — " *xviii* 38
The bridesmaid pale, statuelike, *p*— — *Sisters (E. and E.)* 212
High, self-contain'd, and *p*, — *Guinevere* 406
Passion-pale *P-p* they met And greeted. — " 99
Passive The *p* oxen gaping. — *Amphion* 72
Worried his *p* ear with petty wrongs — *Enoch Arden* 352
when he ceased, in one cold *p* hand — *Lancelot and E.* 1201
p sailor wrecks at last In ever-silent seas ; — *Ancient Sage* 136
Passport no false *p* to that easy realm, — *Aylmer's Field* 183
Past (*adj.*) (*See also* **Past** (verb)) Strange friend, *p*, present, — *In Mem. cxxix* 9
all experience *p* became Consolidate in mind — *Two Voices* 365
Desiring what is mingled with *p* years, — *D. of F. Women* 282
She took the body of my *p* delight, — *Lover's Tale i* 681
Past (*adv.*) seem to flicker *p* thro' sun and shade, — *Ancient Sage* 100
Past (*prep.*) Lame and old, and *p* his time, — *Locksley H., Sixty* 227
Give me your prayers, for he is *past* your prayers, — *Aylmer's Field* 751
Not *past* the living fount of pity in Heaven. — " 752
For it was *past* the time of Easterday. — *Gareth and L.* 186
when old and gray, And *past* desire ! ' — *Last Tournament* 628
old, Gray-hair'd, and *past* desire, — " 653
wind, and *past* his ear Went shrilling, — *Pass of Arthur* 32
raising her Still higher, *past* all peril, — *Lover's Tale i* 394
to be sewer it be *past* 'er time. — *Spinster's S's.* 5
Then home, and *past* the ruin'd mill. — *The Ring* 156
Now *past* her feet the swallow circling flies, — *Prog. of Spring* 44

Past-Pass'd (verb) (*continued*)   And *past* to Enid's tent; *Geraint and E.* 922

So *past* the days.	"	930
they *past* With Arthur to Caerleon upon Usk.	"	945
and they *past* to their own land.	"	955
those three kingless years Have *past*—	*Balin and Balan*	64
so turning side by side They *past*,	"	280
Past eastward from the falling sun.	"	320
For hate and loathing, would have *past* him by;	"	388
She *past*; and Vivien murmur'd after 'Go!	*Merlin and V.*	98
eight years *past*, eight jousts had been,	*Lancelot and E.*	67
Past inward, as she came from out the tower.	"	346
Meanwhile the new companions *past* away	"	399
Arthur to the banquet, dark in mood, *Past*,	"	565
Past to her chamber, and there flung herself	"	609
Thence to the court he *past*;	"	706
Past up the still rich city to his kin,	"	802
past beneath the weirdly-sculptured gates	"	844
and *past* Down thro' the dim rich city to the fields,	"	846
past In either twilight ghost-like to and fro	"	848
ten slow mornings *past*, and on the eleventh	"	1133
Past like a shadow thro' the field,	"	1140
Diamonds to meet them, and they *past* away.	"	1237
slowly *past* the barge Whereon the lily maid	"	1241
Had *pass'd* into the silent life of prayer,	*Holy Grail*	4
the Grail *Past*, and the beam decay'd,	"	122
Fashion'd by Merlin ere he *past* away.	"	168
none might see who bare it, and it *past*.	"	190
showers of flowers Fell as we *past*;	"	349
thence I *past* Far thro' a ruinous city,	"	428
past thro' Pagan realms, and made them mine,	"	478
the sweet Grail Glided and *past*,	"	695
And up into the sounding hall I *past*;	"	827
and the sweet smell of the fields *Past*,	*Pelleas and E.*	6
reach'd Caerleon, ere they *past* to lodging, she,	"	125
he *past*, And heard but his own steps,	"	415
forth he *past*, and mounting on his horse	"	456
with mortal cold *Past* from her;	*Last Tournament*	28
that unhappy child *Past* in her barge:	"	45
When all the goodlier guests are *past* away,	"	158
Our one white day of Innocence hath *past*,	"	218
The leaf is dead, the yearning *past* away:	"	277
Isolt With ruby-circled neck, but evermore *Past*,	"	365
Mark her lord had *past*, the Cornish King,	"	382
lookt So sweet, that halting, in he *past*,	"	388
but turning, *past* and gain'd Tintagil,	"	504
he *past*, Love-loyal to the least wish	*Guinevere*	125
while he *past* the dim-lit woods,	"	251
(When first I learnt thee hidden here) is *past*.	"	539
is also *past*—in part. And all is *past*, the sin	"	542
past To where beyond these voices there is peace.	"	697
when that moan had *past* for evermore,	"	441
Past with thee thro' thy people and their love,	*To the Queen* ii 7
breathless body of her good deeds *past*.	*Lover's Tale* i 217
We *past* from light to dark.	"	516
Past thro' into his citadel, the brain,	"	631
when the woful sentence hath been *past*,	"	788
did strike my forehead as I *past*;	" ii 19
They *past* on, The lordly Phantasms! in their floating folds They *past*	"	98
past and flow'd away To those unreal billows:	"	195
Suddenly came her notice and we *past*,	" iv 154
Past thro' his visions to the burial:	"	357
mounting these He *past* for ever from his native land;	"	387
in the pleasant times that had *past*,	*First Quarrel* 55
Lord Howard *past* away with five ships of war	*The Revenge* 13
Whirl'd by, which, after it had *past* me,	*Sisters (E. and E.)* 86
whirling landaulet For ever *past* me by:	"	115
The morning of our marriage, *past* away—	"	244
past to this ward where the younger children are laid:	*In the Child. Hosp.* 27
and Emmie had *past* away.	"	72
but only a whisper that *past*:	*Def. of Lucknow* 50
On *them* the smell of burning had not *past*.	*Sir J. Oldcastle* 177
and we *past* Over that undersea isle,	*V. of Maeldune* 76
And we *past* to the Isle of Witches	"	97

Past-Pass'd (verb) (*continued*)   So saying, light-foot Iris

pass'd away.	*Achilles over the T.*	1
light to the King till he *past* away	*To Prin. F. of H.*	1
win all praise from all Who *past* it,	*Tiresias*	84
past, in sleep, away By night,	"	203
and *past* Over the range and the change	*The Wreck*	69
I remember I thought, as we *past*,	*Despair*	11
We had *past* from a cheerless night	"	28
I had *past* into perfect quiet at length	"	66
for she *past* from the night to the night.	"	72
past into the Nameless, as a cloud Melts into Heaven.	*Ancient Sage* 233
And *past* the range of Night and Shadow—	"	283
One golden curl, his golden gift, before he *past* away.	*The Flight*	36
The lark has *past* from earth to Heaven	"	62
and thy shadow *past* Before me, crying	*Demeter and P.*	93
breath that *past* With all the cold of winter.	*The Ring*	32
then I *pass'd* Home, and thro' Venice,	"	191
And gave it me, who *pass'd* it down her own,	"	270
spoke no more, but turn'd and *pass'd* away.	"	342
A cold air *pass'd* between us,	"	380
the grating of a sepulchre, *Past* over both.	"	401
face Look'd in upon me like a gleam and *pass'd*,	"	420
Would I had *past* in the morning	*By an Evolution.*	10
She waked a bird of prey that scream'd and *past*;	*Death of Œnone*	87
mixt herself with *him* and *past* in fire.	"	106
there past a crowd With shameless laughter,	*St. Telemachus*	38

Pastern   cream-white mule his *p* set: *Sir L. and Q. G.* 31

Pastime   play'd In his free field, and *p* made,   *Two Voices* 320

You thought to break a country heart For *p*,	*L. C. V. de Vere* 4
Why took ye not your *p*?	*Love and Duty* 28
At our old *p*'s in the hall	*In Mem. xxx* 5
he beats his chair For *p*,	" *lxvi* 14
in a tilt For *p*; yea, he said it:	*Gareth and L.* 543
And *p* both of hawk and hound,	*Marr. of Geraint* 711
who take Their *p* now the trustful King is gone!'	*Lancelot and E.* 101
in one full field Of gracious *p*,	*Holy Grail* 324
Are winners in this *p* of our King.	*Last Tournament* 199
following her old *p* of the brook,	*The Ring* 354

Pastor   being used to find her *p* texts,   *Aylmer's Field* 606

Pastoral   Nor *p* rivulet that swerves To left and right   *In Mem. c.* 14

Upon a *p* slope as fair,	*Maud I xviii* 19
and Peace Pipe on her *p* hillock a languid note,	" *III vi* 24

Pasturage   wither'd holt or tilth or *p*.   *Enoch Arden* 675

Pasture   Thro' crofts and *p*'s wet with dew   *Two Voices* 14

gray twilight pour'd On dewy *p*'s, dewy trees.	*Palace of Art* 86
In tracts of *p* sunny-warm,	"	94
For all the sloping *p* murmur'd,	*Princess, Pro.* 55
Silvery willow, *P* and plowland,	*Merlin and the G.* 54

Pasturing   He pointed out a *p* colt, and said: *The Brook* 136

Pasty   half-cut-down, a *p* costly-made,   *Audley Court* 23

what stick ye round The *p*?   *Gareth and L.* 1073

Pat   *p* The girls upon the cheek,   *Talking Oak* 43

Patch (s)   Or while the *p* was worn;   " 64

Upon my proper *p* of soil   *Amphion* 99

Patch (verb)   three castles *p* my tatter'd coat?   *Princess* ii 416

Patch'd   and refuse *p* with moss.   *Vision of Sin* 212

one was *p* and blurr'd and lustreless   *Marr. of Geraint* 649

Patent   Last night, their mask was *p*,   *Princess* iv 326

Paternoster   *See* **Pather**

Path   (*See also* **Forest-path, Side-path**)   why dare *P*'s in the desert?   *Supp. Confessions* 79

He, stepping down By zig-zag *p*'s,	*M. d'Arthur* 50
Till all the *p*'s were dim,	*Talking Oak* 298
the charm did talk About his *p*,	*Day-Dm., Arrival* 22
To silence from the *p*'s of men;	*L'Envoi* 6
footstep seem'd to fall beside her *p*,	*Enoch Arden* 514
up the steep hill Trod out a *p*:	*Sea Dreams* 121
you planed her *p* To Lady Psyche,	*Princess* iv 315
The *p* of duty was the way to glory: (repeat)	*Ode on Well.* 202, 210
has won His *p* upward, and prevail'd,	" 214
The *p* of duty be the way to glory:	" 224
The *p* by which we twain did go,	*In Mem. xxii* 1
where the *p* we walk'd began To slant	" 9
My *p*'s are in the fields I know,	" *xl* 31
The *p* we came by, thorn and flower,	" *xlvi* 2

Pavilion (*continued*) then this gale Tore my *p* from the tenting-pin, — *Holy Grail* 747
three *p*'s rear'd Above the bushes, gilden-peakt: — *Pelleas and E.* 428
The silk *p*'s of King Arthur raised — *Guinevere* 394
That crown'd the state *p* of the King, — ,, 399
Pavilion'd *See* **Cloud-pavilion'd**
Paw Folded her lion *p*'s, and look'd to Thebes. — *Tiresias* 149
Paw'd *p* his beard, and mutter'd 'catalepsy.' — *Princess i* 20
Kittenlike he roll'd And *p* about her sandal. — ,, iii 182
Pay (*See also* **Paäy**) *p* Meet adoration to my household gods, — *Ulysses* 41
clamouring, 'If we *p*, we starve!' — *Godiva* 15
'If they *p* this tax, they starve.' — ,, 20
half-crown, Which I shall have to *p*? — *Will Water.* 156
Or means to *p* the voice who best could tell — *Enoch Arden* 266
a voice, with which to *p* the debt Of boundless love — *Ode on Well.* 156
Or later, *p* one visit here, — *To F. D. Maurice* 45
Nor *p* but one, but come for many, — ,, 47
a debt, That I never can hope to *p*; — *Maud I xix* 88
No tribute will we *p*:' — *Com. of Arthur* 513
Will *p* thee all thy wages, and to boot. — *Gareth and L.* 1005
And I will *p* you worship; — *Merlin and V.* 228
This father *p*'s his debt with me, — *The Flight* 20
With a purse to *p* for the show. — *Dead Prophet* 8
Paynim But rather proven in his *P* wars — *Balin and Balan* 38
a remnant that were left *P* amid their circles, — *Holy Grail* 664
Troop'd round a *P* harper once, — *Last Tournament* 322
thy *P* bard Had such a mastery of his mystery — ,, 326
Peä 'ere a beän an' yonder a *p*; — *N. Farmer, O. S.* 46
Pluksh!!! the hens i' the *p*'s! — *Village Wife* 124
Peace God gave her *p*; her land reposed; — *To the Queen* 26
And Thou and *p* to earth were born. — *Supp. Confessions* 26
a world of *p* And confidence, day after day; — ,, 29
A haunt of ancient *P*. — *Palace of Art* 88
And let the world have *p* or wars, — ,, 182
the dear old time, and all my *p* of mind; — *May Queen, N. Y's. E.* 6
good man, the clergyman, has told me words of *p*. — ,, *Con.* 2
Is there any *p* In ever climbing up — *Lotos-Eaters, C. S.* 49
The place of him that sleeps in *p*. — *To J. S.* 68
Sleep sweetly, tender heart, in *p*: — ,, 69
Would pace the troubled land, like *P*; — *Love thou thy land* 84
when William died, he died at *p* With all men; — *Dora* 144
breathing health and *p* upon her breast: — *Audley Court* 68
Whose foresight preaches *p*, — *Love and Duty* 34
cross thy thoughts Too sadly for their *p*, — ,, 89
universal *P* Lie like a shaft of light — *Golden Year* 48
Pure lilies of eternal *p*, — *Sir Galahad* 67
Across the whirlwind's heart of *p*, — *The Voyage* 87
And pass his days in *p* among his own. — *Enoch Arden* 147
Philip's true heart, which hunger'd for her *p* — ,, 272
all the warmth, the *p*, the happiness, — ,, 761
Help me not to break in upon her *p*. — ,, 787
sleeps in *p*: and he, poor Philip, — *The Brook* 190
wounded *p* which each had prick'd to death. — *Aylmer's Field* 52
hung With wings of brooding shelter o'er her *p*, — ,, 139
Jilted I was: I say it for your *p*. — ,, 354
Prince of *p*, the Mighty God, — ,, 669
The things belonging to thy *p* and ours! — ,, 740
I sought but *p*; No critic I— — *Princess i* 144
'*p*! and why should I not play The Spartan Mother — ,, ii 282
lead The new light up, and culminate in *p*, — ,, 348
'*P*, you young savage of the Northern wild! — ,, iii 247
P be with her. She is dead. — ,, iv 136
marble Muses, looking *p*. Not *p* she look'd, — ,, 489
P! there are those to avenge us and they come: — ,, 501
resolder'd *p*, whereon Follow'd his tale. — ,, v 47
one The silken *priest* of *p*, one this, — ,, 184
heavy dews Gather'd by night and *p*, — ,, 244
but other thoughts than *P* Burnt in us, — ,, 245
I that prated *p*, when first I heard War-music, — ,, 265
boys Brake on us at our books, and marr'd our *p*, — ,, 395
found fair *p* once more among the sick. — ,, vii 44
plighted troth, and were at *p*. — ,, 83
Far-shadowing from the west, a land of *p*; — ,, *Con.* 42
P, his triumph will be sung — *Ode on Well.* 232
P, it is a day of pain (repeat) — ,, 235, 238

Peace (*continued*) But though we love kind *P* so well, — *Third of Feb.* 9
Who lets once more in *p* the nations meet, — *Ode Inter. Exhib.* 4
The works of *p* with works of war. — ,, 28
And *p* be yours, the *p* of soul in soul! — *W. to Marie Alex.* 47
Between your peoples truth and manful *p*, — ,, 49
mine in a time of *p*, (repeat) — *Grandmother* 89, 94
in this Book, little Annie, the message is one of *P*. — ,, 96
And age is a time of *p*, so it be free from pain, — ,, 97
passes by To some more perfect *p*. — *Requiescat* 8
Calm and deep *p* on this high wold, — *In Mem. xi* 5
Calm and deep *p* in this wide air, — ,,
P and goodwill, goodwill and *p*, *P* and goodwill, — ,, xxviii 11
As daily vexes household *p*, — ,, xxix 2
'Twere best at once to sink to *p*, — ,, xxxiv 13
Days order'd in a wealthy *p*, — ,, xlvi 11
P; come away: the song of woe — ,, lvii 1
P; come away: we do him wrong To sing so wildly: — ,, 3
idly broke the *p* Of hearts that beat from day to day, — ,, lviii 5
But stay'd in *p* with God and man. — ,, lxxx 8
A hundred spirits whisper '*P*.' — ,, lxxxvi 16
and shake The pillars of domestic *p*. — ,, xc 20
My spirit is at *p* with all. — ,, xciv 8
Ring in the thousand years of *p*. — ,, cvi 28
Why do they prate of the blessings of *P*? — *Maud I i* 21
Is it *p* or war? Civil war, as I think, — ,, 27
P sitting under her olive, — ,, 33
P in her vineyard—yes!— — ,, 36
Is it *p* or war? better, war! — ,, 47
if I cannot be gay let a passionless *p* be my lot, — ,, iv 50
P, angry spirit, and let him be! — ,, xiii 44
For I thought the dead had *p*, — ,, II v 15
To have no *p* in the grave, — ,, 16
and *P* Pipe on her pastoral hillock — ,, III vi 9
love of a *p* that was full of wrongs — ,, 40
For the *p*, that I deem'd no *p*, is over and done, — ,, 50
fruitful strifes and rivalries of *p*— — *Ded. of Idylls* 8
nor could I part in *p* Till this were told.' — *Com. of Arthur* 393
P to thee, woman, with thy loves and hates! — *Gareth and L.* 373
as if the world were one Of utter *p*, and love, — ,, 1289
fought Hard with himself, and seem'd at length in *p*. — *Balin and Balan* 239
one said 'Eat in *p*! a liar is he, — ,, 607
'*P*, child! of overpraise and overblame — *Merlin and V.* 90
one had watch'd, and had not held his *p*: — ,, 162
sunn'd The world to *p* again: — ,, 639
To sleek her ruffled *p* of mind, — ,, 899
if I schemed against thy *p* in this, — ,, 930
ravaged woodland yet once more To *p*; — ,, 964
saying, '*P* to thee, Sweet sister,' — *Lancelot and E.* 996
'*P*,' said her father, 'O my child, — ,, 1062
For pity of thine own self, *P*, Lady, *p*: — *Pelleas and E.* 254
Ye know yourselves: how can ye bide at *p*, — ,, 265
But never let me bide one hour at *p*.' — ,, 387
P at his heart, and gazing at a star — ,, 559
'*P* to thine eagle-borne Dead nestling, — *Last Tournament* 33
past To where beyond these voices there is *p*. — *Guinevere* 698
wife and friend Is traitor to my *p*, — *Pass. of Arthur* 25
thou bringest Not *p*, a sword, a fire. — *Sir J. Oldcastle* 36
crowd's roar fell as at the '*P*, be still!' — *Columbus* 13
Might sow and reap in *p*, — *Epilogue* 13
must fight To make true *p* his own, — ,, 27
P, let it be! for I loved him, — *Vastness* 36
Where stood the sheaf of *P*: — *The Ring* 247
Before the feud of Gods had marr'd our *p*, — *Death of Œnone* 32
only conquers men to conquer *p*, — *Akbar's Dream* 15
Truth and *P* And Love and Justice came — ,, 180
Truth, *P*, Love and Justice came and dwelt therein, — ,, 193
Peaceful Her *p* being slowly passes by — *Requiescat* 7
thro' the *p* court she crept And whisper'd: — *Merlin And V.* 139
'Mine enemies Pursue me, but, O *p* Sisterhood, — *Guinevere* 140
And withers on the breast of *p* love; — *Lover's Tale i* 10
My close of earth's experience May prove as *p* as his own. — *Tiresias* 217
in that point of *p* light? — *Locksley H., Sixty* 190
Peacefuller when a balmier breeze curl'd over a *p* sea, — *The Wreck* 133
Peacemaker let the fair white-wing'd *p* fly — *Ode Inter. Exhib.* 34
Peace-offering last Love-offering and *p-o* — *Last Tournament* 748

Peach Solved in the tender blushes of the p ; — *Prog. of Spring* 34
Peacock On the tree-tops a crested p lit, — *Œnone* 104
The p in his laurel bower, — *Day-Dm., Sleep. P.* 15
The parrot scream'd, the p squall'd, — " *Revival* 12
And smooth'd a petted p down with that : — " *Princess ii* 456
Now droops the milkwhite p like a ghost, — " *vii* 180
campanili grew By bays, the p's neck in hue; — *The Daisy* 14
bright and light as the crest Of a p, — *Maud I xvi* 17
placed a p in his pride Before the damsel, — *Gareth and L.* 850
left The damsel by the p in his pride, — " 870
Peacock'd p up with Lancelot's noticing. — " 719
Peacock-yewtree And p-y of the lonely Hall, — *Enoch Arden* 99
The p-y and the lonely Hall, — " 608
Peak (*See also* **Bosom-peak, Eagle-peak**) Twin p's
shadow'd with pine slope — *Leonine Eleg.* 10
Hesper is stayed between the two p's; — " 11
Some blue p's in the distance rose, — *Dying Swan* 11
between The snowy p and snow-white cataract — *Œnone* 211
high on every p a statue seem'd To hang — *Palace of Art* 37
Lotos blooms below the barren p: — *Lotos-Eaters, C. S.* 100
By p's that flamed, or, all in shade, — *The Voyage* 41
The mountain wooded to the p, — *Enoch Arden* 572
climbs a p to gaze O'er land and main, — *Princess vii* 35
THE voice and the P (repeat) — *Voice and the P.* 1, 37
Hast thou no voice, O P, — " 9
'I am the voice of the P, — " 11
The valley, the voice, the p, the star Pass, — " 27
P is high and flush'd At his highest — " 29
P is high, and the stars are high, — " 31
every height comes out, and jutting p — *Spec. of Iliad.* 13
As over Sinaï's of old, — *In Mem. xcvi* 22
the budded p's of the wood are bow'd — *Maud I vi* 4
up to a height, the p Haze-hidden, — *Com. of Arthur* 429
Stream'd to the p, and mingled with the haze — " 435
tipt with lessening p And pinnacle, — *Gareth and L.* 308
A huge pavilion like a mountain p — " 1364
sighs to see the p Sun-flush'd, — *Balin and Balan* 165
a cloud, man-shaped, from mountain p, — *To the Queen ii* 40
isle-side flashing down from the p — *V. of Maeldune* 45
the p of the mountain was apples, — " 63
p sent up one league of fire to the Northern Star; — " 72
For some, descending from the sacred p — *Pref. Son. 19th Cent.* 9
One naked p—the sister of the sun — *Tiresias* 30
two known p's they stand ever spreading — *Parnassus* 11
HAD the fierce ashes of some fiery p — *St. Telemachus* 1
Peak'd A mountain islet pointed and p ; — *The Islet* 15
Peakt *See* **Gilden-peakt**
Peaky Or over hills with p tops engrail'd, — *Palace of Art* 113
The p islet shifted shapes, — *The Voyage* 33
Peal (s) P after p, the British battle broke, — *Buonaparte* 7
With p's of genial clamour sent — *Will Water.* 187
A single p of bells below, — *In Mem. civ* 5
whole wood-world is one full p of praise. — *Balin and Balan* 450
In clanging cadence jangling p on p— — *Lover's Tale iii* 22
p Of laughter drew me thro' the glimmering glades — *Sisters (E. and E.)* 115
Then a p that shakes the portal— — *Locksley H., Sixty* 263
Peal (verb) sweet church bells began to p. — *Two Voices* 408
At this a hundred bells began to p, — *M. d'Arthur, Ep.* 29
the watchman p The sliding season: — *Gardener's D.* 182
shout Of His descending p's from Heaven, — *Romney's R.* 127
Peal'd an answer p from that high land, — *Vision of Sin* 221
And all about us p the nightingale, — *Princess i* 220
old songs that p From knoll to knoll, — *In Mem. xcv* 13
Out of the city a blast of music p. — *Gareth and L.* 238
close upon it p A sharp quick thunder.' — *Holy Grail* 695
the full city p Thee and thy Prince ! — *To the Queen ii* 26
till the great day P on us with that music — *Lover's Tale iv* 65
and whenever their voices p — *V. of Maeldune* 29
thunder of God p over us all the day, — " 113
and p from an organ,— — *The Wreck* 53
Pealing He heard the p of his parish bells; — *Enoch Arden* 615
trumpet in the distance p news Of better, — *Princess iv* 81
single church below the hill Is p, — *In Mem. civ* 4
wild voice p up to the sunny sky, — *Maud I v* 13
'Hark the victor p there !' — *Gareth and L.* 1318

Pear That held the p to the gable-wall. — *Mariana* 4
body slight and round, and like a p In growing, — *Walk. to the Mail* 53
tumbled half the mellowing p's ! — *In Mem. lxxxix* 20
and with golden masses of p, — *V. of Maeldune* 60
Peärky (pert) An' thou was as p as owt, — *Church-warden, etc.* 35
Pearl a brow of p Tress'd with redolent ebony, — *Arabian Nights* 137
In a golden curl With a comb of p, — *The Mermaid* 7
With a comb of p I would comb my hair; — " 10
morning driv'n her plow of p Far furrowing — *Love and Duty* 99
Forth streaming from a braid of p: — *Day-Dm., Sleep B.* 6
now a rain of p's, Or steep-up spout — *Princess, Pro.* 62
shook and fell, an erring p Lost in her bosom: — " *iv* 60
When Time hath sunder'd shell from p.' — *In Mem. lii* 16
in this stormy gulf have found a p — *Maud I xviii* 42
In gloss of satin and glimmer of p's, — " *xxii* 55
Small and pure as a p, — " *II ii* 2
Made with her right a comb of p to part The lists — *Merlin and V.* 244
burst in dancing, and the p's were spilt ; — " 452
But nevermore the same two sister p's — " 454
Yet is there one true line, the p of p's: — " 459
Guinevere, The p of beauty: — *Lancelot and E.* 114
' A red sleeve Broider'd with p's,' — " 373
wore the sleeve Of scarlet, and the p's ; — " 502
sleeve of scarlet, broider'd with great p's, — " 604
carved and cut, and half the p's away, — " 807
So pray you, add my diamonds to her p's ; — " 1224
gateways in a glory like one p— — *Holy Grail* 527
For I have flung thee p's and find thee swine.' — *Last Tournament* 310
since I care not for thy p's. Swine ? — " 314
The Gospel, the Priest's p, flung down to swine— — *Sir J. Oldcastle* 116
and those twelve gates, P— — *Columbus* 87
Pearl-necklace Is like the fair p-n of the Queen, — *Merlin and V.* 451
Pearly Upon her p shoulder leaning cold, — *Œnone* 140
Sleet of diamond-drift and p hail; — *Vision of Sin* 22
Peasant (adj.) Till the p cow shall butt the ' Lion passant ' — *Locksley H., Sixty* 248
Peasant (s) arts of war The p Joan and others ; — *Princess ii* 163
When the wild p rights himself, — " *iv* 385
p's maim the helpless horse, and drive — *Locksley H., Sixty* 95
Pebble Counting the dewy p's, fix'd in thought; — *M. d'Arthur* 84
I babble on the p's. — *The Brook* 42
Counting the dewy p's, fix'd in thought, — *Pass. of Arthur* 252
Peck all wing'd nothings p him dead ! — *Marr. of Geraint* 275
Peculiar When thy p difference Is cancell'd — *Two Voices* 41
Each garlanded with her p flower — *Gardener's D.* 202
Some p mystic grace Made her — *Maud I xiii* 39
And a p treasure, brooking not Exchange — *Lover's Tale i* 447
Ped (paid) he p me back wid the best — *Tomorrow* 42
Pedant held his sceptre like a p's wand — *Princess i* 27
Pedestal Upon an even p with man.' — " *iii* 224
push'd by rude hands from its p, — " *v* 58
seat you sole upon my p Of worship— — *Merlin and V.* 878
Peelè that P the Goddess would wallow — *Kapiolani* 8
handle or gather the berries of P! — " 20
climb to the dwelling of P the Goddess ! — " 22
None but the terrible P remaining — " 28
crying ' I dare her, let P avenge herself ' ! — " 32
Peep (s) birdie say In her nest at p of day ? — *Sea Dreams* 294
baby say, In her bed at p of day ? — " 302
passing one, at the high p of dawn, — *Merlin and V.* 560
Peep (verb) For any male thing but to p at us.' — *Princess, Pro.* 152
Peep'd-peept peep'd in, and saw The boy set up betwixt — *Dora* 130
Peep'd,—but his eyes, before they had their will, — *Godiva* 69
underneath The head of Holofernes peep'd — *Princess iv* 227
thro' the parted silks the tender face Peep'd, — " *vii* 61
Two bright stars Peep'd into the shell. — *Minnie and Winnie* 14
Peept the winsome face of Edith — *Locksley H., Sixty* 260
Peer (s) Could find no statelier than his p's — *Two Voices* 29
'Forerun thy p's, thy time, — " 88
Regard the weakness of thy p's, — *Love thou thy land* 24
drunk delight of battle with my p's, — *Ulysses* 16
in sight of Collatine And all his p's, — *Lucretius* 239
Surprise thee ranging with thy p's. — *In Mem. xliv* 12
Thy spirit in time among thy p's ; — " *xci* 6
to yield thee grace beyond thy p's.' — *Last Tournament* 743

Peer (s) (*continued*) their claim to be thy *p's*; — *To Victor Hugo* 6
Peer (verb) not to pry and *p* on your reserve, — *Princess* iv 419
she *p's* along the tremulous deep, — *Demeter and P.* 14
Peerage the savage yells Of Uther's *p* died, — *Com. of Arthur* 257
Peer'd Or from the crevice *p* about. — *Mariana* 65
I *p* athwart the chancel pane And saw the altar — *The Letters* 3
and of all Who *p* at him so keenly, — *Aylmer's Field* 817
I *p* thro' tomb and cave, — *Demeter and P.* 70
Peereth The frail bluebell *p* over — *A Dirge* 37
Peering thro' the portal-arch *P* askance, — *Merlin and V.* 100
Before a thousand *p* littlenesses, — *Ded. of Idylls* 26
Peerless my glory to have loved One *p*, — *Lancelot and E.* 1091
As thou art a knight *p*.' — " 1282
(Those *p* flowers which in the rudest wind — *Ode to Memory* 24
Peewit *See* **Pewit**
Peg The mantles from the golden *p's* — *Day-Dm., Sleep P.* 19
'Let me screw thee up a *p*: — *Vision of Sin* 87
Peleïan came Into the fair *P* banquet-hall, — *Œnone* 225
Peleïon o'er the great *P's* head Burn'd, — *Achilles over the T.* 28
Peleus Gods Ranged in the halls of *p*, — *Œnone* 81
Pelf dropt the goose, and caught the *p*, — *The Goose* 13
Pelican I saw The *p* on the casque — *Holy Grail* 635
I remember now That *p* on the casque: — " 700
Pellam *P* the King, who held and lost with Lot — *Balin and Balan* 1
P, once A Christless foe of thine — " 96
till castle of a King, the hall Of *P*, — " 332
Then spake the men of *P* crying — " 337
mark'd The portal of King *P's* chapel — " 405
P's feeble cry 'Stay, stay him!' — " 420
King *P's* holy spear, Reputed to be red with
sinless blood, — " 556
'Brother, I dwelt a day in *P's* hall: — " 605
Whom *P* drove away with holy heat. — " 611
Pelleas (a **Knight of the Round Table**) and thro' these
a youth, *P*, — *Pelleas and E.* 5
had *P* for his lady won The golden circlet, — " 13
this new knight, Sir *P* of the isles— — " 17
and slowly *P* drew To that dim day, — " 29
It seem'd to *P* that the fern without Burnt — " 34
P rose, And loosed his horse. — " 60
P gazing thought, 'Is Guinevere herself so beautiful?' — " 69
so did *P* lend All the young beauty of his own soul — " 82
And win me this fine circlet, *P*, — " 128
'O happy world,' thought *P*, — " 136
P look'd Noble among the noble, — " 151
P might obtain his lady's love, — " 161
all day long Sir *P* kept the field With honour: — " 168
and seeing *P* droop, Said Guinevere, — " 178
knights all set their faces home, Sir *P* follow'd. — " 188
'These be the ways of ladies,' *P* thought, — " 209
P overthrew them as they dash'd Against him — " 221
they went, And *P* overthrew them one by one; — " 230
'Nay,' said *P*, 'but forbear; — " 280
And *P* overthrew them, one to three; — " 287
first her anger, leaving *P*, burn'd Full — " 289
P answer'd, 'Lady, for indeed I loved you — " 296
P answer'd, 'O, their wills are hers — " 324
P lent his horse and all his arms, — " 358
I have slain this *P* whom ye hate: — " 372
'Lo! *P* is dead—he told us— — " 377
Lost in a doubt, *P* wandering Waited, — " 392
this lay—Which *P* had heard sung before the Queen, — " 397
did *P* in an utter shame Creep with his shadow — " 440
the poor *p* whom she call'd her fool? — " 474
'Liar, for thou hast not slain This *P*!' — " 491
her ever-veering fancy turn'd To *P*, — " 494
fared it with Sir *P* as with one Who gets a wound — " 528
P, leaping up, Ran thro' the doors and vaulted — " 538
weary steed of *P* floundering flung His rider, — " 574
Sir *P* in brief while Caught his unbroken limbs — " 584
then on *P*, him Who had not greeted her, — " 590
Then she, turning to *P*, 'O young knight, — " 595
P lifted up an eye so fierce She quail'd; — " 601
Pelt *p* me with starry spangles and shells, — *The Merman* 28
That *p* us in the porch with flowers. — *In Mem., Con.* 68

Pelt (*continued*) *p* your offal at her face. — *Locksley H., Sixty* 134
Pelted And *p* with outrageous epithets, — *Aylmer's Field* 286
Pen With such a pencil, such a *p*, — *To E. L.* 6
Penance Betray'd my secret *p*, — *St. S. Stylites* 68
prate Of *p's* I cannot have gone thro', — " 101
power with Heaven From my long *p*: — " 144
From my high nest of *p* here proclaim — " 167
And here I lay this *p* on myself, — *Geraint and E.* 739
And all the *p* the Queen laid upon me — " 854
earth about him everywhere, despite All fast and *p*. — *Holy Grail* 631
if I do not there is *p* given— — *Guinevere* 187
'Heresy.—*P*?' 'Fast, Hairshirt — *Sir J. Oldcastle* 141
Do *p* in his heart, God hears him.' — " 143
Pence (*See also* **Peter's-pence**) Or that eternal want of *p*, — *Will Water.* 43
Thy latter days increased with *p* — " 219
is it shillins an' *p*? — *N. Farmer, N. S.* 42
Even in dreams to the chink of his *p*, — *Maud* I x 43
Pencil Came, drew your *p* from you, — *Gardener's D.* 26
wave of such a breast As never *p* drew. — " 140
'Then I took a *p*, and wrote On the mossy stone, — *Edward Gray* 25
With such a *p*, such a pen, — *To E. L.* 6
Into the shadowing *p's* naked forms — *Lover's Tale* ii 180
Pencill'd *See* **Shadowy-pencill'd, Tender-pencill'd**
Pendent (*See also* **Roof-pendent**) Her *p* hands, and
narrow meagre face — *Aylmer's Field* 813
With many a *p* bell and fragrant star, — *Death of Œnone* 13
Pendragon The dread *P*, Britain's King of kings, — *Lancelot and E.* 424
Came round their great *P*, saying — " 528
Pendragonship The Dragon of the great *P*, (*repeat*) — *Guinevere* 398, 598
Peneïan The long divine *P* pass, — *To E. L.* 3
Pension title, place, or touch Of *p*, — *Love thou thy land* 26
Pension'd Half-sickening of his *p* afternoon, — *Aylmer's Field* 461
Pensive Of *p* thought and aspect pale, — *Margaret* 6
A *p* pair, and you were gay — *Miller's D.* 164
The fulness of the *p* mind; — *Day-Dm., L'Envoi* 48
Edith, whose *p* beauty, perfect else, — *Aylmer's Field* 70
And *p* tendance in the all-weary noons, — *Princess* vii 102
Yet feels, as in a *p* dream, — *In Mem.* lxiv 17
Their *p* tablets round her head, — " Con. 51
Gazing for one *p* moment on that founder — *Locksley H., Sixty* 32
Pent (*See also* **Long-pent**) I lay *P* in a roofless close — *St. S. Stylites* 74
fretful as the wind *P* in a crevice — *Princess* iii 81
Pentagram Some figure like a wizard *p* — *The Brook* 103
Pentecost Hereafter thou, fulfilling *P*, — *Sir J. Oldcastle* 33
Penthouse A snowy *p* for his hollow eyes, — *Merlin and V.* 808
Penuel In the dim tract of *P*. — *Clear-headed friend* 29
People 'She wrought her *p* lasting good; — *To the Queen* 24
Broad-based upon her *p's* will, — " 35
As when a mighty *p* rejoice With shawms, — *Dying Swan* 31
And up and down the *p* go, — *L. of Shalott* i 6
On to God's house the *p* prest: — *Two Voices* 409
The *p* here, a beast of burden slow, — *Palace of Art* 149
I perish by this *p* which I made,— — *M. d'Arthur* 22
speak in the aftertime To all the *p*, — " 108
all the *p* cried, 'Arthur is come again: — " Ep. 23
scarce can hear the *p* hum About the column's base, — *St. S. Stylites* 38
The silly *p* take me for a saint, — " 127
Good *p*, you do ill to kneel to me. — " 133
O Lord, Aid all this foolish *p*; — " 223
by slow prudence to make mild A rugged *p*, — *Ulysses* 37
With the standards of the *p's* — *Locksley Hall* 126
Slowly comes a hungry *p*, — " 135
loved the *p* well, And loathed to see them overtax'd; — *Godiva* 8
but that she would loose The *p*: — " 38
And the *p* loved her much. — *L. of Burleigh* 76
Then her *p*, softly treading, — " 97
He gave the *p* of his best: — *You might have won* 25
The younger *p* making holiday, — *Enoch Arden* 62
happy *p* strowing cried 'Hosanna — " 505
or he himself Moved haunting *p*, — " 604
p talk'd—that it was wholly wise — *Aylmer's Field* 268
p talk'd—The boy might get a notion — " 270
The weakness of a *p* or a house, — " 570
To speak before the *p* of her child, — " 608
hid the Holiest from the *p's* eyes — " 772

Persia (*continued*) a custom in the Orient, friends,—I
read of it in P—   *Lover's Tale iv* 231

Persian (adj.) Gazed on the P girl alone,   *Arabian Nights* 134
Ran down the P, Grecian, Roman lines   *Princess ii* 130

Persian (s) in his behalf Shall I exceed the P,   *Lover's Tale iv* 347

Persistence p turn'd her scorn to wrath.   *Pelleas and E.* 218

Persistent Heart-hiding smile, and gray p eye :   *Guinevere* 64

Person law for *us* ; We paid in p.   *Walk. to the Mail* 86
'The thrall in p may be free in soul,
Done in your maiden's p to yourself :   *Gareth and L.* 165
promises the men who served About my p,   *Marr. of Geraint* 216
Yniol's rusted arms Were on his princely p,   " 454
    " 544

Personal And therefore splenetic, p, base,
Began to chafe as at a p wrong.   *Maud I x* 33
    Enoch Arden 474

Personality The abysmal deeps of P,
Immeasurable Reality ! Infinite P !   *Palace of Art* 223
    De Prof., Human C. 4

Pert *See* **Peärky**

Pest rending earthquake, or the famine, or the p !   *Faith* 4

Persuade I might p myself then   *Maud I x* 56

Persuasion P, no, nor death could alter her :   *Aylmer's Field* 418

Perused conscious of ourselves, P the matting ;   *Princess ii* 68

Peruvian To buy strange shares in some P mine.   *Sea Dreams* 15

Pestle To p a poison'd poison   *Maud I i* 44

Pet (fit of peevishness) ' But in a p she started up,   *Talking Oak* 229

Petal (*See also* **Rose-petal**) p's from blown roses on
the grass,   *Lotos-Eaters, C. S.* 2
two dewdrops on the p shake To the same sweet air,   *Princess vii* 68
' Now sleeps the crimson p,   " 176
Tip-tilted like the p of a flower ;   *Gareth and L.* 591

Peter (*See also* **Pether**) laugh'd, and swore by P and by Paul :   *Godiva* 24
' P had the brush, My P, first : '   *Aylmer's Field* 254
I leap from Satan's foot to P's knee—   *Gareth and L.* 538
sheet Let down to P at his prayers ;   *To E. Fitzgerald* 12
Rome of Cæsar, Rome of P,   *Locksley H., Sixty* 88

Peter's-pence ' Ere yet, in scorn of P-p,   *Talking Oak* 45

Pether (Peter) Till Holy St. P gets up wid his kays   *Tomorrow* 93

Petition make a wild p night and day,   *Princess v* 97
At thy new son, for my p to her.   *Marr. of Geraint* 780
for my strange p I will make Amends   " 817

Petitionary (Claspt hands and that p grace   *The Brook* 112

Petition'd P too for him.   *Princess vi* 320
Queen p for his leave To see the hunt.   *Marr. of Geraint* 154

Petted And smoothed a p peacock down with that :   *Princess ii* 456

Pettish And p cries awoke, and the wan day   *Last Tournament* 214

Petty O, I see thee old and formal, fitted to thy p part,   *Locksley Hall* 93
Worried his passive ear with p wrongs   *Enoch Arden* 352
The p marestail forest, fairy pines,   *Aylmer's Field* 92
A p railway ran : a fire-balloon   *Princess, Pro.* 74
And ' p Ogress,' and ' ungrateful Puss,'   " 157
We cross'd the street and gain'd a p mound   " iv 557
Ah God ! the p fools of rhyme   *Lit Squabbles* 1
And weave their p cells and die.   *In Mem. l* 12
Let cares that p shadows cast,   " cv 13
The p cobwebs we have spun :   " cxxiv 8
For many a p king ere Arthur came   *Com. of Arthur* 5
Drew all their p princedoms under him,   " 18
Colleaguing with a score of p kings,   " 67
Drew in the p princedoms under him,   " 517
That dwarfs the p love of one to one.   *Merlin and V.* 492
And brake the p kings, and fought with Rome,   *Pass. of Arthur* 68

Petulance Seer Would watch her at her p,   *Merlin and V.* 175

Petulancy for her fault she wept Of p ;   " 953

Petulant She brook'd it not ; but wrathful, p,   *Lucretius* 14
nipt her slender nose With p thumb   *Gareth and L.* 750
Whereat the maiden, p, 'Lancelot,   " 1246

Petulantly p she said, ' Ay well—   " 1273

Pew grasping the p's And oaken finials   *Aylmer's Field* 822

Pewit (*See also* **Lapwing**) Returning like the p,   *Will Water.* 230

Phalanx Into that p of the summer spears   *Aylmer's Field* 111

Phantasm white-eyed p's weeping tears of blood,   *Palace of Art* 239
updrawn A fashion and a p of the form   *Lover's Tale i* 646
They past on, The lordly P's !   " ii 99

Phantasmal Cloud-weaver of p hopes and fears,   *To Victor Hugo* 2

Phantom (adj.) Thou shalt hear the ' Never, never,'
whisper'd by the p years,   *Locksley Hall* 83

Phantom (adj.) (*continued*) And p hopes assemble ;   *Will Water.* 30
The p husks of something foully done,   *Lucretius* 160
P sound of blows descending, moan of an enemy massacred,
P wail of women and children, multitudinous agonies.   *Boädicea* 25
Bloodily flow'd the Tamesa rolling p bodies of horses and
men ; Then a p colony smoulder'd on the refluent estuary ;   " 27
a p king, Now looming, and now lost ;   *Com. of Arthur* 430
while the p king Sent out at times a voice ;   " 436
There came a clapping as of p hands.   *Marr. of Geraint* 566
far away The p circle of a moaning sea.   *Pass. of Arthur* 87
there was a p cry that I heard as I tost about,   *In the Child. Hosp.* 63
yet No phantoms, watching from a p shore   *Ancient Sage* 179
The p walls of this illusion fade,   " 181
star that gildest yet this p shore ;   *To Virgil* 26
Far off a p cuckoo cries From out a p hill ;   *Pref Poem, Broth. Son.* 19

Phantom (s) a p two hours old Of a maiden past away,   *Adeline* 18
The p of a wish that once could move,   *The form, the form* 10
The p of a silent song,   *Miller's D.* 71
P's of other forms of rule,   *Love thou thy land* 59
A p made of many p's moved Before him   *Enoch Arden* 602
Beastlier than any p of his kind   *Lucretius* 196
and make One act a p of succession :   *Princess iii* 329
' And all the p, Nature, stands—   *In Mem. iii* 9
Or like to noiseless p's flit :   " xx 16
But mine own p chanting hymns ?   " cviii 10
That abiding p cold.   *Maud II iv* 55
Till I saw the dreary p arise and fly   " III vi 36
But watch'd him have I like a p pass   *Gareth and L.* 1335
' Hark the P of the house That ever shrieks   *Lancelot and E.* 1022
The p of a cup that comes and goes ? '   *Holy Grail* 44
' Nay, monk ! what p ? ' answer'd Percivale.   " 45
To whom I told my p's, and he said :   " 444
Glad that no p vext me more,   " 538
Came ye on none but p's in your quest,   " 562
And women were as p's.   " 566
Who seem'd the p of a Giant in it,   *Guinevere* 602
P!—had the ghastliest That ever lusted for a body,   *Lover's Tale i* 647
I, groaning, from me flung Her empty p :   " ii 206
The p of the whirling landaulet   *Sisters (E. and E.)* 114
shatter'd p of that infinite One,   *De Prof.. Two G.* 47
And all the p's of the dream,   *Tiresias* 195
and yet No p's, watching from a phanton shore   *Ancient Sage* 179
and as the p disappears,   *Locksley H., Sixty* 253
and that rich p of the tower ?   *The Ring* 253

Phantom-fair How faintly-flush'd, how p-f,   *The Daisy* 65

Phantom-warning Should prove the p-w true.   *In Mem. xcii* 12

Pharaoh May P's darkness, folds as dense   *Aylmer's Field* 771

Pharisee These P's, this Caiaphas-Arundel   *Sir J. Oldcastle* 179

Pharos roar that breaks the P from his base   *Princess vi* 339

Phase act Of immolation, any p of death,   " iii 285
out of painful p's wrought There flutters   *In Mem. lxv* 6
And, moved thro' life of lower p,   " Con. 125
every p of ever-heightening life,   *De Prof., Two G.* 7

Pheasant-lord old p-l's, These partridge-breeders   *Aylmer's Field* 381

Phenomenon Arbaces, and P, and the rest,   *The Brook* 162

Philanthropies And nursed by mealy-mouth'd p,   " 94

Philip (*See also* **Philip Ray**) Enoch was host one day, P
the next,   *Enoch Arden* 25
then would P, his blue eyes All flooded   " 31
But P loved in silence ; and the girl Seem'd kinder unto P   " 41
P stay'd (His father lying sick and needing him)   " 64
P look'd, And in their eyes and faces read his doom ;   " 72
P's true heart, which hunger'd for her peace   " 272
P standing up said falteringly ' Annie,   " 284
P ask'd ' Then you will let me, Annie ? '   " 322
P put the boy and girl to school,   " 331
P did not fathom Annie's mind :   " 344
P was her children's all-in-all ;   " 348
call'd him Father P. P gain'd As Enoch lost ;   " 354
they begg'd For Father P (as they call'd him)   " 365
' Come with us Father P ' he denied ;   " 368
So P rested with her well-content ;   " 376
P sitting at her side forgot Her presence,   " 384
P coming somewhat closer spoke.   " 398
God reward you for it, P,   " 425

Philip (*continued*) 'dear *P*, wait a while: If Enoch comes— *Enoch Arden* 430
  P sadly said 'Annie, as I have waited all my life   „   434
  till *P* glancing up Beheld the dead flame   „   440
  P with his eyes Full of that lifelong hunger,   „   463
  Some thought that *P* did but trifle with her: „   475
  And others laugh'd at her and *P* too,   „   477
  P's rosy face contracting grew Careworn and wan;   „   486
  P thought he knew: „   520
  Then her good *P* was her all-in-all,   „   525
  How *P* put her little ones to school,   „   706
  and marriage, and the birth Of *P*'s child: „   709
  Far-blazing from the rear of *P*'s house,   „   727
  P's dwelling fronted on the street,   „   731
  P, the slighted suitor of old times,   „   745
  And say to *P* that I blest him too;   „   886
  Till last by *P*'s farm I flow   *The Brook* 13
  P's farm where brook and river meet.   „   38
  P chatter'd more than brook or bird; Old *P*;   „   51
  And push'd at *P*'s garden-gate.   „   83
  in I went, and call'd old *P* out To show the farm: „   120
  And with me *P*, talking still;   „   164
  when they follow'd us from *P*'s door,   „   167
  Poor *P*, of all his lavish waste of words   „   191

Philip Ray (*See also* **Philip**) *P R* the miller's only son, *Enoch Arden* 13
  I married her who married *P R*.   „   860

Philosopher Be mine a *p*'s life   *Maud I iv* 49
Philosophy Affirming each his own *p*—   *Lucretius* 216
  fair *philosophies* That lift the fancy;   *Princess iii* 340
  And many an old *p* On Argive heights   *In Mem. xxiii* 21
  For fear divine *P* Should push beyond her mark,   „   *liii* 14
  I have had my day and my *philosophies*—   *Last Tournament* 319
  Science, *p*, song—   *The Wreck* 51
  knew no books and no *philosophies*,   *Ancient Sage* 218
  What the *philosophies*, all the sciences,   *Vastness* 31
  each *p* And mood of faith may hold   *Akbar's Dream* 55
  When fine *Philosophies* would fail,   „   140
Philtre brew'd the *p* which had power,   *Lucretius* 16
Phlegethon By the red race of fiery *P*;   *Demeter and P.* 28
Phœnix A fiery *p* rising from the smoke,   *The Ring* 339
Phosphor till *P*, bright As our pure love,   *In Mem. ix* 10
  Bright *P*, fresher for the night,   „   *cxxi* 9
Phosphorescence star of *p* in the calm,   *Audley Court* 87
  Broke with a *p* charming even My lady;   *Aylmer's Field* 116
Phosphorus 'P,' then 'MERIDIES'—'HESPERUS'—   *Gareth and L.* 1204
Phra-bat *P-b* the step; your Pontic coast,   *To Ulysses* 42
Phra-Chai *P-C*, the Shadow of the Best,   „   41
Phrase (*See also* **Boy-phrase**) In *p*'s here and there at
  random,   *Aylmer's Field* 434
  household talk, and *p*'s of the hearth,   *Princess ii* 315
  every *p* well-oil'd, As man's could be;   „   *iii* 133
  Fair speech was his and delicate of *p*,   *Lover's Tale i* 719
  Fair speech was his, and delicate of *p*.   „   *iv* 273
  courtly *p* that masks his malice now—   *The Flight* 30
  that large *p* of yours 'A Star among the stars,'   *Epilogue* 41
  flashing out from many a golden *p*;   *To Virgil* 8
  Have added fulness to the *p*   *To Marq. of Dufferin* 11
Physician a vile *p*, blabbing The case of his patient—   *Maud II v* 36
Piacenza At Lodi, rain, *P*, rain.   *The Daisy* 52
Piano She left the new *p* shut: *Talking Oak* 119
Pibroch Dance to the *p*!—saved!   *Def. of Lucknow* 103
Pick (s) Click with the *p*, coming nearer and nearer   *Def. of Lucknow* 28
Pick (verb) *p* the faded creature from the pool,   *Marr. of Geraint* 671
  p the vicious quitch Of blood and custom   *Geraint and E.* 903
  To dig, *p*, open, find and read the charm: *Merlin and V.* 660
  P's from the colewort a green caterpillar,   *Guinevere* 32
Pickaxe A *p* in her hand: *Sea Dreams* 100
  wait till the point of the *p* be thro'!   *Def. of Lucknow* 27
Pick'd '*p* the eleventh from this hearth   *The Epic* 41
  p offenders from the mass For judgment.   *Princess i* 29
  Hath *p* a ragged-robin from the hedge,   *Marr. of Geraint* 724
  p the lance That pleased him best,   *Geraint and E.* 179
Pickpocket *P*'s, each hand lusting for all   *Maud I i* 22
Picnic Let us *p* there At Audley Court.'   *Audley Court* 2
Pictur (s) The fellers as maäkes them *p*'s,   *Owd Roä* 23
Pictur (verb) to *p* the door-poorch theere,   *Owd Roä* 24

Picture (*See also* **Pictur**) with wide blue eyes As in a *p*.   *M. d'Arthur* 170
  eyes have been intent On that veil'd *p*—   *Gardener's D.* 270
  More like a *p* seemeth all Than those old portraits *Day-Dm., Sleep. P.* 22
  still I wore her *p* by my heart,   *Princess i* 38
  The mimic *p*'s breathing grace,   *In Mem. lxxviii* 11
  I make a *p* in the brain;   „   *lxxx* 9
  still his *p* form'd And grew between her   *Lancelot and E.* 992
  with wide blue eyes As in a *p*.   *Pass. of Arthur* 338
  and fell Slanting upon that *p*,   *Lover's Tale ii* 175
  About a *p* of his lady, taken Some years before,   „   *iv* 216
  And crossing her own *p* as she came,   „   286
  for Emmie, you see, It's all in the *p* there: *In the Child. Hosp.* 50
  In my life there was a *p*,   *Locksley H., Sixty* 15
  I used To prattle to her *p*—   *The Ring* 116
  I see the *p* yet, Mother and child.   *Romney's R.* 80
Pictured From yearlong poring on thy *p* eyes,   *Princess iv* 340
  And grew between her and the *p* wall.   *Lancelot and E.* 993
Picturesque The *p* of man and man.'   *In Mem. lxxxix* 42
  To make old bareness *p* And tuft with grass   „   *cxxviii* 19
Picus snared *P* and Faunus, rustic Gods?   *Lucretius* 182
Pie too noble' he said 'to check at *p*'s,   *Merlin and V.* 126
Pieäce (piece) An' their mashin' their toys to *p*'s   *Spinster's S's.* 88
Piebald Not like the *p* miscellany, man,   *Princess v* 198
Piece (*See also* **Pieäce**) Look what a lovely *p* of
  workmanship!'   *Aylmer's Field* 237
  a rough *p* Of early rigid colour,   „   280
  All over earth, like a *p* of earth,   *Sea Dreams* 99
  earthquake in one day Cracks all to *p*'s,—   *Lucretius* 252
  charr'd and wrinkled *p* of womanhood,   *Princess v* 61
  Cut the Roman boy to *p*'s   *Boädicea* 66
  a *p* of inmost Horticultural art,   *Hendecasyllabics* 19
  I see in part That all, as in some *p* of art,   *In Mem. cxxviii* 23
  to rend the cloth, to rend In *p*'s,   *Gareth and L.* 401
  hew'd great *p*'s of his armour off him,   „   1142
  And high above a *p* of turret stair,   *Marr. of Geraint* 320
  Saw once a great *p* of a promontory,   *Geraint and E.* 162
  heap'd The *p*'s of his armour in one place,   „   374
  his cheek Bulge with the unswallow'd *p*,   „   631
  shadow of some *p* of pointed lace,   *Lancelot and E.* 1174
  p by *p* I learnt the drearier story   *Lover's Tale iv* 146
  a single *p* Weigh'd nigh four thousand Castillanos   *Columbus* 135
Pieced I slept again, and *p* The broken vision: *Sea Dreams* 109
Piecemeal Till all my limbs drop *p*   *St. S. Stylites* 44
  surely would have torn the child *P* among them,   *Com. of Arthur* 218
  if thou doubt, the beasts Will tear thee *p*.'   *Holy Grail* 825
Pied Then all the dry *p* things that be   *The Mermaid* 48
Pier A thousand *p*'s ran into the great Sea.   *Holy Grail* 503
  Dash back that ocean with a *p*,   *Mechanophilus* 5
Pierce Yet could not all creation *p*   *A Character* 5
  watching still To *p* me thro' with pointed light;   *Rosalind* 27
  p The blackest files of clanging fight,   *Kate* 25
  Clear Love would *p* and cleave,   *If I were loved* 6
  Pointed itself to *p*, but sank down shamed   *Lucretius* 63
  p's the liver and blackens the blood;   *The Islet* 35
  P's the keen seraphic flame From orb to orb,   *In Mem. xxx* 27
  And one would *p* an outer ring,   „   *lxxxvii* 27
  With pointed lance as if to *p*, a shape,   *Balin and Balan* 325
  Ascending, *p* the glad and songful air,   *Demeter and P.* 45
Pierced *p* thy heart, my love, my bride,   *Oriana* 42
  heart, *p* thro' with fierce delight,   *Fatima* 34
  Below were men and horses *p* with worms,   *Vision of Sin* 209
  wander from his wits *P* thro' with eyes,   *Princess ii* 441
  maybe *p* to death before mine eyes,   *Marr. of Geraint* 104
  same spear Wherewith the Roman *p* the side of
  Christ.   *Balin and Balan* 114
  and the head *P* thro' his side,   *Lancelot and E.* 490
  thro' those black walls of yew Their talk had *p*,   „   970
  thro' the wind *P* ever a child's cry: *Last Tournament* 17
  dying now *P* by a poison'd dart.   *Death of Œnone* 34
Piercing the high dawn of the royal rose   *Merlin and V.* 739
  from the ground She raised her *p* orbs,   *D. of F. Women* 171
Pierian fire from off a pure *P* altar,   *Parnassus* 17
Piaro and he stabb'd my *P* with this.   *Bandit's Death* 10
  For he reek'd with the blood of *P*;   „   13
Pig great with *p*, wallowing in sun and mud.   *Walk. to the Mail* 88

Pint (*See also* **Point**) Go fetch a *p* of port: — *Will Water.* 4
The *p*, you brought me, was the best — „ 75
No *p* of white or red Had ever half the power — „ 82
To each his perfect *p* of stout, — „ 115
I hold thee dear For this good *p* of port. — „ 212
Wouldn't a *p* a' sarved as well as a quart ? — *North. Cobbler* 99
Pint-pot underneath, A *p-p*, neatly graven. — *Will Water.* 248
Pioneer and the dark *p* is no more ; — *Def. of Lucknow* 29
Pious with sound Of *p* hymns and psalms, — *St. S. Stylites* 34
The Sabbath, *p* variers from the church, — *Sea Dreams* 19
Whose *p* talk, when most his heart was dry, — „ 186
The man, whose *p* hand had built the cross, — *St. Telemachus* 9
Pip ' A thousand *p*'s eat up your sparrow-hawk ! — *Marr. of Geraint* 274
Pipe (cask) the best That ever came from *p*. — *Will Water.* 76
Pipe (musical) (*See also* **Organ-pipes**) ' you pitch the *p* too low : — *Edwin Morris* 52
He set up his forlorn *p*'s, — *Amphion* 22
great organ almost burst his *p*'s, — *Princess* ii 474
earliest *p* of half-awaken'd birds To dying ears, — „ iv 50
make them *p*'s whereon to blow. — *In Mem.* xxi 4
Pipe (tobacco) (*See also* **Cross-pipes**) An' the stink o' 'is *p* i' the 'ouse, — *Spinster's S's.* 100
Pipe (verb) Norland winds *p* down the sea, — *Oriana* 91
tufted plover *p* along the fallow lea, — *May Queen, N. Y's. E.* 18
The bird that *p*'s his lone desire — *You might have won* 31
I would *p* and trill, And cheep and twitter — *Princess* iv 100
Fly to her, and *p* and woo her, — „ 115
children call, and I Thy shepherd *p*, — „ vii 218
And *p* but as the linnets sing : — *In Mem.* xxi 24
And rarely *p*'s the mounted thrush ; — „ xci 2
Where now the seamew *p*'s, — „ cxv 13
and the Devil may *p* to his own. — *Maud* I i 76
Peace *P* on her pastoral hillock — „ III vi 24
Who *p* of nothing but of sparrow-hawks ! — *Marr. of Geraint* 279
Pipe *See also* **Marish-pipe, Water-pipes**
Piped Sometimes the linnet *p* his song : — *Sir L. and Q. G.* 10
On the nigh-naked tree the robin *p* Disconsolate, — *Enoch Arden* 676
song on every spray Of birds that *p* their Valentines, — *Princess* v 239
those white slips Handed her cup and *p*, — *Last Tournament* 296
Piping That with his *p* he may gain — *In Mem.* xxi 11
Like birds of passage *p* up and down, — *Holy Grail* 146
Tityrus *p* underneath his beechen bowers ; — *To Virgil* 14
Pippin while the blackbird on the *p* hung — *Audley Court* 38
pockets as full o' my *p*'s as iver they'd 'owd, — *Church-warden, etc.* 34
Pique feigning *p* at what she call'd — *Princess* v 587
Piracy King impaled him for his *p* ; — *Merlin and V.* 569
Pirate A tawny *p* anchor'd in his port, — „ 558
And since the *p* would not yield her up, — „ 568
Pirouetted Young ashes *p* down — *Amphion* 27
Pish Spat—*p*—the cup was gold, — *Last Tournament* 298
Pit (*See also* **Naphtha-pits**) *p*'s Which some green Christmas crams — *Wan Sculptor* 13
Have scrambled past those *p*'s of fire, — *St. S. Stylites* 184
in the ghastly *p* long since a body was found, — *Maud* I i 5
fled from the place and the *p* and the fear ? — „ 64
lately died, Gone to a blacker *p*, — „ x 6
He laid a cruel snare in a *p* — „ II v 84
comes to the second corpse in the *p* ? — „ 88
Pitch you *p* the pipe too low : — *Edwin Morris* 52
' *P* our pavilion here upon the sward ; — *Princess* iii 346
stones They *p* up straight to heaven : — *Holy Grail* 665
Pitch-blacken'd stump *P-b* sawing the air, — *Last Tournament* 67
Pitch'd (adj. and part.) Arthur reach'd a field-of-battle bright With *p* pavilions of his foe, — *Com. of Arthur* 97
p Beside the Castle Perilous on flat field, — *Gareth and L.* 1362
Pitched (verb) and *p* His tents beside the forest. — *Com. of Arthur* 57
Pitcher sets her *p* underneath the spring, — *Enoch Arden* 207
Piteous *p* was the cry : — *Princess* vi 142
she cast back upon him A *p* glance, — *Aylmer's Field* 284
Pithy Who spoke few words and *p*, — *Princess, Con.* 94
Pitied trust me, Sir, I *p* her. — „ iv 230
last the Queen herself, and *p* her : — *Lancelot and E.* 1269
Pitiful shall we care to be *p* ? — *Boädicea* 32
P sight, wrapp'd in a soldier's cloak, — *Princess* v 56

Pitiful-pitiless Lopping away of the limb by the *p-p* knife,— — *Def. of Lucknow* 85
Pitiless (*See also* **Pitiful-pitiless**) all her *p* avarice, — *Boädicea* 80
Innumerable, *p*, passionless eyes, — *Maud* I xviii 38
Beneath a *p* rush of Autumn rain — *Sisters (E. and E.)* 237
Scribbled or carved upon the *p* stone ; — *Sir J. Oldcastle* 5
He sees not her like anywhere in this *p* world of ours ! — *Charity* 43
Pitted Or from the tiny *p* target blew — *Aylmer's Field* 93
Or little *p* speck in garner'd fruit, — *Merlin and V.* 394
Pity (s) (*See also* **Self-pity**) His books—the more the *p*, so I said— — *Audley Court* 59
a schoolboy ere he grows To *P*— — *Walk. to the Mail* 110
each other for an hour, Till *p* won. — *Godiva* 35
Annie could have wept for *p* of him ; — *Enoch Arden* 467
Nor save for *p* was it hard to take — „ 556
Not past the living fount of *p* in Heaven. — *Aylmer's Field* 752
P, the violet on the tyrant's grave. — „ 845
Who first wrote satire, with no *p* in it. — *Sea Dreams* 202
far aloof From envy, hate and *p*, and spite — *Lucretius* 77
Kill us with *p*, break us with ourselves— — *Princess* iii 258
all prophetic *p*, fling Their pretty maids — „ v 381
Yet *p* for a horse o'er-driven, — *In Mem.* lxiii 1
Without knowledge, without *p*, — *Maud* II iv 53
' Hast thou no *p* upon my loneliness ? — *Gareth and L.* 73
hide with mantling flowers As if for *p* ? ' — „ 1393
Nor dared to waste a perilous *p* on him : — *Geraint and E.* 525
Instead of scornful *p* or pure scorn, — „ 859
Be thine the balm of *p*, — *Merlin and V.* 80
the *p* To find thine own first love once more— — *Holy Grail* 61
p of thine own self, Peace, Lady, peace : — *Pelleas and E.* 25
' *P* on him,' she answer'd, ' a good knight, — „ 38
small *p* upon his horse had he, — „ 540
I, whose vast *p* almost makes me die — *Guinevere* 534
The night in *p* took away my day, — *Lover's Tale* i 612
Lives in the dewy touch of *p* had made — „ 695
Terrible *p*, if one so beautiful Prove, — „ iv 338
look'd at him, first, askance, With *p*— — *The Wreck* 44
Nay, but I am not claiming your *p*: — *Despair* 37
But *p*—the Pagan held it a vice— — „ 41
P for all that aches in the grasp of an idiot power, — „ 43
And *p* for our own selves (repeat) — „ 44, 46
P for all that suffers on land or in air — „ 45
Some half remorseful kind of *p* too— — *The Ring* 375
on stony hearts a fruitless prayer For *p*. — *Death of Œnone* 42
Pity (verb) rather pray for those and *p* them, — *Aylmer's Field* 775
Ah *p*—hint it not in human tones, — *Wan Sculptor* 11
did they *p* me supplicating ? — *Boädicea* 8
there the Queen herself will *p* me, — *Lancelot and E.* 1059
Pitying tax upon themselves, *P* the lonely man, — *Enoch Arden* 664
Sullen, defiant, *p*, wroth, — *Aylmer's Field* 492
My mother *p* made a thousand prayers ; — *Princess* i 21
look'd At the arm'd man sideways, *p* — „ vi 157
Came out of her *p* womanhood, — *Maud* I vi 64
taking the place of the *p* God that should be ! — *Despair* 42
My Miriam nodded with a *p* smile, — *The Ring* 281
Plaäce (place) afoor I coom'd to the *p*. — *N. Farmer, O. S.* 34
hev to be larn'd her awn *p*,' — *Village Wife* 106
Eh ! tha be new to the *p*— — *Spinster's S's.* 3
ya tell'd 'im to knaw his awn *p* — *Church-warden, etc.* 29
Plaäin (plain) thaw soom 'ud 'a thowt ma *p*, An' I wasn't sa *p* i' pink ribbons, — *Spinster's S's.* 16
But niver not speäk *p* out, — *Church-warden, etc.* 49
Plaäte (plate) when she hurl'd a *p* at the cat — „ 25
I gits the *p* fuller o' Soondays — „ 40
Place (s) (*See also* **Dwelling-place, Hiding-place, Landing-place, Living-place, Market-place, Plaäce, Resting-place, Sumner-place, Vivian-place**) Her temple and her *p* of birth, — *Supp. Confessions* 53
I think that pride hath now no *p* Nor sojourn — „ 120
A goodly *p*, a goodly time, (repeat) — *Arabian Nights* 31, 53
Apart from *p*, withholding time, — „ 75
Entranced with that *p* and time, — „ 97
Sole star of all that *p* and time, — „ 152
All the *p* is holy ground ; — *Poet's Mind* 9
swan's death-hymn took the soul Of that waste *p* — *Dying Swan* 22

S*

Placid (*continued*) Crown'd with her highest act the
  p face *Lover's Tale i* 216
  The *p* gleam of sunset after storm ! *Ancient Sage* 133
  With your own shadow in the *p* lake, *Romney's R.* 76
Placing *p* his true hand upon her heart, *Lover's Tale iv* 75
Plagiarised Until he *p* a beart, *Talking Oak* 19
Plagiarist calls her *p* ; I know not what : *Princess iii* 94
Plague (s) (*See also* **Egypt-plague**) Blight and
  famine, *p* and earthquake, *Lotos-Eaters, C. S.* 115
  Remember what a *p* of rain ; *The Daisy* 50
  A *P* upon the people fell, *The Victim* 1
  Help us from famine And *p* and strife ! " 10
  when I spake of famine, *p*, *Tiresias* 60
  an' a trouble an' *p* wi' indoor. *Spinster's S's.* 50
  to stay, Not spread the *p*, the famine ; *Demeter and P.* 134
  leper *p* may scale my skin but never taint my heart ; *Happy* 27
  Your *p* but passes by the touch. " 104
Plague (verb) began To vex and *p* her. *Guinevere* 68
  thou their tool, set on to *p* And play upon, " 359
Plagued *P* her with sore despair. *Palace of Art* 224
  worldly-wise begetters, *p* themselves *Aylmer's Field* 482
  P with a flitting to and fro, *Maud II ii* 33
  We that are *p* with dreams of something sweet *Holy Grail* 625
  to whom Tristram, half *p* by Lancelot's *Last Tournament* 194
Plain (adj.) ' Will thirty seasons render *p* *Two Voices* 82
  Should that *p* fact, as taught by these, " 281
  ' I cannot make this matter *p*, " 343
  Sleeps in the *p* eggs of the nightingale. *Aylmer's Field* 103
  That has but one *p* passage of few notes, *Lancelot and E.* 895
  who himself Besought me to be *p* and blunt, " 1301
  Which lives with blindness, or *p* innocence *Sisters (E. and E.)* 249
  Fair garments, *p* or rich, and fitting close *Akbar's Dream* 131
Plain (adv.) but, Emmie, you tell it him *p*, *In the Child. Hosp.* 57
Plain (s) (*See also* **Battle-plain**, **Ocean-plain**) THE *p* was
  grassy, wild and bare, *Dying Swan* 1
  To stoop the cowslip to the *p*'s, *Rosalind* 16
  By herds upon an endless *p*, *Palace of Art* 74
  droves of swine That range on yonder *p*. " 200
  with dead lips smiled at the twilight *p*, *D. of F. Women* 62
  The wild wind rang from park and *p*, *The Goose* 45
  She glanced across the *p* ; *Talking Oak* 166
  on the ringing *p*'s of windy Troy. *Ulysses* 17
  Clothes and reclothes the happy *p*'s, *Day-Dm., Sleep. P.* 2
  I leave the *p*, I climb the height ; *Sir Galahad* 57
  The maiden Spring upon the *p* *Sir L. and Q. G.* 3
  And fleeter now she skimm'd the *p*'s " 32
  lord of the ringing lists, And all the *p*,— *Princess v* 503
  And had a cousin tumbled on the *p*, " vi 319
  But when we crost the Lombard *p* *The Daisy* 49
  the stars, the seas, the hills and the *p*'s— *High. Pantheism* 1
  winds from off the *p* Roll'd the rich vapour *Spec. of Iliad* 7
  A thousand on the *p* ; " 19
  brightens and darkens down on the *p*. *Window, On the Hill* 2
  Calm and still light on yon great *p* *In Mem. xi* 9
  Imperial halls, or open *p*, " xcviii 29
  The brook shall babble down the *p*, " ci 10
  when their feet were planted on the *p* *Gareth and L.* 187
  Turn'd to the right, and past along the *p* ; " 295
  gazing over *p* and wood ; " 668
  ' O trefoil, sparkling on the rainy *p*, " 1159
  kindled all the *p* and all the wold. *Balin and Balan* 441
  while they rode together down the *p*, *Merlin and V.* 123
  sunlight on the *p* behind a shower : " 403
  they would pare the mountain to the *p*, " 829
  Returning o'er the *p* that then began *Holy Grail* 217
  hill, or *p*, at sea, or flooding ford. " 728
  On some vast *p* before a setting sun, *Guinevere* 77
  You see yon Lombard poplar on the *p*. *Sisters (E. and E.)* 79
  bloom from every vale and *p* *To Mary Boyle* 9
  summer basking in the sultry *p*'s *Prog. of Spring* 77
  hear their words On pathway'd *p*'s ; " 83
  Nor always on the *p*, *Politics* 2
  the black ox of the distant *p*. *On one who ran down Eng.* 4
  ere the mountain rolls into the *p*, *Death of Œnone* 51
Plain *See also* **Plaäin**

Plain-faced gray tower, or *p-f* tabernacle, *Aylmer's Field* 618
Plainness Nay, the *p* of her dresses ? *Maud I xx* 14
Plaintive Then from the *p* mother's teat he took *The Brook* 129
  The *p* cry jarr'd on her ire ; *Princess iv* 393
  ' Yet blame not thou thy *p* song,' *In Mem. lii* 5
  Vext her with *p* memories of the child : *Last Tournament* 29
Plaited (adj.) With *p* alleys of the trailing rose, *Ode to Memory* 106
  Falsehood shall bare her *p* brow : *Clear-headed friend* 11
  Until the *p* ivy-tress had wound *Lover's Tale i* 618
Plaited (verb) she *p* broad and long A strong sword-belt, *Holy Grail* 152
Plan (s) (*See also* **Ground-plan**) Old wishes, ghosts of
  broken *p*'s, *Will Water.* 29
  Enoch lay long-pondering on his *p*'s ; *Enoch Arden* 133
  comes the feebler heiress of your *p*, *Princess iii* 237
  Dismiss me, and I prophesy your *p*, " iv 354
  ' The *p* was mine. I built the nest.' " 365
  she lightens scorn At him that mars her *p*, " v 132
  build some *p* Foursquare to opposition.' " 230
  I scarce am fit for your great *p*'s : " vi 218
  The world-compelling *p* was thine,— *Ode Inter. Exhib.* 10
  And mingles all without a *p* ? *In Mem. xvi* 20
  the boundless *p* That makes you tyrants *Maud I xviii* 36
  a shadow of the planner or the *p* ? *Locksley H., Sixty* 196
  Nature's male and female *p*, *On one who affec. E. M.* 3
Plan (verb) while I *p* and, my hair Is gray *Will Water.* 167
Plane (level surface) Athwart a *p* of molten glass, *In Mem. xv* 11
Plane (tree) under *p* or pine With neighbours *Lucretius* 213
  beneath an emerald *p* Sits Diotima, *Princess iii* 301
  had our wine and chess beneath the *p*'s, " vi 246
Planed you *p* her path To Lady Psyche, " iv 315
Planet I breathed In some new *p* : *Edwin Morris* 115
  O, happy *p*, eastward go ; *Move eastward* 4
  inhabitant Of some clear *p* close upon the Sun, *Princess ii* 36
  eddied into suns, that wheeling cast The *p*'s : " 119
  all the fair young *p* in her hands— " vii 264
  That one fair *p* can produce, *Ode Inter. Exhib.* 24
  songs, that woke The darkness of our *p*, *In Mem. lxxvi* 10
  Whereof the man, that with me trod This *p*, " Con. 138
  Our *p* is one, the suns are many, *Maud I v* 45
  And the *p* of Love is on high, " xxii 8
  A *p* equal to the sun Which cast it, *To E. Fitzgerald* 35
  homeless *p* at length will be wheel'd *Despair* 83
  earthquakes of the *p*'s dawning years. *Locksley H., Sixty* 40
  All their *p*'s whirling round them, " 204
  touch'd on the whole sad *p* of man, *Dead Prophet* 39
  Like some conjectured *p* in mid heaven *To Prin. Beatrice* 20
  Many a *p* by many a sun may roll *Vastness* 2
Plank blind with rage she miss'd the *p*, *Princess iv* 177
  shape it *p* and beam for roof and floor, " vi 46
  Come stepping lightly down the *p*, *In Mem. xiv* 7
Plann'd Below was all mosaic choicely *p* *Palace of Art* 145
Planner a shadow of the *p* or the plan ? *Locksley H., Sixty* 196
Plant (s) Like to the mother *p* in semblance, *The Poet* 23
  frost in your breath Which would blight the *p*'s. *Poet's Mind* 18
  ' The sap dries up : the *p* declines. *Two Voices* 268
  ' Single I grew, like some green *p*, *D. of F. Women* 205
  All creeping *p*'s, a wall of green *Day-Dm., Sleep. P.* 45
  to watch the thirsty *p*'s Imbibing ! *Princess ii* 422
  Wan-sallow as the *p* that feels itself Root-bitten *Gareth and L.* 453
  They will but sicken the sick *p* the more. *Lover's Tale i* 766
  quick as a sensitive *p* to the touch ; *In the Child. Hosp.* 30
  From each fair *p* the blossom choicest-grown *Akbar's Dream* 22
Plant (verb) *P* thou no dusky cypress-tree, *My life is full* 13
  We *p* a solid foot into the Time, *Princess v* 415
  I go to *p* it on his tomb, *In Mem viii* 22
  make all clean, and *p* himself afresh. *Geraint and E.* 905
  That men *p* over graves. *Lover's Tale i* 538
  And *p* on shoulder, hand and knee, *To E. Fitzgerald* 8
Plantagenet The lion-heart, *P*, *Margaret* 34
Plantain hedgehog underneath the *p* bores, *Aylmer's Field* 850
Plantation Is yon *p* where this byway joins *Walk. to the Mail* 4
  He left a small *p* ; *Amphion* 20
  To grow my own *p*. " 100
Planted (*See also* **Palm-planted**) But when we *p* level feet, *Princess iv* 30
  when their feet were *p* on the plain *Gareth and L.* 187

Planted (*continued*)   I was *p* now in a tomb ;   *The Wreck* 37
   O rosetree *p* in my grief,   *Ancient Sage* 163
   off the tree We *p* both together,   *Happy* 14
Plash   *p* of rains, and refuse patch'd with moss.   *Vision of Sin* 212
   many a glancing *p* and sallowy isle,   *Last Tournament* 422
Plash'd   the tide *P*, sapping its worn ribs ;   *Lover's Tale i* 56
Plaster   alum and *p* are sold to the poor   *Maud I i* 39
Plaster'd   almost *p* like a martin's nest   *Holy Grail* 548
Plat   I keep smooth *p's* of fruitful ground,   *The Blackbird* 3
Platan   clear-stemm'd *p's* guard The outlet,   *Arabian Nights* 23
   the thick-leaved *p's* of the vale.   *Princess iii* 175
Plate (*See also* **Plaäte**)   Came out clear *p's* of sapphire mail.   *Two Voices* 12
   Squadrons and squares of men in brazen *p's*,   *D. of F. Women* 33
   Lay your *P* for one minute down,   *To Master of B.* 4
Platform (*See also* **Crag-platform**)   reach'd The grassy
   p on some hill,   *Lover's Tale i* 341
Plato   *P* the wise, and large-brow'd Verulam,   *Palace of Art* 163
   Or lend an ear to *P* where he says,   *Lucretius* 147
   But Homer, *P*, Verulam ;   *Princess ii* 160
   man's ideal Is high in Heaven, and lodged with
   P's God,   *Sisters (E. and E.)* 131
Plaudit   Omar drew Full-handed *p's*   *To E. Fitzgerald* 38
Play (s)   (*See also* **Hand-play**)   At last, tired out with *p*,   *Talking Oak* 206
   That he shouts with his sister at *p*!   *Break, break, etc.* 6
   But now to leaven *p* with profit,   *Princess iv* 149
   Go in and out as if at merry *p*,   *Maud I xviii* 31
   That he left his wine and horses and *p*,   ,,   *xix* 74
   She is weary of dance and *p*.'   ,,   *xxii* 22
   all was joust and *p*, Leaven'd his hall.   *Merlin and V.* 145
   Would watch her at her petulance, and *p*,   ,,   175
   I loved him better than *p* ;   *First Quarrel* 12
   one, Whose life has been no *p* with him   *Columbus* 224
   but that was a perilous *p*,   *V. of Maeldune* 95
   p that they play'd with The children   *Batt. of Brunanburh* 91
   off the crag we clamber'd up in *p*,   *The Flight* 22
   He said it . . . in the *p*.   *Romney's R.* 150
Play (verb)   fingers *p* About his mother's neck,   *Supp. Confessions* 42
   Hither, come hither and frolic and *p* ;   *Sea-Fairies* 18
   at night I would roam abroad and *p*   *The Merman* 11
   lightly vault from the throne and *p*   *The Mermaid* 33
   You needs must *p* such pranks as these.   *L. C. V. de Vere* 64
   'ill merrily glance and *p*,   *May Queen* 39
   Would *p* with flying forms and images,   *Gardener's D.* 60
   ' *P* me no tricks,' said Lord Ronald, (*repeat*)   *Lady Clare* 73, 75
   To *p* their go-between as heretofore   *Aylmer's Field* 523
   why should I not *p* The Spartan Mother with emotion,   *Princess ii* 282
   And *p* the slave to gain the tyranny.   ,,   *iv* 132
   with your long locks *p* the Lion's mane!   ,,   *vi* 164
   And in thy heart the scrawl shall *p*.'   *Sailor Boy* 12
   dart again, and *p* About the prow,   *In Mem. xii* 17
   The tender-pencil'd shadow *p*.   ,,   *xlix* 12
   I'll have leave at times to *p*   ,,   *lix* 11
   You wonder when my fancies *p*   ,,   *lxvi* 2
   He *p's* with threads, he beats his chair   ,,   13
   Or so shall grief with symbols *p*   ,,   *lxxxv* 95
   For him she *p's*, to him she sings   ,,   *xcvii* 29
   It circles round, and fancy *p's*,   *Con.* 81
   And *p* the game of the despot kings,   *Maud I x* 39
   died to live, long as my pulses *p* ;   ,,   *xviii* 66
   With whom he used to *p* at tourney once,   *Gareth and L.* 532
   or the viler devil who *p's* his part,   *Balin and Balan* 300
   you might *p* me falsely, having power,   *Merlin and V* 515
   there he set himself to *p* upon her   *Lancelot and E.* 646
   Abbess and her nuns, To *p* upon me,'   *Guinevere* 310
   set on to plague And *p* upon, and harry me,   ,,   360
   O golden hair, with which I used to *p*   ,,   547
   begins to *p* That air which pleased her   *Lover's Tale i* 20
   How she would smile at 'em, *p* with 'em,   *In the Child. Hosp.* 34
   p the Saul that never will be Paul.   *Sir J. Oldcastle* 103
   tell King Ferdinand who *p's* with me,   *Columbus* 223
   I would *p* my part with the young   *The Wreck* 39
   realist, rhymester, *p* your part,   *Locksley H., Sixty* 139
   and felt An icy breath *p* on me,   *The Ring* 131
   For I used to *p* with the knife,   *Charity* 15
Play'd   'That men with knowledge merely *p*,   *Two Voices* 172

Play'd (*continued*)   when thy father *p* In his free field,   *Two Voices* 319
   For scarce my life with fancy *p*   *Miller's D.* 45
   Here *p*, a tiger, rolling to and fro   *Palace of Art* 151
   with the time we *p*, We spoke of other things ;   *Gardener's D.* 221
   here she came, and round me *p*,   *Talking Oak* 133
   The happy winds upon her *p*,   *Sir L. and Q. G.* 38
   p Among the waste and lumber of the shore,   *Enoch Arden* 15
   the children *p* at keeping house.   ,,   24
   p with him And call'd him Father Philip.   ,,   353
   hand that *p* the patron with her curls.   *Princess, Pro.* 138
   p Charades and riddles as at Christmas here,   ,,   188
   as the beam Of The East, that *p* upon them,   ,,   *v* 259
   He *p* at counsellors and kings,   *In Mem. lxiv* 23
   p A chequer-work of beam and shade Along the hills,   ,,   *lxxii* 14
   Love but *p* with gracious lies,   ,,   *cxxv* 7
   I *p* with the girl when a child ;   *Maud I i* 68
   I have *p* with her when a child ;   ,,   *vi* 87
   And lightnings *p* about it in the storm,   *Gareth and L.* 68
   And only wondering wherefore *p* upon :   ,,   1252
   and took the word and *p* upon it,   *Geraint and E.* 291
   the lovely blue *P* into green,   ,,   689
   She *p* about with slight and sprightly talk,   *Merlin and V.* 171
   Surely I but *p* on Torre?   *Lancelot and E.* 209
   crisping white *P* ever back upon the sloping wave,   *Holy Grail* 382
   ye *p* at ducks and drakes With Arthur's vows   *Last Tournament* 344
   when we *p* together, I loved him   *First Quarrel* 12
   p with The children of Edward.   *Batt. of Brunanburh* 91
Playest   thou *p* that air with Queen Isolt,   *Last Tournament* 263
Playful   with *p* tail Crouch'd fawning in the weed.   *Œnone* 200
Playing   *P* mad pranks along the heathy leas ;   *Circumstance* 2
   p with the blade he prick'd his hand,   *Aylmer's Field* 239
   p, now A twisted snake, and now a rain of pearls,   *Princess, Pro.* 61
   Then that old Seer made answer *p* on him   *Gareth and L.* 252
   And we took to *p* at ball,   *V. of Maeldune* 94
   And we took to *p* at battle,   ,,   95
   foam in the dusk came *p* about our feet.   *Despair* 50
Playmate   Paris, once her *p* on the hills.   *Œnone* 17
   Doubled her own, for want of *p's*,   *Aylmer's Field* 81
   remembering the gay *p* rear'd Among them,   *Death of Œnone* 59
Playwright   Our *P* may show In some fifth Act   *The Play* 3
Plea   King Mused for a little on his *p*,   *Marr. of Geraint* 42
   Be not gull'd by a despot's *p*!   *Riflemen form!* 9
Pleached   *See* **Self-pleached**
Plead   let her *p* in vain ;   *Enoch Arden* 166
   twice I sought to *p* my cause,   *Princess iv* 552
   when I return, will *p* for thee. (*repeat*)   *Gareth and L.* 987, 1052
   Not all in vain may *p*   *Epilogue* 80
   Her sad eyes *p* for my own fame with me   *Romney's R.* 55
Pleaded   Although I *p* tenderly,   *Miller's D.* 135
   on a day When Cyril *p*, Ida came behind   *Princess vii* 78
   And yet hast often *p* for my love—   *Balin and Balan* 571
Pleader   jests, that flash'd about the *p's* room,   *Aylmer's Field* 440
Pleadest   What if Thou *p* still,   *Supp. Confessions* 94
Pleading   a sound Like sleepy counsel *p* ;   *Amphion* 74
   before them paused Hortensia *p* :   *Princess vii* 132
Pleasance   my passion seeks *P* in love-sighs,   *Lilian* 9
   A realm of *p*, many a mound,   *Arabian Nights* 101
Pleasant   And all at once a *p* truth I learn'd,   *The Bridesmaid* 9
   Before I dream'd that *p* dream—   *Miller's D.* 46
   With your feet above my head in the long
   and *p* grass.   *May Queen, N. Y's. E.* 32
   ' Beat quicker, for the time Is *p*, and the woods
   and ways Are *p*,   *On a Mourner* 13
   O ME, my *p* rambles by the lake, (*repeat*)   *Edwin Morris* 1, 13
   Well—were it not a *p* thing   *Day-Dm., L'Envoi* 3
   A *p* hour has passed away   ,,   *Pro.* 2
   By many *p* ways,   *Will Water.* 34
   But for my *p* hour, 'tis gone ;   ,,   179
   Love will make our cottage *p*,   *L. of Burleigh* 15
   made *p* by the baits Of gold and beauty,   *Aylmer's Field* 486
   A *p* game, she thought :   *Princess, Pro.* 194
   tell me *p* tales, and read My sickness   ,,   *ii* 252
   And many a *p* hour with her that's gone,   ,,   *vi* 247
   Often they come to the door in a *p* kind of a dream.   *Grandmother* 82
   So find I every *p* spot In which we two   *In Mem. viii* 9

Plighted (verb) (continued) The heart that never p troth *In Mem. xxvii* 10
Plot (conspiracy) A p, a p, a p, to ruin all!' 'No p, no p,' *Princess ii* 192
man of p's, Craft, poisonous counsels, *Gareth and L.* 431
for fine p's may fail, *Merlin and V.* 820
Plot (of ground) (See also **Diamond-plot**) Or opening
upon level p's Of crowned lilies, *Ode to Memory* 108
Love paced the thymy p's of Paradise, *Love and Death* 2
I steal by lawns and grassy p's, *The Brook* 170
That all the turf was rich in p's *Marr. of Geraint* 660
Why grew we then together in one p? *Lover's Tale ii* 23
pools of salt, and p's of land— *Locksley H., Sixty* 207
Plot (verb) That he p's against me still. *Maud I xix* 81
Plotted He has p against me in this, " 80
Plough-Plow (s) and morning driv'n her plow of pearl *Love and Duty* 99
He praised his ploughs, his cows, his hogs, *The Brook* 125
stood Eight daughters of the plough, *Princess iv* 278
Then those eight mighty daughters of the plough " 550
and those eight daughters of the plough " v 339
an' runn'd plow thruff it an' all, *N. Farmer, O. S.* 42
We could sing a good song at the Plow, (repeat) *North. Cobbler* 18
The steer fell down at the plow *V. of Maeldune* 30
take the suffrage of the plow. *Locksley H., Sixty* 118
an raäved slick thruf by the plow— *Owd Roä* 28
Plough-Plow (verb) an' Thurnaby hoälms to plow! *N. Farmer, O. S.* 52
Who ploughs with pain his native lea *In Mem. lxiv* 25
To whom a space of land is given to plow. *Holy Grail* 907
And plow the Present like a field, *Mechanophilus* 31
Ploughing and Charlie up the hill. *Grandmother* 80
Ploughman in the furrow broke the p's head, *Princess v* 221
Plover tufted p pipe along the fallow lea, *May Queen, N. Y's. E.* 18
There let the wind sweep and the p cry; *Come not, when, etc.* 5
great p's human whistle amazed Her heart, *Geraint and E.* 49
WHY wail you, pretty p? *Happy* 1
Plow See **Plough**
Plow'd (See also **Red-plow'd**) To mix with what he p; *Ancient Sage* 145
Plowing The plowman left his p, and fell down *Holy Grail* 404
Plowland Silvery willow, Pasture and p, *Merlin and the G.* 54
Plowman The p left his plowing, and fell down *Holy Grail* 404
The p passes, bent with pain, *Ancient Sage* 144
Plowmen, Shepherds, have I found, *Locksley H., Sixty* 121
Plowshare it smote the p in the field, *Holy Grail* 403
Pluck 'Hard task, to p resolve,' I cried, *Two Voices* 118
I will p it from my bosom, *Locksley Hall* 66
p's The mortal soul from out immortal hell, *Lucretius* 262
that men may p them from our hearts, *Princess iii* 257
this night should p your palace down; " iv 414
theer's a craw to p wi' tha, Sam: *N. Farmer, N. S.* 5
I p you out of the crannies, *Flower in cran. wall* 2
whose splendour p's The slavish hat *Maud I x* 3
'to p the flower in season;' So says *Merlin and V.* 722
So, brother, p and spare not.' *Lover's Tale i* 351
p from this true breast the locket that I wear, *The Flight* 33
P the mighty from their seat, *Locksley H., Sixty* 133
Pluck'd-Pluckt Devils pluck'd my sleeve, *St. S. Stylites* 171
in a pet she started up, And pluck'd it out, *Talking Oak* 230
Each pluck'd his one foot from the grave *Amphion* 43
he thrice had pluck'd a life From the dread sweep *Enoch Arden* 54
when the children pluck'd at him to go, " 369
left alone he pluck'd her dagger forth *Aylmer's Field* 470
hand from which Livid he pluck'd it forth, " 627
Found a still place, and pluck'd her likeness out; *Princess i* 92
And pluck'd the ripen'd ears, " ii 2
she pluck'd the grass, She flung it from her, " Con. 31
I pluck'd a daisy, I gave it you. *The Daisy* 88
as the cur Pluckt from the cur he fights with, *Gareth and L.* 702
pluck'd the grass There growing longest *Geraint and E.* 256
bone Seems to be pluck'd at by the village boys " 560
he had the gems Pluck'd from the crown, *Lancelot and E.* 57
each as each, Not to be pluck'd asunder; *Holy Grail* 777
touch or see the Holy Grail They might be pluck'd asunder. " 780
That save they could be pluck'd asunder, " 782
pluck'd one way by hate and one by love, *Last Tournament* 539
Lancelot pluck'd him by the heel, *Guinevere* 34
Prince Who scarce had pluck'd his flickering life *To the Queen ii* 5

Plucking P the harmless wild-flower on the hill?— *Maud II i* 3
Pluckt See **Pluck'd**
Pluksh P!!! the hens i' the peäs! *Village Wife* 124
Plum (See also **Sugar-plum**) Glowing with all-colour'd p's *V. of Maeldune* 60
Plumage Conjecture of the p and the form; *Marr. of Geraint* 333
Plume A funeral, with p's and lights *L. of Shalott ii* 31
She saw the helmet and the p, " iii 40
From spur to p a star of tournament, *M. d'Arthur* 223
Ruffles her pure cold p, " 268
Fantastic p or sable pine; *The Voyage* 44
A light-green tuft of p's she bore *Sir L. and Q. G.* 26
The slender coco's drooping crown of p's, *Enoch Arden* 574
till, each, in maiden p We rustled: *Princess i* 202
all about were birds Of sunny p in gilded trellis-work; *Marr. of Geraint* 659
brandish'd p Brushing his instep, *Geraint and E.* 359
underneath a p of lady-fern, Sang, *Balin and Balan* 26
p fall'n from the wing Of that foul bird *Merlin and V.* 727
from spur to p Red as the rising sun *Lancelot and E.* 307
Their p's driv'n backward by the wind " 480
shower and shorn p Went down it. *Last Tournament* 155
fell thick rain, p droopt and mantle clung, " 213
storm and cloud Of shriek and p, " 441
but with p's that mock'd the may, *Guinevere* 22
From spur to p a star of tournament, *Pass. of Arthur* 391
Ruffles her pure cold p, " 436
Plumed pines, that p the craggy ledge *Œnone* 209
Empanoplied and p We enter'd in, *Princess v* 483
a shatter'd archway p with fern; *Marr. of Geraint* 316
green and gold, and p with green *Merlin and V.* 89
Plumelet When rosy p's tuft the larch, *In Mem. xci* 1
Plummet Two p's dropt for one to sound *Princess ii* 176
Plump Grew p and able-bodied; *The Goose* 18
O P head-waiter at The Cock, *Will Water.* 1
One shade more p than common; " 150
blue wood-louse, and the p dormouse, *Window, Winter* 9
As well as the p cheek— *Sisters (E. and E.)* 184
Plump-arm'd A p-a Ostleress and a stable wench *Princess i* 247
Plump'd sweating rosin, p the pine *Amphion* 47
Plumper And cramm'd a p crop; *Will Water.* 124
Plunder (s) is a world of p and prey. *Maud I iv* 24
He found the sack and p of our house *Marr. of Geraint* 694
Earl Doorm with p to the hall. *Geraint and E.* 592
Plunder (verb) I cannot steal or p, no nor beg; " 487
Plunder'd bark had p twenty nameless isles; *Merlin and V.* 559
Plunge (s) thro' the whitening hazels made a p *Enoch Arden* 379
waterfalls Pour'd in a thunderless p *V. of Maeldune* 14
'one p—then quiet for evermore.' *Charity* 16
Plunge (verb) should not p His hand into the bag: *Golden Year* 71
nor rather p at once, Being troubled, *Lucretius* 151
river sloped To p in cataract, *Princess iii* 291
To p old Merlin in the Arabian sea; *Gareth and L.* 211
and the sword That made it p's thro' the wound *Pelleas and E.* 530
she cried, 'P and be lost—ill-fated as they were, *Last Tournament* 40
Not p headforemost from the mountain there, *Lover's Tale iv* 41
P's and heaves at a bank that is daily devour'd *Def. of Lucknow* 39
fearing not to p Thy torch of life *Tiresias* 158
Plunged p Among the bulrush-beds, *M. d'Arthur* 134
but woman-vested as I was P; *Princess iv* 182
P in the battery-smoke Right thro' the line *Light Brigade* 32
slowly rose and p Roaring, *Com. of Arthur* 381
so down among the pines He p; *Gareth and L.* 809
And down the shingly scaur he p, *Lancelot and E.* 53
Seized him, and bound and p him into a cell *Holy Grail* 675
p Among the bulrush beds, *Pass. of Arthur* 302
sea p and fell on the shot-shatter'd navy of Spain, *The Revenge* 117
P in the last fierce charge at Waterloo, *Sisters (E. and E.)* 64
P head down in the sea, *V. of Maeldune* 82
crest of the tides P on the vessel *The Wreck* 90
P up and down, to and fro, *Heavy Brigade* 31
woods P gulf on gulf thro' all their vales *Prog. of Spring* 73
wild horse, anger, p To fling me, *Akbar's Dream* 118
Plunging (See also **Heavy-plunging, Lazy-plunging**)
peoples p thro' the thunder-storm; *Locksley Hall* 126

Plunging (*continued*) p seas draw backward from the land — *Palace of Art* 251
all ablaze too p in the lake Head-foremost— — *The Ring* 251
p down Thro' that disastrous glory, — *St. Telemachus* 28
Ply joint of state, that *plies* Its office, — *Love thou thy land* 47
plies His function of the woodland: — *Lucretius* 45
Poach'd As the p filth that floods the middle street, — *Merlin and V.* 798
Pocket I fun thy p's as full o' my pippins — *Church-warden, etc.* 34
Pock-pitten That great p-p fellow — *Aylmer's Field* 256
Poem (*See also* **Love-poem**) Look, I come to the test, a tiny p — *Hendecasyllabics* 3
Poesy And this poor flower of p — *In Mem. viii* 19
The p of childhood — *Lover's Tale ii* 184
all the sciences, p, varying voices of prayer? — *Vastness* 31
Poet THE p in a golden clime was born, — *The Poet* 1
But one poor p's scroll, — " 55
VEX not thou the p's mind (repeat) — *Poet's Mind* 1, 3
The parson Holmes, the p Everard Hall, — *The Epic* 4
and the p little urged, — " 48
sing Like p's, from the vanity of song? — *Gardener's D.* 100
days were brief Whereof the p's talk, — *Talking Oak* 186
A tongue-tied P in the feverous days, — *Golden Year* 19
Are but as p's' seasons when they flower, — " 28
this is truth the p sings, — *Locksley Hall* 75
To prove myself a p: — *Will Water.* 166
Hours, when the P's words and looks — " 193
You might have won the P's name, — *You might have won* 1
doom Of those that wear the P's crown: — " 10
For now the P cannot die, — " 13
THE rain had fallen, the P arose, — *Poet's Song* 1
fair As ever painter painted, p sang, — *Aylmers' Field* 106
P's, whose thoughts enrich the blood — *Princess ii* 181
held A volume of the P's of her land: — " *vii* 174
such as lurks In some wild P, — *In Mem. xxxiv* 7
read The Tuscan p's on the lawn: — " *lxxxix* 24
passionate heart of the p is whirl'd — *Maud I iv* 39
take withal Thy p's blessing, — *To the Queen ii* 46
Glorious p who never hast written a line, — *To A. Tennyson* 5
word of the p by whom the deeps — *The Wreck* 23
The p whom his Age would quote — *Ancient Sage* 146
Hesper, whom the p call'd the Bringer — *Locksley H., Sixty* 185
P of the happy Tityrus piping underneath — *To Virgil* 13
P of the poet-satyr whom the laughing shepherd — " 15
blackbirds have their wills, The p's too. — *Early Spring* 48
True p, surely to be found When Truth — *Pref. Poem, Broth. Son* 15
'Ave atque Vale' of the P's hopeless woe, Tenderest of Roman p's — *Frater Ave, etc.*
OLD p's foster'd under friendlier skies, — *Poets and their B.* 1
Had swampt the sacred p's with themselves. — " 14
faults your P makes Or many or few, — *To Mary Boyle* 61
P, that evergreen laurel is blasted — *Parnassus* 12
Yes, my wild little P. — *The Throstle* 4
But seldom comes the p here, — *Poets and Critics* 15
Poetess The ancient p singeth, — *Leonine Eleg.* 13
I wish I were Some mighty p, — *Princess, Pro.* 132
Poet-forms The P-f of stronger hours, — *Day-Dm., L'Envoi* 5
Poetic More strong than all p thought; — *In Mem. xxxvi* 12
Poetically 'What, if you drest it up p!' — *Princess, Con.* 6
Poet-like P-l he spoke. — *Edwin Morris* 27
Rather, O ye Gods, P-l, — *Lucretius* 93
Poet-princess P-p with her grand Imaginations — *Princess iii* 273
Poetry poor old P, passing hence, — *Locksley H., Sixty* 249
Poet-satyr Poet of the p-s — *To Virgil* 15
Point (s) clotted into p's and hanging loose, — *M. d'Arthur* 219
sail with Arthur under looming shores, P after p; — " *Ep.* 18
slowly, creeping on from p to p: — *Locksley Hall* 134
And now, the bloodless p reversed, — *The Voyage* 71
talking from the p, he drew him in, — *The Brook* 154
To our p: not war: Lest I lose all.' — *Princess v* 204
touch'd upon the p Where idle boys are cowards — " 308
In conflict with the crash of shivering p's, — " 491
oration flowing free From p to p, — *In Mem. lxxxvii* 33
'Nay, not a p: nor art thou victor here. — *Gareth and L.* 1055
and the p's of lances bicker in it. — *Geraint and E.* 449
p Across the maiden shield of Balan — *Balin and Balan* 558
and faintly-venom'd p's Of slander, — *Merlin and V.* 172

Point (s) (*continued*) It buzzes fiercely round the p; — *Merlin and V.* 432
Touch'd at all p's, except the poplar grove, — *Lancelot and E.* 617
that p where first she saw the King — *Guinevere* 403
clotted into p's and hanging loose, — *Pass. of Arthur* 387
Descending from the p and standing both, — *Lover's Tale i* 411
Confined on p's of faith, — " *ii* 150
Glanced at the p of law, to pass it by, — " *iv* 276
wait till the p of the pickaxe be thro'! — *Def. of Lucknow* 27
Still—could we watch at all p's? — " 49
the p's of the foam in the dusk came — " *Despair* 50
in that p of peaceful light? — *Locksley H., Sixty* 190
p's of the Russian lances arose in the sky; — *Heavy Brigade* 5
All at all p's thou canst not meet, — *Poets and Critics* 7
Point (verb) p thee forward to a distant light, — *Love and Duty* 95
p you out the shadow from the truth! — *Princess i* 84
p to it, and we say, The loyal warmth of Florian — " *ii* 243
To p the term of human strife, — *In Mem. l* 14
A hand that p's, and palled shapes — " *lxx* 7
And then p out the flower or the star? — *Lover's Tale i* 175
An' 'e p's to the bottle o' gin, — *North. Cobbler* 90
lights the clock! the hand p's five— — *The Flight* 94
p and jeer, And gibber at the worm, — *Romney's R.* 136
Point (pint) I've 'ed my p o' aäle ivry noight — *N. Farmer, O. S.* 7
Pointed (adj.) (*See also* **Clear-pointed, Sharp-pointed**) To pierce me thro' with p light; — *Rosalind* 27
By zig-zag paths, and juts of p rock, — *M. d'Arthur* 50
And sketching with her tender p foot — *The Brook* 102
with now a wandering hand And now a p finger, — *Princess v* 270
A mountain islet ... and peak'd; — *The Islet* 15
With p lance as ... to pierce, a shape, — *Balin and Balan* 325
A score with p lances, making at him— — " 401
The shadow of some piece of p lace, — *Lancelot and E.* 1174
By zigzag paths, and juts of p rock, — *Pass. of Arthur* 218
Pointed (verb) 'COURAGE!' he said, and p toward the land, — *Lotos-Eaters* 1
Thereto she p with a laugh, — *D. of F. Women* 159
He p out a pasturing colt, — *The Brook* 136
I follow'd; and at top She p seaward: — *Sea Dreams* 122
P itself to pierce, but sank down shamed — *Lucretius* 63
p on to where A double hill ran up — *Princess iii* 173
For this lost lamb (she p to the child) — " *iv* 361
I tarry for thee,' and p to Mars — *Maud III vi* 13
Stood one who p toward the voice, — *Com. of Arthur* 438
held Her finger up, and p to the dust. — *Geraint and E.* 453
Are scatter'd,' and he p to the field, — " 802
rose And p to the damsel, and the doors. — *Lancelot and E.* 1263
peak'd wings p to the Northern Star. — *Holy Grail* 240
she p downward, 'Look, He haunts me— — *Pelleas and E.* 226
red mark ran All round one finger p straight, — *The Ring* 453
and p to the West, — *St. Telemachus* 25
Pointing p to his drunken sleep, — *Locksley Hall* 81
one was p this way, and one that, — *Pelleas and E.* 58
Point-painted eyes had ever seen, P-p red; — *Balin and Balan* 412
Poise In crystal eddies glance and p, — *Miller's D.* 52
Poised (*See also* **Equal-poised**) court-Galen p his guilt-head cane, — *Princess i* 19
A doom that ever p itself to fall, — *Merlin and V.* 191
Dagonet with one foot p in his hand, — *Last Tournament* 285
Poising And the rainbow hangs on the p wave, — *Sea-Fairies* 29
a p eagle, burns Above the unrisen morrow:' — *Princess iv* 82
Poison (s) Drew forth the p with her balmy breath, — *D. of F. Women* 271
Full of weak p, turnspits for the clown, — *Princess iv* 516
To pestle a poison'd p behind his crimson lights. — *Maud I i* 44
The flowers that run p in their veins. — *Lover's Tale i* 347
naked p's of his heart In his old age.' — " 356
And batten on her p's? Love forbid! — " 777
Cast the p from your bosom, — *Locksley H., Sixty* 241
or shedding p in the fountains of the Will. — " 274
balm May clear the blood from p, — *Death of Œnone* 36
menacing p of intolerant priests, — *Akbar's Dream* 165
Poison (verb) now we p our babes, poor souls! — *Maud II v* 63
Think ye this fellow will p the King's dish? — *Gareth and L.* 471
devil's leaps, and p's half the young. — *Guinevere* 522
Poison'd (adj. and part) (*See also* **Jungle-poison'd**) To pestle a p poison behind his crimson lights. — *Maud I i* 44

Poison'd (adj. and part.) (*continued*) laying his trams in a *p*
gloom Wrought,   *Maud I x 8*
Or make her paler with a *p* rose?   *Merlin and V. 611*
with her flying robe and her *p* rose;   *Vastness 16*
Struck by a *p* arrow in the fight,   *Death of Œnone 26*
I am dying now Pierced by a *p* dart.   „ 34
I am *p* to the heart.   „ 46
Poison'd (verb) an' I doubts they *p* the cow.   *Church-warden, etc. 16*
an' it *p* the cow.   „ 54
Poisoner prov'n themselves *P's*, murderers.   *Sir J. Oldcastle 168*
Poison-flowers The honey of *p-f*   *Maud I iv 56*
Poisoning scorn of Garlon, *p* all his rest,   *Balin and Balan 383*
Poisonous each man walks with his head in a cloud of
p flies.   *Maud I iv 54*
Craft, *p* counsels, wayside ambushings—   *Gareth and L. 432*
until the wholesome flower And *p* grew together,   *Holy Grail 776*
And like a *p* wind I pass to blast And blaze   *Pelleas and E. 569*
On Art with *p* honey stol'n from France,   *To the Queen ii 56*
in every berry and fruit was the *p* pleasure of wine;   *V. of Maeldune 62*
Poland heart of *P* hath not ceased To quiver,   *Poland 3*
Shall I weep if a *P* fall?   *Maud I iv 46*
Polar Is twisting round the *p* star;   *In Mem. ci 12*
P marvels, and a feast Of wonder,   *Ode Inter. Exhib. 20*
Pole (*See also* **May-pole**) True love turn'd round on
fixed *p's*,   *Love thou thy land 5*
Betwixt the slumber of the *p's*,   *In Mem. xcix 18*
Straät as a *p* an' cleän as a flower   *North. Cobbler 8*
happier voyage now Toward no earthly *p*.   *Sir J. Franklin 4*
up to either *p* she smiles,   *Locksley H., Sixty 169*
That wheel between the *p's*.   *Epilogue 21*
New England of the Southern *P*!   *Hands all round 16*
Polish keeps the wear and *p* of the wave.   *Marr. of Geraint 682*
Polish'd The *p* argent of her breast to sight Laid
bare.   *D. of F. Women 158*
Thy care is, under *p* tins,   *Will Water. 227*
Politic Who wants the finer *p* sense   *Maud I vi 47*
With *p* care, with utter gentleness,   *Akbar's Dream 128*
Political A grand *p* dinner To half the squirelings   *Maud I xx 25*
A grand *p* dinner To the men of many acres,   „ 31
In the common deluge drowning old *p* common-
sense!   *Locksley H., Sixty 250*
Politics At wine, in clubs, of art, of *p*;   *Princess, Pro. 161*
The fading *p* of mortal Rome,   „ ii 286
Raving *p*, never at rest—   *Vastness 3*
Pollen'd golden image was *p* head to feet   *V. of Maeldune 49*
Pollio Chanter of the *P*,   *To Virgil 17*
Polluted Lest he should be *p*.   *Balin and Balan 108*
Here looking down on thine *p*,   *Guinevere 555*
he, the King, Call'd me *p*:   „ 620
Scream you are *p* . . .   *Forlorn 28*
Polluting *P*, and imputing her whole self,   *Merlin and V. 803*
And makes me one *p*:   *Guinevere 619*
Pollution enormous *p* Winnow with giant arms   *The Kraken 9*
Polypi
Polytheism *P* and Islám feel after thee.   *Akbar's D., Inscrip. 2*
And vaguer voices of *P* Make but one music,   *Akbar's Dream 150*
Pomp At civic revel and *p* and game, (repeat)   *Ode on Well. 147, 227*
Pond cutting eights that day upon the *p*,   *The Epic 10*
an''stood By the claäy'd-oop *p*,   *Spinster's S's. 24*
I plumpt foot fust i' the *p*;   „ 28
An' 'e niver not fish'd 'is awn *p's*,   *Village Wife 43*
to my *p* to wesh thessens theere—   *Church-warden, etc. 14*
Fur they wesh'd their sins i' *my p*,   „ 16
they leäved their nasty sins i' *my p*,   „ 54
Ponder *p* those three hundred scrolls   *Lucretius 12*
Ponder'd (*See also* **Nine-years-ponder'd**) Paris *p*, and I
cried ' O Paris,   *Œnone 169*
Enid *p* in her heart, and said: (repeat)   *Geraint and E. 64, 130*
Pondering *See* **Long-pondering**
Ponderous till he heard the *p* door Close,   *Aylmer's Field 337*
Our *p* squire will give A grand political dinner   *Maud I xx 24*
Sun Heaved up a *p* arm to strike the fifth,   *Gareth and L. 1045*
Pontic Phra-bat the step; your *P* coast;   *To Ulysses 42*
Pontius *P* and Iscariot by my side   *St. S. Stylites 168*
Poodle a score of pugs And *p's* yell'd   *Edwin Morris 120*
Wheer the *p* runn'd at tha once,   *Spinster's S's. 38*

Pool Over the *p's* in the burn water-gnats   *Leonine Eleg. 8*
Draw down into his vexed *p's*   *Supp. Confessions 133*
marish-flowers that throng The desolate creeks and
p's among,   *Dying Swan 41*
But angled in the higher *p*.   *Miller's D. 64*
sleepy *p* above the dam, The *p* beneath it   „ 99
Touching the sullen *p* below: „ 244
Flash in the *p's* of whirling Simois.   *Œnone 206*
salt *p*, lock'd in with bars of sand,   *Palace of Art 249*
and the bulrush in a *p*.   *May Queen, N. Y's. E. 28*
Down to the *p* and narrow wharf he went,   *Enoch Arden 690*
a hen To her false daughters in the *p*;   *Princess v 329*
is a straight staff bent in a *p*;   *High. Pantheism 16*
the brook, or a *p*, or her window pane,   *Window, On the Hill 4*
That breaks about the dappled *p's*:   *In Mem. xlix 4*
dreams Of goodly supper in the distant *p*,   *Gareth and L. 1187*
Near that old home, a *p* of golden carp;   *Marr. of Geraint 648*
Among his burnish'd brethren of the *p*;   „ 650
Among her burnish'd sisters of the *p*;   „ 655
And tho' she lay dark in the *p*,   „ 657
pick the faded creature from the *p*,   „ 671
Gray swamps and *p's*, waste places   *Geraint and E. 31*
slipt and fell into some *p* or stream,   *Lancelot and E. 214*
A little bitter *p* about a stone   *Guinevere 51*
p's of salt, and plots of land—   *Locksley H., Sixty 207*
That glances from the bottom of the *p*,   *The Ring 371*
Blurr'd like a landskip in a ruffled *p*,—   *Romney's R. 114*
Poonch'd (punched) an' *p* my 'and wi' the hawl,   *North. Cobbler 78*
Poop (pup) an' seeäm'd as blind as a *p*,   *Owd Roä 101*
Poor (adj.) Take, Madam, *this p book of song*;   *To the Queen 17*
But one *p* poet's scroll, and with *his* word   *The Poet 55*
owning but a little more Than beasts, abidest lame
and *p*,   *Two Voices 197*
' Would I had been some maiden coarse and *p* !   *D. of F. Women 253*
I KNEW an old wife lean and *p*,   *The Goose 1*
She in her *p* attire was seen: *Beggar Maid 10*
I grieve to see you *p* and wanting help: *Enoch Arden 406*
had not his *p* heart Spoken with That,   „ 618
' Ay, ay, *p* soul ' said Miriam, ' fear enow !   „ 807
' *P* lad, he died at Florence, quite worn out,   *The Brook 35*
the week Before I parted with *p* Edmund;   „ 78
P fellow, could he help it?   „ 158
and he, *P* Philip, of all his lavish waste of words   „ 191
A splendid presence flattering the *p* roofs   *Aylmer's Field 175*
So they talk'd, *P* children, for their comfort: „ 427
To him that fluster'd his *p* parish wits   „ 521
p child of shame The common care whom no one cared for,   „ 687
long-suffering, meek, Exceeding ' *p* in spirit '—   „ 754
P souls, and knew not what they did,   „ 782
All my *p* scrapings from a dozen years   *Sea Dreams 77*
And my *p* venture but a fleet of glass   „ 138
Nor like *p* Psyche whom she drags in tow.'   *Princess iii 103*
' *P* boy,' she said, ' can he not read—no books?   „ 214
P soul ! I had a maid of honour once;   „ iv 133
O more than *p* men wealth, Than sick men health—   „ 459
Of lands in which at the altar the *p* bride   „ v 377
P weakling ev'n as they are.'   „ vi 310
And some are pretty enough, And some are *p* indeed;   *The Flower 22*
And this *p* flower of poesy Which little cared   *In Mem. viii 19*
Like some *p* girl whose heart is set On one   „ lx 3
But he was rich where I was *p*,   „ lxxix 18
P rivals in a losing game,   „ cii 19
Your father has wealth well-gotten, and I am nameless
and *p*.   *Maud I iv 18*
An eye well-practised in nature, a spirit bounded and *p*;   „ 38
To preach our *p* little army down,   „ x 38
I noticed one of his many rings (For he had many, *p* worm)   „ II ii 69
Courage, *p* heart of stone !   „ iii 1
Courage, *p* stupid heart of stone.—   „ 5
Except that now we poison our babes, *p* souls !   „ v 63
there was ever haunting round the palm A lusty
youth, but *p*,   *Gareth and L. 48*
Am I the cause, I the *p* cause that men Reproach
you,   *Marr. of Geraint 87*
a house Once rich, now *p*, but ever open-door'd.'   „ 302

Poor (*adj.*) (*continued*) At least put off to please me this *p*
  gown,   *Geraint and E.* 679
' In this *p* gown my dear lord found me first,   „   698
In this *p* gown I rode with him to court,   „   700
In this *p* gown he bad me clothe myself,   „   702
And this *p* gown I will not cast aside   „   705
And there, *p* cousin, with your meek blue eyes, *Merlin and V.* 75
P wretch—no friend !—   „   277
And knew no more, nor gave me one *p* word ;   „
More specially should your good knight be *p*, *Lancelot and E.* 956
only the case, Her own *p* work, her empty labour left.   „ 991
More specially were he, she wedded, *p*,   „ 1321
Then said the monk, ' *P* men, when yule is cold, *Holy Grail* 613
blest be Heaven That brought thee here to this *p* house
  of ours   „   617
I, the *p* Pelleas whom she call'd her fool ? *Pelleas and E.* 474
In honour of *p* Innocence the babe, *Last Tournament* 292
To *p* sick people, richer in His eyes   *Guinevere* 684
P Julian—how he rush'd away ;   *Lover's Tale* iv 2
p lad, an' we parted in tears.   *First Quarrel* 20
Seeing forty of our *p* hundred were slain, *The Revenge* 76
—she wrought us harm, *P* soul, not knowing) *Sisters (E. and E.)* 185
sa I knaw'd es 'e'd coom to be ;   *Village Wife* 46
Siver the mou'ds rattled down upo' *p* owd Squire
  i' the wood,   „   95
Quietly sleeping—so quiet, our doctor said ' *P*
  little dear,   *In the Child. Hosp.* 41
that some broken gleam from our *p* earth
  May touch thee,   *Ded. Poem Prin. Alice* 18
Clove into perilous chasms our walls and our *p*
  palisades.   *Def. of Lucknow* 55
hang'd, *p* friends, as rebels And burn'd alive as
  heretics !   *Sir J. Oldcastle* 47
The *p* man's money gone to fat the friar.   „ 150
my *p* thanks ! I am but an alien and a Genovese. *Columbus* 242
A clearer day Than our *p* twilight dawn on earth— *Tiresias* 206
O we *p* orphans of nothing—   *Despair* 33
And we, the *p* earth's dying race,   *Ancient Sage* 178
An' where 'ud the *p* man, thin, cut his bit o' turf
  for the fire ?   *Tomorrow* 65
Wheer the *p* wench drowndid hersen, black Sal, *Spinster's S's.* 25
But fur thy bairns, *p* Steevie, a bouncin' boy an' a gell. „ 83
P old Heraldry, *p* old History, *p* old Poetry,
  passing hence, *Locksley H., Sixty* 249
P old voice of eighty crying after voices that have fled ! „ 251
she cotch'd 'er death o' cowd that night, *p* soul, *Owd Roä* 114
—as this *p* earth's pale history runs,— *Vastness* 3
you an' I Had been abroad for my *p* health so long *The Ring* 101
P nurse ! *Father.* I bad her keep, Like a seal'd book,
  all mention of the ring,   „ 121
P Muriel ! *Father.* Ay, *p* Muriel when you hear
  What follows !   „ 272
O *p* Mother ! And you, *p* desolate Father, and *p* me, „ 302
Each *p* pale cheek a momentary rose—   „ 315
that *p* link With earth is broken, and has left her free, „ 475
This *p* rib-grated dungeon of the holy human ghost, *Happy* 31
Still you wave me off—*p* roses—must I go—   „ 101

Poor (*s*) Nor any *p* about your lands ? *L. C. V. de Vere* 68
He but less loved than Edith, of her *p* : *Aylmer's Field* 167
Last from her own home-circle of the *p*   „ 504
Whose hand at home was gracious to the *p* : *W. to Marie Alex.* 37
Taäke my word for it, Sammy, the *p* in a loomp
  is bad.   *N. Farmer, N. S.* 48
How mend the dwellings, of the *p* ; *To F. D. Maurice* 38
Ring out the feud of rich and *p*, *In Mem.* cvi 11
When the *p* are hovell'd and hustled together, *Maud* I i 34
chalk and alum and plaster are sold to the *p* for bread, „ 39
Laborious for her people and her *p*— *Ded. of Idylls* 35
knights and ladies wept, and rich and *p* Wept, *Holy Grail* 353
When I goäs fur to coomfut the *p* *Spinster's S's.* 108
crowded couch of incest in the warrens of the *p*. *Locksley H., Sixty* 224
                             „ 268
Served the *p*, and built the cottage, *Dead Prophet* 40
The kings and the rich and the *p* ; *On Jub. Q. Victoria* 30
Call your *p* to regale with you, *Church-warden, etc.* 39
an' they maäkes ma a help to the *p*,

Pope And rail'd at all the *P's*, *Sir J. Oldcastle* 165
Poplar (*adj.*) As in a *p* grove when a light wind wakes *Princess* v 13
With young Lavaine into the *p* grove. *Lancelot and E.* 509
Touch'd at all points, except the *p* grove, „ 617
Lavaine across the *p* grove Led to the caves : „ 804
Poplar (*s*) by the *p* tall rivulets babble and fall. *Leonine Eleg.* 4
Hard by a *p* shook alway, *Mariana* 41
The shadow of the *p* fell Upon her bed, „ 55
sound Which to the wooing wind aloof The *p* made, „ 76
The seven elms, the *p's* four *Ode to Memory* 56
The *p's*, in long order due, *Amphion* 37
With blasts which blow the *p* white, *In Mem. lxxii* 3
And *p's* made a noise of falling showers. *Lancelot and E.* 411
wide world's rumour by the grove Of *p's* „ 523
not pass beyond the cape That has the *p* on it : „ 1040
Beyond the *p* and far up the flood, „ 1050
You see yon Lombard *p* on the plain. *Sisters (E. and E.)* 79
And by the *p* vanish'd— „ 110
the *p* and cypress unshaken by storm *V. of Maeldune* 15
Poplartree left Of Balan Balan's near a *p*. *Balin and Balan* 30
Poppy from the craggy ledge the *p* hangs in sleep. *Lotos-Eaters, C. S.* 11
mound That was unsown, where many *poppies* grew. *Dora* 73
More crumpled than a *p* from the sheath, *Princess* v 29
bluebell, kingcup, *p*, glanced About the revels, *Last Tournament* 234
Thro' the fire of the tulip and *p*, *V. of Maeldune* 43
sa much es a *p* along wi' the wheät, *Spinster's S's.* 78
and flush'd as red As *poppies* *The Tourney* 17
Poppy-mingled A land of hops and *p-m* corn, *Aylmer's Field* 31
Poppy-stem Ev'n the dull-blooded *p-s*, *Lover's Tale* i 352
Populace call us Britain's barbarous *p's*, *Boädicea* 7
Here trampled by the *p* underfoot, *Tiresias* 174
famishing *p*, wharves forlorn ; *Vastness* 14
Popular did I take That *p* name of thine to shadow forth *Lucretius* 96
The pretty, *p* name such manhood earns, *Merlin and V.* 787
for this He chill'd the *p* praises of the King *Guinevere* 13
these are the new dark ages, you see, of the *p* press, *Despair* 88
in a *p* torrent of lies upon lies ; *Vastness* 6
Blown into glittering by the *p* breath, *Romney's R.* 49
And you, old *p* Horace, you the wise *Poets and their B.* 5
Porch (*See also* **Door-poorch**) By garden *p'es* on
  the brim,   *Arabian Nights* 16
Or thronging all one *p* of Paradise *Palace of Art* 101
honeysuckle round the *p* has wov'n its wavy bowers, *May Queen* 29
For up the *p* there grew an Eastern rose, *Gardener's D.* 123
The cloudy *p* oft opening on the Sun ? *Love and Duty* 9
' Dark *p*,' I said, ' and silent aisle, *The Letters* 47
Strode from the *p*, tall and erect again. *Aylmer's Field* 825
into rooms which gave Upon a pillar'd *p*, *Princess* i 230
p that sang All round with laurel, „ ii 22
Then summon'd to the *p* we went. „ iii 178
That pelt us in the *p* with flowers. *In Mem., Con.* 68
They leave the *p*, they pass the grave „ 71
I could have linger'd in that *p*, *Lover's Tale* i 186
Porch-pillars *P-p* on the lion resting, *The Daisy* 55
Pore dote and *p* on yonder cloud *In Mem. xv* 16
Pored I *p* upon her letter which I held, *Princess* v 469
Poring *p* over miserable books— *Locksley Hall* 172
Now *p* on the glowworm, now the star, *Princess* iv 211
' From yearlong *p* on thy pictured eyes, „ vii 340
As when a painter, *p* on a face, *Lancelot and E.* 332
he was *p* over his Tables of Trade *The Wreck* 26
Porphyry Nor winks the gold fin in the *p* font : *Princess* vii 178
Port (*demeanour*) modern gentleman Of stateliest *p* ; *M. d'Arthur, Ep.* 23
Port (*harbour*) There lies the *p* ; the vessel puffs *Ulysses* 44
Annie Lee, The prettiest little damsel in the *p*, *Enoch Arden* 12
Ten miles to northward of the narrow *p* „ 102
before she sail'd, Sail'd from this *p*. „ 125
Fearing the lazy gossip of the *p*, „ 335
Then all descended to the *p*, „ 446
By this the lazy gossips of the *p*, „ 472
Told him, with other annals of the *p*, „ 702
And when they buried him the little *p* „ 916
To that fair *p* below the castle Of Queen Theodolind, *The Daisy* 79
And found thee lying in the *p* ; *In Mem. xiv* 4
A tawny pirate anchor'd in his *p*, *Merlin and V.* 558

Port (wine) Go fetch a pint of *p* : — *Will Water.* 4
    But tho' the *p* surpasses praise, — " 77
    I hold thee dear For this good pint of *p*. — " 212

Portal crimson'd all Thy presence and thy *p's*, — *Tithonus* 57
    found at length The garden *p's*. — *Princess iv* 200
    That guard the *p's* of the house ; — *In Mem. xxix* 12
    And doubt beside the *p* waits, — " *xciv* 14
    Lords from Rome before the *p* stood, — *Com. of Arthur* 477
    mark'd The *p* of King Pellam's chapel — *Balin and Balan* 405
    With chasm-like *p's* open to the sea, — *Holy Grail* 815
    saw the postern *p* also wide Yawning ; — *Pelleas and E.* 420
    floods with redundant life Her narrow *p's*. — *Lover's Tale i* 85
    O blossom'd *p* of the lonely house, — " 280
    Forth issuing from his *p's* in the crag — " 430
    Half-entering the *p's*. — " *ii* 123
    Then a peal that shakes the *p*— — *Locksley H., Sixty* 263
    the name A golden *p* to my rhyme : — *To Marq. of Dufferin* 16
    ' Spirit, nearing yon dark *p* at the limit — *God and the Univ.* 4

Portal-arch thro' the *p-a* Peering askance, — *Merlin and V.* 99
Portal-warding Far as the *p-w* lion-whelp, — *Enoch Arden* 98
Porter *I hung with grooms and p's on the bridge,* — *Godiva* 2
Portion *P's* and parcels of the dreadful Past. — *Lotos-Eaters, C. S.* 47
    Ate with young lads his *p* by the door, — *Gareth and L.* 480
    carves A *p* from the solid present, — *Merlin and V.* 462
    A *p* of the pleasant yesterday, — *Lover's Tale i* 122
Portion'd *P* in halves between us, — *Gardener's D.* 5
Portly His double chin, his *p* size, — *Miller's D.* 2
Portrait Than those old *p's* of old kings, — *Day-Dm., Sleep. P.* 23
    Yet hangs his *p* in my father's hall — *Princess ii* 239
    p of his friend Drawn by an artist, — *Sisters (E. and E.)* 134
Portress At break of day the College *P* came : — *Princess ii* 15
    A wakeful *p*, and didst parle with Death,— — *Lover's Tale i* 113
Portugal Was blackening on the slopes of *P*, — *Sisters (E. and E.)* 62
Possess I *will* *p* him or will die. — *Fatima* 39
    What souls *p* themselves so pure, — *In Mem. xxxii* 15
    slay you, and *p* your horse And armour, — *Geraint and E.* 74
Possess'd (*See also* **Half-possess'd, Self-possess'd**) some-
    thing which *p* The darkness of the world, — *Arabian Nights* 71
    For love *p* the atmosphere, — *Miller's D.* 91
    sinful soul *p* of many gifts, — *To——, With Pal. of Art.* 3
    kiss'd her tenderly Not knowing what *p* him : — *Aylmer's Field* 556
    And marvel what *p* my brain ; — *In Mem. xiv* 16
    A rainy cloud *p* the earth, — " *xxx* 3
    The silent snow *p* the earth, — " *lxxviii* 3
Possession ' I take *p* of man's mind and deed. — *Palace of Art* 209
    Enoch would hold *p* for a week : — *Enoch Arden* 27
    reading of the will Before he takes *p* ? — *Lover's Tale i* 677
Possible all Life needs for life is *p* to will— — *Love and Duty* 86
    O that 'twere *p* After long grief and pain — *Maud II iv* 1
    Ah Christ, that it were *p* For one short hour — " 13
Post (s) (*See also* **Sign-post, Woman-post**) quit the *p* Allotted
    by the Gods, — *Lucretius* 148
    thro' twenty *p's* of telegraph They flash'd — *Princess, Pro.* 77
    every man die at his *p* ! (repeat) — *Def. of Lucknow* 10, 13, 52
Post (verb) made a point to *p* with mares ; — *Princess i* 189
Postern the *p* portal also wide Yawning ; — *Pelleas and E.* 420
Postern-gate Deliver'd at a secret *p-g* To Merlin, — *Com. of Arthur* 213
Post-haste His son and heir doth ride *p-h*, — *D. of the O. Year* 31
Postscript came a *p* dash'd across the rest. — *Princess v* 424
Posy went Home with her maiden *p*, — *Maud I xii* 22
Pot (*See also* **Flower-pot, Pint-pot**) Thy latter days
    increased with pence Go down among the *p's* : — *Will Water.* 220
    an' 'e got a brown *p* an' a boän, — *Village Wife* 48
Potato *See* **Taäte**
Potent A *p* voice of Parliament, — *In Mem. cxiii* 11
    No sound is breathed so *p* to coerce, — *Tiresias* 120
Potheen give me a thrifle to dhrink yer health in *p*. — *Tomorrow* 98
Potherbs rights or wrongs like *p's* in the street. — *Princess v* 459
Poultry a larger egg Than modern *p* drop, — *Will Water.* 122
Pounced the bird Who *p* her quarry — *Merlin and V.* 135
Pound wedded her to sixty thousand *p's*, — *Edwin Morris* 126
Pour *P* round mine ears the livelong bleat — *Ode to Memory* 65
    Holy water will I *p* Into every spicy flower — *Poet's Mind* 13
Pour'd beyond the noon a fire Is *p* upon the hills, — *Fatima* 31
    gray twilight *p* On dewy pastures, — *Palace of Art* 85

Pour'd (*continued*) *P* back into my empty soul and frame — *D. of F. Women* 78
    her soft brown hair *P* on one side : — *Gardener's D.* 129
    For me the torrent ever *p* And glisten'd— — *To E. L.* 13
    I had *p* Into the shadowing pencil's — *Lover's Tale ii* 179
    avarice, of your Spain *P* in on all those happy naked
    isles— — *Columbus* 173
    waterfalls *P* in a thunderless plunge — *V. of Maeldune* 14
    From out the sunset *p* an alien race, — *Akbar's Dream* 192
Pouring brooks of hallow'd Israel From craggy
    hollows *p*, — *D. of F. Women* 182
    And England *p* on her foes. — *Ode on Well.* 117
    fountains in the brain, Still *p* thro', — *Lover's Tale i* 84
Poussetting *P* with a sloe-tree : — *Amphion* 44
Pou sto one *P s* whence afterhands May move — *Princess iii* 263
Pouted His own are *p* to a kiss : — *Day-Dm., Sleep. P.* 31
    Perch'd on the *p* blossom of her lips : — *Princess, Pro.* 199
Poverty And lift the household out of *p* ; — *Enoch Arden* 485
    His baby's death, her growing *p*, — " 705
    honest *P*, bare to the bone ; Opulent Avarice, lean as *P* ; — *Vastness* 19
Powder and the *p* was all of it spent ; — *The Revenge* 80
    That grind the glebe to *p* ! — *Tiresias* 95
Power (*See also* **Ocean-power**) arms, or *p* of brain, or
    birth — *To the Queen* 3
    In impotence of fancied *p*. — *A Character* 24
    a name to shake All evil dreams of *p*— — *The Poet* 47
    fill the sea-halls with a voice of *p* ; — *The Merman* 10
    What lit your eyes with tearful *p*, — *Margaret* 3
    Mine be the *p* which ever to its sway — *Mine be the strength* 9
    lest brute *P* be increased, — *Poland* 9
    That once had *p* to rob it of content. — *The form, the form* 8
    How grows the day of human *p* ? ' — *Two Voices* 78
    ' If Nature put not forth her *p* — " 160
    From out my sullen heart a *p* Broke, — " 443
    She to Paris made Proffer of royal *p*, — *Œnone* 111
    Still she spake on and still she spake of *p*, — " 121
    P fitted to the season ; — " 123
    seeing men, in *p* Only, are likest gods, — " 129
    so much the thought of *p* Flatter'd his spirit ; — " 136
    three alone lead life to sovereign *p*. — " 145
    Yet not for *p* (*p* of herself Would come uncall'd for) — *Palace of Art* 246
    without light Or *p* of movement, — *You ask me, why, etc.* 21
    P should make from land to land — *Love thou thy land* 4
    Thro' future time by *p* of thought. — " 64
    sea and air are dark With great contrivances of *P*. — *M. d'Arthur* 122
    Laid widow'd of the *p* in his eye — *St. S. Stylites* 143
    you know I have some *p* with Heaven — " 145
    P goes forth from me. — " 187
    Among the *p's* and princes of this world, — *Talking Oak* 28
    and try If yet he keeps the *p*. — *Tithonus* 70
    happy men that have the *p* to die, — *Godiva* 71
    So the *P's*, who wait On noble deeds, — *Day-Dm., L'Envoi* 8
    The Federations and the *P's* ; — *Will Water.* 21
    Until the charm have *p* to make New lifeblood — " 83
    half the *p* to turn This wheel within my head, — *Vision of Sin* 128
    Faster binds a tyrant's *p* ; — " 217
    ' He had not wholly quench'd his *p* ; — *Enoch Arden* 877
    understand, While I have *p* to speak. — *Aylmer's Field* 287
    Turning beheld the *P's* of the House — " 393
    but he had *p's*, he knew it : — " 452
    and the hands of *p* Were bloodier, — *Lucretius* 16
    the philtre which had *p*, they said, — " 23
    and check'd His *p* to shape: — " 97
    all-generating *p's* and genial heat Of Nature, — *Princess ii* 38
    And so much grace and *p*, breathing down — " 57
    arguing love of knowledge and of *p* ; — " 167
    might grow To use and *p* on this Oasis, — " 475
    organ almost burst his pipes, Groaning for *p*, — " *iv* 335
    To push my rival out of place and *p*. — " *vi* 55
    Autumn, dropping fruits of *p* ; — " *vii* 236
    sought far less for truth than *p* In knowledge : — " 288
    side by side, full-summ'd in all their *p's*, — " *Con.* 13
    —and perhaps they felt their *p*, — " 111
    And gradually the *p's* of the night, — *Ode on Well.* 153
    Confused by brainless mobs and lawless *P's* ; — " 180
    Nor palter'd with Eternal God for *p* ;

Prayer (*continued*) Thrice blest whose lives are faithful *p's*, *In Mem. xxxii* 13
Who built him fanes of fruitless *p*,   " *lvi* 12
breathing a *p* To be friends, to be reconciled ! *Maud I xix* 55
Not a bell was rung, not a *p* was read ;   " *II v* 24
weary her ears with one continuous *p*, *Gareth and L.* 19
only breathe Short fits of *p*, *Geraint and E.* 155
silent life of *p*, Praise, fast, and alms ; *Holy Grail* 4
to *p* and praise She gave herself,   " 76
' might it come To me by *p* and fasting ? '   " 96
and enter'd, and we knelt in *p*.   " 460
And so wear out in almsdeed and in *p* *Guinevere* 687
More things are wrought by *p* Than this world dreams of. *Pass. of Arthur* 415
knowing God, they lift not hands of *p*   " 420
p of many a race and creed, and clime— *To the Queen, ii* 11
That strike across the soul in *p*, *Lover's Tale i* 364
' to seek the Lord Jesus in *p* ; *In the Child. Hosp.* 20
good woman, can *p* set a broken bone ? '   " 20
if our Princes harken'd to my *p*, *Columbus* 100
I send my *p* by night and day—   " 233
sheet Let down to Peter at his *p's* ; *To E. Fitzgerald* 12
Gods, despite of human *p*, Are slower to forgive *Tiresias* 9
I would make my life one *p* *The Wreck* 10
where of old we knelt in *p*, *Locksley H., Sixty* 33
THY *p* was ' Light—more Light— *Epit. on Caxton* 1
the praise And *p* of men, *Demeter and P.* 120
all the sciences, poesy, varying voices of *p*? *Vastness* 31
I that heard, and changed the *p* *Happy* 55
on stony hearts a fruitless *p* For pity. *Death of Œnone* 41
If it be a mosque people murmur the holy *p*, *Akbar's D., Inscrip.* 4
To pray, to do according to the *p*, *Akbar's Dream* 8
but the *p's*, That have no successor in deed,   " 9
Prayerful patient, and *p*, meek, Pale-blooded, *Last Tournament* 607
who am not meek, Pale-blooded, *p*   " 611
Prayer-prelude labour'd thro' His brief *p-p*, *Aylmer's Field* 628
Praying *P* all I can, If prayers will not hush thee, *Lilian* 26
and sinking ships, and *p* hands. *Lotos-Eaters, C. S.* 116
tell her that I died Blessing her, *p* for her, *Enoch Arden* 879
my latest breath Was spent in blessing her and *p* for her.   " 884
p him To speak before the people of her child, *Aylmer's Field* 607
p God will save Thy sailor,— *In Mem. vi* 13
another, a lord of all things, *p* *Maud II v* 32
she was ever *p* the sweet heavens To save *Geraint and E.* 44
p him By that great love they both had borne the dead, *Lover's Tale iv* 180
p that, when I from hence Shall fade *Tiresias* 214
When I was *p* in a storm— *Happy* 80
Preach (*See also* **Preäch**) I will not even *p* to you, *Love and Duty* 39
Whose foresight *p'es* peace, *Love and Duty* 34
Our own experience *p'es*. *Will Water.* 176
he heard his priest *P* an inverted scripture, *Aylmer's Field* 44
Yet who would *p* it as a truth *In Mem. liii* 11
To *p* our poor little army down, *Maud I x* 38
Good, this forward, you that *p* it, *Locksley H., Sixty* 216
Preäch I'd like tha to *p* 'em down, *Church-Warden, etc.* 52
Preach'd *p* An universal culture for the crowd, *Princess, Pro.* 108
Is it you, that *p* in the chapel *Despair* 1
p a Gospel, all men's good ; *Locksley H., Sixty* 89
Preäch'd An' Muggins 'e *p* o' Hell-fire *North. Cobbler* 55
Preacher (*See also* **Wiclif-preacher**) when the *p's* cadence flow'd Softening *Aylmer's Field* 729
p says, our sins should make us sad : *Grandmother* 93
a harm no *p* can heal ; *Maud I iv* 22
Why there ? they came to hear their *p*. *Sir J. Oldcastle* 42
Burnt too, my faithful *p*, Beverley !   " 80
Dooms our unlicensed *p* to the flame,   " 105
p's linger'd o'er his dying words, *St. Telemachus* 75
Preaching (*See also* **A-preächin'**) *p* down a daughter's heart. *Locksley Hall* 94
Not *p* simple Christ to simple men, *Sea Dreams* 21
Preamble prolong Her low *p* all alone, *Palace of Art* 174
tricks and fooleries, O Vivien, the *p* ? *Merlin and V.* 266
Precaution Creeps, no *p* used, among the crowd, *Guinevere* 519
Precedent slowly broadens down From *p* to *p*: *You ask me, why, etc.* 12
That codeless myriad of *p*, *Aylmer's Field* 436

Precedent (*continued*) Swallowing its *p* in victory. [*Lover's Tale i* 763
Precinct did I break Your *p* ; *Princess iv* 422
What, in the *p's* of the chapel-yard, *Merlin and V.* 751
Precious pure quintessences of *p* oils In hollow'd moons of gems, *Palace of Art* 187
Surely a *p* thing, one worthy note, *M. d'Arthur* 89
Thou wouldst betray me for the *p* hilt ;   " 126
ALL *p* things, discover'd late, *Day-Dm., Arrival* 1
To find the *p* morning hours were lost. *Enoch Arden* 302
They knew the *p* things they had to guard : *Third of Feb.* 41
Lo their *p* Roman bantling, *Boädicea* 31
Such *p* relics brought by thee ; *In Mem. xvii* 18
With ' Love's too *p* to be lost,   " *lxv* 3
(Which Maud, like a *p* stone *Maud I xiv* 10
To dissolve the *p* seal on a bond,   " *xix* 45
Surely a *p* thing, one worthy note, *Pass. of Arthur* 257
Thou wouldst betray me for the *p* hilt ;   " 294
The clear brow, bulwark of the *p* brain, *Lover's Tale i* 130
The *p* crystal into which I braided Edwin's hair ! *The Flight* 34
Precipice Among the palms and ferns and *p's* ; *Enoch Arden* 593
Down from the lean and wrinkled *p's*, *Princess iv* 22
breakers boom and blanch on the *p's*, *Boädicea* 76
Went slipping down horrible *p's*, *Geraint and E.* 379
Precipitancy Bearing all down in thy *p*— *Gareth and L.* 8
Precipitate Wheeling with *p* paces To the melody, *Vision of Sin* 37
such a *p* heel, Fledged as it were *Lucretius* 200
Precipitous sweep Of some *p* rivulet to the wave, *Enoch Arden* 587
Precontract ' Our king expects—was there no *p*? *Princess iii* 207
as to *p's*, we move, my friend, At no man's beck,   " 226
I wed with thee ! *I* bound by *p* Your bride,   " *iv* 541
lagg'd in answer loth to render up My *p*,   " *v* 300
Predoom'd most *P* her as unworthy. *Lancelot and E.* 729
Preëminence To assail this gray *p* of man ! *Princess iii* 234
Prefer each *p's* his separate claim, *In Mem. cii* 19
Preference But if there lie a *p* eitherway, *Sisters (E. and E.)* 290
Prefigured ah, you seem All he *p*, *Princess iii* 209
Prejudice Cut *P* against the grain : *Love thou thy land* 22
To leap the rotten pales of *p*, *Princess ii* 142
old-recurring waves of *p* Resmooth to nothing :   " *iii* 240
Prelude (s) (*See also* **Prayer-prelude**) With mellow *p's*, ' We are free.' *The winds, etc.* 4
But with some *p* of disparagement, Read, *The Epic* 49
This *p* has prepared thee. *Gardener's D.* 272
The *p* to some brighter world. *Day-Dm., L'Envoi* 40
Are but the needful *p's* of the truth : *Princess, Con.* 74
Green *p*, April promise, glad new-year *Lover's Tale i* 281
Oftentimes The vision had fair *p's*,   " *ii* 124
by their clash, And *p* on the keys, *Sisters (E. and E.)* 2
Was *p* to the tyranny of all ? *Tiresias* 74
Prelude (verb) And I—my harp would *p* woe— *In Mem. lxxxviii* 9
Preluded sweet breath *P* those melodious *D. of F. Women* 9
Premier city-roar that hails *P* or king ! *Princess, Con.* 102
Prepare but *p*: I speak ; it falls.'   " *ii* 224
Prepared This prelude has *p* thee. *Gardener's D.* 272
The rites *p*, the victim bared, *The Victim* 65
day *p* The daily burden for the back. *In Mem. xxv* 3
let there be *p* a chariot-bier To take me *Lancelot and E.* 1121
Presage after seen The dwarfs of *p*: *Princess iv* 447
No *p*, but the same mistrustful mood *Merlin and V.* 321
Presageful Dark in the glass of some *p* mood,   " 295
That three-days-long *p* gloom of yours   " 320
Prescient at length Prophetical and *p* *Lover's Tale ii* 132
Presence (adj.) That morning in the *p* room I stood *Princess i* 51
Presence (s) The light of thy great *p* ; *Ode to Memory* 32
all the full-faced *p* of the Gods *Œnone* 80
I hate Her *p*, hated both of Gods and men.   " 229
To dwell in *p* of immortal youth, *Tithonus* 21
crimson'd all Thy *p* and thy portals,   " 57
Philip sitting at her side forgot Her *p*, *Enoch Arden* 385
A splendid *p* flattering the poor roofs *Aylmer's Field* 175
Your *p* will be sun in winter, *To F. D. Maurice* 3
gather'd strength and grace And *p*, *In Mem. ciii* 28
in his *p* I attend To hear the tidings   " *cxxvi* 2
As in the *p* of a gracious king. *Gareth and L.* 316
splendour of the *p* of the King Throned,   " 320

Presence (s) (*continued*) Thou hast a pleasant *p*. — *Gareth and L.* 1065
truth if not in Arthur's hall, In Arthur's *p*? — " 1255
faded from the *p* into years Of exile—' — *Balin and Balan* 156
by your state And *p* might have guess'd — *Marr. of Geraint* 431
her gentle *p* at the lists Might well have served — " 795
by thy state And *p* I might guess thee chief of those, — *Lancelot and E.* 183
Ev'n in the *p* of an enemy's fleet, — *Guinevere* 279
Nor yet endured in *p* of His eyes To indue his lustre; — *Lover's Tale i* 423
Next to her *p* whom I loved so well, — " 427
or fold Thy *p* in the silk of sumptuous looms; — *Ancient Sage* 266
Hail ample *p* of a Queen, — *Prog. of Spring* 61
Glanced from our *P* on the face of one, — *Akbar's Dream* 113
Present (adj.) Yet *p* in his natal grove, — *The Daisy* 18
The lowness of the *p* state, — *In Mem. xxiv* 11
Strange friend, past, *p*, and to be; — " *cxix* 9
Yet is my life nor in the *p* time, Nor in the *p* place. — *Lover's Tale i* 116
depth Between is clearer in my life than all Its *p* flow. — " 150
With *p* grief, and made the rhymes, — *Tiresias* 196
Present (gift) 'I can make no marriage *p*: — *L. of Burleigh* 13
Tost over all her *p*'s petulantly: — *Aylmer's Field* 235
A *p*, a great labour of the loom; — *Princess i* 44
Present (time) To glorify the *p*; — *Ode to Memory* 3
Where Past and *P*, wound in one, — *Miller's D.* 197
used Within the *P*, but transfused Thro' future time — *Love thou thy land* 3
noise of life Swarm'd in the golden *p*, — *Gardener's D.* 179
When I clung to all the *p* — *Locksley Hall* 14
A night-long *P* of the Past — *In Mem. lxxi* 3
But in the *p* broke the blow. — " *lxxxv* 56
Thou, like my *p* and my past, — " *cxxi* 19
carves A portion from the solid *p*, — *Merlin and V.* 462
The *P* is the vassal of the Past: — *Lover's Tale i* 119
to this *p* My full-orb'd love has waned not. — " 733
clear-eyed Spirit, Being blunted in the *P*, — " *ii* 131
hold the *P* fatal daughter of the Past, — *Locksley H., Sixty* 105
In the winter of the *P* — *Happy* 70
Her Past became her *P*, — *Death of Œnone* 14
And plow the *P* like a field, — *Mechanophilus* 31
Present (verb) To the young spirit *p* — *Ode to Memory* 73
Each month is various to *p* The world — *Two Voices* 74
With purpose to *p* them to the Queen, — *Lancelot and E.* 69
Presented *p* Maid Or Nymph, or Goddess, — *Princess i* 196
Presentiment But spiritual *p*'s, — *In Mem. xcii* 14
Preserve *P* a broad approach of fame, — *Ode on Well.* 78
Press (newspapers, etc.) 'Fly, happy sails, and bear the *P*; — *Golden Year* 42
That our free *p* should cease to brawl, — *Third of Feb.* 3
His party-secret, fool, to the *p*; — *Maud II v* 35
dark ages, you see, of the popular *p*, — *Despair* 88
the *p* of a thousand cities is prized — *The Dawn* 14
Press (pressure) and knew the *p* return'd, — *Bridesmaid* 12
Press (throng) slanted o'er a *p* Of snowy shoulders, — *Princess iv* 478
Made at me thro' the *p*, — " *v* 522
Press (verb) answer should one *p* his hands? — *Two Voices* 245
whose touch may *p* The maiden's tender palm. — *Talking Oak* 179
p me from the mother's breast. — *Locksley Hall* 90
P'es his without reproof: — *L. of Burleigh* 10
and so *p* in, perforce Of multitude, — *Lucretius* 167
For they *p* in from all the provinces, — *Princess ii* 97
Nor did her father cease to *p* my claim, — " *vii* 87
'*P* this a little closer, sweet, — *Last Tournament* 718
Press'd-Prest *prest* thy hand, and knew the press return'd, — *The Bridesmaid* 12
bosoms *prest* To little harps of gold; — *Sea-Fairies* 3
On to God's house the people *prest*: — *Two Voices* 409
Approaching, *press'd* you heart to heart. — *Miller's D.* 160
He *prest* the blossom of his lips to mine, — *Œnone* 78
my hot lips *prest* Close, close to thine — " 203
kisses *press'd* on Lips Less exquisite than thine.' — *Gardener's D.* 151
The gold-fringed pillow lightly *prest*: — *Day-Dm., Sleep. B.* 22
the daughter *prest* upon her To wed the man — *Enoch Arden* 483
when I *prest* the cause, I learnt that James — *The Brook* 98
to her meek and modest bosom *prest* In agony, — *Aylmer's Field* 416
I *prest* my footsteps into his, — *Lucretius* 118
closer *prest*, denied it not: — *Princess iv* 232
She *prest* and *prest* it on me— — " *v* 283

Press'd-Prest (*continued*) *prest* Their hands, and call'd them dear deliverers, — *Princess vi* 91
where warm hands have *prest* and closed, — *In Mem. xiii* 7
What time his tender palm is *prest* — " *xlv* 2
around him slowly *prest* The people, — *Gareth and L.* 693
All round her *prest* the dark, — *Balin and Balan* 262
And Lancelot ever *prest* upon the maid — *Lancelot and E.* 911
Full of the vision, *prest*: — *Holy Grail* 267
prest together In its green sheath, — *Lover's Tale i* 152
And they *prest*, as they grew, on each other, — *V. of Maeldune* 64
one snowy knee was *prest* Against the margin flowers; — *Tiresias* 42
when we met, you *prest* My hand, and said — *To Mary Boyle* 15
Pressing *P* up against the land, — *Eleänore* 112
Yet *p* on, tho' all in fear to find Sir Gawain — *Gareth and L.* 325
Then *p* day by day thro' Lyonnesse — *Last Tournament* 501
Heart beating time to heart, lip *p* lip, — *Lover's Tale i* 260
Pressure 'Yet seem'd the *p* thrice as sweet — *Talking Oak* 145
in days of difficulty And *p*, — *Enoch Arden* 255
I take the *p* of thine hand. — *In Mem. cxix* 12
Prest *See* **Press'd**
Prester John Or clutch'd the sacred crown of *P J*, — *Columbus* 110
Presumptuous dishonourable, base, *P*! — *Aylmer's Field* 293
nor believe me Too *p*, indolent reviewers. — *Hendecasyllabics* 16
Presumptuously as he deem'd, *p*: — *Balin and Balan* 222
Pretence Our greatest yet with least *p*, — *Ode on Well.* 29
making vain *p* Of gladness, — *In Mem. xxx* 6
Pretender To keep the list low and *p*'s back, — *Merlin and V.* 592
Pretext Light *p*'s drew me — *Gardener's D.* 192
With some *p* of fineness in the meal — *Enoch Arden* 341
some *p* held Of baby troth, invalid, — *Princess v* 397
going to the King, He made this *p*, — *Marr. of Geraint* 33
'And with what face, after my *p* made, — *Lancelot and E.* 141
our true king Will then allow your *p*, — " 153
Had made the *p* of a hindering wound, — " 582
when he learns, Will well allow my *p*, — " 586
Prettier Evelyn is gayer, wittier, *p*, — *Sisters (E. and E.)* 36
The merrier, *p*, wittier, as they talk, — " 286
Prettiest 'Which was *p*, Best-natured?' — *Princess i* 233
The *p* little damsel in the port, — *Enoch Arden* 12
Hers was the *p* prattle, — *In the Child. Hosp.* 31
Prettily How *p* for his own sweet sake — *Maud I vi* 51
Pretty (*See also* **Pratty**) Have all his *p* young ones educated, — *Enoch Arden* 146
Shaking their *p* cabin, hammer and axe, — " 173
This *p*, puny, weakly little one,— — " 195
A *p* face is well, and this is well, — *Edwin Morris* 45
What is their *p* saying? — *Aylmer's Field* 353
worst thought she has Is whiter even than her *p* hand: — " 363
'*P* were the sight If our old halls — *Princess, Pro.* 139
Will crush her *p* maiden fancies dead — " *i* 88
While my little one, while my *p* one, sleeps. — " *iii* 8
Sleep, my little one, sleep, my *p* one, sleep. — " 16
nor *p* babes To be dandled, no, — " *iv* 146
Their *p* maids in the running flood, — " *v* 382
'*P* bud! Lily of the vale! — " *vi* 192
Whither from this *p* home, — *City Child* 2
Whither from this *p* house, — " 7
'O that ye had some brother, *p* one, — *Com. of Arthur* 335
'Are these your *p* tricks and fooleries, — *Merlin and V.* 265
And made a *p* cup of both my hands — " 275
Your *p* sports have brighten'd all again. — " 305
'Thou read the book, my *p* Vivien! — " 667
The *p*, popular name such manhood earns, — " 787
Now made a *p* history to herself — *Lancelot and E.* 18
Handed her cup and piped, the *p* one, — *Last Tournament* 296
'your *p* bud, So blighted here, — *The Ring* 316
WHY wail you, *p* plover? — *Happy* 1
All mine from your *p* blue eyes to your feet, — *Romney's R.* 96
And I blind your *p* blue eyes with a kiss! — " 101
P enough, very *p*! but I was against it — *Grandmother* 7
And some are *p* enough, — *The Flower* 21
Wan, but as *p* as heart can desire, — *In the Child. Hosp.* 40
call'd me es *p* es ony lass i' the Shere; — *Spinster's S's.* 13
An' thou be es *p* a Tabby, — " 14
ye said I wur *p* i' pinks, — " 17

Pretty (continued) Niver wur p, not I, — *Spinster's S's* 21
  Thaw it warn't not me es wur p, — ,, 22
  P anew when ya dresses 'em oop, — ,, 85
Prevail Let her work p. — *In Mem.* cxiv 4
  Let not thy moods p, when I am gone — *Balin and Balan* 140
Prevail'd But why P not thy pure prayers? — *Supp. Confessions* 89
  has won His path upward, and p, — *Ode on Well.* 214
  And now the Barons and the kings p, — *Com. of Arthur* 105
  'Thou hast half p against me,' — *Gareth and L.* 30
  p So far that no caress could win — *Sisters (E. and E.)* 257
Prevailing P in weakness, the coronach stole — *Dying Swan* 26
  not worthy ev'n to speak Of thy p mysteries; — *In Mem.* xxxvii 12
  And her words stole with most p sweetness — *Lover's Tale* i 553
  The King p made his realm:— — *Last Tournament* 651
Prey (s) And stared, with his foot on the p, — *Poet's Song* 12
  biting laws to scare the beasts of p — *Princess* v 393
  The seeming p of cyclic storms, — *In Mem.* cxviii 11
  little wood where I sit is a world of plunder and p. — *Maud* I iv 24
  Bound on a foray, rolling eyes of p, — *Geraint and E.* 538
  bird of rapine whose whole p Is man's good name: — *Merlin and V.* 728
  Beneath the shadow of some bird of p; — *Pelleas and E.* 608
  Round whose sick head all night, like birds of p, — *Last Tournament* 138
Prey (verb) and p By each cold hearth, — *In Mem.* xcviii 17
Price four-field system, and the p of grain; — *Audley Court* 34
  learn the p, and what the p he ask'd, — *The Brook* 142
  the colt would fetch its p; — ,, 149
  to give at last The p of half a realm, — *Lancelot and E.* 1164
  a robe Of samite without p, — *Merlin and V.* 222
  Ev'n by the p that others set upon it, — *Lover's Tale* iv 152
  You have set a p on his head: — *Bandit's Death* 7
Priceless Rich arks with p bones of martyrdom, — *Balin and Balan* 110
  Stared at the p cognizance, and thought — ,, 430
  A p goblet with a p wine Arising, — *Lover's Tale* iv 227
Prick insects p Each leaf into a gall) — *Talking Oak* 69
  To p us on to combat 'Like to like! — *Princess* v 304
  the blood creeps, and the nerves p — *In Mem.* l 2
  plunges thro' the wound again, And p's it deeper: — *Pelleas and E.* 531
  they p's clean thruf to the skin — — *Spinster's S's.* 36
Prick'd p with goads and stings; — *Palace of Art* 150
  like a horse That hears the corn-bin open, p my ears; — *The Epic* 45
  peace which each had p to death. — *Aylmer's Field* 52
  playing with the blade he p his hand, — ,, 239
  while each ear was p to attend A tempest, — *Princess* vi 280
  P by the Papal spur, we rear'd, — *Third of Feb.* 27
  half-way down P thro' the mist; — *Gareth and L.* 194
  And Gareth crying p against the cry; — ,, 1221
  p their light ears, and felt Her low firm voice — *Geraint and E.* 193
  Geraint, who being p In combat with the follower
    of Limours, — ,, 500
  I was p with some reproof, — ,, 890
  p The hauberk to the flesh; — *Balin and Balan* 559
  couch'd their spears and p their steeds, — *Lancelot and E.* 479
  and a spear P sharply his own cuirass, — ,, 489
  All ears were p at once, — ,, 724
  P with incredible pinnacles into heaven. — *Holy Grail* 423
Pricking (Look at it) p a cockney ear. — *Maud* I x 22
Prickle (s) The furzy p fire the dells, — *Two Voices* 71
Prickle (verb) P my skin and catch my breath, — *Maud* I xiv 36
Prickled Gareth's head p beneath his helm; — *Gareth and L.* 1397
Prickly His charger trampling many a p star — *Marr. of Gareth* 313
Pride Is not my human p brought low? — *Supp. Confessions* 14
  And chastisement of human p; That p, the sin
    of devils, — ,, 108
  I think that p hath now no place Nor sojourn in me. — ,, 120
  all the outworks of suspicious p; — *Isabel* 24
  With merriment of kingly p, — *Arabian Nights* 151
  'Self-blinded are you by your p: — *Two Voices* 23
  waste wide Of that abyss, or scornful p! — ,, 120
  Wilt thou find passion, pain or p? — ,, 243
  on herself her serpent p had curl'd. — *Palace of Art* 257
  Your p is yet no mate for mine, — *L. C. V. de Vere* 11
  my brand Excalibur, Which was my p: — *M. d'Arthur* 28
  old Sir Robert's p, His books— — *Audley Court* 58
  shame and p, New things and old, — *Walk. to the Mail* 60
  our p Looks only for a moment whole — *Aylmer's Field* 1

Pride (continued) his p Lay deeper than to wear it as
  his ring— — *Aylmer's Field* 121
  taking p in her, She look'd so sweet, — ,, 554
  a time for these to flaunt their p? — ,, 770
  your Princess cramm'd with erring p, — *Princess* iii 102
  welcome Russian flower, a people's p, — *W. to Marie Alex.* 6
  Ring out false p in place and blood, — *In Mem.* cvi 21
  The proud was half disarm'd of p, — ,, cx 6
  The fire of a foolish p flash'd — *Maud* I iv 16
  We are puppets, Man in his p, — ,, 25
  often a man's own angry p Is cap and bells — ,, vi 61
  thought, is it p, and mused and sigh'd — ,, viii 12
  ' No surely, now it cannot be p.' — ,, 13
  Down with ambition, avarice, p, — ,, x 47
  I to cry out on p Who have won her favour! — ,, xii 17
  Fool that I am to be vext with his p! — ,, xiii 5
  For the keeper was one, so full of p, — ,, II v 79
  shame, p, wrath Slew the May-white: — *Gareth and L.* 656
  placed a peacock in his p Before the damsel, — ,, 850
  The damsel by the peacock in his p, — ,, 870
  And doubling all his master's vice of p, — *Marr. of Geraint* 195
  Then will I fight him, and will break his p, — ,, 221
  fight and break his p, and have it of him. — ,, 416
  That I will break his p and learn his name, — ,, 424
  Refused her his p, then his p awoke; — ,, 448
  But that his p too much despises me: — ,, 464
  In next day's tourney I may break his p.' — ,, 476
  My p is broken: men have seen my fall.' — ,, 578
  my p Is broken down, for Enid sees my fall!' — ,, 589
  For once, when I was up so high in p — *Geraint and E.* 790
  They place their p in Lancelot and the Queen. — *Merlin and V.* 25
  dead love's harsh heir, jealous p? — *Lancelot and E.* 1398
  the heat Of p and glory fired her face; — *Pelleas and E.* 172
  My p in happier summers, at my feet. — *Guinevere* 536
  To whom my false voluptuous p, — ,, 641
  my brand Excalibur, Which was my p: — *Pass. of Arthur* 196
  my house an' my man were my p, — *First Quarrel* 41
  Sir Richard cried in his English p, — *The Revenge* 82
  hesn't the call, nor the mooney, but hes the p, — *Village Wife* 91
  I have only wounded his p— — *The Wreck* 14
  he sail'd the sea to crush the Moslem in his p; — *Locksley H., Sixty* 29
Prideful My nature's p sparkle in the blood — *Geraint and E.* 827
Priest (See also **Soldier-priest**) Speak, if there be a p,
  a man of God, — *St. S. Stylites* 214
  As the p, above his book Leering — *Vision of Sin* 117
  his p Preach an inverted scripture, — *Aylmer's Field* 43
  'Gash thyself, p, and honour thy brute Baäl, — ,, 644
  one The silken p of peace, one this, one that, — *Princess* v 184
  with music, with soldier and with p, — *Ode on Well.* 81
  The P in horror about his altar — *The Victim* 7
  The P went out by heath and hill; — ,, 29
  He seem'd a victim due to the p. The P beheld him, — ,, 36
  For now the P has judged for me.' — ,, 56
  the P was happy, (repeat) — ,, 61, 73
  This faith has many a purer p, — *In Mem.* xxxvii 3
  Delicate-handed p intone; — *Maud* I viii 11
  p, who mumble worship in your quire— — *Balin and Balan* 444
  he had a difference with their p's, — *Holy Grail* 674
  Shone like the countenance of a p of old — *Pelleas and E.* 144
  I was the High P in her holiest place, — *Lover's Tale* i 686
  for your P Labels—to take the king along with
    him— — *Sir J. Oldcastle* 48
  P's Who fear the king's hard common-sense — ,, 65
  Runs in the rut, a coward to the P. — ,, 78
  The Gospel, the P's pearl, flung down to swine— — ,, 116
  What profits an ill P Between me and my God? — ,, 144
  that proud P, That mock-meek mouth of utter
    Antichrist, — ,, 169
  I am damn'd already by the P — ,, 200
  Bantering bridesman, reddening p, — *Forlorn* 33
  when The P pronounced you dead, — *Happy* 50
  P, who join'd you to the dead, — ,, 93
  he buried you, the P; the P is not to blame, — ,, 105
  The menacing poison of intolerant p's, — *Akbar's Dream* 165
  I will find the P and confess. — *Bandit's Death* 18

Priest (*continued*) P's in the name of the Lord passing souls *The Dawn* 4
Priestess O P in the vaults of Death, *In Mem.* iii 2
Priesthood ever and aye the P moan'd, *The Victim* 23
    What said her P? *Kapiolani* 19
    Baffled her p, Broke the Taboo, " 29
Primal grown at last beyond the passions of the p clan? *Locksley H.," Sixty* 93
    Mount and mine, and p wood; *Open I. and C. Exhib.* 6
Prime (*adj.*) On the p labour of thine early days: *Ode to Memory* 94
    P, which I knew; and so we sat and eat *Audley Court* 28
    While the p swallow dips his wing, *Edwin Morris* 145
    Better to clear p forests, heave and thump *Princess* iii 127
    And my p passion in the grave: *In Mem.* lxxxv 76
    from p youth Well-known well-loved. *Lover's Tale* ii 175
    Butter I warrants be p, *Village Wife* 3
Prime (s) golden p Of good Haroun
    Alraschid. *Arabian Nights* 10, 21, 32, 43, 54, 65,
        76, 87, 98, 109, 120, 131, 142, 153
    gray p Make thy grass hoar with early rime. *Two Voices* 65
    could she climb Beyond her own material p? " 378
    Raw from the p, and crushing down his mate; *Princess* ii 121
    about my barren breast In the dead p: " vi 203
    we fought for Freedom from our p, *Third of Feb.* 23
    And at the spiritual p Rewaken *In Mem.* xliii 15
    Dragons of the p, That tare each other " lvi 22
    The colours of the crescent p? " cxvi 4
    shook his wits they wander in his p— *Gareth and L.* 715
    From p to vespers will I chant thy praise *Pelleas and E.* 349
Primrose (*adj.*) Prattling the p fancies of the boy, *The Brook* 19
Primrose (s) p yet is dear, The p of the later year, *In Mem.* lxxxv 118
Prince (*See also* **Lord-prince, Shepherd-prince**) else
    the island p's over-bold *Lotos-Eaters, C. S.* 75
    to greet Troy's wandering p, *On a Mourner* 33
    Among the powers and p's of this world, *St. S. Stylites* 187
    And bring the fated fairy P. *Day-Dm., Sleep.* P. 56
    A fairy P, with joyful eyes, " *Arrival* 7
    P of peace, the Mighty God, *Aylmer's Field* 669
    heads of chiefs and p's fall so fast, " 763
    and be you The P to win her! *Princess, Pro.* 226
    'Then follow me, the P,' I answer'd, " 227
    A p I was, blue-eyed, and fair in face, " i 1
    'You do us, P,' he said, " 120
    would you had her, P, with all my heart, " 126
    She answer'd, 'then ye know the P?' " ii 49
    in me behold the P Your countryman, " 214
    'O Sir, O P, I have no country none; " 218
    be swerved from right to save A p, a brother? " 291
    help my p to gain His rightful bride, " iii 160
    I know the P, I prize his truth: " 232
    tho' your P's love were like a God's, " 248
    'Fair daughter, when we sent the P your way " iv 398
    and like a gentleman. And like a p: " 528
    Arranged the favour, and assumed the P. " 602
    you could not slay Me, nor your p: " v 66
    He seems a gracious and a gallant P, " 213
    We would do much to gratify your P— " 217
    But let your P (our royal word upon it, " 224
    embattled squares, And squadrons of the P, " 247
    P, she can be sweet to those she loves, " 289
    and bore down a P, And Cyril, one. " 518
    Cyril seeing it, push'd against the P, " 533
    there went up a great cry, The P is slain. " vi 26
    on to the tents: take up the P.' " 279
    That you may tend upon him with the p.' " 315
    but the P Her brother came; " 344
    Never, P; You cannot love me.' " vii 337
    Has given our P his own imperial Flower, *W. to Marie Alex.* 4
    A princely people's awful p's, *The Daisy* 39
    in his coffin the P of courtesy lay. *G. of Swainston* 10
    a P indeed, Beyond all titles, *Ded. of Idylls* 41
    his wife Nursed the young p, and rear'd him *Com. of Arthur* 224
    thou art closer to this noble p, " 314
    p his heir, when tall and marriageable, *Gareth and L.* 102
    'P, thou shalt go disguised to Arthur's hall, " 152
    Lancelot answer'd, 'P, O Gareth— " 1236
    Knight, knave, p and fool, I hate thee and for ever.' " 1255

Prince (*continued*) P, Knight, Hail, Knight and P, *Gareth and L.* 1270
    'Nay, P,' she cried, 'God wot, " 1332
    O P, I went for Lancelot first, " 1343
    the P Three times had blown— " 1377
    A tributary p of Devon, *Marr. of Geraint* 2
    Allowing it, the P and Enid rode, " 43
    As of a p whose manhood was all gone, " 59
    Low bow'd the tributary P, and she, " 174
    'Late, late, Sir P,' she said, " 177
    P Had put his horse in motion toward the knight, " 205
    The P's blood spirted upon the scarf, " 208
    'Farewell, fair P,' answer'd the stately Queen. " 224
    P, as Enid past him, fain To follow, " 375
    and while the P and Earl Yet spoke together, " 384
    and prove her heart toward the P.' " 513
    Loudly spake the P, 'Forbear: " 555
    'This noble p who won our earldom back, " 619
    But being so beholden to the P, " 623
    P had found her in her ancient home; " 644
    While ye were talking sweetly with your P, " 698
    Our mended fortunes and a P's bride: " 718
    the P Hath pick'd a ragged-robin from the hedge, " 723
    might shame the P To whom we are beholden; " 726
    we beat him back, As this great P invaded us, " 747
    And did her honour as the P's bride, " 835
    pair Of comrades making slowlier at the P, *Geraint and E.* 167
    'Ye will be all the wealthier,' cried the P. " 221
    P had brought his errant eyes Home from the rock, " 245
    thus he moved the P To laughter and his comrades " 295
    when the P was merry, ask'd Limours. " 297
    the stout P bad him a loud good-night. " 361
    P, without a word, from his horse fell. " 508
    love you, P, with something of the love " 788
    'Follow me, P, to the camp, " 808
    till he saw her Pass into it, turn'd to the P, " 887
    'P, when of late ye pray'd me for " 888
    So spake the King: low bow'd the P, " 920
    call'd him the great P and man of men. " 961
    'P, Art thou so little loyal to thy Queen, *Balin and Balan* 250
    P, we have ridd'n before among the flowers " 272
    thou, Sir P, Wilt surely guide me to the warrior King, " 477
    nor P Nor knight am I, " 483
    a P In the mid might and flourish of his May, *Lancelot and E.* 553
    to whom the P Reported who he was, " 627
    ride no more at random, noble P! " 633
    P Accorded with his wonted courtesy, " 637
    'P, O loyal nephew of our noble King, " 651
    yon proud P who left the quest to me. " 762
    told him all the tale Of King and P, " 824
    P and Lord am I In mine own land, " 916
    And there the heathen P, Arviragus, *Holy Grail* 61
    he knew the P tho' marr'd with dust, *Guinevere* 36
    Sir Lancelot holp To raise the P, " 46
    the P Who scarce had pluck'd his flickering life *To the Queen* ii 4
    full city peal'd Thee and thy P! " 27
    Like to the wild youth of an evil p, *Lover's Tale* i 354
    if our P's harken'd to my prayer, *Columbus* 100
    brought your P's gold enough If left alone! " 105
    native p's slain or slaved, " 174
    A princelier looking man never stept thro' a P's hall. *The Wreck* 16
    now Your fairy P has found you, *The Ring* 69
    One raised the P, one sleek'd the squalid hair, *Death of Œnone* 57
Princedom Drew all their petty p's under him, *Com. of Arthur* 18
    the King Drew in the petty p's under him, " 517
    In his own blood, his p, youth and hopes, *Gareth and L.* 210
    his p lay Close on the borders of a territory, *Marr. of Geraint* 33
    Forgetful of his p and its cares. " 54
Princelier A p looking man never stept thro' a Prince's hall. *The Wreck* 16
Princelike thro' these P his bearing shone; *Marr. of Geraint* 545
Princely And p halls, and farms, and flowing lawns, *Aylmer's Field* 654
    A p people's awful princes, *The Daisy* 39
    Yniol's rusted arms Were on his p person, *Marr. of Geraint* 544
    she gazed upon the man Of p bearing, *Pelleas and E.* 306
    So p, tender, truthful, reverent, pure— *D. of the Duke of C.* 4

Princely-proud too *p-p* To pass thereby;   *Gareth and L.* 162
Princess (*See also* **Maiden-Princess, Poet-princess**) The
  happy *p* follow'd him.   *Day-Dm., Depart.* 8
  I wish That I were some great *p*,   *Princess, Pro.* 134
  'And make her some great *P*, six feet high,   ,, 224
  Heroic seems our *P* as required—   ,, 230
  betroth'd To one, a neighbouring *P*:   ,, i 33
  Who moves about the *P*;   ,, 76
  beauty compass'd in a female form, The *P*;   ,, ii 35
  edge unturnable, our Head, The *P*.   ,, 204
  'Let the *P* judge Of that' she said: ,, 234
  the *P* should have been the Head,   ,, iii 34
  early risen she goes to inform The *P*:   ,, 63
  Not like your *P* cramm'd with erring pride,   ,, 102
  My *p*, O my *p*! true she errs,   ,, 107
  'That afternoon the *P* rode to take The dip   ,, 169
  but with some disdain Answer'd the *P*,   ,, iv 62
  'The Head, the Head, the *P*, O the Head!'   ,, 176
  They haled us to the *P* where she sat High in the hall: ,, 271
  It was not thus, O *P*, in old days: ,, 292
  She ceased: the *P* answer'd coldly, 'Good: ,, 359
  The *P* with her monstrous woman-guard,   ,, 562
  She was a *p* too: and so I swore.   ,, v 295
  A gallant fight, a noble *p*—   ,, Con. 19
  Like our wild *P* with as wise a dream   ,, 69
  Or at thy coming, *P*, everywhere,   *W. to Marie Alex.* 42
  I full oft shall dream I see my *p*   *Marr. of Geraint* 752
  In such apparel as might well beseem His *p*,   ,, 759
  hundred miles of coast, A palace and a *p*,   *Merlin and V.* 589
  hundred miles of coast, The palace and the *p*,   ,, 648
  The *P* of that castle was the one,   *Holy Grail* 578
  And tame thy jailing *p* to thine hand.   *Pelleas and E.* 344
  And marriage with a *p* of that realm,   *Last Tournament* 176
  DEAR *P*, living Power, if that,   *Ded. Poem Prin. Alice* 1
Principle 'Some hidden *p* to move,   *Two Voices* 133
  P's are rain'd in blood;   *Love thou thy land* 80
Print (**s**) (*See also* **Hoof-print, Jewel-print**) take the
  p Of the golden age—   *Maud I* i 29
  (Meaning the *p* that you gave us,   *In the Child. Hosp.* 51
Print (**verb**) hill and wood and field did *p*   *In Mem. lxxix* 7
Prior Archbishop, Bishop, *P*'s, Canons,   *Sir J. Oldcastle* 160
Priory sought A *p* not far off, there lodged,   *Pelleas and E.* 214
Prism Make *p*'s in every carven glass,   *Day-Dm., Sleep. P.* 35
Prison (**adj.**) Sang looking thro' his *p* bars?   *Margaret* 35
Prison (**s**) (*See also* **Shadow-prison**) I kiss'd my boy in the *p*,   *Rizpah* 23
  Flowers to these 'spirits in *p*'   *In the Child. Hosp.* 37
  My *p*, not my fortress, fall away!   *Doubt and Prayer* 12
Prison'd *P*, and kept and coax'd and whistled to—   *Gareth and L.* 14
Prisoner and himself The *p* at the bar,   *Sea Dreams* 176
  A *p*, and the vassal of thy will;   *Pelleas and E.* 241
  Being guiltless, as an innocent *p*,   *Lover's Tale i* 787
  As a vision Unto a haggard *p*,   ,, ii 148
  I read no more the *p*'s mute wail   *Sir J. Oldcastle* 4
Private A *p* life was all his joy,   *Will Water.* 129
  'Is this an hour For *p* sorrow's barren song,   *In Mem. xxi* 14
  For I never whisper'd a *p* affair   *Maud II* v 47
  But the red life spilt for a *p* blow—   ,, 93
Privet (**adj.**) To one green wicket in a *p* hedge;   *Gardener's D.* 1
Privet (**s**) white as *p* when it flowers.   *Walk. to the Mail* 56
Privilege manlike end myself?—our *p*—   *Lucretius* 232
  It was our ancient *p*, my Lords,   *Third of Feb.* 5
Prize (**s**) (*See also* **Tourney-prize**) Ride on! the *p* is near.'   *Sir Galahad* 80
  read and earn our *p*, A golden brooch: *Princess iii* 300
  The *p* of beauty for the fairest there.   *Marr. of Geraint* 485
  He felt, were she the *p* of bodily force,   ,, 541
  two years past have won for thee, The *p* of beauty.'   ,, 555
  tho' you won the *p* of fairest fair,   ,, 719
  shook her pulses, crying 'Look, a *p*!   *Geraint and E.* 123
  since a diamond was the *p*.   *Lancelot and E.* 33
  Proclaiming his the *p*, who wore the sleeve Of scarlet,   ,, 501
  'Advance and take thy *p* The diamond;'   ,, 503
  Prize me no *p*'s, for my *p* is death!   ,, 506
  left his *p* Untaken, crying that his *p* is death.'   ,, 530
  Will deem this *p* of ours is rashly given: ,, 541
  Came not to us, of us to claim the *p*,   ,, 544

Prize (**s**) (*continued*) with you? won he not your *p*?'   *Lancelot and E.* 573
  bore the *p* and could not find The victor,   ,, 629
  'Your *p* the diamond sent you by the King:'   ,, 821
  the *p* A golden circlet and a knightly sword,   *Pelleas and E.* 11
  Saving the goodly sword, his *p*,   ,, 359
  p Of Tristram in the jousts of yesterday,   *Last Tournament* 7
  Innocence the King Gave for a *p*—   ,, 295
  Of one—his name is out of me—the *p*, If *p* she were—   ,, 546
  I mused nor yet endured to take So rich a *p*,   *Lover's Tale iii* 50
Prize (**verb**) should I *p* thee, couldst thou last,   *Will Water.* 203
  I know the Prince, I *p* his truth: *Princess iii* 233
  What dares not Ida do that she should *p* The soldier?   ,, v 174
  sole men we shall *p* in the aftertime,   ,, 412
  p the authentic mother of her mind.   ,, 433
  what the King So *p*'s—overprizes—gentleness.   *Balin and Balan* 184
  'I better *p* The living dog than the dead lion: ,, 584
  prized him more Than who should *p* him   *Merlin and V.* 160
  P me no prizes, for my prize is death!   *Lancelot and E.* 506
  To Canada whom we love and *p*,   *Hands all Round* 19
  my friend, To *p* your various book,   *To Ulysses* 47
  I *p* that soul where man and woman   *On one who effec. E. M.* 2
Prized Or else we loved the man, and *p* his work;   *M. d'Arthur, Ep.* 8
  You *p* my counsel, lived upon my lips: *Princess iv* 293
  p him more Than who should prize him   *Merlin and V.* 159
  No sisters ever *p* each other more.   *Sisters (E. and E.)* 43
  He would open the books that I *p*,   *The Wreck* 21
  is *p* for it smells of the beast,   *The Dawn* 14
Prize-oxen A lord of fat *p-o* and of sheep,   *Princess, Con.* 86
Process widen'd with the *p* of the suns.   *Locksley Hall* 138
  Eternal *p* moving on,   *In Mem. lxxxii* 5
  Who reads thy gradual *p*, Holy Spring.   *Prog. of Spring* 106
Procession Let the long long *p* go,   *Ode on Well.* 15
  I came upon The rear of a *p*,   *Lover's Tale ii* 75
Proclaim From my high nest of penance here *p*   *St. S. Stylites* 167
  '*P* the faults he would not show   *You might have won* 17
  For many and many an age *p*   *Ode on Well.* 226
  let *p* a joust At Camelot,   *Lancelot and E.* 76
  the King Had let *p* a tournament—   *Pelleas and E.* 11
Proclaim'd Spake to the lady with him and *p*,   *Marr. of Geraint* 552
  Arthur's host *P* him Victor, and the day was won.   *Balin and Balan* 90
  p His Master as 'the Sun of Righteousness,'   *Akbar's Dream* 82
Proclaiming *P* Enoch Arden and his woes;   *Enoch Arden* 868
  P social truth shall spread,   *In Mem. cxxvii* 5
  set him in the hall, *P*, 'Here is Uther's heir,   *Com. of Arthur* 230
  P his the prize, who wore the sleeve Of scarlet,   *Lancelot and E.* 501
Proclamation sent His horns of *p* out   *Merlin and V.* 581
Proctor he had breathed the *P*'s dogs;   *Princess, Pro.* 113
  prudes for *p*'s, dowagers for deans,   ,, 141
  Two *P*'s leapt upon us, crying, 'Names:'   ,, iv 259
Procuress *P* to the Lords of Hell.   *In Mem. liii* 16
Prodigal Behind Were realms of upland, *p* in oil,   *Palace of Art* 79
  And *p* of all brain-labour he,   *Aylmer's Field* 447
Prodigies These *p* of myriad nakednesses,   *Lucretius* 156
Prodigious a match as this! Impossible, *p*!'   *Aylmer's Field* 315
  Or Gareth telling some *p* tale Of knights,   *Gareth and L.* 508
Produce (**s**) *P* of your field and flood,   *Open. I. and C. Exhib.* 5
Produce (**verb**) That one fair planet can *p*,   *Ode Inter. Exhib.* 24
Profess seeing they *P* to be none other (repeat)   *Last Tournament* 82, 85
Professor we heard The grave *P*.   *Princess ii* 371
  Sat compass'd with *p*'s: ,, 444
Proffer (**s**) She to Paris made *P* of royal power,   *Œnone* 111
  nor did mine own Refuse her *p*,   *Princess vi* 347
  Made *p* of the league of golden mines,   *Merlin and V.* 646
Proffer (**verb**) *p* these The brethren of our blood   *Princess vi* 70
Proffer'd At one dear knee we *p* vows,   *In Mem. lxxix* 13
  For howsoe'er at first he *p* gold,   *Gareth and L.* 336
Profile Less *p*! turn to me—three-quarter face.   *Romney's R.* 98
Profit (**s**) (*See also* **Self-profit**) With fuller *p*'s lead an
  easier life,   *Enoch Arden* 145
  With daily-dwindling *p*'s held the house;   ,, 696
  But now to leaven play with *p*,   *Princess iv* 149
  The Lady Blanche: much *p*!   ,, vi 239
  Will bloom to *p*, otherwhere.   *In Mem. lxxxii* 12
  What *p* lies in barren faith,   ,, cviii 5
  It surely was my *p* had I known: *Guinevere* 658

Profit (verb) It little *p*'s that an idle king,   *Ulysses* 1
what *p*'s it to put An idle case?   *In Mem. xxxv* 17
what *p*'s me my name Of greatest knight?   *Lancelot and E.* 1413
What *p*'s an ill Priest Between me and my God?   *Sir J. Oldcastle* 144

Profound Passionless, pale, cold face, star-sweet on a gloom *p*;   *Maud I iii* 4

Profulgent An image with *p* brows,   *Supp. Confessions* 145

Progress Our *p* falter to the woman's goal.'   *Princess vi* 127
With statelier *p* to and fro   *In Mem. xcviii* 22
P halts on palsied feet,   *Locksley H., Sixty* 219

Project *p* after *p* rose, and all of them were vain;   *The Flight* 14

Prolong *p* Her low preamble all alone,   *Palace of Art* 173

Promenaded With cypress *p*,   *Amphion* 38

Promise (s) (*See also* **Hand-promise**) Leaving the *p* of my bridal bower,   *D. of F. Women* 218
for the *p* that it closed;   *Locksley Hall* 14
the crescent *p* of my spirit   " 187
With words of *p* in his walk,   *Day-Dm., Arrival* 23
' I am bound: you have my *p*—in a year: *Enoch Arden* 437
stood once more before her face, Claiming her *p*.   " 458
falling in a land Of *p*;   *Princess ii* 140
hold Your *p*: all, I trust, may yet be well.'   " 361
other distance and the hues Of *p*;   " *iv* 87
With *p* of a morn as fair;   *In Mem. lxxxiv* 29
The *p* of the golden hours?   " *lxxxv* 106
Knowing your *p* to me;   *Maud I xxii* 10
Thy *p*, King,' and Arthur glancing at him,   *Gareth and L.* 652
Forgetful of his *p* to the King,   *Marr. of Geraint* 50
Bribed with large *p*'s the men who served   " 453
Woke and bethought her of her *p* given   " 602
He would not leave her, till her *p* given—   " 605
Made *p*, that whatever boon I brought,   " 783
Pelleas might obtain his lady's love, According to her *p*,   *Pelleas and E.* 162
And thou hast given thy *p*,   " 245
With *p* of large light on woods and ways.   " 394
Green prelude, April *p*, glad new-year   *Lover's Tale i* 281
A land of *p*, a land of memory,   " 333
A land of *p* flowing with the milk And honey   " 334
mother broke her *p* to the dead,   *Sisters (E. and E.)* 252
p of blossom, but never a fruit!   *V. of Maeldune* 51
but the *p* had faded away;   *Despair* 27
Be truer to your *p*.   *To Mary Boyle* 5
The still-fulfilling *p* of a light   *Prog. of Spring* 90

Promise (verb) *p* thee The fairest and most loving wife in Greece,'   *Œnone* 186
p (otherwise You perish) as you came,   *Princess ii* 295
who might have shamed us: *p*, all.'   " 299
I *p* you Some palace in our land,   " *iii* 161
King, for hardihood I can *p* thee.   *Gareth and L.* 557
' Now all be dumb, and *p* all of you   *Lover's Tale iv* 351
Didn't you kiss me an' *p*?   *First Quarrel* 53
We will make the Spaniard *p*,   *The Revenge* 94
P me, Miriam not Muriel—she shall have the ring.'   *The Ring* 293

Promise-bounden awed and *p-b* she forbore,   *Enoch Arden* 869

Promised (adj.) (*See also* **Long-promised**) Full to the banks, close on the *p* good.   *Maud I xviii* 6

Promised (verb) And Dora *p*, being meek.   *Dora* 46
and once again She *p*.   *Enoch Arden* 906
she *p* that no force, Persuasion, no,   *Aylmer's Field* 417
What could we else, we *p* each;   *Princess ii* 300
who *p* help, and oozed All o'er with honey'd answer   " *v* 241
she *p* then to be fair.   *Maud I i* 68
He *p* more than ever king has given,   *Merlin and V.* 586
She ceased: her father *p*;   *Lancelot and E.* 1130
those who knew him near the King, And *p* for him: *Pelleas and E.* 16
Lancelot ever *p*, but remain'd,   *Guinevere* 93
' You *p* to find me work near you,   *First Quarrel* 52
an' 'e *p* a son to she,   *Owd Roä* 95
fur I *p* ya'd niver not do it ageän.   *Church-warden, etc.* 32
when he *p* to make me his bride,   *Charity* 11

Promising like a household god *P* empire;   *On a Mourner* 31
Miriam Lane Made such a voluble answer *p* all,   *Enoch Arden* 903

Promontory Lingering about the thymy *promontories*,   *Sea Dreams* 38
Who seems a *p* of rock,   *Will* 8
winds of winter tear an oak on a *p*.   *Boädicea* 77
Saw once a great piece of a *p*,   *Geraint and E.* 162

Prompt as *p* to spring against the pikes,   *Princess iii* 286

Prone Just where the *p* edge of the wood began (repeat)   *Enoch Arden* 67, 373
falling *p* he dug His fingers into the wet earth,   " 779
Against the rush of the air in the *p* swing,   *Aylmer's Field* 86
She veil'd her brows, and *p* she sank,   *Princess v* 107
Thy climbing life, and cherish my *p* year,   *Gareth and L.* 95
p from off her seat she fell,   *Guinevere* 414
in *p* flight By thousands down the crags   *Montenegro* 7

Pronest that most impute a crime Are *p* to it,   *Merlin and V.* 826

Pronounce Nor can *p* upon it If one should ask   *Maud I xx* 16

Pronounced the King *P* a dismal sentence,   *Merlin and V.* 591
All that look'd on her had *p* her dead,   *Lover's Tale iv* 35
himself *p* That my rich gift is wholly mine   " 349
and when The Priest *p* you dead,   *Happy* 50

Proœmion my rich *p* makes Thy glory fly   *Lucretius* 70

Proof To arm in *p*, and guard about   *Supp. Confessions* 65
wall about thy cause With iron-worded *p*,   *To J. M. K.* 9
lest thy heart be put to *p*,   *Locksley Hall* 77
train Of flowery clauses onward to the *p*   *Lucretius* 120
' Come, listen! here is *p* that you were miss'd':   *Princess, Pro.* 177
If we could give them surer, quicker *p*—   " *iii* 282
The *p* and echo of all human fame,   *Ode on Well.* 145
go then, an ye must: only one *p*,   *Gareth and L.* 144
the *p* to prove me to the quick!'   " 150
Tho' yet there lived no *p*,   *Marr. of Geraint* 26
Might well have served for *p* that I was loved,   " 796
As *p* of trust. O Merlin, teach it me.   *Merlin and V.* 331
The great *p* of your love: " 354
prurient for a *p* against the grain   " 487
p of trust—so often ask'd in vain!   " 920
by nine years' *p* we needs must learn   *Lancelot and E.* 62
a *p* That I—even I—at times   *Romney's R.* 92

Proofless Spleen-born, I think, and *p*.   *Merlin and V.* 702

Prop falls A creeper when the *p* is broken,   *Aylmer's Field* 810

Proper Upon my *p* patch of soil To grow my own plantation.   *Amphion* 99
His *p* chop to each.   *Will Water.* 116
this is *p* to the clown, Tho' smock'd, or furr'd   *Princess iv* 246
Till happier times each to her *p* hearth: " *vi* 303
To shroud me from my *p* scorn.   *In Mem. xxvi* 16
He mixing with his *p* sphere,   " *lx* 5
Thy sweetness from its *p* place?   " *lxxxiii* 6
your work is this To hold me from my *p* place,   " *cxvii* 2

Property *See* **Proputty**

Prophecy If aught of *p* be mine,   *Clear-headed friend* 8
At last She rose upon a wind of *p*   *Princess ii* 171
They might not seem thy *prophecies*,   *In Mem. xcii* 13
For the *p* given of old And then not understood,   *Maud II v* 42
A prophet certain of my *p*,   *Marr. of Geraint* 814
Or was there sooth in Arthur's *p*,   *Holy Grail* 709
if ancient *prophecies* Have err'd not,   *Guinevere* 449

Prophesied Approvingly, and *p* his rise: *Aylmer's Field* 474
I have *p*—Strike, thou art worthy   *Gareth and L.* 1137
As holy John had *p* of me,   *Columbus* 21

Prophesy I *p* that I shall die to-night,   *St. S. Stylites* 220
Dismiss me, and I *p* your plan,   *Princess iv* 354
all is lost In what they *p*,   *Epilogue* 65

Prophesying *p* change Beyond all reason: *Princess i* 142
upon me flash'd The power of *p*—   *Tiresias* 57

Prophet (*See also* **World-prophet**) My heart was like a *p* to my heart,   *Gardener's D.* 63
Is there no *p* but the voice that calls   *Aylmer's Field* 741
Cries ' Come up hither,' as a *p* to us?   " 745
fire on a masthead, *P* of storm: *Princess iv* 275
The *p*'s blazon'd on the panes;   *In Mem. lxxxvii* 8
P, curse me the blabbing lip,   *Maud II v* 57
A naked babe, of whom the *P* spake,   *Gareth and L.* 501
A *p* certain of my prophecy,   *Marr. of Geraint* 814
The people call you *p*: let it be: *Merlin and V.* 317
think I show myself Too dark a *p*:   *Holy Grail* 322
For every fiery *p* in old times,   " 876
Was I too dark a *p* when I said   " 889
to some old *p* might have seem'd A vision   *Pelleas and E.* 51
ill *p*'s were they all, Spirits and men: *Guinevere* 272
The *p* and the chariot and the steeds,   *Lover's Tale i* 307
Or *p*'s of them in his fantasy,   " *iv* 12

Prophet (*continued*)   and *p* of the perfect man ;   *De Prof., Two G.* 12
The *p's* beacon burn'd in vain,   *Ancient Sage* 142
And ' The Curse of the *P* ' in Heaven.   *Dead Prophet* 28
Tho' a *p* should have his due,   ,,   50
since he would sit on a *P's* seat,   ,,   53
She tore the *P* after death,   ,,   77
The *p* of his own, my Hubert—   *The Ring* 23
P of the gay time, *P* of the May time, *P* of the roses,   *The Snowdrop* 6
Never a *p* so crazy !   *The Throstle* 10
Issa Ben Mariam, his own *p*,   *Akbar's Dream* 75
he, That other, *p* of their fall,   ,,   82
art *thou* the *P* ? canst *thou* work Miracles ? '   ,,   117
had some *p* spoken true Of all we shall achieve,   *Mechanophilus* 25
Prophetess   have dash'd The passion of the *p* ;   *Princess iv* 140
sang the terrible *p'es*,   *Boädicea* 37
Prophet-eye   *P-e's* may catch a glory   *Making of Man* 6
Prophetic   Mothers,—that, all *p* pity,   *Princess v* 381
Prophetical   at length *P* and prescient   *Lover's Tale ii* 132
Prophet-mind   Self-gather'd in her *p-m*,   *Of old sat Freedom* 6
Propitiated   Taranis be *p*.   *Boädicea* 16
Proportion   gave him mind, the lordiest *P*,   *Two Voices* 20
Propose   I *p* to-night To show you   *Lover's Tale iv* 251
Proposed   Grave doubts and answers here *p*,   *In Mem. xlviii* 3
Propping   in the naked hall, *p* his head,   *Geraint and E.* 581
And found his own dear bride *p* his head,   ,,   584
Proprietress   Is she The sweet *p* a shadow ?   *Princess ii* 415
Propt   my mother, when with brows *P* on thy knees,   *Supp. Confessions* 70
p on beds of amaranth and moly,   *Lotos-Eaters, C. S.* 88
So *p*, worm-eaten, ruinously old,   *Enoch Arden* 693
A broken statue *p* against the wall,   *Princess, Pro.* 99
she, half on her mother *p*, Half-drooping from her,   ,,   *iv* 367
Proputty (Property)   *P*, *p*, *p*—that's what I 'ears 'em   saäy.   *N. Farmer, N.S.* 2
P, *p*, *p*—Sam, thou's an ass for thy paaïns :   ,,   3
P, *p*—woä then woä—   ,,   8
But *p*, *p* sticks, an' *p*, *p* graws.   ,,   16
Woä then, *p*, wiltha ?—   ,,   39
P, *p's* ivrything 'ere,   ,,   43
Coom oop, *p*, *p*—that's what I 'ears 'im saäy—   ,,   59
P, *p*, *p*—canter an' canter awaäy.   ,,   60
Prose (s)   I will work in *p* and rhyme,   *Talking Oak* 289
Let raffs be rife in *p* and rhyme.   *Will Water.* 61
Prose (verb)   they *p* O'er books of travell'd seamen,   *Amphion* 81
Proserpine   Like *P* in Enna, gathering flowers :   *Edwin Morris* 112
Prospect   Large range of *p* had the mother sow,   *Walk. to the Mail* 93
My *p* and horizon gone.   *In Mem. xxxviii* 4
Arise in open *p*—heath and hill,   *Lover's Tale i* 397
Prosper   While yon sun *p's* in the blue,   *The Blackbird* 22
And the third time may *p*,   *M. d'Arthur* 130
and thought He scarce would *p*.   *Princess iii* 76
May she mix With men and *p* !   *In Mem. cxiv* 3
I *p*, circled with thy voice ;   ,,   *cxxx* 15
And the third time may *p*,   *Pass. of Arthur* 298
Prosper'd   throve and *p*: so three years She *p*:   *Palace of Art* 217
so *p* that at last A luckier or a bolder fisherman,   *Enoch Arden* 48
And *p* ; till a rout of saucy boys Brake on us   *Princess v* 394
Hath *p* in the name of Christ,   *Balin and Balan* 99
rich man, That, having always *p* in the world,   *Lover's Tale i* 716
Prosperity   return In such a sunlight of *p*   *Aylmer's Field* 421
Prosperous   lead Thro' *p* floods his holy urn.   *In Mem. ix* 8
While now thy *p* labour fills   ,,   *lxxxv* 25
' Be *p* in this journey, as in all ;   *Marr. of Geraint* 225
Now with *p* auguries Comes at last   *On Jub. Q. Victoria* 9
Prostrate   Sprang from the midriff of a *p* king—   *Aylmer's Field* 16
Protector   call'd him dear *p* in her fright,   *Merlin and V.* 946
Protestant   found her beating the hard *P* doors.   *Sisters (E. and E.)* 240
Protesting   some Vowing, and some *p*), ' what is this ? '   *Holy Grail* 270
Protomartyr   falling, *p* of our cause, Die :   *Princess iv* 505
Proud (adj.)   (*See also* **Princely-proud**)   I know you *p*   to bear your name,   *L. C. V. de Vere* 10
Too *p* to care from whence I came.   ,,   12
languid light of your *p* eyes Is wearied   ,,   59
Be *p* of those strong sons of thine   *England and Amer.* 4
Thought her *p*, and fled over the sea ;   *Edward Gray* 14
Their ancient name ! they *might* be *p* ;   *Aylmer's Field* 378

Proud (adj.) (*continued*)   and mean Vileness, we are   grown so *p*—   *Aylmer's Field* 756
P look'd the lips :   *Princess i* 96
and this *p* watchword rest Of equal ;   ,,   *vii* 300
' O boy, tho' thou art young and *p*,   *Sailor Boy* 7
you wrong your beauty, believe it, in being so *p* ;   *Maud I iv* 17
P on 'im, like, my lad,   *North. Cobbler* 97
Of saner worship sanely *p* ;   *Freedom* 30
My nature was too *p*.   *Happy* 78
three of these *P* in their fantasy call themselves   the Day,   *Gareth and L.* 633
And since the *p* man often is the mean,   *Marr. of Geraint* 449
overthrow My *p* self, and my purpose three years   old,   *Geraint and E.* 849
There to his *p* horse Lancelot turn'd,   *Lancelot and E.* 347
And moved about her palace, *p* and pale.   ,,   614
As yon *p* Prince who left the quest to me.   ,,   762
wherefore would ye look On this *p* fellow again,   ,,   1065
Against the *p* archbishop Arundel—   *Sir J. Oldcastle* 16
that *p* Priest, That mock-meek mouth of utter Antichrist,   ,,   169
Slender warrant had *He* to be *p* of The welcome   *Batt. of Brunanburh* 67
Proud (s)   Which rolling o'er the palaces of the *p*,   *Aylmer's Field* 636
The *p* was half disarm'd of pride,   *In Mem. cx* 6
' Turn, Fortune, turn thy wheel and lower the *p* ;   *Marr. of Geraint* 347
Prouder   She felt her heart grow *p*   *The Goose* 22
Prove   To put together, part and *p*,   *Two Voices* 134
To feel, altho' no tongue can *p*,   ,,   445
You sought to *p* how I could love,   *L. C. V. de Vere* 21
p me what it is I would not do.'   *Godiva* 27
To *p* myself a poet :   *Will Water.* 166
Pale again as death did *p*:   *L. of Burleigh* 66
I fain would *p* A father to your children :   *Enoch Arden* 410
She must *p* true: for, brother,   *Aylmer's Field* 364
call him, love, Before you *p* him, rogue,   *Sea Dreams* 171
Your language *p's* you still the child.   *Princess ii* 58
or *p* The Danaïd of a leaky vase,   ,,   339
I *p* Your knight, and fight your battle,   ,,   *iv* 594
may thy mother *p* As true to thee as false,   ,,   *vi* 203
no truer Time himself Can *p* you,   *A Dedication* 2
Believing where we cannot *p* ;   *In Mem., Pro.* 4
I long to *p* No lapse of moons   ,,   *xxvi* 2
Her care is not to part and *p* ;   ,,   *xlviii* 5
and I shall *p* A meeting somewhere,   ,,   *lxxxv* 98
Should *p* the phantom-warning true.   ,,   *xcii* 12
Let Science *p* we are, and then   ,,   *cxx* 6
Or thou wilt *p* their tool.   *Maud I vi* 59
' Well, if it *p* a girl, the boy   ,,   *vii* 7
' Well, if it *p* a girl, my boy   ,,   15
the proof to *p* me to the quick ! '   *Gareth and L.* 150
and *p* her heart toward the Prince.'   *Marr. of Geraint* 513
I someway *p* such force in her Link'd with such love   ,,   805
That he might *p* her to the uttermost,   *Geraint and E.* 589
Shall I not rather *p* the worse for these ?   *Balin and Balan* 228
We go to *p* it.   Bide ye here the while.'   *Merlin and V.* 97
make me yearn still more to *p* you mine,   ,,   328
That I should *p* it on you unawares,   ,,   340
What other ? for men sought to *p* me vile,   ,,   495
For tho' you should not *p* it upon me,   ,,   687
All—all—the wish to *p* him wholly hers.'   ,,   865
They *p* to him his work :   *Lancelot and E.* 158
p No surer than our falcon yesterday,   ,,   655
Yea, let her *p* me to the uttermost,   *Pelleas and E.* 211
look'd, as he is like to *p*, When Julian goes,   *Lover's Tale iv* 314
Terrible pity, if one so beautiful *P*,   ,,   339
May *p* as peaceful as his own.   *Tiresias* 217
Thou canst not *p* the Nameless, O my son, Nor canst   thou *p* the world thou movest in, Thou canst not *p*   that thou art body alone, Nor canst thou *p* that   thou art spirit alone,   *Ancient Sage* 57
Nor canst thou *p* that thou art both in one :   ,,   61
Thou canst not *p* thou art immortal,   ,,   62
Thou canst not *p* that I, who speak with thee,   ,,   64
Proved   Hadst thou less unworthy *p*—   *Locksley Hall* 63
Before you prove him, rogue, and *p*, forgive.   *Sea Dreams* 171
but him I *p* impossible ;   *Lucretius* 193

Proved (*continued*)   By which our lives are chiefly *p*,   *In Mem.* cv 14
    The truths that never can be *p*   „ cxxxi 10
    nor *p* Since that dark day a day like this;   *Con.* 7
    We have *p* we have hearts in a cause,   *Maud* III vi 55
    p him everyway One of our noblest,   *Geraint and E.* 909
    that also have we *p*;   *Balin and Balan* 34
    Nor is he the wisest man who never *p* himself a fool.   *Locksley H., Sixty* 244
Proven   *See* Prov'n
Provence   hair Studded with one rich *P* rose—   *Lover's Tale* iii 45
Provender   For lust or lusty blood or *p*:   *Lucretius* 198
Proverb   This *p* flashes thro' his head,   *Day-Dm., Arrival* 15
    till their love Shall ripen to a *p*,   *Lover's Tale* i 758
Providence   sermonizing On *p* and trust in Heaven,   *Enoch Arden* 205
Province   they press in from all the *p*'s,   *Princess* ii 97
    O Love, thy *p* were not large,   *In Mem.* xlvi 13
    tho' they sought Thro' all the *p*'s   *Marr. of Geraint* 730
    p with a hundred miles of coast, (repeat)   *Merlin and V.* 588, 647
    leaves Some colder *p* in the North   *The Ring* 481
    and rule thy *P* of the brute.   *By an Evolution.* 16
Proving   converse in the hall, *P* her heart: *Marr. of Geraint* 521
    this cursed charm, Were *p* it on me,   *Merlin and V.* 436
    nothing worthy *p* can be proven,   *Ancient Sage* 66
Prov'n   ' Not *p*' Averill said, or laughingly 'Some other race of Averills'—*p* or no, What cared he?   *Aylmer's Field* 53
    and a laugh Ringing like *p* golden coinage true,   „ 182
    who hath *p* him King Uther's son?   *Com. of Arthur* 69
    Ask'd me to tilt with him, the *p* knight.   *Gareth and L.* 27
    Not *p*, who swept the dust of ruin'd Rome   „ 135
    But justice, so thy say be *p* true.   „ 346
    the first quest: he is not *p*.   „ 582
    O star, my morning dream hath *p* true,   „ 1000
    And horrors only *p* a blooming boy.   „ 1425
    But rather *p* in his Paynim wars Than famous jousts; but see, or *p* or not,   *Balin and Balan* 38
    or a traitor *p*, or hound Beaten,   *Pelleas and E.* 439
    only *p* themselves Prisoners, murderers.   *Sir J. Oldcastle* 167
    nothing worthy proving can be *p*,   *Ancient Sage* 66
    Re-volution has *p* but E-volution   *Beautiful City* 3
Prow   shake The sparkling flints beneath the *p*.   *Arabian Nights* 52
    round about the *p* she wrote *The Lady of Shalott*,   *L. of Shalott* iv 8
    round the *p* they read her name, *The Lady of Shalot*:   „ 44
    Lady's-head upon the *p* Caught the shrill salt,   *The Voyage* 11
    Now nearer to the *p* she seem'd   „ 67
    Sleep, gentle heavens, before the *p*;   *In Mem.* ix 14
    dart again, and play About the *p*,   „ xii 18
    vessel in mid-ocean, her heaved *p* Clambering,   *Lover's Tale* ii 169
    chains for him Who push'd his *p*'s   *Columbus* 24
    their nail'd *p*'s Parted the Norsemen,   *Batt. of Brunanburh* 93
Prowess   whereas I know Your *p*, Arac,   *Princess* v 404
    great deeds Of Lancelot, and his *p* in the lists,   *Lancelot and E.* 82
    His *p* was too wondrous.   „ 542
    learn If his old *p* were in aught decay'd;   „ 584
    acts of *p* done In tournament or tilt,   *Holy Grail* 1
    thought Of all my late-shown *p* in the lists,   „ 362
    Thou thoughtest of thy *p* and thy sins?   „ 455
    here and there a deed Of *p* done   *Guinevere* 459
    In height and *p* more than human,   *Tiresias* 179
Prowest   I chant thy praise As *p* knight and truest lover,   *Pelleas and E.* 350
Prowling   While the Fiend is *p*.   *Forlorn* 66
Proxy-wedded   *p-w* with a bootless calf   *Princess* i 34
Prude   *p*'s for proctors, dowagers for deans,   „ *Pro.* 141
Prudence   a *p* to withhold;   *Isabel* 15
    by slow *p* to make mild A rugged people,   *Ulysses* 36
    Let not your *p*, dearest, drowse,   *Princess* ii 339
Prudent   The *p* partner of his blood   *Two Voices* 415
    these outbuzz'd me so That even our *p* king,   *Columbus* 122
Pruned   Thro' crowded lilac-ambush trimly *p*;   *Gardener's D.* 112
Prurient   *p* for a proof against the grain   *Merlin and V.* 487
    ' In filthy sloughs they roll a *p* skin,   *Palace of Art* 201
Prussian   Last, the *P* trumpet blew;   *Ode on Well.* 127
Pry   not to *p* and peer on your reserve,   *Princess* iv 419
Psalm   with sound Of pious hymns and *p*'s,   *St. S. Stylites* 34
    sound Of solemn *p*'s, and silver litanies   *Princess* ii 477
    Who roll'd the *p* to wintry skies,   *In Mem.* lvi 11

Psalm (*continued*)   As a *p* by a mighty master   *The Wreck* 53
    ' Libera me, Domine!' you sang the *P*,   *Happy* 49
Psyche   Two widows, Lady *P*, Lady Blanche;   *Princess* i 128
    ' Lady Blanche' she said, ' And Lady *P*.'   „ 233
    Which was prettiest, Best-natured ? ' Lady *P*.'   „ 234
    with your own, As Lady *P*'s pupils.'   „ 240
    Lady *P* will harangue The fresh arrivals   „ ii 95
    back again we crost the court To Lady *P*'s: „ 101
    ' Well then, *P*, take my life,   „ 204
    ' having seen And heard the Lady *P*.'   „ 211
    ' Are you that Lady *P*,' I rejoin'd,   „ 237
    ' Are you that *P*,' Florian added,   „ 246
    are you That *P*, wont to bind my throbbing brow,   „ 250
    are you That brother-sister *P*, both in one ?   „ 254
    You were that *P*, but what are you now ? ' (repeat)   „ 255, 277
    ' You are that *P*,' Cyril said,   „ 256
    ' Are you that Lady *P*,' I began,   „ 261
    ' Are you that *P*,' Florian ask'd,   „ 269
    Then Lady *P*, ' Ah—Melissa—you !   „ 330
    While *P* watch'd them, smiling,   „ 365
    you learnt No more from *P*'s lecture,   „ 393
    The long-limb'd lad that had a *P* too,   „ 406
    And dear is sister *P* to my heart,   „ 418
    To rail at Lady *P* and her side.   „ iii 33
    Herself and Lady *P* the two arms;   „ 35
    Lady *P* was the right hand now,   „ 37
    Lady *P* will be crush'd;   „ 63
    Affirms your *P* thieved her theories,   „ 92
    Nor like poor *P* whom she drags in tow.'   „ 103
    then, climbing, Cyril kept With *P*,   „ 355
    P flush'd and wann'd and shook;   „ iv 160
    demanded if her mother knew, Or *P*,   „ 234
    She sent For *P*, but she was not there: „ 237
    she call'd For *P*'s child to cast it from the doors;   „ 238
    And where are *P*, Cyril ? both are fled :   „ 241
    you planed her path To Lady *P*,   „ 316
    ' We thank you, we shall hear of it From Lady *P*:'   „ 329
    later in the night Had come on *P* weeping: „ v 50
    With *P*'s babe, was Ida watching us,   „ 512
    With *P*'s colour round his helmet,   „ 534
    after him Came *P*, sorrowing for Aglaïa.   „ vi 29
    high upon the palace Ida stood With *P*'s babe in arm: „ 31
    while *P* ever stole A little nearer,   „ 132
    Who turn'd half-round to *P* as she sprang   „ 209
    ' Come hither. O *P*,' she cried out,   „ 285
    But *P* tended Florian : with her oft, Melissa came;   „ vii 55
    second suit obtain'd At first with *P*.   „ 72
    Ida came behind Seen but of *P*:   „ 79
Ptarmigan   know The *p* that whitens ere his hour   *Last Tournament* 697
Public   I raged against the *p* liar;   *The Letters* 26
    No *p* life was his on earth,   *You might have won* 23
    Drink we, last, the *p* fool,   *Vision of Sin* 149
    A lidless watcher of the *p* weal,   *Princess* iv 325
    But *p* use required she should be known; And since my oath was ta'en for *p* use,   „ 336
    Till *p* wrong be crumbled into dust,   *Ode on Well.* 167
    They call'd me in the *p* squares   *In Mem.* lxix 11
    Not let any man think for the *p* good,   *Maud* II v 45
    Friend, to be struck by the *p* foe,   „ 89
    That were a *p* merit, far,   „ 91
    And left him lying in the *p* way;   *Geraint and E.* 478
    not the King's—For *p* use: *Lancelot and E.* 60
    I hold that man the worst of *p* foes   *Guinevere* 512
    And leave him in the *p* way to die.   *Lover's Tale* iv 261
    or flamed at a *p* wrong,   *The Wreck* 68
    Thy power, well-used to move the *p* breast.   *To W.C. Macready* 3
    That wanders from the *p* good,   *Freedom* 26
Pucker'd   And shoals of *p* faces drive;   *In Mem.* lxx 10
Puddin'   beslings *p* an' Adam's wine;   *North. Cobbler* 112
Puddled   ' So *p* as it is with favouritism.'   *Princess* iii 146
Puff (s)   Upon the level in little *p*'s of wind,   „ iv 256
Puff (verb)   A wind to *p* your idol-fires,   *Love thou thy land* 69
    the vessel *p*'s her sail.   *Ulysses* 44
Puff'd (adj.)   Where with *p* cheek the belted hunter   *Palace of Art* 63
    behind I heard the *p* pursuer;   *Princess* iv 265

Puff'd (verb) angry gust of wind *P* out his torch   *Merlin and V.* 731
     breaths of anger *p* Her fairy nostril out;   „ 848
     morn That *p* the swaying branches into smoke   *Holy Grail* 15
Pug a score of *p*'s And poodles yell'd   *Edwin Morris* 119
Puissance of her brethren, youths of *p*;   *Princess* i 37
Puissant (*See also* **All-puissant**) round The warrior's *p*
     shoulders Pallas flung   *Achilles over the T.* 3
Pull ' Yet *p* not down my palace towers,   *Palace of Art* 293
     P off, *p* off, the brooch of gold,   *Lady Clare* 39
     tears that make the rose *P* sideways,   *In Mem.* lxxii 11
Pulpit-drone humming of the drowsy *p-d*   *To J. M. K.* 10
Pulpiteer To chapel; where a heated *p*,   *Sea Dreams* 20
Pulsation Hung tranced from all *p*,   *Gardener's D.* 260
     Make me feel the wild *p*   *Locksley Hall* 109
     The wild *p* of her wings;   *In Mem.* xii 4
     The deep *p*'s of the world,   „ xcv 40
Pulse lent The *p* of hope to discontent.   *Two Voices* 450
     Shall strike within thy *p*'s, like a God's,   *Œnone* 162
     stirr'd with languid *p*'s of the oar,   *Gardener's D.* 41
     And her whisper throng'd my *p*'s   *Locksley Hall* 36
     her palfrey's footfall shot Light horrors thro' her *p*'s :   *Godiva* 59
     lent my desire to kneel, and shook My *p*'s,   *Princess* iii 194
     you keep One *p* that beats true woman,   „ vi 180
     p's at the clamouring of her enemy   *Boädicea* 82
     My *p*'s therefore beat again For other friends   *In Mem.* lxxxv 57
     And every *p* of wind and wave Recalls,   „ 73
     measured *p* of racing oars Among the willows;   „ lxxxvii 10
     The *p*'s of a Titan's heart,   „ ciii 32
     force, that keeps A thousand *p*'s dancing,   „ cxxv 16
     my *p*'s closed their gates with a shock   *Maud* I i 15
     Lord of the *p* that is lord of her breast,   „ xvi 13
     died to live, long as my *p*'s play;   „ xviii 66
     Is it gone ? my *p*'s beat—   „ II i 36
     shook her *p*'s, crying, ' Look, a prize !   *Geraint and E.* 123
     and stirs the *p* With devil's leaps,   *Guinevere* 521
     With its true-touched *p*'s in the flow   *Lover's Tale* i 205
     And faints, and hath no *p*, no breath—   „ 268
     Unfrequent, low, as tho' it told its *p*'s ;   „ ii 55
     had lain three days without a *p* :   „ iv 34
     strike Thy youthful *p*'s into rest   *Tiresias* 157
     tho' every *p* would freeze,   *The Flight* 53
     Look how the living *p* of Alla beats   *Akbar's Dream* 41
Pulse (vegetable) eating hoary grain and *p* the steeds,   *Spec. of Iliad* 21
Pulse (verb) began To *p* with such a vehemence   *Lover's Tale* iv 82
     fountain *p*'s high in sunnier jets,   *Prog. of Spring* 54
Pulsing (*See also* **Red-pulsing**) heather-scented air,
     P full man;   *Last Tournament* 692
Pummel dash'd the *p* at the foremost face,   *Balin and Balan* 402
Pun the *p*, the scurrilous tale,—   *Aylmer's Field* 441
Punched *See* **Poonch'd**
Punishment *See* **Pillar-punishment**
Puny This pretty, *p*, weakly little one,—   *Enoch Arden* 195
Pup *See* **Poop**
Pupil Some meeker *p* you must find,   *L. C. V. de Vere* 18
     with your own, As Lady Psyche's *p*'s.'   *Princess* i 240
     A patient range of *p*'s ;   „ ii 104
     angled with them for her *p*'s love;   „ iii 93
Pupilage sons of kings loving in *p*   *Merlin and V.* 517
Puppet *P* to a father's threat,   *Locksley Hall* 42
     We are *p*'s, Man in his pride,   *Maud* I iv 25
Puppy blind and shuddering *puppies*,   *The Brook* 130
Purblind O *P* race of miserable men,   *Geraint and E.* 1
Purchase Yet he hoped to *p* glory,   *The Captain* 17
     To *p* his own boat, and make a home For Annie :   *Enoch Arden* 47
     We sent mine host to *p* female gear;   *Princess* i 199
Purchased *p* his own boat, and made a home For Annie,   *Enoch Arden* 58
Pure (*See also* **Perfect-pure**) ' Her court was *p*; her
     life serene ;   *To the Queen* 25
     But why Prevail'd not thy *p* prayers ?   *Supp. Confessions* 89
     P vestal thoughts in the translucent fane   *Isabel* 4
     Of perfect wifehood and *p* lowlihead.   „ 12
     P silver, underpropt a rich Throne   *Arabian Nights* 145
     As *p* and true as blades of steel.   *Kate* 16
     Pacing with downward eyelids *p*.   *Two Voices* 420
     Disclosed a fruit of *p* Hesperian gold,   *Œnone* 66

Pure (*continued*) *p* law, Commeasure perfect freedom.'   *Œnone* 166
     And *p* quintessences of precious oils   *Palace of Art* 187
     daughter of the warrior Gileadite, A maiden *p* ;   *D. of F. Women* 198
     A man more *p* and bold and just   *To J. S.* 31
     May He within Himself make *p* !   *M. d'Arthur* 245
     Ruffles her *p* cold plume, and takes the flood   „ 268
     all else of heaven was *p* Up to the Sun,   *Gardener's D.* 79
     Gown'd in *p* white, that fitted to the shape—   „ 126
     but what lot is *p* ?   *Walk. to the Mail* 97
     mysterious glimmer steals From thy *p* brows, and
     from thy shoulders *p*,   *Tithonus* 35
     Make Thou my spirit *p* and clear   *St. Agnes' Eve* 9
     To make me *p* of sin.   „ 32
     Because my heart is *p*.   *Sir Galahad* 4
     P spaces clothed in living beams, *P* lilies of eternal peace,   „ 66
     otherwhere *P* sport :   *Princess, Pro.* 81
     ' An open-hearted maiden, true and *p*.   „ iii 98
     But *p* as lines of green that streak the white   „ v 196
     Is not our cause *p* ?   „ 403
     The single *p* and perfect animal,   „ vii 306
     Which he has worn so *p* of blame,   *Ode on Well.* 72
     And *p* as he from taint of craven guile,   „ 135
     And keep the soldier firm, the statesman *p* :   „ 222
     till Phosphor, bright As our *p* love,   *In Mem.* ix 11
     Come then, *p* hands, and bear the head   „ xviii 9
     As *p* and perfect as I say ?   „ xxiv 2
     What souls possess themselves so *p*,   „ xxxii 15
     Her faith thro' form is *p* as thine,   „ xxxiii 9
     And love will last as *p* and whole   „ xliii 13
     How *p* at heart and sound in head,   „ xciv 1
     Perplext in faith, but *p* in deeds,   „ xcvi 9
     To one *p* image of regret.   „ cii 24
     And passion *p* in snowy bloom   „ cix 11
     Flow thro' our deeds and make them *p*,   „ cxxxi 4
     Small and *p* as a pearl,   *Maud* II ii 2
     'Tis a morning *p* and sweet, (repeat)   „ iv 31, 35
     (For I cleaved to a cause that I felt to be *p* and true),   „ III vi 31
     shyly glanced Eyes of *p* women,   *Gareth and L.* 314
     with *p* Affection, and the light of victory,   „ 330
     And *p* nobility of temperament,   *Marr. of Geraint* 212
     Arthur the blameless, *p* as any maid,   *Balin and Balan* 479
     P as our own true Mother is our Queen.'   „ 617
     and the mask of *p* Worn by this court,   *Merlin and V.* 35
     ' This Arthur *p* !   „ 49
     There is no being *p*, My cherub ;   „ 51
     And as it chanced they are happy, being *p*.'   „ 745
     ' A sober man is Percivale and *p* ;   „ 755
     Have all men true and leal, all women *p* ;   „ 794
     and down he sank For the *p* pain,   *Lancelot and E.* 518
     Full many a holy vow and *p* resolve.   „ 879
     And *p* Sir Galahad to uplift the maid ;   „ 1265
     Delicately *p* and marvellously fair,   „ 1369
     P, as you ever wish your knights to be.   „ 1375
     if not so *p* a love Clothes in so *p* a loveliness ?   „ 1383
     Whom Arthur and his knighthood call'd The *P*,   *Holy Grail* 3
     ' I know not, for thy heart is *p* as snow.'   „ 97
     of such a kind, that all of *p* Noble,   „ 773
     Some root of knighthood and *p* nobleness ;   „ 886
     For fair thou art and *p* as Guinevere,   *Pelleas and E.* 44
     P on the virgin forehead of the dawn ;   „ 505
     ' False ! and I held thee *p* as Guinevere.'   „ 522
     ' Am I but false as Guinevere is *p* ?   „ 524
     can Arthur make me *p* As any maiden child ?   *Last Tournament* 692
     could speak Of the *p* heart,   *Guinevere* 502
     Her station, taken everywhere for *p*,   „ 517
     Hereafter in that world where all are *p*   „ 562
     That *p* severity of perfect light—   „ 646
     Then she, for her good deeds and her *p* life,   „ 693
     May He within himself make *p* !   *Pass. of Arthur* 413
     Ruffles her *p* cold plume, and takes the flood   „ 436
     Into a clearer zenith, *p* of cloud.   *Lover's Tale* i 514
     And why was I to darken their *p* love,   „ 727
     Fill'd all with *p* clear fire,   „ ii 146
     That makes the sequel *p* ;   „ iv 157
     Back to the *p* and universal church,   *Sir J. Oldcastle* 71

Pursued (*continued*)   on a sudden rush'd Among us, out of
breath, as one p,   *Princess iv* 375
For that small charm of feature mine, p—   *Merlin and V.* 76
he p her, calling, 'Stay a little!   *Lancelot and E.* 683
Pursuer   behind I heard the puff'd p;   *Princess iv* 265
There the p could pursue no more,   *Pass. of Arthur* 88
Pursuit   body half flung forward in p,   *Aylmer's Field* 587
Pursuivant   burst A spangled p,   *Balin and Balan* 47
Push (*See also* **Shuvv**) p thee forward thro' a life of shocks, *Œnone* 163
P off, and sitting well in order smite   *Ulysses* 58
To p my rival out of place and power.   *Princess iv* 335
Here, p them out at gates.'   " 548
No will p me down to the worm,   *Window, No Answer* 10
Should p beyond her mark,   *In Mem. liii* 15
That p'es us off from the board,   *Maud I iv* 27
Did he p, when he was uncurl'd,   " *II ii* 18
The new leaf ever p'es off the old.   *Balin and Balan* 442
as a hand that p'es thro' the leaf   *Pelleas and E.* 436
p me even In fancy from thy side,   *Last Tournament* 638
drew back His hand to p me from him;   *Lover's Tale* i 93
Push'd   behold thy bride, 'She p me from thee. *Love and Duty* 50
Old writers p the happy season back,—   *Golden Year* 66
And p at Philip's garden-gate.   *The Brook* 83
some were p with lances from the rock,   *Princess, Pro.* 46
child P her flat hand against his face   " *ii* 366
but p alone on foot (For since her horse was lost " *iv* 196
so from her face They p us, down the steps,   " 555
And p by rude hands from its pedestal,   " *v* 58
Cyril seeing it, p against the Prince,   " 533
So p them all unwilling toward the gate. *Gareth and L.* 212
P horse across the foamings of the ford,   " 1040
door, P from without, drave backward   *Geraint and E.* 273
Hath p aside his faithful wife,   *Balin and Balan* 106
P thro' an open casement down, lean'd on it,   " 413
Sir Bors, on entering, p Athwart the throng   *Holy Grail* 752
thought, Why have I p him from me?   *Pelleas and E.* 307
ever p Sir Modred, league by league,   *Pass. of Arthur* 80
p me back again On these deserted sands   *Lover's Tale* i 92
P from his chair of regal heritage,   " 118
deal-box that was p in a corner away,   *First Quarrel* 48
chains for him Who p his prows into the setting sun, *Columbus* 24
a wing p out to the left and a wing to the right, *Heavy Brigade* 15
But she—she p them aside.   *Dead Prophet* 58
Has p toward our faintest sun   *To Ulysses* 23
Pushing   p could move The chair of Idris. *Marr. of Geraint* 542
p his black craft among them all,   *Merlin and V.* 563
Puss   'petty Ogress,' and 'ungrateful P,'   *Princess, Pro.* 157
Put   To p together, part and prove,   *Two Voices* 134
P's forth an arm, and creeps from pine to pine,   *Œnone* 4
and p your hand in mine,   *May Queen, Con.* 23
P forth and feel a gladder clime.'   *On a Mourner* 15
'Bring the dress and p it on her,   *L. of Burleigh* 95
Now let me p the boy and girl to school: *Enoch Arden* 312
Philip the boy and girl to school,   " 331
But she—she p him off—   " 460
Suddenly p her finger on the text,   " 497
How Philip p her little ones to school,   " 706
after that P on more calm and added suppliantly: *Princess vi* 215
He p our lives so far apart   *In Mem. lxxxii* 15
This huckster p down war!   *Maud I x* 44
p force To weary her ears with one continuous prayer. *Gareth and L.* 18
'Thou hast made us lords, and canst not p us down!' " 1132
p on thy worst and meanest dress   *Marr. of Geraint* 130
when she p her horse toward the knight,   " 200
Prince Had p his horse in motion toward the knight, " 206
P on your worst and meanest dress,'   " 848
At least p off to please me this poor gown,   *Geraint and E.* 679
'Thou shalt p the crown to use.   *Balin and Balan* 202
in one moment, she p forth the charm   *Merlin and V.* 967
P's his own baseness in him by default   *Pelleas and E.* 81
strike him! p my hate into your strokes,   " 228
Loathing to p it from herself for ever,   *Lover's Tale* i 214
He softly p his arm about her neck   " *iv* 71
better ha' p my naked hand in a hornets' nest. *First Quarrel* 50
To be hang'd for a thief—and then p away—   *Rizpah* 36

Put (*continued*) never p on the black cap except for the worst *Rizpah* 65
But I p's it inter 'er 'ands   *North. Cobbler* 72
an' p's 'im back i' the light.   " 98
Fur we p's the muck o' the land   *Village Wife* 32
'Emmie, you p out your arms,   *In the Child. Hosp.* 56
but she p thim all to the door.   *Tomorrow* 44
when Molly 'd p out the light,   *Spinster's S's.* 97
Her that shrank, and p me from her,   *Locksley H., Sixty* 264
Thy gay lent-lilies wave and p them by,   *Prog. of Spring* 37
They p him aside for ever,   *Charity* 25
may there be no moaning of the bar, When I p out
to sea,   *Crossing the Bar* 4
Putting   And made a Gardener p in a graff, *Merlin and V.* 479
Puzzle   keep it like a p chest in chest,   " 654
That was a p for Annie.   *In the Child. Hosp.* 55
P. W.   Remains the lean *P. W.* on his tomb: *The Brook* 192
Pyebald   three p's and a roan.   *Walk. to the Mail* 114
Pyramid   The Rhodope, that built the p,   *Princess ii* 82
Pyramidal   Whose eyes from under a p head   *Aylmer's Field* 20
Pyre   wars, and filial faith, and Dido's p;   *To Virgil* 4
The p he burnt in.'—   *The Ring* 340
The woman, gliding toward the p,   *To Master of B.* 18
kindled the p, and all Stood round it,   *Death of Œnone* 65
ask'd Falteringly, 'Who lies on yonder p?'   " 95
'Who burns upon the p?'   " 99
Pyrenean   Beyond the P pines,   *Ode on Well.* 113
Pythagoras   weeks I tried Your table of P, *To E. Fitzgerald* 15

Q

Quaäker (**Quaker**)   I knaw'd a Q feller as often 'as
towd ma this: *N. Farmer, N. S.* 19
Quagmire   follow wandering fires Lost in the q! (repeat) *Holy Grail* 320, 892
Quail (s)   q and pigeon, lark and leveret lay, *Audley Court* 24
Quail (**verb**)   Q not at the fiery mountain,   *Faith* 3
Quail'd   an eye so fierce She q;   *Pelleas and E.* 602
Quaint   bought Q monsters for the market of those times, *Enoch Arden* 539
as q a four-in-hand As you shall see—   *Walk. to the Mail* 113
A crimson to the q Macaw,   *Day-Dm., Pro.* 16
Quaker (*See also* **Quaäker**) Whatever the Q holds, from sin; *Maud II v* 92
Quality   *See* **Quoloty**
Quantity   All in q, careful of my motion, *Hendecasyllabics* 5
Quarrel (s)   Why? What cause of q?   *The Brook* 97
I remember a q I had with your father,   *Grandmother* 21
For, call it lovers' q's, yet I know   *Geraint and E.* 324
In all your q's will I be your knight.   *Lancelot and E.* 961
my q—the first an' the last.   *First Quarrel* 56
I am sorry for all the q   " 87
Quarrel (**verb**)   With time I will not q: *Will Water.* 206
Would q with our lot;   " 226
And pray them not to q for her sake,   *Enoch Arden* 35
I never could q with Harry—   *First Quarrel* 16
Quarrell'd   She and James had q.   *The Brook* 96
if they q, Enoch stronger-made Was master: *Enoch Arden* 30
Before I q with Harry—   *First Quarrel* 56
Had q, till the man repenting sent This ring   *The Ring* 209
Quarried   From scarped cliff and q stone   *In Mem. lvi* 2
Among the q downs of Wight,   *To Ulysses* 32
Quarry (*See also* **Chalk-quarry**) but as a block Left in
the q;   *Princess vii* 231
Nor q trench'd along the hill   *In Mem. c* 11
the bird Who pounced her q and slew it.   *Merlin and V.* 135
Quart   I've 'ed my q ivry market-noight   *N. Farmer, O. S.* 8
Wouldn't a pint a' sarved as well as a q?   *North. Cobbler* 99
Quarter   What is it now? A q to.   *Walk. to the Mail* 10
men brought in whole hogs and q beeves,   *Geraint and E.* 602
Quartering   q your own royal arms of Spain,   *Columbus* 115
Quarter-sessions   A q-s chairman, abler none; *Princess, Con.* 90
Quay   Humm'd like a hive all round the narrow q, *Audley Court* 5
From rock to rock upon the glooming q,   " 84
And I went down unto the q,   *In Mem. xiv* 3
I walked with him down to the q,   *First Quarrel* 20

Queen (s) (*continued*) 'Ay, my *Q*,' he said. 'And thou
hast overthrown him?' 'Ay, my *Q*.'   *Pelleas and E.* 593
If I, the *Q*, May help them, loose thy tongue,   "   599
The *Q* Look'd hard upon her lover,   "   604
Then gave it to his *Q* to rear: the *Q* But coldly
acquiescing,   *Last Tournament* 22
O my *Q*, I muse Why ye not wear on arm,   "   35
Only to yield my *Q* her own again?   "   106
In her high bower the *Q*, Working a tapestry,   "   128
each thro' worship of their *Q* White-robed in honour   "   146
Let be thy fair *Q's* fantasy.   "   197
Be happy in thy fair *Q* as I in mine.'   "   204
Q of Beauty and of love, behold This day my *Q* of
Beauty   "   208
sad eyes, our *Q's* And Lancelot's,   "   222
Beyond all use, that half-amazed, the *Q*,   "   236
gems which Innocence the *Q* Lent to the King,   "   293
the land Was freed, and the *Q* false,   "   339
smoothe And sleek his marriage over to the *Q*.   "   391
Q Graspt it so hard, that all her hand was red.   "   410
glossy-throated grace, Isolt the *Q*.   "   509
hath not our great *Q* My dole of beauty trebled?'   "   557
the great *Q* Have yielded him her love.'   "   564
'Grace, *Q*, for being loved: "   602
First mainly thro' that sullying of our *Q*—   "   682
'Not so, my *Q*,' he said,   "   744
Claspt it and cried 'Thine Order, O my *Q*!'   "   750
look'd and saw The great *Q's* bower was dark,—   "   758
Q who sat betwixt her best Enid,   *Guinevere* 27
Sir Lancelot told This matter to the *Q*,   "   54
Love-loyal to the least wish of the *Q*,   "   126
the stately *Q* abode For many a week,   "   146
when she heard, the *Q* look'd up,   "   164
when first she came, wept the sad *Q*.   "   182
Round that strong castle where he holds the *Q*;   "   194
For his own self, and his own *Q*,   "   197
About the good King and his wicked *Q*, And were I
such a King with such a *Q*,   "   209
Then to her own sad heart mutter'd the *Q*,   "   213
ere the coming of the *Q*.' (repeat)   ", 223, 233
Then thought the *Q* within herself again,   "   224
Before the coming of the sinful *Q*.'   "   270
Then spake the *Q* and somewhat bitterly,   "   271
This evil work of Lancelot and the *Q*?'   "   307
thought the *Q* 'Lo! they have set her on,   "   308
the pale *Q* look'd up and answer'd her,   "   327
To which a mournful answer made the *Q*:   "   341
Such as they are, were you the sinful *Q*.'   "   353
Fired all the pale face of the *Q*,   "   357
stood before the *Q* As tremulously as foam   "   363
when the *Q* had added 'Get thee hence,'   "   366
But when the *Q* immersed in such a trance,   "   401
Rose the pale *Q*, and in her anguish   "   586
and he gave them charge about the *Q*,   "   591
Three *q's* with crowns of gold: *Pass. of Arthur* 366
those three *Q's* Put forth their hands,   "   373
be yon dark *Q's* in yon black boat,   "   452
But thou, my *Q*, Not for itself,   *To the Queen* ii 33
'I have fought for *Q* and Faith   *The Revenge* 101
es wouldn't goä, wi' good gowd o' the *Q*,   *Village Wife* 49
the king, the *q* Bad me be seated.   *Columbus* 10
king, the *q*, Sank from their thrones,   "   14
Ferdinand Hath sign'd it and our Holy Catholic *q*—   "   30
but our *Q* Recall'd me,   "   58
our prudent king, our righteous *q*—   "   122
ghost of our great Catholic *Q* Smiles on me,   "   187
Q of Heaven who seest the souls in Hell   "   216
ready—tho' our Holy Catholic *Q*,   "   228
sorra the *Q* wid her sceptre in sich   *Tomorrow* 35
stood up strait as the *Q* of the world—   "   79
FIRST pledge our *Q* this solemn night,   *Hands all round* 1
Since our *Q* assumed the globe, the sceptre.   *On Jub. Q. Victoria* 3
Q, and Empress of India,   "   6
Q, as true to womanhood as Queenhood,   "   25
Persephone! *Q* of the dead no more—   *Demeter and P.* 18

Queen (s) (*continued*) thou that hast from men, As *Q* of
Death,   *Demeter and P.* 143
Her maiden coming like a *Q*,   *The Ring* 480
Hail ample presence of a *Q*,   *Prog. of Spring* 61
Form in Freedom's name and the *Q's*!   *Riflemen form!* 23
Queen-city To change our dark *Q-c*,   *To Mary Boyle* 65
Queenhood with all grace Of womanhood and *q*,   *Marr. of Geraint* 176
Queen, as true to womanhood as *Q*,   *On Jub. Q. Victoria* 14
Queenly All is gracious, gentle, great and *Q*.   "   14
Quell HE thought to *q* the stubborn hearts of oak,.   *Buonaparte* 1
his great self, Hath force to *q* me.'   *Gareth and L.* 1183
scream of that Wood-devil I came to *q*!'   *Balin and Balan* 548
My yucca, which no winter *q's*,   *To Ulysses* 21
Quelling Move with me toward their *q*,   *Last Tournament* 101
Quench and *q* The red God's anger,   *Tiresias* 157
Gods, To *q*, not hurl the thunderbolt,   *Demeter and P.* 133
Quench'd had not wholly *q* his power: *Vision of Sin* 217
The fame is *q* that I foresaw.   *In Mem. lxxiii* 5
According to his greatness whom she *q*.   *Merlin and V.* 218
that had *q* herself In that assumption   *Sisters (E. and E.)* 233
Their innocent hospitalities *q* in blood,   *Columbus* 176
All diseases *q* by Science,   *Locksley H., Sixty* 163
Quencher You would-be *q's* of the light to be,   *Princess iv* 536
Quenching *q* lake by lake and tarn by tarn   *vii* 40
love of light *q* her fear of pain—   *Sir J. Oldcastle* 190
Query let my *q* pass Unclaim'd,   *The Brook* 104
Answer'd all *queries* touching those at home   *Aylmer's Field* 465
He put the self-same *q*,   *Marr. of Geraint* 269
To all their *queries* answer'd not a word,   *Lover's Tale iv* 333
Quest When I went forth in *q* of truth,   *Supp. Confessions* 141
name Be hidd'n, and give me the first *q*,   *Gareth and L.* 545
'I have given him the first *q*:   "   582
'A boon, Sir King, this *q*!'   "   647
'Bound upon a *q* With horse and arms—   "   708
'Damsel, the *q* is mine.   "   745
I leave not till I finish this fair *q*, Or die therefore.'   "   774
'The *q* is mine; thy kitchen-knave am I,   "   861
'Go therefore,' and so gives the *q* to him—   "   864
'Full pardon, but I follow up the *q*,   "   886
Not fit to cope your *q*.   "   1174
boundless savagery Appal me from the *q*.'   "   1331
The *q* is Lancelot's: give him back the shield.'   "   1344
So large mirth lived and Gareth won the *q*.   "   1426
we rode upon this fatal *q* Of honour,   *Geraint and E.* 703
So claim'd the *q* and rode away,   *Balin and Balan* 138
(His *q* was unaccomplish'd)   "   547
My *q*, meseems, is here.   "   552
And no *q* came, but all was joust and play,   *Merlin and V.* 145
cease not from your *q* until ye find.'   *Lancelot and E.* 548
to sally forth In *q* of whom he knew not,   "   561
Rode with his diamond, wearied of the *q*,   "   616
Reported who he was, and on what *q* Sent,   "   628
And lose the *q* he sent you on,   "   655
let me leave My *q* with you;   "   691
all wearied of the *q* Leapt on his horse,   "   703
ye shall go no more On *q* of mine,   "   717
Lest I be found as faithless in the *q* As yon proud
Prince who left the *q* to me.   "   761
the *q* Assign'd to her not worthy of it,   "   824
ride A twelvemonth and a day in *q* of it,   *Holy Grail* 197
Before ye leave him for this *Q*,   "   325
and cried, 'This *Q* is not for thee.' (repeat)   ", 374, 378
'I am not worthy of the *Q*;'   "   386
Came ye on none but phantoms in your *q*,   "   562
I falter'd from my *q* and vow?   "   568
And the *Q* faded in my heart.   "   600
And ev'n the Holy *Q*, and all but her;   "   610
'Ridest thou then so hotly on a *q* So holy,   "   642
Small heart was his after the Holy *Q*:   "   657
Q and he were in the hands of Heaven.   "   659
and scoff'd at him And this high *Q*   "   668
And those that had gone out upon the *Q*,   "   722
but now—the *Q*, This vision—   "   733
'Gawain, was this *Q* for thee?'   "   740
Who made me sure the *Q* was not for me;   "   743

T

Quest *(continued)* For I was much aweariad of the *Q*: *Holy Grail* 744
nath this *Q* avail'd for thee ?' " 765
all My *q* were but in vain ; " 783
and this *Q* was not for me.' " 852
'Hath Gawain fail'd in any *q* of thine ? " 859
To those who went upon the Holy *Q*, " 890
to fill the gap Left by the Holy *Q*; *Pelleas and E.* 2
Question (s) *(See also* **Test-question**) with *q* unto whom
'twere due: *Œnone* 82
And, smiling, put the *q* by. *Day-Dm., Revival* 32
your *q* now, Which touches on the workman *Princess iii* 321
But then this *q* of your troth remains: " *v* 279
overthrow Of these or those, the *q* settled die.' " 317
In many a subtle *q* versed, *In Mem. xcvi* 6
Nor thro' the *q's* men may try, " *cxxiv* 7
Fixing full eyes of *q* on her face, *Com. of Arthur* 312
And after madness acted *q* ask'd: *Geraint and E.* 813
the *q* rose About the founding of a Table Round, *Merlin and V.* 410
This *q*, so flung down before the guests, *Lover's Tale iv* 268
in the thick of *q* and reply I fled the house, *Sisters (E. and E.)* 157
An' a haxin' ma hawkard *q's*, *Spinster's S's.* 90
Question (verb) 'Twere well to *q* him, and try *Talking Oak* 27
'Thou art but a wild-goose to *q* it.' *Gareth and L.* 36
To *q*, why The sons before the fathers die, *To Marq. of Dufferin* 46
Question'd Doth *q* memory answer not, *Lover's Tale i* 277
or could answer him, If *q*, *Enoch Arden* 654
She, *q* if she knew us men, *Princess iv* 231
q any more Save on the further side ; *Com. of Arthur* 396
A voice clung sobbing till he *q* it, *Last Tournament* 759
then some other *q* if she came From foreign lands, *Lover's Tale i* 330
Questioner Has little time for idle *q's*.' *Marr. of Geraint* 272
Quick (adj.) *(See also* **Too-quick**) —they say that
women are so *q*— *Enoch Arden* 408
The *q* lark's closest-caroll'd strains, *Rosalind* 10
And my thoughts are as *q* and as *q*, *Window, On the Hill* 12
With thy *q* tears that make the rose *In Mem. lxxii* 1
his *q*, instinctive hand Caught at the hilt, *Marr. of Geraint* 209
Thus, after some *q* burst of sudden wrath, *Balin and Balan* 216
so *q* and thick The lightnings here and there *Holy Grail* 493
and close upon it peal'd A sharp *q* thunder.' " 696
Her countenance with *q* and healthful blood— *Lover's Tale i* 97
Q blushes, the sweet dwelling of her eyes *Sisters (E. and E.)* 165
At once The bright *q* smile of Evelyn, " 243
our *q* Evelyn—The merrier, prettier, " 285
Patient of pain tho' as *q* as a sensitive plant *In the Child. Hosp.* 30
So *q*, so capable in soldiership, *Sir J. Oldcastle* 75
Then, after one *q* glance upon the stars, *Akbar's Dream* 3
We are twice as *q*!' *Princess, Pro.* 137
A *q* brunette, well-moulded, falcon-eyed, " *ii* 106
For some cry '*Q*' and some cry 'Slow,' *Politics* 9
Quick (living) That *q* or dead thou holdest me for King. *Pass. of Arthur* 161
Quick (quickset) Rings Eden thro' the budded *q's*, *In Mem. lxxxviii* 2
Now burgeons every maze of *q* " *cxv* 2
Quick (to the quick) I myself, A Tory to the *q*, *Walk. to the Mail* 81
the proof to prove me to the *q*! *Gareth and L.* 150
Quicken mountain *q's* into Nymph and Faun ; *Lucretius* 187
bloodless east began To *q* to the sun, *Marr. of Geraint* 535
Your wailing will not *q* him ; *Geraint and E.* 549
felt my hatred for my Mark *Q* within me, *Last Tournament* 520
Quicken'd Be *q* with a livelier breath, *In Mem. cxxii* 13
Quickening slowly *q* into lower forms ; *Vision of Sin* 210
Quicker Her hands are *q* unto good : *In Mem. xxxiii* 10
If we could give them surer, *q* proof— *Princess iii* 282
It may be, I am *q* of belief Than you believe me, *Lancelot and E.* 1204
Quick-falling *q-f* dew Of fruitful kisses, *Œnone* 204
Quickset-screens Fills out the homely *q-s*, *On a Mourner* 6
Quiet (adj.) *Q*, dispassionate, and cold, *A Character* 28
As waves that up a *q* cove Rolling slide, *Eleänore* 108
A healthy frame, a *q* mind. *Two Voices* 99
Then said the voice, in *q* scorn, " 401
wave that swam Thro' *q* meadows round the mill, *Miller's D.* 98
Rest in a happy place and *q* seats Above the thunder, *Œnone* 131
'Reign thou apart, a *q* king, *Palace of Art* 14
With *q* eyes unfaithful to the truth, *Love and Duty* 94
Here at the *q* limit of the world, *Tithonus* 7

Quiet (adj.) *(continued)* till he find The *q* chamber far
apart. *Day-Dm., Arrival* 28
Let us have a *q* hour, *Vision of Sin* 73
Than aught they fable of the *q* Gods. *Lucretius* 55
pines of Ida shook to see Slide from that *q* heaven of hers, " 87
from some bay-window shake the night ; But all was *q*: *Princess i* 107
Her *q* dream of life this hour may cease. *Requiescat* 6
She desires no isles of the blest, no *q* seats of the just, *Wages* 3
As if the *q* bones were blest Among familiar names *In Mem. xviii* 6
The *q* sense of something lost. " *lxxviii* 8
'I watch thee from the *q* shore ; " *lxxxv* 81
Below me, there, is the village, and looks how *q* and small! *Maud I iv* 7
Be mine a philosopher's life in the *q* woodland ways, " 49
Came glimmering thro' the laurels At the *q* evenfall, " *II iv* 78
Me, that was never a *q* sleeper? " *v* 98
painted battle the war stood Silenced, the living *q* as the dead, *Com. of Arthur* 123
ever fail'd to draw The *q* night into her blood, *Marr. of Geraint* 532
And kiss'd her *q* brows, and saying to her *Lancelot and E.* 1150
my fresh but fixt resolve To pass away into the *q* life, *Holy Grail* 738
But always in the house I heard, " 832
Oh! pleasant breast of waters, *q* bay, Like to a *q* mind in the loud world, *Lover's Tale i* 6
Didst swathe thyself all round Hope's *q* urn For ever? " 100
All this Seems to the *q* daylight of your minds But cloud and smoke, " 296
Why did you sit so *q*? *Rizpah* 14
Quietly sleeping—so *q*, our doctor said *In the Child. Hosp.* 41
It was all of it fair as life, it was all of it as *q* as death, *V. of Maeldune* 20
Silent palaces, *q* fields of eternal sleep ! " 80
By *q* fields, a slowly-dying power, *De Prof.," Two G.* 84
All so *q* the ripple would hardly blanch into spray *The Wreck* 137
Naäy, but the claws o' tha! *q*! *Spinster's S's.* 36
Man is *q* at last As he stands on the heights *By an Evolution.* 19
Quiet (s) For now the noonday *q* holds the hill : *Œnone* 25
Divided in a graceful *q*—paused, *Gardener's D.* 156
And blasting the long *q* of my breast *Lucretius* 162
This look of *q* flatters thus *In Mem. x* 10
Making a treacherous *q* in his heart, *Lancelot and E.* 883
Moan to myself 'one plunge—then *q* for evermore.' *Charity* 16
Quieted Three with good blows he *q*, *Gareth and L.* 813
I was *q*, and slept again. *The Ring* 421
Quieter but I knaws I 'ed led tha a *q* life *Spinster's S's.* 71
Quince As hardly tints the blossom of the *q* *Balin and Balan* 267
Quinquenniad Or gay *q's* would we reap *Day-Dm., L'Envoi* 23
Quinsy 'A *q* choke thy cursed note!' *The Goose* 29
Quintessence As with the *q* of flame, *Arabian Nights* 123
pure *q's* of precious oils In hollow'd moons *Palace of Art* 187
The flower and *q* of change. *Day-Dm., L'Envoi* 24
He had known a man, a *q* of man, *Aylmer's Field* 388
Quintus Calaber *Q C* Somewhat lazily handled *To Master of B.* 7
Quip But all his merry *q's* are o'er. *D. of the O. Year* 29
Tristram, waiting for the *q* to come, *Last Tournament* 260
Quire low-matin chirp hath grown Full *q*, *Love and Duty* 99
O Milan, O the chanting *q's*, *The Daisy* 57
priest, who mumble worship in your *q*— *Balin and Balan* 444
Quirk With twisted *q's* and happy hits, *Will Water.* 189
Quit (leave) *q* the post Allotted by the Gods : *Lucretius* 148
how loth to *q* the land ! *The Flight* 38
Wilt neither *q* the widow'd Crown *To Prin. Beatrice* 15
Quit (repay) ill then should I *q* your brother's love, *Lancelot and E.* 944
Quitch the vicious *q* Of blood and custom *Geraint and E.* 903
Quiver heart of Poland hath not ceased To *q*, *Poland* 4
Willows whiten, aspens *q*, *L. of Shalott i* 10
A thousand moons will *q* ; *A Farewell* 14
sometimes touches but one string That *q's*, *Lover's Tale i* 18
Quiver'd Her eyelid *q* as she spake. *Miller's D.* 144
bright death *q* at the victim's throat ; *D. of F. Women* 115
Trembled and *q*, as the dog, *Pelleas and E.* 284
Q a flying glory on her hair, *Lover's Tale i* 69
Quivering sets all the tops *q*— *Lucretius* 186
Gloom'd the low coast and *q* brine *The Voyage* 42
Tear the noble heart of Britain, leave it gorily *q*? *Boädicea* 12
The rosy *q's* died into the night. *Holy Grail* 123

Quoit *Q*, tennis, ball—no games ?	*Princess* iii 215
Quoloty (quality) Looök 'ow *q* smoiles	*N. Farmer, O. S.* 53
Fur *Q's* hall my friends,	*Church-warden, etc.* 39
Quote —it makes me sick to *q* him—	*Sea Dreams* 159
Love, let me *q* these lines, that you may learn	" 181
Quoted *q* odes, and jewels five-words-long	*Princess* ii 377
Quoting And when the Goan Padre *q* Him,	*Akbar's Dream* 74

R

Raäke (rake) *r* out Hell wi' a small-tooth coämb—	*Village Wife* 76
Raäte (rate) I wur niver agin the *r*.	*N. Farmer, O. S.* 16
an' ageän the toithe an' the *r*,	*Church-warden, etc.* 11
Raäted (scolded) Sally she turn'd a tongue-banger, an'	
r ma,	*North. Cobbler* 23
Raätin (scolding) Robby I gied tha a *r*	*Spinster's S's.* 48
Raäved (tore) an' *r* an' rembled 'um out.	*N. Farmer, O. S.* 32
Raäved (torn) an' *r* slick thruf by the plow—	*Owd Roä* 28
Raävin' (raving) fire was a-raägin' an' *r*	" 110
Rabbit (adj.) A *r* mouth that is ever agape—	*Maud I x* 31
Rabbit (s) The *r* fondles his own harmless face,	*Aylmer's Field* 851
Rabble soft and milky *r* of womankind,	*Princess* iv 309
frantic *r* in half-amaze Stared at him dead,	*St. Telemachus* 71
Race (of persons) (*See also* **Border-race**) Becomes dishonour	
to her *r*—	*Two Voices* 255
Who took a wife, who rear'd his *r*,	" 328
Some legend of a fallen *r* Alone might hint	" 359
WE were two daughters of one *r*:	*The Sisters* 1
Chanted from an ill-used *r* of men	*Lotos-Eaters, C. S.* 120
my *r* Hew'd Ammon, hip and thigh,	*D. of F. Women* 237
To mingle with the human *r*,	*Of old sat Freedom* 10
Unequal laws unto a savage *r*,	*Ulysses* 4
To vary from the kindly *r* of men,	*Tithonus* 29
she shall rear my dusky *r*.	*Locksley Hall* 168
'Some other *r* of Averills'—	*Aylmer's Field* 54
Nor of what *r*, the work;	" 224
and with her the *r* of Aylmer, past.	" 577
Which else had link'd their *r* with times to come—	" 779
I made by these the last of all my *r*,	" 791
And those who sorrow'd o'er a vanish'd *r*,	" 844
a *r* Of giants living, each, a thousand years,	*Princess* iii 268
Then springs the crowning *r* of humankind.	" vii 295
while the *r's* of mankind endure,	*Ode on Well.* 219
Have left the last free *r* with naked coasts !	*Third of Feb.* 40
That 'Loss is common to the *r*'—	*In Mem.* vi 2
Comes out—to some one of his *r*:	" lxxiv 4
Will shelter one of stranger *r*.	" cii 4
Of that great *r*, which is to be,	" ciii 35
The herald of a higher *r*,	" cxviii 14
And throned *r's* may degrade ;	" cxviii 7
Betwixt us and the crowning *r*	*Con.* 128
her father, the wrinkled head of the *r* ?	*Maud I* iv 13
in his force to be Nature's crowning *r*.	" 33
At war with myself and a wretched *r*,	" x 35
On that huge scapegoat of the *r*,	" xiii 42
Strike dead the whole weak *r* of venomous worms,	" II i 46
Beyond the *r* of Britons and of men.	*Com. of Arthur* 331
O PURBLIND *r* of miserable men,	*Geraint and E.* 1
in their chairs set up a stronger *r*	" 940
strange sound of an adulterous *r*,	*Holy Grail* 80
Our *r* and blood, a remnant that were left	" 663
great and sane and simple *r* of brutes	*Pelleas and E.* 480
The prayer of many a *r* and creed, and clime—	*To the Queen* ii 11
Strong with the strength of the *r*	*Def. of Lucknow* 47
Spain once the most chivalric *r* on earth.	*Columbus* 204
I WAS the chief of the *r*—	*V. of Maeldune* 1
boasted he sprang from the oldest *r* upon earth.	" 4
serve This mortal *r* thy kin so well,	*De Prof., Two G.* 16
breathed a *r* of mightier mountaineers.	*Montenegro* 14
one of these, the *r* of Cadmus—	*Tiresias* 134
Motherless evermore an ever-vanishing *r*,	*Despair* 84
we, the poor earth's dying *r*,	*Ancient Sage* 178
for since our dying *r* began,	*Locksley H., Sixty* 65

Race (of persons) (*continued*) Far among the vanish'd *r's*,	*Locksley H., Sixty* 79
to lower the rising *r* of men ;	" 147
All the full-brain, half-brain *r's*,	" 161
a single *r*, a single tongue—	" 165
I would the rising *r* were half as eager	" 228
sunder'd once from all the human *r*,	*To Virgil* 36
souls of men, who grew beyond their *r*,	*Demeter and P.* 140
may roll with the dust of a vanish'd *r*.	*Vastness* 2
As dead from all the human *r*	*Happy* 95
I cull from every faith and *r*	*Akbar's Dream* 68
when creed and *r* Shall bear false witness,	" 97
From out the sunset pour'd an alien *r*,	" 192
there is time for the *r* to grow.	*The Dawn* 20
but, while the *r's* flower and fade,	*Making of Man* 5
Race (course of life, etc.) Till all my widow'd *r* be run ;	*In Mem.* ix 18
Till all my widow'd *r* be run.	" xvii 20
He still outstript me in the *r* ;	" xlii 2
burst All barriers in her onward *r* For power.	" cxiv 14
make one people ere man's *r* be run:	*To Victor Hugo* 11
And I would that my *r* were run,	*The Dreamer* 8
Or ever your *r* be run !	" 30
Race (stream) By the red *r* of fiery Phlegethon ;	*Demeter and P.* 28
Race (verb) and *r* By all the fountains :	*Princess* iv 262
r thro' many a mile Of dense and open,	*Balin and Balan* 423
and hunters *r* The shadowy lion,	*Tiresias* 177
hopes, which *r* the restless blood,	*Prog. of Spring* 115
Raced flew kite, and *r* the purple fly,	*Princess* ii 248
Thro' all the camp and inward *r* the scouts	" v 111
Races and how The *r* went, and who would rent the hall:	*Audley Court* 31
Raceth And *r* freely with his fere,	*Supp. Confessions* 158
Rachel Fairer than *R* by the palmy well,	*Aylmer's Field* 679
Racing Clouds that are *r* above,	*Window, On the Hill* 6
measured pulse of *r* oars Among the willows ;	*In Mem.* lxxxvii 10
He is *r* from heaven to heaven	*The Dreamer* 21
Rack furrowing into light the mounded *r*,	*Love and Duty* 100
As if 'twere drawn asunder by the *r*.	*Lover's Tale* ii 57
save breaking my bones on the *r* ?	*By an Evolution.* 9
Rack'd frame Is *r* with pangs that conquer trust ;	*In Mem. l* 6
I am *r* with pains.	*Columbus* 199
that I, *R* as I am with gout,	" 235
Radiate where the passions meet, Whence *r*:	*In Mem.* lxxxviii 5
Raff Let *r's* be rife in prose and rhyme,	*Will Water.* 61
Rafter slew Till all the *r's* rang with woman-yells,	*Last Tournament* 476
Boardings and *r's* and doors—	*Def. of Lucknow* 67
Rafter'd *See* **Dusky-rafter'd**	
Rag (torn clothes) Her *r's* scarce held together ;	*The Goose* 2
and throng, their *r's* and they The basest,	*Lucretius* 170
all one *r*, disprinced from head to heel,	*Princess* v 30
And him, the lazar, in his *r's* :	*In Mem.* cxxvii 10
put your beauty to this flout and scorn By dressing	
it in *r's* ?	*Geraint and E.* 676
this poor gown, This silken *r*,	" 680
Shaking his hands, as from a lazar's *r*,	*Pelleas and E.* 317
Rag (stone) hornblende, *r* and trap and tuff,	*Princess* iii 362
Rage (s) His early *r* Had force to make me rhyme	*Miller's D.* 192
With inarticulate *r*, and making signs	*Enoch Arden* 640
For blind with *r* she miss'd the plank,	*Princess* iv 177
And I remain on whom to wreak your *r*,	" 350
The captive void of noble *r*,	*In Mem.* xxvii 2
her brother ran in his *r* to the gate,	*Maud II i* 12
that chain'd *r*, which ever yelpt within,	*Balin and Balan* 319
so blind in *r* that unawares He burst his lance	" 328
and dash'd herself Dead in her *r*:	*Tiresias* 153
your faith and a God of eternal *r*,	*Despair* 39
call him dotard in your *r* ?	*Locksley H., Sixty* 9
THIS thing, that thing is the *r*,	*Poets and Critics* 1
Rage (verb) a flame That *r's* in the woodland far	
below,	*Balin and Balan* 234
R like a fire among the noblest names,	*Merlin and V.* 802
Raged I *r* against the public liar ;	*The Letters* 26
am I raging alone as my father *r* in his mood ?	*Maud I i* 53
Rageful Slowly and conscious of the *r* eye That	
watch'd him,	*Aylmer's Field* 336
Nor thou be *r*, like a handled bee,	*Ancient Sage* 269
Ragged The *r* rims of thunder brooding low,	*Palace of Art* 75

Ragged (*continued*)   Pent in a roofless close of *r* stones;   *St. S. Stylites* 74
   babe Too *r* to be fondled on her lap,   *Aylmer's Field* 686
   haunts Would scratch a *r* oval on the sand,   *Gareth and L.* 534
   Hung round with *r* rims and burning folds,—   *Lover's Tale ii* 63
   Upon the morrow, thro' the *r* walls,   "   152
Ragged-robin   Hath pick'd a *r-r* from the hedge,   *Marr. of Geraint* 724
Raging (*See also* **A-raägin'**)   The wind is *r* in turret and
   tree.   *The Sisters* 21
   shot at, slightly hurt, R return'd: *Aylmer's Field* 549
   She heard him *r*, heard him fall;   *Lucretius* 276
   am I *r* alone as my father raged in his mood?   *Maud I i* 53
   shone the Noonday Sun Beyond a *r* shallow.   *Gareth and L.* 1028
Raid   chance of booty from the morning's *r*,   *Geraint and E.* 565
Rail (s)   take their leave, about the garden *r's*.   *Princess, Con.* 38
   In such discourse we gain'd the garden *r's*,   "   80
Rail (verb)   To *r* at Lady Psyche and her side.   "   *iii* 33
   He loved to *r* against it still,   *In Mem. lxxxix* 38
   Who shall *r* Against her beauty?   "   *cxiv* 1
   fight for the good than to *r* at the ill;   *Maud III vi* 57
   For that did never he whereon ye *r*,   *Gareth and L.* 728
   if she had it, would she *r* on me To snare the next,
     and if she have it not So will she *r*.   *Merlin and V.* 810
   Then she began to *r* so bitterly.   *Pelleas and E.* 250
   they *r* At me the Zoroastrian.   *Akbar's Dream* 103
   R at 'Blind Fate' with many a vain 'Alas!'   *Doubt and Prayer* 2
Rail'd (*See also* **Golden-rail'd**)   still she *r* against the
   state of things.   *Princess iii* 84
   r at those Who call'd him the false son   *Guinevere* 287
   And *r* at all the Popes,   *Sir J. Oldcastle* 165
Railer   This *r*, that hath mock'd thee in full hall—   *Gareth and L.* 369
Railing   *r* at thine and thee.   *Balin and Balan* 119
Raillery   feigning pique at what she call'd The *r*,   *Princess iv* 588
Railway   In the steamship, in the *r*,   *Locksley Hall* 166
   A petty *r* ran: a fire-balloon Rose gem-like   *Princess, Pro.* 74
   A *r* there, a tunnel here,   *Mechanophilus* 7
Raiment   in her *r's* hem was traced in flame   *The Poet* 45
   In diverse *r* strange: *Palace of Art* 168
   In *r* white and clean.   *St. Agnes' Eve* 24
   A woman-post in flying *r*.   *Princess iv* 376
   Loosely robed in flying *r*,   *Boädicea* 37
   three fair girls In gilt and rosy *r* came: *Gareth and L.* 927
   His arms, the rosy *r*, and the star.   "   938
   broken wings, torn *r* and loose hair,   "   1208
Rain (s) (*See also* **River-rain**)   R makes music in the tree   *A Dirge* 26
   Wash'd with still *r's* and daisy blossomed;   *Circumstance* 7
   The lightning flash atween the *r's*,   *Rosalind* 12
   From winter *r's* that beat his grave.   *Two Voices* 261
   Autumn *r's* Flash in the pools of whirling Simois.   *Œnone* 205
   With shadow-streaks of *r*.   *Palace of Art* 76
   There will not be a drop of *r*   *May Queen* 35
   Where falls not hail, or *r*, or any snow,   *M. d'Arthur* 260
   beneath a whispering *r* Night slid down   *Gardener's D.* 266
   R, wind, frost, heat, hail, damp,   *St. S. Stylites* 16
   'I swear, by leaf, and wind, and *r*,   *Talking Oak* 81
   Low thunders bring the mellow *r*,   "   279
   when the *r* is on the roof,   *Locksley Hall* 78
   with *r* or hail, or fire or snow;   "   193
   Bullets fell like *r*;   *The Captain* 46
   With ashy *r's*, that spreading made   *The Voyage* 43
   Came in a sun-lit fall of *r*.   *Sir L. and Q. G.* 4
   Old plash of *r's*, and refuse patch'd with moss.   *Vision of Sin* 212
   The *r* had fallen, the Poet arose,   *Poet's Song* 1
   The *r* of heaven, and their own bitter tears, Tears,
     and the careless *r* of heaven,   *Aylmer's Field* 428
   for thrice I heard the *r* Rushing;   *Lucretius* 26
   A twisted snake, and now a *r* of pearls,   *Princess, Pro.* 62
   blowzed with health, and wind, and *r*,   " *iv* 279
   Remember what a plague of *r*;   *The Daisy* 50
   Of *r* at Reggio, *r* at Parma; At Lodi, *r*, Piacenza, *r*.   "   51
   The mist and the *r*, the mist and the *r*!   *Window, No Answer* 1
   And ghastly thro' the drizzling *r*   *In Mem. vii* 11
   A flower beat with *r* and wind,   " *viii* 15
   That takes the sunshine and the *r's*,   " *x* 14
   flakes Of crimson or in emerald *r*.   " *xcviii* 32
   and fed With honey'd *r* and delicate air,   *Maud I xviii* 21

Rain (s) (*continued*)   and the heavens fall in a gentle *r*,   *Maud II i* 41
   'R, *r*, and sun! a rainbow in the sky!'   *Com. of Arthur* 403
   R, *r*, and sun! a rainbow on the lea!   "   406
   R, sun, and *r*! and the free blossom blows: "   409
   Sun, *r*, and sun! and where is he who knows?   "   410
   O rainbow with three colours after *r*,   *Gareth and L.* 1160
   Before the useful trouble of the *r*:   *Geraint and E.* 771
   Or in the noon of dust and driving *r*,   *Merlin and V.* 636
   Then fell thick *r*, plume droopt and mantle clung,   *Last Tournament* 213
   falls not hail, or *r*, or any snow,   *Pass. of Arthur* 428
   and the *r* Had fall'n upon me,   *Lover's Tale i* 622
   few drops of that distressful *r* Fell on my face,   "   698
   As *r* of the midsummer midnight soft,   "   722
   A morning air, sweet after *r*,   " *iii* 3
   An' he took three turns in the *r*,   *First Quarrel* 75
   I find myself drenched with the *r*.   *Rizpah* 8
   Beneath a pitiless rush of Autumn *r*   *Sisters (E. and E.)* 237
   That trees grew downward, *r* fell upward,   *Columbus* 50
   the tundher, an' *r* that fell,   *Tomorrow* 23
   And o'er thee streams the *r*,   *Pref. Poem Broth. Son.* 14
Rain (verb)   R out the heavy mist of tears,   *Love and Duty* 43
   That lightly *r* from ladies' hands.   *Sir Galahad* 12
   To *r* an April of ovation round Their statues,   *Princess vi* 66
   bullets would *r* at our feet—   *Def. of Lucknow* 21
Rainbow (adj.)   And *r* robes, and gems and gemlike eyes,   *Princess iv* 480
   Of his house in a *r* frill?   *Maud II ii* 17
   may roll The *r* hues of heaven about it—   *Romney's R.* 51
Rainbow (s)   the *r* forms and flies on the land   *Sea-Fairies* 25
   And the *r* lives in the curve of the sand;   "   27
   And the *r* hangs on the poising wave,   "   29
   Between the *r* and the sun.   *Margaret* 13
   Broke, like the *r* from the shower.   *Two Voices* 444
   leap the *r's* of the brooks,   *Locksley Hall* 171
   Flung the torrent *r* round: *Vision of Sin* 32
   This flake of *r* flying on the highest   *Princess v* 319
   'Rain, rain, and sun! a *r* in the sky!   *Com. of Arthur* 403
   Rain, rain, and sun! a *r* on the lea!   "   406
   O *r* with three colours after rain,   *Gareth and L.* 1160
   Lay like a *r* fall'n upon the grass,   *Lancelot and E.* 431
   Her smile lit up the *r* on my tears,   *Lover's Tale i* 254
   low down in a *r* deep Silent palaces,   *V. of Maeldune* 79
   Her light makes *r's* in my closing eyes,   *Prog. of Spring* 46
Rain'd   R thro' my sight its overflow   *Two Voices* 45
   Principles are *r* in blood;   *Love thou thy land* 80
   dimly *r* about the leaf Twilights of airy silver,   *Audley Court* 81
   and there *r* a ghastly dew   *Locksley Hall* 123
   a giant's flail, The large blows *r*,   *Princess v* 501
   mine down *r* Their spirit-searching splendours.   *Lover's Tale ii* 146
Raining   Heavily the low sky *r*   *L. of Shalott iv* 4
   Hold swollen clouds from *r*,   *D. of F. Women* 11
Rain-rotten   R-*r* died the wheat,   *Demeter and P.* 112
Rainy   And faint, *r* lights are seen,   *Margaret* 60
   As over *r* mist inclines A gleaming crag   *Two Voices* 188
   The rentroll Cupid of our *r* isles.   *Edwin Morris* 103
   Thro' scudding drifts the *r* Hyades Vext the dim sea: *Ulysses* 10
   The sunny and *r* seasons came and went   *Enoch Arden* 623
   A *r* cloud possess'd the earth,   *In Mem. xxx* 3
   'O trefoil, sparkling on the *r* plain,   *Gareth and L.* 1159
   and thro' the tree Rush'd ever a *r* wind,   *Last Tournament* 16
Raise   Thou wilt never *r* thine head   *A Dirge* 19
   I could *r* One hope that warm'd me   *Two Voices* 121
   R thy soul; Make thine heart ready with thine
     eyes: the time Is come to *r* the veil.   *Gardener's D.* 272
   Most can *r* the flowers now,   *The Flower* 19
   To *r* a cry that lasts not long,   *In Mem. lxxv* 10
   Sir Lancelot holp To *r* the Prince,   *Guinevere* 46
   and could *r* such a battle-cry   *V. of Maeldune* 23
   Tho' some of late would *r* a wind   *Freedom* 35
   R a stately memorial,   *On Jub. Q. Victoria* 44
   R me. I thank you.   *Romney's R.* 60
Raised (adj.)   in your *r* brows I read Some wonder   *Columbus* 1
   my *r* eyelids would not fall,   *Lover's Tale i* 571
Raised (verb)   when I *r* my eyes, above They met   *Miller's D.* 85
   I look'd, Paris had *r* his arm,   *Œnone* 189
   She *r* her piercing orbs,   *D. of F. Women* 171

Ran (*continued*)   Where nymph and god *r* ever round in
gold—   *Lover's Tale iv* 197
and so The little Revenge *r* on   *The Revenge* 33
Revenge *r* on thro' the long sea-lane between.   „ 36
' are you ill ? ' (so *r* The letter)   *Sisters* (*E. and E.*) 185
r Surging and swaying all round us,   *Def. of Lucknow* 37
r into the hearts of my crew,   *V. of Maeldune* 33
fig *r* up from the beach and rioted over the land,   „ 58
By all my ways where'er they *r*,   *Ancient Sage* 157
my life in golden sequence *r*,   *Locksley H., Sixty* 47
sound *r* Thro' palace and cottage door,   *Dead Prophet* 37
red mark *r* All round one finger pointed straight,   *The Ring* 452
dead cords that *r* Dark thro' the mist,   *Death of Œnone* 10
Slipt, and *r* on, and flung himself between   *St. Telemachus* 61
In that vast Oval *r* a shudder of shame.   „ 73
Rancorous   A wounded thing with a *r* cry,   *Maud I x* 34
Rancour   hate the *r* of their castes and creeds,   *Akbar's Dream* 65
Random (*adj.*)   (*See also* **Seeming-random**)   But we must
hood your *r* eyes,   *Rosalind* 37
A *r* arrow from the brain.   *Two Voices* 345
A *r* string Your finer female sense offends.   *Day-Dm., L'Envoi* 1
As dash'd about the drunken leaves The *r* sunshine
lighten'd !   *Amphion* 56
To make me write my *r* rhymes,   *Will Water.* 13
He flash'd his *r* speeches,   „ 198
Whistling a *r* bar of Bonny Doon,   *The Brook* 82
Balmier and nobler from her bath of storm, At *r* ravage ?   *Lucretius* 176
As if to close with Cyril's *r* wish :   *Princess iii* 101
I give you all The *r* scheme as wildly as it rose :   *Con.* 2
For him nor moves the loud world's *r* mock,   *Will* 4
And answering now my *r* stroke   *In Mem. xxxix* 2
Let *r* influences glance,   „ *xlix* 2
With all his rout of *r* followers,   *Geraint and E.* 382
but had ridd'n a *r* round To seek him,   *Lancelot and E.* 630
Or lulling *r* squabbles when they rise,   *Holy Grail* 557
deed Of prowess done redress'd a *r* wrong.   *Guinevere* 459
Along the years of haste and *r* youth Unshatter'd : *De Prof. Two G.* 21
Nor lend an ear to *r* cries,   *Politics* 7
Random (*s*)   as he lay At *r* looking over the brown earth *Pelleas and E.* 32
Random-blown   sank Down on a drift of foliage *r-b*; *Last Tournament* 389
Rang   The bridle bells *r* merrily   *L. of Shalott iii* 13
The wild wind *r* from park and plain,   *The Goose* 45
based His feet on juts of slippery crag that *r*   *M. d'Arthur* 189
So these were wed, and merrily *r* the bells,(repeat) *Enoch Arden* 80, 511
shrill'd and *r*, Till this was ended,   „ 175
Merrily *r* the bells and they were wed   „ 512
That all the houses in the haven *r*.   „ 911
a page or two that *r* With tilt and tourney ;   *Princess, Pro.* 121
with this our banquets *r*;   „ *i* 132
for still my voice *R* false :   „ *iv* 121
With Ida, Ida, Ida, *r* the woods ;   „ 433
R ruin, answer'd full of grief and scorn.   „ *vi* 333
and *r* Beyond the bourn of sunset ;   „ *Con.* 99
And the ringers *r* with a will,   *Grandmother* 58
And round us all the thicket *r*   *In Mem. xxiii* 23
Then echo-like our voices *r*;   „ *xxx* 13
The hall with harp and carol *r*.   „ *ciii* 3
there *r* on a sudden a passionate cry,   *Maud II i* 33
r Clear thro' the open casement of the hall,   *Marr. of Geraint* 327
things that *r* Against the pavement,   *Geraint and E.* 594
R by the white mouth of the violent Glem ;   *Lancelot and E.* 288
Then *r* the shout his lady loved :   *Pelleas and E.* 171
Down *r* the grate of iron thro' the groove,   „ 207
old echoes hidden in the wall *R* out   „ 367
Till all the rafters *r* with woman-yells,   *Last Tournament* 476
based His feet on juts of slippery crag that *r*   *Pass. of Arthur* 357
There r her voice, when the full city   *To the Queen ii* 26
r into the heart and the brain,   *V. of Maeldune* 110
So *r* the clear voice of Æakidès ;   *Achilles over the T.* 21
a voice *r* out in the thunders of Ocean and Heaven   *The Wreck* 88
' Forward ' *r* the voices then,   *Locksley H., Sixty* 77
cry that *r* thro' Hades, Earth, and Heaven !   *Demeter and P.* 33
Weird whispers, bells that *r* without a hand,   *The Ring* 411
r out all down thro' the dell,   *Bandit's Death* 36
was a Scripture that *r* thro' his head,   *The Dreamer* 2

Rang (*continued*)   *R* the stroke, and sprang the blood,   *The Tourney* 9
Range (*s*)   (*See also* **Mountain-range**)   storm Of
running fires and fluid *r*   *Supp. Confessions* 147
And *r* of evil between death and birth,   *If I were loved* 3
Below the *r* of stepping-stones,   *Miller's D.* 54
R's of glimmering vaults with iron grates,   *D. of F. Women* 35
a lyre of widest *r* Struck by all passion,   „ 165
the *r* of lawn and park :   *The Blackbird* 6
over many a *r* Of waning lime the gray cathedral
towers,   *Gardener's D.* 217
Large *r* of prospect had the mother sow,   *Walk. to the Mail* 93
On a *r* of lower feelings   *Locksley Hall* 44
Soft lustre bathes the *r* of urns   *Day-Dm., Sleep. P.* 9
o'er them many a flowing *r* Of vapour   *Depart.* 21
Somewhere beneath his own low *r* of roofs,   *Aylmer's Field* 47
A patient *r* of pupils ;   *Princess ii* 104
the day fled on thro' all Its *r* of duties   „ *iii* 177
Rhymes and rhymes in the *r* of the times !   *Spiteful Letter* 9
Our voices took a higher *r*;   *In Mem. xxx* 21
O, therefore from thy sightless *r*   „ *xciii* 9
There ran a treble *r* of stony shields,—   *Gareth and L.* 407
that gave upon a *r* Of level pavement   „ 666
down that *r* of roses the great Queen Came   *Balin and Balan* 244
Merlin, who knew the *r* of all their arts,   *Merlin and V.* 167
impute themselves, Wanting the mental *r*;   „ 827
A purple *r* of mountain-cones,   *Lover's Tale i* 407
past Over the *r* and the change of the world   *The Wreck* 70
past the *r* of Night and Shadow—   *Ancient Sage* 283
after his brief *r* of blameless days,   *D. of the Duke of C.* 9
Range (*verb*)   So let the wind *r*;   *Nothing will Die* 32
So let the warm winds *r*,   *All Things will Die* 42
Thro' light and shadow thou dost *r*,   *Madeline* 4
' Not less the bee would *r* her cells,   *Two Voices* 70
droves of swine That *r* on yonder plain.   *Palace of Art* 200
Forward, forward let us *r*,   *Locksley Hall* 181
That *r* above the region of the wind,   *Princess, Con.* 112
' My love shall now no further *r*;   *In Mem. lxxxi* 2
That *r* above our mortal state,   „ *lxxxv* 22
To *r* the woods, to roam the park,   „ *Con.* 96
it pleased the King to *r* me close After Sir Galahad); *Holy Grail* 307
To course and *r* thro' all the world,   *Sir J. Oldcastle* 120
Is it well that while we *r* with Science,   *Locksley H., Sixty* 217
The fairy fancies *r*.   *Early Spring* 39
Ranged (*adj.*)   *r* ramparts bright From level meadow-bases *Palace of Art* 6
Than all the *r* reasons of the world.   *Pelleas and E.* 156
Ranged (*verb*)   the solemn palms were *r* Above,   *Arabian Nights* 79
presence of the Gods *R* in the halls of Peleus ;   *Œnone* 81
I *r* too high : what draws me down   *Will Water.* 153
As down the shore he *r*,   *Enoch Arden* 588
gain'd The terrace *r* along the Northern front,   *Princess iii* 118
For now her little ones have *r*;   *In Mem. xxi* 26
tall knights, that *r* about the throne,   *Gareth and L.* 328
R with the Table Round that held the lists,   *Lancelot and E.* 467
And a hundred *r* on the rock   *V. of Maeldune* 82
Small pity for those that have *r*   *Despair* 38
R like a storm or stood like a rock   *Heavy Brigade* 56
He fain had *r* her thro' and thro',   *To Marq. of Dufferin* 23
your eyes Have many a time *r* over when a babe.   *The Ring* 151
so high they *r* about the globe ?   *St. Telemachus* 2
Ranging   My fancy, *r* thro' and thro',   *Day-Dm., L'Envoi* 34
some low fever *r* round to spy The weakness   *Aylmer's Field* 569
That sittest *r* golden hair ;   *In Mem. vi* 26
Surprise thee *r* with thy peers.   „ *xliv* 12
We *r* down this lower track,   „ *xlvi* 1
R and ringing thro' the minds of men,   *Com. of Arthur* 416
Rank (*adj.*)   long, *r*, dark wood-walks drench'd in
dew,   *D. of F. Women* 75
Rank (*line*)   When the *r*'s are roll'd in vapour,   *Locksley Hall* 104
The linden broke her *r*'s   *Amphion* 33
And clad in iron burst the *r*'s of war,   *Princess iv* 504
Should see thy passengers in *r*   *In Mem. xiv* 6
glided winding under *r*'s Of iris,   „ *ciii* 23
The front *r* made a sudden halt ;   *Lover's Tale iii* 29
Rank (*social station*)   To all duties of her *r*:   *L. of Burleigh* 72
Whatever eldest-born of *r* or wealth Might lie   *Aylmer's Field* 484

Rank (social station) (continued)   heart is set On one whose r
    exceeds her own.   *In Mem. lx 4*
    up or down Along the scale of r's,   „ *cxi 2*
    likewise for the high r she had borne,   *Guinevere 695*
Rank (verb)   r you nobly, mingled up with me.   *Princess ii 46*
    She might not r with those detestable   „ *v 457*
    r with the best, Garrick and statelier Kemble,   *To W. C. Macready 6*
Rank'd   made me dream I r with him.   *In Mem. xlii 4*
Rankled   R in him and ruffled all his heart,   *Guinevere 49*
Ransack'd   *See* **Often-ransack'd**
Ransom'd (adj.)   Thy r reason change replies   *In Mem. lxi 2*
Ransom'd (verb)   richer in His eyes Who r us,   *Guinevere 685*
Raphaël   I am not R, Titan—no   *Romney's R. 46*
Rapid (adj.)   Whose free delight, from any height of r flight,   *Rosalind 3*
    Her r laughters wild and shrill,   *Kate 3*
    Clash the darts and on the buckler beat with r unanimous
    hand,   *Boädicea 79*
    gyres R and vast, of hissing spray wind-driven   *Lover's Tale ii 198*
    A long loud clash of r marriage-bells.   „ *iii 23*
Rapid (s)   as the r of life Shoots to the fall—   *A Dedication 3*
    then a brook, With one sharp r,   *Holy Grail 381*
Rapine   For nature is one with r,   *Maud I iv 22*
    the wing Of that foul bird of r   *Merlin and V. 728*
    and the ways Were fill'd with r,   *Guinevere 458*
Rapt   So tranced, so r in ecstasies,   *Eleänore 78*
    R after heaven's starry flight,   *Two Voices 68*
    grunted 'Good!' but we Sat r: *M. d'Arthur, Ep. 5*
    So r, we near'd the house;   *Gardener's D. 142*
    seedsman, r Upon the teeming harvest,   *Golden Year 70*
    And, r thro' many a rosy change,   *Day-Dm., Depart. 23*
    I all r in this, 'Come out,' he said,   *Princess, Pro. 50*
    peal'd the nightingale, R in her song,   „ *i 221*
    They stood, so r, we gazing, came a voice,   „ *ii 318*
    Intent on her, who r in glorious dreams,   „ *442*
    She r upon her subject, he on her: „ *iii 304*
    R to the horrible fall: „ *iv 180*
    Came in long breezes r from inmost south   „ *431*
    Ida spoke not, r upon the child.   „ *vi 220*
    we sat But spoke not, r in nameless reverie,   „ *Con. 108*
    ' R from the fickle and the frail   *In Mem. xxx 25*
    r below Thro' all the dewy-tassell'd wood,   „ *lxxxvi 5*
    Who, but hung to hear The r oration flowing free   „ *lxxxvii 32*
    Tho' r in matters dark and deep   „ *xcvii 19*
    So r I was, they could not win An answer   „ *ciii 49*
    R in the fear and in the wonder of it;   *Marr. of Geraint 529*
    R in this fancy of his Table Round,   *Lancelot and E. 129*
    r By all the sweet and sudden passion of youth   „ *281*
    R on his face as it if were a God's.   „ *356*
    R in sweet talk or lively,   *Guinevere 386*
    Like odour r into the winged wind   *Lover's Tale i 801*
    car Of dark Aïdoneus rising r thee hence.   *Demeter and P. 39*
Raptured   Large dowries doth the r eye   *Ode to Memory 72*
Rare   wintertide shall star The black earth with
    brilliance r.   „ *20*
    wreaths of floating dark upcurl'd, R sunrise flow'd.   *The Poet 36*
    R broidry of the purple clover.   *A Dirge 38*
    O r pale Margaret, (repeat)   *Margaret 2, 55*
    I had hope, by something r To prove myself a poet: *Will Water. 165*
    Should bear a double growth of those r souls,   *Princess ii 160*
    stern and sad (so r the smiles Of sunlight)   *The Daisy 53*
    As some r little rose, a piece of inmost   *Hendecasyllabics 19*
    half-way down r sails, White as white clouds,   *Lover's Tale i 4*
    to reassume The semblance of those r realities   „ *ii 162*
    r or fair Was brought before the guest: „ *iv 203*
    R in Fable or History,   *On Jub. Q. Victoria 5*
Rarer   Your loss is r; for this star   *To J. S. 25*
    Chose the green path that show'd the r foot,   *Lancelot and E. 162*
    And the Critic's r still.   *Poets and Critics 16*
Rascal   Tumbled the tawny r at his feet,   *Aylmer's Field 230*
    Read r in the motions of his back,   *Sea Dreams 167*
Rash   Stern he was and r;   *The Captain 10*
    With a crew that is neither rude nor r,   *The Islet 10*
    the hunter rued His r intrusion, manlike,   *Princess iv 204*
    R were my judgment then,   *Lancelot and E. 239*
    At times her steps are swift and r;   *To Marq. of Dufferin 2*

Rash (continued)   Not swift or r, when late she lent
    The sceptres   *To Marq. of Dufferin 5*
Rashness   if I should do This r,   *Two Voices 392*
Rason (reason)   there's r in all things, yer Honour,   *Tomorrow 6*
Rat   tapt at doors, And rummaged like a r: *Walk. to the Mail 38*
    And curse me the British vermin, the r;   *Maud II v 58*
    Ah little r that borest in the dyke   *Merlin and V. 112*
    Lancelot will be gracious to the r,   „ *120*
    ' Black nest of r's,' he groan'd,   *Pelleas and E. 555*
    Ghoäst moästlins was nobbut a r or a mouse.   *Owd Roä 38*
Rate (*See also* **Raäte, Third-rate**)   Whom all men r as
    kind and hospitable: *Princess i 71*
    I r your chance Almost at naked nothing.'   „ *160*
    Till all men grew to r us at our worth,   „ *iv 145*
    we did not r him then This red-hot iron   „ *v 208*
    Whom all men r the king of courtesy.   *Balin and Balan 257*
Rated (*See also* **Raäted**)   must have r her Beyond all
    tolerance   *Aylmer's Field 380*
    such a one As all day long hath r at her child,   *Gareth and L. 1285*
Rathe (early)   The men of r and riper years: *In Mem. cx 2*
    Till r she rose, half-cheated in the thought   *Lancelot and E. 340*
Ratify   every voice she talk'd with r it,   *Princess v 133*
Rating (*See also* **Raätin**)   like her none the less for r at her!   „ *461*
Rattled   Siver the mou'ds r down upo' poor owd Squire   *Village Wife 95*
Ravage   from her bath of storm, At random r?   *Lucretius 176*
    noise of r wrought by beast and man,   *Gareth and L. 437*
Ravaged   left the r woodland yet once more To peace;   *Merlin and V. 963*
Rave   Let them r. (repeat)   *A Dirge 4, 7, 11, 14, 18, 21,*
    25, 28, 32, 35, 39, 42, 49
    But let them r.   *A Dirge 46*
    ' He will not hear the north-wind r,   *Two Voices 259*
    did seem to mourn and r On alien shores;   *Lotos-Eaters 32*
    For blasts would rise and r and cease,   *The Voyage 85*
    ' Drink, and let the parties r!   *Vision of Sin 123*
    My father r's of death and wreck,   *Sailor Boy 19*
    I heard the voice R over the rocky bar,   *Voice and the P. 6*
    I roar and r for I fall.   „ *12*
    And r at the lie and the liar, ah God, as he used to r.   *Maud I i 60*
    about the shuddering wreck the death-white sea should r,   *The Flight 47*
Raved (*See also* **Raäved**)   nor r And thus foam'd over
    at a rival name: *Balin and Balan 566*
Raven (adj.)   Let darkness keep her r gloss: *In Mem. i 10*
    knew not that which pleased it most, The r ringlet or the
    gold;   *The Ring 166*
Raven (s)   Bark an answer, Britain's r!   *Boädicea 13*
    For a r ever croaks, at my side,   *Maud I vi 57*
    A blot in heaven, the R, flying high, Croak'd,   *Guinevere 133*
    God'll pardon the hell-black r   *Rizpah 39*
    Left for the horny-nibb'd r to rend it,   *Batt. of Brunanburh 108*
    at the croak of a R who crost it,   *Merlin and the G. 24*
Ravening   Again their r eagle rose In anger,   *Ode on Well. 119*
Ravine (mountain-gorge)   brook falling thro' the clov'n r In cataract   *Œnone 8*
    wilt thou snare him in the white r,   *Princess vii 205*
    Or rosy blossom in hot r,   *The Daisy 32*
    Beyond a bridge that spann'd a dry r: *Marr. of Geraint 246*
    Across the bridge that spann'd the dry r.   „ *294*
    Every grim r a garden,   *Locksley H., Sixty 168*
    from out the long r below She heard a wailing cry,   *Death of Œnone 19*
    in front of that r Which drowsed in gloom,   „ *75*
Ravine (rapine)   red in tooth and claw With r,   *In Mem. lvi 16*
Raving (*See also* **Raävin'**)   The wind is r in turret and tree.   *The Sisters 27*
    Now with dug spur and r at himself,   *Balin and Balan 310*
    R of dead men's dust and beating hearts.   *Lover's Tale iv 140*
    tears kill'd the flower, my r's hush'd The bird,   *Demeter and P. 108*
    Roaring London, r Paris,   *Locksley H., Sixty 190*
    R politics, never at rest—   *Vastness 3*
Raving-wild   I was mad, I was r-w,   *Charity 27*
Raw   nor wed R Haste, half-sister to Delay.   *Love thou thy land 96*
    Should see the r mechanic's bloody thumbs   *Walk. to the Mail 75*
    That we should mimic this r fool the world,   „ *106*
    one they knew—R from the nursery—   *Aylmer's Field 264*
    R from the prime, and crushing down his mate;   *Princess ii 121*
    And drill the r world for the march of mind,   *Ode on Well. 168*
    shatter'd talbots, which had left the stones R,   *Holy Grail 720*
    ' I have lighted on a fool, R, yet, so stale!'   *Pelleas and E. 114*

Ray (Philip)   *See* **Philip, Philip Ray**

Ray (s)   lashes like to *r*'s Of darkness,   *Arabian Nights* 136
Make a carcanet of *r*'s,   *Adeline* 59
Thro' lips and eyes in subtle *r*'s.   *Rosalind* 24
neither hide the *r* From those, not blind,   *Love thou thy land* 14
Heaven flash'd a sudden jubilant *r*,   *Ode on Well.* 129
Flame-colour, vert and azure, in three *r*'s,   *Com. of Arthur* 275
gay with gold In streaks and *r*'s,   *Gareth and L.* 911
where morning's earliest *r* Might strike it,   *Lancelot and E.* 5
emerald center'd in a sun Of silver *r*'s,   "   296
shower'd down *R*'s of a mighty circle,   *Lover's Tale* i 418
May send one *r* to thee !   *Ded. Poem Prin. Alice* 14
a *r* red as blood Glanced on the strangled face—   *Bandit's Death* 31
Ray (verb)   *R* round with flames her disk of seed,   *In Mem. ci* 6
Ray'd   His hair, a sun that *r* from off a brow   *Last Tournament* 666
Ray-fringed   *R-f* eyelids of the morn Roof   *Clear-headed friend* 6
Raze   and *r* The blessed tomb of Christ ;   *Columbus* 98
Reach (s)   (*See also* **Eye-reach**) Beside the river's wooded *r*,   *In Mem. lxxi* 13
not learnable, divine, Beyond *my r*.   *Balin and Balan* 176
Reach (verb)   And *r* the law within the law :   *Two Voices* 141
example to mankind, Which few can *r* to.   *St. S. Stylites* 189
r To each his perfect pint of stout,   *Will Water.* 114
r its fatling innocent arms And lazy lingering fingers.   *Princess vi* 138
Deeper than those weird doubts could *r* me,   " *vii* 51
Or *r* a hand thro' time to catch   *In Mem. i* 7
And *r* the glow of southern skies,   " *xii* 10
When Science *r*'es forth her arms   ,, *xxi* 18
R out dead hands to comfort me.   ,, *lxxx* 16
Would *r* us out the shining hand,   ,, *lxxxiv* 43
Thy spirit up to mine can *r* ;   ,, *lxxxv* 82
Or ev'n for intellect to *r*—   ,, *xcv* 47
came the hands That *r* thro' nature,   ,, *cxxiv* 24
until we pass and *r* That other,   *Geraint and E.* 6
Climb first and *r* me down thy hand.   *Sir J. Oldcastle* 204
examples *r* a hand Far thro' all years,   *Tiresias* 126
Earth may *r* her earthly-worst,   *Locksley H., Sixty* 233
In summer if I *r* my day—   *To Ulysses* 9
but echo'd on to *r* Honorius,   *St. Telemachus* 76
Reach'd   music *r* them on the middle sea.   *Sea-Fairies* 6
For ere she *r* upon the tide   *L. of Shalott iv* 33
We *r* a meadow slanting to the North ;   *Gardener's D.* 108
till I *r* The wicket-gate,   ,, 212
and set out, and *r* the farm.   ,, *Dora* 129
we *r* The griffin-guarded gates,   *Audley Court* 14
till we *r* The limit of the hills ;   ,, 82
until she *r* The gateway ;   *Godiva* 50
he *r* the home Where Annie lived and loved him,   *Enoch Arden* 684
we *r* A mountain, like a wall of burs and thorns ;   *Sea Dreams* 118
when the note Had *r* a thunderous fulness,   ,, 214
and with long arms and hands *R* out,   *Princess i* 29
we dropt, And flying *r* the frontier ;   ,, 109
I would have *r* you, had you been Sphered   ,, *iv* 437
he *r* White hands of farewell to my sire,   ,, *v* 232
ere we *r* the highest summit I pluck'd a daisy,   *The Daisy* 87
And *r* the ship and caught the rope,   *Sailor Boy* 3
Mayst seem to have *r* a purer air,   *In Mem. xxxiii* 2
He *r* the glory of a hand,   ,, *lxix* 17
When Arthur *r* a field-of-battle   *Com. of Arthur* 96
But ever when he *r* a hand to climb,   *Gareth and L.* 52
went her way across the bridge, And *r* the town,   *Marr. of Geraint* 384
Thereafter, when I *r* this ruin'd hall,   ,, 785
r a hand, and on his foot She set her own   *Geraint and E.* 759
when they *r* the camp the King himself   ,, 878
Then they *r* a glade,   *Balin and Balan* 460
when they *r* the lists By Camelot in the meadow,   *Lancelot and E.* 428
But when ye *r* The city,   *Holy Grail* 707
O, when we *r* The city,   ,, 715
at the last I *r* a door, A light was in the crannies,   ,, 837
And when they *r* Caerleon, ere they past to lodging,   *Pelleas and E.* 124
r The grassy platform on some hill,   *Lover's Tale i* 340
One hand she *r* to those that came behind,   ,, *iii* 48
Reaching   *r* thro' the night Her other,   *Sea Dreams* 287
One *r* forward drew My burthen from mine arms ;   *Princess iv* 191
Read   (*See also* **Reäd**) giving light To *r* those laws ;   *Isabel* 19
And round the prow they *r* her name,   *L. of Shalott iv* 44

Read (*continued*)   That *r* his spirit blindly wise,   *Two Voices* 287
A love-song I had somewhere *r*,   *Miller's D.* 65
Oh ! teach the orphan-boy to *r*,   *L. C. V. de Vere* 69
I *R*, before my eyelids drop their shade,   *D. of F. Women* 1
R, mouthing out his hollow oes and aes,   *The Epic* 50
it was the tone with which he *r*—   *M. d'Arthur, Ep.* 5
laugh'd, as one that *r* my thought,   *Gardener's D.* 106
Who *r* me rhymes elaborately good,   *Edwin Morris* 20
I *r*, and fled by night, and flying turn'd :   ,, 134
They flapp'd my light out as I *r* :   *St. S. Stylites* 175
But tell me, did she *r* the name   *Talking Oak* 153
They *r* Botanic Treatises,   *Amphion* 77
They *r* in arbours clipt and cut,   ,, 85
' Your riddle is hard to *r*.'   *Lady Clare* 76
I *r* and felt that I was there :   *To E. L.* 8
And in their eyes and faces *r* his doom ;   *Enoch Arden* 73
In those two deaths he *r* God's warning ' wait.'   ,, 571
and *r* Writhing a letter from his child,   *Aylmer's Field* 516
r ; and tore, As if the living passion   ,, 534
R rascal in the motions of his back,   *Sea Dreams* 167
I *r* Of old Sir Ralph a page or two   *Princess, Pro.* 120
We seven stay'd at Christmas up to *r* ;   ,, 178
And there we took one tutor as to *r* :   ,, 179
an officer Rose up, and *r* the statutes,   ,, *ii* 69
r My sickness down to happy dreams ?   ,, 252
In this hand held a volume as to *r*,   ,, 455
' can he not *r*—no books ?   ,, *iii* 214
r and earn our prize, A golden brooch :   ,, 300
Regarding, while she *r*,   ,, *iv* 382
on to me, as who should say ' *R*,' and I *r*—two letters—   ,, 397
So far I *r* ; And then stood up and spoke   ,, 417
I kiss'd it and I *r*.   ,, *v* 373
the maidens came, they talk'd, They sang, they *r* :   ,, *vii* 23
to herself, all in low tones, she *r*.   ,, 175
once more, as low, she *r* :   ,, 191
R my little fable : He that runs may *r*.   *The Flower* 17
Which he may *r* that binds the sheaf,   *In Mem. xxxvi* 13
as he lay and *r* The Tuscan poets on the lawn :   ,, *lxxxix* 23
I *r* Of that glad year which once had been,   ,, *xcv* 21
He *r*'s the secret of the star,   ,, *xcvii* 22
Now sign your names, which shall be *r*,   *Con.* 57
echo of something *R* with a boy's delight,   *Maud I vii* 10
Sat with her, *r* to her, night and day,   ,, *xix* 75
(If I *r* her sweet will right)   ,, *xxi* 10
Not a bell was rung, not a prayer was *r* ;   ,, *II v* 24
Gareth lookt and *r*—In letters   *Gareth and L.* 1201
R but one book, and ever reading grew   *Merlin and V.* 622
To dig, pick, open, find and *r* the charm :   ,, 660
Thou *r* the book, (repeat)   ,, 667, 676
And none can *r* the text, not even I ; And none can
    r the comment but myself ;   ,, 681
Stript off the case, and *r* the naked shield,   *Lancelot and E.* 16
He thinking that he *r* her meaning there,   ,, 86
Lifted her eyes, and *r* his lineaments.   ,, 244
Some *r* the King's face, some the Queen's,   ,, 727
Stoopt, took, brake seal, and *r* it ;   ,, 1271
Thus he *r* ; And ever in the reading,   ,, 1283
looking often from his face who *r* To hers   ,, 1285
Mute of this miracle, so far as I have *r*.   *Holy Grail* 66
ran a scroll Of letters in a tongue no man could *r*.   ,, 171
which oftentime I *r*, Who *r* but on my breviary with ease,   ,, 544
There is a custom in the Orient, friends—I *r* of it in
Persia—   *Lover's Tale iv* 231
this was the letter I *r*—   *First Quarrel* 51
And *r* me a Bible verse of the Lord's good will   *Rizpah* 61
I *r* no more the prisoner's mute wail   *Sir J. Oldcastle* 4
Who *r*'s of begging saints in Scripture ? '   ,, 151
in your raised brows I *r* Some wonder   *Columbus* 1
Who *r*'s your golden Eastern lay,   *To E. Fitzgerald* 4
We had *r* their know-nothing books   *Despair* 55
banquet relish ? let me *r*.   *Ancient Sage* 18
R the wide world's annals, you,   *Locksley H., Sixty* 18
that only those who cannot *r* can rule.   ,, 132
Because you heard the lines I *r*   *Pro. to Gen. Hamley* 17
A storm-worn signpost not to be *r*,   *Dead Prophet* 17

Read (*continued*)   Take, *r* ! and be the faults your Poet
     makes   *To Mary Boyle* 61
     Who *r*'s thy gradual process, Holy Spring.   *Prog. of Spring* 106
     And *r* a Grecian tale re-told,   *To Master of B.* 5
Reäd   a *r*'s wonn sarmin a weeäk,   *N. Farmer, O. S.* 28
     'E *r*'s of a sewèr an' sartan 'oäp   *Village Wife* 92
     like fur to hev soom soort of a sarvice *r*.   *Owd Roä* 12
Reader   make them wealthier in his *r*'s eyes ;   *Poet's and their B.* 4
Readier   And *r*, if the King would hear,   *Columbus* 238
Readin'   Fur atween 'is *r* an' writin'   *Village Wife* 40
Reading   (*See also* **Readin'**)   *R* her perfect features in
     the gloom,   *Gardener's D.* 175
     The modern Muses *r*.   *Amphion* 76
     Yet bitterer from his *r*'s :   *Aylmer's Field* 553
     Read but one book, and ever *r* grew   *Merlin and V.* 622
     And ever in the *r*, lords and dames   *Lancelot and E.* 1284
     heir That scarce can wait the *r* of the will   *Lover's Tale i* 676
Ready   Make thine heart *r* with thine eyes :   *Gardener's D.* 273
     I waited long ; My brows are *r*.   *St. S. Stylites* 206
     The lists were *r*.   Empanoplied   *Princess v* 483
     And *r*, thou, to die with him,   *In Mem. cxxi* 2
     ever *r* to slander and steal ;   *Maud I iv* 19
     R in heart and *r* in hand,   ,, *v* 9
     R to burst in a colour'd flame ;   ,, *vi* 19
     I for three days seen, *r* to fall.   *Merlin and V.* 296
     And while she made her *r* for her ride,   *Lancelot and E.* 779
     and a barge Be *r* on the river,   ,, 1123
     R to spring, waiting a chance :   *Guinevere* 12
     Stands in a wind, *r* to break and fly,   ,, 365
     There were our horses *r* at the doors—   *Lover's Tale iv* 385
     R ! take aim at their leaders—   *Def. of Lucknow* 42
     R, be *r* against the storm ! (repeat)   *Riflemen form !* 6, 20
     R, be *r* to meet the storm ! (repeat)   ,, 13, 27
     Form, be *r* to do or die !   ,, 22
Real   Keeps *r* sorrow far away.   *Margaret* 44
     ' Thou hast not gain'd a *r* height,   *Two Voices* 91
     At half thy *r* worth ?   *Will Water.* 204
     men will say We did not know the *r* light,   *Princess iv* 357
     They hated banter, wish'd for something *r*,   ,, *Con.* 18
     some there be that hold The King a shadow, and
     the city *r* :   *Gareth and L.* 266
     Ideal manhood closed in *r* man,   *To the Queen ii* 38
     Thy frailty counts most *r*,   *Ancient Sage* 51
Realist   Betwixt the mockers and the *r*'s :   *Princess, Con.* 24
     novelist, *r*, rhymester, play your part,   *Locksley H., Sixty* 139
Reality   Thy pain is a *r*.'   *Two Voices* 387
     The semblance of those rare *realities*   *Lover's Tale ii* 162
     Immeasurable *R* !   Infinite Personality !   *De Prof., Human C.* 3
Realm   A *r* of pleasance, many a mound,   *Arabian Nights* 101
     Behind Were *r*'s of upland, prodigal in oil,   *Palace of Art* 79
     shall hold a fretful *r* in awe,   *Locksley Hall* 129
     Were no false passport to that easy *r*,   *Aylmer's Field* 183
     Guarding *r*'s and kings from shame ;   *Ode on Well.* 195
     She enters other *r*'s of love ;   *In Mem. xl* 12
     From the *r*'s of light and song,   *Maud II iv* 82
     over all whose *r*'s to their last isle,   *Ded. of Idylls* 12
     and made a *r*, and reign'd. (repeat)   *Com. of Arthur* 19, 519
     Lords and Barons of his *r* Flash'd forth   ,, 65
     make myself in my own *r* Victor and lord.   ,, 89
     lest the *r* should go to wrack   ,, 208
     So that the *r* has gone to wrack :   ,, 227
     Shall Rome or Heathen rule in Arthur's *r* ?   ,, 485
     swept the dust of ruin'd Rome From off the
     threshold of the *r*,   *Gareth and L.* 136
     ' We sit King, to help the wrong'd Thro' all our *r*.   ,, 372
     wastest moorland of our *r* shall be Safe,   ,, 603
     this Order lives to crush All wrongers of the *R*.   ,, 626
     cleanse this common sewer of all his *r*,   *Marr. of Geraint* 39
     For in that *r* of lawless turbulence,   *Geraint and E.* 521
     cleanse this common sewer of all my *r*,   ,, 895
     Should make an onslaught single on a *r*   ,, 917
     his *r* restored But render'd tributary,   *Balin and Balan* 2
     seeing that thy *r* Hath prosper'd in the name of Christ,   ,, 98
     Roving the trackless *r*'s of Lyonnesse,   *Lancelot and E.* 35
     snare her royal fancy with a boon Worth half her *r*,   ,, 72

T*

Realm (*continued*) Even to the half my *r* beyond the seas,   *Lancelot and E.* 958
     to give at last The price of half a *r*,   ,, 1164
     In mine own *r* beyond the narrow seas,   ,, 1323
     shrine which then in all the *r* Was richest,   ,, 1330
     wild bees That made such honey in his *r*.   *Holy Grail* 215
     for ye know the cries of all my *r*   ,, 315
     past thro' Pagan *r*'s, and made them mine,   ,, 478
     Rode to the lonest tract of all the *r*,   ,, 661
     wholesome *r* is purged of otherwhere,   *Last Tournament* 96
     Or whence the fear lest this my *r*,   ,, 122
     And marriage with a princess of that *r*,   ,, 176
     The King prevailing made his *r* :—   ,, 651
     so the *r* was made ; but then their vows—   ,, 681
     Sir Modred had usurp'd the *r*,   *Guinevere* 154
     King's grief For his own self, and his own Queen, and *r*,   ,, 197
     Grieve with the common grief of all the *r* ? '   ,, 217
     what has fall'n upon the *r* ? '   ,, 275
     kings who drew The knighthood-errant of this *r* and all
     The *r*'s together under me,   ,, 461
     all my *r* Reels back into the beast,   *Pass of Arthur* 25
     And wastes the narrow *r* whereon we move,   ,, 140
     From sunset and sunrise of all thy *r*,   *To the Queen ii* 13
     There in my *r* and even on my throne,   *Lover's Tale i* 593
     Like sounds without the twilight *r* of dreams,   ,, *ii* 120
     and all our breadth of *r*,   *Ded. Poem Prin. Alice* 8
     mightiest, wealthiest *r* on earth,   *Columbus* 205
     Nay—tho' that *r* were in the wrong   *Epilogue* 34
     kings and *r*'s that pass to rise no more ;   *To Virgil* 28
     To those dark millions of her *r* !   *Hands all Round* 18
     recks not to ruin a *r* in her name.   *Vastness* 10
     all her *r* Of sound and smoke,   *To Mary Boyle* 65
     in the heart of this most ancient *r*   *Prog. of Spring* 102
Realm-ruining   Rivals of *r-r* party,   *Locksley H., Sixty* 120
Reap   Sow the seed, and *r* the harvest   *Lotos-Eaters, C. S.* 121
     To-morrow yet would *r* to-day,   *Love thou thy land* 93
     God *r*'s a harvest in me.   *St. S. Stylites* 148
     God *r*'s a harvest in thee.   ,, 149
     r's not harvest of his youthful joys,   *Locksley Hall* 139
     r The flower and quintessence of change.   *Day-Dm., L'Envoi* 23
     perhaps might *r* the applause of Great,   *Princess iii* 262
     r's A truth from one that loves and knows ?   *In Mem. xlii* 11
     And *r*'s the labour of his hands,   ,, *lxiv* 26
     Might sow and *r* in peace,   *Epilogue* 13
     r with me, Earth-mother, in the harvest   *Demeter and P.* 147
     I *r* No revenue from the field of unbelief.   *Akbar's Dream* 66
Reap'd   the reapers *r* And the sun fell, (repeat)   *Dora* 78, 108
Reaper   Only *r*'s, reaping early   *L. of Shalott i* 28
     And by the moon the *r* weary,   ,, 33
     one, the *r*'s at their sultry toil.   *Palace of Art* 77
     the *r*'s reap'd And the sun fell, (repeat)   *Dora* 78, 108
     Once more the *r* in the gleam of dawn   *Demeter and P.* 123
     Homestead and harvest, *R* and gleaner,   *Merlin and the G.* 58
Reaping   Only reapers, *r* early   *L. of Shalott i* 28
     men the workers, ever *r* something new :   *Locksley Hall* 117
Rear (s)   Far-blazing from the *r* of Philip's house,   *Enoch Arden* 727
     I came upon The *r* of a procession,   *Lover's Tale i* 75
     those who led the van, and those in *r*,   ,, *iii* 24
Rear (verb)   she shall *r* my dusky race.   *Locksley Hall* 168
     Her office there to *r*, to teach,   *In Mem. xl* 13
     Then gave it to his Queen to *r* :   *Last Tournament* 22
     Thou—when the nations *r* on high   *Freedom* 27
Rear'd   heart to scathe Flowers thou hadst *r*—   *Supp. Confessions* 84
     Freedom *r* in that august sunrise   *The Poet* 37
     Who took a wife, who *r* his race,   *Two Voices* 328
     ring To tempt the babe, who *r* his creasy arms,   *Enoch Arden* 751
     One *r* a font of stone And drew,   *Princess, Pro.* 59
     and your statues *R*, sung to, when,   ,, *v* 414
     Prick'd by the Papal spur, we *r*,   *Third of Feb.* 27
     r him with her own ; And no man knew.   *Com. of Arthur* 224
     three pavilions *r* Above the bushes, gilden-peakt :   *Pelleas and E.* 428
     than when we had *r* thee on high   *Def. of Lucknow* 3
     a statue, *r* To some great citizen,   *Tiresias* 82
     And dying rose, and *r* her arms,   *The Ring* 222
     remembering the gay playmate *r* Among them,   *Death of Œnone* 59
     sunset glared against a cross *R* on the tumbled ruins   *St. Telemachus* 6

Rear'd (*continued*) stone by stone I *r* a sacred fane,   *Akbar's Dream* 177
Reason (s)   (*See also* **Rason**) Nor any train of *r* keep :   *Two Voices* 50
   ' The end and the beginning vex His *r* :   „ 299
   ' And men, whose *r* long was blind,   „ 370
   He utter'd rhyme and *r*,   *The Goose* 6
   God knows : he has a mint of *r's* :   *The Epic* 33
   We lack not rhymes and *r's*,   *Will Water.* 62
   ' There is no *r* why we should not wed.'   *Enoch Arden* 508
   For save when shutting *r's* up in rhythm,   *Lucretius* 223
   prophesying change Beyond all *r* :   *Princess i* 143
   ' worthy *r's* why she should Bide by this issue :   „ *v* 325
   With *r's* drawn from age and state,   „ 357
   Dark is the world to thee : thyself art the *r* why :   *High. Pantheism* 7
   See thou, that countest *r* ripe   *In Mem. xxxiii* 13
   Thy ransom'd *r* change replies   „ *lxi* 2
   art *r* why I seem to cast a careless eye On souls,   „ *cxii*
   The freezing *r's* colder part,   „ *cxxiv* 14
   And *r* in the chase :   *Com. of Arthur* 168
   Albeit I give no *r* but my wish,   *Marr. of Geraint* 761
   (No *r* given her) she could cast aside   „ 807
   Than all the ranged *r's* of the world.   *Pelleas and E.* 156
   A crueller *r* than a crazy ear,   *Lover's Tale iv* 32
   with goodly rhyme and *r* for it—   *Sisters (E. and E.)* 92
   And not without good *r*, my good son—   „ 287
   Slender *r* had *He* to be glad of The clash   *Batt. of Brunanburh* 76
   This worn-out *R* dying in her house   *Romney's R.* 145
   I can but lift the torch Of *R*   *Akbar's Dream* 121
   And let not *R* fail me,   *Doubt and Prayer* 5
   Must my day be dark by *r*,   *God and the Univ.* 2
Reason (verb) Their's not to *r* why,   *Light Brigade* 14
   I am but a fool to *r* with a fool—   *Last Tournament* 271
Reave like are we to *r* him of his crown   *Gareth and L.* 419
Rebel (adj.) if the *r* subject seek to drag me from the throne,   *By an Evolution.* 15
Rebel (s)   Fire from ten thousand at once of the *r's*   *Def. of Lucknow* 22
   hang't, poor friends, as *r's* And burn'd alive   *Sir J. Oldcastle* 47
   loosed My captives, feed the *r's* of the crown,   *Columbus* 131
Rebell'd till the maid *R* against it,   *Lancelot and E.* 651
Rebellion thirty-nine—Call'd it *r*   *Sir J. Oldcastle* 47
Rebloom'd Gather'd the blossom that *r*,   *Aylmer's Field* 142
Reboant the echoing dance Of *r* whirlwinds,   *Supp. Confessions* 97
Rebuke eighty winters freeze with one *r*   *Ode on Well.* 186
Rebuked I so *r*, reviled, Missaid thee ;   *Gareth and L.* 1164
   Who being still *r*, would answer still   „ 1249
Recall Gods themselves cannot *r* their gifts.'   *Tithonus* 49
   R's, in change of light or gloom,   *In Mem. lxxxv* 74
Recall'd half a night's appliances, *r* Her fluttering life :   *Lover's Tale iv* 93
   but our Queen *R* me,   *Columbus* 59
Receive And then one Heaven *r* us all.   *Supp. Confessions* 32
   but whoso did *r* of them, And taste,   *Lotos-Eaters* 30
   Make broad thy shoulders to *r* my weight,   *M. d'Arthur* 164
   I love the truth ; *R* it ;   *Princess ii* 214
   God accept him, Christ *r* him.   *Ode on Well.* 281
   R, and yield me sanctuary,   *Guinevere* 141
   Make broad thy shoulders to *r* my weight,   *Pass. of Arthur* 332
   Thou didst *r* the growth of pines   *Lover's Tale i* 11
Received I stood like one that had *r* a blow :   *Sea Dreams* 161
   R and gave him welcome there ;   *In Mem. lxxxv* 24
   And many a costly cate, *r* the three.   *Gareth and L.* 849
   R at once and laid aside the gems   *Lancelot and E.* 1202
   in her white arms *R*, and after loved it tenderly,   *Last Tournament* 369
   was *r*, Shorn of its strength,   *Lover's Tale i* 433
   Is presently *r* in a sweet grave Of eglantines,   „ 528
   R unto himself a part of blame,   „ 786
Reciting One walk'd *r* by herself,   *Princess ii* 454
Reck And if ye slay him I *r* not :   *Pelleas and E.* 269
   r's not to ruin a realm in her name.   *Vastness* 10
Reckless A *r* and irreverent knight was he,   *Holy Grail* 856
Reckling there lay the *r*, one But one hour old !   *Merlin and V.* 709
Reckon I *r's* I 'annot sa mooch to larn.   *N. Farmer, O. S.* 13
   summun I *r's* 'ull 'a to wroite,   „ 57
   gross heart Would *r* worth the taking ?   *Merlin and V.* 917
   I *r's* tha'll light of a livin'   *Church-warden, etc.* 47
Reckoning ' Thy *r*, friend ? ' and ere he learnt it,   *Geraint and E.* 408
Reclined On silken cushions half *r* ;   *Eleänore* 126

Reclined (*continued*) In the hollow Lotos-land to live and lie *r* On the hills   *Lotos-Eaters, C. S.* 109
   As by the lattice you *r*,   *Day-Dm., Pro.* 5
Reclining Slowly, with pain, *r* on his arm,   *M. d'Arthur* 168
   Slowly, with pain, *r* on his arm,   *Pass. of Arthur* 336
Reclothes Clothes and *r* the happy plains,   *Day-Dm., Sleep. P.* 2
Recognise scarce can *r* the fields I know ;   *St. S. Stylites* 40
Recollect We do but *r* the dreams that come   *Lucretius* 35
   Unruffling waters *r-c* the shape Of one   *Last Tournament* 369
Recommenced A little ceased, but *r*.   *Two Voices* 318
   Poor fellow, could he help it ? *r*,   *The Brook* 158
   I *r* ; ' Decide not ere you pause.   *Princess iii* 156
   r, and let her tongue Rage like a fire   *Merlin and V.* 801
Reconcile The Gods are hard to *r* :   *Lotos-Eaters, C. S.* 81
Reconciled Nor did mine own, now *r* ;   *Princess vii* 88
   To be friends for her sake, to be *r* ;   *Maud I xix* 50
   breathing a prayer To be friends, to be *r* !   „ 56
   but I—to be *r* ?—No,   *Bandit's Death* 16
Reconcilement difference, *r*, pledges given,   *Gardener's D.* 257
   Quick while I melt ; make *r* sure   *Princess vi* 286
Record Whereof this world holds *r*.   *M. d'Arthur* 16
   What *r*, or what relic of my lord   „ 98
   shaping faithful *r* of the glance That graced   *Gardener's D.* 177
   Sponged and made blank of crimeful *r*   *St. S. Stylites* 158
   in division of the *r's* of the mind :   *Locksley Hall* 69
   Were caught within the *r* of her wrongs,   *Princess v* 143
   Whatever *r* leap to light He never shall be shamed.   *Ode on Well.* 190
   might be left some *r* of the things we said.   *Third of Feb.* 18
   There lives no *r* of reply,   *In Mem. xxxi* 6
   What *r* ? not the sinless years That breathed   „ *lii* 11
   Whereof this world holds *r*.   *Pass. of Arthur* 184
   What *r*, or what relic of my lord   „ 266
Recorded each at other's ear What shall not be *r*—   *Geraint and E.* 635
Recover'd *See* **Now-recover'd**
Recovering And while he lay *r* there,   *Enoch Arden* 108
Recrost my feet *r* the deathful ridge   *Holy Grail* 534
Rector Long since, a bygone *R* of the place,   *Aylmer's Field* 11
Rectory And Averill Averill at the *R* Thrice over ; so that *R* and Hall, Bound in an immemorial intimacy,   „ 37
Recurring (*See also* **Old-recurring, Still-recurring**) *R* and suggesting still !   *Will* 14
   And be found of angel eyes In earth's *r* Paradise.   *Helen's Tower* 12
Red (adj.) (*See also* **Blood-red, Rose-red**) The *r* cheek paling, The strong limbs failing ;   *All Things will Die* 31
   Some *r* heath-flower in the dew,   *Rosalind* 41
   And the *r* cloaks of market girls,   *L. of Shalott ii* 17
   One seem'd all dark and *r*—a tract of sand,   *Palace of Art* 65
   Before the *r* cock crows from the farm upon the hill,   *May Queen, N. Y's. E.* 23
   charmed sunset linger'd low adown In the *r* West :   *Lotos-Eaters* 20
   The dim *r* morn had died, her journey done,   *D. of F. Women* 61
   at the root thro' lush green grasses burn'd The *r* anemone.   „ 72
   We left the dying ebb that faintly lipp'd The flat *r* granite ;   *Audley Court* 13
   And grapes with bunches *r* as blood ;   *Day-Dm., Sleep. P.* 44
   Pale he turn'd and *r*,   *The Captain* 62
   r roofs about a narrow wharf In cluster ;   *Enoch Arden* 3
   When the *r* rose was redder than itself, And York's white rose as *r* as Lancaster's,   *Aylmer's Field* 50
   O there The *r* fruit of an old idolatry—   „ 762
   Fluctuated, as flowers in storm, some *r*, some pale,   *Princess iv* 482
   perforce He yielded, wroth and *r*, with fierce demur :   „ *v* 358
   They mark'd it with the *r* cross to the fall,   „ *vi* 41
   R grief and mother's hunger in her eye,   „ 146
   Or *r* with spirted purple of the vats,   „ *vii* 202
   A *r* sail, or a white ; and far beyond,   *Con.* 47
   The last *r* leaf is whirl'd away,   *In Mem. xv* 3
   Tho' Nature, *r* in tooth and claw With ravine,   „ *lvi* 15
   The *r* fool-fury of the Seine Should pile her barricades   „ *cxxvii* 7
   here on the landward side, by a *r* rock, glimmers the Hall ;   *Maud I iv* 10
   Has a broad-blown comeliness, *r* and white,   „ *xiii* 9
   Till the *r* man dance By his *r* cedar-tree, And the *r* man's babe Leap,   „ *xvii* 17
   The *r* rose cries, ' She is near, she is near ; '   „ *xxii* 63

Red (adj.) (continued) The day comes, a dull r ball Wrapt in
  drifts   *Maud* II iv 65
But the r life spilt for a private blow—   „ v 93
r berries charm the bird, And thee, mine innocent,   *Gareth and L.* 85
who sliced a r life-bubbling way Thro' twenty folds   „ 509
Round as the r eye of an Eagle-owl,   „ 799
Huge on a huge r horse, and all in mail Burnish'd to
  blinding,   „ 1026
Where bread and baken meats and good r wine Of
  Southland,   „ 1190
than r and pale Across the face of Enid hearing her ;   *Marr. of Geraint* 523
Which was the r cock shouting to the light,   *Geraint and E.* 384
At this he turn'd all r and paced his hall,   „ 668
longest lance his eyes had ever seen, Point-
  painted r ;   *Balin and Balan* 412
Reputed to be r with sinless blood,   „ 557
Turn r or pale, would often when they met Sigh
  fully,   *Merlin and V.* 181
from spur to plume R as the rising sun with heathen
  blood,   *Lancelot and E.* 308
A r sleeve Broider'd with pearls,'   „ 372
And shot r fire and shadows thro' the cave,   „ 414
who sat Robed in r samite, easily to be known,   „ 433
What of the knight with the r sleeve ?   „ 621
up a slope of garden, all Of roses white and r,   *Pelleas and E.* 434
in one, R after revel, droned her lurdane knights   „ 430
R Knight Brake in upon me and drave them to
  his tower ;   *Last Tournament* 71
See, the hand Wherewith thou takest this, is r ! '   „ 193
till his Queen Graspt it so hard, that all her hand was r.   „ 411
Then cried the Breton, ' Look, her hand is r !   „ 412
the R Knight heard, and all,   „ 441
r dream Fled with a shout, and that low lodge return'd,   „ 487
tide within R with free chase and heather-scented air,   „ 691
' but the r fruit Grown on a magic oak-tree in mid-heaven,   „ 744
R ruin, and the breaking up of laws,   *Guinevere* 426
blight Lives in the dewy touch of pity had made The
  r rose there a pale one—   *Lover's Tale* i 696
One morning when the upblown billow ran Shoreward
  beneath r clouds,   „ ii 179
Married among the r berries, an' all as merry as
  May—   *First Quarrel* 40
Harsh r hair, big voice, big chest, big merciless
  hands ;   *In the Child. Hosp.* 4
for he look'd so coarse and so r,   „ 7
R in thy birth, redder with household war,   *Sir J. Oldcastle* 53
Redder to be, r rose of Lancaster—   „ 55
And the r passion-flower to the cliffs,   *V. of Maeldune* 39
And r with blood the Crescent reels from fight   *Montenegro* 6
strike Thy youthful pulses into rest and quench The r
  God's anger,   *Tiresias* 158
wi' a niced r faäce, an' es cleän Es a shillin'   *Spinster's S's.* 75
The r ' Blood-eagle ' of liver and heart ;   *Dead Prophet* 71
Fell—and flash'd into the R Sea,   *To Marq. of Dufferin* 44
lighted from below By the r race of fiery Phlegethon ;   *Demeter and P.* 28
Then I seed at 'is faäce wur as r as the Yule-block   *Owd Roä* 56
A r mark ran All round one finger pointed straight,   *The Ring* 452
I well remember that r night When thirty ricks,
  All flaming,   *To Mary Boyle* 35
but close to me to-day As this r rose,   *Roses on the T.* 7
his kisses were r with his crime,   *Bandit's Death* 13
and a ray r as blood Glanced on the strangled face—   „ 31
An' 'e torn'd as r as a stag-tuckey's wattles,   *Church-warden, etc.* 31
flush'd as r As poppies when she crown'd it.   *The Tourney* 16

Red (s) (See also **Rose-red**) As I have seen the rosy r
  flushing in the northern night.   *Locksley Hall* 26
No pint of white or r Had ever half the power to turn   *Will Water.* 82
Blues and r's They talk'd of :   *Aylmer's Field* 251
praised the waning r, and told The vintage—   „ 406
And bickers into r and emerald,   *Princess* v 263
Who tremblest thro' thy darkling r   *In Mem.* xcix 5
And blossom in purple and r.   *Maud* I xxii 74
Breaks from a coppice gemm'd with green and r,   *Marr. of Geraint* 339
' Come to us, O come, come ' in the stormy r of a sky   *V. of Maeldune* 98
Molly Magee, wid the r o' the rose an' the white o' the May,   *Tomorrow* 31

Red (s) (continued) R of the Dawn ! (repeat)   *The Dawn* 1, 6, 21
Is it turning a fainter r ?   *The Dawn* 22
Redan Out yonder. Guard the R !   *Def. of Lucknow* 36
Redcap The r whistled ; and the nightingale   *Gardener's D.* 95
Redcoat our own good r's sank from sight,   *Heavy Brigade* 42
Red-cross A r-c knight for ever kneel'd   *L. of Shalott* iii 6
Redden cheek begins to r thro' the gloom,   *Tithonus* 37
Sad as the last which r's over one   *Princess* iv 46
and his anger r's in the heavens ;   „ 386
He r's what he kisses :   „ v 165
These leaves that r to the fall ;   *In Mem.* xi 14
he r's, cannot speak, So bashful, he !   *Balin and Balan* 519
Redden'd r with no bandit's blood :   *Aylmer's Field* 597
And this was what had r her cheek   *Maud* I xix 65
R at once with sinful,   *Balin and Balan* 558
Miriam r, Muriel clench'd The hand that wore it,   *The Ring* 261
The ring of faces r by the flames   *Death of Œnone* 92
r by that cloud of shame when I . . .   *Akbar's Dream* 64
Reddening Sir Aylmer r from the storm within,   *Aylmer's Field* 322
And r in the furrows of his chin,   *Princess* vi 228
heathen horde, R the sun with smoke and earth   *Com. of Arthur* 37
She r, ' Insolent scullion : I of thee ?   *Gareth and L.* 976
He, r in extremity of delight,   *Geraint and E.* 219
And where it dash'd the r meadow,   *Lucretius* 49
Bantering bridesman, r priest,   *Forlorn* 33
Redder When the red rose was r than itself,   *Aylmer's Field* 50
The whole hill-side was r than a fox.   *Walk. to the Mail* 3
Fair-hair'd and r than a windy morn ;   *Princess, Con.* 91
Shame never made girl r than Gareth joy.   *Gareth and L.* 536
R than any rose, a joy to me,   *Holy Grail* 521
r with household war, Now reddest with the blood
  of holy men, R to be, red rose of Lancaster—   *Sir J. Oldcastle* 53
r than rosiest health or than utterest shame,   *V. of Maeldune* 45
Reddest Now r with the blood of holy men,   *Sir J. Oldcastle* 54
Redeem that From which I would r you :   *Princess* iv 508
Redeem'd R it from the charge of nothingness—   *M. d'Arthur, Ep.* 7
Red-faced But r-f war has rods of steel and fire ;   *Princess* v 118
A r-f bride who knew herself so vile,   *Gareth and L.* 110
Red-hot This r-h iron to be shaped with blows.   *Princess* v 209
Screams of a babe in the r-h palms of a Moloch of
  Tyre,   *The Dawn* 2
Redolent brow of pearl Tressed with r ebony,   *Arabian Nights* 138
Redound not without r Of use and glory to yourselves   *Princess* ii 42
Red-plow'd domes the r-p hills With loving blue ;   *Early Spring* 3
Red-pulsing R-p up thro' Alioth and Alcor,   *Last Tournament* 480
Red-rent arm R-r with hooks of bramble,   *Holy Grail* 211
Redress What hope of answer, or r ?   *In Mem.* lvi 27
Ring in r to all mankind.   „ cvi 12
Redress'd prowess done r a random wrong.   *Guinevere* 459
Redressing Whose glory was, r human wrong ;   *Ded. of Idylls* 9
Than ride abroad r women's wrong,   *Gareth and L.* 866
They ride abroad r human wrongs !   *Merlin and V.* 693
To ride abroad r human wrongs,   *Guinevere* 471
Red-ribb'd r-r ledges drip with a silent horror of blood,   *Maud* I i 3
From the r-r hollow behind the wood,   „ II i 25
Red Sea and flash'd into the R S,   *To Marq. of Dufferin* 44
Redundant floods with r life Her narrow portals.   *Lover's Tale* i 84
Reed Like Indian r's blown from his silver tongue,   *The Poet* 13
the wavy swell of the soughing r's,   *Dying Swan* 38
That sets at twilight in a land of r's.   *Caress'd or chidden* 14
' I heard the ripple washing in the r's,   *M. d'Arthur* 70
And the long ripple washing in the r's.'   „ 117
What r was that on which I leant ?   *In Mem.* lxxxiv 45
Or low morass and whispering r,   „ c 6
ranks Of iris, and the golden r ;   „ ciii 24
And mid-thigh-deep in bulrushes and r,   *Gareth and L.* 810
strange knee rustle thro' her secret r's,   *Balin and Balan* 354
and watch'd The high r wave,   *Lancelot and E.* 1390
Rode far, till o'er the illimitable r,   *Last Tournament* 421
' I heard the ripple washing in the r's,   *Pass. of Arthur* 238
And the long ripple washing in the r's.'   „ 285
A flat malarian world of r and rush !   *Lover's Tale* iv 142
Reed-tops And took the r-t as it went.   *Dying Swan* 10
Reedy Came up from r Simois all alone.   *Œnone* 52
Reef league-long roller thundering on the r,   *Enoch Arden* 584

Reef (*continued*) Down in the water, a long *r* of gold,   *Sea Dreams* 127
Wreck'd on a *r* of visionary gold.'   " 139
In roarings round the coral *r*.   *In Mem. xxxvi* 16
Reek'd For he *r* with the blood of Piero ;   *Bandit's Death* 13
Reel The horse and rider *r* : They *r*, they roll in clanging lists,   *Sir Galahad* 8
We felt the good ship shake and *r*,   *The Voyage* 15
Earth *R's*, and the herdsmen cry ;   *Princess v* 529
R's, as the golden Autumn woodland *r's*   " *vii* 357
When all my spirit *r's* At the shouts,   *Maud II iv* 20
the spear spring, and good horse *r*,   *Gareth and L.* 523
R back into the beast, and be no more ? '   *Last Tournament* 125
all my realm *R's* back into the beast,   *Pass. of Arthur* 26
made the ground *R* under us, and all at once,   *Lover's Tale ii* 194
My brain had begun to *r*—   *In the Child. Hosp.* 60
Backward they *r* like the wave,   *Def. of Lucknow* 43
red with blood the Crescent *r's* from fight   *Montenegro* 6
song-built towers and gates *R*,   *Tiresias* 99
r's not in the storm of warring words,   *Ancient Sage* 70
Reel'd but in the middle aisle *R*,   *Aylmer's Field* 819
part *r* but kept their seats :   *Princess v* 496
R from the sabre-stroke Shatter'd and sunder'd.   *Light Brigade* 35
and *r* Almost to falling from his horse ;   *Pelleas and E.* 23
and the morning star *R* in the smoke,   " 519
And pale he turn'd, and *r*,   *Guinevere* 304
backward *r* the Trojans and allies,   *Achilles over the T.* 31
foeman surged, and waver'd, and *r*   *Heavy Brigade* 62
Reeling Garlon, *r* slowly backward, fell,   *Balin and Balan* 397
Arise and fly The *r* Faun,   *In Mem. cxviii* 26
crooked, *r*, livid, thro' the mist Rose,   *Death of Œnone* 27
Re-father'd stoop'd, *r-f* o'er my wounds.   *Princess vi* 129
Refectory Told us of this in our *r*,   *Holy Grail* 41
Reflect For love *r's* the thing beloved ;   *In Mem. lii* 2
And each *r's* a kindlier day,   " *c* 18
makes Her heart a mirror that *r's* but you.'   *The Ring* 366
Reflected *R*, sends a light on the forgiven.   *Romney's R.* 161
Reflecting Opposed mirrors each *r* each—   *Sonnet To* —— 11
Reflex The mellow'd *r* of a winter moon ;   *Isabel* 29
The *r* of a beauteous form,   *Miller's D.* 77
The *r* of a legend past,   *Day-Dm., Pro.* 11
swims The *r* of a human face.   *In Mem. cviii* 12
depth of an unfathom'd woe *R* of action.   *Lover's Tale i* 747
Refluent a phantom colony smoulder'd on the *r* estuary ;   *Boädicea* 28
Reform *R*, White Rose, Bellerophon,   *The Brook* 161
Let your *r's* for a moment go !   *Riflemen form!* 15
Refraction And such *r* of events   *In Mem. xcii* 15
Refrain we *r* From talk of battles loud and vain,   *Ode on Well.* 246
Refrain'd *r* From ev'n a word.   *Marr. of Geraint* 213
Refresh'd leave thee freer, till thou wake *r*   *Love and Duty* 97
Reft *r* From my dead lord a field with violence :   *Gareth and L.* 334
he *r* us of it Perforce, and left us neither gold nor field.'   " 338
heathen caught and *r* him of his tongue.   *Lancelot and E.* 273
that was *r* of his Folk and his friends   *Batt. of Brunanburh* 69
Refulgent Where some *r* sunset of India   *Milton* 13
Refuse (s) and *r* patch'd with moss.   *Vision of Sin* 212
Refuse (verb) nor did mine own *R* her proffer,   *Princess vi* 347
Refused Nor yet *r* the rose, but granted it,   *Gardener's D.* 160
R her to him, then his pride awoke ;   *Marr. of Geraint* 448
I *r* the hand he gave.   *Locksley H., Sixty* 256
Refusing and thou *r* this Unvenerable   *Tiresias* 131
Regal and a hope The child of *r* compact,   *Princess iv* 421
Of freedom in her *r* seat Of England ;   *In Mem. cix* 14
Push'd from his chair of *r* heritage.   *Lover's Tale i* 118
Regale Call your poor to *r* with you,   *On Jub. Q. Victoria* 30
Regally Make it *r* gorgeous,   " 45
Regard *R* the weakness of thy peers :   *Love thou thy land* 24
R gradation, lest the soul Of Discord   " 67
O blatant Magazines, *r* me rather—   *Hendecasyllabics* 17
Regarded Bedivere Remorsefully *r* thro' his tears,   *M. d'Arthur* 171
daughters in the pool ; for none *R* ;   *Princess v* 330
And many past, but none *r* her,   *Geraint and E.* 520
woman's love, Save one, he *r* not *r*,   *Lancelot and E.* 842
Bedivere Remorsefully *r* thro' his tears,   *Pass. of Arthur* 339
Regarding Droops both his wings, *r* thee,   *Eleänore* 119
any one, *R*, well had deem'd he felt the tale   *Enoch Arden* 711

Regarding (*continued*) silent we with blind surmise *R*,   *Princess iv* 382
Regather co-mates *r* round the mast ;   *Pref. Son. 19th Cent.* 5
Reggio Of rain at *R*, rain at Parma ;   *The Daisy* 51
Region How long this icy-hearted Muscovite Oppress the *r* ? '   *Poland* 11
Within this *r* I subsist,   *You ask me, why, etc.* 2
girt the *r* with high cliff and lawn :   *Vision of Sin* 47
That range above the *r* of the wind,   *Princess, Con.* 112
No wing of wind the *r* swept,   *In Mem. lxxviii* 6
To the *r's* of thy rest ' ?   *Maud II iv* 88
Gawain the while thro' all the *r* round   *Lancelot and E.* 615
fail'd to find him, tho' I rode all round The *r* :   " 710
saw Beneath her feet the *r* far away,   *Lover's Tale i* 395
Register'd Are *r* and calendar'd for saints.   *St. S. Stylites* 132
Regret (s) Love is made a vague *r*.   *Miller's D.* 210
Deep as first love and wild with all *r* ;   *Princess iv* 57
debt Of boundless love and reverence and *r*   *Ode on Well.* 157
So seems it in my deep *r*,   *In Mem. viii* 17
And chains *r* to his decease,   " *xxix* 3
hopes and light *r's* that come Make April   " *xl* 7
O last *r*, *r* can die !   " *lxxviii* 17
To one pure image of *r*.   " *cii* 24
and my *r* Becomes an April violet,   " *cxv* 18
Is it, then, *r* for buried time That keenlier   " *cxvi* 1
Not all *r* : the face will shine Upon me,   " 9
embalm In dying songs a dead *r*,   " *Con.* 14
R is dead, but love is more   " 17
no *r's* for aught that has been,   *Vastness* 23
Regret (verb) and *r* Her parting step,   *Lancelot and E.* 866
Regular Faultily faultless, icily *r*,   *Maud I ii* 6
Them as 'as coäts to their backs an' taäkes their *r* meäls.   *N. Farmer, N. S.* 46
Rehearse 'This truth within thy mind *r*,   *Two Voices* 25
Reign (verb) lips whereon perpetually did *r* The summer calm   *Isabel* 7
I shall *r* for ever over all.'   *Love and Death* 15
'*R* thou apart, a quiet king,   *Palace of Art* 14
you shall *r* The head and heart of all our fair she-world,   *Princess iii* 162
Then *r* the world's great bridals,   " *vii* 294
the wise who think, the wise who *r*,   *Ode Inter. Exhib.* 32
O Soul, the Vision of Him who *r's* ?   *High. Pantheism* 2
What happiness to *r* a lonely king,   *Com. of Arthur* 82
same child,' he said, 'Is he who *r's* ;   " 393
'*R* ye, and live and love,   " 472
' Let the King *r*.' (repeat)   *Com. of Arthur* 484, 487, 490, 493, 496, 499, 502
the worst were that man he that *r's* !   *Guinevere* 523
where I hoped myself to *r* as king,   *Lover's Tale i* 591
When only Day should *r*.'   *Ancient Sage* 244
Reign (s) morning of my *r* Was redden'd by that cloud   *Akbar's Dream* 63
The *R* of the Meek upon earth,   *The Dreamer* 25
Reign'd A kindlier influence *r* ;   *Princess vii* 20
and made a realm, and. *r*. (repeat)   *Com. of Arthur* 19, 519
KING, that hast *r* six hundred years,   *To Dante* 1
when Athens *r* and Rome,   *Freedom* 9
Reigning him, that other, *r* in his place,   *Enoch Arden* 763
And *r* with one will in everything   *Com. of Arthur* 92
Rein (*See also* **Bridle-rein**) sway'd The *r* with dainty finger-tips,   *Sir L. and Q. G.* 41
with slack *r* and careless of himself,   *Balin and Balan* 309
he twitch'd the *r's*, And made his beast   *Pelleas and E.* 550
Will firmly hold the *r*,   *Politics* 5
Rein'd Edyrn *r* his charger at her side,   *Geraint and E.* 820
Re-inspired With youthful fancy *r-i*,   *Ode to Memory* 114
Reissuing whence *r*, robed and crown'd,   *Godiva* 77
Rejected He should not be *r*.   *Aylmer's Field* 422
return'd Leolin's *r* rivals from their suit So often,   " 493
Rejection with hands of wild *r* ' Go ! '—   *Edwin Morris* 124
Rejoice As when a mighty people *r*   *Dying Swan* 31
Than him that said ' *R* ! *r* ! '   *Two Voices* 462
There in her place she did *r*,   *Of old sat Freedom* 5
But Thou *r* with liberal joy,   *England and Amer.* 11
Thus her heart *r's* greatly,   *L. of Burleigh* 41
A people's voice, when they *r* At civic revel   *Ode on Well.* 146
Roll and *r*, jubilant voice,   *W. to Alexandra* 22
O Soul, and let us *r*,   *High. Pantheism* 13

Remember (*continued*) They still *r* what it cost them here,   *The Ring* 201
   I *r* once that being waked By noises in the house—   „ 416
   I brought you, you *r*, these roses,   *Happy* 73
   I well *r* that red night When thirty ricks,   *To Mary Boyle* 35
   I *r* it, a proof That I—   *Romney's R.* 92
Rememberable   Bear witness, that *r* day,   *To the Queen* ii 3
Remember'd (**adj.**)   ' Dear as *r* kisses after death,   *Princess* iv 54
Remember'd (**verb**)   I *r* Everard's college fame   *The Epic* 46
   and *r* one dark hour Here in this wood,   *Enoch Arden* 385
   She *r* that : A pleasant game,   *Princess, Pro.* 193
   I *r* one myself had made,   „ iv 88
   Then I *r* that burnt sorcerer's curse   „ v 475
   Then he *r* her, and how she wept ;   *Geraint and E.* 612
   I—even I—at times *r*,   *Romney's R.* 93
   Then I *r* Arthur's warning word,   *Holy Grail* 598
Rememberest   for thou *r* how In those old days,   *M. d'Arthur* 28
   thou *r* well—one summer dawn—   *Balin and Balan* 505
   for thou *r* how In those old days,   *Pass. of Arthur* 196
   thou *r* what a fury shook Those pillars   *Akbar's Dream* 80
Remembering   *R* its ancient heat.   *Two Voices* 423
   R the day when first she came,   *Dora* 106
   crown of sorrow is *r* happier things.   *Locksley Hall* 76
   fragrant in a heart *r* His former talks with Edith,   *Aylmer's Field* 456
   R her dear Lord who died for all,   *Sea Dreams* 47
   R how we three presented Maid Or Nymph,   *Princess* i 196
   they will beat my girl *R* her mother :   „ v 89
   R his ill-omen'd song,   „ vi 159
   R all his greatness in the Past.   *Ode on Well.* 20
   R all the beauty of that star Which shone   *Ded. of Idylls* 46
   but remembers all, and growls *R*,   *Gareth and L.* 705
   R when first he came on her Drest in that dress,   *Marr. of Geraint* 140
   R how first he came on her,   „ 842
   But she, *r* her old ruin'd hall,   *Geraint and E.* 254
   some token of his Queen Whereon to gaze, *r* her—   *Balin and Balan* 189
   R that dark bower at Camelot,   „ 526
   r Her thought when first she came,   *Guinevere* 181
   r all The love they both have borne me,   *Sisters* (*E. and E.*) 279
   while *r* thee, I lay At thy pale feet   *Ded. Poem Prin. Alice* 19
   R all the golden hours Now silent,   *Tiresias* 210
   r the gay playmate rear'd Among them,   *Death of Œnone* 59
Remembrance   In mute and glad *r*,   *Lover's Tale* ii 186
Remerging   *R* in the general Soul,   *In Mem.* xlvii 4
Remimber (**remember**)   an' meself *r*'s wan night   *Tomorrow* 7
Remiss   ' She had not found me so *r* ;   *Talking Oak* 193
Remit   She takes, when harsher moods *r*,   *In Mem.* xlviii 6
Remnant   a *r* that were left Paynim amid their circles,   *Holy Grail* 663
   and a *r* stays with me. And of this *r* will I leave a part,   *Guinevere* 443
Remodel   why should any man *R* models ?   *The Epic* 38
Remorse   You held your course without *r*,   *L. C. V. de Vere* 45
   all the man was broken with *r* ;   *Dora* 165
   At once without *r* to strike her dead,   *Geraint and E.* 598
   not the one dark hour which brings *r*,   *Merlin and V.* 763
   Dead !—and maybe stung With some *r*,   *The Ring* 454
   For never had I seen her show *r*—   „ 457
   Would the man have a touch of *r*   *Charity* 17
Remorseful   To whom *r* Cyril, ' Yet I pray Take comfort :   *Princess* v 79
   So groan'd Sir Lancelot in *r* pain,   *Lancelot and E.* 1428
   Some half *r* kind of pity too—   *The Ring* 375
Remorseless   But that *r* iron hour Made cypress   *In Mem.* lxxxiv 14
Remote   Beside *r* Shalott. (repeat)   *L. of Shalott* iii 9, 18
Remove   *See* **Remble**
Removed   (*See also* **Rembled**)   Forgive my grief for one *r*,   *In Mem., Pro.* 37
   An awful thought, a life *r*,   „ xiii 10
Rend   cried to *r* the cloth, to *r* In pieces,   *Gareth and L.* 400
   r the cloth and cast it on the hearth.   „ 418
   Left for the horny-nibb'd raven to *r* it,   *Batt. of Brunanburh* 108
Render   ' Will thirty seasons *r* plain   *Two Voices* 82
   left me, statue-like, In act to *r* thanks.   *Gardener's D.* 162
   R him up unscathed :   *Princess* iv 408
   I lagg'd in answer loth to *r* up My precontract,   „ v 299
   R thanks to the Giver, (repeat)   *Ode on Well.* 44, 47
   And *r* him to the mould.   „ 48
   And *r* human love his dues ;   *In Mem.* xxxvii 16
   and *r* All homage to his own darling,   *Maud* I xx 48
   I gave the diamond : she will *r* it ;   *Lancelot and E.* 713

Render (*continued*) Forgetting how to *r* beautiful Her countenance   *Lover's Tale* i 96
Render'd   She *r* answer high :   *D. of F. Women* 202
   Survive in spirits *r* free,   *In Mem.* xxxviii 10
   in my charge, which was not *r* to him ;   *Marr. of Geraint* 452
   Arthur's wars were *r* mystically,   *Lancelot and E.* 801
   Arthur's wars are *r* mystically,   *Holy Grail* 359
Rendering   Not *r* true answer, as beseem'd Thy fëalty,   *M. d'Arthur* 74
   Nor *r* true answer, as beseem'd Thy fëalty,   *Pass. of Arthur* 242
Rending   And *r*, and a blast, and overhead Thunder,   *Holy Grail* 184
   the veil Is *r*, and the Voices of the day   *The Ring* 39
   or the *r* earthquake, or the famine, or the pest !   *Faith* 4
Renegade   and *r*'s, Thieves, bandits,   *Last Tournament* 94
Renew   Would God *r* me from my birth   *Miller's D.* 27
   wilt *r* thy beauty morn by morn ;   *Tithonus* 74
   with the sun and moon *r* their light   *Princess* iii 255
Renew'd   (*See also* **Self-renew'd**)   And bosom beating with a heart *r*.   *Tithonus* 36
   The maid and page *r* their strife,   *Day-Dm., Revival* 13
   a wish *r*, When two years after came a boy   *Enoch Arden* 88
   Many a sad kiss by day by night *r*   „ 161
   Then her new child was as herself *r*,   „ 523
   seem'd For some new death than for a life *r* ;   *Lover's Tale* iv 374
Renown   Of me you shall not win *r* :   *L. C. V. de Vere* 2
   A land of just and old *r*,   *You ask me, why, etc.* 10
   Speak no more of his *r*,   *Ode on Well.* 278
   Who might have chased and claspt *R*   *To Marq. of Dufferin* 29
Renowned   *See* **Far-renowned**
Rent (**tearing**)   Were living nerves to feel the *r* ;   *Aylmer's Field* 536
Rent (**money**)   Howiver was I fur to find my *r*   *Owd Roä* 47
   ' can ya paäy me the *r* to-night ? '   „ 57
Rent (**tore**)   ' An inner impulse *r* the veil   *Two Voices* 10
   r The woodbine wreaths that bind her,   *Amphion* 33
   r The wonder of the loom thro' warp and woof   *Princess* i 61
Rent (**hire**)   how The races went, and who would *r* the hall :   *Audley Court* 31
Rent (**torn**)   *See* **Red-rent**
Rentroll   The *r* Cupid of our rainy isles.   *Edwin Morris* 103
Re-orient   The life *r-o* out of dust,   *In Mem.* cxvi 6
Repaid   money can be *r* ; Not kindness   *Enoch Arden* 320
Repast   For brief *r* or afternoon repose   *Guinevere* 395
   And sitting down to such a base *r*,   *Lover's Tale* iv 134
Repay   Why then he shall *r* me—   *Enoch Arden* 310
   He will *r* you : money can be repaid ;   „ 320
Repeal   ' Ride you naked thro' the town, And I *r* it ; '   *Godiva* 30
Repeat   I must needs *r* for my excuse   *Princess* iii 52
Repeated   *R* muttering ' cast away and lost ; '   *Enoch Arden* 715
Repeating   roll'd his eyes upon her *R* all he wish'd,   „ 905
   simple maid Went half the night *r*, ' Must I die ? '   *Lancelot and E.* 899
   R, till the word we know so well Becomes a wonder,   „ 1028
Repell'd   *R* by the magnet of Art   *The Wreck* 22
Repent   I *r* me of all I did :   *Edward Gray* 23
   voice that calls Doom upon kings, or in the waste ' *R* ' ?   *Aylmer's Field* 742
   The world will not believe a man *r*'s :   *Geraint and E.* 900
   Full seldom doth a man *r*,   „ 902
   ' No light had we : for that we do *r* ;   *Guinevere* 171
   But help me, heaven, for surely I *r*.   „ 372
   let a man *r*, Do penance in his heart,   *Sir J. Oldcastle* 142
   I *r* it o'er his grave—   *Locksley H., Sixty* 255
   I repented and *r*,   *Happy* 85
Repentance   what is true *r* but in thought—   *Guinevere* 373
Repentant   *R* of the word she made him swear,   *Gareth and L.* 527
   ' The souls Of two *r* Lovers guard the ring ; '   *The Ring* 198
Repented   they have told you he never *r* his sin.   *Rizpah* 69
   I *r* and repent,   *Happy* 85
Repenting   till the man *r* sent This ring   *The Ring* 209
Replied   Thereto the silent voice *r* ;   *Two Voices* 22
   He sang his song, and I *r* with mine :   *Audley Court* 56
   Swung themselves, and in low tones *r* ;   *Vision of Sin* 20
   And she *r*, her duty was to speak,   *Princess* iii 151
   Passionate tears Follow'd : the king *r* not :   „ vi 312
   The Spirit of true love *r* ;   *In Mem.* lii 6
   To whom the Queen *r* with drooping eyes,   *Com. of Arthur* 469
   Silent awhile was Gareth, then *r*,   *Gareth and L.* 164
   Then *r* the King : ' Far lovelier in our Lancelot   *Lancelot and E.* 588

Replied (*continued*) Percivale stood near him and *r*, *Pelleas and E.* 523
  his friend *R*, in half a whisper, *Lover's Tale* iv 336
Replieth The hollow grot *r* *Claribel* 20
Reply (s) To which the voice did urge *r* ; *Two Voices* 7
  Kept watch, waiting decision, made *r*. *Œnone* 143
  There comes no murmur of *r*. *Palace of Art* 286
  And my disdain is my *r*. *L. C. V. de Vere* 22
  Oh your sweet eyes, your low *replies* : „ 29
  But since I heard him make *r* *Talking Oak* 25
  In courteous words return'd *r* : *Day-Dm., Revival* 30
  He spoke ; the passion in her moan'd *r* *Enoch Arden* 286
  Their's not to make *r*, *Light Brigade* 13
  There lives no record of *r*, *In Mem. xxxi* 6
  Thy ransom'd reason change *replies* „ lxi 2
  The delight of low *replies*. *Maud II* iv 30
  And hung his head, and halted in *r*, *Geraint and E.* 811
  having no *r*, Gazed at the heaving shoulder, *Merlin and V.* 895
  Stammer'd, and could not make her a *r*. *Pelleas and E.* 85
  gunner made ' Ay, ay,' but the seamen made *r* : *The Revenge* 91
  in the thick of question and *r* *Sisters (E. and E.)* 157
Reply (verb) She *replies*, in accents fainter, *L. of Burleigh* 5
  and the brook, why not ? *replies*. *The Brook* 22
  And my Melpomene *replies*, *In Mem. xxxvii* 9
  Care not thou to *r* : *Maud II* iii 7
  Arthur all at once gone mad *replies*, *Gareth and L.* 863
Replying Blow, let us hear the purple glens *r* : *Princess* iv 11
Report (s) In this *r*, this answer of a king, „ i 70
  If one should bring me this *r*, *In Mem. xiv* 1
  when Yniol made *r* Of that good mother *Marr. of Geraint* 756
  ' Sir King ' they brought *r* ' we hardly found, *Balin and Balan* 94
  And brought *r* of azure lands and fair, „ 168
  angels of our Lord's *r*. *Merlin and V.* 16
Report (verb) Victor his men *R* him ! *Com. of Arthur* 250
Reported still *r* him As closing in himself *Gareth and L.* 1338
  a woodman there *R* of some demon in the woods *Balin and Balan* 124
  R who he was, and on what quest Sent, *Lancelot and E.* 628
Reporting *R* of his vessel China-bound, *Enoch Arden* 122
Repose sick man's room when he taketh *r* *A spirit haunts* 13
  Her manners had not that *r* *L. C. V. de Vere* 39
  For brief repast or afternoon *r* *Guinevere* 395
Reposed *God gave her peace ; her land* r ; *To the Queen* 26
  centuries behind me like a fruitful land *r* ; *Locksley Hall* 13
  A void where heart on heart *r* ; *In Mem. xiii* 6
Reposing His state the king *r* keeps. *Day-Dm., Sleep. P.* 39
Repression what sublime *r* of himself, *Ded. of Idylls* 19
Reproach (s) you may worship me without *r* ; *St. S. Stylites* 193
  all these things fell on her Sharp as *r*. *Enoch Arden* 488
  Thro' light *r'es*, half exprest *In Mem. lxxxv* 15
  He never spake word of *r* to me, *Lancelot and E.* 124
  Mine own name shames me, seeming a *r*, „ 1403
  Seem'd my *r* ? He is not of my kind. *Pelleas and E.* 311
  found my letter upon him, my wail of *r* and scorn ; *Charity* 23
Reproach (verb) the poor cause that men *R* you, *Marr. of Geraint* 88
Reproachful Had floated in with sad *r* eyes, *The Ring* 469
Reprobation Election, Election and *R*— *Rizpah* 73
Reproof I have not lack'd thy mild *r*, *My life is full* 4
  Presses his without *r* : *L. of Burleigh* 10
  I was prick'd with some *r*, *Geraint and E.* 890
  her own *r* At some precipitance in her burial. *Lover's Tale* iv 106
Reprove Was it gentle to *r* her For stealing *Maud I* xx 8
  ' A welfare in thine eye *r's* Our fear *Holy Grail* 726
Republic The vast *R's* that may grow, *Day-Dm., L' Envoi* 15
  Aroused the black *r* on his elms, *Aylmer's Field* 529
  Revolts, *r's*, revolutions, *Princess, Con.* 65
  And crown'd *R's* crowning common-sense, *To the Queen* ii 61
  Kingdoms and *R's* fall, *Locksley H., Sixty* 159
Repulse cloaks the scar of some *r* with lies : *Merlin and V.* 818
Repulsed being *r* By Yniol and yourself, *Geraint and E.* 828
Repute bore a knight of old *r* to the earth, *Lancelot and E.* 492
Reputed *R* to be red with sinless blood, *Balin and Balan* 557
  R the best knight and goodliest man, *Guinevere* 382
Request then at my *r* He brought it ; *The Epic* 47
  ' To what *r* for what strange boon,' *Merlin and V.* 264
Require I should *r* A sign ! *Supp. Confessions* 9
  For this brief idyll would *r* A less diffuse *Tiresias* 188

Required Heroic seems our Princess as *r*— *Princess, Pro.* 230
  But public use *r* she should be known ; „ iv 336
  The men *r* that I should give throughout *Princess Con.* 10
  whom He trusted all things, and of him *r* His
    counsel : *Com. of Arthur* 146
Requiring *R*, tho' I knew it was mine own, *Gardener's D.* 227
  R at her hand the greatest gift, „ 229
Re-reiterated And grant my *r-r* wish, *Merlin and V.* 353
Re-risen content *R-r* in Katie's eyes, *The Brook* 169
Rescue Flights, terrors, sudden *r's*, *Aylmer's Field* 99
Rescued diamonds that I *r* from the tarn, *Last Tournament* 37
  You *r* me—yet—was it well That you came *Despair* 4
Reseated thou *r* in thy place of light, *Guinevere* 525
Resembles And so my wealth *r* thine, *In Mem. lxxix* 17
Reserve not to pry and peer on your *r*, *Princess* iv 419
  Such fine *r* and noble reticence, *Geraint and E.* 860
Reserved from a binn *r* For banquets, *Aylmer's Field* 405
  And in my grief a strength *r*. *In Mem. lxxxv* 52
Resettable gems Moveable and *r* at will, *Lover's Tale* iv 199
Resign'd Asks what thou lackest, thought *r*, *Two Voices* 98
  I pray'd for both, and so I felt *r*, *May Queen, Con.* 31
Resistance to know The limits of *r*, *To Duke of Argyll* 2
Resmooth waves of prejudice *R* to nothing : *Princess* iii 241
Resolder'd *r* peace, whereon Follow'd his tale. „ v 47
Resolute The statesman-warrior, moderate, *r*, *Ode on Well.* 25
Resolution Dispersed his *r* like a cloud. *Lancelot and E.* 884
Resolve ' Hard task, to pluck *r*,' I cried, *Two Voices* 118
  Assurance only breeds *r*.' „ 315
  His *r* Upbore him, and firm faith, *Enoch Arden* 799
  His gazing in on Annie, his *r*, „ 863
  Full many a holy vow and pure *r*. *Lancelot and E.* 879
  my fresh but fixt *r* To pass away into the quiet life, *Holy Grail* 737
Resolve (verb) turn thee round, *r* the doubt ; *In Mem. xliv* 14
  Nor can my dream *r* the doubt : „ lxviii 12
Resolved (adj.) But he was all the more *r* to go, *Lover's Tale* iv 179
  and that self-exile from a land He never would revisit, „ 209
Resolved (verb) start in pain, *R* on noble things, *D. of F. Women* 42
  Here she woke, *R*, sent for him and said *Enoch Arden* 507
Resort To which I most *r*, (repeat) *Will Water.* 2, 210
Resound And solemn chaunts *r* between. *Sir Galahad* 36
  Milton, a name to *r* for ages ; *Milton* 4
Respeck (respect) but I *r's* tha fur that ; ' *North. Cobbler* 90
  fur I *r's* tha,' says 'e ; „ 92
Respect (*See also* **Respeck**) some *r*, however slight, was
    paid To woman, *Princess* ii 136
Response Then did my *r* clearer fall : *Two Voices* 34
Responsive Queenly *r* when the loyal hand *Aylmer's Field* 169
Rest (remainder) Proportion, and, above the *r*, *Two Voices* 20
  ' These words,' I said, ' are like the *r* ; „ 334
  And there the Ionian father of the *r* ; *Palace of Art* 137
  while the *r* were loud in merry-making, *Enoch Arden* 77
  But oft she work'd among the *r* and shook „ 651
  Arbaces, and Phenomenon, and the *r*, *The Brook* 162
  o'er the *r* Arising, did his holy oily best, *Sea Dreams* 194
  who this way runs Before the *r*— *Lucretius* 192
  And sister Lilia with the *r*.' *Princess, Pro.* 52
  Lilia with the *r*, and lady friends „ 97
  ' He began, The *r* would follow, each in turn ; „ 201
  So I began, And the *r* follow'd : „ 244
  and beckon'd us : the *r* Parted ; „ ii 182
  Speak little ; mix not with the *r* ; „ 360
  Electric, chemic laws, and all the *r*, „ 384
  Arriving all confused among the *r* „ iv 224
  half-crush'd among the *r* A dwarf-like Cato cower'd „ vii 125
  nor can I weep for the *r* ; *Grandmother* 19
  Perchance, perchance, among the *r*, *In Mem., Con.* 87
  the *r* Slew on and burnt, crying, *Com. of Arthur* 438
  among the *r* Fierce was the hearth, *Gareth and L.* 1009
  Speak, if ye be not like the *r*, hawk-mad, *Marr. of Geraint* 280
  a name that branches o'er the *r*, *Balin and Balan* 182
  eats And uses, careless of the *r* ; *Merlin and V.* 463
  And being lustily holpen by the *r*, *Lancelot and E.* 496
  one, a fellow-monk among the *r*, Ambrosius, loved him
    much beyond the *r*, *Holy Grail* 8
  Gawain sware, and louder than the *r*.' „ 202

Rest (remainder) (*continued*) My sister's vision, and the *r*,   *Holy Grail* 272
to Bors Beyond the *r* :   " 653
the *r* Spake but of sundry perils in the storm ;   " 760
Thy brotherhood in me and all the *r*,   *Pelleas and E.* 322
But newly-enter'd, taller than the *r*,   *Last Tournament* 169
And trebling all the *r* in value—   *Lover's Tale* iv 200
an' a letter along wi' the *r*,   *First Quarrel* 49
thou'rt like the *r* o' the men,   *North. Cobbler* 63
And the *r* they came aboard us,   *The Revenge* 52
half of the *r* of us maim'd for life   " 77
brain that could think for the *r* ;   *Def. of Lucknow* 20
Old friends outvaluing all the *r*,   *To E. Fitzgerald* 40
An' Shamus along wid the *r*,   *Tomorrow* 44
fur I stuck to tha moor na the *r*,   *Spinster's S's*, 51
r Who made a nation purer through their art.   *To W. C. Macready* 7
the *r* Were crumpled inwards.   *The Ring* 453
London and Paris and all the *r*   *The Dawn* 10

Rest (repose) happiness And perfect *r* so perfect is ;   *Supp. Confessions* 51
In sweet dreams softer than unbroken *r*   *Ode to Memory* 29
Fold thine arms, turn to thy *r*.   *A Dirge* 3
There is no *r* for me below,   *Oriana* 3
Nor unhappy, nor at *r*,   *Adeline* 4
A nobler yearning never broke her *r*   *The form, the form* 2
But long disquiet merged in *r*.   *Two Voices* 249
heart would beat against me, In sorrow and in *r* :   *Miller's D.* 178
Floated her hair or seem'd to float in *r*.   *Œnone* 19
who have attain'd *R* in a happy place   " 131
I kiss'd his eyelids into *r* :   *The Sisters* 19
and the weary are at *r*.   *May Queen, Con.* 60
all things else have *r* from weariness ?   *Lotos-Eaters, C. S.* 14
All things have *r* : (repeat)   " 15, 51
Give us long *r* or death,   " 53
Sleep full of *r* from head to feet ;   *To J. S.* 75
Had *r* by stony hills of Crete.   *On a Mourner* 35
Thou wouldst have caught me up into thy *r*,   *St. S. Stylites* 18
And shadow'd all her *r*—   *Talking Oak* 226
yonder ivied casement, ere I went to *r*,   *Locksley Hall* 7
turn thee on thy pillow : get thee to thy *r* again.   " 86
my latest rival brings thee *r*,   " 89
moving toward the stillness of his *r*.   " 144
A perfect form in perfect *r*.   *Day-Dm., Sleep.* B. 24
That her spirit might have *r*.   *L. of Burleigh* 100
With a nation weeping, and breaking on my *r* ?   *Ode on Well.* 82
tired a little, that's all, and long for *r* ;   *Grandmother* 99
And moan and sink to their *r*.   *Voice and the P.* 16
And waves that sway themselves in *r*,   *In Mem.* xi 18
Nor any want-begotten *r*,   " *xxvii* 12
surely *r* is meet : ' They rest,' we said,   " *xxx* 18
I know that in thy place of *r*   " *lxvii* 2
That wakens at this hour of *r*   " *civ* 6
To the regions of thy *r* ' ?   *Maud* II iv 88
in that hope, dear soul, let trouble have *r*,   " *III vi* 12
Half disarray'd as to her *r*,   *Marr. of Geraint* 516
moving without answer to her *r* She found no *r*,   " 530
scorn of Garlon, poisoning all his *r*,   *Balin and Balan* 383
royal knight, we break on thy sweet *r*,   " 470
I brake upon thy *r*, And now full loth am I   " 499
Arriving at a time of golden *r*,   *Merlin and V.* 142
charm so taught will charm us both to *r*.   " 332
and Love Should have some *r* and pleasure   " 485
Should have small *r* or pleasure in herself,   " 490
R must you have.' ' No *r* for me,'   *Lancelot and E.* 832
' Nay, for near you, fair lord, I am at *r*.'   " 833
And found no ease in turning or in *r* ;   " 901
vext his heart, And marr'd his *r*—   *Pelleas and E.* 399
Hath lain for years at *r*—   *Last Tournament* 94
Farewell ! there is an isle of *r* for thee.   *Pass. of Arthur* 35
But I had been at *r* for evermore.   *Lover's Tale* i 625
and we thought her at *r*,   *In the Child. Hosp.* 40
as he rose from his *r*,   *V. of Maeldune* 85
strike Thy youthful pulses into *r*   *Tiresias* 157
I would that I were gather'd to my *r*,   " 170
let me weep my fill once more, and cry myself to *r* ! To
   r ? to rest and wake no more were better *r* for me,   *The Flight* 6
human offspring this ideal man at *r* ?   *Locksley H., Sixty* 234

Rest (repose) (*continued*) To that which looks
   like *r*,   *Pref. Poem Broth. Son* 6
Raving politics, never at *r*—   *Vastness* 3
Is memory with your Marian gone to *r*,   *To Mary Boyle* 13
and the murderous father at *r*, . . .   *Bandit's Death* 33
blight thy hope or break thy *r*,   *Faith* 2

Rest (s) Go thou to *r*, but ere thou go to *r*   *Marr. of Geraint* 512
Now both are gone to *r*.   *To W. H. Brookfield* 8

Rest (verb) ' The doubt would *r*, I dare not solve.   *Two Voices* 313
Passing the place where each must *r*,   " 410
his shadow on the stone, *R*'s like a shadow,   *Œnone* 28
r thee sure That I shall love thee well   " 159
Oh *r* ye, brother mariners,   *Lotos-Eaters, C. S.* 128
came To *r* beneath thy boughs. (repeat)   *Talking Oak* 36, 156
Where fairer fruit of Love may *r*   " 251
wealth no more shall *r* in mounded heaps,   *Golden Year* 32
I cannot *r* from travel :   *Ulysses* 6
Here *r*'s the sap within the leaf,   *Day-Dm., Sleep. P.* 3
And I desire to *r*.   *Come not, when, etc.* 10
Who will not let his ashes *r* !   *You might have won* 28
and sighing ' Let me *r* ' she said :   *Enoch Arden* 375
Fall back upon a name ! *r*, rot in that !   *Aylmer's Field* 385
Birdie, *r* a little longer,   *Sea Dreams* 297
So she *r*'s a little longer,   " 299
Sleep and *r*, sleep and *r*,   *Princess* iii 9
R, *r*, on mother's breast,   " 11
Said Ida ; ' let us down and *r* ; '   " *iv* 21
and this proud watchword *r* Of equal ;   " *vii* 300
There he shall *r* for ever   *Ode on Well.* 51
To *r* in a golden grove,   *Wages* 9
To *r* beneath the clover sod,   *In Mem.* x 13
Among familiar names to *r*   " *xviii* 7
I sing to him that *r*'s below,   " *xxi* 1
' They *r*,' we said, ' their sleep is sweet,'   " *xxx* 19
And *r*'s upon the Life indeed.   " *xxxii* 8
In endless age ? It *r*'s with God.   " *lxxiii* 12
My heart, tho' widow'd, may not *r*   " *lxxxv* 113
Who *r* to-night beside the sea.   " *Con.* 76
spangle all the happy shores By which they *r*,   " 121
so should he *r* with her, Closed in her castle   *Gareth and L.* 162
R would I not, Sir King, an I were king,   " 597
' I nor mine *R* : so my knighthood keep the vows   " 602
R ! the good house, tho' ruin'd,   *Marr. of Geraint* 378
eye rove in following, or *r* On Enid   " 399
I felt That I could *r*, a rock in ebbs and flows,   " 812
therefore, I do *r*, A prophet certain of my prophecy,   " 813
but to *r* awhile within her court ;   *Geraint and E.* 855
Should *r* and let you *r*, knowing you mine.   *Merlin and V.* 335
r : and Love Should have some rest and pleasure   " 484
after my long voyage I shall *r* ! '   *Lancelot and E.* 1061
' I will *r* here,' I said,   *Holy Grail* 385
as who should say, ' *R* here ; '   " 396
So shook him that he could not *r*,   *Pelleas and E.* 412
but here, Here let me *r* and die,'   " 515
could not *r* for musing how to smoothe   *Last Tournament* 390
' to pass, to sleep, To *r*, to be with her—   *Lover's Tale* iv 64
striding fast, and now Sitting awhile to *r*,   " 88
Travelling that land, and meant to *r* an hour ;   " 133
Come, come, little wife, let it *r*   *First Quarrel* 62
couldn't be idle—my Willy—he never could *r*.   *Rizpah* 27
At times our Britain cannot *r*,   *To Marq. of Dufferin* 1
To rest ? to *r* and wake no more,   *The Flight* 6
He *r*'s content, if his young music   *To Mary Boyle* 63
whether, since our nature cannot *r*,   *Prog. of Spring* 96
And here no longer can I *r* ;   *The Wanderer* 2

Rested where man Hath moor'd and *r* ?   *Supp. Confessions* 125
And *r* from her labours.   *The Goose* 16
So Philip *r* with her well-content ;   *Enoch Arden* 376
There Enoch *r* silent many days.   " 699
and gain'd the hall, and there *R* :   *Princess* vi 353
But *r* with her sweet face satisfied ;   *Marr. of Geraint* 776
She *r*, and her desolation came Upon her,   *Geraint and E.* 518
He *r* well content that all was well.   " 952
But *r* in her fealty, till he crown'd   " 967
Nor *r* thus content, but day by day,   *Lancelot and E.* 13

Rested (*continued*) Wander'd, the while we r:	*Lover's Tale* i 235
Arthur the blameless R The Gleam.	*Merlin and the G.* 74
Resteth but r satisfied, Looking on her	*Lover's Tale* i 159
Resting R weary limbs at last on beds of asphodel.	*Lotos-Eaters, C. S.* 125
Porch-pillars on the lion r,	*The Daisy* 55
Resting-place come again, mother, from out my r-p;	*May Queen, N. Y's. E.* 37
Restless But passionately r came and went,	*Aylmer's Field* 546
and r forefoot plies His function of the woodland:	*Lucretius* 45
swaying upon a r elm Drew the vague glance of Vivien,	*Balin and Balan* 463
To which it made a r heart, he took,	*Lancelot and E.* 550
And men have hopes, which race the r blood,	*Prog. of Spring* 115
Restore ghost of passion that no smiles r—	*The form, the form* 11
Release me, and r me to the ground;	*Tithonus* 72
Restored tho' he built upon the babe r;	*Princess* vii 75
had his realm r But render'd tributary,	*Balin and Balan* 2
Restrain'd Restrain'd him with all manner of device,	*Pelleas and E.* 204
Restrain'd himself quite to the close—	*Lover's Tale* iv 10
Restraining Fierier and stormier from r,	*Balin and Balan* 229
Restraint I spoke without *restraint*,	*Talking Oak* 14
Result (s) The slow r of winter showers:	*Two Voices* 452
Deep-chested music, and to this r.	*The Epic* 51
from age to age With much the same r.	*Walk. to the Mail* 80
and the long r of Time;	*Locksley Hall* 12
But for some true r of good All parties	*Will Water.* 55
victor Hours should scorn The long r of love,	*In Mem.* i 14
self-infolds the large r's Of force	„ lxxiii 15
And that serene r of all.'	„ lxxxv 92
With old r's that look like new;	„ cxxviii 11
O, the r's are simple;	*Merlin and V.* 684
work old laws of Love to fresh r's,	*Prog. of Spring* 85
Result (verb) R in man, be born and think,	*In Mem., Con.* 126
Resume r their life, They would but find	„ xc 6
Retain And so may Place r us still,	„ xlii 5
Which yet r's a memory of its youth,	*Sisters (E. and E.)* 66
Retake stands Vacant, but thou r it,	*Balin and Balan* 79
Retaught R the lesson thou hadst taught,	*England and Amer.* 8
Reticence Such fine reserve and noble r,	*Geraint and E.* 860
Not muffled round with selfish r.	*Merlin and V.* 337
Down with R, down with Reverence—	*Locksley H., Sixty* 142
Retinue The dark r reverencing death	*Aylmer's Field* 842
and so Went forth in long r following up	*Princess* iii 195
and far ahead Of his and her r moving,	*Guinevere* 385
Retire How oft we saw the Sun r,	*The Voyage* 17
And last the dance;—till I r:	*In Mem., Con.* 105
Retired in after life r From brawling storms,	*Ode to Memory* 111
I saw the snare, and I r:	*L. C. V. de Vere* 6
Retiring Ever r thou dost gaze On the prime labour	*Ode to Memory* 93
knights Clash like the coming and r wave,	*Gareth and L.* 522
Re-told And read a Grecian tale r-t,	*To Master of B.* 5
Retreat Ah, for some r Deep in yonder	*Locksley Hall* 153
O joy to him in this r,	*In Mem.* lxxxix 13
Retreated Leolin still R half-aghast,	*Aylmer's Field* 330
The light r, The landskip darken'd,	*Merlin and the G.* 30
Retreating up and down Advancing nor r.	*Sisters (E. and E.)* 179
Retrospect 'Not such as moans about the r,	*Princess* iv 85
yet in r That less than momentary thunder-sketch	*Sisters (E. and E.)* 98
Return (s) (*See also* **Home-return**) Then she went back some paces of r,	*Geraint and E.* 70
with how sweet grace She greeted my r!	*Balin and Balan* 194
tho' my love had no r:	*Lancelot and E.* 1094
I loved you, and my love had no r,	„ 1276
Return (verb) I may r with others there	*Palace of Art* 295
some one said, 'We will r no more;'	*Lotos-Eaters* 43
'I go, but I r: I would I were The pilot	*Audley Court* 71
The fountain had his place r's	*Day-Dm., Sleep. P.* 11
to r When others had been tested)	*Aylmer's Field* 218
and r In such a sunlight of prosperity	„ 420
Returning, as the bird r's, at night,	*Sea Dreams* 43
heard his foot R from pacings in the field,	*Lucretius* 6
back r To where the body sits,	*In Mem.* xii 18
How often she herself r,	„ xl 24
But Death r's an answer sweet:	„ lxxxi 9
Return (verb) (*continued*) r's the dark With no more hope of light.	*Maud* I ix 15
humour of the kings of old R upon me!	*Gareth and L.* 378
R, and meet, and hold him from our eyes,	„ 429
take his horse And arms, and so r him to the King.	„ 956
Myself, when I r, will plead for thee. (repeat)	„ 987, 1052
r, and fetch Fresh victual for these mowers	*Geraint and E.* 224
and r With victual for these men,	„ 239
For the man's love once gone never r's.	„ 333
'Fly, they will r And slay you;	„ 748
And as the cageling newly flown r's,	*Merlin and V.* 901
They prove to him his work: win and r.'	*Lancelot and E.* 158
Rise and take This diamond, and deliver it, and r,	„ 546
And she r's his love in open shame;	„ 1083
Many of you, yea most, R no more:	*Holy Grail* 321
He will r no more.	*Pelleas and E.* 259
Kick'd, he r's: do ye not hate him, ye?	„ 264
the warm hour r's With veer of wind,	*Last Tournament* 230
weep not thou, lest, if thy mate r,	„ 499
And so r's belike within an hour.	„ 531
She is his no more—The dead r's to me,	*Lover's Tale* iv 49
And you shall give me back when he r's.'	„ 112
When he r's, and then will I r,	„ 117
If we should never more r,	*The Flight* 99
Australian dying hopes he shall r,	*Locksley H., Sixty* 70
Return'd prest thy hand, and knew the press r,	*The Bridesmaid* 12
One went, who never hath r.	*To J. S.* 20
And so r unfarrow'd to her sty.	*Walk. to the Mail* 100
Could hope itself r;	*Talking Oak* 12
'Pardy,' r the King, 'but still My joints	*Day-Dm., Revival* 25
In courteous words r reply:	„ 30
when the beauteous hateful isle R upon him,	*Enoch Arden* 618
round again to meet the day When Enoch had r,	„ 823
r Leolin's rejected rivals from their suit	*Aylmer's Field* 492
by a keeper shot at, slightly hurt, Raging r:	„ 549
To whom none spake, half-sick at heart, r.	*Princess* iv 223
The King r from out the wild,	*The Victim* 41
And home to Mary's house r,	*In Mem.* xxxi 2
divine amends For a courtesy not r.	*Maud* I vi 14
pathways for the hunter and the knight And so r.	*Com. of Arthur* 62
r Among the flowers, in May, with Guinevere.	„ 451
she r Indignant to the Queen: (repeat)	*Marr. of Geraint* 201, 413
the boy r And told them of a chamber,	*Geraint and E.* 260
till she woke the sleepers, and r:	„ 404
r The huge Earl Doorm with plunder to the hall.	„ 591
In converse for a little, and r,	„ 882
spirit of his youth r On Arthur's heart;	*Balin and Balan* 21
And lightly so r, and no man knew.	„ 42
till their embassage r.	„ 93
Full courtly, yet not falsely, thus r:	*Lancelot and E.* 236
after two days' tarriance there, r.	„ 569
r To whence I came, the gate of Arthur's wars.'	*Holy Grail* 538
talk And scandal of our table, had r;	„ 650
reach'd The city, found ye all your knights r,	„ 708
scarce r a tithe—	„ 894
these r, But still he kept his watch	*Pelleas and E.* 222
Then turn'd, and so r, and groaning	„ 451
she gazed on Lancelot So soon r,	„ 590
Tristram—late From overseas in Brittany r,	*Last Tournament* 175
one that in them sees himself, r;	„ 370
But left her all as easily, and r.	„ 403
and that low lodge r, Mid-forest,	„ 488
Had been, their wont, a-maying and r,	*Guinevere* 23
'Perchance,' she said, 'r.'	*Lover's Tale* i 581
Then, when her own true spirit had r,	*In the Child. Hosp.* iv 108
Then I r to the ward;	*In the Child. Hosp.* 44
wept with me when I r in chains,	*Columbus* 231
She in wrath R it on her birthday,	*The Ring* 212
We r to his cave—the link was broken—	*Bandit's Death* 29
Returning from the secret shrine R with hot cheek	*Alexander* 14
human things r on themselves Move onward,	*Golden Year* 25
And thee r on thy silver wheels.	*Tithonus* 76
R like the pewit,	*Will Water.* 230
As oft as needed—last, r rich,	*Enoch Arden* 143
His fancy fled before the lazy wind R,	„ 658
Seem'd hope's r rose:	*Aylmer's Field* 559

Rife   With dinning sound my ears are *r*,   *Eleänore* 135
   Let raffs be *r* in prose and rhyme,   *Will Water.* 61
   language *r* With rugged maxims hewn from life ;   *Ode on Well.* 183
Rifle-bullet   Death from their *r-b's*,   *Def. of Lucknow* 14
Rifleman   R, true is your heart,   " 56
   R, high on the roof, hidden there   " 63
   Storm, Storm, *Riflemen* form! (repeat)   *Riflemen form!* 5, 19
   Riflemen, Riflemen, Riflemen form! (repeat)   " 7, 14, 21, 28
   Form, Form, *Riflemen* Form! (repeat)   " 12, 26
Rift (s)   ' It is the little *r* within the lute,   *Merlin and V.* 390
   ' The little *r* within the lover's lute   " 393
   gray heads beneath a gleaming *r*.   *Demeter and P.* 83
   Flattery gilding the *r* in a throne ;   *Vastness* 20
Rift (verb)   R the hills, and roll the waters,   *Locksley Hall* 186
Rifted   (*See also* **Sallow-rifted**)   methought The cloud
   was *r* by a purer gleam   *Akbar's Dream* 78
Rigging   masts and the *r* were lying over the side ;   *The Revenge* 81
   storm grew With a howl and a hoot of the blast In the *r*,   *The Wreck* 92
Right (adj. and adv.)   (*See also* **Half-right**)   whose strong
   r arm debased The throne of Persia,   *Alexander* 1
   The *r* ear, that is fill'd with dust,   *Two Voices* 116
   And I should know if it beat *r*,   *Miller's D.* 179
   Time will set me *r*.'   *Edwin Morris* 88
   My *r* leg chain'd into the crag,   *St. S. Stylites* 73
   For, am I *r*, or am I wrong, (repeat)   *Day-Dm., L'Envoi* 29, 33
   And on the *r*.hand of the hearth he saw Philip,   *Enoch Arden* 744
   But Lady Psyche was the *r* hand now,   *Princess iii* 37
   is not Ida *r*? They worth it?   " 188
   And so I often told her, *r* or wrong,   " 288
   And, *r* or wrong, I care not :   " 290
   she may sit Upon a king's *r* hand in thunderstorms,   " 439
   he That loved me closer than his own *r* eye,   " 531
   And *r* ascension, Heaven knows what ;   " *vi* 257
   she turns Once more to set a ringlet *r* ;   *In Mem. vi* 36
   I cannot see the features or   " *lxx* 1
   And this wise world of ours is mainly *r*.   *Geraint and E.* 901
   ' R was the King! our Lancelot! that true man!'
   ' And *r* was I,'   *Lancelot and E.* 665
   In her *r* hand the lily, in her left The letter—   " 1155
   Power from whose *r* hand the light Of Life issueth,   *Lover's Tale i* 497
   ' you are sure it 'll all come *r*,'   *First Quarrel* 1
   ' Wait a little, my lass, I am sure it 'll all come *r*.'
   (repeat)   " 74, 91
   Steevie be *r* good manners bang thruf   *Spinster's S's.* 66
   It still were *r* to crown with song   *Epilogue* 36
   Death for the *r* cause, death for the wrong cause,   *Vastness* 8
   I worship that *r* hand Which fell'd the foes   *Happy* 41
Right (s)   who stand now, when we should aid the *r*—   *Poland* 13
   because *r* is *r*, to follow *r* Were wisdom   *Œnone* 149
   hers by *r* of full-accomplish'd Fate ;   *Palace of Art* 207
   Who wrench'd their *r's* from thee!   *England and Amer.* 5
   since I knew the *r* And did it ;   *Love and Duty* 29
   we, that prate Of *r's* and wrongs,   *Godiva* 8
   And in the *r's* their name may give,   *Day-Dm., L'Envoi* 54
   ' The man will cleave unto his *r*.'   *Lady Clare* 46
   reigning in his place, Lord of his *r's*   *Enoch Arden* 764
   A talk of college and of ladies' *r's*,   *Princess, Pro.* 233
   be swerved from *r* to save A prince,   " *ii* 290
   Toward that great year of equal mights and *r's*,   " *iv* 74
   To unfurl the maiden banner of our *r's*,   " 503
   What have you done but *r*?   " *v* 65
   As truthful, much that Ida claims as *r*   " 202
   throat's would bawl for civil *r's*, No woman named :   " 387
   With claim on claim from *r* to *r*,   " 417
   r's or wrongs like potherbs in the street.   " 459
   We will be liberal, since our *r's* are won.   " *vi* 68
   wholly scorn'd to help their equal *r's*   " *vii* 233
   All great self-seekers trampling on the *r* :   *Ode on Well.* 187
   only thirsting For the *r*,   " 204
   Maakin' 'em goä together as they've good *r* to do.   *N. Farmer, N. S.* 34
   At you, so careful of the *r*,   *To F. D. Maurice* 10
   Ring in the love of truth and *r*,   *In Mem. cvi* 23
   mine by a *r*, from birth till death.   *Maud I xix* 42
   a war would arise in defence of the *r*,   " *III vi* 19
   in the space to left of her, and *r*,   *Gareth and L.* 224

Right (s) (*continued*)   mocker ending here Turn'd to the *r*,   *Gareth and L.* 295
   Would shape himself a *r*!'   " 348
   bring him here, that I may judge the *r*,   " 380
   mark'd not on his *r* a cavern-chasm   *Balin and Balan* 312
   on his *r* Stood, all of massiest bronze :   " 363
   Made with her *r* a comb of pearl to part The lists   *Merlin and V.* 244
   lightnings here and there to left and *r* Struck,   *Holy Grail* 494
   To *r*? to left? straight forward?   *Pelleas and E.* 67
   as one That doest *r* by gentle and by churl,   *Last Tournament* 74
   King by courtesy, Or King by *r*—   " 342
   What *r's* are his that dare not strike   " 527
   Had Arthur *r* to bind them to himself?   " 684
   For half of their feet to the *r*   *The Revenge* 35
   but sane, if she were in the *r*.   *The Flight* 58
   Follow Light, and do the *R*—   *Locksley H., Sixty* 277
   The ring by *r*, she said, was hers again.   *The Ring* 394
   for the *r's* of an equal humanity,   *Beautiful City* 2
   I still would do the *r* Thro' all the vast dominion   *Akbar's Dream* 13
Right (verb)   When the wild peasant *r's* himself,   *Princess iv* 385
   to fight, to struggle, to *r* the wrong—   *Wages* 3
   ' Bound am I to *r* the wrong'd,   *Gareth and L.* 804
   strength and will to *r* the wrong'd,   *Holy Grail* 309
   And leaving human wrongs to *r* themselves,   " 898
Righteous   Not void of *r* self-applause,   *Two Voices* 146
   That even our prudent king, our *r* queen—   *Columbus* 122
Righteousness   yonder shines The Sun of *R*,   *Enoch Arden* 504
   proclaimed His Master as ' the Sun of *R*,'   *Akbar's Dream* 83
Rightful   help my prince to gain His *r* bride,   *Princess iii* 404
Right-honest   ' All of one mind and all *r-h* friends !   *Geraint and E.* 484
Righting   So I set to *r* the house,   *First Quarrel* 47
Rigid   a rough piece Of early *r* colour,   *Aylmer's Field* 281
Rigtree (beam)   when the *r* was tummlin' in—   *Owd Roä* 115
Riled   Eh but the moor she *r* me,   *North. Cobbler* 30
   Fur if iver thy feyther 'ed *r* me   *Church-warden, etc.* 41
Rill   Like sunshine on a dancing *r*,   *Rosalind* 29
   From old well-heads of haunted *r's* ;   *Eleänore* 16
   Not any song of bird or sound of *r* ;   *D. of F. Women* 66
   ' Go down beside thy native *r*,   *In Mem. xxxvii* 5
   From hidden summits fed with *r's*   " *ciii* 7
   The white-faced halls, the glancing *r's*,   " *Con.* 113
   round with ragged *r's* and burning folds,—   *Lover's Tale ii* 63
Rillet   fall Of diamond *r's* musical,   *Arabian Nights* 48
Rim   ragged *r's* of thunder brooding low,   *Palace of Art* 75
   Beyond their utmost purple *r*, (repeat)   *Day-Dm., Depart.* 6, 30
   the *r* Changed every moment as we flew.   *The Voyage* 27
   ran By sallowy *r's*, arose the labourers' homes,   *Aylmer's Field* 147
   Now pacing mute by ocean's *r* ;   *The Daisy* 21
   Roll'd into light, and turning on its *r's*   *Lancelot and E.* 51
Rime   Make thy grass hoar with early *r*.   *Two Voices* 66
   brows in silent hours become Unnaturally hoar with *r*,   *St. S. Stylites* 166
   the lawn as yet Is hoar with *r*,   *To F. D. Maurice* 42
   the hills are white with *r*.   *The Flight* 4
Rimm'd   length of bright horizon *r* the dark.   *Gardener's D.* 181
Rind   gleaming *r* ingrav'n ' For the most fair,'   *Œnone* 72
   Hard wood I am, and wrinkled *r*,   *Talking Oak* 171
   Is jutting thro' the *r* ;   *Ancient Sage* 122
Rinded   *See* **Golden-rinded**
Ring (encompass)   my followers *r* him round :   *Geraint and E.* 336
Ring (s)   (*See also* **Marriage-ring**)   locks a-drooping twined
   Round thy neck in subtle *r*   *Adeline* 58
   his stedfast shade Sleeps on his luminous *r*.'   *Palace of Art* 16
   they drew into two burning *r's* All beams of Love,   *D. of F. Women* 174
   Five hundred *r's* of years—   *Talking Oak* 84
   ' And even into my inmost *r* A pleasure I discern'd,   " 173
   The dim curls kindle into sunny *r's* ;   *Tithonus* 54
   Grave faces gather'd in a *r*.   *Day-Dm., Sleep. P.* 38
   Closed in a golden *r*.   *Sir L. and Q. G.* 27
   And gave the trinkets and the *r's*,   *The Letters* 21
   Enoch's golden *r* had girt Her finger,   *Enoch Arden* 157
   Dangled a length of ribbon and a *r*   " 750
   fragile bindweed-bells and briony *r's* ;   *The Brook* 203
   Lay deeper than to wear it as his *r*—   *Aylmer's Field* 122
   nor by plight or broken *r* Bound,   " 135
   I'll stake my ruby *r* upon it you did.'   *Princess, Pro.* 170
   a thousand *r's* of Spring In every bole,   " *v* 237

Ring (s) (*continued*) And one would pierce an outer *r*, *In Mem.* lxxxvii 27
The *r* is on, The 'wilt thou' answer'd,   " *Con.* 53
sapphire-spangled marriage *r* of the land? *Maud I* iv 6
I noticed one of his many *r's*   " *II* ii 68
Now over, now beneath her marriage *r*, *Geraint and E.* 259
Spanish fleet with broken sides lay round us all in a *r*; *The Revenge* 71
placed My *r* upon the finger of my bride. *Sisters (E. and E.)* 214
he learnt that I hated the *r* I wore, *The Wreck* 57
diamond necklace dearer than the golden *r*, *Locksley H., Sixty* 21
Prince has found you, take this *r*. *The Ring* 69
This *r* bequeath'd you by your mother,   " 75
The *r* is doubly yours.   " 79
A *r* too which you kiss'd,   " 114
Like a seal'd book, all mention of the *r*,   " 123
while I stoopt To take and kiss the *r*.   " 132
This very *r* Io t'amo?   .. 133
sold This *r* to me, then laugh'd 'the *r* is weird.'   " 195
souls Of two repentant Lovers guard the *r*;'   " 198
'And if you give the *r* to any maid,   . 200
And bind the maid to love you by the *r*; And if the
    r were stolen from the maid,   " 202
sent This *r* 'Io t'amo' to his best beloved,   " 210
half-frenzied by the *r*, He wildly fought   " 213
drew the *r* From his dead finger,   " 217
as the bygone lover thro' this *r* Had sent his cry   " 232
bad the man engrave 'From Walter' on the *r*,   " 236
Some younger hand must have engraven the *r—*   " 238
took the *r*, and flaunted it Before that other   " 243
But coming nearer—Muriel had the *r*—'O Miriam ! have
    you given your *r* to her?   " 259
'O Miriam, if you love me take the *r*!'   " 263
Unclosed the hand, and from it drew the *r*,   " 269
Miriam loved me from the first, Not thro' the *r*; but on
    her marriage-morn, This birthday, death-day, and
    betrothal *r*,   " 275
My *r* too when she comes of age,   " 289
Miriam not Muriel—she shall have the *r*.   " 294
But kept their watch upon the *r* and you.   " 300
'Ever since You sent the fatal *r'*—   " 362
Nor ever ceased to clamour for the *r*; Why had I sent
    the *r* at first to her? Why had I made her love me
    thro' the *r*,   " 389
The *r* by right, she said, was hers again.   " 394
But still she made her outcry for the *r*;   " 403
when the bridegroom murmur'd, 'With this *r*,'   " 439
The guardian of her relics, of *her r*,   " 441
The fatal *r* lay near her;   " 450
had stolen, worn the *r*—Then torn it from her finger,   " 455
from her own hand she had torn the *r* In fright,   " 470
You have the *r* she guarded: " 475
saw The *r* of faces redden'd by the flames *Death of Œnone* 92
and never a *r* for the bride. *Charity* 6

Ring (to resound, etc.) How the merry bluebell *r's*
     Adeline 34
R sudden scritches of the jay, *My life is full* 20
a sound *R's* ever in her ears of armed men. *Œnone* 265
church-bells *r* in the Christmas-morn. *M. d'Arthur,* Ep. 31
R's in mine ears. The steer forgot to graze, *Gardener's D.* 85
did we hear the copses *r*, *Locksley Hall* 35
The shrill bell *r's*, the censer swings, *Sir Galahad* 35
When all the glimmering moorland *r's* *Sir L. and Q. G.* 35
world should *r* of him To shame these mouldy
    Aylmers *Aylmer's Field* 395
R's to the roar of an angel onset— *Milton* 8
'lights and *r's* the gateway bell, *In Mem.* viii 3
Shall *r* with music all the same;   " lxxvii 14
R out, wild bells, to the wild sky,   " cvi 1
R out, wild bells, and let him die.   " 4
R out the old, *r* in the new, *R*, happy bells, across the
    snow: " 5
R out the false, *r* in the true.   " 8
R out the grief that saps the mind,   " 9
R out the feud of rich and poor, *R* in redress to all
    mankind.   " 11
R out a slowly dying cause,   " 13
R in the nobler modes of life,   " 15

Ring (to resound, etc.) (*continued*) *R* out the want. the
    care, the sin, *In Mem.* cvi 17
R out, *r* out my mournful rhymes,   " 19
But *r* the fuller minstrel in.   " 20
R out false pride in place and blood,   " 21
R in the love of truth and right, *R* in the common love
    of good.   " 23
R out old shapes of foul disease; *R* out the narrowing
    lust of gold; *R* out the thousand wars of old, *R* in
    the thousand years of peace.   " 25
R in the valiant man and free,   " 29
R out the darkness of the land, *R* in the Christ that is
    to be.   " 31
Now *r's* the woodland loud and long,   " cxv 5
r's to the yell of the trampled wife, *Maud I* i 38
r's Even in dreams to the chink of his pence,   " x 42
It will *r* in my heart and my ears,   " II i 35
And the woodland echo *r's*,   .. iv 38
But there *r's* on a sudden a passionate cry,   " 47
And heard it *r* as true as tested gold.' *Last Tournament* 284
Four bells instead of one began to *r*, *Lover's Tale* iii 20
in this pavement but shall *r* thy name *Tiresias* 137
R little bells of change From word to word. *Early Spring* 41
if it be a Christian Church, people *r* the bell from
    love to Thee, *Akbar's D., Inscrip.* 4
Ringdove In which the swarthy *r* sat, *Talking Oak* 293
Ring'd white hand whose *r* caress Had wander'd *Balin and Balan* 512
Ringed *R* with the azure world, he stands. *The Eagle* 3
Ringer the *r's* rang with a will, and he gave the *r's* a crown. *Grandmother* 58
Ringing (*See also* **A-ringing, Hollow-ringing**) When
    midnight bells cease *r* suddenly, *D. of F. Women* 247
when the bells were *r*, Allan call'd *Dora* 41
in the *r* of thine ears; *Locksley Hall* 84
Let the great world spin for ever down the *r* grooves
    of change.   " 182
And, *r*, springs from brand and mail; *Sir Galahad* 54
With blissful treble *r* clear. *Sir L. and Q. G.* 22
Once likewise, in the *r* of his ears, *Enoch Arden* 613
R like proven golden coinage true, *Aylmer's Field* 182
but he must—the land was *r* of it—   " 262
with His message *r* in thine ears,   " 666
—Saäint's-daäy—they was *r* the bells. *N. Farmer, N. S.* 13
Maud the delight of the village, the *r* joy of the Hall, *Maud I* i 70
R thro' the valleys,   " xii 10
Clamour and rumble, and *r* and clatter,   " II v 13
Ranging and *r* thro' the minds of men, *Com. of Arthur* 416
r with their serpent hands, *Merlin and V.* 578
R within the fancy had updrawn A fashion *Lover's Tale* i 645
Surely the pibroch of Europe is *r* *Def. of Lucknow* 97
Far on the *r* plains of windy Troy. *Ulysses* 17
He rode the mellay, lord of the *r* lists, *Princess* v 502
those six maids With shrieks and *r* laughter on the
    sand Threw down the bier; *Lover's Tale* iii 32
what a weight of war Rides on those *r* axles ! *Tiresias* 93
Ringlet comb my hair till my *r's* would fall *The Mermaid* 14
Tie up the *r's* on your cheek : *Margaret* 57
For hid in *r's* day and night, *Miller's D.* 173
'Thrice-happy he that may caress The *r's* waving
    balm— *Talking Oak* 178
shower'd the rippled *r's* to her knee; *Godiva* 47
Her full black *r's* downward roll'd, *Day-Dm., Sleep. B.* 12
Blowing the *r* from the braid : *Sir L. and Q. G.* 39
With lengths of yellow *r*, like a girl, *Princess* i 3
turns Once more to set a *r* right; *In Mem.* vi 36
Ere childhood's flaxen *r* turn'd   " lxxix 15
flaxen *r's* of our infancies Wander'd, *Lover's Tale* i 234
Fell on my face, and her long *r's* moved,   " 699
The raven *r* or the gold; *The Ring* 166
Ringleted *See* **Yellow-ringleted**
Ringlet-snake And numbs the Fury's *r-s*, *Lucretius* 262
Riot in many a wild festoon Ran *r*, *Œnone* 101
a noiseless *r* underneath Strikes through the wood, *Lucretius* 185
whereout was roll'd A roar of *r*, *Last Tournament* 426
wallow in fiery *r* and revel On Kilauëä, *Kapiolani* 8
Rioted *r* his life out, and made an end. *Aylmer's Field* 391

Rioted (*continued*) *r* in the city if Cúnobeline ! *Boädicea* 60
There they dwelt and there they *r*; ” 63
and *r* over the land, *V. of Maeldune* 58
Rioting over all the great wood *r* And climbing, *Lover's Tale i* 403
Riotous show'd A *r* confluence of watercourses *Lucretius* 30
She braved a *r* heart in asking for it. *Lancelot and E.* 359
fling Thy royalty back into the *r* fits *Sir J. Oldcastle* 100
Rip *R* your brothers' vices open, *Locksley H., Sixty* 141
Ripe Your *r* lips moved not, but your cheek Flush'd *Miller's D.* 131
when time was *r*, The still affection ” 224
I was *r* for death. *D. of F. Women* 208
And makes the purple lilac *r*, *On a Mourner* 7
Made *r* in Sumner-chace : *Talking Oak* 40
Till all be *r* and rotten. *Will Water.* 16
Half-mused, or reeling *r*, ” 74
' Yes, if the nuts ' he said ' be *r* again : *Enoch Arden* 459
Too *r*, too late ! they come too late *Sea Dreams* 67
See thou, that countest reason *r* *In Mem. xxxiii* 13
Appearing ere the times were *r*, ” *Con.* 139
you may call it a little too *r*, *Maud I ii* 9
shaping an infant *r* for his birth, ” *iv* 34
Ripen flower *r's* in its place, *R's* and fades, *Lotos-Eaters, C. S.* 36
and *r* toward the grave In silence ; *r*, fall, and
cease : ” 51
The unnetted black-hearts *r* dark, *The Blackbird* 7
watch her harvest *r*, her herd increase, *Maud III vi* 25
till their love Shall *r* to a proverb, *Lover's Tale i* 758
Ripen'd And pluck'd the *r* ears, *Princess ii* 2
But woman *r* earlier, and her life ” 154
Ripeness but, when love is grown To *r*, *To J. S.* 15
And gave all *r* to the grain, *In Mem. lxxxi* 11
Riper *r* life may magnetise The baby-oak within. *Talking Oak* 255
Not first, and third, which are a *r* first ? *Sea Dreams* 66
train To *r* growth the mind and will : *In Mem. xlii* 8
The men of rathe and *r* years : ” *cx* 2
Ripple (s) his ridges are not curls And *r's* *Supp. Confessions* 131
watch the crisping *r's* on the beach, *Lotos-Eaters, C. S.* 61
' I heard the *r* washing in the reeds, *M. d'Arthur* 70
And the long *r* washing in the reeds.' ” 117
Stared o'er the *r* feathering from her bows : *Enoch Arden* 544
The seeming-wanton *r* break, *In Mem. xlix* 11
shadowing down the horned flood In *r's*, ” *lxxxvi* 8
' I heard the *r* washing in the reeds, *Pass. of Arthur* 238
And the long *r* washing in the reeds.' ” 285
so quiet the *r* would hardly blanch into spray *The Wreck* 137
Slight *r* on the boundless deep *Ancient Sage* 189
that one *r* on the boundless deep ” 191
Ripple (verb) That *r* round the lonely grange ; *In Mem. xci* 12
rivulet at her feet *R's* on in light and shadow *Maud II iv* 42
Rippled the ringlets to her knee ; *Godiva* 47
which was lined And *r* like an ever-fleeting wave, *Gareth and L.* 215
Rippling ran over The *r* levels of the lake, *Lover's Tale iii* 4
Ripply and ran By *r* shallows of the lisping lake, *Edwin Morris* 98
Rise (s) (*See also* **Moon-rise**) I turning saw, throned
on a flowery *r*, *D. of F. Women* 125
Approvingly, and prophesied his *r* : *Aylmer's Field* 474
upon the *r* And long roll of the Hexameter— *Lucretius* 10
Rise (verb) In roaring he shall *r* and on the surface die. *The Kraken* 15
How could I *r* and come away, *Oriana* 57
R from the feast of sorrow, lady, *Margaret* 62
Pain *r's* up, old pleasures pall. *Two Voices* 164
all day long to fall and *r* Upon her balmy bosom, *Miller's D.* 182
with one mind the Gods *R* up for reverence. *Œnone* 110
I will *r* and go Down into Troy, ” 261
And that sweet incense *r* ? ' *Palace of Art* 44
I would see the sun *r* (repeat) *May Queen, N. Y's. E.* 2, 51
sweeter is the young lamb's voice to me
that cannot *r*, ” *Con.* 6
O look ! the sun begins to *r*, ” 49
threshold of the sun, Never to *r* again. *D. of F. Women* 64
We saw the large white stars *r* one by one, ” 223
And if some dreadful need should *r* *Love thou thy land* 91
let thy voice *R* like a fountain for me *M. d'Arthur* 249
to *r* again Revolving toward fulfilment, *Edwin Morris* 38
and the shadows *r* and fall. *Locksley Hall* 80

Rise (verb) (*continued*) And every hundred years to *r* *Day-Dm., L'Envoi* 7
For blasts would *r* and rave and cease, *The Voyage* 85
and *r* To glass herself in dewy eyes *Move eastward* 6
Are but dust that *r's* up, (repeat) *Vision of Sin* 133, 169
Till thy drooping courage *r*, ” 152
Let me *r* and fly away. *Sea Dreams* 304
The Samian Here *r's* and she speaks *Princess iii* 115
R in the heart, and gather to the eyes, ” *iv* 41
R !' and stoop'd to updrag Melissa : ” 366
they *r* or sink Together, dwarf'd or godlike, ” *vii* 259
A devil *r's* in my heart, *Sailor Boy* 23
That men may *r* on stepping-stones *In Mem. i* 3
And see the sails at distance, ” *xii* 11
To-night the winds begin to *r* ” *xv* 1
cloud That *r's* upward always higher, ” 17
*R,.*happy morn, *r*, holy morn, ” *xxx* 30
When crown'd with blessing she doth *r* ” *xl* 5
Did ever *r* from high to higher ; ” *xli* 2
If any vague desire should *r*, ” *lxxx* 1
An iron welcome when they *r* : ” *xc* 8
of events As often *r's* ere they *r*. ” *xcii* 16
But served the seasons that may *r* ; ” *cxiii* 4
R in the spiritual rock. ” *cxxxi* 3
They *r*, but linger ; it is late ; ” *Con.* 91
And *r*, O moon, from yonder down, ” 109
and thought he would *r* and speak And rave *Maud I i* 59
And there *r's* ever a passionate cry ” *II i* 5
Then I *r*, the eavedrops fall, ” *iv* 62
but at night let go the stone, And *r*, *Gareth and L.* 826
if he *r* no more, I will not look at wine *Geraint and E.* 666
R therefore ; robe yourself in this : ” 685
Rose when they saw the dead man *r*, ” 732
and crying, ' Sirs, *R*, follow ! ' *Balin and Balan* 48
R, my true knight. ” 75
This old sun-worship, boy, will *r* again, ” 457
' *R*, my sweet King, and kiss me on the lips, ” 516
R !' and the damsel bidden *r* arose *Merlin and V.* 68
r, O Gawain, and ride forth and find the knight. *Lancelot and E.* 536
R and take This diamond, and deliver it, ” 545
To *r* hereafter in a stiller flame ” 1319
lulling random squabbles when they *r*, *Holy Grail* 557
' *R*, weakling ; I am Lancelot ; *Pelleas and E.* 582
but *r*, And fly to my strong castle overseas : *Guinevere* 112
yet *r* now, and let us fly, ” 120
r—I hear the steps of Modred in the west, *Pass. of Arthur* 58
let thy voice *R* like a fountain for me ” 417
from the woods That belt it *r* three dark, tall
cypresses,— *Lover's Tale i* 536
and dimly knows His head shall *r* no more : ” 639
laid it in a sepulchre of rock Never to *r* again. ” 684
that strove to *r* From my full heart. ” 711
then I seem'd To *r*, and through the forest-shadow ” *ii* 72
I could not *r* Albeit I strove to follow. ” 97
An' the wind began to *r*, *First Quarrel* 89
My Willy 'ill *r* up whole *Rizpah* 57
wish yon moaning sea would *r* and burst the shore, *The Flight* 11
my mother's ghost would *r*— ” 51
kings and realms that pass to *r* no more ; *To Virgil* 28
heron *r's* from his watch beside the mere, *Happy* 3
in their turn thy warblers *r* on wing. *Prog. of Spring* 108
once again we see thee *r*. *Akbar's D., Hymn* 1
Risen (*See also* **New-risen**, **Re-risen**) Nilus would
have *r* before his time *D. of F. Women* 143
Dora would have *r* and gone to him, *Dora* 77
thus early *r* she goes to inform The Princess : *Princess iii* 62
Has *r* and cleft the soil, ” *vi* 35
those twin brothers, *r* again and whole ; ” *vii* 89
She might have *r* and floated when I saw her. *Holy Grail* 100
sun is rising,' tho' the sun had *r*. ” 408
they have *r* against me in their blood *Pelleas and E.* 461
Lionel, who fain had *r*, but fell again, *Lover's Tale iv* 361
nay but thirty-nine have *r* and stand, *Sir J. Oldcastle* 83
Have we *r* from out the beast, *Locksley H., Sixty* 148
This later light of Love have *r* in vain, *To Prin. Beatrice* 16
Henceforth, as having *r* from out the dead, *Demeter and P.* 144

Risen (*continued*) Not *r* to, she was bolder. — *The Ring* 361
Look, the sun has *r* To flame along — *Romney's R.* 57
vines Which on the touch of heavenly feet had *r*, — *Death of Œnone* 5
Risest *R* thou thus, dim dawn, again, — *In Mem. lxxii* 1
R thou thus, dim dawn, again, — „ *xcix* 1
Rising (*See also* **Ever-rising, Later-rising**) *r*, from her bosom drew Old letters, — *Mariana in the S.* 61
angels *r* and descending met With interchange — *Palace of Art* 143
And of the *r* from the dead, — „ 206
lest the soul Of Discord race the *r* wind; — *Love thou thy land* 68
r bore him thro' the place of tombs. — *M. d'Arthur* 175
made his forehead like the *r* sun High — „ 217
r thro' the mellow shade, — *Locksley Hall* 9
R to no fancy-flies. — *Vision of Sin* 102
R, falling, like a wave, — „ 125
I saw my father's face Grow long and troubled like a *r* moon, — *Princess i* 59
r up Robed in the long night of her deep hair, — „ *iv* 490
Look'd up, and *r* slowly from me, — „ *vi* 151
Last little Lilia, *r* quietly, — „ *Con.* 116
The moon like a rick on fire was *r* — *Grandmother* 39
And *r* up, he rode to Arthur's court, — *Marr. of Geraint* 591
And *r* on the sudden he said, 'Eat! — *Geraint and E.* 614
Azure, an Eagle *r* or, the Sun In dexter chief; — *Merlin and V.* 475
raise the Prince, who *r* twice or thrice — *Guinevere* 46
Will draw me the *r* of the sun, — *Lover's Tale i* 27
for that day Love, *r*, shook his wings, — „ 317
roll *R* and falling— — *The Wreck* 54
the car Of dark Aïdoneus *r* rapt thee hence. — *Demeter and P.* 39
fiery phœnix *r* from the smoke, — *The Ring* 339
O *r* worlds by yonder wood. — *In Mem. cv* 25
Thou standest in the *r* sun, — „ *cxxx* 3
And on the downs a *r* fire: — „ *Con.* 108
And half to the *r* day; — *Maud I xxii* 24
The fires of Hell brake out of thy *r* sun, — *II i* 9
but thought 'The sun is *r*,' tho' the sun had risen. — *Holy Grail* 408
All in the middle of the *r* moon: — „ 636
And *r* bore him thro' the place of tombs. — *Pass. of Arthur* 343
made his forehead like a *r* sun High — „ 385
to lower the *r* race of men; — *Locksley H., Sixty* 147
Yet I would the *r* race were half as eager for the light. — „ 228
Risk and *r* thine all, Life, limbs, — *Gareth and L.* 128
Risk'd (for the man Had *r* his little) — *Sea Dreams* 10
Take not his life: he *r* it for my own; — *Princess v* 407
sweet son, had *r* himself and climb'd, — *Gareth and L.* 60
Risking some knight of mine, *r* his life, — *Geraint and E.* 915
Rite *r's* and forms before his burning eyes — *The Poet* 39
and with solemn *r's* by candle-light— — *Princess v* 292
Worthy of our gorgeous *r's*, — *Ode on Well.* 93
The *r's* prepared, the victim bared, — *The Victim* 65
mingle with your *r's*; Pray and be pray'd for; — *Guinevere* 680
And those lone *r's* I have not seen, — *To Marq. of Dufferin* 39
Ritual And hear the *r* of the dead. — *In Mem. xviii* 12
all else Form, *R*, varying with the tribes of men. — *Akbar's Dream* 125
Rivage From the green *r* many a fall — *Arabian Nights* 47
Rival (adj.) Which fann'd the gardens of that *r* rose — *Aylmer's Field* 455
the King Took, as in *r* heat, to holy things; — *Balin and Balan* 100
nor raved And thus foam'd over at a *r* name: — „ 567
He wildly fought a *r* suitor. — *The Ring* 214
Rival (s) my latest *r* brings thee rest. — *Locksley Hall* 89
Leolin's rejected *r's* from their suit — *Aylmer's Field* 493
Leolin's one strong *r* upon earth; — „ 557
wrathful, petulant, Dreaming some *r*, — *Lucretius* 115
To push my *r* out of place and power. — *Princess iv* 335
Poor *r's* in a losing game, — *In Mem. cii* 19
far away the maid in Astolat, Her guiltless *r*, — *Lancelot and E.* 746
R's of realm-ruining party, — *Locksley H., Sixty* 120
Rivalries fruitful strifes and *r* of peace— — *Ded. of Idylls* 38
Drove me from all vainglories, *r*, — *Holy Grail* 32
Riven within my inmost frame Was *r* in twain: — *Lover's Tale i* 596
Knights were thwack'd and *r*, — *The Tourney* 10
River CLEARLY the blue *r* chimes in its flowing — *All Things will Die* 1
Thoro' the crack-stemm'd pines only the far *r* shines. — *Leonine Eleg.* 2
down a broad canal From the main *r* sluiced, — *Arabian Nights* 26

River (*continued*) A motion from the *r* won Ridged the smooth level, — *Arabian Nights* 34
Flowing like a crystal *r*; — *Poet's Mind* 6
With an inner voice the *r* ran, — *Dying Swan* 5
One willow over the *r* wept, — „ 14
Like some broad *r* rushing down alone, — *Mine be the strength* 2
ON either side the *r* lie Long fields — *L. of Shalott i* 1
By the island in the *r* Flowing down to Camelot. — „ 13
From the *r* winding clearly, — „ 31
There the *r* eddy whirls, — „ *ii* 15
From the bank and from the *r* He flash'd — „ *iii* 33
'Tirra lirra,' by the *r* Sang Sir Lancelot. — „ 35
And down the *r's* dim expanse — „ *iv* 10
full-flowing *r* of speech Came down upon my heart. — *Œnone* 68
one, a full-fed *r* winding slow By herds — *Palace of Art* 73
drew *R's* of melodies; — „ 172
They saw the gleaming *r* seaward flow — *Lotos-Eaters* 14
long bright *r* drawing slowly His waters — „ *C. S.* 92
How fresh the meadows look Above the *r*, — *Walk. to the Mail* 2
willows two and two By *r's* gallopaded. — *Amphion* 40
In curves the yellowing *r* ran, — *Sir L. and Q. G.* 15
A rivulet then a *r*: — *A Farewell* 6
To join the brimming *r*, (repeat) — *The Brook* 32, 48, 64, 183
there the *r*: and there Stands Philip's farm where brook and *r* meet. — „ 37
Runs in a *r* of blood to the sick sea. — *Aylmer's Field* 768
Set in a gleaming *r's* crescent-curve, — *Princess i* 171
We follow'd up the *r* as we rode, — „ 206
and the *r* made a fall Out yonder;' — „ *iii* 172
The *r* as it narrow'd to the hills. — „ 196
we came to where the *r* sloped To plunge — „ 290
They faint on hill or field or *r*: — „ *iv* 14
miss'd the plank, and roll'd In the *r*. — „ 178
combing out her long black hair Damp from the *r*; — „ 277
As waits a *r* level with the dam Ready to burst — „ 473
Let the great *r* take me to the main: — „ *vii* 13
That shines over city and *r*, — *Ode on Well.* 50
Flash, ye cities, in *r's* of fire! — *W. to Alexandra* 19
Beside the *r's* wooded reach, — *In Mem. lxxi* 13
A *r* sliding by the wall. — „ *ciii* 8
his high sun flame, and his *r* billowing ran, — *Maud I iv* 32
a *r* Runs in three loops about her living-place; — *Gareth and L.* 611
Wherethro' the serpent *r* coil'd, they came. — „ 906
Down to the *r*, sink or swim, — „ 1154
O'er the four *r's* the first roses blew, — *Geraint and E.* 764
holding then his court Hard on the *r* — *Lancelot and E.* 75
By the great *r* in a boatman's hut. — „ 278
Up the great *r* in the boatman's boat. — „ 1038
prepared a chariot-bier To take me to the *r*, and a barge Be ready on the *r*, — „ 1122
Sat by the *r* in a cove, and watch'd — „ 1389
and all the sand Swept like a *r*, — *Holy Grail* 800
when I was leaning out Above the *r*— — *Last Tournament* 44
saw the *r's* roll from Paradise! — *Columbus* 27
streaming and shining on Silent *r*, — *Merlin and the G.* 52
River-bank he ran Beside the *r-b*: — *Aylmer's Field* 451
River-bed An empty *r-b* before, — *Mariana in the S.* 6
The *r-b* was dusty-white; — „ 54
River-breeze the soft *r-b*, Which fann'd the gardens — *Aylmer's Field* 454
River-God I am the daughter of a *R-G*, — *Œnone* 38
River-loop So when they touch'd the second *r-l*, — *Gareth and L.* 1025
Lancelot, having swum the *r-l's*— — „ 1216
River-rain Snapt in the rushing of the *r-r* — *Merlin and V.* 958
River-shore Spread the light haze along the *r-s's*, — *Gardener's D.* 264
creep down to the *r-s*, — *Charity* 15
River-sunder'd *r-s* champaign clothed with corn, — *Œnone* 114
River-tide On the misty *r-t*. — *Maud II iv* 67
Riveted the eye Was *r* and charm-bound, — *Lover's Tale ii* 188
Riveting Sat *r* a helmet on his knee, — *Marr. of Geraint* 268
Riving *r* the spirit of man, — *The Poet* 51
A cracking and a *r* of the roofs, — *Holy Grail* 183
Rivulet Down by the poplar tall *r's* babble and fall. — *Leonine Eleg.* 4
r in the flowery dale 'ill merrily glance and play, — *May Queen* 39
Now by some tinkling *r*, — *Sir L. and Q. G.* 29
FLOW down, cold *r*, to the sea, — *A Farewell* 1

Rivulet (*continued*) A *r* then a river: *A Farewell* 6
By dancing *r's* fed his flocks   *To E. L.* 22
sweep Of some precipitous *r* to the wave,   *Enoch Arden* 587
where the *r's* of sweet water ran;   „ 642
Myriads of *r's* hurrying thro' the lawn,   *Princess* vii 220
With many a *r* high against the Sun   *The Islet* 21
Nor pastoral *r* that swerves   *In Mem.* c 14
But the *r* on from the lawn Running down   *Maud* I xiv 29
R crossing my ground,   „ xxi 1
O *R*, born at the Hall,   „ 8
For I heard your *r* fall From the lake   „ xxii 36
the *r* at her feet Ripples on in light and shadow   II iv 41
Fled like a glittering *r* to the tarn :   *Lancelot and E.* 52
one *r* from a tiny cave Came lightening   *Pelleas and E.* 425
She comes ! The loosen'd *r's* run ;   *Prog. of Spring* 9
Roä (dog's name) (*See also* **Roäver**) Naäy, noä mander o' use
   to be callin' 'im *R, R, R,*   *Owd Roä* 1
An' *R* was the dog as knaw'd   „ 8
Fur I wants to tell tha o' *R*   „ 19
Then I call'd out *R, R, R,*   „ 91
R was as good as the Hangel i' saävin' a son   „ 96
' I mun gaw up ageän fur *R*.'   „ 97
an' clemm'd owd *R* by the 'eäd,   „ 99
a-callin' o' *R* till 'e waggled 'is taäil   „ 105
An' I browt *R* round,   „ 113
Roäbin' (robing) a *r* the 'ouse like a Queeän.   *Spinster's S's.* 106
Road (*See also* **Cross-road**) thro' the field the *r* runs by
   To many-tower'd Camelot   *L. of Shalott* i 4
Walking the cold and starless *r* of Death Uncomforted,   *Œnone* 259
and stood by the *r* at the gate.   *Grandmother* 38
Out into the *r* I started, and spoke   „ 43
In ruin, by the mountain *r*;   *The Daisy* 6
And at a sudden swerving of the *r*,   *Geraint and E.* 506
Roam at night I would *r* abroad and play   *The Merman* 11
Too long you *r* and wheel at will ;   *Rosalind* 36
see thee *r*, with tresses unconfined,   *Eleänore* 122
we will no longer *r*.'   *Lotos-Eaters* 45
To those that stay and those that *r*,   *Sailor Boy* 14
Henceforth, wherever thou may'st *r*,   *In Mem.* xvii 9
All winds that *r* the twilight came   „ lxxix 11
To range the woods, to *r* the park,   *Con.* 96
And *r* the goodly places that she knew ;   *Marr. of Geraint* 646
Roam'd the hill Where last we *r* together,   *Lover's Tale* ii 34
For while we *r* along the dreary coast,   „ iv 145
all the summer long we *r* in these wild woods   *The Flight* 79
Roaming Low-flowing breezes are *r*   *Leonine Eleg.* 1
For always *r* with a hungry heart   *Ulysses* 12
A white-hair'd shadow *r* like a dream   *Tithonus* 8
Roan three pyebalds and a *r*.   *Walk. to the Mail* 114
Roar (s) (*See also* **City-roar**) The panther's *r* came muffled,   *Œnone* 214
Heard thro' the living *r*.   *Sea Dreams* 56
' but this tide's *r*, and his,   „ 250
twists the grain with such a *r* that Earth Reels,   *Princess* v 528
The *r* that breaks the Pharos from his base   „ vi 339
Here, in streaming London's central *r*.   *Ode on Well.* 9
The lone glow and long *r* (repeat)   *Voice and the P.* 3, 39
Rings to the *r* of an angel onset—   *Milton* 8
in its broad-flung shipwrecking *r*,   *Maud* I iii 11
whereout was roll'd A *r* of riot,   *Last Tournament* 426
Then at the dry harsh *r* of the great horn,   „ 438
So shook to such a *r* of all the sky,   *To the Queen* ii 20
whom the *r* of Hougoumont Left mightiest   *Def. of Lucknow* 54
R upon *r* in a moment two mines by the enemy   *Columbus* 13
while I spoke The crowd's *r* fell   *The Wreck* 4
My brain is full of the crash of wrecks, and the *r* of waves,   *Despair* 13
thro' the *r* of the breaker a whisper,   *Death of Œnone* 85
By the long torrent's ever-deepen'd *r*,   *St. Telemachus* 67
Then one deep *r* as of a breaking sea,
Roar (verb) below them *r's* The long brook   *Œnone* 7
r rock-thwarted under bellowing caves,   *Palace of Art* 71
' He that *r's* for liberty Faster binds   *Vision of Sin* 127
the sea *r's* Ruin : a fearful night ! '   *Sea Dreams* 80
once or twice I thought to *r*,   *Princess* ii 423
R's as the sea when he welcomes the land,   *W. to Alexandra* 24
I *r* and rave for I fall.   *Voice and the P.* 12

Roar (verb) (*continued*) And *r* from yonder dropping day :   *In Mem.* xv 2
There where the long street *r's*,   „ cxxiii 3
Well *r's* the storm to those that hear   „ cxxvii 3
And molten up, and *r* in flood ;   „ 13
ye seem agape to *r* ! Yea, ramp and *r* at leaving
   of your lord !—   *Gareth and L.* 1306
r An ocean-sounding welcome to one knight,   *Last Tournament* 167
the crowd would *r* For blood, for war,   *Tiresias* 64
and hear the waters *r*, And see the ships   *The Flight* 90
Now thy Forum *r's* no longer,   *To Virgil* 29
Roar'd and above them *r* the pine.   *Aylmer's Field* 431
' No ! ' *R* the rough king,   *Princess* i 87
bones of some vast bulk that lived and *r*   „ iii 294
(thus the King *R*) make yourself a man   „ v 35
R as when the roaring breakers boom   *Boädicea* 76
So Hector spake ; the Trojans *r* applause ;   *Spec. of Iliad* 1
He from beyond the roaring shallow *r*,   *Gareth and L.* 1033
the lake whiten'd and the pinewood *r*,   *Merlin and V.* 637
r And shouted and leapt down upon the fall'n *r*   *Last Tournament* 468
Sir Richard spoke and he laugh'd, and we *r* a hurrah,   *The Revenge* 32
To meet me, *r* my name ;   *Columbus* 10
Roarin' an *r* like judgment daäy.   *Owd Roä* 110
Roaring (*See also* **Roarin'**) In *r* he shall rise and on the
   surface die.   *The Kraken* 15
I hear the *r* of the sea,   *Oriana* 98
The wind is *r* in turret and tree.   *The Sisters* 15
We heard the lion *r* from his den ;   *D. of F. Women* 222
ocean-ridges *r* into cataracts,   *Locksley Hall* 6
mighty wind arises, *r* seaward,   „ 194
heard the foeman's thunder *R* out their doom ;   *The Captain* 42
R to make a third :   *Aylmer's Field* 128
And the *r* of the wheels.   *Maud* II iv 22
slowly rose and plunged *R*,   *Com. of Arthur* 382
He from beyond the *r* shallow roar'd,   *Gareth and L.* 1033
the heavens open'd and blazed again *R*,   *Holy Grail* 517
mast bent and the ravin wind In her sail *r*.   *Lover's Tale* ii 171
And the storm went *r* above us,   *The Wreck* 106
Flung leagues of *r* foam into the gorge   *If I were loved* 13
I whirl like leaves in *r* wind.   *Fatima* 7
plague and earthquake, *r* deeps and fiery sands,   *Lotos-Eaters, C. S.* 115
High over *r* Temple-bar,   *Will Water.* 69
Bows all its ears before the *r* East ;   *Princess* i 237
I take my part Of danger on the *r* sea,   *Sailor Boy* 22
Like the leaf in a *r* whirlwind,   *Boädicea* 59
Roar'd as when the *r* breakers boom and blanch   „ 76
Than if with thee the *r* wells   *In Mem.* x 17
In *r's* round the coral reef.   „ xxxvi 16
up thy vault with *r* sound Climb thy thick noon,   „ lxxii 25
in this *r* moon of daffodil And crocus,   *Pref. Son. 19th Cent.* 7
Watch'd again the hollow ridges *r* into cataracts,   *Locksley H., Sixty* 2
R London, raving Paris,   „ 190
Roasting or bits of *r* ox Moan round the spit—   *Lucretius* 131
Roäver (dog's name) (*See also* **Roä**) Fur I owäs owd
   R moor nor I iver owäd mottal man.   *Owd Roä* 4
Wi' *R* athurt my feeät,   „ 30
cat wur a-sleeäping alongside *R*,   „ 33
I fun it was *R* a-tuggin' an' teärin' my slieäve.   „ 60
I thowt it was *R* a-tuggin' an' teärin' me   „ 66
R was theere i' the chaumber a-yowlin' an' yaupin'   „ 88
Rob (name of man and cat) (*See also* **Robby**) Tommy
   the second, an' Steevie an' *R*.   *Spinster's S's.* 10
R, coom oop 'ere o' my knee.   „ 11
Rob (verb) once had power to *r* it of content.   *The form, the form* 8
They swore that he dare not *r* the mail,   *Rizpah* 30
Robb'd *r* the farmer of his bowl of cream :   *Princess* v 223
Robber There the horde of Roman *r's*   *Boädicea* 18
an onslaught single on a realm Of *r's*,   *Geraint and E.* 918
Robbing I whipt him for *r* an orchard once   *Rizpah* 25
they kill'd him for *r* the mail.   „ 34
Robby (name of man and cat) (*See also* **Rob**) but *R* I
   seed thruf ya theere.   *Spinster's S's.* 14
R, I niver 'a liked tha sa well,   „ 29
R wur fust to be sewer, (repeat)   „ 42, 69
R, I thowt o' tha all the while   „ 43
R I gied tha a raätin that sattled   „ 48

Robby (name of man and cat) (*continued*) But if I 'ed	
married tha, R,	*Spinster's S's.* 54
R, git down wi'tha, wilt tha?	„ 67
Theere! Set it down! Now R!	„ 119
Till R an' Steevie 'es 'ed their lap	„ 121
Robe (s) no blood upon her maiden r's	*The Poet* 41
She threw her royal r's away.	*Palace of Art* 290
(With that she tore her r apart,	*D. of F. Women* 157
the white r and the palm.	*St. S. Stylites* 20
As these white r's are soil'd and dark,	*St. Agnes' Eve* 13
How oft the purple-skirted r	*The Voyage* 21
In r and crown the king stept down,	*Beggar Maid* 5
wove A close-set r of jasmine sown with stars :	*Aylmer's Field* 158
whirl'd her white r like a blossom'd branch	*Princess iv* 179
rainbow r's, and gems and gemlike eyes,	„ 480
he drew Her r to meet his lips,	„ *vi* 156
Her falser self slipt from her like a r,	„ *vii* 161
Till slowly worn her earthly r,	*In Mem. lxxxiv* 33
In a cold white r before me,	*Maud II iv* 19
a r Of samite without price,	*Merlin and V.* 221
down his r the dragon writhed in gold,	*Lancelot and E.* 435
'If I be loved, these are my festal r's,	„ 909
'Take thou my r,' she said,	*Holy Grail* 449
In hanging r or vacant ornament,	*Guinevere* 506
A mystic light flash'd ev'n from her white r	*Lover's Tale i* 370
Robed in those r's of light I must not wear,	„ 671
throwing down his r's, And claspt her hand in his :	„ *iii* 51
with her flying r and her poison'd rose :	*Vastness* 16
Robe (verb) Rise therefore; r yourself in this :	*Geraint and E.* 685
The music that r's it in language	*The Wreck* 24
Robed (*See also* **White-robed**) but r in soften'd light Of	
orient state.	*Ode to Memory* 10
Lying, r in snowy white That loosely flew	*L. of Shalott iv* 19
lying r and crown'd, Worthy a Roman spouse.'	*D. of F. Women* 163
reissuing, r and crown'd, To meet her lord,	*Godiva* 77
hand that r your cottage-walls with flowers	*Aylmer's Field* 698
And r the shoulders in a rosy silk,	*Princess, Pro.* 103
R in the long night of her deep hair,	„ *iv* 491
Loosely r in flying raiment,	*Boädicea* 37
r herself, Help'd by the mother's careful hand	*Marr. of Geraint* 737
And r them in her ancient suit again,	„ 770
R in red samite, easily to be known,	*Lancelot and E.* 433
R in those robes of light I must not wear,	*Lover's Tale i* 671
cliffs all r in lianas that dropt	*The Wreck* 73
R in universal harvest up to either pole	*Locksley H., Sixty* 169
Ilion's lofty temples r in fire,	*To Virgil* 2
r thee in his day from head to feet—	*Demeter and P.* 21
Robert old Sir R's pride, His books—	*Audley Court* 58
slight Sir R with his watery smile	*Edwin Morris* 128
Robin (bird) In the spring a fuller crimson comes upon	
the r's breast;	*Locksley Hall* 17
On the nigh-naked tree the r piped	*Enoch Arden* 676
careful r's eye the delver's toil,	*Marr. of Geraint* 774
careful r's eye the delver's toil;	*Geraint and E.* 431
Robin (Christian name) But R leaning on the bridge	*May Queen* 14
And say to R a kind word,	„ *Con.* 45
Robin *See* **Ragged-robin**	
Robing *See* **Roäbin'**	
Robins (surname) Or a mowt 'a taäen young R—	*N. Farmer, O. S.* 50
Naw, nor a moänt to R—	„ 60
Rock (s) And strike the hard, hard r,	*Supp. Confessions* 116
the mermaids in and out of the r's,	*The Merman* 12
the mermen in and out of the r's;	*The Mermaid* 34
Of ledge or shelf The r rose clear,	*Palace of Art* 10
or a sound Of r's thrown down,	„ 282
zig-zag paths, and juts of pointed r,	*M. d'Arthur* 50
and leveret lay, Like fossils of the r,	*Audley Court* 25
as we sank From r to r upon the glooming quay,	„ 84
upon a r With turrets lichen-gilded like a r :	*Edwin Morris* 7
forged a thousand theories of the r's,	„ 18
he struck his staff against the r's	*Golden Year* 59
lights begin to twinkle from the r's :	*Ulysses* 54
His mantle glitters on the r's—	*Day-Dm., Arrival* 2
The nutmeg r's and isles of clove.	*The Voyage* 40
To him who sat upon the r's,	*To E. L.* 23

Rock (s) (*continued*) Is there no stoning save with	
flint and r ?	*Aylmer's Field* 746
on the foremost r's Touching,	*Sea Dreams* 51
some were push'd with lances from the r,	*Princess, Pro.* 46
The morals, something of the frame, the r,	„ *ii* 382
No r so hard but that a little wave	„ *iii* 154
Glanced like a touch of sunshine on the r's,	„ 357
Each was like a Druid r ;	„ *iv* 280
Part sat like r's : part reel'd but kept their seats :	„ *v* 496
Pharos from his base Had left us r.	„ *vi* 340
for Willy stood like a r.	*Grandmother* 10
Who seems a promontory of r,	*Will* 6
along the valley, by r and cave and tree,	*V. of Cauteretz* 9
My love has talk'd with r's and trees ;	*In Mem. xcvii* 1
Nor runlet tinkling from the r ;	„ *c* 13
Rise in the spiritual r,	„ *cxxxi* 3
There yet lies the r that fell with him	*Maud I i* 8
by a red r, glimmers the Hall ;	„ *iv* 10
Athwart the ledges of r	„ *II ii* 28
smallest r far on the faintest hill,	*Com. of Arthur* 99
As being all bone-shatter'd on the r, Yielded ;	*Gareth and L.* 1050
narrow comb wherein Were slabs of r with figures,	„ 1194
Whose holy hand hath fashion'd on the r	„ 1197
a r in ebbs and flows, Fixt on her faith.	*Marr. of Geraint* 812
knights On horseback, wholly arm'd, behind a r In	
shadow,	*Geraint and E.* 57
I saw three bandits by the r	„ 72
A little town with towers, upon a r,	„ 197
Prince had brought his errant eyes Home from the r,	„ 246
gleam'd on r's Roof-pendent, sharp ;	*Balin and Balan* 314
In the white r a chapel and a hall	*Lancelot and E.* 405
Shape to their fancy's eye from broken r's	„ 1252
A castle like a r upon a r,	*Holy Grail* 814
Far down beneath a winding wall of r	*Last Tournament* 11
zigzag paths, and juts of pointed r,	*Pass. of Arthur* 218
Thro' that r we wound :	*Lover's Tale i* 324
walls of battlemented r Gilded with broom,	„ 399
Shut in the secret chambers of the r	„ 521
laid it in a sepulchre of r Never to rise again.	„ 683
And all the fragments of the living r	„ *ii* 44
I find hard r's, hard life, hard cheer,	*Sir J. Oldcastle* 6
And we left but a naked r,	*V. of Maeldune* 54
And a hundred ranged on the r	„ 101
that smooth r Before it, altar-fashion'd,	*Tiresias* 146
as if she had struck and crash'd on a r ;	*The Wreck* 108
neck Of land running out into r—	*Despair* 10
skull that is left in the r	„ 86
How slowly down the r's he went,	*The Flight* 38
Ranged like a storm or stood like a r	*Heavy Brigade* 56
When seated on a r, and foot to foot	*Romney's R.* 75
Rock (verb) O r upon thy towery-top	*Talking Oak* 265
r the snowy cradle till I died.	*Princess iv* 104
The blind wall r's, and on the trees	*In Mem., Con.* 63
Rock'd R the full-foliaged elms,	„ *xcv* 58
A mountain nest—the pleasure-boat that r,	*Lover's Tale i* 42
Rocket Rush to the roof, sudden r,	*W. to Alexandra* 20
The r molten into flakes	*In Mem. xcviii* 31
Rocking (*See also* **Scarce-rocking**) R with shatter'd spars,	*Buonaparte* 11
Then lightly r baby's cradle	*Enoch Arden* 194
Rock-throne rough r-t Of Freedom !	*Montenegro* 9
Rock-thwarted r-t under bellowing caves,	*Palace of Art* 71
Rocky Lift up thy r face,	*England and Amer.* 12
Dash'd on every r square Their surging charges	*Ode on Well.* 125
How richly down the r dell	*The Daisy* 9
For all along the valley, down thy r bed,	*V. of Cauteretz* 7
I heard the voice Rave over the r bar,	*Voice and the P.* 6
And down a r pathway from the place	*Geraint and E.* 200
And up a r pathway disappear'd,	„ 243
Rod I must brook the r And chastisement	*Supp. Confessions* 107
red-faced war has r's of steel and fire ;	*Princess v* 118
war's avenging r Shall lash all Europe	*To F. D. Maurice* 33
be ruled with r or with knout ?	*Maud I iv* 47
Tho' Sin too oft, when smitten by Thy r,	*Doubt and Prayer* 1
Rode Ere I r into the fight,	*Oriana* 21
He r between the barley-sheaves,	*L. of Shalott iii* 2

Rode (*continued*) As he *r* down to Camelot : (repeat) *L. of Shalott* 14, 23, 32
And as he *r* his armour rung,   „   17
The man, my lover, with whom I *r* sublime   *D. of F. Women* 141
And *r* his hunter down.   *Talking Oak* 104
And far below the Roundhead *r*,   „   299
Then she *r* forth, clothed on with chastity :   *Godiva* 53
The deep air listen'd round her as she *r*,   „   54
she *r* back, clothed on with chastity :   „   65
R thro' the coverts of the deer,   *Sir L. and Q. G.* 21
He *r* a horse with wings, that would have flown,   *Vision of Sin* 3
Who slowly *r* across a wither'd heath,   „   61
They *r* ; they betted ; made a hundred friends,   *Princess, Pro.* 163
We *r* Many a long league back to the North.   ..   *i* 167
follow'd up the river as we *r*, And *r* till midnight   ..   206
' That afternoon the Princess *r* to take   ..   *iii* 169
I *r* beside her and to me she said :   ..   197
we *r* a league beyond, And, o'er a bridge of pinewood   ..   334
Then *r* we with the old king across the lawns   *v* 236
All o'er with honey'd answer as we *r*   ..   242
Back *r* we to my father's camp,   ..   331
as here and everywhere He *r* the mellay,   ..   502
but Arac *r* him down : And Cyril seeing it,   ..   532
R. the six hundred. (repeat)   *Light Brigade* 4, 8, 17, 26
Boldly they *r* and well,   „   23
Then they *r* back, but not Not the six hundred.   „   37
I bow'd to his lady-sister as she *r* by on the moor ;   *Maud I iv* 15
one of the two that *r* at her side Bound for the Hall,   „   *x* 24
r a simple knight among his knights,   *Com. of Arthur* 51
Smite on the sudden, yet *r* on,   „   57
thinking as he *r*, ' Her father said   „   78
A naked babe, and *r* to Merlin's feet,   „   384
Gareth *r* Down the slope street,   *Gareth and L.* 699
thro' silent faces *r* Down the slope city,   „   734
R. on the two, reviler and reviled ;   „   794
Suddenly she that *r* upon his left   „   1319
r In converse till she made her palfrey halt,   „   1359
Prince and Enid *r*, And fifty knights *r* with them,   *Marr. of Geraint* 43
there *r* Full slowly by a knight, lady,   „   186
r, By ups and downs, thro' many a grassy glade   „   235
And onward to the fortress *r* the three,   „   251
Then *r* Geraint, a little spleenful yet,   „   293
Then *r* Geraint into the castle court,   „   312
all unarm'd I *r*, and thought to find Arms   „   417
And rising up, he *r* to Arthur's court,   „   591
claspt and kiss'd her, and they *r* away.   „   825
forth they *r*, but scarce three paces on,   *Geraint and E.* 19
And wildernesses, perilous paths, they *r*:   ..   32
They *r* so slowly and they look'd so pale,   ..   35
for he *r* As if he heard not,   ..   451
Half ridden off with by the thing he *r*,   ..   460
And so *r* on, nor told his gentle wife   ..   503
R. on a mission to the bandit Earl ;   ..   527
In this poor gown I *r* with him to court,   ..   700
now we *r* upon this fatal quest Of honour,   ..   703
cast her arms About him, and at once they *r* away.   ..   762
Tho' thence I *r* all-shamed, hating the life   ..   852
for a space they *r*, And fifty knights *r* with them   ..   953
So claim'd the quest and *r* away,   *Balin and Balan* 138
and *r* The skyless woods, but under open blue   „   292
with droopt brow down the long glades he *r* ;   „   311
damsel-errant, warbling, as she *r* The woodland alleys,   „   438
the knight, with whom I *r*, Hath suffer'd misadventure,   „   475
Yet while they *r* together down the plain,   *Merlin and V.* 123
of old—among the flowers—they *r*.   „   136
and all day long we *r* Thro' the dim land   „   424
He left it with her, when he *r* to tilt   *Lancelot and E.* 30
They rose, heard mass, broke fast, and *r* away :   „   415
all the region round *R* with his diamond,   „   616
A true-love ballad, lightly *r* away.   „   705
fail'd to find him, tho' I *r* all round The region :   „   709
R o'er the long backs of the bushless downs   „   789
To Astolat returning *r* the three.   „   905
Nor bad farewell, but sadly *r* away.   „   987
to this hall full quickly *r* the King,   *Holy Grail* 258
And in he *r*, and up I glanced,   „   262

Rode (*continued*) Queen, Who *r* by Lancelot, wail'd and
shriek'd   *Holy Grail* 356
' And on I *r*, and when I thought my thirst   „   379
on I *r*, and greater was my thirst.   „   401
I *r* on and found a mighty hill,   „   421
And in the strength of this I *r*,   „   476
And maddening what he *r*:   „   641
Sir Bors *R* to the lonest tract of all the realm,   „   661
while they *r*, the meaning in his eyes,   *Pelleas and E.* 109
straight on thro' open door *R* Gawain,   „   383
but *r* Ere midnight to her walls,   „   412
R till the star above the wakening sun,   „   500
Lancelot slowly *r* his warhorse back To Camelot,   „   583
Down the slope city *r*, and sharply turn'd   *Last Tournament* 127
R Tristram toward Lyonnesse and the west.   „   362
Thro' many a league-long bower he *r*.   „   374
Arthur with a hundred spears *R* far,   „   421
Arthur waved them back. Alone he *r*.   „   437
And *r* beneath an ever-showering leaf,   „   492
when first I *r* from our rough Lyonnesse,   „   664
and then they *r* to the divided way,   *Guinevere* 124
And *r* thereto from Lyonnesse, and he said That as he
r, an hour or maybe twain   „   236
R under groves that look'd a paradise   „   389
There *r* an armed warrior to the doors.   „   409
And then he *r* away ; but after this,   *Lover's Tale iv* 126
And thus our lonely lover *r* away,   „   130
and he *r* on ahead, as he waved his blade   *Heavy Brigade* 9
R flashing blow upon blow,   „   32
they *r* like Victors and Lords   „   48
They *r*, or they stood at bay—   „   51
Thou's *r* of 'is back when a babby,   *Owd Roä* 5
you my girl *R* on my shoulder home—   *The Ring* 322
Roger Acton Burnt—good Sir *R A*, my dear friend !   *Sir J. Oldcastle* 79
Rogue unctuous mouth which lured him, *r*,   *Sea Dreams* 14
do not call him, love, Before you prove him, *r*,   „   171
And one the Master, as a *r* in grain   *Princess, Pro.* 116
A *r* of canzonents and serenades.   „   *iv* 135
snubnosed *r* would leap from his counter and till,   *Maud I i* 51
listening *r* hath caught the manner of it.   *Gareth and L.* 778
these caitiff *r*'s Had wreak'd themselves on me ;   „   819
Some meddling *r* has tamper'd with him—   *Lancelot and E.* 128
Roisterer midmost of a rout of *r*'s,   *Geraint and E.* 274
Roky Last in a *r* hollow, belling,   *Last Tournament* 502
Roll (s) (*See also* **Ocean-roll**) upon the rise And long *r* of the
Hexameter—   *Lucretius* 11
Nor ever lowest *r* of thunder moans,   „   108
Now, to the *r* of muffled drums,   *Ode on Well.* 87
R of cannon and clash of arms,   „   116
I hear the *r* of the ages.   *Spiteful Letter* 8
then one low *r* Of Autumn thunder,   *Last Tournament* 152
Rush of Suns, and *r* of systems,   *God. and the Univ.* 3
no discordance in the *r* And march   *D. of the Duke of C.* 14
Roll (verb) (*See also* **Over-roll**) ' In filthy sloughs they
r a prurient skin,   *Palace of Art* 201
trees began to whisper, and the wind began to *r*,   *May Queen, Con.* 27
' This mounting wave will *r* us shoreward soon.'   *Lotos-Eaters* 2
And the great ages onward *r*.   *To J. S.* 72
R onward, leading up the golden year.   *Golden Year* 41
r the waters, flash the lightnings,   *Locksley Hall* 186
the gates *R* back, and far within   *St. Agnes' Eve* 30
They reel, they *r* in clanging lists,   *Sir Galahad* 9
There did a thousand memories *r* upon him,   *Enoch Arden* 724
r thy tender arms Round him,   *Lucretius* 82
Our echoes *r* from soul to soul,   *Princess iv* 15
r The torrents, dash'd to the vale :   „   *v* 349
r the torrent out of dusky doors :   „   *vii* 208
down *r*'s the world In mock heroics   „   *Con.* 63
world on world in myriad myriads *r*   *Ode on Well.* 262
R and rejoice, jubilant voice,   *W. to Alexandra* 22
R as a ground-swell dash'd on the strand,   „   23
And howsoever this wild world may *r*,   *W. to Marie Alex.* 48
two and thirty years were a mist that *r*'s away ;   *V. of Cauteretz* 6
You *r* up away from the light   *Window, Winter* 8
I hear a wizard music *r*,   *In Mem. lxx* 14

Roll (verb) (continued) And r it in another course,   *In Mem. cxiii* 16
The strong imagination r A sphere   „ *cxxii* 6
There r's the deep where grew the tree.   „ *cxxiii* 1
To have her lion r in a silken net   *Maud I vi* 29
swell Of the long waves that r in yonder bay ?   „ *xviii* 63
and the war r down like a wind,   „ *III vi* 54
and when the surface r's,   *Com. of Arthur* 293
sea r's, and all the world is warm'd ? '   *Holy Grail* 672
because they r Thro' such a round in heaven,   „ 685
The years will r into the centuries,   *Guinevere* 626
more than man Which r's the heavens,   *Tiresias* 22
r Rising and falling,   *The Wreck* 53
Nor r thy viands on a luscious tongue   *Ancient Sage* 267
and r their ruins down the slope.   *Locksley H., Sixty* 138
While the silent Heavens r,   „ 203
And when they r their idol down—   *Freedom* 29
may r with the dust of a vanish'd race.   *Vastness* 2
To r her North below thy deepening dome,   *Prog. of Spring* 49
delight To r himself in meadow grass   *Romney's R.* 14
may r The rainbow hues of heaven about it—   „ 50
and r my voice from the summit,   *Parnassus* 6
ere the mountain r's into the plain,   *Death of Œnone* 51
Well if it do not r our way.   *Riflemen form!* 4

Roll'd the tumult of their acclaim is r   *Dying Swan* 33
And all about him r his lustrous eyes ;   *Love and Death* 2
And all the war is r in smoke.'   *Two Voices* 156
I r among the tender flowers :   *Fatima* 11
R round by one fix'd law.   *Palace of Art* 256
R to starboard, r to larboard,   *Lotos-Eaters, C. S.* 106
R on each other, rounded, smooth'd,   *D. of F. Women* 51
Whirl'd by the wind, had r me deep below,   „ 119
' When the next moon was r into the sky,   „ 229
So all day long the noise of battle r   *M. d'Arthur* 1
R in one another's arms,   *Locksley Hall* 58
When the ranks are r in vapour,   „ 104
Her full black ringlets downward r,   *Day-Dm., Sleep. B.* 12
R a sea-haze and whelm'd the world   *Enoch Arden* 672
as the year R itself round again   „ 822
once again he r his eyes upon her   „ 904
and r His hoop to pleasure Edith,   *Aylmer's Field* 84
babies r about Like tumbled fruit in grass ;   *Princess, Pro.* 82
Kittenlike he r And paw'd about her sandal.   „ *iii* 181
miss'd the plank, and r In the river.   „ *iv* 177
slain with laughter r the gilded Squire.   „ *v* 22
giant, Arac, r himself Thrice in the saddle,   „ 274
Part r on the earth and rose again and drew :   „ 497
r With music in the growing breeze of Time,   „ *vi* 55
her eye with slow dilation r Dry flame,   „ 189
the sound of the sorrowing anthem r   *Ode on Well.* 60
Better the waste Atlantic r On her and us   *Third of Feb.* 21
R the rich vapour far into the heaven.   *Spec. of Iliad* 8
Who r the psalm to wintry skies,   *In Mem. lvi* 11
And r the floods in grander space,   „ *ciii* 26
And a sullen thunder is r ;   *Maud II iv* 49
R incense, and there past along the hymns   *Com. of Arthur* 464
the long night hath r away !   „ 483
down his enemy r, And there lay still ;   *Geraint and E.* 160
He r his eyes about the hall,   „ 610
The russet-bearded head r on the floor.   „ 729
a forethought r about his brain,   *Merlin and V.* 230
and r his enemy down, And saved him :   *Lancelot and E.* 26
from the skull the crown R into light,   „ 51
he r his eyes Yet blank from sleep,   „ 819
roofs Of our great hall are r in thunder-smoke !   *Holy Grail* 220
whereout was R a roar of riot,   *Last Tournament* 425
So all day long the noise of battle r   *Pass. of Arthur* 170
And London r one tide of joy   *To the Queen ii* 8
threshold clashing, r Her heaviest thunder—   *Lover's Tale i* 605
And we r upon capes of crocus   *V. of Maeldune* 47
r To meet me long-arm'd vines with grapes   *To E. Fitzgerald* 26
whence he r himself At dead of night—   *Tiresias* 145
And r them around like a cloud,—   *Heavy Brigade* 40
And r his nakedness everyway   *Dead Prophet* 15
once had r you round and round the Sun,   *Poets and their B.* 10
Ghost of Pindar in you R an Olympian ;   *To Prof. Jebb* 4

Roll'd (continued) Till earth has r her latest year—   *To Ulysses* 28
R again back on itself in the tides   *Beautiful City* 4
R them over and over.   *The Tourney* 5
Roller league-long r thundering on the reef,   *Enoch Arden* 584
slowly-ridging r's on the cliffs Clash'd,   *Lover's Tale i* 57
Rollest r from the gorgeous gloom   *In Mem. lxxxvi* 2
Rolling (See also **Crimson-rolling, Far-rolling, Myriad-rolling**)
waves that up a quiet cove R slide,   *Eleänore* 109
r to and fro The heads and crowns   *Palace of Art* 151
R a slumbrous sheet of foam below.   *Lotos-Eaters* 13
holy organ r waves Of sound on roof and floor   *D. of F. Women* 191
her mighty voice Came r on the wind.   *Of old sat Freedom* 8
r as in sleep, Low thunders bring the mellow rain,   *Talking Oak* 278
Enoch r his gray eyes upon her,   *Enoch Arden* 844
and r in his mind Old waifs of rhyme,   *The Brook* 198
Breathed low around the r earth   *The winds, etc.* 3
Is wearied of the r hours.   *L. C. V. de Vere* 60
A r stone of here and everywhere,   *Audley Court* 78
A r organ-harmony Swells up,   *Sir Galahad* 75
Beneath a manelike mass of r gold,   *Aylmer's Field* 68
And r as it were the substance of it   „ 258
Which r o'er the palaces of the proud,   „ 636
Who still'd the r wave of Galilee !   „ 709
And there was r thunder ;   *Sea Dreams* 118
That stays the r Ixionian wheel,   *Lucretius* 261
r thro' the court A long melodious thunder   *Princess ii* 475
Over the r waters go,   „ *iii* 5
Thy voice is heard thro' r drums,   „ *iv* 577
and r words Oration-like.   „ *v* 372
in the centre stood The common men with r eyes ;   „ *vi* 360
fishes turn'd And whiten'd all the r flood ;   *The Victim* 20
Ye watch, like God, the r hours   *In Mem. li* 14
And thunder-music, r, shake The prophet   „ *lxxxvii* 7
Let her great Danube r fair Enwind her isles,   „ *xcviii* 9
To darken on the r brine That breaks the coast.   „ *cvii* 14
Thy voice is on the r air ;   „ *cxxx* 1
And, star and system r past,   „ *Con.* 122
In drifts of smoke before a r wind,   *Com. of Arthur* 434
And mass, and r music, like a queen.   *Lancelot and E.* 1336
wrapt In unremorseful folds of r fire.   *Holy Grail* 261
Thro' the tall oriel on the r sea.   „ 831
light of heaven Burn'd at his lowest in the r year.   *Pass of Arthur* 91
And r far along the gloomy shores   „ 134
When the r eyes of the lighthouse there   *Despair* 9
or the r Thunder, or the rending earthquake,   *Faith* 3
sullen Lethe r doom On them and theirs   *Lit. Squabbles* 11
R on their purple couches   *Boädicea* 62
R her smoke about the Royal mount,   *Gareth and L.* 190
Southwesterns, r ridge on ridge,   „ 1145
Bound on a foray, r eyes of prey,   *Geraint and E.* 538
when they clash'd, R back upon Balin,   *Balin and Balan* 562
R his eyes, a moment stood,   *Pelleas and E.* 581
The moony vapour r round the King,   *Guinevere* 601
Funeral hearses r !   *Forlorn* 68
r of dragons By warble of water,   *Merlin and the G.* 44
R her anger Thro' blasted valley   *Kapiolani* 11

Roman (adj.) My Hercules, my R Antony.   *D. of F. Women* 150
The R soldier found Me lying dead,   „ 161
lying robed and crown'd, Worthy a R spouse.'   „ 164
and the R brows Of Agrippina   *Princess ii* 84
the Persian, Grecian, R lines Of empire,   „ 130
their foreheads drawn in R scowls,   „ *vii* 129
What R strength Turbia show'd In ruin,   *The Daisy* 5
Blacken round the R carrion,   *Boädicea* 14
horde of R robbers mock at a barbarous adversary.   „ 18
hive of R liars worship an emperor-idiot.   „ 19
Lo their precious R bantling,   „ 31
Shall we teach it a R lesson ?   „ 32
Tho' the R eagle shadow thee,   „ 39
Take the hoary R head and shatter it,   „ 65
Cut the R boy to pieces in his lust   „ 66
Ran the land with R slaughter.   „ 84
King Leodogran Groan'd for the R legions   *Com. of Arthur* 34
To drive the heathen from your R wall,   „ 512
for whose love the R Cæsar first Invaded Britain,   *Marr. of Geraint* 745

Root (*continued*)   whose *r* Creeps to the garden water-
    pipes beneath,   *D. of F. Women* 205
The fat earth feed thy branchy *r*,   *Talking Oak* 273
tho' my heart be at the *r*.   *Locksley Hall* 66
And scirrhous *r*'s and tendons.   *Amphion* 64
Soft fruitage, mighty nuts, and nourishing *r*'s ;   *Enoch Arden* 555
fixt As are the *r*'s of earth and base of all ;   *Princess v* 446
hold you here, *r* and all, in my hand,   *Flow. in cran. wall.* 3
What you are, *r* and all,   "   5
Thy *r*'s are wrapt about the bones.   *In Mem. ii* 4
By ashen *r*'s the violets blow.   "   *cxv* 4
for the *r*'s of my hair were stirr'd   *Maud I i* 13
Some *r* of knighthood and pure nobleness ;   *Holy Grail* 886
r's like some black coil of carven snakes,   *Last Tournament* 13
Adown a natural stair of tangled *r*'s,   *Lover's Tale i* 527
His winter chills him to the *r*,   *Ancient Sage* 119
Root-bitten   *R-b* by white lichen,   *Gareth and L.* 454
Rooted   (*See also* **Fast-rooted, Serpent-rooted**)   When *r*
    in the garden of the mind,   *Ode to Memory* 26
' I, *r* here among the groves   *Talking Oak* 181
night and day, and *r* in the fields,   *Com. of Arthur* 24
He *r* out the slothful officer Or guilty,   *Geraint and E.* 938
His honour *r* in dishonour stood,   *Lancelot and E.* 876
jungle *r* in his shatter'd hearth,   *Demeter and P.* 76
Rootless   evermore Seem'd catching at a *r* thorn,   *Geraint and E.* 378
Rope   With hand and *r* we haled the groaning sow,   *Walk. to the Mail* 91
I wore The *r* that haled the buckets   *St. S. Stylites* 64
And reach'd the ship and caught the *r*,   *Sailor Boy* 3
Torn as a sail that leaves the *r* is torn In tempest :   *Holy Grail* 212
Rosa (Monte)   how phantom-fair, Was Monte R,   *The Daisy* 66
Rosalind   bring me my love, *R*.   *Leonine Eleg.* 14
where is my sweet *R* ?   "   16
My *R*, my *R*, (repeat)   *Rosalind* 1, 5
bold and free As you, my falcon *R*.   "   18
Come down, come home, my *R*, My gay young hawk,
    my *R* :   "   33
bind And keep you fast, my *R*, Fast, fast, my wild-
    eyed *R*,   "   43
face again, My *R* in this Arden—   *Sisters (E. and E.)* 119
Rosamond   I am that *R*, whom men call fair,   *D. of F. Women* 251
Rosary (rose-garden)   Thick *rosaries* of scented thorn,   *Arabian Nights* 106
Rosary (string of beads)   amber, ancient *rosaries*,   *Princess, Pro.* 19
Rose (adj.)   the lights, *r*, amber, emerald, blue,   *Palace of Art* 169
Rose (Christian name)   Who had not heard Of *R*, the
    Gardener's daughter ?   *Gardener's D.* 52
but she, a *R* In roses,   "   142
R, on this terrace fifty years ago,   *Roses on the T.* 1
Two words ' My *R* ' set all your face aglow,   "   3
Rose (flower, colour)   (*See also* **Baby-rose, Garden-
rose**)   With plaited alleys of the trailing *r*,   *Ode to Memory* 106
And the year's last *r*.   *A spirit haunts* 20
Bramble *r*'s, faint and pale,   *A Dirge* 30
Some spirit of a crimson *r* In love with thee   *Adeline* 41
Wearing the *r* of womanhood.   *Two Voices* 417
Her cheek had lost the *r*,   *Œnone* 18
her hair Wound with white *r*'s, slept St. Cecily ;   *Palace of Art* 99
petals from blown *r*'s on the grass,   *Lotos-Eaters, C. S.* 2
up the porch there grew an Eastern *r*,   *Gardener's D.* 123
but she, a Rose In *r*'s,   "   143
' Ah, one *r*, One *r*, but one,   "   149
Nor yet refused the *r*, but granted it,   "   160
Kissing the *r* she gave me o'er and o'er,   "   176
then for *r*'s, moss or musk, To grace my city rooms ;   "   193
shut Within the bosom of the *r* ?   *Day-Dm., Moral* 8
With a single *r* in her hair.   *Lady Clare* 60
God made Himself an awful *r* of dawn, (repeat)   *Vision of Sin* 50, 224
The late and early *r*'s from his wall,   *Enoch Arden* 339
the red *r* was redder than itself,   *Aylmer's Field* 50
York's white *r* as red as Lancaster's,   "   51
Which fann'd the gardens of that rival *r*   "   455
Seem'd hope's returning *r* :   "   559
The wilderness shall blossom as the *r*.   "   649
Not ev'n a *r*, were offer'd to thee ?   *Lucretius* 69
In meshes of the jasmine and the *r* :   *Princess i* 219
as tho' there were One *r* in all the world,   "   *ii* 51

Rose (flower, colour) (*continued*)   And sated with the in-
    numerable *r*,   *Princess iii* 122
any *r* of Gulistan Shall burst her veil :   "   *iv* 122
Before me shower'd the *r* in flakes ;   "   264
there's no *r* that's half so dear to them   "   *v* 159
R's and lilies and Canterbury-bells.'   *City Child* 5
some rare little *r*, a piece of inmost Horticultural
    art,   *Hendecasyllabics* 19
R, *r* and clematis, (repeat)   *Window, At the Window* 3, 10
She takes a riband or a *r* ;   *In Mem. vi* 32
quick tears that make the *r* Pull sideways,   "   *lxxii* 10
May breathe, with many *r*'s sweet,   "   *xci* 10
and swung The heavy-folded *r*, and flung The lilies   "   *xcv* 59
And every thought breaks out a *r*.   "   *cxxii* 20
He too foretold the perfect *r*.   "   *Con.* 34
an hour's defect of the *r*,   *Maud I ii* 8
You have but fed on the *r*'s   "   *iv* 60
Maud has a garden of *r*'s   "   *xiv* 1
R's are her cheeks, And a *r* her mouth (repeat)   "   *xvii* 7, 27
' Ah, be Among the *r*'s to-night.'   "   *xxi* 13
And the musk of the *r* is blown.   "   *xxii* 13
All night have the *r*'s heard The flute,   "   13
I said to the *r*, ' The brief night goes In babble   "   27
But mine, but mine,' so I sware to the *r*,   "   31
the soul of the *r* went into my blood,   "   33
the *r* was awake all night for your sake,   "   49
The lilies and *r*'s were all awake,   "   51
Queen *r* of the rosebud garden of girls,   "   53
Queen lily and *r* in one ;   "   56
The red *r* cries ' She is near, she is near ; '   "   63
the white *r* weeps, ' She is late ; '   "   64
All made up of the lily and *r*   "   *II v* 74
I almost fear they are not *r*'s, but blood ;   "   78
O'er the four rivers the first *r*'s blew,   *Geraint and E.* 764
A walk of *r*'s ran from door to door ;   *Balin and Balan* 242
down that range of *r*'s the great Queen Came   "   244
' Sweeter to me ' she said ' this garden *r*   "   269
make her paler with a poison'd *r* ?   *Merlin and V.* 611
To crop his own sweet *r* before the hour ? '   "   725
Till the high dawn piercing the royal *r*   "   739
Redder than any *r*, a joy to me,   *Holy Grail* 521
' A worm within the *r*.'   *Pelleas and E.* 399
' A *r*, but one, none other *r* had I, A *r*, one *r*, and
    this was wondrous fair, One *r*, a *r* that
    gladden'd earth and sky, One *r*, my *r*, that
    sweeten'd all mine air—   "   400
' One *r*, a *r* to gather by and by, One *r*, a *r*, to gather
    and to wear, No *r* but one—what other *r* had I ?
    One *r*, my *r* ; a *r* that will not die,—   "   405
slope of garden, all Of *r*'s white and red,   "   422
and so spilt itself Among the *r*'s,   "   427
colour and the sweetness from the *r*,   *Lover's Tale i* 172
infuse Rich atar in the bosom of the *r*,   "   270
Leaning its *r*'s on my faded eyes.   "   621
made The red *r* there a pale one—   "   696
hair Studded with one rich Provence *r*—   "   *iii* 45
who himself was crown'd With *r*'s,   "   *iv* 297
my *r*, there my allegiance due.   *Sir J. Oldcastle* 59
the blush Of millions of *r*'s   *V. of Maeldune* 44
Rich was the *r* of sunset there,   *The Wreck* 136
Youth began Had set the lily and *r*   *Ancient Sage* 159
My *r* of love for ever gone,   "   161
They made her lily and *r* in one,   *Tomorrow* 31
Molly Magee, wid the red o' the *r*   "   "
Feed the budding *r* of boyhood   *Locksley H., Sixty* 143
FIFTY times the *r* has flower'd and faded,   *On Jub. Q. Victoria* 1
with her flying robe and her poison'd *r* ;   *Vastness* 16
Each poor pale cheek a momentary *r*—   *The Ring* 315
My *r*'s—will he take them *now*—   *Happy* 13
The *r*'s that you cast aside—   "   22
I brought you, you remember, these *r*'s,   "   73
you wave me off—poor *r*'s—must I go—   "   101
gather the *r*'s whenever they blow,   *Romney's R.* 107
close to me to-day As this red *r*,   *Roses on the R.* 7
Prophet of the *r*'s,   *The Snowdrop* 8

Rose (flower, colour) (continued)   Shall the r Cry to the
lotus ' No flower thou ' ?   *Akbar's Dream* 36
Rose (verb)   Some blue peaks in the distance r,   *Dying Swan* 11
Heaven over Heaven r the night,   *Mariana in the S.* 92
At last you r and moved the light,   *Miller's D.* 125
And r, and, with a silent grace Approaching,   „   159
R slowly to a music slowly breathed,   *Œnone* 41
R feud, with question unto whom 'twere due :   „   82
I r up in the silent night :   *The Sisters* 25
Of ledge or shelf The rock r clear,   *Palace of Art* 10
that sweet incense r and never fail'd,   „   45
Here r, an athlete, strong to break or bind   „   153
How sadly, I remember, r the morning of
the year !   *May Queen, Con.* 3
this star R with you thro' a little arc   *To J. S.* 26
so that he r With sacrifice,   *On a Mourner* 33
arm R up from out the bosom of the lake,   *M. d'Arthur* 30
Then quickly r Sir Bedivere, and ran,   „   133
r an arm Clothed in white samite, mystic,   „   143
from the pavement he half r, Slowly,   „   167
from them r A cry that shiver'd to the tingling stars,   „   198
she, that r the tallest of them all And fairest,   „   207
And up we r, and on the spur we went.   *Gardener's D.* 32
but I r up Full of his bliss,   „   210
passion r thro' circumstantial grades   „   240
she r and took The child once more,   *Dora* 80
ere the night we r And saunter'd home   *Audley Court* 79
To some full music r and sank the sun,   *Edwin Morris* 34
I crouch'd on one that r Twenty by measure ;   *St. S. Stylites* 88
When his man-minded offset r To chase the deer   *Talking Oak* 51
flower, she touch'd on, dipt and r,   „   131
we two r, There—closing like an individual life—   *Love and Duty* 78
While Ilion like a mist r into towers.   *Tithonus* 63
There r a noise of striking clocks,   *Day-Dm., Revival* 2
R a ship of France.   *The Captain* 28
So fresh they r in shadow'd swells   *The Letters* 46
R again from where it seem'd to fail,   *Vision of Sin* 24
r and past Bearing a lifelong hunger   *Enoch Arden* 78
Enoch r, Cast his strong arms   „   227
She r, and fixt her swimming eyes upon him,   „   325
r And sent his voice beneath him thro' the wood.   „   443
r And paced Back toward his solitary home again,   „   793
He woke, he r, he spread his arms abroad   „   912
full willingly he r :   *The Brook* 121
R from the clay it work'd in as she past,   *Aylmer's Field* 170
Darkly that day r :   „   609
a full tide R with ground-swell,   *Sea Dreams* 51
a fire-balloon R gem-like up before   *Princess, Pro.* 75
I r and past Thro' the wild woods   „   *i* 90
Whereon a woman-statue r with wings   „   210
She r her height, and said :   „   *ii* 41
an officer R up, and read the statutes,   „   69
She r upon a wind of prophecy Dilating on the future ;   „   171
We r, and each by other drest with care   „   *iii* 19
Stirring a sudden transport r and fell.   „   *iv* 29
on a tripod in the midst A fragrant flame r,   „   34
There r a shriek as of a city sack'd ;   „   165
there r A hubbub in the court of half the maids   „   475
I beheld her, when she r The yesternight,   „   *v* 175
among them r a cry As if to greet the king ;   „   248
On his haunches r the steed,   „   493
Part roll'd on the earth and r again and drew :   „   497
R a nurse of ninety years,   „   *vi* 13
and a day R from the distance on her memory,   „   112
He r, and while each ear was prick'd   „   *vi* 280
nor seem'd it strange that soon He r up whole,   „   *vii* 65
from mine arms she r Glowing all over noble shame ;   „   159
I give you all The random scheme as wildly as it r :   „   *Con.* 2
Then r a little feud betwixt the two,   „   23
And yet to give the story as it r,   „   26
But that there r a shout :   „   36
a shout r again, and made The long line   „   96
Again their ravening eagle r   *Ode on Well.* 119
He r at dawn and, fired with hope,   *Sailor Boy* 1
While I r up against my doom,   *In Mem. cxxii* 2

Rose (verb) (continued) The love that r on stronger wings,   *In Mem. cxxviii* 1
when they r, knighted from kneeling,   *Com. of Arthur* 263
voices, slowly r and plunged Roaring,   „   381
And all at once all round him r in fire,   „   389
He r, and out of slumber calling two   *Gareth and L.* 178
That r between the forest and the field.   „   191
Lot and many another r and fought Against thee,   „   354
R, and high-arching overbrow'd the hearth.   „   408
He r and past ; then Kay, a man of mien   „   452
Sir Gareth call'd him from where he r,   „   645
r High that the highest-crested helm   „   672
Baron set Gareth beside her, but at once she r.   „   852
Fell, as if dead ; but quickly r and drew,   „   967
Death was cast to ground, and slowly r.   „   1403
But when a rumour r about the Queen,   *Marr. of Geraint* 24
But r at last, a single maiden with her,   „   160
from the mason's hand, a fortress r ;   „   244
r a cry That Edyrn's men were on them,   „   638
the maiden r, And left her maiden couch,   „   736
Then r Limours, and looking at his feet,   *Geraint and E.* 302
Anon she r, and stepping lightly,   „   373
And once again she r to look at it,   „   387
R when they saw the dead man rise,   „   732
Then Balin r, and Balan,   *Balin and Balan* 43
His arm half r to strike again, but fell :   „   223
Dishorsed himself, and r again, and fled Far,   „   330
He r, descended, met The scorner in the castle court,   „   386
And Balin r, ' Thither no more !   „   483
he r To leave the hall, and, Vivien following   *Merlin and V.* 31
r Fixt on her hearer's,   „   86
then I r and fled from Arthur's court   „   297
It was the time when first the question r   „   410
He r without a word and parted from her :   „   742
she dislik'd herself at once and r,   „   909
some light jest among them r With laughter   *Lancelot and E.* 178
r And drove him into wastes and solitudes   „   251
rathe she r, half-cheated in the thought   „   340
They r, heard mass, broke fast, and rode away :   „   415
Then flash'd into wild tears, and r again,   „   613
Then r Elaine and glided thro' the fields,   „   843
full meekly r the maid, Stript off the case,   „   978
Then r the dumb old servitor,   „   1153
and r And pointed to the damsel,   „   1262
and she r Opening her arms to meet me,   *Holy Grail* 394
' There r a hill that none but man could climb,   „   489
so that I r and fled, But wail'd and wept,   „   608
when he saw me, r, and bad me hail,   „   725
two great beasts r upright like a man,   „   821
nor that One Who r again :   „   919
Pelleas r, And loosed his horse,   *Pelleas and E.* 60
but r With morning every day,   „   214
they r up, and bound, and brought him in.   „   288
Arthur r and Lancelot follow'd him,   *Last Tournament* 112
She r, and set before him all he will'd ;   „   723
Behind him r a shadow and a shriek—   „   753
aghast the maiden r, White as her veil,   *Guinevere* 362
Then r the King and moved his host by night,   *Pass. of Arthur* 79
and with that wind the tide R,   „   126
an arm R up from out the bosom of the lake,   „   198
Then quickly r Sir Bedivere, and ran,   „   301
r an arm Clothed in white samite, mystic,   „   311
from the pavement he half r, Slowly,   „   335
from them r A cry that shiver'd to the tingling stars,   „   366
she, that r the tallest of them all And fairest,   „   375
the new sun r bringing the new year.   „   469
Whence r as it were breath and steam of gold,   *Lover's Tale i* 402
The fancy stirr'd him so He r and went,   „   *iv* 52
While all the guests in mute amazement r—   „   305
then r up, and with him all his guests   „   359
he r upon their decks, and he cried ;   *The Revenge* 100
she r and fled Beneath a pitiless rush   *Sisters (E. and E.)* 236
Then r the howl of all the cassock'd wolves,   *Sir J. Oldcastle* 158
Who r and doom'd me to the fire.   „   172
Whom once he r from off his throne to greet   *Columbus* 5
then the great ' Laudamus ' r to heaven.   „   18

Rose (verb) (*continued*) each man, as he *r* from his rest,   *V. of Maeldune* 85
THEY *r* to where their sovran eagle sails,   *Montenegro* 1
Then *r* Achilles dear to Zeus ;   *Achilles over the T.* 2
I *r* Following a torrent till its myriad falls   *Tiresias* 36
he *r* as it were on the wings of an eagle   *The Wreck* 69
project after project *r*, and all of them were vain ;   *The Flight* 14
Celtic Demos *r* a Demon,   *Locksley H., Sixty* 90
Step by step we *r* to greatness,—   " 130
truckled and cower'd When he *r* in his wrath,   *Dead Prophet* 63
And dying *r*, and rear'd her arms,   *The Ring* 222
then she *r*, She clung to me with such a hard embrace,   " 434
From under *r* a muffled moan of floods ;   *Prog. of Spring* 70
crooked, reeling, livid, thro' the mist *R*,   *Death of Œnone* 28
She *r* and slowly down,   " 84
Rose-blowing Creeping thro' blossomy rushes and bowers of *r-b* bushes,   *Leonine Eleg.* 3
Rosebud (adj.) Queen rose of the *r* garden of girls,   *Maud I xxii* 53
Rosebud (s) Where on the double *r* droops   *Day-Dm., L'Envoi* 47
A *r* set with little wilful thorns,   *Princess, Pro.* 154
Rose-bush And a *r-b* leans upon,   *Adeline* 14
to train the *r* that I set About the parlour-window   *May Queen, N. Y's. E.* 47
Rose-campion *R-c*, bluebell, kingcup,   *Last Tournament* 234
Rose-carnation And many a *r-c* feed   *In Mem. ci* 7
Rosed darken'd in the west, And *r* in the east :   *Sea Dreams* 40
her white neck Was *r* with indignation :   *Princess vi* 344
Rose-garden For I know her own *r-g*,   *Maud I xx* 41
Rose-hued Flowing beneath her *r-h* zone ;   *Arabian Nights* 140
Rose-leaf Letting the *rose-leaves* fall :   *Claribel* 3
Like a *r-l* I will crush thee,   *Lilian* 29
Rose-lips Thy *r-l* and full blue eyes   *Adeline* 7
Rosemary the boar hath *rosemaries* and bay.   *Gareth and L.* 1074
Rose of Lancaster (*See also* **Lancaster, Roses**) *R o L*, Red in thy birth,   *Sir J. Oldcastle* 52
Redder to be, red *r o L*—   " 55
Rose-petal dust of the *r-p* belongs to the heart   *Akbar's D., Inscrip.* 9
Rose-red (adj.) soon From thy *r-r* lips MY name Floweth ;   *Eleänore* 133
down the long beam stole the Holy Grail, *R-r* with beatings in it,   *Holy Grail* 118
from the star there shot A *r-r* sparkle to the city,   " 530
Rose-red (s) beyond a bridge of treble bow, All in a *r-r* from the west,   *Gareth and L.* 1087
Roses (Wars of the Roses) civil wars and earlier too Among the *R*,   *Sisters (E. and E.)* 76
Rosetree One look'd all *r*, and another wore   *Aylmer's Field* 157
O *r* planted in my grief,   *Ancient Sage* 163
Rosewood ' She left the novel half-uncut Upon the *r* shelf ;   *Talking Oak* 118
Rosier but *r* luck will go With these rich jewels,   *Last Tournament* 45
taller indeed, *R* and comelier, thou—   " 710
Rosiest And all of them redder than *r* health   *V. of Maeldune* 65
Rosin And, sweating *r*, plump'd the pine   *Amphion* 47
Rosy Who lets his *r* fingers play About his mother's neck,   *Supp. Confessions* 42
kiss away the bitter words From off your *r* mouth.   *Rosalind* 51
When Sleep had bound her in his *r* band,   *Caress'd or chidden* 6
Thro' *r* taper fingers drew Her streaming curls   *Mariana in the S.* 15
Winds all the vale in *r* folds,   *Miller's D.* 242
With *r* slender fingers backward drew   *Œnone* 176
Ganymede, his *r* thigh Half-buried in the Eagle's down,   *Palace of Art* 121
Dark faces pale against that *r* flame,   *Lotos-Eaters* 26
' Then flush'd her cheek with *r* light,   *Talking Oak* 165
Coldly thy *r* shadows bathe me,   *Tithonus* 66
As I have seen the *r* red flushing in the northern night.   *Locksley Hall* 26
And, rapt thro' many a *r* change,   *Day-Dm., Depart.* 23
But when the dawn of *r* childhood past,   *Enoch Arden* 37
came a boy to be The *r* idol of her solitudes,   " 90
Philip's *r* face contracting grew Careworn and wan ;   " 486
Stout, *r*, with his babe across his knees,   " 746
This had a *r* sea of gillyflowers About it ;   *Aylmer's Field* 159
And *r* knees and supple roundedness,   *Lucretius* 190
And robed the shoulders in a *r* silk,   *Princess, Pro.* 103
A *r* blonde, and in a college gown,   " *ii* 323

Rosy (*continuea*) all The *r* heights came out above the lawns.   *Princess iii* 365
Or *r* blossom in hot ravine,   *The Daisy* 32
Green-rushing from the *r* thrones of dawn ! (repeat)   *Voice and the P.* 4, 40
A *r* warmth from marge to marge.   *In Mem. xlvi* 16
When *r* plumelets tuft the larch,   " *xci* 1
And left the daisies *r*.   *Maud I xii* 24
R is the West, *R* is the South, (repeat)   " *xvii* 5, 25
three fair girls In gilt and *r* raiment came :   *Gareth and L.* 927
His arms, the *r* raiment, and the star.   " 938
How from the *r* lips of life and love,   *Merlin and V.* 846
With *r* colours leaping on the wall ;   *Holy Grail* 120
The *r* quiverings died into the night.   " 123
her bloom A *r* dawn kindled in stainless heavens,   *Pelleas and E.* 72
Glanced from the *r* forehead of the dawn   " 502
himself was crown'd With roses, none so *r* as himself—   *Lover's Tale iv* 297
Or on your head their *r* feet,   *To E. Fitzgerald* 9
the moon was falling greenish thro' a *r* glow,   *Locksley H., Sixty* 178
made The *r* twilight of a perfect day.   *The Ring* 187
From off the *r* cheek of waking Day.   *Akbar's Dream* 202
Rosy-bright There all in spaces *r-b*   *Mariana in the S.* 89
Rosy-kindled *r-k* with her brother's kiss—   *Lancelot and E.* 393
Rosy-tinted In tufts of *r-t* snow ;   *Two Voices* 60
Rosy-white her light foot Shone *r-w*,   *Œnone* 180
Rot ' Why, if man *r* in dreamless ease,   *Two Voices* 280
Fall back upon a name ! rest, *r* in that !   *Aylmer's Field* 385
   " 200
Rotatory And *r* thumbs on silken knees,   *St. S. Stylites* 41
Rotted my thighs are *r* with the dew ;   "
There the smouldering fire of fever creeps across the *r* floor,   *Locksley H., Sixty* 223
Rotten (*See also* **Rain-rotten**) Till all be ripe and *r*.   *Will Water.* 16
When the *r* woodland drips,   *Vision of Sin* 81
To leap the *r* pales of prejudice,   *Princess ii* 142
when the *r* hustings shake In another month   *Maud I vi* 54
on whom all spears Are *r* sticks !   *Gareth and L.* 1306
r branch Snapt in the rushing of the river-rain   *Merlin and V.* 957
Yea, *r* with a hundred years of death,   *Holy Grail* 496
seeing too much wit Makes the world *r*,   *Last Tournament* 247
What *r* piles uphold their mason-work,   *Sir J. Oldcastle* 67
Better a *r* borough or so Than a *r* fleet   *Riflemen form !* 17
Rotting At the moist rich smell of the *r* leaves,   *A spirit haunts* 17
' At least, not *r* like a weed,   *Two Voices* 142
R on some wild shore with ribs of wreck,   *Princess v* 147
That *r* inward slowly moulders all.   *Merlin and V.* 395
Rough The filter'd tribute of the *r* woodland,   *Ode to Memory* 63
And from a heart as *r* as Esau's hand,   *Godiva* 28
Buss me, thou *r* sketch of man,   *Vision of Sin* 189
And Enoch Arden, a *r* sailor's lad   *Enoch Arden* 14
How many a *r* sea had he weather'd in her !   " 135
a *r* piece Of early rigid colour,   *Aylmer's Field* 280
befool'd and idioted By the *r* amity of the other,   " 591
Dropping the too *r* H in Hell and Heaven,   *Sea Dreams* 196
But your *r* voice (You spoke so loud)   " 280
That ever butted his *r* brother-brute   *Lucretius* 197
Discuss'd his tutor, *r* to common men,   *Princess, Pro.* 114
but ' No ! ' Roar'd the *r* king, ' you shall not ;   " *i* 87
tho' the *r* kex break The starr'd mosaic,   " *iv* 77
At length my Sire, his *r* cheek wet with tears,   " *v* 23
Among piled arms and *r* accoutrements,   " 55
These were the *r* ways of the world till now.   " *vii* 257
Not once or twice in our *r* island story,   *Ode on Well.* 201
Fabric *r*, or fairy-fine,   *Ode Inter. Exhib.* 18
And says he is *r* but kind,   *Maud I xix* 70
R but kind ? yet I know He has plotted against me   " 79
Well, *r* but kind ; why let it be so :   " 83
Is it kind to have made me a grave so *r*,   " *II v* 97
To guard thee on the *r* ways of the world.'   *Com. of Arthur* 336
Lest that *r* humour of the kings of old   *Gareth and L.* 377
' *R*, sudden, And pardonable, worthy to be knight—   " 653
nor *r* face, or voice, Brute bulk of limb,   " 1329
For old am I, and *r* the ways and wild ;   *Marr. of Geraint* 750
Then tending her *r* lord, tho' all unask'd,   *Geraint and E.* 405
In lieu of this *r* beast upon my shield,   *Balin and Balan* 196

Rough (*continued*) And one was *r* with wattling, — *Balin and Balan* 366
Meeker than any child to a *r* nurse, — *Lancelot and E.* 857
she knew right well What the *r* sickness meant, — „ 888
I pray you, use some *r* discourtesy — „ 973
Then the *r* Torre began to heave and move, — „ 1066
I might have put my wits to some *r* use, — „ 1306
r crowd, Hearing he had a difference with their priests, — *Holy Grail* 673
R wives, that laugh'd and scream'd against the gulls, — *Pelleas and E.* 89
Some *r* old knight who knew the worldly way, — „ 192
Her light feet fell on our *r* Lyonnesse, — *Last Tournament* 554
when first I rode from our *r* Lyonnesse, — „ 664
The *r* brier tore my bleeding palms ; — *Lover's Tale* ii 18
In a tone so *r* that I broke into passionate tears, — *The Wreck* 122
r rock-throne Of Freedom ! — *Montenegro* 9
Rougher Here is a story which in *r* shape — *Aylmer's Field* 7
women sang Between the *r* voices of the men, — *Princess, Pro.* 245
the *r* hand Is safer : — „ vi 278
whenever a *r* gust might tumble a stormier wave, — *The Wreck* 131
Roughest A cloth of *r* web, and cast it down, — *Gareth and L.* 683
Rough-redden'd *R-r* with a thousand winter gales, — *Enoch Arden* 95
Rough-ruddy And *r-r* faces Of lowly labour, — *Merlin and the G.* 59
Rough-thicketed *R-t* were the banks and steep ; — *Gareth and L.* 907
Round (adj.) And o'er it many, *r* and small, — *Mariana* 39
We knew the merry world was *r*, — *The Voyage* 7
We know the merry world is *r*, — „ 95
For so the whole *r* earth is every way — *M. d'Arthur* 254
A body slight and *r*, and like a pear — *Walk. to the Mail* 53
Her *r* white shoulder shaken with her sobs, — *Princess* iv 289
For so the whole *r* earth is every way — *Pass. of Arthur* 422
R was their pace at first, but slacken'd soon : — *Geraint and E.* 33
Round (adv.) Shall make the winds blow *R* and *r*, — *Nothing will Die* 24
flashing *r* and *r*, and whirl'd in an arch, — *M. d'Arthur* 138
I'd clasp it *r* so close and tight. — *Miller's D.* 180
And ' while the world runs *r* and *r*,' — *Palace of Art* 13
r and *r* A whirlwind caught and bore us ; — *Lover's Tale* ii 196
Hands all *r* ! (repeat) — *Hands all Round* 9, 21, 33
great name of England, *r* and *r*. (repeat) — „ 12, 36
And all her glorious empire, *r* and *r*. — „ 24
An' the dogs was a-yowlin' all *r*, — *Owd Roä* 107
flashing *r* and *r*, and whirl'd in an arch, — *Pass. of Arthur* 306
Round (prep.) once had roll'd you *r* and *r* the Sun, — *Poets and their B.* 10
Round (s) runs the *r* of life from hour to hour. — *Circumstance* 9
Like the tender amber *r*, — *Margaret* 19
The dark *r* of the dripping wheel, — *Miller's D.* 102
in the *r* of Time Still father Truth ? — *Love and Duty* 4
To yonder argent *r* ; — *St. Agnes' Eve* 16
Comes out a perfect *r*. — *Will Water.* 68
This *r* of green, this orb of flame, — *In Mem.* xxxiv 5
Should move his *r's*, and fusing all — „ xlvii 2
slowly breathing bare The *r* of space, — „ lxxxvi 5
they roll Thro' such a *r* in heaven, — *Holy Grail* 686
Round (verb) Should slowly *r* his orb, — *Eleänore* 91
So *r's* he to a separate mind — *In Mem.* xlv 9
r A higher height, a deeper deep. — „ lxiii 11
Rounded (adj. and part.) clear canal Is *r* to as clear a lake. — *Arabian Nights* 46
Devolved his *r* periods. — *A Character* 18
Roll'd on each other, *r*, smooth'd, — *D. of F. Women* 51
Sweet faces, *r* arms, and bosoms prest To little harps of gold ; — *Sea-Fairies* 3
o'er her *r* form Between the shadows of the vine-bunches — *Œnone* 180
r, smooth'd, and brought Into the gulfs of sleep. — *D. of F. Women* 51
And moves not on the *r* curl. — *Day-Dm., Sleep. B.* 8
O'er ocean-mirrors *r* large, — *In Mem.* xii 9
vizoring up a red And cipher face of *r* foolishness, — *Gareth and L.* 1039
only the *r* moon Thro' the tall oriel on the rolling sea. — *Holy Grail* 830
Rounded (verb) slowly *r* to the east The one black shadow — *Mariana in the S.* 79
And *r* by the stillness of the beach — *Audley Court* 10
The men who met him *r* on their heels — *Pelleas and E.* 142
Roundedness rosy knees and supple *r*, — *Lucretius* 190
Roundel glorious *r* echoing in our ears, — *Merlin and V.* 426
Roundelay Twice or thrice his *r*, (repeat) — *The Owl* i 11, 12
Or carol some old *r*, — *Gareth and L.* 506

Roundelay (*continued*) To dance without a catch, a *r* To dance to.' — *Last Tournament* 250
Rounder softer all her shape And *r* seem'd : — *Princess* vii 137
The *r* cheek had brighten'd into bloom. — *The Ring* 351
Roundest making them An armlet for the *r* arm on earth, — *Lancelot and E.* 1183
Roundhead And far below the *R* rode, — *Talking Oak* 299
Rounding The level waste, the *r* gray. — *Mariana* 44
Round Table (*See also* **Table, Table Round**) But now the whole *R T* is dissolved — *M. d'Arthur* 234
'Have any of our *R T* held their vows ?' — *Pelleas and E.* 533
Have founded my *R T* in the North, — *Last Tournament* 78
The glory of our *R T* is no more.' (repeat) — „ 189, 212
But now the whole *R T* is dissolved — *Pass. of Arthur* 402
Rouse (s) Have a *r* before the morn : (repeat) — *Vision of Sin* 96, 120
Rouse (verb) From deep thought himself he *r's*, — *L. of Burleigh* 21
Roused has *r* the child again. — *Sea Dreams* 281
I am *r* by the wail of a child, — *The Wreck* 7
r a snake that hissing writhed away ; — *Death of Œnone* 88
Rout (s) a *r* of saucy boys Brake on us at our books, — *Princess* v 394
Down on a *r* of craven foresters. — *Gareth and L.* 841
And midmost of a *r* of roisterers, — *Geraint and E.* 274
With all his *r* of random followers, — „ 382
And blindly rush'd on all the *r* behind. — „ 466
whirling *r* Led by those two rush'd into dance, — *Lover's Tale* iii 54
Rout (verb) O sound to *r* the brood of cares, — *In Mem.* lxxxix 17
Rove How young Columbus seem'd to *r*, — *The Daisy* 17
R's from the living brother's face, — *In Mem.* xxxii 7
Let his eye *r* in following, — *Marr. of Geraint* 399
Their lot with ours to *r* the world about ; — *Pref. Son. 19th Cent.* 11
Wild woods in which we *r* no more, — *The Flight* 84
Roved While I *r* about the forest, — *Boädicea* 35
I *r* at random thro' the town, — *In Mem.* lxxxvii 3
Wild woods in which we *r* with him, — *The Flight* 83
Rover and thou hast been a *r* too, — *Last Tournament* 543
Roving When after *r* in the woods — *Miller's D.* 58
R the trackless realms of Lyonnesse, — *Lancelot and E.* 35
Row (s) The streams through many a lilied *r* — *The Winds, etc.* 5
round the cool green courts there ran a *r* Of cloisters, — *Palace of Art* 25
like white sea-birds in a *r*, — *V. of Maeldune* 101
Row (verb) taught me how to skate, to *r*, — *Edwin Morris* 19
he can steer and *r*, and he Will guide me — *Lancelot and E.* 1128
R us out from Desenzano, to your Sirmione *r* ! — *Frater ave, etc.* 1
Row'd and how I *r* across And took it, — *M. d'Arthur* 32
Arthur *r* across and took it— — *Com. of Arthur* 298
and how I *r* across And took it, — *Pass. of Arthur* 200
So they *r*, and there we landed— — *Frater ave, etc.* 2
Rowel He dash'd the *r* into his horse, — *Pelleas and E.* 486
Rowing 'Who, *r* hard against the stream, — *Two Voices* 211
Royal (adj.) (*See also* **Crown-royal**) Victoria,—since your *R* grace — *To the Queen* 5
With *r* frame-work of wrought gold ; — *Ode to Memory* 82
Died the shalott of *r* cheer ; — *L. of Shalott* iv 48
She to Paris made Proffer of *r* power, — *Œnone* 111
paintings of wise men I hung The *r* dais round. — *Palace of Art* 132
She threw her *r* robes away. — „ 290
' By holy rood, a *r* beard !' — *Day-Dm., Revival* 20
Cophetua sware a *r* oath : — *Beggar Maid* 15
From whence the *R* mind, familiar with her, — *Princess* iv 235
(our *r* word upon it, He comes back safe) — „ v 224
Last, Ida's answer, in a *r* hand, — „ 371
Till her people all around the *r* chariot agitated, — *Boädicea* 73
He set his *r* signet there ; — *In Mem.* cxxv 12
Break not, for thou art *R*, but endure, — *Ded. of Idylls* 45
For this an Eagle, a *r* Eagle, laid — *Gareth and L.* 44
Rolling her smoke about the *R* mount, — „ 190
r crown Sparkled, and swaying upon a restless elm — *Balin and Balan* 462
Hail, *r* knight, we break on thy sweet rest, — „ 470
Drove his mail'd heel athwart the *r* crown, — „ 540
Boldness and *r* knighthood of the bird — *Merlin and V.* 134
Till the high dawn piercing the *r* rose — „ 739
but meaning all at once To snare her *r* fancy — *Lancelot and E.* 71
Tho' quartering your own *r* arms of Spain, — *Columbus* 115
Shall the *r* voice be mute ? — *By an Evolution.* 14
Royal (s) O LOYAL to the *r* in thyself, — *To the Queen* ii 1

U

Rule (verb) (*continued*) 'A moral child without the craft to *r*, *Lancelot and E.* 146
as Arthur's Queen I move and *r* :   " 1221
Wed thou our Lady, and *r* over us,   *Holy Grail* 605
King must guard That which he *r's*,   " 906
he knows false, abide and *r* the house :   *Guinevere* 515
I should come again To *r* once more ;   *Pass. of Arthur* 192
The nameless Power, or Powers, that *r*   *Ancient Sage* 29
Night and Shadow *r* below   " 243
only those who cannot read can *r*.   *Locksley H., Sixty* 132
Or Might would *r* alone ;   *Epilogue* 29
thro' the Will of One who knows and *r's*—   *The Ring* 42
and *r* thy Providence of the brute.   *By an Evolution.* 16
For all they *r*—by equal law for all ?   *Akbar's Dream* 110
only let the hand that *r's*, With politic care,   " 127
Power That is not seen and *r's* from far away—   " 138
Ruled captain of my dreams *R* in the eastern sky.   *D. of F. Women* 264
grim Earl, who *r* In Coventry :   *Godiva* 12
Fairer his talk, a tongue that *r* the hour,   *Aylmer's Field* 194
A nation yet, the rulers and the *r*—   *Princess, Con.* 53
There they *r*, and thence they wasted   *Boädicea* 54
infant civilisation be *r* with rod or with knout ?   *Maud I iv* 47
many a petty king ere Arthur came *R* in this isle,   *Com. of Arthur* 6
listen to me, and by me be *r*,   *Geraint and E.* 624
He saw the laws that *r* the tournament   *Last Tournament* 160
if this earth be *r* by Perfect Love,   *D. of the Duke of C.* 8
Ruler *And leave us r's of your blood*   *To the Queen* 21
The deathless *r* of thy dying house   *Aylmer's Field* 661
A nation yet, the *r's* and the ruled—   *Princess, Con.* 53
The name was *r* of the dark—Isolt ?   *Last Tournament* 606
here the faith That made us *r's* ?   *To the Queen ii* 19
What *r's* but the Days and Hours   *Ancient Sage* 95
Unprophetic *r's* they—   *Open. I. and C. Exhib.* 26
Your rule has made the people love Their *r*.   *To Marq. of Dufferin* 7
Ruling And *r* by obeying Nature's powers,   *Ode Inter. Exhib.* 40
Dreams *r* when wit sleeps !   *Balin and Balan* 143
r that which knows To its own harm :   *To the Queen ii* 58
To one, that *r* has increased Her greatness   *To Marq. of Dufferin* 7
Rumble (*See also* **Rummle**) Clamour and *r*, and ringing and clatter,   *Maud II v* 13
Rumbled And round the attics *r*,   *The Goose* 46
Rumbling *See* **Roomlin'**
Rummage from what side The blindfold *r*   *Balin and Balan* 416
Rummaged tapt at doors, And *r* like a rat :   *Walk. to the Mail* 38
Rummle (**rumble**) I eärd the bricks an' the baulks *r* down   *Owd Roä* 109
Rumour empty breath And *r's* of a doubt ?   *M. d'Arthur* 100
Wife-hunting, as the *r* ran, was he :   *Aylmer's Field* 212
down the wind With *r*,   " 496
With *r* of Prince Arac hard at hand.   *Princess v* 112
let the turbid streams of *r* flow   *Ode on Well.* 181
months ran on and *r* of battle grew,   *Maud III vi* 29
Sir, there be many *r's* on this head :   *Com. of Arthur* 178
But when a *r* rose about the Queen,   *Marr. of Geraint* 24
Vext at a *r* issued from herself   *Merlin and V.* 153
A *r* runs, she took him for the King,   " 776
Hid from the wide world's *r* by the grove   *Lancelot and E.* 522
I hear of *r's* flying thro' your court.   " 1190
let *r's* be : When did not *r's* fly ?   " 1193
This night, a *r* wildly blown about Came,   *Guinevere* 153
Less noble, being, as all *r* runs,   " 339
but empty breath And *r's* of a doubt ?   *Pass. of Arthur* 268
somewhere in the North, as *R* sang   *Sir J. Oldcastle* 56
Run (s) so quick the *r*, We felt the good ship   *The Voyage* 14
Lies the hawk's cast, the mole has made his *r*,   *Aylmer's Field* 849
Run (verb) *r* short pains Thro' his warm heart ;   *Supp. Confessions* 161
WHEN cats *r* home and light is come, '   *The Owl i* 1
trenched waters *r* from sky to sky ;   *Ode to Memory* 104
R's up the ridged sea.   *Sea-Fairies* 39
And then the tears *r* down my cheek,   *Oriana* 69
So *r's* the round of life from hour to hour.   *Circumstance* 9
would *r* to and fro, and hide and seek,   *The Mermaid* 35
r thro' every change of sharp and flat,   *Caress'd or chidden* 4
And thro' the field the road *r's* by   *L. of Shalott i* 4
Thro' the wave that *r's* for ever By the island   " 12
'while the world *r's* round and round,'   *Palace of Art* 13
r before the fluttering tongues of fire ;   *D. of F. Women* 30

Run (verb) (*continued*) where the bay *r's* up its latest horn.   *Audley Court* 11
can *r* My faith beyond my practice into his :   *Edwin Morris* 53
The Sun will *r* his orbit,   *Love and Duty* 22
one increasing purpose *r's*,   *Locksley Hall* 137
they shall dive, and they shall *r*,   " 169
The vilest herb that *r's* to seed   *Amphion* 95
Against its fountain upward *r's*   *Will Water.* 35
To make my blood *r* quicker,   " 110
Where the bloody conduit *r's*,   *Vision of Sin* 144
he clamour'd from a casement, '*R*'   *The Brook* 85
'*R*, Katie !' Katie never ran :   " 87
R's in a river of blood to the sick sea.   *Aylmer's Field* 768
enter'd one Of those dark caves that *r* beneath the cliffs.   *Sea Dreams* 90
who this way *r's* Before the rest—   *Lucretius* 191
Feyther *r* oop to the farm, an' I *r's* oop to the mill ;   *N. Farmer, N. S.* 54
An' I'll *r* oop to the brig,   " 55
He that *r's* may read.   *The Flower* 18
Cataract brooks to the ocean *r*,   *The Islet* 17
'The stars,' she whispers, 'blindly *r* ;   *In Mem. iii* 5
Till all my widow'd race be *r* ;   " *ix* 18
Till all my widow'd race be *r*.   " *xvii* 20
So *r's* my dream : but what am I ?   " *liv* 17
R out your measured arcs,   " *cv* 27
For every grain of sand that *r's*,   " *cxvii* 9
I hear thee where the waters *r* ;   " *cxxx* 2
And letting a dangerous thought *r* wild   *Maud I xix* 52
long-lanced battle let their horses *r*.   *Com. of Arthur* 104
a river *R's* in three loops about her living-place ;   *Gareth and L.* 612
these be for the snare (So *r's* thy fancy)   " 1082
Shot from behind me, *r* along the ground ;   *Balin and Balan* 374
rumour *r's*, she took him for the King,   *Merlin and V.* 776
let his eyes *R* thro' the peopled gallery   *Lancelot and E.* 430
being snapt—We *r* more counter to the soul   *Last Tournament* 659
being, as all rumour *r's*, The most disloyal friend   *Guinevere* 339
flowers that *r* poison in their veins.   *Lover's Tale i* 347
the sight *r* over Upon his steely gyves ;   " *ii* 156
r's out when ya breäks the shell.   *Village Wife* 4
It is charged and we fire, and they *r*.   *Def. of Lucknow* 68
R's in the rut, a coward to the Priest.   *Sir J. Oldcastle* 78
make one people ere man's race be *r* :   *To Victor Hugo* 11
as I saw the white sail *r*, And darken,   *The Flight* 39
May we find, as ages *r*,   *Open I. and C. Exhib.* 11
but I knaws they *r's* upo' four,—   *Owd Roä* 17
' Ya mun *r* fur the lether.   " 77
Sa I *r's* to the yard fur a lether,   " 82
as this poor earth's pale history *r's*,—   *Vastness* 3
She comes ! The loosen'd rivulets *r* ;   *Prog. of Spring* 9
And I would that my race were *r*,   *The Dreamer* 8
Or ever your race be *r* !   " 30
Helter-skelter *r's* the age ;   *Poets and Critics* 2
Rung Loud, loud *r* out the bugle's brays,   *Oriana* 48
And as he rode his armour *r*,   *L. of Shalott iii* 17
The distant battle flash'd and *r*.   *Two Voices* 126
Not a bell was *r*, not a prayer was read ;   *Maud II v* 26
Runlet And *r's* babbling down the glen.   *Mariana in the S.* 44
Nor *r* tinkling from the rock ;   *In Mem. c* 13
Runn'd (ran) an' *r* plow thruff it an' all,   *N. Farmer, O. S.* 42
An' 'e niver *r* arter the fox,   *Village Wife* 41
An' sarvints *r* in an' out,   " 56
the poodle *r* at tha once, an' thou *r*   *Spinster's S's.* 38
an' the Freeä Traäde *r* 'i my 'ead,   *Owd Roä* 54
Haäfe o' the parish *r* oop   " 115
Runnel The babbling *r* crispeth,   *Claribel* 19
dashing in the spring Had liveried   *Lover's Tale ii* 49
fallen Prone by the dashing *r* on the grass.   " 101
Runnin' sthrames *r* down at the back o' the glin   *Tomorrow* 24
Running (*See also* **Runnin'**) Him *r* on thus hopefully she heard,   *Enoch Arden* 201
know his babes were *r* wild Like colts   " 304
While you were *r* down the sands,   *Sea Dreams* 265
Of *r* fires and fluid range Of lawless airs,   *Supp. Confessions* 147
Betwixt the green brink and the *r* foam,   *Sea-Fairies* 2
a stable wench Came *r* at the call,   *Princess i* 227
The second was my father's *r* thus :   " *iv* 406

Running (*continued*) fling Their pretty maids in the *r* flood,   *Princess v* 382
All *r* on one way to the home of my love,   *Window, On the Hill* 8
You are all *r* on, and I stand on the slope   " 9
R down to my own dark wood ;   *Maud I xiv* 30
for *r* sharply with thy spit Down on a rout   *Gareth and L.* 840
And *r* down the Soul, a Shape that fled   " 1207
R too vehemently to break upon it.   *Marr. of Geraint* 78
and by fountains *r* wine,   *Last Tournament* 141
perchance of streams *R* far on within its inmost halls,   *Lover's Tale i* 523
the mad little craft *R* on and on,   *The Revenge* 39
highway *r* by it leaves a breadth Of sward   *Sisters (E. and E.)* 80
r out below Thro' the fire   *V. of Maeldune* 42
neck Of land *r* out into rock—   *Despair* 10
dark little worlds *r* round them were worlds   " 18
r after a shadow of good ;   " 92
Runnymede Is this the manly strain of *R* ?   *Third of Feb.* 34
Rush (s) thro' blossomy *r'es* and bowers   *Leonine Eleg.* 3
the *r* of the air in the prone swing,   *Aylmer's Field* 86
the shrieking *r* of the wainscot mouse,   *Maud I vi* 71
Follow'd a *r* of eagle's wings,   *Last Tournament* 417
A flat malarian world of reed and *r* !   *Lover's Tale iv* 142
Beneath a pitiless *r* of Autumn rain   *Sisters (E. and E.)* 237
The *r* of the javelins,   *Batt. of Brunanburh* 88
R of Suns, and roll of systems,   *God and the Univ.* 3
Rush (verb) those, who clench their nerves to *r*   *Love and Duty* 77
To *r* abroad all round the little haven,   *Enoch Arden* 867
A thousand arms and *r'es* to the Sun.   *Princess vi* 37
R to the roof, sudden rocket,   *W. to Alexandra* 3
would *r* on a thousand lances and die—   *V. of Maeldune* 24
Rush'd And out spirits *r* together   *Locksley Hall* 38
We *r* into each other's arms.   *The Letters* 40
A wind arose and *r* upon the South,   *Princess i* 97
on a sudden *r* Among us, out of breath,   " *iv* 374
I am his dearest ! ' *r* on the knife,   *The Victim* 72
And blindly *r* on all the rout behind.   *Geraint and E.* 466
thro' the tree *R* ever a rainy wind,   *Last Tournament* 16
R into dance, and like wild Bacchanals   *Lover's Tale iii* 25
whirling rout Led by those two *r* into dance,   " 55
Poor Julian—how he *r* away ;   " *iv* 2
R each at each with a cry,   " 373
Rushing (*See also* **Green-rushing, Upward-rushing**) The
    shadow *r* up the sea,   *Rosalind* 11
Like some broad river *r* down alone,   *Mine be the strength* 2
The milldam *r* down with noise,   *Miller's D.* 50
whisper of the south-wind *r* warm,   *Locksley Hall* 125
Far purelier in his *r's* to and fro,   *Aylmer's Field* 458
My lady's Indian kinsman *r* in,   " 593
A *r* tempest of the wrath of God   " 757
for thrice I heard the rain *R* ;   *Lucretius* 27
r battle-bolt sang from the three-decker   *Maud I i* 50
we rode Thro' the dim land against a *r* wind,   *Merlin and V.* 425
rotten branch Snapt in the *r* of the river-rain   " 957
Lancelot, who *r* outward lionlike Leapt on him,   *Guinevere* 107
Blaze by the *r* brook or silent well.   " 400
the storm *r* over the down,   *Rizpah* 6
I am flung from the *r* tide of the world   *The Wreck* 6
hellish heat of a wretched life *r* back thro' the veins ?   *Despair* 68
Rushy Or dimple in the dark of *r* coves,   *Ode to Memory* 60
Russet She clad herself in a *r* gown,   *Lady Clare* 57
An old storm-beaten, *r*, many-stain'd Pavilion,   *Gareth and L.* 1113
Broad-faced with under-fringe of *r* beard,   *Geraint and E.* 537
And took his *r* beard between his teeth ;   " 713
Russet-bearded The *r-b* head roll'd on the floor.   " 729
Russia *R* bursts our Indian barrier,   *Locksley H., Sixty* 115
Russian (adj.) And welcome *R* flower, a people's pride,   *W. to Marie Alex.* 6
the points of the *R* lances arose in the sky ;   *Heavy Brigade* 5
In the heart of the *R* hordes,   " 50
Russian (s) Cossack and *R* Reel'd   *Light Brigade* 34
thousands of *R's*, Thousands of horsemen,   *Heavy Brigade* 2
Rust (s) fearing *r* or soilure fashion'd for it   *Lancelot and E.* 7
That keeps the *r* of murder on the walls—   *Guinevere* 74
Rust (verb) lest we *r* in ease.   *Love thou thy land* 42
To *r* unburnish'd, not to shine in use !   *Ulysses* 23
the cannon-bullet *r* on a slothful shore,   *Maud III vi* 26
Rusted (adj.) The *r* nails fell from the knots   *Mariana* 3

Rusted (adj.) (*continued*) Yniol's *r* arms Were on his
    princely person,   *Marr. of Geraint* 543
Rusted (verb) when the bracken *r* on their crags,   *Edwin Morris* 100
Rustic Not by the well-known stream and *r* spire,   *The Brook* 188
that in the garden snared Picus and Faunus, *r* Gods ?   *Lucretius* 182
We dropt with evening on a *r* town   *Princess i* 170
a *r* tower Half-lost in belts of hop and breadths of wheat;   " *Con.* 44
The rich Virgilian *r* measure Of Lari Maxume,   *The Daisy* 75
Ye think the *r* cackle of your bourg   *Marr. of Geraint* 276
They take the *r* murmur of their bourg   " 419
sound and honest, *r* Squire,   *Locksley H., Sixty* 239
Rustiest drew The *r* iron of old fighters' hearts ;   *Merlin and V.* 574
Rusting Forgotten, *r* on his iron hills,   *Princess v* 146
Rustle (verb) Sweet-Gale *r* round the shelving keel ;   *Edwin Morris* 110
heard In the dead hush the papers that she held *R* :   *Princess iv* 391
A strange knee *r* thro' her secret reeds,   *Balin and Balan* 354
Rustle (s) Past, as a *r* or twitter in the wood   *Last Tournament* 365
Rustled each, in maiden plumes We *r* :   *Princess i* 203
Rustling *r* thro' The low and bloomed foliage,   *Arabian Nights* 12
And *r* once at night about the place,   *Aylmer's Field* 547
Rusty Anchors of *r* fluke, and boats updrawn ;   *Enoch Arden* 18
Ah, let the *r* theme alone !   *Will Water.* 177
I think they should not wear our *r* gowns,   *Princess, Pro.* 143
I grate on *r* hinges here :   " *i* 86
but old And *r*, old and *r*, Prince Geraint,   *Marr. of Geraint* 478
Cries of the partridge like a *r* key   *Lover's Tale ii* 115
Rut same old *r* would deepen year by year ;   *Aylmer's Field* 34
Runs in the *r*, a coward to the Priest.   *Sir J. Oldcastle* 78
Ruth (proper name) Fairer than *R* among the fields of
    corn,   *Aylmer's Field* 680
Ruth methinks Some *r* is mine for thee.   *Gareth and L.* 895
r began to work Against his anger in him,   *Geraint and E.* 101
Geraint Had *r* again on Enid looking pale :   " 203
Then with another humorous *r* remark'd   " 250
Ruthless As *r* as a baby with a worm,   *Walk. to the Mail* 108
And gathering *r* gold—   *Columbus* 135
r Mussulman Who flings his bowstrung Harem in the
    sea,   *Romney's R.* 134
Rye Long fields of barley and of *r*,   *L. of Shalott i* 2

S

Saäilor (sailor) what *s's* a' seëan an' a' doon ;   *North. Cobbler* 4
Saäint's-daäy (Saints-day) *S-d*—they was ringing the
    bells.   *N. Farmer, N. S.* 13
Saäle (sale) fetch'd nigh to nowt at the *s*,   *Village Wife* 73
Saäme (lard) An' I niver puts *s* i' *my* butter,   " 119
Saätan (Satan) like *S* as fell Down out o' heaven   *North. Cobbler* 57
Saäve (save) wur it nobbut to *s* my life ;   " 84
I may *s* mysen yit.'   *Village Wife* 66
she beäld ' Ya mun *s* little Dick,   *Owd Roä* 81
Saävin' (saving) in *s* a son fur me.   " 96
Saäy (say) use to *s* the things that a do.   *N. Farmer, O. S.* 6
I thowt a 'ad summut to *s*,   " 19
I weänt *s* men be loiars,   " 27
—that's what I 'ears 'em *s*.   " *N. S.* 2
—that's what I 'ears 'im *s*—   " 59
Feyther 'ud *s* I wur ugly es sin,   *Spinster's S's.* 15
when they 'ev'n't a word to *s*.   " 102
Saäyin' (saying) an' wur niver sa nigh *s* Yis.   " 32
an' *s* ondecent things,   " 90
Sabæan Dripping with *S* spice   *Adeline* 53
Sabbath (adj.) ' Behold, it is the *S* morn.'   *Two Voices* 402
Sabbath (s) Half God's good *s*,   *To J. M. K.* 11
The *s's* of Eternity, One *s* deep and wide—   *St Agnes' Eve* 33
fixt the *S*. Darkly that day rose :   *Aylmer's Field* 609
woke, and went the next, The *S*,   *Sea Dreams* 19
On that loud *s* shook the spoiler   *Ode on Well.* 123
Sabbath-drawler art no *s-d* of old saws,   *To J. M. K.* 5
Sabine she That taught the *S* how to rule,   *Princess ii* 79
Sable Fantastic plume or *s* pine ;   *The Voyage* 44
    The towering car, the *s* steeds :   *Ode on Well.* 55

Sadder   She, as her carol *s* grew,   *Mariana in the S.* 13
Poor Fancy *s* than a single star,   *Caress'd or chidden* 13
s age begins To war against ill uses of a life,   *Gareth and L.* 1129
Saddle   Arac, roll'd himself Thrice in the *s*,   *Princess* v 275
I so shook him in the *s*, he said,   *Gareth and L.* 29
And lets me from the *s* ;'   *Lancelot and E.* 94
Then crush'd the *s* with his thighs,   *Pelleas and E.* 459
drew The foe from the *s* and threw   *Heavy Brigade* 54
Saddle-bow   A cavalier from off his *s-b*,   *D. of F. Women* 46
But when it glitter'd o'er the *s-b*,   *Gareth and L.* 1119
Saddle-leather   Thick-jewell'd shone the *s-l*,   *L. of Shalott* iii 20
Sadness   Can I but relive in *s* ?   *Locksley Hall* 107
memories roll upon him, Unspeakable for *s*.   *Enoch Arden* 725
But *s* on the soul of Ida fell,   *Princess* vii 29
Or *s* in the summer moons ?   *In Mem. lxxxiii* 8
s flings Her shadow on the blaze of kings :   *,, xcviii* 18
spake with such a *s* and so low We heard not   *Holy Grail* 42
Thou majestic in thy *s* at the doubtful doom   *To Virgil* 23
All her tale of *s*,   *Forlorn* 80
may there be no *s* of farewell,   *Crossing the Bar* 11
Saesneg   Vailing a sudden eyelid with his hard 'Dim *S*'
   passes,   *Sir J. Oldcastle* 21
Safe   giving *s* pledge of fruits,   *Ode to Memory* 18
S, damsel, as the centre of this hall.   *Gareth and L.* 604
The loneliest ways are *s* from shore to shore.   *Last Tournament* 103
So all the ways were *s* from shore to shore,   *,,* 485
(our royal word upon it, He comes back *s*)   *Princess* v 225
might be *s* our censures to withdraw ;   *Third of Feb.* 11
Safer   the rougher hand Is *s* :   *Princess* vi 279
Sagest   some were left of those Held *s*,   *,,* 382
Sagramore   What say ye then to sweet Sir *S*,   *Merlin and V.* 721
Sahib   At once the costly *S* yielded to her.   *Aylmer's Field* 233
Said   I *s* that 'all the years invent ;   *Two Voices* 73
when I have *s* goodnight for evermore,   *May Queen, N. Y's. E.* 41
I know not what was *s* ;   *Con.* 34
He thought that nothing new was *s*, or else Something
   so *s* 'twas nothing—   *The Epic* 30
Eustace painted her, And *s* to me,   *Gardener's D.* 21
And if I *s* that Fancy, led by Love,   *,,* 59
he *s* That he was wrong to cross his father   *Dora* 147
'Tis *s* he had a tuneful tongue,   *Amphion* 17
'Cruel, cruel the words I *s* !   *Edward Gray* 17
She told me all her friends had *s* ;   *The Letters* 25
I have ever *s* You chose the best among us—   *Enoch Arden* 292
' This miller's wife ' He *s* to Miriam   *,,* 805
life in him Could scarce be *s* to flourish,   *The Brook* 12
so like her ? so they *s* on board.   *,,* 223
and he meant, he *s* he meant,   *Sea Dreams* 178
For so, my mother *s*, the story ran.   *Princess* i 11
He *s* there was a compact ; that was true :   *,,* 47
I *s* no, Yet being an easy man,   *,,* 148
some *s* their heads were less :   *,, ii* 147
it shall be *s*, These women were too barbarous,   *,,* 297
much I might have *s*, but that my zone   *,,* 420
(For so they *s* themselves) inosculated ;   *,, iii* 89
I thought on all the wrathful king had *s*,   *,, v* 473
so it seem'd, or so they *s* to me,   *,, vi* 22
She *s* you had a heart—   *,,* 234
All people *s* she had authority—   *,,* 238
all, they *s*, as earnest as the close ?   *,, Con.* 21
left some record of the things we *s*.   *Third of Feb.* 18
for he seldom *s* me nay :   *Grandmother* 69
I thowt a *s* whot a owt to 'a *s*   *N. Farmer, O. S.* 20
thaw summun *s* it in 'aäste :   *,,* 27
The people *s*, a weed.   *The Flower* 4
Somebody *s* that she'd say no ; (repeat)   *Window, Letter 7,* 14
The lesser griefs that may be *s*,   *In Mem. xx* 1
And all he *s* of things divine,   *,, xxxvii* 3
To dying lips is all he *s*),   *,,* 20
Could I have *s* while he was here,   *,, lxxxi* 1
s The dawn, the dawn,' and died away ;   *,, xcv* 60
Whatever I have *s* or sung,   *,, cxxv* 1
And how she look'd, and what he *s*,   *,, Con.* 99
How strange was what she *s*,   *Maud I xix* 34
whether there were truth in anything *S* by these three,   *Com. of Arthur* 243

Said (*continued*)   For pastime ; yea, he *s* it : joust can I.   *Gareth and L.* 543
You *s* your say ; Mine answer was my deed.   *,,* 1174
She told him all that Earl Limours had *s*,   *Geraint and E.* 391
I have *s*. Not so—not all.   *Balin and Balan* 69
s a light came from her when she moved :   *Merlin and V.* 567
What *s* the happy sire ?   *,,* 710
we hear it *s* That men go down before your spear   *Lancelot and E.* 148
I *s* That if I went and if I fought and won it   *,,* 215
one *s* to the other, ' Lo ! What is he ?   *,,* 470
being weak in body *s* no more ;   *,,* 839
We heard not half of what he *s*.   *Holy Grail* 43
asking him, ' What *s* the King ?   *,,* 204
what *s* each, and what the King ?   *,,* 710
one most holy saint, who wept and *s*,   *,,* 781
Was I too dark a prophet when I *s*   *,,* 889
There she that seem'd the chief among them *s*,   *Pelleas and E.* 62
I know not what I would '—but *s* to her,   *Last Tournament* 498
went To-day for three days' hunting—as he *s*—   *,,* 530
But openly she spake and *s* to her,   *Guinevere* 226
So *s* my father, and himself was knight   *,,* 234
and he *s* That as he rode,   *,,* 236
So *s* my father—yea, and furthermore,   *,,* 250
S the good nuns would check her gadding tongue   *,,* 313
as he *s*, that once was loving hearts,   *Lover's Tale iv* 68
An' once I *s* to the Missis,   *North. Cobbler* 11
Miss Annie she *s* it wur draäins,   *Village Wife* 103
This tongue that wagg'd They *s*   *Sir J. Oldcastle* 15
and I heard a voice that *s*   *Tiresias* 48
' He *s* he would meet me tomorra !'   *Tomorrow* 80
ye *s* I wur pretty i' pinks,   *Spinster's S's.* 17
She *s*, that you and I Had been abroad   *The Ring* 100
He *s* it . . . in the play.   *Romney's R.* 150
Sa I warrants 'e niver *s* haafe wot 'e thowt,   *Church-warden, etc.* 18
She *s* with a sudden glow On her patient face   *Charity* 35
What *s* her Priesthood ?   *Kapiolani* 19
Said (Abû)   *See* Abû Saïd
Sail (*s*)   And the whirring *s* goes round, (repeat)   *The Owl* i 4
In the silken *s* of infancy,   *Arabian Nights* 2
come hither and furl your *s's*,   *Sea-Fairies* 16
Mariner, mariner, furl your *s's*,   *,,* 21
surf wind-scatter'd over *s's* and masts,   *D. of F. Women* 31
barge with oar and *s* Moved from the brink,   *M. d'Arthur* 265
' Fly, happy happy *s's*, and bear the Press ;   *Golden Year* 42
the vessel puffs her *s* :   *Ulysses* 44
argosies of magic *s's*,   *Locksley Hall* 121
Dry sang the tackle, sang the *s* :   *The Voyage* 10
And never *s* of ours was furl'd,   *,,* 81
whence were those that drove the *s*   *,,* 86
to the last dip of the vanishing *s*   *Enoch Arden* 245
waiting for a *s* : No *s* from day to day,   *,,* 590
scarlet shafts of sunrise—but no *s*.   *,,* 599
Crying with a loud voice ' A *s* ! a *s* !   *,,* 913
all the *s's* were darken'd in the west,   *Sea Dreams* 39
boat Tacks, and the slacken'd *s* flaps,   *Princess ii* 186
Silver *s's* all out of the west   *,, iii* 14
' Fresh as the first beam glittering on a *s*,   *,, iv* 44
trim our *s's*, and let old bygones be,   *,,* 69
the seas ; A red *s*, or a white ;   *,, Con.* 47
With a satin *s* of a ruby glow,   *The Islet* 13
And see the *s's* at distance rise,   *In Mem. xii* 11
glance about the approaching *s's*,   *,, xiii* 18
And milkier every milky *s*   *,, cxv* 11
far-off *s* is blown by the breeze   *Maud I iv* 4
And white *s's* flying on the yellow sea ;   *Marr. of Geraint* 829
one side had sea And ship and *s* and angels   *Balin and Balan* 365
She took the helm and he the *s* ;   *Merlin and V.* 200
Torn as a *s* that leaves the rope   *Holy Grail* 212
had he set the *s*, or had the boat Become   *,,* 518
the barge with oar and *s* Moved from the brink,   *Pass. of Arthur* 433
and half-way down rare *s's*,   *Lover's Tale i* 4
the *s* Will draw me to the rising of the sun,   *,,* 26
the ravin wind In her *s* roaring.   *,, ii* 171
Took the breath from our *s's*, and we stay'd.   *The Revenge* 42
Till it smote on their hulls and their *s's*   *,,* 116
look yonder,' he cried, ' a *s* '   *The Wreck* 121

Sail (s) (*continued*) as I saw the white s run, And darken,   *The Flight* 39
And sunshine on that s at last   ,, 92
Sail (verb) s with Arthur under looming shores,   *M. d'Arthur, Ep.* 17
purpose holds To s beyond the sunset,   *Ulysses* 60
On sleeping wings they s.   *Sir Galahad* 44
And we might s for evermore.   *The Voyage* 8
We seem'd s into the Sun !   ,, 16
And we may s for evermore.   ,, 96
Annie, the ship I s in passes here   *Enoch Arden* 214
Abiding with me till I s   *In Mem. cxxv* 13
All night the shining vapour s   ,, *Con.* 111
I have seen the good ship s Keel upward,   *Gareth and L.* 253
ready to s forth on one last voyage.   *Columbus* 237
THEY rose to where their sovran eagle s's,   *Montenegro* 1
and s to help them in the war ;   *Achilles over the T.* 13
We sail'd wherever ship could s,   *Hands all Round* 29
Sail'd (*See also* **Full-sail'd, Silken-sail'd**) SLOW s the
weary mariners and saw,   *Sea-Fairies* 1
throne of Indian Cama slowly s   *Palace of Art* 115
weeks before she s, S from this port.   *Enoch Arden* 124
prosperously The ship 'Good Fortune,'   ,, 527
in that harbour whence he s before.   ,, 666
s, Full-blown, before us into rooms   *Princess i* 228
And those fair hills I s below,   *In Mem. xcviii* 2
And he s away from Flores   *The Revenge* 23
away she s with her loss and long'd for her own ;   ,, 111
made West East, and s the Dragon's mouth,   *Columbus* 25
I s On my first voyage, harass'd by the frights   ,, 66
—we s on a Friday morn—   *V. of Maeldune* 7
we s away. (repeat)   ,, 26, 70, 114
and we s with our wounded away.   ,, 36
and in anger we s away.   ,, 54
and away we s, and we past Over that undersea isle,   ,, 76
we slew and we s away.   ,, 96
and hastily s away.   ,, 104
Saint who had s with St. Brendan of yore,   ,, 115
and sadly we s away.   ,, 126
he s the sea to crush the Moslem in his pride ;   *Locksley H., Sixty* 29
We s wherever ship could sail,   *Hands all Round* 29
Sailest S the placid ocean-plains   *In Mem. ix* 2
Sailing (*See also* **A-sailing**) S under palmy highlands
Far within the South.   *The Captain* 23
With here a blossom s,   *The Brook* 56
S along before a gloomy cloud   *Sea Dreams* 124
The s moon in creek and cove ;   *In Mem. ci* 16
S from Ireland.   *Last Tournament* 555
Sailor (adj.) O well for the s lad,   *Break, break, etc.* 7
In s fashion roughly sermonizing On providence   *Enoch Arden* 204
Gone our s son thy father, Leonard early lost at
sea ;   *Locksley H., Sixty* 55
Sailor (s) (*See also* **Saäilor**) S's bold and true.   *The Captain* 8
And Enoch Arden, a rough s's lad   *Enoch Arden* 14
and made himself Full s ;   ,, 54
A shipwreck'd s, waiting for a sail :   ,, 590
The greatest s since our world began.   *Ode on Well.* 86
praying God will save Thy s,—   *In Mem. vi* 14
I see the s at the wheel.   ,, *x* 4
Thou bring'st the s to his wife,   ,, 5
passive s wrecks at last In ever-silent seas ;   *Ancient Sage* 136
Desolate as that s, whom the storm Had parted   *The Ring* 307
Sailorless Desolate offing, s harbours,   *Vastness* 14
Sailor-soul and thou, Heroic s-s,   *Sir J. Franklin* 2
Saint (s) (*See also* **Francis of Assisi**) meed of s's, the
white robe and the palm.   *St. S. Stylites* 20
Who may be made a s, if I fail here ?   ,, 48
thou and all the s's Enjoy themselves   ,, 105
To Christ, the Virgin Mother, and the s's ;   ,, 112
The silly people take me for a s,   ,, 127
Are register'd and calendar'd for s's.   ,, 132
It may be, no one, even among the s's,   ,, 138
This is not told of any. They were s's.   ,, 151
Yea, crown'd a s. They shout, 'Behold a s !'   ,, 153
I am gather'd to the glorious s's.   ,, 197
Ah ! let me not be fool'd, sweet s's :   ,, 212
Than Papist unto S.   *Talking Oak* 16

Saint (s) (*continued*) statues, king or s, or founder fell ;   *Sea Dreams* 224
My mother was as mild as any s,   *Princess i* 22
Swear by S something—   ,, *v* 293
Like a S's glory up in heaven : but she No s—
inexorable—no tenderness—   ,, 514
your mother, now a s with s's.   ,, *vi* 233
arrived, by Dubric the high s,   *Com. of Arthur* 453
For by the hands of Dubric, the high s,   *Marr. of Geraint* 838
oft I talk'd with Dubric, the high s,   *Geraint and E.* 865
descended from the S Arimathæan Joseph ;   *Balin and Balan* 101
I saw That maiden S who stands with lily   ,, 261
scarce could spy the Christ for S's,   ,, 409
but all the maiden S's,   ,, 520
the good s Arimathæan Joseph, journeying   *Holy Grail* 50
larger, tho' the goal of all the s's—   ,, 528
I spake To one most holy s,   ,, 781
crying, 'Praise the patient s's,   *Last Tournament* 217
I thank the s's, I am not great.   *Guinevere* 199
Who wast, as is the conscience of a s   ,, 639
Who reads of begging s's in Scripture ? '   *Sir J. Oldcastle* 151
And we came to the Isle of a S   *V. of Maeldune* 115
Wid his blessed Marthyrs an' S's ; '   *Tomorrow* 58
an' S's an' Marthyrs galore,   ,, 95
I cried to the S's to avenge me.   *Bandit's Death* 14
But thanks to the Blessed S's   ,, 40
Saint (verb) lower voices s me from above.   *St. S. Stylites* 154
St. Brendan   *See* **Brendan**
St. Cecily   *See* **Cecily**
St. Francis of Assisi   *See* **Francis of Assisi**
St. Paul   *See* **Paul**
Saintdom grasp the hope I hold Of s,   *St. S. Stylites* 6
Saint-like women smile with s-l glances   *Supp. Confessions* 22
Saintly The s youth, the spotless lamb of Christ,   *Merlin and V.* 749
Therefore I communed with a s man,   *Holy Grail* 742
Saint's-day   *See* **Saäint's-daäy**
Saith s not Holy Writ the same ? '—   *Merlin and V.* 52
He, that s it, hath o'erstept   *Lover's Tale i* 101
Sake 'Yet must I love her for your s ;   *Miller's D.* 142
Nor would I break for your sweet s   *L. C. V. de Vere* 13
for his s I bred His daughter Dora :   *Dora* 19
for the s of him that's gone, (repeat)   *Dora* 62, 70, 94
for your s, the woman that he chose,   ,, 63
may be, for her own dear s but this,   *Edwin Morris* 141
pray them not to quarrel for her s,   *Enoch Arden* 35
for Annie's s, Fearing the lazy gossip   ,, 334
for God's s,' he answer'd, 'both our s's,   ,, 509
Katie, what I suffer'd for your s !   *The Brook* 119
How prettily for his own sweet s   *Maud I vi* 51
To be friends for her s, to be reconciled ;   ,, *xix* 50
And for your sweet s to yours ;   ,, 91
the rose was awake all night for your s,   ,, *xxii* 49
rather for the s of me, their King,   *Gareth and L.* 571
the deed's s my knighthood do the deed,   ,, 572
for the deed's s have I done the deed,   ,, 832
Balan answer'd ' For the s Of glory ;   *Balin and Balan* 32
And were it only for the giver's s,   *Lover's Tale iv* 364
freedom, or the s of those they loved,   *Sir J. Oldcastle* 186
I know Less for its own than for the s   *To E. Fitzgerald* 52
sorrow that I bear is sorrow for his s.   *The Flight* 64
will you sicken for her s ?   *Locksley H., Sixty* 17
God stay me there, if only for your s,   *Romney's R.* 34
for my s, According to my word ? '   ,, 129
Sal (*See also* **Sally**) black S, es 'ed been disgraäced ?   *Spinster's S's.* 25
Salamanca Were you at S ? No.   *Columbus* 40
Sale   *See* **Saäle**
Saleem heart is for my son, S, my heir,—   *Akbar's Dream* 171
on the sudden, and with a cry ' S '   ,, 184
Salient beneath Its s springs, and far apart,   *Supp. Confessions* 56
Do beating hearts of s springs Keep measure   *Adeline* 26
Salique fulmined out her scorn of laws S   *Princess ii* 133
Sallow (adj.) (*See also* **Wan-sallow**) With s scraps of
manuscript,   *To E. Fitzgerald* 48
Sallow (s) satin-shining palm On s's   *Merlin and V.* 225
Sallow-rifted the s-r glooms Of evening,   *Lancelot and E.* 1002
Sallow-skin Many a livid one, many a s-s—   *Batt. of Brunanburh* 106

Sallowy ran By *s* rims, arose the labourers' homes, *Aylmer's Field* 147
And many a glancing plash and *s* isle, *Last Tournament* 422
Sally (proper name) (*See also* **Sal**) to 's chooch afoor moy *S* wur deäd, *N. Farmer, O. S.* 17
Waäit till our *S* cooms in, *North. Cobbler* 1
That *S* she turn'd a tongue-banger, „ 23
S she wesh'd foäks' cloäths to keep the wolf fro' the door, „ 29
wheer *S*'s owd stockin' wur 'id, „ 31
an' I gied our *S* a kick, „ 36
I seeäd that our *S* went laämed Cos' o' the kick as I gied 'er, „ 39
An' *S* wur sloomy an' draggle „ 41
then I minded our *S* sa pratty an' neät an' sweeät, „ 43
' I mun gie tha a kiss,' an' *S* says ' Noä, thou moänt,' „ 51
gied 'er a kiss, an' then anoother, an' *S* says ' doänt ! ' „ 52
upo' coomin' awaäy *S* gied me a kiss ov 'ersen. „ 56
fur to kick our *S* as kep the wolf fro' the door, „ 59
an' *S* looökt up an' she said, ' I'll upowd it tha weänt „ 62
' That caps owt,' says *S*, an' saw she begins to cry, „ 71
' *S*,' says I, ' Stan' 'im theer i' the naäme o' the Lord „ 72
An' *S* she tell'd it about, an' foäk „ 81
an' if *S* be left aloän, „ 105
'Ere be my father, an' *S* an' Tommy, an' we be a-goin to dine, „ 111
weänt shed a drop on 'is blood, noä, not fur *S*'s oän kin. „ 114
Sally (a rush) I make a sudden *s*, *The Brook* 24
our *sallies*, their lying alarms, *Def. of Lucknow* 75
Sally (verb) the cave From which he *sallies*, *Balin and Balan* 132
all at once should *s* out upon me, *Geraint and E.* 149
Wroth that the King's command to *s* forth *Lancelot and E.* 560
Sallying *s* thro' the gate, Had beat her foes *Princess, Pro.* 33
s thro' the gates, and caught his hair, „ v 340
In blood-red armour, howl'd to the King, *Last Tournament* 443
Saloon Or, in a shadowy *s*, *Eleänore* 125
Salt (adj.) And in the middle of the green *s* sea *Mine be the strength* 7
A still *s* pool, lock'd in with bars of sand, *Palace of Art* 249
The *s* sea-water passes by, *In Mem. xix* 6
old dwarf-elm That turns its back on the *s* blast, *Pelleas and E.* 544
Salt (s) stony drought and steaming *s*; *Mariana in the S.* 40
Caught the shrill *s*, and sheer'd the gale. *The Voyage* 12
By shards and scurf of *s*, *Vision of Sin* 211
The city sparkles like a grain of *s*. *Will* 20
she has neither savour nor *s*, *Maud I ii* 2
pools of *s*, and plots of land— *Locksley H., Sixty* 207
Salute (s) Take my *s*,' unknightly with flat hand, *Geraint and E.* 717
Salute (verb) Many a merry face *S*'s them— *In Mem., Con.* 67
I *s* thee, Mantovano, *To Virgil* 37
Salvation and lost *S* for a sketch. *Romney's R.* 139
Salve Our Britain cannot a tyrant o'er. *Third of Feb.* 20
Salver fruitage golden-rinded On golden *s*'s, *Eleänore* 34
Chalice and *s*, wines that, Heaven knows when, *Lover's Tale iv* 193
Sam (*See also* **Sammy**) *S*, thou's an ass for thy paaïns: *N. Farmer, N. S.* 3
theer's a craw to pluck wi' tha, *S*: „ 5
Same (*See also* **Self-same**) In the *s* circle we revolve. *Two Voices* 314
Living together under the *s* roof, *To* ——, *With Pal. of Art* 12
and still The *s* old sore breaks out from age to age With much the *s* result. *Walk. to the Mail* 79
and that *s* song of his He told me; *Golden Year* 7
This *s* grand year is ever at the doors.' „ 74
A sleepy land, where under the *s* wheel The *s* old rut *Aylmer's Field* 33
thunders of the house Had fallen first, was Edith that *s* night; „ 279
Then she told it, having dream'd Of that *s* coast. *Sea Dreams* 207
So stood that *s* fair creature at the door. *Princess ii* 329
Would this *s* mock-love, and this Mock-Hymen „ iv 143
Than when two dewdrops on the petal shake To the *s* sweet air, „ vii 69
The *s* sweet forms in either mind. *In Mem. lxxix* 8
For us the *s* cold streamlet curl'd „ 9
and all about The *s* gray flats again, „ lxxxvii 13
and that *s* night, the night of the new year, *Com. of Arthur* 209
' And this *s* child,' he said, ' Is he who reigns; „ 392
Then that *s* day there past into the hall *Gareth and L.* 587
But that *s* strength which threw the Morning Star „ 1108
that *s* spear Wherewith the Roman pierced the side of Christ. *Balin and Balan* 113

Same (*continued*) ' What, wear ye still that *s* crown-scandalous ? ' *Balin and Balan* 390
for early that *s* day, Scaped thro' a cavern from a bandit hold, *Holy Grail* 206
stood beside thee even now, the *s*. *Balin and Balan* 613
and felt The *s*, but not the *s*; *In Mem. lxxvii* 14
saith not Holy Writ the *s* ? '— *Merlin and V.* 52
Sameness With weary *s* in the rhymes, *Miller's D.* 70
Samian whene'er she moves The *S* Herè rises *Princess iii* 115
Samite Clothed in white *s*, mystic, wonderful, (repeat) *M. d'Arthur* 31, 144, 159
Clothed in white *s*, mystic, wonderful. *Com. of Arthur* 285
a robe Of *s* without price, *Merlin and V.* 222
King, who sat Robed in red *s*, *Lancelot and E.* 433
Pall'd all its length in blackest *s*, „ 1142
Clothed in white *s* or a luminous cloud. *Holy Grail* 513
All pall'd in crimson *s*, „ 847
hung with folds of pure White *s*, *Last Tournament* 141
Clothed in white *s*, mystic, wonderful, (repeat) *Pass. of Arthur* 199, 312, 327
Sammy (*See also* **Sam**) Me an' thy muther, *S*, 'as beän a-talkin *N. Farmer, N. S.* 9
fur, *S*, 'e married fur luvv. „ 32
an', *S*, I'm blest If it isn't the saäme oop yonder, „ 43
Taäke my word for it, *S*, „ 48
Thim's my noätions, *S*, wheerby I means to stick; „ 57
Sanctimonious as a rogue in grain Veneer'd with *s* theory. *Princess, Pro.* 117
Sanction dare not ev'n by silence *s* lies. *Third of Feb.* 10
Sanction'd *See* **Mitre-sanction'd**
Sanctities And darken'd *s* with song.' *In Mem. xxxvii* 24
Sanctuary crowds in column'd *sanctuaries*; *D. of F. Women* 22
behold our *s* Is violate, our laws broken: *Princess vi* 59
So was their *s* violated, „ vii 16
For I will draw me into *s*, *Guinevere* 121
yield me *s*, nor ask Her name to whom ye yield it, „ 141
S granted To bandit, thief, assassin— *Sir J. Oldcastle* 112
Sand purl o'er matted cress and ribbed *s*, *Ode to Memory* 59
rainbow lives in the curve of the *s*; *Sea-Fairies* 27
the brine against the Coptic *s*'s. *Buonaparte* 8
In glaring *s* and inlets bright. *Mariana in the S.* 8
to where the sky Dipt down to sea and *s*'s. *Palace of Art* 32
seem'd all dark and red—a tract of *s*, „ 65
salt pool, lock'd in with bars of *s*, „ 249
sat them down upon the yellow *s*, *Lotos-Eaters* 37
roaring deeps and fiery *s*'s, „ C. S. 115
foam-flakes scud along the level *s*, *D. of F. Women* 39
Should fill and choke with golden *s*— *You ask me, why, etc.* 24
I might as well have traced it in the *s*'s; *Audley Court* 50
ran itself in golden *s*'s. *Locksley Hall* 32
By *s*'s and steaming flats, and floods *The Voyage* 45
in the chasm are foam and yellow *s*'s; *Enoch Arden* 2
built their castles of dissolving *s* „ 19
All *s* and cliff and deep-inrunning cave, *Sea Dreams* 17
now on *s* they walk'd, and now on cliff, „ 37
While you were running down the *s*'s, „ 265
May only make that footprint upon *s* *Princess iii* 239
Tall as a figure lengthen'd on the *s* „ vi 161
suck the blinding splendour from the *s*, „ vii 39
Tumbles a billow on chalk and *s*; *To F. D. Maurice* 24
Toiling in immeasureable *s*, *Will* 16
' The *s*'s and yeasty surges mix In caves *Sailor Boy* 9
For every grain of *s* that runs, *In Mem. cxvii* 9
Low on the *s* and loud on the stone *Maud I xxii* 25
a tap Of my finger-nail on the *s*, „ II ii 22
scratch a ragged oval on the *s*, *Gareth and L.* 534
Come slipping o'er their shadows on the *s*, *Geraint and E.* 471
the *s* danced at the bottom of it. *Balin and Balan* 27
touching Breton *s*'s, they disembark'd. *Merlin and V* 202
Glass'd in the slippery *s* before it breaks ? „ 293
in a land of *s* and thorns, (repeat) *Holy Grail* 376, 390
wearying in a land of *s* and thorns. „ 420
and all the *s* Swept like a river, „ 799
Far over *s*'s marbled with moon and cloud, *Last Tournament* 466
They found a naked child upon the *s*'s *Guinevere* 293
mountains ended in a coast Of ever-shifting *s*, *Pass. of Arthur* 86

Sand (*continued*) On the waste *s* by the waste sea they
   closed. | *Pass of Arthur* 92
A deathwhite mist slept over *s* and sea: | " 95
these deserted *s*'s of barren life. | *Lover's Tale i* 93
heats of the blinding noons Beat from the concave *s*; | " 140
leaves Low banks of yellow *s*; | " 535
upon the *s*'s Insensibly I drew her name, | " *ii* 6
shrieks and ringing laughter on the *s* | " *iii* 32
melon lay like a little sun on the tawny *s*, | *V. of Maeldune* 57
and pranced on the wrecks in the *s* below, | " 102
that bay with the colour'd *s*— | *The Wreck* 135
in the chapel there looking over the *s*? | *Despair* 1
'Lightly step over the *s*'s! | " 47
his boat was on the *s*; | *The Flight* 37
chains of mountains, grains of *s* | *Locksley H., Sixty* 208
airs from where the deep, All down the *s*, | *Early Spring* 22
dash'd half dead on barren *s*'s, | *The Ring* 309
I know not, your Arabian *s*'s; | *To Ulysses* 35
Are blinding desert *s*; | *Akbar's Dream* 30
Sandal (shoe) he roll'd And paw'd about her *s*. | *Princess iii* 182
Sandal (wood) toys in lava, fans Of *s*, | " *Pro.* 19
Sandal'd *See* Silken-sandal'd
Sandbank some dismal *s* far at sea, | *Lover's Tale i* 809
Sand-built a *s-b* ridge Of heaped hills | *Ode to Memory* 97
Sand-erased disgraced For ever—thee (thy pathway *s-e*) | *Alexander* 5
Sandhill In this gap between the *s*'s, | *Locksley H., Sixty* 176
Sand-shore the waste *s-s*'s of Trath Treroit, | *Lancelot and E.* 301
Sandy Locksley Hall, that in the distance overlooks the
   s tracts, | *Locksley Hall* 5
I make the netted sunbeam dance Against my *s* shallows. | *The Brook* 177
and watch The *s* footprint harden into stone.' | *Princess iii* 270
on *s* beaches A milky-bell'd amaryllis blew. | *The Daisy* 15
Unloved, by many a *s* bar, | *In Mem. ci* 9
half the morning have I paced these *s* tracts, | *Locksley H., Sixty* 1
Sane I woke *s*, but well-nigh close to death | *Princess vii* 119
O great and *s* and simple race of brutes | *Pelleas and E.* 480
Till crowds at length be *s* | *Ode on Well.* 169
but *s*, if she were in the right. | *The Flight* 58
Saner Of *s* worship sanely proud; | *Freedom* 30
A simpler, *s* lesson might he learn | *Prog. of Spring* 105
Sanest valorous, *S* and most obedient; | *Geraint and E.* 911
Sang (*See also* Sing'd) *S* looking thro' his prison bars? | *Margaret* 35
'Tirra lirra,' by the river *S* Sir Lancelot. | *L. of Shalott iii* 36
'Ah,' she *s*, 'to be all alone, (repeat) | *Mariana in the S.* 11, 23
S to the stillness, till the mountain-shade | *Œnone* 21
they *s*, 'Our island home Is far beyond the wave'; | *Lotos-Eaters* 44
'Glory to God,' she *s*, and past afar, | *D. of F. Women* 242
and over them the sea-wind *s* Shrill, | *M. d'Arthur* 48
nightingale *S* loud, as tho' he were the bird of day. | *Gardener's D.* 96
clapt his hand in mine and *s*— | *Audley Court* 39
He *s* his song, and I replied with mine: | " 56
So *s* we each to either, Francis Hale, | " 74
An angel stand and watch me, as I *s*. | *St. S. Stylites* 35
s to me the whole Of those three stanzas | *Talking Oak* 134
Dry *s* the tackle, *s* the sail. | *The Voyage* 10
a couple, fair As ever painter painted, poet *s*, | *Aylmer's Field* 106
sway'd The cradle, while she *s* this baby song. | *Sea Dreams* 292
So *s* the gallant glorious chronicle; | *Princess, Pro.* 49
the women *s* Between the rougher voices of the men, | " 244
Beyond all reason: these the women *s*; | " *i* 143
thro' the porch that *s* All round with laurel, | " *ii* 22
With whom I *s* about the morning hills, | " 247
maid, Of those beside her, smote her harp, and *s*. | " *iv* 38
the tear, She *s* of, shook and fell, | " 60
part made long since, and part Now while I *s*, | " 91
So Lilia *s*: we thought her half-possess'd, | " 585
Like that great dame of Lapidoth she *s*. | " *vi* 142
Violet, she that *s* the mournful song, | " 318
maidens came, they talk'd, They *s*, they read: | " *vii* 23
What pleasure lives in height (the shepherd *s*) | " 193
something in the ballads which they *s*, | " *Con.* 14
Nightingales *s* in his woods: | *G. of Swainston* 6
Nightingales warbled and *s* Of a passion | " 8
in flying raiment, *s* the terrible prophetesses, | *Boädicea* 37
many an old philosophy On Argive heights divinely *s*, | *In Mem. xxiii* 22

Sang (*continued*) A merry song we *s* with him Last year:
   impetuously we *s*: | *In Mem. xxx* 15
we *s*: 'They do not die Nor lose their mortal sympathy, | " 22
While now we *s* old songs that peal'd | " *xcv* 13
They *s* of what is wise and good And graceful. | " *ciii* 10
In the centre stood A statue veil'd, to which they *s*; | " 12
s from the three-decker out of the foam, | *Maud I i* 50
Birds in our wood *s* Ringing thro' the valleys, | " *xii* 9
Arthur's knighthood *s* before the King:— | *Com. of Arthur* 481
s the knighthood, moving to their hall. | " 503
And then she *s*, 'O morning star' | *Gareth and L.* 995
the song that Enid *s* was one Of Fortune | *Marr. of Geraint* 345
From underneath a plume of lady-fern, *S*, | *Balin and Balan* 27
they drank and some one *s*, Sweet-voiced, | " 85
But, Vivien, when you *s* me that sweet rhyme, I felt | *Merlin and V.* 434
And *s* it: sweetly could she make and sing. | *Lancelot and E.* 1006
Then Tristram laughing caught the harp, and *s*: | *Last Tournament* 730
Whereat full willingly *s* the little maid. | *Guinevere* 167
So *s* the novice, while full passionately, | " 180
S Arthur's glorious wars, and *s* the King | " 286
then, he *s*, The twain together well might change | " 300
and over them the sea-wind *s* Shrill, | *Pass. of Arthur* 216
And *s* aloud the matin-song of life. | *Lover's Tale i* 232
If somewhere in the North, as Rumour *s* | *Sir J. Oldcastle* 56
And we *s* of the triumphs of Finn, | *V. of Maeldune* 88
more than he that *s* the Works and Days, | *To Virgil* 6
I *s* the song, 'are bride And bridegroom.' | *The Ring* 25
'Libera me, Domine!' you *s* the Psalm, | *Happy* 49
And *s* the married 'nos' for the solitary 'me.' | " 56
Wed to the melody, *S* thro' the world; | *Merlin and the G.* 98
Last year you *s* it as gladly. | *The Throstle* 6
Sanguine *S* he was: a but less vivid hue | *Aylmer's Field* 64
s Lazarus felt a vacant hand Fill with *his* purse. | *To Mary Boyle* 31
Sank I *s* In cool soft turf upon the bank, | *Arabian Nights* 95
And, while day *s* or mounted higher, | *Palace of Art* 46
Her slow full words *s* thro' the silence drear, | *D. of F. Women* 121
as we *s* From rock to rock upon the glooming quay, | *Audley Court* 83
To some full music rose and *s* the sun, | *Edwin Morris* 34
She *s* her head upon her arm | *Talking Oak* 207
Tho' at times her spirit *s*: | *L. of Burleigh* 70
s As into sleep again. | *Aylmer's Field* 591
but *s* down shamed At all that beauty; | *Lucretius* 63
leaning deep in broider'd down we *s* Our elbows: | *Princess iv* 32
but again She veil'd her brows, and prone she *s*, | " *v* 107
And down dead-heavy *s* her curls, | " *vi* 147
after *s* and *s* And, into mournful twilight mellowing, | " 190
I *s* and slept, Fill'd thro' and thro' with Love, | " *vii* 171
voice Choked, and her forehead *s* upon her hands, | " 247
A bitter day that early *s* | *In Mem. cvii* 2
show'd themselves against the sky, and *s*. | *Marr. of Geraint* 240
S her sweet head upon her gentle breast; | " 527
half his blood burst forth, and down he *s* For the
   pure pain, | *Lancelot and E.* 517
s Down on a drift of foliage random-blown; | *Last Tournament* 388
s his head in mire, and slimed themselves: | " 471
breakers of the outer sea *S* powerless, | *Lover's Tale i* 9
s his body with honour down into the deep, | *The Revenge* 109
king, the queen, *S* from their thrones, | *Columbus* 15
when drowning hope *S* all but out of sight, | " 157
And the roof *s* in on the hearth, | *V. of Maeldune* 32
And his white hair *s* to his heels | " 118
till the glorious creature *S* to his setting. | *Batt. of Brunanburh* 30
when our good redcoats *s* from sight, | *Heavy Brigade* 42
Where I *s* with the body at times | *By an Evolution.* 18
Became a shadow, *s* and disappear'd, | *Death of Œnone* 50
Then her head *s*, she slept, | " 78
San Philip delay'd By their mountain-like *S P* | *The Revenge* 40
the great *S P* hung above us like a cloud | " 43
But anon the great *S P*, she bethought | " 50
San Salvador I changed the name; *S S* I call'd it; | *Columbus* 76
Sap (s) 'The *s* dries up: the plant declines. | *Two Voices* 268
But yet my *s* was stirr'd: | *Talking Oak* 172
Here rests the *s* within the leaf, | *Day-Dm., Sleep. P.* 3
say rather, was my growth, My inward *s*, | *Lover's Tale i* 166
Sap (verb) Ring out the grief that *s*'s the mind, | *In Mem. cvi* 9

U*

Sap (verb) (*continued*) and *s*'s The fealty of our friends,   *Guinevere* 520
tides of onset *s* Our seven high gates,   *Tiresias* 91
Sapience And glean your scatter'd *s*.'   *Princess ii* 259
Sapless staring eye glazed o'er with *s* days,   *Love and Duty* 16
Sapling a promontory, That had a *s* growing on it,   *Geraint and E.* 163
  And there lie still, and yet *s* grew :   " 165
Sapphire (adj.) Came out clear plates of *s* mail.   *Two Voices* 12
Sapphire (s) A purer *s* melts into the sea.   *Maud I xviii* 52
  from jasper, *s*, Chalcedony, emerald,   *Columbus* 83
Sapphire-spangled The silent *s-s* marriage ring   *Maud I iv* 6
Sappho arts of grace *S* and others   *Princess ii* 164
Sapping tide Plash'd, *s* its worn ribs,   *Lover's Tale i* 56
Sappy Are neither green nor *s* ;   *Amphion* 90
  And when the *s* field and wood   *My life is full* 16
Saracen to lead A new crusade against the *S*,   *Columbus* 103
  to lead One last crusade against the *S*,   " 239
Sardius *s*, Chrysolite, beryl, topaz,   " 84
Sardonically *See* **Half-sardonically**
Sardonyx Beneath branch-work of costly *s*   *Palace of Art* 95
  Chalcedony, emerald, *s*, sardius, Chrysolite,   *Columbus* 84
Sarmin (sermon) But 'e reäds wonn *s* a weeäk,   *N. Farmer, O. S.* 28
Sartin-sewer (certain-sure) *S-s* I beä,   " 59
Sarve (serve) —an' it *s*'s ye right.   *Spinster's S's.* 121
Sarved (served) Wouldn't a pint a' *s* as well as a
  quart ?   *North. Cobbler* 99
  But I *s* 'em wi' butter an' heggs   *Village Wife* 114
  an' *s* by my oän little lass,   *Spinster's S's.* 103
  An' 'e *s* me sa well when 'e lived,   *Owd Roä* 11
Sarvice (service) like fur to hev soom soort of a *s* reäd.   " 12
Sarvint (servant) An' *s*'s runn'd in an' out,   *Village Wife* 56
Sassenach ' Goin' to cut the *S* whate '   *Tomorrow* 14
  ' niver crasst over say to the *S* whate ;   " 48
  that's betther nor cuttin' the *S* whate   " 94
Sat (*See also* **Sate**) Fancy came at her pillow *s*,   *Caress'd or chidden* 5
  He *s* upon the knees of men In days   *Two Voices* 323
  I ceased, and *s* as one forlorn.   " 400
  I came and *s* Below the chestnuts,   *Miller's D.* 59
  As near this door you *s* apart,   " 158
  With down-dropt eyes I *s* alone :   *Œnone* 57
  panther's roar came muffled, while I *s* Low in the valley.   " 214
  S smiling, babe in arm.   *Palace of Art* 96
  She *s* betwixt the shining Oriels,   " 159
  Flash'd thro' her as she *s* alone,   " 214
  They *s* them down upon the yellow sand,   *Lotos-Eaters* 37
  we *s* as God by God :   *D. of F. Women* 142
  Of old *s* Freedom on the heights,   *Of old sat Freedom* 1
  and I *s* round the wassail-bowl,   *The Epic* 5
  waked with silence, grunted ' Good ! ' but we *S*
  rapt :   *M. d'Arthur, Ep.* 5
  Eustace might have *s* for Hercules ;   *Gardener's D.* 7
  There *s* we down upon a garden mound,   " 214
  Mary *s* And look'd with tears upon her boy,   *Dora* 56
  and *s* upon a mound That was unsown,   " 72
  took The child once more, and *s* upon the mound ;   " 81
  so we *s* and eat And talk'd old matters over ;   *Audley Court* 28
  In which the swarthy ringdove *s*,   *Talking Oak* 293
  the night In which we *s* together and alone,   *Love and Duty* 60
  Wherever he *s* down and sung   *Amphion* 19
  To-day I *s* for an hour and wept,   *Edward Gray* 11
  Where *s* a company with heated eyes,   *Vision of Sin* 7
  Narrowing in to where they *s* assembled   " 16
  To him who *s* upon the rocks,   *To E. L.* 23
  And he *s* him down in a lonely place,   *Poet's Song* 5
  S often in the seaward-gazing gorge,   *Enoch Arden* 589
  There he *s* down gazing on all below ;   " 723
  S anger-charm'd from sorrow, soldier-like,   *Aylmer's Field* 728
  gentle hearted wife *S* shuddering at the ruin   *Sea Dreams* 30
  S at his table ; drank his costly wines ;   " 74
  And near the light a giant woman *s*,   " 98
  and I *s* down and wrote, In such a hand   *Princess i* 235
  There at a board by tome and paper *s*,   " *ii* 32
  There *s* along the forms, like morning doves   " 102
  We *s* : the Lady glanced :   " 111
  fawn Came flying while you *s* beside the well ?   " 271
  In each we *s*, we heard The grave Professor.   " 370

Sat (*continued*) *S* compass'd with professors :   *Princess ii* 444
  but we three *S* muffled like the Fates ;   " 467
  haled us to the Princess where she *s* High in the hall :   " *iv* 271
  up she *s*, And raised the cloak from brows   " *v* 72
  Part *s* like rocks : part reel'd but kept their seats :   " 496
  I lay still, and with me oft she *s* :   " *vii* 91
  by axe and eagle *s*, With all their foreheads   " 128
  palm to palm she *s* : the dew Dwelt in her eyes,   " 135
  Or in their silent influence as they *s*,   " *Con.* 15
  she *s*, she pluck'd the grass, She flung it from her,   " 31
  But we went back to the Abbey, and *s* on,   " 106
  we *s* But spoke not, rapt in nameless reverie,   " 107
  Turn'd as he *s*, and struck the keys   *The Islet* 7
  all night upon the bridge of war *S* glorying ;   *Spec. of Iliad* 10
  S fifty in the blaze of burning fire ;   " 20
  There *s* the Shadow fear'd of man ;   *In Mem. xxii* 12
  I myself, who *s* apart And watch'd them,   " *ciii* 29
  While I, thy nearest, *s* apart,   " *cx* 13
  And *s* by a pillar alone ;   *Maud I viii* 2
  S with her, read to her, night and day,   " *xix* 75
  Bleys Laid magic by, and *s* him down, and wrote
  All things   *Com. of Arthur* 156
  King Made feast for, saying, as they *s* at meat,   " 247
  and Arthur *s* Crown'd on the daïs,   " 257
  S down beside him, ate and then began.   *Gareth and L.* 872
  Enid woke and *s* beside the couch,   " 247
  S riveting a helmet on his knee,   *Marr. of Geraint* 79
  There musing *s* the hoary-headed Earl,   " 268
  So for long hours *s* Enid by her lord,   *Geraint and E.* 295
  none spake word, but all *s* down at once,   " 580
  ' Tell me your names ; why *s* ye by the well ? '   *Balin and Balan* 604
  Methought that if we *s* beside the well,   " 50
  they *s*, And cup clash'd cup ;   " 65
  Balin *s* Close-bower'd in that garden nigh the hall.   " 84
  saw The fountain where they *s* together,   " 240
  (She *s* beside the banquet nearest Mark),   " 291
  Among her damsels broidering *s*, heard,   *Merlin and V.* 18
  slided up his knee and *s*,   " 138
  And found a fair young squire who *s* alone,   " 239
  while she *s*, half-falling from his knees,   " 472
  King, who *s* Robed in red samite,   *Lancelot and E.* 904
  There from his charger down he slid, and *s*,   " 432
  then from where he *s* At Arthur's right,   " 510
  Queen, who *s* With lips severely placid,   " 551
  S on his knee, stroked his gray face   " 739
  So in her tower alone the maiden *s* :   " 749
  There *s* the lifelong creature of the house,   " 989
  S by the river in a cove,   " 1143
  and as they *s* Beneath a world-old yew-tree,   *Holy Grail* 1389
  once by misadvertence Merlin *s* In his own chair,   " 12
  as there we *s*, we heard A cracking and a riving   " 175
  and fair the house whereby she *s*,   " 182
  there *s* Arthur on the daïs-throne,   " 392
  and as he *s* In hall at old Caerleon,   *Pelleas and E.* 721
  each one *s*, Tho' served with choice from air,   " 2
  Full-arm'd upon his charger all day long *S* by the walls,   " 148
  children *s* in white with cups of gold,   *Last Tournament* 217
  S their great umpire, looking o'er the lists.   " 142
  them that round it *s* with golden cups   " 159
  Down in a casement *s*, A low sea-sunset glorying   " 289
  Drain'd of her force, again she *s*,   " 507
  Here one black, mute midsummer night I *s*,   " 540
  s There in the holy house at Almesbury Weeping,   *Guinevere* 612
  saw the Queen who *s* betwixt her best Enid,   " 1
  Low on the border of her couch they *s*   " 27
  She *s*, Stiff-stricken, listening :   " 101
  And lo, he *s* on horseback at the door !   " 411
  All day I *s* within the cavern-mouth,   *Lover's Tale ii* 589
  day waned : Alone I *s* with her :   " 37
  I CAME one day and *s* among the stones   " 140
  I never *S* at a costlier :   " *iii* 1
  s as if in chains—to whom he said :   " *iv* 188
  I had *s* three nights by the child—   " 362
  s each on the lap of the breeze ;   *In the Child. Hosp.* 59
  as we *s* by the gurgle of springs,   *V. of Maeldune* 38
  " 89

Sat (*continued*)   once when I *S* all alone, revolving   *Ancient Sage* 230
I *s* beside her dying, and she gaspt :   *The Ring* 287
I *s* beneath a solitude of snow ;   *Prog. of Spring* 71
Œnone *s* within the cave from out   *Death of Œnone* 1
Œnone *s* Not moving,   ,,   74
He stumbled in, and *s* Blinded ;   *St. Telemachus* 48
she *s* day and night by my bed,   *Charity* 33

Satan (*See also* **Saätan**)   ' *S* take The old women and their shadows !   *Princess v* 33
I leap from *S*'s foot to Peter's knee—   *Gareth and L.* 538
Or some black wether of St. *S*'s fold.   *Merlin and V.* 750
Where one of *S*'s shepherdesses caught   ,,   758
Make their last head like *S* in the North.   *Last Tournament* 98
But Michaël trampling *S* ;   ,,   673
A stranger as welcome as *S*—   *Charity* 26

Satan-haunted   This *S-h* ruin, this little city of sewers,   *Happy* 34
Sate (sat)   Round the hall where I *s*,   *The Mermaid* 26
Sate (to gratify)   things fair to *s* my various eyes !   *Palace of Art* 193
Sated   And *s* with the innumerable rose,   *Princess iii* 122
Satiate   Nor Arac, *s* with his victory.   ,, *vii* 90
Satiated   but *s* at length Came to the ruins.   ,, *Pro.* 90
an anger, not by blood to be *s*.   *Boädicea* 12
With meats and wines, and *s* their hearts—   *Last Tournament* 725
Satin (adj.)   dipt Beneath the *s* dome and enter'd in,   *Princess iv* 31
With a *s* sail of a ruby glow,   *The Islet* 13
Satin (s)   A tent of *s*, elaborately wrought   *Princess iii* 348
In gloss of *s* and glimmer of pearls,   *Maud I xxii* 55
Satin-shining   In colour like the *s-s* palm   *Merlin and V.* 224
Satin-wood   Erect behind a desk of *s-w*,   *Princess ii* 105
Satire   How like you this old *s* ? '   *Sea Dreams* 198
Who first wrote *s*, with no pity in it.   ,, 202
shafts Of gentle *s*, kin to charity,   *Princess ii* 469
Satisfied   Look to thy wants, and send thee *s*—   *Gareth and L.* 434
But rested with her sweet face *s* ;   *Marr. of Geraint* 776
And Geraint look'd and was not *s*.   *Geraint and E.* 435
s With what himself had done so graciously,   ,, 644
But when at last his doubts were *s*,   *Lover's Tale iv* 84
Satisfy   And *s* my soul with kissing her !   *Princess v* 103
Satrap   when her *S* bled At Issus by the Syrian gates,   *Alexander* 2
Sattle (settle)   An' *s* their ends upo stools   *Owd Roä* 24
Sattled (settled)   an' *s* 'ersen o' my knee,   *North. Cobbler* 79
I gied tha a raätin that *s* thy coortin o' me.   *Spinster's S's.* 48
Saturate   Tho' soak'd and *s*, out and out,   *Will Water.* 87
foul adulteries That *s* soul with body.   *Aylmer's Field* 377
Saturn   while *S* whirls, his stedfast shade   *Palace of Art* 15
Satyr   A *s*, a *s*, see—Follows ;   *Lucretius* 192
Glorifying clown and *s* ;   *Princess v* 187
Satyr-shape   Or in his coarsest *S-s*   *In Mem. xxxv* 22
Saucy   With a heaved shoulder and a *s* smile,   *Aylmer's Field* 466
They flash'd a *s* message to and fro   *Princess, Pro.* 78
till a rout of *s* boys Brake on us at our books,   ,, *v* 394
forced Sweet love on pranks of *s* boyhood :   ,, *vii* 344
Saul   play the *S* that never will be Paul.   *Sir J. Oldcastle* 103
Saunter   to those that *s* in the broad   *Aylmer's Field* 744
Saunter'd   we rose And *s* home beneath a moon,   *Audley Court* 80
Savage (adj.)   I mete and dole Unequal laws unto a *s* race,   *Ulysses* 4
I will take some *s* woman, she shall rear my dusky race.   *Locksley Hall* 168
For I was near him when the *s* yells Of Uther's peerage died,   *Com. of Arthur* 256
Balin, ' the *S* '—that addition thine—   *Balin and Balan* 53
here I dwell *S* among the *s* woods, here die—   ,, 486
Chaste, frugal, *s*, arm'd by day and night   *Montenegro* 3
Savage (s)   Mated with a squalid *s*—   *Locksley Hall* 177
' Peace, you young *s* of the Northern wild !   *Princess iii* 247
Savagery   A huge man-beast of boundless *s*.   *Gareth and L.* 637
Brute bulk of limb, or boundless *s*   ,, 1330
and tooth'd with grinning *s*.'   *Balin and Balan* 197
Save (*See also* **Saäve**)   who can *s* But will not ?   *Supp. Confessions* 90
And *s* me lest I die ? '   *Palace of Art* 288
died To *s* her father's vow ;   *D. of F. Women* 196
Dora stored what little she could *s*,   *Dora* 52
To *s* her little finger from a scratch   *Edwin Morris* 63
Jesus, if thou wilt not *s* my soul,   *St. S. Stylites* 46

Save (*continued*)   To *s* from shame and thrall :   *Sir Galahad* 16
And vex the unhappy dust thou wouldst not *s*.   *Come not, when, etc.* 4
wish To *s* all earnings to the uttermost,   *Enoch Arden* 86
be pray'd ' *S* them from this, whatever comes to me.'   ,, 118
To *s* the offence of charitable,   ,, 342
hope of life approach To *s* the life despair'd of,   ,, 831
(I thought I could have died to *s* it)   *Sea Dreams* 134
be swerved from right to *s* A prince, a brother ?   *Princess ii* 290
And *s* the one true seed of freedom   *Ode on Well.* 162
For, saving that, ye help to *s* mankind   ,, 166
But as he *s*'s or serves the state.   ,, 200
her father was not the man to *s*,   *Grandmother* 5
O mother, praying God will *s* Thy sailor,—   *In Mem. vi* 13
And, influence-rich to sooth and *s*,   ,, *lxxx* 14
If lowliness could *s* her.   *Maud I xii* 20
I know it the one bright thing to *s* My yet young life   ,, *xvi* 20
To *s* from some slight shame one simple girl.   ,, *xviii* 45
a monster unsubduable Of any *s* of him whom I call'd—   *Gareth and L.* 859
S that the dome was purple, and above, Crimson,   ,, 912
To *s* her dear lord whole from any wound.   *Geraint and E.* 45
I *s* a life dearer to me than mine.'   ,, 138
Truly *s* for fears, My fears for thee,   *Balin and Balan* 146
I that fain had died To *s* thy life,   ,, 600
I fly to thee. *S*, *s* me thou—   *Merlin and V.* 78
Merlin, tho' you do not love me, *s*, Yet *s* me ! '   ,, 944
' *S* your great self, fair lord ; '   *Lancelot and E.* 320
' If I lose myself, I myself ! '   *Holy Grail* 178
Thou hast not lost thyself to *s* thyself As Galahad.'   ,, 456
And *s* it even in extremes,   *Guinevere* 67
To *s* his blood from scandal,   ,, 514
S for some whisper of the seething seas,   *Pass. of Arthur* 121
And all the senses weaken'd, *s* in that,   *Lover's Tale i* 127
s in that Where to have been one had been   ,, *ii* 26
but to *s* my soul, that is all your desire :   *Rizpah* 77
happier using the knife than in trying to *s* the limb,   *In the Child. Hosp.* 6
for it never could *s* us a life.   *Def. of Lucknow* 86
before their Gods, And wailing ' *S* us.'   *Tiresias* 106
to the Faith that *s*'s,   *The Wreck* 3
would you *s* A madman to vex you with wretched words,   *Despair* 107
Pierced by a poison'd dart. *S* me.   *Death of Œnone* 34
Take it, and *s* me from it !   *Bandit's Death* 38
darken'd with doubts of a Faith that *s*'s,   *The Dreamer* 11
Saved   Who may be *s* ? who is it may be *s* ?   *St. S. Stylites* 47
Can I work miracles and not be *s* ?   ,, 150
It cannot be but that I shall be *s* ;   ,, 152
every hour is *s* From that eternal silence,   *Ulysses* 26
' Thou shalt not be *s* by works :   *Vision of Sin* 91
' A sail ! a sail ! *s* ; '   *Enoch Arden* 914
you may yet be *s*, and therefore fly :   *Princess iii* 64
You *s* our life : we owe you bitter thanks :   ,, *iv* 531
' He *s* my life : my brother slew him for it.'   ,, *vi* 108
let the land whose hearths he *s* from shame   *Ode on Well.* 225
how the King had *s* his life In battle twice,—   *Gareth and L.* 493
Good now, ye have *s* a life Worth somewhat   ,, 827
the lord whose life he *s* Had, some brief space,   ,, 888
There was I broken down : there was I *s* :   *Geraint and E.* 851
and roll'd his enemy down, And *s* him—   *Lancelot and E.* 827
Told him that her fine care had *s* his life.   ,, 863
That *s* her many times, not fail—   *To the Queen ii* 62
fed, and cherish'd him, and *s* his life.   *Lover's Tale iv* 264
Who thrust him out, or him who *s* his life ? '   ,, 267
service of the one so *s* was due All to the saver—   ,, 279
Dance to the pibroch !—*s* ! we are *s* !   *Def. of Lucknow* 103
S by the valour of Havelock, *s*   ,, 104
' Heresy—Not shriven, not *s* ? '   *Sir J. Oldcastle* 144
they had *s* many hundreds from wreck—   *Despair* 10
Does it matter how many they *s* ?   ,, 12
and you *s* me, a valueless life   ,, 61
S when your life was wreck'd !   *The Ring* 305
Saver   And *s* of my life ;   *Gareth and L.* 879
The *s* of my life.'   ,, 884
service of the one so saved was due All to the *s*—   *Lover's Tale iv* 280

Saw (verb) (*continued*)   *s* That Death was cast to ground,   *Gareth and L.* 1402

He look'd and *s* that all was ruinous.	*Marr. of Geraint*	315
For if he be the knight whom late I *s*	"	406
I *s* you moving by me on the bridge,	"	429
For this dear child, because I never *s*,	"	497
And looking round he *s* not Enid there,	"	506
Men *s* the goodly hills of Somerset,	"	828
By the flat meadow, till she *s* them come ;	"	832
I *s* three bandits by the rock Waiting to fall on you,	*Geraint and E.*	72
S once a great piece of a promontory,	"	162
When now they *s* their bulwark fallen,	"	168
In former days you *s* me favourably.	"	315
when she *s* him ride More near by many a rood	"	441
turning round she *s* Dust, and the points of lances	..	448
Who *s* the chargers of the two that fell	"	481
Rose when they *s* the dead man rise,	"	732
But *s* me not, or mark'd not if you *s* ;	"	870
for a minute, till he *s* her Pass into it,	"	886
he *s* not whence, Strikes from behind.	*Balin and Balan*	130
We *s* the hoof-print of a horse, no more.'	"	133
once he *s* the thrall His passion half had gauntleted	"	219
As if he *s* not, glanced aside,	"	248
Last night methought I *s* That maiden Saint	"	260
s The fountain where they sat together,	"	290
I *s* the flash of him but yestereven.	"	303
s, With pointed lance as if to pierce, a shape,	"	324
That *s* to-day the shadow of a spear,	"	373
in simple nakedness, *S* them embrace :	"	519
' I *s* the little elf-god eyeless once	*Merlin and V.*	249
I look'd, and *s* you following still,	"	299
gloom'd Your fancy when ye *s* me following you,	"	326
Because I *s* you sad, to comfort you.	"	441
He *s* two cities in a thousand boats	"	561
men Became a crystal, and he *s* them thro' it,	"	630
Nor *s* she save the King, who wrought the charm,	"	643
s The knights, the court, the King,	"	874
since he *s* The slow tear creep from her closed eyelid	"	905
raised his eyes and *s* The tree that shone white-listed	"	938
s Fired from the west, far on a hill,	*Lancelot and E.*	167
I *s* him, after, stand High on a heap of slain,	"	306
I never *s* his like : there lives No greater leader.'	"	316
s The maiden standing in the dewy light.	"	351
till he *s* Which were the weaker ;	"	461
when he *s* the Queen, embracing ask'd,	"	570
Gawain *s* Sir Lancelot's azure lions,	"	662
Whom when she *s*, ' Lavaine,' she cried,	"	794
there first she *s* the casque Of Lancelot on the wall :	"	805
Then she that *s* him lying unsleek, unshorn,	"	815
Lancelot *s* that she withheld her wish,	"	920
s One of her house, and sent him to the Queen	"	1167
s with a sidelong eye The shadow of some piece	"	1173
wild Queen, who *s* not, burst away To weep	"	1244
s the barge that brought her moving down,	"	1391
But who first *s* the holy thing to-day ? '	*Holy Grail*	67
She might have risen and floated when I *s* her.	"	100
s the bright boy-knight, and bound it on him,	"	156
found and *s* it, as the nun My sister *s* it ;	"	198
Some little of this marvel he too *s*,	"	216
s The golden dragon sparkling over all :	"	262
I heard the sound, I *s* the light,	"	280
I sware a vow to follow it till I *s*.'	"	282
s the Holy Grail, I *s* the Holy Grail	"	290
s deep lawns, and then a brook,	"	380
I *s* That man had once dwelt there ;	"	429
I *s* The holy elements alone ;	"	462
but he, ' *S* ye no more ? I, Galahad, *s* the Grail, The Holy Grail,	"	464
I *s* the fiery face as of a child That smote itself	"	466
At once I *s* him far on the great Sea,	"	510
If boat it were—I *s* not whence it came.	"	515
again Roaring, I *s* him like a silver star—	"	517
I *s* the least of little stars Down on the waste,	"	524
I *s* the spiritual city and all her spires	"	526
S ye none beside, None of your knights ?'	"	631
I *s* The pelican on the casque of our Sir Bors	"	634

Saw (verb) (*continued*)   Who, when he *s* me, rose, and bad

me hail,	*Holy Grail*	725
turn'd to whom at first He *s* not,	"	752
I may not speak of it : I *s* it ; '	"	759
But nothing in the sounding hall I *s*,	"	828
yet methought I *s* the Holy Grail,	"	846
I had sworn I *s* That which I *s* ; but what I *s* was veil'd And cover'd ;	"	850
And as ye *s* it ye have spoken truth.	"	880
My greatest hardly will believe he *s* ;	"	896
but *s* Near him a mound of even-sloping side,	*Pelleas and E.*	24
glancing thro' the hoary boles, he *s*,	"	50
She that *s* him cried, ' Damsels—	"	188
But *s* the postern portal also wide Yawning ;	"	420
hiss, snake—I *s* him there—	"	471
he *s* High up in heaven the hall that Merlin built,	"	552
He glanced and *s* the stately galleries,	*Last Tournament*	145
He *s* the laws that ruled the tournament	"	160
as the water Moab *s* Come round by the East,	"	482
look'd and *s* The great Queen's bower was dark,—	"	757
s the Queen who sat betwixt her best Enid,	*Guinevere*	27
and more than this He *s* not,	"	30
He *s* them—headland after headland flame	"	243
the golden days In which she *s* him first,	"	381
Came to that point where first she *s* the King	"	403
she *s*, Wet with the mists and smitten by the lights,	"	596
she look'd and *s* The novice, weeping,	"	663
I *s* One lying in the dust at Almesbury,	*Pass. of Arthur*	76
since he *s* not whom he fought.	"	99
Look'd up for heaven, and only *s* the mist ;	"	112
But when he *s* the wonder of the hilt,	"	253
I never *s*, Nor shall see, here or elsewhere,	"	321
s, Straining his eyes beneath an arch of hand,	"	463
thought he *s*, the speck that bare the King,	"	465
Before he *s* my day my father died, And he was happy that he *s* it not ;	*Lover's Tale i*	191
looking back, we *s* The clefts and openings	"	329
she *s* Beneath her feet the region far away,	"	394
And *s* the motion of all other things ;	"	574
I *s* There, where I hoped myself to reign	"	590
I *s* the moonlight glitter on their tears—	"	697
But cast a parting glance at me, you *s*,	"	iv 4
he *s* His lady with the moonlight on her face ;	"	56
when I *s* her (and I thought him crazed,	"	163
Julian goes, the lord of all he *s*.	"	315
I, by Lionel sitting, *s* his face Fire,	"	322
s The bridesmaid pale, statuelike,	*Sisters (E. and E.)*	211
when I *s* him come in at the door,	*In the Child. Hosp.*	2
we *s* the rivers roll from Paradise !	*Columbus*	27
and I *s* The glory of the Lord flash up,	"	81
I *s* that we could not stay,	*V. of Maeldune*	35
I *s* him and let him be.	"	128
He *s* not his daughter—he blest her :	*To Prin. F. of H.*	3
meanings ambush'd under all they *s*,	*Tiresias*	5
There in a secret olive-glade I *s* Pallas Athene	"	39
mask that I *s* so amazed me,	*The Wreck*	117
I *s* that a boat was nearing us—	"	123
as I *s* the white sail run, And darken,	*The Flight*	39
who *s* the death, but kept the deck,	*Locksley H., Sixty*	63
You *s* the league-long rampart-fire	*Pro. to Gen. Hamley*	27
A sudden nightingale *S* thee,	*Demeter and P.*	12
crocus-purple hour That *s* thee vanish.	"	51
I *s* the tiger in the ruin'd fane	"	79
but trace of thee I *s* not ;	"	81
I never *s* it yet so all ablaze	*The Ring*	81
stretch'd my hands As if I *s* her ;	"	117
We *s* far off an old forsaken house,	"	155
And *s* the world fly by me like a dream,	"	180
one day came And *s* you, shook her head,	"	313
and once we only *s* Your gilded vane,	"	330
the matron *s* That hinted love was only wasted bait,	"	359
Who *s* you kneel beside your bier,	*Happy*	54
And him I *s* but once again,	"	79
I *s* beyond their silent tops The steaming marshes	*Prog. of Spring*	74
I *s*, whenever In passing it glanced upon	*Merlin and the G.*	102

Saw (verb) (*continued*)   she *s* Him, climbing toward her

with the golden fruit,	*Death of Œnone* 14
and *s* The ring of faces redden'd by the flames	,, 91
Thou, thou—I *s* thee fall before me,	*Akbar's Dream* 185
on a sudden we *s* your soldiers crossing the ridge,	*Bandit's Death* 21
An' *s* by the Graäce o' the Lord,	*Church-warden, etc.* 42
S them lie confounded,	*The Tourney* 14

Sawdust   Or elbow-deep in *s*, slept,   *Will Water.* 99

Sawest   Who never *s* Caerleon upon Usk—   *Balin and Balan* 570

  Thou *s* a glory growing on the night,   *Epit. on Caxton* 2

Sawing   stump Pitch-blacken'd *s* the air,   *Last Tournament* 67

Sawn   *s* In twain beneath the ribs ;   *St. S. Stylites* 52

Saxon (*See also* **West-Saxons, West-Saxon-land**) *S*

and Norman and Dane are we,	*W. to Alexandra* 3
For *S* or Dane or Norman we,	,, 31
S and Angle from Over the broad billow	*Batt. of Brunanburh* 118
Noble the *S* who hurl'd at his Idol	*Kapiolani* 4

Say (s) (*See also* **Saäy**) Give me my fling, and let me

say my *s*.	*Aylmer's Field* 399
men are bold and strongly say their *s* :—	*W. to Marie Alex.* 32
Say thou thy *s*, and I will do my deed.	*Gareth and L.* 901
You said your *s* ; Mine answer was my deed.	,, 1174
I am Lancelot ; say thy *s*.'	*Pelleas and E.* 582

Say (verb)   *May* children of our children *s*,

	To the Queen 23
Men *s* that Thou Didst die for me,	*Supp. Confessions* 2
still as I comb'd I would sing and *s*,	*The Mermaid* 12
What they *s* betwixt their wings ?	*Adeline* 29
She has heard a whisper *s*,	*L. of Shalott* ii 3
she *s*'s A fire dances before her,	*Œnone* 263
but I care not what they *s*,	*May Queen* 19
They *s* he's dying all for love,	,, 21
They *s* his heart is breaking, mother—	,, 22
I shall hearken what you *s*,	*May Queen, N. Y's. E.* 39
And *s* to Robin a kind word,	,, *Con.* 45
Yet something I did wish to *s* :	*To J. S.* 60
Is this enough to *s* That my desire,	*Gardener's D.* 236
He *s*'s that he will never see me more.'	*Dora* 116
I scarce have other music : yet *s* on	*Edwin Morris* 57
They *s* that they are heal'd.	*St. S. Stylites* 146
I do not *s* But that a time may come—	,, 189
S thou, whereon I carved her name,	*Talking Oak* 33
Will some one *s*, Then why not ill for good ?	*Love and Duty* 27
How *s* you ? we have slept, my lords.	*Day-Dm., Revival* 21
As who shall *s* me nay :	*Will Water.* 92
S's to her that loves him well,	*L. of Burleigh* 22
She was more fair than words can *s*	*Beggar Maid* 2
And *s* she would be little wife to both.	*Enoch Arden* 36
still foreboding ' what would Enoch *s* ? '	,, 253
Him and his children not to *s* me nay—	,, 308
they *s* that women are so quick—	,, 408
And *s* to Philip that I blest him too ;	,, 886
Far as we track ourselves—I *s* that this—	*Aylmer's Field* 306
And you shall *s* that having spoken with me,	,, 311
Jilted I was : I *s* it for your peace.	,, 354
Give me my fling, and let me *s* my say.'	,, 399
How many will *s* 'forgive,'	*Sea Dreams* 60
What does little birdie *s* In her nest	,, 293
What does little baby *s*, In her bed at peep of day ?	,, 301
No matter ; we will *s* whatever comes.	*Princess, Pro.* 239
I, Who am not mine, *s*, live :	,, ii 223
She *s*'s the Princess should have been the Head,	,, iii 34
in the second place, Some *s* the third—	,, 158
Your Highness might have seem'd the thing you *s*.'	,, 202
S to her, I do but wanton in the South,	,, iv 109
and to shame That which he *s*'s he loves :	,, 249
let me *s* but this, That many a famous man and woman,	,, 444
as they *s* The seal does music ;	,, 455
when they *s* The child is hers ;	,, v 86
and yet they *s* that still You love her.	,, 122
How *s* you, war or not ? '	,, 124
neither seem'd there more to *s* :	,, 330
S one soft word and let me part forgiven.'	,, vi 219
said you had a heart—I heard her *s* it—	,, 234
Far, how far no tongue can *s*,	*Ode Inter. Exhib.* 30
men are bold and strongly *s* their say :—	*W. to Marie Alex.* 32

Say (verb) (*continued*)   and Willy, you *s*, is gone.

	Grandmother 8
S's that I moänt 'a naw moor aäle.	*N. Farmer, O. S.* 3
Doctors, they knaws nowt, fur a *s*'s what's naw-	
ways true :	,, 5
an' a *s*'s it eäsy an' freeä	,, 25
S's to thessén naw doubt ' what a man a beä sewer-loy !'	,, 54
Sin' I mun doy I mun doy, thaw loife they *s*'s is sweet,	,, 63
thy muther *s*'s thou wants to marry the lass,	,, *N. S.* 37
Somebody said that she'd *s* no ; (repeat)	*Window, Letter* 7, 14
As pure and perfect as I *s* ?	*In Mem.* xxiv 2
Whatever fickle tongues may *s*.	,, xxvi 4
Or so methinks the dead would *s* ;	,, lxxxv 94
Except, like them, thou too canst *s*,	,, xciv 7
Whate'er the faithless people *s*.	,, xcvii 16
And yet myself have heard him *s*,	,, xcviii 20
They *s*, The solid earth whereon we tread	,, cxviii 7
One *s*'s, we are villains all.	*Maud I* i 17
And *s*'s he is rough but kind,	,, xix 70
O then, what then shall I *s*?—	,, 92
what will the old man *s*? (repeat)	*Maud II* v 83, 87
But *s*, these four, Who be they ?	*Gareth and L.* 626
' *S* thou thy say, and I will do my deed.'	,, 901
tell him what I think and what they *s*.	*Marr. of Geraint* 90
ye look so scared at what I *s* :	*Geraint and E.* 339
what *s* ye, shall we strip him there Your lover ?	,, 488
Enid could not *s* one tender word,	,, 746
some *do s* that our Sir Garlon too Hath learn'd	
black magic,	*Balin and Balan* 304
' Who are wise in love Love most, *s* least,'	*Merlin and V.* 248
Yet you are wise who *s* it ;	,, 252
' *S*'s she not well ? and there is more—	,, 450
proof against the grain Of him ye *s* ye love :	,, 488
Should try this charm on whom ye *s* ye love.'	,, 525
What dare the full-fed liars *s* of me ?	,, 692
' O ay, what *s* ye to Sir Valence,	,, 705
What *s* ye then to sweet Sir Sagramore,	,, 721
What *s* ye then to fair Sir Percivale	,, 747
' O ay ; what *s* ye to Sir Lancelot,	,, 769
What did the wanton *s* ?	,, 812
heathen, who, some *s*, shall rule the land	*Lancelot and E.* 65
I might *s* that I had seen.'	,, 427
if I could believe the things you *s*	,, 1097
For so they *s*, these books of ours,	*Holy Grail* 65
Our Lady *s*'s it, and we well believe :	,, 604
and yet I should be shamed to *s* it—	*Pelleas and E.* 189
I will *s* That I have slain thee.	,, 345
Blowing his bugle as who should *s* him nay.'	,, 381
I am Lancelot ; *s* thy say.'	,, 582
and *s* My tower is full of harlots, like his court,	*Last Tournament* 80
s My knights are all adulterers like his own,	,, 83
and *s* his hour is come, The heathen are upon him,	,, 86
Swine, *s* ? swine, goats, asses, rams and geese	,, 321
Lied, *s* ye ? Nay, but learnt,	,, 656
himself would *s* Sir Lancelot had the noblest ;	*Guinevere* 319
Not to break in on what I *s* by word Or whisper,	*Lover's Tale* iv 352
The men would *s* of the maids,	*First Quarrel* 28
But *s* nothing hard of my boy,	*Rizpah* 22
he had something further to *s*,	,, 43
I charge you never to *s* that I laid him	,, 58
You *s* that you can do it as willingly	*Sisters (E. and E.)* 70
but I know that I heard him *s*	*In the Child. Hosp.* 21
' He *s*'s I shall never live thro' it,	,, 47
S that His day is done ! Ah why should we care	
what they *s*?	,, 71
What did he *s*, My frighted Wiclif-preacher	*Sir J. Oldcastle* 37
Then some one standing by my grave will *s*,	*Columbus* 209
is a man to be loved by the women they *s*.	*The Wreck* 18
' Tho' some have gleams or so they *s*	*Ancient Sage* 214
write ten lines, they *s*, At dawn,	*Poets and their B.* 2
s That here the torpid mummy wheat	*To Prof. Jebb* 4
What did she *s* ?	*The Ring* 99
and seem'd to *s* ' Again.'	*The Ring* 154
You *s* your body is so foul—	*Happy* 25
Yet ' Alla,' *s*'s their sacred book, ' is Love,'	*Akbar's Dream* 73
WHAT am I doing, you *s* to me,	*Charity* 1

Sayest 'Tis Kate—She *s* what she will: *Kate* 6
   as thou *s*, a Fairy King And Fairy Queens   *Gareth and L.* 258
   as thou *s*, it is enchanted, son,   "   263
Saying (part.) (*See also* **Saäyin'**) *s* that which pleased him,
   for he smiled.   *Enoch Arden* 757
   S this, The woman half turn'd round   *Sea Dreams* 285
   and I (Pardon me *s* it) were much loth   *Princess i* 156
   So *s* from the court we paced,   " *iii* 117
   Shame might befall Melissa, knowing, *s* not she knew :   " 148
   S in odour and colour, ' Ah, be Among the roses   *Maud I xxi* 12
   King Made feast for, *s*, as they sat at meat,   *Com. of Arthur* 247
   s this the seer Went thro' the strait   " 394
   s thou wert basely born.   *Gareth and L.* 355
   Reproach you, *s* all your force is gone ?   *Marr. of Geraint* 88
   s all his force Is melted into mere effeminacy ?   " 106
   So *s*, from the carven flower above,   *Lancelot and E.* 549
   hopes are mine,' and *s* that, she choked,   " 607
   S which she seized, And, thro' the casement   " 1233
   s to me That Guinevere had sinn'd against the
   highest,   *Last Tournament* 569
   ev'n in *s* this, Her memory from old habit   *Guinevere* 378
   And well for thee, *s* in my dark hour,   *Pass. of Arthur* 159
   What am I *s* ? and what are *you* ?   *Rizpah* 11
   So *s*, light-foot Iris pass'd away.   *Achilles over the T.* 1
   What art thou *s* ? ' And was not Alla   *Akbar's Dream* 86
Saying (s) A *s*, hard to shape in act ;   *Love thou thy land* 49
   a *s* learnt, In days far-off,   *Tithonus* 47
   What is their pretty *s* ? jilted, is it ?   *Aylmer's Field* 353
   dark *s's* from of old Ranging and ringing   *Com. of Arthur* 415
   thy foul *s's* fought for me :   *Gareth and L.* 1180
   And mirthful *s's*, children of the place,   *Holy Grail* 555
   a *s* that anger'd her.   *Last Tournament* 628
Scabbard when she show'd the wealthy *s*,   *Aylmer's Field* 236
Scaffold (*See also* **Death-scaffold**) *S's*, still sheets of
   water,   *D. of F. Women* 34
Scald That let the bantling *s* at home,   *Princess v* 458
Scale (for weighing) fortunes, justlier balanced, *s* with *s*,'   *ii* 66
   takes it up, And topples down the *s's* ;   " *v* 445
   While slowly falling as a *s* that falls,   *Marr. of Geraint* 525
Scale (graduated series) Along the *s* of ranks, thro' all,   *In Mem. cxi* 2
Scale (of armour) splendours and the golden *s* Of harness,   *Princess v* 41
Scale (proportion) Because the *s* is infinite.   *Two Voices* 93
Scale (verb) she that out of Lethe *s's* with man   *Princess vii* 261
   To *s* the heaven's highest height,   *In Mem. cviii* 7
   to *s* the highest of the heights With some strange hope   *Tiresias* 28
   The leper plague may *s* my skin   *Happy* 27
Scaled Suddenly *s* the light.   *Palace of Art* 8
   And *s* in sheets of wasteful foam,   *Sea Dreams* 53
   Shall find the toppling crags of Duty *s*   *Ode on Well.* 215
   s with help a hundred feet Up from the base :   *Balin and Balan* 170
   High with the last line *s* her voice,   *Lancelot and E.* 1019
   The spiring stone that *s* about her tower,   *Last Tournament* 511
   I *s* the buoyant highway of the birds,   *Prog. of Spring* 80
Scaling Tho' *s* slow from grade to grade ;   *Two Voices* 174
   But after *s* half the weary down,   *Enoch Arden* 372
   crag and tree *S*, Sir Lancelot from the perilous nest,   *Last Tournament* 18
Scalp From *s* to sole one slough and crust   *St. S. Stylites* 2
   Beat into my *s* and my brain,   *Maud II v* 10
Scan I *s* him now Beastlier than any phantom   *Lucretius* 195
   We needs must *s* him from head to feet   *Dead Prophet* 55
Scandal Begins the *s* and the cry :   *You might have won* 16
   Old *s's* buried now seem decads deep In other *s's*
   that have lived and died, And left the living *s*
   that shall die—   *Aylmer's Field* 442
   You'll have no *s* while you dine,   *To F. D. Maurice* 17
   like a city, with gossip, *s*, and spite ;   *Maud I iv* 8
   Nun as she was, the *s* of the Court,   *Holy Grail* 78
   once the talk And *s* of our table, had return'd ;   " 650
   To spy some secret *s* if he might,   *Guinevere* 26
   make the smouldering *s* break and blaze Before the people,   " 91
   To save his blood from *s*,   " 514
   him The causer of that *s*, fought and fell ;   *The Ring* 215
   While *s* is mouthing a bloodless name   *The Dawn* 12
Scandalous (*See also* **Crown-scandalous**) To smoke the
   s hive of those wild bees   *Holy Grail* 214

Scandalous (*continued*) I have scared you pale with my *s* talk,   *Despair* 111
Scant 'Tis life, whereof our nerves are *s*,   *Two Voices* 397
   But work was *s* in the Isle,   *First Quarrel* 43
Scanty Gain'd for her own a *s* sustenance,   *Enoch Arden* 259
   Thus earn'd a *s* living for himself :   " 818
Scape who may slay or *s* the three,   *Gareth and L.* 641
   Pray for him that he *s* the doom of fire,   *Guinevere* 347
Scaped *S* thro' a cavern from a bandit hold,   *Holy Grail* 207
'Scaped (escaped) by this way I *'s* them.   *St. S. Stylites* 179
Scapegoat On that huge *s* of the race,   *Maud I xiii* 42
Scar O sweet and far from cliff and *s*   *Princess iv* 9
   cloaks the *s* of some repulse with lies ;   *Merlin and V.* 818
Scarce upon the game, how *s* it was This season ;   *Audley Court* 32
   I *s* can ask it thee for hate,   *Gareth and L.* 361
   He *s* is knight, yea but half-man,   " 1176
   But *s* could see, as now we see,   *Epilogue* 48
   But *s* of such majestic mien   *Freedom* 6
   I *s* have learnt the title of your book,   *The Ring* 126
   saw you kneel beside your bier, and weeping *s* could see ;   *Happy* 54
   Altho' months have *s* begun,   *To Ulysses* 22
   we *s* can spell The Alif of Thine alphabet   *Akbar's Dream* 30
Scarce-believable many a *s-b* excuse,   *Enoch Arden* 469
Scarce-credited *S-c* at first but more and more,   " 648
Scarce-rocking *S-r*, her full-busted figure-head   " 543
Scare *s* church-harpies from the master's feast ;   *To J. M. K.* 3
   Why wilt thou ever *s* me with thy tears,   *Tithonus* 46
   To *s* the fowl from fruit :   *Princess ii* 228
   biting laws to *s* the beasts of prey   " *v* 393
   You cannot *s* me ; nor rough face,   *Gareth and L.* 1329
   shadow of my spear had been enow To *s* them from
   me once ;   *Holy Grail* 792
Scarecrow Empty *s's*, I and you !   *Vision of Sin* 94
Scared (*See also* **Skeärd**) ' O ' she cried, *S* as it were,   *Enoch Arden* 430
   But *s* with threats of jail and halter   *Aylmer's Field* 520
   he heard her speak ; She *s* him ;   *Princess i* 186
   To lag behind, *s* by the cry they made,   " *v* 94
   The king is *s*, the soldier will not fight,   " *Con.* 60
   and this music now Hath *s* them both,   *Gareth and L.* 251
   foemen *s*, like that false pair who turn'd   *Geraint and E.* 176
   Nor need ye look so *s* at what I say :   " 339
   So, *s* but at the motion of the man,   " 476
   beauteous beast *S* by the noise upstarted   *Merlin and V.* 480
   some are *s*, who mark, Or wisely or unwisely,   *To the Queen ii* 48
   Do you think I was *s* by the bones ?   *Rizpah* 55
   I have *s* you pale with my scandalous talk,   *Despair* 111
   that the foälk be sa *s* at,   *Spinster's S's.* 24
   My people too were *s* with eerie sounds,   *The Ring* 408
Scarf One sitting on a crimson *s* unroll'd,   *D. of F. Women* 126
   Dark as a funeral *s* from stem to stern,   *M. d'Arthur* 194
   A *s* of orange round the stony helm,   *Princess, Pro.* 102
   palace-front Alive with fluttering *s's* and ladies' eyes,   " *v* 509
   A purple *s*, at either end whereof   *Marr. of Geraint* 169
   Prince's blood spirted upon the *s*,   " 208
   Yniol caught His purple *s*, and held,   " 377
   Dark as a funeral *s* from stem to stern,   *Pass. of Arthur* 362
Scarfskin not a hair Ruffled upon the *s*,   *Aylmer's Field* 660
Scarlet (adj.) The sunrise broken into *s* shafts   *Enoch Arden* 592
   and again The *s* shafts of sunrise—but no sail.   " 599
   and fulminated Against the *s* woman and her creed ;   *Sea Dreams* 23
   her *s* sleeve, Tho' carved and cut,   *Lancelot and E.* 806
   The steaming marshes of the *s* cranes,   *Prog. of Spring* 75
Scarlet (s) who wore the sleeve Of *s*, and the pearls ;   *Lancelot and E.* 502
   upon his helm A sleeve of *s*, broider'd   " 604
   Hued with the *s* of a fierce sunrise,   *Lover's Tale i* 353
   crimson and *s* of berries that flamed   *V. of Maeldune* 61
Scarlet-mingled And hills and *s-m* woods   *The Voyage* 47
Scarlett *S* and *S's* three hundred were riding by   *Heavy Brigade* 4
Scarlett's Brigade three hundred of *S B* !'   " 45
Scarped From *s* cliff and quarried stone   *In Mem. lvi* 2
Scarr'd *S* with a hundred wintry watercourses—   *Holy Grail* 490
Scathe What Devil had the heart to *s*   *Supn. Confessions* 83
   as God's high gift from *s* and wrong,   *Guinevere* 494
   given my life To help his own from *s*,   *Sir J. Oldcastle* 63
Scathed down in a furrow *s* with flame :   *The Victim* 22
Scatter we will *s* all our maids Till happier times   *Princess vi* 302

Scatter (continued) S the blossom under her feet ! — *W. to Alexandra* 9
Disband himself, and s all his powers, — *Geraint and E.* 798
would s the ghosts of the Past, — *Despair* 23
s's on her throat the sparks of dew, — *Prog. of Spring* 58
Scatter'd (See also Wind-scatter'd) 'Tho' thou wert s to the wind, — *Two Voices* 32
The twinkling laurel s silver lights. — *Gardener's D.* 118
Or s blanching on the grass. — *Day-Dm., Arrival* 12
were s Blood and brains of men. — *The Captain* 47
huts At random s, each a nest in bloom. — *Aylmer's Field* 150
dear diminutives S all over the vocabulary — „ 540
And glean your s sapience' — *Princess ii* 259
Yet how to bind the s scheme of seven Together in one sheaf ? — „ *Con.* 8
A thresher with his flail had s them. — *Gareth and L.* 842
And s all they had to all the winds ; — *Marr. of Geraint* 635
All s thro' the houses of the town ; — „ 695
strown With gold and s coinage, — *Geraint and E.* 26
' and lo, the powers of Doorm Are s,' — „ 802
One from the bandit s in the field, — „ 818
He lightly s theirs and brought her off — *Merlin and V.* 564
And some with s jewels, — *Last Tournament* 148
books are s from hand to hand— — *Despair* 93
Her dauntless army s, and so small, — *The Fleet* 11
band will be s now their gallant captain is dead, — *Bandit's Death* 41
Scattering (See also Ever-scattering) Time, a maniac s dust, — *In Mem. l* 7
Scaur down the shingly s he plunged, — *Lancelot and E.* 53
Scene all but sicken at the shifting s's. — *The Play* 2
Scent I s it twenty-fold.' — *Gareth and L.* 995
Scented (See also Heather-scented) Thick rosaries of s thorn, — *Arabian Nights* 106
Thro' half-open lattices Coming in the s breeze, — *Eleänore* 24
Sceptre A crown, a s, and a throne ! — *Ode to Memory* 121
To whom I leave the s and the isle— — *Ulysses* 34
He held his s like a pedant's wand — *Princess i* 27
O would I had his s for one hour ! — „ *iv* 538
sorra the Queen wid her s in sich an illigant han', — *Tomorrow* 35
millions under one Imperial s now, — *Locksley H., Sixty* 117
lent The s's of her West, her East, — *To Marq. of Dufferin* 6
Since our Queen assumed the globe, the s. — *On Jub. Q. Victoria* 3
Hold the s, Human Soul, — *By an Evolution.* 16
Sceptre-staff till thy hand Fail from the s-s. — *Œnone* 126
Scheme noble s Grew up from seed we two long since had sown', — *Princess iv* 309
She ask'd but space and fairplay for her s ; — „ *v* 282
I give you all The random s as wildly as it rose : — „ *Con.* 2
how to bind the scatter'd s of seven Together — „ 8
s that had left us flaccid and drain'd. — *Maud I i* 20
When the s's and all the systems, — *Locksley H., Sixty* 159
Schemed s and wrought Until I overturn'd him ; — *Geraint and E.* 829
That if I s against thy peace in this, — *Merlin and V.* 930
Scheming At your simple s . . . — *Forlorn* 16
Schism Now hawking at Geology and s ; — *The Epic* 16
Scholar (See also Scholard) but the s ran Before the master, — *Com. of Arthur* 154
Youthful ! youth and age are s's yet — *Locksley H., Sixty* 243
Scholard (scholar) Fur Squire wur a Varsity s, — *Village Wife* 25
Fur thou be a big s now — *Church-warden, etc.* 22
School (See also Surgery-school) Completion in a painful s ; — *Love thou thy land* 58
I was at s—a college in the South : — *Walk. to the Mail* 83
As in the Latin song I learnt at s, — *Edwin Morris* 79
Thro' the courts, the camps, the s's, — *Vision of Sin* 104
Now let me put the boy and girl to s ; — *Enoch Arden* 312
Then Philip put the boy and girl to s, — „ 331
How Philip put her little ones to s, — „ 706
For there are s's for all.' — *Princess iii* 305
From art, from nature, from the s's, — *In Mem. xlix* 1
The flippant put himself to s — „ *cx* 10
smiles at one That is not of his s, nor any s — *Merlin and V.* 663
scholars yet but in the lower s, — *Locksley H., Sixty* 243
raised the s, and drain'd the fen. — „ 268
lost in the gloom of doubts that darken the s's ; — *Vastness* 11
Schoolbooks In our s we say, — *The Brook* 9
Schoolboy (adj.) not the s heat, The blind hysterics of the Celt : — *In Mem. cix* 15

Schoolboy (s) As cruel as a s ere he grows To Pity— — *Walk. to the Mail* 109
No graver than a s's' barring out ; — *Princess, Con.* 66
School'd whom Gideon s with briers. — *Buonaparte* 14
Science (See also Half-science) truths of S waiting to be caught— — *Golden Year* 17
With the fairy tales of s, — *Locksley Hall* 12
S moves, but slowly slowly, — 134
And wake on s grown to more, — *Day-Dm., L'Envoi* 10
Mastering the lawless s of our law, — *Aylmer's Field* 435
so that sport Went hand in hand with S ; — *Princess, Pro.* 80
Two plummets dropt for one to sound the abyss Of s, — „ *ii* 177
And every Muse tumbled a s in. — „ 399
mixt with inmost terms Of art and s : — „ 447
Two great statues, Art And S, — „ *iv* 201
Where S, Art, and Labour have outpour'd — *Ode Inter. Exhib.* 5
When S reaches forth her arms — *In Mem. xxi* 18
Let S prove we are, and then What matters S unto men, — „ *cxx* 6
man of s himself is fonder of glory, — *Maud I iv* 37
gleam Of letters, dear to S, dear to Art, — *Ded. of Idylls* 40
The simples and the s of that time, — *Lancelot and E.* 862
touching on all things great, S, philosophy, song— — *The Wreck* 51
Till the Sun and the Moon of our s — *Despair* 91
All diseases quench'd by S, — *Locksley H., Sixty* 163
Is it well that while we range with S, — „ 217
S grows and Beauty dwindles— — 246
Fifty years of ever-brightening S ! — *On Jub. Q. Victoria* 53
What the philosophies, all the s's, — *Vastness* 31
tracks Of s making toward Thy Perfectness — *Akbar's Dream* 29
Scion Nor cared for seed or s ! — *Amphion* 12
Scirrhous And s roots and tendons. — 64
Scoff (s) I met with s, I met with scorns — *In Mem. lxix* 9
Scoff (verb) Began to s and jeer and babble of him — *Marr. of Geraint* 58
Scoff'd and s at him And this high Quest — *Holy Grail* 667
Scolded See Raäted
Scolding (See also Raätin') Half-parted from a weak and s hinge, — *The Brook* 84
Scoop'd had s himself In the white rock a chapel — *Lancelot and E.* 404
On the other side Is s a cavern — *Lover's Tale i* 517
Scoor (score) an' soä is s's o' gells, — *N. Farmer, N. S.* 14
Scope shall have s and breathing space — *Locksley Hall* 167
Scorch'd Shot out of them, and s me that I woke. — *Lucretius* 66
Score (See also Scoor) Colleaguing with a s of petty kings, — *Com. of Arthur* 67
and his winters were fifteen s, — *V. of Maeldune* 116
Scorn (s) (See also Self-scorn) Patient of ill, and death, and s, — *Supp. Confessions* 4
To hold a common s of death ! — „ 34
CLEAR-HEADED friend, whose joyful s, — *Clear-headed friend* 1
Dower'd with the hate of hate, the s of s, — *The Poet* 3
' And cruel love, whose end is s, — *Mariana in the S.* 70
Then said the voice, in quiet s, — *Two Voices* 401
Were wisdom in the s of consequence.' — *Œnone* 150
from which mood was born S of herself ; — *Palace of Art* 231
grief became A solemn s of ills. — *D. of F. Women* 228
Turning to s with lips divine The falsehood — *Of old sat Freedom* 23
' Ere yet, in s of Peter's-pence, — *Talking Oak* 45
passion were a target for their s ; — *Locksley Hall* 146
Shall it not be s to me — „ 147
nodding, as in s, He parted, with great strides — *Godiva* 30
I trow they did not part in s : — *Lady Clare* 5
He laugh'd a laugh of merry s : — „ 81
But laws of nature were our s. — *The Voyage* 84
Mingle madness, mingle s ! — *Vision of Sin* 204
bent as he was To make disproof of s, — *Aylmer's Field* 446
striking on huge stumbling-blocks of s — „ 538
From envy, hate and pity, and spite and s, — *Lucretius* 77
She fulmined out her s of laws Salique — *Princess ii* 133
sacred from the blight Of ancient influence and s. — „ 169
' lest some classic Angel speak In s of us, — „ *iii* 71
she lightens s At him that mars her plan, — „ *v* 131
but brooding turn The book of s, — *Princess v* 142
the king in bitter s Drew from my neck — „ *vi* 109
answer'd full of grief and s. — „ 333
and after praise and s, As one who feels — *A Dedication* 6
To shroud me from my proper s. — *In Mem. xxvi* 16

Scorn (s) (*continued*   I met with scoffs, I met with *s*'s   *In Mem.* lxix 9
You say, but with no touch of *s*,   „ xcvi 1
Why then my *s* might well descend   „ cxviii 21
With a glassy smile his brutal *s*—   *Maud* I vi 49
Sir Kay beside the door Mutter'd in *s* of Gareth   *Gareth and L.* 706
The King in utter *s* Of thee and thy much folly   „ 918
' A kitchen-knave, and sent in *s* of me: Such fight   not I, but answer *s* with *s*.   „ 952
Would handle *s*, or yield you,   „ 1173
put your beauty to this flout and *s*   *Geraint and E.* 675
Instead or scornful pity or pure *s*,   „ 859
The *s* of Garlon, poisoning all his rest,   *Balin and Balan* 383
those large eyes, the haunts of *s*,   *Pelleas and E.* 75
persistence turn'd her *s* to wrath.   „ 218
Gawain answer'd kindly tho' in *s*,   „ 333
and these Full knightly without *s*;   *Guinevere* 39
No knight of Arthur's noblest dealt in *s*;   „ 40
S was allow'd as part of his defect,   „ 43
hers Would be for evermore a name of *s*.   „ 61
And mine will ever be a name of *s*.   „ 627
Softness breeding *s* of simple life,   *To the Queen* ii 53
to love and to live for, glanced at in *s*!   *The Wreck* 35
shaft of *s* that once had stung   *Ancient Sage* 131
laughing sober fact to *s*,   *Locksley H., Sixty* 109
Not only to slight praise but suffer *s*;   *To Duke of Argyll* 4
made him leper to compass him with *s*—   *Happy* 16
my wail of reproach and *s*;   *Charity* 23
Scorn (verb)   or if you *s* to lay it, Yourself,   *Princess* vi 183
' They that *s* the tribes and call us   *Boädicea* 7
victor Hours should *s* The long result of love,   *In Mem.* i 13
Then these were such as men might *s*:   „ xlviii 4
Scorn'd, to be scorn'd by one that I *s*,   *Maud* I xiii 1
' Wherefore did the King *S* me ?   *Gareth and L.* 738
' Girl, for I see ye *s* my courtesies,   *Geraint and E.* 671
monk and nun, ye *s* the world's desire,   *Balin and Balan* 445
touching fame, howe'er ye *s* my song,   *Merlin and V.* 444
—we *s* them, but they sting.'   *Lancelot and E.* 139
look On this proud fellow again, who *s*'s us all?'   „ 1065
I must not *s* myself : he loves me still.   *Guinevere* 673
To one who knows I *s* him.   *The Flight* 29
whom most I loathe, to honour whom I *s*?   „ 50
You *s* my Mother's warning,   *The Ring* 326
do you *s* me when you tell me, O my lord,   *Happy* 23
Scorn'd   cursed and *s*, and bruised with stones: *Two Voices* 222
Comfort? comfort *s* of devils?   *Locksley Hall* 75
s to help their equal rights Against the sons   *Princess* vii 233
S, to be *s* by one that I scorn,   *Maud* I xiii 1
and thought the King *S* me and mine;   *Gareth and L.* 1166
And doubtful whether I and mine be *s*.   „ 1253
Scorner   not a *s* of your sex But venerator,   *Princess* iv 422
He rose, descended, met The *s* in the castle court,   *Balin and Balan* 387
O *s* of the party cry That wanders   *Freedom* 25
Scornful   waste wide Of that abyss, or *s* pride !   *Two Voices* 120
All barr'd with long white cloud the *s* crags,   *Palace of Art* 83
But she, with sick and *s* looks averse,   *D. of F. Women* 101
In *s* stillness gazing as they past;   *Com. of Arthur* 478
Instead of *s* pity or pure scorn,   *Geraint and E.* 859
She broke into a little *s* laugh: *Lancelot and E.* 120
Scorning   He utter'd words of *s*;   *The Goose* 42
Enoch set himself, *S* an alms, to work   *Enoch Arden* 812
and they too smiled, *S* him;   *Pelleas and E.* 97
Scorpion   *s* crawling over naked skulls;—   *Demeter and P.* 78
Scorpion-worm   Sware by the *s-w* that twists   *Last Tournament* 451
Scotsman   Bow'd the spoiler, Bent the *S*,   *Batt. of Brunanburh* 21
There was the *S* Weary of war.   „ 35
numberless numbers, Shipmen and *Scotsmen*.   „ 55
Scott (**Sir Walter**)   O great and gallant *S*,   *Bandit's Death* 1
Scoundrel (adj.)   seeing what a door for *s* scum I open'd to   the West,   *Columbus* 170
Scoundrel (s)   stammering ' *s* ' out of teeth that   *Aylmer's Field* 328
And *s* in the supple-sliding knee.'   *Sea Dreams* 168
Scour   to scream, to burnish, and to *s*,   *Princess* iv 520
Scour'd   whistle of the youth who *s* His master's   armour;   *Marr. of Geraint* 257
And *s* into the coppices and was lost,   *Geraint and E.* 534

Scourge   Mortify Your flesh, like me, with *s*'s   *St. S. Stylites* 180
bride Gives her harsh groom for bridal-gift a *s*;   *Princess* v 378
' a *s* am I To lash the treasons of the Table Round.'   *Pelleas and E.* 565
' Heresy.—Penance ? ' ' Fast, Hairshirt and *s*—   *Sir J. Oldcastle* 142
some beneath the *s*, Some over-labour'd,   *Columbus* 177
The slave, the *s*, the chain;   *Freedom* 12
Scourged   Aurelius Emrys would have *s* thee dead,   *Gareth and L.* 375
Scouring   told him, *s* still, ' The sparrow-hawk !'   *Marr. of Geraint* 260
Scout   inward raced the *s*'s With rumour   *Princess* v 111
is it true what was told by the *s*,   *Def. of Lucknow* 95
Scouted   put by, *s* by court and king—   *Columbus* 165
Scowl   foreheads drawn in Roman *s*'s,   *Princess* vii 129
Scowl'd   *s* At their great lord.   *Aylmer's Field* 724
Scrambled   Have *s* past those pits of fire,   *St. S. Stylites* 184
Scrap   *s*'s of thundrous Epic lilted out   *Princess* ii 375
faded rhymes and *s*'s of ancient crones,   *Lover's Tale* i 289
With sallow *s*'s of manuscript,   *To E. Fitzgerald* 48
a *s*, clipt out of the ' deaths ' in a paper, fell.   *The Wreck* 146
Scrape   The four-handed mole chipt *s*   *My life is full* 20
Scraped   (*See also* **Scrawm'd**)   I *s* the lichen from it: *The Brook* 193
Scraping   With strumming and with *s*,   *Amphion* 70
All my poor *s*'s from a dozen years Of dust   *Sea Dreams* 77
Scratby   niver swap Owlby an' *S*   *Church-warden, etc.* 44
Scratch (s)   save her little finger from a *s*   *Edwin Morris* 63
And every *s* a lance had made upon it,   *Lancelot and E.* 20
Scratch (verb)   And *s* the very dead for spite: *Lit. Squabbles* 8
Would a *s* ragged oval on the sand,   *Gareth and L.* 534
They would *s* him up—   *Rizpah* 59
Scratch'd   (*See also* **Scratted**)   *S*, bitten, blinded,   marr'd me   *Last Tournament* 526
Scratted (scratched)   he scrawm'd an' *s* my faäce like a cat   *North. Cobbler* 22
' e gied—I be fear'd fur to tell tha 'ow much—fur an   owd *s* stoän,   *Village Wife* 47
Scrawl   in thy heart the *s* shall play.'   *Sailor Boy* 12
Scrawl'd   The butler drank, the steward *s*,   *Day-Dm., Revival* 10
s A ' Miriam ' that might seem a ' Muriel ';   *The Ring* 240
Scrawm'd (scraped)   he *s* an's cratted my faäce like a cat,   *North. Cobbler* 22
Scream (s)   Now to the *s* of a madden'd beach   *Maud* I iii 12
s of that Wood-devil I came to quell ! '   *Balin and Balan* 548
S's of a babe in the red-hot palms   *The Dawn* 2
Scream (verb)   To tramp, *to s*, to burnish,   *Princess* iv 520
Let the fierce east *s* thro' your eyelet-holes,   *Pelleas and E.* 469
S you are polluted . . .   *Forlorn* 28
Scream'd   The parrot *s*, the peacock squall'd,   *Day-Dm., Revival* 4
wives, that laugh'd and *s* against the gulls,   *Pelleas and E.* 89
waked a bird of prey that *s* and past;   *Death of Œnone* 87
Screeäd (shriek'd)   an' *s* like a Howl gone wud—   *Owd Roä* 76
Screen   (*See also* **Ivy-screen, Quickset-screens**)   neither   of them stands behind the *s* of thy truth.   *Akbar's D., Inscrip.* 7
Screw   ' Let me *s* thee up a peg: *Vision of Sin* 87
' *S* not the chord too sharply lest it snap.'   *Aylmer's Field* 469
Scribbled   every margin *s*, crost, and cramm'd   *Merlin and V.* 677
S or carved upon the pitiless stone;   *Sir J. Oldcastle* 5
Scrimp   Master *s*'s his haggard semptress of her daily   bread,   *Locksley H., Sixty* 221
Scrip   lucky rhymes to him were *s* and share,   *The Brook* 4
Scriptur (scripture)   them words be i' *S*—   *Owd Roä* 15
Or like tother Hangel i' *S*   „ 94
Scripture   (*See also* **Scriptur**)   he heard his priest Preach   an inverted *s*,   *Aylmer's Field* 44
Who reads of begging saints in *S* ? '   *Sir J. Oldcastle* 151
woman ruin'd the world, as God's own *s*'s tell,   *Charity* 3
was a *S* that rang thro' his head,   *The Dreamer* 2
Scritch   Ring sudden *s*'es of the jay,   *My life is full* 20
Scroll   (*See also* **Title-scroll**)   An open *s*, Before him lay :   *The Poet* 8
But one poor poet's *s*,   „ 55
ponder those three hundred *s*'s Left by the Teacher,   *Lucretius* 12
The seal was Cupid bent above a *s*,   *Princess* i 242
she crush'd The *s*'s together, made a sudden turn   „ iv 394
Sun In dexter chief; the *s* ' I follow fame.'   *Merlin and V.* 476
like a serpent, ran a *s* Of letters   *Holy Grail* 170
fiery *s* written over with lamentation and woe.   *Despair* 20
in his hand A *s* of verse—   *Ancient Sage* 6
Scroob'd (scrubbed)   es it couldn't be *s* awaäy,   *Village Wife* 39
Scrubbed   See **Scroob'd**

Second (adj.) (continued) The s brother in their fool's
    parable— *Gareth and L.* 1004
So when they touch'd the s river-loop, " 1025
To seek a s favour at his hands. *Marr. of Geraint* 626
Then went Sir Bedivere the s time *Pass. of Arthur* 250
And hid Excalibur the s time, " 279
Obedient to her s master now ; *Lover's Tale* iv 343
You'll make her its s mother ! *First Quarrel* 71
and in the s year was born A s— *Sisters (E. and E.)* 269
Felt within themselves the sacred passion of the
    s life. *Locksley H., Sixty* 68
No s cloudless honeymoon was mine. *The Ring* 382
Second (s) ashes and all fire again Thrice in a s, *Lover's Tale* iv 324
Second-hand fit us like a nature s-h ; *Walk to the Mail* 65
Second-sight The s-s of some Astræan age, *Princess* ii 443
Secret (adj.) From many a wondrous grot and s cell *The Kraken* 8
Only they saw thee from the s shrine *Alexander* 13
and close it up With s death for ever. *Wan Sculptor* 13
and made appear Still-lighted in a s shrine, *Mariana in the S.* 18
' Yet,' said the s voice, ' some time, Sooner or later, *Two Voices* 64
' But heard, by s transport led, " 214
doors that bar The s bridal chambers of the heart, *Gardener's D.* 249
Then by some s shrine I ride ; *Sir Galahad* 29
S wrath like smother'd fuel Burnt in each man's blood. *The Captain* 15
And s laughter tickled all my soul. *Princess* iv 267
considering everywhere Her s meaning in her deeds, *In Mem.* lv 10
A s sweetness in the stream, " lxiv 20
Thy passion clasps a s joy : " lxxxviii 8
all as soon as born Deliver'd at a s postern-gate *Com. of Arthur* 213
She answer'd, ' These be s things,' " 318
That God hath told the King a s word. " 489
In whom high God hath breathed a s thing. " 501
A strange knee rustle thro' her s reeds, *Balin and Balan* 354
This fair wife-worship cloaks a s shame ? " 360
To spy some s scandal if he might, *Guinevere* 26
Shut in the s chambers of the rock. *Lover's Tale* i 521
and not rather A sacred, s, unapproached woe, " 679
Then Julian made a s sign to me " iv 284
strange dream to me To mind me of the s vow I made *Columbus* 92
There in a s olive-glade I saw Pallas Athene *Tiresias* 39
Wild flowers of the s woods. *The Flight* 82
Patient—the s splendour of the brooks. *Prog. of Spring* 21
Secret (s) (*See also* **Party-secret**) What know we of
    the s of a man ? *Walk. to the Mail* 104
On s's of the brain, the stars, *Day-Dm., L'Envoi* 11
' But keep the s for your life, *Lady Clare* 34
' But keep the s all ye can.' " 42
' Woman, I have a s—only swear, *Enoch Arden* 837
abyss Of science, and the s's of the mind : *Princess* ii 177
the snake, My s, seem'd to stir within my breast ; " iii 44
And holy s's of this microcosm. " 313
S's of the sullen mine, *Ode Inter. Exhib.* 16
charms Her s from the latest moon ? ' *In Mem.* xxi 20
And all the s of the Spring " xxiii 19
He reads the s of the star, " xcvii 22
after-years Will learn the s of our Arthur's birth.' *Com. of Arthur* 159
learnt their elemental s's, powers And forces ; *Merlin and V.* 632
familiar friend Might well have kept his s. *Lancelot and E.* 593
her heart's sad s blazed itself In the heart's colours " 836
And every homely s in their hearts, *Holy Grail* 552
kept our holy faith among her kin In s, " 698
For all the s of her inmost heart, *Lover's Tale* i 588
Not know ? with such a s to be known. " iv 121
and the s of the Gods. *Tiresias* 8
Secretest with echoing feet he threaded The s walks
    of fame ; *The Poet* 10
Sect I care not what the s's may brawl. *Palace of Art* 210
To cleave a creed in s's and cries, *In Mem.* cxxviii 15
every splinter'd fraction of a s Will clamour *Akbar's Dream* 33
Secular on whom The s emancipation turns Of half this
    world, *Princess* ii 289
lighten thro' The s abyss to come, *In Mem.* lxxvi 6
Secure And in their double love s, *Two Voices* 418
Lie still, dry dust, s of change. *To J. S.* 76
as from men s Amid their marshes, *Last Tournament* 426

Secure (continued) look down and up, Serene, s, *Early Spring* 28
Sedate The chancellor, s and vain, *Day-Dm., Revival* 29
Sedge whisper'd ' Asses' ears,' among the s, *Princess* ii 113
Seduced harlot-like S me from you, *Romney's R.* 116
See (*See also* **Seeä**) S ! our friends are all forsaking *All Things will Die* 18
For even and morn Ye will never s Thro' eternity. " 45
Hither, come hither and s ; *Sea-Fairies* 28
thro' the windows we shall s The nakedness *Deserted House* 10
I s thy beauty gradually unfold, *Eleänore* 70
I seem to s Thought folded over thought, " 83
I s thee roam, with tresses unconfined, " 122
as far on as eye could s. *If I were loved* 14
Thine eyes so wept that they could hardly s ; *The Bridesmaid* 2
There she s's the highway near *L. of Shalott* ii 13
Like to some branch of stars we s " iii 11
' Still s's the sacred morning spread *Two Voices* 80
' I s the end, and know the good.' " 432
You scarce could s the grass for flowers. " 453
I s the wealthy miller yet, *Miller's D.* 1
In yonder chair I s him sit, " 9
I s his gray eyes twinkle yet At his own jest— " 11
And s the minnows everywhere In crystal eddies " 51
The doubt my mother would not s ; " 154
and s thy Paris judge of gods.' *Œnone* 90
never more Shall lone Œnone s the morning mist Sweep
    thro' them ; never s them overlaid With narrow moon-
    lit slips " 216
O happy heaven, how canst thou s my face ? " 236
I dimly s My far-off doubtful purpose, " 250
O the Earl was fair to s ! (repeat) *The Sisters* 6, 12, 18, 24, 30, 36
Houris bow'd to s The dying Islamite, *Palace of Art* 102
Which you had hardly cared to s. *L. C. V. de Vere* 32
whom think ye should I s, *May Queen* 13
you'll be there too, mother, to s me made the Queen ; " 26
I would s the sun rise upon the glad New-
    year. (repeat) *May Queen, N. Y's. E.* 2, 51
It is the last New-Year that I shall ever s, " 3
never s The blossom on the blackthorn, " 7
I long to s a flower so before the day I die. " 16
never s me more in the long gray fields " 26
And you'll come sometimes and s me " 30
Tho' you'll not s me, mother, " 38
s me carried out from the threshold of the door ; " 42
Don't let Effie come to s me " 43
hear and s the far-off sparkling brine, *Lotos-Eaters, C. S.* 98
Waiting to s me die. *D. of F. Women* 112
O me, that I should ever s the light ! " 254
He will not s the dawn of day. *D. of the O. Year* 11
A jollier year we shall not s. " 20
To s him die, across the waste " 30
I will s before I die The palms and temples *You ask me, why, etc.* 27
Watch what I s, and lightly bring thee word.' *M. d'Arthur* 123
I s thee what thou art, " 123
' Now s I by thine eyes that this is done. " 149
Nor shall s, here or elsewhere, till I die, " 154
now I s the true old times are dead, " 229
If thou should'st never s my face again, " 246
in itself the day we went To s her. *Gardener's D.* 76
I would wish to s My grandchild on my knees before I die : *Dora* 12
he may s the boy, And bless him " 69
Allan said, ' I s it is a trick Got up betwixt you " 95
But go you hence, and never s me more.' " 100
He says that he will never s me more.' " 116
Whose house is that I s ? *Walk. to the Mail* 11
eyes Should s the raw mechanic's bloody thumbs " 75
I s the moulder'd Abbey-walls, *Talking Oak* 3
when I s the woodman lift His axe to slay my kin. " 235
Then not to dare to s ! *Love and Duty* 38
And s the great Achilles, whom we knew. *Ulysses* 64
Thou seëst all things, thou wilt s my grave : *Tithonus* 73
far as human eye could s ; (repeat) *Locksley Hall* 15, 119
O, I s thee old and formal, " 93
S's in heaven the light of London " 114
O, I s the crescent promise " 187
And loathed to s them overtax'd ; *Godiva* 9

See (*continued*) *S* what I *s*, be thou where I have been,   *Balin and Balan* 572
I scarce can *s* thee now. Goodnight!   ,, 621
I *s* thee now no more.   ,, 624
Nor could he *s* but him who wrought the charm   *Merlin and V.* 212
s you not, dear love, That such a mood as that,   ,, 324
that no man could *s* her more,   ,, 642
S's what his fair bride is and does,   ,, 782
s Her godlike head crown'd with spiritual fire,   ,, 836
ask you not to *s* the shield he left,   *Lancelot and E.* 653
an ye will it let me *s* the shield.'   ,, 661
'Going? and we shall never *s* you more.   ,, 926
to *s* your face, To serve you,   ,, 938
'Not to be with you, not to *s* your face—   ,, 946
To *s* that she be buried worshipfully.'   ,, 1329
to *s* The maiden buried, not as one unknown,   ,, 1333
if a man Could touch or *s* it, he was heal'd   *Holy Grail* 55
for thou shalt *s* what I have seen,   ,, 160
none might *s* who bare it, and it past.   ,, 190
But since I did not *s* the Holy Thing,   ,, 281
What go ye into the wilderness to *s*?'   ,, 287
one hath seen, and all the blind will *s*.   ,, 313
what thy sister taught me first to *s*,   ,, 469
thou shalt *s* the vision when I go.'   ,, 484
On either hand, as far as eye could *s*,   ,, 498
Which never eyes on earth again shall *s*.   ,, 532
if ever loyal man and true Could *s* it,   ,, 757
cannot *s* for slime, Slime of the ditch: ,, 771
could I touch or *s* the Holy Grail   ,, 779
Being too blind to have desire to *s*.   ,, 872
'*S*! look at mine! but wilt thou fight   *Pelleas and E.* 127
Content am I so that I *s* thy face But once a day: ,, 243
from the vermin that he *s*'s Before him,   ,, 285
Vex not yourself: ye will not *s* me more.'   ,, 304
Thus to be bounden, so to *s* her face,   ,, 326
Let me be bounden, I shall *s* her face;   ,, 331
S, the hand Wherewith thou takest this,   *Last Tournament* 192
Tuwhoo! do ye *s* it? do ye *s* the star?'   ,, 346
'Nay, nor will: I *s* it and hear.   ,, 348
shape Of one that in them *s*'s himself,   ,, 370
forgotten all in my strong joy To *s* thee—   ,, 583
Who *s* your tender grace and stateliness.   *Guinevere* 190
sworn never to *s* him more, To *s* him more.'   ,, 376
pity almost makes me die To *s* thee,   ,, 535
Never lie by thy side; *s* thee no more—   ,, 579
I might *s* his face, and not be seen.'   ,, 588
so she did not *s* the face,   ,, 595
now I *s* thee what thou art,   ,, 648
We needs must love the highest when we *s* it,   ,, 660
And have not power to *s* it as it is: *Pass. of Arthur* 20
because we *s* not to the close',   ,, 21
one last act of knighthood shalt thou *s*   ,, 163
Watch what I *s*, and lightly bring thee word.'   ,, 212
I *s* thee what thou art,   ,, 291
'Now *s* I by thine eyes that this is done.   ,, 317
Nor shall *s*, here or elsewhere, till I die,   ,, 322
now I *s* the true old times are dead,   ,, 397
thou should'st never *s* my face again,   ,, 414
S, sirs, Even now the Goddess of the Past,   *Lover's Tale i* 15
Chink'd as you *s*, and seam'd—   ,, 131
Waiting to *s* some blessed shape in heaven,   ,, 312
FROM that time forth I would not *s* her more;   ,, ii 1
in her you *s* That faithful servant   ,, iv 341
to *s* if work could be found;   *First Quarrel* 44
When I cannot *s* my own hand,   *Rizpah* 7
Couldn't *s* 'im, we 'eärd 'im   *North. Cobbler* 47
'Doesn't tha *s* 'im, she axes, 'fur I can *s* 'im?'   ,, 49
For *s*—this wine—the grape from whence   *Sisters (E. and E.)* 61
That time I did *s*,   ,, 90
when she thought I did not *s*—   ,, 166
The Lord has so *much* to *s* to!   *In the Child Hosp.* 57
and we went to *s* to the child.   ,, 68
perchance the neighbours round May *s*,   *Achilles over the T.* 13
Whom yet I *s* as there you sit   *To E. Fitzgerald* 5
strange hope to *s* the nearer God.   *Tiresias* 29
eyes, that cannot *s* thine own, *S* this,   ,, 108

See (*continued*) *S*, we were nursed in the drear night-fold   *Despair* 21
s's and stirs the surface-shadow   *Ancient Sage* 38
s's the Best that glimmers thro' the Worst,   ,, 72
Who *s* not what they do?'   ,, 81
s The high-heaven dawn of more than mortal day   ,, 283
waken every morning to that face I loathe to *s*:   *The Flight* 8
And *s* the ships from out the West   ,, 91
I seem to *s* a new-dug grave up yonder by the yew!   ,, 98
people 'ud *s* it that wint in to mass—   *Tomorrow* 74
Thou *s*'s that i' spite o' the men   *Spinster's S's.* 11
guide us thro' the days I shall not *s*?   *Locksley H., Sixty* 158
whence you *s* the Locksley tower,   ,, 176
and even where you *s* her now—   ,, 179
We should *s* the Globe we groan in,   ,, 188
Man or Mind that *s*'s a shadow   ,, 196
those nearest us whom we neither *s* nor name,   ,, 272
s the highest Human Nature is divine.   ,, 276
But scarce could *s*, as now we *s*,   *Epilogue* 48
all in vain As far as man can *s*,   ,, 69
Shall we *s* to it, I and you?   *Dead Prophet* 52
'*S*, what a little heart,' she said,   ,, 75
both our Houses, may they *s* Beyond the borough   *Hands all Round* 2
those gilt gauds men-children swarm to *s*.   *To W. C. Macready* 11
For, *s*, thy foot has touch'd it;   *Demeter and P.* 48
Will *s* me by the landmark far away,   ,, 124
s no more The Stone, the Wheel,   ,, 149
I couldn't *s* fur the smoäke   *Owd Roä* 87
not shown To dazzle all that *s* them?   *The Ring* 144
that *s*'s A thousand squares of corn and meadow,   ,, 148
and cried 'I *s* him, Io t'amo, Io t'amo.'   ,, 223
'*S*!—Found in a chink of that old moulder'd floor!'   ,, 279
and *s* beneath our feet The mist of autumn   ,, 328
In all the world my dear one *s*'s but you—   ,, 364
as a man Who *s*'s his face in water,   ,, 370
till she *s*'s Her maiden coming like a Queen,   ,, 479
He *s* me, waves me from him.   *Happy* 19
and weeping scarce could *s*;   ,, 54
S, I sinn'd but for a moment.   ,, 85
And *s* my cedar green, and there My giant ilex   *To Ulysses* 17
gladly *s* I thro' the wavering flakes   *Prog. of Spring* 29
Beyond the darker hour to *s* the bright,   ,, 88
The best in me that *s*'s the worst in me, And groans
   to *s* it, finds no comfort there.   *Romney's R.* 44
S, there is hardly a daisy.   *The Throstle* 12
O GOD in every temple I *s* people that *s* thee,   *Akbar's D., Inscrip.* 1
once again we *s* thee rise.   *Hymn* 1
SIR, do you *s* this dagger?   *Bandit's Death* 5
He *s*'s not her like anywhere in this pitiless world   *Charity* 43
And *s* and shape and do.   *Mechanophilus* 4
I hope to *s* my Pilot face to face   *Crossing the Bar* 15
Seeä (**see**) when they *s*'s ma a passin' boy,   *N. Farmer, O. S.* 53
if tha *s*'s 'im an' smells 'im   *North. Cobbler* 66
I browt what tha *s*'s stannin' theer,   ,, 70
Seeä'd (**saw**) *S* her todaäy goä by—   *N. Farmer, N. S.* 13
Seeäd I *s* that our Sally went laämed   *North. Cobbler* 39
S nobbut the smile o' the sun   ,, 50
Seeäd (**seed**) an' some on it down i' *s*.   *N. Farmer, O. S.* 40
Seeädin' (**seeding**) wool of a thistle a-flyin' an' tha
haäted to see;   *Spinster's S's.* 79
Seeäm (**seem**) 'E *s*'s naw moor nor watter,   *North. Cobbler* 76
Seeäm'd (**seemed**) an' *s* as blind as a poop,   *Owd Roä* 101
Seed (*See also* **Arrow-seed, Seeäd**) having sown some
generous *s*,   *Two Voices* 143
Sow the *s*, and reap the harvest   *Lotos-Eaters, C. S.* 121
Bear of men and growth of minds.   *Love thou thy land* 20
That sought to sow themselves like winged *s*'s,   *Gardener's D.* 65
Not only we, the latest *s* of Time,   *Godiva* 5
Nor cared for *s* or scion!   *Amphion* 12
The vilest herb that runs to *s*   ,, 95
But in my words were *s*'s of fire.   *The Letters* 28
and thus a noble scheme Grew up from *s*   *Princess iv* 310
the *s*, The little *s* they laugh'd at in the dark,   ,, vi 33
save the one true *s* of freedom sown   *Ode on Well.* 162
Once in a golden hour I cast to earth a *s*.   *The Flower* 2
thieves from o'er the wall Stole the *s* by night.   ,, 12

Seed (continued) For all have got the s. *The Flower* 20
And finding that of fifty s's *In Mem.* lv 11
This bitter s among mankind ; „ xc 4
Ray round with flames her disk of s, „ ci 6
Long sleeps the summer in the s; „ cv 26
is but s Of what in them is flower „ *Con.* 135
three gray linnets wrangle for the s: *Guinevere* 255
winds, Laden with thistledown and s's *Lover's Tale* ii 13
Eastern gauze With s's of gold— „ iv 292
for I loathe The s of Cadmus— *Tiresias* 117
Daughter of the s of Cain, *Forlorn* 39
Accomplish that blind model in the s, *Prog. of Spring* 114
Seed (saw) nor 'e niver not s to owt, *Village Wife* 51
but Robby I s thruf ya theere. *Spinster's S's.* 14
Fur I s that Steevie wur coomin', „ 40
fur I s that it couldn't be, „ 47
Fur I s the beck coomin' down *Owd Roä* 40
I s at 'is faäce wur as red as the Yule-block „ 56
then I s 'er a-cryin', I did. „ 80
'at summun s i' the flaäme, „ 94
Ay, an' ya s the Bishop. *Church-warden, etc.* 17
An' keeäper 'e s ya an roon'd, „ 28
Seed (seen) I niver ha s it sa white wi' the Maäy *Village Wife* 80
An' they niver 'ed s sich ivin' *Owd Roä* 26
See'd (saw) white wi' the Maäy es I s it to-year— *Village Wife* 80
See'd (seen) boooks, I ha' s 'em, belong'd to the Squire, „ 71
Seeded Across the silent s meadow-grass Borne, *Pelleas and E.* 561
Seeding *See* **Seeädin'**
Seedling as Nature packs Her blossom or her s, *Enoch Arden* 179
Seedsman s, rapt Upon the teeming harvest, *Golden Year* 70
Seeing (*See also* **All-seeing**) S all his own mischance— *L. of Shalott* iv 12
s men, in power Only, are likest gods, *Œnone* 129
s not That Beauty, Good, and Knowledge, To——, *With Pal. of Art* 9
Averill s How low his brother's mood had fallen, *Aylmer's Field* 403
we should find the land Worth s ; *Princess* iii 172
S I saw not, hearing not I heard : „ vi 19
s either sex alone Is half itself, „ vii 301
And our s is not sight. *Voice and the P.* 36
S his gewgaw castle shine, *Maud* I x 18
her men, S the mighty swarm about their walls, *Com. of Arthur* 200
S that ye be grown too weak and old „ 511
s the city is built To music, *Gareth and L.* 276
s he hath sent us cloth of gold, „ 428
s who had work'd Lustier than any, „ 695
And s now thy words are fair, „ 1181
S he never rides abroad by day ; „ 1334
And all the three were silent s, „ 1362
And s them so tender and so close, *Marr. of Geraint* 22
And s one so gay in purple silks, „ 284
And s her so sweet and serviceable, „ 393
s I have sworn That I will break his pride „ 423
Danced in his bosom, s better days. „ 505
Then s cloud upon the mother's brow, „ 777
Arthur s ask'd ' Tell me your names ; *Balin and Balan* 49
s that thy realm Hath prosper'd in the name of Christ, „ 98
Balin first woke, and s that true face, „ 590
And s me, with a great voice he cried, *Lancelot and E.* 309
s that ye forget Obedience is the courtesy „ 717
S it is no more Sir Lancelot's fault „ 1075
Yet, s you desire your child to live, „ 1095
S I never stray'd beyond the cell, *Holy Grail* 628
s that the King must guard That which he rules, „ 905
and s Pelleas droop, Said Guinevere, *Pelleas and E.* 178
so went back, and s them yet in sleep „ 445
s they profess To be none other (repeat) *Last Tournament* 82, 85
s too much wit Makes the world rotten, „ 246
Let be thy Mark, s he is not thine.' „ 522
Flatter me rather, s me so weak, „ 642
S it is not bounded save by love.' „ 703
S forty of our poor hundred were slain, *The Revenge* 76
s what a door for scoundrel scum I open'd *Columbus* 170
Seek When my passion s's Pleasance *Lilian* 8
What wantest thou ? whom dost thou s, *Oriana* 71
We would run to and fro, and hide and s, *The Mermaid* 35
And seem to find, but still to s. *Two Voices* 96

Seek (continued) I s a warmer sky, *You ask me, why, etc.* 26
'Tis not too late to s a newer world. *Ulysses* 57
to s, to find, and not to yield. „ 70
To those that s them issue forth ; *Day-Dm., Arrival* 2
He comes, scarce knowing what he s's : „ 17
' O s my father's court with me, „ *Depart.* 27
childless mother went to s her child ; *Aylmer's Field* 829
' Hist O Hist,' he said, ' They s us : *Princess* iv 219
where you s the common love of these, „ vi 172
He s's at least Upon the last *In Mem.* xlvii 12
s A friendship for the years to come. „ lxxxv 79
But s's to beat in time with one „ 115
To s thee on the mystic deeps, „ cxxv 14
And so that he find what he went to s, *Maud* I xvi 3
I will s thee out Some comfortable bride *Gareth and L.* 93
twelvemonth and a day, nor s my name. „ 446
S, till we find.' „ 1279
I s a harbourage for the night.' *Marr. of Geraint* 299
To s a second favour at his hands. „ 626
had ridd'n a random round To s him, *Lancelot and E.* 631
my craven s's To wreck thee villainously : *Last Tournament* 548
' to s the Lord Jesus in prayer; *In the Child. Hosp.* 158
made by me, may s to unbury me, *Columbus* 206
sworn to s If any golden harbour *Pref. Son. 19th Cent.* 12
then so keen to s The meanings ambush'd *Tiresias* 4
the rebel subject s to drag me from the throne, *By an Evolution.* 15
Seeker *See* **Self-seeker**
Seeking in s to undo One riddle, *Two Voices* 232
S a tavern which of old he knew, *Enoch Arden* 691
For love or fear, or s favour of us, *Marr. of Geraint* 700
weak beast s to help herself By striking *Merlin and V.* 498
Seeling Diet and s, jesses, leash „ 125
Seem (*See also* **Seeäm**) And children all s full of Thee ! *Supp. Confessions* 21
things that s, And things that be, „ 173
I s to see Thought folded over thought, *Eleänore* 83
or s To lapse far back in some confused dream *Sonnet To ——* 2
' He s's to hear a Heavenly Friend, *Two Voices* 295
' Moreover, something is or s's, „ 379
So sweet it s's with thee to walk, *Miller's D.* 29
It s's in after-dinner talk „ 31
I may s, As in the nights of old, „ 165
would s to award it thine, *Œnone* 73
Howe'er it be, it s's to me, *L. C. V. de Vere* 53
And now it s's as hard to stay, *May Queen, Con.* 10
O sweet and strange it s's to me, „ 53
s to mourn and rave On alien shores ; *Lotos-Eaters* 32
It s's I broke a close with force and arms : *Edwin Morris* 131
She s's a part of those fresh days to me ; „ 142
So s's she to the boy. *Talking Oak* 108
' So strange it s's to me. *Lady Clare* 52
Evermore she s's to gaze On that cottage *L. of Burleigh* 34
I s so foolish and so broken down. *Enoch Arden* 245
s's, as I re-listen to it, *The Brook* 18
My mother, as it s's you did, „ 225
I s to be ungraciousness itself.' *Aylmer's Field* 245
King of the East altho' he s, *Lucretius* 133
s's some unseen monster lays His vast and filthy hands „ 219
since the nobler pleasure s's to fade. „ 230
I would be that for ever which I s, *Princess* ii 257
Methinks he s's no better than a girl ; „ iii 218
I s no more : I want forgiveness too : „ vi 290
That s to keep her up but drag her down— „ vii 270
I s A mockery to my own self. „ 336
Mourn, for to us he s's the last, *Ode on Well.* 19
Who s's a promontory of rock, *Will* 6
tho' He be not that which He s's? *High. Pantheism* 3
So s's it in my deep regret, *In Mem.* viii 17
I s to meet their least desire, „ lxxxiv 17
I s to love thee more and more. „ cxxx 12
It s's that I am happy, *Maud* I xviii 50
undercurrent woe That s's to draw— „ 84
indeed He s's to me Scarce other *Ded. of Idylls* 6
I s as nothing in the mighty world, *Com. of Arthur* 87
there is nothing in it as it s's Saving the King; *Gareth and L.* 264

Seem (*continued*) *s's* Wellnigh as long as thou art
    statured tall!   *Gareth and L.* 281
see ye not how weak and hungerworn I *s*—   ,, 444
S I not as tender to him As any mother?   ,, 1283
ye *s* agape to roar!   ,, 1306
For tho' it *s's* my spurs are yet to win,   *Marr. of Geraint* 128
Who *s's* no bolder than a beaten hound;   *Geraint and E.* 61
who sits apart, And *s's* so lonely?'   ,, 300
It *s's* another voice in other groves;   *Balin and Balan* 215
s's a flame That rages in the woodland far below,   ,, 233
For thanks it *s* till now neglected,   *Merlin and V.* 308
makes you *s* less noble than yourself,   ,, 322
since ye *s* the Master of all Art,   ,, 468
That *s* a sword beneath a belt of three,   ,, 510
wreathen round it made it *s* his own;   ,, 735
My father, howsoe'er I *s* to you,   *Lancelot and E.* 1092
but *s* Mute of this miracle,   *Holy Grail* 65
Until this earth he walks on *s's* not earth,   ,, 912
mine the blame that oft I *s* as he   *Last Tournament* 115
the glance That only *s's* half-loyal to command,—   ,, 118
Behold, I *s* but King among the dead.'   *Pass. of Arthur* 146
(For they *s* many and my most of life,   *Lover's Tale i* 185
All this *S's* to the quiet daylight of your minds   ,, 296
S's but a cobweb filament to link   ,, 376
tho' she *s* so like the one you lost,   ,, iv 365
eyes frown: the lips *S* but a gash.   *Sisters (E. and E.)* 107
s Like would-be guests an hour too late,   *Tiresias* 197
brain was drunk with the water, it *s's*;   *Despair* 65
s to flicker past thro' sun and shade,   *Ancient Sage* 100
I *s* to see a new-dug grave up yonder   *The Flight* 98
s's to me now like a bit of yisther-day   *Tomorrow* 8
The days that *s* to-day,   *Pref. Poem Broth. S.* 24
A 'Miriam' that might *s* a 'Muriel';   *The Ring* 241
May *s* the black ox of the distant plain.   *To one who ran down Eng.* 4
I *s* no longer like a lonely man   *Akbar's Dream* 20
But such a tide as moving *s's* asleep,   *Crossing the Bar* 5

Seem'd (*See also* **Seeäm'd**) In sleep she *s* to walk forlorn,   *Mariana* 30
s to shake The sparkling flints   *Arabian Nights* 51
there *s* Hundreds of crescents on the roof   ,, 128
And *s* knee-deep in mountain grass,   *Mariana in the S.* 42
Such *s* the whisper at my side: *Two Voices* 439
There *s* no room for sense of wrong;   ,, 456
S half-within and half-without,   *Miller's D.* 7
Floated her hair or *s* to float in rest.   *Œnone* 19
on every peak a statue *s* To hang on tiptoe,   *Palace of Art* 37
One *s* all dark and red—a tract of sand,   ,, 65
You *s* to hear them climb and fall   ,, 70
without light Or power of movement, *s* my soul,   ,, 246
It *s* so hard at first, mother,   *May Queen, Con.* 9
s to go right up to Heaven and die   ,, 40
In which it *s* always afternoon.   *Lotos-Eaters* 4
A land where all things *s* the same !   ,, 24
And deep-asleep he *s*, yet all awake,   ,, 35
Most weary *s* the sea, weary the oar,   ,, 41
I started once, or *s* to start in pain,   *D. of F. Women* 41
in her throat Her voice *s* distant,   *To J. S* 55
there *s* A touch of something false,   *Edwin Morris* 73
'Yet *s* the pressure thrice as sweet   *Talking Oak* 145
how hard it *s* to me, When eyes,   *Love and Duty* 35
he *s* To his great heart none other than a God !   *Tithonus* 13
We *s* to sail into the Sun!   *The Voyage* 67
Now nearer to the prow she *s*   ,, 67
She *s* a part of joyous Spring: *Sir L. and Q. G.* 23
Rose again from where it *s* to fail,   *Vision of Sin* 24
the girl *S* kinder unto Philip than to him;   *Enoch Arden* 42
He *s*, as in a nightmare of the night,   ,, 114
while Annie *s* to hear Her own death-scaffold raising,   ,, 174
for Enoch *s* to them Uncertain as a vision   ,, 355
A footstep *s* to fall beside her path,   ,, 514
There often as he watch'd or *s* to watch,   ,, 600
idiotlike it *s*, With inarticulate rage,   ,, 639
it *s* he saw No pale sheet-lightnings from afar,   *Aylmer's Field* 725
Fought with what *s* my own uncharity,   *Sea Dreams* 73
That *s* a fleet of jewels under me,   ,, 123
for it *s* A void was made in Nature;   *Lucretius* 36

Seem'd (*continued*) I *s* to move among a world of ghosts,   *Princess i* 17
the snake, My secret, *s* to stir within my breast;   ,, iii 44
I *s* to move among a world of ghosts;   ,, iv 561
neither *s* there more to say: ,, v 330
and *s* to charm from thence The wrath   ,, 436
I *s* to move in old memorial tilts,   ,, 479
Yet it *s* a dream, I dream'd Of fighting.   ,, 492
For so it *s*, or so they said to me,   ,, vi 27
pitying as it *s*, Or self-involved ;   ,, 157
nor *s* it strange that soon He rose up whole,   ,, vii 64
meek *S* the full lips, and mild the luminous eyes,   ,, 226
Had ever *s* to wrestle with burlesque,   ,, Con. 16
He is gone who *s* so great.—   *Ode on Well.* 271
That *s* to touch it in leaf: *In Mem. lxix* 18
The gentleness he *s* to be,   ,, cxi 12
Best *s* the thing he was, and join'd   ,, 13
tho' there often *s* to live A contradiction   ,, cxxv 3
If Maud were all that she *s*, (repeat)   *Maud I vi* 36, 92
S her light foot along the garden walk,   ,, xviii 9
Ever and ever afresh they *s* to grow.   ,, II i 28
sad At times he *s*, and sad with him was I,   *Com. of Arthur* 353
high upon the dreary deeps It *s* in heaven,   ,, 374
it *s* The dragon-boughts and elvish emblemings   *Gareth and L.* 232
that ev'n to him they *s* to move.   ,, 237
all Naked it *s*, and glowing in the broad   ,, 1088
for he *s* as one That all in later,   ,, 1128
so Gareth *s* to strike Vainly,   ,, 1133
s The dress that now she look'd on   *Marr. of Geraint* 612
But evermore it *s* an easier thing   *Geraint and E.* 108
Whereof one *s* far larger than her lord,   ,, 122
and *s* So justified by that necessity,   ,, 395
How far beyond him Lancelot *s* to move,   *Balin and Balan* 172
The music in him *s* to change,   ,, 217
fought Hard with himself, and *s* at length in peace.   ,, 239
Ev'n when they *s* unloveable,   *Merlin and V.* 176
The man so wrought on ever *s* to lie   ,, 208
s a lovely baleful star Veil'd in gray vapour;   ,, 262
You *s* that wave about to break upon me   ,, 302
course of life that *s* so flowery to me   ,, 880
he *s* the goodliest man That ever among ladies   *Lancelot and E.* 254
He *s* to me another Lancelot—   ,, 534
When some brave deed *s* to be done in vain,   *Holy Grail* 274
s to me the Lord of all the world,   ,, 414
s Shoutings of all the sons of God :   ,, 508
in a dream I *s* to climb For ever: ,, 836
It *s* to Pelleas that the fern without   *Pelleas and E.* 34
have *s* A vision hovering on a sea of fire,   ,, 51
she that *s* the chief among them said,   ,, 62
She might have *s* a toy to trifle with,   ,, 76
S my reproach ? He is not of my kind.   ,, 311
hard his eyes ; harder his heart *S* ;   ,, 513
S those far-rolling, westward-smiling seas,   *Last Tournament* 587
he *s* to me no man, But Michaël trampling Satan ;   ,, 672
from the dawn it *s* there came,   *Pass. of Arthur* 457
It *s* to keep its sweetness to itself, Yet was not
    the less sweet for that it *s* ?   *Lover's Tale i* 154
the sunshine *s* to brood More warmly   ,, 327
s a gossamer filament up in air,   ,, 413
I died then, I had not *s* to die,   ,, 494
I *s* the only part of Time stood still,   ,, 573
then it *s* as tho' a link Of some tight chain   ,, 594
and then I *s* to hear Its murmur,   ,, 634
The spirit *s* to flag from thought to thought,   ,, ii 51
motions of my heart *s* far within me,   ,, 54
then I *s* To rise, and through the forest-shadow   ,, 71
at his feet I *s* to faint and fall,   ,, 96
it *s* By that which follow'd—   ,, iv 21
Found, as it *s*, a skeleton alone,   ,, 139
such a feast, ill-suited as it *s* To such a time,   ,, 207
S stepping out of darkness with a smile.   ,, 220
veil, that *s* no more than gilded air,   ,, 290
cry, that rather *s* For some new death   ,, 373
Often I *s* unhappy, and often as happy too,   *First Quarrel* 31
We *s* like ships i' the Channel   ,, 42
to be found Long after, as it *s*,   *Sisters (E. and E.)* 111

Sell (*continued*) And yet to *s* her—then with what she brought   *Enoch Arden* 137
  s her, those good parents, for her good.   *Aylmer's Field* 483
  An' pigs didn't *s* at fall,   *Church-warden, etc.* 5
Seller (*See also* **Absolution-seller**) belongs to the
  heart of the perfume *s*.   *Akbar's D., Inscrip.* 9
Semblance Like to the mother plant in *s*,   *The Poet* 23
  edict of the will to reassume The *s*   *Lover's Tale ii* 162
Semicircle Leapt in a *s*, and lit on earth ;   *Balin and Balan* 414
  the *s* Of dark-blue waters and the narrow fringe   *Lover's Tale i* 37
Semi-jealousy A flash of *s-j* clear'd it to her.   *Aylmer's Field* 189
Semi-smile *s-s* As at a strong conclusion—   *Lover's Tale iv* 281
Sempstress Master scrimps his haggard *s* of her daily
  bread,   *Locksley H., Sixty* 221
Sen (**self**) 'E seeäms naw moor nor watter, an' 'e's
  the Divil's oän *s*.'   *North. Cobbler* 76
  An' Squire, his oän very *s*, walks down fro' the 'All to see,   ,,   91
  An' 'e'd wrote an owd book, his awn *s*,   *Village Wife* 46
  An' I'd voät fur 'im, my oän *s*, if 'e could but stan fur the
  Shere.   *Owd Roä* 14
Send—I *s* you here a sort of allegory,   *To ——, With Pal. of Art* 1
  fear'd To *s* abroad a shrill and terrible cry,   *Enoch Arden* 768
  he would *s* a hundred thousand men,   *Princess i* 64
  unless you *s* us back Our son,   ,, *iv* 415
  'Sdeath ! but we will *s* to her,'   ,, *v* 324
  You *s* a flash to the sun.   *Window, Marr. Morn.* 2
  But *s* it slackly from the string ;   *In Mem. lxxxvii* 26
  and *s* thee satisfied—   *Gareth and L.* 434
  delays his purport till thou *s* To do the battle with him,   ,,   618
  they *s* That strength of anger thro' mine arms,   ,,   947
  render'd tributary, fail'd of late To *s* his tribute ;   *Balin and Balan* 4
  I undertake them as we pass, And *s* them to thee ?'   ,,   15
  King will *s* thee his own leech—   ,,   275
  s One flash, that, missing all things else,   *Merlin and V.* 931
  of us to claim the prize, Ourselves will *s* it after.   *Lancelot and E.* 545
  This will he *s* or come for :   ,,   635
  I pray him, *s* a sudden Angel down   ,,   1424
  If God would *s* the vision, well :   *Holy Grail* 658
  she *s* her delegate to thrall These fighting hands   *Pelleas and E.* 336
  S ! bid him come ; ' but Lionel was away—   *Lover's Tale iv* 101
  but *s* me notice of him When he returns,   ,,   116
  you used to *s* her the flowers ;   *In the Child. Hosp.* 33
  May *s* one ray to thee !   *Ded. Poem Prin. Alice* 14
  I *s* my prayer by night and day—   *Columbus* 233
  ninth moon, that *s's* the hidden sun   *De Prof., Two G.* 33
  I *s* a birthday line Of greeting ;   *To E. Fitzgerald* 45
  S no such light upon the ways of men   *Tiresias* 161
  s the day into the darken'd heart ;   *Ancient Sage* 261
  S the drain into the fountain,   *Locksley H., Sixty* 144
  ' *S* them no more, for evermore.   *Dead Prophet* 3
  I fail'd To *s* my life thro' olive-yard   *Demeter and P.* 110
  To *s* the moon into the night and break   ,,   135
  Shalt ever *s* thy life along with mine   ,,   145
  bad the man engrave ' From Walter ' on the ring, and *s* it—   *The Ring* 236
  And *s* her home to you rejoicing.   ,,   320
  and *s* A gift of slenderer value,   *To Ulysses* 47
  Take then this spring-flower I *s*,   *To Mary Boyle* 19
  Reflected, *s's* a light on the forgiven.   *Romney's R.* 161
  dust *s* up a steam of human blood,   *St. Telemachus* 53
Sendest O THOU, that *s* out the man To rule   *England and Amer.* 1
  when thou *s* thy free soul thro' heaven,   *Ancient Sage* 47
Seneschal Then came Sir Kay, the *s*, and cried,   *Gareth and L.* 367
  let Kay the *s* Look to thy wants,   ,,   433
  ' Sir *S*, Sleuth-hound thou knowest, and gray,   ,,   461
  But Kay the *s*, who loved him not,   ,,   483
  Sir Kay, the *s*, would come Blustering upon them,   ,,   513
  S, No mellow master of the meats and drinks !   ,,   559
  page, and maid, and squire, and *s*,   *Marr. of Geraint* 710
  Arthur turn'd to Kay the *s*,   *Last Tournament* 89
Sennight three rich *s's* more, my love for her.   *Edwin Morris* 30
Sense (*See also* **Common-sense**) did all confound Her *s* ;   *Mariana* 77
  feedeth The *s's* with a still delight   *Margaret* 17
  Controlleth all the soul and *s*   *Eleänore* 115
  Is cancell'd in the world of *s* ?'   *Two Voices* 42
  Unmanacled from bonds of *s*,   ,,   236
  ' The simple *s's* crown'd his head :   ,,   277

Sense (*continued*) By which he doubts against the *s* ?   *Two Voices* 285
  There seem'd no room for *s* of wrong ;   ,,   456
  Lord of the *s's* five :   *Palace of Art* 180
  Slowly my *s* undazzled.   *D. of F. Women* 177
  Flutter'd about my *s's* and my soul ;   *Gardener's D.* 67
  Or have they any *s* of why they sing ?   ,,   101
  He lost the *s* that handles daily life—   *Walk. to the Mail* 22
  weigh'd Upon my brain, my *s's* and my soul !   *Love and Duty* 44
  If the *s* is hard To alien ears,   ,,   51
  the common *s* of most shall hold   *Locksley Hall* 129
  cancell'd a *s* misused :   *Godiva* 72
  Your finer female *s* offends.   *Day-Dm., L'Envoi* 2
  I grow in worth, and wit, and *s*,   *Will Water.* 41
  it was a crime Of *s* avenged by *s*   *Vision of Sin* 214
  crime of *s* became The crime of malice,   ,,   215
  less of sentiment than *s* Had Katie ;   *The Brook* 91
  a *s* Of meanness in her unresisting life.   *Aylmer's Field* 800
  And such a *s*, when first I fronted him,   *Sea Dreams* 70
  s of wrong had touch'd her face With colour)   *Princess, Pro.* 219
  Or master'd by the *s* of sport,   ,, *iv* 156
  I broke the letter of it to keep the *s*.   ,,   338
  I grant in her some *s* of shame,   ,,   349
  ' Nay, nay, you spake but *s* ' Said Gama.   ,, *v* 206
  Love to sloughs That swallow common *s*,   ,,   442
  Or own one port of *s* not flint to prayer,   ,, *vi* 182
  My haunting *s* of hollow shows :   ,, *vii* 349
  Some *s* of duty, something of a faith,   ,, *Con.* 54
  Joänes, as 'ant not a 'aäpoth o' *s*,   *N. Farmer, O. S.* 49
  moor s' i' one o' 'is legs nor in all thy braaïns.   ,, *N. S.* 4
  Unfetter'd by the *s* of crime,   *In Mem. xxvii* 7
  an awful *s* Of one mute Shadow watching all.   ,, *xxx* 7
  the hoarding *s* Gives out at times   ,, *xliv* 6
  Drug down the blindfold *s* of wrong   ,, *lxxi* 7
  The quiet *s* of something lost.   ,, *lxxviii* 8
  The *s* of human will demands   ,, *lxxxv* 39
  O tell me where the *s's* mix,   ,, *lxxxviii* 3
  Where all the nerve of *s* is numb ;   ,, *xciii* 7
  Cry thro' the *s* to hearten trust   ,, *cxvi* 7
  Who wants the finer politic *s*   *Maud I vi* 47
  Suddenly strike on a sharper *s*   ,, *II ii* 63
  sent him from his *s's* : let me go.'   *Gareth and L.* 71
  whether some false *s* in her own self   *Marr. of Geraint* 800
  such a *s* might make her long for court   ,,   803
  with every *s* as false and foul   *Merlin and V.* 797
  conscience of a saint Among his warring *s's*,   *Guinevere* 640
  and shadowing *S* at war with Soul,   *To the Queen ii* 37
  all the *s's* weaken'd, save in that,   *Lover's Tale i* 127
  scarce can tune his high majestic *s*   ,,   475
  No longer in the dearest *s* of mine—   ,,   587
  Entering all the avenues of *s*   ,,   630
  And now first heard with any *s* of pain,   ,,   709
  Falling in whispers on the *s*,   ,,   720
  A shameful *s* as of a cleaving crime—   ,,   794
  face was flash'd thro' *s* and soul   *Sisters (E. and E.)* 109
  Scarce feels the *s's* break away   *Ancient Sage* 152
  Await the last and largest *s*   ,,   180
  soul and *s* in city slime ?   *Locksley H., Sixty* 144
  moor good *s* na the Parliament man   *Owd Roä* 13
  His crime was of the *s's* ;   *Romney's R.* 151
  Why not bask amid the *s's*   *By an Evolution.* 6
  wi' a hoonderd haäcre o' *s*—   *Church-warden, etc.* 22
Senseless O *s* cataract, Bearing all down in thy
  precipitancy—   *Gareth and L.* 7
  The little *s*, worthless, wordless babe,   *The Ring* 304
Sensible worth the life That made it *s*.   *Lover's Tale i* 800
Sensitive Or the least little delicate aquiline curve in
  a *s* nose,   *Maud I ii* 10
  Patient of pain tho' as quick as a *s* plant to
  the touch ;   *In the Child. Hosp.* 30
Sensual Bursts of great heart and slips in *s* mire,   *Princess v* 199
  Arise and fly The reeling Faun, the *s* feast ;   *In Mem. cxviii* 26
  For such a supersensual *s* bond   *Merlin and V.* 109
  Nor own'd a *s* wish,   ,,   628
Sensuous Makes noble thro' the *s* organism   *Princess ii* 87
  Be near me when the *s* frame Is rack'd   *In Mem. l* 5

Sent   *s* it them by stealth, nor did they know Who *s* it ;   *Dora* 53
She *s* a note, the seal an *Elle vous suit,*   *Edwin Morris* 105
She *s* her voice thro' all the holt   *Talking Oak* 123
She *s* a herald forth, And bade him cry,   *Godiva* 35
With peals of genial clamour *s*   *Will Water.* 187
yet he *s* Gifts by the children,   *Enoch Arden* 337
s his voice beneath him thro' the wood.   ,, 444
s for him and said wildly to him   ,, 507
And *s* her sweetly by the golden isles,   ,, 536
They *s* a crew that landing burst away   ,, 634
he *s* the bailiff to the farm To learn   *The Brook* 141
S to the harrow'd brother, praying him   *Aylmer's Field* 607
but every roof *S* out a listener   ,, 614
S like the twelve-divided concubine   ,, 759
s out a cry Which mixt with little Margaret's,   *Sea Dreams* 245
My father *s* ambassadors with furs   *Princess* i 199
We *s* mine host to purchase female gear ;   ,, 199
I gave the letter to be *s* with dawn ;   ,, 245
s For Psyche, but she was not there ;   ,, iv 236
s for Blanche to accuse her face to face ;   ,, 239
S out a bitter bleating for its dam ;   ,, 392
when we *s* the Prince your way We knew not   ,, 398
some one *s* beneath his vaulted palm   ,, v 31
found He thrice had *s* a herald to the gates,   ,, 332
S from a dewy breast a cry for light :   ,, vii 253
A soul on highest mission *s,*   *In Mem. cxiii* 10
My Maud has *s* it by thee   *Maud* I xxi 9
the King *S* to him, saying, ' Arise,   *Com. of Arthur* 44
he *s* Ulfius, and Brastias, and Bedivere,   ,, 135
Died but of late, and *s* his cry to me,   ,, 361
while the phantom king *S* out at times a voice ;   ,, 437
Leodogran awoke, and *s* Ulfius and Brastias and Bedivere,   ,, 444
That *S* him from his senses : let me go.   *Gareth and L.* 71
seeing he hath *s* us cloth of gold,   ,, 428
s, Between the in-crescent and de-crescent moon,   ,, 528
s her wish that I would yield thee thine.   ,, 551
thy much folly hath *s* thee here His kitchen-knave :   ,, 919
' A kitchen-knave, and *s* in scorn of me :   ,, 952
and say His kitchen-knave hath *s* thee.   ,, 985
and Gareth *s* him to the King.   ,, 1051
Had *s* her coming champion, waited him.   ,, 1192
Had *s* thee down before a lesser spear,   ,, 1244
S all his heart and breath thro' all the horn.   ,, 1369
s Her maiden to demand it of the dwarf ;   *Marr. of Geraint* 192
S her own maiden to demand the name,   ,, 411
S forth a sudden sharp and bitter cry,   *Geraint and E.* 722
s a thousand men To till the wastes,   ,, 941
ye be *s* for by the King,' They follow'd ;   *Balin and Balan* 48
wrath *S* me a three-years' exile from thine eyes.   ,, 59
the hall Of him to whom ye *s* us, Pellam,   ,, 96
being jealous, that he *s* His horns of proclamation out   *Merlin and V.* 580
Reported who he was, and on what quest *S,*   *Lancelot and E.* 629
And lose the quest he *s* you on,   ,, 655
' Your prize the diamond *s* you by the King : '   ,, 821
the tale Of King and Prince, the diamond *s,*   ,, 824
and toward even *S* for his shield :   ,, 978
he saw One of her house, and *s* him to the Queen   ,, 1168
' For on a day she *s* to speak with me.   *Holy Grail* 101
She *s* the deathless passion in her eyes   ,, 163
S hands upon him, as to tear him,   *Pelleas and E.* 521
golden grove Appearing, *s* his fancy back   *Last Tournament* 380
then what folly had *s* him overseas   ,, 394
That *s* the face of all the marsh aloft   ,, 439
the voice about his feet *S* up an answer,   ,, 761
s a deep sea-voice thro' all the land,   *Guinevere* 247
S notes of preparation manifold,   *Lover's Tale* i 207
and *s* his soul Into the songs of birds,   ,, 320
s my cry Thro' the blank night to Him   ,, 751
S such a flame into his face,   ,, iv 177
s at once to Lionel, praying him By that great love   ,, 180
he *s,* an' the father agreed ;   *First Quarrel* 18
And then he *s* me a letter,   ,, 85
Better have *s* Our Edith thro' the glories   *Sisters (E. and E.)* 224
'OUSE-KEEPER *s* tha my lass,   *Village Wife* 1

Sent *(continued)* But he *s* a chill to my heart   *In the Child. Hosp.* 2
The Lord had *s* this bright,   *Columbus* 91
They *s* me out *his* tool, Bovadilla,   ,, 127
we have *s* them very fiends from Hell ;   ,, 184
Thrice from the dyke he *s* his mighty shout,   *Achilles over the T.* 30
S the shadow of Himself,   *Locksley H., Sixty* 211
Sons and brothers that have *s,*   *Open. I. and C. Exhib.* 3
the man repenting *s* This ring " Io t'amo " to his best beloved, And *s* it on her birthday.   *The Ring* 209
Had *s* his cry for her forgiveness,   ,, 233
Muriel's mother *s,* And sure am I,   ,, 311
' Ever since You *s* the fatal ring '—I told her ' *s* To Miriam,'   ,, 262
Why had I *s* the ring at first to her ?   ,, 390
s him charr'd and blasted to the deathless fire   *Happy* 84
I *s* him a desolate wail and a curse,   *Charity* 14
I *s* him back what he gave,—   ,, 19
Sentence And mystic *s* spoke ;—   *Talking Oak* 294
I hear the *s* that he speaks ;   *In Mem. lxxx* 10
there he broke the *s* in his heart Abruptly,   *Geraint and E.* 41
the King Pronounced a dismal *s,*   *Merlin and V.* 591
when the woful *s* hath been past,   *Lover's Tale* i 788
Sentiment less of *s* than sense Had Katie ;   *The Brook* 91
A classic lecture, rich in *s,*   *Princess* ii 374
Sentinel And hear at times a *s*   *In Mem. cxxvi* 9
to be soldier all day and be *s* all thro' the night—   *Def. of Lucknow* 74
Separate So rounds he to a *s* mind   *In Mem. xlv* 9
That each, who seems a *s* whole,   ,, xlvii 1
and is Eternal, *s* from fears :   ,, lxxxv 66
And each prefers his *s* claim,   ,, cii 18
And all the *s* Edens of this earth,   *Lover's Tale* i 551
September on your third *S* birthday   *The Ring* 130
Your fifth *S* birthday.   ,, 423
Sepulchral Like echoes in *s* halls,   *In Mem. lviii* 2
Sepulchre *(See also* **Bosom-sepulchre***)* Gross darkness of the inner *s*   *D. of F. Women* 67
While thou, a meteor of the *s,*   *Lover's Tale* i 99
laid it in a *s* of rock Never to rise again.   ,, 683
He raised her softly from the *s,*   ,, iv 85
There came two voices from the *S,*   *Columbus* 95
And free the Holy *S* from thrall.   ,, 104
And save the Holy *S* from thrall.   ,, 240
icy breath, As from the grating of a *s,*   *The Ring* 400
Sequel *S* of guerdon could not alter me To fairer.   *Œnone* 153
' The *s* of to-day unsolders all   *M. d'Arthur* 14
Of love that never found his earthly close, What *s* ?   *Love and Duty* 2
For love in *s* works with fate,   *Day-Dm., Arrival* 3
I shudder at the *s,* but I go.'   *Princess* ii 236
the *s* of the tale Had touch'd her ;   ,, *Con.* 30
' The *s* of to-day unsolders all   *Pass. of Arthur* 182
the soul : *That* makes the *s* pure ;   *Lover's Tale* iv 157
Beginning at the *s* know no more.   ,, 158
Sequence And in the fatal *s* of this world   *Ancient Sage* 274
for forty years my life in golden *s* ran,   *Locksley H., Sixty* 47
Seraglio iron grates, And hush'd *s's.*   *D. of F. Women* 36
Seraph there was Milton like a *s* strong,   *Palace of Art* 133
Pontius and Iscariot by my side Show'd like fair *s's.*   *St. S. Stylites* 169
Seraphic Pierces the keen *s* flame From orb to orb,   *In Mem. xxx* 27
S intellect and force To seize and throw the doubts   ,, cix 5
Sere *(See also* **Sear***)* in the rudest wind Never grow *s,*   *Ode to Memory* 25
Shrank one sick willow *s* and small.   *Mariana in the S.* 53
And, tho' his violet sicken into *s,*   *Prog. of Spring* 25
Serenade A rogue of canzonets and *s's.*   *Princess* iv 135
Serene ' Her court was pure ; her life *s ;*   *To the Queen* 25
S with argent-lidded eyes Amorous,   *Arabian Nights* 135
S, imperial Eleänore. (repeat)   *Eleänore* 81, 121
My mother, looks as whole as some *s*   *Princess* v 193
And that *s* result of all.'   *In Mem. lxxxv* 92
O heart, look down and up *S,* secure,   *Early Spring* 28
Serenest Now towering o'er him in *s* air,   *Lucretius* 178
Serf Who made the *s* a man, and burst his chain—   *W. to Marie Alex.* 3
Serious Her bright hair blown about the *s* face   *Lancelot and E.* 392
Sermon See **Sarmin.**
Sermonizing In sailor fashion roughly *s*   *Enoch Arden* 204
Serpent *(adj.)* Back on herself her *s* pride had curl'd.   *Palace of Art* 257
in whom all evil fancies clung Like *s* eggs together,   *Enoch Arden* 480

Serpent (adj.) (*continued*) Wherethro' the *s* river coil'd,
they came. | *Gareth and L.* 906
ringing with their *s* hands, | *Merlin and V.* 578
Every tiger madness muzzled, every *s* passion
kill'd, | *Locksley H., Sixty* 167
all the *s* vines Which on the touch of heavenly feet
had risen, | *Death of Œnone* 4
Serpent (s) Gliding with equal crowns two *s's* led | *Alexander* 6
Like birds the charming *s* draws, | *In Mem. xxxiv* 14
Nor cared the *s* at thy side | " *cx* 7
whose souls the old *s* long had drawn Down, | *Geraint and E.* 632
like a *s*, ran a scroll Of letters | *Holy Grail* 170
Let the trampled *s* show you | *Locksley H., Sixty* 242
The *s* coil'd about his broken shaft, | *Demeter and P.* 77
Serpent-rooted seated on a *s-r* beech, | *The Brook* 135
Serpent-throated long horn And *s-t* bugle, | *Princess v* 253
Serpent-wanded *s-w* power Draw downward into Hades | *Demeter and P.* 25
Servant (*See also* **Sarvint**) rummaged like a rat : no
s stay'd : | *Walk. to the Mail* 38
and gull'd Our *s's*, wrong'd and lied | *Princess iv* 540
Are but as *s's* in a house | *In Mem. xx* 3
s's of the Morning-Star, approach, | *Gareth and L.* 924
He had a faithful *s*, one who loved | *Lover's Tale iv* 256
Who found the dying *s*, took him home, | " 263
That faithful *s* whom we spoke about, | " 342
Serve (*See also* **Sarve**) Would *s* his kind in deed and
word, | *Love thou thy land* 86
Who'd *s* the state ? for if I carved my name | *Audley Court* 48
To *s* the hot-and-hot ; | *Will Water.* 228
I'll *s* you better in a strait ; | *Princess i* 85
all things *s* their time Toward that great year | " *iv* 73
fellow-worker be, When time should *s* ; | " 309
We two will *s* them both in aiding her— | " *vii* 268
Who never sold the truth to *s* the hour, | *Ode on Well.* 179
But as he saves or *s's* the state. | " 200
But better *s's* a wholesome law, | *In Mem. xlviii* 10
May *s* to curl a maiden's locks, | " *lxxvii* 7
hire thyself to *s* for meats and drinks | *Gareth and L.* 153
thou shalt *s* a twelvemonth and a day.' | " 157
s with scullions and with kitchen-knaves ; | " 170
grant me to *s* For meat and drink among thy
kitchen-knaves | " 444
' So that ye do not *s* me sparrow-hawks | *Marr. of Geraint* 304
Endures not that her guest should *s* himself.' | " 379
because their hall must also *s* For kitchen, | " 390
s thee costlier than with mowers' fare.' | *Geraint and E.* 231
attendance, page or maid, To *s* you— | " 323
a glance will *s*—the liars ! | *Merlin and V.* 111
Being but ampler means to *s* mankind, | " 489
to see your face, To *s* you, | *Lancelot and E.* 939
To *s* as model for the mighty world, | *Guinevere* 465
Had died almost to *s* them any way, | *Lover's Tale iv* 124
O how could I *s* in the wards | *In the Child. Hosp.* 24
s This mortal race thy kin so well, | *De Prof., Two G.* 15
make the passing shadow *s* thy will. | *Ancient Sage* 110
To *s* her myriads and the State,— | *To Marq. of Dufferin* 24
and *s* that Infinite Within us, | *Akbar's Dream* 145
Served (*See also* **Sarved**) So sitting, *s* by man and maid, | *The Goose* 21
or fruits and cream *S* in the weeping elm ; | *Gardener's D.* 195
he *s* a year On board a merchantman, | *Enoch Arden* 52
master of that ship Enoch had *s* in, | " 120
s, Long since, a bygone Rector of the place, | *Aylmer's Field* 10
and *s* With female hands and hospitality.' | *Princess vi* 95
' We *s* thee here,' they said, ' so long, | *In Mem. ciii* 47
But *s* the seasons that may rise ; | " *cxiii* 4
' If I in aught have *s* thee well, | *Com. of Arthur* 138
s King Uther thro' his magic art ; | " 151
Merlin ever *s* about the King, Uther, | " 365
But ever meekly *s* the King in thee ? | *Gareth and L.* 729
Bribed with large promises the men who *s* About
my person, | *Marr. of Geraint* 453
Might well have *s* for proof that I was loved, | " 796
s a little to disedge The sharpness | *Geraint and E.* 189
one sat, Tho' *s* with choice from air, | *Pelleas and E.* 149
Who *s* him well with those white hands of hers, | *Last Tournament* 400

Served (*continued*) They *s* their use, their time ; | *Last Tournament* 676
meat he long'd for *s* By hands unseen ; | *Guinevere* 265
Infinite Love that has *s* us so well ? | *Despair* 95
S the poor, and built the cottage, | *Locksley H., Sixty* 268
Dead, who had *s* his time, | *Dead Prophet* 9
Service (*See also* **Sarvice**) while the tender *s* made thee
weep, | *The Bridesmaid* 10
' to find Another *s* such as this.' | *In Mem. xx* 8
All kind of *s* with a noble ease | *Gareth and L.* 489
knave that doth thee *s* as full knight | " 1016
Grateful to Prince Geraint for *s* done, | *Marr. of Geraint* 15
s done so graciously would bind The two together ; | " 790
did him *s* as a squire ; | *Geraint and E.* 406
(I speak as one Speaks of a *s* done him) | " 848
Now weary of my *s* and devoir, | *Lancelot and E.* 118
Such *s* have ye done me, that I make My will | " 915
vain and rude With proffer of unwish'd-for *s's*) | *Lover's Tale i* 629
should this first master claim His *s*, | " *iv* 266
The *s* of the one so saved was due All to the
saver— | " 279
Gain'd in the *s* of His Highness, | *Columbus* 236
Serviceable And seeing her so sweet and *s*, | *Marr. of Geraint* 393
to be sweet and *s* To noble knights in sickness, | *Lancelot and E.* 767
Servile and *s* to a shrewish tongue ! | *Locksley Hall* 42
Master of half a *s* shire, | *Maud I x* 10
Serving And loved me *s* in my father's hall : | *Geraint and E.* 699
to splinter it into feuds *S* his traitorous end ; | *Guinevere* 19
Serving-man As just and mere a *s-m* | *Will Water.* 151
there brake a *s* Flying from out of the black wood, | *Gareth and L.* 801
Servitor Loyal, the dumb old *s*, | *Lancelot and E.* 1144
Then rose the dumb old *s*, and the dead, | " 1153
Session in *s* on their roofs Approved him, | *The Brook* 127
Leapt from her *s* on his lap, | *Merlin and V.* 844
Set (adj.) The *s* gray life, and apathetic end. | *Love and Duty* 18
One *s* slow bell will seem to toll The passing | *In Mem. lvii* 10
Set (s) with others of our *s*, Five others : | *Princess, Pro.* 8
O wretched *s* of sparrows, one and all, | *Marr. of Geraint* 278
Two *s's* of three laden with jingling arms, | *Geraint and E.* 188
with *s* of sun Their fires flame thickly, | *Achilles over the T.* 10
Set (verb) (*See also* **Sit**) The sun is just about to *s*, | *Margaret* 58
As tho' a star, in inmost heaven *s*, | *Eleänore* 89
That *s's* at twilight in a land of reeds. | *Caress'd or chidden* 14
be *s* In midst of knowledge, | *Two Voices* 89
' Why not *s* forth, if I should do This rashness, | " 391
you had *s*, That morning, on the casement-edge | *Miller's D.* 81
Many suns arise and *s*. | " 205
To-night I saw the sun *s* : he *s* | *May Queen, N. Y's. E.* 5
S in all lights by many minds, | *Love thou thy land* 35
I have *s* my heart upon a match. | *Dora* 14
I will *s* him in my uncle's eye Among the wheat ; | " 67
women kiss'd Each other, and *s* out, | " 129
saw The boy *s* up betwixt his grandsire's knees, | " 131
Allan *s* him down, and Mary said : | " 139
I *s* the words, and added names I knew. | *Audley Court* 61
S's out, and meets a friend who hails him, | *Walk. to the Mail* 42
Time will *s* me right.' | *Edwin Morris* 88
They *s* an ancient creditor to work : | " 130
all the current of my being *s's* to thee.' | *Locksley Hall* 24
promise of my spirit hath not *s*. | " 187
He *s* up his forlorn pipes, | *Amphion* 22
You *s* before chance-comers, | *Will Water.* 6
And *s* in Heaven's third story, | " 70
S thy hoary fancies free ; | *Vision of Sin* 156
Enoch *s* A purpose evermore before his eyes, | *Enoch Arden* 44
s Annie forth in trade With all that seamen | " 138
s his hand To fit their little streetward sitting-room | " 169
village girl, Who *s's* her pitcher underneath the spring, | " 207
S her sad will no less to chime with his, | " 248
He *s* himself beside her, saying to her : | " 290
where he fixt his heart he *s* his hand | " 294
Suddenly *s* it wide to find a sign, | " 496
S in this Eden of all plenteousness, | " 561
Enoch *s* himself, Scorning an alms, to work | " 811
fairy foreland *s* With willow-weed and mallow. | *The Brook* 45
Have also *s* his many-shielded tree ? | *Aylmer's Field* 48

Set (verb) (*continued*) He never yet had *s* his daughter
forth | *Aylmer's Field* 347
and one was *s* to watch The watcher, | „ 551
'*S* them up! they shall not fall!' | *Sea Dreams* 227
I had *s* my heart on your forgiving him | „ 269
s's all the tops quivering— | *Lucretius* 186
show'd the house, Greek, *s* with busts: | *Princess, Pro.* 11
rosebud *s* with little wilful thorns, | „ 154
S in a gleaming river's crescent-curve, | „ i 171
when we *s* our hand To this great work, | „ ii 59
Till toward the centre *s* the starry tides, | „ 117
You need not *s* your thoughts in rubric | „ iii 50
but we *S* forth to climb; | „ 354
foot shone like a jewel *s* In the dark crag: | „ 358
Blow, bugle, blow, *s* the wild echoes flying, (repeat) | „ iv 5, 17
Norway sun *S* into sunrise; | „ 576
S in a cataract on an island-crag, | „ v 347
I *s* my face Against all men, | „ 388
S his child upon her knee— | „ vi 14
Till at the last she *s* herself to man, | „ vii 285
and roughly *s* His Briton in blown seas | *Ode on Well.* 154
Sun *s*'s, moon *s*'s, | *Window, When* 3
Once more to *s* a ringlet right; | *In Mem.* vi 36
Since our first Sun arose and *s*. | „ xxiv 8
That *s*'s the past in this relief? | „ 12
On thy Parnassus *s* thy feet, | „ xxxvii 6
And *s* there forth, for thou art mine, | „ lix 13
'Like some poor girl whose heart is *s* | „ lx 3
I would *s* their pains at ease. | „ lxiii 8
Whate'er thy hands are *s* to do | „ lxv 19
And in a moment *s* thy face | „ lxxvi 2
His credit thus shall *s* me free; | „ lxxx 13
my feet are *s* To leave the pleasant fields | „ cii 21
S light by narrower perfectness. | „ cxii 4
She *s* her forward countenance And leaps | „ cxiv 6
He *s* his royal signet there; | „ cxxv 12
But now *s* out: the noon is near, | *Con.* 41
make my heart as a millstone, *s* my face as a flint, | *Maud I* i 31
S in the heart of the carven gloom, | „ xiv 11
He *s*'s the jewel-print of your feet, | „ xxii 41
Till God's love *s* Thee at his side again! | *Ded. of Idylls* 55
So when the King had *s* his banner broad, | *Com. of Arthur* 101
Brought Arthur forth, and *s* him in the hall,
Proclaiming, | „ 229
thereupon the King *S* two before him. | *Gareth and L.* 104
Southward they *s* their faces. | „ 182
s To turn the broach, draw water, or hew wood, | „ 485
Arthur's men are *s* along the wood; | „ 788
Gareth loosed his bonds and on free feet *S* him, | „ 818
and the Baron *s* Gareth beside her, | „ 851
further wrong Than *s* him on his feet, | „ 955
Which *s* the horror higher? | „ 1394
and *s* foot upon his breast, | *Marr. of Geraint* 574
When my dear child is *s* forth at her best, | „ 728
in charge of whom? a girl: *s* on.' | *Geraint and E.* 125
then *s* down His basket, | „ 209
on his foot She *s* her own and climb'd; | „ 760
s his foot upon me, and give me life. | „ 850
in their chairs *s* up a stronger race | „ 940
Lest we should *s* one truer on his throne. | *Balin and Balan* 7
beside The carolling water *s* themselves again, | „ 44
s himself To learn what Arthur meant by courtesy, | „ 157
See now, I *s* thee high on vantage ground, | „ 534
after that, she *s* herself to gain Him, | *Merlin and V.* 165
If ye know, *S* up the charge ye know, | „ 703
and caught, And *s* it on his head, | *Lancelot and E.* 54
And *s* it in this damsel's golden hair, | „ 205
S every gilded parapet shuddering; | „ 299
more amazed Than if seven men had *s* upon him, | „ 351
in the costly canopy o'er him *s*, | „ 443
kith and kin, not knowing, *s* upon him; | „ 599
he *s* himself to play upon her With sallying wit, | „ 646
S in her hand a lily, o'er her hung The silken case | „ 1148
s betwixt With many a mystic symbol, | *Holy Grail* 232
s the sail, or had the boat Become a living creature | „ 518

Set (verb) (*continued*) while I tarried, every day she *s* A
banquet | *Holy Grail* 588
s his name High on all hills, | *Last Tournament* 336
ye *s* yourself To babble about him, | „ 339
and *s* me far In the gray distance, | „ 639
She rose, and *s* before him all he will'd; | „ 723
Lancelot got her horse, *S* her thereon, | *Guinevere* 123
thought the Queen 'Lo! they have *s* her on, | „ 308
thou their tool, *s* on to plague And play upon, | „ 359
Which are as gems *s* in my memory, | *Lover's Tale* i 291
Ev'n by the price that others *s* upon it, | „ iv 152
He brings and *s*'s before him in rich guise | „ 247
So I *s* to righting the house, | *First Quarrel* 47
they *s* him so high That all the ships | *Rizpah* 37
little of us left by the time this sun be *s*.' | *The Revenge* 28
Had *s* the blossom of her health again, | *Sisters (E. and E.)* 151
will she never *s* her sister free?' | „ 218
good woman, can prayer *s* a broken bone?' | *In the Child. Hosp.* 20
hour and the wine Had *s* the wits aflame. | *Sir J. Oldcastle* 95
A thousand marks are *s* upon my head. | „ 195
S thee in light till time shall be no more? | *Columbus* 150
s me climbing icy capes And glaciers, | *To E. Fitzgerald* 25
Had *s* the lily and rose By all my ways | *Ancient Sage* 156
s The lamps alight, and call For golden music, | „ 195
some that never *s*, but pass From sight and night | „ 202
ye *s* me heart batin' to music wid ivery word! | *Tomorrow* 34
ye'll niver *s* eyes an the face | „ 50
stick oop thy back, an' *s* oop thy taäil, | *Spinster's S's.* 31
as if they was *s* upo' springs, | „ 89
Theere! *S* it down! Now Robby! | „ 118
but *s* no meek ones in their place; | *Locksley H., Sixty* 133
S the feet above the brain | „ 136
S the maiden fancies wallowing | „ 145
S the sphere of all the boundless Heavens | „ 210
Nor this way will you *s* your name | *Epilogue* 1
S the mountain aflame to-night, | *On Jub. Q. Victoria* 16
And *s* the mother waking in amaze | *Demeter and P.* 57
an' *s*'s 'im ageän the wall, | *Owd Roä* 82
Nor ever cared to *s* you on her knee, | *The Ring* 386
And *s* a crueller mark than Cain's on him, | *Happy* 18
—from the bush we both had *s*— | „ 102
pine which here The warrior of Caprera *s*, | *To Ulysses* 26
'My Rose' *s* all your faces aglow, | *Roses on the T.* 3
s his face By waste and field and town | *St. Telemachus* 29
You have *s* a price on his head: | *Bandit's Death* 7
calls to them 'S yourselves free!' | *Kapiolani* 3

Set *See also* **Close-set, Deep-set, Hard-set, High-set, Silver-set, Solid-set, Stately-set, Stiff-set, Thick-set**

Setting *s* round thy first experiment | *Ode to Memory* 81
It was when the moon was *s*; | *May Queen, Con.* 26
s wide the doors that bar The secret bridal chambers | *Gardener's D.* 248
s the how much before the how, | *Golden Year* 11
at *s* forth The Biscay, roughly ridging eastward, | *Enoch Arden* 528
Music's golden sea *S* toward eternity, | *Ode on Well.* 253
And in the *s* thou art fair | *In Mem.* cxxx 4
S this knave, Lord Baron, at my side. | *Gareth and L.* 854
Who push'd his prows into the *s* sun, | *Columbus* 24
And a hush with the *s* sun. | *Maud I* xxii 18
Now half to the *s* moon are gone, | „ 23
On some vast plain before a *s* sun, | *Guinevere* 77
Down those loud waters, like a *s* star, | *Lover's Tale* i 59
s, when Even descended, the very sunset aflame | *V. of Maeldune* 66
glorious creature Sank to his *s*. | *Batt. of Brunanburh* 30
up that lane of light into the *s* sun. | *The Flight* 40
Charity *s* the martyr aflame; | *Vastness* 9
his The words, and mine the *s*. | *The Ring* 24
And while the moon was *s*. | *Forlorn* 84
Those cobras ever *s* up their hoods— | *Akbar's Dream* 166

Settle (s) Down on an oaken *s* in the hall, | *Geraint and E.* 573
Settle (verb) (*See also* **Sattle**) 'Tis hard to *s* order
once again. | *Lotos-Eaters, C. S.* 82
the cloud that *s*'s round his birth Hath lifted | *Gareth and L.* 130
ere they *s* for the night. | *Marr. of Geraint* 250
s's, beaten back, and beaten back *S*'s, | *Merlin and V.* 371
Nor *s*'s into hueless gray, | *To Marq. of Dufferin* 50

Settled (*See also* **Sattled**) A land of *s* government, *You ask me, why, etc.* 9
Until I woke, and found him *s* down   *The Epic* 17
seem but to be Weak symbols of the *s* bliss,   *Miller's D.* 233
wheeling round The central wish, until we *s* there. *Gardener's D.* 225
And loosely *s* into form.   *Day-Dm., Pro.* 12
Nothing to mar the sober majesties Of *s*, sweet, Epicurean
  life.   *Lucretius* 218
s in her eyes, The green malignant light   *Princess iii* 131
on my spirits *S* a gentle cloud of melancholy ;   „   *iv* 570
by overthrow Of these or those, the question *s* die.'   „   *v* 317
Now looking to some *s* end,   *In Mem. lxxxv* 97
to her old perch back, and *s* there.   *Merlin and V.* 903
Waiting to see the *s* countenance Of her I loved, *Lover's Tale iii* 39
Settling *s* circled all the lists.   *Marr. of Geraint* 547
Seven (adj.) The *s* elms, the poplars four   *Ode to Memory* 56
s happy years, *S* happy years of health and competence, *Enoch Arden* 82
In those far-off *s* happy years were born ;   „   686
till the Bear had wheel'd Thro' a great arc his *s* slow
  suns.   *Princess iv* 213
and more amazed Than if *s* men had set upon him, *Lancelot and E.* 351
thro' the gap The *s* clear stars of Arthur's Table
  Round—   *Holy Grail* 684
Across the *s* clear stars—O grace to me—   „   692
S days I drove along the dreary deep,   „   808
S strong Earls of the army of Anlaf   *Batt. of Brunanburh* 53
I can hear Too plainly what full tides of onset sap Our
  s high gates,   *Tiresias* 92
His fingers were so stiffen'd by the frost Of *s* and ninety
  winters,   *The Ring* 240
Seven (s) It should 'a been 'ere by *s*,   *Spinster's S's.* 114
Sevenfold Would slowly trail himself *s*   *The Mermaid* 25
and so We forged a *s* story.   *Princess, Pro.* 202
Seven-headed *S-h* monsters only made to kill Time   „   204
Seven-months' A *s-m* babe had been a truer gift. *Merlin and V.* 711
Seventeen petitionary grace Of sweet *s*   *The Brook* 113
Maud is not *s*,   *Maud I xii* 15
Seventh Like a beam of the *s* Heaven, down to my side,   „   *xiv* 21
on the *s* night I heard the shingle grinding   *Holy Grail* 810
Seventimes-heated a heat As from a *s-h* furnace,   „   843
Seventy *S* years ago, my darling, *s* years ago. (repeat) *Grandmother* 24, 56
Hallus aloän wi' 'is boooks, thaw nigh upo' *s* year. *Village Wife* 27
Seventy-five While you have touch'd at *s-f*, *To E. Fitzgerald* 44
Seventy-four And I am nearing *s-f*,   „   43
Seventy-seven To you that are *s-s*,   *June Bracken, etc.* 6
Several I bump'd the ice into three *s* stars,   *The Epic* 12
Sever'd Her lips are *s* as to speak :   *Day-Dm., Sleep. P.* 30
Severe The grave, *s* Genovese of old.   *The Daisy* 40
across him came a cloud Of melancholy *s*,   *Lancelot and E.* 325
Severer *S* in the logic of a life ?   *Princess v* 190
Severity That pure *s* of perfect light—   *Guinevere* 646
Severn The Danube to the *S* gave   *In Mem. xix* 1
There twice a day the *S* fills ;   „   5
fifty knights rode with them, to the shores Of *S*,
  and they past to their own land ;   *Marr. of Geraint* 45
fifty knights rode with them to the shores Of *S*,
  and they past to their own land.   *Geraint and E.* 955
Seville Let us bang these dogs of *S*,   *The Revenge* 30
Sew Or teach the orphan girl to *s*,   *L. C. V. de Vere* 70
Sewer cleanse this common *s* of all his realm, *Marr. of Geraint* 39
cleanse this common *s* of all my realm,   *Geraint and E.* 895
with the drainage of your *s* ;   *Locksley H., Sixty* 143
Or the foulest *s* of the town—   *Dead Prophet* 48
this little city of *s's*,   *Happy* 34
Sewer (sure) But I beänt that *s* es the Lord, *Village Wife* 93
Naäy to be *s* it be past 'er time.   *Spinster's S's.* 5
I wur *s* that it couldn't be true ;   „   20
Robby wur fust to be *s*,   „   69
Sex ' No more of love ; your *s* is known :   *The Letters* 29
Madam—if I know your *s*,   *Vision of Sin* 181
If our old halls could change their *s*,   *Princess, Pro.* 140
not a scorner of your *s* But venerator,   „   *iv* 422
She wrongs herself, her *s*, and me,   „   *v* 117
either *s* alone Is half itself,   „   *vii* 301
hustled together, each *s*, like swine,   *Maud I i* 34
Shaäky (shaky) Nasty an' snaggy an' *s*,   *North. Cobbler* 78

Shaame (shame) an which was a *s* to be seen ;   *Village Wife* 50
Shaämed (ashamed) I be bafe *s* on it now,   *North. Cobbler* 17
we was *s* to cross Gigglesby Greeän,   *Spinster's S's.* 33
niver done nowt to be *s* on,   *Owd Roä* 10
Shackle The *s's* of an old love straiten'd him, *Lancelot and E.* 875
Shadda (shadow) Shamus O'Shea was yer *s*,   *Tomorrow* 38
Shade (*See also* **Mountain-shade**) From the long alley's
  latticed *s*   *Arabian Nights* 112
Life eminent creates the *s* of death ;   *Love and Death* 13
Your sorrow, only sorrow's *s*,   *Margaret* 43
lavish lights, and floating *s's* :   *Eleänore* 12
There in a silent *s* of laurel brown   *Alexander* 9
' Let me not cast in endless *s*   *Two Voices* 5
A merry boy in sun and *s* ?   „   321
when in the chestnut *s* I found the blue Forget-me-not. *Miller's D.* 201
Untouch'd with any *s* of years,   „   219
stedfast *s* Sleeps on his luminous ring.'   *Palace of Art* 15
And hollow *s's* enclosing hearts of flame,   „   241
You'll bury me, my mother, just beneath
  the hawthorn *s*,   *May Queen, N. Y's. E.* 29
I READ, before my eyelids dropt their *s*,   *D. of F. Women* 1
A cedar spread his dark-green layers of *s*.   *Gardener's D.* 116
trembled on her waist—Ah, happy *s*—   „   132
Half light, half *s*, She stood,   „   140
Danced into light, and died into the *s* ;   „   203
House in the *s* of comfortable roofs,   *St. S. Stylites* 107
What's here ? a shape, a *s*,   „   202
' Yet, since I first could cast a *s*,   *Talking Oak* 85
rising thro' the mellow *s*,   *Locksley Hall* 9
Breadths of tropic *s* and palms in cluster,   „   160
This whole wide earth of light and *s*   *Will Water.* 67
One *s* more plump than common ;   „   150
By peaks that flamed, or, all in *s*,   *The Voyage* 41
As fast she fled thro' sun and *s*,   *Sir L. and Q. G.* 37
Slided, they moving under *s* :   *Princess vi* 82
Thine are these orbs of light and *s* ;   *In Mem., Pro.* 5
there no *s* can last In that deep dawn   *.. xlvi* 5
What slender *s* of doubt may flit,   „   *xlviii* 7
The *s* by which my life was crost,   „   *lxvi* 5
play'd A chequer-work of beam and *s*   „   *lxxii* 15
No visual *s* of some one lost,   „   *xciii* 5
And every span of *s* that steals,   „   *cxvii* 10
The sport of random sun and *s*.   „   *Con.* 24
A *s* falls on us like the dark   „   93
The *s* of passing thought,   „   102
And touch with *s* the bridal doors,   „   117
never light and *s* Coursed one another   *Marr. of Geraint* 521
our fortune swerved from sun to *s*,   „   714
behold In the first shallow *s* of a deep wood, *Geraint and E.* 119
There is no *s* or fold of mystery   *Lover's Tale i* 182
Boughs on each side, laden with wholesome *s*,   „   230
All day I watch'd the floating isles of *s*,   „   *ii* 5
seem to flicker past thro' sun and *s*,   *Ancient Sage* 100
and yet no *s* of doubt,   „   235
mantle, every *s* of glancing green,   *Prog. of Spring* 63
And light, with more or less of *s*,   *Akbar's Dream* 46
a glory slowly gaining on the *s*,   *Making of Man* 6
Shaded (*See also* **Sun-shaded**) To light her *s* eye ; *Talking Oak* 218
Shading that other gazed, *S* his eyes   *Lover's Tale i* 306
Shadow (s) (*See also* **Citron-shadow, Forest-shadow,
  Half-shadow, Shadda, Surface-shadow**) on
his light there falls A *s*,   *Supp. Confessions* 164
Were fixed *s's* of thy fixed mood,   *Isabel* 9
She saw the gusty *s* sway.   *Mariana* 52
The *s* of the poplar fell Upon her bed,   „   55
Thro' light and *s* thou dost range,   *Madeline* 4
S's of the silver birk Sweep the green   *A Dirge* 5
Light and *s* ever wander O'er the green   „   12
Thou art the *s* of life,   *Love and Death* 10
The *s* passeth when the tree shall fall,   „   14
The *s* rushing up the sea,   *Rosalind* 11
S's of the world appear.   *L. of Shalott ii* 12
' I am half-sick of *s's*,'   „   35
WITH one black *s* at its feet,   *Mariana in the S.* 1
The one black *s* from the wall.   „   80

X

Shame (verb) (continued) 'Nay father, nay good
  father, *s* me not   *Lancelot and E.* 207
Mine own name *s*'s me,   ,,   1403
my brother, Why wilt thou *s* me to confess   *Holy Grail* 567
Nor let me *s* my father's memory,   *Guinevere* 318
whereof we lately heard A strain to *s* us   *To the Queen ii* 15
Our sons will *s* our own ;   *Mechanophilus* 22

Shamed (*See also* **All-shamed**) I am *s* thro' all my—
  nature   *Locksley Hall* 148
Far too naked to be *s* !   *Vision of Sin* 190
but sank down *s* At all that beauty ;   *Lucretius* 63
Pardon, I am *s* That I must needs repeat   *Princess iii* 51
He never shall be *s*.   *Ode on Well.* 191
Nor *s* to bawl himself a kitchen-knave.   *Gareth and L.* 717
the new knight Had fear he might be *s* ;   ,,   1044
S am I that I so rebuked,   ,,   1164
S ! care not ! thy foul sayings fought for me :   ,,   1180
she ask'd him, '*S* and overthrown,   ,,   1227
S had I been, and sad—O Lancelot—thou !'   ,,   1245
O damsel, be you wise To call him *s*,   ,,   1260
Then were ye *s*, and, worse,   *Marr. of Geraint* 726
'I have *s* thee so that now thou shamest me,   *Balin and Balan* 431
and yet I should be *s* to say it   *Pelleas and E.* 189
'The end is come, And I am *s* for ever ;'   *Guinevere* 111
S in their souls.   *Batt. of Brunanburh* 99
a child Had *s* me at it—   *Romney's R.* 112

Shameful This is a *s* thing for men to lie.   *M. d'Arthur* 78
Dabbling a shameless hand with *s* jest,   *Princess iii* 314
And with a *s* swiftness,   *Com. of Arthur* 205
Or seeming *s*—for what shame in love,   *Merlin and V.* 861
Then came thy *s* sin with Lancelot   *Guinevere* 487
in his agony conceives A *s* sense as of a cleaving
  crime—   *Lover's Tale i* 794

Shamefulness Arthur were the child of *s*,   *Com. of Arthur* 239

Shameless Ah *s* ! for he did but sing A song   *You might have won* 21
s noon Was clash'd and hammer'd from a hundred towers,   *Godiva* 74
will she fling herself, *S* upon me ?   *Lucretius* 203
Dabbling a *s* hand with shameful jest,   *Princess iii* 314
'Lo the *s* ones, who take Their pastime   *Lancelot and E.* 100
Anon there past a crowd With *s* laughter,   *St. Telemachus* 39

Shamest shamed thee so that now thou *s* me,   *Balin and Balan* 431

Shamus (*See also* **Shamus O'Shea**) An' *S* along wid the
  rest,   *Tomorrow* 44

Shamus O'Shea (*See also* **Shamus**) Dhrinkin' yer health
  wid *S O'S*   ,,   12
An' *S O'S* was yer shadda,   ,,   38
S O'S that has now ten childer,   ,,   85

Shape (s) A gleaming *s* she floated by,   *L. of Shalott iv* 39
A cloud that gather'd *s* :   *Œnone* 42
tears of angels to the perfect *s* of man.   *To* ——, *With Pal. of Art* 19
O *s*'s and hues that please me well !   *Palace of Art* 194
in dark corners of her palace stood Uncertain *s*'s ;   ,,   238
So *s* chased *s* as swift as,   *D. of F. Women* 1
Gown'd in pure white, that fitted to the *s*—   *Gardener's D.* 126
What's here ? a *s*, a shade,   *St. S. Stylites* 202
Ten thousand broken lights and *s*'s,   *Will Water.* 59
The peaky islet shifted *s*'s,   *The Voyage* 33
Suffused them, sitting, lying, languid *s*'s,   *Vision of Sin* 12
Here is a story which in rougher *s*   *Aylmer's Field* 7
In such a *s* dost thou behold thy God.   ,,   657
And twisted *s*'s of lust, unspeakable,   *Lucretius* 157
cloud may stoop from heaven and take the *s*   *Princess vii* 2
Titanic *s*'s, they cramm'd The forum,   ,,   124
softer all her *s* And rounder seem'd :   ,,   136
And *s*'s and hues of Art divine !   *Ode Inter. Exhib.* 22
Those niched *s*'s of noble mould,   *The Daisy* 38
palled *s*'s In shadowy thoroughfares   *In Mem. lxx* 7
And wheel'd or lit the filmy *s*'s   ,,   *xcv* 10
The *s* of him I loved, and love   ,,   *ciii* 14
Ring out old *s*'s of foul disease ;   ,,   *cvi* 25
with the shocks of doom To *s* and use.   ,,   *cxviii* 25
To a lord, a captain, a padded *s*,   *Maud I x* 29
a ship, the *s* thereof A dragon wing'd,   *Com. of Arthur* 374
S that fled With broken wings,   *Gareth and L* 1207
With pointed lance as if to pierce, a *s*,   *Balin and Balan* 325

Shape (s) (continued) The *s* and colour of a mind and life,   *Lancelot and E.* 335
her *s* From forehead down to foot, perfect—   ,,   641
around Great angels, awful *s*'s, and wings and eyes.   *Holy Grail* 848
slender was her hand and small her *s* ;   *Pelleas and E.* 74
Unruffling waters re-collect the *s*   *Last Tournament* 369
morning shadows huger than the *s*'s That cast them,   *To the Queen* 63
Waiting to see some blessed *s* in heaven,   *Lover's Tale i* 312
shadows of dawn on the beautiful *s*'s,   *V. of Maeldune* 99
two *s*'s high over the sacred fountain,   *Parnassus* 9
s with wings Came sweeping by him,   *St. Telemachus* 24
The *s* with wings.   ,,   38
æon pass and touch him into *s* ?   *Making of Man* 4

Shape (verb) thoughts Do *s* themselves within me,   *Œnone* 247
A saying, hard to *s* in act ;   *Love thou thy land* 47
that which *s*'s it to some perfect end.   *Love and Duty* 26
To *s* the song for your delight   *Day-Dm., Ep.* 6
and check'd His power to *s* :   *Lucretius* 23
Our weakness somehow *s*'s the shadow, Time ;   *Princess iii* 330
s it plank and beam for roof and floor,   ,,   *vi* 46
And *s* the whisper of the throne ;   *In Mem. lxiv* 12
Then fancy *s*'s, as fancy can,   ,,   *lxxx* 5
s His action like the greater ape,   ,,   *cxx* 10
Like clouds they *s* themselves and go.   ,,   *cxxiii* 8
Would *s* himself a right !'   *Gareth and L.* 348
face that men *S* to their fancy's eye   *Lancelot and E.* 1252
But had not force to *s* it as he would,   *Pass. of Arthur* 15
Ye cannot *s* Fancy so fair as is this   *Lover's Tale i* 547
Was my sight drunk that it did *s* to me   ,,   642
Virtue must *s* itself in deed,   *Tiresias* 86
and *s* it at the last According to the Highest   *Ancient Sage* 89
S your heart to front the hour,   *Locksley H., Sixty* 106
You that *s* for Eternity,   *On Jub. Q. Victoria* 43
And see and *s* and do.   *Mechanophilus* 4

Shaped (*See also* **Bow-shaped, Man-shaped**) *s* The city's ancient
  legend into this :—   *Godiva* 3
S her heart with woman's meekness   *L. of Burleigh* 71
This red-hot iron to be *s* with blows.   *Princess v* 209
s, it seems, By God for thee alone,   *Lancelot and E.* 1366
foot was on a stool *S* as a dragon ;   *Last Tournament* 672
S by the audible and visible,   *Lover's Tale ii* 104
motion lives Be prosperously *s*,   *De Prof., Two G.* 20
Who *s* the forms, obey them,   *Akbar's Dream* 143

Shaping 'By *s* some august decree,   *To the Queen* 33
'Here sits he *s* wings to fly :   *Two Voices* 289
s faithful record of the glance That graced   *Gardener's D.* 177
And one the *s* of a star ;   *In Mem. ciii* 36
s an infant ripe for its birth,   *Maud I iv* 34
S their way toward Dyflen again,   *Batt. of Brunanburh* 98

Shard By *s*'s and scurf of salt,   *Vision of Sin* 211
dash'd Your cities into *s*'s with catapults,   *Princess v* 138

Share (s) rhymes to him were scrip and *s*,   *The Brook* 4
To buy strange *s*'s in some Peruvian mine.   *Sea Dreams* 15
O then to ask her of my *s*'s,   ,,   115
Then beast and man had had their *s* of me :   *Com. of Arthur* 163
Who leaving *s* in furrow come to see   *Gareth and L.* 243
dividend, consol, and—*s*   *The Wreck* 30

Share (verb) Now could you *s* your thought ;   *Princess vi* 252
s's with man His nights, his days,   ,,   *vii* 262
Who stay to *s* the morning feast,   *In Mem., Con.* 75
him who had ceased to *s* her heart,   *Maud I xix* 30
For ye shall *s* my earldom with me, girl,   *Geraint and E.* 626
and to *s* Their marriage-banquet.   *The Ring* 430
To *s* his living death with him,   *Happy* 8

Shared one sorrow and she *s* it not ?   *Aylmer's Field* 702
I *s* with her in whom myself remains.   *Lover's Tale i* 248
all my griefs were *s* with thee,   *Pref. Poem Broth. S.* 25

Sharer *S*'s of our glorious past,   *Open. I. and C. Exhib.* 31

Sharp (adj.) Edged with *s* laughter, cuts atwain   *Clear-headed friend* 2
When the *s* clear twang of the golden chords   *Sea-Fairies* 38
S and few, but seeming-bitter From excess   *Rosalind* 31
bright and *s* As edges of the scymetar.   *Kate* 11
And utterly consumed with *s* distress,   *Lotos-Eaters, C. S* 13
I made my dagger *s* and bright.   *The Sisters* 26
He thought of that *s* look, Mother, I gave him
  yesterday,   *May Queen* 15

Sharp (adj.) (continued) All those *s* fancies, by down-
  lapsing thought | *D. of F. Women* 49
  With that *s* sound the white dawn's creeping beams, | " 261
  His face is growing *s* and thin. | *D. of the O. Year* 46
  all these things fell on her *S* as reproach. | *Enoch Arden* 488
  dying, gleam'd on rocks Roof-pendent, *s*; | *Balin and Balan* 315
  s breaths of anger puff'd Her fairy nostril out; | *Merlin and V.* 848
  Thro' her own side she felt the *s* lance go; | *Lancelot and E.* 624
  dame Came suddenly on the Queen with the *s* news. | " 730
  With one *s* rapid, where the crisping white | *Holy Grail* 381
  close upon it peal'd A *s* quick thunder.' | " 696
  As the *s* wind that ruffles all day long | *Guinevere* 50
  On that *s* ridge of utmost doom ride highly | *Lover's Tale i* 805
  S is the fire of assault, | *Def. of Lucknow* 57
  'Ya mun saäve little Dick, an' be *s* about it an' all,' | *Owd Roä* 81
Sharp (s) thro' every change of *s* and flat; | *Caress'd or chidden* 4
  In little *s's* and trebles, | *The Brook* 40
Sharpen'd Are *s* to a needle's end; | *In Mem. lxxvi* 4
  and ice Makes daggers at the *s* eaves, | " *cvii* 8
  his aims Were *s* by strong hate for Lancelot. | *Guinevere* 20
Sharper she was *s* than an eastern wind, | *Audley Court* 53
  Suddenly strike on a *s* sense For a shell, | *Maud II ii* 63
Sharpest Upon the last and *s* height, | *In Mem. xlvii* 13
  Shall *s* pathos blight us, knowing all | *Love and Duty* 85
Sharp-headed busy fret Of that *s-h* worm begins | *Supp. Confessions* 186
Sharpness *s* of that pain about her heart: | *Geraint and E.* 190
Sharp-pointed He! where is some *s-p* thing? | *The Flight* 72
Sharp-smitten *S-s* with the dint of armed heels— | *M. d'Arthur* 190
  S-s with the dint of armed heels— | *Pass. of Arthur* 358
Shatter And *s*, when the storms are black, | *England and Amer.* 13
  Would *s* all the happiness of the hearth. | *Enoch Arden* 770
  Take the hoary Roman head and *s* it, | *Boädicea* 65
  ere the onward whirlwind *s* it, | *Lover's Tale i* 451
  shake with her thunders and *s* her island, | *Kapiolani* 10
Shatter'd (See also **Still-shatter'd**) Spars were splinter'd,
  decks were *s*, | *The Captain* 45
  S into one earthquake in one day | *Lucretius* 251
  arms were *s* to the shoulder blade. | *Princess vi* 52
  from the sabre-stroke *S* and sunder'd. | *Light Brigade* 36
  some were sunk and many were *s*, | *The Revenge* 61
  Rocking with *s* spars, with sudden fires Flamed over: | *Buonaparte* 11
  And loosed the *s* casque, and chafed his hands, | *M. d'Arthur* 209
  So like a *s* column lay the King; | " 221
  And these are the *s* stalks, | *In Mem. lxxxii* 7
  On a horror of *s* limbs and a wretched swindler's lie? | *Maud I i* 56
  Here stood a *s* archway plumed with fern; | *Marr. of Geraint* 316
  And one with *s* fingers dangling lame, | *Last Tournament* 60
  the crash Of battleaxes on *s* helms, | *Pass. of Arthur* 110
  And loosed the *s* casque, and chafed his hands, | " 377
  So like a *s* column lay the King; | " 389
  a stream Flies with a *s* foam along the chasm. | *Lover's Tale i* 383
  Gilded with broom, or *s* into spires, | " 400
  but *s* nerve, Yet haunting Julian, | " *iv* 105
  And *s* phantom of that infinite One, | *De Prof., Two G.* 47
  Wreck'd—your train: or all but wreck'd? a *s*
  wheel? a vicious boy | *Locksley H., Sixty* 215
  The jungle rooted in his *s* hearth, | *Demeter and P.* 76
  Spurning a *s* fragment of the God, | *St. Telemachus* 16
Shattering (See also **Shrine-shattering**) plunge in cataract,
  s on black blocks | *Princess iii* 291
  The *s* trumpet shrilleth high, | *Sir Galahad* 5
  I rode, *S* all evil customs everywhere, | *Holy Grail* 477
Shaw (show) an' 'e *s's* it to me, | *North. Cobbler* 85
Shawm With *s's*, and with cymbals, | *Dying Swan* 32
Sheaf (See also **Autumn-sheaf, Barley-sheaves**) Piling
  sheaves in uplands airy, | *L. of Shalott i* 34
  In front they bound the *sheaves*. | *Palace of Art* 78
  THE varying year with blade and *s* | *Day-Dm., Sleep. P.* 1
  bind the scatter'd scheme of seven Together in one *s*? | *Princess, Con.* 9
  Which he may read that binds the *s*, | *In Mem. xxxvi* 13
  And whirl the ungarner'd *s* afar, | " *lxxii* 23
  Where stood the *s* of Peace: | *The Ring* 247
Shear I did but a *s* feather, | *Princess v* 541
Sheath (See also **Flower-sheath**) New from its silken *s*. | *D. of F. Women* 60
  A dagger, in rich *s* with jewels on it | *Aylmer's Field* 220

Sheath (continued) More crumpled than a poppy from the *s*, | *Princess v* 29
  tearing out of *s* The brand, Sir Balin with a
  fiery ' Ha! | *Balin and Balan* 392
  when, prest together In its green *s*, | *Lover's Tale i* 153
Sheathe To draw, to *s* a useless sword, | *In Mem. cxxviii* 13
Sheathing To *s* splendours and the golden scale | *Princess v* 41
Sheba That *S* came to ask of Solomon.' | " *ii* 346
  For Solomon may come to *S* yet.' | " 349
Shebeen (grog-shop) wid Shamus O'Shea at Katty's *s*; | *Tomorrow* 12
  he says to me wanst, at Katty's *s*, | " 63
Shed (s) broken *s's* look'd sad and strange: | *Mariana* 5
  Became no better than a broken *s*, | *Holy Grail* 398
  boäth slinkt 'oäm by the brokken *s* | *Spinster's S's.* 37
  An' tha squeedg'd my 'and i' the *s*, | " 39
Shed (verb) They have not *s* a many tears, | *Miller's D.* 221
  Yet tears they *s*: they had their part | " 223
  I thought that all the blood by Sylla *s* | *Lucretius* 47
  dry up these tears *S* for the love of Love; | *Lover's Tale i* 781
  I weänt a *s* a drop on 'is blood, | *North. Cobbler* 114
  since Sylvester *s* the venom of world-wealth | *Sir J. Oldcastle* 166
Shedding *s* poison in the fountains of the Will. | *Locksley H., Sixty* 274
Sheeny And many a *s* summer-morn, | *Arabian Nights* 5
  Hues of the silken *s* woof | *Madeline* 22
  Love wept and spread his *s* vans for flight; | *Love and Death* 8
Sheep livelong bleat Of the thick-fleeced *s* | *Ode to Memory* 66
  are men better than *s* or goats | *M. d'Arthur* 250
  A lord of fat prize-oxen and of *s*, | *Princess, Con.* 86
  oxen from the city, and goodly *s* In haste they drove, | *Spec. of Iliad* 4
  As well as ever shepherd knew his *s*, | *Holy Grail* 551
  Old milky fables of the wolf and *s*, | *Pelleas and E.* 196
  are men better than *s* or goats | *Pass. of Arthur* 418
Sheepcot or from *s* or king's-hall, | *Gareth and L.* 467
Sheepwalk Or *s* up the windy wold; | *In Mem. c* 8
Sheer Revenge ran on *s* into the heart of the foe, | *The Revenge* 33
  Stock-still for *s* amazement. | *Will Water.* 136
Sheer-astounded And *s-a* were the charioteers | *Achilles over the T.* 26
Sheer'd Caught the shrill salt, and *s* the gale. | *The Voyage* 12
Sheet (adj.) In the middle leaps a fountain Like *s* lightning, | *Poet's Mind* 25
Sheet (s) I wrapt his body in the *s*, | *The Sisters* 34
  Rolling a slumbrous *s* of foam below. | *Lotos-Eaters* 13
  Scaffolds, still *s's* of water, | *D. of F. Women* 24
  See that *s's* are on my bed; | *Vision of Sin* 68
  falls Of water, *s's* of summer glass, | *To E. L.* 2
  And scaled in *s's* of wasteful foam, | *Sea Dreams* 15
  A music out of *s* and shroud, | *In Mem. ciii* 54
  s's of hyacinth That seem'd the heavens | *Guinevere* 390
  Whatever moved in that full *s* | *To E Fitzgerald* 11
Sheeted *See* **Silver-sheeted**
Sheet-lightnings saw No pale *s-l* from afar, | *Aylmer's Field* 726
Sheik but I know it—*his*, the hoary *S*, | *Akbar's Dream* 90
Shelf Of ledge or *s* The rock rose clear, | *Palace of Art* 9
  Upon the rosewood *s*; | *Talking Oak* 118
  With *s* and corner for the goods and stores. | *Enoch Arden* 171
  That strikes by night a craggy *s*, | *In Mem. xvi* 13
  see your Art still shrined in human *shelves*, | *Poets and their B.* 11
  Laid in the *s* | *To Mary Boyle* 24
Shell (See also **Egg-shell**) A walk with vary-colour'd *s's* | *Arabian Nights* 57
  They freshen the silvery-crimson *s's*, | *Sea-Fairies* 13
  pelt me with starry spangles and *s's*, | *The Merman* 28
  broad sea-wolds in the crimson *s's*, | *The Mermaid* 36
  Jewel or *s*, or starry ore, | *Eleänore* 20
  when the *s* Divides threefold to show the fruit
  (repeat) | *The Brook* 72, 207
  the bird, the fish, the *s*, the flower, | *Princess iii* 383
  Storm'd at with shot and *s* (repeat) | *Light Brigade* 22, 43
  MINNIE and Winnie Slept in a *s*. | *Minnie and Winnie* 2
  Pink was the *s* within, Silver without; | " 5
  stars Peep'd into the *s*. | " 14
  Should toss with tangle and with *s's*. | *In Mem. x* 20
  Time hath sunder'd *s* from pearl.' | " *lii* 16
  The ruin'd *s's* of hollow towers? | " *lxxvi* 16
  See what a lovely *s*, | *Maud II ii* 1
  For a *s*, or a flower, little things | " 64
  How fast they hold like colours of a *s* | *Marr. of Geraint* 681
  hast broken *s*, Art yet half-yolk, | *Balin and Balan* 568

X*

Shot (verb) (continued)) pine *s* aloft from the crag — *V. of Maeldune* 16
Men of the Northland *S* over shield. — *Batt. of Brunanburh* 34
'Ud 'a *s* his own sowl dead — *Tomorrow* 40
A light *s* upward on them from the lake. — *The Ring* 256

Shotted *See* **Heavy-shotted**

Shoulder over his left *s* laugh'd at thee, — *The Bridesmaid* 7
a leopard-skin Droop'd from his *s*, — *Œnone* 59
Upon her pearly *s* leaning cold, — „ 140
golden round her lucid throat And *s*: — „ 179
From off her *s* backward borne: — *Palace of Art* 118
clapt his hand On Everard's *s*, — *The Epic* 22
Make broad thy *s*'s to receive my weight, — *M. d'Arthur* 164
O'er both his *s*'s drew the languid hands, — „ 174
From thy pure brows, and from thy *s*'s pure, — *Tithonus* 35
Till over thy dark *s* glow Thy silver sister-world, — *Move eastward* 5
Naiads oar'd A glimmering *s* — *To E. L.* 17
With a heaved *s* and a saucy smile, — *Aylmer's Field* 466
Among the honest *s*'s of the crowd, — *Sea Dreams* 166
And robed the *s*'s in a rosy silk, — *Princess, Pro.* 103
Her round white *s* shaken with her sobs, — „ iv 289
lanes of splendour slanted o'er a press Of snowy *s*'s, — „ 479
But on my *s* hung their heavy hands, — „ 553
Leapt from the dewy *s*'s of the Earth, — „ v 43
Down on the *s*'s of the twain, his men, — *Gareth and L.* 440
On either shining *s* laid a hand, — *Marr. of Geraint* 518
and the squire Chafing his *s*: — *Geraint and E.* 27
letting her left hand Droop from his mighty *s*, — *Merlin and V.* 243
Gazed at the heaving *s*, and the face Hand-hidden, — „ 896
Lancelot turn'd, and smooth'd The glossy *s*, — *Lancelot and E.* 348
Each gript a *s*, and I stood between; — *Holy Grail* 822
Make broad thy *s*'s to receive my weight, — *Pass. of Arthur* 332
O'er both his *s*'s drew the languid hands, — „ 342
warrior's puissant *s*'s Pallas flung — *Achilles over the T.* 3
And plant on *s*, hand and knee, — *To E. Fitzgerald* 8
lay thine uphill *s* to the wheel, — *Ancient Sage* 279
fur the merk's o' thy *s* yit; — *Owd Roä* 90
you my girl Rode on my *s* home— — *The Ring* 322

Shoulder Blade (*See also* **Blade**) arms were shatter'd to the *s b*, — *Princess* vi 52

Shoulder'd (*See also* **Broad-shoulder'd**) Then we *s* thro' the swarm, — *Audley Court* 9
in the cellars merry bloated things *S* the spigot, — *Guinevere* 268

Shoulder-slipt they shock'd, and Kay Fell *s-s*, — *Gareth and L.* 759

Shout (s) Herod, when the *s* was in his ears, — *Palace of Art* 219
shall the braggart *s* For some blind glimpse — *Love and Duty* 5
But that there rose a *s*: — *Princess, Con.* 36
a *s* rose again, and made The long line — „ 96
a *s* More joyful than the city-roar — „ 100
And caught once more the distant *s*, — *In Mem.* lxxxvii 9
At the *s*'s, the leagues of lights, — *Maud II* iv 21
And *s*'s, and clarions shrilling unto blood, — *Com. of Arthur* 103
voice As dreadful as the *s* of one who sees — „ 117
s's Ascended, and there brake a servingman — *Gareth and L.* 800
whereupon Their common *s* in chorus, — *Balin and Balan* 87
Then rang the *s* his lady loved: — *Pelleas and E.* 171
the red dream Fled with a *s*, — *Last Tournament* 488
s's of heathen and the traitor knights, — *Pass. of Arthur* 113
on a sudden the garrison utter a jubilant *s*, — *Def. of Lucknow* 98
from the dyke he sent his mighty *s*, — *Achilles over the T.* 30
jingle of bits, *S*'s, arrows, — *Tiresias* 94
an' maäkin' ma deaf wi' their *s*'s, — *Spinster's S*'s 88
gallop up with a cheer and a *s*, — *Heavy Brigade* 61
the *s* Of His descending peals from Heaven, — *Romney's R.* 126

Shout (verb) hark! they *s* 'St. Simeon Stylites.' — *St. S. Stylites* 146
They *s*, 'Behold a saint!' — „ 153
That he *s*'s with his sister at play! — *Break, break, etc.* 8
S Icenian, Catieuchlanian, *s* Coritanian, — *Boädicea* 57
dying while they *s* her name. — *Locksley H., Sixty* 128

Shouted Till I struck out and *s*; — *Princess* v 540
But I heard it *s* at once from the top — *Maud II* v 50
Then the third brother *s* o'er the bridge, — *Gareth and L.* 1096
Lancelot *s*, 'Stay me not! — *Holy Grail* 643
'No name, no name,' he *s*, 'a scourge am I — *Pelleas and E.* 565
roar'd And *s* and leapt down upon the fall'n; — *Last Tournament* 469
Till they *s* along with the shouting — *V. of Maeldune* 34

Shouted (*continued*) standing, *s*, and Pallas far away — *Achilles over the T.* 17
lighted on him there, And *s*, — *Death of Œnone* 56

Shouting Heard the heavens fill with *s*, — *Locksley Hall* 123
With a loyal people *s* a battle cry, — *Maud III* vi 35
thro' lanes of *s* Gareth rode Down the slope street, — *Gareth and L.* 699
Which was the red cock *s* to the light, — *Geraint and E.* 384
S, 'Sir Galahad and Sir Percivale!' — *Holy Grail* 337
seem'd *S*'s of all the sons of God: — „ 509
and *s*'s and soundings to arms, — *Def. of Lucknow* 76
And we came to the Isle of *S*, — *V. of Maeldune* 27
And the *s* of these wild birds — „ 33
Till they shouted along with the *s* — „ 34

Shove *See* **Shuvv**

Shovell'd *s* up into some bloody trench — *Audley Court* 42

Show (s) Thou comest not with *s*'s of flaunting vines — *Ode to Memory* 48
Had made him talk for *s*; — *Will Water.* 196
Princess Ida seem'd a hollow *s*, — *Princess* iii 185
camp and college turn'd to hollow *s*'s; — „ v 478
They did but look like hollow *s*'s; — „ vii 134
My haunting sense of mutual *s*'s: — „ 349
hang'd him in chains for a *s*— — *Rizpah* 35
With a purse to pay for the *s*. — *Dead Prophet* 8

Show (verb) (*See also* **Shaw**) Nor canst thou *s* the dead are dead. — *Two Voices* 267
Some one might *s* it at a joust of arms, — *M. d'Arthur* 102
S me the man hath suffer'd more than I. — *St. S. Stylites* 49
That *s* the year is turn'd. — *Talking Oak* 176
and *s*'s At distance like a little wood; — *Day-Dm., Sleep. P.* 41
And all that else the years will *s*, — „ *L'Envoi* 13
s you slips of all that grows — *Amphion* 83
So *s*'s my soul before the Lamb, — *St. Agnes' Eve* 17
Shall *s* thee past to Heaven: — *Will Water.* 246
All he *s*'s her makes him dearer: — *L. of Burleigh* 33
'Proclaim the faults he would not *s*: — *You might have won* 17
Divides threefold to *s* the fruit within. (*Repeat*) — *The Brook* 73, 208
call'd old Philip out To *s* the farm: — „ 121
into Darnley chase To *s* Sir Arthur's deer. — „ 133
'*S* me the books!' — *Sea Dreams* 148
these I thought my dream would *s* to me, — *Lucretius* 51
and *s* That life is not as idle ore, — *In Mem.* cxviii 19
That *will s* itself without. — *Maud II* iv 61
To *s* that who may slay or scape the three, — *Gareth and L.* 641
to *s* His loathing of our Order and the Queen. — *Balin and Balan* 550
think I *s* myself Too dark a prophet: — *Holy Grail* 321
babble about him, all to *s* your wit— — *Last Tournament* 340
Bear with me for the last time while I *s*, — *Guinevere* 454
Some one might *s* it at a joust of arms, — *Pass. of Arthur* 270
and *s* us That we are surely heard. — *Lover's Tale* i 364
he brings And *s*'s them whatsoever he accounts — „ iv 233
'O my heart's lord, would I could *s* you,' he says, — „ 250
I propose to-night To *s* you what is dearest to my heart, — „ 252
while I *s* you all my heart.' — „ 353
s us that the world is wholly fair. — *Ancient Sage* 182
Let the trampled serpent *s* you — *Locksley H., Sixty* 242
never had I seen her *s* remorse— — *The Ring* 457
Our Playwright may *s* In some fifth Act — *The Play* 3
I will *s* it you by-and-by. — *Bandit's Death* 8

Show'd the world Like one great garden *s*, — *The Poet* 34
One *s* an iron coast and angry waves. — *Palace of Art* 69
for he *s* me all the sin. — *May Queen, Con.* 17
Pontius and Iscariot by my side *S* like fair seraphs. — *St. S. Stylites* 169
S her the fairy footings on the grass, — *Aylmer's Field* 90
And when she *s* the wealthy scabbard, — „ 236
s their eyes Glaring, and passionate looks, — *Sea Dreams* 235
and *s* A riotous confluence of watercourses — *Lucretius* 29
s the house, Greek, set with busts: — *Princess, Pro.* 10
s the late-writ letters of the king. — „ i 175
He *s* a tent A stone-shot off: — „ v 53
What Roman strength Turbia *s* — *The Daisy* 5
Who *s* a token of distress? — *In Mem.* lxxviii 13
And *s* him in the fountain fresh — „ lxxxv 26
knight Had visor up, and *s* a youthful face, — *Marr. of Geraint* 189
s themselves against the sky, and sank. — „ 240
For while the mother *s* it, — „ 636
And *s* an empty tent allotted her, — *Geraint and E.* 885
This gray King *S* us a shrine — *Balin and Balan* 109

Show'd (continued) This woodman s the cave From which he sallies, — *Balin and Balan* 131

gems Pluck'd from the crown, and s them to his knights, — *Lancelot and E.* 57

Chose the green path that s the rarer foot, — „ 162

And s him, like a vermin in its hole, — *Last Tournament* 165

And s them both the ruby-chain, — „ 409

in the light's last glimmer Tristram s — „ 739

s he drank beyond his use ; — *Lover's Tale iv* 228

s Turning my way, the loveliest face — *Sisters (E. and E.)* 86

Shower (s) (*See also* **Thunder-shower**) sweet s's Of festal flowers, — *Ode to Memory* 77

These in every s creep Thro' the green — *A Dirge* 33

Like moonlight on a falling s ? — *Margaret* 4

like the rainbow from the s, — *Two Voices* 444

The slow result of winter s's : — „ 452

I thirsted for the brooks, the s's : — *Fatima* 10

I'll take the s's as they fall, — *Amphion* 101

Perfume and flowers fall in s's, — *Sir Galahad* 11

The gentle s, the smell of dying leaves, — *Enoch Arden* 611

s's of random sweet on maid and man. — *Princess vii* 86

Briton in blown seas and storming s's, — *Ode on Well.* 155

s and storm and blast Had blown the lake — *The Daisy* 70

daisy close Her crimson fringes to the s ; — *In Mem. lxxii* 12

Sweet after s's, ambrosial air, — „ *lxxxvi* 1

in the sudden sun Between two s's, — *Gareth and L.* 389

Was cared as much for as a summer s ; — *Geraint and E.* 523

Like sunlight on the plain behind a s : — *Merlin and V.* 403

poplars made a noise of falling s's. — *Lancelot and E.* 411

poplars with their noise of falling s's, — „ 523

s's of flowers Fell as we past ; — *Holy Grail* 348

and s and shorn plume Went down it. — *Last Tournament* 155

with Queen Isolt Against a s, — „ 379

Showing a s of blood in a field noir, — „ 433

the wind and the s and the snow. — *Rizpah* 68

from out the west in shadowing s's, — *Sisters (E. and E.)* 7

Thro' the blotting mist, the blinding s's, — „ 18

Stony s's Of that ear-stunning hail of Arês — *Tiresias* 95

from a day of driving s's— — *Locksley H., Sixty* 259

Before them fleets the s, — *Early Spring* 13

a s of stones that stoned him dead, — *St. Telemachus* 68

Shower (verb) Down s the gambolling waterfalls — *Sea-Fairies* 10

s the fiery grain Of freedom broadcast — *Princess v* 421

S's slanting light upon the dolorous wave. — *Lover's Tale i* 811

Shower'd (adj.) To enrich the threshold of the night With s largess of delight — *In Mem. xxix* 7

Shower'd (verb) s the rippled ringlets to her knee ; — *Godiva* 47

s His oriental gifts on everyone And most on Edith : — *Aylmer's Field* 213

Before me s the rose in flakes ; — *Princess iv* 264

Lavish Honour s all her stars, — *Ode on Well.* 196

s down Rays of a mighty circle, — *Lover's Tale i* 417

Showerful in a s spring Stared at the spate. — *Gareth and L.* 2

Showering (*See also* **Ever-showering**) S thy gleaned wealth into my open breast — *Ode to Memory* 23

s wide Sleet of diamond-drift and pearly hail ; — *Vision of Sin* 21

fountains spouted up and s down In meshes — *Princess i* 218

Showery Grow green beneath the s gray, — *My life is full* 17

dew'd with s drops, Up-clomb the shadowy pine — *Lotos-Eaters* 17

last, she fixt A s glance upon her aunt, — *Princess, Con.* 33

Showing (*See also* **A-Shawin'**) S a gaudy summer-morn, — *Palace of Art* 62

she pointed with a laugh, (S the aspick's bite.) — *D. of F. Women* 160

S a shower of blood in a field noir, — *Last Tournament* 433

Not only s ? and he himself pronounced — *Lover's Tale iv* 349

And s them, souls have wings ! — *Dead Prophet* 12

Shown (*See also* **Late-shown**) Half s, are broken and withdrawn. — *Two Voices* 306

and s the truth betimes, That old true filth, — *Merlin and V.* 46

after he hath s him gems or gold, — *Lover's Tale iv* 246

France had s a light to all men, — *Locksley H., Sixty* 89

not s To dazzle all that see them ? — *The Ring* 143

Shrank S one sick willow sere and small. — *Mariana in the S.* 53

Enid s far back into herself, — *Geraint and E.* 607

his charger at her side, She s a little. — „ 821

and he s and wail'd, ' Is the Queen false ? ' — *Pelleas and E.* 531

He s and howl'd, and from his brow drew back — *Lover's Tale ii* 92

Shrank (continued) her weight S in my grasp, — *Lover's Tale ii* 203

I turn'd : my heart S in me, — „ *iii* 38

Her that s, and put me from her, — *Locksley H., Sixty* 264

Shrew woodland thing, Or s, or weasel, — *Gareth and L.* 749

Shrewdest a sting of s pain Ran shrivelling thro' me, — *St. S. Stylites* 198

Shrewdness nor compensating the want By s, — *Enoch Arden* 251

Shrewish Puppet to a father's threat, and servile to a s tongue ! — *Locksley Hall* 42

Shriek (s) (*See also* **Flittermouse-shriek**) myriad s of wheeling ocean-fowl, — *Enoch Arden* 583

the keen s ' Yes love, yes, Edith, yes,' — *Aylmer's Field* 582

their s's Ran highest up the gamut, — *Sea Dreams* 232

One s of hate would jar all the hymns of heaven : — „ 259

Dislik'd with s's and laughter : — *Princess, Pro.* 70

yonder, s's and strange experiments — „ 235

the whispers, and the s's Of the wild woods together ; — „ *i* 98

There rose a s as of a city sack'd ; — „ *iv* 165

another s, ' The Head, the Head, the Princess, — „ 175

A kingdom topples over with a s — „ *Con.* 62

The shrill-edged s of a mother — *Maud I i* 16

there was *love* in the passionate s, — „ 57

And all in passion uttering a dry s, — *Geraint and E.* 461

Unearthlier than all s of bird or beast, — *Balin and Balan* 545

clapt her hands Together with a wailing s, — *Merlin and V.* 867

Lancelot gave A marvellous great s — *Lancelot and E.* 516

upward-rushing storm and cloud Of s and plume, — *Last Tournament* 441

Behind him rose a shadow and a s— — „ 753

s's and ringing laughter on the sand — *Lover's Tale iii* 32

wail came borne in the s of a growing wind, — *The Wreck* 87

s for the rights of an equal humanity, — *Beautiful City* 2

she heard The s of some lost life — *Death of Œnone* 90

arose The s and curse of trampled millions, — *Akbar's Dream* 190

Shriek (verb) if any came near I would call, and s, — *The Mermaid* 38

S out ' I hate you, Enoch,' — *Enoch Arden* 33

and s ' You are not Ida ; ' — *Princess vii* 94

That s and sweat in pigmy wars — *Lit. Squabbles* 2

shall s if a Hungary fail ? — *Maud I iv* 46

That ever s's before a death, — *Lancelot and E.* 1023

and s's After the Christ, — *Pass. of Arthur* 110

glance the tits, and s the jays, — *Prog. of Spring* 15

If every single star Should s its claim — *Akbar's Dream* 43

Shriek'd (*See also* **Screeäd**) mouse Behind the mouldering wainscot s, — *Mariana* 64

' No voice,' she s in that lone hall, — *Palace of Art* 258

Again they s the burthen—' Him ! ' — *Edwin Morris* 123

' A ship of fools,' he s in spite, — *The Voyage* 77

For sideways up he swung his arms, and s — *Sea Dreams* 24

s That she but meant to win him back, — *Lucretius* 278

Daintily she s And wrung it. — *Princess, Pro.* 175

' Boys ! ' s the old king, — „ *v* 328

s The virgin marble under iron heels : — „ *vi* 350

Yell'd and s between her daughters (repeat) — *Boädicea* 6, 72

s against his creed— — *In Mem. lvi* 16

His helmet as to slay him, but she s, — *Gareth and L.* 979

S to the stranger, ' Slay not a dead man ! ' — *Geraint and E.* 779

moved so much the more, and s again, — „ 782

s out ' Traitor ' to the unhearing wall, — *Lancelot and E.* 612

Who rode by Lancelot, wail'd and s aloud, — *Holy Grail* 356

The words of Arthur flying s, arose, — *Last Tournament* 139

Who s and wail'd, the three whereat we gazed — *Pass. of Arthur* 453

Aloud she s : My heart was cloven with pain ; — *Lover's Tale ii* 199

s and slaked the light with blood. — *Locksley H., Sixty* 90

s, and started from my side— — „ 264

One s ' The fires of Hell ! ' — *Dead Prophet* 80

when I learnt it at last, I s, — *Charity* 37

Shrieking fell The woman s at his feet, — *Aylmer's Field* 811

And s ' I am his dearest, I— — *The Victim* 71

And the s rush of the wainscot mouse, — *Maud I vi* 71

s out ' O fool ! ' the harlot leapt Adown the forest, — *Merlin and V.* 972

On whom the women s " Atheist " flung Filth — *Akbar's Dream* 91

Shrift And number'd bead, and s, — *Talking Oak* 46

Wrapt in her grief, for housel or for s, — *Guinevere* 149

Shrike the sparrow spear'd by the s, — *Maud I iv* 23

Shrill (adj.) And the s winds were up and away, — *Mariana* 50

Shrill (adj.) (continued) *S* music reach'd them on the middle
  sea. *Sea-Fairies* 6
  Springing alone With a *s* inner sound, *The Mermaid* 20
  Her rapid laughters wild and *s*, *Kate* 3
  Lest their *s* happy laughter come to me *Œnone* 258
  over them the sea-wind sang *S*, chill, *M. d'Arthur* 49
  The *s* bell rings, the censer swings, *Sir Galahad* 35
  The Lady's-head upon the prow Caught the *s* salt, *The Voyage* 12
  and fear'd To send abroad a *s* and terrible cry, *Enoch Arden* 768
  S, till the comrade of his chambers woke, *Aylmer's Field* 583
  she lifted up a voice Of *s* command, *Death of Œnone* 99
Shrill (adv.) Thereat she suddenly laugh'd and *s*, *Balin and Balan* 493
  over them the sea-wind sang *S*, chill, *Pass. of Arthur* 217
Shrill (verb) wind, that *s*'s All night in a waste land, *M. d'Arthur* 201
  her whinny *s*'s From tile to scullery, *Princess* v 452
  wind that *s*'s All night in a waste land, *Pass. of Arthur* 369
  like the clear voice When a trumpet *s*'s, *Achilles over the T.* 19
Shrill-edged The *s-e* shriek of a mother *Maud* I i 16
Shrill'd (*s* the cotton-spinning chorus); *Edwin Morris* 122
  And *s* his tinsel shaft. *Talking Oak* 68
  s and rang, Till this was ended, *Enoch Arden* 175
  merrily-blowing *s* the martial fife ; *Princess* v 251
  Shot up and *s* in flickering gyres, " vii 46
  And she athwart the shallow *s* again, *Gareth and L.* 1035
  she tower'd her bells, Tone under tone, *s* ; *Merlin and V.* 132
  Dagonet clapt his hands and *s*, *Last Tournament* 353
  down the long wind the dream *S* ; *Pass. of Arthur* 41
  all the night an answer *s*, *Demeter and P.* 61
Shrilleth The shattering trumpet *s* high, *Sir Galahad* 5
Shrilling (*See also* **Sudden-shrilling**) nipt her slender nose
  With petulant thumb and finger, *s*, ' Hence ! *Gareth and L.* 750
  she *s* ' Let me die ! ' *Lancelot and E.* 1026
  in a voice *S* along the hall to Arthur, *Holy Grail* 289
  and past his ear Went *s*, ' Hollow, *Pass. of Arthur* 33
  With *s* shafts of subtle wit. *Clear-headed friend* 13
  At times too *s* in her angrier moods, *The Ring* 395
  Thin as the batlike *s*'s of the Dead *Death of Œnone* 21
  wind of the Night *s* out Desolation and wrong *The Dreamer* 15
Shrilly The *s* whinnyings of the team of Hell, *Demeter and P.* 44
Shrine (*See also* **Altar-shrine**) By Bagdat's *s*'s of fretted
  gold, *Arabian Nights* 7
  From one censer in one *s*, *Eleänore* 59
  they saw thee from the secret *s* *Alexander* 13
  Still-lighted in a secret *s*, *Mariana in the S.* 18
  Going before to some far *s*, *On a Mourner* 17
  from the ruin'd *s* he stept And in the moon *M. d'Arthur* 45
  And you may carve a *s* about my dust, *St. S. Stylites* 195
  My knees are bow'd in crypt and *s* : *Sir Galahad* 18
  Then by some secret *s* I ride " 29
  The desecrated *s*, the trampled year, *Princess* v 127
  two Sware at the *s* of Christ a deathless love : *Com. of Arthur* 466
  when they left the *s* Great Lords from Rome " 476
  Show'd us a *s* wherein were wonders— *Balin and Balan* 109
  Saint who stands with lily in hand In yonder *s*. " 262
  but while he stared about the *s*, " 408
  that *s* which then in all the realm Was richest, *Lancelot and E.* 1330
  The Holy Grail, descend upon the *s* : *Holy Grail* 465
  lie before your *s*'s ; Do each low office *Guinevere* 681
  from the ruin'd *s* he stept, And in the moon *Pass. of Arthur* 213
  So that they pass not to the *s* of sound. *Lover's Tale* i 470
  lay me in some *s* of this old Spain, *Columbus* 207
  Falling about their *s*'s before their Gods, *Tiresias* 105
Shrined Methinks my friend is richly *s* ; *In Mem. lvii* 7
  see your Art still *s* in human shelves, *Poets and their B.* 11
  S him within the temple of her heart, *The Ring* 219
Shrine-doors *s-d* burst thro' with heated blasts *D. of F. Women* 29
Shrine-shattering *S-s* earthquake, fire, flood, thunderbolt, *Tiresias* 61
Shrink It would *s* to the earth if you came in. *Poet's Mind* 37
  Smite, *s* not, spare not. *St. S. Stylites* 181
  nor *s* For fear our solid aim be dissipated *Princess* iii 265
  her small goodman *S*'s in his arm-chair " v 454
  Nor make a snail's horn *s* for wantonness ; *Ancient Sage* 272
Shrive let me *s* me clean, and die.' *Lancelot and E.* 1100
  s myself No, not to an Apostle.' *Sir J. Oldcastle* 146
Shrivel Lightning may *s* the laurel of Cæsar, *Parnassus* 4

Shrivell'd Were *s* into darkness in his head, *Godiva* 70
  Wine is good for *s* lips, *Vision of Sin* 79
  Is *s* in a fruitless fire, *In Mem. liv* 11
  kernel of the *s* fruit Is jutting thro' the rind ; *Ancient Sage* 121
Shrivelling sting of shrewdest pain Ran *s* thro' me, *St. S. Stylites* 199
Shriven ' Heresy—Not *s*, not saved ? ' *Sir J. Oldcastle* 144
Shroud (s) (*See also* **Hammock-shroud**) Nor was the
  night thy *s*. *Ode to Memory* 28
  A music out of sheet and *s*, *In Mem. ciii* 54
  bird with a warble plaintively sweet Perch'd on the *s*'s, *The Wreck* 82
Shroud (verb) *s* this great sin from all ! *Aylmer's Field* 773
  To *s* me from my proper scorn. *In Mem. xxvi* 16
  mist of autumn gather from your lake, And *s* the tower ; *The Ring* 330
Shrouded *See* **Half-shrouded**
Shrub (*See also* **Laurel-shrubs**) Tall orient *s*'s, and
  obelisks *Arabian Nights* 107
Shrunk *S* like a fairy changeling lay the mage ; *Com. of Arthur* 363
  s by usage into commonest commonplace ! *Locksley H., Sixty* 76
Shtreet (street) whiniver ye walkt in the *s*, *Tomorrow* 37
Shudder (s) her child !—a *s* comes Across me : *Œnone* 253
  In that vast Oval ran a *s* of shame. *St. Telemachus* 73
Shudder (verb) I *s* at the sequel, but I go.' *Princess* ii 236
  We *s* but to dream our maids should ape " iii 309
  Nor *s*'s at the gulfs beneath, *In Mem. xli* 15
  O ye stars that *s* over me, *Com. of Arthur* 83
  ' I *s*, some one steps across my grave ; ' *Guinevere* 57
  So let me, if you do not *s* at me, " 675
  yet it shook me, that my frame would *s*, *Lover's Tale* ii 56
  heart of motherhood Within me *s*, *Demeter and P.* 42
  I *s* at the Christian and the stake ; *Akbar's Dream* 72
Shudder'd *s*, lest a cry Should break his sleep *Walk. to the Mail* 73
  ' Why—these—*are*—men : ' I *s* : *Princess* iii 58
  all dabbled with the blood Of his own son, *s*, " vi 105
  Yet I *s* and thought like a fool *Maud* I xiv 38
  Then *s*, as the village wife who cries *Guinevere* 56
  For the whole isle *s* and shook *V. of Maeldune* 74
Shudderest *S* when I strain my sight, *Fatima* 3
Shuddering delight and *s* took hold of all my mind, *May Queen, Con.* 35
  he knew not wherefore, started up *S*, *Enoch Arden* 617
  from the plaintive mother's teat he took Her blind
  and *s* puppies, *The Brook* 130
  Sat *s* at the ruin of a world ; *Sea Dreams* 30
  And *s* fled from room to room, *Princess* vi 370
  Set every gilded parapet *s* ; *Lancelot and E.* 299
  and thought With *s*, ' Hark the Phantom 1022
  There in the *s* moonlight brought its face *Lover's Tale* i 650
  till one of them Said, *s*, ' Her spectre ! ' " iv 335
  shrill-edged shriek of a mother divide the *s* night. *Maud* I i 16
  In the *s* dawn, behold, " II iv 52
  bruised and butted with the *s* War-thunder of iron rams ; *Tiresias* 99
  about the *s* wreck the death-white sea should rave, *The Flight* 47
Shuffled for the roots of my hair were stirr'd By a *s* step, *Maud* I i 14
Shun on our dead self, nor *s* to do it, *Princess* iii 221
  My drooping memory will not *s* The foaming grape *In Mem., Con.* 79
  s the wild ways of the lawless tribe. *Geraint and E.* 608
  do not *s* To speak the wish most near to your
  true heart ; *Lancelot and E.* 913
  Would *s* to break those bounds of courtesy " 1220
  did not *s* to smite me in worse way, *Guinevere* 435
  Nor *s* to call me sister, " 676
  She used to *s* the wailing babe, *The Ring* 358
Shunn'd But Enoch *s* the middle walk *Enoch Arden* 738
  thence That which he better might have *s*, " 740
  nor broke, nor *s* a soldier's death, *Princess, Pro.* 38
  had not *s* the death, No, not the soldier's : " v 178
Shushan brawl at *S* underneath the palms.' " iii 230
Shut (*See also* **Half-shut**) I *s* my life from happier chance. *Two Voices* 54
  I *s* my sight for fear : *Œnone* 188
  And he that *s*'s Love out, in turn shall be
  S out from Love, *To ——, With Pal. of Art* 14
  S up as in a crumbling tomb, *Palace of Art* 273
  Two handfuls of white dust, *s* in an urn of brass ! *Lotos-Eaters, C. S.* 68
  She left the new piano *s* : *Talking Oak* 119
  said he lived *s* up within himself, *Golden Year* 9
  all Should keep within, door *s*, and window barr'd. *Godiva* 41

Shut (*continued*)   is there any moral *s* Within the bosom of the rose ? — *Day-Dm., Moral* 7
By squares of tropic summer *s* — *Amphion* 87
gentle creature *s* from all Her charitable use, — *Aylmer's Field* 565
To one deep chamber *s* from sound, — *Princess* vi 376
an' 'e 'ant got *s* on 'em yet. — *N. Farmer, N. S.* 30
Now, sometimes in my sorrow *s*, — *In Mem.* xxiii 1
Were *s* between me and the sound : — „ xxviii 8
Or been in narrowest working *s*, — „ xxxv 20
God *s* the doorways of his head. — „ xliv 4
A gulf that ever *s*'s and gapes, — „ lxx 6
I will not *s* me from my kind, — „ cviii 1
' O little maid, *s* in by nunnery walls. — *Guinevere* 227
s me round with narrowing nunnery-walls. — „ 671
little hour was bound *S* in from Time, — *Lover's Tale* i 438
S in the secret chambers of the rock. — „ 521
I was *s* up with Grief ; — „ 680
They seized me and *s* me up : — *Rizpah* 46
The daisy will *s* to the shadow, — *The Wreck* 38
Shutter   Close the door, the *s*'s close, — *Deserted House* 9
Shutting   when *s* reasons up in rhythm, — *Lucretius* 223
Shuvv (Shove)   wi' noän to lend 'im a *s*, — *N. Farmer, N. S.* 31
Shy   (*See also* **Half-shy**)   ' *S* she was, and I thought her cold ; — *Edward Gray* 13
A little *s* at first, but by and by We twain, — *Princess* v 45
Fine of the fine, and *s* of the *s* ? — *Window, Letter* 2
Ay or no, from *s* of the *s* ? — „ 10
but he look'd at me sidelong and *s*, — *First Quarrel* 35
Shyness   It is my *s*, or my self-distrust, — *Edwin Morris* 86
Sibilation   He with a long low *s*, stared — *Princess* i 176
Sicilian   as the great *S* called Calliope — *Lucretius* 93
Sick (adj.)   (*See also* **Half-sick**)   thought, ' My life is *s* of single sleep : — *The Bridesmaid* 13
' I am half *s* of shadows,' — *L. of Shalott* ii 35
' *S* art thou—a divided will Still heaping — *Two Voices* 106
King is *s*, and knows not what he does. — *M. d'Arthur* 97
s of home went overseas for change. — *Walk. to the Mail* 24
This girl, for whom your heart is *s*, — *Talking Oak* 71
half the crew are *s* or dead, — *The Voyage* 92
blind or lame or *s* or sound, — „ 93
but I am *s* of Time, And I desire to rest. — *Come not, when, etc.* 9
(His father lying *s* and needing him) — *Enoch Arden* 65
As lightly as a *s* man's chamber-door, — „ 776
—it makes me *s* to quote him— — *Sea Dreams* 159
S for the hollies and the yews of home— — *Princess, Pro.* 187
you that talk'd The trash that made me *s*, — „ ii 394
Were you *s*, ourself Would tend upon you. — „ iii 320
The land is *s*, the people diseased, — *The Victim* 45
S for thy stubborn hardihood, — *In Mem.* ii 14
heart is *s*, And all the wheels of Being slow. — „ l 3
I am *s* of the Hall and the hill, I am *s* of the moor — *Maud* I i 61
S, am I *s* of a jealous dread ? — „ x 1
S, *s* to the heart of life, am I. — „ 36
his essences turn'd the live air *s*, — „ xiii 11
S once, with a fear of worse, — „ xix 73
S of a nameless fear, — „ II ii 44
Art thou sad ? or *s* ? — *Balin and Balan* 274
S ? or for any matter anger'd at me ? ' — „ 276
we maidens often laugh When *s* at heart, — „ 498
Spake (for she had been *s*) to Guinevere, ' Are you so *s*, my Queen, you cannot move — *Lancelot and E.* 78
' Stay with me, I am *s* ; — „ 87
' Love, are you yet *s* ? ' — „ 571
sound not wonted in a place so still Woke the *s* knight, — „ 819
Milder than any mother to a *s* child, — „ 858
And the *s* man forgot her simple blush, — „ 864
that other world Another world for the *s* man ; — „ 874
for what force is yours to go So far, being *s* ? — „ 1064
all too faint and *s* am I For anger : — „ 1086
King is *s*, and knows not what he does. — *Pass. of Arthur* 265
Floats from his *s* and filmed eyes, — *Supp. Confessions* 166
As a *s* man's room when he taketh repose — *A spirit haunts* 14
steady glare Shrank one *s* willow sere and small. — *Mariana in the S.* 53

Sick (adj.) (*continued*)   And here once more like some *s* man declined, — *Palace of Art* 155
But she, with *s* and scornful looks averse, — *D. of F. Women* 101
Teach that *s* heart the stronger choice, — *On a Mourner* 18
How often placed upon the *s* man's brow — *Aylmer's Field* 700
Runs in a river of blood to the *s* sea. — „ 768
The *s* weak beast seeking to help herself — *Merlin and V.* 498
Round whose *s* head all night, like birds of prey, — *Last Tournament* 138
and distribute dole To poor *s* people, — *Guinevere* 684
A body journeying onward, *s* with toil, — *Lover's Tale* i 124
lisp'd To kisses of the wind, that, *s* with love, — „ 545
They will but sicken the *s* plant the more. — „ 766
He falling, *s*, and seeming close on death, — „ iv 258
And the half my men are *s*. — *The Revenge* 6
But I've ninety men and more that are lying *s* ashore. — „ 10
But Sir Richard bore in hand all his *s* men — „ 15
s men down in the hold were most of them stark and cold, — „ 79
Some birds are *s* and sullen when they moult. — *Sisters (E. and E.)* 73
and *s* For shadow—not one bush — *Tiresias* 35
in amaze To find her *s* one whole ; — *Demeter and P.* 58
Doänt maäke thysen *s* wi' the caäke. — *Owd Roä* 34
Is he *s* your mate like mine ? — *Happy* 2
Sick (s)   Low voices with the ministering hand Hung round the *s* : — *Princess* vii 22
And found fair peace once more among the *s*. — „ 44
cheating the *s* of a few last gasps, — *Maud* I i 43
With her hundred fighters on deck, and her ninety *s* below ; — *The Revenge* 34
S from the hospital echo them, — *Def. of Lucknow* 100
Sicken   Here at least, where nature *s*'s, — *Locksley Hall* 153
I hate, abhor, spit, *s* at him ; — *Lucretius* 199
Or *s* with ill-usage, — *Princess* v 86
' A time to *s* and to swoon, — *In Mem.* xxi 17
loss So pains him that he *s*'s nigh to death ; — *Geraint and E.* 499
They will but *s* the sick plant the more. — *Lover's Tale* i 766
will you *s* for her sake ? — *Locksley H., Sixty* 17
that *s* at your lawless din, — „ 149
tho' thy violet *s* into sere, — *Prog. of Spring* 25
all but *s* at the shifting scenes. — *The Play* 2
Sicken'd   Which *s* every living bloom, — *In Mem.* lxxii 7
successful war On all the youth, they *s* ; — *Merlin and V.* 572
by and by she *s* of the farce, — *The Ring* 383
Sickening   (*See also* **Half-sickening**)   But *s* of a vague disease, — *L. C. V. de Vere* 62
once again the *s* game ; — *Locksley H., Sixty* 127
Sickle   ere the silver *s* of that month — *Princess* i 101
Sicklier   sickly-born and grew Yet *s*, — *Enoch Arden* 262
Like echoes from beyond a hollow, came Her *s* iteration. — *Aylmer's Field* 299
Sickly   And far away into the *s* light, — *The Kraken* 7
Cursed be the *s* forms that err from honest Nature's rule ! — *Locksley Hall* 61
Bore him another son, a *s* one : — *Enoch Arden* 109
Nursing the *s* babe, her latest-born. — „ 150
But for the third, the *s* one, who slept — „ 230
bearing hardly more Than his own shadow in a *s* sun. — *Aylmer's Field* 30
Sickly-born   Now the third child was *s-b* — *Enoch Arden* 261
Sickness   (*See also* **Mid-sickness**)   ' Some turn this *s* yet might take, — *Two Voices* 55
a languor came Upon him, gentle *s*, — *Enoch Arden* 824
and read My *s* down to happy dreams ? — *Princess* ii 253
and due To languid limbs and *s* ; — „ vi 377
serviceable To noble knights in *s*, — *Lancelot and E.* 768
as but born of *s*, could not live : — „ 880
she knew right well What the rough *s* meant, — „ 888
Side   (*See also* **Cliff-side, Fountain-side, Hill-side, Island-sides, Mountain-side, Water-side**)   faintest sunlights flee About his shadowy *s*'s : — *The Kraken* 5
Madonna-wise on either *s* her head ; — *Isabel* 6
Six columns, three on either *s*, — *Arabian Nights* 144
and Thought have gone away *S* by *s*, — *Deserted House* 2
Wander from the *s* of the morn, — *Adeline* 52
the couple standing *s* by *s*, — *The Bridesmaid* 5
On either *s* the river lie Long fields — *L. of Shalott* i 1
The mirror crack'd from *s* to *s* ; — „ iii 43

Side (*continued*) Such seem'd the whisper at my *s* :   *Two Voices* 439
the piney *s*'s Of this long glen.   *Œnone* 93
And Effie on the other *s*,   *May Queen, Con.* 24
and thrust The dagger thro' her *s*.'   *D. of F. Women* 260
I lived up there on yonder mountain *s*.   *St. S. Stylites* 72
On one *s* lay the Ocean, and on one Lay a great
     water,   *M. d'Arthur* 11
That only by thy *s* Will I to Olive plight   *Talking Oak* 282
clamber'd half way up The counter *s* ;   *Golden Year* 7
Had cast upon its crusty *s*   *Will Water.* 103
S by *s* beneath the water Crew and Captain lie ;   *The Captain* 67
Fading slowly from his *s* :   *L. of Burleigh* 86
Philip sitting at her *s* forgot Her presence,   *Enoch Arden* 384
On either *s* the hearth, indignant :   *Aylmer's Field* 288
To glance and shift about her slippery *s*'s,   *Lucretius* 189
The very *s*'s of the grave itself shall pass,   ,, 257
With that he drove the knife into his *s* :   ,, 275
lovelier than their names, Grew *s* by *s* ;   *Princess, Pro.* 13
Whichever *s* be Victor,   ,, *ii* 231
To rail at Lady Psyche and her *s*.   ,, *iii* 33
That when our *s* was vanquish'd and my cause   ,, *vi* 24
and fain had slept at his *s*.   *Grandmother* 74
Should still be near us at our *s* ?   *In Mem. li* 2
' Thou canst not move me from thy *s*,   ,, *lii* 7
A great ship left her shining *s*'s.   ,, *ciii* 40
Up the *s* I went, And fell in silence   ,, 43
moving *s* by *s* With wisdom,   ,, *cxiv* 19
grave That to-day its sunny *s*.   ,, *Con.* 72
And here on the landward *s*,   *Maud I iv* 10
For a raven ever croaks, at my *s*,   ,, *vi* 57
There were two at her *s*,   ,, *ix* 9
Was not one of the two at her *s*   ,, *x* 2
For one of the two that rode at her *s*   ,, 24
To the sweeter blood by the other *s* ;   ,. *xiii* 34
of the seventh Heaven, down to my *s*,   ,, *xiv* 21
Would he have that hole in his *s* ?   *II v* 82
Up to my throne, and *s* by *s* with me ?   *Com. of Arthur* 81
At once from either *s*, with trumpet-blast,   ,, 102
Not ever to be question'd any more Save on the
     further *s* ;   ,, 397
Wept from her *s*'s as water flowing away ;   *Gareth and L.* 217
midway down the *s* of that long hall A stately pile,—   ,, 404
Setting this knave, Lord Baron, at my *s*.   ,, 854
on the further *s* Arose a silk pavilion,   ,, 909
lead no longer ; ride thou at my *s* ;   ,, 1157
' Not at my *s*. I charge thee ride before,   *Geraint and E.* 14
Bow'd at her *s* and utter'd whisperingly :   ,, 305
so turning *s* by *s* They past,   *Balin and Balan* 279
one *s* had sea And ship and sail and angels   ,, 364
harkening from what *s* The blindfold rummage   ,, 415
Like its own mists to all the mountain *s* :   *Lancelot and E.* 38
He up the *s*, sweating with agony,   ,, 490
parted from the jousts Hurt in the *s*,'   ,, 623
Thro' her own *s* she felt the sharp lance go ;   ,, 624
All in an oriel on the summer *s*,   ,, 1177
thou hast been in battle by my *s*,   ,, 1358
after heaven, on our dull *s* of death,   ,, 1382
Your places being vacant at my *s*,   *Holy Grail* 317
fail'd from my *s*, nor come Cover'd.   ,, 470
Stood near it but a lion on each *s*   ,, 817
Near him a mound of even-sloping *s*,   *Pelleas and E.* 25
from her *s* Restrain'd him with all manner of device,   ,, 203
and he call'd, ' I strike upon thy *s*—   ,, 279
on the hither *s* of that loud morn   *Last Tournament* 56
push me even In fancy from thy *s*,   ,, 639
Never lie by thy *s* ; see thee no more—   *Guinevere* 579
On one *s* lay the Ocean, and on one Lay a great
     water,   *Pass. of Arthur* 179
dimplings of the wave, That blanch'd upon its *s*.   *Lover's Tale i* 45
and shot forth Boughs on each *s*,   ,, 230
On the other *s*, the moon, Half-melted   ,, 420
Love wraps his wings on either *s* the heart,   ,, 467
On the other *s* Is scoop'd a cavern   ,, 516
they are mine—not theirs—they had moved in my *s*.   *Rizpah* 54

Side (*continued*) was wounded again in the *s* and the
     head,   *The Revenge* 68
Spanish fleet with broken *s*'s   ,, 71
masts and the rigging were lying over the *s* ;   ,, 81
sewer an' sartan 'oäp o' the tother *s* ;   *Village Wife* 92
as ocean on every *s* Plunges   *Def. of Lucknow* 38
a merry tale That shook our *s*'s—   *Sir J. Oldcastle* 92
swept in a cataract off from her *s*'s,   *V. of Maeldune* 111
They lower'd me down the *s*,   *The Wreck* 90
you bawl'd the dark *s* of your faith   ,, 125
and we lean'd to the darker *s*—   *Despair* 39
Cleave ever to the sunnier *s* of doubt,   ,, 55
When he will tear me from your *s*,   *Ancient Sage* 68
Wild flowers blowing *s* by *s*   *The Flight* 19
shriek'd, and started from my *s*—   ,, 81
Lies upon this *s*, lies upon that *s*,   *Locksley H., Sixty* 264
die with him *s* by *s* ?   *Vastness* 5
my faithful counsellor, Sit by my *s*.   *Happy* 8
tho' sitting close at his *s*.   *Akbar's Dream* 19
   Charity 22

Sided *See* **Many-sided**

Sidelong And *s* glances at my father's grief,   *Princess vii* 107
saw with a *s* eye The shadow of some piece of
     pointed lace,   *Lancelot and E.* 1173
but he look'd at me *s* and shy,   *First Quarrel* 35
but often in the *s* eyes a gleam of all things ill—   *The Flight* 31

Side-path By one *s-p*, from simple truth ;   *To Marq. of Dufferin* 28

Sideway *s*'s he let them glance At Enid,   *Geraint and E.* 246

Siding Wheedling and *s* with them !   *Princess v* 158

Sidled I *s* awaäy an' awaäy   *Spinster's S's.* 28

Siege in the ghastly *s* of Lucknow—   *Def. of Lucknow* 4
Merlin call'd it ' The *S* perilous,'   *Holy Grail* 172

Sift *s* his doubtings to the last,   *Com. of Arthur* 311

Sifted (And heedfully I *s* all my thought)   *St. S. Stylites* 56
Every heart, when *s* well,   *Vision of Sin* 112
Thro' her this matter might be *s* clean.'   *Princess i* 80
thou hast seen me strain'd And *s* to the utmost,   *Pelleas and E.* 248

Sigh (s) (*See also* **Love-sighs**) wasting odorous *s*'s All
     night long   *Adeline* 43
Kate will not hear of lovers' *s*'s.   *Kate* 20
With her laughter or her *s*'s,   *Miller's D.* 184
my voice was thick with *s*'s   *D. of F. Women* 109
in *s*'s Which perfect Joy, perplex'd   *Gardener's D.* 254
A welcome mix'd with *s*'s.   *Talking Oak* 212
shaken with a sudden storm of *s*'s—   *Locksley Hall* 27
With half a *s* she turn'd the key,   *The Letters* 18
from my breast the involuntary *s* Brake,   *Princess iii* 191
The bosom with long *s* labour'd ;   ,, *vii* 225
Love would answer with a *s*,   *In Mem. xxxv* 13
Nor feed with *s*'s a passing wind :   ,, *cviii* 4
And in my thoughts with scarce a *s*   ,, *cxix* 11
young lord-lover, what *s*'s are those,   *Maud I xxii* 29
Half the night I waste in *s*'s,   ,, *II iv* 23
songs, *S*'s, and slow smiles, and golden
     eloquence   *Lancelot and E.* 649

Sigh (verb) you may hear him sob and *s*   *A spirit haunts* 5
shook the wave as the wind did *s* ;   *Dying Swan* 15
' To breathe and loathe, to live and *s*,   *Two Voices* 104
But here will *s* thine alder tree,   *A Farewell* 9
She *s*'s amid her narrow days,   *In Mem. lx* 10
and *s* The full new life that feeds thy breath   ,, *lxxxvi* 9
That whenever a March-wind *s*'s   *Maud I xxii* 40
s's to see the peak Sun-flush'd,   *Balin and Balan* 165
would often when they met *S* fully,   *Merlin and V.* 182
to *s*, and to stretch and yawn,   *V. of Maeldune* 91
s's after many a vanish'd face,   *Vastness* 1
silver year should cease to mourn and *s*—   *To Mary Boyle* 57

Sigh'd when I heard my name *S* forth with life   *D. of F. Women* 154
So *s* the King, Muttering and murmuring at his
     ear,   *M. d'Arthur* 178
they that heard it *s*,   *Vision of Sin* 18
Cold ev'n to her, she *s* ;   *Princess vi* 102
I *s* : a touch Came round my wrist,   ,, *vii* 137
Long have I *s* for a calm :   *Maud I ii* 1
thought, is it pride, and mused and *s*   ,, *viii* 12

Sigh'd (continued) They's for the dawn and thee. *Maud I xxii 52*
s and smiled the hoary-headed Earl, *Marr. of Geraint 307*
came upon him, and he s ; *Geraint and E. 249*
S, as a boy lame-born beneath a height, *Balin and Balan 164*
s ' Was I not better there with him ? ' *" 291*
anon S all as suddenly. *" 494*
Again she s ' Pardon, sweet lord ! *" 496*
s in passing, ' Lancelot, Forgive me ; *Lancelot and E. 1350*
and knew not that she s. *Last Tournament 130*
S, and began to gather heart again, *Guinevere 368*
s to find Her journey done, glanced at him, *" 404*
So s the King, Muttering and murmuring at his
 ear, *Pass. of Arthur 346*
I s, as the low dark hull dipt *The Wreck 127*
but I wept alone, and s *Happy 69*
Sigheth But the solemn oak-tree s, *Claribel 4*
Sighing the winter winds are wearily s : *D. of the O. Year 2*
all her force Fail'd her ; and s, ' Let me rest ' she
 said : *Enoch Arden 375*
by them went The enamour'd air s, *Princess vi 79*
S she spoke ' I fear They will not.' *" vii 297*
again s she spoke : ' A dream That once was mine ! *" 309*
O, art thou s for Lebanon *Maud I xviii 15*
S for Lebanon, Dark cedar, *" 17*
Shaking her head at her son and s *" xix 24*
turn'd S, and feign'd a sleep until he slept. *Lancelot and E. 842*
S weariedly, as one Who sits and gazes *Last Tournament 156*
Sight (See also **Second-sight**) talking to himself, first
 met his s : *Love and Death 6*
While blissful tears blinded my s *Oriana 23*
Even in her s he loved so well ? *Margaret 40*
I cannot veil, or droop my s, *Eleänore 87*
To weave the mirror's magic s's, *L. of Shalott ii 29*
Rain'd thro' my s its overflow. *Two Voices 45*
Shudderest when I strain my s, *Fatima 7*
Bursts into blossom in his s. *" 35*
I shut my s for fear : *Œnone 188*
where'er she turn'd her s The airy hand confusion
 wrought, *Palace of Art 225*
polish'd argent of her breast to s *D. of F. Women 158*
tell o'er Each little sound and s. *" 277*
a s to make an old man young. *Gardener's D. 141*
Love at first s, first-born *" 189*
But not a creature was in s : *Talking Oak 167*
trembling, pass'd in music out of s. *Locksley Hall 34*
And wasn't it a s to see, *Amphion 49*
How fresh was every s and sound *The Voyage 5*
while I breathed in s of haven, *The Brook 157*
out of s, and sink Past earthquake— *Lucretius 152*
in s of Collatine And all his peers, *" 238*
strange was the s to me ; *Princess, Pro. 54*
Strange was the s and smacking of the time ; *" 89*
' Pretty were the s If our old halls could change *" 139*
a s to shake The midriff of despair with laughter, *" i 200*
Pitiful s, wrapp'd in a soldier's cloak, *" v 56*
And our seeing is not s. *Voice and the P. 36*
like to him whose s is lost ; *In Mem. lxvi 8*
Forgot his weakness in thy s. *" cx 4*
by this my love has closed her s *Maud I xviii 67*
So the last s that Enid had of home *Geraint and E. 24*
and stood Stiff as a viper frozen ; loathsome s, *Merlin and V. 845*
A s ye love to look on.' *Lancelot and E. 83*
and the sorrow dimm'd her s, *" 889*
these have seen according to their s. *Holy Grail 875*
that if the King Had seen the s *" 904*
the s Of her rich beauty made him at one glance *Pelleas and E. 237*
goal of this great world Lies beyond s : *To the Queen ii 60*
s that throbs and aches beneath my touch, *Lover's Tale i 33*
Was my s drunk that it did shape to me *" 642*
vanish'd from my s Beneath the bower *" ii 42*
and the s run over Upon his steely gyves ; *" 156*
the s of this So frighted our good friend, *" iv 382*
till the Spaniard came in s, *The Revenge 23*
Love at first s May seem— *Sisters (E. and E.) 91*
How could I bear with the s's *In the Child. Hosp. 25*

Sight (continued) hope Sank all but out of s, *Columbus 157*
flourish'd up beyond s, *V. of Maeldune 15*
Ruddy thro' both the roofs of s, *Tiresias 3*
Son, in the hidden world of s, *" 51*
but pass From s and night to lose themselves *Ancient Sage 203*
boäth on us kep out o' s o' the winders *Spinster's S's. 35*
our own good redcoats sank from s, *Heavy Brigade 42*
She clear'd her s, she arose, *Dead Prophet 31*
Young again you grow Out of s. *The Ring 12*
I am not keen of s, *" 258*
Nor ever let you gambol in her s, *" 387*
pass on ! the s confuses— *Parnassus 15*
WHAT s so lured him thro' the fields *Far—far—away 1*
RALPH would fight in Edith's s, *The Tourney 1*
Sighted (See also **Far-sighted**) we have s fifty-three ! ' *The Revenge 3*
Sightless O, therefore from thy s range *In Mem. xciii 9*
in yonder living blue The lark becomes a s song. *" cxv 8*
Sign (s) I should require A s ! *Supp. Confessions 10*
Scarce outward s's of joy arise, *" 49*
And heaven's mazed s's stood still *Clear-headed friend 28*
Know I not Death ? the outward s's ? *Two Voices 270*
and I will tell the s. *May Queen, Con. 24*
I thought, I take it for a s. *" 38*
By s's or groans or tears ; *D. of F. Women 284*
For surer s had follow'd, either hand, *M. d'Arthur 76*
A s betwixt the meadow and the cloud, *St. S. Stylites 14*
A s to many a staring shire *Will Water. 189*
' If my heart by s's can tell, *L. of Burleigh 2*
Pray'd for a s ' my Enoch is he gone ? ' *Enoch Arden 491*
Suddenly set it wide to find a s, *" 496*
and making s's They knew not what : *" 640*
And swang besides on many a windy s— *Aylmer's Field 19*
There stood a bust of Pallas for a s, *Princess i 222*
And cannot speak, nor move, nor make one s, *" vii 153*
Till the Sun drop, dead, from the s's.' *" 245*
I waste my heart in s's : let be. *" 359*
Are they not s and symbol *High. Pantheism 6*
shield was blank and bare without a s Saving the
 name beneath ; *Gareth and L. 414*
With no more s of reverence than a beard. *Merlin and V. 279*
Thy holy nun and thou have seen a s— *Holy Grail 295*
A s to maim this Order which I made. *" 297*
An out-door s of all the warmth within, *" 704*
if indeed there came a s from heaven, *" 873*
on all hills, and in the s's of heaven.' *Last Tournament 337*
With s's and miracles and wonders, *Guinevere 222*
Or what of s's and wonders, but the s's *" 229*
the land was full of s's And wonders *" 232*
Not even thy wise father with his s's *" 274*
For surer s had follow'd, either hand, *Pass. of Arthur 244*
Or wisely or unwisely, s's of storm, *To the Queen ii 49*
Then Julian made a secret s to me *Lover's Tale iv 284*
Then waving us a s to seat ourselves, *" 320*
this fleshly s That thou art thou— *De Prof., Two G. 40*
And yet what s of aught that lies *Ancient Sage 25*
that take Some warrior for a s *Pro. to Gen. Hamley 14*
Sign (verb) Now s your names, which shall be read, *In Mem., Con. 57*
Signal An idle s, for the brittle fleet *Sea Dreams 133*
Sign'd The names are s, and overhead *In Mem., Con. 60*
s To those two sons to pass, and let them be. *Com. of Arthur 318*
Ferdinand Hath s it and our Holy Catholic queen— *Columbus 30*
Signet (adj.) Airing a snowy hand and s gem, *Princess i 121*
Signet (s) He set his royal s there ; *In Mem. cxxv 12*
Sign-post storm-worn s-p not to be read, *Dead Prophet 17*
Silence (s) All night the s seems to flow *Oriana 86*
And crystal s creeping down, *Two Voices 86*
One deep, deep s all ! ' *Palace of Art 260*
and ripen toward the grave In s ; *Lotos-Eaters, C. S. 52*
Her slow full words sank thro' the s drear, *D. of F. Women 121*
That only s suiteth best. *To J. S. 64*
Thro' s and the trembling stars *On a Mourner 28*
And waked with s, grunted ' Good ! ' *M. d'Arthur, Ep. 4*
There was s in the room ; *Dora 157*
every hour is saved From that eternal s, *Ulysses 27*
ever thus thou growest beautiful In s, *Tithonus 44*

Silence (s) (*continued*) To *s* from the paths of men ;   *Day-Dm., L'Envoi* 6
But Philip loved in *s* ;   *Enoch Arden* 41
let my query pass Unclaim'd, in flushing *s*,   *The Brook* 105
Vocal, with here and there a *s*,   *Aylmer's Field* 146
face to face With twenty months of *s*,   " 567
a louder one Was all but *s*—   " 697
he felt the *s* of his house About him,   " 830
escaped His keepers, and the *s* which he felt,   " 839
And silenced by that *s* lay the wife,   *Sea Dreams* 46
him we gave a costly bribe To guerdon *s*,   *Princess i* 204
We dare not ev'n by *s* sanction lies.   *Third of Feb.* 10
We feel, at least, that *s* here were sin,   " 37
S, till I be silent too.   *In Mem. xiii* 8
And makes a *s* in the hills.   " *xix* 8
And *s* follow'd, and we wept.   " *xxx* 20
So here shall *s* guard thy fame ;   " *lxxv* 17
They haunt the *s* of the breast,   " *xciv* 9
And strangely on the *s* broke   " *xcv* 25
And fell in *s* on his neck :   " *ciii* 44
And, tho' in *s*, wishing joy.   " *Con.* 88
Till a *s* fell with the waking bird,   *Maud I xxii* 17
I wish Your warning or your *s* ?   *Geraint and E.* 77
Debating his command of *s* given,   " 366
Then breaking his command of *s* given,   " 390
In *s*, did him service as a squire ;   " 406
blind wave feeling round his long sea-hall In *s* :   *Merlin and V.* 233
let me think *S* is wisdom :   " 253
such a *s* is more wise than kind.'   " 289
grew darker toward the storm In *s*,   " 891
Dark-splendid, speaking in the *s*,   *Lancelot and E.* 338
standing near the shield In *s*,   " 395
Now bolden'd by the *s* of his King,—   *Holy Grail* 857
Then a long *s* came upon the hall,   *Pelleas and E.* 609
little maid, who brook'd No *s*, brake it,   *Guinevere* 160
I cry my cry in *s*,   " 201
howsoever much they may desire *S*,   " 207
then came *s*, then a voice,   " 419
after wail Of suffering, *s* follows,   *Pass. of Arthur* 119
They stood before his throne in *s*,   " 455
till helpless death And *s* made him bold—   *Lover's Tale iv* 73
Evelyn clung In utter *s* for so long,   *Sisters (E. and E.)* 217
Found *s* in the hollows underneath.   *Tiresias* 38
only heard in *s* from the *s* of a tomb.   *Locksley H., Sixty* 74
Death and *S* hold their own.   " 237
Swallow'd in Vastness, lost in *S*,   *Vastness* 34
And found a corpse and *s*,   *The Ring* 217
That icy winter *s*—how it froze you   *Happy* 71
In *s* wept upon the flowerless earth.   *Death of Œnone* 9
A *s* follow'd as of death,   *St. Telemachus* 65
then once more a *s* as of death.   " 69
Silence (verb) ever widening slowly *s* all.   *Merlin and V.* 392
Them surely can I *s* with all ease.   *Lancelot and E.* 109
Silenced *s* by that silence lay the wife,   *Sea Dreams* 46
S for ever—craven—a man of plots,   *Gareth and L.* 431
Silent (*See also* **All-silent, Ever-silent**) Losing his fire and
active might In a *s* meditation,   *Eleänore* 105
There in a *s* shade of laurel brown   *Alexander* 9
And the *s* isle imbowers The Lady of Shalott.   *L. of Shalott* i 17
For often thro' the *s* nights A funeral,   " *ii* 30
S into Camelot.   " *iv* 41
And *s* in its dusty vines :   *Mariana in the S.* 4
And deepening thro' the *s* spheres   " 91
Thereto the *s* voice replied ;   *Two Voices* 22
'Still sees the sacred morning spread The *s* summit
overhead.   " 81
The phantom of a *s* song,   *Miller's D.* 71
And rose, and, with a *s* grace Approaching,   " 159
The grasshopper is *s* in the grass :   *Œnone* 26
O *s* faces of the Great and Wise¹   *Palace of Art* 195
Three *s* pinnacles of aged snow,   *Lotos-Eaters* 16
Drops in a *s* autumn night.   " *C. S.* 34
Lower'd softly with a threefold cord of love Down
to a *s* grave.   *D. of F. Women* 212
I rose up in the *s* night :   *The Sisters* 25
a *s* cousin stole Upon us and departed :   *Edwin Morris* 115

Silent (*continued*) I, whose bald brows in *s* hours become
Unnaturally hoar with rime,   *St. S. Stylites* 165
Roll'd in one another's arms, and *s* in a last embrace,   *Locksley Hall* 58
He gazes on the *s* dead :   *Day-Dm., Arrival* 13
I pledge her *s* at the board ;   *Will Water.* 25
And watch'd by *s* gentlemen,   " 231
'Dark porch,' I said, 'and *s* aisle,   *The Letters* 47
A deedful life, a *s* voice :   *You might have won* 8
And lived a life of *s* melancholy.   *Enoch Arden* 260
Her own son Was *s*, tho' he often look'd his wish ;   " 482
Till *s* in her oriental haven.   " 537
The *s* water slipping from the hills,   " 633
There Enoch rested *s* many days.   " 699
and ever bears about A *s* court of justice in his breast,   *Sea Dreams* 174
Too often, in that *s* court of yours—   " 183
Why were you *s* when I spoke to-night ?   " 268
question'd if she knew us men, at first Was *s* ;   *Princess iv* 232
s we with blind surmise Regarding,   " 381
glaring with his whelpless eye, *S*;   " *vi* 100
stood Erect and *s*, striking with her glance   " 152
all *s*, save When armour clash'd or jingled,   " 362
Lay *s* in the muffled cage of life :   " *vii* 47
s light Slept on the painted walls,   " 120
Now slides the *s* meteor on, and leaves   " 184
Or in their *s* influence as they sat,   " *Con.* 15
Thro' all the *s* spaces of the worlds,   " 114
His voice is *s* in your council-hall   *Ode on Well.* 174
and whatever tempests lour For ever *s* ; even if they
broke In thunder, *s* ;   " 176
O *s* father of our Kings to be   *Ode Inter. Exhib.* 7
Where oleanders flush'd the bed Of *s* torrents,   *The Daisy* 34
I stood among the *s* statues,   " 63
And look'd at by the *s* stars :   *Lit. Squabbles* 4
But thou wert *s* in heaven,   *Voice and the P.* 7
So the *s* colony hearing her tumultuous adversaries   *Boädicea* 78
Silence, till I be *s* too.   *In Mem. xiii* 8
Sat *s*, looking each at each.   " *xxx* 12
Her eyes are homes of *s* prayer,   " *xxxii* 1
And *s* traces of the past Be all the colour of the flower :   " *xliii* 2
The *s* snow possess'd the earth,   " *lxxviii* 3
And *s* under other snows :   " *cv* 6
The red-ribb'd ledges drip with a *s* horror of blood,   *Maud I i* 3
Love for the *s* thing that had made false haste to the
grave—   " 58
The *s* sapphire-spangled marriage ring of the land ?   " *iv* 6
When I was wont to meet her In the *s* woody places   " *II iv* 6
But is ever the one thing *s* here.   " *v* 68
That like a *s* lightning under the stars   " *III vi* 9
he is gone : We know him now : all narrow jealousies
Are *s*;   *Ded. of Idylls* 17
on thro' *s* faces rode Down the slope city,   *Gareth and L.* 734
And Gareth *s* gazed upon the knight,   " 933
S the *s* field They traversed.   " 1313
And all the three were *s* seeing,   " 1362
Worn by the feet that now were *s*,   *Marr. of Geraint* 321
Her mother *s* too, nor helping her,   " 768
I am *s* then, And ask no kiss ;'   *Merlin and V.* 253
We could not keep him *s*,   " 416
For *s*, tho' he greeted her, she stood Rapt on his
face   *Lancelot and E.* 355
from his face who read To hers which lay so *s*,   " 1286
Had pass'd into the *s* life of prayer,   *Holy Grail* 4
Lancelot left The hall long *s*,   " 854
Cares but to pass into the *s* life.   " 899
Hot was the night and *s* ;   *Pelleas and E.* 395
Across the *s* seeded meadow-grass Borne,   " 561
Speak, Lancelot, thou art *s* :   *Last Tournament* 107
It makes a *s* music up in heaven,   " 349
With *s* smiles of slow disparagement ;   *Guinevere* 14
bow'd down upon her hands *S*, until the little maid,   " 159
Blaze by the rushing brook or *s* well.   " 400
witness, too, the *s* cry, The prayer of many a race
and creed,   *To the Queen ii* 10
one string That quivers, and is *s*,   *Lover's Tale i* 18
till the things familiar to her youth Had made a *s* answer :   " *iv* 96

Silver (verb) linger there To s all the valleys — *Tiresias* 32
Silver-chiming from the central fountain's flow Fall'n s-c, *Arabian Nights* 51
Silver-chorded Her warm breath floated in the utterance
  Of s-c tones : — *Lover's Tale ii* 142
Silver-clear A little whisper s-c, — *Two Voices* 428
Silver-coasted O saviour of the s-c isle, — *Ode on Well.* 136
Silver-fair glancing heavenward on a star so s-f, *Locksley H., Sixty* 191
Silver-green All s-g with gnarled bark : — *Mariana* 42
Silvering See **Early-silvering**
Silver-misty they saw the s-m morn Rolling her smoke *Gareth and L.* 189
Silver-set near his tomb a feast Shone, s-s ; — *Princess, Pro.* 106
Silver-sheeted curving round The s-s bay ; — *Lover's Tale ii* 76
Silver-shining s-s armour starry-clear ; — *Holy Grail* 511
Silver-smiling s-s Venus ere she fell — *Lover's Tale i* 61
Silver-treble S-t laughter trilleth : — *Lilian* 24
Silvery (See also **Olive-silvery**) s marish-flowers that
    throng The desolate creeks — *Dying Swan* 40
  Whose s spikes are nighest the sea. — *The Mermaid* 37
  one s cloud Had lost his way between — *Œnone* 92
  With many a s waterbreak Above the golden gravel, *The Brook* 61
  'Fear not, isle of blowing woodland, isle of s parapets ! *Boädicea* 38
  all the s gossamers That twinkle into green and gold : *In Mem. xi* 7
  o'er the sky The s haze of summer drawn ; — " *xcv* 4
  S willow, Pasture and plowland, — *Merlin and the G.* 53
  Long as the s vapour in daylight — *Kapiolani* 16
Silvery-crimson They freshen the s-c shells, — *Sea-Fairies* 15
Silvery-streak'd overstream'd and s-s — *The Islet* 20
Simeon (See also **Simeon Stylites, Stylites**) 'Fall down,
    O S : thou hast suffer'd — *St. S. Stylites* 99
  Courage, St. S ! This dull chrysalis Cracks — " 155
  I, S of the pillar, by surname Stylites, among men ; I, S, " 161
  I, S, whose brain the sunshine bakes ; — " 164
Simeon Stylites (See also **Simeon, Stylites**) hark ! they
    shout 'St. S S.' — " 147
Similitude dream To states of mystical s ; *Sonnet To —— 4
Simois Came up from reedy S all alone. — *Œnone* 52
  Flash in the pools of whirling S. — " 206
Simper s and set their voices lower, — *Maud I x* 15
Simple (adj.) (See also **Cunning-simple**) 'The s senses
    crown'd his head : — *Two Voices* 277
  Not s as a thing that dies. — " 288
  A s maiden in her flower Is worth a hundred
    coats-of-arms. — *L. C. V. de Vere* 15
  And s faith than Norman blood. — " 56
  As s folk that knew not their own minds, *Enoch Arden* 478
  Not preaching s Christ to s men, — *Sea Dreams* 21
  And on a s village green ; — *In Mem. lxiv* 4
  He mixt in all our s sports ; — " *lxxxix* 10
  He seems to slight her s heart. — " *xcvii* 20
  Or s stile from mead to mead, — " *c* 7
  Like some of the s great ones gone For ever *Maud I x* 61
  To save from some slight shame one s girl. — " *xviii* 45
  But rode a s knight among his knights, *Com. of Arthur* 51
  Enid easily believed, Like s noble natures, — " 261
  thou from Arthur's hall, and yet So s ! *Geraint and E.* 875
  Is mere white truth in s nakedness, *Balin and Balan* 358
  O, the results are s ; a mere child Might use it — " 518
  'Such be for queens, and not for s maids.' *Merlin and V.* 684
  Full s was her answer, 'What know I ? *Lancelot and E.* 231
  In the heart's colours and on her s face ; — " 671
  And the sick man forgot her s blush, — " 837
  Will sing the s passage o'er and o'er — " 864
  so the s maid Went half the night repeating, — " 896
  'Ah s heart and sweet, Ye loved me, damsel, — " 898
  And this high Quest as at a s thing : — " 1393
  O great and sane and s race of brutes *Holy Grail* 668
  So dame and damsel cast the s white, *Pelleas and E.* 480
  signs And s miracles of thy nunnery ?' *Last Tournament* 232
  'The s, fearful child Meant nothing, *Guinevere* 230
  For I, being s, thought to work His will, — " 369
  And Softness breeding scorn of s life, *Pass. of Arthur* 22
  Loosed from their s thrall they had flow'd abroad, *To the Queen ii* 53
  told it me all at once, as s as any child, *Lover's Tale i* 703
  Because the s mother work'd upon By Edith *First Quarrel* 58
    Sisters (E. and E.) 206

Simple (adj.) (continued) By one side-path, from
    s truth ; — *To Marq. of Dufferin* 28
  Thro' manifold effect of s powers— *Prog. of Spring* 86
  A s, saner lesson might he learn — " 105
  There is laughter down in Hell At your s scheming . . . *Forlorn* 16
Simple (s) the hermit, skill'd in all The s's *Lancelot and E.* 862
Simple-hearted seeming-injured s-h thing *Merlin and V.* 902
Simpler guilt, S than any child, — *Guinevere* 371
  A temple, neither Pagod, Mosque, nor Church, But
    loftier, s, always open-door'd *Akbar's Dream* 179
Simple-seeming Our s-s Abbess and her nuns, *Guinevere* 309
Simplicity In his s sublime. — *Ode on Well.* 34
Sin (s) my s was as a thorn Among the thorns *Supp. Confessions* 5
  That pride, the s of devils, stood Betwixt me — " 109
  and my s's Be unremember'd, — " 181
  you are foul with s ; — *Poet's Mind* 36
  What is it that will take away my s, *Palace of Art* 287
  for he show'd me all the s — *May Queen, Con.* 17
  From scalp to sole one slough and crust of s, *St. S. Stylites* 11
  Have mercy, Lord, and take away my s. — " 8
  Than were those lead-like tons of s, — " 25
  Have mercy, mercy : take away my s. — " 45
  subdue this home Of s, my flesh, — " 58
  Have mercy, mercy ! cover all my s. — " 84
  O mercy, mercy ! wash away my s. — " 120
  A sinful man, conceived and born in s : — " 122
  On the coals I lay, A vessel full of s : — " 170
  S itself be found The cloudy porch *Love and Duty* 8
  To make me pure of s. — *St. Agnes' Eve* 32
  from the palace came a child of s, *Vision of Sin* 5
  shroud this great s from all ! *Aylmer's Field* 773
  the s That neither God nor man can well forgive, *Sea Dreams* 62
  The s's of emptiness, gossip and spite *Princess ii* 92
  We feel, at least, that silence here were s, *Third of Feb.* 37
  says, our s's should make us sad : *Grandmother* 93
  An' a towd ma my s's, *N. Farmer, O. S.* 11
  We might discuss the Northern s *To F. D. Maurice* 29
  The wages of s is death ! — *Wages* 6
  Forgive what seem'd my s in me, *In Mem., Pro.* 33
  I sometimes hold it half a s — " *v* 1
  Thou fail not in a world of s, — " *xxxiii* 15
  And holds it s and shame to draw — " *xlviii* 11
  That life is dash'd with flecks of s. — " *lii* 14
  To pangs of nature, s's of will, — " *liv* 3
  Ring out the want, the care, the s, — " *cvi* 17
  And heap'd the whole inherited s *Maud I xiii* 41
  Not touch on her father's s : — " *xix* 17
  Whatever the Quaker holds, from s ; — *II v* 92
  that best blood it is a s to spill.' *Gareth and L.* 600
  The s that practice burns into the blood, *Merlin and V.* 762
  She with a face, bright as for s forgiven, *Lancelot and E.* 1102
  Such s in words Perchance — " 1188
  To make men worse by making my s known ? Or
    s seem less, the sinner seeming great ? — " 1417
  S against Arthur and the Table Round, *Holy Grail* 79
  'And he to whom she told her s's, or what Her all but
    utter whiteness held for s, — " 83
  Holy Grail would come again ; But s broke out. — " 93
  'This madness has come on us for our s's.' — " 357
  thoughtest of thy prowess and thy s ? — " 455
  Happier are those that welter in their s, — " 770
  in me lived a s So strange, of such a kind, — " 772
  twined and clung Round that one s, — " 775
  And in the great sea wash away my s.' — " 806
  And but for all my madness and my s, — " 849
  Twine round one s, whatever it might be, — " 883
  If here be comfort, and if ours be s, Crown'd
    warrant had we for the crowning s *Last Tournament* 575
  'Mine be the shame ; mine was the s : *Guinevere* 112
  The s's that made the past so pleasant — " 375
  and as yet no s was dream'd,) — " 388
  the s which thou hast sinn'd. — " 455
  Then came thy shameful s with Lancelot ; — " 487
  Then came the s of Tristram and Isolt ; — " 488
  As in the golden days before thy s. — " 500

Single (*continued*) And thought, ' My life is sick of *s* sleep : | *The Bridesmaid* 13
' *S* I grew, like some green plant, | *D. of F. Women* 205
induce a time When *s* thought is civil crime, | *You ask me, why, etc.* 19
s note From that deep chord which Hampden smote | *England and Amer.* 18
A *s* stream of all her soft brown hair | *Gardener's D.* 128
And spake not of it to a *s* soul, | *St. S. Stylites* 66
With a *s* rose in her hair. | *Lady Clare* 60
That wilderness of *s* instances, | *Aylmer's Field* 437
a cave Of touchwood, with a *s* flourishing spray. | " 512
than by *s* act Of immolation, | *Princess iii* 284
made the *s* jewel on her brow Burn like the mystic fire | " *iv* 273
A *s* band of gold about her hair, | " *v* 513
The *s* pure and perfect animal, | " *vii* 306
And his compass is but of a *s* note, | *The Islet* 28
Be tenants of a *s* breast, | *In Mem. xvi* 3
Love would cleave in twain The lading of a *s* pain, | " *xxv* 11
So careless of the *s* life ; | " *lv* 8
No *s* tear, no mark of pain : | " *lxxviii* 14
And take us as a *s* soul. | " *lxxxiv* 44
A *s* church below the hill Is pealing, | " *civ* 3
A *s* peal of bells below, | " 5
A *s* murmur in the breast, | " 7
this a bridge of *s* arc Took at a leap ; | *Gareth and L.* 908
But rose at last, a *s* maiden with her, | *Marr. of Geraint* 160
Made but a *s* bound, and with a sweep of it | *Geraint and E.* 727
Should make an onslaught *s* on a realm | " 917
a *s* misty star, Which is the second in a line of stars | *Merlin and V.* 508
a *s* glance of them Will govern a whole life | *Lover's Tale i* 75
' What can it matter, my lass, what I did wi' my *s* life ? | *First Quarrel* 59
a *s* piece Weigh'd nigh four thousand Castillanos | *Columbus* 135
His fathers have slain thy fathers in war or in *s* strife, | *V. of Maeldune* 121
This double seeming of the *s* world !— | *Ancient Sage* 105
Earth at last a warless world, a *s* race, a *s* tongue— | *Locksley H., Sixty* 165
There a *s* sordid attic holds the living and the dead. | " 222
Mother weeps At that white funeral of the *s* life, | *Prin. Beatrice* 9
If every *s* star Should shriek its claim | *Akbar's Dream* 42
Singleness Arthur bound them not to *s* | *Merlin and V.* 28
Singular I have heard, I know not whence, of the *s* beauty of Maud ; | *Maud I i* 67
Sink I cannot *s* So far—far down, | *My life is full* 8
And while he *s's* or swells | *Talking Oak* 270
wholly out of sight, and *s* Past earthquake— | *Lucretius* 152
' There *s's* the nebulous star we call the Sun, | *Princess iv* 19
That *s's* with all we love below the verge ; | " 47
they rise or *s* Together, dwarf'd or godlike, | " *vii* 259
And moan and *s* to their rest. | *Voice and the P.* 16
And *s* again into sleep.' | " 24
And staggers blindly ere she *s* ? | *In Mem. xvi* 14
So much the vital spirits *s* | " *xx* 18
'Twere best at once to *s* to peace, | " *xxxiv* 13
When in the down I *s* my head, | " *lxviii* 1
And the great Æon *s's* in blood, | " *cxxvii* 16
A gloomy-gladed hollow slowly *s* To westward— | *Gareth and L.* 797
Down to the river, *s* or swim, | " 1154
we scarce can *s* as low : | *Merlin and V.* 813
By fire, to *s* into the abyss again ; | *Pass. of Arthur* 83
S me the ship, Master Gunner—*s* her, split her in twain ! | *The Revenge* 89
s Thy fleurs-de-lys in slime again, | *Sir J. Oldcastle* 98
Sinking and *s* ships, and praying hands. | *Lotos-Eaters, C. S.* 116
To follow knowledge like a *s* star, | *Ulysses* 31
The voice of Britain, or a *s* land, | *To the Queen ii* 24
I kiss'd him, I clung to the *s* form, | *The Wreck* 105
' We are *s*, and yet there's hope : | " 121
slowly *s* now into the ground, | *Locksley H., Sixty* 27
and *s* with the *s* wreck, | " 64
Sinless their *s* faith, A maiden moon that sparkles on a sty, | *Princess v* 185
not the *s* years That breathed beneath the Syrian blue : | *In Mem. lii* 11
Reputed to be red with *s* blood, | *Balin and Balan* 557

Sinn'd I have *s*, for it was all thro' me | *Dora* 60
Alas, my child, I *s* for thee.' | *Lady Clare* 50
s in grosser lips Beyond all pardon— | *Princess iv* 251
And that he *s* is not believable ; | *Merlin and V.* 760
but if he *s*, The sin that practice burns | " 761
Guinevere had *s* against the highest, | *Last Tournament* 570
Ev'n for thy sake, the sin which thou hast *s*. | *Guinevere* 455
drawing foul ensample from fair names, *S* also, | " 491
And all is past, the sin is *s*, | " 543
And in the flesh thou hast *s* ; | " 554
S thro' an animal vileness, | *The Wreck* 42
thunders of Ocean and Heaven ' Thou hast *s*.' | " 88
See, I *s* but for a moment, | *Happy* 85
And—well, if I *s* last night, | *Bandit's Death* 18
Sinner I am a *s* viler than you all. | *St. S. Stylites* 135
In haunts of hungry *s's*, | *Will Water.* 222
Thou hast been a *s* too : | *Vision of Sin* 92
Or sin seem less, the *s* seeming great ? | *Lancelot and E.* 1418
Sin ? O yes—we are *s's*, I know— | *Rizpah* 60
Sinning Another *s* on such heights with one, | *Lancelot and E.* 248
Sipt *S* wine from silver, praising God, | *Will Water.* 127
Sir these great *S's* Give up their parks | *Princess, Con.* 102
Sire to die For God and for my *s* ! | *D. of F. Women* 232
That we are wiser than our *s's*. | *Love thou thy land* 72
I read—two letters—one her *s's*. | *Princess iv* 397
At length my *S*, his rough cheek wet with tears, | " *v* 23
reach'd White hands of farewell to my *s*, | " 233
' O *S*,' she said, ' he lives : | " *vi* 122
then brake out my *s*, Lifting his grim head | " 271
Were those your *s's* who fought at Lewes ? | *Third of Feb.* 33
yet-loved *s* would make Confusion worse | *In Mem. xc* 18
thou that slewest the *s* hast left the son. | *Gareth and L.* 360
What said the happy *s* ? | *Merlin and V.* 710
Siren O sister, *S's* tho' they be, were such | *Princess ii* 198
Sirius as the fiery *S* alters hue, | " *v* 262
Sirmio ' O venusta *S* ! ' | *Frater Ave, etc.* 2
all-but-island, olive-silvery *S* ! | " 9
Sirmione Row us from Desenzano, to your *S* row ! | " 1
Sister (*adj.*) same two *s* pearls Ran down the silken thread | *Merlin and V.* 454
Sister (*s*) (*See also* **Brother-sister, Foster-sister, Half-sister, Lady-sister, Mock-sister, Star-sisters, Twin-sister**) Thy *s* smiled and said, ' No tears for me ! | *The Bridesmaid* 3
three *s's* That doat upon each other, | *To ——, With Pal. of Art* 10
To greet their fairer *s's* of the East. | *Gardener's D.* 188
Stole from her *s* Sorrow. | " 256
Sleep, Ellen, folded in thy *s's* arm, | *Audley Court* 63
he shouts with his *s* at play ! | *Break, break, etc.* 6
' I have a *s* at the foreign court, | *Princess i* 75
' My *s*.' ' Comely, too, by all that's fair,' | " *ii* 114
she cried, ' My brother !' ' Well, my *s*.' | " 188
O *s*, Sirens tho' they be, were such As chanted | " 198
Here lies a brother by a s slain, | " 208
when your *s* came she won the heart Of Ida : | " *iii* 87
To compass our dear *s's'* liberties.' | " 288
Shall croak thee *s*, or the meadow-crake | " *iv* 124
' Lift up your head, sweet *s* : | " *v* 64
all about his motion clung The shadow of his *s*, | " 258
and in our noble *s's* cause ? | " 312
My *s's* crying, ' Stay for shame ; ' | *Sailor Boy* 18
Old *s's* of a day gone by, | *In Mem. xxix* 13
Leave thou thy *s* when she prays, | " *xxxiii* 5
A guest, or happy *s*, sung, | " *lxxxix* 26
Has not his *s* smiled on me ? | *Maud I xiii* 45
Hath ever like a loyal *s* cleaved To Arthur,— | *Com. of Arthur* 191
closer to this noble prince, Being his own dear *s* ; ' | " 315
' And therefore Arthur's *s* ? ' ask'd the King. | " 317
a knight To combat for my *s*, Lyonors, | *Gareth and L.* 608
as any knight Toward thy *s's* freeing.' | " 1018
Among her burnish'd *s's* of the pool ; | *Marr. of Geraint* 655
Would call her friend and *s*, sweet Elaine, | *Lancelot and E.* 865
' Ah *s*,' answer'd Lancelot, ' what is this ? ' | " 931
came her brethren saying, ' Peace to thee, Sweet *s*,' | " 997
To whom the gentle *s* made reply, | " 1073
' *S*, farewell for ever,' and again ' Farewell, sweet *s*,' | " 1151

Sitting (continued) am I s here so stunn'd and still,   *Maud II i 2*
his good mates Lying or s round him,   *Gareth and L. 512*
There on a day, he s high in hall,   *Marr. of Geraint 147*
And knew her s sad and solitary.   *Geraint and E. 282*
Balin and Balan s statuelike,   *Balin and Balan 24*
as makes The white swan-mother, s,   " 353
s in thine own hall, canst endure To mouth   " 378
Sir Lancelot, s in my place Enchair'd to-morrow,   *Last Tournament 103*
s in the deeps Upon the hidden bases of the hills.'   *Pass. of Arthur 273*
And s down upon the golden moss,   *Lover's Tale i 540*
now striding fast, and now S awhile to rest,   " iv 88
And s down to such a base repast,   " 134
'There is more than one Here s who desires it   " 242
I, by Lionel s, saw his face Fire,   " 322
But Julian, s by her, answer'd all :   " 340
The face of one there s opposite,   *Sisters (E. and E.) 88*
summer days upon deck, s hand in hand—   *The Wreck 64*
children in a sunbeam s on the ribs of wreck.   *Locksley H., Sixty 14*
left within the shadow s on the wreck alone.   " 16
Who 's on green sofas contemplate The torment   *Akbar's Dream 48*
wife was unharm'd, tho' s close to his side.   *Charity 22*
Sitting-room To fit their little streetward s-r   *Enoch Arden 170*
Six S columns, three on either side,   *Arabian Nights 144*
high S cubits, and three years on one of twelve ;   *St. S. Stylites 87*
' And make her some great Princess, s feet high,   *Princess, Pro. 224*
S hundred maidens clad in purest white,   " ii 472
S thousand years of fear have made you   " iv 507
Among s boys, head under head, and look'd   *Con. 83*
And s feet two, as I think, he stands ;   *Maud I xiii 10*
Saw s tall men haling a seventh along,   *Gareth and L. 811*
S stately virgins, all in white, upbare   *Lover's Tale ii 77*
Save those s virgins which upheld the bier,   " 84
those s maids With shrieks and ringing laughter   " iii 31
An' he wrote ' I ha' s weeks' work, little wife,   *First Quarrel 45*
I ha' s weeks' work in Jersey an' go to-night   " 88
We are s ships of the line ;   *The Revenge 7*
KING, that hast reign'd s hundred years,   *To Dante 1*
S foot deep of burial mould Will dull their comments !   *Romney's R. 125*
Six hundred Rode the s h. (repeat)   *Light Brigade 4, 8, 17, 26*
rode back, but not Not the s h.   " 38
All that was left of them, Left of s h.   " 49
Honour the Light Brigade, Noble s h !   " 55
Sixpence Be shot for s in a battle-field,   *Audley Court 41*
Sixty in one month They wedded her to s thousand pounds,   *Edwin Morris 126*
when every hour Must sweat her s minutes to the death,   *Golden Year 69*
And s feet the fountain leapt.   *Day-Dm., Revival 8*
Here we met, our latest meeting—Amy—s years ago—   *Locksley H., Sixty 177*
Strove for s widow'd years to help his homelier brother men,   " 267
thro' this midnight breaks the sun Of s years away,   *Pref. Poem Broth. Son. 22*
Size His double chin, his portly s,   *Miller's D. 2*
This weight and s, this heart and eyes,   *Sir Galahad 71*
For often fineness compensated s ;   *Princess ii 149*
Skate taught me how to s, to row, to swim,   *Edwin Morris 19*
Skater Like the s on ice that hardly bears him,   *Hendecasyllabics 6*
Skeärd (scared) an' tellin' me not to be s,   *Owd Roä 85*
Skeleton make the carcase a s,   *Boädicea 14*
And bears a s figured on his arms,   *Gareth and L. 640*
Flash'd the bare-grinning s of death !   *Merlin and V. 847*
unawares Had trodden that crown'd s,   *Lancelot and E. 49*
Gaunt as it were the s of himself, (repeat)   " 764, 816
Not from the s of a brother-slayer,   *Last Tournament 47*
Found, as it seem'd, a s alone,   *Lover's Tale iv 139*
But that half s, like a barren ghost   *The Ring 227*
Skelpt (overturned) she s ma haäfe ower i' the chair,   *Owd Roä 76*
Sketch (*See also* **Thunder-sketch**) No matter what the s might be ;   *Ode to Memory 95*
Buss me, thou rough s of man,   *Vision of Sin 189*
s'es rude and faint.   *Aylmer's Field 100*
and lost Salvation for a s.   *Romney's R. 139*
Sketch'd Miriam s and Muriel threw the fly ;   *The Ring 159*

Sketcher I was a s then : See here,   *Edwin Morris 4*
Sketching s with her slender pointed foot   *The Brook 102*
Skiff drive Thro' utter dark a full-sail'd s,   *Supp. Confessions 95*
Skill (*See also* **Tourney-skill**) Nor mine the sweetness or the s,   *In Mem. cx 17*
with force and s To strive, to fashion,   " *cxiii 6*
fill up the gap where force might fail With s and fineness.   *Gareth and L. 1353*
And might of limb, but mainly use and s,   *Last Tournament 198*
now leaving to the s Of others their old craft   *Pref. Son. 19th Cent. 2*
As we surpass our fathers' s,   *Mechanophilus 21*
Skill'd O s to sing of Time or Eternity,   *Milton 2*
in a moment—at one touch Of that s spear,   *Gareth and L. 1223*
the hermit, s in all The simples and the science   *Lancelot and E. 861*
to keep So s a nurse about you always—   *The Ring 374*
Skim dip Their wings in tears, and s away.   *In Mem. xlviii 3*
Before her s's the jubilant woodpecker,   *Prog. of Spring 16*
Skimm'd fleeter now she s the plains   *Sir L. and Q. G. 32*
Skimming S down to Camelot :   *L. of Shalott i 23*
Among my s swallows   *The Brook 175*
Skin (s) (*See also* **Sallow-skin**) a leopard s Droop'd from his shoulder,   *Œnone 58*
A million wrinkles carved his s ;   *Palace of Art 138*
' In filthy sloughs they roll a prurient s,   " 201
a s As clean and white as privet when it flowers.   *Walk. to the Mail 55*
a scratch No deeper than the s :   *Edwin Morris 64*
Until the ulcer, eating thro' my s,   *St. S. Stylites 67*
We fret, we fume, would shift our s's,   *Will Water. 225*
s's of wine, and piles of grapes.   *Vision of Sin 13*
Tattoo'd or woaded, winter-clad in s's,   *Princess ii 120*
hunt them for the beauty of their s's ;   " v 156
Prickle my s and catch my breath,   *Maud I xiv 36*
wrapt in harden'd s's That fit him like his own ;   *Gareth and L. 1093*
His arms are old, he trusts the harden'd s—   " 1139
But lash'd in vain against the harden'd s,   " 1143
the s Clung but to crate and basket,   *Merlin and V. 624*
he was all wet thro' to the s,   *First Quarrel 76*
they pricks cleän thruf to the s—   *Spinster's S's. 36*
Shallow s of green and azure—   *Locksley H., Sixty 208*
' Small blemish upon the s !   *Dead Prophet 66*
The leper plague may scale my s   *Happy 27*
Skin (verb) like a man That s the wild beast after slaying him,   *Geraint and E. 93*
Skip ' Why s ye so, Sir Fool ? ' (repeat)   *Last Tournament 9, 243*
belike I s To know myself the wisest knight   " 247
S to the broken music of my brains   " 258
Arthur and the angels hear, And then we s.'   " 351
Skipping Dagonet, s, ' Arthur, the King's ;   " 262
Skipt But when the twangling ended, s again ; And being ask'd, ' Why s ye not, Sir Fool ? '   " 255
Skirt (s) Brightening the s's of a long cloud,   *M. d'Arthur 54*
thro' the gray s's of a lifting squall   *Enoch Arden 829*
thro' warp and woof From s to s ;   *Princess i 63*
your ingress here Upon the s and fringe of our fair land,   " v 219
upon the s's of Time, Sit side by side,   " vii 287
Imagined more than seen, the s's of France.   *Con. 48*
fusing all The s's of self again,   *In Mem. xlvii 3*
And grasps the s's of happy chance,   " lxiv 3
s's are loosen'd by the breaking storm,   *Geraint and E. 459*
the gloomy s's Of Celidon the forest ;   *Lancelot and E. 291*
Tho' somewhat draggled at the s.   *Last Tournament 219*
Brightening the s's of a long cloud,   *Pass. of Arthur 222*
Skirt (verb) oft when sundown s's the moor   *In Mem. xli 17*
Skirted *See* **Purple-skirted**
Skull Is but modell'd on a s.   *Vision of Sin 178*
thy foot Is on the s which thou hast made.   *In Mem., Pro. 8*
And wears a helmet mounted with a s,   *Gareth and L. 639*
with one stroke Sir Gareth split the s.   " 1404
clove the helm As throughly as the s ;   " 1407
I smote upon the naked s A thrall of thine in open hall,   *Balin and Balan 55*
and the s Brake from the nape, and from the s the crown Roll'd into light,   *Lancelot and E. 49*
Black as the harlot's heart—hollow as a s !   *Pelleas and E. 468*
fossil s that is left in the rocks   *Despair 86*

Skull (*continued*)   which for thee But holds a *s*,   *Ancient Sage* 255
whin I crackd his *s* for her sake,   *Tomorrow* 41
tower of eighty thousand human *s's*,   *Locksley H., Sixty* 82
scorpion crawling over naked *s's* ;—   *Demeter and P.* 78

Sky   wind be aweary of blowing Over the *s* ?   *Nothing will Die* 4
south winds are blowing Over the *s*.   *All Things will Die* 4
When thickest dark did trance the *s*,   *Mariana* 18
trenched waters ran from *s* to *s*,   *Ode to Memory* 104
WITH a half-glance upon the *s*   *A Character* 1
Sunn'd by those orient *skies* ;   *The Poet* 42
And white against the cold-white *s*,   *Dying Swan* 12
Thou comest atween me and the *skies*,   *Oriana* 75
When thou gazest at the *skies* ?   *Adeline* 50
Stoops at all game that wing the *skies*,   *Rosalind* 4
Too long you keep the upper *skies* ;   ,, 35
Grow golden all about the *s* ;   *Eleänore* 101
That clothe the wold and meet the *s* ;   *L. of Shalott* i 3
Heavily the low *s* raining   ,, iv 4
The *skies* stoop down in their desire ;   *Fatima* 32
All naked in a sultry *s*,   ,, 37
to where the *s* Dipt down to sea and sands.   *Palace of Art* 31
Sole as a flying star shot thro' the *s*   ,, 123
violet, that comes beneath the *skies*,   *May Queen, Con.* 5
Music that brings sweet sleep down from the blissful *skies*.   *Lotos-Eaters, C. S.* 7
Hateful is the dark-blue *s*,   ,, 39
the next moon was roll'd into the *s*,   *D. of F. Women* 229
Ruled in the eastern *s*.   ,, 264
To every land beneath the *skies*,   *On a Mourner* 3
I seek a warmer *s*, And I will see before I die   *You ask me, why, etc.* 26
whatever *s* Bear seed of men and growth of minds.   *Love thou thy land* 19
mellow moons and happy *skies*,   *Locksley Hall* 159
He travels far from other *skies*—   *Day-Dm., Arrival* 5
pure and clear As are the frosty *skies*,   *St. Agnes' Eve* 10
The clouds are broken in the *s*,   *Sir Galahad* 73
As shines the moon in clouded *skies*,   *Beggar Maid* 9
Flutter'd headlong from the *s*.   *Vision of Sin* 45
O love, they die in yon rich *s*,   *Princess* iv 13
When your *skies* change again :   ,, vi 278
To happy havens under all the *s*,   *Ode Inter. Exhib.* 35
This nurseling of another's   *The Daisy* 98
or to bask in a summer *s* :   *Wages* 9
A web is wov'n across the *s* ;   *In Mem.* iii 6
And reach the glow of southern *skies*,   ,, xii 10
The rooks are blown about the *skies* ;   ,, xv 4
Thro' circles of the bounding *s*,   ,, xvii 6
Tho' always under alter'd *skies*   ,, xxxviii 2
The baby new to earth and *s*,   ,, xlv 1
Who roll'd the psalm to wintry *skies*,   ,, lvi 11
For pastime, dreaming of the *s* ;   ,, lxvi 14
And sow the *s* with flying boughs,   ,, lxxii 24
o'er the *s* The silvery haze of summer drawn ;   ,, xcv 3
And bats went round in fragrant *skies*,   ,, 9
Where first we gazed upon the *s* ;   ,, cii 2
Ring out, wild bells, to the wild *s*,   ,, cvi 1
Of sorrow under human *skies* :   ,, cviii 14
happy birds, that change their *s* To build and brood ;   ,, cxv 15
The brute earth lightens to the *s*,   ,, cxxvii 15
wild voice pealing up to the sunny *s*,   *Maud* I v 13
makes you tyrants in your iron *skies*,   ,, xviii 37
The countercharm of space and hollow *s*,   ,, 43
On a bed of daffodil *s*,   ,, xxii 10
dawn of Eden bright over earth and *s*,   ,, II i 8
The delight of early *skies* ;   ,, iv 25
presently thereafter follow'd calm, Free *s* and stars :   *Com. of Arthur* 392
' Rain, rain, and sun ! a rainbow in the *s* !   ,, 403
' O birds, that warble to the morning *s*,   *Gareth and L.* 1075
show'd themselves against the *s*, and sank.   *Marr. of Geraint* 240
stormy crests that smoke against the *skies*,   *Lancelot and E.* 484
Totter'd toward each other in the *s*,   *Holy Grail* 343
One rose, a rose that gladden'd earth and *s*,   *Pelleas and E.* 402
So shook to such a roar of all the *s*,   *Last Tournament* 621
White as white clouds, floated from *s* to *s*.   *Lover's Tale* i 5
But still I kept my eyes upon the *s*.   ,, 572

Sky (*continued*)   Like to a low-hung and a fiery *s*   *Lover's Tale* ii 61
The snow and the *s* so bright—   *Rizpah* 83
Far from out a *s* for ever bright,   *Sisters (E. and E.)* 19
or a deluge of cataract *skies*,   *Def. of Lucknow* 81
brought out a broad *s* Of dawning over—   *Columbus* 77
from the *s* to the blue of the sea ;   *V. of Maeldune* 46
O come, come ' in the stormy red of a *s*   ,, 98
ship stood still, and the *skies* were blue,   *The Wreck* 115
sparkled and shone in the *s*,   *Despair* 15
How summer-bright are yonder *skies*,   *Ancient Sage* 23
blue of *s* and sea, the green of earth,   ,, 41
points of Russian lances arose in the *s* ;   *Heavy Brigade* 5
World-isles in lonely *skies*,   *Epilogue* 55
From *skies* of glass A Jacob's ladder   *Early Spring* 8
now to these unsummer'd *skies*   *Pref. Poem Broth. Son.* 17
To England under Indian *skies*,   *Hands all Round* 17
Glorying between sea and *s*,   *Open. I. and C. Exhib.* 18
OLD poets foster'd under friendlier *skies*,   *Poets and their B.* 1
Self-darken'd in the *s*, descending slow !   *Prog. of Spring* 28
once were gayer than a dawning *s*   *Death of Œnone* 12
in thine ever-changing *skies*.   *Akbar's D., Hymn* 4
—not a star in the *s*—   *Bandit's Death* 25
my wings That I may soar the *s*,   *Mechanophilus* 10
Far as the Future vaults her *skies*,   ,, 17
A VOICE spake out of the *skies*   *Voice spake, etc.* 1

Skylark   By some wild *s's* matin song.   *Miller's D.* 40
Skyless   and rode The *s* woods,   *Balin and Balan* 293
Slaäpe (**Slap ? Slippery ?**)   *s* down i' the squad an' the muck: *North. Cobbler* 20
Slab   Were *s's* of rock with figures,   *Gareth and L.* 1194
S after *s*, their faces forward all,   ,, 1206
Slack   Now with *s* rein and careless of himself,   *Balin and Balan* 309
Slacken   I saw it and grieved—to *s* and to cool ;   *Princess* iv 299
Slacken'd   His bow-string *s*, languid Love,   *Eleänore* 117
till as when a boat Tacks, and the *s* sail flaps,   *Princess* ii 186
Round was their pace at first, but *s* soon :   *Geraint and E.* 33
Slag   foreground black with stones and *s's*,   *Palace of Art* 81
Slain   (*See also* **Arrow-slain**)   With thine own weapon art thou *s*,   *Two Voices* 311
Here lies a brother by a sister s,   *Princess* ii 208
s with laughter roll'd the gilded Squire.   ,, v 22
went up a great cry, The Prince is *s*.   ,, vi 26
make her as the man, Sweet Love were *s* :   ,, vii 277
And overthrown was Gorloïs and *s*.   *Com. of Arthur* 197
Far as thou mayest, he be nor ta'en nor *s*.'   *Gareth and L.* 586
S by himself, shall enter endless night.   ,, 642
Thou hast overthrown and *s* thy master—   ,, 769
If both be *s*, I am rid of thee ;   ,, 790
but have ye *s* The damsel's champion ? '   ,, 1098
the huge Earl lay *s* within his hall.   *Geraint and E.* 806
I should have *s* your father,   ,, 838
foully *s* And villainously !   *Balin and Balan* 135
had I crown'd With my *s* self the heaps of whom I slew—   ,, 178
' Lo ! he hath *s* some brother-knight,   ,, 549
As after furious battle turfs the *s*   *Merlin and V.* 657
And each had *s* his brother at a blow ;   *Lancelot and E.* 41
I saw him, after, stand High on a heap of *s*,   ,, 307
I will say That I have *s* thee.   *Pelleas and E.* 346
I have *s* this Pelleas whom ye hate :   ,, 372
' Liar, for thou hast not *s* This Pelleas ! here he stood, and might have *s* Me and thyself.'   ,, 490
he shrieked, ' my will is to be *s*,'   ,, 579
Maim'd me and maul'd, and would outright have *s*,   *Last Tournament* 75
S was the brother of my paramour By a knight   ,, 448
but many a knight was *s* ;   *Guinevere* 438
thro' my sin to slay and to be *s* !   ,, 613
Slew him, and all but *s* himself, he fell.   *Pass. of Arthur* 169
Seeing forty of our poor hundred were *s*,   *The Revenge* 76
Their kindly native princes *s* or slaved,   *Columbus* 174
s my father the day before I was born.   *V. of Maeldune* 8
s thy fathers in war or in single strife,   ,, 121
s my fathers have *s* his fathers,   ,, 122
Thy father had *s* his father,   ,, 123
The man that had *s* my father.   ,, 128

Slain (continued) *S* by the sword-edge— *Batt. of Brunanburh* 113
blade that had *s* my husband thrice thro' his breast. *Bandit's Death* 34
Slake 'Let her go! her thirst she *s's* *Vision of Sin* 143
Slaked the hermit *s* my burning thirst, *Holy Grail* 461
shriek'd and *s* the light with blood. *Locksley H., Sixty* 90
Slander (s) Thee nor carketh care nor *s*; *A Dirge* 8
'Thro' *s*, meanest spawn of Hell— *The Letters* 33
And women's *s* is the worst, " 34
sins of emptiness, gossip and spite And *s*, *Princess ii* 93
The civic *s* and the spite; *In Mem. cvi* 22
spake no *s*, nor listen'd to it; *Ded. of Idylls* 10
Whenever *s* breathed against the King— *Com. of Arthur* 177
He sow'd a *s* in the common ear, *Marr. of Geraint* 450
vivid smiles, and faintly-venom'd points Of *s*, *Merlin and V.* 173
these are *s's*: never yet Was noble man *Lancelot and E.* 1087
To speak no *s*, no, nor listen to it, *Guinevere* 472
S, her shadow, sowing the nettle *Vastness* 22
Slander (verb) Come to the hollow heart they *s* so! *Princess vi* 288
Jenny, to *s* me, who knew what Jenny had been! *Grandmother* 35
ever ready to *s* and steal; *Maud I iv* 19
Slander'd he thought, had *s* Leolin to him. *Aylmer's Field* 350
To judge between my *s* self and me— *Columbus* 125
Slandering And she to be coming and *s* me, *Grandmother* 27
Slanderous All for a *s* story, that cost me many a tear. " 22
Slant *S* down the snowy sward, *St. Agnes' Eve* 6
That huddling *s* in furrow-cloven falls *Princess vii* 207
To *s* the fifth autumnal slope, *In Mem. xxii* 10
That God would ever *s* His bolt from falling *Happy* 81
The *s* seas leaning on the mangrove copse, *Prog. of Spring* 76
Slanted a beam Had *s* forward, falling in a land Of promise; *Princess ii* 139
Long lanes of splendour *s* o'er a press *iv* 478
Slanting reach'd a meadow *s* to the North; *Gardener's D.* 108
On every *s* terrace-lawn. *Day-Dm., Sleep. P.* 10
And lash'd it at the base with *s* storm; *Merlin and V.* 635
Showers *s* light upon the dolorous wave. *Lover's Tale i* 811
and fell *S* upon that picture, *ii* 175
Slap *See* **Slaäpe**
Slate On the lecture *s* The circle rounded *Princess ii* 371
lies a ridge of *s* across the ford; *Gareth and L.* 1056
Slated roofs of *s* hideousness! *Locksley H., Sixty* 246
Slate-quarry I heard them blast The steep *s-q*, *Golden Year* 76
Slaughter Dismal error! fearful *s*! *The Captain* 65
Had beat her foes with *s* from her walls. *Princess, Pro.* 34
drove her foes with *s* from her walls, " 123
Ran the land with Roman *s*, *Boädicea* 84
In perils of battle On places of *s*— *Batt. of Brunanburh* 86
Never had huger *S* of heroes " 112
Slaughter-house makes a steaming *s-h* of Rome. *Lucretius* 84
Slav *S*, Teuton, Kelt, I count them all My friends *Epilogue* 18
Slave Of child, and wife, and *s*; *Lotos-Eaters* 40
Drink deep, until the habits of the *s*, *Princess ii* 91
And play the *s* to gain the tyranny. *iv* 132
For ever *s's* at home and fools abroad.' *v* 521
—or brought her chain'd, a *s*, *v* 139
if ye fail, Give ye the *s* mine order *Pelleas and E.* 270
Artificer and subject, lord and *s*, *Lover's Tale ii* 103
bow'd myself down as a *s* to his intellectual throne, *The Wreck* 66
I was the lonely *s* of an often-wandering mind; " 130
who bought me for his *s*: *The Flight* 19
Those that in barbarian burials kill'd the *s*, *Locksley H., Sixty* 67
Now the Rome of *s's* hath perish'd, *To Virgil* 33
The *s*, the scourge, the chain; *Freedom* 12
Man is but the *s* of Fate. *Death of Œnone* 44
Three *s's* were trailing a dead lion away, *St. Telemachus* 47
no *s's* of a four-footed will? *The Dawn* 18
wearied of Autocrats, Anarchs, and *S's*, *The Dreamer* 10
Slaved Their kindly native princes slain or *s*, *Columbus* 174
Slavish plucks The *s* hat from the villager's head? *Maud I x* 4
Slay I will arise and *s* thee with my hands.' *M. d'Arthur* 132
I see the woodman lift His axe *s* my kin. *Talking Oak* 236
As I might *s* this child, if good need were, *Princess ii* 287
Within me, that except you *s* me here, *iv* 453
you could not *s* Me, nor your prince, *v* 65
Give me to right her wrong, and *s* the man.' *Gareth and L.* 366
lay him low and *s* him not, " 379

Slay (continued) To show that who may *s* or scape the three, *Gareth and L.* 641
hard by here is one will overthrow And *s* thee: " 897
See that he fall not on thee suddenly, And *s* thee unarm'd: " 922
Gareth there unlaced His helmet as to *s* him, " 979
as to *s* One nobler than thyself.' " 980
and crying, 'Knight, *S* me not: " 1410
hoped to *s* him somewhere on the stream, " 1419
we will *s* him and will have his horse And armour, *Geraint and E.* 62
they would *s* you, and possess your horse And armour, " 74
'Fly, they will return And *s* you; " 749
Shriek'd to the stranger '*S* not a dead man!' " 779
'O cousin, *s* not him who gave you life.' " 783
I thought my thirst Would *s* me, *Holy Grail* 380
And if ye *s* him I reck not: *Pelleas and E.* 269
It may be ye shall *s* him in his bonds.' " 272
'I will go back, and *s* them where they lie.' " 444
'What! *s* a sleeping knight? " 448
'Thou art false as Hell: *s* me: " 576
'*S* then,' he shriek'd, 'my will is to be slain,' " 579
Begin to *s* the folk, and spoil the land.' *Guinevere* 137
Gone thro' my sin to *s* and to be slain! " 613
I will arise and *s* thee with my hands.' *Pass. of Arthur* 300
drew His sword on his fellow to *s* him, *V. of Maeldune* 68
Freedom, free to *s* herself, *Locksley H., Sixty* 128
Slayer *See* **Brother-slayer, Shadow-slayer**
Slaying For, be he wroth even to *s* me, *Geraint and E.* 67
That skins the wild beast after *s* him, " 93
Sleeäp (sleep) an' dussn't not *s* i' the 'ouse, *Owd Roä* 37
Sleeäpin (sleeping) an' *s* still as a stoän, " 30
Sleek (adj.) With chisell'd features clear and *s*. *A Character* 30
And, issuing shorn and *s*, *Talking Oak* 42
S Odalisques, or oracles of mode, *Princess ii* 77
The *s* and shining creatures of the chase, *v* 155
Sleek (verb) To *s* her ruffled peace of mind, *Merlin and V.* 899
And *s* his marriage over to the Queen. *Last Tournament* 391
Sleek'd smooth'd his chin and *s* his hair, *A Character* 11
one *s* the squalid hair, One kiss'd his hand, *Death of Œnone* 57
Sleeker *s* shall he shine than any hog.' *Gareth and L.* 460
and all the world, Had been the *s* for it: *Lancelot and E.* 250
equal baseness lived in *s* times With smoother men: *Princess v* 385
Sleep (s) in her first *s* earth breathes sleep: *Leonine Eleg.* 7
dreamless, uninvaded *s* The Kraken sleepeth: *The Kraken* 3
lie Battening upon huge seaworms in his *s*, " 12
In *s* she seem'd to walk forlorn, *Mariana* 30
as in *s* I sank In cool soft turf upon the bank, *Arabian Nights* 95
From his coiled *s's* in the central deeps *The Mermaid* 24
S had bound her in his rosy band, *Caress'd or chidden* 6
'My life is sick of single *s*: *The Bridesmaid* 13
She breathed in a *s* lower moan, *Mariana in the S.* 45
Each morn my *s* was broken thro' *Miller's D.* 39
Softer than *s*—all things in order stored, *Palace of Art* 87
Music that brings sweet *s* down from the blissful skies. *Lotos-Eaters, C. S.* 7
from the craggy ledge the poppy hangs in *s*. " 11
and brought Into the gulfs of *s*. *D. of F. Women* 52
'We drank the Libyan Sun to *s*, " 145
dissolved the mystery Of folded *s*. " 263
than I from *s* To gather and tell o'er " 275
Such a *s* They sleep—the men I loved. *M. d'Arthur* 16
yet in *s* I seem'd To sail with Arthur " *Ep.* 16
And in her bosom bore the baby, *S*. *Gardener's D.* 268
lest a cry Should break his *s* by night, *Walk. to the Mail* 74
Or in the night, after a little *s*, I wake: *St. S. Stylites* 113
But, rolling as in *s*, Low thunders *Talking Oak* 278
pointing to his drunken *s*, *Locksley Hall* 81
'O eyes long laid in happy *s*!' *Day-Dm., Depart.* 17
'O happy *s*, that lightly fled!' " 18
'O happy kiss, that woke thy *s*!' " 19
So sleeping, so aroused from *s* " *L'Envoi* 21
Yet sleeps a dreamless *s* to me; A *s* by kisses undissolved, " 50
Charier of *s*, and wine, and exercise, *Aylmer's Field* 448
And came upon him half-arisen from *s*, " 584
rough amity of the other, sank As into *s* again. " 592
He also sleeps—another *s* than ours. *Sea Dreams* 310

Sleep (s) (*continued*) let your *s* for this one night be sound :   *Sea Dreams* 315
Echo answer'd in her *s* From hollow fields: *Princess, Pro.* 66
tinged with wan from lack of *s*,   ,, *iii* 25
hand That nursed her, more than infants in their *s*.   ,, *vii* 54
Fill'd thro' and thro' with Love, a happy *s*.   ,, 172
And sink again into *s*.'   *Voice and the P.* 24
To *S* I give my powers away;   *In Mem.* iv 1
Calm on the seas, and silver *s*,   ,, *xi* 17
A late-lost form that *s* reveals,   ,, *xiii* 2
That sleeps or wears the mask of *s*,   ,, *xviii* 10
'They rest,' we said, 'their *s* is sweet,'   ,, *xxx* 19
If *S* and Death be truly one,   ,, *xliii* 1
S, Death's twin-brother, times my breath ; *S*, Death's twin-brother, knows not Death,   .. *lxviii* 2
That foolish *s* transfers to thee.   ,, 16
S, kinsman thou to death and trance   ,, *lxxi* 1
And *S* must lie down arm'd,   *Maud* I i 41
Knew that the death-white curtain meant but *s*,   ,, *xiv* 37
thought like a fool of the *s* of death.   ,, 38
O moon, that layest all to *s* again,   *Gareth and L.* 1061
and all his life Past into *s*;   ,, 1281
'Sound *s* be thine!'   ,, 1282
and slept the *s* With Balin,   *Balin and Balan* 631
full Of noble things, and held her from her *s*.   *Lancelot and E.* 339
he roll'd his eyes Yet blank from *s*,   ,, 820
and feign'd a *s* until he slept.   ,, 842
malice on the placid lip Froz'n by sweet *s*,   *Pelleas and E.* 433
went back, and seeing them yet in *s* Said, 'Ye, that so dishallow the holy *s*, Your *s* is death,'   ,, 445
And gulf'd his griefs in inmost *s*;   ,, 516
Such a *s* They sleep—the men I loved.   *Pass. of Arthur* 184
but were a part of *s*,   *Lover's Tale* ii 117
And murmur at the low-dropt eaves of *s*,   ,, 122
wind from the lands they had ruin'd awoke from *s*,   *The Revenge* 112
My *s* was broken besides with dreams   *In the Child. Hosp.* 65
Silent palaces, quiet fields of eternal *s* !   *V. of Maeldune* 80
past, in *s*, away By night,   *Tiresias* 203
till we long'd for eternal *s*.   *Despair* 46
first dark hour of his last *s* alone.   *Locksley H., Sixty* 238
Is breathing in his *s*,   *Early Spring* 23
in *s* I said 'All praise to Alla   *Akbar's Dream* 197
I could make *S* Death, if I would—   *Bandit's Death* 32

Sleep (verb) (*See also* **Sleeäp**) Ox Feeds in the herb, and *s*'s,   *Supp. Confessions* 151
I *s* forgotten, I wake forlorn.'   *Mariana in the S.* 36
'Thine anguish will not let thee *s*,   *Two Voices* 49
'Go, vexed Spirit, *s* in trust;   ,, 115
his stedfast shade *S*'s on his luminous ring.'   *Palace of Art* 16
They graze and wallow, breed and *s*;   ,, 202
I *s* so sound all night, mother,   *May Queen* 9
The place of him that *s*'s in peace.   *To J. S.* 68
S sweetly, tender heart, in peace :   ,, 69
S, holy spirit, blessed soul,   ,, 70
S till the end, true soul and sweet.   ,, 73
S full of rest from head to feet ;   ,, 75
Such a sleep They *s*—the men I loved.   *M. d'Arthur* 17
home I went, but could not *s* for joy,   *Gardener's D.* 174
'*S*, Ellen Aubrey, *s*, and dream of me :   *Audley Court* 62
S, Ellen, folded in thy sister's arm,   ,, 63
'*S*, Ellen, folded in Emilia's arm';   ,, 65
'*S*, breathing health and peace upon her breast :   ,, 68
S, breathing love and trust against her lip :   ,, 69
S, Ellen Aubrey, love, and dream of me.'   ,, 73
To walk, to sit, to *s*, to wake, to breathe.'   *Edwin Morris* 40
'We *s* and wake and *s*, but all things move;   *Golden Year* 22
and *s*, and feed, and know not me.   *Ulysses* 5
Each baron at the banquet *s*'s,   *Day-Dm., Sleep. P.* 37
She *s*'s: her breathings are not heard   ,, *Sleep. B.* 17
She *s*'s: on either hand upswells   ,, 21
She *s*'s, nor dreams, but ever dwells   ,, 23
'I'd *s* another hundred years,   ,, *Depart.* 9
And learn the world, and *s* again ;   ,, *L'Envoi* 8
To *s* thro' terms of mighty wars,   ,, 9
Yet *s*'s a dreamless sleep to me ;   ,, 50
And *s* beneath his pillar'd light !   *The Voyage* 20

Sleep (verb) (*continued*) 'Wake him not; let him *s*;   *Enoch Arden* 233
one night it chanced That Annie could not *s*,   ,, 490
My dearest brother, Edmund, *s*'s,   *The Brook* 187
s's in peace : and he, Poor Philip,   ,, 190
S's in the plain eggs of the nightingale.   *Aylmer's Field* 103
S, little birdie, *s*! will she not *s* Without her 'little birdie' ? well then, *s*, And I will sing you 'birdie.'   *Sea Dreams* 282
Baby, *s* a little longer,   ,, 305
If she *s*'s a little longer,   ,, 307
'She *s*'s; let us too, let all evil, *s*. He also *s*'s—another sleep than ours.   ,, 309
And I shall *s* the sounder !'   ,, 312
While my little one, while my pretty one, *s*'s.   *Princess* iii 8
S and rest, *s* and rest,   ,, 9
S, my little one, *s*, my pretty one, *s*.   ,, 16
'Now *s*'s the crimson petal,   ,, *vii* 176
S, little ladies! And they slept well.   *Minnie and Winnie* 3
S, little ladies! Wake not soon !   ,, 9
Behold me, for I cannot *s*,   *In Mem. vii* 6
S, gentle heavens, before the prow ;   ,, *ix* 14
S, gentle winds, as he *s*'s now,   ,, 15
That *s*'s or wears the mask of sleep,   ,, *xviii* 10
I *s* till dusk is dipt in gray :   ,, *lxvii* 12
Long *s*'s the summer in the seed ;   ,, *cv* 26
Whatever wisdom *s* with thee.   ,, *cviii* 16
Yet how much wisdom *s*'s with thee   ,, *cxiii* 2
I come once more ; the city *s*'s;   ,, *cxix* 3
and *s* Encompass'd by his faithful guard,   ,, *cxxvi* 7
sound cause to *s* hast thou.   *Gareth and L.* 1282
Dreams ruling when wit *s*'s!   *Balin and Balan* 143
Look how she *s*'s—the Fairy Queen.   *Lancelot and E.* 1255
Such a sleep They *s*—the men I loved.   *Pass. of Arthur* 184
'It was my wish,' he said, 'to pass, to *s*,   *Lover's Tale* iv 63
'Do I wake or *s*?   ,, 78
do not *s*, my sister dear! How *can* you *s*?   *The Flight* 1
who? who? my father *s*'s!   ,, 69
s's the gleam of dying day.   *Locksley H., Sixty* 42
meant to *s* her hundred summers out   *The Ring* 66
'*S*, little blossom, my honey, my bliss !   *Romney's R.* 99
I blind your pretty blue eyes with a kiss ! *S*!'   ,, 102
then he yawn'd, for the wretch *could*'s,   *Bandit's Death* 30

Sleeper That watch the *s*'s from the wall.   *Day-Dm., Sleep. P.* 24
Me, that was never a quiet *s*?   *Maud* II v 98
Beat, till she woke the *s*,   *Geraint and E.* 404
Stirs up again in the heart of the *s*,   *Vastness* 18

Sleepeth uninvaded sleep The Kraken *s*:   *The Kraken* 4
when the air *S* over all the heaven,   *Eleänore* 39

Sleepin' As the Holy Mother o' Glory that smiles at her *s* child—   *Tomorrow* 26

Sleeping (*See also* **A-sleeäpin', Sleeäpin, Sleepin'**) you were *s*; and I said, 'It's not for them :   *May Queen, Con.* 37
And *s*, haply dream her arm is mine.   *Audley Court* 64
As thunder-drops fall on a *s* sea.   *D. of F. Women* 122
So *s*, so aroused from sleep   *Day-Dm., L'Envoi* 21
On *s* wings they sail.   *Sir Galahad* 44
while the two were *s*, a full tide Rose   *Sea Dreams* 50
Their *s* silver thro' the hills ;   *In Mem., Con.* 116
on a summer morn (They *s* each by either)   *Marr. of Geraint* 70
You thought me *s*, but I heard you say,   *Geraint and E.* 741
Not dead; he stirs !—but *s*.   *Balin and Balan* 469
A stone is flung into some *s* tarn,   *Pelleas and E.* 93
'What ! slay a *s* knight ?   ,, 448
There left it, and them *s*;   ,, 453
There came on Arthur *s*, Gawain kill'd   *Pass. of Arthur* 30
and in the *s* mere below Blood-red.   *Holy Grail* 475
Wherein we nested *s* or awake,   *Lover's Tale* i 231
Quietly *s*—so quiet, our doctor said   *In the Child. Hosp.* 41
And stir the *s* earth, and wake The bloom   *Ancient Sage* 93
ARE you *s*? have you forgotten ?   *The Flight* 1
While the house is *s*.   *Forlorn* 42
Who found me at sunrise *S*,   *Merlin and the G.* 13

Sleeping-night That was my *s-n*,   *In the Child. Hosp.* 61

Sleepy The *s* pool above the dam,   *Miller's D.* 99
He laugh'd and I, tho' *s*, like a horse   *The Epic* 44
a sound Like *s* counsel pleading ;   *Amphion* 74

Sleepy (*continued*) A *s* light upon their brows and lips— *Vision of Sin* 9
A *s* land, where under the same wheel *Aylmer's Field* 33
so *s* was the land. ,, 45
Sleet frost, heat, hail, damp, and *s*, and snow ; *St. S. Stylites* 16
S of diamond-drift and pearly hail ; *Vision of Sin* 22
Sleeve (*See also* **Slieäve**) Devils pluck'd my *s*, *St. S. Stylites* 171
' A red *s* Broider'd with pearls,' *Lancelot and E.* 372
his the prize, who wore the *s* Of scarlet, ,, 501
upon his helm A *s* of scarlet, ,, 604
What of the knight with the red *s* ? ,, 621
he wore your *s* : Would he break faith with one ,, 684
but I lighted on the maid Whose *s* he wore ; ,, 711
her scarlet *s*, Tho' carved and cut, ,, 806
Down on his helm, from which her *s* had gone. ,, 982
Slender **Caress'd** or chidden by the *s* hand, *Caress'd or chidden* 1
With rosy *s* fingers backward drew *Œnone* 176
Betwixt the *s* shafts were blazon'd fair *Palace of Art* 167
s stream Along the cliff to fall and pause *Lotos-Eaters* 8
The *s* coco's drooping crown of plumes, *Enoch Arden* 574
And sketching with her *s* pointed foot *The Brook* 102
Their *s* household fortunes (for the man *Sea Dreams* 9
What *s* campanili grew By bays, *The Daisy* 13
How best to help the *s* store, *To F. D. Maurice* 37
What *s* shade of doubt may flit, *In Mem. xlviii* 7
I kiss'd her *s* hand, *Maud I xii* 13
The *s* acacia would not shake ,, *xxii* 45
lightly was her *s* nose Tip-tilted like the petal of a
flower ; *Gareth and L.* 591
nipt her *s* nose With petulant thumb and finger, ,, 749
Crimson, a *s* banneret fluttering. ,, 913
The *s* entertainment of a house Once rich, *Marr. of Geraint* 300
s sound As from a distance beyond distance *Holy Grail* 111
A *s* page about her father's hall, And she a *s* maiden, ,, 581
And *s* was her hand and small her shape ; *Pelleas and E.* 74
Flow back again unto my *s* spring *Lover's Tale i* 147
S warrant had *He* to be proud of The welcome *Batt. of Brunanburh* 66
S reason had *He* to be glad of The clash ,, 76
O *s* lily waving there, *Ancient Sage* 167
That all the Thrones are clouded by your loss,
Were *s* solace. *D. of the Duke of C.* 7
Slenderer and send A *s* gift of *s* value, mine. *To Ulysses* 48
Slender-shafted A *s-s* Pine Lost footing, fell, *Gareth and L.* 3
Slep (**slept**) Thou *s* i' the chaumber above us, *Owd Roä* 49
gell o' the farm 'at *s* wi' tha ,, 51
An' I *s* i' my chair hup-on-end, ,, 54
An' I *s* i' my chair ageän ,, 65
Slept (*See also* **Slep**) A sluice with blacken'd waters *s*, *Mariana* 38
Adown to where the water *s*. *Arabian Nights* 30
The tangled water-courses *s*, *Dying Swan* 19
Till now at noon she *s* again, *Mariana in the S.* 41
Touch'd by his feet the daisy *s*. *Two Voices* 276
s St. Cecily ; An angel look'd at her. *Palace of Art* 99
I linger'd there Till every daisy *s*, *Gardener's D.* 165
How say you ? we have *s*, my lords. *Day-Dm., Revival* 21
Or elbow-deep in sawdust, *s*, *Will Water.* 99
Ascending tired, heavily *s* till morn. *Enoch Arden* 181
for the third, the sickly one, who *s* ,, 230
she closed the Book and *s* : When lo! ,, 499
s, woke, and went the next, The Sabbath, *Sea Dreams* 18
up the stream In fancy, till I *s* again, ,, 109
' Your own will be the sweeter,' and they *s*. ,, 318
Her maiden babe, a double April old, Aglaïa *s*. *Princess ii* 111
silent light *S* on the painted walls, ,, *vii* 121
I sank and *s*, Fill'd thro' and thro' with Love, ,, 171
and fain had *s* at his side. *Grandmother* 74
Of Queen Theodolind, where we *s* ; *The Daisy* 80
Or hardly *s*, but watch'd awake ,, 81
Minnie and Winnie *S* in a shell. *Minnie and Winnie* 2
Sleep, little ladies! And they *s* well. ,, 4
This year I *s* and woke with pain, *In Mem. xxviii* 13
But over all things brooding *s* ,, *lxxviii* 7
God's finger touch'd him, and he *s*. ,, *lxxxv* 20
That landlike *s* along the deep. ,, *ciii* 56
and *s*, and saw, Dreaming, a slope of land *Com. of Arthur* 427
Geraint Woke where he *s* in the high hall, *Marr. of Geraint* 755

Slept (*continued*) and *s* the sleep With Balin, *Balin and Balan* 631
wearied out made for the couch and *s*, *Merlin and V.* 736
And either *s*, nor knew of other there ; ,, 738
yielded, told her all the charm, and *s*. ,, 966
when they gain'd the cell wherein he *s*, *Lancelot and E.* 811
and feign'd a sleep until he *s*. ,, 842
s that night for pleasure in his blood, *Pelleas and E.* 138
if she *s*, she dream'd An awful dream ; *Guinevere* 75
A deathwhite mist *s* over sand and sea : *Pass. of Arthur* 95
he pray'd for both : he *s* Dreaming of both : *Lover's Tale i* 227
we *s* In the same cradle always, face to face ,, 258
I was quieted, and *s* again. *The Ring* 421
Then her head sank, she *s*, *Death of Œnone* 78
he *s* Ay, till dawn stole into the cave. *Bandit's Death* 30
Sleuth-hound *S-h* thou knowest, and gray, *Gareth and L.* 462
Slew And *s* him with your noble birth. *L. C. V. de Vere* 48
tho' I *s* thee with my hand ! *Locksley Hall* 56
own traditions God, and *s* the Lord, *Aylmer's Field* 795
S both his sons : and I, shall I, *Princess ii* 288
' He saved my life : my brother *s* him for it.' ,, *vi* 108
s the beast, and fell'd The forest, *Com. of Arthur* 59
the rest *S* on and burnt, crying, ,, 439
pride, wrath *S* the May-white. *Gareth and L.* 657
and stunn'd the twain Or *s* them, *Geraint and E.* 92
tho' he *s* them one by one, ,, 918
my hand Was gauntleted, half *s* him ; *Balin and Balan* 178
With my slain self the heaps of whom I *s*— ,, 178
Who pounced her quarry and *s* it. *Merlin and V.* 135
will ye let him in ? He *s* him ! *Pelleas and E.* 379
s Till all the rafters rang with woman-yells, *Last Tournament* 475
friend *s* friend not knowing whom he *s* ; *Pass. of Arthur* 101
S him, and all but slain himself, he fell. ,, 169
if Affection Living *s* Love, *Lover's Tale ii* 31
drove them, and smote them, and *s*, *Def. of Lucknow* 71
and seized one another and *s* ; *V. of Maeldune* 34
and ever they struck and they *s* ; ,, 68
we *s* and we sail'd away. ,, 96
For the one half *s* the other, ,, 114
S with the sword-edge There by Brunanburh, *Batt. of Brunanburh* 9
blanch the bones of whom she *s*, *Tiresias* 150
kill'd the slave, and *s* the wife *Locksley H., Sixty* 67
Struck with the sword-hand and *s*, *Heavy Brigade* 52
Slewest thine own hand thou *s* my dear lord, *Gareth and L.* 352
Which thou that *s* the sire hast left the son. ,, 360
Slice I will *s* him handless by the wrist, *Pelleas and E.* 338
Sliced who *s* a red life-bubbling way *Gareth and L.* 509
Slid The sullen answer *s* betwixt : *Two Voices* 226
Night *s* down one long stream of sighing wind, *Gardener's D.* 267
Another *s*, a sunny fleck, *Talking Oak* 223
like a creeping sunbeam, *s* From pillar unto pillar, *Godiva* 49
The snake of gold *s* from her hair, *Merlin and V.* 888
There from his charger down he *s*, *Lancelot and E.* 510
S from my hands, when I was leaning *Last Tournament* 43
Slide waves that up a quiet cove Rolling *s*, *Eleänore* 109
S the heavy barges trail'd *L. of Shalott i* 20
I fear to *s* from bad to worse. *Two Voices* 231
S's the bird o'er lustrous woodland, *Locksley Hall* 162
As down dark tides the glory *s's*, *Sir Galahad* 47
I *s* by hazel covers ; *The Brook* 171
I slip, I *s*, I gloom, I glance, ,, 174
S from that quiet heaven of hers, *Lucretius* 87
as the waterlily starts and *s's* Upon the level *Princess iv* 255
Now *s's* the silent meteor on, ,, *vii* 184
S from the bosom of the stars. *In Mem. xvii* 16
that making *s* apart Their dusk wing-cases, *Gareth and L.* 686
s From the long shore-cliff's windy walls *Geraint and E.* 163
Spring *s's* hither o'er the Southern sea, *Prog. of Spring* 2
Slided over them the tremulous isles of light *S*, *Princess vi* 82
Writhed toward him, *s* up his knee and sat, *Merlin and V.* 239
S The Gleam. *Merlin and the G.* 61
Sliding (*See also* **Supple-sliding**) all that night I heard
the watchman peal The *s* season : *Gardener's D.* 183
And o'er them many a *s* star, *Day-Dm., Depart.* 14
Dream in the *s* tides. *Requiescat* 4
All night no ruder air perplex Thy *s* keel *In Mem. ix* 10

Sliding (*continued*) Unconscious of the *s* hour, — *In Mem. xliii* 5
A river *s* by the wall. — „ *ciii* 8
Come *s* out of her sacred glove, — *Maud I vi* 85
Went *s* down so easily, and fell, — *Gareth and L.* 1224
On to the palace-doorway *s*, paused. — *Lancelot and E.* 1246
and *s* down the blacken'd marsh Blood-red, — *Holy Grail* 473
Slieäve (sleeve) Roäver a-tuggin' an' teärin' my *s*. — *Owd Roä* 60
Slight (adj.) 'You're too *s* and fickle,' I said, — *Edward Gray* 19
S was his answer 'Well—I care not for it:' — *Aylmer's Field* 238
When some respect, however, *s*, was paid To woman, — *Princess ii* 136
for such, my friend, We hold them *s*: — „ *iv* 127
No doubt, for *s* delay, remain'd among us — „ 331
We are fools and *s*; — *In Mem., Pro.* 29
How dimly character'd and *s*, — „ *lxi* 6
To save from some *s* shame one simple girl. — *Maud I xviii* 45
S, to be crush'd with a tap Of my finger-nail — „ *II ii* 21
For ah! the *s* coquette, she cannot love, — *The form, the form* 12
'The *s* she-slips of loyal blood, — *Talking Oak* 57
A body *s* and round, and like a pear In growing, — *Walk. to the Mail* 53
And *s* Sir Robert with his watery smile — *Edwin Morris* 128
She play'd about with *s* and sprightly talk. — *Merlin and V.* 171
For, grant me some *s* power upon your fate, — „ 333
Flush'd slightly at the *s* disparagement — *Lancelot and E.* 234
I am not made of so *s* elements. — *Guinevere* 510
and death at our *s* barricade, — *Def. of Lucknow* 15
S ripple on the boundless deep That moves, — *Ancient Sage* 189
Future glimpse and fade Thro' some *s* spell, — *Early Spring* 32
Slight (s) To look at her with *s*, and say — *Mariana in the S.* 66
bare in bitter grudge The *s's* of Arthur and his Table, — *Merlin and V.* 7
Slight (verb) and yet you dared To *s* it. — *Dora* 99
he will teach him hardness, and to *s* His mother; — „ 120
he will learn to *s* his father's memory; — „ 153
Wherefore *s* me not wholly, — *Hendecasyllabics* 15
He seems to *s* her simple heart. — *In Mem. xcvii* 20
A song that *s's* the coming care, — „ *xcix* 10
Why *s* your King, And lose the quest — *Lancelot and E.* 654
I, would *s* our marriage oath: — *Happy* 89
Slighted saw Philip, the *s* suitor of old times, — *Enoch Arden* 745
Going? I am old and *s*: — *Columbus* 241
Slighter Yours has been a *s* ailment, — *Locksley H., Sixty* 17
Near us Edith's holy shadow, smiling at the *s* ghost. — „ 54
Slightest The *s* air of song shall breathe — *In Mem. xlix* 7
Slightly Flush'd *s* at the slight disparagement — *Lancelot and E.* 234
Slight-natured If she be small, *s-n*, miserable, — *Princess vii* 265
Slime That tare each other in their *s*, — *In Mem. lvi* 23
that cannot see for *s*, *S* of the ditch: — *Holy Grail* 771
sink Thy fleurs-de-lys in *s* again, — *Sir J. Oldcastle* 99
soul and sense in city *s*? — *Locksley H., Sixty* 218
labour'd in lifting them out of *s*, — *Dead Prophet* 11
Slimed snake-like *s* his victim ere he gorged; — *Sea Dreams* 193
And sank his head in mire, and *s* themselves — *Last Tournament* 471
Slink As boys that *s* From ferule — *Princess v* 37
a coward *s's* from what he fears To cope with, — *Pelleas and E.* 438
Slip (s) (*See also* **She-slip**) narrow moon-lit *s's* of silver cloud, — *Œnone* 218
And show you *s's* of all that grows — *Amphion* 83
Bursts of great heart and *s's* in sensual mire, — *Princess v* 199
those white *s's* Handed her cup and piped, — *Last Tournament* 295
there was but a *s* of a moon, — *Tomorrow* 9
Slip (verb) Could *s* its bark and walk. — *Talking Oak* 188
'Sometimes I let a sunbeam *s*, — „ 217
Or *s* between the ridges, — *The Brook* 28
I *s*, I slide, I gloom, I glance, — „ 174
to *s* away To-day, to-morrow, soon: — *Princess ii* 296
And *s* at once all-fragrant into one: — „ *vii* 70
And *s's* into the bosom of the lake: — „ 187
and *s* Into my bosom and be lost in me.' — „ 188
Sun comes, moon comes, Time *s's* away. — *Window, When* 2
I *s* the thoughts of life and death; — *In Mem. cxxii* 16
I will not let his name *S* from my lips — *Marr. of Geraint* 446
and by and by *S's* into golden cloud, — „ 736
Slipper fit to wear your *s* for a glove. — *Geraint and E.* 623
Slippery (*See also* **Slaäpe**) as he based His feet on juts of *s* crag — *M. d'Arthur* 189
To glance and shift about her *s* sides, — *Lucretius* 189
Glass'd in the *s* sand before it breaks? — *Merlin and V.* 293

Slippery (*continued*) And that it was too *s* to be held, — *Lancelot and E.* 213
as he based His feet on juts of *s* crag — *Pass. of Arthur* 357
hath o'erstept The *s* footing of his narrow wit, — *Lover's Tale i* 102
Slipping The *s* thro' from state to state. — *Two Voices* 351
three times *s* from the outer edge, — *The Epic* 11
The silent water *s* from the hills, — *Enoch Arden* 633
and then Went *s* down horrible precipices, — *Geraint and E.* 379
Come *s* o'er their shadows on the sand, — „ 471
Went *s* back upon the golden days — *Guinevere* 380
Slip-shod '*S-s* waiter, lank and sour, — *Vision of Sin* 71
Slipt (*See also* **Shoulder-slipt**) 'Tis gone: a thousand such have *s* — *Will Water.* 181
The snake *s* under a spray, — *Poet's Song* 10
And *s* aside, and like a wounded life — *Enoch Arden* 75
by mischance he *s* and fell: — „ 106
Till half-another year had *s* away. — „ 471
She *s* across the summer of the world, — „ 531
S into ashes, and was found no more. — *Aylmer's Field* 6
S o'er those lazy limits down the wind — „ 495
out I *s* Into a land all sun and blossom, — *Sea Dreams* 100
And I *s* out: but whither will you now? — *Princess iv* 240
S round and in the dark invested you, — „ 404
And blossom-fragrant *s* the heavy dews — „ *v* 243
Her falser self *s* from her like a robe, — „ *vii* 161
The hoof of his horse *s* in the stream, — *Gareth and L.* 1046
like a silver shadow *s* away Thro' the dim land; — *Merlin and V.* 423
the braid *S* and uncoil'd itself, — „ 889
And *s* and fell into some pool or stream, — *Lancelot and E.* 214
Who lost the hern we *s* her at, — „ 657
Lightly, her suit allow'd, she *s* away, — „ 778
At once she *s* like water to the floor. — „ 830
Heavy as it was, a great stone *s* and fell, — *Holy Grail* 680
S, and ran on, and flung himself between — *St. Telemachus* 61
Slit And Uther *s* thy tongue; — *Gareth and L.* 376
Slither'd I *s* an' hurted my huck, — *North. Cobbler* 19
Sloe blackthorn-blossom fades and falls and leaves the bitter *s*, — *The Flight* 15
betwixt the whitening *s* And kingcup blaze, — *To Mary Boyle* 25
Sloe-tree Poussetting with a *s-t*: — *Amphion* 44
Sloomy (sluggish) An' Sally wur *s* an' draggle — *North. Cobbler* 41
Slope (adj.) when the crisp *s* waves After a tempest, — *Supp. Confessions* 126
Took horse, descended the *s* street, — *Gareth and L.* 662
thro' lanes of shouting Gareth rode Down the *s* street, — „ 700
on thro' silent faces rode Down the *s* city, — „ 735
Down the *s* city rode, and sharply turn'd — *Last Tournament* 127
Slope (s) (*See also* **Hill-slope**) his native *s*, Where he was wont to leap — *Supp. Confessions* 164
And on the *s*, an absent fool, — *Miller's D.* 62
Upon the freshly-flower'd *s*. — „ 112
The downward *s* to death. — *D. of F. Women* 16
There, on a *s* of orchard, Francis laid — *Audley Court* 20
At last I heard a voice upon the *s* — *Vision of Sin* 219
And many a *s* was rich in bloom — *To E. L.* 20
drew, from butts of water on the *s*, — *Princess, Pro.* 60
Blot out the *s* of sea from verge to shore, — „ *vii* 38
we climb'd The *s* to Vivian-place, — „ *Con.* 40
From *s* to *s* thro' distant ferns, — „ 99
and I stand on the *s* of the hill, — *Window, On the Hill* 9
Follow them down the *s*! — „ 16
To slant the fifth autumnal *s*, — *In Mem. xxii* 10
Becomes on Fortune's crowning *s* — „ *lxiv* 14
Upon a pastoral *s* as fair, — *Maud I xviii* 19
on the *s* The sword rose, the hind fell, — *Com. of Arthur* 431
after one long *s* was mounted, saw, Bowl-shaped, — *Gareth and L.* 795
I was halfway down the *s* to Hell, — *Geraint and E.* 791
up a *s* of garden, all Of roses white and red, — *Pelleas and E.* 421
purple *s's* of mountain flowers Pass — *Last Tournament* 229
Was blackening on the *s's* of Portugal, — *Sisters (E. and E.)* 62
and roll their ruins down the *s*. — *Locksley H., Sixty* 138
Thro' the great gray *s* of men, — *Heavy Brigade* 17
and flamed On one huge *s* beyond, — *St. Telemachus* 8
Slope (verb) peaks shadow'd with pine *s* to the dark hyaline. — *Leonine Eleg.* 10
the summits *s* Beyond the furthest flights — *Two Voices* 184
swimming vapour *s's* athwart the glen, — *Œnone* 3
leave The monstrous ledges there to *s*, — *Princess vii* 212

Slope (verb) (*continued*)   That *s* thro' darkness up to God,   *In Mem. lv* 16
··· As *s's* a wild brook o'er a little stone,   *Marr. of Geraint* 77
Sloped the mountain-shade *S* downward to her seat   *Œnone* 22
we came to where the river *s* To plunge   *Princess iii* 290
down from this a lordly stairway *s*   *Gareth and L.* 669
arms on which the standing muscle *s*,   *Marr. of Geraint* 76
till the morning light *S* thro' the pines,   *Lover's Tale i* 264
breakers on the shore *S* into louder surf :   "   *iii* 15
Sloping (*See also* **Even-sloping, Onward-sloping**) Was *s*
toward his western bower.   *Mariana* 80
s of the moon-lit sward Was damask-work,   *Arabian Nights* 27
great Orion *s* slowly to the West.   *Locksley Hall* 8
s down to make Arms for his chair,   *Lancelot and E.* 437
In some fair space of *s* greens   *Palace of Art* 106
For all the *s* pasture murmur'd, sown   *Princess, Pro.* 55
Who, smitten by the dusty *s* beam,   *Marr. of Geraint* 262
crisping white Play'd ever back upon the *s* wave,   *Holy Grail* 382
the *s* seas Hung in mid-heaven,   *Lover's Tale i* 3
Slot But at the *s* or fewmets of a deer,   *Last Tournament* 371
Sloth But stagnates in the weeds of *s* ;   *In Mem. xxvii* 11
Slothful Inwrapt tenfold in *s* shame,   *Palace of Art* 262
But wink no more in *s* overtrust.   *Ode on Well.* 170
Nor the cannon-bullet rust on a *s* shore,   *Maud III vi* 26
He rooted out the *s* officer Or guilty,   *Geraint and E.* 938
Slough (*See also* **Woman-slough**) 'In filthy *s's* they roll
a prurient skin,   *Palace of Art* 201
From scalp to sole one *s* and crust of sin,   *St. S. Stylites* 2
mountain there has cast his cloudy *s*,   *Lucretius* 177
dazzled by the wildfire Love to *s's* That swallow
common sense,   *Princess v* 441
times in the *s's* of a low desire,   *By an Evolution.* 18
Slow (*See also* **Too-slow**) The *s* clock ticking, and the sound   *Mariana* 74
So full, so deep, so *s*,   *Eleänore* 95
The *s* result of winter showers :   *Two Voices* 452
The *s* wise smile that, round about   *Miller's D.* 5
Her *s* full words sank thro' the silence drear,   *D. of F. Women* 121
Nor swift nor *s* to change, but firm :   *Love thou thy land* 31
A league of grass, wash'd by a *s* broad stream,   *Gardener's D.* 40
If I may measure time by yon *s* light,   *St. S. Stylites* 94
I hardly, with *s* steps, With *s*, faint steps,   "   182
my heart so *s* To feel it !   *Love and Duty* 34
The *s* sweet hours that bring us all things good, The
s sad hours that bring us all things ill,   "   57
by *s* prudence to make mild A rugged people,   *Ulysses* 36
The long day wanes : the *s* moon climbs :   "   55
his long wooing her, Her *s* consent, and marriage,   *Enoch Arden* 708
By *s* approaches, than by single act   *Princess iii* 284
till the Bear had wheel'd Thro' a great arc his seven *s*
suns.   "   *iv* 213
At first her eye with *s* dilation roll'd   "   *vi* 189
Lead out the pageant : sad and *s*,   *Ode on Well.* 13
The sound of streams that swift or *s*   *In Mem. xxxv* 10
And all the wheels of Being *s*   "   *l* 4
One set *s* bell will seem to toll   "   *lvii* 10
With *s* steps from out An old storm-beaten,   *Gareth and L.* 1112
the great Queen Came with *s* steps,   *Balin and Balan* 245
Here her *s* sweet eyes Fear-tremulous,   *Merlin and V.* 85
The *s* tear creep from her closed eyelid yet,   "   906
Sighs, and *s* smiles, and golden eloquence   *Lancelot and E.* 649
But ten *s* mornings past, and on the eleventh   "   1133
Then with a *s* smile turn'd the lady round   *Pelleas and E.* 91
Spread the *s* smile thro' all her company.   "   95
and there, with *s* sad steps Ascending,   *Last Tournament* 143
With silent smiles of *s* disparagement ;   *Guinevere* 14
Methought by *s* degrees the sullen bell Toll'd quicker,   *Lover's Tale iii* 13
Some thro' age and *s* diseases,   *Locksley H., Sixty* 46
Æonian Evolution, swift or *s*, Thro' all the Spheres—   *The Ring* 44
But after ten *s* weeks her fix'd intent,   "   345
Slow-arching crest of some *s-a* wave,   *Last Tournament* 462
Slow-develop'd A *s-d* strength awaits Completion   *Love thou thy land* 57
Slow-dropping *S-d* veils of thinnest lawn,   *Lotos-Eaters* 11
Slower Are *s* to forgive than human kings.   *Tiresias* 10
And *s* and fainter, Old and weary,   *Merlin and the G.* 99
Slow-falling westward—under yon *s-f* star,   *Akbar's Dream* 152
Slow-flaming Would seem *s-f* crimson fires   *Palace of Art* 50

Slowly Ring out a *s* dying cause,   *In Mem. cvi* 13
out of the darkness Silent and *s*   *Merlin and the G.* 82
Slowly-dying (*See also* **Slowly**) and winks behind
a *s-d* fire.   *Locksley Hall* 136
By quiet fields, a *s-d* power,   *De Prof., Two G.* 24
Slowly-fading The *s-f* mistress of the world,   *Com. of Arthur* 505
Slowly-grown if our *s-g* And crown'd Republic's
crowning common-sense,   *To the Queen ii* 60
Slowly-mellowing thro' the *s-m* avenues   *Last Tournament* 360
Slowly-painful More *s-p* to subdue this home Of sin,   *St. S. Stylites* 57
Slowly-ridging The *s-r* rollers on the cliffs Clash'd,   *Lover's Tale i* 57
Slowly-thickening I see the *s-t* chestnut towers   *Prog. of Spring* 42
Slowly-waning and deckt in *s-w* hues,   *Gareth and L.* 1195
Slow-measure have moved *s-m* to my tune,   *Last Tournament* 282
Slow-moving *S-m* as a wave against the wind,   *Lover's Tale iv* 293
Slow-worm *s-w* creeps, and the thin weasel   *Aylmer's Field* 852
Sludge tends her bristled grunters in the *s* :'   *Princess v* 27
Sluggard I have been the *s*, and I ride apace,   *Holy Grail* 644
Sluggish (*See also* **Sloomy**) Mere fellowship of *s* moods,   *In Mem. xxxv* 21
Sluice A *s* with blacken'd waters slept,   *Mariana* 38
Sluiced canal From the main river *s*,   *Arabian Nights* 26
Slumber (*s*) hum of swarming bees Into dreamful *s* lull'd.   *Eleänore* 30
in its place My heart a charmed *s* keeps,   "   128
Nor steep our brows in *s's* holy balm ;   *Lotos-Eaters, C. S.* 21
surely, *s* is more sweet than toil,   "   126
As thro' the *s* of the globe   *The Voyage* 23
Betwixt the *s* of the poles,   *In Mem. xcix* 18
Breaking a *s* in which all spleenful folly   *Maud I iii* 2
I envied your sweet *s*,   *The Flight* 9
Slumber (verb) *S's* not like a mountain tarn ?   *Supp. Confessions* 129
And the kindly earth shall *s*,   *Locksley Hall* 130
In some long trance should *s* on ;   *In Mem. xliii* 4
Slumber'd the garden-bowers and grots *S* :   *Arabian Nights* 79
While Enoch *s* motionless and pale,   *Enoch Arden* 908
Slumbering Winnow with giant arms the *s* green.   *The Kraken* 10
Red after revel, droned her lurdane knights *S*,   *Pelleas and E.* 431
Who slowly paced among the *s* host,   *Pass. of Arthur* 7
Slumbrous The *s* wave outwelleth,   *Claribel* 18
if a bolt of fire Would rive the *s* summer noon   *Supp. Confessions* 11
Rolling a *s* sheet of foam below.   *Lotos-Eaters* 13
The *s* light is rich and warm,   *Day-Dm., Sleep. B.* 7
Slung from his blazon'd baldric *s*   *L. of Shalott iii* 15
Slur seem'd to *s* With garrulous ease   *Princess i* 163
how men *s* him, saying all his force Is melted   *Marr. of Geraint* 106
Slurring and *s* the days gone by,   *Maud I i* 33
Slushin' *s* down fro' the bank to the beck,   *Owd Roä* 41
Slut *See* **Trollope**
Sly *See* **Half-sly**
Smack'd Their nectar *s* of hemlock on the lips,   *Demeter and P.* 104
Smacking the sight and *s* of the time ;   *Princess, Pro.* 89
Small o'er it many, round and *s*,   *Mariana* 39
Nothing but the *s* cold worm Fretteth   *A Dirge* 9
A STILL *s* voice spake unto me,   *Two Voices* 1
Then to the still *s* voice I said ;   "   4
He left a *s* plantation   *Amphion* 20
great and *s*, Went nutting to the hazels.   *Enoch Arden* 63
With one *s* gate that open'd on the waste,   "   733
For which his gains were dock'd, however *s* : *S* were
his gains,   *Sea Dreams* 7
the master took *S* notice, or austerely,   *Lucretius* 8
His name was Gama ; crack'd and *s* his voice,   *Princess i* 114
heads were less : Some men's were *s* ;   "   *ii* 148
her *s* goodman Shrinks in his arm-chair   "   *v* 453
So said the *s* king moved beyond his wont.   "   *vi* 265
here and there the *s* bright head,   "   *vii* 58
she found a *s* Sweet Idyl,   "   190
If she be *s*, slight-natured,   "   265
When one *s* touch of Charity Could lift   *Lit. Squabbles* 13
the village, and looks how quiet and *s* !   *Maud I iv* 7
S and pure as a pearl,   "   *II ii* 2
S, but a work divine,   "   23
by Mark the King For that *s* charm of feature mine,   *Merlin and V.* 76
grieving that their greatest are so *s*,   "   833
Rejoice, *s* man, in this *s* world of mine,   *Holy Grail* 559
S heart was his after the Holy Quest :   "   657

Small (*continued*) ' And then, with *s* adventure met, Sir Bors   *Holy Grail* 660
And slender was her hand and *s* her shape ;   *Pelleas and E.* 74
and if he fly us, *S* matter ! let him.'   „ 200
And mindful of her *s* and cruel hand,   „ 201
s pity upon his horse had he,   „ 540
The twelve *s* damosels white as Innocence,   *Last Tournament* 291
and cast thee back Thine own *s* saw,   „ 712
s violence done Rankled in him and ruffled   *Guinevere* 48
But let my words, the words of one so *s*,   „ 185
Of that *s* bay, which out to open main   *Lover's Tale i* 435
The *s* sweet face was flush'd,   *The Wreck* 60
With all the peoples, great and *s*,   *Epilogue* 20
' *S* blemish upon the skin !   *Dead Prophet* 66
Her dauntless army scatter'd, and so *s*,   *The Fleet* 11
At times the *s* black fly upon the pane   *To One who ran down Eng.* 3
Smaller   O God, that I had loved a *s* man !   *Merlin and V.* 872
Hid under grace, as in a *s* time,   *Lancelot and E.* 264
I am thine husband—not a *s* soul,   *Guinevere* 566
When I was *s* than the statuette   *The Ring* 109
Smallest   he saw The *s* rock far on the faintest hill,   *Com. of Arthur* 99
O *s* among peoples !   *Montenegro* 9
Smash   (*See also* **Mash**)   *S* the bottle to smithers,   *North. Cobbler* 104
Smashed   *See* **Mash'd**
Smashing   *See* **Mashin'**
Smear'd   shining hair Was *s* with earth,   *Holy Grail* 210
Their idol *s* with blood,   *Freedom* 28
Smell (**s**)   moist rich *s* of the rotting leaves,   *A spirit haunts* 17
The *s* of violets, hidden in the green,   *D. of F. Women* 77
The gentle shower, the *s* of dying leaves,   *Enoch Arden* 611
A great black swamp and of an evil *s*,   *Holy Grail* 499
and the sweet *s* of the fields Past,   *Pelleas and E.* 5
wind Came wooingly with woodbine *s*'s.   *Lover's Tale ii* 36
blew Coolness and moisture and all *s*'s of bud And foliage   *iii* 5
and the loathsome *s*'s of disease   *In the Child. Hosp.* 25
On them the *s* of burning had not past.   *Sir J. Oldcastle* 177
sympathies, how frail, In sound and *s* !   *Early Spring* 36
Smell (**verb**)   rarely *s*'s the new-mown hay,   *The Owl i* 9
I *s* the meadow in the street;   *In Mem. cxix* 4
as one That *s*'s a foul-flesh'd agaric in the holt,   *Gareth and L.* 747
how sweetly *s*'s the honeysuckle In the hush'd night,   „ 1287
if tha seeäs 'im an' *s*'s 'im   *North. Cobbler* 66
is prized for it *s*'s of the beast,   *The Dawn* 14
Smell'd   Fur 'e *s* like a herse a-singein',   *Owd Roä* 101
Smellest   thou *s* all of kitchen-grease.   *Gareth and L.* 751
Thou *s* all of kitchen as before.'   „ 771
Nay—for thou *s* of the kitchen still.   „ 843
Smelling   (*See also* **Ocean-smelling**, **Sweet-smelling**)   *S* of musk and of insolence,   *Maud I vi* 45
over-full Of sweetness, and in *s* of itself,   *Lover's Tale i* 272
Smelt   Hesperian gold, That *s* ambrosially,   *Œnone* 67
S of the coming summer, as one large cloud   *Gardener's D.* 78
Brought out a dusky loaf that *s* of home,   *Audley Court* 22
Smile (**s**)   deep and clear are thine Of wealthy *s*'s : but who may know Whether *s* or frown be fleeter ?
Whether *s* or frown be sweeter,   *Madeline* 11
Thy *s* and frown are not aloof From one another,   „ 19
heart entanglest In a golden-netted *s* ;   „ 41
Hollow *s* and frozen sneer Come not here.   *Poet's Mind* 10
Wherefore those faint *s*'s of thine,   *Adeline* 21
Wherefore that faint *s* of thine,   „ 38
Hence that look and *s* of thine,   „ 63
The very *s* before you speak,   *Margaret* 14
Comes out thy deep ambrosial *s*.   *Eleänore* 74
ghost of passion that no *s*'s restore—   *The form, the form* 11
The slow wise *s* that, round about   *Miller's D.* 5
She with a subtle *s* in her mild eyes,   *Œnone* 184
She, flashing forth a haughty *s*,   *D. of F. Women* 129
slight Sir Robert with his watery *s*   *Edwin Morris* 128
thou grant mine asking with a *s*,   *Tithonus* 16
With one *s* of still defiance   *The Captain* 59
With tears and *s*'s from heaven again   *Sir L. and Q. G.* 2
With half-allowing *s*'s for all the world,   *Aylmer's Field* 120
Sir Aylmer half forgot his lazy *s* Of patron   „ 197
With a heaved shoulder and a saucy *s*,   „ 466

Smile (**s**) (*continued*)   Never one kindly *s*, one kindly word :   *Aylmer's Field* 564
with the fat affectionate *s* That makes the widow lean.   *Sea Dreams* 155
s that like a wrinkling wind On glassy water   *Princess i* 115
She paused, and added with a haughtier *s*,   „ *iii* 225
shot from crooked lips a haggard *s*.   „ *iv* 364
s, that look'd A stroke of cruel sunshine   „ 523
common light of *s*'s at our disguise   „ *v* 271
doubtful *s* dwelt like a clouded moon   „ *vi* 270
' Ay so,' said Ida with a bitter *s*,   „ 316
blush and *s*, a medicine in themselves   „ *vii* 62
(so rare the *s*'s Of sunlight)   *The Daisy* 53
Is matter for a flying *s*.   *In Mem. lxii* 12
In glance and *s*, and clasp and kiss,   „ *lxxxiv* 7
I know it, and smile a hard-set *s*,   *Maud I iv* 20
touch'd my hand with a *s* so sweet,   „ *vi* 12
And *s* as sunny as cold,   „ 24
And her *s* were all that I dream'd,   „ 37
And her *s* had all that I dream'd,   „ 93
But a *s* could make it sweet. (repeat)   „ *I vi* 39, 95
With a glassy *s* his brutal scorn—   „ 49
Perhaps the *s* and tender tone   „ 63
The sun look'd out with a *s*   „ *ix* 3
' I shall assay,' said Gareth with a *s* That madden'd her,   *Gareth and L.* 783
' Turn, Fortune, turn thy wheel with *s* or frown ;   *Marr. of Geraint* 350
With frequent *s* and nod departing found,   „ 515
when he mark'd his high sweet *s* In passing,   *Balin and Balan* 160
slight and sprightly talk, And vivid *s*'s,   *Merlin and V.* 172
when the living *s* Died from his lips,   *Lancelot and E.* 323
he bound Her token on his helmet, with a *s*   „ 374
Sighs, and slow *s*'s, and golden eloquence   „ 649
Smiled with his lips—a *s* beneath a cloud,   *Holy Grail* 705
with a slow *s* turn'd the lady round   *Pelleas and E.* 91
With silent *s*'s of slow disparagement ;   *Guinevere* 14
Heart-hiding *s*, and gray persistent eye :   „ 64
Flicker'd like doubtful *s*'s about her lips,   *Lover's Tale i* 68
when I wept, Her *s* lit up the rainbow on my tears,   „ 254
her love did clothe itself in *s*'s About his lips !   „ 658
her lips were sunder'd With *s*'s of tranquil bliss,   „ *ii* 143
bond and seal Of friendship, spoken of with tearful *s*'s ;   „ 182
stepping out of darkness with a *s*.   „ *iv* 220
—adding, with a *s*, The first for many weeks—   „ 280
Seeäd nobbut the *s* o' the sun   *North. Cobbler* 50
The bright quick *s* of Evelyn,   *Sisters (E. and E.)* 243
and the *s*, and the comforting eye—   *In the Child. Hosp.* 12
And greet it with a kindly *s*   *To E. Fitzgerald* 4
bask'd in the light of a dowerless *s*,   *The Wreck* 45
But wakes a dotard *s*.'   *Ancient Sage* 132
The cruel *s*, the courtly phrase that masks   *The Flight* 30
If greeted by your classic *s*,   *To Prof. Jebb.* 10
Miriam nodded with a pitying *s*,   *The Ring* 281
Nor ever cheer'd you with a kindly *s*,   „ 388
in the tearful splendour of her *s*'s   *Prog. of Spring* 41
Smile (**verb**)   (*See also* **Smoile**)   women *s* with saint-like glances   *Supp. Confessions* 22
S at the claims of long descent.   *L. C. V. de Vere* 52
Where they *s* in secret, looking over wasted lands,   *Lotos-Eaters, C. S.* 114
But they *s*, they find a music centred   „ 117
' No fair Hebrew boy Shall *s* away my maiden blame   *D. of F. Women* 214
He will not *s*—not speak to me Once more.   *To J. S.* 21
Did they *s* on him.   *The Captain* 56
The very graves appear'd to *s*,   *The Letters* 45
Seeing with how great ease Nature can *s*,   *Lucretius* 174
empire upon empire *s* to-day,   *W. to Marie Alex.* 33
I know it, and *s* a hard-set smile,   *Maud I iv* 20
S sweetly, thou ! my love hath smiled on me.'   *Gareth and L.* 1001
S and we *s*, the lords of many lands ;   *Marr. of Geraint* 353
Frown and we *s*, the lords of our own hands ;   „ 354
S at him, as he deem'd, presumptuously :   *Balin and Balan* 222
To make her *s*, her golden ankle-bells.   *Merlin and V.* 579
smiling as a master *s*'s at one That is not of his school,   „ 662
you yourself will *s* at your own self   *Lancelot and E.* 951

Smile (verb) (*continued*) I shall never make thee *s* again.' *Last Tournament* 762
    They *s* upon me, till, remembering all   *Sisters* (*E. and E.*) 279
    How she would *s* at 'em, play with 'em,   *In the Child. Hosp.* 34
    thine Imperial mother *s* again,   *Ded. Poem Prin. Alice* 13
    ghost of our great Catholic Queen *S*'s on me,   *Columbus* 188
    s's at her sleepin' child—   *Tomorrow* 26
    up to either pole she *s*'s,   *Locksley H., Sixty* 169
    Where man, nor only Nature *s*'s ;   *To Ulysses* 39
Smiled who *s* when she was torn in three ;   *Poland* 12
    Thy sister *s* and said, ' No tears for me !   *The Bridesmaid* 3
    And now and then he gravely *s*.   *Two Voices* 414
    He *s*, and opening out his milk-white palm   *Œnone* 65
    And somewhat grimly *s*.   *Palace of Art* 136
    At me you *s*, but unbeguiled I saw the snare,   *L. C. V. de Vere* 5
    with dead lips *s* at the twilight plain,   *D. of F. Women* 62
    She faintly *s*, she hardly moved ;   *The Letters* 14
    that which pleased him, for he *s*.   *Enoch Arden* 757
    He look'd upon my crown and *s* :   *In Mem. lxix* 16
    Has not his sister *s* on me ?   *Maud I xiii* 45
    with a kindly hand on Gareth's arm *S* the great
        King,   *Gareth and L.* 579
    Smile sweetly, thou ! my love hath *s* on me.'   ,, 1001
    twice my love hath *s* on me.' (repeat)   ,, 1062, 1077
    thrice my love hath *s* on me.'   ,, 1161
    Then sigh'd and *s* the hoary-headed Earl,   *Marr. of Geraint* 307
    He spoke : the mother *s*, but half in tears,   ,, 823
    Then like a stormy sunlight *s* Geraint,   *Geraint and E.* 480
    From being *s* at happier in themselves   *Balin and Balan* 163
    Whereat she *s* and turn'd her to the King,   ,, 201
    Garlon, hissing ; then he sourly *s*.   ,, 355
    Sunnily she *s* ' And even in this lone wood,   ,, 528
    till he sadly *s* : ' To what request for what strange
        boon,'   *Merlin and V.* 263
    S at each other, while the Queen,   *Lancelot and E.* 739
    But fast asleep, and lay as tho' she *s*.   ,, 1161
    S with his lips—a smile beneath a cloud,   *Holy Grail* 705
    and they too *s*, Scorning him,   *Pelleas and E.* 96
    Full sharply smote his knees, and *s*,   *Guinevere* 47
    An' he *s* at me, ' Ain't you, my love ?   *First Quarrel* 62
    the sun *s* out far over the summer sea,   *The Revenge* 70
    An' Squire 'e *s* an' 'e *s* (repeat)   *Village Wife* 61, 88
    an' 'e *s*, fur 'e hedn't naw friend,   ,, 89
    it seem'd she stood by me and *s*,   *In the Child. Hosp.* 67
    it coo'd to the Mother and *s*.   *The Wreck* 60
    an' Hiven in its glory, *s*,   *Tomorrow* 25
    looking still as if she *s*,   *Locksley H., Sixty* 35
    shook her head, and patted yours, And *s*,   *The Ring* 314
Smiler Thou faint *s*, Adeline ?   *Adeline* 48
Smilest Thou *s*, but thou dost not speak,   *Oriana* 68
    Thou that faintly *s* still,   *Adeline* 15
    And *s*, knowing all is well.   *In Mem. cxxvii* 20
    ' O morning star that *s* in the blue,   *Gareth and L.* 999
Smiling (*See also* **A-smilin', Silver-smiling, Westward-smiling**)
    S, never speaks ;   *Lilian* 12
    S, frowning, evermore, (repeat)   *Madeline* 8, 25
    Faintly *s* Adeline ,   *Adeline* 2
    Thought folded over thought, *s* asleep,   *Eleánore* 84
    Sat *s*, babe in arm.   *Palace of Art* 96
    Eustace turn'd, and *s* said to me,   *Gardener's D.* 97
    And, *s*, put the question by.   *Day-Dm., Revival* 32
    And one said *s* ' Pretty were the sight   *Princess, Pro.* 139
    Took both his hands, and *s* faintly said :   ,, *ii* 304
    While Psyche watch'd them, *s*,   ,, 365
    but *s* ' Not for thee,' she said,   ,, *iv* 121
    Then turn'd the noble damsel *s* at him,   *Gareth and L.* 1188
    And, gravely *s*, lifted her from horse,   *Geraint and E.* 883
    And Vivien answer'd, *s* scornfully,   *Merlin and V.* 37
    And Vivien answer'd *s* saucily, (repeat)   ,, 268, 651
    And Vivien answer'd *s* mournfully : (repeat)   ,, 311, 438
    And Vivien answer'd *s* as in wrath :   ,, 526
    And *s* as a master smiles at one That is not of his school,   ,, 662
    while the king Would listen *s*.   *Lancelot and E.* 116
    ' So ye will grace me,' answer'd Lancelot, *S* a moment,   ,, 224
    with *s* face arose, With *s* face and frowning heart,   ,, 552
    past the barge Whereon the lily maid of Astolat Lay *s*,   ,, 1243

Smiling (*continued*) To whom Sir Tristram *s*, ' I am here.   *Last Tournament* 521
    made garlands of the selfsame flower, Which she
        took *s*,   *Lover's Tale i* 344
    a light Of *s* welcome round her lips—   ,, *iii* 46
    s at the slighter ghost.   *Locksley H., Sixty* 54
    s downward at this earthlier earth of ours,   ,, 183
    as the low dark hull dipt under the *s* main,   *The Wreck* 127
Smirk'd The parson *s* and nodded.   *The Goose* 20
Smit *s* with freër light shall slowly melt   *Golden Year* 33
    S with exceeding sorrow unto Death.   *Lover's Tale i* 601
Smite Tho' one should *s* him on the cheek,   *Two Voices* 251
    S, shrink not, spare not.   *St. S. Stylites* 181
    his footsteps *s* the threshold stairs Of life—   ,, 191
    sitting well in order *s* The sounding furrows ;   *Ulysses* 58
    S on the sudden, yet rode on,   *Com. of Arthur* 57
    Utterly *s* the heathen underfoot,   ,, 423
    This air that *s*'s his forehead is not air But vision—   *Holy Grail* 914
    That did not shun to *s* me in worse way,   *Guinevere* 435
Smither (*piece*) Smash the bottle to *s*'s,   *North. Cobbler* 104
Smitten (*See also* **Sharp-smitten, Sun-smitten**) I am so
    deeply *s* thro' the helm   *M. d'Arthur* 25
    Aidless, alone, and *s* thro' the helm.   ,, 41
    A Memnon *s* with the morning Sun.'   *Princess iii* 116
    Who, *s* by the dusty sloping beam,   *Marr. of Geraint* 262
    Then from the *s* surface flash'd, as it were,   *Lancelot and E.* 1236
    Pray Heaven, they be not *s* by the bolt.'   *Holy Grail* 221
    And, when I would have *s* them,   ,, 823
    young life Being *s* in mid heaven with mortal
        cold   *Last Tournament* 27
    Wet with the mists and *s* by the lights,   *Guinevere* 597
    I am so deeply *s* thro' the helm   *Pass. of Arthur* 193
    Aidless, alone, and *s* thro' the helm—   ,, 209
    Tho' *S* too oft, when *s* by Thy rod,   *Doubt and Prayer* 1
Smoäke (*smoke*) I couldn't see fur the *s*   *Owd Roä* 87
Smoäkin' (*smoking*) Guzzlin' an' soäkin' an' *s*   *North. Cobbler* 24
    An' *s* an' thinkin' o' things   *Owd Roä* 34
Smock'd Tho' *s*, or furr'd and purpled,   *Princess iv* 247
Smoile (*smile*) Looök 'ow quoloty *s*'s   *N. Farmer, O. S.* 53
Smoke (s) (*See also* **Sea-smoke, Smoäke, Thunder-smoke, Water-smoke**) With thunders, and with lightnings,
    and with *s*,—   *Buonaparte* 6
    And all the war is roll'd in *s*.'   *Two Voices* 156
    And like a downward *s*, the slender stream   *Lotos-Eaters* 8
    A land of streams ! some, like a downward *s*,   ,, 10
    Beneath its drift of *s* ;   *Talking Oak* 6
    thro' the *s* The blight of low desires—   *Aylmer's Field* 672
    A *s* go up thro' which I loom to her   *Princess v* 193
    Athwart the *s* of burning weeds.   ,, *vii* 358
    Where, far from noise and *s* of town,   *To F. D. Maurice* 13
    like the *s* in a hurricane whirl'd.   *Boädicea* 59
    With fruitful cloud and living *s*,   *In Mem. xxxix* 3
    streets were black with *s* and frost,   ,, *lxix* 3
    Wrapt in drifts of lurid *s*   *Maud II vi* 66
    Reddening the sun with *s* and earth with blood,   *Com. of Arthur* 37
    In drifts of *s* before a rolling wind,   ,, 434
    walks thro' fire will hardly heed the *s*.   *Gareth and L.* 143
    Rolling her *s* about the Royal mount,   ,, 190
    ' Out of the *s*, at once I leap from Satan's foot   ,, 537
    Out of the *s* he came, and so my lance Hold,   ,, 722
    if the King awaken from his craze, Into the *s* again.'   ,, 725
    puff'd the swaying branches into *s*   *Holy Grail* 15
    their foreheads grimed with *s*, and sear'd,   ,, 265
    the morning star Reel'd in the *s*,   *Pelleas and E.* 519
    daylight of your minds But cloud and *s*,   *Lover's Tale i* 297
    Dark thro' the *s* and the sulphur   *Def. of Lucknow* 33
    Dark with the *s* of human sacrifice,   *Sir J. Oldcastle* 84
    when a *s* from a city goes to heaven   *Achilles over the T.* 7
    He is only a cloud and a *s*   *Despair* 29
    ' A fiery phœnix rising from the *s*,   *The Ring* 339
    all her realm Of sound and *s*,   *To Mary Boyle* 66
    s of war's volcano burst again From hoary deeps   *Prog. of Spring* 97
Smoke (verb) The long way *s* beneath him in his fear ;   *Geraint and E.* 532
    stormy crests that *s* against the skies,   *Lancelot and E.* 484
    I have seen this yew-tree *s*, Spring after spring,   *Holy Grail* 18
    went To *s* the scandalous hive of those wild bees   ,, 214

Snivel   I that heard her whine And *s*,   *Last Tournament* 450
Snorin'   ' What arta *s* theere fur ?   *Owd Roä* 68
Snow   (*See also* **Snaw**)   rites and form before his burning
   eyes Melted like *s*.   *The Poet* 40
   Shone out their crowning *s's*.   *Dying Swan* 13
   When the long dun wolds are ribb'd with *s*,   *Oriana* 5
   thorn will blow In tufts of rosy-tinted *s* ;   *Two Voices* 60
   solitary morning smote The streaks of virgin *s*.   *Œnone* 56
   And highest, *s* and fire.   *Palace of Art* 84
   I wish the *s* would melt and the sun come
     out   *May Queen, N. Y's. E.* 15
   Three silent pinnacles of aged *s*,   *Lotos-Eaters* 16
   FULL knee-deep lies the winter *s*,   *D. of the O. Year* 1
   over the *s* I heard just now the crowing cock.   „ 37
   Where falls not hail, or rain, or any *s*,   *M. d'Arthur* 260
   wind, frost, heat, hail, damp, and sleet, and *s* ;   *St. S. Stylites* 16
   with rain or hail, or fire or *s* ;   *Locksley Hall* 193
   DEEP on the convent-roof the *s's*   *St. Agnes' Eve* 1
   The streets are dumb with *s*.   *Sir Galahad* 52
   Nor ever falls the least white star of *s*,   *Lucretius* 107
   like the flakes In a fall of *s*,   „ 167
   From flower to flower, from *s* to *s* :   *In Mem. xxii* 4
   The silent *s* possess'd the earth,   „ *lxxviii* 3
   And silent under other *s's* :   „ *cv* 6
   Ring, happy bells, across the *s* :   „ *cvi* 6
   Now fades the last long streak of *s*,   „ *cxv* 1
   yet thou art but swollen with cold *s's*   *Gareth and L.* 9
   glittering star of morn Parts from a bank of *s*,   *Marr. of Geraint* 735
   ' I know not, for thy heart is pure as *s*.'   *Holy Grail* 97
   like a bank Of maiden *s* mingled with sparks   *Last Tournament* 149
   cold Falls on the mountain in midsummer *s's*,   „ 228
   Where falls not hail, or rain, or any *s*,   *Pass. of Arthur* 428
   like cold *s*, it melteth in the source   *Lover's Tale i* 783
   and the full moon stares at the *s*.   *Rizpah* 4
   the wind and the shower and the *s*.   „ 68
   The *s* and the sky so bright—   „ 83
   mountain was lilies in lieu of *s*,   *V. of Maeldune* 41
   kiss fell chill as a flake of *s* on the cheek :   *The Wreck* 32
   And cap our age with *s* ? '   *Ancient Sage* 98
   was as light as *s* an the lan',   *Tomorrow* 36
   hair was as white as the *s* an a grave.   „ 60
   high hill-passes of stainless *s*,   *Dead Prophet* 47
   blanching apricot like *s* in *s*.   *Prog. of Spring* 30
   I sat beneath a solitude of *s* ;   „ 71
   Where am I ? *s* on all the hills !   *Romney's R.* 12
   I have climb'd to the *s's* of Age,   *By an Evolution.* 17
Snow-cold   Over her *s-c* breast and angry cheek   *Œnone* 142
Snowdon   we that day had been Up *S* ;   *Golden Year* 4
Snowdrop   to live till the *s's* come again :   *May Queen, N. Y's. E.* 14
   To die before the *s* came,   „ *Con.* 4
   Or this first *s* of the year   *St. Agnes' Eve* 11
   the white Of the first *s's* inner leaves ;   *Princess v* 197
   The *s* only, flowering thro' the year,   *Last Tournament* 220
   Like *s's*, pure !   *Early Spring* 30
   Wavers on her thin stem the *s* cold   *Prog. of Spring* 3
Snow'd   A hundred winters *s* upon his breast,   *Palace of Art* 4
   Tore the king's letter, *s* it down,   *Princess i* 61
Snowflake   like a *s* in the hand,   *Lover's Tale iii* 38
Snowlike   Down to the least sparkle of a cloth   *Sisters (E. and E.)* 117
Snow-limb'd   the *s-l* Eve from whom she came.   *Maud I xviii* 28
Snowshoe   Claymore and *s*, toys in lava,   *Princess, Pro.* 18
Snow-white   The snowy peak and *s-w* cataract   *Œnone* 211
Snowy   Lying, robed in *s* white   *L. of Shalott iv* 19
   between The *s* peak and snow-white cataract   *Œnone* 211
   Slant down the *s* sward,   *St. Agnes' Eve* 6
   Fair gleams the *s* altar-cloth,   *Sir Galahad* 33
   Airing a *s* hand and signet gem,   *Princess i* 121
   And *s* summits old in story :   „ *iv* 2
   Would rock the *s* cradle till I died.   „ 104
   as flies A troop of *s* doves athwart the dusk,   „ 168
   Long lanes of splendour slanted o'er a press Of *s* shoulders,   „ 479
   And *s* dells in a golden air,   *The Daisy* 68
   And up the *s* Splugen drew,   „ 86
   And passion pure in *s* bloom   *In Mem. cix* 11
   made A *s* penthouse for his hollow eyes,   *Merlin and V.* 808

Snowy (*continued*)   one *s* knee was prest Against the margin
   flowers ;   *Tiresias* 42
Snowy-banded   The *s-b*, dilettante,   *Maud I viii* 10
Snubnosed   smooth-faced *s* rogue would leap from his
   counter   *i* 51
Snuff   An' 'is noäse sa grufted wi' *s*   *Village Wife* 39
Soäber (sober)   Thaw thou was es *s* es daäy,   *Spinster's S's.* 75
Soak   City children *s* and blacken   *Locksley H., Sixty* 218
Soak'd   Tho' *s* and saturate, out and out,   *Will Water.* 87
Soäk'd   Moother 'ed beän sa *s* wi' the thaw   *Owd Roä* 113
Soäkin   Guzzlin' an' *s* an' smoäkin'   *North. Cobbler* 24
Soaking (*See also* **Soäkin'**)   I *s* here in winter wet—   *To Ulysses* 6
Soar   she answered, ' Ay, And men to *s* : '   *Lover's Tale i* 305
   my wings That I may *s* the sky,   *Mechanophilus* 10
Soaring   from my vapour-girdle *s* forth   *Prog. of Spring* 79
Sob (s)   all at once the old man burst in *s's* :—   *Dora* 158
   shaken with her *s's*, Melissa knelt ;   *Princess iv* 289
   dark crowd moves, and there are *s's*   *Ode on Well.* 268
   her false voice made way, broken with *s's* :   *Merlin and V.* 857
   And bluster into stormy *s's* and say,   *Lancelot and E.* 1067
Sob (verb)   hear him *s* and sigh In the walks ;   *A spirit haunts* 5
   and to clamour, mourn and *s*,   *St. S. Stylites* 6
Sobb'd   for three hours he *s* o'er William's child   *Dora* 167
   And *s*, and you *s* with it,   *Princess ii* 273
   he *s* and he wept, And cursed himself ;   *Bandit's Death* 29
Sobbing   See, there is one of us *s*,   *Maud II v* 30
   A voice clung *s* till he question'd it,   *Last Tournament* 759
   Set up an answer, *s*, ' I am thy fool,   „ 761
Sober (*See also* **Soäber**)   Nothing to mar the *s* majesties
   Of settled,   *Lucretius* 217
   That *s* freedom out of which there springs   *Ode on Well.* 164
   A *s* man, among his boys,   *In Mem. liii* 2
   ' A *s* man is Percivale and pure ;   *Merlin and V.* 755
   Envy wears the mask of Love, and, laughing
   s fact to scorn,   *Locksley H., Sixty* 109
   I heard the *s* rook And carrion crow cry   *The Ring* 173
Soberer-hued   Autumn-changed, *S-h* Gold again.   *The Oak* 9
Sober-suited   That *s-s* Freedom chose,   *You ask me, why, etc.* 6
Social   Cursed be the *s* wants that sin against the
   strength of youth !   *Locksley Hall* 59
   Cursed be the *s* lies that warp us from the living
   truth !   „ 60
   To pass with all our *s* ties   *Day-Dm., L'Envoi* 5
   ' Have patience,' I replied, ' ourselves are full
   Of *s* wrong ;   *Princess, Con.* 73
   For ' ground in yonder *s* mill We rub each other's
   angles down,   *In Mem. lxxxix* 39
   and join'd Each office of the *s* hour   „ *cxi* 14
   Proclaiming *s* truth shall spread,   „ *cxxvii* 5
Society   *See* **She-society**
Socratic   Or threaded some *S* dream ;   *In Mem. lxxxix* 36
Sod   The blackness round the tombing *s*,   *On a Mourner* 27
   mouldering with the dull earth's mouldering *s*,   *Palace of Art* 261
   To rest beneath the clover *s*,   *In Mem. x* 13
   after *s* and shingle ceased to fly Behind her,   *Gareth and L.* 761
   And over hard and soft, striking the *s*   *Pelleas and E.* 498
   nor the *s* Draw from my death Thy living flower   *Doubt and Prayer* 5
Sodden   Men, women, on their *s* faces,   *Last Tournament* 474
Sofa   And broider'd *s's* on each side :   *Arabian Nights* 19
   Who ' sitting on green *s's* contemplate   *Akbar's Dream* 48
Soft   (*See also* **Silk-soft**)   as in sleep I sank In cool *s*
   turf upon the bank,   *Arabian Nights* 96
   S are the moss-beds under the sea ;   *The Merman* 39
   things that are forked, and horned, and *s*,   *The Mermaid* 53
   A single stream of all her *s* brown häir Pour'd on
   one side :   *Gardener's D.* 128
   The *s* wind blowing over meadowy holms   *Edwin Morris* 95
   thro' *s* degrees Subdue them to the useful and the good.   *Ulysses* 32
   A *s* air fans the cloud apart ;   *Tithonus* 32
   S lustre bathes the range of urns On every
   slanting terrace-lawn.   *Day-Dm., Sleep. P.* 9
   S fruitage, mighty nuts, and nourishing roots ;   *Enoch Arden* 555
   half-embraced the basket cradle-head With one *s* arm,   *Sea Dreams* 290
   saw The *s* white vapour streak the crowned towers   *Princess iii* 344
   and so Laid the *s* babe in his hard-mailed hands.   „ *vi* 208

Soft (continued) Say one *s* word and let me part forgiven.' *Princess vi* 219
The *s* and milky rabble of womankind,   " 309
glow Of your *s* splendours that you look so bright ? *Maud I xviii* 79
massacring Man, woman, lad and girl—yea, the *s* babe ! *Gareth and L.* 1341
And over hard and *s*, striking the sod From out the *s*, the spark from off the hard, *Pelleas and E.* 498
And thine is more to me—*s*, gracious, kind— *Last Tournament* 560
one *s* lap Pillow'd us both : *Lover's Tale i* 235
As rain of the midsummer midnight *s*,   " 722
s winds, Laden with thistledown and seeds of flowers,   " *ii* 12
Ah—you, that have lived so *s*, *Rizpah* 17
Hallus a *s* un Squire ! an' 'e smiled, *Village Wife* 89
About the *s* Mediterranean shores, *Sir J. Oldcastle* 30
Tha thowt tha would marry ma, did tha ? but that wur a bit ower *s*, *Spinster's S's.* 74
She turn'd, and in her *s* imperial way *The Ring* 267
Soften And *s* as if to a girl, *Maud I x* 16
Steel me with patience ! *s* me with grief ! *Doubt and Prayer* 9
Soften'd but robed in *s* light Of orient state. *Ode to Memory* 10
whom waitest thou With thy *s*, shadow'd brow, *Adeline* 46
Like *s* airs that blowing steal, *Two Voices* 406
and the brazen fool Was *s*, *In Mem. cx* 12
Softening *S* thro' all the gentle attributes *Aylmer's Field* 730
Softer *S* than sleep—all things in order *Palace of Art* 87
' who could think The *s* Adams of your Academe, *Princess ii* 197
and *s* all her shape And rounder seem'd :   " *vii* 136
When the far-off sail is blown by the breeze of a *s* clime, *Maud I iv* 4
Softly-shadow'd Glows forth each *s-s* arm *Day-Dm., Sleep. B.* 13
Softness *S* breeding scorn of simple life, *To the Queen ii* 53
Soil (s) Fast-rooted in the fruitful *s*. *Lotos-Eaters, C. S.* 38
ill-used race of men that cleave the *s*,   " 120
That numbers forty cubits from the *s*. *St. S. Stylites* 91
Upon my proper patch of *s* *Amphion* 99
Know you no song, the true growth of your *s*, *Princess iv* 150
Has risen and cleft the *s*,   " *vi* 35
The *s*, left barren, scarce had grown *In Mem. liii* 7
three were clad like tillers of the *s*. *Gareth and L.* 181
Gareth, ' We be tillers of the *s*,   " 242
Soil (verb) evil thought may *s* thy children's blood ; *Ancient Sage* 275
Soil'd When, *s* with noble dust, he hears *Two Voices* 152
As these white robes are *s* and dark, *St. Agnes' Eve* 13
And *s* with all ignoble use. *In Mem. cxi* 24
Soiling *s* another, Annie, will never make *Grandmother* 36
Soilure fearing rust or *s* fashion'd for it *Lancelot and E.* 7
'**Soize** (assize) Noäks wur 'ang'd for it oop at 's— *N. Farmer, O. S.* 36
Solace (s) Vain *s* ! Memory standing near *To J. S.* 53
Nay, but Nature brings thee *s* ; *Locksley Hall* 87
A doubtful gleam of *s* lives. *In Mem. xxxviii* 8
And in that *s* can I sing,   " *lxv* 5
From his great hoard of happiness distill'd Some drops of *s* ; *Lover's Tale i* 715
S at least—before he left his home.   " *iv* 7
In his own well, draw *s* as he may. *Tiresias* 89
Nay, you were my one *s* ; *The Ring* 310
Were tender *s*. Yet be comforted ; *D. of the Duke of C.* 7
Solace (verb) A little hint to *s* woe, *Two Voices* 433
Solaced Whom Averill *s* as he might, *Aylmer's Field* 343
Sold (See also **Sowd**) Himself unto himself he *s*, *A Character* 26
Nor *s* his heart to idle moans, *Two Voices* 221
he's abroad : the place is to be *s*. *Walk. to the Mail* 16
S him unto shame. *The Captain* 60
s her wares for less Than what she gave in buying what she *s* : *Enoch Arden* 255
The horse he drove, the boat he *s*,   " 609
' That was the four-year-old I *s* the Squire.' *The Brook* 137
Where our Caucasians let themselves be *s*. *Aylmer's Field* 349
never the truth to serve the hour, *Ode on Well.* 179
chalk and alum and plaster are *s* to the poor for bread, *Maud I i* 39
being *s* and *s* had bought them bread : *Marr. of Geraint* 641
S the crown-farms for all but nothing, *Columbus* 132
nearing his own hundred, *s* This ring to me, *The Ring* 194
Soldan he, the fierce *S* of Egypt, *Columbus* 98
Soldier (adj.) No more in *s* fashion will he greet *Ode on Well.* 21

Soldier (s) (See also **Patriot-soldier, Woman-soldier**)
The Roman *s* found Me lying dead, *D. of F. Women* 161
men like *s*'s may not quit the post *Lucretius* 148
nor broke, nor shunn'd a *s*'s death, *Princess, Pro.* 38
Pitiful sight, wrapp'd in a *s*'s cloak,   " *v* 56
The *s* ? No : What dares not Ida do that she should prize The *s* ?   " 173
not shunn'd the death, No, not the *s*'s :   " 179
one loves the *s*, one The silken priest   " 183
The king is scared, the *s* will not fight,   " *Con.* 60
banner and with music, with *s* and with priest, *Ode on Well.* 81
To thee the greatest *s* comes ;   " 88
So great a *s* taught us there,   " 131
And keep the *s* firm, the statesman pure :   " 222
the *s* knew Some one had blunder'd : *Light Brigade* 11
were the *s*'s wont to hear His voice in battle, *Geraint and E.* 174
The King should have made him a *s*, *Rizpah* 28
Thousands of their *s*'s look'd down *The Revenge* 37
that brave *s*, down the terrible ridge *Sisters (E. and E.)* 63
they shall know we are *s*'s and men ! *Def. of Lucknow* 41
to be *s* all day and be sentinel all thro' the night—   " 74
Were *s*'s to her heart's desire, *Pro. to Gen. Hamley* 25
My *s* of the Cross ? it is he and he indeed ! *Happy* 12
we saw your *s*'s crossing the ridge, *Bandit's Death* 21
Soldier-brother *S-b*'s bridal orange-bloom *Ded. Poem Prin. Alice* 11
Soldier-city led Threading the *s-c*, *Princess v* 7
Soldier-laddie violin Struck up with *S-l*,   " *Pro.* 86
Soldierlike anger-charm'd from sorrow, *s*, *Aylmer's Field* 728
Soldierly His own, tho' keen and bold and *s*   " 192
Soldier-priest A latter Luther, and a *s-p* *To "J. M. K.* 2
Soldiership mind, So quick, so capable in *s*, *Sir J. Oldcastle* 75
Sole (adj.) *S* star of all that place and time, *Arabian Nights* 152
Thy *s* delight is, sitting still, *The Blackbird* 10
S star of phosphorescence in the calm, *Audley Court* 87
The *s* succeeder to their wealth, their lands, *Aylmer's Field* 294
you the *s* men to be mingled with our cause, *Princess v* 411
The *s* men we shall prize in the aftertime,   " 412
S comfort of my dark hour, when a world   " *vi* 194
Nor Britain's one *s* God be the millionaire : *Maud III vi* 22
And since he kept his mind on one *s* aim, *Merlin and V.* 626
To seat you *s* upon my pedestal Of worship—   " 878
S Queen of Beauty and of love, *Last Tournament* 208
his one true knight—*S* follower of the vows '—   " 303
And I stood *s* beside the vacant bier. *Lover's Tale iii* 58
My *s* memorial Of Edith—no, the other,— *Sisters (E. and E.)* 107
Sole (s) (See also **Baby-sole**) From scalp to *s* one slough and crust *St. S. Stylites* 2
Solecism Chimeras, crotchets, Christmas *s*'s, *Princess, Pro.* 203
Solemn (See also **Mock-solemn**) But the *s* oak-tree sigheth, *Claribel* 4
the *s* palms were ranged Above, *Arabian Nights* 79
Yet not the less held she her *s* mirth, *Palace of Art* 215
and grief became A *s* scorn of ills. *D. of F. Women* 228
With *s* gibe did Eustace banter me *Gardener's D.* 168
And hear me swear a *s* oath, *Talking Oak* 281
And *s* chaunts resound between. *Sir Galahad* 36
Heroic, for a hero lies beneath, Grave, *s* !' *Princess, Pro.* 213
At last a *s* grace Concluded,   " *ii* 452
Of *s* psalms, and silver litanies,   " 477
'Sdeath—and with *s* rites by candle-light—   " *v* 292
And drove us, last, to quite a *s* close—   " *Con.* 17
Too comic for the *s* things they are, Too *s* for the comic touches in them,   " 67
For such a wise humility As befits a *s* fane : *Ode on Well.* 250
A *s* gladness even crown'd The purple brows of Olivet. *In Mem. xxxi* 11
O *s* ghost, O crowned soul !   " *lxxxv* 36
And hold it *s* to the past.   " *cv* 16
And I will make a *s* offering of you *Lover's Tale iv* 118
And Julian made a *s* feast :   " 187
Well then—our *s* feast—we ate and drank,   " 221
decked them out As for a *s* sacrifice of love—   " 301
FIRST pledge our Queen this *s* night, *Hands all Round* 1
Solemnity watching here At this, our great *s*. *Ode on Well.* 244
And Lancelot's, at this night's *s* *Last Tournament* 223
Solemnly And *s* as when ye sware to him,   " 647
Solent Harry went over the *S* to see if work *First Quarrel* 44

Y

Son (*continued*)   for I have loved you more as *s* Than

brother,	*Aylmer's Field* 351
Born of a village girl, carpenter's *s*,	„ 668
but some, *S*'s of the glebe, with other frowns	„ 723
visiting the *s*,—the *s* A Walter too,—	*Princess, Pro.* 7
Slew both his *s*'s: and I, shall I,	„ ii 288
she that has a *s* And sees him err:	„ iii 260
And here he keeps me hostage for his *s*.'	„ iv 405
' You have our *s* : touch not a hair of his head :	„ 407
unless you send us back Our *s*, on the instant,	„ 416
We did but keep you surety for our *s*,	„ v 25
then took the king His three broad *s*'s ;	„ 269
dabbled with the blood Of his own *s*,	„ vi 105
were half fool'd to let you tend our *s*,	„ 274
O sire, Grant me your *s*, to nurse,	„ 298
Against the *s*'s of men, and barbarous laws.	„ vii 234
' nor blame Too much the *s*'s of men and barbarous laws ;	„ 256
The Tory member's elder *s*,	„ *Con.* 50
thanks to the Giver, England, for thy *s*.	*Ode on Well.* 45
For this is England's greatest *s*,	„ 95
What England was, shall her true *s*'s forget?	*Third of Feb.* 44
S of him with whom we strove for power—	*W. to Marie Alex.* 1
Gone for a minute, my *s*,	*Grandmother* 103
They have taken our *s*,	*The Victim* 49
We have his dearest, His only *s*!'	„ 64
Strong *S* of God, immortal Love,	*In Mem., Pro.* 1
Who pledgest now thy gallant *s* ;	„ vi 10
Dear as the mother to thy *s*,	„ ix 19
All knowledge that the *s*'s of flesh	„ lxxxv 27
Yea, tho' their *s*'s were none of these,	„ xc 17
Shaking her head at her *s* and sighing	*Maud* I xix 24
Who dares foreshadow for an only *s*	*Ded. of Idylls* 29
Or how should England dreaming of *his s*'s	„ 31
The love of all Thy *s*'s encompass Thee,	„ 52
Who cried, ' He is not Uther's *s* '—	*Com. of Arthur* 43
who hath proven him King Uther's *s*?	„ 70
This is the *s* of Gorloïs, not the King,	„ 73
This is the *s* of Anton, not the King.'	„ 74
daughter saving to a king, And a king's *s*?'—	„ 144
Hold ye this Arthur for King Uther's *s*?'	„ 172
—but a *s* she had not borne.	„ 192
s of Gorloïs he, Or else the child of Anton,	„ 232
Or born the *s* of Gorloïs, after death, Or Uther's *s*,	
and born before his time,	„ 240
Gawain and young Modred, her two *s*'s,	„ 244
and sign'd To those two *s*'s to pass,	„ 319
No *s* of Uther, and no king of ours ;'	„ 440
The last tall *s* of Lot and Bellicent,	*Gareth and L.* 1
' True love, sweet *s*, had risk'd himself	„ 60
Stay, my best *s*! ye are yet more boy than man.'	„ 98
' Sweet *s*, for there be many who deem him not,	„ 121
lifted but a little. Stay, sweet *s*.'	„ 131
Found her *s*'s will unwaveringly one,	„ 141
when her *s* Beheld his only way to glory	„ 158
Thy *s* am I, And since thou art my mother,	„ 166
saying, ' Who be ye, my *s*'s?'	„ 241
' *S*, I have seen the good ship sail Keel upward,	„ 253
And Fairy Queens have built the city, *s* ;	„ 259
as thou sayest, it is enchanted, *s*,	„ 263
my husband's brother had my *s* Thrall'd in his castle,	„ 357
thou that slewest the sire hast left the *s*.	„ 360
Kill the foul thief, and wreak me for my *s*.'	„ 363
Arms for her *s*, and loosed him from his vow.	„ 530
' *S*, the good mother let me know thee here,	„ 550
lay Among the ashes and wedded the King's *s*.'	„ 904
s Of old King Lot and good Queen Bellicent,	„ 1230
' Whither, fair *s* ?' to whom Geraint replied,	*Marr. of Geraint* 298
Rest! the good house, tho' ruin'd, O my *s*,	„ 378
be not wroth or grieved At thy new *s*,	„ 780
Know well that Envy calls you Devil's *s*,	*Merlin and V.* 467
And then did Envy call me Devil's *s*:	„ 497
(As *s*'s of kings loving in pupilage	„ 517
With two strong *s*'s, Sir Torre and Sir Lavaine,	*Lancelot and E.* 174
Hurt in his first tilt with my *s*,	„ 196
But I, my *s*'s and little daughter fled	„ 276

Son (*continued*)   furthermore Our *s* is with him ;

	Lancelot and E. 636
s's Born to the glory of thy name and fame,	„ 1371
' Thou art fair, my child, As a king's,'	„ 1410
but some Call'd him a *s* of Lancelot,	*Holy Grail* 144
' O *s*, thou hast not true humility.	„ 445
seem'd Shoutings of all the *s*'s of God:	„ 509
Who call'd him the false *s* of Gorloïs:	*Guinevere* 288
strike against the man they call My sister's *s*—	„ 573
Are loyal to their own far *s*'s,	*To the Queen* ii 28
And grovel and grope for my *s*	*Rizpah* 8
I'll none of it, said my *s*.	„ 32
know you worthy everyway To be my *s*,	*Sisters (E. and E.)* 49
my good *s*—Is yet untouch'd:	„ 287
but 'e leäved it to Charlie 'is *s*,	*Village Wife* 42
An' 'e calls fur 'is *s*,	„ 62
But Squire wur afear'd o' 'is *s*,	„ 63
Sa feyther an' *s* was buried together,	„ 90
the fourth Was like the *S* of God!	*Sir J. Oldcastle* 176
we, We and our *s*'s for ever.	*Columbus* 29
was it otherwise With thine own *S* ?'	„ 154
Stay, my *s* Is here anon: my *s*	„ 218
To younger England in the boy my *s*.	*To Victor Hugo* 14
S's of Edward with hammer'd brands.	*Batt. of Brunanburh* 14
Leaving his *s* too Lost in the carnage,	„ 72
my *s*, who dipt In some forgotten book	*To E. Fitzgerald* 46
My *s*, the Gods, despite of human prayer,	*Tiresias* 9
fathers call'd The Gods own *s*.	„ 17
S, in the hidden world of sight,	„ 51
My *s*, No sound is breathed so potent to coerce,	„ 119
Thither, my *s*, and there Thou,	„ 163
the *s*'s of a winterless day.	*The Wreck* 74
one *s* had forged on his father and fled,	*Despair* 69
but, *s*, the source is higher,	*Ancient Sage* 10
I am wearied of our city, *s*,	„ 15
To me, my *s*, more mystic than myself,	„ 45
Thou canst not prove the Nameless, O my *s*,	„ 57
nay my *s*, Thou canst not prove that I,	„ 63
But some in yonder city hold, my *s*,	„ 82
The wife, the *s*'s, who love him best	„ 125
My *s*, the world is dark with griefs and graves,	„ 171
If utter darkness closed the day, my *s*—	„ 199
more, my *s*! for more than once when I Sat all alone,	„ 229
such counter-terms, my *s*, Are border-races,	„ 250
Gone your sailor *s* thy father,	*Locksley H., Sixty* 55
S's of God, and kings of men	„ 122
To all our noble *s*'s, the strong New England	*Hands all Round* 15
S's and brothers that have sent,	*Open I. and C. Exhib.* 3
The mother featured in the *s* ;	„ 12
Britain fought her *s*'s of yore—	„ 21
' *S*'s, be welded each and all,	„ 36
why The *s*'s before the fathers die,	*To Marq. of Dufferin* 47
summun 'ed hax'd fur a *s*, an' 'e promised a *s*	*Owd Roä* 95
i' saävin' a *s* fur me.	„ 96
Tell my *s*—O let me lean my head upon your breast.	*Romney's R.* 153
Dying in childbirth of dead *s*'s.	*Akbar's Dream* 12
heart is for my *s*, Saleem, mine heir,—	„ 171
watch'd my *s*, And those that follow'd,	„ 187
In a while I bore him a *s*,	*Bandit's Death* 15
Glared on at the murder'd *s*,	„ 33
Our *s*'s will shame our own ;	*Mechanophilus* 22

Song (*See* e*also* **Battle-song, Death-song, Drinking-song, Love-song, Matin-song, War-song**) Take, Madam,

this poor book of *s* ;	*To the Queen* 17
Her *s* the lintwhite swelleth,	*Claribel* 15
And it sings a *s* of undying love ;	*Poet's Mind* 33
Were flooded over with eddying *s*.	*Dying Swan* 42
What *s*'s below the waning stars	*Margaret* 33
Hear a *s* that echoes cheerly	*L. of Shalott* i 30
They heard her singing her last *s*,	„ iv 26
Singing in her *s* she died,	„ 35
The woods were fill'd so full with *s*,	*Two Voices* 455
sleep was broken thro' By some wild skylark's matin *s*.	*Miller's D.* 40
The phantom of a silent *s*,	„ 71
Ah, well—but sing the foolish *s* I gave you,	„ 161
So sing that other *s* I made,	„ 199

Songless (continued) She hears the lark within the *s* egg, *Ancient Sage* 76

Songster Catullus, whose dead *s* never dies ; *Poets and their B.* 8

Sonorous Echoing all night to that *s* flow *Palace of Art* 27

Soon There will come a witness *s* *Forlorn* 25
Will it ever ? late or *s* ? *Locksley H., Sixty* 173

Soon (sun) ' Cast awaäy on a disolut land wi' a vartical *s* ! ' *North. Cobbler* 3

Soonday (Sunday) I gits the plaäte fuller o' *S's* *Church-warden, etc.* 40

Sooner I'd *s* fold an icy corpse dead *The Flight* 54

Soort (sort) Naw *s* o' koind o' use to saäy the things like fur to hev soom *s* of a sarvice reäd. *N. Farmer, O. S.* 6
Owd Roä 12

Soofläke (The *s* of so many a summer still *Sea Dreams* 35

Sooth Good *s* ! I hold He scarce is knight, *Gareth and L.* 1175
' for in *s* These ancient books— *Holy Grail* 540
Or was there *s* in Arthur's prophecy, ,, 709

Soothe How *should* I *s* you anyway, *To J. S.* 58
S him with thy finer fancies, *Locksley Hall* 54
One spiritual doubt she did not *s* ? *Aylmer's Field* 704
O for thy voice to *s* and bless ! *In Mem. lvi* 26
And, influence-rich to *s* and save, ,, *lxxx* 15
hurt Whom she would *s*, *Guinevere* 355

Soothed This fiat somewhat *s* himself *Aylmer's Field* 26
underwent The *s* yoke of kitchen-vassalage ; *Gareth and L.* 479

Sooty Low-cowering shall the *S* sit ; *Clear-headed friend* 10
Dark-brow'd *s*, come not anear ; *Poet's Mind* 8

Sophist That every *s* can lime. *Love thou thy land* 12

Sophister Some *s*, whom a far-off grandsire burnt *Princess i* 6

Sorcerer I have no *s's* malison on me, ,, *ii* 410
I remember'd that burnt *s's* curse ,, *v* 475

Sorcery drave the heathen hence by *s* And Merlin's glamour.' *Gareth and L.* 204
Whom thou by *s* or unhappiness Or some device, ,, 997
Device and *s* and unhappiness— ,, 1235

Sordid Love, that endures not *s* ends, *Love thou thy land* 6
Till I well could weep for a time so *s* and mean, *Maud I v* 17
There a single *s* attic holds the living and the dead. *Locksley H., Sixty* 222

Sore (adj.) (See also **Foot-sore**) Plagued her with *s* despair. *Palace of Art* 224
S task to hearts worn out by many wars *Lotos-Eaters, C. S.* 86

Sore (s) old *s* breaks out from age to age *Walk. to the Mail* 79

Sorrow (s) waste place with joy Hidden in *s* : *Dying Swan* 23
delight Of dainty *s* without sound, *Margaret* 18
Your *s*, only *s's* shade, Keeps real *s* far away. ,, 43
Rise from the feast of *s*, lady, ,, 62
' Whatever crazy *s* saith, *Two Voices* 394
her heart would beat against me, In *s* and in rest : *Miller's D.* 178
they had their part Of *s* : ,, 224
build up all My *s* with my song, *Œnone* 40
Still from one *s* to another thrown : *Lotos-Eaters, C. S.* 18
The star-like *s's* of immortal eyes, *D. of F. Women* 91
Stole from her sister *S*. *Gardener's D.* 256
this high dial, which my *s* crowns— *St. S. Stylites* 95
a *s's* crown of *s* is remembering *Locksley Hall* 76
When you came in my *s* broke me down ; *Enoch Arden* 317
Had you one *s* and she shared it not ? *Aylmer's Field* 702
Sat anger-charm'd from *s*, soldier-like, ,, 728
Their own gray hairs with *s* to the grave— ,, 777
Her crampt-up *s* pain'd her, ,, 800
Nor sound of human *s* mounts to mar *Lucretius* 109
And *s* darkens hamlet and hall. *Ode on Well.* 7
And makes it a *s* to be.' *The Islet* 36
O *S*, cruel fellowship, *In Mem. iii* 1
Or *s* such a changeling be ? ,, *xvi* 4
I brim with *s* drowning song. ,, *xix* 12
For private *s's* barren song, ,, *xxi* 14
Now, sometimes in my *s* shut, ,, *xxiii* 1
They bring me *s* touch'd with joy, ,, *xxviii* 19
But *S*—fixt upon the dead, ,, *xxxix* 8
If these brief lays, of *S* born, ,, *xlviii* 1
Ay me, the *s* deepens down, ,, *xlix* 14
O *S*, wilt thou live with me No casual mistress, ,, *lix* 1
O *S*, wilt thou rule my blood, ,, 5
O *s*, then can *s* wane ? ,, *lxxviii* 15
Delayest the *s* in my blood, ,, *lxxxiii* 14

Sorrow (s) (continued) trust in things above Be dimm'd of *s*, *In Mem. lxxxv* 10
take what fruit may be Of *s* under human skies : ,, *cviii* 14
'Tis held that *s* makes us wise, ,, 15
'Tis held that *s* makes us wise ; ,, *cxiii* 1
Yet less of *s* lives in me ,, *cxvi* 13
Would there be *s* for *me* ? *Maud I i* 57
But *s* seize me if ever that light ,, *iv* 12
and the *s* dimm'd her sight, *Lancelot and E.* 889
Comfort your *s's* ; for they do not flow *Guinevere* 188
weigh your *s's* with our lord the King's, ,, 191
Stay'd on the cloud of *s* ; *Lover's Tale i* 255
Smit with exceeding *s* unto Death. ,, 601
s of my spirit Was of so wide a compass ,, *ii* 134
chiefly to my *s* by the Church, *Columbus* 56
he heal'd me with *s* for evermore. *The Wreck* 58
the *s* that I bear is *s* for *his* sake. *The Flight* 64
Sorrowing with the *s's* of the lowest ! *On Jub. Q. Victoria* 27
From sin thro' *s* into Thee we pass *Doubt and Prayer* 3

Sorrow (verb) who most have cause to *s* for her— *Aylmer's Field* 678
And he should *s* o'er my state *In Mem. xiv* 15
I feel it, when I *s* most ; ,, *xxvii* 14
I *s* after The delight of early skies ; *Maud II iv* 24
In a wakeful doze I *s* For the hand, ,, 26

Sorrow'd those who *s* o'er a vanish'd race, *Aylmer's Field* 844
I felt it, when I *s* most, *In Mem. lxxxv* 2
Love mourn'd long, and *s* after Hope ; *Lover's Tale i* 819

Sorrowest O *s* thou, pale Painter, for the past, *Wan Sculptor* 3

Sorrowing after him Came Psyche, *s* for Aglaïa. *Princess vi* 29
Went *s* in a pause I dared not break ; ,, *vii* 249
s Lancelot should have stoop'd so low, *Lancelot and E.* 732
and *s* for our Lancelot, *Holy Grail* 648
And let the *s* crowd about it grow, *Ode on Well.* 16
And the sound of the *s* anthem roll'd ,, 60
S with the sorrows of the lowest ! *On Jub. Q. Victoria* 27

Sorry an' *s* when he was away, *First Quarrel* 11
I am *s* for all the quarrel an' *s* ,, 87

Sort (See also **Soort**) older *s*, and murmur'd that their May *Princess ii* 463
fused with female grace In such a *s*, *In Mem. cix* 18
' Ay, truly of a truth, And in a *s*, *Gareth and L.* 838

Sottin' ' *S* thy braäins Guzzlin' an' soäkin' *North. Cobbler* 23

Soudan Now somewhere dead far in the waste *S*, *Epit. on Gordon* 2

Soughing And the wavy swell of the *s* reeds, *Dying Swan* 38

Sought Still moving after truth long *s*, *Two Voices* 62
You *s* to prove how I could love, *L. C. V. de Vere* 21
I *s* to strike Into that wondrous track *D. of F. Women* 278
That *s* to sow themselves like winged seeds, *Gardener's D.* 65
She *s* her lord, and found him, *Godiva* 16
s and found a witch Who brew'd the philtre *Lucretius* 15
I *s* but peace ; No critic I— *Princess i* 144
grace Concluded, and we *s* the gardens : ,, *ii* 453
some hid and *s* In the orange thickets : ,, 459
twice I *s* to plead my cause, ,, *iv* 552
and I—I *s* for one—All people said she had authority— ,, *vi* 552
s far less for truth than power In knowledge : ,, *vii* 236
one that *s* but Duty's iron crown *Ode on Well.* 122
whereon he *s* The King alone, and found, *Gareth and L.* 540
when they *s* and found, Sir Gareth drank and ate, ,, 1279
though they *s* Thro' all the provinces *Marr. of Geraint* 729
after, when we *s* The tribute, answer'd *Balin and Balan* 115
And Arthur, when Sir Balin *s* him, said ,, 198
King, who *s* to win my love Thro' evil ways : ,, 474
a wanton damsel came, And *s* for Garlon at the castle-gates, ,, 610
And Vivien ever *s* to work the charm *Merlin and V.* 215
What other ? for men *s* to prove me vile, ,, 495
darkness falling, *s* A priory not far off, *Pelleas and E.* 213
s To make disruption in the Table Round *Guinevere* 16
nor *s*, Wrapt in her grief, for housel ,, 148
At last she *s* out Memory, and they trod *Lover's Tale i* 820
Chiefly I *s* the cavern and the hill ,, *ii* 33
Hath *s* the tribute of a verse from me, *To Dante* 5
at home if I *s* for a kindly caress, *The Wreck* 31
The Count who *s* to snap the bond *Happy* 61

Soul (continued)   That strike across the _s_ in prayer,   _Lover's Tale_ i 364
my life, love, _s_, spirit, and heart and strength.   "   460
And _s_ and heart and body are all at ease :   "   556
Come like an angel to a damned _s_,   "   673
Memory fed the _s_ of Love with tears.   "   822
a strong sympathy Shook all my _s_: "   ii 89
all at once, _s_, life And breath and motion,   "   194
This love is of the brain, the mind, the _s_: "   iv 156
' body and _s_ And life and limbs,   "   282
but to save _my_ s, that is all your desire : Do you think
  I care for _my_ s   _Rizpah_ 77
face was flash'd thro' sense and _s_   _Sisters_ (E. and E.) 109
—wrought us harm, Poor _s_, not knowing)   "   185
a thousand lives To save his _s_.   _Sir J. Oldcastle_ 64
How now, my _s_, we do not heed the fire ?   "   191
' O _s_ of little faith, slow to believe !   _Columbus_ 147
who seest the _s_'s in Hell And purgatory,   "   216
Shamed in their _s_'s.   _Batt. of Brunanburh_ 99
make my life one prayer for a _s_ that died in his sin,   _The Wreck_ 10
for Mother, the voice was the voice of the _s_ ;   "   54
the sun of the _s_ made day in the dark   "   55
a huge sea smote every _s_ from the decks   "   109
No _s_ in the heaven above, no _s_ on the earth below,   _Despair_ 19
Come from the brute, poor _s_'s—no _s_'s—   "   36
if the _s_'s of men were immortal,   "   99
thou sendest thy free _s_ thro' heaven,   _Ancient Sage_ 47
daughter yield her life, heart, _s_ to one—   _The Flight_ 28
She bad us love, like _s_'s in Heaven,   "   88
shadow of Himself, the boundless, thro' the
  human _s_ ;   _Locksley H., Sixty_ 211
_s_ and sense in city slime ?   "   218
Worthier _s_ was he than I am,   "   239
count them all My friends and brother _s_'s,   _Epilogue_ 19
And showing them, _s_'s have wings !   _Dead Prophet_ 12
As a lord of the Human _s_,   "   54
While yet thy fresh and virgin _s_   _Freedom_ 2
Till every _S_ be free ;   "   20
One with Britain, heart and _s_ !   _Open. I. and C. Exhib._ 38
A _s_ that, watch'd from earliest youth,   _To Marq. of Dufferin_ 25
And _s_'s of men, who grew beyond their race,   _Demeter and P._ 140
cotch'd 'er death o' cowd that night, poor _s_, i' the straw.   _Owd Roä_ 114
and you the _s_ of Truth In Hubert ?   _The Ring_ 62
' The _s_'s Of two repentant Lovers guard the ring ; '   "   197
wall of solid flesh that comes between your _s_ and mine,   _Happy_ 35
_s_ in _s_ and light in light,   "   39
So wed thee with my _s_, that I may mark   _Prog. of Spring_ 92
Lord let the house of a brute to the _s_ of a man,   _By an Evolution._ 1
my _s_ uncertain, or a fable,   "   5
Hold the sceptre, Human _S_,   "   16
prize that _s_ where man and woman meet,   _On One who Eff. E. M._ 2
thoughts that lift the _s_ of men,   _To Master of B._ 14
And bravest _s_ for counsellor and friend.   _Akbar's Dream_ 69
guess at the love of a _s_ for a _s_ ?   _Charity_ 30
passing _s_'s thro' fire to the fire,   _The Dawn_ 4
bodies and _s_'s go down in a common wreck,   "   13
Men, with a heart and a _s_,   "   18

Soul-stricken   _S_-s at their kindness to him,   _Aylmer's Field_ 525
Sound (adj.)   So healthy, _s_, and clear and whole,   _Miller's D._ 15
What ails us, who are _s_,   _Walk. to the Mail_ 105
But, blind or lame or sick or _s_,   _The Voyage_ 93
Looks only for a moment whole and _s_ ;   _Aylmer's Field_ 2
let your sleep for this one night be _s_ :   _Sea Dreams_ 315
If that hypothesis of theirs be _s_'   _Princess_ iv 20
felt it _s_ and whole from head to foot,   "   vi 211
Or, if we held the doctrine _s_   _In Mem._ liii 9
How pure at heart and _s_ in head,   "   xciv 1
' _S_ sleep be thine ! _s_ cause to sleep hast thou.   _Gareth and L._ 1282
Worthier soul was he than I am, _s_ and honest,   _Locksley H., Sixty_ 239
Sound (s)   the _s_ Which to the wooing wind aloof   _Mariana_ 74
Full of the city's stilly _s_,   _Arabian Nights_ 103
no more of mirth Is here or merry-making _s_.   _Deserted House_ 14
Springing alone With a shrill inner _s_,   _The Mermaid_ 20
Of dainty sorrow without _s_,   _Margaret_ 18
With dinning _s_ my ears are rife,   _Eleänore_ 135
Died the _s_ of royal cheer ;   _L. of Shalott_ iv 48

Sound (s) (continued)   There came a _s_ as of the sea ;   _Mariana in the S._ 8
I hear Dead _s_'s at night come from the inmost hills,   _Œnone_ 246
a _s_ Rings ever in her ears of armed men.   "   264
Moved of themselves, with silver _s_ ;   _Palace of Art_ 130
seem'd to hear the dully _s_ Of human footsteps fall.   "   275
or a _s_ Of rocks thrown down,   "   281
With _s_'s that echo still.   _D. of F. Women_ 8
I heard _s_'s of insult, shame, and wrong,   "   19
Not any song or bird or _s_ of rill ;   "   66
and fill'd with light The interval of _s_.   "   172
Hearing the holy organ rolling waves Of _s_   "   192
With that sharp _s_ the white dawn's creeping beams,   "   261
and tell o'er Each little _s_ and sight.   "   277
Parson, sent to sleep with _s_, And waked with silence,   _M. d'Arthur, Ep._ 3
That with the _s_ I woke, and heard   "   30
In _s_ of funeral or of marriage bells ;   _Gardener's D._ 36
hour just flown, that morn with all its _s_,   "   83
Delighted with the freshness and the _s_.   _Edwin Morris_ 99
with _s_ Of pious hymns and psalms,   _St. S. Stylites_ 33
' I took the swarming _s_ of life—   _Talking Oak_ 213
south-breeze around thee blow The _s_ of minster bells.   "   272
and the winds are laid with _s_.   _Locksley Hall_ 104
And bade him cry, with _s_ of trumpet,   _Godiva_ 36
With twelve great shocks of _s_,   "   74
no _s_ is made, Not even of a gnat that sings.   _Day-Dm., Sleep. P._ 20
a _s_ Like sleepy counsel pleading ;   _Amphion_ 73
A gentle _s_, an awful light !   _Sir Galahad_ 41
How fresh was every sight and _s_   _The Voyage_ 5
By grassy capes with fuller _s_   _Sir L. and Q. G._ 14
There comes a _s_ of marriage bells.   _The Letters_ 48
Then methought I heard a mellow _s_,   _Vision of Sin_ 14
Ran into its giddiest whirl of _s_,   "   29
And the _s_ of a voice that is still !   _Break, break, etc._ 12
and find A sort of absolution in the _s_   _Sea Dreams_ 61
Nor of human sorrow mounts to mar   _Lucretius_ 109
melodious thunder to the _s_ Of solemn psalms,   _Princess_ ii 476
hundred doors To one deep chamber shut from _s_,   "   vi 376
That afternoon a _s_ arose of hoof And chariot,   "   379
and sweet is every _s_, Sweeter thy voice, but every _s_
  is sweet ;   "   vii 218
Let the _s_ of those he wrought for,   _Ode on Well._ 10
the _s_ of the sorrowing anthem roll'd   "   60
In that dread _s_ to the great name,   "   71
compass'd round with turbulent _s_,   _Will_ 7
_S_'s of the great sea Wander'd about.   _Minnie and Winnie_ 7
Phantom _s_ of blows descending,   _Boädicea_ 25
When was a harsher _s_ ever heard,   _Trans. of Homer_ 3
Calm is the morn without a _s_,   _In Mem._ xi 1
door Were shut between me and the _s_ :   "   xxviii 8
The streets were fill'd with joyful _s_,   "   xxxi 10
The _s_ of streams that swift or slow   "   xxxv 10
' The _s_ of that forgetful shore   "   14
And up thy vault with roaring _s_   "   lxxii 25
O _s_ to rout the brood of cares,   "   lxxxix 17
and growing upon me without a _s_,   _Maud_ I iii 7
I heard no _s_ where I stood But the rivulet   "   xiv 28
To the _s_ of dancing music and flutes :   "   II v 76
and the _s_ was good to Gareth's ear.   _Gareth and L._ 312
but heard instead A sudden _s_ of hoofs,   _Marr. of Geraint_ 164
the tender _s_ of his own voice And sweet self-pity,   _Geraint and E._ 348
_s_ of many a heavily-galloping hoof Smote on her ear,   "   447
Such a _s_ (for Arthur's knights Were hated strangers   _Balin and Balan_ 351
_s_ not wonted in a place so still Woke the sick
  knight,   _Lancelot and E._ 818
Lancelot knew the little clinking _s_ ;   "   983
And the strange _s_ of an adulterous race,   _Holy Grail_ 80
I heard a _s_ As of a silver horn from o'er the hills   "   108
slender _s_ As from a distance beyond distance grew   "   111
I heard the _s_, I saw the light,   "   280
heavens Were shaken with the motion and the _s_.   "   801
Suddenly waken'd with a _s_ of talk   _Pelleas and E._ 48
but a _s_ Of Gawain ever coming, and this lay—   "   395
' A _s_ is in his ears ' ?   _Last Tournament_ 116
_S_'s, as if some fair city were one voice   _Pass. of Arthur_ 460
we loved The _s_ of one-another's voices   _Lover's Tale_ i 256

Sound (s) (*continued*) great pine shook with lonely *s*'s of joy *Lover's Tale i* 325
So that they pass not to the shrine of *s*. „ 470
I too have heard a *s*— „ 522
Her words did of their meaning borrow *s*, „ 568
With such a *s* as when an iceberg splits „ 603
for the *s* Of that dear voice so musically low, „ 707
for the *s* Of the loud stream was pleasant, „ *ii* 34
All crisped *s*'s of wave and leaf and wind, „ 106
Like *s*'s without the twilight realm of dreams, „ 120
No *s* is breathed so potent to coerce, *Tiresias* 120
sweet *s* ran Thro' palace and cottage door, *Dead Prophet* 37
sympathies, how frail, In *s* and smell! *Early Spring* 36
one drear *s* I have not heard, *To Marq. of Dufferin* 40
A *s* of anger like a distant storm. *The Ring* 119
My people too were scared with eerie *s*'s, „ 408
all her realm Of *s* and smoke, *To Mary Boyle* 66
A *s* from far away, No louder than a bee *Romney's R.* 81
What *s* was dearest in his native dells? *Far—far—away* 4
THERE is a *s* of thunder afar, *Riflemen form!* 1
Be not deaf to the *s* that warns, „ 8
Too full for *s* and foam, *Crossing the Bar* 6
Sound (verb) the waterfall Which ever *s*'s and shines *Ode to Memory* 52
how thy name may *s* Will vex thee lying underground? *Two Voices* 110
The wind *s*'s like a silver wire, *Fatima* 29
S all night long, in falling thro' the dell, *D. of F. Women* 183
when you want me, *s* upon the bugle-horn, *Locksley Hall* 2
Like strangers' voices here they *s*, *In Mem. civ* 9
S on a dreadful trumpet, summoning her; *Geraint and E.* 383
rhythm *s* for ever of Imperial Rome— *To Virgil* 32
that would *s* so mean That all the dead, *Romney's R.* 131
S's happier than the merriest marriage-bell. *D. of the Duke of C.* 11
Sound (fathom) Two plummets dropt for one to *s* the abyss Of science. *Princess ii* 176
Sounded (*See also* **Far-sounded**) Then the voice Of Ida *s*, issuing ordinance: „ *vi* 373
from the castle a cry *S* across the court, *Balin and Balan* 400
The sudden trumpet *s* as in a dream *Last Tournament* 151
bound Not by the *s* letter of the word, *Sisters (E. and E.)* 162
thunder of the brook *S* 'Œnone'; *Death of Œnone* 24
Sounder Of *s* leaf than I can claim; *You might have won* 4
I have stumbled back again Into the common day, the *s* self. *Romney's R.* 33
Sounding (*See also* **Long-sounding, Ocean-sounding, Sea-sounding**) my merry comrades call me, *s* on the bugle-horn, *Locksley Hall* 145
Breathing and *s* beauteous battle, *Princess v* 161
The great city is wide; *Maud II iv* 64
Made answer, *s* like a distant horn. *Guinevere* 249
and shoutings and *s*'s to arms, *Def. of Lucknow* 76
The pillar'd dusk of *s* sycamores, *Audley Court* 16
and sitting well in order smite The *s* furrows; *Ulysses* 59
into the *s* hall I past; But nothing in the *s* hall I saw, *Holy Grail* 827
a little silver cloud Over the *s* seas: *Lover's Tale iii* 37
ear-stunning hail of Arês crash Along the *s* walls. *Tiresias* 97
while the golden lyre Is ever *s* in heroic ears „ 181
Well be grateful for the *s* watchword 'Evolution' here, *Locksley H., Sixty* 198
and alarms *S* 'To arms! to arms!' *Prog. of Spring* 104
S for ever and ever thro' Earth *Parnassus* 7
'*S* for ever and ever?' pass on! „ 15
Sour 'Slip-shod waiter, lank and *s*, *Vision of Sin* 71
A little grain of conscience made him *s*.' „ 218
Come, thou art crabb'd and *s*: *Last Tournament* 272
All out like a long life to a *s* end— „ 288
Source A teardrop trembled from its *s*, *Talking Oak* 161
Like torrents from a mountain *s* *The Letters* 39
Prayer from a living *s* within the will, *Enoch Arden* 801
The very *s* and fount of Day *In Mem. xxiv* 3
it melteth in the *s* Of these sad tears, *Lover's Tale i* 783
but, son, the *s* is higher, *Ancient Sage* 10
Soured she *s* To what she is: *Walk. to the Mail* 61
South by day and night, From North to *S*, *Rosalind* 48
Warmly and broadly the *s* winds are blowing *All Things will Die* 3
For look, the sunset, *s* and north, *Miller's D.* 241
Of that long desert to the *s*. *Fatima* 14

South (*continued*) Four courts I made, East, West and *S* and North, *Palace of Art* 21
The palms and temples of the *S*. *You ask me, why* 28
I was at school—a college in the *S*: *Walk. to the Mail* 83
Sailing under palmy highlands Far within the *S*. *The Captain* 24
As fast we fleeted to the *S*: *The Voyage* 4
Came murmurs of her beauty from the *S*, *Princess i* 36
That bright and fierce and fickle is the *S*, „ *iv* 97
Say to her, I do but wanton in the *S*, „ 109
And brief the moon of beauty in the *S*. „ 113
long breezes rapt from inmost *s* „ 431
My fancy fled to the *S* again. *The Daisy* 108
To North, *S*, East, and West; *Voice and the P.* 14
Thine the North and thine the *S* *Boädicea* 44
Down in the *s* is a flash and a groan: *Window, Gone.* 8
Rosy is the West, Rosy is the *S*, (repeat) *Maud I xvii* 6, 26
And looking to the *S*, and fed With honey'd rain „ *xviii* 20
All the west And ev'n unto the middle *s* *Lover's Tale i* 415
Who whilome spakest to the *S* in Greek *Sir J. Oldcastle* 29
'From the *S* I bring you balm, *Prog. of Spring* 66
Storm in the *S* that darkens the day! *Riflemen form!* 2
South-breeze The full *s-b* around thee blow *Talking Oak* 271
Southern The lavish growths of *s* Mexico. *Mine be the strength* 14
Would still be dear beyond the *s* hills: *Princess ii* 265
Between the Northern and the *S* morn.' „ *v* 423
In lands of palm and *s* pine; *The Daisy* 2
And reach the glow of *s* skies, *In Mem. xii* 10
New England of the *S* Pole! *Hands all Round* 16
So fair in *s* sunshine bathed, *Freedom* 5
Fair Spring slides hither o'er the *S* sea, *Prog. of Spring* 2
Southland meats and good red wine Of *S*, *Gareth and L.* 1191
South-sea-isle under worse than *S-s-i* taboo, *Princess* 278
Southward *S* they set their faces. *Gareth and L.* 182
South-west the *s-w* that blowing Bala lake *Geraint and E.* 929
South-western loud *S*'s, rolling ridge on ridge, *Gareth and L.* 1145
South-wind whisper of the *s-w* rushing warm, *Locksley Hall* 125
Sovereign These three alone lead life to *s* power. *Œnone* 145
Creation minted in the golden moods Of *s* artists; *Princess v* 195
Sovran THEY rose to where their *s* eagle sails, *Montenegro* 1
Sow (s) He had a *s*, sir. *Walk. to the Mail* 86
With hand and rope we haled the groaning *s*, „ 91
Large range of prospect had the mother *s*, „ 93
As never *s* was higher in this world— „ 96
all the swine were *s*'s; And all the dogs'— *Princess i* 192
Sow (verb) (*See also* **Saw**) He *s* himself on every wind. *Two Voices* 294
S the seed, and reap the harvest *Lotos-Eaters, C. S.* 121
sought to *s* themselves like winged seeds, *Gardener's D.* 65
and *s* The dust of continents to be; *In Mem. xxxv* 11
And *s* the sky with flying boughs, „ *lxxii* 24
Might *s* and reap in peace, *Epilogue* 13
Sowd (sold) why shouldn't thy boooks be *s*? *Village Wife* 69
Sow'd *S* all their mystic gulfs with fleeting stars; *Gardener's D.* 262
s her name and kept it green In living letters, *Aylmer's Field* 88
S it far and wide By every town and tower, *The Flower* 1
He *s* a slander in the common ear, *Marr. of Geraint* 450
Sow-droonk (very drunk) Soä *s-d* that tha doesn not touch thy 'at to the Squire;' *North. Cobbler* 25
Sowing *s* hedgerow texts and passing by, *Aylmer's Field* 171
Dispensing harvest, *s* the To-be, *Princess vii* 289
And *s* one ill hint from ear to ear, *Merlin and V.* 143
s the nettle on all the laurel'd graves of the Great; *Vastness* 22
Sowl (soul) 'Ud 'a shot his own *s* dead *Tomorrow* 40
Sown But, having *s* some generous seed, *Two Voices* 143
another wore A close-set robe of jasmine *s* with stars: *Aylmer's Field* 158
murmur'd, *s* With happy faces and with holiday. *Princess, Pro.* 55
Grew up from seed we two long since had *s*; „ *iv* 310
save the one true seed of freedom *s* *Ode on Well.* 162
S in a wrinkle of the monstrous hill, *Will* 19
That had the wild oat not been *s*, *In Mem. liii* 6
Among the dead and *s* upon the wind— *Merlin and V.* 45
Space (*See also* **Breathing-space**) Oh! narrow, narrow was the *s*, *Oriana* 46
Overlook a *s* of flowers, *L. of Shalott i* 16
But Lancelot mused a little *s*; „ *iv* 51

Space (*continued*)   all in *s*'s rosy-bright Large Hesper

glitter'd	*Mariana in the S.* 89
Free *s* for every human doubt,	*Two Voices* 137
In some fair *s* of sloping greens Lay,	*Palace of Art* 106
Hath time and *s* to work and spread.	*You ask me, why,* etc. 16
The ever-silent *s*'s of the East,	*Tithonus* 9
shall have scope and breathing *s*	*Locksley Hall* 167
Pure *s*'s clothed in living beams,	*Sir Galahad* 66
The *s* was narrow,— having order'd all	*Enoch Arden* 177
little *s* was left between the horns,	*Princess* iv 207
ask'd but *s* and fairplay for her scheme ;	,, v 282
leave her *s* to burgeon out of all Within her—	,, vii 271
Thro' all the silent *s*'s of the worlds,	,, *Con.* 114
The height, the *s*, the gloom,	*The Daisy* 59
starry heavens of *s* Are sharpen'd to a needle's end ;	*In Mem.* lxxvi 3
slowly breathing bare The round of *s*,	,, lxxxvi 5
And roll'd the floods in grander *s*,	,, ciii 26
And whispers to the worlds of *s*,	,, cxxvi 11
countercharm of *s* and hollow sky,	*Maud* I xviii 43
It is but for a little *s* I go :	,, 75
And after these King Arthur for a *s*,	*Com. of Arthur* 16
Arthur and his knighthood for a *s* Were all one will,	,, 515
And in the *s* to left of her, and right,	*Gareth and L.* 224
Gareth for so long a *s* Stared at the figures,	,, 231
some brief *s*, convey'd them on their way	,, 889
Then for a *s*, and under cloud that grew	,, 1358
Painted, who stare at open *s*,	*Geraint and E.* 268
Thence after tarrying for a *s* they rode,	,, 953
bode among them yet a little *s*	*Lancelot and E.* 921
the hind To whom a *s* of land is given to plow.	*Holy Grail* 907
But for a mile all round was open *s*,	*Pelleas and E.* 28
Then at Caerleon for a *s*—	,, 176
and either knight Drew back a *s*,	,, 573
Held for a *s* 'twixt cloud and wave,	*Lover's Tale* i 417
finite-infinite *s* In finite-infinite Time—	*De Prof., Two G.* 45
will be wheel'd thro' the silence of *s*,	*Despair* 83
triumphs over time and *s*,	*Locksley H., Sixty* 75
The man in *S* and Time,	*Epilogue* 49
s Of blank earth-baldness clothes itself afresh,	*Demeter and P.* 48
Fill out the *s*'s by the barren tiles.	*Prog. of Spring* 43

Spacious   A *s* garden full of flowering weeds,

	To ——, With Pal. of Art 4
'My *s* mansion built for me,	*Palace of Art* 234
The *s* times of great Elizabeth	*D. of F. Women* 7
And flowing odour of the *s* air,	*Lover's Tale* i 478

Spade   death while we stoop'd to the *s*,   *Def. of Lucknow* 16

Spain   To these Inquisition dogs and the devildoms of *S*.'   *The Revenge* 12

that they were not left to *S*,	,, 20
not into the hands of *S*!'	,, 90
had holden the power and glory of *S* so cheap	,, 106
sea plunged and fell on the shot-shatter'd navy of *S*,	,, 117
more empire to the kings Of *S* than all battles !	*Columbus* 23
Eighteen long years of waste, seven in your *S*,	,, 36
We fronted there the learning of all *S*,	,, 41
thought to turn my face from *S*,	,, 57
When *S* was waging war against the Moor—	,, 93
I strove myself with *S* against the Moor.	,, 94
if *S* should oust The Moslem from her limit,	,, 96
Blue blood of *S*, Tho' quartering your own royal arms of *S*,	,, 114
blue blood and black blood of *S*,	,, 116
S Pour'd in on all those happy naked isles—	,, 172
Their babies at the breast for hate of *S*—	,, 180
hard memorials of our truth to *S*	,, 196
S once the most chivalric race on earth, *S*	,, 204
To lay me in some shrine of this old *S*, Or in that vaster	
S I leave to *S*.	,, 207
I sorrow for that kindly child of *S*	,, 212
S in his blood and the Jew—	*The Wreck* 15
No! father, *S*, but Hubert brings me home	*The Ring* 59

Spake   When angels *s* to men aloud,   *Supp. Confessions* 25

He *s* of beauty : that the dull Saw no divinity in grass,	*A Character* 7
He *s* of virtue : not the gods More purely,	,, 13
when she *s*, Her words did gather thunder	*The Poet* 48
A **still** small voice *s* unto me,	*Two Voices* 1
It *s*, moreover, in my mind :	,, 31
Again the voice *s* unto me :	,, 46

Y*

Spake (*continued*)   Her eyelid quiver'd as she *s*.

	Miller's D. 144
Still she *s* on and still she *s* of power,	*Œnone* 121
She *s* some certain truths of you.	*L. C. V. de Vere* 36
and if his fellow *s*, His voice was thin,	*Lotos-Eaters* 33
I heard Him, for He *s*,	*D. of F. Women* 227
So *s* he, clouded with his own conceit,	*M. d'Arthur* 110
And *s*, 'Be wise : not easily forgiven Are those,	*Gardener's D.* 247
And *s* not of it to a single soul,	*St. S. Stylites* 66
While I *s* then, a sting of shrewdest pain	,, 198
some one *s*: 'Behold ! it was a crime	*Vision of Sin* 213
while they *s*, I saw my father's face	*Princess* i 58
And on the fourth I *s* of why we came,	,, 119
companion yestermorn ; Unwillingly we *s*.'	,, iii 200
'but to one of whom we *s* Your Highness	,, 201
She *s* With kindled eyes :	,, 333
To whom none *s*, half-sick at heart,	,, iv 223
Stood up and *s*, an affluent orator.	,, 291
roughly *s* My father, 'Tut, you know them not,	,, v 150
To such as her ! if Cyril *s* her true,	,, 168
'Nay, nay, you *s* but sense'	,, 206
So Hector *s*; the Trojans roar'd applause ;	*Spec. of Iliad* 1
Yea, tho' it *s* and made appeal	*In Mem.* xcii 4
Yea, tho' it *s* and bared to view	,, 9
Dumb is that tower which *s* so loud,	,, *Con.* 106
s no slander, no, nor listen'd to it ;	*Ded. of Idylls* 10
Then *s* the hoary chamberlain and said,	*Com. of Arthur* 148
when he *s* and cheer'd his Table Round	,, 267
s sweet words, and comforted my heart,	,, 349
Lash'd at the wizard as he *s* the word,	,, 388
She *s* and King Leodogran rejoiced,	,, 425
holy Dubric spread his hands and *s*,	,, 471
had the thing I *s* of been Mere gold—	*Gareth and L.* 65
But slowly *s* the mother looking at him,	,, 151
Gareth *s* Anger'd, 'Old Master,	,, 279
With all good cheer, He *s* and laugh'd,	,, 302
Nay, for *s* too fool-like :	,, 472
Lancelot ever *s* him pleasantly,	,, 482
A naked babe, of whom the Prophet *s*,	,, 501
when the damsel *s* contemptuously,	,, 806
Gareth sharply *s*, 'None ! for the deed's sake	,, 831
So she *s*. A league beyond the wood,	,, 845
Sir Gareth *s*, 'Lead, and I follow.'	,, 890
He *s*; and all at fiery speed the two Shock'd	,, 962
s 'Methought, Knave, when I watch'd thee striking	,, 991
advanced The monster, and then paused, and *s* no word.	,, 1385
But Gareth *s* and all indignantly,	,, 1386
he *s* no word ; Which set the horror higher :	,, 1393
But none *s* word except the hoary Earl :	*Marr. of Geraint* 369
So *s* the kindly-hearted Earl,	,, 514
S to the lady with him and proclaim'd,	,, 552
Loudly *s* the Prince, 'Forbear :	,, 555
He *s*, and past away, But left two brawny spearmen,	*Geraint and E.* 557
none *s* word, but all sat down at once,	,, 604
She *s* so low he hardly heard her speak,	,, 643
s, 'Go thou with him and him and bring it to us,	*Balin and Balan* 5
And *s* no word until the shadow turn'd ;	,, 45
Then *s* the men of Pellam crying 'Lord,	,, 337
Sir Balin *s* not word, But snatch'd	,, 553
he kiss'd it, moan'd and *s*;	,, 598
S (for she had been sick) to Guinevere,	*Lancelot and E.* 78
He never *s* word of reproach to me,	,, 124
hath come Despite the wound he *s* of,	,, 566
He *s* and parted. Wroth, but all in awe,	,, 719
Then *s* the lily maid of Astolat—	,, 1085
Arthur *s* among them, 'Let her tomb Be costly,	,, 1339
S thro' the limbs and in the voice—	*Holy Grail* 23
But *s* with such a sadness and so low	,, 42
S often with her of the Holy Grail	,, 86
leaving the pale nun, I *s* of this To all men ;	,, 129
as she *s* She sent the deathless passion in her eyes	,, 162
Then *s* the monk Ambrosius,	,, 203
King *S* to me, being nearest, 'Percivale,'	,, 268
'While thus he *s*, his eye, dwelling on mine,	,, 485
Sir Bors it was Who *s* so low and sadly	,, 701
the rest *S* but of sundry perils in the storm ;	,, 761

Spake (*continued*) Then I *s* To one most holy saint, who wept   *Holy Grail* 780
'And *s* I not too truly, O my knights?'   „ 888
s the King: 'I knew not all he meant.'   „ 920
and when she *s* to him, Stammer'd,   *Pelleas and E.* 84
Yet with good cheer he *s*, 'Behold me, Lady,   „ 240
She *s*; and at her will they couch'd their spears,   „ 273
While thus he *s*, she gazed upon the man   „ 305
then *s*: 'Rise, weakling; I am Lancelot;   „ 581
saw the laws that ruled the tournament Broken, but
   s not;   *Last Tournament* 161
Tristram, *s* not any word, But bode his hour,   „ 385
and *s* To Tristram, as he knelt before her,   „ 540
And, saddening on the sudden, *s* Isolt,   „ 581
once or twice I *s* thy name aloud.   „ 615
while she *s*, Mindful of what he brought   „ 714
when she came to Almesbury she *s* There to the nuns,   *Guinevere* 138
But openly she *s* and said to her,   „ 226
To play upon me,' and bowed her head nor *s*.   „ 310
As at a friend's voice, and he *s* again: „ 531
while he *s* to these his helm was lower'd,   „ 593
Except he mock'd me when he *s* of hope;   „ 631
Arthur woke and call'd, 'Who *s*?   *Pass. of Arthur* 46
This heard the bold Sir Bedivere and *s*:   „ 50
Then *s* King Arthur to Sir Bedivere: (repeat)   „ 65, 136
Then *s* the bold Sir Bedivere: „ 147
Then *s* the King: 'My house hath been my doom.   „ 154
So *s* he, clouded with his own conceit,   „ 278
she *s* on, for I did name no wish, (repeat)   *Lover's Tale* i 578, 583
ask'd, Unanswer'd, since I *s* not;   „ 707
Or this, or somewhat like to this, I *s*,   „ 772
Within the summer-house of which I *s*,   „ ii 167
Then *s* Sir Richard Grenville: *The Revenge* 8
he *s* to me, 'O Maeldune, let be this purpose   *V. of Maeldune* 119
when I *s* of famine, plague,   *Tiresias* 60
never *s* with man, And never named the Name'—   *Ancient Sage* 55
Well *s* thy brother in his hymn to heaven   *Akbar's Dream* 27
A VOICE *s* out of the skies   *Voice spake, etc.* 1

Spake (*speak*) She began to *s* to herself,   *Tomorrow* 54
Spakest he were the swine thou *s* of,   *Holy Grail* 885
Who whilome *s* to the South in Greek   *Sir J. Oldcastle* 29
Spakin' (*speaking*) HER, that yer Honour was *s*' to?   *Tomorrow* 1
Span (*s*) every *s* of shade that steals,   *In Mem. cxvii* 10
Span (*verb*) She strove to *s* my waist: *Talking Oak* 138
Span (*See also* **Spick-span-new**)
Spangle (*s*) the *s* dances in bight and bay,   *Sea-Fairies* 24
They would pelt me with starry *s*'s and shells,   *The Merman* 28
Spangle (*verb*) To *s* all the happy shores   *In Mem., Con.* 120
Spangled (*See also* **Sapphire-spangled**) Flung inward
   over *s* floors,   *Arabian Nights* 116
from a fringe of coppice round them burst A *s*
   pursuivant,   *Balin and Balan* 47
Spaniard till the *S* came in sight,   *The Revenge* 23
We will make the *S* promise,   „ 94
Spanish '*S* ships of war at sea!   „ 3
Four galleons drew away From the *S* fleet that day,   „ 47
S fleet with broken sides lay round us   „ 71
stately *S* men to their flagship bore him then,   „ 97
wives and children *S* concubines,   *Columbus* 175
Spank (*strike*) An' 'e *s*'s 'is 'and into mine,   *North. Cobbler* 92
Spanless and grown a bulk Of *s* girth,   *Princess vi* 36
Spann'd Beyond a bridge that *s* a dry ravine: *Marr. of Geraint* 246
Across the bridge that *s* the dry ravine.   „ 294
Spar Rocking with shatter'd *s*'s,   *Buonaparte* 11
S's were splinter'd, (repeat)   *The Captain* 45, 49
Buoy'd upon floating tackle and broken *s*'s,   *Enoch Arden* 551
Spare (*adj.*) But far too *s* of flesh.'   *Talking Oak* 92
Except the *s* chance-gift of those that came   *St. S. Stylites* 78
Spare (*verb*) But, if thou *s* to fling Excalibur,   *M. d'Arthur* 131
Smite, shrink not, *s* not.   *St. S. Stylites* 181
one little kindly word, Not one to *s* her: *Princess vi* 259
we will not *s* the tyrant one hard word.   *Third of Feb.* 42
whatever tempest mars Mid-ocean, *s* thee, sacred bark;   *In Mem. xvii* 14
And yet I *s* them sympathy,   „ *lxiii* 7
A little *s* the night I loved,   „ *cv* 15
If the wolf *s* me, weep my life away,   *Merlin and V.* 885

Spare (*verb*) (*continued*) But, if thou *s* to fling Excalibur,   *Pass. of Arthur* 299
So, brother, pluck and *s* not.'   *Lover's Tale* i 351
As if they knew your diet *s*'s   *To E. Fitzgerald* 10
hallus to hax of a man how much to *s* or to spend;   *Spinster's S's.* 111
S not now to be bountiful,   *On Jub. Q. Victoria* 29
Spared Yet, tho' I *s* thee all the spring,   *The Blackbird* 9
and they *s* To ask it.   *Guinevere* 144
He *s* to lift his hand against the King   „ 437
And the Lord hath *s* our lives.   *The Revenge* 93
Hast *s* the flesh of thousands,   *Happy* 17
Sparhawk (*See also* **Sparrow-hawk**) Sometimes the *s*,
   wheel'd along,   *Sir L. and Q. G.* 12
Sparing *S* not any of Those that with Anlaf,   *Batt. of Brunanburh* 45
Spark the haft twinkled with diamond *s*'s,   *M. d'Arthur* 56
As this pale taper's earthly *s*,   *St. Agnes' Eve* 15
She lit the *s* within my throat,   *Will Water.* 109
Mix'd with cunning *s*'s of hell.   *Vision of Sin* 114
a delicate *s* Of glowing and growing light   *Maud I vi* 15
Like a sudden *s* Struck vainly in the night,   „ ix 13
a *s* of will Not to be trampled out.   „ II ii 56
the soft, the *s* from off the hard,   *Pelleas and E.* 499
snow mingled with *s*'s of fire.   *Last Tournament* 149
the haft twinkled with diamond *s*'s,   *Pass. of Arthur* 224
match'd with ours Were Sun to *s*—   *Ancient Sage* 238
scatters on her throat the *s*'s of dew,   *Prog. of Spring* 58
new developments, whatever *s*   „ 94
WILL my tiny *s* of being wholly vanish   *God and the Univ.* 1
Sparkle (*s*) That sent a blast of *s*'s up the flue: *M. d'Arthur, Ep.* 15
With one green *s* ever and anon   *Audley Court* 88
Caught the *s*'s, and in circles,   *Vision of Sin* 30
Like *s*'s in the stone Aventurine.   *Gareth and L.* 930
make My nature's prideful *s* in the blood   *Geraint and E.* 827
from the star there shot A rose-red *s* to the city,   *Holy Grail* 530
an' 'e shined like a *s* o' fire.   *North. Cobbler* 48
to the snowlike *s* of a cloth   *Sisters (E. and E.)* 117
Sparkle (*verb*) I wake: the chill stars *s*;   *St. S. Stylites* 114
The silver vessels *s* clean,   *Sir Galahad* 34
And *s* out among the fern,   *The Brook* 25
stretch'd forefinger of all Time *S* for ever;   *Princess ii* 379
A maiden moon that *s* on a sty,   „ v 186
The city *s*'s like a grain of salt.   *Will* 20
wont to glance and *s* like a gem Of fifty facets;   *Geraint and E.* 294
while she watch'd their arms far-off *S*,   *Lancelot and E.* 396
heats that spring and *s* out Among us   *Holy Grail* 33
Sparkled shield, That *s* on the yellow field,   *L. of Shalott iii* 8
And *s* keen with frost against the hilt: *M. d'Arthur* 55
From Allan's watch, and *s* far away;   *Dora* 15
cups and silver on the burnish'd board *S* and shone;   *Enoch Arden* 743
when some heat of difference *s* out,   *Aylmer's Field* 705
The yule-log *s* keen with frost,   *In Mem. lxxviii* 5
royal crown *S*, and swaying upon a restless elm   *Balin and Balan* 463
pride and glory fired her face; her eye *S*;   *Pelleas and E.* 173
And *s* keen with frost against the hilt: *Pass. of Arthur* 223
jewels Of many generations of his house *S* and flash'd,   *Lover's Tale iv* 300
s and shone in the sky,   *Despair* 15
but, however they *s* and shone,   „ 17
What *s* there? whose hand was that?   *The Ring* 257
Sparkling the snows Are *s* to the moon: *St Agnes' Eve* 2
The *s* flints beneath the prow.   *Arabian Nights* 52
who often saw The splendour *s* from aloft,   *Gareth and L.* 49
Only to hear and see the far-off *s* brine,   *Lotos-Eaters, C. S.* 98
'O trefoil, *s* on the rainy plain,   *Gareth and L.* 1159
and saw The golden dragon *s* over all: *Holy Grail* 263
To sit a star upon the *s* spire;   *Princess vii* 197
Sparkling-fresh hue Is so *s-f* to view,   *Rosalind* 40
Sparrow The *s*'s chirrup on the roof,   *Mariana* 73
very *s*'s in the hedge Scarce answer   *Amphion* 67
And swallow and *s* and throstle,   *Window, Ay* 14
the *s* spear'd by the shrike,   *Maud I iv* 23
O wretched set of *s*'s, one and all,   *Marr. of Geraint* 278
Sparrow-grass an' my oän bed o' *s-g*,   *Spinster's S's.* 104
Sparrow-hawk (*See also* **Sparhawk**) Who told him,
   scouring still, 'The *s-h*!'   *Marr. of Geraint* 260
Who answer'd gruffly, 'Ugh! the *s-h*.'   „ 265
'Friend, he that labours for the *s-h*   „ 271

Sparrow-hawk (continued) 'A thousand pips eat up your *s-h*!　　*Marr. of Geraint* 274
Who pipe of nothing but of *s-h's*!　　,, 279
'So that ye do not serve me *s-h's*　　,, 304
To curse this hedgerow thief, the *s-h*:　　,, 309
'This *s-h*, what is he? tell me of him.　　,, 404
The second was your foe, the *s-h*,　　,, 444
if the *s-h*, this nephew, fight In next day's tourney　　,, 475
And over that a golden *s-h*,　　,, 484
Has earn'd himself the name of *s-h*.　　,, 492
And over that the golden *s-h*.　　,, 550
Spartan　play The *S* Mother with emotion,　　*Princess ii* 283
Spasm　in these *s's* that grind Bone against bone.　　*Columbus* 220
The tiger *s's* tear his chest,　　*Ancient Sage* 123
Spat　*S*—pish—the cup was gold,　　*Last Tournament* 298
Spate　in a showerful spring Stared at the *s*.　　*Gareth and L.* 3
Spawn　'Thro' slander, meanest *s* of Hell—　　*The Letters* 33
Speak　(*See also* **Spake, Speäk**)　Hark! death is calling While I *s* to ye,　　*All Things will Die* 29
Smiling, never *s's*!　　*Lilian* 12
kiss sweet kisses, and *s* sweet words:　　*Sea-Fairies* 34
Thou smilest, but thou dost not *s*,　　*Margaret* 14
The very smile before you *s*,　　,, 56
Come down, come down, and hear me *s*:　　,, 56
If one but *s's* or hems or stirs his chair,　　*Sonnet to* —— 5
'Twere better not to breathe or *s*,　　*Two Voices* 94
And on the mouth, he will not *s*.　　,, 252
'I may not *s* of what I know.'　　,, 435
But when at last I dared to *s*,　　*Miller's D.* 129
Hear me, for I will *s*, and build up all　　*Œnone* 39
for it may be That, while I *s* of it,　　,, 43
that I might *s* my mind, And tell her to her face　　,, 227
Tho' I cannot *s* a word,　　*May Queen, N. Y's. E.* 39
And then did something *s* to me—　　,, Con. 34
Resolved on noble things, and strove to *s*,　　*D. of F. Women* 42
'Still strove to *s*: my voice was thick　　,, 109
And tread softly and *s* low,　　*D. of the O. Year* 4
And tho' his foes *s* ill of him,　　,, 22
S out before you die.　　,, 45
He will not smile—not *s* to me Once more.　　*To J. S.* 21
A man says *s* the thing he will;　　*You ask me, why, etc.* 8
some old man *s* in the aftertime To all the people,　　*M. d'Arthur* 107
S out: what is it thou hast heard,　　,, 150
if you *s* with him that was my son,　　*Dora* 43
S! is there any of you halt or maim'd?　　*St. S. Stylites* 142
let him *s* his wish.　　,, 144
S, if there be a priest, a man of God,　　,, 214
To alien ears, I did not *s* to these—　　*Love and Duty* 52
was it not well to *s*, To have spoken once?　　,, 55
s, and *s* the truth to me,　　*Locksley Hall* 23
sweetly did she *s* and move:　　,, 71
O LADY FLORA, let me *s*:　　*Day-Dm., Pro.* 1
Her lips are sever'd as to *s*:　　,, *Sleep. P.* 30
S a little, Ellen Adair!'　　*Edward Gray* 24
Said Lady Clare 'that ye *s* so wild?'　　*Lady Clare* 22
'I *s* the truth: you are my child.　　,, 24
I *s* the truth, as I live by bread!　　,, 26
'I will *s* out, for I dare not lie.　　,, 38
And they *s* in gentle murmur,　　*L. of Burleigh* 49
I came to *s* to you of what he wish'd,　　*Enoch Arden* 291
'Tired, Annie?' for she did not *s* a word.　　,, 390
Should still be living; well then—let me *s*:　　,, 405
Lets none, who *s's* with Him, seem all alone,　　,, 620
But turning now and then to *s* with him,　　,, 755
My children too! must I not *s* to these?　　,, 788
mark me and understand, While I have power to *s*.　　,, 877
To *s* before the people of her child,　　*Aylmer's Field* 608
Friends, I was bid to *s* of such a one　　,, 677
—of him I was not bid to *s*—　　,, 710
'Love, forgive him:' but he did not *s*;　　*Sea Dreams* 45
My tongue Trips, or I *s* profanely.　　*Lucretius* 74
yet, to *s* the truth, I rate your chance　　*Princess i* 160
Had given us letters, was he bound to *s*?　　,, 181
he heard her *s*; She scared him; life!　　,, 185
scarce could hear each other *s* for noise　　,, 215

Speak (continued)　Not for three years to *s* with any men;　　*Princess ii* 72
my vow Binds me to *s*, and O that iron will,　　,, 202
but prepare: I *s*; it falls.'　　,, 224
S little; mix not with the rest;　　,, 360
Abate the stride, which *s's* of man,　　,, 429
some classic Angel *s* In scorn of us,　　,, *iii* 70
she *s's* A Memnon smitten with the morning Sun.'　　,, 115
And she replied, her duty was to *s*,　　,, 151
s, and let the topic die.'　　,, 205
That surely she will *s*; if not, then I:　　,, *iv* 344
made a sudden turn As if to *s*,　　,, 395
there she lies, But will not *s*, nor stir.'　　,, *v* 52
and she of whom you *s*, My mother,　　,, 192
ride with us to our lines, And *s* with Arac:　　,, 226
So often that I *s* as having seen.　　,, *vi* 21
Or to her, your dearest,　　,, 185
yet *s* to me, Say one soft word and let us part forgiven.'　　,, 218
Is it kind? *S* to her I say:　　,, 249
Help, father, brother, help; *s* to the king:　　,, 305
cannot *s*, nor move, nor make one sign,　　,, *vii* 153
S no more of his renown,　　*Ode on Well.* 278
My Lords, we heard you *s*　　*Third of Feb.* 1
As long as we remain, we must *s* free,　　,, 13
But the one voice in Europe: we *must s*;　　,, 16
let her *s* of you well or ill;　　*Grandmother* 51
'but I needs must *s* my mind,　　,, 53
S to Him thou for He hears,　　*High. Pantheism* 11
They should *s* to me without a welcome,　　*Hendecasyllabics* 11
And I can *s* a little then.　　*In Mem. xix* 16
Who *s* their feeling as it is,　　,, *xx* 5
And sometimes harshly will he *s*:　　,, *xxi* 6
Behold, ye *s* an idle thing:　　,, 21
Urania *s's* with darken'd brow:　　,, *xxxvii* 1
'I am not worthy ev'n to *s*　　,, 11
My guardian angel will *s* out In that high place,　　,, *xliv* 15
Nor *s* it, knowing Death has made　　,, *lxxiv* 11
I hear the sentence that he *s's*;　　,, *lxxx* 10
We cannot hear each other *s*.　　,, *lxxxii* 16
A part of stillness, yearns to *s*:　　,, *lxxxv* 78
Still *s* to me of me and mine:　　,, *cxvi* 12
thought he would rise and *s* And rave at the lie　　*Maud I i* 59
But this is the day when I must *s*,　　,, *xvi* 7
I am sure I did but *s* Of my mother's faded cheek　　,, *xix* 18
To *s* of the mother she loved As one scarce less forlorn,　　,, 27
Chid her, and forbid her to *s* To me,　　,, 63
But *s* to her all things holy and high,　　,, *II ii* 78
for she never *s's* her mind,　　,, *v* 67
as he *s's* who tells the tale—　　*Com. of Arthur* 95
speech ye *s* yourself, 'Cast me away!'　　,, 304
hear him *s* before he left his life.　　,, 362
S of the King;　　,, 419
nor sees, nor hears, nor *s's*, nor knows.　　*Gareth and L.* 81
Live pure, *s* true, right wrong,　　,, 118
And heard him Kingly *s*, and doubted him　　,, 125
King will doom me when I *s*.'　　,, 324
My deeds will *s*: it is but for a day.'　　,, 577
I but *s* for thine avail, The saver of my life.'　　,, 883
I *am* the cause, because I dare not *s*　　*Marr. of Geraint* 89
Thou art not worthy ev'n to *s* of him:'　　,, 199
S, if ye be not like the rest, hawk-mad,　　,, 280
S!' Whereat the armourer turning all amazed　　,, 282
They would not hear me *s*:　　,, 421
Nor *s* I now from foolish flattery;　　,, 433
Nor did she lift an eye nor *s* a word,　　,, 528
Whatever happens, not to *s* to me,　　*Geraint and E.* 17
If he would only *s* and tell me of it.'　　,, 54
I laid upon you, not to *s* to me,　　,, 78
That she *could s* whom his own ear had heard　　,, 113
Needs must I *s*, and tho' he kill me for it,　　,, 137
'Have I leave to *s*?' He said,　　,, 140
and *s* To your good damsel there who sits apart,　　,, 298
'Get her to *s*: she doth not *s* to me.'　　,, 301
Ye sit apart, you do not *s* to him,　　,, 321
dumbly *s's* Your story, that this man loves you　　,, 328
Good, *s* the word: my followers ring him round:　　,, 336

Spire (*continued*)   I saw the spiritual city and all her *s's*
And gateways   *Holy Grail* 526
Gilded with broom, or shatter'd into *s's*,   *Lover's Tale* i 400
overhead The aërial poplar wave, an amber *s*.   *Sisters (E. and E.)* 84
topmost *s* of the mountain was lilies in lieu of
snow,   *V. of Maeldune* 41
and pigmy spites of the village *s*;   *Vastness* 25
Spired   cypress-cones That *s* above the wood;   *Lover's Tale* ii 332
every topmost pine *S* into bluest heaven,   *Death of Œnone* 69
Spiring   *s* stone that scaled about her tower,   *Last Tournament* 511
Spirit   The boastings of my *s* still?   *Supp. Confessions* 15
S of happiness And perfect rest so inward is;   ,,   50
And the clear *s* shining thro'.   ,,   76
My judgment, and my *s* whirls,   ,,   137
O *s* and heart made desolate!   ,,   189
thoughts in the translucent fane Of her still *s*;   *Isabel* 5
To the young *s* present   *Ode to Memory* 73
A *S* haunts the year's last hours   *A spirit haunts* 1
Life in dead stones, or *s* in air;   *A Character* 9
riving the *s* of man,   *The Poet* 51
Some *s* of a crimson rose In love   *Adeline* 41
Your is the calmed sea,   *Margaret* 25
Touch'd by thy *s's* mellowness,   *Eleänore* 103
Kate hath a *s* ever strung Like a new bow,   *Kate* 10
MINE be the strength of *s*, full and free,   *Mine be the strength* 1
by degrees May into uncongenial *s's* flow;   ,,   11
She thought, 'My *s* is here alone,   *Mariana in the S.* 47
'Go, vexed *S*, sleep in trust;   *Two Voices* 115
That read his *s* blindly wise,   ,,   287
For all the *s* is his own.   *Miller's D.* 190
who wrought Two *s's* to one equal mind—   ,,   236
In my dry brain my *s* soon,   *Fatima* 26
the thought of power Flatter'd his *s*;   *Œnone* 137
Music that gentlier on the *s* lies,   *Lotos-Eaters, C. S.* 5
Nor harken what the inner *s* sings,   ,,   22
lend our hearts and *s's* wholly To the influence   ,,   63
Sweetens the *s* still.   *D. of F. Women* 236
Drawn from the *s* thro' the brain,   *To J. S.* 38
Sleep, holy *s*, blessed soul,   ,,   70
Whose *s's* falter in the mist,   *You ask me, why, etc.* 3
The *S* of the years to come Yearning to mix   *Love thou thy land* 55
And in thy *s* with thee fought—   *England and Amer.* 9
Juliet, she So light of foot, so light of *s*—   *Gardener's D.* 14
that crush'd My *s* flat before thee.   *St. S. Stylites* 26
And this gray *s* yearning in desire   *Ulysses* 30
All the *s* deeply dawning in the dark   *Locksley Hall* 28
And our *s's* rush'd together   ,,   38
And his *s* leaps within him to be gone   ,,   115
crescent promise of my *s* hath not set.   ,,   187
To *s's* folded in the womb.   *Day-Dm., Sleep. P.* 8
His *s* flutters like a lark,   ,, *Arrival* 29
Make Thou my *s* pure and clear   *St. Agnes' Eve* 9
My *s* before Thee;   ,,   18
My *s* beats her mortal bars,   *Sir Galahad* 46
And her *s* changed within.   *L. of Burleigh* 64
Tho' at times her *s* sank: ,,   70
That her *s* might have rest.   ,,   100
I found My *s's* in the golden age.   *To E. L.* 12
So lifted up in *s* he moved away.   *Enoch Arden* 330
Call'd all her vital *s's* into each ear   *Aylmer's Field* 201
But they that cast her *s* into flesh.   ,,   481
meek, Exceeding ' poor in *s* '—   ,,   754
with shameful jest, Encarnalize their *s's*:   *Princess* iii 315
force and growth Of *s* than to junketing   ,, iv 142
on my *s's* Settled a gentle cloud of melancholy;   ,,   569
My *s* closed with Ida's at the lips;   ,, vii 158
Touch a *s* among things divine,   *Ode on Well.* 139
and *S* with *S* can meet—   *High. Pantheism* 11
hear it, *S* of Cássivélaún!   *Boädicea* 20
A *S*, not a breathing voice.   *In Mem.* xiii 12
For I in *s* saw thee move   ,, xvii 5
So much the vital *s's* sink   ,, xx 18
But they my troubled *s* rule,   ,, xxviii 17
Survive in *s's* render'd free,   ,, xxxviii 10
And look on *S's* breathed away,   ,, xl 2

Spirit (*continued*)   Thy *s* ere our fatal loss   *In Mem.* xli 1
That stir the *s's* inner deeps,   ,, xlii 10
And every *s's* folded bloom   ,, xliii 2
Before the *s's* fade away,   ,, xlvii 14
The *S* of true love replied;   ,, lii 6
' What keeps a *s* wholly true   ,, 9
The *s* does but mean the breath   ,, lvi 7
My *s* loved and loves him yet,   ,, lx 2
I loved thee, *S*, and love,   ,, lxi 11
From state to state the *s* walks;   ,, lxxxii 6
Thy *s* should fail from off the globe;   ,, lxxxiv 36
Thy *s* up to mine can reach;   ,, lxxxv 82
A hundred *s's* whisper ' Peace.'   ,, lxxxvi 16
fierce extremes employ Thy *s's*   ,, lxxxviii 6
I know Thy *s* in time among thy peers;   ,, xci 6
No *s* ever brake the band   ,, xciii 2
But he, the *S* himself, may come   ,, 6
S to *S*, Ghost to Ghost.   ,, 8
call The *s's* from their golden day,   ,, xciv 6
My *s* is at peace with all.   ,, 8
And of my *s* as of a wife.   ,, xcvii 8
Two *s's* of a diverse love   ,, cii 7
Thro' which the *s* breathes no more?   ,, cv 20
The churl in *s*, up or down   ,, cxi 1
The churl in *s*, howe'er he veil   ,, 5
But in my *s* will I dwell,   ,, cxiii 9
He breathed the *s* of the song;   ,, cxxv 10
While thou, dear *s*, happy star,   ,, cxxvii 18
Let all my genial *s's* advance   ,, Con. 77
And lust of gain, in the *s* of Cain,   *Maud* I i 23
And the *s* of murder works   ,, 40
eye well-practised in nature, a *s* bounded and poor;   ,, iv 38
Peace, angry *s*, and let him be!   ,, xiii 44
When all my *s* reels At the shouts,   ,, II iv 20
Would the happy *s* descend,   ,, 81
like a household *S* at the walls Beat,   *Geraint and E.* 403
light-wing'd *s* of his youth return'd   *Balin and Balan* 21
his evil *s* upon him leapt,   ,, 537
whimpering of the *s* of the child,   *Last Tournament* 418
heard the *S's* of the waste and weald   *Guinevere* 129
Himself beheld three *s's* mad with joy   ,, 252
so glad were *s's* and men   ,, 269
ill prophets were they all, *S's* and men: ,, 273
When round him bent the *s's* of the hills   ,, 283
Thou art light, To which my *s* leaneth   *Lover's Tale* i 104
and his *s* From bitterness of death.   ,, 142
Which to the imprison'd *s* of the child,   ,, 204
while i gazed My *s* leap'd as with those thrills   ,, 363
S of Love! that lithe hour was bound   ,, 437
life, love, soul, *s*, and heart and strength.   ,, 460
O innocent of *s*—let my heart Break rather—   ,, 737
s seem'd to flag from thought to thought,   ,, ii 51
clear-eyed *S*, Being blunted in the Present,   ,, 130
sorrow of my *s* Was of so wide a compass   ,, 134
Moved with one *s* round about the bay,   ,, iii 17
when her own true *s* had return'd,   ,, iv 108
With a joyful *s* I Sir Richard Grenville die!'   *The Revenge* 103
Flowers to these ' *s's* in prison '   *In the Child. Hosp.* 37
Whereon the *S* of God moves as he will—   *De Prof., Two G.* 28
Out of the deep, *S*, out of the deep,   ,, 32
S half-lost In thine own shadow   ,, 39
Nor canst thou prove that thou art *s* alone,   *Ancient Sage* 60
And some new *S* o'erbear the old,   *Epilogue* 14
out the fleshless world of *s's*,   *The Ring* 228
Her *s* hovering by the church,   ,, 478
fashion'd and worship a *S* of Evil,   *Kapiolani* 1
' *S*, nearing yon dark portal   *God and the Univ.* 4
Spirited   *See* **Tender-spirited**
Spirit-searching   thro' mine down rain'd Their *s-s*
splendours.   *Lover's Tale* ii 147
Spirit-thrilling   Those *s-t* eyes so keen and beautiful: *Ode to Memory* 39
Spiritual (*adj.*)   (*See also* **Half-spiritual**)   *S* Adeline?
(repeat)   *Adeline* 22, 64
One *s* doubt she did not soothe?   *Aylmer's Field* 704
And at the *s* prime Rewaken with the dawning soul.   *In Mem.* xliii 15

Spiritual (adj.) *(continued)* That loved to handle *s* strife,   *In Mem.* lxxxv 54
But *s* presentiments,   „   xcii 14
Rise in the *s* rock,   „   cxxxi 3
Flow'd from the *s* lily that she held.   *Balin and Balan* 264
see Her godlike head crown'd with *s* fire,   *Merlin and V.* 837
and waste the *s* strength Within us,   *Holy Grail* 35
one will crown thee king Far in the *s* city:'   „   162
one will crown me king Far in the *s* city;   „   483
I saw the *s* city and all her spires   „   526
grim faces came and went Before her, or a vague *s* fear—   *Guinevere* 71
the babe She lean'd to from her *S* sphere,   *The Ring* 484
The beauty that endures on the *S* height,   *Happy* 37
The Christians own a *S* Head;   *Akbar's Dream* 153
Spiritual (s)   *S* in Nature's market-place—   „   135
Spirt   upjetted in *s*'s of wild sea-smoke,   *Sea Dreams* 52
Spirted (adj.)   Or red with *s* purple of the vats,   *Princess* vii 202
Spirted (verb)   Prince's blood *s* upon the scarf,   *Marr. of Geraint* 208
Spit   bits of roasting ox Moan round the *s*—   *Lucretius* 132
Sir Scullion, canst thou use that *s* of thine?   *Gareth and L.* 791
Scullion, for running sharply with thy *s*   „   840
these be for the *s*, Larding and basting.   „   1082
Spit (verb)   I hate, abhor, *s*, sicken at him;   *Lucretius* 199
Spite *(See also* **Monkey-spite)** Delicious *s*'s and darling angers,   *Madeline* 6
half in love, half *s*, he woo'd and wed   *Dora* 39
Fill'd I was with folly and *s*,   *Edward Gray* 15
' A ship of fools,' he shriek'd in *s*,   *The Voyage* 77
envy, hate and pity, and *s* and scorn,   *Lucretius* 77
sins of emptiness, gossip and *s* And slander,   *Princess* ii 92
Should all our churchmen foam in *s*   *To F. D. Maurice* 9
How I hate the *s*'s and the follies !   *Spiteful Letter* 24
And scratch the very dead for *s*:   *Lit. Squabbles* 8
The civic slander and the *s*;   *In Mem.* cvi 22
Nor ever narrowness or *s*,   „   cxi 17
a city, with gossip, scandal and *s*;   *Maud I* iv 8
His face, as I grant, in *s* of *s*,   „   xiii 8
to see your beauty marr'd Thro' evil *s*:   *Pelleas and E.* 299
Marr'd tho' it be with *s* and mockery   „   327
tho' she hath me bounden but in *s*,   „   329
when I were so crazy wi' *s*,   *First Quarrel* 73
craft and madness, lust and *s*,   *Locksley H., Sixty* 189
pigmy *s*'s of the village spire;   *Vastness* 25
Spiteful   And with it a *s* letter.   *Spiteful Letter* 2
all hearts Applauded, and the *s* whisper died: *Geraint and E.* 958
Spitting   split the mother's heart *S* the child,   *Com. of Arthur* 39
s at their vows and thee.   *Pass. of Arthur* 62
Splash   and the *s* and stir Of fountains   *Princess* i 217
Splash'd   *s* and dyed The strong White Horse   *Holy Grail* 311
And a hundred *s* from the ledges,   *V. of Maeldune* 103
Spleen   They are fill'd with idle *s*;   *Vision of Sin* 124
cook'd his *s*, Communing with his captains   *Princess* i 66
with the least little touch of *s*.   *Maud I* ii 11
Geraint flash'd into sudden *s*:   *Marr. of Geraint* 273
is your *s* froth'd out, or have ye more ? '   *Merlin and V.* 767
Spleen-born   *S-b*, I think, and proofless.   „   702
Spleenful   Breaking a slumber in which all *s* folly was drown'd,   *Maud I* iii 2
rode Geraint, a little *s* yet,   *Marr. of Geraint* 293
Splendid *(See also* **Dark-splendid)** Sees whatever fair and *s* Lay betwixt his home   *L. of Burleigh* 27
A *s* presence flattering the poor roofs   *Aylmer's Field* 175
The meteor of a *s* season, she,   „   205
Till all the people cried, ' *S* is the flower.'   *The Flower* 16
Such *s* purpose in his eyes,   *In Mem.* lvi 10
There has fallen a *s* tear From the passion-flower   *Maud I* xxii 59
And shine in the sudden making of *s* names,   „   III vi 47
So *s* in his acts and his attire,   *Marr. of Geraint* 620
Display'd a *s* silk of foreign loom,   *Geraint and E.* 687
Splendour   A sudden *s* from behind Flush'd   *Arabian Nights* 81
The maiden's *s*'s of the morning star   *D. of F. Women* 55
Made lightnings in the *s* of the moon,   *M. d'Arthur* 137
The *s* falls on castle walls   *Princess* iv 1
Long lanes of *s* slanted o'er a press   „   478
sheathing *s*'s and the golden scale Of harness,   „   v 41
A flying *s* out of brass and steel,   „   vi 365
suck the blinding *s* from the sand,   „   vii 39

Splendour *(continued)*   height and cold, the *s* of the hills ?   *Princess* vii 194
and a stifled *s* and gloom.   *High. Pantheism* 10
And blurr'd the *s* of the sun;   *In Mem.* lxxii 8
All her *s* seems No livelier   „   xcviii 6
And breaking let the *s* fall   „   Con. 119
I saw the treasured *s*, her hand,   *Maud I* vi 84
new-made lord, whose *s* plucks The slavish hat   „   x 3
nearer to the glow Of your soft *s*'s   „   xviii 79
Queen Maud in all her *s*.   „   xx 50
And a dewy *s* falls On the little flower   „   II iv 32
past and leaves The Crown a lonely *s*.   *Ded. of Idylls* 49
often saw The *s* sparkling from aloft,   *Gareth and L.* 49
s of the presence of the King Throned,   „   320
daily fronted him In some fresh *s*;   *Marr. of Geraint* 14
Made a low *s* in the world,   „   598
she could cast aside A *s* dear to women,   „   808
And on the *s* came, flashing me blind;   *Holy Grail* 413
Made lightnings in the *s* of the moon,   *Pass. of Arthur* 305
We paused amid the *s*.   *Lover's Tale* i 414
mine down rain'd Their spirit-searching *s*'s.   „   ii 147
glory in all The *s*'s and the voices of the world !   *Ancient Sage* 177
native to that *s* or in Mars,   *Locksley H., Sixty* 187
And *s*'s of the morning land,   *Open. I. and C. Exhib.* 8
the secret *s* of the brooks.   *Prog. of Spring* 21
But in the tearful *s* of her smiles   „   41
All her *s* fail'd To lure those eyes   *St. Telemachus* 35
Splenetic   And therefore *s*, personal, base,   *Maud I* x 33
Splinter (s)   into fiery *s*'s leapt the lance,   *Princess* v 494
With darted spikes and *s*'s of the wood   *Merlin and V.* 937
Splinter (verb)   gay navy there should *s* on it,   *Sea Dreams* 131
and to *s* it into feuds Serving his traitorous end;   *Guinevere* 18
Splinter'd   All night the *s* crags that wall the dell   *D. of F. Women* 187
The *s* spear-shafts crack and fly,   *Sir Galahad* 7
Spars were *s*, (repeat)   *The Captain* 45, 49
A lance that *s* like an icicle,   *Geraint and E.* 89
Crack'd basilisks, and *s* cockatrices,   *Holy Grail* 718
Then, sputtering thro' the hedge of *s* teeth,   *Last Tournament* 65
For every *s* fraction of a sect Will clamour   *Akbar's Dream* 33
Splintering *(See also* **Lance-splintering)** the blade flew *S* in six,   *Balin and Balan* 396
and the *s* spear, the hard mail hewn,   *Pass. of Arthur* 108
Split   upon the corn-laws, where we *s*,   *Audley Court* 35
the wild figtree *s* Their monstrous idols,   *Princess* iv 79
takes, and breaks, and cracks, and *s*'s,   „   v 527
spike that mother's heart Spitting the child,   *Com. of Arthur* 38
with one stroke Sir Gareth *s* the skull.   *Gareth and L.* 1404
earthquake shivering to your base *S* you,   *Pelleas and E.* 466
an iceberg *s*'s From cope to base—   *Lover's Tale* i 603
sink her, *s* her in twain !   *The Revenge* 89
Splugen   And up the snowy *S* drew,   *The Daisy* 86
Spoil (s) *(See also* **Ocean-spoil)** the children laden with their *s*;   *Enoch Arden* 445
Spoil (verb)   and *s*'s My bliss in being;   *Lucretius* 221
Begin to slay the folk, and *s* the land.'   *Guinevere* 137
Spoil'd   still the foeman *s* and burn'd,   *The Victim* 17
Because the twain had *s* her carcanet.   *Last Tournament* 419
Spoiler   loud sabbath shook the *s* down;   *Ode on Well.* 123
Bow'd the *s*, Bent the Scotsman,   *Batt. of Brunanburh* 20
Spoilt   You have *s* this child;   *Princess* v 116
thou hast *s* the purpose of my life.   *Guinevere* 453
Spoke   I *s*, but answer came there none: *Two Voices* 425
She *s* at large of many things, And at the last she *s* of me;   *Miller's D.* 155
Last night, when some one *s* his name,   *Fatima* 15
She *s* and laugh'd: I shut my sight   *Œnone* 188
S slowly in her place.   *D. of F. Women* 92
We *s* of other things; we coursed about   *Gardener's D.* 222
in that time and place, I *s* to her,   „   226
I *s*, while Audley feast Humm'd like a hive   *Audley Court* 4
Poet-like he. *s*   *Edwin Morris* 27
Or this or something like to this he *s*.   „   41
I *s* her name alone.   „   68
Whether he *s* too largely;   „   73
So *s* I knowing not the things that were.   „   89

Spoke (*continued*) I s without restraint,　*Talking Oak* 14
And mystic sentence s;　„ 294
He s; and high above, I heard them blast　*Golden Year* 75
yawn'd, and rubb'd his face, and s,　*Day-Dm., Revival* 19
Sweet Emma Moreland s to me:　*Edward Gray* 5
I s with heart, and heat and force,　*The Letters* 37
and Enoch s his love, But Philip loved in silence;　*Enoch Arden* 40
till the morrow, when he s.　„ 156
Philip coming somewhat closer s.　„ 398
Then answer'd Annie; tenderly she s:　„ 422
Saying gently 'Annie, when I s to you,　„ 448
There Enoch s no word to any one,　„ 667
He said to Miriam 'that you s about,　„ 805
and so fell back and s no more.　„ 914
Of sweet seventeen subdued me ere she s)　*The Brook* 113
while she s, I saw where James Made toward us,　„ 116
I know not, for he s not,　*Aylmer's Field* 213
While thus he s, his hearers wept;　„ 722
s with me on the shore;　*Sea Dreams* 264
Why were you silent when I s to-night?　„ 268
your rough voice (You s so loud)　„ 281
Petulant she s, and at herself she laugh'd;　*Princess, Pro.* 153
Thus he s, Part banter, part affection.　„ 166
At last I s. 'My father, let me go.　„ i 68
She s, and bowing waved Dismissal:　„ ii 99
s of those That lay at wine with Lar and Lucumo;　„ 128
it was duty s, not I.　„ 308
I s of war to come and many deaths,　„ iii 150
She s and turn'd her sumptuous head　„ iv 152
I s not then at first, but watch'd　„ 339
And then stood up and s impetuously.　„ 418
being caught feign death, S not, nor stirr'd.　„ v 109
Yet she neither s nor moved.　„ vi 8
Ida s not, rapt upon the child.　„ 220
Ida s not, gazing on the ground,　„ 227
But Ida stood nor s, drain'd of her force　„ vi 266
Old studies fail'd; seldom she s:　„ vii 31
Hortensia s against the tax;　„ 127
Who s few words and pithy,　„ Con. 94
But s not, rapt in nameless reverie,　„ 108
He s among you, and the Man who s;　*Ode on Well.* 178
Who never s against a foe?　„ 185
I started, and s I scarce knew how;　*Grandmother* 43
Till I with as fierce an anger s,　*Maud II i* 17
s of a hope for the world in the coming wars—　„ *III vi* 11
Perforce she stay'd, and overtaken s.　*Gareth and L.* 764
Half inwardly, half audibly she s,　*Marr. of Geraint* 109
He s and fell to work again.　„ 292
Prince and Earl Yet s together,　„ 385
if he s at all, would break perforce　*Geraint and E.* 12
He s, and one among his gentlewomen　„ 686
He s, and Enid easily believed,　„ 874
he s Closed his death-drowsing eyes,　*Ba'in and Balan* 630
He s in words part heard,　*Merlin and V.* 839
Lancelot s And answer'd him at full,　*Lancelot and E.* 285*
He s, and vanish'd suddenly from the field　„ 508
s, he answer'd not, Or short and coldly,　„ 886
passionately she s: 'I have gone mad.　„ 930
While he s She neither blush'd nor shook,　„ 964
thus he s, half turn'd away, the Queen　„ 1197
Then freely s Sir Lancelot to them all:　„ 1289
and even as he s Fell into dust,　*Holy Grail* 435
s, and taking all his younger knights,　*Last Tournament* 126
He s, he turn'd, then, flinging round her neck,　„ 749
S loudly even into my inmost heart　*Lover's Tale i* 428
she s 'Here! and how came I here?'　„ iv 96
What was it? for our lover seldom s,　„ 225
That faithful servant whom we s about,　„ 342
Sir Richard s and he laugh'd,　*The Revenge* 32
I s it—told her of my passion,　*Sisters (E. and E.)* 146
when we parted, Edith s no word,　„ 215
while I s The crowd's roar fell　*Columbus* 12
When he s of his tropical home　*The Wreck* 71
And he s not—only the storm;　„ 103

Spoke (*continued*) For He s, or it seem'd that He s,　*Despair* 26
'Ah God' tho' I felt as I s　„ 52
From darkness into daylight, turn'd and s.　*Ancient Sage* 8
We s of what has been Most marvellous　*Pro. to Gen. Hamley* 10
for he s and the people heard,　*Dead Prophet* 33
No voice for either s within my heart　*The Ring* 162
And s no more, but turn'd and pass'd away.　„ 342
Spoken (*See also* **Fairest-spoken, Fair-spoken, Free-spoken, Low-spoken**) High things were s there,　*Alexander* 12
would have s, but be found not words,　*M. d'Arthur* 172
was it not well to speak, To have s once?　*Love and Duty* 56
Down they dropt—no word was s—　*The Captain* 51
I would have s, And warn'd that madman　*Vision of Sin* 55
had not his poor heart S with That,　*Enoch Arden* 619
you shall say that having s with me,　*Aylmer's Field* 311
so she would have s, but there rose A hubbub　*Princess iv* 475
And every s tongue should lord you.　„ 544
And out of hauntings of my s love,　„ vii 109
sweet soul, had hardly s a word,　*Maud II i* 11
Hath s also, not in jest,　*Com. of Arthur* 420
he fain had s to her, And loosed in words　*Geraint and E.* 105
I heard He had s evil of me;　*Balin and Balan* 58
Said Arthur 'Thou hast ever s truth;　„ 73
half her realm, had never s word.　*Lancelot and E.* 117
is there more? Has Arthur s aught?　„ 117
Then every evil word I had s once,　*Holy Grail* 371
as ye saw it ye have s truth.　„ 880
would have s, but he found not words;　*Pass. of Arthur* 340
s of with tearful smiles;　*Lover's Tale ii* 182
To one who had not s, Lionel.　„ iv 272
The spectre that will speak if s to.　„ 337
Than ha' s as kind as you did,　*First Quarrel* 73
you never have s a word.　*Rizpah* 14
When was age so cramm'd with menace? madness? written, s lies?　*Locksley H., Sixty* 108
in every language I hear s, people praise thee,　*Akbar's D., Inscrip.* 1
And had some prophet s true　*Mechanophilus* 25
Sponge Huge s's of millennial growth　*The Kraken* 4
Sponged S and made blank of crimeful record　*St. S. Stylites* 158
Spongy-wet Is hoar with rime, or s-w;　*To F. D. Maurice* 42
Sport (s) But take it—earnest wed with s,　*Day-Dm., Ep.* 11
so that s Went hand in hand with Science; otherwise Pure:　*Princess, Pro.* 79
Lilia, wild with s, Half child half woman　„ 100
Or master'd by the sense of s,　„ iv 156
—the striplings!—for their s!—　„ v 399
The s half-science, fill me with a faith,　„ Con. 76
Me the s of ribald Veterans,　*Boädicea* 50
He mixt in all our simple s's;　*In Mem. lxxxix* 10
and loud With s and song, in booth and tent,　„ xcviii 28
The s of random sun and shade.　„ Con. 24
Or when the thralls had s among themselves,　*Gareth and L.* 516
Began to break her s's with graver fits,　*Merlin and V.* 180
Your pretty s's have brighten'd all again.　„ 305
• Brake up their s's, then slowly to her bower Parted,　*Last Tournament* 238
on love And s and tilts and pleasure,　*Guinevere* 387
Sport (*verb*) came To s beneath thy boughs.　*Talking Oak* 100
And hence, indeed, she s's with words,　*In Mem. xlviii* 9
Spot A s of dull stagnation, without light　*Palace of Art* 245
So find I every pleasant s　*In Mem. viii* 9
Spotless The saintly youth, the s lamb of Christ,　*Merlin and V.* 749
Spousal and one The later-rising Sun of s Love,　*Prin. Beatrice* 6
Spouse Worthy a Roman s.'　*D. of F. Women* 164
Came Hope and Memory, s and bride,　*On a Mourner* 23
If ever maid or s, As fair as my Olivia,　*Talking Oak* 34
With only Fame for s and your great deeds　*Princess iii* 242
Spout (s) little wide-mouth'd heads upon the s　*Godiva* 56
s whereon the gilded ball Danced like a wisp:　*Princess, Pro.* 63
Spout (*verb*) S from the maiden fountain in her heart.　*Lucretius* 240
Spouted that sonorous flow Of s fountain-floods.　*Palace of Art* 28
golden gorge of dragons s forth　„ 23
monster s his foam-fountains in the sea.　*Lotos-Eaters, C. S.* 107
Till the fountain s, showering wide　*Vision of Sin* 21
fountains s up and showering down　*Princess i* 218

Spouting as a stream that *s* from a cliff   *Guinevere* 608
Sprang Who *s* from English blood !   *England and Amer.* 10
S from the midriff of a prostrate king—   *Aylmer's Field* 16
s No dragon warriors from Cadmean teeth,   *Lucretius* 49
yell'd again Half-suffocated, and *s* up,   „ 58
And from it *s* the Commonwealth,   „ 241
Out I *s* from glow to gloom :   *Princess iv* 178
And out of stricken helmets *s* the fire.   „ *v* 495
turn'd half-round to Psyche as she *s* To meet it,   „ *vi* 209
To the altar-stone she *s* alone,   *The Victim* 67
S up for ever at a touch,   *In Mem. cxii* 10
Gawain went, and breaking into song *S* out,   *Com. of Arthur* 321
He laugh'd ; he *s*.   *Gareth and L.* 537
but forth that other *s*, And, all unknightlike,   „ 1149
s the happier day from underground ;   „ 1421
ground his teeth together, *s* with a yell,   *Balin and Balan* 538
the blood *S* to her face and fill'd her with delight;   *Lancelot and E.* 377
An outraged maiden *s* into the hall   *Holy Grail* 208
rotten with a hundred years of death, *S* into fire :   „ 497
S into fire and vanish'd,   „ 506
I burst the chain, I *s* into the boat.   „ 807
Forth *s* Gawain, and loosed him from his bonds,   *Pelleas and E.* 315
S from the door into the dark.   „ 603
but *s* Thro' open doors, and swording right   *Last Tournament* 472
current to the fountain whence it *s*,—   *Lover's Tale i* 503
S up a friendship that may help us yet.   „ *iv* 144
he *s* from the oldest race upon earth.   *V. of Maeldune* 4
s without leaf or a thorn from the bush ;   „ 44
A panther *s* across her path,   *Death of Œnone* 89
Turn'd him again to boy, for up he *s*,   *St. Telemachus* 58
I *s* from my seat, I wept,   *Charity* 37
Rang the stroke, and *s* the blood,   *The Tourney* 9
Spray (foam) tender curving lines of creamy *s* ;   *Lotos-Eaters, C. S.* 62
Torn from the fringe of *s*.   *D. of F. Women* 40
of hissing *s* wind-driven Far thro' the dizzy dark.   *Lover's Tale ii* 198
and bosom'd the burst of the *s*,   *V. of Maeldune* 103
the ripple would hardly blanch into *s*   *The Wreck* 137
Spray (twig) (*See also* **Holly-spray**) From *s*, and branch, and stem,   *Talking Oak* 190
The snake slipt under a *s*,   *Poet's Song* 10
touchwood, with a single flourishing *s*.   *Aylmer's Field* 512
a song on every *s* Of birds that piped   *Princess v* 238
faces flat against the panes, *S's* grated,   *Balin and Balan* 345
Blinkt the white morn, *s's* grated,   „ 385
Spread (*See also* **Gravel-spread**) *s* his sheeny vans for flight ;   *Love and Death* 8
' Still sees the sacred morning *s*   *Two Voices* 80
That every cloud, that *s's* above And veileth love,   „ 446
Hath time and space to work and *s*.   *You ask me, why, etc.* 16
So muscular he *s*, so broad of breast.   *Gardener's D.* 8
A cedar *s* his dark-green layers of shade.   „ 116
S the light haze along the river-shores,   „ 264
hope ere death *S's* more and more   *St. S. Stylites* 157
The life that *s's* in them,   *Talking Oak* 192
' Then close and dark my arms I *s*,   „ 225
S upward till thy boughs discern   „ 247
light shall *s*, and man be liker man   *Golden Year* 35
But o'er the dark a glory *s's*,   *Sir Galahad* 55
To *s* into the perfect fan,   *Sir L. and Q. G.* 17
The chap-fallen circle *s's* :   *Vision of Sin* 172
He woke, he rose, he *s* his arms abroad   *Enoch Arden* 912
To *s* the Word by which himself had thriven.'   *Sea Dreams* 197
and the branches thereupon *S* out at top,   *Princess iv* 206
A rampant heresy, such as if it *s*   „ 411
S thy full wings, and waft him o'er.   *In Mem. ix* 4
s his mantle dark and cold,   „ *xxii* 14
Proclaiming social truth shall *s*,   „ *cxxvii* 5
And o'er the friths that branch and *s*   „ *Con.* 115
over whom thy darkness must have *s*   *Maud I xviii* 25
Dubric *s* his hands and spake,   *Com. of Arthur* 471
boil'd the flesh, and *s* the board,   *Marr. of Geraint* 391
S the slow smile thro' all her company.   *Pelleas and E.* 95
Lower down *S's* out a little lake,   *Lover's Tale i* 534
I *s* mine arms, God's work, I said,   *Sir J. Oldcastle* 136

Spread (*continued*) call'd the heavens a hide, a tent *S* over earth,   *Columbus* 48
hope was mine to *s* the Catholic faith,   „ 230
to stay, Not *s* the plague, the famine;   *Demeter and P.* 134
and to *s* the Divine Faith Like calming oil   *Akbar's Dream* 159
Spreadeth Which the moon about her *s*,   *Margaret* 20
Spreading *s* made Fantastic plume or sable pine;   *The Voyage* 43
peaks they stand ever *s* and heightening ;   *Parnassus* 11
Sprig Blow, flute, and stir the stiff-set *s's*,   *Amphion* 63
s's of summer laid between the folds,   *Marr. of Geraint* 138
Sprightly at first She play'd about with slight and *s* talk,   *Merlin and V.* 171
Spring (elastic contrivance) a-joompin' about ma as if they was set upo' *s's*,   *Spinster's S's.* 89
Spring (fountain) Life of the fountain there, beneath Its salient *s's*,   *Supp. Confessions* 56
Do beating hearts of salient *s's*   *Adeline* 26
Fresh-water *s's* come up through bitter brine.   *If I were loved* 8
The *s's* of life, the depths of awe,   *Two Voices* 140
Who sets her pitcher underneath the *s*,   *Enoch Arden* 207
(If Death so taste Lethean *s's*),   *In Mem. xliv* 10
While yet beside its vocal *s's*   „ *lxiv* 22
Nor ever drank the inviolate *s*   „ *xc* 2
The bitter *s's* of anger and fear ;   *Maud I x* 49
Brethren, to right and left the *s*,   *Balin and Balan* 25
In mine own lady palms I cull'd the *s*   *Merlin and V.* 273
Flow back again unto my slender *s*   *Lover's Tale i* 147
runnel in the *s* Had liveried them all over.   „ *ii* 49
as we sat by the gurgle of *s's*,   *V. of Maeldune* 89
who found Beside the *s's* of Dircê,   *Tiresias* 14
the *s's* Of Dircê laving yonder battle-plain,   „ 138
Spring (rise) 'tween the *s* and downfall of the light,   *St. S. Stylites* 110
Spring (season) But *s*, a new comer, A *s* rich and strange,   *Nothing will Die* 21
S will come never more.   *All Things will Die* 15
the breathing *s* Of Hope and Youth.   *The Poet* 27
S Letters cowslips on the hill ?   *Adeline* 61
Sweet as new buds in *S*.   *D. of F. Women* 272
Yet, tho' I spared thee all the *s*,   *The Blackbird* 9
Caught in the frozen palms of *S*.   „ 24
But in these latter *s's* I saw   *Talking Oak* 75
Like those blind motions of the *S*,   „ 175
In the *S* a fuller crimson comes upon the robin's breast;   *Locksley Hall* 17
In the *S* the wanton lapwing gets himself another crest ;   „ 18
In the *S* a livelier iris changes on the burnish'd dove ;   „ 19
In the *S* a young man's fancy lightly turns to thoughts of love.   „ 20
throng'd my pulses with the fullness of the *S*.   „ 36
The maiden *S* upon the plain   *Sir L. and Q. G.* 3
She seem'd a part of joyous *S* ;   „ 23
a thousand rings of *S* In every bole,   *Princess v* 237
Shall strip a hundred hollows bare of *S*,   „ *vi* 65
My *s* is all the nearer,   *Window, Winter* 17
S is here with leaf and grass :   „ *No Answer* 23
And all the secret of the *S*   *In Mem. xxiii* 19
The herald melodies of *s*,   „ *xxxviii* 6
And men the flies of latter *s*,   „ *l* 10
And every winter change to *s*.   „ *liv* 16
I dream'd there would be *S* no more,   „ *lxix* 1
S that swells the narrow brooks,   „ *lxxxv* 70
As not unlike to that of *S*.   „ 120
and in my breast *S* wakens too ;   „ *cxv* 18
in a showerful *s* Stared at the spate.   *Gareth and L.* 2
Hath earnest in it of far *s's* to be.   *Merlin and V.* 557
I have seen this yew-tree smoke, *S* after *s*,   *Holy Grail* 19
the *s* Pour with such sudden deluges of light   *Lover's Tale i* 314
recalling fragrance and the green Of the dead *s* :   „ 724
are all they can know of the *s*,   *In the Child. Hosp.* 37
For the *S* and the middle Summer sat   *V. of Maeldune* 38
winter sunset fairer than a morn of *S*.   *Locksley H., Sixty* 22
S and Summer and Autumn and Winter,   *Vastness* 29
spring-flower I send, This song of *s*,   *To Mary Boyle* 20
S slides hither o'er the Southern sea,   *Prog. of Spring* 2
Come, *S*, for now from all the dripping eaves   „ 5
Come, *S* ! She comes on waste and wood,   „ 22

Spring (season) (*continued*)   Come, *S* ! She comes, and
    Earth is glad   *Prog. of Spring* 48
    reads thy gradual process, Holy *S.*   ” 106
    Bright in *S*, Living gold ;   *The Oak* 4
Spring (verb)   It *s*'s on a level of bowery lawn,   *Poet's Mind* 31
    ringing, *s*'s from brand and mail ;   *Sir Galahad* 54
    she whose elfin prancer *s*'s By night   *Sir L. and Q. G.* 33
    a tiger-cat In act to *s*.   *Princess ii* 451
    We were as prompt to *s* against the pikes,   ” iii 286
    Then *s*'s the crowning race of humankind.   ” vii 295
    sober freedom out of which there *s*'s   *Ode on Well.* 164
    Lo, as a dove when up she *s*'s   *In Mem. xii* 1
    Let him, the wiser man who *s*'s Hereafter,   ” cxx 9
    the spear *s*, and good horse reel,   *Gareth and L.* 523
    I *s* Like flame from ashes.'   ” 545
    I *s* from loftier lineage than thine own.'   ” 961
    and dips and *s*'s For ever ;   ” 1146
    earthly heats that *s* and sparkle out   *Holy Grail* 33
    shivers, ere he *s*'s and kills.   *Pelleas and E.* 286
    Ready to *s*, waiting a chance :   *Guinevere* 12
    Wilt *s* to me, and claim me thine,   ” 565
    flowers o' Jeroosilim blossom an' *s* from the grass,   *Tomorrow* 89
    S from his fallen God,   *Demeter and P.* 80
    For Thought into the outward *s*'s,   *Mechanophilus* 11
Spring-flower   ' *S-F's* ' ! While you still delay   *To Mary Boyle* 7
    ' I come with your *s-f's*.'   ” 17
    Take then this *s-f* I send,   ” 19
Springing   took root, and *s* forth anew   *The Poet* 21
    S alone With a shrill inner sound,   *The Mermaid* 19
    Gareth, lightly *s* from his knees,   *Gareth and L.* 556
    Smote by the fresh beam of the *s* east ;   *M. d'Arthur* 214
    Smote by the fresh beam of the *s* east ;   *Pass. of Arthur* 382
    Fresh *s* from her fountains in the brain,   *Lover's Tale i* 83
    From buried grain thro' *s* blade,   *Demeter and P.* 146
Sprinkled   sheath with jewels on it *S* about in gold   *Aylmer's Field* 221
    and the blood Was *s* on your kirtle,   *Princess ii* 274
    The household Fury *s* with blood   *Maud I xix* 32
    the chillness of the *s* brook Smote on my brows,   *Lover's Tale i* 633
Sprouted   manlike, but his brows Had *s*,   *Marr. of Geraint* 314
    Of *s* thistle on the broken stones   *Princess iv* 205
Sprung   The tall flag-flowers when they *s*   *Miller's D.* 53
    but the foe *s* his mine many times,   *Def. of Lucknow* 31
    two mines by the enemy *s*   ” 54
Spun   wheels of Time *S* round in station,   *Love and Duty* 76
    The petty cobwebs we have *s* :   *In Mem. cxxiv* 8
Spur (s)   From *s* to plume a star of tournament,   *M. d'Arthur* 223
    up we rose, and on the *s* we went.   *Gardener's D.* 32
    on the *s* she fled ; and more We know not,—   *Princess i* 151
    Prick'd by the Papal *s*, we rear'd,   *Third of Feb.* 27
    For tho' it seems my *s*'s are yet to win,   *Marr. of Geraint* 80
    Now with dug *s* and raving at himself,   *Balin and Balan* 310
    from *s* to plume Red as the rising sun   *Lancelot and E.* 307
    Set lance in rest, strike *s*,   ” 456
    that dishonour done the gilded *s*,   *Last Tournament* 435
    From *s* to plume a star of tournament,   *Pass. of Arthur* 391
Spur (verb)   desire That *s*'s an imitative will.   *In Mem. cx* 20
Spurge   milk From burning *s*, honey from hornet-combs,   *Last Tournament* 357
Spurn   would not *s* Good counsel of good friends,   *Sir J. Oldcastle* 145
    ' The heart of the father will *s* her,'   *The Wreck* 99
    let them *s* me from the doors,   *The Flight* 55
    The mango *s* the melon at his foot ?   *Akbar's Dream* 39
Spurn'd   *S* by this heir of the liar—   *Maud I xix* 78
    I So mock'd, so *s*, so baited two whole days—   *Sir J. Oldcastle* 163
Spurner   trickster And *s* of treaties   *Batt. of Brunanburh* 80
Spurning   *S* a shatter'd fragment of the God,   *St. Telemachus* 16
Spurr'd   But *s* at heart with fieriest energy   *To J. M. K.* 7
    glaring, by his own stale devil *s*,   *Aylmer's Field* 290
    last I *s* ; I felt my veins Stretch with fierce heat ;   *Princess v* 537
    take my charger, fresh, Not to be *s*,   *Gareth and L.* 1301
    S with his terrible war-cry ;   *Geraint and E.* 170
    what knight soever *s* Against us,   *Balin and Balan* 66
    And toward him *s*, and hail'd him,   *Holy Grail* 637
    And you *s* your fiery horse,   *Happy* 76
Spurt   A sudden *s* of woman's jealousy,—   *Merlin and V.* 524
Sputtering   *s* thro' the hedge of splinter'd teeth,   *Last Tournament* 65

Spy (s)   harry me, petty *s* And traitress.'   *Guinevere* 360
    what are *you* ? do you come as a *s* ?   *Rizpah* 11
    yes—a lady—none of their *spies*—   ” 15
    Death—for their *spies* were among us,   *Def. of Lucknow* 19
Spy (verb)   Whither fly ye, what game *s* ye,   *Rosalind* 8
    get you a seaman's glass, *S* out my face,   *Enoch Arden* 216
    to *s* The weakness of a people or a house,   *Aylmer's Field* 569
    embower the nest, Some boy would *s* it.'   *Princess, Pro.* 148
    he scarce could *s* the Christ for Saints;   *Balin and Balan* 409
    To *s* some secret scandal if he might,   *Guinevere* 26
    she thought, ' He *spies* a field of death ;   ” 134
    they would *s* us out of the town.   *Rizpah* 5
    She *spies* the summer thro' the winter bud,   *Ancient Sage* 74
    She offens 'ud *s* summut wrong   *Owd Roä* 70
    I *s* nor term nor bound.   *Mechanophilus* 20
Squabble   lulling random *s*'s when they rise,   *Holy Grail* 557
Squad (mud)   neck-an-crop soomtimes slaäpe down i'
    the *s*   *North. Cobbler* 20
    as iver traäpes'd i' the *s*.   *Owd Roä* 72
Squadron   *S*'s and squares of men in brazen plates,   *D. of F. Women* 33
    embattled squares, And *s*'s of the Prince,   *Princess v* 247
Squalid   Mated with a *s* savage—what to me were sun
    or clime ?   *Locksley Hall* 177
    one sleek'd the *s* hair, One kiss'd his hand,   *Death of Œnone* 57
Squall   *s* nor storm Could keep me from that Eden   *Gardener's D.* 190
    thro' the gray skirts of a lifting *s*   *Enoch Arden* 829
Squall'd   The parrot scream'd, the peacock *s*,   *Day-Dm., Revival* 12
Square   (*See also* **Garden-square**)   and *s*'s of men in
    brazen plates,   *D. of F. Women* 33
    All the land in flowery *s*'s,   *Gardener's D.* 76
    By *s*'s of tropic summer shut   *Amphion* 87
    The ruddy *s* of comfortable light,   *Enoch Arden* 726
    Flourish'd a little garden *s* and wall'd :   ” 734
    Muses of the cube and *s*,   *Princess, Pro.* 180
    casement slowly grows a glimmering *s* ;   ” iv 52
    embattled *s*'s, And squadrons of the Prince,   ” v 246
    Dash'd on every rocky *s* Their surging charges   *Ode on Well.* 125
    They call'd me in the public *s*'s   *In Mem. lxix* 11
    maze of quick About the flowering *s*'s,   ” cxv 3
    And I loathe the *s*'s and streets,   *Maud II iv* 92
    The massive *s* of his heroic breast,   *Marr. of Geraint* 75
    A *s* of text that looks a little blot,   *Merlin and V.* 671
    And every *s* of text an awful charm,   ” 673
    A thousand *s*'s of corn and meadow,   *The Ring* 149
    And from the thousand *s*'s,   ” 153
Squared   In each a *s* lawn, wherefrom The golden gorge
    of dragons   *Palace of Art* 22
Square-set   A *s-s* man and honest ;   *Holy Grail* 703
Squaw   Nor stunted *s*'s of West or East ;   *Princess ii* 78
Squealing   *See* **A-squeälin'**
Squeedg'd (squeezed)   An' tha *s* my 'and i' the shed,   *Spinster's S's.* 39
Squeezed   (*See also* **Squeedg'd**)   he had *s* himself
    betwixt the bars,   *Princess, Pro.* 112
Squench   I'll coom an' I'll *s* the light,   *Owd Roä* 117
Squire   (*See also* **Squoire**)   Late-left an orphan of the *s*,   *Miller's D.* 34
    ' That was the four-year-old I sold the *S*.'   *The Brook* 137
    the *S* had seen the colt at grass,   ” 139
    slain with laughter roll'd the gilded *S*.   *Princess v* 22
    Our ponderous *s* will give A grand political dinner   *Maud I xx* 24
    Gareth hearing from a *s* of Lot   *Gareth and L.* 531
    shook his drowsy *s* awake and cried,   *Marr. of Geraint* 125
    page, and maid, and *s*, and seneschal,   ” 710
    Hung at his belt, and hurl'd it toward the *s*.   *Geraint and E.* 23
    and the *s* Chafing his shoulder :   ” 26
    In silence, did him service as a *s* ;   ” 406
    Vivien, with her *S*.   *Balin and Balan* 439
    Then turning to her *S* ' This fire of Heaven,   ” 456
    Drew the vague glance of Vivien, and her *S*,   ” 464
    and my *s* Hath in him small defence ;   ” 476
    But snatch'd a sudden buckler from the *S*,   ” 554
    Then to her *S* mutter'd the damsel ' Fools !   ” 564
    And when the *S* had loosed them,   ” 575
    Then the gentle *S* ' I hold them happy,   ” 580
    And found a fair young *s* who sat alone,   *Merlin and V.* 472
    twice to-day. I am your *s* !'   *Lancelot and E.* 384

Squire (*continued*) and their three *s*'s across their feet: *Pelleas and E.* 431
doesn not touch thy 'at to the *S* ; ' *North. Cobbler* 25
An' *S*, his oän very sen, walks down fro' the 'All   „ 91
fur New *S* coom'd last night. *Village Wife* 1
I liked the owd *S* an' 'is gells   „ 6
the *S* an' 'is darters an' me,   „ 7
new *S*'s coom'd wi' 'is taäil in 'is 'and, an' owd *S*'s gone. (repeat) .. 14, 121
We'd anew o' that wi' the *S*,   „ 24
Fur *S* wur a Varsity scholard,   „ 25
An' *S* wur hallus a-smilin',   „ 33
ivry darter o' *S*'s hed her awn ridin-erse   „ 35
An' *S* 'e smiled an' 'e smiled (repeat) .. 61, 88
But *S* wur afear'd o' 'is son,   „ 63
boooks, I ha' see'd 'em, belong'd to the *S*,   „ 71
And *S* were at Charlie ageän   „ 74
Hallus a soft un *S* !   „ 89
rattled down upo' poor owd *S* i' the wood,   „ 95
Fur I'd ha done owt for the *S*   „ 112
sound and honest, rustic *S*, *Locksley H., Sixty* 239
Till I dreäm'd 'at *S* walkt in, an' I says to him
' *S*, ya're laäte,' *Owd Roä* 55
an' not the faults o' the *S*. *Church-warden, etc.* 46
Squireling political dinner To half the *s*'s near ; *Maud I xx* 26
Squirrel And snared the *s* of the glen ? *Princess ii* 249
merry linnet knew me, The *s* knew me, *Lover's Tale ii* 16
While *s*'s from our fiery beech *Pro. to Gen. Hamley* 3
Squoire (**Squire**) Thaw a knaws I hallus voäted wi' *S* *N. Farmer, O. S.* 15
wi' haäte hoonderd haäcre o' *S*'s,   „ 44
An' *S* 'ull be sa mad an' all—   „ 47
I 'a managed for *S* coom Michaelmas thutty year.   „ 48
Fur they knaws what I beän to *S*   „ 55
I done moy duty by *S*   „ 56
S's i' Lunnon, an' summun I reckons   „ 57
Staäin'd (**stained**) An' the taäble *s* wi' 'is aäle, *Spinster's S's.* 99
Staäte (**state**) voäted wi' Squoire an' choorch an' *s*, *N. Farmer, O. S.* 15
I thowt shall I chaänge my *s* ? *Spinster's S's.* 44
I thowt if the *S* was a gawin' *Owd Roä* 45
'Staäte (**estate**) Fur 's be i' taäil, my lass : *Village Wife* 15
I've gotten the *S* by the taäil   „ 68
Stab (s) deathful *s*'s were dealt apace, *Oriana* 50
Stab (verb) little boys begin to shoot and *s*, *Princess, Con.* 61
I was not going to *s* you, *Bandit's Death* 5
Stabb'd They should have *s* me where I lay, (repeat) *Oriana* 55, 60
Three times I *s* him thro' and thro'. *The Sisters* 29
She would have *s* him ; *Merlin and V.* 853
' *S* thro' the heart's affections to the heart !   „ 868
bride who *s* her bridegroom on her bridal night— *The Flight* 57
and he *s* my Piero with this. *Bandit's Death* 10
Stable a *s* wench Came running at the call, *Princess i* 226
they ran To loose him at the *s*'s, *Aylmer's Field* 126
brute rejoicing in my hounds, and in my *s*, *By an Evolution.* 7
Staff (*See also* **Sceptre-staff**) he struck his *s* against the rocks *Golden Year* 59
is a straight *s* bent in a pool ; *High. Pantheism* 16
Shot thro' the *s* or the halyard, *Def. of Lucknow* 5
the carven *s*—and last the light, *Columbus* 74
Stage actor mouth his last upon the *s*. *Locksley H., Sixty* 152
this Earth, a *s* so gloom'd with woe *The Play* 1
Stagger ' I *s* in the stream : *Princess vi* 321
And *s*'s blindly ere she sink ? *In Mem. xvi* 14
I *s* at the Koràn and the sword. *Akbar's Dream* 71
Stagger'd *S* and shook, holding the branch, *Enoch Arden* 767
s thy strong Gawain in a tilt For pastime ; *Gareth and L.* 542
Into the hall *s*, his visage ribb'd *Last Tournament* 57
the ship *s* under a thunderous shock, *The Wreck* 107
shock upon shock *S* the mass from without, *Heavy Brigade* 59
Staggering and *s* back With stroke on stroke *Princess v* 522
Staghorn-moss brought you down A length of *s-m*, *Romney's R.* 79
Stagnant A black yew gloom'd the *s* air, *The Letters* 2
Stagnate But *s*'s in the weeds of sloth : *In Mem. xxvii* 11
As one that let foul wrong *s* and be, *Geraint and E.* 891
Stagnation A spot of dull *s*, without light *Palace of Art* 245
Stag-tuckey (**turkey-cock**) An' 'e torn'd as red as a *s-t*'s wattles, *Churchwarden, etc,* 31

Staid (*See also* **Stay'd**) I had not *s* so long to tell you all, *Gardener's D.* 242
Staid (adj.) Altho' a grave and *s* God-fearing man, *Enoch Arden* 112
Stain (s) Some *s* or blemish in a name of note, *Merlin and V.* 832
to have loved One peerless, without *s* : *Lancelot and E.* 1091
Stain (verb) And I, ' Can clouds of nature *s* *In Mem. lxxxv* 85
Stain'd (*See also* **Staäin'd, Many-stain'd**) deep-set windows, *s* and traced, *Palace of Art* 49
Stainless But she, a *s* wife to Gorloïs, *Com. of Arthur* 194
King That morn was married, while in *s* white,   „ 456
Would mar their charm of *s* maidenhood.' *Balin and Balan* 268
Thy blessing, *s* King ! *Merlin and V.* 54
O Heaven's own white Earth-angel, *s* bride of *s* King— .. 81
A *s* man beside a *s* maid ;   „ 737
Arthur, blameless King and *s* man ? '   „ 779
O selfless man and *s* gentleman,   „ 792
her bloom A rosy dawn kindled in *s* heavens, *Pelleas and E.* 72
White-robed in honour of the *s* child, *Last Tournament* 147
Thro' her high hill-passes of *s* snow, *Dead Prophet* 47
Stair (*See also* **Altar-stairs, Tower-stairs**) Broad-based flights of marble *s*'s *Arabian Nights* 117
The rock rose clear, or winding *s*. *Palace of Art* 10
up the corkscrew *s* With hand and rope *Walk. to the Mail* 90
his footsteps smite the threshold *s*'s *St. S. Stylites* 191
adown the *s* Stole on ; *Godiva* 48
His golden feet on those empurpled *s*'s *Lucretius* 135
And up a flight of *s*'s into the hall. *Princess ii* 31
A column'd entry shone and marble *s*'s,   „ *v* 364
And me they bore up the broad *s*'s,   „ *vi* 374
And high above a piece of turret *s*, *Marr. of Geraint* 320
All up the marble *s*, tier over tier, *Lancelot and E.* 1248
Then from the boat I leapt, and up the *s*'s. *Holy Grail* 819
Or ghostly footfall echoing on the *s*. *Guinevere* 507
Adown a natural *s* of tangled roots, *Lover's Tale i* 527
and climb'd The moulder'd *s*'s   „ *iv* 137
I stood upon the *s*'s of Paradise. *Sisters (E. and E.)* 144
as far as the head of the *s*, *In the Child. Hosp.* 43
A stealthy foot upon the *s* ! *The Flight* 70
an' the mud o' 'is boots o' the *s*'s, *Spinster's S's.* 99
tummled up *s*'s, fur I 'eärd 'im, *Owd Roä* 63
' But the *s*'s is afire,' she said ;   „ 80
And glided lightly down the *s*'s, *St. Telemachus* 59
Stairway down from this a lordly *s* sloped *Gareth and L.* 669
The *s* to the hall ; and look'd and saw *Last Tournament* 757
Stake (verb) I'll *s* my ruby ring upon it you did.' *Princess, Pro.* 170
Stake (s) To the thumbscrew and the *s*, *The Revenge* 21
And the *s* and the cross-road, fool, *Despair* 116
I shudder at the Christian and the *s* ; *Akbar's Dream* 72
Stale a fool, Raw, yet so *s* ! ' *Pelleas and E.* 114
Him, glaring, by his own *s* devil spurr'd, *Aylmer's Field* 290
Staled *S* by frequence, shrunk by usage *Locksley H., Sixty* 76
Stalk Earthward he boweth the heavy *s*'s *A spirit haunts* 7
And these are but the shatter'd *s*'s, *In Mem. lxxxii* 7
Stall and even beasts have *s*'s, *St. S. Stylites* 109
The *s*'s are void, the doors are wide, *Sir Galahad* 31
A man upon a *s* may find, *In Mem. lxxvii* 9
Take him to *s*, and give him corn, *Marr. of Geraint* 371
Enid took his charger to the *s* ;   „ 382
Stall'd *s* his horse, and strode across the court, *Balin and Balan* 341
Stalling chamber for the night, And *s* for the horses, *Geraint and E.* 239
Stalwart On free feet Set him, a *s* Baron, Arthur's friend. *Gareth and L.*
but afterwards He made a *s* knight. *Merlin and V.* 482
Stamford-town Burleigh-house by *S-t*. *L. of Burleigh* 92
Stammer That made my tongue so *s* and trip *Maud I vi* 83
left him leave to *s*, ' Is it indeed ? ' *Lancelot and E.* 420
Stammer'd I *s* that I knew him—could have wish'd— *Princess iii* 206
and when she spake to him, *S*, *Pelleas and E.* 85
Stammering *s* ' scoundrel ' out of teeth that ground *Aylmer's Field* 328
deafen'd with the *s* cracks and claps That follow'd, *Merlin and V.* 942
on the border of her couch they sat *S* and staring. *Guinevere* 102
Stamp Which *s*'s the caste of Vere de Vere. *L. C. V. de Vere* 40
meant to *s* him with her master's mark ; *Merlin and V.* 266
I could *s* my image on her heart ! *Sisters (E. and E.)* 195
Stamp'd-Stampt And the leaf is *stamp'd* in clay. *Vision of Sin* 82
Stampt all into defacement, *Balin and Balan* 541
Stamp'd with the image of the King ; *Holy Grail* 27

Star (s) (*continued*) happy *s's* above them seem to brighten | *May Queen* 34
up to Heaven and die among the *s's*. | „ *Con.* 40
Sung by the morning *s* of song, | *D. of F. Women* 3
Peopled the hollow dark, like burning *s's*, | „ 18
maiden splendours of the morning *s* Shook | „ 55
We saw the large white *s's* rise one by one, | „ 223
this *s* Rose with you thro' a little arc | *To J. S.* 25
While the *s's* burn, the moons increase, | „ 71
Thro' silence and the trembling *s's* | *On a Mourner* 28
if Nature's evil *s* Drive men in manhood, | *Love thou thy land* 73
I bump'd the ice into three several *s's*, | *The Epic* 12
cry that shiver'd to the tingling *s's*, | *M. d'Arthur* 199
From spur to plume a *s* of tournament, | „ 223
ere a *s* can wink, beheld her there. | *Gardener's D.* 122
Love's white *s* Beam'd thro' the thicken'd cedar | „ 165
Sow'd all their mystic gulfs with fleeting *s's*; | „ 262
Sole *s* of phosphorescence in the calm, | *Audley Court* 87
I wake: the still *s's* sparkle; | *St. S. Stylites* 114
paused Among her *s's* to hear us; *s's* that hung Love-charm'd | *Love and Duty* 74
To follow knowledge like a sinking *s*, | *Ulysses* 31
and the baths Of all the western *s's*, | „ 61
Close over us, the silver *s*, | *Tithonus* 25
Ere yet they blind the *s's*, | „ 39
And o'er them many a sliding *s*, | *Day-Dm., Depart.* 13
On secrets of the brain, the *s's*, | „ *L'Envoi* 11
Draw me, thy bride, a glittering *s*, | *St. Agnes' Eve* 23
And star-like mingles with the *s's*. | *Sir Galahad* 48
New *s's* all night above the brim | *The Voyage* 25
We parted: sweetly gleam'd the *s's*, | *The Letters* 41
the great *s's* that globed themselves | *Enoch Arden* 597
I murmur under moon and *s's* In brambly wildernesses; | *The Brook* 178
and holds her head to other *s's*, | „ 195
Shone like a mystic *s* between the less | *Aylmer's Field* 72
A close-set robe of jasmine sown with *s's*: | „ 158
S to *s* vibrates light: may soul to soul | „ 578
such a *s* of morning in their blue, | „ 692
'if every *s* in heaven Can make it fair: | *Sea Dreams* 83
then I saw one lovely *s* Larger and larger. | „ 93
crown'd with *s's* and high among the *s's*,— | „ 241
Nor ever falls the least white *s* of snow, | *Lucretius* 107
For on my cradle shone the Northern *s*. | *Princess i* 4
dry old man, without a *s*, Not like a king: | „ 117
four wing'd horses dark against the *s's*; | „ 211
In shining draperies, headed like a *s*, | „ *ii* 109
glorious names Were fewer, scatter'd *s's*, | „ 156
The *s*, the bird, the fish, the shell, | „ 383
Morn in the white wake of the morning *s* | „ *iii* 17
'There sinks the nebulous *s* we call the Sun, | „ *iv* 19
Now poring on the glowworm, now the *s*, | „ 211
leader wildswan in among the *s's* Would clang it, | „ 434
those three *s's* of the airy Giant's zone, | „ *v* 260
The tops shall strike from *s* to *s*, | „ *vi* 57
S after *s*, arose and fell; but I, | „ *vii* 50
Now lies the Earth all Danaë to the *s's*, | „ 182
To sit a *s* upon the sparkling spire; | „ 197
Lavish Honour shower'd all her *s's*, | *Ode on Well.* 196
Brought from under every *s*, | *Ode Inter. Exhib.* 25
Melt into *s's* for the land's desire! | *W. to Alexandra* 21
And whistled to the morning *s*. | *Sailor Boy* 4
Two bright *s's* Peep'd into the shell. | *Minnie and Winnie* 13
And look'd at by the silent *s's*: | *Lit. Squabbles* 4
THE sun, the moon, the *s's*, the seas, | *High. Pantheism* 1
Earth, these solid *s's*, this weight of body | „ 5
Above thee glided the *s*. | *Voice and the P.* 8
The valley, the voice, the peak, the *s* Pass, | „ 27
Peak is high, and the *s's* are high, | „ 31
the *s's* about the moon Look beautiful, | *Spec. of Iliad* 11
the *s's* Shine, and the Shepherd gladdens in his heart: | „ 15
Taken the *s's* from the night | *Window, Gone* 5
And you are his morning *s*. | *Marr. Morn.* 12
'The *s's*,' she whispers, 'blindly run; | *In Mem. iii* 5
Slide from the bosom of the *s's*. | „ *xvii* 16
And orb into the perfect *s* | „ *xxiv* 15
Look also, Love, a brooding *s*, | „ *xlvi* 15

Star (s) (*continued*) And grapples with his evil *s*; | *In Mem. lxiv* 8
Thro' clouds that drench the morning *s*, | „ *lxxii* 22
To where in yonder orient *s* | „ *lxxxvi* 15
Before the crimson-circled *s* | „ *lxxxix* 47
He reads the secret of the *s*, | „ *xcvii* 22
Is twisting round the polar *s*; | „ *ci* 12
And one the shaping of a *s*; | „ *ciii* 36
A sphere of *s's* about my soul, | „ *cxxii* 7
While thou, dear spirit, happy *s*, | „ *cxxvii* 18
But tho' I seem in *s* and flower | „ *cxxx* 6
And brighten like the *s* that shook | *Con.* 31
And, *s* and system rolling past, | „ 122
sorrow seize me if ever that light be my leading *s*! | *Maud I iv* 12
you fair *s's* that crown a happy day | „ *xviii* 30
Beat, happy *s's*, timing with things below, | „ 81
like a silent lightning under the *s's* | „ *III vi* 9
Remembering all the beauty of that *s* | *Ded. of Idylls* 46
O ye *s's* that shudder over me, | *Com. of Arthur* 83
And even in high day the morning *s*. | „ 100
thereafter follow'd calm, Free sky and *s's*: | „ 392
wholesome *s's* of love; | *Gareth and L.* 314
honour shining like the dewy *s* Of dawn, | „ 329
and thereon the morning *s*, | „ 932
His arms, the rosy raiment, and the *s*. | „ 938
And he that bore The *s*, when mounted, | „ 951
And then she sang, 'O morning *s*' | „ 996
'O morning *s* that smilest in the blue, O *s*, my morning dream hath proven true, | „ 999
That named himself the *S* of Evening, | „ 1090
'No *s* of thine, but shot from Arthur's heaven | „ 1100
so wilt thou, Sir *S*; Art thou not old?' | „ 1103
that same strength which threw the Morning *S* | „ 1108
a shield whereon the *S* of Even Half-tarnish'd | „ 1117
and when he saw the *s* Gleam, | „ 1218
s shot: 'Lo,' said Gareth, 'the foe falls!' | „ 1317
cloud that grew To thunder-gloom palling all *s's*, | „ 1359
now by night With moon and trembling *s's*, | *Marr. of Geraint* 8
His charger trampling many a prickly *s* | „ 313
as the white and glittering *s* of morn | „ 734
'Enid, the pilot *s* of my lone life, | *Geraint and E.* 306
Kiss'd the white *s* upon his noble front, | „ 757
or touch at night the northern *s*; | *Balin and Balan* 166
rather seem'd a lovely baleful *s* | *Merlin and V.* 262
misty *s*, Which is the second in a line of *s's* | „ 508
Of some vast charm concluded in that *s* | „ 512
Her seer, her bard, her silver *s* of eve, | „ 954
like a *s* in blackest night. | *Lancelot and E.* 1243
And peak'd wings pointed to the Northern *S*. | *Holy Grail* 240
like a flying *s* Led on the gray-hair'd wisdom | „ 452
I saw him like a silver *s*— | „ 517
I saw the least of little *s's* Down on the waste, and straight beyond the *s* I saw the spiritual city | „ 524
from the *s* there shot A rose-red sparkle | „ 529
which can trace The wandering of the *s's*, | „ 667
The seven clear *s's* of Arthur's Table Round— | „ 684
a round in heaven, we named the *s's*, | „ 686
Across the seven clear *s's*—O grace to me— | „ 692
Rode the *s* above the wakening sun, | *Pelleas and E.* 500
'O sweet *s*, Pure on the virgin forehead | „ 504
and the morning *s* Reel'd in the smoke, | „ 518
Peace at his heart, and gazing at a *s* | „ 559
Dost thou know the *s* We call the harp | *Last Tournament* 332
do ye see it? do ye see the *s*?' | „ 346
The night was dark; the true *s* set. Isolt! | „ 605
s in heaven, a *s* within the mere! Ay, ay, O ay,—a *s* | „ 732
And one was water, and one *s* was fire, | „ 736
'I found Him in the shining of the *s's*, | *Pass. of Arthur* 9
cry that shiver'd to the tingling *s's*, | „ 367
From spur to plume a *s* of tournament, | „ 391
lucid chambers of the morning *s*, | *Lover's Tale i* 28
Down those loud waters, like a setting *s*, | „ 59
Their Notions and their brightness from the *s's*, And then point out the flower or the *s*? | „ 174
Under the selfsame aspect of the *s's*, | „ 199
Suck'd into oneness like a little *s* | „ 308

Started (*continued*) and Balin *s* from his bower. *Balin and Balan* 280
Sideways he *s* from the path, and saw, „ 324
Yet blank from sleep, she *s* to him, *Lancelot and E.* 820
s thro' mid air Bearing an eagle's nest: *Last Tournament* 14
Flush'd, *s*, met him at the doors, „ 512
an' I *s* awaäy like a shot, *North. Cobbler* 69
shriek'd, and *s* from my side— *Locksley H., Sixty* 264

Starting *S* up at once, As from a dismal dream *Lover's Tale i* 747
then *s*, thought His dreams had come again. „ *iv* 77

Startled neither self-possess'd Nor *s*, *Gardener's D.* 155
Life was *s* from the tender love *Lover's Tale i* 616

Starve clamouring, 'If we pay, we *s*!' *Godiva* 15
'If they pay this tax, they *s*.' „ 20
s not thou this fire within thy blood, *Balin and Balan* 453
The first discoverer *s's*—his followers, *Columbus* 166
When all men *s*, the wild mob's million feet *The Fleet* 18

Starved (*See also* **Self-starved**) my husband's brother had my son Thrall'd in his castle, and hath *s* him dead; *Gareth and L.* 358
s the wild beast that was linkt with thee eighty years back. *By an Evolution.* 11

State (*adj.*) That crown'd the *s* pavilion of the King, *Guinevere* 399

State (*body politic*) (*See also* **Staäte**) Tho' every channel of the *S* *You ask me, why, etc.* 23
And work, a joint of *s*, that plies Its office, *Love thou thy land* 47
New Majesties of mighty *S's*— „ 60
'Who'd serve the *s*? for if I carved my name *Audley Court* 48
Visions of a perfect *S*: *Vision of Sin* 148
the *s*, The total chronicles of man, *Princess ii* 380
But as he saves or serves the *s*. *Ode on Well.* 200
No little German *s* are we, *Third of Feb.* 15
To mould a mighty *s's* decrees, *In Mem. lxiv* 11
Or touch'd the changes of the *s*, „ *lxxxix* 35
the *s* has done it and thrice as well: *Maud I x* 40
In silver tissue talking things of *s*; *Marr. of Geraint* 663
people's praise From thine own *S*, *Ded. Poem Prin. Alice* 8
bring on both the yoke Of stronger *s's*, *Tiresias* 70
Break the *S*, the Church, the Throne, *Locksley H., Sixty* 138
We founded many a mighty *s*; *Hands all Round* 30
Were she . . . a fallen *s*? *The Fleet* 10
In our ancient *S*, *Open. I. and C. Exhib.* 16
To serve her myriads and the *S*,— *To Marq. of Dufferin* 24
and men at the helm of *s*— *The Wreck* 49

State (*condition*) Thrice happy *s* again to be The trustful infant on the knee! *Supp. Confessions* 40
O damned vacillating *s*! „ 190
in some confused dream To *s's* of mystical similitude; *Sonnet to ——* 4
The slipping thro' from *s* to *s*, *Two Voices* 351
'So might we, if our *s* were such As one before, „ 355
Such doubts and fears were common to her *s*, *Enoch Arden* 521
Roman lines Of empire, and the woman's *s* in each, *Princess ii* 131
still she rail'd against the *s* of things. „ *iii* 84
As in some mystic middle *s* I lay, „ *vi* 18
Charity Could lift them nearer God-like *s* *Lit. Squabbles* 14
And he should sorrow o'er my *s* *In Mem. xv* 15
The lowness of the present *s*, „ *xxiv* 11
If, in thy second *s* sublime, „ *lxi* 1
From *s* to *s* the spirit walks; „ *lxxxii* 6
That range above our mortal *s*, „ *lxxxv* 22
Who first had found and loved her in a *s* Of broken fortunes, *Marr. of Geraint* 12
dazed and dumb With passing thro' at once from *s* to *s*, *Demeter and P.* 7
nearing yon dark portal at the limit of thy human *s*, *God and the Univ.* 4

State (*chair of state*) His *s* the king reposing keeps. *Day-Dm., Sleep. P.* 39
Summon'd out She kept her *s*, *Princess iii* 229

State (*dignity*) overflowing revenue Wherewith to embellish, *Œnone* 113
Built for pleasure and for *s*. *L. of Burleigh* 32
Here he lives in *s* and bounty, „ 57
There she walks in her *s* And tends upon bed and bower, *Maud I xiv* 3
all his land and wealth and *s* were hers. *Holy Grail* 587

State (*mien*) and by your *s* And presence might have guess'd you one *Marr. of Geraint* 430
for by thy *s* And Presence I might guess thee chief of those, *Lancelot and E.* 182

State (*pomp*) Where we withdrew from summer heats and *s*, *Princess vi* 245
I go in *s* to court, to meet the Queen. *Lancelot and E.* 1124
Led his dear lady to a chair of *s*. *Lover's Tale iv* 321

State (*rank*) And bow'd her *s* to them, that they might grow *Princess ii* 166
With reasons drawn from age and *s*, „ *v* 357
we believe him Something far advanced in *S*, *Ode on Well.* 275
And, for himself was of the greater *s*, *Gareth and L.* 395
As Mark would sully the low *s* of churl: „ 427

State (*splendour*) but robed in soften'd light Of orient *s*. *Ode to Memory* 11

Statelier (*adj.*) Then comes the *s* Eden back to men: *Princess vii* 293
With *s* progress to and fro The double tides of chariots flow *In Mem. xcviii* 22
Garrick and *s* Kemble, and the rest *To W. C. Macready* 7
Then, with a melody Stronger and *s*, *Merlin and the G.* 63

Statelier (*s*) Could find no *s* than his peers *Two Voices* 29

Stateliest sit the best and *s* of the land? *Lucretius* 172
King Arthur, like a modern gentleman Of *s* port; *M. d'Arthur, Ep.* 23
nor end of mine, *S*, for thee! *Princess vii* 170
Adored her, as the *s* and the best *Marr. of Geraint* 20
and as the *s* under heaven. *Holy Grail* 224
Wielder of the *s* measure ever moulded by the lips of man. *To Virgil* 39

Stateliness harmony Of thy swan-like *s*, *Eleänore* 47
Who see your tender grace and *s*. *Guinevere* 190

Stately The *s* flower of female fortitude, *Isabel* 11
deep myrrh-thickets blowing round The *s* cedar, *Arabian Nights* 105
maid, whose *s* brow The dew-impearled winds of dawn *Ode to Memory* 13
To throng with *s* blooms the breathing spring *The Poet* 27
To her full height her *s* stature draws; *D. of F. Women* 102
all the decks were dense with *s* forms Black-stoled, *M. d'Arthur* 196
Many an evening by the waters did we watch the *s* ships, *Locksley Hall* 37
s ships go on To their haven under the hill; *Break, break, etc.* 9
long convolvuluses That coil'd around the *s* stems, *Enoch Arden* 577
Stept thro' the *s* minuet of those days: *Aylmer's Field* 207
we stroll'd For half the day thro' *s* theatres *Princess ii* 369
standing like a *s* Pine Set in a cataract on an island-crag, „ *v* 346
leader of the herd That holds a *s* fretwork to the Sun, „ *vi* 86
crimson-hued the *s* palm-woods Whisper in odorous heights *Milton* 15
But she is tall and *s*. *Maud I xii* 16
From mother unto mother, *s* bride, *W. to Marie Alex.* 9
Camelot, a city of shadowy palaces And *s*, *Gareth and L.* 304
midway down the side of that long hall A *s* pile,— „ 405
'Farewell, fair Prince,' answer'd the *s* Queen. *Marr. of Geraint* 224
And there be made known to the *s*, „ 607
came A *s* queen whose name was Guinevere, „ 667
His princess, or indeed the *s* Queen, „ 759
And moving out they found the *s* horse, *Geraint and E.* 752
Manners so kind, yet *s*, such a grace Of tenderest courtesy, „ 861
Being mirthful he, but in a *s* kind— *Lancelot and E.* 322
Whereon a hundred *s* beeches grew, *Pelleas and E.* 26
He glanced and saw the *s* galleries, *Last Tournament* 145
So the *s* Queen abode For many a week, unknown, *Guinevere* 146
all the decks were dense with *s* forms, Black-stoled, *Pass. of Arthur* 364
A *s* mountain nymph she look'd! *Lover's Tale i* 359
in front of which Six *s* virgins, all in white, „ *ii* 77
s vestibules To caves and shows of Death: „ 125
the *s* Spanish men to their flagship bore him then, *The Revenge* 97
s and tall—A princelier looking man never stept thro' a Prince's hall. *The Wreck* 15
Raise a *s* memorial, Make it regally gorgeous, *On Jub. Q. Victoria* 44
S purposes, valour in battle, *Vastness* 7
Edith bow'd her *s* head, *The Tourney* 13

Stately-gentle nay Being so *s-g*, *Balin and Balan* 192

Stately-set the fair hall-ceiling *s-s* *Palace of Art* 141

State-oracle O friends, our chief *s-o* is mute: *Ode on Well.* 23

States (**United**) He's gone to the *S's*, aroon, *Tomorrow* 49

Statesman (*See also* **Statesman-warrior**) 'And statesmen at her council met *To the Queen* 29
No blazon'd *s* he, nor king. *You might have won* 24
O *Statesmen*, guard us, guard the eye, *Ode on Well.* 160
keep the soldier firm, the *s* pure: „ 222

Stephen (the speaker's lover) we fondled it, *S* and I, But it died,	*The Wreck* 83
' O *S*, I love you, I love you, and yet '—	" 101
' O *S*,' I moan'd, ' I am coming to thee	" 132
Stepmother you hear Far-off, is Muriel—your *s's* voice.	*The Ring* 139
Your Mother and *s-m*—	" 146
Steppe golden news along the *s's* is blown,	*W. to Marie Alex.* 11
Steppeth *S* from Heaven to Heaven, from light to light,	*Lover's Tale i* 512
Stepping (*See also* **A-steppin'**) He, *s* down By zig-zag paths,	*M. d'Arthur* 49
Come *s* lightly down the plank,	*In Mem. xiv* 7
she rose, and *s* lightly, heap'd The pieces	*Geraint and E.* 373
He, *s* down By zigzag paths,	*Pass. of Arthur* 217
Seem'd *s* out of darkness with a smile.	*Lover's Tale iv* 220
Stepping-stones Below the range of *s-s*,	*Miller's D.* 54
That men may rise on *s-s*	*In Mem. i* 3
Stept When forth there *s* a foeman tall,	*Oriana* 33
Then *s* she down thro' town and field	*Of old sat Freedom* 9
from the ruin'd shrine he *s*	*M. d'Arthur* 45
And out I *s*, and up I crept :	*Edwin Morris* 111
S forward on a firmer leg,	*Will Water.* 123
Down *s* Lord Ronald from his tower :	*Lady Clare* 65
In robe and crown the king *s* down,	*Beggar Maid* 5
S the long-hair'd long-bearded solitary,	*Enoch Arden* 637
S thro' the stately minuet of those days :	*Aylmer's Field* 207
Then *s* a buxom hostess forth,	*Princess i* 223
Lightly to the warrior *s*,	" *vi* 10
a healthful people *s* As in the presence	*Gareth and L.* 315
And inward to the wall ; he *s* behind ;	*Balin and Balan* 406
found a little boat, and *s* into it ;	*Merlin and V.* 198
close behind them *s* the lily maid Elaine,	*Lancelot and E.* 176
into that rude hall *S* with all grace,	" 263
from the ruin'd shrine he *s*,	*Pass. of Arthur* 213
the man who stood with me *S* gaily forward,	*Lover's Tale iii* 51
From wall to dyke he *s*,	*Achilles over the T.* 15
princelier looking man never *s* thro' a Prince's hall.	*The Wreck* 16
she *s* an the chapel-green,	*Tomorrow* 27
Christ-like creature that ever *s* on the ground.	*Charity* 32
Sterling most, of *s* worth, is what Our own experience preaches.	*Will Water.* 175
Stern (adj.) Or gay, or grave, or sweet, or *s*,	*Palace of Art* 91
The *s* black-bearded kings with wolfish eyes,	*D. of F. Women* 111
S he was and rash ;	*The Captain* 10
Grave, florid, *s*, as far as eye could see,	*Sea Dreams* 219
s and sad (so rare the smiles Of sunlight)	*The Daisy* 53
The *s* were mild when thou wert by,	*In Mem. cx* 9
S too at times, and then I loved him not,	*Com. of Arthur* 354
To such a *s* and iron-clashing close,	*Merlin and V.* 419
Stern (s) Dark as a funeral scarf from stem to *s*,	*M. d'Arthur* 194
from stem to *s* Bright with a shining people	*Com. of Arthur* 375
Dark as a funeral scarf from stem to *s*,	*Pass. of Arthur* 362
Steward The wrinkled *s* at his task,	*Day-Dm., Sleep. P.* 27
The butler drank, the *s* scrawl'd,	" *Revival* 10
'Tis but a *s* of the can,	*Will Water.* 149
Sthrame (stream) comin' down be the *s*,	*Tomorrow* 7
s's runnin' down at the back o' the glin	" 24
Stick (s) on whom all spears Are rotten *s's* !	*Gareth and L.* 1306
an' swear'd as I'd break ivry	*North. Cobbler* 35
Molly kem limpin' up wid her *s*,	*Tomorrow* 77
stannin' theere o' the brokken *s* ;	*Owd Roä* 25
Stick (verb) And on thy ribs the limpet *s's*	*Sailor Boy* 11
But proputty, proputty *s's*,	*N. Farmer, N. S.* 16
a villain fitter to *s* swine Than ride abroad	*Gareth and L.* 865
Thim's my noätions, Sammy, wheerby I means to *s* ;	*N. Farmer, N. S.* 57
what *s* ye round The pasty ?	*Gareth and L.* 1072
s oop thy back, an' set oop thy taäil,	*Spinster's S's.* 31
if t'one *s* alongside t'uther	*Church-warden, etc.* 10
Sa I *s's* like the ivin as long as I lives	" 15
Stiff While my *s* spine can hold my weary head,	*St. S. Stylites* 43
wet With drenching dews, or *s* with cracking frost.	" 115
' but still My joints are somewhat *s* or so.	*Day-Dm., Revival* 26
That stood from out a *s* brocade in which,	*Aylmer's Field* 204
see how you stand *S* as Lot's wife,	*Princess vi* 241

Stiff (*continued*) and stood *S* as a viper frozen ;	*Merlin and V.* 845
That whistled *s* and dry about the marge.	*Pass. of Arthur* 232
That whistled *s* and dry about the marge.	*M. d'Arthur* 64
Stiffen And, lest I *s* into stone,	*In Mem. cviii* 2
Stiffen'd His fingers were so *s* by the frost	*The Ring* 239
Stiffening Sir Aylmer Aylmer slowly *s* spoke :	*Aylmer's Field* 273
Stiffer My nerves have dealt with *s*.	*Will Water.* 78
Stiff-set Blow, flute, and stir the *s-s* sprigs,	*Amphion* 63
Stiff-stricken She sat *S-s*, listening ;	*Guinevere* 412
Stifled She whisper'd, with a *s* moan	*Mariana in the S.* 57
Making Him broken gleams, and a *s* splendour and gloom.	*High. Pantheism* 10
breathless burthen of low-folded heavens *S* and chill'd at once ;	*Aylmer's Field* 613
my strangled vanity Utter'd a *s* cry—	*Sisters (E. and E.)* 200
Stile So Lawrence Aylmer, seated on a *s*	*The Brook* 197
S's where we stay'd to be kind,	*Window, Marr. Morn.* 7
By meadow and *s* and wood,	" 14
Over the meadows and *s's*,	" 22
Or simple *s* from mead to mead,	*In Mem. c* 7
That ever bided tryst at village *s*,	*Merlin and V.* 378
Still Pure vestal thoughts in the translucent fane Of her *s* spirit ;	*Isabel* 5
Wash'd with *s* rains and daisy blossomed ;	*Circumstance* 7
senses with a *s* delight Of dainty sorrow	*Margaret* 17
Falling into a *s* delight,	*Eleänore* 106
Come only, when the days are *s*,	*My life is full* 23
A *S* small voice spake unto me,	*Two Voices* 1
Then to the *s* small voice I said ;	" 4
In her *s* place the morning wept :	" 275
The *s* voice laugh'd. ' I talk,' said he,	" 385
The pool beneath it never *s*,	*Miller's D.* 100
s affection of the heart Became an outward breathing type,	" 225
fit for every mood And change of my *s* soul.	*Palace of Art* 60
' I marvel if my *s* delight In this great house	" 190
A *s* salt pool, lock'd in with bars of sand,	" 249
All the valley, mother, 'ill be fresh and green and *s*,	*May Queen* 37
When you are warm-asleep, mother, and all the world is *s*.	*May Queen, N. Y's. E.* 24
Or night-dews on *s* waters between walls	*Lotos-Eaters, C. S.* 3
Scaffolds, *s* sheets of water, divers woes,	*D. of F. Women* 34
not so deadly *s* As that wide forest.	" 68
Thy sole delight is, sitting *s*,	*The Blackbird* 10
One after one, thro' that *s* garden pass'd ;	*Gardener's D.* 201
By this *s* hearth, among these barren crags,	*Ulysses* 2
With one smile of *s* defiance Sold him	*The Captain* 59
detaching, fold by fold, From those *s* heights,	*Vision of Sin* 52
And the sound of a voice that is *s* !	*Break, break, etc.* 12
face All-kindled by a *s* and sacred fire,	*Enoch Arden* 71
Found a *s* place, and pluck'd her likeness out ;	*Princess i* 92
doubtful smile dwelt like a clouded moon In a *s* water ·	" *vi* 271
strong on his legs, but *s* on his tongue !	*Grandmother* 13
I look'd at the *s* little body—	" 66
Calm and *s* light on yon great plain	*In Mem. xi* 9
The moon is hid ; the night is *s* ;	" *xxviii* 2
So that *s* garden of the souls In many a figured leaf	" *xliii* 10
The fruitful hours of *s* increase ;	" *xlvi* 10
When all his active powers are *s*,	" *lxiv* 18
Looks thy fair face and makes it *s*.	" *lxx* 16
And fluctuate all the *s* perfume,	" *xcv* 56
The moon is hid, the night is *s* ;	" *civ* 2
One *s* strong man in a blatant land,	*Maud I x* 63
Why am I sitting here so stunn'd and *s*,	" *II i* 2
Always I long to creep Into some *s* cavern deep,	" *iv* 96
the two Left the *s* King, and passing forth	*Com. of Arthur* 369
A STORM was coming, and the winds were *s*,	*Merlin and V.* 1
Past up the *s* rich city to his kin,	*Lancelot and E.* 802
Speaking a *s* good-morrow with her eyes.	" 1033
As hard and *s* as is the face that men	" 1251
then came a night *S* as the day was loud ;	*Holy Grail* 683
Who yells Here in the *s* sweet summer night,	*Pelleas and E.* 473
Clung to the dead earth, and the land was *s*.	*Guinevere* 8
took and bare him off, And all was *s* :	" 110
There came a day as *s* as heaven,	" 292

Stol'n (*continued*) and *s* away To dreamful wastes   *Maud I xviii* 68

(Who hearing her own name had *s* away)   *Marr. of Geraint* 507

Some lost, some *s*, some as relics kept.   *Merlin and V.* 453

Art with poisonous honey *s* from France,   *To the Queen ii* 56

And if the ring were *s* from the maid,   *The Ring* 203

had *s*, worn the ring—Then torn it from her finger,   „ 455

Stomach Less having *s* for it than desire   *Geraint and E.* 213

Stomach'd *See* **Faint-stomach'd**

Stomacher He cleft me thro' the *s*;   *Princess ii* 407

Stone (*See also* **Altar-stone, Foundation-stone, Stepping-stones, Stoän**) Life in dead *s's*, or spirit in air;   *A Character* 9

cursed and scorn'd, and bruised with *s's*:   *Two Voices* 222

The lizard, with his shadow on the *s*,   *Œnone* 27

Ev'n on this hand, and sitting on this *s*?   „ 233

one a foreground black with *s's* and slags,   *Palace of Art* 81

song Throb thro' the ribbed *s*;   „ 176

A rolling *s* of here and everywhere,   *Audley Court* 78

Till all my limbs drop piecemeal from the *s*,   *St. S. Stylites* 44

I lay Pent in a roofless close of ragged *s's*;   „ 74

On the mossy *s*, as I lay,   *Edward Gray* 26

' Bitterly wept I over the *s*:   „ 33

Tread a measure on the *s's*,   *Vision of Sin* 180

On thy cold gray *s's*, O Sea!   *Break, break, etc.* 2

His eyes upon the *s's*, he reach'd the home   *Enoch Arden* 684

or one *s* Left on another,   *Aylmer's Field* 788

men of flesh and blood, and men of *s*,   *Sea Dreams* 237

on the pavement lay Carved *s's* of the Abbey-ruin   *Princess, Pro.* 14

One rear'd a font of *s* And drew,   „ *iii* 271

and watch The sandy footprint harden into *s*.'   „ *iii* 271

Old Yew, which graspest at the *s's*   *In Mem. ii* 1

Dark yew, that graspest at the *s's*   „ *xxxix* 2

From scarped cliff and quarried *s*   „ *lvi* 2

And, lest I stiffen into *s*,   „ *cviii* 2

On a heart half-turn'd to *s*.   *Maud I vi* 78

O heart of *s*, are you flesh,   „ 79

Wept over her, carved in *s*;   „ *viii* 4

(Which Maud, like a precious *s* Set in the heart   „ *xiv* 10

Low on the sand and loud on the *s*   „ *xxii* 25

Courage, poor heart of *s*!   „ *II iii* 1

Courage, poor stupid heart of *s*.—   „ 5

Of ancient kings who did their days in *s*;   *Gareth and L.* 305

by two yards in casting bar or *s* Was counted best;   „ 518

A *s* about his neck to drown him in it.   „ 812

Gareth loosed the *s* From off his neck,   „ 814

and with a *s* about his neck;   „ 823

but at night let go the *s*, And rise,   „ 825

Like sparkles in the *s* Avanturine.   „ 930

Hurl'd as a *s* from out of a catapult   „ 965

slopes a wild brook o'er a little *s*,   *Marr. of Geraint* 77

star Of sprouted thistle on the broken *s's*.   „ 314

suck'd the joining of the *s's*, and look'd A knot,   „ 324

Right o'er a mount of newly-fallen *s's*   „ 361

blade flew Splintering in six, and clinkt upon the *s's*.   *Balin and Balan* 396

when she heard his horse upon the *s's*,   *Lancelot and E.* 980

With knees of adoration wore the *s*;   *Holy Grail* 71

and the *s's* They pitch up straight to heaven: „ 664

bound and plunged him into a cell Of great piled *s's*;   „ 676

Heavy as it was, a great *s* slipt and fell,   „ 680

shatter'd talbots, which had left the *s's* Raw,   „ 719

s is flung into some sleeping tarn,   *Pelleas and E.* 93

spiring *s* that scaled about her tower,   *Last Tournament* 511

A little bitter pool about a *s*   *Guinevere* 51

I CAME one day and sat among the *s's*   *Lover's Tale iii* 1

you are just as hard as a *s*.   *Rizpah* 80

Scribbled or carved upon the pitiless *s*;   *Sir J. Oldcastle* 5

and we took to throwing the *s*,   *V. of Maeldune* 94

One was of smooth-cut *s*,   „ 106

There were some for the clean-cut *s*,   „ 112

Beyond all work of those who carve the *s*,   *Tiresias* 53

No *s* is fitted in yon marble girth   „ 135

and mute below the chancel *s's*,   *Locksley H., Sixty* 43

Tho' carved in harder *s*—   *Epilogue* 53

I am mortal *s* and lime.   *Helen's Tower* 6

and see no more The *S*, the Wheel,   *Demeter and P.* 150

Stone (*continued*) a *s*, That glances from the bottom of the pool,   *The Ring* 370

a shower of *s's* that stoned him dead,   *St. Telemachus* 68

I dream'd That *s* by *s* I rear'd a sacred fane,   *Akbar's Dream* 177

loosen, *s* from *s*, All my fair work;   „ 188

Who fitted *s* to *s* again, and Truth, Peace,   „ 193

Stone (*disease*) Past earthquake—ay, and gout and *s*,   *Lucretius* 153

Stone-cast About a *s-c* from the wall   *Mariana* 37

Stoned either they were *s*, or crucified,   *St. S. Stylites* 51

a shower of stones that *s* him dead,   *St. Telemachus* 68

Stone-deaf *See* **Stoän-deäf**

Stone-shot He show'd a tent A *s-s* off;   *Princess v* 54

Stonest O thou that *s*, hadst thou understood   *Aylmer's Field* 739

Stoning no *s* save with flint and rock?   „ 746

Stony On *s* drought and steaming salt;   *Mariana in the S.* 40

lion on your old *s* gates Is not more cold to you than I.   *L. C. V. de Vere* 23

while all the fleet Had rest by *s* hills of Crete.   *On a Mourner* 35

Better the narrow brain, the *s* heart,   *Love and Duty* 15

I chatter over *s* ways,   *The Brook* 39

Before the *s* face of Time,   *Lit. Squabbles* 3

had wound A scarf of orange round the *s* helm,   *Princess, Pro.* 102

chattering *s* names Of shale and hornblende,   „ *iii* 361

the fangs Shall move the *s* bases of the world.   „ *vi* 58

Gorgonised me from head to foot With a *s* British stare.   *Maud I xiii* 22

There ran a treble range of *s* shields,—   *Gareth and L.* 407

S showers Of that ear-stunning hail of Arès   *Tiresias* 95

Gods Avenge on *s* hearts a fruitless prayer   *Death of Œnone* 41

Stood *s* Betwixt me and the light of God!   *Supp. Confessions* 109

at last *s* out This excellence and solid form   „ 148

heaven's mazed signs *s* still In the   *Clear-headed friend* 28

And *s* aloof from other minds   *A Character* 23

She *s* upon the castle wall,   *Oriana* 28

you *s* Between the rainbow and the sun.   *Margaret* 21

Pallas where she *s* Somewhat apart,   *Œnone* 137

Full of great rooms and small the palace *s*,   *Palace of Art* 57

in dark corners of her palace *s* Uncertain shapes;   „ 237

That *s* against the wall.   „ 244

Join'd not, but *s*, and standing saw   „ 254

Full-faced above the valley *s* the moon;   *Lotos-Eaters* 7

silent pinnacles of aged snow, *S* sunset flush'd: „ 17

I appeal'd To one that *s* beside.   *D. of F. Women* 100

so *s* I, when that flow Of music left the lips   „ 194

She lock'd her lips: she left me where I *s*:   „ 241

Losing her carol I *s* pensively,   „ 245

That *s* on a dark strait of barren land.   *M. d'Arthur* 10

both his eyes were dazzled, as he *s*,   „ 59

Long *s* Sir Bedivere Revolving many memories,   „ 269

those that *s* upon the hills behind Repeated—   „ *Ep.* 25

s, Leaning his horns into the neighbour field,   *Gardener's D.* 86

Holding the bush, to fix it back, she *s*,   „ 127

Half light, half shade, She *s*,   „ 141

to Mary's house, and *s* Upon the threshold.   *Dora* 110

and while we *s* like fools Embracing,   *Edwin Morris* 118

brothers of the weather *s* Stock-still   *Will Water.* 135

O and proudly *s* she up!   *Lady Clare* 77

He turn'd and kiss'd her where she *s*:   „ 82

STILL on the tower *s* the vane,   *The Letters* 1

wild hawk *s* with the down on his beak,   *Poet's Song* 11

and while he *s* on deck Waving,   *Enoch Arden* 243

there he *s* once more before her face,   „ 457

Her son, who *s* beside her tall and strong,   „ 756

There *s* a maiden near, Waiting to pass.   *The Brook* 204

S from his walls and wing'd his entry-gates   *Aylmer's Field* 18

That *s* from out a stiff brocade in which,   „ 204

under his own lintel *s* Storming with lifted hands,   „ 331

to the lychgate, where his chariot *s*,   „ 824

I *s* like one that had received a blow: *Sea Dreams* 161

s out the breasts, The breasts of Helen,   *Lucretius* 60

in the presence room *s* With Cyril   *Princess i* 51

There *s* a bust of Pallas for a sign,   „ 222

while They *s*, so rapt, we gazing, came a voice,   „ *ii* 318

saw The Lady Blanche's daughter where she *s*,   „ 321

So *s* that same fair creature at the door.   „ 329

There while we *s* beside the fount,   „ *iii* 23

Stood (*continued*) She *s* Among her maidens, higher by the
　head,　　　　　　　　　　　　　　　　　*Princess iii* 178
s, Engirt with many a florid maiden-cheek,　　.. 349
Alone I *s* With Florian, cursing Cyril,　　　.. *iv* 170
There *s* her maidens glimmeringly group'd　　.. 190
Lady Blanche erect *S* up and spake,　　　　.. 291
You *s* in your light and darken'd mine.　　　.. 314
And then *s* up and spoke impetuously.　　　.. 418
high above them *s* The placid marble Muses,　.. 488
I *s* and seem'd to hear, As in a poplar grove　*v* 12
storming in extremes, *S* for her cause,　　　.. 177
high upon the palace Ida *s* With Psyche's babe　*vi* 30
So *s* the unhappy mother open-mouth'd,　　.. 143
rising slowly from me, *s* Erect and silent,　.. 151
But Ida *s* nor spoke, drain'd of her force　　.. 266
had you *s* by us, The roar that breaks the Pharos　.. 338
in the centre *s* The common men with rolling eyes;　.. 359
And there we saw Sir Walter where he *s*,　.. *Con.* 81
now him, of those. That *s* the nearest—　　.. 93
Which *s* four-square to all the winds that blew!　*Ode on Well.* 39
Where he greatly *s* at bay,　　　　　　　.. 106
for Willy *s* like a rock.　　　　　　*Grandmother* 10
and *s* by the road at the gate.　　　　　" 38
Willy *s* up like a man,　　　　　　　" 45
I *s* among the silent statues,　　　　*The Daisy* 63
In the centre *s* A statue veil'd,'　　　*In Mem. ciii* 11
S up and answer'd 'I have felt.'　　　　" *cxxiv* 16
He *s* on the path a little aside;　　　*Maud I xiii* 7
And *s* by her garden-gate;　　　　　.. *xiv* 6
I thought as I *s*, if a hand, as white　　.. 17
And long by the garden lake I *s*,　　　" *xxii* 35
For front to front in an hour we *s*,　　" *II i* 23
And I *s* on a giant deck and mix'd my breath　" *III vi* 34
Guinevere *S* by the castle walls to watch him pass;　*Com. of Arthur* 48
Who *s* in silence near his throne,　　　.. 277
'And near him *s* the Lady of the Lake,　.. 283
S one who pointed toward the voice,　　.. 438
but the King *s* out in heaven, Crown'd.　.. 443
his knights *S* round him, and rejoicing in his joy.　.. 459
The Lady of the Lake *s*: all her dress Wept　*Gareth and L.* 216
near it *s* The two that out of north　　.. 678
Hear me—this morn I *s* in Arthur's hall,　.. 855
Who *s* a moment, ere his horse was brought,　.. 934
The Lady Lyonors at a window *s*,　　　.. 1375
And *s* behind, and waited on the three.　*Marr. of Geraint* 392
And Enid *s* aside to wait the event,　*Geraint and E.* 153
When now they saw their bulwark fallen, *s*;　.. 168
Was in a manner pleased, and turning, *s*.　.. 456
While the great charger *s*, grieved like a man.　.. 535
on his right *S*, all of massiest bronze	*Balin and Balan* 364
the one Who *s* beside thee even now,　　" 613
arose And *s* with folded hands and downward eyes	*Merlin and V.* 69
Queen who *s* All glittering like May sunshine　.. 87
and *s* Stiff as a viper frozen;　　　　.. 844
and *s*, A virtuous gentlewoman deeply wrong'd,　.. 910
Lancelot, where he *s* beside the King.	*Lancelot and E.* 85
she drew Nearer and *s*.　　　　　.. 350
For silent, tho' he greeted her, she *s*　.. 355
His honour rooted in dishonour *s*,　　.. 876
but deadly-pale *S* grasping what was nearest,　.. 966
all the place whereon she was green;　　.. 1200
There two *s* arm'd, and kept the door;　" 1247
In our great hall there *s* a vacant chair,	*Holy Grail* 167
And staring each at other like dumb men *S*,　.. 194
And those that had not, *s* before the King,　., 724
and there, half-hidden by him, *s*,　　.. 754
there was none *S* near it but a lion on each side　.. 817
Breast-high in that bright line of bracken *s*:	*Pelleas and E.* 56
he *s* There on the castle-bridge once more,　.. 442
here he *s*, and might have slain Me and thyself.'　.. 491
But Percivale *s* near him and replied,　.. 523
Rolling his eyes, a moment *s*, then spake:　.. 581
And while they *s* without the doors,	*Last Tournament* 113
there with gibes and flickering mockeries *S*,　" 187
while he twangled little Dagonet *s* Quiet　" 252

Stood (*continued*) moved slow-measure to my tune,
　Not *s* stockstill.　　　　　　*Last Tournament* 283
machicolated tower That *s* with open doors,　.. 425
near me *s*, In fuming sulphur blue and green,　.. 616
strong man-breasted things *s* from the sea,　*Guinevere* 246
s before the Queen As tremulously as foam　.. 363
near him the sad nuns with each a light *S*,　.. 591
That *s* on a dark strait of barren land:	*Pass. of Arthur* 178
That both his eyes were dazzled as he *s*,　.. 227
Long *s* Sir Bedivere Revolving many memories,　.. 437
They *s* before his throne in silence,　　.. 455
Were drunk into the inmost blue, we *s*,	*Lover's Tale i* 309
near'd the bay, For there the Temple *s*.　.. 339
and *s* A solid glory on her bright black hair;　.. 366
Half-melted into thin blue air, *s* still　.. 421
For bliss *s* round me like the light of Heaven,—　.. 495
I seem'd the only part of Time *s* still,　.. 573
forms which ever *s* Within the magic cirque　.. *ii* 158
the man who *s* with me Stept gaily forward,　.. *iii* 50
And I *s* stole beside the vacant bier.　　.. 58
Before the board, there paused and *s*,　.. *iv* 307
I *s* upon the stairs of Paradise.	*Sisters (E. and E.)* 144
Death while we *s* with the musket,	*Def. of Lucknow* 16
s on each of the loftiest capes,	*V. of Maeldune* 100
he *s*, nor join'd The Achæans—	*Achilles over the T.* 15
S out before a darkness, crying ' Thebes,	*Tiresias* 115
and the ship *s* still, and the skies were blue,	*The Wreck* 115
ruin'd by *him*, by *him*, I *s* there, naked, amazed	*Despair* 77
An' Dan *s* there for a minute,	*Tomorrow* 22
s up strait as the Queen of the world—　.. 79
an' *s* By the claäy'd-oop pond,	*Spinster's S's.* 23
I feel'd thy arm es I *s* wur a-creeäpin　.. 26
often I and Amy in the mouldering aisle
　have *s*,	*Locksley H., Sixty* 31
There again I *s* to-day,　　　　　.. 33
Here we *s* and claspt each other,　　.. 180
They rode, or they *s* at bay—	*Heavy Brigade* 51
Ranged like a storm or *s* like a rock　.. 56
s stark by the dead; And behind him,	*Dead Prophet* 19
wife and his child *s* by him in tears,　" 57
An' then as I *s* i' the doorwaäy,	*Owd Roä* 42
Where *s* the sheaf of Peace:	*The Ring* 247
who were those that *s* between The tower　.. 252
whose hand was that ? they *s* So close together.　.. 257
Even from myself ? stand ? *s* . . . no more.	*Romney's R.* 66
s Before the great Madonna-masterpieces　.. 85
kindled the pyre, and all *S* round it,	*Death of Œnone* 66
But while we *s* rejoicing, I and thou,	*Akbar's Dream* 182
An' ya *s* oop naäkt i' the beck,	*Church-warden, etc.* 29

Stook (stuck) *S* to his taäil they did,	*N. Farmer, N. S.* 30
Stool Perch'd like a crow upon a three-legg'd *s*,	*Audley Court* 45
his foot was on a *s* Shaped as a dragon;	*Last Tournament* 671
An' sattle their ends upo *s's*	*Owd Roä* 24
Stoop *S's* at all game that wing the skies,	*Rosalind* 4
To *s* the cowslip to the plains,　　　　"
The skies *s* down in their desire;	*Fatima* 32
I could not *s* to such a mind.	*L. C. V. de Vere* 20
Enormous elm-tree-boles did *s* and lean	*D. of F. Women* 57
He *s's*—to kiss her—on his knee.	*Day-Dm., Arrival* 30
The cloud may *s* from heaven and take the shape	*Princess vii* 2
S down and seem to kiss me ere I die.'　" 150
To *s* and kiss the tender little thumb,	*Marr. of Geraint* 395
watch the time, and eagle-like *S* at thy will	*Balin and Balan* 536
I said to her, ' A day for Gods to *s*,'	*Lover's Tale i* 304
A clamorous cuckoo *s's* to meet her hand;	*Prog. of Spring* 45

Stoop'd-Stoopt He *stoop'd* and clutch'd him, fair and
　good,	*Will Water.* 133
And o'er her second father *stoopt* a girl,	*Enoch Arden* 747
stoop'd. To drench his dark locks in the gurgling wave	*Princess iv* 186
Rise ! ' and *stoop'd* to updrag Melissa:　.. 366
when a boy, you *stoop'd* to me From all high places,　.. 429
My father *stoop'd*, re-father'd o'er my wounds.　.. *vi* 129
She turn'd ; she paused ; She *stoop'd* ;　" *vii* 155
rode to Merlin's feet, Who *stoopt* and caught the
　babe,	*Com. of Arthur* 385

Stoop'd-Stoopt (*continued*) and *stoop'd* With a low
  whinny toward the pair : | *Geraint and E.* 755
sorrowing Lancelot should have *stoop'd* so low, | *Lancelot and E.* 732
Stoopt, took, break seal, and read it ; | " 1271
I *stoop'd*, I gather'd the wild herbs, | *Lover's Tale i* 341
and death while we *stoopt* to the spade, | *Def. of Lucknow* 16
dreamer *stoopt* and kiss'd her marble brow. | *Locksley H., Sixty* 38
while I *stoopt* To raise and kiss the ring. | *The Ring* 131

Stopt   The swallow *s* as he hunted the fly, | *Poet's Song* 9
All of a sudden he *s* : | *Grandmother* 41
S, and then with a riding whip | *Maud I xiii* 18
when he *s* we long'd to hurl together, | *Merlin and V.* 420

Store (s)   then with what she brought Buy goods and
  s's— | *Enoch Arden* 138
Bought Annie goods and *s's*, and set his hand | ,, 169
With shelf and corner for the goods and *s's*. | ,, 171
How best to help the slender *s*, | *To F. D. Maurice* 37
Love, then, had hope of richer *s* : | *In Mem. lxxxi* 5
We wish them *s* of happy days. | *Con.* 84
With *s* of rich apparel, sumptuous fare, | *Marr. of Geraint* 709
of whate'er The Future had in *s* : | *Lover's Tale ii* 133

Store (verb)   For some three suns to *s* and hoard myself, | *Ulysses* 29
Stored   all things in order *s*, | *Palace of Art* 87
S in some treasure-house of mighty kings, | *M. d'Arthur* 101
Dora *s* what little she could save, | *Dora* 52
honeycomb of eloquence *S* from all flowers ? | *Edwin Morris* 27
I *s* it full of rich memorial : | *Princess v* 391
In this wide hall with earth's invention *s*, | *Ode Inter. Exhib.* 2
S in some treasure-house of mighty kings, | *Pass. of Arthur* 269
summers are *s* in the sunlight still, | *The Dawn* 19

Storied   where sweetest sunlight falls Upon the *s* walls ; | *Ode to Memory* 86
with love far-brought From out the *s* Past, | *Love thou thy land* 2

Storing   *S* yearly little dues of wheat, | *Lotos-Eaters, C. S.* 122

Stork   Went by me, like a *s* : | *Talking Oak* 56

Storm   (See also **Thunder-storm**)   as from the *s* Of
  running fires and fluid range | *Supp. Confessions* 146
Whither in after life retired From brawling *s's*, | *Ode to Memory* 112
And shatter, when the *s's* are black, | *England and Amer.* 13
Henceforward squall nor *s* Could keep me | *Gardener's D.* 190
I turn'd once more, close-button'd to the *s* ; | *Edwin Morris* 136
Battering the gates of heaven with *s's* of prayer, | *St. S. Stylites* 7
shaken with a sudden *s* of sighs— | *Locksley Hall* 27
But blessed forms in whistling *s's* | *Sir Galahad* 59
S, such as drove her under moonless heavens | *Enoch Arden* 547
like a *s* he came, And shook the house, and like
  a *s* he went. | *Aylmer's Field* 215
Caught in a burst of unexpected *s*, | ,, 285
Sir Aylmer reddening from the *s* within, | ,, 322
but presently Wept like a *s* ; | ,, 403
sheet-lightnings from afar, but fork'd Of the near *s*, | ,, 727
but when the wordy *s* Had ended, | *Sea Dreams* 31
' *S* in the night ! for thrice I heard the rain | *Lucretius* 26
' *S*, and what dreams, ye holy Gods, | ,, 33
Balmier and nobler from her bath of *s*, | ,, 175
The green malignant light of coming *s*. | *Princess iii* 132
mystic fire on a mast-head, Prophet of *s* : | ,, iv 275
Fluctuated, as flowers in *s*, some red, | ,, 482
On me, me, me, the *s* first breaks : | ,, 499
When *s* is on the heights, | ,, v 348
at which the *s* Of galloping hoofs bare on the ridge | ,, 488
Let our girls flit, Till the *s* die ! | ,, vi 338
Tho' all the *s* of Europe on us break ; | *Third of Feb.* 14
s and blast Had blown the lake beyond his limit, | *The Daisy* 70
And a *s* never wakes on the lonely sea, | *The Islet* 33
a cloud in my heart, and a *s* in the air ! | *Window, Gone* 6
No is trouble and cloud and *s*, | ,, *No Answer* 8
The touch of change in calm or *s* : | *In Mem. xvi* 6
O thou that after toil and *s* | ,, *xxxiii* 1
And lash with *s* the streaming pane ? | ,, *lxxii* 4
The *s* their high-built organs make, | ,, *lxxxvii* 6
A pillar stedfast in the *s*, | ,, *cxiii* 12
The seeming prey of cyclic *s's*, | ,, *cxviii* 11
Well roars the *s* to those that hear A deeper voice
  across the *s*, | ,, *cxxvii* 3
should burst and drown with deluging *s's* | *Maud II i* 42

Storm (*continued*)   whatsoever *s* May shake the world, | *Com. of Arthur* 292
And lightnings play'd about it in the *s*, | *Gareth and L.* 68
A censer, either worn with wind and *s* ; | ,, 222
world's loud whisper breaking into *s*, | *Marr. of Geraint* 27
Turn thy wild wheel thro' sunshine, *s*, and cloud ; | ,, 348
Whose skirts are loosen'd by the breaking *s*, | *Geraint and E.* 459
A *S* was coming, but the winds were still, | *Merlin and V.* 1
A minstrel of Caerleon by strong *s* | ,, 9
s Brake on the mountain and I cared not for it. | ,, 502
And lash'd it at the base with slanting *s* ; | ,, 635
dark wood grew darker toward the *s* In silence, | ,, 890
' Come from the *s*,' and having no reply, | ,, 895
(For now the *s* was close above them) | ,, 935
Till now the *s*, its burst of passion spent, | ,, 961
(Sea was her wrath, yet working after *s*) | *Lancelot and E.* 1309
S at the top, and when we gain'd it, *s* Round us and
  death ; | *Holy Grail* 491
Spake but of sundry perils in the *s* ; | ,, 761
upward-rushing *s* and cloud Of shriek and plume, | *Last Tournament* 440
When that *s* of anger brake From Guinevere, | *Guinevere* 361
Or wisely or unwisely, signs of *s*, | *To the Queen ii* 49
mind Lies folded, often sweeps athwart in *s*— | *Lover's Tale i* 50
S, sunset, glows and glories of the moon | ,, ii 110
my lost love Symbol'd in *s*. | ,, 185
sway and whirl Of the *s* dropt to windless calm, | ,, 207
and the *s* rushing over the down, | *Rizpah* 6
when the *s* on the downs began, | ,, 71
A moonless night with *s*— | *Sisters (E. and E.)* 96
bleat of a lamb in the *s* and the darkness
  without ; | *In the Child. Hosp.* 64
S at the Water-gate ! *s* at the Bailey-gate ! *s*, and
  it ran | *Def. of Lucknow* 37
in days Of doubt and cloud and *s*, | *Columbus* 156
the poplar and cypress unshaken by *s* | *V. of Maeldune* 15
ridges drew the cloud and brake the *s* | *Montenegro* 13
driven by *s* and sin and death to the ancient fold, | *The Wreck* 2
I would hide from the *s* without, I would flee from
  the *s* within, | ,, 9
great *s* grew with a howl and a hoot | ,, 91
And he spoke not—only the *s* ; till after a little, | ,, 103
the *s* went roaring above us, and he—was out of the *s*. | ,, 106
the *s* and the days went by, but I knew no more— | ,, 111
And gone—that day of the *s*— | ,, 148
She reels not in the *s* of warring words, | *Ancient Sage* 70
The placid gleam of sunset after *s* ! | ,, 133
But wirrah ! the *s* that night— | *Tomorrow* 23
Ranged like a *s* or stood like a rock | *Heavy Brigade* 56
And glared at a coming *s*. | *Dead Prophet* 24
s's Of Autumn swept across the city, | *Demeter and P.* 70
A sound of anger like a distant *s*. | *The Ring* 119
The *s*, you hear Far-off, is Muriel— | ,, 138
One year without a *s*, or even a cloud ; | ,, 284
whom the *s* Had parted from his comrade | ,, 307
When the *s's* are blowing. | *Forlorn* 6
When I was praying in a *s*— | *Happy* 80
And bring or chase the *s*, | *Mechanophilus* 14
S in the South that darkens the day ! | *Riflemen form !* 2
S of battle and thunder of war ! | ,, 3
S, *S*, Riflemen form ! (repeat) | ,, 5, 19
Ready, be ready against the *s* ! (repeat) | ,, 6, 20
Ready, be ready to meet the *s* ! (repeat) | ,, 13, 27

Storm-beaten   With slow steps from out An old *s-b*,
  russet, | *Gareth and L.* 1113

Storm'd   *S* in orbs of song, a growing gale ; | *Vision of Sin* 25
and *s* At the Oppian law. | *Princess vii* 123
S at with shot and shell (repeat) | *Light Brigade* 22, 43

Stormier   Fiercer and *s* from restraining, | *Balin and Balan* 229
For whenever a rougher gust might tumble a *s* wave, | *The Wreck* 131

Storming   *s* a hill-fort of thieves He got it ; | *Aylmer's Field* 225
under his own lintel stood *S* with lifted hands, | ,, 332
and *s* in extremes, Stood for her cause, | *Princess v* 176
roughly set His Briton in blown seas and *s* showers, | *Ode on Well.* 155

Stormless   pass With all fair theories only made to gild
  A *s* summer. | *Princess ii* 234

Storm-strengthen'd   of grain *S-s* on a windy site, | *Gareth and L.* 692

Storm-worn   A *s-w* signpost not to be read,   *Dead Prophet* 17
Stormy   IN the *s* east-wind straining,   *L. of Shalott* iv 1
It is a *s* season.'   *The Goose* 8
It is a *s* morning.'   *„* 44
When down the *s* crescent goes,   *Sir Galahad* 25
There must be *s* weather;   *Will Water.* 54
overboard one *s* night He cast his body,   *The Voyage* 79
As of some fire against a *s* cloud,   *Princess* iv 384
'We fear, indeed, you spent a *s* time   *„ v* 121
Morning arises *s* and pale,   *Maud I* vi 1
Who in this *s* gulf have found a pearl   *„ xviii* 42
To catch a friend of mine one *s* day;   *„ II v* 85
Then like a *s* sunlight smiled Geraint,   *Geraint and E.* 480
with all Its *s* crests that smoke against the skies,   *Lancelot and E.* 484
And bluster into *s* sobs and say,   *„* 1067
thro' a *s* glare, a heat As from a seventimes-heated furnace,   *Holy Grail* 842
years Have hollow'd out a deep and *s* strait   *Lover's Tale* i 24
again this heaven *s* Crash'd in the shingle: *„* ii 53
'Come to us, O come, come' in the *s* red of a sky   *V. of Maeldune* 98
S voice of France! Who dost not love our England—   *To Victor Hugo* 8
spear and helmet tipt With *s* light as on a mast at sea,   *Tiresias* 114
After all the *s* changes shall we find a changeless May?   *Locksley H., Sixty* 156
Forward, let the *s* moment fly and mingle with the Past.   *„* 279
stood like a rock In the wave of a *s* day;   *Heavy Brigade* 57
Muses cried with a *s* cry 'Send them no more,   *Dead Prophet* 2
Like calming oil on all their *s* creeds,   *Akbar's Dream* 160
Story   (*See also* **Island-story**)   make the name Of his vessel great in *s*,   *The Captain* 19
—all the *s* of his house.   *Enoch Arden* 704
Here is a *s* which in rougher shape   *Aylmer's Field* 7
but as he told The *s*, storming a hill-fort   *„* 225
and so We forged a sevenfold *s*.   *Princess, Pro.* 202
And here I give the *s* and the songs.   *„* 247
For so, my mother said, the *s* ran.   *„ i* 11
And snowy summits old in *s*:   *„ iv* 2
And yet to give the *s* as it rose,   *„ Con.* 26
Till in all lands and thro' all human *s*   *Ode on Well.* 223
All for a slanderous *s*,   *Grandmother* 22
Hear the child's *s*.'   *Gareth and L.* 39
Hear yet once more the *s* of the child.   *„* 100
dumbly speaks Your *s*, that this man loves you no more.   *Geraint and E.* 329
And let the *s* of her dolorous voyage   *Lancelot and E.* 1343
THAT *s* which the bold Sir Bedivere   *Pass. of Arthur* 1
A woful man (for so the *s* went)   *Lover's Tale* i 379
I learnt the drearier *s* of his life;   *„ iv* 147
then began the *s* of his love As here to-day,   *„* 354
I told your wayside *s* to my mother   *Sisters (E. and E.)* 189
tell them all The *s* of my voyage,   *Columbus* 12
Story (floor)   And set in Heaven's third *s*,   *Will Water.* 70
Stout (adj.)   *S*, rosy, with his babe across his knees;   *Enoch Arden* 746
'ye are overfine To mar *s* knaves with foolish courtesies:'   *Gareth and L.* 733
And the *s* Prince bad him a loud good-night.   *Geraint and E.* 361
that had need Of a good *s* lad at his farm;   *First Quarrel* 18
Stout (s)   To each his perfect pint of *s*,   *Will Water.* 115
Stow'd   Or *s*, when classic Canning died,   *„* 101
Straänge (strange)   *S* an' cowd fur the time!   *Village Wife* 21
S an' unheppen Miss Lucy!   *„* 100
S an' owd-farran'd the 'ouse,   *Owd Roä* 21
Straät (straight)   *S* as a pole an' cleän as a flower   *North. Cobbler* 44
Straddling   *s* on the butts While the wine ran: *Guinevere* 268
Straight   (*See also* **Straät, Strait, Straït**)   'If *s* thy track, or if oblique,   *Two Voices* 193
To the pale-green sea-groves *s* and high,   *The Merman* 19
S, but as lissome as a hazel wand;   *The Brook* 70
Should, as by miracle, grow *s* and fair—   *Aylmer's Field* 676
For all we have power to see is a *s* staff bent in a pool;   *High. Pantheism* 16
All round one finger pointed *s*,   *The Ring* 453
Strain (s)   quick lark's closest-caroll' *s*'s,   *Rosalind* 10
An echo from a measured *s*,   *Miller's D.* 66

Strain (s) (*continued*)   Is this the manly *s* of Runnymede?   *Third of Feb.* 34
I scarce could brook the *s* and stir   *In Mem.* xv 12
A *s* to shame us 'keep you to yourselves;   *To the Queen* ii 15
Strain (verb)   cords that bind and *s* The heart   *Clear-headed Friend* 4
Shudderest when I *s* my sight,   *Fatima* 3
s to make an inch of room For their sweet selves,   *Lit. Squabbles* 9
Strain'd   A little in the late encounter *s*,   *Geraint and E.* 158
thou hast seen me *s* And sifted to the utmost,   *Pelleas and E.* 247
Straining   IN the stormy east-wind *s*,   *L. of Shalott* iv 1
but s ev'n his uttermost Cast,   *Gareth and L.* 1152
S his eyes beneath an arch of hand,   *Pass. of Arthur* 464
Strait (adj.)   Bound them by so *s* vows to his own self,   *Com. of Arthur* 262
Went thro' the *s* and dreadful pass of death,   *„* 395
Strait (s)   That stood on a dark *s* of barren land.   *M. d'Arthur* 10
I'll serve you better in a *s*;   *Princess* i 85
hovering o'er the dolorous *s* To the other shore,   *In Mem.* lxxxiv 39
That stood on a dark *s* of barren land.   *Pass. of Arthur* 178
years Have hollow'd out a deep and stormy *s*   *Lover's Tale* i 24
wreaths of all that would advance, Beyond our *s*,   *To Victor Hugo* 6
Strait (straight)   stood up *s* as the Queen of the world—   *Tomorrow* 79
Straït   fur I'll looök my hennemy *s* i' the faäce,   *North. Cobbler* 74
Strait-besieged   being *s-b* By this wild king   *Princess, Pro.* 36
Straiten'd (adj.)   Cursed be the gold that gilds the *s* forehead of the fool!   *Locksley Hall* 62
Straiten'd (verb)   shackles of an old love *s* him,   *Lancelot and E.* 875
Strait-laced   *S-l*, but all-too-full in bud   *Talking Oak* 59
Straitlier   But *s* bound am I to bide with thee.'   *Gareth and L.* 805
Strand (shore)   as a ground-swell dash'd on the *s*,   *W. to Alexandra* 23
Here on the Breton *s*!   *Maud II* ii 29
fringe Of that great breaker, sweeping up the *s*,   *Com. of Arthur* 387
He seem'd to pace the *s* of Brittany   *Last Tournament* 407
Before Isolt of Brittany on the *s*,   *„* 589
Strand (thread)   'The dusky *s* of Death inwoven here   *Maud I* xviii 60
Stranded   For sure no gladlier does the *s* wreck   *Enoch Arden* 828
Stranding   *s* on an isle at morn Rich,   *„* 552
Strange   (*See also* **Straänge**)   A spring rich and *s*,   *Nothing will Die* 22
The broken sheds look'd sad and *s*:   *Mariana* 5
Like that *s* angel which of old,   *Clear-headed friend* 24
Sudden glances, sweet and *s*,   *Madeline* 5
With a music *s* and manifold,   *Dying Swan* 29
At such *s* war with something good,   *Two Voices* 302
shafts were blazon'd fair In diverse raiment *s*:   *Palace of Art* 168
As in *s* lands a traveller walking slow,   *„* 277
You put *s* memories in my head.   *L. C. V. de Vere* 26
O sweet and *s* it seems to me,   *May Queen, Con.* 53
Our sons inherit us: our looks are *s*:   *Lotos-Eaters, C. S.* 73
'Tis *s* that those we lean on most,   *To J. S.* 9
Nothing comes to thee new or *s*.   *„* 74
Among new men, *s* faces, other minds.'   *M. d'Arthur* 238
Like that *s* song I heard Apollo sing,   *Tithonus* 62
Thro' sunny decads new and *s*,   *Day-Dm., L'Envoi* 22
'So *s* it seems to me.   *Lady Clare* 52
'That were *s*. What surname?'   *The Brook* 211
she grieved In her *s* dream, she knew not why,   *Sea Dreams* 230
She brought *s* news.   *„* 267
s was the sight to me;   *Princess, Pro.* 54
S was the sight and smacking of the time;   *„* 89
And, yonder, shrieks and *s* experiments   *„* 235
An old and *s* affection of the house.   *„ i* 13
On a sudden my *s* seizure came Upon me,   *„ iii* 183
we give you, being *s*, A license: speak,   *„* 204
If that *s* Poet-princess with her grand Imaginations   *„* 273
'Ah, sad and *s* as in dark summer dawns   *„ iv* 49
So sad, so *s*, the days that are no more.   *„* 53
and *s* experiences Unmeet for ladies.   *„* 158
you spent a stormy time With our *s* girl: *„ v* 122
And how the *s* betrothment was to end: *„* 474
That all things grew more tragic and more *s*;   *„ vi* 23
nor seem'd it *s* that soon He rose up whole,   *„ vii* 64
I have heard Of your *s* doubts: *„* 336
I moved as in a *s* diagonal,   *„ Con.* 27
For now so *s* do these things seem,   *In Mem.* xiii 15
I should not feel it to be *s*.   *„* xiv 20
But thou art turn'd to something *s*,   *„* xli 5
The days that grow to something *s*,   *„* lxxi 11

Strange (*continued*) and *s* Was love's dumb cry defying
change   *In Mem. xcv* 26
S friend, past, present, and to be ;   ,, *cxxix* 9
S, that I hear two men,   *Maud I vii* 13
How *s* was what she said,   ,, *xix* 34
S, that I felt so gay, *S*, that *I* tried to-day   .. *xx* 1
S, that the mind, when fraught With a passion   ,, *II ii* 58
terror grew Of that *s* bright and dreadful thing,   *Marr. of Geraint* 616
And for my *s* petition I will make Amends   ,, 817
ye surely have endured *S* chances here alone ; '   *Geraint and E.* 810
there be two *s* knights Who sit near Camelot   *Balin and Balan* 10
A *s* knee rustle thro' her secret reeds,   ,, 354
' To what request for what *s* boon,'   *Merlin and V.* 264
Boon, ay, there was a boon, one not so *s*—   .. 287
And take this boon so *s* and not so *s*.'   .. 310
' O not so *s* as my long asking it, Not yet so *s* as you
yourself are *s*, Nor half so *s* as that dark mood of
yours.   ,, 312
nothing wild or *s*, Or seeming shameful—   ,, 860
—this, however, My latest :   *Lancelot and E.* 1112
An end to this ! A *s* one !   ,, 1223
And the *s* sound of an adulterous race,   *Holy Grail* 80
And crimson in the belt a *s* device,   .. 154
And carven with *s* figures ;   ,, 169
So *s*, and rich, and dim ;   .. 342
Among the *s* devices of our kings   ,, 730
but in me lived a sin So *s*,   ,, 773
S as to some old prophet might have seem'd   *Pelleas and E.* 51
and *s* knights From the four winds came in :   ,, 147
Then ran across her memory the *s* rhyme   *Last Tournament* 131
he heard *S* music, and he paused, and turning—   *Guinevere* 239
Among new men, *s* faces, other minds.'   *Pass. of Arthur* 406
All—all but one ; and *s* to me, and sweet, Sweet
thro' *s* years to know that   *Lover's Tale i* 243
And Hate is *s* beneath the roof of Love.   ,, 779
Made *s* division of its suffering With her,   ,, *ii* 128
Wonder'd at some *s* light in Julian's eyes   ,, *iv* 205
such a feast So rich, so *s*, and stranger ev'n than rich,   ,, 211
I never yet beheld a thing so *s*, Sad, sweet, and *s*
together—   ,, 303
thence Down to this last *s* hour in his own hall ;   ,, 358
S fur to goä fur to think what saäilors   *North. Cobbler* 4
On whom I brought a *s* unhappiness,   *Sisters (E. and E.)* 89
and for a face Gone in a moment—*s*.   ,, 94
Selfish, *s* ! What dwarfs are men !   ,, 198
The Lord had sent this bright, *s* dream to me   *Columbus* 91
With some *s* hope to see the nearer God.   *Tiresias* 29
The *s* misfeaturing mask that I saw so amazed me,   *The Wreck* 117
I touch'd my limbs, the limbs Were *s* not mine—   *Ancient Sage* 235
S ! She used to shun the wailing babe,   *The Ring* 357
Strangeness feels a glimmering in his dream.   *The Brook* 216
Stranger (*adj. and s*) Two *s*'s meeting at a festival :   *Circumstance* 3
There strode a *s* to the door, (repeat)   *The Goose* 3, 39
And God forget the *s* ! '   ,, 56
s's at my hearth Not welcome,   *Lucretius* 158
The first-fruits of the *s* :   *Princess ii* 44
Moreover ' seize the *s*'s ' is the cry.   ,, *iv* 220
And Love has led thee to the *s* land,   *W. to Marie Alex.* 31
Will shelter one of *s* race,   *In Mem. cii* 4
And answer'd, ' Pardon me, O *s* knight ;   *Marr. of Geraint* 286
Queen demanded as by chance ' Know ye the *s*
woman ? '   *Merlin and V.* 129
Flush'd slightly at the slight disparagement Before
the *s* knight,   *Lancelot and E.* 235
landscape grow Familiar to the *s*'s child ;   *In Mem. ci* 20
Like *s*'s' voices here they sound,   ,, *civ* 9
We live within the *s*'s land,   ,, *cv* 3
Why mockest thou the *s* that hath been   *Gareth and L.* 283
A *s* meeting them had surely thought   *Geraint and E.* 34
Shriek'd to the *s* ' Slay not a dead man ! '   ,, 779
(for Arthur's knights Were hated *s*'s in the hall)   *Balin and Balan* 352
I bid the *s* welcome.   *Merlin and V.* 270
Yet *s*'s to the tongue, and with blunt stump   *Last Tournament* 66
A *s* as welcome as Satan—   *Charity* 26
Stranger (*compar.*) nor *s* seem'd that hearts So gentle,   *Princess vii* 66

Stranger (*compar.*) (*continued*) such a feast So rich, so
strange, and *s* ev'n than rich,   *Lover's Tale iv* 211
And *s* yet, at one end of the hall   ,, 213
S than earth has ever seen ;   *The Ring* 38
Strange-statued under the *s-s* gate, Where Arthur's
wars   *Lancelot and E.* 800
Strangled felt, despite his mail, *S*,   *Gareth and L.* 1152
and then A *s* titter,   *Princess v* 16
my *s* vanity Utter'd a stifled cry—   *Sisters (E. and E.)* 199
and a ray red as Blood Glanced on the *s* face—   *Bandit's Death* 32
Strata dip of certain *s* to the North.   *Princess iii* 170
Straw lance Broken, and his Excalibur a *s*.'   *Last Tournament* 88
cotch'd 'er death o' cowd that night, poor soul,
i' the *s*.   *Owd Roä* 114
Stray Beyond the bounding hill to *s*,   *In Mem. lxxxix* 30
In lands where not a memory *s*'s,   ,, *civ* 10
Stray'd Thy feet have *s* in after hours   ,, *cii* 14
Nor ever *s* beyond the pale :   *Holy Grail* 21
Seeing I never *s* beyond the cell,   · ,, 628
Streak (*s*) (*See also* **Shadow-streak**) solitary morning smote
The *s*'s of virgin snow.   *Œnone* 56
Now fades the last long *s* of snow,   *In Mem. cxv* 1
gay with gold In *s*'s and rays,   *Gareth and L.* 911
winds Laid the long night in silver *s*'s and bars,   *Lover's Tale ii* 112
The first gray *s* of earliest summer-dawn,   *Ancient Sage* 220
Streak (*verb*) white vapour *s* the crowned towers   *Princess iii* 344
But pure as lines of green that *s* the white   ,, *v* 196
Streak'd (*See also* **Silvery-streak'd**) *s* or starr'd at intervals
With falling brook   *Lover's Tale i* 404
Stream (*s*) (*See also* **Atom-stream, Gulf-stream, Sthrame**)
WHEN will the *s* be aweary of flowing   *Nothing will Die* 1
The *s* flows, The wind blows,   ,, 9
The *s* will cease to flow ;   *All Things will Die* 9
The *s*'s through many a lilied row   *The winds, etc.* 5
A clear *s* flowing with a muddy one,   *Isabel* 30
And the far-off *s* is dumb.   *The Owl i* 3
The leaping *s*, the very wind,   *Rosalind* 14
Like two *s*'s of incense free From one censer   *Eleänore* 58
The broad *s* in his banks complaining,   *L. of Shalott iv* 3
The broad *s* bore her far away,   ,, 17
the babble of the *s* Fell, and, without,   *Mariana in the S.* 51
' Who, rowing hard against the *s*,   *Two Voices* 211
Like those long mosses in the *s*.   *Miller's D.* 48
Beside the mill-wheel in the *s*,   ,, 167
Between the loud *s* and the trembling stars.   *Œnone* 219
like a downward smoke, the slender *s*   *Lotos-Eaters* 8
A land of *s*'s ! some, like a downward smoke,   ,, 10
in the *s* the long-leaved flowers weep,   ,, *C. S.* 10
How sweet it were, hearing the downward *s*,   ,, 54
A league of grass, wash'd by a slow broad *s*,   *Gardener's D.* 40
A single *s* of all her soft brown hair   ,, 128
Night slid down one long *s* of sighing wind,   ,, 267
In many *s*'s to fatten lower lands,   *Golden Year* 34
And all the long-pent *s* of life   *Day-Dm., Revival* 15
burst away In search of *s* or fount,   *Enoch Arden* 635
Not by the well-known *s* and rustic spire,   *The Brook* 188
Bright with the sun upon the *s* beyond :   *Sea Dreams* 97
drifting up the *s* In fancy, till I slept again,   ,, 108
Before two *s*'s of light from wall to wall,   *Princess ii* 473
s's that float us each and all To the issue,   ,, *iv* 70
' I stagger in the *s* :   ,, *vi* 321
I strove against the *s* and all in vain :   ,, *vii* 12
The shimmering glimpses of a *s* ;   ,, *Con.* 46
Who let the turbid *s*'s of rumour flow   *Ode on Well.* 181
ALL along the valley, *s* that flashest white,   *V. of Cauteretz* 1
many a fire between the ships and *s*   *Spec. of Iliad* 17
The sound of *s*'s that swift or slow   *In Mem. xxxv* 10
A secret sweetness in the *s*,   ,, *lxiv* 20
We talk'd : the *s* beneath us ran,   ,, *lxxxix* 43
On winding *s* or distant sea ;   ,, *cxv* 12
The market boat is on the *s*,   ,, *cxxi* 13
With never an end to the *s* of passing feet,   *Maud II v* 11
the *s* Full, narrow ; this a bridge of single arc   *Gareth and L.* 907
and in the *s* beneath him, shone Immingled   ,, 935
hoof of his horse slipt in the *s*, the *s* Descended,   ,, 1046

Stream (s) (*continued*) Well hast thou done ; for all the

s is freed,	*Gareth and L.* 1267
They hoped to slay him somewhere on the s,	„ 1419
And slipt and fell into some pool or s,	*Lancelot and E.* 214
to that s whereon the barge, Pall'd all its length	„ 1141
of Arthur's palace toward the s, They met,	„ 1178
and down they flash'd, and smote the s.	„ 1235
barge that brought her moving down, Far-off, a blot upon the s,	„ 1392
I walking to and fro beside a s	*Holy Grail* 592
served with choice from air, land, s, and sea,	*Pelleas and E.* 149
as a s that spouting from a cliff Fails in mid air,	*Guinevere* 608
The s of life, one s, one life, one blood,	*Lover's Tale i* 239
As mountain s's Our bloods ran free :	„ 326
a s Flies with a shatter'd foam along the chasm.	„ 382
s, Forth issuing from his portals in the crag	„ 429
perchance of s's Running far on within	„ 522
the sound Of the loud s was pleasant,	„ *ii* 35
lest the s should issue pure.	*Locksley H., Sixty* 144
And borne along by that full s of men,	*St. Telemachus* 43

Stream (verb) A thousand suns will s on thee,

	A Farewell 13
S's o'er a rich ambrosial ocean isle,	*Milton* 14
And crowds that s from yawning doors,	*In Mem. lxx* 9
In the long breeze that s's to thy delicious East,	*Maud I xviii* 16
S's thro' the twelve great battles of our King.	*Holy Grail* 250
S's like a cloud, man-shaped,	*To the Queen ii* 40
And o'er thee s' the rain,	*Pref. Poem Broth. Son.* 14

Stream'd s Upon the mooned domes aloof In inmost Bagdat,

	Arabian Nights 126
Across the mountain s below In misty folds,	*Palace of Art* 34
S onward, lost their edges,	*D. of F. Women* 50
And, s thro' many a golden bar,	*Day-Dm., Depart.* 15
The vine s out to follow,	*Amphion* 46
How swiftly s ye by the bark !	*The Voyage* 50
And in we s Among the columns,	*Princess ii* 434
I likewise, and in groups they s away.	„ *Con.* 105
S to the peak, and mingled with the haze	*Com. of Arthur* 435
half the pearls away, S from it still ;	*Lancelot and E.* 808
S thro' my cell a cold and silver beam,	*Holy Grail* 116
And all the pavement s with massacre :	*Last Tournament* 477

Streamer Shot like a s of the northern morn,

	M. d'Arthur 139
Shot like a s of the northern morn,	*Pass. of Arthur* 307

Streaming (*See also* **Down-streaming**) Forth s from a braid of pearl;

	Day-Dm., Sleep. B. 6
The torrent vineyard s fell To meet the sun	*The Daisy* 10
And lash with storm the s pane ?	*In Mem. lxxii* 4
On leagues of odour s far,	„ *lxxxvi* 14
And high in heaven the s cloud,	„ *Con.* 107
—all her bright hair s down—	*Lancelot and E.* 1156
people, from the high door s, brake Disorderly,	„ 1347
hill and wood Went ever s by him till the gloom,	*Pelleas and E.* 548
Up or down the s wind ?	*Rosalind* 9
In many a s torrent back,	*England and Amer.* 14
What sequel ? S eyes and breaking hearts ?	*Love and Duty* 2
Struck out the s mountain-side,	*Lucretius* 29
And down the s crystal dropt ;	*Princess vii* 165
Here, in s London's central roar.	*Ode on Well.* 9
Hath left crag-carven o'er the s Gelt—	*Gareth and L.* 1203
grayly draped With s grass, appear'd,	*Balin and Balan* 333
and thro' the gap Glimmer'd the s scud :	*Holy Grail* 682
Crook and turn upon itself in many a backward s curve.	*Locksley H., Sixty* 236
and aloft the glare Flies s,	*Achilles over the T.* 12
And s and shining on Silent river,	*Merlin and the G.* 51

Streamlet For us the same cold s curl'd

	In Mem. lxxix 9

Streeät (**street**) yon laädy a-steppin' along the s,

	North. Cobbler 107

Street (*See also* **Shtreet, Streeät**) till noon no foot should pace the s,

	Godiva 39
The s's are dumb with snow.	*Sir Galahad* 52
Till, where the s grows straiter,	*Will Water.* 142
He pass'd by the town and out of the s,	*Poet's Song* 2
long s climbs to one tall-tower'd mill,	*Enoch Arden* 5
narrow s that clamber'd toward the mill.	„ 60
From distant corners of the s they ran	„ 349
The climbing s, the mill, the leafy lanes,	„ 607

Street (*continued*) Then down the long s having slowly stolen, *Enoch Arden* 682

For Philip's dwelling fronted on the s,	„ 731
All down the long and narrow s he went	„ 795
I mind him coming down the s ;	„ 847
'yesterday I met him suddenly in the s,	*Sea Dreams* 146
then my eyes Pursued him down the s,	„ 165
A little s half garden and half house ;	*Princess i* 214
heave and thump A league of s in summer solstice down,	„ *iii* 128
We cross'd the s and gain'd a petty mound	„ *iv* 557
brawl Their rights or wrongs like potherbs in the s.	„ *v* 459
With lifted hand the gazer in the s.	*Ode on Well.* 22
Welcome her, thundering cheer of the s !	*W. to Alexandra* 7
Till, in a narrow s and dim,	*The Daisy* 22
Here in the long unlovely s,	*In Mem. vii* 2
On the bald s breaks the blank day.	„ 12
The field, the chamber and the s,	„ *viii* 11
The s's were fill'd with joyful sound,	„ *xxxi* 10
The s's were black with smoke and frost,	„ *lxix* 3
I smell the meadow in the s ;	„ *cxix* 4
There where the long s roars,	„ *cxxiii* 3
At the head of the village s,	*Maud I vi* 10
For only once, in the village s,	„ *xiii* 26
In the chamber or the s, ·	„ *II iv* 83
I loathe the squares and s's,	„ 92
Only a yard beneath the s,	„ *v* 7
Took horse, descended the slope s, and past	*Gareth and L.* 662
Gareth rode Down the slope s,	„ 700
Beheld the long s of a little town	*Marr. of Geraint* 242
And down the long s riding wearily,	„ 254
On a sudden, many a voice along the s,	*Geraint and E.* 270
That glance of theirs, but for the s,	*Merlin and V.* 105
As the poach'd filth that floods the middle s,	„ 798
Met foreheads all along the s	*Holy Grail* 344
in middle s the Queen, Who rode by Lancelot,	„ 355
from over the breadth of a s,	*Def. of Lucknow* 23
and, yelling with the yelling s,	*Locksley H., Sixty* 135
maidens by the thousand on the s.	„ 220
would it matter so much if I came on the s ?	*Charity* 8

Streetward To fit their little s sitting-room *Enoch Arden* 170

Streetway a s hung with folds of pure White samite, *Last Tournament* 140

Strength The unsunn'd freshness of my s, *Supp. Confessions* 140

MINE be the s of spirit,	*Mine be the strength* 1
Than cry for s, remaining weak,	*Two Voices* 95
'What, is not this my place of s,'	*Palace of Art* 233
With all my s I pray'd for both,	*May Queen, Con.* 31
S came to me that equall'd my desire.	*D. of F. Women* 230
s of some diffusive thought Hath time	*You ask me, why, etc.* 15
A slow-develop'd s awaits Completion	*Love thou thy land* 57
We are not now that s which in old days	*Ulysses* 66
that sin against the s of youth !	*Locksley Hall* 59
My s is as the s of ten,	*Sir Galahad* 3
aid me, give me s Not to tell her,	*Enoch Arden* 785
and truth and love are s,	*Aylmer's Field* 365
I wonder'd at her s, and ask'd her of it :	*Sea Dreams* 113
He took advantage of his s to be First in the field :	*Princess ii* 152
O fall'n at length that tower of s	*Ode on Well.* 38
What Roman s Turbia show'd In ruin,	*The Daisy* 5
Corrupts the s of heaven-descended Will,	*Will* 11
And in my grief a s reserved.	*In Mem. lxxxv* 52
He fought his doubts and gather'd s,	„ *xcvi* 13
The maidens gather'd s and grace	„ *ciii* 27
Blow trumpet ! live the s and die the lust !	*Com. of Arthur* 492
thro' that s the King Drew in the petty princedoms	„ 516
Have s and wit, in my good mother's hall	*Gareth and L.* 12
That s of anger thro' mine arms,	„ 948
same s which threw the Morning Star	„ 1108
As closing in himself the s of ten,	„ 1339
'Fool, for thou hast, men say, the s of ten,	„ 1387
And s against all odds, and what the King	*Balin and Balan* 183
they lifted up Their eager faces, wondering at the s,	*Merlin and V.* 133
and waste the spiritual s Within us,	*Holy Grail* 35
said he, ' but men With s and will to right the wrong'd,	„ 309
may count The yet-unbroken s of all his knights,	„ 326
for a s Was in us from the vision,	„ 333
And in the s of this I rode,	„ 476

Z

Strength (continued)   and in the s of this Come victor.   *Holy Grail* 480
S of heart And might of limb,   *Last Tournament* 197
chance and craft and s in single fights,   *Pass. of Arthur* 106
image, like a charm of light and s Upon the waters,   *Lover's Tale i* 91
Fierce in the s of far descent, a stream   ,,   382
Shorn of its s, into the sympathy Of that small bay,   ,,   434
With my life, love, soul, spirit, and heart and s.   ,,   460
In confidence of unabated s,   ,,   511
when s is shock'd With torment,   ,,   ii 150
Strong with the s of the race to command,   *Def. of Lucknow* 47
and the s To mould it into action pure as theirs.   *Tiresias* 128
That old s and constancy Which has made your fathers great   *Open. I. and C. Exhib.* 14
Trunk and bough, Naked s.   *The Oak* 15
A sudden s from heaven,   *St. Telemachus* 56
Strengthen S me, enlighten me ! (repeat)   *Ode to Memory* 5, 43, 122
Strengthen'd *See* **Storm-strengthen'd**
Stretch The garden s'es southward.   *Gardener's D.* 115
I felt my veins S with fierce heat ;   *Princess* v 538
I s lame hands of faith, and grope,   *In Mem.* lv 17
But free to s his limbs in lawful fight,   *Geraint and E.* 754
at length we began to be weary, to sigh, and to s and yawn,   *V. of Maeldune* 91
Stretch'd S wide and wild the waste enormous marsh   *Ode to Memory* 101
s out beneath the pine.   *Lotos-Eaters, C. S.* 99
lad s out And babbled for the golden seal,   *Dora* 134
his long arms s as to grasp a flyer;   *Aylmer's Field* 588
jewels five-words long That on the s forefinger of all Time Sparkle   *Princess* ii 378
Thereat the Lady s a vulture throat,   ,,   iv 363
She s her arms and call'd Across the tumult   ,,   496
arms S under all the cornice and upheld :   *Gareth and L.* 219
drunkard, as he s from horse To strike him,   *Last Tournament* 459
she s out her arms and cried aloud 'Oh Arthur !'   *Guinevere* 606
—s my hands As if I saw her ;   *The Ring* 116
Stretching A bounded field, nor s far ;   *In Mem.* xlvi 14
Lets down his other leg, and s,   *Gareth and L.* 1186
Strew *See* **Strow**
Strewn S in the entry of the moaning cave ;   *Lover's Tale iii* 2
Stricken (*See also* **Awe-stricken, Horror-stricken, Panic-stricken, Spear-stricken, Sun-stricken, Well-stricken, Wonder-stricken**) And, s by an angel's hand,   *Sir Galahad* 69
And out of s helmets sprang the fire.   *Princess* v 495
Was cancell'd, s thro' with doubt.   *In Mem.* xcv 44
knave-knight, well s, O good knight-knave— then were I s blind That minute,   *Gareth and L.* 1135
With all her damsels, he was s mute ;   *Lancelot and E.* 426
And have but s with the sword in vain ;   *Pelleas and E.* 251
I might have s a lusty stroke for him,   *Pass. of Arthur* 23
I was the chief of the race—he had s my father dead—   *Sir J. Oldcastle* 69
Stride (s) He parted, with great s among his dogs.   *V. of Maeldune* 1
Abate the s, which speaks of man,   *Godiva* 31
the Prince, as Enid past him, fain To follow, strode a s,   *Princess* ii 429
Stride (verb) hard heir s's about their lands,   *Marr. of Geraint* 376
Stridest warrior-wise thou s thro' his halls   *In Mem.* xc 15
Striding now s fast, and now Sitting awhile   *Last Tournament* 517
Strife To hear the murmur of the s,   *Lover's Tale iv* 87
'Waiting to strive a happy s,   *Margaret* 23
The flattery and the s,   *Two Voices* 130
Ev'n now we hear with inward s   *D. of F. Women* 148
pulsation that I felt before the s,   *Love thou thy land* 53
The maid and page renew'd their s,   *Locksley Hall* 109
Half fearful that, with self at s,   *Day-Dm., Revival* 13
'Help us from famine And plague and s !   *Will Water.* 161
To point the term of human s,   *The Victim* 10
Are God and Nature then at s,   *In Mem.* l 14
That loved to handle spiritual s,   ,,   lv 5
And ancient forms of party s ;   ,,   lxxxv 54
To fruitful s's and rivalries of peace—   ,,   cvi 14
And see my dear lord wounded in the s,   *Ded. of Idylls* 38
In the crash of the cannonades and the desperate s ;   *Marr. of Geraint* 103
slain thy fathers in war or in single s,   *The Revenge* 78
weary was I of the travel, the trouble, the s and the sin,   *V. of Maeldune* 121   ,,   129

Strife (continued) Theirs that so often in S with their enemies   *Batt. of Brunanburh* 18
Strike (*See also* **Spank**) grow awry From roots which s so deep ?   *Supp. Confessions* 78
God would move And s the hard, hard rock,   ,,   116
And strongly s to left and right,   *Kate* 27
Shadows thou dost s, Embracing cloud,   *Two Voices* 194
Shall s within thy pulses, like a God's,   *Œnone* 162
As when a great thought s's along the brain,   *D. of F. Women* 43
I sought to s Into that wondrous track of dreams   ,,   278
Would s, and firmly, and one stroke :   *Love thou thy land* 92
earth feed thy branchy root, That under deeply s's !   *Talking Oak* 274
till he madly s's Against it, and beats out his weary life.   *Enoch Arden* 729
S thro' a finer element of her own ?   *Aylmer's Field* 579
when she s's thro' the thick blood Of cattle,   *Lucretius* 98
a noiseless riot underneath S's thro' the wood,   ,,   186
And s's him dead for thine and thee.   *Princess* iv 584
Stir in us as to s :   ,,   v 268
Fight and fight well : s and s home.   ,,   409
shadowing down the champaign till it s's   ,,   526
The tops shall s from star to star,   ,,   vi 57
Look up, and let thy nature s on mine,   ,,   vii 351
Should s a sudden hand in mine,   *In Mem.* xiv 11
The sunbeam s's along the world :   ,,   xv 8
That s's by night a craggy shelf,   ,,   xvi 13
And s his being into bounds,   ,,   Con. 124
And s, if he could, were it but with his   *Maud I i* 52
Arise, my God, and s, for we hold Thee just,   ,,   II i 45
S dead the whole weak race of venomous worms,   ,,   46
Suddenly s on a sharper sense For a shell,   ,,   ii 52
Then to s him and lay him low,   ,,   v 90
'Take thou and s !   *Com. of Arthur* 307
'S for the King and live !   ,,   488
'S for the King and die !   ,,   494
Accursed, who s's nor lets the hand be seen !   *Gareth and L.* 435
Sun Heaved up a ponderous arm to s the fifth,   ,,   1045
so Gareth seem'd to s Vainly,   ,,   1133
I have prophesied—S, thou art worthy of the Table Round—   ,,   1138
S—s—the wind will never change again.'   ,,   1140
Lancelot thro' his warm blood felt Ice s,   ,,   1399
At once without remorse to s her dead,   *Geraint and E.* 109
dawn ascending lets the day S where it clung :   ,,   693
tongues he saw not whence, S's from behind.   *Balin and Balan* 131
His arm half rose to s again, but fell :   ,,   223
I yet should s upon a sudden means To dig,   *Merlin and V.* 659
placed where morning's earliest ray Might s it,   *Lancelot and E.* 6
Set lance in rest, s spur, suddenly move,   ,,   456
I fear me, that will s my blossom dead.   ,,   971
Then will I s at him and s him down,   ,,   1070
Give me good fortune, I will s him dead,   ,,   1071
S down the lusty and long practised knight,   ,,   1360
S from the sea ; and from the star there shot   *Holy Grail* 529
This light that s's his eyeball is not light,   ,,   913
Down ! s him ! put my hate into your strokes,   *Pelleas and E.* 228
No men to s ? Fall on him all at once,   ,,   268
and he call'd, 'I s upon thy side—   ,,   279
drunkard, as he stretch'd from horse To s him,   *Last Tournament* 460
What rights are his that dare not s for them ?   ,,   527
Where I must s against the man they call   *Guinevere* 572
and s him dead, and meet myself Death,   ,,   575
stroke That s's them dead is as my death to me.   *Pass. of Arthur* 74
thrills of bliss That s across the soul in prayer,   *Lover's Tale i* 364
hemlock, Brow-high, did s my forehead as I past ;   ,,   ii 19
live to fight again and to s another blow.'   *The Revenge* 95
I swore I would s off his head.   *V. of Maeldune* 2
let thine own hand s Thy youthful pulses   *Tiresias* 156
hand points five—O me—it s's the hour—   *The Flight* 94
'I will s' said he 'The stars with head sublime,'   *Epilogue* 46
aiming at an all but hopeless mark To s it, struck ;   *The Ring* 347
S upward thro' the shadow'   ,,   372
Thou wilt s Thy glory thro' the day.   *Doubt and Prayer* 14
Strikest but thou s a strong stroke,   *Gareth and L.* 877
Ay, knave, because thou s as a knight,   ,,   1020

Strikin' an' theere—it be s height—   *Spinster's S's.* 114
   waäit till tha 'eärs it be s the hour.   *Owd Roä* 18
Striking (*See also* **Strikin'**) blow Before him, s on my brow.   *Fatima* 25
   There rose a noise of s clocks,   *Day-Dm., Revival* 2
   Now s on huge stumbling-blocks of scorn   *Aylmer's Field* 538
   s with her glance, The mother, me, the child ;   *Princess vi* 152
   Struck for the throne, and s found his doom.   *Com. of Arthur* 325
   when I watch'd thee s on the bridge   *Gareth and L.* 992
   watch his mightful hand s great blows At caitiffs   *Marr. of Geraint* 99
   And strongly s out her limbs awoke ;   *Geraint and E.* 380
   beast seeking to help herself By s at her better,   *Merlin and V.* 499
   And over hard and soft, s the sod   *Pelleas and E.* 498
   S the last stroke with Excalibur,   *Pass. of Arthur* 168
   Thunderless lightnings s under sea   *To the Queen ii* 12
   S the hospital wall, crashing thro' it,   *Def. of Lucknow* 18
String (*See also* **Bow-string, Leading-strings**) Shall it not
   be scorn to me to harp on such a moulder'd s?   *Locksley Hall* 147
   But send it slackly from the s ;   *In Mem. lxxxvii* 26
   I cannot all command the s's ;   „ *lxxxviii* 10
   and sometimes touches but one s That quivers,   *Lover's Tale i* 17
   coostom flitted awaäy like a kite wi' a brokken s.   *North. Cobbler* 28
Strip Shall s a hundred hollows bare of Spring,   *Princess vi* 65
   shall we s him there Your lover?   *Geraint and E.* 488
   blacksmith 'e s's me the thick ov 'is airm,   *North. Cobbler* 85
   s your own foul passions bare ;   *Locksley H., Sixty* 141
Stripe Blackening against the dead-green s's   *Pelleas and E.* 554
   The last long s of waning crimson gloom,   *Ancient Sage* 221
Striped dropping bitter tears against his brow S with
   dark blood :   *M. d'Arthur* 212
   dropping bitter tears against a brow S with dark
   blood :   *Pass. of Arthur* 380
Stripling the s's !—for their sport !—I tamed my leopards :   *Princess v* 399
   'The years that made the s wise   *Ancient Sage* 111
Stript our long walks were s as bare as brooms,   *Princess, Pro.* 184
   S from the three dead wolves of woman born   *Geraint and E.* 94
   entering barr'd her door, S off the case,   *Lancelot and E.* 16
   meekly rose the maid, S off the case,   „ 979
   His friends had s him bare,   *Dead Prophet* 14
Strive s To reconcile me with thy God.   *Supp. Confessions* 101
   'Waiting to s a happy strife,   *Two Voices* 130
   And s and wrestle with thee till I die :   *St. S. Stylites* 119
   strong in will To s, to seek, to find,   *Ulysses* 70
   But for one hour, O Love, I s To keep   *In Mem. xxxv* 6
   When on the gloom I s to paint The face I know ;   „ *lxx* 2
   To s, to fashion, to fulfil—   „ *cxiii* 7
   s Again for glory, while the golden lyre   *Tiresias* 179
Striven 'I cannot hide that some have s,   *Two Voices* 208
   These two have s half the day,   *In Mem. cii* 17
   With sword we have not s ;   *Gareth and L.* 1264
   lily maid had s to make him cheer,   *Lancelot and E.* 327
Stroäk (stroke) Naäy—let ma s tha down   *Spinster's S's.* 53
Stroäkin (stroking) Ye was s ma down wi' the 'air,   „ 19
Strode There s a stranger to the door, (repeat)   *The Goose* 3, 39
   So s he back slow to the wounded King.   *M. d'Arthur* 65
   And so s back slow to the wounded King.   „ 112
   But the other swiftly s from ridge to ridge,   „ 181
   where he s About the hall, among his dogs,   *Godiva* 16
   S from the porch, tall and erect again.   *Aylmer's Field* 825
   S in, and claim'd their tribute as of yore.   *Com. of Arthur* 506
   Then s a good knight forward,   *Gareth and L.* 364
   Sir Gareth s, and saw without the door   „ 676
   Prince, as Enid past him, fain To follow, s a stride,   *Marr. of Geraint* 376
   s the brute Earl up and down his hall,   *Geraint and E.* 712
   stall'd his horse, and s across the court,   *Balin and Balan* 341
   shook his hair, s off, and buzz'd abroad   *Lancelot and E.* 722
   So s he back slow to the wounded King.   *Pass. of Arthur* 233
   And so s back slow to the wounded King.   „ 280
   But the other swiftly s from ridge to ridge,   „ 349
Stroke (*See also* **Sabre-stroke, Stroäk, Sword-stroke**)
   'Then dying of a mortal s,   *Two Voices* 154
   Would strike, and firmly, and one s :   *Love thou thy land* 92
   A s of cruel sunshine on the cliff,   *Princess iv* 524
   mutual pardon ask'd and given For s and song,   „ *v* 47
   With s on s the horse and horseman, came   „ 523
   two-cell'd heart beating, with one full s, Life.'   „ *vii* 307

Stroke (*continued*) answering now my random s With
   fruitful cloud   *In Mem. xxxix* 2
   Struck for himself an evil s ;   *Maud II i* 21
   but thou strikest a strong s, For strong thou art   *Gareth and L.* 877
   one s Laid him that clove it grovelling on the ground.   „ 971
   four s's they struck With sword, and these were mighty ;   „ 1042
   But with one s Sir Gareth split the skull.   „ 1404
   Short fits of prayer, at every s a breath.   *Geraint and E.* 155
   God's mercy, what a s was there !   *Lancelot and E.* 24
   For twenty s's of the blood,   „ 720
   When have I stinted s in foughten field ?   *Holy Grail* 860
   strike him ! put my hate into your s's,   *Pelleas and E.* 228
   the s That strikes them dead is as my death to me.   *Pass. of Arthur* 73
   Striking the last s with Excalibur,   „ 168
   I might have stricken a lusty s for him,   *Sir J. Oldcastle* 69
   Not one s firm.   *Romney's R.* 115
   Rang the s, and sprang the blood,   *The Tourney* 9
Stroked Sat on his knee, s his gray face   *Lancelot and E.* 749
Stroking *See* **A-stroäkin, Stroäkin**
Stroll all that from the town would s,   *Talking Oak* 53
Stroll'd then we s For half the day thro' stately theatres   *Princess ii* 368
Strong The s limbs failing ;   *All Things will Die* 32
   Great in faith, and s Against the grief of
   circumstance   *Supp. Confessions* 91
   whose s right arm debased The throne of Persia,   *Alexander* 1
   For there was Milton like a seraph s,   *Palace of Art* 133
   s to break or bind All force in bonds   „ 153
   Whereof the s foundation-stones were laid   „ 235
   tale of little meaning tho' the words are s ;   *Lotos-Eaters, C. S.* 119
   as s gales Hold swollen clouds from raining,   *D. of F. Women* 10
   Thro' many agents making s,   *Love thou thy land* 39
   S mother of a Lion-line, Be proud of those s sons
   of thine   *England and Amer.* 3
   I was s and hale of body then ;   *St. S. Stylites* 3
   words That make a man feel s in speaking truth ;   *Love and Duty* 70
   s in will To strive, to seek, to find,   *Ulysses* 69
   But thy s Hours indignant work'd their wills,   *Tithonus* 18
   The s tempestuous treble throbb'd and palpitated ;   *Vision of Sin* 28
   Cast his s arms about his drooping wife,   *Enoch Arden* 228
   You chose the best among us—a s man :   „ 293
   Her son, who stood beside her tall and s,   „ 756
   So past the s heroic soul away.   „ 915
   One whom the s sons of the world despise ;   *The Brook* 3
   To make disproof of scorn, and s in hopes,   *Aylmer's Field* 446
   that one kiss Was Leolin's one s rival upon earth :   „ 557
   But she with her s feet up the steep hill   *Sea Dreams* 120
   And mould a generation s to move   *Princess v* 416
   S, supple, sinew-corded, apt at arms ;   „ 535
   'O fair and s and terrible !   „ *vi* 163
   Ruddy and white, and s on his legs,   *Grandmother* 2
   S of his hands, and s on his legs,   „ 13
   WELL for him whose will is s !   *Will* 1
   S Son of God, immortal Love,   *In Mem., Pro.* 1
   More s than all poetic thought ;   „ *xxxvi* 12
   Then bring an opiate trebly s,   „ *lxxi* 6
   For thou wert s as thou wert true ?   „ *lxxiii* 4
   The wish too s for words to name ;   „ *xciii* 14
   Than some s bond which is to be.   „ *cxvi* 16
   The s imagination roll A sphere of stars   „ *cxxii* 6
   And if the words were sweet and s   „ *cxxv* 11
   But, I fear, the new s wine of love,   *Maud I vi* 82
   S in the power that all men adore,   „ *x* 14
   One still s man in a blatant land,   „ 63
   So many those that hate him, and so s,   *Com. of Arthur* 251
   One was fair, s, arm'd—But to be won by force—   *Gareth and L.* 104
   'I have stagger'd thy s Gawain in a tilt For pastime ;   „ 542
   Morning-Star, and Noon-Sun, and Evening-Star, Being
   s fools ;   „ 635
   but thou strikest a s stroke, For s thou art and goodly
   therewithal,   „ 877
   'O Sun' (not this s fool whom thou, Sir Knave,   „ 1058
   And heated the s warrior in his dreams ;   *Marr. of Geraint* 72
   And the s passion in her made her weep   „ 110
   and the blood Of their s bodies, flowing,   „ 569
   With streaming grass, appear'd, low-built but s ;   *Balin and Balan* 333

Strong (*continued*) A minstrel of Caerleon by *s* storm Blown
  into shelter   *Merlin and V*. 9
but God Broke the *s* lance, and roll'd his enemy
  down,   *Lancelot and E*. 26
found the Lord of Astolat With two *s* sons,   „   174
When the *s* neighings of the wild white Horse   „   298
S men, and wrathful that a stranger knight   „   468
Gawain, surnamed The Courteous, fair and *s*,   „   555
out of this she plaited broad and long A *s* sword-belt, *Holy Grail* 153
dyed The *s* White Horse in his own heathen blood—   „   312
How my *s* lance had beaten down the knights,   „   363
their wise men Were *s* in that old magic   „   666
had felt the sun Beat like a *s* knight on his helm, *Pelleas and E*. 23
beholding him so *s*, she thought That peradventure
  he will fight   „   117
'O the *s* hand,' she said, 'See! look at mine!   „   126
so by that *s* hand of his The sword and golden circlet   „   169
Then let the *s* hand, which had overthrown   „   234
O towers so *s*, Huge, solid,   „   463
his *s* hands gript And dinted the gilt dragons *Last Tournament* 181
'I had forgotten all in my *s* joy To see thee—   „   582
all his aims Were sharpen'd by *s* hate for Lancelot *Guinevere* 20
And fly to my *s* castle overseas: „   112
Round that *s* castle where he holds the Queen;   „   194
And *s* man-breasted things stood from the sea,   „   246
a *s* sympathy Shook all my soul! *Lover's Tale ii* 88
a semi-smile As at a *s* conclusion—   „ *iv* 282
S with the strength of the race to command, *Def. of Lucknow* 47
Seven *s* Earls of the army of Anlaf *Batt. of Brunanburh* 53
There was a *s* sea-current would sweep us *Despair* 51
S in will and rich in wisdom, *Locksley H., Sixty* 49
Would my granite girth were *s* As either love, *Helen's Tower* 7
The century's three *s* eights have met *To Ulysses* 7
Stronger Teach that sick heart the *s* choice, *On a Mourner* 18
Then wax'd her anger *s*.   *The Goose* 30
The Poet-forms of *s* hours, *Day-Dm., L'Envoi* 14
Till the little wings are *s*. *Sea Dreams* 298
Till the little limbs are *s*.   „ 306
Eight daughters of the plough, *s* than men, *Princess iv* 278
But tougher, heavier, *s*, he that smote   „ *v* 536
Love and Nature, there are two more terrible And *s*.   „ *vi* 166
Are mine for the moment *s*? *Spiteful Letter* 10
he came at length To find a *s* faith his own; *In Mem. xcvi* 17
The love that rose on *s* wings,   „ *cxxviii* 1
suddenly, sweeter, my heart beat *s* And thicker, *Maud I viii* 8
Then with a *s* buffet he clove the helm *Gareth and L*. 1405
My malice is no deeper than a moat, No *s* than a
  wall: *Geraint and E*. 341
in their chairs set up a *s* race With hearts   „ 940
Yea, shook this newer, *s* hall of ours, *Holy Grail* 731
then he hurl'd into it Against the *s*; *Lancelot and E*. 463
The vast occasion of our *s* life— *Columbus* 35
and bring on both the yoke Of *s* states, *Tiresias* 70
Pining for the *s* heart that once had beat beside
  her own.   *Locksley H., Sixty* 58
With *s* life from day to day; *Hands all Round* 6
Tho' you'll ne'er be *s*; *Forlorn* 62
Then, with a melody *S* and statelier, *Merlin and the G*. 63
Stronger-made Enoch *s-m* Was master: *Enoch Arden* 30
Strongest Is this enough to say That my desire, like all
  s hopes,   *Gardener's D*. 237
where two fight The *s* wins, *Aylmer's Field* 365
Cries to Weakest as to *S*, *Locksley H., Sixty* 110
my *s* wish Falls flat before your least unwillingness. *Romney's R*. 71
Stronglier And Gareth hearing ever *s* smote, *Gareth and L*. 1141
Strong-wing'd THESE lame hexameters the *s-w* music
  of Homer!   *Trans. of Homer* 1
Strove Resolved on noble things, and *s* to speak, *D. of F. Women* 42
blinded with my tears, Still *s* to speak: „ 109
She *s* to span my waist: *Talking Oak* 138
Not unbecoming men that *s* with Gods. *Ulysses* 53
That *s* in other days to pass, *Day-Dm., Arrival* 10
So she *s* against her weakness, *L. of Burleigh* 69
And still they *s* and wrangled: *Sea Dreams* 229
S to buffet to land in vain. *Princess iv* 185

Strove (*continued*) I *s* against the stream and all in vain: *Princess vii* 12
Son of him with whom we *s* for power— *W. to Marie Alex*. 1
Shall be for whose applause I *s*, *In Mem. li* 5
But ever *s* to make it true: „ *xcvi* 8
And while she wept, and I *s* to be cool, *Maud II i* 15
lords Drew back in wrath, and Arthur *s* with
  Rome.   *Com. of Arthur* 514
yet he *s* To learn the graces of their Table, *Balin and Balan* 237
I yearn'd and *s* To tear the twain asunder *Holy Grail* 785
when we *s* in youth, And brake the petty kings, *Pass. of Arthur* 107
I *s* to disengage myself, but fail'd, *Lover's Tale i* 692
thou *s* to rise From my full heart.   „ *ii* 711
I could not rise Albeit I *s* to follow.   „ *ii* 98
I *s* myself with Spain against the Moor. *Columbus* 94
for whenever we *s* to speak Our voices *V. of Maeldune* 21
But ever I fail'd to please him, however I *s* to please— *The Wreck* 28
S for sixty widow'd years to help *Locksley H., Sixty* 267
S yonder mountain flat, *Mechanophilus* 6
Strow And *s*'s her lights below, *St. Agnes' Eve* 2
Strowing the happy people *s* cried 'Hosanna *Enoch Arden* 505
S balm, or shedding poison in the fountains *Locksley H., Sixty* 274
Strown (*See also* **Strewn**, **Star-strown**) And would have *s*
  it, and are fall'n themselves. *Princess vi* 42
s with gold and scatter'd coinage, *Geraint and E*. 25
loosely *s* with crags: We mounted slowly; *Lover's Tale i* 384
Hath still'd the blast and *s* the wave, *Freedom* 34
Struck light *S* up against the blinding wall. *Mariana in the S*. 56
S thro' with pangs of hell. *Palace of Art* 220
a lyre of widest range *S* by all passion, *D. of F. Women* 166
And *s* upon the corn-laws, where we split, *Audley Court* 35
he *s* his staff against the rocks And broke it,— *Golden Year* 59
Then *s* it thrice, and, no one opening, *Enoch Arden* 279
Started from bed, and *s* herself a light,   „ 494
S out the streaming mountain-side, *Lucretius* 29
Whose death-blow *s* the dateless doom of kings,   „ 236
twangling violin *S* up with Soldier-laddie, *Princess, Pro*. 86
I *s* in: 'Albeit so mask'd, Madam,   „ *ii* 212
'you wrong him more than I That *s* him: „ *iv* 246
She *s* such warbling fury thro' the words;   „ 586
Till I *s* out and shouted;   „ *v* 540
our enemies have fall'n, have fall'n: they *s*;   „ *vi* 48
while the day, Descending, *s* athwart the hall,   „ 364
and flying *s* With showers of random sweet   „ *vii* 53
That if to-night our greatness were *s* dead, *Third of Feb*. 17
s the keys There at his right with a sudden crash, *The Islet* 7
I hear the bell *s* in the night: *In Mem. x* 2
When the dark hand *s* down thro' time,   „ *lxxii* 19
Like a sudden spark *S* vainly in the night, *Maud I ix* 14
And he *s* me, madman, over the face, *S* me before the
  languid fool,   „ *II i* 18
S for himself an evil stroke;   „ 21
Friend, to be *s* by the public foe,   „ *v* 89
afterward *S* for the throne, and striking found his
  doom.   *Com. of Arthur* 325
four strokes they *s* With sword, and these were
  mighty: *Gareth and L*. 1042
S at her with his whip, (repeat) *Marr. of Geraint* 201, 413
S at him with his whip, and cut his cheek.   „ 207
S thro' the bulky bandit's corselet home, *Geraint and E*. 159
Earl Doorm *s* with a knife's haft   „ 600
In those fierce wars, *s* hard— *Balin and Balan* 177
Dragg'd him, and *s*, but from the castle a cry   „ 399
s Furrowing a giant oak, and javelining *Merlin and V*. 935
S up and lived along the milky roofs; *Lancelot and E*. 409
lightnings here and there to left and right *S*, *Holy Grail* 495
moon *S* from an open grating overhead *Lover's Tale iv* 60
bullet *s* him that was dressing it suddenly dead, *The Revenge* 67
and ever they *s* and they slew *V. of Maeldune* 68
S for their hoards and their hearths *Batt. of Brunanburh* 19
as if she had *s* and crash'd on a rock; *The Wreck* 108
S hard at the tender heart of the mother, *Despair* 74
S with the sword-hand and slew, *Heavy Brigade* 52
aiming at an all but hopeless mark To strike it, *s*; *The Ring* 347
Be *s* from out the clash of warring wills; *Prog. of Spring* 95
S by a poison'd arrow in the fight, *Death of Œnone* 26

Struck (*continued*)   every dawn *S* from him his own shadow on to Rome.   *St. Telemachus* 33
S to the left and *s* to the right   *The Tourney* 4
Struggle (s)   The *s* of standards,   *Batt. of Brunanburh* 87
Struggle (verb)   Glory of Virtue, to fight, to *s*,   *Wages* 3
   ruby-chain, and both Began to *s* for it,   *Last Tournament* 410
Struggled   boy that cried aloud And *s* hard.   *Dora* 102
Strumming   With *s* and with scraping,   *Amphion* 70
Strung   Kate hath a spirit ever *s*   *Kate* 10
Stubb'd (**hoed**)   an' I 'a *s* Thurnaby waäste.   *N. Farmer, O. S.* 28
   But I *s* 'um oop wi' the lot,   "   32
   an' I meän'd to 'a *s* it at fall,   "   41
Stubble   Fire in a dry *s* a nine-days' wonder   *Lancelot and E.* 735
Stubborn   HE thought to quell the *s* hearts of oak,   *Buonaparte* 1
   '*S*, but she may sit Upon a king's right hand   *Princess v* 438
   He shall find the *s* thistle bursting   *Ode on Well.* 206
   Sick for thy *s* hardihood,   *In Mem. ii* 14
Stubborn-shafted   Before a gloom of *s-s* oaks,   *Geraint and E.* 120
Stuck (*See also* **Stook**)   *S*; and he clamour'd from a casement,   *The Brook* 85
   s out The bones of some vast bulk that lived   *Princess iii* 293
   Hoänly Miss Annie were saw *s* oop,   *Village Wife* 59
   fur I *s* to tha moor na the rest,   *Spinster's S's.* 51
   I couldn't a' *s* by my word.   "   96
Studded   others *s* wide With disks and tiars,   *Arabian Nights* 63
   her hair *S* with one rich Provence rose—   *Lover's Tale iii* 45
Student   Drove in upon the *s* once or twice,   *Aylmer's Field* 462
   Hers more than half the *s's*, all the love.   *Princess iii* 39
   What *s* came but that you planed her path   " *iv* 315
   To cramp the *s* at his desk,   *In Mem. cxxviii* 18
Study   Back would he to his *studies,*   *Aylmer's Field* 394
   Old *studies* fail'd; seldom she spoke: *Princess vii* 31
Stuff (s)   and chairs, And all his household *s*;   *Walk. to the Mail* 40
   Man is made of solid *s*.   *Edwin Morris* 49
   'What *s* is this!   Old writers push'd the happy season   *Golden Year* 65
   household *s*, Live chattels, mincers   *Princess iv* 514
Stuff (verb)   *S* his ribs with mouldy hay.   *Vision of Sin* 66
Stumble   my mind *S's*, and all my faculties are lamed   *Lucretius* 123
Stumbled   Ran Gaffer, *s* Gammer.   *The Goose* 34
   We *s* on a stationary voice,   *Princess v* 2
   Part *s* mixt with floundering horses.   " 498
   lies a ridge of slate across the ford; His horse thereon *s*—   *Gareth and L.* 1057
   horse, Arising wearily at a fallen oak, *S* headlong,   *Balin and Balan* 426
   I *S* on deck, half mad.   *The Wreck* 118
   I have *s* back again Into the common day,   *Romney's R.* 32
   He *s* in, and sat Blinded: *St. Telemachus* 48
Stumbling   *S* across the market to his death,   *Aylmer's Field* 820
   our horses *s* as they trode On heaps of ruin,   *Holy Grail* 716
Stumbling-block   striking on huge *s-b's* of scorn   *Pelleas and E.* 339
Stump   And let my lady sear the *s* for him,
   A *s* of oak half-dead, From roots like some black coil   *Last Tournament* 12
   with blunt *s* Pitch-blacken'd sawing the air,   " 66
Stump'd   with clamour bowl'd And *s* the wicket;   *Princess, Pro.* 82
Stung   poisoning all his rest, *S* him in dreams.   *Balin and Balan* 384
   S by his loss had vanish'd, none knew where.   *Lover's Tale iv* 102
   'The shaft of scorn that once had *s*   *Ancient Sage* 131
   Dead!—and maybe *s* With some remorse,   *The Ring* 454
Stunn'd   And *s* me from my power to think   *In Mem. xvi* 15
   I sitting here so *s* and still,   *Maud II i* 2
   and *s* the twain Or slew them,   *Geraint and E.* 91
   and so left him *s* or dead,   " 464
   hurl'd him headlong, and he fell *S*,   *Guinevere* 109
Stunning   *See* **Ear-stunning**
Stunt (**obstinate**)   Do'ant be *s*: taäke time: *N. Farmer, N. S.* 17
Stunted   I lived for years a *s* sunless life;   *Aylmer's Field* 357
   Nor *s* squaws of West or East;   *Princess ii* 78
Stupid   Courage, poor *s* heart of stone.—   *Maud II iii* 5
   She felt so blunt and *s* at the heart: *Geraint and E.* 747
   O *s* child!   Yet you are wise who say it;   *Merlin and V.* 251
   with such a *s* heart To interpret ear and eye,   *Lancelot and E.* 941
   then at the last they found I had grown so *s* and still   *Rizpah* 49
Sty   so return'd unfarrow'd to her *s*.   *Walk. to the Mail* 100
   A maiden moon that sparkles on a *s*,   *Princess v* 186

Style   take the *s* of those heroic times ?   *The Epic* 35
   What *s* could suit?   *Princess, Con.* 9
Styled   *See* **Self-styled**
Stylites   (*See also* **Simeon, Simeon Stylites**)   Simeon of the pillar, by surname, *S*, among men;   *St. S. Stylites* 162
Subdue   to *s* this home Of sin, my flesh,   " 57
   S them to the useful and the good.   *Ulysses* 38
   foil'd at the last by the handful they could not *s*;   *Def. of Lucknow* 44
   he thought he could *s* me to his will.   *Happy* 64
Subdued   I *s* me to my father's will;   *D. of F. Women* 234
   grace Of sweet seventeen *s* me ere she spoke)   *The Brook* 113
   S me somewhat to that gentleness,   *Geraint and E.* 867
Subject (adj.)   *s* to the season or the mood,   *Aylmer's Field* 71
Subject (s)   knowledge of his art Held me above the *s*,   *D. of F. Women* 10
   we coursed about The *s* most at heart,   *Gardener's D.* 223
   She rapt upon her *s*, he on her: *Princess iii* 304
   My *s* with my *s's* under him,   *Geraint and E.* 916
   'Queen? *s*? but I see not what I see.   *Balin and Balan* 281
   mine image, The *s* of thy power, be cold in her,   *Lover's Tale i* 782
   Artificer and *s*, lord and slave,   " *ii* 103
   if the rebel *s* seek to drag me from the throne,   *By an Evolution.* 15
Sublime   my lover, with whom I rode *s* On Fortune's neck: *D. of F. Women* 141
   ' Name and fame ! to fly *s* Thro' the courts,   *Vision of Sin* 103
   raillery, or grotesque, or false *s*—   *Princess iv* 588
   In his simplicity *s*.   *Ode on Well.* 34
   nourishing a youth *s* With the fairy tales of science,   *Locksley Hall* 11
   If, in thy second state *s*,   *In Mem. lxi* 1
   With what *s* repression of himself,   *Ded. of Idylls* 19
   Farewell, Macready; moral, grave, *s*;   *To W. C. Macready* 12
   'The stars with head *s*,'   *Epilogue* 47
Submit   *S*, and hear the judgment of the King.'   *Geraint and E.* 799
Submitting   *S* all things to desire.   *In Mem. cxiv* 11
Subscribed   which hastily *s*, We enter'd on the boards: *Princess ii* 73
Subserve   Or but *s's* another's gain.   *In Mem. liv* 12
Subsist   Within this region I *s*,   *You ask me, why, etc.* 2
Substance   island princes over-bold Have eat our *s*,   *Lotos-Eaters, C. S.* 76
   And rolling as it were the *s* of it   *Aylmer's Field* 258
   none of all our blood should know The shadow from the *s*,   *Princess i* 9
   do I chase The *s* or the shadow?   " *ii* 409
   everywhere I know the *s* when I see it.   " 413
   spirit flash not all at once from out This shadow into *S*—   *Ded. Poem Prin. Alice* 6
   shadow leave the *S* in the brooding light   *Happy* 99
Subtil   Her *s*, warm, and golden breath,   *Supp. Confessions* 60
Subtilising   *See* **All-subtilising**
Subtle   A *s*, sudden flame,   *Madeline* 28
   With shrilling shafts of *s* wit.   *Clear-headed friend* 13
   Round thy neck in *s* ring   *Adeline* 58
   Thro' lips and eyes in *s* rays.   *Rosalind* 24
   She with a *s* smile in her mild eyes,   *Œnone* 184
   All *s* thought, all curious fears,   *In Mem. xxxii* 9
   one indeed I knew In many a *s* question versed,   " *xcvi* 6
   he that like a *s* beast Lay couchant with his eyes   *Guinevere* 10
   the *s* beast, Would track her guilt until he found,   " 59
   I knew Of no more *s* master under heaven   " 478
   Works of *s* brain and hand,   *Open. I. and C. Exhib.* 7
   How a *s* at tierce and quart of mind   *In Mem., W. G. Ward* 5
Subtle-paced   silver flow Of *s-p* counsel   *Isabel* 21
Subtler   Who knows a *s* magic than his own—   *Com. of Arthur* 284
Subtlest   Myriads of topaz-lights, and jacinth-work Of *s* jewellery.   *M. d'Arthur* 58
   Myriads of topaz-lights, and jacinth-work Of *s* jewellery.   *Pass. of Arthur* 226
Subtle-thoughted   *S-t*, myriad-minded.   *Ode to Memory* 118
Suburb   (*See also* **Wheat-suburb**)   By park and *s* under brown Of lustier leaves;   *In Mem. xcviii* 24
   mitre-sanction'd harlot draws his clerks Into the *s*—   *Sir J. Oldcastle* 107
   OLD FITZ, who from your *s* grange,   *To E. Fitzgerald* 1
Succeed   ' I know that age to age *s's*,   *Two Voices* 205
   'The many fail: the one *s's*.'   *Day-Dm., Arrival* 16
   pushes us off from the board, and others ever *s*?   *Maud I iv* 27
   That after many changes may *s* Life,   *Prog. of Spring* 116
Succeeder   The sole *s* to their wealth,   *Aylmer's Field* 294

Successful   Waged such unwilling tho' *s* war On all the
youth,   *Merlin and V.* 571
Succession   make One act a phantom of *s*:   *Princess iii* 329
Successor   be dissipated By frail *s*'s.   "   267
but the prayers, That have no *s* in deed,   *Akbar's Dream* 10
Such   Kings have no *s* couch as thine,   *A Dirge* 40
You move not in *s* solitudes,   *Margaret* 45
At *s* strange war with something good,   *Two Voices* 302
And they that know *s* things—   *Princess i* 144
In *s* discourse we gain'd the garden rails,   " *Con.* 80
With *s* compelling cause to grieve   *In Mem. xxix* 1
I had *s* reverence for his blame.   " *li* 6
And *s* refraction of events As often rises ere they rise.   " *xcii* 15
thy darkness must have spread With *s* delight as theirs
of old,   *Maud I xviii* 26
' Lord, there is no *s* city anywhere,   *Gareth and L.* 206
for the King Will bind thee by *s* vows,   "   270
lash'd at each So often and with *s* blows,   *Marr. of Geraint* 564
Such-wise   In *s-w*, that no man could see her   *Merlin and V.* 642
Suck   from all things *s* Marrow of mirth   *Will Water.* 213
s the blinding splendour from the sand,   *Princess vii* 39
I should *s* Lies like sweet wines :   *Last Tournament* 644
an' they *s*'s the muck fro' the grass.   *Village Wife* 32
the babe Will *s* in with his milk hereafter—   *Columbus* 38
Suck'd   Have *s* and gather'd into one   *Talking Oak* 191
S from the dark heart of the long hills   *Princess v* 349
And *s* from out the distant gloom   *In Mem. xcv* 53
four fools have *s* their allegory From these damp
walls,   *Gareth and L.* 1199
And *s* the joining of the stones,   *Marr. of Geraint* 324
S into oneness like a little star   *Lover's Tale i* 308
Had *s* the fire of some forgotten sun,   " *iv* 194
My baby, the bones that had *s* me,   *Rizpah* 53
Sucking   sometimes *S* the damps for drink,   *St. S. Stylites* 77
Flaying the roofs and *s* up the drains,   *Princess v* 525
s The foul steam of the grave to thicken by it,   *Lover's Tale i* 648
Suckling   fierce teat To Human *s*'s ;   *Com. of Arthur* 29
Sudden   *S* glances, sweet and strange,   *Madeline* 5
A subtle, *s* flame,   "   28
A *s* splendour from behind Flush'd   *Arabian Nights* 81
in thee Is nothing *s*, nothing single ;   *Eleänore* 57
Ring *s* scritches of the jay,   *My life is full* 20
with *s* fires Flamed over :   *Buonaparte* 11
And, isled in *s* seas of light,   *Fatima* 33
Because with *s* motion from the ground   *D. of F. Women* 170
But I have *s* touches, and can run   *Edwin Morris* 53
her bosom shaken with a *s* storm of sighs—   *Locksley Hall* 27
A *s* hubbub shook the hall,   *Day-Dm., Revival* 7
Hurt in that night of *s* ruin and wreck,   *Enoch Arden* 564
I make a *s* sally,   *The Brook* 24
with a *s* execration drove The footstool   *Aylmer's Field* 326
Who entering fill'd the house with *s* light.   "   682
Paled at a *s* twitch of his iron mouth ;   "   732
Stirring a *s* transport rose and fell.   *Princess iv* 29
Up in one night and due to *s* sun :   "   312
made a *s* turn As if to speak,   "   394
for spite of doubts And *s* ghostly shadowings   "   572
Entering, the *s* light Dazed me half-blind :   " *v* 11
But yonder, whiff ! there comes a *s* heat,   " *Con.* 58
Heaven flash'd a *s* jubilant ray,   *Ode on Well.* 129
Rush to the roof, and higher   *W. to Alexandra* 20
There at his right with a *s* crash,   *The Islet* 8
For on them brake the *s* foe,   *The Victim* 4
He caught her away with a *s* cry ;   "   69
Should strike a *s* hand in mine,   *In Mem. xiv* 11
' My *s* frost was *s* gain,   " *lxxxi* 10
Like a *s* spark Struck vainly in the night,   *Maud I ix* 13
and my Delight Had a *s* desire,   " *xiv* 20
And shine in the *s* making of splendid names,   " *III vi* 47
A field of charlock in the *s* sun   *Gareth and L.* 388
like a *s* wind Among dead leaves.   "   514
' Rough, *s*, And pardonable, worthy to be knight—   "   653
but heard instead A *s* sound of hoofs.   *Marr. of Geraint* 164
Whereat Geraint flash'd into *s* spleen :   "   273
And loosed in words of *s* fire the wrath   *Geraint and E.* 106

Sudden (*continued*)   cried Geraint for wine and goodly
cheer To feed the *s* guest,   *Geraint and E.* 284
All to be there against a *s* need ;   "   375
And at a *s* swerving of the road,   "   506
Sent forth a *s* sharp and bitter cry,   "   722
Thus, after some quick burst of *s* wrath,   *Balin and Balan* 217
But snatch'd a *s* buckler from the Squire,   "   554
boat Drave with a *s* wind across the deeps,   *Merlin and V.* 201
or else A *s* spurt of woman's jealousy,—   "   524
Might feel some *s* turn of anger born   "   531
I yet should strike upon a *s* means To dig,   "   659
rapt By all the sweet and *s* passion of youth   *Lancelot and E.* 282
Then made a *s* step to the gate, and there—   "   391
I pray him, send a *s* Angel down To seize me   "   1424
power To lay the *s* heads of violence flat,   *Holy Grail* 310
And all her form shone forth with *s* light   "   45C
coming out of gloom Was dazzled by the *s* light,   *Pelleas and E.* 105
The *s* trumpet sounded as in a dream   *Last Tournament* 151
And, saddening on the *s*, spake Isolt,   "   581
For here a *s* flush of wrathful heat   *Guinevere* 356
Pour with such *s* deluges of light   *Lover's Tale i* 315
For in the *s* anguish of her heart   "   702
all at once The front rank made a *s* halt ;   " *iii* 29
woods upon the hill Waved with a *s* gust   "   34
And, making there a *s* light, beheld   " *iv* 53
Found that the *s* wail his lady made Dwelt   "   149
I knew Some *s* vivid pleasure hit him there.   "   178
Vailing a *s* eyelid with his hard ' Dim Saesneg'   *Sir J. Oldcastle* 20
I felt On a *s* I know not what,   *The Ring* 32
No *s* heaven, nor *s* hell, for man,   "   41
and a *s* face Look'd in upon me like a gleam   "   419
A *s* nightingale Saw thee, and flash'd   *Demeter and P.* 11
The *s* fire from Heaven had dash'd him dead,   *Happy* 83
on a *s* he, Paris, no longer beauteous as a God,   *Death of Œnone* 24
And on the *s*, and with a cry ' Saleem'   *Akbar's Dream* 184
Then on a *s* we saw your soldiers crossing the ridge,   *Bandit's Death* 21
She said with a *s* glow On her patient face   *Charity* 35
Sudden-beaming   a *s-b* tenderness Of manners   *Lancelot and E.* 322
Sudden-curved   drops down A *s-c* frown: *Madeline* 35
Sudden-flaring   With *s-f* manes Those two great beasts   *Holy Grail* 820
Suddenly   I came among you here so *s*,   *Marr. of Geraint* 794
Sudden-shrilling   Lilia woke with *s-s* mirth An echo   *Princess, Pro.* 216
Sue   *s* me, and woo me, and flatter me,   *The Mermaid* 43
Not one word ; No ! tho' your father *s*'s :   *Princess vi* 240
Suffer   they *s*—some, 'tis whisper'd—down in hell *S*
endless anguish,   *Lotos-Eaters, C. S.* 123
woman well as not as we, But *s*'s change of frame.   *Princess v* 463
He *s*'s, but he will not *s* long ;   *Will* 2
He *s*'s, but he cannot *s* wrong :   "   3
I do not *s* in a dream ;   *In Mem. xiii* 14
When all that seems shall *s* shock,   " *cxxxi* 2
Had suffer'd, or should *s* any taint In nature :   *Marr. of Geraint* 31
my lord thro' me should *s* shame.   "   101
I seem to *s* nothing heart or limb,   "   472
Than that my lord should *s* loss or shame.'   *Geraint and E.* 69
I *s* from the things before me,   *Balin and Balan* 284
passionate moment would not *s* that—   *Lover's Tale iv* 356
Men will forget what we *s* and not what we do.   *Def. of Lucknow* 73
I *s* all as much As they do—   *Columbus* 217
Sufferance   See **Long-sufferance**
Suffer'd   but all hath *s* change :   *Lotos-Eaters, C. S.* 71
Show me the man hath *s* more than I.   *St. S. Stylites* 49
thou hast *s* long For ages and for ages ! '   "   99
I have enjoy'd Greatly, have *s* greatly,   *Ulysses* 8
Truly, she herself had *s* —   *Locksley Hall* 96
' O Katie, what I *s* for your sake !   *The Brook* 119
Who loved, who *s* countless ills,   *In Mem. lvi* 17
and loved and did, And hoped, and *s*,   " *Con.* 135
Had *s*, or should suffer any taint In nature :   *Marr. of Geraint* 31
That each had *s* some exceeding wrong.   *Geraint and E.* 36
knight, with whom I rode, Hath *s* misadventure.   *Balin and Balan* 476
' None wrought, but *s* much, an orphan maid !   *Merlin and V.* 71
Yet who had done, or who had *s* wrong ?   *Lover's Tale i* 726
Suffering   (*See also* **Long-suffering**)   I go, weak from *s*
here :   *Two Voices* 238

Sumptuous (*continued*) Thy presence in the silk of *s* looms ;   *Ancient Sage* 266
Sumptuously and *s* According to his fashion,   *Geraint and E.* 284
Sun (*s*)   (*See also* **Noon-Sun, Soon**)   as the tree Stands in
   the *s* and shadows all beneath,   *Love and Death* 11
Like a lily which the *s* Looks thro'   *Adeline* 12
tho' you stood Between the rainbow and the *s*.   *Margaret* 13
The *s* is just about to set,   ,, 58
grow To a full face, there like a *s* remain Fix'd—   *Eleänore* 92
The *s* came dazzling thro' the leaves,   *L. of Shalott* iii 3
A merry boy in *s* and shade ?   *Two Voices* 321
Many *s's* arise and set.   *Miller's D.* 205
O *s*, that from thy noonday height   *Fatima* 2
While this great bow will waver in the *s*,   *Palace of Art* 43
I would see the *s* rise upon the glad New-
   year. (repeat)   *May Queen, N. Y's. E.* 2, 51
To-night I saw the *s* set :   ,, 5
I wish the snow would melt and the *s* come
   out on high :   ,, 15
In the early early morning the summer *s* 'ill
   shine,   ,, 22
It seem'd so hard at first, mother, to leave
   the blessed *s*,   *Con.* 9
O look ! the *s* begins to rise,   ,, 49
voice, that now is speaking, may be beyond
   the *s*—   ,, 54
Between the *s* and moon upon the shore ;   *Lotos-Eaters* 38
Half-fall'n across the threshold of the *s*,   *D. of F. Women* 63
We drank the Libyan *S* to sleep,   ,, 145
While yon *s* prospers in the blue,   *The Blackbird* 22
That broods above the fallen *s*,   *To J. S.* 51
That made his forehead like a rising *s*   *M. d'Arthur* 217
but all else of heaven was pure Up to the *S*,   *Gardener's D.* 80
the *s* fell, and all the land was dark. (repeat)—   *Dora* 79, 109
Lay great with pig, wallowing in *s* and mud.   *Walk. to the Mail* 88
To some full music rose and sank the *s*,   *Edwin Morris* 34
The cloudy porch oft opening on the *S* ?   *Love and Duty* 9
The *S* will run his orbit, and the Moon Her circle.   ,, 22
The *S* flies forward to his brother *S* ;   *Golden Year* 23
For some three *s's* to store and hoard   *Ulysses* 29
widen'd with the process of the *s's*.   *Locksley Hall* 138
hurl their lances in the *s* ;   ,, 170
what to me were *s* or clime ?   ,, 177
flash the lightnings, weigh the *S*—   ,, 186
Thro' many an hour of summer *s's*,   *Will Water.* 33
To keep the best man under the *s*   *Lady Clare* 31
We seem'd to sail into the *S* !   *The Voyage* 16
How oft we saw the *S* retire,   ,, 17
As fast she fled thro' *s* and shade,   *Sir L. and Q. G.* 37
A thousand *s's* will stream on thee,   *A Farewell* 13
Close to the *s* in lonely lands,   *The Eagle* 2
As when the *s*, a crescent of eclipse,   *Vision of Sin* 10
A light wind blew from the gates of the *s*,   *Poet's Song* 3
new warmth of life's ascending *s* Was felt by either,   *Enoch Arden* 38
Cuts off the fiery highway of the *s*,   ,, 130
Under a palm-tree, over him the *S* :   ,, 501
yonder shines The *S* of Righteousness,   ,, 504
We turn'd our foreheads from the falling *s*,   *The Brook* 165
found the *s* of sweet content Re-risen in Katie's eyes,   ,, 168
bearing hardly more Than his own shadow in a
   sickly *s*.   *Aylmer's Field* 30
' Let not the *s* go down upon your wrath,'   *Sea Dreams* 44
Bright with the *s* upon the stream beyond :   ,, 97
out I slipt Into a land all *s* and blossom,   ,, 101
another of our Gods, the *S*, Apollo, Delius,   *Lucretius* 124
how the *s* delights To glance and shift about   ,, 188
until the set of *s* Up to the people :   *Princess, Pro.* 2
inhabitant Of some clear planet close upon the *S*,   ,, ii 36
set the starry tides, And eddied into *s's*,   ,, 118
A Memnon smitten with the morning *S*.'   ,, iii 116
They with the *s* and moon renew their light   ,, 255
white vapour streak the crowned towers Built to the *S* : '   ,, 345
till the *S* Grew broader toward his death and fell,   ,, 363
' There sinks the nebulous star we call the *S*,   ,, iv 19
And brief the *s* of summer in the North,   ,, 112
till the Bear had wheel'd Thro' a great arc his seven slow *s's*.   ,, 213

Z*

Sun (*s*) (*continued*) Up in one night and due to sudden *s* :   *Princess* iv 312
Sees the midsummer, midnight, Norway *s* Set into
   sunrise ;   ,, 575
issued in the *s*, that now Leapt from the dewy shoulders   ,, v 42
lays on every side A thousand arms and rushes to the *S*.   ,, vi 37
leader of the herd That holds a stately fretwork to the *S*,   ,, 86
So drench'd it is with tempest, to the *s*,   ,, vii 142
Till the *S* drop, dead, from the signs.'   ,, 245
underneath another *s*, Warring on a later day,   *Ode on Well.* 101
To which our God Himself is moon and *s*.   ,, 217
To meet the *s* and sunny waters,   *The Daisy* 11
Your presence will be *s* in winter,   *To F. D. Maurice* 3
With many a rivulet high against the *S*   *The Islet* 21
Wake, little ladies, The *s* is aloft !   *Minnie and Winnie* 20
THE *s*, the moon, the stars, the seas,   *High. Pantheism* 1
stars from the night and the *s* from the day !   *Window, Gone* 5
S comes, moon comes,   ,, *When* 1
S sets, moon sets,   ,, 3
Blaze upon her window, *s*,   ,, 15
You send a flash to the *s*.   *Window, Marr. Morn* 2
Nor branding summer *s's* avail   *In Mem.* ii 11
And murmurs from the dying *s* :   ,, iii 8
Since our first *S* arose and set.   ,, xxiv 8
And blurr'd the splendour of the *s* ;   ,, lxxii 8
And, while we breathe beneath the *s*,   ,, lxxv 14
s by *s* the happy days Descend below   ,, lxxxiv 27
And all the courses of the *s's*.   ,, cxvii 12
Sad Hesper o'er the buried *s* And ready,   ,, cxxi 1
I found Him not in world or *s*,   ,, cxxiv 5
Thou standest in the rising *s*,   ,, cxxx 3
The sport of random *s* and shade.   ,, *Con.* 24
To meet and greet a whiter *s* ;   ,, 78
For him did his high *s* flame,   *Maud I* iv 32
Our planet is one, the *s's* are many,   ,, 45
No *s*, but a wannish glare In fold upon fold   ,, vi 2
s look'd out with a smile Betwixt the cloud   ,, ix 3
Something flash'd in the *s*,   ,, 10
To faint in the light of the *s* that she loves,   ,, xxii 11
To the flowers, and be their *s*.   ,, 58
fires of Hell brake out of thy rising *s*,   ,, *II* i 9
And noble thought be freër under the *s*,   ,, *III* vi 48
heathen horde, Reddening the *s* with smoke and
   earth with blood,   *Com. of Arthur* 37
and fell'd The forest, letting in the *s*,   ,, 60
' Rain, rain, and *s* ! a rainbow in the sky !   ,, 403
Rain, rain, and *s* ! a rainbow on the lea !   ,, 406
Rain, *s*, and rain ! and the free blossom blows :   ,, 409
S, rain, and *s* ! and where is he who knows ?   ,, 410
The *S* of May descended on their King,   ,, 462
paced a city all on fire With *s* and cloth of gold,   ,, 480
' Blow, for our *S* is mighty in his May !   ,, 497
Blow, for our *S* is mightier day by day !   ,, 498
ever-highering eagle-circles up To the great *S* of Glory,   *Gareth and L.* 22
field of charlock in the sudden *s* Between two showers,   ,, 389
shone the Noonday *S* Beyond a raging shallow.   ,, 1027
flash'd the fierce shield, All *s* ;   ,, 1031
' Ugh ! ' cried the *S*, and vizoring up a red   ,, 1038
the *S* Heaved up a ponderous arm to strike the fifth,   ,, 1044
the stream Descended, and the *S* was wash'd away.   ,, 1047
' O *S* ' (not this strong fool whom thou, Sir Knave,   ,, 1058
S, that wakenest all to bliss or pain,   ,, 1060
' O dewy flowers that open to the *s*,   ,, 1066
new *s* Beat thro' the blindless casement   *Marr. of Geraint* 70
Will clothe her for her bridals like the *s*.'   ,, 231
wound Bare to the *s*, and monstrous ivy-stems   ,, 322
pale and bloodless east began To quicken to the *s*, arose,   ,, 535
But since our fortune swerved from *s* to shade,   ,, 714
Herself would clothe her like the *s* in Heaven.   ,, 784
And clothed her for her bridals like the *s* ;   ,, 836
watch'd the *s* blaze on the turning scythe,   *Geraint and E.* 252
But while the *s* yet beat a dewy blade,   ,, 446
But lift a shining hand against the *s*,   ,, 473
Had bared her forehead to the blistering *s*,   ,, 51*
And bear him hence out of this cruel *s* ?   ,, 544
there the Queen array'd me like the *s* :   *Geraint and E.* 701

Sung (continued)   Among the tents I paused and *s*,   *Two Voices* 125
' I *s* the joyful Pæan clear,   „ 127
S by the morning star of song,   *D. of F. Women* 3
anthem *s*, is charm'd and tied To where he stands,—   „ 193
And, wheresoever I am *s* or told In aftertime,   *M. d'Arthur* 34
falser than all songs have *s*,   *Locksley Hall* 41
Wherever he sat down and *s*   *Amphion* 19
nightingale thought, ' I have *s* many songs,   *Poet's Song* 13
s to, when, this gad-fly brush'd aside,   *Princess v* 414
Peace, his triumph will be *s* By some   *Ode on Well.* 232
We *s*, tho' every eye was dim,   *In Mem. xxx* 14
S by a long-forgotten mind.   „ *lxxvii* 12
A guest, or happy sister, *s*,   „ *lxxxix* 26
One whispers, ' Here thy boyhood *s*   „ *cii* 9
Whatever I have said or *s*,   „ *cxxv* 1
song that once I heard By this huge oak, *s* nearly
    where we sit :   *Merlin and V.* 406
' O crueller than was ever told in tale, Or *s* in song !   „ 859
And one hath *s* and all the dumb will sing.   *Holy Grail* 301
more Than any have *s* thee living,   *Pelleas and E.* 351
Pelleas had heard *s* before the Queen,   „ 397
many a noble war-song had he *s*,   *Guinevere* 278
And, wheresoever I am *s* or told In aftertime,   *Pass. of Arthur* 202
we whirl'd giddily ; the wind *S* ;   *Lover's Tale ii* 202
Noble ! he *s*, and the sweet sound ran   *Dead Prophet* 37
And he *s* not alone of an old sun set,   „ 41
men ater supper 'ed *s* their songs an' 'ed 'ed their beer,   *Owd Roä* 35

Sunk   some were *s* and many were shatter'd,   *The Revenge* 61
Have we *s* below them ?   *Locksley H., Sixty* 95

Sunless   I lived for years a stunted *s* life ;   *Aylmer's Field* 357
S and moonless, utter light—but no !   *Columbus* 90
Sun-flame or *s* frost,   *Epilogue* 66
The *s* halls of Hades into Heaven ?   *Demeter and P.* 136
In seas of Death and *s* gulfs of Doubt.   *Pref. Son. 19th Cent.* 14
And thro' the *s* winter morning-mist   *Death of Œnone* 8

Sunlight   faintest *s*'s flee About his shadowy sides :   *The Kraken* 4
Place it, where sweetest *s* falls   *Ode to Memory* 85
The *s* driving down the lea,   *Rosalind* 13
His broad clear brow in *s* glow'd ;   *L. of Shalott iii* 28
as *s* drinketh dew.   *Fatima* 21
Floated the glowing *s*'s, as she moved.   *Œnone* 182
Are as moonlight unto *s*,   *Locksley Hall* 152
and return In such a *s* of prosperity   *Aylmer's Field* 421
(so rare the smiles Of *s*)   *The Daisy* 54
And the *s* broke from her lip ?   *Maud I vi* 86
Then like a stormy *s* smiled Geraint,   *Geraint and E.* 480
Like *s* on the plain behind a shower :   *Merlin and V.* 403
Crown'd with *s*—over darkness—   *Locksley H., Sixty* 92
Yet the moonlight is the *s*,   „ 182
Not of the *s*, Not of the moonlight,   *Merlin and the G.* 120
million of summers are stored in the *s* still,   *The Dawn* 19
And the *s* that is gone !   *Silent Voices* 6

Sunlike   make your Enid burst *S* from cloud—   *Marr. of Geraint* 789

Sun-lit   The s-l almond-blossom shakes—   *To the Queen* 16
maiden Spring upon the plain Came in a s-l fall of
    rain.   *Sir L. and Q. G.* 4
There the *s* ocean tosses O'er them mouldering,   *The Captain* 69

Sunn'd   *S* by those orient skies ;   *The Poet* 42
day dwelt on her brows, and *s* Her violet eyes,   *Gardener's D.* 136
S itself on his breast and his hands.   *Maud I xiii* 13
cairn'd mountain was a shadow, *s* The world to
    peace again :   *Merlin and V.* 638
had *s* The morning of our marriage,   *Sisters (E. and E.)* 243
S with a summer of milder heat.   *To Prof. Jebb* 8

Sunnee   warms the blood of Shiah and *S*,   *Akbar's Dream* 107

Sunnier   Cleave ever to the *s* side of doubt,   *Ancient Sage* 68
The fountain pulses high in *s* jets,   *Prog. of Spring* 54

Sunning   *S* himself in a waste field alone—   *Aylmer's Field* 9
Shine out, little head, *s* over with curls,   *Maud I xxii* 57

Sunny   And shadow'd coves on a *s* shore,   *Eleänore* 18
but his *s* hair Cluster'd about his temples   *Œnone* 59
Another slid, a *s* fleck,   *Talking Oak* 223
saw The dim curls kindle into *s* rings ;   *Tithonus* 54
Thro' *s* decads new and strange,   *Day-Dm., L'Envoi* 22
The *s* and rainy seasons came and went   *Enoch Arden* 623

Sunny (continued)   Bright was that afternoon, *S* but chill ;   *Enoch Arden* 670
S tokens of the Line,   *Ode Inter. Exhib.* 19
To meet the sun and *s* waters,   *The Daisy* 11
they pass the grave That has to-day its *s* side.   *In Mem., Con.* 72
And wild voice pealing up to the *s* sky,   *Maud I v* 13
And feet like *s* gems on an English green,   „ *vi* 23
What if with her *s* hair, And smile as *s* as cold,   „ 14
birds Of *s* plume in gilded trellis-work ;   *Marr. of Geraint* 659
But heaven had meant it for a *s* one :   *Holy Grail* 706
To make it wholly thine on *s* days.   *Lover's Tale i* 14

Sunny-sweet   Of tower or duomo, *s-s*,   *The Daisy* 46

Sunny-warm   In tracts of pasture *s-w*,   *Palace of Art* 94

Sunrise (adj.)   At his highest with *s* fire ;   *Voice and the P.* 30

Sunrise (s)   Rare *s* flow'd.   *The Poet* 36
And Freedom rear'd in that august *s*   „ 37
look'd upon the breath Of the lilies at *s* ?   *Adeline* 37
heath-flower in the dew, Touch'd with *s*.   *Rosalind* 42
lights of sunset and of *s* mix'd In that brief night ;   *Love and Duty* 72
every day The *s* broken into scarlet shafts   *Enoch Arden* 592
The scarlet shafts of *s*—but no sail.   „ 599
Her stature more than mortal in the burst Of *s*,   *Princess, Pro.* 41
Norway sun Set into *s* ;   „ *iv* 576
came from out a mountain-cleft Toward the *s*,   *Gareth and L.* 261
level pavement where the King would pace At *s*,   „ 668
light of Heaven varies, now At *s*, now at sunset,   *Marr. of Geraint* 7
flame At *s* till the people in far fields,   *Holy Grail* 243
Damsels in divers colours like the cloud Of sunset
    and *s*,   *Pelleas and E.* 54
From sunset and *s* of all thy realm,   *To the Queen ii* 13
Hued with the scarlet of a fierce *s*,   *Lover's Tale i* 353
Star of the morning, Hope in the *s* ;   *Vastness* 15
Who found me at *s* Sleeping,   *Merlin and the G.* 12
One from the *S* Dawn'd on His people,   *Kapiolani* 24

Sunset (adj.)   Back to the *s* bound of Lyonnesse—   *Pass. of Arthur* 81

Sunset (s)   (See also **Sea-sunset**)   Breathes low between
    the *s* and the moon ;   *Eleänore* 124
the *s*, south and north, Winds all the vale   *Miller's D.* 241
charmed *s* linger'd low adown In the red West :   *Lotos-Eaters* 19
lights of *s* and of sunrise mix'd In that brief night ;   *Love and Duty* 72
for my purpose holds To sail beyond the *s*,   *Ulysses* 60
and leave Yon orange *s* waning slow :   *Move eastward* 2
the gates were closed At *s*,   *Princess, Con.* 37
and rang Beyond the bourn of *s* ;   „ 100
Where some refulgent *s* of India   *Milton* 13
when the *s* burn'd On the blossom'd gable-ends   *Maud I vi* 8
Under the half-dead *s* glared—   *Gareth and L.* 800
light of Heaven varies, now At sunrise, now at *s*,   *Marr. of Geraint* 7
Damsels in divers colours like the cloud Of *s* and
    sunrise,   *Pelleas and E.* 54
The wide-wing'd *s* of the misty marsh   *Last Tournament* 423
an hour or maybe twain After the *s*,   *Guinevere* 238
From *s* and sunrise of all thy realm,   *To the Queen ii* 13
that shot the *s* In lightnings round me ;   *Lover's Tale i* 442
Storm, *s*, glows and glories of the moon   „ *ii* 110
setting, when Even descended, the very *s* aflame ;   *V. of Maeldune* 66
Rich was the rose of *s* there,   *The Wreck* 136
The placid gleam of *s* after storm !   *Ancient Sage* 133
She that finds a winter *s*   *Locksley H., Sixty* 22
As if perpetual *s* linger'd there,   *The Ring* 83
The *s* blazed along the wall of Troy,   *Death of Œnone* 77
The wrathful *s* glared against a cross   *St. Telemachus* 5
Following a hundred *s*'s, and the sphere   „ 31
From out the *s* pour'd an alien race,   *Akbar's Dream* 192
S and evening star,   *Crossing the Bar* 1

Sunset-flush'd   pinnacles of aged snow, Stood *s-f*   *Lotos-Eaters* 17

Sun-shaded   *S-s* in the heat of dusty fights)   *Princess ii* 241

Sunshine   Like *s* on a dancing rill,   *Rosalind* 29
where broad *s* laves The lawn by some cathedral,   *D. of F. Women* 189
Simeon, whose brain the *s* bakes ;   *St. S. Stylites* 164
frolic welcome took The thunder and the *s*,   *Ulysses* 48
The random *s* lighten'd !   *Amphion* 56
Autumn's mock *s* of the faded woods   *Aylmer's Field* 610
past In *s* : right across its track there lay,   *Sea Dreams* 126
Many a little hand Glanced like a touch of *s* on the
    rocks,   *Princess iii* 357

Sunshine (*continued*) A stroke of cruel *s* on the cliff,   *Princess iv* 524
When the tide ebbs in *s*,   „ *vi* 162
clover sod, That takes the *s* and the rains,   *In Mem. x* 14
Turn thy wild wheel thro' *s*, storm and cloud;   *Marr. of Geraint* 348
This was the *s* that hath given the man   *Balin and Balan* 181
glittering like May *s* on May leaves   *Merlin and V.* 88
and the *s* came along with him.   *Pelleas and E.* 6
s seem'd to brood More warmly on the heart   *Lover's Tale i* 327
s on that sail at last which brings our Edwin home.   *The Flight* 92
So fair in southern *s* bathed,   *Freedom* 5
THE gleam of household *s* ends,   *The Wanderer* 1
Sun-smitten *S-s* Alps before me lay.   *The Daisy* 62
Sun-star great *S-s* of morningtide,   *Batt. of Brunanburh* 26
Sun-steep'd *S-s* at noon, and in the moon   *Lotos-Eaters, C. S.* 29
Sun-stricken fell *S-s*, and that other lived alone.   *Enoch Arden* 570
Sun-worship Their sweet *s-w* ?   *Gareth and L.* 1081
This old *s-w*, boy, will rise again,   *Balin and Balan* 457
Superhuman Thrice multiplied by *s* pangs,   *St. S. Stylites* 11
Superlative ' Most dearest ' be a true *s*—   *Sisters (E. and E.)* 292
Supersede one deep love doth *s* All other,   *In Mem. xxxii* 5
Supersensual For such a *s* sensual bond   *Merlin and V.* 109
Superstition was paid To woman, *s* all awry: *Princess ii* 137
Supper And after *s*, on a bed,   *The Sisters* 16
dreams Of goodly *s* in the distant pool,   *Gareth and L.* 1187
' So that ye do not serve me sparrow-hawks For *s*,   *Marr. of Geraint* 305
cup itself, from which our Lord Drank at the last sad *s*   *Holy Grail* 47
How oft the Cantab *s*, host and guest,   *To W. H. Brookfield* 4
Fur the men ater *s*'ed sung their songs   *Owd Roä* 35
Supple *s*, sinew-corded, apt at arms;   *Princess v* 535
And rosy knees and *s* roundedness,   *Lucretius* 190
Supple-sinew'd Iron jointed, *s-s*, they shall dive,   *Locksley Hall* 169
Supple-sliding scoundrel in the *s-s* knee.'   *Sea Dreams* 168
Supplest and Death will freeze the *s* limbs—   *Happy* 46
Suppliant many another *s* crying came   *Gareth and L.* 436
look'd and saw The novice, weeping, *s*,   *Guinevere* 664
Supplicated shall I brook to be *s* ?   *Boädicea* 9
Supplicating Besought him, *s*, if he cared   *Enoch Arden* 163
would they listen, did they pity me *s* ?   *Boädicea* 8
Supplication With *s* both of knees and tongue :   *Holy Grail* 602
Supplied And he *s* my want the more   *In Mem. lxxix* 19
Supporter like *s's* on a shield, Bow-back'd   *Princess iv* 358
Or two wild men *s's* of a shield,   *Geraint and E.* 267
Suppose ' Good soul ! *s* I grant it thee,   *Two Voices* 38
Suppression *See* **Self-suppression**
Supremacy In knowledge of their own *s*.'   *Œnone* 133
Supreme every legend fair Which the *s* Caucasian mind   *Palace of Art* 126
Supt The kitchen brewis that was ever *s*   *Gareth and L.* 781
Sure (*See also* **Sewer**) Not make him *s* that he shall cease ?   *Two Voices* 282
' Ah ! *s* within him and without,   „ 307
'Mid onward-sloping motions infinite Making for one *s* goal.   *Palace of Art* 248
rest thee *s* That I shall love thee well   *Œnone* 159
To be *s* the preacher says,   *Grandmother* 93
' Fool,' he answer'd, ' death is *s*   *Sailor Boy* 13
Bound for the Hall, I am *s* was he :   *Maud I x* 25
I am quite quite *s* That there is one to love me ;   „ *xi* 10
O Maud were *s* of Heaven If lowliness could save her.   „ *xii* 19
Most *s* am I, quite *s*, he is not dead.'   *Geraint and E.* 545
they do not flow From evil done ; right *s* am I of that,   *Guinevere* 189
' you are *s* it 'll all come right,'   *First Quarrel* 1
I am *s* it 'll all come right.' (repeat)   „ 74, 91
lit by *s* hands,—With thunders, and with lightnings,   *Buonaparte* 5
He means me I'm *s* to be happy   *Rizpah* 76
well, I am not *s*—But if there lie a preference   *Sisters (E. and E.)* 289
let come what will ; at last the end is *s*,   *The Flight* 103
And *s* am I, by Muriel, one day came And saw you,   *The Ring* 312
I am all but *s* I have—in Kendal church—   *Romney's R.* 19
For you forgive me, you are *s* of that—   „ 160
Surely I am not *s* one of those Caught by the flower   *The Ring* 343
How *s* glidest thou from March to May,   *Prog. of Spring* 109
Surer For *s* sign had follow'd, either hand,   *M. d'Arthur* 76

Surer (*continued*) If we could give them *s*, quicker proof—   *Princess iii* 282
For *s* sign had follow'd, either hand,   *Pass. of Arthur* 244
Surety We did but keep you *s* for our son,   *Princess v* 25
Surf White *s* wind-scatter'd over sails and masts,   *D. of F. Women* 31
like a wader in the *s*, Beyond the brook,   *The Brook* 117
the breakers on the shore Sloped into louder *s* :   *Lover's Tale iii* 15
again the stormy *s* Crash'd in the shingle :   „ 53
Surface (*adj.*) Then, for the *s* eye, that only doats   *The Ring* 163
Surface (*s*) In roaring he shall rise and on the *s* die.   *The Kraken* 15
But ere he dipt the *s*, rose an arm   *M. d'Arthur* 143
And down my *s* crept.   *Talking Oak* 162
These flashes on the *s* are not he.   *Princess iv* 253
To make the sullen *s* crisp.   *In Mem. xlix* 8
when the *s* rolls, Hath power to walk the waters   *Com. of Arthur* 293
Then from the smitten *s* flash'd,   *Lancelot and E.* 1236
But ere he dipt the *s*, rose an arm   *Pass. of Arthur* 311
Who with his head below the *s* dropt   *Lover's Tale i* 636
You, what the cultured *s* grows,   *Mechanophilus* 33
Surface-shadow sees and stirs the *s-s*   *Ancient Sage* 38
Surge tho' the *s* Of some new deluge   *If I were loved* 11
when the *s* was seething free,   *Lotos-Eaters, C. S.* 106
sands and yeasty *s's* mix In caves   *Sailor Boy* 9
I heard the shingle grinding in the *s*,   *Holy Grail* 811
the *s* fell From thunder into whispers ;   *Lover's Tale iii* 30
Surged foeman *s*, and waver'd, and reel'd   *Heavy Brigade* 62
Surgery-school Fresh from the *s-s's* of France   *In the Child. Hosp.* 3
Surging In middle ocean meets the *s* shock,   *Will* 8
Their *s* charges foam'd themselves away ;   *Ode on Well.* 126
and it ran *S* and swaying all round us,   *Def. of Lucknow* 38
Surly And there the *s* village-churls,   *L. of Shalott ii* 16
And humm'd a *s* hymn.   *Talking Oak* 300
Surmise silent, we with blind *s* Regarding,   *Princess iv* 381
Surname Simeon of the pillar, by *s* Stylites,   *St. S. Stylites* 161
' Katie.' ' That were strange. What *s* ? '   *The Brook* 212
wrote Name, *s*, all as clear as noon,   *The Ring* 237
Surpass But tho' the port *s'es* praise,   *Will Water.* 77
As we *s* our fathers' skill,   *Mechanophilus* 21
Surprise (*s*) with *s* Froze my swift speech :   *D. of F. Women* 89
With some *s* and thrice as much disdain Turn'd,   *Marr. of Geraint* 557
But kept it for a sweet *s* at morn. Yea, truly is it not a sweet *s* ?   703
Surprise (*verb*) *S* thee ranging with thy peers.   *In Mem. xliv* 12
Surrender ' Never *s*, I charge you,   *Def. of Lucknow* 10
Survive *S* in spirits render'd free,   *In Mem. xxxviii* 10
Suspend And he *s's* his converse with a friend,   *Marr. of Geraint* 340
Suspicion A vague *s* of the breast :   *Two Voices* 356
There gleam'd a vague *s* in his eyes :   *Lancelot and E.* 127
Suspicious *S* that her nature had a taint.   *Marr. of Geraint* 68
Thro' all the outworks of *s* pride ;   *Isabel* 24
Sussex Green *S* fading into blue   *Pro. to Gen. Hamley* 7
Sustain bad him with good heart *s* himself—   *Aylmer's Field* 544
Sustain'd Be dimm'd of sorrow, or *s* ;   *In Mem. lxxxv* 10
Sustaining They tremble, the *s* crags :   „ *cxxvii* 11
Sustenance Gain'd for her own a scanty *s*,   *Enoch Arden* 259
No want was there of human *s*,   „ 554
One *s*, which, still as thought grew large,   *Lover's Tale i* 240
Súttee were seen or heard Fires of *S*,   *Akbar's Dream* 196
Swallies (**swallow**) whin they *s* the man intire !   *Tomorrow* 66
Swallow (*s*) Above in the wind was the *s*,   *Dying Swan* 16
the *s* 'ill come back again with summer   *May Queen. N. Y's. E.* 19
While the prime *s* dips his wing,   *Edwin Morris* 145
The *s* stopt as he hunted the fly,   *Poet's Song* 9
I glance, Among my skimming *s's* ;   *The Brook* 175
Where they like *s's* coming out of time   *Princess ii* 431
I watch'd the *s* winging south From mine own land,   „ *iv* 89
' O *S*, flying, flying South,   „ 93
O tell her, *S*, thou that knowest each,   „ 96
' O *S*, *S*, if I could follow, and light   „ 99
' O tell her, *S*, that thy brood is flown :   „ 108
' O *S*, flying from the golden woods,   „ 114
And *s* and sparrow and throstle,   *Window, Ay* 14
The Mayfly is torn by *s*,   *Maud I iv* 23
' The *s* and the swift are near akin,   *Com. of Arthur* 313
For Knowledge is the *s* on the lake   *Ancient Sage* 37
Hubert brings me home With April and the *s*.   *The Ring* 60

Swear (continued)   'I s (and else may insects prick Each leaf   *Talking Oak* 69
'I s, by leaf, and wind, and rain,   ,,   81
And hear me s a solemn oath,   ,,   281
I have a secret—only s, Before I tell you—s upon the
book Not to reveal it,   *Enoch Arden* 837
'S' added Enoch sternly 'on the book.'   ,,   842
I s you shall not make them out of mine.   *Aylmer's Field* 301
she made me s it—'Sdeath—   *Princess v* 291
S by St. something—I forget her name—   ,,   293
I s to you, lawful and lawless war   *Maud II v* 94
but, so thou dread to s, Pass not beneath this
gateway,   *Gareth and L.* 272
Repentant of the word she made him s,   ,,   527
I s thou canst not fling the fourth.'   ,,   1327
I s it would not ruffle me so much   *Geraint and E.* 150
I s I will not ask your meaning in it :   ,,   743
But ere I leave thee let me s once more   *Merlin and V.* 929
I s by truth and knighthood that I gave   *Lancelot and E.* 1297
But by mine eyes and by mine ears I s,   *Holy Grail* 864
Will ye not lie? not s, as there ye kneel,   *Last Tournament* 646
I say, S to me thou wilt love me ev'n when old,   ,,   652
Than had we never sworn. I s no more.   ,,   660
lay their hands in mine and s To reverence the King,   *Guinevere* 467
where is he can s But that some broken gleam   *Ded. Poem Prin. Alice* 17
O my lord, I s to you I heard his voice   *Columbus* 145
I s and s forsworn To love him most,   *The Flight* 49
and s the brain is in the feet.   *Locksley H., Sixty* 136
who shall s it cannot be?   ,,   269
Sweär an' 'e s's, an' 'e says to 'im 'Noa.   *Village Wife* 67
Ye niver 'eärd Steevie s 'cep' it wur at a dog   *Spinster's S's.* 60
Sweär'd (swore) an' s as I'd breäk ivry stick   *North. Cobbler* 35
Sweärin S agean, you Toms,   *Spinster's S's.* 59
Swearing (See also **Sweärin**)   s he had glamour enow In
his own blood,   *Gareth and L.* 209
And s men to vows impossible,   *Lancelot and E.* 130
Sweat bloody thumbs S on his blazon'd chairs ;   *Walk. to the Mail* 76
every hour Must s her sixty minutes to the death,   *Golden Year* 69
That shriek and s in pigmy wars   *Lit. Squabbles* 2
S, writhings, anguish, labouring of the lungs   *Pass. of Arthur* 115
Sweating And, s rosin, plump'd the pine   *Amphion* 47
With a weird bright eye, s and trembling,   *Aylmer's Field* 585
Then loosed their s horses from the yoke,   *Spec. of Iliad* 2
Went s underneath a sack of corn,   *Marr. of Geraint* 263
He up the side, s with agony, got,   *Lancelot and E.* 494
Sweeät (sweet) sa pratty an' neät an' s,   *North. Cobbler* 43
sa pratty, an' feät, an' neät, an' s?   ,,   108
Sweep (s) and a s Of richest pauses,   *Eleänore* 65
The parson taking wide and wider s's,   *The Epic* 14
by many a s Of meadow smooth from aftermath   *Audley Court* 13
From the dread s of the down-streaming seas :   *Enoch Arden* 55
or the s Of some precipitous rivulet   ,,   586
The s of scythe in morning dew,   *In Mem. lxxxix* 18
Made but a single bound, and with a s of it   *Geraint and E.* 727
Sweep (verb) S the green that folds thy grave.   *A Dirge* 6
Would s the tracts of day and night.   *Two Voices* 69
never more Shall lone Œnone see the morning mist S
thro' them ;   *Œnone* 217
we s into the younger day :   *Locksley Hall* 183
Who s the crossings, wet or dry,   *Will Water.* 47
those long swells of breaker s The nutmeg rocks   *The Voyage* 39
There let the wind s and the plover cry ;   *Come not, when, etc.* 5
That s's with all its autumn bowers,   *In Mem. xi* 10
We heard them s the winter land ;   ,, *xxx* 10
while the wind began to s A music   ,, *ciii* 53
But s's away as out we pass To range the woods,   ,, *Con.* 95
to s In ever-highering eagle-circles   *Gareth and L.* 20
And s me from my hold upon the world,   *Merlin and V.* 303
heard the hollow-ringing heavens s Over him till by
miracle—   *Holy Grail* 678
S's suddenly all its half-moulder'd chords   *Lover's Tale i* 19
often s's athwart in storm—   ,,   50
sea-current would s us out to the main.   *Despair* 51
Sweeping (See also **Earth-sweeping**, **Long-sweeping**)   And
with a s of the arm,   *A Character* 16
passion s thro' me left me dry,   *Locksley Hall* 131

Sweeping (continued) S the frothfly from the fescue brush'd   *Aylmer's Field* 530
Of that great breaker, s up the strand,   *Com. of Arthur* 387
sudden gust that s down Took the edges of the pall,   *Lover's Tale iii* 34
shape with wings Came s by him,   *St. Telemachus* 25
Sweet (See also **Heaven-sweet**, **Lowly-sweet**, **May-sweet**,
Perfect-sweet, **Star-sweet**, **Sunny-sweet**, **Sweeät**)
False-eyed Hesper, unkind, where is my s Rosalind ?   *Leonine Eleg.* 16
How s to have a common faith !   *Supp. Confessions* 33
S in their utmost bitterness,   ,,   117
S lips whereon perpetually did reign The summer calm   *Isabel* 7
She could not look on the s heaven,   *Mariana* 15
Sudden glances, s and strange,   *Madeline* 5
vaults of pillar'd palm, Imprisoning s's,   *Arabian Nights* 40
In s dreams softer than unbroken rest   *Ode to Memory* 29
With music and s showers Of festal flowers,   ,,   77
S faces, rounded arms, and bosoms prest   *Sea-Fairies* 3
And s is the colour of cove and cave, And s shall your
welcome be :   ,,   30
We will kiss s kisses, and speak s words :   ,,   34
O pale, pale face so s and meek,   *Oriana* 66
O S pale Margaret, (repeat)   *Margaret 1*, 54
Your melancholy s and frail   ,,   7
'His little daughter, whose s face He kiss'd,   *Two Voices* 253
The s church bells began to peal.   ,,   408
These three made unity so s,   ,,   421
'What is it thou knowest, s voice ?'   ,,   440
My own s Alice, we must die.   *Miller's D.* 18
So s it seems with thee to walk,   ,,   29
S Alice, if I told her all ?'   ,,   120
A trifle, s ! which true love spells—   ,,   187
S gales, as from deep gardens, blow   *Fatima* 24
And that s incense rise ? '   *Palace of Art* 44
For that s incense rose and never fail'd,   ,,   45
Or gay, or grave, or s, or stern,   ,,   91
Or s Europa's mantle blew unclasp'd,   ,,   117
Making s close of his delicious toils—   ,,   185
Nor would I break for your s sake   *L. C. V. de Vere* 13
Oh your s eyes, your low replies :   ,,   29
by the meadow-trenches blow the faint s cuckoo-flowers ;   *May Queen* 30
O s is the new violet,   *May Queen, Con.* 5
And s is all the land about,   ,,   7
O s and strange it seems to me,   ,,   53
THERE is s music here that softer falls   *Lotos-Eaters, C. S.* 1
Music that brings s sleep down from the blissful skies.   ,,   7
How s it were, hearing the downward stream,   ,,   54
How s (while warm airs lull us, blowing lowly)   ,,   89
Only to hear were s,   ,,   99
Surely, surely, slumber is more s than toil,   ,,   126
And s it was to dream of Fatherland,   *Lotos-Eaters* 39
whose s breath Preluded those melodious bursts   *D. of F. Women* 5
S as new buds in Spring.   ,,   272
Failing to give the bitter of the s,   ,,   286
Sleep till the end, true soul and s.   *To J. S.* 73
and stirr'd her lips For some s answer,   *Gardener's D.* 159
Of that which came between, more s than each,   ,,   252
My s, wild, fresh three quarters of a year,   *Edwin Morris* 2
made it s To walk, to sit, to sleep, to wake,   ,,   39
Then low and s I whistled thrice ;   ,,   113
S ! s ! spikenard, and balm, and frankincense.   *St. S. Stylites* 211
Ah ! let me not be fool'd, s saints :   ,,   212
'Yet seem'd the pressure thrice as s   *Talking Oak* 145
The slow s hours that bring us all things good,   *Love and Duty* 57
Thy s eyes brighten slowly close to mine,   *Tithonus* 38
Whispering I knew not what of wild and s,   ,,   61
How s are looks that ladies bend   *Sir Galahad* 13
S Emma Moreland of yonder town   *Edward Gray* 1
S Emma Moreland spoke to me :   ,,   5
'S Emma Moreland, love no more   ,,   7
I buried her like my own s child,   *Lady Clare* 27
colour flushes Her s face from brow to chin :   *L. of Burleigh* 62
So s a face, such angel grace,   *Beggar Maid* 13
Who make it seem more s to be   *You might have won* 29
And chanted a melody loud and s,   *Poet's Song* 6
To where the rivulets of s water ran ;   *Enoch Arden* 642
'If I might look on her s face again   ,,   718

Sweet (*continued*)   Like fountains of *s* water in the sea,   *Enoch Arden* 803
Or ev'n the *s* half-English Neilgherry air   *The Brook* 17
'*S* Katie, once I did her a good turn,   „   74
Of *s* seventeen subdued me ere she spoke)   „   113
Arrived and found the sun of *s* content Re-risen   „   168
I move the *s* forget-me-nots   „   172
her *s* face and faith Held him from that: *Aylmer's Field* 392
She look'd so *s*, he kiss'd her tenderly   „   555
'That was then your dream,' she said, 'Not sad, but *s*.'   *Sea Dreams* 106
'So *s*, I lay,' said he, 'And mused upon it,   „   107
Their wildest wailings never out of tune With that *s* note;   „   232
Nothing to mar the sober majesties Of settled, *s*,
     Epicurean life.   *Lucretius* 218
And *s* girl-graduates in their golden hair.   *Princess, Pro.* 142
And *s* as English air could make her,   „   155
S thoughts would swarm as bees about their queen.   „ i 40
We remember love ourselves In our *s* youth: „   123
S household talk, and phrases of the hearth,   „ ii 315
Is she The *s* proprietress a shadow?   „   415
S and low, *s* and low,   „ iii 1
'What pardon, *s* Melissa, for a blush?'   „   66
'O how *s*' I said (For I was half-oblivious of my mask)   „   337
O *s* and far from cliff and scar   „ iv 9
And *s* as those by hopeless fancy feign'd   „   55
So *s* a voice and vague, fatal to men,   „   64
Like some *s* sculpture draped from head to foot,   „ v 57
'Lift up your head, *s* sister: lie not thus.   „   64
S is it to have done the thing one ought,   „   67
My one *s* child, whom I shall see no more!   „   83
My babe, my *s* Aglaïa, my one child: „   101
Twice as magnetic to *s* influences Of earth and heaven?   „   191
'We remember love ourself In our *s* youth;   „   208
Prince, she can be *s* to those she loves,   „   289
'*S* my child, I live for thee.'   „ vi 16
by and by *S* order lived again with other laws: „ vii 19
two dewdrops on the petal shake To the same *s* air,   „   69
showers of random *s* on maid and man.   „   86
And call her *s*, as if in irony,   „   97
nor more *S* Ida: palm to palm she sat: „   135
'If you be, what I think you, some *s* dream,   „   145
only, if a dream, *S* dream, be perfect.   „   149
she found a small *S* Idyl, and once more, as low,
     she read: „   191
and *s* is every sound, Sweeter thy voice, but every
     sound is *s*;   „   218
she had fail'd In *s* humility; had fail'd in all;   „   229
could we make her as the man, *S* Love were slain: „   277
lives A drowning life, besotted in *s* self,   „   314
forced *S* love on pranks of saucy boyhood: „   344
Lay thy *s* hands in mine and trust to me.'   „   366
Uplift a thousand voices full and *s*,   *Ode Inter. Exhib.* 1
Welcome her, all things youthful and *s*,   *W. to Alexandra* 8
he turn'd, and I saw his eyes all wet, in the *s* moon-
     shine: *Grandmother* 49
There lay the *s* little body that never had drawn a breath.   „   62
Sin' I mun doy I mun doy, thaw loife they says
     is *s*,   *N. Farmer, O. S.* 63
thou's *s* upo' parson's lass—   „ *N. S.* 11
For a score of *s* little summers or so?'   *The Islet* 2
The *s* little wife of the singer said,   „ 3
To a little Eden on earth that I know,   „ 14
And strain to make an inch of room For their *s*
     selves,   *Lit. Squabbles* 10
honouring your *s* faith in him, May trust himself;   *A Dedication* 5
O lights, are you flying over her *s* little face?   *Window, On the Hill* 13
Where is another *s* as my *s*,   „ *Letter* 1
Claspt on her seal, my *s*!   „ *Answer* 2
O *s* and bitter in a breath,   *In Mem.* iii 3
Thro' four *s* years arose and fell,   „ xxii 3
'They rest,' we said, 'their sleep is *s*,'   „ xxx 19
I strive To keep so *s* a thing alive:'   „ xxxv 7
hear thy laurel whisper *s* About the ledges of the hill.'   „ xxxvii 7
S soul, do with me as thou wilt;   „ lxv 1
To utter love more *s* than praise.   „ lxvii 16
The same *s* forms in either mind.   „ lxix 8

Sweet (*continued*)   But Death returns an answer *s*:   *In Mem.* lxxxi 9
O *s* new-year delaying long;   „ lxxxiii 2
S after showers, ambrosial air,   „ lxxxvi 1
Wild bird, whose warble, liquid *s*,   „ lxxxviii 1
regret for buried time That keenlier in *s* April wakes,   „ cxvi 2
Desire of nearness doubly *s*;   „ cxvii 6
S Hesper-Phosphor, double name   „ cxxi 17
And if the words were *s* and strong   „ cxxv 11
S human hand and lips and eye;   „ cxxix 6
Maud with her *s* purse-mouth when my father dangled
     the grapes,   *Maud I* i 71
And she touch'd my hand with a smile so *s*,   „ vi 12
But a smile could make it *s*. (repeat)   „ 39, 95
How prettily for his own *s* sake   „ 51
What some have found so *s*;   „ xi 4
Let the *s* heavens endure,   „ 8
Maud is as true as Maud is *s*:   „ xiii 32
Think I may hold dominion *s*,   „ xvi 12
In our low world, where yet 'tis *s* to live.   „ xviii 48
silver knell Of twelve *s* hours that past in bridal white,   „ 65
Seal'd her mine from her first *s* breath.   „ xix 41
That, if left uncancell'd, had been so *s*:   „ 46
And for your *s* sake to yours;   „ 91
(If I read her *s* will right)   „ xxi 1
From the meadow your walks have left so *s*   „ xxii 39
She is coming, my own, my *s*;   „ 67
For she, *s* soul, had hardly spoken a word,   „ *II* i 11
'Tis a morning pure and *s*, (repeat)   „ iv 31, 35
'Take me, *s*, To the regions of thy rest'?   „ 87
S nature gilded by the gracious gleam Of letters,   *Ded. of Idylls* 39
Call him baseborn, and since his ways are *s*,   *Com. of Arthur* 180
friends Of Arthur, gazing on him, tall, with bright
     S faces,   „ 279
And spake *s* words, and comforted my heart,   „ 349
But *s* again, and then I loved him well.   „ 355
S mother, do ye love the child?'   *Gareth and L.* 35
so the boy, *S* mother, neither clomb,   „ 56
'True love, *s* son, had risk'd himself and climb'd,   „ 60
S is the chase: „ 93
'*S* son, for there be many who deem him not,   „ 121
Stay, *s* son.'   „ 131
Rather than—O *s* heaven!   „ 741
S lord, how like a noble knight he talks!   „ 777
Their *s* sun-worship? these be for the snare   „ 1081
He compass'd her with *s* observances And worship,   *Marr. of Geraint* 48
in the *s* face of her Whom he loves most,   „ 122
Lost in *s* dreams, and dreaming of her love For
     Lancelot,   „ 158
Singing; and as the *s* voice of a bird,   „ 329
So the *s* voice of Enid moved Geraint;   „ 334
And Enid brought *s* cakes to make them cheer,   „ 388
And seeing her so *s* and serviceable,   „ 393
Sank her *s* head upon her gentle breast;   „ 527
And softly to her own *s* heart she said: „ 618
S heaven, how much I shall discredit him!   „ 621
But kept it for a *s* surprise at morn. Yea, truly is
     it not a *s* surprise?   „ 703
But rested with her *s* face satisfied;   „ 776
In words whose echo lasts, they were so *s*,   „ 782
To compass her with *s* observances,   *Geraint and E.* 39
And she was ever praying the *s* heavens To save her
     dear lord   „ 44
But keep a touch of *s* civility Here in the heart   „ 312
tender sound of his own voice And *s* self-pity,   „ 349
But ended with apology so *s*,   „ 394
'Your *s* faces make good fellows fools And traitors.   „ 399
S lady, never since I first drew breath Have I beheld   „ 619
breath Of her *s* tendance hovering over him,   „ 926
but when he mark'd his high *s* smile In passing,   *Balin and Balan* 160
and with how *s* grace She greeted my return!   „ 193
Hail, royal knight, we break on thy *s* rest,   „ 470
Again she sigh'd 'Pardon, *s* lord!   „ 497
'Rise, my *s* King, and kiss me on the lips,   „ 516
S lord, ye do right well to whisper this.   „ 529
Here her slow *s* eyes Fear-tremulous,   *Merlin and V.* 85

Sweet (*continued*)   With dark *s* hints of some who prized
    him more   *Merlin and V.* 159
But, Vivien, when you sang me that *s* rhyme,   ,,   434
S were the days when I was all unknown,   ,,   501
Those twelve *s* moons confused his fatherhood.'   ,,   712
What say ye then to *s* Sir Sagramore,   ,,   721
To crop his own *s* rose before the hour?'   ,,   725
And they, *s* soul, that most impute a crime Are
    pronest to it,   ,,   825
rapt By all the *s* and sudden passion of youth   *Lancelot and E.* 282
She needs must bid farewell to *s* Lavaine.   ,,   341
' Ah my *s* lord Sir Lancelot,' said Lavaine,   ,,   512
For if you love, it will be *s* to give it; And if he
    love, it will be *s* to have it   ,,   692
S father, will you let me lose my wits?'   ,,   752
S father, I behold him in my dreams   ,,   763
to be *s* and serviceable To noble knights in sickness,   ,,   767
Would call her friend and sister, *s* Elaine,   ,,   865
arraying her *s* self In that wherein she deem'd she
    look'd her best,   ,,   906
I had been wedded earlier, *s* Elaine: ,,   935
for true you are and *s* Beyond mine old belief in
    womanhood,   ,,   954
' Peace to thee, *S* sister,'   ,,   997
' *S* is true love tho' given in vain, in vain; And *s*
    is death who puts an end to pain: ,,   1007
' Love, art thou *s*? then bitter death must be:
    Love, thou art bitter; *s* is death to me.   ,,   1010
' *S* love, that seems not made to fade away, *S*
    death, that seems to make us loveless clay,   ,,   1013
' *S* brothers, yesternight I seem'd a curious little
    maid again,   ,,   1034
S father, all too faint and sick am I For anger: ,,   1086
' *S* father, and bid call the ghostly man Hither,   ,,   1099
' O *s* father, tender and true, Deny me not,' she said—   ,,   1110
' Farewell, *s* sister,' parted all in tears.   ,,   1152
Ah simple heart and *s*, Ye loved me, damsel,   ,,   1393
But the *s* vision of the Holy Grail   *Holy Grail* 31
' *S* brother, I have seen the Holy Grail: ,,   107
' But she, the wan *s* maiden, shore away   ,,   149
We that are plagued with dreams of something *s*   ,,   625
the *s* Grail Glided and past, and close upon it peal'd   ,,   694
A *s* voice singing in the topmost tower To the eastward: ,,   834
and the *s* smell of the fields Past,   *Pelleas and E.* 5
their malice on the placid lip Froz'n by *s* sleep,   ,,   433
Who yells Here in the still *s* summer night, but I—   ,,   473
' O *s* star, Pure on the virgin forehead of the dawn!'   ,,   504
Till the *s* heavens have fill'd it from the heights   ,,   510
But the *s* body of a maiden babe.   *Last Tournament* 48
New loves are *s* as those that went before: ,,   280
that desert lodge to Tristram lookt So *s*,   ,,   388
the *s* name Allured him first, and then the maid herself,   ,,   398
If this be *s*, to sin in leading-strings,   ,,   574
thy *s* memories Of Tristram in that year he was away.'   ,,   579
To pine and waste in those *s* memories.   ,,   598
' May God be with thee, *s*, when old and gray,   ,,   627
' May God be with thee, *s*, when thou art old, And
    s no more to me !'   ,,   629
that I should suck Lies like *s* wines :   ,,   645
' Press this a little closer, *s*,   ,,   718
' Have we not heard the bridegroom is so *s* ?   *Guinevere* 177
Ah *s* lady, the King's grief For his own self,   ,,   196
' and, *s* lady, if I seem To vex an ear too sad to
    listen to me,   ,,   314
As I could think, *s* lady, yours would be Such as they are,   ,,   352
Rapt in *s* talk or lively, all on love And sport   ,,   386
Thou hast not made my life so *s* to me,   ,,   451
To lead *s* lives in purest chastity.   ,,   474
yet in him keeps A draught of that *s* fountain that
    he loves,   *Lover's Tale i* 141
Yet was not the less *s* for that it seem'd ?   ,,   155
All—all but one ; and strange to me, and *s*, *S*
    thro' strange years to come   ,,   243
Still to believe it—'tis so *s* a thought,   ,,   275
Absorbing all the incense of *s* thoughts   ,,   469

Sweet (*continued*)   Is presently received in a *s* grave Of
    eglantines,   *Lover's Tale i* 528
Held converse *s* and low—low converse *s*,   ,,   541
It was so happy an hour, so *s* a place,   ,,   558
At first her voice was very *s* and low,   ,,   563
A morning air, *s* after rain, ran over The rippling
    levels   *iii* 3
That will not hear my call, however *s*,   *iv* 160
So the *s* figure folded round with night   ,,   219
Sad, *s*, and strange together—floated in—   ,,   304
A *s* voice that—you scarce could better that.   *Sisters (E. and E.)* 14
the *s* eyes frown : the lips Seem but a gash.   ,,   106
And all her *s* self-sacrifice and death.   ,,   255
his voice was low as from other worlds, and his
    eyes were *s*,   *V. of Maeldune* 117
For that *s* mother land which gave them birth   *Tiresias* 122
The small *s* face was flush'd,   *The Wreck* 60
Ten long *s* summer days upon deck,   ,,   64
one morning a bird with a warble plaintively *s*   ,,   81
' Ten long *s* summer days ' of fever,   ,,   147
she was always loyal and *s*—   *Despair* 49
The morning with such music, would never be so *s* !   *The Flight* 66
O *s*, they tell me that the world is hard,   ,,   101
Achora, yer laste little whishper was *s* as the lilt of a
    bird !   *Tomorrow* 33
I calls 'em arter the fellers es once was *s* upo' me ?   *Spinster's S's.* 4
I remember how you kiss'd the miniature with
    those *s* eyes.   *Locksley H., Sixty* 12
S St. Francis of Assisi, would that he were here again,   ,,   100
the *s* sound ran Thro' palace and cottage door,   *Dead Prophet* 37
S Catullus's all-but-island, olive-silvery Sirmio !   *Frater Ave, etc.* 9
torpid mummy wheat Of Egypt bore a grain as *s*   *To Prof. Jebb* 6
In your *s* babe she finds but you—   *The Ring* 365
Beat upon mine ! you are mine, my *s* ! All mine from
    your pretty blue eyes to your feet, My *s*.'   *Romney's R.* 95
And find the white heather wherever you go, My *s*.'   ,,   7
' wasting the *s* summer hours ' ?   *Charity* 1
All very well just now to be calling me darling and *s*,   ,,   7
Sing thou low or loud or *s*,   *Poets and Critics* 6

Sweet-'arts (sweet-hearts)   Lucy wur laäme o' one leg,
    s-a she niver 'ed none—   *Village Wife* 99
MILK for my *s-a*, Bess !   *Spinster's S's.* 1
S-a ! Molly belike may 'a lighted to-night upo' one.   ,,   7
S-a ! thanks to the Lord that I niver not listen'd
    to noän !   ,,   8
An' noän of my four *s-a* 'ud 'a let me 'a hed my
    oän waäy,   ,,   101

Sweeten   *S's* the spirit still.   *D. of F. Women* 236
They freshen and *s* the wards   *In the Child. Hosp.* 38

Sweeten'd   Lo ! *s* with the summer light,   *Lotos-Eaters, C. S.* 32
One rose, my rose, that *s* all mine air—   *Pelleas and E.* 403

Sweeter   Whether smile or frown be *s*,   *Madeline* 13
And *s* is the young lamb's voice   *May Queen, Con.* 1
And *s* far is death than life to me   ,,   8
There came a *s* token when the night and morning
    meet ;   ,,   22
s than the dream Dream'd by a happy man,   *Gardener's D.* 71
' Your own will be the *s*,'   *Sea Dreams* 318
S thy voice, but every sound is sweet ;   *Princess vii* 219
' *S* to me ' she said ' this garden rose   *Balin and Balan* 269
s still The wild-wood hyacinth and the bloom of May.   ,,   270
I know not which is *s*, no, not I. (repeat)   *Lancelot and E.* 1009, 1015
O Love, if death be *s*, let me die.   ,,   1012
O *s* than all memories of thee,   *Last Tournament* 585
Then—while a s music wakes,   *To the Queen* 13
Chaunteth not the brooding bee *S* tones than calumny ?   *A Dirge* 17
Drip *s* dews than traitor's tear.   ,,   24
You could not light upon a *s* thing :   *Walk. to the Mail* 52
Ah, *s* to be drunk with loss,   *In Mem. i* 11
s seems To rest beneath the clover sod,   ,,   *x* 12
With *s* manners, purer laws.   ,,   *cvi* 16
can a *s* chance ever come to me here ?   *Maud I i* 62
To the *s* blood by the other side ;   ,,   *xiii* 34
For nothing can be *s* Than maiden Maud in either.   ,,   *xx* 21
Mixt with kisses *s s* Than anything on earth.   ,,   *II iv* 9

Sweeter (continued) And s than the bride of Cassivelaun,   *Marr. of Geraint* 744
And you, that wear a wreath of s bay,   *Poets and their B.* 7
Sweetest The s lady of the time,   *Arabian Nights* 141
where s sunlight falls Upon the storied walls ;   *Ode to Memory* 85
Then her s meal she makes On the first-born of her sons.   *Vision of Sin* 145
' The mother of the s little maid,   *Princess ii* 279
The passing of the s soul That ever look'd with human eyes.   *In Mem. lvii* 11
tiny-trumpeting gnat can break our dream When s ;   *Lancelot and E.* 138
love of man and woman when they love their best, Closest and s,   " 870
Sweet-Gale S-G rustle round the shelving keel ;   *Edwin Morris* 110
Sweetheart (*See also* **Sweet-'arts**) ' S, I love you so well   *Grandmother* 50
' S '—this was the letter—   *First Quarrel* 51
Sweet-hearted S-h, you, whose light-blue eyes   *In Mem. xcvi* 2
Sweetness Now folds the lily all her s up,   *Princess vii* 186
   " 281
He gain in s and in moral height,   *In Mem. xxxv* 15
Will change my s more and more,   " *lxiv* 20
A secret s in the stream,   " *lxxxiii* 6
Thy s from its proper place ?   " *cx* 17
Nor mine the s or the skill,   *Maud I v* 24
For your s hardly leaves me a choice   " *xiii* 33
Tho' I fancy her s only due   *Holy Grail* 623
Foregoing all her s, like a weed.   " 626
dreams of something sweet Beyond all s   *Lover's Tale i* 154
It seem'd to keep its s to itself,   " 171
Can ye take off the s from the flower, The colour and the s from the rose,   " 272
and over-full Of s, and in smelling of itself,   " 355
wild youth of an evil prince, Is without s,   " 531
But taken with the s of the place,   " 553
her words stole with most prevailing s Into my heart,   " *ii* 155
And with the excess of s and of awe,   *Ancient Sage* 226
Desolate s—far and far away—   *The Brook* 122
Sweet-smelling led me thro' the short s-s lanes   *Balin and Balan* 86
Sweet-voiced S-v, a song of welcome,   *Dying Swan* 38
Swell (s) (*See also* **Ground-swell**) And the wavy s of the soughing reeds,   *Palace of Art* 33
From those four jets four currents in one s   *May Queen, Con.* 9
up the valley came a s of music on the wind.   *The Voyage* 39
those long s's of breaker sweep The nutmeg rocks   *The Letters* 46
So fresh they rose in shadow'd s's   *To E. L.* 18
on the s The silver lily heaved and fell ;   *The Daisy* 12
That only heaved with a summer s.   *Maud I xviii* 62
only the s Of the long waves that roll
Swell (verb) above him s Huge sponges of millennial growth   *The Kraken* 5
thick with white bells the clover-hill s's   *Sea-Fairies* 14
Or sometimes they s and move,   *Eleänore* 111
And while he sinks or s's   *Talking Oak* 270
S's up, and shakes and falls.   *Sir Galahad* 76
s On some dark shore just seen that it was rich.   *Princess i* 248
S out and fail, as if a door Were shut   *In Mem. xxviii* 7
Spring that s's the narrow brooks,   " *lxxxv* 70
   The Voyage 13
Swell'd The broad seas s to meet the keel,   *Sea Dreams* 211
low musical note S up and died ; and, as it s, a ridge Of breaker issued from the belt,   " 222
past into the belt and s again Slowly to music :   *Princess iv* 319
But still her lists were s and mine were lean ;   *Maud I xiv* 31
voice of the long sea-wave as it s   *Claribel* 15
Swelleth Her song the lintwhite s,   *Sea Dreams* 87
Swelling Of such a tide s toward the land,   *Gardener's D.* 246
Swept And with a flying finger s my lips,   *Day-Dm., Revival* 6
A breeze thro' all the garden s behind ;   *The Voyage* 14
swell'd to meet the keel, And s behind ;   " 80
He cast his body, and on we s.   *Sea Dreams* 89
S with it to the shore, and enter'd one   " 236
and s away The men of flesh and blood,   *Ode on Well.* 130
down we s and charged and overthrew.   *In Mem. lxxviii* 6
No wing of wind the region s,   *Gareth and L.* 135
s the dust of ruin'd Rome From off the threshold   " 177
voice S bellowing thro' the darkness on to dawn,   "
and all the sand S like a river,   *Holy Grail* 800
S like a torrent of gems from the sky   *V. of Maeldune* 46

Swept (continued) and s in a cataract off from her sides,   *The Wreck* 90
And deed and song alike are s Away,   *Epilogue* 67
she s The dust of earth from her knee.   *Dead Prophet* 31
in the storms Of Autumn s across the city,   *Demeter and P.* 71
Swerve S from her duty to herself and us—   *Aylmer's Field* 304
line of the approaching rookery s From the elms,   *Princess, Con.* 97
Nor pastoral rivulet that s's   *In Mem. c* 14
made his beast that better knew it, s   *Pelleas and E.* 551
remember how the course of Time will s,   *Locksley H., Sixty* 235
Swerved be s from right to save A prince,   *Princess ii* 290
And so my passion hath not s   *In Mem. lxxxv* 49
they s and brake Flying, and Arthur call'd   *Com. of Arthur* 119
But since our fortune s from sun to shade,   *Marr. of Geraint* 714
And Holy Church, from whom I never s   *Columbus* 63
Had never s for craft or fear,   *To Marq. of Dufferin* 27
Swerving And at a sudden s of the road,   *Geraint and E.* 506
' One night my pathway s east,   *Holy Grail* 634
Swift (a bird) The swallow and the s are near akin,   *Com. of Arthur* 313
Swift (adj.) but seeming-bitter From excess of s delight.   *Rosalind* 32
' Not less s souls that yearn for light,   *Two Voices* 67
From my s blood that went and came   *Fatima* 16
Her loveliness with shame and with surprise Froze my s speech :   *D. of F. Women* 90
Not s nor slow to change, out firm :   *Love thou thy land* 31
This way and that dividing the s mind,   *M. d'Arthur* 60
The sound of streams that s or slow   *In Mem. xxxv* 10
This way and that dividing the s mind,   *Pass. of Arthur* 228
At times her steps are s and rash ;   *To Marq. of Dufferin* 2
Not s or rash, when late she lent   " 5
Æonian Evolution, s or slow, Thro' all the Spheres—   *The Ring* 44
Swifter With s movement and in purer light   *Isabel* 32
Moved with one spirit round about the bay, Trod s steps ;   *Lover's Tale iii* 18
Swiftness And with a shameful s :   *Com. of Arthur* 205
And with exceeding s ran the boat,   *Holy Grail* 514
borne With more than mortal s,   *Lover's Tale ii* 73
Swim ' High up the vapours fold and s :   *Two Voices* 262
taught me how to skate, to row, to s,   *Edwin Morris* 19
A light before me s's,   *Sir Galahad* 26
The mystic glory s's away :   *In Mem. lxvii* 9
And on the depths of death there s's   " *cviii* 11
Down to the river, sink or s,   *Gareth and L.* 1154
read but on my breviary with ease, Till my head s's ;   *Holy Grail* 546
Swimming The s vapour slopes athwart the glen,   *Œnone* 3
She rose, and fixt her s eyes upon him,   *Enoch Arden* 325
Sun Burst from a s fleece of winter gray,   *Demeter and P.* 20
Swindler and a wretched s's lie ?   *Maud I i* 56
Swine I watch the darkening droves of s   *Palace of Art* 199
Upon her tower, the Niobe of s,   *Walk. to the Mail* 99
all the s were sows, And all the dogs'—   *Princess i* 192
poor as hovell'd and hustled together, each sex, like s.   *Maud I* 34
a villain fitter to stick s Than ride abroad   *Gareth and L.* 865
one of all the drove should touch me : s ! '   *Merlin and V.* 699
S in the mud, that cannot see for slime,   *Holy Grail* 771
Save that he were the s thou spakest of,   " 885
Lord, I was tending s, and the Red Knight   *Last Tournament* 71
Who knew thee s enow before I came,   " 304
less than s, A naked aught—yet s I hold thee still,   " 308
For I have flung thee pearls and find thee s.'   " 310
S ? I have wallow'd, I have wash'd—   " 315
S, say ye ? s, goats, asses, rams and geese   " 321
' Then were s, goats, asses, geese The wiser fools,   " 325
Priest's pearl, flung down to s—The s,   *Sir J. Oldcastle* 116
my lord is lower than his oxen or his s.   *Locksley H., Sixty* 126
Swine-flesh men may taste S-f, drink wine ;   *Akbar's Dream* 54
Swineherd the s's malkin in the mast ?   *Last Tournament* 632
Swing (s) the rush of the air in the prone s,   *Aylmer's Field* 86
Swing (verb) s's the trailer from the crag ;   *Locksley Hall* 162
The shrill bell rings, the censer s's,   *Sir Galahad* 35
thrones and peoples are as waifs that s,   *W. to Marie Alex.* 26
where they s the Locksley shield,   *Locksley H., Sixty* 247
Swollen thou art but s with cold snows   *Gareth and L.* 9
as strong gales Hold s clouds from raining,   *D. of F. Women* 11
And blew the s cheek of a trumpeter,   *Princess ii* 364
On yon s brook that bubbles fast By meadows   *In Mem. xcix* 6

Swung (continued) A goodly brother of the Table
Round S by the neck : — *Last Tournament* 432
Tristram show'd And s the ruby carcanet. — „ 740
S round the lighted lantern of the hall ; — *Guinevere* 262
Great garlands s and blossom'd ; — *Lover's Tale iv* 191
Sycamore The pillar'd dusk of sounding s's, — *Audley Court* 16
   with all thy breadth and height Of foliage,
   towering s ; — *In Mem. lxxxix* 4
   The large leaves of the s, — „ *xcv* 55
Sylla all the blood by S shed Came driving — *Lucretius* 47
Syllable Faltering, would break its s's, — *Love and Duty* 39
   Be cabin'd up in words and s's, — *Lover's Tale i* 480
   While her words, s by s, — „ 575
   Choked all the s's, that strove to rise — „ 711
Sylvester ever since S shed the venom of world-wealth — *Sir J. Oldcastle* 166
Symbol Weak s's of the settled bliss, — *Miller's D.* 233
   Are they not sign and s of thy division — *High. Pantheism* 6
   Or so shall grief with s's play — *In Mem. lxxxv* 95
   Mute s's of a joyful morn, — „ *Con.* 58
   The golden s of his kinglihood, — *Com. of Arthur* 50
   With many a mystic s, gird the hall : — *Holy Grail* 233
   Three cypresses, s's of mortal woe, — *Lover's Tale i* 537
   The word that is the s of myself, — *Ancient Sage* 231
   All the suns—are these but s's of innumerable
   man, — *Locksley H., Sixty* 195
   Institute, Rich in s, in ornament, — *On Jub. Q. Victoria* 47
   Shiah and Sunnee, S the Eternal ! — *Akbar's Dream* 108
Symbol'd As if the living passion s there — *Aylmer's Field* 535
Symmetry s Of thy floating gracefulness, — *Eleänore* 49
   long desired A certain miracle of s, — *Gardener's D.* 11
Sympathise growing coarse to s with clay. — *Locksley Hall* 46
Sympathy trembling thro' the dew Of dainty-woeful
   sympathies. — *Margaret* 53
   that plies Its office, moved with s. — *Love thou thy land* 48
   Nor lose their mortal s, — *In Mem. xxx* 23
   And yet I spare them s, — „ *lxiii* 7
   Some painless s with pain ? ' — „ *lxxxv* 88
   into the s Of that small bay, — *Lover's Tale i* 434
   and S hew'd out The bosom-sepulchre of S ? — „ *ii* 31
   a strong s Shook all my soul ! — „ 88
   And *sympathies*, how frail, In sound and smell ! — *Early Spring* 35
Syrian when her Satrap bled At Issus by the S gates. — *Alexander* 3
   years That breathed beneath the S blue ! — *In Mem. lii* 12
System A dust of s's and of creeds. — *Two Voices* 207
   The four-field s, and the price of grain ; — *Audley Court* 34
   hated by the wise, to law S and empire ? — *Love and Duty* 8
   you block and bar Your heart with s — *Princess iv* 463
   a world Of traitorous friend and broken s — „ *vi* 195
   Our little s's have their day ; — *In Mem., Pro.* 17
   And, star and s rolling past, — „ *Con.* 122
   When the schemes and all the s's, — *Locksley H., Sixty* 159
   Rush of Suns, and roll of s's, — *God and the Univ.* 3

T

Taäble (table) I mash'd the t's an' chairs, — *North. Cobbler* 37
   An' the t staäin'd wi' 'is aäle, — *Spinster's S's.* 99
Taäen (taken) A mowt 'a t owd Joänes, — *N. Farmer, O. S.* 49
   Or a mowt 'a t young Robins— — „ 50
   And 'a t to the bottle beside, — *Spinster's S's.* 56
   fur I could 'a t to tha well, — „ 81
Taäil (entail) Stook to his t they did, — *N. Farmer, N. S.* 30
   new Squire's coom'd wi' 'is t in 'is 'and, (repeat) — *Village Wife* 14, 121
   Fur 'staäte be i' t, my lass : — „ 15
   and the next un he taäkes the t.' — „ 18
   An' the gells, they hedn't naw t's, — „ 29
   That 'is t were soä tied up — „ 30
   ' Lad, thou mun cut off thy t, — „ 64
   if thou'll 'gree to cut off thy t — „ 66
   I've gotten the 'staäte by the — „ 68
   to git 'im to cut off 'is t. — „ 74
   an' 'e wouldn't cut off the t. — „ 78

Taäil (entail) (continued) theer wur a hend o' the t, fur 'e
   lost 'is t i' the beck, — *Village Wife* 86
   Sa 'is t wur lost an 'is booöks wur gone — „ 87
Taäil (tail) stick oop thy back, an' set oop thy t, — *Spinster's S's.* 31
   Steevie be right good manners bang thruf to the tip
   o' the t. — „ 66
   Sa I likes 'em best wi' t's — „ 102
   an' 'e'd niver not down wi' 'is t, — *Owd Roä* 9
   till 'e waggled 'is t fur a bit, — „ 105
Taäil'd (draggle) t in an owd turn gown, — *North. Cobbler* 41
Taäilor (tailor) An' once I fowt wi' the T— — „ 21
Taäke (take) But godamoighty a moost t meä an' t — *N. Farmer, O. S.* 51
   Do'ant be stunt : t time : — „ *N. S.* 17
   coäts to their backs an' t's their regular meäls. — „ 46
   T my word for it, Sammy, the poor in a loomp is bad. — „ 48
   and then I t's to the drink. — *North. Cobbler* 16
   hev 'im a-buried wi'mma an' t 'im afoor the Throän. — „ 106
   and the next un he t's the taäil.' — *Village Wife* 18
   Sa I didn't not t it kindly ov owd Miss Annie — „ 109
   Can't ye t pattern by Steevie ? — *Spinster's S's.* 65
   Parson 'e 'ears on it all, an' then t's kindly to me, — *Church-warden, etc.* 37
Taäked (took) I t 'im at fust fur deäd, — *Owd Roä* 100
Taäkin (taking) ' The amoighty's a t o' you to
   'issén, (repeat) — *N. Farmer, O. S.* 10, 26
   I'll gie tha a bit o' my mind an' tha weant be t
   offence, — *Church-warden, etc.* 21
Taäle (tale) an a's hallus i' the owd t ; — *N. Farmer, O. S.* 66
Taäste (taste) if I cared to t, — *North. Cobbler* 101
   T another drop o' the wine— — *Village Wife* 120
Taäte (potato) Baäcon an' t's, an' a beslings puddin' — *North. Cobbler* 112
   Whoäts or tonups or t's— — *Village Wife* 26
Tabby An' thou be es pretty a T, — *Spinster's S's.* 14
   thou be es 'ansom a t es iver patted a mouse. — „ 70
Tabernacle left Their own gray tower, or plain-faced t, — *Aylmer's Field* 618
Table (See also **Round Table, Taäble, Table Round**) Till
   all the t's danced again, — *The Goose* 47
   Until King Arthur's t, man by man, — *M. d'Arthur* 3
   But now the whole ROUND r is dissolved — „ 234
   And thrumming on the t : — *Will Water.* 160
   Sat at his t ; drank his costly wines ; — *Sea Dreams* 74
   on the t's every clime and age Jumbled together ; — *Princess, Pro.* 16
   drank in cups of emerald, there at t's of ebony lay, — *Boädicea* 61
   ' I well believe You be of Arthur's T,' — *Gareth and L.* 836
   yet he strove To learn the graces of their T, — *Balin and Balan* 238
   to thy guest, Me, me of Arthur's T. — „ 380
   and break the King And all his T.' — „ 459
   The slights of Arthur and his T, — *Merlin and V.* 7
   laid aside the gems There on a t near her, — *Lancelot and E.* 1203
   All the great t of our Arthur closed — *Holy Grail* 329
   once the talk And scandal of our t, — „ 650
   nothing in the sounding hall I saw, No bench nor t, — „ 829
   whom late our Arthur made Knight of his t ; — *Pelleas and E.* 320
   or being one Of our free-spoken T — „ 526
   ' Have any of our Round T held their vows ? ' — „ 533
   that I Have founded my Round T in the North, — *Last Tournament* 78
   The glory of our Round T is no more.' (repeat) — „ 189, 212
   hurl'd The t's over and the wines, — „ 475
   he was answer'd softly by the King And all his T. — *Guinevere* 45
   said my father, and himself was knight Of the great T— — „ 235
   Until King Arthur's T, man by man, — *Pass. of Arthur* 172
   But now the whole Round T is dissolved — „ 402
   Their favourite—which I call ' The T's Turned.' — *Sisters (E. and E.)* 3
   weeks I tried Your t of Pythagoras, — *To E. Fitzgerald* 15
   poring over his T's of Trade and Finance ; — *The Wreck* 26
   Laid on her t overnight, was gone ; — *The Ring* 277
Table-knight Some hold he was a t-k — *Last Tournament* 69
Table-land Are close upon the shining t-l's — *Ode on Well.* 216
Table Round (See also **Round Table, Table**) And thro'
   the puissance of his T R, — *Com. of Arthur* 17
   when he spake and cheer'd his T R — „ 267
   And all this Order of thy T R — „ 474
   Strike, thou art worthy of the T R— — *Gareth and L.* 1138
   Hail, Knight and Prince, and of our T R !' — „ 1271
   one Of that great order of the T R, — *Marr. of Geraint* 3
   Now, made a knight of Arthur's T R, — *Geraint and E.* 793

Talk (verb) *(continued)* For one half-hour, and let him *t* to
me ! ' *The Brook* 115
the days That most she loves to *t* of, „ 226
We did but *t* you over, pledge you all *Princess, Pro.* 185
Or down the fiery gulf as *t* of it, „ iii 287
You *t* almost like Ida : *she* can *t* ; „ v 210
But you *t* kindlier : we esteem you for it.— „ 212
And I too, *t*, and lose the touch I *t* of. *Lit. Squabbles* 11
While now we *t* as once we talk'd *In Mem. lxxi* 9
To *t* them o'er, to wish them here, „ xc 11
Be cheerful-minded, *t* and treat „ cvii 19
And *t* of others that are wed, „ Con. 98
I trust that I did not *t* (repeat) *Maud I* xix 12, 16
Sweet lord, how like a noble knight he *t's* ! *Gareth and L.* 777
Up then, ride with me ! *T* not of shame ! *Balin and Balan* 523
Too curious Vivien, tho' you *t* of trust, *Merlin and V.* 358
Yea, if ye *t* of trust I tell you this, „ 360
And heard their voices *t* behind the wall, „ 631
Of whom the people *t* mysteriously, *Lancelot and E.* 425
fool,' he said, ' ye *t* Fool's treason : *Last Tournament* 351
As even here they *t* at Almesbury *Guinevere* 208
T of lost hopes and broken heart ! *Lover's Tale* iv 176
The merrier, prettier, wittier, as they *t*, *Sisters (E. and E.)* 286
lasses 'ud *t* o' their Missis's waäys, *Village Wife* 57
play with 'em, *t* to 'em hours after hours ! *In the Child. Hosp.* 34
thou hast come to *t* our isle. *Sir J. Oldcastle* 32
Fur moäst of 'em *t's* ageän tithe, *Church-warden, etc.* 52

Talk'd-Talkt so we sat and eat And *talk'd* old matters
over ; *Audley Court* 29
For oft I *talk'd* with him apart, *Talking Oak* 17
She *talk'd* as if her love were dead, *The Letters* 27
Blues and reds They *talk'd* of : *Aylmer's Field* 252
For people *talk'd*—that it was wholly wise „ 268
people *talk'd*—The boy might get a notion into him ; „ 270
So they *talk'd*, Poor children, for their comfort : „ 426
wrinkled benchers often *talk'd* of him Approvingly, „ 473
But while they *talk'd*, above their heads I saw *Princess, Pro.* 118
they *talk'd* At wine, in clubs, of art, of politics ; „ 160
And while I walk'd and *talk'd* as heretofore, „ i 16
you that *talk'd* The trash that made me sick, „ ii 393
She answer'd sharply that I *talk'd* astray. „ iii 140
we are not *talk'd* to thus : „ 250
(And every voice she *talk'd* with ratify it, „ v 133
Her that *talk'd* down the fifty wisest men ; „ 294
she you walk'd with, she You *talk'd* with, „ vi 255
the maidens came, they *talk'd*, They sang, „ vii 22
That hears his burial *talk'd* of by his friends, „ 152
While now we talk as once we *talk'd* *In Mem. lxxi* 9
We *talk'd* : the stream beneath us ran, „ lxxxix 43
My love has *talk'd* with rocks and trees ; „ xcvii 1
And oft I *talk'd* with Dubric, the high saint, *Geraint and E.* 865
And I, when often they have *talk'd* of love, *Lancelot and E.* 673
for they *talk'd*, Meseem'd, of what they knew not ; „ 674
And all the damsels *talk'd* confusedly, *Pelleas and E.* 57
Fur hoffens we *talkt* o' my darter *Village Wife* 10
An' the Missis *talk'd* o' the lasses.— „ 58

Talketh Who *t* with thee, Adeline ? *Adeline* 24
Talkin' Thou's beän *t'* to muther, *N. Farmer, N. S.* 10
Es I should be *t* ageän 'em, *Village Wife* 110
Talking *(See also* **A-talkin'**, **Talkin'***)* walking all alone
beneath a yew, And *t* to himself, *Love and Death* 6
heard them *t*, his long-bounden tongue Was loosen'd, *Enoch Arden* 644
And, *t* from the point, he drew him in, *The Brook* 154
And with me Philip, *t* still ; „ 164
I thought her half-right *t* of her wrongs ; *Princess* v 285
Drinking and *t* of me ; *Maud I* vii 6
I hear two men, Somewhere, *t* of me ; „ 14
In silver tissue *t* things of state ; *Marr. of Geraint* 663
While he were *t* sweetly with your Prince, „ 698
thither came the village girls And linger'd *t*, *Pelleas and E.* 509
Now *t* of their woodland paradise, *Last Tournament* 726

Talkt *See* **Talk'd**
Tall Down by the poplar *t* rivulets babble and fall. *Leonine Eleg.* 4
T orient shrubs, and obelisks *Arabian Nights* 107
When forth there stept a foeman *t*, *Oriana* 33

Tall *(continued)* The arching limes are *t* and shady, *Margaret* 59
The *t* flag-flowers when they sprung *Miller's D.* 53
My *t* dark pines, that plumed the craggy ledge *Œnone* 209
Till Charles's Wain came out above the *t* white
chimney-tops. *May Queen, N. Y's. E.* 12
The building rook 'll caw from the windy *t* elm-tree, „ 17
heroes *t* Dislodging pinnacle and parapet *D. of F. Women* 25
A daughter of the gods, divinely *t*, „ 87
Patient on this *t* pillar I have borne *St. S. Stylites* 15
To watch the three t spires ; *Godiva* 3
flour From his *t* mill that whistled on the waste. *Enoch Arden* 343
A later but a loftier Annie Lee, Fair-hair'd and *t*, „ 749
Her son, who stood beside her *t* and strong, „ 756
And his own children *t* and beautiful, „ 762
help'd At lading and unlading the *t* barks, „ 816
T and erect, but bending from his height *Aylmer's Field* 119
A perilous meeting under the *t* pines „ 414
follow'd out *T* and erect, but in the middle aisle „ 818
Strode from the porch, *t* and erect again. „ 825
What ! are the ladies of your land so *t* ? ' *Princess* ii 47
o'er him grew *T* as a figure lengthen'd on the sand „ vi 161
those *t* columns drown'd In silken fluctuation „ 354
One *t* Agavè above the lake. *The Daisy* 84
Then it grew so *t* It wore a crown of light, *The Flower* 9
But she is *t* and stately. *Maud I* xii 16
friends Of Arthur, gazing on him, *t*, *Com. of Arthur* 278
THE last *t* son of Lot and Bellicent, *Gareth and L.* 1
follow the deer By these *t* firs and our fast-falling burns ; „ 91
The prince his heir, when *t* and marriageable, „ 102
Wellnigh as long as thou art statured *t* ! „ 282
but in all the listening eyes Of those *t* knights, „ 328
Saw six *t* men haling a seventh along, „ 811
(not that *t* felon there Whom thou by sorcery „ 996
Then Enid was aware of three *t* knights On
horseback, *Geraint and E.* 56
rounded moon Thro' the *t* oriel on the rolling sea. *Holy Grail* 831
By those whom God had made full-limb'd and *t*, *Guinevere* 42
Come dashing down on a *t* wayside flower, „ 253
and swum with balanced wings To some *t*
mountain : *Lover's Tale* i 303
rise three dark, *t* cypresses,— „ 536
As the *t* ship, that many a dreary year „ 808
years went over till I that was little had grown so *t*, *First Quarrel* 27
I had grown so handsome and *t*— „ 37
as it seem'd, beneath the *t* Tree-bowers, *Sisters (E. and E.)* 111
—dark visaged, stately and *t*— *The Wreck* 15
Shamus O'Shea that has now ten childer, hansome
an' *t*, *Tomorrow* 85

Taller a hart *T* than all his fellows, *Marr. of Geraint* 150
But newly-enter'd, *t* than the rest, *Last Tournament* 169
he is Lancelot—*t* indeed, Rosier and comelier, „ 709
T than all the Muses, and huger than all the
mountain ? *Parnassus* 10

Tallest she, that rose the *t* of them all And fairest, *M. d'Arthur* 207
last tall son of Lot and Bellicent, And *t*, Gareth, *Gareth and L.* 2
In glassy bays among her *t* towers.' *Œnone* 119
They came, they cut away my *t* pines, „ 208
she, that rose the *t* of all And fairest, *Pass. of Arthur* 175

Tall-tower'd long street climbs to one *t-t* mill ; *Enoch Arden* 5
Tallyho Black Bess, Tantivy, *T*, *The Brook* 160
Talon and swoops The Vulture, beak and *t*, *Princess* v 383
their ever-ravening eagle's beak and *t* *Boädicea* 11
And all unscarr'd from beak or *t*, *Last Tournament* 20
Tamarisk The stately cedar, *t's*, *Arabian Nights* 105
from a *t* near Two Proctors leapt upon us, *Princess* iv 258
Tame (adj.) The helpless life so wild that it was *t*. *Enoch Arden* 557
With two *t* leopards couch'd beside her throne, *Princess* ii 33
her foot on one Of those *t* leopards. „ iii 181
' Being a goose and rather *t* than wild, *Gareth and L.* 38
Tut : he was *t* and meek enow with me, „ 718
were all as *t* I mean, as noble, *Merlin and V.* 607
Tame (verb) nor *t* and tutor with mine eye *D. of F. Women* 138
I tamed my leopards : shall I not *t* these ? *Princess* v 400
And *t* thy jailing princess to thine hand. *Pelleas and E.* 344
Tamed I *t* my leopards : shall I not tame these ? *Princess* v 400

Tamesa (Thames) Bloodily flow'd the *T* rolling phantom bodies *Boädicea* 27
Tamper embassies of love, To *t* with the feelings, *Gardener's D.* 19
Tamper'd Some meddling rogue has *t* with him— *Lancelot and E.* 128
   And *t* with the Lords of the White Horse, *Guinevere* 15
Tangle (s) Should toss with *t* and with shells. *In Mem. x* 20
Tangle (verb) cuts atwain The knots that *t* human creeds, *Clear-headed friend* 3
Tangled (adj. and part.) The *t* water-courses slept, *Dying Swan* 19
   Glitter like a swarm of fire-flies *t* in a silver braid. *Locksley Hall* 10
   Two in the *t* business of the world, *Princess ii* 174
   passing lightly Adown a natural stair of *t* roots, *Lover's Tale i* 527
Tantivy Black Bess, *T*, Tallyho, *The Brook* 160
Tap (a touch) crush'd with a *t* Of my finger-na *Maud II ii* 21
Tap (tap-room) Thou'll goä sniffin' about the *t* *North. Cobbler* 64
   I weänt goä sniffin' about the *t.*' " 67
Taper (adj.) If my lips should dare to kiss Thy *t* fingers amorously, *Madeline* 44
   Thro' rosy *t* fingers drew Her streaming curls *Mariana in the S.* 15
Taper (s) A million *t's* flaring bright *Arabian Nights* 124
   I knew your *t* far away, *Miller's D.* 109
   Her *t* glimmer'd in the lake below: *Edwin Morris* 135
   As this pale *t's* earthly spark, *St. Agnes' Eve* 15
   The *t's* burning fair. *Sir Galahad* 32
   And calm that let the *t's* burn Unwavering: *In Mem. xcv* 5
   fingers of a hand Before a burning *t*, *Holy Grail* 694
Tapestry Working a *t*, lifted up her head, *Last Tournament* 129
Tapping Leisurely *t* a glossy boot, *Maud I xiii* 19
Tapt whined in lobbies, *t* at doors, *Walk. to the Mail* 37
   She *t* her tiny silken-sandal'd foot: *Princess, Pro.* 150
Taranis *T* be propitiated. *Boädicea* 16
Tare That *t* each other in their slime, *In Mem. lvi* 23
   And when his anger *t* him, *Gareth and L.* 1340
Target passion were a *t* for their scorn: *Locksley Hall* 146
   Or from the tiny pitted *t* blew *Aylmer's Field* 93
Tarn Slumbers not like a mountain *t* ? *Supp. Confessions* 129
   And quenching lake by lake and *t* by *t* *Princess vii* 40
   Far over the blue *t's* and hazy seas, *Gareth and L.* 499
   Had found a glen, gray boulder and black *t*. *Lancelot and E.* 36
   A horror lived about the *t*, and clave " 37
   Fled like a glittering rivulet to the *t*: " 52
   A stone is flung into some sleeping *t*, *Pelleas and E.* 93
   Those diamonds that I rescued from the *t*, *Last Tournament* 37
Tarnish'd (*See also* **Half-tarnish'd**) Mark hath *t* the great name of king, *Gareth and L.* 426
Tarquin brooking not the *T* in her veins, *Lucretius* 237
Tarriance after two days' *t* there, return'd. *Lancelot and E.* 569
Tarried And while I *t*, every day she set *Holy Grail* 588
   Where once I *t* for a while, *To E. Fitzgerald* 2
Tarry ' He dared not *t*,' men will say, *Two Voices* 101
   I must go : I dare not *t*,' *Princess iii* 95
   Knowing I *t* for thee,' *Maud III vi* 13
   Would he could *t* with us here awhile, *Marr. of Geraint* 622
   Yet if he could but *t* a day or two, " 627
   For if thou *t* we shall meet again, *Guinevere* 89
Tarrying after *t* for a space they rode, *Geraint and E.* 953
Tartar at thy name the *T* tents are stirr'd ; *W. to Marie Alex.* 12
   thine own land had bow'd to *T* hordes " 23
Task (s) ' Hard *t*, to pluck resolve,' I cried, *Two Voices* 118
   Sore *t* to hearts worn out by many wars *Lotos-Eaters, C. S.* 86
   Deliver not the *t's* of might To weakness, *Love thou thy land* 13
   The wrinkled steward at his *t*, *Day-Dm., Sleep. P.* 27
   I take myself to *t* ; *Will Water.* 162
   came Cyril, and yawning ' O hard *t*,' he cried ; *Princess iii* 124
   or hew wood, Or grosser *t's* ; *Gareth and L.* 487
   kiss the child That does the *t* assign'd, *Lancelot and E.* 829
Task (verb) as we *t* ourselves To learn a language *Aylmer's Field* 432
Tassel-hung In native hazels *t-h.*' *In Mem. cii* 12
Tassell'd *See* **Dewy-tassell'd**
Taste (s) Made all our *t's* and fancies like, *Lover's Tale i* 242
Taste (verb) (*See also* **Taäste**) but whoso did receive of them, And *t*, *Lotos-Eaters* 31
   (If Death so *t* Lethean springs), *In Mem. xliv* 10
   She *t* the fruit before the blossom falls, *Ancient Sage* 75
   that men may *t* Swine-flesh, drink wine ; *Akbar's Dream* 53
Tasted He *t* love with half his mind, *In Mem. xc* 1

Tasted (*continued*) Nor ever touch'd fierce wine, nor *t* flesh, *Merlin and V.* 627
   till I *t* flesh again One night *To E. Fitzgerald* 20
Tattoo'd then the man ; *T* or woaded, *Princess ii* 120
Taught (*See also* **Larn'd**) We *t* him lowlier moods, *Buonaparte* 9
   at Trafalgar yet once more We *t* him : 13
   Should that plain fact, as *t* by these, *Two Voices* 281
   He *t* me all the mercy, *May Queen, Con.* 17
   Retaught the lesson thou hadst *t*, *England and Amer.* 8
   I must be *t* my duty, and by you ! *Dora* 97
   Who *t* me how to skate, to row, to swim, *Edwin Morris* 19
   leaders of their Institute *T* them with facts. *Princess, Pro.* 59
   And I would teach them all that men are *t* ; " 136
   but she That *t* the Sabine how to rule, " *ii* 79
   Here might they learn whatever men were *t* : " 146
   And whatsoever can be *t* and known ; " 385
   what woman *t* you this ? ' " *vii* 310
   With those deep voices our dead captain *t* The tyrant, *Ode on Well.* 69
   So great a soldier *t* us there, " 131
   Bleys, Who *t* him magic ; *Com. of Arthur* 154
   The charm so *t* will charm us both to rest. *Merlin and V.* 332
   then he *t* the King to charm the Queen " 641
   never yet Hath what thy sister *t* me first to see, *Holy Grail* 469
   My knighthood *t* me this— *Last Tournament* 658
   began to hum An air the nuns had *t* her ; *Guinevere* 163
   should he not be *t*, Ev'n by the price *Lover's Tale iv* 151
   I *t* myself as I could To make a good wife *First Quarrel* 29
   Who *t* me in childhood, *Merlin and the G.* 115
   Thou knowest, *T* by some God, *Death of Œnone* 35
Taunt (s) A *t* that clench'd his purpose like a blow ! *Princess v* 306
Taunt (verb) I know it ; *T* me no more : " *vi* 301
Tavern Seeking a *t* which of old he knew, *Enoch Arden* 691
Tavern-catch To troll a careless, careless *t-c* *Princess iv* 157
Tavern-door sent From many a *t-d*, *Will Water.* 188
Tavern-fellow My boon companion, *t-f*— *Sir J. Oldcastle* 90
Tavern-hour The *t-h's* of mighty wits— *Will Water.* 191
Taw boy That knuckled at the *t* : " 132
Tawnier the swan's Is *t* than her cygnet's : *Lancelot and E.* 1185
Tawny to tear away Their *t* clusters, *Enoch Arden* 382
   Tumbled the *t* rascal at his feet, *Aylmer's Field* 230
   warm melon lay like a little sun on the *t* sand, *V. of Maeldune* 57
Tax Honour,' she said, ' and homage, *t* and toll, *Œnone* 116
   for when he laid a *t* Upon his town, *Godiva* 13
   ' If they pay this *t*, they starve.' " 20
   she took the *t* away And built herself " 78
   Levied a kindly *t* upon themselves, *Enoch Arden* 663
   Hortensia spoke against the *t* ; *Princess vii* 127
Ta-year (this year, to-year) (*See also* **To-year**) Done it *t-y* I meän'd, *N. Farmer, O. S.* 42
   fur a lot on 'em coom'd *t-y*— *Church-warden, etc.* 13
Tea an' offens we hed 'em to *t*. *Village Wife* 56
Teach Oh *t* me yet Somewhat before the heavy clod *Supp. Confessions* 183
   T me the nothingness of things. *A Character* 4
   Oh ! *t* the orphan boy to read, Or *t* the orphan-girl to sew, *L. C. V. de Vere* 69
   T that sick heart the stronger choice, *On a Mourner* 18
   For he will *t* him hardness, *Dora* 120
   And, as tradition *t'es*, *Amphion* 26
   And others' follies *t* us not, *Will Water.* 173
   Nor much their wisdom *t'es* ; " 174
   And I would *t* them all that men are taught ; *Princess, Pro.* 136
   Shall we *t* it a Roman lesson ? *Boädicea* 32
   Come Time, and *t* me, many years, *In Mem. xiii* 13
   My own dim life should *t* me this, " *xxxiv* 1
   Her office there to rear, to *t*, " *xl* 13
   And *t* true life to fight with mortal wrongs. *Maud I xviii* 54
   As proof of trust. O Merlin, *t* it me. *Merlin and V.* 331
   To find a wizard who might *t* the King " 583
   But high thought, and amiable words *Guinevere* 481
   Ev'n the homely farm can *t* us *Locksley H., Sixty* 26
   T your flatter'd kings that only those who cannot read " 132
   I too would *t* the man Beyond the darker hour *Prog. of Spring* 87
Teacher Left by the *T*, whom he held divine. *Lucretius* 13
   Blest be the Voice of the *T* *Kapiolani* 2

Teaching *t* him that died Of hemlock ; | *Princess* iii 302
Teacup-times In *t-t* of hood and hoop, | *Talking Oak* 63
Team (*See also* **Teäm**) and the wild *t* Which love thee, | *Tithonus* 39
I hear them too—they sing to their *t* : | *Grandmother* 81
The *t* is loosen'd from the wain, | *In Mem. cxxi* 5
And see'st the moving of the *t*. | „ 16
The shrilly whinnyings of the *t* of Hell, | *Demeter and P.* 44
Teäm blessed feälds wi' the Divil's oän *t*. | *N. Farmer, O. S.* 62
Tear (s) Would issue *t's* of penitence | *Supp. Confessions* 118
Her *t's* fell with the dews at even ; | *Mariana* 13
Her *t's* fell ere the dews were dried ; | „ 14
Crocodiles wept *t's* for thee ; | *A Dirge* 22
woodbine and eglatere Drip sweeter dews than traitor's *t*. | „ 24
While blissful *t's* blinded my sight | *Oriana* 23
And then the *t's* run down my cheek, | „ 69
I feel the *t's* of blood arise | „ 77
A matter to be wept with *t's* of blood ! | *Poland* 14
A moment came the tenderness of *t's*, | *The form, the form* 9
My *t's*, no *t's* of Love, are flowing fast, | *Wan Sculptor* 7
No *t's* of love, but *t's* that Love can die. | „ 8
Thy sister smiled and said, ' No *t's* for me ! | *The Bridesmaid* 3
I loved thee for the *t* thou couldst not hide, | „ 11
The home of woe without a *t*. | *Mariana in the S.* 20
Larger Hesper glitter'd on her *t's*, | „ 90
' Whose eyes are dim with glorious *t's*, | *Two Voices* 151
And dews, that would have fall'n in *t's*, | *Miller's D.* 151
Eyes with idle *t's* are wet. | „ 211
They have not shed a many *t's*, | „ 221
Yet *t's* they shed : they had their part Of sorrow : | „ 223
My eyes are full of *t's*, my heart of love, | *Œnone* 31
water'd it with *t's* ? O happy *t's*, | „ 234
And never can be sunder'd without *t's*. *To* ——, *With Pal. of Art* 13
and temper'd with the *t's* Of angels | „ 18
white-eyed phantasms weeping *t's* of blood, | *Palace of Art* 239
And ever unrelieved by dismal *t's*, | „ 271
embraces of our wives And their warm *t's* : | *Lotos-Eaters, C. S.* 71
Charged both mine eyes with *t's*. | *D. of F. Women* 13
I, blinded with my *t's*, ' Still strove to speak : | „ 108
She ceased in *t's*, fallen from hope and trust : | „ 257
By sighs or groans or *t's* ; | „ 284
and a *t* Dropt on the letters as I wrote. | *To J. S.* 55
May perpetual youth Keep dry their light from *t's* ; | *Of old sat Freedom* 20
Him Sir Bedivere Remorsefully regarded thro' his *t's*, | *M. d'Arthur* 171
dropping bitter *t's* against his brow | „ 211
Mary sat And look'd with *t's* upon her boy, | *Dora* 57
When eyes, love-languid thro' half *t's* | *Love and Duty* 36
Rain out the heavy mist of *t's*, | „ 43
burn'd upon its object thro' such *t's* As flow but once a life. | „ 63
those tremulous eyes that fill with *t's* | *Tithonus* 26
and thy *t's* are on my cheek. | „ 45
Why wilt thou ever scare me with thy *t's*, | „ 46
to the *t's* that thou wilt weep. | *Locksley Hall* 82
She told him of their *t's*, And pray'd him, | *Godiva* 19
With *t's* and smiles from heaven again | *Sir L. and Q. G.* 2
To drop thy foolish *t's* upon my grave, | *Come not, when, etc.* 2
What there is in loving *t's*, | *Vision of Sin* 161
eyes All flooded with the helpless wrath of *t's*, | *Enoch Arden* 32
But manifold entreaties, many a *t*, | „ 160
Fast flow'd the current of her easy *t's*, | „ 865
Who dabbling in the fount of fictive *t's*, | *The Brook* 93
their own bitter *t's*, *T's*, and the careless rain | *Aylmer's Field* 428
Deity false in human-amorous *t's* ; | *Lucretius* 90
And kiss'd again with *t's*. | *Princess* ii 5
And kiss again with *t's*. | „ 9
We kiss'd again with *t's*. | „ 14
round her dewy eyes The circled Iris of a night of *t's* ; | „ iii 27
She bow'd as if to veil a noble *t* ; | „ 289
' *T's*, idle *t's*, I know not what they mean, | „ iv 39
T's from the depth of some divine despair | „ 40
the *t*, She sang of, shook and fell, | „ 59
At length my Sire, his rough cheek wet with *t's*, | „ v 23
Like summer tempest came her *t's*— | „ vi 15

Tear (s) (*continued*) The leaves were wet with women's *t's* : | *Princess* vi 39
Passionate *t's* Follow'd : the king replied not : | „ 311
Love, like an Alpine harebell hung with *t's* | „ vii 115
a touch Came round my wrist, and *t's* upon my hand | „ 138
dark crowd moves, and there are sobs and *t's* : | *Ode on Well.* 268
All for a slanderous story, that cost me many a *t*. | *Grandmother* 22
time to catch The far-off interest of *t's* ? | *In Mem. i* 8
Break, thou deep vase of chilling *t's*, | „ iv 11
T's of the widower, when he sees | „ xiii 1
Mine eyes have leisure for their *t's* ; | „ 16
When fill'd with *t's* that cannot fall, | „ xix 11
And *t's* that at their fountain freeze ; | „ xx 12
With costly spikenard and with *t's*. | „ xxxii 12
And *t's* are on the mother's face, | „ xl 10
dip Their wings in *t's*, and skim away. | „ xlviii 16
motions blindly drown The bases of my life in *t's*. | „ xlix 16
grieve Thy brethren with a fruitless *t* ? | „ lviii 10
With thy quick *t's* that make the rose Pull sideways, | „ lxxii 10
No single *t*, no mark of pain : | „ lxxviii 14
But with long use her *t's* are dry. | „ 20
To pledge them with a kindly *t*, | „ xc 10
And dipt in baths of hissing *t's*, | „ cxviii 23
There has fallen a splendid *t* | *Maud I* xxii 59
Shall shake its threaded *t's* in the wind no more. | „ III vi 28
I consecrate with *t's*—These Idylls. | *Ded. of Idylls* 4
Enforced she was to wed him in her *t's*, | *Com. of Arthur* 204
comforted my heart, And dried my *t's*, | „ 350
True *t's* upon his broad and naked breast, | *Marr. of Geraint* 111
the mother smiled, but half in *t's*, | „ 823
Ye mar a comely face with idiot *t's*. | *Geraint and E.* 550
And felt the warm *t's* falling on his face ; | „ 586
Made answer, either eyelid wet with *t's* | *Merlin and V.* 379
So sweetly gleam'd her eyes behind her *t's* | „ 402
The slow *t* creep from her closed eyelid yet, | „ 906
Then flash'd into wild *t's*, and rose again, | *Lancelot and E.* 613
' Farewell, sweet sister,' parted all in *t's*. | „ 1152
grant my worship of it Words, as we grant grief *t's*. | „ 1188
and the *t's* were in his eyes. | *Holy Grail* 759
and my *t's* have brought me good : | *Guinevere* 202
Made my *t's* burn—is also past—part. | „ 542
Him Sir Bedivere Remorsefully regarded thro' his *t's*, | *Pass. of Arthur* 339
And dropping bitter *t's* against a brow | „ 379
Her smile lit up the rainbow on my *t's*, | *Lover's Tale i* 254
and mine Were dim with floating *t's*, | „ 442
I saw the moonlight glitter on their *t's*— | „ 697
The dew of *t's* in an unwholesome dew, | „ 765
if thou be'st Love, dry up these *t's* | „ 780
it melteth in the source Of these sad *t's*, | „ 784
And Memory fed the soul of Love with *t's*. | „ 822
I flung myself upon him In *t's* and cries : | „ ii 90
poor lad, an' we parted in *t's*. | *First Quarrel* 20
Edith spoke no word, She wept no *t*, | *Sisters (E. and E.)* 216
it often moved me to *t's*, | *In the Child. Hosp.* 31
hand of the Highlander wet with their *t's* ! | *Def. of Lucknow* 102
Sank from their thrones, and melted into *t's*, | *Columbus* 15
Lord of human *t's* ; Child-lover ; | *To Victor Hugo* 3
I felt one warm *t* fall upon it. | *Tiresias* 167
a tone so rough that I broke into passionate *t's*, | *The Wreck* 122
But vain the *t's* for darken'd years As laughter over wine, And vain the laughter as the *t's*, | *Ancient Sage* 183
all night I pray'd with *t's*, | *The Flight* 17
I watch'd her at mass lettin' down the *t*, | *Tomorrow* 29
the follies, furies, curses, passionate *t's*, | *Locksley H., Sixty* 39
wife and his child stood by him in *t's* | *Dead Prophet* 57
her *t's* Are half of pleasure, half of pain— | *To Prin. Beatrice* 10
My quick *t's* kill'd the flower, | *Demeter and P.* 108
So glad ? no *t* for him, who left you wealth, | *The Ring* 188
And then the *t* fell, the voice broke. | „ 367
Blister'd every word with *t's*, | *Forlorn* 81
Are they *t's* ? For me— | *Romney's R.* 26
Tear (verb) To *t* his heart before the crowd ! | *You might have won* 36
to *t* away Their tawny clusters, | *Enoch Arden* 381
T the noble heart of Britain, | *Boädicea* 12
the winds of winter *t* an oak on a promontory. | „ 77

Ten (adj.) (*continued*)   And once for *t* long weeks I tried
   Your table of Pythagoras,   *To E. Fitzgerald* 14
T long sweet summer days upon deck,   *The Wreck* 64
T long days of summer and sin—   ,, 77
' *T* long sweet summer days ' of fever,   ,, 147
An' Shamus O'Shea that has now *t* childer,   *Tomorrow* 85
Let us hush this cry of ' Forward ' till *t* thousand
   years have gone.   *Locksley H., Sixty* 78
Old Virgil who would write *t* lines,   *Poets and their B.* 2
Ull he fun' upo' four short legs *t* times fur one upo' two.   *Owd Roä* 16
T year sin—Naäy—naäy !   ,, 20
Too laäte—but it's all ower now—hall hower—an' *t* year sin ;   ,, 116
For *t* thousand years Old and new ?   *The Ring* 19
But after *t* slow weeks her fix'd intent,   ,, 345

Ten (s)   Warless ? when her *t*'s are thousands,   *Locksley H., Sixty* 171
Tenant   Careless *t*'s they !
As well as with his *t*, Jocky Dawes.   *Walk. to the Mail* 28
thither flock'd at noon His *t*'s, wife and child,   *Princess, Pro.* 4
Be *t*'s of a single breast,   *In Mem. xvi* 3
Tenanted   We bought the farm we *t* before.   *The Brook* 222
Tend   Live happy ; *t* thy flowers ;   *Love and Duty* 87
Were you sick, ourself Would *t* upon you.   *Princess iii* 321
That *t*'s her bristled grunters in the sludge : '   ,, *v* 27
we will *t* on him Like one of these ;   ,, *vi* 124
And were half fool'd to let you *t* our son,   ,, 274
That you may *t* upon him with the prince.'   ,, 315
And *t*'s upon bed and bower,   *Maud I xiv* 4
' O I that wasted time to *t* upon her,   *Geraint and E.* 38
and *t* him curiously Like a king's heir,   *Last Tournament* 90
Henceforward too, the Powers that *t* the soul,   *Guinevere* 65
Tendance   nor from her *t* turn'd Into the world without ;   *Gardener's D.* 144
And pensive *t* in the all-weary noons,   *Princess vii* 102
breath Of her sweet *t* hovering over him,   *Geraint and E.* 926
Tended   *t* by Pure vestal thoughts in the translucent fane   *Isabel* 3
tend thy flowers ; be *t* by My blessing !   *Love and Duty* 87
But Psyche *t* Florian : with her oft, Melissa came ;   *Princess vii* 55
And *t* her like a nurse.   *Maud I xix* 76
That still had *t* on him from his birth,   *Gareth and L.* 179
And Enid *t* on him there ;   *Geraint and E.* 924
and every day she *t* him,   *Lancelot and E.* 850
women who *t* the hospital bed,   *Def. of Lucknow* 81
Tender   Like the *t* amber round,   *Margaret* 19
For while the *t* service made thee weep,   *The Bridesmaid* 10
And oft I heard the *t* dove   *Miller's D.* 41
I roll'd among the *t* flowers :   *Fatima* 11
And *t* curving lines of creamy spray ;   *Lotos-Eaters, C. S.* 62
Sleep sweetly, *t* heart, in peace :   *To J. S.* 69
cushions of whose touch may press The maiden's *t* palm.   *Talking Oak* 180
for a *t* voice will cry.   *Locksley Hall* 87
But the *t* grace of a day that is dead   *Break, break, etc.* 15
On a sudden a low breath Of *t* air made tremble   *The Brook* 202
The *t* pink five-beaded baby-soles,   *Aylmer's Field* 186
nor from *t* hearts, And those who sorrow'd o'er a vanish'd race,   ,, 843
Where she, who kept a *t* Christian hope,   *Sea Dreams* 41
Made havock among those *t* cells,   *Lucretius* 22
roll thy *t* arms Round him,   ,, 82
And dark and true and *t* is the North.   *Princess iv* 98
Delaying as the *t* ash delays To clothe herself,   ,, 106
Like *t* things that being caught feign death,   ,, *v* 108
there the *t* orphan hands Felt at my heart,   ,, 435
t ministries Of female hands and hospitality.   ,, *vi* 72
Steps with a *t* foot, light as on air,   ,, 88
Or thro' the parted silks the *t* face Peep'd,   ,, *vii* 60
Not perfect, nay, but full of *t* wants,   ,, 319
Mighty Seaman, *t* and true,   *Ode on Well.* 134
Rolling on their purple couches in their *t* effeminacy.   *Boädicea* 62
That breathe a thousand *t* vows,   *In Mem. xx* 2
hopes and light regrets that come Make April of her *t* eyes,   ,, *xl* 8
What time his *t* palm is prest   ,, *xlv* 2
whose light-blue eyes Are *t* over drowning flies,   ,, *xcvi* 3
The *t* blossom flutter down, Unloved,   ,, *ci* 3
With *t* gloom the roof, the wall ;   ,, *Con.* 118

Tender (*continued*)   Perhaps the smile and *t* tone Came out
   of her pitying womanhood,   *Maud I vi* 63
And dream of her beauty with *t* dread,   ,, *xvi* 14
For, Maud, so *t* and true,   ,, *xix* 85
My own dove with the *t* eye ?   ,, *II iv* 46
Seem I not as *t* to him As any mother ?   *Gareth and L.* 1283
And seeing them so *t* and so close,   *Marr. of Geraint* 22
To stoop and kiss the *t* little thumb,   ,, 395
' Mother, a maiden is a *t* thing,   ,, 510
and felt Her low firm voice and *t* government.   *Geraint and E.* 194
At this the *t* sound of his own voice   ,, 348
And Enid could not say one *t* word,   ,, 746
I think ye hardly know the *t* rhyme   *Merlin and V.* 383
O Master, do ye love my *t* rhyme ? '   ,, 399
So *t* was her voice, so fair her face,   ,, 401
Then Merlin to his own heart, loathing, said :
   ' O true and *t* !   ,, 791
Yet with all ease, so *t* was the work :   *Lancelot and E.* 442
Utter'd a little *t* dolorous cry.   ,, 817
' O sweet father, *t* and true, Deny me not,'   ,, 1110
This *t* rhyme, and evermore the doubt,   *Pelleas and E.* 410
Who see your *t* grace and stateliness.   *Guinevere* 190
and all The careful burthen of our *t* years   *Lover's Tale i* 222
Frail Life was startled from the *t* love   ,, 616
' Never the heart among women,' he said, ' more *t* and true.'   *The Wreck* 96
Struck hard at the *t* heart of the mother,   *Despair* 74
Sun of dawn That brightens thro' the Mother's *t* eyes,   *Prin. Beatrice* 4
Woman to her inmost heart, and woman to her *t* feet,   *Locksley H., Sixty* 50
Legend or true ? so *t* should be true !   *The Ring* 224
Solved in the *t* blushes of the peach,   *Prog. of Spring* 34
slowly moving again to a melody Yearningly *t*,   *Merlin and the G.* 91
So princely, *t*, truthful, reverent, pure—   *D. of the Duke of C.* 4
Tenderer   surely with a love Far *t* than my Queen's.   *Lancelot and E.* 1395
Tenderest   The fancy's *t* eddy wreathe,   *In Mem. xlix* 6
such a grace Of *t* courtesy,   *Geraint and E.* 862
T of Roman poets nineteen-hundred years ago,   *Frater Ave, etc.* 6
in wife and woman I found The *t* Christ-like creature   *Charity* 32
Tenderest-hearted   Vivien, like the *t-h* maid   *Merlin and V.* 377
Tenderest-touching   by *t-t* terms, To sleek her ruffled peace   ,, 898
Tenderly   in what limits, and how *t* ;   *Ded. of Idylls* 20
Tender-natured   Gone thy *t-n* mother, wearying to be left alone,   *Locksley H., Sixty* 57
Tenderness   A moment came the *t* of tears,   *The form, the form* 9
decent not to fail In offices of *t*,   *Ulysses* 41
His bashfulness and *t* at war,   *Enoch Arden* 289
So gracious was her tact and *t* :   *Princess i* 24
That lute and flute fantastic *t*,   ,, *iv* 129
No saint—inexorable—no *t*—   ,, *v* 515
The *t*, not yours, that could not kill,   ,, *vi* 186
T touch by touch, and last,   ,, *vii* 114
that might express All-comprehensive *t*,   *In Mem. lxxxv* 47
A face of *t* might be feign'd,   *Maud I vi* 52
Thro' that great *t* for Guinevere,   *Marr. of Geraint* 30
There brake a sudden-beaming *t* Of manners   *Lancelot and E.* 328
His *t* of manner, and chaste awe,   *Pelleas and E.* 110
offices Of watchful care and trembling *t*.   *Lover's Tale i* 226
Tender-pencil'd   The *t-p* shadow play.   *In Mem. xlix* 12
Tender-spirited   The low-voiced, *t-s* Lionel.   *Lover's Tale i* 655
Tending   *t* her rough lord, tho' all unask'd,   *Geraint and E.* 405
Tendon   And scirrhous roots and *t*'s.   *Amphion* 64
Teneriffe   great flame-banner borne by *T*,   *Columbus* 69
Tenfold-complicated   abyss Of *t-c* change,   *In Mem. xciii* 12
Ten-hundred-fold   Pain heap'd *t-h-f* to this, were still Less burthen, by *t-h-f*,   *St. S. Stylites* 23
Tennis   Quoit, *t*, ball—no games ?   *Princess iii* 215
Tenor   My blood an even *t* kept,   *In Mem. lxxxv* 17
Tent   Among the *t*'s I paused and sung,   *Two Voices* 125
they raised A *t* of satin, elaborately wrought   *Princess iii* 348
No bigger than a glow-worm shone the *t*   ,, *iv* 25
They bore her back into the *t* :   ,, 193
blazon'd lions o'er the imperial *t*   ,, *v* 9
He show'd a *t* A stone-shot off :   ,, 53

Tent *(continued)* lie in the *t*'s with coarse mankind, — *Princess vi* 69
You shall not lie in the *t*'s but here, — „ 94
on to the *t*'s : take up the Prince.' — „ 279
And at thy name the Tartar *t*'s are stirr'd ; — *W. to Marie Alex.* 12
and loud With sport and song, in booth and *t*, — *In Mem. xcviii* 28
and pitch'd His *t*'s beside the forest. — *Com. of Arthur* 58
And show'd an empty *t* allotted her, — *Geraint and E.* 885
And past to Enid's *t* ; and thither came — „ 922
Heard in his *t* the moanings of the King : — *Pass. of Arthur* 8
the heavens a hide, a *t* Spread over earth, — *Columbus* 47
Tented The *t* winter-field was broken up — *Aylmer's Field* 110
Ten-thousand The bearded Victor of *t-t* hymns, — *Princess iii* 352
Ten-times And make, as *t-t* worthier to be thine — *Balin and Balan* 68
Tenting-pin Tore my pavilion from the *t-p*, — *Holy Grail* 747
Term (academic) save for college-times Or Temple-eaten *t*'s, — *Aylmer's Field* 105
caught the blossom of the flying *t*'s, — *Princess, Pro.* 164
Term (of time) To sleep thro' *t*'s of mighty wars, — *Day-Dm., L'Envoi* 9
days Were clipt by horror from his *t* of life. — *Aylmer's Field* 603
To point the *t* of human strife, — *In Mem. l* 14
Pass we then A *t* of eighteen years. — *Lover's Tale i* 287
Clung closer to us for a longer *t* — *Columbus* 197
five-fold thy *t* Of years, I lay ; — *Tiresias* 33
I spy nor *t* nor bound. — *Mechanophilus* 20
Term (word, etc.) *(See also* **Counter-term**) Not master'd by some modern *t* ; — *Love thou thy land* 30
mixt with inmost *t*'s Of art and science : — *Princess ii* 446
Heap'd on her *t*'s of disgrace, — *Maud II i* 14
may merit well Your *t* of overstrain'd. — *Merlin and V.* 535
Then thrice essay'd, by tenderest-touching *t*'s, — „ 898
after that vile *t* of yours, I find with grief ! — „ 921
Terrace The *t* ranged along the Northern front, — *Princess iii* 118
I paced the *t*, till the Bear had wheel'd — „ *iv* 212
The moonlight touching o'er a *t* — *The Daisy* 83
I used to walk This *T*—morbid, — *The Ring* 168
ROSE, on this *t* fifty years ago, — *Roses on the T.* 1
which on our *t* here Glows in the blue — „ 7
Terrace-lawn On every slanting *t-l.* — *Day-Dm., Sleep. P.* 10
Terrible fear'd To send abroad a shrill and *t* cry, — *Enoch Arden* 768
recollect the dreams that come Just ere the waking : *t* ! — *Lucretius* 36
' O fair and strong and *t* ! — *Princess vi* 163
Love and Nature, these are two more *t* And stronger. — „ 165
sang the *t* prophetesses. — *Boädicea* 37
Spurr'd with their *t* war-cry ; — *Geraint and E.* 170
T pity, if one so beautiful Prove, — *Lover's Tale iv* 338
down the *t* ridge Plunged in the last fierce charge — *Sisters (E. and E.)* 63
These are Astronomy and Geology, *t* Muses ! — *Parnassus* 16
None but the *t* Peelè remaining — *Kapiolani* 28
Territorial *See* **Lord-territorial**
Territory You lying close upon his *t*, — *Princess iv* 403
they wasted all the flourishing *t*, — *Boädicea* 54
And Arthur gave him back his *t*, — *Gareth and L.* 78
his princedom lay Close on the borders of a *t*, — *Marr. of Geraint* 34
loves to know When men of mark are in his *t* : — *Geraint and E.* 229
Led from the *t* of false Limours — „ 437
Endow you with broad land and *t* — *Lancelot and E.* 957
Estate them with large land and *t* — „ 1322
Terror HE that only rules by *t* — *The Captain* 1
Brook'd not the expectant *t* of her heart, — *Enoch Arden* 493
wreck, Flights, *t*'s, sudden rescues, — *Aylmer's Field* 99
But must, to make the *t* of thee more, — *Gareth and L.* 1389
Then those that did not blink the *t*, — „ 1402
still she look'd, and still the *t* grew — *Marr. of Geraint* 615
leech forsake the dying bed for *t* of his life ? — *Happy* 98
WHEN from the *t*'s of Nature a people — *Kapiolani* 1
Test (s) I come to the *t*, a tiny poem — *Hendecasyllabics* 3
Test (verb) defying change To *t* his worth ; — *In Mem. xcv* 28
Well, we shall *t* thee farther ; — *Merlin and V.* 94
Tested to return When others had been *t*) — *Aylmer's Field* 219
And heard it ring as true as *t* gold.' — *Last Tournament* 284
Testify Yes, as the dead we weep for *t*— — *Aylmer's Field* 747
For I must live to *t* by fire. — *Sir J. Oldcastle* 206
Testimony To this I call my friends in *t*, — *Lancelot and E.* 1299
to the basement of the tower For *t* ; — *Guinevere* 105

Test-question That was their main *t-q*— — *Sir J. Oldcastle* 155
Tether'd How can ye keep me *t* to you— — *Gareth and L.* 115
should be *T* to these dead pillars of the Church— — *Sir J. Oldcastle* 121
Teuton *T* or Celt, or whatever we be, — *W. to Alexandra* 32
Slav, *T*, Kelt, I count them all My friends — *Epilogue* 18
Tew (a worry) *(See also* **Tued**) at fust she wur all in a *t*, — *North. Cobbler* 53
Text Suddenly put her finger on the *t*, — *Enoch Arden* 497
Not sowing hedgerow *t*'s and passing by, — *Aylmer's Field* 171
And being used to find her pastor *t*'s, — „ 606
Christian hope, Haunting a holy *t*, — *Sea Dreams* 42
the maiden Aunt Took this fair day for *t*, — *Princess, Pro.* 108
And the parson made it his *t* that week, — *Grandmother* 29
A square of *t* that looks a little blot, The *t* no larger than the limbs of fleas ; And every square of *t* an awful charm, — *Merlin and V.* 671
And none can read the *t*, not even I ; — „ 681
Thack (thatch) an' thou runn'd oop o' the *t* ; — *Spinster's S's.* 38
Thames *(See also* **Tamesa**) Came crowing over *T*. — *Will Water.* 140
Thank Light on a broken word to *t* him with. — *Enoch Arden* 347
I fear'd To meet a cold ' We *t* you, — *Princess iv* 328
T Him who isled us here, and roughly set — *Ode on Well.* 154
t God that I keep my eyes. — *Grandmother* 106
And *t* the Lord I am King Arthur's fool. — *Last Tournament* 320
I *t* the saints, I am not great. — *Guinevere* 199
I would *t* him, the other is dead, — *Despair* 70
' *t* God that I hevn't naw cauf o' my oän.' — *Spinster's S's.* 116
We *t* thee with our voice, — *To W. C. Macready* 4
I *t* him. I am happy, happy. — *Happy* 107
Raise me. I *t* you. — *Romney's R.* 60
Thanked God be *t* !' said Alice the nurse, — *Lady Clare* 17
Assumed that she had *t* him, adding, — *Geraint and E.* 646
Thankful Not *t* that his troubles are no more. — *Lucretius* 143
Thanks statue-like, In act to render *t*. — *Gardener's D.* 162
A thousand *t* for what I learn — *Talking Oak* 203
I do forgive him !' ' *T*, my love,' — *Sea Dreams* 317
Their debt of *t* to her who first had dared — *Princess ii* 141
But ' *T*,' she answer'd ' Go : — „ 357
you have our *t* for all : — „ *iv* 528
You saved our life : we owe you bitter *t* : — „ 531
To lighten this great clog of *t*, — „ *vi* 126
with an eye that swum in *t* ; — „ 210
Render *t* to the Giver, (repeat) — *Ode on Well.* 44, 47
For this, for all, we weep our *t* to thee ! — *Open. Inter. Exhib.* 9
T, for the fiend best knows whether — *Maud I i* 75
' *T*, venerable friend,' replied Geraint ; — *Marr. of Geraint* 303
maybe, shall have learn'd to lisp you *t*.' — „ 822
to which She answer'd, ' *T*, my lord ; ' — *Geraint and E.* 264
my *t*, For these have broken up my melancholy.' — *Merlin and V.* 266
I bid the stranger welcome. *T* at last ! — „ 270
O no more *t* than might a goat have given your feet before her own ? And yet no *t* : — „ 278
next For *t* it seems till now neglected, — „ 285
T, but you work against your own desire ; — *Lancelot and E.* 1096
And love, and boundless *t*— — *Lover's Tale iv* 382
an' arn'd naw *t* fur 'er paäins. — *Village Wife* 12
my poor *t* ! I am but an alien and a Genovese. — *Columbus* 242
Yield thee full *t* for thy full courtesy — *To Victor Hugo* 13
t to the Lord that I never not listen'd to noän ! — *Spinster's S's.* 8
would yield full *t* to you For your rich gift, — *To Ulysses* 33
But *t* to the Blessed Saints that I came — *Bandit's Death* 40
Thatch *(See also* **Thack**) Weeded and worn the ancient *t* — *Mariana* 7
And the cock hath sung beneath the *t* — *The Owl i* 10
doves That sun their milky bosoms on the *t*, — *Princess ii* 103
It sees itself from *t* to base — *Requiescat* 3
and drive Innocent cattle under *t*, — *Locksley H., Sixty* 96
Thatch'd They built, and *t* with leaves of palm, — *Enoch Arden* 558
Thaw (verb) *T* this male nature to some touch — *Princess vi* 306
And *t*'s the cold, and fills The flower — *Early Spring* 45
Thaw (s) an' the daäle was all of a *t*, — *Owd Roä* 39
Moother 'ed beän sa soäk'd wi' the *t* — „ 113
Theatre stately *t*'s Bench'd crescent-wise. — *Princess ii* 369
Thebes in thy virtue lies The saving of our *T* ; — *Tiresias* 110
crying ' *T*, Thy *T*. shall fall and perish, — „ 115
will murmur thee To thine own *T*, while *T* thro' thee shall stand — „ 141

Thebes (*continued*) Folded her lion paws, and look'd to T.   *Tiresias* 149
Theft and you, will you call it a *t*?—   *Rizpah* 52
The *t* were death or madness to the thief,   *The Ring* 204
Theme Seem but the *t* of writers,   *Edwin Morris* 48
Ah, let the rusty *t* alone !   *Will Water.* 177
warming with her *t* She fulmined out her scorn   *Princess* ii 132
Whereat we glanced from *t* to *t*,   *In Mem. lxxix* 33
Then (*See also* **Thin**) Break into ' *T*'s ' and ' Whens '   *Ancient Sage* 104
Theodolind castle Of Queen *T*, where we slept ;   *The Daisy* 80
Theory forged a thousand *theories* of the rocks,   *Edwin Morris* 18
as a rogue in grain Veneer'd with sanctimonious *t*.   *Princess, Pro.* 117
They fed her *theories*, in and out of place   ,, i 129
pass With all fair *theories* only made to gild   ,, ii 233
my mother still Affirms your Psyche thieved her
theories,   ,, iii 92
For she was cramm'd with *theories* out of books,   ,, *Con.* 35
Thermopylæ these in our *T* shall stand,   *Third of Feb.* 47
Thesis The *t* which thy words intend—   *Two Voices* 338
Thessalian Or that *T* growth,   *Talking Oak* 292
Thew nor ever had I seen Such *t*'s of men :   *Princess v* 256
Nor lose the wrestling *t*'s that throw the world ;   ,, vii 282
I felt the *t*'s of Anakim,   *In Mem. ciii* 31
Thick (*See also* **Jewel-thick**) *faults were* t *as dust In vacant*
chambers,   *To the Queen* 18
t with white bells the clover-hill swells   *Sea-Fairies* 14
chestnuts near, that hung In masses *t* with milky
cones.   *Miller's D.* 56
t as Autumn rains Flash in the pools   *Œnone* 205
my voice was *t* with sighs As in a dream.   *D. of F. Women* 109
with a grosser film made *t* These heavy, horny eyes.   *St. S. Stylites* 200
We gaih'd the mother-city *t* with towers,   *Princess* i 112
snowy shoulders, *t* as herded ewes,   ,, iv 479
T rosaries of scented thorn,   *Arabian Nights* 106
And thro' *t* veils to apprehend   *Two Voices* 296
from beneath Whose *t* mysterious boughs in the dark morn *Œnone* 213
when she strikes thro' the *t* blood Of cattle,   *Lucretius* 98
Climb thy *t* noon, disastrous day ;   *In Mem. lxxii* 26
So *t* with lowings of the herds,   ,, xcix 3
t By ashen roots the violets blow.   ,, cxv 3
Then fell *t* rain, plume droopt and mantle clung, *Last Tournament* 213
Thro' the *t* night I hear the trumpet blow :   *Guinevere* 569
T with wet words, and many a beast therein,   *Com. of Arthur* 21
so quick and *t* The lightnings here and there   *Holy Grail* 493
Thicken'd (*adj.*) (*See also* **Grape-thicken'd**) Love's
white star Beam'd thro' the *t* cedar in the dusk.   *Gardener's D.* 166
Thicken'd (*verb*) A clamour *t*, mixt with inmost terms   *Princess* ii 446
Thickening *See* **Slowly-thickening**
Thicker *T* the drizzle grew, deeper the gloom ;   *Enoch Arden* 679
Now thinner, and now *t*, like the flakes   *Lucretius* 166
and mingled with the haze And made it *t* ;   *Com. of Arthur* 436
t down the front With jewels than the sward   *Geraint and E.* 689
T than drops from thunder,   *Holy Grail* 348
Then spoke King Arthur, drawing *t* breath :   *M. d'Arthur* 148
my heart beat stronger And *t*,   *Maud I viii* 9
Then spoke King Arthur, drawing *t* breath :   *Pass. of Arthur* 316
Thickest When *t* dark did trance the sky,   *Mariana* 18
Among the *t* and bore down a Prince,   *Princess v* 518
Thicket (*See also* **Elder-thicket, Myrrh-thicket**) Athwart the
t lone :   *Claribel* 10
Or the dry *t*'s, I could meet with her   *Œnone* 223
No branchy *t* shelter yields ;   *Sir Galahad* 58
some hid and sought In the orange *t*'s :   *Princess* ii 460
round us all the *t* rang To many a flute   *In Mem. xxiii* 23
and the *t* closed Behind her,   *Merlin and V.* 973
Across my garden ! and the *t* stirs,   *Prog. of Spring* 53
Thicketed *See* **Rough-thicketed**
Thick-fleeced livelong bleat Of the *t-f* sheep   *Ode to Memory* 66
Thick-jewell'd *T-j* shone the saddle-leather,   *L. of Shalott* iii 20
Thick-leaved oak-tree sigheth, *T-l*, ambrosial,   *Claribel* 5
Beyond the *t-l* platans of the vale.   *Princess* iii 175
Thick-moted When the *t-m* sunbeam lay   *Mariana* 78
Thick-set from thy topmost head The *t-s* hazel dies ;   *Will Water.* 234
Thick-twined cave to cave thro' the *t-t* vine—   *Lotos-Eaters, C. S.* 95
Thief therefore turning softly like a *t*,   *Enoch Arden* 771
storming a hill-fort of *thieves* He got it ;   *Aylmer's Field* 225

Thief (*continued*) But *thieves* from o'er the wall Stole the seed   *The Flower* 11
Kill the foul *t*, and wreak me for my son.'   *Gareth and L.* 363
wood is nigh as full of *thieves* as leaves :   ,, 789
for my wont hath ever been To catch my *t*,   ,, 822
To curse this hedgerow *t*, the sparrow-hawk :   *Marr. of Geraint* 309
Who now no more a vassal to the *t*,   *Geraint and E.* 753
Thieves, bandits, leavings of confusion,   *Last Tournament* 95
To be hang'd for a *t*—and then put away—   *Rizpah* 36
Sanctuary granted To bandit, *t*, assassin—   *Sir J. Oldcastle* 113
theft were death or madness to the *t*,   *The Ring* 204
Thieved my mother still Affirms your Psyche *t* her theories, *Princess iii* 92
Thigh (*See also* **Mid-thigh-deep**) flush'd Ganymede, his
rosy *t* Half-buried   *Palace of Art* 121
it is written that my race Hew'd Ammon, hip and *t*,   *D. of F. Women* 238
And both my *t*'s are rotted with the dew ;   *St. S. Stylites* 41
Ramp in the field, he smote his *t*, and mock'd :   *Lancelot and E.* 664
Then crush'd the saddle with his *t*'s,   *Pelleas and E.* 459
Thimbleby Noäks or *T*—toäner 'ed shot 'um   *N. Farmer, O. S.* 35
Thin (*adj.*) if his fellow spake, His voice was *t*,   *Lotos-Eaters* 34
His face is growing sharp and *t*.   *D. of the O. Year* 46
O hark, O hear ! how *t* and clear,   *Princess iv* 7
When it slowly grew so *t*,   *Maud I xix* 20
Tho' Modred biting his *t* lips was mute,   *Gareth and L.* 31
the moon, Half-melted into *t* blue air,   *Lover's Tale i* 421
and her *t* hands crost on her breast—   *In the Child. Hosp.* 39
Wavers on her *t* stem the snowdrop cold   *Prog. of Spring* 3
Hath ever and anon a note so *t*   *Balin and Balan* 214
T as the batlike shrillings of the Dead   *Death of Œnone* 21
Thin (*verb*) or would seem to *t* her in a day,   ⸸ *Aylmer's Field* 76
waters break Whitening for half a league, and *t*
themselves,   *Last Tournament* 465
Thin (*then*) An' where 'ud the poor man, *t*, cut his bit o'
turf for the fire ?   *Tomorrow* 65
Thing All *t*'s will change (repeat)   *Nothing will Die* 15, 38
Yet all *t*'s must die.   *All Things will Die* 8
For all *t*'s must die. (repeat)   ,, 13, 49
All *t*'s must die.   ,, 14
All *t*'s were born.   ,, 47
that Hesperus all *t*'s bringeth,   *Leonine Eleg.* 13
And trust and hope till *t*'s should cease,   *Supp. Confessions* 31
and *t*'s that seem, And *t*'s that be,   ,, 173
Teach me the nothingness of *t*'s.   *A 'Character* 4
all the dry pied *t*'s that be In the hueless mosses   *The Mermaid* 48
All *t*'s that are forked, and horned,   ,, 53
From all *t*'s outward thou have won A tearful grace,   *Margaret* 11
But good *t*'s have not kept aloof,   *My life is full, etc.* 2
High *t*'s were spoken there,   *Alexander* 12
' Lord, how long shall these *t*'s be ?   *Poland* 9
Will learn new *t*'s when I am not.'   *Two Voices* 63
There is no other *t* express'd But long disquiet   ,, 248
' These *t*'s are wrapt in doubt and dread,   ,, 266
Not simple as a *t* that dies.   ,, 288
many *t*'s perplex, With motions, checks,   ,, 299
He may not do the *t* he would.   ,, 303
She spoke at large of many *t*'s,   *Miller's D.* 155
all *t*'s in order stored, A haunt of ancient Peace.   *Palace of Art* 87
' O all *t*'s fair to sate my various eyes !   ,, 193
But all these *t*'s have ceased to be,   *May Queen, Con.* 48
A land where all *t*'s always seem'd the same !   *Lotos-Eaters* 24
While all *t*'s else have rest from weariness ?   ,, *C. S.* 14
All *t*'s have rest : why should we toil alone,   ,, 15
We only toil, who are the first of *t*'s,   ,, 16
the roof and crown of *t*'s ?   ,, 24
All *t*'s are taken from us,   ,, 46
All *t*'s have rest, and ripen toward the grave   ,, 51
And our great deeds, as half-forgotten *t*'s.   ,, 78
to start in pain, Resolved on noble *t*'s,   *D. of F. Women* 42
How beautiful a *t* it was to die For God   ,, 231
A man may speak the *t* he will ;   *You ask me, why, etc.* 8
keep a *t*, its use will come.   *The Epic* 42
A little *t* may harm a wounded man.   *M. d'Arthur* 42
This is a shameful *t* for men to lie.   ,, 78
and do the *t* I bad thee, watch,   ,, 80
Such a precious *t*, one worthy note,   ,, 89
More *t*'s are wrought by prayer Than this world dreams of. ,, 247

Thing (*continued*) ' Come With all good *t's*, and war
  shall be no more.'   *M. d'Arthur, Ep.* 28
We spoke of other *t's* ; we coursed about   *Gardener's D.* 222
and thought Hard *t's* of Dora.   *Dora* 58
And all the *t's* that had been.   ,, 107
(For they had pack'd the *t* among the beds,)   *Walk. to the Mail* 44
You could not light upon a sweeter *t* :   ,, 52
betwixt shame and pride, New *t's* and old,   .. 61
should have seen him wince As from a venomous *t* :   72
spoke I knowing not the *t's* that were.   *Edwin Morris* 89
slow sweet hours that bring us all *t's* good, The
  slow sad hours that bring us all *t's* ill, And all
  good *t's* from evil,   *Love and Duty* 57
' We sleep and wake and sleep, but all *t's* move ;   *Golden Year* 22
human *t's* returning on themselves Move onward,   ,, 25
something more, A bringer of new *t's* ;   *Ulysses* 28
Thou seëst all *t's*, thou wilt see my grave :   *Tithonus* 73
easy *t's* to understand—   *Locksley Hall* 55
sorrow's crown of sorrow is remembering happier *t's*.   ,, 76
but earnest of the *t's* that they shall do :   ,, 118
all *t's* here are out of joint :   .. 133
to have loved so slight a *t*.   .. 148
Howsoever these *t's* be, a long farewell   189
Here all *t's* in their place remain,   *Day-Dm., Sleep. P.* 53
ALL precious *t's*, discover'd late,   ,, *Arrival* 1
Well—were it not a pleasant *t* To fall asleep   ,, *L'Envoi* 3
nor take Half-views of men and *t's*.   *Will Water.* 52
If old *t's*, there are new ;   ,, 58
I look at all *t's* as they are,   ,, 71
Like all good *t's* on earth !   ,, 202
I hold it good, good *t's* should pass :   ,, 205
thou shalt from all *t's* suck Marrow   ,, 213
She will order all *t's* duly,   *L. of Burleigh* 39
As looks a father on the *t's* Of his dead son,   *The Letters* 23
Callest thou that *t* a leg ?   *Vision of Sin* 89
Tomohrit, Athos, all *t's* fair,   *To E. L.* 5
came a change, as all *t's* human change.   *Enoch Arden* 101
turn'd The current of his talk to graver *t's*.   .. 203
he set his hand To do the *t* he will'd,   ,, 295
Annie, there is a *t* upon my mind,   ,, 399
and all these *t's* fell on her Sharp as reproach.   ,, 487
he himself Moved haunting people, *t's* and places,   ,, 604
Because *t's* seen are mightier than *t's* heard,   ,, 766
Almost to all *t's* could he turn his hand.   ,, 813
Nor could he understand how money breeds, Thought
  it a dead *t* ; yet himself could make The *t* that is not
  as the *t* that is.   *The Brook* 7
And how it was the *t* his daughter wish'd,   ,, 140
Re-risen in Katie's eyes, and all *t's* well.   ,, 169
Took joyful note of all *t's* joyful,   *Aylmer's Field* 67
And neither loved nor liked the *t* he heard.   ,, 250
T's in an Aylmer deem'd impossible,   ,, 305
The *t's* belonging to thy peace and ours !   ,, 740
is it a light *t* That I, their guest, their host,   ,, 789
all *t's* work together for the good Of those '—   *Sea Dreams* 158
Another and another frame of *t's* For ever :   *Lucretius* 42
Which *t's* appear the work of mighty Gods.   ,, 102
universal culture for the crowd, And all *t's*   *Princess, Pro.* 110
made it death For any male *t* but to peep at us.'   ,, 152
And they that know such, *t's*—   ,, *i* 144
not to answer, Madam, all those hard *t's*   ,, *ii* 345
And two dear *t's* are one of double worth,   ,, 419
And still she rail'd against the state of *t's*.   ,, *iii* 84
One mind in all *t's* :   ,, 91
For all *t's* were and were not.   ,, 189
Your Highness might have seem'd the *t* you say.'   ,, 202
for all *t's* serve their time Toward that great
  year   ,, *iv* 73
To harm the *t* that trusts him,   ,, 248
And all *t's* were and were not.   ,, 567
Sweet is it to have done the *t* one ought,   ,, *v* 67
Like tender *t's* that being caught feign death,   ,, 108
As he that does the *t* they dare not do,   ,, 160
I myself, What know I of these *t's* ?   ,, 284
That all *t's* grew more tragic and more strange ;   ,, *vi* 23

Thing (*continued*) May these *t's* be ! ' Sighing she spoke
  ' I fear They will not.'   *Princess vii* 296
trust in all *t's* high Comes easy to him,   ,, 329
Too comic for the solemn *t's* they are,   .. *Con.* 67
If aught of *t's* that here befall Touch a spirit among
  t's divine,   *Ode on Well.* 138
let all good *t's* await Him who cares not to be great,   ,, 198
There might be left some record of the *t's* we said.   *Third of Feb.* 18
They knew the precious *t's* they had to guard :   ,, 41
Welcome her, all *t's* youthful and sweet,   *W. to Alexandra* 8
And all *t's* look'd half-dead,   *Grandmother* 34
and look'd the *t* that he meant ;   ,, 45
laughing at *t's* that have long gone by.   .. 92
o' use to saäy the *t's* that a do.   *N. Farmer, O. S.* 6
On them and theirs and all *t's* here :   *Lit. Squabbles* 12
Of their dead selves to higher *t's*.   *In Mem. i* 4
And shall I take a *t* so blind,   .. *iii* 13
like a guilty *t* I creep At earliest morning   *vii* 7
For now so strange do these *t's* seem,   .. *xiii* 15
And ask a thousand *t's* of home ;   .. *xiv* 12
Behold, ye speak an idle *t* :   .. *xxi* 21
hardly worth my while to choose Of *t's* all mortal,   .. *xxxiv* 11
To keep so sweet a *t* alive : '   .. *xxxv* 7
And all he said of *t's* divine,   .. *xxxvii* 18
Shall count new *t's* as dear as old :   .. *xl* 28
May some dim touch of earthly *t's*   .. *xliv* 11
And other than the *t's* I touch.'   .. *xlv* 8
For love reflects the *t* beloved :   .. *lii* 2
How should he love a *t* so low ? '   .. *lx* 16
So little done, such *t's* to be,   .. *lxxiii* 2
In fitting aptest words to *t's*,   ,, *lxxv* 6
But over all *t's* brooding slept   .. *lxxviii* 7
whether trust in *t's* above Be dimm'd of sorrow,   .. *lxxxv* 9
Where all *t's* round me breathed of him.   ,, 32
these *t's* pass, and I shall prove A meeting somewhere,   .. 98
The glory of the sum of *t's*   ,, *lxxxviii* 11
And he, he knows a thousand *t's*.   .. *xcvii* 32
talk and treat Of all *t's* ev'n as he were by ;   ,, *cvii* 20
Best seem'd the *t* he was, and join'd   ,, *cxi* 13
Submitting all *t's* to desire.   ,, *cxiv* 8
But I was *born* to other *t's*.   ,, *cxx* 12
Thou watchest all *t's* ever dim And dimmer,   ,, *cxxi* 3
I cannot think the *t* farewell.   ,, *cxxiii* 12
That sees the course of human *t's*.   ,, *cxxviii* 4
Love for the silent *t* that had made false haste   *Maud I i* 58
cannot I be Like *t's* of the season gay,   ,, *iv* 3
A wounded *t* with a rancorous cry,   ,, *x* 34
This broad-brimm'd hawker of holy *t's*,   .. 41
Her mother has been a *t* complete,   ,, *xiii* 35
I know it the one bright *t* to save   ,, *xvi* 20
Had given her word to a *t* so low ?   ,, 27
Beat, happy stars, timing with *t's* below,   ,, *xviii* 81
I have cursed him even to lifeless *t's*)   ,, *xix* 15
For a shell, or a flower, little *t's*   .. *II ii* 64
Comfort her, comfort her, all *t's* good,   ,, 75
But speak to her all *t's* holy and high,   ,, 78
another, a lord of all *t's*, praying   ,, *v* 32
But is ever the one *t* silent here.   ,, 68
I come to be grateful at last for a little *t* :   .. *III vi* 3
in a weary world my one *t* bright ;   ,, 17
his chamberlain, to whom He trusted all *t's*,   *Com. of Arthur* 146
wrote All *t's* and whatsoever Merlin did   .. 157
She answer'd, ' These be secret *t's*,'   .. 318
and ask'd him if these *t's* were truth—   ,, 398
King In whom high God hath breathed a secret *t*.   ,, 501
and thence swoop Down upon all *t's* base,   *Gareth and L.* 23
had the *t* I spake of been Mere gold—   ,, 65
New *t's* and old co-twisted, as if Time Were
  nothing,   .. 226
and flash'd as those Dull-coated *t's*,   ,, 686
And deems it carrion of some woodland *t*,   ,, 748
these *t's* he told the King.   *Marr. of Geraint* 151
And may you light on all *t's* that you love,   ,, 226
His dwarf, a vicious under-shapen *t*,   ,, 412
' Mother, a maiden is a tender *t*,   ,, 510

Thing (*continued*) ' These two *t*'s shalt thou do, or else thou diest. — *Marr. of Geraint* 580

These two *t*'s shalt thou do, or thou shalt die.' And Edyrn answer'd, ' These *t*'s will I do, — ,, 586
In silver tissue talking *t*'s of state ; — ,, 663
But evermore it seem'd an easier *t* — *Geraint and E.* 108
Tho' men may bicker with the *t*'s they love, — ,, 325
What *t* soever ye may hear, or see, — ,, 415
Half ridden off with by the *t* he rode, — ,, 460
Each hurling down a heap of *t*'s that rang — ,, 594
I never yet beheld a *t* so pale. — ,, 615
I will do the *t* I have not done, — ,, 625
or what had been those gracious *t*'s, — ,, 636
As of a wild *t* taken in the trap, — ,, 723
Took, as in rival heat, to holy *t*'s ; — *Balin and Balan* 100
I suffer from the *t*'s before me, — ,, 284
he defileth heavenly *t*'s With earthly uses ' — ,, 421
' The fire of Heaven is lord of all *t*'s good, — ,, 452
My mind involved yourself the nearest *t* — *Merlin and V.* 300
unashamed, On all *t*'s all day long, — ,, 666
But when the *t* was blazed about the court, — ,, 743
To *t*'s with every sense as false and foul — ,, 797
The seeming-injured simple-hearted *t* — ,, 902
In truth, but one *t* now—better have died — ,, 918
One flash, that, missing all *t*'s else, — ,, 932
speaking in the silence, full Of noble *t*'s, — *Lancelot and E.* 339
Lavaine gaped upon him As on a *t* miraculous, — ,, 453
For if I could believe the *t*'s you say — ,, 1097
in half disdain At love, life, all *t*'s, — *Holy Grail* 39
But who first saw the holy *t* to-day ? ' — ,, 67
glanced and shot Only to holy *t*'s ; — ,, 76
So now the Holy *T* is here again Among us. — ,, 124
But since I did not see the Holy *T*, — ,, 281
all these *t*'s at once Fell into dust, — ,, 388
the Lord of all *t*'s made Himself Naked of glory — ,, 447
thy sister taught me first to see, This Holy *T*, — ,, 470
And this high Quest as at a simple *t*: — ,, 668
' Gawain, and blinder unto holy *t*'s — ,, 870
strong man-breasted *t*'s stood from the sea, — *Guinevere* 246
in the cellars merry bloated *t*'s Shoulder'd the spigot, — ,, 267
A little *t* may harm a wounded man : — *Pass. of Arthur* 210
This is a shameful *t* for men to lie. — ,, 246
and do the *t* I bade thee, watch, — ,, 248
Surely a precious *t*, one worthy note, — ,, 257
More *t*'s are wrought by prayer Than this world dreams of. — ,, 415
Moved from the cloud of unforgotten *t*'s, — *Lover's Tale* i 48
Once or twice she told me (For I remember all *t*'s) — ,, 346
And saw the motion of all other *t*'s ; — ,, 574
Why were we one in all *t*'s, — ,, ii 26
till the *t*'s familiar to her youth Had made — ,, iv 95
I never yet beheld a *t* so strange, — ,, 303
Of all *t*'s upon earth the dearest to me.' — ,, 319
That which of all *t*'s is the dearest to me, — ,, 348
I that hold them both Dearest of all *t*'s— — *Sisters (E. and E.)* 289
that ever such *t*'s should be ! — *In the Child. Hosp.* 10
God's free air, and hope of better *t*'s. — *Sir J. Oldcastle* 10
wroth at *t*'s of old—No fault of mine. — ,, 21
greatness and touching on all *t*'s great, — *The Wreck* 50
some have gleams or so they say Of more than mortal *t*'s. — *Ancient Sage* 215
in the sidelong eyes a gleam of all *t*'s ill— — *The Flight* 31
He ! where is some sharp-pointed *t* ? — ,, 72
there's rason in all *t*'s, yer Honour, — *Tomorrow* 6
That a man be a durty *t* an' a trouble — *Spinster's S's.* 50
an' saäyin' ondecent *t*'s, — ,, 90
Bringer home of all good *t*'s. — *Locksley H., Sixty* 185
All good *t*'s may move in Hesper, — ,, 186
the Heavenly Power Makes all *t*'s new, (repeat) — *Early Spring* 2, 44
Expecting all *t*'s in an hour— — *Freedom* 39
Fair *t*'s are slow to fade away, — *To Prof. Jebb* 1
An' smoäkin' an' thinkin' o' *t*'s— — *Owd Roä* 34
A thousand *t*'s are hidden still — *Mechanophilus* 23
This *t*, that *t* is the rage, — *Poets and Critics* 1

Think *T* my belief would stronger grow ! — *Supp. Confessions* 13
I *t* that pride hath now no place Nor sojourn in me. — ,, 120
I walk, I dare not *t* of thee, — *Oriana* 93
' *T* you this mould of hopes and fears — *Two Voices* 28
Thou canst not *t*, but thou wilt weep. — ,, 51
When she would *t*, where'er she turn'd — *Palace of Art* 225
As I came up the valley whom *t* ye should I see, — *May Queen* 13
low i' the mould and *t* no more of me. — *May Queen, N. Y's. E.* 4
often with you when you *t* I'm far away. — ,, 40
I *t* it can't be long before I find release ; — *Con.* 11
So now I *t* my time is near. I trust it is. — ,, 41
I *t* that we Shall never more, — *M. d'Arthur* 17
T you they sing Like poets, — *Gardener's D.* 99
Consider, William : take a month to *t*, — *Dora* 29
And, now I *t*, he shall not have the boy, — ,, 119
Edwin, do not *t* yourself alone Of all men happy. — *Edwin Morris* 77
I have, I *t*,—Heaven knows—as much within ; — ,, 82
I *t* that I have borne as much as this— — *St. S. Stylites* 92
Ha ! ha ! They *t* that I am somewhat. — ,, 126
let me *t* 'tis well for thee and me— — *Love and Duty* 32
t not they are glazed with wine. — *Locksley Hall* 51
Can I *t* of her as dead, — ,, 73
' What wonder, if he *t*'s me fair ? ' — *Day-Dm., Ep.* 4
I *t* he came like Ganymede, — *Will Water* 119
And I *t* thou lov'st me well.' — *L. of Burleigh* 4
I remember, when I *t*, — *Vision of Sin* 77
I *t* we know the hue Of that cap upon her brows. — ,, 141
I *t* your kindness breaks me down ; — *Enoch Arden* 318
I do *t* They love me as a father : — ,, 411
T upon it : For I am well-to-do— — ,, 417
I *t* I have not three days more to live ; — ,, 851
t—For people talk'd—that it was wholly wise — *Aylmer's Field* 267
To *t* that in our often-ransack'd world — *Sea Dreams* 129
I *t* they should not wear our rusty gowns, — *Princess, Pro.* 143
I *t* the year in which our olives fail'd — ,, i 125
I confess with right) you *t* me bound In some sort, — ,, 158
' who could *t* The softer Adams of your Academe, — ,, ii 196
I *t* no more of deadly lurks therein, — ,, 226
Nor *t* I bear that heart within my breast, — ,, 334
What *t* you of it, Florian ? — ,, 408
You grant me license : might I use it ? *t* ; — ,, iii 235
I almost *t* That idiot legend credible. — ,, v 152
for since you *t* me touch'd In honour— — ,, 401
indeed I *t* Our chiefest comfort is the little child — ,, 429
to *t* I might be something to them, — ,, vi 200
And *t* that you might mix his draught with death, — ,, 277
—verily I *t* to win.' — ,, 329
' If you be, what I *t* you, some sweet dream, — ,, vii 145
O ye, the wise who *t*, the wise who reign, — *Ode Inter. Exhib.* 32
you *t* I am hard and cold ; — *Grandmother* 17
Time to *t* on it then ; for thou'll — *N. Farmer, N. S.* 7
an' we boäth on us *t*'s tha an ass. (repeat) — ,, 12, 38
She's a beauty thou *t*'s— — ,, 14
I *t* not much of yours or of mine, — *Spiteful Letter* 7
He *t*'s he was not made to die ; — *In Mem., Pro.* 11
And stunn'd me from my power to *t* — ,, xvi 15
To see the vacant chair, and *t* ' How good ! how kind ! — ,, xx 19
And *t*, that somewhere in the waste — ,, xxii 19
He looks so cold : she *t*'s him kind. — ,, xcvii 24
I *t* once more he seems to die. — ,, c 20
And *t* of early days and thee, — ,, cxix 8
I *t* we are not wholly brain, — ,, cxx 2
I cannot *t* the thing farewell. — ,, cxxiii 12
Result in man, be born and *t*, — *Con.* 126
Bound for the Hall, and I *t* for a bride. — *Maud* I x 26
And six feet two, as I *t*, he stands ; — ,, xiii 10
Shall I not take care of all that I *t*, — ,, xv 7
T I may hold dominion sweet, — ,, xvi 12
shook my heart to *t* she comes once more ; — ,, xviii 10
t that it well Might drown all life in the eye,— — ,, II ii 60
Not let any man *t* for the public good, — ,, v 45
I could even weep to *t* of it ; — ,, 86
Yea, but ye—*t* ye this king— — *Com. of Arthur* 250
T ye this fellow will poison the King's dish ? — *Gareth and L.* 471
And tell him what I *t* and what they say. — *Marr. of Geraint* 90

Think (continued)   And yet not dare to tell him what I t,   *Marr. of Geraint* 105
   Ye t the rustic cackle of your bourg   ,,   276
   Moves him to t what kind of bird it is That sings   ,,   331
   To t or say, ' There is the nightingale ; '   ,,   342
   Let never maiden t, however fair,   ,,   721
   let me t Silence is wisdom :   *Merlin and V.* 252
   O, if you t this wickedness in me,   ,,   339
   but t or not, By Heaven that hears I tell you   ,,   342
   because I t, However wise, ye hardly know me yet.'   ,,   354
   I t ye hardly know the tender rhyme   ,,   383
   O Vivien, For you, methinks you t you love me well ;   ,,   483
   However well ye t ye love me now   ,,   516
   Spleen-born, I t, and proofless.   ,,   702
   Farewell ; t gently of me, for I fear   ,,   926
   there, I t, So ye will learn the courtesies of the court,   *Lancelot and E.* 698
   sure I t this fruit is hung too high   ,,   774
   ye t I show myself Too dark a prophet :   *Holy Grail* 321
   to t of Modred's dusty fall,   *Guinevere* 55
   As I could t, sweet lady, yours would be   ,,   352
   Not ev'n in inmost thought to t again   ,,   374
   but rather t How sad it were for Arthur,   ,,   495
   t not, tho' thou wouldst not love thy lord,   ,,   508
   Yet t not that I come to urge thy crimes,   ,,   532
   what hope ?   I t there was a hope,   ,,   630
   I t that we Shall never more,   *Pass. of Arthur* 185
   (They told her somewhat rashly as I t)   *Lover's Tale iv* 98
   Do you t I was scared by the bones ?   *Rizpah* 55
   Do you t that I care for *my* soul   ,,   78
   I t that you mean to be kind,   ,,   81
   t what saäilors a' seëan an' a' doon ;   *North. Cobbler* 4
   as 'appy as 'art could t,   ,,   15
   yet she t's She sees you when she hears.   *Sisters (E. and E.)* 192
   I t this gross hard-seeming world   ,,   229
   I t I likewise love your Edith most.   ,,   293
   t he was one of those who would break   *In the Child. Hosp.* 8
   bullet broke thro' the brain that could t for the rest ;   *Def. of Lucknow* 20
   I beänt sich a fool as ye t's ;   *Spinster's S's.* 18
   I t's as I'd like fur to hev   *Owd Roä* 12
   I t's leästwaäys as I wasn't afeärd ;   ,,   86
   thaw I didn't haäfe t as 'e'd 'ear,   ,,   91
   tho' I t I hated him less,   *Bandit's Death* 17
Thinketh   then t, ' I have found A new land,   *Palace of Art* 283
Thinkin'   An' smoäkin' an' t' o' things—   *Owd Roä* 34
Thinking (See also **Half-thinking, Thinkin'**)   for three hours he sobb'd o'er William's child *T* of William.   *Dora* 168
   Still downward t ' dead or dead to me ! '   *Enoch Arden* 689
   Enoch t ' after I am gone,   ,,   834
   t that her clear germander eye Droopt   *Sea Dreams* 4
   And t of the days that are no more.   *Princess iv* 43
   She flung it from her, t ;   ,, *Con.* 32
   t, ' here to-day,' Or ' here to-morrow   *In Mem. vi* 23
   And t ' this will please him best,'   ,,   31
   Looking, t of all I have lost ;   *Maud II ii* 46
   t as he rode, ' Her father said That there between   *Com. of Arthur* 78
   t, that if ever yet was wife True to her lord,   *Marr. of Geraint* 46
   Geraint, now t that he heard The noble hart at bay,   ,,   232
   He t that he read her meaning there,   *Lancelot and E.* 86
   t ' Is it Lancelot who has come Despite the wound   ,,   565
Thinn'd   T, or would seem to thin her in a day.   *Aylmer's Field* 76
   councils t, And armies waned, for magnet-like she drew   *Merlin and V.* 572
Thinner   Then her cheek was pale and t   *Locksley Hall* 21
   they fly Now t, and now thicker, like the flakes   *Lucretius* 166
   And t, clearer, farther going !   *Princess iv* 8
   Our voices were t and fainter   *V. of Maeldune* 22
Thinnest   Slow-dropping veils of t lawn, did go ;   *Lotos-Eaters* 11
   Which is t ? thine or mine ?   *Vision of Sin* 90
Third   And set in Heaven's t story,   *Will Water.* 70
   t child was sickly-born and grew Yet sicklier,   *Enoch Arden* 261
   Then the t night after this,   ,,   907
   There stands the t fool of their allegory.'   *Gareth and L.* 1085
   Then the t brother shouted o'er the bridge,   ,,   1096
   And on the t day will again be here,   *Marr. of Geraint* 222

AA

Third (continued)   But when the t day from the hunting-morn   *Marr. of Geraint* 597
   So bent he seem'd on going the t day,   ,,   604
   Bent as he seem'd on going this t day,   ,,   625
   hope The t night hence will bring thee news of gold.'   *Pelleas and E.* 357
   t night brought a moon With promise of large light   ,,   393
   THOU t great Canning, stand among our best   *Epit. on Stratford* 1
   I brought you to that chamber on your t September birthday   *The Ring* 129
Third-rate   Some t-r isle half-lost among her seas ?   *To the Queen ii* 25
Thirst   In hungers and in t's, fevers and cold,   *St. S. Stylites* 12
   her t she slakes Where the bloody conduit runs,   *Vision of Sin* 143
   and when I thought my t Would slay me,   *Holy Grail* 379
   ' And on I rode, and greater was my t.   ,,   401
   there the hermit slaked my burning t,   ,,   461
   with t in the middle-day heat.   *V. of Maeldune* 50
Thirsted   I t for the brooks, the showers :   *Fatima* 10
Thirsteth   He that t, come and drink !   *Sir J. Oldcastle* 134
Thirsting   only t For the right,   *Ode on Well.* 203
   and I was left alone, And t,   *Holy Grail* 390
Thirsty   O to watch the t plants Imbibing !   *Princess ii* 422
   And I was t even unto death ;   *Holy Grail* 377
Thirty (See also **Thutty**)   ' Will t seasons render plain   *Two Voices* 82
   But t moons, one honeymoon to that,   *Edwin Morris* 29
   larded with the steam Of t thousand dinners.   *Will Water.* 224
   By t hills I hurry down,   *The Brook* 27
   I walk'd with one I loved two and t years ago.   *V. of Cauteretz* 4
   The two and t years were a mist that rolls away ;   ,,   6
   I well remember that red night When t ricks, All flaming,   *To Mary Boyle* 36
Thistle   I could not move a t ;   *Amphion* 66
   Let there be t's, there are grapes ;   *Will Water.* 57
   stubborn t bursting Into glossy purples,   *Ode on Well.* 206
   many a prickly star Of sprouted t   *Marr. of Geraint* 314
   Figs out of t's, silk from bristles,   *Last Tournament* 356
   flower, That shook beneath them, as the t shakes   *Guinevere* 254
   the wool of a t a-flyin' an' seeädin'   *Spinster's S's.* 13
   Are figs of t's ? or grapes of thorns ?   *Riflemen form !* 10
Thistledown   soft winds, Laden with t   *Lover's Tale ii* 13
Thomas Howard (See also **Howard**)   Then sware Lord T H :   *The Revenge* 4
Thor   To T and Odin lifted a hand :   *The Victim* 8
Thorn (See also **Thurn**)   my sin was as a t Among the t's   *Supp. Confessions* 5
   Thick rosaries of scented t,   *Arabian Nights* 106
   I know That all about the t will blow   *Two Voices* 59
   as a t Turns from the sea ;   *Audley Court* 51
   like me, with scourges and with t's ;   *St. S. Stylites* 180
   T's, ivies, woodbine, mistletoes,   *Day-Dm., Sleep. P.* 43
   we reach'd A mountain, like a wall of burs and t's ;   *Sea Dreams* 119
   A rosebud set with little wilful t's,   *Princess, Pro.* 154
   Shadow and shine is life, little Annie, flower and t.   *Grandmother* 60
   I have heard of t's and briers.   *Window, Marr. Morn.* 20
   Over the t's and briers,   ,,   21
   The path we came by, t and flower,   *In Mem. xlvi* 2
   I took the t's to bind my brows,   ,, *lxix* 7
   The fool that wears a crown of t's :   ,,   12
   bristles all the brakes and t's   ,, *cvii* 9
   evermore Seem'd catching at a rootless t,   *Geraint and E.* 378
   T's of the crown and shivers of the cross,   *Balin and Balan* 111
   where the winter t Blossoms at Christmas,   *Holy Grail* 377
   in a land of sand and t's, (repeat)   ,,   376, 390
   And wearying in a land of sand and t's.   ,,   420
   I cared not for the t's ; the t's were there.   *Pelleas and E.* 404
   fall on its own t's—if this be true—   *Lover's Tale i* 273
   Its knotted t's thro' my unpaining brows,   ,,   620
   roses that sprang without leaf or a t from the bush ;   *V. of Maeldune* 44
   Are figs of thistles ? or grapes of t's ?   *Riflemen form !* 10
Thornless   thy great Forefathers of the t garden,   *Maud I xviii* 27
Thorny   Are wither'd in the t close,   *Day-Dm., Arrival* 11
   I found a wood with t boughs :   *In Mem. lxix* 6
Thorough-edged   t-e intellect to part Error from crime ;   *Isabel* 14
Thoroughfare   In shadowy t's of thought ;   *In Mem. lxx* 8
   He left the barren-beaten t,   *Lancelot and E.* 161
Thorpe   But he, by farmstead, t and spire,   *Will Water.* 137

Thorpe (*continued*)   By twenty *thorps*, a little town,   *The Brook* 29
Then *t* and byre arose in fire,   *The Victim* 3
Down to the little *t* that lies so close,   *Holy Grail* 547
Thought (s)   (*See also* **Thowt**)   He hath no *t* of
     coming woes;   *Supp. Confessions* 47
tended by Pure vestal *t's* in the translucent fane   *Isabel* 4
Small *t* was there of life's distress;   *Ode to Memory* 37
The viewless arrows of his *t's* were headed   *The Poet* 11
LIFE and *T* have gone away Side by side,   *Deserted House* 1
for Life and *T* Here no longer dwell;   ,, 17
mortal dower Of pensive *t* and aspect pale,   *Margaret* 6
who can tell The last wild *t* of Chatelet,   ,, 37
Moulded thy baby *t*.   *Eleänore* 5
And flattering thy childish *t*   ,, 13
T and motion mingle, Mingle ever.   ,, 60
I seem to see *T* folded over *t*, smiling asleep,   ,, 84
T seems to come and go In thy large eyes,   ,, 96
Our *t* gave answer each to each,   *Sonnet to ——* 10
' And men, thro' novel spheres of *t*   *Two Voices* 61
Asks what thou lackest, *t* resign'd,   ,, 98
Fruitful of further *t* and deed,   ,, 144
but overtakes Far *t* with music that it makes: ,, 438
mind was brought To anchor by one gloomy *t*;   ,, 459
I least should breathe a *t* of pain.   *Miller's D.* 26
With blessings beyond hope or *t*,   ,, 237
so much the *t* of power Flatter'd his spirit;   *Œnone* 136
for fiery *t's* Do shape themselves within me,   ,, 246
and divided quite The kingdom of her *t*.   *Palace of Art* 228
As when a great *t* strikes along the brain,   *D. of F. Women* 43
by down-lapsing *t* Stream'd onward,   ,, 49
' It comforts me in this one *t* to dwell,   ,, 233
deep Gold-mines of *t* to lift the hidden ore   ,, 274
strength of some diffusive *t* Hath time and
     space   *You ask me, why, etc.* 15
When single *t* is civil crime,   ,, 19
Thro' future time by power of *t*.   *Love thou thy land* 4
Wherever *T* hath wedded Fact.   ,, 52
Counting the dewy pebbles, fix'd in *t*;   *M. d'Arthur* 84
His own *t* drove him, like a goad.   ,, 185
all kinds of *t*, That verged upon them,   *Gardener's D.* 70
These birds have joyful *t's*.   ,, 99
Lightly he laugh'd, as one that read my *t*,   ,, 106
A *t* would fill my eyes with happy dew;   ,, 197
or should have, for a *t* or two,   *Edwin Morris* 83
(And heedfully I sifted all my *t*)   *St. S. Stylites* 56
Should my Shadow cross thy *t's*   *Love and Duty* 88
tho' the times, when some new *t* can bud,   *Golden Year* 27
Beyond the utmost bound of human *t*.   *Ulysses* 32
Spring a young man's fancy lightly turns to *t's* of love.   *Locksley Hall* 20
touch him with thy lighter *t*.   ,, 54
t's of men are widen'd with the process of the suns.   ,, 138
in the railway, in the *t's* that shake mankind.   ,, 166
And would you have the *t* I had,   *Day-Dm., Pro.* 13
And *t* and time be born again,   ,, *Sleep. P.* 50
From deep *t* himself he rouses,   *L. of Burleigh* 21
Whited *t* and cleanly life As the priest,   *Vision of Sin* 116
utter The *t's* that arise in me.   *Break, break, etc.* 4
So the *t* Haunted and harass'd him,   *Enoch Arden* 719
There speech and *t* and nature fail'd a little,   ,, 792
Her all of *t* and bearing hardly more   *Aylmer's Field* 29
worst *t* she has Is whiter even than her pretty hand :   ,, 362
Is it so true that second *t's* are best ?   *Sea Dreams* 65
Sweet *t's* would swarm as bees about their queen.   *Princess i* 40
A *t* flash'd thro' me which I clothed in act,   ,, 195
whose *t's* enrich the blood of the world.'   ,, *ii* 181
And all her *t's* as fair within her eyes,   ,, 326
You need not set your *t's* in rubric thus   ,, *iii* 50
And she broke out interpreting my *t's* :   ,, 275
And live, perforce, from *t* to *t*,   ,, 328
tost on *t's* that changed from hue to hue,   ,, *iv* 210
to those *t's* that wait On you, their centre :   ,, 443
not a *t*, a touch, But pure as lines of green   ,, *v* 195
but other *t's* than Peace Burnt in us,   ,, 245
Now could you share your *t*;   ,, *vi* 252
A shining furrow, as thy *t's* in me.   ,, *vii* 185

Thought (s) (*continued*) and always *t* in *t*, Purpose in purpose, *Princess vii* 304
Beyond all *t* into the Heaven of Heavens.   ,, *Con.* 115
And the *t* of a man is higher.   *Voice and the P.* 32
And my *t's* are as quick and as quick,   *Window, On the Hill* 12
And with the *t* her colour burns ;   *In Mem. vi* 34
An awful *t*, a life removed,   ,, *xiii* 10
And *T* leapt out to wed with *T* Ere *T* could wed
     itself with Speech ;   ,, *xxiii* 15
Nor other *t* her mind admits   ,, *xxxii* 2
All subtle *t*, all curious fears,   ,, 9
More strong than all poetic *t* ;   ,, *xxxvi* 12
The lightest wave of *t* shall lisp,   ,, *xlix* 5
and moved Upon the topmost froth of *t*.   ,, *lii* 4
There flutters up a happy *t*,   ,, *lxv* 7
In shadowy thoroughfares of *t* ;   ,, *lxx* 8
A grief as deep as life or *t*,   ,, *lxxx* 7
And fix my *t's* on all the glow   ,, *lxxxiv* 3
Leaving great legacies of *t*,   ,, 35
Whose life, whose *t's* were little worth,   ,, *lxxxv* 30
I find not yet one lonely *t*   ,, *xc* 23
Should be the man whose *t* would hold   ,, *xciv* 3
About empyreal heights of *t*,   ,, *xcv* 38
sway'd In vassal tides that follow'd *t*.   ,, *cxii* 16
And in my *t's* with scarce a sigh   ,, *cxix* 11
I slip the *t's* of life and death ;   ,, *cxxii* 16
And every *t* breaks out a rose.   ,, 20
shade of passing *t*, the wealth Of words and wit,   ,, *Con.* 102
wrong Done but in *t* to your beauty,   *Maud I iii* 6
And letting a dangerous *t* run wild   ,, *xix* 52
And noble *t* be freër under the sun,   ,, *III vi* 48
Another *t* was mine ;   *Marr. of Geraint* 793
Grant me pardon for my *t's* :   ,, 816
They hated her, who took no *t* of them,   *Geraint and E.* 639
and heard in *t* Their lavish comment   *Merlin and V.* 150
So grated down and filed away with *t*,   ,, 623
rathe the rose, half-cheated in the *t*   *Lancelot and E.* 340
And every evil *t* I had thought of old,   *Holy Grail* 372
remembering Her *t* when first she came,   *Guinevere* 182
what is true repentance but in *t*—Not ev'n in inmost *t*
     to think   373
grew half-guilty in her *t's* again,   ,, 408
But teach high *t*, and amiable words   ,, 481
wrath which forced my *t's* on that fierce law,   ,, 537
Counting the dewy pebbles, fixed in *t* ;   *Pass. of Arthur* 252
His own *t* drove him like a goad.   ,, 353
Leapt like a passing *t* across her eyes ;   *Lover's Tale i* 70
And length of days, and immortality Of *t*,   ,, 106
One sustenance, which, still as *t* grew large, Still larger
     moulding all the house of *t*,   ,, 240
At *t* of which my whole soul languishes   ,, 267
Still to believe it—'tis so sweet a *t*,   ,, 275
tell you how I hoard in *t* The faded rhymes   ,, 288
A graceful *t* of hers Grav'n on my fancy !   ,, 357
Absorbing all the incense of sweet *t's*   ,, 469
Oh friend, *t's* deep and heavy as these   ,, 688
The brightness of a burning *t*,   ,, 743
The spirit seem'd to flag from *t* to *t*,   ,, *ii* 51
Alway the inaudible invisible *t*,   ,, 102
burst through the cloud of *t* Keen, irrepressible.   ,, 164
T's of the breezes of May blowing   *Def. of Lucknow* 83
That Lenten fare makes Lenten *t*,   *To E. Fitzgerald* 31
thin minds, who creep from *t* to *t*,   *Ancient Sage* 103
Do-well will follow *t*,   ,, 273
An evil *t* may soil thy children's blood ;   ,, 275
I am old, and think gray *t's*,   *Locksley H., Sixty* 155
To *t's* that lift the soul of men,   *To Master of B.* 14
For *t* into the outward springs,   *Mechanophilus* 11
Thought (verb)   (*See also* **Thowt**)   HE *t* to quell the
     stubborn hearts   *Buonaparte* 1
And *t*, ' My life is sick of single sleep :   *The Bridesmaid* 13
She *t*, ' My spirit is here alone,   *Mariana in the S.* 47
I cast me down, nor *t* of you,   *Miller's D.* 63
My mother *t*, What ails the boy ?   ,, 93
And ' by that lamp,' I *t*, ' she sits !'   ,, 114
she *t* I might have look'd a little higher ;   ,, 139

Threaded (*adj.*) (*See also* **Crimson-threaded**) from the
  bastion'd walls Like *t* spiders, one by one, we dropt,   *Princess i* 108
  Shall shake its *t* tears in the wind no more.   *Maud III vi* 28
Threaded (*verb*) he *t* The secretest walks of fame :   *The Poet* 9
  Or *t* some Socratic dream ;   *In Mem. lxxxix* 36
Threading led *T* the soldier-city,   *Princess v* 7
Threat Puppet to a father's *t*,   *Locksley Hall* 42
  But scared with *t's* of jail and halter   *Aylmer's Field* 520
  Our Boanerges with his *t's* of doom,   *Sea Dreams* 251
  I hear the violent *t's* you do not hear,   *Geraint and E.* 420
  after hours of search and doubt and *t's*, And hubbub,   *The Ring* 278
Threaten'd Had wink'd and *t* darkness,   *M. d'Arthur, Ep.* 2
Three (*adj.*) (*See also* **Fifty-three, Three Hundred**) She
  made *t* paces thro' the room,   *L. of Shalott iii* 38
  T fingers round the old silver cup—   *Miller's D.* 10
  Or those *t* chestnuts near, that hung   ,,   55
  T times I stabb'd him thro' and thro'.   *The Sisters* 29
  brandish'd him *T* times, and drew him under in
    the mere.' (repeat)   *M. d'Arthur* 146, 161
  Not tho' I live *t* lives of mortal men,   ,,   155
  by these *T* Queens with crowns of gold—   ,,   198
  There those *t* Queens Put forth their hands,   ,,   205
  to *t* arches of a bridge Crown'd with the minster-towers.   *Gardener's D.* 43
  And in the compass of *t* little words,   ,,   232
  And for *t* hours he sobb'd o'er William's child   *Dora* 167
  T winters, that my soul might grow to thee,   *St. S. Stylites* 71
  and *t* years on one of twelve ; And twice *t* years I
    crouch'd on one that rose   ,,   87
  Is *t* times worth them all ;   *Talking Oak* 72
  those *t* stanzas that you made About my " giant bole ; "   ,,   135
  For some *t* suns to store and hoard myself,   *Ulysses* 29
  To watch the *t* tall spires ;   *Godiva* 4
  T fair children first she bore him,   *L. of Burleigh* 87
  I think I have not *t* days more to live ;   *Enoch Arden* 851
  he past To turn and ponder those *t* hundred scrolls   *Lucretius* 12
  One babe was theirs, a Margaret, *t* years old :   *Sea Dreams* 3
  The lady of *t* castles in that land :   *Princess i* 79
  ' *T* ladies of the Northern empire pray   ,,   238
  Not for *t* years to correspond with home ; Not for *t* years
    to cross the liberties ; Not for *t* years to speak with
    any men ;   ,,   *ii* 70
  To give *t* gallant gentlemen to death.'   ,,   335
  Till like *t* horses that have broken fence,   ,,   386
  For dear are those *t* castles to my wants,   ,,   417
  Descended to the court that lay *t* parts In shadow,   ,,   *iii* 20
  being herself *T* times more noble than *t* score of men,   ,,   109
  And our *t* lives.   ,,   142
  Now, scarce *t* paces measured from the mound,   ,,   *v* 1
  A smoke go up thro' which I loom to her *T* times a
    monster :   ,,   131
  anon to meet us lightly pranced *T* captains out ;   ,,   255
  made them glance Like those *t* stars of the airy Giant's
    zone,   ,,   260
  then took the king His *t* broad sons ;   ,,   269
  t times he went : The first, be blew and blew,   ,,   335
  Shadows of *t* dead men (repeat)   *G. of Swainston* 3, 5
  T dead men have I loved and thou art last of the three.   ,,   15
  Tho' I since then have number'd o'er Some thrice *t*
    years :   *In Mem., Con.* 10
  cataract seas that snap The *t* decker's oaken spine   *Maud II ii* 27
  Flame-colour, vert and azure, in *t* rays, One
    falling upon each of *t* fair queens,   *Com. of Arthur* 275
  over all High on the top were those *t* Queens,   *Gareth and L.* 229
  a river Runs in *t* loops about her living-place ; And
    o'er it are *t* passings, and *t* knights   ,,   612
  t fair girls In gilt and rosy raiment came :   ,,   926
  O rainbow with *t* colours after rain,   ,,   1160
  but when the Prince *T* times had blown—   ,,   1378
  Slay we not : my *t* brethren bad me do it,   ,,   1410
  night Before her birthday, *t* sad years ago,   *Marr. of Geraint* 633
  And forth they rode, but scarce *t* paces on,   *Geraint and E.* 19
  Then Enid was aware of *t* tall knights On horseback,   ,,   56
  I saw *t* bandits by the rock Waiting to fall on you,   ,,   72
  Stript from the *t* dead wolves of woman born The *t*
    gay suits of armour   ,,   94

Three (*adj.*) (*continued*) *T* other horsemen waiting,
    wholly arm'd,   *Geraint and E.* 121
  ' There lurk *t* villains yonder in the wood,   ,,   142
  Their *t* gay suits of armour, each from each,   ,,   181
  and my purpose *t* years old,   ,,   849
  those *t* kingless years Have past—   *Balin and Balan* 63
  for but *t* brief moons had glanced away   ,,   154
  Had I for *t* days seen, ready to fall.   *Merlin and V.* 296
  So to the Gate of the *t* Queens we came,   *Holy Grail* 358
  T knights were thereamong ; and they too smiled,   *Pelleas and E.* 96
  Then glanced askew at those *t* knights of hers,   ,,   134
  And those *t* knights all set their faces home,   ,,   187
  Then calling her *t* knights, she charged them,   ,,   219
  while walking on the walls With her *t* knights,   ,,   226
  Give me *t* days to melt her fancy,   ,,   356
  So those *t* days, aimless about the land,   ,,   391
  Then was he ware of *t* pavilions rear'd   ,,   428
  and their *t* squires across their feet :   ,,   431
  hence he went To-day for *t* days' hunting—   *Last Tournament* 530
  Himself beheld *t* spirits mad with joy   *Guinevere* 252
  When *t* gray linnets wrangle for the seed :   ,,   255
  lived For *t* brief years, and there,   ,,   697
  brandish'd him *T* times, and drew him under
    in the mere. (repeat)   *Pass. of Arthur* 314, 329
  Not tho' I live *t* lives of mortal men,   ,,   323
  by these *T* Queens with crowns of gold :   ,,   366
  There those *t* Queens Put forth their hands,   ,,   373
  from the woods That belt it rise *t* dark, tall
    cypresses,—*T* cypresses,   *Lover's Tale i* 536
  Fixing my eyes on those *t* cypress-cones   *ii* 38
  The mountain, the *t* cypresses, the cave,   ,,   109
  Dead—and had lain *t* days without a pulse :   *iv* 34
  An' he took *t* turns in the rain,   *First Quarrel* 75
  which our house has held *T* hundred years—   *Sisters (E. and E.)* 53
  I had sat *t* nights by the child   *In the Child. Hosp.* 59
  And we stay'd *t* days, and we gorged   *V. of Maeldune* 67
  T days since, *t* more dark days of the Godless gloom   *Despair* 6
  Those *t* hundred millions under one Imperial
    sceptre now,   *Locksley H., Sixty* 117
  came On *t* gray heads beneath a gleaming rift.   *Demeter and P.* 83
  T dark ones in the shadow with thy King.   ,,   122
  those *t* sweet Italian words,   *The Ring* 406
  The century's *t* strong eights have met   *To Ulysses* 7
  T slaves were trailing a dead lion away,   *St. Telemachus* 47
  Thro' those *t* words would haunt him when a boy,   *Far—far—away* 8
Three (*s*) Three dead men have I loved and thou art
    last of the *t*.   *G. of Swainston* 15
Three-days-long That *t-d-l* presageful gloom of yours   *Merlin and V.* 320
Three-decker rushing battle-bolt sang from the *t-d*   *Maud I i* 50
  cataract seas that snap The *t d's* oaken spine   *II ii* 27
Threefold Lower'd softly with a *t* cord of love   *D. of F. Women* 211
Three hundred THE charge of the gallant *t h*,   *Heavy Brigade* 1
  Scarlett and Scarlett's *t h* were riding by   ,,   4
  gallant *t h* whose glory will never die—   ,,   10
  Gallopt the gallant *t h*, the Heavy Brigade.   ,,   25
  ' Lost are the gallant *t h* of Scarlett's Brigade ! '   ,,   45
  Glory to all the *t h*, and all the Brigade !   ,,   66
Three-months-old On corpses *t-m-o* at noon she came,   *Palace of Art* 243
Three-parts-sick *t-p-s* With strumming and with scraping,   *Amphion* 69
Three-times-three The crowning cup, the *t-t-t*,   *In Mem., Con.* 104
Three-years Sent me a *t-y* exile from thine eyes.   *Balin and Balan* 59
Thresher *t* with his flail had scatter'd them.   *Gareth and L.* 842
Threshing-floor by the lonely *t-f*,   *Demeter and P.* 126
Threshold (*adj.*) footsteps smite the *t* stairs Of life—   *St. S. Stylites* 191
Threshold (*s*) and on her *t* lie Howling in
    outer darkness.   *To ——, With Pal. of Art* 15
  see me carried out from the *t* of the door ;   *May Queen, N. Y's. E.* 42
  Corpses across the *t* ;   *D. of F. Women* 25
  Half-fall'n across the *t* of the sun,   ,,   63
  Dora went to Mary's house, and stood Upon the *t*.   *Dora* 111
  That float about the *t* of an age,   *Golden Year* 16
  wrinkled feet Upon thy glimmering *t's*,   *Tithonus* 68
  And burn the *t* of the night,   *The Voyage* 18
  And seldom crost her *t*,   *Enoch Arden* 337
  dark retinue reverencing death At golden *t's* ;   *Aylmer's Field* 843

Threshold (s) (*continued*)   come thou down And find him ;

by the happy *t*, he,	*Princess vii 200*
Upon the *t* of the mind ?	*In Mem. iii 16*
guest To enrich the *t* of the night	„ *xxix 6*
From off the *t* of the realm,	*Gareth and L. 136*
Here on the *t* of our enterprise.	„ *298*
Was all the marble *t* flashing,	*Geraint and E. 25*
With all her golden *t's* clashing,	*Lover's Tale i 605*
Love passeth not the *t* of cold Hate,	„ *778*
Falls on the *t* of her native land,	*Demeter and P. 3*

Threw (*See also* **Thraw'd**) She *t* her royal robes away.

	Palace of Art 290
clutch'd the sword, And strongly wheel'd and *t* it.	*M. d'Arthur 136*
heavier, stronger, he that smote And *t* him :	*Princess v 537*
t the kings Carádos, Urien, Cradlemont of Wales,	*Com. of Arthur 111*
Mounted in arms, *t* up their caps	*Gareth and L. 697*
same strength which *t* the Morning Star Can throw the Evening.'	„ *1108*
Lancelot !—thine the hand That *t* me ?	„ *1242*
By overthrowing me you *t* me higher.	*Geraint and E. 792*
clutch'd the sword, And strongly wheel'd and *t* it.	*Pass. of Arthur 304*
on the sand *T* down the bier ;	*Lover's Tale iii 33*
I *t* myself all abroad—	*The Wreck 39*
and *t* Underfoot there in the fray—	*Heavy Brigade 54*
Miriam sketch'd and Muriel *t* the fly ;	*The Ring 159*
She *t* the fly for me ;	„ *355*
how long—till you *t* me aside !	*Charity 5*

Thrice   *T* happy state again to be   *Supp. Confessions 40*

Thrice-beaten   weakling, and *t-b* hound :   *Pelleas and E. 291*

Thrice-happy   *T-h* days ! The flower of each,   *Edwin Morris 68*

   ' *T-h* he that may caress The ringlet's   *Talking Oak 177*

Thrice-turn'd   chew'd The *t-t* cud of wrath,   *Princess i 66*

Thrid   To *t* the musky-circled mazes,   „   *iv 261*

   He *t's* the labyrinth of the mind,   *In Mem. xcvii 11*

Thridded   I *t* the black heart of all the woods,   *Demeter and P. 69*

Thridding   *T* the sombre boskage of the wood,   *D. of F. Women 243*

Thried (**tried**)   I *t* her meself av the bird 'ud come   *Tomorrow 45*

Thrift   like the little *t*, Trembled in perilous places   *Sea Dreams 10*

Thrifty   *t* too beyond her age.   *Dora 16*

   Earn well the *t* months, nor wed Raw Haste,   *Love thou thy land 95*

Thrill   His country's war-song *t* his ears :   *Two Voices 153*

   Me mightier transports move and *t* ;   *Sir Galahad 22*

   My spirit leap'd as with those *t's* of bliss   *Lover's Tale i 363*

   with some electric *t* A cold air pass'd between us,   *The Ring 379*

Thrill'd   a clear under-tone *T* thro' mine ears   *D. of F. Women 82*

   T thro' the woods ; and Balan lurking there   *Balin and Balan 546*

Thrilleth   Thro' my very heart it *t*   *Lilian 22*

Thrilling   *See* **Spirit-thrilling**

Thrive   those Fresh faces, that would *t*   *Talking Oak 50*

Thriven   Word by which himself had *t*.'   *Sea Dreams 197*

   That on dumb death had *t* ;   *Dead Prophet 26*

Throän (**throne**)   an' taäke 'im afoor the *T*.   *North. Cobbler 106*

   an' sits o' the Bishop's *T*.   *Church-warden, etc. 20*

Throat   golden round her lucid *t* And shoulder :

From cheek and *t* and chin.	*Œnone 178*
But there was that across his *t*	*Palace of Art 140*
bright death quiver'd at the victim's *t* ;	*L. C. V. de Vere 31*
and in her *t* Her voice seem'd distant,	*D. of F. Women 115*
' Go, take the goose, and wring her *t*,	*To J. S. 54*
All *t's* that gurgle sweet !	*The Goose 31*
She lit the spark within my *t*,	*Talking Oak 266*
Faltering and fluttering in her *t*,	*Will Water. 109*
Make liquid treble of that bassoon, my *t* ;	*Princess ii 187*
Thereat the Lady stretch'd a vulture *t*,	„ *426*
Millions of *t's* would bawl for civil rights,	„ *iv 363*
Tho' niggard *t's* of Manchester may bawl,	„ *v 387*
There is but one bird with a musical *t*,	*Third of Feb. 43*
And flood a fresher *t* with song.	*The Islet 27*
cobweb woven across the cannon's *t*	*In Mem. lxxxiii 16*
bared the knotted column of his *t*,	*Maud III vi 27*
many-winter'd fleece of *t* and chin.	*Marr. of Geraint 74*
felt the knot Climb in her *t*,	*Merlin and V. 841*
' Taliessin is our fullest *t* of song,	*Lancelot and E. 741*
The naked sword athwart their naked *t's*,	*Holy Grail 300*
the sword of the tourney across her *t*.	*Pelleas and E. 452*
	„ *455*
that felt the cold touch on her *t*,	„ *488*

Throat (*continued*)   The warm white apple of her *t*,

he bow'd to kiss the jewell'd *t*,	*Last Tournament 717*
	„ *751*
yea to him Who hacks his mother's *t*—	*Sir J. Oldcastle 114*
Sorra the silent *t* but we hard it	*Tomorrow 84*
scatters on her *t* the sparks of dew,	*Prog. of Spring 58*
you will not deny my sultry *t* One draught	*Romney's R. 22*
He gript it so hard by the *t*	*Bandit's Death 28*

Throated   *See* **Glossy-throated, Hundred-throated, Serpent-throated, Yellow-throated.**

Throb (s)   Perchance, to lull the *t's* of pain,   *The Daisy 105*

Throb (verb)   and *t's* Thro' earth, and all her graves,   *Romney's R. 127*

   T thro' the ribbed stone ;   *Palace of Art 176*

   The sight that *t's* and aches beneath my touch,   *Lover's Tale i 33*

Throbb'd   Till the war-drum *t* no longer,   *Locksley Hall 127*

   tempestuous treble *t* and palpitated ;   *Vision of Sin 28*

   T thunder thro' the palace floors,   *Princess vii 104*

   brows that shook and *t* From temple unto temple.   *Lover's Tale iii 7*

Throbbing   *T* thro' all thy heat and light,   *Fatima 4*

   Her heart is like a *t* star.   *Kate 9*

   When last with *t* heart I came To rest   *Talking Oak 155*

   A footstep, a low *t* in the walls,   *The Ring 409*

Throe   coughs, aches, stitches, ulcerous *t's*   *St. S. Stylites 13*

   Travail, and *t's* and agonies of the life,   *Com. of Arthur 76*

Throne (*See also* **Bosom-throne, Dais-throne, Rock-throne, Throän**) Which kept her *t* unshaken still,

	To the Queen 34
underpropt a rich *T* of the massive ore,	*Arabian Nights 146*
to own A crown, a sceptre, and a *t* !	*Ode to Memory 121*
With a crown of gold, On a *t* ?	*The Merman 7*
With a comb of pearl, On a *t* ?	*The Mermaid 8*
Over the *t* In the midst of the hall ;	„ *21*
lightly vault from the *t* and play With the mermen	„ *33*
Thou from a *t* Mounted in heaven	*To J. M. K. 12*
whose strong right arm debased The *t* of Persia,	*Alexander 2*
The *t* of Indian Cama slowly sail'd	*Palace of Art 115*
bells Began to chime. She took her *t* :	„ *158*
held she her solemn mirth, And intellectual *t*.	„ *216*
two tame leopards couch'd beside her *t*,	*Princess ii 33*
glittering bergs of ice, *T* after *t*,	„ *iv 72*
the crowd dividing clove An advent to the *t* :	„ *284*
and winged Her transit to the *t*,	„ *378*
at the further end Was Ida by the *t*,	„ *vi 357*
And barking for the *t's* of kings	*Ode on Well. 121*
Betwixt a people and their ancient *t*,	„ *163*
joy to the people and joy to the *t*,	*W. to Alexandra 29*
English Harold gave its *t* a shock,	*W. to Marie Alex. 24*
t's and peoples are as waifs that swing,	„ *26*
Green-rushing from the rosy *t's* of dawn !	
(repeat)	*Voice and the P. 4, 40*
The chairs and *t's* of civil power ?	*In Mem. xxi 16*
And shape the whisper of the *t* ;	„ *lxiv 12*
thousand battles, and shaking a hundred *t's*.	*Maud I i 48*
In that fierce light which beats upon a *t*,	*Ded. of Idylls 27*
from this land of beasts Up to my *t*,	*Com. of Arthur 248*
' A doubtful *t* is ice on summer seas.	„ *277*
Who stood in silence near his *t*,	„ *325*
same that afterward Struck for the *t*,	*Gareth and L. 328*
those tall knights, that ranged about the *t*,	„ *390*
Which down he laid before the *t*, and knelt,	*Balin and Balan 7*
Lest we should set one truer on his *t*.	*Last Tournament 162*
a knight cast down Before his *t*	*Guinevere 11*
Lay couchant with his eyes upon the *t*,	*Pass. of Arthur 160*
When all the purport of my *t* hath fail'd,	„ *455*
They stood before his *t* in silence,	*To the Queen ii 30*
and her *t* In our vast Orient,	*Lover's Tale i 593*
There in my realm and even on my *t*,	*Columbus 5*
Whom once he rose from off his *t* to greet	„ *15*
the king, the queen, Sank from their *t's*,	*V. of Maeldune 59*
the mountain arose like a jewell'd *t*	*The Wreck 66*
as a slave to his intellectual *t*,	*Locksley H., Sixty 138*
Break the State, the Church, the *T*,	*To Prin. Beatrice 14*
seen the loneliness of earthly *t's*,	*Open. I. and C. Exhib. 39*
One life, one flag, one fleet, one *T* ! '	*Vastness 20*
Flattery gilding the rift in a *t* ;	*By an Evolution. 15*
rebel subject seek to drag me from the *t*,	*D. of the Duke of C. 6*
all the *T's* are clouded by your loss,	

Throned (*See also* **Low-throned**) wisdom-bred And *t* of
  wisdom— *Œnone* 124
I turning saw, *t* on a flowery rise, *D. of F. Women* 125
And *t* races may degrade ; *In Mem. cxxviii* 7
splendour of the presence of the King *T*, *Gareth and L.* 321
That victor of the Pagan *t* in hall— *Last Tournament* 665
Throng (s) in among the *t's* of men : *Locksley Hall* 116
And pinch their brethren in the *t*, *Lit. Squabbles* 7
A head with kindling eyes above the *t*, *Gareth and L.* 646
from out of kitchen came The thralls in *t*,   695
push'd Athwart the *t* to Lancelot, *Holy Grail* 753
Throng (verb) To *t* with stately blooms *The Poet* 27
marish-flowers that *t* The desolate creeks *Dying Swan* 40
and *t*, their rags and they The basest, *Lucretius* 170
the people *t* The chairs and thrones *In Mem. xxi* 15
Throng'd (*See also* **Mast-throng'd**) And her whisper *t*
  my pulses *Locksley Hall* 36
Every gate is *t* with suitors,   101
In their own darkness, *t* into the moon. *Pelleas and E.* 458
Their people *t* about them from the hall, *Sisters (E. and E.)* 156
a crowd *T* the waste field about the city gates : *Sir J. Oldcastle* 40
Thronging Or *t* all one porch of Paradise *Palace of Art* 101
Till *t* in and in, to where they waited, *Vision of Sin* 26
as *t* fancies come To boys and girls *Lover's Tale* i 554
Throstle *And thro' wild March the* t *calls,* *To the Queen* 14
The callow *t* lispeth. *Claribel* 17
Sometimes the *t* whistled strong : *Sir L. and Q. G.* 11
And swallow and sparrow and *t*, *Window, Ay* 14
blackbirds have their wills, The *t's* too. *Early Spring* 6
Throve And so she *t* and prosper'd *Palace of Art* 217
that on which it *t* Falls off, *To J. S.* 15
But *t* not in her trade, not being bred To barter, *Enoch Arden* 249
And in it *t* an ancient evergreen,   735
Who *t* and branch'd from clime to clime, *In Mem. cxviii* 13
And all this *t* until I wedded thee, *Guinevere* 484
Throw I would *t* to them back in mine *The Merman* 31
dividing the swift mind, In act to *t* : *M. d'Arthur* 61
Nor lose the wrestling thews that *t* the world ; *Princess* vii 282
To seize and *t* the doubts of man ; *In Mem. cix* 6
being but knave, I *t* thine enemies.' *Gareth and L.* 1023
Morning Star Can *t* the Evening.'   1109
dividing the swift mind, In act to *t* : *Pass. of Arthur* 229
Throwing *t* down his robes, And claspt her hand *Lover's Tale* i 51
and we took to the stone, *V. of Maeldune* 94
Thrown selfsame impulse wherewith he was *t* *Mine be the strength* 3
thunder, or a sound Of rocks *t* down, *Palace of Art* 282
Still from one sorrow to another *t* : *Lotos-Eaters, C. S.* 18
broad-limb'd Gods at random *t* By fountain-urns ;— *To E. L.* 15
the shiver of dancing leaves is *t* *Maud* I vi 73
knight of Arthur, here lie *t* by whom I know not, *Gareth and L.* 1233
Out, sword ; we are *t* !'   1236
T have I been, nor once, but many a time.   1261
Thrue (true) yer Honour's the *t* ould blood *Tomorrow* 5
Thrum to flaunt, to dress, to dance, to *t*, *Princess* iv 519
Thrumm'd who *t* On such a wire as musically *Last Tournament* 322
Thrumming And *t* on the table : *Will Water.* 160
Thrush (*See also* **Mavis**) rarely pipes the mounted *t* ; *In Mem. xci* 2
Thrust (s) here a *t* that might have kill'd, *Lancelot and E.* 25
Thrust (verb) and *t* The dagger thro' her side.' *D. of F. Women* 259
Who *t* him in the hollows of his arm, *Dora* 132
And with grim laughter *t* us out at gates. *Princess* iv 556
T in between ; but Arac rode him down :   v 532
For into a shallow grave they are *t*, *Maud* II v 6
And *t* the dish before her, crying, ' Eat.' *Geraint and E.* 655
Unbind him now, And *t* him out of doors ; *Pelleas and E.* 257
and unbound, and *t* him from the gate.   260
Far less to bind, your victor, and *t* him out,   293
but *t* him bounden out of door.   314
Or *t* the heathen from the Roman wall, *Pass. of Arthur* 69
portion of the pleasant yesterday, *T* forward on
  to-day *Lover's Tale* i 123
Had *t* his wife and child and dash'd   380
him Who *t* him out, or him who saved his life ?'   iv 267
Thrusteth My tough lance *t* sure, *Sir Galahad* 2
Thud the hollow-beaten mosses *t* *Balin and Balan* 321

Thumb his nice eyes Should see the raw mechanic's
  bloody *t's* *Walk. to the Mail* 75
And rotatory *t's* on silken knees, *Aylmer's Field* 200
nipt her slender nose With petulant *t* and finger, *Gareth and L.* 750
stoop and kiss the tender little *t*, *Marr. of Geraint* 395
Thumbscrew To the *t* and the stake, *The Revenge* 21
Thump heave and *t* A league of street *Princess* iii 127
Thunder (s) (*See also* **Battle-thunder, Tundher, War-**
  thunder) BELOW the *t's* of the upper deep ; *The Kraken* 1
Her words did gather *t* as they ran, *The Poet* 49
And as the lightning to the *t* Which follows it,   50
Ever brightening With a low melodious *t* ; *Poet's Mind* 27
Low *t* and light in the magic night— *The Merman* 23
With *t's*, and with lightnings, *Buonaparte* 6
Rest in a happy place and quiet seats Above the *t*, *Œnone* 132
The ragged rims Of *t* brooding low, *Palace of Art* 75
t, or a sound of rocks thrown down,   281
And *t* on the everlasting hills. *D. of F. Women* 226
The *t's* breaking at her feet : *Of old sat Freedom* 2
Black'd with thy branding *t*, *St. S. Stylites* 76
Low *t's* bring the mellow rain, *Talking Oak* 279
frolic welcome took The *t* and the sunshine, *Ulysses* 48
But they heard the foeman's *t* *The Captain* 41
for on her the *t's* of the house Had fallen *Aylmer's Field* 278
flood, fire, earthquake, *t*, wrought Such waste   639
Dead claps of *t* from within the cliffs *Sea Dreams* 55
And there was rolling *t* ;   118
Nor ever lowest roll of *t* moans, *Lucretius* 108
A long melodious *t* to the sound Of solemn psalms, *Princess* ii 476
shattering on black blocks A breadth of *t*.   iii 292
with the crash of shivering points, And *t*.   v 492
Throbb'd *t* thro' the palace floors,   vii 104
even if they broke In *t*, silent ; *Ode on Well.* 177
Welcome her, *t's* of fort and of fleet ! *W. to Alexandra* 6
if he thunder by law the *t* is yet His voice. *High. Pantheism* 14
T, a flying fire in heaven, *Boädicea* 24
And a sullen *t* is roll'd ; *Maud* II iv 49
Made lightnings and great *t's* over him, *Com. of Arthur* 108
break perforce Upon a head so dear in *t*, said : *Geraint and E.* 13
crash of the near cataract hears The drumming *t*   173
The hard earth shake, and a low *t* of arms. *Lancelot and E.* 460
and overhead *T*, and in the *t* was a cry. *Holy Grail* 185
Thicker than drops from *t*,   348
the heavens Open'd and blazed with *t*   508
and close upon it peal'd A sharp quick *t*.'   696
then one low roll Of Autumn *t*, *Last Tournament* 153
thresholds clashing, roll'd Her heaviest *t*— *Lover's Tale* i 606
the surge fell From *t* into whispers ;   iii 31
I heard his voice between The *t's* *Columbus* 146
t of God peal'd over us all the day, *V. of Maeldune* 113
a voice rang out in the *t's* of Ocean and Heaven *The Wreck* 88
Full-handed *t's* often have confessed Thy
  power, *To W. C. Macready* 2
Are there *t's* moaning in the distance ? *On Jub. Q. Victoria* 66
Till the *t's* pass, the spectres vanish,   69
Downward *t* in hollow and glen, *To Master of B.* 16
Across the downward *t* of the brook *Death of Œnone* 23
or shake with her *t's* and shatter her island, *Kapiolani* 10
THERE is a sound of *t* afar, *Riflemen form !* 1
Storm of battle and *t* of war !   3
and hew'd Like broad oaks with *t*. *The Tourney* 11
at the shipwreck, or the rolling *T*,, *Faith* 4
Thunder (verb) That not one moment ceased to *t*, *Sea Dreams* 125
And the volleying cannon *t* his loss ; *Ode on Well.* 62
T ' Anathema,' friend, at you ; *To F. D. Maurice* 8
if He *t* by law the thunder is yet His voice. *High. Pantheism* 14
Thunderbolt in its breast a *t*. *Locksley Hall* 192
And like a *t* he falls. *The Eagle* 6
and once the flash of a *t*— *Lucretius* 27
And, falling on them like a *t*, *Princess, Pro.* 43
the *t* Hangs silent ; but prepare : I speak ;   ii 223
I dare All these male *t's* :   iv 500
Whence the *t* will fall Long and loud, *The Revenge* 44
Shrine-shattering earthquake, fire, flood, *t*, *Tiresias* 61
Burst like a *t*, Crash'd like a hurricane, *Heavy Brigade* 27

Tilt (knightly exercise) (*continued*)   on love And sport and *t's*
and pleasure,   *Guinevere* 387
Tilt (verb)   Himself would *t* it out among the lads :   *Princess* v 355
Ask'd me to *t* with him, the proven knight.   *Gareth and L.* 27
Who *t* for lady's love and glory here,   ,, 740
But in this tournament can no man *t*,   *Marr. of Geraint* 480
And *t's* with my good nephew thereupon,   ,, 488
He left it with her, when he rode to *t*   *Lancelot and E.* 30
to *t* against the knights There at Caerleon,   *Pelleas and E.* 65
t with a lance Becomes thee well—   *Last Tournament* 636
Tilted   *See* **Tip-tilted**
Tilth   wither'd holt or *t* or pasturage.   *Enoch Arden* 675
and so by *t* and grange, And vines,   *Princess* i 110
t and vineyard, hive and horse and herd ;   *To Virgil* 10
Tilting-field   In open battle or the *t-f* (repeat)   *Guinevere* 330, 332
Timber   And fiddled in the *t* !   *Amphion* 16
Timber-crost   A front of *t-c* antiquity,   *Enoch Arden* 692
Timbrel   With *t* and with song.   *D. of F. Women* 200
Time (s)   (*See also* **Bridal-time, College-time, Cradle-time, Ten-times, Toime**)   *yield you* t *To make demand of modern rhyme*   *To the Queen* 10
Nine *t's* goes the passing bell :   *All Things will Die* 35
In a *t*, Of which he wots not,   *Supp. Confessions* 160
The tide of *t* flow'd back with me, The forward-flowing tide of *t*;   *Arabian Nights* 3
In sooth it was a goodly *t*;   ,, 20
A goodly place, a goodly *t*, (repeat)   ,, 31, 53
A goodly *t*, For it was in the golden prime   ,, 42
fed the *t* With odour in the golden prime   ,, 64
Apart from place, withholding *t*,   ,, 75
A lovely *t*, For it was in the golden prime   ,, 86
Entranced with that place and *t*,   ,, 97
Graven with emblems of the *t*,   ,, 108
After the fashion of the *t*,   ,, 119
night new-risen, that marvellous *t*   ,, 130
The sweetest lady of the *t*,   ,, 141
Sole star of all that place and *t*,   ,, 152
What *t* the amber morn Forth gushes   *Ode to Memory* 70
WHAT *t* the mighty moon was gathering light   *Love and Death* 1
That tho' I knew not in what *t* or place,   *Sonnet to* —— 12
said the secret voice, ' some a *t*, Sooner or later,   *Two Voices* 64
' Forerun thy peers, thy, *t*, and let Thy feet,   ,, 88
memory of the wither'd leaf In endless *t*   ,, 113
What *t* the foeman's line is broke,   ,, 155
' For memory dealing but with *t*,   ,, 376
Beat *t* to nothing in my head   *Miller's D.* 67
That went and came a thousand *t's*.   ,, 72
when *t* was ripe, The still affection of the heart   ,, 224
from that *t* to this I am alone,   *Œnone* 193
My love hath told me so a thousand *t's*.   ,, 197
Hath he not sworn his love a thousand *t's*,   ,, 231
Three *t's* I stabb'd him thro' and thro'.   *The Sisters* 29
the *t's* of every land So wrought,   *Palace of Art* 147
What *t* I watch the darkening droves of swine   ,, 199
But dreadful *t*, dreadful eternity,   ,, 267
And ever worse with growing *t*,   ,, 270
You know so ill to deal with *t*,   *L. C. V. de Vere* 63
If *t* be heavy on your hands,   ,, 66
To-morrow 'ill be the happiest *t* of all the glad New-year; (repeat)   *May Queen* 2, 42
The good old year, the dear old *t*,   ,, *N. Y's. E.* 6
A thousand *t's* I blest him,   ,, *Con.* 16
And if it comes three *t's*, I thought,   ,, 38
So now I think my *t* is near.   ,, 41
T driveth onward fast,   *Lotos-Eaters, C. S.* 43
The spacious *t's* of great Elizabeth   *D. of F. Women* 7
The *t's* when I remember to have been   ,, 79
wood is all thine own, Until the end of *t*.'   ,, 84
The Nilus would have risen before his *t*   ,, 143
This is the curse of *t*. Alas !   *To J. S.* 17
' Beat quicker, for the *t* Is pleasant,   *On a Mourner* 12
Hath *t* and space to work and spread.   *You ask me, why, etc.* 16
induce a *t* When single thought is civil crime,   ,, 18
transfused Thro' future *t* by power of thought.   *Love thou thy land* 4
But pamper not a hasty *t*,   ,, 9

AA*

Time (s) (*continued*)   For all the past of *T* reveals A bridal dawn   *Love thou thy land* 50
And this be true, till *T* shall close,   ,, 79
' Why take the style of those heroic *t's* ?   *The Epic* 35
For nature brings not back the Mastodon, Nor we those *t's*;   ,, 37
Shall never more, at any future *t*,   *M. d'Arthur* 18
And hid Excalibur the second *t*,   ,, 111
brandish'd him Three *t's*, and drew him under in the mere. (repeat)   ,, 146, 161
'tis *t* that I were gone.   ,, 163
I see the true old *t's* are dead,   ,, 229
Such *t's* have been not since the light   ,, 232
cock crew loud; as at that *t* of year The lusty bird   ,, *Ep.* 10
we listen'd ; with the *t* we play'd,   *Gardener's D.* 221
Then, in that *t* and place, I spoke to her,   ,, 226
And in that *t* and place she answer'd me,   ,, 231
the *t* Is come to raise the veil.   ,, 273
But in my *t* a father's word was law,   *Dora* 27
and in harvest *t* he died.   ,, 55
T will set me right.'   *Edwin Morris* 88
for so long a *t*, If I may measure *t*   *St. S. Stylites* 93
Heaven, and Earth, and *T* are choked.   ,, 104
Bow down one thousand and two hundred *t's*, To Christ,   ,, 111
I do not say But that a *t* may come—   ,, 190
Yet I do not say, that *t* is at the doors   ,, 192
' But could I, as in *t's* foregone,   *Talking Oak* 189
Shall Error in the round of *t* Still father Truth ?   *Love and Duty* 4
O three *t's* less unworthy !   ,, 20
Wait; my faith is large in *T*,   ,, 25
when a hundred *t's* In that last kiss,   ,, 66
all the wheels of *T* Spun round in station,   ,, 75
' Ah tho' the *t's*, when some new thought can bud,   *Golden Year* 27
Not in our *t*, nor in our children's *t*,   ,, 55
all *t's* I have enjoy'd Greatly,   *Ulysses* 7
Made weak by *t* and fate, but strong in will   ,, 69
fairy tales of science, and the long result of *T* ;   *Locksley Hall* 12
Love took up the glass of *T*,   ,, 31
in the foremost files of *t*—   ,, 178
Not only we, the latest seed of *T*,   *Godiva* 5
And thought and *t* be born again,   *Day-Dm., Sleep. P.* 50
And in the morning of the *t's*.   ,, *L'Envoi* 20
For since the *t* when Adam first Embraced his Eve   ,, 41
How goes the *t* ? 'Tis five o'clock.   *Will Water.* 15
Nor add and alter, many *t's*,   ,, 63
on this whirligig of *T* We circle   ,, 206
With *t* I will not quarrel :   *Lady Clare* 1
IT was the *t* when lilies blow,   *L. of Burleigh* 70
Tho' at *t's* her spirit sank ;   ,, 88
Then before her *t* she died.   *The Voyage* 51
At *t's* the whole sea burn'd, at *t's*   ,, 53
At *t's* a carven craft would shoot   *Come not, when, etc.* 9
Wed whom thou wilt, but I am sick of *T*,   *Vision of Sin* 105
Is to be the ball of *T*,   ,, 214
crime Of sense avenged by sense that wore with *t*.'   *Enoch Arden* 26
at *t's* Enoch would hold possession for a week :   ,, 104
Enoch at *t's* to go by land or sea ;   ,, 466
' Take your own, Annie, take your own *t*.'   ,, 539
bought Quaint monsters for the market of those *t's*,   ,, 745
saw Philip, the slighted suitor of old *t's*,   ,, 811
Lord has call'd me she shall know, I wait His *t*,'   *The Brook* 13
touch'd On such a *t* as goes before the leaf,   *Aylmer's Field* 452
and then indeed Harder the *t's* were,   ,, 463
Ran a Malayan amuck against the *t's*,   ,, 601
Beholding how the years which are not *T's* Had blasted him—   ,, 769
Is this a *t* to madden madness then ?   ,, 770
Was this a *t* for these to flaunt their pride ?   ,, 779
Which else had link'd their race with *t's* to come—   *Lucretius* 18
this, at *t's*, she mingled with his drink,   *Princess, Pro.* 15
Huge Ammonites, and the first bones of *T* ;   ,, 89
Strange was the sight and smacking of the *t* ;   ,, 93
one wide chasm of *t* and frost they gave The park,   ,, 205
monsters only made to kill *T* by the fire in winter.'   ,, 210
A tale for summer as befits the *t*,   ,, 210

Time (s) (*continued*) something made to suit with *T* and
 place,   *Princess Pro.* 231
From *t* to *t*, some ballad or a song   ,, 241
still from *t* to *t* Came murmurs of her beauty ,, *i* 35
Some future *t*, if so indeed you will,   ,, *ii* 64
on the stretch'd forefinger of all *T* Sparkle for ever: ,, 378
like swallows coming out of *t*   ,, 431
your great name flow on with broadening *t* ,, *iii* 164
Our weakness somehow shapes the shadow, *T* ; ,, 330
all things serve their *t* Toward that great year ,, *iv* 73
What *t* I watch'd the swallow winging south ,, 89
Like the Ithacensian suitors in old *t*, ,, 118
they mind us of the *t* When we made bricks in Egypt. ,, 127
those were gracious *t's*.   ,, 297
fellow-worker be, When *t* should serve; ,, 309
I that have wasted here health, wealth, and *t*, ,, 352
drunkard's football, laughing-stocks of *T*, ,, 517
you spent a stormy *t* With our strange girl : ,, *v* 121
three *t's* he went: The first, he blew and blew, ,, 335
equal baseness lived in sleeker *t's*.   ,, 385
We plant a solid foot into the *T*,   ,, 415
roll'd With music in the growing breeze of *T*, ,, *vi* 56
we will scatter all our maids Till happier *t's* ,, 303
many a maiden passing home Till happier *t's*; ,, 381
call'd On flying *T* from all their silver tongues— ,, *vii* 105
Much had she learnt in little *t*.   ,, 240
these twain, upon the skirts of *T*, Sit side by side, ,, 287
Give it *T* To learn its limbs :   ,, *Con.* 78
Give up their parks some dozen *t's* a year ,, 103
Foremost captain of his *t*,   *Ode on Well.* 31
For many a *t* in many a clime His captain's-ear ,, 64
That Jenny had tript in her *t*: *Grandmother* 26
was the first *t*, too, that ever I thought of death. ,, 61
I could not weep—my own *t* seem'd so near. ,, 72
mine is a *t* of peace, (repeat)   ,, 89, 94
And age is a *t* of peace,   ,, 97
What *t* have I to be vext?   ,, 104
T to think on it then,   *N. Farmer, N. S.* 7
Do'ant be stunt: taäke *t*:   ,, 17
But ill for him who, bettering not with *t*, *Will* 10
Rhymes and rhymes in the range of the *t's* ! *Spiteful Letter* 9
But this is the *t* of hollies.   ,, 22
Before the stony face of *T*,   *Lit. Squabbles* 3
no truer *T* himself Can prove you, *A Dedication* 1
O skill'd to sing of *T* or Eternity,   *Milton* 2
Sun comes, moon comes, *T* slips away. *Window, When* 2
Or reach a hand thro' *t* to catch *In Mem. i* 7
Come *T*, and teach me, many years, ,, *xiii* 13
My fancies *t* to rise on wing,   ,, 17
' A *t* to sicken and to swoon,   ,, *xxi* 17
And all was good that *T* could bring, ,, *xxiii* 18
envy not the beast that takes His license in the field of *t*, ,, *xxvii* 28
The *t* draws near the birth of Christ; ,, *xxviii* 1
Why should they miss their yearly due Before their *t* ? ,, *xxix* 16
As when he loved me here in *T*,   ,, *xliii* 14
What *t* his tender palm is prest   ,, *xlv* 2
A lifelong tract of *t* reveal'd;   ,, *xlvi* 9
And *T*, a maniac scattering dust,   ,, *l* 7
When *T* hath sunder'd shell from pearl.' ,, *lii* 16
The perfect flower of human *t*;   ,, *lxi* 4
When the dark hand struck down thro' *t*, ,, *lxxii* 19
Foreshorten'd in the tract of *t* ?   ,, *lxxvii* 4
What *t* mine own might also flee, ,, *lxxxiv* 37
Shall gather in the cycled *t's*.   ,, *lxxxv* 28
such A friendship as had master'd *T* ; ,, 64
Which masters *T* indeed, and is Eternal, ,, 65
Thy spirit in *t* among thy peers ;   ,, *xci* 6
Æonian music measuring out The steps of *T*— ,, *xcv* 42
The *t* draws near the birth of Christ; ,, *civ* 1
There in due *t* the woodbine blows, ,, *cv* 7
For change of place, like growth of *t*, ,, 11
The faithless coldness of the *t's*;   ,, *cvi* 18
The *t* admits not flowers or leaves   ,, *cvii* 5
Becoming, when the *t* has birth,   ,, *cxiii* 14
Is it, then, regret for buried *t*   ,, *cxvi* 1

Time (s) (*continued*) Contemplate all this work of *T*, *In Mem. cxviii* 1
If so he type this work of *t*   ,, 16
vast eddies in the flood Of onward *t* ,, *cxxviii* 6
As echoes out of weaker *t's*,   ,, *Con.* 22
But they must go, the *t* draws on,   ,, 89
Appearing ere the *t's* were ripe,   ,, 139
I remember the *t*, for the roots of my hair *Maud I i* 13
I well could weep for a *t* so sordid and mean, ,, *v* 17
My yet young life in the wilds of *T*, ,, *xvi* 21
She is but dead, and the *t* is at hand ,, *II iii* 8
Wretchedest age, since *T* began,   ,, *v* 21
My mood is changed, for it fell at a *t* of year ,, *III vi* 4
' It is *t*, it is *t*, O passionate heart,   ,, 30
' It is *t*, O passionate heart and morbid eye. ,, 32
Hereafter, thro' all *t's*, Albert the Good. *Ded. of Idylls* 43
from *t* to *t* the heathen host Swarm'd overseas, *Com. of Arthur* 8
ye know that in King Uther's *t* The prince ,, 185
all before his *t* Was Arthur born,   ,, 211
Of Uther's son, and born before his *t*, ,, 241
the *t* to cast away Is yet far-off.'   ,, 307
And many a *t* he came, and evermore ,, 351
and sad At *t's* he seem'd, and sad with him was I, ,, 353
 Stern too at *t's*, and then I loved him not, ,, 353
answer'd me In riddling triplets of old *t*, ,, 402
and Merlin in our *t* Hath spoken also, ,, 419
while the phantom king Sent out at *t's* a voice ; ,, 437
The fair beginners of a nobler *t*,   ,, 457
For it was past the *t* of Easterday. *Gareth and L.* 186
At *t's* the summit of the high city flash'd ; At *t's* the
 spires and turrets half-way down Prick'd thro' the
 mist ; at *t's* the great gate shone Only, ,, 192
New things and old co-twisted, as if *T* Were nothing, ,, 226
the King hath past his *t*—   ,, 709
Lion and stoat have isled together, knave, In *t* of flood. ,, 894
Thou shakest in thy fear: there yet is *t*: ,, 940
Far liefer had I fight a score of *t's*   ,, 944
So many a *t* he vaulted up again ;   ,, 1125
The war of *T* against the soul of man. ,, 1198
Thrown have I been, nor once, but many a *t*. ,, 1261
but when the Prince Three *t's* had blown— ,, 1378
And he that told the tale in older *t's*   ,, 1427
Has little *t* for idle questioners.' *Marr. of Geraint* 272
And there is scantly *t* for half the work. ,, 288
Tho' having seen all beauties of our *t*, ,, 498
Constrain'd us, but a better *t* has come; ,, 716
' O I that wasted *t* to tend upon her, *Geraint and E.* 38
in scarce longer *t* Than at Caerleon   ,, 115
cursing their lost *t*, and the dead man, ,, 576
cry of children, Enids and Geraints Of *t's* to be ; ,, 966
Groan'd, and at *t's* would mutter, *Balin and Balan* 173
From whence to watch the *t*,   ,, 535
Many a *t* As once—of old—among the flowers— *Merlin and V.* 135
Arriving at a *t* of golden rest,   ,, 142
the most famous man of all those *t's*, ,, 166
at *t's* Would flatter his own wish in age for love, ,, 184
for thus at *t's* He waver'd;   ,, 186
Upon the great Enchanter of the *T*, ,, 216
It was the *t* when first the question rose ,, 410
nine tithes of *t's* Face-flatterer and backbiter ,, 823
when the *t* drew nigh Spake (for she had been sick) *Lancelot and E.* 77
Had marr'd his face, and mark'd it ere his *t*. ,, 247
with half disdain Hid under grace, as in a smaller *t*, ,, 264
Yea, twenty *t's* I thought him Lancelot— ,, 535
Fare you well A thousand *t's*—a thousand *t's* farewell ! ,, 696
at *t's* Brain-feverous in his heat and agony, ,, 853
The simples and the science of that *t*, ,, 862
drave her ere her *t* across the fields   ,, 890
he answer'd ' ten *t's* nay ! This is not love: ,, 948
and at *t's*, So touch'd were they,   ,, 1286
many a *t* have watch'd thee at the tilt ,, 1359
then the *t's* Grew to such evil that the holy cup *Holy Grail* 56
each of these a hundred winters old, From our Lord's *t*. ,, 89
beam of light seven *t's* more clear than day: ,, 187
But my *t* is hard at hand, And hence I go; ,, 481
Embraced me, and so kiss'd me the first *t*, ,, 596

Time (s) (*continued*) For every fiery prophet in old *t's*, *Holy Grail* 876
Come, as they will, and many a *t* they come, „ 911
'In happy *t* behold our pilot-star! *Pelleas and E.* 63
So for the last *t* she was gracious to him. „ 175
Modred thought, 'The *t* is hard at hand.' „ 610
in *t* the carcanet Vext her with plaintive memories *Last Tournament* 28
They served their use, their *t*; „ 676
Many a *t* for hours, Beside the placid breathings *Guinevere* 68
till her *t* To tell you:' „ 142
(for the *t* Was maytime, and as yet no sin „ 387
Bear with me for the last *t* while I show, „ 454
And be the fair beginning of a *t*. „ 466
Dwelt with them, till in *t* their Abbess died. „ 692
Shall never more, at any future *t*, *Pass. of Arthur* 186
And hid Excalibur the second *t*, „ 279
caught him by the hilt, and brandish'd him Three *t's*, (repeat) „ 314, 329
'tis *t* that I were gone. „ 331
For now I see the true old *t's* are dead, „ 397
Such *t's* have been not since the light „ 400
Touch'd by the adulterous finger of a *t* *To the Queen* ii 43
That saved her many *t's*, not fail— „ 62
For *T* and Grief abode too long with Life, *Lover's Tale* i 107
So *T* and Grief did beckon unto Death, „ 110
Yet is my life nor in the present *t*, „ 116
Heart beating *t* to heart, lip pressing lip, „ 260
that little hour was bound Shut in from *T*, „ 438
strait girth of *T* Inswathe the fulness of Eternity. „ 482
To centre in this place and *t*. „ 552
And heralded the distance of this *t*! „ 562
I seem'd the only part of *T* stood still, „ 573
Long *t* entrancement held me. „ 626
From that *t* forth I would not see her more; „ ii 1
(As I have seen them many a hundred *t's*) „ 145
ill-suited as it seem'd To such a *t*, „ iv 208
Laud me not Before my *t*, but hear me to the close. „ 243
Those were the pleasant *t's*, *First Quarrel* 41
in the pleasant *t's* that had past, „ 55
I was near my *t* wi' the boy, „ 82
little of us left by the *t* this sun be set.' *The Revenge* 28
For a dozen *t's* they came with their pikes and musqueteers,
And a dozen *t's* we shook 'em off „ 53
That *t* I did not see. *Sisters* (E. and E.) 90
Sträänge an' cowd fur the *t*! *Village Wife* 21
but the foe sprung his mine many *t's*, *Def. of Lucknow* 31
(My good friend By this *t* should be with me.) *Sir J. Oldcastle* 139
Set thee in light till *t* shall be no more? *Columbus* 150
Towers of a happier *t*, low down in a rainbow deep *V. of Maeldune* 79
O never was *t* so good! „ 87
And we came in an evil *t* to the Isle „ 105
finite-infinite space In finite-infinite *T*— *De Prof., Two G.* 46
the lost light of those dawn-golden *t's*, *To W. H. Brookfield* 7
for the sake Of one recalling gracious *t's*, *To E. Fitzgerald* 53
And mixt the dream of classic *t's* *Tiresias* 194
To women, the flower of the *t*, *The Wreck* 49
glory and shame dying out for ever in endless *t*, *Despair* 75
I have had some glimmer, at *t's*, „ 103
A Thousand summers ere the *t* of Christ *Ancient Sage* 1
cock has crow'd already once, he crows before his *t*; *The Flight* 3
Not he, not yet! and *t* to act— „ 73
many's the *t* that I watch'd her at mass *Tomorrow* 29
fur it mun be the *t* about now When Molly *Spinster's S's.* 1
Naäy to be sewer it be past 'er *t*. „ 5
triumphs over *t* and space, *Locksley H., Sixty* 75
Then, and here in Edward's *t*, „ 83
we range with Science, glorying in the *T*, „ 217
Lame and old, and past his *t*, „ 227
remember how the course of *T* will swerve, „ 235
The man in Space and *T*, *Epilogue* 49
Dead, who had served his *t*, *Dead Prophet* 9
Love is in and out of *t*, *Helen's Tower* 5
'Light—more Light—while *T* shall last!' *Epit. on Caxton* 1
At *t's* our Britain cannot rest, At *t's* her steps are swift and rash; *To Marq. of Dufferin* 1
But since your name will grow with *T*, „ 13

Time (s) (*continued*) Fifty *t's* the rose has flower'd and faded, Fifty *t's* the golden harvest fallen, *On Jub. Q. Victoria* 1
drew down before his *t* Sickening, *Demeter and P.* 114
fun' upo' four short legs ten *t's* fur one upo' two. *Owd Roä* 16
I thowt o' the good owd *t's* 'at was goan, „ 43
an' the *t's* 'at was coomin' on; „ 44
a jubilant challenge to *T* and to Fate; *Vastness* 21
Twelve *t's* in the year Bring me bliss, *The Ring* 5
Moon, you fade at *t's* From the night. „ 9
landscape which your eyes Have many a *t* ranged over „ 151
At *t's* too shrilling in her angrier moods, „ 395
Up, get up, the *t* is short, *Forlorn* 73
I tolerant of the colder *t*, *To Ulysses* 13
As I shall be forgotten by old *T*, *To Mary Boyle* 23
When Dives loathed the *t's*, „ 29
in their *t* thy warblers rise on wing. *Prog. of Spring* 108
The true Alcestis of the *t*. *Romney's R.* 91
a proof That I—even I—at *t's* remember'd you. „ 93
I sank with the body at *t's* in the sloughs *By an Evolution.* 18
At *t's* the small black fly upon the pane *To one who ran down Eng.* 3
Ever as of old *t*, Solitary firstling, *The Snowdrop* 3
Coming in the cold *t*, Prophet of the gay *t*, Prophet of the May *t*, „ 5
But in due *t* for every Mussulmân, *Akbar's Dream* 24
Still—at *t's* A doubt, a fear,— „ 168
even As in the *t* before; „ 191
in the flame that measures *T*! „ Hymn 8
They heard, they bided their *t*. *Bandit's Death* 14
there is *t* for the race to grow. *The Dawn* 20
that Eternal Harmony Whereto the worlds beat *t*, *D. of the Duke of C.* 16
For tho' from out our bourne of *T* and Place *Crossing the Bar* 13
Time (verb) Death's twin-brother, *t's* my breath; *In Mem.* lxviii 2
Timeless Kneel adoring Him the *T* *Akbar's D., Hymn* 8
Timid and said to him With *t* firmness, *Geraint and E.* 140
Amy loved me, Amy fail'd me, Amy was a *t* child; *Locksley H., Sixty* 19
Timing happy stars, *t* with things below, *Maud* I xviii 81
Timour-Mammon *T-M* grins on a pile of children's bones, „ i 46
Timur *T* built his ghastly tower of eighty *Locksley H., Sixty* 82
Tin polish'd *t's*, To serve the hot-and-hot; *Will Water.* 227
Tinct blazon'd on the shield In their own *t*, *Lancelot and E.* 10
Tinged *t* with wan from lack of sleep, *Princess* iii 25
Tingle and the nerves prick And *t*: *In Mem.* l 3
Tingling A cry that shiver'd to the *t* stars, *M. d'Arthur* 199
A cry that shiver'd to the *t* stars, *Pass. of Arthur* 367
Tinkled *See* Low-tinkled
Tinkling Now by some *t* rivulet, *Sir L. and Q. G.* 29
Nor rivulet *t* from the rock; *In Mem.* c 13
Here at the head of a *t* fall, *Maud* I xxi 6
Tinsel And shrill'd his *t* shaft. *Talking Oak* 68
Light coin, the *t* clink of compliment. *Princess* ii 55
Tint (s) days have vanish'd, tone and *t*, *In Mem.* xliv 5
Tint (verb) As light a flush As hardly *t's* the blossom *Balin and Balan* 267
Tintagil held *T* castle by the Cornish sea, *Com. of Arthur* 187
Uther in his wrath and heat besieged Ygerne within *T*, „ 199
on the night When Uther in *T* past away „ 367
by strong storm Blown into shelter at *T*, *Merlin and V.* 10
Perchance in lone *T* far from all The tonguesters *Last Tournament* 392
turning, past and gain'd *T*, half in sea, „ 505
sands Of dark *T* by the Cornish sea; *Guinevere* 294
Tinted *See* Rosy-tinted
Tiny Claps her *t* hands above me, *Lilian* 4
Annie from her baby's forehead clipt A *t* curl, and gave it *Enoch Arden* 236
Or from the *t* pitted target blew *Aylmer's Field* 93
She tapt her *t* silken-sandal'd foot: *Princess, Pro.* 150
a *t* poem All composed in a metre of Catullus, *Hendecasyllabics* 3
The *t* cell is forlorn, *Maud* II ii 13
Save that one rivulet from a *t* cave *Pelleas and E.* 425
whereon There tript a hundred *t* silver deer, *Last Tournament* 171
t fist Had graspt a daisy from your Mother's grave— *The Ring* 322
The starling claps his *t* castanets. *Prog. of Spring* 56
Will my *t* spark of being wholly vanish *God and the Univ.* 1
Tiny-trumpeting The *t-t* gnat can break our dream *Lancelot and E.* 137

Tip (*See also* **Finger-tips**) thro' her to the *t*'s of her
long hands,   *Princess ii* 40
Thy gloom is kindled at the *t*'s,   *In Mem. xxxix* 11
Tipmost to *t* lance and topmost helm,   *Last Tournament* 442
Tipt And *t* with frost-like spires.   *Palace of Art* 52
with their fires Love *t* his keenest darts ;   *D. of F. Women* 173
t with lessening peak And pinnacle,   *Gareth and L.* 308
and *t* With trenchant steel,   " 692
spear and helmet *t* With stormy light   *Tiresias* 113
Tip-tilted *T-t* like the petal of a flower ;   *Gareth and L.* 591
Tiptoe on every peak a statue seem'd To hang on *t*,   *Palace of Art* 38
On *t* seem'd to touch upon a sphere   *Princess vii* 324
Tire Bore and forebore, and did not *t*,   *Two Voices* 218
For a love that never *t*'s ?   *Window, Marr. Morn.* 18
But mine the love that will not *t*,   *In Mem. cx* 18
Tired *t* out With cutting eights that day   *The Epic* 9
Than *t* eyelids upon *t* eyes ;   *Lotos-Eaters, C. S.* 6
At last, *t* out with play,   *Talking Oak* 206
Ascending *t*, heavily slept till morn.   *Enoch Arden* 181
' *T*, Annie ? ' for she did not speak a word.   " 390
' *T* ? ' but her face had fall'n upon her hands ;   " 391
T of so much within our little life,   *Lucretius* 226
I began to be *t* a little,   *Grandmother* 74
I seem to be *t* a little,   " 99
Tirra lirra ' *T l*,' by the river Sang Sir Lancelot.   *L. of Shalott iii* 35
Tissue In silver *t* talking things of state ;   *Marr. of Geraint* 663
Tit tumble the blossom, the mad little *t*'s !   *Window, Ay* 9
T's, wrens, and all wing'd nothings peck   *Marr. of Geraint* 275
glance the *t*'s, and shriek the jays,   *Prog. of Spring* 15
Titan (adj.) Whose *T* angels, Gabriel, Abdiel,   *Milton* 5
Titan (s) The pulses of a *T*'s heart ;   *In Mem. ciii* 32
Weird *T* by thy winter weight of years   *To Victor Hugo* 7
Titanic *T* forces taking birth In divers seasons,   *Day Dm., L'Envoi* 17
T shapes, they cramm'd The forum,   *Princess vii* 124
Tithe (church rate) (*See also* **Toithe**) paid our *t*'s in the
days that are gone,   *Maud II v* 23
Fur moäst on 'em talks ageän *t*,   *Church-warden, etc.* 52
Tithe (tenth part) nine *t*'s of times Face-flatterer and
backbiter   *Merlin and V.* 823
Wasted and worn, and but a *t* of them,   *Holy Grail* 723
And a lean Order—scarce return'd a *t*—   " 894
When I landed again, with a *t* of my men,   *V. of Maeldune* 130
Titian I am not Raphaël, *T*—no   *Romney's R.* 46
Titianic in hues to dim The *T* Flora.   *Gardener's D.* 171
Title Nor toil for *t*, place, or touch Of pension,   *Love thou thy land* 93
New as his *t*, built last year,   *Maud I x* 19
a Prince indeed, Beyond all *t*'s,   *Ded. of Idylls* 42
her name And *t*, ' Queen of Beauty,'   *Pelleas and E.* 116
heirless flaw In his throne's *t*   *Sir J. Oldcastle* 73
Our *t*, which we never mean to yield,   *Columbus* 32
scarce have learnt the *t* of your book,   *The Ring* 126
Title-scroll *t-s*'s and gorgeous heraldries.   *Aylmer's Field* 656
Titmouse *t* hope to win her With his chirrup   *Maud I xx* 29
Titter and then A strangled *t*,   *Princess v* 16
Tityrus Poet of the happy *T* piping underneath   *To Virgil* 13
To-and-fro commenced A *t-a-f*, so pacing   *Princess iii* 302
'Toättler (teetotaler) Doctor's a '*t*, lass,   *N. Farmer, O. S.* 66
To-be Dispensing harvest, sowing the *T-b*,   *Princess vii* 289
Thro' all the secular *t-b*,   *In Mem. xli* 23
To-come and all the rich *t-c* Reels,   *Princess vii* 356
To-daay (to-day) As I says to my missis *t-d*,   *Church-warden, etc.* 25
Todaäy (to-day) Seeäd her *t* goä by—   *N. Farmer, N. S.* 13
To-day (*See also* **To-daay, Todaäy**) To-morrow yet
would reap *t-d*,   *Love thou thy land* 93
' *T-d* I saw the dragon-fly   *Two Voices* 8
Herè comes *t-d*, Pallas and Aphroditè,   *Œnone* 85
I care not if I go *t-d*.   *May Queen, Con.* 43
' The sequel of *t-d* unsolders all   *M. d'Arthur* 14
I die here *T-d*, and whole years long,   *St. S. Stylites* 54
T-d I sat for an hour and wept,   *Edward Gray* 11
Cruelly came they back *t-d* :   " 18
T-d the Lady Psyche will harangue   *Princess ii* 95
to slip away *T-d*, to-morrow, gone ;   " 297
And told me she would answer us *t-d*,   " *iii* 166
Let us dream our dream *t-d*.   *Ode Inter. Exhib.* 31

To-day (*continued*) See, empire upon empire
smiles *t-d*,   *W. to Marie Alex.* 33
All along the valley, while I walk'd *t-d*,   *V. of Cauteretz* 5
Be merry, all birds, *t-d*,   *Window, Ay* 1
thinking ' here *t-d*,' Or ' here to-morrow   *In Mem. vi* 23
That thou hadst touch'd the land *t-d*,   " *xiv* 2
Nor will it lessen from *t-d* ;   " *lix* 10
T-d they count as kindred souls ;   " *xcix* 19
That has *t-d* its sunny side.   *Con.* 72
T-d the grave is bright for me,   " 73
Strange, that I tried *t-d* To beguile her   *Maud I xx* 2
So well thine arm hath wrought for me *t-d*.'   *Com. of Arthur* 127
By this King Arthur as by thee *t-d*,   " 162
' Forward ! and *t-d* I charge you,   *Geraint and E.* 413
A man of thine *t-d* Abash'd us both,   *Balin and Balan* 70
' Eyes have I That saw *t-d* the shadow of a spear,   " 373
He cares not for me : only here *t-d*   *Lancelot and E.* 126
grace to me,' She answer'd, ' twice *t-d*.   " 384
So great a knight as we have seen *t-d*—   " 533
speak your wish, Seeing I go *t-d* : '   " 925
But who first saw the holy thing *t-d* ? '   *Holy Grail* 67
hence he went *T-d* for three days' hunting—   *Last Tournament* 530
' The sequel of *t-d* unsolders all   *Pass. of Arthur* 182
Thrust froward on *t-d* and out of place ;   *Lover's Tale i* 123
As here *t-d*, but not so wordily—   " *iv* 355
' O worms and maggots of *t-d*   *Ancient Sage* 210
T-d ? but what of yesterday ?   " 216
There again I stood *t-d*,   *Locksley H., Sixty* 33
Here *t-d* was Amy with me,   " 53
Those eyes the blue *t-d*,   *Epilogue* 9
happier lot Than ours, who rhyme *t-d*,   " 51
The days that seem *t-d*,   *Pref. Poem Broth. Son.* 24
Miriam, breaks her latest earthy link With me *t-d*.   *The Ring* 48
For I myself would tell you all *t-d*.   " 124
' She too might speak *t-d*,'   " 125
Ay, *t-d* ! I brought you to that chamber   " 128
but close to me *t-d* As this red rose,   *Roses on the T.* 6
T-d, before you turn again To thoughts   *To Master of B.* 13
and wield The forces of *t-d*,   *Mechanophilus* 30
Toddle Poor little life that *t*'s half an hour   *Lucretius* 228
Toil (s) But enter not the *t* of life.   *Margaret* 24
And one, the reapers at their sultry *t*.   *Palace of Art* 77
Making sweet close of his delicious *t*'s—   " 185
Ripens and fades, and falls, and hath no *t*,   *Lotos-Eaters, C. S.* 37
and reap the harvest with enduring *t*,   " 121
surely, slumber is more sweet than *t*,   " 126
a Rose In roses, mingled with her fragrant *t*,   *Gardener's D.* 143
Old age hath yet his honour and his *t* ;   *Ulysses* 50
I must work thro' months of *t*,   *Amphion* 97
And mutual love and honourable *t* ;   *Enoch Arden* 83
On with *t* of heart and knees and hands,   *Ode on Well.* 212
O thou that after *t* and storm   *In Mem. xxxiii* 1
Is *t* cöoperant to an end.   " *cxxviii* 10
As careful robins eye the delver's *t*,   *Marr. of Geraint* 774
As careful robins eye the delver's *t* ;   *Geraint and E.* 431
body journeying onward, sick with *t*.   *Lover's Tale i* 124
T and ineffable weariness,   *Def. of Lucknow* 90
If night, what barren *t* to be !   *Tiresias* 207
Toil (verb) I said, ' I *t* beneath the curse,   *Two Voices* 229
why should we *t* alone, We only *t*,   *Lotos-Eaters, C. S.* 15
Why should we only *t*,   " 24
Nor *t* for title, place, or touch Of pension,   *Love thou thy land* 93
Who *t*'s across the middle moonlit nights,   *Lover's Tale i* 138
Toil'd *T* onward, prick'd with goads and stings ;   *Palace of Art* 150
Souls that have *t*, and wrought,   *Ulysses* 46
t Mastering the lawless science of our law,   *Aylmer's Field* 434
Has often *t* to clothe your little ones ;   " 699
Toiling late and soon Spins, *t* out his own cocoon.   *Two Voices* 180
A motion *t* in the gloom—   *Love thou thy land* 54
T in immeasurable sand,   *Will* 16
Of loyal vassals *t* for their liege.   *Com. of Arthur* 282
Toime (time) i' the woost o' *t*'s I wur niver   *N. Farmer, O. S.* 16
Toithe (tithe) an's *t* were due, an' I gied it in hond ;   " 11
an' ageän the *t* an' the raäte,   *Church-warden, etc.* 11
Token There came a sweeter *t* when the night   *May Queen, Con.* 22

Token (*continued*) There came a mystic *t* from the king | *Edwin Morris* 132
It will moreover be a *t* to her, That I am he.' | *Enoch Arden* 900
Sunny *t's* of the Line, | *Ode Inter. Exhib.* 19
Who show'd a *t* of distress ? | *In Mem. lxxviii* 13
In *t* of true heart and feälty. | *Gareth and L.* 399
pray the King To let me bear some *t* of his
  Queen | *Balin and Balan* 188
Thro' memory of that *t* on the shield | „ 369
then he bound Her *t* on h s helmet, | *Lancelot and E.* 374
know When these have worn their *t's* : | „ 769

Told (*See also* **Re-told, Tell'd, Tould, Towd**) I *t* thee—
  hardly nigher made, | *Two Voices* 173
Sweet Alice, if I *t* her all ?' | *Miller's D.* 120
My love hath *t* me so a thousand times. | *Œnone* 197
the clergyman, has *t* me words of peace. | *May Queen, Con.* 12
wheresoever I am sung or *t* In aftertime, | *M. d'Arthur* 34
And *t* me I should love. | *Gardener's D.* 64
The cuckoo *t* his name to all the hills ; | „ 93
This is not *t* of any. They were saints. | *St. S. Stylites* 151
And *t* him of my choice, | *Talking Oak* 18
and that same song of his He *t* me ; | *Golden Year* 8
She *t* him of their tears, And pray'd him, | *Godiva* 19
And *t* him all her nurse's tale. | *Lady Clare* 80
She *t* me all her friends had said ; | *The Letters* 25
T him, with other annals of the port, | *Enoch Arden* 702
tho' Miriam Lane had *t* him all, | „ 765
Then he *t* her of his voyage, His wreck, | „ 861
' She *t* me. She and James had quarrell'd. | *The Brook* 96
he *t* a long long-winded tale Of how the Squire | „ 138
And been himself a part of what he *t*. | *Aylmer's Field* 12
t her fairy-tales, Show'd her the fairy footings | „ 89
as he *t* The story, storming a hill-fort | „ 224
praised the waning red, and *t* The vintage— | „ 406
Then she *t* it, having dream'd Of that same coast. | *Sea Dreams* 206
My golden work in which I *t* a truth | *Lucretius* 260
but we, unworthier, *t* Of college : | *Princess, Pro.* 110
And often *t* a tale from mouth to mouth | „ 191
have him back Who *t* the ' Winter's tale ' | „ 238
But your example pilot, *t* her all. | „ iii 137
But such extremes, I *t* her, well might harm | „ 144
And *t* me she would answer us to-day, | „ 166
How came you here ?' I *t* him : | „ iv 221
And me none *t* : not less to an eye like mine | „ 324
you had gone to her, She *t*, perforce ; | „ 330
Go : Cyril *t* us all.' | „ v 36
now a pointed finger, *t* them all : | „ 270
And so I often *t* her, right or wrong, | „ 288
I *t* the king that I was pledged To fight | „ 352
if I saw not, yet they *t* me all | „ vi 20
who might have *t*, For she was cramm'd | „ Con. 34
you *t* us all That England's honest censure | *Third of Feb.* 1
It *t* of England then to me, | *The Daisy* 89
These have *t* us all their anger | *Boädicea* 23
There was one who watch'd and *t* me— | „ 30
He *t* it not ; or something seal'd | *In Mem. xxxi* 15
And tell them all they would have *t*, | „ xl 25
He *t* me, lives in any crowd, | „ xcviii 26
Since first he *t* me that he loved | „ Con. 6
What if he had *t* her yestermorn | *Maud I vi* 50
Who *t* him we were there ? | „ II v 52
Horrible, hateful, monstrous, not to be *t* ; | „ III vi 41
when I enter'd *t* me that himself And Merlin | *Com. of Arthur* 364
nor could I part in peace Till this were *t*.' | „ 394
That God hath *t* the King a secret word. | „ 489
Take thou the truth as thou hast *t* it me. | *Gareth and L.* 257
t, How once the wandering forester at dawn, | „ 497
he sought The king alone, and found, and *t* him all. | „ 541
And *t* him of a cavern hard at hand, | „ 1189
turning to Lynette he *t* The tale of Gareth, | „ 1272
And he that *t* the tale in older times | „ 1427
But he, that *t* it later, says Lynette. | „ 1429
T Enid, and they sadden'd her the more : | *Marr. of Geraint* 64
journey to her, as himself Had *t* her, | „ 144
these things he *t* the King. | „ 151
Who *t* him, scouring still, ' The sparrow-hawk !' | „ 260

Told (*continued*) And *t* her all their converse in the hall, | *Marr. of Geraint* 520
journey toward her, as himself Had *t* her, | „ 846
the boy return'd And *t* them of a chamber, | *Geraint and E.* 261
t Free tales, and took the word and play'd | „ 290
She *t* him all that Earl Limours had said, | „ 391
nor *t* his gentle wife What ail'd him, | „ 503
then he plainlier *t* How the huge Earl lay slain | „ 805
therewithal (for thus he *t* us) brought | *Balin and Balan* 112
Then Balan *t* him brokenly, and in gasps, | „ 603
this good knight *T* me, that twice a wanton damsel | „ 609
For Merlin once had *t* her of a charm, | *Merlin and V.* 205
Than when I *t* you first of such a charm. | „ 359
Too much I trusted when I *t* you that, | „ 361
' O crueller than was ever *t* in tale, | „ 858
t her all the charm, and slept. | „ 966
What is it ? and she *t* him ' A red sleeve
  Broider'd with pearls,' | *Lancelot and E.* 372
Than Lancelot *t* me of a common talk | „ 577
there *t* the King What the King knew, | „ 706
But when the maid had *t* him all her tale, | „ 798
And when the maid had *t* him all the tale | „ 823
T him that her fine care had saved his life. | „ 863
I *t* her that her love Was but the flash of youth, | „ 1317
T us of this in our refectory, | *Holy Grail* 41
And he to whom she *t* her sins, or what | „ 83
' O brother, when I *t* him what had chanced, | „ 271
To whom I *t* my phantoms, and he said : | „ 444
T him he follow'd—almost Arthur's words— | „ 669
So when I *t* him all thyself hast heard, | „ 736
' Lo ! Pelleas is dead—he *t* us— | *Pelleas and E.* 377
Sir Lancelot *t* This matter to the Queen, | *Guinevere* 53
Vivien, lurking, heard. She *t* Sir Modred. | „ 99
Nor with them mix'd, nor *t* her name, | „ 148
and the tales Which my good father *t* me, | „ 317
T, when the man was no more than a voice | *Pass. of Arthur* 3
wheresoever I am sung or *t* In aftertime, | „ 202
Once or twice she *t* me (For I remember all
  things) | *Lover's Tale i* 345
The wind *T* a lovetale beside us, | „ 543
What marvel my Camilla *t* me all ? (repeat) | „ 557, 579
She *t* me all her love : she shall not weep. | „ 742
Unfrequent, low, as tho' it *t* its pulses ; | „ ii 55
Some one had *t* me she was dead, | „ 70
I *t* him all my love, How I had loved her | „ 90
but of this I deem As of the visions that he *t*— | „ iv 23
(They *t* her somewhat rashly as I think) | „ 98
(I *t* you that he had his golden hour), | „ 206
till he *t* me that so many years had gone by, | *First Quarrel* 36
An' he *t* it me all at once, as simple as any child, | „ 58
and he never has *t* me a lie. | *Rizpah* 24
I *t* them my tale, God's own truth— | „ 33
they have *t* you he never repented his sin. | „ 69
Then *t* them of his wars, and of his wound. | *Sisters (E. and E.)* 60
I *t* your wayside story to my mother And Evelyn | „ 189
And *t* the living daughter with what love | „ 253
' All the more need,' I *t* him, | *In the Child. Hosp.* 18
their marksmen were *t* of our best, | *Def. of Lucknow* 19
is it true what was *t* by the scout, | „ 95
tale, that *t* to me, When but thine age, | *Tiresias* 18
souls of men were immortal, as men have been *t*, | *Despair* 99
And then he *t* their legend : | *The Ring* 206
I *t* her ' sent To Miriam,' | „ 362
I *t* her of my vow, | „ 401
I have *t* you my tale. Get you gone. | *Charity* 44

Told-of and cursed the tale, The *t-o*, | *Balin and Balan* 543

Tolerance must have rated her Beyond all *t*. | *Aylmer's Field* 381
This Gama swamp'd in lazy *t*. | *Princess v* 443

Tolerant *T* of what he half disdain'd, | *Merlin and V.* 178
I *t* of the colder time, | *To Ulysses* 13

Toll (s) ' Honour,' she said, ' and homage, tax and *t*, | *Œnone* 116
With silks, and fruits, and spices, clear of *t*, | *Golden Year* 45
The *t* of funeral in an Angel ear | *D. of the Duke of C.* 10

Toll (*verb*) *T* ye the church-bell sad and slow, | *D. of the O. Year* 3
One set slow bell will seem to *t* | *In Mem. lvii* 10
Would you could *t* me out of life, | *Lover's Tale iv* 30

Toll (verb) (*continued*) when they *t* the Chapel bell ! *Locksley H., Sixty* 261
Toll'd like a bell *T* by an earthquake in a trembling
  tower,   *Princess vi* 332
  Let the bell be *t*. (repeat)   *Ode on Well.* 46, 53, 58
  by slow degrees the sullen bell *T* quicker,   *Lover's Tale iii* 14
Tolling thence at intervals A low bell *t*.
                ,,   *ii* 83
  Then came on me The hollow *t* of the bell,   ,,   *iii* 10
  Heard yet once more the *t* bell,   ,,   *iv* 29
  For that low knell *t* his lady dead—   ,,   33
  t of his funeral bell Broke on my Pagan Paradise,   *Tiresias* 192
  Bridal bells with *t* ! . . .   *Forlorn* 70
Tom (name of men and cats) (*See also* **Tommy**) *T*, lig
  theere o' the cushion, an' tother *T* 'ere o' the mat. *Spinster's S's.* 94
  Sweäring agean, you *T's*,   ,,   59
Tomb Shut up as in a crumbling *t*,   *Palace of Art* 273
  And in the moon athwart the place of *t's*,   *M. d'Arthur* 46
  rising bore him thro' the place of *t's*.   ,,   175
  Shall hold their orgies at your *t*.   *You might have won* 12
  Remains the lean P. W. on his *t* :   *The Brook* 192
  her, that is the womb and *t* of all,   *Lucretius* 244
  near his *t* a feast Shone, silver-set ;   *Princess, Pro.* 105
  her empty glove upon the *t* Lay by her   ,,   *iv* 596
  I go to plant it on his *t*,   *In Mem. viii* 22
  In that deep dawn behind the *t*,   ,,   *xlvi* 6
  My old affection of the *t*, (repeat)   ,, *lxxxv* 75, 77
  As it were a duty done to the *t*,   *Maud I xix* 49
  ' Let her *t* Be costly, and her image thereupon, *Lancelot and E.* 1339
  all true hearts be blazon'd on her *t* In letters gold
    and azure ! '   ,,   1344
  And in the moon athwart the place of *t's*,   *Pass. of Arthur* 214
  rising bore him thro' the place of *t's*.   ,,   343
  break down and raze The blessed *t* of Christ ;   *Columbus* 99
  I was planted now in a *t* ;   *The Wreck* 37
  And growing, on her *t*,   *Ancient Sage* 164
  heard in silence from the silence of a *t*. *Locksley H., Sixty* 74
  Angel seated in the vacant *t*.   ,,   278
  I peer'd thro' *t* and cave,   *Demeter and P.* 70
  ' Among the *t's* in this damp vale of yours !   *The Ring* 325
Tombing The blackness round the *t* sod,   *On a Mourner* 27
Tome at a board by *t* and paper sat,   *Princess ii* 32
Tommy (lovers and cats) (*See also* **Tom**) *T* the fust, an' *T*
  the second,   *Spinster's S's.* 10
  and one o' the *Tommies* beside.   ,,   40
  I mun part them *Tommies*—   ,,   92
  Hed I married the *Tommies*—O Lord,   ,,   95
  To loove an' obaäy the *Tommies* !   ,,   96
  You *Tommies* shall waäit to-night   ,,   120
Tommy (name of boy) *T's* faäce be as fresh as a codlin *North. Cobbler* 110
  'Ere be our Sally an' *T*,   ,,   111
Tomohrit *T*, Athos, all things fair,   *To E. L.* 5
Tomorra (to-morrow) ye gev her the top of the mornin', ' *T* '
  says she.   *Tomorrow* 3
  I'll meet you agin *t*,' says she,   ,,   16
  ye'll meet me *t* ? '   ' *T, t*, Machree ! '   ,,   18
  an' whishper, an' say ' *T, T* ! '   ,,   55
  ' *T, T*,' she says, an' she didn't intind   ,,   59
  ' He said he would meet me *t* ! '   ,,   80
To-morrow (*See also* **Morrow, Tomorra**) I come *t-m* morn.
  ' I go, but I return :   *Audley Court* 70
  We two will wed *t-m* morn,   *Lady Clare* 87
  We hold a tourney here *t-m* morn,   *Marr. of Geraint* 287
  T-m 'ill be the happiest time of all the glad New-
    year ; (repeat)   *May Queen* 2, 42
  Effie shall go with me *t-m* to the green,   ,,   25
  T-m 'ill be of all the year the maddest merriest day,   ,,   43
  T-m yet would reap to-day,   *Love thou thy land* 93
  ' *T-m* he weds with me.'   *Lady Clare* 16
  to slip away To-day, *t-m*, soon :   *Princess ii* 297
  ' *T-m*, love, *t-m*, And that's an age away.'   *Window, When* 13
  thinking, ' here to-day,' Or ' here *t-m*   *In Mem. vi* 24
  But *t-m*, if we live,   *Maud I xx* 23
  Lancelot, sitting in my place Enchair'd *t-m*,   *Last Tournament* 104
  Hail, King !   *T-m* thou shalt pass away.   *Pass. of Arthur* 34
  I'll come for an hour *t-m*,   *First Quarrel* 46
  Nurse, I must do it *t-m* ;   *In the Child. Hosp.* 42

To-morrow (*continued*) Not to-night in Locksley
  Hall—*t-m*—   *Locksley H., Sixty* 214
  Here to-night, the Hall *t-m*,   ,,   261
Tomyris bronze valves, emboss'd with *T*   *Princess v* 365
Ton Than were those lead-like *t's* of sin,   *St. S. Stylites* 25
  San Philip that, of fifteen hundred *t's*,   *The Revenge* 40
Tone (*See also* **Under-tone**) Wears all day a fainter *t*.   *The Owl ii* 7
  Sweeter *t's* than calumny ?   *A Dirge* 17
  Ah pity—hint it not in human *t's*,   *Wan Sculptor* 11
  ' O cruel heart,' she changed her *t*,   *Mariana in the S.* 69
  ' He heeded not reviling *t's*,   *Two Voices* 220
  All day the wind breathes low with mellower *t* : *Lotos-Eaters, C. S.* 102
  fall down and glance From *t* to *t*,   *D. of F. Women* 167
  it was the *t* with which he read—   *M. d'Arthur, Ep.* 5
  Swung themselves, and in low *t's* replied ;   *Vision of Sin* 20
  There to herself, all in low *t's*, she read.   *Princess vii* 175
  To one clear harp in divers *t's*,   *In Mem. i* 2
  With all the music in her *t*,   ,,   *iii* 10
  The days have vanish'd, *t* and tint,   ,,   *xliv* 5
  He past ; a soul of nobler *t* :   ,,   *lx* 1
  Perhaps the smile and tender *t*   *Maud I vi* 63
  Then the King in low deep *t's*,   *Com. of Arthur* 260
  she tower'd her bells, *T* under *t*, shrill'd ;   *Merlin and V.* 132
  Then came her father, saying in low *t's*,   *Lancelot and E.* 994
  Is this the *t* of empire ?   *To the Queen ii* 18
  in the utterance Of silver-chorded *t's* :   *Lover's Tale ii* 142
  a *t* so rough that I broke into passionate tears,   *The Wreck* 122
Toned *See* **Full-toned, Heavenly-toned, Low-toned, Richest-toned**
Tongue (s) Thou of the many *t's*, the myriad eyes !   *Ode to Memory* 47
  Like Indian reeds blown from his silver *t*,   *The Poet* 13
  My tremulous *t* faltereth,   *Eleänore* 136
  For Kate hath an unbridled *t*,   *Kate* 7
  ' When, wide in soul and bold of *t*,   *Two Voices* 124
  Blowing a noise of *t's* and deeds,   ,,   206
  To feel, altho' no *t* can prove,   ,,   445
  That run before the fluttering *t's* of fire ;   *D. of F. Women* 30
  A golden bill ! the silver *t*,   *The Blackbird* 13
  and servile to a shrewish *t* !   *Locksley Hall* 42
  'Tis said he had a tuneful *t*,   *Amphion* 17
  Let me loose thy *t* with wine !   *Vision of Sin* 88
  ' Fear not thou to loose thy *t* ;   ,,   155
  But in a *t* no man can understand ;   ,,   222
  I would that my *t* could utter The thoughts   *Break, break, etc.* 3
  his long-bounden *t* Was loosen'd,   *Enoch Arden* 644
  Fairer his talk, a *t* that ruled the hour,   *Aylmer's Field* 194
  My *t* Trips, or I speak profanely,   *Lucretius* 73
  Not in this frequence can I lend full *t*,   *Princess iv* 442
  And every spoken *t* should lord you.   ,,   544
  On flying Time from all their silver *t's*—   ,,   *vii* 105
  his triumph will be sung By some yet unmoulded *t*   *Ode on Well.* 233
  Far, how far no *t* can say,   *Ode Inter. Exhib.* 30
  strong on his legs, but still of his *t* !   *Grandmother* 13
  t is a fire as you know, my dear, the *t*   ,,   28
  Whatever fickle *t's* may say.   *In Mem. xxvi* 4
  To flicker with his double *t*.   ,,   *cx* 8
  seem'd to live A contradiction on the *t*,   ,,   *cxxv* 4
  That made my *t* so stammer and trip   *Maud I vi* 83
  With the evil *t* and the evil ear,   ,,   *x* 51
  Let not my *t* be a thrall to my eye,   ,,   *xvi* 32
  words, Beyond my *t* to tell thee—   *Com. of Arthur* 269
  Graven in the oldest *t* of all this world,   ,,   302
  And Uther slit thy *t* !   *Gareth and L.* 376
  I curse the *t* that all thro' yesterday Reviled thee,   ,,   1322
  as a man upon his *t* May break it,   *Geraint and E.* 42
  man, who driven by evil *t's* From all his fellows, *Balin and Balan* 125
  as the man in life Was wounded by blind *t's* he saw
    not   ,,   130
  Woods have *t's*, As walls have ears :   ,,   530
  neither eyes nor *t*—O stupid child !   *Merlin and V.* 251
  yet, methinks Thy *t* has tript a little :   ,,   602
  and let her *t* Rage like a fire   ,,   801
  heathen caught and reft him of his *t*.   *Lancelot and E.* 273
  prick'd at once, all *t's* were loosed :   ,,   724
  such a *t* To blare its own interpretation—   ,,   942
  rain a scroll Of letters in a *t* no man could read.   *Holy Grail* 171

Took (*continued*) *T*, as in rival heat, to holy things; | *Balin and Balan* 100
He *t* the selfsame track as Balan, | „ 290
She *t* the helm and he the sail; | *Merlin and V.* 200
I *t* his brush and blotted out the bird, | „ 478
A rumour runs, she *t* him for the King, | „ 776
and suddenly she *t* To bitter weeping | „ 854
blood of the wizard at her touch *T* gayer colours, | „ 950
Then of the crowd ye *t* no more account | *Lancelot and E.* 105
She still *t* note that when the living smile Died | „ 323
and *t* the shield, There kept it, | „ 397
he *t*, And gave, the diamond: | „ 550
So those two brethren from the chariot *t* | „ 1146
Stoopt, *t*, brake seal, and read it; | „ 1271
And *t* both ear and eye; and o'er the brook | *Holy Grail* 383
and *t* Gawain's, and said, 'Bétray me not, but help— | *Pelleas and E.* 359
brought A maiden babe; which Arthur pitying *t*, | *Last Tournament* 21
'He *t* them and he drave them to his tower— | „ 68
and his creatures *t* and bare him off, | *Guinevere* 109
that *t* Full easily all impressions from below, | „ 641
She said: they *t* her to themselves; | „ 690
I row'd across And *t* it, and have worn it, | *Pass. of Arthur* 201
Then *t* with care, and kneeling on one knee, | „ 341
Put forth their hands, and *t* the King, | „ 374
made garlands of the selfsame flower, Which she *t* smiling, | *Lover's Tale i* 344
The night in pity *t* away my day, | „ 612
She *t* the body of my past delight, | „ 681
sorrow of my spirit Was of so wide a compass it *t* in | „ *ii* 135
sudden gust that sweeping down *T* the edges of the pall, | „ *iii* 35
t him home, And fed, and cherish'd him, | „ *iv* 263
An' he *t* three turns in the rain, | *First Quarrel* 75
he *t* no life, but he *t* one purse, | *Rizpah* 31
T the breath from our sails, | *The Revenge* 42
So *t* her thence, and brought her here, | *Sisters (E. and E.)* 267
Annie, the heldest, I niver not *t* to she: | *Village Wife* 8
t and hang'd, *T*, hang'd and burnt— | *Sir J. Oldcastle* 45
Who *t* the world so easily heretofore, | „ 89
Who *t* us for the very Gods from Heaven, | *Columbus* 183
And we *t* to playing at ball, and we *t* to throwing the stone, | *V. of Maeldune* 94
And we *t* to playing at battle, | „ 95
I *t* it, he made it a cage, | *The Wreck* 83
They *t* us abroad: the crew were gentle, | „ 129
t and kiss'd me, and again He kiss'd me; | *The Flight* 23
Christian conquerors *t* and flung | *Locksley H., Sixty* 84
You *t* me to that chamber in the tower, | *The Ring* 111
t the ring, and flaunted it Before that other | „ 243
I *t*, I left you there; I came, | „ 347
I *t* And chafed the freezing hand. | „ 451
you *t* them tho' you frown'd; | *Happy* 74

Tool (*See also* **Edge-tools, Garden-tools, Harvest-tool**)
Made Him his catspaw and the Cross his *t*, | *Sea Dreams* 190
Or thou wilt prove their *t*. | *Maud I vi* 59
thou their *t*, set on to plague And play upon, | *Guinevere* 359
He had brought his ghastly *t*'s: | *In the Child. Hosp.* 69
Down, you idle *t*'s, Stampt into dust— | *Romney's R.* 112
Too-officious Life (like a wanton *t-o* friend, | *Lover's Tale i* 627
Too-quick Down hill '*T-q*,' the chain. | *Politics* 12
Too-slow Up hill '*T-s*' will need the whip, | „ 11
Tooth my *teeth*, which now are dropt away, | *St. S. Stylites* 30
stammering 'scoundrel' out of *teeth* that ground | *Aylmer's Field* 328
sprang No dragon warriors from Cadmean *teeth*, | *Lucretius* 50
But in the *teeth* of clench'd antagonisms | *Princess iv* 465
captains flash'd their glittering *teeth*, | „ *v* 20
red in *t* and claw With ravine, | *In Mem. lvi* 15
And took his russet beard between his *teeth*; | *Geraint and E.* 713
He ground his *teeth* together, | *Balin and Balan* 538
thro' the hedge of splinter'd *teeth*, | *Last Tournament* 65
teeth of Hell flay bare and gnash thee flat !— | „ 444
Tooth'd (*See also* **Gap-tooth'd**) and *t* with grinning savagery.' | *Balin and Balan* 197
Toothed And every kiss of *t* wheels, | *In Mem. cxvii* 11

Top (*See also* **Chimney-top, Mountain-top, Reed-tops, Towery-top**) Or over hills with peaky *t*'s engrail'd, | *Palace of Art* 113
' will you climb the *t* of Art. | *Gardener's D.* 169
and here it comes With five at *t*: | *Walk. to the Mail* 113
Strikes through the wood, sets all the *t*'s quivering— | *Lucretius* 186
The *t*'s shall strike from star to star, | *Princess vi* 57
I climb'd to the *t* of the garth, | *Grandmother* 38
A lion ramps at the *t*, | *Maud I xiv* 7
shouted at once from the *t* of the house; | „ *II v* 50
High on the *t* were those three Queens, | *Gareth and L.* 229
Till lost in blowing trees and *t*'s of towers; | „ 670
saw, Bowl-shaped, thro' *t*'s of many thousand pines | „ 796
And on the *t*, a city wall'd: | *Holy Grail* 422
but found at *t* No man, nor any voice. | „ 427
and on the naked mountain *t* Blood-red, | „ 474
Storm at the *t*, and when we gain'd it, | „ 491
Climb'd to the high *t* of the garden-wall | *Guinevere* 25
Flying at *t* of the roofs in the ghastly siege | *Def. of Lucknow* 4
ye gev her the *t* of the mornin', | *Tomorrow* 3
I mashes the winder hin, when I gits to the *t*, | *Owd Roä* 83
I saw beyond their silent *t*'s The steaming marshes | *Prog. of Spring* 74
THERE on the *t* of the down, | *June Bracken, etc.* 1
an' coom'd to the *t* o' the tree, | *Church-warden, etc.* 38
Topaz sardius, Chrysolite, beryl, *t*, | *Columbus* 85
Topaz-lights Myriads of *t-l*, and jacinth-work | *M. d'Arthur* 57
Myriads of *i-l*, and jacinth-work | *Pass. of Arthur* 225
Topic speak, and let the *t* die.' | *Princess iii* 205
Topmost Behind the valley *t* Gargarus Stands up | *Œnone* 10
And thro' the *t* Oriels' coloured flame | *Palace of Art* 161
Whose *t* branches can discern The roofs of Sumner-place ! | *Talking Oak* 31
Long may thy *t* branch discern The roofs of Sumner-place ! | „ 151
High up, the *t* palace spire. | *Day-Dm., Sleep. P.* 48
The *t* elm-tree gather'd green | *Sir L. and Q. G.* 8
and moved Upon the *t* froth of thought. | *In Mem. lii* 4
A sweet voice singing in the *t* tower To the eastward: | *Holy Grail* 834
Even to tipmost lance and *t* helm, | *Last Tournament* 442
HERE far away, seen from the *t* cliff, | *Lover's Tale i* 1
ever upon the *t* roof our banner of England blew. (repeat) | *Def. of Lucknow* 6, 30, 45, 60, 94
That ever upon the *t* roof our banner in India blew. | 72
Cried from the *t* summit with human voices and words: | *V. of Maeldune* 28
And the *t* spire of the mountain was lilies in lieu of snow, | „ 41
and every *t* pine Spired into bluest heaven, | *Death of Œnone* 68
The *t*—a chest there, by which you knelt— | *The Ring* 112
Topple Will *t* to the trumpet down, | *Princess ii* 232
And *t*'s down the scales; | „ *v* 445
A kingdom *t*'s over with a shriek Like an old woman, | „ *Con.* 62
And *t*'s round the dreary west, | *In Mem. xv* 19
I can *t* over a hundred such. | *Gareth and L.* 651
Toppled The spires of ice are *t* down, | *In Mem. cxxvii* 12
Toppling And *t* over all antagonism | *Marr. of Arthur* 491
Shall find the *t* crags of Duty scaled | *Ode on Well.* 215
And, *t* over all antagonism, | *Geraint and E.* 834
Topsy-turvy solid turrets *t-t* in air: | *Gareth and L.* 255
Torch gust of wind Puff'd out his *t* | *Merlin and V.* 731
not to plunge Thy *t* of life in darkness, | *Tiresias* 159
I can but lift the *t* Of Reason | *Akbar's Dream* 120
Tore (*See also* **Out-tore, Raäved**) (With that she *t* her robe apart, | *D. of F. Women* 157
With wakes of fire we *t* the dark; | *The Voyage* 52
t, As if the living passion symbol'd there | *Aylmer's Field* 534
ran in, Beat breast, *t* hair, | *Lucretius* 277
T the king's letter, snow'd it down, | *Princess i* 61
Took half-amazed, and in her lion's mood *T* open, | „ *iv* 381
T from the branch, and cast on earth, | *Balin and Balan* 539
Leaf after leaf, and *t*, and cast them off, | *Lancelot and E.* 1199
then this gale *T* my pavilion from the tenting-pin, | *Holy Grail* 747
The rough brier *t* my bleeding palms; | *Lover's Tale ii* 18
And we *t* up the flowers by the million | *V. of Maeldune* 53

Tore (*continued*)   She crouch'd, she *t* him part from part,   *Dead Prophet* 69
   She *t* the Prophet after death,   "   77
Torment   when strength is shock'd With *t*,   *Lover's Tale ii* 151
   and infinite *t* of flies,   *Def. of Lucknow* 82
   all the hateful fires Of *t*,   *Demeter and P.* 152
   contemplate The *t* of the damn'd'   *Akbar's Dream* 49
Tormented   *See* **Long-tormented**
Torn (*See also* **Raäved, Teär'd, Turn**) who smiled when she
   was *t* in three ;   *Poland* 12
   T from the fringe of spray.   *D. of F. Women* 40
   All the air was *t* in sunder,   *The Captain* 43
   I was drench'd with ooze, and *t* with briers,   *Princess v* 28
   and the household flower *T* from the lintel—   "   129
   her blooming mantle *t*,   "   *vi* 145
   The Mayfly is *t* by the swallow,   *Maud I iv* 23
   By which our houses are *t* :   "   *xix* 33
   a Shape that fled With broken wings, *t* raiment   *Gareth and L.* 1208
   would have *t* the child Piecemeal among them,   *Com. of Arthur* 217
   T as a sail that leaves the rope is *t* In tempest :   *Holy Grail* 212
   Then *t* it from her finger,   *The Ring* 456
   from her own hand she had *t* the ring In fright,   "   470
Torn'd (**turned**)   An' 'e *t* as red as a stag-tuckey's
   wattles,   *Church-warden, etc.* 31
Torpid   That here the *t* mummy wheat Of Egypt   *To Prof. Jebb.* 5
Torre   two strong sons, Sir *T* and Sir Lavaine,   *Lancelot and E.* 174
   ' Here is *T's* ! Hurt in his first tilt was my son Sir *T.*   "   195
   added plain Sir *T*, ' Yea, since I cannot use it,   "   198
   Surely I but play'd on *T* :   "   209
   Then far away with good Sir *T* for guide   "   788
   He amazed, ' *T* and Elaine ! why here ?   "   796
   Then turn'd Sir *T*, and being in his moods   "   799
   Then the rough *T* began to heave and move,   "   1066
Torrent (*adj.*)   ' The *t* brooks of hallow'd Israel   *D. of F. Women* 181
   Flung the *t* rainbow round :   *Vision of Sin* 32
   The *t* vineyard streaming fell   *The Daisy* 10
   That listens near a *t* mountain-brook,   *Geraint and E.* 171
Torrent (*s*)   Far-off the *t* call'd me from the cleft :   *Œnone* 54
   She heard the *t's* meet.   *Of old sat Freedom* 4
   In many a streaming *t* back,   *England and Amer.* 14
   Like *t's* from a mountain source   *The Letters* 39
   For me the *t* ever pour'd And glisten'd—   *To E. L.* 13
   And *t's* of her myriad universe,   *Lucretius* 39
   roll The *t's*, dash'd to the vale :   *Princess v* 350
   To roll the *t* out of dusky doors :   "   *vii* 208
   let the *t* dance thee down To find him in the valley ;   "   209
   oleanders flush'd the bed Of silent *t's*,   *The Daisy* 34
   must fain have *t's*, lakes, Hills,   *Sisters (E. and E.)* 221
   Swept like a *t* of gems from the sky   *V. of Maeldune* 46
   Following a *t* till its myriad falls   *Tiresias* 37
   in a popular *t* of lies upon lies ;   *Vastness* 6
   Of cataract music Of falling *t's*,   *Merlin and the G.* 47
   By the long *t's* ever-deepen'd roar,   *Death of Œnone* 85
Torrent-bow   floating as they fell Lit up a *t-b.*   *Palace of Art* 36
Tortoise   Upon the *t* creeping to the wall ;   *D. of F. Women* 27
Torture   *T* and trouble in vain,—   *Def. of Lucknow* 86
   Why should we bear with an hour of *t*,   *Despair* 81
Tortured   a twitch of pain *T* her mouth,   *Princess vi* 106
   Me they seized and me they *t*,   *Boädicea* 49
Tory (*adj.*)   The *T* member's elder son,   *Princess, Con.* 50
Tory (*s*)   I myself, A *T* to the quick,   *Walk. to the Mail* 81
   Let Whig and *T* stir their blood ;   *Will Water.* 53
   A gathering of the *T*,   *Maud I xx* 33
Toss   There the sunlit ocean *t'es*   *The Captain* 69
   That *t'es* at the harbour-mouth ;   *The Voyage* 2
   Should it with tangle and with shells.   *In Mem. x* 20
   but wherefore *t* me this Like a dry bone   *Last Tournament* 195
   and *t* them away with a yawn,   *The Wreck* 21
Tossing   *t* up A cloud of incense of all odour   *Palace of Art* 84
Tost (*See also* **Trouble-tost**)   Had *t* his ball and flown his
   kite,   *Aylmer's Field* 84
   T over all her presents petulantly :   "   235
   Discuss'd a doubt and *t* it to and fro :   *Princess ii* 445
   others *t* a ball Above the fountain-jets,   "   460
   t on thoughts that changed from hue to hue,   "   *iv* 210
   Elaine, and heard her name so *t* about,   *Lancelot and E.* 233

Tost (*continued*)   was a phantom cry that I heard as
   I *t* about,   *In the Child. Hosp.* 63
   The sacred relics *t* about the floor—   *The Ring* 447
Total   The *t* chronicles of man, the mind,   *Princess ii* 381
   The *t* world since life began ;   *In Mem. xliii* 12
Tother (**other**)   'E reäds of a sewer an' sartan 'oäp o' the
   t side ;   *Village Wife* 92
   Or like *t* Hangel i' Scriptur   *Owd Roä* 94
Totter   Till she began to *t*,   *Sea Dreams* 244
   what is it ? there ? yon arbutus *T's* ;   *Lucretius* 185
Totter'd   roofs *T* toward each other in the sky,   *Holy Grail* 343
Tottering   yester-even, suddenly giddily *t*—   *Boädicea* 29
Touch (*s*)   And weary with a finger's *t*   *Clear-headed friend* 22
   Nor toil for title, place, or *t* Of pension,   *Love thou thy land* 25
   Perhaps some modern *t'es* here and there   *M. d'Arthur, Ep.* 6
   Such *t'es* are but embassies of love,   *Gardener's D.* 18
   But I have sudden *t'es*, and can run My faith   *Edwin Morris* 53
   there seem'd A *t* of something false,   "   74
   My sense of *t* is something coarse,   *Talking Oak* 163
   The cushions of whose *t* may press   "   179
   Baby fingers, waxen *t'es*,   *Locksley Hall* 90
   A *T*, a kiss ! the charm was snapt   *Day-Dm., Revival* 1
   O for the *t* of a vanish'd hand,   *Break, break, etc.* 11
   Which at a *t* of light, an air of heaven,   *Aylmer's Field* 5
   so finely, that a troublous *t* Thinn'd,   "   75
   hand Glanced like a *t* of sunshine on the rocks,   *Princess iii* 357
   To whom the *t* of all mischance but came   "   *iv* 573
   not a thought, a *t*, But pure as lines of green   "   *v* 195
   some *t* of that Which kills me with myself,   "   *vi* 306
   No more, dear love, for at a *t* I yield ;   "   *vii* 14
   Tenderness *t* by *t*, and last, to these,   "   114
   a *t* Came round my wrist, and tears upon my hand   "   137
   Too solemn for the comic *t'es* in them,   *Con.* 68
   When one small *t* of Charity   *Lit. Squabbles* 13
   And I too, talk, and lose the *t* I talk of.   "   17
   And I perceived no *t* of change,   *In Mem. xiv* 17
   The *t* of change in calm or storm ;   "   *xvi* 6
   A *t* of shame upon her cheek :   "   *xxxvii* 10
   May some dim *t* of earthly things   "   *xliv* 11
   If such a dreamy *t* should fall,   "   13
   You say, but with no *t* of scorn,   "   *xcvi* 1
   Sprang up for ever at a *t*,   "   *cxii* 10
   old place will be gilt by the *t* of a millionaire :   *Maud I i* 66
   heart-free, with the least little *t* of spleen.   "   *ii* 11
   A *t* of their office might have sufficed,   "   *II v* 27
   in a moment—at one *t* Of that skill'd spear,   *Gareth and L.* 1222
   But keep a *t* of sweet civility   *Geraint and E.* 312
   The pale blood of the wizard at her *t*   *Merlin and V.* 949
   For who loves me must have a *t* of earth ;   *Lancelot and E.* 133
   That men go down before your spear at a *t*,   "   149
   save it be some far-off *t* Of greatness   "   450
   That men went down before his spear at a *t*,   "   578
   Courtesy with a *t* of traitor in it,   "   639
   she, that felt the cold *t* on her throat,   *Pelleas and E.* 488
   I'll hold thou hast some *t* Of music,   *Last Tournament* 313
   The sight that throbs and aches beneath my *t*,   *Lover's Tale i* 33
   quick as a sensitive plant to the *t* ;   *In the Child. Hosp.* 30
   Your plague but passes by the *t*.   *Happy* 104
   Who feel no *t* of my temptation,   *Romney's R.* 121
   vines Which on the *t* of heavenly feet   *Death of Œnone* 5
   Would the man have a *t* of remorse   *Charity* 17
Touch (*verb*)   For those two likes might meet and *t*.   *Two Voices* 357
   That *t'es* me with mystic gleams,   "   380
   I'd *t* her neck so warm and white.   *Miller's D.* 174
   touch'd with some new grace Or seem'd to *t* her,   *Gardener's D.* 205
   came To *t* my body and be heal'd, and live :   *St. S. Stylites* 79
   It may be we shall *t* the Happy Isles,   *Ulysses* 63
   t him with thy lighter thought.   *Locksley Hall* 54
   love no more Can *t* the heart of Edward Gray.   *Edward Gray* 8
   And *t* upon the master-chord   *Will Water.* 27
   So,—from afar,—*t* as at once ?   *Aylmer's Field* 580
   O Goddess, like ourselves *T*, and be touch'd,   *Lucretius* 81
   We *t* on our dead self, nor shun to do it,   *Princess iii* 221
   Which *t'es* on the workman and his work.   "   322
   ' You have our son : *t* not a hair of his head :   "   *iv* 407

Touch (verb) (*continued*) seem'd to *t* upon a sphere Too gross to tread, *Princess* vii 324
T a spirit among things divine, *Ode on Well.* 139
To *t* thy thousand years of gloom : *In Mem.* ii 12
O Father, *t* the east, and light ,, *xxx* 31
And other than the things I *t*.' ,, *xlv* 8
That seem'd to *t* it into leaf : ,, *lxix* 18
T thy dull goal of joyless gray, ,, *lxxii* 27
Descend, and *t*, and enter ; ,, *xciii* 13
And *t* with shade the bridal doors, ,, *Con.* 117
Not *t* on her father's sin? *Maud* I xix 17
We will not *t* upon him ev'n in jest.' *Marr. of Geraint* 311
or *t* at night the northern star ; *Balin and Balan* 166
T flax with flame—a glance will serve— *Merlin and V.* 111
but *t* it with a sword, It buzzes fiercely ,, 431
Not one of all the drove should *t* me : ,, 699
if a man Could *t* or see it, he was heal'd at once, *Holy Grail* 55
Nor aught we blow with breath, or *t* with hand, ,, 114
if I find the Holy Grail itself And *t* it, ,, 439
That could I *t* or see the Holy Grail ,, 779
'Yet, take him, ye that scarce are fit to *t*, *Pelleas and E.* 292
Save that to *t* a harp, tilt with a lance *Last Tournament* 636
had let one finger lightly *t* The warm white apple ,, 716
I cannot *t* thy lips, they are not mine, *Guinevere* 551
sometimes *t'es* but one string That quivers, *Lover's Tale* i 17
doesn't *t* thy 'at to the Squire ;' *North. Cobbler* 25
But they dared not *t* us again, *The Revenge* 72
gleam from our poor earth May *t* thee, *Ded. Poem Prin. Alice* 19
fleeted far and fast To *t* all shores, *Pref. Son. 19th Cent.* 2
I *t* thy world again— *Ancient Sage* 249
Earth would never *t* her worst, *Locksley H., Sixty* 270
Did he *t* me on the lips ? *Happy* 66
Human forgiveness *t'es* heaven, and thence— *Romney's R.* 159
for *t* after æon pass and *t* him into shape ? *Making of Man* 4

Touch'd (*See also* **True-touched**) *T* with a somewhat darker hue, *Margaret* 50
heath-flower in the dew, *T* with sunrise. *Rosalind* 42
T by thy spirit's mellowness, *Eleänore* 103
T by his feet the daisy slept. *Two Voices* 276
T ; and I knew no more.' *D. of F. Women* 116
ere it *t* a foot, that might have danced *Gardener's D.* 133
each in passing *t* with some new grace ,, 204
Then *t* upon the game, how scarce it was *Audley Court* 32
The flower, she *t* on, dipt and rose, *Talking Oak* 131
Are *t*, are turn'd to finest air. *Sir Galahad* 72
Then the music *t* the gates and died ; *Vision of Sin* 23
When that cold vapour *t* the palace gate, ,, 58
And ere he *t* his one-and-twentieth May *Enoch Arden* 57
t On such a time as goes before the leaf, *The Brook* 12
for the second death Scarce *t* her *Aylmer's Field* 605
And oaken finials till he *t* the door ; ,, 823
T, clink'd, and clash'd, and vanish'd, *Sea Dreams* 135
O Goddess, like ourselves Touch, and be *t*, *Lucretius* 81
(A little sense of wrong had *t* her face With colour) *Princess, Pro.* 219
t on Mahomet With much contempt, ,, ii 134
the Muses' heads were *t* Above the darkness ,, iii 21
t upon the point Where idle boys are cowards ,, v 308
for since you think me *t* In honour— ,, 401
the sequel of the tale Had *t* her ; ,, *Con.* 31
That thou hadst *t* the land to-day, *In Mem.* xiv 2
God's finger *t* him, and he slept. ,, *lxxxv* 20
Or *t* the changes of the state, ,, *lxxxix* 35
The dead man *t* me from the past. ,, *xcv* 34
Who *t* a jarring lyre at first, ,, *xcvi* 7
Nor harp be *t*, nor flute be blown ; ,, *cv* 22
But *t* with no ascetic gloom ; ,, *cix* 10
she *t* my hand with a smile so sweet, *Maud* I vi 12
For her feet have *t* the meadows ,, *xii* 23
I find whenever she *t* on me ,, *xix* 59
Mage at Arthur's Court, Knowing all arts, had *t*, *Gareth and L.* 307
So when they *t* the second river-loop, ,, 1025
rose to look at it, But *t* it unawares : *Geraint and E.* 388
Nor ever *t* fierce wine, nor tasted flesh, *Merlin and V.* 627
T at all points, except the poplar grove, *Lancelot and E.* 617
at times, So *t* were they, half-thinking ,, 1287

Touch'd (*continued*) but when I *t* her, lo ! she, too, Fell into dust *Holy Grail* 396
up I went and *t* him, and he, too, Fell into dust, ,, 418
I *t* The chapel-doors at dawn I know ; ,, 535
Out of the dark, just as the lips had *t*, *Last Tournament* 752
its shadow flew Before it, till it *t* her, *Guinevere* 80
T by the adulterous finger of a time *To the Queen* ii 43
and *t* far-off His mountain-altars, *Lover's Tale* i 321
Thy fires from heaven had *t* it, ,, 439
But all from these to where she *t* on earth, ,, iv 167
our lover seldom spoke, Scarce *t* the meats ; ,, 226
we came to the Silent Isle that we never had *t* at before, *V. of Maeldune* 11
dark orb *T* with earth's light— *De Prof., Two G.* 10
you have *t* at seventy-five, *To E. Fitzgerald* 44
I *t* my limbs, the limbs Were strange *Ancient Sage* 234
t on the whole sad planet of man, *Dead Prophet* 39
For, see, thy foot has *t* it ; *Demeter and P.* 48
T at the golden Cross *Merlin and the G.* 67
If the lips were *t* with fire *Parnassus* 17
he *t* his goal, The Christian city. *St. Telemachus* 34

Touching (*See also* **Tenderest-touching**) *T* the sullen pool below : *Miller's D.* 244
our spirits rush'd together at the *t* of the lips. *Locksley Hall* 38
Answer'd all queries *t* those at home *Aylmer's Field* 465
which, on the foremost rocks *t*, upjetted *Sea Dreams* 52
moonlight *t* o'er a terrace One tall Agavè *The Daisy* 83
T her guilty love for Lancelot, *Marr. of Geraint* 25
And *t* Breton sands, they disembark'd. *Merlin and V.* 202
And *t* fame, howe'er ye scorn my song, ,, 444
crown'd with spiritual fire, And *t* other worlds. ,, 838
and *t* on all things great, *The Wreck* 50

Touchwood a cave Of *t*, with a single flourishing spray. *Aylmer's Field* 512
the stem Less grain than *t*, *Princess* iv 333

Touchwood-dust Raking in that millennial *t-d* *Aylmer's Field* 514

Tough My *t* lance thrusteth sure, *Sir Galahad* 2
t, Strong, supple, sinew-corded, *Princess* v 534

Tougher *t*, heavier, stronger, he that smote ,, 536

Tould (**told**) Call'd from her cabin an' *t* her *Tomorrow* 20
I *t* yer Honour whativer I hard an' seen, ,, 97

Tour last summer on a *t* in Wales : *Golden Year* 2

Tournament From spur to plume a star of *t*, *M. d'Arthur* 223
For Lancelot was the first in *T*, *Gareth and L.* 495
Forgetful of the tilt and *t*, *Marr. of Geraint* 52
But in this *t* can no man tilt, ,, 480
And victor at the tilt and *t*, *Geraint and E.* 960
and acts of prowess done In *t* or tilt, *Holy Grail* 2
heard the King had let proclaim a *t*— *Pelleas and E.* 11
And this was call'd ' The *T* of Youth :' ,, 158
But when the morning of a *t*, *Last Tournament* 134
in mockery call'd The *T* of the Dead Innocence, ,, 136
He saw the laws that ruled the *t* Broken, ,, 160
From spur to plume a star of *t*, *Pass. of Arthur* 391
Flash'd on the *T*, *Merlin and the G.* 69

Tourney (s) a page or two that rang With tilt and *t* ; *Princess, Pro.* 122
pledged To fight in *t* for my bride, ,, v 353
With whom he used to play at *t* once, *Gareth and L.* 532
beside The field of *t*, murmuring ' kitchen-knave.' ,, 664
But by the field of *t* lingering yet ,, 736
We hold a *t* here to-morrow morn, *Marr. of Geraint* 287
this nephew, fight In next day's *t* ,, 476
—will you wear My favour at this *t* ?' *Lancelot and E.* 362
closed And clash'd in such a *t* and so full, *Holy Grail* 330
and remain Lord of the *t*. *Pelleas and E.* 163
The circlet of the *t* round her brows, And the sword of the *t* across her throat. 454

Tourney (verb) But meant once more perchance to *t* in it. *Lancelot and E.* 810

Tourney-fall In those brain-stunning shocks, and *t-f's*, *Gareth and L.* 89

Tourney-prize And make them, an thou wilt a *t-p*. *Last Tournament* 32
And won by Tristram as a *t-p*, ,, 746

Tourney-skill no room was there For lance or *t-s* : *Gareth and L.* 1042

Tow Nor like poor Psyche whom she drags in *t*.' *Princess* iii 103

Towd (**told**) An' a *t* ma my sins, *N. Farmer, O. S.* 11
knawed a Quaäker fellow as often 'as *t* ma this : *N. S.* 19
I knaws the law, I does, for the lawyer ha *t* it me. *Village Wife* 16

Towd (told) (*continued*)   the lawyer he *t* it me That ʼis taäil

were soä tied up

es it beänt not fit to be *t* !   ”   108

Tower (s)   (*See also* **Beacon-tower, Church-tower, Cloud-tower, Convent-tower, Minster-tower**)

flee By town, and *t*, and hill, and cape,   *Mine be the Strength* 6

Four gray walls, and four gray *t's*,   *L. of Shalott* i 15

Under *t* and balcony,   *iv* 37

Tho' watching from a ruin'd *t*   *Two Voices* 77

Below the city's eastern *t's*:   *Fatima* 9

In glassy bays among her tallest *t's.*'   *Œnone* 119

in the *t's* I placed great bells that swung,   *Palace of Art* 129

' Yet pull not down my palace *t's*,   ”   293

You pine among your halls and *t's:*   *L. C. V. de Vere* 58

grape-loaded vines that glow Beneath the battled *t*.   *D. of F. Women* 220

range Of waning lime the gray cathedral *t's*,   *Gardener's D.* 218

By night we dragg'd her to the college *t*   *Walk. to the Mail* 89

left alone Upon her *t*, the Niobe of swine,   ”   99

O flourish high, with leafy *t's*,   *Talking Oak* 197

While Ilion like a mist rose into *t's*.   *Tithonus* 63

clash'd and hammer'd from a hundred *t's*,   *Godiva* 75

Here droops the banner on the *t*,   *Day-Dm., Sleep.* P. 15

Down stept Lord Ronald from his *t*:   *Lady Clare* 65

STILL on the *t* stood the vane,   *The Letters* 1

but now The broken base of a black *t*,   *Aylmer's Field* 511

left Their own gray *t*, or plain-faced tabernacle,   ”   618

We gain'd the mother-city thick with *t's*,   *Princess* i 112

soft white vapour streak the crowned *t's*   *iii* 344

she You talk'd with, whole nights long, up in the *t*,   *vi* 255

Toll'd by an earthquake in a trembling *t*,   ”   332

here and there a rustic *t* Half-lost in belts   ” *Con.* 44

Before a *t* of crimson holly-hoaks,   ”   82

O fall'n at length that *t* of strength   *Ode on Well.* 38

Breaking their mailed fleets and armed *t's*,   *Ode Inter. Exhib.* 39

Flags, flutter out upon turret and *t's* !   *W. to Alexandra* 15

Or *t*, or high hill-convent,   *The Daisy* 29

Of *t*, or duomo, sunny-sweet, Or palace,   ”   46

Sow'd it far and wide By every town and *t*,   *The Flower* 14

stream Of Xanthus blazed before the *t's* of Troy,   *Spec. of Iliad* 18

And crowded farms and lessening *t's*,   *In Mem.* xi 11

And wildly dash'd on *t* and tree   ” *xv* 7

And *t's* fall'n as soon as built—   ” *xxvi* 8

The ruin'd shells of hollow *t's* ?   ” *lxxvi* 16

And tuft with grass a feudal *t*;   ” *cxxviii* 20

Dumb is that *t* which spake so loud,   ” *Con.* 106

everyone that owns a *t* The Lord for half a league.   *Gareth and L.* 595

stairway sloped Till lost in blowing trees and tops of *t's*;   ”   670

His *t's* where that day a feast had been Held   ”   847

And here had fall'n a great part of a *t*,   *Marr. of Geraint* 317

Guinevere had climb'd The giant *t*,   ”   827

beheld A little town with *t's*, upon a rock,   *Geraint and E.* 197

A home of bats, in every *t* an owl.   *Balin and Balan* 336

By the great *t*—Caerleon upon Usk—   ”   506

I thought the great *t* would crash down on both—   ”   515

huge and old It look'd a *t* of ivied masonwork,   *Merlin and V.* 4

Closed in the four walls of a hollow *t*, (repeat)   ” 209, 543

crows Hung like a cloud above the gateway *t's*.'   ”   599

High in her chamber up a *t* to the east   *Lancelot and E.* 3

climb'd That eastern *t*, and entering barr'd her door,   ”   15

Fired from the west, far on a hill, the *t's*.   ”   168

Lavaine Past inward, as she came from out the *t*.   ”   346

Then to her *t* she climb'd, and took the shield,   ”   397

And thus they bore her swooning to her *t*.   ”   968

So in her *t* alone the maiden sat: ”   989

fiery dawning wild with wind That shook her *t*,   ”   1021

T after *t*, spire beyond spire,   *Holy Grail* 229

Behold, the enchanted *t's* of Carbonek,   ”   813

sweet voice singing in the topmost *t* To the eastward: ”   834

great *t* fill'd with eyes Up to the summit,   *Pelleas and E.* 166

from the *t* above him cried Ettarre,   ”   231

beneath the shadow of those *t's* A villainy,   ”   276

Up ran a score of damsels to the *t*;   ”   368

mounting on his horse Stared at her *t's*   ”   457

O *t's* so strong, Huge, solid,   ”   463

Beside that *t* where Percivale was cowl'd,   ”   501

Tower (s) (*continued*)   From Camelot in among the faded

fields To furthest *t's*;   *Last Tournament* 54

' He took them and he drave them to his *t*—   ”   68

Brake in upon me and drave them to his *t*;   ”   72

My *t* is full of harlots, like his court,   ”   81

Glared on a huge machicolated *t* That stood   ”   424

High on a grim dead tree before the *t*,   ”   430

echoing yell with yell, they fired the *t*;   ”   478

and high on land, A crown of *t's*.   ”   506

feet of Tristram grind The spiring stone that scaled about her *t*,   ”   511

westward-smiling seas, Watch'd from this *t*.   ”   588

then this crown of *t's* So shook to such a roar   ”   620

Modred brought His creatures to the basement of the *t*   *Guinevere* 104

T's of a happier time, low down in a rainbow deep   *V. of Maeldune* 79

And we came in an evil time to the Isle of the Double *T's*,   ”   105

And the daws flew out of the *T's*   ”   109

and all took sides with the *T's*,   ”   111

the song-built *t's* and gates Reel,   *Tiresias* 98

And trees like the *t's* of a minster,   *The Wreck* 74

ghastly *t* of eighty thousand human skulls,   *Locksley H., Sixty* 82

In this gap between the sandhills, whence you see the Locksley *t*,   ”   176

Just above the gateway *t*,   ”   179

HELEN'S *T*, here I stand,   *Helen's Tower* 1

Why do you look so gravely at the *t*?   *The Ring* 80

And how the birds that circle round the *t*   ”   85

That chamber in the *t*.   ”   94

You took me to that chamber in the *t*,   ”   111

when the *t* as now Was all ablaze with crimson   ”   249

between The *t* and that rich phantom of the *t*?   ”   253

mist of autumn gather from your lake, And shroud the *t*;   ”   330

up the *t*—an icy air Fled by me.   ”   445

T and altar trembling . . .   *Forlorn* 34

I see the slowly-thickening chestnut *t's*   *Prog. of Spring* 42

Tower (verb)   *T*, as the deep-domed empyrean   *Milton* 7

The chestnut *t's* in his bloom: *Voice and the P.* 18

Tower'd (adj.)   (*See also* **Tall-tower'd, Many-tower'd**) the river winding clearly, Down to *t* Camelot;   *L. of Shalott* i 32

page in crimson clad, Goes by to *t* Camelot: ” *ii* 23

Heavily the low sky raining Over *t* Camelot;   ” *iv* 5

From Mizpeh's *t* gate with welcome light,   *D. of F. Women* 199

Tower'd (verb)   the pale head of him, who *t* Above them,   *Aylmer's Field* 623

she *t*; her bells, Tone under tone, shrill'd ;   *Merlin and V.* 131

Towering   Now *t* o'er him in serenest air,   *Lucretius* 178

And a reverent people behold The *t* car,   *Ode on Well.* 55

with all thy breadth and height Of foliage, *t* sycamore ;   *In Mem.* lxxxix 4

for the *t* crest of the tides Plunged on the vessel   *The Wreck* 89

Tower-stairs   she stole Down the long *t-s*,   *Lancelot and E.* 343

Towery-top   O rock upon thy *t-p*   *Talking Oak* 265

Town   (*See also* **County town**)   flee By *t*, and tower, and hill,   *Mine be the strength* 6

and out of every smouldering *t* Cries to Thee,   *Poland* 5

Flood with full daylight glebe and *t*?   *Two Voices* 87

From many an inland *t* and haven large,   *Œnone* 117

flying star shot thro' the sky Above the pillar'd *t*.   *Palace of Art* 124

For pastime, ere you went to *t*.   *L. C. V. de Vere* 4

Clanging fights, and flaming *t's*,   *Lotos-Eaters, C. S.* 116

That bore a lady from a leaguer'd *t*;   *D. of F. Women* 47

Then stept she down thro' *t* and field   *Of old sat Freedom* 9

The *t* was hush'd beneath us: *Audley Court* 85

' And all that from the *t* would stroll,   *Talking Oak* 53

the fair Was holden at the *t*;   ”   102

The music from the *t*—   ”   214

for when he laid a tax Upon his *t*,   *Godiva* 14

answer'd, ' Ride you naked thro' the *t*,   ”   29

Thro' dreaming *t's* I go,   *Sir Galahad* 50

SWEET Emma Moreland of yonder *t*   *Edward Gray* 1

High *t's* on hills were dimly seen,   *The Voyage* 34

He pass'd by the *t* and out of the street,   *Poet's Song* 2

' Did you know Enoch Arden of this *t* ? '   *Enoch Arden* 845

By twenty thorps, a little *t*,   *The Brook* 29

One of our *t*, but later by an hour   *Sea Dreams* 263

Thro' the wild woods that hung about the *t*;   *Princess* i 91

Town (*continued*)   Cat-footed thro' the *t* and half in dread | *Princess i* 104
We dropt with evening on a rustic *t* | „ 170
man and woman, *t* And landskip, have I heard of, | „ *iv* 445
Where, far from noise and smoke of *t*, | *To F. D. Maurice* 13
Sow'd it far and wide By every *t* and tower, | *The Flower* 14
I wander'd from the noisy *t*, | *In Mem. lxix* 5
I roved at random thro' the *t*, | .. *lxxxvii* 3
The dust and din and steam of *t*: | „ *lxxxix* 8
But if I praised the busy *t*, | „ 37
That not in any mother *t* | „ *xcviii* 21
And pass the silent-lighted *t*, | „ *Con.* 112
Last week came one to the county *t*, | *Maud I x* 37
His heart in the gross mud-honey of *t*, | „ *xvi* 5
the worth of half a *t*, A warhorse of the best, | *Gareth and L.* 677
Beheld the long street of a little *t* | *Marr. of Geraint* 242
And out of *t* and valley came a noise | .. 247
'What means the tumult in the *t*?' | „ 259
Go to the *t* and buy us flesh and wine; | „ 372
went her way across the bridge, And reach'd the *t*, | „ 384
Ride into that new fortress by your *t*, | „ 407
and thought to find Arms in your *t*, | „ 418
Raised my own *t* against me in the night | „ 457
knights And ladies came, and by and by the *t* Flow'd in, | .. 546
Went Yniol thro' the *t*, and everywhere He found the sack' and plunder of our house All scatter'd thro' the houses of the *t*; | „ 693
beheld A little *t* with towers, upon a rock, | *Geraint and E.* 197
And then I chanced upon a goodly *t* | *Holy Grail* 573
they would spy us out of the *t*. | *Rizpah* 5
and beat Thro' all the homely *t* | *Columbus* 83
Blown by the fierce beleaguerers of a *t*, | *Achilles over the T.* 20
Or the foulest sewer of the *t*— | *Dead Prophet* 48
illuminate All your *t's* for a festival, | *On Jub. Q. Victoria* 19
you still delay to take Your leave of *T*, | *To Mary Boyle* 2
DEAR Master in our classic *t*, | *To Master of B.* 1
waste and field and *t* of alien tongue, | *St. Telemachus* 30
tha *mun* speäk hout to the Baptises here i' the *t*, | *Church-warden, etc.* 51
Toy   *t's* in lava, fans Of sandal, | *Princess, Pro.* 18
The tricks, which make us *t's* of men, | „ *ii* 63
might have seem'd a *t* to trifle with, | *Pelleas and E.* 76
An' their mashin' their *t's* to pieäces | *Spinster's S's.* 88
To-year   niver ha seed it sa white wi' the Maäy es I see'd it *t-y*— | *Village Wife* 80
Traäde (trade)   Burn i' *t* | *Church-warden, etc.* 18
an' the Freeä *T* runn'd 'i my 'ead, | *Owd Roä* 54
Traäpes'd (trapesed, trudged)   as iver *t* i' the squad. | „ 72
Trace (s)   And silent *t's* of the past | *In Mem. xliii* 7
but *t* of thee I saw not; | *Demeter and P.* 80
Trace (verb)   old magic which can *t* The wandering of the stars, | *Holy Grail* 666
fail'd to *t* him thro' the flesh and blood | *Last Tournament* 686
to *t* On paler heavens the branching grace | *To Ulysses* 14
Traced   in her raiment's hem was *t* in flame | *The Poet* 45
Likewise the deep-set windows, stain'd and *t*, | *Palace of Art* 49
I might as well have *t* it in the sands; | *Audley Court* 50
Till as he *t* a faintly-shadow'd track, | *Lancelot and E.* 165
and in the dark of mine Is *t* with flame. | *Lover's Tale i* 298
Trachyte   trap and tuff, Amygdaloid and *t*, | *Princess iii* 363
Track (s)   'If straight thy *t*, or if oblique, | *Two Voices* 193
strike Into that wondrous *t* of dreams again! | *D. of F. Women* 279
right across its *t* there lay, | *Sea Dreams* 126
the *t* Whereon with equal feet we fared; | *In Mem. xxv* 1
We ranging down this lower *t*, | „ *xlvi* 1
Enid leading down the *t's* Thro' which he bad her lead | *Geraint and E.* 28
He took the selfsame *t* as Balan, | *Balin and Balan* 290
Till as he traced a faintly-shadow'd *t*, | *Lancelot and E.* 165
Troubled the *t* of the host that we hated, | *Batt. of Brunanburh* 40
All the *t's* Of science making toward | *Akbar's Dream* 28
Forward to the starry *t* Glimmering | *Silent Voices* 8
Track (verb)   impossible, Far as we *t* ourselves— | *Aylmer's Field* 306
snares to *t* Suggestion to her inmost cell. | *In Mem. xcv* 31
I will *t* this vermin to their earths: | *Marr. of Geraint* 217
swore That I would *t* this caitiff to his hold, | „ 415
the subtle beast, Would *t* her guilt until he found, | *Guinevere* 60
Track'd   And *t* you still on classic ground, | *To E. L.* 10
'So,' thought Geraint, 'I have *t* him to his earth.' | *Marr. of Geraint* 253

Trackless   Roving the *t* realms of Lyonnesse, | *Lancelot and E.* 35
Tract (s)   (*See also* **Mountain-tract**) In the dim *t* of Penuel. | *Clear-headed friend* 29
Would sweep the *t's* of day and night. | *Two Voices* 69
One seem'd all dark and red—a *t* of sand, | *Palace of Art* 65
In *t's* of pasture sunny-warm, | „ 94
And many a *t* of palm and rice, | „ 114
Faith from *t's* no feet have trod, | *On a Mourner* 29
overlooks the sandy *t's*, | *Locksley Hall* 5
Which led by *t's* that pleased us well, | *In Mem. xxii* 2
A lifelong *t* of time reveal'd; | .. *xlvi* 9
Foreshorten'd in the *t* of time? | „ *lxxvii* 4
And *t's* of calm from tempest made, | .. *cxii* 14
In *t's* of fluent heat began, | „ *cxviii* 9
thro' all this *t* of years Wearing the white flower | *Ded. of Idylls* 24
so there grew great *t's* of wilderness, | *Com. of Arthur* 10
Sir Bors Rode to the lonest *t* of all the realm, | *Holy Grail* 661
half the morning have I paced these sandy *t's*, | *Locksley H., Sixty* 1
Trade (s)   (*See also* **Traäde**) Another hand crept too across his *t* | *Enoch Arden* 110
set Annie forth in *t* With all that seamen | „ 138
But throve not in her *t*, not being bred To barter, | „ 249
poring over his Tables of *T* and Finance, | *The Wreck* 26
Or *T* re-frain the Powers From war | *Epilogue* 15
T flying over a thousand seas with her spice | *Vastness* 13
Trade (verb)   Should he not *t* himself out yonder? | *Enoch Arden* 141
Traded   There Enoch *t* for himself, | „ 538
Trader   Never comes the *t*, never floats | *Locksley Hall* 161
Tradesman   faith in a *t's* ware or his word? | *Maud I i* 26
Tradition   as *t* teaches, Young ashes pirouetted | *Amphion* 26
made Their own *t's* God, and slew the Lord, | *Aylmer's Field* 795
He thwarting their *t* of Himself, | *Sir J. Oldcastle* 181
Trafalgar   at *T* yet once more We taught him: | *Buonaparte* 12
Tragedian   great *T*, that had quench'd herself | *Sisters (E. and E.)* 233
Tragic   (*See also* **Over-tragic**) That all things grew more *t* | *Princess vi* 23
Trail (s)   They hunt old *t's*' said Cyril 'very well; | „ *ii* 390
Trail (verb)   Would slowly *t* himself sevenfold | *The Mermaid* 25
Clasp her window, *t* and twine! | *Window, At the Wind.* 2
T and twine and clasp and kiss, | „ 4
Trail'd   heavy barges *t* By slow horses; | *L. of Shalott i* 20
T himself up on one knee: | *Princess vi* 155
By a shuffled step, by a dead weight *t*, | *Maud I i* 14
Trailer   bell-like flower Of fragrant *t's*, | *Eleänore* 38
swings the *t* from the crag; | *Locksley Hall* 162
the *t* mantles all the mouldering bricks— | *Locksley H., Sixty* 257
Trailing   Some bearded meteor, *t* light, | *L. of Shalott iii* 26
With plaited alleys of the *t* rose, | *Ode to Memory* 106
Three slaves were *t* a dead lion away, | *St. Telemachus* 47
Train (of dress)   Or old-world *t's*, upheld at court | *Day-Dm., Ep.* 9
Train (ordered sequence)   Nor any *t* of reason keep: | *Two Voices* 50
lead my Memmius in a *t* Of flowery clauses | *Lucretius* 119
'Last of the *t*, a moral leper, I, | *Princess iv* 222
A hundred maids in *t* across the Park. | „ *vi* 76
behind, A *t* of dames: by axe and eagle sat, | „ *vii* 128
And all the *t* of bounteous hours | *In Mem. lxxxiv* 30
Train (railway)   *I* waited for the *t* at Coventry; | *Godiva* 1
Wreck'd—your *t*—or all but wreck'd? | *Locksley H., Sixty* 215
Two *t's* clash'd: then and there | *Charity* 21
Train (verb)   to *t* the rose-bush that I set | *May Queen, N. Y's. E.* 47
t To riper growth the mind and will: | *In Mem. xliii* 7
Train'd   given us a fair falcon which he *t*; | *Merlin and V.* 96
Training   The bearing and the *t* of a child | *Princess v* 465
Their talk was all of *t*, terms of art, | *Merlin and V.* 124
Trait   From talk of war to *t's* of pleasantry— | *Lancelot and E.* 321
Traitor (adj.)   And shouts of heathen and the *t* knights, | *Pass. of Arthur* 113
Sir Lancelot, friend *T* or true? | *Merlin and V.* 770
Traitor (s)   (*See also* **Thraithur**) Drip sweeter dews than *t's* tear. | *A Dirge* 24
So foul a *t* to myself and her, | *Aylmer's Field* 319
'See that there be no *t's* in your camp: We seem a nest of *t's*— | *Princess v* 425
Dear *t*, too much loved, why? | „ *vi* 293
For ever since when *t* to the King | *Gareth and L.* 76
changed and came to loathe His crime of *t*, | *Marr. of Geraint* 594
And all thro' that young *t*, | „ 715
'Your sweet faces make good fellows fools And *t's*. | *Geraint and E.* 400

Traitor (s) (*continued*) Fools prate, and perish *t's*. — *Balin and Balan* 530
shriek'd out '*T*' to the unhearing wall, — *Lancelot and E.* 612
Courtesy with a touch of *t* in it, — „ 639
a coward slinks from what he fears To cope with, or a *t* proven, — *Pelleas and E.* 439
'*T*, come out, ye are trapt at last,' — *Guinevere* 106
Modred whom he left in charge of all, The *t*— — „ 196
If this false *t* have displaced his lord, — „ 216
heathen, and knights, *T's*— — „ 575
I lean'd in wife and friend Is *t* to my peace, — *Pass. of Arthur* 25
Modred, unharm'd, the *t* of thine house.' — „ 153
But call not thou this *t* of my house — „ 155
her own true eyes Are *t's* to her; — *Sisters (E. and E.)* 285
who can tell but the *t's* had won? — *Def. of Lucknow* 66
but to call men *t's* May make men *t's*. — *Sir J. Oldcastle* 50
That *t* to King Richard and the truth, — „ 171
T and trickster And spurner of treaties— — *Batt. of Brunanburh* 79
God the *t's* hope confound! (repeat) — *Hands all Round* 10, 22, 34
Traitor-hearted unkind, untrue, Unknightly, *t-h*! — *M. d'Arthur* 120
unkind, untrue, Unknightly, *t-h*! — *Pass. of Arthur* 288
Traitorous when a world Of *t* friend and broken system — *Princess vi* 195
to splinter it into feuds Serving his *t* end; — *Guinevere* 19
Ever the day with its *t* death from the loopholes around, — *Def. of Lucknow* 79
Traitress nip me flat, If I be such a *t* — *Merlin and V.* 351
and harry me, petty spy And *t*.' — *Guinevere* 361
Tram laying his *t's* in a poison'd gloom — *Maud I x* 8
Tramp (a vagrant) an' gied the *t's* goin' by— — *Village Wife* 33
Tramp (sound) *t* of the hornfooted horse That grind — *Tiresias* 94
Tramp (verb) To *t*, to scream, to burnish, — *Princess iv* 520
Trample To *t* round my fallen head, — *Come not, when, etc.* 3
I *t* on your offers and on you: — *Princess iv* 546
on my chargers, *t* them under us.' — *Boädicea* 69
Behold me overturn and *t* on him. — *Geraint and E.* 843
And *t's* on the goodly shield to show — *Balin and Balan* 550
'*T* me, Dear feet, that I have follow'd — *Merlin and V.* 226
and burns the feet would *t* it to dust. — *The Flight* 68
Trampled (adj.) I was left a *t* orphan, — *Locksley Hall* 156
The desecrated shrine, the *t* year, — *Princess v* 127
Till the filthy by-lane rings to the yell of the *t* wife, — *Maud I i* 38
Let the *t* serpent show you that you have not lived in vain. — *Locksley H., Sixty* 242
arose The shriek and curse of *t* millions, — *Akbar's Dream* 190
Trampled (verb) And *t* under by the last and least — *Poland* 2
She *t* some beneath her horses' heels, — *Princess, Pro.* 44
a spark of will Not to be *t* out. — *Maud II ii* 57
and why *T* ye thus on that which bare the Crown?' — *Balin and Balan* 602
There *t* out his face from being known, — *Last Tournament* 470
man's word, Here *t* by the populace underfoot, — *Tiresias* 174
Trampling *t* the flowers With clamour. — *Princess v* 247
All great self-seekers *t* on the right: — *Ode on Well.* 187
hollow *t's* up and down And muffled voices heard, — *Gareth and L.* 1372
His charger *t* many a prickly star — *Marr. of Geraint* 313
But Michaël *t* Satan; — *Last Tournament* 673
Trance (s) I muse, as in a *t*, (repeat) — *Eleänore* 72, 75
Like some bold seër in a *t*, — *L. of Shalott iv* 11
'As here we find in *t's*, men Forget the dream that happens then, Until they fall in *t* again. — *Two Voices* 352
who clasp'd in her last *t* Her murder'd father's head, — *D. of F. Women* 266
The *t* gave way To those caresses, — *Love and Duty* 65
I could no more, but lay like one in *t*, — *Princess vii* 151
In some long *t* should slumber on; — *In Mem. xliii* 4
Sleep, kinsman thou to death and *t* And madness, — „ lxxi 1
At length my *t* Was cancell'd, — „ xcv 43
But when the Queen immersed in such a *t*, — *Guinevere* 401
led on with light *t* In *t's* and in visions: — *Lover's Tale i* 78
Thro' dreams by night and *t's* of the day, — *Sisters (E. and E.)* 274
Till I woke from the *t*, — *The Wreck* 115
following, as in *t*, the silent cry. — *Death of Œnone* 86
Trance (verb) When thickest dark did *t* the sky, — *Mariana* 18
Tranced (*See also* **Deep-tranced**) So *t*, so rapt in ecstasies, — *Eleänore* 72
No *t* summer calm is thine, — *Madeline* 2
Hung *t* from all pulsation, — *Gardener's D.* 260

Tranced (*continued*) On either side her *t* form Forth streaming — *Day-Dm., Sleep. B.* 5
nature fail'd a little, And he lay *t*; — *Enoch Arden* 793
We stood *t* in long embraces Mixt with kisses — *Maud II iv* 8
Tranquil her lips were sunder'd With smiles of *t* bliss, — *Lover's Tale ii* 143
Tranquillity O Thou, Passionless bride, divine *T*, — *Lucretius* 266
Marr'd her friend's aim with pale *t*. — *Lancelot and E.* 733
Transfer That foolish sleep *t's* to thee. — *In Mem. lxviii* 16
t The whole I felt for him to you. — *lxxxv* 103
Transferr'd my dull agony, Ideally to her *t*, — *Lover's Tale ii* 137
Transfigured When we shall stand *t*, — *Happy* 38
Transfixt So lay the man *t*. — *Geraint and E.* 166
Transfused but *t* Thro' future time by power — *Love thou thy land* 3
Transgress *T* his ample bound to some new crown:— — *Poland* 8
Transgression So for every light *t* — *The Captain* 11
Transient Away we stole, and *t* in a trice — *Princess v* 39
But knows no more of *t* form In her deep self, — *In Mem. xvi* 7
Womanlike, taking revenge too deep for a *t* wrong — *Maud I iii* 5
And wordy trucklings to the *t* hour, — *To the Queen ii* 51
And the *t* trouble of drowning, — *Despair* 67
Transit and wing'd Her *t* to the throne, — *Princess iv* 378
Transitory and a *t* word Made knight or churl or child — *Balin and Balan* 161
Translucent Pure vestal thoughts in the *t* fane — *Isabel* 4
Transmitter The one *t* of their ancient name, — *Aylmer's Field* 296
Transparent That dimples thro' *t* cheek, — *Margaret* 15
Transplanted I know *t* human worth Will bloom to profit, — *In Mem. lxxxii* 11
Transplanting And Methods of *t* trees — *Amphion* 79
Transport 'But heard, by secret *t* led, — *Two Voices* 214
Me mightier *t's* move and thrill; — *Sir Galahad* 22
Stirring a sudden *t* rose and fell. — *Princess iv* 29
     — „ *iii* 362
Trap (rock) hornblende, rag and *t* and tuff, — „ *iii* 362
Trap (snare) As of a wild thing taken in the *t*, — *Geraint and E.* 723
Trap (verb) Christ the bait to *t* his dupe — *Sea Dreams* 191
Trapesed *See* **Traäpes'd**
Trapper Which sees the *t* coming thro' the wood. — *Geraint and E.* 724
Trapt (adorned) there she found her palfrey *t* — *Godiva* 51
On horses, and the horses richly *t* — *Pelleas and E.* 55
Trapt (caught) 'Traitor, come out, ye are *t* at last,' — *Guinevere* 106
Trash you that talk'd The *t* that made me sick, — *Princess ii* 394
'O *t*' he said, 'but with a kernel in it. — „ 395
Trath Treroit down the waste sand-shores of *T T*, — *Lancelot and E.* 301
Travail *T*, and throes and agonies of the life, — *Com. of Arthur* 76
Camilla's *t* came Upon her, — *Lover's Tale iv* 127
Travel (s) I cannot rest from *t*: — *Ulysses* 6
if it had not been For a chance of *t*, — *Maud I ii* 8
overtoil'd By that day's grief and *t*, — *Geraint and E.* 377
O weary was I of the *t*, — *V. of Maeldune* 129
Travel (verb) blasts of balm To one that *t's* quickly, — *Gardener's D.* 69
He *t's* far from other skies— — *Day-Dm., Arrival* 5
here and there a foamy flake Upon me, as I *t* — *The Brook* 60
Travell'd how they prose O'er books of *t* seamen, — *Amphion* 82
And *t* men from foreign lands; — *In Mem. x* 6
Traveller in strange lands a *t* walking slow, — *Palace of Art* 277
The *t* hears me now and then, — *In Mem. xxi* 5
Traveller's-joy Was parcel-bearded with the *t-j* — *Aylmer's Field* 153
Travelling quite worn out, *T* to Naples. — *The Brook* 36
His kinsman *t* on his own affair — *Merlin and V.* 717
myself was then *T* that land, — *Lover's Tale iv* 133
Traversed Silent the silent field They *t*. — *Gareth and L.* 1314
blossom-dust of those Deep meadows we had *t*, — *Merlin and V.* 283
Treachery Making a *t* quiet in his heart, — *Lancelot and E.* 883
Treachery tript on such conjectural *t*— — *Merlin and V.* 348
fevers, fights, Mutinies, *treacheries*— — *Columbus* 226
Tread (s) Were it ever so airy a *t*, — *Maud I xxii* 68
Tread (verb) And *t* softly and speak low, — *D. of the O. Year* 4
ere the hateful crow shall *t* The corners — *Will Water.* 235
While he *t's* with footstep firmer, — *L. of Burleigh* 51
Freedom, gaily doth she *t*; — *Vision of Sin* 136
T a measure on the stones, — „ 180
The wisp that flickers where no foot can *t*.' — *Princess iv* 358
And *t* you out for ever: — „ *vi* 176
seem'd to touch upon a sphere Too gross to *t*, — „ *vii* 325
The solid earth whereon we *t* — *In Mem. cxviii* 8
t me down And I will kiss you for it;' — *Merlin and V.* 228
You that would not *t* on a worm — *Forlorn* 45

True (adj.) (continued) The burning brain from the *t* heart, *Margaret* 39
As pure and *t* as blades of steel. *Kate* 16
Our thought gave answer each to each, so *t*— *Sonnet to* —— 10
For ' Love,' they said, ' must needs be *t*, *Mariana in the S.* 63
A trifle, sweet ! which *t* love spells—*T* love interprets—
 right alone. *Miller's D.* 187
T wife, Round my *t* heart thine arms entwine „ 215
For ever and for ever with those just souls and *t*— *May Queen, Con.* 55
He gave me a friend, and a *t* true-love, *D. of the O. Year* 13
and my *t* breast Bleedeth for both ; *To J. S.* 62
Sleep till the end, *t* soul and sweet. „ 73
T love turn'd round on fixed poles, *Love thou thy land* 5
And this be *t*, till Time shall close, „ 79
Not rendering *t* answer, as beseem'd Thy fëalty, *M. d'Arthur* 74
For now I see the *t* old times are dead, „ 229
Yet this is also *t*, that, long before *Gardener's D.* 61
'Tis *t*, we met ; one hour I had, no more : *Edwin Morris* 104
In days far-off, on that dark earth, be *t* ? *Tithonus* 48
But for some *t* result of good All parties *Will Water.* 55
He loves me for my own *t* worth, *Lady Clare* 11
O mother,' she said, ' if this be *t*, „ 30
Sailors bold and *t*. *The Captain* 8
Philip's *t* heart, which hunger'd for her peace *Enoch Arden* 272
and *t* love Crown'd after trial ; *Aylmer's Field* 99
Ringing like proven golden coinage *t*, „ 182
She must prove *t* : for, brother, „ 364
Is it so *t* that second thoughts are best ? *Sea Dreams* 65
So false, he partly took himself for *t* ; „ 185
T Devils with no ear, they howl in tune „ 260
' *T* ' indeed ! One of our town, „ 262
' *T*,' she said, ' We doubt not that. *Princess, Pro.* 168
And bites it for *t* heart and not for harm, „ 174
that was *t* : But then she had a will ; „ i 47
' An open-hearted maiden, *t* and pure. „ iii 98
My princess, O my princess ! *t* she errs, „ 107
T—we had limed ourselves With open eyes, „ 142
nor is it Wiser to weep a *t* occasion lost, „ iv 68
And dark and *t* and tender is the North. „ 98
She wept her *t* eyes blind for such a one, „ 134
Know you no song, the *t* growth of your soil, „ 150
In us *t* growth, in her a Jonah's gourd, „ 311
gentleness To such as her ! if Cyril spake her *t*, „ v 168
T woman : but you clash them all in one, „ 180
As *t* to thee as false, false, false to me ! „ vi 204
It was ill counsel had misled the girl To vex *t* hearts : „ vii 242
in *t* marriage lies Nor equal, nor unequal : „ 302
O iron nerve to *t* occasion *t*, *Ode on Well.* 37
Mighty Seaman, tender and *t*, „ 134
And save the one *t* seed of freedom sown „ 162
Until we doubt not that for one so *t* „ 255
What England was, shall her *t* sons forget ? *Third of Feb.* 44
Doctors, they knaws nowt, fur a says what's
 nawways *t* : *N. Farmer, O. S.* 5
Dreams are *t* while they last, *High. Pantheism* 4
DEAR, near and *t*—no truer Time himself *A Dedication* 1
And flashes into false and *t*, *In Mem. xvi* 19
In more of life *t* life no more And Love „ xxvi 11
I hold it *t*, whate'er befall ; „ xxvii 13
The Spirit of *t* love replied ; „ lii 6
' What keeps a spirit wholly *t* „ 9
For thou wert strong as thou wert *t* ? „ lxxiii 4
O *t* in word, and tried in deed, „ lxxxv 5
If not so fresh, with love as *t*, „ 101
Should prove the phantom-warning *t*. „ xcii 12
But ever strove to make it *t* : „ xcvi 8
And dream my dream, and hold it *t* ; „ cxxiii 10
O *t* and tried, so well and long, *Con.* 1
She might by a *t* descent be untrue ; And Maud is
 as *t* as Maud is sweet : *Maud I xiii* 31
And teach *t* life to fight with mortal wrongs. „ xviii 54
But the *t* blood spilt had in it a heat „ xix 44
For, Maud, so tende and *t*, „ 85
Come out to your own *t* lover, That your *t* lover
 may see Your glory also, „ xx 46
To find the arms of my *t* love Round me „ II iv 3

True (adj.) (continued) (For I cleaved to a cause that I felt
 to be pure and *t*), *Maud III vi* 31
' O King ! ' she cried, ' and I will tell thee *t* : *Com. of Arthur* 339
' *T* love, sweet son, had risk'd himself *Gareth and L.* 60
but this was all of that *t* steel, „ 66
Her own *t* Gareth was too princely-proud „ 161
In token of *t* heart and fëalty. „ 399
Enid loved the Queen, and with *t* heart Adored her, *Marr. of Geraint* 19
that if ever yet was wife *T* to her lord, „ 47
O me, I fear that I am no *t* wife.' „ 108
T tears upon his broad and naked breast, „ 111
And that she fear'd she was not a *t* wife. „ 114
' Well said, *t* heart,' replied Geraint, „ 474
As I will make her truly my *t* wife.' „ 503
To dress her beautifully and keep her *t* '— *Geraint and E.* 40
The one *t* lover whom you ever own d, „ 344
Nor let her *t* hand falter, nor blue eye Moisten, „ 512
I heard you say, that you were no *t* wife : „ 742
with your own *t* eyes Beheld the man you loved „ 846
Rise, my *t* knight. *Balin and Balan* 75
Balin first woke, and seeing that *t* face, „ 590
Pure as our own *t* Mother is our Queen.' „ 617
Goodnight, *t* brother.' (repeat) „ 626, 628
To worship woman as *t* wife beyond *Merlin and V.* 23
That old *t* filth, and bottom of the well, „ 47
And half believe her *t* : „ 186
and half believed her *t*, (repeat) „ 400, 893
Yet is there one *t* line, took the pearl of pearls : „ 459
And Vivien, frowning in *t* anger, said : „ 691
friend Traitor or *t* ? „ 770
' O *t* and tender ! O my liege and King ! „ 791
Have all men *t* and leal, all women pure ! „ 794
So love be *t*, and not as yours is— „ 862
O, I, that flattering my *t* passion, „ 874
our *t* King Will then allow your pretext, *Lancelot and E.* 152
And found it *t*, and answer'd, ' *T*, my child. „ 370
Dearer to young hearts than their own praise, „ 419
' Our *t* Arthur, when he learns, „ 585
T, indeed, Albeit I know my knights fantastical, „ 593
our Lancelot ! that *t* man ! ' „ 665
I know not if I know what *t* love is, „ 676
Must our *t* man change like a leaf at last ? „ 686
And faith unfaithful kept him falsely *t*. „ 877
To speak the wish most near to your *t* heart ; „ 914
And then will I, for *t* you are and sweet „ 954
' Sweet is *t* love tho' given in vain, „ 1007
And folded, ' O sweet father, tender and *t*, „ 1110
And therefore my *t* love has been my death. „ 1277
for good she was and *t*, „ 1292
For all *t* hearts be blazon'd on her tomb „ 1344
like to coins, Some, some light, *Holy Grail* 26
' O son, thou hast not *t* humility, „ 445
' Hail, Bors ! if ever loyal man and *t* Could see it, „ 756
Dishonour'd all for trial of *t* love— *Pelleas and E.* 477
as the one *t* knight on earth, And only lover ; „ 494
' Is the King *t* ? ' ' The King ! ' said Percivale. „ 535
And harken if my music be not *t*. *Last Tournament* 274
And heard it ring as *t* as tested gold.' „ 284
' Fear God : honour the King—his one *t*
 knight— „ 302
The night was dark ; the *t* star set. „ 605
For what is *t* repentance but in thought— *Guinevere* 373
T men who love me still, for whom I live, „ 445
Too wholly *t* to dream untruth in thee, „ 541
My own *t* lord ! how dare I call him mine ? „ 617
Not rendering *t* answer, as beseem'd Thy fëalty, *Pass. of Arthur* 242
For now I see the *t* old times are dead, „ 397
And that *t* North, whereof we lately heard *To the Queen ii* 14
If this be *t*, At thought of which my whole soul *Lover's Tale i* 266
It fall on its own thorns—if this be *t*— „ 273
But, placing his *t* hand upon her heart, „ iv 75
Then, when her own *t* spirit had return'd, „ 108
I ha' been as *t* to you as ever a man to his wife ; *First Quarrel* 60
' You said that you hated me, Ellen, but that isn't
 t, you know ; „ 79

Trust (s) (*continued*) Should have in it an absoluter	
t To make	*Lancelot and E.* 1192
and his *t* that Heaven Will blow the tempest	*To the Queen* ii 46
My lily of truth and *t*—	*Ancient Sage* 160
Trust (verb) *I could t Your kindness.*	*To the Queen* 19
' *T* me, in bliss I shall abide	*Palace of Art* 18
To make him *t* his modest worth,	*L. C. V. de Vere* 46
T me, Clara Vere de Vere,	„ 49
I think my time is near. I *t* it is.	*May Queen, Con.* 41
I *t* That I am whole, and clean,	*St. S. Stylites* 212
t me on my word, Hard wood I am,	*Talking Oak* 170
T me, cousin, all the current of my being	*Locksley Hall* 24
He *t*'s to lent on something fair ;	*Day-Dm., Arrival* 20
Henceforth I *t* the man alone,	*The Letters* 31
And *t* me while I turn'd the page,	*To E. L.* 9
Raw from the nursery—who could *t* a child ?	*Aylmer's Field* 264
first I fronted him, Said, ' *T* him not ; '	*Sea Dreams* 71
' I *t* you,' said that other ' for we two	*Princess* ii 336
all, I *t*, may yet be well.'	„ 361
' O friend, we *t* that you esteem'd us not Too harsh	„ iii 198
To harm the thing that *t*'s him,	„ iv 248
nest of traitors—none to *t* Since our arms fail'd—	„ v 426
I *t* that there is no one hurt to death,	„ vi 242
And *t*, not love, you less.	„ 296
Lay thy sweet hands in mine and *t* to me.'	„ vii 366
May I himself ; and after praise and scorn,	*A Dedication* 6
And yet we *t* it comes from thee,	*In Mem., Pro.* 23
I *t* he lives in thee,	„ 39
Yet if some voice that man could *t*	„ xxxv 1
Nor dare she *t* a larger lay,	„ xlviii 13
Oh yet we *t* that somehow good	„ liv 1
I can but *t* that good shall fall At last—	„ 14
And faintly *t* the larger hope.	„ lv 20
But *t* that those we call the dead	„ cxviii 5
I *t* I have not wasted breath :	„ cxx 1
To one that with us works, and, *t*,	„ cxxxi 8
For I *t* if an enemy's fleet came yonder	*Maud* I i 49
I *t* that it is not so.	„ xvi 30
I *t* that I did not talk (repeat)	„ xix 12, 16
Let chance what will, I *t* thee to the death.'	*Com. of Arthur* 134
thy chief man Sir Lancelot whom he *t*'s to overthrow,	*Gareth and L.* 620
His arms are old, he *t*'s the harden'd skin—	„ 1139
Canst thou not *t* the limbs thy God hath given,	„ 1388
' *t* me not at all or all in all.' (repeat) *Merlin and V.* 384, 398, 449	
I *t* That you *t* me in your own nobleness,	*Lancelot and E.* 1194
I *t* We are green in Heaven's eyes ;	*Holy Grail* 37
T me, long ago I should have died,	*Lover's Tale* i 86
says The common voice, if one may *t* it :	*Sisters (E. and E.)* 37
T the Hand of Light will lead her people,	*On Jub. Q. Victoria* 68
To make him *t* his life, and give His fealty	*The Wanderer* 11
Trusted some sick man declined, And *t* any cure.	*Palace of Art* 156
t as he was with her, The sole succeeder	*Aylmer's Field* 293
fool ! and I him *t* with all, All my poor scrapings	*Sea Dreams* 76
Who *t* God was love indeed	*In Mem.* lvi 13
his chamberlain, to whom He *t* all things,	*Com. of Arthur* 146
t his liege-lord Would yield him this large honour	*Gareth and L.* 396
Too much I *t* when I told you that,	*Merlin and V.* 361
Yea, by God's rood, I *t* you too much.'	„ 376
Have I not sworn ? I am not *t*.	„ 527
A woman and not *t*,	„ 530
To have *t* me as he hath *t* thee.	*Lancelot and E.* 591
Trustee came *T*'s and Aunts and Uncles.	*Edwin Morris* 121
Trustful The *t* infant on the knee !	*Supp. Confessions* 41
the child would twine A *t* hand,	*In Mem.* cix 19
who take Their pastime now the *t* King is gone ! '	*Lancelot and E.* 101
And *t* courtesies of household life,	*Guinevere* 86
Truthful, *t*, looking upward to the practised hustings-liar ;	*Locksley H., Sixty* 123
Our kindlier, *t* Jaques, past away !	*To W. H. Brookfield* 11
Trusting *T* no longer that earthly flower	*Despair* 35
Truth When I went forth in quest of *t*,	*Supp. Confessions* 141
T may stand forth unmoved of change,	„ 144
Fair-fronted *T* shall droop not now	*Clear-headed friend* 12

Truth (*continued*) Weak *T* a-leaning on her crutch,	
Wan, wasted *T* in her utmost need.	*Clear-headed friend* 18
to fling The winged shafts of *t*,	*The Poet* 26
Thus *t* was multiplied on *t*,	„ 33
And all at once a pleasant *t* I learn'd,	*The Bridesmaid* 9
' This *t* within thy mind rehearse,	*Two Voices* 25
Still moving after *t* long sought,	„ 62
Named man, may hope some *t* to find,	„ 176
' Cry, faint not : either *T* is born	„ 181
was there Not less than *t* design'd.	*Palace of Art* 92
She spake some certain *t*'s of you.	*L. C. V. de Vere* 36
In *t*, How *should* I soothe you anyway,	*To J. S.* 57
Her open eyes desire the *t*.	*Of old sat Freedom* 17
To follow flying steps of *T*	*Love thou thy land* 75
a *t* Looks freshest in the fashion of the day :	*The Epic.* 31
Begin to feel the *t* and stir of day,	*M. d'Arthur, Ep.* 19
Shall Error in the round of time Still father *T* ?	*Love and Duty* 5
That make a man feel strong in speaking *t* ;	„ 70
With quiet eyes unfaithful to the *t*,	„ 94
Like *t*'s of Science waiting to be caught—	*Golden Year* 17
Amy, speak, and speak the *t* to me,	*Locksley Hall* 23
Cursed be the social lies that warp us from the living *t* !	„ 60
this is the poet sings,	„ 75
Bring *t* that sways the soul of men ?	*Day-Dm., Sleep. P.* 52
Nor finds a closer *t* than this All-graceful head,	„ *L'Envoi* 37
The *t*, that flies the flowing can,	*Will Water.* 171
' I speak the *t* : you are my child.	*Lady Clare* 24
I speak the *t*, as I live by bread !	„ 26
Trying his *t* and his long-sufferance,	*Enoch Arden* 470
and *t* and love are strength, And you are happy :	*Aylmer's Field* 365
To make a *t* less harsh, I often grew Tired	*Lucretius* 225
My golden work in which I told a *t*	„ 260
point you out the shadow from the *t* !	*Princess* i 84
yet, to speak the *t*, I rate your chance	„ 160
' Albeit so mask'd, Madam, I love the *t* ;	„ ii 213
So my mother clutch'd The *t* at once,	„ iii 61
wears her error like a crown To blind the *t* and me :	„ 112
I know the Prince, I prize his *t* :	„ 233
and dream and *t* Flow'd from me ;	„ v 541
call her hard and cold which seem'd a *t* :	„ vii 98
sought far less for *t* than power In knowledge :	„ 236
dreams Are but the needful preludes of the *t* :	„ *Con.* 74
never sold the *t* to serve the hour,	*Ode on Well.* 179
Between your peoples *t* and manful peace,	*W. to Marie Alex.* 49
That a lie which is half a *t*	*Grandmother* 30
But a lie which is part a *t*	„ 32
I know for a *t*, there's none of them	„ 85
So I pray you tell the *t* to me.	*The Victim* 48
Forgive them where they fail in *t*,	*In Mem., Pro.* 43
I HELD it *t*, with him who sings	„ i 1
To which she links a *t* divine !	„ xxxiii 12
Tho' *t*'s in manhood darkly join,	„ xxxvi 1
Where *t* in closest words shall fail,	„ 6
When *t* embodied in a tale Shall enter	„ 7
Of comfort clasp'd in *t* reveal'd ;	„ xxxvii 22
reaps A *t* from one that loves and knows ?	„ xlii 12
Yet who would preach it as a *t*	„ liii 12
I wake, and I discern the *t* ;	„ lxviii 14
This *t* came borne with bier and pall,	„ lxxxv 1
Ring in the love of *t* and right,	„ cvi 23
Nor dream of human love and *t*,	„ cxviii 3
Because he felt so fix'd in *t* :	„ cxxv 8
Proclaiming social *t* shall spread,	„ cxxvii 5
The *t*'s that never can be proved	„ cxxxi 10
I have walk'd awake with *T*.	*Maud* I xix 4
whether there were *t* in anything Said by these three,	*Com. of Arthur* 242
and ask'd him if these things were *t*—	„ 398
And *t* is this to me, and that to thee ;	„ 407
And *t* or clothed or naked let it be.	„ 408
but tell thou these the *t*.'	*Gareth and L.* 251
And here is *t* ; but an it please thee not, Take thou the *t* as thou hast told it me.	„ 256
beard That looks as white as utter *t*,	„ 281
' Ay, truly of a *t*, And in a sort,	„ 837

Truth (*continued*) Where should be *t* if not in Arthur's hall, *Gareth and L.* 1254
Arms ? *t* ! I know not : all are wanted here. *Marr. of Geraint* 289
t, good *t*, I know not, save, ,, 290
Said Arthur ' Thou hast ever spoken *t* ; *Balin and Balan* 73
' Nay ' said the churl, ' our devil is a *t*, ,, 302
But thou art man, and canst abide a *t*, ,, 501
lightest word Is mere white *t* in simple nakedness, ,, 518
Breathed in a dismal whisper ' Is it *t*.' ,, 527
and shown the *t* betimes, That old true filth, and bottom of the well, Where *T* is hidden. *Merlin and V.* 46
for shall I tell you *t* ? You seem'd that wave ,, 301
By Heaven that hears I tell you the clean *t*, ,, 343
He brought, not found it therefore : take the *t*.' ,, 719
In *t*, but one thing now— ,, 918
Urged him to speak against the *t*, *Lancelot and E.* 92
In lieu of idly dallying with the *t*, ,, 590
I swear by *t* and knighthood that I gave No cause, ,, 1297
And as ye saw it ye have spoken *t*. *Holy Grail* 880
And love of *t*, and all that makes a man. *Guinevere* 483
yet, in *t*, Fair speech was his and delicate of phrase, *Lover's Tale i* 718
told them my tale, God's own *t*— *Rizpah* 34
That traitor to King Richard and the *t*, *Sir J. Oldcastle* 171
showing courts and kings a *t* *Columbus* 37
morning-star to the full round of *t*. ,, 44
and murmur down *T* in the distance— ,, 121
These hard memorials of our *t* to Spain ,, 196
And speak the *t* that no man may believe.' *Tiresias* 50
I speak the *t* Believe I speak it, ,, 155
My lily of *t* and trust— *Ancient Sage* 160
every heart that loves with *t* is equal to endure. *The Flight* 104
T, for *T* is *T*, he worshipt, *Locksley H., Sixty* 59
T for *t*, and good for good ! ,, 71
these would feel and follow *T* ,, 119
led by Justice, Love, and *T* ; ,, 161
For man is a lover of *T*, *Dead Prophet* 44
Yet a *t* is a *t*,' she cried. ,, 60
surely to be found When *T* is found again. *Pref. Poem Broth. Son.* 16
By one side-path, from simple *t* ; *To Marq. of Dufferin* 28
and you the soul of *T* In Hubert ? *The Ring* 62
Grafted on half a *t* ; *Romney's R.* 42
One *t* will damn me with the mindless mob, ,, 120
neither of them stands behind the screen of thy *t*. *Akbar's D., Inscrip.* 7
held His people by the bridle-rein of *T*. *Akbar's Dream* 85
and Love The net of *t* ? ' ,, 88
Thro' after ages in the love of *T*, The *t* of Love. ,, 101
nurse my children on the milk of *T*, ,, 162
T and Peace And Love and Justice came and dwelt therein ; ,, 180
T, Peace, Love and Justice came and dwelt therein, ,, 193
violates virgin *T* for a coin or a cheque. *The Dawn* 15
And I clash with an iron *T*, *The Dreamer* 6
Truthful half as good, as kind, As *t*, *Princess v* 202
This *t* change in thee has kill'd it. ,, *vii* 350
The *t* King will doom me when I speak.' *Gareth and L.* 324
T, trustful, looking upward to the practised hustings-liar ; *Locksley H., Sixty* 123
So princely, tender, *t*, reverent, pure— *D. of the Duke of C.* 4
Truthless *t* violence mourn'd by the Wise, *Vastness* 5
Truth-lover *T-l* was our English Duke, *Ode on Well.* 189
Truth-speaking *T-s*, brave, good livers, *Gareth and L.* 424
Truth-teller *T-t* was our England's Alfred named ; *Ode on Well.* 188
Try 'Twere well to question him, and *t* *Talking Oak* 27
Nor thro' the questions men may *t*, *In Mem. cxxiv* 7
Like him who *tries* the bridge he fears may fail, *Geraint and E.* 303
Should *t* this charm on whom ye say ye love.' *Merlin and V.* 525
should ye *t* him with a merry one *Pelleas and E.* 198
Trying *T* his truth and his long-sufferance, *Enoch Arden* 470
And *t* to pass to the sea ; *Maud I xxi* 7
happier using the knife than in *t* to save the limb, *In the Child. Hosp.* 6
Tryst That ever bided *t* at village stile, *Merlin and V.* 378
Tsernogora Great *T* ! never since thine own *Montenegro* 12
Tudor-chimnied a *T-c* bulk Of mellow brickwork *Edwin Morris* 11

Tued (*worried*) (*See also* **Tew**) But 'e *t* and moil'd issén deäd, *N. Farmer, N. S.* 52
Tuff hornblende, rag and trap and *t*, *Princess iii* 362
Tuft (**s**) In *t's* of rosy-tinted snow ; *Two Voices* 60
Behind yon whispering *t* of oldest pine, *Œnone* 88
A light-green *t* of plumes she bore *Sir L. and Q. G.* 26
Tuft (**verb**) When rosy plumelets *t* the larch, *In Mem. xci* 1
And *t* with grass a feudal tower ; ,, *cxxviii* 20
Tufted And the *t* plover pipe along the fallow lea, *May Queen, N. Y's. E.* 18
Filling with purple gloom the vacancies Between the *t* hills, *Lover's Tale i* 2
Tugging *See* **A-tuggin**
Tuk (**took**) Father Molowny he *t* her in han', *Tomorrow* 55
Tulip sometimes a Dutch love For *t's* ; *Gardener's D.* 193
Deep *t's* dash'd with fiery dew, *In Mem. lxxxiii* 11
Thro' the fire of the *t* and poppy, *V. of Maeldune* 43
Tumble (**s**) after a long *t* about the Cape *Enoch Arden* 532
Should I flounder awhile without a *t* *Hendacasyllabics* 9
Maud with her venturous climbings and *t's* *Maud I i* 69
Tumble (**verb**) Lest he should swoon and *t* *Enoch Arden* 774
' They mounted, Ganymedes, To *t*, Vulcans, *Princess iii* 72
T's a billow on chalk and sand ; *To F. D. Maurice* 24
Hard, hard, hard is it, only not to *t*, *Hendecasyllabics* 13
Look how they *t* the blossom, the mad little tits ! *Window, Ay* 9
Dark bulks that *t* half alive, *In Mem. lxx* 11
like a crag that *t's* from the cliff, *Marr. of Geraint* 318
a rougher gust might *t* a stormier wave, *The Wreck* 131
Tumbled (**adj. and part.**) Among the fragments *t* from the glens, *Œnone* 222
babies roll'd about Like *t* fruit in grass ; *Princess, Pro.* 83
And had a cousin *t* on the plain, ,, *vi* 319
Among the *t* fragments of the hills.' *Lancelot and E.* 1427
Rear'd on the *t* ruins of an old fane *St. Telemachus* 6
Tumbled (**verb**) (*See also* **Tummled**) And half the chimneys *t*. *The Goose* 48
T the tawny rascal at his feet, *Aylmer's Field* 230
you *t* down and broke The glass *Sea Dreams* 141
And every Muse *t* a science in. *Princess ii* 399
And *t* on the purple footcloth, ,, *iv* 286
And *t* half the mellowing pears ! *In Mem. lxxxix* 20
That *t* in the Godless deep ; ,, *cxxiv* 12
then in the mere beside *T* it ; *Gareth and L.* 816
And *t* back into the kitchen-knave, ,, 1228
To hang whatever knight of thine I fought And *t*. *Last Tournament* 454
She *t* his helpless corpse about. *Dead Prophet* 65
Tumbling (*See also* **Tummlin'**) *T* the hollow helmets of the fallen, *Pass. of Arthur* 132
Tummled (**tumbled**) An' I *t* athurt the craädle *North. Cobbler* 35
t up stairs, fur I 'eärd 'im, *Owd Roä* 63
Tummlin' (**tumbling**) when the rigtree was *t'* in— ,, 115
Tumult the *t* of their acclaim is roll'd *Dying Swan* 33
Laid by the *t* of the fight. *Margaret* 26
and the *t* of my life ; *Locksley Hall* 110
in an hour Of civic *t* jam the doors, *Lucretius* 169
call'd Across the *t* and the *t* fell. *Princess iv* 497
The cataract and the *t* and the kings ,, 564
Is wrought with *t* of acclaim. *In Mem. lxxv* 20
And saw the *t* of the halls ; ,, *lxxxvii* 4
O'erlook'st the *t* from afar, ,, *cxxvii* 19
For a *t* shakes the city, *Maud II iv* 50
' What means the *t* in the town ? ' *Marr. of Geraint* 259
And ate with *t* in the naked hall, *Geraint and E.* 605
(Because the hall was all in *t*— *Holy Grail* 269
Tumultuous So the silent colony hearing her *t* adversaries *Boädicea* 78
Tumultuously *t* Down thro' the whitening hazels *Enoch Arden* 378
Tundher (**thunder**) *t*, an' rain that fell, *Tomorrow* 23
Tune (**s**) wildest wailings never out of *t* *Sea Dreams* 231
howl in *t* With nothing but the Devil ! ' ,, 260
Their hearts of old have beat in *t*, *In Mem. xcvii* 10
To the dancers dancing in *t* ; *Maud I xxii* 16
' Ye might have moved slow-measure to my *t*, *Last Tournament* 282
and learn'd To lisp in *t* together ; *Lover's Tale i* 258
MIDNIGHT—in no midsummer *t* ; *Pref. Poem Broth. Son.* 1
Tune (**verb**) Who scarce can *t* his high majestic sense *Lover's Tale i* 475
Tuned *See* **Full-tuned**

Tuwhoo (continued) *T*, tuwhit, tuwhit, t-o-o. — *The Owl* ii 14
T ! do you see it ? do ye see the star ? ' — *Last Tournament* 346
Twain yearn'd and strove To tear the *t* asunder — *Holy Grail* 786
when I knew the *t* Would each waste each, — *Tiresias* 68
Twang (s) sharp clear *t* of the golden chords — *Sea-Fairies* 38
Twang (verb) *T* out, my fiddle ! shake the twigs ! — *Amphion* 61
Twanging Clear as the *t* of a harp. — *Kate* 8
Fly *t* headless arrows at the hearts, — *Princess* ii 402
Twangled Then he *t* on his harp, And while he *t* — *Last Tournament* 251
Twangling while the *t* violin Struck up with Soldier-laddie, — *Princess*, Pro. 85
But when the *t* ended, skipt again ; — *Last Tournament* 255
Twelve ' he burnt His epic, his King Arthur, some books '— *The Epic* 28
these *t* books of mine Were faint Homeric echoes, — „ 38
With *t* great shocks of sound, — *Godiva* 74
silver knell Of *t* sweet hours that past — *Maud* I xviii 65
in *t* great battles overcame The heathen hordes, — *Com. of Arthur* 518
With all the passion of a *t* hours' fast.' — *Marr. of Geraint* 306
made Those banners of *t* battles overhead — *Balin and Balan* 88
Those *t* sweet moons confused his fatherhood.' — *Merlin and V.* 712
Where *t* great windows blazon Arthur's wars, — *Holy Grail* 248
Streams thro' the *t* great battles of our King. — „ 250
Knights that in *t* great battles splash'd and dyed — „ 311
The *t* small damosels white as Innocence, — *Last Tournament* 291
In *t* great battles ruining overthrown. — *Guinevere* 432
ten or *t* good paces or more. — *Def. of Lucknow* 62
—and those *t* gates, Pearl!—and I woke, — *Columbus* 86
as ye used to do *t* year sin' ! — *Spinster's S's.* 59
T times in the year Bring me bliss, — *The Ring* 5
Twelve-divided Sent like the *t-d* concubine — *Aylmer's Field* 759
Twelvemonth thou shalt serve a *t* and a day.' — *Gareth and L.* 157
meat and drink among thy kitchen-knaves A *t* and a day, — „ 446
would ride A *t* and a day in quest of it, — *Holy Grail* 196
My *t* and a day were pleasant to me.' — „ 750
Twenty By *t* thorps, a little town, — *The Brook* 29
For here I came, *t* years back— — „ 77
About these meadows, *t* years ago.' — „ 220
wealth enough for theirs For *t* matches. — *Aylmer's Field* 370
Why *t* boys and girls should marry on it, — „ 371
So old, that *t* years before, a part Falling — „ 508
face to face With *t* months of silence, — „ 567
And there thro' *t* posts of telegraph — *Princess*, Pro. 77
or so she look'd, Of *t* summers. — „ ii 108
And cheep and twitter *t* million loves. — „ iv 101
There was not his like that year in *t* parishes round. — *Grandmother* 12
Time to think on it then ; for thou'll be *t* to weeäk. — *N. Farmer, N. S.* 7
Thro' *t* folds of twisted dragon, — *Gareth and L.* 510
Old, with the might and breath of *t* boys.' — „ 1106
ten-times worthier to be thine Than *t* Balins, — *Balin and Balan* 69
Whose bark had plunder'd *t* nameless isles ; — *Merlin and V.* 559
O ay, it is but *t* pages long, — „ 668
Yea, *t* times I thought him Lancelot— — *Lancelot and E.* 535
For *t* strokes of the blood, without a word, — „ 720
' I had liefer *t* years Skip to the broken music — *Last Tournament* 257
I sarved 'em wi' butter an' heggs fur huppuds o' *t* year. — *Village Wife* 114
still for *t* years Bound by the golden cord — *The Ring* 428
But if *t* million of summers are stored in the sunlight still, — *The Dawn* 19
Twenty-five so bitter When I am but *t-f* ? — *Maud* I vi 34
Twenty-fold I scent it *t-f*.' — *Gareth and L.* 995
Twice And *t* three years I crouch'd on one — *St. S. Stylites* 88
Twig Twang out, my fiddle ! shake the *t's* ! — *Amphion* 61
low bushes dip their *t's* in foam, — *Prog. of Spring* 51
Twilight (adj.) Long alleys falling down to *t* grots, — *Ode to Memory* 107
Than our poor *t* dawn on earth— — *Tiresias* 206
Twilight (s) In the purple *t's* under the sea ; — *The Mermaid* 44
That sets at *t* in a land of reeds. — *Caress'd or chidden* 14
About him broods the *t* dim : — *Two Voices* 263
gray *t* pour'd On dewy pastures, dewy trees, — *Palace of Art* 85
rain'd about the leaf *T's* of airy silver, — *Audley Court* 82
And either *t* and the day between ; — *Edwin Morris* 37
And beat the *t* into flakes of fire. — *Tithonus* 42
Pilots of the purple *t*, — *Locksley Hall* 122
The *t* melted into morn. — *Day-Dm., Depart.* 16
The *t* died into the dark. — „ 24
purple-skirted robe Of *t* slowly downward drawn, — *The Voyage* 22
November day Was growing duller *t*, — *Enoch Arden* 722
And, into mournful *t* mellowing, — *Princess* vi 191

Twilight (s) (continued) And *t* dawn'd ; and morn by morn the lark — *Princess* vii 45
And *t* gloom'd ; and broader-grown the bowers — „ vii 48
Deepening the courts of *t* broke them up — „ Con. 113
I watch the *t* falling brown — *To F. D. Maurice* 14
The *t* of eternal day. — *In Mem.* l 16
All winds that roam the *t* came — *In Mem.* lxxix 11
When it was falling, — *Maud* I xii 2
thro' the feeble *t* of this world Groping, — *Geraint and E.* 5
when the gloom Of *t* deepens round it, — *Balin and Balan* 233
day by day she past In either *t* ghost-like to and fro — *Lancelot and E.* 849
Thro' that green-glooming *t* of the grove, — *Pelleas and E.* 33
day Grew drearier toward *t* falling, — *Pass. of Arthur* 123
The rosy *t* of a perfect day. — *The Ring* 187
T and evening bell, — *Crossing the Bar* 9
Twin (adj.) *T* peaks shadow'd with pine slope to the dark hyaline. — *Leonine Eleg.* 10
nor yet Did those *t* brothers, risen again and whole ; — *Princess* vii 89
Twin (s) nor the *t's* Her brethren, tho' they love her, — „ i 153
two crowned *t's*, Commerce and conquest, — „ v 420
A lusty brace Of *t's* may weed her of her folly. — „ 464
Henceforth that mystic bond betwixt the *t's*—
Did I not tell you they were *t's* ?— — *Sisters (E. and E.)* 256
Twin-brother Sleep, Death's *t-b*, (repeat) — *In Mem.* lxviii 2, 3
Twine (s) reverend beard Of grisly *t*, — *Princess* vi 104
Twine (verb) Clasp her window, trail and *t* ! — *Window, At the Window* 2
Trail and *t* and clasp and kiss, — „ 4
the child would to *t* A trustful hand, — *In Mem.* cix 18
Began to move, seethe, *t* and curl : — *Gareth and L.* 234
T round one sin, whatever it might be, — *Holy Grail* 883
soul *t's* and mingles with the growths — *Lover's Tale* i 132
Twined (See also **Thick-twined**) locks a-drooping *t* Round thy neck — *Adeline* 57
leaning on a fragrant *t* with vine, — *Œnone* 20
Behind his ankle *t* her hollow feet — *Merlin and V.* 240
knightly in me *t* and clung Round that one sin, — *Holy Grail* 774
an' *t* like a band o' haäy. — *Owd Roä* 22
and this you *t* About her cap. — *Romney's R.* 79
Twinkle (s) There is not left a *t* of a fin — *Geraint and E.* 474
Then with a ribald *t* in his bleak eyes— — *The Ring* 199
Twinkle (verb) I see his gray eyes *t* yet — *Miller's D.* 11
The lights begin to *t* from the rocks : — *Ulysses* 54
That *t* into green and gold : — *In Mem.* xi 8
A livelier emerald *t's* in the grass, — *Maud* I xviii 51
Twinkled For all the haft *t* with diamond sparks, — *M. d'Arthur* 56
T the innumerable ear and tail. — *The Brook* 134
Echo'd the walls ; a light *t* ; — *Gareth and L.* 1370
For all the haft *t* with diamond sparks, — *Pass. of Arthur* 224
Twinkling momently The *t* laurel scatter'd silver lights. — *Gardener's D.* 118
Till at thy chuckled note, Thou *t* bird, — *Early Spring* 38
Twinn'd *t* as horse's ear and eye. — *Princess* i 57
Twin-sister Margaret, than your *t-s*, Adeline. — *Margaret* 48
like *t-s's* grew, *T-s's* differently beautiful. — *Edwin Morris* 32
Twist (s) A *t* of gold was round her hair ; — *Merlin and V.* 221
Twist (verb) Would *t* his girdle tight, and pat — *Talking Oak* 43
And *t's* the grain with such a roar — *Princess* v 528
Sware by the scorpion-worm that *t's* in hell, — *Last Tournament* 451
Twisted (See also **A-twizzen'd, Co-twisted**) A million tapers flaring bright From *t* silvers — *Arabian Nights* 125
T as tight as I could knot the noose ; — *St. S. Stylites* 65
With *t* quirks and happy hits, — *Will Water.* 189
Now on some *t* ivy-net, — *Sir L. and Q. G.* 28
how the words Have *t* back upon themselves, — *Aylmer's Field* 755
And *t* shapes of lust, unspeakable, — *Lucretius* 157
now A *t* snake, and now a rain of pearls, — *Princess*, Pro. 62
Thro' twenty folds of *t* dragon, — *Gareth and L.* 510
T hard in fierce embraces, — *Vision of Sin* 40
Winking his eyes, and *t* all his face. — *Lancelot and E.* 1145
and this *t* in mortal agony — *Locksley H., Sixty* 98
Twisting Is *t* round the polar star ; — *In Mem.* ci 12
Twit to *t* me with the cause ! — *Lover's Tale* i 661
Twitch Paled at a sudden *t* of his iron mouth ; — *Aylmer's Field* 732
a *t* of pain Tortured her mouth, — *Princess* vi 105
Twitch'd *t* the reins, And made his beast — *Pelleas and E.* 550
Then his pale face *t* ; — *The Wreck* 101
Twitter (verb) cheep and *t* twenty million loves. — *Princess* iv 101

Twitter (s)   as a rustle or *t* in the wood Made dull his
inner,   *Last Tournament* 365

Two   Low-throned Hesper is stayed between the *t* peaks ;   *Leonine Eleg.* 11
With Cyril and with Florian, my *t* friends :   *Princess* i 52
T widows, Lady Psyche, Lady Blanche ;   ,,   128
With *t* tame leopards couch'd beside her throne,   ,. ii 33
' everywhere *T* heads in council, *t* beside the hearth,
  T in the tangled business of the world, *T* in the
  liberal offices of life, *T* plummets dropt for one to
  sound the abyss   ,, 173
And *t* dear things are one of double worth,   ,, 419
Before *t* streams of light from wall to wall,   ,, 473
Herself and Lady Psyche the *t* arms ;   ,, iii 35
' Read,' and I read—*t* letters—one her sire's.   ,, iv 397
Till one of those *t* brothers, half aside   ,, v 302
Down From those *t* bulks at Arac's side,   ,, 499
So those *t* foes above my fallen life,   ,, vi 130
T women faster welded in one love   ,, 253
the *t* great cats Close by her,   ,, 357
From those *t* hosts that lay beside the walls,   ,, 383
Than when *t* dewdrops on the petal shake   ,, vii 68
wherein were wrought *T* grand designs ;   ,, 122
I walk'd with one I loved *t* and thirty years ago.   *V. of Cauteretz* 4
t and thirty years were a mist that rolls away ;   ,, 6
T dead men have I known   *G. of Swainston* 11
T dead men have I loved   ,, 13
T bright stars Peep'd into the shell.   *Minnie and Winnie* 13
T little hands that meet, (repeat)   *Window, Answer* 1, 4
With Gawain and young Modred, her *t* sons,   *Com. of Arthur* 244
sign'd To those *t* sons to pass, and let them be.   ,, 319
field of charlock in the sudden sun Between *t* showers,   *Gareth and L.* 389
by *t* yards in casting bar or stone Was counted best ;   ,, 518
Now *t* great entries open'd from the hall,   ,, 665
T forks are fixt into the meadow ground,   *Marr. of Geraint* 482
What I these *t* years past have won for thee,   ,, 554
' These *t* things shalt thou do, (repeat)   ,, 580, 586
And made it of *t* colours ;   *Geraint and E.* 292
And we will live like *t* birds in one nest,   ,, 627
But Enid in their going had *t* fears,   ,, 817
But nevermore the same *t* sister pearls   *Merlin and V.* 454
He saw *t* cities in a thousand boats   ,, 561
And *t* fair babes, and went to distant lands ;   ,, 707
For here *t* brothers, one a king, had met   *Lancelot and E.* 39
With *t* strong sons, Sir Torre and Sir Lavaine,   ,, 174
from the carven-work behind him crept *T* dragons gilded,   ,, 437
after *t* days' tarriance there, return'd.   ,, 569
those *t* brethren slowly with bent brows Accompanying,   ,, 1138
So those *t* brethren from the chariot took   ,, 1146
Those *t* great beasts rose upright like a man,   *Holy Grail* 821
So from each Of those *t* pillars which from earth   *Lover's Tale* i 220
at one end of the hall *T* great funereal curtains,   ,, iv 214
On a sudden after *t* Italian years   *Sisters (E. and E.)* 150
then *t* weeks—no more—she joined,   ,, 271
Roar upon roar in a moment *t* mines by the enemy   *Def. of Lucknow* 54
Lord give thou power to thy *t* witnesses !   *Sir J. Oldcastle* 81
I So mock'd, so spurn'd, so baited *t* whole days—   ,, 163
so might there be *T* Adams, *t* mankinds,   *Columbus* 54
There came *t* voices from the Sepulchre, *T* friars crying
  that if Spain should oust   ,, 95
T voices heard on earth no more ;   *To E. Fitzgerald* 41
' His *t* wild woodland flowers.'   *The Flight* 80
I' a kep' thruf thick an' thin my *t* 'oonderd a-year
  to mysen ;   *Spinster's S's.* 12
Thou 'ed wellnigh purr'd ma awaäy fro' my oän *t*
  'oonderd a-year.   ,, 58
Like some conjectured planet in mid heaven Between
  t Suns,   *Prin. Beatrice* 21
An' the Heagle 'as hed *t* heäds stannin' theere   *Owd Roä* 25
' The souls Of *t* repentant Lovers guard the ring ; '   *The Ring* 198
T lovers parted by a scurrilous tale Had quarrell'd,   ,, 208
T lovers parted by no scurrilous tale—   ,, 427
—those *t* Ghost lovers— *Father.* Lovers yet—   ,, 459
What be those *t* shapes high over the sacred fountain,   *Parnassus* 9
t known peaks they stand ever spreading   ,, 11
T words, ' *My Rose* ' set all your face aglow,   *Roses on the T.* 3
T trains clash'd : then and there he was crush'd   *Charity* 21

Two-cell'd   The *t-c* heart beating, with one full stroke,   *Princess* vii 307
Twofold   One *t* mightier than the other was,   *Lover's Tale* i 211
Twofooted   *T* at the limit of his chain,   *Aylmer's Field* 127
Twy-natured   *T-n* is no nature :   *Lucretius* 194
Type (s)   Tho' all her fairest forms are *t's* of thee,   *Isabel* 39
' That *t* of Perfect in his mind   *Two Voices* 292
Became an outward breathing *t,*   *Miller's D.* 226
carved cross-bones, the *t's* of Death,   *Will Water.* 245
And ev'n for want of such a *t.*   *In Mem. xxxiii* 16
So careful of the *t* she seems,   ,, lv 7
' So careful of the *t* ? ' but no.   ,, lvi 3
She cries, ' A thousand *t's* are gone :   ,, Con. 138
man, that with me trod This planet, was a noble *t*   *Maud II* iv 58
Pass, thou deathlike *t* of pain,   ,,
Type (verb)   ' Dear, but let us *t* them now   *Princess* vii 299
If so he *t* this work of time   *In Mem. cxviii* 16
Which *t's* all Nature's male and female   *On One who aff. E. M.* 3
Tyrannous   And fused together in the *t* light—   *Lover's Tale* ii 67
Tyranny   And play the slave to gain the *t.*   *Princess* iv 132
Thought on all her evil *tyrannies,*   *Boädicea* 80
Out of evil evil flourishes, out of *t t* buds.   ,, 83
iron *t* now should bend or cease,   *Maud III* vi 37
My warning that the *t* of one Was prelude to
  the *t* of all ? My counsel that the *t* of all Led
  backward to the *t* of one ?   *Tiresias* 73
Tyrant (adj.)   Caught in a great old *t* spider's web,   *Merlin and V.* 259
No father now, the *t* vassal of a *t* vice !   *The Flight* 25
Tyrant (s)   Faster binds a *t's* power ; And the *t's* cruel
  glee Forces on the freer hour,   *Vision of Sin* 128
Pity, the violet on the *t's* grave.   *Aylmer's Field* 845
' Kill him now, The *t* !   *Princess, Pro.* 207
our dead captain taught The *t,*   *Ode on Well.* 70
Our Britain cannot salve a *t* o'er.   *Third of Feb.* 42
we will not spare the *t* one hard word.   ,,
makes you *t's* in your iron skies,   *Maud I* xviii 37
Than hardest *t's* in their day of power,   *Geraint and E.* 695
Have turn'd to *t's* when they came to power)   *Merlin and V.* 518
Gone the *t* of my youth,   *Locksley H., Sixty* 43
WARRIOR of God, man's friend, and *t's* foe,   *Epit. on Gordon* 1
Tyre   Against the guiltless heirs of him from *T,*   *Tiresias* 12
red-hot palms of a Moloch of *T,*   *The Dawn* 2
Tyrol   A cap of *T* borrow'd from the hall,   *Princess* iv 601

U

Udder   Nosing the mother's *u,*   *Lucretius* 100
Udder'd   *See* **Deep-udder'd**
Ugly   (*See also* **Hugly**)   Feyther 'ud saäy I wur *u* es sin,   *Spinster's S's.* 15
Ulama   our *U,* Who " sitting on green sofas   *Akbar's Dream* 47
Ulcer   the *u,* eating thro' my skin,   *St. S. Stylites* 67
Ulcerous   aches, stitches, *u* throes and cramps,   ,, 13
Ulfius (**a Knight of the Round Table**)   *U,* and
  Brastias, and Bedivere, (repeat)   *Com. of Arthur* 136, 165
And *U* and Brastias answer'd, ' Ay.'   ,, 173
Ulric   Where noble *U* dwells forlorn,   *Happy* 10
Who whisper'd me ' your *U* loves '—   ,, 62
' Let us revenge ourselves, your *U* woos my wife '—   ,, 63
Ultramontane   Most generous of all *U's,* Ward,   *In Mem., W. G. Ward* 4
Ulysses   *U,* much-experienced man,   *To Ulysses* 1
Umpire   by common voice, Elected *u,*   *Œnone* 85
Sat their great *u,* looking o'er the lists.   *Last Tournament* 159
Unabated   In confidence of *u* strength,   *Lover's Tale* i 511
Unaccomplish'd   The hope of *u* years   *In Mem. xci* 7
and Balan lurking there (His quest was *u*)   *Balin and Balan* 547
Unanimous   Clash the darts and on the buckler beat with
  rapid *u* hand,   *Boädicea* 79
Unannounced   My lady's Indian kinsman *u*   *Aylmer's Field* 190
Unanswer'd   *U,* since I spake not ;   *Lover's Tale* i 707
Unapproached   Shelter'd his *u* mysteries :   *Alexander* 11
not rather A sacred, secret, *u* woe,   *Lover's Tale* i 679
Unarm'd   the lawless warrior paced *U,*   *Gareth and L.* 915
See that he fall not on thee suddenly, And slay thee *u* :   ,, 922
For tho' I ride *u,* I do not doubt To find,   *Marr. of Geraint* 218

BB

Understand (*continued*) The words were hard to *u*.   *In Mem. lxix* 20
   ' I cannot *u* : I love.'   "   *xcvii* 36
   What is, and no man *u's* ;   "   *cxxiv* 22
   nursed at ease and brought to *u* A sad astrology,   *Maud I xviii* 35
   Thou canst not *u* That thou art left for ever alone :   "   *II iii* 3
   I hold a finger up ; They *u*:   *Geraint and E.* 338
   But you are man, you well can *u*   *Merlin and V.* 697
   these can never know thee, They cannot *u* me.   *Lover's Tale i* 286
   if you shall fail to *u* What England is,   *The Fleet* 1
   Now first we stand and *u*,   *Mechanophilus* 1
Understandest Nor *u* bound nor boundlessness,   *Ancient Sage* 48
Understanding *u* all the foolish work Of Fancy,   *Princess vi* 116
Understond (**understand**) I kep 'um, my lass, tha
   mun *u* ;   *N. Farmer, O. S.* 23
Understood A notice faintly *u*,   *Two Voices* 431
   O thou that stonest, hadst thou *u*   *Aylmer's Field* 739
   The land, he *u*, for miles about Was till'd by women ;   *Princess i* 191
   Loved deeplier, darklier *u* ;   *In Mem. cxxix* 10
   the prophecy given of old And then not *u*,   *Maud II v* 43
   And best by her that bore her *u*.   *Marr. of Geraint* 511
Undertake Wilt thou *I u* them as we pass,   *Balin and Balan* 14
Under-tone And from within me a clear *u-t*   *D. of F. Women* 81
Underwent Did more, and *u*, and overcame,   *Godiva* 10
   Gareth all for glory *u* The sooty yoke of kitchen-
   vassalage ;   *Gareth and L.* 478
Underworld That brings our friends up from the *u*,   *Princess iv* 45
Undescried tho' *u*, Winning its way with extreme gentleness   *Isabel* 22
Undevelopt For woman is not *u* man,   *Princess vii* 275
Undherstan' (**understand**) ' me dear, av I *u*,'   *Tomorrow* 56
Undimmed And holdeth his *u* forehead far   *Lover's Tale i* 513
Undiscover'd And thine in *u* lands.   *In Mem. xl* 32
Undissolved A sleep by kisses *u*,   *Day-Dm., L'Envoi* 51
Undo Thoroughly to *u*,   *Lilian* 11
   in seeking to *u* One riddle, and to find the true,   *Two Voices* 232
   To know her beauty might half *u* it.   *Maud I xvi* 19
   fineness, Lancelot, some fine day *U* thee not—   *Gareth and L.* 477
   And never could *u* it : ask no more :   *Merlin and V.* 686
Undoing flattery and the craft Which were my *u* . . .   *Forlorn* 4
Undone What harm, *u* ? deep harm to disobey,   *M. d'Arthur* 93
   What harm, *u* ? Deep harm to disobey,   *Pass. of Arthur* 261
Undrainable labour'd mine *u* of ore.   *Œnone* 115
Undress'd wear an *u* goatskin on my back ;   *St. S. Stylites* 116
Undulated *u* The banner : anon to meet us   *Princess v* 253
Undulation cries, And *u's* to and fro.   *In Mem. cxiii* 20
Undying Clear, without heat, *u*,   *Isabel* 3
   And it sings a song of love ;   *Poet's Mind* 33
   with *u* bliss In knowledge of their own supremacy.'   *Œnone* 132
Unearn'd doubtless, all *u* by noble deeds.   *Balin and Balan* 471
Unearthlier *U* than all shriek of bird or beast,   "   545
Unequal in true marriage lies Nor equal, nor *u* :   *Princess vii* 303
   I mete and dole *U* laws unto a savage race,   *Ulysses* 4
Unexhausted bloodily fall the battle-axe, *u*,   *Boädicea* 56
Unexpected as one Caught in a burst of *u* storm,   *Aylmer's Field* 285
Unexpress'd I leave thy praises *u*   *In Mem. lxxv* 1
Unfair Who shall call me ungentle, *u*,   *Maud I xiii* 14
Unfaith Faith and *u* can ne'er be equal powers :   *Merlin and V.* 388
   U in aught is want of faith in all.   "   389
Unfaithful With quiet eyes *u* to the truth,   *Love and Duty* 94
   And faith *u* kept him falsely true.   *Lancelot and E.* 877
Unfamiliar But *u* Arno, and the dome Of Brunelleschi ;   *The Brook* 189
Unfarrow'd And so return'd *u* to her sty.   *Walk. to the Mail* 100
Unfathom'd There on the depth of an *u* woe   *Lover's Tale i* 746
Unfelt shock of gloom had fall'n *U*,   "   506
   U by the sense of crime,   *In Mem. xxvii* 7
Unfinish'd work is left *U*—if I go.   *Lucretius* 104
Unfit *U* for earth, *u* for heaven,   *St. S. Stylites* 3
Unfold I see thy beauty gradually *u*,   *Eleänore* 70
   And like a flower that cannot all *u*,   *Princess vii* 141
Unfolding hour by hour *u* woodbine leaves   *Prog. of Spring* 7
Unforgotten Moved from the cloud of *u* things,   *Lover's Tale i* 48
Unfrequent *U*, low, as tho' it told its pulses ;   "   *ii* 55
Unfriendly *U* of your parted guest.   *The Wanderer* 4
Unfrowardly thou canst not bide, *u*,   *Pelleas and E.* 597
Unfulfill'd O therefore that the *u* desire,   *Tiresias* 79
Unfurl *u* the maiden banner of our rights,   *Princess iv* 503

Unfurnish'd *U* brows, tempestuous tongues—   *Freedom* 38
Ungainliness mocking at the much *u*,   *Last Tournament* 728
Ungainly *See* **Unheppen**
Ungarner'd And whirl the *u* sheaf afar,   *In Mem. lxxii* 23
Ungather'd To-night *u* let us leave   "   *cv* 1
Ungenerous ' *U*, dishonourable, base,   *Aylmer's Field* 292
Ungentle Who shall call me *u*, unfair,   *Maud I xiii* 14
   to be gentle than *u* with you ;   *Geraint and E.* 716
   The most *u* knight in Arthur's hall.'   *Gareth and L.* 757
Ungracious I am more *u* ev'n than you,   *Aylmer's Field* 247
   A bird's-eye-view of all the *u* past ;   *Princess ii* 125
   ' *U* !' answer'd Florian ; ' have you learnt   "   392
   We knew not your *u* laws,   "   *iv* 399
Ungraciousness I seem to be *u* itself.'   *Aylmer's Field* 245
Ungrateful Not all *u* to thine ear.   *In Mem. xxxviii* 12
   And ' petty Ogress,' and ' *u* Puss,'   *Princess, Pro.* 157
Unguent heal'd Thy hurt and heart with *u* and
   caress—   *Last Tournament* 595
Unhail'd *u* The shallop flitteth silken-sail'd   *L. of Shalott i* 21
Unhallow'd But all is new *u* ground.   *In Mem. civ* 12
Unhanded High things were spoken there, *u* down ;   *Alexander* 12
Unhappiness by some device Full cowardly, or by
   mere *u*,   *Gareth and L.* 768
   by sorcery or *u* Or some device, hast foully overthrown),   "   997
   Hast overthrown thro' mere *u*),   "   1059
   all thro' mere *u*—   "   1234
   Device and sorcery and *u*—   "   1235
   thro' the mere *u* Of one who came to help thee,   "   1237
   Else must I die thro' mine *u*.'   *Pelleas and E.* 332
   On whom I brought a strange *u*,   *Sisters (E. and E.)* 89
Unhappy Nor *u*, nor at rest,   *Adeline* 4
   There are enough *u* on this earth,   *Œnone* 239
   he turn'd His face and pass'd—*u* that I am !   *Dora* 151
   The spindlings look *u*.   *Amphion* 92
   He was not all *u*. His resolve Upbore him,   *Enoch Arden* 799
   Not all *u*, having loved God's best And greatest,   *Lancelot and E.* 1093
   made The happy and the *u* love,   *Lover's Tale i* 753
   Often I seem'd *u*, and often as happy too,   *First Quarrel* 31
   In the dead *u* night, and when the rain is on the
   roof.   *Locksley Hall* 78
   And vex the *u* dust thou wouldst not save.   *Come not, when, etc.* 4
   So stood the *u* mother open-mouth'd,   *Princess vi* 143
   Confused me like the *u* bark   *In Mem. xvi* 12
   So sadly lost on that *u* night ;   *Marr. of Geraint* 689
   that *u* child Past in her barge :   *Last Tournament* 44
   wail For ever woke the *u* Past again,   *Sisters (E. and E.)* 263
   has it come to this, O *u* creature ?   *Forlorn* 44
Unharm'd yonder stands, Modred, *u*,   *Pass. of Arthur* 153
   But the new-wedded wife was *u*,   *Charity* 22
Unheard grief of circumstance Wert thou, and
   yet *u*.   *Supp. Confessions* 93
   behold them unbeheld, *u* Hear all,   *Œnone* 89
   They were modulated so To *u* melody,   *Eleänore* 64
   And dies *u* within his tree,   *You might have won* 32
Unhearing shriek'd out ' Traitor ' to the *u* wall,   *Lancelot and E.* 612
Unheeded *U* : and detaching, fold by fold,   *Vision of Sin* 51
   U : and I thought I would have spoken,   "   55
Unheedful or as once we met *U*,   *Gardener's D.* 266
Unheppen (**ungainly**) Straänge an' *u* Miss Lucy !   *Village Wife* 100
Unhooded and *u* casting off The goodly falcon   *Merlin and V.* 130
Unicorn hornless *u's*, Crack'd basilisks,   *Holy Grail* 717
Unimpassion'd Beneath a pale and *u* moon,   *Aylmer's Field* 334
Uninvaded *u* sleep The Kraken sleepeth :   *The Kraken* 3
Uninvited The Abominable, that *u* came   *Œnone* 224
Union Should banded *u's* persecute Opinion,   *You ask me, why, etc.* 17
   our knights at feast Have pledged us in this *u*,   *Lancelot and E.* 115
   Here's to your happy *u* with my child !   *Sisters (E. and E.)* 68
   power to fuse My myriads into *u* under one ;   *Akbar's Dream* 157
Unison All your voices in *u*,   *On Jub. Q. Victoria* 63
Unity These three made *u* so sweet,   *Two Voices* 421
   It was but *u* of place   *In Mem. xlii* 3
Universal and *u* Peace Lie like a shaft of light   *Golden Year* 48
   the kindly earth shall slumber, lapt in *u* law.   *Locksley Hall* 130
   from it preach'd An *u* culture for the crowd,   *Princess, Pro.* 109
   sad and slow, As fits an *u* woe,   *Ode on Well.* 14

Universal (*continued*) And praise the invisible *u*
Lord, | *Ode Inter. Exhib.* 3
The voices of our *u* sea | *W. to Marie Alex.* 16
led my friend Back to the pure and *u* church, | *Sir J. Oldcastle* 71
Robed in *u* harvest up to either pole she smiles,
U ocean softly washing all her warless Isles, | *Locksley H., Sixty* 169
Thou that seëst *U* Nature moved by *U* Mind ; | *To Virgil* 21
Our Shakespeare's bland and *u* eye Dwells | *To W. C. Macready* 13

Universe wanderings Of this most intricate *U* | *A Character* 3
That in a boundless *u* Is boundless better, | *Two Voices* 26
knowing not the *u*, I fear to slide from bad to worse. | „ 230
atom-streams And torrents of her myriad *u*, | *Lucretius* 39
And fleeting thro' the boundless *u*, | „ 161
Quite sunder'd from the moving *U*, | *Princess vii* 52
suns of the limitless *U* sparkled and shone | *Despair* 15

University (*See also* **Varsity**) All wild to found an *U* For
maidens, | *Princess i* 150

Unjust and yet Pardon—too harsh, *u*. | *Columbus* 199
Unkept vintage, yet *u*, Had relish fiery-new, | *Will Water.* 97
Unkind False-eyed Hesper, *u*, | *Leonine Eleg.* 16
Ah, miserable and *u*, untrue, | *M. d'Arthur* 119
be jealous and hard and *u*.' | *Grandmother* 54
' Ah, miserable and *u*, untrue, | *Pass. of Arthur* 287
Unkindliness Kill'd with unutterable *u*.' | *Merlin and V.* 886
Unkinglike wall them up perforce in mine—
unwise, *U* ;— | *Akbar's Dream* 63
Unknightlike all *u*, writhed his wiry arms Around
him, | *Gareth and L.* 1150
Unknightly *U*, traitor-hearted ! Woe is me ! | *M. d'Arthur* 120
u with flat hand, However lightly, | *Geraint and E.* 717
U, traitor-hearted ! Woe is me ! | *Pass. of Arthur* 288
Unknit God *u's* the riddle of the one, | *Lover's Tale i* 181
Unknown And left a want *u* before ; | *Miller's D.* 228
hears the low Moan of an *u* sea ; | *Palace of Art* 280
His wife, an *u* artist's orphan child— | *Sea Dreams* 2
remain'd among us In our young nursery still *u*, | *Princess iv* 332
Known and *u* ; human, divine, | *In Mem. cxxix* 5
Sweet were the days when I was all *u*, | *Merlin and V.* 501
your great name, This conquers : hide it therefore ;
go *u* : Win ! | *Lancelot and E.* 151
Known as they are, to me they are *u*.' | „ 186
But since I go to joust as one *u* At Camelot | „ 190
That he might joust *u* of all, | „ 583
The maiden buried, not as one *u*, | „ 1334
Queen abode For many a week, *u*, among the nuns ; | *Guinevere* 147
With some revenge—even to itself *u*,— | *Lover's Tale ii* 127
Shall fade with him into the *u*, | *Tiresias* 215
Unlaborious *u* earth and oarless sea ; | *To Virgil* 20
Unlaced *u* my casque And grovell'd on my body, | *Princess vi* 27
Gareth there *u* His helmet as to slay him, | *Gareth and L.* 978
Unlading At lading and *u* the tall barks, | *Enoch Arden* 816
Unlamed to find his charger yet *u*, | *Balin and Balan* 428
Unlawful *U* and disloyal brotherhood— | *Sisters (E. and E.)* 174
Unlearn'd In grief I am not all *u* ; | *To J. S.* 18
Unled (His gentle charger following him *u*) | *Geraint and E.* 571
Unlicensed Dooms our *u* preacher to the flame, | *Sir J. Oldcastle* 105
Unlifted *U* was the clinking latch ; | *Mariana* 6
Unlike O happy tears, and how *u* to these ! | *Œnone* 235
Said Ida, tremulously, ' so all *u*— | *Princess vii* 333
As not *u* to that of Spring. | *In Mem. lxxxv* 120
With miracles and marvels like to these, Not all *u* ; | *Holy Grail* 544
Unlikeness As his *u* fitted mine. | *In Mem. lxxix* 20
Unlimited The Heavenly-unmeasured or *u* Love, | *Lover's Tale i* 474
Unloveable Ev'n when they seem'd *u*, | *Merlin and V.* 176
Unloved *U*, that beech will gather brown, | *In Mem. ci* 3
U, the sun-flower, shining fair, | „ 5
U, by many a sandy bar, | „ 9
Unlovely I stand Here in the long *u* street, | „ vii 2
Unloverlike most *u*, Since in his absence | *Lover's Tale i* 424
Unmanacled *U* from bonds of sense, | *Two Voices* 236
Unmann'd but that my zone *U* me : | *Princess ii* 421
Unmannerly *U*, with prattling and the tales | *Guinevere* 316
Unmark'd Enwind her isles, *u* of me : | *In Mem. xcviii* 10
Unmarried But Dora lived *u* till her death. | *Dora* 172
Sir Lancelot worshipt no *u* girl | *Merlin and V.* 12

Unmeasured (*See also* **Heavenly-unmeasured**) clamouring
etiquette to death, *U* mirth ; | *Princess v* 18
Unmeet and strange experiences *U* for ladies. | „ iv 159
Maud, you milkwhite fawn, you are all *u* for a wife. | *Maud I iv* 57
Unmelodious Saying ' An *u* name to thee, | *Balin and Balan* 52
Unmockingly *U* the mocker ending here | *Gareth and L.* 294
Unmortised The feet *u* from their ankle-bones | *Merlin and V.* 552
Unmoulded By some yet *u* tongue | *Ode on Well.* 233
Unmoved With such and so *u* a majesty | *Lancelot and E.* 1170
Unmown deep inlay Of braided blooms *u*, | *Arabian Nights* 29
Unnetted The *u* black-hearts ripen dark, | *The Blackbird* 7
Unnoticed For that *u* failing in herself, | *Geraint and E.* 47
Unnumber'd *U* and enormous polypi | *The Kraken* 9
Unopen'd and dash'd *U* at her feet : | *Princess iv* 471
Unpaining driven Its knotted thorns thro' my *u* brows, | *Lover's Tale i* 620
Unpalsied *U* when he met with Death, | *In Mem. cxxviii* 2
Unparallel'd That various wilderness a tissue of
light *U*. | *Lover's Tale i* 420
Unpeopled Whose crime had half *u* Ilion, | *Death of Œnone* 61
Unperceived Love, *u*, A more ideal Artist | *Gardener's D.* 24
stole from court With Cyril and with Florian, *u*, | *Princess i* 103
Unpiloted *U* i' the echoing dance Of reboant
whirlwinds, | *Supp. Confessions* 96
Unpitied *U*: for he groped as blind, | *Aylmer's Field* 821
Unprofitable if a king demand An act *u*, | *M. d'Arthur* 96
if a king demand An act *u*, | *Pass. of Arthur* 264
Unprogressive Cries of *u* dotage ere the dotard fall
asleep, | *Locksley H., Sixty* 153
Unprophetic *U* rulers they— | *Open. I. and C. Exhib.* 26
Unproportion'd So *u* to the dwelling-place,) | *Lover's Tale i* 187
Unproven and every younger knight, *U*, | *Holy Grail* 304
Unquenched Like Stephen, an *u* fire. | *Two Voices* 219
Unquestion'd ample rule *U*, | *Œnone* 112
Unquiet But, for the *u* heart and brain, | *In Mem. v* 5
Unreal but these *u* ways Seem but the theme | *Edwin Morris* 47
past and flow'd away To those *u* billows : | *Lover's Tale ii* 196
Unrecorded a wife as you Should vanish *u*. | *Romney's R.* 69
Unrecording Thro' troops of *u* friends, | *You might have won* 7
Unrelieved and ever *u* by dismal tears, | *Palace of Art* 271
Unremember'd and my sins Be *u*, | *Supp. Confessions* 182
Unremorseful wrapt In *u* folds of rolling fire. | *Holy Grail* 261
Unrepress'd Ceasing not, mingled, *u*, | *Arabian Nights* 74
Unresisting and a sense Of meanness in her *u* life. | *Aylmer's Field* 801
Unrest but the Naiad Throbbing in mild *u* | *Leonine Eleg.* 12
The wild *u* that lives in woe | *In Mem. xv* 15
Can calm despair and wild *u* | „ xvi 2
Unreveal'd The rest remaineth *u* ; | „ xxxi 14
Unriddled Shall be *u* by and by. | *Miller's D.* 20
Unrisen a poising eagle, burns Above the *u* morrow :' | *Princess iv* 83
—over darkness—from the still *u* sun. | *Locksley H., Sixty* 92
Unroll'd One sitting on a crimson scarf *u* ; | *D. of F. Women* 126
hail once more to the banner of battle *u* ! | *Maud III vi* 42
Unruffling *U* waters re-collect the shape | *Last Tournament* 369
Unsaid And what I see I leave *u*, | *In Mem. lxxiv* 10
Unsay *U* it, unswear ! | *Last Tournament* 641
Unscarr'd And all *u* from beak or talon, | „ 20
Unscathed Render him up *u* : | *Princess iv* 408
Unseal'd Falling, *u* our eyelids, and we woke | *Lover's Tale i* 265
Unseen Then leaping out upon them *u* | *The Merman* 33
the dark East, *U*, is brightening to his bridal morn. | *Gardener's D.* 73
Her face was evermore *u*, | *The Voyage* 61
And far, in forest-deeps *u*, | *Sir L. and Q. G.* 7
Had his dark hour *u*, and rose and past | *Enoch Arden* 78
But now it seems some *u* monster lays | *Lucretius* 219
Into the *u* for ever,—till that hour, | „ 259
or are moved by an *u* hand at a game | *Maud I iv* 26
His love, *u* but felt, o'ershadow Thee, | *Ded. of Idylls* 51
Merlin, who, they say, can walk *U* at pleasure— | *Com. of Arthur* 348
with her feet *u* Crush'd the wild passion | *Lancelot and E.* 741
for *u*, But taken with the sweetness of the place, | *Lover's Tale i* 530
Unshadowable *u* in words, Themselves but shadows | *Ancient Sage* 238
Unshaken Which kept her throne *u* still, | *To the Queen* 34
Thro' open doors of Ida stationed there *U*, | *Princess v* 344
Unshatter'd haste and random youth *U* ; | *De Prof., Two G.* 22
Unshorn she that saw him lying unsleek, *u*, | *Lancelot and E.* 815

Unskill'd   And let the younger and *u* go by   *Lancelot and E.* 1361
Unsleek   she that saw him lying *u*, unshorn,   „   815
Unsolder   sequel of to-day *u*'s all The goodliest fellowship   *M. d'Arthur* 14
   sequel of to-day *u*'s all The goodliest fellowship   *Pass. of Arthur* 182
Unsown   sat upon a mound That was *u*,   *Dora* 73
Unspeakable   memories roll upon him, *U* for sadness.   *Enoch Arden* 725
   And twisted shapes of lust, *u*,   *Lucretius* 157
   A sacred, secret, unapproached woe, *U* ?   *Lover's Tale i* 680
   Dying, ' *U* ' he wrote ' Their kindness,'   *To Marq. of Dufferin* 35
Unstain'd   A lovelier life, a more *u*, than his !   *Ded. of Idylls* 30
Unsubduable   The last a monster *u*   *Gareth and L.* 858
Unsubject   *U* to confusion,   *Will Water.* 86
Unsummer'd   And, now to these *u* skies   *Pref. Poem Broth. Son.* 17
Unsunn'd   The *u* freshness of my strength,   *Supp. Confessions* 140
Unsunny   O damsel, wearing this *u* face   *Pelleas and E.* 180
Unswallow'd   brawny spearman let his cheek Bulge with the *u* piece,   *Geraint and E.* 631
Unswear   Unsay it, *u* !   *Last Tournament* 641
Unsweet   Is faith as vague as all *u* :   *In Mem. xlvii* 5
Untaken   and hath left his prize *U*,   *Lancelot and E.* 531
Untarnish'd   name will yet remain *U* as before ;   *Marr. of Geraint* 501
Untidy   *See* **Hugger-mugger**
'Untin' (hunting)   an' was '*u*' arter the men,   *Village Wife* 36
Untold   Nor left *u* the craft herself had used ;   *Geraint and E.* 393
Untouch'd   *U* with any shade of years,   *Miller's D.* 219
   my good son—Is yet *u* :   *Sisters (E. and E.)* 288
Untravell'd   experience is an arch wherethro' Gleams that *u* world,   *Ulysses* 20
Untrue   Ah, miserable and unkind, *u*,   *M. d'Arthur* 119
   I wrong the grave with fears *u*,   *In Mem. li* 9
   She might by a true descent be *u* ;   *Maud I xiii* 31
   ' Ah, miserable and unkind, *u*,   *Pass. of Arthur* 287
Untruth   never had a glimpse of mine *u*,   *Lancelot and E.* 125
   Too wholly true to dream *u* in thee,   *Guinevere* 541
Untuneful   That her voice *u* grown,   *The Owl ii* 6
Unused   *U* example from the grave   *In Mem. lxxx* 15
Unvenerable   *U* will thy memory be   *Tiresias* 132
Unvext   *u* She slipt across the summer   *Enoch Arden* 530
Unwatch'd   *U*, the garden bough shall sway,   *In Mem. ci* 1
Unwavering   calm that let the tapers burn *U* :   „ *xcv* 6
Unwedded   I was wife, and thou *U* :   *Guinevere* 120
Unwilling   Waged such *u* tho' successful war   *Merlin and V.* 571
   The lady never made *u* war With those fine eyes :   „   603
Unwillingly   *See* **Half-unwillingly**
Unwillingness   wish Falls flat before your least *u*.   *Romney's R.* 72
Unwise   What wonder I was all *u*,   *Day-Dm., Ep.* 5
   wall them up perforce in mine—*u*, Unkinglike ;—   *Akbar's Dream* 62
Unwisely   wisely or *u*, signs of storm,   *To the Queen ii* 49
Unwish'd   That you came *u* for, uncall'd,   *Despair* 5
Unwish'd-for   With proffer of *u-f* services)   *Lover's Tale i* 629
Unwitty   If these *u* wandering wits of mine,   *Merlin and V.* 346
Unwonted   Should kiss with an *u* gentleness.   *Lover's Tale i* 739
Unwoo'd   palms were ranged Above, *u* of summer wind :   *Arabian Nights* 80
Unworldly   My friend, the most *u* of mankind,   *In Mem. W. G. Ward* 3
Unworthier   but we, *u*, told Of college :   *Princess, Pro.* 110
Unworthily   some *u* ; their sinless faith,   „ *v* 185
Unworthiness   lay Contemplating her own *u* ;   *Marr. of Geraint* 533
Unworthy   O three times less *u* !   *Love and Duty* 20
   Hadst thou less *u* proved—   *Locksley Hall* 63
   Vext with *u* madness, and deform'd.   *Aylmer's Field* 335
   chiefest comfort is the little child Of one *u* mother;   *Princess v* 431
   On some *u* heart with joy,   *In Mem. lxii* 7
   but most Predoom'd her as *u*.   *Lancelot and E.* 729
Unwounded   To find him yet *u* after fight,   *Geraint and E.* 371
Unwove   Wove and *u* it, till the boy return'd   „   260
Up   *See* **Steep-up**
Upbare   *u* A broad earth-sweeping pall of whitest lawn,   *Lover's Tale ii* 77
Upbearing   A leaning and *u* parasite,   *Isabel* 34
Upblown   *u* billow ran Shoreward beneath red clouds,   *Lover's Tale ii* 178
Upbore   His resolve *U* him, and firm faith,   *Enoch Arden* 800
   but her deep love *U* her ;   *Lancelot and E.* 861
Upbreaking   the heavens *u* thro' the earth,   *Guinevere* 391

Up-clomb   *U-c* the shadowy pine above the woven copse.   *Lotos-Eaters* 18
Upcurl'd   wreaths of floating dark *u*,   *The Poet* 35
Updrag   Rise ! ' and stoop'd to *u* Melissa :   *Princess iv* 366
Updrawn   Anchors of rusty fluke, and boats *u* ;   *Enoch Arden* 18
Upheaven   land of old *u* from the abyss By fire,   *Pass. of Arthur* 82
Upheld   under all the cornice and *u* :   *Gareth and L.* 219
Uphill   lay thine *u* shoulder to the wheel,   *Ancient Sage* 279
Uphold   (*See also* **Upowd**)   didst *u* me on my lonely isle,   *Enoch Arden* 783
   U me,   *Guinevere* 470
   To break the heathen and *u* the Christ,   *Lover's Tale i* 168
   Which yet *u*'s my life, and evermore   „   220
   two pillars which from earth *u* Our childhood,   „
   Genius of that hour which dost *u* Thy coronal of glory   487
Upjetted   *u* in spirts of wild sea-smoke,   *Sea Dreams* 52
Upland   Piling sheaves in *u*'s airy,   *L. of Shalott i* 34
   Behind Were realms of *u*, prodigal in oil,   *Palace of Art* 79
Uplift   *U* a thousand voices full and sweet,   *Ode Inter. Exhib.* 1
   A lever to *u* the earth   *In Mem. cxiii* 15
   And pure Sir Galahad to *u* the maid ;   *Lancelot and E.* 1265
Uplifted   *U* was the clinking latch ;   *Mariana* 6
   The bold Sir Bedivere *u* him,   *M. d'Arthur* 6
   U high in heart and hope are we,   *Ode on Well.* 254
   And been thereby *u*, should thro' me,   *Balin and Balan* 491
   The bold Sir Bedivere *u* him,   *Pass. of Arthur* 175
Uplooking   *u* and almost Waiting to see some blessed shape   *Lover's Tale i* 311
Up-on-end   *See* **Hup-on-end**
Upowd (uphold)   ' I'll *u* it tha weänt ;   *North. Cobbler* 63
Upper   BELOW the thunders of the *u* deep ;   *The Kraken* 1
   Old footsteps trod the *u* floors,   *Mariana* 67
   Too long you keep the *u* skies ;   *Rosalind* 35
   Now gnaw'd his under, now his *u* lip,   *Geraint and E.* 669
Uprear'd   And in his chair himself *u*,   *Day-Dm., Revival* 18
   Or whence the fear fest this my realm, *u*,   *Last Tournament* 122
Upright   *U* and flush'd before him :   *Merlin and V.* 912
   but scarcely could stand *u*,   *V. of Maeldune* 73
Uprising   The knife *u* toward the blow   *The Victim* 66
Uproar   not without an *u* made by those Who cried,   *Com. of Arthur* 42
Uprose   *u* the mystic mountain-range ;   *Vision of Sin* 208
Upshoot   All round a hedge *u*'s, and shows   *Day-Sm., Sleep. P.* 41
Upside   *See* **Hupside**
Upsprang   gain'd her castle, *u* the bridge,   *Pelleas and E.* 206
Upsprung   In closest coverture *u*,   *Arabian Nights* 68
Upstarted   Scared by the noise *u* at our feet,   *Merlin and V.* 422
Upstay'd   Bent o'er me, and my neck his arm *u*.   *Lover's Tale i* 690
Upswell   *u*'s The gold-fringed pillow lightly prest :   *Day-Dm., Sleep. B.* 21
Upward   Strike *u* thro' the shadow ;   *The Ring* 372
   Tho' following with an *u* mind   *In Mem. xli* 21
Upward-rushing   ever *u-r* storm and cloud Of shriek and plume,   *Last Tournament* 440
Urania   *U* speaks with darken'd brow :   *In Mem. xxxvii* 1
Uranian   o'er his head *U* Venus hung,   *Princess i* 243
Urge   To which the voice did *u* reply :   *Two Voices* 7
   ' Yet think not that I come to *u* thy crimes,   *Guinevere* 532
   U him to foreign war.   *Sir J. Oldcastle* 68
Urged   brought it ; and the poet little *u*,   *The Epic* 48
   I *u* the fierce inscription on the gate,   *Princess iii* 141
   Lancelot on him *u* All the devisings   *Gareth and L.* 1348
   U him to speak against the truth,   *Lancelot and E.* 92
Urien   then his brother king, *U*, assail'd him :   *Com. of Arthur* 36
   Carádos, *U*, Cradlemont of Wales,   „   112
Urim   rich With jewels, elfin *U*, on the hilt,   „   298
Urn   (*See also* **Fountain-urns**)   From fluted vase, and brazen *u*   *Arabian Nights* 60
   Drawing into his narrow earthen *u*,   *Ode to Memory* 61
   white dust, shut in an *u* of brass !   *Lotos-Eaters, C. S.* 68
   Soft lustre bathes the range of *u*'s   *Day-Dm., Sleep. P.* 9
   Found lying with his *u*'s and ornaments,   *Aylmer's Field* 4
   and with great *u*'s of flowers.   *Princess ii* 26
   Thro' prosperous floods his holy *u*.   *In Mem. ix* 8
   And on the board the fluttering *u* :   „ *xcv* 8
   An angel watching an *u* Wept   *Maud I viii* 3
   swathe thyself all round Hope's quiet *u* For ever ?   *Lover's Tale i* 100
   immerging, each, his *u* In his own well,   *Tiresias* 88

'Urry (hurry)   Naay sit down—naw *'u*—sa cowd !—   *Village Wife* 20

Usage (*See also* **Ill-usage**) tenfold dearer by the
    power Of intermitted *u* ;   *Marr. of Geraint* 811
    And lose thy life by *u* of thy sting ;   *Ancient Sage* 270
    shrunk by *u* into commonest commonplace !   *Locksley H., Sixty* 76

Use (s)   keep a thing, its *u* will come.   *The Epic* 42
    ' God made the woman for the *u* of man,   *Edwin Morris* 91
    To rust unburnish'd, not to shine in *u* !   *Ulysses* 23
    to what *u*'s shall we put The wildweed-flower   *Day-Dm., Moral* 5
    So 'twere to cramp its *u*, if I Should hook   ,, 15
    gentle creature shut from all Her charitable *u*,   *Aylmer's Field* 566
    too late ! they come too late for *u*.   *Sea Dreams* 67
    or of older *u* All-seeing Hyperion—   *Lucretius* 125
    From childly wont and ancient *u* I call—   ,, 209
    redound Of *u* and glory to yourselves ye come,   *Princess ii* 43
    might grow To *u* and power on this Oasis,   ,, 167
    public *u* required she should be known ;   ,, *iv* 336
    since my oath was ta'en for public *u*,   ,, 337
    And boats and bridges for the *u* of men.   ,, *vi* 47
    What *u* to keep them here—now ?   ,, 304
    void was her *u*, And she as one that climbs a peak   ,, *vii* 34
    All of beauty, all of *u*,   *Ode Inter. Exhib.* 23
    Naw soort o' koind o' *u* to saäy   *N. Farmer, O. S.* 6
    ' O wife, what *u* to answer now ?   *The Victim* 55
    A *u* in measured language lies ;   *In Mem. v* 6
    Make one wreath more for *U* and Wont,   ,, *xxix* 11
    And learns the *u* of ' I,' and ' me,'   ,, *xlv* 6
    This *u* may lie in blood and breath,   ,, 13
    But with long *u* her tears are dry.   ,, *lxxviii* 20
    because he bare The *u* of virtue out of earth :   ,, *lxxxii* 10
    Has broke the bond of dying *u*.   ,, *cv* 12
    And soil'd with all ignoble *u*.   ,, *cxi* 24
    batter'd with the shocks of doom To shape and *u*.   ,, *cxviii* 25
    And thrice the gold for Uther's *u* thereof,   *Gareth and L.* 344
    To war against ill *u*'s of a life,   ,, 1130
    I will make *u* of all the power I have.   *Gareth and E.* 345
    (tho' I count it of small *u* To charge you)   ,, 416
    ' Thou shalt put the crown to *u*.   *Balin and Balan* 202
    he defileth heavenly things With earthly *u*'s'—   ,, 422
    lost to life and *u* and name and fame. (repeat)   *Merlin and V.* 214, 970
    My *u* and name and fame.   ,, 304
    Upon my life and *u* and name and fame,   ,, 374
    With this for motto, ' Rather *u* than fame.'   ,, 480
    U gave me Fame at first, and Fame again
      Increasing gave me *u*.   ,, 493
    I rather dread the loss of *u* than fame ;   ,, 519
    and she lay as dead, And lost all *u* of life :   ,, 645
    kingdom's, not the King's—For public *u* :   *Lancelot and E.* 60
    ourselves shall grow In *u* of arms and manhood,   ,, 64
    I might have put my wits to some rough *u*,   ,, 1306
    Now grown a part of me : that what *u* in it ?   ,, 1416
    ' It is not Arthur's *u* To hunt by moonlight ; '   *Holy Grail* 110
    heart And might of limb, but mainly *u* and skill,   *Last Tournament* 198
    and with mirth so loud Beyond all *u*,   ,, 236
    Arthur deign'd not *u* of word or sword,   ,, 458
    They served their *u*, their time ;   ,, 676
    or what *u* To know her father left us   *Lover's Tale i* 292
    for henceforth what *u* were words to me !   ,, 609
    show'd he drank beyond his *u* ;   ,, *iv* 228
    What *u* to brood ? this life of mingled pains   *To Mary Boyle* 49

Use (verb)   and *u* Her influence on the mind,   *Will Water.* 11
    You grant me license ; might I *u* it ?   *Princess iii* 235
    to *u* A little patience ere I die ;   *In Mem. xxxiv* 11
    before my lance if lance Were mine to *u*—   *Gareth and L.* 7
    And answer'd with such craft as women *u*,   *Geraint and E.* 352
    u Both grace and will to pick the vicious quitch   ,, 902
    eats And *u*'s, careless of the rest ;   *Merlin and V.* 463
    Might *u* it to the harm of anyone,   ,, 685
    since I cannot *u* it, ye may have it.'   *Lancelot and E.* 199
    I pray you, *u* some rough discourtesy   ,, 973
    Besought me to be plain and blunt, and *u*,   ,, 1301
    who cared Only to *u* his own,   *Lover's Tale iv* 312
    my Leonard, *u* and not abuse your day,   *Locksley H., Sixty* 265

Used   (*See also* **Ill-used**) out the storied Past, and
    u Within the Present,   *Love thou thy land* 2

Used (*continued*)   *U* all her fiery will, and smote Her life   *Will Water.* 111
    And she the left, or not, or seldom *u* ;   *Princess iii* 38
    But great is song *U* to great ends :   ,, *iv* 138
    Fatherly fears—you *u* us courteously—   ,, *v* 216
    It is all *u* up for that.   *Maud II v* 64
    Am much too gentle, have not *u* my power :   *Marr. of Geraint* 467
    Nor left untold the craft herself had *u* ;   *Geraint and E.* 393
    ' Enid, I have *u* you worse than that dead man ;   ,, 735
    wrought too long with delegated hands, Not *u* mine
      own :   ,, 894
    So *u* as I, My daily wonder is,   *Merlin and V.* 535
    This was the one discourtesy that he *u*.   *Lancelot and E.* 988

Used (accustomed)   We are *u* to that :   *Princess iii* 277

Used (was or were accustomed)   Musing on him that
    u to fill it for her,   *Enoch Arden* 208
    ah God, as he *u* to rave.   *Maud I i* 60
    full of wolves, where he *u* to lie ;   ,, *II v* 54
    With whom he *u* to play at tourney once,   *Gareth and L.* 532
    whom he *u* To harry and hustle.   ,, 706
    when I am gone Who *u* to lay them !   *Balin and Balan* 141
    golden hair, with which I *u* to play Not knowing !   *Guinevere* 547
    as ye *u* to do twelve year sin' !   *Spinster's S's.* 59
    you *u* to call me once The lonely maiden-Princess   *The Ring* 115
    as I *u* To prattle to her picture—   ,, 167
    I *u* to walk This Terrace—morbid,   ,, 358
    She *u* to shun the wailing gale,   *Death of Œnone* 2
    she *u* to gaze Down at the Troad ;   *Charity* 15
    For I *u* to play with the knife,

Useful   Should hook it to some *u* end.   *Day-Dm., Moral* 16
    So never took that *u* name in vain,   *Sea Dreams* 189
    Before the *u* trouble of the rain ·   *Geraint and E.* 771
    Subdue them to the *u* and the good.   *Ulysses* 38

Useless   To draw, to sheathe a *u* sword,   *In Mem. cxxviii* 13
    these blind hands were *u* in their wars.   *Tiresias* 78
    This *u* hand ! I felt one warm tear fall upon it.   ,, 166

Usherest   Who *u* in the dolorous hour   *In Mem. lxxii* 9

Using   like the hand, and grew With *u* ;   *Princess ii* 151

Usk   Held court at old Caerleon upon *U*.   *Marr. of Geraint* 146
    Took horse, and forded *U*, and gain'd the wood ;   ,, 161
    but up the vale of *U*, By the flat meadow,   ,, 831
    the full-tided *U*, Before he turn to fall seaward   *Geraint and E.* 116
    they past With Arthur to Caerleon upon *U*.   ,, 946
    By the great tower—Caerleon upon *U*—   *Balin and Balan* 506
    Who never sawest Caerleon upon *U*—   ,, 570
    the flat field by the shore of *U* Holden :   *Pelleas and E.* 164

Usurp'd   Sir Modred had *u* the realm,   *Guinevere* 154

Usury   kiss for kiss, With *u* thereto.'   *Talking Oak* 196

Uther   Or mythic *U*'s deeply-wounded son   *Palace of Art* 105
    And after him King *U* fought and died,   *Com. of Arthur* 14
    Who cried, ' He is not *U*'s son '—   ,, 43
    who hath proven him King *U*'s son ?   ,, 70
    Are like to those of *U* whom we knew.   ,, 72
    wise man that served King *U* thro' his magic art ;   ,, 152
    Hold ye this Arthur for King *U*'s son ? '   ,, 172
    for ye know that in King *U*'s time   ,, 185
    And *U* cast upon her eyes of love :   ,, 193
    That Gorloïs and King *U* went to war :   ,, 196
    Then *U* in his wrath and heat besieged Ygerne   ,, 198
    Left her and fled, and U enter'd in,   ,, 201
    King *U* died himself, Moaning and wailing for an heir   ,, 206
    And many hated *U* for the sake Of Gorloïs.   ,, 220
    an old knight And ancient friend of *U* ;   ,, 223
    ' Here is *U*'s heir, your king,'   ,, 230
    Or *U*'s son, and born before his time,   ,, 241
    near him when the savage yells Of *U*'s peerage died,   ,, 257
    and dark was *U* too, Wellnigh to blackness ;   ,, 329
    Merlin ever served about the King, *U*, before he died ;
      and on the night When *U* in Tintagil past away   ,, 366
    ' The King ! Here is an heir for *U* ! '   ,, 386
    No son of *U*, and no king of ours ; '   ,, 440
    Thy father, *U*, reft From my dead lord a field   *Gareth and L.* 334
    And thrice the gold for *U*'s use thereof,   ,, 344
    A knight of *U* in the Barons' war,   ,, 353
    And *U* slit thy tongue :   ,, 376
    whom *U* left in charge Long since,   *Geraint and E.* 933

Utmost   Sweet in their *u* bitterness,   *Supp. Confessions* 117
Wan, wasted Truth in her *u* need.   *Clear-headed friend* 19
Beyond the *u* bound of human thought.   *Ulysses* 32
Beyond their *u* purple rim, (repeat)   *Day-Dm., Depart.* 6, 30
as for *u* grief or shame ;   *Merlin and V.* 897
His party, knights of *u* North and West,   *Lancelot and E.* 526
when thou hast seen me strain'd And sifted to the *u*,   *Pelleas and E.* 248
On that sharp ridge of *u* doom ride highly   *Lover's Tale i* 805

Utter (adj.)   seest me drive Thro' *u* dark a full-sail'd skiff,   *Supp. Confessions* 95
silence seems to flow Beside me in my *u* woe,   *Oriana* 87
' Then, then, from *u* gloom stood out the breasts,   *Lucretius* 60
reverence thine own beard That looks as white as *u* truth,   *Gareth and L.* 281
my knights are sworn to vows Of *u* hardihood, *u* gentleness, And, loving, *u* faithfulness in love,   ,, 553
The King in *u* scorn Of thee and thy much folly   ,, 918
as if the world were one Of *u* peace, and love, and gentleness !   ,, 1289
Geraint, from *u* courtesy, forbore.   *Marr. of Geraint* 381
Then Enid, in her *u* helplessness,   *Geraint and E.* 719
So passionate for an *u* purity   *Merlin and V.* 26
or what Her all but *u* whiteness held for sin,   *Holy Grail* 84
did Pelleas in an *u* shame Creep with his shadow thro' the court again,   *Pelleas and E.* 440
That here in *u* dark I swoon'd away,   *Last Tournament* 622
You lose yourself in *u* ignorance ;   *Lover's Tale i* 79
Why in the *u* stillness of the soul   ,, 276
All thro' the livelong hours of *u* dark,   ,, 810
but round my Evelyn clung In *u* silence for so long,   *Sisters (E. and E.)* 217
That mock-meek mouth of *u* Antichrist,   *Sir J. Oldcastle* 170
Sunless and moonless, *u* light—but no !   *Columbus* 90
If *u* darkness closed the day, my son—   *Ancient Sage* 199
Sons of God, and kings of men in *u* nobleness of mind,   *Locksley H., Sixty* 122
Were *u* darkness—one, the Sun of dawn   *Prin. Beatrice* 3
lost in *u* grief I fail'd To send my life   *Demeter and P.* 109
And *u* knowledge is but *u* love—   *The Ring* 43
colour'd bubble bursts above the abyss Of Darkness, *u* Lethe,   *Romney's R.* 53
With politic care, with *u* gentleness,   *Akbar's Dream* 128

Utter (verb)   I would that my tongue could *u* *U* your jubilee, steeple and spire !   *Break, Break, etc.* 3 / *W. to Alexandra* 17
To *u* love more sweet than praise.   *In Mem. lxxvii* 16
what dream ye when they *u* forth May-music   *Gareth and L.* 1079
on a sudden the garrison *u* a jubilant shout,   *Def. of Lucknow* 98

Utterance   glided thro' all change Of liveliest *u*,   *D. of F. Women* 168
in sighs Which perfect Joy, perplex'd for *u*,   *Gardener's D.* 255
Gave *u* by the yearning of an eye,   *Love and Duty* 62
As if to speak, but, *u* failing her,   *Princess iv* 395
told us all their anger in miraculous *u's*,   *Boädicea* 23
His broken *u's* and bashfulness,   *Pelleas and E.* 111
Went on in passionate *u* :   *Guinevere* 611
her gracious lips Did lend such gentle *u*,   *Lover's Tale i* 457
As if she were afraid of *u* ;   ,, 564
breath floated in the *u* Of silver-chorded tones :   ,, *ii* 141

Utter'd   brows Of him that *u* nothing base ;   *To the Queen* 8
He *u* rhyme and reason,   *The Goose* 6
He *u* words of scorning ;   ,, 42
Caught up the whole of love and *u* it,   *Love and Duty* 82
And there the tale he *u* brokenly,   *Enoch Arden* 647
She nor swoon'd, nor *u* cry :   *Princess vi* 2
on her Fixt my faint eyes, and *u* whisperingly :   ,, *vii* 144
Bow'd at her side and *u* whisperingly :   *Geraint and E.* 305
To whom the woodman *u* wonderingly   *Balin and Balan* 297
But when Sir Garlon *u* mocking-wise   ,, 389
While he *u* this, Low to her own heart   *Lancelot and E.* 318
U a little tender dolorous cry.   ,, 817
Lancelot kneeling *u*, ' Queen, Lady, my liege,   ,, 1179
For when had Lancelot *u* aught so gross   *Last Tournament* 631
my strangled vanity *U* a stifled cry—   *Sisters (E. and E.)* 200
Before the first ' I will ' was *u*,   ,, 211
you heard the lines I read Nor *u* word of blame,   *Pro. to Gen. Hamley* 18

Utter'd *(continued)*   heart of this most ancient realm A hateful voice be *u*,   *Prog. of Spring* 103
till the little one *u* a cry.   *Bandit's Death* 26
Utterest   all of them redder than rosiest health or than *u* shame,   *V. of Maeldune* 65
Uttering   all in passion *u* a dry shriek,   *Geraint and E.* 461
lock up my tongue From *u* freely what I freely hear ?   *Last Tournament* 694
brook'd No silence, brake it, *u* ' Late ! so late ! What hour,   *Guinevere* 160
And *u* this the King Made at the man :   *Pass. of Arthur* 164
Utterly   and brake it *u* to the hilt.   *Gareth and L.* 1148
Uttermost (adj.)   Is He not yonder in those *u* Parts of the morning ?   *Enoch Arden* 223
And *u* obedience to the King.'   *Gareth and L.* 555
For *u* obedience make demand   ,, 558
In *u* obedience to the King.   ,, 833
Uttermost (s)   To hoard all savings to the *u*,   *Enoch Arden* 46
wish To save all earnings to the *u*,   ,, 86
So aid me Heaven when at mine *u*,   *Marr. of Geraint* 502
That he might prove her to the *u*,   *Geraint and E.* 589
Fasted and pray'd even to the *u*,   *Holy Grail* 132
Yea, let her prove me to the *u*, For loyal to the *u* am I.'   *Pelleas and E.* 211
when the guest Is loved and honour'd to the *u*.   *Lover's Tale iv* 245
you are honour'd now Ev'n to the *u* :   ,, 317
Uxoriousness   And molten down in mere *u*.   *Marr. of Geraint* 60
past the people's talk And accusation of *u*   ,, 83

V

Vaäin (vain)   an' I beänt not *v*,   *Spinster's S's.* 15
An' I beänt not *v*, but I knaws   ,, 71
Vacancy   we shall see The nakedness and *v*   *Deserted House* 11
gloom the *vacancies* Between the tufted hills,   *Lover's Tale i* 2
Vacant   *In v chambers, I could trust Your kindness.*   *To the Queen* 19
And, last, you fix'd a *v* stare,   *L. C. V. de Vere* 47
v of our glorious gains,   *Locksley Hall* 175
Will haunt the *v* cup :   *Will Water.* 172
I cry to *v* chairs and widow'd walls,   *Aylmer's Field* 720
Whence follows many a *v* pang ;   *Princess ii* 403
Perchance, to charm a *v* brain,   *The Daisy* 106
And *v* chaff well meant for grain.   *In Mem. iv* 3
vital spirits sink To see the *v* chair,   ,, *xx* 19
Of *v* darkness and to cease.   ,, *xxxiv* 16
And *v* yearning, tho' with might   ,, *cviii* 6
stands *V*, but thou retake it, mine again ! '   *Balin and Balan* 79
In our great hall there stood a *v* chair,   *Holy Grail* 167
Your places being *v* at my side,   ,, 317
In hanging robe or *v* ornament,   *Guinevere* 506
And I stood sole beside the *v* bier.   *Lover's Tale iii* 58
Till you find the deathless Angel seated in the *v* tomb.   *Locksley H., Sixty* 278
And sanguine Lazarus felt a *v* hand   *To Mary Boyle* 31
Vacillating   O damned *v* state !   *Supp. Confessions* 190
in my good mother's hall Linger with *v* obedience,   *Gareth and L.* 13
Vagrant   And *v* melodies the winds which bore   *The Poet* 17
' If all be dark, *v* voice,' I said,   *Two Voices* 265
A *v* suspicion of the breast :   ,, 336
: Some *v* emotion of delight   ,, 361
Love is made a *v* regret.   *Miller's D.* 210
But sickening of a *v* disease,   *L. C. V. de Vere* 62
But *v* in vapour, hard to mark ;   *Love thou thy land* 62
And *v* desires, like fitful blasts of balm   *Gardener's D.* 68
I shook her breast with *v* alarms—   *The Letters* 38
And therewithal an answer *v* as wind ;   *Princess i* 45
moulder'd lodges of the Past So sweet a voice and *v*,   ,, *iv* 64
as babies for the moon, *V* brightness ;   ,, 429
To that *v* fear implied in death ;   *In Mem. xli* 14
Is faith as *v* as all unsweet :   ,, *xlvii* 5
If any *v* desire should rise,   ,, *lxxx* 1
V words ! but ah, how hard to frame   ,, *xcv* 45

Vagrant (continued)   v desire That spurs an imitative will.   *In Mem.* cx 19
   swaying upon a restless elm Drew the v glance of
     Vivien,   *Balin and Balan* 464
   To one at least, who hath not children, v,   *Merlin and V.* 506
   ' You breathe but accusation vast and v,   „ 701
   There gleam'd a v suspicion in his eyes :   *Lancelot and E.* 127
   came and went Before her, or a v spiritual fear—   *Guinevere* 71
   Laziness, v love-longings, the bright May,   *Sisters* (E. and E.) 128
   What v world-whisper, mystic pain or joy,   *Far—far—away* 7
   Till, led by dream and v desire,   *To Master of B.* 17
Vaguer   v voices of Polytheism Make but one music,   *Akbar's Dream* 150
Vail   her hand Grasp'd, made her v her eyes :   *Guinevere* 663
Vail'd   He look'd but once, and v his eyes again.   *Last Tournament* 150
Vain (adj.)   (See also **Vaäin**)   Of knitted purport, all
   were v.   *Two Voices* 168
   The chancellor, sedate and v,   *Day-Dm., Revival* 29
   blank And waste it seem'd and v ;   *Princess* vii 43
   From talk of battles loud and v,   *Ode on Well.* 247
   V solace ! Memory standing near   *To J. S.* 53
   No v libation to the Muse,   *Will Water.* 9
   Who will not *hear* denial, v and rude   *Lover's Tale* i 628
   like a v rich man, That, having always prosper'd   „ 715
   ' But v the tears for darken'd years   *Ancient Sage* 183
   And v the laughter as the tears,   „ 185
   Rail at ' Blind Fate ' with many a v ' Alas ! '   *Doubt and Prayer* 2
   Help thy v worlds to bear thy light.   *In Mem.,* Pro. 32
   making v pretence Of gladness,   „ xxx 6
   That not a moth with v desire   „ liv 10
   At night she weeps, ' How v am I !   „ lx 15
   With fifty Mays, thy songs are v ;   „ lxxvi 14
   Thy likeness, I might count it v   „ xcii 2
   Half-grown as yet, a child, and v—   „ cxiv 9
   man of science himself is fonder of glory, and v,   *Maud* I iv 37
   She murmur'd, ' V, in vain : it cannot be.   *Lancelot and E.* 892
   project after project rose, and all of them were v ;   *The Flight* 14
   I was jealous, anger'd, v,   *Happy* 66
   May your fears be v !   *To One who ran down Eng.* 2
Vain (s)   I would shoot, howe'er in v,   *Two Voices* 344
   Her and her children, let her plead in v;   *Enoch Arden* 166
   Borrow'd a glass, but all in v :   „ 240
   If all be not in v ;   *In Mem.* cxiv 18
   the Queen, who long had sought in v To break him   *Gareth and L.* 139
   Foredooming all his trouble was in v,   „ 1127
   that ye blew your boast in v ? '   „ 1229
   To sleek her ruffled peace of mind, in v.   *Merlin and V.* 899
   That proof of trust—so often ask'd in v !   „ 920
   She murmur'd, ' Vain, in v : it cannot be.   *Lancelot and E.* 892
   When some brave deed seem'd to be done in v,   *Holy Grail* 274
   all My quest were but in v ;   „ 783
   And now his chair desires him here in v,   „ 901
   her life Wasted and pined, desiring him in v.   *Pelleas and E.* 496
   have but stricken with the sword in v ;   *Pass. of Arthur* 23
   And we had not fought them in v,   *The Revenge* 74
   Torture and trouble in v,—   *Def. of Lucknow* 86
   Or you may drive in v,—   *Politics* 8
   But the Bandit had woo'd me in v,   *Bandit's Death* 10
Vainglorious   Nothing of the vulgar, or v,   *On Jub. Q. Victoria* 13
Vainglory   Drove me from all *vainglories*,   *Holy Grail* 32
Vainlier   v than a hen To her false daughters   *Princess* v 328
Vale   Winds all the v in rosy folds,   *Miller's D.* 242
   THERE lies a v in Ida,   *Œnone* 1
   many a v And river-sunder'd champaign   „ 113
   Lay, dozing in the v of Avalon,   *Palace of Art* 107
   ' Make me a cottage in the v,'   „ 291
   and many a winding v And meadow,   *Lotos-Eaters* 22
   Beyond the thick-leaved platans of the v.   *Princess* iii 175
   roll The torrents, dash'd to the v :   „ v 350
   ' Pretty bud ! Lily of the v !   „ vi 193
   come ; for all the v's Await thee ;   „ vii 215
   Light, so low in the v You flash and lighten
     afar,   *Window, Marr. Morn.* 9
   The flocks are whiter down the v,   *In Mem.* cxv 10
   up the v of Usk, By the flat meadow,   *Marr. of Geraint* 831
   ' And thence I dropt into a lowly v,   *Holy Grail* 440
   and where the v Was lowest, found a chapel,   „ 441

Vale (continued)   Re-makes itself, and flashes down the v—   *Guinevere* 610
   By thousands down the crags and thro' the v's.   *Montenegro* 8
   and every way the v's Wind,   *Tiresias* 182
   A gleam from yonder v,   *Early Spring* 33
   in this pleasant v we stand again,   *Demeter and P.* 34
   ' Among the tombs in this damp v of yours !   *The Ring* 325
   Our vernal bloom from every v and plain   *To Mary Boyle* 9
   gulf on gulf thro' all their v's below.   *Prog. of Spring* 73
   But when she gain'd the broader v,   *Death of Œnone* 91
   Came that ' Ave atque V ' of the Poet's   *Frater Ave, etc.* 5
   ' Frater Ave atque V '—as we wander'd to and fro   „ 7
Valence   ' O ay, what say ye to Sir V,   *Merlin and V.* 705
   Sir V wedded with an outland dame :   „ 714
   Was charged by V to bring home the child.   „ 718
Valentine   birds that piped their V's,   *Princess* v 239
Valiant   Ring in the v man and free,   *In Mem.* cvi 29
   ' I have fought for Queen and Faith like a v man
     and true,   *The Revenge* 101
   they stared at the dead that had been so v and true,   „ 105
Valkyrian   ourself have often tried V hymns,   *Princess* iv 139
Valley   (See also **Island-valley**)   the broad v dimm'd
   in the gloaming :   *Leonine Eleg.* 1
   or fills The horned v's all about,   *Supp. Confessions* 152
   lovelier Than all the v's of Ionian hills.   *Œnone* 2
   Behind the v topmost Gargarus Stands up   „ 10
   panther's roar came muffled, while I sat Low in the v.   „ 215
   In this green v, under this green hill,   „ 232
   As I came up the v whom think ye should I see,   *May Queen* 13
   All the v, mother, 'ill be fresh and green   „ 37
   up the v came a swell of music on the wind.   „ Con. 32
   And up the v came again the music on the wind.   „ 36
   Wild flowers in the v for other hands than mine.   „ 52
   Full-faced above the v stood the moon ;   *Lotos-Eaters* 7
   bolts are hurl'd Far below them in the v's,   „ C. S. 112
   others in Elysian v's dwell,   „ 124
   The v's of grape-loaded vines that glow   *D. of F. Women* 219
   Where yon dark v's wind forlorn,   *On a Mourner* 22
   I lived In the white convent down the v there,   *St. S. Stylites* 62
   from the v's underneath Came little copses   *Amphion* 31
   From some delightful v.   *Will Water.* 120
   To bicker down a v.   *The Brook* 26
   fought their last below, Was climbing up the v ;   *Aylmer's Field* 228
   come, for Love is of the v, come, For Love is of the
     v, come thou down   *Princess* vii 198
   let the torrent dance thee down To find him in the v ;   „ 210
   turning saw The happy v's, half in light,   „ Con. 41
   Follow'd up in v and glen With blare of bugle,   *Ode on Well.* 114
   All in the v of Death Rode the six hundred.   *Light Brigade* 3
   Into the v of Death Rode the six hundred. (repeat)   „ 7, 16
   A thousand shadowy-pencill'd v's   *The Daisy* 67
   ALL along the v, stream that flashest white,   *V. of Cauteretz* 1
   All along the v, where thy waters flow,   „ 3
   All along the v, while I walk'd to-day,   „ 5
   For all along the v, down thy rocky bed,   „ 7
   And all along the v, by rock and cave and tree,   „ 9
   Above the v's of palm and pine.'   *The Islet* 23
   The v, the voice, the peak,   *Voice and the P.* 27
   and jutting peak And v,   *Spec. of Iliad* 14
   Fly to the light in the v below—   *Window, Letter* 12
   Ringing thro' the v's,   *Maud* I xii 10
   And the v's of Paradise.   „ xxii 44
   Flee down the v before he get to horse.   *Gareth and L.* 941
   thro' many a grassy glade And v,   *Marr. of Geraint* 237
   long street of a little town In a long v,   „ 243
   And out of town and v came a noise   „ 247
   That glooms his v, sighs to see the peak Sun-
     flush'd,   *Balin and Balan* 165
   fill'd With the blue v and the glistening brooks,   *Lover's Tale* i 331
   men dropt dead in the v's   *V. of Maeldune* 31
   To silver all the v's with her shafts—   *Tiresias* 32
   horsemen, drew to the v—and stay'd ;   *Heavy Brigade* 3
   When over the v, In early summers,   *Merlin and the G.* 17
   Drew to the v Named of the Shadow,   „ 86
   while we dwelt Together in this v—   *Death of Œnone* 30
   Thro' blasted v and flaring forest   *Kapiolani* 12

Valorous many a *v* legionary, — *Boädicea* 85
  our most *v*, Sanest and most obedient : — *Geraint and E.* 910
  a *v* weapon in olden England ! — *Kapiolani* 4
Valour *V* and charity more and more. — *To F. D. Maurice* 40
  courtesy wins woman all as well As *v* may, — *Last Tournament* 708
  Stately purposes, *v* in battle, — *Vastness* 7
Value To loyal hearts the *v* of all gifts — *Lancelot and E.* 1214
  The *v* of that jewel he had to guard ? — *Lover's Tale iv* 153
  And trebling all the rest in *v*— — „ 200
  A gift of slenderer *v*, mine. — *To Ulysses* 48
Valued he knew the man and *v* him. — *Enoch Arden* 121
Valueless and you saved me, a *v* life, — *Despair* 61
Valuing *V* the giddy pleasure of the eyes. — *M. d'Arthur* 128
  V the giddy pleasure of the eyes. — *Pass. of Arthur* 296
Valve and betwixt were *v's* Of open-work — *Princess iv* 202
  marble stairs, And great bronze *v's*, — „ *v* 365
  Descending, burst the great bronze *v's*, — „ *vi* 75
Van Love wept and spread his sheeny *v's* for flight ; — *Love and Death* 8
  Then those who led the *v*, and those in rear, — *Lover's Tale iii* 24
Van Diemen grows From England to *V D.* — *Amphion* 84
Vane not the County Member's with the *v* : — *Walk. to the Mail* 12
  STILL on the tower stood the *v*, — *The Letters* 1
  Waverings of every *v* with every wind, — *To the Queen ii* 50
  and once we only saw Your gilded *v*, — *The Ring* 331
Vanish So *v* friendships only made in wine. — *Geraint and E.* 479
  and pass And *v* in the woods ; — *Balin and Balan* 327
  Dreamlike, should on the sudden *v*, — *Holy Grail* 260
  From less to less and *v* into light. — *Pass. of Arthur* 468
  madden'd the peoples would *v* at last, — *Despair* 24
  And ever vanishing, never *v'es*, — *Ancient Sage* 44
  thy world Might *v* like thy shadow in the dark. — „ 52
  The hope I catch at *v'es* and youth — *The Flight* 16
  But Song will *v* in the Vast; — *Epilogue* 40
  Till shadows *v* in the Light of Light. — *Epit. on Caxton* 4
  Will *v* and give place to the beauty — *Happy* 36
  ere it *v'es* Over the margin, — *Merlin and the G.* 128
  if such a wife as you Should *v* unrecorded. — *Romney's R.* 69
  Let the golden Iliad *v*, — *Parnassus* 20
  v in your deeps and heights ? — *God and the Univ.* 1
Vanish'd (adj. and part.) But O for the touch of a *v* hand, — *Break, break, etc.* 11
  And those who sorrow'd o'er a *v* race, — *Aylmer's Field* 844
  But since it pleased a *v* eye, — *In Mem. viii* 21
  And, thy dark freight, a *v* life. — „ *x* 8
  The days have *v*, tone and tint, — „ *xliv* 5
  And thou hast *v* from thine own — *Pref. Poem Broth. Son.* 5
  Far among the *v* races, old Assyrian kings would flay — *Locksley H., Sixty* 79
  All I loved are *v* voices, all my steps are on the dead. — „ 252
  When, in the *v* year, You saw the league-long rampart-fire — *Pro. to Gen. Hamley* 26
  Light among the *v* ages ; — *To Virgil* 25
  Stung by his loss had *v*, none knew where. — *Lover's Tale iv* 102
  MANY a hearth upon our dark globe sighs after many a *v* face, — *Vastness* 1
  Many a planet by many a sun may roll with the dust of a *v* race. — „ 2
  Arthur had *v* I knew not whither, — *Merlin and the G.* 77
  Has *v* in the shadow cast by Death. — *D. of the Duke of C.* 3
Vanish'd (verb) she cast back upon him A piteous glance, and *v*. — *Aylmer's Field* 284
  clink'd, and clash'd, and *v*, and I woke, — *Sea Dreams* 135
  v panic-stricken, like a shoal Of darting fish, — *Geraint and E.* 468
  Until they *v* by the fairy well — *Merlin and V.* 428
  And *v*, and his book came down to me.' — „ 650
  v suddenly from the field With young Lavaine — *Lancelot and E.* 508
  every bridge as quickly as he crost Sprang into fire and *v*, — *Holy Grail* 506
  now there is a lion in the way.' So *v*." — „ 646
  bounded forth and *v* thro' the night. — *Pelleas and E.* 487
  Or ev'n a fall'n feather, *v* again. — *Last Tournament* 372
  watch'd them till they *v* from my sight — *Lover's Tale ii* 42
  flash'd thro' sense and soul And by the poplar *v*— — *Sisters (E. and E.)* 110
  power over Hell till it utterly *v* away. — *Despair* 102
  when the white fog *v* like a ghost Before the day, — *Death of Œnone* 67

Vanish'd (verb) (continued) before him *V* shadow-like Gods and Goddesses, — *Kapiolani* 26
Vanishing (*See also* **Ever-vanishing**) grave itself shall pass, — *Lucretius* 258
  V, atom and void, — *Lucretius* 258
  to the last dip of the *v* sail She watch'd it, — *Enoch Arden* 245
  And ever *v*, never vanishes, — *Ancient Sage* 44
Vanity Oh ! *v* ! Death waits at the door. — *All Things will Die* 16
  they sing Like poets, from the *v* of song ? — *Gardener's D.* 100
  thy *v* so shot up It frighted all free fool — *Last Tournament* 306
  my strangled *v* Utter'd a stifled cry— — *Sisters (E. and E.)* 199
Vanquish knew that Love can *v* Death, — *D. of F. Women* 269
Vanquish'd when our side was *v* and my cause For ever lost, — *Princess vi* 24
  We *v*, you the Victor of your will. — „ 167
  Victor from *v* issues at the last, — *Gareth and L.* 1262
Vantage I set thee high on *v* ground, — *Balin and Balan* 534
Vantage-ground With such a *v-g* for nobleness ! — *Aylmer's Field* 387
  nor a *v-g* For pleasure — *Ded. of Idylls* 23
Vapid But languidly adjust My *v* vegetable loves — *Talking Oak* 183
Vapour ' High up the *v's* fold and swim— — *Two Voices* 262
  swimming *v* slopes athwart the glen, — *Œnone* 3
  But vague in *v*, hard to mark ; — *Love thou thy land* 62
  The *v's* weep their burthen to the ground, — *Tithonus* 2
  When the ranks are roll'd in *v*, — *Locksley Hall* 104
  Comes a *v* from the margin, — „ 191
  Faint shadows, *v's* lightly curl'd, — *Day-Dm., Sleep. P.* 5
  flowing range Of *v* buoy'd the crescent-bark, — „ *Depart.* 22
  My breath to heaven like *v* goes : — *St. Agnes' Eve* 3
  In crystal *v* everywhere — *Sir L. and Q. G.* 5
  A *v* heavy, hueless, formless, cold, — *Vision of Sin* 53
  When that cold *v* touch'd the palace gate, — „ 58
  A belt, it seem'd, of luminous *v*, lay, — *Sea Dreams* 209
  saw The soft white *v* streak the crowned towers — *Princess iii* 344
  Roll'd the rich *v* far into the heaven. — *Spec. of Iliad* 8
  Behind a purple-frosty bank Of *v*, — *In Mem. cvii* 4
  All night the shining *v* sail — „ *Con.* 111
  yellow *v's* choke The great city sounding wide ; — *Maud II iv* 63
  a lovely baleful star Veil'd in gray *v* ; — *Merlin and V.* 263
  The moony *v* rolling round the King, — *Guinevere* 601
  silvery *v* in daylight Over the mountain Floats, — *Kapiolani* 16
Vapour-braided And sweet the *v-b* blue, — *The Letters* 42
Vapour-girdle from my *v-g* soaring forth — *Prog. of Spring* 79
Vapour-swathed forehead *v-s* In meadows ever green ; — *Freedom* 7
Variable Then follow'd calms, and then winds *v*, — *Enoch Arden* 545
Varied With all the *v* changes of the dark, — *Edwin Morris* 36
  The coming year's great good and *v* ills, — *Prog. of Spring* 93
Varier pious *v's* from the church, To chapel ; — *Sea Dreams* 19
Varieties (Beauty seen In all *v* of mould and mind) — *To ——, With Pal. of Art* 7
Various Each month is *v* to present The world — *Two Voices* 74
  All *v*, each a perfect whole From living Nature, — *Palace of Art* 58
  ' O all things fair to sate my *v* eyes ! — „ 193
  So beautiful, vast, *v*, — *Ancient Sage* 84
  foremost in thy *v* gallery Place it, — *Ode to Memory* 84
  That *v* wilderness a tissue of light — *Lover's Tale i* 419
  To prize your *v* book, and send A gift — *To Ulysses* 47
Varmint (vermin) ' Gaw up ageän fur the *v* ? ' — *Owd Roä* 98
Varnish'd once more in *v* glory shine Thy stars — *Prog. of Spring* 38
Varsity (university) 'e coom'd to the parish wi' lots o' *V* debt, — *N. Farmer, N. S.* 29
  Fur Squire wur a *V* scholard, — *Village Wife* 25
Vertical (vertical) ' Cast awaäy on a disolut land wi' a *v* soon ! ' — *North. Cobbler* 3
Vary To *v* from the kindly race of men, — *Tithonus* 29
  violet *varies* from the lily as far As oak from elm : — *Princess v* 182
  And as the light of Heaven *varies*, — *Marr. of Geraint* 6
  so loved Geraint To make her beauty *v* day by day, — „ 9
  value of all gifts Must *v* as the giver's. — *Lancelot and E.* 1215
  V like the leaves and flowers, — *Poets and Critics* 4
Vary-colour'd A walk in *v-c* shells — *Arabian Nights* 57
Varying *v* to and fro, We know not wherefore ; — *Aylmer's Field* 73
  Form, Ritual, *v* with the tribes of men. — *Akbar's Dream* 125
  Ever *v* Madeline. (repeat) — *Madeline 3, 18, 27*
  THE *v* year with blade and sheaf — *Day-Dm., Sleep. P.* 1
  By many a *v* influence and so long. — *Princess vi* 267

Varying (continued) poesy, *v* voices of prayer ? — *Vastness* 31
Vase From fluted *v*, and brazen urn In order, — *Arabian Nights* 60
from *v's* in the hall Flowers of all heavens, — *Princess, Pro.* 11
or prove The Danaïd of a leaky *v*, — „ *ii* 340
Break, thou deep *v* of chilling tears, — *In Mem. iv* 11
Years that make And break the *v* of clay, — *Ancient Sage* 92
Vashti O *V*, noble *V* ! Summon'd out She kept her state, — *Princess iii* 228
Vassal.) In *v* tides that follow'd thought. — *In Mem. cxii* 16
Delivering, that his lord, the *v* king, — *Gareth and L.* 391
follow'd up by her *v* legion of fools ; — *Vastness* 12
Vassal (s) Not *v's* to be beat, nor pretty babes — *Princess iv* 146
And makes it *v* unto love : — *In Mem. xlviii* 8
feeble *v's* of wine and anger and lust, — *Maud II i* 43
loyal *v's* toiling for their liege. — *Com. of Arthur* 282
Doorm, whom his shaking *v's* call'd the Bull, — *Geraint and E.* 439
Who now no more a *v* to the thief, — „ 753
But work as *v* to the larger love, — *Merlin and V.* 491
A prisoner, and the *v* of thy will ; — *Pelleas and E.* 241
The Present is the *v* of the Past ; — *Lover's Tale i* 119
And make thy gold thy *v* not thy king, — *Ancient Sage* 259
the tyrant *v* of a tyrant vice ! — *The Flight* 25
Vassalage *See* **Kitchen-vassalage**
Vast (adj.) *V* images in glimmering dawn, — *Two Voices* 305
The *v* Republics that may grow, — *Day-Dm., L'Envoi* 15
But, all his *v* heart sherris-warm'd, — *Will Water.* 197
The *v* Akrokeraunian walls, — *To E. L.* 4
and fell In *v* sea-cataracts— — *Sea Dreams* 54
lays His *v* and filthy hands upon my will, — *Lucretius* 220
then how a *v* a work To assail this gray — *Princess iii* 233
The bones of some *v* bulk that lived — „ 294
the *v* designs Of his labour'd rampart-lines, — *Ode on Well.* 104
And in the *v* cathedral leave him, — „ 280
fur I luvv'd 'er a *v* sight moor fur it : — *N. Farmer, N. S.* 36
Drops in his *v* and wandering grave. — *In Mem. vi* 16
His own *v* shadow glory-crown'd ; — „ *xcvii* 3
No doubt *v* eddies in the flood — „ *cxxviii* 5
for a *v* speculation had fail'd — *Maud I i* 9
whose *v* wit And hundred winters — *Com. of Arthur* 280
drew The *v* and shaggy mantle of his beard — *Merlin and V.* 256
but I dreamt Of some *v* charm concluded — „ 512
Drew the *v* eyelid of an inky cloud, — „ 634
And whelm all this beneath as *v* a mound — „ 656
' You breathe but accusation *v* and vague, — „ 701
The *v* necessity of heart and hand. — „ 925
Brake from the *v* oriel-embowering vine — *Lancelot and E.* 1198
Then Arthur made *v* banquets, and strange knights — *Pelleas and E.* 147
On some *v* plain before a setting sun, — *Guinevere* 77
I, whose *v* pity almost makes me die — „ 534
who broke The *v* design and purpose of the King. — „ 670
and her throne In our *v* Orient, and one isle, — *To the Queen ii* 31
mighty gyres Rapid and *v*, — *Lover's Tale ii* 198
The *v* occasion of our stronger life— — *Columbus* 35
So beautiful, *v*, various, so beyond — *Ancient Sage* 84
The *v* sun-clusters' gather'd blaze, — *Epilogue* 54
In that *v* Oval ran a shudder of shame. — *St. Telemachus* 73
Thro' all the *v* dominion which a sword, — *Akbar's Dream* 14
Vast (s) Thine own shall wither in the *v*, — *In Mem. lxxvi* 11
A soul shall draw from out the *v* — „ *Con.* 123
But Song will vanish in the *V* ; — *Epilogue* 40
Vaster May make one music as before, But *v*. — *In Mem., Pro.* 29
What *v* dream can hit the mood Of Love — „ *xlvii* 11
As, unto *v* motions bound, — „ *lxiii* 10
And still as *v* grew the shore — „ *ciii* 25
My love is *v* passion now ; — „ *cxxx* 10
Or in that *v* Spain I leave to Spain. — *Columbus* 208
Sway'd by *v* ebbs and flows than can be known — *Locksley H., Sixty* 194
Vastness In *v* and in mystery, — *In Mem. xcvii* 7
Swallow'd in *V*, lost in Silence, — *Vastness* 34
Vat flask of cider from his father's *v's*, — *Audley Court* 27
red with spirted purple of the *v's*, — *Princess vii* 202
Vault (s) Imbower'd *v's* of pillar'd palm, — *Arabian Nights* 39
Nor any cloud would cross the *v*, — *Mariana in the S.* 38
Ranges of glimmering *v's* with iron grates, — *D. of F. Women* 35
O Priestess in the *v's* of Death, — *In Mem. iii* 2
In *v's* and catacombs, they fell ; — „ *lviii* 4

Vault (s) (continued) up thy *v* with roaring sound Climb thy thick noon, — *In Mem. lxxii* 25
Far beneath a blazing *v*, — *Will* 18
from the deep *v* where the heart of Hope Fell into dust, — *Lover's Tale i* 94
And laid her in the *v* of her own kin. — „ *iv* 39
entering the dim *v*, And, making there a sudden light, — „ 52
Then at the far end of the *v* he saw His lady — „ 56
Drown'd in the gloom and horror of the *v*. — „ 62
Vault (verb) lightly *v* from the throne and play — *The Mermaid* 33
Far as the Future *v's* her skies, — *Mechanophilus* 17
Vaulted (*See also* **Hollow-vaulted, Long-vaulted, Over-vaulted**) *V* o'er the dark-blue sea. — *Lotos-Eaters, C. S.* 40
Then some one sent beneath his *v* palm — *Princess v* 31
So many a time he *v* up again ; — *Gareth and L.* 1125
And *v* on his horse, and so they crash'd In onset, — *Balin and Balan* 555
Ran thro' the doors and *v* on his horse And fled : — *Pelleas and E.* 539
v upon him, And rode beneath an ever-showering leaf, — *Last Tournament* 491
Vauntcourier that one *V* to this *double* ? — *Lover's Tale ii* 30
Vaunted and *v* our kith and our kin, — *V. of Maeldune* 47
Veer the warm hour returns With *v* of wind, — *Last Tournament* 231
Veering (*See also* **Ever-veering**) bird that still is *v* there Above his four gold letters, — *The Ring* 332
By *v* passion fann'd, — *Madeline* 29
Vegetable But languidly adjust My vapid *v* loves — *Talking Oak* 183
Veil (s) inner impulse rent the *v* Of his old husk : — *Two Voices* 10
thro' thick *v's* to apprehend A labour — „ 296
Slow-dropping *v's* of thinnest lawn, — *Lotos-Eaters* 11
the time Is come to raise the *v*. — *Gardener's D.* 274
And draws the *v* from hidden worth. — *Day-Dm., Arrival* 4
rose of Gulistan Shall burst her *v* : — *Princess iv* 123
From orb to orb, from *v* to *v*.' — *In Mem. xxx* 28
Behind the *v*, behind the *v*, — „ *lvi* 28
A lucid *v* from coast to coast, — „ *lxvii* 14
We heard behind the woodbine *v* — „ *lxxxix* 50
an Isis hid by the *v*. — *Maud I iv* 43
A faded mantle and a faded *v*, — *Marr. of Geraint* 135
And in her *v* enfolded, manchet bread. — „ 389
And tearing off her *v* of faded silk — *Geraint and E.* 514
I knew the *v* had been withdrawn. — *Holy Grail* 522
aghast the maiden arose, White as her *v*, — *Guinevere* 363
from under this A *v*, that seemed no more than gilded air, — *Lover's Tale iv* 290
our mortal *v* And shatter'd phantom — *De Prof., Two G.* 46
the *v* is rending, and the Voices of the day — *The Ring* 38
She comes to dress me in my bridal *v*. — „ 98
But the bridal *v*—Your nurse is waiting. — „ 488
Veil (verb) I cannot *v*, or droop my sight, — *Eleänore* 87
gleams of good that broke From either side, nor *v* his eyes : — *Love thou thy land* 90
She bow'd as if to *v* a noble tear ; — *Princess iii* 289
v His want in forms for fashion's sake, — *In Mem. cxi* 5
Well might I wish to *v* her wickedness, — *Guinevere* 211
and now He *v's* His flesh in bread, — *Sir J. Oldcastle* 156
Murder would not *v* your sin, — *Forlorn* 49
Veil'd (*See also* **Willow-veil'd**) eyes have been intent On that *v* picture—*v*, for what it holds — *Gardener's D.* 270
That *v* the world with jaundice, — *Walk. to the Mail* 20
he *v* His face with the other, and at once, — *Aylmer's Field* 808
again She *v* her brows, and prone she sank, — *Princess v* 107
In the centre stood A statue *v*, to which they sang ; And, withal, tho' *v*, was known to me, — *In Mem. ciii* 12
seem'd a lovely baleful star *V* in gray vapour ; — *Merlin and V.* 263
but what I saw was *v* And cover'd ; — *Holy Grail* 851
walk'd abreast with me, and *v* his brow, — *Lover's Tale ii* 86
I walk'd behind with one who *v* his brow. — „ *iii* 12
' He *v* Himself in flesh, — *Sir J. Oldcastle* 156
Veileth every cloud, that spreads above And *v* love, — *Two Voices* 447
Veilless He drove the dust against her *v* eyes : — *Geraint and E.* 529
Vein (s) (*See also* **Willow-veil'd**) Life shoots and glances thro' your *v's*, — *Rosalind* 22
a languid fire creeps Thro' my *v's* — *Eleänore* 131
you can talk : yours is a kindly *v* : — *Edwin Morris* 81
Here stays the blood along the *v's*. — *Day-Dm., Sleep P.* 4

BB*

Vein (s) *(continued)* brooking not the Tarquin in her *v's*,   *Lucretius* 237
The summer of the vine in all his *v's*—   *Princess* i 183
But branches current yet in kindred *v's*.'   ,,   ii 245
From out a common *v* of memory Sweet household talk,   ,,   314
I felt my *v's* Stretch with fierce heat ;   ,,   v 537
half the wolf's-milk curdled in their *v's*,   ,,   vii 130
now the wine made summer in his *v's*,   *Marr. of Geraint* 398
his forehead *v's* Bloated, and branch'd ;   *Balin and Balan* 391
The flowers that run poison in their *v's*.   *Lover's Tale* i 347
Burst *v*, snap sinew, and crack heart,   *Sir J. Oldcastle* 123
heat of a wretched life rushing back thro' the *v's* ?   *Despair* 68
Vein (verb) all the gold That *v's* the world   *Princess* iv 543
Velvet (adj.) added fulness to the phrase Of
'Gauntlet in the *v* glove.'   *To Marq. of Dufferin* 12
Velvet (s) dusted *v's* have much need of thee :   *To J. M. K.* 4
Black *v* of the costliest—   *Aylmer's Field* 804
Veneer'd *V* with sanctimonious theory.   *Princess, Pro.* 117
Venerable ' Thanks, *v* friend,' replied Geraint ;   *Marr. of Geraint* 303
Among the Roses, the more *v*.   *Sisters (E. and E.)* 76
Venerator not a scorner of your sex But *v*,   *Princess* iv 423
Vengeance ' Is this thy *v*, holy Venus,   *Lucretius* 67
What hinders me To take such bloody *v* on you both ?— *Princess* iv 534
when he told us ' *V* is mine ! '   *V. of Maeldune* 120
Venial Or seeming-genial *v* fault,   *Will* 13
Venice then I pass'd Home, and thro' *V*,   *The Ring* 192
Venom Not one to flirt a *v* at her eyes,   *Merlin and V.* 609
Venom'd *See* **Faintly-venom'd**
Venomous You should have seen him wince As from
a *v* thing,   *Walk. to the Mail* 72
Strike dead the whole weak race of *v* worms,   *Maud* II i 46
Venture my poor *v* but a fleet of glass   *Sea Dreams* 138
would *v* to give him the nay ?   *The Wreck* 17
Ventured Alone at home, nor *v* out alone.   *Enoch Arden* 517
And boldly *v* on the liberties.   *Princess* i 205
or half the world Had *v*—   *Gareth and L.* 65
Venturous Maud with her *v* climbings   *Maud* I i 69
Venus ' Is this thy vengeance, holy *V*,   *Lucretius* 67
And o'er his head Uranian *V* hung,   *Princess* i 243
And silver-smiling *V* ere she fell   *Lover's Tale* i 61
V near her ! smiling downward   *Locksley H., Sixty* 183
Hesper—*V*—were we native to that splendour   ,,   187
Veragua thunders in the black *V* nights,   *Columbus* 146
Verbiage This barren *v*, current among men,   *Princess* ii 54
Vere de Vere *(See also* **Clara Vere de Vere)** repose
Which stamps the caste of *V d V*,   *L. C. V. de Vere* 40
Verge Float by you on the *v* of night.   *Margaret* 31
That lent broad *v* to distant lands,   *Palace of Art* 30
hull Look'd one black dot against the *v* of dawn,   *M. d'Arthur* 271
May from *v* to *v*, And May with me from head to
heel.   *Gardener's D.* 80
That sinks with all we love below the *v* ;   *Princess* iv 47
Blot out the slope of sea from *v* to shore,   ,,   vii 38
And on the low dark *v* of life   *In Mem.* l 15
hull Look'd one black dot against the *v* of dawn,   *Pass. of Arthur* 439
Each way from *v* to *v* a Holy Land,   *Lover's Tale* i 337
dipping his head low beneath the *v*,   ,,   509
Verged kinds of thought, That *v* upon them,   *Gardener's D.* 71
Veriest The *v* beauties of the work appear   *Sisters (E. and E.)* 105
Sworn to be *v* ice of pureness.   *Sir J. Oldcastle* 108
Vermeil-white near her, like a blossom *v-w*,   *Marr. of Geraint* 364
Vermin (adj.) and the *v* voices here May buzz so
loud—   *Lancelot and E.* 138
Vermin (s) *(See also* **Varmint)** As fancies like the *v* in
a nut   *Princess* vi 263
curse me the British *v*, the rat ;   *Maud* II v 58
and then like *v* here Drown him,   *Gareth and L.* 822
I will track this *v* to their earths :   *Marr. of Geraint* 217
from the *v* that he sees Before him,   *Pelleas and E.* 285
show'd him, like a *v* in its hole,   *Last Tournament* 165
Vernal till all Our *v* bloom from every vale   *To Mary Boyle* 9
Broaden the glowing isles of *v* blue.   *Prog. of Spring* 60
Versatility The grace and *v* of the man !   *Lancelot and E.* 472
Verse How may full-sail'd *v* express,   *Eleänore* 44
invade Even with a *v* your holy woe.   *To J. S.* 8
another which you had, I mean of *v*   *The Epic* 26

Verse *(continued)* gave the *v* ' Behold, Your house is
left unto you desolate ! '   *Aylmer's Field* 628
great Sicilian called Calliope to grace his golden *v*—   *Lucretius* 94
In *v* that brings myself relief,   *In Mem. lxxv* 2
Take one *v* more—the lady speaks   *Merlin and V.* 445
the name at the head of my *v* is thine.   *To A. Tennyson* 6
read me a Bible *v* of the Lord's good will   *Rizpah* 61
sought the tribute of a *v* from me,   *To Dante* 5
in his hand A scroll of *v*—   *Ancient Sage* 6
patriot-soldier take His meed of fame in *v* ;   *Epilogue* 33
Versed In many a subtle question *v*,   *In Mem. xcvi* 6
Version which I know no *v* done In English   *To E. Fitzgerald* 5
Vert Flame-colour, *v* and azure, in three rays,   *Com. of Arthur* 275
Vertical *See* **Vartical**
Verulam (Lord, Francis Bacon) Plato the wise, and large-
brow'd *V*,   *Palace of Art* 163
But Homer, Plato, *V* ;   *Princess* ii 160
Verulam (Roman Colony) London, *V*, Cámulodúne.   *Boädicea* 86
Very The *v* graves appear'd to smile,   *The Letters* 45
And some that men were in the *v* walls,   *Princess* iv 485
The *v* source and fount of Day   *In Mem. xxiv* 3
But brake his *v* heart in pining for it,   *Gareth and L.* 57
I fear'd The *v* fountains of her life were chill'd ; *Sisters (E. and E.)* 266
when Even descended, the *v* sunset aflame ;   *V. of Maeldune* 66
This *v* ring Io t'amo ?   *The Ring* 133
Vesper From prime to *v's* will I chant   *Pelleas and E.* 349
Vessel On the coals I lay, A *v* full of sin :   *St. S. Stylites* 170
There lies the port ; the *v* puffs her sail :   *Ulysses* 44
The silver *v's* sparkle clean,   *Sir Galahad* 34
to make the name Of his *v* great in story,   *The Captain* 19
Reporting of his *v* China-bound,   *Enoch Arden* 122
Waving, the moment and the *v* past.   ,,   244
The *v* scarce sea-worthy ;   ,,   656
And o'er his head the Holy *V* hung (repeat)   *Holy Grail* 512, 520
And to the Holy *V* of the Grail.'   ,,   840
one A *v* in mid-ocean, her heaved prow Clambering, *Lover's Tale* ii 169
when all at once That painted *v*,   ,,   191
Tho' his *v* was all but a wreck ;   *The Revenge* 64
Fleeted his *v* to sea with the king in it,   *Batt. of Brunanburh* 64
crest of the tides Plunged on the *v*   *The Wreck* 90
Launch your *v*, And crowd your canvas,   *Merlin and the G.* 126
Vestal tended by Pure *v* thoughts in the translucent fane   *Isabel* 4
love-whispers may not breathe Within this *v* limit,   *Princess* ii 222
in the *V* entry shriek'd The virgin marble   ,,   vi 350
the flower of all their *v* knighthood,   *Balin and Balan* 508
Vested *See* **Woman-vested**
Vestibule *v's* To caves and shows of Death :   *Lover's Tale* ii 125
Veteran Me the sport of ribald *V's*,   *Boädicea* 50
Vex *V* not thou the poet's mind (repeat)   *Poet's Mind* 1, 3
Will *v* thee lying underground ?   *Two Voices* 111
' The end and the beginning *v* His reason :   ,,   298
to *v* me with his father's eyes !   *Œnone* 255
And an eye shall *v* thee,   *Locksley Hall* 85
I will not *v* my bosom :   *Amphion* 102
want of pence, Which *v'es* public men,   *Will Water.* 44
v the unhappy dust thou wouldst not save.   *Come not, when, etc.* 4
And it would *v* him even in his grave,   *Enoch Arden* 303
For my dead face would *v* her after-life.   ,,   891
Ere you were born to *v* us ?   *Princess* iv 248
ill counsel had misled the girl To *v* true hearts :   ,,   vii 242
As daily *v'es* household peace,   *In Mem. xxix* 2
I *v* my heart with fancies dim :   ,,   xlii 1
Let this not *v* thee, noble heart !   ,,   lxxix 2
An old song *v'es* my ear ;   *Maud* II ii 47
boys Who love to *v* him eating,   *Geraint and E.* 561
V not yourself : ye will not see me more.'   *Pelleas and E.* 304
began To *v* and plague her.   *Guinevere* 68
I seem To *v* an ear too sad to listen to me,   ,,   315
And *v* them with my darkness ?   *Lover's Tale* i 732
A madman or to you with wretched words,   *Despair* 108
To *v* the noon with fiery gems,   *Ancient Sage* 265
Vexed-Vext *Vex'd* with a morbid devil in his blood   *Walk. to the Mail* 19
The farmer *vext* packs up his beds and chairs,   ,,   39
Draw down into his *vexed* pools   *Supp. Confessions* 133
The *vexed* eddies of its wayward brother :   *Isabel* 33

Vexed-Vext (*continued*) ' Go, *vexed* Spirit, sleep in trust ; *Two Voices* 115
scudding drifts the rainy Hyades *Vext* the dim sea : *Ulysses* 11
if he come again, *vext* will he be To find *Enoch Arden* 301
And James departed *vext* with him and her.' *The Brook* 110
Vext with unworthy madness, and deform'd. *Aylmer's Field* 335
Then their eyes *vext* her ; " 802
they *vext* the souls of deans ; *Princess, Pro.* 162
I stood With Florian, cursing Cyril, *vext* at heart, " *iv* 171
What time have I to be *vext* ? *Grandmother* 104
Fool that I am to be *vext* with his pride ! *Maud I xiii* 5
Vext with lawyers and harass'd with debt ; " *xix* 22
But he *vext* her and perplext her " *xx* 6
Vext with waste dreams ? *Com. of Arthur* 85
bitterness and grief That *vext* his mother, " 211
And *vext* his day, but blesses him asleep— *Gareth and L.* 1286
A little *vext* at losing of the hunt, *Marr. of Geraint* 234
' No, no,' said Enid, *vext*, ' I will not eat *Geraint and E.* 656
Vext at a rumour issued from herself *Merlin and V.* 153
Then Lancelot *vext* at having lied in vain : *Lancelot and E.* 102
He seem'd so sullen, *vext* he could not go : " 210
Glad that no phantom *vext* me more, *Holy Grail* 538
vext his heart, And marr'd his rest— *Pelleas and E.* 398
carcanet *Vext* her with plaintive memories of the child : *Last Tournament* 29
I should evermore be *vext* with thee *Guinevere* 505
Vext me a bit, till he told me *First Quarrel* 36
to have *vext* myself And all in vain for her— *Sisters (E. and E.)* 200
Never since I was nurse, had I been so grieved and so *vext* ! *In the Child. Hosp.* 45
Vext, that you thought your Mother came to me ? *The Ring* 140
A demon *vext* me, The light retreated, *Merlin and the G.* 29
Vexillary In letters like to those the *v* *Gareth and L.* 1202
Vexing O Mary, Mary ! *V* you with words ! *Romney's R.* 29
Vext *See* **Vexed**
Vial A man with knobs and wires and *v's* *Princess, Pro.* 65
Viand Lay out the *v's*.' " *iii* 347
before us glow'd Fruit, blossom, *v*, amber wine, " *iv* 35
many a *v* left, And many a costly cate, *Gareth and L.* 848
Nor roll thy *v's* on a luscious tongue, *Ancient Sage* 267
Vibrate chord which Hampden smote Will *v* to the doom. *England and Amer.* 20
Star to star *v's* light : *Aylmer's Field* 578
In the Queen's shadow, *v* on the walls, *Lancelot and E.* 1175
Vicar Rome's *V* in our Indies ? *Columbus* 195
Vice Or crush her, like a *v* of blood, *In Mem. iii* 15
heart of the poet is whirl'd into folly and *v*. *Maud I iv* 39
And doubling all his master's *v* of pride, *Marr. of Geraint* 195
stirr'd this *v* in you which ruin'd man *Merlin and V.* 362
I call it,—well, I will not call it *v* : " 368
They fain would make you Master of all *v*.' " 469
bagpipes, revelling, devil's-dances, *v*. *Sir J. Oldcastle* 149
But pity—the Pagan held it a *v*— *Despair* 41
the tyrant vassal of a tyrant *v* ! *The Flight* 25
Rip your brothers' *v's* open, *Locksley H., Sixty* 141
Viceregal Your *v* days Have added fulness *To Marq. of Dufferin* 10
Vicious Who being *v*, old and irritable, *Marr. of Geraint* 194
His dwarf, a *v* under-shapen thing, " 412
Both grace and will to pick the *v* quitch *Geraint and E.* 903
a shatter'd wheel ? a *v* boy *Locksley H., Sixty* 215
Vicisti Galilæe often mutter low ' *V G* '; louder again,
Spurning a shatter'd fragment of the God, ' *V G* !' *St. Telemachus* 15
Victim (*See also* **Fellow-victim**) death quiver'd at the *v's* throat ; *D. of F. Women* 115
snake-like slimed his *v* ere he gorged ; *Sea Dreams* 193
And dress the *v* to the offering up. *Princess iv* 130
He seem'd a *v* due to the priest. *The Victim* 36
Priest was happy, His *v* won ; " 62
The rites prepared, the *v* bared, " 65
Till the *v* hear within and yearn *Boädicea* 58
One took him for a *v* of Earl Doorm, *Geraint and E.* 524
If not, the *v's* flowers before he fall.' *Lancelot and E.* 910
lurks, listens, fears his *v* may have fled— *The Flight* 71
A virgin *v* to his memory, *The Ring* 221
O you that can flatter your *v's*, *Charity* 29
Victor (adj.) Than that the *v* Hours should scorn *In Mem. i* 13

Victor (s) (*See also* **World-victor**) Whichever side be *V*, in the halloo *Princess ii* 231
The bearded *V* of ten-thousand hymns, " *iii* 352
We vanquish'd, you the *V* of your will. " *vi* 167
great World-victor's *v* will be seen no more. *Ode on Well.* 42
And *V* he must ever be. " 258
And fawn at a *v's* feet. *Maud I vi* 30
nor make myself in my own realm *V* and lord. *Com. of Arthur* 90
V his men Report him ! " 249
' Nay, not a point : nor art thou *v* here. *Gareth and L.* 1055
And *v* of the bridges and the ford, .. 1232
V from vanquish'd issues at the last, .. 1262
Who doubts thee *v* ? .. 1296
' Hark the *v* pealing there ! ' .. 1318
I watch'd thee *v* in the joust, .. 1356
On whom the *v*, to confound them more, *Geraint and E.* 169
And *v* at the tilt and tournament, .. 960
Arthur's host Proclaim'd him *V*, *Balin and Balan* 90
bore the prize and could not find The *v*, *Lancelot and E.* 630
and in the strength of this Come *v*. *Holy Grail* 481
Far less to bind, your *v*, and thrust him out, *Pelleas and E.* 293
for when our King Was *v* wellnigh day by day, *Last Tournament* 335
beheld That *v* of the Pagan throned in hall— .. 665
V in Drama, *V* in Romance, *To Victor Hugo* 1
iron-hearted *v's* they. *Locksley H., Sixty* 80
But they rode like *V's* and Lords *Heavy Brigade* 48
the Light is *V*, and the darkness Dawns *On Jub. Q. Victoria* 70
Victoria *V,—since your Royal grace* *To the Queen* 5
Victory Not Arac, satiate with his *v*. *Princess vii* 90
Bellowing *v*, bellowing doom : *Ode on Well.* 66
down their statue of *V* fell. *Boädicea* 30
and there cometh a *v* now. " 46
with pure Affection, and the light of *v*, *Gareth and L.* 331
Whether ye wish me *v* or defeat, *Geraint and E.* 80
in steepness overcome, And *victories* of ascent, *Lover's Tale i* 387
Swallowing its precedent in *v*. " 763
trumpets of *v*, groans of defeat ; *Vastness* 8
Victual in his hand Bare *v* for the mowers : *Geraint and E.* 202
Geraint Ate all the mowers' *v* unawares, " 215
fetch Fresh *v* for these mowers of our Earl ; " 225
and return With *v* for these men, " 240
Vied Sappho and others *v* with any man : *Princess ii* 164
Vienna That in *V's* fatal walls *In Mem. lxxxv* 19
I have not seen, I will not see *V* ; " *xcviii* 12
View (*See also* **Half-views**) full in *v*, Death, walking all alone *Love and Death* 4
whose brilliant hue Is so sparkling-fresh to *v*, *Rosalind* 40
When thus he met his mother's *v*, *L. C. V. de Vere* 34
Half-invisible to the *v*, *Vision of Sin* 36
here were telescopes For azure *v's* ; *Princess, Pro.* 68
Her early Heaven, her happy *v's* ; *In Mem. xxxiii* 6
But somewhere, out of human *v*, " *lxxv* 18
Yea, tho' it spake and buried *v* " *xcii* 9
to reprove her For stealing out of *v* *Maud I xx* 9
lands in your *v* From this bay window— *Sisters (E. and E.)* 51
loved the *v* Long-known and loved by me, *Pro. to Gen. Hamley* 5
She held them up to the *v* ; *Dead Prophet* 72
but the goodly *v* Was now one blank, *Death of Œnone* 3
View'd suffering *v* had been Extremest pain ; *Lover's Tale ii* 129
Viewless The *v* arrows of his thoughts were headed *The Poet* 11
Vignette In bright *v's*, and each complete, *The Daisy* 45
Vigorous with the growths Of *v* early days, *Lover's Tale i* 133
Vigorously So *v* yet mildly, that all hearts *Geraint and E.* 957
Vigour So that my *v*, wedded to thy blood, *Œnone* 161
The faith, the *v*, bold to dwell *In Mem. xcv* 29
Yourself shall see my *v* is not lost.' *Geraint and E.* 82
Vile And yonder a *v* physician, *Maud II v* 36
A little at the *v* occasion, rode, *Marr. of Geraint* 235
' This is more *v*,' he made reply, *Two Voices* 103
v it were For some three suns to store *Ulysses* 28
Hired animalisms, *v* as those that made *Lucretius* 53
A red-faced bride who knew herself so *v*, *Gareth and L.* 110
for men sought to prove me *v*, *Merlin and V.* 495
How justly, after that *v* term of yours, " 921
climb'd The moulder'd stairs (for everything was *v*) *Lover's Tale iv* 137

Vile (*continued*)   *V*, so near the ghost Himself,   *The Ring* 230
Vileness   mean *V*, we are grown so proud—   *Aylmer's Field* 756
   No inner *v* that we dread ?   *In Mem. li* 4
   Sinn'd thro' an animal *v*,   *The Wreck* 42
Viler   I am a sinner *v* than you all.   *St. S. Stylites* 135
   or the *v* devil who plays his part,   *Balin and Balan* 300
   of a kind The *v*, as underhand,   *Maud I i* 28
Vilest   The *v* herb that runs to seed   *Amphion* 95
Village (*adj.*)   Looks down upon the *v* spire :   *Miller's D.* 36
   I saw the *v* lights below ;   ” 108
   Why come you drest like a *v* maid,   *Lady Clare* 67
   ' If I come drest like a *v* maid,   ” 69
   At the head of the *v* street,   *Maud I vi* 10
   She came to the *v* church,   ” *viii* 1
   For only once, in the *v* street,   ” *xiii* 26
   maid That ever bided tryst at *v* stile,   *Merlin and V.* 378
   came the *v* girls And linger'd talking,   *Pelleas and E.* 508
   ' A hignorant *v* wife as 'ud hev to be larn'd   *Village Wife* 106
   and pigmy spites of the *v* spire;   *Vastness* 25
   And darkness in the *v* yew.   *Two Voices* 273
   And a *v* maiden she.   *L. of Burleigh* 8
   Leads her to the *v* altar,   ” 11
   as the *v* girl Who sets her pitcher underneath   *Enoch Arden* 206
   Born of a *v* girl, carpenter's son,   *Aylmer's Field* 668
   And on a simple *v* green ;   *In Mem. lxiv* 4
   Thou hear'st the *v* hammer clink,   ” *cxxi* 15
   By *v* eyes as yet unborn ;   ” *Con.* 59
   Seems to be pluck'd at by the *v* boys   *Geraint and E.* 560
   as the *v* wife who cries ' I shudder,   *Guinevere* 56
   having climb'd one step beyond Our *v* miseries,   *Ancient Sage* 207
Village (s)   (*See also* **Sea-village**)   Two children in two
   neighbour *v's*   *Circumstance* 1
   Where almost all the *v* had one name ;   *Aylmer's Field* 35
   The little *v* looks forlorn ;   *In Mem. lx* 9
   Maud the delight of the *v*,   *Maud I i* 70
   Below me, there, is the *v*,   ” *iv* 7
   For one from out his *v* lately climb'd   *Balin and Balan* 167
   tho' he tried the *v's* round,   *First Quarrel* 43
Village-churls   And there the surly *v-c*,   *L. of Shalott ii* 16
Villager   slavish hat from the *v's* head ?   *Maud I x* 4
Villain (*adj.*)   Low down thro' *v* kitchen-vassalage,   *Gareth and L.* 160
Villain (s)   One says, we are *v's* all.   *Maud I i* 17
   How the *v* lifted up his voice,   *Gareth and L.* 716
   a *v* fitter to stick swine Than ride abroad   ” 865
   ' There lurk three *v's* yonder in the wood,   *Geraint and E.* 142
Villainous   the *v* centre-bits Grind on the wakeful ear   *Maud I i* 41
Villainously   foully slain And *v* !   *Balin and Balan* 136
Villainy   *V* somewhere ! whose ?   One says,   *Maud I i* 17
   And I will tell him all their *v*.   *Geraint and E.* 132
   My violence, and my *v*, come to shame.'   *Balin and Balan* 492
   beneath the shadow of those towers A *v*, three
   to one :   *Pelleas and E.* 277
   So Gawain, looking at the *v* done, Forbore,   ” 282
   lust, *V*, violence, avarice, of your Spain   *Columbus* 172
Vine   (*See also* **Briony-vine**)   comest not with shows
   of flaunting *v's*   *Ode to Memory* 48
   And silent in its dusty *v's* :   *Mariana in the S.* 4
   leaning on a fragment twined with *v*,   *Œnone* 20
   And overhead the wandering ivy and *v*,   ” 99
   From cave to cave thro' the thick-twined *v*—   *Lotos-Eaters, C. S.* 95
   valleys of grape-loaded *v's* that glow   *D. of F. Women* 219
   And chimneys muffled in the leafy *v*.   *Audley Court* 19
   Old elms came breaking from the *v*,   *Amphion* 45
   The *v* stream'd out to follow,   ” 46
   from a bower of *v* and honeysuckle :   *Aylmer's Field* 156
   and so by tilth and grange, And *v's*,   *Princess i* 111
   The summer of the *v* in all his veins—   ” 183
   we two Were always friends, none closer, elm and *v* :   ” *ii* 337
   At last I hook'd my ankle in a *v*,   ” *iv* 268
   Or foxlike in the *v* ;   ” *vii* 203
   Beating from the wasted *v's*   *Ode on Well.* 109
   Of olive, aloe, and maize and *v*.   *The Daisy* 4
   Mixt with myrtle and clad with *v*,   *The Islet* 19
   V, *v*, and eglantine, (repeat)   *Window, At the Window* 1, 8
   and go By summer belts of wheat and *v*   *In Mem. xcviii* 4

Vine (*continued*)   Queen Brake from the vast oriel-
   embowering *v*   *Lancelot and E.* 1198
   berries that flamed upon bine and *v*,   *V. of Maeldune* 61
   v's with grapes Of Eshcol hugeness ;   *To E. Fitzgerald* 27
   they tell me, now in flowing *v's*—   *Tiresias* 144
   send my life thro' olive-yard and *v* And golden
   grain,   *Demeter and P.* 110
   spinning at your wheel beside the *v*—   *Romney's R.* 5
   serpent *v's* Which on the touch of heavenly feet   *Death of Œnone* 4
Vine-bunches   Between the shadows of the *v-b*   *Œnone* 181
Vine-clad   an oriel on the summer side, *V-c*,   *Lancelot and E.* 1178
Vineyard   Peace in her *v*—yes !—   *Maud I i* 36
   torrent *v* streaming fell To meet the sun   *The Daisy* 10
   tilth and *v*, hive and horse and herd ;   *To Virgil* 10
Vinous   And softly, thro' a *v* mist,   *Will Water.* 39
Vintage   Whether the *v*, yet unkept,   ” 97
   praised the waning red, and told The *v*—   *Aylmer's Field* 407
   Whom they with meats and *v* of their best   *Lancelot and E.* 266
   with her spice and her *v*, her silk and her corn ;   *Vastness* 13
Violate   behold our sanctuary Is *v*, our laws broken :   *Princess vi* 60
   And that she now perforce must *v* it,   *Geraint and E.* 367
   Which flesh and blood perforce would *v* :   *Last Tournament* 689
   v's virgin Truth for a coin or a cheque.   *The Dawn* 15
Violated   So was their sanctuary *v*,   *Princess vii* 16
Violating   Not *v* the bond of like to like.'   *Lancelot and E.* 241
Violator   mine of ruffian *v's* !   *Boädicea* 50
Violence   Moved with *v*, changed in hue,   *Vision of Sin* 34
   and shriek'd ' Thus, thus with *v*,   *Sea Dreams* 25
   ' Thus with *v* Shall Babylon be cast into the sea ;   ” 27
   Uther, reft From my dead lord a field with *v* :   *Gareth and L.* 335
   Was nigh to burst with *v* of the beat,   ” 763
   And snatch me from him as by *v* ;   *Geraint and E.* 357
   And bare her by main *v* to the board,   ” 654
   Edyrn wrought upon himself After a life of *v*,   ” 913
   For I that did that *v* to thy thrall,   *Balin and Balan* 61
   forget My heats and *v's* ?   ” 190
   So this will help him of his *v's* ! '   ” 205
   Moaning ' My *v's*, my *v's* ! '   ” 435
   My *v*, and my villainy, come to shame.'   ” 492
   power To lay the sudden heads of *v* flat,   *Holy Grail* 310
   with *v* The sword was dash'd from out my hand,   ” 825
   From flat confusion and brute *v's*,   *Last Tournament* 124
   small *v* done Rankled in him and ruffled   *Guinevere* 48
   Villainy, *v*, avarice, of your Spain   *Columbus* 172
   truthless *v* mourn'd by the Wise,   *Vastness* 5
Violent   I hear the *v* threats you do not hear,   *Geraint and E.* 420
   Rang by the white mouth of the *v* Glem ;   *Lancelot and E.* 288
Violet (*adj.*)   and sunn'd Her *v* eyes,   *Gardener's D.* 137
   For large her *v* eyes look'd,   *Pelleas and E.* 71
Violet (**Christian Name**)   *V*, she that sang the mournful
   song,   *Princess vi* 318
Violet (**flower, colour**)   With what voice the *v* woos   *Adeline* 31
   V, amaracus, and asphodel, Lotos and lilies :   *Œnone* 97
   from the *v's* her light foot Shone rosy-white,   ” 179
   To die before the snowdrop came, and now the *v's*
   here.   *May Queen, Con.* 4
   O sweet is the new *v*, that comes beneath the skies,   ” 5
   The smell of *v's*, hidden in the green,   *D. of F. Women* 77
   The *v* of a legend blow Among the chops   *Will Water.* 147
   In mosses mixt with *v* Her cream-white mule   *Sir L. and Q. G.* 30
   Pity, the *v* on the tyrant's grave.   *Aylmer's Field* 845
   The *v* varies from the lily as far As oak from elm :   *Princess v* 182
   Crocus, anemone, *v*,   *To F. D. Maurice* 44
   The *v* of his native land.   *In Mem. xviii* 4
   A wither'd *v* is her bliss :   ” *xcvii* 26
   The *v* comes, but we are gone.   ” *cv* 8
   By ashen roots the *v's* blow.   ” *cxv* 4
   and my regret Becomes an April *v*,   ” 19
   jewel-print of your feet In *v's* blue as your eyes,   *Maud I xxii* 42
   with earliest *v's* And lavish carol   *Lover's Tale i* 282
   And, tho' thy *v* sicken into sere,   *Prog. of Spring* 25
Violet-hooded   Epic lilted out By *v-h* Doctors,   *Princess ii* 376
Violin   twangling *v* Struck up with Soldier-laddie,   ” *Pro.* 85
   All night have the roses heard The flute, *v*, bassoon ;   *Maud I xxii* 14
Viper   fling it like a *v* off, and shriek   *Princess vii* 94

Voyage (*continued*)   this *v* by the grace of God Will bring
     fair weather   *Enoch Arden* 190
And dull the *v* was with long delays,   „ 655
Then he told her of his *v*, His wreck,   „ 861
And after my long *v* I shall rest ! ’   *Lancelot and E.* 1061
And let the story of her dolorous *v*   „ 1343
and tell them all The story of my *v*,   *Columbus* 12
I sail’d On my first *v*, harrass’d by the frights   „ 67
Who fain had pledged her jewels on my first *v*,   „ 229
yet Am ready to sail forth on one last *v*.   „ 237
Art passing on thine happier *v* now   *Sir J. Franklin* 3
Vulcan   mounted, Ganymedes, To tumble, *V*’s,   *Princess* iii 72
Vulgar   Nothing of the *v*, or vainglorious,   *On Jub. Q. Victoria* 13
Vulture (adj.)   Threat the Lady stretch’d a *v* throat,   *Princess* iv 363
Vulture (s)   For whom the carrion *v* waits   *You might have won* 35
     swoops The *v*, beak and talon, at the heart   *Princess* v 383
Vulturous   Then glided a *v* Beldam forth,   *Dead Prophet* 25

W

Waäist (**waist**)   wur a-creeäpin’ about my *w* ;   *Spinster’s S’s.* 26
Waäit (**wait**)   *W* till our Sally cooms in,   *North. Cobbler* 1
     You Tommies shall *w* to-night   *Spinster’s S’s.* 120
     but *w* till tha ’eärs it be strikin’ the hour.   *Owd Roä* 18
Waäked (**waked**)   An’ when I *w* i’ the murnin’   *North. Cobbler* 39
     To be horder’d about, an’ *w*,   *Spinster’s S’s.* 97
     Then I *w* an’ I fun it was Roäver   *Owd Roä* 60
Waäste (**waste**)   D’ya moind the *w*, my lass ?   *N. Farmer, O. S.* 29
     Dubbut looök at the *w* :   „ 37
     an’ I ’a stubb’d Thurnaby *w*.   „ 28
Waäy (**way**)   in anoother kind of a *w*,   *North. Cobbler* 96
     lasses ’ud talk o’ their Missis’s *w*’s,   *Village Wife* 57
     ’ud ’a let me ’a hed my oän *w*   *Spinster’s S’s.* 101
     An’ ’ed goän their *w*’s ;   *Owd Roä* 36
     I wur gawin’ that *w* to the bad,   „ 71
     wind blawin’ hard tother *w*,   „ 104
     rummle down when the roof gev *w*,   „ 109
     I fun that it warn’t not the gaäinist *w* to the
     narra Gaäte.   *Church-warden, etc.* 12
Wader   James Made toward us, like a *w* in the surf,   *The Brook* 117
Waft (s)   crosses With one *w* of the wing.   *The Captain* 72
     like the *w* of an Angel’s wing.   *In the Child. Hosp.* 38
Waft (verb)   Yet *w* me from the harbour-mouth,   *You ask me, why, etc.* 25
     Spread thy full wings, and *w* him o’er.   *In Mem.* ix 4
Wafted   the woodbine spices are *w* abroad,   *Maud* I xxii 7
Wag   kings Began to *w* their baldness up and down,   *Princess* v 19
     The palsy *w*’s his head ;   *Ancient Sage* 124
Wage   I *w* not any feud with Death   *In Mem.* lxxxii 1
     ‘ Behold, for these have sworn To *w* my wars,   *Com. of Arthur* 508
     To *w* grim war against Sir Lancelot there,   *Guinevere* 193
     I *w* His wars, and now I pass and die.   *Pass. of Arthur* 12
Waged   *W* such unwilling tho’ successful war   *Merlin and V.* 571
Wages   The *w* of sin is death : if the *w* of Virtue be dust,   *Wages* 6
     Give her the *w* of going on,   „ 10
     Will pay thee all thy *w*, and to boot.   *Gareth and L.* 1005
     ‘ The *w* of sin is death,’   *The Wreck* 93
     I need no *w* of shame.   *Charity* 40
Wage-work   comfort after their *w-w* is done,   *Com. of Arthur* 418
Wagg’d   Till his eye darken’d and his helmet *w* ;   *Geraint and E.* 505
     This tongue that *w* They said with such   *Sir J. Oldcastle* 14
Waggled   till ’e *w* ’is taäil fur a bit,   *Owd Roä* 105
Waging   and ever *w* war Each upon other,   *Com. of Arthur* 6
     while the King Was *w* war on Lancelot :   *Guinevere* 156
     From *w* bitter war with him :   „ 434
Waif   rolling in his mind Old *w*’s of rhyme,   *The Brook* 199
     thrones and peoples are as *w*’s that swing,   *W. to Marie Alex.* 26
     flung from the rushing tide of the world as a *w* of shame,   *The Wreck* 6
Wail (s)   gets for greeting but a *w* of pain ;   *Lucretius* 138
     Phantom *w* of women and children,   *Boädicea* 26
     whose dying eyes Were closed with *w*,   *In Mem.* xc 6
     then with a childlike *w*, And drawing down   *Balin and Balan* 596
     wife and child with *w* Pass to new lords ;   *Pass. of Arthur* 44
     as by some deathbed after *w* Of suffering,   „ 118

Wail (s) (*continued*)   a *w* That seeming something, yet
     was nothing,   *Lover’s Tale* iv 103
the sudden *w* his lady made Dwelt in his fancy :   „ 149
the mother’s garrulous *w* For ever woke   *Sisters (E. and E.)* 262
I read no more the prisoner’s mute *w*   *Sir J. Oldcastle* 4
I am roused by the *w* of a child,   *The Wreck* 7
w came borne in the shriek of a growing wind,   „ 87
and the *w* Of a beaten babe,   „ 122
Let be thy *w* and help thy fellow men,   *Ancient Sage* 258
Among the *w* of midnight winds,   *Demeter and P.* 59
As we forget our *w* at being born.   *The Ring* 465
nor *w* of baby-wife, Or Indian widow ;   *Akbar’s Dream* 196
I sent him a desolate *w* and a curse,   *Charity* 14
my *w* of reproach and scorn ;   „ 23
To the *w* of my winds,   *The Dreamer* 13
thought that he answer’d her *w* with a song—   „ 16
Wail (verb)   Here it is only the mew that *w*’s ;   *Sea-Fairies* 19
     Cease to *w* and brawl !   *Two Voices* 199
     the Dead March *w*’s in the people’s ears :   *Ode on Well.* 267
     if he be not dead, Why *w* ye for him thus ?   *Geraint and E.* 547
     wherefore *w* for one, Who put your beauty   „ 674
     burst away To weep and *w* in secret ;   *Lancelot and E.* 1245
     beneath a winding wall of rock Heard a child *w*.   *Last Tournament* 12
     and *w* their way From cloud to cloud,   *Pass. of Arthur* 39
     At once began to wander and to *w*,   *Lover’s Tale* iv 99
     Whereat the very babe began to *w* ? ’   „ 375
     The wind that ’ill *w* like a child   *Rizpah* 72
     And they *w* to thee :   *Tiresias* 107
     Wherefore do ye *w* ? ’   *Demeter and P.* 60
     ‘ We know not, and we know not why we *w*.’   „ 62
     WHY *w* you, pretty plover ?   *Happy* 1
Wail’d   *w* and woke The mother, and the father suddenly
     cried,   *Sea Dreams* 57
     fell on him, Clasp’d, kiss’d him, *w* :   *Lucretius* 280
     and *w* about with mews.   *Princess* iv 282
     They wept and *w*, but led the way   *In Mem.* ciii 18
     the wind like a broken worldling *w*,   *Maud* I i 11
     Cast herself down, knelt to the Queen, and *w*.   *Merlin and V.* 66
     Queen, Who rode by Lancelot, *w* and shriek’d   *Holy Grail* 356
     But *w* and wept, and hated mine own self,   „ 609
     and he shrank and *w*, ‘ Is the Queen false ? ’   *Pelleas and E.* 531
     Queens in yon black boat, Who shriek’d and *w*,   *Pass. of Arthur* 453
     finds the fountain where they *w* ‘ Mirage ’ !   *Ancient Sage* 77
     So the Shadow *w*. Then I, Earth-Goddess,   *Demeter and P.* 101
     and the dream *W* in her, when she woke   *Death of Œnone* 82
Wailest   who *w* being born And banish’d   *De Prof., Two G.* 41
Wailing   (*See also* **Keenin’**)   And on the mere the *w*
     died away.   *M. d’Arthur* 272
     To ailing wife or *w* infancy Or old bedridden palsy,—   *Aylmer’s Field* 177
     After much *w*, hush’d itself at last   „ 542
     Their wildest *w*’s never out of tune   *Sea Dreams* 231
     they hate to hear me like a wind *W* for ever,   *Princess* v 99
     Moaning and *w* for an heir (repeat)   *Com. of Arthur* 207, 368
     Your *w* will not quicken him :   *Geraint and E.* 549
     clapt her hands Together with a *w* shriek,   *Merlin and V.* 867
     the owls *W* had power upon her,   *Lancelot and E.* 1001
     And on the mere the *w* died away.   *Pass. of Arthur* 440
     W, *w*, *w*, the wind over land and sea—   *Rizpah* 1
     before their Gods, And *w* ‘ Save us.’   *Tiresias* 106
     hear in one dark room a *w*,   *Locksley H., Sixty* 262
     She used to shun the *w* babe,   *The Ring* 358
     O the night, When the owls are *w* !   *Forlorn* 30
     She heard a *w* cry, that seem’d at first   *Death of Œnone* 20
Wailingly   Voice of the Earth went *w* past him   *The Dreamer* 3
Wain   or when the lesser *w* Is twisting   *In Mem.* ci 11
     The team is loosen’d from the *w*,   „ cxxi 5
Wainscot (adj.)   And the shrieking rush of the *w* mouse,   *Maud* I vi 71
Wainscot (s)   Behind the mouldering *w* shriek’d,   *Mariana* 64
Waist (*See also* **Waäist**)   the girdle About her dainty
     dainty *w*,   *Miller’s D.* 176
     You should have clung to Fulvia’s *w*,   *D. of F. Women* 259
     Lovingly lower, trembled on her *w*—   *Gardener’s D.* 131
     She strove to span my *w* :   *Talking Oak* 138
     And round her *w* she felt it fold,   *Day-Dm., Depart.* 2
     And held her round the knees against his **w,**   *Princess* ii 363

Wake (verb) (*continued*) But *w*'s a dotard smile.' — *Ancient Sage* 132
to rest and *w* no more were better rest for me, — *The Flight* 7
how early would I *w* ! — " 63
Before a kiss should *w* her. — *The Ring* 67
I rais'd her, call'd her ' Muriel, Muriel *w* ! ' — " 449
his young music *w*'s A wish in you — *To Mary Boyle* 63
an answer ' *W* Thou deedless dreamer, — *St. Telemachus* 20
great shock may *w* a palsied limb, — " 57
Waked (*See also* **Waäked**) to sleep with sound, And *w*
  with silence, — *M. d'Arthur, Ep.* 4
w at dead of night, I heard a sound — *Holy Grail* 108
He *w* for both : he pray'd for both : — *Lover's Tale i* 227
I remember once that being *w* By noises in the house— — *The Ring* 416
She *w* a bird of prey that scream'd and past ; — *Death of Œnone* 87
Wakeful Beginning, and the *w* bird ; — *In Mem. cxxi* 11
Grind on the *w* ear in the hush of the moonless nights, — *Maud I i* 42
Before he *w* mother heard him, went. — *Gareth and L.* 180
A *w* portress, and didst parle with Death,— — *Lover's Tale i* 113
Wakefulness After a night of feverous *w*, — *Enoch Arden* 231
Waken (*See also* **Wakken**) The fire-fly *w*'s : *w* thou
  with me. — *Princess vii* 179
That *w*'s at this hour of rest — *In Mem. civ* 6
and in my breast Spring *w*'s too ; — " *cxv* 18
Than to *w* every morning to that face I loathe — *The Flight* 8
Waken'd the first matin-song hath *w* loud — *Ode to Memory* 68
What eyes, like thine, have *w* hopes, — *Day-Dm., L'Envoi* 45
For thrice I *w* after dreams. — *Lucretius* 34
Till at the last he *w* from his swoon, — *Geraint and E.* 583
A way by love that *w* love within, — *Holy Grail* 11
Suddenly *w* with a sound of talk — *Pelleas and E.* 48
Wakenest Who *w* with thy balmy breath — *In Mem. xcix* 13
Sun, that *w* all to bliss or pain, — *Gareth and L.* 1060
Wakening Gareth, *w*, fiercely clutch'd the shield ; — " 1304
Rode till the star above the *w* sun, — *Pelleas and E.* 500
Waking *W* she heard the night-fowl crow : — *Mariana* 26
If you're *w* call me early, — *May Queen, N. Y's. E.* 1
if you're *w*, call me, call me early, — " 52
the dreams that come Just ere the *w* : — *Lucretius* 36
And, truly, *w* dreams were, more or less, — *Princess i* 12
W laughter in indolent reviewers. — *Hendecasyllabics* 8
Till a silence fell with the *w* bird, — *Maud I xxii* 17
But come to her *w*, find her asleep, — " *II ii* 81
And Enid started *w*, with her heart — *Marr. of Geraint* 674
Tristram *w*, the red dream Fled with a shout, — *Last Tournament* 487
set the mother *w* in amaze To find her sick — *Demeter and P.* 57
From off the rosy cheek of *w* Day. — *Akbar's Dream* 202
Wakken (waken) I couldn't *w* 'im oop, — *Owd Roä* 104
Wales It was last summer on a tour in *W* : — *Golden Year* 2
Urien, Cradlemont of *W*, Claudias, — *Com. of Arthur* 112
ears for Christ in this wild field of *W*— — *Sir J. Oldcastle* 13
Walk (s) (*See also* **Garden-walks, Wood-walk**) A *w* with
  vary-colour'd shells — *Arabian Nights* 57
you may hear him sob and sigh In the *w*'s ; — *A spirit haunts* 6
with echoing feet he threaded The secretest *w*'s of fame : — *The Poet* 10
said Death, ' these *w*'s are mine.' — *Love and Death* 7
yielding, gave into a grassy *w* — *Gardener's D.* 111
last night's gale had caught, And blown across the *w*. — " 125
With words of promise in his *w*, — *Day-Dm., Arrival* 23
and all round it ran a *w* Of shingle, and a *w* divided it : — *Enoch Arden* 736
Enoch shunn'd the middle *w* and stole — " 738
Katie somewhere in the *w*'s below, — *The Brook* 86
Would often, in his *w*'s with Edith, claim — *Aylmer's Field* 61
our long *w*'s were stript as bare as brooms, — *Princess, Pro.* 184
the chapel bells Call'd us : we left the *w*'s ; — " *ii* 471
Dropt on the sward, and up the linden *w*'s, — " *iv* 209
Nor waves the cypress in the palace *w* ; — " *vii* 177
Or *w*'s in Boboli's ducal bowers. — *The Daisy* 44
Shadows of three dead men Walk'd in the *w*'s with me, — *G. of Swainston* 4
In those deserted *w*'s, may find — *In Mem. viii* 14
partner in the flowery *w* Of letters, — " *lxxxiv* 22
Up that long *w* of limes I past — " *lxxxvii* 15
That saw thro' all the Muses' *w*, — " *cix* 4
her light foot along the garden *w*, — *Maud I xviii* 9
I did not talk To gentle Maud in our *w* — " *xix* 13
From the meadow your *w*'s have left so sweet — " *xxii* 39

Walk (s) (*continued*) Glanced at the doors or gambol'd
  down the *w*'s ; — *Marr. of Geraint* 665
A *w* of roses ran from door to door ; A *w* of lilies
  crost it to the bower : — *Balin and Balan* 242
paced The long white *w* of lilies toward the bower. — " 249
she stole upon my *w*, And calling me the greatest — *Holy Grail* 594
How oft with him we paced that *w* of limes, — *To W. H. Brookfield* 6
an' they goäs fur a *w*, — *Spinster's S's.* 85
He dreams of that long *w* thro' desert life — *To Mary Boyle* 55
Walk (verb) In sleep she seem'd to *w* forlorn, — *Mariana* 30
I *w*, I dare not think of thee, — *Oriana* 93
W's forgotten, and is forlorn.' — *Mariana in the S.* 48
So sweet it seems with thee to *w*, — *Miller's D.* 29
made it sweet To *w*, to sit, to sleep, to wake, — *Edwin Morris* 40
Could slip its bark and *w*. — *Talking Oak* 188
But any man that *w*'s the mead, — *Day-Dm., Moral* 9
Katie *w*'s By the long wash of Australasian seas — *The Brook* 193
Averill *w* So freely with his daughter ? — *Aylmer's Field* 269
nor cares to *w* With Death and Morning — *Princess vii* 203
O we will *w* this world, Yoked in all exercise — " 360
He that *w*'s it, only thirsting For the right, — *Ode on Well.* 203
Nor follow, tho' I *w* in haste, — *In Mem. xxii* 18
That nothing *w*'s with aimless feet ; — " *liv* 5
I *w* as ere I walk'd forlorn, — " *lxviii* 5
From state to state the spirit *w*'s ; — " *lxxxii* 6
to *w* all day like the sultan of old — *Maud I iv* 42
each man *w*'s with his head in a cloud of poisonous flies — " 54
There she *w*'s in her state — " *xiv* 3
the Powers who *w* the world Made lightnings — *Com. of Arthur* 107
Hath power to *w* the waters like our Lord. — " 294
Merlin, who, they say, can *w* Unseen at pleasure— — " 347
I will *w* thro' fire, Mother, to gain it— — *Gareth and L.* 133
' Will ye *w* thro' fire ? Who *w*'s thro' fire will
  hardly heed the smoke. — " 142
w with me, and move To music with thine Order — *Balin and Balan* 76
Until this earth he *w*'s on seems not earth, — *Holy Grail* 912
W your dim cloister, and distribute dole — *Guinevere* 683
Who *w* before thee, ever turning round — *Lover's Tale i* 490
his wont to *w* Between the going light — " 663
Where Love could *w* with banish'd Hope — " 813
w's down fro' the' All to see, — *North. Cobbler* 91
To *w* within the glory of the Lord — *Columbus* 89
lies all in the way that you *w*. — *Despair* 112
An' maäybe they'll *w* upo' two — *Owd Roä* 17
Thraldom who *w*'s with the banner of Freedom, — *Vastness* 10
I used to *w* This Terrace— — *The Ring* 167
We often *w* In open sun, and see beneath our feet — " 327
Walk'd–Walkt One *walk'd* between his wife and child, — *Two Voices* 412
The little maiden *walk'd* demure, — " 419
But, as he *walk'd*, King Arthur panted hard, — *M. d'Arthur* 176
and looking, as he *walk'd*, Larger than human — " 182
I'M glad I *walk'd*. How fresh the meadows look — *Walk. to the Mail* 1
what home ? had he a home ? His home, he *walk'd*. — *Enoch Arden* 669
for she *walk'd* Wearing the light yoke — *Aylmer's Field* 707
So now on sand they *walk'd*, and now on cliff, — *Sea Dreams* 37
And that the woman *walk'd* upon the brink : — " 112
And while I *walk'd* and talk'd as heretofore, — *Princess i* 16
there One *walk'd* reciting by herself, — " *ii* 454
she you *walk'd* with, she You talk'd with, — " *vi* 254
Walk'd at their will, and everything was changed. — " 384
I *walk'd* with one I loved Two and thirty years ago. — *V. of Cauteretz* 4
while I *walk'd* to-day, The two and thirty years — " 5
Shadows of three dead men *Walk'd* in the walks — *G. of Swainston* 4
where the path we *walk'd* began To slant — *In Mem. xxii* 9
I walk as ere I *walk'd* forlorn, — " *lxviii* 5
In walking as of old we *walk'd* — " *lxxi* 12
Where first he *walk'd* when claspt in clay ? — " *xciii* 4
out he *walk'd* when the wind like a broken — *Maud I i* 11
Walk'd in a wintry wind by a ghastly glimmer, — " *iii* 13
I have *walk'd* awake with Truth. — " *xix* 4
He *walk'd* with dreams and darkness, — *Merlin and V.* 190
For all that *walk'd*, or crept, or perch'd, or flew. — *Last Tournament* 367
But, as he *walk'd*, King Arthur panted hard, — *Pass. of Arthur* 344
and looking, as he *walk'd*, Larger than human — " 350
same old paths where Love had *walk'd* with Hope, — *Lover's Tale i* 821

Walk'd-Walkt (*continued*) One *walk'd* abreast with me, and veil'd his brow, *Lover's Tale ii* 86

I *walk'd* behind with one who veil'd his brow. „ *iii* 12

and while I *walk'd* with these In marvel „ 18

I *walked* with him down to the quay, *First Quarrel* 20

Fur Molly the long un she *walkt* awaäy *Village Wife* 97

I *walk'd* with our kindly old doctor *In the Child. Hosp.* 43

men *Walk'd* like the fly on ceilings? *Columbus* 51

whiniver ye *walkt* in the shtreet, *Tomorrow* 37

Fur I *walk'd* wi' tha all the way hoam *Spinster's S's.* 32

Till I dreäm'd 'at Squire *walkt* in, *Owd Roä* 55

Walking (*See also* **A-walkin'**) Death, *w* all alone beneath a yew, *Love and Death* 5

W the cold and starless road of Death *Œnone* 259

As in strange lands a traveller *w* slow, *Palace of Art* 277

Beauty and anguish *w* hand in hand *D. of F. Women* 15

W about the gardens and the halls Of Camelot, *M. d'Arthur* 20

Met me *w* on yonder way, *Edward Gray* 2

W up and pacing down, *L. of Burleigh* 90

Would care no more for Leolin's *w* with her *Aylmer's Field* 124

In *w* as of old we walk'd *In Mem. lxxi* 12

I was *w* a mile, More than a mile *Maud I ix* 1

She is *w* in the meadow, „ *II iv* 37

For once, when Arthur *w* all alone, *Merlin and V.* 152

one fair morn, I *w* to and fro beside a stream *Holy Grail* 592

once, A week beyond, while *w* on the walls *Pelleas and E.* 225

W about the gardens and the halls Of Camelot, *Pass. of Arthur* 188

Brute that is *w* and haunting us yet, *The Dawn* 23

Walkt *See* **Walk'd-Walkt**

Wall (s) (*See also* **Abbey-wall, Castle-wall, Cottage-walls, Gable-wall, Garden-wall, Mountain-wall, Nunnery-walls, Palace-walls, Shield-wall**) About a stone-cast from the *w* *Mariana* 37

A pillar of white light upon the *w* *Ode to Memory* 53

sunlight falls Upon the storied *w's* ; „ 86

She stood upon the castle *w*, *Oriana* 28

Atween me and the castle *w*, „ 35

Two lovers whispering by an orchard *w* ; *Circumstance* 4

When from her wooden *w's*,— *Buonaparte* 5

Four gray *w's*, and four gray towers, *L. of Shalott i* 15

Struck up against the blinding *w*. *Mariana in the S.* 56

The one black shadow from the *w*. „ 80

as yonder *w's* Rose slowly to a music *Œnone* 40

bellowing caves, Beneath the windy *w*. *Palace of Art* 72

That stood against the *w*. „ 244

girt round With blackness as a solid *w*, „ 274

between *w's* Of shadowy granite, *Lotos-Eaters, C. S.* 3

Upon the tortoise creeping to the *w* ; *D. of F. Women* 27

All thine, against the garden *w*. *The Blackbird* 8

its *w's* And chimneys muffled in the leafy vine. *Audley Court* 18

and thou art staring at the *w*, *Locksley Hall* 79

the blind *w's* Were full of chinks and holes ; *Godiva* 59

Gleam thro' the Gothic archway in the *w*. „ 64

That watch the sleepers from the *w*. *Day-Dm., Sleep. P.* 24

All creeping plants, a *w* of green Close-matted, „ 45

He watches from his mountain *w*, *The Eagle* 5

The vast Akrokeraunian *w's*, *To E. L.* 4

But turn'd her own toward the *w* and wept. *Enoch Arden* 283

Then Annie with her brows against the *w* „ 314

The late and early roses from his *w*, „ 339

compass'd round by the blind *w* of night „ 492

blown across her ghostly *w* : „ 661

and stole Up by the *w*, behind the yew ; „ 739

Stood from his *w's* and wing'd his entry-gates *Aylmer's Field* 18

I cry to vacant chairs and widow'd *w's*, „ 720

Staring for ever from their gilded *w's* „ 833

A mountain, like a *w* of burs and thorns ; *Sea Dreams* 119

higher on the *w's*, Betwixt the monstrous horns *Princess, Pro.* 22

Had beat her foes with slaughter from her *w's*. „ 34

some were whelm'd with missiles of the *w*, „ 45

A broken statue propt against the *w*, „ 99

That drove her foes with slaughter from her *w's*, „ 123

from the bastion *w's* Like threaded spiders, „ *i* 107

The foundress of the Babylonian *w*, „ *ii* 80

Before two streams of light from *w* to *w*, „ 473

The splendour falls on castle *w's* „ *iv* 1

Wall (s) (*continued*) And some that men were in the very *w's*, *Princess iv* 485

By glimmering lanes and *w's* of canvas „ *v* 6

From those two hosts that lay beside the *w's*, „ *vi* 383

cloud Drag inward from the deeps, a *w* of night, „ *vii* 37

silent light Slept on the painted *w's*, „ 121

the *w's* Blacken'd about us, bats wheel'd, „ *Con.* 109

Your cannons moulder on the seaward *w* ; *Ode on Well.* 173

But thieves from o'er the *w* Stole the seed by night. *The Flower* 11

FLOWER in the crannied *w*, *Flow. in cran. wall* 1

Is vocal in its wooded *w's* : *In Mem. xix* 14

There comes a glory on the *w's* : „ *lxvii* 4

That in Vienna's fatal *w's* „ *lxxxv* 19

I past beside the reverend *w's* „ *lxxxvii* 1

A river sliding by the *w*. „ *ciii* 8

The blind *w* rocks, and on the trees „ *Con.* 63

With tender gloom the roof, the *w* ; „ 118

little flower that clings To the turrets and the *w's* ; *Maud II iv* 34

and Guinevere Stood by the castle *w's* *Com. of Arthur* 48

Seeing the mighty swarm about their *w's*, „ 200

To drive the heathen from your Roman *w*, „ 512

fools have suck'd their allegory From these damp *w's*, *Gareth and L.* 1200

Echo'd the *w's* ; a light twinkled ; „ 1370

And enter'd, and were lost behind the *w's*. *Marr. of Geraint* 252

ivy-stems Claspt the gray *w's* with hairy-fibred arms, „ 323

now and then from distant *w's* There came a clapping „ 565

slide From the long shore-cliff's windy *w's* *Geraint and E.* 164

Push'd from without, drave backward to the *w*, „ 273

No stronger than a *w* : there is the keep ; „ 341

like a household Spirit at the *w's* Beat, „ 403

Along the *w's* and down the board ; *Balin and Balan* 84

the *w's* Of that low church he built at Glastonbury. „ 366

portal of King Pellam's chapel wide And inward to the *w* ; „ 406

rummage buried in the *w's* Might echo, „ 416

Woods have tongues, As *w's* have ears : „ 531

Closed in the four *w's* of a hollow tower, (repeat) *Merlin and V.* 209, 543

And many a wizard brow bleach'd on the *w's* : „ 597

to him the *w* That sunders ghosts and shadow-casting men „ 628

And heard their voices talk behind the *w*, „ 631

and she watch'd him from her *w's*. „ 775

' Traitor ' to the unhearing *w*, *Lancelot and E.* 612

first she saw the casque Of Lancelot on the *w* : „ 806

to whom thro' those black *w's* of yew „ 969

And grew between her and the pictured *w*. „ 993

In the Queen's shadow, vibrate on the *w's*, „ 1175

Till all the white *w's* of my cell were dyed With rosy colours leaping on the *w* ; *Holy Grail* 119

from the *w's* The rosy quiverings died into the night. „ 122

necks Of dragons clinging to the crazy *w's*, „ 347

plaster'd like a martin's nest To these old *w's*— „ 549

painting on the *w* Or shield of knight ; „ 829

upon his charger all day long Sat by the *w's*, *Pelleas and E.* 217

' Out ! And drive him from the *w's*.' „ 220

still he kept his watch beneath the *w*. „ 223

while walking on the *w's* With her three knights, „ 225

And drive him from my *w's*.' „ 229

loosed him from his bonds, And flung them o'er the *w's* ; „ 316

Then bounded forward to the castle *w's*, „ 363

That all the echoes hidden in the *w* Rang out „ 366

there he waits below the *w*, Blowing his bugle „ 380

but rode Ere midnight to her *w's*, „ 413

Far down beneath a winding *w* of rock *Last Tournament* 11

So from the high *w* and the flowering grove *Guinevere* 33

That keeps the rust of murder on the *w's*— „ 74

Or thrust the heathen from the Roman *w*, *Pass. of Arthur* 69

Or build a *w* betwixt my life and love, *Lover's Tale i* 176

And steep-down *w's* of battlemented rock „ 399

thro' the ragged *w's*, All unawares „ *ii* 152

from an open grating overhead High in the *w*, „ *iv* 61

—in the night by the churchyard *w*. *Rizpah* 56

it is coming—shaking the *w's*— „ 85

fell, Striking the hospital *w*, crashing *Def. of Lucknow* 18

into perilous chasms our *w's* and our poor palisades. „ 55

War (s) (*continued*) As one would sing the death of *w*,   *In Mem. ciii* 33
Ring out the thousand *w's* of old,   „ *cvi* 27
heart of the citizen hissing in *w*   *Maud I i* 24
Is it peace or *w*? Civil *w*, as I think,   „ 27
Is it peace or *w*? better *w*! loud *w* by land and by sea,
    W with a thousand battles,   „ 47
At *w* with myself and a wretched race,   „ *x* 35
This huckster put down *w*! can he tell Whether *w* be
    a cause or a consequence?   „ 44
For each is at *w* with mankind.   „ 52
I swear to you, lawful and lawless *w*   *II v* 94
spoke of a hope for the world in the coming *w's*—   „ *III vi* 11
I thought that a *w* would arise in defence of the right,   „ 19
flames The blood-red blossom of *w*   „ 53
and the *w* roll down like a wind,   „ 54
Commingled with the gloom of imminent *w*,   *Ded. of Idylls* 13
Far-sighted summoner of *W* and Waste   „ 37
and ever waging *w* Each upon other,   *Com. of Arthur* 6
Lords and Barons of his realm Flash'd forth and
    into *w*:   „ 66
as here and there that *w* Went swaying;   „ 106
So like a painted battle the *w* stood Silenced,   „ 122
Do these your lords stir up the heat of *w*,   „ 169
That Gorloïs and King Uther went to *w*:   „ 196
lords Banded, and so brake out in open *w*.'   „ 237
for these have sworn To wage my *w's*,   „ 508
mine innocent, the jousts, the *w's*,   *Gareth and L.* 86
Were Arthur's *w's* in weird devices done,   „ 225
A knight of Uther in the Barons' *w*,   „ 353
ye know we stay'd their hands From *w*   „ 422
w of Time against the soul of man.   „ 1198
who held and lost with Lot In that first *w*,   *Balin and Balan* 2
But rather proven in his Paynim *w's*   „ 38
In those fierce *w's*, struck hard—   „ 177
Waged such unwilling tho' successful *w*   *Merlin and V.* 571
The lady never made *unwilling w*   „ 603
you know Of Arthur's glorious *w's*.'   *Lancelot and E.* 285
then the *w* That thunder'd in and out   „ 290
nor cares For triumph in our mimic *w's*,   „ 312
Yet in this heathen *w* the fire of God Fills him: „ 315
From talk of *w* to traits of pleasantry—   „ 321
Where Arthur's *w's* were render'd mystically,   „ 801
Where twelve great windows blazon Arthur's *w's*,   *Holy Grail* 248
perchance, when all our *w's* are done,   „ 256
Where Arthur's *w's* are rendered mystically,   „ 359
To whence I came, the gate of Arthur's *w's*.'   „ 539
I came late, the heathen *w's* were o'er,   *Last Tournament* 269
while the King Was waging *w* on Lancelot: *Guinevere* 156
To wage grim *w* against Sir Lancelot there,   „ 193
that night the bard Sang Arthur's glorious *w's*,   „ 286
From waging bitter *w* with him: „ 434
I waged His *w's*, and now I pass and die.   *Pass. of Arthur* 12
Gawain kill'd In Lancelot's *w*,   „ 31
Around a king returning from his *w's*.   „ 461
and shadowing Sense at *w* with Soul,   *To the Queen ii* 37
That hover'd between *w* and wantonness,   „ 44
' Spanish ships of *w* at sea!   *The Revenge* 3
past away with five ships of *w* that day,   „ 13
Then told them of his *w's*, and of his wound.   *Sisters (E. and E.)* 60
mine that stirr'd Among our civil *w's*   „ 75
Red in thy birth, redder with household *w*,   *Sir J. Oldcastle* 53
Urge him to foreign *w*.   „ 68
Spain was waging *w* against the Moor—   *Columbus* 93
slain thy fathers in *w* or in single strife,   *V. of Maeldune* 121
There was the Scotsman Weary of *w*,   *Batt. of Brunanburh* 36
Mangled to morsels, A youngster in *w*!   „ 74
own in his own West-Saxon-land, Glad of the *w*.   „ 104
men contend in grievous *w* From their own city,   *Achilles over the T.* 9
and sail to help them in the *w*;   „ 13
the crowd would roar For blood, for *w*,   *Tiresias* 65
these blind hands were useless in their *w's*.   „ 78
a weight of *w* Rides on those ringing axles!   „ 92
whose one bliss Is *w*, and human sacrifice—   „ 112
holding, each its own By endless *w*:   *Ancient Sage* 252
w will die out late then.   *Locksley H., Sixty* 173

War (s) (*continued*) Could we dream of *w's* and
    carnage,   *Locksley H., Sixty* 189
Most marvellous in the *w's* your own   *Pro. to Gen. Hamley* 11
You praise when you should blame The barbarian of *w's*.   *Epilogue* 5
I would that *w's* would cease,   „ 11
Or Trade re-frain the Powers From *w*   „ 16
who loves *W* for *W's* own sake Is fool,   „ 30
w's, and filial faith, and Dido's pyre;   *To Virgil* 4
An' the munney they maäde by the *w*,   *Owd Roä* 44
' A warrior's crest above the cloud of *w* '—   *The Ring* 338
You were parting for the *w*,   *Happy* 74
You parted for the Holy *W* without a word to me,   „ 77
The smoke of *w's* volcano burst again   *Prog. of Spring* 97
bolt of *w* dashing down upon cities   *The Dawn* 8
Storm of battle and thunder of *w*!   *Riflemen form!* 3
War (verb) To *w* with falsehood to the knife,   *Two Voices* 131
What pleasure can we have To *w* with evil?   *Lotos-Eaters, C. S.* 49
To *w* against ill uses of a life,   *Gareth and L.* 1130
To *w* against my people and my knights.   *Pass. of Arthur* 71
War (was) An' I went wheer munny *w*—   *N. Farmer, N. S.* 21
Warble (s) at first to the ear The *w* was low,   *Dying Swan* 24
Wild bird, whose *w*, liquid sweet,   *In Mem. lxxxviii* 1
a bird with a *w* plaintively sweet Perch'd   *The Wreck* 81
And rolling of dragons By *w* of water,   *Merlin and the G.* 45
Warble (verb) thou may'st *w*, eat and dwell.   *The Blackbird* 4
Than he that *w's* long and loud   *You might have won* 33
W, O bugle, and trumpet, blare!   *W. to Alexandra* 14
' O birds, that *w* to the morning sky, O birds that
    w as the day goes by,   *Gareth and L.* 1075
birds Begin to *w* yonder in the budding   *The Flight* 61
The blackcap *w's*, and the turtle purrs,   *Prog. of Spring* 55
O *w* unchidden, unbidden!   *The Throstle* 14
Warbled NIGHTINGALES *w* without,   *G. of Swainston* 1
Nightingales *w* and sang Of a passion   „ 8
That she *w* alone in her joy!   *Maud I x* 55
Warbler Dan Chaucer, the first *w*,   *D. of F. Women* 5
in their time thy *w's* rise on wing.   *Prog. of Spring* 108
Warbling springs By night to eery *w's*,   *Sir L. and Q. G.* 34
She struck such *w* fury thro' the words;   *Princess iv* 586
Her *w* voice, a lyre of widest range   *D. of F. Women* 165
damsel-errant, *w*, as she rode The woodland
    alleys,   *Balin and Balan* 438
War-cry Spurr'd with his terrible *w-c*;   *Geraint and E.* 170
Ward (surname) generous of all Untramontanes, *W*,   *In Mem., W. G. Ward* 4
Ward (minor) and a selfish uncle's *w*.   *Locksley Hall* 156
Ward (of a hospital) Here was a boy in the *w*,   *In the Child. Hosp.* 13
O how could I serve in the *w*   „ 24
past to this *w* where the younger children are laid: „ 27
They freshen and sweeten the *w's*   „ 38
Then I return'd to the *w*;   „ 44
such a lot of beds in the *w*!'   „ 54
caught when a nurse in a hospital *w*.   *Charity* 41
Ward (guard) Keep watch and *w*, (repeat)   *Maud I vi* 58
why shine ye here so low? Thy *w* is higher up: *Gareth and L.* 1098
Warded For each had *w* either in the fight,   *Com. of Arthur* 131
Warder The *w's* of the growing hour,   *Love thou thy land* 61
Old *w* of these buried bones,   *In Mem. xxxix* 1
War-drum Till the *w-d* throbb'd no longer,   *Locksley Hall* 127
Ware (adj.) they were *w* That all the decks were dense   *M. d'Arthur* 195
Then was I *w* of one that on me moved   *Holy Grail* 409
He woke, and being *w* of some one nigh,   *Pelleas and E.* 520
they were *w* That all the decks were dense   *Pass. of Arthur* 363
Ware (s) As when a hawker hawks his *w's*.   *The Blackbird* 20
sold her *w's* for less Than what she gave   *Enoch Arden* 255
faith in a tradesman's *w* or his word?   *Maud I i* 26
Ware (verb) *w* their ladies' colours on the casque,   *Last Tournament* 184
War-field Earls of the army of Anlaf Fell on
    the *w-f*,   *Batt. of Brunanburh* 54
    „ 78
War-glaive The clash of the *w-g*—   „
War-harden'd Kissing the *w-h* hand of the Highlander   *Def. of Lucknow* 102
War-hawk Gave to the garbaging *w-h* to gorge it,   *Batt. of Brunanburh* 109
War-horse On burnish'd hooves his *w-h* trode;   *L. of Shalott iii* 29
A *w* of the best, and near it stood   *Gareth and L.* 1401
Death's dark *w-h* bounded forward with him.   „ 1401
and thence Taking my *w-h* from the holy man,   *Holy Grail* 537

War-horse (*continued*) Lancelot slowly rode his *w* back
To Camelot, *Pelleas and E.* 583
He whistled his good *w* left to graze *Last Tournament* 490
waiting by the doors the *w* neigh'd *Guinevere* 530
War-knife—The welcome of *war-knives*— *Batt. of Brunanburh* 68
Warless Earth at last a *w* world, a single race, *Locksley H., Sixty* 165
W ? when her tens are thousands, „ 171
—who can fancy *w* men ? „ 172
W ? war will die out late then. „ 173
Warm (adj.) Ice with the *w* blood mixing ; *All Things will Die* 33
So let the *w* winds range, „ 42
Her subtil, *w*, and golden breath, *Supp. Confessions* 60
run short pains Thro' his *w* heart ; „ 162
Ev'n as the *w* gulf-stream of Florida *Mine be the strength* 12
As when a sunbeam wavers *w* Within the dark *Miller's D.* 79
I'd touch her neck so *w* and white. „ 174
From her *w* brows and bosom her deep hair *Œnone* 177
dear the last embraces of our wives And
their *w* tears : *Lotos-Eaters, C. S.* 71
(while *w* airs lull us, blowing lowly) „ 89
For Nature also, cold and *w*, *Love thou thy land* 37
' Here, take the goose, and keep you *w*, *The Goose* 7
' So keep you cold, or keep you *w*, „ 43
And one *w* gust, full-fed with perfume, *Gardener's D.* 113
we dragg'd her to the college tower From
her *w* bed, *Walk. to the Mail* 90
eat wholesome food, And wear *w* clothes, *St. S. Stylites* 109
'Tis little more : the day was *w* ; *Talking Oak* 205
world-wide whisper of the south-wind rushing *w*, *Locksley Hall* 125
The slumbrous light is rich and *w*, *Day-Dm., Sleep. B.* 7
' The birds were *w*, the birds were *w* upon him ; *Aylmer's Field* 260
From where his worldless heart had kept it *w*, „ 471
And, where *w* hands have prest and closed, *In Mem. xiii* 7
O heart, with kindliest motion *w*, „ *lxxxv* 34
'Twas well, indeed, when *w* with wine, „ *xc* 9
But where the sunbeam broodeth *w*, „ *xci* 14
Nor bowl of wassail mantle *w* ; „ *cv* 18
A life in civic action *w*, „ *cxiii* 9
Kept itself *w* in the heart of my dreams, *Maud I vi* 18
Sir Lancelot thro' his *w* blood felt Ice strike, *Gareth and L.* 1398
shall wear your costly gift Beside your own *w*
hearth, *Marr. of Geraint* 820
And felt the *w* tears falling on his face ; *Geraint and E.* 586
Not to be bound, save by white bonds and *w*, *Pelleas and E.* 353
W with a gracious parting from the Queen, „ 558
till the *w* hour returns With veer of wind, *Last Tournament* 230
The *w* white apple of her throat, „ 717
neither Love, *W* in the heart, his cradle, *Lover's Tale i* 158
Constraining it with kisses close and *w*, „ 468
Her *w* breath floated in the utterance „ *ii* 141
' O, you *w* heart,' he moan'd, „ *iv* 76
w melon lay like a little sun on the tawny sand, *V. of Maeldune* 57
This useless hand ! I felt one *w* tear fall upon it. *Tiresias* 167
Low *w* winds had gently breathed us away *The Wreck* 63
W as the crocus cup, *Early Spring* 29
W enew theere sewer-ly, *Owd Roä* 111
often while her lips Were *w* upon my cheek, *The Ring* 399
Warm (verb) Roof-haunting martins *w* their eggs : *Day-Dm., Sleep. P.* 17
New life-blood *w* the bosom, *Will Water.* 22
That *w*'s another living breast. *In Mem. lxxxv* 116
to *w* My cold heart with a friend : *Holy Grail* 618
Cold words from one I had hoped to *w* so far *Sisters (E. and E.)* 194
And *w*'s the child's awakening world— *To Prin. Beatrice* 5
the long day of knowledge grows and *w*'s, *Prog. of Spring* 101
And *w*'s the blood of Shiah and Sunnee, *Akbar's Dream* 107
Warm-asleep When you are *w-a*, mother, *May Queen, N. Y's. E.* 24
Warm-blue The *w-b* breathings of a hidden hearth *Aylmer's Field* 155
Warm'd (*See also* **Sherris-warm'd**) One hope that *w* me
in the days *Two Voices* 122
And in crystal cases. *Amphion* 88
W with his wines, or taking pride in her, *Aylmer's Field* 554
Too ragged to be fondled on her lap, *W* at her bosom ? „ 687
And hearts are *w* and faces bloom, *In Mem., Con.* 82
Took gayer colours, like an opal *w*. *Merlin and V.* 950
And the sea rolls, and all the world is *w* ? ' *Holy Grail* 672

Warm'd (*continued*) *w* but by the heart Within
them, *Akbar's Dream* 132
Warmer Wild wind ! I seek a *w* sky, *You ask me, why, etc.* 26
We came to *w* waves, and deep Across *The Voyage* 37
Is a clot of *w* dust, *Vision of Sin* 113
You turn'd your *w* currents all to her, *Princess iv* 301
Warmest Brimm'd with delirious draughts of *w* life. *Eleänore* 139
Warming Alone and *w* his five wits, (repeat) *The Owl i* 6, 13
w with her theme She fulmined out her scorn *Princess ii* 132
but *w* as he went, Glanced at the point of law, *Lover's Tale iv* 275
Warmth (*See also* **Mid-warmth**) So full of summer *w*,
so glad, *Miller's D.* 14
And doubled his own *w* against her lips, *Gardener's D.* 138
The *w* it thence shall win To riper life *Talking Oak* 254
And the *w* of hand in hand. *Vision of Sin* 162
new *w* of life's ascending sun Was felt *Enoch Arden* 38
And all the *w*, the peace, the happiness, „ 761
Having the *w* and muscle of the heart, *Aylmer's Field* 180
and turning to the *w* The tender pink „ 185
The loyal *w* of Florian is not cold, *Princess ii* 244
helpless *w* about my barren breast In the dead prime : „ *vi* 202
broke A genial *w* and light once more, „ 282
A rosy *w* from marge to marge *In Mem. xlvi* 16
A central *w* diffusing bliss In glance and smile, „ *lxxxiv* 6
underfoot the herb was dry ; And genial *w* ; „ *xcv* 3
A *w* within the breast would melt „ *cxxiv* 13
all the kindly *w* of Arthur's hall *Balin and Balan* 236
For we that want the *w* of double life, *Holy Grail* 624
An out-door sign of all the *w* within, „ 704
I yearn'd for *w* and colour which I found *Guinevere* 647
With hated *w* of apprehensiveness. *Lover's Tale i* 632
for the cold Without, and *w* within me, *To E. Fitzgerald* 29
ranged from the narrow *w* of your fold, *Despair* 38
light and genial *w* of double day. *To Prin. Beatrice* 22
With all the *w* of summer. *The Ring* 30
Thy *w*'s from bud to bud Accomplish *Prog. of Spring* 113
Beyond all hopes of *w*, by Œnone sat Not moving, *Death of Œnone* 14
Express him also by their *w* of love *Akbar's Dream* 109
War-music when first I heard *W-m*, *Princess v* 266
Warn part against himself To *w* us off, *Love and Duty* 46
Something divine to *w* them of their foes : *Sea Dreams* 69
And fearing waved my arm to *w* them off ; „ 132
from him flits to *w* A far-off friendship *Demeter and P.* 89
Be not deaf to the sound that *w*'s, *Riflemen form !* 8
Warn'd spoken, And *w* that madman ere it grew too late : *Vision of Sin* 56
An awful voice within had *w* him hence *Princess v* 338
Balan *w*, and went ; Balin remain'd : *Balin and Balan* 153
w me of their fierce design Against my house, *Lancelot and E.* 274
Warning (*See also* **Phantom-warning**) Take *w* ! he that
will not sing *The Blackbird* 21
For by the *w* of the Holy Ghost, *St. S. Stylites* 219
In those two deaths he read God's *w* ' wait.' *Enoch Arden* 571
nail me like a weasel on a grange For *w* : *Princess ii* 206
Did I wish Your *w* or your silence ? *Geraint and E.* 77
Then not to give you *w*, that seems hard ; „ 422
yet to give him *w*, for he rode As if he heard not, „ 451
Take *w* : yonder man is surely dead ; „ 672
' Thereafter, the dark *w* of our King, *Holy Grail* 368
Then I remember'd Arthur's word, „ 598
Some *w*—sent divinely—as it seem'd *Lover's Tale iv* 21
Who ever turn'd upon his heel to hear My *w* *Tiresias* 73
You scorn my Mother's *w*, *The Ring* 326
Warp (s) wonder of the loom thro' *w* and woof *Princess i* 62
Warp (verb) lies that *w* us from the living truth ! *Locksley Hall* 60
' Ye are green wood, see ye *w* not. *Princess ii* 75
I loved thee first, That *w*'s the wit.' *Merlin and V.* 61
Warp'd Walter *w* his mouth at this To something *Princess, Pro.* 214
Warrant (s) Crown'd *w* had we for the crowning sin *Last Tournament* 576
Slender *w* had *He* to be proud of *Batt. of Brunanburh* 66
Warrant (verb) I *w*, man, that we shall bring you round.' *Enoch Arden* 841
Butter I *w*'s be prime, an' I *w*'s the heggs be as well, *Village Wife* 3
I *w* ye soom fine daäy— *Spinster's S's.* 63
Sa I *w*'s 'e niver said haafe wot 'e thowt, *Church-warden, etc.* 18
Warren And waster than a *w* : *Amphion* 4
couch of incest in the *w*'s of the poor. *Locksley H., Sixty* 224

Warring   *W* on a later day,   *Ode on Well.* 102
conscience of a saint Among his *w* senses,   *Guinevere* 640
She reels not in the storm of *w* words,   *Ancient Sage* 70
Be struck from out the clash of *w* wills ;   *Prog. of Spring* 95
Thro' all the *w* world of Hindustan   *Akbar's Dream* 26
Warrior (adj.)   *Could give the* w *kings of old,*   *To the Queen* 4
The daughter of the *w* Gileadite,   *D. of F. Women* 197
Wilt surely guide me to the *w* King,   *Balin and Balan* 478
Warrior (s)   (*See also* **Statesman-warrior**)   *W* of God,
    whose strong right arm   *Alexander* 1
And like a *w* overthrown ;   *Two Voices* 150
sprang No dragon *w's* from Cadmean teeth,   *Lucretius* 50
made the old *w* from his ivied nook Glow   *Princess, Pro.* 104
about their heads I saw The feudal *w* lady-clad ;   ,,   119
in thunder-storms, And breed up *w's* !   ,,   v 440
Home they brought her *w* dead :   ,,   vi 1
Lightly to the *w* stept,   ,,   10
And happy *w's*, and immortal names,   ,,   93
Come, a grace to me !   I am your *w* :   ,,   224
W's carry the *w's* pall,   *Ode on Well.* 6
GLORY of *w*, glory of orator,   *Wages* 1
laugh'd upon his *w* whom he loved And honour'd
    most.   *Com. of Arthur* 125
and his *w's* cried, ' Be thou the king,   ,,   258
charg'd his *w* whom he loved And honour'd most,   ,,   447
therebefore the lawless *w* paced Unarm'd,   *Gareth and L.* 914
And heated the strong *w* in his dreams ;   *Marr. of Geraint* 72
At which the *w* in his obstinacy,   *Geraint and E.* 454
vanish'd by the fairy well That laughs at iron— as
    our *w's* did—   *Merlin and V.* 429
And on the third are *w's*, perfect men,   *Holy Grail* 236
dreading worse than shame Her *w* Tristram,   *Last Tournament* 385
There rode an armed *w* to the doors.   *Guinevere* 409
w's beating back the swarm Of Turkish Islam   *Montenegro* 10
W's over the Weltering waters   *Batt. of Brunanburh* 47
and round The *w's* puissant shoulders   *Achilles over the T.* 3
The *w* hath forgot his arms,   *Ancient Sage* 138
Lies the *w*, my forefather,   *Locksley H., Sixty* 28
Dead the *w*, dead his glory,   ,,   30
Indian *w's* dream of ampler hunting grounds   ,,   69
old-world inns that take Some *w* for a sign   *Pro. to Gen. Hamley* 14
realm were in the wrong For which her *w's* bleed,   *Epilogue* 35
right to crown with song The *w's* noble deed—   ,,   37
W of God, man's friend,   *Epit. on Gordon* 1
the shadowy *w* glide Along the silent field   *Demeter and P.* 152
A *w's* crest above the cloud of war '—   *The Ring* 338
My *w* of the Holy Cross and of the conquering sword,   *Happy* 7
pine which here The *w* of Caprera set,   *To Ulysses* 26
Find her *w* Stark and dark in his funeral fire.   *To Master of B.* 19
The wounded *w* climbs from Troy to thee.   *Death of Œnone* 39
Warrior-king   the *w-k's*, In height and prowess   *Tiresias* 178
Warrior-wise   *w-w* thou stridest thro' his halls   *Last Tournament* 517
Warship   Fled to his *w* :   *Batt. of Brunanburh* 59
War-song   His country's *w-s* thrill his ears :   *Two Voices* 153
Full many a noble *w-s* had he sung,   *Guinevere* 278
Wart   Were it but for a *w* or a mole ? '   *Dead Prophet* 56
War-thunder   shuddering *W-t* of iron rams ;   *Tiresias* 100
War-worker   *w-w's* who Harried the Welshman,   *Batt. of Brunanburh* 121
Was   (*See also* **War**)   For *w*, and is, and will be, are
    but is ;   *Princess iii* 324
And now the *W*, the Might-have been,   *To Marq. of Dufferin* 38
Who am, and *w*, and will be his, his own   *Happy* 7
Wash (s)   Katie walks By the long *w* of Australasian seas   *The Brook* 194
Wash (verb)   (*See also* **Wesh**)   O mercy, mercy ! *w*
    away my sin.   *St. S. Stylites* 120
It may be that the gulfs will *w* us down :   *Ulysses* 62
And in the great sea *w* away my sin.'   *Holy Grail* 806
Wash'd   (*See also* **Fresh-washed, Wesh'd**)   *W* with still
    rains and daisy blossomed ;   *Circumstance* 7
A league of grass, *w* by a slow broad stream,   *Gardener's D.* 40
daily left The little footprint daily *w* away.   *Enoch Arden* 22
shone Their morions, *w* with morning,   *Princess v* 264
stream Descended, and the Sun was *w* away.   *Gareth and L.* 1047
I have wallow'd, I have *w*—   *Last Tournament* 315
an I wallow'd, then I *w*—   ,,   318

Wash'd (*continued*)   *w* up from out the deep ?   *Last Tournament* 685
anon the wanton billow *w* Them over,   *Lover's Tale ii* 9
Washer   *See* **Dish-washer**
Washing   I heard the ripple *w* in the reeds,   *M. d'Arthur* 70
And the long ripple *w* in the reeds.'   ,,   117
I heard the ripple *w* in the reeds,   *Pass. of Arthur* 238
And the long ripple *w* in the reeds.'   ,,   285
Universal ocean softly *w* all her warless Isles   *Locksley H., Sixty* 170
Wasp   *W's* in our good hive,   *Princess iv* 535
Wassail   pledge you all In *w* ;   ,, *Pro.* 186
Nor bowl of *w* mantle warm ;   *In Mem. cv* 18
Wassail-bowl   The host, and I sat round the *w-b*,   *The Epic* 5
I,' quoth Everard, ' by the *w-b*.'   ,,   23
Waste (adj.)   Stretch'd wide and wild the *w* enormous
    marsh,   *Ode to Memory* 101
swan's death-hymn took the soul Of that *w* place
    with joy   *Dying Swan* 22
' From emptiness and the *w* wide Of that abyss,   *Two Voices* 119
like a wind, that shrills All night in a *w* land,   *M. d'Arthur* 202
Fly o'er *w* fens and windy fields.   *Sir Galahad* 60
Down the *w* waters day and night,   *The Voyage* 58
Sunning himself in a *w* field alone—   *Aylmer's Field* 9
To the *w* deeps together.   *Sea Dreams* 238
blank And *w* it seem'd and vain ;   *Princess vii* 43
Better the *w* Atlantic roll'd On her   *Third of Feb.* 21
From out *w* places comes a cry,   *In Mem. iii* 7
And thus the land of Cameliard was *w*,   *Com. of Arthur* 20
Vext with *w* dreams ?   ,,   85
Gray swamps and pools, *w* places of the hern,   *Geraint and E.* 31
To the *w* earldom of another earl,   ,,   438
O'er these *w* downs whereon I lost myself,   *Lancelot and E.* 225
And down the *w* sand-shores of Trath Treroit,   ,,   301
Lords of *w* marshes, kings of desolate isles,   ,,   527
And whipt me into *w* fields far away ;   *Holy Grail* 788
For out of the *w* islands had he come,   *Pelleas and E.* 86
Better the King's *w* hearth and aching heart   *Guinevere* 524
On the *w* sand by the *w* sea they closed.   *Pass. of Arthur* 92
like a wind that shrills All night in a *w* land,   ,,   370
Forthgazing on the *w* and open sea,   *Lover's Tale ii* 177
And all the land was *w* and solitary :   ,, *iv* 125
a crowd Throng'd the *w* field about the city gates :   *Sir J. Oldcastle* 40
Some lodge within the *w* sea-dunes,   *The Flight* 90
Now somewhere dead far in the *w* Soudan,   *Epit. on Gordon* 2
Waste (s)   (*See also* **Waäste**)   The level *w*, the rounding gray.   *Mariana* 44
Ammonian Oasis in the *w*.   *Alexander* 8
across the *w* His son and heir doth ride   *D. of the O. Year* 30
play'd Among the *w* and lumber of the shore,   *Enoch Arden* 16
babes were running wild Like colts about the *w*.   ,,   305
flour From his tall mill that whistled on the *w*.   ,,   343
With one small gate that open'd on the *w*,   ,,   733
and came out upon the *w*.   *The Brook* 191
of all his lavish *w* of words   ,,   777
wrought Such *w* and havock as the idolatries,   *Aylmer's Field* 640
Doom upon kings, or in the *w* ' Repent ' ?   ,,   742
and molten on the *w* Becomes a cloud :   *Princess iv* 72
that somewhere in the *w* The Shadow sits   *In Mem. xxii* 19
dreamful *w's* where footless fancies dwell   *Maud I xviii* 69
Far-sighted summoner of War and *W*   *Ded. of Idylls* 37
glancing round the *w* she fear'd   *Geraint and E* 50
and she drove them thro' the *w*.   ,,   100
Here in the heart of *w* and wilderness.   ,,   313
and sent a thousand men To till the *w's*,   ,,   942
The sad sea-sounding *w's* of Lyonesse—   *Merlin and V.* 74
rose And drove him into *w's* and solitudes For ,
    agony,   *Lancelot and E.* 252
I saw the least of little stars Down on the *w*,   *Holy Grail* 525
Fled all night long by glimmering *w* and weald, And
    heard the Spirits of the *w* and weald   *Guinevere* 128
or doth all that haunts the *w* and wild Mourn,   *Pass. of Arthur* 48
In praise to God who led me thro' the *w*.   *Columbus* 17
turn'd, And fled by many a *w*,   *Demeter and P.* 74
She comes on *w* and wood, On farm and field :   *Prog. of Spring* 22
By *w* and field and town of alien tongue,   *St. Telemachus* 30
Waste (verb)   if I *w* words now, in truth You must
    blame Love.   *Miller's D.* 191

Waste (verb) (*continued*) The sea *w's* all: but let me live
my life. *Audley Court* 51
To *w* his whole heart in one kiss *Sir L. and Q. G.* 44
That like a broken purpose *w* in air : So *w* not thou ;
but come ; *Princess vii* 214
Forgive me, I *w* my heart in signs : let be. „ 359
Half the night I *w* in sighs, *Maud II iv* 23
Nor dared to *w* a perilous pity on him : *Geraint and E.* 525
Speak therefore : shall I *w* myself in vain ? ' *Lancelot and E.* 670
and *w* the spiritual strength Within us, *Holy Grail* 35
her too hast thou left To pine and *w* *Last Tournament* 598
when I knew the twain Would each *w* each, *Tiresias* 69
Ill To *w* this earth began— *Epilogue* 23
Wasted (adj. and part.) My heart is *w* with my woe, *Oriana* 1
Wan, *w* Truth in her utmost need. *Clear-headed friend* 19
Where they smile in secret, looking over *w*
lands, *Lotos-Eaters, C. S.* 114
I that have *w* here health, wealth, and time, *Princess iv* 352
And wordless broodings on the *w* cheek— „ *vii* 112
Beating from the *w* vines Back to France *Ode on Well.* 109
Confusions of a *w* youth ; *In Mem., Pro.* 42
I trust I have not *w* breath : „ *cxx* 1
Thro' the hubbub of the market I steal, a *w* frame, *Maud II iv* 69
W so often by the heathen hordes, *Holy Grail* 244
W and worn, and but a tithe of them, „ 723
But when the matron saw That hinted love was only
w bait, *The Ring* 360
You that lie with *w* lungs Waiting for your summons . . . *Forlorn* 21
Wasted (verb) Last night I *w* hateful hours *Fatima* 8
And beat me down and marr'd and *w* me, *Tithonus* 19
He *w* hours with Averill. *Aylmer's Field* 109
There they ruled, and thence they *w* *Boädicea* 54
waging war Each upon other, *w* all the land ; *Com. of Arthur* 7
' O I that *w* time to tend upon her, *Geraint and E.* 38
and thro' her love her life *W* and pined, *Pelleas and E.* 496
Wasteful And scaled in sheets of *w* foam, *Sea Dreams* 53
disciple, richly garb'd, but worn From *w* living,
follow'd— *Ancient Sage* 5
Waster And *w* than a warren : *Amphion* 4
Wastest The *w* moorland of our realm shall be Safe, *Gareth and L.* 603
Wasting *w* odorous sighs All night long *Adeline* 43
leapt To greet her, *w* his forgotten heart, *Aylmer's Field* 689
' *w* the sweet summer hours ' ? *Charity* 1
Watch (s) (*See also* **Death-watch**) Kept *w*, waiting decision, *Œnone* 143
wan was her cheek With hollow *w*, *Princess vi* 145
And *w'es* in the dead, the dark, „ *vii* 103
Come : not in *w'es* of the night, *In Mem. xci* 13
Keep *w* and ward, keep *w* and ward, *Maud I vi* 58
did Enid, keeping *w*, behold In the first shallow
shade *Geraint and E.* 118
still he kept his *w* beneath the wall. *Pelleas and E.* 223
Wide open were the gates, And no *w* kept ; „ 415
But kept their *w* upon the ring and you. *The Ring* 300
heron rises from his *w* beside the mere, *Happy* 3
Watch (time-piece) seal, that hung From Allan's *w*, *Dora* 136
Watch (verb) I *w* thy grace ; and in its place *Eleänore* 127
Fancy *w'es* in the wilderness, *Caress'd or chidden* 12
I *w* the darkening droves of swine *Palace of Art* 199
To *w* the crisping ripples on the beach, *Lotos-Eaters, C. S.* 61
To *w* the long bright river drawing slowly „ 92
To *w* the emerald-colour'd water falling „ 96
W what main-currents draw the years : *Love thou thy land* 21
W what thou seëst, and lightly bring me word.' *M. d'Arthur* 38
W what I see, and lightly bring thee word.' „ 44
I bad thee, *w*, and lightly bring me word.' „ 81
saw An angel stand and *w* me, as I sang. *St. S. Stylites* 35
I used to *w*—if I be he that watch'd— *Tithonus* 52
did we *w* the stately ships, *Locksley Hall* 37
To w the three tall spires ; *Godiva* 3
That *w* the sleepers from the wall. *Day-Dm., Sleep. P.* 24
He *w'es* from his mountain walls, *The Eagle* 5
dewy eyes That *w* me from the glen below. *Move Eastward* 8
built their castles of dissolving sand To *w* them
overflow'd, *Enoch Arden* 20
There often as he watch'd or seem'd to *w*, „ 600

Watch (verb) (*continued*) ' Good,' said his friend,
' but *w* !' *Aylmer's Field* 275
and one was set to *w* The watcher, „ 551
and *w* A full sea glazed with muffled moonlight, *Princess i* 247
O to *w* the thirsty plants Imbibing ! „ *ii* 422
Or seem'd to *w* the dancing bubble, „ *iii* 24
and *w* The sandy footprint harden into stone.' „ 270
I *w* the twilight falling brown *To F. D. Maurice* 14
if that eye which *w'es* guilt And goodness, *In Mem. xxvi* 5
And those wild eyes that *w* the wave „ *xxxvi* 15
Ye *w*, like God, the rolling hours „ *li* 14
So may'st thou *w* me where I weep, „ *lxiii* 2
To those that *w* it more and more, „ *lxxiv* 2
' I *w* thee from the quiet shore, „ *lxxxv* 81
For who was left to *w* her but I ? *Maud I xix* 10
And *w* her harvest ripen, her herd increase, „ *III vi* 25
Guinevere Stood by the castle walls to *w* him pass ; *Com. of Arthur* 48
w his mightful hand striking great blows *Marr. of Geraint* 95
last bethought her how she used to *w*, „ 647
Not dare to *w* the combat, *Geraint and E.* 154
Geraint Waving an angry hand as who should say
' Ye *w* me,' 445
From whence to *w* the time, and eagle-like *Balin and Balan* 535
the Seer Would *w* her at her petulance, *Merlin and V.* 175
and laugh As those that *w* a kitten ; „ 177
And *w* the curl'd white of the coming wave „ 292
while women *w* Who wins, who falls ; *Holy Grail* 34
' There he *w'es* yet, There like a dog *Pelleas and E.* 262
W what thou seëst, and lightly bring me word.' *Pass. of Arthur* 206
W what I see, and lightly bring thee word.' „ 212
I bad thee, *w*, and lightly bring me word.' „ 249
I could not *w* her for four— *In the Child. Hosp.* 59
Still—could we *w* at all points ? *Def. of Lucknow* 49
w the chariot whirl About the goal again, *Tiresias* 176
Or *w* the waving pine which here *To Ulysses* 25
' Father and Mother will *w* you grow '— (repeat) *Romney's R.* 104, 106
Christian faces *w* Man murder man. *St. Telemachus* 55
Watch'd She *w* my crest among them all, *Oriana* 30
In lazy mood I *w* the little circles die ; *Miller's D.* 74
I *w* the little flutterings, „ 153
And *w* by weeping queens. *Palace of Art* 108
I used to watch—if I be he that *w*— *Tithonus* 52
And *w* by silent gentlemen, *Will Water.* 231
Maiden, I have *w* thee daily, *L. of Burleigh* 3
to the last dip of the vanishing sail She *w* it, *Enoch Arden* 246
There often as he *w* or seem'd to watch, „ 600
Miriam *w* and dozed at intervals, „ 909
They parted, and Sir Alymer Aylmer *w*. *Aylmer's Field* 277
conscious of the rageful eye That *w* him, „ 337
Or made occasion, being strictly *w*, „ 478
and groves of pines, *W* even there ; „ 551
and Sir Aylmer *w* them all, „ 552
the wife, who *w* his face, Paled at a sudden twitch „ 731
and *w* it lying bathed In the green gleam *Princess i* 93
While Psyche *w* them, smiling, „ *ii* 365
and *w* Or seem'd to watch the dancing bubble, „ *iii* 23
I *w* the swallow winging south „ *iv* 89
but *w* them well, Saw that they kept apart, „ 339
but *w* awake A cypress in the moonlight shake, *The Daisy* 81
There was one who *w* and told me, *Boädicea* 30
And I myself, who sat apart And *w* them, *In Mem. ciii* 30
That *w* her on her nurse's arm, „ *Con.* 46
and *w* the great sea fall, Wave after wave, *Com. of Arthur* 378
and *w* him from the gates : „ 449
Then she that *w* him, ' Wherefore stare ye so ? *Gareth and L.* 939
Knave, when I *w* thee striking on the bridge „ 992
But *w* him have I like a phantom pass „ 1335
Yet have I *w* thee victor in the joust, „ 1356
While he that *w* her sadden *Marr. of Geraint* 67
he *w* The being he loved best in all the world, *Geraint and E.* 102
And *w* the sun blaze on the turning scythe, „ 252
Eyes too that long have *w* how Lancelot draws *Balin and Balan* 375
Queen Among her damsels broidering sat, heard, *w*
And whisper'd : *Merlin and V.* 138
one had *w*, and had not held his peace : „ 162

Water'd   Seal'd it with kisses ? *w* it with tears ?   *Œnone* 234
Waterfall   Thou wert not nursed by the *w*   *Ode to Memory* 51
   Down shower the gambolling *w's*   *Sea-Fairies* 10
   w's Pour'd in a thunderless plunge   *V. of Maeldune* 13
Waterflag   There in the many-knotted *w's*,   *M. d'Arthur* 63
   There in the many-knotted *w's*,   *Pass. of Arthur* 231
Waterfowl   they ride away—to hawk For *w.*   *Merlin and V.* 108
Water-gate   Storm at the *W-g* !   *Def. of Lucknow* 37
Water-gnat   in the burn *w-g's* murmur and mourn.   *Leonine Eleg.* 8
Water-lily   She saw the *w-l* bloom,   *L. of Shalott iii* 39
   But as the *w* starts and slides Upon the level   *Princess iv* 255
Waterloo   in sawdust, slept, As old as *W* ;   *Will Water.* 100
   In that world-earthquake, *W* !   *Ode on Well.* 133
   nobler work to do Than when he fought at *W*,   " 257
   Plunged in the last fierce charge at *W*,   *Sisters (E. and E.)* 64
Water-pipes   Creeps to the garden *w-p* beneath,   *D. of F. Women* 206
Water-side   The first house by the *w-s*,   *L. of Shalott iv* 34
Water-smoke   thousand wreaths of dangling *w-s*,   *Princess vii* 213
Water-sodden   Dagonet stood Quiet as any *w-s* log   *Last Tournament* 253
Water-world   Thro' his dim *w-w* ?   *Maud II ii* 20
Watery   slight Sir Robert with his *w* smile   *Edwin Morris* 128
   ' That weak and *w* nature love you ? No !   *The Ring* 396
Watter (water)   'E seeäms naw moor nor *w*,   *North. Cobbler* 76
   some on 'em said it wur *w—*   " 83
   thou can't graw this upo' *w* ! '   " 86
Wattle   he built with *w's* from the marsh   *Holy Grail* 63
   An' 'e torn'd as red as a stag-tuckey's *w's*,   *Church-warden, etc.* 31
Wattled   bleat Of the thick-fleeced sheep from *w* folds,   *Ode to Memory* 66
Wattling   And one was rough with *w*,   *Balin and Balan* 366
Wave (s)   (*See also* **Sea-wave**)   The slumbrous *w* outwelleth,   *Claribel* 18
   when the crisp slope *w's* After a tempest,   *Supp. Confessions* 126
   And the blue *w* beat the shore ;   *All Things will Die* 43
   the rainbow hangs on the poising *w*,   *Sea-Fairies* 29
   And shook the *w* as the wind did sigh ;   *Dying Swan* 15
   But the *w* would make music above us afar—   *The Merman* 22
   adown the steep like a *w* I would leap   *The Mermaid* 39
   As *w's* that up a quiet cove Rolling slide,   *Eleänore* 108
   Thro' the *w* that runs for ever By the island   *L. of Shalott i* 12
   I loved the brimming *w* that swam   *Miller's D.* 97
   One show'd an iron coast and angry *w's*.   *Palace of Art* 69
   swallow 'ill come back again with summer o'er the *w*,   *May Queen, N. Y's. E.* 19
   ' This mounting *w* will roll us shoreward soon.'   *Lotos-Eaters* 2
   gushing far far away did seem to mourn   " 31
   ' Our island home Is far beyond the *w* ;   " 45
   In ever climbing up the climbing *w* ?   " *C. S.* 50
   wind and *w* and oar ;   " 127
   holy organ rolling *w's* Of sound on roof and floor   *D. of F. Women* 191
   on the bounteous *w* of such a breast   *Gardener's D.* 139
   Came wet-shod alder from the *w*,   *Amphion* 41
   We came to warmer *w's*, and deep   *The Voyage* 37
   on *w's* that idly burst Like Heavenly Hope   " 69
   Thy tribute *w* deliver :   *A Farewell* 2
   Rising, falling, like a *w*,   *Vision of Sin* 125
   And *w's* of shadow went over the wheat,   *Poet's Song* 4
   sweep Of some precipitous rivulet to the *w*,   *Enoch Arden* 587
   Who still'd the rolling *w* of Galilee !   *Aylmer's Field* 709
   that great *w* Returning, while none mark'd it,   *Sea Dreams* 233
   No rock so hard but that a little *w*   *Princess iii* 154
   old-recurring *w's* of prejudice Resmooth   " 240
   drench his dark locks in the gurgling *w* Mid-channel.   " *iv* 187
   like a beacon-tower above the *w's* Of tempest,   " 493
   Naked, a double light in air and *w*,   " *vii* 167
   Nor all Calamity's hugest *w's* confound,   *Will* 5
   W's on a diamond shingle dash,   *The Islet* 16
   And *w's* that sway themselves in rest,   *In Mem. xi* 18
   And in the hearing of the *w*.   " *xix* 4
   the *w* again Is vocal in its wooded walls ;   " 13
   And those wild eyes that watch the *w*   " *xxxvi* 15
   The lightest *w* of thought shall lisp,   " *xlix* 5
   And every pulse of wind and *w* Recalls,   " *lxxxv* 73
   Or cool'd within the glooming *w* ;   " *lxxxix* 45
   Upon the thousand *w's* of wheat,   " *xci* 11
   Till all my blood, a fuller *w*,   " *cxxii* 12
   scream of a madden'd beach dragg'd down by the *w*,   *Maud I iii* 12

Wave (s (*continued*) the long *w's* that roll in yonder bay ?   *Maud I xviii* 63
   W after *w*, each mightier than the last,   *Com. of Arthur* 379
   and all the *w* was in a flame : And down the *w* and in the flame was borne A naked babe,   " 383
   And rippled like an ever-fleeting *w*,   *Gareth and L.* 215
   Clash like the coming and retiring *w*,   " 522
   Comes flying over many a windy *w* To Britain,   *Marr. of Geraint* 337
   For the great *w* that echoes round the world ;   " 420
   That keeps the wear and polish of the *w*.   " 682
   blind *w* feeling round his long sea-hall   *Merlin and V.* 232
   watch the curl'd white of the coming *w*   " 292
   Ev'n such a *w*, but not so pleasurable,   " 294
   You seem'd that *w* about to break upon me   " 302
   as a wild *w* in the wide North-sea,   *Lancelot and E.* 482
   Play'd ever back upon the sloping *w*,   *Holy Grail* 382
   The heathen—but that ever-climbing *w*,   *Last Tournament* 92
   as the crest of some slow-arching *w*,   " 462
   Between the steep cliff and the coming *w* ;   *Guinevere* 280
   But after tempest, when the long *w* broke   " 290
   only the wan *w* Brake in among dead faces,   *Pass. of Arthur* 129
   Upon the dappled dimplings of the *w*,   *Lover's Tale i* 44
   Held for a space 'twixt cloud and *w*,   " 417
   Showers slanting light upon the dolorous *w*.   " 811
   All crisped sounds of *w* and leaf and wind,   " *ii* 106
   Slow-moving as a *w* against the wind,   " *iii* 293
   a *w* like the *w* that is raised by an earthquake grew,   *The Revenge* 115
   Backward they reel like the *w*, like the *w*   *Def. of Lucknow* 43
   And we gazed at the wandering *w*   *V. of Maeldune* 89
   and the roar of *w's*,   *The Wreck* 3
   rougher gust might tumble a stormier *w*,   " 131
   But the blind *w* cast me ashore,   *Despair* 61
   Or if lip were laid to lip on the pillows of the *w*.   *The Flight* 48
   like a rock In the *w* of a stormy day ;   *Heavy Brigade* 57
   Hath still'd the blast and strown the *w*,   *Freedom* 34
   And ask'd the *w's* that moan about the world   *Demeter and P.* 64
   fill the hollows between *w* and *w* ;   *Akbar's Dream* 161
   and the moan of my *w* I whirl,   *The Dreamer* 13
Wave (verb)   But who hath seen her *w* her hand ?   *L. of Shalott i* 24
   W's all its lazy lilies, and creeps on,   *Gardener's D.* 42
   bottom agates seem to *w* and float   *Princess ii* 327
   Nor *w's* the cypress in the palace walk ;   " *vii* 177
   And, since the grasses round me *w*,   *In Mem. xxi* 2
   Sat by the river in a cove, and watch'd The high reed *w*,   *Lancelot and E.* 1390
   watching overhead The aërial poplar *w*,   *Sisters (E. and E.)* 84
   He sees me, *w's* me from him.   *Happy* 19
   You need not *w* me from you.   " 20
   Still you *w* me off—poor roses—   " 101
   Thy gay lent-lilies *w* and put them by,   *Prog. of Spring* 37
Waved   caught His bundle, *w* his hand, and went his way.   *Enoch Arden* 238
   And fearing *w* my arm to warn them off ;   *Sea Dreams* 132
   She spoke, and bowing *w* Dismissal :   *Princess ii* 99
   She, ending, *w* her hands :   " *iv* 522
   She *w* to me with her hand.   *Maud I ix* 8
   The wrist is parted from the hand that *w*,   *Merlin and V.* 551
   yet he glanced not up, nor *w* his hand,   *Lancelot and E.* 986
   Arthur *w* them back. Alone he rode.   *Last Tournament* 437
   woods upon the hill *W* with a sudden gust   *Lover's Tale iii* 34
   w his blade To the gallant three hundred   *Heavy Brigade* 9
Waver   As when a sunbeam *w's* warm   *Miller's D.* 79
   While this great bow will *w* in the sun,   *Palace of Art* 43
   The gas-light *w's* dimmer ;   *Will Water.* 38
   W's on her thin stem the snowdrop cold   *Prog. of Spring* 2
   A blood-red awning *w* overhead,   *St. Telemachus* 52
Waver'd   The crowds, the temples, *w*, and the shore ;   *D. of F. Women* 114
   for thus at times He *w* ;   *Merlin and V.* 187
   Here, too, my love *W* at anchor with me,   *Lover's Tale i* 65
   W and floated—which was less than Hope,   " 452
   foeman surged, and *w*, and reel'd Up the hill,   *Heavy Brigade* 62
Wavering   and, *w* Lovingly lower, trembled on her waist—Ah, happy shade—and still went *w* down,   *Gardener's D.* 130
   From the high tree the blossom *w* fell,   *Princess vi* 80
   W's of every vane with every wind,   *To the Queen ii* 50

Way (*continued*)   So all the *w's* were safe from shore
     to shore,   *Last Tournament* 485
     Mark's *w*, my soul !—but eat not thou with Mark,   ,,   532
     So, pluck'd one *w* by hate and one by love,   ,,   539
     Mark's *w's* to steal behind one in the dark—   ,,   618
     And cast him as a worm upon the *w*,   *Guinevere* 35
     And then they rode to the divided *w*,   ,,   124
     That did not shun to smite me in worse *w*,   ,,   435
     and the *w's* Were filled with rapine,   ,,   457
     But in His *w's* with men I find Him not.   *Pass. of Arthur* 11
     and wail their *w* From cloud to cloud,   ,,   39
     find or feel a *w* Thro' this blind haze,   ,,   75
     And God fulfils himself in many *w's*,   ,,   409
     I am going a long *w* With these thou seëst—   ,,   424
     that *w* my wish leads me evermore Still to
     believe it—   *Lover's Tale* i 274
     Each *w* from verge to verge a Holy Land,   ,,   337
     effect weigh'd seas upon my head To come my *w* !   ,,   661
     Was not the land as free thro' all her *w's*   ,,   662
     Could that be more because he came my *w* ?   ,,   666
     Why should he not come my *w* if he would ?   ,,   667
     why *should* he come my *w* Robed in those robes   ,,   670
     what gleam on those black *w's* Where Love   ,,   812
     Had died almost to serve them any *w*,   ,,   iv 124
     And leave him in the public *w* to die.   ,,   261
     And balanced either *w* by each,   ,,   269
     he patted my hand in his gentle *w*,   *First Quarrel* 67
     and now you may go your *w*.   *Rizpah* 20
     Turning my *w*, the loveliest face on earth.   *Sisters (E. and E.)* 87
     Flower into fortune—our world's *w*—   *Columbus* 167
     sometimes wish I had never led the *w*.   ,,   186
     Shaping their *w* toward Dyflen again,   *Batt. of Brunanburh* 98
     moves unseen among the *w's* of men.   *Tiresias* 24
     Send no such light upon the *w's* of men   ,,   161
     and every *w* the vales Wind,   ,,   182
     By all my *w's* where'er they ran,   *Ancient Sage* 157
     he—some one—this *w* creeps—   *The Flight* 70
     and Suns along their fiery *w*,   *Locksley H., Sixty* 203
     know them, follow him who led the *w*,   ,,   266
     Nor this *w* will you set your name   *Epilogue* 1
     Yon myriad-worlded *w*—   ,,   53
     Well, One *w* for Miriam.   *The Ring* 73
     She turn'd, and in her soft imperial *w*   ,,   267
     I am the Perfect *W*, All else is to perdition.'   *Akbar's Dream* 34
     Here on this bank in *some w* live the life   ,,   144
     Will you move a little that *w* ?   *Charity* 20
     Well if it do not roll our *w*.   *Riflemen form !* 4
     Toward the lowland *w's* behind me,   *Silent Voices* 5

Wayfaring-tree   Black holly, and white-flower'd *w-t* !   *Sir J. Oldcastle* 130

Wayside   Craft, poisonous counsels, *w* ambushings—   *Gareth and L.* 432
     The *w* blossoms open to the blaze.   *Balin and Balan* 449
     Come dashing down on a tall *w* flower,   *Guinevere* 253
     I told your *w* story to my mother   *Sisters (E. and E.)* 189

Wayward—The vexed eddies of its *w* brother :   *Isabel* 33
     I have been wild and *w*, but you'll forgive me
     now ;   *May Queen, N. Y's. E.* 33
     Or something of a *w* modern mind   *Edwin Morris* 87
     I went thro' many *w* moods   *Day-Dm., Pro.* 6
     No more shall *w* grief abuse The genial hour   *In Mem. cv* 9
     And yet so wild and *w* that my dream—   *Akbar's Dream* 172

Waywardness   At any gentle damsel's *w*.   *Gareth and L.* 1179

Way-worn   Foot-sore, *w-w*, at length   *St. Telemachus* 34

Weak (*adj.*)   *W* Truth a-leaning on her crutch,   *Clear-headed friend* 18
     Than cry for strength, remaining *w*,   *Two Voices* 95
     ' For I go, *w* from suffering here :   ,,   238
     W symbols of the settled bliss,   *Miller's D.* 233
     And in my *w*, lean arms I lift the cross,   *St. S. Stylites* 118
     Made *w* by time and fate, but strong in will   *Ulysses* 69
     Pass on, *w* heart, and leave me where I lie :   *Come not, when, etc.* 11
     Half-parted from a *w* and scolding hinge,   *The Brook* 84
     Full of *w* poison, turnspits for the clown,   *Princess iv* 516
     ' This fellow would make weakness *w*,   *In Mem. xxi* 7
     Strike dead the whole *w* race of venomous worms,   *Maud II i* 46
     Seeing that ye be grown too *w* and old   *Com. of Arthur* 511
     For see ye not how *w* and hungerworn I seem—   *Gareth and L.* 443

Weak (*adj.*) (*continued*)   The sick *w* beast seeking to
     help herself   *Merlin and V.* 498
     And being *w* in body said no more ;   *Lancelot and E.* 839
     Flatter me rather, seeing me so *w*,   *Last Tournament* 642
     Of eyes too *w* to look upon the light ;   *Lover's Tale* i 614
     An' Hetty wur *w* i' the hattics,   *Village Wife* 101
     being woman and *w*, His formal kiss fell   *The Wreck* 31
     ' That and watery nature love you ?   No !   *The Ring* 396

Weak (*s*)   if from Arthur's hall, To help the *w*.   *Balin and Balan* 473

Weaken'd   And all the senses *w*, save in that,   *Lover's Tale* i 127
     ' Muriel's health Had *w*, nursing little Miriam.   *The Ring* 357

Weakening   gentle sickness, gradually *W* the man,   *Enoch Arden* 825

Weaker   Words *w* than your grief would make   *To J. S.* 65
     And ever *w* grows thro' acted crime,   *Will* 12
     ' I might forget my *w* lot ;   *Two Voices* 367
     songs I made As echoes out of *w* times,   *In Mem., Con.* 22
     till he saw Which were the *w* ;   *Lancelot and E.* 462

Weakest   Cries to *W* as to Strongest,   *Locksley H., Sixty* 110

Weakling   Poor *w* ev'n as they are.'   *Princess vi* 310
     Of craven, *w*, and thrice-beaten hound :   *Pelleas and E.* 291
     ' Rise, *w* ; I am Lancelot ; say thy say.'   ,,   582

Weakly   This pretty, puny, *w* little one,   *Enoch Arden* 195

Weakness   my own *w* fools My judgment,   *Supp. Confessions* 136
     Prevailing in *w*, the coronach stole   *Dying Swan* 26
     Deliver not the tasks of might To *w*,   *Love thou thy land* 14
     Regard the *w* of thy peers :   ,,   24
     W to be wroth with *w* !   *Locksley Hall* 149
     So she strove against her *w*,   *L. of Burleigh* 69
     That was your hour of *w*.   *Enoch Arden* 449
     And Enoch bore his *w* cheerfully.   ,,   827
     to spy The *w* of a people or a house,   *Aylmer's Field* 570
     Our *w* somehow shapes the shadow,   *Princess iii* 330
     And hatred of her *w*, blent with shame.   ,,   vii 30
     but well-nigh close to death For *w* :   ,,   120
     ' This fellow would make *w* weak,   *In Mem. xxi* 7
     my passion hath not swerved To works of *w*,   ,,   lxxxv 50
     Forgot his *w* in thy sight.   ,,   cx 4
     those Whom *w* or necessity have cramp'd   *Tiresias* 87

Weal   (*See also* **Dogwhip-weals**)   he for the common *w*,   *Princess ii* 285
     The fading politics   ,,   iv 325
     A lidless watcher of the public *w*,   *In Mem. cxxix* 2
     So far, so near in woe and *w* ;   *Marr. of Geraint* 799
     Be moulded by your wishes for her *w* ;   *Ancient Sage* 96
     Hours That cancel *w* with woe.

Weald   Fled all night long by glimmering waste and *w*, And
     heard the Spirits of the waste and *w*   *Guinevere* 128
     That gray beast, the wolf of the *w*.   *Batt. of Brunanburh* 110

Wealth   (*See also* **World-wealth**)   Showering thy gleaned
     w into my open breast   *Ode to Memory* 23
     The choicest *w* of all the earth,   *Eleänore* 19
     In glowing health, with boundless *w*,   *L. C. V. de Vere* 61
     ' When *w* no more shall rest in mounded heaps,   *Golden Year* 32
     The sole succeeder to their *w*, their lands,   *Aylmer's Field* 294
     heiress, *w*, Their *w*, their heiress ! *w* enough was
     theirs For twenty matches.   ,,   368
     May beat a pathway out to *w* and fame.   ,,   439
     Whatever eldest-born of rank or *w*   ,,   484
     I that have wasted here health, *w*, and time,   *Princess iv* 352
     O more than poor men *w*, Than sick men health—   ,,   459
     Abide : thy *w* is gather'd in,   *In Mem. lii* 15
     And so my *w* resembles thine,   ,,   lxxix 17
     the *w* Of words and wit, the double health,   ,,   Con. 102
     Your father has *w* well-gotten,   *Maud I iv* 18
     joy that blazed itself in woodland *w* Of leaf,   *Balin and Balan* 82
     all his land and *w* and state were hers.   *Holy Grail* 587
     And gave herself and all her *w* to me.   ,,   597
     all the *w* and all the woe ?   *Guinevere* 344
     And so much *w* as God had charged her with—   *Lover's Tale* i 213
     when all my *w* Flash'd from me in a moment   ,,   668
     Whatever *w* I brought from that new world   *Columbus* 101
     with the wisdom and *w* of his own,   *The Wreck* 65
     W with his wines and his wedded harlots,   *Vastness* 19
     kinsman, dying, summon'd me to Rome—He left me *w*—   *The Ring* 179
     no tear for him, who left you *w*,   ,,   188
     The *w* of tropic bower and brake ;   *To Ulysses* 37

Wealth (*continued*) Youth and Health, and birth
and w,   *By an Evolution.* 8
Wealthier and himself Be wealthy still, ay w.   *Aylmer's Field* 373
Then closed her access to the w farms,   " 503
Then were I w than a leash of kings.'   *Gareth and L.* 51
' Ye will be all the w,' (repeat)   *Geraint and E.* 221, 412
A w life than heretofore with these And Balin,   *Balin and Balan* 92
w—w—hour by hour !   *To the Queen* ii 23
Jilted for a w ! w ?   *Locksley H., Sixty* 11
To make them w in his readers' eyes ;   *Poets and their B.* 4
Wealthiest Spain then the mightiest, w realm on earth,   *Columbus* 205
Wealthy Revealings deep and clear are thine Of w smiles :   *Madeline* 11
I SEE the w miller yet,   *Miller's D.* 1
Like w men who care not how they give.   *Tithonus* 17
Where the w nobles dwell.'   *L. of Burleigh* 24
And when she show'd the w scabbard,
and himself Be w still, ay wealthier.   *Aylmer's Field* 236
                                          " 373
Days order'd in a w peace,   *In Mem. xlvi* 11
W with wandering lines of mount and mere,   *Holy Grail* 252
Hold her a w bride within thine arms,   " 621
Tho' w enough to have bask'd in the light   *The Wreck* 45
Weapon With thine own w art thou slain,   *Two Voices* 311
wearing neither hunting-dress Nor w,   *Marr. of Geraint* 166
The wielding of w's—   *Batt. of Brunanburh* 90
a valorous w in olden England !   *Kapiolani* 4
Wear (s) keeps the w and polish of the wave.   *Marr. of Geraint* 682
Wear (verb) W's all day a fainter tone.   *The Owl* ii 7
And King-like w's the crown ;   *Of old sat Freedom* 16
eat wholesome food, And w warm clothes,   *St. S. Stylites* 109
w an undress'd goatskin on my back ;   " 116
shall w Alternate leaf and acorn-ball   *Talking Oak* 286
This mortal armour that I w,   *Sir Galahad* 70
Of those that w the Poet's crown :   *You might have won* 116
spears That soon should w the garland ;   *Aylmer's Field* 112
his pride Lay deeper than to w it as his ring—   " 122
I think they should not w our rusty gowns,'   *Princess, Pro.* 143
than w Those lilies, better blush   " iii 67
And so she w's her error like a crown   " 111
he w's a truer crown Than any wreath   *Ode on Well.* 276
bear the head That sleeps or w's the mask of sleep,   *In Mem. xviii* 10
When first she w's her orange-flower !   " xl 4
Who w's his manhood hale and green :   " liii 4
The fool that w's a crown of thorns :   " lxix 12
Come, w the forms by which I know   " xci 5
But ill for him that w's a crown,   " cxxvii 9
And Maud will w her jewels,   *Maud I xx* 27
And w's a helmet mounted with a skull,   *Gareth and L.* 639
your fair child shall w your costly gift   *Marr. of Geraint* 819
Were fit to w your slipper for a glove.   *Geraint and E.* 623
Why w ye this crown-royal upon shield ? '   *Balin and Balan* 338
' Why w ye that crown-royal ? '   " 348
' What, w ye still that same crown-scandalous ? '   " 390
this maid Might w as fair a jewel as is on earth,   *Lancelot and E.* 240
That he should w her favour at the tilt.   " 358
will you w My favour at this tourney ? '   " 361
Well, I will w it : fetch it out to me :   " 371
One rose, a rose, to gather and to w,   *Pelleas and E.* 406
Why w you not w on arm, or neck, or zone   *Last Tournament* 38
Lancelot won, methought, for thee to w.'   " 38
W black and white, and be a nun like you,   *Guinevere* 677
And so w not in almsdeed and in prayer   " 687
Robed in those robes of light I must not w,   *Lover's Tale* i 671
pluck from this true breast the locket that I w,   *The Flight* 33
Envy w's the mask of Love,   *Locksley H., Sixty* 109
I should w my crown entire   *Helen's Tower* 9
you, that w a wreath of sweeter bay,   *Poets and their B.* 7
I myself Am half afraid to w it.   *The Ring* 472
and w's the leper's weed ?   *Happy* 10
Wear'd (spent) I w it o' liquor, I did.   *North. Cobbler* 32
Wearied Is w of the rolling hours.   *L. C. V. de Vere* 60
Smoothing the w mind :   *Leonine Eleg.* 14
And closing eaves of w eyes I sleep till dusk   *In Mem. lxvii* 11
I felt Thy manhood thro' that w lance of thine.   *Gareth and L.* 1266
and Balin's horse Was w to the death,   *Balin and Balan* 561
And w out made for the couch and slept,   *Merlin and V.* 736

Wearied (*continued*) Wounded and w needs must he
be near.   *Lancelot and E.* 538
Rode with his diamond, w of the quest,   " 616
To seek him, and had w of the search.   " 631
all w of the quest Leapt on his horse,   " 703
' Alas,' he said, ' your ride hath w you.   " 831
I am w of our city, son,   *Ancient Sage* 15
And w of Autocrats, Anarchs, and Slaves,   *The Dreamer* 10
Wearier Thro' weary and yet ever w hours,   *Aylmer's Field* 828
Wearieth Gaiety without eclipse, W me,   *Lilian* 21
Weariness all things else have rest from w ?   *Lotos-Eaters, C. S.* 14
As all but empty heart and w   *Geraint and E.* 652
Settles, till one could yield for w :   *Merlin and V.* 372
wan day Went glooming down in wet and w :   *Last Tournament* 215
Toil and ineffable w, faltering hopes of relief,   *Def. of Lucknow* 90
those three sweet Italian words, became a w.   *The Ring* 407
He, all but deaf thro' age and w,   *St. Telemachus* 41
Wearing And w on my swarthy brows The garland   *Kate* 23
W the rose of womanhood.   *Two Voices* 417
W the light yoke of that Lord of love,   *Aylmer's Field* 708
W his wisdom lightly, like the fruit   *A Dedication* 12
w all that weight Of learning lightly   *In Mem., Con.* 39
W the white flower of a blameless life, .   *Ded. of Idylls* 25
w neither hunting-dress Nor weapon,   *Marr. of Geraint* 165
in w mine Needs must be lesser likelihood,   *Lancelot and E.* 366
damsel, w this unsunny face To him who won   *Pelleas and E.* 180
And w but a holly-spray for crest,   *Last Tournament* 172
I, w but the garland of a day,   *To Dante* 6
Weary (adj.) (*See also* **Heart-weary**) O w life ! O
w death !   *Supp. Confessions* 188
w with a finger's touch Those writhed limbs   *Clear-headed friend* 22
From brawling storms, From w wind,   *Ode to Memory* 113
SLOW sail'd the w mariners and saw,   *Sea-Fairies* 1
Ever the w wind went on,   *Dying Swan* 9
A w, w way I go, Oriana.   *Oriana* 89
My life is full of w days,   *My life is full* 1
Which some green Christmas crams with w bones.   *Wan Sculptor* 14
And by the moon the reaper w,   *L. of Shalott* i 33
give me grace To help me of my w load.'   *Mariana in the S.* 30
With w sameness in the rhymes,   *Miller's D.* 70
Breathing like one that hath a w dream.   *Lotos-Eaters* 6
but evermore Most w seem'd the sea, w the oar, W the
wandering fields of barren foam.   " 41
Resting w limbs at last on beds of asphodel.   " C. S. 125
While my stiff spine can hold my w head,   *St. S. Stylites* 43
Twice ten long w w years to this,   " 90
since I heard him make reply Is many a w hour ;   *Talking Oak* 26
It may be my lord is w,   *Locksley Hall* 53
And wherefore did he go this w way,   *Enoch Arden* 296
But after scaling half the w down,   " 372
and beats out his w life.   " 730
Beating it in upon his w brain,   " 796
all about the fields you caught His w daylong chirping,   *The Brook* 53
Thro' w and yet ever wearier hours,   *Aylmer's Field* 828
For many w moons before we came,   *Princess* iii 319
Panted from w sides ' King, you are free ! '   " v 24
When ill and w, alone and cold,   *The Daisy* 96
And o'er a w sultry land,   *Will* 17
That it makes one w to hear.'   *The Islet* 29
With w steps I loiter on,   *In Mem. xxxviii* 1
She is w of dance and play.'   *Maud I xxii* 24
However w, a spark of will Not to be trampled out.   " II ii 56
That has been in a w world my one thing bright ;   " III vi 17
and thy good horse And thou are w ;   *Gareth and L.* 1265
My lord is w with the fight before,   *Geraint and E.* 133
Leave me to-night : I am w to the death.'   " 358
I am w of her.'   *Merlin and V.* 838
Now w of my service and devoir,   *Lancelot and E.* 118
but so w were his limbs, that he,   *Pelleas and E.* 513
at once The w steed of Pelleas floundering   " 574
The white light of the w moon above,   *Lover's Tale* i 640
But many w moons I lived alone—   *Sisters (E. and E.)* 12
Over all this w world of ours,   " ii 2
But at length we began to be w,   *V. of Maeldune* 91
O w was I of the travel,   " 129

Weary (adj.) *(continued)* There was the Scotsman *W*
 of war. *Batt. of Brunanburh* 36
 Old and *w*, But eager to follow, *Merlin and the G.* 100
 Good, I am never *w* painting you. *Romney's R.* 3
 O *w* one, has it begun ? *The Dreamer* 26
Weary (s) And the wicked cease from troubling, and
 the *w* are at rest. *May Queen, Con.* 60
 Let the *w* be comforted, *On Jub. Q. Victoria* 34
Weary (verb) Nor could I *w*, heart or limb, *In Mem. xxv* 9
 till the ear *Wearies* to hear it, *Lancelot and E.* 898
Wearying And *w* in a land of sand and thorns. *Holy Grail* 420
 Gone thy tender-natured mother, *w* to be left
 alone, *Locksley H., Sixty* 57
Weasel the thin *w* there Follows the mouse, *Aylmer's Field* 852
 nail me like a *w* on a grange For warning : *Princess ii* 205
 deems it carrion of some woodland thing, Or shrew,
 or *w*, *Gareth and L.* 749
Weather (adj.) huge sea-castles heaving upon the *w* bow. *The Revenge* 24
Weather (s) Careless both of wind and *w*, *Rosalind* 7
 All in the blue unclouded *w* *L. of Shalott iii* 19
 And it was windy *w*. (repeat) *The Goose* 4, 40
 There must be stormy *w* ; *Will Water.* 54
 His brothers of the *w* stood Stock-still „ 135
 Will bring fair *w* yet to all of us. *Enoch Arden* 191
 Passing with the *w*, *Window, Spring* 6
 water began to heave and the *w* to moan, *The Revenge* 113
 Nasty, casselty *w* ! *Church-warden, etc.* 2
Weather-beaten Denying not these *w-b* limbs *St. S. Stylites* 19
 His large gray eyes and *w-b* face *Enoch Arden* 70
Weathercock'd Whose blazing wyvern *w* the spire, *Aylmer's Field* 17
Weather'd many a rough sea had he *w* in her ! *Enoch Arden* 135
Weave THERE she *w's* by night and day *L. of Shalott ii* 1
 To *w* the mirror's magic sights, „ 29
 Than any wreath that man can *w* him. *Ode on Well.* 277
 With trembling fingers did we *w* *In Mem. xxx* 1
 And *w* their petty cells and die. „ *l* 12
 Again at Christmas did we *w* „ *lxxviii* 1
 She meant to *w* me a snare *Maud I vi* 25
Weaver *See* **Cloud-weaver**
Weaveth And so she *w* steadily, *L. of Shalott ii* 7
Weaving *w* over That various wilderness *Lover's Tale i* 418
Web A magic *w* with colours gay. *L. of Shalott ii* 2
 in her *w* she still delights To weave „ 28
 She left the *w*, she left the loom, „ *iii* 37
 Out flew the *w* and floated wide ; „ 42
 and takes the flood With swarthy *w's*. *M. d'Arthur* 269
 Who wove coarse *w's* to snare her purity, *Aylmer's Field* 780
 A *w* is wov'n across the sky ; *In Mem. iii* 6
 A cloth of roughest *w*, and cast it down, *Gareth and L.* 683
 Caught in a great old tyrant spider's *w*, *Merlin and V.* 259
 and takes the flood With swarthy *w's*. *Pass. of Arthur* 437
Wed young spirit present When first she is *w* ; *Ode to Memory* 74
 Came two young lovers lately *w* ; *L. of Shalott ii* 34
 And I was young—too young to *w* : *Miller's D.* 141
 nor *w* Raw Haste, half-sister to Delay. *Love thou thy land* 95
 he woo'd and *w* A labourer's daughter, *Dora* 39
 But take it—earnest *w* with sport, *Day-Dm., Ep.* 11
 They two will *w* the morrow morn : *Lady Clare* 7
 ' To-morrow he *w's* with me.' „ 16
 We two will *w* to-morrow morn, „ 87
 That she wore when she was *w*.' *L. of Burleigh* 96
 In the dress that she was *w* in, „ 99
 W whom thou wilt, but I am sick of Time, *Come not, when, etc.* 9
 It is long before you *w*. *Vision of Sin* 70
 So these were *w*, and merrily rang the bells,
 (repeat) *Enoch Arden* 80, 511
 To *w* the man so dear to all of them „ 484
 ' There is no reason why we should not *w*.' „ 508
 So you will *w* me, let it be at once.' „ 510
 Merrily rang the bells and they were *w* „ 512
 when the days drew nigh that I should *w*, *Princess i* 41
 certain, would not *w*. „ 50
 we purposed with ourself Never to *w*. „ *ii* 61
 I *w* with thee ! I bound by precontract „ *iv* 541
 Besides, the woman I is not as we, „ *v* 462

Wed *(continued)* She needs must *w* him for her own
 good name ; *Princess vii* 74
 On the day that follow'd the day she was *w*, *The Islet* 4
 Thought leapt out to *w* with Thought Ere Thought
 could *w* itself with Speech ; *In Mem. xxiii* 15
 But lives to *w* an equal mind ; „ *lxii* 8
 And talk of others that are *w*, „ *Con.* 98
 Enforced she was to *w* him in her tears, *Com. of Arthur* 204
 he needs Must *w* that other, whom no man desired, *Gareth and L.* 109
 break her will, and make her *w* with him : „ 617
 whom she trusts to overthrow, Then *w*, with glory :
 but she will not *w* Save whom she loveth, „ 621
 And live to *w* with her whom first you love : But
 ere you *w* with any, bring your bride, *Marr. of Geraint* 227
 when it *w's* with manhood, makes a man. *Geraint and E.* 868
 ' Had I chosen to *w*, I had been wedded earlier, *Lancelot and E.* 934
 W thou our Lady, and rule over us, *Holy Grail* 605
 but could I *w* her Loving the other ? *Sisters (E. and E.)* 167
 and *w's* me to my grave. *The Flight* 20
 not Love but Hate that *w's* a bride against her will ; „ 32
 W him ! I will not *w* him, „ 55
 when Hubert *w's* in you The heart of Love, *The Ring* 61
 So *w* thee with my soul, *Prog. of Spring* 92
 W to the melody, Sang thro' the world ; *Merlin and the G.* 97
Wedded (adj. and part.) *(See also* **New-wedded, Proxy-wedded***)*
 So that my vigour, *w* to thy blood, *Œnone* 161
 Dear is the memory of our *w* lives, *Lotos-Eaters, C. S.* 96
 Wherever Thought hath *w* Fact. *Love thou thy land* 52
 there Unclasp'd the *w* eagles of her belt, *Godiva* 43
 LUCILIA, *w* to Lucretius, found Her master cold ; *Lucretius* 1
 but she says (God help her) she was *w* to a fool ; *Princess iii* 83
 I had been *w* wife, I knew mankind, „ *vi* 327
 So Willy and I were *w* : I wore a lilac gown ; *Grandmother* 57
 Ay is the song of the *w* spheres, *Window, No Answer* 7
 Was *w* with a winsome wife, Ygerne : *Com. of Arthur* 188
 And there be *w* with all ceremony. *Marr. of Geraint* 608
 They twain were *w* with all ceremony. „ 839
 Seeing that ye are *w* to a man, *Geraint and E.* 425
 I had been *w* earlier, sweet Elaine : *Lancelot and E.* 935
 And one had *w* her, and he was dead, *Holy Grail* 586
 until himself had thought He loved her also, *w*
 easily, *Last Tournament* 402
 ' He has *w* her,' she said, Not said, but hiss'd it : „ 619
 but Lionel and the girl Were *w*, *Lover's Tale iv* 14
 ' get them *w* ' would he say. *Sisters (E. and E.)* 52
 Wealth with his wines and his *w* harlots ; *Vastness* 19
 ' I take thee Muriel for my *w* wife '— *The Ring* 377
Wedded (verb) and in one month They *w* her to sixty
 thousand pounds, *Edwin Morris* 126
 Who *w* with a nobleman from thence : *Princess i* 77
 who lay Among the ashes and *w* the King's son.' *Gareth and L.* 904
 Says that Sir Gareth *w* Lyonors, „ 1428
 Sir Valence *w* with an outland dame : *Merlin and V.* 714
 ' Queen, she would not be content Save that I *w*
 her, *Lancelot and E.* 1315
 More specially were he, she *w*, poor, „ 1321
 W her ? Fought in her father's battles ? *Last Tournament* 591
 And all this throve before I *w* thee, *Guinevere* 484
Wedged *W* themselves in between horse and horse, *Heavy Brigade* 22
Wedlock welded in one love Than pairs of *w* ; *Princess vi* 254
 The boy was born in *w*, *First Quarrel* 6
Weeäk (week) But 'e reäds wonn sarmin a *w*, *N. Farmer, O. S.* 28
 for thou'll be twenty to *w*. „ *N. S.* 7
Weed (dress) In words, like *w's*, I'll wrap me o'er, *In Mem. v* 9
 But stagnates in the *w's* of sloth : „ *xxvii* 11
 This silken rag, this beggar woman's *w* ; *Geraint and E.* 680
 And wears the leper's *w* ? *Happy* 10
Weed (plant) *(See also* **Willow-weed***)* creeping mosses and
 clambering *w's*, *Dying Swan* 36
 At least, not rotting like a *w*, *Two Voices* 162
 Crouch'd fawning in the *w*. *Œnone* 201
 A spacious garden full of flowering *w's*, *To* ——, *With Pal. of Art* 4
 Better to me the meanest *w* That blows *Amphion* 93
 Athwart the smoke of burning *w's*. *Princess vii* 358
 The people said, a *w*. *The Flower* 4

Weed (plant) (*continued*)   again the people Call it but

a w.	*The Flower* 24
Is dim, or will be dim, with w's :	*In Mem. lxxiii* 10
hurl'd it from him Among the forest w's,	*Balin and Balan* 542
' I once was looking for a magic w,	*Merlin and V.* 471
Foregoing all her sweetness, like a w.	*Holy Grail* 623
Half overtrailed with a wanton w,	*Lover's Tale i* 525

Weed (verb)   brace Of twins may w her of her folly. *Princess v* 464

As I will w this land before I go.	*Geraint and E.* 907
as now Men w the white horse on the Berkshire hills	,, 936

Weeded   W and worn the ancient thatch   *Mariana* 7

Weeding   Edyrn has done it, w all his heart   *Geraint and E.* 906

Weedy   the wind Still westward, and the w seas—   *Columbus* 72

Week (*See also* **Weeäk**)   whole w's and months, and early

and late,	*The Sisters* 10
For many w's about my loins I wore	*St. S. Stylites* 63
Enoch would hold possession for a w :	*Enoch Arden* 27
There yet were many w's before she sail'd,	,, 124
In that same w when Annie buried it,	,, 271
the w Before I parted with poor Edmund ;	*The Brook* 77
They lost their w's,	*Princess, Pro.* 162
harangue The fresh arrivals of the w before ;	,, ii 96
she had nursed me there from w to w :	,, vii 239
' Here's a leg for a babe of a w ! '	*Grandmother* 11
And the parson made it his text that w,	,, 29
Willy had not been down to the farm for a w and a day ;	,, 33
' A w hence, a w hence.'	*Window, When* 9
W after w : the days go by :	*In Mem. xvii* 7
He bears the burthen of the w's	,, lxxx 11
Last w came one to the county town,	*Maud I x* 37
He may stay for a year who has gone for a w :	,, xvi 6
But in the w's that follow'd,	*Gareth and L.* 526
And all that w was old Caerleon gay,	*Marr. of Geraint* 837
many w's a troop of carrion crows Hung	*Merlin and V.* 598
for many a w Hid from the wide world's rumour	*Lancelot and E.* 521
many among us many a w Fasted and pray'd	*Holy Grail* 131
once, A w beyond, while walking on the walls	*Pelleas and E.* 225
after this, a w beyond, again She call'd them,	,, 261
Queen abode For many a w, unknown,	*Guinevere* 147
days will grow to w's, the w's to months,	,, 624
adding, with a smile, The first for many w's—	*Lover's Tale iv* 281
' I ha' six w's' work, little wife,	*First Quarrel* 45
I ha' six w's' work in Jersey	,, 88
then two w's—no more—she join'd,	*Sisters (E. and E.)* 271
for ten long w's I tried Your table of Pythagoras,	*To E. Fitzgerald* 14
all but yours—A w betwixt—	*The Ring* 249
But after ten slow w's her fix'd intent,	,, 345
after a w—no more—A stranger as welcome	*Charity* 25

Weep (*See also* **Blubber'd**)   Prythee w, May Lilian ! (repeat) *Lilian* 19, 25

W on : beyond his object Love can last : His object

lives : more cause to w have I :	*Wan Sculptor* 5
For while the tender service made thee w,	*The Bridesmaid* 10
Who'll w for thy deficiency ?	*Two Voices* 39
Thou canst not think, but thou wilt w.	,, 51
Nay, nay, you must not w,	*May Queen, N. Y's. E.* 35
in the stream the long-leaved flowers w,	*Lotos-Eaters, C. S.* 10
I will not tell you not to w.	*To J. S.* 36
' W, weeping dulls the inward pain.'	,, 40
Let her will Be done—to w or not to w.	,, 44
The vapours w their burthen to the ground,	*Tithonus* 2
to the tears that thou wilt w.	*Locksley Hall* 82
at this The little wife would w for company,	*Enoch Arden* 34
Yes, as the dead we w for testify—	*Aylmer's Field* 747
Wiser to w a true occasion lost,	*Princess iv* 68
' She must w or she will die.'	,, vi 4
kiss her ; take her hand, she w's :	,, 225
For this, for all, we w our thanks to thee !	*Ode Inter. Exhib.* 9
I cannot w for Willy, nor can I w for the rest ;	*Grandmother* 67
For Willy I cannot w,	,, 72
I could not w—my own time seem'd so near.	,, 102
But how can I w for Willy,	*In Mem. xiii* 5
Which w a loss for ever new,	,, 9
Which w the comrade of my choice,	,, xviii 11
And come, whatever loves to w,	,, xx 6
And w the fulness from the mind :	

CC

Weep (*continued*)   At night she w's, ' How vain am I !

	In Mem. lx 15
So mayst thou watch me where I w,	,, lxiii 9
He loves her yet, she will not w,	,, xcvii 18
not as one that w's I come once more ;	,, cxix 2
Shall I w if a Poland fall ?	*Maud I iv* 46
Till I well could w for a time so sordid and mean,	,, v 17
And the white rose w's, ' She is late ; '	,, xxii 64
There to w, and w, and w My whole soul out	,, II iv 97
Yet now I could even w to think of it ;	,, v 86
a light shall darken, and many shall w	,, III vi 43
strong passion in her made her w	*Marr. of Geraint* 110
said to his own heart, ' She w's for me ' : (repeat)	*Geraint and E.* 587, 590
God's curse, it makes me mad to see you w.	,, 616
were I dead who is it would w for me ?	,, 618
she did not w, But o'er her meek eyes	,, 768
When sick at heart, when rather we should w.	*Balan and Balan* 498
If the wolf spare me, w my life away,	*Merlin and V.* 885
burst away To w and wail in secret	*Lancelot and E.* 1245
' Why w ye ? ' ' Lord,' she said,	*Last Tournament* 494
' Yet w not thou, lest, if thy mate return,	,, 499
Sing, and unbind my heart that I may w.'	*Guinevere* 166
' O pray you, noble lady, w no more ;	,, 184
they cannot w behind a cloud :	,, 207
And w for her who drew him to his doom.'	,, 348
What had *she* done to w ? Why should *she* w ?	*Lover's Tale i* 736
She told me all her love : she shall not w.	,, 742
When I beheld her w so ruefully ;	,, 773
I felt myself ready to w For I knew not what,	*The Wreck* 51
and there I began to w,	,, 93
For all that laugh, and all that w	*Ancient Sage* 187
let me w my fill once more, and cry myself to rest !	*The Flight* 6
Mother w's At that white funeral of the single life,	*To Prin. Beatrice* 8

Weepest   WAN Sculptor, w thou to take the cast *Wan Sculptor* 1

Weeping   And w then she made her moan, *Mariana in the S.* 93

And watch'd by w queens.	*Palace of Art* 108
white-eyed phantasms w tears of blood,	,, 239
' Weep, w dulls the inward pain.'	*To J. S.* 40
or fruits and cream Served in the w elm ;	*Gardener's D.* 195
w, ' I have loved thee long.'	*Locksley Hall* 30
Bitterly w I turn'd away : (repeat)	*Edward Gray* 6, 34
W, w late and early,	*L. of Burleigh* 89
and departed for him ;	*Enoch Arden* 246
Then Annie w answer'd ' I am bound.'	,, 451
later in the night Had come on Psyche w :	*Princess v* 50
With a nation w, and breaking on my rest ?	*Ode on Well.* 82
Within was w for thee :	*G. of Swainston* 2
And linger w on the marge,	*In Mem. xii* 12
To hear her w by his grave ?	,, xxxi 4
A mother w, and I hear her say,	*Com. of Arthur* 334
woman w, ' Nay, my lord, The field was pleasant	*Gareth and L.* 341
W for some gay knight in Arthur's hall.'	*Marr. of Geraint* 118
A woman w for her murder'd mate	*Geraint and E.* 522
suddenly she took To bitter w like a beaten child,	
A long, long w, not consolable.	*Merlin and V.* 855
one lone woman, w near a cross, Stay'd him.	*Last Tournament* 493
sat There in the holy house at Almesbury W,	*Guinevere* 3
There kiss'd, and parted w :	,, 125
she look'd and saw The novice, w,	,, 664
beheld the holy nuns All round her, w ;	,, 667
he was loud in w and in praise Of her,	*Lover's Tale ii* 87
He left us w in the woods ;	*The Flight* 37
and w scarce could see ;	*Happy* 54

Weigh   before the heavy clod W's on me, *Supp. Confessions* 185

lightly w's With thee unto thee	*Ode to Memory* 90
W heavy on my eyelids : let me die.	*Œnone* 244
flash the lightnings, w the Sun.	*Locksley Hall* 186
w Whether thou wilt not with thy damsel	*Gareth and L.* 880
w your sorrows with our lord the King's,	*Guinevere* 191

Weigh'd   Why are we w upon with heaviness, *Lotos-Eaters, C. S.* 12

heavy mist of tears, that w Upon my brain,	*Love and Duty* 43
But a trouble w upon her,	*L. of Burleigh* 77
why, the causes w, Fatherly fears—	*Princess v* 215
w the necks Of dragons clinging to the crazy walls,	*Holy Grail* 346
while I w thy heart with one Too wholly true	*Guinevere* 540
the effect w seas upon my head	*Lover's Tale i* 660

Weigh'd (continued) The whole land w him down as
Ætna does — *Lover's Tale iv* 17
—his loss W on him yet—   "   275
single piece W nigh four thousand Castillanos—so They
tell me—w him down into the abysm— *Columbus* 136
Weighest Thou w heavy on the heart within, *Œnone* 243
Weighing And w find them less ; *Guinevere* 192
Weight O happy earth, how canst thou bear my w ? *Œnone* 237
Make broad thy shoulders to receive my w, *M. d'Arthur* 164
will have w to drag thee down. *Locksley Hall* 48
This w and size, this heart and eyes, *Sir Galahad* 71
Is it the w of that half-crown, *Will Water.* 155
Appraised his w and fondled father-like, *Enoch Arden* 154
dead w of the dead leaf bore it down :   "   678
The w of all the hopes of half the world, *Princess iv* 184
Caryatids, lifted up A w of emblem,   "   202
their heavy hands, The w of destiny :   "   554
When the man wants w, the woman takes it up,   "   v 444
This nightmare w of gratitude,   "   vi 300
Then us they lifted up, dead w's,   "   338
Once the w and fate of Europe hung. *Ode on Well.* 240
these solid stars, this w of body and limb, *High. Pantheism* 5
A w of nerves without a mind, *In Mem. xii* 7
I loved the w I had to bear,   "   xxv 7
And falling with my w of cares   "   lv 14
Can hang no w upon my heart   "   lxiii 3
wearing all that w Of learning lightly   "   Con. 39
By a shuffled step, by a dead w trail'd, *Maud I i* 14
The lighter by the loss of his w ;   "   xvi 2
By the loss of that dead w,   "   xix 99
When w is added only grain by grain, *Marr. of Geraint* 526
Make broad thy shoulders to receive my w, *Pass. of Arthur* 332
The w as if of age upon my limbs, *Lover's Tale i* 125
her w Shrank in my grasp,   "   ii 202
commission one of w and worth To judge *Columbus* 124
w of war Rides on those ringing axles ! *Tiresias* 92
noise of falling w's that never fell, *The Ring* 410
Less w now for the ladder-of-heaven *By an Evolution.* 12
and the w that dragg'd at my hand ; *Bandit's Death* 39
Weighted cognizance on shield W it down, *Balin and Balan* 225
Weightier his mind Half buried in some w argument, *Lucretius* 9
Weird With a w bright eye, sweating and trembling, *Aylmer's Field* 585
Myself too had w seizures, Heaven knows what : *Princess i* 14
' what, if these w seizures come Upon you   "   82
strange seizure came Upon me, the w vision of our house :   "   iii 184
came On a sudden the w seizure and the doubt :   "   iv 560
And like a flash the w affection came :   "   v 477
Deeper than those w doubts could reach me,   "   vii 51
Were Arthur's wars in w devices done, *Gareth and L.* 225
past The w white gate, and paused without,   "   663
That w yell, Unearthlier than all shriek of bird *Balin and Balan* 544
Moreover, that w legend of his birth, *Last Tournament* 669
Then, ere that last w battle in the west, *Pass. of Arthur* 29
Like this last, dim, w battle of the west.   "   94
And therewithal came on him the w rhyme,   "   444
And something w and wild about it all : *Lover's Tale iv* 224
W Titan by thy winter weight of years *To Victor Hugo* 7
since The key to that w casket, which for thee *Ancient Sage* 254
then laugh'd ' the ring is w.' And w and worn and
wizard-like was he. ' Why w ? ' I ask'd him ; *The Ring* 195
W whispers, bells that rang without a hand,   "   411
Weirdly-sculptured And past beneath the w-s gates *Lancelot and E.* 844
Welcome (inter. and adj.) Should come most w, seeing men, *Œnone* 129
Each enter'd like a w guest. *Two Voices* 411
W, fellow-citizens, *Vision of Sin* 173
From Mizpeh's tower'd gate with w light, *D. of F. Women* 199
But she—you will be w—O, come in ! ' *The Brook* 228
lastly there At Christmas ; ever w at the Hall, *Aylmer's Field* 114
strangers at my hearth Not w, *Lucretius* 159
Which brings no more a w guest *In Mem. xxix* 5
And w Russian flower, a people's pride, *W. to Marie Alex.* 6
Cried to me climbing, ' W, Percivale ! *Holy Grail* 425
Cold, but as w as free airs of heaven *Sisters (E. and E.)* 197
W, w with one voice ! *Open. I. and C. Exhib.* 1
says to tha ' keeap 'em, an' w ' *Church-warden, etc.* 36

Welcome (inter. and adj.) (continued) A stranger as w as
Satan— *Charity* 26
Welcome (s) And sweet shall your w be : *Sea-Fairies* 31
A w mix'd with sighs. *Talking Oak* 212
Farewell, like endless w, lived and died. *Love and Duty* 68
with a frolic w took The thunder and the sunshine, *Ulysses* 47
To greet his hearty w heartily ; *Enoch Arden* 350
' We give you w : not without redound *Princess ii* 42
glowing full-faced w, she Began to address us,   "   183
Less w find among us, if you came Among us,   "   ii 354
W, farewell, and w for the year To follow :   "   Con. 95
O give him w, this is he Worthy *Ode on Well.* 92
all of us Danes in our w of thee, *W. to Alexandra* 4
We are each all Dane in our w of thee,   "   33
Yet one lay-hearth would give you w *To F. D. Maurice* 11
They should speak to me not without a w, *Hendecasyllabics* 11
Received and gave him w there ; *In Mem. lxxxv* 24
An iron w when they rise :   "   xc 8
means of goodly w, flesh and wine. *Marr. of Geraint* 387
Embraced her with all w as a friend,   "   834
In the mid-warmth of w and graspt hand, *Geraint and E.* 280
Sweet-voiced, a song of w, *Balin and Balan* 86
Witness their flowery w.   "   145
I bid the stranger w. *Merlin and V.* 270
roar An ocean-sounding w to one knight, *Last Tournament* 168
and loud leagues of man And w ! *To the Queen ii* 10
a light Of smiling w round her lips— *Lover's Tale iii* 46
and a noise of w at the doors— *Sisters (E. and E.)* 149
made the rhymes, That miss'd his living w, *Tiresias* 197
and flash'd into frolic of song And w ; *Demeter and P.* 13
where the loyal bells Clash w— *The Ring* 483
MANY, many w's, February fair-maid, (repeat) *Snowdrop* 1, 9
Welcome (verb) · W her, thunders of fort and of fleet !
W her, thundering cheer of the street ! W her,
all things youthful and sweet, *W. to Alexandra* 6
W her, w her, all that is ours !   "   13
Roar as the sea when he w's the land, And w her,
w the land's desire,   "   24
And all the gentle court will w me, *Lancelot and E.* 1060
Up leaps the lark, gone wild to w her, *Prog. of Spring* 14
Welcomed Not beat him back, but w him *Marr. of Geraint* 748
Welded Two women faster w in one love *Princess* 253
' Sons, be w each and all, *Open. I. and C. Exhib.* 36
Welfare How much their w is a passion to us. *Princess iii* 281
' A w in thine eye reproves Our fear *Holy Grail* 726
In your w we rejoice, *Open. I. and C. Exhib.* 7
Well (adj. and adv.) Nor would I now be w, mother, *May Queen, Con.* 19
A pretty face is w, and this is w, *Edwin Morris* 45
'Tis w ; 'tis something ; we may stand *In Mem. xviii* 1
O true and tried, so w and long,   "   Con. 1
O father ! O God ! was it w ?— *Maud I i* 6
Let all be w, be w.   "   xviii 85
He rested w content that all was w. *Geraint and E.* 952
Speak, Lancelot, thou art silent : is it w ? ' *Last Tournament* 107
Sir Lancelot answer'd, ' It is w :   "   108
Else, for the King has will'd it, it is w.'   "   111
King Turn'd to him saying, ' Is it then so w ?   "   114
Election, Election and Reprobation—it's all very w. *Rizpah* 73
but I be maäin glad to seeä tha sa 'arty an' w. *North. Cobbler* 2
an' I knaws, as knaws tha sa w,   "   65
And, Robby, I niver 'a liked tha sa w, *Spinster's S's.* 29
or I mowt 'a liked tha sa w,   "   42
is it w to wish you joy ? Is it w that while we
range with Science, *Locksley H., Sixty* 216
all's w that ends w, (repeat) *The Dreamer* 19, 23, 27, 32
Well (s) (See also **Castle-well, Dropping-wells**) As a Naiad in
a w, Looking at the set of day. *Adeline* 16
Come from the w's where he did lie. *Two Voices* 9
Fresh as the foam, new-bathed in Paphian w's, *Œnone* 175
rope that haled the buckets from the w, *St. S. Stylites* 64
Fairer than Rachel by the palmy w, *Aylmer's Field* 679
fawn Came flying while you sat beside the w ? *Princess ii* 271
Or by denial flush her babbling w's   "   v 334
Than if with thee the roaring w's *In Mem. x* 17
Or dive below the w's of Death ?   "   cviii 8

Went (*continued*)   as here and there that war *W*
 swaying ;   *Com. of Arthur* 107
Gawain *w*, and breaking into song Sprang out,   „   320
' How he *w* down,' said Gareth, ' as a false knight   *Gareth and L.* 5
Gareth *w*, and hovering round her chair   „   33
Before the wakeful mother heard him, *w*.   ‥   180
Then those who *w* with Gareth were amazed,   ‥   197
W sliding down so easily, and fell,   ‥   1224
a page Who came and *w*, and still reported   ‥   1338
O Prince, I *w* for Lancelot first,   ‥   1343
W sweating underneath a sack of corn,   *Marr. of Geraint* 263
And after *w* her way across the bridge,   „   383
lords and ladies of the high court *w*   „   662
W Yniol thro' the town,   „   693
Yniol with that hard message *w* ;   „   763
Then she *w* back some paces of return,   *Geraint and E.* 70
' Yea, my kind lord,' said the glad youth, and *w*, „   241
And told them of a chamber, and they *w* ;   „   261
and then *W* slipping down horrible precipices,   „   379
W Enid with her sullen follower on.   „   440
' Enough,' he said, ' I follow,' and they *w*.   „   816
But *w* apart with Edyrn, whom he held   „   881
blameless King *w* forth and cast his eyes   „   932
he arm'd himself and *w*,   *Balin and Balan* 22
So Balan warn'd, and *w* ; Balin remain'd :   „   153
Fixt in her will, and so the seasons *w*.   *Merlin and V.* 188
that old man *W* back to his old wild,   „   649
two fair babes, and *w* to distant lands ;   „   707
Sir Lancelot *w* ambassador, at first,   „   774
her hand half-clench'd *W* faltering sideways downward „   850
Her eyes and neck glittering *w* and came ;   „   960
King Glanced first at him, then her, and *w* his way. *Lancelot and E.* 95
That *if* I *w* and *if* I fought and won it   „   216
So all in wrath he got to horse and *w* ;   „   563
men *w* down before his spear at a touch,   „   578
So that he *w* sore wounded from the field :   „   600
and *w* To all the winds ? '   „   657
and carolling as he *w* A true-love ballad,   „   704
the simple maid *W* half the night repeating,   „   899
Lancelot, who coldly *w*, nor bad me one :   „   1057
Oar'd by the dumb, *w* upward with the flood—   „   1154
slowly *w* The marshall'd Order of their Table Round, „   1331
he *w*, And at the inrunning of a little brook   „   1387
when the dead *W* wandering o'er Moriah—   *Holy Grail* 50
King arose and *w* To smoke the scandalous hive   „   213
And up I *w* and touch'd him, and he, too,   „   418
That smote itself into the bread, and *w* ;   „   467
Then, when the day began to wane, we *w*.   ‥   488
all my heart *W* after her with longing :   „   583
And forth I *w*, and while I yearn'd and strove   „   785
To those who went the Holy Quest,   „   890
' Lead then,' she said ; and thro' the woods they *w*. *Pelleas and E.* 108
Glanced down upon her, turn'd and *w* her way.   „   185
they *w*, And Pelleas overthrew them one by one ;   ‥   229
w on, and found, Here too, all hush'd below   „   423
so *w* back, and seeing them yet in sleep   „   445
hill and wood *W* ever streaming by him   „   548
and shower and shorn plume *W* down it.   *Last Tournament* 156
New loves are sweet as those that *w* before ;   „   280
name *W* wandering somewhere darkling in his mind.   „   457
hence he *w* To-day for three days' hunting—   „   529
I sware, Being amazed : but this *w* by—   „   674
sharply smote his knees, and smiled, and *w* : *Guinevere* 47
grim faces came and *w* Before her,   „   70
W slipping back upon the golden days   ‥   380
W on in passionate utterance   „   611
and past his ear *W* shrilling, ' Hollow, hollow *Pass. of Arthur* 33
w Sir Bedevere the second time Across the ridge,   „   250
And lightly *w* the other to the King.   „   315
A woful man (for so the story *w*)   *Lover's Tale i* 379
those that *w* with me, And those that held   „   *iii* 15
The fancy stirr'd him so He rose and *w*,   „   *iv* 52
The light was but a flash, and *w* again.   „   55
but warming as he *w*, Glanced at the point of **law,** „ 275
And years *w* over till I that was little   *First Quarrel* 27

Went (*continued*)   Harry *w* over the Solent to see if work *First Quarrel* 44
an' he turn'd *his* face an' he *w*.   „   84
the boat *w* down that night— (repeat)   „   92
I kiss'd my boy in the prison, before he *w* out to die. *Rizpah* 23
she bethought herself and *w*   *The Revenge* 50
the sun *w* down, and the stars came out   „   56
the night *w* down, and the sun smiled   „   70
Revenge herself *w* down by the island crags   „   118
Far off we *w*. My God, I would not live   *Sisters (E. and E.)* 228
Not thaw ya *w* fur to raäke out Hell   *Village Wife* 76
es soon es they *w* awaäy, Fur, lawks ! 'ow I cried
 when they *w*,   „   110
So he *w*. And we past to this ward   *In the Child." Hosp.* 27
and we *w* to see to the child.   „   68
And round it *w* and, thro' it,   *V. of Maeldune* 19
W to his own in his own West-Saxon-land, *Batt. of Brunanburh* 103
And the storm *w* roaring above us,   *The Wreck* 106
the storm and the days *w* by, but I knew no more—   „   111
stars *w* down across the gleaming pane,   *The Flight* 13
How slowly down the rocks he *w*,   „   38
w in search of thee Thro' many a palace,   *Demeter and P.* 54
I fetcht 'im a kick an' 'e *w*.   *Owd Roä* 62
I came, I *w*, was happier day by day ;   *The Ring* 348
I parted from her, and I *w* alone.   „   437
Voice of the Earth *w* wailingly past   *The Dreamer* 3
Ralph *w* down like a fire to the fight   *The Tourney* 3

Wept   She *w*, ' I am aweary, aweary,   *Mariana* 83
One willow over the river *w*,   *Dying Swan* 14
Crocodiles *w* tears for thee ;   *A Dirge* 22
Love *w* and spread his sheeny vans for flight ; *Love and Death* 8
A matter to be *w* with tears of blood !   *Poland* 14
Thine eyes so *w* that they could hardly see ; *The Bridesmaid* 2
I *w* ' Tho' I should die, I know   *Two Voices* 58
To perish, *w* for, honour'd, known,   „   149
In her still place the morning *w* :   „   275
and took the King, and *w*.   *M. d'Arthur* 206
She bow'd down And *w* in secret ;   *Dora* 108
But I believe she *w*.   *Talking Oak* 164
To-day I sat for an hour and *w*,   *Edward Gray* 11
' Bitterly *w* I over the stone :   „   33
' A ship of fools,' he sneer'd and *w*.   *The Voyage* 78
But turn'd her own toward the wall and *w*. *Enoch Arden* 283
Annie could have *w* for pity of him ;   „   467
but presently *W* like a storm :   *Aylmer's Field* 403
While thus he spoke, his hearers *w* ;   „   722
her that o'er her wounded hunter *w*   *Lucretius* 89
blood Was sprinkled on your kirtle, and you *w*. *Princess ii* 274
That was fawn's blood, not brother's, yet you *w*. „ 275
' My fault ! ' she *w* ' my fault !   „   *iii* 30
She *w* her true eyes blind for such a one,   „   *iv* 134
Yet she neither moved nor *w*.   „   *vi* 12
Down thro' her limbs a drooping languor *w* :   „   268
I could have *w* with the best. (repeat) *Grandmother* 20, 100
I had not *w*, little Annie, not since I had been a wife ;
 But I *w* like a child that day,   „   63
But I *w* like a child for the child that was dead „ 68
Thou comest, much *w* for :   *In Mem. xvii* 1
And silence follow'd, and we *w*.   „   *xxx* 20
They *w* and wail'd, but led the way   „ *ciii* 18
W over her, carved in stone :   *Maud I viii* 4
And while she *w*, and I strove to be cool,   „   *II i* 15
And *w*, and wish'd that I were dead ;   *Com. of Arthur* 345
all her dress *W* from her sides as water *Gareth and L.* 217
Lady Lyonors wrung her hands and *w*,   „   1395
' was it for him she *w* In Devon ? '   *Geraint and E.* 397
and she *w* beside the way.   „   519
Then he remember'd her, and how she *w* ;   „   612
braid Slipt and uncoil'd itself, she *w* afresh, *Merlin and V.* 889
and for her fault she *w* Of petulancy   „   952
W, looking often from his face who read   *Lancelot and E.* 1285
The knights and ladies *w*, and rich and poor *W*, *Holy Grail* 353
But wail'd and *w*, and hated mine own self,   „   609
To one most holy saint, who *w* and said,   „   781
he would have *w*, but felt his eyes Harder *Pelleas and E.* 506
when first she came, *w* the sad **Queen.** *Guinevere* 182

Wept (*continued*) her heart was loosed Within her, and she *w*   *Guinevere* 668
and took the King, and *w*.   *Pass. of Arthur* 374
when I *w*, Her smile lit up the rainbow on my tears,   *Lover's Tale i* 253
' He casts me out,' she *w*, ' and goes '   „ *iv* 103
Edith spoke no word, She *w* no tear,   *Sisters (E. and E.)* 216
Who *w* with me when I return'd in chains,   *Columbus* 231
She knelt—' We worship him '—all but *w*—   *Dead Prophet* 29
but I *w* alone, and sigh'd In the winter   *Happy* 69
The spear of ice has *w* itself away,   *Prog. of Spring* 6
In silence *w* upon the flowerless earth.   *Death of Œnone* 9
he sobb'd and he *w*, And cursed himself ;   *Bandit's Death* 29
I *w*, and I kiss'd her hands,   *Charity* 38
Wesh (wash)   to *my* pond to *w* thessens theere—   *Churchwarden, etc.* 14
Wesh'd (washed)   Sally she *w* foälks' cloäths   *North. Cobbler* 29
An' the babby's faäce wurn't *w*   „ 42
Tommy's faäce be as fresh as a codlin *w* i' the dew.   „ 110
Fur they *w* their sins i' *my* pond,   *Church-warden, etc.* 16
West (adj.)   Four courts I made, East, *W* and South and
North,   *Palace of Art* 21
wet *w* wind and the world will go on. (repeat) *Window, No Answer* 6, 12
Wet *w* wind how you blow, you blow !   „ 14
wet *w* wind and the world may go on.   „ 18
why, you shiver tho' the wind is *w*   *The Ring* 29
West (s)   (*See also* **South-west**)   sunset linger'd low adown
In the red *W* :   *Lotos-Eaters* 20
Across a hazy glimmer of the *w*,   *Gardener's D.* 219
Orion sloping slowly to the *W*.   *Locksley Hall* 8
The blaze upon the waters to the *w* ;   *Enoch Arden* 596
Here in the woman-markets of the *w*,   *Aylmer's Field* 348
Till all the sails were darken'd in the *w*,   *Sea Dreams* 39
Nor stunted squaws of *W* or East,   *Princess ii* 78
Silver sails all out of the *w*   „ *iii* 14
and half Far-shadowing from the *w*,   „ *Con.* 42
and a feast Of wonder, out of *W* and East,   *Ode Inter. Exhib.* 21
So now thy fuller life is in the *w*,   *W. to Marie Alex.* 36
voices go To North, South, East, and *W* ;   *Voice and the P.* 14
Flown to the east or the *w*,   *Window, Gone* 7
And topples round the dreary *w*,   *In Mem. xv* 19
By that broad water of the *w*,   „ *lxvii* 3
And East and *W*, without a breath,   „ *xcv* 62
Rosy is the *W*, Rosy is the South, (repeat)   *Maud I xvii* 5, 25
Blush it thro' the *W* ; (repeat)   „ 16, 24
Blush from *W* to East, Blush from East to *W*, Till
the *W* is East,   „ 21
Orion's grave low down in the *w*,   „ *III vi* 8
Will there be dawn in *W* and eve in East ?   *Gareth and L.* 712
All in a rose-red from the *w*,   „ 1087
he saw Fired from the *w*, far on a hill,   *Lancelot and E.* 168
The flower of all the *w* and all the world,   „ 249
knights of utmost North and *W*,   „ 526
And also one to the *w*, and counter to it, And blank :   *Holy Grail* 254
Rode Tristram toward Lyonnesse and the *w*.   *Last Tournament* 362
Far on into the rich heart of the *w* :   *Guinevere* 244
Far down to that great battle in the *w*,   „ 571
ere that last weird battle in the *w*,   *Pass. of Arthur* 29
I hear the steps of Modred in the *w*,   „ 59
' Far other is this battle in the *w* Whereto we move,   „ 66
this last, dim, weird battle of the *w*.   „ 94
forego The darkness of that battle in the *W*,   *To the Queen ii* 65
Mixt with the gorgeous *w* the lighthouse shone,   *Lover's Tale i* 60
Framing the mighty landscape to the *w*,   „ 406
All the *w* And ev'n unto the middle south   „ 414
Ran amber toward the *w*, and nigh the sea   „ 432
Far from out the *w* in shadowing showers,   *Sisters (E. and E.)* 7
made *W* East, and sail'd the Dragon's mouth,   *Columbus* 25
a door for scoundrel scum I open'd to the *W*,   „ 171
till the labourless day dipt under the *W* ;   *V. of Maeldune* 86
we watch'd the sun fade from us thro' the *W*.   *The Flight* 41
And see the ships from out the *W*   „ 91
And behind him, low in the *W*,   *Dead Prophet* 20
Here silent in our Minster of the *W*   *Epit. on Stratford* 3
That young eagle of the *W*   *Open. I. and C. Exhib.* 28
The golden keys of East and *W*.   *To Marq. of Dufferin* 4
she lent The sceptres of her *W*, her East,   „ 6
hoary deeps that belt the changeful *W*,   *Prog. of Spring* 98

West (s) (*continued*)   drowsed in gloom, self-darken'd
from the *w*,   *Death of Œnone* 76
' Is earth On fire to the *W* ?   *St. Telemachus* 19
shape with wings Came sweeping by him, and pointed
to the *W*,   „ 25
Western   day Was sloping toward his *w* bower.   *Mariana* 80
baths Of all the *w* stars, until I die.   *Ulysses* 61
Wind of the *w* sea, (repeat)   *Princess iii* 2, 4
West-Indian   lands at home and abroad in a rich *W-I* isle ;   *The Wreck* 46
West Indies   *See* **Indies**
West-Saxon-land   Went to his own in his own
W-S-l,   *Batt. of Brunanburh* 103
West-Saxons   We the *W-S*,   „ 37
Westward   gloomy-gladed hollow slowly sink To *w*—   *Gareth and L.* 798
For on their march to *w*, Bedivere,   *Pass. of Arthur* 6
and the wind Still *w*, and the weedy seas—   *Columbus* 72
There *w*—under yon slow-falling star,   *Akbar's Dream* 152
Westward-smiling   far-rolling, *w-s* seas,   *Last Tournament* 587
Westward-wheeling   sphere Of *w-w* stars ;   *St. Telemachus* 32
Westward-winding   From the *w-w* flood,   *Margaret* 9
Wet (adj.)   (*See also* **Spongy-wet**)   Thro' crofts and pastures
w with dew   *Two Voices* 14
Eyes with idle tears are *w*.   *Miller's D.* 211
I am *w* With drenching dews,   *St. S. Stylites* 114
Who sweep the crossings, *w* or dry,   *Will Water.* 47
so that falling prone he dug His fingers into the *w*
earth,   *Enoch Arden* 780
Made *w* the crafty crowsfoot round his eye ;   *Sea Dreams* 187
my Sire, his rough cheek *w* with tears,   *Princess v* 23
The leaves were *w* with women's tears :   „ *vi* 39
I saw his eyes all *w*, in the sweet moonshine :   *Grandmother* 49
w west wind and the world will go on.
(repeat)   *Window, No Answer* 6, 12
W west wind how you blow, you blow !   „ 14
w west wind and the world may go on.   „ 18
often I caught her with eyes all *w*,   *Maud I xix* 23
Thick with *w* woods, and many a beast therein,   *Com. of Arthur* 21
came a forester of Dean, *W* from the woods,   *Marr. of Geraint* 149
Made answer, either eyelid *w* with tears :   *Merlin and V.* 379
Brake with a *w* wind blowing, Lancelot,   *Last Tournament* 137
W with the mists and smitten by the lights,   *Guinevere* 597
he was all *w* thro' to the skin,   *First Quarrel* 76
hand of the Highlander *w* with their tears !   *Def. of Lucknow* 102
These *w* black passes and foam-churning chasms—   *Sir J. Oldcastle* 9
dhry eye thin but was *w* for the frinds that was gone !   *Tomorrow* 83
Wet (s)   The wind and the *w*, the wind and the *w* !   *Window, No Answer* 13
Woods where we hid from the *w*,   „ *Marr. Morn.* 6
day Went glooming down in *w* and weariness :   *Last Tournament* 215
An' I never said 'off wi' the *w*,'   *First Quarrel* 77
I soaking here in winter *w*—   *To Ulysses* 6
Wether   Or some black *w* of St. Satan's fold.   *Merlin and V.* 750
Wet-shod   Came *w-s* alder from the wave,   *Amphion* 41
Wharf   Out upon the *w*'s they came,   *L. of Shalott iv* 42
red roofs about a narrow *w* In cluster ;   *Enoch Arden* 3
Down to the pool and narrow *w* he went,   „ 690
famishing populace, *wharves* forlorn ;   *Vastness* 14
Whate (wheat)   ' Goin' to cut the Sassenach *w* '   *Tomorrow* 14
' niver crasst over say to the Sassenach *w* ;   „ 48
betther nor cuttin' the Sassenach *w* '   „ 94
What's my thought   *w m t* and *when* and *where*
and *how*,   *Princess, Pro.* 190
Whatsoever   For *w* knight against us came   *Balin and Balan* 35
Wheat   (*See also* **Whate, Wheät**)   Storing yearly little
dues of *w*, and wine and oil ;   *Lotos-Eaters, C. S.* 122
I will set him in my uncle's eye Among the *w* ;   *Dora* 68
and went her way Across the *w*,   „ 72
And waves of shadow went over the *w*,   *Poet's Song* 4
Half-lost in belts of hop and breadths of *w* ;   *Princess, Con.* 45
Upon the thousand waves of *w*,   *In Mem. xci* 11
and go By summer belts of *w* and vine   „ *xcviii* 4
Thou that singest *w* and woodland,   *To Virgil* 9
torpid mummy *w* Of Egypt bore a grain as sweet   *To Prof. Jebb* 5
Rain-rotten died the *w*, the barley-spears   *Demeter and P.* 112
Wheät   sa much es a poppy along wi' the *w*,   *Spinster's S's.* 78
if the Staäte was a gawin' to let in furriners' *w*,   *Owd Roä* 45

Wheat-suburb   sweet-smelling lanes Of his *w-s*,   *The Brook* 123
Wheedle   And *w* a world that loves him not,   *Maud II v* 39
Wheedling   *W* and siding with them !   *Princess v* 158
Wheel (s)   (*See also* **Mill-wheel**)   The dark round of the
   dripping *w*,   *Miller's D.* 102
all the *w's* of Time Spun round in station,   *Love and Duty* 75
And thee returning on thy silver *w's*.   *Tithonus* 76
men, that in the flying of a *w* Cry down the past,   *Godiva* 6
power to turn This *w* within my head,   *Will Water.* 84
land, where under the same *w* The same old rut   *Aylmer's Field* 33
That stays the rolling Ixionian *w*,   *Lucretius* 261
The common hate with the revolving *w*   *Princess vi* 173
And he call'd ' Left *w* into line ! '   *Heavy Brigade* 6
Loom and *w* and enginery,   *Ode Inter. Exhib.* 15
I stay'd the *w's* at Cogoletto,   *The Daisy* 23
I see the sailor at the *w*.   *In Mem. x* 4
And all the *w's* of Being slow.   ” *l* 4
And every kiss of toothed *w's*,   ” *cxvii* 11
The last *w* echoes away.   *Maud I xxii* 26
And the roaring of the *w's*.   ” *II iv* 22
And the *w's* go over my head,   ” *v* 4
song that Enid sang was one Of Fortune and her *w*,   *Marr. of Geraint* 346
' Turn, Fortune, turn thy *w* and lower the proud ;   ” 347
Turn thy wild *w* thro' sunshine, storm, and cloud ;   ” 348
Thy *w* and thee we neither love nor hate. (repeat)   ” 349, 358
' Turn, Fortune, turn thy *w* with smile or frown ;   ” 350
With that wild *w* we go not up or down ;   ” 351
' Turn, turn thy *w* above the staring crowd ;   ” 356
Thy *w* and thou are shadows in the cloud ;   ” 357
I heard *W's*, and a noise of welcome at the
   doors—   *Sisters* (E. and E.) 149
And lay thine uphill shoulder to the *w*,   *Ancient Sage* 279
a shatter'd *w* ? a vicious boy !   *Locksley H., Sixty* 215
and see no more The Stone, the *W*,   *Demeter and P.* 150
Or spinning at your *w* beside the vine—   *Romney's R.* 5
WE move, the *w* must always move,   *Politics* 1
Wheel (verb)   Too long you roam and *w* at will ;   *Rosalind* 36
And *w's* the circled dance,   *In Mem. xcviii* 30
Unto the thundersong that *w's* the spheres,   *Lover's Tale i* 476
That *w* between the poles.   *Epilogue* 21
round her forehead *w's* the woodland dove,   *Prog. of Spring* 57
Wheel'd   (*See also* **Low-wheel'd**)   clutch'd the sword, And
   strongly *w* and threw it.   *M. d'Arthur* 136
Earth follows *w* in her ellipse ;   *Golden Year* 24
Sometimes the sparhawk, *w* along,   *Sir L. and Q. G.* 12
Bear had *w* Thro' a great arc his seven slow suns.   *Princess iv* 212
bats *w*, and owls whoop'd,   *Con.* 110
w on Europe-shadowing wings,   *Ode on Well.* 120
w or lit the filmy shapes That haunt the dusk,   *In Mem. xcv* 10
W round on either heel, Dagonet replied,   *Last Tournament* 244
w and broke Flying, and, link'd again, and *w* and broke
   Flying,   *Guinevere* 257
clutch'd the sword, And strongly *w* and threw it.   *Pass. of Arthur* 304
planet at length will be *w* thro' the silence of space,   *Despair* 83
and they *w* and obey'd.   *Heavy Brigade* 6
Wheeling   (*See also* **Westward-wheeling**)   with both hands
   I flung him, *w* him,   *M. d'Arthur* 157
w round The central wish,   *Gardener's D.* 224
The myriad shriek of *w* ocean-fowl,   *Enoch Arden* 583
W with precipitate paces To the melody,   *Vision of Sin* 37
eddied into suns, that *w* cast The planets :   *Princess ii* 118
with both hands I flung him, *w* him,   *Pass. of Arthur* 325
Glance at the *w* Orb of change,   *To E. Fitzgerald* 3
Whelm   or to *w* All of them in one massacre ?   *Lucretius* 206
And *w* all this beneath as vast a mound   *Merlin and V.* 656
Whelm'd   Roll'd a sea-haze and *w* the world in gray ;   *Enoch Arden* 672
some were in with missiles of the wall,   *Princess, Pro.* 45
Whelp   (*See also* **Lion-whelp**)   bones for his o'ergrown
   w to crack ;   *Maud II v* 55
Whelpless   glaring with his *w* eye, Silent ;   *Princess vi* 99
When and where and how   *what's my thought* and *when* and
   where and *how*,   ” *Pro.* 190
Whens   Break into ' Thens ' and ' *W* '   *Ancient Sage* 104
Wherewithal   having *w*, And in the fallow leisure of my
   life   *Audley Court* 76

Wherewithal (*continued*)   for the *w* To give his babes a
   better bringing-up   *Enoch Arden* 298
Whiff   yonder, *w* ! there comes a sudden heat,   *Princess, Con.* 58
Whig   Let *W* and Tory stir their blood ;   *Will Water.* 53
While   we might make it worth his *w*.   *Princess i* 184
'Twere hardly worth my *w* to choose   *In Mem. xxxiv* 10
Bide ye here the *w*.'   *Merlin and V.* 97
Pelleas in brief *w* Caught his unbroken limbs   *Pelleas and E.* 584
Whim   hurt to death, For your wild *w*;   *Princess iv* 243
Whimper   Who love her still, and *w*,   *Romney's R.* 117
Whimpering   then A *w* of the spirit of the child,   *Last Tournament* 138
Whine (s)   colt-like whinny and with hoggish *w*   *St. S. Stylites* 177
Whine (verb)   I that heard her *w* And snivel,   *Last Tournament* 449
Whined   ghost, that shook The curtains, *w* in lobbies,   *Walk. to the Mail* 31
canker'd boughs without *W* in the wood ;   *Balin and Balan* 346
and old boughs, *W* in the wood.   ” 386
Whinny   colt-like *w* and with hoggish whine   *St. S. Stylites* 177
her *w* shrills From tile to scullery,   *Princess v* 452
and stoop'd With a low *w* toward the pair :   *Geraint and E.* 756
Whinnying   At which her palfrey *w* lifted heel,   ” 533
thence The shrilly *w's* of the team of Hell,   *Demeter and P.* 44
Whip   Stopt, and then with a riding *w*   *Maud I xiii* 18
Struck at her with his *w*, (repeat)   *Marr. of Geraint* 201, 413
Struck at him with his *w*, and cut his cheek.   ” 207
Up hill ' Too-slow ' will need the *w*,   *Politics* 11
Whipt   And *w* me into the waste fields far away ;   *Holy Grail* 788
I *w* him for robbing an orchard once   *Rizpah* 25
Whirl (s)   Ran into its giddiest *w* of sound,   *Vision of Sin* 29
sway and *w* Of the storm dropt to windless calm,   *Lover's Tale ii* 206
Whirl (verb)   My judgment, and my spirit *w's*,   *Supp. Confessions* 137
There the river eddy *w's*,   *L. of Shalott ii* 15
I *w* like leaves in roaring wind.   *Fatima* 7
while Saturn *w's*, his stedfast shade   *Palace of Art* 15
W's her to me : but will she fling herself,   *Lucretius* 202
And *w* the ungarner'd sheaf afar,   *In Mem lxxii* 23
w the dust of harlots round and round   *Pelleas and E.* 470
watch the chariot *w* About the goal again,   *Tiresias* 176
I *w*, and I follow the Sun.'   *The Dreamer* 14
W, and follow the Sun ! (repeat)   ” 20, 24, 28, 32
Whirl'd   No sword Of wrath her right arm *w*,   *The Poet* 54
heavy-plunging foam, *W* by the wind,   *D. of F. Women* 119
flashing round and round, and *w* in an arch,   *M. d'Arthur* 138
w her white robe like a blossom'd branch   *Princess iv* 179
She *w* them on to me, as who should say   ” 396
like the smoke in a hurricane *w*   *Boädicea* 59
The last red leaf is *w* away,   *In Mem. xv* 2
and *w* About empyreal heights of thought,   ” *xcv* 37
heart of the poet is *w* into folly and vice.   *Maud I iv* 39
Pine Lost footing, fell, and so was *w* away.   *Gareth and L.* 4
flashing round and round, and *w* in an arch,   *Pass. of Arthur* 306
we *w* giddily ; the wind Sung   *Lover's Tale ii* 201
An open landaulet *W* by, which,   *Sisters* (E. and E.) 86
W for a million æons thro' the vast Waste dawn   *De Prof., Two G.* 3
full-maned horses *w* The chariots backward,   *Achilles over the T.* 24
Whirligig   As on this *w* of Time We circle   *Will Water.* 63
Whirling   All their planets *w* round them,   *Locksley H., Sixty* 204
Yet in the *w* dances as we went,   *The form, the form* 5
Flash in the pools of *w* Simois.   *Œnone* 206
part were drown'd within the *w* brook :   *Princess, Pro.* 47
w rout Led by those two rush'd into dance,   *Lover's Tale iii* 54
phantom of the *w* landaulet For ever past me by :   *Sisters* (E. and E.) 114
W their sabres in circles of light !   *Heavy Brigade* 34
Whirlwind   the echoing dance Of reboant *w's*,   *Supp. Confessions* 97
And loud the Norland *w's* blow,   *Oriana* 6
And a *w* clear'd the larder :   *The Goose* 52
Across the *w's* heart of peace,   *The Voyage* 87
And bring her in a *w* :   *Princess i* 65
Like the leaf in a roaring *w*,   *Boädicea* 59
A moment, ere the onward *w* shatter it,   *Lover's Tale i* 451
round and round A *w* caught and bore us ;   ” *ii* 197
a *w* blow these woods, as never blew before.   *The Flight* 12
Whirr   See **Dorhawk-whirr**
Whirring   And the *w* sail goes round, (repeat)   *The Owl i* 4, 5
Whishper (**whisper**) (**s**)   laste little *w* was sweet as the
   lilt of a bird !   *Tomorrow* 33

Whishper (verb)   the crathur, an' *w*, an' say   *Tomorrow* 54
Whisker   his watery smile And educated *w*.   *Edwin Morris* 129
   Ay, roob thy *w's* ageàn ma,   *Spinster's S's.* 81
Whisky   *See* **Crathur'**
Whisper (s)   (*See also* **Love-whispers, Whishper, World-whisper**)   She has heard a *w* say,   *L. of Shalott* ii 3
   A little *w* silver-clear,   *Two Voices* 428
   A hint, a *w* breathing low,   ,, 434
   Such seem'd the *w* at my side :   ,, 439
   In *w's*, like the *w's* of the leaves   *Gardener's D.* 253
   And her *w* throng'd my pulses   *Locksley Hall* 36
   w of the south-wind rushing warm,   ,, 125
   a *w* on her ear, She knew not what ;   *Enoch Arden* 515
   w of huge trees that branch'd And blossom'd   ,, 585
   Again in deeper inward *w's* ' lost ! '   ,, 716
   A *w* half reveal'd her to herself.   *Aylmer's Field* 144
   But honçying at the *w* of a lord ;   *Princess, Pro.* 115
   shook the songs, the *w's*, and the shrieks   ,, i 98
   o'er the imperial tent *W's* of war.   ,, v 10
   Would lisp in honey'd *w's* of this monstrous fraud !   *Third of Feb.* 36
   and my prayer Was as the *w* of an air   *In Mem. xvii* 3
   And shape the *w* of the throne ;   ,, *lxiv* 12
   In *w's* of the beauteous world.   ,, *lxxix* 12
   This haunting *w* makes me faint,   ,, *lxxxi* 7
   And lightly does the *w* fall ;   ,, *lxxxv* 89
   world's loud *w* breaking into storm,   *Marr. of Geraint* 27
   all hearts Applauded, and the spiteful *w* died :   *Geraint and E.* 958
   Breathed in a dismal *w* ' It is truth.'   *Balin and Balan* 527
   He spoke in words part heard, in *w's* part,   *Merlin and V.* 839
   whose lightest *w* moved him more   *Pelleas and E.* 155
   A murmuring *w* thro' the nunnery ran,   *Guinevere* 410
   Save for some *w* of the seething seas,   *Pass. of Arthur* 121
   Falling in *w* on the sense,   *Lover's Tale* i 720
   the surge fell From thunder into *w's* ;   ,, iii 31
   Surely, but for a *w*, ' Go not yet,'   ,, iv 20
   He knew the meaning of the *w* now,   ,, 43
   But his friend Replied, in half a *w*,   ,, 336
   Not to break in on what I say by word Or *w*,   ,, 353
   There was a *w* among us, but only a *w*   *Def. of Lucknow* 50
   thro' the roar of the breaker a *w*,   *Despair* 13
   A breath, a *w*—some divine farewell—   *Ancient Sage* 225
   Weird *w's*, bells that rang without a hand,   *The Ring* 411
   A *w* from his dawn of life ?   *Far—far—away* 10
   And at his ear he heard a *w* ' Rome '   *St. Telemachus* 26

Whisper (verb)   (*See also* **Whishper**)   all day long you sit between Joy and woe, and *w* each.   *Margaret* 64
   And at my headstone what a *w* low,   *My life is full* 24
   Listening, *w's* ' 'Tis the fairy Lady of Shalott.'   *L. of Shalott* i 35
   While those full chestnuts *w* by.   *Miller's D.* 168
   The trees began to *w*, and the wind began to roll,   *May Queen, Con.* 27
   Not *w*, any murmur of complaint.   *St. S. Stylites* 22
   O *w* to your glass, and say,   *Day-Dm., Ep.* 3
   And *w* lovely words, and use Her influence   *Will Water.* 11
   In her ear he *w's* gaily,   *L. of Burleigh* 1
   Heard the good mother softly *w*   *Aylmer's Field* 187
   W in odorous heights of even.   *Milton* 16
   What *w's* from thy lying lip ?   *In Mem. iii* 4
   ' The stars,' she *w's*, ' blindly run ;   ,, 5
   And hear thy laurel *w* sweet   ,, *xxxvii* 7
   A hundred spirits *w* ' Peace.'   ,, *lxxxvi* 16
   One *w's*, ' Here thy boyhood sung   ,, *cii* 9
   And *w's* to the worlds of space,   ,, *cxxvi* 11
   We *w*, and hint, and chuckle,   *Maud* I iv 29
   And the lily *w's*, ' I wait.'   ,, *xxii* 66
   Sweet lord, ye do right well to *w* this.   *Balin and Balan* 529
   Edith pray'd me not to *w* of it.   *Sisters (E. and E.)* 207
   She *w's*, ' From the South I bring you balm,   *Prog. of Spring* 66
   I hear a death-bed Angel *w* ' Hope.'   *Romney's R.* 148

Whisper'd (adj. and part.)   (*See also* **Half-whisper'd**) To hear each other's *w* speech ;   *Lotos-Eaters, C. S.* 59
   and they suffer—some, 'tis *w*—down in hell   ,, 123
   Thou shalt hear the ' Never, never,' *w* by the phantom years,   *Locksley Hall* 83
   And *w* voices at his ear.   *Day-Dm., Arrival* 24
   A *w* jest to some one near him, ' Look,   *Princess* v 32

Whisper'd (adj. and part.) (*continued*)   By a shuffled step, by a dead weight trail'd, by a *w* fright,   *Maud* I i 14
   Love drew in her breath In that close kiss, and drunk her *w* tales.   *Lover's Tale* i 817
Whisper (verb)   She *w*, with a stifled moan what he *w* under Heaven None else could understand ;   *Mariana in the S.* 57
   W, ' Listen to my despair :   *Talking Oak* 21
   Cyril *w* ; ' Take me with you too.'   *Edward Gray* 22
   no livelier than the dame That *w* ' Asses' ears,'   *Princess* i 81
   ' Come,' he *w* to her ' Lift up your head,   ,, ii 113
   What *w* from her lying lips ?   ,, v 63
   ' The fault was mine,' he *w*, ' fly ! '   *In Mem. xxxix* 10
   For I never *w* a private affair   *Maud* II i 30
   Lifted an arm, and softly *w*, ' There.'   ,, v 47
   sat, heard, watch'd And *w* : thro' the peaceful court she crept And *w* :   *Gareth and L.* 1361
   Or *w* in the corner ? do ye know it ? '   *Merlin and V.* 139
   half-awake he *w*, ' Where ? O where ?   ,, 772
   For all that ample woodland *w* ' debt,'   *Pelleas and E.* 41
   Who *w* me ' your Ulric loves '—   *The Ring* 170
   Master *w* ' Follow the Gleam.'   *Happy* 62
   I *w* ' give it to me,' but he would not   *Merlin and the G.* 33
       Bandit's Death 27
Whisperer   and the swarm Of female *w's* :   *Princess* vi 356
Whispering   within the cave Behind yon *w* tuft of oldest pine,   *Œnone* 88
   beneath a *w* rain Night slid down one long stream   *Gardener's D.* 266
   Or low morass and *w* reed,   *In Mem. c* 6
   these few lanes of elm And *w* oak.   *To Mary Boyle* 68
   W to each other half in fear,   *Sea-Fairies* 5
   Two lovers *w* by an orchard wall ;   *Circumstance* 4
   W I knew not what of wild and sweet,   *Tithonus* 61
   or, *w*, play'd A chequer-work of beam   *In Mem. lxxii* 14
   turn'd to each other, *w*, all dismay'd,   *Heavy Brigade* 44
Whistle (s)   Scarce answer to my *w* ;   *Amphion* 68
   And bustling *w* of the youth   *Marr. of Geraint* 257
   great plover's human *w* amazed Her heart,   *Geraint and E.* 49
Whistle (verb)   *W* back the parrot's call,   *Locksley Hall* 171
   Then would he *w* rapid as any lark,   *Gareth and L.* 505
   But if my neighbour *w* answers him—   *Lover's Tale* iv 161
Whistled   waterflags, That *w* stiff and dry about the marge.   *M. d'Arthur* 64
   redcap *w* ; and the nightingale Sang loud,   *Gardener's D.* 95
   Then low and sweet I *w* thrice ;   *Edwin Morris* 113
   Sometimes the throstle *w* strong :   *Sir L. and Q. G.* 11
   flour From his tall mill that *w* on the waste.   *Enoch Arden* 343
   And *w* to the morning star.   *Sailor Boy* 4
   And while he *w* long and loud   ,, 5
   Prison'd, and kept and coax'd and *w* to—   *Gareth and L.* 14
   He *w* his good warhorse left to graze   *Last Tournament* 490
   waterflags, That *w* stiff and dry about the marge.   *Pass. of Arthur* 232
Whistling   *W* a random bar of Bonny Doon,   *The Brook* 82
   But blessed forms in *w* storms   *Sir Galahad* 59
   Half *w* and half singing a coarse song,   *Geraint and E.* 528
Whit   Not a *w* of thy tuwhoo,   *The Owl* ii 10
   And *w*, *w*, *w*, in the bush beside me   *Grandmother* 40
   and never a *w* more wise The fourth,   *Gareth and L.* 635
White (adj.)   *See also* **Cold-white, Death-white, Dusty-white, Lily-white, May-white, Milk-white, Milky-white, Rosy-white, Snow-white, Vermeil-white, Winter-white**)
   And *w* against the cold-white sky,   *Dying Swan* 12
   One after another the *w* clouds are fleeting ;   *All Things will Die* 9
   In the *w* curtain, to and fro,   *Mariana* 51
   The *w* owl in the belfry sits. (repeat)   *The Owl* i 7, 14
   Flinging the gloom of yesternight On the *w* day ;   *Ode to Memory* 10
   A pillar of *w* light upon the wall Of purple cliffs,   ,, 53
   thick with *w* bells the clover-hill swells   *Sea-Fairies* 14
   The *w* chalk-quarry from the hill   *Miller's D.* 115
   The lanes, you know, were *w* with may,   ,, 130
   I'd touch her neck so warm and *w*.   ,, 174
   All barr'd with long *w* cloud the scornful crags,   *Palace of Art* 83
   her hair Wound with *w* roses, slept St. Cecily ;   ,, 99
   seas draw backward from the land Their moon-led waters *w*.   ,, 252
   Till Charles's Wain came out above the tall *w* chimney-tops.   *May Queen, N. Y's. E.* 12

White (adj.) (*continued*) Two handfuls of *w* dust, shut
  in an urn of brass !   *Lotos- Eaters, C. S.* 68
W surf wind-scatter'd over sails and masts,   *D. of F. Women* 31
' I would the *w* cold heavy-plunging foam,   ,, 118
' The light *w* cloud swam over us.   ,, 221
We saw the large *w* stars rise one by one,   ,, 223
With that sharp sound the *w* dawn's creeping beams, ,, 261
She caught the *w* goose by the leg,   *The Goose* 9
more the *w* goose laid It clack'd and cackled louder. ,, 23
Clothed in *w* samite, mystic, wonderful,
  (repeat)   *M. d'Arthur* 31, 144, 159
for all his face was *w* And colourless,   ,, 212
Love's *w* star Beam'd thro' the thicken'd cedar *Gardener's D.* 165
As clean and *w* as privet when it flowers. *Walk. to the Mail* 56
The meed of saints, the *w* robe and the palm. *St. S. Stylites* 20
I lived In the *w* convent down the valley there, ,, 62
As these *w* robes are soil'd and dark, *St. Agnes' Eve* 13
In raiment *w* and clean.   ,, 24
or following up And flying the *w* breaker. *Enoch Arden* 21
Enoch's *w* horse, and Enoch's ocean-spoil ,, 93
And York's *w* rose as red as Lancaster's, *Aylmer's Field* 51
Nor ever falls the least *w* star of snow, *Lucretius* 107
Morn in the *w* wake of the morning star *Princess iii* 17
saw The soft *w* vapour streak the crowned towers ,, 344
There whirl'd her *w* robe like a blossom'd branch ,, *iv* 179
Her round *w* shoulder shaken with her sobs, ,, 289
Here he reach'd *W* hands of farewell to my sire, ,, *v* 233
very nape of her *w* neck Was rosed with indignation : ,, *vi* 343
' Now sleeps the crimson petal, now the *w* ; ,, *vii* 176
Nor wilt thou snare him in the *w* ravine, ,, 205
A red sail, or a *w* ; and far beyond, *Con.* 47
Ruddy and *w*, and strong on his legs, he looks like a
  man.   *Grandmother* 2
We loved that hall, tho' *w* and cold, *The Daisy* 37
ALL along the valley, stream that flashest *w*, *V. of Cauteretz* 1
With blasts that blow the poplar *w*, *In Mem. lxxii* 3
The *w* kine glimmer'd, and the trees (repeat) ,, *xcv* 15, 51
Has a broad-blown comeliness, red and *w*, *Maud I xiii* 9
if a hand, as *w* As ocean-foam in the moon, ,, *xiv* 17
The *w* lake-blossom fell into the lake. ,, *xxii* 47
And the *w* rose weeps, ' She is late ; ' ,, 64
It lightly winds and steals In a cold *w* robe before me, ,, *II iv* 19
Wearing the *w* flower of a blameless life, *Ded. of Idylls* 25
Clothed in *w* samite, mystic, wonderful. *Com. of Arthur* 285
' Blow trumpet, for the world is *w* with May ; ,, 482
reverence thine own beard That looks as *w* as utter
  truth,   *Gareth and L.* 281
Our one *w* lie sits like a little ghost ,, 297
plant that feels itself Root-bitten by *w* lichen, ,, 454
past The weird *w* gate, and paused without, ,, 663
With *w* breast-bone, and barren ribs of Death, ,, 1382
often with her own *w* hands Array'd and deck'd
  her,   *Marr. of Geraint* 16
W from the mason's hand, (repeat) ,, 244, 408
Then, as the *w* and glittering star of morn ,, 734
And *w* sails flying on the yellow sea ; ,, 829
Betwixt the cressy islets *w* in flower ; *Geraint and E.* 475
she Kiss'd the *w* star upon his noble front, ,, 757
Men weed the *w* horse on the Berkshire hills ,, 936
and paced The long *w* walk of lilies toward the
  bower.   *Balin and Balan* 249
as makes The *w* swan-mother, sitting, ,, 353
and dim thro' leaves Blinkt the *w* morn, ,, 385
And mumbled that *w* hand whose ring'd caress ,, 512
whose lightest word Is mere *w* truth in simple
  nakedness,   ,, 518
O Heaven's own *w* Earth-angel, *Merlin and V.* 80
As clean as blood of babes, as *w* as milk : ,, 344
Ran down the silken thread to kiss each other On her
  w neck—   ,, 456
A maid so smooth, so *w*, so wonderful, ,, 566
Is thy *w* blamelessness accounted blame ! ' ,, 799
bare-grinning skeleton of death ! *W* was her cheek ; ,, 848
Rang by the *w* mouth of the violent Glem ; *Lancelot and E.* 288
When the strong neighings of the wild *w* Horse ,, 298

White (adj.) (*continued*) In the *w* rock a chapel and
  a hall On massive columns, *Lancelot and E.* 405
And innocently extending her *w* arms, ,, 932
Till all the *w* walls of my cell were dyed *Holy Grail* 119
ever moved Among us in *w* armour, Galahad. ,, 135
dyed The strong *W* Horse in his own heathen blood— ,, 312
Not to be bound, save by *w* bonds and warm, *Pelleas and E.* 353
up a slope of garden, all Of roses and red, ,, 422
in her *w* arms Received, and after loved it
  tenderly,   *Last Tournament* 23
down a streetway hung with folds of pure *W* samite, ,, 141
Isolt the *w*—Sir Tristram of the Woods— ,, 177
Our one *w* day of Innocence hath past, ,, 218
The twelve small damosels *w* as Innocence, ,, 291
one of those *w* slips Handed her cup and piped, ,, 295
' Isolt Of the *w* hands ' they call'd her : ,, 398
Who served him well with those *w* hands of hers, ,, 400
Is all as cool and *w* as any flower.' ,, 416
there Belted his body with her *w* embrace, ,, 513
Calling me thy *w* hind, and saying to me ,, 569
The warm *w* apple of her throat, ,, 717
The *w* mist, like a face-cloth to the face, *Guinevere* 7
And in the light the *w* mermaiden swam, ,, 245
aghast the maiden rose, *W* as her veil, ,, 363
who leagues With Lords of the *W* Horse, heathen, ,, 574
when the man was no more than a voice In the *w*
  winter of his age,   *Pass. of Arthur* 4
Clothed in *w* samite, mystic, wonderful, (repeat) ,, 199, 312, 327
for all his face was *w* And colourless, ,, 380
W as *w* clouds, floated from sky to sky. *Lover's Tale i* 5
Or when the *w* heats of the blinding noons ,, 139
A mystic light flash'd ev'n from her *w* robe ,, 370
then came in The *w* light of the weary moon above, ,, 640
But the boy was born i' trouble, an' looks so wan an'
  so *w* :   *First Quarrel* 2
I niver ha seed it sa *w* wi' the Maäy es I see'd it
  to-year—   *Village Wife* 80
Fur I thowt it wur Charlie's ghoäst i' the derk, fur
  it looökt sa *w*.   ,, 82
Blessing the wholesome *w* faces of Havelock's good
  fusileers,   *Def. of Lucknow* 101
And a hundred ranged on the rock like *w* sea-birds *V. of Maeldune* 101
And his *w* hair sank to his heels and his *w* beard
  fell to his feet,   ,, 118
NOT here ! the *w* North has thy bones ; *Sir J. Franklin* 1
The broad *w* brow of the Isle— *The Wreck* 135
the hills are *w* with rime. *The Flight* 4
all my life was darken'd, as I saw the *w* sail run, ,, 39
an' her hair was as *w* as the snow an a grave. *Tomorrow* 60
All in *w* Italian marble, looking still as if she
  smiled,   *Locksley H., Sixty* 35
Mother weeps At that *w* funeral of the single life, *Prin. Beatrice* 9
dwell For nine *w* moons of each whole year with me, *Demeter and P.* 121
Of a Christmas Eäve, an' as cowd as this, an' the midders
  as *w*,   *Owd Roä* 31
Flies back in fragrant breezes to display A tunic *w* as
  May !   *Prog. of Spring* 65
And find the *w* heather wherever you go, *Romney's R.* 108
my *w* heather only blooms in heaven ,, 110
And on this *w* midwinter day— *To Master of B.* 9
But when the *w* fog vanish'd like a ghost *Death of Œnone* 67
And now that I am *w*, and you are gray, *Roses on the T.* 4
White (s) (*See also* **May-white**) Lying, robed in
  snowy *w*   *L. of Shalott iv* 19
He thought I was a ghost, mother, for I was all
  in *w*,   *May Queen* 17
Gown'd in pure *w*, that fitted to the shape— *Gardener's D.* 126
Which charts us all in its coarse blacks or *w*'s, *Walk. to the Mail* 107
With folded feet, in stoles of *w*, *Sir Galahad* 43
No pint of *w* or red Had ever half the power *Will Water.* 82
Six hundred maidens clad in purest *w*, *Princess ii* 472
But pure as lines of green that streak the *w* ,, *v* 196
Of twelve sweet hours that past in bridal *w*, *Maud I xviii* 6
King That morn was married, while in stainless *w*, *Com. of Arthur* 456
Muriel and Miriam, each in *w*, and like May-blossoms *The Ring* 254

White (s) (*continued*)   And watch the curl'd *w* of
  the coming wave | *Merlin and V.* 292
and she herself in *w* All but her face, | *Lancelot and E.* 1158
where the crisping *w* Play'd ever back upon the
  sloping wave, | *Holy Grail* 381
Where children sat in *w* with cups of gold, | *Last Tournament* 142
all the purple slopes of mountain flowers Pass
  under *w*, | ,, 230
So dame and damsel cast the simple *w*, | ,, 232
Wear black and *w*, and be a nun like you, | *Guinevere* 677
in front of which Six stately virgins, all in *w*, | *Lover's Tale* i 77
Leapt lightly clad in bridal *w*— | ,, iii 44
might be borne in *w* To burial or to burning, | *Ancient Sage* 207
Molly Magee, wid the red o' the rose an' the *w* o'
  the May, | *Tomorrow* 31
All his virtues—I forgive them—black in *w* above
  his bones. | *Locksley H., Sixty* 44
White-breasted *w-b* like a star Fronting the dawn | *Œnone* 57
Whited *W* thought and cleanly life As the priest, | *Vision of Sin* 116
White-eyed *w-e* phantasms weeping tears of blood, | *Palace of Art* 239
White-faced The *w-f* halls, the glancing rills, | *In Mem., Con.* 113
White-favour'd And those *w-f* horses wait ; | ,, 90
White-flower'd saw The *w-f* elder-thicket from the field | *Godiva* 63
Black holly, and *w-f* wayfaring-tree ! | *Sir J. Oldcastle* 130
White-hair'd A *w-h* shadow roaming like a dream | *Tithonus* 8
White-headed I this old *w-h* dreamer stoopt | *Locksley H., Sixty* 38
White-hooved Leading a jet-black goat white-horn'd, *w-h*, | *Œnone* 51
White-horn'd Leading a jet-black goat *w-h*, white-hooved, | ,, 51
White-listed tree that shone *w-l* thro' the gloom. | *Merlin and V.* 939
Whiten Willows *w*, aspens quiver, | *L. of Shalott* i 10
The ptarmigan that *w's* ere his hour | *Last Tournament* 697
Whiten'd (adj. and part.) Part black, part *w* with the
  bones of men, | *Holy Grail* 500
The meal-sacks on the *w* floor, | *Miller's D.* 101
Whiten'd (verb) And *w* all the rolling flood ; | *The Victim* 20
When the lake *w* and the pinewood roar'd, | *Merlin and V.* 637
Whiteness all but utter *w* held for sin, | *Holy Grail* 84
Whitening Down thro' the *w* hazels made a plunge | *Enoch Arden* 379
after the great waters break *W* for half a league, | *Last Tournament* 465
A rhyme that flower'd betwixt the *w* sloe | *To Mary Boyle* 25
Whiter Is *w* even than her pretty hand : | *Aylmer's Field* 363
The flocks are *w* down the vale, | *In Mem. cxv* 10
To meet and greet a *w* sun ; | ,, *Con.* 78
And *w* than the mist that all day long | *Pass. of Arthur* 137
White-robed *W-r* in honour of the stainless child, | *Last Tournament* 147
White Rose *W R*, Bellerophon, the Jilt, | *The Brook* 161
Whitest With *w* honey in fairy gardens cull'd— | *Eleänore* 26
The very *w* lamb in all my fold Loves you : | *Aylmer's Field* 361
A broad earth-sweeping pall of *w* lawn, | *Lover's Tale* ii 78
White-tail'd Left for the *w-t* eagle to tear it | *Batt. of Brunanburh* 107
White-wing'd let the fair *w-w* peacemaker fly | *Ode Inter. Exhib.* 34
Whither Arthur had vanish'd I knew not *w*, | *Merlin and the G.* 78
Whitsuntide Arthur on the *W* before Held court | *Marr. of Geraint* 145
And this was on the last year's *W*. | ,, 840
Whizz'd An arrow *w* to the right, one to the left, | *Balin and Balan* 419
Whoäts (oats) *W* or tonups or taätes— | *Village Wife* 26
Whole (adj.) (*See also* '*Ole*) Oft lose *w* years of darker
  mind. | *Two Voices* 372
So healthy, sound, and clear and *w*, | *Miller's D.* 15
With one long kiss my *w* soul thro' My lips, | *Fatima* 20
My *w* soul waiting silently, | ,, 36
W weeks and months, and early and late, | *The Sisters* 10
And blessings on his *w* life long, | *May Queen, Con.* 14
But now the *w* ROUND TABLE is dissolved | *M. d'Arthur* 234
I, that day, Saw her no more, | *Gardener's D.* 163
But this *w* hour your eyes have been intent | ,, 269
but I die here To-day, and *w* years long, a life
  of death. | *St. S. Stylites* 54
If it may be, fast *W* Lents, and pray. | ,, 182
I trust That I am *w*, and clean, and meet for Heaven. | ,, 213
This *w* wide earth of light and shade, | *Will Water.* 67
At times the *w* sea burn'd, at times | *The Voyage* 51
To waste his *w* heart in one kiss Upon her perfect
  lips. | *Sir L. and Q. G.* 44
our pride Looks only for a moment *w* and sound ; | *Aylmer's Field* 2

Whole (adj.) (*continued*) for fear This *w* foundation ruin, | *Princess* ii 341
sphered *W* in ourselves and owed to none. | ,, iv 148
unless you send us back Our son, on the instant, *w*.' | ,, 416
but half Without you ; with you, *w* ; | ,, 461
My mother, looks as *w* as some serene | ,, v 193
and slips in sensual mire, But *w* and one : | ,, v 200
Then felt it sound and *w* from head to foot, | ,, vi 211
she You talk'd with, *w* nights long, up in the tower, | ,, 255
nor seem'd it strange that soon He rose up *w*, | ,, vii 65
nor yet Did those twin brothers, risen again and *w* ; | ,, 89
And keeps our Britain, *w* within herself, | ,, *Con.* 52
I wish they were a *w* Atlantic broad.' | ,, 71
W in himself, a common good, | *Ode on Well.* 26
keep our noble England *w*, | ,, 161
And love will last as pure and *w* | *In Mem. xliii* 13
That so my pleasure may be *w* ; | ,, *lxxi* 8
To which the *w* creation moves. | ,, *Con.* 144
Has our *w* earth gone nearer to the glow | *Maud* I xviii 78
Strike dead the *w* weak race of venomous worms, | ,, II i 46
and weep My *w* soul out to thee. | ,, iv 98
W, like a crag that tumbles from the cliff, | *Marr. of Geraint* 318
To save her dear lord *w* from any wound. | *Geraint and E.* 45
And men brought in *w* hogs and quarter beeves, | ,, 602
Then, when Geraint was *w* again, | ,, 945
The *w* wood-world is one full peal of praise. | *Balin and Balan* 450
Polluting, and imputing her *w* self, | *Merlin and V.* 803
the one passionate love Of her *w* life ; | ,, 956
' Sir King, mine ancient wound is hardly *w*, | *Lancelot and E.* 93
Right fain were I to learn this knight were *w*, | ,, 772
Whereof he should be quickly *w*, | ,, 853
But when Sir Lancelot's deadly hurt was *w*, | ,, 904
Yet still thy life is *w*, and still I live Who love
  thee ; | *Pass. of Arthur* 150
But now the *w* Round Table is dissolved | ,, 402
For so the *w* round earth is every way | ,, 422
single glance of them Will govern a *w* life from
  birth to death, | *Lover's Tale* i 76
At thought of which my *w* soul languishes | ,, 267
The *w* land weigh'd him down as Ætna does The Giant
  of Mythology : | ,, iv 17
Ship after ship, the *w* night long, (repeat) | *The Revenge* 58, 59, 60
And the *w* sea plunged and fell on the shot-
  shatter'd navy of Spain, | ,, 117
So mock'd, so spurn'd, so baited two *w* days— | *Sir J. Oldcastle* 163
And the *w* isle-side flashing down from the peak | *V. of Maeldune* 45
For the *w* isle shudder'd and shook like a man | ,, 74
Out of His *w* World-self and all in all— | *De Prof., Two G.* 49
For he touch'd on the *w* sad planet of man, | *Dead Prophet* 39
dwell For nine white moons of each *w* year with me, | *Demeter and P.* 121
When thou shalt dwell the *w* bright year with me, | ,, 139
National hatreds of *w* generations, | *Vastness* 25
Whole (s) All various, each a perfect *w* From living
  Nature, | *Palace of Art* 58
Is bodied forth the second *w*. | *Love thou thy land* 66
That each, who seems a separate *w*, | *In Mem. xlvii* 1
The wish, that of the living *w* | ,, lv 1
Boundless inward, in the atom, boundless
  outward, in the *W*. | *Locksley H., Sixty* 212
be welded each and all, Into one imperial *w*, | *Open. I. and C. Exhib.* 37
Wholeness He that in his Catholic *w* | *Locksley H., Sixty* 101
Wholesale You need not set your thoughts in rubric
  thus For *w* comment.' | *Princess* iii 51
Wholesome You changed a *w* heart to gall. | *L. C. V. de Vere* 44
eat *w* food, And wear warm clothes, | *St. S. Stylites* 108
That mock'd the *w* human heart, | *The Letters* 10
But honest talk and *w* wine, | *To F. D. Maurice* 18
But better serves a *w* law, | *In Mem. xlviii* 10
glanced Eyes of pure women, *w* stars of love ; | *Gareth and L.* 314
None ; or the *w* boon of gyve and gag.' | ,, 370
But now the *w* music of the wood | *Balin and Balan* 436
until the *w* flower And poisonous grew together, | *Holy Grail* 775
Such as the *w* mothers tell their boys. | *Pelleas and E.* 197
whom The *w* realm is purged of otherwhere, | *Last Tournament* 96
O ay—the *w* madness of an hour— | ,, 675
Boughs on each side, laden with *w* shade, | *Lover's Tale* i 230

CC*

Wild (adj.) (*continued*)   Drove it in *w* disarray,   *Heavy Brigade* 60
w mob's million feet Will kick you from your place,   *The Fleet* 18
Yea, for some *w* hope was mine That,   *The Ring* 135
Up leaps the lark, gone *w* to welcome her,   *Prog. of Spring* 14
I am *w* again!   The coals of fire you heap   *Romney's R.* 140
starved the *w* beast that was linkt with thee   *By an Evolution.* 11
In some fifth Act what this *w* Drama means.   *The Play* 4
Yes, my little Poet.   *The Throstle* 4
w heather round me and over me June's high blue,   *June Bracken, etc.* 2
these Are like *w* brutes new-caged—   *Akbar's Dream* 50
w horse, anger, plunged To fling me,   „ 118
And yet so *w* and wayward that my dream—   „ 172
Wild (s)   flight from out your bookless *w's*   *Princess ii* 56
'Peace, you young savage of the Northern *w*!   „ *iii* 247
thro' those dark gates across the *w* That no man knows.   „ *vii* 362
The King was hunting in the *w*;   *The Victim* 30
The King return'd from out the *w*,   „ 41
Till from the garden and the *w*   *In Mem. ci* 17
My yet young life in the *w's* of Time,   *Maud I xvi* 21
then he cried again, 'To the *w's*!'   *Geraint and E.* 28
a meadow gemlike chased In the brown *w*,   „ 199
Who lived alone in a great *w* on grass;   *Merlin and V.* 621
that old man Went back to his old *w*,   „ 649
But he by *w* and way, for half the night,   *Pelleas and E.* 497
doth all that haunts the waste and *w* Mourn,   *Pass. of Arthur* 48
Wildbeast (*See also* **Wild**)   felt the blind *w* of force,   *Princess v* 266
Wild-bird (*See also* **Wild**)   From the groves within The *w-b's* din.   *Poet's Mind* 21
Nor bruised the *w's* egg.   *Lover's Tale ii* 21
Wilder   And some are *w* comrades,   *Pref. Son. 19th Cent.* 12
Wilderness   As manna on my *w*,   *Supp. Confessions* 114
And Fancy watches in the *w*,   *Caress'd or chidden* 12
I murmur under moon and stars In brambly *w'es*   *The Brook* 179
That *w* of single instances,   *Aylmer's Field* 437
The *w* shall blossom as the rose.   „ 649
Hide, hide them, million-myrtled *w*,   *Lucretius* 204
And vines, and blowing bosks of *w*,   *Princess i* 111
wolf and wolfkin, from the *w*, wallow in it,   *Boädicea* 15
w, full of wolves, where he used to lie;   *Maud II v* 54
And so there grew great tracts of *w*,   *Com. of Arthur* 10
'I will forth into the *w*;   *Marr. of Geraint* 127
And *w'es*, perilous paths, they rode: *Geraint and E.* 32
Here in the heart of waste and *w*.   „ 313
What go ye into the *w* to see?'   *Holy Grail* 287
weaving over That various *w* a tissue of light   *Lover's Tale i* 419
But God is with me in this *w*,   *Sir J. Oldcastle* 8
Over a *w* Gliding,   *Merlin and the G.* 36
then A hiss as from a *w* of snakes,   *St. Telemachus* 66
Wildest   Their *w* wailings never out of tune   *Sea Dreams* 231
maybe *w* dreams Are but the needful preludes   *Princess, Con.* 73
Something other than the *w* modern guess   *Locksley H., Sixty* 232
Wild-eyed (adj.)   My bright-eyed, *w-e* falcon,   *Rosalind* 6
Fast, fast, my *w-e* Rosalind.   „ 44
Wildfire   Be dazzled by the *w* Love   *Princess v* 441
Wild-flower (adj.)   I had lived a *w-f* life,   *The Wreck* 37
Wild-flower (s) (*See also* **Wild**)   Plucking the harmless *w-f* on the hill?—   *Maud II i* 3
Yet trod I not the *w* in my path,   *Lover's Tale ii* 20
Wild-goose   'Thou art but a *w-g* to question it.'   *Gareth and L.* 36
Wilding   And like a crag was gay with *w* flowers: *Marr. of Geraint* 319
Wildness   His *w*, and the chances of the dark.'   *Princess iv* 244
Wild-swan (*See also* **Wild**)   made the *w-s* pause in her cloud,   *Poet's Song* 7
leader *w* in among the stars Would clang it,   *Princess iv* 434
Wildweed-flower   The *w-f* that simply blows?   *Day-Dm., Moral* 6
Wild-wide   found the world, Staring *w-w*;   *Balin and Balan* 596
Wild Will   *W W*, Black Bess, Tantivy,   *The Brook* 160
Wild-wood (*See also* **Wild**)   sweeter still The *w-w* hyacinth   *Balin and Balan* 271
Wile   *w* the length from languorous hours,   *Princess vii* 63
Wilful   To make her thrice as *w* as before.'   *Lancelot and E.* 206
'Father, you call me *w*, and the fault Is yours   „ 750
Being so very *w* you must go.' (repeat)   „ 777, 781
'Being so very *w* you must die.'   „ 783
A rosebud set with little *w* thorns,   *Princess, Pro.* 154
Wiliest   of her court The *w* and the worst;   *Guinevere* 29
Will (s)   *Broad-based upon her people's w*,   *To the Queen* 35

Will (s) (*continued*)   My Lord, if so it be Thy *w*.'   *Supp. Confessions* 106
The marvel of the everlasting *w*,   *The Poet* 7
Chasing itself at its own wild *w*,   *Dying Swan* 17
Then let wise Nature work her *w*,   *My life is full* 21
'Sick art thou—a divided *w* Still heaping   *Two Voices* 106
full-grown *w*, Circled thro' all experiences,   *Œnone* 165
and yet His *w* be done!   *May Queen, Con.* 10
yet it chafes me that I could not bend One *w*;   *D. of F. Women* 138
That I subdued me to my father's *w*;   „ 234
Let her *w* Be done—to weep   *To J. S.* 43
With one wide *W* that closes thine.   *On a Mourner* 20
power in his eye That bow'd the *w*.   *M. d'Arthur* 123
Now Dora felt her uncle's *w* in all,   *Dora* 5
My home is none of yours.   My *w* is law.'   „ 45
more from ignorance than *w*   *Walk. to the Mail* 110
knowing all Life needs for life is possible to *w*—   *Love and Duty* 86
strong in *w* To strive, to seek, to find,   *Ulysses* 69
thy strong Hours indignant work'd their *w's*,   *Tithonus* 18
his eyes, before they had their *w*,   *Godiva* 69
A virgin heart in work and *w*.   *Sir Galahad* 24
Against her father's and mother's *w*:   *Edward Gray* 10
Used all her fiery *w*, and smote Her life   *Will Water.* 111
Annie fought against his *w*:   *Enoch Arden* 158
So grieving held his *w*, and bore it thro'.   „ 167
Set her sad *w* no less to chime with his,   „ 248
Prayer from a living source within the *w*,   „ 801
His vast and filthy hands upon my *w*,   *Lucretius* 220
Dash them anew together at her *w*   „ 247
laid about them at their *w's* and died;   *Princess, Pro.* 31
But then she had a *w*; was he to blame?   „ *i* 48
O that iron *w*, That axelike edge unturnable,   „ *ii* 202
nor pretty babes To be dandled, no, but living *w's*,   „ *iv* 147
'sdeath! against my father's *w*.'   „ *v* 298
yet her *w* Bred *w* in me to overcome it or fall.   „ 350
since my *w* Seal'd not the bond—   „ 398
Her iron *w* was broken in her mind;   „ *vi* 117
you the Victor of your *w*.   „ 167
Purpose in purpose, *w* in *w*,   „ *vii* 305
Make and break, and work their *w*;   *Ode on Well.* 261
Whose *w* is lord thro' all this world-domain—   *W. to Marie Alex.* 2
But I wish'd it had been God's *w* that I,   *Grandmother* 73
O **well** for him whose *w* is strong!   *Will* 1
Corrupts the strength of heaven-descended *W*,   „ 11
Thither at their *w* they haled   *Boädicea* 55
Our *w's* are ours, we know not how;   *In Mem, Pro.* 15
Our *w's* are ours, to make them thine.   „ 16
My *w* is bondsman to the dark;   „ *iv* 2
With morning wakes the *w*, and cries,   „ 15
That I could wing my *w* with might   „ *xli* 10
To riper growth the mind and *w*:   „ *xlii* 8
To pangs of nature, sins of *w*,   „ *liv* 3
Till all at once beyond the *w*   „ *lxx* 13
The sense of human *w* demands   „ *lxxxv* 39
vague desire That spurs an imitative *w*.   „ *cx* 20
O living *w* that shalt endure   „ *cxxxi* 1
whose gentle *w* has changed my fate,   *Maud I xviii* 23
For shall not Maud have her *w*?   „ *xix* 84
(If I read her sweet *w* right)   „ *xxi* 10
Void of the little living *w*   „ *II ii* 14
However weary, a spark of *w* Not to be trampled out.   „ 56
cannot will my *w*, nor work my work Wholly,   *Com. of Arthur* 88
And reigning with one *w* in everything   „ 92
thou dost His *w*, The Maker's,   *Gareth and L.* 10
A knight of Arthur, working out his *w*,   „ 24
Found her son's *w* unwaveringly one,   „ 141
I therefore yield me freely to thy *w*;   „ 168
and so besieges her To break her *w*,   „ 617
I compel all creatures to my *w*.' (repeat)   *Geraint and E.* 629, 673
and the wine will change your *w*.'   „ 663
use Both grace and *w* to pick the vicious quitch   „ 903
and brake my boast.   Thy *w*?'   *Balin and Balan* 72
eagle-like Stoop at thy *w* on Lancelot and the Queen.'   „ 536
Fixt in her *w*, and so the seasons went.   *Merlin and V.* 188
Without the *w* to lift their eyes,   „ 836
and the fault Is yours who let me have my *w*,   *Lancelot and E.* 751

Win (continued) w's, tho' dash'd with death He reddens — *Princess* v 164
if we fail, we fail, And if we w, we fail: — ,, 323
And on the 'Follow, follow, thou shalt w:' — ,, 472
W you the hearts of women; — ,, vi 171
—verily I think to w.' — ,, 329
Emperor, Ottoman, which shall w: — *To F. D. Maurice* 32
That out of words a comfort w; — *In Mem.* xx 10
the past will always w A glory from its being far; — ,, xxiv 13
they could not w An answer from my lips, — ,, ciii 49
And the titmouse hope to w her — *Maud* I xx 29
Belike he w's it as the better man: — *Gareth and L.* 1346
To dash against mine enemy and to w. — ,, 1355
For tho' it seems my spurs are yet to w, — *Marr. of Geraint* 128
I know men: nor will ye w him back, — *Geraint and E.* 332
who sought to w my love Thro' evil ways: — *Balin and Balan* 474
Vivien had not done to w his trust — *Merlin and V.* 863
W! by this kiss you will: — *Lancelot and E.* 152
They prove to him his work : w and return.' — ,, 158
Joust for it, and w, and bring it in an hour, — ,, 204
W shall I not, but do my best to w: — ,, 221
And you shall w this diamond, — ,, 227
To w his honour and to make his name, — ,, 1362
while women watch Who w's, who falls; — *Holy Grail* 35
and they would w thee—teem, — ,, 541
he will fight for me, And w the circlet: — *Pelleas and E.* 119
And w me this fine circlet, Pelleas, — ,, 128
he cried, 'Ay! wilt thou if I w?' 'Ay, that will I,' — ,, 131
purest of thy knights May w them — *Last Tournament* 50
For courtesy w's woman all as well As valour may, — ,, 707
Yet so my path was clear To w the sister. — *Sisters (E. and E.)* 203
no caress could w my wife Back to that passionate answer — ,, 258
w all praise from all Who past it, — *Tiresias* 83
To w her back before I die— — *Romney's R.* 118

Wince You should have seen him w — *Walk. to the Mail* 71

Wind (s) (*See also* **East-wind, March-wind, Night-wind, North-wind, Sea-wind, South-wind**)
When will the w be aweary of blowing — *Nothing will Die* 3
The stream flows, The w blows, — ,, 10
Shall make the w's blow Round and round, — ,, 23
So let the w range; — ,, 32
south w's are blowing Over the sky. — *All Things will Die* 3
The w will cease to blow; — ,, 10
Nor the w on the hill. — ,, 26
So let the warm w's range, — ,, 42
W's creep; dews fall chilly: — *Leonine Eleg.* 7
THE w's, as at their hour of birth, — *The winds, etc.* 1
Till cold w's woke the gray-eyed morn — *Mariana* 31
the shrill w's were up and away, — ,, 50
wild w's bound within their cell, — ,, 54
sound Which to the wooing w aloof The poplar made, — ,, 75
palms were ranged Above, unwoo'd of summer w: — *Arabian Nights* 80
The dew-impearled w's of dawn have kiss'd, — *Ode to Memory* 14
flowers which in the rudest w Never grow sere, — ,, 24
From brawling storms, From weary w, — ,, 113
w's Blew his own praises in his eyes, — *A Character* 21
the w's which bore Them earthward — *The Poet* 17
Bright as light, and clear as w. — *Poet's Mind* 7
Ever the weary w went on, — *Dying Swan* 9
shook the wave as the w did sigh; — ,, 15
Above in the w was the swallow, — ,, 16
W's were blowing, waters flowing, — *Oriana* 14
When Norland w's pipe down the sea, — ,, 91
Lovest thou the doleful w — *Adeline* 49
Careless both of w and weather, — *Rosalind* 7
Up or down the streaming w? — ,, 9
The leaping stream, the very w, — ,, 14
the amorous, odorous w Breathes low — *Eleänore* 123
'Tho' thou wert scatter'd to the w, — *Two Voices* 32
He sows himself on every w. — ,, 294
And, in the pauses of the w, — *Miller's D.* 122
I whirl like leaves in roaring w. — *Fatima* 7
The w sounds like a silver wire, — ,, 29
Rests like a shadow, and the w's are dead. — *Œnone* 28
the foam-bow brightens When the w blows the foam, — ,, 62

Wind (s) (continued) a w arose, And overhead the wandering ivy — *Œnone* 98
The w is blowing in turret and tree. (repeat) — *The Sisters* 3, 33
The w is howling in turret and tree. — ,, 9
The w is roaring in turret and tree. — ,, 15
The w is raging in turret and tree. — ,, 21
The w is raving in turret and tree. — ,, 27
And hoary to the w. — *Palace of Art* 80
trees began to whisper, and the w began to roll, — *May Queen, Con.* 27
up the valley came a swell of music on the w. — ,, 32
up the valley again the music on the w. — ,, 36
With w's upon the branch, — *Lotos-Eaters, C. S.* 27
All day the w breathes low with mellower tone: — ,, 102
w and wave and oar, — ,, 127
Bluster the w's and tides the self-same way, — *D. of F. Women* 38
Whirl'd by the w, had roll'd me deep below, — ,, 119
And the winter w's are wearily sighing— — *D. of the O. Year* 2
THE w, that beats the mountain, blows — *To J. S.* 1
God's ordinance Of Death is blown in every w;' — ,, 46
waft me from the harbour mouth, Wild w! — *You ask me, why, etc.* 26
voice Came rolling on the w. — *Of old sat Freedom* 8
Make knowledge circle with the w's; — *Love thou thy land* 17
lest the soul Of Discord race the rising w; — ,, 68
A w to puff your idol-fires, — ,, 69
The wild w rang from park and plain, — *The Goose* 45
like a w, that shrills All night in a waste land, — *M. d'Arthur* 201
Nor ever w blows loudly; — ,, 261
Beneath a broad and equal-blowing w, — *Gardener's D.* 77
Night slid down one long stream of sighing w, — ,, 267
But she was sharper than an eastern w, — *Audley Court* 53
soft w blowing over meadowy holms And alders, — *Edwin Morris* 95
Rain, w, frost, heat, hail, — *St. S. Stylites* 16
Till that wild w made work — *Talking Oak* 54
'I swear, by leaf, and w, and rain, — ,, 81
'A light w chased her on the wing, — ,, 125
light as any w that blows So fleetly — ,, 129
and the w's are laid with sound. — *Locksley Hall* 104
For the mighty w arises, roaring seaward, — ,, 194
As w's from all the compass shift and blow, — *Godiva* 33
And all the low w hardly breathed for fear. — ,, 55
And many a merry w was borne, — *Day-Dm., Depart.* 14
And the w did blow; — *The Captain* 34
The happy w's upon her play'd, — *Sir L. and Q. G.* 38
There let the w sweep and the plover cry; — *Come not, when, etc.* 5
A light w blew from the gates of the sun, — *Poet's Song* 3
Then follow'd calms, and then w's variable, — *Enoch Arden* 545
blown by baffling w's, Like the Good Fortune, — ,, 628
His fancy fled before the lazy w — ,, 657
the w blew; The rain of heaven, — *Aylmer's Field* 427
o'er those lazy limits down the w With rumour, — ,, 495
Where never creeps a cloud, or moves a w, — *Lucretius* 106
Like linnets in the pauses of the w: — *Princess, Pro.* 246
And therewithal an answer vague as w: — ,, i 45
A w arose and rush'd upon the South, — ,, 97
smile that like a wrinkling w On glassy water — ,, 115
She rose upon a w of prophecy — ,, ii 171
W of the western sea, (repeat) — ,, iii 2, 4
often fretful as the w Pent in a crevice: — ,, 80
Upon the level in little puffs of w, — ,, iv 256
Huge women blowzed with health, and w, and rain, — ,, 279
light w wakes A lisping of the innumerous leaf — ,, v 13
Until they hate to hear me like a w — ,, 98
That range above the region of the w, — ,, Con. 112
four-square to all the w's that blew! — *Ode on Well.* 39
Yell'd as when the w's of winter tear an oak — *Boädicea* 77
w's from off the plain Roll'd the rich vapour — *Spec. of Iliad* 7
moon Look beautiful, when all the w's are laid, — ,, 12
the w's are up in the morning? (repeat) — *Window, On the Hill* 5, 10, 15, 20
w's and lights and shadows that cannot be still, — ,, 7
wet west w and the world will go on. (repeat) — ,, *No Answer* 6, 12
The w and the wet, the w and the wet! — ,, 13
Wet west w how you blow, you blow! — ,, 14
wet west w and the world may go on. — ,, 18
W's are loud and you are dumb, — ,, 19
W's are loud and w's will pass! — ,, 22

Wind (s) (*continued*)   A flower beat with rain and *w*,   *In Mem. viii* 15
Sleep, gentle *w*'s, as he sleeps now,   ,,   *ix* 15
To-night the *w*'s begin to rise And roar   ,,   *xv* 1
Each voice four changes on the *w*,   ,,   *xxviii* 9
We paused: the *w*'s were in the beech: ,,   *xxx* 9
But blame not thou the *w*'s that make   ,,   *xlix* 10
No wing of *w* the region swept,   ,,   *lxxviii* 6
All *w*'s that roam the twilight came   ,,   *lxxix* 11
And every pulse of *w* and wave   ,,   *lxxxv* 73
I hear a *w* Of memory murmuring the past.   ,,   *xcii* 7
while the *w* began to sweep A music   ,,   *ciii* 53
Nor feed with sighs a passing *w*:   ,,   *cviii* 4
the *w* like a broken worldling wail'd,   *Maud I i* 11
Walk'd in a wintry *w* by a ghastly glimmer,   ,,   *iii* 13
shake its threaded tears in the *w* no more.   ,, *III vi* 28
and the war roll down like a *w*,   ,,   54
In drifts of smoke before a rolling *w*,   *Com. of Arthur* 434
When waken'd by the *w* which with full voice   *Gareth and L.* 176
A censer, either worn with *w* and storm;   ,,   222
like a sudden *w* Among dead leaves,   ,,   514
but the *w* hath changed: I scent it twenty-fold.'   ,,   994
'Hath not the good *w*, damsel, changed again?   ,,   1054
the *w* will never change again.'   ,,   1140
And scatter'd all they had to all the *w*'s: *Marr. of Geraint* 635
A **storm** was coming, but the *w*'s were still,   *Merlin and V.* 1
Among the dead and sown upon the *w*—   ,,   45
Drave with a sudden *w* across the deeps,   ,,   201
Thro' the dim land against a rushing *w*,   ,,   425
An angry gust of *w* Puff'd out his torch   ,,   730
Their plumes driv'n backward by the *w* they made   *Lancelot and E.* 480
and went To all the *w*'s?'   ,,   658
glooms Of evening, and the moanings of the *w*.   ,,   1003
All in a fiery dawning wild with *w*   ,,   1020
the sun Shone, and the *w* blew, thro' her,   *Holy Grail* 99
Such as no *w* could move: ,,   681
And the *w* fell, and on the seventh night   ,,   810
strange knights From the four *w*'s came in: *Pelleas and E.* 148
like a poisonous *w* I pass to blast   ,,   569
thro' the tree Rush'd ever a rainy *w*, and thro' the *w* Pierced ever a child's cry: *Last Tournament* 16
Brake with a wet *w* blowing, Lancelot,   ,,   137
And ever the *w* blew, and yellowing leaf   ,,   154
till the warm hour returns With veer of *w*,   ,,   231
and the *w* among the boughs.   ,,   489
' Ay, ay, O ay—the *w*'s that bend the brier !   ,,   731
O ay—the *w*'s that bow the grass !   ,,   735
O ay—the *w*'s that move the mere.'   ,,   738
As the sharp *w* that ruffles all day long   *Guinevere* 50
Till in the cold *w* that foreruns the morn,   ,,   132
Stands in a *w*, ready to break and fly,   ,,   365
ghost of Gawain blown Along a wandering *w*,   *Pass. of Arthur* 32
And I am blown along a wandering *w*,   ,,   36
down the long *w* the dream Shrill'd ;   ,,   40
O light upon the *w*, Thine, Gawain, was the voice—   ,,   46
came A bitter *w*, clear from the North, and blew The mist aside, and with that *w* the tide Rose,   ,,   124
like a *w* that shrills All night in a waste land,   ,,   369
Nor ever *w* blows loudly ;   ,,   429
Waverings of every vane with every *w*,   *To the Queen ii* 50
charged the *w*'s With spiced May-sweets   *Lover's Tale i* 317
And shot itself into the singing *w*'s ;   ,,   369
thence one night, when all the *w*'s were loud,   ,,   378
The *w* Told a lovetale beside us,   ,,   542
waters answering lisp'd To kisses of the *w*, that,   ,,   545
The *w* had blown above me,   ,,   622
hour died Like odour rapt into the winged *w*   ,,   801
soft *w*'s, Laden with thistledown and seeds   ,, *ii* 12
the *w* Came wooingly with woodbine smells.   ,,   35
All crisped sounds of wave and leaf and *w*,   ,,   106
silent-creeping *w*'s Laid the long night   ,,   111
mast bent and the ravin *w* In her sail roaring.   ,,   170
we whirl'd giddily : the *w* Sung,   ,,   201
Slow-moving as a wave against the *w*,   ,, *iv* 293
like ships i' the Channel a-sailing with *w* an' tide.   *First Quarrel* 42
An' the *w* began to rise,   ,,   89

Wind (s) (*continued*)   wailing, wailing, the *w* over land and sea—   *Rizpah* 1
Willy's voice in the *w*, ' O mother,   ,,   2
and the *w* and the shower and the snow.   ,,   68
The *w* that 'ill wail like a child   ,,   72
for my Willy's voice in the *w*—   ,,   82
coostom ageän draw'd in like a *w* fro' far an' wide,   *North. Cobbler* 93
When a *w* from the lands they had ruin'd   *The Revenge* 112
and the *w* Still westward, and the weedy seas—   *Columbus* 71
the *w*'s were dead for heat ;   *Tiresias* 34
warm *w*'s had gently breathed us away from the land—   *The Wreck* 63
orphan wail came borne in the shriek of a growing *w*,   ,,   87
some of late would raise a *w* To sing thee to thy grave,   *Freedom* 35
Among the wail of midnight *w*'s,   *Demeter and P.* 59
w blawin' hard tother waäy, an' the *w* wasn't like to turn.   *Owd Roä* 104
you shiver tho' the *w* is west   *The Ring* 29
one silent voice Came on the *w*,   ,,   154
changest, breathing it, the sullen *w*,   *Prog. of Spring* 110
when all but the *w*'s were dead,   *The Dreamer* 1
To the wail of my *w*'s,   ,,   13
Was it only the *w* of the Night shrilling   ,,   15
Wind (verb)   *W*'s all the vale in rosy folds,   *Miller's D.* 242
Where yon dark valleys *w* forlorn,   *On a Mourner* 22
More close and close his footsteps *w* :   *Day-Dm., Arrival* 25
I *w* about, and in and out,   *The Brook* 55
w And double in and out the boles,   *Princess iv* 261
Still onward *w*'s the dreary way ;   *In Mem. xxvi* 1
And *w*'s their curls about his hand :   ,,   *lxvi* 12
It lightly *w*'s and steals In a cold white robe   *Maud II iv* 18
and every way the vales *W*,   *Tiresias* 183
And *w* the front of youth with flowers,   *Ancient Sage* 97
Wind-driven   spray *w-d* Far thro' the dizzy dark.   *Lover's Tale ii* 198
Winded   (*See also* **Long-winded**)   And *w* it, and that so musically   *Pelleas and E.* 365
the lilies like the glaciers *w* down,   *V. of Maeldune* 42
Winder (**window**)   Stan' 'im theer i' the *w*,   *North. Cobbler* 75
out o' sight o' the *w*'s o' Gigglesby Hinn—   *Spinster's S's.* 35
I claums an' I mashes the *w* hin,   *Owd Roä* 83
wi' my bairn i' 'is mouth to the *w*   ,,   92
I claumb'd up ageän to the *w*,   ,,   99
Wind-footed   fled *W-f* to the steeple in the woods,   *Lover's Tale iii* 56
Wind-hover (**kestrel**)   as long As the *w-h* hangs in balance,   *Aylmer's Field* 321
Winding   (*See also* **Westward-winding**)   From the river *w* clearly,   *L. of Shalott i* 31
she sees the highway near *W* down to Camelot :   ,,   *ii* 14
we paused About the *w*'s of the marge   *Edwin Morris* 94
Low voluptuous music *w* trembled,   *Vision of Sin* 17
w under woodbine bowers,   *The Brook* 88
We glided *w* under ranks Of iris,   *In Mem. ciii* 23
The rock rose clear, or *w* stair.   *Palace of Art* 10
a full-fed river *w* slow By herds upon an endless plain,   ,,   73
and many a *w* vale And meadow,   *Lotos-Eaters* 22
The Lotos blows by every *w* creek :   ,, *C. S.* 101
On open main or *w* shore ;   *The Voyage* 6
the lawns And *w* glades high up like ways to Heaven,   *Enoch Arden* 573
On *w* stream or distant sea ;   *In Mem. cxv* 12
Far down beneath a *w* wall of rock   *Last Tournament* 11
She chanted snatches of mysterious hymns Heard on the *w* waters,   *Lancelot and E.* 1408
Windle (**drifted snow**)   all on 'em bolster'd oop wi' the *w* that night ;   *Owd Roä* 32
Windless   Who might'st have heaved a *w* flame Up the deep East,   *In Mem. lxxii* 13
all the sway and whirl Of the storm dropt to *w* calm,   *Lover's Tale ii* 207
Windmill   an' thy *w* oop o' the croft,   *Spinster's S's.* 73
Window (**adj.**)   Oh is it the brook, or a pool, or her *w* pane,   *Window, On the Hill* 4
And never a glimpse of her *w* pane ?   ,,   *No Answer* 3
on the *w* ledge, Close underneath his eyes,   *Lancelot and E.* 1239
Window (s)   (*See also* **Bay-window, Cabin-window, Parlour-window, Winder**)   The fourscore *w*'s all alight   *Arabian Nights* 122
Leaving doors and *w*'s wide :   *Deserted House* 3
In the *w*'s is no light ;   ,,   6

Window (s) (*continued*) Or thro' the *w's* we shall see The
   nakedness | *Deserted House* 10
the deep-set *w's*, stain'd and traced, | *Palace of Art* 49
forms that pass'd at *w's* and on roofs | *D. of F. Women* 23
Reveal'd their shining *w's* : | *Gardener's D.* 220
all Should keep within, door shut, and *w* barr'd. | *Godiva* 41
Saw from his *w's* nothing save his own— | *Aylmer's Field* 21
so To the open *w* moved, remaining there | *Princess* iv 492
The giant *w's'* blazon'd fires, | *The Daisy* 58
Clasp her *w*, trail and twine ! | *Window, At the Window* 2
Blaze upon her *w*, sun, | "   *When* 15
were laid On the hasp of the *w*, | *Maud* I xiv 19
The Lady Lyonors at a *w* stood, | *Gareth and L.* 1375
glancing on the *w*, when the gloom Of twilight | *Balin and Balan* 232
Where twelve great *w's* blazon Arthur's wars, | *Holy Grail* 248
lands in your view From this bay *w*— | *Sisters (E. and E.)* 52
May leave the *w's* blinded, | *Romney's R.* 146
Window-bars it came, and close beside the *w-b*, | *May Queen, Con.* 39
Window-pane Oh is it the brook, or a pool, or her *w p*, | *Window, On the Hill* 4
I follow them down to the *w-p* of my dear, | "   17
And never a glimpse of her *w p* ! | "   *No Answer* 3
Wind-scatter'd surf *w-s* over sails and masts, | *D. of F. Women* 31
Windy Beneath the *w* wall. | *Palace of Art* 72
building rook 'll caw from the *w* tall elm-
   tree, | *May Queen, N. Y's. E.* 17
And it was *w* weather. (repeat) | *The Goose* 4, 40
you hear The *w* clanging of the minster clock ; | *Gardener's D.* 38
Far on the ringing plains of *w* Troy. | *Ulysses* 17
Fly o'er waste fens and *w* fields. | *Sir Galahad* 60
By Ellen's grave, on the *w* hill. | *Edward Gray* 12
All the *w* ways of men Are but dust that rises
   up, (repeat) | *Vision of Sin* 132, 168
And swang besides on many a *w* sign— | *Aylmer's Field* 19
That climb into the *w* halls of heaven : | *Lucretius* 136
ere the *w* jest Had labour'd down within | *Princess* v 272
Fair-hair'd and redder than a *w* morn ; | "   *Con.* 91
Flames, on the *w* headland flare ! | *W. to Alexandra* 16
Or sheepwalk up the *w* wold ; | *In Mem.* c 8
Uncared for, gird the *w* grove, | "   ci 13
of grain Storm-strengthen'd on a *w* site, | *Gareth and L.* 692
Comes flying over many a *w* wave To Britain, | *Marr. of Geraint* 337
Swung from his brand a *w* buffet out Once, | *Geraint and E.* 90
slide From the long shore-cliff's *w* walls | "   164
And all the *w* clamour of the daws | "   255
On sallows in the *w* gleams of March : | *Merlin and V.* 225
On some wild down above the *w* deep, | "   658
Wine (*See also* **Adam's wine, Cowslip wine**) our
   friends at forsaking The *w* and the merry-
   making. | *All Things will Die* 19
Across the walnuts and the *w*— | *Miller's D.* 32
little dues of wheat, and *w* and oil ; | *Lotos-Eaters, C. S.* 122
think not they are glazed with *w*. | *Locksley Hall* 51
as moonlight unto sunlight, and as water unto *w*— | "   152
And beaker brimm'd with noble *w*. | *Day-Dm., Sleep. P.* 36
she comes and dips Her laurel in the *w*, | *Will Water.* 18
Sipt *w* from silver, praising God, | "   127
By heaps of gourds, and skins of *w*, | *Vision of Sin* 13
Bring me spices, bring me *w* ; | "   76
W is good for shrivell'd lips, | "   79
Let me loose thy tongue with *w* : | "   88
Charier of sleep, and *w*, and exercise, | *Aylmer's Field* 448
Warm'd with his *w's*, or taking pride in her, | "   554
Sat at his table ; drank his costly *w's* ; | *Sea Dreams* 74
they talk'd At *w*, in clubs, of art, of politics ; | *Princess, Pro.* 161
call'd mine host To council, plied him with his
   richest *w's*, | "   i 174
those That lay at *w* with Lar and Lucumo ; | "   ii 129
Fruit, blossom, viand, amber *w*, | "   iv 35
not a death's-head at the *w*.' | "   vi 246
And had our *w* and chess beneath the planes, | *Ode Inter. Exhib.* 17
Steel and gold, and corn and *w*, | *To F. D. Maurice* 18
But honest talk and wholesome *w*, | *Spec. of Iliad* 5
honey-hearted *w* And bread from out the houses | *In Mem.* xxxvii 19
(And dear to me as sacred *w* To dying lips | "   xc 9
'Twas well, indeed, when warm with *w*, | "

Wine (*continued*) fetch the *w*, Arrange the board and brim
   the glass ; | *In Mem.* cvii 15
yes !—but a company forges the *w*. | *Maud* I i 36
I fear, the new strong *w* of love, | "   vi 82
Betrothed us over their *w*, | "   xix 39
That he left his *w* and horses and play, | "   74
brief night goes In babble and revel and *w*. | "   xxii 28
feeble vassals of *w* and anger and lust, | "   II i 43
baken meats and good red *w* Of Southland, | *Gareth and L.* 1190
Go to the town and buy us flesh and *w* ; | *Marr. of Geraint* 372
means of goodly welcome, flesh and *w*. | "   387
For now the *w* made summer in his veins, | "   398
A creature wholly given to brawls and *w*, | "   441
cried Geraint for *w* and goodly cheer | *Geraint and E.* 283
And *w* and food were brought, | "   289
When *w* and free companions kindled him, | "   293
So vanish friendships only made in *w*. | "   479
call'd for flesh and *w* to feed his spears. | "   601
(And fill'd a horn with *w* and held it to her,) | "   659
Drink therefore and the *w* will change your will.' | "   663
I will not look at *w* until I die.' | "   667
Nor ever touch'd fierce *w*, nor tasted flesh, | *Merlin and V.* 627
They sit with knife in meat and *w* in horn ! | "   694
But once in life was fluster'd with new *w*, | "   756
and by fountains running *w*, | *Last Tournament* 141
did ye mark that fountain yesterday Made to
   run *w* ?— | "   287
To hand the *w* to whosoever came— | "   290
hurl'd The tables over and the *w's*, | "   475
that I should suck Lies like sweet *w's* : | "   645
meat, *W*, *w*—and I will love thee to the death, | "   720
these had comforted the blood With meats and *w's*, | "   725
straddling on the butts While the *w* ran : | *Guinevere* 269
Till, drunk with its own *w*, | *Lover's Tale* i 271
w's that, Heaven knows when, Had suck'd the fire | "   iv 193
the *w's* being of such nobleness | "   222
priceless goblet with a priceless *w* Arising, | "   227
Crazy with laughter and babble and earth's new *w*, | *To A. Tennyson* 2
For see—this *w*—the grape from whence | *Sisters (E. and E.)* 61
hev a glass o' cowslip *w* ! | *Village Wife* 5
Droonk wi' the Quoloty's *w*, | "   77
Taäste another drop o' the *w*— | "   120
the wild hour and the *w* Had set the wits aflame. | *Sir J. Oldcastle* 94
riotous fits Of *w* and harlotry— | "   101
was the poisonous pleasure of *w*, | *V. of Maeldune* 62
of a hand giving bread and *w*, | *The Wreck* 114
As laughter over *w*, | *Ancient Sage* 184
' Yet *w* and laughter friends ! | "   195
Nor drown thyself with flies in honied *w* ; | "   268
guest may make True cheer with honest *w*— | *Pro. to Gen. Hamley* 16
Wealth with his *w's* and his wedded harlots ; | *Vastness* 19
and choice of women and of *w's* ? | *By an Evolution.* 8
men may taste Swine-flesh, drink *w* ; | *Akbar's Dream* 54
one of those Who mix the *w's* of heresy | "   174
brag to his fellow rakes of his conquest over the *w* ? | *Charity* 18
Wine-flask The *w-f* lying couch'd in moss, | *In Mem.* lxxxix 44
Wine-heated Moist as they were, *w-h* from the feast ; | *Geraint and E.* 351
Wing (s) (*See also* **Ankle-wing**) What they say betwixt
   their *w's* ? | *Adeline* 29
And clip your *w's*, and make you love : | *Rosalind* 45
Droops both his *w's*, regarding thee, | *Eleänore* 119
' He dried his *w's* : like gauze they grew ; | *Two Voices* 13
' Here sits he shaping *w's* to fly : | "   289
fold our *w's*, And cease from wanderings, | *Lotos-Eaters, C. S.* 19
crested bird That claps his *w's* at dawn. | *D. of F. Women* 180
hearts and feeble *w's* That every sophister | *Love thou thy land* 11
lime a summer home of murmurous *w's*. | *Gardener's D.* 48
O'er the mute city stole with folded *w's*, Distilling
   odours | 186
While the prime swallow dips his *w*, | *Edwin Morris* 145
This dull chrysalis Cracks into shining *w's*, | *St. S. Stylites* 156
' A light wind chased her on the *w*, | *Talking Oak* 125
On sleeping *w's* they sail. | *Sir Galahad* 44
W's flutter, voices hover clear : | "   78
Tho' fortune clip my *w's*, | *Will Water.* 50

Wing (**s**) (*continued*)   seabird crosses With one waft of
    the w.   *The Captain* 72
He rode a horse with w's,   *Vision of Sin* 3
hung With w's of brooding shelter o'er her peace,   *Aylmer's Field* 139
So often, that the folly taking w's
     " 494
Till the little w's are stronger.   *Sea Dreams* 298
Whereon a woman-statue rose with w's   *Princess i* 210
wheel'd on Europe-shadowing w's,   *Ode on Well.* 120
you have gotten the w's of love,   *Window, Ay* 15
Spread thy full w's, and waft him o'er   *In Mem. ix* 4
The wild pulsation of her w's ;   " *xii* 4
My fancies time to rise on w,   " *xiii* 17
that dip Their w's in tears, and skim away.   " *xlviii* 16
Self-balanced on a lightsome w :   " *lxv* 8
Take w's of fancy, and ascend,   " *lxxvi* 1
Take w's of foresight ; lighten thro'   " 5
No w of wind the region swept,   " *lxxviii* 6
Or eagle's w, or insect's eye ;   " *cxxvi* 6
The love that rose on stronger w's,   " *cxxviii* 1
My life has crept so long on a broken w   *Maud III vi* 1
a Shape that fled With broken w's,   *Gareth and L.* 1208
and w's Moved in her ivy,   *Marr. of Geraint* 598
made his feet W's thro' a glimmering gallery,   *Balin and Balan* 404
To catch a loathly plume fall'n from the w   *Merlin and V.* 727
And on the fourth are men with growing w's,   *Holy Grail* 237
And peak'd w's pointed to the Northern Star.   " 240
And both the w's are made of gold,   " 242
Became a living creature clad with w's ?   " 519
Half-wrench'd a golden w ;   " 733
Great angels, awful shapes, and w's and eyes.   " 848
Follow'd a rush of eagle's w's,   *Last Tournament* 417
swum with balanced w's To some tall mountain :   *Lover's Tale i* 302
Love, rising, shook his w's, and charged the winds   " 317
Love wraps his w's on either side the heart,   " 467
like the waft of an Angel's w ;   *In the Child. Hosp.* 38
The moth will singe her w's,   *Sir J. Oldcastle* 189
Sphinx, with w's drawn back,   *Tiresias* 148
rose as it were on the w's of an eagle   *The Wreck* 69
Without their hope of w's ! '   *Ancient Sage* 211
w push'd out to the left and a w to the right,   *Heavy Brigade* 15
Russian crowd Folded its w's   " 39
And showing them, souls have w's !   *Dead Prophet* 12
in their turn thy warblers rise on w.   *Prog. of Spring* 108
a shape with w's Came sweeping by him,   *St. Telemachus* 24
The shape with w's.   " 38
Bring me my horse ?—my horse ? my w's   *Mechanophilus* 9

Wing (**verb**)   Stoops at all game that w the skies,   *Rosalind* 4
Far as the wild swan w's, to where the sky   *Palace of Art* 31
That I could w my will with might   *In Mem. xli* 10

Wing-case   slide apart Their dusk w-c's,   *Gareth and L.* 687

Wing'd (*See also* **Black-wing'd, Light-wing'd, Strong-wing'd, White-wing'd, Wide-wing'd**)   arrows of his thoughts
    were headed And w with flame,   *The Poet* 12
bravely furnish'd all abroad to fling The w shafts of truth,   " 26
That sought to sow themselves like w seeds,   *Gardener's D.* 65
Stood from his walls and w his entry-gates   *Aylmer's Field* 18
From four w horses dark against the stars ;   *Princess i* 211
and w Her transit to the throne,   " *iv* 377
Or keeps his w affections clipt with crime :   " *vii* 316
Not making his high place the lawless perch Of w
    ambitions,   *Ded. of Idylls* 23
Tits, wrens, and all w nothings peck him dead !   *Marr. of Geraint* 275
Like odour rapt into the w mind   *Lover's Tale i* 801

Winging   What time I watch'd the swallow w   *Princess iv* 89

Wink (**s**)   Till with a w his dream was changed,   *Com. of Arthur* 441
(For in a w the false love turns to hate)   *Merlin and V.* 852

Wink (**verb**)   ere a star can w, beheld her there.   *Gardener's D.* 122
one that nods and w's behind a slowly dying fire.   *Locksley Hall* 136
W at our advent : help my prince to gain   *Princess iii* 160
Nor w's the gold fin in the porphyry font :   " *vii* 178
But w no more in slothful overtrust.   *Ode on Well.* 170
' Man ! is he man at all, who knows and w's ?   Sees
    what his fair bride is and does, and w's ?   *Merlin and V.* 781

Wink'd   last light, that long Had w and threaten'd
    darkness,   *M. d'Arthur, Ep.* 2

Wink'd (*continued*)   which for bribe had w at wrong,   *Geraint and E.* 939
Mutinies, treacheries—w at, and condoned—   *Columbus* 226

Winking   The landscape w thro' the heat :   *In Mem. lxxxix* 16
W his eyes, and twisted all his face.   *Lancelot and E.* 1145

Winner   Are w's in this pastime of our King.   *Last Tournament* 199

Winnie   MINNIE and W Slept in a shell.   *Minnie and Winnie* 1

Winning   W its way with extreme gentleness   *Isabel* 23
To all the people, w reverence.   *M. d'Arthur* 108
If such be worth the w now,   *You might have won* 2
w easy grace, No doubt, for slight delay,   *Princess iv* 330
a good mother, a good wife, Worth w ;   " *v* 167
To all the people, w reverence.   *Pass. of Arthur* 276

Winnow   enormous polypi W with giant arms   *The Kraken* 10

Winsome   Was wedded with a w wife, Ygerne :   *Com. of Arthur* 188
Peept the w face of Edith like a flower   *Locksley H., Sixty* 260

Wint (**went**)   an' thin w into the dark.   *Tomorrow* 22
people 'ud see it that w in to mass—   " 74

Winter (**adj.**)   (*See also* **Midwinter**)   The mellow'd reflex of a w
    moon ;   *Isabel* 29
From w rains that beat his grave.   *Two Voices* 261
The slow result of w showers :   " 452
FULL knee-deep lies the w snow, And the w winds
    are wearily sighing :   *D. of the O. Year* 1
Among the mountains by the w sea ;   *M. d'Arthur* 2
w moon, Brightening the skirts of a long cloud,   " 53
And the long glories of the w moon.   " 192
And like an oaken stock in w woods,   *Golden Year* 62
Made orphan by a w shipwreck,   *Enoch Arden* 15
face, Rough-redden'd with a thousand w gales,   " 95
Mock-Hymen were laid up like w bats,   *Princess iv* 144
Which in our w woodland looks a flower.   *A Dedication* 13
We heard them sweep the w land ;   *In Mem. xxx* 10
Glastonbury, where the w thorn Blossoms at
    Christmas,   *Holy Grail* 52
Among the mountains by the w sea ;   *Pass. of Arthur* 171
w moon, Brightening the skirts of a long cloud,   " 221
And the long glories of the w moon.   " 360
The stillness of the dead world's w dawn   " 442
Weird Titan by thy w weight of years   *To Victor Hugo* 7
She spies the summer thro' the w bud,   *Ancient Sage* 74
She that finds a w sunset fairer than a morn of
    Spring.   *Locksley H., Sixty* 22
Dumb on the w heath he lay.   *Dead Prophet* 13
Sun Burst from a swimming fleece of w gray,   *Demeter and P.* 20
and Ætna kept her w snow.   " 115
That icy w silence—how it froze you   " *Happy* 71
I soaking here in w wet—   *To Ulysses* 6
Who love the w woods, to trace On paler heavens   " 14
thro' the sunless w morning-mist In silence wept   *Death of Œnone* 8

Winter (**s**)   (*See also* **Midwinter, Summer-winter**)   'Tis
    the world's w ;   *Nothing will Die* 17
A hundred w's snow'd upon his breast,   *Palace of Art* 139
where the moving isles of w shock By night,   *M. d'Arthur* 140
Three w's, that my soul might grow to thee,   *St. S. Stylites* 71
monsters only made to kill Time by the fire in w.'   *Princess, Pro.* 205
' Why not a summer's as a w's tale ?   " 209
we should have him back Who told the ' W's tale '   " 238
Those w's of abeyance all worn out,   " *iv* 440
Whose eighty w's freeze with one rebuke   *Ode on Well.* 186
Your presence will be sun in w,   *To F. D. Maurice* 3
To break the blast of w, stand ;   " 22
Yell'd as when the winds of w   *Boädicea* 77
Till growing w's lay me low ;   *In Mem. xl* 30
And every w change to spring.   " *liv* 16
As in the w's left behind,   " *lxxviii* 9
Merlin, whose vast wit And hundred w's   *Com. of Arthur* 281
A man wellnigh a hundred w's old,   *Holy Grail* 85
And each of these a hundred w's old,   " 88
man was no more than a voice In the white w of his
    age,   *Pass. of Arthur* 4
seen where the moving isles of w shock By night,   " 308
and his w's were fifteen score,   *V. of Maeldune* 116
His w chills him to the root,   *Ancient Sage* 119
Eighty w's leave the dog too lame to follow   *Locksley H., Sixty* 226
Spring and Summer and Autumn and W,   *Vastness* 29

Winter (s) *(continued)* a breath that past With all the cold
  of *w*.   *The Ring* 33
  fingers were so stiffen'd by the frost Of seven and
    ninety *w*'s,   ,, 240
  sigh'd In the *w* of the Present for the summer of the
    Past ;   *Happy* 70
  My yucca, which no *w* quells,   *To Ulysses* 21
  To wallow in that *w* of the hills.   *Romney's R.* 15
  And all the *w*'s are hidden.   *The Throstle* 16
  In a hundred, a thousand *w*'s ?   *The Dawn* 24
Winter-black One night when earth was *w-b*   *To E. Fitzgerald* 21
Winter-clad Tattoo'd or woaded, *w-c* in skins,   *Princess ii* 120
Winter'd *See* **Many-winter'd**
Winter-field The tented *w-f* was broken up   *Aylmer's Field* 110
     The Wreck 74
Winterless the sons of a *w* day.   *Ode to Memory* 19
Wintertide in *w* shall star The black earth
  Would make the world as blank as *W-t.*   *Last Tournament* 221
Winter-white by age as *w-w* As mine is now,   *Tiresias* 19
Wintry So she, and turn'd askance a *w* eye :   *Princess vi* 329
  Who roll'd the psalm to *w* skies,   *In Mem. lvi* 11
  Walk'd in a *w* wind by a ghastly glimmer,   *Maud I iii* 13
  Scarr'd with a hundred *w* water-courses—   *Holy Grail* 490
  Gleam, that had waned to a *w* glimmer On icy
    fallow   *Merlin and the G.* 83
Wiped Why 'edn't tha *w* thy shoes ?   *Spinster's S's.* 46
Wire The wind sounds like a silver *w*,   *Fatima* 29
  The parrot in his gilded *w*'s.   *Day-Dm., Sleep. P.* 16
  A man with knobs and *w*'s and vials fired A
    cannon :   *Princess, Pro.* 65
  Up thro' gilt *w*'s a crafty loving eye,   ,, 172
  who thrumm'd On such a *w* as musically   *Last Tournament* 323
Wirer The nightly *w* of their innocent hare   *Aylmer's Field* 490
Wiry writhed his *w* arms Around him,   *Gareth and L.* 1150
Wisdom her raiment's hem was traced in flame *W*,   *The Poet* 46
  Could his dark *w* find it out,   *Two Voices* 308
  wisdom-bred And throned of *w*—   *Œnone* 124
  Were *w* in the scorn of consequence.'   ,, 150
  stay'd the Ausonian king to hear Of *w*   *Palace of Art* 112
  The *w* of a thousand years Is in them.   *Of old sat Freedom* 18
  flower of knowledge changed to fruit Of *w*.   *Love and Duty* 25
  Knowledge comes, but *w* lingers, (repeat)   *Locksley Hall* 141, 143
  Not much their *w* teaches ;   *Will Water.* 174
  yet for all your *w* well know I That I shall look   *Enoch Arden* 211
  a tigress with a gossamer, Were *w* to it.'   *Princess v* 171
  bearing and the training of a child Is woman's *w*.'   ,, 466
  Wearing his *w* lightly, like the fruit   *A Dedication* 12
  And in thy *w* make me wise.   *In Mem. Pro.* 44
  For *W* dealt with mortal powers,   ,, *xxxvi* 5
  There must be *w* with great Death :   ,, *li* 11
  Whatever *w* sleep with thee.   ,, *cviii* 16
  Nor let thy *w* make me wise.   ,, *cix* 24
  High *w* holds my *w* less,   ,, *cxii* 1
  Yet how much *w* sleeps with thee   ,, *cxiii* 2
  moving side by side With *w*,   ,, *cxiv* 20
  But *W* heavenly of the soul.   ,, 22
  let me think Silence is *w* :   *Merlin and V.* 253
  ' And lo, I clothe myself with *w*,   ,, 255
  till he let his *w* go For ease of heart,   ,, 892
  Led on the gray-hair'd *w* of the east ;   *Holy Grail* 453
  with the *w* and wealth of his own,   *The Wreck* 65
  Strong in will and rich in *w*,   *Locksley H., Sixty* 49
  and take their *w* for your friend.   ,, 104
  Pillory *W* in your markets,   ,, 134
  move to such a goal As *W* hopes to gain,   *Politics* 4
  ' Thy glory baffles *w*.   *Akbar's Dream* 28
Wisdom-bred *w-b* And throned of wisdom—   *Œnone* 123
Wise (adj.) That read his spirit blindly *w*,   *Two Voices* 287
  The slow *w* smile that, round about   *Miller's D.* 5
  No one can be more *w* than destiny.   *D. of F. Women* 94
  with choice paintings of *w* men I hung The royal
    dais round.   *Palace of Art* 131
  Great Nature is more *w* than I :   *To J. S.* 35
  ' Be *w* : not easily forgiven Are those,   *Gardener's D.* 247
  Therefore comes it we are *w*.   *Vision of Sin* 100
  ' O Enoch, you are *w* ; And yet for all your wisdom   *Enoch Arden* 210

Wise (adj.) *(continued)* wholly *w* To let that handsome
  fellow   *Aylmer's Field* 268
  Should I not call her *w*, who made me *w* ?   *Princess ii* 396
  Lady Psyche, younger, not so *w*,   ,, *iv* 316
  Like our wild Princess with as *w* a dream   ,, *Con.* 69
  Attain the *w* indifference of the wise ;   *A Dedication* 8
  For such a *w* humility As befits a solemn fane :   *Ode on Well.* 249
  And in thy wisdom make me *w*.   *In Mem., Pro.* 44
  If thou wilt have me *w* and good.   ,, *lix* 8
  She darkly feels him great and *w*,   ,, *xcvii* 34
  They sang of what is *w* and good   ,, *ciii* 10
  'Tis held that sorrow makes us *w*,   ,, *cviii* 15
  Nor let thy wisdom make me *w*.   ,, *cix* 24
  'Tis held that sorrow makes us *w* ;   ,, *cxiii* 1
  But that blind clamour made me *w* ;   ,, *cxxiv* 18
  Were it not *w* if I fled from the place   *Maud I i* 64
  How modest, kindly, all-accomplish'd, *w*,   *Ded. of Idylls* 18
  we have heard from our *w* man at home To North-
    ward,   *Gareth and L.* 201
  and never a whit more *w* The fourth,   ,, 635
  O damsel, be you *w* To call him shamed,   ,, 1259
  whether very *w* Or very foolish ;   *Marr. of Geraint* 469
  ' Yea so,' said he, ' do it : be not too *w* ;   *Geraint and E.* 424
  And this *w* world of ours is mainly right.   ,, 901
  And our *w* Queen, if knowing that I know,   *Merlin and V.* 121
  ' Who are *w* in love Love most, say least,'   ,, 247
  Yet you are *w* who say it ;   ,, 252
  surely ye are *w*, But such a silence is more *w* than
    kind.'   ,, 288
  However *w*, ye hardly know me yet.'   ,, 355
  ' I never was less *w*, however *w*,   ,, 357
  ' Are ye so *w* ? ye were not once so *w*,   *Lancelot and E.* 103
  their *w* men Were strong in that old magic   *Holy Grail* 665
  the heart that was *w* !   *The Wreck* 56
  By which thou wilt abide, if thou be *w*,   *Ancient Sage* 35
  wherefore thou be *w*, Cleave ever to the sunnier side   ,, 67
  But thou be *w* in this dream-world of ours,   ,, 108
  years that made the stripling *w* Undo their work again,   ,, 111
  yet perhaps she was not *w* ;   *Locksley H., Sixty* 11
  if dynamite and revolver leave you courage to be *w* :   ,, 107
  PATRIOT Statesman, be thou *w* to know   *To Duke of Argyll* 1
  Then let *w* Nature work her will,   *My life is full* 21
  Merlin, the *w* man that ever served King Uther   *Com. of Arthur* 151
  Not even thy *w* father with his signs   *Guinevere* 274
  ' If I,' said the *w* little Annie, ' was you,   *In the Child. Hosp.* 48
  Achæans—honouring his *w* mother's word—   *Achilles over the T.* 16
  To cast *w* words among the multitude   *Tiresias* 66
  but thou art *w* enough, Tho' young to love thy wiser,   ,, 153
  w man's word, Here trampled by the populace   ,, 173
  In what they prophesy, our *w* men,   *Epilogue* 65
  Horace, you the *w* Adviser of the nine-years-ponder'd
    lay,   *Poets and their B.* 5
  VOICE spake out of the skies To a just man and
    a *w*—   *Voice spake, etc.* 2
Wise (s) to its sway Will win the *w* at once,   *Mine be the strength* 10
  O silent faces of the Great and *W*,   *Palace of Art* 195
  Not yet the *w* of heart would cease   *Love thou thy land* 81
  her least remark was worth The experience of the *w*.   *Edwin Morris* 66
  Thro' madness, hated by the *w*,   *Love and Duty* 7
  Yearn'd after by the wisest of the *w*,   *Lucretius* 267
  Among the *w* and the bold.   *Ode on Well.* 57
  War, who breaks the converse of the *w* ;   *Third of Feb.* 8
  the *w* who think, the *w* who reign,   *Ode Inter. Exhib.* 32
  God is law, say the *w* ;   *High. Pantheism* 13
  Attain the wise indifference of the *w* ;   *A Dedication* 8
  With all the circle of the *w*,   *In Mem. lxi* 3
  Thy likeness to the *w* below,   ,, *lxxiv* 7
  truthless violence mourn'd by the *W*,   *Vastness* 5
Wise *See* **Broken-wise, Crescent-wise, Dropwise, Earthly-wise,**
  Elsewise, Heavenly-wise, Madonna-wise, Mocking-wise,
  Over-wise, Warrior-wise, Worldly-wise
Wisely Or *w* or unwisely, signs of storm,   *To the Queen ii* 49
     Love thou thy land 72
Wiser That we are *w* than our sires.   *Enoch Arden* 433
  Surely I shall be *w* in a year :   *Princess iv* 68
  nor is it *W* to weep a true occasion lost,

Wiser (*continued*) dismiss'd in shame to live No *w* than
   their mothers,   *Princess* iv 514
A young man will be *w* by and by ;   *Com. of Arthur* 404
As children learn, be thou *W* for falling !   *Balin and Balan* 76
fierce beast found A *w* than herself,   *Tiresias* 152
thou art wise enough, Tho' young, to love thy *w*,   „   154
W there than you, that crowning barren Death   *Locksley H., Sixty* 61
But you have made the *w* choice,   *You might have won* 5
Let him, the *w* man who springs Hereafter,   *In Mem. cxx* 9
like a stoic, or like A *w* epicurean,   *Maud I* iv 21
' Belike for lack of *w* company ;   *Last Tournament* 245
' Then were swine, goats, asses, geese The *w* fools,   „   326

Wisest Yearn'd after by the *w* of the wise,   *Lucretius* 267
' Madam, he the *w* man Feasted the woman *w* then,   *Princess ii* 350
Her that talk'd down the fifty *w* men ;   „   *v* 294
To know myself the *w* knight of all.'   *Last Tournament* 248
Nor is he the *w* man who never proved himself
   a fool.   *Locksley H., Sixty* 244
Doubt no longer that the Highest is the *w* and the best,   *Faith* 1

Wish (s) phantom of a *w* that once could move,   *The form, the form* 10
wheeling round The central *w*,   *Gardener's D.* 225
And let me have an answer to my *w* ;   *Dora* 30
let him speak his *w*.   *St. S. Stylites* 144
Old *w'es*, ghosts of broken plans,   *Will Water.* 29
the noble *w* To save all earnings to the uttermost,   *Enoch Arden* 85
a *w* renew'd, When two years after came a boy   „   88
his had been, or yours : that was his *w*.   „   300
He oft denied his heart his dearest *w*,   „   336
He laugh'd, and yielded readily to their *w*,   „   370
son Was silent, tho' he often look'd his *w* ;   „   482
this wild king to force her to his *w*,   *Princess, Pro.* 37
As if to close with Cyril's random *w* :   „   *iii* 101
But led by golden *w'es*, and a hope   „   *iv* 420
Tell my *w* to her dewy blue eye :   *Window, Letter* 13
And ever met him on his way With *w'es*,   *In Mem. vi* 22
The *w*, that of the living whole   „   *lv* 1
That cries against my *w* for thee.   „   *xc* 24
The *w* too strong for words to name ;   „   *xciii* 14
sent her that I would yield thee thine.   *Gareth and L.* 551
knight art thou To the King's best *w*.   „   1259
Albeit I give no reason but my *w*,   *Marr. of Geraint* 761
Be moulded by your *w'es* for her weal ;   „   799
I know Your *w*, and would obey ;   *Geraint and E.* 419
Beholding how ye butt against my *w*,   „   677
at times Would flatter his own *w* in age for love,   *Merlin and V.* 185
And grant my re-iterated *w*,   „   353
Nor own'd a sensual *w*,   „   628
the *w* to prove him wholly hers.'   „   865
Love-loyal to the least *w* of the Queen   *Lancelot and E.* 89
To speak the *w* most near to your true heart ;   „   914
And Lancelot saw that she withheld her *w*,   „   920
' Delay no longer, speak your *w*,   „   924
And there I woke, but still the *w* remain'd.   „   1048
and sent him to the Queen Bearing his *w*,   „   1169
that he wellnigh deem'd His *w* by hers was
   echo'd ;   *Pelleas and E.* 121
Love-loyal to the least *w* of the Queen   *Guinevere* 126
way my *w* leads me evermore Still to believe it—   *Lover's Tale i* 274
But she spake on, for I did name no *w*,   „   578
But she spake on, for I did name no *w*, No *w*—no
   hope.   „   583
' It was my *w*,' he said, ' to pass, to sleep,   „   *iv* 63
such her dying *w*—Given on the morning   *The Ring* 76
if his young music wakes A *w* in you   *To Mary Boyle* 64
my strongest *w* Falls flat before your least unwillingness.   *Romney's R.* 71

Wish (verb) Where she would ever *w* to dwell,   *Supp. Confessions* 54
they *w* to charm Pallas and Juno sitting by :   *A Character* 14
I *w* that somewhere in the ruin'd folds,   *Œnone* 221
only *w* to live till the snowdrops come again :   *May Queen, N. Y's. E.* 14
I *w* the snow would melt and the sun come out   „   15
Yet something I did *w* to say :   *To J. S.* 60
I would *w* to see My grandchild on my knees   *Dora* 12
Is it well to *w* thee happy ?—   *Locksley Hall* 43
I cannot help you as I *w* to do Unless—   *Enoch Arden* 407
I *w* you for my wife.   „   410

Wish (verb) (*continued*) do I *w*—What ?—that the bush
   were leafless ?   *Lucretius* 205
I *w* I were Some mighty poetess,   *Princess, Pro.* 131
O I *w* That I were some great princess,   „   133
I could not help it, did not *w* :   „   *ii* 332
that *w'es* at a dance to change The music—   „   *iv* 589
I *w* it Gentle as freedom '—   „   *vi* 205
I *w* she had not yielded ! '   „   *Con.* 5
I *w* they were a whole Atlantic broad.'   „   71
To talk them o'er, to *w* them here,   *In Mem. xc* 11
We *w* them store of happy days   „   *Con.* 84
I *w* I could hear again The chivalrous battle-song   *Maud I x* 53
And *w'es* me to approve him,   „   *xix* 71
She did not *w* to blame him—   „   *xx* 5
I have not fall'n so low as some would *w*.   *Marr. of Geraint* 129
' Did I *w* Your warning or your silence ?   *Geraint and E.* 76
Whether ye *w* me victory or defeat,   „   80
Then said Geraint, ' I *w* no better fare :   „   232
make me *w* still more to learn this charm   *Merlin and V.* 329
I well could *w* a cobweb for the gnat,   „   370
Pure, as you ever *w* your knights to be.   *Lancelot and E.* 1375
Well—can I *w* her any huger wrong   *Last Tournament* 596
Well might I *w* to veil her wickedness,   *Guinevere* 211
an' I *w* I was dead—   *First Quarrel* 52
died o' your going away, an' I *w* that I had.'   „   54
I too *w* that I had—in the pleasant times   „   55
best And oldest friend, your Uncle, *w'es* it,   *Sisters (E. and E.)* 47
Could sometimes *w* I had never led the way.   *Columbus* 186
I *W* I were in the years of old,   *Tiresias* 1
And *w* the dead, as happier than ourselves   *Ancient Sage* 205
I could *w* yon moaning sea would rise   *The Flight* 11
is it well to *w* you joy ?   *Locksley H., Sixty* 216
W me joy ! Father. What need to *w* when Hubert
   weds in you The heart of Love,   *The Ring* 60
' He is fled—I *w* him dead—   *Forlorn* 1

Wish'd She *w* me happy, but she thought   *Miller's D.* 139
I have *w* this marriage, night and day,   *Dora* 21
' I *w* myself the fair young beech   *Talking Oak* 141
and I *w* for Leonard there,   *Golden Year* 4
' I came to speak to you of what he *w*,   *Enoch Arden* 291
roll'd his eyes upon her Repeating all he *w*,   „   905
And how it was the thing his daughter *w*,   *The Brook* 140
I *w* my voice A rushing tempest   *Aylmer's Field* 756
They *w* to marry ; they could rule a house ;   *Princess ii* 465
I stammer'd that I knew him—could have *w*—   „   *iii* 206
Because he might have *w* it—   „   *vi* 275
They hated banter, *w* for something real,   „   *Con.* 18
But I *w* it had been God's will that I,   *Grandmother* 73
I almost *w* no more to wake,   *In Mem. xxviii* 14
And wept, and *w* that I were dead ;   *Com. of Arthur* 345
w The Prince had found her in her ancient home ;   *Marr. of Geraint* 643
W it had been my mother,   *Lancelot and E.* 674
and I *w*, yet *w* her not to speak ;   *Lover's Tale i* 577
But I niver not *w* fur childer,   *Spinster's S's.* 84

Wishing And, tho' in silence, *w* joy.   *In Mem., Con.* 88
Wisp the gilded ball Danced like a *w* :   *Princess, Pro.* 64
w that flickers where no foot can tread.'   „   *iv* 358
the *w* that gleams On Lethe in the eyes of Death.   *In Mem. xcviii* 7
Wistful ' Then I fixt My *w* eyes on two fair images,   *Sea Dreams* 240
mother's eye Full of the *w* fear that he would go,   *Gareth and L.* 173
Wit With shrilling shafts of subtle *w*.   *Clear-headed friend* 38
Alone and warming his five *w's*, (repeat)   *The Owl i* 6, 13
The fruitful *w* Cleaving, took root,   *The Poet* 20
With thy shallow *w* :   *Poet's Mind* 2
O the dalliance and the *w*,   *D. of F. Women* 147
I grow in worth, and *w*, and sense,   *Will Water.* 41
The tavern-hours of mighty *w's*—   „   191
Thro' which a few, by *w* or fortune led,   *Aylmer's Field* 438
gave To him that fluster'd his poor parish *w's*   „   521
How might a man not wander from his *w's*   *Princess ii* 440
the wealth Of words and *w*,   *In Mem., Con.* 103
Merlin, whose vast *w* And hundred winters   *Com. of Arthur* 280
An old man's *w* may wander ere he die.   „   405
Have strength and *w*, in my good mother's hall   *Gareth and L.* 12
shook his *w's* they wander in his prime—   „   715

Wit (continued) but, being knave, Hast mazed my *w*:   *Gareth and L.* 1170
Dreams ruling when *w* sleeps !   *Balin and Balan* 143
I loved thee first, That warps the *w*.'   *Merlin and V.* 61
If these unwitty wandering *w's* of mine,   „ 346
I fain had given them greater *w's* :   „ 496
added, of her *w*, A border fantasy of branch and flower,   *Lancelot and E.* 10
but listen to me, If I must find you *w* :   „ 148
set himself to play upon her With sallying *w*,   „ 647
Sweet father, will you let me lose my *w's* ?'   „ 752
' Ye will not lose your *w's* for dear Lavaine :   „ 755
I might have put my *w's* to some rough use,   „ 1306
Beast too, as lacking human *w*—   *Pelleas and E.* 476
seeing too much *w* Makes the world rotten,   *Last Tournament* 246
To babble about him, all to show your *w*—   „ 340
The slippery footing of his narrow *w*,   *Lover's Tale i* 102
wild hour and the wine Had set the *w's* aflame.   *Sir J. Oldcastle* 95
But her *w's* wor dead, an' her hair was as white   *Tomorrow* 60
Witch sought and found a *w* Who brew'd the philtre   *Lucretius* 15
And we past to the Isle of *W'es*   *V. of Maeldune* 97
For a wild *w* naked as heaven stood   „ 100
Witch-elm *W-e's* that counterchange the floor   *In Mem. lxxxix* 1
Withdraw ' To pass, when Life her light *w's*,   *Two Voices* 145
Else I *w* favour and countenance   *Aylmer's Field* 307
It might be safe our censures to *w* ;   *Third of Feb.* 11
still *w* themselves Quite into the deep soul,   *Lover's Tale i* 81
if the Nameless should *w* from all   *Ancient Sage* 50
Withdrawing *W* by the counter door to that   *Aylmer's Field* 282
Withdrawn (*See also* **Long-withdrawn**) Half shown, are broken and *w*.   *Two Voices* 306
Deep in the garden lake *w*.   *Day-Dm., Sleep. P.* 12
every morning, far *w* Beyond the darkness   *Vision of Sin* 48
on the glimmering limit far *w*   „ 223
Far into heaven, *w*,   *Voice and the P.* 38
Death in the living waters, and *w*,   *Merlin and V.* 148
I knew the veil had been *w*.   *Holy Grail* 522
Withdrew As she *w* into the golden cloud,   *Œnone* 191
Where we *w* from summer heats and state,   *Princess vi* 245
W themselves from me and night,   *In Mem. xcv* 18
Wither *W* beneath the palate, and the heart Faints,   *D. of F. Women* 287
I *w* slowly in thine arms,   *Tithonus* 6
lest I *w* by despair.   *Locksley Hall* 98
And the individual *w's*,   „ 142
Now for me the woods may *w*,   „ 190
Thine own shall *w* in the vast,   *In Mem. lxxvi* 11
as anger falls aside And *w's* on the breast   *Lover's Tale i* 10
He *w's* marrow and mind;   *Ancient Sage* 120
laurel of Cæsar, but mind would not *w*.   *Parnassus* 4
Wither'd parch'd and *w*, deaf and blind,   *Fatima* 6
My suit had *w*, nipt to death by him   *Edwin Morris* 101
Are *w* in the thorny close,   *Day-Dm., Arrival* 11
The naked Three, were *w* long ago,   *Death of Œnone* 7
' What drug can make A *w* palsy cease to shake ?'   *Two Voices* 57
' The memory of the *w* leaf In endless time   „ 112
like the *w* moon Smote by the fresh beam of the springing east;   *M. d'Arthur* 213
The *w* Misses! how they prose O'er books   *Amphion* 81
Who slowly rode across a *w* heath,   *Vision of Sin* 61
Ruin'd trunks on *w* forks,   „ 93
to left and right Of *w* holt or tilth or pasturage.   *Enoch Arden* 675
A *w* violet is her bliss: *In Mem. xcvii* 26
as the worm draws in the *w* leaf And makes it earth,   *Geraint and E.* 633
Danced like a *w* leaf before the hall. (repeat)   *Last Tournament* 4, 242
like the *w* moon Smote by the fresh beam of the springing east;   *Pass. of Arthur* 381
And pale and fibrous as a *w* leaf,   *Lover's Tale i* 422
Withering O LOVE, Love, Love! O *w* might!   *Fatima* 1
Withheld Lancelot saw that she *w* her wish,   *Lancelot and E.* 920
w His older and his mightier from the lists;   *Pelleas and E.* 159
Withhold a prudence to *w*;   *Isabel* 15
Withholding Apart from place, *w* time,   *Arabian Nights* 75
Within *See* **Half-within**
Without *See* **Half-without**
Withstand caught By that you swore to *w*?   *Maud I vi* 80
Frail, but of force to *w*,   „ *II ii* 24

Witness (s) (*See also* **Eye-witness**) Bear *w*, if I could have found a way   *St. S. Stylites* 55
in truth (thou wilt bear *w* here)   „ 129
thine own *w* that thou bringest Not peace,   *Sir J. Oldcastle* 35
Lord give thou power to thy two *w'es* !   „ 81
Bear *w* you, that yesterday   *To Prof. Jebb.* 2
' Who was *w* of the crime?   *Forlorn* 7
There will come a *w* soon Hard to be confuted,   „ 25
when creed and race Shall bear false *w*,   *Akbar's Dream* 98
Witness (verb) Yes, as your moanings *w*,   *Aylmer's Field* 749
W their flowery welcome.   *Balin and Balan* 145
Wittier Evelyn is gayer, *w*, prettier,   *Sisters (E. and E.)* 36
our quick Evelyn—The merrier, prettier, *w*,   „ 286
Witty grew So *w* that ye play'd at ducks and drakes   *Last Tournament* 344
Wizard (adj.) Some figure like a *w* pentagram   *The Brook* 103
I hear a *w* music roll,   *In Mem. lxx* 14
The *w* lightnings deeply glow,   „ *cxxii* 19
Wizard (s) Lash'd at the *w* as he spake the word,   *Com. of Arthur* 388
The people call'd him *W*;   *Merlin and V.* 170
To find a *w* who might teach the King   „ 583
but did they find A *w*? Tell me, was he like to thee?'   „ 613
The gentle *w* cast a shielding arm.   „ 908
pale blood of the *w* at her touch Took gayer colours,   „ 949
Mighty the *W* Who found me at sunrise   *Merlin and the G.* 11
Wizard-like And weird and worn and *w-l* was he.   *The Ring* 196
Woä (stop) *W*—theer's a craw to pluck wi' tha, Sam: *N. Farmer, N. S.* 5
—*w* then *w*—let ma 'ear mysén speäk.   „ 8
W then, proputty, wiltha?—   „ 39
W then, wiltha? dangtha!—   „ 40
Woaded Tattoo'd or *w*, winter-clad in skins,   *Princess ii* 120
Woe He hath no thought of coming *w's*;   *Supp. Confessions* 47
My heart is wasted with my *w*,   *Oriana* 1
silence seems to flow Beside me in my utter *w*,   „ 87
all day long you sit between Joy and *w*,   *Margaret* 64
The home of *w* without a tear.   *Mariana in the S.* 20
A little hint to solace *w*,   *Two Voices* 433
My heart may wander from its deeper *w*.   *Œnone* 44
Or hearing would not hear me, *w* is me !   „ 171
still sheets of water, divers *w's*,   *D. of F. Women* 34
That makes my only *w*.   „ 136
Even with a verse your holy *w*.   *To J. S.* 8
Proclaiming Enoch Arden and his *w's*;   *Enoch Arden* 868
As fits an universal *w*,   *Ode on Well.* 14
it cost me a world of *w*,   *Grandmother* 23
To bear thro' Heaven a tale of *w*,   *In Mem. xii* 2
And standing, muffled round with *w*,   „ *xiv* 5
The wild unrest that lives in *w*   „ *xv* 15
Peace ; come away: the song of *w*   „ *lvii* 1
Likewise the imaginative *w*,   „ *lxxv* 53
And I—my harp would prelude *w*—   „ *lxxxviii* 9
Or, crown'd with attributes of *w*   „ *cxvii* 18
So far, so near in *w* and weal;   „ *cxix* 2
for some dark undercurrent *w* That seems to draw—   *Maud I xviii* 83
Wrought for his house an irredeemable *w* ;   *II i* 22
' O brother' answer'd Balin ' *w* is me!   *Balin and Balan* 618
' *W* is me, my knights,' he cried,   *Holy Grail* 275
all the wealth and all the *w*?   *Guinevere* 344
we came To what our people call ' The Hill of *W*.'   *Lover's Tale i* 374
Three cypresses, symbols of mortal *w*,   „ 537
A sacred, secret, unapproached *w*,   „ 679
on the depth of an unfathom'd *w* Reflex of action.   „ 746
were worlds of *w* like our own—   *Despair* 18
scroll written over with lamentation and *w*.   „ 20
had some glimmer, at times, in my gloomiest *w*,   „ 103
Days and Hours That cancel weal with *w*,   *Ancient Sage* 96
and youth is turn'd to *w*.   *The Flight* 16
this Earth, a stage so gloom'd with *w*   *The Play* 1
' *W* to this island if ever a woman (repeat)   *Kapiolani* 20, 22
Woful (*See also* **Dainty-woeful**) A *w* man (for so the story went)   *Lover's Tale i* 379
when the *w* sentence hath been past,   „ 788
Embathing all with wild and *w* hues,   „ *ii* 64
Woild (wild) Down i' the *w* 'enemies afoor I coom'd to the plaäce.   *N. Farmer, O. S.* 34
Woke Till cold winds *w* the gray-eyed morn   *Mariana* 31

Woke (*continued*) Ind to Ind, but in far daylight *w*,   *Buonaparte* 4
And *w* her with a lay from fairy land.   *Caress'd or chidden* 8
She *w*: the babble of the stream Fell,   *Mariana in the S.* 51
Until I *w*, and found him settled down   *The Epic* 17
That with the sound I *w*, and heard   *M. d'Arthur, Ep.* 30
'O happy kiss, that *w* thy sleep!'   *Day-Dm., Depart.* 19
In him *w*, With his first babe's first cry,   *Enoch Arden* 84
Here she *w*, Resolved, sent for him   „ 506
He *w*, he rose, he spread his arms abroad   „ 912
out a despot dream The father panting *w*,   *Aylmer's Field* 528
till the comrade of his chambers *w*,   „ 583
slept, *w*, and went the next, The Sabbath,   *Sea Dreams* 18
wail'd and *w* The mother,   „ 57
I *w*, I heard the clash so clearly.   „ 135
mixt with little Margaret's, and I *w*,   „ 246
After a tempest *w* upon a morn   *Lucretius* 24
Shot out of them, and scorch'd me that I *w*.   „ 66
Lilia *w* with sudden-shrilling mirth   *Princess, Pro.* 216
w Desire in me to infuse my tale of love   *v* 239
And ere I *w* it was the point of noon,   „ 482
Last I *w* sane, but well-nigh close to death   *vii* 119
Deep in the night I *w*: she, near me,   „ 173
That early *w* to feed her little ones,   „ 252
This year I slept and *w* with pain,   *In Mem. xxviii* 13
songs, that *w* The darkness of our planet,   „ *lxxvi* 9
Enid *w* and sat beside the couch,   *Marr. of Geraint* 79
W and bethought her of her promise given   „ 602
Geraint *W* where he slept in the high hall,   „ 755
Beat, till she *w* the sleepers.   *Geraint and E.* 404
Balin first *w*, and seeing that true face,   *Balin and Balan* 590
W the sick knight, and while he roll'd his eyes   *Lancelot and E.* 819
There bode the night: but *w* with dawn,   „ 846
there I *w*, but still the wish remain'd.   „ 1048
damsel,' answer'd he, 'I *w* from dreams;   *Pelleas and E.* 104
He *w*, and being ware of some one nigh,   „ 520
And *w* again in utter dark, and cried,   *Last Tournament* 623
Far cities burnt, and with a cry she *w*.   *Guinevere* 83
Arthur *w* and call'd, 'Who spake?   *Pass. of Arthur* 45
and we *w* To gaze upon each other.   *Lover's Tale i* 265
when I *w*, Something she ask'd, I know not what,   „ 705
I dozed; I *w*. An open landaulet Whirl'd by,   *Sisters (E. and E.)* 85
wail For ever *w* the unhappy Past again,   „ 263
I *w*, and thought—death—I shall die—   *Columbus* 87
and *w* These eyes, now dull, but then so keen   *Tiresias* 3
Till I *w* from the trance,   *The Wreck* 115
I *w* to all of truest in myself,   *The Ring* 182
w me And learn'd me Magic!   *Merlin and the G.* 13
dream Wail'd in her, when she *w* beneath the stars.   *Death of Œnone* 82
His dream became a deed that *w* the world,   *St. Telemachus* 70

Wold (*See also* **Sea-wold, Wowd**) sheep from wattled
folds, Upon the ridged *w's*,   *Ode to Memory* 67
the long dun *w's* are ribb'd with snow,   *Oriana* 5
That clothe the *w* and meet the sky;   *L. of Shalott i* 3
And oft in ramblings on the *w*,   *Miller's D.* 105
From off the *w* I came, and lay   „ 111
To yon old mill across the *w's*;   „ 240
from the dry dark *w* the summer airs blow cool   *May Queen, N. Y's. E.* 27
blows More softly round the open *w*,   *To J. S.* 2
Calm and deep peace on this high *w*,   *In Mem. xi* 5
Or sheepwalk up the windy *w*;   „ *c* 8
And kindled all the plain and all the *w*.   *Balin and Balan* 441

Wolf By shores that darken with the gathering *w*,   *Aylmer's Field* 767
a *w* within the fold! A pack of *wolves*!   *Princess ii* 190
Then came these *wolves: they* knew her: „ *iv* 321
Kite and kestrel, *w* and wolfkin,   *Boädicea* 15
A gray old *w* and a lean.   *Maud I xiii* 28
Not that gray old *w*, for he came not back From the
wilderness, full of *wolves*,   „ *II v* 53
dog, and *w* and boar and bear Came night and day,   *Com. of Arthur* 23
the *w* would steal The children and devour,   „ 26
grew up to wolflike men, Worse than the *wolves*.   „ 33
Stript from the three dead *wolves* of woman born   *Geraint and E.* 94
drew from those dead *wolves* Their three gay suits   „ 180
And waiting to be treated like a *w*,   „ 857
And find that it had been the *w's* indeed: „ 864

Wolf (*continued*) heard them pass like *wolves*
Howling;   *Balin and Balan* 407
let the *wolves'* black maws ensepulchre   „ 487
'Leave them to the *wolves*.'   „ 588
If the *w* spare me, weep my life away,   *Merlin and V.* 885
Old milky fables of the *w* and sheep,   *Pelleas and E.* 196
Let the fox bark, let the *w* yell.   „ 472
'Why then let men couple at once with *wolves*.   „ 536
Sally she wesh'd foälks' cloäths to keep the *w* fro' the
door,   *North. Cobbler* 29
Meä fur to kick our Sally as kep the *w* fro' the door,   „ 59
the howl of all the cassock'd *wolves*,   *Sir J. Oldcastle* 158
That gray beast, the *w* of the weald.   *Batt. of Brunanburh* 110
When the *wolves* are howling.   *Forlorn* 72
Wolfish stern black-bearded kings with *w* eyes,   *D. of F. Women* 111
Wolfkin Kite and kestrel, wolf and *w*,   *Boädicea* 15
Wolf-like they grew up to *w-l* men, Worse than the
wolves.   *Com. of Arthur* 32
Wolfskin mighty hands Lay naked on the *w*,   *Lancelot and E.* 813
Wolf's-milk half the *w-m* curdled in their veins,   *Princess vii* 130
Wolseley foe was driven, And *W* overthrew Arâbi,   *Pro. to Gen. Hamley* 30
Woman (*See also* **Beggar-woman, Countrywoman,**
Gentlewoman, Lay-women, Man-woman And
women smile with saint-like glances   *Supp. Confessions* 22
my ancient love With the Greek *w*.   *Œnone* 261
'The Legend of Good *Women*' long ago Sung   *D. of F. Women* 2
This *w* was the cause.   „ 104
the greatest gift, A *w's* heart,   *Gardener's D.* 230
for your sake, the *w* that he chose,   *Dora* 63
Got up betwixt you and the *w* there.   „ 96
So the *women* kiss'd Each other, and set out,   „ 128
I woo'd a *w* once, But she was sharper   *Audley Court* 52
A *w* like a butt, and harsh as crabs.   *Walk. to the Mail* 49
God made the *w* for the man, (repeat)   *Edwin Morris* 43, 50
'God made the *w* for the use of man,   *Locksley Hall* 149
w's pleasure, *w's* pain—   „ 151
W is the lesser man,   „ 151
I will take some savage *w*,   „ 168
The *w* of a thousand summers back,   *Godiva* 11
As just and mere a serving-man As any born of *w*.   *Will Water.* 152
Shaped her heart with *w's* meekness   *L. of Burleigh* 71
The *w* cannot be believed.   *The Letters* 32
And *women's* slander is the worst,   „ 34
Scarce could the *w* when he came upon her,   *Enoch Arden* 345
they say that *women* are so quick—   „ 408
'*W*, I have a secret—only swear,   „ 837
'Dead,' clamour'd the good *w*,   „ 840
At which the *w* gave A half-incredulous,   „ 852
As the *w* heard, Fast flow'd the current   „ 864
'*W*, disturb me not now at the last,   „ 874
the shame The *w* should have borne,   *Aylmer's Field* 356
fell The *w* shrieking at his feet,   „ 811
fulminated Against the scarlet *w* and her creed;   *Sea Dreams* 23
And near the light a giant *w* sat,   „ 98
that the *w* walked upon the brink: „ 112
the *w* honest Work;   „ 137
That which I ask'd the *w* in my dream.   „ 147
Came men and *women* in dark clusters round,   „ 226
The *w* half turn'd round from him she loved,   „ 286
when the *w* heard his foot Return from pacings   *Lucretius* 5
'O miracle of *women*,' said the book,   *Princess, Pro.* 35
Half child half *w* as she was,   „ 101
'lives there such a *w* now?'   „ 126
'There are thousands now Such *women*,   „ 128
the rest follow'd: and the *women* sang   „ 244
loved to live alone Among her *women*;   *i* 50
The *w* were an equal to the man.   „ 131
they must lose the child, assume The *w*:   „ 138
these the *women* sang   „ 143
for miles about Was till'd by *women*;   „ 192
and the *w's* state in each, How far from just;   *ii* 131
respect, however slight was paid To *w*,   „ 137
but that which made *W* and man.   „ 145
But *w* ripen'd earlier, and her life Was longer;   „ 154
Plato, Verulam; even so With *w*:   „ 161

Woman-guard Princess with her monstrous w-g,   *Princess* iv 562
Womanhood Wearing the rose of w.   *Two Voices* 417
O miracle of noble w!'   *Princess, Pro.* 48
A charr'd and wrinkled piece of w,   „ v 61
All that not harms distinctive w.   „ vii 274
Came out of her pitying w,   *Maud* I vi 64
and with all grace Of w and queenhood,   *Marr. of Geraint* 176
Could call him (were it not for w)   *Merlin and V.* 786
Beyond mine old belief in w,   *Lancelot and E.* 955
And round her limbs, mature in w;   *Pelleas and E.* 73
A woman in her w as great As he was in his manhood,   *Guinevere* 299
Beyond all dreams of Godlike w,   *Tiresias* 54
Queen, as true to w as Queenhood,   *On Jub. Q. Victoria* 25
Womankind *All for the common good of* w.'   *Princess* ii 209
I take her for the flower of w,   „ v 287
The soft and milky rabble of w,   „ vi 309
faith in w Beats with his blood,   „ vii 328
Womanlike W, taking revenge too deep   *Maud* I iii 5
Woman-man man-woman is not w-m.   *On One who eff. E. M.* 4
Woman-markets Here in the w-m of the west,   *Aylmer's Field* 348
Woman-post A w-p in flying raiment.   *Princess* iv 376
Woman's-heart Break not, O w-h, but still endure;   *Ded. of Idylls* 44
Woman-slough what was left of faded w-s   *Princess* v 40
Woman-soldier My w-s, gallant Kate,   *Kate* 15
Woman-statue Whereon a w-s rose with wings   *Princess* i 210
Woman-vested but w-v as I was Plunged;   „ iv 181
Woman-world w-w Of wives and mothers.   *The Ring* 486
Woman-worshipper The w-w? Yea, God's curse,   *Last Tournament* 447
Woman-yell slew Till all the rafters rang with w-y's,   „ 476
Womb To spirits folded in the w.   *Day-Dm., Sleep. P.* 8
Let her, that is the w and tomb of all,   *Lucretius* 244
can remember Love in the w,   *Lover's Tale* i 159
within her w that had left her ill content;   *The Revenge* 51
Won (*See also* **Hard-won, Well-won**) A motion from the river w Ridged the smooth level,   *Arabian Nights* 34
things outward You have w A tearful grace,   *Margaret* 11
'That w his praises night and morn?'   *Mariana in the S.* 34
I w his love, I brought hi.n home.   *The Sisters* 14
You might have w the Poet's name,   *You might have won* 1
but w mysterious way Thro' the seal'd ear   *Aylmer's Field* 695
when your sister came she w the heart Of Ida?   *Princess* iii 87
Imaginations might at all be w.   „ 274
thus I w Your mother, a good mother,   „ v 165
w it with a day Blanch'd in our annals,   „ vi 62
We will be liberal, since our rights are w.   „ 68
Clash'd with his fiery few and w;   *Ode on Well.* 100
has w His path upward, and prevail'd,   „ 213
Priest was happy, His victim w: *The Victim* 62
Faint heart never w—   *Window, The Answer* 9
Who have w her favour!   *Maud* I xii 18
fair, strong, arm'd—But to be w by force—   *Gareth and L.* 105
That save he w the first by force,   „ 108
So large mirth lived and Gareth w the quest.   „ 1426
Has ever w it for the lady with him,   *Marr. of Geraint* 490
What I these two years past have w for thee,   „ 554
'This noble prince who w our earldom back,   „ 619
For tho' ye w the prize of fairest fair,   „ 719
Proclaim'd him Victor, and the day was w.   *Balin and Balan* 90
Had Lancelot w the diamond of the year, With purpose to present them to the Queen, When all were w;   *Lancelot and E.* 68
That *if* I went and *if* I fought and w it   „ 216
W by the mellow voice before she look'd,   „ 243
'Lo, Sire, our knight, thro' whom we w the day,   „ 529
'Was he not with you? w he not your prize?'   „ 573
What of the knight with the red sleeve? 'He w.'   „ 621
Hard-won and hardly w with bruise and blow,   „ 1165
Take, what I had not w except for you,   „ 1181
Pelleas for his lady w The golden circlet,   *Pelleas and E.* 13
wearing this unsunny face To him who w thee glory!'   „ 181
My Queen, he had not w.'   „ 183
yea and he that w The circlet?   „ 320
their wills are hers For whom I w the circlet;   „ 325
Lancelot w methought, for thee to wear.'   *Last Tournament* 38

Won (*continued*) So Tristram w, and Lancelot gave, the gems, Not speaking other word than 'Hast thou w?   *Last Tournament* 190
And w by Tristram as a tourney-prize,   „ 746
years of noble deeds, Until they w her;   *Guinevere* 477
attracted, w, Married, made one with,   *Lover's Tale* i 133
We have w great glory, my men!   *The Revenge* 85
Whom I woo'd and w.   *Sisters (E. and E.)* 204
who can tell but the traitors had w?   *Def. of Lucknow* 66
till his Word Had w him a noble name.   *Dead Prophet* 36
'Take comfort you have w the Painter's fame,'   *Romney's R.* 43
sword, That only conquers men to conquer peace, Has w me.   *Akbar's Dream* 16
And less will be lost than w.   *The Dreamer* 22
Won (one) (*See also* **Wonn**) I minds when i' How-laby beck w daäy   *Church-warden, etc.* 27
Wonder (s) Ever the w waxeth more and more,   *Sonnet to —* 6
What w, if in noble heat Those men thine arms   *England and Amer.* 6
But when he saw the w of the hilt,   *M. d'Arthur* 85
'this w keeps the house.'   *Gardener's D.* 119
this w, dead, become Mere highway dust?   *Love and Duty* 10
The w of the eagle were the less,   *Golden Year* 39
and all the w that would be.—(repeat)   *Locksley Hall* 16, 120
For there are greater w's there.'   *Day-Dm., Depart.* 28
'What w, if he thinks me fair?' What w I was all unwise,   „ *Ep.* 4
'It is no w,' said the lords,   *Beggar Maid* 7
and rent The w of the loom thro' warp and woof   *Princess* i 62
a feast Of w, out of West and East,   *Ode Inter. Exhib.* 21
The w's that have come to thee,   *In Mem.* xli 22
skill'd spear, the w of the world—   *Gareth and L.* 1223
w's ye have done; Miracles ye cannot: „ 1324
Rapt in the fear and in the w of it;   *Marr. of Geraint* 529
Show'd us a shrine wherein were w's—   *Balin and Balan* 109
My daily w is, I love at all.   *Merlin and V.* 536
What w, being jealous, that he sent   „ 580
Fire in dry stubble a nine-days' w flared: *Lancelot and E.* 1029
Becomes a w, and we know not why,   „ 1029
Expectant of the w that would be.   *Holy Grail* 133
With signs and miracles and w's,   *Guinevere* 222
Or what of signs and w's,   „ 229
the land was full of signs And w's   „ 233
thy wise father with his signs And w's,   „ 275
But when he saw the w of the hilt,   *Pass. of Arthur* 253
Your w of the boiling lake;   *To Ulysses* 40
What w! I decreed That even the dog was clean,   *Akbar's Dream* 52
The w's were so wildly new,   *Mechanophilus* 27
Wonder (verb) riving the spirit of man, Making earth w,   *The Poet* 52
And, while now she w's blindly,   *L. of Burleigh* 53
swallows coming out of time Will w why they came: *Princess* ii 432
I w he went so young.   *Grandmother* 14
You w when my fancies play   *In Mem.* lxvi 2
'But wherefore would ye men should w at you?   *Gareth and L.* 570
But there the fine Gawain will w at me,   *Lancelot and E.* 1054
Heated am I? you—you w—   *Locksley H., Sixty* 151
Wonder'd I w at the bounteous hours,   *Two Voices* 451
I w, while I paced along: „ 454
I w at her strength, and ask'd her of it: *Sea Dreams* 113
what kind of tales did men tell men, She w,   *Princess, Pro.* 197
All the world w: (repeat)   *Light Brigade* 31, 52
with such blows, that all the crowd W,   *Marr. of Geraint* 565
Then came the fine Gawain and w at her,   *Lancelot and E.* 1267
men who met him rounded on their heels And w   *Pelleas and E.* 143
W at some strange light in Julian's eyes   *Lover's Tale* iv 205
Wonderful Clothed in white samite, mystic, w, (repeat)   *M. d'Arthur* 31, 144, 159
W, Prince of peace, the Mighty God,   *Aylmer's Field* 669
Clothed in white samite, mystic, w.   *Com. of Arthur* 285
This work of his is great and w.   *Geraint and E.* 898
A thousand-fold more great and w   „ 914
felt His work was neither great nor w,   „ 921
A maid so smooth, so white, so w,   *Merlin and V.* 566
Beyond all knowing of them, w,   *Holy Grail* 104
Clothed in white samite, mystic, w, (repeat)   *Pass. of Arthur* 199, 312, 327
W cures he had done, O yes,   *In the Child. Hosp.* 5

Wonderful (*continued*)   sun of the soul made day in the
   dark of his *w* eyes.   *The Wreck* 55
Wondering   *w*, ask'd her 'Are you from the farm?'   *The Brook* 209
   And only *w* wherefore play'd upon: *Gareth and L.* 1252
   lifted up Their eager faces, *w* at the strength,   *Merlin and V.* 133
   I sat, Lonely, but musing on thee, *w* where,   *Last Tournament* 613
Wonderingly   *w* she gazed on Lancelot So soon return'd,   *Pelleas and E.* 589
Wonder-stricken   kiss'd his *w-s* little ones;   *Enoch Arden* 229
Wondrous   From many a *w* grot and secret cell   *The Kraken* 8
   strike Into that *w* track of dreams again,   *D. of F. Women* 279
   O thou *w* Mother-Age!   *Locksley Hall* 108
   yet her cheek Kept colour: *w*!   *Aylmer's Field* 506
   His prowess was too *w*.   *Lancelot and E.* 542
   w one Who passes thro' the vision of the night—   " 1405
Wonn (**one**)   (*See also* **Won**)   But 'e reäds *w* sarmin
   a weeäk,   *N. Farmer, O. S.* 28
Wont (**s**)   From childly *w* and ancient use I call—   *Lucretius* 209
   'tis her *w* from night to night To rail   *Princess iii* 32
   So said the small king moved beyond his *w*.   " *vi* 265
   Make one wreath more for Use and *W*,   *In Mem. xxix* 11
   He laugh'd as is his *w*, and answer'd   *Com. of Arthur* 401
   my *w* hath ever been To catch my thief,   *Gareth and L.* 821
   Such is my *w*, as those, who know me, know.'   *Lancelot and E.* 365
   such his *w*, as we, that know him, know.'   " 475
   He wore, against his *w*, upon his helm   " 603
   Lancelot sad beyond his *w*, to see The maiden buried,   " 1333
   Had been, their *w*, a-maying and return'd,   *Guinevere* 283
Wont (**adj.**)   Where he was *w* to leap and climb,   *Supp. Confessions* 165
   Psyche, *w* to bind my throbbing brow,   *Princess ii* 250
   In which we two were *w* to meet,   *In Mem. viii* 10
   When I was *w* to meet her In the silent woody places   *Maud II iv* 5
   soldiers *w* to hear His voice in battle,   *Geraint and E.* 174
   w to glance and sparkle like a gem Of fifty facets;   " 294
Wonted   As year by year the labourer tills His *w* glebe,   *In Mem. ci* 22
   To this the courteous Prince Accorded with his *w*
   courtesy,   *Lancelot and E.* 638
   The sound not *w* in a place so still   " 818
   And miss the *w* number of my knights,   *Guinevere* 498
   when he miss'd The *w* steam of sacrifice,   *Demeter and P.* 119
Woo   Thee to *w* to thy tuwhit, (repeat)   *The Owl ii* 11
   They would sue me, and *w* me, and flatter me,   *The Mermaid* 43
   W me, and win me, and marry me,   " 46
   With what voice the violet *w's*   *Adeline* 31
   And once again to *w* thee mine—   *Miller's D.* 30
   I *w* thee not with gifts.   *Œnone* 152
   There's many a bolder lad 'll *w* me   *May Queen* 23
   gold and beauty, wooing him to *w*.   *Aylmer's Field* 487
   thus I *w* thee roughly, for thou carest not How roughly
   men may *w* thee so they win—   *Lucretius* 272
   Fly to her, and pipe and *w* her,   *Princess iv* 115
   these men came to *w* Your Highness—   " *vi* 328
   I *w* your love; I count it crime   *In Mem. lxxxv* 61
   One is come to *w* her.   *Maud I xii* 28
   whitens ere this hour *W's* his own end;   *Last Tournament* 698
   W her and gain her then: *Sisters (E. and E.)* 39
   'Let us revenge ourselves, your Ulric *w's* my wife'—   *Happy* 63
Wood (**trees**)   (*See also* **Cedar-wood, Palmwood, Pine-wood,**
   Yew-wood)   the *w's* that belt the gray hill-side,   *Ode to Memory* 55
   From the evening-lighted *w*,   *Margaret* 10
   field and *w* Grow green beneath the showery gray,   *My life is full* 16
   The pale yellow *w's* were waning,   *L. of Shalott iv* 2
   The *w's* were fill'd so full with song,   *Two Voices* 455
   When after roving in the *w's*   *Miller's D.* 58
   cloisters, branch'd like mighty *w's*,   *Palace of Art* 26
   Lo! in the middle of the *w*,   *Lotos-Eaters, C. S.* 25
   I had wander'd far In an old *w*:   *D. of F. Women* 54
   'Pass freely thro': the *w* is all thine own,   " 83
   I have no men to govern in this *w*:   " 135
   Thridding the sombre boskage of the *w*,   " 243
   and the *w's* and ways Are pleasant,   *On a Mourner* 13
   From the *w's* Came voices of the well-contented doves.   *Gardener's D.* 88
   And like an oaken stock in winter *w's*,   *Golden Year* 62
   The *w's* decay, the *w's* decay and fall,   *Tithonus* 1
   Now for me the *w's* may wither,   *Locksley Hall* 190
   A summer crisp with shining *w's*.   *Day-Dm., Pro.* 8

Wood (**trees**) (*continued*)   and shows At distance
   like a little *w*;   *Day-Dm., Sleep. P.* 42
   Summer *w's*, about them blowing,   *L. of Burleigh* 19
   And hills and scarlet-mingled *w's*   *The Voyage* 47
   where the prone edge of the *w* began (repeat)   *Enoch Arden* 67, 373
   Crept down into the hollows of the *w*;   " 76
   To go with others, nutting to the *w*,   " 363
   calling, here and there, about the *w*.   " 383
   remember'd one dark hour Here in this *w*,   " 386
   How merry they are down yonder in the *w*.   " 389
   sent his voice beneath him thro' the *w*.   " 444
   all the *w* stands in a mist of green,   *The Brook* 14
   Autumn's mock sunshine of the faded *w's*   *Aylmer's Field* 610
   I rose and past Thro' the wild *w's*   *Princess i* 91
   and the shrieks Of the wild *w's* together;   " 99
   O'er it shook the *w's*, And danced the colour,   " *iii* 292
   when all the *w's* are green?   " *iv* 107
   'O Swallow, flying from the golden *w's*,   " 114
   Across the *w's*, and less from Indian craft   " 198
   With Ida, Ida, Ida, rang the *w's*,   " 433
   mused on that wild morning in the *w's*,   " *v* 471
   strikes On a *w*, and takes, and breaks,   " 527
   half-open'd bell of the *w's*!   " *vi* 193
   Nightingales sang in his *w's*:   *G. of Swainston* 6
   And a worm is there in the lonely *w*,   *The Islet* 34
   And cattle died, and deer in *w*,   *The Victim* 18
   And *w's* are sear, And fires burn clear,   *Window, Winter* 3
   The *w's* are all the searer.   " 14
   Oh, the *w's* and the meadows, *W's* where we hid
   from the wet,   " *Marr. Morn.* 5
   By meadow and stile and *w*,   " 14
   That never knew the summer *w's*:   *In Mem. xxvii* 4
   And bask'd and batten'd in the *w*;   " *xxxv* 24
   I found a *w* with thorny boughs: " *lxix* 6
   hill and *w* and field did print The same sweet forms   " *lxxix* 7
   noise of rooks, That gather in the waning *w's*,   " *lxxxv* 72
   Thro' all the dewy-tassell'd *w*,   " *lxxxvi* 6
   With banquet in the distant *w's*;   " *lxxxix* 32
   Of rising worlds by yonder *w*.   " *cv* 25
   Above the *w* which grides and clangs   " *cvii* 11
   To range the *w's*, to roam the park,   *Con.* 96
   I HATE the dreadful hollow behind the little *w*,   *Maud I i* 1
   little *w* where I sit is a world of plunder   " *iv* 24
   the budded peaks of the *w* are bow'd   " *vi* 4
   Here half-hid in the gleaming *w*,   " 69
   Where was Maud? in our *w*;   " *xii* 5
   Birds in our *w* sang   " 9
   Running down to my own dark *w*;   " *xiv* 30
   From the lake to the meadow and on to the *w*,   " *xxii* 37
   Our *w*, that is dearer than all;   " 38
   From the red-ribb'd hollow behind the *w*,   " *II i* 25
   Then glided out of the joyous *w*   " 31
   Thick with wet *w's*, and many a beast therein,   *Com. of Arthur* 21
   gazing over plain and *w*;   *Gareth and L.* 668
   Down the long avenues of a boundless *w*,   " 785
   Where Arthur's men are set along the *w*; The *w* is
   nigh as full of thieves as leaves: " 788
   Flying from out of the black *w*,   " 802
   somewhat as the cleanser of this *w*.   " 828
   So she spake. A league beyond the *w*,   " 845
   damsel's headlong error thro' the *w*—   " 1215
   a forester of Dean, Wet from the *w's*,   *Marr. of Geraint* 149
   Took horse, and forded Usk, and gain'd the *w*; '   " 161
   At last they issued from the world of *w*,   " 238
   In the first shallow shade of a deep *w*,   *Geraint and E.* 119
   'There lurk three villains yonder in the *w*,   " 142
   'And if there were an hundred in the *w*,   " 147
   and she drove them thro' the *w*.   " 185
   keep them in the wild ways of the *w*,   " 187
   thro' the green gloom of the *w* they past,   " 195
   Which sees the trapper coming thro' the *w*.   " 724
   in those deep *w's* we found A knight   *Balin and Balan* 120
   Reported of some demon in the *w's* Was once a man,   " 124
   who will hunt for me This demon of the *w's*?'   " 137
   and rode The skyless *w's*, but under open blue   " 293

Wood (trees) (*continued*)   thou couldst lay the Devil

of these *w's*	*Balin and Balan* 298
and pass And vanish in the *w's*;	,, 327
the canker'd boughs without Whined in the *w*;	,, 346
and old boughs Whined in the *w*.	,, 386
and turn'd aside into the *w's*,	,, 433
the wholesome music of the *w* Was dumb'd	,, 436
Before another *w*, the royal crown Sparkled,	,, 462
yonder lies one dead within the *w*.	,, 468
I dwell Savage among the savage *w's*,	,, 486
she smiled ' And even in this lone *w*, Sweet lord,	,, 528
W's have tongues, As walls have ears:	,, 530
shriek of bird or beast, Thrill'd thro' the *w's*;	,, 546
'She dwells among the *w's*' he said	,, 614
the wild *w's* of Broceliande, (repeat)	*Merlin and V.* 2, 204
Who meant to eat her up in that wild *w*	,, 260
and all thro' this wild *w* And all this morning	,, 285
chase a creature that was current then In these wild *w's*,	,, 409
And all thro' following you to this wild *w*,	,, 440
the dark *w* grew darker toward the storm	,, 890
dwelt among the *w's* By the great river	*Lancelot and E.* 277
As happy as when we dwelt among the *w's*,	,, 1036
And laughter at the limit of the *w*,	*Pelleas and E.* 49
Again she said, 'O wild and of the *w's*,	,, 99
'Lead then,' she said; and thro' the *w's* they went.	,, 108
Other than when I found her in the *w's*:	,, 328
Rang out like hollow *w's* at hunting-tide.	,, 367
With promise of large light on *w's* and ways.	,, 394
hill and *w* Went ever streaming by him	,, 547
At Camelot, high above the yellowing *w's*,	*Last Tournament* 3
Sir Tristram of the *W's*—Whom Lancelot knew,	,, 177
The *w's* are hush'd, their music is no more:	,, 276
I made it in the *w's*. And heard it ring	,, 283
avenues And solitary passes of the *w*	,, 361
as a rustle or twitter in the *w* Made dull his inner,	,, 365
and when thou passest any *w* Close vizor,	,, 534
vows—I am a woodman of the *w's*,	,, 699
Next morning, while he past the dim-lit *w's*,	*Guinevere* 251
over all the great *w* rioting And climbing,	*Lover's Tale i* 403
and from the *w's* That belt it rise three dark,	,, 535
three cypress-cones That spired above the *w*;	,, *ii* 39
From out the yellow *w's* upon the hill	,, 80
The cloud-pavilion'd element,	,, 108
foliage from the dark and dripping *w's*	,, *iii* 6
Fled onward to the steeple in the *w's*:	,, 26
the *w's* upon the hill Waved with a sudden gust	,, 33
fled Wind-footed to the steeple in the *w's*,	,, 56
What matter? there are others in the *w*.	,, *iv* 162
From column on to column, as in a *w*,	,, 189
rattled down upo' poor owd Squire i' the *w*,	*Village Wife* 95
a whirlwind blow these *w's*, as never blew	*The Flight* 12
These ancient *w's*, this Hall at last will go—	,, 27
He left us weeping in the *w's*;	,, 37
all the summer long we roam'd in these wild *w's*	,, 79
Wild flowers of the secret *w's*,	,, 82
Wild *w's* in which we roved with him,	,, 83
Wild *w's* in which we rove no more,	,, 84
foälk be sa scared at, i' Gigglesby *w*,	*Spinsters S's.* 24
stars are from their hands Flung thro' the *w's*,	*Early Spring* 18
The *w's* with living airs How softly fann'd,	,, 19
Mount and mine, and primal *w*;	*Open. I. and C. Exhib.* 6
thridded the black heart of all the *w's*,	*Demeter and P.* 69
you used to call me once The lonely maiden-Princess of the *w*,	*The Ring* 65
Who love the winter *w's*, to trace	*To Ulysses* 14
She comes on waste and *w*, On farm and field:	*Prog. of Spring* 22
w's Plunged gulf on gulf thro' all their vales below.	,, 72
found Paris, a naked babe, among the *w's* Of Ida,	*Death of Œnone* 54
on man in the tropical *w*,	*The Dawn* 3

Wood (substance) (*See also*, **Pinewood, Satin-wood**)

Hard *w* I am, and wrinkled rind,	*Talking Oak* 171
a noiseless riot underneath Strikes thro' the *w*,	*Lucretius* 186
'Ye are green *w*, see ye warp not.	*Princess ii* 75
draw water, or hew *w*, Or grosser tasks;	*Gareth and L.* 486

Wood (substance) (*continued*)   Had carved himself a

knightly shield of *w*,	*Merlin and V.* 473
javelining With darted spikes and splinters of the *w*	,, 937
To thee, dead *w*, I bow not head nor knees.	*Sir J. Oldcastle* 128
fell'd the foes before you as the woodman fells the *w*,	*Happy* 42

Woodbine (adj.)   rent The *w* wreaths that bind her, | *Amphion* 34

And the *w* spices are wafted abroad,	*Maud I xxii* 5
wind Came wooingly with *w* smells,	*Lover's Tale ii* 36
And hour by hour unfolding *w* leaves	*Prog. of Spring* 7

Woodbine (s)   *w* and eglatere Drip sweeter dews | *A Dirge* 23

And tell me if the *w's* blow.	*My life is full* 25
as sweet As *w's* fragile hold,	*Talking Oak* 146
Thorns, ivies, *w*, mistletoes,	*Day-Dm., Sleep. P.* 43
There in due time the *w* blows,	*In Mem. cv* 7
my oän door-poorch wi' the *w* an' jessmine	*Spinster's S's.* 105

Woodcraft   Look to thy *w*,' and so leaving him, | *Balin and Balan* 308

Wood-devil   scream of that *W-d* I came to quell!' | ,,   548

Wood-dove   Deeply the *w-d* coos; | *Leonine Eleg.* 6

Wooded (*See also* **Deep-wooded**)   The mountain *w* to

the peak,	*Enoch Arden* 572
And hollow lined and *w* to the lips,	*Lover's Tale i* 398
the wave again Is vocal in its *w* walls;	*In Mem. xix* 14
Beside the river's *w* reach,	,, *lxxi* 13

Wooden   When from her *w* walls,—lit by sure hands,— | *Buonaparte* 5

Woodland (adj.)   Be mine a philosopher's life in the quiet *w*

ways,	*Maud I iv* 49
Gathering *w* lilies, Myriads blow together.	,, *xii* 7
And the *w* echo rings;	,, *II iv* 38
And deem it carrion of some *w* thing,	*Gareth and L.* 748
With joy that blazed itself in *w* wealth	*Balin and Balan* 82
A damsel-errant, warbling, as she rode The *w* alleys,	,, 439
Now talking of their *w* paradise	*Last Tournament* 726
My Edwin loved to call us then 'His two wild *w* flowers.'	*The Flight* 80
While round her brows a *w* culver flits,	*Prog. of Spring* 18
Still round her forehead wheels the *w* dove,	,, 57
Hear thy myriad laureates hail thee monarch in their *w* rhyme.	*Akbar's D., Hymn* 6

Woodland (s)   filter'd tribute of the rough *w*, | *Ode to Memory* 63

In firry *w's* making moan;	*Miller's D.* 42
Slides the bird o'er lustrous *w*,	*Locksley Hall* 162
That grows within the *w*.	*Amphion* 8
When the rotten *w* drips,	*Vision of Sin* 81
ILLYRIAN *w's*, echoing falls Of water,	*To E. L.* 1
the broad *w* parcell'd into farms;	*Aylmer's Field* 847
forefoot plies His function of the *w*:	*Lucretius* 46
as the golden Autumn *w* reels Athwart the smoke	*Princess vii* 357
Which in our winter *w* looks a flower.	*A Dedication* 13
'Fear not, isle of blowing *w*,	*Boädicea* 38
Made the noise of frosty *w's*,	,, 75
And *w's* holy to the dead;	*In Mem. xcix* 8
Now rings the *w* loud and long,	,, *cxv* 5
flying gold of the ruin'd *w's* drove thro' the air.	*Maud I i* 12
a flame That rages in the *w* far below,	*Balin and Balan* 234
left the ravaged *w* yet once more To peace;	*Merlin and V.* 963
Over all the *w's* flooded bowers,	*Sisters (E. and E.)* 20
Thou that singest wheat and *w*,	*To Virgil* 9
For all that ample *w* whisper'd ' debt,'	*The Ring* 170
and glancing at Elf of the *w*,	*Merlin and the G.* 38

Wood-louse   blue *w-l*, and the plump dormouse, | *Windov, Winter* 9

Woodman   see the *w* lift His axe to slay my kin. | *Talking Oak* 235

they came, The *woodmen* with their axes:	*Princess vi* 44
a *w* there Reported of some demon in the woods	*Balin and Balan* 123
This *w* show'd the cave From which he sallies,	,, 131
Came on the hoarhead at a bough	,, 294
To whom the *w* utter'd wonderingly	,, 297
vows—I am *w* of the woods,	*Last Tournament* 699
fell'd the foes before you as the *w* fells the wood,	*Happy* 42

Wood-nymph   a foot-fall, ere he saw The *w-n*, | *Palace of Art* 111

Woodpecker   As laughters of the *w* | *Kate* 4

An echo like a ghostly *w*,	*Princess, Pro.* 217
Before her skims the jubilant *w*,	*Prog. of Spring* 16

Wood-walk   dark *w-w's* drench'd in dew, | *D. of F. Women* 75

Wood-way   green *w-w's*, and eyes among the leaves; | *Pelleas and E.* 139

Woodwork   Fled ever thro' the *w*, till they found | *Lancelot and E.* 440

Wood-world   *w-w* is one full peal of praise. | *Balin and Balan* 450

Woody	To the *w* hollows in which we meet	*Maud I xxii* 43
	In the silent *w* places By the home that gave me birth,	,, *II iv* 6
Woo'd	folded leaf is *w* from out the bud	*Lotos-Eaters, C. S.* 26
	he *w* and wed A labourer's daughter,	*Dora* 39
	who would love? I *w* a woman once,	*Audley Court* 52
	Drunk even when he *w*;	*Marr. of Geraint* 442
	how he *w* The waters, and the waters answering	*Lover's Tale i* 543
	I *w* her then, nor unsuccessfully,	*Sisters (E. and E.)* 125
	Whom I *w* and won.	,, 204
	But the Bandit had *w* me in vain,	*Bandit's Death* 10
Wooest	*W* not, nor vainly wranglest;	*Madeline* 38
Woof	Hues of the silken sheeny *w*	,, 22
	thro' warp and *w* From skirt to skirt;	*Princess i* 62
Wooing	his long *w* her, Her slow consent,	*Enoch Arden* 707
	baits Of gold and beauty, *w* him to woo.	*Aylmer's Field* 487
	All my *w* is done.	*Window, Marr. Morn.* 4
	Edith had welcomed my brief *w* of her,	*Sisters (E. and E.)* 254
	sound Which to the *w* wind aloof The poplar made,	*Mariana* 75
Wool	Like footsteps upon *w*.	*Œnone* 250
	needs it we should cram our ears with *w*	*Princess iv* 65
	w of a thistle a-flyin' an' seeädin'	*Spinster's S's.* 79
	but *w's* looking oop my how.	*Church-warden, etc.* 6
Woolly	And *w* breasts and beaded eyes;	*In Mem. xcv* 12
Woorse (worse)	*W* nor a far-welter'd yowe :	*N. Farmer, N. S.* 32
Woost (worst)	And i' the *w* o' toimes	,, *O. S.* 16
Word	(*See also* **Watch-word**) Shot thro' and thro' with cunning *w's*.	*Clear-headed friend* 17
	Her *w's* did gather thunder as they ran,	*The Poet* 49
	So was their meaning to her *w's*.	,, 53
	and with *his w* She shook the world.	,, 55
	kiss sweet kisses, and speak sweet *w's*:	*Sea-Fairies* 34
	Wild *w's* wander here and there :	*A Dirge* 43
	And your *w's* are seeming-bitter	*Rosalind* 30
	And kiss away the bitter *w's*	,, 50
	How may measur'd *w's* adore The full-flowing harmony	*Eleänore* 45
	'These *w's*,' I said, 'are like the rest;	*Two Voices* 334
	The thesis which thy *w's* intend—	,, 338
	if I waste *w's* now, in truth You must blame Love.	*Miller's D.* 191
	With blessings which no *w's* can find.	,, 238
	Indeed I heard one bitter *w*	*L. C. V. de Vere* 37
	Tho' I cannot speak a *w*, I shall harken	*May Queen, N. Y's.* 39
	the clergyman, has told me *w's* of peace.	,, *Con.* 12
	say to Robin a kind *w*, and tell him not to fret;	,, 45
	little meaning tho' the *w's* are strong ;	*Lotos-Eaters, C. S.* 119
	Her slow full *w's* sank thro' the silence drear,	*D. of F. Women* 121
	My *w's* leapt forth : 'Heaven heads the count of crimes	,, 201
	Because all *w's*, tho' cull'd with choicest art,	,, 285
	I had not dared to flow In these *w's* toward you,	*To J. S.* 7
	W's weaker than your grief would make	,, 65
	But gentle *w's* are always gain:	*Love thou thy land* 23
	Would serve his kind in deed and *w*,	,, 86
	He utter'd *w's* of scorning;	*The Goose* 42
	Watch what thou seëst, and lightly bring me *w*.'	*M. d'Arthur* 38
	Watch what I see, and lightly bring thee *w*.'	,, 44
	I bad thee, watch, and lightly bring me *w*.'	,, 81
	would have spoken, but he found not *w's*,	,, 172
	(My *w's* were half in earnest, half in jest,)	*Gardener's D.* 23
	A *w* could bring the colour to my cheek ;	,, 196
	And in the compass of three little *w's*,	,, 232
	Here, then, my *w's* have end.	,, 250
	he and I Had once hard *w's*, and parted,	*Dora* 18
	But in my time a father's *w* was law,	,, 27
	Or change a *w* with her he calls his wife,	,, 44
	You knew my *w* was law, and yet you dared	,, 98
	I set the *w's*, and added names I knew.	*Audley Court* 61
	Caught *in flagrante*—what's the Latin ?—	*Walk. to the Mail* 34
	And well his *w's* became him :	*Edwin Morris* 25
	Were not his *w's* delicious,	,, 71
	That, trust me on my *w*,	*Talking Oak* 170
	w's That make a man feel strong in speaking truth;	*Love and Duty* 69
	These measured *w's*, my work of yestermorn.	*Golden Year* 21
	but I *know* my *w's* are wild,	*Locksley Hall* 173
	And order'd *w's* asunder fly.	*Day-Dm., Pro.* 20
	With *w's* of promise in his walk,	,, *Arrival* 23

Word (*continued*)	The barons swore, with many *w's*,	*Day-Dm., Revival* 23
	In courteous *w's* return'd reply :	,, 30
	'Cruel, cruel the *w's* I said !	*Edward Gray* 17
	And whisper lovely *w's*, and use	*Will Water.* 11
	Hours, when the Poet's *w's* and looks	,, 193
	For I am yours in *w* and in deed.	*Lady Clare* 74
	Down they dropt—no *w* was spoken—	*The Captain* 51
	She was more fair than a *w's* can say :	*Beggar Maid* 2
	But in my *w's* were seeds of fire.	*The Letters* 28
	Light on a broken *w* to thank him with.	*Enoch Arden* 347
	for she did not speak a *w*.	,, 390
	Ev'n as she dwelt upon his latest *w's*,	,, 454
	Enoch spoke no *w* to any one,	,, 667
	for Enoch hung A moment on her *w's*,	,, 873
	Poor Philip, of all his lavish waste of *w's*	*The Brook* 191
	were *w's*, As meted by his measure of himself,	*Aylmer's Field* 315
	Never one kindly smile, one kindly *w*:	,, 564
	how the *w's* Have twisted back upon themselves,	,, 754
	his one *w* was 'desolate;'	,, 836
	but not a *w*; she shook her head.	*Sea Dreams* 116
	To spread the *W* by which himself had thriven.'	,, 197
	Of Heliconian honey in living *w's*,	*Lucretius* 224
	'Doubt my *w* again !' he said.	*Princess, Pro.* 176
	At those high *w's*, we conscious of ourselves,	,, *ii* 67
	at these *w's* the snake, My secret,	,, *iii* 32
	(for still My mother went revolving on the *w*)	,, 54
	Then came these dreadful *w's* out one by one,	,, 57
	The truth at once, but with no *w* from me ;	,, 61
	She struck such warbling fury thro' the *w's*;	,, *iv* 586
	(our royal *w* upon it, He comes back safe)	,, *v* 224
	Arac's *w* is thrice As ours with Ida :	,, 226
	roll'd himself Thrice in the saddle, then burst out in *w's*.	,, 275
	And you shall have her answer by the *w*.'	,, 327
	and rolling *w's* Oration-like.	,, 372
	at the happy *w* 'he lives' My father stoop'd,	,, *vi* 128
	Say one soft *w* and let me part forgiven.'	,, 219
	Not one *w*? not one?	,, 231
	Not one *w*; No ! tho' your father sues :	,, 239
	A *w*, but one, one little kindly *w*,	,, 258
	king her father charm'd Her wounded soul with *w's*:	,, 346
	Like perfect music unto noble *w's*;	,, *vii* 286
	It seems you love to cheat yourself with *w's*:	,, 334
	The *w's* are mostly mine :	,, *Con.* 3
	Who spoke few *w's* and pithy, such as closed Welcome,	,, 94
	To fling whate'er we felt, not fearing, into *w's*.	*Third of Feb.* 6
	we will not spare the tyrant one hard *w*.	,, 42
	Taäke my *w* for it, Sammy,	*N. Farmer, N. S.* 48
	To put in *w's* the grief I feel; For *w's*, like Nature, half reveal	*In Mem. v* 2
	In *w's*, like weeds, I'll wrap me o'er,	,, 9
	What *w's* are these have fall'n from me ?	,, *xvi* 1
	The *w's* that are not heard again.	,, *xviii* 20
	That out of *w's* a comfort win;	,, *xx* 10
	Where truth in closest *w's* shall fail,	,, *xxxvi* 6
	And so the *W* had breath, and wrought	,, 9
	And hence, indeed, she sports with *w's*,	,, *xlviii* 9
	My *w's* are only *w's*, and moved	,, *lii* 3
	In those sad *w's* I took farewell :	,, *lviii* 1
	The *w's* were hard to understand.	,, *lxix* 20
	In fitting aptest *w's* to things,	,, *lxxv* 6
	O true in *w*, and tried in deed.	,, *lxxxv* 5
	Your *w's* have virtue such as draws	,, 13
	But in dear *w's* of human speech	,, 83
	The wish too strong for *w's* to name ;	,, *xciii* 14
	strangely on the silence broke The silent-speaking *w's*,	,, *xcv* 26
	So *w* by *w*, and line by line,	,, 33
	Vague *w's*! but ah, how hard to frame	,, 45
	And if the *w's* were sweet and strong	,, *cxxv* 11
	To change the bearing of a *w*,	,, *cxxviii* 16
	living *w's* of life Breathed in her ear.	,, *Con.* 52
	the wealth Of *w's* and wit, the double health,	,, 103
	faith in a tradesman's ware or his *w* ?	*Maud I i* 26
	Dare I bid her abide by her *w* ?	,, *xvi* 25
	Had given her *w* to a thing so low ?	,, 27
	Can break her *w* were it even for me ?	,, 29

Wordless (*continued*)   And *w* broodings on the wasted
    cheek—   *Princess* vii 112
Wordy   but when the *w* storm Had ended,   *Sea Dreams* 31
And keen thro' *w* snares to track Suggestion   *In Mem.* xcv 31
And *w* trucklings to the transient hour,   *To the Queen* ii 51
Wore   (*See also* **Ware, Weär'd**)   For many weeks about
    my loins I *w*   *St. S. Stylites* 63
That she *w* when she was wed.'   *L. of Burleigh* 96
A gown of grass-green silk she *w*,   *Sir L. and Q. G.* 24
She *w* the colours I approved.   *The Letters* 16
crime Of sense avenged by sense that *w* with time.'   *Vision of Sin* 214
another *w* A close-set robe of jasmine   *Aylmer's Field* 157
And still I *w* her picture by my heart,   *Princess* i 38
I *w* a lilac gown;   *Grandmother* 57
it grew so tall It *w* a crown of light,   *The Flower* 10
Never morning *w* To evening,   *In Mem.* vi 7
I *w* them like a civic crown: „ lxix 8
In which of old I *w* the gown;   „ lxxxvii 2
since he neither *w* on helm or shield   *Com. of Arthur* 49
three gay suits of armour which they *w*,   *Geraint and E.* 95
his the prize, who *w* the sleeve Of scarlet,   *Lancelot and E.* 501
He *w*, against his wont, upon his helm   „ 603
he *w* your sleeve: Would he break faith   „ 684
but I lighted on the maid Whose sleeve he *w*;   „ 711
With knees of adoration *w* the stone,   *Holy Grail* 71
all she *w* Torn as a sail that leaves the rope   „ 211
And beauty such as never woman *w*,   *Guinevere* 549
She deem'd I *w* a brother's mind: *Lover's Tale* i 741
he learnt that I hated the ring I *w*,   *The Wreck* 57
w it till her death, Shrined him within the temple   *The Ring* 218
Muriel clench'd The hand that *w* it,   „ 262
That ever *w* a Christian marriage-ring.   *Romney's R.* 36
Work (s)   (*See also* **Branch - work, Chequer - work,**
Damask-work, Frame-work, Handmaid-work,
Jacinth-work, Mat-work, Trellis-work, Works and
Days)   At his *w* you may hear him sob and sigh   *A spirit haunts* 5
Now is done thy long day's *w*;   *A Dirge* 1
Grave mother of majestic *w*'s,   *Of old sat Freedom* 13
Thy *w* is thine—The single note   *England and Amer.* 18
we loved the man, and prized his *w*;   *M. d'Arthur*, Ep. 8
'Tis not your *w*, but Love's.   *Gardener's D.* 24
and he left his men at *w*, And came and said: *Dora* 86
Till that wild wind made *w*   *Talking Oak* 54
To that man My *w* shall answer,   *Love and Duty* 29
These measured words, my *w* of yestermorn.   *Golden Year* 21
He works his *w*, I mine.   *Ulysses* 43
Some *w* of noble note, may yet be done,   „ 52
A virgin heart in *w* and will.   *Sir Galahad* 24
'Thou shalt not be saved by *w*'s: *Vision of Sin* 91
Nor of what race, the *w*;   *Aylmer's Field* 224
Small were his gains, and hard his *w*;   *Sea Dreams* 8
the woman honest *W*;   „ 137
Which things appear the *w* of mighty Gods.   *Lucretius* 102
and if I go *my w* is left Unfinish'd—*if* I go.   „ 103
when we set our hand To this great *w*,   *Princess* ii 60
Your own *w* marr'd: „ 230
and silver litanies, The *w* of Ida,   „ 478
how vast a *w* To assail this gray preëminence   „ iii 233
That we might see our own *w* out,   „ 270
as the workman and his *w*, That practice betters?'   „ 298
Which touches on the workman and his *w*.   „ 322
and known at last (my *w*)   „ iv 347
understanding all the foolish *w* Of Fancy,   „ vi 116
The treble *w*'s, the vast designs   *Ode on Well.* 104
Whose life was *w*, whose language rife   „ 183
Such was he: his *w* is done.   „ 218
There must be other nobler *w* to do   „ 256
The *w*'s of peace with *w*'s of war.   *Ode Inter. Exhib.* 19
Fur *w* mun 'a gone to the gittin'   *N. Farmer, N. S.* 50
burn the palaces, break the *w*'s of the statuary,   *Boädicea* 64
Man, her last *w*, who seem'd so fair,   *In Mem.* lvi 9
I shall pass; my *w* will fail.   „ lvii 8
my passion hath not swerved To *w*'s of weakness,   „ lxxxv 50
Let her *w* prevail.   „ cxiv 4
O days and hours, your *w* is this   „ cxvii 1

Work (s) (*continued*)   Contemplate all this *w* of Time,   *In Mem.* cxviii 1
If so he type this *w* of time Within himself,   „ 16
By thee the world's great *w* is heard Beginning,   „ cxxi 10
the *w*'s of the men of mind,   *Maud* I i 25
Awe-stricken breaths at a *w* divine,   „ x 17
Frail, but a *w* divine,   „ II ii 4
Small, but a *w* divine,   „ 23
There is none that does his *w*, not one;   „ v 26
cannot will my will, nor work my *w* Wholly,   *Com. of Arthur* 88
Man am I grown, a man's *w* must I do.   *Gareth and L.* 116
rich in emblem and the *w* Of ancient kings   „ 304
Thralls to your *w* again,   „ 710
with back turn'd, and bow'd above his *w*,   *Marr. of Geraint* 267
And there is scantly time for half the *w*.   „ 288
He spoke and fell to *w* again.   „ 292
the *w* To both appear'd so costly,   „ 637
This *w* of his is great and wonderful.   *Geraint and E.* 898
This *w* of Edyrn wrought upon himself   „ 912
felt His *w* was neither great nor wonderful,   „ 921
Yet needs must work my *w*.   *Merlin and V.* 505
They prove to him his *w*:   *Lancelot and E.* 158
Yet with all ease, so tender was the *w*:   „ 442
Her own poor *w*, her empty labour, left.   „ 991
Before his *w* be done,   *Holy Grail* 909
I will be leal to thee and work thy *w*,   *Pelleas and E.* 343
This evil of Lancelot and the Queen?   *Guinevere* 307
and with my *w* thus Crown'd her clear forehead.   *Lover's Tale* i 344
But *w* was scant in the Isle,   *First Quarrel* 43
to see if *w* could be found;   „ 44
'I ha' six weeks' *w*, little wife,   „ 45
'You promised to find me *w* near you,   „ 52
'I've gotten my *w* to do;   „ 85
I ha' six weeks' *w* in Jersey   „ 88
couldn't do naw *w* an' all,   *North. Cobbler* 77
where the *w*'s of the Lord are reveal'd   *In the Child. Hosp.* 35
Frail were the *w*'s that defended the hold   *Def. of Lucknow* 7
Beyond all *w* of those who carve the stone,   *Tiresias* 53
beyond All *w* of man, yet, like all *w* of man,   *Ancient Sage* 85
Undo their *w* again, And leave him,   „ 112
aisier av they lived be an Irish bog.   *Tomorrow* 72
but 'a left me the *w* to do,   *Spinster's S's.* 55
of the chasm between *W* and Ideal?   *Romney's R.* 64
now thy long day's *w* hath ceased,   *Epit. on Stratford* 2
W's of subtle brain and hand,   *Open I. and C. Exhib.* 7
Whose Faith and *W*'s were bells of full accord,   *In Mem., W. G. Ward* 2
loosen, stone from stone, All my fair *w*;   *Akbar's Dream* 189
Work (**literary production**)   Botanic Treatises, And *W*'s
    on Gardening   *Amphion* 78
My golden *w* in which I told a truth   *Lucretius* 260
Work (**verb**)   Then let wise Nature *w* her will,   *My life is full* 21
Hath time and space to *w* and spread.   *You ask me, why, etc.* 16
And *w*, a joint of state, that plies Its office,   *Love thou thy land* 47
but *w* in hues to dim The Titianic Flora.   *Gardener's D.* 170
And hired himself to *w* within the fields;   *Dora* 38
Mary, let me live and *w* with you: „ 115
w for William's child, until he grows Of age,   „ 126
Can I *w* miracles and not be saved?   *St. S. Stylites* 150
I will *w* in prose and rhyme,   *Talking Oak* 289
w itself Thro' madness, hated by the wise,   *Love and Duty* 6
That unto him who *w*'s, and feels he *w*'s,   *Golden Year* 73
He *w*'s his work, I mine.   *Ulysses* 43
For love in sequel *w*'s with fate,   *Day-Dm., Arrival* 3
I must *w* thro' months of toil,   *Amphion* 97
All parties *w* together.   *Will Water.* 56
Who needs would *w* for Annie to the last,   *Enoch Arden* 180
Scorning an alms, to *w* whereby to live.   „ 812
but labour for himself, *W* without hope,   „ 820
all things *w* together for the good Of those'—   *Sea Dreams* 158
Embrace our aims: *w* out your freedom.   *Princess* ii 89
nor would we *w* for fame;   „ iii 261
But in the shadow will we *w*,   „ 331
but *w* no more alone! Our place is much: „ vii 266
Make and break, and *w* their will;   *Ode on Well.* 261
And all men *w* in noble brotherhood,   *Ode Inter. Exhib.* 38
w's Without a conscience or an aim.   *In Mem.* xxxiv 7

Work (verb) (*continued*) To one that with us *w*'s, and trust, — *In Mem. cxxxi* 8
spirit of murder *w*'s in the very means of life, — *Maud* I i 40
cannot will my will, nor *w* my work Wholly, — *Com. of Arthur* 88
and we will *w* thy will Who love thee.' — " 259
but an he *w*, Like any pigeon will I cram — *Gareth and L.* 458
Myself would *w* eye dim, and finger lame, — *Marr. of Geraint* 628
ruth began to *w* Against his anger in him, — *Geraint and E.* 101
Vivien ever sought to *w* the charm — *Merlin and V.* 215
But *w* as vassal to the larger love, — " 491
You needs must *w* my work. — " 505
To all the foulness that they *w*. — " 785
Thanks, but you *w* against your own desire; — *Lancelot and E.* 1096
Or hers or mine, mine now to *w* my will— — " 1231
to whom I vow'd That I would *w* — *Holy Grail* 784
As let these caitiffs on thee *w* their will?' — *Pelleas and E.* 323
I will be leal to thee and *w* thy work, — " 343
I, being simple, thought to *w* His will, — *Pass. of Arthur* 22
And life and limbs, all his to *w* his will.' — *Lover's Tale* iv 283
an' I *w* an' I wait to the end. — *First Quarrel* 7
gave All but free leave for all to *w* the mines, — *Columbus* 133
I am not yet too old to *w* his will— — " 161
hourly *w* their brother insect wrong, — *Locksley H., Sixty* 202
To *w* old laws of Love to fresh results, — *Prog. of Spring* 85
art *thou* the Prophet? canst *thou w* Miracles?' — *Akbar's Dream* 117
Meanwhile, my brothers, *w*, and wield — *Mechanophilus* 29
Hold thine own, and *w* thy will! — *Poets and Critics* 13

Work'd-Workt But my full heart, that *work'd* below, — *Two Voices* 44
And they say then that I *work'd* miracles, — *St. S. Stylites* 80
thy strong Hours indignant *work'd* their wills, — *Tithonus* 18
But oft he *work'd* among the rest and shook — *Enoch Arden* 651
Rose from the clay it *work'd* in as she past, — *Aylmer's Field* 170
seeing who had *work'd* Lustier than any, — *Gareth and L.* 695
I ha' *work'd* for him fifteen years, — *First Quarrel* 7
He *workt* me the daisy chain— — " 13
a girl, a hussy, that *workt* with him up at the farm, — " 24
but the creatures had *worked* their will. — *Rizpah* 50
Because the simple mother *work'd* upon By Edith — *Sisters (E. and E.)* 206
This power hath *work'd* no good to aught that lives, — *Tiresias* 77

Worker (*See also* **Fellow-worker, War-worker**) Men, my brothers, men the *w*'s, — *Locksley Hall* 117

Working (*See also* **Still-working**) A labour *w* to an end. — *Two Voices* 297
Life, that, *w* strongly, binds— — *Love thou thy land* 34
Him, like the *w* bee in blossom-dust, — *Enoch Arden* 366
' It came,' she said, ' by *w* in the mines:' — *Sea Dreams* 114
The jest and earnest *w* side by side, — *Princess* iv 563
Or been in narrowest *w* shut, — *In Mem.* xxxv 20
His being *w* in mine own, — " lxxxv 43
Move upward, *w* out the beast, — " cxviii 27
A knight of Arthur, *w* out his will, — *Gareth and L.* 24
(Sea was her wrath, yet *w* after storm) — *Lancelot and E.* 1309
Queen, *W* a tapestry, lifted up her head, — *Last Tournament* 129
Demos end in *w* its own doom. — *Locksley H., Sixty* 114

Workman Which wrought us, as the *w* and his work, — *Princess* iii 298
Which touches on the *w* and his work. — " 322
Workmen up at the Hall!— — *Maud* I i 65

Workmanship I admire Joints of cunning *w*. — *Vision of Sin* 186
' Look what a lovely piece of *w*!' — *Aylmer's Field* 237

Works and Days more than he that sang the *W a D*, — *To Virgil* 6
Workt *See* **Work'd**
Wo'ld (world) Tha mun tackle the sins o' the *W*, — *Church-warden, etc.* 46
World (*See also* **Dream-world, Half-world, New-world, Old-world, Shadow-world, She-world, Sister-world, Water-world, Wo'ld, Woman-world, Wood-world**) 'Tis the *w*'s winter; — *Nothing will Die* 17
The *w* was never made; — " 30
a *w* of peace And confidence, day after day; — *Supp. Confessions* 29
w hath not another (Tho' all her fairest forms — *Isabel* 38
which possess'd The darkness of the *w*, — *Arabian Nights* 72
the *w* Like one great garden show'd, — *The Poet* 33
and with *his* word She shook the *w*. — " 56
All the *w* o'er, (repeat) — *Sea-Fairies* 41
Roof'd the *w* with doubt and fear, — *Eleänore* 99
Kate saith ' the *w* is void of might.' — *Kate* 17

World (*continued*) All the inner, all the outer *w* of pain — *If I were loved* 5
Shadows of the *w* appear. — *L. of Shalott* ii 12
I said ' When first the *w* began, — *Two Voices* 16
Look up thro' night: the *w* is wide. — " 24
Is cancell'd in the *w* of sense?' — " 42
to present The *w* with some development. — " 75
And full of dealings with the *w*? — *Miller's D.* 8
There's somewhat in this *w* amiss — " 19
' while the *w* runs round and round,' — *Palace of Art* 13
cycles of the human tale Of this wide *w*, — " 147
And let the *w* have peace or wars, — " 182
' No voice breaks thro' the stillness of this *w*: — " 259
and all the *w* is still. — *May Queen, N. Y's. E.* 24
girdled with the gleaming *w*: — *Lotos-Eaters, C. S.* 113
gently comes the *w* to those That are cast — *To J. S.* 3
harmonies of law The growing *w* assume, — *England and Amer.* 17
general decay of faith Right thro' the *w*, — *The Epic* 19
famous knights Whereof this *w* holds record. — *M. d'Arthur* 16
Or hath come, since the making of the *w*. — " 203
Which was an image of the mighty *w*; — " 235
Lest one good custom should corrupt the *w*. — " 242
More things are wrought by prayer Than this *w* dreams of. — " 248
Not wholly in the busy *w*, nor quite Beyond it, — *Gardener's D.* 33
And Beauty such a mistress of the *w*. — " 58
nor from her tendance turn'd Into the *w* without; — " 145
to hold From thence thro' all the *w*'s: — " 182
That veil'd the *w* with jaundice. — *Walk. to the Mail* 20
That these two parties still divide the *w*— — " 77
As never sow was higher in this *w*— — " 96
we should mimic this raw fool the *w*, — " 106
for the good and increase of the *w*.' (repeat) — *Edwin Morris* 51, 92
Among the powers and princes of this *w*, — *St. S. Stylites* 187
O this *w*'s curse,—beloved but hated— — *Love and Duty* 47
If all the *w* were falcons, what of that? — *Golden Year* 38
like the second *w* to us that live; — " 56
arch wherethro' Gleams that untravell'd *w*, — *Ulysses* 20
'Tis not too late to seek a newer *w*. — " 57
Here at the quiet limit of the *w*, — *Tithonus* 7
comes A glimpse of that dark *w* where I was born. — " 33
Saw the Vision of the *w*, (repeat) — *Locksley Hall* 16, 120
the Federation of the *w*. — " 128
and the *w* is more and more. — " 142
Let the great *w* spin for ever — " 182
Like hints and echoes of the *w* — *Day-Dm., Sleep. P.* 7
In that new *w* which is the old: — " *Depart.* 4
Thro' all the *w* she follow'd him. — " 32
And learn the *w*, and sleep again; — " *L'Envoi* 8
The prelude to some brighter *w*. — " 40
And all the *w* go by them. — *Will Water.* 48
Ah yet, tho' all the *w* forsake, — " 49
We knew the merry *w* was round, — *The Voyage* 7
We lov'd the glories of the *w*, — " 83
We know the merry *w* is round, — " 95
Ring'd with the azure *w*, he stands. — *The Eagle* 3
And my mockeries of the *w*. — *Vision of Sin* 202
he sings of what the *w* will be When the years — *Poet's Song* 15
not to see the *w*—For pleasure? — *Enoch Arden* 297
She slipt across the summer of the *w*, — " 531
She passing thro' the summer *w* again, — " 534
And glories of the broad belt of the *w*, — " 579
Roll'd a sea-haze and whelm'd the *w* in gray; — " 672
And beating up thro' all the bitter *w*, — " 802
One whom the strong sons of the *w* despise; — *The Brook* 3
Too fresh and fair in our sad *w*'s best bloom, — " 218
With half-allowing smiles for all the *w*, — *Aylmer's Field* 120
the *w* should ring of him To shame these — " 395
And fain had haled him out into the *w*, — " 467
Against the desolations of the *w*. — " 634
Eight that were left to make a purer *w*— — " 638
To blow these sacrifices thro' the *w*— — " 758
Doubtless our narrow *w* must canvass it: — " 774
And left their memories a *w*'s curse— — " 796
wife Sat shuddering at the ruin of a *w*; — *Sea Dreams* 30
' What a *w*,' I thought, ' To live in!' — " 94
think that in our often-ransack'd *w* — " 129

World (*continued*) The lucid interspace of *w* and *w*,   *Lucretius* 105
I seem'd to move among a *w* of ghosts,   *Princess i* 17
One rose in all the *w*, your Highness that,   ,,   *ii* 51
'This *w* was once a fluid haze of light,   ,,   116
Two in the tangled business of the *w*,   ,,   174
Poets, whose thoughts enrich the blood of the *w*.'   ,,   181
secular emancipation turns Of half this *w*,   ,,   290
A blessing on her labours for the *w*.   ,,   479
whence after-hands May move the *w*,   ,,   *iii* 264
weight of all the hopes of half the *w*,   ,,   *iv* 184
women kick against their Lords Thro' all the *w*,   ,,   413
dam Ready to burst and flood the *w* with foam: ,,   474
tho' all the gold That veins the *w* were pack'd   ,,   543
I seem'd to move among a *w* of ghosts;   ,,   561
The wrath I nursed against the *w*:   ,,   *v* 437
Shall move the stony bases of the *w*.   ,,   *vi* 58
when a *w* Of traitorous friend and broken system   ,,   194
and tarn by tarn Expunge the *w*:   ,,   *vii* 41
So blacken'd all her *w* in secret,   ,,   42
I believed that in the living *w* My spirit closed   ,,   157
notice of a change in the dark *w* Was lispt   ,,   250
These were the rough ways of the *w* till now.   ,,   257
Nor lose the wrestling thews that throw the *w*;   ,,   282
Then reign the *w's* great bridals,   ,,   294
Immersed in rich foreshadowings of the *w*,   ,,   312
O we will walk this *w*, Yoked in all exercise   ,,   360
and down rolls the *w* In mock heroics   ,, *Con.* 63
This fine old *w* of ours is but a child   ,,   77
Thro' all the silent spaces of the *w's*,   ,,   114
The greatest sailor since our *w* began.   *Ode on Well.* 86
And drill the raw *w* for the march of mind,   ,,   168
Thro' either babbling *w* of high and low;   ,,   182
Tho' *w* on *w* in myriad myriads roll Round us,   ,,   262
hold against the *w* this honour of the land.   *Third of Feb.* 48
All the *w* wonder'd: (repeat)   *Light Brigade* 31, 52
diviner air Breathe thro' the *w* and change   *W. to Marie Alex.* 44
And howsoever this wild *w* may roll,   ,,   48
it cost me a *w* of woe,   *Grandmother* 23
For him nor moves thel oud *w's* random mock,   *Will* 4
Dark is the *w* to thee: *High. Pantheism* 7
As one who feels the immeasurable *w*,   *A Dedication* 7
wet west wind and the *w* will go on. (repeat) *Window, No Answer* 6, 12
wet west wind and the *w* may go on.   ,,   18
Over the *w* to the end of it   *Marr. Morn.* 23
Help thy vain *w's* to bear thy light.   *In Mem., Pro.* 32
The sunbeam strikes along the *w*:   ,,   *xv* 8
Science reaches forth her arms To feel from *w* to *w*,   ,,   *xxi* 19
Thou fail not in a *w* of sin,   ,,   *xxxiii* 15
The total *w* since life began;   ,,   *xliii* 12
Upon the great *w's* altar-stairs   ,,   *lv* 15
breathes a novel *w*, while the His other passion   ,,   *lxii* 9
The centre of a *w's* desire;   ,,   *lxiv* 16
So many *w's*, so much to do,   ,,   *lxxiii* 1
The *w* which credits what is done Is cold to all   ,,   *lxxv* 15
In whispers of the beauteous *w*.   ,,   *lxxix* 12
The deep pulsations of the *w*,   ,,   *xcv* 40
Of rising *w's* by yonder wood.   ,,   *cv* 25
I would the great *w* grew like thee,   ,,   *cxiv* 25
In that which made the *w* so fair.   ,,   *cxvi* 8
the *w's* great work is heard Beginning,   ,,   *cxxi* 10
I found Him not in *w* or sun,   ,,   *cxxiv* 5
And whispers to the *w's* of space,   ,,   *cxxvi* 11
And mingle all the *w* with thee.   ,,   *cxxix* 12
and let the *w* have its way: *Maud I iv* 21
wood where I sit is a *w* of plunder and prey.   ,,   24
Who knows the ways of the *w*,   ,,   44
the suns are many, the *w* is wide.   ,,   45
I have not made the *w*,   ,,   48
From the long-neck'd geese of the *w*   ,,   52
If I find the *w* so bitter   ,,   *vi* 33
Then the *w* were not so bitter (repeat)   ,,   38, 94
a *w* in which I have hardly mixt,   ,,   76
More life to Love than is or ever was In our low *w*,   ,,   *xviii* 48
A *w* of trouble within!   ,,   *xix* 25
makes us loud in the *w* of the dead;   ,,   *II v* 25

World (*continued*) a *w* that loves him not, For it is but a
   w of the dead.   *Maud II v* 39
She comes from another stiller *w* of the dead,   ,,   70
Fairer than aught in the *w* beside,   ,,   73
spoke of a hope for the *w* in the coming wars—   ,, *III vi* 11
in a weary *w* my one thing bright;   ,,   17
His loss drew like eclipse, Darkening the *w*.   *Ded. of Idylls* 15
I seem as nothing in the mighty *w*,   *Com. of Arthur* 87
And power on this dead *w* to make it live.'   ,,   94
the *w* Was all so clear about him,   ,,   97
the Powers who walk the *w* Made lightnings   ,,   107
deems himself alone And all the *w* asleep,   ,,   119
whatsoever storms May shake the *w*,   ,,   293
Graven in the oldest tongue of all this *w*,   ,,   302
To guard thee on the rough ways of the *w*.'   ,,   336
And hated this fair *w* and all therein,   ,,   344
live and love, and make the *w* Other,   ,,   472
'Blow trumpet, for the *w* is white with May;   ,,   482
Blow thro' the living *w*—   ,,   484
The slowly-fading mistress of the *w*,   ,,   505
working out his will, To cleanse the *w*.   *Gareth and L.* 25
or half the *w* Had ventured—   ,,   64
that skill'd spear, the wonder of the *w*—   ,,   1223
if the *w* were one Of utter peace, and love,   ,,   1288
And stay the *w* from Lady Lyonors.   ,,   1412
The *w's* loud whisper breaking into storm,   *Marr. of Geraint* 27
At caitiffs and at wrongers of the *w*.   ,,   96
At last they issued from the *w* of wood.   ,,   238
cackle of your bourg The murmur of the *w*!   ,,   277
the great wave that echoes round the *w*;   ,,   420
Made a low splendour in the *w*,   ,,   598
thro' the feeble twilight of this *w* Groping,   *Geraint and E.* 5
The being he loved best in all the *w*,   ,,   103
As the gray dawn stole o'er the dewy *w*,   ,,   385
Henceforth in all the *w* at anything,   ,,   649
The *w* will not believe a man repents: And this wise
   w of ours is mainly right.   ,,   900
I have quite foregone All matters of this *w*:   *Balin and Balan* 117
the Queen, and all the *w* Made music,   ,,   210
Old monk and fool, ye scorn the *w's* desire,   ,,   445
all at once they found the *w*, Staring wild-wide;   ,,   595
as Arthur in the highest Leaven'd the *w*,   *Merlin and V.* 141
Dear feet, that I have follow'd thro' the *w*,   ,.   227
And sweep me from my hold upon the *w*,   ,,   303
Who have to learn themselves and all the *w*,   ..   365
noble deeds, the flower of all the *w*.   ,,   413
I well believe that all about this *w*   ,,   541
sunn'd The *w* to peace again.   ..   639
The brute *w* howling forced them into bonds,   ,,   744
And touching other *w's*.   ,,   838
the place which now Is this *w's* hugest,   *Lancelot and E.* 76
flower of all the west and all the *w*,   ,,   249
Hid from the wide *w's* rumour by the grove Of poplars   .,   522
this and that other *w* Another *w* for the sick man;   ..   873
To serve you, and to follow you thro' the *w*.'   ,,   939
'Nay, the *w*, the *w*, All ear and eye,   ..   940
'For Lancelot and the Queen and all the *w*,   ,,   1107
Then might she follow me thro' the *w*,   ,,   1316
For never have I known the *w* without,   *Holy Grail* 20
And heal the *w* of all their wickedness!   ,,   94
and all the *w* be heal'd.'   ,,   128
Then flash'd a yellow gleam across the *w*,   ,,   402
And seem'd to me the Lord of all the *w*,   ,,   414
Rejoice, small man, in this small *w* of mine,   ,.   559
the sea rolls, and all the *w* is warm'd? '   ,,   672
'O happy, *w*,' thought Pelleas, ' all, meseems,   *Pelleas and E.* 136
Than all the ranged reasons of the *w*.   ,,   156
That follows on the turning of the *w*,   ,,   549
brother, thou nor I have made the *w*;   *Last Tournament* 203
Would make the *w* as blank as Winter-tide.   ,,   221
seeing too much wit Makes the *w* rotten,   ,,   247
the *w* Is flesh and shadow—   ,,   315
Who fain had clipt free manhood from the *w*—   ,,   446
The wide *w* laughs at it. And worldling of the *w*
   am I, and know The ptarmigan   ,,   695

Worm (*continued*) for the life of the *w* and the fly? — *Wages* 7
No will push me down to the *w*, — *Window, No Answer* 10
That not a *w* is cloven in vain; — *In Mem. liv* 9
Strike dead the whole weak race of venomous *w's*, — *Maud II i* 46
many rings (For he had many, poor *w*) — „ *ii* 69
Wroth to be wroth at such a *w*, — *Marr. of Geraint* 213
as the *w* draws in the wither'd leaf — *Geraint and E.* 633
And the high purpose broken by the *w*. — *Merlin and V.* 196
' A *w* within the rose.' — *Pelleas and E.* 399
He dies who loves it,—if the *w* be there.' — „ 409
And cast him as a *w* upon the way; — *Guinevere* 35
The guess of a *w* in the dust — *Despair* 30
Of a *w* as it writhes in a world — „ 31
Of a dying *w* in a world, — „ 32
When the *w* shall have writhed its last, — „ 85
' O *w's* and maggots of to-day — *Ancient Sage* 210
a *w* which writhes all day, and at night Stirs up — *Vastness* 17
You that would not tread on a *w* — *Forlorn* 45
flesh at last is filth on which the *w* will feast; — *Happy* 30
point and jeer, And gibber at the *w*, — *Romney's R.* 137
Worm-canker'd Distill'd from some *w-c* homily; — *To J. M. K.* 6
Worm-eaten So propt, *w-e*, ruinously old, — *Enoch Arden* 693
Wormwood banquet, where the meats became As *w*, — *Lancelot and E.* 744
Wormwood-bitter were *w-b* to me. — *Balin and Balan* 64
Worn (*See also* **Fever-worn, Storm-worn, Wave-worn, Way-worn, Well-worn, World-worn**) Weeded and *w* the
    ancient thatch — *Mariana* 7
both Brake into hall together, *w* and pale. — *Pelleas and E.* 587
where the tide Plash'd, sapping its *w* ribs; — *Lover's Tale* i
plaited ivy-tress had wound Round my *w* limbs, — „ 619
And weird and *w* and wizard-like was he. — *The Ring* 196
hearts *w* out by many wars And eyes grown
  dim — *Lotos-Eater's, C. S.* 86
took it, and have it *w*, like a king: — *M. d'Arthur* 33
theme of writers, and indeed W threadbare. — *Edwin Morris* 49
Or while the patch was *w*; — *Talking Oak* 64
Till now the dark was *w*, — *Love and Duty* 71
he died at Florence, quite *w* out, — *The Brook* 35
Those winters of abeyance all *w* out, — *Princess iv* 440
Which he has *w* so pure of blame, — *Ode on Well.* 72
Till slowly *w* her earthly robe, — *In Mem. lxxxiv* 33
A censer, either *w* with wind and storm; — *Gareth and L.* 222
W by the feet that now were silent, — *Marr. of Geraint* 321
It never yet was *w*, I trow: — „ 683
I myself unwillingly have *w* My faded suit, — „ 705
and the mask of pure W by this court, — *Merlin and V.* 36
King Had on his cuirass *w* our Lady's Head, — *Lancelot and E.* 294
w Favour of any lady in the lists. (repeat) — „ 363, 473
When these have *w* their tokens; — „ 769
Wasted and *w*, and but a tithe of them, — *Holy Grail* 723
took it, and have it *w*, like a king; — *Pass. of Arthur* 201
richly garb'd, but *w* From wasteful living, — *Ancient Sage* 4
Never *w* by a worthier, — *On Jub. Q. Victoria* 8
had stolen, *w* the ring—Then torn it from her finger, — *The Ring* 455
I have *w* them year by year— — *Happy* 102
Worn-out while the *w-o* clerk Brow-beats his desk — *To J. M. K.* 11
This *w-o* Reason dying in her house — *Romney's R.* 145
Worried W his passive ear with petty wrongs — *Enoch Arden* 352
Worry (*See also* **Tew, Tued**) a dog am I, To *w*, and not
  to flee— — *Gareth and L.* 1015
Worse (*See also* **Woorse, Wuss**) Is boundless better,
  boundless *w*. — *Two Voices* 27
I fear to slide from bad to *w*. — „ 231
And ever *w* with growing time, — *Palace of Art* 270
There *is* confusion *w* than death, — *Lotos-Eaters, C. S.* 83
laughingly Would hint at *w* in either. — *Enoch Arden* 481
if griefs Like his have *w* or better, — „ 741
the song Might have been *w* and sinn'd — *Princess iv* 251
some cold reverence *w* than were she dead. — „ *v* 92
Or pines in sad experience *w* than death, — „ *vii* 315
Far *w* than any death to me.' — *Sailor Boy* 24
Hexameters no *w* than daring Germany gave us, — *Trans. of Homer* 5
would make Confusion *w* than death, — *In Mem. xc* 19
better or *w* Than the heart of the citizen — *Maud I i* 23
fiend best knows whether woman or man be the *w*. — „ 75

DD

Worse (*continued*) Sick once, with a fear of *w*, — *Maud I xix* 73
grew up to wolflike men, W than the wolves. — *Com. of Arthur* 33
A *w* were better; yet no *w* would I. — *Gareth and L.* 17
for *w* than being fool'd Of others, — „ 1274
Shall I not rather prove the *w* for these? — *Balin and Balan* 228
Kill'd with a word *w* than a life of blows! — *Merlin and V.* 870
To make men *w* by making my sin known? — *Lancelot and E.* 1417
That did not shun to smite me in *w* way, — *Guinevere* 435
and expectancy of *w* Upon the morrow, — *Lover's Tale ii* 151
The *w* for her, for me! was I content? — *Sisters (E. and E.)* 126
I am handled *w* than had I been a Moor, — *Columbus* 107
which was crueller? which was *w* — *Locksley H., Sixty* 88
War for War's own sake Is fool, or crazed, or *w*; — *Epilogue* 31
cuckoo of a *w* July Is calling thro' the dark: — *Pref. Poem Broth. Son.* 11
and paced his land In fear of *w*, — *To Mary Boyle* 30
of the mind Mine; *w*, cold, calculated. — *Romney's R.* 152
Worse-confounded Babel, woman-built, And *w-c*: — *Princess iv* 488
Worship (s) (*See also* **Sun-worship, Wife-worship**) deck'd
  her out For *w* without end; — „ *vii* 169
compass'd her with sweet observances And *w*, — *Marr. of Geraint* 49
But this *w* of the Queen, — *Balin and Balan* 179
' Old priest, who mumble *w* in your quire— — „ 444
And I will pay you *w*; — *Merlin and V.* 228
To seat you sole upon my pedestal Of *w*— — „ 879
now my loyal *w* is allow'd Of all men: — *Lancelot and E.* 110
yet O grant my *w* of it Words, — „ 1187
It will be to thy *w*, as my knight, — „ 1327
Dame, damsel, each thro' *w* of their Queen — *Last Tournament* 146
There crown'd with *w*— — *Tiresias* 175
Of saner *w* sanely proud; — *Freedom* 30
that *w* which is Fear, Henceforth, — *Demeter and P.* 143
harvest hymns of Earth The *w* which is Love, — „ 149
in all Man-modes of *w*; — *Akbar's Dream* 47
Worship (verb) That here come those that *w* me? — *St. S. Stylites* 125
When you may *w* me without reproach; — „ 193
Crown thyself, worm, and *w* thine own lusts!— — *Aylmer's Field* 650
He *w's* your ideal:' she replied: — *Princess ii* 52
hive of Roman liars *w* an emperor-idiot. — *Boädicea* 19
To wage my wars, and *w* me their King; — *Com. of Arthur* 508
' Fair damsel, you should *w* me the more, — *Gareth and L.* 1022
Her likewise would I *w* an I might. — *Balin and Balan* 185
The Queen we *w*, Lancelot, I, and all, — „ 349
To *w* woman as true wife beyond — *Merlin and V.* 23
And beasts themselves would *w*; — „ 575
For Lancelot's kith and kin so *w* him — *Holy Grail* 651
' Fair damsels, each to him who *w's* each — *Last Tournament* 207
And *w* her by years of noble deeds, — *Guinevere* 476
There also will I *w* thee as King. — *Pass. of Arthur* 149
I anger'd Arundel asking me To *w* Holy Cross! — *Sir J. Oldcastle* 136
She knelt—' We *w* him '— — *Dead Prophet* 29
I *w* that right hand Which fell'd the foes — *Happy* 41
both, to *w* Alla, but the prayers, — *Akbar's Dream* 9
I let men *w* as they will, — „ 66
a peopie have fashion'd and *w* a Spirit — *Kapiolani* 1
Worshipfully Sir Lavaine did well and *w*; — *Lancelot and E.* 491
would I reward thee *w*. — *Gareth and L.* 829
Worshipp'd-Worship And *worshipt* their own darkness in
  the Highest? — *Aylmer's Field* 643
Sir Lancelot *worship* no unmarried girl — *Merlin and V.* 12
and him his new-made knight *Worshipt*, — *Pelleas and E.* 155
Thy name is ever *worshipp'd* among hours! — *Lover's Tale i* 493
Truth, for Truth is Truth, he *worshipt*, — *Locksley H., Sixty* 59
once I *worshipt* all too well this creature — *Happy* 45
Worshipper (*See also* **Woman-worshipper**) outlast thy Deity?
  Deity? nay, thy *w's*. — *Lucretius* 73
Worst (*See also* **Earthly-worst, Woost**) ' Never, dearest,
  never: here I brave the *w*:' — *Edwin Morris* 118
And women's slander is the *w*, — *The Letters* 34
His *w* he kept, his best he gave. — *You might have won* 26
' His deeds yet live, the *w* is yet to come. — *Sea Dreams* 314
of her court The wiliest and the *w*; — *Guinevere* 29
I hold that man the *w* of public foes — „ 512
W of the *w* were that man he that reigns! — „ 523
An' *she* wasn't one o' the *w*.' — *First Quarrel* 61
never put on the black cap except for the *w* of the *w*, — *Rizpah* 65

Wounded (adj. and part.) (*continued*) Hath gone sore

w, and hath left his prize	*Lancelot and E.* 530
W and wearied needs must he be near.	„ 538
So that he went sore w from the field :	„ 600
deals comfortable words To hearts w for ever;	*Lover's Tale i* 718
he was w again in the side and the head,	*The Revenge* 68
I have only w his pride—	*The Wreck* 14
A little thing may harm a w man.	*M. d'Arthur* 42
So strode he back slow to the w King.	„ 65
And so strode back slow to the w King.	„ 112
like a w life Crept down into the hollows of the wood;	*Enoch Arden* 75
when like a w life He crept into the shadow :	„ 386
Nor her that o'er her w hunter wept	*Lucretius* 89
lordly creature floated on To where her w brethren lay;	*Princess vi* 90
king her father charm'd Her w soul with words :	„ 346
shining in upon the w man With blush and smile,	„ *vii* 61
A w thing with a rancorous cry,	*Maud I x* 34
Kay near him groaning like a w bull—	*Gareth and L.* 648
A little thing may harm a w man;	*Pass. of Arthur* 210
So strode he back slow to the w King.	„ 233
And so strode back slow to the w King.	„ 280
Fought in her father's battles? w there?	*Last Tournament* 592
The w warrior climbs from Troy to thee.	*Death of Œnone* 39

Wounded (s) Death to the dying, and wounds to the w, *Def. of Lucknow* 17

and we sail'd with our w away.   *V. of Maeldune* 36

Wounded (verb) brought Her own claw back, and w her

own heart.   *Merlin and V.* 500

Wounding The w cords that bind and strain   *Clear-headed friend* 4

Wove Who w coarse webs to snare her purity,   *Aylmer's Field* 780

beneath her marriage ring, W and unwove it,	*Geraint and E.* 260
w with silver thread And crimson in the belt	*Holy Grail* 153
So I w Ev'n the dull-blooded poppy-stem,	*Lover's Tale i* 351

Wov'n honeysuckle round the porch has w its wavy bowers, *May Queen* 29

music winding trembled, W in circles:	*Vision of Sin* 18
A web is w across the sky;	*In Mem. iii* 6
The kiss, The w arms, seem but to be Weak symbols	*Miller's D.* 232
Up-clomb the shadowy pine above the w copse.	*Lotos-Eaters* 18
Thro' many a w acanthus-wreath divine!	„ *C. S.* 97
With w paces and with waving arms,	*Merlin and V.* 207
Of w paces and of waving hands, (repeat)	„ 330, 968
cobweb w across the cannon's throat	*Maud III vi* 27
Burst from the garland I had w,	*Lover's Tale i* 366

Wowd (wold) tha'll light of a livin' somewheers i'

the W or the Fen,   *Church-warden, etc.* 47

Wrack lest the realm should go to w.   *Com. of Arthur* 208

So that the realm has gone to w: „ 227

Wraith O hollow w of dying fame,   *In Mem. lxxiii* 13

The ghastly W of one that I know;	*Maud II i* 32
And w's of the mountain,	*Merlin and the G.* 43
Rose, like the w of his dead self,	*Death of Œnone* 28

Wrangle three gray linnets for the seed :   *Guinevere* 255

Wrangled And still they strove and w: *Sea Dreams* 229

and jangled and w in vain,   *V. of Maeldune* 109

Wranglest Wooest not, nor vainly w;   *Madeline* 38

Wrangling And haunted by the w daw;   *In Mem. c* 12

Wrap When a blanket w's the day,   *Vision of Sin* 80

In words, like weeds, I'll w me o'er,	*In Mem. v* 9
Love w's his wings on either side the heart,	*Lover's Tale i* 467
Now w's her close, now arching leaves her bare	*Prog. of Spring* 12

Wrapp'd-Wrapt (*See also* **Happt**) *Wrapt* in dense cloud

from base to cope.   *Two Voices* 186

'These things are *wrapt* in doubt and dread,	„ 266
I *wrapt* his body in the sheet,	*The Sisters* 34
Pitiful sight, *wrapp'd* in a soldier's cloak,	*Princess v* 56
The roots are *wrapt* about the bones.	*In Mem. ii* 4
And *wrapt* thee formless in the fold,	„ *xxii* 15
Wrapt in a cloak, as I saw him,	*Maud I i* 59
Wrapt in drifts of lurid smoke	„ *II vi* 66
'Not naked, only *wrapt* in harden'd skins	*Gareth and L.* 1093
Then brought a mantle down and *wrapt* her in it,	*Marr. of Geraint* 824
wrapt In unremorseful folds of rolling fire.	*Holy Grail* 260
Wrapt in her grief, for housel or for shrift,	*Guinevere* 149

Wrapping He w her all over with the cloak He came in, *Lover's Tale iv* 86

Wrapt *See* **Wrapp'd**

Wrath No sword Of w her right arm whirl'd,   *The Poet* 54

Wrath (*continued*) To whom replied King Arthur, much

in w:	*M. d'Arthur* 118
Secret w like smother'd fuel	*The Captain* 15
Shame and w his heart confounded,	„ 61
And then we met in w and wrong,	*The Letters* 11
eyes All flooded with the helpless w of tears,	*Enoch Arden* 32
How sweetly would she glide between your w's,	*Aylmer's Field* 706
A rushing tempest of the w of God	„ 757
'Let not the sun go down upon your w,'	*Sea Dreams* 44
Except his w were wreak'd on wretched man,	*Lucretius* 128
troubled like a rising moon, Inflamed with w:	*Princess i* 60
then he chew'd The thrice-turn'd cud of w,	„ 66
And heated thro' and thro' with w and love,	„ *iv* 163
The w I nursed against the world :	„ *v* 437
The w that garners in my heart	*In Mem. lxxxii* 14
And like a man in w the heart	*cxxiv* 15
God's just w shall be wreak'd on a giant liar;	*Maud III vi* 45
Then Uther in his w and heat besieged	*Com. of Arthur* 198
so those great lords Drew back in w,	„ 514
on the damsel's forehead shame, pride, w Slew the	
May-white;	*Gareth and L.* 656
by this entry fled The damsel in her w,	„ 675
loosed in words of sudden fire the w	*Geraint and E.* 106
Another, flying from the w of Doorm	„ 530
thy just w Sent me a three-years' exile	*Balin and Balan* 58
after some quick burst of sudden w,	„ 216
My father hath begotten me in his w.	„ 283
And Vivien answer'd smiling as in w:	*Merlin and V.* 526
And Vivien answer'd frowning yet in w:	„ 768
So all in w he got to horse and went;	*Lancelot and E.* 563
(Sea was her w, yet working after storm)	„ 1309
this persistence turn'd her scorn to w.	*Pelleas and E.* 218
Thereon her w became a hate;	„ 224
'I am w and shame and hate and evil fame,	„ 568
Until he groan'd for w—	*Last Tournament* 183
The w which forced my thoughts on that fierce law,	*Guinevere* 537
To whom replied King Arthur, much in w:	*Pass. of Arthur* 286
When he rose in his w,	*Dead Prophet* 63
She in w Return'd it on her birthday,	*The Ring* 211

Wrathful but w, petulant, Dreaming some rival,   *Lucretius* 14

While Enoch was abroad on w seas,	*Enoch Arden* 91
cheek and blossom brake the w bloom	*Princess iv* 383
I thought on all the w king had said,	„ *v* 473
Now set a w Dian's moon on flame,	„ *vi* 368
He made a w answer: 'Did I wish Your warning	*Geraint and E.* 76
To which he flung a w answer back:	„ 146
he but gave a w groan, Saying,	„ 398
That makes me passing w;	*Merlin and V.* 341
'Nay, Master, be not w with your maid;	„ 380
Strong men, and w that a stranger knight	*Lancelot and E.* 468
a sudden flush of w heat Fired all the pale face	*Guinevere* 356
w thunder of God peal'd over us all the day,	*V. of Maeldune* 113
The w sunset glared against a cross	*St. Telemachus* 5

Wreak I remain on whom to w your rage,   *Princess iv* 350

I w The wrath that garners	*In Mem. lxxxii* 13
Kill the foul thief, and w me for my son.'	*Gareth and L.* 363

Wreak'd Except his wrath were w on wretched man, *Lucretius* 128

God's just wrath shall be w on a giant liar;	*Maud III vi* 45
these caitiff rogues Had w themselves on me;	*Gareth and L.* 820
thou hast w his justice on his foes,	„ 1268

Wreath (*See also* **Acanthus-wreath, Ivy-wreath**) thro' the w's

of floating dark upcurl'd,	*The Poet* 35
Lit light in w's and anadems,	*Palace of Art* 186
made a little w of all the flowers	*Dora* 82
The w of flowers fell At Dora's feet.	„ 102
In w about her hair.	*Talking Oak* 288
and rent The woodbine w's that bind her,	*Amphion* 34
In her right a civic w,	*Vision of Sin* 137
lapt in w's of glowworm light The mellow breaker	*Princess iv* 435
'for this wild w of air, This flake of rainbow	„ *v* 318
thousand w's of dangling water-smoke,	„ *vii* 213
any w that man can weave him.	*Ode on Well.* 277
But when the w of March has blossom'd,	*To F. D. Maurice* 43
Make one w more for Use and Wont,	*In Mem. xxix* 11
The head hath miss'd an earthly w:	„ *lxxiii* 6

Wreath (*continued*) thine The *w* of beauty, thine the
crown of power, — *Merlin and V.* 79
A *w* of airy dancers hand-in-hand — *Guinevere* 261
—its *w*'s of dripping green— — *Lover's Tale* i 39
Darkening the *w*'s of all that would advance, — *To Victor Hugo* 5
This *w*, above his honour'd head, — *Tiresias* 213
I caught the *w* that was flung. — *The Wreck* 40
Or Love with *w*'s of flowers. — *Epilogue* 17
And you, that wear a *w* of sweeter bay, — *Poets and their B.* 7
Wreath'd (*See also* **New-wreathed**) Love's arms were
w about the neck of Hope, — *Lover's Tale* i 815
Beneath the bower of *w* eglantines : — ,, ii 43
W round the bier with garlands : — ,, 79
the belted hunter blew His *w* bugle-horn. — *Palace of Art* 64
around his head The glorious goddess *w* a golden
cloud, — *Achilles over the T.* 5
Wreathe Now *w* thy cap with doleful crape, — *My life is full* 14
The fancy's tenderest eddy *w*, — *In Mem. xlix* 6
To *w* a crown not only for the king — *Akbar's Dream* 23
Wreathen (*See also* **Mist-wreathen**) the sculptured
ornament That *w* round it — *Merlin and V.* 735
Wreck (s) Hurt in that night of sudden ruin and *w*, — *Enoch Arden* 564
sure no gladlier does the stranded *w* — ,, 828
his voyage, His *w*, his lonely life, — ,, 862
battle, bold adventure, dungeon, *w*, — *Aylmer's Field* 98
the father suddenly cried, 'A *w*, a *w* !' — *Sea Dreams* 59
Rotting on some wild shore with ribs of *w*, — *Princess* v 147
My father raves of death and *w*, — *Sailor Boy* 19
Tho' his vessel was all but a *w* ; — *The Revenge* 64
pranced on the *w*'s in the sand below, — *V. of Maeldune* 102
My brain is full of the crash of *w*'s, — *The Wreck* 4
My life itself is a *w*, — ,, 5
the one man left on the *w*— — ,, 119
they had saved many hundreds from *w*— — *Despair* 10
about the shuddering *w* the death-white sea — *The Flight* 47
children in a sunbeam sitting on the ribs of *w*. — *Locksley H., Sixty* 14
I was left within the shadow sitting on the *w* alone. — ,, 16
and sinking with the sinking *w*, — ,, 64
Like some old *w* on some indrawing sea, — *St. Telemachus* 44
bodies and souls go down in a common *w*, — *The Dawn* 13
Wreck (verb) sought'st to *w* my mortal ark, — *Two Voices* 389
May *w* itself without the pilot's guilt, — *Aylmer's Field* 716
my craven seeks To *w* thee villainously : — *Last Tournament*
love is wreck'd—if Love can *w*— — *Lover's Tale* i 804
passive sailor *w*'s at last In ever-silent seas ; — *Ancient Sage* 136
Wreck'd *W* on a reef of visionary gold.' — *Sea Dreams* 139
when their love is *w*—if Love can wreck— — *Lover's Tale* i 804
we are all of us *w* at last— — *Despair* 12
W—your train—or all but *w* ? — *Locksley H., Sixty* 215
Saved when your life was *w* ! — *The Ring* 305
Wren 'Shall eagles not be eagles ? *w*'s be *w*'s ? — *Golden Year* 37
And you my *w* with a crown of gold, You my
queen of the *w*'s ! You the queen of the *w*'s— — *Window, Spring* 11
I'll be the King of the Queen of the *w*'s, — ,, 15
The fire-crown'd king of the *w*'s, — ,, A y 8
flit like the king of the *w*'s with a crown of fire. — ,, 16
Tits, *w*'s, and all wing'd nothings — *Marr. of Geraint* 275
Wrench'd (*See also* **Half-wrench'd**) Who *w* their
rights from thee ! — *England and Amer.* 5
and *w* with pains Gain'd in the service — *Columbus* 235
dearer ghost had— *Father.* —*w* it away. — *The Ring* 468
Wrenching *W* it backward into his ; — *Lucretius* 221
Wrestle strive and *w* with thee till I die : — *St. S. Stylites* 119
Had ever seem'd to *w* with burlesque. — *Princess, Con.* 16
Wrestled *W* with wandering Israel, — *Clear-headed friend* 26
Wrestling Nor lose the *w* thews that throw the world ; — *Princess* vii 282
Wretch Poor *w*—no friend !— — *Merlin and V.* 75
W you must abide it . . . — *Forlorn* 52
then he yawn'd, for the *w* could sleep,— — *Bandit's Death* 30
Wretched Except his wrath were wreak'd on *w* man, — *Lucretius* 128
And *w* age—and worst disease of all, — ,, 155
'*W* boy, How saw you not the inscription on the gate, — *Princess* ii 193
On a horror of shatter'd limbs and a *w* swindler's lie ? — *Maud* I i 56
A *w* vote may be gain'd. — ,, vi 56
At war with myself and a *w* race, — ,, x 35

Wretched (*continued*) Yea ev'n of *w* meat and drink, — *Maud* I xv 8
May God make me more *w* Than ever I have been yet ! — ,, xix 94
O *w* set of sparrows, one and all, — *Marr. of Geraint* 278
and your *w* dress, A *w* insult on you, — *Geraint and E.* 327
pains Of the hellish heat of a *w* life — *Despair* 68
A madman to vex you with *w* words, — ,, 108
Wretchedest *W* age, since Time began, — *Maud* II v 21
Wretchedness But bode his hour, devising *w*. — *Last Tournament* 386
Wrigglesby beck Loook thou theer wheer *W b* cooms
out by the 'll ! — *N. Farmer, N. S.* 53
Wring take the goose, and *w* her throat, — *The Goose* 31
Wrinkle Whose *w*'s gather'd on his face, — *Two Voices* 329
The busy *w*'s round his eyes ? — *Miller's D.* 6
A million *w*'s carved his skin ; — *Palace of Art* 138
Sown in a *w* of the monstrous hill, — *Will* 19
Wrinkled (*See also* **Myriad-wrinkled**) Hard wood I am,
and *w* rind, — *Talking Oak* 171
cold my *w* feet Upon thy glimmering thresholds, — *Tithonus* 67
and there The *w* steward at his task, — *Day-Dm., Sleep. P.* 27
The *w* sea beneath him crawls ; — *The Eagle* 4
' *W* ostler, grim and thin ! — *Vision of Sin* 63
w benchers often talk'd of him Approvingly, — *Aylmer's Field* 473
Down from the lean and *w* precipices, — *Princess* iv 22
A charr'd and *w* piece of womanhood, — ,, v 61
When have I bow'd to her father, the *w* head of the race ? — *Maud* I iv 13
God help the *w* children that are Christ's — *Sisters (E. and E.)* 183
Wrinkling But bland the smile that like a *w* wind — *Princess* i 115
Wrist I sigh'd : a touch Came round my *w*, — ,, vii 138
The *w* is parted from the hand that waved, — *Merlin and V.* 551
But I will slice him handless by the *w*, — *Pelleas and E.* 338
Writ (s) saith not Holy *W* the same ?'— — *Merlin and V.* 52
Perhaps, like him of Cana in Holy *W*, — *Holy Grail* 762
Writ (verb) *W* in a language that has long gone by. — *Merlin and V.* 674
wrote The letter she devised ; which being *w* And
folded, — *Lancelot and E.* 1109
old writers Have *w* of in histories— — *Batt. of Brunanburh* 115
Write (*See also* **Wroite**) To make me *w* my random rhymes, — *Will Water.* 13
you shall *w*, and not to her, but me : — *Aylmer's Field* 310
' *W* to me ! They loved me, — ,, 422
Shall I *w* to her ? shall I go ? — *Window, Letter* 5
One *w*'s, that 'Other friends remain,' — *In Mem.* vi 1
Besought Lavaine to *w* as she devised A letter, — *Lancelot and E.* 1103
Old Virgil who would *w* ten lines, — *Poets and their B.* 2
Writer Seem but the theme of *w*'s, — *Edwin Morris* 48
Old *w*'s push'd the happy season back,— — *Golden Year* 66
old *w*'s Have writ of in histories— — *Batt. of Brunanburh* 114
Writhe a worm which *w*'s all day, — *Vastness* 17
Writhed (adj. and part.) Those *w* limbs of lightning
speed ; — *Clear-headed friend* 23
When the worm shall have *w* its last, — *Despair* 85
Writhed (verb) *w* his wiry arms Around him, till he felt, — *Gareth and L.* 1150
W toward him, slided up his knee and sat, — *Merlin and V.* 239
down his robe the dragon *w* in gold, — *Lancelot and E.* 435
Down on the great King's couch, and *w* upon it, — ,, 610
She roused a snake that hissing *w* away ; — *Death of Œnone* 88
Writhen *See* **Battle-writhen**
Writhing read *W* a letter from his child, — *Aylmer's Field* 517
w barbarous lineäments, — *Boädicea* 74
Sweat, *w*'s, anguish, labouring of the lungs — *Pass. of Arthur* 115
Writin' atween 'is reädin' an' *w* 'e snifft — *Village Wife* 40
Writing (*See also* **Writin'**) crazed myself over their horrible
infidel *w*'s ? — *Despair* 87
Written (*See also* **Wrote**) it is *w* that my race
Hew'd Ammon, — *D. of F. Women* 237
w as she found Or made occasion, — *Aylmer's Field* 477
And Willy's wife has *w* : (repeat) — *Grandmother* 3, 105
And something *w*, something thought ; — *In Mem.* vi 20
And *w* in the speech ye speak yourself, — *Com. of Arthur* 304
' Ye have the book : the charm is *w* in it ; — *Merlin and V.* 652
oft I seem as he Of whom was *w*, — *Last Tournament* 116
Glorious poet who never hast *w* a line, — *To A. Tennyson* 5
I am *w* in the Lamb's own Book of Life — *Columbus* 88
scroll *w* over with lamentation and woe. — *Despair* 20
Wroite (write) summun I reckons 'ull 'a to *w*, — *N. Farmer, O. S.* 57
Wrong (adj.) he was *w* to cross his father thus : — *Dora* 148

Wrong (adj.) (*continued*) His nerves were *w.* *Walk. to the Mail* 105
am I right, or am I *w*, (repeat) *Day-Dm., L'Envoi* 29, 33
What! I am not all as *w* As a bitter jest *Vision of Sin* 197
I was *w*, I am always bound to you, *Enoch Arden* 449
'Would I—was it *w*?' *The Brook* 111
And so I often told her, right or *w.* *Princess v* 288
And, right or *w*, I care not: this is all, „ 290
Death for the right cause, death for the *w* cause, *Vastness* 8
She offens 'ud spy summut *w* *Owd Roä* 70
W there! The painter's fame? *Romney's R.* 48
Wrong (s) There seem'd no room for sense of *w*; *Two Voices* 456
lamentation and an ancient tale of *w*, *Lotos-Eaters, C. S.* 118
I heard sounds of insult, shame, and *w*, *D. of F. Women* 19
'I have hid my feelings, fearing they should do me *w*;' *Locksley Hall* 29
we, that prate Of rights and *w*'s, *Godiva* 8
He that only rules by terror Doeth grievous *w.* *The Captain* 2
Hush'd all the groves from fear of *w*: *Sir L. and Q. G.* 13
And then we met in wrath and *w*, *The Letters* 11
Worried his passive ear with petty *w*'s Or pleasures, *Enoch Arden* 474
Began to chafe as at a personal *w*. „ 474
if he did that *w* you charge him with, *Sea Dreams* 279
He can do no more *w*: forgive him, „ 311
(A little sense of *w* had touch'd her face *Princess, Pro.* 219
Bow'd on her palms and folded up from *w*, „ iv 288
Came all in haste to hinder *w*, „ 401
Tho' man, yet human, whatsoe'er your *w*'s, „ 425
Torn from the lintel—all the common *w*— „ v 129
chance Were caught within the record of her *w*'s, „ 143
I thought her half-right talking of her *w*'s; „ 285
brawl Their rights or *w*'s like potherbs in the street. „ 459
' ourselves are full Of social *w*; „ Con. 73
Till public *w* be crumbled into dust, *Ode on Well.* 167
He suffers, but he cannot suffer *w*: *Will* 3
My name in song has done him much *w*, *Spiteful Letter* 3
to fight, to struggle, to right the *w*— *Wages* 3
Nor human frailty do me *w*. *In Mem. lii* 8
we do him *w* To sing so wildly: „ lvii 3
Drug down the blindfold sense of *w* „ lxxi 7
Thou doest expectant nature *w*; „ lxxxiii 3
Bewail'd their lot; I did them *w*: „ ciii 46
taking revenge too deep for a transient *w* *Maud I iii* 5
She would not do herself this great *w*, „ x 57
teach true life to fight with mortal *w*'s. „ xviii 54
Or to say 'Forgive the *w*,' „ II iv 86
peace that was full of *w*'s and shames, „ III vi 40
Whose glory was, redressing human *w*; *Ded. of Idylls* 9
speak true, right *w*, follow the King— *Gareth and L.* 118
from the *w*'s his father did Would shape himself „ 347
Give me to right her *w*, and slay the man.' „ 366
Than ride abroad redressing women's *w*, „ 866
For this were shame to do him further *w* „ 954
To noble hearts who see but acts of *w*: *Marr. of Geraint* 438
That each had suffer'd some exceeding *w*. *Geraint and E.* 36
smoulder'd *w* that burnt him all within; „ 107
worse than that dead man; Done you more *w*: „ 736
As one that let foul *w* stagnate and be, „ 891
which for bribe had wink'd at *w*, „ 939
Once for *w* done you by confusion, *Merlin and V.* 307
And see, yourself have own'd ye did me *w*. „ 316
They ride abroad redressing human *w*'s! „ 693
many a year have done despite and *w* *Lancelot and E.* 1209
leaving human *w*'s to right themselves, *Holy Grail* 898
Well—can I wish her any huger *w* *Last Tournament* 596
deed Of prowess done redress'd a random *w*. *Guinevere* 459
To ride abroad redressing human *w*'s, „ 471
Yet who had done, or who had suffer'd *w*? *Lover's Tale i* 726
No, no, you are doing me *w*! *First Quarrel* 4
Loving the other? do her that great *w*? *Sisters (E. and E.)* 168
than have done one another a *w*. *V. of Maeldune* 6
or flamed at a public *w*, *The Wreck* 68
that hourly work their brother insect *w*, *Locksley H., Sixty* 202
tho' that realm were in the *w* *Epilogue* 34
I wrought thee bitter *w*, but thou forgive, *Death of Œnone* 43
wind of the Night shrilling out Desolation and *w* *The Dreamer* 15

Wrong (verb) he that *w*'s his friend *W*'s himself *Sea Dreams* 172
'you *w* him more than I That struck him: *Princess iv* 245
She *w*'s herself, her sex, and me, „ v 117
You *w* yourselves—the woman is so hard „ vi 222
I *w* the grave with fears untrue: *In Mem. li* 9
O child, you *w* your beauty, believe it, *Maud I iv* 17
dream That any of these would *w* thee, *w*'s thyself. *Balin and Balan* 144
—nay, but I *w* him, *Lover's Tale iv* 73
You *w* me, passionate little friend. *Epilogue* 10
I can *w* thee now no more, Œnone, *Death of Œnone* 80
Wrong'd (part.) I knew thee *w.* I brake upon thy rest, *Balin and Balan* 499
How had I *w* you? surely ye are wise, *Merlin and V.* 288
A virtuous gentlewoman deeply *w*, „ 911
'Can he be *w* who is not ev'n his own, *Last Tournament* 524
May'st thou never be *w* by the name *To A. Tennyson* 7
I never have *w* his heart, *The Wreck* 14
Wrong'd (s) to help the *w* Thro' all our realm. *Gareth and L.* 371
Then Gareth, 'Bound am I to right the *w*, „ 804
With strength and will to right the *w*, *Holy Grail* 309
Wrong'd (verb) *w* and lied and thwarted us— *Princess v* 540
judge their cause from her That *w* it, „ vii 236
he never *w* his bride. I know the tale. *Merlin and V.* 729
Hears he now the Voice that *w* him? *Locksley H., Sixty* 269
Wronger this Order lives to crush All *w*'s of the Realm. *Gareth and L.* 626
At caitiffs and at *w*'s of the world. *Marr. of Geraint* 96
Brutes are the brutes are not your *w*'s— *Locksley H., Sixty* 97
Wrote round about the prow she *w* *L. of Shalott iv* 8
W, 'Mene, mene,' and divided quite *Palace of Art* 227
and a tear Dropt on the letters as I *w.* *To J. S.* 56
I *w* I know not what. In truth, „ 57
you shall have that song which Leonard *w*: *Golden Year* 1
'Then I took a pencil, and *w* On the mossy stone, *Edward Gray* 25
tho' Averill *w* And bad him with good heart *Aylmer's Field* 543
Who first *w* satire, with no pity in it. *Sea Dreams* 202
then, Sir, awful odes she *w*, Too awful, *Princess i* 138
and I sat down and *w*, In such a hand „ 235
take this and pray that he Who *w* it, *A Dedication* 5
and sat him down, and *w* All things *Com. of Arthur* 156
Then he *w* The letter she devised; *Lancelot and E.* 1209
An' he *w* 'I ha' six weeks' work, *First Quarrel* 45
an' sorry for what she *w*, „ 87
Edith *w*: 'My mother bids me ask' *Sisters (E. and E.)* 180
and besides, The great Augustine *w* *Columbus* 52
I *w* to the nurse Who had borne my flower *The Wreck* 142
He knows not ev'n the book he *w*, *Ancient Sage* 148
he *w* 'Their kindness,' and he *w* no more; *To Marq. of Dufferin* 35
w Name, surname, all as clear as noon, *The Ring* 236
Up she got, and *w* him all, *Forlorn* 79
Wrote (written) An' 'e'd *w* an owd book, his awn sen, *Village Wife* 46
Wroth (*See also* Half-wroth) Then the old man Was *w*, *Dora* 25
Weakness to be *w* with weakness! *Locksley Hall* 149
Sullen, defiant, pitying, *w*, *Aylmer's Field* 492
perforce He yielded, *w* and red, with fierce demur: *Princess v* 358
A third is *w*: 'Is this an hour For private sorrow's *In Mem. xxi* 13
W to be *w* at such a worm, *Marr. of Geraint* 213
my new mother, be not *w* or grieved At thy new son, „ 779
For, be he *w* even to slaying me, *Geraint and E.* 67
it made him *w* the more That she *could* speak „ 112
neither dame nor damsel then *W* at a lover's loss? *Merlin and V.* 607
W at himself. Not willing to be known, *Lancelot and E.* 160
W that the King's command to sally forth „ 560
W, but all in awe, For twenty strokes „ 719
Fret not yourself, dear brother, nor be *w*, „ 1074
And *w* at Tristram and the lawless jousts, *Last Tournament* 237
is the Demon-god *W* at his fall?' *St. Telemachus* 20
Wrought 'She *w* her people lasting good; *To the Queen* 24
And all so variously *w*, *Two Voices* 457
With royal frame-work of *w* gold; *Ode to Memory* 82
who *w* Two spirits to one equal mind— *Miller's D.* 235
times of every land So *w*, they will not fail. *Palace of Art* 148
she turn'd her sight The airy hand confusion *w*, „ 226
But by degrees to fulness *w* *You ask me, why, etc.* 14
W by the lonely maiden of the Lake. *M. d'Arthur* 104
Nine years she *w* it, sitting in the deeps „ 105

Yearn (*continued*) A part of stillness, *y*'s to speak : *In Mem. lxxxv 78*
but made me *y* For larger glimpses *Tiresias 20*
and the miser would *y* for his gold, *Despair 100*
Y, and clasp the hands and murmur, *Locksley H., Sixty 192*
y to lay my loving head upon your leprous breast. *Happy 26*
Yearn'd While still I *y* for human praise. *Two Voices 123*
And *y* toward William ; but the youth, *Dora 6*
But Enoch *y* to see her face again ; *Enoch Arden 717*
While in her heart she *y* incessantly *„ 866*
Y after by the wisest of the wise, *Lucretius 267*
y To hear her weeping by his grave ? *In Mem. xxxi 3*
And *y* to burst the folded gloom, *„ cxxii 3*
he *y* to make complete The tale of diamonds *Lancelot and E. 90*
Sprang into fire and vanish'd, tho' I *y* To follow ; *Holy Grail 506*
I *y* and strove To tear the twain asunder *„ 785*
now *y* to shake The burthen off his heart *Last Tournament 179*
I *y* for warmth and colour which I found In Lancelot *Guinevere 647*
I *y* For his voice again, *The Wreck 103*
To lure those eyes that only *y* to see, *St. Telemachus 36*
Yearning (*See also* **Heart-yearning**) A nobler *y* never
broke her rest *The form, the form 2*
Some *y* toward the lamps of night ; *Two Voices 363*
In *y*'s that can never be exprest By signs *D. of F. Women 283*
Y to mix himself with Life. *Love thou thy land 56*
Gave utterance by the *y* of an eye, *Love and Duty 62*
gray spirit *y* in desire To follow knowledge *Ulysses 30*
team Which love thee, *y* for thy yoke, *Tithonus 40*
Y for the large excitement *Locksley Hall 111*
profit lies in barren faith, And vacant *y*, *In Mem. cviii 6*
Less *y* for the friendship fled, *„ cxvi 15*
The leaf is dead, the *y* past away : *Last Tournament 277*
y's ?—ay ! for, hour by hour, *„ 583*
Deeper than any *y*'s after thee *„ 586*
The boundless *y* of the Prophet's heart— *Tiresias 81*
Yearningly moving again to a melody *Y* tender, *Merlin and the G. 91*
Yeasty ' The sands and *y* surges mix *Sailor Boy 9*
Yell (s) (*See also* **Counter-yell, Woman-yell**) rings to
the *y* of the trampled wife, *Maud I i 38*
I was near him when the savage *y*'s *Com. of Arthur 256*
He ground his teeth together, sprang with a *y*, *Balin and Balan 538*
weird *y*, Unearthlier than all shriek of bird *„ 544*
echoing *y* with *y*, they fired the tower, *Last Tournament 478*
volley on volley, and *y* upon *y*— *Def. of Lucknow 34*
Thro' all the *y*'s and counter-yells *To Duke of Argyll 8*
dog : it was chain'd, but its horrible *y* *Bandit's Death 35*
Yell (verb) Let the fox bark, let the wolf *y*. *Pelleas and E. 472*
Who *y*'s Here in the still sweet summer night, *„ 472*
Fiend would *y*, the grave would yawn, *The Flight 51*
Yell'd score of pugs And poodles *y* within, *Edwin Morris 120*
y and round me drove In narrowing circles till I *y* again *Lucretius 56*
they made a halt ; The horses *y* ; *Princess v 250*
Y and shriek'd between her daughters (repeat) *Boädicea 6, 72*
Y as when the winds of winter tear an oak *„ 77*
' Fight therefore,' *y* the youth, *Pelleas and E. 572*
caged beast *Y*, as he *y* of yore for Christian blood. *St. Telemachus 46*
Y ' hast *thou* brought us down a new Korân *Akbar's Dream 116*
Yelling and fled *Y* as from a spectre, *Geraint and E. 733*
and, *y* with the *y* street, *Locksley H., Sixty 135*
Yellow (adj.) (*See also* **Dim-yellow**) That sparkled on
the *y* field, *L. of Shalott iii 8*
The pale *y* woods were waning, *„ iv 2*
and the *y* down Border'd with palm, *Lotos-Eaters 21*
They sat them down upon the *y* sand, *„ 37*
turning *y* Falls, and floats adown the air. *„ C. S. 30*
Round and round the spicy downs the *y* Lotos-dust
is blown. *„ 104*
And in the chasm are foam and *y* sands ; *Enoch Arden 2*
And here upon a *y* eyelid fall'n *Lucretius 141*
With lengths of *y* ringlet, like a girl, *Princess i 3*
Yet the *y* leaf hates the greener leaf, *Spiteful Letter 15*
y vapours choke The great city sounding wide ; *Maud II iv 63*
And white sails flying on the *y* sea ; But not to
goodly hill or *y* sea *Marr. of Geraint 82?*
Then flash'd a *y* gleam across the world, *Holy Grail 402*
little lake, that, flooding, leaves Low banks of *y* sand ; *Lover's Tale i 535*

DD*

Yellow (adj.) (*continued*) From out the *y* woods upon the hill *Lover's Tale ii 80*
Yellow (s) Shot over with purple, and green, and *y*. *Dying Swan 20*
Yellow-banded Or the *y-b* bees, *Eleänore 22*
Yellowing Dwelling amid these *y* bowers : *A spirit haunts 2*
In curves the *y* river ran, *Sir L. and Q. G. 15*
At Camelot, high above the *y* woods, *Last Tournament 3*
and *y* leaf And gloom and gleam, *„ 154*
High over all the *y* Autumn-tide, *„ 241*
OUR birches *y* and from each The light leaf
falling fast, *Pro. to Gen. Hamley 1*
Yellow-ringleted Thither at their will they haled the
y-r Britoness— *Boädicea 55*
Yellow-throated And *y-t* nestling in the nest. *Lancelot and E. 12*
Yelp (s) With inward *y* and restless forefoot *Lucretius 45*
But I hear no *y* of the beast, *By an Evolution. 19*
Yelp (verb) Lean-headed Eagles *y* alone, *Princess vii 211*
felt the goodly hounds *Y* at his heart, *Last Tournament 504*
Yelp'd-Yelpt Then *yelp'd* the cur, and yawl'd the cat ; *The Goose 33*
that chain'd rage, which ever *yelpt* within, *Balin and Balan 319*
Yelping *See* **Yaupin'**
Yeoman And let the foolish *y* go. *L. C. V. de Vere 72*
A mockery to the *yoemen* over ale, *Aylmer's Field 497*
Yerl (earl) Then 'e married a greät *Y*'s darter, *Church-warden, etc. 20*
Yes (*See also* **Yis**) keen shriek ' *Y* love, *y*, Edith, *y*,' *Aylmer's Field 582*
When the happy *Y* Falters from her lips, *Maud I xvii 9*
brightens at the clash of ' *Y* ' and ' No,' *Ancient Sage 71*
Yester —and *y* afternoon I dream'd,— *Akbar's Dream 169*
Yesterday (*See also* **Yisther-day**) for *y*, When I past by, a wild
and wanton pard, *Œnone 198*
sharp look, mother, I gave him *y*, *May Queen 15*
And now, As tho' 'twere *y*, *Gardener's D. 82*
' Where were you *y* ? Whose child is that ? *Dora 87*
' O *y*, you know, the fair Was holden at the town ; *Talking Oak 101*
' *y* I met him suddenly in the street, *Sea Dreams 145*
I curse the tongue that all thro' *y* Reviled thee, *Gareth and L. 1322*
But *y* you never open'd lip, *Merlin and V. 271*
the prize Of Tristram in the jousts of *y*, *Last Tournament 286*
' Friend, did ye mark that fountain *y* *„ 286*
A portion of the pleasant *y*, *Lover's Tale i 122*
To-day ? but what of *y* ? *Ancient Sage 216*
that *y* From out the Ghost of Pindar *To Prof. Jebb 2*
I climb'd the hill with Hubert *y*, *The Ring 152*
O the grief when *y* They bore the Cross *Happy 47*
Found *y*—forgotten mine own rhyme *To Mary Boyle 21*
Yester-eve But light-foot Iris brought it *y-e*, *Œnone 83*
Where all but *y-e* was dusky-dry. *Lucretius 32*
and *y-e*, While ye were talking sweetly *Marr. of Geraint 697*
And *y-e* I would not tell you of it, *„ 702*
Yester-even Lastly yonder *y-e*, *Boädicea 29*
I saw the flash of him but *y*. *Balin and Balan 303*
Yestermorn These measured words, my work of *y*. *Golden Year 21*
Too harsh to your companion *y* ; *Princess iii 199*
Long-closeted with her the *y*, *„ iv 322*
What if he had to'd her *y* *Maud I vi 50*
saw him ride More near by many a rood than *y*, *Geraint and E. 442*
tho' mine own ears heard you *y*— *„ 740*
Had I not dream'd I loved her *y* ? *Sisters (E. and E.) 169*
Who breaking in upon us *y*, *Akbar's Dream 114*
Yesternight Thy tuwhoos of *y*, *The Owl ii 2*
Flinging the gloom of *y* On the white day ; *Ode to Memory 9*
I beheld her, when she rose The *y*, *Princess v 176*
' Sweet brothers, *y* I seem'd a curious little maid *Lancelot and E. 1034*
for, *y*, To me, the great God Arês, *Tiresias 110*
Yet-loved the *y-l* sire would make Confusion *In Mem. xc 18*
Yet-unblazon'd Returning brought the *y-u* shield, *Lancelot and E. 379*
Yet-unbroken count The *y-u* strength of all his knights, *Holy Grail 326*
Yet-warm and now lies there A *y-w* corpse, *Gareth and L. 80*
Yew Death, walking all alone beneath a *y*, *Love and Death 5*
And darkness in the village. *Two Voices 273*
Came *y*'s, a dismal coterie ; *Amphion 42*
A black *y* gloom'd the stagnant air, *The Letters 2*
and stole Up by the wall, behind the *y* ; *Enoch Arden 739*
Sick for the hollies and the *y*'s of home— *Princess, Pro. 187*
Old *Y*, which graspest at the stones *In Mem. ii 1*
Dark *y*, that graspest at the stones *„ xxxix 4*

A CONCORDANCE TO THE DRAMATIC WORKS

OF

ALFRED, LORD TENNYSON.

A

A that all the louts to whom Their *A* B C is darkness,   *Queen Mary* III iv 35

Aäle (ale) They ha' broached a barrel of *a* i' the long barn,   *Prom. of May* I 426

Abbacy From all the vacant sees and *abbacies*,   *Becket* I iii 652

Abbess I think our *A* knew it and allow'd it.   „ v ii 95

Abbey The kingliest *A* in all Christian lands,   *Harold* III i 204
He shelter'd in the *A* of Pontigny.   *Becket* II i 84
Hard as the stones of his *a*.   *Foresters* I ii 270

Abbeyland new Lords Are quieted with their sop of *A's*,   *Queen Mary* III i 142

Abbot there were *A's*—but they did not bring their women;   *Becket* III iii 135
sits and eats his heart for want of money to pay the *A*.   *Foresters* I i 5
he borrowed the monies from the *A* of York, the Sheriff's brother. And if they be not paid back at the end of the year, the land goes to the *A*.   „ I i 68
Those two thousand marks lent me by the *A*   „ I i 264
I believed this *A* of the party of King Richard,   „ I i 266
Or I forfeit my land to the *A*.   „ I ii 152
You shall wait for mine till Sir Richard has paid the *A*.   „ I ii 232
I fear this *A* is a heart of flint,   „ I ii 268
I ran into my debt to the *A*, Two thousand marks in gold.   „ II i 463
We spoil'd the prior, friar, *a*, monk,   „ III 167
Then that bond he hath Of the *A*—   „ IV 85
I have sent to the *A* and justiciary.   „ IV 87
The *A* of York and his justiciary.   „ IV 334
it was agreed when you borrowed these monies from the *A*   „ IV 467
these monies should be paid in to the *A* at York,   „ IV 507
Save for this maiden and thy brother *A*,   „ IV 633
You, my lord *A*, you Justiciary, I made you *A*, you Justiciary :   „ IV 841
Our rebel *A* then shall join your hands,   „ IV 933
Here *A*, Sheriff—no—no, Robin Hood.   „ IV 989

Abeär (bear) I can't *a* to think on 'er now,   *Prom. of May* II 32
I can't *a* to see her.   „ III 758

Abel light darkness, *A* Cain, The soul the body,   *Becket* I iii 715

Abetting They say, his wife was knowing and *a*.   *Harold* II ii 307

Abhor all of us *a* The venomous, bestial, devilish revolt   *Queen Mary* II ii 286
and refuse, Reject him, and *a* him.   „ IV iii 279
—the whole world *A* you;   *Becket* v iii 184

Abide You must *a* my judgment, and my father's,   *Queen Mary* v i 145
and on thee, Edith, if thou *a* it,—   *Harold* III i 317
King will not *a* thee with thy cross.   *Becket* I iii 488
then he called me a rude naäme, and I can't *a* 'im.   *Prom. of May* II 159
but he wur so rough wi' ma, I couldn't *a* 'im.   „ III 104
as the good Sally says, 'I can't *a* him'—   „ III 174
If it be her ghoäst, we mun *a* it.   „ III 460
but *a* with me who love thee.   *Foresters* II i 602

Ability Hath he the large *a* of the Emperor?   *Queen Mary* I v 323
Hath he the large *a* of his father?   „ I v 438

Able The man is *a* enough—no lack of wit,   *Foresters* I ii 103

Abler while in Normanland God speaks thro' *a* voices,   *Harold* I i 167

Abolish to cancel and *a* all bonds of human allegiance,   *Queen Mary* v iv 49

Abroach Not set myself *a* And run my mind out   *The Cup* I ii 106

Abrogation Towards the *a* and repeal Of all such laws   *Queen Mary* III iii 141

Absalom Deal gently with the young man *A*.   *Becket* I iii 757

Absence Which in his *a* had been all my wealth.   *Queen Mary* I v 361
But since mine *a* will not be for long,   „ III vi 216
Thine *a* well may seem a want of care.   *Harold* I i 322
and you look thin and pale. Is it for his *a*?   *Prom. of May* I 782
this world Is brighter for his *a* as that other Is darker for his presence.   „ II 458
but can he trace me Thro' five years' *a*,   „ II 615

Absolution Pole, to give us all that holy *a* which—— *First Citizen.* Old Bourne to the life ! *Second Citizen.* Holy *a* !   *Queen Mary* I iii 28
Legate's coming To bring us *a* from the Pope.   „ III i 432
To take this *a* from your lips,   „ III ii 116
Thro' this most reverend Father, *a*,   „ III iii 148
Stigand shall give me *a* for it—   *Harold* III i 798
Hast thou had *a* for thine oath ?   „ III i 212
Stigand hath given me *a* for it.   „ III i 213
Not I, the Pope. Ask *him* for *a*.   *Becket* v ii 379

Absolve commission from the Pope To *a* thee   *Queen Mary* III ii 53
He by His mercy *a* you !   „ III iii 209
Do here *a* you and deliver you And every one of you,   „ III iii 214
Cannot the Pope *a* thee if thou sign ?   *Becket* I iii 230
A the left-hand thief and damn the right ?   „ II ii 392
Forgive me and *a* me, holy father.   „ II ii 441
Son, I *a* thee in the name of God.   „ II ii 442
He shall *a* you . . . you shall have redress.   „ v i 86
Our Becket, who will not *a* the Bishops.   „ v i 223
he shall *a* The bishops—they but did my will—   „ v i 253
Oh, if you have, *a* him !   „ v ii 131
to *a* the bishops Whom you have excommunicated.   „ v ii 376
Save that you will *a* the bishops.   „ v iii 120

Absolved Tut, tut, I have *a* thee :   *Harold* II i 104

A-burnin' Queen Mary gwoes on *a-b* and *a-b*,   *Queen Mary* IV iii 523
A-b, and *a-b*, and a-makin'   „ IV 531

Abused Her name is much *a* among these traitors.   „ III ii 110
Modest maiden lily *a*,   *Foresters* II ii 158

A-bussin' (kissing) thou and me *a-b* o' one another t'other side o' the haäycock,   *Prom. of May* II 231

Abysm Steam'd upward from the undescendible *A*.   *Harold* I i 16

Abyss rough road That breaks off short into the *a's*—   *Prom. of May* I 230

A-callin' they ha' ta'en the body up inter your chaumber, and they be all *a-c* for ye.   „ II 571

Accept France would not *a* her for a bride   *Queen Mary* I ii 67
beseech Your Highness to *a* our lowliest thanks   „ II ii 131
tell him That I *a* the diadem of Galatia—   *The Cup* II 158
So I would, Robin, if any man would *a* her.   *Foresters* III 74
A this horn ! if e'er thou be assail'd   IV 423
  Harold III i 348

Acceptable more the love, the more *a* The sacrifice nobler The victim was, the more *a* Might be the sacrifice.   *The Falcon* 880

Accepting For that would seem *a* of your love.   „ 739

Accepting (*continued*) Have I done wisely, then, in *a* him? *Prom. of May* III 184
Access A stranger monk desires *a* to you. *Becket* v ii 65
Mine enemies barr'd all *a* to the boy.   „   v ii 451
Accomplish'd to see my solemn vow *A*. *Harold* III i 308
The purpose of my being is *a*, *The Falcon* 926
To-day he hath *a* his thirtieth birthday, *Foresters* I i 298
Account There's half an angel wrong'd in your *a*; *Queen Mary* v iii 2
King Demands a strict *a* of all those revenues *Becket* I i 650
dead; gone to his *a*—dead and buried. *Prom. of May* III 145
Then by thine own *a* thou shouldst be mine. *Foresters* IV 1038
Accruing Judgment, and pain *a* thereupon; *Queen Mary* III iii 219
Accursed my men Hold that the shipwreckt are *a* of God;— *Harold* II i 100
for the two were fellow-prisoners So many years in yon *a* Tower— *Queen Mary* I iv 200
With that vile Cranmer in the *a* lie Of good Queen Catharine's divorce—   „   III iv 231
'We pray continually for the death Of our *a* Queen and Cardinal Pole.'   „   v ii 181
Nay, ev'n the *a* heathen Saladeen—— Strike! *Becket* I ii 251
Accuse Lest men *a* you of indifference To all faiths, *Queen Mary* III iv 223
Shall these *a* him to a foreign prince?   „   IV i 24
must *A* himself, excuse himself; *The Cup* II 115
Accused 'If any cleric be *a* of felony, the Church shall not protect him; *Becket* I iii 87
Accuser appear before the Pope, And answer thine *a*'s . . .   „   I iii 603
Achage his *a*, and his breakage, if that were all: *Queen Mary* I i 128
Ache full of *a*'s and broken before his day.   „   I i 124
Against the moral excess No physical *a*, *Becket* I i 382
Acies *A*, *A* Prona sternatur! *Harold* v i 581
Acknowledge and *a* The primacy of the Pope? *Queen Mary* III iii 107
Acknowledged Mary hath *a* you her heir.   „   v iii 30
She knew me, and *a* me her heir,   „   v v 255
A-coomin' (**coming**) I seed that one cow o' thine i' the pinfold ageän as I wur *a-c* 'ere. *Prom. of May* I 191
Acorn On nuts and *a*'s, ha! Or the King's deer? *Foresters* IV 882
Acre (**seaport**) like the woman at *A* when the Turk shot her   „   II i 307
Acre (**land**) (*See also* **Haäcre, Ten-aäcre**) her advowsons, granges, farms, And goodly *a*'s— *Becket* I i 163
I took it For some three thousand *a*'s. *Prom. of May* I 614
Acrid Ah, what an *a* wine has Luther brew'd! *Queen Mary* IV iii 545
Acrisius Danaë has escaped again Her tower, and her *A*— *Becket* I i 396
A-crying and they was all *a-c* out at the bad times, *Prom. of May* I 138
Act (**s**) he begs you to forget it As scarce his *a*:— *The Cup* II 53
Act (**verb**) (*See also* **Re-act**) that these may *a* On Harold when they meet. *Harold* II ii 91
King would a servitor and hand a dish to his son; *Becket* III iii 139
Veiling one sin to a another. *Prom. of May* III 773
Actable Is naked truth *a* in true life? *Harold* III i 109
Acted why should not the parable of our blessed Lord be *a* again? *Becket* I iv 77
Who made the second mitre play the first, And *a* me?   „   III iii 213
Well *a*, was it? A comedy meant to seem a tragedy—   „   IV ii 321
and *a* on would yield A nobler breed *The Falcon* 753
Acting tear it all to pieces, never dream'd Of *a* on it. *The Cup* I ii 248
No! *a*, playing on me, both of them. *Prom. of May* III 693
Action (*See also* **Re-action**) *A* and re-action, The miserable see-saw of our child-world, *Queen Mary* IV iii 384
Act of Parliament they be both bastards by *A o P* and Council.   „   I i 24
Corroborate by your *a*'s *o P*:   „   II ii 173
Actor Should play the second *a* in this pageant   „   III iii 13
A-cum (**come**) there wur an owld lord *a-c* to dine wi' un,   „   IV iii 504
Adage there's An old world English *a* to the point.   „   IV i 175
Adam-clay Cleaving to your original *A-c*,   „   IV iii 418
Add Leave it with him and *a* a gold mark thereto. *Foresters* III 210
Added the clauses A To that same treaty *Queen Mary* III iii 68
Adder To the deaf *a* thee, that wilt not dance *Harold* I i 385
the Norman *a* Hath bitten us; we are poison'd: „   III i 38
he that lookt a fangless one, Issues a venomous *a*. *Becket* I iii 453
Addled Eggs? *Filippo*. One, but *a*. *The Falcon* 129
Address (**s**) All hangs on her *a*, And upon you, Lord Mayor. *Queen Mary* II ii 55
he gave me no *a*, and there was no word of marriage; *Prom. of May* III 332

Address (**verb**) She will *a* your guilds and companies. *Queen Mary* II ii 15
Adieu Both be happy, and *a* for ever and for evermore—*a*. *Foresters* II ii 196
Adit Here His turtle builds; his exit is our *a*: *Becket* III ii 7
Adjudge at this time *A* him to the death. *Queen Mary* IV iii 38
Admiral Her freaks and frolics with the late Lord *A*?   „   I iv 20
Admiration begets An *a* and an indignation,   „   III iv 170
Admired But having now *a* it long enough, *Becket* IV ii 262
'To the *a* Camma, wife of Sinnatus, the Tetrarch, *The Cup* I i 36
'To the *a* Camma,—beheld you afar off—   „   I i 70
Admit Ay, gentle friend, *a* them. I will go. *Queen Mary* I ii 110
A-doing What be he *a-d* here ten mile an' moor fro' a raäil? *Prom. of May* I 209
Adore and *a* This Vicar of their Vicar. *Queen Mary* III iii 243
Adorer an *a* of our great goddess, Artemis, *The Cup* I i 38
Adulterous *A* to the very heart of Hell. *Queen Mary* v v 163
A dog! (repeat) *The Cup* I iii 108, 122
Adultery She seethed with such *adulteries*, *Queen Mary* IV iv 189
Advance *A* our Standard of the Warrior, *Harold* IV i 248
told me he would *a* me to the service of a great lady, *Becket* III i 123
He has a friend there will *a* the monies, *Foresters* II i 628
There was no room to *a* or to retire.   „   IV 534
A, *a*! (repeat)   „   IV 735, 761
Advanced *A* thee at his instance by the Jews, *Becket* I iii 643
Advantage To be of rich *a* to our realm, *Queen Mary* II ii 235
I, that taking The Fiend's *a* of a throne, *Becket* I i 152
We have him at last; we have him at *a*. *Foresters* II i 415
O no, we took *A* of the letter—   „   IV 621
Advent To celebrate this *a* of our King!   „   IV 1048
Advice With our *a* and in our company, *Queen Mary* I iii 150
and your Grace, So you will take *a* of mine,   „   v 301
and by the *a* of his Government.' *Becket* I iii 9
Advise I would *a* That we should thoroughly *Queen Mary* III iv 194
A him: speak him sweetly, he will hear thee. *Harold* I i 116
could do No other than this way a the king   „   v i 281
Advised The Queen is ill *a*: *Queen Mary* I iv 5
He cannot dream that *I a* the war;   „   v ii 57
But you *a* the Pope. *Becket* v ii 380
Advising On any man's *a* but your own.   „   v ii 551
Advowson have graspt Her livings, her *a*'s,   „   I i 161
'All causes of *a*'s and presentations,   „   I iii 79
A-dying I ha' three sisters *a-d* at home o' the sweating sickness.   „   I iv 246
Æsop Inverted *Æ*—mountain out of mouse. *Queen Mary* II i 67
Afeard (**afraid**) I was *a* it was the ghost, your worship. *Foresters* II i 225
I am mortally *a* o' thee, thou big man,   „   IV 316
Affable you were bland And *a* to men of all estates, *Queen Mary* III vi 81
Affair His Highness is so vex'd with strange *a*'s— *Mary*. That his own wife is no *a* of his.   „   v ii 560
Has let his farm, all his *a*'s, I fear, *Prom. of May* II 420
for I must hence upon The King's *a*. *Foresters* IV 1058
Affect Her Majesty Hears you *a* the Prince— *Queen Mary* I iv 82
what shall I call it, *a* her thine own self. *Becket, Pro.* 513
Your lordship *a*'s the unwavering perpendicular;   „   II ii 325
Affection old *a* master'd you, You falter'd into tears.   „   v ii 143
from you except Return of his *a*— *The Falcon* 717
and her *a*'s Will flower toward the light *Prom. of May* I 484
Affinity the man, the woman, Following their best *affinities*,   „   I 523
Affirm and *a*'s The Queen has forfeited her right *Queen Mary* v i 289
Affright yet the word *A*'s me somewhat: „   I iv 9
Doth this *a* thee? *Harold* I i 23
Affrighted scurrying of a rat *A* me, *Queen Mary* III v 144
A-fobbing (**to put off**) hallus *a-f* ma off, tho' ye knaws I love ye. *Prom. of May* I 108
A-follering (**following**) then back ageän, *a-f* my oän shadder—   „   I 371
Afraid (*See also* **Afear'd, Half-afraid**) I was *a* of her, and I hid myself.   „   I 551
I am half *a* to pass.   „   II 328
Be not *a* of me, For these are no conventional flourishes.   „   II 561
After And that this noble realm thro' *a* years May in this unity *Queen Mary* III iii 156
and all thy flock should catch An *a* ague-fit of trembling. *Becket* III iii 33
After-dinner Not now, not now—with *a-d* grace. *Foresters* IV 937

After-life man perceives that The lost gleam of an *a-l* *Prom. of May* I 503
   greater nearness to the birthday Of the *a-l*, *Foresters* II i 45
After-marriage link rusts with the breath of the first *a-m*
   kiss, *Becket, Pro.* 362
Afternoon (*See also* **Arternoon**) The clamour'd darling of
   their *a*! *The Cup* II 125
   You had better attend to your hayfield. Good *a*. *Prom. of May* II 123
   Good *a*, my friends. ,, III 20
Agatha ask his forgiveness before he dies.—SISTER *A*.'
   Sister *A* is right. ,, III 402
A-gawin' (going) Be thou *a-g* to the long barn? ,, I 1
Age (*See also* **Lisping-age**) tho' by your *a*, And by
   your looks you are not worth the having, *Queen Mary* I iv 12
   Song flies you know For *a's*. ,, II i 82
   it is an *a* Of brief life, and brief purpose, ,, III iv 412
   'what am I, Cranmer, against whole *a's*?' ,, IV ii 104
   gray dawn Of an old *a* that never will be mine ,, v ii 235
   From child to child, from Pope to Pope, from *a* to *a*, *Harold* I iii 249
   he would be mine *a* Had he lived now; *Becket* I iii 249
   A, orphans, and babe-breasting mothers, ,, II i 72
   Will enter on the larger golden *a*; *Prom. of May* I 590
   may not those, who march Before their *a*, ,, II 633
   I could make his *a* A comfort to him— ,, II 661
   your Father must be now in extreme old *a*. ,, III 400
   poor Steer looks The very type of *A* in a picture, ,, III 514
   Some hollow-hearted from exceeding *a*— *Foresters* III 97
Aged How doubly *a* this Queen of ours hath grown *Queen Mary* v i 227
A-getting he makes moan that all be *a-g* cold. *Becket* I iv 61
   when I was *a-g* o' bluebells for your ladyship's nose
   to smell on— ,, III i 161
A-gittin' and my missus *a-g* ower 'er lyin'-in. *Prom. of May* III 74
A-glorifying our master been *a-g* and a-velveting and
   a-silking himself, *The Falcon* 98
A-going We be *a-g* home after our supper in all humbleness, *Becket* I iv 206
Agony Fire—inch by inch to die in *a*! *Queen Mary* IV iv 223
   in her *a* The mother came upon her— ,, v iv 19
   star That dances in it as mad with *a*! *Harold* I i 9
   all promises Made in our *a* for help from heaven? ,, II i 288
   Only this morning in his *a* *Foresters* IV 453
Agree (*See also* **'Grees**) *A* with him quickly again, even
   for the sake of the Church. *Becket* II ii 376
Agreed are well *a* That those old statutes touching
   Lollardism *Queen Mary* III iv 6
   it was *a* when you borrowed these monies from the
   Abbot *Foresters* IV 465
A-groänin' He's been a-moänin' and *a-g* in 'is sleep, *Prom. of May* III 411
Ague Harvestless autumns, horrible *a's*, plague *Queen Mary* v 98
   Wet, famine, *a*, fever, storm, wreck, wrath,— ,, v v 108
Ague-fit thy flock should catch An after *a-f* of trembling. *Becket* III iii 33
A-harrowin' Hodge 'ud ha' been *a-h* o' white peasen
   i' the outfield *Queen Mary* IV iii 492
A-hawking *A-h, a-h*! If I sit, I grow fat. *Becket, Pro.* 413
   ride *a-h* with the help of the men. *Foresters* I i 213
A-hell-fire and sets the church-tower over there all *a-h-f*
   as it were? *Becket* III iii 51
A-hunting King's verdurer caught him *a-h* in the forest, ,, I iv 95
Aid (s) But with Cecil's *a* And others, *Queen Mary* v v 279
Aid (verb) as I love The people! whom God *a*! ,, v iii 36
   Believing I should ever *a* the Church. *Becket, Pro.* 417
Ail What *a's* you? *Harold*. Speak. *Prom. of May* III 661
Ailmer (John, Bishop of London) *A* and Bullingham,
   and hundreds more; *Queen Mary* I ii 11
Aim stateliest deer in all the herd—Beyond his *a*— ,, v ii 427
   I am *not* Beyond his *a*, or was not. ,, v ii 450
   man that hath to foil a murderous *a* May, surely, play
   with words. *Harold* II ii 417
   Their *a* is ever at that which flies highest— *Foresters* I i 261
   Mine eye most true to one hair's-breadth of *a*. ,, IV 695
Aim'd spoil and sackage *a* at by these rebels, *Queen Mary* II ii 248
   but failure it may be Of all we *a* at. *Becket* I i 383
   The point you *a* at, and pray God she prove ,, II ii 77
Aiming in *a* at your love, It may be sometimes ,, v ii 35
Air (atmosphere) Like universal *a* and sunshine! *Queen Mary* III ii 182
   A and sunshine. I would we had you, ,, v ii 605
   Free *a*! free field! *Harold* II ii 230

Air (atmosphere) (*continued*) he flings His brand in *a* and
   catches it again, *Harold* v i 494
   and fling them out to the free *a*. *Becket* I i 288
   Blurt thy free mind to the *a*? ,, I iii 239
   when I flee from this For a gasp of freer *a*, ,, II i 29
   Let all the *a* reel into a mist of odour, *The Cup* II 185
   give him limbs, then *a*, and send him forth ,, II 261
   come as freely as heaven's *a* and mother's milk? *Foresters* I i 210
   We should be free as *a* in the wild wood— ,, I iii 124
   I breathe Heaven's *a*, and Heaven looks down on me, ,, IV 725
   if ye cannot breathe but woodland *a*, ,, IV 953
'Air (hair) I ha' heärd 'im a-gawin' on 'ud make your
   '*a*—God bless it!—stan' on end. *Prom. of May* I 135
Air (strain of music) Play the *a*, Little John. *Foresters* III 418
   A and word, my lady, are maid and man. ,, III 419
Aisle (*See also* **Minster-aisle**) The nave and *a's* all
   empty as a fool's jest! *Queen Mary* IV iii 286
   Did not a man's voice ring along the *a*, *Becket* v ii 151
Alarm my master hears with much *a*, *Queen Mary* I v 250
   Have you had any *a*? no stranger? *Becket* III i 28
Alarum clang and clash *a* as we pass, *Queen Mary* II 230
A-laughin' I'd like to leather 'im black and blue, and
   she to be *a-l* at it. *Prom. of May* II 596
Alberighi (Federigo degli) *See* **Federigo degli Alberighi**
Alchemic and jealousy Hath in it an *a* force to fuse *Queen Mary* III vi 181
Alchemy backward-working *a* Should change this gold to
   silver, *Foresters* IV 39
Alder We parted like the brook yonder about the *a*
   island, *Prom. of May* I 773
   ,, II 535
Alder-island Close by that *a-i* in your brook, ,, II 535
Aldred (Archbishop of York) take, sign it, Stigand, *A*! *Harold* III i 198
   Sign it, ,, III i 226
   Ask it of *A*. ,, IV i 241
   Come, *A*, join our hands before the hosts, ,, IV i 241
**Aldwyth (daughter of Alfgar and widow of Griffyth, King of
   Wales)** The Lady *A* Was here to-day, ,, I ii 34
   not like *A* . . . For which I strangely love him. Should
   not England Love *A*, ,, I ii 175
   Courage, noble *A*! ,, I ii 183
   They say thou art to wed the Lady *A*. ,, II ii 108
   A! *A*! (repeat) ,, IV i 19, 25
   A, Harold, *A*! ,, IV i 132
   His conqueror conquer'd *A*. ,, IV i 218
   A, *A*, Canst thou love me, ,, IV i 225
   Harold, Harold and *A*! ,, IV i 244
   Hail! Harold! *A*! hail, bridegroom and bride! ,, IV iii 1
   Hail, Harold, *A*! Bridegroom and bride! ,, IV iii 42
   Leave them! and thee too, *A*, ,, IV iii 227
Ale (*See also* **Aäle**) Brain-dizzied with a draught of
   morning *a*. *Queen Mary* II i 72
   and she brew'd the best *a* in all Glo'ster, *Becket* III i 197
   I am misty with my thimbleful of *a*. *Foresters* IV 278
   The king's good health in *a* and Malvoisie. ,, IV 968
Ale-house spent all your last Saturday's wages at
   the *a-h*; *Prom. of May* III 79
Alençon hast thou never heard His savagery at *A*,— *Harold* II ii 382
Alfgar (Earl of Mercia) (*See also* **Half-Alfgar**) light enough
   for *A's* house To strike thee down ,, I i 307
   It means the lifting of the house of *A*. ,, I i 473
   feuds that part The sons of Godwin from the sons of *A* ,, I ii 181
   Godwin still at feud with *A*, And *A* hates King Harold. ,, IV i 124
Alfred (the Great, King of the West Saxons) They blinded
   my young kinsman, *A*— ,, II ii 511
   And that my wife descends from *A*? ,, II ii 594
   tell me tales Of *A* and of Athelstan the Great ,, IV i 74
   Less than a star among the goldenest hours Of *A*, ,, IV iii 52
   A Was England. Ethelred was nothing. ,, v i 373
Alfwig Abbot *A*, Leofric, and all the monks ,, v i 445
   sure this body Is *A*, the king's uncle. ,, v ii 68
Alice (a Lady in Waiting to Queen Mary) Shall *A* sing
   you One of her pleasant songs? *A*, my child,
   Bring us your lute. *Queen Mary* v ii 354
Alien Philip's no sudden *a*—the Queen's husband, ,, III iii 42
   forfeited her right to reign By marriage with an *a*— ,, v i 291
   So strange among them—such an *a* there, *The Cup* II 143

Alight (lighted) Last night, I dream'd the faggots
were a,   *Queen Mary* IV ii 2
Alighted *See* **Lighted**
A-limpin' I seed tha *a-l* up just now wi' the roomatics
i' the knee.   *Prom. of May* I 384
Alington Ah, gray old castle of *A*,   *Queen Mary* II i 243
Alive (*See also* **Half-alive**) become Hideously *a* again
from head to heel,   ,,   IV iii 447
while famished rats Eat them *a*.   ,,   V ii 198
Dead or *a* you cannot make him happy.   ,,   V v 71
And flay me all *a*.   *Harold* IV i 191
All (*See also* **All-but-nothing**, **All-in-all**, **Hall**) Long
live Queen Mary ! down with *a* traitors !   *Queen Mary* I i 66
but *a* things here At court are known ;   ,,   I iv 56
but God hath sent me here To take such order with *a*
heretics   ,,   I v 34
now that *a* traitors Against our royal state have lost
the heads   ,,   III iv 2
The devil take *a* boots were ever made Since man went
barefoot.   ,,   III v 197
But held from you *a* papers sent by Rome,   ,,   V ii 45
That *a* day long hath wrought his father's work,   ,,   V ii 118
Methinks I am *a* angel, that I bear it Without more
ruffling.   ,,   V iii 3
But by *a* Saints— *Leofwin.* Barring the Norman !   *Harold* V i 224
and *a* left-handedness and under-handedness.   *Becket, Pro.* 340
Father, I am so tender to *a* hardness !   ,,   I i 316
Mine enemies barr'd *a* access to the boy.   ,,   V ii 451
Lady, I say it with *a* gentleness,   *The Cup* I iii 99
And fill *a* hearts with fatness and the lust Of plenty—   ,,   II 272
Richer than *a* the wide world-wealth of May,   *The Falcon* 466
A Quietist taking *a* things easily—why—   *Prom. of May* I 290
I've hed the long barn cleared out of *a* the machines,   ,,   I 451
Who leaves me *a* his land at Littlechester,   ,,   I 511
drest like a gentleman, too. ,Damn *a* gentlemen, says I !   ,,   II 579
and they both love me—I am *a* in *a* to both ;   ,,   III 213
a in *a* to one another from the time when we first peeped   ,,   III 273
Push'd from *a* doors as if we bore the plague,   ,,   III 804
but go about to come at their love with *a* manner of
homages,   *Foresters* I i 102
Sleep, happy soul ! *a* life will sleep at last.   ,,   I iii 48
in the name of *a* our woodmen, present her with this
oaken chaplet as Queen of the wood,   ,,   III 57
Out upon *a* hard-hearted maidenhood !   ,,   IV 50
And *a* I love, Robin, and *a* his men,   ,,   IV 722
Are *a* our guests here ?   ,,   IV 993
All-but-nothing if *a-b-n* be anything, and one plate of
dried prunes *a-b-n*,   *The Falcon* 134
Allegiance promise full *A* and obedience to the
death.   *Queen Mary* II ii 169
to cancel and abolish all bonds of human *a*,   ,,   IV v 50
Lay hands of full *a* in thy Lord's And crave his mercy,   *Harold* V i 16
thou hast sworn a voluntary *a* to him ?   *Becket Pro.* 439
Allen (a farm labourer) so, *A*, I may as well begin
with you.   *Prom. of May* III 29
I spoke of your names, *A*,   ,,   III 35
But, *A*, tho' you can't read,   ,,   III 42
What is all this, *A* ?   ,,   III 123
Allen (Sally) *See* **Sally Allen**
Allendale The warrior Earl of *A*,   *Foresters* I i 6
Alley so many *a*'s, crossings, Paths, avenues—   *Becket* IV ii 6
Alliance Have you *a*'s ? Bithynia, Pontus, Paphlagonia ?   *The Cup* I ii 99
Break thine *a* with this faithless John,   *Foresters* IV 323
Allied Art thou for Richard, or *a* to John ? *Richard.* I
am *a* to John.   ,,   IV 135
for how canst thou be thus *a* With John,   ,,   IV 350
All-in-all (*See also* **All**) Their Flemish go-between
And *a-i-a*.   *Queen Mary* III vi 5
Allow your Highness will *a* Some spice of wisdom   ,,   III iv 133
His Highness and myself (so you *a* us)   ,,   III iv 324
rage of one who hates a truth He cannot but *a*.   ,,   III vi 145
A me the same answer as before—   ,,   V i 237
world *a*'s I fall no inch Behind this Becket,   *Becket* V i 39
A me, sir, to pass you.   *Prom. of May* II 354
A me to go with you to the farm.   ,,   II 574

Allowance I can make *a* for thee,   *Queen Mary* I v 326
Make no *a* for the naked truth.   ,,   I v 328
To make *a* for their rougher fashions,   *Harold* II ii 8
easier then for you to make *A* for a mother—
ready To make *a*'s, and mighty slow To feel
offences.   *Prom. of May* III 629
Allow'd tho' a stranger fain would be *a* To join the hunt.   *The Cup* I i 196
I think our Abbess knew it and *a* it.   *Becket* V ii 95
All-prepared The best of all not *a-p* to die.   ,,   V ii 564
All-royal Look rather thou *a-r* as when first I met thee.   ,,   II i 46
Almighty floated downward from the throne Of God *A*.   *Harold* I i 19
Harold and God *A* !   ,,   I v 526
Almoner This *A* hath tasted Henry's gold.   *Becket* I i 294
Almost *See* **Ommost**
Alms his wealth A fountain of perennial *a*—   *Queen Mary* II ii 385
she holds it in Free and perpetual *a*,   *Becket* I iii 680
boldness of this hand hath won it Love's *a*,   ,,   I 184
pale beggar-woman seeking *a* For her sick son,   *The Falcon* 853
sweet saints bless your worship for your *a* to the old
woman !   *Foresters* II i 364
O your honour, I pray you too to give me an *a*.   ,,   II i 390
Almshouses Part shall go to the *a* at Nottingham,   ,,   II 206
Aloän (alone) Let ma *a* afoor foälk, wilt tha ?   *Prom. of May* II 213
I tell'd tha to let ma *a* !   ,,   II 229
I can't let tha *a* if I would, Sally.   ,,   II 233
A-lodgin' What dost a knaw o' this Mr Hedgar as be
a-l' wi' ye ?   ,,   I 200
A-lolluping (hanging down) tongue on un cum *a-l*
out o' 'is mouth as black as a rat.   *Queen Mary* IV iii 519
Alone (*See also* **Aloän**) And think not we shall be *a*—   ,,   II 191
and not *a* from this, Likewise from any other,   ,,   II 236
Harold Hear the king's music, all *a* with him,   *Harold* I ii 194
I leave thee to thy talk with him *a* ;   ,,   II i 324
And Wulfnoth is *a* in Normandy,   ,,   III i 81
The Church *a* hath eyes—and now I see That I was
blind—   *Becket* II i 436
So many happy hours *a* together,   ,,   III iii 39
That I would speak with you once more *a*.   ,,   III iii 41
Can I speak with you *A*, my father ?   ,,   V ii 70
will you have it *a*, Or with these listeners near you ?   ,,   V ii 304
We are all *a* with him.   ,,   V ii 312
A I do it.   ,,   V ii 459
Too early to be here *a* with thee ;   *The Cup* I iii 82
Can I not speak with you once more *a* ?   *The Falcon* 689
Ay, the dear nurse will leave you *a* ;   ,,   703
Let him *a* ! A worthy messenger !   *Foresters* I iii 84
Thou art *a* in the silence of the forest   ,,   IV 630
Let him *a a* while. He loves the chivalry of his single arm.   ,,   IV 784
A-lookin' then a-scrattin upon a bit o' paäper, then
a-l ageän ;   *Prom. of May* I 203
I'd like to drag 'im thruff the herse-pond, and she
to be *a-l* at it.   ,,   II 594
Alphabetical (*See also* **Halfabitical**) but he sent me an *a*
list of those that remain,   ,,   III 28
Alphege (Archbishop of Canterbury) St. Denis of France
and St. *A* of England,   *Becket* V iii 165
Altar (*See also* **Haltar**) Our *a* is a mound of dead
men's clay,   *Queen Mary* V ii 161
a dead man Rose from behind the *a*,   *Harold* I ii 79
let our high *a* Stand where their standard fell . . .   ,,   V ii 139
look how the table steams, like a heathen *a* ; nay, like
the *a* at Jerusalem,   *Becket* I iv 69
he hath made his bed between the *a*'s,   ,,   I iv 264
You on this side the *a*. You on that.   *The Cup* I. 254
Altar-flame Rouse the dead *a-f*, fling in the spices,   ,,   II 182
Alter every tongue *A*'s it passing,   *Queen Mary* III v 36
Altered He is much *a* ; but I trust that your return—   *Prom. of May* III 420
Alva (Duke) The Duke Of *A*, an iron soldier.   *Queen Mary* III i 194
for their heresies, *A*, they will fight ;   ,,   III ii 204
Duke *A* will but touch him on the horns,   ,,   V i 155
For *A* is true son of the true church—   ,,   V i 159
Always *See* **Hallus**
A-makin' and *a-m'* o' volk madder and madder ;   ,,   IV iii 532
Amaze one step in the dark beyond Our expectation,
that *a*'s us.   *The Cup* I i 213

Amazed (*See also* **Maäzed**) Madam, I am *a*:   *Queen Mary* I v 308
brake into woman-tears, Ev'n Gardiner, all *a*,   ,,   I v 566
were much *a* To find as fair a sun   ,,   III ii 21
Why lookest thou so *a*?   *Foresters* I i 130
Ambassador King of France, Noailles the *A*,   *Queen Mary* I v 239
The *A* from France, your Grace.   ,,   I v 239
Who waits? *Usher.* The *A* of Spain,   ,,   I v 342
Ambition The proud *a's* of Elizabeth,   ,,   II i 169
For hath not thine *a* set the Church This day   *Becket* I iii 584
that *a* Is like the sea wave,   *The Cup* I iii 137
a, pride So bloat and redden his face—   ,,   II 169
Ambush Where have you lain in *a* all the morning?   *Prom. of May* I 544
Amen Serve God and both your Majesties.
   Voices. A.   *Queen Mary* III iii 160
They groan *a*; they swarm into the fire   ,,   v ii 110
A. Come on.   ,,   v iv 9
A to all Your wish, and further.   ,,   v iv 28
Deserts! *A* to what? Whose deserts?   ,,   v iv 30
Amenable Like other lords *a* to law.   *Becket, Pro.* 25
Amends They make *a* for the tails.   *Queen Mary* III i 227
I make thee full *a*.   *Becket* III iii 219
To make *a* I come this day to break my fast   *The Cup* 275
I cannot find the word—forgive it—*A*.   *Prom. of May* III 791
Amiss I know I have done *a*, have been a fool.   *Foresters* II ii 51
Amity Are now once more at perfect *a*.   *Becket* III iii 229
Amnesty more of olive-branch and *a* For foes at home—   ,,   v ii 15
A-moänin' He's been *a-m* and a-groänin' in 'is sleep,   *Prom. of May* III 411
Amomum Nard, Cinnamon, *a*, benzoin.   *The Cup* IV 184
Amorous If I tried her and la—she's *a*.   *Queen Mary* I iv 17
nor yet so *a* That I must needs be husbanded,   ,,   II ii 215
a Of good old red sound liberal Gascon wine: *Becket, Pro.* 99
Amount How much might that *a* to, my lord Leicester?   ,,   I iii 655
Amour Thomas, lord Not only of your vassals but *a's*,   ,,   IV i 205
Amourist he, your rustic *a*, The polish'd Damon   *Prom. of May* III 561
Amphisbæna Two vipers of one breed—an *a*, Each
   end a sting: *Queen Mary* III iv 39
Ampler Farewell, Madam, God grant you *a* mercy
   at your call   ,,   IV i 189
Amplier *A* than any field on our poor earth   ,,   III 197
Amulet that are *a's* against all The kisses of all kind   *Harold* I ii 112
Mine *a* . . . This last . . .   ,,   I ii 124
Anabaptist world-hating beast, A haggard *A*.   *Queen Mary* II ii 92
Anathema He is pronounced *a*.   ,,   IV i 187
The Pope's *A*—the Holy Rood That bow'd to me   *Harold* v i 382
and let them be *a*, And all that speak for them *a*.   *Becket* I i 170
I charge thee, upon pain of mine *a*,   ,,   I iii 719
Go, lest I blast thee with *a*,   ,,   IV i 287
gone to the King And taken our *a* with him.   ,,   v ii 8
Anathematise (*See also* **De-Anathematise**) I would *a* him.   ,,   I iii 314
I will not seal.   ,,   v i 4
Anathematised Cursed and *a* us right and left,   ,,   v i 4
Anatomized *a* The flowers for her—   *Prom. of May* II 302
Ancestor bowl my *a* Fetch'd from the farthest east—   *The Falcon* 484
Ancestral lest the crown should be Shorn of *a* splendour.   *Becket* I iii 157
Anchor such a one Was without rudder, *a*, compass—   *Prom. of May* III 534
Ancient Who now recalls her to His *a* fold.   *Queen Mary* III iii 167
Which frights you back into the *a* faith;   ,,   IV ii 143
he stood More like an *a* father of the Church,   ,,   IV iii 598
And for these Royal customs, These *a* Royal customs—
   they *are* Royal,   *Becket* I i 167
These *a* laws and customs of the realm. (repeat)   ,,   I iii 7, 18
For I was musing on an *a* saw,   ,,   v ii 538
It is our *a* custom in Galatia   *The Cup* II 358
Andrew, St. *See* **St. Andrew**
Andrew's Laughs at the last red leaf, and *A* Day.   *Queen Mary* III iii 87
Anew Why, tha looks haäle *a* to last to a hoonderd.   *Prom. of May* I 354
Angel Let the great *a* of the church come with him;   *Queen Mary* I v 377
As an *a* among *a's*.   ,,   I v 449
His friends—as *A's* I received 'em,   ,,   I v 625
flocks of swans, As fair and white as *a's*;   ,,   III ii 16
True, and I am the *A* of the Pope.   ,,   III ii 144
how the blessed *a's* who rejoice Over one saved   ,,   III iii 180
There's half an *a* wrong'd in your account; Methinks
   I am all *a*,   ,,   v iii 1
May the great *a's* join their wings,   ,,   v iv 6

Angel (*continued*) Then a great *A* past along the highest   *Harold* III i 134
great *A* rose And past again along   ,,   III i 153
Are those the blessed *a's* quiring, father?   ,,   v i 472
Whisper! God's *a's* only know it. Ha!   ,,   v ii 31
will be reflected in the spiritual body among the *a's*.   *Becket, Pro.* 398
So now he bears the standard of the *a's*.   ,,   I iii 497
till it break Into young *a's*.   ,,   v ii 257
face of an *a* and the heart of a—that's too positive!   *The Falcon* 86
Seem my good *a* who may help me from it.   *Prom. of May* II 388
God's good *A* Help him back hither,   *Foresters* I ii 10
Thou comest a very *a* out of heaven.   ,,   II i 105
I am but an *a* by reflected light.   ,,   II i 108
Your heaven is vacant of your *a*.   ,,   II i 109
Anger (s) no more rein upon thine *a* Than any child!   *Queen Mary* III iv 303
The King is quick to *a*; if thou anger him,   *Becket* I iii 165
betwixt thine Appeal, and Henry's *a*, yield.   ,,   I iii 623
Our brother's *a* puts him, Poor man,   ,,   II i 234
When I was in mine *a* with King Louis,   ,,   III iii 257
A noble *a*! but Antonius To-morrow   *The Cup* I v 95
My five-years' *a* cannot die at once,   *Prom. of May* II 462
Anger (verb) The King is quick to anger; if thou *a* him,   *Becket* I iii 165
Nay—go. What! will you *a* me?   ,,   II i 209
King plucks out their eyes Who *a* him,   ,,   IV i 407
talk not of cows. You *a* the spirit.   *Foresters* II i 330
A the scritch-owl.   ,,   II i 331
A brave old fellow but he *a's* me.   ,,   II i 471
Away, away, wife, wilt thou *a* him?   ,,   II i 255
Anger'd And if her people, *a* thereupon,   *Queen Mary* I iii 90
That had *a* me Had I been William.   *Harold* II ii 386
How he flamed When Tostig's *a* earldom flung him,   ,,   III i 54
Tostig, poor brother, Art *thou* so *a*?   ,,   v i 274
I deny not That I was somewhat *a*.   *Becket* IV ii 351
and yet You know me easily *a*.   ,,   v i 84
But *a* at their flaunting of our flag,   *The Falcon* 628
I have *a* your good nurse;   ,,   706
he kneels! he has *a* the foul witch,   *Foresters* II i 670
Angerest Thou *a* me, man: I do not jest.   *Becket, Pro.* 299
Angle *A*, Jute, Dane, Saxon, Norman,   *Harold* II ii 762
yet he held that Dane, Jute, *A*, Saxon,   ,,   IV i 77
As once he bore the standard of the *A's*,   *Becket* I iii 495
Angler's Home Close by that alder-island in your
   brook 'The *A H*.'   *Prom. of May* II 536
Anglia Pereant, pereant, *A* precatur.   *Harold* v i 534
Angliae Hostis per *A* Plagas bacchatur;   ,,   v i 510
Angliam Hostis in *A* Ruit prædator.   ,,   v i 506
Angry Thro' all her *a* chronicles hereafter By loss of
   Calais.   *Queen Mary* v ii 304
Animal What, is not man a hunting *a*?   *Foresters* IV 224
Anjou (**French province**) When I am out in Normandy
   or *A*.   *Becket, Pro.* 144
We take her from her secret bower in *A*   ,,   *Pro.* 182
A hundred, too, from Normandy and *A*:   ,,   II ii 174
My *A* bower was scarce as beautiful.   ,,   III i 52
Glancing at the days when his father was only
   Earl of *A*,   ,,   III iii 150
Anne (**Christian name**) He loved the Lady *A*;   *Foresters* I i 7
Anne (**Queen**) Queen *A* loved him. All the women
   loved him.   *Queen Mary* II i 33
Anne (**Wharton**) (*See also* **Anne Wharton**) and the
   Lady *A* Bow'd to the Pyx;   ,,   I v 41
wherefore bow ye not, says Lady *A*,   ,,   I v 46
Anne Wharton (*See also* **Anne**) with her Lady *A W*,
   and the Lady Anne   ,,   I v 41
Annex'd and the legateship *A* to Canterbury—   ,,   v ii 37
Another —a recantation Of Cranmer at the stake.   ,,   IV iii 299
There! there! *a* paper!   ,,   v ii 329
revolt? A new Northumberland, *a* Wyatt?   ,,   v v 188
for what right had he to get himself wrecked on *a*
   man's land?   *Harold* II i 60
a hill Or fort, or city, took it,   ,,   IV i 49
With whom I fought *a* fight than this Of Stamford-bridge.   ,,   IV iii 23
And then *a* wood, and in the midst A garden and
   my Rosamund.   *Becket, Pro.* 168
You bad me take revenge *a* way—   ,,   IV ii 153
There is yet *a* old woman.   *Foresters* II i 244

Apostolic And from the *A* see of Rome ;   *Queen Mary* III iii 127
   by your intercession May from the *A* see obtain,   ,,   III iii 147
   And we by that authority *A* Given unto us, his
   Legate,   ,,   III iii 210
Appall'd And yet I seem *a*—on such a sudden   *Becket* I i 137
Appeal for their sake who stagger betwixt thine *A*,   ,,   I i 623
   make *a* To all the archbishops, bishops,   ,,   v ii 403
Appeal'd You were sent for, You were *a* to,   *Queen Mary* IV iv 256
   I *a* to the Sister again, her answer—   *Prom. of May* III 394
Appear doth *a* this marriage is the least Of all their
   quarrel.   *Queen Mary* II ii 154
   And cite thee to *a* before the Pope,   *Becket* I iii 602
Appearance for *a* sake, stay with the Queen.   *Queen Mary* II 137
'Appen (happen) To be true to each other,
   let '*a* what maäy, (repeat)   *Prom. of May* II 206, 236, 257
Appertaining myself Half beast and fool as *a* to it ;   *Queen Mary* IV iii 415
Applaud I say Ye would *a* that Norman   *Harold* II ii 539
Apple (adj.) No, not that way—here, under the *a* tree.   *Prom. of May* I 83
Apple (s) cut out the rotten from your *a*, Your *a* eats   *Queen Mary* II ii 6
   That bears not its own *a's*.   ,,   I i 23
   if I had been Eve i' the garden I shouldn't ha'
   minded the *a*, for what's an *a*,   *Becket* I i 140
   you have robb'd poor father Of ten good *a's*.   *Prom. of May* I 616
Appoint Or he the bridegroom may *a* ?   *Becket* I iii 687
Appointed He, whom the Father had *a* Head Of all
   his church,   *Queen Mary* III iii 206
   the King, till another be *a*, shall receive the revenues
   thereof,'   *Becket* I iii 101
Appreciation commend them to your ladyship's most
   peculiar *a*.   *The Falcon* 568
Apprehend ' Whosoever will *a* the traitor Thomas
   Wyatt   *Queen Mary* II iii 59
   Which you would scarce *a* of :   ,,   v iii 63
Approve I am happy you *a* it.   *Prom. of May* III 624
Approved the Emperor *A* you, and when last he
   wrote,   *Queen Mary* III vi 77
   When I was made Archbishop, he *a* me.   ,,   v ii 86
Appurtenance so descend again with some of her
   ladyship's own *a's* ?   *The Falcon* 417
'Appy (happy) They can't be many, my dear, but I
   'oäpes they'll be '*a*.   *Prom. of May* I 353
Apricot walnut, *a*, Vine, cypress, poplar, myrtle,   *The Cup* I i 2
April (adj.) Like *A* sap to the topmost tree,   *Foresters* I iii 24
April (s) I was but fourteen and an *A* then.   *Becket* I i 279
Apt And *a* at arms and shrewd in policy.   *Foresters* II ii 104
Aquitaine (a French province) but our sun in *A* lasts
   longer. I would I were in *A* again—   *Becket*, Pro. 328
   ' Eleanor of *A*, Eleanor of England !   ,,   IV ii 241
   To take my life might lose him *A*.   ,,   IV ii 396
   Of England ? Say of *A*. I am no Queen of England.   ,,   v i 100
   I will go live and die in *A*. (repeat)   ,,   v i 109, 143
   Ha, you of *A* ! O you of *A* ! You were but *A* to
   Louis—no wife ; You are only *A* to me—   ,,   v i 114
   I be wife to one That only wedded me for *A* ?   ,,   v i 121
   And what would my own *A* say to that ?   ,,   v i 182
Arab I had it from an *A* soldan, who,   *Queen Mary* III v 300
Araby free wing The world were all one *A*.   *Queen Mary* III v 210
Aragon (a Spanish province) The voices of Castille
   and *A*,   ,,   v i 43
   O Saint of *A*, with that sweet worn smile   ,,   v v 198
Arbour *See* **Harbour**
Archbishop (*See also* **Chancellor-Archbishop. Dis-
   Archbishop**) The false *a* fawning on him,   ,,   I v 30
   That when I was *a* held with me.   ,,   IV iv 160
   Chief prelate of our Church, *a*,   ,,   IV iii 70
   burnin' o' the owld *a* 'll burn the Pwoap   ,,   IV iii 535
   When I was made *A*, he approved me.   ,,   v ii 85
   Did ye not outlaw your *a* Robert,   *Harold* I i 56
   Ask *our A*. Stigand should know the purposes of
   Heaven.   ,,   I i 63
   A Robert ! Robert the *A* !   ,,   II ii 528
   No, nor *a*, nor my confessor yet.   *Becket*, Pro. 84
   Why—look—is this a sleeve For an *a* ?   ,,   Pro. 251
   A more awful one. Make *me a* !   ,,   Pro. 289
   Me *A* ! God's favour and king's favour   ,,   Pro. 293

Archbishop (*continued*) My liege, the good *A* is no more.   *Becket*, Pro. 392
   And this plebeian like to be *A* !   ,,   Pro. 459
   A ? I can see further into a man   ,,   Pro. 462
   but the Chancellor's and the *A's* Together   ,,   I i 23
   Make an *A* of a soldier ?   ,,   I i 41
   ' My young *A*—thou wouldst make A stately *A* ! '   ,,   I i 65
   And how been made *A* hadst thou told him,   ,,   I i 121
   The *A* ! *Becket.* Ay ! what wouldst thou,   ,,   I i 185
   Come, come, my lord *A* ;   ,,   I i 201
   can I be under him As Chancellor ? as *A* over him ?   ,,   I i 349
   my Lord *A*, 'Tis known you are midwinter to all
   women,   ,,   I ii 26
   first *a* fled, And York lay barren for a hundred years.   ,,   I iii 53
   Is it thy will, My lord *A*,   ,,   I iii 272
   Loyally and with good faith, my lord *A* ?   ,,   I iii 279
   My lord *A*, thou hast yet to seal.   ,,   I iii 306
   Say that a cleric murder'd an *a*,   ,,   I iii 399
   Hoped, were he chosen *a*,   ,,   I iii 442
   Now as *A* goest against the King ;   ,,   I iii 530
   and no forsworn *A* Shall helm the Church.   ,,   I iii 597
   To see the proud *A* mutilated.   ,,   I iii 614
   Know that when made *A* I was freed,   ,,   I iii 707
   That none should wrong or injure your *A*.   ,,   I iii 755
   My lord *A*, wilt thou permit us—   ,,   I iv 5
   My lord *A*, may I come in with my poor friend,
   my dog ?   ,,   I iv 93
   Is the *A* a thief who gives thee thy supper ?   ,,   I iv 115
   if the barons and bishops hadn't been a-sitting
   on the *A*.   ,,   I iv 128
   Where is my lord *A* ?   ,,   I iv 184
   for the *A* loves humbleness, my lord ;   ,,   I iv 208
   the *A* washed my feet o' Tuesday.   ,,   I iv 234
   for the *A* likes the smell on it,   ,,   I iv 240
   I bring the taint on it along wi' me, for the *A* likes it,   ,,   I iv 253
   for to-night ye have saved our *A* !   ,,   I iv 257
   My friends, the *A* bids you good night.   ,,   I iv 261
   then to be made *A* and go against the King   ,,   II i 237
   nor our *A* Stagger on the slope decks   ,,   II ii 105
   Blessed be the Lord *A*, who hath withstood   ,,   II ii 275
   My dear Lord *A*, I learn but now   ,,   II ii 426
   God bless the great *A* !   ,,   II ii 452
   you had safelier have slain an *a* than a she-goat :   ,,   III iii 68
   What more, my lord *A* ? What more, Thomas ?   ,,   III iii 217
   But kinglike fought the proud *a*,—   ,,   IV vi 438
   Down with King Henry ! up with the *A* !   ,,   v i 261
   I told him I was bound to see the *A* ;   ,,   v ii 100
   she had seen the *A* once, So mild, so kind.   ,,   v ii 119
   No, daughter, you mistake our good *A* !   ,,   v ii 138
   How the good *A* reddens !   ,,   v ii 298
   To all the *a's*, bishops, prelates, barons,   ,,   v ii 404
   My vassals—and yet threaten your *A* In his own
   house.   ,,   v iii 505
   Here is the great *A* ! He lives ! he lives !   ,,   v iii 29
   my lord *A*, A score of knights all arm'd   ,,   v iii 70
   Where is the *A*, Thomas Becket ?   ,,   v iii 109
   Strike our *A* in his own cathedral !   ,,   v iii 180
   the great *A* ! Does he breathe ? No ?   ,,   v iii 202
   they plunder—yea, ev'n bishops, Yea, ev'n *a's*—   *Foresters* IV 911
Archbishoprick as his successor in the *a*.   *Becket*, Pro. 402
   From out his grave to this *a*.   ,,   Pro. 420
   and chosen me For this thy great *a*,   ,,   I i 91
   Save from the throne of thine *a* ?   ,,   I i 119
   I care not for thy new *a*.   ,,   I i 217
   Shall I forget my new *a*   ,,   I i 220
   It well befits thy new *a* To take the vagabond woman   ,,   I i 225
   Found two *a's*, London and York ?   ,,   I iii 50
   King Would throne me in the great *A* :   ,,   I iii 694
Archdeacon The Pope and that *A* Hildebrand His
   master,   *Harold* III ii 144
Archiepiscopari but *Nolo A*, my good friend,   *Becket*, Pro. 286
Archiepiscopally As magnificently and *a* as our Thomas
   would have done :   ,,   III iii 87
A-reädin' arter she'd been *a-r* me the letter wi' 'er
   voice a-shaäkin',   *Prom. of May* II 128
Argue and I can't *a* upon it ;   *Queen Mary* I i 55

Ash (cinder) (*See also* **Ashes**) fain had calcined all
  Northumbria To one black *a*,   *Harold* III i 57
Ash (tree) (*See also* **Ashtree**) And wattled thick with *a* and
  willow-wands ;   „   v i 190
  This is the hottest of it : hold, *a* ! hold, willow !   „   v i 628
  I remember, Scarlet hacking down A hollow *a*,   *Foresters* II ii 96
A-shaäkin' (**shaking**) arter she'd been a-reädin' me
  the letter wi' 'er voice *a-s*,   *Prom. of May* II 129
Ashamed (*See also* **Shaämed**) I am a that I am
  Bagenhall, English.   *Queen Mary* III iii 248
  Thou mak'st me much a That I was for a moment
  wroth at thee.   „   III iv 305
  Till I myself was half *a* for him.   „   IV iv 171
  I am a to lift my eyes to heaven,   „   IV iii 127
  you yourself are *a* of me, and I do not wonder at it. *Prom. of May* II 269
  I fall before thee, clasp Thy knees. I am *a*.   *Foresters* II i 600
Ashes (*See also* **Ash**) those *a* Which all must be.   *The Cup* I iii 134
  to such a heat As burns a wrong to *a*,   *Foresters* II i 700
Ashridge means to counsel your withdrawing to A, *Queen Mary* I iv 226
  Permission of her Highness to retire To A,   „   I iv 237
Ashtree (*See also* **Ash, Eshtree**) always told Father
  that the huge old *a* there would cause an
  accident some day ;   *Prom. of May* III 244
A-silking (**dressing in silk**) master been a-glorifying
  and a-velveting and *a-s* himself,   *The Falcon* 99
A-sitting if the barons and bishops hadn't been *a-s* on the
  Archbishop.   *Becket* I iv 128
  Didn't I spy 'em *a-s* i' the woodbine harbour
  togither ?   *Prom. of May* I 124
Ask (*See also* **Ax**) Why do you *a* ? you know it. *Queen Mary* I iv 34
  A thou Lord Leofwin what he thinks of this !   *Harold* I i 40
  A it of King Edward !   „   I i 78
  a of *me* Who had my pallium from an Antipope !   „   I i 81
  A our broad Earl.   „   I i 90
  I *a* thee, wilt thou help me to the crown ?   „   II ii 627
  A me for this at thy most need, son Harold,   „   III i 225
  A it of Aldred.   „   III ii 46
  A me not, Lest I should yield it,   „   v i 16
  I *a* again When had the Lateran and the Holy Father   „   v i 451
  I have a power—would Harold *a* me for it—   *Becket* I i 320
  I a no more. Heaven bless thee ! hence !   „   III i 6
  That which you *a* me Till better times.   „   III i 79
  What did you *a* her ?   „   v ii 379
  Not I, the Pope. A *him* for absolution.   „   v ii 458
  I a no leave of king, or mortal man,   *The Cup* I ii 26
  You will not easily make me credit that. *Phœbe.* A her.   *The Falcon* 220
  His falcon, and I come to a for his falcon,   „   234
  How can I *a* for his falcon ?   „   244
  Yet if I *a*, He loves me, and he knows I know   „   264
  How can I, dare I, *a* him for his falcon ?   „   299
  Yet I come To *a* a gift.   „   778
  for the gift I *a* for, to *my* mind   „   788
  love for my dying boy, Moves me to *a* it of you.   „   805
  Will pardon me for asking what I *a*. *Prom. of May* II 393
  Might I *a* your name ? *Harold.* Harold.   „   III 401
  Go back to him and a his forgiveness before he dies.—   *Foresters* I i 54
  I *a* you all, did none of you love young Walter Lea ?
  will you answer me a question ? *Marian.* Any that
  you may *a*.   „   I ii 137
  A question that every true man *a's* of a woman once
  in his life.   „   I ii 139
  we be beggars, we come to *a* o' you. We ha' nothing.   „   III 190
  bond he hath Of the Abbot—wilt thou *a* him for it ?   „   IV 85
  I fear to *a* who left us even now.   „   IV 808
Ask'd (*See also* **Axed, Haxed**) And by their answers
  to the question *a*,   *Queen Mary* II ii 153
  a him, childlike : ' Will you take it off   „   III i 401
  they clapt their hands Upon their swords when *a* ;   „   v i 174
  when he *a* for England ?   *Harold* IV viii 110
  Was there not someone *a* me for forgiveness ?   „   v ii 82
  I *a* the way. *Rosamund.* I think so.   *Becket* II i 62
  I but *a* her One question, and she primm'd her mouth   „   III i 73
  a our mother if I could keep a quiet tongue i' my head,   „   III i 118
  I *a* A ribbon from her hair to bind it with ;   *The Falcon* 358
  you *a* to eat with me.   „   868

Ask'd (*continued*) And *a* me what I could not answer. *Prom. of May* I 555
  and I *a* her once more to help me,   „   III 387
  I would ha' given my whole body to the King had
  he *a* for it,   *Foresters* II i 306
  criedst ' I yield ' almost before the thing was *a*,   „   II i 567
Asking Have for thine *a* aught that I can give, *Queen Mary* III iii 7
  Will pardon me for a what I ask.   *The Falcon* 805
  a his consent—you wish'd me—   *Prom. of May* III 493
Asleep wholesome medicine here Puts that belief *a*.   *Becket* IV ii 52
  Shall I find you *a* when I come back ?   „   IV ii 64
  with as little pain As it is to fall *a*.   *Prom. of May* II 342
  The sick lady here might have been *a*.   „   III 344
  Some hunter in day-dreams or half *a*   *Foresters* IV 1088
A-spitting you'll set the Divil's Tower *a-s*, *Queen Mary* II iii 103
A-spreading and *a-s* to catch her eye for a dozen year, *The Falcon* 100
Ass with an *a's*, not a horse's head,   „   v i 284
  Sir Thomas Stafford, a bull-headed *a*,   „   IV ii 34
Assail And might *a* you passing through the street, *Becket* v ii 251
  To *a* our Holy Mother lest she brood Too long   *Foresters* IV 423
Assail'd if e'er thou be *a* In any of our forests,   *The Cup* I i 177
  woman's fealty when *A* by Craft and Love.   *Becket* v ii 522
Assassin even now You seem the least *a* of the four. *Queen Mary* v i 147
Assaulted my house hath been *a*,   „   III iii 114
Assembled And Commons here in Parliament *a*,   *Harold* II ii 126
Assembly But there the great A choose their king, *Queen Mary* II ii 206
Assent This marriage had the *a* of those   „   III i 311
  Thine is a half voice and a lean *a*.   *Becket* I iii 195
  That were but as the shadow of an *a*.
Assertion *See* **Self-assertion**
Assessor But his *a* in the throne,   *Queen Mary* I v 501
Assize *See* **'Size**
Assure I do *a* you, that it must be look'd to :   „   v i 2
  I do most earnestly *a* you that Your likeness— *Prom. of May* II 563
Assured Art thou *a* By this, that Harold loves but Edith ? *Harold* I ii 209
A-steälin' cotched 'im once *a-s* coäls an' I sent fur 'im, *Prom. of May* I 412
Astride with the Holy Father *a* of it down upon his own
  head.   *Becket* III iii 77
Asunder here I gash myself *a* from the King,   „   I i 175
A-supping be we not *a-s* with the head of the family ?   „   I iv 178
  They be dead while I be *a-s*.   „   I iv 247
A-sweäring I be afeard I shall set him *a-s* like
  onythink.   *Prom. of May* III 359
At (hat) We fun' 'im out a-walkin' i' West Field wi'
  a white '*a*,   „   III 135
A-talkin' What feller wur it as '*a*' been *a-t* fur haäfe
  an hour wi' my Dora ?   „   II 576
A-telling Robin the Earl, is always *a-t* us that every man, *Foresters* I i 95
Atheling (a **Saxon prince**) The *A* is nearest to the throne. *Harold* II ii 569
  So that ye will not crown the *A* ?   „   II ii 598
  Who inherits ? Edgar the *A* ?   „   III i 240
Athelstan (**King of the English**) and tell me tales Of
  Alfred and of *A* the Great   „   IV i 74
  Or *A*, or English Ironside Who fought with Knut,   „   IV iii 53
A-top and your worship *a-t* of it.   *Queen Mary* II i 66
A-tryin' if she weänt listen to me when I be *a-t* to
  saäve 'er—   *Prom. of May* II 694
Attainder Ye have reversed the *a* laid on us *Queen Mary* III iii 194
       „   III ii 54
Attainted Thou hast disgraced me and *a* me,   *Foresters* I iii 57
  Thou, Robin Hood Earl of Huntingdon, art *a* *Queen Mary* I iii 152
Attend so you well *a* to the king's moves,   „   III iv 431
  I *a* the Queen To crave most humble pardon—   *Becket* v ii 598
  You should *a* the office, give them heart.   „   v ii 607
  He said, ' *A* the office.' *Becket.* A the office ? *Prom. of May* II 122
  You had better *a* to your hayfield.
  I am sorry Mr. Steer still continues too unwell to
  a to you,   „   III 22
  ' I am sorry that we could not *a* your Grace's party
  on the 10th ! '   „   III 313
Attendance must we dance *a* all the day ?   *Foresters* IV 551
Attending I've been *a* on his deathbed and his burial. *Prom. of May* II 4
Attraction fine *a's* and repulses, the delicacies,   *Becket,* Pro. 499
Audience Your *a* is concluded, sir.   *Queen Mary* I v 337
Aught (*See also* **Ought, Owt**) Have you *a* else to tell me ? „   v iii 100
Augustine *See* **Austin**
Aureole Sees ever such an *a* round the Queen,   „   v ii 413

Austin (Augustine, first Archbishop of Canterbury) *Gregory*
  bid St. *A* here Found two archbishopricks,   *Becket* I iii 48
  bravest in our roll of Primates down From *A*—   „ v ii 59
Author This *a*, with his charm of simple style   *Prom. of May* I 223
Authority Under and with your Majesties' *authorities*, *Queen Mary* III iii 138
  we by that *a* Apostolic Given unto us,   „ iii 210
  And under his *a*—I depart.   *Becket* I iii 728
  Not punish of your own *a*?   „ v ii 450
  I would stand Clothed with the full *a* of Rome,   „ v ii 493
Automatic all but proving man An *a* series of sensations, *Prom. of May* I 226
Autumn (adj.) Sick as an *a* swallow for a voyage, *Harold* I i 101
Autumn (s) Harvestless *a's*, horrible agues, plague— *Queen Mary* v i 98
Avarice shakes at mortal kings—her vacillation, *A*, craft— *Becket* II ii 407
A-velveting (dressing in velvet) master been a-glorifying
  and *a-v* and a-silking himself,   *The Falcon* 98
Avenge Who will *a* me of mine enemies— *Queen Mary* III ii 166
Avenged that blighted vow Which God *a* to-day. *Harold* v i 157
Avenue —so many alleys, crossings, Paths, *a's*— *Becket* IV iv 7
A-vire (on fire) and a set un all *a-v*, so 'z the tongue *Queen Mary* IV iii 518
Avoid I may as well *a* him.   *Prom. of May* II 619
Avouch I dare *a* you'd stand up for yourself, *Queen Mary* II ii 360
Await My lord ! the Duke *a's* thee at the banquet. *Harold* II ii 805
Awaked (*See also* **Half-waked**) He hath *a* ! he
  hath *a* !   *Queen Mary* III ii 156
Awaken Love will hover round the flowers when
  they first *a*;   „ v ii 371
Awaken'd It seems her Highness hath *a*.   „ v ii 522
Awakening *See* **New-wakening**
A-walkin' we fun' 'im out *a-w* i' West Field wi' a
  white 'at,   *Prom. of May* III 134
Award Thou shalt receive the penitent thief's *a*, *Queen Mary* IV iii 87
Awe —they cannot speak—for *a*;   *Harold* I i 33
Awful A more *a* one. Make *me* archbishop !   *Becket, Pro.* 288
Awry Nothing; but ' come, come, come,' and all *a*, *Queen Mary* v v 16
Ax (ask) Shall I foller 'er and *a* 'er to maäke it up ? *Prom. of May* II 131
Axe (*See also* **Battle-axe, War-axe**) there is *a* and
  cord.   *Queen Mary* III iv 47
  How oft the falling *a*, that never fell,   „ III v 134
  I have a mind to brain thee with mine *a*. *Harold* II i 74
  Our *a's* lighten with a single flash   „ v i 537
  Against the shifting blaze of Harold's *a* !   „ v i 587
  score of knights all arm'd with swords and *a's*— *Becket* v iii 72
Axed (asked) when I *a* 'im why, he telled me 'at
  sweet'arts   *Prom. of May* II 155
  an' *a* ma to be 'is little sweet'art,   „ III 120
Axle rear and run And break both neck and *a*. *Harold* I i 374

B

Baaby (baby) to get her *b* born;   *Queen Mary* IV iii 524
Baaed black sheep *b* to the miller's ewe-lamb, *Becket* I iv 162
Baäker (baker) and *B*, thaw I sticks to hoäm-maäde— *Prom. of May* I 448
Baal The priests of *B* tread her underfoot— *Becket* III iii 179
Babble (*See also* **Bird-babble**) *B* in bower Under the
  rose !   „ III i 96
  Thou art cold thyself To *b* of their coldness. *Queen Mary* v ii 292
  And doth so bound and *b* all the way   „ v 86
  convene This conference but to *b* of our wives ? *Becket* II ii 90
  Not while the rivulet *b's* by the door, *Foresters* III i 321
Babbled I follow'd You and the child : he *b* all the way. *Becket* IV iv 140
Babe but your king stole her a *b* from Scotland *Queen Mary* I v 291
  her *b* in arms Had felt the faltering   „ III 80
  The Queen hath felt the motion of her *b* !   „ III ii 214
  baptized in fire, the *b* Might be in fire for ever.   „ IV iv 23
  The *b* enwomb'd and at the breast is cursed, *Harold* I v 65
  B's, orphans, mothers ! is that royal, Sire ? *Becket* II i 80
  Out of the mouths of *b's* and sucklings, praise !   „ II ii 278
  Will greet us as our *b's* in Paradise.   „ v ii 225
  I had once A boy who died a *b*;   *The Cup* I ii 149
  be curious About the welfare of their *b's*,   „ I ii 362
  O Thou that slayest the *b* within the womb   „ II 279
Babe-breasting Age, orphans, and *b-b* mothers— *Becket* II i 72

Baby (adj.) some waxen doll Thy *b* eyes have rested on,
  belike ;   *Queen Mary* I v 9
  whose *b* eye Saw them sufficient.   *Harold* III ii 65
Baby (s) (*See also* **Baaby**) strike Their hearts, and hold
  their *babies* up to it.   „ I i 35
  That's all nonsense, you know, such a *b* as you are. *Prom. of May* I 785
  King, thy god-father, gave it thee when a *b*. *Foresters* I i 286
Babyhood Was she not betroth'd in her *b* to the Great
  Emperor   *Queen Mary* I i 118
Baby-king Stirring her *b-k* against me ? ha ! *Becket* v i 106
Bacchatur Hostis per Angliae Plagas *b*;   *Harold* v i 511
Bachelor *See* **Batchelor**
Back bald o' the *b*, and bursten at the toes, *Queen Mary* I i 52
  show'd his *b* Before I read his face.   „ II i 132
  scorn'd the man, Or lash'd his rascal *b*, *Harold* II i 507
  but the *b* methought was Rosamund— *Becket, Pro.* 470
  be bound Behind the *b* like laymen-criminals ?   „ I iii 96
  so dusted his *b* with the meal in his sack,   „ I iv 174
  wi' bare *b's*, but the *b's* 'ud ha' countenanced one another, „ III i 147
  Can't you hear that you are saying behind his *b* *The Falcon* 107
  nor behind your lordship's *b*,   „ 113
  When I vaulted on his *b*,   *Foresters* II ii 150
  which longs to break itself across their *b's*.   „ IV v 918
Backbone Stiff as the very *b* of heresy. *Queen Mary* I v 44
Back'd *B* by the power of France, and landing here,   „ III i 447
Back'd *See* **Broken-back'd**
Backward courtesy which hath less loyalty in it than
  the *b* scrape of the clown's heel— *Becket* III iii 143
  my child is so young, So *b* too ;   „ II ii 85
Backwardness Hath rated for some *b* *Queen Mary* IV iii 307
Backward-working if his *b-w* alchemy Should change *Foresters* IV 38
Bad (adj.) I will take Such order with all *b*, heretical
  books   *Queen Mary* IV i 95
  Eh, my rheumatizy be that *b* howiver be I to win
   to the burnin'.   „ IV iii 474
  Eh, but I do know ez Pwoaps and vires be *b* things ;   „ IV iii 501
  And love to hear *b* tales of Philip.   „ IV 429
  for the people do say that his is *b* beyond all reckoning, *Becket* III i 175
  There are good fairies and *b* fairies, and sometimes she
   cries, and can't sleep sound o' nights because of the
   b fairies.   „ IV i 29
  Very *b*. Somebody struck him.   „ IV i 50
  and they was all a-crying out at the *b* times, *Prom. of May* I 139
  But I taäkes 'im fur a *b* lot and a burn fool,   „ I 153
  Thruf slush an' squad When roäds was *b*,   „ II 310
  And what harm will that do you, so that you do
   not copy his *b* manners ?   „ III 361
  It be one o' my *b* daäys.   „ III 465
  You heard him say it was one of his *b* days.   „ III 469
  It is almost the last of my *b* days, I think.   „ III 471
  We be fairies of the wood, We be neither *b* nor good. *Foresters* II ii 119
  Robin, I do, but I have a *b* wife.   „ III 70
  they put it upon me because I have a *b* wife.   „ III 437
Bad-bade (verb) *Bad* you so softly with your heretics
  here,   *Queen Mary* I v 392
  Bad me to tell you that she counts on you   „ II ii 104
  Cranmer. Fly would he not, when all men *bad* him fly.   „ III i 171
  I *bad* my chaplain, Castro, preach Against these burnings. „ III vi 73
  And *bad* me have good courage ;   „ IV ii 8
  bad the king Who doted on him, *Harold* IV i 101
  Edward *bad* me spare thee.   „ IV ii 11
  And *bad* me seal against the rights of the Church, *Becket* I iii 312
  I *bad* them clear A royal pleasaunce for thee,   „ II i 127
  Thy true King *bad* thee be A fisher of men ;   „ II ii 285
  bad me whatever I saw not to speak one word,   „ III i 132
  You *bad* me take revenge another way—   „ IV ii 152
  life which Henry *bad* me Guard from the stroke   „ IV ii 269
  He *bad* me put her into a nunnery—   „ v i 214
  Bade me beware Of John :   *Foresters* I ii 255
Badger highback'd polecat, the wild boar, The burrow-
  ing *b*—   I iii 121
Baffle We'll *b* them, I warrant.   *Becket* I i 299
Bag We'll dust him from a *b* of Spanish gold. *Queen Mary* I v 421
Bagenhall (*See also* **Ralph, Ralph Bagenhall**) *B*, I see The
  Tudor green and white.   „ III i 179

Baron (*continued*) Yea, heard the churl against the *b*— *Becket* I iii 365
Did not your *b's* draw their swords against me? ,, I iii 501
The King and all his *b's*—— *Becket*. Judgment! *B's*! ,, I iii 683
B's of England and of Normandy, ,, I iii 741
Ay, my lord, and divers other earls and *b's*. ,, I iv 59
these earls and *b's*, that clung to me, ,, I iv 66
They shall henceforward be my earls and *b's*— ,, I iv 87
if the *b's* and bishops hadn't been a-sitting on the Archbishop. ,, I iv 127
Summon your *b's*; take their counsel: ,, v i 74
for he did his best To break the *b's*, ,, v i 235
To all the archbishops, bishops, prelates, *b's*, ,, v i 405
So that our *B's* bring his baseness under. *Foresters* I ii 117
horn, that scares The *B* at the torture of his churls, ,, III 106
these proud priests, and these *B's*, Devils, ,, III 126
Baronage confirm it now Before our gather'd Norman *b*, *Harold* II ii 695
A bulwark against Throne and *B*. *Becket* I i 17
Baron-brute These be those *b-b's* That havock'd all the land ,, I i 240
Baronial Among my thralls in my *b* hall *Foresters* II i 61
Barony The Church should hold her *baronies* of me, *Becket* Pro. 24
In fee and *b* of the King. ,, I iii 675
I hold Nothing in fee and *b* of the King. ,, I iii 678
Barr'd Mine enemies *b* all access to the boy. ,, vi 451
Not if I *b* thee up in thy chamber. *Foresters* I i 314
Barrel They ha' broached a *b* of aäle i' the long barn, *Prom. of May* 426
Barren 'The King hath wearied of his *b* bride.' *Queen Mary* III vi 140
Is God's best dew upon the *b* field. ,, v i 102
Then for thy *b* jest Take thou mine answer in bare common-place— *Becket*, Pro. 281
And York lay *b* for a hundred years. ,, I iii 54
like a *b* shore That grew salt weeds, *The Cup* II 231
Barricade Their horse are thronging to the *b's*; *Harold* i 547
They thunder again upon the *b's*. ,, v i 626
Barrin' and *b* the wet, Hodge 'ud ha' been a-harrowin' *Queen Mary* IV iii 491
b the wind, Dumble wur blow'd wi' the wind, ,, IV iii 493
Barring (*See also* **Barrin'**) But by all Saints— *Leofwin*.
B the Norman! *Harold* v i 225
Barton, Elizabeth *See* **Joan of Kent**
Base were all as *b* as—who shall I say—Fitzurse and his following— *Becket* III iii 307
His own true people cast him from their doors Like a *b* coin. *The Cup* I ii 353
Baseness and great *b* loathed as an exception: *Becket* III iii 304
Would bow to such a *b* as would make me ,, vi 234
So that our Barons bring his *b* under. *Foresters* I ii 117
hands Of these same Moors thro' nature's *b*, ,, II i 564
That *b* which for fear or monies, ,, I i 706
Baser lower and *b* Than even I can well believe you. *Prom. of May* III 814
Bashful eyes So *b* that you look'd no higher? *Queen Mary* III i 65
Our *b* Legate, saw'st not how he flush'd? ,, III iv 350
Was yet too *b* to return for it? *The Falcon* 540
Basket *See* **Lobster-basket**
Basle Zurich, Worms, Geneva, *B*— *Queen Mary* I ii 3
Bass This burst and *b* of loyal harmony, ,, II ii 285
Bastard (adj.) then the *b* sprout, My sister, is far fairer than myself. *Queen Mary* I v 71
A *b* hate born of a former love. *Becket* II i 174
Bastard (s) It means a *b* *Queen Mary* I i 13
Why, didn't the Parliament make her a *b*? ,, I i 16
Then which is the *b*? ,, I i 22
they be both *b's* by Act of Parliament and Council. ,, I i 24
Parliament can make every true-born man of us a *b*. ,, I i 28
Old Nokes, can't it make thee a *b*? ,, I i 47
and so they can't make me a *b*. ,, I i 49
But if Parliament can make the Queen a *b*, *Harold* II ii 773
Juggler and *b*—*b*—he hates that most—William the tanner's *b*! ,, III ii 155
And given thy realm of England to the *b*. ,, III ii 155
Then for the *b* Six feet and nothing more! ,, IV iii 115
The tanner's *b*! ,, IV iii 173
hath borne at times A *b* false as William. ,, v i 176
Ay, my girl, no tricks in him—No *b* he! ,, v i 403
We can't all of us be as pretty as thou art—little *b* *Becket* IV i 39
thereupon he call'd my children *b's*. ,, IV ii 45

Bastard (s) (*continued*) Then is thy pretty boy a *b*? *Becket* IV ii 113
This in thy bosom, fool, And after in thy *b's*! ,, IV ii 258
Bastardise And done your best to *b* our Queen, *Queen Mary* III iv 238
Bastard-making that was afore *b-m* began. ,, I i 44
Bastardy What are you cackling of *b* under ,, I i 59
Bat What's here? a dead *b* in the fairy ring— *Foresters* II ii 93
a *b* flew out at him In the clear noon, ,, II ii 96
Crush'd my *b* whereon I flew! ,, II ii 146
Batchelor And out upon all simple *b*! ,, v 52
Bathe To *b* this sacred pavement with my blood. *Becket* v iii 131
Battel we should have better *b's* at home. *Foresters* I i 58
Batter Began to *b* at your English Church, *Queen Mary* IV iv 186
Battering *B* the doors, and breaking thro' the walls? *Becket* v ii 626
Battle (*See also* **Mid-battle**) or wave And wind at their old *b*: *Queen Mary* I v 357
Hark, there is *b* at the palace gates, ,, II iv 47
I myself Will down into the *b* and there bide ,, II iv 85
and hurl'd our *b's* Into the heart of Spain; ,, III i 108
many English in your ranks To help your *b*. ,, v i 112
I had heard of him in *b* over seas, ,, v v 33
For thou hast done the *b* in my cause; *Harold* II ii 555
To do the *b* for me here in England, ,, IV ii 70
than his league With Norway, and this *b*. ,, IV iii 89
and had my constant 'No' For all but instant *b*. ,, v i 7
After the *b*—after the *b*. Go. ,, v i 362
Whose life was all one *b*, incarnate war, ,, v i 397
Waste not thy might before the *b*! ,, v i 416
I will bear thy blessing into the *b* ,, v i 435
until I find Which way the *b* balance. ,, v i 461
O God of *b's*, make their wall of shields ,, v i 478
Look out upon the *b*—is he safe? (repeat) ,, v i 484, 654
O God of *b's*, make his battle-axe keen ,, v i 562
O God of *b's*, they are three to one, ,, v i 575
Look out upon the *b*! ,, v i 624
build a church to God Here on the hill of *b*; ,, v i 138
Since I knew *b*, And that was from my boyhood, ,, v i 174
Lest there be *b* between Heaven and Earth, *Becket* II ii 226
The glory and grief of *b* won or lost *The Cup* I ii 161
a rumour then That you were kill'd in *b*. *The Falcon* 382
having his right hand Lamed in the *b*, ,, 445
The story of your *b* and your wound. ,, 594
in this same *b* We had been beaten— ,, 602
I tear away The leaves were darken'd by the *b* ,, 913
if he had not gone to fight the king's *b's*, *Foresters* I i 57
I saved his life once in *b*. ,, I i 273
Battle-axe they With their good *b's* will do you right *Queen Mary* IV iv 66
And strike among them with thy *b-a* *Harold* I ii 89
b-a Was out of place; that should have been the bow.— ,, I ii 105
With nothing but my *b-a* and him To spatter his brains! ,, II ii 779
were man's to have held The *b-a* by thee! ,, IV iii 13
and our *b-a's* broken The Raven's wing, ,, IV iii 64
we must use our *b-a* to-day. ,, v i 205
My *b-a* against your voices. ,, v i 265
And Loathing wield a Saxon *b-a*— ,, v i 414
Cowl, helm; and crozier, *b-a*. ,, v i 444
make his *b-a* keen As thine own sharp-dividing justice, ,, v i 563
Battled I would have *b* for it to the death. *Foresters* I i 664
Battle-field and seen the red of the *b-f*, *The Falcon* 549
Battle-hymns ghostly horn Blowing continually, and faint *b-h*, *Harold* III i 373
Battlement flung them streaming over the *b's* ,, II ii 391
Bawl When shall your parish-parson *b* our banns *Prom. of May* I 685
Bay (arm of the sea) *b's* And havens filling with a blissful sea. *The Cup* II 235
And over this Robin Hood's *b*! *Foresters* II ii 177
Bay (verb) Tho' all the world should *b* like winter wolves. *Queen Mary* II ii 361
how those Roman wolfdogs howl and *b* him! ,, IV iii 355
Bayeux I saw him coming with his brother Odo The *B* bishop, *Harold* II ii 348
from Guy To mine own hearth at *B*, ,, II ii 43
Beach drave and crack'd His boat on Ponthieu *b*; ,, II ii 36
They stood on Dover *b* to murder me, *Becket* v ii 436
A child's sand-castle on the *b* *The Cup* I ii 254
And the great breaker beats upon the *b*! *Foresters* I ii 324

Bead Counts his old *b's*, and hath forgotten thee. — *Harold* II ii 447
  they are but blue *b's*—my Piero, — *The Falcon* 48
Beak His buzzard *b* and deep-incavern'd eyes — *Queen Mary* I iv 266
Beam (*See also* **Side-beam**) so the *b's* of both may
  shine upon us, — ,, III iv 20
  My grayhounds fleeting like a *b* of light, — *Harold* I ii 129
  That *b* of dawn upon the opening flower, — *Foresters* IV 3
Beaming his fine-cut face bowing and *b* with all that
  courtesy — *Becket* III iii 141
  Her bright face *b* starlike down upon me — *Prom. of May* II 248
Bear (s) Like the rough *b* beneath the tree, — *Harold* I i 327
  No, my *b*, thou hast not. — *Becket, Pro.* 497
  O drunken ribaldry ! Out, beast ! out, *b* ! — ,, I i 231
  Dares the *b* slouch into the lion's den ? — ,, IV ii 282
Bear (verb) (*See also* **Abeär**) You needs must *b* it
  hardly. — *Queen Mary* I iv 36
  B witness, Renard, that I live and die — ,, II iv 41
  The tree that only *b's* dead fruit is gone. — ,, III i 19
  That *b's* not its own apples. — ,, III i 23
  How should he *b* a bridegroom out of Spain ? — ,, III iii 25
  How should he *b* the headship of the Pope ? — ,, III iii 29
  I think the Queen may never *b* a child ; — ,, IV v 231
  Lose the sweet hope that I may *b* a prince. — ,, III vi 201
  I could mould myself To *b* your going better ; — ,, III vi 236
  yet what hatred Christian men *B* to each other, — ,, IV iii 184
  that I *b* it Without more ruffling. — ,, v iii 3
  And Tostig is not stout enough to *b* it. — *Harold* I i 402
  And thy love ?   Aldwyth. As much as thou canst *b*. — ,, I i 484
  I can *b* all, And not be giddy. — ,, I i 485
  Let all men *b* witness of our bond ! — ,, II ii 698
  That mortal men should *b* their earthly heats — ,, v i 283
  I will *b* thy blessing into the battle — ,, v i 434
  B me true witness—only for this once— — ,, v ii 115
  My punishment is more than I can *b*.— — ,, v ii 202
  Together more than mortal man can *b*. — *Becket* I i 24
  Permit me, my good lord, to *b* it for thee, — ,, I i 490
  So now he *b's* the standard of the angels. — ,, I i 496
  I am the Dean of the province : let me *b* it. — ,, I iii 499
  Wherefore dost thou presume to *b* thy cross, — ,, I iii 504
  Let York *b* his to mate with Canterbury. — ,, I iii 512
  But with Walter Map, — ,, II ii 307
  —The Cross !—who *b's* my Cross before me ? — ,, v ii 610
  Would that I could *b* thy cross indeed ! — ,, v ii 614
  It *b's* an evil savour among women. — *The Cup* I iii 86
  body of that dead traitor Sinnatus.   *B* him away. — ,, I iii 181
  the love I *b* to thee Glow thro' thy veins ? — ,, II 426
  The love I *b* to thee Glows thro' my veins — ,, II 428
  I *b* with him no longer. — *The Falcon* 884
  And he will have to *b* with it as he may. — ,, 887
  But if it be so we must *b* with John. — *Foresters* I i 102
  Risk not the love I *b* thee for a girl. — ,, IV 742
  It is the King Who *b's* all down. — ,, IV 784
Beard (s) tell me, did you ever Sigh for a *b* ? — *Queen Mary* IV 609
  Dare-devils, that would eat fire and spit it out At
  Philip's *b* : — ,, III i 158
  but he hath a yellow *b*. — ,, III i 216
  A fine *b*, Bonner, a very full fine. — ,, III iv 338
  His long white *b*, which he had never shaven — ,, IV vi 592
  Your Philip hath gold hair and golden *b* ; — ,, v iii 57
  The rosy face, and long down-silvering *b*, — *Harold* III i 47
  The rosy face and long down-silvering *b*— — ,, IV i 262
  The tan of southern summers and the *b* ? — *Prom. of May* II 618
  thy father will not grace our feast With his white *b*
  to-day. — *Foresters* IV 81
Beard (verb) A bold heart yours to *b* that raging mob ! — *Queen Mary* I iii 96
Bearer The King may rend the *b* limb from limb. — *Becket* I i 378
  He all but pluck'd the *b's* eyes away. — ,, I iii 11
Bearing (adj. and part.) I, *b* this great ensign, make it
  clear — ,, I iii 544
  wherewithal he cleft the tree From off the *b* trunk, — *Harold* III i 138
  —the stream is *b* us all down, — *Foresters* I i 239
Bearing (bringing forth) To go twelve months in *b* of
  a child ? — *Queen Mary* III vi 91
  Her fierce desire of *b* him a child, — ,, IV iii 429
  Since she lost hope of *b* us a child ? — ,, v i 229

Bearing (mien) Philip shows Some of the *b* of your
  blue blood— — *Queen Mary* I v 434
  His *b* is so courtly-delicate ; — ,, III iv 397
Beast (*See also* **Beast-body, Wild-beast**) pounce like
  a wild *b* out of his cage to worry Cranmer. — ,, I i 88
  world-hating *b*, A haggard Anabaptist. — ,, II ii 91
  but I thought he was a *b*. — ,, III i 221
  Bonner cannot out-Bonner his own self—*B* !— — ,, IV vi 28
  Because these islanders are brutal *b's* ? — ,, III vi 153
  and in itself a *b*. — ,, IV i 33
  creep down into some dark hole Like a hurt *b*, — ,, IV i 142
  Stand watching a sick *b* before he dies ? — ,, IV iii 7
  the *b* might roar his claim To being in God's image, — ,, IV iii 367
  I conclude the King a *b* ; Verily a lion if you
  will—the world A most obedient *b* and fool—
  myself Half *b* and fool as appertaining to it ; — ,, IV iii 412
  Thou's thy way wi' man and *b*, Tib. — ,, IV iii 499
  like a timorous *b* of prey Out of the bush — *Harold* I ii 212
  The wolf ! the *b* ! — ,, II iii 301
  O drunken ribaldry ! Out, *b* ! out, bear ! — *Becket* I i 231
  Poor *b*, poor *b* ! set him down. — ,, I iv 105
  Like the wild *b*—if you can call it love. — ,, IV vi 121
  The world God made—even the *b*—the bird ! — ,, v ii 243
  Ay, still a lover of the *b* and bird ? — ,, v ii 246
  How should *you* guess What manner of *b* it is ? — *The Cup* I ii 371
  leaves him A *b* of prey in the dark, — *Prom. of May* I 505
Beast-body this *b-b* That God has plunged my soul in— — *Becket* II i 149
Beastly These *b* swine make such a grunting here, — *Queen Mary* I iii 12
Beat I can play well, and I shall *b* you there. — ,, I iii 129
  Make all tongues praise and all hearts *b* for you. — ,, I v 118
  which every now and then *B's* me half dead : — ,, I v 525
  whether It *b's* hard at this marriage. — ,, III i 39
  for to-day My heart *b's* twenty, — ,, III ii 59
  Your father had a will that *b* men down ; Your
  father had a brain that *b* men down— — ,, IV i 108
  God will *b* down the fury of the flame, — ,, IV iii 98
  I wonder at tha', it *b's* me ! — ,, IV iii 499
  You *b* upon the rock. — ,, v i 210
  How Harold used to *b* him ! — *Harold* I i 432
  Leofwin would often fight me, and I *b* him. — ,, I i 434
  only pulsed for Griffyth, *b* For his pursuer. — ,, II ii 151
  or the sword that *b's* them down. — ,, II ii 136
  There somewhere *b's* an English pulse in thee ! — ,, II ii 266
  let him flap The wings that *b* down Wales ? — ,, IV i 247
  I should *b* Thy kingship as my bishop — *Becket, Pro.* 90
  Yet my fingers itch to *b* him into nothing. — ,, I iv 229
  best heart that ever *B* for one woman. — *The Falcon* 668
  No other heart Of such magnificence in courtesy *B's*—
  out of heaven. — ,, 724
  would you *b* a man for his brother's fault ? — *Prom. of May* III 154
  broke the heart That only *b* for you ; — ,, III 763
  the great breaker *b's* upon the beach ! — *Foresters* II i 323
  That thou mightst *b* him down at quarterstaff ! — ,, IV 517
  Will chill the hearts that *b* for Robin Hood ! — ,, IV 1064
Beaten You are *b*. — *Becket, Pro.* 45
  I loathe being *b* ; had I fixt my fancy Upon the
  game I should have *b* thee, — ,, Pro. 49
  beat Thy kingship as my bishop hath *b* it. — ,, Pro. 91
  who hath *b* down my foes. — ,, Pro. 253
  Becket hath *b* thee again— — ,, Pro. 314
  in this same battle We had been *b*— — *The Falcon* 603
  Our Robin *b*, pleading for his life ! — *Foresters* II i 674
  Lusty bracken *b* flat, — ,, II ii 154
  Sit here by me, where the most *b* track Runs thro'
  the forest, — ,, III 89
  Or else be bound and *b*. (repeat) — ,, III 370, 390
Beating the rain *b* in my face all the way, — *Prom. of May* III 367
Beautiful I left her lying still and *b*, More *b* — *Queen Mary* v v 261
  O *b* ! May I have it as mine, — *Becket* III i 297
  My Anjou bower was scarce as *b*. — ,, III i 52
  The Lady Camma, Wise I am sure as she is *b*, — *The Cup* I ii 139
  She b : sleek as a miller's mouse ! Meal enough,
  meat enough, well fed ; but *b*—bah ! — *The Falcon* 164
  you look as *b* this morning as the very Madonna — ,, 198
  A lady that was *b* as day Sat by me — ,, 349

Beautiful (*continued*) And she was the most *b* of all ; Then but fifteen, and still as *b*.   *The Falcon* 353

Come, give me your hand and kiss me This *b* May-morning.   *Prom. of May* I 565

The most *b* May we have had for many years !   ,, I 566

And here Is the most *b* morning of this May.   ,, I 569

You, the most *b* blossom of the May,   ,, I 574

all the world is *b* If we were happy,   ,, I 577

How *b* His manners are, and how unlike the farmer's !   ,, II 530

no maids like English maids So *b* as they be.   *Foresters* II i 20

And love is joyful, innocent, *b*,   ,, II ii 64

Beauty a head So full of grace and *b* !   *Queen Mary* I v 64

B passes like a breath and love is lost in loathing :   ,, v ii 365

She hath won upon our people thro' her *b*,   *Harold* IV i 23

cowling and clouding up That fatal star, thy *B*,   *Becket* I i 312

Your answer, *b* !   ,, IV ii 53

She calls you *b*, but I don't like her looks.   ,, IV ii 61

my sleeping-draught May bloat thy *b* out of shape,   ,, IV ii 170

By thy leave, *b*. Ay, the same !   ,, IV ii 203

marvell'd at Our unfamiliar *beauties* of the west ;   ,, IV ii 303

You have *b*,—O great *b*,—and Antonius,   *The Cup* I ii 297

for her *b*, stateliness, and power, Was chosen Priestess   ,, II 16

To-day, my *b*, thou must dash us down   *The Falcon* 152

With other *beauties* on a mountain meadow,   ,, 351

I whisper'd, Let me crown you Queen of *B*,   ,, 361

crown you Again with the same crown my Queen of *B*.   ,, 916

like the Moslem *beauties* waiting To clasp their lovers   *Prom. of May* I 246

—her main law Whereby she grows in *b*—   ,, I 283

prize The pearl of *B*, even if I found it   ,, III 601

and if her *beauties* answer their report.   *Forsters* II i 27

Becamest when thou *b* Man in the Flesh,   *Queen Mary* IV iii 140

Beck (*brook*) leästwaäys they niver cooms 'ere but fur the trout i' our *b*,   *Prom. of May* I 213

Becket (**Chancellor of England, 1154-1162 Archbishop of Canterbury, 1162-1170**) (*See also* **Dare - Becket, Godstow - Becket, Thomas, Thomas Becket, Thomas of Canterbury**)

As proud as *B*.   *Queen Mary* III i 332

You would not have him murder'd as *B* was ?   ,, III i 334

the arm within Is *B's*, which hath beaten down my foes.   *Becket, Pro.* 253

The chart is not mine, but *B's* : take it, Thomas.   .. Pro. 311

B ! O—ay—and these chessmen on the floor—   ,, Pro. 312

B hath beaten thee again—   ,, Pro. 314

Ha, *B* ! thou rememberest our talk !   ,, Pro. 404

this *B*, her father's friend, like enough staved us   ,, Pro. 517

B, I am the oldest of the Templars ;   ,, I iii 247

Behold thy father kneeling to thee, *B*.   ,, I iii 253

And *B* had my bosom on all this ;   ,, I iii 433

Our Lord *B's* our great sitting-hen cock,   ,, I iv 125

B, beware of the knife !   ,, I iv 133

B shall be king, and the Holy Father shall be king,   ,, I iv 269

With *B* ? I have but one hour with thee—   ,, II i 23

Why thou, my bird, thou pipest *B*, *B*—   ,, II i 32

Must be the nightmare breaking on my peace with ' *B.*'   ,, II i 38

We have but one bond, her hate of *B*.   ,, II i 166

Nay ! nay ! what art thou muttering ? I hate *B* ?   ,, II i 168

'Tis true what *B* told me, that the mother   ,, II ii 9

and *B*—*B* should crown him were he crown'd at all :   ,, II ii 16

Brother of France, what shall be done with *B* ?   ,, II ii 65

Master *B*, you That owe to me your power over me—sure to wake As great a wrath in *B*—   *Rosamund.*   ,, II ii 151

Always *B* !   ,, III i 88

Henry—*B* tells him this—To take my life   ,, IV ii 394

But *B* ever moves against a king.   ,, v 25

world allows I fall no inch Behind this *B*,   ,, v 40

B hath trodden on us like worms,   ,, v 60

scarcely dare to bless the good we eat Because of *B*.   ,, v 72

I know—could swear—as long as *B* breathes,   ,, v 76

The brideless *B* is thy king and mine !   ,, v i 107

B is like enough to make all his.   ,, v i 134

Methought I had recover'd of the *B*,   ,, v i 137

Why do you thrust this *B* on me again ?   ,, v i 155

Lest *B* thrust you even from your throne.   ,, v i 159

Your *B* knew the secret of your bower.   ,, v i 177

Becket (*continued*) Our *B*, who will not absolve the Bishops.   *Becket* v i 222

I think ye four have cause to love this *B*.   ,, v i 225

You are no King's men—you—you—you are *B's* men.   ,, v i 259

What say ye there of *B* ?   ,, v ii 56

B, it is too late.   ,, v ii 526

Where is the traitor *B* ?   ,, v iii 103

Becket (Gilbert) *See* **Gilbert Becket**

Beckon the right hand still *B's* me hence.   *Queen Mary* v v 138

Becomes nay, it well *b* him.   ,, I v 436

Bed (*See also* **Down, Flower-bed**) As tho' the nightmare never left her *b*.   ,, I v 606

Spain in our ships, in our forts, in our houses, in our *b's* ?   ,, II i 180

No Spain in our *b's*—   ,, II i 182

and the *b's* I know. I hate Spain.   ,, II i 184

on a soft *b*, in a closed room, with light,   ,, IV iv 36

gather'd one From out a *b* of thick forget-me-nots,   ,, v v 94

It lies beside thee, king, upon thy *b*.   *Harold* III i 196

get thee to thine own *b*.   *Becket* I i 8

he hath made his *b* between the altars,   ,, I iv 264

My *b*, where ev'n the slave is private—   ,, v i 251

I measured his foot wi' the mark i' the *b*, but it wouldn't fit   *Prom. of May* I 414

seen us that wild morning when we found Her *b* unslept in,   ,, II 471

Strike up a song, my friends, and then to *b*.   *Foresters* I iii 31

Bedingfield (Sir Henry) *See* **Henry, Henry Bedingfield**

Bedroom We found a letter in your *b* torn into bits.   *Prom. of May* III 323

Bee As the first flower no *b* has ever tried: *Queen Mary* I iv 63

Are you the *b* to try me ?   ,, I iv 64

b's, If any creeping life invade their hive   ,, III iii 53

your wise *b's* had stung him first to death.   ,, III iii 64

The people are as thick as *b's* below, They hum like *b's*,—   *Harold* I i 31

B mustn't buzz, Whoop—but he knows. (repeat)   *Becket* III i 98, 239

So rare the household honeymaking *b*,   ,, v ii 218

As happy as the *b's* there at their honey   *Prom. of May* I 606

Swarm to thy voice like *b's* to the brass pan.   *Foresters* I iii 108

B's rather, flying to the flower for honey.   ,, IV 12

The *b* buzz'd up in the heat.   ,, IV 14

And the *b* buzz'd down from the heat.   ,, IV 20

And the *b* buzz'd up in the cold   ,, IV 27

And the *b* buzz'd off in the cold.   ,, IV 33

And yet in tune with Nature and the *b's*.   ,, IV 44

Thy *b* should buzz about the Court of John.   ,,

Beech Pine, *b* and plane, oak, walnut,   *The Cup* I i 1

Beef and there is a piece of *b* like a house-side,   *Prom. of May* I 793

Beelzebub By Mahound I could dine with *B* !   *Foresters* IV 971

Beer Owd Steer gi'es nubbut cowd tea to 'is men, and owd Dobson gi'es *b*.   *Prom. of May* II 225

But I'd like owd Steer's cowd tea better nor Dobson's *b*.   ,, II 227

That *b* be as good fur 'erses as men.   ,, II 315

The *b's* gotten oop into my 'eäd.   ,, II 320

worked at all the worse upon the cold tea than you would have done upon the *b* ?   ,, III 57

but we'd ha' worked better upo' the *b*.   ,, III 60

Beeswax By bonds of *b*, like your creeping thing ;   *Queen Mary* III iii 62

Beetle *B's* jewel armour crack'd,   *Foresters* II i 160

Befall No ill *b* on him or thee when I Am gone.   *Becket* II i 260

get you hence in haste Lest worse *b* you.   ,, IV ii 28

Befit It well *b's* thy new archbishoprick   ,, I i 225

Befitting But ill *b* such a festal day   *Foresters* I iii 37

Beg You are to *b* the people to pray for you ;   *Queen Mary* IV ii 76

—there to *b*, starve, die—   *Becket* II i 74

I will *b* my bread along the world   ,, IV ii 103

he *b's* you to forget it As scarce his act :—   *The Cup* II 51

Dare *b* him to receive his diamonds back.—   *The Falcon* 262

Beget sire *b's* Not half his likeness in the son.   *Queen Mary* II i 54

b's An admiration and an indignation,   ,, III iv 169

Beggar (**s**) How should a baron love a *b* on horseback,   *Becket, Pro.* 444

half-rag, half-sore,—*b's*, poor rogues   ,, I iv 82

If the King hold his purpose, I am myself a *b*.   ,, I iv 90

—like some loud *b* at thy gate—   ,, II i 180

mastiff, That all but kill'd the *b*,   *Prom. of May* I 559

Beggar (s) (*continued*)   but if he do not I and thou are
but *b's*.   *Foresters* I i 200
Canst thou endure to be a *b* whose whole life   „   I i 205
Here come three *b's*.   „   III 187
we be *b's*, we come to ask o' you. We ha' nothing.   „   III 189
B's, you are sturdy rogues that should be set to work.   „   III 196
How much for a *b* ?   „   III 216
will you not hear one of these *b's'* catches ?   „   III 405
by St. Mary these *b's* and these friars shall join you.   „   III 417
Beggar (verb)   Down to the devil with this bond that *b's* me !   „   I i 340
Beggared   She has *b* him.   *The Falcon* 157
He hath become so *b*, that his falcon   „   229
We will be *b* then and be true to the King.   *Foresters* I i 201
Beggarly   This *b* life, This poor, flat, hedged-in field—   *Prom. of May* II 343
Beggar-woman   rags Of some pale *b-w* seeking alms   *The Falcon* 852
Begin   old Gospeller, sour as midwinter, *B* with him.   *Queen Mary* I iii 41
But he *b's* to flutter.   *Harold* II 3
He *b's* at top with me :   *Becket* I iii 617
so, Allen, I may as well *b* with you.   *Prom. of May* II 30
Beginning   In your old place ? and vespers are *b*.   *Becket* V i 597
Begone   Do, and *b* !   „   I i 233
Begun   hath *b* to re-edify the true temple—   *Queen Mary* I v 109
Your people have *b* to learn your worth.   „   I v 109
she hath *b* Her life-long prayer for thee.   *Harold* III i 323
Behalf   Stood out against the King in your *b*,   *Queen Mary* IV i 126
Behaviour   I promise you that if you forget yourself
in your *b* to this gentleman,   *Prom. of May* I 162
Behold   *B* him— *People.* Oh, unhappy sight !   *Queen Mary* IV iii 1
B him, brethren : he hath cause to weep !—   „   IV iii 13
Beholden   Thanks, Sir Thomas, we be *b* to you,   „   II iii 121
Thou art much *b* to this foot of mine,   „   III ii 49
But I am much *b* to your King.   „   V iii 99
I am much *b* to the King, your master.   „   V iii 111
We should be all the more *b* to him.   *Foresters* IV 292
Being   From the dim dawn of *B*—   *Prom. of May* I 281
Belated   I and my friend, this monk, were here *b*,   *Foresters* I iii 193
Belief   wholesome medicine here Puts that *b* asleep.   *Becket* IV ii 52
Believe   He *did b* the bond incestuous.   *Queen Mary* I ii 77
I do *b* she'd yield.   „   I iv 22
I *b* you mine ; And so you may continue mine,   „   I iv 136
I myself *B* it will be better for your welfare.   „   I v 254
I do *b* he help Northumberland Against me.   „   I v 278
I do *b*, I have dusted some already,   „   I v 423
some *b* that he will go beyond him.   „   I v 440
his fault So thoroughly to *b* in his own self.   „   II ii 386
Yet thoroughly to *b* in one's own self,   „   II ii 387
I *b* Sir Thomas Stafford ?   „   III i 31
And I, by God, *b* myself a man.   „   III i 168
I *b* so, cousin.   „   III ii 72
who not *B's* the Pope, nor any of them *b*—   „   III iii 238
I do *b* in God, Father of all ;   „   IV iii 228
men Have hardly known what to *b*, or whether They
should *b* in anything ;   „   IV iii 405
I hear unhappy rumours—nay, I say not, I *b*.   „   V i 36
And I *b*, Spite of your melancholy Sir Nicholas,   „   V ii 326
I do *b* I lamed his Majesty's For a day or two,   „   V ii 471
He had his gracious moment, Altho' you'll not *b* me.   „   V v 39
Lord Leofwin, dost thou *b*, that these Three rods   *Harold* I i 43
an honest world Will not *b* them.   „   I i 348
And makes *b* that he *b's* my word—   „   II ii 668
For they will not *b* thee—as I *b*.   „   II ii 696
But that my barons might *b* thy word,   „   II ii 725
I do *b* My old crook'd spine would bud   „   III i 23
b that lying And ruling men are fatal twins   „   III i 126
prayers go up as fast as my tears fall, I well *b*,   „   III i 167
Let not our great king *B* us sullen—   „   IV i 7
b thee The veriest Galahad of old Arthur's hall.   *Becket, Pro.* 128
I do *b* thee, then. I am the man.   „   I i 135
Do you *b* that you are married to him ? (repeat)   „   IV ii 46,54
I *should b* it. *Eleanor.* You must not *b* it,   „   IV ii 48
Do you b it ? I pray you then to take my sleeping-
draught ;   „   IV ii 68
Do you hear me ? *B* or no, I care not.   „   IV ii 353
I b him The bravest in our roll of Primates   „   V ii 57
But she would not *b* me, and she wish'd   „   V ii 116

Believe (*continued*)   You will *b* Now that he never struck
the stag—   *The Cup* I ii 429
he prays you to *b* him. *Camma.* I pray him to *b*—
that I *b* him.   „   II 55
I scarce *b* it ! *Elisabetta.* Shame upon her then !   *The Falcon* 517
I doänt *b* he's iver a 'eart under his waistcoat.   *Prom. of May* I 130
they that love do not *b* that death Will part them.   „   I 662
My father's death, Let her *b* it mine ;   „   II 454
I do *b* I lost my heart to him the very first time we
met,   „   III 283
I do *b* I could forgive—well, almost anything—   „   III 630
lower and baser Than even I can well *b* you.   „   III 815
but I *b* there lives No man who truly loves   *Foresters* II i 74
I *b* She came with me into the forest here.   „   II i 484
I *b* thou fell'st into the hands Of these same Moors   „   II i 562
b There came some evil fairy at my birth And cursed
me,   „   II ii 107
I *b* thee, thou art a good fellow, though a friar.   „   III 341
O my good liege, we did *b* you dead.   „   II 846
Believed   His friends would praise him, I *b* 'em,   *Queen Mary* I v 623
Stigand *b* he knew not what he spake.   *Harold* III ii 61
—some *b* she was his paramour.   „   v ii 102
b that Rome Made war upon the peoples not the Gods.   *The Cup* II ii 58
I *b* thee to be too solemn and formal to be a ruffler.   *Foresters* I i 168
I *b* this Abbot of the party of King Richard,   „   I i 266
Believer   as I am a true *b* in true love myself,   „   I i 162
Believing   *B* I should ever aid the Church—   *Becket, Pro.* 417
b That I should go against the Church with him,   „   I i 91
b that our brother Had wrong'd you ;   „   II ii 237
Theer ye goäs ageän, Miss niver *b* owt I says to
ye—   *Prom. of May* I 107
Bell   (*See also* **Minster-bell**)   The *b's* are ringing at
Maidstone.   *Queen Mary* II i 18
The *b's* must ring ; Te Deums must be sung ;   „   III ii 211
Toll of a *b*, Stroke of a clock,   „   III v 142
clash'd their *b's*, Shot off their lying cannon,   „   IV vi 96
A passing *b* toll'd in a dying ear—   „   V ii 41
And hear my peregrine and her *b's* in heaven ; And
other *b's* on earth,   *Harold* I ii 131
Our scouts have heard the tinkle of their *b's*.   „   V i 221
like the gravedigger's child I have heard of, trying
to ring the *b*,   *Becket* III iii 74
—the *b's* rang out even to deafening,   „   V ii 363
Bell-silencing   black, *b-s*, anti-marrying, burial-hindering
interdict   „   III iii 54
Belly   since the Sheriff left me naught but an empty *b*,   *Foresters* II i 279
Belonging   His kin, all his *b's*, overseas ;   *Becket* IV ii 11
Of and *b* to the King of England,   „   IV ii 23
I am mine own self Of and *b* to the King.   „   IV ii 30
King Hath divers ofs and ons, ofs and *b's*,   „   IV ii 32
It is the cup *b* our own Temple.   *The Cup* II 345
B's, paramours, whom it pleases him   *Becket* IV ii 35
Beloved   *See* **Well-beloved**
Bench   There is a *b*. Come, wilt thou sit ?   *Becket* II i 124
Help me to move this *b* for him into the sun.   *Prom. of May* I 81
Doubtless, like judges of another *b*,   *Foresters* III 153
Bend   seeks To *b* the laws to his own will,   *Queen Mary* II ii 184
Bended   and we'll pray for you all on our *b* knees.   „   II iii 109
and we'll pray for you on our *b* knees till our
lives' end.   „   II iii 122
Benedict   O blessed saint, O glorious *B*,—   *Becket* V iii 2
Benedicta   Ave Maria, gratia plena, *B* tu in
mulieribus.   *Queen Mary* III ii 1
Benedictus   Sit *b* fructus ventris tui !'   „   III ii 83
Bent   (*See also* **Bow-bent**)   *b* to his saddle-bow, As if to
win the man   „   II ii 310
Benzoin   Nard, Cinnamon, amomum, *b*.   *The Cup* II 184
Bequeath   Edward might *b* the crown Of England,   *Queen Mary* I ii 26
Berkeley (Sir Maurice)   *See* **Maurice Berkeley**
Berkhamstead   Due from his castles of *B* and Eye   *Becket* I iii 628
Beset   O Renard, I am much *b*,   *Queen Mary* I v 385
I should be hard *b* with thy fourscore.   *Foresters* IV 179
Beside   lost and found together, None *b* them.   *Harold* III ii 8
' I am *b* thee.'   „   III ii 14
Besotted   One half *b* in religious rites.   *The Cup* I i 74

Best (adj.) Dumble's the *b* milcher in Islip.
    (repeat)   *Queen Mary* IV iii 478, 497
  The blood and sweat of heretics at the stake
    Is God's *b* dew upon the barren field. ,,   v i 102
  You had *b* go home. What are you? ,,   v iv 43
  Noble Gurth! *B* son of Godwin!   *Harold* v i 135
  Serve my *b* friend and make him my worst foe; *Becket* I iii 567
  Only my *b* bower-maiden died of late, ,,   III i 67
  Stain'd with the blood of the *b* heart that ever Beat
    for one woman.   *The Falcon* 667
  yet that might be The *b* way out of it, *Prom. of May* I 476
  Then the man, the woman, Following their *b* affinities, ,,   I 523
  this is a true woodman's bow of the *b* yew-wood to
    slay the deer.   *Foresters* II i 393
  Heaven looks down on me, And smiles at my *b* meanings, ,, IV 727
Best (s) I do my most and *b*.   *Queen Mary* II ii 24
  it is a day to test your health Ev'n at the *b*: ,, IV ii 118
  You have done your *b*. *Pole.* Have done my *b*, ,, v ii 115
  But thou canst hear the *b* and wisest of us. *Harold* I i 300
  I have done me *b*. I am not learn'd. *Becket* II i 24
  it's all for the *b*, come when they will— *The Falcon* 201
  I and Filippo here had done our *b*, ,, 607
Bested See **Ill-bested**
Bestial all of us abhor The venomous, *b*, devilish
    revolt Of Thomas Wyatt. *Queen Mary* II ii 287
  Did ye not cast with *b* violence Our holy Norman
    bishops down   *Harold* I i 49
  O *b*! O how unlike our goodly Sinnatus. *The Cup* II 172
Bethink And now, I do *b* me, thou wast by *Foresters* II i 540
Betray Before he would *b* it. *Becket* II i 268
  And if you should *b* me to your husband— *The Cup* I ii 242
  Will *you* *b* him by this order? ,, I ii 244
  And I will not *b* you. ,, I ii 316
  for fear or monies, might *B* me to the wild Prince. *Foresters* I i 708
  For those of thine own band who would *b* thee? ,, IV 833
Betray'd Cast off, *b*, defamed, *Queen Mary* I v 26
  They have *b* the treason of their hearts: ,, II ii 156
  Thou hast *b* us on these rocks of thine! *Harold* II i 23
  O Wulfnoth, Wulfnoth, brother, thou hast *b* me! ,, II ii 802
  Herbert, Herbert, have I *b* the Church? *Becket* I iii 284
  But thou the shepherd hast *b* the sheep, ,, I iii 524
  hast *b* Thy father to the losing of his land. *Foresters* II i 569
Betroth In order to *b* her to your Dauphin. *Queen Mary* I v 293
Betrothal (adj.) it was her own *B* ring. *Foresters* I ii 295
  Thou hast robb'd my girl of her *b* ring. ,, II i 586
Betrothal (s) Of her *b* to the Emperor Charles, *Queen Mary* v v 233
Betroth'd Was she not *b* in her babyhood to the
    Great Emperor   ,, I i 118
  and presently That I and Harold are *b*— *Harold* I ii 223
Betrothing Hapless beginning of woman happy in *b*! *Queen Mary* v ii 364
Better and I myself Believe it will be *b* for your welfare. ,, I iv 254
  He must deserve his surname *b*. ,, III ii 197
  A *b* and a worse—he is here To persecute, ,, III iv 114
  I could mould myself To bear your going *b*; ,, III vi 236
  The *b* for him. He burns in Purgatory, not in Hell. ,, IV i 55
  There is no hope of *b* left for him, ,, IV ii 79
  Our Daisy's cheeses be *b*. ,, IV iii 484
  I thought you knew me *b*. ,, v ii 186
  I am not well, but it will *b* me, ,, v ii 554
  I wish her Highness *b*. ,, v ii 615
  Nay! *B* die than lie! *Harold* I i 158
  Because I love the Norman *b*—no, ,, I i 171
  and left me time And peace for prayer to gain a *b* one. ,, I i 220
  B die than lie! ,, II ii 281
  Is it not *b* still to speak the truth? ,, II ii 373
  B methinks have slain the man at once! ,, II ii 498
  Who hath a *b* claim then to the crown ,, II ii 596
  b die Than credit this, for death is death, ,, III ii 77
  Hadst thou been braver, I had *b* braved All— ,, III ii 178
  the king like his own man, No *b*; ,, IV iii 59
  I could pity this poor world myself that it is no *b*
    ordered.   *Becket*, Pro. 366
  Friend, am I so much *b* than thyself ,, I i 3
  You have had the *b* of us In secular matters. ,, II ii 80
  B have been A fisherman at Bosham, my good Herbert, ,, II ii 290

Better (*continued*) I cannot answer it Till *b* times, *Becket* III i 3
  That which you ask me Till *b* times. ,, III i 7
  And I thought if it were the King's brother he had
    a *b* bride than the King, ,, III i 173
  b Than raised to take a life which Henry bad me ,, IV ii 267
  Why then *B* perhaps to speak with them apart. ,, IV iii 310
  to submit at once Is *b* than a wholly-hopeless war, *The Cup* II ii 141
  I meant thee to have follow'd—*b* thus. ,, II 498
  that's positive again—that's *b*! *The Falcon* 95
  and *b* late than never—but come when they will— ,, 199
  '*B* a man without riches, than riches without a man.' ,, 751
  Hath served me *b* than her living— ,, 901
  Betting *b*, Mr. Dobson. *Prom. of May* I 69
  B step out of his road, then, for he's walking to us, ,, I 218
  I'm sorry for it, for, tho' he never comes to church,
    I thought *b* of him. ,, I 261
  Niver man 'ed *b* friends, and I will saäy niver
    master 'ed *b* men: ,, I 322
  thaw I says it mysen, niver men 'ed a *b* master— ,, I 327
  So much the *b*, so much the *b*. ,, I 435
  B and higher than Nature, we might be As happy as
    the bees   ,, I 604
  Noä; I knaws a deäl *b* now. ,, II 26
  You had *b* attend to your hayfield. ,, II 122
  knaw'd *b* nor to cast her sister's misfortin inter 'er
    teeth   ,, II 127
  But I'd like owd Steer's cowd tea *b* nor Dobson's beer. ,, II 227
  b death With our first wail than life— ,, II 289
  Why, you look *b*. *Eva.* And I feel so much *b*, ,, III 220
  it might have been *b* for her, for him, and for you. ,, III 251
  B for me! That's good. How *b* for me? ,, III 253
  B not. Has he offered you marriage, this gentleman? ,, III 289
  but you seem somewhat *b* to-day. ,, III 322
  if you cram me crop-full I be little *b* than Famine in
    the picture,   *Foresters* I i 47
  we should have *b* battels at home. ,, I i 58
  Till *b* times. *Robin.* But if the *b* times should never
    come?   ,, I ii 286
  Why then I will be *b* than the time. ,, I ii 291
  Would it be *b* for thee in the wood? ,, I iii 140
  Am I worse or *b*? I am outlaw'd. ,, II i 49
  and all the *b* For this free forest-life, ,, II i 59
  B than heart-sick, friar. ,, IV 674
Bevell'd That all was planed and *b* smooth again, *Becket* v i 138
Beware *B*, Lord Legate, of a heavier crime Than
    heresy is itself; *b*, I say, Lest men accuse
    you of indifference   *Queen Mary* III iv 221
  Ay, ay, *b* of France. ,, IV iii 434
Bewitch'd And thought thou wert *b*. *Foresters* II i 684
Bible they have their *b's* burnt. The *b* is the priest's. *Queen Mary* III i 284
  Look to your *B*, Paget! we are fallen. ,, III iv 80
  And may not read your *B*, ,, III iv 83
  never merry world In England, since the *B* came
    among us.   ,, v v 241
  Till all men have their *B*, rich and poor. ,, v v 248
Bid the Lord Chancellor. *Mary.* *B* him come in. ,, I v 97
  B him come in. Good morning, Sir de Noailles. ,, I v 241
  Gregory *b* St. Austin here Found two archbishopricks, *Becket* I iii 48
  And *b* him re-create me, Gilbert Foliot. ,, I iii 152
  My friends, the Archbishop *b's* you good night. ,, I iv 261
  he sends me to *b* you this night pray for him ,, I iv 265
  you *b* me go, and I'll have my ball anyhow. ,, IV ii 63
  B their old bond farewell with smiles, not tears; *Prom. of May* I 524
  Do not till I *b* you. *Eva.* No, Philip, no. ,, I 732
  Will *b* you welcome, and will listen to you. ,, II 522
  I Titania *b* you flit, *Foresters* II ii 126
Bidd'n and *b* him Charge one against a thousand, *Queen Mary* IV iii 308
  Was not my lord of Leicester *b* to our supper? *Becket* I iv 56
Bide and there *b* The upshot of my quarrel, *Queen Mary* II iv 85
  and a wur so owld a couldn't *b* vor his dinner, but
    a had to *b* howsomiver, ,, IV iii 505
  But now I cannot *b*. ,, v i 93
  Ay, so your Grace would *b* a moment yet. ,, v i 547
  And *b* the doom of God. *Harold* v i 61
  tho' I can drink wine I cannot *b* water, *Becket* I iv 220

Bide (*continued*) in Nottingham they say There *b's* a
  foul witch | *Foresters* II i 203
  But how then if I will not *b* to be search'd? | „   IV 168
Bided so they *b* on and on till vour o' the clock, | *Queen Mary* IV iii 509
Biding So sick am I with *b* for this child. | „   III vi 89
Big his *b* baldness, That irritable forelock which he rubs, | „   I iv 264
  Is that it? That's a *b* lot of money. | „   II iii 62
  Map, tho' you make your butt too *b*, you overshoot it. | *Becket* III iii 122
  be i' the long barn by one o'clock, fur he'll gie us a *b*
  dinner, | *Prom. of May* I 9
  and a plum-pudding as *b* as the round haystack. | „   I 794
  and I wur hallus scaäred by a *b* word; | „   III 33
  and wheere the *b* eshtree cuts athurt it, | „   III 94
  I am mortally afear'd o' thee, thou *b* man, | *Foresters* IV 317
Bigger *B* in our small world than thou art. | *Becket* V i 128
  Not yet, but here comes one of *b* mould. | *Foresters* IV 115
Bigot To be nor mad, nor *b*—have a mind— | *Queen Mary* V v 216
Bill (beak) gaping *b's* in the home-nest Piping for
  bread— | *Becket* II ii 300
  No bird? *Filippo.* Half a tit and a hern's *b*. | *The Falcon* 131
Bill (document) In several *b's* and declarations, | *Queen Mary* IV i 48
  ay; if Bonner have not forged the *b's*. | „   IV i 51
Billing nor priestly king to cross Their *b's* ere they nest. | *Harold* III ii 95
Bind To *b* me first by oaths I could not keep, | *Queen Mary* I v 557
  And *b* him in from harming of their combs, | „   III iii 57
  Which *b's* us friendship-fast for ever! | *Harold* II i 162
  The shackles that will *b* me to the wall. | „   II ii 410
  And I would *b* thee more, | „   II ii 559
  b a score All in one faggot, snap it over knee, | „   IV i 57
  bound To that necessity which *b's* us down; | „   V i 108
  Tho' she that *b's* the bond, herself should see | *Becket* I ii 76
  I will *b* up his wounds with my napkin. | „   I iv 106
  striving still to break or *b* The spiritual giant | „   IV ii 443
  I ask'd A ribbon from her hair to *b* it with; | *The Falcon* 359
  if you *will b* love to one for ever, | *Prom. of May* I 644
  Thou hast risk'd thy life for mine: *b* these two men. | *Foresters* IV 894
Bird (*See also* **Sea-bird**) These *b's* of passage come
  before their time: | *Queen Mary* I iii 75
  To kiss and cuff among the *b's* and flowers— | „   III v 258
  I never breathed it to a *b* in the eaves, | „   V ii 454
  I whistle to the *b* has broken cage, And all in vain. | „   V v 19
  let fly the *b* within the hand, To catch the *b* again | *Harold* II ii 65
  Poor *b* of passage! so I was; but, father, | *Becket* I i 253
  Bar the *b* From following the fled summer— | „   I i 258
  To guard this *b* of passage to her cage; | „   I i 329
  b that moults sings the same song again, | „   I iii 447
  I wrong the *b*; she leaves only the nest she built, | „   I iv 45
  thou, my *b*, thou pipest Becket, Becket— | „   II i 32
  B mustn't tell, Whoop—he can see. (repeat) | *Becket* III i 106, 254
  I have lived, poor *b*, from cage to cage, | *Becket* III i 222
  The world God made—even the beast—the *b*! | „   V ii 244
  Ay, still a lover of the beast and *b*? | „   V ii 246
  See, see, my white *b* stepping toward the snare. | *The Cup* I iii 35
  Hear that, my *b*! Art thou not jealous of her? | *The Falcon* 5
  Buss me, my *b*! | „   29
  No *b*? *Filippo.* Half a tit and a hern's bill. | „   130
  A noble *b*, each perfect of the breed. | „   320
  What do you rate her at? *Count.* My *b*? | „   323
  Nothing but my brave *b*, my noble falcon, | „   873
  dying of my noble *b* Hath served me better than her living— | „   900
  all in all to one another from the time when we
  first peeped into the *b's* nest, | *Prom. of May* III 274
  barred the way to her chamber, like a *b* in a cage. | *Foresters* I i 315
  tree-Cupids half-way up in heaven, The *b's*— | „   III 37
  And all the *b's* that sing When all the leaves are green; | „   III 440
  And live with us and the *b's* in the green wood. | „   IV 325
  Let the *b's* sing, and do you dance to their song. | „   IV 556
  All the *b's* in merry Sherwood sing and sing him home
  again. | „   IV 1109
Bird-babble *B-b* for my falcon! Let it pass. | *The Falcon* 38
Bird-echoing Their long *b-e* minster-aisles,— | *Becket* III i 44
Birdlime I think there may be *b* here for me; | *Queen Mary* IV v 227
Bird-Robin If my man-Robin were but a *b-R*, | *Foresters* III 39
Birth every rebel *b* That passes out of embryo. | *Queen Mary* III vi 51
  We have the man that rail'd against thy *b*. | *Harold* II ii 486

Birth (*continued*) The child, a thread within the house
  of *b*, | *The Cup* II 260
  There came some evil fairy at my *b* | *Foresters* II ii 108
Birthdaäy (birthday) Why, o' coorse, fur it be the owd
  man's *b*. | *Prom. of May* I 6
  Owd Steer wur afeärd she wouldn't be back i' time
  to keep his *b*, | „   I 18
  I be coomed to keep his *b* an' all. | „   I 76
  —to celebrate my *b* i' this fashion. | „   I 321
Birthday (adj.) A *b* welcome! happy days and many! | *Harold* V i 431
Birthday (s) (*See also* **Birthdaäy**) My father on a *b*
  gave it me, | *Queen Mary* I v 527
  Plots and feuds! This is my ninetieth *b*. (repeat) | *Harold* IV i 121, 127
  Thy death!—to-day! Is it not thy *b*? | „   V i 429
  hath kinglike fought and fallen, His *b*, too. | „   V ii 126
  I came back to keep his *b*. | *Prom. of May* I 74
  but is not to-day his *b*? | *Foresters* I i 219
  that thou keepest a record of his *b's*? | „   I i 222
  To-day he hath accomplished his thirtieth *b*, | „   I i 298
  last time When I shall hold my *b* in this hall: | „   I ii 89
  Cloud not thy *b* with one fear for me. | „   I ii 126
  I am only merry for an hour or two Upon a *b*: | „   I iii 12
  It is my *b*. | „   II i 35
  greater nearness to the *b* Of the after-life, | „   I 44
Birthplace Bosham, my good Herbert, Thy *b*— | *Becket* II ii 293
Bishop (ecclesiastic) our *B's* from their sees Or fled,
  they say, or flying— | *Queen Mary* I ii 3
  —and now that your good *b*, Bonner, | „   I iii 35
  Why, my lord *B*? (repeat) | „   I iv 223, 227
  Some six or seven *B's*, diamonds, pearls, | „   III i 52
  I am but of the laity, my Lord *B*, | „   III iv 81
  Thou Christian *B*, thou Lord Chancellor Of England! | „   III iv 300
  Tut, Master *B*, Our bashful Legate, | „   III iv 349
  B Thirlby, And my Lord Paget and Lord William
  Howard, | „   IV i 4
  These are but natural graces, my good *B*, | „   IV i 177
  'I wunt dine,' says my Lord *B*, | „   IV iii 507
  'Now,' says the *B*, says he, 'we'll gwo to dinner;' | „   IV iii 513
  Our holy Norman *b's* down from all Their thrones in
  England? | *Harold* I i 50
  I saw him coming with his brother Odo The Bayeux *b*, | „   II ii 348
  thou art but deacon, not yet *b*, | *Becket*, Pro. 83
  beat Thy kingship as my *b* hath beaten it. | „   Pro. 91
  Hell take thy *b* then, and my kingship too! | „   Pro. 93
  Barons and *b's* of our realm of England, | „   I iii 336
  B's—York, London, Chichester, Westminster— | „   I iii 385
  where our *b's* And our great lords will sit in judgment | „   I iii 548
  What say the *b's*? | „   I iii 589
  —and these craven *b's*! | „   I iv 92
  if the barons and *b's* hadn't been a-sitting on the
  Archbishop. | „   I iv 127
  Knights, *b's*, earls, this London spawn— | „   II ii 143
  Our Becket, who will not absolve the *B's*. | „   V i 223
  he shall absolve The *b's*—they but did my will— | „   V i 254
  to absolve the *b's* Whom you have excommunicated. | „   V ii 376
  To all the archbishops, *b's*, prelates, barons, | „   V ii 404
  Save that you will absolve the *b's*. | „   V iii 120
  they plunder—yea, ev'n *b's*, Yea, ev'n archbishops— | *Foresters* IV 910
Bishop (chess) My liege, I move my *b*. | *Becket*, Pro. 28
  you see my *b* Hath brought your king to a standstill. | „   Pro. 43
  Why, there then—down go *b* and king together. | „   Pro. 47
Bishoprick fill'd All offices, all *b's* with English— | *Harold* II ii 535
  Saving thro' Norman *b's*— | „   II ii 538
  'When a *b* falls vacant, the King, | *Becket* I iii 99
  And let another take his *b*! | „   II ii 260
Bit (s) smash all our *b's* o' things worse than Philip
  o' Spain. | *Queen Mary* II iii 104
  Beänt Miss Eva gone off a *b* of 'er good looks o'
  laäte? *Man.* Noä, not a *b*. | *Prom. of May* I 33
  fur owd Dobson 'll gie us a *b* o' supper. | „   II 217
  Taäke one o' the young 'uns fust, Miss, fur I be a *b*
  deaf, | „   III 32
  We found a letter in your bedroom torn into *b's*. | „   III 324
  b by *b*—for she promised secrecy—I told her all. | „   III 379
Bit (verb) if a mad dog *b* your hand, my Lord, | *Queen Mary* III iv 204

Bit (verb) (*continued*) And *b* his shield, and dash'd it on the
ground,   *Harold* v i 405
And I was *b* by a mad dog o' Friday,   *Becket* i iv 217
Bite (s) The mad *b* Must have the cautery—   *Queen Mary* iii iv 275
Bite (verb) to turn and *b* the hand Would help thee   *Harold* i i 381
and I want to *b*, I want to *b*,   *Becket* i iv 221
Well, well, well! I *b* my tongue.   *The Falcon* 624
Bithynia Have you alliances? *B*, Pontus, Paphlagonia?   *The Cup* i ii 100
Bitten Would you not chop the *b* finger off,   *Queen Mary* iii iv 206
the Norman adder Hath *b* us; we are poison'd: *Harold* iii i 39
Bitter (adj.) Before these *b* statutes be requicken'd.   *Queen Mary* iii v 197
And, whether it bring you *b* news or sweet,   „ iii v 201
Hath, like a brief and *b* winter's day,   „ iv iii 430
And thrust his right into the *b* flame;   „ iv iii 610
bound me too With *b* obligation to the Count—   *Harold* ii ii 221
To plunge into this *b* world again—   *Becket* v ii 81
on a Tuesday pass'd From England into *b* banishment;   „ v ii 289
Bitter (s) The *b* in the sweet.   *Queen Mary* i v 235
Bitterer And mine a *b* illegitimate hate,   *Becket* iii iii 173
Bitterness She hath wean'd me from it with such *b*.   *Harold* iv ii 28
Bitters and I put the *b* on my breast to wean him,   *The Falcon* 189
your ladyship has given him *b* enough in this world,   „ 192
B before dinner, my lady, to give you a relish.   *Foresters* iii 434
Blaäme (blame) but summun else—*b't* if I beänt!   *Prom. of May* ii 140
Black I see but the *b* night, and hear the wolf.   *Queen Mary* v 413
It roll'd as *b* as death;   „ ii iii 20
four guns gaped at me, *B*, silent mouths;   „ ii iii 32
or you'll make the White Tower a *b* 'un for us this blessed day.   „ ii iii 100
These *b* dog-Dons Garb themselves bravely.   „ iii i 189
I thought this Philip had been one of those *b* devils of Spain,   „ iii i 215
Those damp, *b*, dead Nights in the Tower;   „ iii v 138
so 'z the tongue on un cum a-lolluping out o' 'is mouth as *b* as a rat.   „ iv iii 519
A drinker of *b*, strong, volcanic wines,   „ v iii 93
lash'd to death, or lie Famishing in *b* cells,   „ v ii 196
For twenty miles, where the *b* crow flies five,   „ v v 84
Ay, but thou liest as loud as the *b* herring-pond behind thee.   *Harold* ii i 26
He fain had calcined all Northumbria To one *b* ash,   „ iii i 57
Night, as *b* as a raven's feather;   „ iii ii 6
And thou, my carrier-pigeon of *b* news,   „ iv iii 233
I have an inherited loathing of these *b* sheep of the Papacy.   *Becket, Pro.* 461
Is *b* and white at once, and comes to nought.   „ i iii 32
The *b* sheep baaed to the miller's ewe-lamb,   „ i iv 162
B sheep, quoth she, too *b* a sin for me. And what said the *b* sheep, my masters? We can make a *b* sin white.   „ i iv 165
That he made the *b* sheep white.   „ i iv 176
Out from among us; thou art our *b* sheep.   „ i iv 181
Then I saw Thy high *b* steed among the flaming furze,   „ ii i 55
How ghostly sounds that horn in the *b* wood!   „ iii ii 17
Do you see that great *b* cloud that hath come over the sun   „ iii iii 46
It is this *b*, bell-silencing, anti-marrying,   „ iii iii 54
Who else, with this *b* thunderbolt of Rome Above him,   *The Cup* i ii 265
poor worm, crawl down thine own *b* hole To the lowest Hell.   „ ii 495
heat and fire Of life will bring them out, and *b* enough,   *Prom. of May* ii 287
I'd like to leather 'im *b* and blue,   „ ii 595
and the *b* river Flow'd thro' my dreams—   „ ii 649
It mun be true, fur it wur i' print as *b* as owt.   „ ii 731
the river, *b*, slimy, swirling under me in the lamplight,   „ iii 369
these lilies to lighten Sir Richard's *b* room,   *Foresters* i i 3
Sour milk and *b* bread.   „ ii i 272
They might be harder upon thee, if met in a *b* lane at midnight: „ iii 224
The *b* fiend grip her!   „ iii 380
B news, *b* news from Nottingham!   „ iii 446
Black-blooded You are too *b-b*.   *Queen Mary* iii i 126

Black-blooded (*continued*) Yea, you yourself, altho' you are *b-b*:   *Queen Mary* iii i 166
You call me too *b-b*—   „ iii i 347
He grovels to the Church when he's *b-b*,   *Becket* iv ii 437
Blacken I will hide my face, *B* and gipsyfy it;   „ iv ii 100
Whose lava-torrents blast and *b* a province   *The Cup* ii 302
Blackest Traced in the *b* text of Hell—   *Queen Mary* iii i 426
Black-faced Philip and the *b-f* swarms of Spain,   „ ii i 98
Blackness I see the *b* of my dungeon loom   *Harold* ii ii 405
thirty feet below the smiling day—In *b*—   „ ii ii 431
But what a blotch of *b* underneath!   *The Cup* i ii 398
Blacksmith and *B*, thaw he niver shoes a herse to my likings;   *Prom. of May* i 447
Blade take heed! The *b* is keen as death.   *Queen Mary* v v 175
When every baron ground his *b* in blood;   *Becket* i iii 349
Blaise (Bishop of Sebaste) To the chapel of St. *B* beneath the roof!   „ v iii 82
Blame (*See also* **Blaäme**) His foes would *b* him, and I scorned 'em,   *Queen Mary* i v 624
it is the Pope Will be to *b*—not thou.   *Becket* iii iii 222
I was to *b*—the love you said you bore me—   *The Falcon* 857
Blamed Praised, where you should have *b* him,   *Queen Mary* i v 600
Blameless condemn The *b* exile?   *Becket* ii ii 396
Blanch And *b* the crowd with horror.   *The Cup* ii 154
Blanch'd A doll-face *b* and bloodless,   *Becket* iv ii 175
Bland you were *b* And affable to men of all estates,   *Queen Mary* iv ii 80
Blank It seems that we shall fly These bald, *b* fields,   „ iii v 252
A poor philosopher who call'd the mind Of children a *b* page,   *Prom. of May* ii 282
Blanketed who dream'd us *b* In ever-closing fog,   *Queen Mary* iii ii 20
Blared *B* from the heights of all the thrones of her kings,   *Becket* v ii 489
Blasphemous Monstrous! *b*! She ought to burn.   *Queen Mary* v 57
Blasphemy terms Of Satan, liars, *b*, Antichrist,   „ i ii 95
Blast (s) (*See also* **Thunder-blast**) The *b* that came So suddenly hath fallen as suddenly   *Harold* ii i 12
Put thou the comet and this *b* together—   .. ii i 15
Which hunted *him* when that un-Saxon *b*,   „ ii i 31
showers of blood are blown Before a never ending *b*,   .. iii i 395
The sign in heaven—the sudden *b* at sea—   „ v i 378
Blast (verb) Would'st thou not burn and *b* them   *Queen Mary* iii iv 282
if yon weird sign Not *b* us in our dreams.—   *Harold* i i 122
b your infants, dash The torch of war among your standing corn,   „ ii ii 747
will *b* and blind you like a curse.   *Becket* i iv 39
To *b* my realms with excommunication And interdict.   „ ii ii 52
Go, lest I *b* thee with anathema,   „ iv ii 287
—and *b* the king and me,   *The Cup* ii 152
Whose lava-torrents blast and blacken a province   „ ii 302
That *b* our natural passions into pains!   *Prom. af May* ii 724
when they look at a maid they *b* her.   *Foresters* i i 257
Blatant But lack of happiness in a *b* wife.   „ i iii 132
Blaze (s) hiss Against the *b* they cannot quench—   *Harold* iii i 396
Against the shifting *b* of Harold's axe!   „ v 587
Blaze (verb) banner, *B* like a night of fatal stars   *Becket* iv i 251
But *b* not out before the Frenchmen here.   *Becket* iii iii 221
Blazed *B* false upon her heart.   *Queen Mary* iii i 70
Blazing A sacred cup saved from a *b* shrine   *The Cup* ii 54
Bleak and those *b* manners thaw,   *Queen Mary* iii ii 160
fierce forekings had clench'd their pirate hides To the *b* church doors,   *Harold* iv iii 37
Bled He had been hurt, And *b* beneath his armour.   *Foresters* ii ii 5
Bless and I return As Peter, but to *b* thee: *Queen Mary* ii ii 56
And may God *b* you, Thirlby!   „ iv ii 197
God *b* him!   „ iv iii 256
owld lord fell to 's meat wi' a will, God *b* un!   „ iv iii 515
Let all thy people *b* thee!   *Harold* i ii 184
And *b* the Queen of England.   „ i ii 207
And even as I should *b* thee saving mine,   „ ii ii 651
God *b* thee, wedded daughter. *Queen*. *B* thou too That brother whom I love beyond the rest,   „ iii i 293
All the sweet Saints *b* him!   „ iii i 298
I ask no more. Heaven *b* thee! hence!   *Becket* i i 321
Wilt thou not say, ' God *b* you,' ere we go? *Becket*. God *b* you all!   „ i iv 33
and see it mounting to Heaven, my God *b* you,   „ i iv 38

Bless (*continued*)   beggars, poor rogues (Heaven *b* 'em)   *Becket* I iv 83
God *b* the great Archbishop !   ,,   II ii 451
all on us ha' had to go, *b* the Saints, wi' bare backs,   ,,   III i 146
We scarcely dare to *b* the food we eat   ,,   v i 70
To *b* thine enemies—— *Becket.* Ay, mine, not Heaven's.   ,,   v ii 24
God *b* him for it.   ,,   v ii 146
hear us, O Mother, hear us, and *b* us !   *The Cup* II 2
Why, *b* the saints !   *The Falcon* 171
and *b* your sweet face, you look as beautiful   ,,   197
I ha' heärd 'im a-gawin' on 'ud make your 'air— God *b* it !—stan' on end.   *Prom. of May* I 135
The Lord *b* boath on 'em !   ,,   I 341
—the Lord *b* 'er—'er oän sen;   ,,   II 40
God *b* our well-beloved Robin, Earl of Huntingdon.   *Foresters* I i 247
sweet saints *b* your worship for your alms to the old woman !   ,,   II i 363
those poor serfs whom we have served will *b* us,   ,,   IV 1075

Blessed-Blest   The *blessed* Mary's a-passing !   *Queen Mary* I i 36
Holy Virgin, Plead with thy *blessed* Son ;   ,,   I v 85
or you'll make the White Tower a black 'un for us this *blessed* day.   ,,   II iii 101
Oh how the *blessed* angels who rejoice   ,,   III iii 180
And God hath *blest* or cursed me with a nose—   ,,   III v 178
And Thy most *blessed* Son's, who died for man.   ,,   IV iii 154
Have I not heard them mock the *blessed* Host In songs so lewd,   ,,   IV iii 365
' O *blessed* relics !' ' O Holy Peter !'   *Harold* I ii 169
Nay then, we be liker the *blessed* Apostles ;   ,,   II i 33
Yet the curse is on him For swearing falsely by those *blessed* bones.   ,,   III i 246
have sent him back A holy gonfanon, and a *blessed* hair Of Peter,   ,,   III ii 148
Thou swarest falsely by our *blessed* bones,   ,,   v i 259
Are those the *blessed* angels quiring, father ?   ,,   v i 472
Yea, by the *Blessed* Virgin !   *Becket, Pro.* 520
Blessed is he that cometh in the name of the Lord !   ,,   I iii 758
That is the parable of our *blessed* Lord. *Becket.* And why should not the parable of our *blessed* Lord be acted again ?   ,,   I iv 75
Blessed be the Lord Archbishop, who hath withstood two Kings   ,,   II ii 274
Thanks to the *blessed* Magdalen, whose day it is.   ,,   III iii 171
Man's help ! but we, we have the *Blessed* Virgin For worship,   ,,   v ii 219
O *blessed* saint, O glorious Benedict,—   ,,   v iii 1
Row to the *blessed* Isles ! the *blessed* Isles !—   *The Cup* II 525
in hope that the saints would send us this *blessed* morning ;   *The Falcon* 186
they are made by the *blessed* saints—these marriages.   ,,   203
It served me for a *blessed* rosary.   ,,   632
more *blessed* were the rags Of some pale beggar-woman seeking alms For her sick son,   ,,   850
but I wur so ta'en up wi' leädin' the owd man about all the *blessed* murnin'   *Prom. of May* III 3
For all the blessed souls in heaven Are both forgivers and forgiven.'   ,,   III 10
O brook, that brawlest merrily by Thro' fields that once were *blest*,   ,,   III 202
for the sake of the great *blessed* Mother in heaven,   *Foresters* I i 96
I keep it For holy vows made to the *blessed* Saints Not pleasures,   ,,   I ii 175
My mother, For whose sake, and the *blessed* Queen of Heaven,   ,,   II i 38
Devils, that make this *blessed* England hell.   ,,   III 127
That by the *blessed* Mother no man,   ,,   III 239
Our Lady's *blessed* shrines throughout the land Be all the richer for us.   ,,   IV 1079

Blessing (part.)   pauper, who had died in his misery *b* God,   *Prom. of May* III 378

Blessing (s)   I will bear thy *b* into the battle   *Harold* v 434
Was not the people's *b* as we past Heart-comfort   *Becket* I i 12
Nay, father, first thy *b*.   ,,   I i 317
Our humblest thanks for your *b*.   ,,   I iv 42
But that might bring a Roman *b* on us.   *The Cup* II 372
This *b* is for Synorix and for me.   ,,   II 376

Blessing (s) (*continued*)   *B*'s on your pretty voice, Miss Dora.   *Prom. of May* I 63
and the old woman's *b* with them to the last fringe.   *Foresters* II i 195
The silent *b* of one honest man Is heard in heaven—   ,,   III 321
Thou shalt pronounce the *b* of the Church   ,,   IV 927

Blest   *See* **Blessed**

Blew   Rose never *b* that equall'd such a bud.   *Queen Mary* III 373
Until the powder suddenly *b* him dead.   ,,   IV iii 340
Of Provence *b* you to your English throne;   *Becket* v i 123

Blighted   till that *b* vow Which God avenged to-day.   *Harold* v ii 155

Blind (adj.)   (*See also* **Stone-blind**)   Are you *b* ?   *Queen Mary* I iv 151
She, with her poor *b* hands feeling—' where is it ?   ,,   III i 407
with offal thrown Into the *b* sea of forgetfulness.   ,,   III iii 193
There is a movement there, A *b* one—   *Harold* I i 355
now I see That I was *b*—suffer the phrase—   *Becket* II ii 438
' What are we, says the *b* old man in Lear ?   *Prom. of May* I 262
I would taäke the owd *b* man to my oän fireside.   ,,   II 74
What was that ? my poor *b* father—   ,,   II 566
Poor *b* Father's little guide, Milly,   ,,   III 231
niver been surprised but once i' my life, and I went *b* upon it.   ,,   III 440
That Love is *b*, but thou hast proven it true.   *Foresters* II i 644

Blind (verb)   It frights the traitor more to maim and *b*.   *Harold* II 504
Say that he *b* thee and tear out thy tongue.   *Becket* I iii 615
will blast and *b* you like a curse.   ,,   I iv 40

Blinded   into some more costly stone Than ever *b* eye.   *Queen Mary* I v 371
No, no ; her innocent blood had *b* me.   ,,   III i 346
They *b* my young kinsman, Alfred—   *Harold* II ii 511
be sure they be, but he *b* 'em for all that,   *Becket* II i 128
Not caught, maim'd, *b* him.   *The Cup* II i 271
and the hunters, if caught, are *b*, or worse than *b*.   *Foresters* IV 226

Blindfold   was a pity to *b* such eyes as mine,   *Becket* I i 127

Blindness   and my father's breaking down, and his *b*.   *Prom. of May* II 70
My father stricken with his first paralysis, And then with *b*—   ,,   II 482
And cheer his *b* with a traveller's tales ?   ,,   II 515

Blissful   bounteous bays And havens filling with a *b* sea.   *The Cup* II 236

Bloat   my sleeping-draught May *b* thy beauty out of shape,   *Becket* IV ii 170
ambition, pride So *b* and redden his face—   *The Cup* II 170

Block (s)   The Tower ! the *b* !   *Queen Mary* IV 470
Like that poor heart, Northumberland, at the *b*.   ,,   II ii 334
Who changed not colour when she saw the *b*,   ,,   III i 400
To say ' I did not ?' and my rod's the *b*.   ,,   III v 130
My heart is no such *b* as Bonner's is: ,,   IV ii 174
like the bloodless head Fall'n on the *b*,   ,,   v ii 11

Block (verb)   How can I come When you so *b* the entry ?   *Becket* v iii 37

Block'd   All passes *b*.   *Harold* II ii 317

Blood   of royal *b*, of splendid feature,   *Queen Mary* I i 111
Why not ?   I am king's *b*.   ,,   I iii 105
I am the noblest *b* in Europe, Madam,   ,,   I iv 84
I have sworn upon the body and *b* of Christ   ,,   I v 215
Some of the bearing of your blue *b*—   ,,   I v 434
Your houses fired—your gutters bubbling *b*—   ,,   II ii 280
Scarlet, as if her feet were wash'd in *b*,   ,,   III i 62
No, no ; her innocent *b* had blinded me.   ,,   III i 346
Her dark dead *b* is in my heart with mine.   ,,   III i 349
Her dark dead *b* that ever moves with mine   ,,   III i 352
trusted God would save her thro' the *b* Of Jesus Christ   ,,   III i 387
a little letting of the *b*.   ,,   III ii 40
With His own *b*, and wash'd us from our sins,   ,,   III iii 203
Nay, I know They hunt my *b*.   ,,   III v 78
' Martyr's *b*—seed of the Church.'   ,,   IV i 146
b and sweat of heretics at the stake Is God's best dew   ,,   v i 100
And panting for my *b* as I go by.   ,,   v ii 219
Some few of Gothic *b* have golden hair,   ,,   v iii 60
sure she hates thee, Pants for thy *b*.   *Harold* I ii 39
the *b* That should have only pulsed for Griffyth,   ,,   I ii 149
She hath but *b* enough to live, not love.—   ,,   I ii 161
shown And redden'd with his people's *b*   ,,   I ii 243
' This Harold is not of the royal *b*,   ,,   II ii 354
Thou art of my *b*, and so methinks, my boy,   ,,   II ii 449
helpless folk Are wash'd away, wailing, in their own *b*—   ,,   II ii 472
Dabble your hearths with your own *b*.   ,,   II ii 751
Where they eat dead men's flesh, and drink their *b*.   ,,   II ii 808
he soak'd the trunk with human *b*,   ,,   III i 143

Blood (*continued*)   thus baptized in *b* Grew ever high and
higher,   *Harold* III i 147
Senlac ! Sanguelac, The Lake of *B* !   „   III i 386
showers of *b* are blown Before a never ending blast,   „   III i 393
A sea of *b*—we are drown'd in *b*—   „   III i 398
Mixing our *b's*, that thence a king may rise   „   IV i 142
Trampling thy mother's bosom into *b* ?   „   IV ii 26
sight of Danish *b* Might serve an end not English—   „   IV iii 97
did the dead man call it—Sanguelac, The lake of *b* ?   „   V i 185
Praise the Saints.   It is over.   No more *b* !   „   V ii 195
Ay ! *b*, perchance, except thou see to her.   *Becket*, Pro. 175
Heart-comfort and a balsam to thy *b* ?   „   I i 14
like Egypt's plague, had fill'd All things with *b* ;   „   I iii 346
When every baron ground his blade in *b* ;   „   I iii 350
household dough was kneaded up with *b* ;   „   I iii 352
The millwheel turn'd in *b* ;   „   I iii 353
God redden your pale *b* !   But mine is human-red ;   „   I iv 35
there be those about our King who would have thy *b*.'   „   I iv 55
Which it will quench in *b* !   „   IV ii 192
not life shot up in *b*, But death drawn in ;—   „   IV ii 381
Save him, his *b* would darken Henry's name ;   „   V iii 10
To bathe this sacred pavement with my *b*.   „   V iii 132
hand Red with the sacred *b* of Sinnatus ?   *The Cup* II 84
Hot *b*, ambition, pride So bloat and redden   „   II 169
Wine Ran down the marble and lookt like *b*, like *b*.   „   II 205
frost That help'd to check the flowing of the *b*.   *The Falcon* 646
Stain'd with the *b* of the best heart that ever Beat   „   666
servants Are all but flesh and *b* with those they serve.   „   709
would not crush The fly that drew her *b* ;   *Prom. of May* II 494
We Steers are of old *b*, tho' we be fallen.   „   III 604
thro' the *b* the wine leaps to the brain   *Foresters* I iii 22
Red with his own and enemy's *b*—   „   II i 32
soul of the woods hath stricken thro' my *b*,   „   II i 67
one of those mercenaries that suck the *b* of England.   „   II i 175
I wouldn't have thy *b* on my hearth.   „   II i 356
clothes itself In maiden flesh and *b*,   „   III 117
And thou wouldst run more wine than *b*.   „   III 338
Boldness is in the *b*, Truth in the bottle.   „   IV 240

Blooded   *See* **Black-blooded, Blue-blooded, Hot-blooded,**
    Norman-blooded, Red-blooded
Bloodier   Why, she's grown *b* !   *Queen Mary* III i 416
Bloodless   And look'd as *b*.   „   II ii 84
What makes thy favour like the *b* head Fall'n on
the block,   „   V ii 19
mortal men should bear their earthly heats Into
yon *b* world,   *Harold* V i 285
A doll-face blanch'd and *b*,   *Becket* IV ii 175
Blood-red   that these Three rods of *b-r* fire up yonder   *Harold* I i 44
This *b-r* line ?   *Henry.*   Ay ! blood, perchance,   *Becket*, Pro. 174
Bloody   King's courts would use thee worse than thy dog
—they are too *b*.   „   I iv 103
Bloom (s)   To me, tho' all your *b* has died away,   *The Falcon* 468
Bloom (verb)   You *b* again, dead mountain-meadow flowers.'   „   470
Blossom   (*See also* **Myrtle-blossom**)   She to shut up my *b* in
the dark !   *Harold* I ii 62
one fancy hath taken root, and borne *b* too,   *Becket*, Pro. 481
were more than I buzzing round the *b*—   „   Pro. 522
wither'd wreath is of more worth to me Than all the *b*,   *The Falcon* 339
never saw The land so rich in *b* as this year.   „   342
tree that my lord himself planted here in the *b* of his
boyhood—   „   563
dead garland Will break once more into the living *b*.   „   920
The *b* had open'd on every bough ;   *Prom. of May* I 42
Look how full of rosy *b* it is.   „   I 84
Theer be redder *b's* nor them, Miss Dora.   „   I 85
they'll hev' a fine cider-crop to-year if the *b* 'owds.   „   I 316
You, the most beautiful *b* of the May.   „   I 574
happy as the bees there at their honey In these sweet *b's*.   „   I 607
But, look, how wasteful of the *b* you are !   „   I 612
upon me Thro' that rich cloud of *b*.   „   II 250
the *b* of his youth, Has faded, falling fruitless—   „   II 332
I that held the orange *b* Dark as the yew ?   „   II 629
whose whole life hath been folded like a *b* in the sheath,   *Foresters* I i 206
I thank you, noble sir, the very *b* Of bandits.   „   III 247
they that suffer by him call the *b* Of bandits.   „   IV 372

Blossom'd   sow'd therein The seed of Hate, it *b*
Charity.   *Queen Mary* IV i 172
That ever *b* on this English isle.   *Foresters* I ii 124
Blossoming   And a salt wind burnt the *b* trees ;   *Prom. of May* I 57
Blot   I'll have the paper back—*b* out my name.   *Becket* I iii 286
Blotch   But what a *b* of blackness underneath !   *The Cup* I ii 398
Blotted   (*See also* **Self-blotted**)   And *b* by her tears.
This cannot last.   *Queen Mary* V v 17
if a state submit At once, she may be *b* out   *The Cup* I ii 157
That desolate letter, *b* with her tears,   *Prom. of May* II 475
Blow (s)   *b's*—Hark, there is battle at the palace
gates,   *Queen Mary* II iv 46
To strike too soon is oft to miss the *b*.   „   III vi 72
The *b* that brains the horseman cleaves the horse,   *Harold* V i 593
Nor ever strike him *b* for *b* ;   *Prom. of May* III 6
Blow (verb)   *b* this Philip and all Your trouble to the
dogstar   *Queen Mary* I iv 290
Daisies grow again, Kingcups *b* again,   „   III v 90
Which way does it *b* ?   *Harold* II ii 151
b the trumpet, priest ! .   „   III i 188
we must fight.   How *b's* the wind ?   „   III iii 135
William's or his own As wind *b's*, or tide flows : .   „   V i 163
As one that *b's* the coal to cool the fire.   *Becket* V ii 548
Where do they *b*, Mr. Dobson ?   *Prom. of May* I 87
b upon it Three mots, this fashion—listen !   *Foresters* IV 424
Wait till he *b* the horn.   „   IV 787
I *b* the horn against this rascal rout !   „   IV 794
Blow'd   but Dumble wur *b* wi' the wind,   *Queen Mary* IV iii 477
barrin' the wind, Dumble wur *b* wi' the wind,   „   IV iii 494
Blowest   Thou *b* hot and cold.   Where is she then ?   *Foresters* I 490
Why *b* thou not the horn ?   „   IV 790
Blowing   there are trumpets *b* now : what is it ?   *Queen Mary* IV ii 13
Why are the trumpets *b*, Father Cole ?   „   IV ii 23
B for England, ha ?   Not yet.   *Harold* II ii 152
The cold, white lily *b* in her cell :   „   III i 274
A ghostly horn *B* continually,   „   III i 373
Were the great trumpet *b* doomsday dawn,   „   V i 227
B the world against me,   *Becket* V ii 491
Not like the vintage *b* round your castle.   *The Falcon* 579
Blown   fate hath *b* me hither, bound me too   *Harold* II ii 219
showers of blood are *b* Before a never ending blast,   „   III i 394
He hath *b* himself as red as fire with curses. .   „   V i 86
B everyway with every gust and wreck On any
rock,   *Prom. of May* III 536
Her face on flame, her red hair all *b* back,   *Queen Mary* II ii 70
for any rough sea *B* by the breath of kings.   *Becket* II ii 108
B like a true son of the woods.   *Foresters* IV 427
Blubber'd   knelt And *b* like a lad,   *Queen Mary* III i 150
Blue   Philip shows Some of the bearing of your *b*
blood—   „   I v 434
This old thing here, they are but *b* beads—my Piero,   *The Falcon* 48
And your eyes be as *b* as—   *Prom. of May* I 91
Noä, Miss Dora ; as *b* as— (repeat)   „   I 95, 99
The sky ? or the sea on a *b* day ? *Dobson.* Naäy
then.   I meän'd they be as *b* as violets.   „   I 101
An' the midders all mow'd, an' the sky sa *b*—
(repeat)   *Prom. of May* II 177, 189, 201
I'd like to leather 'im black and *b*,   *Prom. of May* II 595
Bluebell   *B*, harebell, speedwell, bluebottle,   „   I 97
when I was a-getting o' *b's* for your ladyship's nose to
smell on—   *Becket* III i 162
Blue-blooded   this fine *b-b* Courtenay seems Too
princely for a pawn.   *Queen Mary* I iii 165
Bluebottle   speedwell, *b*, succory, forget-me-not ?   *Prom. of May* I 98
Bluff   He comes, a rough, *b*, simple-looking fellow.   *The Cup* I i 173
Blunt   Ever a rough, *b*, and uncourtly fellow—   *Queen Mary* V v 120
Blur   would not *b* A moth's wing by the touching ;   *Prom. of May* II 491
Blurt   But if thou *b* thy curse among our folk,   *Harold* V i 89
B thy free mind to the air ?   *Becket* I iii 239
Blush   Make *b* the maiden-white of our tall cliffs,   *Harold* II ii 332
Blush'd   That heaven wept and earth *b*.   *Queen Mary* III iv 193
every doorway *b*, Dash'd red with that unhallow'd
passover ;   *Becket* I iii 347
Bluster (verb)   Come, you *b*, Antony !   *Queen Mary* II ii 118
Bluster (s)   One of much outdoor *b*.   „   II ii 381

Book (*continued*)   same *b* You wrote against my
Lord of Winchester ;   *Queen Mary* IV iii 264
I hold by all I wrote within that *b*.   „   IV iii 275
thank'd her father sweetly for his *b* Against that godless German.   „   V v 237
There is a pleasant fable in old *b's*,   *Harold* IV i 56
fur him as be handy wi' a *b* bean't but haäfe a hand at a pitchfork.   *Prom. of May* I 188
for he's walking to us, and with a *b* in his hand.   „   I 220
I'll git the *b* ageän, and larn mysen the rest,   „   III 12
Bookman   A *b*, flying from the heat and tussle,   *Queen Mary* III iv 251
Boon (adj.)   My comrade, *b* companion, my co-reveller,   *Becket* I iii 460
Boon (s)   Wyatt, but now you promised me a *b*.   *Queen Mary* IV i 130
My life is not so happy, no such *b*,   „   IV i 130
And after those twelve years a *b*, my king,   *Harold* I i 226
And afterwards a *b* to crave of you.   *The Falcon* 712
to let me know the *b* By granting which,   „   766
First, king, a *b* !   *Foresters* IV 945
Boook (book)   An' I haätes *b's* an' all, fur they puts foälk off the owd waäys.   *Prom. of May* I 221
Boot   Your *b's* are from the horses.   *Queen Mary* III v 180
O God, sir, do you look upon your *b's*,   „   III v 191
I thought not on my *b's* ; The devil take all *b's*   „   III v 196
seeäms to me the mark wur maäde by a Lunnon *b*.   *Prom. of May* I 416
and I think ye weärs a Lunnon *b*.   „   I 461
Boot (in addition)   A man of this world and the next to *b*.   *Becket, Pro.* 259
and the weight of the church to *b* on my shoulders,   *Foresters* II ii 58
Booth   citizens Stood each before his shut-up *b*,   *Queen Mary* II ii 63
Booty   a troop, Laden with *b* and with a flag of ours   *The Falcon* 612
Bore   I never found he *b* me any spite.   *Queen Mary* V ii 474
Of this dead King, who never *b* revenge.   *Harold* V ii 85
My mother, ere she *b* me, Dream'd that twelve stars   *Becket* I i 45
When Canterbury hardly *b* a name.   „   I iii 60
As once he *b* the standard of the Angles,   „   I iii 494
—the love you said you *b* me—   *The Falcon* 858
Push'd from all doors as if we *b* the plague,   *Prom. of May* III 804
Born (*See also* **Burn, English-born, Galatian-born, Half-born, True-born**)   thou was *b* i' the tail end of old Harry the Seventh.   *Queen Mary* I i 42
I was *b* true man at five in the forenoon   „   I i 45
I was *b* of a true man and a ring'd wife,   „   I i 54
True, Mary was *b*, But France would not accept her for a bride As being *b* from incest ;   „   I ii 66
Yea, were there issue *b* to her,   „   I v 301
Would I had been *B* Spaniard !   „   III iii 246
If such a prince were *b* and you not here !   „   III vi 203
I should be here if such a prince were *b*.   „   III vi 206
to get her baaby *b* ;   „   IV iii 524
in her agony The mother came upon her—a child was *b*—   „   V iv 21
wise and holy men That shall be *b* hereafter.   *Harold* III i 210
laughter in old Rome Before a Pope was *b*,   „   III i 165
Not made but *b*, like the great king of all,   „   IV i 85
Wild was he, *b* so : but the plots against him   „   IV i 110
for a spark Of self-disdain *b* in me   „   V i 302
My day when I was *b*.   „   V ii 122
I was *b* with it, and sulphur won't bring it out o' me.   *Becket* I iv 232
Love that is *b* of the deep coming up with the sun from the sea. (repeat)   „   I i 9, 19
A bastard hate *b* of a former love.   „   I i 174
I had sooner have been *b* a Mussulman—   „   II ii 145
And this no wife has *b* you four brave sons,   „   V i 125
On a Tuesday was I *b*,   „   V ii 284
Because thou wast *b* excommunicate.   „   V ii 472
slayest the babe within the womb Or in the being *b*,   *The Cup* II 280
wasn't my lady *b* with a golden spoon in her ladyship's mouth.   *The Falcon* 401
left his heir, *B*, happily, with some sense of art,   *Prom. of May* I 497
though fortune had *b* you into the estate of a gentleman,   „   II 120
O this mortal house, Which we are *b* into,   „   II 274
Yet I, *b* here, not only love the country,   „   II 544
Wasn't Miss Vavasour, our schoolmistress at Littlechester, a lady *b* ?   „   III 299
shamed of her among The ladies, *b* his equals.   „   III 582
—they were *b* and bred on it—it was their mother—   *Foresters* I i 332

Born (*continued*)   saints were so kind to both on us that he was dead before he was *b*.   *Foresters* II i 374
Borne (*See also* **Shield-borne**)   And their strong torment bravely *b*,   *Queen Mary* III iv 168
they see not how they are *b*, Nor whither.   „   IV iii 410
Good for good hath *b* at times   *Harold* V i 174
one fancy hath taken root, and *b* blossom too,   *Becket, Pro.* 481
You had not *b* it, no, not for a day.   „   II ii 305
Borrowed   he *b* the monies from the Abbot of York, the Sheriff's brother.   *Foresters* I i 67
it was agreed when you *b* these monies from the Abbot   „   IV 466
Bosham   To-morrow—first to *B*, then to Flanders.   *Harold* I ii 239
Better have been A fisherman at *B*, my good Herbert,   *Becket* II ii 292
Bosom (adj.)   Should fly like *b* friends when needed most.   *The Falcon* 527
Bosom (s)   come to cast herself On loyal hearts and *b's*,   *Queen Mary* III i 263
received into the *b* And unity of Universal Church ;   „   III iii 154
we restore you to the *b* And unity of Universal Church.   „   III iii 220
And put it in my *b*, and all at once I felt his arms   „   V v 98
Trampling thy mother's *b* into blood ?   *Harold* IV ii 26
twelve stars fell glittering out of heaven Into her *b*.   *Becket* I i 433
And Becket had my *b* on all this ;   ..   I iii 433
To rest upon thy *b* and forget him—   „   II i 31
Beware of opening out thy *b* to it,   „   III iii 30
that *b* never Heaved under the King's hand   „   IV ii 188
This in thy *b*, fool, And after in thy bastard's !   „   IV ii 257
Bottle   like a *b* full up to the cork, or as hollow as a kex,   *Foresters* IV 210
He hath got it from the *b*, noble knight.   „   IV 237
Boldness out of the *b* !   „   IV 239
Boldness is in the blood, Truth in the *b*.   „   IV 241
so she glided up into the heart O' the *b*,   „   IV 245
Bottom   not even Hope Left at the *b* !   *Prom. of May* II 349
We are almost at the *b* of the well—   „   III 161
as they call it so truly, to the grave at the *b*,   „   III 193
why did you write ' Seek me at the *b* of the river ' ?   „   III 364
Hoäm ? fro' the *b* o' the river ?   „   III 443
She lay so long at the *b* of her well   *Foresters* IV 242
The deer fell dead to the *b*,   „   IV 543
Bough   shot out sidelong *b's* across the deep   *Harold* II i 150
Were there no *b's* to hang on, Rivers to drown in ?   *The Cup* I ii 77
The blossom had open'd on every *b* ;   *Prom. of May* I 42
The tawny squirrel vaulting thro' the *b's*,   *Foresters* I iii 118
Bought (*See also* **Bowt**)   God rest his honest soul, he *b* 'em for me,   *The Falcon* 49
She rich enough to have *b* it for herself !   „   62
But the King hath *b* half the College of Redhats.   *Becket* II ii 373
Bound (limit)   More like a school-boy that hath broken *b's*,   *Queen Mary* I v 171
Put on your hood and see me to the *b's*.   *Becket* I i 95
That your own people cast you from their *b's*,   *The Cup* I i 138
Bound (part)   if I save him, he and his Are *b* to me—   *Queen Mary* II iv 125
and when her innocent eyes were *b*,   „   III i 406
Philip by these articles is *b* From stirring hand or foot   „   III iii 59
b me too With bitter obligation to the Count—   *Harold* II ii 219
I am doubly *b* to thee . . .   „   II ii 557
Ay ! No !—he hath not *b* me by an oath—   „   II ii 660
I mean to be a liar—I am not *b*—   „   II ii 797
we be not *b* by the king's voice In making of a king,   „   II i 236
Rood itself were *b* To that necessity which binds us down ;   „   V i 107
to whom thou art *b* By Holy Church.   *Becket, Pro.* 67
be *b* Behind the back like laymen-criminals ?   „   I iii 95
For which the King was *b* security.   „   I iii 645
I am *b* For that one hour to stay with good King Louis,   „   III iii 246
Or else be *b* and beaten. (repeat)   *Foresters* III 370, 390
Bound (past of bind)   chain, Wherewith they *b* him to the stake,   *Queen Mary* IV iii 596
And *b* me by his love to secrecy Till his own time.   *Becket* III i 228
but I *b* the seller To silence,   *The Falcon* 72
I *b* myself, and by a solemn vow,   „   679
Bound (verb)   And doth so *b* and babble all the way   *Queen Mary* V v 86
Wherever the horn sound, and the buck *b*,   *Foresters* III 346
Wherever the buck *b*, and the horn sound,   „   III 355
Bounden   ruler of a land Is *b* by his power and place to see   *Queen Mary* III iv 212
and would myself Be *b* to thee more.   *Harold* II ii 561

Bounden (*continued*) The crime be on his head—not *b*—no.   *Harold* II ii 670

Being *b* by my coronation oath To do men justice.   *Becket* I iii 396

holy Palmer, *b* by a vow not to show his face,   *Foresters* I ii 236

Boundless I always hated *b* arrogance.   *Becket* v i 12

Here crawling in this *b* Nature.   *Prom. of May* III 637

Bounteous the *b* bays And havens filling with a blissful sea.   *The Cup* II 234

Bourne I cannot catch what Father *B* is saying.   *Queen Mary* I iii 14

Old *B* to the life !   ,,   I iii 30

Bout Come now, I fain would have a *b* with thee.   *Foresters* II i 552

but thyself Shalt play a *b* with me,   ,,   IV 252

I am overbreathed, Friar, by my two *b's* at quarter-staff.   ,,   IV 267

Bow (s) (*See also* **Saddle-bow**) battle-axe Was out of place ; it should have been the *b*.—   *Harold* I ii 107

and Death has drawn the *b*—   ,,   I i 401

Give him a *b* and arrows—follow—follow.   *The Cup* I i 208

shoot almost as closely with the *b* as the great Earl himself.   *Foresters* I i 216

but who be those three yonder with *b's* ?—   ,,   II i 172

who art more bow-bent than the very *b* thou carriest ?   ,,   II i 378

This is no *b* to hit nightingales ; this is a true woodman's *b* of the best yew-wood to slay the deer.   ,,   II i 391

Take thou my *b* and arrow and compel them to pay toll.   ,,   III 263

Give me my *b* and arrows.   ,,   IV 603

Bow (verb) wherefore *b* ye not, says Lady Anne   *Queen Mary* I v 45

Lords and Commons will *b* down before him—   ,,   III i 433

He *b's*, he bares his head, he is coming hither.   *Becket* III iii 34

or I Would *b* to such a baseness as would make me   ,,   IV ii 234

But crowns must *b* when mitres sit so high.   ,,   IV ii 297

Life yields to death and wisdom *b's* to Fate,   *The Cup* II 89

Bow-bent who art more *b-b* than the very bow thou carriest ?   ,,   II i 378

Bow'd (part. and adj.) over his *b* shoulder Scowl'd that world-hated and world-hating beast,   *Queen Mary* II ii 89

Men now are *b* and old, the doctors tell you,   ,,   III iv 408

Now, even now, when *b* before my time,   ,,   v ii 64

They told me that the Holy Rood had lean'd And *b* above me ;   *Harold* v i 104

b To the earth he came from, to the grave he goes to,   *Prom. of May* III 514

B to the dust beneath the burthen of sin.   ,,   III 521

Had she but *b* herself to meet the wave   *Becket* IV ii 388

Bow'd (verb) and the Lady Anne *B* to the Pyx ;   *Queen Mary* I v 42

all the rest of England *b* theirs to the Norman,   ,,   II i 160

Whether it *b* at all but in their fancy ; Or if it *b*,   *Harold* II i 109

the Holy Rood That *b* to me at Waltham—   ,,   v i 383

Bowel bury her Even in the *b's* of the earth   *Foresters* III 462

Bower (*See also* **Haveringatte-bower, Vine-bower**) I have built a secret *b* in England, Thomas,   *Becket, Pro.* 153

take her from her secret *b* in Anjou And pass her to her secret *b* in England.   ,,   *Pro.* 181

This chart with the red line ! her *b* ! whose *b* ?   ,,   *Pro.* 308

one rose will outblossom the rest, one rose in a *b*.   ,,   *Pro.* 346

chart with the red line—thou sawest it—her *b*.   *Fitzurse.* Rosamund's ?   ,,   *Pro.* 428

To pass thee to thy secret *b* to-morrow.   ,,   I i 249

Must speed you to your *b* at once.   ,,   I i 291

heard her cry ' Where is this *b* of mine ? '   ,,   I ii 42

With the red line—' her *b*.'   ,,   I ii 62

thou my golden dream of Love's own *b*,   ,,   II i 35

Thine enemy knows the secret of my *b*.   ,,   II i 265

warder of the *b* hath given himself Of late to wine.   ,,   III i 30

Springs from the loneliness of my poor *b*,   ,,   III i 41

My Anjou *b* was scarce as beautiful.   ,,   III i 52

Babble in *b* Under the rose !   ,,   III i 96

Kiss in the *b*, Tit on the tree !   ,,   III i 104

John of Salisbury committed The secret of the *b*,   ,,   III iii 6

Know you not this *b* is secret,   ,,   IV ii 22

Found out her secret *b* and murder'd her.   ,,   v i 175

Your Becket knew the secret of your *b*.   ,,   v i 178

The monk's disguise thou gavest me for my *b* :   ,,   v ii 94

When first he meets his maiden in a *b*.   *The Cup* I iii 42

I have lodged my pretty Katekin in her *b*.   *Foresters* II i 418

Bowering-in myrtle, *b-i* The city where she dwells.   *The Cup* I i 3

Bower-maiden Only my best *b-m* died of late,   *Becket* III i 67

Bowing his fine-cut face *b* and beaming with all that courtesy   ,,   III iii 141

Bowl *b* my ancestor Fetch'd from the farthest east—   *The Falcon* 483

as she has broken My china *b*.   ,,   524

Bowl'd no man yet has ever *b* me down.   *Foresters* IV 288

more of a man than to be *b* over like a ninepin.   ,,   IV 304

Bowman Our *bowmen* are so true They strike the deer   ,,   IV 524

Bowstring By arrow and by *b*,   ,,   III 442

Bowt (**bought**) an' it belongs to the Steers ageän : I *b* it back ageän ;   *Prom. of May* III 452

Boxed if you *b* the Pope's ears with a purse, you might stagger him,   *Becket* II ii 370

Boy (*See also* **School-boy**) After him *b's* ! and pelt him from the city.   *Queen Mary* I iii 85

while the *b* she held Mimick'd and piped her   ,,   II ii 72

So wife-like humble to the trivial *b*   ,,   III i 364

seven-years' friend was with me, my young *b* ;   ,,   III iii 48

the *b* Not out of him—but neither cold,   ,,   v ii 480

I am eleven years older than he, Poor *b* !   ,,   v v 47

That was a lusty *b* of twenty-seven ;   ,,   v v 48

Why—how they fought when *b's*—   *Harold* I i 430

Why, *b's* will fight. Leofwin would often fight me,   ,,   I i 433

The *b* would fist me hard, and when we fought   ,,   I i 444

Thou art the Queen ; ye are *b* and girl no more :   ,,   I i 455

stuff'd him with fears that these may act Father. *William.* Well, *b*.   ,,   II ii 90

,,   II ii 104

Why, *b* ? *Rufus.* Because I broke The horse's leg—   ,,   II ii 108

methinks, my *b*, Thy fears infect me beyond reason.   ,,   II ii 450

B, thou hast forgotten That thou art English.   ,,   II ii 473

I have lost the *b* who play'd at ball with me,   ,,   IV iii 21

How the *b* grows !   *Becket* II i 217

Dost thou know, my *b*, what it is to be Chancellor of England ?   ,,   II i 231

It is, my *b*, to side with the King when Chancellor,   ,,   II i 235

Here is a ball, my *b*, thy world,   ,,   II i 244

A pretty lusty *b*. *Rosamund.* So like to thee ;   ,,   II i 247

I spoke of late to the *b*, he answer'd me,   ,,   II ii 5

I love thy mother, my pretty *b*.   ,,   IV i 45

The *b* so late ; pray God, he be not lost.   ,,   IV ii 1

Geoffrey, my *b*, I saw the ball you lost   ,,   IV ii 56

—let me go With my young *b*,   ,,   IV ii 98

beg my bread along the world With my young *b*,   ,,   IV ii 104

Then is thy pretty *b* a bastard ?   ,,   IV ii 112

I will fly with my sweet *b* to heaven,   ,,   IV ii 237

Even when you both were *b's* at Theobald's.   ,,   v i 10

How fares thy pretty *b*, the little Geoffrey ?   ,,   v ii 167

Mine enemies barr'd all access to the *b*.   ,,   v ii 452

B, dost thou know the house of Sinnatus ?   *The Cup* I i 49

My *b*, Take thou this letter and this cup   ,,   I i 60

Why, whither runs the *b* ?   ,,   I i 70

I had once A *b* who died a babe ;   ,,   I ii 149

As helplessly as some unbearded *b's*   ,,   I iii 40

or after slayest him As *b* or man,   ,,   II 281

O my sick *b* ! My daily fading Florio,   *The Falcon* 235

But my—No, no ! not yet—   ,,   303

That bright inheritor of your eyes—your *b* ?   ,,   307

How charm'd he was ! what wonder ?—A gallant *b*,   ,,   319

love for thy dying *b*, Moves me to ask it of you.   ,,   787

How often has my sick *b* yearn'd for this !   ,,   829

The *b* may die : more blessed were the rags   ,,   850

Our men and *b's* would hoot him, stone him,   *Prom. of May* IV 425

the *b* was taken prisoner by the Moors.   *Foresters* I i 60

Come, *b* ! 'tis but to see if thou canst fence.   ,,   II i 571

I am like a *b* now going to be whipt ;   ,,   II ii 50

' This *b* will never wed the maid he loves,   ,,   II ii 111

Boyhood knew battle, And that was from my *b*,   *Harold* v ii 175

tree that my lord himself planted here in the blossom of his *b*—   *The Falcon* 564

Boy-king *b-k*, with his fast-fading eyes Fixt hard   *Queen Mary* II ii 30

Brace Out of the church, you *b* of cursed crones,   ,,   IV iii 539

Braced Are *b* and brazen'd up with Christmas wines   *Becket* v ii 423

Bracelet A man may hang gold *b's* on a bush,   *Harold* II i 87

Bracken Lusty *b* beaten flat,   *Foresters* II ii 154

Bragging is he *b* still that he will come — *Harold* IV iii 124
Brain (s) what, have you eyes, ears, *b*'s? — *Queen Mary* II i 97
   Your father had a *b* that beat men down— — „ IV i 110
   With nothing but my battle-axe and him To spatter
   his *b*'s! — *Harold* II ii 781
   All my *b* is full of sleep. — *The Cup* I ii 445
   thro' the blood the wine leaps to the *b* — *Foresters* I ii 23
   if you care to drag your *b*'s for such a minnow. — „ II i 323
Brain (verb) I have a mind to *b* thee with mine axe. — *Harold* II i 73
   blow that *b*'s the horseman cleaves the horse, — „ v 593
Brain-dazing After the long *b-d* colloquies, — *Queen Mary* IV ii 92
Brain-dizzied *B-d* with a draught of morning ale. — „ II i 71
Brain'd Methought they would have *b* me with it, John. — *Becket* v ii 612
Brainless over this the *b* loons That cannot spell
   Esaïas from St. Paul, — *Queen Mary* III i 280
Brake (*See also* **Broke**) those hard men *b* into woman-
   tears, Ev'n Gardiner, — „ I v 564
   some fool that once *B* bread with us, perhaps : — „ III v 45
   Who *b* into Lord Tostig's treasure-house — *Harold* II i 114
   Before these bandits *b* into your presence. — *Becket* v ii 556
Branch (*See also* **Olive-branch**) Would'st thou not
   burn and blast them root and *b* ? — *Queen Mary* III iv 283
Brand (a sword) flings His *b* in air and catches it again, — *Harold* v i 494
Brand (verb) So *b*'s me in the stare of Christendom
   A heretic ! — *Queen Mary* v ii 62
Brandish With hands too limp to *b* iron— — *Harold* v i 449
Brandish'd *See* **Treble-brandish'd**
Brass Swarm to thy voice like bees to the *b* pan. — *Foresters* I iii 108
Brat The washerwoman's *b* ! — *Harold* IV iii 172
Brave (adj.) For all that, Most honest, *b*, and skilful ; — *Queen Mary* II ii 383
   No, girl ; most *b* and loyal, *b* and loyal. — „ II iv 11
   b Lord William Thrust him from Ludgate, — „ II iv 91
   There's a *b* man, if any. — „ III i 175
   Might it not be the other side rejoicing In his *b* end ? — „ IV iii 358
   that our *b* English Had sallied out from Calais — „ v ii 255
   B, wary, sane to the heart of her— — „ v v 224
   And being *b* he must be subtly cow'd, — *Harold* II ii 75
   thou, *b* banner, Blaze like a night of fatal stars — „ IV i 250
   No, no—*b* Gurth, one gash from brow to knee ! — „ v i 70
   Hate him ? as *b* a soldier as Henry and a goodlier
   man ? — *Becket, Pro.* 436
   And this no wife has born you four *b* sons, — „ v i 125
   Why said you not as much to my *b* Sinnatus ? — *The Cup* I ii 260
   B—ay—too *b*, too over-confident, — „ I ii 261
   a *b* one Which you shall see to-morrow. — „ I ii 431
   That this *b* heart of mine should shake me so, — „ I ii 138
   I am sure that more than one *b* fellow owed His death — *The Falcon* 633
   Nothing but my *b* bird, my noble falcon, — „ 873
   She struck him, my *b* Marian, struck the Prince, — *Foresters* II i 134
   A *b* old fellow but he angers me. — „ II i 471
   he As gentle as he's *b*— — „ II i 659
   I know not, can I trust myself With your *b* band ? — „ II i 704
   Honour to thee, *b* Marian, and thy Kate. — „ III 299
   For our *b* Robin is a man indeed. — „ IV 1037
Brave (verb) Nay, nay, my lord, thou must not *b* the King. — *Becket* I iii 515
   I must hence to *b* The Pope, King Louis, and this
   turbulent priest. — „ II i 311
   To break the barons, and now *b*'s the King. — „ v i 235
   I dare not *b* my brother, Break with my kin. — *The Falcon* 255
   I cannot *b* my brother—but be sure — „ 741
Braved Hadst thou been braver, I had better *b* All— — *Harold* III ii 179
Brave-hearted My *b-h* Rose ! Hath he ever been to see
   thee ? — *Becket* II i 287
Braver Hadst thou been *b*, I had better braved All— — *Harold* III ii 178
Bravest *b* in our roll of Primates down From Austin— — *Becket* v ii 58
   the *b* English heart Since Hereward the Wake — *Foresters* II i 686
Brawl (s) witness the *b*'s, the gibbets. — *Queen Mary* v i 85
   Peace, friends ! what idle *b* is this ? — *Becket* I ii 3
   Wakening such *b*'s and loud disturbances In England, — „ v ii 352
   brazen'd up with Christmas wines For any murderous *b*. — „ v ii 425
   yet they prate Of mine, my *b*'s, when those, — „ v ii 427
   This last to rid thee of a world of *b*'s ! — „ v iii 199
   His grandsire struck my grandsire in a *b* At Florence, — *The Falcon* 251
Brawl (verb) You *b* beyond the question ; speak,
   Lord Legate ! — *Queen Mary* III iv 97

Brawler torn Down the strong wave of *b*'s. — *Queen Mary* III i 186
   Even this *b* of harsh truths— — *Foresters* IV 948
Brawlest O brook, that *b* merrily by — *Prom. of May* III 201
Brazen'd Are braced and *b* up with Christmas wines — *Becket* v ii 423
Bread (*See also* **Manchet-bread**) when the traitor wife
   came out for *b* — *Queen Mary* III i 12
   fool that once Brake *b* with us, perhaps : — „ III v 45
   Fed with rank *b* that crawl'd upon the tongue, — „ IV iii 442
   had they remained true to me whose *b* they have
   partaken. — *Becket* I iv 150
   live by the King's venison and the *b* o' the Lord, — „ I iv 272
   gaping bills in the home-nest Piping for *b*— — „ II ii 301
   and to win my own *b*, — „ III i 118
   I will beg my *b* along the world With my young boy, — „ IV iii 103
   The slave that eat my *b* has kick'd his King ! — „ v i 242
   How oft in coming hast thou broken *b* ? — *Harold* IV iii 200
   No *b* ? *Filippo.* Half a breakfast for a rat ! — *The Falcon* 122
   Sour milk and black *b*. — *Foresters* II i 272
   and her *b* is beyond me : and the milk—faugh ! — „ II i 292
   In the sweat of thy brow, says Holy Writ, shalt thou
   eat *b*, — „ IV 202
Breadth What *b*, height, strength—torrents of eddying
   bark ! — „ III 94
Break draw back your heads and your horns before I *b*
   them, — *Queen Mary* I i 5
   Pray God he do not be the first to *b* them, — „ I v 269
   It *b*'s my heart to hear her moan at night — „ I v 603
   These Kentish ploughmen cannot *b* the guards. — „ II iv 17
   The King of France will help to *b* it. — „ III i 105
   Beheld our rough forefathers *b* their Gods, — „ III ii 120
   You must *b* them or they *b* you. — „ III ii 205
   B's into feather'd merriments, — „ III v 13
   Whose colours in a moment *b* and fly, — „ IV iii 169
   Whose colours in a moment *b* and fly ! ' — „ v 206
   And *b* your paces in, and make you tame ; — „ v iii 121
   to *b* down all kingship and queenship, — „ v iv 47
   for thy brother *b*'s us With over-taxing— — *Harold* I i 109
   lest they rear and run And *b* both neck and axle. — „ I i 374
   close as our shield-wall, Who *b*'s us then ? — „ I i 400
   to swear Vows that he dare not *b*. — „ II ii 77
   —it was mine own to *b* ; — „ II ii 111
   I like to have my toys, and *b* them too. — „ II ii 112
   And may I *b* his legs ? — „ II ii 115
   Tho' scarce at ease ; for, save our meshes *b*, — „ II ii 141
   Or is it the same sin to *b* my work As *b* mine oath ? — „ II ii 664
   Enough ! Thou wilt not *b* it ! — „ II ii 753
   Ye take a stick, and *b* it ; — „ IV i 57
   Who made this Britain England, *b* the North : — „ IV iii 154
   B the banquet up . . . Ye four ! — „ IV iii 231
   our shield wall—Wall—*b* it not—*b* not—*b*— — „ v i 233
   made too good an use of Holy Church To *b* her close ! — „ v i 314
   he holp the King to *b* down our castles, — *Becket, Pro.* 447
   it is the will of God To *b* me, — „ I iii 292
   Nay, if I cannot *b* him as the prelate, — „ I iii 333
   If pretty Geoffrey do not *b* his own, — „ IV ii 177
   striving still to *b* or bind The spiritual giant — „ IV ii 442
   And *b* the soul from earth. — „ v i 44
   for he did his best To *b* the barons, — „ v i 235
   till it *b* Into young angels. — „ v ii 256
   Antonius would not suffer me to *b* Into the sanctuary. — *The Cup* I iii 120
   They will *b* in the earth— I am sinking— — „ II 477
   I dare not brave my brother, *B* with my kin. — *The Falcon* 257
   I come this day to *b* my fast with you. — „ 276
   I did it, my lord : it is broken ! — „ 494
   How shall I *b* it to him ? how shall I tell him ? — „ 848
   I *b* with him for ever ! — „ 889
   dead garland Will *b* once more into the living blossom. — „ 919
   She *will b* fence. I can't keep her in order. — *Prom. of May* I 194
   rough road That *b*'s off short into the abysses— — „ I 230
   There ! let me *b* some off for you. — „ I 609
   B's thro' them, and so flies away for ever ; — „ I 650
   If that should *b* before we meet again ? — „ I 755
   B ! nay, but call for Philip when you will, — „ I 757
   And as ready to *b* it again. — „ III 86
   I think That I should *b* my heart, — „ III 556

Break (*continued*)   I would *b* through them all, like the
   King of England.   *Foresters* I i 325
I will *b* thy sconce with my quarterstaff.   ,,   I ii 75
Who *b's* the stillness of the morning thus ?   ,,   I iii 50
Why *b* you thus upon my lonely hour ?   ,,   II i 93
b it all to pieces, as you *b* the poor,   ,,   II i 285
he would *b*, Far as he might, the power of John—   .   II i 695
To *b* our band and scatter us to the winds.   ,,   III 453
The chief of these outlaws who *b* the law ?   ,,   IV 141
being out of the law how should we *b* the law ? if we
   broke into it again we should *b* the law,   ,,   IV 145
B thine alliance with this faithless John,   ,,   IV 323
I cannot *b* it, Robin, if I wish'd.   ,,   IV 327
Then on the instant I will *b* thy head.   ,,   IV 680
That thou wilt *b* our forest laws again   ,,   IV 888
They *b* thy forest laws—nay, by the rood   ,,   IV 907
which longs to *b* itself across their backs.   ,,   IV 918
And have thy fees, and *b* the law no more.   ,,   IV 955
Breakage   his achage and his *b*, if that were all :   *Queen Mary* I i 128
we never use it For fear of *b*—   *The Falcon* 487
Breaker   the great *b* beats upon the beach !   *Foresters* I i 323
Breakfast   No bread ?   *Filippo.*   Half a *b* for a rat !   *The Falcon* 123
Call him back and say I come to *b* with him.   ,,   213
Holy Mother !   To *b* !   ,,   215
Breaking (*part.*)   (*See also* **Bond-breaking**)   Is guiltier
   keeping this, than *b* it.   *Harold* III i 231
the nightmare *b* on my peace ' With Becket.'   *Becket* II i 36
O God ! some dreadful truth is *b* on me—   ,,   III i 266
B already from thy noviciate To plunge   ,,   v i 79
Battering the doors, and *b* thro' the walls ?   ,,   v ii 626
Fairy realm is *b* down   *Foresters* II ii 134
Breaking (*s*)   His *b* with Northumberland broke
   Northumberland.   *Queen Mary* II iv 13
A day may save a heart from *b* too.   ,,   II vi 241
what with the fear of *b* it, I did break it,   *The Falcon* 494
and my father's *b* down, and his blindness.   *Prom. of May* II 69
Breast (*s*)   natural brother Of the same roof, same *b*.   *Queen Mary* IV iii 191
The babe enwomb'd and at the *b* is cursed,   *Harold* v i 65
Parthian shaft of a forlorn Cupid at the King's left *b*,   *Becket, Pro.* 340
On this left *b* before so hard a heart,   ,,   *Pro.* 375
I put the bitters on my *b* to wean him,   *The Falcon* 190
but in the sweat of thy brow, and thy *b*,   *Foresters* IV 203
Breast (*verb*)   there make strength to *b* Whatever chance,   *Harold* v i 127
Breasted   *See* **Many-breasted**
Breath   Did not his last *b* Clear Courtenay   *Queen Mary* III i 134
All her *b* should, incenselike, Rise to the heavens   ,,   III iii 163
it takes my *b* :   ,,   III v 190
All that is gracious in the *b* of heaven   ,,   III vi 224
Pray with one *b*, one heart, one soul for me.   ,,   IV iii 104
Beauty passes like a *b* and love is lost in loathing :   ,,   v ii 365
He hath swoon'd !   Death ? . . . no, as yet a *b*.   *Harold* III i 319
A *b* that fleets beyond this iron world,   ,,   III ii 197
link rusts with the *b* of the first after-marriage kiss,   *Becket, Pro.* 361
there stole into the city a *b* Full of the meadows,   ,,   I i 262
—John, and out of *b* !   ,,   I i 389
and they do say the very *b* catches.   ,,   I iv 222
stay it But for a *b*.   ,,   II ii 178
any rough sea Blown by the *b* of kings.   ,,   II ii 108
Thou whose *b* Is balmy wind to robe   *The Cup* II 264
Breathe   let them sit.   I must have time to *b*.   *Queen Mary* I v 546
that she *b's* in England Is life and lungs   ,,   III vi 49
And every soul of man that *b's* therein.   ,,   III vi 107
B the free wind from off our Saxon downs,   *Harold* III ii 186
for the sake Of any king that *b's*.   *Becket* II ii 221
I know—could swear—as long as Becket *b's*,   ,,   v i 77
And *b* one prayer for my liege-lord the King,   ,,   v ii 191
the great Archbishop !   Does he *b* ?   No ?   ,,   v iii 203
That I might *b* for a moment free of shield   *Foresters* IV 128
I *b* Heaven's air, and Heaven looks down on me,   ,,   IV 725
Then, if ye cannot *b* but woodland air,   ,,   IV 952
Breathed   (*See also* **Over-breathed**)   Girl never *b* to
   rival such a rose ;   *Queen Mary* III i 372
I never *b* it to a bird in the eaves,   ,,   v ii 453
since I *b*, A houseless head beneath the sun   *Foresters* II i 63
lips that never *b* Love's falsehood to true maid   ,,   IV 72

Breathing (*part.*)   *B* an easy gladness . . . not like
   Aldwyth . . .   *Harold* I ii 174
Breathing (*s*)   Like sun-gilt *b's* on a frosty dawn—   *Queen Mary* v iii 50
Or in the balmy *b's* of the night,   *Foresters* IV 1068
Breathing-time   But in this narrow *b-t* of life   *The Cup* I i 29
Breathing-while   a *b-w* To rest upon thy bosom   *Becket* II i 29
Breathless   lying chain'd In *b* dungeons over steam-
   ing sewers,   *Queen Mary* IV iii 440
Bred   *That b* the doubt ! but I am wiser now . . .   *Harold* v ii 111
Tho' I *b* thee The full-train'd marvel   *The Falcon* 24
—they were born and *b* on it—it was their mother—   *Foresters* I i 332
Traitors are rarely *b* Save under traitor kings.   ,,   II i 80
only they that be *b* in it can find their way a-nights in it.   ,,   II i 264
Breed (*s*)   Two vipers of one *b*—an amphisbæna,   *Queen Mary* III iv 39
Thy *b* will die with thee, and mine with me :   *The Falcon* 18
A noble bird, each perfect of the *b*.   ,,   320
A nobler *b* of men and women.   ,,   755
Breed (*verb*)   And if I *b* confusion anyway—
   world would grow mouldy, would only *b* the past   *Queen Mary* I iii 93
   again.   *Becket, Pro.* 410
And if my pleasure *b* another's pain,   *Prom. of May* I 278
Breeding   (*See also* **Fever-breeding**)   In *b* godless
   vermin.   *Queen Mary* III iv 329
b A fierce resolve and fixt heart-hate   ,,   III vi 31
Breeze   which a *b* of May Took ever and anon,   *The Cup* II ii 406
Brethren   (*See also* **Brother**)   Behold him, *b* : he
   hath cause to weep !—   *Queen Mary* IV iii 13
I pray you all to live together Like *b* ;   ,,   IV iii 182
seeming not as *b*, But mortal foes !   ,,   IV iii 185
Hear him, my good *b*.   ,,   IV iii 227
Join hands, let *b* dwell in unity ;   *Harold* I i 397
To help us from their *b* yonder ?   ,,   II i 221
Can ye not Be *b* ?   Godwin still at feud with Alfgar,   ,,   IV i 123
Have thy two *b* sent their forces in ?   ,,   v i 342
have I fought men Like Harold and his *b*,   ,,   v ii 179
Stay, Dine with my *b* here,   *Foresters* IV 346
Brett (*adherent of Wyatt*)   You know that after The
   Captain *B*,   *Queen Mary* II ii 26
B, when the Duke of Norfolk moved against us   ,,   II iii 1
for which I love thee, *B*.   ,,   II iii 6
Last night I climb'd into the gate-house, *B*,   ,,   II iii 15
Brevity   Tit, for love and *b*,   *Foresters* II ii 128
Brew   To sing, love, marry, churn, *b*, bake, and die,   *Queen Mary* III v 111
b from out This Godstow-Becket intermeddling   *Becket* II ii 455
I can bake and I can *b*,   *Foresters* I 215
Brew'd   what an acrid wine has Luther *b*,   *Queen Mary* IV iii 545
and she *b* the best ale in all Glo'ster,   *Becket* III i 196
Briar   Wi' the *b* sa green, an' the willer sa graäy,   *Prom. of May* II 186
Bribe   *b's* our nobles with her gold,   *Queen Mary* II i 202
but they *b* Each other, and so often,   *Harold* I i 346
—*b* all the Cardinals—   *Becket* II ii 473
Bribed   Except this old hag have been *b* to lie.   *Robin.*
   We old hags should be *b* to speak truth,   *Foresters* II ii 235
Brickwork   This labyrinthine *b* maze in maze,   *Becket, Pro.* 166
Bridal   tore away My marriage ring, and rent my *b* veil ;   *Harold* I ii 80
Like the Love-goddess, with no *b* veil,   *Prom. of May* I 596
Bride   France would not accept her for a *b*   *Queen Mary* I ii 68
Were I in Devon with my wedded *b*,   ,,   I iv 119
Had mark'd her for my brother Edward's *b* ;   ,,   I v 290
I live and die The true and faithful *b* of Philip—   ,,   II iv 43
To purchase for Himself a stainless *b* ;   ,,   III iii 205
White as the light, the spotless *b* of Christ,   ,,   III iv 199
King hath wearied of his barren *b*.'   ,,   III vi 141
there is one Death stands behind the *B*—   ,,   v ii 168
B of the mightiest sovereign upon earth ?   ,,   v ii 544
Hail !   Harold !   Aldwyth ! hail, bridegroom and *b* !   *Harold* IV iii 2
Hail, Harold, Aldwyth !   Bridegroom and *b* !   ,,   IV iii 43
Full thanks for your fair greeting of my *b* !   ,,   IV iii 47
I could not : Thou art my *b* !   ,,   v i 322
Who but the bridegroom dares to judge the *b*.   *Becket* I iii 686
thought if it were the King's brother he had a better *b*
   than the King,   ,,   III i 173
I had dream'd I was the *b* of England, and a queen.   ,,   v i 103
while you dream'd you were the *b* of England,—   ,,   v i 105
and our Mother Church for *b* ;   ,,   v ii 222

Bride (*continued*) And Camma for my *b*—The people
love her—   *The Cup* I iii 152
   I am the *b* of Death, and only Marry the dead.   ,,   II 28
   The king should pace on purple to his *b*,   ,,   II 190
   She too—she too—the *b* ! the Queen ! and I—   ,,   II 467
   An outlaw's *b* may not be wife in law.   *Foresters* II ii 90
   This other, willy-nilly, for his *b*.   ,,   IV 768
Bridegroom (*See also* **Groom**) How should he bear a
b out of Spain ?   *Queen Mary* III iii 25
   But softly as a *b* to his own.   *Harold* II i 758
   Hail ! Harold ! Aldwyth ! hail, *b* and bride !   ,,   IV iii 2
   Hail, Harold, Aldwyth ! *B* and bride !   ,,   IV iii 43
   Who but the *b* dares to judge the bride. Or he the *b*
may appoint ?   *Becket* I iii 685
Brideless The *b* Becket is thy king and mine :   ,,   v i 107
Bridesmaid Our *b*'s are not lovely—Disappointment, *Queen Mary* v ii 154
Bridge And broken *b*, or spavin'd horse,   ,,   I v 355
   thro' thine help we are come to London *B* ;   ,,   II iii 9
   On over London *B* We cannot : stay we cannot ;   ,,   II iii 41
   we must round By Kingston *B*.   ,,   II iii 48
   And then a brook, a *b* ;   *Becket, Pro.* 164
   This *b* again ! How often have I stood With Eva
here !   *Prom. of May* II 295
   madman, is it, Gesticulating there upon the *b* ?   ,,   II 327
   I dozed upon the *b*, and the black river   ,,   II 649
   dead midnight when I came upon the *b* ;   ,,   III 369
Bridged and brooks Were *b* and damm'd with dead, *Harold* III ii 130
Brief it is an age Of *b* life, and *b* purpose, and *b*
patience, As I have shown to-day.   *Queen Mary* III iv 413
   Care more for our *b* life in their wet land,   ,,   III vi 62
   Latimer Had a *b* end—not Ridley.   ,,   IV ii 225
   in *b*, so miserable,   ,,   IV iii 78
   Hath, like a *b* and bitter winter's day,   ,,   IV iii 430
   Suffer not That my *b* reign in England be defamed   ,,   v ii 302
Brief-sighted And warble those *b-s* eyes of hers ?   ,,   III vi 155
   B-s tho' they be, I have seen them,   ,,   III vi 157
Bright And dazzled men and deafen'd by some *b* Loud
venture,   ,,   III i 452
   the *b* sky cleave To the very feet of God,   *Harold* II ii 741
   the *b* link rusts with the breath of the first after-
marriage kiss,   *Becket, Pro.* 361
   Gleam upon gloom, *B* as my dream,   ,,   III i 278
   To-day they are fixt and *b*—   *The Cup* II 20
   Ay, how is he, That *b* inheritor of your eyes—your
boy ?   *The Falcon* 306
   And the day's *b* like a friend,   *Prom. of May* I 79
   I remember Her *b* face beaming starlike down upon me   ,,   II 248
   To sleep ! to sleep ! The long *b* day is done,   *Foresters* I iii 41
   So now the forest lawns are all as *b* As ways to heaven,   ,,   II 631
Brighten or it is but past That *b*'s in retiring ?   *Prom. of May* II 645
Brighter Cousin Pole, You are fresh from *b* lands. *Queen Mary* III iv 322
   this world Is *b* for his absence as that other Is
darker for his presence.   *Prom. of May* II 458
   but if you Can tell me anything of our sweet Eva
When in her *b* girlhood,   ,,   II 521
Brightest In Britain's calendar the *b* day   *Queen Mary* III ii 118
Brim Fill to the *b*.   *Foresters* III 343
   To the *b* and over till the green earth   ,,   III 349
Brimming green field Beside the *b* Medway,   *Queen Mary* II i 244
Bring I do but *b* the message, know no more.   ,,   I iv 228
   I'll have one mark it And *b* it me.   ,,   I v 373
   messenger Who *b*'s that letter which we waited for—   ,,   I v 586
   This marriage should *b* loss or danger to you,   ,,   II ii 227
   Find out his name and *b* it to me   ,,   III i 253
   Legate's coming To *b* us absolution from the Pope.   ,,   III i 432
   second actor in this pageant That *b*'s him in ;   ,,   III iii 15
   To *b* the heretic to the stake,   ,,   III iv 9
   ' I come not to *b* peace but a sword ' ?   ,,   III iv 88
   sends His careful dog to *b* them to the fold.   ,,   III iv 105
   And, whether it be your bitter news or sweet,   ,,   III v 201
   b it Home to the leisure wisdom of his Queen,   ,,   III vi 22
   lo ! thou art reclaim'd ; He *b*'s thee home :   ,,   IV iii 84
   you *b* the smoke Of Cranmer's burning with you.   ,,   IV iii 560
   B's the new learning back.   ,,   v i 202
   My liege, I *b* you goodly tidings.   ,,   v i 279

Bring (*continued*) Why do you *b* me these ?   *Queen Mary* v ii 185
   Why do they *b* me these ?   ,,   v ii 198
   he may *b* you news from Philip.   ,,   v ii 229
   I *b* your Majesty such grievous news I grieve to *b* it.   ,,   v ii 239
   Alice, my child, *B* us your lute.   ,,   v ii 357
   No, no, he *b*'s a letter.   ,,   v ii 548
   to read the letter which you *b*. *Feria.* Madam, I *b*
no letter. *Mary.* How ! no letter ?   ,,   v ii 556
   that I am in state to *b* forth death—   ,,   v ii 592
   I pray thee, let me hence and *b* him home.   *Harold* I i 241
   thunder may *b* down That which the flash   ,,   II i 234
   I want thy voice with him to *b* him round ;   ,,   II ii 73
   make A league with William, so to *b* him back ?   ,,   II ii 461
   wilt thou *b* another, Edith, upon his head ?   ,,   III i 260
   B not thy hollowness On our full feast.   ,,   IV iii 203
   b her to the level of the dust, so that the King— *Becket, Pro.* 530
   And *b* us all to shame ?   ,,   I ii 38
   If Canterbury *b* his cross to court,   ,,   I iii 511
   I was born with it, and sulphur won't *b* it out o' me.   ,,   I iv 233
   I *b* the taint on it along wi' me, for the Archbishop likes it,   ,,   I iv 252
   till the weight of Germany or the gold of England *b*'s
one of them down to the dust—   ,,   II ii 364
   there were Abbots—but they did not *b* their women ;   ,,   III iii 135
   To *b* her to the dust ...   ,,   IV ii 154
   we *b* a message from the King Beyond the water ;   ,,   v ii 301
   Moon *b* him home, *b* him home Safe from the dark and
the cold, Home, sweet moon, *b* him home,   *The Cup* I ii 5
   B me The costly wines we use in marriages.   ,,   II 364
   But that might *b* a Roman blessing on us.   ,,   II 371
   Lady, you *b* your light into my cottage   *The Falcon* 283
   look for 'im, Eva, and *b* 'im to the barn.   *Prom. of May* I 438
   but I thowt I'd *b* tha them roses fust.   ,,   II 50
   And *b* us to confusion.   ,,   II 279
   the heat and fire Of life will *b* them out,   ,,   II 287
   Let me *b* you in here where there is still full daylight.   ,,   III 217
   and the man must *b* it out of her.   *Foresters* I i 118
   So that our Barons *b* his baseness under.   ,,   I ii 117
   I trust he *b*'s us news of the King's coming.   ,,   I iii 53
   To *b* their counter-bond into the forest.   ,,   IV 89
   I *b* the bond.   ,,   IV 109
   I can *b* down Fourscore tall fellows on thee.   ,,   IV 175
   Shall I not after him and *b* him back ?   ,,   IV 812
Bristle So that he *b* himself against my will.   *Harold* II ii 19
Bristled monarch mane *B* about his quick ears—   *The Cup* I ii 121
Britain In *B*'s calendar the brightest day   *Queen Mary* III ii 118
   sons of those Who made this *B* England,   *Harold* IV iii 154
Brito (Richard de) (knight of King Henry II.'s household)
(*See also* **De Brito, Richard**) France ! Ha ! De
Morville, Tracy, *B*—fled is he ?   *Becket* I iv 199
Brittany brought Thy war with *B* to a goodlier close *Harold* II ii 49
   one that should be grateful to me overseas, a Count in *B*— *Foresters* I i 271
Broach *See* **Abroach**
Broached They ha' *b* a barrel of aäle i' the long barn, *Prom. of May* I 426
Broad What it means ? Ask our *b* Earl.   *Harold* I i 90
   he is *b* and honest, Breathing an easy gladness. . . .   ,,   I i 172
Brocade —O he Flamed in *b*—   *Queen Mary* I i 76
Broider these poor hands but sew, Spin, *b*—   *Harold* IV iii 11
   maidens who can only *b* and mayhap ride a-hawking *Foresters* I i 213
Broke (*See also* **Brake**) When Henry *b* the carcase of
your church   *Queen Mary* I v 397
   His breaking with Northumberland *b* Northumberland.   ,,   II iv 13
   Charing Cross ; the rebels *b* us there,   ,,   II iv 76
   Because I *b* The horse's leg—   *Harold* II ii 109
   I trod upon him even now, my lord, in my hurry,
and *b* him.   *The Falcon* 410
   Immanuel Goldsmiths was *b* into o' Monday night, *Prom. of May* I 392
   b the heart That only beat for you ;   ,,   III 761
   I have shelter'd some that *b* the forest laws.   *Foresters* I iii 70
   She *b* my head on Tuesday with a dish.   ,,   I iii 133
   if we *b* into it again we should break the law,   ,,   IV 145
   This young warrior *B* his prison   ,,   IV 999
Broken (*See also* **Brokken, Neck-broken**) I hear that
he too is full of aches and *b* before his day.   *Queen Mary* I i 125
   that *b*, out you flutter Thro' the new world,   ,,   I iv 52
   More like a school-boy that hath *b* bounds,   ,,   I i 171

Brother (*continued*) Thou art her *b*, and her voice is thine, *Foresters* II i 478

Thou art Her *b*—I forgive thee. Come be thou My *b* too. „ II i 516

O thou unworthy *b* of my dear Marian ! „ II i 538

That such a *b*—*she* marry the Sheriff ! „ II i 550

go not yet, stay with us, and when thy *b*— „ II i 641

to dream that he My *b*, my dear Walter— „ II i 652

See, thou hast wrong'd my *b* and myself. „ II i 665

Ha, *b*. Toll, my dear ? the toll of love. „ III 270

For so this maid would wed our *b*, „ IV 483

When Richard comes he is soft enough to pardon His *b* ; „ IV 748

What ! go to slay his *b*, and make *me* The monkey „ IV 804

Thou art tann'd almost beyond my knowing, *b*. „ IV 1016

Brotherhood lustiest and lousiest of this Cain's *b*, answer. *Becket* I iv 185

find The common *b* of man has been Wrong'd *Prom. of May* III 543

Brother-like That is not *b-l*. *Foresters* II i 504

Brought (*See also* **Browt**) and he *b* his doubts And fears to me. *Queen Mary* I ii 74

And *b* us back the mass. „ I v 184

Hast thou *B* me the letter which thine Emperor promised „ I v 347

cause that hath *b* us together is not the cause „ II i 161

They have *b* it in large measure on themselves. „ IV iii 363

Indian shawl That Philip *b* me in our happy days !— „ V ii 540

Madam, I *b* My King's congratulations ; „ V ii 569

b Thy war with Brittany to a goodlier close *Harold* II ii 48

And *b* the sunder'd tree again, „ III i 144

Alas ! poor man, *His* promise *b* in on me. „ III i 338

being *b* before the courts of the Church, *Becket, Pro.* 12

my bishop Hath *b* your king to a standstill. „ Pro. 44

I *b* them In the wood, and set them here. „ II i 130

My liege, what hast thou *b* me ? „ II i 223

I *b* not ev'n my crucifix. *Henry*. Take this. „ II i 295

and so *b* me no-hows as I may say, „ II i 129

Your old child *b* me hither ! „ IV ii 13

B me again to her own city ?— *The Cup* I i 14

but this day has *b* A great occasion. *The Falcon* 488

I think I never can be *b* to love any man. *Prom. of May* II 78

Superstitious fool, What *b* me here ? „ II 351

now that you have been *b* to us as it were from the grave, „ III 235

If marriage ever *b* a woman happiness „ III 639

Thro' that dishonour which you *b* upon us, „ III 765

could be *b* to love me As I loved you— „ III 779

new term *B* from the sacred East, his harem ? *Foresters* IV 705

like the man In Holy Writ, who *b* his talent back ; „ IV 981

Brow The *b's* unwrinkled as a summer mere.— *Harold* II i 48

—brave Gurth, one gash from *b* to knee ! „ II i 71

There's no jest on the *b's* of Herbert there. *Becket, Pro.* 390

Life on the face, the *b's*—clear innocence ! „ II i 195

Ay, and his *b's* are thine ; „ II i 218

bust of Juno and the *b's* and eyes Of Venus ; *The Cup* I i 120

In the sweat of thy *b*, says Holy Writ, shalt thou eat bread, but in the sweat of thy *b* *Foresters* IV 201

Browt (**brought**) I ha' *b* these roses to ye—I forgits what they calls 'em, *Prom. of May* II 14

so I allus *b* soom on 'em to her ; „ II 20

to saäy he's *b* some of Miss Eva's roses „ III 346

Bruised as having been so *b* By Harold, King of Norway ; *Harold* IV i 9

B ; but no bones broken. *Prom. of May* III 242

Honest daisy deadly *b*, *Foresters* II ii 156

And *b* him almost to the death, „ III 361

Brunanburg What's *B* To Stamford-bridge ? *Harold* III iii 142

And chanting that old song of *B* „ V i 215

Brush (s) with some sense of art, to live By *b* and pencil. *Prom. of May* I 499

Brush (verb) and *b* This Wyatt from our shoulders, *Queen Mary* II ii 293

Her cap would *b* his heels. „ II 14

Brussels We meet at *B*. „ III vi 215

Brutal Because these islanders are *b* beasts ? „ III vi 153

almost *b*, and matched with my Harold *Prom. of May* III 175

Curse on your *b* strength ! „ III 732

Brute (adj.) Brook for an hour such *b* malignity ? *Queen Mary* IV iii 544

Brute (s) (*See also* **Baron-brute**) Mutilated, poor *b*, my sumpter-mule. *Becket* V ii 440

Bubble Many so dote upon this *b* world, *Queen Mary* IV iii 168

'O *b* world, Whose colours in a moment break and fly ! ' „ V ii 204

Bubbled you so *b* over with hot terms Of Satan, „ I ii 94

Buck *B* ; deer, as you call it. *Becket* I iv 139

Wherever the horn sound, and the *b* bound, *Foresters* III 345

Wherever the *b* bound, and the horn sound, „ III 355

Buckingham (**Duke of**) And I the race of murder'd *B*— *Queen Mary* III i 454

Bud (s) Rose never blew that equall'd such a *b*. „ III i 373

that shoots New *b's* to heaven, *Foresters* III i 26

Bud (verb) court is always May, *b's* out in masques, *Queen Mary* III v 11

believe My old crook'd spine would *b* out two young wings *Harold* III i 24

Buffet (s) I will give thee a *b* on the face. *Foresters* I i 146

Then thou shalt play the game of *b's* with us. „ IV 259

I give thee A *b*, and thou me. „ IV 263

Buffet (verb) you stroke me on one cheek, *B* the other. *Queen Mary* II i 118

Build Too gross to be thrust out, will *b* him round, „ III iii 55

help to *b* a throne Out-towering hers of France . . . *Harold* II ii 763

I vow to *b* a church to God Here on the hill of battle ; „ V ii 137

Here His turtle *b's* ; his exit is our adit : *Becket* III ii 7

as she was helping to *b* the mound against the city. *Foresters* III 309

would cower to any Of mortal *b*. „ II i 690

whose return *B's* up our house again ? „ IV 1009

Builded (*See also* **Built**) I have *b* the great church of Holy Peter : *Harold* I i 179

Builder she leaves only the nest she built, they leave the *b*. *Becket* I iv 47

Built (*See also* **Builded**) They have *b* their castles here ; *Harold* III i 36

I have *b* the Lord a house—(repeat) *Harold* III i 178, 180, 186

loftiest minster ever *b* To Holy Peter in our English isle ! *Harold* III i 206

I have *b* a secret bower in England, Thomas, *Becket, Pro.* 153

I wrong the bird ; she leaves only the nest she *b*, „ I iv 46

Bull-headed Sir Thomas Stafford, a *b-h* ass, *Queen Mary* V i 284

Bullingham (**Nicholas, afterwards Bishop of Worcester**) Ailmer and *B*, and hundreds more ; „ I ii 11

Bullock I'd like to fell 'im as deäd as a *b* ! *Prom. of May* II 597

Bully Keep silence, *b* friar, before the King. *Foresters* IV 919

Bulrush Had I a *b* now in this right hand For sceptre, „ II 76

Bulwark A *b* against Throne and Baronage. *Becket* I i 17

Burgher My *b's* son—Nay, if I cannot break „ I iii 331

Burgundy all France, all *B*, Poitou, all Christendom *Harold* III ii 149

Burial We will not give him A Christian *b* : „ V ii 154

I've been attending on his deathbed and his *b*. *Prom. of May* IV 4

Burial-hindering bell-silencing, anti-marrying, *b-h* interdict *Becket* III iii 55

Buried (part. and adj.) boil'd, *b* alive, worried by dogs ; *Queen Mary* II i 210

There lies a treasure *b* down in Ely. *Harold* III i 11

Let me be *b* there, and all our kings, „ III i 208

Buried (verb) traitor-brother, Tostig, him Reverently we *b*. „ IV iii 85

Burn but I and my old woman 'ud *b* upon it, *Queen Mary* I i 56

her hate Will *b* till you are burn'd. „ I ii 59

I wrote it, and God grant me power to *b* ! „ I ii 99

Monstrous ! blasphemous ! She ought to *b*. „ I v 58

and *b* the throne Where you should sit with Philip : „ I v 509

Let the dead letter *b* ! „ III iii 44

If we could *b* out heresy, my Lord Paget, „ III iv 53

yet I would not say *B* ! and we cannot *b* whole towns ; „ III iv 175

many of them Would *b*—have burnt each other ; „ III iv 217

Would'st thou not *b* and blast them root and branch ? „ III iv 282

He'll *b* a diocese to prove his orthodoxy. „ III iv 353

Smiles that *b* men. „ III iv 404

they play with fire as children do, And *b* the house. „ III vi 30

Gardiner *b's*, And Bonner *b's* ; „ III vi 59

Did not More die, and Fisher ? he must *b*. „ IV i 53

The better for him. He *b's* in Purgatory, not in Hell. „ IV i 56

The heretic must *b*. „ IV i 123

But if you *b* him,—well, your Highness knows „ IV i 144

It were more merciful to *b* him now. „ IV i 153

Philip's will, and mine, that he should *b*. „ IV i 186

It is against all precedent to *b* One who recants ; „ IV ii 49

Well, *b* me or not *b* me I am fixt ; „ IV ii 54

Will they *b* me, Thirlby ? „ IV ii 181

And they will surely *b* me ? „ IV ii 190

Burn (*continued*)   he was deliver'd To the secular arm
to *b*;   *Queen Mary* IV ii 214
You shall *b* too, B first when I am burnt.   „   IV ii 220
What sort of brothers then be those that lust To *b*
each other ?   „   IV iii 198
And watch a good man *b*.   „   IV iii 293
all her burnins' 'ill never *b* out the hypocrisy   „   IV iii 525
There's nought but the vire of God's hell ez can *b*
out that.   „   IV iii 527
'll *b* the Pwoap out o' this 'ere land vor iver and iver. „   IV iii 535
B more !   *Mary.*   I will, I will ; and you will stay ? „   v i 103
They know nothing ; They *b* for nothing.   „   v ii 114
Thou hast burnt others, do thou *b* thyself, Or I will
b thee ; '   „   v ii 176
Seize him and *b* him for a Lutheran.   „   v ii 245
How her hand *b's* ! (repeat)   „   v ii 552, 616
Gardiner *b's* Already ; but to pay them full in kind,   „   v iv 13
sir, in Guernsey, I watch'd a woman *b* ;   „   v iv 18
And *b* the tares with unquenchable fire !   *B* !—
Fie, what a savour !   „   v v 114
but take back thy ring.   It *b's* my hand—   *Harold* III ii 186
They *b* themselves *within*-door.   *Becket* I i 289
grow to such a heat As *b's* a wrong to ashes,   *Foresters* II i 700
Burn (born)   But I taäkes 'im fur a bad lot and a *b*
fool,   *Prom. of May* I 153
but I taäkes 'im for a Lunnun swindler, and a *b* fool.   „   I 309
b a plowman, and now, as far as money goäs,   „   I 330
afoor ony o' ye wur *b*—ye all knaws the ten aäcre—   „   I 366
but I were *b* afoor schoolin-time.   „   III 40
Burn'd   (*See also* **Burnt**)   her hate Will burn till you
are *b*.   *Queen Mary* I ii 59
b, boil'd, buried alive, worried by dogs ;   „   II i 210
Hooper *b* Three-quarters of an hour.   „   IV ii 226
hand ! '   So held it till it all was *b*,   „   IV ii 615
Burner   are profitless to the *b's*, And help the other side. „   IV ii 219
My fancy takes the *b's* part,   „   IV ii 231
Burnin'   my rheumatizy be that bad howiver be I to
win to the *b*.   „   IV iii 474
wi' dree hard eggs for a good pleace at the *b* ;   „   IV iii 490
but all her *b's* 'ill niver burn out the hypocrisy   „   IV iii 524
the *b* o' the owld archbishop 'll burn   „   IV iii 535
Burning (part.)   (*See also* **A-burnin'**)   Ridley was longer *b* ;
but he died As manfully   „   IV iii 342
Burning (s)   (*See also* **Burnin'**)   bad my chaplain, Castro,
preach Against these *b's*.   „   III vi 75
His learning makes his *b* the more just.   „   IV i 159
these *b's* will not help The purpose of the faith ;   „   IV ii 183
'twas you That sign'd the *b* of poor Joan of Kent ;   „   IV ii 206
these *b's*, As Thirlby says, are profitless to the burners, „   IV ii 217
You have not gone to see the *b* ?   „   IV iii 290
I warrant you they talk about the *b*.   „   IV iii 463
you bring the smoke Of Cranmer's *b* with you.   „   IV iii 562
this cup rescued from the *b* of one of her shrines   *The Cup* I i 41
Burnish'd   I'll have it *b* firelike ;   *Queen Mary* I v 373
I flash out at times Of festival like *b* summer-flies, *Foresters* II i 276
Burnt   (*See also* **Burn'd**)   I'll have you flogg'd and *b* too, *Queen Mary* I i 60
she said that no one in her time should be *b* for heresy. „   I i 97
I'll have their bibles *b*.   The bible is the priest's.   „   III i 285
many of them Would burn—have *b* each other ;   „   III iv 217
It would have *b* both speakers.   „   III vi 164
Burn first when I am *b*.   „   IV ii 222
my hand shall first be *b* ; So I may come to the fire.   „   IV iii 250
When we had come where Ridley *b* with Latimer,   „   IV iii 585
Thou hast *b* others, do thou burn thyself,   „   v ii 176
hands that write them should be *b* clean off As Cranmer's, „   v ii 191
Gardiner, out of love for him, *B* it,   „   v ii 503
We have but *b* The heretic priest,   „   v v 105
Sir, you were *b* for heresy, not for treason,   „   v v 139
sacred shrine By chance was *b* along with it.   *The Cup* I ii 66
And a salt wind *b* the blossoming trees ;   *Prom. of May* I 57
Burrow   far-off *b* where the King Would miss her and
for ever.   *Becket* IV ii 158
Burrowing   the wild boar, The *b* badger—   *Foresters* III i 121
Burst (adj.)   And like a river in flood thro' a *b* dam   *Harold* II ii 466
Burst (s)   This *b* and bass of loyal harmony, *Queen Mary* II ii 285

Burst (verb)   (*See also* **Bust**)   in that last inhospitable
plunge Our boat hath *b* her ribs ;   *Harold* II i 3
Hot-headed fools—to *b* the wall of shields !   „   v i 612
Fly, fly, my lord, before they *b* the doors !   *Becket* v iii 56
Bursten   *b* at the toes, and down at heels.   *Queen Mary* I i 52
Burthen (load)   the monk-king, Louis, our former *b*, *Becket* IV iii 306
One slow, fat, white, a *b* of the hearth ;   „   v ii 211
grave he goes to, Beneath the *b* of years.   *Prom. of May* III 517
Bow'd to the dust beneath the *b* of sin.   „   III 521
Burthen (refrain)   That is the *b* of it—lost and found   *Harold* III ii 9
Bury   *B* him and his paramour together.   *Foresters* II i 312
b me in the mound, says the woman.   „   vii 150
let him *b* her Even in the bowels of the earth   „   III 461
Bush   like a timorous beast of prey Out of the *b* by night ? *Harold* I ii 214
A man may hang gold bracelets on a *b*,   „   II i 88
To catch the bird again within the *b* !   „   II ii 67
A nest in a *b*.   *Becket.*   And where, my liege ? *Becket, Pro.* 155
stray'd From love's clear path into the common *b*,   „   III i 248
Miss Eva, she set the *b* by my dairy winder   *Prom. of May* II 18
Softly ! softly ! there may be a thief in every *b*. *Foresters* I 368
Crouch all into the *b* !   „   IV 596
Business (adj.)   whether thou be Hedgar, or Hedgar's
b man,   *Prom. of May* II 735
Business (s)   pray'd me to confess In Wyatt's *b*, *Queen Mary* III v 167
Your Grace's *b* will not suffer, sire,   „   III vi 244
Sire, the *b* Of thy whole kingdom waits me :   *Becket, Pro.* 277
Well, *b*.   I must leave you, love, to-day.   *Prom. of May* I 624
for as I used to transact all his *b* for him,   „   II 719
whether thou be Hedgar, or Hedgar's business man,
thou hesn't naw *b* 'ere wi' *my* Dora,   „   II 735
I trust I may be able by-and-by to help you in the
b of the farm ;   „   III 223
That *b* which we have in Nottingham—   *Foresters* III 229
And may your *b* thrive in Nottingham !   „   III 244
Buss   *B* me, my bird !   *The Falcon* 28
Bussing   *See* **A-bussin'**
Bust   *b* of Juno and the brows and eyes Of Venus ; *The Cup* I i 120
Bust (burst)   he be fit to *b* hissen wi' spites and
jalousies.   *Prom. of May* II 164
Let 'im *b* hissen, then, for owt *I* cares.   „   II 166
Bustle   gather your men—Myself must *b*.   *Queen Mary* II iv 374
Butcher   they call me now, The scourge and *b*   „   v ii 106
What, Mr. Dobson ?   A *b's* frock ?   *Prom. of May* I 94
Butt   This Barbarossa *b's* him from his chair, *Becket, Pro.* 217
Butter   Our Daisy's *b's* as good 'z hern.   *Queen Mary* IV iii 481
the making of your *b*, and the managing of your
poultry ?   *Prom. of May* I 93
Butterfly   like a *b* in a chrysalis, You spent your life ; *Queen Mary* I iv 51
but now I called you *b*.   „   I iv 66
I love not to be called a *b* : Why do you call me *b* ?   „   I iv 68
Wi' the *butterflies* out, and the swallers at plaäy, *Prom. of May* II 198
waded in the brook, ran after the *butterflies*,   „   III 275
Buy   Gardiner *b's* them With Philip's gold.   *Queen Mary* I i 144
B you their cheeses, and they'll side with you ;   „   IV iii 548
if we *will b* diamond necklaces To please our lady, *The Falcon* 44
And sold thine own To *b* it for her.   „   77
but I couldn't *b* my darter back ageän when she
lost hersen,   *Prom. of May* III 453
How hadst thou then the means to *b* a cow ?   *Foresters* I 304
Would *b* me for a thousand marks in gold—   „   IV 652
Who thought to *b* your marrying me with gold.   „   IV 718
Buzz (s)   Little doubt This *b* will soon be silenced ; *Queen Mary* v i 293
We make but one hour's *b*,   *Foresters* II i 277
Buzz (verb)   Bee mustn't *b*, Whoop—but ne knows.
(repeat)   *Becket* III i 98, 240
Thy bee should *b* about the Court of John.   *Foresters* IV 44
Buzzard (adj.)   His *b* beak and deep-incavern'd eyes *Queen Mary* I v 266
Buzzard (s)   Hawk, *b*, jay, the mavis and the merle, *Foresters* I iii 115
Buzzed   Were freely *b* among them.   *Queen Mary* II ii 98
The bee *b* up in the heat.   *Foresters* IV 14
And the bee *b* down from the heat.   „   IV 20
And the bee *b* up in the cold   „   IV 21
And the bee *b* off in the cold.   „   IV 27
Buzzing   were more than I *b* round the blossom— *Becket, Pro.* 521
For ever *b* at your lady's face.   *Foresters* IV 11

EE*

By-and-by   I trust I shall forgive him—*b-a-b*—not now.   *Prom. of May* II 466
She said herself She would forgive him, *b-a-b*, not now—For her own sake *then*, if not for mine—not now—But *b-a-b*.   „   II 681
B-a-b—eh, lad, dosta knaw this paäper?   „   II 686
Eh, lad, dosta knaw what tha meäns wi' *b-a-b* ?   „   II 691
then, *b-a-b*, if she weänt listen to me when I be a-tryin' to saäve 'er—   „   II 693
I trust I may be able *b-a-b* to help you in the business of the farm;   „   III 222
Let me rest. I'll call you *b a b*.   *Becket* v i 90
Byblow   The Falaise *b* !   *Harold* IV iii 174
Bygone (adj.)   and smile At *b* things till that eternal peace.   *The Cup* I iii 172
Bygone (s)   Let *b's* be *b's*. Go home ! Good-night !   *Prom. of May* III 156
By-thing   These are *b-t's* In the great cause.   *Becket* III iii 11
The *b-t's* of the Lord Are the wrong'd innocences   „   III iii 13
Byway   The leprous flutterings of the *b*,   *Queen Mary* IV iii 76
From all the hidden *b-w's* of the world   *Becket* III iii 15
Byword   I am a *b*. Heretic and rebel Point at me   *Queen Mary* V ii 316

C

Cabin   Show me some cave or *c* where I may rest   *Foresters* II i 130
Cackling   What are you *c* of bastardy under   *Queen Mary* I i 58
Cadaver   Perinde ac *c*—as the priest says,   „   I iv 180
Cade   And he will prove an Iden to this *C*,   „   II ii 369
Cæsar   (*See also* Scizzars)   kindly rendering Of ' Render unto *C*.'   *Harold* III ii 168
the first Christian *C* drew to the East   „   v i 22
make the soil For *C's*, Cromwells, and Napoleons   *Prom. of May* III 593
Cage   pounce like a wild beast out of his *c*   *Queen Mary* I i 88
It is the heat and narrowness of the *c*   „   III v 207
I whistle to the bird has broken *c*, And all in vain.   „   v v 20
To guard this bird of passage to her *c* ;   *Becket* I i 329
I have lived, poor bird, from *c* to *c*,   „   III i 222
fondest pair of doves will jar, Ev'n in a *c* of gold,   „   IV ii 42
barred thee up in thy chamber, like a bird in a *c*.   *Foresters* I i 315
Cage (verb)   Catch the wild cat, *c* him, and when he springs   *Queen Mary* v v 65
Cain   And mark'd me ev'n as *C*,   „   III ii 55
light darkness, Abel *C*, The soul the body,   *Becket* I iii 716
Thou the lustiest and lousiest of this *C's* brotherhood, answer.   „   I iv 185
With *C's* answer, my lord. Am I his keeper ? Thou shouldst call him *C*, not me.   „   I iv 186
With *C* belike, in the land of Nod,   „   I iv 195
Caitiff   From councillor to *c*—fallen so low,   *Queen Mary* IV iii 75
Ay, go in peace, *c, c* !   *Becket* I iii 735
Cake   He speaks As if it were a *c* of gingerbread.   „   II i 230
Caked   And *c* and plaster'd with a hundred mires,   *Harold* IV iii 177
Calais   withdraw Part of our garrison at *C*. Mary. *C* !   *Queen Mary* IV i 123
take mine eyes, mine heart, But do not lose me *C*.   „   I v 129
C is but ill-garrison'd, in Guisnes   „   v i 4
Or you will lose your *C*.   „   v i 11
And you must look to *C* when I go.   „   v i 17
Is *C* taken ?   „   v ii 27
sharper harm to England and to Rome, Than *C* taken.   „   v ii 30
Madam, *C* is taken.   „   v ii 241
that our brave English Had sallied out from *C*   „   v ii 256
Let every craft that carries sail and gun Steer toward *C*.   „   v ii 276
Ah ! much heresy Shelter'd in *C*.   „   v ii 299
angry chronicles hereafter By loss of *C*. Grant me *C*.   „   v ii 305
C gone—Guisnes gone, too—and Philip gone !   „   v v 22
you will find written Two names, Philip and *C* ;   „   v v 155
Calcined   fain had *c* all Northumbria To one black ash,   *Harold* I i 56
Calculated   —all seen,—all *c*, All known by Rome.   *The Cup* I ii 255
Calender   In Britain's *c* the brightest day   *Queen Mary* III ii 118
Calf (of the leg)   Prick 'em in the *calves* with the arrow-points—prick 'em in the *calves*.   *Foresters* IV 560
Prick him in the *calves* !   „   IV 567
Calf (young of the cow, etc.)   By God's death, thou shalt stick him like a *c* !   *Becket* I iii 184
but Salisbury was a *c* cowed by Mother Church,   „   III iii 95

Calf (young of the cow, etc.) (*continued*)   the fatting of your *calves*, the making of your butter,   *Prom. of May* II 93
Calixtus (the first, Pope)   The day of St. *C*, and the day,   *Harold* v i 121
Call (s)   There's no *c* As yet for me ;   *Queen Mary* II i 24
and no *c* for sonnet-sorting now,   „   II i 59
God grant you ampler mercy at your *c*   „   IV i 189
Heaven curse him if he come not at your *c* !   *Prom. of May* I 765
He did it so well there was no *c* for me.   *Foresters* II i 548
Call (verb)   let me *c* her our second Virgin Mary,   *Queen Mary* I iii 57
C him a Knight, That, with an ass's,   „   I iii 167
Why do you *c* me butterfly ?   „   I iv 69
They *c* him cold, Haughty, ay, worse.   „   I v 431
I do not love your Grace should *c* me coward.   „   II iv 89
Why do they *c* him so ?   „   III i 199
I cannot tell you why they *c* him so.   „   III i 205
You *c* me too black-blooded—   „   III i 347
William the Silent They *c* him—   „   III ii 193
Or a high-dropsy, as the doctors *c* it.   „   III ii 225
We come not to compel, but *c* again ;   „   III iii 187
c they not The one true faith, a loathsome idol-worship ?   „   III iv 218
And let him *c* me truckler.   „   III iv 355
Nor shame to *c* it nature.   „   III v 77
New learning as they *c* it ;   „   IV i 78
Ay—gentle as they *c* you—live or die !   „   IV ii 161
Did I *c* him heretic ? A huge heresiarch !   „   IV iii 45
if thou *c* on God and all the saints,   „   IV iii 96
so past martyr-like—Martyr I may not *c* him—   „   IV iii 625
Ay, ay ; but many voices *c* me hence.   „   v i 32
What voices *c* you Dearer than mine   „   v i 36
He *c's* us worse than Jews, Moors, Saracens.   „   v i 150
they *c* me now, The scourge and butcher of their English church.   „   v ii 104
They *c* him away : Ye do him wrong,   *Harold* I ii 14
C it to temporize ; and not to lie ;   „   II ii 415
They *c* me near, for I am close to thee   „   III i 6
C me not King, but Harold.   „   III ii 33
He *c's* us little !   „   IV i 41
Somewhere hard at hand. *C* and she comes.   „   IV i 186
What did the dead man *c* it—Sanguelac,   „   v i 184
C when the Norman moves—   „   v i 229
C not for help from me. I knew him not.   „   v ii 54
what shall I *c* it, affect her thine own self.   *Becket*, *Pro.* 513
As Canterbury *c's* them, wandering clouds,   „   I iii 70
Or constitutions, or whate'er ye *c* them,   „   I iii 138
C in the poor from the streets, and let them feast.   „   I iv 72
C in the poor !   „   I iv 78
C them in, I say.   „   I iv 85
Buck ; deer, as you *c* it.   „   I iv 139
Thou shouldst *c* him Cain, not me.   „   I iv 188
I'll *c* thee little Geoffrey. *C* him !   „   II i 214
See if our pious—what shall I *c* him, John ?—   „   II ii 38
Ay, ay, good brother, They *c* you the Monk-King.   „   II ii 73
Who *c's* me ? she That was my wife,   „   II ii 74
if the city be sick, and I cannot *c* the kennel sweet,   „   II ii 348
They *c* thee John the Swearer.   „   II ii 462
whom you *c*—fancy—my husband's brother's wife.   „   III i 202
They *c* her—But she lives secret, you see.   „   IV i 11
What does she *c* him ? Geoffrey. My liege.   „   IV i 18
whom it pleases him To *c* his wives ;   „   IV ii 37
She *c's* you beauty, but I don't like her looks.   „   IV ii 61
Like the wild beast—if you can *c* it love.   „   IV ii 121
Let me rest. I'll *c* you by and by.   „   v i 90
Then you have done it, and I *c* *you* cruel.   „   v ii 135
I know not why You *c* these old things back   „   v ii 270
c's you oversea To answer for it in his Norman courts.   „   v ii 354
Who is our guest ? Sinnatus. Strato he *c's* himself.   *The Cup* I ii 48
they *c* it so in Rome. Sinnatus. Province !   „   II i 93
C first upon the Goddess, Synorix.   „   II 256
I *c* thee To make my marriage prosper to my wish !   „   II 307
I *c* on our own Goddess in our own Temple.   „   II 314
Speak freely, tho' to *c* a madman mad   *The Falcon* 81
if your lordship care to *c* for it.   „   139
C him back and say I come to breakfast with him.   „   211
my nobleness Of nature, as you deign to *c* it,   „   811
he cooms up, and he *c's* out among our oän men,   *Prom. of May* I 139

Careless (*continued*)   like a *c* sleeper in the down;   *Foresters* I ii 207
Caress   in some lewd *c* Has wheedled it off the King's neck   *Becket* IV ii 200
Carew (*See also* **Peter Carew**)   I do not hear from *C* or the Duke Of Suffolk,   *Queen Mary* II i 2
    C stirs In Devon: „   II i 4
    I must not move Until I hear from *C* and the Duke.   „   II i 122
    C is there, and Thomas Stafford there.   „   v i 125
Carle   little help without our Saxon *c*'s Against Hardrada.   *Harold* IV i 35
Carlos   But is Don *C* such a goodly match?   *Queen Mary* v iii 86
    Don *C*, Madam, is but twelve years old.   „   v iii 87
    Don *C*? Madam, if you marry Philip,   „   v iii 117
Carnage   So packt with *c* that the dykes and brooks   *Harold* III ii 128
Carpet   Lay down the Lydian *c*'s for the king.   *The Cup* II 187
Carried   Bonner, it will be *c*.   *Queen Mary* III iv 405
    I ha' *c* him ever so many miles in my arms,   *Becket* IV i 98
    drop The mud I *c*, like yon brook,   „   II i 159
    c off the casks, Kill'd half the crew,   „   v ii 442
    one shock upon the field when all The harvest has been *c*.   *The Falcon* 302
    you kept your veil too close for that when they *c* you in;   *Prom. of May* III 227
Carrier-pigeon   And thou, my *c-p* of black news,   *Harold* IV iii 233
Carriest   who art more bow-bent than the very bow thou *c*?   *Foresters* II 379
Carrion (*adj.*)   didst thou ever see a *c* crow Stand watching a sick beast   *Queen Mary* IV iii 6
    and dumb'd his *c* croak From the gray sea for ever.   *Harold* IV iii 65
    I'd think na moor o' maäkin' an end o' tha nor a *c* craw—   *Prom. of May* II 697
Carrion (*s*)   And rolls himself in *c* like a dog.   *Queen Mary* I v 169
Carrion-nosing   Made even the *c-n* mongrel vomit   „   IV iii 448
Carrot   Like a *c*'s, as thou say'st, and English *c*'s better   „   III 218
Carry   I trust that he will *c* you well to-day,   „   I iv 145
    For all that I can *c* it in my head.   „   II i 88
    If you can *c* your head upon your shoulders.   „   II i 89
    I fear you come to *c* it off my shoulders,   „   II i 91
    that every Spaniard *carries* a tail like a devil   „   III i 223
    Let every craft that *carries* sail and gun   „   v ii 275
    C her off among you;   *Becket*, Pro. 524
    We shall be overwhelm'd. Seize him and *c* him!   „   v iii 142
    C fresh rushes into the dining-hall,   *Foresters* I i 80
    C her off, and let the old man die.   „   IV 677
    Seize him and truss him up, and *c* her off.   „   IV 690
    Seize her and *c* her off into my castle.   „   IV 738
Cart   fur she tell'd ma to taäke the *c* to Littlechester.   *Prom. of May* II 322
    Dan Smith's *c* hes runned ower a laädy i' the holler laäne.   „   II 568
    Besides it was you that were driving the *c*—   „   II 88
    our horse and our little *c*—   *Foresters* II i 192
Carter   our *c*'s and our shepherds Still find a comfort there. *Harold*. *C*'s and shepherds!   *Prom. of May* III 527
    „   II 138
Cartwhip   and doänt laäy my *c* athurt 'is shou'ders,   *Queen Mary* II iv 110
Carve   And *c* my coat upon the walls again!   *Foresters* I i 42
    to *c* One lone hour from it,   *Harold* v i 512
Casa   *C* crematur, Pastor fugatur   *Queen Mary* IV iii 167
Case   And first I say it is a grievous *c*,   *Becket* II i 347
    Is that my *c*? so if the city be sick,   „   III iii 67
    as the *c* stood, you had safelier have slain an archbishop than a she-goat:
Casement   moonlight *c*'s pattern'd on the wall,   *Queen Mary* v v 9
    Ay! yonder is her *c*.   *Prom. of May* II 246
    storm and shower lashing Her *c*,   „   II 473
    Then I would drop from the *c*, like a spider.   *Foresters* I i 317
Cask   carried off the *c*'s, Kill'd have the crew,   *Becket* v ii 443
    c of wine whereof we plunder'd The Norman prelate?   *Foresters* III 306
Casket   Close as a miser's *c*. Listen: *Queen Mary* I iv 108
    Hand me the *c* with my father's sonnets.   „   II i 43
Cast   *C* off, betray'd, defamed, divorced, forlorn!   „   I v 26
    C myself down upon my knees before them,   „   I v 562
    come to *c* herself On loyal hearts and bosoms,   „   II ii 261
    She *c* on him a vassal smile of love,   „   II i 98
    pine in Italy that *c* its shadow Athwart a cataract;   „   III iv 136
    to *c* myself Upon the good Queen's mercy;   „   III v 167
    and then *C* on the dunghill naked,   „   IV iii 446
    The Pope would *c* the Spaniard out of Naples: „   v i 148

Cast (*continued*)   His early follies *c* into his teeth,   *Queen Mary* v ii 124
    C it o'er again.   „   v iii 4
    Did ye not *c* with bestial violence   *Harold* I i 49
    I *c* me down prone, praying;   „   v i 100
    I *c* upon the side of Canterbury—   *Becket* I i 155
    Let either *c* him away like a dead dog!   „   II ii 257
    black cloud that hath come over the sun and *c* us all into shadow?   „   III iii 47
    your own people *c* you from their bounds,   *The Cup* I i 137
    His own true people *c* him from their doors   „   I ii 351
    I cannot help the mould that I was *c* in.   „   I iii 25
    Might *c* my largess of it to the crowd!   „   II 224
    knaw'd better nor to *c* her sister's misfortin inter 'er teeth   *Prom. of May* II 127
    Be not so *c* down, my sweet Eva.   „   III 468
    Would you *c* An eye of favour on me,   *Foresters* I ii 216
    That if I *c* an eye of favour on him,   „   I ii 261
    to *c* All threadbare household habit,   „   I iii 111
    C them into our treasury, the beggars' mites,   „   III 204
Castaly   wells of *C* are not wasted upon the desert.   *Becket*, Pro. 387
Castille   voices of *C* and Aragon, Granada,   *Queen Mary* v i 42
Castle (*adj.*)   All in the *c* garden,   *Foresters* I i 10
Castle (*s*)   (*See also* **Sand-castle**)   Ah, gray old *c* of Alington,   *Queen Mary* II i 243
    They have built their *c*'s here;   *Harold* III i 36
    he holp the King to break down our *c*'s,   *Becket*, Pro. 447
    De Tracy and De Brito, from our *c*.   „   I i 278
    Lord Fitzurse reported this In passing to the *C* even now.   „   I ii 13
    You are going to the *C*,   „   I ii 45
    My drift is to the *C*, Where I shall meet the Barons   „   I ii 83
    To the *C*? *De Broc*. Ay!   „   I ii 86
    thou, De Broc, that holdest Saltwood *C*—   „   I iii 160
    Due from his *c*'s of Berkhamstead and Eye   „   I iii 628
    Here is a missive left at the gate by one from the *c*.   „   I iv 50
    Our *c*, my lord, belongs to Canterbury.   „   II ii 261
    cursed those De Brocs That hold our Saltwood *C*   „   II ii 269
    Perchance the fierce De Brocs from Saltwood *C*,   „   v ii 249
    dungeon'd the other half In Pevensey *C*—   „   v ii 446
    Undo the doors: the Church is not a *c*:   „   v iii 63
    came back last night with her son to the *c*.   *The Falcon* 4
    there is Monna Giovanna coming down the hill from the *c*.   „   161
    mount with your lordship's leave to her ladyship's *c*,   „   414
    Not like the vintage blowing round your *c*.   „   580
    Shall I return to the *c* with you?   „   793
    I would set my men-at-arms to oppose thee, like the Lord of the *C*.   *Foresters* I i 324
    and seeing the hospitable lights in your *c*,   „   I i 195
    he hath seized On half the royal *c*'s.   „   I iii 83
    whereon she struck him, And fled into the *c*.   „   II i 118
    Seize her and carry her off into my *c*.   „   IV 738
    Thy *c*? (repeat)   *Foresters* IV 739, 743
Castro   I bad my chaplain, *C*, preach Against these burnings.   *Queen Mary* III vi 73
Cat   Catch the wild *c*, cage him, and when he springs   „   v v 65
    He hath as much of *c* as tiger in him.   *Harold* I i 154
    Milk? *Filippo*. Three laps for a *c*!   *The Falcon* 125
    And a *c* to the cream, and a rat to the cheese;   *Prom. of May* I 53
    If a *c* may look at a king, may not a friar speak to one?   *Foresters* IV 921
Cataract (*See also* **Winter-cataracts**)   A pine in Italy that cast its shadow Athwart a *c*; firm stood the pine—The *c* shook the shadow.   *Queen Mary* III iv 137
    c typed the headlong plunge and fall Of heresy   „   III iv 140
Catch   I cannot *c* what Father Bourne is saying.   „   I iii 14
    We have our spies abroad to *c* her tripping,   „   I v 468
    there's no Renard here to '*c* her tripping.' *C* me who can; yet, sometime I have wish'd That I were caught,   „   III v 159
    C the wild cat, cage him, and when he springs   „   v v 65
    Fellow, dost thou *c* crabs?   *Harold* I i 66
    I have a mind that thou shalt *c* no more.   „   II i 71
    To *c* the bird again within the bush!   „   II ii 67
    flings His brand in air and *c*'es it again,   „   v i 494
    You *c* 'em, so, Softly, and fling them out to the free air.   *Becket* I i 286

Catch (*continued*)   and they do say the very breath *c'es.*   *Becket* I iv 222
   thy flock should *c* An after ague-fit of trembling.   ,, III iii 32
   Take thy one chance ;   *C* at the last straw.   ,, IV ii 221
   and a-spreading to *c* her eye for a dozen year,   *The Falcon* 100
   c A glimpse of them and of their fairy Queen—   *Foresters* II 102
   And *c* the winding of a phantom horn.   ,, IV 1091
Catechize   But who art thou to *c* me—   ,, III 14
Catharine   (*first queen of Henry VIII.*)   you divorced
   Queen *C* and her father;   *Queen Mary* I ii 57
   accursed lie Of good Queen *C's* divorce—   ,, III iv 232
Cathedral   nor any ground but English, Where his *c*
   stands.   *Becket* III iii 262
   Take refuge in your own *c*, (repeat)   ,, v ii 584, 590
   Strike our Archbishop in his own *c* !   ,, v iii 180
Catholic (*adj.*)   But if this Philip, the proud *C*
   prince,   *Queen Mary* I iv 280
   where you gave your hand To this great *C* King.   ,, III ii 92
   Can we not have the *C* church as well   ,, III iii 97
   Which in the *C* garden are as flowers,   ,, IV i 178
   Have you remain'd in the true *C* faith I left you
   in ?   *Cranmer.*   In the true *C* faith,   ,, IV ii 17
   Yet wherefore should he die that hath return'd To
   the one *C* Universal Church,   ,, IV iii 21
   In every article of the *C* faith,   ,, IV iii 230
   Peters, you know me *C*, but English.   ,, IV iii 566
   The Queen of Scots at least is *C*.   *Philip.*   Ay,
   Madam, *C* ;   ,, v i 195
   But—he would have me *C* of Rome,   ,, v iii 93
Catholic (*s*)   for we are many of us *C's*, but few
   Papists,   ,, I i 114
   a pious *C*, Mumbling and mixing up in his scared
   prayers   ,, II ii 85
   there be some disloyal *C's*, And many heretics loyal;   ,, III iv 43
   tho' a *C*, I would not, For the pure honour of our
   common nature,   ,, IV iii 296
   I do hold The *C*, if he have the greater right,   ,, IV iii 382
   Peters, my gentleman, an honest *C*,   ,, IV iii 553
   It is a saying among the *C's*.   ,, v v 245
Cattle   Hath harried mine own *c*—God confound him !   *Harold* IV iii 190
Caught   (*See also* **Cotched**)   And then if *c*, to the
   Tower.   *Queen Mary* I v 469
   sometime I have wish'd That I were *c*,   ,, III v 163
   He *c* a chill in the lagoons of Venice,   ,, v ii 515
   if I *c* them, they should hang Cliff-gibbeted   *Harold* II i 95
   I shame to quote 'em—*c*, my lord,   *Becket* I ii 7
   King's verdurer *c* him a-hunting in the forest,   ,, I iv 95
   Not *c*, maim'd, blinded him.   *The Cup* I ii 271
   when you put it in green, and your stack *c* fire.   *Prom. of May* II 56
   I am outlaw'd, and if *c*, I die.   *Foresters* I iii 163
   He *c* her round the waist,   ,, II i 116
   You *c* a lonely woodman of our band,   ,, III 359
   and the hunters, if *c*, are blinded, or worse than blinded.   ,, IV 226
Cause (*s*)   you had time and *c* enough To sicken   *Queen Mary* I v 23
   the *c* that hath brought us together is not the *c*   ,, II ii 160
   under colour Of such a *c* as hath no colour,   ,, II ii 183
   This was the *c*, and hence the judgment on her.   ,, III iv 187
   Crave, in the same *c*, hearing of your Grace.   ,, IV i 8
   Behold him, brethren : he hath *c* to weep !—   ,, IV iii 14
   thro' the fear of death Gave up his *c*,   ,, IV iii 28
   there *c's* Wherefore our Queen and Council   ,, IV iii 35
   Much less shall others in like *c* escape,   ,, IV iii 62
   I come to the great *c* that weighs Upon my conscience   ,, IV iii 237
   I will move then in your *c* again,   ,, v i 178
   and mine own natural man (It was God's *c*) ;   ,, v ii 104
   We fought like great states for grave *c* ;   *Harold* I i 441
   I have given her *c*—I fear no woman.   ,, I ii 41
   For thou hast done the battle in my *c* ;   ,, II ii 555
   Refer my *c*, my crown to Rome ! . . .   ,, v i 1
   ' All *c's* of advowsons and presentations,   *Becket* I iii 78
   For the King's pleasure rather than God's *c*   ,, I iii 698
   My lord, We have claspt your *c*,   ,, II ii 237
   That in thy *c* were stirr'd against King Henry,   ,, II ii 429
   These are by-things In the great *c*.   ,, III iii 12
   as one That mars a *c* with over-violence.   ,, IV iii 327
   In mine own *c* I strove against him there,   ,, v i 14

Cause (*s*) (*continued*)   And in thy *c* I strive against him now.   *Becket* v i 16
   I do commend my *c* to God, the Virgin,   ,, v iii 163
   not so much for the *c* as for the Earl.   *Foresters* I ii 38
   I cannot sleep o' nights by *c* on 'em.   ,, II i 384
   What rightful *c* could grow to such a heat   ,, II i 698
   I can defend my *c* against the traitors   ,, IV 898
Cause (*verb*)   always told Father that the huge old
   ashtree there would *c* an accident some
   day ;   *Prom. of May* III 245
Causest   Who *c* the safe earth to shudder and gape,   *The Cup* II 298
Cautery   mad bite Must have the *c*—tell him—   *Queen Mary* III iv 276
Cavalier   And Counts, and sixty Spanish *c's*,   ,, III i 51
Cave   seven sleepers in the *c* at Ephesus Have turn'd   *Harold* I i 192
   As find a hare's form in a lion's *c*.   *Becket* I iii 177
   Show me some *c* or cabin where I may rest.   *Foresters* II i 130
Cawved (*calved*)   Hes the cow *c* ?   *Dora.*   No,
   Father.   *Prom. of May* III 427
Cease   When will ye *c* to plot against my house ?   *Harold* IV i 161
   when I *c* To care for thee as ever !   *Becket* I i 121
   Well, well, until they *c* to go together,   *Foresters* II ii 67
Ceased   Until your throne had *c* to tremble.   *Queen Mary* I v 393
Cecil (**William, Baron Burghley, Queen Elizabeth's chief
   Minister**)   *C* . . . God guide me lest I lose the
   way.   ,, v v 209
   But with *C's* aid And others,   ,, v v 279
Cedar   now you are enclosed with boards of *c*,   ,, III ii 102
Cede   now and then to *c* A point to her demand ?   ,, III vi 169
Ceded   father *c* Naples, that the son Being a King,   ,, III i 74
Ceiling   under no *c* but the cloud that wept on them,   ,, v iv 39
Celebrate   —*c*—to *c* my birthdaäy i' this fashion.   *Prom. of May* I 321
   To *c* this advent of our King !   *Foresters* IV 1048
Celibate   Dan John, how much we lose, we *c's*,   *Becket* v ii 197
Cell   lash'd to death, or lie Famishing in black *c's*,   *Queen Mary* IV vi 196
   The cold, white lily blowing in her *c* :   *Harold* III i 274
   In cold, white *c's* beneath an icy moon—   ,, v i 325
Cellar   Our *c* is hard by.   Take him, good Little John,   *Foresters* II i 468
Censure   (*See also* **Church-censure**)   release from
   danger of all *c's* Of Holy Church   *Queen Mary* III iii 151
   All schism, and from all and every *c*,   ,, III iii 217
   I refuse to stand By the King's *c*,   *Becket* I iii 723
   pass the *c's* of the Church On those that crown'd   ,, v i 390
Centaur   That *C* of a monstrous Commonweal,   *Queen Mary* III iv 163
Central   Not ev'n the *c* diamond, worth, I think,   *Becket* v i 164
Centre   Henceforth a *c* of the living faith.   *Queen Mary* III i 155
   And oublietted in the *c*—No !   *Becket* IV ii 150
   weight of the very land itself, Down to the
   inmost *c*.   *Foresters* IV 1027
Century   fire that flashes out again From *c* to *c*,   *The Cup* I ii 167
Ceremony   Why do you palter with the *c* ?   ,, II 420
   But wherefore slur the perfect *c* ?   ,, II 431
Certain   I am not *c* but that Philibert Shall be the
   man ;   *Queen Mary* v i 263
   because I am not *c* : You understand, Feria.   ,, v i 268
   Would freely canvass *c* Lutheranisms.   ,, v ii 76
   I came on *c* wholesome usages,   *Becket* I iii 412
   No, no ! we have *c* news he died in prison.   *Foresters* IV 778
Chafe   Why *c* me then ?   *Harold* I i 296
Chain (*s*)   this golden *c*—My father on a birthday   *Queen Mary* I v 526
   c, Wherewith they bound him to the stake,   ,, IV iii 595
   here is a golden *c* I will give thee   *Becket* I v 40
   Thou art happier than thy king.   Put him in *c's*.   *Foresters* IV 838
Chain (*verb*)   This *c's* me to your service,   *Queen Mary* I v 537
   To *c* the free guest to the banquet-board ;   *Harold* II ii 193
   if he be conspirator, Rome will *c*, Or slay him.   *The Cup* I i 18
Chain'd   lying *c* In breathless dungeons over steam-
   ing sewers,   *Queen Mary* IV iii 439
Chair   (*See also* **Cheer**)   How deathly pale !—a *c*, your
   Highness.   ,, I v 636
   same *c*, Or rather throne of purple, on the deck.   ,, III ii 7
   The Eternal Peter of the changeless *c*,   ,, III iv 380
   Out friends, the Normans, help to shake his *c*.   *Harold* I i 86
   sat within the Norman *c* A ruler all for England—   ,, II i 533
   This Barbarossa butts him from his *c*,   *Becket, Pro.* 217
   let me place this *c* for your ladyship.   *The Falcon* 178
Chair'd   yea, and thou *C* in his place.   *Harold* I ii 247

Charge (to enjoin) (*continued*) Back ! back ! I *c* thee, back ! *Foresters* II i 425
Charge (to accuse) dare you *c* the King with treachery ? *Becket* v ii 396
Charge (to rush) and bidd'n him *C* one against a thousand, *Queen Mary* IV iii 309
Charged (enjoined) no, nor if the Pope, *C* him to do it— ,, IV iii 558
He *c* me not to question any of those About me. *Becket* II i 210
Charged (filled) Tho' *c* with all the wet of all the west. *Harold* II ii 188
C with the weight of heaven wherefrom they fall ! ,, v i 567
one So *c* with tongue, that every thread of thought *Becket* v ii 205
Charing Cross From *C C* ; the rebels broke us there, *Queen Mary* II iv 75
Charity sow'd therein The seed of Hate, it blossom'd *C*. ,, IV i 172
Let them flow forth in *c*, ,, IV iii 208
To rival him in Christian *c*. *Becket* III iii 233
Your Christian's Christian *c* ! ,, v ii 476
Perhaps you judge him With feeble *c* : *The Cup* I ii 186
Charles (V., King of Spain, Emperor) rumour that *C*, the master of the world, *Queen Mary* I i 104
He is every way a lesser man than *C*. ,, I v 330
My master, *C*, Bad you go softly with your heretics ,, I v 391
And *C*, the lord of this low world, is gone ; ,, v v 54
prattling to her mother Of her betrothal to the Emperor *C*, ,, v v 233
Charm (s) To draw him nearer with a *c* Like thine to thine. *Harold* I ii 8
more than one brave fellow owed His death to the *c* in it. *The Falcon* 635
with his *c* of simple style And close dialectic, *Prom. of May* I 223
And *her c* Of voice is also yours ; ,, II 380
and the country Has many *c*'s, ,, II 541
Might have more *c* for me than all the country. ,, II 553
True soul of the Saxon churl for whom their song has no *c*. *Foresters* II i 386
Charm (verb) In hope to *c* them from their hate of Spain. *Queen Mary* III vi 82
May serve to *c* the tiger out of him. *Harold* I i 153
kiss that *c*'s thine eyelids into sleep, ,, I ii 139
I do not then *c* this secret out of our loyal Thomas, *Becket*, Pro. 466
how to *c* and waste the hearts of men. *Foresters* II i 502
Charm'd that wilt not dance However wisely *c*. *Harold* I i 387
When you have *c* our general into mercy, *The Cup* I ii 311
How *c* he was ! what wonder ?—A gallant boy, *The Falcon* 318
ruddiest cheek That ever *c* the plowman of your wolds *Prom. of May* III 488
Charon Not be my *C* to the counter side ? *Queen Mary* III ii 149
Chart This *c* here mark'd ' *Her Bower*,' *Becket*, Pro. 160
but this Draws thro' the *c* to her. ,, Pro. 173
This *c* with the red line ! her bower ! ,, Pro. 308
The *c* is not mine, but Becket's : take it, Thomas. ,, Pro. 310
Fitzurse, that *c* with the red line—thou sawest it— ,, Pro. 427
c which Henry gave you With the red line— ,, I ii 60
Charter Your rights and *c*'s hobnail'd into slush— *Queen Mary* II ii 278
Where is the *c* of our Westminster ? *Harold* II i 194
Chase (s) thyself wast wont To love the *c* : ,, I i 228
More sacred than his forests for the *c* ? *Becket* IV ii 25
running down the *c* is kindlier sport Ev'n than the death. ,, IV ii 213
climb The mountain opposite and watch the *c*. *The Cup* I i 118
I am a life-long lover of the *c*, ,, I i 195
Roused by the clamour of the *c* he woke, ,, I i 117
Chased *C* deer-like up his mountains, *Harold* I ii 148
would have *c* the stag to-day In the full face *The Cup* I ii 267
I am *c* by my foes. *Foresters* II i 184
Chasm o'er the *c* I saw Lord William Howard *Queen Mary* II iii 28
and flatten in her closing *c* Domed cities, hear. *The Cup* II 300
Chaste *C* as your Grace ! *Queen Mary* I v 456
Your Grace hath a most *c* and loving wife. ,, III vi 129
The Queen of Philip should be *c*. ,, III vi 132
no wives like English wives So fair and *c* as they be. *Foresters* I i 16
Chasten'd So thou be *c* by thy banishment, *Harold* IV ii 50
Chastest Thro' *c* honour of the Decalogue *Becket* v 206
Chattel thou art dispossessed of all thy lands, goods, and *c*'s ; *Foresters* I iii 60
Chaumber (chamber) winder at the end o' the passage, that goäs by thy *c*. *Prom. of May* I 397
Did 'e git into thy *c* ? ,, I 400
they ha' ta'en the body up inter your *c*, ,, II 570
By haäfe a scoor o' naämes—out o' the *c*. ,, III 730

Chaumber (chamber) (*continued*) Out o' the *c* ! I'll mash tha into nowt. *Prom. of May* III 734
Out o' the *c*, dang tha ! ,, III 737
Check I never knew thee *c* thy will for ought *Harold* II ii 120
C—you move so wildly. *Becket*, Pro. 40
frost That help'd to *c* the flowing of the blood. *The Falcon* 645
Cheek you stroke me on one *c*, Buffet the other. *Queen Mary* II i 117
' Wyatt,' as red as she In hair and *c* ; ,, II ii 76
gave me a great pat o' the *c* for a pretty wench, *Becket* I i 125
a *c* like a peach and a heart like the stone in it— *The Falcon* 93
ruddiest *c* That ever charm'd the plowman of your wolds *Prom. of May* III 487
Here—give me one sharp pinch upon the *c* *Foresters* IV 1012
Cheeked *See* **Red-cheek'd**
Cheer (s) good *c* ! thou art Harold, I am Edith ! *Harold* v i 391
You, Strato, make good *c* till I return. *The Cup* I ii 20?
Yeas, yeas ! Three *c*'s for Mr. Steer ! *Prom. of May* I 455
Cheer (verb) And *c* his blindness with a traveller's tales ? ,, II 515
Cheer (chair) they wunt set i' the Lord's *c* o' that daäy. *Queen Mary* IV iii 470
Cheerful He, with a *c* smile, as one whose mind Is all made up, ,, IV iii 587
Cheerless Your people are as *c* as your clime ; ,, v i 83
For me, whose *c* Houris after death Are Night and Silence, *Prom. of May* I 249
Cheese Our Daisy's *c*'s be better. *Queen Mary* IV iii 484
Buy you their *c*'s, and they'll side with you ; ,, IV iii 548
C ! *Filippo*. A supper for twelve mites. *The Falcon* 126
And a cat to the cream, and a rat to the *c* ; *Prom. of May* I 54
Cherish'd *c* him Who thief-like fled from his own church *Becket* II ii 155
Cherubim golden *c* With twenty-cubit wings *Harold* II i 183
Chess The Game of *C*. (repeat) *Queen Mary* I iii 127
Strange game of *c* ! a King That with her own powers ,, I iii 161
Chessmen and these *c* on the floor— *Becket*, Pro. 313
Chest Did the *c* move ! did it move ? *Harold* II ii 799
Chichester Bishops—York, London, *C*, Westminster— *Becket* I iii 385
Chief (adj.) *C* prelate of our Church, archbishop, first In Council, *Queen Mary* IV iii 70
Before the Prince and *c* Justiciary, *Becket* II i 709
Did not some old Greek Say death was the *c* good ? *The Cup* II 515
Chief (s) The *c* of these outlaws who break the law ? *Foresters* IV 141
Child (*See also* **Childer, Children**) of the good Lady Jane as a poor innocent *c* *Queen Mary* I i 94
c by *c*, you know, Were momentary sparkles ,, I ii 71
I think she entreats me like a *c*. ,, I iii 112
she is but a *c*. We do not kill the *c* for doing that ,, I v 61
the *c* obey'd her father. ,, I v 493
perchance A *c* more innocent than Lady Jane. ,, I v 502
nursery-cocker'd *c* will jeer at aught ,, II ii 394
He is *c* and fool, and traitor to the State. ,, II ii 403
That if the Queen should die without a *c*, ,, III iii 75
no more rein upon thine anger Than any *c* ! ,, III iv 304
Threaten the *c* ; ' I'll scourge you if you did it : ' ,, III v 126
What weapon hath the *c*, save his soft tongue, ,, III v 128
I think the Queen may never bear a *c* ; ,, III v 232
So sick am I with biding for this *c*. Is it the fashion in this clime for women To go twelve months in bearing of a *c* ? ,, III vi 89
Her fierce desire of bearing him a *c*, ,, IV viii 429
Since she lost hope of bearing us a *c* ? ,, v i 230
Alice, my *c*, Bring us your lute. ,, v i 356
But the *c* came not, and the husband came not ; ,, v i 581
in her agony The mother came upon her—a *c* was born— ,, v iv 20
Now the spoilt *c* sways both. *Harold* I i 453
my *c* ; Thou hast misread this merry dream of thine, ,, I ii 97
tenfold, than this fearful *c* can do ; ,, I ii 143
But sickly, slight, half-witted and a *c*, ,, II ii 572
From *c* to *c*, from Pope to Pope, from age to age, ,, v 329
widow And orphan *c*, whom one of thy wild barons— *Becket*, Pro. 188
And when I was a *c*, The Virgin, ,, I i 52
The *c* Is there already. *Rosamund*. Yes—the *c*— the *c*— ,, I i 292
Who misuses a dog would misuse a *c*— ,, I iv 109
Why, the *c* will drown himself. ,, II i 322

Child (*continued*) And one fair *c* to fondle ! *Becket* III i 12
the *c* We waited for so long—heaven's gift at last— ,, III i 13
But then the *c* *is* such a *c*. ,, III i 20
what's an apple, you know, save to a *c*, and I'm no *c*, ,, III i 141
like the gravedigger's *c* I have heard of, trying to ring
the bell, ,, III iii 73
Thou art the prettiest *c* I ever saw. ,, IV i 7
Your own *c* brought me hither ! ,, IV ii 13
C, I am mine own self Of and belonging to the King. ,, IV ii 29
so it chances, *c*, That I am his main paramour, ,, IV ii 38
—my *c* is so young, So backward too ; ,, IV ii 84
But the *c* is so young. You have children—his ; And
mine is the King's *c* ; ,, IV ii 89
I follow'd You and the *c* : he babbled all the way. ,, IV ii 140
and make Thy body loathsome even to thy *c* ; ,, IV ii 172
The *c* . . No . . . mercy ! No ! ,, IV ii 185
His *c* and mine own soul, and so return. ,, V i 193
Lacking the love of woman and of *c*. ,, V iii 9
Save him, he saved my life, he saved my *c*, ,, V iii 9
A *c*'s sand-castle on the beach For the next wave— *The Cup* I i 253
that dost inspire the germ with life, The *c*, ,, II 259
and she, A girl, a *c*, then but fifteen, *The Falcon* 537
My one *c* Florio lying still so sick, ,, 678
best way out of it, if the *c* could keep Her counsel. *Prom. of May* I 476
when the man, The *c* of evolution, flings aside ,, I 585
C, do you love me now ? ,, I 640
For ever, you foolish *c* ! What's come over you ? ,, I 771
Ay, *c* ; and you look thin and pale. ,, I 781
Well, my *c*, let us join them. ,, I 796
So the *c* grow to manhood : ,, II 289
—she was his favourite *c*— ,, II 419
Our old nurse crying as if for her own *c*, ,, II 480
so that you do not copy his bad manners ? Go, *c*. ,, III 362
' My dear *C*,—I can do no more for you. ,, III 397
C, read a little history, you will find ,, III 542
C, can't you see ? Tell them to fly for a doctor. ,, III 711
A *c*, and all as trustful as a *c* ! ,, III 759
C, thou shouldst marry one who will pay the mortgage. *Foresters* I i 279
by this Holy Cross Which good King Richard gave me
when a *c*— ,, I ii 311
Nor leave a *c* behind him ' ,, II ii 113
Has never glanced upon me when a *c*. ,, IV 5
C, thou shalt wed him, Or thine old father will go mad— ,, IV 643
Childer (children) theer be a thousand i' the parish,
taäkin' in the women and *c*; *Prom. of May* I 146
Them be what they larns the *c*' at school, ,, III 39
Childhood Away from Philip, Back in her *c*— *Queen Mary* V v 231
Childish No—the *c* fist That cannot strike again. *Harold* III 30
Childless 'Tis written, ' They shall be *c*.' *Queen Mary* II ii 65
Evil for good, it seems, Is oft as *c* of the good *Harold* V i 172
Than all my *c* wealth, if mine must die. *The Falcon* 855
Childlike ask'd him, *c* : ' Will you take it off *Queen Mary* III i 401
great motion of laughter among us, part real,
part *c*, *Becket* III iii 155
part *c* again—when we felt we had laughed too long ,, III iii 159
Childlike-jealous And *c-j* of him again— *Queen Mary* V v 234
Children (*See also* **Child, Childer**) These princes are
like *c*, must be physick'd, ,, I v 234
Dumb *c* of my father, that will speak ,, II i 77
cannot tell How mothers love their *c* ; ,, II ii 190
naturally may love his people As these their *c* ; ,, II ii 193
The man had *c*, and he whined for those. ,, II iii 335
Away ! Women and *c* ! ,, III iii 97
So that we may, as *c* penitent, ,, III iii 153
Watch'd *c* playing at *their* life to be, ,, III iv 63
They had not reach'd right reason ; little *c* ! ,, III iv 73
wholesome scripture, ' Little *c*, Love one another.' ,, III iv 85
but they play with fire as *c* do, And burn the house. ,, III vi 28
His *c* and his concubine, belike. ,, IV i 165
To the poor flock—to women and to *c*— ,, IV ii 159
fire seem To those three *c* like a pleasant dew. ,, IV iii 91
burnt The heretic priest, workmen, and women and *c*. ,, V v 107
Old, miserable, diseased, Incapable of *c*. ,, V v 179
That tread the kings their *c* under-heel— *Becket, Pro.* 213
and her *c*—canst thou not—that secret matter ,, Pro. 486

Children (*continued*) my *c*, your prayers will do more
for me *Becket* I iv 143
And thereupon he call'd my *c* bastards. ,, IV ii 44
You have *c*—his ; And mine is the King's child ; ,, IV ii 90
new-made *c* Of our imperial mother see the show. *The Cup* II 164
More specially sick *c*, have strange fancies, *The Falcon* 817
who call'd the mind Of *c* a blank page, *Prom. of May* II 282
they tell me that you—and you have six *c*— ,, III 77
and when the *c* grew too old for me, ,, III 386
love that *c* owe to both I give To him alone. *Foresters* IV 7
Child-world The miserable see-saw of our *c-w*, *Queen Mary* IV iii 385
Chill (*adj.*) Come, come, you are *c* here ; ,, I 275
wherefore waste your heart In looking on a *c* and
changeless Past ? *Prom. of May* II 504
Chill (*s*) He caught a *c* in the lagoons of Venice, *Queen Mary* V ii 515
Chill (*verb*) —your north *c*'s me. *Becket, Pro.* 330
Will *c* the hearts that beat for Robin Hood ! *Foresters* IV 1064
Chilled He warmed to you to-day, and you have *c* him
again. *Becket* II ii 375
Chime fawn upon him ? *C* in with all ? *Harold* I ii 167
Low words best *c* with this solemnity. *The Cup* II 217
world is beautiful If we were happy, and could *c* in
with it. *Prom. of May* I 578
Chin both her knees drawn upward to her *c*. *Queen Mary* V ii 392
Not in my *c*, I hope ! That threatens double. *Becket* II i 250
China as she has broken My *c* bowl. *The Falcon* 524
Chink (*crevice*) A twilight conscience lighted thro' a *c* ; *Harold* III i 66
—a *c*—he's out, Gone ! *Becket* I i 259
Chink (*verb*) wholesome use of these To *c* against the
Norman, *Harold* III i 22
Chirp we will *c* among our vines, and smile *The Cup* I iii 170
Chivalry yet I hate him for his want of *c*. *Foresters* I ii 107
He loves the *c* of his single arm. ,, IV 786
Choice The *c* of England is the voice of England.
William. I will be king of England by the
laws, The *c*, and voice of England. *Harold* II ii 128
Tostig's banishment, and *c* of Morcar, ,, IV i 104
To do with England's *c* of her own king ? ,, V i 19
weight down all free *c* beneath the throne. *Becket* I iii 118
The wiser *c*, because my sleeping-draught ,, IV ii 168
Choir To the *c*, to the *c* ! *Becket*. Shall I too pass to
the *c*, ,, V iii 73
Choose not so set on wedlock as to *c* But where I
list, *Queen Mary* II ii 214
dead I cannot *c* but love her. ,, III i 340
Pray God the people *c* thee for their king ! *Harold* I i 314
there the great Assembly *c* their king, ,, II ii 127
C therefore whether thou wilt have thy conscience ,, II ii 282
c A hundred of the wisest heads from England, *Becket* II ii 170
Still *c* Barabbas rather than the Christ, ,, II ii 390
Choosing old Northumbrian crown, And kings of our
own *c*, *Harold* IV i 33
Chop Would you not *c* the bitten finger off, *Queen Mary* IV iv 206
Chord touch No *c* in me that would not answer *The Falcon* 456
Chosen thought I might be *c* Pope, But then withdrew it. *Queen Mary* V ii 82
coming from the people, And *c* by the people— *Harold* V i 387
c by his people And fighting for his people ! ,, V i 490
and *c* me For this thy great archbishoprick, *Becket* I i 90
Hoped, were he *c* archbishop, ,, I iii 442
for her beauty, stateliness, and power, Was *c* Priestess *The Cup* II 17
Christ (*See also* **Christ Jesus, Jesus Christ**) And stand
within the porch, and *C* with me : *Queen Mary* I ii 51
and kindled with the palms of *C* ! ,, I v 94
sworn upon the body and blood of *C* I'll none
but Philip. ,, I v 215
And keep with *C* and conscience— ,, I v 558
And clasp the faith in *C* ; ,, III ii 122
what saith *C* ? ' Compel them to come in.' ,, III iv 29
White as the light, the spotless bride of *C*, ,, III iv 200
Like *C* himself on Tabor, ,, III iv 201
And be with *C* the Lord in Paradise. ,, IV iii 88
Either to live with *C* in Heaven with joy, ,, IV iii 220
seen the true men of *C* lying famine-dead by scores, ,, V iv 38
the one King, the *C*, and all things in common, ,, V iv 53

Church (s) (*continued*) now the glory of the *C* Hath
 swallow'd up the glory of the King;   *Becket* I iii 665
Whatever the *C* owns—she holds it in Free and
 perpetual alms,   ,, I iii 679
The soul the body, and the *C* the Throne, ,, I iii 717
The King, these customs, all the *C*, ,, I iii 726
The *C* is ever at variance with the kings, ,, I iv 78
Were the *C* king, it would be otherwise. ,, I iv 104
for the sake of the *C* itself, if not for my own, ,, I iv 153
And I have been as royal with the *C*. ,, II i 83
Shrink from me, like a daughter of the *C*. ,, II i 278
Quarrel of Crown and *C*—to rend again. ,, II ii 56
We never hounded on the State at home To spoil the *C*. ,, II ii 97
Holy *C* May rock, but will not wreck, ,, II ii 102
Who thief-like fled from his own *c* by night, ,, II ii 156
all the *C* of France Decide on their decision, ,, II ii 176
thanks of Holy *C* are due to those That went before us ,, II ii 190
we grant the *C* King over this world's kings, ,, II ii 242
—the green field—the gray *c*— ,, II ii 296
Agree with him quickly again, even for the sake of the *C*. ,, II ii 378
The *C* alone hath eyes—and now I see That I was
 blind—   ,, II ii 436
Perish she, I, all, before The *C* should suffer wrong! ,, III iii 20
I have been more for the King than the *C* in this
 matter—yea, even for the sake of the *C*: ,, III iii 65
so violated the immemorial usage of the *C*, ,, III iii 73
half-hanged himself in the rope of the *C*, or rather
 pulled all the *C*   ,, III iii 76
but Salisbury was a calf cowed by Mother *C*, ,, III iii 96
puffed out such an incense of unctuosity into the
 nostrils of our Gods of *C* and State, ,, III iii 116
hurl the dread ban of the *C* on those ,, III iii 210
The State will die, the *C* can never die. ,, III iii 336
God's grace and Holy *C* deliver'd us. ,, IV ii 309
He grovels to the *C* when he's black-blooded, ,, IV ii 436
The *C* is all—the crime to be a king. ,, V i 26
I have overshot My duties to our Holy Mother *C*, ,, V i 38
Are push'd from out communion of the *C*. ,, V i 59
Hath used the full authority of his *C* ,, V i 207
The *C*! the *C*! God's eyes! I would the *C* were down
 in hell!   ,, V i 216
crying On Holy *C* to thunder out her rights ,, V ii 31
she would not believe me, and she wish'd The *C* were
 king: ,, V ii 118
and our Mother *C* for bride; ,, V ii 221
Divide me from the mother *c* of England, My Canterbury. ,, V ii 360
chants and hymns In all the *c'es*, ,, V ii 367
pass the censures of the *C* On those that crown'd young
 Henry   ,, V ii 391
my dream foretold my martyrdom In mine own *c*. ,, V ii 634
Undo the doors: the *c* is not a castle: ,, V iii 62
Seen by the *C* in heaven, the *C* on earth— ,, V iii 98
Except they make submission to the *C*. ,, V iii 123
—for thy *C*, O Lord—Into thy hands, ,, V iii 194
tho' he never comes to *c*, I thought better of him. *Prom. of May* I 261
Thrones, *c'es*, ranks, traditions, customs, ,, I 519
Ring, trinket of the *C*, ,, I 598
Not in our *c*—I think I scarce could hold my head up ,, I 688
and the weight of the *c* to boot on my shoulders, *Foresters* I ii 58
weight of the flesh at odd times overbalance the
 weight of the *c*, ,, I ii 62
which a pious son of the *C* gave me this morning ,, III 281
Thou hast roll'd over the *C* militant ,, IV 272
C and Law, halt and pay toll! ,, IV 429
When the *C* and the law have forgotten God's music, ,, IV 554
Beware, O King, the vengeance of the *C*. ,, IV 914
let me execute the vengeance of the *C* upon them. ,, IV 916
the vengeance of the *C*! Thou shalt pronounce the
 blessing of the *C* ,, IV 926
Church-bond that stale *C-b* which link'd me with him *Becket* IV ii 447
Church-censure I fear *C-c's* like your King. ,, IV ii 434
Church-land We have given the *c-l's* back: *Queen Mary* V i 171
Churchless Back from her *c* commerce with the King *Becket* IV ii 332
Churchman her needle perfect, and her learning
 Beyond the *churchmen*; *Queen Mary* III i 362

Churchman (*continued*) being English *c* How should
 he bear the headship of the Pope? *Queen Mary* III iii 28
And by the *c's* pitiless doom of fire, ,, III iv 49
lives Of many among your *churchmen* were so foul ,, III iv 191
Statesman not *C* he. *Becket, Pro.* 450
thou, that art *c* too In a fashion, *Foresters* IV 410
Church-policy State-policy and *c-p* are conjoint, *Queen Mary* III ii 73
Church-tower sets the *c-t* over there all a-hell-fire as
 it were? *Becket* III iii 51
Churchwarden *C* be a coomin, thaw me and 'im we
 niver 'grees about the tithe; *Prom. of May* I 443
Churl Thine, thine, or King or *c*! *Harold* III ii 37
he speaks to a noble as tho' he were a *c*, and to a *c Becket, Pro.* 455
 C! I will have thee frighted into France, ,, I ii 93
Yea, heard the *c* against the baron— ,, I iii 365
Lout, *c*, clown! *Prom. of May* III 739
True soul of the Saxon *c* for whom song has no
 charm. *Foresters* II i 386
scares The Baron at the torture of his *c's*, ,, III 106
Churn To sing, love, marry, *c*, brew, bake, and die, *Queen Mary* III v 111
Cider-crop they'll hev' a fine *c-c* to-year if the blossom
 'owds. *Prom. of May* I 316
Cinder I wish some thunderbolt Would make this
 Cole a *c*, *Queen Mary* IV vii 11
lava-torrents blast and blacken a province To a *c*,
 hear. *The Cup* II 304
Cinnamon Nard, *C*, amomum, benzoin. ,, II 184
Cipher Ha! Courtenay's *c*. *Queen Mary* II i 134
Circe Our woodland *C* that hath witch'd the King? *Becket* III ii 32
Circling See, first, a *c* wood, ,, *Pro.* 161
Circumbendibuses all manner of homages, and observ-
 ances, and *c*. *Foresters* I i 103
Circumstance The painful *c's* which I heard— *Prom. of May* II 402
Cistercian as I hate the dirty gap in the face of a *C* monk, *Becket* II ii 381
Cite And *c* thee to appear before the Pope, ,, I iii 602
Cited He hath *c* me to Rome, for heresy, *Queen Mary* V ii 42
Citizen (*See also* **Fellow-citizen**) *c's* Stood each before
 his shut-up booth, ,, II ii 62
With execrating execrable eyes, Glared at the *c*. ,, II ii 68
we pray That we, you true and loyal *c's*, ,, II ii 135
And see the *c's* arm'd. Good day; ,, II ii 378
Ay, and for Gardiner! being English *c*, ,, III ii 24
The *c's* heir hath conquer'd me For the moment. *Becket* II ii 60
Our gallant *c's* murder'd all in vain, *The Cup* I ii 142
Would clap his honest *c's* on the back, ,, I ii 358
Here comes a *c*, and I think his wife. *Foresters* III 227
City After him, boys! and pelt him from the *c*. *Queen Mary* I iii 86
make Your *c* loyal, and be the mightiest man ,, II ii 19
How look'd the *c* When now you past it? ,, II ii 57
Like our Council, Your *c* is divided. ,, II ii 60
So I say Your *c* is divided, ,, II ii 99
on you, In your own *c*, as her right, my Lord, ,, II ii 106
I leave Lord William Howard in your *c*, ,, II ii 245
We thank your Lordship and your loyal *c*. ,, II ii 301
I have notice from our partisans Within the *c* ,, II iii 52
scum And offal of the *c* would not change Estates
 with him; ,, IV iii 77
Saints to scatter sparks of plague Thro' all your *cities*, *Harold* II ii 747
A hill, a fort, a *c*—that reach'd a hand ,, IV i 44
another hill Or fort, or *c*, took it, ,, IV i 50
Would God she were—no, here within the *c*. *Becket, Pro.* 180
Last night I followed a woman in the *c* here. ,, *Pro.* 469
there stole into the *c* a breath Full of the meadows, ,, I i 261
where to seek? I have been about the *c*. ,, I i 398
I made him porcelain from the clay of the *c*— ,, I iii 439
if the *c* be sick, and I cannot call the kennel sweet, ,, II ii 348
plagues That smite the *c* spare the solitudes. ,, V ii 173
My lord, the *c* is full of armed men. ,, V ii 187
she told us of arm'd men Here in the *c*. ,, V ii 228
These arm'd men in the *c*, these fierce faces— ,, V iii 3
myrtle, bowering-in The *c* where she dwells. *The Cup* I i 14
Brought me again to her own *c*?— ,, I i 42
in a *c* thro' which he past with the Roman army: ,, I ii 56
in some *c* where Antonius past. ,, I ii 62
Most like the *c* rose against Antonius, ,, I ii 62

City (continued) The Roman is encampt without your c— *The Cup* I ii 84
The camp is half a league without the c; „ I iii 90
and flatten in her closing chasm Domed cities, hear. „ II 301
as she was helping to build the mound against the c. *Foresters* I i 309

Civil Would perish on the c slaughter-field, *Queen Mary* III i 118
The c wars are gone for evermore: „ III v 150
for that would drag The cleric before the c judgment-seat, *Becket* I iii 84

Civil-spoken He's a Somersetshire man, and a very c-s gentleman. *Prom. of May* I 207
' Good daäy then, Dobson ! ' C-s i'deed ! „ I 301

Claim (s) beast might roar his c To being in God's image, *Queen Mary* IV iii 368
know'st my c on England Thro' Edward's promise: *Harold* II ii 12
Who hath a better c then to the crown „ II ii 596
Wilt thou uphold my c ? „ II ii 603

Claim (verb) the people C as their natural leader— *Queen Mary* I iv 210
Foliot may c the pall For London too. *Becket* I iii 55

Claim'd C some of our crown lands for Canterbury— „ I iii 458

Clamour Roused by the c of the chase he woke, *The Cup* I ii 117
with no fear Of the world's gossiping c, *Prom. of May* I 528

Clamour'd The c darling of their afternoon ! *The Cup* II 125

Clan The weakness and the dissonance of our c's, „ I i 24
' I go to fight in Scotland With many a savage c ; ' *Foresters* I i 15

Clang every parish tower Shall c and clash *Queen Mary* II i 230
Iron on iron c, *Harold* IV iii 160

Clank c The shackles that will bind me to the wall. „ II i 409

Clap Except I c thee into prison here, *Becket* V i 110
Would c his honest citizens on the back, *The Cup* I ii 358

Clapt (adj.) we shall hear him presently with c wing Crow over Barbarossa— *Becket* II ii 49

Clapt (verb) Which a young lust had c upon the back, *Queen Mary* IV iii 401
they c their hands Upon their swords when ask'd ; „ V i 172
wicked sister c her hands and laugh'd ; *Harold* V ii 48
i' the poorch as soon as he c eyes of 'er. *Prom. of May* I 23

Clarence (lady in waiting to Queen Mary) C, they hate me ; even when I speak *Queen Mary* V ii 214
he may bring you news from Philip. *Mary.* So, C. „ V ii 230
C, C, what have I done ? „ V ii 338
Our C there Sees ever such an aureole „ V ii 412

Clash (s) cries, and c'es, and the groans of men ; *Harold* III i 375

Clash (verb) every parish tower Shall clang and c *Queen Mary* II i 230
Let all the steeples c, „ III ii 237
If ever, as heaven grant, we c with Spain, „ IV iii 346
Smooth thou my way, before he c with me ; *Harold* II ii 69
sing, Asaph ! c The cymbal, Heman ! „ III i 187
and king's favour might so c That thou and I— *Becket, Pro.* 296

Clash'd c their bells, Shot off their lying cannon, *Queen Mary* V vi 95
Tho' earth's last earthquake c the minster-bells, *Becket* V iii 41

Clashing Ye make this c for no love o' the customs „ I iii 136
Sceptre and crozier c, and the mitre Grappling „ II i 25
Less c with their priests— „ II i 147
C of swords—three upon one, and that one our Robin ! *Foresters* II i 419

Clasp And c the faith in Christ ; *Queen Mary* III ii 122
c a hand Red with the sacred blood of Sinnatus ? *The Cup* II 82
waiting To c their lovers by the golden gates. *Prom. of May* I 248
I fall before thee, c Thy knees. *Foresters* II i 599
I thought I saw thee c and kiss a man „ II ii 72
Thou see me c and kiss a man indeed, „ II ii 76
Fancied he saw thee c and kiss a man. „ III 23
I have seen thee c and kiss a man indeed, „ IV 1035

Claspt Then c the cross, and pass'd away in peace. *Queen Mary* V v 259
My lord, We have c your cause, *Becket* II ii 237

Clause the c's added To that same treaty *Queen Mary* III iii 67

Claw Such hold-fast c's that you perforce *Becket* II ii 86

Clay (See also **Adam-clay**) Statesmen that are wise Shape a necessity, as a sculptor c, *Queen Mary* III iii 33
Our altar is a mound of dead men's c, „ V ii 162
I made him porcelain from the c of the city— *Becket* I iii 438

Clean (See also **Cleän**) And cried I was not c, what should I care ? *Queen Mary* V ii 324
May plaister his c name with scurrilous rhymes ! *Becket* I i 308
that Is c against God's honour— „ II ii 163
Only see your cloth be c. *The Falcon* 420

Cleän The feller's c daäzed, an' maäzed, an' maäted, *Prom. of May* II 728

Cleanse we should thoroughly c the Church within *Queen Mary* III iv 195

Clear (adj.) Stand back, keep a c lane ! *Queen Mary* I i 2
In c and open day were congruent With that vile Cranmer „ III iv 230
So from a c sky falls the thunderbolt ! „ V iii 115
I think that they would Molochize them too, To have the heavens c. *Harold* I i 38
Like on the face, the brows—c innocence ! *Becket* II i 195
Hath he stray'd From love's c path into the common bush, „ III i 247
a bat flew out at him In the c noon, and hook'd him by the hair, *Foresters* II ii 97

Clear (verb) his last breath C Courtenay and the Princess *Queen Mary* III i 135
I bad them c A royal pleasaunce for thee, *Becket* II i 127
I say that those Who went before us did not wholly c The deadly growths of earth, „ II ii 202
Fasts, disciplines that c the spiritual eye, „ V i 42

Clear'd The king, the lords, the people c him of it. *Harold* II ii 522
I've hed the long barn c out of all the machines, *Prom. of May* I 451

Clearer gray dawn Of an old age that never will be mine Is all the c seen. *Queen Mary* V 236

Cleave (to adhere) and c unto each other As man and wife ? „ V ii 137
in hope the crown Would c to me that but obey'd *Becket* V i 50
—if I win her love, They too will c to me, *The Cup* I ii 154
I'll c to you rich or poor. *Foresters* I i 155
C to him, father ! he will come home at last. „ I i 197

Cleave (to divide) bright sky c To the very feet of God, *Harold* II ii 742
C heaven, and send thy saints that I may say „ II ii 785
blow that brains the horseman c's the horse, „ V i 593

Cleaved thro' all this quarrel I still have c to the crown, *Becket* V i 48

Cleaving Is like the c of a heart ; *Queen Mary* III vi 196
C to your original Adam-clay, „ IV vii 418

Cleft c the tree From off the bearing trunk, *Harold* III i 137
And c the Moslem turban at my side. *Foresters* IV 1001

Clench'd fierce forekings had c their pirate hides *Harold* IV iii 35

Cleric A c lately poison'd his own mother, *Becket, Pro.* 10
whether between laymen or c's, shall be tried in the King's court.' „ I iii 80
would drag The c before the civil judgment-seat, „ I iii 84
' If any c be accused of felony, the Church shall not protect him ; „ I iii 86
A c violated The daughter of his host, „ I iii 382
Say that a c murder'd an archbishop, „ I iii 399
the lady holds the c Lovelier than any soldier, „ V i 193
Your c hath your lady. „ V i 200
Lifted our produce, driven our c's out— „ V ii 432

Clever And speak for him after—you that are so c ! *Prom. of May* I 620

Cliff Make blush the maiden-white of our tall c's, *Harold* II ii 333
make their wall of shields Firm as thy c's, „ V i 480
voice of the deep as it hollows the c's of the land. *Becket* II i 4

Cliff-gibbeted they should hang C-g for sea-marks ; *Harold* II i 97

Clifford (See also **Rosamund, Rosamund de Clifford**) and it minded me Of the sweet woods of C, *Becket* I i 264
The mouth is only C, my dear father. „ II ii 220
I am a C, My son a C and Plantagenet. „ IV ii 226

Climb we will c The mountain opposite and watch the chase. *The Cup* I i 116
He c's the throne. Hot blood, ambition, „ II 168

Climb'd Have I c back into the primal church, *Queen Mary* I ii 49
Last night I c into the gate-house, Brett, „ III iii 14
Hath c the throne and almost clutch'd the crown ; *Becket, Pro.* 21
That hath c up to nobler company. „ I i 351
his politic Holiness Hath all but c the Roman perch „ II ii 46

Clime Is it the fashion in this c for women *Queen Mary* III vi 90
Your people are as cheerless as your c ; „ V i 84

Cling now thy love to mine Will c more close, „ III iii 160
C to their love ; for, now the sons of Godwin *Harold* I i 324
women C to the conquer'd, if they love, „ IV i 213
I c to you all the more. *Foresters* I i 160
Your names will c like ivy to the wood. „ IV 1085

Clinging c thus Felt the remorseless outdraught *Harold* II i 7
c to thee Closer than ever. *Becket* II i 285

Clip rather than so c The flowery robe of Hymen, *The Cup* II 435

Clipt The common barber c your hair, *Queen Mary* IV ii 131

Cloak like his c, his manners want the nap „ III v 69

Cloak (*continued*)   Wrap them together in a purple *c*   *Harold* v ii 158
   A ragged *c* for saddle—he, he, he,   *Becket* v i 248
Clock   Toll of a bell, Stroke of a *c*,   *Queen Mary* III v 143
   so they bided on and on till vour o' the *c*,   ,,   IV iii 510
Cloister   Thou art *my* nun, thy *c* in mine arms.   *Harold* I ii 63
   then would find Her nest within the *c*,   ,,   IV i 234
   Get thou into thy *c* as the king Will'd it: ,,   v i 309
   Those arm'd men in the *c*.   *Becket* v iii 50
Cloister'd   She must be *c* somehow, lest the king   *Harold* I ii 157
   The silent, *c*, solitary life,   ,,   III i 277
Cloistral   Retiring into *c* solitude   *Queen Mary* III vi 209
Close (adj. and adv.)   Can you be *c*? *Elizabeth*. Can you, my Lord? *Courtenay*. *C* as a miser's casket. Listen: I iv 106
   They call me near, for I am *c* to thee And England—   *Harold* III i 6
   with his charm of simple style And *c* dialectic,   *Prom. of May* I 225
   From the farm Here, *c* at hand.   ,,   II 361
   C by that alder-island in your brook,   ,,   II 535
   you kept your veil too *c* for that when they carried you in;   ,,   III 227
   but call Kate when you will, for I am *c* at hand.   *Foresters* III 50
Close (an end)   Gone narrowing down and darkening to a *c*.   *Queen Mary* IV iii 432
   war with Brittany to a goodlier *c* Than else had been,   *Harold* II ii 49
   And never a flower at the *c*; (repeat)   *Becket*, Pro. 332, 342
Close (verb)   all too much at odds to *c* at once   *Queen Mary* I v 632
   Tell her to come and *c* my dying eyes,   ,,   v ii 599
   tell the cooks to *c* The doors of all the offices below.   ,,   v v 116
   To make all England one, to *c* all feuds,   *Harold* IV i 141
   Over! the sweet summer *c's*, (repeat)   *Becket*, Pro. 302, 324, 331
   that the rift he made May *c* between us,   ,,   II ii 132
   C the great gate—ho, there—upon the town.   ,,   v ii 529
   Will *c* with me that to submit at once   *The Cup* I ii 148
   c not yet the door upon a night That looks half day.   ,,   I ii 387
   She—*c* the Temple door. Let her not fly.   ,,   II 460
   and warm hands *c* with warm hands,   *Foresters* I iii 20
Closed (adj. and part.)   on a soft bed, in a *c* room, with light, fire, physic, tendance;   *Queen Mary* v iv 36
   Thro' all *c* doors a dreadful whisper crept   *Becket* v ii 88
   or *c* For ever in a Moorish tower.   *Foresters* II i 655
Closed (verb)   King *c* with me last July That I should pass   *Becket* v ii 388
Closer   Might it not Be the rough preface of some *c* bond?   *Queen Mary* I iv 48
   So that your sister were but look'd to *c*.   ,,   I v 461
   Hast thou not mark'd—come *c* to mine ear— clinging to thee *C* than ever.   *Becket* II i 286
   Why, an old woman can shoot *c* than you two.   *Foresters* II i 400
Closet   listening In some dark *c*,   *Queen Mary* v ii 217
   Get thee into the *c* there,   *Foresters* II i 215
Closing   gulf and flatten in her *c* chasm Domed cities, hear.   *The Cup* II 300
Cloth (*See also* **Cloth of gold, Dust-cloth**)   Only see your *c* be clean.   *The Falcon* 420
   see your *c* be white as snow!   ,,   498
Clothe   His faith shall *c* the world that will be his,   *Queen Mary* III ii 180
   And tropes are good to *c* a naked truth,   ,,   III iv 150
   c's itself In maiden flesh and blood,   *Foresters* III 115
Clothed   stand *C* with the full authority of Rome,   *Becket* II ii 493
   C with the mystic silver of her moon.   *Foresters* II i 608
Cloth of gold   That royal commonplace too, *c o g*,   *Queen Mary* III i 54
Cloud (s)   (*See also* **Thunder-cloud**)   then King Harry look'd from out a *c*,   ,,   IV ii 7
   under no ceiling but the *c* that wept on them,   ,,   v iv 40
   be as the shadow of a *c* Crossing your light.   *Harold* II ii 177
   Come, Harold, shake the *c* off!   ,,   III i 74
   Fall, *c*, and fill the house—   ,,   III i 190
   Customs, traditions,—*c's* that come and go;   *Becket* I iii 22
   As Canterbury calls them, wandering *c's*,   ,,   I iii 71
   My sun, no *c*! Let there not be one frown in this one hour.   ,,   II i 42
   Out of the *c*, my Sun—out of the eclipse   ,,   II i 202
   black *c* that hath come over the sun and cast   ,,   III iii 64
   King at last is fairly scared by this *c*—this interdict.   *The Falcon* 7
   My princess of the *c*, my plumed purveyor   *Prom. of May* II 250
   upon me Thro' that rich *c* of blossom.   *Foresters* I ii 319
   And the white *c* is roll'd along the sky!   ,,   II i 28
   Flung by the golden mantle of the *c*,   ,,   II i 28

Cloud (verb)   *C* not thy birthday with one fear for me.   *Foresters* I ii 125
Cloudless   But *c* heavens which we have found together   *The Cup* I ii 415
Clown   Their A B C is darkness, *c's* and grooms May read it!   *Queen Mary* III iv 35
   one that pares his nails; to me? the *c*!   ,,   III v 66
   Insolent *c*. Shall I smite him   *Becket* I iv 223
   less loyalty in it than the backward scrape of the *c's* heel—   ,,   III iii 144
   parish-parson bawl our banns Before your gaping *c's*?   *Prom. of May* I 687
   How the *c* glared at me! that Dobbins, is it,   ,,   II 611
   Lout, churl, *c*!   ,,   III 739
Club   *See* **War-club**
Cluckt   The hen *c* late by the white farm gate,   ,,   I 38
Clumsy   O the *c* word! *Robin*. Take thou this light kiss for thy *c* word.   *Foresters* III 133
   You lovers are such *c* summer-flies   ,,   IV 10
Clung   these earls and barons, that *c* to me,   *Becket* I iv 66
Clutch   Here is one would *c* Our pretty Marian for his paramour,   *Foresters* IV 766
Clutch'd   and almost *c* the crown;   *Becket*, Pro. 22
Coal   (*See also* **Coäl**)   As one that blows the *c* to cool the fire.   ,,   v ii 549
   my father and I forgave you stealing our *c's*.   *Prom. of May* III 69
Coäl   cotched 'im once a-steälin' *c's* an' I sent fur 'im,   ,,   I 412
Coalscuttle   fell ageän *c* an my kneeä gev waäy   ,,   I 403
Coarse   This hard *c* man of old hath crouch'd to me   *Queen Mary* IV ii 169
   but neither cold, *c*, cruel, And more than all—   ,,   v ii 481
Coarseness   This *c* is a want of phantasy.   ,,   v ii 438
Coat   And carve my *c* upon the walls again!   ,,   II iv 110
   This Gardiner turn'd his *c* in Henry's time;   ,,   III iii 17
   Down with him, tear his *c* from his back.   *Foresters* I iii 73
Cobbled   for mine own father Was great, and *c*.   *Harold* IV i 91
Cobbler   the psalm-singing weavers, *c's*, scum—   *Queen Mary* III iv 290
Cock   Our Lord Becket's our great sitting-hen *c*,   *Becket* I iv 126
   He was the *c* o' the walk;   *Foresters* II i 320
Cockboat   he look'd the Great Harry, You but his *c*;   *Queen Mary* v ii 147
Cocker'd   *See* **Nursery-cocker'd**
Cockerel   thou'rt no such *c* thyself,   ,,   I i 41
Cockle-shell   Scuttle his *c-s*?   *Harold* IV iii 142
Cocksbody   It must be thus; and yet, *c*!   *Queen Mary* III iii 4
   He's here, and king, or will be—yet *c*!   ,,   III iii 45
Codlin   as sleek and as round-about as a mellow *c*.   *Foresters* I i 43
Coesnon   from the liquid sands of *C* Haled   *Harold* II i 56
Coffin   like Mahound's *c* hung between heaven and earth—   *Becket* III i 361
Cognisant   told Sir Maurice there was one *C* of this,   *Queen Mary* II iv 100
   Wyatt did confess the Princess *C* thereof,   ,,   II iv 113
Coif   Disguise me—thy gown and thy *c*.   *Foresters* II i 187
   Ay, ay, gown, *c*, and petticoat,   ,,   II i 194
Coil'd   And *c* himself about her sacred waist.   *Harold* I i 71
Coin   He can but read the king's face on his *c's*.   *Becket* II ii 470
   Spare not thy tongue! be lavish with our *c's*,   *The Cup* I ii 353
   cast him from their doors Like a base *c*.   *Foresters* III 173
   Then after we have eased them of their *c's*   *Becket* II ii 123
Co-king   *C-k's* we were, and made the laws together.   *Queen Mary* I v 196
Cold (adj.)   (*See also* **Cowd, Ice-cold**)   Madam, me- thinks a *c* face and a haughty.   ,,   I v 333
   If *c*, his life is pure.   ,,   I v 431
   They call him *c*, Haughty, ay, worse.   ,,   I v 620
   know that whether A wind be warm or *c*,   ,,   v ii 26
   Ay, and then as *c* as ever. Is Calais taken?   ,,   v ii 281
   Ah, Madam, but your people are so *c*;   ,,   v ii 290
   Thou art *c* thyself To babble of their coldness.   ,,   v ii 481
   but neither *c*, coarse, cruel, And more than all—.   *Harold* III i 274
   The *c*, white lily blowing in her cell: ,,   v i 151
   Vying a tear with our *c* dews,   ,,   v i 325
   In *c*, white cells beneath an icy moon—   *Becket* I i 384
   John of Salisbury Hath often laid a *c* hand on my heats,   ,,   I iv 62
   he makes moan that all be a-getting *c*.   ,,   I iv 64
   C after warm, winter after summer,   ,,   I iv 68
   frosted off me by the first *c* frown of the King. *C*, but look how the table steams.   ,,   II ii 126
   You are too *c* to know the fashion of it.   ,,   III iii 153
   And when the *c* corners of the King's mouth began To thaw,   *The Cup* I iii 128
   To warm the *c* bounds of our dying life

Cold (adj.) (continued) It is but thin and *c*, Not like the vintage — *The Falcon* 578
Why, what a *c* grasp is thine— — *Foresters* I ii 242
Thou blowest hot and *c*. Where is she then? — „ II i 490
What makes you seem so *c* to Robin, lady? — „ III 1
What makes thee think I seem so *c* to Robin? — „ III 4
In the *c* water that she lost her voice, — „ IV 243
Did you find that you worked at all the worse upon the *c* tea — *Prom. of May* III 56

Cold (s) bring him home Safe from the dark and the *c*, — *The Cup* I ii 6
O heavens! the very letters seem to shake With *c*, — *The Falcon* 449
And the bee buzz'd up in the *c*. — *Foresters* IV 21
And the bee buzz'd off in the *c*. — „ IV 27

Colder To-day I almost fear'd your kiss was *c*— — *Becket* III i 18

Cold-manner'd *c-m* friend may strangely do us The truest service, — *The Falcon* 642

Coldness Thou art cold thyself To babble of their *c*. — *Queen Mary* V ii 292
God's revenge upon this realm For narrowness and *c*: — *Harold* I i 174

Cole Why are the trumpets blowing, Father *C*? — *Queen Mary* IV ii 24
I wish some thunderbolt Would make this *C* a cinder, — „ IV iii 11

Collar on his neck a *c*, Gold, thick with diamonds; — „ III i 79

Colleagued yet the Pope is now *c* with France; — „ V i 140

Collect *c* the fleet; Let every craft that carries — „ V ii 273
Morcar, *c* thy men; Edwin, my friend— — *Harold* IV i 256

College But the King hath bought half the *C* of Redhats. — *Becket* III ii 374

Colloquy After the long brain-dazing *colloquies*, — *Queen Mary* IV ii 92
Her Highness is too ill for *c*. — „ V ii 613

Colossal Your father was a man Of such *c* kinghood, — „ IV i 101

Colour (s) under *c* Of such a cause as hath no *c*, — „ II ii 182
The *c* freely play'd into her face, — „ II ii 321
Who changed not *c* when she saw the block, — „ III i 399
The *c's* of our Queen are green and white, — „ III v 5
Whose *c's* in a moment break and fly, — „ IV vi 169
declare to you my very faith Without all *c*. — „ VII iii 226
Whose *c's* in a moment break and fly!' — „ V ii 206
A *c*, which has colour'd all my life, — *The Falcon* 364
C Flows thro' my life again, — *Prom. of May* II 666
He wore thy *c's* once at a tourney. — *Foresters* I i 250

Colour (verb) She *c's*! *Dora*. Sir! — *Prom. of May* II 559

Colour'd A colour, which has *c* all my life, — *The Falcon* 364

Colt *c* winced and whinnied and flung up her heels; — *Becket, Pro.* 514
Be the *c* deäd? *Dora*. No, Father. — *Prom. of May* III 429
deer from a dog, or a *c* from a gad-fly, — *Foresters* II i 434

Column For smooth stone *c's* of the sanctuary, — *Harold* II i 101
hurls the victor's *c* down with him That crowns it, — *The Cup* II 295

Co-mate *C-m's* we were, and had our sport together, — *Becket* II ii 121

Comb And bind him in from harming of their *c's*. — *Queen Mary* III iii 58

Combat My lords, is this a *c* or a council? — *Becket* I iii 133

Come (See also **A-cum, Coom, Coomed**) They love thee, and thou canst not *c* to harm. — *Queen Mary* I iii 67
These birds of passage *c* before their time: — „ I iii 75
And in the whirl of change may *c* to be one. — „ I iii 107
Prince of fluff and feather *c* To woo you, — „ I iv 163
This *c's* of parleying with my Lord of Devon. — „ I iv 251
Your time will *c*. *Elizabeth*. I think my time will *c*. — „ I iv 255
C, *c*, I will go with you to the Queen. — „ I iv 297
Madam, the Lord Chancellor. *Mary*. Bid him *c* in. — „ I v 97
C you to tell me this, my Lord? — „ I v 106
Bid him *c* in. Good morning, Sir de Noailles. — „ I v 241
Let the great angel of the church *c* with him; — „ I v 377
To save your crown that it must *c* to this. — „ I v 479
No, Renard; it must never *c* to this. — „ I v 482
he will not *c* Till she be gone. — „ I v 512
For Philip *c's*, one hand in mine, — „ I v 515
No, say I *c*. I won by boldness once. — „ I v 547
Why *c's* that old fox-Fleming back again? — „ I v 581
Her Highness *c's*. — „ I v 635
No new news that Philip *c's* to wed Mary, — „ II i 16
Ay, for the Saints are *c* to reign again. — „ II i 21
I fear you *c* to carry it off my shoulders, — „ II i 91
C locusting upon us, eat us up, — „ II i 101
C, you bluster, Antony! — „ II i 118
and if Philip *c* to be King, O, my God! — „ II i 199
C, now, you're sonnetting again. — „ II i 247

Come (continued) I trust the Queen *c's* hither with her guards. — *Queen Mary* II ii 1
One word before she *c's*. — „ II ii 109
Queen had written her word to *c* to court: — „ II ii 117
Here *c's* her Royal Grace. — „ II ii 126
In mine own person am I *c* to you, — „ II ii 142
Your lawful Prince hath *c* to cast herself — „ II ii 261
C, sirs, we prate; hence all— — „ II ii 372
Wyatt *c's* to Southwark; — „ II ii 374
thro' thine help we are *c* to London Bridge; — „ II iii 8
make Those that we *c* to serve our sharpest foes? — „ II iii 77
we know that ye be *c* to kill the Queen, — „ II iii 108
I have not *c* to kill the Queen Or here or there: — „ II iii 116
Whence *c* you, sir? — „ II iv 74
Philip would not *c* Till Guildford Dudley — „ II iv 136
An hour will *c* When they will sweep her from the seas. — „ III i 161
here they *c*—a pale horse for Death — „ III i 234
The Queen *c's* first, Mary and Philip. — „ III i 299
C to me to-morrow.— — „ III i 320
He *c's*, and my star rises. — „ III ii 167
Oh, Philip, *c* with me; — „ III ii 185
Nay *c* with me—one moment! — „ III ii 189
We *c* not to condemn, but reconcile; We *c* not to compel, but call again; We *c* not to destroy, but edify; — „ III iii 186
what saith Christ? 'Compel them to *c* in.' — „ III iv 30
' I *c* not to bring peace but a sword'? — „ III iv 88
The end's not *c*. *Pole*. No—nor this way will *c*, — „ III iv 110
I *c* for counsel and ye give me feuds, — „ III iv 307
pray Heaven That you may see according to our sight. *C*, cousin. — „ III iv 332
C, *c*, the morsel stuck—this Cardinal's fault— — „ III iv 375
Rogers and Ferrar, for their time is *c*, — „ III iv 425
not like a word, That *c's* and goes in uttering. — „ III v 30
Is like a word that *c's* from olden days, — „ III v 34
But there hath some one *c*; — „ III v 82
C, Robin, Robin, *C* and kiss me now; — „ III v 99
C behind and kiss me milking the cow! — „ III v 105
Rose hand in hand, and whisper'd, '*c* away! — „ III v 148
Thou last of all the Tudors, *c* away! — „ III v 151
When next there *c's* a missive from the Queen — „ III v 182
For I will *c* no nearer to your Grace; — „ III v 200
You know I never *c* till I be call'd. — „ III v 215
C, *c*, the worst! — „ III v 219
You are to *c* to Court on the instant; — „ III v 223
C, *c*, you are chill here; — „ III v 275
the fools, of this fair prince to *c*; — „ III vi 100
As else we might be—here she *c's*. — „ III vi 190
Here *c* the Cranmerites! — „ IV i 40
Cranmer, I *c* to question you again; — „ IV ii 15
refusing none That *c* to Thee for succour, unto Thee, Therefore, I *c*; — „ IV iii 132
forasmuch as I have *c* To the last end of life, — „ IV iii 217
I *c* to the great cause that weighs Upon my conscience — „ IV iii 236
So I may *c* to the fire. — „ IV iii 251
So that she *c* to rule us. — „ IV iii 390
When we had *c* where Ridley burnt with Latimer, — „ IV iii 585
C out, my Lord, it is a world of fools. — „ IV iii 639
Knows where he nested—ever *c's* again. — „ V i 6
I am faint with fear that you will *c* no more. — „ V i 30
Sire, I obey you. *C* quickly. — „ V i 221
Hast thou not mark'd—*c* closer to mine ear— — „ V i 225
When back he *c's* at evening hath the door — „ V ii 120
they *c* back upon my dreams. — „ V ii 188
what good could *c* of that? — „ V ii 309
And says, he will *c* quickly. — „ V ii 565
you said more; You said he would *c* quickly. — „ V ii 575
And yet he will *c* quickly . . . — „ V ii 583
And tell him that I know he *c's* no more. — „ V ii 589
Tell her to *c* and close my dying eyes, — „ V ii 599
Amen. *C* on. — „ V iv 9
' I am dying, Philip; *c* to me.' — „ V v 3
Nothing; but ' *c*, *c*, *c*,' and all awry, — „ V v 15
I cannot doubt but that he *c's* again; — „ V v 26
No, Philip *c's* and goes, but never goes. — „ V v 150

Come (*continued*)   *C* thou down. Lie there.   *Queen Mary* v v 179
Madam, your royal sister *c's* to see you.   "   v v 192
C, *c*! as yet thou art not gone so wild   *Harold* i i 298
C, *c*, Join hands, let brethren dwell in unity;   "   i i 395
Love is *c* with a song and a smile,   "   i ii 10
I will demand his ward From Edward when I *c* again.   "   i ii 60
C, thou shalt dream no more such dreams;   "   i ii 108
tho' I would not That it should *c* to that.   "   i ii 227
Not to *c* back till Tostig shall have shown   "   i ii 241
Here *c's* the would-be what I will be . . .   "   ii ii 138
the lark sings, the sweet stars *c* and go,   "   ii ii 434
I will not hear thee—William *c's*.   "   ii ii 480
C hither, I have a power;   "   ii i 5
C, Harold, shake the cloud off!   "   iii i 73
Spare and forbear him, Harold, if he *c's*!   "   iii i 300
Pray God that *c* not suddenly!   "   iii i 364
not so with us—No wings to *c* and go.   "   iii ii 99
Ill news hath *c*! Our hapless brother,   "   iii ii 120
—the Pope Is man and *c's* as God.   "   iii ii 174
This brother *c's* to save Your land from waste;   "   iv i 94
Somewhere hard at hand. Call and she *c's*.   "   iv i 186
Who is it *c's* this way? Tostig?   "   iv ii 1
I *c* for mine own Earldom, my Northumbria;   "   iv ii 29
C back with him. Know what thou dost;   "   iv ii 47
C thou back, and be Once more a son of Godwin.   "   iv ii 59
Nay then, *c* thou back to us!   "   iv ii 64
bragging still that he will *c* To thrust our Harold's throne   "   iv iii 125
Let him *c*! let him *c*.   "   iv iii 132
Cram thy crop full, but *c* when thou art call'd.   "   iv iii 234
C yet once more, from where I am at peace,   "   v i 238
There is one *C* as Goliath came of yore—   "   v i 493
And thou art *c* to rob them of their rings!   "   v ii 36
C, *c*, thou art but deacon, not yet bishop,   *Becket*, Pro. 82
C, *c*, I love thee and I know thee, I know thee,   Pro. 95
C, I would give her to thy care in England   "   Pro. 142
Whatever *c* between us? *Becket*. What should *c*
  Between us, Henry?   "   Pro. 194
Well—whatever *c* between us.   "   Pro. 199
C to me-morrow.   "   Pro. 410
C with me. Let me learn at full The manner of his
  death,   "   Pro. 424
and if there ever *c* feud between Church and Crown,   "   Pro. 464
C, *c*, my lord Archbishop;   "   i i 201
O brother!—I may *c* to martyrdom.   "   i i 361
Customs, traditions,—clouds that *c* and go;   "   i iii 22
Is black and white at once, and *c's* to nought.   "   i iii 32
but an he *c* to Saltwood, By God's death,   "   i iii 182
should harm *c* of it, it is the Pope Will be to blame—   "   i iii 220
snake that sloughs *c's* out a snake again.   "   i iii 449
Arm'd with thy cross, to *c* before the King?   "   i iii 509
The King's 'God's eyes!' *c* now so thick and fast,   "   i iii 609
C on, on *c*! it is not fit for us To see the proud Arch-
  bishop mutilated.   "   i iii 613
My lord, I *c* unwillingly.   "   i iii 648
may I *c* in with my poor friend, my dog?   "   i iv 93
C, *c*! thou hadst thy share on her.   "   i iv 123
I must fly to France to-night. *C* with me.   "   i iv 154
C, you filthy knaves, let us pass.   "   i iv 203
There is a bench. *C*, wilt thou sit?   "   ii i 124
no hand to mate with *her*, If it should *c* to that.   "   ii i 191
C, *c*, mine hour!   "   ii i 212
The word should *c* from him.   "   ii ii 134
I pray you *c* and take it.   "   ii ii 263
For here he *c's* to comment on the time.   "   ii ii 308
No one *c's*, Nor foe nor friend;   "   iii i 37
Always Becket! He always *c's* between us.   "   iii i 90
for here *c's* my lady, and, my lady,   "   iii i 153
if it should *c* to that!—To that—to what?   "   iii i 259
when the horn sounds she *c's* out as a wolf.   "   iii ii 23
black cloud that hath *c* over the sun and cast us all
  into shadow?   "   iii iii 46
so that the smell of their own roast had not *c* across it—   "   iii iii 120
from those, as I said before, there may *c* a conflagration—   "   iii iii 164
ere Pope or King Had *c* between us!   "   iii iii 268
That perfect trust may *c* again between us,   "   iii iii 351

Come (*continued*)   *C* to me, little one. How camest thou
  hither?   *Becket* iv i 3
Ay, but some one *c's* to see her now and then.   "   iv i 15
C, here is a golden chain I will give thee   "   iv i 40
C along, then? we shall see the silk here and there,   "   iv i 55
I sent this Margery, and she *c's* not back; I sent another,
  and she *c's* not back.   "   iv ii 3
C with me, love, And I will love thee . . .   "   iv ii 154
C hither, man; stand there.   "   iv ii 219
C thou with me to Godstow nunnery,   "   iv ii 366
What! Is the end *c*?   "   v i 148
C you to confess?   "   v ii 71
Hark! Is it they? *C*!   "   v iii 15
C, then, with us to vespers.   "   v iii 34
How can I *c* When you so block the entry?   "   v iii 36
C in, my friends, *c* in!   "   v iii 68
C with us—nay—thou art our prisoner—*c*!   "   v iii 143
C; as he said, thou art our prisoner.   "   v iii 155
You *c* here with your soldiers to enforce   *The Cup* i i 75
Stand aside, Stand aside; here she *c's*!   "   i i 105
He *c's*, a rough, bluff, simple-looking fellow.   "   i i 172
c upon *her* Again, perhaps, to-day—*her*.   "   i i 179
Nay, here he *c's*.   "   i ii 25
C, *c*, we will not quarrel about the stag.   "   i ii 38
Think,—torture,—death,—and *c*.   "   i ii 314
C, *c*, could he deny it? What did he say?   "   i ii 344
If I be not back in half an hour, *C* after me.   "   i ii 439
Will she *c* to me Now that she knows me Synorix?   "   i iii 19
Nay, she will not *c*.   "   i iii 31
Why *c* we now? Whom shall we seize upon?   "   i iii 177
C once more to me Before the crowning,—   "   ii 78
Let him *c*—a legion with him, if he will.   "   ii 250
Why *c's* he not to meet me?   "   ii 528
C, *c*, Filippo, what is there in the larder?   *The Falcon* 117
I knew it would *c* to this. (repeat)   "   156, 174
I always knew it would *c* to this! (repeat)   "   158, 175
C in, Madonna, *c* in.   "   176
—but *c* when they will—then or now—it's all for the
  best, *c* when they will—   "   200
Call him back and say I *c* to breakfast with him.   "   213
His falcon, and I *c* to ask for his falcon,   "   220
I *c* this day to break my fast with you.   "   276
Yet I *c* To ask a gift.   "   298
That seem'd to *c* and go.   "   650
who *c's* To rob you of your one delight on earth.   "   827
tho' he never *c's* to church, I thought better of
  him.   *Prom. of May* i 261
when Thought *C's* down among the crowd,   i 501
Heaven curse him if he *c* not at your call!   i 764
For ever, you foolish child! What's *c* over you?   i 772
to *c* together again in a moment and to go on together
  again,   i 774
C, then, and make them happy in the long barn,   i 790
What are you? Where do you *c* from?   ii 359
The body!—Heavens! I *c*!   ii 572
C, you will set all right again,   ii 658
if the farming-men be *c* for their wages, to send them
  up to me.   iii 16
C, *c*, you worked well enough,   iii 61
that you did not *c* into the hayfield.   iii 82
C, *c*, keep a good heart!   iii 252
not forgotten his promise to *c* when I called him.   iii 330
Well, Milly, why do you *c* in so roughly?   iii 342
a Sister of Mercy, *c* from the death-bed of a pauper,   iii 376
She would have persuaded me to *c* back here,   iii 384
Must to *c* in our spring-and-winter world   iii 510
C, *c*, my girl, enough Of this strange talk.   iii 619
C, *c*, why do ye loiter here?   *Foresters* i i 79
to *c* at their love with all manner of homages,   i i 102
'You have *c* for you saw Wealth coming,'   i i 152
Cleave to him, father! he will *c* home at last.   i i 198
have *c* as freely as heaven's air and mother's milk?   i i 302
Say, we will *c*.   i ii 26
I *c* here to see this daughter of Sir Richard of the Lea   i ii 26
the Earl and Sir Richard *c* this way.   i ii 148

Come (*continued*) I cannot answer thee till Richard *c*.
  Sheriff. And when he *c's*? *Marian.* Well, you
  must wait till then.   *Foresters* I ii 221
C away, daughter.   „   I ii 283
But if the better times should never *c*?   „   I ii 288
And if the worst time *c*?   „   I ii 290
Have they *c* for me? Here is the witch's hut.   „   II i 177
C in, *c* in; I would give my life for thee,   „   II i 188
C in, *c* in. *John.* Why did ye keep us at the door so long? „   II i 222
He will *c* to the gibbet at last.   „   II i 328
And here *c's* another.   „   II i 399
C now, I fain would have a bout with thee.   „   II i 552
C to him. *Marian.* O my poor father !   „   II ii 7
there *c's* a deputation From our finikin fairy nation.   „   II ii 144
warm thy heart to Little John. Look where he *c's* !   „   III 46
we be beggars, we *c* to ask o' you. We ha' nothing.   „   III 190
Here *c's* a citizen, and I think his wife.   „   III 227
and I pray you to *c* between us again,   „   III 413
c between me and my Kate and make us one again.   „   III 422
So *c, c* !' 'Hum !'   „   IV 18
But *c, c* !' 'Hum !'   „   IV 25
Till thou thyself shalt *c* to sing it—in time.   „   IV 36
thou seest the land has *c* between us, And my sick father
  here has *c* between us And this rich Sheriff too has *c*
  between us;   „   IV 53
But will they *c*?   „   IV 91
if they *c* I will not tear the bond,   „   IV 97
but here *c's* one of bigger mould.   „   IV 114
Rogue, we *c* not alone.   „   IV 573
save King Richard, when he *c's*, forbid me.   „   IV 665
C, girl, thou shalt along with us on the instant.   „   IV 678
You, Prince, our king to *c*—   „   IV 696
When Richard *c's* he is soft enough to pardon His brother ; „   IV 746
and she will not marry till Richard *c*.   „   IV 773
But look, who *c's*?   „   IV 977
C from out That oak-tree !   „   IV 996
Comedy A *c* meant to seem a tragedy—   *Becket* IV ii 322
  players In such a *c* as our court of Provence   „   V i 189
Comelier She looks *c* than ordinary to-day;   *Queen Mary* I i 70
Comely (*See also* **Coomly**) Master Dobson, you are a *c*
  man to look at.   *Prom. of May* I 156
Comest Why *c* thou like a death's head at my feast ?   *Foresters* II ii 210
  Thou *c* a very angel out of heaven.   „   II i 105
Comet and look upon my face, Not on the *c*.   *Harold* I i 27
  That were too small a matter for a *c* !   „   I i 471
Too small ! a *c* would not show for that !   „   I i 474
Put thou the *c* and the blast together—   „   II i 15
Your *c* came and went.   „   III i 359
Cometh Blessed is he that *c* in the name of the Lord !   *Becket* I iii 758
Comfort (*See also* **Heart-comfort**) And it would be
  your *c*, as I trust;   *Queen Mary* II ii 225
when last he wrote, declared His *c* in your Grace   „   III vi 79
I could make his age A *c* to him—   *Prom. of May* II 662
our carters and our shepherds Still find a *c* there.   „   III 529
Comfortable set up your broken images ; Be *c* to me.   *Queen Mary* V ii 301
Comforted Be *c*. Thou art the man—   *Becket* I i 132
Coming (adj. and part.) (*See also* **A-coomin'**, **Coomin**)
  Prince of Spain *c* to wed our Queen ?   *Queen Mary* I iii 83
Gardiner, *c* with the Queen, And meeting Pembroke,   „   II ii 309
same tide Which, *c* with our coming, seem'd to smile   „   II iii 22
They are *c* now.   „   III i 181
Legate's *c* To bring us absolution from the Pope.   „   III i 431
there's the face *c* on here of one Who knows me.   „   III i 470
I fain would hear him *c* ! . . .   *Harold* II ii 5
leave them for a year, and *c* back Find them again.   „   II 89
I saw him *c* with his brother Odo The Bayeux bishop,   „   II ii 347
Not *c* fiercely like a conqueror, now,   „   II ii 757
First of a line that *c* from the people,   „   V i 386
why, then it is my will—Is he *c*?   *Becket* I iii 474
voice *c* up with the voice of the deep from the strand,
  One *c* up with a song   „   II i 5
Love that is born of the deep *c* up with the sun from
  the sea. (repeat)   „   II i 9, 19
Some dreadful thing is *c* on me.   „   III i 267
He bows, he bares his head, he is *c* hither.   „   III iii 34

Coming (adj. and part.) (*continued*) Is he *c*? I thought I
  heard A footstep.   *The Cup* I ii 10
I fear some strange and evil chance *C* upon me,   „   I iii 76
walk with me we needs must meet Antonius *c*,   „   I iii 93
Thou—*c* my way too—Camma—good-night.   „   II 492
there is Monna Giovanna *c* down the hill from the
  castle.   *The Falcon* 160
C to visit my lord, for the first time in her life too !   „   169
I'm *c* down, Mr. Dobson.   *Prom. of May* I 45
But see they are *c* out for the dance already.   „   I 795
Hark, Dora, some one is *c*.   „   III 339
' You have come for you saw Wealth *c*,'   *Foresters* I i 152
But they are *c* hither for the dance—   „   I ii 52
but the twilight of the *c* day already glimmers in the east.   „   I ii 247
Is *c* with a swarm of mercenaries To break our band   „   III 452
mark'd if those two knaves from York be *c*?   „   IV 113
Coming (s) At his *c* Your star will rise.   *Queen Mary* I v 410
at once may know The wherefore of this *c*,   „   II iii 138
same tide Which, coming with our *c*, seem'd to smile   „   II iii 22
I have changed a word with him In *c*,   „   III iv 16
and think of this in your *c*. 'MARY THE QUEEN.'   „   III vi 219
How oft in *c* hast thou broken bread ?   *Harold* IV iii 199
with my lady's *c* that had so flurried me,   *The Falcon* 492
I trust he brings us news of the King's *c*.   *Foresters* I iii 54
To warn us of his *c* !   „   III 458
We told the Prince and the Sheriff of our *c*.   „   IV 576
Command (s) so my Lord of Pembroke in *c* Of all her
  force be safe ;   *Queen Mary* II ii 305
Lord Pembroke in *c* of all our force   „   II iv 3
I have the Count's *c's* to follow thee.   *Harold* II ii 235
I have the Count's *c's*.   „   II ii 239
But by the King's *c* are written down,   *Becket* I iii 72
by the King's *c* I, John of Oxford,   „   I iii 74
Now, sirs, the King's *c's* !   „   V ii 322
Command (verb) Her Grace the Queen *c's* you to the
  Tower.   *Queen Mary* III iii 270
and *c* That kiss my due when subject   *Harold* III ii 41
The king *c's* thee, woman !   „   V i 340
Power now from Harold to *c* thee hence   „   V i 456
King *c's* you upon pain of death,   *Becket* I iii 752
C's you to be dutiful and leal To your young King   „   V ii 325
King *c's* you to absolve the bishops   „   V ii 375
King *c's* you. We are all King's men.   „   V ii 383
How if the King *c* it ?   *Foresters* IV 868
Commandment Obey my first and last *c*. Go !   *Harold* V i 359
They have broken the *c* of the king !   „   V i 614
she kept the seventh *c* better than some I know on,   *Becket* III i 194
Commend He *c's* me now From out his grave   *Pro.* 418
when thou seest him next, *C* me to thy friend.   „   I i 324
I do *c* my cause to God, the Virgin,   „   V i 163
c them to your ladyship's most peculiar appreciation.   *The Falcon* 567
Commendation his last words were a *c* of Thomas Becket   *Becket, Pro.* 401
Commended It has been much *c* as a medicine.   *The Falcon* 587
Comment here he comes to *c* on the time.   *Becket* II ii 308
Commerce Back from her churchless *c* with the King   „   IV ii 332
Commission That hastes with full *c* from the Pope   *Queen Mary* II i 51
That our *c* is to heal, not harm,   „   III iii 185
Our letters of *c* will declare this plainlier.   „   III iii 222
Commission'd Thou art *c* to Elizabeth, And not to me !   „   IV i 594
I have *c* thee to save the man :   *Harold* II ii 98
Commissioner You would not cap the Pope's *c*—   *Queen Mary* IV ii 123
Commit to whom The king, my father, did *c* his
  trust ;   „   II ii 208
Committed John of Salisbury *c* The secret of the bower,   *Becket* III iii 4
Common (adj.) the tongue yet quiver'd with the jest
  When the head leapt—so *c* !   *Queen Mary* I v 477
And thro' this *c* knot and bond of love,   „   II ii 198
The *c* barber clipt your hair,   „   IV i 131
For the pure honour of our *c* nature,   „   IV iii 297
Things that seem jerk'd out of the *c* rut Of Nature   *Harold* I i 137
Now must I send thee as a *c* friend   *Becket* I i 341
when murder *c* As nature's death,   „   I iii 343
Hath he stray'd From love's clear path into the *c* bush,   „   III i 247
Lost in the *c* good, the *c* wrong,   „   V ii 40

Common (adj.) (continued) you will find The c
brotherhood of man has been Wrong'd — *Prom. of May* III 543
Common (s) lanker than an old horse turned out to die on
the c. — *Foresters* I i 52
Commoner Should we so doat on courage, were it c? — *Queen Mary* II ii 340
Commonplace That royal c too, cloth of gold, — „ III i 54
Take thou mine answer in bare c— — *Becket, Pro.* 282
Commons however the Council and the C may fence — *Queen Mary* II i 171
Lords and C will bow down before him— — „ III i 433
And C here in Parliament assembled, — „ III iii 114
Commonweal That Centaur of a monstrous C, — „ III iv 163
Commonwealth to play The tyrant, or in c or church. — „ I v 191
Communion It is but a c, not a mass: (repeat) — „ IV ii 56, 111
you have put so many of the King's household out
of c, — *Becket* III iii 311
Are push'd from out c of the Church. — „ v i 58
Communist I that have been call'd a Socialist, A C,
a Nihilist,— — *Prom. of May* III 585
Companion Leave me now, Will you, c to myself,
sir? — *Queen Mary* III v 212
My comrade, boon c, my co-reveller, — *Becket* I iii 460
His one c here—nay, I have heard That, — *The Falcon* 225
Company With our advice and in our c, — *Queen Mary* II ii 151
She will address your guilds and *companies*. — „ II ii 15
and these our *companies* And guilds of London, — „ II ii 128
I, Lord Mayor Of London, and our guilds and *companies*. — „ II ii 141
Three voices from our guilds and *companies*! — „ II ii 256
With all your trades, and guilds, and *companies*. — „ II ii 297
That hath climb'd up to nobler c. — *Becket* I iii 351
Oh, do not damn yourself for c! — „ v ii 523
Ay, prune our c of thine own and go! — *The Falcon* 695
Compass (s) such a one Was without rudder, anchor,
c— — *Prom. of May* III 534
Compass (verb) To c which I wrote myself to Rome, — *Queen Mary* IV i 49
Not small for thee, if thou canst c it. — *Harold* I i 477
Compel We come not to c, but call again; — *Queen Mary* III iii 187
what saith Christ? ' C them to come in.' — „ III iv 29
for the sake of Sinnatus your husband, I must c you. — *The Cup* I iii 102
Take thou my bow and arrow and c them to pay toll. — *Foresters* III 263
Complain If this be so, c to your young King, — *Becket* v ii 448
Complexion The peoples are unlike as their c; — *Queen Mary* v i 89
Compliment Mere c's and wishes. — „ v ii 596
Comport And how did Roger of York c himself? — *Becket* III iii 85
Compose to c the event In some such form as least — *Queen Mary* I v 223
Compromise But—if let be—balance and c; — „ v v 223
Compurgation freed himself By oath and c — *Harold* II ii 520
Comrade My c, boon companion, my co-reveller, — *Becket* I iii 460
My c of the house, and of the field. — *The Falcon* 875
C's, I thank you for your loyalty, — *Foresters* III 78
Conciliation No more feuds, but peace, Peace and c! — *The Falcon* 911
Conclude I c the King a beast; Verily a lion — *Queen Mary* IV iii 411
Concluded Your audience is c, sir. — „ I v 337
Concubine His children and his c, belike. — „ IV i 165
Condemn We come not to c, but reconcile; — „ III iii 186
c The blameless exile?— — *Becket* II ii 395
The King c's your excommunicating— — „ v i 317
If the King C us without trial, — *Foresters* IV 902
Condemn'd said she was c to die for treason; — *Queen Mary* III i 377
Condition Nay—but there be c's, easy ones, — *Harold* II ii 206
C's? What c's? pay him back His ransom? — „ II ii 212
I must not hence Save on c's. — „ II ii 262
Obey the Count's c's, my good friend. — „ II ii 276
But on c's. Canst thou guess at them? — „ II ii 343
Conduct (*See also* **Safe-conduct**) They have given me
a safe c: — *Queen Mary* I ii 101
Conduit The c painted—the nine worthies—ay! — „ III i 258
Confer and c with her ladyship's seneschal, — *The Falcon* 415
Conference We'll have no private c. Welcome to
England! — *Queen Mary* v iii 13
convene This c but to babble of our wives? — *Becket* I i 90
Confess Wyatt did c the Princess Cognisant thereof, — *Queen Mary* II iv 111
Went on his knees, and pray'd me to c In Wyatt's
business, — „ III v 166
c Your faith before all hearers; — „ IV ii 79
Thou shalt c all thy sweet sins to me. — *Becket* II i 291

Confess (continued) Come, c, good brother, — *Becket* II ii 82
Come you to c? — „ v ii 71
I'll be bound to c her love to him at last. — *The Falcon* 172
Confessed Father Philip that has c our mother for twenty
years, — *Becket* III i 111
Confession Shamed a too trustful widow whom you heard
In her c; — *Foresters* III 387
Confessor Saving my c and my cousin Pole. — *Queen Mary* v ii 527
No, nor archbishop, nor my c yet. — *Becket, Pro.* 84
for I should find An easy father c in thee. — „ *Pro.* 88
And it is so lonely here—no c. — „ II i 290
Thou art the Earl's c and shouldst know. — *Foresters* I i 55
Confident *See* **Over-confident**
Confirm Thy naked word thy bond! c it now Before — *Harold* II ii 693
Name him; the Holy Father will c him. — *Becket, Pro.* 245
Confirm'd By Heaven's grace, I am more and more c. — *Queen Mary* IV ii 22
Confiscate C lands, goods, money— — „ II i 102
Conflagration that hath squeezed out this side-smile
upon Canterbury, whereof may come c. — *Becket* III i 58
from those, as I said before, there may come a c— — „ III iii 165
Confound Their Graces, our disgraces! God c them! — *Queen Mary* II i 415
and weave the web That may c thee yet. — *Harold* I i 212
Hath harried mine own cattle—God c him! — „ IV iii 190
Confounded Lest you should be c with it. — *Queen Mary* I iv 178
I am c by thee. Go in peace. — *Becket* III i 731
Confounder A shaker and c of the realm; — *Queen Mary* IV iii 40
Confuse C her not; she hath begun Her life-long prayer. — *Harold* III i 322
Confused Myself c with parting from the King. — *Becket* II i 237
Confusion And if I breed c anyway— — *Queen Mary* I iii 93
I have heard the Normans Count upon this c— — *Harold* II ii 459
see c fall On thee and on thine house. — „ II ii 489
that had found a King Who ranged c's, — *Becket* I iii 371
I see it—some c, Some strange mistake. — „ II i 234
And bring us to c. — *Prom. of May* II 279
C!—Ah well, well! — „ III 508
Congratulate Kiss and c me, my good Kate. — *Foresters* IV 1033
Congratulation Madam, I brought My King's c's; — *Queen Mary* v ii 570
Congruent In clear and open day were c With that vile
Cranmer — „ III iv 230
Conjecture (s) My liege, to your c. — *Becket* I ii 50
Conjecture (verb) If Mary will not hear us—well—c— — *Queen Mary* I iv 117
Conjoint State-policy and church-policy and c, — „ III i 73
Conjured C the mightier Harold from his North — *Harold* IV ii 68
Conquer He told me I should c:— — „ IV i 263
And told me we should c. — „ IV i 267
Conquer'd and when we fought I c, — „ I i 446
we are Danes, Who c what we walk on, — „ IV i 38
and women Cling to the c, if they love, — „ IV i 213
His conqueror c Aldwyth. — „ IV i 218
when at thy side He c with thee. — „ IV ii 29
chanting that old song of Brunanburg Where England c. — „ v i 216
citizen's heir hath c me For the moment. — *Becket* II ii 60
Conqueror Not coming fiercely like a c, now, — *Harold* II ii 757
If not, they cannot hate the c. — „ IV i 215
His c conquer'd Aldwyth. — „ IV i 218
York crown'd the C—not Canterbury. — *Becket* III iii 197
—fight out the good fight—die C. — „ v iii 191
And swallow'd in the c's chronicle. — *The Cup* I ii 158
Conscience And keep with Christ and c— — *Queen Mary* I v 558
Convicted by their c, arrant cowards, — „ II ii 9
This was against her c—would be murder! — „ III i 418
which God's hand Wrote on her c, — „ III i 422
cause that weighs Upon my c more than anything — „ IV iii 238
have thy c White as a maiden's hand, — *Harold* II ii 283
A c for his own soul, not his realm; — „ III i 63
A twilight c lighted thro' a chink; — „ III i 65
That scared the dying c of the king, — „ v i 211
Who like my c never lets me be. — *Becket* v ii 75
—the crowd would call it c— — *Prom. of May* II 638
What pricks thee save it be thy c, man? — *Foresters* IV 626
Consecrate sware To c my virgin here to heaven— — *Harold* IV i 276
Consent (s) with the c of our lord the King, and by the
advice — *Becket* I iii 111
Consent (verb) I would never C thereto, nor marry
while I live; — *Queen Mary* II ii 231

Consent (verb) (*continued*)   Ay . . . if the Witan will *c* to
this.   *Harold* II ii 616
Consider   Pray—*c*—   *Queen Mary* I iv 141
But as to Philip and your Grace—*c*,—   ,,   v iii 65
Consistory   In full *c*, When I was made Archbishop,   ,,   v ii 84
Consonant   As may be *c* with mortality.   ,,   IV iii 419
Consort   I dream'd I was the *c* of a king,   *Becket* v i 144
Conspiracy   With some *c* against the wolf.   *The Cup* I ii 16
There will be more *conspiracies*, I fear.   *Queen Mary* IV iii 433
This is the fifth *c* hatch'd in France;   ,,   v i 297
Rome has a glimpse of this *c*;   *The Cup* I ii 233
Conspirator   But if he be *c*, Rome will chain, Or slay him.   ,,   I i 18
Rome never yet hath spar'd *c*.   ,,   I ii 234
Constancy   draws From you, and from my *c* to you.   *The Falcon* 812
Constant   callous with a *c* stripe, Unwoundable.   *Queen Mary* v v 171
and had my *c* ' No ' For all but instant battle.   *Harold* v i 6
Constitution   for no love o' the customs, Or *c's*,   *Becket* I iii 138
Content (adj.)   Must be *c* with that; and so, farewell.   *Queen Mary* IV iv 271
They smile as if *c* with one another.   ,,   III i 210
So the wine run, and there be revelry, *C* am I.   ,,   III ii 237
Is now *c* to grant you full forgiveness,   ,,   IV iv 389
I am *c*, For thou art truthful,   *Harold* II ii 644
Decide on their decision, I am *c*.   *Becket* II i 178
Let him do the same to me—I am *c*.   ,,   II ii 182
No woman but should be *c* with that—   ,,   III i 11
Content (verb)   *C* you, Madam; You must abide my
judgment,   *Queen Mary* v i 144
Let it *c* you now There is no woman that I love   *Becket* III i 7
Continue   And so you may *c* mine, farewell   *Queen Mary* I iv 137
I am sorry Mr. Steer still *c's* too unwell to attend
to you,   *Prom. of May* III 22
Continuing   So poisoning the Church, so long *c*,   *Queen Mary* IV viii 48
Control   but I am Tudor, And shall *c* them.   ,,   I v 176
Controversy   I here deliver all this *c* Into your royal hands.   *Becket* II ii 136
Convene   did we *c* This conference but to babble of our wives?   ,,   II ii 89
Convent   praised The *c* and lone life—within the pale—   *Harold* I ii 47
What monk of what *c* art thou?   *Foresters* II 205
Conventional   Then, if we needs must be *c*,   *Prom. of May* I 684
For these are no *c* flourishes.   ,,   II 562
Conventionalism   *C*, Who shrieks by day at what she
does by night,   ,,   I 531
Conversion   He is glorified In thy *c*:   *Queen Mary* IV iii 83
doubt The man's *c* and remorse of heart,   ,,   IV iii 108
Converted   Ay, that am I, new *c*,   ,,   I iii 47
Convicted   *C* by their conscience, arrant cowards,   ,,   II ii 9
Coo   Ringdoves *c* again, All things woo again.   ,,   III v 103
Coo'd   The stock-dove *c* at the fall of night,   *Prom. of May* I 41
And the stock-dove *c*, till a kite dropt down,   ,,   I 55
Cook   tell the *c's* to close The doors of all the offices
below.   *Queen Mary* v v 116
But the hour is past, and our brother, Master *C*,   *Becket* I iv 60
Cookery   I know your Norman *c* is so spiced,   *Harold* II ii 810
Cool (adj.)   *C* as the light in old decaying wood;   *Queen Mary* IV ii 5
Cool (verb)   As one that blows the coal to *c* the fire.   *Becket* v i 549
Noä, not yet.   Let 'er *c* upon it.   *Prom. of May* II 132
Cooler   What power this *c* sun of England hath   *Queen Mary* III iv 327
Coöm (come)   Why *c* awaäy, then, to the long barn.   *Prom. of May* I 35
he *c's* up, and he calls out among our oän men,   ,,   I 139
and see that all be right and reg'lar fur 'em afoor he *c*.   ,,   I 170
leästwaäys they niver *c's* 'ere but fur the trout i' our beck,   ,,   I 212
but, c, *c*! let's be gawin.   ,,   I 425
C along then, all the rest o' ye!   ,,   I 442
C, *c*, that's a good un.   ,,   I 467
but if iver I *c's* upo' Gentleman Hedgar ageän,   ,,   II 136
Why, *c* then, owd feller, I'll tell it to you;   ,,   II 202
now she be fallen out wi' ma, and I can't *c* at 'er.   ,,   II 601
How *c* thou to be sa like 'im, then?   ,,   II 712
An' ow *c* thou by the letter to 'im?   ,,   II 716
she moänt *c* here.   What would her mother saäy?   ,,   III 458
but he'll *c* up if ye lets 'im.   ,,   III 481
Coömberland (Cumberland)   An' how did ye leäve the owd
uncle i' *C*?   ,,   I 68
So the owd uncle i' *C* be deäd, Miss Dora,   ,,   II 1
Coom'd (came)   I *c* upon 'im t'other daäy lookin' at the
coontry,   ,,   I 201

Coom'd (came) (*continued*)   afoor I *c* up he got thruff
the winder ageän.   *Prom. of May* I 405
He *c* up to me yisterdaäy i' the haäyfield,   ,,   II 150
when owd Dobson *c* upo' us?   ,,   II 232
Coomed (come)   Miss Dora be *c* back, then?   ,,   I 13
I be *c* to keep his birthdaäy an' all.   ,,   I 75
I warrants ye'll think moor o' this young Squire Edgar
as ha' *c* among us—   ,,   I 110
you be *c*—what's the newspaäper word, Wilson?   ,,   I 319
darters to marry gentlefoälk, and see what's *c* on it.   ,,   III 117
The owd man's *c* ageän to 'issen,   ,,   III 702
Coomin (coming)   Churchwarden be a *c*, thaw me and 'im
we niver 'grees about the tithe: ,,   I 443
'ow should I see to laäme the laädy, and meä *c* along
pretty sharp an' all?   ,,   III 96
Coomly (comely)   *C*, says she.   I niver thowt o' mysen i'
that waäy,';   ,,   I 175
' *C* to look at,' says she—but she said it spiteful-
like.   To look at—yeas, ' *c* ';   ,,   I 179
Coontry (country)   I coom'd upon 'im t'other daäy lookin'
at the *c*,   ,,   I 202
Cope   How should we *c* with John?   *Foresters* I iii 79
I cannot *c* with him: my wrist is strain'd.   ,,   IV 312
Coppice   saw your ladyship a-parting wi' him even now i'
the *c*,   *Becket* III i 161
Copse   how he fells The mortal *c* of faces!   *Harold* v i 589
Copy   so that you do not *c* his bad manners?   *Prom. of May* III 361
Cord   there is axe and *c*.   *Queen Mary* III iv 47
Each of us has an arrow on the *c*;   *Foresters* IV 607
I am here, my arrow on the *c*   ,,   IV 733
Core   For thou and thine are Roman to the *c*.   *Queen Mary* III ii 230
Sound at the *c* as we are.   *Foresters* III 102
Co-rebels   from the charge Of being his *c-r's*?   *Queen Mary* III i 137
Co-reveller   My comrade, boon companion, my *c-r*,   *Becket* I iii 460
Cork   like a bottle full up to the *c*, or as hollow as a kex,   *Foresters* IV 210
Corn   dash The torch of war among your standing *c*,   *Harold* II ii 750
Much *c*, repeopled towns, a realm again.   *Becket* I iii 377
Corner   do not you Be seen in *c's* with my Lord of
Devon.   *Queen Mary* I iv 154
And whisking round a *c*, show'd his back   ,,   II i 131
skulk into *c's* Like rabbits to their holes.   ,,   II iv 55
The hog hath tumbled himself into some *c*,   *Becket* I i 370
the cold *c's* of the King's mouth began to thaw,   ,,   III iii 153
Cornhill   Where dost thou live?   *Man*.   In *C*.   *Queen Mary* III i 317
Cornwall   *C's* hand or Leicester's: they write marvellously
alike.   *Becket* I iv 51
Cornwallis (Sir Thomas)   Sent *C* and Hastings to the
traitor,   *Queen Mary* II ii 31
Coronation (adj.)   Being bounden by my *c* oath To do men
justice.   *Becket* I iii 396
Coronation (s)   would make his *c* void By cursing those   ,,   v iii 329
Corpore   *Gratior in pulchro c virtus*.   ,,   v ii 542
Corpse   *c* thou whelmest with thine earth is cursed,   *Harold* v i 67
Corpse-candles   *C-c* gliding over nameless graves—   ,,   v ii 381
Corridor   My window look'd upon the *c*;   *Queen Mary* v ii 459
I was in the *c*, I saw him coming with his brother   *Harold* II ii 346
Corroborate   *C* by your acts of Parliament—   *Queen Mary* II ii 173
Corrupt   Manners be so *c*, and these are the days of Prince
John.   *Foresters* I i 177
Corruption   Against the huge *c's* of the Church,   *Queen Mary* IV iv 100
sucking thro' fools' ears The flatteries of *c*—   *Becket* I iii 362
Cost (s)   be The one man, he shall be so to his *c*.   *Queen Mary* III iii 276
Cost (verb)   some secret that may *c* Philip his life.   ,,   III i 201
' After his kind it *c's* him nothing,'   ,,   IV i 173
Costly   into some more *c* stone Than ever blinded eye.   ,,   IV v 370
Well—Well—too *c* to be left or lost.   *Becket* II v 299
Bring me The *c* wines we use in marriages.   *The Cup* II 365
And this last *c* gift to mine own self,   *The Falcon* 228
Cotched (caught)   my kneä gev waäy or I'd ha' *c* 'im,   *Prom. of May* I 404
c 'im once a-steälin' coäls an' I sent fur 'im,   ,,   I 412
'A *c* ma about the waaist, Miss,   ,,   III 118
Cottage (adj.)   while the smoke floats from the *c* roof,   *Foresters* I ii 318
Cottage (s)   Stops and stares at our *c*.   *The Falcon* 162
Welcome to this poor *c*, my dear lady.   ,,   270
And welcome turns a *c* to a palace.   ,,   273

Cottage (s) (*continued*) Lady, you bring your light into
my *c* — *The Falcon* 284
My palace wanting you was but a *c*; My *c*, while you
grace it, is a palace. — ,, 287
In *c* or in palace, being still Beyond your fortunes, — ,, 289
you could whitewash that *c* of yours — *Prom. of May* III 43
Make for the *c* then ! — *Foresters* II i 210
Couch'd with mine old hound *C* at my hearth. — *Queen Mary* III i 46
Cough No fever, *c*, croup, sickness ? — *Becket* V ii 169
Could How *c* you—Oh, how *c* you ?—nay, how *c* I ? — *Prom. of May* I 716
Council (adj.) I hear them stirring in the *C* Chamber. — *Queen Mary* I v 628
Council (s) both bastards by Act of Parliament and *C*. — ,, I i 25
the *c* and all her people wish her to marry. — ,, I i 112
Those that are now her Privy *C*, sign'd Before me : — ,, I ii 22
She cannot pass her traitor *c* by, — ,, I ii 40
The *C*, people, Parliament against him ; — ,, I v 78
we will leave all this, sir, to our *c*. — ,, I v 318
Your *C* is in Session, please your Majesty. — ,, I v 543
And when the *C* would not crown me— — ,, I v 555
An instant Ay or No ! the *C* sits. — ,, I v 591
The *C* ! *Mary*. Ay ! My Philip is all mine. — ,, I v 639
Gardiner knows, but the *C* are all at odds, — ,, II i 139
however the *C* and the Commons may fence round
his power — ,, II i 171
The *C*, the Court itself, is on our side. — ,, II i 192
And four of her poor *C* too, my Lord, — ,, II ii 42
What do and say Your *C* at this hour ? — ,, II ii 46
The *C*, The Parliament as well, are troubled waters; — ,, II ii 49
Like our *C*, Your city is divided. — ,, II ii 59
But we sent divers of our *C* to them, — ,, II ii 152
theretoward unadvised Of all our Privy *C* ; — ,, II ii 205
heard One of your *C* fleer and jeer at him. — ,, II ii 393
Lord Paget Waits to present our *C* to the Legate. — ,, III ii 98
And she impress her wrongs upon her *C*, — ,, III vi 184
Cranmer, it is decided by the *C* That you to-day — ,, IV ii 26
Or seek to rescue me. I thank the *C*. — ,, IV ii 39
I must obey the Queen and *C*, man. — ,, IV ii 164
causes Wherefore our Queen and *C* at this time — ,, IV iii 36
which our Queen And *C* at this present — ,, IV iii 56
first In *C*, second person in the realm, — ,, IV iii 72
came to sue Your *C* and yourself to declare war.
(*repeat*) — ,, v 108, 114
Alas ! the *C* will not hear of war. — ,, v 163
the *C* (I have talked with some already) are for war. — ,, v 294
Tell my mind to the *C*—to the Parliament : — ,, v ii 288
Then our great *C* wait to crown the King — *Harold* III i 3
Siding with our great *C* against Tostig, — ,, III i 59
Nay—but the *c*, and the king himself, — ,, III i 170
And our great *C* wait to crown thee King. — ,, III i 406
Thou gavest thy voice against me in the *C*— — ,, IV ii 78
I, John of Oxford, The President of this *C*, — *Becket* I iii 76
My lords, is this a combat or a *c* ? — ,, I iii 134
whene'er your royal rights Are mooted in our *c's*— — ,, I iii 431
Let us go in to the *C*, where our bishops — ,, I iii 547
Councillor Place and displace our *c's*, — *Queen Mary* II ii 160
Your faithful friend and trusty *c*. — ,, IV i 89
From *c* to caitiff—fallen so low, — ,, IV ii 75
is it then with thy goodwill that I Proceed against
thine evil *c's*, — *Becket* III iii 209
It may be they were evil *c's*. — ,, III iii 216
Counsel (advice) I follow your good *c*, gracious uncle. — *Queen Mary* I iv 186
She hath harken'd evil *c*— — ,, I v 54
So would your cousin, Cardinal Pole ; ill *c* ! — ,, I v 406
I come for *c* and ye give me feuds, — ,, III iv 307
Good *c* yours—No one in waiting ? — ,, v v 202
Good *c* truly ! I heard from my Northumbria
yesterday. — *Harold* I i 330
Good *c* tho' scarce needed. — ,, I i 376
My one grain of good *c* which you will not swallow. — *Becket* II ii 379
second grain of good *c* I ever proffered thee, — ,, III iii 318
Summon your barons ; take their *c* : — ,, v i 75
a man may take good *c* Ev'n from his foe. — ,, v ii 3
Counsel (deliberation) You should have taken *c* with your
friends — ,, v ii 555
My *c* is already taken, John. — ,, v ii 560

Counsel (deliberation) (*continued*) Have shut you
from our *c's*. — *Queen Mary* III iv 320
Counsel (secret) if the child could keep Her *c*. — *Prom. of May* I 478
Counsel (verb) means to *c* your withdrawing To
Ashridge, — *Queen Mary* I iv 224
Till when, my Lords, I *c* tolerance. — ,, IV iii 203
Harold, I do not *c* thee to lie. — *Harold* II ii 416
O good son Louis, do not *c* me, — *Becket* II ii 219
Counsell'd Emperor *c* me to fly to Flanders. — *Queen Mary* I v 549
I had *c* him To rest from vain resistance. — *The Cup* 413
Counsellor who am your friend And ever faithful *c*, — *Queen Mary* I v 135
Count (s) and *C's*, and sixty Spanish cavaliers, — ,, III i 51
I might dare to tell her that the *C*— — ,, v ii 524
What *C* ? *Magdalen*. The Count de Feria, — ,, v ii 530
Sir *C*, to read the letter which you bring. — ,, v ii 555
My Lord *C* ? Her Highness is too ill for colloquy. — ,, v ii 612
I shine ! What else, Sir *C* ? — ,, v iii 17
Is not the Norman *C* thy friend and mine ? — *Harold* I i 247
C of the Normans, thou hast ransom'd us, — ,, II ii 157
C, I thank thee, but had rather Breathe the free wind — ,, II ii 184
With bitter obligation to the *C*— — ,, II ii 221
I have the *C's* commands to follow thee. — ,, II ii 234
I have the *C's* commands. — ,, II ii 239
'Tis the good *C's* care for thee ! — ,, II ii 251
Obey the *C's* conditions, my good friend. — ,, II ii 276
C ! if there sat within the Norman chair — ,, II ii 532
Sir *C*, He had but one foot, — ,, II ii 674
I, the *C*—the King—Thy friend— — ,, II ii 753
perjury-mongering *C* Hath made too good an use — ,, v i 311
The Norman *C* is down. — ,, v i 553
Can I speak with the *C* ? — *The Falcon* 180
Where is the *C* ? *Elisabetta*. Just gone To fly his
falcon, — ,, 208
'Get the *C* to give me his falcon, — ,, 241
' I should be well again If the good *C* would give me——' — ,, 838
There is one that should be grateful to me overseas, a
C in Brittany— — *Foresters* I i 271
Count (verb) (I *c* it as a kind of virtue in him, — *Queen Mary* I iv 193
she *c's* on you And on myself as her two hands ; — ,, II ii 104
As for the Pope I *c* him Antichrist, — ,, IV iii 277
C's his old beads, and hath forgotten thee. — *Harold* II ii 447
I have heard the Normans *C* upon this confusion— — ,, II ii 459
Take and slay me, I say, Or I shall *c* thee fool. — ,, IV ii 16
tho' I *c* Henry honest enough, yet when fear creeps — *Becket* III iii 60
Why now I *c* it all but miracle, — *The Cup* III 37
However, staying not to *c* how many, — *The Falcon* 627
C the money and see if it's all right. — *Prom. of May* III 64
Count-crab and our great *C-c* will make his nippers — *Harold* I i 76
Counted When all men *c* Harold would be king, — ,, v ii 132
Countenanced but the backs 'ud ha' *c* one another, — *Becket* III i 147
Counter not Spear into pruning-hook—the—*c* way— — *Harold* v i 442
Counter-bond To bring their *c-b* into the forest. — *Foresters* IV 89
Counterpoint Veer to the *c*, and jealousy — *Queen Mary* III vi 180
Country (adj.) Far liefer had I in my *c* hall — ,, III i 43
She means to counsel your withdrawing To
Ashridge, or some other *c* house. — ,, I iv 226
Country (s) (*See also* **Coontry**) there's no glory Like
his who saves his *c* : — ,, II i 110
I swear you do your *c* wrong, Sir Ralph. — ,, II i 153
and the *c* Has many charms, — *Prom. of May* ii 540
not only love the *c*, But its inhabitants too ; — ,, II 545
Might have more charm for me than all the *c*. — ,, II 554
to save his *c*, and the liberties of his people ! — *Foresters* I i 246
You are those that tramp the *c*, — ,, III 198
Countryfolk Not leave these *c* at court. — *Becket* I i 129
Countryman —home your banish'd *c*. — *Queen Mary* III ii 31
Earls, Thanes, and all our *countrymen* ! — *Harold* IV iii 48
Country-wives poor garrulous *c-w*. — *Queen Mary* iv iii 547
County is not the cause of a *c* or a shire, — ,, II i 162
and make Musters in all the *counties* ; — ,, v ii 272
went abroad Thro' all my *counties*, — *Becket* I iii 363
Couple as the new-made *c* Came from the Minster, — *Queen Mary* III i 94
They hunt in *c's*, and when they look at a maid — *Foresters* I i 256
Courage *C*, sir, *That* makes or man or woman — *Queen Mary* II ii 328
Should we so doat on *c*, were it commoner ? — ,, II ii 339

Courage (*continued*) All greed, no faith, no *c*!   *Queen Mary* III i 146
And bad me have good *c*;   „ IV ii 8
Have *c*, your reward is Heaven itself.   „ V ii 108
C, noble Aldwyth!   *Harold* I ii 182
C, *c*! and all will go well.   *Prom. of May* III 215
Course So far my *c*, albeit not glassy-smooth,   *Becket* I iii 379
sat Thro' every sensual *c* of that full feast   *Prom. of May* II 254
Court (s) (*See also* **Hampton Court**) You've but a dull
life in this maiden *c*,   *Queen Mary* I iii 114
And certain of his *c*.   „ I iii 133
out all things here At *c* are known;   „ I iv 58
I freed him from the Tower, placed him at *C*;   „ I v 164
You have sent her from the *c*,   „ I v 462
heard Slanders against Prince Philip in our *C*?   „ I v 571
a fine courtier of the old *C*, old Sir Thomas. *Wyatt*.
Courtier of many *c*'s,   „ II i 46
The Council, the *C* itself, is on our side.   „ II i 192
Queen had written her word to come to *c*:   „ II ii 118
Before our own High *C* of Parliament,   „ II ii 234
Your *c*'s of justice will determine that.   „ II iv 130
But *c* is always May, buds out in masques,   „ III v 11
his manners want the nap And gloss of *c*;   „ III v 71
You are to come to *C* on the instant;   „ III v 223
you want the sun That shines at *c*;   „ III v 277
trifling royally With some fair dame of *c*,   „ III vi 160
The foreign *c*'s report him in his manner   „ III ii 175
scarce touch'd or tasted The splendours of our *C*.   *Harold* II ii 175
Am I in danger in this *c*?   „ II ii 237
being brought before the *c*'s of the Church,   *Becket, Pro.* 12
My *C*'s of Love would have held thee guiltless of love—   „ *Pro.* 498
whether between laymen or clerics, shall be tried in the
King's *c*.'   „ I iii 81
he shall answer to the summons of the King's *c* to be
tried therein.'   „ I iii 89
the King shall summon the chapter of that church to *c*,   „ I iii 110
sat in mine own *c*'s Judging my judges,   „ I iii 368
Ye haled this tonsured devil into your *c*'s;   „ I iii 388
If Canterbury bring his cross to *c*,   „ I iii 511
The King's *c*'s would use thee worse than thy dog—   „ I iv 102
Not leave these countryfolk at *c*.   „ I iv 129
you are known Thro' all the *c*'s of Christendom   „ IV ii 325
such a comedy as our *c* of Provence Had laugh'd at.   „ V i 189
The fellow that on a lame jade came to *c*,   *Harold* V i 247
I said it was the King's *c*'s, not the King;   „ V ii 114
calls you oversea To answer for it in his Norman *c*'s.   „ V ii 355
The bee should buzz about the *C* of John.   *Foresters* IV 44
ye shall with us to *c*.   „ IV 951
And we must hence to the King's *c*.   „ IV 1050
Court (verb) Why will you *c* it By self-exposure?   *Becket* I i 281
Courtenay (**Earl of Devon**) (*See also* **Devon** (**Earl of**))
C, to be made Earl of Devon,   *Queen Mary* I i 110
Son *C*, wilt thou see the holy father Murdered   „ I iii 63
A *C*! a *C*!   „ I iii 74
this fine blue-blooded *C* seems Too princely for a pawn.   „ I iii 165
A *C* of Devon, and her cousin.   „ I iv 86
I charge you, Tell *C* nothing.   „ I iv 192
Hath taken to this *C*.   „ I iv 201
And when your Highness talks of *C*—   „ I v 198
C, Save that he fears he might be crack'd in using,
Ha! *C*'s cipher.   „ II i 6
The names of Wyatt, Elizabeth, *C*,   „ II i 134
die with those That are no cowards and no *C*'s.   „ II ii 95
breath Clear *C* and the Princess from the charge   „ IV iv 87
So they have sent poor *C* over sea.   „ III i 135
C, belike— *Mary*. A fool and featherhead!   „ III v 2
with full proof Of *C*'s treason?   „ V i 127
   „ V ii 499
Courteous a man Of such colossal kinghood, yet so *c*,   „ IV i 101
C enough too when he wills;   *Foresters* I ii 105
Courteousness They shall be handled with all *c*.   „ IV 102
Courtesan He wrecks his health and wealth on *c*'s,   *Queen Mary* I v 168
There may be *c*'s for aught I know   *The Cup* I ii 192
Courtesy But lest we turn the scale of *c*   *Harold* II ii 164
that *c* which hath less loyalty in it than   *Becket* III iii 142
Might not your *c* stoop to hand it me?   „ IV ii 295
yet of his *c* Entreats he may be present   *The Cup* II 247

Courtesy (*continued*) you are still the king Of *c* and
liberality.   *The Falcon* 293
I trust I still maintain my *c*;   „ 295
No other heart Of such magnificence in *c*   „ 723
turn back at times, and make *C* to custom?   *Prom. of May* II 635
thou didst repent thy *c* even in the doing it.   *Foresters* I ii 243
Richard's the king of *c*,   „ IV 363
I could but sneak and smile and call it *c*,   „ IV 367
And that is only *c* by *c*—But Robin is a thief of *c*   „ IV 369
There—to be a thief of *c*—   „ IV 374
Courtier He was a fine *c*, he; Queen Anne loved him.   *Queen Mary* II i 33
a fine *c* of the old Court, old Sir Thomas. *Wyatt*.
   „ II i 45
and a favourer Of players, and a *c*,   *Becket* I i 79
Courtly He said it was not *c* to stand helmeted Before
the Queen.   *Queen Mary* V v 35
Courtly-delicate His bearing is so *c-d*.   „ III iv 397
Cousin (*See also* **Dear-cousin, Legate-cousin, Side-cousin,
Royal-cousin**) again to her *c* Reginald Pole, now
Cardinal;   „ I i 123
but you, *c*, are fresh and sweet As the first flower   „ I iv 61
A Courtenay of Devon, and her *c*.   „ I iv 86
Nay, pout not, *c*.   „ I iv 134
So would your *c*, Cardinal Pole;   „ I v 405
with what haste I might To save my royal *c*.   „ II iv 78
Loyal and royal *c*, humblest thanks.   „ III i 3
We heard that you were sick in Flanders, *c*.   „ III ii 34
c, as the heathen giant Had but to touch the ground,   „ III ii 42
My heart beats twenty, when I see you *c*. Ah, gentle *c*,   „ III ii 60
True, good *c* Pole; And there were also those   „ III ii 68
I believe so, *c*.   „ III ii 72
No, *c*, happy—Happy to see you;   „ III ii 86
Sweet *c*, you forget That long low minster   „ III ii 89
True, *c*, I am happy.   „ III ii 113
Our good Queen's *c*—dallying over seas   „ III iv 292
see according to our sight. Come, *c*.   „ III iv 332
C, there hath chanced A sharper harm   „ V ii 28
And so must you, good *c*;—   „ V ii 39
I knew it, *c*, But held from you all papers sent by Rome,   „ V ii 44
To sleep, to die—I shall die of it, *c*.   „ V ii 128
Poor *c*! Have not I been the fast friend of your life   „ V ii 132
Ah, *c*, I remember How I would dandle you upon my
knee   „ V ii 140
Peace, *c*, peace! I am sad at heart myself.   „ V ii 159
Your pardon, Sweet *c*, and farewell!   „ V ii 204
Thou knowest I am his *c*,   *Harold* II i 593
seem at most Sweet guests, or foreign *c*'s,   *Becket* II i 135
Cover (s) I saw the *c*'s laying. *Philip*. Let us
have it.   *Queen Mary* III vi 258
'Will your Ladyship ride to *c* to-day?   *Prom. of May* III 310
Cover (verb) That *c*'s all.   *Queen Mary* V ii 542
I saw the hand of Tostig *c* it.   *Harold* IV iii 82
Coverdale (**Bishop of Exeter**) Poinet, Barlow, Bale,
Scory, *C*;   *Queen Mary* I ii 7
Coveted your hand Will be much *c*! What a delicate
one!   „ V iii 44
Covetousness 'Lust, Prodigality, *C*, Craft,   *Prom. of May* II 284
Cow with my hands Milking the *c*? (repeat)   *Queen Mary* III v 88, 95, 102
you came and kiss'd me milking the *c*. (repeat)   *Queen Mary* III v 91, 98
Come behind and kiss me milking the *c*!   „ III v 105
the *c* kick'd, and all her milk was spilt.   „ III v 266
I had kept My Robins and my *c*'s in sweeter order   „ III v 270
The maid to her dairy came in from the *c*,   *Prom. of May* I 40
I seed that one *c* o' thine i' the pinfold ageän   „ I 190
An' if tha can't keep thy one *c* i' horder,   „ I 197
take to the milking of your *c*'s, the fatting of your
calves,   „ II 92
Hes the *c* cawved? *Dora*. No, Father.   „ III 427
Thou hast a *c* then, hast thou?   *Foresters* II i 298
How hadst thou then the means to buy a *c*?   „ II i 304
but the *c*? *Robin*. She was given me.   „ II i 314
That *c* was mine. I have lost a *c* from my meadow.   „ II i 325
O sweet sir, talk not of *c*'s.   „ II i 330
wouldst bar me fro' the milk o' my *c*,   „ II i 355
or the *c* that jumped over the moon.   „ II i 435

Damn'd my Lord, He is *d* enough already. *Queen Mary* II ii 407
and brooks Were bridged and *d* with dead, *Harold* III ii 130
Damon The polish'd *D* of your pastoral here, *Prom. of May* III 562
Damp hand, *D* with the sweat of death, *Queen Mary* I ii 33
Those *d*, black, dead Nights in the Tower; dead— „ III v 137
Damsel I love him as a *d* of his day *Foresters* I i 227
if ever A Norman *d* fell into our hands, „ III 181
You hide this *d* in your forest here, „ IV 476
D, is this the truth? *Marian.* Ay, noble knight. „ IV 769
Danaë included *D* has escaped again Her tower, *Becket* I i 395
Dance (s) (*See also* **Diamond-dance**) Have you been looking at the '*D* of Death'? *Queen Mary* V ii 170
Two sisters gliding in an equal *d*, *Becket* I iii 444
She saw it at a *d*, upon a neck Less lovely *The Falcon* 54
and the lads and lasses 'ull hev a *d*. *Prom. of May* I 428
But see they were coming out for the *d* already. „ I 796
But they are coming hither for the *d*— *Foresters* I ii 53
Dance (verb) Till the sun *d*, as upon Easter Day. *Queen Mary* III ii 238
and *d* into the sun That shines on princes. „ III v 252
And wear my crown, and *d* upon my grave. „ V ii 601
star That *d's* in it as mad with agony! *Harold* I i 9
that wilt not *d* However wisely charm'd. „ I i 386
D! small heart have I to *d*. *Prom. of May* I 429
weight of the church to boot on my shoulders, I would *d* too. *Foresters* I ii 59
Go now and ask the maid to *d* with thee, „ I ii 185
Pretty mistress, will you *d*? „ I ii 204
What? must we *d* attendance all the day? „ IV 550
D! ay, by all the saints and all the devils ye shall *d*. „ IV 552
they shall *d* to the music of the wild wood. Let the birds sing, and do you *d* to their song. „ IV 555
Rouge, I am full of gout. I cannot *d*. „ IV 563
for by my life, you shall *d* till he can. „ IV 566
Prick him where thou wilt, so that he *d*. „ IV 572
Let us hang, so thou *d* meanwhile; „ IV 581
Take care, take care! I *d*—I will *d*—I *d*. „ IV 586
Dancing I watch'd you *d* once With your huge father; *Queen Mary* V ii 143
I should seem to be *d* upon a grave. *Prom. of May* I 431
Dandle I would *d* you upon my knee At lisping-age. *Queen Mary* V ii 141
Dane Angle, Jute, *D*, Saxon, Norman, *Harold* II ii 763
we are *D's*, Who conquer'd what we walk on, „ IV i 37
Thou art but a West Saxon: *we* are *D's*! *Harold.* My mother is a *D*, and I am English; „ IV i 53
Athelstan the Great Who drove you *D's*; and yet he held That *D*, Jute, Angle, Saxon, „ IV i 75
or Knut who coming *D* Died English. „ IV iii 55
Dang (damn) 'Good daäy, Dobbins.' *D* tha! *Prom. of May* II 742
Out o' the chaumber, *d* tha „ III 73
Danger But your own state is full of *d* here. *Queen Mary* I iv 169
This marriage should bring loss or *d* to you, „ II ii 227
release from *d* of all censures Of Holy Church „ III iii 150
How dense a fold of *d* nets him round, *Harold* II ii 17
Am I in *d* in this court? „ II ii 236
And take the Church's *d* on myself. *Becket* I ii 72
is there *d*? *Camma.* Nay, None that I know: *The Cup* I ii 440
Dangerous therefore is he *d*. *Queen Mary* I iv 161
he is *d* everyway. „ I iv 164
Not every *d* that way, my good uncle. „ I iv 166
Altho' we grant when kings are *d* *Becket* I ii 67
Dangle You ought to *d* up there among the crows. *Foresters* III 366
Dangled The traitor husband *d* at the door, *Queen Mary* III i 10
Daniel I am the messenger of God, His Norman *D*! *Harold* V i 35
Danish that sight of *D* blood Might serve an end not English— „ IV iii 96
Dan Smith (farm labourer) *D S*, fur I cotched 'im once a-steälin' coäls *Prom. of May* I 411
D S's cart hes runned ower a laädy i' the holler laäne, „ II 567
D S, my father and I forgave you stealing our coals. „ III 68
But, *D S*, they tell me that you— „ III 76
Dare I *d* not leave my post. *Queen Mary* I ii 55
for all that I *d* not stay. „ I ii 102
I cannot, and I *d* not, „ I v 49
Yet others are that *d* the stake and fire, „ III iv 167
Before I *d* to glance upon your Grace. „ III v 186
This last—I *d* not read it her. „ V ii 183
Dare (*continued*) How *d* you say it? *Queen Mary* V ii 379
I might *d* to tell her that the Count— „ V ii 523
The Queen is dying, or you *d* not say it. „ V v 251
I *d* not well be seen in talk with thee. *Harold* II ii 481
I *d* not. *Harold.* Scared by the church— „ III ii 86
I *d* not wear it. *Harold.* But I *d*. God with thee! „ III ii 187
If one may *d* to speak the truth, „ IV i 108
D's the bear slouch into the lion's den? *Becket* IV ii 282
I *d* not, sir! Throne him—and then the marriage— *The Cup* II 155
D beg him to receive his diamonds back—How can I, *d* I, *The Falcon* 262
I do not *d*, like an old friend, to shake it. *Prom. of May* II 526
That I *d* not tell how much I love him. „ III 287
Dare-Becket only there was a dare-devil in his eye—I should say a *d-B*. *Becket* III iii 89
Dared If they *d* To harm you, I would blow *Queen Mary* I iv 289
Ev'n that young girl who *d* to wear your crown? *Mary.* *D*? nay, not so; „ I v 491
How *d* he? *Magdalen.* Stupid soldiers oft are bold. „ V ii 444
Nobles we *d* not touch. „ V v 104
Which even Peter had not *d*? *Becket* II ii 395
How *d* you? Know you not this bower is secret, „ IV ii 21
He *d* not—liar! yet, yet I remember— „ V i 211
May they not say you *d* not show yourself „ V ii 594
but to-day I *d* not—so much weaker, *The Falcon* 832
Dare-devil *D-d's*, that would eat fire and spit it out *Queen Mary* III i 156
only there was a *d-d* in his eye—I should say a dare-Becket. *Becket* III iii 88
Daring ice-cold—no dash of *d* in him. *Queen Mary* I v 331
Dark (adj.) For I foresee *d* days. „ I v 275
true enough Her *d* dead blood is in my heart with mine. „ III i 349
Her *d* dead blood that ever moves with mine „ III i 352
He can but creep down into some *d* hole „ IV i 140
listening In some *d* closet, some long gallery, „ V ii 217
D among gems and gold; *Harold* IV i 249
My fatal oath—the dead Saints—the *d* dreams— „ V i 380
Gloom upon gleam, *D* as my doom— *Becket* III i 282
Have track'd the King to this *d* inland wood; „ III ii 3
And far on in the *d* heart of the wood „ III ii 47
D even from a side glance of the moon, „ IV ii 148
Growing *d* too—but light enough to row. *The Cup* II 523
What, I that held the orange blossom *D* as the yew? *Prom. of May* II 631
Ye sees the holler laäne be hallus sa *d* i' the arternoon, „ III 93
How *d* your room is! „ III 217
even if I found it *D* with the soot of slums. „ III 602
our King is gone, the light Of these *d* hours; *Foresters* I ii 85
O look! before the shadow of these *d* oaks „ II i 604
A maiden now Were ill-bested in these *d* days of John, „ II ii 45
In this *d* wood when all was in our power „ III 182
Dark (s) Your master works against me in the *d*. *Queen Mary* I v 277
She to shut up my blossom in the *d*! *Harold* I ii 62
I am in the *d*. *Becket* III i 221
one step in the *d* beyond Our expectation, *The Cup* I i 212
Safe from the *d* and the cold, „ I ii 6
I runned arter thief i' the *d*, *Prom. of May* I 403
leaves him A beast of prey in the *d*, „ I 505
Death As against Life! all, all, into the *d*— „ II 338
and saäy it to ye afoor *d*; „ III 14
Darken Save him, his blood would *d* Henry's name; *Becket* V iii 10
Darken'd I tear away The leaves were *d* by the battle— *The Falcon* 913
Darkening Gone narrowing down and *d* to a close. *Queen Mary* IV iii 431
Darker Thy Duke will seem the *d*. Hence, I follow. *Harold* II ii 817
They told me, from the farm—and *d* news. *Prom. of May* II 408
this world Is brighter for his absence as that other Is *d* for his presence. „ II 459
Darkness He stirs within the *d*! *Queen Mary* III ii 158
that all the louts to whom Their A B C is *d*, „ III iv 35
—the Lord hath dwelt In *d*. *Harold* III i 180
As gold Outvalues dross, light *d*, *Becket* I iii 715
Could shine away the *d* of that gap „ III i 59
Stumble not in the *d*, Lest they should seize thee. „ V iii 79
And fear not I should stumble in the *d*, Not tho' it be their hour, the power of *d*, But my hour too, the power of light in *d*! „ V iii 92

Darkness (*continued*)   I am not in the *d*, but the light,   *Becket* v iii 97
in the gulf Of never-dawning *d*?   *Prom. of May* I 542
lie down there together in the *d* which would seem
   but for a moment,   „   III 194
but this new moon, I fear, Is *d*.   *Foresters* I ii 87
And *d* rises from the fallen sun.   „   I iii 42
You see the *d* thro' the lighter leaf.   „   IV 975
Darling   His village *d* in some lewd caress   *Becket* IV ii 200
The clamour *d* of their afternoon!   *The Cup* II 125
She has disappear'd, poor *d*, from the world—   *Prom. of May* II 410
Darn   necklaces To please our lady, we must *d*,   *The Falcon* 45
Darning   What art thou doing there? *Elisabetta*. D
   your lordship.   „   41
Dart   To hide the scar left by thy Parthian *d*.   *Becket, Pro.* 377
Darter (**daughter**)   I ha' nine *d's* i' the spital that be dead   I iv 249
to turn out boäth my *d's* right down fine laädies.   *Prom. of May* I 336
Thy feyther eddicated his *d's* to marry gentlefoälk,   „   II 116
but I couldn't buy my *d* back ageän when she lost
   hersen,   „   III 453
Dash (s)   ice-cold—no *d* of daring in him.   *Queen Mary* I v 331
Dash (**verb**)   *d* The torch of war among your standing
   corn,   *Harold* II ii 748
wields His war-club, *d'es* it on Gurth,   „   v 640
I *d* myself to pieces—I stay myself—   *Becket* II ii 150
d thyself against me that I may slay thee!   „   IV ii 195
thou must *d* us down Our dinner from the skies.   *The Falcon* 152
Dash'd (**rushed**)   We mounted, and we *d* into the heart
   of 'em.   „   629
Dash'd (**sprinkled**)   then he *d* and drench'd, He dyed,   *Harold* III i 140
D red with that unhallow'd passover;   *Becket* I iii 348
Dash'd (**threw**)   insolent shot that *d* the seas Upon us,   *Queen Mary* v i 57
bit his shield, and *d* it on the ground,   *Harold* I v 405
Dash'd (**thrown**)   wines Of wedding had been *d* into the
   cups Of victory,   „   IV iii 7
Daub   This is a *d* to Philip.   *Queen Mary* I v 447
Daughter (*See also* **Darter**)   Mary, the lawful and
   legitimate *d* of Harry the Eighth!   „   I i 8
(I have a *d* in her service who reported it)   „   I i 76
my *d* said that when there rose a talk of the late
   rebellion,   „   I i 91
I am Harry's *d*, Tudor, and not Fear.   „   II iv 52
'Hail, *D* of God, and saver of the faith.   „   III ii 82
I am Harry's *d*:   „   III v 117
Who knows if Boleyn's *d* be my sister?   „   v v 194
God bless thee, wedded *d*.   *Harold* III i 293
so will I, *d*, until I find Which way the battle balance.   „   v i 459
No, *d*, but the canons out of Waltham,   „   v i 474
Look, *d*, look.   *Edith*.   Nay, father, look for *me*!   „   v i 535
No, *d*, no—they fall behind the horse—   „   v i 545
A cleric violated The *d* of his host,   *Becket* I iii 383
Shrink from me, like a *d* of the Church.   „   II i 277
like the Greek king when his *d* was sacrificed,   „   III iii 105
The *d* of Zion lies beside the way—   „   III iii 177
D, the world hath trick'd thee.   Leave it, *d*; Come
   thou with me to Godstow nunnery,   „   IV ii 364
I am grieved, my *d*.   „   v ii 83
D, *d*, Deal not with things you know not.   „   v ii 132
No, *d*, you mistake our good Archbishop;   „   v ii 137
D, my time is short, I shall not do it.   „   v ii 157
Liker the King.   *Becket*.   No, *d*,   „   v ii 182
Tho' you are a gentleman, I but a farmer's *d*—   *Prom. of May* I 668
—a *d* of the fields, This Dora!   „   II 622
shamed of his poor farmer's *d* among the ladies in his
   drawing-room?   „   III 294
if a gentleman Should wed a farmer's *d*,   „   III 579
only there was left A second *d*,   „   III 772
I come here to see this *d* of Sir Richard of the Lea   *Foresters* I ii 26
Come away, *d*.   „   I ii 283
then each man That owns a wife or *d*,   „   III 460
dishonour The *d's* and the wives of your own faction—   „   IV 698
Daunted   What, *d* by a garrulous, arrogant girl!   „   IV 736
Dauphin   In order to betroth her to your *D*.   *Queen Mary* I v 293
Mary of Scotland, married to your *D*,   „   I v 296
your Scottish namesake marrying The *D*,   „   v i 136
The Queen of Scots is married to the *D*,   „   v v 53

David   gloom of Saul Was lighten'd by young *D's* harp.   *Queen Mary* v ii 359
And no *D* To meet him?   *Harold* v i 496
Dawn (s)   If Ludgate can be reach'd by *d* to-morrow.   *Queen Mary* II iii 53
gray *d* Of an old age that never will be mine   „   v ii 234
Like sun-gilt breathings on a frosty *d*—   „   v iii 51
Shall see the dewy kiss of *d* no more   *Harold* II ii 331
by dead Norway without dream or *d*!   „   IV iii 122
Were the great trumpet blowing doomsday *d*,   „   v i 228
wind of the *d* that I hear in the pine overhead?   *Becket* II i 1
In the gray *d* before the Temple doors.   *The Cup* I ii 295
I rise to-morrow In the gray *d*,   „   I ii 434
Hang'd at mid-day, their traitor of the *d*   „   II 124
From the dim *d* of Being—   *Prom. of May* I 281
That beam of *d* upon the opening flower,   *Foresters* IV 3
yet I think these oaks at *d* and even,   „   IV 1067
Dawn (**verb**)   day of peril that *d's* darkly and drearily   *Becket* I iv 145
Dawning (*See also* **Never-dawning**)   The islands
   call'd into the *d* church Out of the dead,   *Queen Mary* III iii 172
Day (*See also* **Daay, Gala-day, Good-day, Mid-day,
   Saint's-day**)   too full of aches and broken
   before his *d*.   „   I i 125
I have seen enough for this *d*.   „   I i 131
For I foresee dark *d's*.   *Mary*.   And so do I, sir;   „   I v 275
and be the mightiest man This *d* in England.   „   II ii 20
I trust this *d*, thro' God, I have saved the crown.   „   II ii 302
And see the citizens arm'd.   Good *d*; good *d*.   „   II ii 378
a black 'un for us this blessed *d*.   „   III ii 101
the brightest *d* Beheld our rough forefathers   „   III ii 119
Might not St. Andrew's be her happiest *d*?   *Mary*.
   Then these shall meet upon St. Andrew's *d*.   „   III ii 124
Till the sun dance, as upon Easter *D*.   „   III ii 238
St. Andrew's *d*; sit close, sit close, we are friends.   „   III iii 1
Laughs at the last red leaf, and Andrew's *D*.   „   III iii 87
Should not this *d* be held in after years   „   III iii 89
This is the loveliest *d* that ever smiled On England.   „   III iii 161
I found One *d*, a wholesome scripture,   „   III iv 84
In clear and open *d* were congruent With that vile
   Cranmer   „   III iv 230
Is like a word that comes from olden *d's*,   „   III iv 34
Queen hath been three *d's* in tears For Philip's
   going,   „   III vi 12
Still Parleying with Renard, all the *d* with Renard,   „   III vi 116
And scarce a greeting all the *d* for me—   „   III vi 118
Methinks that would you tarry one *d* more   „   III vi 233
Madam, a *d* may sink or save a realm.   *Mary*.   A
   d may save a heart from breaking too.   *Philip*.
   Well, Simon Renard, shall we two?   *Renard*.
   Your Grace's business will not suffer, sire, For
   one *d* more, so far as I can tell.   *Philip*.   Then
   one *d* more to please her Majesty.   „   III vi 238
Good *d*, old friend; what, you look somewhat worn;   „   IV ii 115
yet it is a *d* to test your health   „   IV ii 117
Win thro' this *d* with honour to yourself,   „   IV ii 165
It is a *d* of rain.   „   IV ii 229
Hath, like a brief and bitter winter's *d*,   „   IV iii 430
Expectant of the rack from *d* to *d*,   „   IV iii 437
What a *d*, what a *d*! nigh upo' judgement daay   „   IV iii 467
What, not one *d*?   „   v i 209
That all *d* long hath wrought his father's work,   „   v ii 118
believe I lamed his Majesty's For a *d* or two,   „   v ii 472
Indian shawl That Philip brought me in our happy
   d's?   „   v ii 541
On all the road from Dover, *d* and night; On all
   the road from Harwich, night and *d*;   „   v ii 577
as in the *d* of the first church, when Christ Jesus
   was King.   „   v iv 54
Ah, those *d's* Were happy.   „   v v 239
These meteors came and went before our *d*,   *Harold* I i 132
wilt thou fly my falcons this fair *d*?   „   II ii 147
Down thirty feet below the smiling *d*—   „   II ii 430
in thy father's *d* They blinded my young kinsman,   „   II ii 510
O friends, I shall not overlive the *d*.   „   III i 233
Lost, lost, the light of *d*,   „   III ii 12
The *d* is won!   „   IV i 270
the *d*, Our *d* beside the Derwent will not shine   „   IV iii 49

Day (*continued*) guest, As haggard as a fast of forty *d's*, *Harold* IV iii 176
I have ridden night and *d* from Pevensey— „ IV iii 192
but leave this *d* to me. „ v i 128
Because I loved thee in my mortal *d*, „ v i 240
I am dead as Death this *d* to ought of earth's „ v i 425
that happy *d*! A birthday welcome! happy *d's* and many! „ v i 430
Stigand, O father, have we won the *d*? „ v i 544
and enough of death for this one *d*, The *d* of St. Calixtus, and the *d*, My *d* „ v ii 120
His *d*, with all his rooftree ringing 'Harold,' „ v ii 129
A sauce-deviser for thy *d's* of fish, *Becket, Pro.* 98
Follow me this Rosamund *d* and night, „ *Pro.* 506
Thou art wearied out With this *d's* work, „ I i 7
That havock'd all the land in Stephen's *d*. „ I i 243
O rare, a whole long *d* of open field. „ I i 296
made the twilight *d*, „ I iii 372
Lost in desuetude, of my grandsire's *d*, „ I iii 414
set the Church This *d* between the hammer and the anvil— „ I iii 585
Grant me one *d* To ponder these demands. „ I iii 668
d of peril that dawns darkly and drearily „ I iv 144
yea, and in the *d* of judgment also, „ I iv 147
that be dead ten times o'er i' one *d* wi' the putrid fever; „ I iv 251
Like sudden night in the main glare of *d*. „ II i 58
decide on what was customary In olden *d's*, „ II ii 176
but this *d* he proffer'd peace. „ II ii 239
You had not borne it, no, not for a *d*. „ II ii 305
In the great *d* against the wronger. „ III iii 17
Glancing at the *d's* when his father was only Earl of Anjou, „ III iii 149
Thanks to the blessed Magdalen, whose *d* it is. „ III iii 172
out with Henry in the *d's* When Henry loved me, „ v ii 231
What *d* of the week? Tuesday? „ v ii 281
to people heaven in the great *d* When God makes up his jewels. „ v ii 496
Do they not fight the Great Fiend *d* by *d*? „ v ii 586
Fair Sir, a happy *d* to you! *The Cup* I i 188
I have had a weary *d* in watching you. „ I ii 40
close not yet the door upon a night That looks half *d*. „ I ii 389
This very *d* the Romans crown him king „ II 63
He wills you then this *d* to marry him, „ II 66
And join your life this *d* with his, „ II 135
to make the *d* memorial, when Synorix, first King, „ II 439
This all too happy *d*, crown—queen at once. „ II 451
been on my knees every *d* for these half-dozen years *The Falcon* 184
I come this *d* to break my fast with you. „ 276
A lady that was beautiful as *d* Sat by me „ 349
but this *d* has brought A great occasion. „ 487
so much worse For last *d's* journey. „ 834
And the *d's* bright like a friend, but the wind east like an enemy. *Prom. of May* I 79
The sky? or the sea on a blue *d*? „ I 102
Good *d*! *Wilson*. Good *d*, sir. „ I 294
Good *d*, then, Dobson. „ I 299
Many happy returns of the *d*, father. „ I 351
Who shrieks by *d* at what she does by night, „ I 532
and it seems to me nobbut t'other *d*. „ II 7
My name is Harold! Good *d*, Dobbins! „ II 726
always told Father that the huge old ashtree there would cause an accident some *d*; „ III 245
may drop off any *d*, any hour. You must see at once. „ III 407
You heard him say it was one of his bad *d's*. „ III 469
It is almost the last of my bad *d's*, I think. „ III 472
.Or ever the *d* began, *Foresters* I i 11
and these are the *d's* of Prince John. „ I i 177
I love him as a damsel of his *d* „ I i 227
Sufficient for the *d*, dear father! „ I i 343
twilight of the coming *d* already glimmers in the east. „ I ii 247
But ill befitting such a festal *d* „ I iii 37
To sleep! to sleep! The long bright *d* is done, „ I iii 41
Whate'er thy joys, they vanish with the *d*; „ I iii 44
There is no land like England Where'er the light of *d* be; (repeat) *Foresters* II i 2, 6, 14, 18
king of *d* hath stept from off his throne, *Foresters* II i 26

Day (*continued*) Perchance this *d* may sink so gloriously, *Foresters* II i 31
Whene'er this *d* should come about, „ II i 41
A maiden now Were ill-bested in these dark *d's* of John, „ II ii 45
In the night, in the *d*, „ II i 182
Dear, in these *d's* of Norman license, „ III 177
having lived For twenty *d's* and nights in mail, „ IV 124
Not having broken fast the livelong *d*— „ IV 186
must we dance attendance all the *d*? „ IV 551
Daybreak Send the Great Seal by *d*. *Becket* I i 405
Day-dream Some hunter in *d-d's* or half asleep *Foresters* IV 1088
Daylight (adj.) Hath shock'd me back into the *d* truth *Queen Mary* III v 135
Daylight (s) Let me bring you in here where there is still full *d*. *Prom. of May* III 218
Dazed (*See also* **Daäzed**) Edward wakes!—*D*—he hath seen a vision. *Harold* III i 131
Dazing *See* **Brain-dazing**
Deacon (*See also* **Cardinal-deacon**) thou art but *d*, not yet bishop, *Becket, Pro.* 83
Dead (adj.) (*See also* **Deäd, Famine-dead**) You know your Latin—quiet as a *d* body. *Queen Mary* I iv 181
Quiet as a *d* body. „ I iv 187
which every now and then Beats me half *d*: „ I v 525
When I and thou and all rebellions lie *D* bodies „ II i 80
The tree that only bears *d* fruit is gone. „ III i 19
Sir, this *d* fruit was ripening overmuch, And had to be removed lest living Spain Should sicken at *d* England. *Stafford*. Not so *d*, But that a shock may rouse her. „ III i 25
d I cannot choose but love her. „ III i 339
true enough Her dark *d* blood is in my heart with mine. „ III i 349
Her dark *d* blood that ever moves with mine „ III i 352
And unto no *d* world; but Lambeth palace, „ III i 153
The islands call'd into the dawning church Out of the *d*, deep night „ III iii 173
should be No longer a *d* letter, but requicken'd. „ III iv 10
Let the *d* letter live.' „ III iv 33
Let the *d* letter burn! „ III iv 40
d—with the fear of death Too *d* ev'n for a death-watch! „ III v 139
my faith would seem *D* or half-drown'd, „ IV ii 98
Until the power suddenly blew him *d*. „ IV iii 341
The parson from his own spire swung out *d*, „ IV iii 376
Our altar is a mound of *d* men's clay, „ v ii 161
A letter which the Count de Noailles wrote To that *d* traitor Wyatt, „ v ii 498
Let *d* things rest. „ v ii 506
Tell him at last I know his love is *d*, „ v ii 591
D or alive you cannot make him happy. „ v v 71
Women, when I am *d*, Open my heart, „ v v 152
The Queen is *d*. „ v v 252
For my *d* father's loyalty to thee? *Harold* I i 240
a *d* man Rose from behind the altar, „ I ii 78
saw the church all fill'd With *d* men upright from their graves, and all The *d* men made at thee to murder thee, „ I ii 83
The shadows of a hundred fat *d* deer For *d* men's ghosts. „ I ii 103
Where they eat *d* men's flesh, and drink their blood. „ II ii 807
Dry as an old wood-fungus on a *d* tree, „ III i 8
and sell not thou Our living passion for a *d* man's dream; „ III ii 60
Our dear, *d*, traitor-brother, Tostig, „ IV iii 83
How ran that answer which King Harold gave To his *d* namesake, „ IV iii 110
Sound sleep to the man Here by *d* Norway „ IV iii 122
By God, we thought him *d*— „ IV iii 148
What did the *d* man call it—Sanguelac, „ v i 184
My fatal oath—the *d* Saints—the dark dreams— „ v i 380
I am *d* as Death this day to ought of earth's „ v i 425
They are stripping the *d* bodies naked yonder, „ v ii 34
I tell thee, girl, I am seeking my *d* Harold, „ v ii 43
being the true wife Of this *d* King, who never bore revenge. „ v ii 85
And this *d* king's Who, king or not, „ v ii 123
Pluck the *d* woman off the *d* man, Malet! „ v ii 144
D is he, my Queen? *Becket, Pro.* 368
A *d* man's dying wish should be of weight. „ *Pro.* 422
We wait but the King's word to strike thee *d*. „ I iii 167
They be *d* while I be a-supping. „ I iv 247
that be *d* ten times o'er i' one day wi' the putrid fever; „ I iv 250

De Brito (knight of King Henry II.'s household) (*See also* Brito, Richard) De Tracy—even that flint *D B*.   *Becket, Pro.* 523
De Tracy and *D B*, from our castle.   „   I i 278
De Broc   thou, *D B*, that holdest Saltwood Castle—   „   I iii 160
cursed those *D B's* That hold our Saltwood Castle   II ii 267
Perchance the fierce *D B's* from Saltwood Castle,   „   v ii 249
your friends, those ruffians, the *D B's*,   „   v ii 435
And one of the *D B's* is with them,   „   v ii 572
Debt   Your pious wish to pay King Edward's *d's*,   *Queen Mary* I v 112
Pray'd me to pay her *d's*, and keep the Faith;   „   v v 257
—thou art drowned in *d*—   *Becket, Pro.* 491
every bond and *d* and obligation Incurr'd as Chancellor.   „   I iii 710
but the ill success of the farm, and the *d's*,   *Prom. of May* II 69
I would pay My brother all his *d*   *Foresters* I ii 218
For whom I ran into my *d* to the Abbot,   „   II i 462
No, not an hour: the *d* is due to-day.   „   IV 448
he Would pay us all the *d* at once,   „   IV 485
The *d* hath not been paid.   „   IV 612
Decalogue   Thro' chastest honour of the *D*   *Becket* v i 206
Decaying   Cool as the light in old *d* wood;   *Queen Mary* IV ii 5
Decent   We be more like scarecrows in a field than *d* serving men;   *Foresters* I i 35
Decide   *d* on what was customary In olden days,   *Becket* II ii 175
all the Church of France *D* on their decision,   „   II ii 178
Decided   Cranmer, it is *d* by the Council   *Queen Mary* IV ii 178
Decision   all the Church of France Decide on their *d*,   *Becket* II ii 178
Deck   Stand on the *d* and spread his wings for sail!   *Queen Mary* I v 379
same chair, Or rather throne of purple, on the *d*.   „   III ii 8
Stagger on the slope *d's* for any rough sea   *Becket* II ii 106
Declaration   In several bills and *d's*,   *Queen Mary* IV i 48
Declare   *d* our penitence and grief For our long schism   „   III iii 128
Our letters of commission will *d* this plainlier.   „   III iii 222
D the Queen's right to the throne;   „   IV ii 78
I shall *d* to you my very faith Without all colour.   „   IV iii 225
came to sue Your Council and yourself to *d* war. (repeat)   „   v 108, 116
Declared   when last he wrote, *d* His comfort in your Grace   „   III vi 78
As I have many a time *d* to you—   *The Cup* II 48
Decline   *d* The judgment of the King?   *Becket* I iii 675
Decree   sanction your *d* Of Tostig's banishment,   *Harold* IV i 103
Deed   With golden *d's* and iron strokes that brought   „   II ii 47
Some said it was thy father's *d*.   *Harold*. They lied.   „   II ii 513
Nothing, so thy promise be thy *d*.   *Becket* III iii 224
The *d's* done—Away!   „   v iii 207
Deem   needs must *d* This love by you return'd as heartily,   *Queen Mary* II ii 196
Who *d's* it a most just and holy war.   „   v i 147
Deeming   *D* him one that thro' the fear of death   „   IV iii 26
Deep (adj. and adv.)   *D*—I shall fathom him.   „   I iii 158
islands call'd into the dawning church Out of the dead, *d* night of heathendom,   „   III iii 173
And crying, in his *d* voice, more than once,   „   IV iii 611
strike hard and *d* into The prey they are rending from her—   „   v ii 267
There thou prick'st me *d*.   *Harold* II ii 424
Drink and drink *d*—our marriage will be fruitful.
Drink and drink *d*, and thou wilt make me happy.   *The Cup* II 380
We lie too *d* down in the shadow here.   *The Falcon* 581
I only wish This pool were *d* enough,   *Prom. of May* II 304
Lead us thou to some *d* glen,   *Foresters* II ii 168
Deep (s)   outdraught of the *d* Haul like a great strong fellow   *Harold* IV i 10
boughs across the *d* That dropt themselves,   „   III i 151
voice of the *d* as it hollows the cliffs of the land.   *Becket* II i 3
voice coming up with the voice of the *d* from the strand,   „   II i 6
Love that is born of the *d* coming up with the sun from the sea. (repeat)   „   II i 9, 19
And the great *d's* were broken up again,   „   v iii 43
Deep-down   And deeper still the *d-d* oubliette,   *Harold* II ii 428
Deeper   see *D* into the mysteries of heaven   „   I i 200
D still.   *Wulfnoth*. And *d* still the deep-down oubliette,   „   II ii 427
that tempest which will set it trembling Only to base it *d*.   *Becket, Pro.* 210
Deepest   Sunk in the *d* pit of pauperism,   *Prom. of May* III 803

Deep-incavern'd   His buzzard-beak and *d-i* eyes Half fright me.   *Queen Mary* I iv 266
Deer   You are the stateliest *d* in all the herd—   „   vi 425
The shadows of a hundred fat red *d*   *Harold* I ii 103
Buck; *d*, as you call it.   *Becket* I iv 139
This Canterbury, like a wounded *d*,   „   II i 21
Huntsman, and hound, and *d* were all neck-broken!   *The Cup* II ii 23
That hold by Richard, tho' they kill his *d*.   *Foresters* I iii 101
The *d*, the highback'd polecat, the wild boar.   „   I iii 119
true woodman's bow of the best yew-wood to slay the *d*.   „   II i 393
Robin, like a *d* from a dog,   „   II i 433
By all the *d* that spring Thro' wood and lawn   „   III 424
Gone, like a *d* that hath escaped thine arrow!   „   IV 60
What *d* when I have mark'd him ever yet Escaped   „   IV 62
They strike the *d* at once to death—   „   IV 525
He drove his knife into the heart of the *d*, The *d* fell dead to the bottom,   „   IV 542
On nuts and acorns, ha! Or the King's *d*?   „   IV 884
Deer-like   Chased *d-l* up his mountains,   *Harold* I ii 148
Defamed   betray'd, *d*, divorced, forlorn!   *Queen Mary* I v 26
Suffer not That my brief reign in England be *d*   „   v ii 302
Defeat   What! are thy people sullen from *d*?   *Harold* IV i 2
and now but shuns The semblance of *d*;   *Becket* I iii 191
Defect   We hold by his defiance, not his *d*.   „   II ii 218
Defective   seeing they were men *D* or excessive,   „   II ii 213
Nay, if they were *d* as St. Peter Denying Christ,   „   II ii 215
Defence   or any harm done to the people if my jest be in *d* of the Truth?   „   II ii 340
And private hates with our *d* of Heaven.   „   v ii 52
Spare this *d*, dear brother.   „   v iii 168
Whereas in wars of freedom and *d*   *The Cup* I ii 160
Defend   I pray you, Do not *d* yourself.   *Becket* II ii 112
Except she could *d* her innocence.   *Foresters* II ii 47
I can *d* my cause against the traitors   „   IV 898
Defender   The great unborn *d* of the Faith,   *Queen Mary* III ii 165
Till Truth herself be shamed of her *d*.   *Becket* II ii 345
Defensoribus   *Non* d *istis*, Walter Map.   „   II ii 346
Defiance   We hold by his *d*, not his defect.   „   II ii 218
Defied   who yet *d* the tyrant,   „   II ii 216
—kinglike *D* the Pope, and, like his kingly sires,   „   IV ii 440
Defy   I hate thee, and despise thee, and *d* thee.   *Harold* IV ii 79
Boldness out of the bottle! I *d* thee.   *Foresters* IV 239
Nay, I *d* thee still.   „   IV 276
Degradation   scarce have spoken with you Since when?—your *d*.   *Queen Mary* IV ii 120
papers by my hand Sign'd since my *d*—   „   IV iii 244
What doth hard murder care For *d*?   *Becket* III ii 394
Degrade   and *d* the realm By seeking justice   *Queen Mary* IV i 18
D, imprison him—Not death for death.   *Becket* I iii 400
Degraded   the courts of the Church, They but *d* him.   „   Pro. 14
ye but *d* him Where I had hang'd him.   „   I iii 391
Degree   There stands a man, once of so high *d*,   *Queen Mary* IV iii 69
Dei   Ha—Verbum *D*—verbum—word of God!   „   III i 262
Deign   my nobleness Of nature, as you *d* to call it,   *The Falcon* 811
Who *d* to honour this my thirtieth year,   *Foresters* I ii 79
If you will *d* to tread a measure with me.   „   I ii 132
Deign'd   Who never *d* to shine into my palace.   *The Falcon* 285
The diamonds that you never *d* to wear.   „   761
Dejiciatur   Equus cum equite *D*!   *Harold* v i 580
Delay   *D* is death to thee, ruin to England.   „   II ii 717
Delicacy   repulses, the *delicacies*, the subtleties.   *Becket, Pro.* 500
Delicate   (*See also* **Courtly-delicate**) your hand Will be much coveted! What a *d* one!   *Queen Mary* v iii 44
Be men less *d* than the Devil himself?   *Harold* III i 116
I have been a lover of wines, and *d* meats,   *Becket* I i 76
That's a *d* Latin lay Of Walter Map: „   v i 191
I am none of your *d* Norman maidens   *Foresters* I i 212
Delicate-footed   the *d-f* creature Came stepping o'er him,   „   IV 535
Delight (s)   comes To rob you of your one *d* on earth.   *The Falcon* 828
but I Take some *d* in sketching,   *Prom. of May* II 539
Delight (verb)   *D* to wallow in the grossness of it,   *Becket* II ii 343
Delighted   Affrighted me, and then *d* me,   *Queen Mary* III v 144
Deliver   Do here absolve you and *d* you And every one of you,   „   III iii 214
wouldst *d* Canterbury To our King's hands again,   *Becket* I iii 580

Deliver (*continued*)   I here *d* all this controversy Into
    your royal hands.   *Becket* II ii 136
    I might *d* all things to thy hand—   ,,   III iii 270
Delivered   'The Queen of England is *d* of a dead
    dog!'   *Queen Mary* III ii 219
    he was *d* To the secular arm to burn;   ,,   IV ii 213
    God's grace and Holy Church *d* us.   *Becket* IV ii 309
    are *d* here in the wild wood an hour after noon.   *Foresters* IV 509
Demand (s)   then to cede A point to her *d*?   *Queen Mary* III vi 170
    Grant me one day To ponder these *d*'s.   *Becket* I iii 669
Demand (verb)   I will *d* his ward From Edward   *Harold* I ii 58
    the King *d*'s three hundred marks,   *Becket* I iii 626
    the King *d*'s seven hundred marks,   ,,   I iii 634
    the King *d*'s five hundred marks,   ,,   I iii 641
    King *D*'s a strict account of all those revenues   ,,   I iii 650
    Antonius To-morrow will *d* your tribute—   *The Cup* II ii 97
Demanded   *d* Possession of her person and the Tower.   *Queen Mary* III vi 40
Demi-Norman   our dear England Is *d*-*N*.   *Harold* III i 41
De-miracled   fish, they *d*-*m* the miraculous draught,   *Becket* III iii 124
Democracy   when the tide Of full *d* has overwhelm'd
    This Old world,   *Prom. of May* I 593
    When the great *D* Makes a new world—   ,,   I 670
De Morville (knight of the household of King Henry II.)
    (*See also* **Hugh**)   France! Ha! *D M*, Tracy,
    Brito—fled is he?   *Becket* I iv 198
    D M, I had thought so well of you;   ,,   v ii 519
    This wanton here.   *D M*, Hold her away.   ,,   v iii 171
Den   Who dragg'd the scatter'd limbs into their *d*.   *Queen Mary* I v 402
    hottest hold in all the devil's *d*   ,,   v iv 15
    Dares the bear slouch into the lion's *d*?   *Becket* II iii 282
Denial   Treble *d* of the tongue of flesh,   *Harold* III i 281
Denied   Renard *d* her, Ev'n now to me.   *Queen Mary* III vi 2
    or more *D* the Holy Father!   ,,   III iv 248
    St. Peter in his time of fear *D* his Master,   ,,   III iv 264
    Albeit I have *d* him.   ,,   IV ii 236
    Nay, but, my Lord, he *d* purgatory.   ,,   IV iii 629
    Would not—if penitent—have *d* him *her* Forgive-
    ness.   *Prom. of May* ii 496
Denis (Bishop of Paris and Patron Saint of France)   St. *D*,
    that thou shouldst not.   *Becket*, Pro. 89
    By St. *D*——   *De Brito*.   Ay, by St. *D*, now will he
    flame out, And lose his head as old St. *D* did.   ,,   v ii 477
    St. *D* of France and St. Alphege of England,   ,,   v iii 165
Denmark   the King of *D* is with us;   *Queen Mary* II i 195
Dense   How *d* a fold of danger nets him round,   *Harold* II ii 17
Deny   I *d* not to have been Your faithful friend   *Queen Mary* IV i 88
    against the Norseman, If thou *d* them this.   *Harold* IV i 159
    D not thou God's honour for a king.   *Becket* II ii 424
    Nay, I *d* not That I was somewhat anger'd.   ,,   IV ii 350
    Come, come, could he *d* it?   What did he say?   *The Cup* I ii 345
    can *d* Nothing to you that you require of him.   *The Falcon* 717
Denying   if they were defective as St. Peter *D* Christ,   *Becket* II i 216
Depart   And under his authority—I *d*.   ,,   I iii 728
Departed   And presently all rose, and so *d*.   *The Falcon* 367
Depend   all *d*'s Upon the skill and swiftness   *Queen Mary* I iii 142
    All *d*'s on me—Father, this poor girl,   *Prom. of May* ii 211
Deputation   comes a *d* From our finikin fairy nation.   *Foresters* II i 144
Derwent   Where lie the Norsemen? on the *D*?   *Harold* IV i 253
    Our day beside the *D* will not shine   ,,   IV iii 50
Descend   *D*'s the ruthless Norman—   ,,   II ii 467
    And that my wife *d*'s from Alfred?   ,,   II ii 594
    the second curse *D* upon thine head,   ,,   III ii 49
    Scatter thy people home, *d* the hill,   ,,   v i 10
    so *d* again with some of her ladyship's own
    appurtenances?   *The Falcon* 416
Descending   as the soul *d* out of heaven Into a body
    generate.   *Queen Mary* IV i 35
Desert (merit)   fierier than fire To yield them their *d*'s.   ,,   v iv 27
    D's!   Amen to what?   Whose *d*'s?   ,,   v iv 30
Desert (waste)   wells of Castaly are not wasted upon the *d*.   *Becket*, Pro. 388
Deserve   He must *d* his surname better.   *Queen Mary* III ii 197
    that worship for me which Heaven knows I ill *d*—   *Foresters* I iii 162
Designer   See **Dish-designer**
Desire (s)   She had no *d* for that, and wrung her
    hands,   *Queen Mary* III i 384

Desire (s) (*continued*)   And hot *d* to imitate;   *Queen Mary* III iv 171
    Her fierce *d* of bearing him a child,   ,,   IV iii 429
    O yield them all their *d*!   *The Cup* II 8
    and no need Of veiling their *d*'s.   *Prom. of May* I 530
    The love of freedom, the *d* of God,   *Foresters* II i 68
Desire (verb)   My people hate me and *d* my death,   *Queen Mary* v ii 345
    My husband hates me, and *d*'s my death.   ,,   v ii 348
    I hate myself, and I *d* my death.   ,,   v ii 351
    A stranger monk *d*'s access to you.   *Becket* v ii 65
Desolate   That *d* letter, blotted with her tears,   *Prom. of May* II 475
Despair   I am almost in.   *Queen Mary* I v 385
    Shall I *d* then?—God forbid!   ,,   III 129
    but O girl, girl, I am almost in *d*.   *Foresters* I i 263
Despair'd   I had *d* of thee—that sent me crazed.   ,,   v 1021
Despise   Those of the wrong side will *d* the man,   *Queen Mary* IV iii 25
    Make us *d* it at odd hours, my Lord.   ,,   IV iii 386
    I hate thee, and *d* thee, and defy thee.   *Harold* IV ii 79
Despite   *d* his fearful heresies, I loved the man,   *Queen Mary* IV iii 633
    And *he* hath learnt, *d* the tiger in him,   *Harold* I i 147
    d his kingly promise given To our own self of pardon,   *Becket* II ii 431
Despondency   When left alone in my *d*,   *Queen Mary* IV ii 95
Destiny   Moved in the iron grooves of *D*?   Remorse
    then is a part of *D*,   *Prom. of May* II 267
Destroy   We come not to *d*, but edify;   *Queen Mary* III iii 188
    Take heed, lest he *d* thee utterly.   *Becket* I iii 13
    Wilt thou *d* the Church in fighting for it,   ,,   I iii 36
Desuetude   wholesome usages, Lost in *d*,   ,,   I iii 413
Determine   Your courts of justice will *d* that.   *Queen Mary* II iv 131
Dethrone   Arise against her and *d* the Queen—   ,,   I iii 91
De Tracy (Sir William, knight of the household of King
    Henry II.)   (*See also* **Tracy**)   *D T*—even that
    flint De Brito.   *Becket*, Pro. 522
    D T and De Brito, from our castle.   ,,   I i 278
Deum   bells must ring; Te *D*'s must be sung;   *Queen Mary* III ii 211
Deus   Jacta tonitrua *D* bellator!   *Harold* v i 570
    Fulmina, fulmina *D* vastator!   ,,   v i 574
Device   put some fresh *d* in lieu of it—   *Queen Mary* III i 268
    but follow'd the *d* of those Her nearest kin: ,,   III i 379
Devil   (*See also* **Dare-devil, Divil**)   has offer'd her his
    son Philip, the Pope and the *D*.   ,,   I i 106
    all Your trouble to the dogstar and the *d*.   ,,   I iv 292
    His foes—the *D* had suborn'd 'em,   ,,   I v 626
    ordnance On the White Tower and on the *D*'s Tower,   ,,   II iii 44
    Philip had been one of those black *d*'s of Spain,   ,,   III i 215
    that every Spaniard carries a tale like a *d*   ,,   III i 224
    Death and the *D*—if he find I have one—   ,,   III i 231
    a pale horse for Death and Gardiner for the *D*.   ,,   III i 235
    Not for the seven *d*'s to enter in?   ,,   III ii 140
    d take all boots were ever made Since man went
    barefoot.   ,,   III v 197
    Or to be still in pain with *d*'s in hell;   ,,   IV iii 222
    With all his *d*'s doctrines;   ,,   IV iii 278
    Pole Will tell you that the *d* helpt them thro' it.   ,,   IV iii 352
    give the *D* his due, I never found he bore me any
    spite   ,,   v ii 472
    I were whole *d* if I wrong'd you, Madam.   ,,   v iii 6
    hottest hold in all the *d*'s den   ,,   v iv 15
    wrath of Heaven hath three tails, The *d* only one.   *Harold* I i 62
    Fishermen? *d*'s!   Who, while ye fish for men with your
    false fires, Let the great *D* fish for your own souls.   ,,   II i 29
    Like Jonah, than have known there were such *d*'s.   ,,   II i 39
    would make the hard earth rive To the very *D*'s horns,   ,,   II ii 741
    Be men less delicate than the *D* himself? I thought that
    naked Truth would shame the *D* The *D* is so modest.   ,,   III i 117
    A lying *d* Hath haunted me—   ,,   v i 317
    Ye haled this tonsured *d* into your courts;   *Becket* I iii 387
    Forty thousand marks! forty thousand *d*'s—   ,,   I iv 91
    Saving the *D*'s honour, his yes and no.   ,,   II ii 142
    if this *if* be like the *D*'s ' *if* Thou wilt fall down and
    worship me.'   ,,   III iii 285
    O *d*, can I free her from the grave?   ,,   v 185
    Down to the *d* with this bond that beggars me!   *Foresters* I i 340
    By all the *d*'s in and out of Hell!   ,,   II ii 27
    proud priests, and these Barons, *D*'s,   ,,   III 127
    And wake the *D*, and I may sicken by 'em.   ,,   III 325

Devil (*continued*)   by all the saints and all the *d*'s ye shall
dance.   *Foresters* IV 553
Or, like the *D*'s they are, straight up from Hell.   „   IV 594

Devilish   all of us abhor The venomous, bestial, *d*
revolt Of Thomas Wyatt.   *Queen Mary* II ii 287

Devilry   What game, what juggle, what *d* are you playing?   *Becket* v i 153

Devilstow   Into Godstow, into Hellstow, *D*!   „   v i 215

Devon (**County**)   Were I in *D* with my wedded bride,   *Queen Mary* I iv 119
Carew stirs In *D*:   „   II i 6
should be in *D* too.   „   II i 11

Devon (**Earl of**)   (*See also* **Courtenay**)   Courtenay, to
be made Earl of *D*,   „   I i 111
Good-day, my Lord of *D*;   „   I iii 95
What are you musing on, my Lord of *D*?   „   I iv 27
This dress was made me as the Earl of *D* To take
my seat in;   „   I iv 73
A Courtenay of *D*, and her cousin.   „   I iv 86
Was that my Lord of *D*? do not you Be seen in
corners with my Lord of *D*.   „   I iv 152
What was my Lord of *D* telling you?   „   I iv 183
This comes of parleying with my Lord of *D*.   „   I iv 252
But our young Earl of *D*— *Mary*. Earl of *D*?
I freed him from the Tower, placed him at Court;
I made him Earl of *D*, and—the fool—   „   I v 161
My Lord of *D* is a pretty man.   „   I v 614
and party thereunto, My Lord of *D*.   „   II iv 101
not now and save the life Of *D*:   „   II iv 124
could have wedded that poor youth, My Lord of *D*—   „   v ii 477
Lord *D*, girls! what are you whispering here?   „   v ii 485

Devour   run in upon her and *d* her, one and all   *Becket, Pro.* 525

Dew   To those three children like a pleasant *d*.   *Queen Mary* IV iii 92
Is God's best *d* upon the barren field.   „   v i 102
Vying a tear with our cold *d*'s,   *Harold* v i 151
hath the fire in her face and the *d* in her eyes.   *Foresters* I i 167
Found him dead and drench'd in *d*,   „   II ii 147

Dewy   I Shall see the *d* kiss of dawn no more   *Harold* II ii 331

Diadem   He sends you This *d* of the first Galatian Queen,   *The Cup* II 132
tell him That I accept the *d* of Galatia—   „   II 158

Diagonalise   if he move at all, Heaven stay him, is fain to
d. *Herbert*. *D*! thou art a word-monger. Our
Thomas never will *d*. Thou art a jester and a verse-
maker. *D*!   *Becket* II ii 330

Dialectic   with his charm of simple style And close *d*,   *Prom. of May* I 225

Diamond (*adj.*)   if we *will* buy *d* necklaces To please our lady,   *The Falcon* 44

Diamond (*s*)   set it round with gold, with pearl, with *d*.   *Queen Mary* IV 376
Some six or seven Bishops, *d*'s, pearls,   „   III i 52
A *d*, And Philip's gift, as proof of Philip's love,   „   III i 66
on his neck a collar, Gold, thick with *d*'s;   „   III i 80
Cut with a *d*; so to last like truth.   „   III v 25
Not ev'n the central *d*, worth, I think,   *Becket* v i 164
Dare beg him to receive his *d*'s back—   *The Falcon* 262
Then I require you to take back your *d*'s—   „   720
But have you ever worn my *d*'s?   „   737
The *d*'s that you never deign'd to wear.   „   761
I cannot keep your *d*'s, for the gift I ask for,   „   776
These *d*'s are both yours and mine—   „   903

Diamond-dance   ripples twinkled at their *d-d*,   *Queen Mary* III ii 10

Dian   Behold a pretty *D* of the wood,   *Foresters* III 267

Diana   Our Artemis Has vanquish'd their *D*.   *The Cup* II 457

Dickon   here's little *D*, and little Robin, and little
Jenny—   *Queen Mary* II iii 112
This paper, *D*. I found it fluttering at the palace
gates:—   „   III ii 217

Die   Fly and farewell, and let me *d* the death.   „   I ii 106
order with all heretics That it shall be, before I *d*,   „   I v 35
D like the torn fox dumb,   „   II ii 331
I live and *d* The true and faithful bride of Philip—   „   II iv 42
or *d* with those That are no cowards and no Courtenays.   „   II iv 86
And Lady Jane had left us. *Mary*. They shall *d*. *Renard*.
And your so loving sister? *Mary*. She shall *d*.   *Queen Mary* II iv 140
Did not Lord Suffolk *d* like a true man?   „   III i 164
Did you see her *d*?   „   III i 344
said she was condemn'd to *d* for treason;   „   III i 377
light of this new learning wanes and *d*'s: „   III ii 173
That if the Queen should *d* without a child,   „   III iii 74

FF*

Die (*continued*)   Thou knowest we had to dodge, or
duck, or *d*;   *Queen Mary* III iv 358
To sing, love, marry, churn, brew, bake, and *d*,   „   III v 112
says she will live And *d* true maid—   „   III vi 46
Did not More *d*, and Fisher? he must burn.   „   IV i 52
and hide himself and *d*;   „   IV i 143
—they give the poor who *d*.   „   IV ii 53
Ay—gentle as they call you—live or *d*?   „   IV ii 162
Fire—inch by inch to *d* in agony!   „   IV ii 223
Stand watching a sick beast before he *d*'s?   „   IV iii 8
Yet—It is expedient for one man to *d*, Yea, for the
people, lest the people *d*. Yet wherefore should
he *d* that hath return'd   „   IV iii 17
therefore he must *d*, For warning and example.   „   IV iii 51
Hurls his soil'd life against the pikes and *d*'s.   „   IV iii 312
howsoever hero-like the man *D*'s in the fire,   „   IV iii 325
And you saw Latimer and Ridley *d*?   „   IV iii 328
Did he *d* bravely? Tell me that, or leave All else
untold.   „   IV vii 568
To sleep, to *d*—I shall *d* of it, cousin.   „   v ii 127
I may *d* Before I read it. Let me see him at once.   „   v ii 549
Make me full fain to live and *d* a maid.   „   v iii 98
Nay! Better *d* than lie!   *Harold* I i 158
Better *d* than lie!   „   II ii 281
Forgive me, brother, I will live here and *d*.   „   II ii 804
better *d* Than credit this, for death is death,   „   III ii 78
Blaze like a night of fatal stars on those Who read
their doom and *d*.   „   IV i 252
till her voice *D* with the world.   „   IV iii 76
To tell thee thou shalt *d* on Senlac hill—   „   v i 241
I shall *d*—I *d* for England then, who lived for England
—What nobler? men must *d*.   „   v i 267
live or *d*, I would I were among them!   „   v i 463
honeymoon is the gall of love; he *d*'s of his
honeymoon.   *Becket, Pro.* 365
old men must *d*, or the world would grow mouldy,   „   Pro. 409
Lo! I must out or *d*. *Becket*. Or out *and d*.   „   i 268
For we would live and *d* for thee, my lord,   „   i ii 16
Strike, and I *d* the death of martyrdom;   „   i iii 168
—there to beg, starve, *d*—   „   II i 75
you still move against him, you may have no less than
to *d* for it;   „   III iii 326
To *d* for it—I live to *d* for it, I *d* to live for it. The
State will *d*, the Church can never *d*. The
King's not like to *d* for that which *d*'s; But
I must *d* for that which never *d*'s.   „   III iii 334
I am not so happy I could not *d* myself,   „   IV i 87
I am to *d* then, tho' there stand beside thee   „   IV ii 228
both of us will *d*, And I will fly with my sweet boy   „   IV ii 236
I will go live and *d* in Aquitaine. (repeat)   „   v i 109, 142
The chances of his life, just ere he *d*'s.   „   v ii 274
foremost of their files, who *d* For God,   „   v ii 495
I am prepared to *d*.   „   v ii 562
The best of all not all-prepared to *d*.   „   v ii 564
D with him, and be glorified together.   „   v iii 31
And *d* upon the Patriarchal throne Of all my predecessors?   „   v iii 75
whole world Abhor you; ye will *d* the death of dogs!   „   v iii 184
—fight out the good fight—*d* Conqueror.   „   v iii 190
I'd sooner *d* than do it.   *The Cup* I ii 224
A woman I could live and *d* for. What! *D* for a
woman, what new faith is this?   „   I iii 65
I will be faithful to thee till thou *d*.   „   II 330
to live And *d* together.   „   II 444
Thy breed will *d* with thee, and mine with me: *The Falcon* 18
The boy may *d*: more blessed were the rags   „   850
Than all my childless wealth, if mine must *d*.   „   856
She had to *d* for it—she died for you.   „   877
'Let us eat and drink, for to-morrow we *d*.'   *Prom. of May* I 260
I shall go mad for utter shame and *d*.   „   I 682
And poor old father not *d* miserable.   „   I 722
My five-years' anger cannot *d* at once,   „   II 463
and father Will not *d* miserable.'   „   II 660
Go back to him and ask his forgiveness before he *d*'s.—   „   III 402
I would almost *d* to have it! *Dora*. And he may *d*
before he gives it;   „   III 405

Die (*continued*) d, and make the soil For Cæsars, Cromwells, | *Prom. of May* III 591
lanker than an old horse turned out to d on the common. | *Foresters* I i 52
O Lord, I will live and d for King Richard— | „ I ii 37
I am outlaw'd, and if caught, I d. | „ I iii 163
But if you follow me, you may d with me. | „ I iii 166
We will live and d with thee, (repeat) | „ I iii 168
That we would d for a Queen— | „ III 444
and if thou prick me there I shall d. | „ IV 570
Carry her off, and let the old man d. | „ IV 677
He d's who dares to touch there. | „ IV 734

Died doubtless you can tell me how she d? | *Queen Mary* III i 357
And Thy most blessed Son's, who d for man. | „ IV iii 154
he d As manfully and boldly, and, 'fore God, | „ IV iii 342
Until they d of rotted limbs; | „ IV iii 445
My Lord, he d most bravely. | „ IV iii 570
Ay, and with him who d Alone in Italy. | „ V ii 507
caught a chill in the lagoons of Venice, And d in Padua. *Mary.* D in the true faith? | „ V ii 516
That she would see your Grace before she—d. | „ V ii 105
or Knut who coming Dane D English. | *Harold* IV iii 56
Drink to the dead who d for us, the living Who fought and would have d, | „ IV iii 69
ran in upon us And d so, | „ V i 411
remembering One who d for thee, | *Becket* I i 307
Only my best bower-maiden d of late, | „ III i 68
She d of leprosy. | „ V ii 268
I had once A boy who d a babe; | *The Cup* I i 149
To me, tho' all your bloom has d away, | *The Falcon* 468
She had to die for it—she d for you, | „ 877
Oh, yes, indeed, I would have d for you. | *Prom. of May* I 714
pauper, who had d in his misery blessing God, | „ III 378
when the mistress d, and I appealed to the Sister again, | „ III 393
we have certain news he d in prison. | *Foresters* IV 778

Dies Illa Their 'd I,' which will test their sect. | *Queen Mary* III iv 428
Dies Iræ Their hour is hard at hand, their 'd I,' | „ III iv 426
Differing where the man and the woman, only d as the stronger and the weaker, | *Prom. of May* III 190
Dig Or I will d thee with my dagger. | *Queen Mary* III iii 96
And d it from the root for ever. | *Becket* IV ii 77
Dilated Seem'd thro' that dim d world of hers, | *Queen Mary* II ii 324
Dim (adj.) Seem'd thro' that d dilated world of hers, | „ II ii 324
You droop in your d London. | „ V ii 609
Mine eyes are d: what hath she written? read. | „ V v 1
Well—is not that the course of Nature too, From the d dawn of Being— | *Prom. of May* I 281
Dim (verb) Rather than d the splendour of his crown | *Becket* V iii 343
Dimple silver Were dear as gold, the wrinkle as the d. | *Foresters* IV 43
Dine there wur an owld lord a-cum to d wi' un, | *Queen Mary* IV iii 504
' I wunt d,' says my Lord Bishop, | „ IV iii 507
He wishes you to d along with us, | *Prom. of May* I 618
Stay, D with my brethren here, | *Foresters* IV 346
bonds From these three men, and let them d with us, | „ IV 963
By Mahound I could d with Beelzebub! | „ IV 971
there's yet one other: I will not d without him. | „ IV 996
Dined let that wait till we have d. | „ IV 992
Dingle And loves and dotes on every d of it. | „ IV 390
Dining-hall Carry fresh rushes into the d-h, | „ I i 81
Dinner (*See also* **After-dinner**) and a wur so owld a couldn't bide vor his d, | *Queen Mary* IV iii 506
' Now,' says the Bishop, says he, ' we'll gwo to d;' | „ IV iii 513
thou must dash us down Our d from the skies. | *The Falcon* 154
his falcon Ev'n wins his d for him in the field. | „ 231
fur he'll gie us a big d, | *Prom. of May* I 9
there wudn't be a d for nawbody, and I should ha' lost the pig. | „ I 149
the farming men 'ull hev their d i' the long barn, | „ I 166
Why if Steer han't haxed schoolmaster to d, | „ I 185
and we'll git 'im to speechify for us arter d. | „ I 440
his monies, his oxen, his d's, himself. | *Foresters* I i 234
I love my d—but I can fast, I can fast; | „ I ii 64
Bitters before d, my lady, to give you a relish. | „ III 434
he that pays not for his d must fight for it. | „ IV 200
thou fight at quarterstaff for thy d with our Robin, | „ IV 208
So now which way to the d? | „ IV 972

Diocese He'll burn a d to prove his orthodoxy. | *Queen Mary* III iv 353
Wasted our d, outraged our tenants, | *Becket* V ii 431
Dip A lake that d's in William As well as Harold. | *Harold* V i 186
Dipping Have I been d into this again | *Prom. of May* I 292
Dipt d your sovereign head Thro' these low doors, | *The Falcon* 866
Directed Half a score of them, all d to me— | *Prom. of May* II 722
Dirty as I hate the d gap in the face of a Cistercian monk, | *Becket* II ii 381
Disaffected The d, heretics, reformers, Look to you | *Queen Mary* I iv 170
Disappear my voice Is martyr'd mute, and this man d's, | *Becket* III iii 350
Disappear'd She has d, They told me, from the farm— | *Prom. of May* I 406
She has d, poor darling, from the world— | „ II 409
Disappointment D, Ingratitude, Injustice, Evil-tongue, | *Queen Mary* V ii 154
Dis-archbishop after that, We had to d-a and unlord, | „ IV ii 128
Disarm Is it not easy to d a woman? | *The Cup* I iii 106
Disastrous And fared so ill in this d world. | *Queen Mary* III iv 344
Discipline d's that clear the spiritual eye, | *Becket* V i 42
Disconsolate I pray you be not so d; | *Queen Mary* V ii 129
Discontent Hath made me king of all the d | *Foresters* I i 87
Discourage to d and lay lame The plots of France, | *Queen Mary* V i 187
Discourtesy I shall remember this D. | *Becket* I i 239
Discrown Who did d thine husband, unqueen thee? | *Harold* IV v 193
Disdain (*See also* **Self-disdain**) for I much d thee, but if ever Thou see me clasp | *Foresters* II ii 74
Diseased Old, miserable, d, Incapable of children. | *Queen Mary* V v 178
Disgrace Their Graces, our d's! God confound them! | „ III i 414
Disgraced Thou hast d me and attainted me, | „ III ii 54
Why do you so my-lord me, Who am d? | „ IV ii 177
D, dishonour'd!—not by them, | „ IV ii 200
Disguise (s) No! the d was perfect. Let's away. | „ I ii 186
The monk's d thou gavest me for my bower: | *Becket* V ii 93
Shall I be known? is my d perfect? | *Foresters* I ii 18
Disguise (verb) D me—thy gown and thy coif. | *Queen Mary* III i 33
Disguised I am ill d. | *Becket* I i 297
Ay, but go d. | *Foresters* I i 410
Thou art no old woman—thou art d— | „ II i 680
this is Maid Marian Flying from John—d. | „ II 680
Dish which cannot tell A good d from a bad, | *Becket, Pro.* 106
Ye have eaten of my d and drunken of my cup for a dozen years. | „ I iv 29
King would act servitor and hand a d to his son; | „ III iii 139
She broke my head on Tuesday with a d. | *Foresters* I iii 134
Dish-designer A d-d, and most amorous | *Becket, Pro.* 99
Dishonour (s) —did D to our wives. | *The Cup* I ii 184
willing wives enough To feel d, honour. | „ I ii 189
courteous for aught I know Whose life is one d. | „ I ii 194
Thro' that d which you brought upon us, | *Prom. of May* III 765
Dishonour (verb) you that d The daughters and wives of your own faction— | *Foresters* IV 697
Dishonour'd Disgraced, d!—not by them, | *Queen Mary* IV ii 200
old man, Seven-fold d even in the sight Of thine own sectaries— | „ V v 133
I have not d thee—I trust I have not; | *Becket* I i 354
Dislocation And lamed and maim'd to d, | „ IV ii 267
Disloyal Yet there be some d Catholics, | *Queen Mary* III iv 42
Disobedience and grief For our long schism and d, | „ III iii 129
Disobey and that you might not seem To d his Holiness. | „ V ii 53
Dispense the Pope could d with his Cardinalate, | „ I i 127
Displace Place and d our councillors, | „ II ii 160
Displease sheathe your swords, ye will d the King. | *Becket* I iii 179
For whatsoever may d him— | „ II i 162
Something that would d me. | „ III i 245
If the phrase ' Return' d you, we will say— | *The Falcon* 729
Dispoped From one whom they d? | *Harold* III i 107
Dispossessed thou art d of all thy lands, goods, and chattels; | *Foresters* I i 59
Disruption shake the North With earthquake and d— | *Harold* I ii 200
Dissemble D not; play the plain Christian man. | *Queen Mary* IV iii 267
I did d, but the hour has come For utter truth and plainness; | „ IV iii 272
Dissembler Liar! d! traitor! to the fire! | „ IV iii 259
Dissoluteness our John By his Norman arrogance and d, | *Foresters* I i 85
Dissolved The bond between the kingdoms be d; | *Queen Mary* III iii 77
The worldly bond between us is d, | *Becket* I i 347

Doll-face A *d-f* blanch'd and bloodless,   *Becket* IV ii 175
Domed gulf and flatten in her closing chasm *D* cities, hear. *The Cup* II 301
Domine Illorum, *D*, Scutum scindatur !   *Harold* v i 508
  Illos trucida, *D*.   v i 515
Dominion realm Of England, and *d's* of the same, *Queen Mary* III iii 117
  all the realm And its *d's* from all heresy,   „   III iii 216
  To leave the Pope *d* in the West.   *Harold* v i 23
Don Carlos *See* **Carlos**
Doom (s) some great *d* when God's just hour Peals— *Queen Mary* I iv 261
  Into the deathless hell which is their *d*   „   III iii 75
  And by the churchman's pitiless *d* of fire,   „   III iv 49
  Reversed his *d*, and that you might not seem   „   v ii 51
  Hapless *d* of woman happy in betrothing !   „   v ii 364
  mean The *d* of England and the wrath of Heaven ? *Harold* I i 46
  War there, my son ? is that the *d* of England ?   „   I i 125
  Why not the *d* of all the world as well ?   „   I i 127
  Crying ' the *d* of England,' and at once He stood „   III i 134
  along the highest crying ' The *d* of England ! '— „   III i 157
  Blaze like a night of fatal stars on those Who read their
    d and die.   „   IV i 252
  And bide the *d* of God.   „   v i 61
  If I fall, I fall—The *d* of God !   „   v i 136
  And not on thee—nor England—fall God's *d* !   „   v i 371
  And front the *d* of God.   „   v i 436
  the man shall seal, Or I will seal his *d*. *Becket* I iii 331
  Dark as my *d*—   „   III i 282
  To draw you and your husband to your *d*. *The Cup* I ii 223
  thy *d* and mine—Thou—coming my way too— „   I 490
Doom (verb) stroke that *d's* thee after death To wail *Becket* IV ii 270
Doomsday (adj.) Were the great trumpet blowing *d* dawn, *Harold* v i 227
Doomsday (s) Till *d* melt it.   *Queen Mary* III v 51
Door (*See also* **Hall-door, In-door, Within-door**) The
    traitor husband dangled at the *d*,   „   III i 10
  hath the *d* Shut on him by the father whom he loved, „   v ii 121
  tell the cooks to close The *d's* of all the offices below. „   v v 117
  arm'd men Ever keep watch beside my chamber *d*, *Harold* II ii 245
  clench'd their pirate hides To the bleak church *d's*, „   IV iii 37
  move as true with me To the *d* of death.   „   v ii 186
  I saw that *d* Close even now upon the woman. *Becket* I i 202
  when he hears a *d* open in the house and thinks ' the
    master.'   „   III iii 98
  Thro' all closed *d's* a dreadful whisper crept   „   v ii 88
  No, look ! the *d* is open: let him be.   „   v ii 315
  Battering the *d's*, and breaking thro' the walls ?   „   v ii 626
  Shut the *d's* ! We will not have him slain   „   v iii 53
  Fly, fly, my lord, before they burst the *d's* !   „   v iii 57
  Undo the *d's* : the church is not a castle !   „   v iii 62
  Take thou this cup and leave it at her *d's*. *The Cup* I ii 68
  In the gray dawn before the Temple *d's*.   „   I ii 295
  this *d* Opens upon the forest ! Out, begone !   „   I ii 328
  His own true people cast him from their *d's*,   „   I ii 352
  close not yet the *d* upon a night That looks half day. „   I ii 387
  Fling wide the *d's* and let the new-made children   „   II 163
  She—close the Temple *d*. Let her not fly.   „   II 460
  and dipt your sovereign head Thro' these low *d's*, *The Falcon* 868
  Push'd from all *d's* as if we bore the plague, *Prom. of May* III 804
  As Wealth walk'd in at the *d*.   *Foresters* I i 151
  Poverty crept thro' the *d*.   „   I i 157
  Not while the rivulet babbles by the *d*,   „   I ii 322
  open, or I will drive the *d* from the door-post   „   II i 220
  Why did ye keep us at the *d* so long ?   „   II i 224
Door-post open, or I will drive the door from the *d-p*. „   II i 220
  I will fasten thee to thine own *d-p*   „   II i 403
Doorway when every *d* blush'd, Dash'd red *Becket* I iii 346
Dora (daughter of Farmer Steer) (*See also* **Dora Steer**)
  an' Miss *D*, an' Miss Eva, an' all !   *Prom. of May* I 11
  Miss *D* be coomed back, then ?   „   I 12
  Blessings on your pretty voice, Miss *D*.   „   I 64
  Theer be redder blossoms nor them, Miss *D*.   „   I 86
  Under your eyes, Miss *D*,   „   I 89
  Noä, Miss *D* ; as blue as— (repeat)   „   I 95, 99
  He'll be arter you now, Miss *D*.   „   I 119
  And I tells ye what, Miss *D*: he's no respect for the
    Queen,   „   I 131
  I thank you for that, Miss *D*, onyhow.   „   I 158

Dora (daughter of Farmer Steer) (*continued*) They say
  your sister, *D*, has return'd,   *Prom. of May* I 546
  Oh, *D*, *D*, how long you have been away from home ! „   I 767
  So the owd uncle i' Coomberland be dead, Miss *D*, „   II 2
  Not like me, Miss *D* ; and I ha' brout these roses to ye— „   II 13
  and now she be gone, will ye taäke 'em, Miss *D* ? „   II 21
  an' weänt ye taäke 'em now, Miss *D*,   „   II 41
  I feel sewer, Miss *D*, that I ha' been noän too sudden wi' you, „   II 60
  ' Dearest *D*, I have lost myself,   „   II 83
  Are you—you are—that *D*, The sister.   „   II 363
  Miss *D*, Dan Smith's cart hes runned ower a laädy „   II 567
  What feller wur it as 'a' been a-talkin' fur haäfe an hour
    wi' my *D* ?   „   II 576
  a-plaäyin' the saäme gaäme wi' my *D*—   „   II 591
  —a daughter of the fields, This *D* !   „   II 624
  if ye be goin' to sarve our *D* as ye sarved our Eva— „   II 692
  What hasta been saäyin' to my *D* ?   „   II 704
  thou hesn't naw business 'ere with my *D*, as I knaws on, „   II 736
  Miss *D*, meä and my maätes, us three, we wants to hev
    three words wi' ye.   „   III 124
  Has anyone found me out, *D* ?   „   III 225
  See *D* ; you yourself are shamed of me,   „   III 268
  and I love him so much—   *Eva*.   Poor *D* !   „   III 286
  O *D*, he signed himself ' Yours gratefully '—fancy, *D*, „   III 333
  Hark ! *D*, some one is coming.   „   III 339
  Oh, *D*, *D* !   „   III 425
  Miss *D* ! Miss *D* !   *Dora*.   Quiet ! quiet !   „   III 475
  You are pale, my *D* ! but the ruddiest cheek   „   III 486
  D, If marriage ever brought a woman happiness   „   III 638
  O *D*, *D* !   „   III 787
Dora Steer (*See also* **Dora**) doänt tha knaw he be sweet upo' *D S*, „   II 161
  kill'd her oän sister, or she beänt *D S*.   „   II 605
Dotage love her less For such a *d* upon such a man. *Queen Mary* v ii 421
  Stigand, unriddle This vision, canst thou ?   *Stigand*. *D* ! *Harold* I i 176
Dote Many so *d* upon this bubble world, *Queen Mary* IV iii 168
  The old man *d's*.   *Foresters* II ii 83
  And loves and *d's* on every dingle of it.   „   IV 390
Doted bad the king Who *d* on him,   *Harold* IV i 103
Doter A *d* on white pheasant-flesh at feasts, *Becket, Pro.* 97
Double (adj.) this *d* thundercloud That lours on England— *Harold* II ii 159
Double (s) Fight thou with thine own *d*, not with me, „   IV iii 168
  would dare the chance Of *d*, or losing all. *The Cup* I ii 148
Doubly I am *d* bound to thee . . .   *Harold* II ii 557
Doubt (s) he brought his *d's* And fears to me. *Queen Mary* I ii 75
  Which found me full of foolish *d's*,   „   I v 530
  but there are *d's*.   „   II ii 307
  all my *d's* I fling from me like dust,   *Becket* I i 148
Doubt (verb) I *d* it not, Madam, most loyal. *Queen Mary* I iv 248
  D not they will be speedily overthrown.   „   II ii 200
  I not *d* that God will give me strength,   „   IV ii 234
  lest anyone among you *d* The man's conversion   „   IV iii 107
  I cannot *d* but that he comes again;   „   v v 26
  Thanks, truthful Earl ; I did not *d* thy word, *Harold* II ii 724
  what is it you *d* ?   Behold your peace at hand. *Becket* II ii 199
  Wherefore should you *d* it ?   *The Cup* I ii 340
  I *d* not they are yours.   *The Falcon* 721
  I *d* not, I *d* not, and though I be down in the mouth, *Foresters* I ii 43
Doubted ay, but mighty doctors *d* there. *Queen Mary* IV i 84
Dough household *d* was kneaded up with blood ; *Becket* I iii 351
Dove (*See also* **Stock-dove**) *d*, who flutters Between thee
    and the porch,   *Harold* IV i 230
  But since the fondest pair of *d's* will jar, *Becket* IV ii 40
Dovecote Our *d* flown !   I cannot tell why monks „   v ii 580
Dover Your Majesty shall go to *D* with me, *Queen Mary* III vi 218
  To *D* ? no, I am too feeble.   „   III vi 220
  On all the road from *D*, day and night ;   „   v ii 577
  We could not move from *D* to the Humber *Harold* II ii 536
  They stood on *D* beach to murder me, *Becket* v ii 436
Down (adj.) (*See also* **Deep-down**) and bursten at the
    toes, and *d* at heels.   *Queen Mary* I i 53
  ha ! he is *d* !   *Edith*.   He *d*.   Who *d* ?   *Stigand*.   The
    Norman Count is *d*.   *Harold* v i 551
Down (bed) like a careless sleeper in the *d* ; *Foresters* I i 207
  And make *D* for their heads to heaven ! *Queen Mary* v iv 8
Down (hill) Breathe the free wind from off our Saxon *d's*, *Harold* II ii 187

Downfall   The *d* of so many simple souls,   *Queen Mary* I ii 54
Downfallen   *d* and debased From councillor to caitiff—   ,,   IV iii 74
Down-silvering   The rosy face, and long *d-s* beard,   *Harold* III i 46
   The rosy face, and long *d-s* beard—   ,,   IV i 261
Down-sweeping   *d-s* to the chain, Wherewith they
   bound   *Queen Mary* IV iii 594
Downward   One *d* plunge of his paw would rend away   *Becket* IV ii 283
Doze   He *d's*. I have left her watching him.   *Foresters* II ii 80
Dozed   I *d* upon the bridge, and the black river   *Prom. of May* II 649
Dozen   (*See also* **Half-dozen**) And drunken of my cup for
   a *d* years.   *Becket* I iv 30
   a-peacocking and a-spreading to catch her eye for a *d*
   year,   *The Falcon* 101
Drag   To *d* us with them. Fishermen? devils !   *Harold* II i 28
   would *d* The cleric before the civil judgment-seat,   *Becket* I iii 83
   Nay, *d* me not. We must not seem to fly.   ,,   v ii 636
   I will not only touch, but *d* thee hence.   ,,   v iii 152
   The women of the Temple *d* her in.   *The Cup* I iii 118
   I'd like to *d* 'im thruff the herse-pond, and she to
   be a-lookin' at it.   *Prom. of May* II 593
   They d the river for her ! no, not they !   ,,   III 694
   if you care to *d* your brains for such a minnow.   *Foresters* II i 323
Dragg'd   Who *d* the scatter'd limbs into their den.   *Queen Mary* I v 401
   and we *d* The Littlechester river all in vain :   *Prom. of May* II 413
Dragon   Our Wessex *d* flies beyond the Humber,   *Harold* IV i 3
   Set forth our golden *D*,   ,,   v i 245
   by the *d* of St. George, we shall Do some injustice,   *Foresters* IV 939
Drain   And *d's* the heart and marrow from a man.   ,,   II i 672
Drain'd   thou hast *d* them shallow by thy tolls,   *Harold* I i 319
   I have almost *d* the cup—A few drops left.   *The Cup* II 385
Draught   (*See also* **Sleeping-draught**) Brain-dizzied
   with a *d* of morning ale.   *Queen Mary* II i 71
   they de-miracled the miraculous *d*,   *Becket* III iii 124
   No not a *d* of milk, no not an egg,   *The Falcon* 871
   drink Her health along with us in this rich *d*,   *Foresters* 352
Drave   (*See also* **Drove**) *d* and crack'd His boat on Ponthieu
   beach ;   *Harold* II ii 34
Draw   *d* back your heads and your horns before I break
   them,   *Queen Mary* I i 4
   D with your sails from our poor land,   ,,   III vi 226
   where Edward *d's* A faint foot hither,   *Harold* I i 143
   To *d* him nearer with a charm Like thine to thine.   ,,   II ii 7
   D nearer,—I was in the corridor,   ,,   II ii 345
   D thou to London, there make strength   ,,   v i 126
   but this *D's* thro' the chart to her.   *Becket, Pro.* 173
   Did not your barons *d* their swords against me ?   ,,   I iii 501
   we pray you, *d* yourself from under The wings of France.   ,,   II ii 247
   lest ye should *d* together like two ships in a calm.   ,,   III ii 297
   To *d* you and your husband to your doom.   *The Cup* I ii 222
   d's From you, and from my constancy to you.   *The Falcon* 811
   If thou *d* one inch nearer,   *Foresters* I i 145
   I will not harm thee. *D* !   ,,   II i 556
   'tis but to see if thou canst fence. *D* !   ,,   II i 573
Drawbridge   I'll have the *d* hewn into the Thames,   *Queen Mary* II iv 376
   They had hewn the *d* down into the river.   ,,   II iii 18
   I would hoist the *d*, like thy master.   *Foresters* I i 319
Drawing-room   shamed of his poor farmer's daughter
   among the ladies in his *d-r* ?   *Prom. of May* III 295
   Shamed of me in a *d-r* ! (repeat)   ,,   III 296, 307
Drawl'd   fat fool ! He *d* and prated so,   *Harold* IV ii 41
Drawn   Will he be *d* to her ?   *Queen Mary* I v 73
   fain have some fresh treaty *d* between you.   ,,   I v 361
   I say they have *d* the fire On their own heads :   ,,   IV iii 379
   In some dark closet, some long gallery, *d*,   ,,   v ii 218
   With both her knees *d* upward to her chin.   ,,   v ii 391
   hath mainly *d* itself From lack of Tostig—   *Harold* III i 167
   fill'd the quiver, and Death has *d* the bow—   ,,   III i 401
   Hast not thou *d* the short straw ?   *Becket* I iv 3
   not life shot up in blood, But death *d* in ;—   ,,   IV ii 382
   We are almost at the bottom of the well ; little
   more to be, *d* from it—   *Prom. of May* III 162
Dread (**adj.**)   And hurl the *d* ban of the Church on those   *Becket* III iii 210
Dread (**s**)   not for *d* Of these alone, but from the fear
   of Him   *Queen Mary* IV iii 178
Dread (**verb**)   lied like a lad That *d's* the pendent scourge,   *Harold* II ii 658

Dread (**verb**) (*continued*)   They fear you slain : they *d* they
   know not what.   *Becket* v ii 600
Dreadful   And *d* shadows strove upon the hill,   *Harold* III i 377
   O God ! some *d* truth is breaking on me—Some thing
   is coming on me.   *Becket* III i 265
   Thro' all closed doors a *d* whisper crept   ,,   v ii 88
   Left but one *d* line to say, that we Should find her
   in the river ;   *Prom. of May* II 411
   that *d* night ! that lonely walk to Littlechester,   ,,   III 366
Dreading   But *d* God's revenge upon this realm   *Harold* I i 172
Dream (**s**)   (*See also* **Day-dream, Love-dream**) men-at-
   arms Guard my poor *d's* for England.   *Queen Mary* I v 154
   It was a *d*; I must not dream, not wink,   ,,   III v 153
   they come back upon my *d's*.   ,,   v ii 189
   Wide of the mark ev'n for a madman's *d*.   ,,   v iii 82
   Nor let Priests' talk, or *d* of worlds to be,   ,,   v v 217
   if yon weird sign Not blast us in our *d's*.—   *Harold* I i 122
   An evil *d* that ever came and went—   ,,   I ii 70
   what a *d*! *Harold.* Well, well,—a *d*—no more !   ,,   I ii 91
   Did not Heaven speak to men in *d's* of old ?   ,,   I ii 95
   Thou hast misread this merry *d* of thine,   ,,   I ii 98
   Come, thou shalt dream no more such *d's*;   ,,   I ii 108
   upon thine eyelids, to shut in A happier *d*.   ,,   II i 127
   Our living passion for a dead man's *d*;   ,,   III ii 60
   Last night King Edward came to me in *d's*—
   (repeat)   *Harold* IV i 259, 266
   I am no woman to put faith in *d's*.   ,,   IV i 264
   by dead Norway without *d* or dawn !   ,,   IV iii 122
   only *d's*—where mine own self Takes part   ,,   v i 298
   My fatal oath—the dead Saints—the dark *d's*—   ,,   v i 381
   D, Or prophecy, that ?   *Becket* I i 55
   Well, *d* and prophecy both.   ,,   I i 57
   thou my golden *d* of Love's own bower,   ,,   II i 34
   Bright as my *d*,   ,,   II i 278
   my *d* foretold my martyrdom In mine own church.   ,,   v ii 632
   the black river Flow'd thro' my *d's*—if *d's* they
   were.   *Prom. of May* II 651
   which is my *d* of a true marriage.   ,,   III 179
   I have freed myself From all such *d's*   ,,   III 595
Dream (**verb**)   It was a dream ; I must not *d*, not
   wink,   *Queen Mary* III v 154
   He cannot *d* that *I* advised the war ;   ,,   v ii 57
   Come, thou shalt *d* no more such dreams ;   *Harold* I ii 108
   Good-night, and *d* thyself Their chosen Earl.   ,,   I ii 248
   Who knows I may not *d* myself their king !   ,,   I ii 251
   He sees me not—and yet he *d's* of me,   ,,   II ii 144
   I did not *d* then I should be king.—   ,,   III i 270
   king can scarcely *d* that we, who know   ,,   IV i 163
   Tell him the Saints are nobler than he *d's*,   ,,   v i 56
   that none may *d* I go against God's honour—   *Becket* II ii 167
   D of it, then, all the way back,   *Foresters* I i 140
   to *d* that he My brother, my dear Walter—   ,,   II i 651
   You dared to *d* That our great Earl,   ,,   II i 685
   I fear I *d*.   ,,   IV 1010
Dream'd   who *d* us blanketed In ever-closing fog,   *Queen Mary* III ii 19
   Not *d* of by the rabidest gospeller.   ,,   III vi 138
   Last night, I *d* the faggots were alight,   ,,   IV ii 1
   and I *d* that I loved Louis of France : and I loved
   Henry of England, and Henry of England *d* that
   he loved me ;   *Becket, Pro.* 356
   D that twelve stars fell glittering out of heaven,   ,,   I i 46
   who never saw nor *d* of such a banquet.   ,,   I iv 84
   I had *d* I was the bride of England, and a queen,   ,,   v 102
   while you *d* you were the bride of England,—   ,,   v 104
   I *d* I was the consort of a king,   ,,   v 144
   This mountain shepherd never *d* of Rome.   *The Cup* I ii 17
   tear it all to pieces, never *d* Of acting on it.   ,,   I ii 247
   Who knows that he had ever *d* of flying ?   *Prom. of May* I 654
   cuirass in this forest where I *d* That all was peace—   *Foresters* IV 130
Dreaming   old enough To scare me into *d*,   *Queen Mary* IV 103
   I am *d* ; for the past Look'd thro' the present,   *Prom. of May* II 639
   I was *d* of it all the way hither.   *Foresters* I i 139
Dree (**three**)   and awaay betimes wi' *d* hard eggs for
   a good pleace at the burnin' ;   *Queen Mary* IV iii 489
Drench'd   then he dash'd and *d*, He dyed,   *Harold* III i 141

Drench'd (*continued*)   Found him dead and *d* in dew,   *Foresters* II ii 147
Dress   This *d* was made me as the Earl of Devon   *Queen Mary* I iv 72
I wear beneath my *d* A shirt of mail: ,,   I v 145
And what was Mary's *d*?   ,,   III i 56
I was too sorry for the woman To mark the *d.*   ,,   III i 59
Arrange my *d*—the gorgeous Indian shawl   ,,   v ii 538
if I hadn't a sprig o' wickentree sewn into my *d,*   *Foresters* II i 250
Drest   —*d* like a gentleman, too.   Damn all gentlemen, says I !   *Prom. of May* II 578
O graves in daisies *d,*   ,,   III 204
Drew   He *d* this shaft against me to the head,   *Queen Mary* v ii 80
Earl, the first Christian Cæsar *d* to the East   *Harold* v i 22
thereupon, methought, He *d* toward me,   *Becket* I i 102
loveliest life that ever *d* the light From heaven   *The Cup* I iii 56
D here the richest lot from Fate,   ,,   II 442
would not crush The fly that *d* her blood ;   *Prom. of May* II 494
Robin fancied me a man, And *d* his sword upon me,   *Foresters* II 21
Drewest   And never *d* sword to help the old man   ,,   II 541
Drift   That is your *d.*   *Queen Mary* I v 305
And queens also !   What is your *d*?   *Becket.*   My *d* is to the Castle,   *Becket* I ii 82
I see your *d* . . . it may be so . . .   ,,   v i 82
Drill   how should thy one tooth *d* thro' this ?   *Foresters* II i 276
Drill-sergeant   yet are we now *d-s* to his lordship's lettuces,   *The Falcon* 550
Drink   thou could'st *d* in Spain if I remember.   *Queen Mary* II 38
eat dead men's flesh, and *d* their blood.   *Harold* II iii 808
D to the dead who died for us,   ,,   IV iii 69
tho' I can *d* wine I cannot bide water,   *Becket* I iv 220
which the more you *d,* The more you thirst—yea—*d* too much,   *The Cup* I iii 139
That Synorix should *d* from his own cup.   ,,   II 353
They two should *d* together from one cup.   ,,   II 361
See here, I fill it.   Will you *d,* my lord ?   ,,   II 367
make libation to the Goddess, And now I *d.*   ,,   II 378
D and *d* deep—our marriage will be fruitful.   *D* and *d* deep, and thou wilt make me happy.   ,,   II 380
' Let us eat and *d,* for to-morrow we die.'   *Prom. of May* I 259
D to the Lion-heart Every one !   *Foresters* I ii 5
Here, here—a cup of wine—*d* and begone !   ,,   I iii 89
Shall *d* the health of our new woodland Queen.   ,,   III 314
till the green earth *d* Her health along with us   ,,   III 350
D to the health of our new Queen o' the woods,   ,,   III 368
We *d* the health of thy new Queen o' the woods.   ,,   III 372
D to the Queen o' the woods,   ,,   III 388
And lie with us among the flowers, and—*d*—   ,,   IV 966
Drinker   A *d* of black, strong, volcanic wines,   *Queen Mary* v ii 93
Drive   Do you mean to *d* me mad ?   ,,   v ii 200
applaud that Norman who should *d* The stranger   *Harold* II 540
and yet I saw thee *d* him up his hills—   ,,   IV i 211
he join'd with thee To *d* me outlaw'd.   ,,   IV ii 14
Follow them, follow them, *d* them to the sea !   ,,   v i 602
Louis Returning, ah ! to *d* thee from his realm.   *Becket* II ii 418
as men Have done on rafts of wreck—it *d's* you mad.   *The Cup* I iii 142
and I'd *d* the plow straäit as a line   *Prom. of May* I 369
open, or I will *d* the door from the door-post.   *Foresters* II i 220
Driven   The guards are all *d* in,   *Queen Mary* II iv 54
and *d* back The Frenchmen from their trenches ?   ,,   v ii 256
eat it like the serpent, and be *d* out of her paradise.   *Becket,* Pro. 533
Lifted our produce, *d* our clerics out—   ,,   v ii 432
mine own dagger *d* by Synorix found   *The Cup* II 86
Have our loud pastimes *d* them all away ?   *Foresters* II ii 105
Driving   it was you that were *d* the cart—   *Prom. of May* III 87
Droop   faith that seem'd to *d* will feel your light,   *Queen Mary* III iv 22
You *d* in your dim London.   ,,   v 609
Drooping   and maiden moon Our *d* Queen should know !   ,,   v ii 457
Drop (s)   And putrid water, every *d* a worm,   ,,   IV iii 444
tho' the *d* may hollow out the dead stone.   *Becket* III 314
I have almost drain'd the cup—A few *d's* left.   *The Cup* II 386
niver touched a *d* of owt till my oän wedding-daäy,   *Prom. of May* I 362
p'raps ye hears 'at I soomtimes taäkes a *d* too much ;   ,,   II 108
voice a-shaäkin', and the *d* in 'er eye.   ,,   II 130
Drop (verb)   His in whose hand she *d's* ;   *Queen Mary* III i 112
not *d* the mask before The masquerade is over—   ,,   III vi 109
d the mud I carried, like yon brook,   *Becket* II i 158

Drop (verb) (*continued*)   may *d* off any day, any hour. You must see him at once.   *Prom. of May* III 407
Then I would *d* from the casement, like a spider.   *Foresters* I 316
Dropsy   (*See also* **High-dropsy**)   but I hear she hath a *d,* lad,   *Queen Mary* III ii 224
Fie on her *d,* so she have a *d* !   ,,   III ii 226
Dropt   Have I *d* it ?   I have but shown a loathing face   ,,   III vi 112
dog that snapt the shadow, *d* the bone.—   *Harold* I ii 188
boughs across the deep That *d* themselves,   ,,   III i 152
He sat down there And *d* it in his hands,   *Becket* I iii 324
royal promise might have *d* into thy mouth   ,,   III iii 276
and *d* Their streamers earthward,   *The Cup* I 404
And the stock-dove coo'd, till a kite *d* down,   *Prom. of May* I 55
dosta knaw this paäper ?   Ye *d* it upo' the road.   ,,   II 687
Wealth *d* out of the window,   *Foresters* I 156
Dross   As gold Outvalues *d,* light darkness,   *Becket* I iii 715
Drove   (*See also* **Drave**)   When he we speak of *d* the window back,   *Queen Mary* v ii 464
my father *d* the Normans out Of England ?—   *Harold* I i 251
thou and he *d* our good Normans out From England,   ,,   II ii 524
Athelstan the Great Who *d* you Danes—   ,,   IV i 75
my father *d* him and his friends, De Tracy   *Becket* I i 276
d me From out her memory.   *Prom. of May* II 404
My lord John, In wrath because you *d* him from the forest,   *Foresters* III 450
He *d* his knife into the heart of the deer,   ,,   IV 541
Drown   Why, the child will *d* himself.   *Becket* II i 322
but these arm'd men—will *you d* yourself?   ,,   v ii 276
even *d* you In the good regard of Rome.   *The Cup* I i 150
Were there no boughs to hang on, Rivers to *d* in ?   ,,   I i 79
Must all Galatia hang or *d* herself ?   ,,   I ii 87
d all poor self-passion in the sense Of public good ?   ,,   II 101
how often justice *d's* Between the law and the letter of the law !   *Foresters* IV 512
Drown'd   (*See also* **Half-drown'd**)   A sea of blood—we are *d* in blood—   *Harold* III i 398
The curse of England ! these are *d* in wassail,   ,,   IV iii 223
—thou art *d* in debt—   *Becket,* Pro. 491
all *d* in love And glittering at full tide—   *The Cup* II 233
Drowning   The *d* man, they say, remembers all The chances of his life,   *Becket* v i 272
Drudge   went into service—the *d* of a lodging-house—   *Prom. of May* III 392
Drug (s)   *D's*—but he knows they cannot help me—   *Queen Mary* v v 60
Drug (verb)   and science now could *d* and balm us   *Prom. of May* III 339
Drunk   has *d* and gambled out All that he had,   *Queen Mary* II iii 87
Make themselves *d* and mad,   ,,   III i 282
and our marriage and thy glory Been *d* together !   *Harold* IV iii 9
Old dog, Thou art *d,* old dog !   ,,   IV iii 164
Too *d* to fight with thee !   ,,   IV iii 165
Thou hast *d* deep enough to make me happy.   *The Cup* II 424
Have I not of the same cup with thee ?   ,,   II 463
you were stupid *d* all Sunday, and so ill in consequence all Monday,   *Prom. of May* III 80
Is he deaf, or dumb, or daft, or *d* belike ?   *Foresters* II i 208
Drunken   My Lord, the world is like a *d* man,   *Queen Mary* IV iii 393
O *d* ribaldry !   Out, beast ! out, bear !   *Becket* I i 230
Ye have eaten of my dish and *d* of my cup for a dozen years.   ,,   I iv 30
Drunkenness   to snore away his *d* Into the sober headache,—   ,,   I i 371
Dry   *D* as an old wood-fungus on a dead tree,   *Harold* III i 8
if you follow Not the *d* light of Rome's straight-going policy,   *The Cup* I i 145
Duchy   You have her *D,* The point you aim'd at,   *Becket* I ii 76
You did your best or worst to keep her *D.*   ,,   II ii 84
Duck   Thou knowest we had to dodge, or *d,* or die ;   *Queen Mary* III iv 357
Duck'd   Or I will have you *d* !   ,,   IV iii 540
Dudley (Guildford)   *See* **Guildford Dudley**
Due (adj.)   *D* from his castles of Berkhamstead and Eye   *Becket* I iii 628
thanks of Holy Church are *d* to those That went   ,,   II ii 190
According to the canon's pardon To him that so repents,   *Queen Mary* IV iii 33
No, not an hour : the debt is *d* to-day.   *Foresters* IV 448
Due (s)   command That kiss my *d* when subject,   *Harold* III ii 42
Dug   *D* from the grave that yawns for us beyond ;   *Queen Mary* v ii 163
I *d* mine into My old fast friend the shore,   *Harold* II i 6
The trenches *d,* the palisades uprear'd   ,,   v i 189

Duke   The *D* hath gone to Leicester;   *Queen Mary* II i 4
Until I hear from Carew and the *D*.   ,,   II i 122
it is thought the *D* will be taken.   ,,   II i 136
Is Peter Carew fled?   Is the *D* taken?   ,,   II i 142
Ay, if *D's*, and Earls, And Counts,   ,,   III i 50
Our *D* is all between thee and the sea, Our *D* is all
   about thee like a God;   *Harold* II ii 314
yield this iron-mooded *D* To let me go.   ,,   II ii 340
My lord! the *D* awaits thee at the banquet.   ,,   II ii 805
Thy *D* will seem the darker. Hence, I follow.   ,,   II ii 817
a hundred Gold pieces once were offer'd by the *D*.   *The Falcon* 325
Dulcimer   Organ and pipe, and *d*, chants and hymns   *Becket* v 365
Dull   You've but a *d* life in this maiden court,   *Queen Mary* I iii 113
Sin is too *d* to see beyond himself.   ,,   v ii 441
Magdalen, sin is bold as well as *d*.   ,,   v ii 443
we were *d* enough at first, but in the end we flourished
   out   *Becket* III iii 136
Dulness   part real, part childlike, to be freed from the *d*—   ,,   III iii 156
Dumb (adj.)   and he pray'd them *d*, and thus I dumb thee
   too,   *Harold* I ii 22
be not wroth at the *d* parchment.   *Foresters* I i 342
Is he deaf, or *d*, or daft, or drunk belike?   ,,   I ii 208
D children of my father, that will speak   *Queen Mary* II i 77
Die like the torn fox *d*,   ,,   II ii 331
Dumb (verb)   and he pray'd them dumb, and thus I *d*
   thee too,   *Harold* I ii 24
Dumb'd   *d* his carrion croak From the gray sea for ever.   ,,   IV iii 65
Dumbfounded   and your heresy *D* half of us.   *Queen Mary* IV ii 127
Dumble (name of a cow)   but *D* wur blow'd wi' the
   wind, and *D's*   ,,   IV iii 476
barrin' the wind, *D* wur blow'd wi' the wind,   ,,   IV iii 493
D's the best milcher in Islip.   ,,   IV iii 496
Dungeon   In breathless *d's* over steaming sewers,   ,,   IV iii 440
blackness of my *d* loom Across their lamps of revel,   *Harold* II ii 406
Dungeon'd   *d* the other half In Pevensey Castle—   *Becket* v ii 444
Dunghill   But on the heretic *d* only weeds. *Howard*.   *Queen Mary* IV i 180
Such weeds make *d's* gracious.   *Queen Mary* IV i 180
and then Cast on the *d* naked,   ,,   IV iii 446
Dunstan (Archbishop of Canterbury)   by St. *D*, old St.
   Thor—By God, we thought him dead—   *Harold* IV iii 146
Durham   Deans Of Christchurch, *D*, Exeter, and Wells—   *Queen Mary* I ii 9
Dust (s)   (*See also* **Gold-dust**)   Will front their cry and
   shatter them into *d*.   ,,   II iv 6
Who rub their fawning noses in the *d*,   ,,   III iii 242
char us back again into the *d* We spring from.   ,,   III v 55
A low voice from the *d* and from the grave   ,,   v ii 385
bring her to the level of the *d*, so that the King—   *Becket*, Pro. 531
all my doubts I fling from me like *d*,   ,,   I i 149
till the weight of Germany or the gold of England
   brings one of them down to the *d*—   ,,   II ii 365
leave Lateran and Vatican in one *d* of gold—   ,,   II ii 475
To bring her to the *d* . . .   ,,   v ii 154
Bow'd to the *d* beneath the burthen of sin.   *Prom. of May* III 521
Dust (verb)   We'll *d* him from a bag of Spanish gold.   *Queen Mary* I v 421
Dust-cloth   slut whose fairest linen seems Foul as her *d-c*,   *Becket* v ii 203
Dusted   I do believe, I have *d* some already,   *Queen Mary* IV iii 423
so *d* his back with the meal in his sack,   *Becket* I iv 174
Dutchman   And the *D*, Now laughing at some jest?   *Queen Mary* III i 195
Duteous   being ever *d* to the King,   *Becket* III iv 464
Dutiful   Commands you to be *d* and leal To your young King   ,,   v v 325
Duty   the *d* which as Legate He owes himself,   *Queen Mary* III iv 401
I feel it but a *d*—you will find in it Pleasure as
   well as *d*,   ,,   III iv 429
Morcar, it is all but *d* in her To hate me;   *Harold* IV i 153
I have overshot My *duties* to our Holy Mother Church,   *Becket* v i 38
Dwarf   Till famine *d* the race—   ,,   I iii 356
Dwell   in Normanland God speaks thro' abler voices, as He
   d's In statelier shrines.   *Harold* I i 167
Join hands, let brethren *d* in unity;   ,,   i i 397
Care *d* with me for ever,   *Becket* II i 120
myrtle, bowering-in The city where she *d's*.   *The Cup* I i 4
never I trust to roam So far again, but *d* among his
   own.   *Foresters* IV 1100
Dwelt   the Lord hath *d* In darkness.   *Harold* III i 179
Nor *d* alone, like a soft lord of the East,   *Becket* I iii 358

Dwelt (continued)   So *d* on that they rose and darken'd
   Heaven.   *Becket* II ii 205
If Synorix, who has *d* three years in Rome   *The Cup* I ii 175
Dyed   He *d*, he soak'd the trunk with human blood,   *Harold* III i 142
Dying (adj. and part.)   (*See also* **A-dying**)   A passing
   bell toll'd in a *d* ear—   *Queen Mary* v ii 41
Tell her to come and close my *d* eyes,   ,,   v ii 600
They say she's *d*.   *First*.   So is Cardinal Pole.   ,,   v iv 4
' I am *d*, Philip; come to me.'   ,,   v v 3
The Queen is *d*, or you dare not say it.   ,,   v v 250
That never English monarch *d* left England so little.   ,,   v v 277
Sleeping or *d* there?   If this be death,   *Harold* III i 1
when thro' his *d* sense Shrills 'lost thro'' thee.'   ,,   III i 33
No, but to please our *d* king,   ,,   III i 328
Your second-sighted man That scared the *d* conscience of
   the king,   ,,   v i 211
And fighting for And *d* for the people—   ,,   I i 389
So then our good Archbishop Theobald Lies *d*.   *Becket*, Pro. 3
Who shall crown him?   Canterbury is *d*.   ,,   Pro. 240
A dead man's *d* wish should be of weight.   ,,   Pro. 422
You will do much To rake out all old *d* heats,   ,,   II ii 114
To warm the cold bounds of our *d* life   *The Cup* I iii 128
Love? it *is* love, love for my *d* boy,   *The Falcon* 787
I reverence all women, bad me, *d*,   *Foresters* II i 40
Speak not.   I wait upon a *d* father.   ,,   IV 611
Dying (s)   the *d* of my noble bird Hath served me better
   than her living—   *The Falcon* 900
Dyke   the *d's* and brooks Were bridged and damn'd with
   dead,   *Harold* III ii 128

E

E   See here—an interwoven H and *E* !   *Harold* I ii 57
Each   an amphisbæna, *E* end a sting: *Queen Mary* III iv 40
we two Might make one flesh, and cleave unto *e*
   other   ,,   v ii 138
but they bribe *E* other, and so often,   *Harold* I i 347
We never kept a secret from *e* other;   *Prom. of May* I 552
and prattled to *e* other that we would marry fine
   gentlemen,   ,,   III 276
E man for his own.   *Foresters* I iii 105
But shout and echo play'd into *e* other   ,,   II i 258
Nor care to leap into *e* other's arms.   ,,   III 7
where twelve Can stand upright, nor touch *e* other.   ,,   III 310
then *e* man That owns a wife or daughter,   ,,   III 458
'Eäd (head)   it be i' *my* natur to knock 'im o' the '*e* now;   *Prom. of May* I 288
The beer's gotten oop into my '*e*.   ,,   II 320
says the master goäs cleän off his '*e* when he 'eärs
   the naäme on 'im;   ,,   III 132
Eagle   My sight is *e*, but the strife so thick—   *Harold* I i 627
Eagle-height   At such an *e-h* I stand and see   *Becket* I i 139
Eagle-like   swoop down upon him *E-l*, lightning-like—   *The Falcon* 14
Ear   Your *e*; You shall be Queen.   *Queen Mary* I iv 121
what, have you eyes, *e's*, brains?   ,,   II i 97
I have *e's* to hear.   *Gardiner*.   Ay, rascal, if I
   leave thee *e's* to hear.   ,,   III i 250
thou shalt lose thine *e's* and find thy tongue,   ,,   III i 256
Repeat your recantation in the *e's* Of all men,   ,,   IV iii 193
Hast thou not mark'd—come closer to mine *e*—   ,,   v i 226
A passing bell toll'd in a dying *e*—   ,,   v ii 41
but those heavenly *e's* have heard,   *Harold* III i 258
would deign to lend an *e* Not overscornful,   ,,   IV i 136
Thou didst possess thyself of Edward's *e*   ,,   v i 345
And where, my liege?   *Henry*.   Thine *e*.   *Becket*, Pro. 157
Good *e's* too !   ,,   I ii 44
My lord, thine *e* !   I have the *e* of the Pope.   ,,   I iii 199
sucking thro' fools' *e's* The flatteries of corruption—   ,,   I iii 361
if you boxed the Pope's *e's* with a purse, you might
   stagger him,   ,,   II ii 370
They say that walls have *e's*;   ,,   IV ii 80
You have lost The *e* of the King.   ,,   IV ii 355
monarch mane Bristled about his quick *e's*—   *The Cup* I ii 121

Ear (*continued*)   For your *e* only—I love you—   *The Cup* I ii 217

'Eär (hear)   says the master goäs cleän off his 'eäd
when he '*e's* the naäme on 'im;   *Prom. of May* III 132

'Eärd (heard)   Well, I never '*e* the likes o' that afoor.   „   I 255

Why, Wilson, tha '*e* 'im thysen—   „   I 302

Earl   Ay, if Dukes, and *E's*, And Counts,   *Queen Mary* III i 50

this young *E* was sent on foreign travel,   „   v ii 489

Ask our broad *E*.   *Harold* I i 90

Art thou sick, good *E* ?   „   I i 100

When camest thou hither ?   *Gamel.* To-day, good *E*.   „   I i 106

The King hath made me *E* ; make me not fool !   Nor
make the King a fool, who made me *E* !   „   I i 288

Who made the King who made thee, make thee.   „   I i 295

Tostig, Edward hath made him *E* :   „   I ii 186

Follow my lead, and I will make thee.   „   I ii 217

Good-night, and dream thyself Their chosen *E*.   „   I ii 249

E first, and after that Who knows I may not dream myself
their king !   „   I ii 250

E, wilt thou fly my falcons this fair day ?   „   II ii 146

Thy valour and thy value, noble *e*.   „   II ii 202

Look not amazed, fair *e* !   „   II ii 494

And I will make thee my great *E* of *E's*,   „   II ii 629

Thou must swear absolutely, noble *E*.   „   II ii 716

Thanks, truthful *E* ; I did not doubt thy word,   „   II ii 723

Who make thy good their own—all England, *E*.   „   III i 331

E's and Thanes ! Full thanks for your fair greeting of
my bride !   *E's*, Thanes, and all our countrymen !   „   IV iii 45

E, the first Christian Cæsar drew to the East   „   v i 21

So !—did he ?—*E*—I have a mind to play The William   „   v i 25

E—ay—thou art but a messenger of William.   „   v i 29

Ay, my lord, and divers other *e's* and barons.   *Becket* I iv 59

golden leaves, these *e's* and barons, that clung to me,   „   I iv 66

They shall henceforward be my *e's* and barons—   „   I iv 86

Knights, bishops, *e's*, this London spawn—   „   II ii 143

The lady gave a rose to the *E*, (repeat)   *Foresters* I i 12, 105

The lady gave her hand to the *E*, (repeat)   „   I i 16, 92

'Farewell, farewell, my warrior *E* ! '   „   I i 18

She gave a weeping kiss to the *E*, (repeat)   „   I i 20, 119

never was an *E* so true a friend of the people   „   I i 188

A gallant *E*. I love him as I hate John.   „   I i 190

shoot almost as closely with the bow as the great *E*
himself.   „   I i 217

so flustered me that I forgot my message from the *E*.   „   I i 297

I am a silent man myself, and all the more wonder
at our *E*.   „   I ii 36

not so much for the cause as for the *E*.   O Lord,
I am easily led by words, but I think the *E*
hath right.   Scarlet, hath not the *E* right ?   „   I ii 39

I will swear by the head of the *E*.   „   I ii 45

Thou Much, miller's son, hath not the *E* right ?   „   I ii 47

but for all that I will swear the *E* hath right.   „   I ii 51

Thou art the *E's* confessor and shouldst know.   „   I ii 55

the *E* and Sir Richard come this way.   „   I ii 147

And learn from her if she do love this *E*.   „   I ii 188

Ay, noble *E*, and never part with it.   „   I ii 303

Robin, *E*—   *Robin.* Let be the *E*.   „   I iii 93

You dared to dream That our great *E*,   „   II i 686

E——   *Robin.* Nay, no *E* am I.   I am English yeoman..   „   III 129

But, *E*, if thou be he——   *Friar Tuck.* Fine him !
fine him ! he hath called plain Robin an *e*.   „   IV 148

Robin, Earl of Huntingdon, For *E* thou art again,   „   IV 830

Earldom   yet hear ! thine *e*, Tostig,   *Harold* I i 303

I would it went as well as with mine *e*.   „   I i 337

I have to make report of my good *e* To the good king   „   I i 406

It means the fall of Tostig from his *e*.   „   I i 469

In mine *e* A man may hang gold bracelets   „   II i 86

Thou art a mighty man In thine own *e* !   „   II i 93

We have few prisoners in mine *e* there,   „   II ii 687

ever-jarring *E's* move To music and in order—   „   II ii 760

he flamed When Tostig's anger'd *e* flung him,   „   II i 54

I come for mine own *E*, my Northumbria ;   „   IV ii 29

be chasten'd by thy banishment, Some easier *e*.   „   IV ii 51

Fain had I kept thine *e* in thy hands   „   v i 275

Earlier   O higher, holier, *e*, purer church,   *Queen Mary* IV ii 108

Early   Not here as yet.   You are too *e* for him.   *The Cup* I iii 50

Early (*continued*)   As I said before, you are still too *e*.
Camma. Too *e* to be here alone with thee ;   *The Cup* I iii 81

His *e* follies cast into his teeth,   *Queen Mary* v ii 124

Earn'd   Hast thou not fought for it, and *e* it ?   *Foresters* IV 345

Earshot   Stand out of *e* then,   *Harold* II ii 240

'Eart (heart)   I doänt believe he's iver a '*e* under his
waistcoat.   *Prom. of May* I 130

Earth   To him within there who made Heaven and *E* ?   *Queen Mary* I v 48

in his scared prayers Heaven and *e's* Maries ;   „   II ii 88

Between the two most high-set thrones on *e*,   „   III ii 107

Amplier than any field on our poor *e*   „   III iii 197

With heaven for *e*.   „   III iii 201

Julius, God's Vicar and Viceregent upon *e*,   „   III iii 213

That heaven wept and *e* blush'd.   „   III iv 193

God upon *e* ? what more ?   „   III iv 383

As Cranmer hath, came to the fire on *e*.   „   IV i 61

On *e* ; but saved in heaven By your recanting.   „   IV i 178

I have offended against heaven and *e*   „   IV iii 124

And I can find no refuge upon *e*.   „   IV iii 128

You are the mightiest monarch upon *e*,   „   v i 52

Bride of the mightiest sovereign upon *e* ?   „   v ii 545

Should make the mightiest empire *e* has known.   „   v ii 70

for heaven's credit Makes it on *e* :   *Harold* I i 142

In heaven signs !   Signs upon *e* !   „   I i 160

Not stagger'd by this ominous *e* and heaven : But
heaven and *e* are threads   „   I i 207

And other bells on *e*, which yet are heavens ;   „   I ii 133

would make the hard *e* rive To the very Devil's horns,   „   II ii 740

let *e* rive, gulf in These cursed Normans—   „   II ii 781

And signs on *e* !   Knowest thou Senlac hill ?   „   III i 360

'Seven feet of English *e*, or something more,   „   IV iii 112

corpse thou whelmest with thine *e* is cursed,   „   v i 68

dead as Death this day to ought of *e*   „   I 426

Is not the Church the visible Lord on *e* ?   *Becket* I iii 93

Lest there be battle between Heaven and *E*, And *E*
should get the better—   „   I iii 227

and when ye shall hear it is poured out upon *e*,   „   I iv 37

did not wholly clear The deadly growths of *e*,   „   II ii 203

like Mahound's coffin hung between heaven and *e*—   „   II ii 362

E's falses are heaven's truths.   „   III iii 348

cry out for thee Who art too pure for *e*.   „   IV ii 134

And break the soul from *e*.   „   v i 44

She sends it back, as being dead to *e*,   „   v i 171

Flash sometimes out of *e* against the heavens.   „   v iii 37

Tho' all the loud-lung'd trumpets upon *e*   „   v ii 488

Too late on *e* may be too soon in hell.   „   v ii 528

Tho' *e's* last earthquake clash'd the minster-bells,   „   v iii 41

Seen by the Church in Heaven, the Church on *e*—   „   v iii 99

Will the *e* gape and swallow us ?   „   v iii 205

and enrich *E* with her shadow !   *The Cup* I iii 60

Who causest the safe *e* to shudder and gape,   „   II 298

They will break in the *e*—I am sinking—   „   II 477

Thou art the last friend left me upon *e*—   *The Falcon* 32

Outvalues all the jewels upon *e*.   „   779

comes To rob you of your one delight on *e*.   „   828

For all the souls on *e* that live To be forgiven   *Prom. of May* III 7

bow'd To the *e* he came from,   „   III 515

fiercest storm That ever made *e* tremble—   „   III 798

for the love of his own little mother on *e*,   *Foresters* I i 98

it answers, I am thine to the very heart of the *e*—   „   I i 337

till the green *e* drink Her health along with us   „   III 350

bury her Even in the bowels of the *e*   „   III 462

Earthly   Is it possible That mortal men should bear their *e*
heats   *Harold* v i 283

unsubject to Our *e* sceptre.   *Becket* I iii 681

Earthquake   and underfoot An *e* ;   *Queen Mary* IV iii 399

shake the North With *e* and disruption—   *Harold* I ii 200

midriff-shaken even to tears, as springs gush out
after *e's*—   *Becket* III iii 163

Tho' earth's last *e* clash'd the minster-bells,   „   v iii 41

Earthware   one piece of *e* to serve the salad in to my
lady,   *The Falcon* 481

Earthworm   What poor *e's* are all and each of us,   *Prom. of May* III 635

Ease   Tho' scarce at *e* ; for, save our meshes break,   *Harold* II ii 140

Eased   Then after we have *e* them of their coins   *Foresters* III 172

Easier Thy life at home Is *e* than mine here.   *Harold* I i 97
So thou be chasten'd by thy banishment, Some *e* earldom.   „ IV ii 51
which we Inheriting reap an *e* harvest.   *Becket* II ii 194
It might be *e* then for you to make Allowance for a
  mother—   *The Falcon* 825
East (adj.) but the wind *e* like an enemy.   *Prom. of May* I 80
East (s) (*See also* **North-east**) And all the fair spice-
  islands of the *E.*   *Queen Mary* V i 50
the first Christian Cæsar drew to the *E*   *Harold* V i 22
dwelt alone, like a soft lord of the *E*,   *Becket* I iii 359
We fought in the *E*, And felt the sun of Antioch   „ II ii 92
Whose doings are a horror to the *e*, A hissing in the west!' „ IV ii 244
bowl my ancestor Fetch'd from the farthest *e*—   *The Falcon* 485
twilight of the coming day already glimmers in the *e.*   *Foresters* I ii 248
new term Brought from the sacred *E*, his harem?   „ IV 705
Easter Till the sun dance, as upon *E* Day.   *Queen Mary* III ii 238
Eastern We have had our leagues of old with *E* kings.   *The Cup* I ii 102
men will call him An *E* tyrant, not an English king.   *Foresters* IV 904
Easy (*See also* **Eäsy**) Breathing an *e* gladness . . . not
  like Aldwyth . . .   *Harold* I ii 174
Nay—but there be conditions, *e* ones,   „ II ii 206
'*e*'—that were *e*—nay—No money-lover he!   „ II ii 214
for I should find An *e* father confessor in thee.   *Becket, Pro.* 88
Rest you *e*, For I am *e* to keep. I shall not fly.   „ V ii 512
Is it not *e* to disarm a woman?   *The Cup* I iii 106
then you would know it is not So *e* to forgive—   *Prom. of May* II 486
Eäsy Maäke thysen *e*. I'll hev the winder naäiled up,   „ I 419
I could put all that o' one side a anew.   „ II 111
Eat I couldn't *e* in Spain, I couldn't sleep in Spain.   *Queen Mary* II i 36
Come locusting upon us, *e* us up,   „ II ii 101
Your apple *e*'s the better. Let them go.   „ II ii 7
Dare-devils, that would *e* fire and spit it out   „ III i 156
while famish'd rats *E* them alive.   „ IV 198
Where they *e* dead men's flesh,   *Harold* II ii 807
Sit down, sit down, and *e*,   „ IV iii 207
Let her *e* it like the serpent,   *Becket, Pro.* 532
We scarcely dare to bless the food we *e*   „ V 71
slave that *e* my bread has kick'd his King!   „ V i 242
I could not *e*, sleep, pray: „ V i 92
Sit and *e*, And take a hunter's vengeance   *The Cup* I ii 42
Will you not *e* a little?   „ I ii 425
Will you not *e* with me, my lord?   *The Falcon* 570
I can *e* no more!   „ 670
you ask'd to *e* with me.   „ 868
'Let us *e* and drink, for to-morrow we die.'   *Prom. of May* I 259
sits and *e*'s his heart for want of money to pay the
  Abbot.   *Foresters* I i 4
I came To *e* him up and make an end of him.   „ II i 125
Well, set them forth. I could *e* anything.   „ II i 274
before you can *e* it you must hack it with a hatchet,   „ III i 284
Something to *e*. *Robin.* And thou shalt have it, man.   „ IV 187
in the sweat of thy brow, says Holy Writ, shalt thou *e*
  bread,   „ IV 202
in the fear of thy life shalt thou *e* the King's venison—   „ IV 206
Eaten Ye have *e* of my dish and drunken of my cup for a
  dozen years.   *Becket* I iv 29
—we have *e*—we are heated. Wine!   *The Cup* I ii 45
Not *e* anything.   *The Falcon* 674
she that has *e* the yolk is scarce like to swallow the shell. „ 704
Eating (*See also* **Word-eating**) so thou be Squeamish at *e*
  the King's venison.   *Foresters* IV 194
'Eaven (heaven) Granny says marriages be maäde
  i' '*e*.   *Prom. of May* III 709
Eaves I never breathed it to a bird in the *e*,   *Queen Mary* V i 454
Echo (s) But shout and *e* play'd into each other   *Foresters* II i 258
The wood is full of *e*'es, owls, elfs,   „ II i 262
When horn and *e* ring,   „ III 428
I am but the *e* of the lips of love.   „ IV 892
Echo (verb) my wish *E*'es your Majesty's. *Pole.* It
  shall be so.   *Queen Mary* III iii 93
Mine *e*'es both your Graces';   „ III iii 95
yells of thief And rogue and liar *e* down in Hell,   *Foresters* III 324
Echo'd The trumpets of the fight had *e* down,   *The Falcon* 605
Echoing *See* **Bird-echoing**
Eclipse out of the *e* Narrowing my golden hour!   *Becket* II i 202

Eddicated (educated) Thy feyther *e* his darters to marry
  gentlefoälk,   *Prom. of May* II 115
I *e* boäth on 'em to marry gentlemen,   „ III 454
Eddying torrents of *e* bark!   *Foresters* III 95
Eden To make this Sherwood *E* o'er again,   „ II i 168
Ederunt *Sederunt principes, e pauperes.*   *Becket* I iv 132
Edgar (afterwards Mr. Harold) *See also* **Harold, Hedgar,
  Philip, Philip Edgar, Philip Harold, Philip
  Hedgar**) I warrants ye'll think moor o' this
  young Squire *E* as ha' coomed among us—   *Prom. of May* I 110
Wheer be Mr. *E*? about the premises?   „ I 432
where is this Mr. *E* whom you praised so in your
  first letters?   „ I 776
I thought Mr. *E* the best of men, and he has proved
  himself the worst.   „ II 85
that villain, *E*, If he should ever show his face   „ II 422
What *E*? *Dora.* Philip Edgar of Toft Hall   „ II 437
This *E*, then, is living? *Harold.* Living? well—   „ II 443
But she hates *E*. May not this Dobbins, or some
  other, spy *E* in Harold?   „ II 672
then she will forgive *E* for Harold's sake.   „ II 679
Nor am I *E*, my good fellow.   „ II 701
Mr. *E*? *Allen.* Theer, Miss! You ha' naämed 'im—   „ III 141
She must be crying '*E*' in her sleep. *Harold.* Who
  must be crying out '*E*' in her sleep?   „ III 653
Happy! What? *E*? Is it so?   „ III 668
Edgar (the Atheling) Who inherits? *E* the Atheling?   *Harold* III i 240
Edge (*See also* **Knife-edge**) Shall I smite him with the *e* of
  the sword?   *Becket* I iv 224
Edify (*See also* **Re-edify**) We come not to destroy,
  but *e*;   *Queen Mary* III iii 188
Edith (ward of King Edward, the Confessor) Art thou assured
  By this, that Harold loves but *E*?   *Harold* I i 210
Then for thine *E*?   „ II ii 422
I know the Norman license—thine own *E*—   „ II ii 478
Harold, if thou love thine *E*, ay.   „ II ii 622
wilt thou bring another, *E*, upon his head?   „ III i 262
and on thee, *E*, if thou abide it,—   „ III i 317
Look up! look up! *E*!   „ III i 321
E, Tho' somewhat less a king to my true self   „ III ii 52
Good even, gentle *E*.   „ III ii 118
E, Hadst thou been braver, I had better braved All—   „ III ii 177
E, *E*, Get thou into thy cloister as the king Will'd it: „ V i 308
E, The sign in heaven—the sudden blast at sea—   „ V i 377
E, if I, the last English King of England—   „ V i 383
thou art Harold, I am *E*!   „ V i 392
O *E*, thou here?   „ V ii 1
O *E*, if I ever wrought against thee,   „ V ii 21
O *E*, *E*, I have lost both crown And husband.   „ V ii 38
E, *E*— *Edith.* What was he like,   „ V ii 51
Edmund (King of the East English, martyred in 870) By
  St. *E* I overmeasure him.   „ IV iii 119
Educated *See* **Eddicated**
Edward (the Confessor) Ask it of King *E*!   „ I i 78
look, where *E* draws A faint foot hither,   „ I i 143
E loves him, so Ye hate him.   „ I i 427
E's prayers Were deafen'd and he pray'd them dumb,   „ I ii 21
foes in *E*'s hall To league against thy weal.   „ I ii 32
she held with *E*, At least methought she held with
  holy *E*,   „ I ii 50
I will demand his ward From *E* when I come again.   „ I ii 60
Our wild Tostig, *E* hath made him Earl: „ I ii 186
thine host in England when I went To visit *E*.   „ II ii 6
know'st my claim on England Thro' *E*'s promise: „ II ii 13
did *E* know of this?   „ II ii 304
Then let me hence With Wulfnoth to King *E*.   „ II ii 563
And hath King *E* not pronounced his heir?   „ II ii 575
if that but hung upon King *E*'s will.   „ II ii 601
According as King *E* promises.   „ II ii 714
Thou art English, *E* too is English now,   „ III i 28
E wakes!—Dazed—he hath seen a vision.   „ III i 129
And *E* would have sent a host against you,   „ IV i 99
Since Griffyth's head was sent To *E*,   „ IV i 222
Last night King *E* came to me in dreams—
  (repeat)   *Harold* IV i 259, 265

Edward (the Confessor) (continued) Take and slay me, For
E loved me. Harold. E bad me spare thee. Tostig.
I hate King E, for he join'd with thee To drive me
outlaw'd.   Harold iv ii 10
Of Alfred, or of E his great son,   ,,   iv iii 52
They know King E's promise and thine—thine. ,, v i 45
Not know that E cancell'd his own promise ? ,, v i 51
Thou didst possess thyself of E's ear   ,, v i 345
Edward (the First) In William's time, in our first
E's time,   Queen Mary iii iii 226
Edward (the Fourth) Who's a-passing ? King E or
King Richard ?   ,, i i 32
Edward (the Sixth) our young E might bequeath the
crown Of England,   ,, i ii 26
Yet I stood out, till E sent for me.   ,, i ii 29
Have we not heard of her in E's time,   ,, i iv 18
Your pious wish to pay King E's debts,   ,, i v 111
Had mark'd her for my brother E's bride ; ,, i·v 289
Did she not In Henry's time and E's ?   ,, iii iv 132
imprisonment, my Lord, Under young E.   ,, iii iv 244
Edwin (Earl of Mercia) Morcar and E have stirr'd up the
Thanes   Harold ii ii 288
have overthrown Morcar and E.   ,, iii ii 132
Again ! Morcar ! E ! What do they mean ? ,, iv i 133
Morcar and E, When will ye cease to plot   ,, iv i 160
Morcar and E, will ye, if I yield,   ,, iv i 175
Morcar and E, will ye upon oath, Help us   ,, iv i 179
E, my friend—Thou lingerest.—Gurth,—   ,, iv i 256
Gurth, Leofwin, Morcar, E !   ,, iv iii 221
Eel wriggle out of them like an e When the time serves. Becket ii ii 187
Effaced he is e, Self-blotted out ;   Queen Mary iv i 137
Egg wi' dree hard e's for a good pleace at the
burnin' ;   ,, iv iii 490
sat Stone-dead upon a heap of ice-cold e's. Becket v ii 240
brood Too long o'er this hard e, the world,   ,, v ii 253
E's. Filippo. One, but addled.   The Falcon 128
No not a draught of milk, no not an e,   872
and each of 'em as full of meat as an e,   Foresters i i 42
or the shambles-oak, or a weasel-sucked e,   ,, iv 212
Egg-bald may give that e-b head The tap that silences. Harold v i 90
Egypt like E's plague, had fill'd All things with blood ; Becket i iii 344
I heard a saying in E, that ambition   The Cup i iii 137
tho' the fire should run along the ground, As once
it did in E.   Prom. of May i 705
Eight Seventeen—and knew e languages— Queen Mary iii i 359
Eighty His e years Look'd somewhat crooked on him
in his frieze ;   ,, iv iii 331
Either You were the one sole man in e house ,, iii iii 253
I am the one sole man in e house,   ,, iii iii 266
true To e function, holding it ;   Becket ii iii 538
Yea, since he flouts the will of e realm,   ,, ii ii 256
Oh, no, not e way, nor any way   ,, v iii 86
Elbow fray'd i' the knees, and out at e, Queen Mary i i 52
look at our suits, out at knee, out at e. Foresters i i 33
Elbowing and almost e her, So else they stood, Queen Mary ii ii 76
Elder Made younger e son, violated the whole Tradition Prom. of May i 494
Eleanor (of Aquitaine, Queen of England) so this
Rosamund, my true heart-wife, Not E ! Becket, Pro. 132
and the soul of E from hell-fire.   ,, Pro. 151
secret out of our loyal Thomas, I am not E. ,, Pro. 467
and made Our waning E all but love me !   ,, ii ii 458
Oh, Queen E. Yes, my lady ;   ,, iii i 203
E, E, have I Not heard ill things of her   ,, iii i 230
'E of Aquitaine, E of England ! Murder'd by that
adulteress E,   ,, iv ii 241
Why should I swear, E, who am, or was,   ,, iv ii 403
Election dost thou think the King Forced mine e ? Herbert.
I do think the King Was potent in the e,   ,, i i 127
the e shall be made in the Chapel Royal,   ,, i iii 110
was thine own e so canonical, Good father ? ,, i iii 120
Eleven I am e years older than he is. Queen Mary i v 68
I am e years older than he,   ,, v v 46
Elf The wood is full of echoes, owls, e's, Foresters i i 263
E, with spiteful heart and eye,   ,, ii ii 172
Elfin Nay, an please your E Grace,   ,, ii ii 132

Elisabetta (nurse to Count Federigo degli Alberighi) you
Would find it stain'd—— Count. Silence, E ! The Falcon 665
Elizabeth (Princess, afterwards Queen of England) No ;
it was the Lady E.   Queen Mary i i 18
the Lady E is the more noble and royal.   ,, i i 72
I mean the Lady E.   ,, i i 75
be no peace for Mary till E lose her head.'   ,, i iii 5
' Long live E the Queen !'   ,, i iii 8
And get the swine to shout E.   ,, i iii 39
we'll have no pope here while the Lady E lives. ,, i iii 44
we'll have no virgins here—we'll have the Lady E ! ,, i iii 62
If E lose her head—That makes for France.   ,, i iii 88
married The mother of E—a heretic Ev'n as she is ; ,, i v 32
Wyatt, shall we proclaim E ?   ,, ii i 239
The names of Wyatt, E, Courtenay,   ,, ii ii 94
E—Her name is much abused among those traitors. ,, ii ii 109
whom did you say ? Messenger. E ? Your Royal sister. ,, ii iv 116
Can I strike E ?—not now and save the life Of Devon : ,, ii iv 123
The proud ambitions of E,   ,, iii ii 169
Quoth E, prisoner.   ,, iv v 21
this re-action not re-act Yet fiercelier under Queen E, ,, iv iii 389
You must proclaim E your heir. (repeat)   ,, v 191, 204
E, How fair and royal—like a Queen, indeed ? ,, v i 234
E—To Philibert of Savoy, as you know,   ,, v i 246
Thou art commission'd to E, and not to me !   ,, v ii 594
A cry ! What's that ? E ? revolt ?   ,, v v 187
God save E, the Queen of England !   ,, v v 283
Elizabeth Barton See **Joan of Kent**
Ely (Bishop [Thirlby] of) My Lord of E, this. After a
riot We hang the leaders, Queen Mary iv i 72
Ely (city) There lies a treasure buried down in E: Harold ii i 11
Emboss'd many-breasted mother Artemis E upon it. The Cup ii 341
Embrace on thee remains the curse, Harold, if thou
e her :   Harold iii i 316
great and sound policy that : I could e him for it : Becket, Pro. 452
for who could e such an armful of joy ?   Foresters i ii 70
Wilt thou e thy sweetheart 'fore my face ?   ,, ii i 28
I E thee with the kisses of the soul.   ,, iii 143
E me, Marian, and thou, good Kate,   ,, iv 1031
Embroilment may come a crash and e as in Stephen's
time ;   Becket, Pro. 485
Embryo every rebel birth That passes out of e. Queen Mary iii vi 52
Emerald English Garter, studded with great e's, ,, iii i 85
Emperor (s) betroth'd in her babyhood to the Great E ,, i i 119
Most goodly, Kinglike and an E's son,—   ,, i v 2
Hath he the large ability of the E ?   ,, i v 324
letter which thine E promised Long since,   ,, i v 348
I am English Queen, not Roman E.   ,, i v 504
The E counsell'd me to fly to Flanders.   ,, i v 549
I fear the E much misvalued me.   ,, iii ii 76
The E's highness happily symboll'd   ,, iii ii 108
treaty which the e sent us Were mainly Gardiner's ; ,, iii iii 69
And the E Approved you, and when last he wrote, ,, iii vi 76
prattling to her mother Of her betrothal to the E
Charles,   ,, v v 233
prest upon By the fierce E and his Antipope. Becket i iii 203
When he hath shaken off the E,   ,, i iii 244
you have traffick'd Between the E and the Pope, ,, ii ii 68
Threaten our junction with the E—   ,, ii ii 471
Empire Should make the mightiest e earth has
known.   Queen Mary v iii 70
the first Fell, and the next became an E. Harold iv i 51
push'd one way by the E and another by England, Becket ii i 327
his poor tonsure A crown of E.   ,, v i 196
Employ E us, heat us, quicken us, help us, The Cup i iii 131
Empress But—shamed of you, my E ! Prom. of May iii 599
Emptiness I had but e to set before you, The Falcon 870
course of that full feast That leaves but e. Prom. of May ii 256
Empty Most fruitful, yet, indeed, an e rind, Queen Mary iii ii 202
nave and aisles all e as a fool's jest !   ,, iv iii 286
Why then the throne is e. Who inherits ? Harold iii i 235
since the Sheriff left me naught but an e belly, Foresters ii i 279
Encampt The Roman is e without your city— The Cup i ii 83
Enchanted the people Believe the wood e. Becket iii i 36
Enclosed now you are e with boards of cedar, Queen Mary iii ii 101

Encumbered E as we are, who would lend us anything? *Prom. of May* III 162

End (s) born i' the tail e of old Harry the Seventh. *Queen Mary* I i 42
Look to you as the one to crown their e's. ,, I iv 172
She fear'd it might unman him for his e. ,, III i 368
to what e? For yet the faith is not established there.
Gardiner. The e's not come. *Pole.* No—nor this
way will come, Seeing there lie two ways to every e, ,, III iv 108
Latimer Had a brief e—not Ridley. ,, IV ii 225
as I have come To the last e of life, ,, IV iii 218
Might it not be the other side rejoicing In his brave e? ,, IV iii 358
Who cannot move straight to his e— ,, IV iii 394
sight of Danish blood Might serve an e not English— *Harold* IV iii 98
And to what e? *Becket* I ii 63
and to speak truth, nigh at the e of our last crust, ,, III i 114
an' it 'ud be well for me in the e, ,, III i 134
but in the e we flourished out into a merriment; ,, III i 137
What! Is the e come? ,, v i 148
The e is mine. ,, v i 151
If once our e's are gain'd? *The Cup* I i 32
harm at times, may even Hasten their e. *The Falcon* 823
At the e of the daäy, For the last loäd hoäm?
(repeat) *Prom. of May* II 183, 194
Till the e of the daäy And the last loäd hoäm. ,, II 208
Till the e o' the daäy An' the last loäd hoäm?' (repeat) .. II 238, 292
To the e o' the daäy An' the last loäd hoäm.' ,, II 259
I came To eat him up and make an e of him. *Foresters* II i 125
at the far e of the glade I see two figures ,, IV 332
To his own unprincely e's. ,, IV 716

End (verb) Ay, if he do not e in smoke again. *Becket* II ii 315
So e all passions. Then what use in passions? *The Cup* I iii 126
Ended all things lived and e honestly. *Queen Mary* III v 115
Thou shalt not go. I have not e with thee. *Becket, Pro.* 305
That was not the way I e it first— ,, *Pro.* 335
Our forest games are e, our free life, *Foresters* IV 1049
Ending (adj.) showers of blood are blown Before a never e blast, *Harold* III i 395
Ending (s) Other reasons There be for this man's e, *Queen Mary* IV iii 54
misreport His e to the glory of their church. ,, IV iii 327
Endure Canst thou e to be a beggar *Foresters* I i 204
Enemy Thou speakest of the e of thy king. *Queen Mary* I v 327
Stand fast against our enemies and yours, ,, II ii 242
Makes enemies for himself and for his king; ,, II ii 399
Who will avenge me of mine enemies ,, III ii 166
But he was evermore mine e, ,, v ii 91
Thou hast given it to the e of our house. *Harold* IV ii 31
So perish all the enemies of Harold! ,, v i 504
So perish all the enemies of England! ,, v i 554
Be sweet to her, she has many enemies. *Becket* I i 404
Is he thy e? Henry. He? who? ay! *Rosamund.*
Thine e knows the secret of my bower. ,, II i 262
To bless thine enemies—— *Becket.* Ay, mine, not Heaven's. ,, v ii 25
Mine enemies barr'd all access to the boy. ,, v ii 451
My lord, we force you from your enemies. ,, v iii 24
Henceforth I am thy mortal e. *The Cup* I ii 330
I was but wounded by the e there And then imprison'd. *The Falcon* 388
day's bright like a friend, but the wind east like an e. *Prom. of May* I 80
They say, we should forgive our enemies. ,, II 432
Red with his own and e's blood— *Foresters* II i 32
Enforce to e The long-withholden tribute: *The Cup* I i 76
Enframed powers of the house of Godwin Are not e in thee. *Harold* I i 317
Engelram de Trie mightiest knight of France, Sir E d T,— *Becket* I iii 748
England Edward might bequeath the crown Of E, *Queen Mary* I ii 28
not to yield His Church of E to the Papal wolf And Mary; ,, I ii 36
—for to wed with Spain Would treble E— ,, I v 76
I am Queen of E; take mine eyes, ,, I v 127
Would I marry Prince Philip, if all E hate him? ,, I v 139
Is it E, or a party? Now, your answer. ,, I v 142
men-at-arms Guard my poor dreams for E. ,, I v 154
if this Philip be the titular king Of E, ,, I v 255
—after me Is heir of E; ,, I v 286
Would make our E, France; Mary of E, joining hands with Spain, ,, I v 297

England (continued) Heir of this E and the Netherlands! *Queen Mary* I v 418
Men of Kent; E of E; ,, II i 157
all the rest of E bow'd theirs to the Norman, ,, II i 159
county or a shire, but of this E, ,, II i 163
he will be King, King of E, my masters; ,, II i 173
and be the mightiest man This day in E. ,, II ii 20
my father was the rightful heir Of E, ,, II ii 171
or impair in any way This royal state of E, ,, II ii 230
The Queen of E—or the Kentish Squire? ,, II ii 269
The Queen of E or the rabble of Kent? ,, II ii 273
'Who knows?' I am for E. ,, II ii 412
They are the flower of E; set the gates wide. ,, II iv 70
lest living Spain Should sicken at dead E. ,, III i 28
I came to feel the pulse of E, ,, III i 37
E now Is but a ball chuck'd between France and Spain, ,, III i 109
'The Queen of E is delivered of a dead dog!' ,, III ii 219
Presenting the whole body of this realm Of E, ,, III iii 117
This is the loveliest day that ever smiled On E. ,, III iii 163
But stretch it wider; say when E fell. ,, III iii 261
Perchance in E, loves her like a son. ,, III iii 267
We reck not tho' we lost this crown of E—Ay! tho'
it were ten E's? ,, III iv 56
Thou Christian Bishop, thou Lord Chancellor Of E! ,, III iv 302
What power this cooler sun of E hath ,, III iv 327
She troubles E: that she breathes in E ,, III vi 49
I cannot be True to this realm of E ,, IV i 27
made us lower our kingly flag To yours of E. ,, v i 60
lower his flag To that of E in the seas of E. ,, v i 66
Being Queen of E, I have none other. ,, v i 69
he would weld France, E, Scotland, ,, v i 137
They say your wars are not the wars of E. ,, v i 166
The King of France the King of E too. ,, v i 198
sharper harm to E and to Rome, Than Calais taken. ,, v ii 29
Send out: let E as of old Rise lionlike, ,, v ii 265
I do much fear that E will not care. ,, v ii 282
Suffer not That my brief reign in E be defamed ,, v ii 302
Your E is as loyal as myself. ,, v ii 328
remember what you said When last you came to E? ,, v ii 568
Welcome to E! ,, v iii 14
What hinders but that Spain and E join'd, ,, v iii 68
Spain would be E on her seas, and E Mistress of the Indies. ,, v iii 72
E Will be the Mistress of the Indies yet, ,, v iii 76
never merry world In E, since the Bible came among us. ,, v v 241
It never will be merry world in E, ,, v v 247
That never English monarch dying left E so little. ,, v v 278
—we will make E great. ,, v v 281
God save Elizabeth, the Queen of E! ,, v v 284
Yon grimly-glaring, treble-brandish'd scourge Of E! *Harold* I i 5
mean The doom of E and the wrath of Heaven? ,, I i 46
bishops down from all Their thrones in E! ,, I i 51
is this pendent hell in heaven A harm to E? ,, I i 77
he may tell thee, I am a harm to E. ,, I i 80
War there, my son? is that the doom of E? ,, I i 126
For all the world sees it as well as E. ,, I i 130
but after I am gone Woe, woe to E! ,, I i 190
E loves thee for it. ,, I i 221
my father drove the Normans out Of E?— ,, I i 253
Be there not fair woods and fields In E? ,, I i 263
sons of Godwin Sit topmost in the field of E, ,, I ii 326
Griffyth I hated; why not hate the foe Of E? ,, I ii 146
If he were King of E, I his queen, ,, I ii 154
Should not I Love Aldwyth, ,, I ii 177
Pronounced his heir of E, ,, I ii 195
Peace-lover is our Harold for the sake Of E's wholeness— ,, I ii 198
And bless the Queen of E. ,, I ii 207
a whale to a whelk we have swallowed the King of E. ,, II i 45
thine host in E when I went To visit Edward. ,, II ii 4
know'st my claim on E Thro' Edward's promise: ,, II ii 12
I want his voice in E for the crown, ,, II ii 71
E our own Thro' Harold's help, ,, II ii 77
Who shall be kings of E. I am heir Of E ,, II ii 124
The choice of E is the voice of E. *William.* I will be king of E by the laws, The choice, and voice of E. ,, II ii 128

English (*continued*)   That never *E* monarch dying
    left England so little.   *Queen Mary* v v 277
There somewhere beats an *E* pulse in thee !   *Harold* II ii 266
Boy, thou hast forgotten That thou art *E*.   „   III ii 475
Thou art *E*, Edward too is *E* now,   „   III i 28
To Holy Peter in our *E* isle !   „   III i 207
My mother is a Dane, and I am *E* ;   „   IV i 55
Seven feet of *E* land, or something more,   „   IV ii 54
   or *E* Ironside Who fought with Knut, or Knut who
    coming Dane Died *E*.   „   IV iii 53
sight of Danish blood Might serve an end not *E*—   „   IV iii 98
'Seven feet of *E* earth, or something more,   „   IV iii 112
Edith, if I, the last *E* King of England—   „   v i 384
I do not hear our *E* war-cry.   „   v i 651
I held it with him in his *E* halls,   „   v ii 128
And where is she ?   There in her *E* nest ?   *Becket, Pro.* 178
Of Provence blew you to your *E* throne ;   „   v i 123
That ever blossom'd on this *E* isle ?   *Foresters* I ii 124
There are no hearts like *E* hearts   „   II i 3
There are no wives like *E* wives   „   II i 15
There are no maids like *E* maids   „   II i 19
the bravest *E* heart Since Hereward the Wake,   „   II i 686
Nay, no Earl am I.   I am *E* yeoman.   „   III i 131
when Our *E* maidens are their prey,   „   III i 179
men will call him An Eastern tyrant, not an *E* king.   „   IV 904
Look ; can you make it *E* ?   *Queen Mary* I i 127
Word of God In *E* !   „   III i 280
said the Miserere Mei—But all in *E*, mark you ;   „   III i 392
These Spaniel-Spaniard *E* of the time,   „   III iii 240
I am ashamed that I am Bagenhall, *E*.   „   III iii 249
Peters, you know me Catholic, but *E*.   „   IV iii 567
Howard is all *E* !   „   v i 61
there are many *E* in your ranks To help your battle.   „   v i 110
that our brave *E* Had sallied out from Calais   „   v i 255
one who fill'd All offices, all bishopricks with *E*—   *Harold* II ii 535
That art half *E*.   Take them away !   „   v ii 135
fought men Like Harold and his brethren, and his guard
   Of *E*.   „   v ii 181
Make them again one people — Norman, *E* ; And *E*,
   Norman ;   „   v ii 189
That's the *E* of it.   *Becket* I iv 275
Not on French ground, nor any ground but *E*,   „   III iii 261
and your own name Of Harold sounds so *E* and
   so old   *Prom. of May* III 610

English-born   Shame, shame, my masters ! are you
   E-b,   *Queen Mary* I iii 70
Englishman   You are shy and proud like *Englishmen*,   „   II ii 257
Here swings a Spaniard—there an *E* ;   „   v i 87
Sailing from France, with thirty *Englishmen*,   „   v i 285
There are no men like *Englishmen*   *Foresters* II i 7
Englishwoman   Malet, thy mother was an *E* ;   *Harold* II ii 265
Enlisted   *See* 'Listed
Enliven   We might *e* you.   *Queen Mary* I iii 119
Enough   (*See also* **Anew**)   *E*, my Lords.   It is God's
   will, the Holy Father's will,   „   IV i 183
The prison fare is good *e* for me.   „   IV i 42
old *e* To scare me into dreaming, ' what am I,   „   IV ii 102
E !   Thou wilt not break it !   *Harold* II ii 752
wouldst tug thy Cupid till his ribs cracked—*e* of this.   *Becket, Pro.* 505
E, my lord, *e* !   „   I iii 740
E, my lord.   *Becket*.   More than *e*.   „   I iii 749
They are plagues *e* in-door.   „   II ii 91
Ay, ay ! the King humbles himself *e*.   „   II ii 185
But thou art like *e* to make him thine.   *Eleanor*.
   Becket is like *e* to make all his.   „   v i 132
their spites at Rome, Is like *e* to cancel them,   *The Cup* I i 92
That is *e*, Farmer Dobson.   *Prom. of May* II 118
E !   *Dora*.   It seem'd so ; only there was left A
   second daughter,   „   III 769
Enrich   and *e* Earth with her shadow !   *The Cup* I iii 59
Ensign   I, bearing this great *e*, make it clear   *Becket* I iii 544
Entanglement   I must free myself from this *e*.   *Prom. of May* I 480
Enter   Not for the seven devils to *e* in ?   *Queen Mary* III ii 140
   ' How hard it is For the rich man to *e* into
    Heaven ; '   „   IV iii 205

Enter (*continued*)   Ah !—let him *e*.   Nay, you need
   not go :   *Queen Mary* v iii 10
Why not ?   Let him *e*.   *The Cup* II 39
Will *e* on the larger golden age ;   *Prom. of May* I 590
Enter'd   spirit of the twelve Apostles *e* Into thy making.   *Becket* I 50
There was a man just now that *e* here ?   *Foresters* II i 240
Entertain'd   Maintain'd, and *e* us royally !   *Harold* II ii 159
Entertainment   My lord, we thank you for your *e*.   *The Falcon* 859
I fear you scarce Will thank me for your *e* now.   „   882
Entreat   does your gracious Queen *e* you kinglike ?
   Courtenay.   'Fore God, I think she *e*'s like a
   child.   *Queen Mary* I iii 110
Poor Wulfnoth ! do they not *e* thee well ?   *Harold* II ii 404
Madam, we will *e* thee with all honour.   „   v ii 199
my good lord, I do *e* thee—sign.   *Becket* I iii 185
E's he may be present at our marriage.   *The Cup* II 248
Entreaty   Still plied him with *e* and reproach :   *Queen Mary* III 577
Entrenchment   A good *e* for a perilous hour !   *Harold* III i 363
Entry   How can I come When you so block the *e* ?   *Becket* v iii 37
Envied   I *e* Sinnatus when he married her.   *The Cup* I i 129
Envy   Spite, ignorance, *e*, Yea, honesty too,   *Becket* II i 100
Enwomb'd   The babe *e* and at the breast is cursed,   *Harold* v i 65
Ephesian   Artemis, Artemis, hear her, *E* Artemis !   *The Cup* II 311
Ephesus   seven sleepers in the cave at *E* Have turn'd   *Harold* I i 192
Episcopari   Nolo *e*.   *Becket, Pro.* 284
Epitaph   And, like the stone-cut *e*,   *Queen Mary* IV iii 163
Equal (**adj.**)   I am not *e* to it yet.   *Prom. of May* III 239
We have heard Of thy just, mild, and *e* governance ;   *Harold* III ii 690
Two sisters gliding at an *e* dance,   *Becket* I iii 444
Equal (**s**)   never since have met Her *e* for pure innocence   *Prom. of May* II 372
shamed of her among The ladies, born his *e*'s.   „   III 582
Equall'd   Rose never blew that *e* such a bud.   *Queen Mary* I 373
Eques   *E* cum pedite Præpediatur !   *Harold* v i 529
Equite   Equus cum *e* Dejiciatur !   „   v i 579
Equus cum *e*. Præcipitatur.   „   v i 598
Equity   and golden provinces So that were done in *e*.   *Becket* v i 348
Equus   *E* cum equite Dejiciatur !   *Harold* v i 579
E cum equite Præcipitatur.   „   v i 598
Err   And there *e*'s ; As he hath ever err'd   *Queen Mary* IV i 30
Err'd   As he hath ever *e* thro' vanity.   „   IV i 31
I have *e* with him ; with him I have recanted.   „   IV i 66
Thought that I knew him, *e* thro' love of him,   *Becket* I iii 440
Error   Repentant of his *e*'s ?   *Queen Mary* IV iii 22
'Erse (**horse**)   That beer be as good fur '*e*'s as men.   *Prom. of May* II 315
Esaïas   loons cannot spell *E* from St. Paul,   *Queen Mary* III i 281
Escape   (*See also* '**Scape**)   Much less shall others in
   like cause *e*,   „   IV iii 63
Who will be martyr when he might *e*.   *Becket* v ii 280
Escaped   (*See also* **Scaped**)   Danaë has *e* again Her tower,
   and her Acrisius—   „   I i 395
She hath *e*.   *The Cup* I iii 121
This is my son but late *e* from prison,   *Foresters* II i 460
Gone, like a deer that hath *e* thine arrow !   *Robin*.
   What deer when I have mark'd him ever yet *E*
   mine arrow ?   „   IV 60
Escaping   charge you that ye keep This traitor from *e*.   *Becket* v i 511
Eshtree (**ash-tree**)   wheere the big *e* cuts athurt it,   *Prom. of May* III 94
Especial   A token of His more *e* Grace ;   *Queen Mary* III iii 170
Our old friend Cranmer, Your more *e* love,   „   III iv 418
Essex   she was passing Some chapel down in *E*,   „   I v 40
Established   For yet the faith is not *e* there.   „   III iv 109
Estate (**condition**)   bland And affable to men of all *e*'s,   „   III vi 81
offal of the city would not change *E*'s with him ;   „   IV iii 78
Estate (**property**)   that holdest thine *e*'s In fee and
   barony   *Becket* I iii 674
Esteem'd   Who not alone *e* it honourable,   *Queen Mary* II ii 209
Estimation   Doth not the *fewness* of anything make the
   fulness of it in *e* ?   *Becket* III iii 303
Eternal   The *E* Peter of the changeless chair,   *Queen Mary* III iv 380
our grim Walhalla, *E* war,   *Harold* III ii 75
wing'd souls flying Beyond all change and in the
   e distance   „   III ii 101
Who stands aghast at her *e* self   *Becket* II 404
Then with one quick short stab—*e* peace.   *The Cup* I iii 124
and smile At bygone things till that *e* peace.   „   I iii 173

Face (s) *(continued)*   I have but shown a loathing *f*
to you,   *Queen Mary* III vi 113
See how the tears run down his fatherly *f*.   ,,   IV iii 4
wash'd his hands and all his *f* therein,   ,,   IV iii 338
and look upon my *f*, Not on the comet.   *Harold* I i 26
I cannot read the *f* of heaven;   ,,   I i 67
He can but read the king's *f* on his coins. *Stigand.* Ay,
ay, young lord, *there* the king's *f* is power.   ,,   I i 71
send thy saints that I may say Ev'n to their *f's*,   ,,   II ii 787
The rosy *f*, and long down-silvering beard,   ,,   III i 46
turn not thou Thy *f* away,   ,,   III ii 40
The rosy *f* and long down-silvering beard—   ,,   IV i 261
he hath risen again—he bares his *f*—   ,,   V i 557
how he fells The mortal copse of *f's*!   ,,   V i 589
They have so maim'd and murder'd all his *f*   ,,   V ii 77
I left him with peace on his *f*—   *Becket,* Pro. 396
Her *f* was veiled, but the back methought   ,,   Pro. 469
Exile me from the *f* of Theobald.   ,,   I iii 43
when he sign'd, his *f* was stormy-red—   ,,   I iii 320
Flung the Great Seal of England in my *f*—   ,,   I iii 457
he licks my *f* and moans and cries out against the King.   ,,   I iv 99
and glass The faithful *f* of heaven—   ,,   II i 161
Life on the *f*, the brows—clear innocence !   ,,   II i 195
who hath withstood two Kings to their *f's* for the
honour of God.   ,,   II ii 276
as I hate the dirty gap in the *f* of a Cistercian monk,   ,,   II ii 381
or I couldn't look your ladyship i' the *f*,   ,,   III i 196
and to read the *f's* of men at a great show.   ,,   III iii 83
ran a twitch across his *f* as who should say   ,,   III iii 94
and once he strove to hide his *f*,   ,,   III iii 104
his fine-cut *f* bowing and beaming with all that courtesy   ,,   III iii 141
scared the red rose from your *f* Into your heart ?   ,,   IV ii 74
I will hide my *f*, Blacken and gipsyfy it;   ,,   IV ii 99
Nay, what uncomely *f's*, could he see you!   ,,   V i 201
These arm'd men in the city, these fierce *f's*—   ,,   V iii 4
We will not have him slain before our *f*.   ,,   V iii 55
shun To meet her *f* to *f* at once !   *The Cup* I i 59
brows and eyes Of Venus; *f* and form unmatchable !   ,,   I i 122
She—no, not ev'n my *f*.   ,,   I i 132
Who are with him ?   I see no *f* that knows me.   ,,   I i 183
In the full *f* of all the Roman camp ?   ,,   I ii 269
Only one, And he perhaps mistaken in the *f*.   ,,   I ii 343
His *f* was not malignant, and he said   ,,   I ii 451
ambition, pride So bloat and redden his *f*—   ,,   II 170
far as the *f* goes A goodlier-looking man   ,,   II 175
f of an angel and the heart of a—that's too positive !   *The Falcon* 86
what you see you are saying afore his *f* ?   *Count.* Let
him—he never spares me to my *f* !   *Filippo.* No,
my lord, I never spare your lordship to your lordship's *f*,   ,,   108
nor to round about and back to your lordship's *f* again,   ,,   115
and bless your sweet *f*, you look as beautiful   ,,   197
colour'd all my life, Flush'd in her *f*;   ,,   365
one sweet *f* Crown'd with the wreath.   ,,   648
her affections Will flower toward the light in some
new *f*.   *Prom. of May* I 487
Her bright *f* beaming starlike down upon me   ,,   II 248
If he should ever show his *f* among us,   ,,   II 423
the rain beating in my *f* all the way,   ,,   III 367
' Go home ; ' but I hadn't the heart or *f* to do it.   ,,   III 389
I will give thee a buffet on the *f*.   *Foresters* I i 146
hath the fire in her *f* and the dew in her eyes.   ,,   I i 167
How she looks up at him, how she holds her *f* !   ,,   I ii 145
Why wearest thou thy cowl to hide thy *f* ?   ,,   I ii 207
bounden by a vow not to show his *f*,   ,,   I ii 237
I hate hidden *f's*. (repeat)   ,,   I ii 245, 251
and old *f's* Press round us, and warm hands   ,,   I iii 19
Her *f* is thine, and if thou be as gentle   ,,   II i 480
Wilt thou embrace thy sweetheart 'fore my *f* ?   ,,   II ii 29
Never Ob before his *f*.   ,,   II ii 133
For ever buzzing at your lady's *f*.   ,,   IV 11
It is not he—his *f*—tho' very like—   ,,   IV 777
And scruplest not to flaunt it to our *f*   ,,   IV 887
Face (verb)   *f* me out of all My regal rights.   *Becket* II ii 165
Faced   *See* **Black-faced, Red-faced**

Facile   be *f* to my hands.   Now is my time.   *Becket,* Pro. 218
Facility   translated that hard heart into our Provençal
facilities,   ,,   Pro. 381
to spare us the hardness of your *f* ?   ,,   Pro. 386
Faction   There is a *f* risen again for Tostig,   *Harold* IV i 172
Our anti-Roman *f* ?   *The Cup* I ii 197
I have enough—their anti-Roman *f*.   ,,   I ii 201
dishonour The daughters and the wives of your
own *f*—   *Foresters* IV 699
Fade   *f* Into the deathless hell which is their doom   *Queen Mary* III ii 174
we *f* and are forsaken—   ,,   V ii 374
Faded   Flower, she !   Half *f* !   ,,   I iv 61
this *f* ribbon was the mode In Florence ten years back.   *The Falcon* 421
blossom of his youth, Has *f*, falling fruitless—   *Prom. of May* II 334
Fading   (*See also* **Fast-fading**)   O my sick boy !   My daily
f Florio,   *The Falcon* 236
Faggot   then, who lights the *f* ?   Not the full faith,   *Queen Mary* III iv 123
Last night, I dream'd the *f's* were alight,   ,,   IV ii 2
Will my *f's* Be wet as his were ?   ,,   IV ii 228
bind a score All in one *f*, snap it over knee,   *Harold* IV i 58
Faggot-band   Snap not the *f-b* then.   ,,   IV i 66
Fail   I *f* Where he was fullest: *Queen Mary* II i 55
All traitors *f* like Tostig !   *Harold* IV iii 79
Solders a race together—yea—tho' they *f*,   *The Cup* I ii 163
Lest he should *f* to pay these thousand marks   *Foresters* IV 454
Fail'd   Few things have *f* to which I set my will.   *Queen Mary* II ii 22
Wyatt was a good soldier, yet he *f*,   ,,   III i 132
On my last voyage—but the wind has *f*—   *The Cup* II 522
We ever *f* to light upon thy son.   *Foresters* IV 984
Failing   F her, my Lord, Doth not as great   *Queen Mary* I iv 94
Failure   but *f* it may be Of all we aim'd at.   *Becket* I i 382
Fain   Make me full *f* to live and die a maid.   *Queen Mary* V iii 98
Faint   I am somewhat *f* With our long talk.   ,,   i v 520
I am *f* with fear that you will come no more.   ,,   v 30
but look, where Edward draws A *f* foot hither,   *Harold* I i 144
Tostig, I am *f* again.   ,,   I i 266
A ghostly horn Blowing continually, and *f* battle-hymns,   ,,   I i 373
I am *f* and sleepy.   Leave me.   *Becket* III i 208
I am very *f*.   I must lie down.   *Prom. of May* III 472
' I am *f* for your honey, my sweet.'   *Foresters* IV 15
Move me no more !   I am sick and *f* with pain !   ,,   IV 599
Fainted   O she has *f*.   Sister, Eva, sister !   *Prom. of May* III 672
Fair   Even so, *f* lady.   *Queen Mary* I iv 97
left about Like loosely-scatter'd jewels, in *f* order,   ,,   I 28
As *f* and white as angels;   ,,   III ii 16
were much amazed To find as *f* a sun as might have
flash'd   ,,   III ii 22
you perchance were trifling royally With some *f*
dame of court,   ,,   III vi 160
And all the *f* spice-islands of the East.   ,,   v i 49
How *f* and royal—like a Queen, indeed ?   ,,   v i 235
F island star !   ,,   v iii 15
Were you in Spain, this fine *f* gossamer gold—   ,,   v iii 48
I never look'd upon so *f* a likeness   ,,   v v 28
Be there not *f* woods and fields In England ?   *Harold* I i 261
Then fling mine own *f* person in the gap A sacrifice to
Harold,   ,,   I ii 202
then a *f* life And bless the Queen of England.   ,,   I ii 206
Earl, wilt thou fly my falcons this *f* day ?   ,,   II ii 146
So thou, *f* friend, will take them easily.   ,,   II ii 207
Not ever *f* for England ?   ,,   II ii 258
Obey him, speak him *f*,   ,,   II ii 318
O speak him *f*, Harold, for thine own sake.   ,,   II ii 395
Look not amazed, *f* earl !   ,,   II ii 494
The wind is *f* For England now . . .   ,,   II ii 766
Full thanks for your *f* greeting of my bride !   ,,   IV iii 46
Good royal customs—had them written *f*   *Becket* I iii 416
And one *f* child to fondle !   ,,   III ii 12
F Sir, a happy day to you !   *The Cup* I i 188
Leaving your *f* Marian alone here.   *Foresters* I ii 154
There are no wives like English wives So *f* and chaste
as they be.   ,,   II i 16
Fare you well, *f* lady !   ,,   III 243
but see *f* play Betwixt them and Sir Richard—   ,,   IV 98
But thou art *f* as ever, my sweet sister,   ,,   IV 1017

Fairer   My sister, is far *f* than myself.   *Queen Mary* I v 72
How look'd the Queen?   *Bagenhall.*   No *f* for her
   jewels.   "   III i 92
and the flowers Are all the *f.*   *Becket, Pro.* 117
Fairest   but of this England, in whose crown our Kent
   is the *f* jewel.   *Queen Mary* II i 163
Find one a slut whose *f* linen seems Foul   *Becket* v ii 202
Who art the *f* flower of maidenhood   *Foresters* I ii 123
Fair-hair'd   little *f-h* Norman maid Lived in my mother's
   house: *Becket* v ii 259
Fairly   My King would know if you be *f* served,   *Queen Mary* v iii 20
Fairy (adj.)   What's here?   A dead bat in the *f* ring—   *Foresters* II ii 93
A glimpse of them and of their *f* Queen—   "   II ii 103
F realm is breaking down   "   II ii 134
there comes a deputation From our finikin *f* nation.   "   II ii 145
Fairy (s)   wish before the word Is man's good *F*—   *Queen Mary* I iv 240
I thought if I followed it I should find the *fairies.*
   Eleanor.   I am the *f*, pretty one, a good *f* to
   thy mother.   *Becket* IV i 24
There are good *fairies* and bad *fairies*,   "   IV i 28
can't sleep sound o' nights because of the bad *fairies.*   "   IV i 31
I am her good *f*.   *Geoffrey.*   But you don't look like a
   good *f.*   Mother does.   "   IV i 34
And leave you alone with the good *f.*   "   IV ii 61
She may have lighted on your *fairies* here,   *Foresters* II i 496
My men say The *fairies* haunt this glade;—   "   II ii 101
There came some evil *f* at my birth   "   II ii 108
Evil *f*! do you hear?   "   II ii 116
We be *fairies* of the wood,   "   II ii 118
When the *f* slights the crown.   "   II ii 135
Fairy-ring   And now be skipping in their *f-r's*,   "   II i 497
Faith   My flight were such a scandal to the *f*,   *Queen Mary* I ii 53
long divided in itself, and sever'd from the *f*,   "   I iii 22
Bonner, who hath lain so long under bonds for the *f*—   "   I iii 36
Art thou of the true *f*, fellow,   "   I iii 45
No, being of the true *f* with myself.   "   I v 74
we two will lead The living waters of the *F* again   "   I v 88
But here's some Hebrew.   *F*, I half forgot it.   "   II i 125
Good *f*, I was too sorry for the woman   "   I 57
All greed, no *f*, no courage!   "   III i 145
'Hail, Daughter of God, and saver of the *f.*   "   III ii 82
And clasp the *f* in Christ;   "   III ii 122
Henceforth a centre of the living *f.*   "   III ii 155
The great unborn defender of the *F*,   "   III ii 165
His *f* shall clothe the world that will be his,   "   III ii 180
f that seem'd to droop will feel your light,   "   III iv 22
track of the true *f* Your lapses are far seen.   "   III iv 94
For yet the *f* is not established there.   "   III iv 109
because to persecute Makes a *f* hated, and is further-
   more No perfect witness of a perfect *f*   "   III iv 116
Not the full *f*, no, but the lurking doubt.   "   III iv 124
When *f* is wavering makes the waverer pass   "   III iv 157
call they not The one true *f*, a loathsome idol-worship?   "   III iv 219
accuse you of indifference To all *f's*, all religion;   "   III iv 224
the Queen, the Holy Father, The *f* itself.   "   III vi 35
Upon the *f* and honour of a Spaniard,   "   III vi 254
Have you remain'd in the true Catholic *f* I left you
   in?   *Cranmer.*   In the true Catholic *f*,   "   IV ii 17
confess Your *f* before all hearers;   "   IV ii 80
my *f* would seem Dead or half-drown'd,   "   IV ii 96
Which frights you back into the ancient *f*;   "   IV ii 144
Power hath been given you to try *f* by fire—   "   IV ii 153
these burnings will not help The purpose of the *f*;   "   IV ii 185
he seal his *f* In sight of all with flaming martyrdom.   "   IV iii 28
proclaim Your true undoubted *f*, that all may hear.   "   IV iii 114
declare to you my very *f* Without all colour.   "   IV iii 225
In every article of the Catholic *f*,   "   IV iii 230
No *f* with heretics, my Lord!   "   IV iii 458
Died in the true *f*?   "   v ii 518
sunk rocks; no passionate *f*—   "   v v 222
Pray'd me to pay her debts, and keep the *F*;   "   v v 258
What's up is *f*, what's down is heresy.   *Harold* I i 84
yet to us, in *f*, A happy one—   "   III i 200
That runs thro' all the *f's* of all the world.   "   III i 352
all the *f's* Of this grown world of ours,   "   III ii 64

Faith (continued)   Loyally and with good *f*, my lord
   Archbishop?   *Becket* I iii 278
with all that loyalty and good *f* Thou still   "   I iii 281
Mail'd in the perfect panoply of *f*,   "   I vii 494
Die for a woman, what new *f* is this?   *The Cup* I iii 67
learnt at last that all His old-world *f*,   *Prom. of May* II 332
—will he ever be of one *f* with his wife?   "   III 178
Beware, man, lest thou lose thy *f* in me.   *Foresters* I ii 179
on the *f* and honour of a king The land is his again.   "   IV 851
Faithful   who am your friend And ever *f* counsellor,   *Queen Mary* I iv 135
that I live and die That true and *f* bride of Philip—   "   II iv 43
Your *f* friend and trusty councillor.   "   II i 89
Have done my best, and, as a *f* son,   "   v ii 117
herself should see That king's are *f* to their marriage vow.   *Becket* I ii 78
A *f* traitress to thy royal fame.   "   II i 97
and glass The *f* face of heaven—   "   II i 161
and be to Rome More *f* than a Roman.   *The Cup* I i 103
This very day the Romans crown him king For all his
   f services to Rome.   "   II 65
Our Antonius, Our *f* friend of Rome,   "   II 244
I will be *f* to thee till thou die.   "   II 330
Faithless   Break thine alliance with this *f* John,   *Foresters* IV 323
Falaise   The *F* byblow!   *Harold* IV iii 174
Falcon   wilt thou fly my *f's* this fair day?   II 146
Bird-babble for my *f*!   Let it pass.   *The Falcon* 38
Just gone To fly his *f.*   "   210
His *f*, and I come to ask for his *f*,   "   219
his *f* Ev'n wins his dinner for him in the field.   "   230
How can I ask for his *f*?   "   234
'Get the Count to give me his *f*,   "   242
How can I, dare I, ask him for his *f*?   "   264
and once you let him fly your *f.*   "   317
His *F.*   *Count.*   My *f*!   *Giovanna.*   Yes, your *f*, Federigo!   "   840
Nothing but my brave bird, my noble *f*,   "   874
Falconry   The full-train'd marvel of all *f*,   "   25
plunge and *f* Of heresy to the pit: *Queen Mary* III iv 141
Fall (s)   have I that I am fixt, Fixt beyond *f*;   "   IV ii 90
It means the *f* of Tostig from his earldom.   *Harold* I i 468
Except it be a soft one, And undereaten to the *f.*   "   I ii 123
Do you still suffer from your *f* in the hollow
   lane?   *Prom. of May* III 241
She said 'It's the *f* of the year,   *Foresters* IV 24
Fall (verb)   Hast thou let *f* those papers in the palace?   *Queen Mary* I iii 1
No—being traitor Her head will *f*:   "   I v 60
let Rebellion Roar till throne rock, and crown *f.*   "   II i 145
hoped to *f* Into the wide-spread arms of fealty,   "   II ii 263
Like dogs that set to watch their master's gate, *F*,   "   III iv 311
in the daylight truth That it may *f* to-day!   "   III v 137
If war should *f* between yourself and France;   "   v i 9
So from a clear sky *f's* the thunderbolt!   "   v iii 115
Come *f* not foul on me.   *Harold* I i 460
see confusion *f* On thee and on thine house.   "   II ii 489
My prayers go up as fast as my tears *f*,   "   III i 166
F, cloud, and fill the house—   "   III i 190
And on it *f's* the shadow of the priest;   "   III ii 70
If the king *f*, may not the kingdom *f*?   But if I *f*, I *f*,   "   v i 123
If I *f*, I *f*—The doom of God!   "   v i 135
I cannot *f* into a falser world—   "   v i 271
And not on thee—nor England—*f* God's doom!   "   v i 370
F's—and another *f's.*   "   v i 500
No, daughter, no—they *f* behind the horse—   "   v i 545
As thine own bolts that *f* on crimeful heads   "   v i 565
Charged with the weight of heaven wherefrom they *f*!   "   v i 568
They *f* on those within the palisade!   "   v i 668
As seeming his, not mine, and *f* abroad.   *Becket, Pro.* 228
God make not thee, but thy foes,   *Becket.*   I fell.
   Why?   Why did He smite me?   What?   Shall
   I *f* off—to please the King once more?   "   I i 107
Thou canst not *f* that way.   "   I i 115
'When a bishoprick *f's* vacant, the King,   "   I iii 100
When thieves *f* out, honest men—   "   I iv 114
When honest men *f* out, thieves—   "   I iv 118
Shame *f* on those who gave it a dog's name—   "   II i 141
the sea-creek—the petty rill That *f's* into it—   "   II ii 295
Devil's 'if Thou wilt *f* down and worship me.'   "   III iii 286

Fall (verb) *(continued)* I could *f* down, and worship thee,
  my Thomas,   *Becket* III iii 288
Go. See that you do not *f* in. Go.   ,,   IV ii 59
world allows I *f* no inch Behind this Becket,   ,,   v i 39
Ready to *f* at Henry's word or yours—   ,,   v ii 486
I heard in Rome, This tributary crown may *f* to you. *The Cup* I i 97
So *f*'s the throne of an hour.   ,,   II 486
with as little pain As it is to *f* asleep.   *Prom. of May* II 342
But for the slender help that I can give, F into ruin. ,, II 422
I *f* before thee, clasp Thy knees.   *Foresters* II i 598
When heaven *f*'s, I may light on such a lark !   ,, III 12
he *f*'s And knows no more.   ,,   IV 526
Fallen (*See also* **Flesh-fallen**) He hath *f* out of favour
  with the Queen.   *Queen Mary* I iv 156
We are *f*, and as I think, Never to rise again. ,, III i 123
of all censures Of Holy Church that we be *f* into, ,, III iii 152
we are *f* creatures; Look to your Bible, Paget ! we are *f*. ,, III iv 80
You sit upon this *f* Cranmer's throne;   ,, IV i 114
How are the mighty *f*, Master Cranmer !   ,, IV ii 146
From councillor to caitiff—*f* so low,   ,, IV iii 75
That should have *f*, and may rise again.   ,, v ii 6
like the bloodless head F on the block,   ,, v ii 21
Love will fly the *f* leaf, and not be overtaken; ,, v ii 372
blast that came So suddenly hath *f* as suddenly— *Harold* II i 14
Many are *f* At Stamford-bridge . . .   ,, IV ii 214
Gurth hath leapt upon him And slain him: he hath *f*. ,, v i 634
Glory to God in the Highest ! *f*, *f* !   ,, v i 636
hath kinglike fought and *f*, His birthday, too. ,, v ii 125
spouse of the Great King, thy King, hath *f*— *Becket* III iii 176
The folds have *f* from the mystery,   ,, v ii 8
he hath *f* Into a sickness, and it troubles me. *The Falcon* 309
thaw I may ha' *f* out wi' ye sometimes, *Prom. of May* I 324
and now she be *f* out wi' ma, and I can't coom at 'er. ,, II 600
We Steers are of old blood, tho' we be *f*.   ,, II 605
And darkness rises from the *f* sun.   *Foresters* I iii 42
Or haply *f* a victim to the wolf.   ,, I 509
we have *f* into the hands Of Robin Hood. (repeat) ,, III 232, 297
my lady, Kate and I have *f* out again,   ,, III 412
Falling How oft the *f* axe, that never fell, *Queen Mary* III v 134
not to-night—the night is *f*.   *Becket* III ii 52
blossom of his youth, Has faded, *f* fruitless— *Prom. of May* II 334
Fallow —our *f*'s till'd, Much corn, *Becket* I iii 376
False (adj. and adv.) The *f* archbishop fawning on him, *Queen Mary* I v 30
O madam, if this Pembroke should be *f* ?   ,, II iv 10
F to Northumberland, is he *f* to me ?   ,, II iv 39
tho' a true one, Blazed *f* upon her heart.   ,, III i 70
And whether this flash of news be *f* or true, ,, III ii 234
No pardon !—Why that was *f*:   ,, v v 136
Who, while ye fish for men with your *f* fires, *Harold* II i 31
So less chance for *f* keepers.   ,, II ii 688
Good for good hath borne at times A bastard *f* as
  William.   ,, v i 176
Thou hast been *f* to England and to me !— ,, v i 349
As . . . in some sort . . . I have been *f* to thee. ,, v i 352
He that was *f* in oath to me, it seems Was *f* to his own
  wife.   ,, v ii 151
And that the *f* Northumbrian held aloof, ,, v ii 165
F to myself—it is the will of God (repeat) *Becket* I iii 290, 328
F to himself, but ten-fold *f* to me !   ,, I iii 472
F figure, Map would say.   ,, III iii 346
F oath on holy cross—for thou must leave him
  To-day,   ,, IV ii 209
Robin, I ever held that saying *f* That Love is blind, *Foresters* I i 643
No, no, *f* knight, thou canst not hide thyself ,, II i 23
False (s) Earth's *f*'s are heaven's truths. *Becket* III iii 348
Falsehood lips that never breathed Love's *f* to true maid *Foresters* IV 73
Falsely when I sware F to him, the falser Norman, *Harold* v i 303
Falser I cannot fall into a *f* world— ,, v i 271
when I sware Falsely to him, the *f* Norman, ,, v i 303
Falter And yet methinks he *f*'s: *Queen Mary* IV iii 398
He *f*'s, ha ? 'fore God, we change and change ; ,, III iv 406
Falter'd old affection master'd you, You *f* into tears. *Becket* v ii 145
Faltering felt the *f* of his mother's heart, *Queen Mary* II ii 82
Fame A faithful traitress to thy royal *f*. *Henry.* F ! what
  care I for *f* ?   *Becket* II i 98

Fame *(continued)* F of to-day is infamy to-morrow ; Infamy
  of to-day is *f* to-morrow :   *Becket* II i 103
—thy *f* too : I say that should be royal. ,, II i 109
You heed not how you soil her maiden *f*, *Foresters* IV 480
Familiar Yea, some *f* spirit must have help'd him.
  William. Woe knave to thy *f* and to thee ! *Harold* II ii 679
Family Be we not of the *f* ? be we not a-supping with the
  head of the *f* ?   *Becket* I iv 178
for I am closely related to the dead man's *f*. *Prom. of May* II 715
It is the trick of the *f*, my lord. *Foresters* I iii 151
Famine Wet, *f*, ague, fever, storm, wreck, wrath,— *Queen Mary* v v 108
War, waste, plague, *f*, all malignities. *Harold* I i 466
F is fear, were it but Of being starved. ,, IV iii 204
Till *f* dwarft the race—   *Becket* I iii 356
if you cram me crop-full I am little better than F in the
  picture,   *Foresters* I i 47
Famine-dead seen the true men of Christ lying *f-d* by
  scores,   *Queen Mary* v iv 38
Famine-stricken Laid *f-s* at the gates of Death— *Prom. of May* III 807
Famine-wasted Who wander *f-w* thro' the world. *Becket* III iii 188
Famish'd I am footsore and *f* therewithal. *Foresters* II i 267
while *f* rats Eat them alive. *Queen Mary* v ii 196
Famishing lash'd to death, or lie F in black cells, ,, v i 196
Fan (s) that his *f* may thoroughly purge his floor. ,, III iv 369
Fan (verb) it serves to *f* A kindled fire. ,, I v 620
Fancied Have you *f* yourself in love with him ? *Prom. of May* I 783
Why, my good Robin *f* me a man, *Foresters* III 20
F he saw thee clasp and kiss a man. *Kate.* Well, if
  he f that I fancy a man Other than *him*, ,, III 23
Fancy (s) My *f* takes the burner's part, . *Queen Mary* IV ii 231
this ghastly glare May heat their *fancies*. *Harold* I i 310
Who sow'd this *f* here among the people ? ,, IV i 147
Whether it bow'd at all but in their *f* ; ,, v i 109
had I fixt my *f* Upon the game I should have beaten
  thee,   *Becket, Pro.* 50
And thy thoughts, thy, *fancies* ? ,, *Pro.* 118
I speak after my *fancies*, for I am a Troubadour, ,, *Pro.* 347
would she were but his paramour, for men tire of their
  fancies ; but I fear this one *f* hath taken root, ,, *Pro.* 480
That you may feed your *f* on the glory of it, *The Cup* II 133
And all Thro' following of my *f*. *The Falcon* 144
specially sick children, have strange *fancies*, ,, 818
I have ta'en a sudden *f* to thee. *Foresters* IV 422
Fancy (verb) You must *f* that which follow'd, *Queen Mary* III i 409
Can I *f* him kneeling with me, and uttering *Prom. of May* III 179
if *he* fancied that I *f* a man Other than *him*, *Foresters* II 25
Fancy-ridd'n known a semi-madman in my time So *f-r*) *Queen Mary* II i 11
Fancy-sick F-*s* ; these things are done, ,, III vii 453
Fangless he that lookt a *f* one, Issues a venomous adder. *Becket* I iii 451
Fanny F be the naäme i' the song, but I swopt it
  fur *she*.   *Prom. of May* II 211
Far (*See also* **Var**) My sister, is *f* fairer than myself. *Queen Mary* I v 72
F liefer had I in my country hall Been reading some
  old book,   ,, III i 43
and rooted in *f* isles Beyond my seeing : *Harold* III i 152
at the *f* end of the glade I see two figures crawling up
  the hill.   *Foresters* IV 331
Farce comedy meant to seem a tragedy—A feint, a *f*. *Becket* IV ii 323
You have spoilt the *f*. ,, IV ii 337
There was the *f*, the feint—not mine. ,, IV ii 377
Fare (s) The prison *f* is good enough for me. *Queen Mary* IV ii 42
Fare (verb) F you well, Sir Ralph. ,, II ii 409
I must leave you. F you well, ,, III i 473
How *f*'s thy pretty boy, the little Geoffrey ? *Becket* v ii 167
F you well. *Synorix.* Farewell ! *The Cup* I i 158
Sir Richard and my Lady Marian *f* wellnigh as sparely
  as their people.   *Foresters* I i 31
Where is she ? and how *f*'s she ? ,, II i 106
F you well, fair lady ! ,, III 242
Fared And *f* so ill in this disastrous world. *Queen Mary* v ii 344
Farewell (adj.) she means to make A *f* present to your
  grace.   ,, I iv 245
Farewell (s) heard She would not take a last *f* of him, ,, III i 367
Farewell (verb, and inter.) *f*, and fly. *Cranmer.* Fly
  and *f*,   ,, I ii 103

Farewell (verb, and inter.) (*continued*) And so you may
continue mine, *f*,   *Queen Mary* I iv 137
Must be content with that; and so, *f*.   „   I v 271
F. I am somewhat faint With our long talk.   „   I v 519
F, and trust me, Philip is yours.   „   I v 539
F, your Graces.   „   III ii 146
F, Madam, God grant you ampler mercy   „   IV i 188
For a little space, *f*;   „   IV ii 46
Have you good hopes of mercy! So, *f*.   „   IV ii 87
Your pardon, Sweet cousin, and *f*!   „   v ii 204
F, my king. *Harold.* Not yet, but then—my queen. *Harold* I ii 137
F for ever!   „   IV ii 81
F! *Harold.* Not yet. Stay.   „   v i 336
Stigand will see thee safe, And so—*F*.   „   v i 420
F! I am dead as Death this day to ought of earth's   „   v i 424
F! *Becket.* *F*, friends! *f*, swallows!   *Becket* I iv 43
that will swallow anything. *F*.   „   II ii 383
And so *f* until we meet in England.   „ III iii 236
f, my lord. *Becket.* *F*, my liege!   „ III iii 271
F! I must follow the King.   „ III iii 329
Ev'n so : but think not of the King : *f*!   „   v ii 186
city is full of armed men. *Becket.* Ev'n so : *f*!   „   v ii 189
Fare you well. *Synorix.* *F*!   *The Cup* I i 160
Remember! Away—*f*! *Camma.* *F*!   „   I iii 115
Nothing more, *f*.   *Prom. of May* I 749
' *F, f,* my warrior Earl!'   *Foresters* I i 18
We thank you, and *f*. *Robin.* *F, f*.   „   I ii 249
F, Sir Richard : *f*, sweet Marian.   „   I ii 284
F, good fellows !   „   III 86
F at once, for I must hence upon The King's affair.   „   IV 341
F! I left mine horse and armour with a Squire,   „   IV 413
Blown like a true son of the woods. *F*!   „   IV 428
Meanwhile, *f* Old friends, old patriarch oaks.   „   IV 1053
Far-eyed My *f-e* queen of the winds—   *The Falcon* 9
Farm (adj.) The hen cluckt late by the white *f* gate,   *Prom. of May* I 38
Farm (s) her advowsons, granges, *f*'s, And goodly acres—   *Becket* I i 162
but the ill success of the *f*, and the debts,   *Prom. of May* II 68
S'iver I mun git along back to the *f*,   „   II 321
From the *f* here, close at hand.   „   II 360
I met her first at a *f* in Cumberland—Her uncle's.   „   II 396
She has disappear'd, They told me, from the *f*—   „   II 407
Has left his *f*, all his affairs, I fear,   „   II 420
hunt him With pitchforks off the *f*,   „   II 427
Allow me to go with you to the *f*.   „   II 574
rose From the foul flood and pointed toward the *f*,   „   II 654
The work of the *f* will go on still, but for how long ?   „   III 159
Father, this poor girl, the *f*, everything ;   „   III 212
I trust I may be able by-and-by to help you in the
business of the *f*;   „   III 223
And in the winter I will fire their *f*'s.   *Foresters* IV 95
Farm (verb) feller couldn't find a Mister in his mouth
fur me, as *f*'s five hoonderd haäcre.   *Prom. of May* I 303
Farmer When theer wur a meeting o' *f*'s at Littlechester   „   I 137
Tho' you are a gentleman, I but a *f*'s daughter—   „   I 668
F, you should be in the hayfield looking after your
men ;   „   II 46
How beautiful His manners are, and how unlike the *f*'s!   „   II 532
shamed of his poor *f*'s daughter among the ladies in
his drawing-room ?   „   III 294
if a gentleman Should wed a *f*'s daughter,   „   III 579
Farm-gate She gave her hand, unask'd, at the *f-g*;   „   II 626
Farming Miss, the *f* men 'ull hev their dinner i' the
long barn,   „   I 165
Farming-men if the *f-m* be come for their wages, to send
them up to me.   „   III 15
Farmstead and scare lonely maidens at the *f*.   *Foresters* III 201
Far-off I have a *f-o* burrow where the King Would miss
her and for ever.   *Becket* IV ii 158
Farther Your Grace's policy hath a *f* flight Than
mine   *Queen Mary* I v 312
Farthest that flower'd bowl my ancestor Fetch'd from the
f east—   *The Falcon* 485
Fashion red and white, the *f* of our land.   *Queen Mary* I v 10
Is it the *f* of this clime for women   „   III vi 90
Will in some lying *f* misreport His ending   „   IV iii 326

Fashion (*continued*) the dead were found Sitting, and
in this *f*;   *Queen Mary* v ii 397
To make allowance for their rougher *f*'s,   *Harold* II ii 9
You are too cold to know the *f* of it.   *Becket* II ii 126
Or scarce would smile that *f*.   „   III iii 28
—to celebrate my birthdaäy i' this *f*.   *Prom. of May* I 322
your Ladyship hath sung the old proverb out of *f*.   *Foresters* I i 164
that he may see The *f* of it.   „   IV 254
thou, that art churchman too In a *f*,   „   IV 412
blow upon it Three mots, this *f*—listen !   „   IV 425
Fashion'd (*See also* **Old-fashioned**) I have had it *f*, see, to
meet my hand.   *Harold* v i 422
Fast (adj. and adv.) (*See also* **Hold-fast, Friendship-fast**)
Do ye stand *f* by that which ye resolved ?   *Queen Mary* III iii 103
Have not I been the *f* friend of your life   „   v ii 133
I dug mine into My old *f* friend the shore,   *Harold* II i 7
come now so thick and *f*,   *Becket* I iii 610
Fast (s) If *f* and prayer, the lacerating scourge—   „   I iii 303
He fast ! is that an arm of *f*?   „   I iii 520
In scourgings, macerations, mortifyings, *F*'s,   „   v i 42
I come this day to break my *f* with you.   *The Falcon* 276
I have broken My *f* already.   „   575
Not having broken *f* the livelong day—   *Foresters* IV 186
Fast (verb) Your Foliot *f*'s and fawns too much for me.   *Becket, Pro.* 264
He *f*'s, they say, this mitred Hercules ! *He f*! is that
an arm of fast ?   „   I iii 518
F, scourge thyself, and mortify thy flesh,   „   I iii 539
I love my dinner—but I can *f*, I can *f*;   *Foresters* I i 64
Fasten I will *f* thee to mine own door-post   „   II i 403
Fasten'd And that myself was *f* to the stake,   *Queen Mary* IV ii 3
not at the moment who had *f* About his throat—   *The Cup* I 50
Faster *F* than ivy. Must I hack her arms off ?   *Harold* v ii 146
Come in, my friends, come in ! Nay; *f, f*!   *Becket* v iii 69
Fastest I am thy *f* friend in Normandy.   *Harold* II ii 556
Fasting A life of prayer and *f* well may see   *Harold* I i 199
Fat The shadows of a hundred *f* dead deer   „   I ii 103
The slow, *f* fool ! He drawl'd and prated so,   „   IV ii 40
A-hawking, a-hawking ! If I sit, I grow *f*.   *Becket, Pro.* 414
One slow, *f*, white, a burthen of the hearth ;   „   v ii 211
That fine, *f*, hook-nosed uncle of mine, old Harold, *Prom. of May* I 509
Fatal ruling men are *f* twins that cannot Move one with-
out the other.   *Harold* III i 127
Blaze like a night of *f* stars on those Who read   „   IV i 251
My *f* oath—the dead Saints—the dark dreams—   „   v 380
cowling and clouding up That *f* star, thy Beauty,   *Becket* I i 312
Fatality foul *fatalities* That blast our natural passions *Prom. of May* III 723
Fate *f* Which hunted *him* when that un-Saxon blast,   *Harold* I i 29
f hath blown me hither, bound me too   „   II ii 219
She is my *f*—else wherefore has my *f*   *The Cup* I i 12
I fling all that upon my *f*, my star.   „   I iii 27
Life yields to death and wisdom bows to *F*,   „   II 90
The wheel of *F* has roll'd me to the top.   „   II 221
Drew here the richest lot from *F*,   „   II 442
is it thou ? the *F*'s are throned, not we—   „   II 488
He had my *f* for it, Poison'd.   „   II 516
Fated Rome is *f* To rule the world.   „   II 415
Father (s) (*See also* **Feyther, God-father**) Let *f* alone,
my masters !   *Queen Mary* I i 38
child who had but obeyed her *f*;   „   I i 95
putting by his *f*'s will.   „   I ii 28
you divorced Queen Catharine and her *f*;   „   I ii 57
Courtenay, wilt thou see the holy *f* Murder'd before
thy face ?   „   I iii 64
Your royal *f* (For so they say) was all pure lily   „   I v 19
as tho' My *f* and my brother had not lived.   „   I v 36
for doing that His *f* whipt him into doing—   „   I v 63
My hard *f* hated me ;   „   I v 80
my royal *f*, To make the crown of Scotland one with ours,   „   I v 286
Hath he the large ability of his *f* ?   „   I v 439
thing Was no such scarecrow in your *f*'s time.   „   I v 473
the child obey'd her *f*. Spite of her tears her *f* forced
it on her.   „   I v 494
My *f* on a birthday gave it me, And I have broken with
my *f*—   „   I v 527

Father (s) (continued)   were a pious work To string
 my f's sonnets,   *Queen Mary* II i 27
Hand me the casket with my f's sonnets. ,, II i 44
Dumb children of my f, that will speak ,, II i 77
I know Spain.   I have been there with my f; ,, II ii 167
my f was the rightful heir Of England, ,, II ii 170
to whom The king, my f, did commit his trust; ,, II ii 208
The f ceded Naples, that the son Being a King, ,, III i 74
Against the Holy F's primacy,   ,, III iii 131
Thro' this most reverend F, absolution, ,, III iii 148
He, whom the F hath appointed Head ,, III iii 206
or more Denied the Holy F!   ,, III iv 248
As once the Holy F did with mine, ,, III v 243
Before my f married my good mother,— ,, III v 245
Against the King, the Queen, the Holy F, ,, III vi 33
What your imperial f said, my liege, ,, III vi 56
you know my f, Retiring into cloistral solitude ,, III vi 208
The Holy F in a secular kingdom Is as the soul ,, IV i 34
Cranmer is head and f of these heresies, ,, IV i 76
Your f was a man Of such colossal kinghood, ,, IV i 100
Your f had a will that beat men down; Your f had a
 brain that beat men down—   ,, IV i 108
It is God's will, the Holy F's will, ,, IV i 184
As if he had been the Holy F, sat And judged it. ,, IV iii 44
O God, F of Heaven !   O Son of God, ,, IV iii 117
O God the F, not for little sins   ,, IV iii 143
Forgive me, F, for no merit of mine, ,, IV iii 152
I do believe in God, F of all;   ,, IV iii 228
stood More like an ancient f of the Church, ,, IV iii 598
You must abide my judgment, and my f's, ,, v i 146
And yet I must obey the Holy F, ,, v ii 38
That all day long hath wrought his f's work, ,, v ii 118
Shut on him by the f whom he loved, ,, v ii 122
I watch'd you dancing once With your huge f; ,, v ii 145
O would I were My f for an hour ! ,, v ii 294
We have made war upon the Holy F All for your sake: ,, v ii 307
No, Madam, not against the Holy F, ,, v ii 312
There was an old-world tomb beside my f's, ,, v ii 394
My sister's marriage, and my f's marriages, ,, v iii 96
It was his f's policy against France. ,, v v 45
Holy F Has ta'en the legateship from our cousin Pole— ,, v v 125
She thank'd her f sweetly for his book ,, v v 236
O f, mock not at a public fear, *Harold* I i 74
For my dead f's loyalty to thee ? ,, I i 240
my f drove the Normans out Of England ?— ,, I i 251
F. William. Well, boy.   ,, II ii 103
But for my f I love Normandy. ,, II ii 270
in thy f's day They blinded my young kinsman,
 Alfred—ay, Some said it was thy f's deed. ,, II ii 510
Thank thee, f!   Thou art English, ,, III i 27
Harold, shake the cloud off ! Harold.   Can I, f? ,, III i 75
I have heard a saying of thy f Godwin, ,, III i 111
F, we so loved— Aldred.   The more the love, ,, III i 345
Hush, f, hush !   ,, III i 389
for this cow-herd, like my f,   ,, IV i 80
for mine own f Was great, and cobbled. ,, IV i 90
Holy F Hath given this realm of England to the Norman. ,, v i 12
Holy F To do with England's choice of her own king ? ,, v i 17
What power, holy f?   ,, v i 454
Are those the blessed angels quiring, f? ,, v i 473
Ay, good f.   ,, v i 516
Look, daughter, look. Edith.   Nay, f, look for *me* ! ,, v i 536
Stigand, O f, have we won the day ? ,, v i 543
The Holy F strangled him with a hair Of Peter ,, v ii 45
the Holy F, while This Barbarossa butts him, from
 his chair,   *Becket,* Pro. 215
Name him; the Holy F will confirm him. ,, Pro. 244
Becket, her f's friend, like enough staved ,, Pro. 517
Save me, f, hide me—they follow me— ,, I i 181
but, f, They say that you are wise in winged things, ,, I i 254
my f drove him and his friends, De Tracy and De Brito, ,, I i 276
F, I am so tender to all hardness !   Nay, f, ,, I i 315
Wedded ? Rosamund.   F!   ,, I i 319
O, holy f, when thou seest him next, ,, I i 322
and lay My crozier in the Holy F's hands, ,, I iii 125

Father (s) (continued)   Have I the orders of the Holy F ? *Becket* I iii 233
The secret whisper of the Holy F. ,, I iii 236
I knew thy f; he would be mine age Had he lived now; ,, I iii 249
think of me as thy f!   Behold thy f kneeling ,, I iii 251
F, I am the youngest of the Templars, ,, I iii 260
Sons sit in judgment on their f!— ,, I iii 552
Becket shall be king, and the Holy F shall be king, ,, I iv 270
The mouth is only Clifford, my dear f. ,, II i 221
I would that thou hadst been the Holy F. ,, II ii 398
I am the King, his f, And I will look to it. ,, III i 26
Hath not thy F left us to ourselves ? ,, III i 271
with the Holy f astride of it down upon his own head. ,, III iii 77
f's eye was so tender it would have called ,, III iii 101
Glancing at the days when his f was only Earl of Anjou, ,, III iii 150
nay, Geoffrey Plantaganet, thine own husband's f— ,, IV ii 250
His f gave him to my care, and I Became his second f: ,, v ii 335
And love him next after my lord his f. ,, v ii 342
scare me from my loyalty To God and to the Holy F. ,, v ii 483
He is not yet ascended to the F. ,, v iii 150
and send him forth The glory of his f— *The Cup* II 263
happy was the prodigal son, For he return'd to the
 rich f;   *The Falcon* 142
Many happy returns of the day, f. *Prom. of May* I 351
Did 'e git into thy chaumber ? Eva.   F! ,, I 401
No, no, f!   Towser'll tear him all to pieces. ,, I 423
I hate Traditions, ever since my narrow f, ,, I 492
Oh, Philip, F heard you last night. ,, I 557
you have robb'd poor f Of ten good apples. ,, I 615
nor f, Sister, nor you, shall ever see me more. ,, I 675
And poor old f not die miserable. ,, I 722
make them happy in the long barn, for f is in his glory, ,, I 792
mentioned her name too suddenly before my f. ,, II 24
and my f's breaking down, and his blindness. ,, II 69
I have lost myself, and am lost for ever to you and
 my poor f.   ,, II 85
my poor f, utterly broken down By losing her— ,, II 417
My f's death, Let her believe it mine; ,, II 453
My f stricken with his first paralysis, ,, II 481
Might I call Upon your f—   ,, II 513
I cannot Well answer for my f; ,, II 519
What was that ? my poor blind f— ,, II 566
and f Will not die miserable.'   ,, II 659
my f and I forgave you stealing our coals. ,, III 68
which F, for a whole life, has been getting together, ,, III 165
F, this poor girl, the farm, everything; ,, III 211
Poor blind F's little guide, Milly, ,, III 231
will you not speak with F to-day ? ,, III 237
always told F that the huge old ashtree ,, III 243
he will be willing that you and F should live with us; ,, III 261
That last was my F's fault, poor man. ,, III 279
And then—what would F say ? ,, III 390
your F must be now in extreme old age. ,, III 400
Don't you long for F's forgiveness ! ,, III 404
You must not expect to find our F as he was five years
 ago.   ,, III 419
Hes the cow cawved ? Dora.   No, F. ,, III 428
Be the colt deäd ? Dora. No, F. ,, III 430
Well, F, I have a surprise for you. ,, III 438
No, F, that was a mistake. She's here again. ,, III 445
lost hersen i' the river. Dora. No. F, she's here. ,, III 457
speaking with Your f, asking his consent— ,, III 493
state Of my poor f puts me out of heart. ,, III 504
I told you—My f.   ,, III 574
he, the f, Thro' that dishonour which you brought
 Marian ! Marian.   F!   *Foresters* I i 180
Cleave to him, f! he will come home at last. ,, I i 197
Tut, f!   I am none of your delicate Norman maidens ,, I i 211
F, you see this cross?   ,, I i 284
prays your ladyship and your ladyship's f to be present
 at his banquet to-night.   ,, I i 300
I wish you and your ladyship's f a most exceeding good
 morning.   ,, I i 309
and my own f—they were born and bred on it— ,, I i 331
Take it again, dear f, be not wroth ,, I i 341
Sufficient for the day, dear f !   ,, I i 343

Father (s) (*continued*) My lord, myself and my good *f* pray	*Foresters* I ii 127
Not her, the *f's* power upon her.	„ I iii 9
Much, the miller's son, I knew thy *f*:	„ I iii 147
but my *f* will not lose his land,	„ II i 522
betray'd Thy *f* to the losing of his land.	„ II i 570
your good *f* had his draught of wine	„ II ii 1
O my poor *f*!	„ II ii 8
O lead me to my *f*! (repeat)	„ II ii 22, 48
She will not marry till her *f* yield.	„ II ii 82
There is a fence I cannot overleap, *My f's* will.	„ III 10
And were my kindly *f* sound again,	„ III 81
He was my *f*, mother, both in one.	„ IV 6
And my sick *f* here has come between us	„ IV 55
Quiet, quiet! or I will to my *f*.	„ IV 78
thy *f* will not grace our feast With his white beard to-day. „	IV 79
Here is my *f's* bond.	„ IV 463
You scheme against her *f's* weal and hers,	„ IV 481
I remain Beside my *F's* litter.	„ IV 605
Speak not. I wait upon a dying *f*.	„ IV 611
It seems thy *f's* land is forfeited.	„ IV 640
thou shalt wed him, Or thine old *f* will go mad—	„ IV 645
F, I cannot marry till Richard comes.	„ IV 648
the Sheriff, *f*, Would buy me for a thousand marks	„ IV 651
But pity for a *f*, it may be,	„ IV 659
I grieve to say it was thy *f's* son.	„ IV 811
Art thou my son? *Walter Lea.* I am, good *f*,	„ IV 1020
Father (verb) No—murder *f's* murder:	*Queen Mary* III i 335
Fathered had I *f* him I had given him more of the rod than the sceptre.	*Becket* III iii 110
all the souls we saved and *f* here Will greet us	„ v ii 223
Father-king And the *f-k*?	„ III iii 100
Father-like Julius the Third Was ever just, and mild, and *f-l*;	*Queen Mary* v ii 31
Fatherly See how the tears run down his *f* face.	„ IV iii 4
Fathom Deep—I shall *f* him.	„ III i 158
Thou stirrest up a grief thou canst not *f*.	„ III iv 299
Fatness fill all hearts with *f* and the lust Of plenty—	*The Cup* II 272
Fatter yonder's *f* game for you Than this old gaping gurgoyle:	*Queen Mary* I iii 79
Fatting the *f* of your calves, the making of your butter,	*Prom. of May* II 92
Faugh *F*! we shall all be poisoned. Let us go.	*Becket* I iv 243
Fault his *f* So thoroughly to believe in his own self.	*Queen Mary* II ii 385
—this Cardinal's *f*—I have gulpt it down.	„ III iv 376
To veil the *f* of my most outward foe	„ IV i 106
O God the Son, Not for slight *f's* alone,	„ IV iii 139
not *his f*, if our two houses Be less than brothers.	*Harold* VI i 129
And yet she plagues me too—no *f* in her—	*Becket*, Pro. 59
he had his *f's*, For which I would have laid	„ v i 337
the *f*, mebbe, wur as much mine as yours;	*Prom. of May* I 325
Be that my *f*?	„ II 89
making us feel guilty Of her own *f's*.	„ II 270
would you beat a man for his brother's *f*?	„ III 155
That last was my Father's *f*, poor man.	„ III 280
Faultless The *f* Gardiner!	*Queen Mary* III iv 96
Faulty Some of my former friends Would find my logic *f*;	*Prom. of May* II 665
Favour He hath fallen out of *f* with the Queen.	*Queen Mary* I v 156
What makes thy *f* like the bloodless head	„ v ii 19
God's *f* and king's *f* might so clash	*Becket*, Pro. 295
So that your grant me one slight *f*.	„ I ii 58
Would you cast An eye of *f* on me,	*Foresters* I ii 217
That if I cast an eye of *f* on him,	„ I ii 262
Favour'd he would pay The mortgage if she *f* him.	„ I iii 7
Favourer Because they think me *f* of this marriage.	*Queen Mary* I v 156
and a *f* Of players, and a courtier,	*Becket* I i 78
Favourite utterly broken down By losing her—she was his *f* child—	*Prom. of May* II 418
for you know, my dear, you were always his *f*—	„ II 423
Fawn *f* upon him? Chime in with all?	*Harold* I ii 165
Your Foliot fasts and *f's* too much for me.	*Becket*, Pro. 264
f upon him For thy life and thy son's.	„ IV ii 224
Fawning The false Archbishop *f* on him,	*Queen Mary* I v 30
Who rub their *f* noses in the dust,	„ III iii 242

Fay To a land where the *f*,	*Foresters* II ii 180
Fealty Into the wide-spread arms of *f*,	*Queen Mary* II ii 264
F to the King, obedience to thyself?	*Becket* I iii 587
That goes against our *f* to the King.	„ v ii 508
Not one to keep a woman's *f*	*The Cup* I i 176
Fear (s) he brought his doubts And *f's* to me.	*Queen Mary* I ii 76
Skips every way, from levity or from *f*.	„ I iii 170
There lies your *f*. That is your drift.	„ I v 304
I am Harry's daughter, Tudor, and not *F*.	„ II iv 53
St. Peter in his time of *f* Denied his Master,	„ III iv 263
my father married my good mother,—For *f* of Spain.	„ IV v 247
from the *f* of Him Whose ministers they be to govern you.	IV iii 179
O father, mock not at a public *f*,	*Harold* I i 75
That's a truer *f*!	„ II i 66
stuff'd the boy with *f's* that these may act	„ II ii 90
Thy *f's* infect me beyond reason. Peace!	„ II ii 451
Famine is *f*, were it but Of being starved.	„ IV iii 204
Yet if a *f*, Or shadow of a *f*,	„ v i 114
To lodge a *f* in Thomas Becket's heart	*Becket* I iii 176
Nay—no *f*! More like is he to excommunicate me.	„ II i 269
yet what *f*? the people Believe the wood enchanted.	„ III i 35
f creeps in at the front, honesty steals out at the back,	„ III iii 61
No *f*! *Grim.* No *f*, my lord.	„ v ii 578
from maiden *f's* Or reverential love for him I loved,	*The Cup* II 196
I do remember your first-marriage *f's*.	„ II 207
I have no *f's* at this my second marriage.	„ II 208
Fear (verb) I *f*, I *f*, I see you, Dear friend,	*Queen Mary* I ii 102
dull life in this maiden court, I *f*, my Lord?	„ I iii 115
She *f's* the Lords may side with you	„ I iv 158
Do not *f* it. Of that hereafter.	„ I v 130
Courtenay, Save that he *f's* he might be crack'd in using,	” II i 7
I *f* the mine is fired before the time.	„ II i 123
I *f* we be too few, Sir Thomas,	„ II i 224
and I *f* One scruple, this or that way,	„ II ii 99
And *f* them not. I *f* them not.	„ II ii 243
how to cross it balks me. I *f* we cannot.	„ II iii 10
I *f* the Emperor much misvalued me.	„ III ii 76
This Howard, whom they *f*, what was he saying?	„ III vi 54
nor *f* but that to-day Thou shalt receive	„ IV i 84
There will be more conspiracies, I *f*.	„ IV iii 433
I do much *f* that England will not care.	„ v i 282
I have given her cause—I *f* no woman.	*Harold* I ii 42
Why then of England. Madam, *f* us not,	„ v ii 97
that I *f* the Queen would have her life.	*Becket*, Pro. 61
We *f* that he may reave thee of thine own.	„ I iii 611
I *f* Church-censures like your King.	„ IV ii 434
They *f* you slain: they dread they know not what.	„ v ii 600
Tut—*f* me not; I ever had my victories among women.	*The Cup* I i 152
I *f* not. *Synorix.* Then do not tell him.	„ II ii 308
Yes, my lord, I *f* not. I will answer for you.	*Foresters* II ii 32
And *f* not thou! Each of us has an arrow on the cord;	„ IV 606
Fear'd She *f* it might unman him for his end.	*Queen Mary* I i 368
Cannot? Even so! I *f* as much.	*The Falcon* 846
Fearful Paget, despite his *f* heresies, I loved the man,	*Queen Mary* IV iii 633
whose *f* Priest Sits winking at the license of a king,	*Becket* I ii 65
More, tenfold, than this *f* child can do;	*Harold* I ii 143
thou Wast ever *f*.	„ II ii 351
Too *f* still!	„ II ii 412
Fearing *f* for her, sent a secret missive,	*Queen Mary* II ii 121
Feast (s) No sacrifice, but a life-giving *f*!	„ IV ii 112
Bring not thy hollowness On our full *f*.	*Harold* IV iii 204
A doter on white pheasant-flesh at *f's*,	*Becket*, Pro. 97
I would that every man made *f* to-day	*The Cup* II 225
of that full *f* That leaves but emptiness.	*Prom. of May* II 255
Why comest thou like a death's head at my *f*?	*Foresters* I ii 211
And join your *f's* and all your forest games	„ III 84
thy father will not grace our *f* With his white beard to-day. „	IV 80
Our *f* is yonder, spread beneath an oak,	„ IV 189
Feast (verb) Call in the poor from the streets, and let them *f*.	*Becket* IV ii 73
Feed, *f*, and be merry.	„ I iv 151
Feather if this Prince of fluff and *f* come	*Queen Mary* I iv 162
Night, as black as a raven's *f*;	*Harold* III ii 6
strike, make his *f's* Glance in mid heaven.	*The Falcon* 15
We cannot flaunt it in new *f's* now:	„ 42

Feather'd Breaks into *f* merriments, and flowers   *Queen Mary* III v 13
Featherhead Courtenay, belike— *Mary.* A fool and *f* !   „   v i 128
Feature of royal blood, of splendid *f*,   „   I i 112
   equal for pure innocence of nature, And loveliness
   of *f*.   *Prom. of May* II 373
Featureless play'd at ball with And kick'd it *f*—   *The Cup* II 128
Fed swoll'n and *f* With indraughts and side-currents,   *Queen Mary* II i 233
   F with rank bread that crawl'd upon the tongue,   „   IV iii 442
   pray for him who hath *f* you in the wilderness.   *Becket* I iv 266
   Meal enough, meat enough, well *f* ;   *The Falcon* 166
   You be *f* with tit-bits, you,   *Foresters* I i 24
   I am *f* with tit-bits no more than you are,   „   I i 27
   those pale mouths which we have *f* will praise us—   „   IV 1076
Federigo (*See also* **Federigo degli Alberighi**) my Lord *F*,
   he hath fallen Into a sickness,   *The Falcon* 309
   My lord *F*, Can I not speak with you once more   „   687
   Yes, your falcon, *F* !   „   843
   O *F*, *F*, I love you ! Spite of ten thousand brothers, *F*.   „   897
   And I am happy ! *Giovanna.* And I too, *F*.   „   928
Federigo degli Alberighi Poor *F d A* Takes nothing in return   „   715
Fee (s) In *f* and barony of the King,   *Becket* I iii 675
   I hold Nothing in *f* and barony of the King.   „   I iii 678
   Take *f*'s of tyranny, wink at sacrilege,   „   II ii 394
   And have thy *f*'s, and break the law no more.   *Foresters* IV 955
Fee (verb) he will *f* thee as freely as he will wrench   *Harold* I i 57
   if you cared To *f* an over-opulent superstition,   *Prom. of May* I 693
Feeble To Dover ? no, I am too *f*.   *Queen Mary* III vi 221
   If Rome be *f*, then should I be firm.   *Becket* I iii 140
   Perhaps you judge him With *f* charity :   *The Cup* I ii 186
   Shall I tell her he is dead ? No ; she is still too *f*.   *Prom. of May* III 338
Feed *F*, feast, and be merry.   *Becket* I iv 151
   So that the fool King Louis *f* them not.   „   II i 76
   that the sheep May *f* in peace.   „   III iii 346
   That you may *f* your fancy on the glory of it,   *The Cup* I ii 133
Feeder a *f* Of dogs and hawks, and apes,   *Becket* I i 79
Feel I came to the pulse of England,   *Queen Mary* III iv 37
   faith that seem'd to droop will *f* your light,   „   III iv 22
   I *f* it but a duty—you will find in it Pleasure   „   III iv 429
   your Grace, your Grace, I *f* so happy :   „   V 250
   And it were well, if thou shouldst let him *f*,   *Harold* II ii 16
   I can *f* for thee. *Eleanor.* Thou *f* for me !—   *Becket, Pro.* 472
   The man shall *f* that I can strike him yet.   „   II i 78
   And *f* it too.   „   III iii 48
   willing wives enough To *f* dishonour, honour.   *The Cup* I ii 189
   Will *f* no shame to give themselves the lie.   „   I 117
   Dost thou not *f* the love I bear to thee   „   II 426
   As years go on, he *f*'s them press upon him,   *Prom. of May* I 647
   I *f* sewer, Miss Dora, that I ha' been noän too
   sudden wi' you,   „   II 59
   I *f* so much better, that I trust I may be able   „   III 221
   As yet I scarcely *f* it mine.   „   III 613
   and mighty slow To *f* offences.   „   III 630
   churchman too In a fashion, and shouldst *f* with him.   *Foresters* IV 412
   he will, He will—he *f*'s it in his head.   „   IV 646
   That I may *f* thou art no phantom—   „   IV 1013
Feeling with her poor blind hands *f*—'where is it ?   *Queen Mary* II i 407
   F my native land beneath my foot,   „   III ii 47
Feel'st thou *f* into the hands Of these same Moors   *Foresters* II i 562
   when thou *f* with me The ghost returns to Marian,   „   III 113
Feigning *F* to treat with him about her marriage—   *Queen Mary* II ii 33
Feint comedy meant to seem a tragedy—A *f*, a farce.   *Becket* IV iv 323
   There was the farce, the *f*—not mine. And yet I am
   all but sure my dagger was a *f* Till the worm
   turn'd—   „   IV ii 377
   —*this* was no *f* then ? no.   „   IV ii 383
   No, for it came to nothing—only a *f*.   „   IV ii 398
   I'll swear to mine own self it was a *f*.   „   IV ii 402
Fell Who stood upright when both houses *f*.
   Bagenhall. The houses *f* ! *Officer.* I mean
   the houses knelt   *Queen Mary* III iii 255
   But stretch it wider ; say when England *f*.   „   III iii 262
   God's righteous judgment *f* upon you   „   III iv 240
   nay, his noble mother's, Head *f*—   „   III iv 296
   How oft the falling axe, that never *f*,   „   III v 134
   owld lord *f* to 's meat wi' a will, God bless un !   „   IV iii 514

Fell (*continued*) Like Peter's when he *f*, and thou wilt   *Harold* III i 283
   the first *F*, and the next became an Empire.   „   IV i 51
   Hail to the living who fought, the dead who *f* !   „   IV iii 106
   how he *f*'s The mortal copse of faces !   „   V i 588
   Then all the dead *f* on him.   „   V ii 50
   Here *f* the truest, manliest hearts of England.   „   V ii 58
   Before he *f* into the snare of Guy ;   „   V ii 131
   high altar Stand where their standard *f* . . .   „   V ii 140
   Every man about his king *F* where he stood.   „   V ii 182
   twelve stars *f* glittering out of heaven Into her bosom.   *Becket* I i 46
   smote me down upon the Minster floor. I *f*.   „   I i 105
   I *f*. Why fall ? Why did He smite me ?   „   I i 108
   they mock'd us and we *f* upon 'em,   „   I ii 15
   names of those who fought and *f* are like   *The Cup* I i 164
   F with her motion as she rose, and she,   *The Falcon* 536
   how long we strove before Our horses *f* beneath us,   „   639
   'er an' the owd man they *f* a kissin' o' one another   *Prom. of May* I 21
   f ageän coalscuttle and my kneeä gev waäy   „   I 403
   as I telled 'er to-daäy when she *f* foul   „   II 582
   I'd like to *f* 'im as deäd as a bullock !   „   II 597
   if ever A Norman damsel *f* into our hands,   *Foresters* III 181
   The deer *f* dead to the bottom, and the man *F* with him,   „   IV 543
Feller (**fellow**) the *f* couldn't find a Mister in his mouth
   fur me,   *Prom. of May* I 302
   Why, coom then, owd *f*, I'll tell it to you ;   „   II 202
   What *f* wur it as 'a' been a-talkin'   „   II 575
   thaw the *f*'s gone and maäde such a litter of his faäce.   „   II 588
Fellow (*See also* **Feller**) Art thou of the true faith, *f*,   *Queen Mary* I iii 46
   Divers honest *f*'s,   „   I iii 120
   I will be there ; the *f*'s at his tricks—   „   I iii 157
   A goodlier-looking *f* than this Philip.   „   I iv 3
   and I warrant this fine *f*'s life.   „   II iii 84
   I know some lusty *f*'s there in France.   „   III i 128
   Ay ! *f*, what ! Stand staring at me !   „   III i 286
   Ever a rough, blunt, and uncourtly *f*—   „   V v 120
   Haul like a great strong *f* at my legs,   *Harold* II i 11
   F, dost thou catch crabs ?   „   II i 65
   my *f*'s know that I am all one scale like a fish.   *Becket* I iv 212
   The *f* that on a lame jade came to court,   „   V i 246
   He comes, a rough, bluff, simple-looking *f*.   *The Cup* I i 173
   I tell thee, my good *f*, *My* arrow struck the stag.   *The Falcon* 282
   I will, I will. Poor *f* !   „   634
   more than one brave *f* owed His death to the charm in it.   „   691
   You hear, Filippo ? My good *f*, go !   *Prom. of May* II 702
   Nor am I Edgar, my good *f*.   *Foresters* I i 91
   Poor *f*'s !
   there is a lot of wild *f*'s in Sherwood Forest who hold
   by King Richard,   „   I ii 73
   good *f*'s there in merry Sherwood That hold by Richard,   „   I iii 98
   A brave old *f* but he angers me.   „   II i 471
   Farewell, good *f*'s !   „   III 87
   I believe thee, thou art a good *f*, though a friar.   „   III 342
   Thou payest easily, like a good *f*,   „   IV 156
   I can bring down Fourscore tall *f*'s on thee.   „   IV 177
   now I love thee mightily, thou tall *f*.   „   IV 322
   Were some strong *f* here in the wild wood,   „   IV 515
   man of ours Up in the North, a goodly *f* too,   „   IV 530
Fellow-citizen Swear with me, noble *f-c*'s, all,   *Queen Mary* II i 296
Fellow-prisoner Thus Gardiner—for the two were *f-p*'s   „   I iv 198
Fellow-pupil Were not our *f-p*'s all ladies ?   *Prom. of May* III 299
Fellow-trickster one should be This William's *f-t*'s ;—   *Harold* III i 77
Felony 'If any cleric be accused of *f*, the Church   *Becket* I iii 87
Felt I have *f* within me Stirrings of some great doom   *Queen Mary* I iv 259
   babe in arms Had *f* the faltering of his mother's heart,   „   II 82
   The Queen hath *f* the motion of her babe !   „   III ii 213
   and the power They *f* in killing.   „   III iv 76
   if I knew you *f* this parting, Philip, As I do !   „   III vi 251
   I *f* his arms about me, and his lips—   „   V v 99
   Hate not one who *f* Some pity for thy hater !   *Harold* I ii 43
   F the remorseless outdraught of the deep   „   II i 9
   I *f* it in the middle of that fierce fight   „   IV iii 183
   And *f* the sun of Antioch scald our mail,   *Becket* II ii 93
   we *f* we had laughed too long and could not stay
   ourselves—   „   III iii 160

Fierce (*continued*) sorely prest upon By the *f* Emperor and his Antipope.   *Becket* I iii 203
  Perchance the *f* De Brocs from Saltwood Castle,   ,, v ii 249
  These arm'd men in the city, these *f* faces—   ,, v iii 3
  may not be seized With some *f* passion,   *Prom. of May* II 336

Fiercelier Heaven help that this re-action not re-act Yet *f* under Queen Elizabeth,   *Queen Mary* IV iii 389

Fiercest Out in the *f* storm That ever made earth tremble—   *Prom. of May* III 796

Fierier That ever make him *f*.   *Queen Mary* v ii 95
  something *f* than fire To yield them their deserts.   ,, v iv 26

Fieriest And all her *f* partisans—are pale Before my star !   ,, III iii 170

Fiery And then our *f* Tostig, while thy hands Are palsied here,   *Harold* II ii 453

Fiery-choleric And hates the Spaniard—*f-c*.   *Queen Mary* v ii 92

Fifth This is the *f* conspiracy hatch'd in France ;   ,, v i 297

Fifty We may have left their *f* less by five.   *The Falcon* 625
  F leagues Of woodland hear and know my horn,   *Foresters* III 102

Fight (s) I have fought the *f* and go—   *Harold* I i 184
  I fought another *f* than this Of Stamford-bridge.   ,, IV iii 23
  I felt it in the middle of that fierce *f* At Stamford-bridge.   ,, IV iii 184
  power to balk Thy puissance in this *f*   ,, v i 119
  I can no more—fight out the good *f*—die Conqueror.   *Becket* v iii 189
  in the front rank of the *f* With scarce a pang.   *The Cup* I ii 154
  The trumpets of the *f* had echo'd down,   *The Falcon* 605
  and with a flag of ours Ta'en in the *f*—   ,, 613

Fight (verb) who went with your train bands To *f* with Wyatt,   *Queen Mary* II i 28
  Is he so safe to *f* upon her side ?   ,, II ii 313
  I trust that you would *f* along with us.   ,, III i 457
  would you not *f* then ? *Bagenhall.* I think I should *f* then.   ,, III i 466
  for their heresies, Alva, they will *f*;   ,, III ii 204
  Paget, You stand up here to *f* for heresy,   ,, III iv 92
  I'll *f* it on the threshold of the grave.   ,, v v 189
  boys will *f*. Leofwin would often *f* me,   *Harold* I i 433
  Even old Gurth would *f*.   ,, I i 436
  Normans up To *f* for thee again !   ,, II ii 59
  Well then, we must *f*. How blows the wind ?   ,, III ii 134
  He hath cursed thee, and all those who *f* for thee,   ,, IV iii 153
  Too drunk to *f* with thee !   ,, IV iii 165
  F thou with thine own double, not with me,   ,, IV iii 167
  How should the people *f* When the king flies ?   ,, v 137
  Not *f*—tho' somehow traitor to the King—   *Becket* I i 112
  'I mean to *f* mine utmost for the Church,   ,, I i 123
  make it clear Under what Prince I *f*.   ,, I iii 545
  F for the Church, and set the Church against me !   ,, I iii 569
  we daren't *f* you with our crutches,   ,, I iv 210
  Do they not *f* the Great Fiend day by day ?   ,, v ii 585
  I can no more—*f* out the good fight—die Conqueror.   ,, v iii 189
  We cannot *f* imperial Rome,   *The Cup* II 92
  'I go to *f* in Scotland With many a savage clan;'   *Foresters* I i 14
  if he had not gone to *f* the king's battles,   ,, I i 57
  if he dare to *f* at all, would *f* for his rents,   ,, I i 232
  f's not for himself but for the people of England.   ,, I i 236
  I would *f* with any man but thee.   ,, II i 557
  No, Sir Earl, I will not *f* to-day.   ,, II i 575
  Well, I will *f* to-morrow.   ,, II i 577
  he that pays not for his dinner must *f* for it.   ,, IV 200
  thou *f* at quarterstaff for thy dinner with our Robin,   ,, IV 207

Fighteth The soul who *f* on thy side is cursed,   *Harold* v i 69

Fighting And *f* for And dying for the people—   ,, v i 388
  chosen by his people And *f* for his people !   ,, v i 491
  Wilt thou destroy the Church in *f* for it,   *Becket* I iii 36
  they were *f* for her to-day in the street.   ,, I iv 160
  to help the old man When he was *f*.   *Foresters* II i 543
  Were *f* underhand unholy wars   ,, IV 821

Figure to keep the *f* moist and make it hold water,   *Becket* III iii 165
  False *f*, Map would say.   ,, III iii 346
  —a mere *f*. Let it go by.   *Foresters* IV 221
  No *f*, no fiction, Robin.   ,, IV 222
  I see two *f*'s crawling up the hill.   ,, IV 333

Filch a fox may *f* a hen by night,   *Queen Mary* III v 157
  f the linen from the hawthorn,   *Foresters* III 198

Fili Salva *F*, Salva Spiritus,   *Harold* v i 468

Filippo (foster brother to Count Federigo degli Alberighi)
  Sh—sh—*F* ! (repeat)   *The Falcon* 96, 105
  Come, come, *F*, what is there in the larder ?   ,, 117
  out of those scraps and shreds *F* spoke of.   ,, 148
  Away, *F* !   ,, 155
  What is it, *F* ? *Filippo.* Spoons, your lordship.   ,, 396
  I thank thee, good *F*.   ,, 554
  so I, *F*, being, with your ladyship's pardon,   ,, 564
  F ! *Giovanna.* Will you not eat with me,   ,, 569
  Wine ! *F*, wine !   ,, 577
  F ! will you take the word out of your master's own mouth ?   ,, 597
  I and *F* here had done our best,   ,, 607
  F ! *Count.* A troop of horse—   ,, 616
  And we kill'd 'em by the score. *Elisabetta.* *F* !   ,, 622
  See, my lady ! *Giovanna.* I see, *F* !   ,, 655
  And why, *F* ?   ,, 658
  tree that his lordship—— *Giovanna.* Not now, *F*.   ,, 686
  You hear, *F* ? My good fellow, go !   ,, 690
  But the prunes that your lordship—— *Elisabetta.* *F* !——   ,, 694
  F ! *Filippo.* Well, well ! the women !   ,, 697

Fill no foreign prince or priest Should *f* my throne,   *Queen Mary* III v 237
  suddenly *f* With such fierce fire—   ,, III vi 161
  And we will *f* thee full of Norman sun,   *Harold* II ii 180
  and *f* the sky With free sea-laughter—   ,, II ii 336
  Fall, cloud, and *f* the house—   ,, III i 190
  God of truth *F* all thine hours with peace !—   ,, v i 316
  Thou art the man to *f* out the Church robe ;   *Becket*, Pro. 262
  And *f* all hearts with fatness and the lust   *The Cup* II 272
  See here, I *f* it. Will you drink, my lord ?   ,, II 366
  F to the brim.   *Foresters* III 343

Fill'd saw the church all *f* With dead men   *Harold* I ii 82
  one who *f* All offices, all bishopricks with English—   ,, II ii 534
  God Has *f* the quiver, and Death has drawn the bow—   ,, II ii 400
  ' And when the vacancy is to be *f* up,   *Becket* I iii 108
  like Egypt's plague, had *f* All things with blood ;   ,, I iii 345

Filthy Come, you *f* knaves, let us pass.   ,, I iv 203
  What *f* tools our Senate works with !   *The Cup* I i 156

Find Whose play is all to *f* herself a King.   *Queen Mary* I iii 164
  And *f*'s you statues.   ,, II ii 265
  Death and the Devil—if he *f* I have one—   ,, III i 232
  F out his name and bring it me.   ,, III i 253
  thou shalt lose thine ears and *f* thy tongue,   ,, III i 256
  amazed To *f* as fair a sun as might have flash'd   ,, III ii 22
  Did you *f* a scripture, ' I come not to bring   ,, IV iv 87
  Till, by St. James, I *f* myself the fool.   ,, III vi 101
  And I can *f* no refuge upon earth.   ,, IV iii 128
  I shall *f* Heaven or else hell ready to swallow me,   ,, IV iii 223
  And I have often found them. *Mary.* *F* me one !   ,, v ii 223
  you will *f* written Two names, Philip and Calais ;   ,, v v 153
  You will *f* Philip only, policy, policy,—   ,, v v 158
  To *f* the sweet refreshment of the Saints.   *Harold* I i 177
  and coming back *F* them again.   ,, II ii 91
  And, brother, we will *f* a way,' said he—   ,, II ii 367
  To *f* a means whereby the curse might glance   ,, III i 342
  then would *f* Her nest within the cloister,   ,, IV i 233
  Know what thou dost ; and we may *f* for thee,   ,, IV ii 48
  until I *f* Which way the battle balance.   ,, v 460
  Harold slain ?—I cannot *f* his body.   ,, v ii 20
  Go further hence and *f* him.   ,, v ii 60
  for I should *f* An easy father confessor in thee.   *Becket*, Pro. 87
  Thou wilt *f* her Back in her lodging.   ,, I i 399
  As *f* a hare's form in a lion's cave.   ,, I iii 177
  Shall I *f* you one ?   ,, I iv 24
  makes after it too To *f* it.   ,, I i 322
  To *f* my stray sheep back within the fold.   ,, III iii 355
  I thought if I followed it I should *f* the fairies.   ,, IV i 24
  but I don't know if I can *f* the way back again.   ,, IV i 48
  Shall I *f* you asleep when I come back ?   ,, IV ii 64
  this will *f* it there, And dig it from the root   ,, IV ii 75
  We *f* that it is mightier than it seems—   ,, IV ii 263
  Follow us, my son, and we will *f* it for thee—   ,, IV ii 373
  F one a slut whose fairest linen seems Foul   ,, v ii 202
  Here, here, here will you *f* me.   ,, v ii 514
  To *f* Antonius here.   *The Cup* I iii 55

Find (*continued*) or at least shall *f* him There in the camp.   *The Cup* I iii 93
Whose winter-cataracts *f* a realm and leave it   „   II 305
I sought him and I could not *f* him.   „   II 397
To *f* one shock upon the field when all The harvest   *The Falcon* 301
If a written scroll That seems to run in rhymings.   „   431
you Would *f* it stain'd——   *Count.* Silence, Elisabetta !   „   664
Lady, I *f* you a shrewd bargainer.   „   757
But you will *f* me a shrewd bargainer still.   „   774
An' how d'ye *f* the owd man 'ere ?   *Prom. of May* I 71
feller couldn't *f* a Mister in his mouth fur me,   „   I 302
You never *f* one for me, Mr. Dobson.   „   I 305
or you may *f* me at the bottom of the river.—   „   II 88
that we Should *f* me in the river ?   „   II 412
Some of my former friends Would *f* my logic faulty ;   „   II 665
Did you *f* that you worked at all the worse   „   III 55
You must not expect to *f* our Father as he was five
 years ago.   „   III 419
our carters and our shepherds Still *f* a comfort there.   „   III 529
you will *f* The common brotherhood of man   „   III 542
I cannot *f* the word—forgive it—Amends.   „   III 789
only they that be bred in it can *f* their way a-nights
 in it.   *Foresters* II i 265
Your worship may *f* another rhyme if you care   „   II i 322
Sheriff, thou wilt *f* me at Nottingham.   *Sheriff.* If
 anywhere, I shall *f* thee in hell.   „   IV 801

Fine (*adj.*) If you have falsely painted your *f* Prince ;   *Queen Mary* I v 598
Carew stirs In Devon : that *f* porcelain Courtenay,   „   II i 6
Ay, why not, Sir Thomas ? He was a *f* courtier, he ;   „   II i 33
a *f* courtier of the old Court, old Sir Thomas.   „   II i 45
Ay, and I warrant this *f* fellow's life.   „   II iii 83
Lord ! they be *f* ; I never stitch'd none such.   „   III i 226
F eyes—but melancholy, irresolute—A *f* beard,
 Bonner, a very full *f* beard.   „   III iv 337
Of such *f* mould, that if you sow'd therein The seed
 of Hate,   „   IV i 170
Were you in Spain, this *f* fair gossamer gold—   „   V iii 48
Is it so *f* ? Troth, some have said so.   „   V iii 53
but therein Sunk rocks—they need *f* steering—   „   V v 214
the *f* attractions and repulses, the delicacies,   *Becket,* Pro. 499
Now let the King's *f* game look to itself.   „   III ii 44
My lord, we know you proud of your *f* hand,   „   IV ii 261
Here's a *f* salad for my lady ;   *The Falcon* 546
Here's a *f* fowl for my lady ;   „   556
And here are *f* fruits for my lady—   „   561
Well, I reckons they'll hev' a *f* cider-crop to-year   *Prom. of May* I 316
but I ha taäen good care to turn out boäth my
 darters right down *f* laädies.   „   I 337
That *f*, fat, hook-nosed uncle of mine, old Harold,   „   I 509
sometimes been moved to tears by a chapter of *f*
 writing in a novel ;   „   III 209
and prattled to each other that we would marry *f*
 gentlemen,   „   III 277
Ay, how *f* they be in their liveries,   *Foresters* I i 40
Because thou sayest such *f* things of women,   „   I iii 137

Fine (*s*) A round *f* likelier. Your pardon.   *Queen Mary* III iv 279
A *f*, a *f* ! he hath called plain Robin Hood a lord.   *Foresters* III 214
A *f* ! a *f* ! He hath called plain Robin a king.   „   IV 217

Fine (*verb*) *F* him ! *f* him ! he hath called plain Robin an
 earl.   „   IV 150

Fine-cut his *f-c* face bowing and beaming with all that
 courtesy   *Becket* III iii 141

Finer Margery ? no, that's a *f* thing there. How it
 glitters !   „   IV i 2

Finger populace, With *f's* pointed like so many
 daggers,   *Queen Mary* I v 149
I wear Upon this *f),* ye did promise full Allegiance   „   II ii 168
Would you not chop the bitten *f* off,   „   III iv 206
You have a gold ring on your *f*,   „   V iv 32
A lesson worth *F* and thumb—thus   *Harold* I ii 55
How their pointed *f's* Glared at me !   „   II ii 790
his *f* on her harp (I heard him more than once)   *Becket* IV iv 203
Yet my *f's* itch to beat him into nothing.   „   IV iii
Ay, and I left two *f's* there for dead.   *The Falcon* 653
ye'll think more on 'is little *f* than hall my hand
 at the haltar.   *Prom. of May* I 112
to pass it down A *f* of that hand   *Foresters* I ii 299

Finger (*continued*) she swore it never Should leave her *f*.   *Foresters* II i 593
Finger'd The cardinals have *f* Henry's gold.   *Becket* I iii 295
Fingernail and he's as like the King as *f* to *f*,   „   III i 165
Finger-point I Scraped from your *f-p's* the holy oil ;   *Queen Mary* IV ii 132
Finikin there comes a deputation From our *f* fairy
 nation.   *Foresters* II ii 145
Finish I am your Legate ; please you let me *f*.   *Queen Mary* IV iv 180
Finish'd It is *f*. (repeat)   *Harold* III i 177, 203, 211
They are *f*. *Synorix.* How !   *The Cup* II 422
Have you not *f*, my lord ?   *Foresters* II i 341

Fire (*s*) (*See also* **A-hell-fire, A-vire, Fool-fire, Hell-fire,
 Vire**) practise on my life, By poison, *f*, shot,   *Queen Mary* I iv 285
Stamp out the *f*, or this Will smoulder and re-flame,   „   I v 508
it serves to fan A kindled *f*.   „   I v 621
the rack, the thumbscrew, the stake, the *f*.   „   II i 201
Dare-devils, that would eat *f* and spit it out   „   III i 156
Rascal !—this land is like a hill of *f*,   „   III i 321
I will show *f* on my side—stake and *f*—   „   III i 327
Let the dead letter live ! Trace it in *f*,   „   III iv 34
by the churchman's pitiless doom of *f*,   „   III iv 50
Yet others are that dare the stake and *f*,   „   III iv 167
I am on *f* until I see them flame.   „   III iv 287
Or a second *f*, Like that which lately crackled   „   III v 52
but of this *f* he says, Nay swears,   „   III v 71
but they play with *f* as children do,   „   III vi 28
you may strike *f* from her, Not hope to melt her.   „   III vi 38
suddenly fill With such fierce *f*—had it been *f* indeed   „   III vi 162
As Cranmer hath, came to the *f* on earth.   „   IV i 60
Power hath been given you to try faith by *f*—   „   IV i 154
F—inch by inch to die in agony !   „   IV i 223
makes The *f* seem crueller than it is.   „   IV ii 233
Remember how God made the fierce *f* seem   „   IV iii 89
The patience of St. Lawrence in the *f*.   „   IV iii 95
So I may come to the *f*.   „   IV iii 251
Liar ! dissembler ! traitor ! to the *f* !   „   IV iii 259
Harm him not, harm him not ! have him to the *f* !   „   IV iii 285
howsoever hero-like the man Dies in the *f*,   „   IV iii 325
I say they have drawn the *f* On their own heads :   „   IV iii 380
To whom the *f* were welcome,   „   IV iii 438
Who follow'd with the crowd to Cranmer's *f*.   „   IV iii 555
they swarm into the *f* Like flies—for what ? no
 dogma.   „   V ii 111
sir, they hurl'd it back into the *f*, That, being but
 baptized in *f*, the babe Might be in *f* for ever.   „   V iv 22
something fierier than *f* To yield them their deserts.   „   V iv 26
in a closed room, with light, *f*, physic, tendance ;   „   V iv 37
And burn the tares with unquenchable *f* !   „   V v 114
that these Three rods of blood-red *f* up yonder   *Harold* I i 44
For if the North take *f*, I should be back ;   „   I ii 67
while ye fish for men with your false *f's*,   „   II i 31
hath blown himself as red as *f* with curses.   „   V i 87
the *f*, the light, The spirit of the twelve Apostles   *Becket* I i 49
Make it so hard to save a moth from the *f* ?   „   I i 284
Set all on *f* against him !   „   I ii 89
the *f*, when first kindled, said to the smoke,   „   II ii 317
As one that blows the coal to cool the *f*.   „   V ii 549
Is that the cup you rescued from the *f* ?   *The Cup* I i 71
like A bank'd-up *f* that flashes out again   „   I ii 166
to the wave, to the glebe, to the *f* !   „   II 4
a red *f* woke in the heart of the town,   *Prom. of May* I 50
tho' they *f* should run along the ground,   „   I 703
when you put it in green, and your stack caught *f*.   „   II 56
heat and *f* Of life will bring them out,   „   II 286
She hath the *f* in her face and the dew in her eyes.   *Foresters* I i 166
mantle of the cloud, And sets, a naked *f*.   „   II i 29
Who melts a waxen image by the *f*,   „   II i 671

Fire (*verb*) Upon their lake of Garda, *f* the Thames ;   *Queen Mary* III ii 23
And in the winter I will *f* their farms.   *Foresters* IV 95

Fired so in this pause, before The mine be *f*,   *Queen Mary* II i 26
I fear the mine is *f* before the time.   „   II i 123
The mine is *f*, and I will speak to them.   „   II i 155
Your houses *f*—your gutters bubbling blood—   „   II i 280
city rose against Antonius, Whereon he *f* it,   *The Cup* I ii 64

Firelike I'll have it burnish'd *f* ;   *Queen Mary* I v 374
Fireside I would taäke the owd blind man to my oä͞ ;.   *Prom. of May* II 74
Firm make their wall of shields *F* as thy cliffs,   *Harold* V v 480

Firm *(continued)* by thy wisdom Hast kept it *f* from shaking ;   *Becket, Pro.* 204

If Rome be feeble, then should I be *f*.   ,,   I iii 241

My hand is *f*, Mine eye most true to one hair's-breadth of aim.   *Foresters* IV 693

First (adj.) are fresh and sweet As the *f* flower no bee has ever tried.   *Queen Mary* I iv 63

and your worship the *f* man in Kent and Christendom,   ,,   III i 64

In William's time, in our *f* Edward's time,   ,,   III iii 226

as in the day of the *f* church, when Christ Jesus was King.   ,,   V iv 55

Earl, the *f* Christian Cæsar drew to the East   *Harold* V i 21

wherefore now Obey my *f* and last commandment. Go !   ,,   V i 359

the bright link rusts with the breath of the *f* after-marriage kiss,   *Becket, Pro.* 362

The *f* archbishop fled, And York lay barren for a hundred years.   ,,   I iii 53

frosted off me by the *f* cold frown of the King.   ,,   I iv 67

But Hereford, you know, crown'd the *f* Henry.   ,,   III iii 202

To the fond arms of her *f* love, Fitzurse,   ,,   IV ii 334

You kiss'd me there For the *f* time.   *The Cup* I ii 419

F kiss. There then. You talk almost as if it Might be the last.   ,,   I ii 421

He sends you This diadem of the *f* Galatian Queen,   ,,   II 132

when Synorix, *f* King, Camma, *f* Queen o' the Realm,   ,,   II 440

Coming to visit my lord, for the *f* time in her life too !   *The Falcon* 170

I lay them for the *f* time round your neck.   ,,   907

But where is this Mr. Edgar whom you praised so in your *f* letters ?   *Prom. of May* I 777

better death With our *f* wail than life—   ,,   II 291

My father stricken with his *f* paralysis,   ,,   II 481

as they are arranged here according to their *f* letters.   ,,   III 37

I do believe I lost my heart to him the very *f* time we met,   ,,   III 284

shall I give her the *f* kiss ? O sweet Kate, my *f* love, the *f* kiss, the *f* kiss !   *Foresters* I i 126

but I came to give thee the *f* kiss, and thou hast given it me.   ,,   I i 132

does it matter so much if the maid give the *f* kiss ?

Little John. I cannot tell, but I had sooner have given thee the *f* kiss.   ,,   I i 136

if a man and a maid love one another, may the maid give the *f* kiss ?   ,,   I i 173

You shall give me the *f* kiss.   ,,   I ii 227

The *f* part—made before you came among us—   ,,   III 435

First (s) We strove against the papacy from the *f*,   *Queen Mary* III iii 225

Who knew it from the *f*.   ,,   VI 114

First-marriage I do remember your *f-m* fears.   *The Cup* II 206

Fish (s) I had liefer that the *f* had swallowed me,   *Harold* II i 36

Rolf, what *f* did swallow Jonah ? *Rolf.* A whale !   ,,   II i 41

A sauce-deviser for thy days of *f*,   *Becket, Pro.* 98

my fellows know that I am all one scale like a *f*.   ,,   I iv 213

as to the *f*, they de-miracled the miraculous draught,   ,,   III iii 123

Fish (verb) while ye *f* for men with your false fires, Let the great Devil *f* for your own souls.   *Harold* II i 30

But 'e doänt *f* neither.   *Prom. of May* I 214

Well, it's no sin in a gentleman not to *f*.   ,,   I 216

Fisher Apostles ; *they* were *f*'s of men,   *Harold* II i 34

Thy true King bad thee be A *f* of men ;   *Becket* II i 286

Fisher (John, Bishop of Rochester) Did not More die, and *F* ? he must burn.   *Queen Mary* IV i 52

Fisherman We be *fishermen* ; I came to see after my nets.   *Harold* II i 27

Fishermen ? devils ! Who, while ye fish for men   ,,   II i 29

Better have been A *f* at Bosham, my good Herbert,   *Becket* II ii 292

Fist (s) and plunge His foreign *f* into our island Church   *Queen Mary* III iv 364

the childish *f* That cannot strike again.   *Harold* III iii 30

Fist (verb) The boy would *f* me hard, and when we fought   ,,   I i 444

Fit (adj.) Is the King's treasury A *f* place for the monies of the Church,   *Becket* I iii 105

it is not *f* for us To see the proud Archbishop mutilated.   ,,   I iii 613

he be *f* to bust hissen wi' spites and jalousies.   *Prom. of May* II 164

Fit (verb) I measured his foot wi' the mark i' the bed, but it wouldn't *f*   ,,   I 414

Fit *See also* **Ague-fit**

Fitter thousand times *F* for this grand function.   *Becket, Pro.* 293

Fitzurse (Reginald, knight of Henry II.'s household) (*See also* **Reginald, Reginald Fitzurse**) *F*, that chart with the red line—   *Becket Pro.* 427

what hast thou to do with this *F* ?   ,,   I i 271

And watch *F*, and if he follow thee,   ,,   I i 330

No footfall—no *F*. We have seen her home.   ,,   I i 367

Lord *F* reported this In passing to the Castle   ,,   I ii 12

F—Becket. Nay, let him be.   ,,   I ii 23

My lord, *F* beheld her in your lodging.   ,,   I ii 33

Cursed *F*, and all the rest of them   ,,   II ii 271

—*F* and his following—who would look down upon them ?   ,,   III iii 308

F, The running down the chase is kindlier   ,,   IV ii 212

Kneel to thy lord *F* ; Crouch even because thou hatest him ;   ,,   IV ii 222

My lord *F*—— *Becket.* He too ! what dost thou here ?   ,,   IV ii 280

You have wrong'd *F*. I speak not of myself.   ,,   IV ii 328

fond arms of her first love, *F*, Who swore to marry her.   ,,   IV ii 335

Five that she met the Queen at Wanstead with *f* hundred horse,   *Queen Mary* I i 78

God's righteous judgment fell upon you In your *f* years of imprisonment,   ,,   III iv 242

My lord, the King demands *f* hundred marks,   *Becket* I iii 641

Monks, knights, *f* hundred, that were there and heard.   ,,   V ii 406

F hundred ! *Count.* Say fifty !   *The Falcon* 618

the feller couldn't find a Mister in his mouth fur me, as farms *f* hoonderd haäcre.   *Prom. of May* I 304

It be *f* year sin' ye went afoor to him,   ,,   II 5

We have been in such grief these *f* years,   ,,   II 67

Poor sister, I had it *f* years ago.   ,,   II 82

but can he trace me Thro' *f* years' absence,   ,,   II 615

Him as did the mischief here, *f* year' sin'.   ,,   III 140

You must not expect to find our Father as he was *f* years ago.   ,,   III 420

F years of shame and suffering broke the heart   ,,   III 761

and can make *F* quarts pass into a thimble.   *Foresters* IV 283

Nay, my tongue tript—*f* hundred marks for use.   ,,   IV 499

Five-fold and they rate the land *f-f* The worth of the mortgage,   ,,   I i 149

Five-years' My *f-y* anger cannot die at once,   *Prom. of May* IV 462

Fixt with his fast-fading eyes *F* hard on mine,   *Queen Mary* I ii 31

Well, burn me or not burn me I am *f* ;   ,,   IV ii 55

have I that I am *f*, *F* beyond fall ;   ,,   VI ii 89

had I *f* my fancy Upon the game I should   *Becket, Pro.* 49

To-day they are *f* and bright—they look straight out.   *The Cup* II 20

Flag made us lower our kingly *f* To yours of England.   *Queen Mary* V i 59

must lower his *f* To that of England in the seas of England.   ,,   V i 65

Our *f* hath floated for two hundred years Is France again.   ,,   V ii 261

and with a *f* of ours Ta'en in the fight—   *The Falcon* 612

But anger'd at their flaunting of our *f*,   ,,   628

Flame (s) (*See also* **Altar-flame, Re-flame**) Here was a young mother, Her face on *f*,   *Queen Mary* II ii 70

And found it all a visionary—   ,,   IV ii 4

God will beat down the fury of the *f*,   ,,   IV iii 98

gather'd with his hands the starting *f*,   ,,   IV iii 337

And thrust his right into the bitter *f* ;   ,,   IV iii 610

before The *f* had reach'd his body ;   ,,   IV iii 614

Unmoving in the greatness of the *f*,   ,,   IV iii 622

and cannot scape the *f*.   *Harold* I i 13

Fling not thy soul into the *f*'s of hell.   *Becket* II i 316

dooms thee after death To wail in deathless *f*.   ,,   IV ii 272

He miss the searching *f* of purgatory,   ,,   VII 13

Flame (verb) I am on fire until I see them *f*.   *Queen Mary* III iv 288

'Tis out—mine *f*.   ,,   V v 124

by St. Denis, now will he *f* out, And lose his head   *Becket* VI 479

Flamed —O he *F* in brocade—   *Queen Mary* III i 76

How he *f* When Tostig's anger'd earldom   *Harold* III i 53

Flaming In sight of all with *f* martyrdom   *Queen Mary* IV iii 29

What with this *f* horror overhead ?   *Harold* I i 231

Then I saw Thy high black steed among the *f* furze,   *Becket* II i 55

Flanders prince is known in Spain, in *F*,   *Queen Mary* I v 207

Emperor counsell'd me to fly to *F*.   ,,   V 550

We heard that you w⸺ sick in *F*, cousin.   ,,   III ii 34

Flanders (*continued*) Why then to F. I will hawk and hunt
In F.   *Harold* I i 258
To follow thee to F! Must thou go?   ,, I ii 27
kisses of all kind of womankind In F,   ,, I ii 114
To-morrow—first to Bosham, then to F.   ,, I ii 240
Flap let him *f* The wings that beat down Wales!   *Queen Mary* III i 283
Flare fly out and *f* Into rebellions.   *Queen Mary* III i 283
It glares in heaven, it *f*'s upon the Thames,   *Harold* I i 29
Flash (s) whether this *f* of news be false or true,   *Queen Mary* III ii 234
It is the *f* that murders, the poor thunder   *Harold* I ii 231
That which the *f* hath stricken.   ,, I ii 235
Our axes lighten with a single *f*   ,, v i 538
lest there should be *f*'es And fulminations   *Becket, Pro.* 221
whose quick *f* splits The mid-sea mast,   *The Cup* II 293
Flash (verb) Thou shalt *f* it secretly Among the good   *Harold* I ii 219
I will both F And thunder for thee.   ,, I ii 228
F sometimes out of earth against the heavens,   *Becket* II 37
fire that *f*'es out again From century to century,   *The Cup* I ii 166
though my men and I *f* out at times Of festival   *Foresters* I ii 274
Flash'd as might have *f* Upon their lake of Garda,   *Queen Mary* III i 22
to stay his hand Before he *f* the bolt.   *Becket* II i 275
And when he *f* it Shrink from me,   ,, II i 276
Tho' all the swords in England *f* above me   ,, v ii 484
noblest light That ever *f* across my life,   *Foresters* III 142
The hunter's passion *f* into the man,   ,, IV 539
Flashing I see the *f* of the gates of pearl—   *Harold* I i 186
Flask and mine old *f* of wine Beside me,   *Queen Mary* III i 46
send you down a *f* or two Of that same vintage?   *Falcon* 585
Flat (adj.) but tramples *f* Whatever thwarts him;   *Harold* II ii 379
and a foot to stamp it . . . . F.   ,, v ii 194
This beggarly life, This poor, *f*, hedged-in field—   *Prom. of May* II 344
Lusty bracken beaten *f*, Queen.   *Foresters* II 154
Flat (s) No, nor with the *f* of it either.   *Becket* I iv 225
Flatten gulf and *f* in her closing chasm Domed cities,   *The Cup* II 90
Flatter You know to *f* ladies.   *Queen Mary* I iv 98
I am safe enough; no man need *f* me.   ,, II i 317
Will not thy body rebel, man, if thou *f* it?   *Becket, Pro.* 103
—*f* And fright the Pope?   ,, II ii 472
You *f* me. Dear Eva Was always thought the
prettier.   *Prom. of May* II 378
Flatter'd Flutter'd or *f* by your notice of her,   *The Falcon* 538
Flattering As if to win the man by *f* him.   *Queen Mary* II ii 312
Flattery sucking thro' fools' ears The *flatteries* of corruption—   *Becket* I iii 362
Flaunt We cannot *f* it in new feathers now: *The Falcon* 42
And scruplest not to *f* it to our face   *Foresters* IV 887
Flaunting But anger'd at their *f* of our flag,   *The Falcon* 628
Flay And *f* me all alive.   *Harold* IV i 191
Flay'd starved, maim'd, flogg'd, *f*, burn'd,   *Queen Mary* III i 210
Flaying Horrible! *f*, scourging, crucifying—   *The Cup* I ii 235
Flea like a *f* That might have leapt upon us   *Queen Mary* II ii 294
Fled (adj. and part.) our Bishops from their sees Or
f, they say, or flying—   ,, I ii 5
' Sir Peter Carew *f* to France;   ,, II i 135
Is Peter Carew *f*? Is the Duke taken?   ,, II i 142
Bar the bird From following the *f* summer—   *Becket* I i 259
France! Ha! De Morville, Tracy, Brito—*f* is he?   ,, I iv 199
Love that can shape or can shatter a life till the life shall
have *f*?   ,, II i 12
Has *f* our presence and our feeding-grounds.   ,, II ii 22
Fled (verb) Left him and *f*; and thou that would'st
be King,   *Queen Mary* II iv 82
first archbishop *f*, And York lay barren   *Becket* I iii 53
Who thief-like *f* from his own church by night,   ,, II ii 156
I *f*, and found thy name a charm to get me Food,   ,, v ii 96
Once I *f*—Never again, and you—   *The Cup* II 14
Since Camma *f* from Synorix to our Temple,   *Foresters* II i 118
whereon she struck him, And *f* into the castle.   ,, III 142
for Oberon *f* away Twenty thousand leagues to-day.   *Queen Mary* IV iii 126
Flee Then whither should I *f* for any help?   *Harold* I ii 147
Griffyth when I saw him *f*, Chased deer-like   *Becket* II i 27
when I *f* from this For a gasp of freer air,   ,, v iii 126
then you are a dead man; *f*!   *Queen Mary* III i 82
Fleece hanging down from this The Golden F—   *Queen Mary* III i 82
Fleer heard One of your Council *f* and jeer at him.   ,, II ii 393
The statesman that shall jeer and *f* at men,   ,, II ii 397
Fleet (s) Mine is the *f* and all the power at sea—   ,, I iv 287

Fleet (s) (*continued*) To seize upon the forts and *f*,   *Queen Mary* III i 464
Hold office in the household, *f*, forts, army;   ,, III iii 72
and the French *f* Rule in the narrow seas.   ,, v i 6
collect the *f*; Let every craft that carries   v ii 274
Fleet (verb) A breath that *f*'s beyond this iron world,   *Harold* III ii 197
Fleeted and makes it Foam over all the *f* wealth of kings   *The Cup* II 289
Fleeth fowl that *f* o'er thy field is cursed,   *Harold* v i 73
Fleeting My grayhounds *f* like a beam of light,   ,, I ii 129
Fleming See *Fox-Fleming*
Flemish Their F go-between And all-in-all.   *Queen Mary* III vi 4
Flesh (*See also* **Pheasant-flesh**) with right reason,
flies that prick the *f*.   ,, III iv 71
The soft and tremulous coward in the *f*?   ,, IV ii 107
when thou becamest Man in the F,   ,, IV iii 141
it was thought we two Might make one *f*,   ,, v ii 137
we were not made One *f* in happiness, no happiness
here; But now we are made one *f* in misery;   ,, v ii 150
Where they eat dead men's *f*,   *Harold* II ii 808
Treble denial of the tongue of *f*,   ,, III i 282
Fast, scourge thyself, and mortify thy *f*,   *Becket* I iii 540
And as for the *f* at table, a whole Peter's sheet,   ,, III iii 128
That I would touch no *f* till he were well   *The Falcon* 680
servants Are all but *f* and blood with those they serve.   ,, 709
And these take *f* again with our own *f*,   *Prom. of May* II 277
weight of the *f* at odd times overbalance the weight
of the church,   *Foresters* I ii 61
and as to other frailties of the *f*—   ,, I ii 65
clothes itself In maiden *f* and blood,   ,, III ii 117
Flesh-fallen Look! am I not Work-wan, *f-f*?   *Harold* I i 99
Flew in a narrow path. A plover *f* before thee.   *Becket* I i 54
a bat *f* out at him In the clear noon,   *Foresters* II ii 96
Crush'd my bat whereon I *f*!   ,, II ii 146
Flickering Pertest of our *f* mob,   ,, II ii 130
Fliest stay, fool, and tell me why thou *f*.   *Becket* III ii 35
Flight My *f* were such a scandal to the faith,   *Queen Mary* I ii 53
hath a farther *f* Than mine into the future.   ,, I v 312
Fling We *f* ourselves on you, my Lord.   ,, II i 48
why *f* back the stone he strikes me with?   ,, IV ii 150
Then *f* mine own fair person in the gap   *Harold* I ii 202
he *f*'s His brand in air and catches it again,   ,, v i 493
all my doubts I *f* from me like dust,   *Becket* I i 148
and *f* them out to the free air.   ,, I i 287
F not thy soul into the flames of hell: ,, I i 316
I *f* all that upon my fate, my star.   *The Cup* I ii 27
F wide the doors and let the new-made children   ,, II 163
f in the spices, Nard, Cinnamon, amomum,   ,, II 183
child of evolution, *f*'s aside His swaddling-bands,   *Prom. of May* I 585
To *f* myself over, when I heard a voice,   ,, III 374
Flint in all this, my Lord, her Majesty Is *f* of *f*,   *Queen Mary* III vi 38
All your voices Are waves on *f*,   ,, v i 122
crawl over knife-edge *f* Barefoot,   *Becket* I i 272
I fear this Abbot is a heart of *f*,   *Foresters* I ii 269
Flit We must *f* for evermore.   ,, II ii 123
I Titania bid you *f*,   ,, II ii 126
Float while the smoke *f*'s from the cottage roof,   ,, I ii 317
Floated *f* downward from the throne Of God Almighty.   *Harold* I i 17
Our flag hath *f* for two hundred years Is France
again.   *Queen Mary* v ii 261
Floating gonfanon of Holy Peter F above their helmets—   *Harold* v i 550
Flock (s) your *f*'s of swans, As fair and white as angels;   *Queen Mary* III ii 14
doth not kill The sheep that wander from his *f*,   ,, III iv 103
To the poor *f*—to women and to children—   ,, IV ii 158
and all thy *f* should catch An after ague-fit   *Becket* III iii 31
Shatter you all to pieces if ye harm One of my *f*!   ,, v iii 136
Home with the *f* to the fold—   *The Cup* I ii 8
Flock (verb) —thousands will *f* to us.   *Queen Mary* III i 192
Flogg'd I'll have you *f* and burnt too,   ,, I i 60
starved, maim'd, *f*, flay'd, burn'd,   ,, III i 210
Flood some mischance of *f*, And broken bridge,   ,, v ii 354
like a river in thro' a burst dam   *Harold* II ii 465
had in it Wales, Her *f*'s, her woods, her hills: ,, IV i 207
from that *f* will rise the New,   *Prom. of May* I 594
She rose From the foul *f* and pointed toward the farm,   ,, II 653
Floor that his fan may thoroughly purge his *f*.   *Queen Mary* III iv 370
these chessmen on the *f*—the king's crown broken!   *Becket, Pro.* 313
And smote me down upon the Minster *f*.   ,, I i 104

Foot (*continued*) bright sky cleave To the very *feet* of God,   *Harold* II ii 743
Seven *feet* of English land, or something more,   „ IV ii 54
' Seven *feet* of English earth, or something more,   „ IV iii 112
Then for the bastard Six *feet* and nothing more !   „ IV iii 116
Our guardsman hath but toil'd his hand and *f*, I hand, *f*,   „ v i 201
They turn on the pursuer, horse against *f*,   „ v i 609
and a *f* to stamp it . . . Flat.   „ v ii 192
the Archbishop washed my *feet* o' Tuesday.   *Becket* I iv 234
My bank Of wild-flowers. At thy *feet* !   „ II i 126
if Thomas have not flung himself at the King's *feet*.   „ III iii 169
o'erleaps a jutting rock And shoots three hundred *feet*.   *The Cup* I i 111
tho' Rome may set A free *f* where she will,   „ II 246
My *feet* are tons of lead, They will break   „ II 476
but he left the mark of 'is *f* i' the flower-bed ;   *Prom. of May* I 409
I measured his *f* wi' the mark i' the bed,   „ I 413
I thinks I'd like to taäke the measure o' your *f*.   „ I 464
is a gentleman ? *Dora*. That he is, from head to *f*.   „ III 282
land now And wealth, And lay both at your *feet*.   „ III 616
whenever I set my own *f* on it I say to it,   *Foresters* I i 335
Far from solid *f* of men,   „ II ii 169

Footed *See* **Delicate-footed, Four-footed**
Footfall No *f*—no Fitzurse. We have seen her home.   *Becket* I i 367
Footsore I am *f* and famish'd therewithal.   *Foresters* I i 266
Footstep I thought I heard A *f*.   *The Cup* I ii 12
Footstool There let them lie, your *f* !   *Queen Mary* II iv 121
For *See* **Vor, Vor't**
Forage To leave the foe no *f*.   *Harold* v i 133
Foraging I am *f* For Norway's army.   „ IV ii 5
Forbad So royal that the Queen *f* you wearing it.   *Queen Mary* I iv 77
The King *f* it. True, my liege.   *Foresters* IV 865
Forbear Spare and *f* him, Harold, if he comes !   *Harold* III i 299
How long shall we *f* him ?   *Becket* v ii 417
Forbid Shall I despair then ?—God *f* !   *Queen Mary* IV iii 129
No, God *f* ! *Henry*. No ! God *f* !   *Becket* III ii 222
God *f* ! (repeat)   *Foresters* I ii 93, 100
Ay God *f*, But if it be so we must bear with John.   „ I ii 101
save King Richard, when he comes, *f* me.   „ IV 665
if the King *f* thy marrying With Robin,   „ IV 874
Forbidden loved within the pale *f* By Holy Church :   *Harold* III ii 23
Force (s) in full *f* Roll upon London.   *Queen Mary* II i 235
so my Lord of Pembroke in command Of all her *f* be safe,   „ II i 306
Lord Pembroke in command of all our *f*   „ III iv 4
jealousy Hath in it an alchemic *f* to fuse   „ III vi 181
No power mine To hold their *f* together . . .   *Harold* IV iii 213
Have thy two brethren sent their *f*'s in ?   „ v i 342
Then there's no *f* in thee !   „ v i 344
' A GALATIAN SERVING BY *F* IN THE ROMAN LEGION.'   *The Cup* I ii 47
' A GALATIAN SERVING BY *F* IN THE ROMAN LEGION.'   „ I ii 75
Serve by *f* ? No *f* Could make me serve by *f*.   „ I ii 79
The *f* of Rome a thousand-fold our own.   „ I ii 85
Force (verb) Why do you *f* me thus against my will ?
Grim. My lord, we *f* you from your enemies.
Becket. As you would *f* a king from being crown'd. *John of Salisbury*. We must not *f* the crown of martyrdom.   *Becket* v iii 21
I could not *f* or wheedle to my will.   *The Cup* I iii 167
Forced Spite of her tears her father *f* it on her.   *Queen Mary* I v 495
so 'z we was *f* to stick her,   „ IV iii 494
When being *f* aloof from all my guard,   *Harold* IV iii 15
dost thou think the King *F* mine election ?   *Becket* I i 127
see you yon side-beam that is *f* from under it,   „ III iii 50
Forefather Beheld our rough *f*'s break their Gods,   *Queen Mary* III ii 120
Foreign My *f* friends, who dream'd us blanketed In ever-closing fog,   „ III ii 19
That Gardiner, once so one with all of us Against this *f* marriage,   „ III iii 7
and plunge His *f* fist into our island Church   „ III iv 364
no *f* prince or priest Should fill my throne,   „ III v 235
A long petition from the *f* exiles To spare the life of Cranmer.   „ IV i 3
Shall these accuse him to a *f* prince ?   „ IV i 24
That Cranmer may withdraw to *f* parts,   „ IV i 45
This same petition of the *f* exiles For Cranmer's life.   „ IV i 193

Foreign (*continued*) how it chanced That this young Earl was sent on *f* travel,   *Queen Mary* v ii 489
The *f* courts report him in his manner Noble   „ v ii 511
that seem at most Sweet guests, or *f* cousins,   *Becket* II i 135
Foreigner that no *f* Hold office in the household,   *Queen Mary* III iii 71
Forekings fierce *f* had clench'd their private hides   *Harold* IV iii 35
Forelead twin sister of the morning star, *F* the sun.   *The Cup* I iii 47
Forelock That irritable *f* which he rubs,   *Queen Mary* I iv 265
what hath fluster'd Gardiner ? how he rubs His *f* !   „ III iv 13
Foremost First of the *f* of their files, who die For God,   *Becket* I i 495
F in England and in Normandy ;   *Harold* II ii 631
Forenoon I was born true man at five in the *f*   *Queen Mary* I i 46
Foresee For I *f* dark days. *Mary*. And so do I, sir ;   „ I v 275
and there was Lambert ; Who can *f* himself ?   „ IV ii 216
Foreseeing *F*, with whate'er unwillingness,   „ I v 253
Foreshorten That so *f*'s greatness.   „ III v 41
Forespeak I can *f* your speaking.   „ I v 137
Forest (adj.) The King keeps his *f* head of game here,   *Becket* III i 37
I have shelter'd some that broke the *f* laws.   *Foresters* I iii 70
up thro' all the *f* land North to the Tyne :   „ II i 88
So now the *f* lawns are all as bright As ways to heaven,   „ II i 630
And join our feasts and all your *f* games   „ III 85
It is our *f* custom they should revel Along with Robin.   „ III 174
Have ye glanced down thro' all the *f* ways   „ IV 111
Ay, ay, Robin, but let him know our *f* laws :   „ IV 199
Hast broken all our Norman *f* laws,   „ IV 886
That thou wilt break our *f* laws again   „ IV 888
They break thy *f* laws—nay, by the rood   „ IV 907
Our *f* games are ended, our free life,   „ IV 1049
Forest (s) King's verdurer caught him a-hunting in the *f*,   *Becket* I iv 96
More sacred than his *f*'s for the chase ?   „ IV ii 24
this door Opens upon the *f* ! Out, begone !   *The Cup* I ii 329
there is a lot of wild fellows in Sherwood *f* who hold by King Richard.   *Foresters* I ii 73
In Sherwood *F*. I have heard of them.   „ I iii 102
I believe She came with me into the *f* here. *Robin*. She follow'd thee into the *f* here ?   „ II i 485
myself Would guide you thro' the *f* to the sea.   „ II i 638
out of the *f* and over the hills and away,   „ II ii 175
most beaten track Runs thro' the *f*,   „ III 90
My lord John, In wrath because you drove him from the *f*,   „ III 451
To bring their counter-bond into the *f*.   „ IV 90
cuirass in this *f* where I dream'd That all was peace—   „ IV 130
Thou art the king of the *f*,   „ IV 232
if e'er thou be assail'd In any of our *f*'s,   „ IV 424
Thou told'st us we should meet him in the *f*,   „ IV 440
You hide this damsel in your *f* here,   „ IV 476
Thou art alone in the silence of the *f*   „ IV 631
Thou Robin shalt be ranger of this *f*,   „ IV 954
We leave but happy memories to the *f*.   „ IV 1071
Forester He was a *f* good ;   „ II i 319
Forest-horn if I wind This *f-h* of mine   „ IV 175
Forest-life and all the better For this free *f-l*,   „ II i 60
Foretold my dream *f* my martyrdom In mine own church.   *Becket* v ii 632
Forfeit Or I *f* my land to the Abbot.   *Foresters* I ii 151
if they were not repaid within a limited time your land should be *f*.   „ IV 469
Forfeited affirms The Queen has *f* her right to reign   *Queen Mary* v i 290
It seems thy father's land is *f*.   *Foresters* IV 640
Forgave my father and I *f* you stealing our coals.   *Prom. of May* III 69
—her last word *F*—and I forgive you.   „ III 811
Forged ay ; if Bonner have not *f* the bills.   *Queen Mary* IV i 51
Forget (*See also* **Forgit**) you *f* That long low minster where you gave your hand   „ III ii 89
may God *F* me at most need when I *f* Her foul divorce—   „ IV i 80
if that May make your Grace *f* yourself a little.   „ v v 81
Shall I *f* my new archbishoprick   *Becket* I i 220
To rest upon thy bosom and *f* him—   „ II i 31
Forgetting that *F*'s me too.   „ II i 50
You were. I never *f* anything.   „ v ii 413
he begs you to *f* As scarce his act :—   *The Cup* II 51
I promise you that if you *f* yourself in your behaviour to this gentleman,   *Prom. of May* I 161
I am old and *f*. Was Prince John there ?   *Foresters* I i 251

Fought (*continued*) Give me that hand which *f* for Richard there. *Foresters* IV 1029
Foul lives Of many among your churchmen were so *f* *Queen Mary* III iv 192
may God Forget me at most need when I forget Her *f* divorce— „ IV i 81
F maggots crawling in a fester'd vice ! „ V v 161
I free From this *f* charge— *Harold* II ii 518
a *f* stream Thro' fever-breeding levels,— *Becket* II ii 154
slut whose fairest linen seems *F* as her dust-cloth, „ V ii 203
She rose From the *f* flood and pointed toward the farm, *Prom. of May* II 653
all the *f* fatalities That blast our natural passions into pains ! „ III 723
in Nottingham they say There bides a *f* witch somewhere hereabout. *Foresters* II i 203
he has anger'd the *f* witch, „ i 670
slut whose fairest linen seems *F* as her dust-cloth, *Becket* V ii 203
Found (*See also* **Fun**') All my hope is now It may be *f* a scandal. *Queen Mary* I v 231
Which *f* me full of foolish doubts, „ I v 530
Happily or not, It *f* her sick indeed. „ II ii 124
I've *f* this paper ; pray your worship read it ; „ II iii 55
We *f* him, your worship, a plundering „ II iii 72
I *f* it fluttering at the palace gates :— „ III ii 218
yet I *f* One day, a wholesome scripture, „ III iv 83
And *f* it all a visionary flame, „ IV ii 4
I have *f* thee and not leave thee any more. „ IV ii 109
Have *f* a real presence in the stake, „ IV ii 142
so long continuing, Hath *f* his pardon ; „ IV iii 50
libellous papers which I *f* Strewn in your palace. „ V ii 172
And I have often *f* them. *Mary.* Find me one ! „ V ii 222
God pardon me ! I have never yet *f* one. „ V ii 335
and the dead were *f* Sitting, and in this fashion ; „ V ii 396
I never *f* he bore me any spite. „ V v 144
Have you *f* mercy there, Grant it me here : „ V v 144
If he *f* me thus, Harold might hate me ; *Harold* I ii 171
I *f* him all a noble host should be. „ II ii 10
because we *f* him A Norman of the Normans. „ II ii 581
Both were lost and *f* together, „ III ii 7
lost and *f* Together in the cruel river Swale „ III ii 9
Tho' we be lost and be *f* together.' „ III ii 21
I have *f* him, I am happy. „ V ii 81
That I have *f* it here again ? „ V ii 116
He *f* me once alone. Nay—nay—I cannot Tell you : *Becket* I i 274
They said—her Grace's people—thou wast *f*— „ I ii 6
that had *f* a King Who ranged confusions, „ I iii 369
I *f* a hundred ghastly murders done By men, „ I iii 407
and went on till I *f* the light and the lady, „ IV ii 18
He is easily *f* again. „ IV ii 67
F out her secret bower and murder'd her. „ V i 175
f thy name a charm to get me Food, roof, and rest. „ V ii 96
have *f* together In our three married years ! *The Cup* I ii 416
we *f* a goat-herd's hut and shared His fruits „ I ii 426
I never *f* the woman I could not force or wheedle „ I iii 165
f All good in the true heart of Sinnatus, „ II 86
If you had *f* him plotting against Rome, „ II 406
But had I *f* him plotting, I had counsell'd „ II 412
chaplet on the grass, And there I *f* it. *The Falcon* 370
I have *f* it once again In your own self. *Prom. of May* II 375
seen us that wild morning when we *f* Her bed unslept in, „ II 470
Has anyone *f* me out, Dora ? „ III 225
We *f* a letter in your bedroom torn into bits. „ III 323
even if I *f* it Dark with the soot of slums. „ III 601
I *f* this white doe wandering thro' the wood, *Foresters* I 95
F him dead and drench'd in dew, „ II ii 147
the warm wine, and *f* it again. „ IV 245
I never *f* one traitor in my band. „ IV 836
Foundation Waltham, my *f* For men who serve the neighbour, *Harold* V i 97
The king's *f*, that have follow'd him. „ V i 476
Fountain (**adj.**) Were seated sadly at a *f* side, *The Falcon* 610
Fountain (**s**) his wealth A *f* of perennial alms— *Queen Mary* II ii 385
Four (*See also* **Vour**) *f* guns gaped at me, Black, silent mouths : „ II iii 30
I know Some three or *f* poor priests a thousand times Fitter *Becket, Pro.* 291

GG*

Four (*continued*) And this no wife has born you *f* brave sons, *Becket* V i 125
There then, *f* hundred marks. *Foresters* IV 497
Four-and-twenty We will away in *f-a-t* hours, „ I iii 91
Four-footed all manner of game, and *f-f* things, and fowls— *Becket* III iii 130
Fourscore This forest-horn of mine I can bring down *F* tall fellows on thee. *Foresters* IV 177
Fowl (*See also* **Wild-fowl**) The *f* that fleeth o'er thy field is cursed, *Harold* V i 73
all manner of game, and four-footed things, and *f*'s— *Becket* III iii 131
Here's a fine *f* for my lady ; *The Falcon* 556
Fox Die like the torn *f* dumb, *Queen Mary* II ii 331
a *f* may filch a hen by night, „ V 157
a *f* from the glen ran away with the hen, *Prom. of May* I 51
Fox-Fleming Why comes that old *f-F* back again ? *Queen Mary* I v 581
Foxglove Past the bank Of *f*, then to left by that one yew. *Foresters* IV 974
Fox-lion sorrow'd for my random promise given To yon *f-l*. *Harold* III i 270
Fragment or whether England Be shatter'd into *f*'s. „ II ii 286
Frail his *f* transparent hand, Damp with the sweat of death, *Queen Mary* I ii 31
Frailer At least mine own is *f*: you are laming it. *Becket* IV ii 264
Frailty and as to other *frailties* of the flesh— *Foresters* II 65
Frailty *F* would not accept her for a bride *Queen Mary* I ii 67
France *F* would not accept her for a bride *Queen Mary* I ii 67
That makes for *F*. (repeat) *Queen Mary* I iii 89, 92, 94
But we play with Henry, King of *F*, *Queen Mary* I iii 132
The King of *F*, Noailles the Ambassador, „ I iv 110
Our one point on the main, the gate of *F* ! „ I v 126
The Ambassador from *F*, your Grace. „ I v 239
Would make our England, *F*; „ I v 297
Would be too strong for *F*. „ I v 300
I must needs wish all good things for *F*. „ I v 310
'Sir Peter Carew fled to *F*: „ II i 135
The King of *F* is with us ; „ II i 195
The King of *F* will help to break it. *Bagenhall.*
F ! We once had half of *F*, „ III i 105
England now Is but a ball chuck'd between *F* and Spain, „ III i 110
I know some lusty fellows there in *F*. „ III i 129
Back'd by the power of *F*, and landing here, „ III i 447
Not so well holpen in our wars with *F*, „ III vi 189
Ay, ay, beware of *F*. „ IV iii 434
If war should fall between yourself and *F*; „ V i 10
To declare war against the King of *F*. „ V i 117
soon or late you must have war with *F*; „ V i 122
he would weld *F*, England, Scotland, „ V i 140
yet the Pope is now colleagued with *F*; „ V i 189
to discourage and lay lame The plots of *F*, „ V i 198
The King of *F* the King of England too. „ V i 198
There *will* be war with *F*, at last, my liege ; „ V i 283
Sailing from *F*, with thirty Englishmen, „ V i 285
This is the fifth conspiracy hatch'd in *F*; „ V i 298
Our flag hath floated for two hundred years Is *F* again. „ V ii 263
You did but help King Philip's war with *F*, „ V ii 314
As far as *F*, and into Philip's heart. „ V iii 18
It was his father's policy against *F*. „ V v 45
help to build a throne Out-towering hers of *F* . . . *Harold* II ii 765
and all *F*, all Burgundy, Poitou, all Christendom „ II ii 149
Louis of *F* loved me, and I dreamed that I loved Louis of *F*: *Becket, Pro.* 355
I will have thee frighted into *F*, „ I ii 94
I mean to cross the sea to *F*, „ I iii 124
Thou knowest he was forced to fly to *F*; „ I iii 205
But I that threw the mightiest knight of *F*, „ I iii 747
' Fly at once to *F*, to King Louis of *F*: „ I iv 53
I must fly to *F* to-night. „ I iv 154
or in the land of *F* for aught I know. „ I iv 196
F ! Ha ! De Morville, Tracy, Brito—fled is he ? „ I iv 198
one who lives for thee Out there in *F* ? „ II i 310
Brother of *F*, what shall be done with Becket ? „ II ii 64
claws that you perforce again Shrank into *F*. „ II ii 88
Brother of *F*, you have taken, „ II ii 154
all the Church of *F* Decide on their decision, „ II ii 177
we pray you, draw yourself from under The wings of *F*. „ II ii 249

France (continued)   I am glad that F hath scouted him
  at last :   *Becket* II ii 252
  you have quenched the warmth of F toward you,   „   II ii 311
  The wine and wealth of all our F are yours ;   „   II ii 446
  have I Not heard ill things of her in F ?   Oh, she's
  The Queen of F.   „   III i 231
  My Lords of F and England, My friend of Canterbury   „   III iii 227
  we will to F and be Beforehand with the King,   „   IV ii 453
  For once in F the King had been so harsh,   „   V ii 139
  St. Denis of F and St. Alphege of England,   „   V iii 165

Franche-Comté (a French province)   voices of F-C, and
  the Netherlands,   *Queen Mary* V i 45
Frange   Illorum lanceas F Creator !   *Harold* V i 584
Frankfort   To Strasburg, Antwerp, F, Zurich,   *Queen Mary* I ii 2
Fray'd   f i' the knees, and out at elbow,   „   I i 51
Freak   Her f's and frolics with the late Lord Admiral ?   „   I iv 20
Free (adj.)   (*See also* **Tongue-free**)   To make f spoil and
  havock of your goods.   „   II ii 186
  but we can save your Grace.   The river still is f.   „   IV iv 25
  he is f enough in talk, But tells me nothing.   „   III ii 193
  That jail you from f life, bar you from death.   „   III v 172
  with f wing The world were all one Araby.   „   III v 208
  but had rather Breathe the f wind from off our Saxon
  downs,   *Harold* II ii 186
  To chain the f guest to the banquet-board ;   „   II ii 193
  F air ! f field !   „   II ii 230
  and fill the sky With f sea-laughter.   „   II ii 337
  Should they not know f England crowns herself ?   „   V i 47
  Softly, and fling them out to the f air.   *Becket* I i 287
  And weight down all f choice beneath the throne,   „   I iii 118
  couldst thou always Blurt thy f mind to the air ?   „   I iii 239
  she holds it in F and perpetual alms,   „   I iii 680
  To speak without stammering and like a f man ?   „   I iv 8
  but God and his f wind grant your lordship a happy
  home-return   „   III iii 327
  Give me the poison ; set me f of him !   „   IV ii 165
  The power of life in death to make her f !   „   V iii 101
  tho' Rome may set A f foot where she will,   *The Cup* II 246
  While, had you left him f use of his wings,   *Prom. of May* I 652
  for the moment, Will leave me a f field.   „   II 456
  We should be f as air in the wild wood—   *Foresters* I iii 124
  And these will strike for England And man and maid
  be f   „   II 10
  And these shall wed with freemen, And all their sons be f,   „   II 12
  and all the better For this f forest-life,   „   II i 60
  That I might breathe for a moment f of shield And cuirass   „   IV 128
  Friends, your f sports have swallow'd my f hour.   „   IV 339
  while our Robin's life Hangs by a thread, but he is a
  f man.   „   IV 385
  Our forest games are ended, our f life,   „   IV 1049
Free (verb)   I f From this foul charge—   *Harold* II ii 517
  Take thee, or f thee, F thee or slay thee,   „   IV ii 17
  if thou light upon her—f me from her ?   *Becket*, Pro. 493
  First, f thy captive from *her* hopeless prison,   „   V i 183
  O devil, can I f her from the grave ?   „   V i 185
  That sought to f the tomb-place of the King   *Foresters* IV 408
Freed   Duke of Suffolk lately f from prison,   *Queen Mary* I iii 121
  Earl of Devon ?   I f him from the Tower,   „   V i 163
  he f himself By oath and compurgation from the charge.   *Harold* II ii 519
  Know that when made Archbishop I was f,   *Becket* I iii 708
  part real, part childlike, to be f from the dulness—   „   III i 156
  I have f myself From all such dreams,   *Prom. of May* III 594
Freedom   Whereas in wars of f and defence   *The Cup* I ii 160
  The love of f, the desire of God,   *Foresters* I 68
  maiden f which Would never brook the tyrant.   „   III 119
Freeing   For f my friend Bagenhall from the Tower ;   *Queen Mary* III vi 7
Freely   that more f than your formal priest,   *Prom. of May* III 632
Freeman   wrench'd All hearts of *freemen* from thee.   *Harold* V 279
  And these shall wed with *freemen*,   *Foresters* II 21
Freer   and when I flee from this For a gasp of f air,   *Becket* II i 216
Free-will   now the stronger motive, Misnamed f-w—   *Prom. of May* II 637
Freeze   And, lest we f in mortal apathy,   *The Cup* I iii 130
French (adj.)   F, I must needs wish all goods things for
  France.   *Queen Mary* I v 309
  The F King winks at it.   „   III i 160

French (adj.) (continued)   not mix us any way With
  his F wars—   *Queen Mary* III iii 79
  and the F fleet Rule in the narrow seas.   „   V i 6
  Swine, sheep, ox—here's a F supper.   *Becket* I iv 113
  Not on F ground, nor any ground but English,   „   III iii 260
French (s)   it threatens us no more Than F or Norman.   *Harold* I i 135
  talk a little F like a lady ; play a little like a lady ?   *Prom. of May* III 303
Frenchman   You must be sweet and supple, like a F.   *Queen Mary* I v 276
  and driven back The *Frenchmen* from their trenches ?   „   V ii 258
  But blaze not out before the *Frenchmen* here.   *Becket* III iii 221
Frequency   and so cannot suffer by the rule of f.   „   III iii 319
Fresh   but you, cousin, are f and sweet As the first
  flower   *Queen Mary* I iv 61
  Would fain have some f treaty drawn between you.   „   I v 261
  Mary. Why some f treaty ?   „   I v 261
  And put some f device in lieu of it—   „   III i 268
  Cousin Pole, You are f from brighter lands.   „   III iv 322
  Carry f rushes into the dining-hall,   *Foresters* I i 80
Friar   (*See also* **Fool-friar**)   Of those two f's ever in
  my prison,   *Queen Mary* IV ii 94
  as he walk'd the Spanish f's Still plied him   „   IV iii 576
  f's Plied him, but Cranmer only shook his head,   „   IV iii 600
  overbalance the weight of the church, ha f ?   *Foresters* I ii 62
  Quick, f, follow them :   „   II i 429
  Nay, nay, but softly, lest they spy thee, f !   „   II i 438
  We spoil'd the prior, f, abbot, monk,   „   III 167
  Here come three f's.   „   III 256
  Thou and thy woman are a match for three f's.   „   III 262
  How should poor f's have money ?   „   III 276
  These f's, thieves, and liars, Shall drink   „   III 312
  I believe thee, thou art a good fellow, though a f.   „   III 342
  by St. Mary these beggars and these f's shall join you.   „   III 417
  This f is of much boldness, noble captain.   „   IV 234
  I am overbreathed, F, by my two bouts at quarterstaff.   „   IV 267
  our f is so holy That he's a miracle-monger,   „   IV 280
  Keep silence, bully f, before the King.   „   IV 919
  If a cat may look at a king, may not a f speak to one ?   „   IV 922
  —I trust Half truths, good f :   „   IV 950
  You, good f, You Much, you Scarlet, you dear Little John,   „   IV 1082
Friar Tuck (follower of Robin Hood)   coming hither for the
  dance—be they not, F T ?   „   I i 54
  Besides, tho' F T might make us one,   „   II ii 88
Friday   And I was bit by a mad dog o' F.   *Becket* I iv 218
Friend   fear, I see you, Dear f, for the last time ;   *Queen Mary* I ii 103
  Ay, gentle f, admit them.   I will go.   „   I ii 110
  By the mass, old f, we'll have no pope here   „   I iii 42
  Unless my f's and mirrors lie to me,   „   I iv 2
  Queen Is both my foe and yours : we should be f's.   „   I iv 43
  Not many f's are mine, except indeed Among the many.   „   I iv 135
  Speak not thereof—no, not to your best f,   „   I iv 177
  who am your f And ever faithful counsellor,   „   I v 134
  call'd my f's together, Struck home and won.   „   I v 552
  His f's would praise him, I believed 'em,   „   I v 623
  His f's—as Angels I received 'em,   „   I v 625
  You as poor a critic As an honest f—   „   II i 116
  No, my f ; war *for* the Queen's Grace—   „   II i 188
  world as yet, my f, Is not half-waked ;   „   II i 227
  Ay, ay, my f ; not read it ?   „   II iii 64
  My f's, I have not come to kill the Queen   „   II iii 116
  Be happy, I am your f.   „   II iii 123
  hath shut the gates On f and foe.   „   II iv 62
  My foreign f's, who dream'd us blanketed   „   III ii 19
  St. Andrew's day ; sit close, sit close, we are f's.   „   III iii 2
  My seven-years' f was with me, my young boy ;   „   III iii 417
  Our old f Cranmer, Your more especial love,   „   III iv 416
  To reach the hand of mercy to my f.   „   IV i 65
  why my f Should meet with lesser mercy   „   IV i 69
  Your faithful f and trusty councillor.   „   IV i 89
  Without a f, a book, my faith would seem Dead   „   IV ii 96
  Or am I slandering my most inward f,   „   IV ii 105
  Good day, old f ; what, you look somewhat worn ;   „   IV ii 115
  F for so long time of a mighty King ;   „   IV iii 73
  And I and learned f's among ourselves   „   V ii 74
  Have not I been the fast f of your life Since mine began,   „   V ii 133
  He is my good f, and I would keep him so ;   „   V iii 91

Friend (*continued*) F, tho' so late, it is not safe to
  preach.   *Queen Mary* v iv 41
Our *f's*, the Normans, holp to shake his chair.   *Harold* i i 85
Stand by him, mine old *f*,   ,,   i i 113
Is not the Norman Count thy *f* and mine ?   ,,   i i 247
F's, in that last inhospitable plunge   ,,   ii i 1
I dug mine into My old fast *f* the shore,   ,,   ii i 7
Thou art his *f*: thou know'st my claim on England   ,,   ii ii 11
he shall be my dear As well as thine,   ,,   ii ii 80
So thou, fair *f*, will take them easily.   ,,   ii ii 207
Obey the Count's conditions, my good *f*.   ,,   ii ii 277
I am thy fastest *f* in Normandy.   ,,   ii ii 556
Be careful of thine answer, my good *f*.   ,,   ii ii 605
Harold, I am thy *f*, one life with thee,   ,,   ii ii 649
My *f*, thou hast gone too far to palter now.   ,,   ii ii 706
I, the Count—the King—Thy *f*—   ,,   ii ii 755
O *f's*, I shall not overlive the day.   ,,   iii i 232
Edwin, my *f*—Thou lingerest.—Gurth,—   ,,   iv i 257
F's, had I been here, Without too large self-lauding   ,,   iv ii 85
King Loves not as statesman, but true lover and *f*.   *Becket*, Pro. 81
Nolo Archiepiscopari, my good *f*, Is quite another
  matter.   ,,   Pro. 286
Becket, her father's *f*, like enough staved   ,,   Pro. 518
F, am I so much better than thyself   ,,   i i 3
Henry the King hath been my *f*, my brother,   ,,   i i 87
my father drove him and his *f's*, De Tracy   ,,   i i 277
when thou seest him next, Commend me to thy *f*.
  What *f*?   *Rosamund*.   The King.   ,,   i i 324
My *f*, the King ! . . . O thou Great Seal of England,
  Given me by my dear *f* the King of England—   ,,   i i 335
Now must I send thee as a common *f* To tell the King,
  my *f*, I am against him. We are *f's* no more :   ,,   i i 342
Go therefore like a *f* slighted by one   ,,   i i 350
O, my dear *f*, the King ! O brother !—   ,,   i i 359
Peace, fools !   *Becket*.   Peace, *f's* !   ,,   i ii 2
Serve my best *f* and make him my worst foe ;   ,,   i iii 567
Farewell, *f's* ! farewell, swallows !   ,,   i iv 44
may I come in with my poor *f*, my dog ?   ,,   i iv 94
My *f's*, the Archbishop bids you good night.   ,,   i iv 261
Be *f's* with him again—I do beseech thee.   ,,   ii i 21
But since he cursed My *f's* at Veselay,   ,,   ii i 89
I kneel to thee—be *f's* with him again.   ,,   ii i 317
Be, both, the *f's* you were.   *Henry*.   The *f's* we were !
  Co-mates we were,   ,,   ii ii 119
No one comes, Nor foe nor *f*;   ,,   iii i 38
My *f* of Canterbury and myself Are now once more   ,,   iii iii 228
It must be so, my *f*!   ,,   iii iii 342
Soon as she learnt I was a *f* of thine,   ,,   v ii 110
Why they, your *f's*, those ruffians, the De Brocs,   ,,   v ii 434
My two good *f's*, What matters murder'd here,   ,,   v ii 629
Come in, my *f's*, come in !   ,,   v iii 68
Some *f's* of mine would speak with me without.   *The Cup* ii 202
my *f's* may spy him And slay him as he runs.   ,,   ii 390
Our Antonius, Our faithful *f* of Rome,   ,,   ii 244
Thou art the last *f* left me upon earth—   *The Falcon* 31
No, no—a *f* of hers.   ,,   59
For fear of losing more than *f*, a son ;   ,,   332
Should fly like bosom *f's* when needed most.   ,,   527
cold-manner'd *f* may strangely do us The truest service,   ,,   642
day's bright like a *f*, but the wind east like an
  enemy.   *Prom. of May* i 79
forget yourself in your behaviour to this gentleman,
  my father's *f*,   ,,   i 163
Niver man 'ed better *f's*, and I will saäy niver master
  'ed better men :   ,,   i 323
I trust, my dear, we shall be always *f's*.   ,,   i 632
After all that has gone between us—*f's* ! What,
  only *f's* ?   ,,   i 634
All that has gone between us Should surely make us *f's*.   ,,   i 638
I do not dare, like an old *f*, to shake it.   ,,   ii 526
Some of my former *f's* Would find my logic faulty ;   ,,   ii 664
But, O dear *f*, If thro' the want of any—   ,,   iii 549
a *f* just now, One that has been much wrong'd,   ,,   iii 574
so true a *f* of the people as Lord Robin of
  Huntingdon.   *Foresters* i i 188

Friend (*continued*) This Robin, this Earl of Huntingdon
  —he is a *f* of Richard,   *Foresters* i i 282
My guests and *f's*, Sir Richard,   ,,   i ii 77
Dost thou mistrust me ? Am I not thy *f* ?   ,,   i ii 178
as I *am* thy *f*, I promise thee to make this Marian
  thine.   ,,   i ii 182
I and my *f*, this monk, were here belated,   ,,   i ii 193
Sheriff, thy *f*, this monk, is but a statue.   ,,   i ii 233
F's, I am only merry for an hour or two   ,,   i iii 10
Strike up a song, my *f's*, and then to bed.   ,,   i iii 30
Ah dear Robin ? ah noble captain, *f* of the poor !   ,,   ii i 182
Nay—that, my *f*, I am sure I did not say.   ,,   ii i 488
He has a *f* there will advance the monies,   ,,   ii i 628
We never robb'd one *f* of the true King.   ,,   iii 157
Robin, the people's *f*, the King o' the woods !   ,,   iii 347
F's, your free sports have swallow'd my free hour.   ,,   iv 339
Meanwhile, farewell Old *f's*, old patriarch oaks.   ,,   iv 1054

Friendly-fiendly with that *f-f* smile of his,   *Harold* iii i 86
Friendship hatred of another to us Is no true bond
  of *f*.   *Queen Mary* i iv 46
I hate a split between old *f's*   *Becket* ii ii 380
No *f* sacred, values neither man Nor woman   *Foresters* iv 713
Friendship-fast Which binds us *f-f* for ever !   *Harold* ii ii 162
Frieze Look'd somewhat crooked on him in his *f*;   *Queen Mary* iv iii 333
Fright (s) what maäkes tha sa white ?   *Eva*.   F,
  father !   *Prom. of May* i 418
Since Tostig came with Norway—*f* not love.   *Harold* iv i 173
Fright (verb) and deep-incavern'd eyes Half *f* me.   *Queen Mary* i iv 268
Which *f's* you back into the ancient faith ;   ,,   iv ii 143
They *f* not me.   *Harold* i i 39
It *f's* the traitor more to maim and blind.   ,,   ii ii 503
—flatter And *f* the Pope—   *Becket* ii ii 473
I see now Your purpose is to *f* me—   ,,   iv ii 180
Why do you jest with me, and try To *f* me ?   *Prom. of May* i 666
I am not deaf : you *f* me.   ,,   ii 660
To *f* the wild hawk passing overhead,   *Foresters* iii 318
Frighted Are *f* back to Tostig.   *Harold* iv i 119
I will have thee *f* into France,   *Becket* ii ii 143
Fringe Some golden *f* of gorgeousness beyond Old use,   *The Cup* ii 438
old woman's blessing with them to the last *f*.   *Foresters* ii i 196
Frith (John) But you were never raised to plead for F,   *Queen Mary* iv ii 211
Frock What, Mr. Dobson ? A butcher's *f* ?   *Prom. of May* i 94
Frog Quash'd my *f* that used to quack   *Foresters* ii ii 149
Frolic Her freaks and *f's* with the late Lord Admiral ?   *Queen Mary* iv 20
After my *f* with his tenant's girl,   *Prom. of May* i 493
Can have *f* and play.   *Foresters* ii ii 183
From See **Vro'**
Front (adj.) Would set him in the *f* rank of the fight   *The Cup* i i 153
Front (verb) That is Your question, and I *f* it with
  another :   *Queen Mary* i v 141
Will *f* their cry and shatter them into dust.   ,,   ii iv 5
And *f* the doom of God.   *Harold* v i 436
I'll *f* him, cross to cross.   *Becket* i iii 481
Frost had a touch of *f* That help'd to check   *The Falcon* 644
How few *f's* Will chill the hearts   *Foresters* iv 1063
Frosted *f* off me by the first cold frown of the King.   *Becket* i iv 67
Frosty Like sun-gilt breathings on a *f* dawn—   *Queen Mary* v iii 50
Frown (s) frosted off me by the first cold *f* of the King.   *Becket* i iv 67
Let there not be one *f* in this one hour.   ,,   ii i 43
Frown (verb) should not *f* as Power, but smile   *Harold* i i 365
However kings and queens may *f* on thee.   *Becket* ii i 19
Frowned The King hath *f* upon me.   ,,   i iv 25
he *f* ' No mate for her, if it should come to that '—   ,,   iii i 258
Frozen snow had *f* round her, and she sat Stone-dead   ,,   v ii 237
Fructus Sit benedictus *f* ventris tui !'   *Queen Mary* iii ii 83
Fruit should leave Some *f* of mine own body after me,   ,,   ii ii 223
The tree that only bears dead *f* is gone.   ,,   iii i 19
this dead *f* was ripening overmuch,   ,,   iii i 25
Can render thanks in *f* for being sown,   ,,   iii i 198
when the full *f* of the royal promise might have dropt   *Becket* iii iii 275
and shared His *f's* and milk.   Liar !   *The Cup* i ii 428
strows our *f's*, and lays Our golden grain,   ,,   ii 285
And here are fine *f's* for my lady.   *The Falcon* 561
Fruitful Most *f*, yet, indeed, an empty rind,   *Queen Mary* iii ii 202
Drink and drink deep—our marriage will be *f*.   *The Cup* ii 381

Gallery And I will out upon the *g.*   *Queen Mary* II iv 49
In some dark closet, some long *g*, drawn,   ,,   v ii 217
Galley more than one Row'd in that *g*—Gardiner to wit,   ,,   IV i 87
Galley-slave now, perhaps, Fetter'd and lash'd, a *g-s,*   *Foresters* II i 654
Gallop (s) On the *g*, on the *g*, Robin, like a deer   ,,   II i 432
Gallop (verb) 'at I tell'd 'em to *g* 'im.   *Prom. of May* III 433
Gallows What ! the *g* ?   *Queen Mary* II i 24
Gamble *G* thyself at once out of my sight,   ,,   II iii 95
Gambled has drunk and *g* out All that he had,   ,,   II iii 87
He has *g* for his life, and lost, he hangs.   ,,   II iii 91
Game (pastime) (*See also* **Gaäme**) The *G* of Chess.
(repeat)   ,,   I iii 127
such a *g*, sir, were whole years a playing.   ,,   I iii 139
Strange *g* of chess ! a King That with her own pawns   ,,   I iii 161
Simon Renard spy not out our *g* Too early.   ,,   I iii 173
With whom they play'd their *g* against the king !   *Harold* v ii 13
fixt my fancy Upon the *g* I should have beaten thee,   *Becket, Pro.* 51
a perilous *g* For men to play with God.   ,,   II ii 70
Is this a *g* for thee to play at ? Away.   *Foresters* II i 426
All our *g*'s be put to rout.   ,,   II ii 166
And join your feasts and all your forest *g*'s   ,,   III 85
Then thou shalt play the *g* of buffets with us.   ,,   IV 259
Our forest *g*'s are ended, our free life,   ,,   IV 1049
Game (thing hunted) fatter *g* for you Than this old
gaping gurgoyle :   *Queen Mary* I iii 80
well train'd, and easily call'd Off from the *g.*   *Becket, Pro.* 121
When they ran down the *g* and worried it.   ,,   *Pro.* 123
The King keeps his forest head of *g* here,   ,,   III ii 37
let the King's fine *g* look to itself.   ,,   III ii 44
with all manner of *g*, and four-footed things, and fowls—   ,,   III iii 130
No rushing on the *g*—the net,—the net.   *The Cup* I i 170
And I may strike your *g* when you are gone.   ,,   I ii 36
I must lure my *g* into the camp.   ,,   I ii 64
You run down your *g*, We ours. What pity have
you for your *g* ?   *Foresters* IV 520
Gamekeeper Have I not seen the *g*, the groom,   *Queen Mary* IV iii 371
Gamel (a Northumbrian Thane) *G*, son of Orm, What
thinkest thou this means ? (repeat)   *Harold* I i 20, 463
Hail, *G*, son of Orm,   ,,   I i 91
Albeit no rolling stone, my good friend *G*,   ,,   I i 94
Is the North quiet, *G* ?   ,,   I i 107
I trust he may do well, this *G*,   ,,   I ii 190
that was his guest, *G*, the son of Orm :   *Foresters* II ii 299
murder'd thine own guest, the son of Orm, *G*,   ,,   IV ii 39
Gamester no such *g* As, having won the stake,   *The Cup* I iii 145
Gangrene this rag fro' the *g* i' my leg.   *Becket* I iv 237
and *g*'s, and running sores, praise ye the Lord,   ,,   I iv 255
Gap Sheep at the *g* which Gardiner takes,   *Queen Mary* III iii 236
Then fling mine own fair person in the *g*   *Harold* I ii 202
as I hate the dirty *g* in the face of a Cistercian monk,   *Becket* II ii 381
Could snaw away the darkness of that *g*   ,,   i 60
thaw he niver mended that *g* i' the glebe fence   *Prom. of May* I 446
Gape These fields are only green, they make me *g.*   *Queen Mary* III v 8
Will the earth *g* and swallow us ?   *Becket* v 205
causest the safe earth to shudder and *g*,   *The Cup* II 299
throat might *g* before the tongue could cry who ?   *Foresters* III 225
Gaped four guns *g* at me, Black, silent mouths :   *Queen Mary* III iii 31
The nurses yawn'd, the cradle *g*,   ,,   III vi 93
Gaping yonder's fatter game for you Than this old *g*
gurgoyle :   ,,   I iii 81
Stand staring at me ! shout, you *g* rogue !   ,,   III i 288
The pretty *g* bills in the home-nest Piping for bread—   *Becket* II ii 300
When shall your parish-parson bawl our banns
Before your *g* clowns ?   *Prom. of May* I 687
Garb These black dog-Dons *G* themselves bravely.   *Queen Mary* III i 190
Garcia (Villa) *See* **Villa Garcia**
Garda might have flash'd Upon their lake of *G*,   ,,   III ii 23
Garden (adj.) I love them More than the *g* flowers,   *Becket* II i 133
matched with my Harold is like a hedge thistle
by a *g* rose.   *Prom. of May* III 176
Garden (s) were as glowing-gay As regal *g*'s ;   *Queen Mary* III ii 14
Which in the Catholic *g* are as flowers,   ,,   IV i 178
and in the midst A *g* and my Rosamund.   *Becket, Pro.* 169
into a *g* and not into the world,   ,,   III i 131
not to speak one word, for that's the rule o' the *g*,   ,,   III i 138

Garden (s) (continued) if I had been Eve i' the *g* I shouldn't
ha' minded the apple,   *Becket* III i 139
the knights are arming in the *g* Beneath the sycamore.   ,,   v ii 569
There sprouts a salad in the *g* still.   *The Falcon* 149
I haven't seen Eva yet. Is she anywhere in the *g* ?   *Prom. of May* I 47
All in the castle *g*,   *Foresters* I i 10
Stole on her, she was walking in the *g*,   ,,   II i 113
The serpent that had crept into the *g*   ,,   II i 137
Gardener the groom, *G*, and huntsman, in the
parson's place,   *Queen Mary* IV iii 373
Garden-stuff profess to be great in green things and
in *g-s.*   *The Falcon* 552
Gardiner (Bishop of Winchester and Lord Chancellor)
(*See also* **Out-Gardiners, Stephen Gardiner**) *G*
for one, who is to be made Lord Chancellor,   *Queen Mary* I i 86
so that *G* And Simon Renard spy not out our game   ,,   I iii 172
Thus *G*—for the two were fellow-prisoners   ,,   I iv 198
He hath no fence when *G* questions him ;   ,,   I iv 204
this fierce old *G*—his big baldness,   ,,   I iv 263
G is against him ; The Council,   ,,   I v 76
It then remains for your poor *G*,   ,,   I v 220
Paget is ours. *G* perchance is ours ;   ,,   I v 386
brake into woman-tears, Ev'n *G*, all amazed,   ,,   I v 566
G knows, but the Council are all at odds,   ,,   II i 138
I hear that *G*, coming with the Queen,   ,,   II ii 308
G buys them With Philip's gold.   ,,   III i 143
a pale horse for Death and *G* for the Devil.   ,,   II 1235
how strange That *G*, once so one with all   ,,   III iii 6
This *G* turn'd his coat in Henry's time ;   ,,   III iii 16
Ay, and for *G* ! being English citizen,   ,,   III iii 23
which the emperor sent us Were mainly *G*'s :   ,,   III iii 71
Mary would have it ; and this *G* follows ;   ,,   III iii 230
Philip would have it ; and this *G* follows !   ,,   III iii 233
Sheep at the gap which *G* takes,   ,,   III iii 236
what hath fluster'd *G* ? how he rubs His forelock !   ,,   III iv 12
The faultless *G* !   ,,   III iv 96
G would have my head.   ,,   III v 118
The gray rogue, *G*, Went on his knees,   ,,   v 165
G out-Gardiners *G* in his heat,   ,,   III vi 25
G burns, And Bonner burns   ,,   III vi 58
more than one Row'd in that galley—*G* to wit,   ,,   IV i 87
summun towld summun o' owld Bishop *G*'s end ;   ,,   IV iii 503
G wur struck down like by the hand o' God   ,,   IV iii 515
did not *G* intercept A letter which the Count de
Noailles wrote   ,,   v ii 494
Some say that *G*, out of love for him,   ,,   v ii 501
G burns Already ; but to pay them full in kind,   ,,   v v 13
Garland (*See also* **Marriage-garland**) your ladyship were
not Too proud to look upon the *g*,   *The Falcon* 663
dead *G* Will break once more into the living blossom.   ,,   918
Garner *g* the wheat ; And burn the tares   *Queen Mary* v v 113
Garnish'd We have had it swept and *g* after him.   ,,   III 139
Garrison we might withdraw Part of our *g* at Calais.   ,,   I v 123
Garrison'd *See* **Ill-garrison'd**
Garrulous poor *g* country-wives.   *Queen Mary* IV iii 547
What, daunted by a *g*, arrogant girl !   *Foresters* IV 736
Garter English *G*, studded with great emeralds,   *Queen Mary* I i 84
Gascon amorous Of good old red sound liberal *G* wine :   *Becket, Pro.* 100
when the *G* wine mounts to my head,   ,,   *Pro.* 113
Plunder'd the vessel full of *G* wine,   ,,   v ii 441
Gash (s) —brave Gurth, one *g* from brow to knee !   *Harold* v ii 70
Gash (verb) here I *g* myself asunder from the King,   *Becket* I i 175
Gash'd Son, husband, brother *g* to death in vain,   *The Cup* I ii 143
Gasp when I flee from this For a *g* of freer air,   *Becket* II i 29
Gasping ' No, madam,' he said, *G* ;   *Queen Mary* III i 405
Gate (*See also* **Farm-gate**) Our one point on the
main, *g* of France !   ,,   I v 125
At the park *g* he hovers with our guards.   ,,   II iv 15
Hark, there is battle at the palace *g*'s,   ,,   II iv 47
they have shut the *g*'s !   ,,   II iv 59
hath shut the *g*'s On friend and foe.   ,,   II iv 61
cry To have the *g*'s set wide again,   ,,   II iv 65
They are the flower of England ; set the *g*'s wide.   ,,   II iv 70
How oft hath Peter knock'd at Mary's *g* !   ,,   III ii 63
Open, Ye everlasting *g*'s !   ,,   III ii 183

Gate (*continued*)   I found it fluttering at the palace
   g's :—   *Queen Mary* III ii 218
   Like dogs that set to watch their master's *g*,   „   III iv 310
   I see the flashing of the *g's* of pearl—   *Harold* I i 186
   my men will guard you to the *g's*.   *Becket* I i 403
   Here is a missive left at the *g* by one from the castle.   „   I iv 50
   —like some loud beggar at thy *g*—   „   II i 181
   Close the great *g*—ho, there—upon the town.   „   v ii 530
   Was not the great *g* shut ?   „   v iii 137
   waiting To clasp their lovers by the golden *g's*.   *Prom. of May* I 248
   Laid famine-stricken at the *g's* of Death—   „   III 807
Gate-house   Last night I climb'd into the *g-h*, Brett,   *Queen Mary* II iii 15
Gateway   *g* to the mainland over which Our flag hath
   floated   „   v ii 260
Gather   *g* your men—Myself must bustle.   „   II ii 372
   g all From sixteen years to sixty ;   „   v ii 272
Gathered   these our companies And guilds of London,
   g here,   „   II ii 129
   And *g* with his hands the starting flame,   „   IV iii 336
   I *g* from the Queen That she would see your Grace   „   v iii 102
   g one From out a bed of thick forget-me-nots,   „   v v 92
   Was not the year when this was *g* richer ?   *The Falcon* 345
   confirm it now Before our *g* Norman baronage,   *Harold* II ii 695
Gaul   That we Galatians are both Greek and *G*.   *The Cup* I i 204
Gave   (*See also* **Gev, Gie'd**)   That *g* her royal crown to
   Lady Jane.   *Queen Mary* I i 19
   My father on a birthday *g* it me,   „   I v 527
   and in that passion *G* me my Crown.   „   I v 568
   where you *g* your hand To this great Catholic King.   „   III iv 90
   thro' the fear of death *G* up his cause,   „   IV iii 28
   Whereat Lord Williams *g* a sudden cry :—   „   IV iii 604
   G up the ghost ; and so past martyr-like—   „   IV iii 623
   reft me of that legateship Which Julius *g* me,   „   v ii 35
   Look'd hard and sweet at me, and *g* it me.   „   v v 95
   To the good king who *g* it—not to you—   *Harold* I i 407
   G his shorn smile the lie.   ..   II ii 226
   God *g* us to divide us from the wolf !   „   IV iii 101
   answer which King Harold *g* To his dead namesake,   „   IV iii 109
   He *g* him all the kingdoms of the West.   „   v i 24
   and the King *g* it to his Chancellor.   *Becket, Pro.* 431
   G me the golden keys of Paradise.   „   I i 54
   We *g* thee to the charge of John of Salisbury,   „   I i 247
   chart which Henry *g* you With the red line—   „   I i 61
   King Stephen *g* Many of the crown lands   „   I iii 149
   Shame fall on those who *g* it a dog's name—   „   II i 141
   and *g* me a great pat o' the cheek for a pretty wench,   „   II i 125
   save King Henry *g* thee first the kiss of peace.   „   III iii 253
   By very God, the cross I *g* the King !   „   IV ii 199
   life Saved as by miracle alone with Him Who *g* it.   „   IV iii 369
   I *g* it you, and you your paramour ;   „   v i 168
   His father *g* him to my care,   „   v ii 335
   and open arms To him who *g* it ;   *The Cup* I i 85
   He *g* me his hand :   *The Falcon* 836
   she that *g* herself to me so easily   *Prom. of May* I 746
   She *g* her hand, unask'd, at the farm-gate ;   „   II 625
   he *g* me no address, and there was no word of marriage ;   „   III 332
   The lady *g* a rose to the Earl, (repeat)   *Foresters* I i 12, 105
   The lady *g* her hand to the Earl, (repeat)   „   I i 16, 92
   She *g* a weeping kiss to the Earl, (repeat)   „   I i 20, 119
   the man had given her a rose and she *g* him another.   „   I i 111
   King, thy god-father, *g* it thee when a baby.   „   I i 286
   This ring my mother *g* me :   „   I ii 293
   by this Holy Cross Which good King Richard *g* me
   when a child—   „   I ii 310
   g me this morning on my setting forth.   „   II 281
Gavest   They have taken away the toy thou *g* me,   *Harold* II ii 106
   Thou *g* thy voice against me in the Council—   „   IV ii 77
   Thou *g* thy voice against me in my life,   „   v i 252
   The monk's disguise thou *g* me for my bower :   *Becket* v ii 93
Gawin (*going*)   but coom, coom ! let's be *g*.   *Prom. of May* I 425
   Do ye think I be *g'* to tell it to you,   „   II 190
Gay   (*See also* **Gaäy, Glowing-gay**)   Why do you go
   so *g* then ?   *Queen Mary* I iv 70
   Dearer than when you made your mountain *g*,   *The Falcon* 464
Gear   Have you had enough Of all this *g* ?   *Queen Mary* III i 88

Gee oop (a call to horses to start)   *G o* ! whoä !
   G o ! whoä ! (repeat)   *Prom. of May* II 307, 317
Gel (*girl*)   they be two o' the purtiest *g's* ye can
   see of a summer murnin'.   „   I 30
   Eva's saäke.   Yeas.   Poor *g*, poor *g* !   „   II 32
   Taäke me awaäy, little *g*.   It be one o' my
   bad daäys.   „   III 465
Gem   Standard of the Warrior, Dark among *g's* and
   gold ;   *Harold* IV i 249
Gemini   Nay, by St. *G*, I ha' two ;   *Foresters* II i 277
General   whom the *g* He looks to and he leans on as
   his God,   *Queen Mary* IV iii 305
   Poor lads, they see not what the *g* sees,   „   v ii 447
   When you have charm'd our *g* into mercy,   *The Cup* I ii 311
Generate   Is as the soul descending out of heaven Into
   a body ;   *Queen Mary* IV i 36
Generous   You are *g*, but it cannot be.   *Prom. of May* II 76
Geneva   Zurich, Worms, *G*, Basle—   *Queen Mary* I i 3
Genial   I know that I am *g*, I would be Happy,   *The Cup* I iii 28
Genius   There is a trade of *g*, there's glory !   *Foresters* IV 375
Gentle   O, kind and *g* master, the Queen's Officers   *Queen Mary* I i 107
   Ay, *g* friend, admit them.   I will go.   „   I i 110
   Peruse it ; is it not goodly, ay, and *g* ?   „   I v 195
   Ah, *g* cousin, since your Herod's death,   „   III ii 61
   if you knew him As I do, ever *g*, and so gracious,   „   IV i 156
   Ay—*g* as they call you—live or die !   „   IV iii 161
   and see, he smiles and goes, *g* as in life.   „   v v 147
   A *g*, gracious, pure and saintly man !   *Harold* II ii 584
   Good even, *g* Edith.   „   III ii 118
   Well, well, we will be *g* with him, gracious—   *Becket* II ii 128
   He is *g*, tho' a Roman.   *The Cup* II 502
   tho' you are good and *g*, Yet if thro' any want—   *Prom. of May* III 539
   if thou be as *g* Give me some news of my sweet
   Marian.   *Foresters* II i 480
   he *As g* as he's brave—that such as he   „   II i 659
Gentlefoälk (gentlefolk)   We laäys out o' the waäy fur
   g altogither—   *Prom. of May* I 211
   Thy feyther eddicated his darters to marry *g*,   ..   II 116
   I should ha' thowt they'd hed anew o' *g*,   „   II 581
   The Steers was all *g's* i' the owd times, an' I worked
   early an' laäte to make 'em all *g's* ageän.   „   III 447
Gentleman   he says he's a poor *g*.   Wyatt.   *G* ! a
   thief !   *Queen Mary* II iii 74
   and *g* he was.   We have been glad together ;   „   II iii 89
   Take thy poor *g* !   „   II iii 94
   But you, my Lord, a polish'd *g*,   „   III iv 250
   Out, girl ! you wrong a noble *g*.   „   III v 68
   Peters, my *g*, an honest Catholic,   „   IV iii 553
   I have small hope of the *g* out in my great toe.   *The Falcon* 657
   I promise you that if you forget yourself in your
   behaviour to this *g*,   *Prom. of May* I 162
   He's a Somersetshire man, and a very civil-spoken
   g.   Dobson.   *G* !   „   I 207
   Well, it's no sin in a *g* not to fish.   „   I 215
   and now, as far as money goäs, I be a *g*,   „   I 332
   while I wur maäkin' mysen a *g*,   „   I 335
   Tho' you are a *g*, I but a farmer's daughter—   „   I 666
   and you, a *g*, Told me to trust you :   „   I 708
   And I would loove tha moor nor ony *g* 'ud loove tha.   „   II 105
   though fortune had born you into the estate of a *g*,   „   II 121
   drest like a *g*, too.   Damn all *gentlemen*, says I !   „   II 579
   and prattled to each other that we would marry
   fine *gentlemen*,   „   III 277
   And this lover of yours—this Mr. Harold—is a *g* ?   „   III 281
   Has he offered you marriage, this *g* ?   „   III 290
   I eddicated boäth on 'em to marry *gentlemen*,   „   III 455
   that if a *g* Should wed a farmer's daughter,   „   III 578
   you are tenfold more a *g*,   „   III 742
   He may be prince ; he is not *g*.   *Foresters* IV 685
Gentlemen-at-arms   your *g-a-a*, If this be not your
   Grace's order,   *Queen Mary* II iv 62
Gentleness   Lady, I say it with all *g*,   *The Cup* I iii 99
   G, Low words best chime with this solemnity.   „   II 216
   sure am I that of your *g* You will forgive him.   *Prom. of May* II 488
   She, you mourn for, seem'd A miracle of *g*—   „   II 491

Gentlier my liege, To deal with heresy *g*. — *Queen Mary* III vi 58

Geoffrey (son of Rosamund and Henry) (*See also* **Geoffrey Plantagenet, Plantagenet**) I'll call thee little *G*.
　Henry. Call him ! *Rosamund. G* ! — *Becket* II i 214
　if little *G* have not tost His ball into the brook ! — „ II i 319
　the child will drown himself. *Rosamund. G* ! *G* ! — „ II i 324
　G ! *Geoffrey*. What are you crying for, — „ III i 268
　G, the pain thou hast put me to ! — „ IV i 10
　G, my boy, I saw the ball you lost in the fork — „ IV ii 56
　If pretty *G* do not break his own, — „ IV ii 177
　How fares thy pretty boy, the little *G* ? — „ v ii 168

Geoffrey Plantagenet nay, *G P*, thine own husband's father— — „ IV ii 249

George (patron saint of England) by the dragon of St. *G*, we shall Do some injustice, — *Foresters* IV 939

Germ O Thou, that dost inspire the *g* with life, — *The Cup* II 258

German for his book Against that godless *G*. — *Queen Mary* v v 238

Germany till the weight of *G* or the gold of England brings one of them down to the dust— — *Becket* II ii 363

Gesticulating madman, is it, *G* there upon the bridge ? — *Prom. of May* II 327

Get (*See also* **Git**) if I can *g* near enough I shall judge with my own eyes — *Queen Mary* I i 133
　And *g* the swine to shout Elizabeth. — „ i iii 39
　But so I *g* the laws against the heretic, — „ III i 323
　to *g* her baaby born ; — „ IV iii 523
　G you home at once. — „ v iv 63
　Till thou wouldst *g* him all apart, — *Harold* I i 447
　G thee gone ! He means the thing he says. — „ v i 83
　G thou into thy cloister as the king Will'd it : — „ v i 309
　g thee to thine own bed. — *Becket* I i 7
　G ye hence, Tell what I say to the King. — „ I iii 563
　G you hence ! a man passed in there to-day : — „ III vi 24
　g you hence in haste Lest worse befall you. — „ IV vi 26
　found thy name a charm to *g* Food, roof, and rest. — „ v ii 97
　G thee back to thy nunnery with all haste ; — „ v i 163
　g you back ! go on with the office. — „ v iii 32
　What can I do—what can I *g* for thee ? He answers,
　‘ *G* the Count to give me his falcon, — *The Falcon* 239
　next time you waste them at a pot-house you *g* no more from me. — *Prom. of May* III 100
　Sir Richard must scrape and scrape till he *g* to the land again. — *Foresters* I i 79
　G thee into the closet there, — „ II i 214

Getting (*See also* **A-getting**) *G* better, Mr. Dobson. — *Prom. of May* I 69
　which Father, for a whole life, has been *g* together, — „ III 166

Gev (gave) fell ageän coalscuttle and my kneeä *g* waäy — *Prom. of May* I 404

Ghastly how grim and *g* looks her Grace, — *Queen Mary* v ii 390
　nay, this *g* glare May heat their fancies, — *Harold* I i 308
　Strange and *g* in the gloom And shadowing — „ III iii 157
　from your *g* oubliette I send my voice across the narrow seas— — „ v i 245
　I found a hundred *g* murders done By men, — *Becket* I iii 407

Ghittern that I can touch The *g* to some purpose. — *The Falcon* 799

Ghoäst (ghost) If it be her *g*, we mun abide it. We can't keep a *g* out. — *Prom. of May* III 460

Ghost (*See also* **Ghoäst**) The *g*'s of Luther and Zuinglius fade Into the deathless hell — *Queen Mary* III ii 174
　Gave up the *g* ; and so past martyr-like— — „ IV iii 623
　shadows of a hundred fat dead deer For dead men's *g*'s. — *Harold* I ii 104
　One *g* of all the *g*'s—as yet so new, — *The Cup* II 141
　haunted by The *g*'s of the dead passions — *Prom. of May* II 275
　To see her grave ? her *g* ? Her *g* is everyway — „ II 352
　I was afear'd it was the *g*, your worship. *Prince John. G* ! did one in white pass ? — *Foresters* II i 226
　oafs, *g*'s o' the mist, wills-o'-the-wisp ; — „ II i 263
　Love himself Seems but a *g*, but when thou feel'st with me The *g* returns — „ III 113
　They must have sprung like *G*'s from underground, — „ IV 592

Ghostly A *g* horn Blowing continually, and faint battle-hymns, — *Harold* III i 372
　at Pontigny came to me The *g* warning of my martyrdom ; — *Becket* v ii 292
　and make a *g* wail ever and anon to scare 'em. — *Foresters* II i 215

Giant (adj.) He, and the *g* King of Norway, Harold Hardrada, — *Harold* III ii 122

Giant (s) \as the heathen *g* Had but to touch the ground, — *Queen Mary* III ii 43
　or something more, Seeing he is a *g*. — *Harold* IV ii 56
　or something more, Seeing he is a *g* ! ' — „ IV iii 114
　spiritual *g* with our island laws And customs, — *Becket* IV ii 444

Giant-king Their *g-k*, a mightier man-in-arms — *Harold* v i 399

Gibbet In every London street a *g* stood. — *Queen Mary* II i 7
　witness the brawls, the *g*'s. — „ v i 86
　He will come to the *g* at last ? — *Foresters* II i 328

Gibbeted *See* **Cliff-gibbeted**

Giddy I can bear all, And not be *g*. — *Harold* I i 486

Gie (give) fur he'll *g* us a big dinner, — *Prom. of May* I 9

Gi'e (give) and s'pose I kills my pig, and *g*'s it among 'em, — „ I 147
　Weänt ye *g* me a kind answer at last ? — „ II 63
　fur owd Dobson 'll *g* us a bit o' supper. — „ II 216
　Owd Steer *g*'s nubbut cowd tea to '*is* men, and owd Dobson *g*'s beer. — „ II 223
　G us a buss fust, lass. — „ II 228
　d'ye think I'd *g* 'em the fever ? — „ III 49
　and wheere the big eshtree cuts athurt it, it *g*'s a turn like, — „ III 95

Gie'd (gave) but I hallus *g* soom on 'em to Miss Eva — „ II 15

Gift A diamond, And Philip's *g*, as proof of Philip's love, — *Queen Mary* III i 67
　An honest *g*, by all the Saints, — *Harold* I i 344
　thro' The random *g*'s of careless kings, — *Becket* I i 159
　Then he took back not only Stephen's *g*'s, — „ I iii 154
　I thought it was a *g* ; — „ I iii 646
　Shall God's good *g*'s be wasted ? — „ I iv 71
　child We waited for so long—heaven's *g* at last— — „ III i 14
　A strange *g* sent to me to-day. — *The Cup* I ii 52
　is another sacred to the Goddess, The *g* of Synorix ; — „ II 347
　In honour of his *g* and of our marriage, — „ II 351
　And this last costly *g* to mine own self, — *The Falcon* 228
　Yet I come To ask a *g*. — „ 299
　g I ask for, to *my* mind and at this present — „ 777

Gig and he sent me wi' the *g* to Littlechester to fetch 'er — *Prom. of May* I 20

Gilbert Becket (father of Thomas Becket) me, Thomas, son Of *G B*, London Merchant. — *Becket* II ii 231

Gilbert Foliot (Bishop of London) (*See also* **Foliot**) There's *G F*. Henry. He ! too thin, too thin. — „ *Pro.* 260
　But hast thou heard this cry of *G F* — „ I i 36
　Ay, For *G F* held himself the man. — „ I i 43
　If it were not, *G F*, I mean to cross the sea to France, — „ I iii 123
　And bid him re-create me, *G F*. — „ I iii 126
　Thou still hast owed thy father, *G F*. — „ I iii 276
　Thou still hast shown thy primate, *G F*. — „ I iii 282
　G F, A worldly follower of the worldly strong. — „ I iii 541
　Cursed be John of Oxford, Roger of York, And *G F* ! — „ II ii 267

Gild It *g*'s the greatest wronger of his peace, — *Queen Mary* v II 415

Gilded over His *g* ark of mummy-saints, — *Harold* v i 304

Gilt *See* **Sun-gilt**

Gingerbread He speaks As if it were a cake of *g*. — *Becket* II i 230

Giovanna (*See also* **Monna Giovanna**) the Lady *G*, who hath been away so long, — *The Falcon* 2
　G here ! Ay, ruffle thyself—*be* jealous ! — „ 21
　yet if *G* Be here again—No, no ! — „ 27
　G, my dear lady, in this same battle — „ 601
　G, dear *G*, I that once The wildest — „ 806
　Yes, *G*, But he will keep his love to you for ever ! — „ 891

Gipsyfy I will hide my face, Blacken and *g* it ; — *Becket* IV ii 100

Gipsy-stuff Life on the hand is naked *g-s*. — „ I 194

Girl (*See also* **Gall, Gel**) A king to be,—is he not noble, *g* ? — *Queen Mary* I v 4
　that young *g* who dared to wear your crown ? — „ I v 491
　G ; hast thou ever heard Slanders against Prince Philip — „ I v 569
　No, *g* ; most brave and loyal, — „ II iv 11
　G never breathed to rival such a rose ; — „ III i 372
　There's whitethorn, *g*. — „ III v 9
　But truth of story, which I glanced at, *g*, — „ III v 33
　Out, *g* ! you wrong a noble gentleman. — „ III v 67

Girl (*continued*) Lord Devon, *g's* ! what are you
  whispering here? | *Queen Mary* v ii 485
I could not, *g*, Not this way— | „ v v 170
That art the Queen ; ye are boy and *g* no more : | *Harold* i i 455
My *g*, what was it ? | „ i ii 73
My *g*, thou hast been weeping : | „ iii ii 38
thou art not A holy sister yet, my *g*, | „ iii ii 82
Ay, my *g*, no tricks in him— | „ v i 401
I tell thee, *g*, I am seeking my dead Harold. | „ v ii 42
Not true, my *g*, here is the Queen ! | „ v ii 91
Where is he, *g* ? | *The Cup* i i 106
My *g*, I am the bride of Death, | „ ii 28
My *g*, At times this oracle of great Artemis | „ ii 32
and she, A *g*, a child, then but fifteen, | *The Falcon* 537
After my frolic with his tenant's *g*, | *Prom. of May* i 493
may not a *g's* love-dream have too much romance in it | .. iii 184
Father, this poor *g*, the farm, everything ; | „ iii 211
Can't a *g* when she loves her husband, and he her, | „ iii 304
I heard a voice, '*G*, what are you doing there ?' | „ iii 375
Come, come, my *g*, enough Of this strange talk. | „ iii 619
and is flustered by a *g's* kiss. | *Foresters* i i 186
but O *g*, *g*, I am almost in despair. | „ i i 262
Thou hast robb'd my *g* of her betrothal ring. | „ ii i 586
to mistrust the *g* you say you love Is to mistrust your
  own love for your *g* ! | „ ii ii 57
Come, *g*, thou shalt along with us on the instant. | „ iv 678
What, daunted by a garrulous, arrogant *g* ! | „ iv 737
Risk not the love I bear thee for a *g*. | „ iv 742

Girlhood tell me anything of our sweet Eva When in
  her brighter *g*, | *Prom. of May* ii 521

Git (**get**) Did 'e *g* into thy chaumber ? | „ i 399
an' we'll *g* 'im to speechify for us arter dinner. | „ i 439
G along wi' ye, do ! | „ ii 235
S'iver I mun *g* along back to the farm, | „ ii 321
I mun *g* out on 'is waäy now, or I shall be the
  death on 'im. | „ ii 609
I'll *g* the book ageän, and larn mysen the rest, | „ iii 12

Give (*See also* **Gie**, **Gi'e**, **Gi'ed**) to *g* us all that holy
  absolution which— | *Queen Mary* i iii 28
grant me my prayer: *G* me my Philip ; | „ i v 87
G it me quick. | „ i v 592
Have for thine asking aught that I can *g*, | .. ii iii 7
G me a piece of paper ! | „ ii iii 66
boldness, which will *g* my followers boldness. | „ ii iii 71
'You will *g* me my true crown at last, | „ ii i 395
I come for counsel and ye *g* me feuds, | „ iii iv 307
I will *g* your message. | „ iii vi 40
Ay, but to *g* the poor. | „ iv i 43
To *g* the poor—they *g* the poor who die. | „ iv ii 52
It is the last. *Cranmer. G* it me, then. | „ iv ii 65
I not doubt that God will *g* me strength, | „ iv ii 234
Or *g* thee saintly strength to undergo. | „ iv iii 99
For death *g's* life's last word a power to live, | „ iv iii 161
G to the poor, Ye *g* to God. | „ iv iii 212
G me the lute. He hates me ! | „ v ii 362
g the Devil his due, I never found he bore me
  any spite. | „ v ii 472
in happy state To *g* him an heir male. | „ v ii 573
Ay, ever *g* yourselves your own good word. | *Harold* i i 342
As much as I can *g* thee, man ; | „ i i 479
thou didst stand by her and *g* her thy crabs, | „ ii i 49
And I'll *g* her my crabs again, | „ ii i 52
would *g* his kingly voice To me as his successor. | „ ii ii 588
G me thy keys. | „ ii ii 681
Stigand shall *g* me absolution for it— | „ ii ii 798
I may *g* that egg-bald head The tap that silences. | „ v i 90
I *g* my voice against thee from the grave— | „ v i 254
We *g* our voice against thee out of heaven ! | „ v i 260
We will not *g* him A Christian burial : | „ v ii 153
I would *g* her to thy care in England | *Becket*, Pro. 143
G him a bone, *g* him a bone ! | „ i iv 107
Is the Archbishop a thief who *g's* thee thy supper ? | „ i iv 116
Something good, or thou wouldst not *g* it me. | „ ii i 234
but *g* it me, and I promise thee not to turn the world | „ ii i 241
Kind of the witch to *g* thee warning tho'. | „ iii ii 29

Give (*continued*) *G* me thy hand. My Lords of France
  and England, | *Becket* iii iii 225
I sware I would not *g* the kiss of peace, | „ iii iii 259
here is a golden chain I will *g* thee | „ iv i 40
G her to me. | „ iv ii 135
G her to me to make my honeymoon. | „ iv ii 142
G me the poison ; set me free of him ! | „ iv ii 164
G to the King the things that are the King's, | „ v ii 461
You should attend the office, *g* them heart. | „ v ii 598
I *g* you here an order To seize upon him. | *The Cup* i i 163
G him a bow and arrows—follow—follow. | „ i i 208
Will feel no shame to *g* themselves the lie. | „ ii 117
And *g* him limbs, then air, and send him forth | „ ii 261
G it me again. It is the cup belonging our own Temple. | „ ii 343
Well, Madam, I will *g* your message to him. | *The Falcon* 217
'Get the Count to *g* me his falcon, | „ 241
I *g* it my sick son, and if you be Not quite recover'd | „ 589
I can *g* my time To him that is a part of you, | „ 790
If the good Count would *g* me——' *Count. G* me. | „ 838
G her a month or two, and her affections | *Prom. of May* i 484
Come, *g* me your hand and kiss me | „ i 563
But for the slender help that I can *g*, | „ ii 421
But *g* me first your hand : | „ ii 525
And he may die before he *g's* it ; | „ iii 407
will *g* him, as they say, a new lease of life. | „ iii 423
G me your arm. Lead me back again. | „ iii 473
I *g* him back to you again. | „ iii 675
shall I *g* her the first kiss ? | *Foresters* i i 126
I came to *g* the first kiss, and thou hast given
  it me. | „ i i 132
matter so much if the maid *g* the first kiss ? | „ i i 136
now thou hast given me the man's kiss, let me *g*
  thee the maid's. | „ i i 143
I will *g* thee a buffet on the face. | „ i i 146
Wilt thou not *g* me rather the little rose for Little John ? | „ i i 147
may the maid *g* the first kiss ? | „ i i 173
said that whenever I married he would *g* me away, | „ i i 288
there is no other man that shall *g* me away. | „ i i 291
I would *g* thee any gold So that myself | „ i ii 165
You shall *g* me the first kiss. | „ i ii 227
G me thy hand and tell him— | „ i ii 241
what we wring from them we *g* the poor. | „ ii i 56
I would *g* my life for thee, | „ ii i 189
I can spell the hand. *G* me thine. | „ ii i 351
I will *g* thee a silver penny if thou wilt show | „ ii i 359
O your honour, I pray you too to *g* me an alms. | „ ii i 389
G me a draught of wine. | „ ii i 458
Take him, good Little John, and *g* him wine. | „ ii i 469
G me some news of my sweet Marian. | „ ii i 481
G me thy glove upon it. | „ ii i 579
G it me, by heaven, Or I will force it from thee. | „ ii i 593
g us guides To lead us thro' the windings of the wood. | „ ii i 632
'Sell all thou hast and *g* it to the poor ; ' Take all
  they have and *g* it to thyself ! | „ iii 169
Bitters before dinner, my lady, to *g* you a relish. | „ iii 435
love that children owe to both I *g* To him alone. | „ iv 7
G me thy hand on that ? *Marian.* Take it. | „ iv 66
I am glad of it. *G* him back his gold again. | „ iv 182
that will *g* thee a new zest for it, | „ iv 208
G him the quarterstaff. | „ iv 250
I *g* thee A buffet, and thou me. | „ iv 262
G me thy hand, Much ; I love thee. At him, Scarlet ! | „ iv 309
G him another month, and he will pay it. *Justiciary.*
  We cannot *g* a month. | „ iv 443
G me my bow and arrows. | „ iv 603
g me one sharp pinch upon the cheek | „ iv 1011
G me that hand which fought for Richard there. | „ iv 1029

Given They have *g* me a safe conduct : | *Queen Mary* i ii 100
g A token of His more especial Grace ; | „ iii iii 169
God hath *g* Grace to repent and sorrow for their
  schism ; | „ iii iii 176
we by that authority Apostolic *G* unto us, | „ iii iii 211
God hath *g* your Grace a nose, or not, | „ iii v 203
Power hath been *g* you to try faith by fire— | „ iv ii 153
Done right against the promise of this Queen Twice *g*. | „ iv iii 457

Given (*continued*) We have *g* the church-lands back : *Queen Mary* v i 170
I have *g* her cause—I fear no woman.   *Harold* ii 40
God and the sea have *g* thee to our hands—   „ II ii 548
Stigand hath *g* me absolution for it.   „ II i 213
sorrow'd for my random promise *g* To yon fox-lion.   „ III i 269
king Hath *g* his virgin lamb to Holy Church   „ II i 334
And *g* thy realm of England to the bastard.   „ III ii 154
Thou hast *g* it to the enemy of our house.   „ IV ii 31
Holy Father Hath *g* this realm of England to the Norman.   „ v i 13
G me by my dear friend the King of England—   *Becket* I i 337
I pray God I haven't *g* thee my leprosy,   „ I iv 214
kingly promise *g* To our own self of pardon,   „ II i 432
warder of the bower hath *g* himself Of late to wine.   „ III i 30
had I fathered him I had *g* him more of the rod than the sceptre.   „ III iii 110
I think, time *g*, I could have talk'd   „ IV ii 311
had she but *g* Plain answer to plain query ?   „ IV ii 385
your ladyship has *g* him bitters enough in this world,   *The Falcon* 192
the man had *g* her a rose and she gave him another.   *Foresters* I i 110
I came to give thee the first kiss, and thou hast *g* it me.   „ I i 138
but I had sooner have *g* thee the first kiss.   „ I i 138
now thou hast *g* me the man's kiss, let me give thee the maid's.   „ I i 143
g my whole body to the King had *he* asked for it,   „ II i 305
but the cow ? *Robin.* She was *g* me.   „ II i 315
Giver if *g* And taker be but honest !   *Harold* I i 345
if She knew the *g*; but I bound the seller   *The Falcon* 72
Giving (*See also* **Life-giving**) My liberality perforce is dead Thro' lack of means of *g*.   „ 297
Glad We have been *g* together; let him live.   *Queen Mary* II iii 90
Cranmer, be thou *g*. This is the work of God.   „ IV iii 81
g to wreak our spite on the rosefaced minion   *Becket, Pro.* 528
I am *g* that France hath scouted him at last :   „ II ii 251
She will be *g* at last to wear my crown.   *The Cup* I iii 168
I am *g* I shall not see it.   „ II 512
an' owd Dobson should be *g* on it.   *Prom. of May* II 147
I am *g* it pleases you ;   „ II 543
There, I am *g* my nonsense has made you smile !   „ II 314
if this life of ours Be a good *g* thing,   *Foresters* I iii 13
I am *g* of it. Give him back his gold again.   „ IV 182
Glade My men say The fairies haunt this *g*;—   „ II ii 101
See that men be set Along the *g*'s and passes of the wood   „ III 457
Look, Robin, at the far end of the *g*   „ IV 332
Gladness Breathing an easy *g* . . . not like Aldwyth . . . *Harold* I ii 174
Glance (s) Philip with a *g* of some distaste,   *Queen Mary* III i 99
No *g* yet Of the Northumbrian helmet on the heath ? *Harold* v i 142
Dark even from a side *g* of the moon,   *Becket* IV i 148
to 'scape The *g* of John—   *Foresters* IV 463
Glance (verb) Before I dare to *g* upon your Grace. *Queen Mary* v v 186
whereby the curse might *g* From thee and England. *Harold* III i 343
Tho' in one moment she should *g* away,   *Foresters* I ii 161
Glanced But truth of story, which I *g* at, girl, *Queen Mary* III v 33
Has never *g* upon me when a child.   *Foresters* IV 5
Have ye *g* down thro' all the forest ways   „ IV 110
Glancing a Boleyn, too, *G* across the Tudor *Queen Mary* v v 228
Then, *g* thro' the story of this realm,   *Becket* I iii 410
now and then *g* about him like a thief at night   „ III iii 97
G at the days when his father was only Earl of Anjou,   „ III iii 149
Glare (s) this ghastly *g* May heat their fancies. *Harold* I i 309
from the squint Of lust and *g* of malice.   *Becket* I i 313
Like sudden night in the main *g* of day.   „ II i 57
Glare (verb) It *g*'s in heaven, it flares upon the Thames, *Harold* I i 29
for thine eyes *G* stupid-wild with wine.   „ II i
Glared execrable eyes, *G* at the citizen.   *Queen Mary* II ii 68
How their pointed fingers *G* at me !   *Harold* II ii 791
How the clown *g* at me ! that Dobbins, is it, *Prom. of May* II 611
Glaring *See* **Grimly-glaring**
Glass (barometer) weather's well anew, but the *g* be a bit shaäky.   *Prom. of May* II 51
Glass (substance) and my poor chronicle Is but of *g*. *Queen Mary* III v 47
fuse the *g*, And char us back again into the dust   „ III v 54
Glass (verb) and *g* The faithful face of heaven—   *Becket* II i 160
Glasses (spectacles) You see thro' warping *g*. *Queen Mary* I v 212
Glassy-smooth So far my course, albeit not *g-s*, *Becket* I iii 379
Gleam *G* upon gloom,   „ III i 277

Gleam (*continued*) Gloom upon *g*,   *Becket* III i 281
I never spied in thee one *g* of grace.   „ v ii 474
man perceives that The lost *g* of an after-life *Prom. of May* I 503
This world of mud, on all its idiot *g*'s Of pleasure,   „ III 722
Gleaming There lodged a *g* grimness in his eyes, *Harold* II ii 224
Glebe (adj.) thaw he niver mended that gap i' the *g* fence   *Prom. of May* I 446
Glebe (s) to the wave, to the *g*, to the fire ! *The Cup* II 4
Glen a fox from the *g* ran away with the hen, *Prom. of May* I 51
Lead us thou to some deep *g*,   *Foresters* II ii 168
Glide Seem'd as a happy miracle to make *g*— *Queen Mary* III ii 30
There is an arm'd man ever *g*'s behind ! *Harold* II i 247
G like a light across these woodland ways ! *Foresters* II i 159
Glided so she *g* up into the heart O' the bottle,   „ IV 244
Gliding Corpse-candles *g* over nameless graves— *Harold* III i 381
Two sisters *g* in an equal dance,   *Becket* I iii 444
Glimmer twilight of the coming day already *g*'s in the east.   *Foresters* I ii 248
Glimmering One coming up with a song in the flush of the *g* red ?   *Becket* II i 8
Glimpse Rome has a *g* of this conspiracy ; *The Cup* I ii 233
catch A *g* of them and of their fairy Queen— *Foresters* II ii 103
Glitter He *g*'s on the crowning of the hill. *Harold* v i 488
that's a finer thing there. How it *g*'s ! *Becket* IV i 2
Glittering all drown'd in love And *g* at full tide— *The Cup* II 234
Gloom I crept along the *g* and saw   *Queen Mary* III iii 17
g of Saul Was lighten'd by young David's harp.   „ v ii 358
Strange and ghastly in the *g*   *Harold* III iii 158
Gleam upon *g*,   *Becket* III i 277
G upon gleam,   „ III i 281
Glorified He is *g* In thy conversion : *Queen Mary* IV iii 82
But that Thy name by man be *g*,   „ IV iii 153
Die with him, and be *g* together.   *Becket* v iii 31
Glorify God grant me grace to *g* my God ! *Queen Mary* IV iii 166
Glorifying *See* **A-glorifying**
Glorious O blessed saint, O *g* Benedict,— *Becket* v iii 1
Glory there's no *g* Like his who saves his country : *Queen Mary* v i 109
But for the wealth and *g* of our realm,   „ II ii 210
misreport His ending to *g* of their church.   „ III iii 327
I have wrought miracles—to God the *g*— *Harold* I i 182
and our marriage and thy *g* Been drunk together !   „ IV iii 8
whether it symbol'd ruin Or *g*, who shall tell ?   „ v i 111
G to God in the Highest ! fallen, fallen !   „ v i 636
All I had I lavish'd for the *g* of the King; I shone from him, for him, his *g*, his Reflection : now the *g* of the Church Hath swallow'd up the *g* of the King;   *Becket* I iii 663
Power and great *g*—for thy Church, O Lord—   „ v iii 194
The *g* and grief of battle won or lost *The Cup* I ii 161
Hear thy priestesses hymn thy *g* !   „ II 7
That you may feed your fancy on the *g* of it,   „ II 134
and send him forth The *g* of his father—   „ II 263
make them happy in the long barn, for father is in his *g*,   *Prom. of May* I 792
There is a trade of genius, there's *g* ! *Foresters* IV 375
Gloss his manners want the nap And *g* of court ; *Queen Mary* v v 71
Glo'ster (Gloucester) and she brew'd the best ale in all *G*, *Becket* III 197
Glove Give me thy *g* upon it.   *Foresters* II i 579
A pair of *g*'s, a pair of *g*'s, sir; ha ? *Queen Mary* III i 270
The man shall paint a pair of *g*'s.   „ III i 274
Glow Dost thou not feel the love I bear to thee *G* thro' thy veins ? *Synorix.* The love I bear to thee *G*'s thro' my veins   *The Cup* II 427
Glowing-gay were as *g-g* As regal gardens ; *Queen Mary* III ii 12
Glowworm yellow silk here and there, and it looked pretty like a *g*,   *Becket* IV i 23
No, by wisp and *g*, no.   *Foresters* II ii 136
Glum What maäkes 'im allus sa *g* ? *Sally Allen.* *G* ! he be wuss nor *g*.   *Prom. of May* II 148
  Foresters III 92
Gnarl'd hundreds of huge oaks, *G*—   *Harold* I ii 71
Gnat A *g* that vext thy pillow !   *Foresters* I i 88
Gnawed The rats have *g* 'em already. *Queen Mary* I ii 83
Go (*See also* **Goä, Gwo**) God be with you ! *G*.   „ I ii 111
gentle friend, admit them. I will *g*.   „ I iii 98
My mother said, *G* up ; and up I went.

Go (*continued*) there are messengers That *g* between
us.   *Queen Mary* I iii 138
g zigzag, now would settle Upon this flower,   "   I iv 54
Why do you *g* so gay then?   "   I iv 70
Come, come, I will *g* with you to the Queen.   "   I iv 297
Your people, and I *g* with them so far,   "   I v 188
Bad you *g* softly with your heretics here,   "   I v 392
some believe that he will *g* beyond him.   "   I v 441
she *goes*, I warrant, not to hear the nightingales,   "   I v 463
Your apple eats the better. Let them *g*. They *g*
like those old Pharisees in John   "   II ii 7
Sir Thomas, pray you *g* away,   "   II iii 99
Don't ye now *g* to think that we be for Philip o' Spain.   "   II iii 105
come to save you all, And I'll *g* further off.   "   II iii 119
Pray you *g* on. (*repeat*)   "   III i 374, 389
I will *g* with you to the waterside.   "   III ii 148
No, my Lord Legate, the Lord Chancellor *goes*.   "   III ii 152
His sceptre shall *g* forth from Ind to Ind !   "   III ii 177
We might *g* softlier than with crimson rowel   "   III iv 182
And if he *g* not with you—   "   III iv 348
not like a word, That comes and *goes* in uttering.   "   III v 30
leisure wisdom of his Queen, Before he *g*,   "   III vi 24
for women To *g* twelve months in bearing   "   III vi 91
And *goes* to-morrow.   "   III vi 119
O Philip ! Nay, must you *g* indeed ?   "   III vi 192
But must you *g* ?   "   III vi 207
Your Majesty shall *g* to Dover with me,   "   III vi 218
I will *g* to Greenwich, So you will have me with you;   "   III vi 221
hang the leaders, let their following *g*.   "   IV i 75
you must look to Calais when I *g*. *Mary*. G? must
you *g*, indeed—   "   V i 17
G in, I pray you.   "   V i 214
Say *g*; but only say it lovingly.   "   V i 216
And panting for my blood as I *g* by.   "   V ii 219
Ah !—let him enter. Nay, you need not *g*:   "   V iii 11
You had best *g* home. What are you ?   "   V iv 43
Why, you long-winded— Sir, you *g* beyond me.   "   V iv 58
Good night ! G home. Besides, you curse so loud,   "   V iv 61
Thou light a torch that never will *g* out!   "   V v 122
see, he smiles and *goes*, Gentle as in life. *Alice.*
Madam, who *goes* ? King Philip ? *Mary*. No,
Philip comes and *goes*, but never *goes*.   "   V v 146
before I *g*, To find the sweet refreshment of the Saints.   *Harold* I i 176
I have fought the fight and *g*—   "   I i 185
if it pass. G not to Normandy—*g* not to Normandy.   "   I i 235
I pray thee, do not *g* to Normandy.   "   I i 249
Harold, I will not yield thee leave to *g*.   "   I i 257
G—the Saints Pilot and prosper all thy wandering   "   I i 263
How *goes* it then with thy Northumbria ?   "   I i 332
To follow thee to Flanders ! Must thou *g* ?   "   I ii 28
When Harold *goes* and Tostig, shall I play   "   I ii 163
And when doth Harold *g* ? *Morcar.* To-morrow—
—I will *g* with thee to-morrow—   "   I ii 238
   "   II ii 204
' I pray you do not *g* to Normandy.'   "   II ii 218
G not to Normandy— (*repeat*)   "   II ii 327
yield this iron-mooded Duke To let me *g*.   "   II ii 341
'Marry, the Saints must *g* along with us,   "   II ii 365
the lark sings, the sweet stars come and *g*,   "   II ii 435
Or lash'd his rascal back, and let him *g*.   "   II ii 507
And let him *g* ? To slander thee again !   "   II ii 508
My prayers *g* up as fast as my tears fall,   "   III i 166
not so with us—No wings to come and *g*.   "   III ii 99
I am weary—*g*: make me not wroth with thee !   "   V i 31
Gurth, Leofwin, *g* once more about the hill—   "   V i 182
G round once more; See all be sound and whole.   "   V i 192
Leave me. No more—Pardon on both sides—G !   "   V i 354
Obey my first and last commandment. G !   "   V i 359
After the battle—after the battle. G. *Aldwyth.* I *g*.   "   V i 363
G further hence and find him.   "   V ii 60
business Of thy whole kingdom waits me: let me *g*.   *Becket,* Pro. 279
Thou shalt not *g*. I have not ended with thee.   "   Pro. 305
Follow me this Rosamund day and night, whithersoever
she *goes*;   "   Pro. 507
That I should *g* against the Church with him, And I
shall *g* against him with the Church,   "   I i 93

Go (*continued*) G home, and sleep thy wine off, for thine eyes   *Becket* I i 212
What shall it be ? I'll *g* as a nun.   "   I i 301
G like a monk, cowling and clouding up   "   I i 311
G therefore like a friend slighted by one   "   I i 350
Not slighted—all but moan'd for: thou must *g*.   "   I i 353
G with her—at once—To-night—   "   I i 400
G, *g*—no more of this !   "   I ii 20
Customs, traditions,—clouds that come and *g*;   "   I iii 23
for if thou *g* against thy King, Then must he likewise
g against thy King,   "   I iii 207
Let us *g* in to the Council, where our bishops   "   I iii 547
I am confounded by thee. G in peace.   "   I iii 731
Ay, *g* in peace, caitiff, caitiff !   "   I iii 735
No; yet all but all. G, *g* !   "   I iv 28
Wilt thou not say, 'God bless you,' ere we *g* ?   "   I iv 33
Well, then, how does it *g* ?   "   I iv 118
we shall all be poisoned. Let us *g*.   "   I iv 244
I'll *g* back again. I hain't half done yet.   "   I iv 258
then to be made Archbishop and *g* against the King   "   II i 237
G try it, play.   "   II i 246
I must *g*; but when thou layest thy lip To this,   "   II i 305
Mince and *g* back ! his politic Holiness   "   II ii 45
that none may dream I *g* against God's honour—   "   II ii 168
said to the smoke, 'G up, my son, straight to Heaven.'
And the smoke said, 'I *g*;'   "   II ii 318
it was in him to *g* up straight if the time had been quieter.   "   II ii 324
there they *g*—both backs are turn'd to me—   "   II ii 453
I *g* to have young Henry crown'd by York.   "   II ii 478
Must you *g*, my liege, So suddenly ?   "   III i 84
all on us ha' had to *g*, bless the Saints,   "   III i 146
G, you shall tell me of her some other time.   "   III i 190
Nay—*g*. What ! will you anger me ?   "   III i 208
I hear Margery : I'll *g* play with her.   "   III i 274
I *g* myself—so many alleys,   "   IV ii 6
G. See that you do not fall in. G.   "   IV ii 58
you bid me *g*, and I'll have my ball anyhow.   "   IV ii 63
let me *g* With my young boy, and I will hide my face,   "   IV ii 97
Wilt thou *g* with him ? he will marry thee.   "   IV ii 162
The worm ! shall I let her *g* ?   "   IV ii 197
G, lest I blast thee with anathema,   "   IV ii 287
Lest I remember thee to the lion, *g*.   "   IV ii 292
rather *g* beyond In scourgings, macerations, mortifyings,   "   V i 40
That *goes* against our fealty to the King.   "   V ii 508
Valour and holy life should *g* together.   "   V ii 587
I *g* to meet my King !   "   V ii 620
It is God's will. G on.   "   V ii 635
get you back ! *g* on with the office.   "   V iii 33
Back, I say ! G on with the office.   "   V iii 39
I will *g* out and meet them.   "   V iii 52
Wake me before you *g*, I'll after you—   *The Cup* I ii 447
Shall I *g* ? Shall I *g* ? Death, torture—   "   I ii 452
I *g*, but I will have my dagger with me.   "   I ii 457
whither *g* you now ? *Camma.* To lodge this cup   "   I iii 51
Pray you, G on with the marriage rites.   "   II 399
G on with the marriage rites.   "   II 421
I will *g* To meet him, crown'd ?   "   II 518
There *goes* a musical score along with them,   *The Falcon* 452
That seem'd to come and *g*.   "   650
You hear, Filippo ? My good fellow, *g* !   "   691
Ay, prune our company of thine own and *g* !   "   696
I *g*. Master Dobson, did you hear what I said ?   *Prom. of May* I 171
to come together again in a moment and to *g* on
together again,   "   I 775
Now I must *g*.   "   II 524
Allow me to *g* with you to the farm.   "   II 574
Let bygones be bygones. G home ! Good-night !   "   III 157
Courage, courage ! and all will *g* well.   "   III 215
so that you do not copy his bad manners ? G, child.   "   III 362
'G home ;' but I hadn't the heart or face to do it.   "   III 389
G back to him and ask his forgiveness before he dies.—   "   III 401
You see she is lamed, and cannot *g* down to him.   "   III 416
to the grave he *goes* to, Beneath the burthen of years.   "   III 516
Than even I can well believe you, G !   "   III 815
'I *g* to fight in Scotland With many a savage clan;'   *Foresters* I i 14
I am all but sure of him. I will *g* to him.   "   I i 276

Go (continued)   but I know not if I will let thee *g*.
    Marian. I mean to *g*.   *Foresters* I i 312
Well, thou shalt *g*, but O the land ! the land !   ”   I i 327
More water *goes* by the mill than the miller wots of,
   and more *goes* to make right   ”   I ii 48
G now and ask the maid to dance with thee,   ”   I ii 185
What say you ? shall we *g* ?   ”   I iii 126
Then, Scarlet, thou at least wilt *g* with me.   ”   I iii 145
G with him. I will talk with thee anon.   ”   II i 132
I saw a *g* in, my lord.   ”   II i 207
let me *g* to make the mound : bury me in the mound,   ”   II i 311
Shall we not *g* ?   ”   II i 349
I pray thee *g*, *g*, for tho' thou wouldst bar   ”   II i 354
there *goes* one in the moonlight. Shoot !   ”   II i 394
Missed ! There *goes* another. Shoot, Sheriff !   ”   II i 397
But *g* not yet, stay with us, and when thy brother—   ”   II i 640
Yet are they twins and always *g* together. *Kate.*
    Well, well, until they cease to *g* together,   ”   II ii 66
Wherefore, wherefore should we *g*   ”   II ii 125
Only wherefore should we *g* ?   ”   II ii 137
One half of this shall *g* to those they have wrong'd,   ”   III 303
—a mere figure. Let it by.   ”   IV 221
is not he that *goes* against the king and the law   ”   IV 229
I *g* to Nottingham.   ”   IV 799
What ! *g* to slay his brother, and make *me*   ”   IV 804
Goä (go) Theer ye *g's* ageän, Miss,   *Prom. of May* I 106
But let that *g* by.   ”   I 199
noän o' the parishes *g's* by that naäme 'ereabouts.   ”   I 268
and now, as far as money *g's*, I be a gentleman,   ”   I 331
winder at the end o' the passage, that *g's* by thy
   chaumber.   ”   I 397
Theer she *g's* ! Shall I foller 'er and ax 'er   ”   II 130
I weänt *g* to owd Dobson ;   ”   II 218
and wants a hand, and I'll *g* to him.   ”   II 222
Scizzars an' Pumpy was good uns to *g* (repeat)   ”   II 308, 319
says the master *g's* cleän off his 'eäd when he 'eärs the
   naäme on 'im ;   ”   II 132
I warrants that ye *g's* By haäfe a scoor o' naämes—   ”   III 728
Goal I see the *g* and half the way to it.—   *Harold* I ii 196
in the racing toward this golden *g* He turns   ”   II ii 377
Goat See **Scape-goat, She-goat**
Goat-herd we found a *g-h's* hut and shared   *The Cup* I ii 426
Go-between Their Flemish *g-b* And all-in-all   *Queen Mary* III vi 4
God (s) (See also **Warrior-god**) *G* save her Grace ;   ”   I i 66
By *G's* light a noble creature, right royal !   ”   I i 68
G be with you. Go.   ”   I ii 82
I wrote it, and *G* grant me power to burn !   ”   I ii 98
I thank my *G* it is too late to fly.   ”   I ii 112
'Fore *G*, I think she entreats me like a child.   ”   I iii 111
some great doom when *G's* just hour Peals—   ”   I iv 261
my good mother came (*G* rest her soul)   ”   I v 11
O, just *G* ! Sweet mother,   ”   I v 22
G hath sent me here To take such order with all
   heretics   ”   I v 33
I am all thanks To *G* and to your Grace :   ”   I v 186
Pray *G* he do not be the first to break them,   ”   I v 269
G change the pebble which his kingly foot   ”   I v 368
G lay the waves and strow the storms at sea,   ”   I v 381
I pray *G* No woman ever love you,   ”   I v 601
By *G*, you are as poor a poet, Wyatt,   ”   II i 113
and if Philip come to be King, O, my *G* !   ”   II i 200
Or—if the Lord *G* will it—on the stake.   ”   II i 251
—'fore *G*, the rogues—   ”   II ii 96
G send her well ; Here comes her Royal Grace.   ”   II ii 125
I thank *G*, I have lived a virgin, and I noway doubt
   But that with *G's* grace, I can live so still. Yet
   if it might please *G* that I should leave Some fruit   ”   II ii 217
Speak ! in the name of *G* ?   ”   II ii 272
I trust this day, thro' *G*, I have saved the crown.   ”   II ii 302
But o' *G's* mercy don't ye kill the Queen here,   ”   II iii 110
And I, by *G*, believe myself a man.   ”   III i 168
G save their Graces ! (repeat)   *Queen Mary* III i 177, ” 187, 342, 412
G's passion ! knave, thy name ?   *Queen Mary* III i 248
Ha — Verbum Dei — verbum — word of *G* ! *G's*
   passion ! do you know the knave that painted it ?   ”   III i 263

God (s) (continued) Word of *G* In English !   *Queen Mary* III i 279
trusted *G* would save her thro' the blood   ”   III i 386
Their Graces, our disgraces ! *G* confound them !   ”   III i 415
which *G's* hand Wrote on her conscience,   ”   III i 421
But all is well ; 'twas ev'n the will of *G*,   ”   III i 77
' Hail, Daughter of *G*, and saver of the faith.   ”   III ii 82
Beheld our rough forefathers break their *G's*,   ”   III ii 121
Serve *G* and both your Majesties.   ”   III iii 159
G to this realm hath given A token   ”   III iii 168
first whom *G* hath given Grace to repent   ”   III iii 175
By him who sack'd the house of *G* ;   ”   III iii 195
Julius, *G's* Vicar and Viceregent upon earth,   ”   III iii 213
Trembled for her own *g's*, for these were trembling—   ”   III iv 128
For which *G's* righteous judgment fell upon you   ”   III iv 240
Nay, *G's* passion, before me ! speak !   ”   III iv 285
G upon earth ! what more ? what would you have ?   ”   III iv 383
He falters, ha ? 'fore *G*, we change and change ;   ”   III iv 406
G grant it last, And witness to your Grace's innocence,   ”   III v 49
G save the Queen !   ”   III v 170
G hath blest or cursed me with a nose—   ”   III v 178
O *G*, sir, do you look upon your boots,—   ”   III v 191
G hath given your Grace a nose, or not,   ”   III v 203
Pray *G*, we 'scape the sunstroke.   ”   III v 279
These are the means *G* works with,   ”   III vi 68
To whom he owes his loyalty after *G*,   ”   IV i 23
may *G* Forget me at most need when I forget Her
   foul divorce—   ”   IV i 79
It is *G's* will, the Holy Father's will,   ”   IV i 184
G grant you ampler mercy at your call   ”   IV i 189
May *G* help you Thro' that hard hour ! *Cranmer.*
   And may *G* bless you, Thirlby !   ”   IV ii 195
I not doubt that *G* will give me strength,   ”   IV ii 234
Cranmer, be thou glad. This is the work of *G*.   ”   IV iii 82
Remember how *G* made the fierce fire   ”   IV iii 89
if thou call on *G* and all the saints, *G* will beat
   down the fury of the flame,   ”   IV iii 96
O *G*, Father of Heaven ! O Son of *G*, Redeemer
   of the world !   ”   IV iii 116
Three persons and one *G*, have mercy on me,   ”   IV iii 121
Shall I despair then ?—*G* forbid ! O *G*. For thou
   art merciful, refusing none That come to Thee   ”   IV iii 129
O Lord *G*, although my sins be great,   ”   IV iii 135
O *G* the Son, Not for slight faults alone,   ”   IV iii 138
O *G* the Father, not for little sins   ”   IV iii 143
truth of *G*, which I have proven and known.   ”   IV iii 149
G grant me grace to glorify my *G* !   ”   IV iii 166
' Love of this world is hatred against *G*.' Again,
   I pray you all that, next to *G*,   ”   IV iii 174
Albeit he think himself at home with *G*,   ”   IV iii 193
Give to the poor, Ye give to *G*.   ”   IV iii 214
I do believe in *G*, Father of all ;   ”   IV iii 256
G bless him !   ”   IV iii 306
He looks to and he leans on as his *G*,   ”   IV iii 343
died As manfully and boldly, and, 'fore *G*,   ”   IV iii 369
beast might roar his claim To being in *G's* image,
owld lord fell to 's meat wi' a will, *G* bless un !   ”   IV iii 515
   but Gardiner wur struck down like by the hand
   o' *G*
There's nought but the vire of *G's* hell ez can burn
   out him.   ”   IV iii 527
Why then to heaven, and *G* ha' mercy on him.   ”   IV iii 631
Is *G's* best dew upon the barren field.   ”   V i 102
and therefore *G* Is hard upon the people.   ”   V i 175
and mine own natural man (It was *G's* cause) ;   ”   V ii 104
I hoped I had served *G* with all my might !   ”   V ii 296
G pardon me ! I had never yet found one.   ”   V ii 334
Mother of *G*, Thou knowest never woman   ”   V ii 341
G help me, but methinks I love her less   ”   V ii 420
by *G's* providence a good stout staff Lay near me ;   ”   V ii 468
light enough, *G* knows, And mixt with Wyatt's
   rising—   ”   V iii 36
as I love The people ! whom *G* aid !   ”   V iii 106
G's death ! and wherefore spake you not before ?   ”   V iii 119
Then I and he will snaffle your ' *G's* death,'   ”   V iii 123
G's death, forsooth—you do not know King Philip.

God (s) (*continued*)   *G* curse her and her Legate !   *Queen Mary* v iv 12

cries continually with sweat and tears to the Lord *G*	„ v iv 46
Poor enough in *G's* grace !	„ v v 50
I trust that *G* will make you happy yet.	„ v v 76
O *G* ! I have been too slack, too slack ;	„ v v 100
but by *G's* grace, We'll follow Philip's leading,	„ v v 111
Ay, Madam, but o' *G's* mercy—	„ v v 165
O *G*, I have kill'd my Philip !	„ v v 180
G guide me lest I lose the way.	„ v v 209
she loved much : pray *G* she be forgiven.	„ v v 271
Bagenhall. *G* save the Crown ! the Papacy is no more.	„ v v 283
G save the Queen !	„ v v 288
floated downward from the throne Of *G* Almighty.	*Harold* I i 19
in Normanland *G* speaks thro' abler voices,	„ I i 167
But dreading *G's* revenge upon this realm	„ I i 172
I have wrought miracles—to *G* the glory—	„ I i 181
Pray *G* the people choose thee for their king !	„ I i 314
that the shipwreckt are accursed of *G* :—	„ II i 101
by the splendour of *G*, no guest of mine.	„ II ii 26
My *G*, I should be there.	„ II ii 310
Our Duke is all about thee like a *G* ;	„ II ii 316
G and the sea have given thee to our hands—	„ II ii 548
bright sky cleave To the very feet of *G*,	„ II ii 743
O *G*, that I were in some wide, waste field	„ II ii 777
That sun may *G* speed !	„ III i 72
G bless thee, wedded daughter.	„ III i 293
for the king Is holy, and hath talk'd with *G*,	„ III i 355
Pray *G* that come not suddenly !	„ III i 364
G Has fill'd the quiver, and Death has drawn the bow—	„ III i 399
O *G* ! I cannot help it, but at times	„ III ii 63
when that which reign'd Call'd itself *G*.—	„ III ii 167
The Lord was *G* and came as man—the Pope Is man and comes as *G*.—	„ III ii 172
But I dare. *G* with thee !	„ III ii 188
G help me ! I know nothing—	„ III ii 193
in the name of the great *G*, so be it !	„ IV i 240
peace with what *G* gave us to divide us	„ IV iii 101
Here's to him, sink or swim ! *Thane.* *G* sink him !	„ IV iii 135
By *G*, we thought him dead—	„ IV iii 148
Hath harried mine own cattle—*G* confound him !	„ IV iii 190
And all the Heavens and very *G* : they heard—	„ v i 43
Tell him that *G* is nobler than the Saints,	„ v i 57
And bide the doom of *G*.	„ v i 61
If I fall, I fall—The doom of *G* !	„ v i 136
A snatch of sleep were like the peace of *G*.	„ v i 181
great *G* of truth Fill all thine hours with peace !—	„ v i 315
And not on thee—nor England—fall *G's* doom !	„ v i 371
And front the doom of *G*.	„ v i 436
O *G* of battles, make their wall of shields	„ v i 478
G save King Harold !	„ v i 489
Harold and *G* Almighty !	„ v i 526
O *G* of battles, make his battle-axe keen	„ v i 562
O *G* of battles, they are three to one,	„ v i 575
O *G*, the *G* of truth hath heard my cry.	„ v i 600
Glory to *G* in the Highest ! fallen, fallen !	„ v i 636
Whisper ! *G's* angels only know it.	„ v ii 31
my *G*, They have so maim'd and murder'd all his face	„ v ii 75
build a church to *G* Here on the hill of battle ;	„ v ii 137
till that blighted vow Which *G* avenged to-day.	„ v ii 157
by the splendour of *G*—have I fought men	„ v ii 177
pray *G* My Normans may but move as true	„ v ii 183
I would to *G* thou wert, for I should find	*Becket,* Pro. 86
Men are *G's* trees, and women are *G's* flowers ;	„ Pro. 111
No, my liege, no !—not once—in *G's* name, no !	„ Pro. 126
G's eyes ! I know all that—	„ Pro. 148
Would *G* she were—no, here within the city.	„ Pro. 179
G's favour and king's favour might so clash	„ Pro. 295
G's eyes ! what a lovely cross !	„ Pro. 370
And spake to the Lord *G*, and said,	„ I i 74
' O Lord my *G*, Henry the King hath been my friend,	„ I i 86
G make not thee, but thy foes, fall.	„ I i 106
'Fore *G*, I am a mightier man than thou.	„ I i 223
By *G's* death, thou shalt stick him like a calf !	„ I iii 183

God (s) (*continued*)   it is the will of *G* To break me,   *Becket* I iii 291

' False to myself ! It is the will of *G* ! ' *Henry.*	
G's will be what it will,	„ I iii 328
The King's will and *G's* will and justice ;	„ I iii 420
G's eyes ! I had meant to make him all but king.	„ I iii 464
The will of *G*—why, then it is my will—	„ I iii 473
The King's ' *G's* eyes ! ' come now so thick and fast,	„ I iii 609
For the King's pleasure rather than *G's* cause	„ I iii 697
G from me withdraws Himself, And the King too.	„ I iii 701
That thou obey, not me, but *G* in me,	„ I iii 721
Wilt thou not say, ' *G* bless you, 'ere we go ?	
Becket. ' *G* bless you all ! *G* redden your pale blood ! But mine is human-red ;	„ I iv 33
and see it mounting to Heaven, my *G* bless you,	„ I iv 38
Shall *G's* good gifts be wasted ?	„ I iv 70
his paws are past help. *G* help him.	„ I iv 111
dawns darkly and drearily over the house of *G*—	„ I iv 146
I pray *G* I haven't given thee my leprosy,	„ I iv 214
this beast-body That *G* has plunged my soul in—	„ II i 150
May *G* grant No ill befall or him or thee	„ II i 259
by *G's* eyes, we will not have him crown'd.	„ II ii 3
a perilous game For men to play with *G*.	„ II ii 71
and pray *G* she prove True wife to you.	„ II ii 77
Saving *G's* honour !	„ II ii 140
—that Is clean against *G's* honour—	„ II ii 163
that none may dream I go against *G's* honour—	„ II ii 168
Would *G* they had torn up all By the hard root,	„ II ii 207
to suppress *G's* honour for the sake Of any king that breathes. No, *G* forbid ! Henry. No ! *G* forbid !	„ II ii 220
No *G* but one, and Mahound is his prophet.	„ II ii 225
you shall have None other *G* but me—	„ II ii 229
who hath withstood two Kings to their faces for the honour of *G*—	„ II ii 277
I pray *G* pardon mine infirmity.	„ II ii 353
Yet they both love *G*.	„ II ii 376
O *G*, how many an innocent Has left his bones	„ II ii 407
Deny not thou *G's* honour for a king.	„ II ii 424
surrendering *G's* honour to the pleasure of a man.	„ II ii 440
Son, I absolve thee in the name of *G*.	„ II ii 443
G bless the great Archbishop !	„ II ii 451
G help her, That she was sworn to silence.	„ III i 77
G help her, she had 'em from her mother,	„ III i 185
O *G* ! some dreadful truth is breaking on me—	„ III i 265
puffed out such an incense of unctuosity into the nostrils of our *G's* of Church and State,	„ III iii 116
before *G* I promise you the King hath many	„ III iii 321
G and his free wind grant your lordship a happy home-return	„ III iii 326
The boy so late ; pray *G*, he be not lost.	„ IV ii 2
and *G* will be our guide.	„ IV ii 104
By very *G*, the cross I gave the King !	„ IV ii 199
Strike ! I challenge thee to meet me before *G*.	„ IV ii 254
G's grace and Holy Church deliver'd us.	„ IV ii 309
If *G* would take him in some sudden way—	„ v i 93
My liege, the Queen of England. *Henry.* *G's* eyes !	„ v i 98
The Church ! the Church ! *G's* eyes !	„ v i 217
Thou hast waged *G's* wars against the King ;	„ v ii 46
York against Canterbury, York against *G* !	„ v ii 67
G bless him for it.	„ v ii 146
G save him from all sickness of the soul !	„ v ii 174
this mother, runs thro' all The world *G* made—	„ v ii 243
G help thee !	„ v ii 296
things that are the King's, And those of *G* to *G*.	„ v ii 463
scare me from my loyalty To *G* and to the Holy Father.	„ v ii 483
foremost of their files, who die For *G*,	„ v ii 496
to people heaven in the great day When *G* makes up his jewels.	„ v ii 497
G's will be done ! (repeat)	*Becket* v ii 565, 567
It is *G's* will. Go on.	*Becket* v ii 634
No traitor to the King, but Priest of *G*,	„ v iii 113
G pardon thee and these, but *G's* full curse	„ v iii 133
I do commend my cause to *G*, the Virgin,	„ v iii 163
O *G*, O noble knights, O sacrilege !	„ v iii 178
O *G's* ! She is my fate—	*The Cup* I ii 11
Rome Made war upon the peoples not the *G's*.	„ I ii 61

God (s) (*continued*) to victory—I hope so—Like phantoms
 of the G's. *The Cup* I ii 170
for by the G's I seem Strange to myself. ,, I iii 76
to the fullest in the sight Of all the G's. ,, II 434
O all ye G's—Jupiter !—Jupiter ! ,, II 453
Dost thou cry out upon the G's of Rome ? ,, II 455
by the G's of Rome and all the world, ,, II 465
G rest his honest soul, he bought 'em for me, *The Falcon* 49
I ha' heard 'im a-gawin' on 'ud make your 'air—
 G bless it !—stan' on end. *Prom. of May* I 135
As flies to the G's ; they kill us for their sport. ,, I 264
The G's ! but they, the shadows of ourselves, ,, I 270
He, following his own instincts as his G, ,, I 589
O my G, if man be only A willy-nilly current of
 sensations— ,, II 261
At Michaelmas, Miss, please G. ,, III 113
pauper, who had died in his misery blessing G, ,, III 378
—the heart, O G !—the poor young heart ,, III 679
G bless our well-beloved Robin, Earl of Huntingdon. *Foresters* I i 247
And I will follow thee, and G help us both. ,, I i 278
G's good Angel Help him back hither, ,, I ii 10
G forbid ! (repeat) ,, I ii 93, 100
Ay G forbid, But if it be so we must bear with John. ,, I ii 101
The love of freedom, the desire of G, ,, II i 68
My G, thou art the very woman who waits ,, II i 101
for, G help us, we lie by nature. ,, II i 237
Is she not here with thee ? *Robin.* Would G she were ! ,, II i 493
My G—That such a brother— ,, II i 549
O G ! What sparkles in the moonlight on thy hand ? ,, II i 581
O G, I would the letter of the law ,, IV 514
When the Church and the law have forgotten G's
 music, ,, IV 555
Take the left leg for the love of G. ,, IV 578
by that same love of G we will hang *thee*, ,, IV 582
—G help the mark— ,, IV 714
G save the King ! ,, IV 857
God (verb) How the good priest g's himself ! *Becket* V iii 149
God-bless-her Cried no G-b-h to the Lady Jane, *Queen Mary* III iv 45
Goddess (*See also* **Love-goddess**) himself an adorer of our
 great g, Artemis, *The Cup* I i 38
cup saved from a blazing shrine Of our great G, ,, I i 56
I love you—for your love to the great G. ,, I ii 219
Wherefrom we make libation to the G ,, II 201
Call first upon the G, Synorix. ,, II 256
G, whose storm-voice Unsockets the strong oak, ,, II 281
I call on our own G in our own Temple. ,, II 314
Here is another sacred to the G, The gift of Synorix ;
 and the G, ,, II 346
Making libation to the G. ,, II 364
See first I make libation to the G, ,, II 377
Libation to the G. ,, II 387
Why then the G hears. ,, II 388
God-father King, thy g-f, gave it thee when a baby. *Foresters* I i 285
Godless this cooler sun of England hath In breed-
 ing g vermin. *Queen Mary* III iv 329
She thank'd her father sweetly for his book
 Against that g German. ,, V v 238
Godric More likely G. *Harold* V i 66
Godstow (adj.) Come thou with me to G nunnery, *Becket* IV ii 366
To put her into G nunnery. (repeat) ,, V ii 208, 209
Godstow (s) Into G, into Hellstow, Devilstow ! ,, V i 215
Godstow-Becket This G-B intermeddling such ,, IV ii 457
Godwin (Earl of the West Saxons) (*See also* **Half-Godwin**)
 powers of the house of G Are not enframed in thee. *Harold* I i 316
sons of G Sit topmost in the field of England, ,, I i 325
Unwholesome talk For G's house ! ,, I i 391
feuds that part The sons of G from the sons of Alfgar ,, II i 180
Am I Harold, Harold, son Of our great G ? ,, II ii 793
Remain a hostage for the loyalty Of G's house.' ,, III i 91
I have heard a saying of thy father G, ,, III i 112
There spake G, Who hated all the Normans ; ,, III i 251
G still at feud with Alfgar, ,, IV i 123
That is noble ! That sounds of G. ,, IV ii 58
Come thou back, and be Once more a son of G. ,, IV ii 60
Thou hast no passion for the House of G— ,, IV ii 73

Godwin (Earl of the West Saxons) (*continued*) Noble Gurth !
 Best son of G ! *Harold* V i 135
advise the king Against the race of G. ,, V i 282
and the race of G Hath ruin'd G. ,, V i 293
Goest And waste the land about thee as thou g, ,, V i 131
Thou g beyond thyself in petulancy ! *Becket* I iii 65
Now as Archbishop g against the King ; ,, I iii 530
Going (part.) (*See also* **A-gawin', A-going, Gawin,**
 Straight-going) g now to the Tower to loose
 the prisoners *Queen Mary* I i 108
Well, I am g. ,, III vi 171
He can but stay a moment : he is g. *Harold* I ii 4
Oh ! that thou wert not g ! ,, I ii 75
You are g to the Castle, *Becket* II ii 45
G to the Holy Land to Richard ! *Foresters* I ii 240
Going (s) three days in tears For Philip's g— *Queen Mary* III vi 14
I could mould myself To bear your g better ; ,, III vi 236
And you will stay your g ? ,, V i 186
Then it is done ; but you will stay your g ,, V i 206
Gold Velvet and g. This dress was made me ,, I iv 71
set it round with g, with pearl, with diamond. ,, I v 375
We'll dust him from a bag of Spanish g. ,, I v 422
not with g, But dearest links of love. ,, I v 538
Spain moves, bribes our nobles with her g, ,, II i 203
on his neck a collar, G, thick with diamonds ; ,, III i 80
Gardiner buys them With Philip's g. ,, III i 145
Were you in Spain, this fine fair gossamer g— ,, V iii 49
Your Philip hath g hair and golden beard ; ,, V iii 56
You have a g ring on your finger, ,, V iv 32
In mine earldom A man may hang g bracelets on
 a bush, *Harold* II i 87
if not with g, With golden deeds and iron strokes ,, II ii 46
jewel of St. Pancratius Woven into the g. ,, II ii 701
Red g—a hundred purses—yea, and more ! ,, III i 18
Standard of the Warrior, Dark among gems and g ; ,, IV i 249
thou shalt have our love, our silence, and our g— *Becket,* Pro. 492
This Almoner hath tasted Henry's g. The cardinals
 have finger'd Henry's. ,, I iii 294
As g Outvalues dross, light darkness, ,, I iii 714
till the weight of Germany or the g of England ,, II ii 364
leave Lateran and Vatican in one dust of g— ,, II ii 475
she sits naked by a great heap of g in the middle of
 the wood, ,, III ii 21
No—no g. Mother says g spoils all. Love is the
 only g. ,, IV i 42
fondest pair of doves will jar, Ev'n in a cage of g, ,, V ii 42
I would that happiness were g, *The Cup* II 223
a hundred G pieces once were offer'd by the Duke. *The Falcon* 324
ransomed for two thousand marks in g. *Foresters* I i 65
nor of the g, nor the man who took out the g : ,, I i 74
I have lost my g, I have lost my son, ,, I i 338
Good Prince, art thou in need of any g ? *Prince John.*
 G ? why ? not now. *Sheriff.* I would give thee any
 g So that myself ,, I ii 163
I ran into my debt to the Abbot, Two thousand marks
 in g. ,, II i 464
These two have forty g marks between them, Robin. ,, III 202
Leave it with him and add a g mark thereto. ,, III 211
Take his penny and leave him his g mark. ,, III 218
I have one mark in g which a pious son of the Church ,, III 280
Well, as he said, one mark in g. ,, III 285
One mark in g. ,, III 287
they have each ten marks in g. ,, III 292
alchemy Should change this g to silver, why, the silver
 Were dear as g, ,, IV 40
But being o' John's side we must have thy g. ,, IV 158
I am glad of it. Give him back his g again. ,, IV 183
But I had liefer than this g again— ,, IV 185
Would buy me for a thousand marks in g— ,, IV 653
Much lighter than a thousand marks in g ; ,, IV 658
Is weightier than a thousand marks in g. ,, IV 661
Who thought to buy your marrying me with g. ,, IV 719
Here is thy g again. I am sorry for it. ,, IV 985
The g—my son—my g, my son, the land— ,, IV 987
Gold-dust For that is Philip's g-d, and adore *Queen Mary* III iii 243

Good (*continued*)   Have you *g* hopes of mercy !   So, farewell. *Queen Mary* IV ii 86

G hopes, not theirs, have I that I am fixt, Fixt beyond fall ; „ IV ii 88

G day, old friend ; what, you look somewhat worn ; „ IV ii 115

Weep not, *g* Thirlby. „ IV ii 172

G people, every man at time of death Would fain set forth „ IV iii 156

But do you *g* to all As much as in you lieth. „ IV iii 186

Hear him, my *g* brethren. „ IV iii 227

And watch a *g* man burn. „ IV iii 293

Out Daisy's as *g* 'z her. „ IV iii 479

Our Daisy's butter's as *g* 'z hern. „ IV iii 481

for a *g* pleace at the burnin' ; „ IV iii 489

I wish you a *g* morning, *g* Sir Nicholas : „ v 13

So far, *g*.   I say I came to sue your Council and yourself „ v 113

G, now ; methinks my Queen is like enough To leave me by and by. „ v i 241

G !   Renard, I will stay then. „ v i 305

And so must you, *g* cousin ;—worse than all, „ v ii 39

What said you, my *g* lord, that our brave English „ v ii 254

what *g* could come of that ? „ v ii 309

G Lord ! how grim and ghastly looks her Grace, „ v ii 389

But by God's providence a *g* stout staff Lay near me ; „ v ii 468

He is my *g* friend, and I would keep him so ; „ v iii 91

Ah, *g* neighbour, There should be something fiercer than fire „ v iv 24

G night !   Go home.   Besides, you curse so loud, „ v iv 61

Nay, dearest lady, see your *g* physician. „ v v 59

G counsel yours—No one in waiting ?   still, „ v v 202

How is the *g* Queen now ? „ v v 229

Albeit no rolling stone, my *g* friend Gamel, *Harold* i i 93

To-day, *g* Earl. „ i i 106

Deeper into the mysteries of heaven Than thou, *g* brother. „ i i 201

What lies upon the mind of our *g* king „ i i 269

Like the rough bear beneath the tree, *g* brother, „ i i 328

G counsel truly !   I heard from my Northumbria yesterday. „ i i 330

Ay, ever give yourselves your own *g* word. „ i i 343

G again !   *G* counsel tho' scarce needed. „ i i 375

I have to make report of my *g* earldom To the *g* king who gave it— „ i i 406

Nay, my *g* sister— „ i i 462

Thou shalt flash it secretly Among the *g* Northumbrian folk, „ i ii 220

Help the *g* ship, showing the sunken rock, „ ii ii 100

G !   But lest we turn the scale of courtesy „ ii ii 163

'Tis the *g* Count's care for thee ! „ ii ii 251

Obey the Count's conditions, my *g* friend. „ ii ii 276

our *g* King Kneels mumbling some old bone— „ ii ii 467

But thou and he drove our *g* Normans out From England, „ ii ii 525

Be careful of thine answer, my *g* friend. „ ii ii 605

G, *g*, and thou wilt help me to the crown ? „ ii ii 613

G brother, By all the truths that ever priest hath preach'd, „ iii i 96

Sign it, my *g* son Harold, Gurth, and Leofwin, „ iii i 199

and those Who make thy *g* their own— „ iii i 330

O *g* son !   That knowledge made him all the carefuller „ iii i 339

I know all Sussex ;   A *g* entrenchment for a perilous hour ! „ iii i 363

Where all *g* things are lost, where Tostig lost The *g* hearts of his people. „ iii ii 28

G even, my *g* brother !   *Gurth*.   *G* even, gentle Edith.   *Edith*.   *G* even, Gurth. „ iii ii 116

The *G* Shepherd !   Take this, and render that. „ iii ii 169

when our *g* hive Needs every sting to save it. „ iv i 17

So the *g* king would deign to lend an ear Not overscornful, „ iv i 135

With *g* will ;   Yes, take the Sacrament upon it, king. „ iv i 182

We never—oh ! *g* Morcar, speak for us, „ iv i 216

Evil for *g*, it seems, Is oft as childless of the *g* as evil For evil. „ v i 171

G for *g* hath borne at times A bastard false as William. „ v i 174

I will, *g* brother. „ v i 199

perjury-mongering Count Hath made too *g* an use of Holy Church „ v i 312

Good (*continued*)   Yea so, *g* cheer ! thou art Harold, I am Edith ! *Harold* v i 391

Lo ! our *g* Gurth hath smitten him to the death. „ v i 502

Ay, *g* father. „ v i 516

So then our *g* Archbishop Theobald Lies dying. *Becket*, Pro. 1

and most amorous Of *g* old red sound liberal Gascon wine : „ Pro. 100

That palate is insane which cannot tell A *g* dish from a bad, „ Pro. 106

G dogs, my liege, well train'd, „ Pro. 119

My *g* liege, if a man Wastes himself among women, „ Pro. 136

but *Nolo Archiepiscopari*, my *g* friend, „ Pro. 286

My liege, the *g* Archbishop is no more. „ Pro. 392

The *g* old man would sometimes have his jest— „ i i 61

Our *g* John Must speed you to your bower at once. „ i i 290

What, not *g* enough Even to play at nun ? „ i i 303

G night !   *g* night ! „ i i 313

Send the Great Seal by daybreak.   Both, *g* night ! „ i i 406

He had *g* eyes ! „ i ii 38

G ears too ! „ i ii 44

Ay, *g* Madam ! „ i ii 90

And with *g* reason too, „ i iii 58

And was thine own election so canonical, *G* father ? „ i iii 122

O my *g* lord, I do entreat thee—sign. „ i iii 185

Loyally and with *g* faith, my lord Archbishop ? „ i iii 278

O ay, with all that loyalty and *g* faith „ i iii 281

G royal cousins—had them written fair For John of Oxford „ i iii 415

Permit me, my *g* lord, to bear it for thee, „ i iii 490

O my *g* lord Leicester, The King and I were brothers. „ i iii 660

Shall God's *g* gifts be wasted ? „ i iv 71

My friends, the Archbishop bids you *g* night. „ i iv 261

Something *g*, or thou wouldst not give it me. „ ii ii 233

Ay, ay, *g* brother, They call you the Monk-King. „ ii ii 72

Come, confess, *g* brother, „ ii ii 82

O *g* son Louis, do not counsel me, „ ii ii 219

my *g* lord, We that are kings are something in this world, „ ii ii 244

Better have been A fisherman at Bosham, my *g* Herbert, „ ii ii 292

My one grain of *g* counsel which you will not swallow. „ ii ii 378

Long live the *g* King Louis ! „ ii ii 451

I am bound For that one hour to stay with *g* King Louis, „ iii iii 247

This is the second grain of *g* counsel I ever proffered thee, „ iii iii 318

I am the fairy, pretty one, a *g* fairy to thy mother. „ iv i 26

There are *g* fairies and bad fairies, „ iv i 28

I am her *g* fairy.   *Geoffrey*.   But you don't look like a *g* fairy. „ iv i 34

And leave you alone with the *g* fairy. „ iv ii 61

My *g* Fitzurse, The running down the chase is kindlier sport „ iv ii 211

that our *g* Henry Says many a thing in sudden heats, „ iv ii 275

when I strove To work against her license for her *g*, „ iv ii 341

York and myself, and our *g* Salisbury here, „ v i 56

Yes : a man may take *g* counsel Ev'n from his foe. „ v ii 3

when he lets his whole self go Lost in the common *g*, „ v ii 40

I know him ;   our *g* John of Salisbury. „ v ii 77

No, daughter, you mistake our *g* Archbishop ; „ v ii 138

How the *g* Archbishop reddens ! „ v ii 298

O my *g* lord, Speak with them privately on this hereafter. „ v ii 418

G !   let them arm. „ v ii 571

My two *g* friends, What matters murder'd here, or murder'd there ? „ v ii 629

How the *g* priest gods himself ! „ v iii 148

ye will die the death of dogs ! Nay, nay, *g* Tracy. „ v iii 185

I can no more—fight out the *g* fight—die Conqueror. „ v iii 189

may even drown you In the *g* regard of Rome. *The Cup* i i 151

I tell thee, my *g* fellow, *My* arrow struck the stag. „ i ii 27

My *g* Lord Sinnatus, I once was at the hunting of a lion. „ i ii 115

You, Strato, make *g* cheer till I return. „ i ii 205

G !   *Camma*.   If I be not back in half an hour, Come after me. „ i ii 436

Or, *g*, or wise, that you should clasp a hand „ ii 82

G ! mine own dagger driven by Synorix found All *g* in the true heart of Sinnatus, „ ii 85

Gorgeous   the *g* Indian shawl That Philip brought
me in our happy days!—   *Queen Mary* v ii 538
Gorgeousness   Some golden fringe of *g* beyond   *The Cup* ii 438
Gospeller   and the Hot *G's* will go mad upon it.   *Queen Mary* i i 115
Yon gray old *G*, sour as midwinter,   „   i iii 40
Not dream'd of by the rabidest *g*.   „   iii vi 138
there be two old gossips—*g's*, I take it;   „   iv iii 460
There are Hot *G's* even among our guards—   „   v v 102
Gossamer   Were you in Spain, this fine fair *g* gold—   „   v iii 48
Gossip   Hist! there be two old *g's*—gospellers,   „   iv iii 460
Gossiping   with no fear Of the world's *g* clamour,   *Prom. of May* i 528
Got   And I *g* it. I woke Sir Henry—   *Queen Mary* iii v 59
afoor I coomed up he *g* thruff the winder ageän.
Eva.   *G* thro' the window again?   *Prom. of May* i 405
Then she *g* me a place as nursery governess,   „   iii 385
Gothic   Some few of *G* blood have golden hair,   *Queen Mary* v iii 60
Gotten   Owd Steer's *g* all his grass down and wants a
hand,   *Prom. of May* ii 221
The beer's *g* oop into my 'eäd,   „   ii 320
Gout   small hope of the gentleman *g* in my great toe.   *The Falcon* 657
' I hope your Lordship is quite recovered of
your *g*?'   *Prom. of May* iii 309
Rogue, I am full of *g*. I cannot dance.   *Foresters* iv 562
Sweat out your *g*, friend, for by my life,   „   iv 565
Govern   Whose ministers they be to *g* you.   *Queen Mary* iv iii 180
Ye *g* milder men.   *Harold* i 339
Governance   Against thy brother Tostig's *g*;   „   ii ii 290
We have heard Of thy just, mild, and equal *g*;   „   ii ii 690
Governess   Then she got me a place as a nursery *g*,   *Prom. of May* iii 385
Government   We have made them milder by just *g*.   *Harold* i i 341
and by the advice of his *G*.'   *Becket* i iii 113
Gown   Disguise me—thy *g* and thy coif.   *Foresters* i i 186
Ay, ay, *g*, coif, and petticoat,   „   ii i 194
Graäy (gray)   Wi' the briar sa green, an' the willer
sa *g*,   *Prom. of May* ii 187
Grace (s)   (*See also* **Herb-of-grace**) God save her *G*;   *Queen Mary* i,i 67
whether her *G* incline to this splendid scion of
Plantagenet.   „   i i 134
The Queen would see your *G* upon the moment.   „   i iv 222
Your *G* will hear her reasons from herself.   „   i iv 230
Whereof 'tis like enough she means to make A farewell
present to your G.   „   i iv 245
Goodly enough, your *G*, and yet, methinks, I have seen
goodlier.   „   i v 5
By your *G's* leave Your royal mother came of Spain,   „   i v 15
I cannot, and I dare not, tell your *G* What Lady Jane
replied.   „   i v 49
—a head So full of *g* and beauty!   „   i v 64
I say your *G* is loved.   „   i v 131
I am all thanks To God and to your *G*:   „   i v 186
Hath your *G* so sworn?   „   i v 217
In some such form as least may harm your *G*.   „   i v 226
your *G* And kingdom will be suck'd into the war,   „   i v 256
Nay, pure phantasy, your *G*.   „   i v 280
but I protest Your *G's* policy hath a farther flight   „   i v 312
Who waits? *Usher.* The Ambassador of Spain, your *G*.   „   i v 343
Nay, your *G*, it hath not reach'd me.   „   i v 351
You are happy in him there, Chaste as your *G*!   „   i v 456
What slanders? I, your *G*; no, never. *Mary.* Nothing?
Alice. Never, your *G*.   „   i v 572
I scarce had left your *G's* presence   „   i v 583
must we levy war against the Queen's *G*? *Wyatt.* No,
my friend, war *for* the Queen's *G*—to save her from
herself and Philip—   „   ii i 187
When will her *G* be here?   „   ii ii 13
Here comes her Royal *G*.   „   ii ii 126
But that with God's *G*, I can live so still.   „   ii ii 219
but we can save your *G*. The river still is free.   „   ii iv 24
No, no, your *G*; see there the arrows flying.   „   ii iv 50
The porter, please your *G*, hath shut the gates On friend
and foe. Your gentlemen-at-arms, If this be not your
G's order,   „   ii iv 61
I do not love your *G* should call me coward. *Messenger.*
Over, your *G*, all crush'd;   „   ii iv 88
God save their *G's*. (repeat).   *Queen Mary* iii i 178, 187, 343, 413

Grace (s) (*continued*)   Seventeen—a rose of *g*!   *Queen Mary* iii i 371
Their *G's*, our disgraces! God confound them!   „   iii i 415
Farewell, your *G's*.   „   iii ii 146
Mine echoes both your *G's*;   „   iii iii 96
Lo! once again God to this realm hath given A token
of His more especial *G*;   „   iii iii 170
G to repent and sorrow for their schism;   „   iii iii 177
their two *G's* Do so dear-cousin and royal-cousin him,   „   iii iv 398
Why do they keep us here? Why still suspect your *G*?   „   iii v 17
And witness to your *G's* innocence.   „   iii v 50
Before I dare to glance upon your *G*.   „   iii v 186
See, I lay it here, For I will come no nearer to your *G*;   „   iii v 200
And God hath given your *G* a nose, or not,   „   iii v 203
O Lord! your *G*, your *G*,   „   iii v 248
And had your *G* a Robin?   „   iii v 273
A *g* to me! Mercy, that herb-of-grace,   „   iii vi 9
when last he wrote, declared His comfort in your *G*   „   iii vi 79
Your *G* hath a most chaste and loving wife.   „   iii vi 129
Your *G's* business will not suffer, sire,   „   iii vi 244
Crave, in the same cause, hearing of your *G*.   „   iv i 9
Health to your *G*! Good morrow, my Lord Cardinal;
We make our humble prayer unto your *G*   „   iv i 41
Ay, ay, your *G*; but it was never seen That any one
recanting thus at full,   „   iv i 57
These are but natural *g's*, my good Bishop.   „   iv i 176
After this, Your *G* will hardly care to overlook   „   iv i 192
By Heaven's *g*, I am more and more confirm'd.   „   iv ii 21
Sire, if your *G* hath mark'd it, so have I.   „   v i 231
That if your *G* hath mark'd her, so have I.   „   v i 239
and your *G*, So you will take advice of mine,   „   v i 300
Your *G* hath been More merciful to many a rebel head   „   v ii 4
what sin Beyond all *g*, all pardon?   „   v ii 340
Your *G* hath a low voice.   „   v ii 378
Good Lord! how grim and ghastly looks her *G*,   „   v ii 390
Ay, so your *G* would bide a moment yet.   „   v ii 546
I trust your *G* is well.   „   v ii 551
But shall I take some message from your *G*?   „   v ii 597
Then I may say your *G* will see your sister? Your
G is too low-spirited.   „   v ii 603
But as to Philip and your *G*—consider,—   „   v iii 64
I gather'd from the Queen That she would see your
G before she—died.   „   v iii 104
Poor enough in God's *g*!   „   v v 50
I will, if that May make your *G* forget yourself a little.   „   v v 81
by God's *g*, We'll follow Philip's leading,   „   v v 111
I never spied in thee one gleam of *g*.   *Becket* v ii 474
Is strength less strong when hand-in-hand with *g*?   „   v ii 541
and ' your *G*' are all growing old-fashioned   *Prom. of May* iii 318
So winsome in her *g* and gaiety,   „   iii 754
Nay, an please your Elfin *G*,   *Foresters* ii ii 132
For if he did me the good *g* to kick me   „   iv 364
Not now, not now—with after-dinner *g*.   „   iv 938
Grace (verb)   To *g* his memory.   *Queen Mary* ii i 31
My cottage, while you *g* it, is a palace.   *The Falcon* 288
thy father will not *g* our feast With his white beard
to-day.   *Foresters* iv 80
Graced   Much *g* are we that our Queen Rome in you   *The Cup* ii 335
Graceless   That were a *g* hospitality To chain the free quest   *Harold* ii ii 192
Gracious   seeing that our *g* Virgin Queen hath—   *Queen Mary* i iii 23
—and since our *G* Queen, let me call her our second
Virgin Mary,   „   i iii 56
But does your *g* Queen entreat you kinglike?   „   i iii 109
I follow your good counsel, *g* uncle.   „   i iv 186
would that mine Were half as *g*!   „   i v 66
A *g* guard Truly; shame on them! they have shut the
gates!   „   ii iv 56
That by your *g* means and intercession   „   iii iii 121
and there watch All that is *g* in the breath of heaven   „   iii vi 224
O, Madam, if you knew him As I do, ever gentle, and so *g*,   „   iv i 156
Such weeds make dunghills *g*.   „   iv i 182
He had his *g* moment, Altho' you'll not believe me.   „   v v 37
A gentle, *g*, pure, and saintly man!   *Harold* ii ii 584
Well, well, we will be gentle with him, *g*—Most *g*.   *Becket* ii ii 129
will not your Holiness Vouchsafe a *g* answer to your
Queen?   „   iv ii 359

Gracious (*continued*) So *g* toward women, never yet Flung
    back a woman's prayer.   *The Cup* I ii 299
    And be you *G* enough to let me know the boon   *The Falcon* 765
    It will be all the more *g* of her if she do.   *Foresters* I i 175
Grafted And *g* on the hard-grain'd stock of Spain— *Queen Mary* IV iii 426
Grain (corn) And roll the golden oceans of our *g*, *The Cup* II 269
    strows our fruits, and lays Our golden *g*,   „ II 287
    and why ye have so few *g*'s to peck at.   *Foresters* I i 77
Grain (particle) My one *g* of good counsel which you will
    not swallow.   *Becket* II ii 378
    second *g* of good counsel I ever proffered thee,   „ III iii 317
Grain'd *See* **Hard-grain'd**
Gramercy *G* for thy preachment !   *Foresters* IV 397
Granada *G*, Naples, Sicily, and Milan,—   *Queen Mary* V i 44
Grand a thousand times Fitter for this *g* function.   *Becket, Pro.* 293
Grandfather My *g*—of him They say, that women— *Prom. of May* II 271
    my great great great *g*, my great great *g*, my great *g*,
    my *g*, and my own father—   *Foresters* I i 329
Grandsire Lost in desuetude, of my *g*'s day—   *Becket* I iii 413
    His *g* struck my *g* in a brawl At Florence, and my *g*
    stabb'd   *The Falcon* 250
Grandson only *g* To Wulfnoth, a poor cow-herd. *Harold* IV i 69
    cottage of yours where your *g* had the fever. *Prom. of May* III 44
Grange her advowsons, *g*'s, farms, And goodly acres— *Becket* I i 161
Granny *G* says marriages be maäde i' 'eaven. *Prom. of May* III 709
Grant I wrote it, and God *g* me power to burn ! *Queen Mary* I ii 98
    g me my prayer: Give me my Philip;   „ I v 85
    Sir Thomas, we may *g* the wine.   „ II i 40
    Is now content to *g* you full forgiveness,   „ III iv 389
    God *g* it last, And witness to your Grace's innocence, „ III v 49
    God *g* your ampler mercy at your call   „ IV i 189
    God *g* me grace to glorify my God !   „ IV iii 166
    If ever, as heaven *g*, we clash with Spain,   „ IV iii 346
    By loss of Calais. *G* me Calais.   „ V iii 305
    Have you found mercy there, *G* it me here: „ V v 145
    So that you *g* me one slight favour.   *Becket* I ii 58
    we *g* when kings are dangerous The Church must play „ I i 67
    he would *g* thee The crown itself.   „ I iii 29
    G me one day To ponder these demands.   „ I iii 667
    May God *g* No ill befall or him or thee   „ II i 259
    we *g* the Church King over this world's kings,   „ II ii 241
    God and his free wind *g* your lordship a happy home-return „ III iii 327
    By granting which, if aught be mine to *g*,   *The Falcon* 768
    Then they would *g* you what they call a licence *Prom. of May* I 694
Granted Old Sir Thomas always *g* the wine.   *Queen Mary* II i 42
    Why, good ! what then ? *g* !—   „ III iv 78
    It shall be *g* him, my king;   *Harold* III i 227
Granting let me know the boon By *g* which,   *The Falcon* 767
Grape These *g*'s are for the house of Sinnatus— *The Cup* I i 51
    may this mouth Never suck *g* again,   *Foresters* IV 394
Grape-bunches sway the long *g-b* of our vines, *The Cup* II 270
Grapple stand beside thee One who might *g* with thy
    dagger,   *Becket* IV ii 230
    He would *g* with a lion like the King,   *Foresters* I i 185
Grappling and the mitre *G* the crown—   *Becket* II i 27
Grasp (s) in his *g* a sword Of lightnings,   *Harold* III i 136
    Why, what a cold *g* is thine—   *Foresters* III i 242
Grasp (verb) should have a hand To *g* the world with, *Harold* V ii 192
Graspt have *g* Her livings, her advowsons,   *Becket* I i 160
Grass balmy wind to robe our hills with *g*,   *The Cup* II 266
    she had thrown my chaplet on the *g*,   *The Falcon* 369
    Had she not thrown my chaplet on the *g*,   „ 378
    if you'd like to measure your own length upon the *g*. *Prom. of May* I 466
    Owd Steer's gotten all his *g* down and wants a hand, „ II 221
Grasshopper *G*, *g*, Whoop—you can hear.   *Becket* I ii 102
Grateful All the church is *g*.   *Queen Mary* I v 179
    Most loyal and most *g* to the Queen.   „ V iii 25
    You should be *g* to my master, too.   „ V iii 27
    And *g* to the hand that shielded him,   *Harold* II ii 586
    —am *g* for thine honest oath,   „ II ii 755
    For which she should be duly *g*.   *Becket* I ii 74
    I should be *g*—He hath not excommunicated *me*. „ V ii 470
    g that I show'd her The weakness   *The Cup* I i 21
    and the Goddess, being For this most *g*,   „ II 349
    That one, then, should be *g* for your preference. *Prom. of May* II 556

Grateful (*continued*) one that should be *g* to me overseas,
    a Count in Brittany—   *Foresters* I i 270
    so you would make it two I should be *g*.   „ III 195
Gratefully O Dora, he signed himself 'Yours *g*'—
    fancy, Dora, '*g*' ! 'Yours *g*' !   *Prom. of May* III 334
Gratefulness If ever man by bonds of *g*—   *Becket* I iii 435
Gratia Ave Maria, *g* plena, Benedicta tu in mulieribus. *Queen Mary* III ii 1
Grating Close to the *g* on a winter morn   *The Falcon* 441
Gratior *G* in pulchro corpore virtus.   *Becket* V ii 542
Grave (adj.) look'd As grim and *g* as from a funeral. *Queen Mary* II ii 65
    We fought like great states for *g* cause;   *Harold* I i 440
Grave (s) Dug from the *g* that yawns for us beyond; *Queen Mary* I iii 163
    A low voice from the dust and from the *g*   „ V ii 386
    And wear my crown, and dance upon my *g*.   „ V ii 602
    I'll fight it on the threshold of the *g*.   „ V v 190
    With dead men upright from their *g*'s,   *Harold* I ii 83
    And thou art upright in thy living *g*,   „ II ii 440
    Corpse-candles gliding over nameless *g*'s—   „ III i 382
    I give my voice against thee from the *g*—   „ V i 255
    He commends me now From out his *g*   *Becket, Pro.* 420
    And I shall live to trample on thy *g*.   „ I 95
    spire of Holy Church may prick the *g*'s—   „ I iii 554
    O devil, can I free her from the *g*?   „ V i 186
    I should seem to be dancing upon a *g*.   *Prom. of May* I 431
    And *he* would hear you even from the *g*.   „ I 763
    I told her I should hear her from the *g*.   „ II 245
    To see her *g* ? her ghost ?   „ II 352
    as they call it so truly, to the *g* at the bottom,   „ III 193
    O *g*'s in daisies drest,   „ III 204
    But now that you have been brought to us as it were
    from the *g*,   „ III 235
    to the *g* he goes to, Beneath the burthen of years. „ III 515
    stillness in the *g* By the last trumpet.   *Foresters* II i 47
Gravedigger like the *g*'s child I have heard of, trying to
    ring the bell,   *Becket* III iii 73
Graveness Had put off levity and put *g* on.   *Queen Mary* V ii 510
Gray (*See also* **Graäy**) Yon *g* old Gospeller, sour as
    midwinter,   „ I iii 40
    he loved the more His own *g* towers,   „ II i 49
    Ah, *g* old castle of Alington, green field Beside the
    brimming Medway,   „ II i 243
    And scared the *g* old porter and his wife.   „ II iii 16
    The *g* rogue, Gardiner, Work on his knees,   „ IV v 164
    And the *g* dawn Of an old age that never will be mine „ V ii 234
    and dumb'd his carrion croak From the *g* sea for ever. *Harold* IV iii 67
    the green field—the *g* church—   *Becket* II i 296
    He will pass to-morrow In the *g* dawn before the
    Temple doors.   *The Cup* I i 295
    I rise to-morrow In the *g* dawn, and take this holy cup „ I ii 434
    And *g* before his time as thou art, Much.   *Foresters* I iii 149
    By arrow and *g* goosewing,   „ III 427
Grayhound My *g*'s fleeting like a beam of light, *Harold* II ii 129
Graze would not *g* The Prince of Spain.   *Queen Mary* I v 453
Grazing Our horses *g* by us, when a troop,   *The Falcon* 611
Greasy so *g*, and smell so vilely that my Lady Marian *Foresters* I i 82
    that very word '*g*' hath a kind of unction in it,   „ I i 86
Great Was she not betroth'd in her babyhood to the *G*
    Emperor himself ?   *Queen Mary* I i 118
    How folly ? a *g* party in the state Wills me to wed
    her.   „ I iv 91
    Doth not as *g* a party in the state Will you to wed me ? „ I iv 95
    Is no *g* party in the state as yet.   „ I iv 102
    G, said you ? nay, you shall be *g*. I love you,   „ I iv 103
    I have felt within me Stirrings of some *g* doom when
    God's just hour Peals—   „ I iv 261
    Let the *g* angel of the church come with him;   „ I v 377
    Spain in all the *g* offices of state;   „ II i 178
    were to do *G* things, my Lord.   „ II ii 390
    and round his knee, misplaced, Our English Garter,
    studded with *g* emeralds,   „ III i 84
    where you gave your hand To this *g* Catholic King. „ III i 92
    The *g* unborn defender of the Faith,   „ III ii 165
    Ay, sir; Inherit the *G* Silence.   „ III ii 199
    Saying, O Lord God, although my sins be *g*, For thy
    g mercy have mercy !   „ IV iii 136

Green (s) Bagenhall, I see The Tudor *g* and white.   *Queen Mary* III i 180
The colours of our Queen are *g* and white,   „   III v 5
father's eye was so tender it would have called a goose off the *g*,   *Becket* III iii 103
Greenwich I will go to G, So you will have me   *Queen Mary* III vi 221
Greenwood Beneath the *g* tree. (repeat)   *Foresters* I i 12, 24
'Grees (agree) thaw me and 'im we niver '*g* about the tithe ;   *Prom. of May* I 444
Greet Wessex dragon flies beyond the Humber, No voice to *g* it.   *Harold* IV i 5
Will *g* us as our babes in Paradise.   *Becket* v ii 225
And music there to *g* my lord the king.   *The Cup* II 191
Greeting Makes he his mouth of holy *g*.   *Queen Mary* III ii 80
And scarce a *g* all the day for me—   „   III vi 118
Full thanks for your fair *g* of my bride !   *Harold* IV iii 46
G and health from Synorix ! (repeat)   *The Cup* II 40, 130
Gregory (Pope) no croucher to the *Gregories* That tread the kings   *Becket, Pro.* 212
G bid St. Austin here Found two archbishopricks,   „   i iii 48
Not to a G of my throning ! No.   „   v i 33
Gresham (Sir Thomas) *See* **Thomas Gresham**
Grew thus baptized in blood G ever high and higher,   *Harold* III i 148
like a barren shore That *g* salt weeds,   *The Cup* II 232
mountain flowers *g* thickly round about.   *The Falcon* 355
and when the children *g* too old for me,   *Prom. of May* III 386
Grex Pastor fugatur G trucidatur—   *Harold* v i 514
Grey (Lady Jane) *See* **Jane**
Grief Thou stirrest up a *g* thou canst not fathom.   *Queen Mary* III iv 298
mine own, a *g* To show the scar for ever—   *Becket* I i 177
O *g* for the promise of May, (repeat)   *Prom. of May* I 59, 60, 750, 752
We have been in such *g* these five years,   *Prom. of May* II 66
how should I, with this *g* still at my heart,   „   III 91
One that has been much wrong'd, whose *g*'s are mine,   „   III 577
Whate'er thy *g*'s, in sleep they fade away.   *Foresters* I iii 45
Grieve Death would not *g* him more.   *Queen Mary* IV i 25
I bring your Majesty such grievous news I *g* to bring it   „   v ii 241
I *g* I cannot; but, indeed—   *Prom. of May* I 621
I *g* I am the Raven who croaks it.   *Foresters* III 447
I *g* to say it was thy father's son.   „   IV 810
Grieved I am vastly *g* to leave your Majesty.   *Queen Mary* III vi 255
I am *g* to know as much.   *Becket, Pro.* 4
I am *g*, my daughter.   „   IV 82
The Sheriff—I am *g* it was the Sheriff ;   *Foresters* II i 449
Grievous And first I say it is a *g* case,   *Queen Mary* IV iii 167
I bring your Majesty such *g* news I grieve to bring it.   „   v ii 240
in their mood May work them *g* harm at times,   *The Falcon* 821
Griffyth (King of Wales) *G* I hated: why not hate the foe Of England ? *G* when I saw him flee, Chased deer-like up his mountains, all the blood That should have only pulsed for G,   *Harold* I ii 145
Since G's head was sent To Edward,   „   IV i 221
With a love Passing thy love for G ?   „   I 357
Grim (adj.) look'd As *g* and grave as from a funeral.   *Queen Mary* II ii 65
how *g* and ghastly looks her Grace,   „   v ii 389
Our cancell'd warrior-gods, our *g* Walhalla,   *Harold* IV iii 73
Grim (a monk) Thou art but yesterday from Cambridge, G;   *Becket* v ii 55
Grimly-glaring Yon *g-g*, treble-brandish'd scourge Of England !   *Harold* I i 3
Grimness There lodged a gleaming *g* in his eyes,   „   II ii 224
Grip The black fiend *g* her ?   *Foresters* III 380
Griping and *g* mine, Whisper'd me,   *Queen Mary* I i 34
Grisly Spite of this *g* star ye three must gall Poor Tostig.   *Harold* I i 418
Groan (s) cries, and clashes, and the *g*'s of men ;   „   III i 375
Misheard their snores for *g*'s.   „   v i 213
Groan (verb) They *g* amen ; they swarm into the fire   *Queen Mary* v ii 110
Groan'd crept Up even to the tonsure, and he *g*,   *Becket* I iii 327
Groaning *See* **A-groänin'**
Groining The *g* hid the heavens ;   *Foresters* II i 62
Groom (a servant) clowns and *g*'s May read it !   *Queen Mary* III iv 36
the *g*, Gardener, and huntsman, in the parson's place,   „   IV iii 372
Groom (bridegroom) (*See also* **Bridegroom**) there is one Death stands behind the G,   „   v ii 166

Groove Moved in the iron *g*'s of Destiny ?   *Prom. of May* II 267
Gross invade their hive Too *g* to be thrust out,   *Queen Mary* III iii 55
Who so bolster'd up The *g* King's headship of the Church,   „   III iv 246
your Priests G, worldly, simoniacal, unlearn'd !   *Harold* I i 162
Grossness Delight to wallow in the *g* of it,   *Becket* II ii 343
Ground We but seek Some settled *g* for peace   *Queen Mary* I v 315
as the heathen giant Had but to touch the *g*,   „   III ii 44
bit his shield, and dash'd it on the *g*,   *Harold* v i 406
tho' the fire should run along the *g*,   *Prom. of May* I 704
Not while the swallow skims along the *g*,   *Foresters* I ii 314
Group Many such *g*'s.   *Queen Mary* II ii 93
Grove Oh look,—yon *g* upon the mountain,   *The Cup* I iii 1
Grovel He *g*'s to the Church when he's black-blooded,   *Becket* IV ii 436
Grow I shall *g* into it—I shall be the Tower.   *Queen Mary* II iv 105
Daisies *g* again, Kingcups blow again,   „   IV 89
Perhaps our vines will *g* the better for it.   *Harold* I i 68
If e'er the Norman *g* too hard for thee,   „   III i 12
old men must die, or the world would *g* mouldy,   *Becket, Pro.* 409
If I sit, I *g* fat.   „   *Pro.* 414
How the boy *g*'s !   „   II i 217
—her main law Whereby she *g*'s in beauty—   *Prom. of May* I 283
So the child *g* to manhood :   „   II 289
What rightful cause could *g* to such a heat   *Foresters* II i 698
Growing G dark too—but light enough to row.   *The Cup* II 523
I have heard that 'your Lordship,' and 'your Ladyship,' and 'your Grace' are all *g* old-fashioned !   *Prom. of May* III 318
He hath been hurt, was *g* whole again,   *Foresters* IV 451
Grown Why, she's *g* bloodier !   *Queen Mary* III i 416
How doubly aged this Queen of ours hath *g*   „   v i 228
all the faiths Of this *g* world of ours,   *Harold* III ii 65
were he living And *g* to man and Sinnatus will'd it,   *The Cup* I ii 151
Growth did not wholly clear The deadly *g*'s of earth,   *Becket* II ii 203
Grudge tho' I *g* the pretty jewel, that I Have worn,   *Prom. of May* I 473
Grunting These beastly swine make such a *g* here,   *Queen Mary* I iii 12
Guard (s) I trust the Queen comes hither with her *g*'s.   „   II ii 2
I must set The *g* at Ludgate.   „   II ii 409
I saw Lord William Howard By torchlight, and his *g* ;   „   II iii 30
At the park gate he hovers with our *g*'s.   „   II iv 16
These Kentish ploughmen cannot break the *g*'s.   „   II iv 18
broken thro' the *g*'s And gone to Ludgate.   „   II iv 20
The *g*'s are all driven in, skulk into corners   „   II iv 54
A gracious *g* Truly ; shame on them !   „   II iv 57
And tear you piecemeal : so you have a *g*.   „   IV vi 37
There are Hot Gospellers even among our *g*'s—   „   v v 103
When being forced aloof from all my *g*,   *Harold* IV iii 16
fought men Like Harold and his brethren, and his *g* Of English.   „   v ii 180
I have my *g* about me.   *The Cup* I iii 14
Guard (verb) men-at-arms G my poor dreams for England.   *Queen Mary* I v 154
To *g* and keep you whole and safe   „   II ii 246
The lion needs but roar to *g* his young ;   „   III v 123
not the living rock Which *g*'s the land.   *Harold* I ii 121
voice of any people is the sword That *g*'s them,   „   II ii 136
to *g* the land for which He did forswear himself—   „   v ii 161
To *g* this bird of passage to her cage ;   *Becket* I i 329
my men will *g* you to the gates.   „   I i 402
G from the stroke that dooms thee after death high Heaven *g* thee from his wantonness,   „   IV ii 270
And there be men-at-arms to *g* her.   *Foresters* I ii 121
  „   II i 158
Guarded The men that *g* England to the South   *Harold* IV iii 209
Guardsman Our *g* hath but toil'd his hand and foot,   „   v i 200
Our *guardsmen* have slept well, since we came in ?   „   v i 207
Guernsey in G, I watch'd a woman burn ;   *Queen Mary* v iv 16
Guess G what they be. *Edith.* He cannot *g* who knows.   *Harold* I ii 135
But on conditions. Canst thou *g* at them ?   „   II ii 343
might chance—perchance—To *g* their meaning.   „   IV i 139
How should *you g* What manner of beast it is ?   *The Cup* I ii 370
if but to *g* what flowers Had made it ;   *The Falcon* 429
Guess'd You are more than *g* at as a heretic,   *Queen Mary* III iv 93

H

Hail'd As we past, Some *h*, some hiss'd us. *Queen Mary* II ii 61

Hair (*See also* **'Air**) her red *h* all blown back, She shrilling   II ii 70

as red as she In *h* and cheek ;   II ii 76

The common barber clipt your *h*,   IV ii 131

No *h* is harm'd.   v i 161

and held up by the *h* ?   v ii 22

Let me first put up your *h* ;   v ii 232

Philip ! quick ! loop up my *h* !   v ii 535

Your Philip hath gold *h* and golden beard ; There must be ladies many with *h* like mine. *Feria.*   v iii 56

Some few of Gothic blood have golden *h*, *Harold* III i 371

Heard, heard— *Harold.* The wind in his *h* ? III i 148

and a blessed *h* Of Peter, and all France, v ii 46

Holy Father strangled him with a *h* Of Peter, *The Falcon* 359

I ask'd A ribbon from her *h* to bind it with ; *Foresters* II ii 98

a bat flew out at him In the clear noon, and hook'd him by the *h*,

Hair'd *See* **Fair-hair'd**

Hair's-breadth Mine eye most true to one *h-b* of aim.   IV 694

Hale (robust) *See* **Haäle**

Hale (verb) stop the heretic's mouth ! *H* him away ! *Queen Mary* IV iii 283

H him hence ! *Harold* II i 108

Haled *H* thy shore-swallow'd, armour'd Normans II ii 57

Ye *h* this tonsured devil into your courts ; *Becket* I iii 387

Half (*See also* **Haäfe**) Flower, she ! *H* faded ! *Queen Mary* I iv 61

His buzzard beak and deep-incavern'd eyes *H* fright me. I iv 268

and the remission Of *h* that subsidy levied on the people, I v 115

which every now and then Beats me *h* dead : I v 525

The sire begets Not *h* his likeness in the son. II i 55

And the *h* sight which makes her look so stern, II ii 322

'tis not written *H* plain enough. II iii 66

Thine is a *h* voice and a lean assent. III i 311

Out crept a wasp, with *h* the swarm behind. III i 49

one *h* Will flutter here, one there. III vi 196

Till I myself was *h* ashamed for him. IV iv 171

myself *H* beast and fool as appertaining to it ; IV iii 415

There's *h* an angel wrong'd in your account ; v iii 1

I say not this, as being *H* Norman-blooded, *Harold* I i 169

That marriage was *h* sin. I ii 53

I see the goal and *h* the way to it.— I ii 196

And yon huge keep that hinders *h* the heaven. II ii 228

Better leave undone Than do by *halves*— II ii 496

Thou art *h* English. Take them away ! v ii 135

an' I be *h* dog already by this token, *Becket* I iv 259

I'll go back again. I hain't *h* done yet. I iv 259

or foreign cousins, not *h* speaking The language of the land. II i 135

Not *h* her hand—no hand to mate with *her*, II i 189

But the King hath bought *h* the College of Redhats. II ii 374

Trodden one *h* dead ; one *h*, but half-alive, v i 63

He loses *h* the meed of martyrdom Who will be martyr when he might escape. v ii 278

Hugh, I know well thou hast but *h* a heart v iii 129

They are thronging in to vespers—*h* the town. v iii 139

One *h* besotted in religious rites. *The Cup* I i 74

close not yet the door upon a night That looks *h* day. I i 389

If I be not back in *h* an hour, Come after me. I ii 438

How many of you are there ? *Publius.* Some *h* a score. I iii 13

The camp is *h* a league without the city ; I iii 89

Beside this temple *h* a year ago ? II 393

H a breakfast for a rat ! *The Falcon* 123

H a tit and a hern's bill. 131

Have we not *h* a score of silver spoons ? *Filippo.* *H* o' one, my lord ! *Count.* How *h* of one ? 405

H an hour late ! why are you loitering here ? *Prom. of May* II 324

I am *h* afraid to pass. II 328

H a score of them, all directed to me— II 721

could it look But *h* as lovely. III 491

they have trodden it for *h* a thousand years, *Foresters* I i 333

and he hath seized On *h* the royal castles. I iii 83

Half (*continued*) I have paid him *h*. That other thousand— *Foresters* II i 465

I trust *H* truths, good friar : IV 950

Some hunter in day-dreams or *h* asleep. IV 1088

Halfabitical (alphabetical) *H* ! Taäke one o' the young 'uns fust, *Prom. of May* III 31

Half-afraid Still I am *h-a* to meet her now. I 488

Half-Alfgar thence a king may rise Half-Godwin and *h-A*, *Harold* IV i 144

Half-alive one half, but *h-a*, Cries to the King. *Becket* I v 64

Half-born I must—I will !—Crush it *h-b* ! *Harold* I i 359

Half-dozen for I've been on my knees every day for these *h-d* years *The Falcon* 185

Half-drown'd my faith would seem Dead or *h-d*, *Queen Mary* IV ii 98

Half-Godwin thence a king may rise *H-G* and half-Alfgar, *Harold* IV i 144

Half-hanged he hath *h-h* himself in the rope of the Church, *Becket* III iii 75

Half-rag *h-r*, half-sore—beggars, poor rogues I iv 81

Half-ruin'd The house *h-r* ere the lease be out ; *Queen Mary* v vi 66

Half-shamed I seem *h-a* at times to be so tall. v ii 423

Half-sore half-rag, *h-s*—beggars, poor rogues *Becket* I iv. 81

Half-Spanish Hard-natured Queen, *h-S* in herself, *Queen Mary* IV iii 424

Half-waked world as yet, my friend, Is not *h-w* ; II i 228

Half-way I am *h-w* down the slope—will no man stay me ? *Becket* II ii 148

Those sweet tree-Cupids *h-w* up in heaven, *Foresters* III 35

Half-witted *H-w* and a witch to boot ! II i 375

But sickly, slight, *h-w* and a child, *Harold* II ii 571

Halidome By my *h* I felt him at my leg still. *Foresters* IV 627

Hall (*See also* **Dining-hall**) Far liefer had I in my country *h* *Queen Mary* III i 43

Is this a place To wail in, Madam, what ! a public *h*. v i 213

foes in Edward's *h* To league against thy weal. *Harold* I ii 32

And Tostig in his own *h* on suspicion II ii 295

At banquet in this *h*, and hearing me— IV iii 93

I held it with him in his English *h's*, v ii 128

The veriest Galahad of old Arthur's *h*. *Becket*, Pro. 129

In mine own *h*, and sucking thro' fools' ears I iii 360

trumpets in the *h's*, Sobs, laughter, cries : v ii 367

Philip Edgar of Toft *H* in Somerset. *Prom. of May* II 438

One Philip Edgar of Toft *H* in Somerset Is lately dead. II 445

I have been telling her of the death of one Philip Edgar of Toft *H*, Somerset. II 706

' O' the 17th, Philip Edgar, o' Toft *H*, Soomerset.' II 712

last time When I shall hold my birthday in this *h* : *Foresters* I ii 90

sat Among my thralls in my baronial *h* II i 61

Hall (**all**) ye'll think more on 'is little finger than *h* my hand at the haltar. *Prom. of May* I 112

Hall-door Shut the *h-d's*. *Becket* v ii 532

Hallus (always) Foälks doesn't *h* knaw thessens ; *Prom. of May* I 28

h a-fobbing ma off, tho' ye knaws I love ye. I 107

thaw 'e knaws I was *h* ageän heving schoolmaster i' the parish ! I 186

h hup at sunrise, and I'd drive the plow straäit as a line I 368

H about the premises ! I 434

but I *h* gi'ed soom on 'em to Miss Eva at this time o' year. II 15

But *h* ud stop at the Vine-an'-the-Hop, II 311

and I wur *h* scaäred by a big word ; III 33

Ye sees the holler laäne be *h* sa dark i' the arternoon, III 93

Halt That business which we have in Nottingham—— *Little John. H* ! *Foresters* III 231

Church and Law, *h* and pay toll ! IV 429

Haltar (altar) ye'll think more on 'is little finger than hall my hand at the *h*. *Prom. of May* I 113

Haman will hang as high As *H*. *Foresters* IV 752

Hammer (s) Anvil on *h* bang— *Harold* IV iii 161

H on anvil, *h* on anvil. IV iii 162

set the Church This day between the *h* and the anvil— *Becket* I iii 585

Hampton Court In *H C* My window look'd upon the corridor ; *Queen Mary* v ii 458

Hand (s) (*See also* **Left-hand**) took her *h*, call'd her sweet sister, I i 80

h, Damp with the sweat of death, I ii 32

Hand (s) (*continued*) I love you, Lay my life in
  your *h's*. *Queen Mary* I iv 105
I left her with rich jewels in her *h*, „ I iv 242
Mary of England, joining *h's* with Spain, „ I v 298
a formal offer of the *h* Of Philip ? „ I v 349
For Philip comes, one *h* in mine, „ I v 515
The formal offer of Prince Philip's *h*. „ I v 588
counts on you And on myself as her two *h's* ; „ II ii 105
And arm and strike as with one *h*, „ II ii 292
I feel most goodly heart and *h*, „ II ii 352
His in whose *h* she drops ; „ III i 112
I cannot lift my *h's* unto my head. „ III i 240
See there be others that can use their *h's*. „ III i 243
She had no desire for that, and wrung her *h's*, „ III i 385
with her poor blind *h's* feeling—' where is it ? „ III i 407
which God's *h* Wrote on her conscience, „ III i 421
where you gave your *h* To this great Catholic King. „ III iii 91
From stirring *h* or foot to wrong the realm. „ III iii 60
The sword Is in her Grace's *h* to smite with. „ III iv 90
What, if a mad dog bit your *h*, my Lord, „ III iv 205
Their hour is hard at *h*, „ III iv 426
with my *h's* Milking the cow ? (repeat) *Queen Mary* III v 87, 94, 101
Rose *h* in *h*, and whisper'd, ' come away ! *Queen Mary* III v 148
By seeking justice at a stranger's *h* „ IV i 20
To reach the *h* of mercy to my friend. „ IV i 65
By mine own self—by mine own *h* ! O thin-
  skinn'd *h* and jutting veins, „ IV ii 203
papers by my *h* Sign'd since my degradation—by
  this *h* „ IV iii 243
since my *h* offended, having written Against my
  heart, my *h* shall first be burnt, So I may come
  to the fire. „ IV iii 247
gather'd with his *h's* the starting flame, And wash'd
  his *h's* and all his face therein, „ IV iii 336
Gardiner wur struck down like by the *h* o' God „ IV iii 516
I could see that many silent *h's* Came from the crowd „ IV iii 582
Then Cranmer lifted his left *h* to heaven, „ IV iii 608
' This hath offended—this unworthy *h* ! ' „ IV iii 614
they clapt their *h's* Upon their swords when ask'd ; „ V i 173
The *h's* that write them should be burnt clean off „ V ii 190
And, like a thief, push'd in his royal *h* ; „ V ii 467
How her *h* burns ! (repeat) „ V ii 552, 616
your *h* Will be much coveted ! What a delicate
  one ! „ V iii 43
King in armour there, his *h* Upon his helmet. „ V v 30
there is the right *h* still Beckons me hence. „ V v 137
To sleek and supple himself to the king's *h*. *Harold* I i 150
Our Tostig loves the *h* and not the man. „ I i 156
to turn and bite the *h* Would help thee „ I i 382
Join *h's*, let brethren dwell in unity ; „ I i 397
I have but bark'd my *h's*. „ II i 5
Run thou to Count Guy ; he is hard at *h*. „ II i 55
let fly the bird within the *h*, „ II ii 66
Thou hast but seen how Norman *h's* can strike, „ II ii 171
have thy conscience White as a maiden's *h*, „ II ii 284
He tore their eyes out, sliced their *h's* away, „ II ii 389
while thy *h's* Are palsied here, „ II ii 454
God and the sea have given thee to our *h's*— „ II ii 549
And grateful to the *h* that shielded him, „ II ii 586
Lay thou thy *h* upon this golden pall ! „ II ii 699
but take back thy ring. It burns my *h*— „ III ii 186
that reach'd a *h* Down to the field beneath it, „ IV i 44
Somewhere hard at *h*. Call and she comes. „ IV i 185
join our *h's* before the hosts, That all may see. „ IV i 241
these poor *h's* but sew, Spin, broider— „ IV iii 9
I saw the *h* of Tostig cover it. „ IV iii 81
Cannot *h's* which had the strength To shove „ IV iii 136
And be thy *h* as winter on the field, „ V i 132
Our guardsman hath but toil'd his *h* and foot, I *h*,
  foot, „ V i 201
Fain had I kept thine earldom in thy *h's* „ V i 276
I have had it fashion'd, see, to melt my *h*. „ V i 423
Stigand, With *h's* too limp to brandish iron— „ V i 449
wicked sister clapt her *h's* and laugh'd ; „ V ii 48
we should have a *h* To grasp the world with, „ V ii 191

Hand (s) (*continued*) be facile to my *h's*. Now is my
  time. *Becket, Pro.* 219
Thou hast but to hold out thy *h*. „ *Pro.* 412
He sued my *h*. I shook at him. „ I i 273
May the *h* that next Inherits thee be but as true „ I i 357
Hath often laid a cold *h* on my heats, „ I i 384
Church must play into the *h's* of kings ; „ I ii 68
Shall *h's* that do create the Lord be bound „ I iii 94
lay My crozier in the Holy Father's *h's*, „ I iii 125
For, like a son, I lift my *h's* to thee. „ I iii 264
He sat down there And dropt it in his *h's*, „ I iii 324
wouldst deliver Canterbury To our King's *h's* again, „ I iii 581
Which came into thy *h's* when Chancellor. „ I iii 653
Cornwall's *h* or Leicester's : they write marvellously
  alike. „ I iv 51
if thou hast not laid *h's* upon me ! „ I iv 212
let the *h* of one To whom thy voice is all her music, „ II i 176
happy boldness of this *h* hath won it Love's alms, „ II i 182
Not half her *h*—no *h* to mate with her, „ II i 189
Life on the *h* is naked gipsy-stuff ; „ II i 193
to stay his *h* Before he flash'd the bolt. „ II i 274
I here deliver all this controversy Into your royal *h's*. „ II ii 137
primm'd her mouth and put Her *h's* together— „ II i 76
Give me thy *h*. My Lords of France and England, „ III iii 226
I might deliver all things to thy *h*— „ III iii 270
bosom never Heaved under the King's *h* „ IV ii 189
My lord, we know you proud of your fine *h*, „ IV ii 261
so still I reach'd my *h* and touch'd ; „ V ii 235
I cannot bear a *h* upon my person, „ V iii 20
At the right *h* of Power— „ V iii 193
Into Thy *h's*, O Lord—into Thy *h's* !— „ V iii 196
There is my *h*—if such a league there be. *The Cup* I ii 103
For I have always play'd into their *h's*, „ I iii 150
More than once You have refused his *h*. „ II 43
clasp a *h* Red with the sacred blood of Sinnatus ? „ II 83
So shook within my *h*, that the red wine Ran down „ II 202
See here—I stretch my *h* out—hold it there. „ II 210
and my *h's* are too sleepy To lift it off. „ II 530
Shame on her that she took it at thy *h's*, *The Falcon* 61
The pleasure of his eyes—boast of his *h*— „ 222
who could trace a *h* So wild and staggering ? „ 438
having right *h* Lamed in the battle, „ 444
He gave me his *h* : „ 836
ye'll think more on 'is little finger than hall my *h*
  at the haltar. *Prom. of May* I 112
fur him as be handy wi' a book bean't but haäfe
  a *h* at a pitchfork. „ I 188
he's walking to us, and with a book in his *h*. „ I 220
storm is hard at *h* will sweep away Thrones, „ I 517
Come, give me your *h* and kiss me „ I 564
Owd Steer's gotten all his grass down and wants
  a *h*, „ II 222
From the farm Here, close at *h*. „ II 361
what full *h's*, may be Waiting you in the distance ? „ II 510
But give me first your *h* : „ II 525
She gave her *h*, unask'd, at the farm-gate ; „ II 625
should walk *h* in *h* together down this valley of
  tears, „ III 191
The lady gave her *h* to the Earl, The maid her *h* to
  the man. (repeat) *Foresters* I i 16, 92
That is no true man's *h*. I hate hidden faces. „ I ii 245
A finger of that *h* which should be mine „ I ii 299
and warm *h's* close with warm *h's*, „ I iii 20
Your *h's*, your *h's* ! „ I iii 127
Your *h's* again. „ I iii 164
old hag tho' I be, I can spell the *h*. „ II i 351
And capering *h* in *h* with Oberon „ II i 498
fell'st into the *h's* Of these same Moors „ II i 563
What sparkles in the moonlight on thy *h* ? „ II i 583
O hold thy *h* ! this is our Marian. „ II ii 36
call Kate when you will, for I am close at *h*. „ III 51
bulrush now in this right *h* For sceptre, „ III 76
all that live By their own *h's*, the labourer, the
  poor priest ; „ III 165
if ever A Norman damsel fell into our *h's*, „ III 181

Happy (continued) Make her *h*, then, and I forgive
  you. *Dora.* H ! *Prom. of May* III 666
So *h* in herself and in her home— „ III 756
As *h* as any of those that went before. *Foresters* I ii 129
—my ring—I am *h*—should be *h*. „ I iii 2
Sleep, *h* soul ! all life will sleep at last. „ I iii 48
Both be *h*, and adieu for ever and for evermore— „ II ii 196
Shall I be *h* ? *H* vision, stay. „ II ii 199
Could live as *h* as the larks in heaven, „ III 82
We leave but *h* memories to the forest. „ IV 1070
I am most *h*—Art thou not mine ?—and *h* that
  our King „ IV 1096
Harass'd Why am I follow'd, haunted, *h*, watch'd ? *Harold* II ii 248
Harbour At last a *h* opens ; but therein Sunk
  rocks— *Queen Mary* V v 213
Harbour (arbour) Didn't I spy 'em a-sitting i' the
  woodbine *h* togither ? *Prom. of May* I 125
Hard (*See also* **Stone-hard**) That's a *h* word,
  legitimate ; what does it mean ? *Queen Mary* I i 11
My *h* father hated me ; „ I v 80
And that were *h* upon you, my Lord Chancellor. „ I v 158
And those *h* men brake into woman-tears, „ I v 564
the provinces Are *h* to rule and must be hardly ruled ; „ III ii 201
You are *h* to please. „ III iv 154
Their hour is *h* at hand, their ' dies Iræ,' „ III iv 426
H upon both. „ III v 18
This *h* coarse man of old hath crouch'd to me „ IV ii 169
May God help you Thro' that *h* hour ! „ IV ii 196
' How *h* it is For the rich man to enter into Heaven ; '
  Let all rich men remember that *h* word. „ IV iii 203
and awaay betimes wi' dree *h* eggs for a good
  pleace at the burnin' ; „ IV iii 489
and therefore God Is *h* upon the people. „ V i 176
strike *h* and deep into The prey they are rending
  from her— „ V ii 267
Look'd *h* and sweet at me, and gave it me. „ V v 95
Tostig says true ; my son, thou art too *h*, *Harold* I i 206
The boy would fist me *h*, and when we fought I
  conquer'd, „ I i 444
Run thou to Count Guy ; he is *h* at hand. „ II i 55
would make the *h* earth rive To the very Devil's
  horns, „ II ii 739
If e'er the Norman grow too *h* for thee, „ III i 12
a war-crash, and so *h*, So loud, that, by St. Dunstan,
  old St. Thor— „ IV iii 145
Harsh is the news ! *h* is our honeymoon ! „ IV iii 229
Take it and wear it on that *h* heart of yours—there. *Becket,* Pro. 373
On this left breast before so *h* a heart, „ Pro. 376
Nay, if I took and translated that *h* heart into our
  Provençal facilities. „ Pro. 380
Make it so *h* to save a moth from the fire ? „ I i 283
What doth *h* murder care For degradation ? „ I iii 393
Would God they had torn up all By the *h* root, „ II ii 209
To assail our Holy Mother lest she brood Too long
  o'er this *h* egg, „ V ii 253
it is thou Hath set me this *h* task, *The Falcon* 237
It will be *h*, I fear, To find one shock upon the field „ 300
She smiles at him—how *h* the woman is ! „ 661
My brother ! my brother ! „ 895
The storm is *h* at hand will sweep away Thrones, *Prom. of May* I 517
I fear this Abbot is a heart of flint, *H* as the stones
  of his abbey. *Foresters* I ii 270
Our cellar is *h* by. Take him, good Little John, and
  give him wine. „ II i 468
Art thou not *h* upon them, my good Robin ? „ III 221
I should be *h* beset with thy fourscore. „ IV 179
Harder might be *h* upon thee, if met in a black lane „ III 223
Hardest The *h*, cruellest people in the world, *Queen Mary* II i 100
Hard-grain'd And grafted on the *h-g* stock of Spain— „ IV iii 426
Hard-hearted Out upon all *h-h* maidenhood ! *Foresters* IV 50
Hard-natured *H-n* Queen, half-Spanish in herself, *Queen Mary* IV iii 424
Hardness spare us the *h* of your facility ? *Becket,* Pro. 386
Father, I am so tender to all *h* ! „ I i 316
Hardrada (King of Norway) (*See also* **Harold**) the giant
  King of Norway, Harold *H*— *Harold* III ii 123

Hardrada (King of Norway) (continued) little help without
  our Saxon carles Against *H*. *Harold* IV i 36
striking at *H* and his madmen I had wish'd „ IV iii 17
May all invaders perish like *H* ! „ IV iii 78
Hard Tillery (artillery) 'Listed for a soädger, Miss, i'
  the Queen's Real *H T*. *Prom. of May* III 109
Hardy Too *h* with thy king ! *Harold* I i 198
Hare As find a *h's* form in a lion's cave. *Becket* I iii 177
Venison, and wild boar, *h*, geese, *Foresters* IV 191
Harebell Bluebell, *h*, speedwell, bluebottle, *Prom. of May* I 97
Harem new term Brought from the sacred East, his *h* ? *Foresters* IV 705
Harfleur To-morrow we will ride with thee to *H*, *Harold* II ii 196
To-morrow will we ride with thee to *H*. „ II ii 648
To-morrow will I ride with thee to *H*. „ II ii 770
For when I rode with William down to *H*, „ III i 83
Hark *H* ! the trumpets. *Queen Mary* I i 64
H, there is battle at the palace gates, „ II iv 47
H, how those Roman wolfdogs howl and bay him ! „ IV iii 354
H ! Madam ! *Eleanore.* Ay, *Becket* III i 14
H ! Is it they ? Coming ! „ V iii 15
The murderers, *h* ! Let us hide ! „ V iii 46
H ! Dora, some one is coming. *Prom. of May* III 339
Harken'd She hath *h* evil counsel— *Queen Mary* I v 54
Harlot She play the *h* ! never. „ III vi 136
They are so much holier than their *h's* son *Harold* V ii 11
kill with knife or venom One of his slanderous *h's* ? *Becket* IV ii 411
Harm (s) and thou canst not come to *h*. *Queen Mary* I iii 68
sharper h to England and to Rome, Than Calais taken. „ V ii 29
What *h* ? She hath but blood enough to live, *Harold* I ii 160
He meant no *h* nor damage to the Church. *Becket* I iii 216
and should *h* come of it, it is the Pope Will be to
  blame— „ I iii 220
or any *h* done to the people if my jest be in defence
  of the Truth ? „ II ii 339
I never meant you *h* in any way. „ IV ii 106
May work them grievous *h* at times, *The Falcon* 821
And what *h* will that do you, *Prom. of May* III 360
Harm (verb) If they dared To *h* you, I would blow
  this Philip *Queen Mary* I iv 290
In some such form as least may *h* your Grace. „ I v 225
That our commission is to heal, not *h* ; „ III iii 185
Than you would *h* your loving natural brother „ IV iii 189
H him not, *h* him not ! have him to the fire ! „ IV iii 284
scorn'd her too much To *h* her. *Becket* IV iii 394
God's full curse Shatter you all to pieces if ye *h* One of
  my flock ! „ V iii 135
They shall not *h* My guest within my house. *The Cup* I iii 248
It is but pastime—nay, I will not *h* thee. *Foresters* II i 554
Came stepping o'er him, so as not to *h* him— „ IV 538
Harm'd No hair is *h*. *Queen Mary* V i 161
the poor thunder Never *h* head. *Harold* I ii 233
Harming And bind him in from *h* of their combs. *Queen Mary* III iii 57
came and went before our day, Not *h* any : *Harold* I i 133
Harmony This burst and bass of loyal *h*, *Queen Mary* II ii 285
Harold (Earl of Wessex, afterwards King of England) (*See
  also* **Harold the Saxon**) *H*, I will not yield thee
  leave to go. *Harold* I i 256
Son *H*, I will in and pray for thee. „ I i 267
My wise head-shaking *H* ? „ I i 361
H always hated him. „ I i 429
How *H* used to beat him ! „ I i 432
lest the king Should yield his ward to *H's* will. „ I ii 159
When *H* goes and Tostig, shall I play The craftier Tostig
  with him ? „ I ii 163
If he found me thus, *H* might hate me ; „ I ii 172
H Hear the king's music, all alone with him, „ I ii 193
Peace-lover is our *H* for the sake Of England's „ I ii 197
A sacrifice to *H*, a peace-offering, „ I ii 203
thou assured By this, that *H* loves but Edith ? „ I ii 210
that I—That *H* loves me—yea, and presently That I and
  H are betroth'd—and last—Perchance that *H* wrongs me ; „ I ii 222
And when doth *H* go ? *Morcar.* To-morrow— „ I ii 237
H ? Earl of Wessex ! „ II i 82
Fly thou to William ; tell him we have *H*. „ II i 111
they are not like to league With *H* against *me*. „ II ii 54

Harold (Earl of Wessex, afterwards King of England) *(continued)*

England our own Thro' H's help,	*Harold* II ii 79
that these may act On H when they meet.	„ II ii 92
I can but love this noble, honest H.	„ II ii 95
Yea, lord H.	„ II ii 243
Thou canst not, H; Our Duke is all between thee	„ II ii 313
'This H is not of the royal blood,	„ II ii 354
O speak him fair, H, for thine own sake.	„ II ii 395
H, I do not counsel thee to lie.	„ II ii 416
H, for my sake and for thine own!	„ II ii 607
H, if thou love thine Edith, ay.	„ II ii 622
H, I am thy friend, one life with thee,	„ II ii 649
Am I H, H, son Of our great Godwin?	„ II ii 791
Ask me for this at thy most need, son H,	„ III i 15
Come, H, shake the cloud off!	„ III i 73
Let H serve for Tostig! *Queen.* H served Tostig so ill, he cannot serve for Tostig!	„ III i 159
H? Gurth, where am I?	„ III i 193
Sign it, my good son H, Gurth, and Leofwin,	„ III i 199
No, no, but H. I love him:	„ III i 241
but their Saints Have heard thee, H.	„ III i 254
Spare and forbear him, H, if he comes!	„ III i 299
And let him pass unscathed; he loves me, H!	„ III i 302
on the remains the curse, H, if thou embrace her:	„ III i 316
noble H, I would thou couldst have sworn.	„ III i 325
It is H! H the King! *Harold.* Call me not King, but H.	„ III ii 31
H, H! *Harold.* The voice of Gurth!	„ III ii 114
can but pray For H—pray, pray, pray—	„ III ii 195
but our help Is H, king of England.	„ IV i 11
Hear King H! he says true!	„ IV i 60
And Alfgar hates King H.	„ IV i 125
Old man, H Hates nothing;	„ IV i 128
Aldwyth, H, Aldwyth!	„ IV i 132
Thine own meaning, H, To make all England one,	„ IV i 140
H, H and Aldwyth!	„ IV i 244
Forward! Forward! H and Holy Cross!	„ IV i 269
O brother, brother, O H!	„ IV ii 63
Conjured the mightier H from his North	„ IV ii 68
Hail! H! Aldwyth! hail, bridegroom and bride!	„ IV iii 1
Hail, H, Aldwyth! Bridegroom and bride!	„ IV iii 42
answer which King H gave To his dead namesake,	„ IV iii 109
'To thrust our H's throne from under him?	„ IV iii 126
Thou hast lost thine even temper, brother H!	„ V i 95
A lake that dips in William As well as H.	„ V i 187
Son H, I thy King, who came before To tell thee	„ V i 234
O hapless H! King but for an hour!	„ V i 258
O H! husband! Shall we meet again?	„ V i 360
England Is but her king, and thou art H!	„ V i 376
thou art H, I am Edith!	„ V i 392
H and Holy Cross! (repeat)	*Harold* V i 439, 519, 662
I have a power—would H ask me for it—	*Harold* V i 451
Power now from H to command thee hence	„ V i 455
God save King H!	„ V i 489
So perish all the enemies of H!	„ V i 505
H and God Almighty!	„ V i 526
Against the shifting blaze of H's axe!	„ V i 587
Look out upon the hill—is H there?	„ V i 670
O H, H—Our H—we shall never see him more.	„ V ii 2
H slain? I cannot find his body.	„ V ii 18
I tell thee, girl, I am seeking my dead H.	„ V ii 43
H? Oh no—nay, if it were—my God,	„ V ii 74
And what body is this? *Edith.* H, thy better!	„ V ii 88
with all his rooftree ringing ' H,'	„ V ii 130
When all men counted H would be king, And H	„ V ii 132
have I fought men Like H and his brethren,	„ V ii 179

Harold (King of Norway) *(See also* **Hardrada***)* the giant King of Norway, H Hardrada—

	„ III ii 123
as having been so bruised By H, king of Norway;	„ IV i 10

Harold (Mr. Philip Edgar) *(See also* **'Arold, Edgar, Philip, Philip Edgar, Philip Harold, Philip Hedgar***)* That fine, fat, hook-nosed uncle of mine, old H,

	Prom. of May I 510
Not H! ' Philip Edgar, Philip Edgar!'	„ II 240
Might I ask your name? *Harold.* H.	„ II 394

Harold (Mr. Philip Edgar) *(continued)* Nay—now—not one, for I am Philip H.

	Prom. of May II 451
Dobbins, or some other, spy Edgar in H? Well then, I must make her Love H first, and then she will forgive Edgar for H's sake.	„ II 675
Half a score of them, all directed to me—H.	„ II 723
My name is H! Good day, Dobbins!	„ II 726
an' whether thou calls thysen Hedgar or H,	„ II 738
matched with my H is like a hedge thistle by a garden rose.	„ III 175
And this lover of yours—this Mr. H—is a gentleman?	„ III 281
your own name Of H sounds so English	„ III 610
Master Hedgar, H, or whativer They calls ye,	„ III 726

Harold the Saxon (Earl of Wessex, afterwards King of England) *(See also* **Harold***)* have loved H t S, or Hereward the Wake.

	Foresters I i 228

Ha Rou H R! H R! (repeat)   *Harold* V i 437, 528, 631, 650, 661, 664

Harp (s) his finger on her h (I heard him more than once) *Harold* IV i 204

gloom of Saul Was lighten'd by young David's h.   *Queen Mary* V ii 359

Harp (verb) That he should h this way on Normandy?   *Harold* I i 270

Harried Hath h mine own cattle—God confound him!   „ IV iii 190

Harrowing *See* **A-harrowin'**

Harry (great ship) he look'd the Great H, You but his cockboat;

	Queen Mary V ii 146

Harry (Henry) Bolingbroke such a one As H B hath a lure in it.

	„ I iv 10
H o B Had holpen Richard's tottering throne to stand, Could H have foreseen that all our nobles	„ III i 112

Harry (Henry the Eighth) *(See also* **Henry***)* Mary, the lawful and legitimate daughter of H the Eighth!

	„ I i 9
Our sovereign Lady by King H's will;	„ II ii 268
I am H's daughter, Tudor, and not Fear.	„ II iv 52
But then what's here? King H with a scroll.	„ III i 260
I am H's daughter:	„ III v 116
then King H look'd from out a cloud,	„ IV ii 6

Harry (Henry the Seventh) born i' the tail end of old H the Seventh.

	I i 43
born true man at five in the forenoon i' the tail of old H,	I i 46

Harry (Henry the Sixth?) It's H! *Third Citizen.* It's Queen.

	I i 34

Harsh H is the news! hard is our honeymoon!   *Harold* IV iii 229

but my voice is h here, not in tune,   *Becket, Pro.* 349

For once in France The King had been so h,   „ IV i 140

Even this brawler of h truths—   *Foresters* IV 948

Hartist (artist) What's a h? I doänt believe he's iver *Prom. of May* I 129

Harvest (adj.) the h moon is the ripening of the harvest, *Becket, Pro.* 362

Harvest (s) Were scatter'd to the h . . .   *Harold* IV iii 211

which we Inheriting reap an easier h.   *Becket* II ii 194

find one shock upon the field when all The h has been carried.

	The Falcon 302

Harvestless H autumns, horrible agues, plague—   *Queen Mary* V i 98

Harwich On all the road from H, night and day;   „ V ii 579

Haste (s) with what h I might To save my royal cousin.   „ II iv 77

in h put off the rags They had mock'd his misery with,   „ IV iii 589

Haste (verb) That h's with full commission from the Pope   „ III ii 51

Hasten harm at times, may even H their end.   *The Falcon* 823

Hastings (Francis, second Earl of Huntingdon) Sent Cornwallis and H to the traitor,

	Queen Mary II ii 31

Hastings (town in Sussex) lay them both upon the waste sea-shore At H,

	Harold V ii 161

Hat *See* **'At**

Hatch But h you some new treason in the woods.   *Queen Mary* I v 465

Hatch'd This is the fifth conspiracy h in France;   „ I i 297

Hatchet before you can eat it you must hack it with a h, *Foresters* II i 285

Hate (s) *(See also* **Heart-hate***)* her h Will burn till you are burn'd.

	Queen Mary I ii 58
In hope to charm them from their h of Spain.	„ III vi 82
to fuse Almost into one metal love and h,—	„ III vi 182
sow'd therein The seed of H, it blossom'd Charity.	„ IV i 172
carrion-nosing mongrel vomit With h and horror.	„ IV iii 450
when she touch'd on thee, She stammer'd in her h;	*Harold* I ii 37
If H can kill, And Loathing wield a Saxon battle-axe—	„ V i 412
his, a h Not ever to be heal'd.	*Becket* I i 178
We have but one bond, her h of Becket.	„ II i 165

Hate (s) (continued) And mine a bitterer illegitimate h, A bastard h — *Becket* II i 173
That sow this h between my lord and me! — ,, II ii 272
I follow out my h and thy revenge. — ,, IV i 151
And private h's with our defence of Heaven. — ,, V ii 52
and all her loves and h's Sink again into chaos. — *Foresters* I ii 329

Hate (verb) (*See also* **Haäte**) this bald priest, and she that h's me, — *Queen Mary* I iv 282
My sister cowers and h's me. — ,, I v 83
Would I marry Prince Philip, if all England h him? — ,, I v 139
Lord of Devon is a pretty man. I h him. — ,, I v 616
no old news that all men h it. — ,, II i 17
and the beds I know. I h Spain. — ,, II i 185
Ay, since you h the telling it. — ,, III i 89
With all the rage of one who h's a truth — ,, III vi 143
H me and mine: — ,, V i 85
They h me also for my love to you, My Philip; — ,, V i 95
He h's Philip; He is all Italian, and he h's the Spaniard; — ,, V ii 54
but I know it of old, he h's me too; — ,, V ii 60
And h's the Spaniard—fiery-choleric, — ,, V ii 92
Clarence, they h me; even while I speak — ,, V ii 214
' Your people h you as your husband h's you.' — ,, V ii 336
My people h me and desire my death. — ,, V ii 345
My husband h's me, and desires my death. — ,, V ii 347
I h myself, and I desire my death. — ,, V ii 351
Give me the lute. He h's me! — ,, V ii 363
Even for that he h's me. — ,, V ii 380
Edward loves him, so Ye h him. — *Harold* I ii 9
I am sure she h's thee, Pants for thy blood. — ,, I ii 38
H not one who felt Some pity for thy hater! — ,, I ii 43
H him? I could love him More, — ,, I ii 141
Griffyth I hated: why not h the foe Of England? — ,, I ii 145
If he found me thus, Harold might h me; — ,, I ii 172
many among our Norman lords H have the for this, — ,, II ii 546
Juggler and bastard—bastard—he h's that most— — ,, II ii 773
Our sister h's us for his banishment; — ,, III i 78
And Alfgar h's King Harold. — ,, IV i 125
Old man, Harold H's nothing; — ,, IV i 129
Morcar, it is all but duty in her To h me; I have heard she h's me. — ,, IV i 154
If not, they cannot h the conqueror. — ,, IV i 215
I h King Edward, for he join'd with thee — ,, IV ii 12
I h myself for all things that I do. — ,, IV ii 45
I h thee, and despise thee, and defy thee. — ,, IV ii 79
I loved him as I h This liar who made me liar. — ,, V i 411
how your Grace must h him. *Eleanor.* H him? — *Becket, Pro.* 434
break down our castles, for the which I h him. — ,, *Pro.* 448
The Church will h him. — ,, I iii 566
He h's my will, not me. — ,, II ii 27
I h a split between old friendships as I h the dirty gap — ,, II ii 380
I h him for his insolence to all. — ,, V i 226
I h him for I h him is my reason, And yet I h him for a hypocrite. — ,, V i 230
I h the man! What filthy tools our Senate — *The Cup* I i 155
I could h her for it But that she is distracted. — ,, II 178
My brother h's him, scorns The noblest-natured man — *The Falcon* 257
I h tears. Marriage is but an old tradition. I h Traditions, ever since my narrow father, — *Prom. of May* I 489
It seems to me that I h men, ever since my sister left us. — ,, II 79
But she h's Edgar. — ,, II 672
Scorn! I h scorn! A soul with no religion— — ,, II 531
A gallant Earl. I love him as I h John. — *Foresters* I i 191
yet I h him for his want of chivalry. — ,, I ii 107
I h him, I h the man. I may not h the King — ,, I ii 113
Beware of John! *Marian.* I h him. — ,, I ii 215
I h hidden faces. (repeat) — ,, I ii 245, 250

Hated (*See also* **World-hated**) My hard father h me; — *Queen Mary* I v 81
My brother rather h me — ,, I i 18
Old Sir Thomas would have h it. — ,, I i 18
So h here! I watch'd a hive of late; — ,, III iii 46
because to persecute Makes a faith h, — ,, III iv 116
Harold always h him. — *Harold* I i 429
Griffyth I h: why not hate the foe Of England? — ,, I ii 145
There spake Godwin, Who h all the Normans; — ,, III i 252

Hated (continued) Out, beast monk! I ever h monks. — *Harold* V i 76
Roger of York, you always h him, — *Becket* V i 9
I always h boundless arrogance. — ,, V i 12
I held for Richard, and I h John. — *Foresters* II i 52
Hateful make her as h to herself and to the King, — *Becket, Pro.* 526
Fool! I will make thee h to thy King. — ,, I ii 92
Save from some h cantrip of thine own. — ,, V i 140
Hate-philtre such A strong h-p as may madden him— — ,, IV ii 458
Hater Hate not one who felt Some pity for thy h! — *Harold* I ii 44
Hatest Thou h him, h him. — ,, III i 172
Crouch even because thou h him; — *Becket* IV ii 223
Hating *See* **World-hating**
Hatred the h of another to us Is no true bond — *Queen Mary* I iv 44
h of the doctrines Of those who rule, which h by and by Involves the ruler — ,, III iv 159
'Love of this world is h against God.' — ,, IV iii 173
yet what h Christian men Bear to each other, — ,, IV iii 182
Haughtiness have marked the h of their nobles; — ,, II i 168
Haughty Madam, methinks a cold face and a h. — ,, I v 197
They call him cold, H, ay, worse. — ,, I v 432
Why, ev'n the h prince, Northumberland, — ,, III i 147
Haul H like a great strong fellow at my legs, — *Harold* II i 11
Haunt There h some Papist ruffians hereabout — *Queen Mary* III v 174
My men say The fairies h this glade;— — *Foresters* II ii 101
Haunted Why am I follow'd, h, harrass'd, — *Harold* II ii 248
A lying devil Hath h me— — ,, V i 318
is h by The ghosts of the dead passions of dead men; — *Prom. of May* II 274
Haven looking to the happy h Where he shall rest — *Queen Mary* IV viii 579
bays And h's filling with a blissful sea. — *The Cup* II ii 236
Haveringatte-Bower nightingales in H-B Sang out — *Harold* I ii 18
Havings Your h wasted by the scythe and spade— — *Queen Mary* III ii 276
Havock To make free spoil and h of your goods. — ,, II ii 186
Havock'd That h all the land in Stephen's day. — *Becket* I i 242
Hawk (s) Sick for an idle week of h and hound — *Harold* I i 103
a feeder Of dogs and h's, and apes, — *Becket* I i 80
H, buzzard, jay, the mavis and the merle, — *Foresters* I iii 115
To fright the wild h passing overhead, — ,, III 318
Hawk (verb) and hunt and h beyond the seas! — *Harold* I i 229
I will h and hunt In Flanders. — ,, I i 259
had past me by To hunt and h elsewhere, — ,, II ii 28
Hawking (*See also* **A-hawking**) Gone h on the Nene, — *Becket* I iii 2
when he came last year To see me h, he was well enough: — *The Falcon* 313
Hawking-phrases then I taught him all our h-p. — ,, 314
Hawthorn filch the linen from the h, — *Foresters* III 199
Haxed (asked) Why if Steer han't h schoolmaster to dinner, — *Prom. of May* I 185
Hay *See* **Haäy**
Haycock *See* **Haäycock**
Hayfield (*See also* **Haäyfield**) you should be in the h looking after your men; — *Prom. of May* II 47
You had better attend to your h. — ,, II 123
that you did not come into the h. — ,, III 82
You are as good as a man in the h. — ,, III 106
Haystack and a plum-pudding as big as the round h. — ,, I 794
Head (s) (*See also* **'Eäd**) draw back your h's and your horns — *Queen Mary* I i 4
be no peace for Mary till Elizabeth lose her h.' — ,, I iii 5
If Elizabeth lose her h— — ,, I iii 88
with an ass's, not a horse's h, — ,, I iii 169
Stand further off, or you may lose your h. *Courtenay.* — ,, I iv 129
I have a h to lose for your sweet sake. — ,, I v 60
No—being traitor Her h will fall: — ,, I v 63
a h So full of grace and beauty! — ,, I v 477
When the h leapt—so common! — ,, II i 88
For all that I can carry it in my h. — ,, II i 89
If you can carry your h upon your shoulders. — ,, II ii 146
I'll have my h set higher in the state; — ,, II ii 250
Have made strong h against ourselves and you. — ,, III i 240
I cannot lift my hands unto my h. — ,, III iii 207
He, whom the Father hath appointed H — ,, III iii 246
I had held my h up then. — ,, III iii 278
What! will she have my h? — ,, III iii 278
lost the h's Wherewith they plotted in their treasonous malice, — ,, III iv 3

Hear (*continued*) And love to *h* bad tales of Philip. *Queen Mary* v ii 429
Much changed, I *h*, Had put off levity   „ v ii 509
There's the Queen's light. I *h* she cannot live.   „ v iv 11
you curse so loud, The watch will *h* you.   „ v iv 63
speak him sweetly, he will *h* thee.   *Harold* I i 117
When didst thou *h* from thy Northumbria? *Tostig*.
     When did I *h* aught but this ' *When* ' from thee?   „ I i 281
But thou canst *h* the best and wisest of us.   „ I i 300
yet *h*! thine earldom, Tostig, hath been a kingdom.   „ I i 303
I fain would *h* him coming! . . .   „ I ii 5
And *h* my peregrine and her bells in heaven;   „ I ii 131
Harold *H* the king's music, all alone with him,   „ I ii 194
Come, Malet, let us *h*!   „ II ii 211
No more! I will not *h* thee—William comes.   „ II ii 479
We *h* he hath not long to live.   „ II ii 565
H King Harold! he says true!   „ IV i 60
I *h* no more. *Margot.* *H* me again—for the last time.   „ v i 7
H me again! Our Saints have moved the Church   „ v i 39
H it thro' me.   „ v i 62
I do not *h* our English war-cry.   „ v i 651
That thou wilt *h* no more o' the customs. *Becket* I iii 255
Dost thou not *h*?   „ I iii 267
till I *h* from the Pope I will suspend myself   „ I iii 299
Art thou deaf? *Becket.* I *h* you. *Hilary.* Dost thou
     h those others? *Becket.* Ay!   „ I iii 605
H first thy sentence! The King and all his lords—
     Becket. Son, first *h* me.   „ I iii 670
Nay, but *h* thy judgment.   „ I iii 682
H me son. As gold Outvalues dross,   „ I iii 713
and when ye shall *h* it is poured out upon earth,   „ I iv 36
wind of the dawn that I *h* in the pine overhead?   „ II i 1
I will not *h*.   „ II i 211
we shall *h* him presently with clapt wing   „ II ii 48
Out! I *h* no more.   „ II ii 233
Grasshopper, grasshopper, Whoop—you can *h*.   „ III i 103
I did not *h* aright,   „ III i 235
I would not *h* him.   „ III i 257
I *h* Margery: I'll go play with her.   „ III i 274
I holla'd to him, but he didn't *h* me: „ III ii 26
I *h* the yelping of the hounds of hell.   „ III ii 48
when he *h's* a door open in the house and thinks ' the
     master.'   „ III iii 98
Did you *h* the young King's quip?   „ III iii 146
The King shall never *h* of me again,   „ IV ii 102
Do you *h* me? Believe or no, I care not.   „ IV ii 352
Threats! threats! ye *h* him.   „ v ii 465
You *h* them, brother John;   „ v ii 534
Can you not *h* them yonder like a storm,   „ v ii 624
Do you *h* that? strike, strike.   „ v iii 161
Artemis, Artemis, *h* us, O Mother, *h* us, and bless us! *The Cup* II 1
H thy people who praise thee!   „ II 5
H thy priestesses hymn thy glory!   „ II 7
Artemis, Artemis, *h* him, Ionian Artemis!   „ II 277
all the fleeted wealth of kings And peoples, *h*.   „ II 290
hurls the victor's column down with him That crowns it, *h*.   „ II 297
gulf and flatten in her closing chasm Domed cities, *h*.   „ II 301
     Whose lava-torrents blast and blacken a province
     To a cinder, *h*. Whose winter-cataracts find a
     realm and leave it A waste of rock and ruin, *h*.   „ II 301
Artemis, Artemis, *h* her, Ephesian Artemis! *Camma*.
     Artemis, Artemis, *h* me, Galatian Artemis!   „ II 310
Why then the Goddess *h's*.   „ II 388
H that, my bird! Art thou not jealous of her? *The Falcon* 5
h that you are saying behind his back   „ 106
by your leave if you would *h* the rest, The writing.   „ 529
H that, my lady! (repeat)   „ 636, 652
You *h*, Filippo? My good fellow, go!   „ 690
Master Dobson, did you *h* what I said? *Prom. of May* I 172
Heaven *h's* you, Philip Edgar!   „ I 760
And *he* would *h* you even from the grave.   „ I 762
p'raps ye *h's* 'at I soomtimes taäkes a drop too much;   „ II 107
I told her I should *h* her from the grave.   „ II 244
You—did *you h* a cry?   „ III 652
Sweet, do you *h* me?   „ III 678
You wrong me there! *h*, *h* me!   „ III 775

Hear (*continued*) You *h*! *Sheriff.* Yes, my lord, fear not. *Foresters* I ii 31
but no! We *h* he is in prison.   „ II i 34
Did we not *h* the two would pass this way?   „ II i 197
Ay, do you *h*? There may be murder done.   „ II i 339
Evil fairy! do you *h*?   „ II ii 116
Up with you, all of you, out of it! *h* and obey.   „ II ii 184
Fifty leagues Of woodland *h* and know my horn,   „ III 104
will you not *h* one of these beggars' catches?   „ III 405
You *h* your Queen, obey!   „ III 464
Will *h* our arrows whizzing overhead,   „ IV 1090
Heard (*See also* 'Eärd, Heärd, Heerd) Have we not *h*
     of her in Edward's time, *Queen Mary* I iv 18
I have *h*, the tongue yet quiver'd with the jest   „ I v 475
hast thou ever *h* Slanders against Prince Philip   „ I v 569
but I have *h* a thousand such.   „ I v 579
and your worship's name *h* into Maidstone market,   „ II i 63
I have *h* One of your Council fleer and jeer   „ II ii 392
I had *h* that every Spaniard carries   „ III i 222
h She would not take a last farewell of him,   „ III i 366
We *h* that you were sick in Flanders, cousin.   „ III ii 33
Methinks the good land *h* me,   „ III i 57
I *h* An angel cry ' There is more joy in Heaven,'—   „ IV ii 9
yet have *h* Of all their wretchedness.   „ IV iii 211
Our prayers are *h*!   „ IV iii 255
Have I not *h* them mock the blessed Host   „ IV iii 365
And *h* these two, there might be sport for him.   „ v ii 212
I never *h* him utter worse of you   „ v ii 431
If ever I *h* a madman,—let's away!   „ v iv 56
I had *h* of him in battle over seas,   „ v v 33
I *h* from my Northumbria yesterday. *Harold* I i 331
I *h* from thy Northumberland to-day.   „ I i 350
And he spoke—I *h* him—   „ II i 353
hast thou never *h* His savagery at Alençon,—   „ II i 381
I have *h* the Normans Count upon this confusion—   „ II i 457
We have *h* Of thy just, mild, and equal governance;   „ II ii 689
Would he *h* me! O God, that I were in some wide,   „ II ii 776
I have *h* a saying of thy father Godwin,   „ III i 111
but their Saints Have *h* thee, Harold.   „ III i 254
but those heavenly ears have *h*,   „ III i 259
H, *h*— *Harold.* The wind in his hair?   „ III i 370
that Archdeacon Hildebrand His master, *h* him,   „ III ii 146
I have *h* she hates me.   „ IV i 154
Ye *h* one witness even now.   „ IV i 170
his finger on her harp (I *h* him more than once)   „ IV i 205
but our old Thor *H* his own thunder again,   „ IV iii 150
H how the war-horn sang,   „ IV iii 157
H how the shield-wall rang,   „ IV iii 159
And all the Heavens and very God: they *h*—   „ v i 44
who made And *h* thee swear—   „ v i 121
Nor seen, nor *h*; thine,   „ v i 161
Our scouts have *h* the tinkle of their bells.   „ v i 220
O God, the God of truth hath *h* my cry.   „ v i 601
And I am *h*.   „ v i 635
hast thou *h* this cry of Gilbert Foliot *Becket* I i 36
I *h* him swear revenge.   „ I i 280
And *h* her cry ' Where is this bower of mine? '   „ I ii 42
I have *h* him say He means no more;   „ I iii 191
Yea, *h* the churl against the baron—   „ I iii 365
have *h* say that if you boxed the Pope's ears   „ II ii 369
have I Not *h* ill things of her in France?   „ III i 231
like the gravedigger's child I have *h* of, trying to ring the
     bell,   „ III iii 74
But I *h* say he had had a stroke, or you'd have *h* his horn   „ iv i 53
I have *h* of such that range from love to love,   „ IV ii 119
I have *h* of such—yea, even among those   „ IV ii 123
Have you *h* Raymond of Poitou, thine own uncle—   „ IV ii 246
I *h* your savage cry.   „ IV ii 320
knights, five hundred, that were there and *h*. Nay,
     you yourself were there: you *h* yourself.   „ v ii 407
I *h* in Rome, This tributary crown may fall to you. *The Cup* I i 95
I have *h* them say in Rome,   „ I i 136
I thought I *h* a footstep.   „ I ii 11
you *h* him on the letter.   „ I ii 279
I *h* a saying in Egypt, that ambition Is like the sea wave,   „ I iii 137
I never *h* of this request of thine.   „ II 394

Heard (*continued*) I have *h* these poisons May be walk'd down. — *The Cup* II 474

I have *h* That, thro' his late magnificence — *The Falcon* 226

Oh, Philip, Father *h* you last night. — *Prom. of May* I 557

I have *h* of you. The likeness Is very striking. — „ II 364

I never *h* her mention you. — „ II 395

The painful circumstances which I *h*— — „ II 402

I never *h* that he had a brother. — „ III 152

I have *h* that ' your Lordship,' and ' your Ladyship,' and ' your Grace ' are all growing old-fashioned ! — „ III 316

I *h* a voice, ' Girl, what are you doing there ? ' — „ III 375

You *h* him say it was one of his bad days. — „ III 469

I have *h* the Steers Had land in Saxon times ; — „ III 607

I may be outlaw'd, I have *h* a rumour. — *Foresters* I i 91

I *h* this Sheriff tell her he would pay — „ I iii 5

I have *h* of them. Have they no leader ? — „ I iii 103

I have *h* him swear he will be even wi' thee. — „ II i 344

silent blessing of one honest man Is *h* in heaven— — „ III 322

Shamed a too trustful widow whom you *h* In her confession ; — „ III 386

I have *h* 'em in the market at Mansfield. — „ III 406

We *h* Sir Richard Lea was here with Robin. — „ IV 978

Heärd I ha' *h* 'im a-gawin' on 'ud make your 'air— God bless it !—stan' on end. — *Prom. of May* I 134

and I *h* the winder—that's the winder at the end o' the passage, — „ I 395

Heardst He said (thou *h* him) that I must not — *Harold* II ii 260

Hearer confess Your faith before all *h's* ; — *Queen Mary* IV ii 80

Hearing Crave, in the same cause, *h* of your Grace. — „ IV i 8

At banquet in this hall, and *h* me— — *Harold* IV ii 93

If *h*, would have spurn'd her ; — *Becket* IV ii 346

the man himself, When *h* of that piteous death, — *Prom. of May* II 500

Heart (*See also* '**Eart, Lion-heart**) A bold *h* yours to beard that raging mob ! — *Queen Mary* I iii 96

I meant True matters of the *h*. — „ I iv 100

My h, my Lord, Is no great party in the state — „ I iv 101

I have the jewel of a loyal *h*. — „ I iv 247

You've a bold *h* ; keep it so. — „ I iv 269

Make all tongues praise and all *h's* beat for you. — „ I v 117

take mine eyes, mine *h*, But do not lose me Calais. — „ I v 128

I am not Queen Of mine own *h*, — „ I v 523

It breaks my *h* to hear her moan at night — „ I v 603

felt the faltering of his mother's *h*, — „ II ii 83

I scarce have *h* to mingle in this matter, — „ II ii 113

They have betray'd the treason of their *h's* : — „ II ii 157

come to cast herself On loyal *h's* and bosoms, — „ II ii 263

never whine Like that poor *h*, Northumberland, — „ II ii 333

I feel most goodly *h* and hand, — „ II ii 352

And hast not *h* nor honour. — „ II iv 84

Blazed false upon her *h*. — „ III i 70

and hurl'd our battles Into the *h* of Spain ; — „ III i 109

Her dark dead blood is in my *h* with mine. — „ III i 349

If you have *h* to do it ! — „ III i 411

to-day My *h* beats twenty, when I see you, cousin. — „ III i 59

Is like the cleaving of a *h* ; — „ III vi 196

A day may save a *h* from breaking too. — „ III vi 240

beget A kindness from him, for his *h* was rich, — „ IV i 169

My *h* is no such block as Bonner's is : — „ IV ii 174

Pray with one breath, one *h*, one soul for me. — „ IV iii 104

doubt The man's conversion and remorse of *h*, — „ IV iii 109

Against the truth I knew within my *h*, — „ IV iii 241

since my hand offended, having written Against my *h*, — „ IV iii 249

That might live always in the sun's warm *h*, — „ V i 23

Reginald Pole, what news hath plagued my *h* ? — „ V ii 18

I am sad at *h* myself. — „ V ii 159

I used to love the Queen with all my *h*— — „ V ii 419

As far as France, and into Philip's *h*. — „ V iii 19

Women, when I am dead, Open my *h*, — „ V v 153

Adulterous to the very *h* of Hell. — „ V v 163

Brave, wary, sane to the *h* of her— — „ V v 224

I swear I have no *h* To be your Queen. — „ V v 264

strike Their *h's*, and hold their babies up to it. — *Harold* I i 35

will make his nippers meet in thine *h* ; — „ II i 77

It is the arrow of death in his own *h*— — „ III i 405

where Tostig lost The good *h's* of his people. — „ III ii 30

Heart (*continued*) hand and foot, I hand, foot, *h* and head. — *Harold* V i 202

violent will that wrench'd All *h's* of freemen from thee. — „ V i 279

Here fell the truest, manliest *h's* of England. — „ V ii 58

Take it and wear it on that hard *h* of yours— — *Becket, Pro.* 373

On this left breast before so hard a *h*, — „ *Pro.* 376

translated that hard *h* into our Provençal facilities, — „ *Pro.* 380

That the *h* were lost in the rhyme and the matter — „ *Pro.* 383

My *h* is full of tears—I have no answer. — „ *Pro.* 406

His *h* so gall'd with thine ingratitude, — „ I iii 4

To lodge a fear in Thomas Becket's *h* — „ I iii 176

That my poor heretic *h* would excommunicate — „ II i 283

And push'd our lances into Saracen *h's*. — „ II ii 95

in the dark *h* of the wood I hear the yelping — „ III ii 47

That health of *h*, once ours, — „ III iii 266

scared the red rose from your face Into your *h* ? — „ IV i 75

While this but leaves me with a broken *h*, — „ IV ii 174

shall not I, the Queen, Tear out her *h*— — „ IV ii 409

and send Her whole *h's* heat into it, — „ V ii 255

full mid-summer in those honest *h's*. — „ V ii 374

You should attend the office, give them *h*. — „ V ii 599

I know well thou hast but half a *h* — „ V iii 130

I thank you from my *h*. — *The Cup* I ii 211

Yea,—with our eyes,—our *h's*, — „ I ii 412

That this brave *h* of mine should shake me so, — „ I iii 38

I have it in my *h*—to the Temple—fly— — „ I iii 111

found All good in the true *h* of Sinnatus, — „ II 87

I have no *h* to do it. — „ II 166

As in the midmost *h* of Paradise. — „ II 186

fill all *h's* with fatness and the lust Of plenty— — „ II 272

The stately widow has no *h* for me. — *The Falcon* 30

you that have the face of an angel and the *h* of a—that's too positive ! You that have a score of lovers and have not a *h* for any of them— — „ 87

and *not* a *h* like the jewel in it— — „ 91

cheek like a peach and a *h* like the stone in it— — „ 93

Pride of his *h*—the solace of his hours— — „ 223

I had no *h* to part with her for money. — „ 326

We mounted, and we dash'd into the *h* of 'em. — „ 630

best *h* that ever Beat for one woman. — „ 667

No other *h* Of such magnificence in courtesy — „ 722

a red fire woke in the *h* of the town, — *Prom. of May* I 50

small *h* have I to dance. — „ I 429

Keep up your *h* until we meet again. — „ I 754

I wear it next my *h*. — „ II 82

how should I, with this grief still at my *h*, — „ II 91

O sir, you seem to have a *h* ; — „ II 468

But wherefore waste your *h* In looking — „ II 503

the man has doubtless a good *h*, and a true and lasting love for me : — „ III 171

Come, come, keep a good *h* ! — „ III 253

I do believe I lost my *h* to him the very first time we met, — „ III 283

' Go home ; ' but I hadn't the *h* or face to do it. — „ III 389

What is it Has put you out of *h* ? — „ III 501

It puts me in *h* Again to see you ; but indeed the state Of my poor father puts me out of *h*. — „ III 502

I think That I should break my *h*, — „ III 556

—the *h*, O God !—the poor young *h* Broken — „ III 679

broke the *h* That only beat for you ; — „ III 762

sits and eats his *h* for want of money to pay the Abbot. — *Foresters* I i 4

but I keep a good *h* and make the most of it, — „ I i 28

it answers, I am thine to the very *h* of the earth— — „ I i 337

I fear this Abbot is a *h* of flint, — „ I ii 268

when I loved A maid with all my *h* — „ I ii 297

Sleep, mournful *h*, and let the past be past ! — „ I iii 47

There are no *h's* like English *h's* Such *h's* of oak — „ II i 3

I have shot her thro' the *h*. *Kate.* He lies, my lord. I have shot *him* thro' the *h*. — „ II i 98

That I had shot *him* thro' the *h*, — „ II i 123

my *h* so down in my heels that if I stay, I can't run. — „ II i 346

how to charm and waste the *h's* of men. — „ II i 502

And drains the *h* and marrow from a man. — „ II i 672

the bravest English *h* Since Hereward the Wake, — „ II i 687

Elf, with spiteful *h* and eye, — „ II ii 172

Heart (*continued*) And that would quite unman him, *h* and soul.   *Foresters* III 30

And let them warm thy *h* to Little John.   ,,   III 44

but I hold thee The husband of my *h*,   ,,   III 140

and thy legs, and thy *h*, and thy liver,   ,,   IV 204

or the head of a fool, or the *h* of Prince John,   ,,   IV 213

so she glided up into the *h* O' the bottle,   ,,   IV 244

flung His life, *h*, soul into those holy wars   ,,   IV 407

He drove his knife into the *h* of the deer,   ,,   IV 541

A woman's *h* is but a little thing,   ,,   IV 656

Will chill the *h*'s that beat for Robin Hood !   ,,   IV 1064

Heartache what headache ? *H*, perchance ;   *Queen Mary* I iv 149

Heart-comfort *H-c* and a balsam to thy blood ?   *Becket* I i 14

Hearted *See* **Brave-hearted, Great-hearted, Hard-hearted, High-hearted, Hollow-hearted, Poor-hearted**

Heartedest *See* **Human-heartedest**

Hearth with mine old hound Couch'd at my *h*   *Queen Mary* III i 46

The stranger at his *h*, and all his house—   ,,   IV i 163

King Henry warms your traitors at his *h*.   ,,   V i 124

Translating his captivity from Guy To mine own *h* at Bayeux,   *Harold* II i 43

Dabble your *h*'s with our own blood.   ,,   II ii 751

son of Orm, Gamel, at thine own *h*.   ,,   IV ii 39

none could sit By his own *h* in peace ;   *Becket* I iii 342

a son stone-blind Sat by his mother's *h* :   ,,   V ii 106

One slow, fat, white, a burthen of the *h* ;   ,,   V ii 212

I wouldn't have thy blood on my *h*.   *Foresters* II i 356

Heart-hate fierce resolve and fixt *h-h* in men   *Queen Mary* III vi 32

Heart-sick Better than *h-s*, friar.   *Foresters* IV 674

Heart-wife so this Rosamund, my true *h-w*, Not Eleanor.   *Becket, Pro.* 130

Heat (s) There must be *h*—there must be *h* enough   *Queen Mary* III iv 26

A bookman, flying from the *h* and tussle,   ,,   III iv 251

It is the *h* and narrowness of the cage   ,,   III v 207

Gardiner out-Gardiners Gardiner in his *h*,   ,,   III vi 26

men should bear their earthly *h*'s Into yon bloodless world,   *Harold* V i 284

Hath often laid a cold hand on my *h*'s,   *Becket* I i 384

Besides, we came away in such a *h*,   ,,   II i 294

do much To rake out all old dying *h*'s,   ,,   II ii 114

Hell's own *h* So dwelt on that they rose   ,,   II ii 204

Henry Says many a thing in sudden *h*'s,   ,,   IV ii 276

and send Her whole heart's *h* into it,   ,,   V ii 255

h and fire Of life will bring them out,   *Prom. of May* II 285

In that great *h* to wed her to the Sheriff   *Foresters* II i 584

The bee buzz'd up in the *h*.   ,,   IV 14

And the bee buzz'd down from the *h*.   ,,   IV 20

Heat (verb) this ghastly glare May *h* their fancies.   *Harold* I i 310

secret matter which would *h* the King against thee.   *Becket, Pro.* 487

Why should you *h* yourself for such as these ?   ,,   V ii 544

Employ us, *h* us, quicken us, help us,   *The Cup* I iii 131

How few Junes Will *h* our pulses quicker ?   *Foresters* IV 1062

Heated —we have eaten—we are *h*. Wine !   *The Cup* I ii 46

Heath ten thousand men on Penenden *H* all calling after   *Queen Mary* II i 61

They roar for you On Penenden *H*,   ,,   II i 106

fifty That follow'd me from Penenden *H* in hope   ,,   II i 151

Of the Northumbrian helmet on the *h* ?   *Harold* V i 145

No, but a shoal of wives upon the *h*,   ,,   V i 147

Heath (Sir Nicholas) *See* **Nicholas, Nicholas Heath**

Heathen (adj.) Ay, cousin, as the *h* giant Had but to touch the ground,   *Queen Mary* III ii 43

The *h* priesthood of a *h* creed !   *Becket* I iii 63

Cold, but look how the table steams, like a *h* altar ;   ,,   I iv 69

Heathen (s) Why do the *h* rage ?   ,,   V ii 628

Heathendom Out of the deep, deep night of *h*,   *Queen Mary* III iii 173

Heathenism that Lucullus or Apicius might have sniffed it in their Hades of *h*,   *Becket* III iii 118

Heather Walk'd at night on the misty *h* ;   *Harold* III iii 113

Heaved that bosom never *H* under the King's hand   *Becket* IV ii 189

Heaven (*See also* **'Eaven**) To him within there who made *H* and Earth?   *Queen Mary* I v 47

banks rolling incense, as of old, To *h*,   ,,   I v 93

Yea, by *H*, The text—Your Highness knows it,   ,,   I v 450

in his scared prayers *H* and earth's Maries ;   ,,   II ii 88

Heaven (*continued*) Ah, *h* ! *Pole.* Unwell, your Grace ?   *Queen Mary* III ii 84

Rise to the *h*'s in grateful praise of Him   ,,   III iii 165

With *h* for earth.   ,,   III iii 201

That *h* wept and earth blush'd.   ,,   III iv 193

pray *H* That you may see according to our sight.   ,,   III iv 330

To yield the remnant of his years to *h*,   ,,   III vi 211

All that is gracious in the breath of *h*   ,,   III vi 225

soul descending out of *h* Into a body generate.   ,,   IV i 35

An angel cry ' There is more joy in *H*,'—   ,,   IV ii 11

By *H*'s grace, I am more and more confirm'd.   ,,   IV ii 21

On earth ; but saved in *h* By your recanting.   ,,   IV ii 179

O God, Father of *H* ! O Son of God,   ,,   IV iii 124

I have offended against *h* and earth   ,,   IV iii 124

I am ashamed to lift my eyes to *h*,   ,,   IV iii 127

' How hard it is For the rich man to enter into *H* ; '   ,,   IV iii 205

Either to live with Christ in *H* with joy,   ,,   IV iii 220

find *H* or else hell ready to swallow me,   ,,   IV iii 224

If ever, as *h* grant, we clash with Spain,   ,,   IV iii 346

H help that this re-action not re-act   ,,   IV iii 388

Then Cranmer lifted his left hand to *h*,   ,,   IV iii 609

Why then to *h*, and God ha' mercy on him.   ,,   IV iii 631

Have courage, your reward is *H* itself.   ,,   V ii 109

and make Down for their heads to *h* !   ,,   V iv 8

It glares in *h*, it flares upon the Thames,   *Harold* I i 29

To have the *h*'s clear.   ,,   I i 38

mean The doom of England and the wrath of *H* ?   ,,   I i 47

Why should not *H* be wroth ?   ,,   I i 53

Is there no reason for the wrath of *H* ? *Leofwin.* Why then the wrath of *H* hath three tails, The devil only one.   ,,   I i 59

Stigand should know the purposes of *H*. *Stigand.* Not I. I cannot read the face of *h* ;   ,,   I i 65

is this pendent hell in *h* A harm to England ?   ,,   I i 76

religious fool, Who, seeing war in *h*, for *h*'s credit   ,,   I i 140

In *h* signs ! Signs upon earth !   ,,   I i 159

see Deeper into the mysteries of *h* Than thou,   ,,   I i 200

Not stagger'd by this ominous earth and *h* : But *h* and earth are threads   ,,   I i 208

Did not *H* speak to men in dreams of old ?   ,,   I ii 94

and her bells in *h* ; And other bells on earth, which yet are *h*'s ;   ,,   I ii 132

thunder moulded in high *h* To serve the Norman purpose,   ,,   II ii 33

yon huge keep that hinders half the *h*.   ,,   II ii 229

Cleave *h*, and send thy saints that I may say   ,,   II ii 785

two young wings To fly to *h* straight with.   ,,   III i 26

swear To consecrate my virgin here to *h*—   ,,   III i 276

all promises Made in our agony for help from *h* ?   ,,   III i 288

more the love, the more acceptable The sacrifice of both your loves to *h*. No sacrifice to *h*, no help from *h* ;   ,,   III i 349

there are signs in *h*—   ,,   III i 358

H yield us more ! for better,   ,,   III ii 71

Yon *h* is wroth with *thee* ?   ,,   V 39

And all the *H*'s and very God : they heard—   ,,   V 43

a sigh With these low-moaning *h*'s.   ,,   V i 152

We give our voice against thee out of *h* !   ,,   V i 261

The sign in *h*—the sudden blast at sea—   ,,   V i 378

Charged with the weight of *h* wherefrom they fall !   ,,   V i 567

Ye that are now of *h*, and see beyond   ,,   V i 618

The Norman sends his arrows up to *H*,   ,,   V i 667

twelve stars fell glittering out of *h* Into her bosom.   *Becket* I i 47

Why should not *H* have so inspired the King ?   ,,   I i 130

I ask no more. *H* bless thee ! hence !   ,,   I i 321

Lest there be battle between *H* and Earth,   ,,   I iii 226

Strong—not in mine own self, but *H* ;   ,,   I iii 537

and see it mounting to *H*, my God bless you,   ,,   I iv 38

beggars, poor rogues (*H* bless 'em)   ,,   I iv 83

and glass The faithful face of *h*—   ,,   II i 161

dwelt on that they rose and darken'd *H*.   ,,   II ii 206

said to the smoke, ' Go up, my son, straight to *H*.'   ,,   II ii 319

if he move at all, *H* stay him, is fain to diagonalise.   ,,   II ii 329

like Mahound's coffin hung between *h* and earth—   ,,   II ii 362

child We waited for so long—*h*'s gift at last—   ,,   III i 14

Heaven (*continued*)   All praise to *H*, and sweet St.
Magdalen !   *Becket* iii iii 234
Earth's falses are *h's* truths.   ,,   iii iii 348
H help you ; get you hence in haste   ,,   iv ii 26
thy true home—the *h's*—cry out for thee   ,,   iv ii 132
I will fly with my sweet boy to *h*,   ,,   iv ii 238
To bless thine enemies—— *Becket.* Ay, mine, not *H's.* ,,   v ii 26
lightnings that we think are only *H's* Flash sometimes
out of earth against the *h's*.   ,,   v ii 36
And private hates with our defence of *H*.   ,,   v ii 53
to people *h* in the great day When God makes up
his jewels.   ,,   v ii 496
He is not here—Not yet, thank *h*. O save him !   ,,   v iii 17
Shall not *H* be served Tho' earth's last earthquake   ,,   v iii 39
Seen by the Church in *H*, the Church on earth—   ,,   v iii 98
open'd out The purple zone of hill and *h* ;   *The Cup* i ii 408
cloudless *h* which we have found together   ,,   i ii 415
drew the light From *h* to brood upon her,   ,,   i iii 58
strike, make his feathers Glance in mid *h*.   *The Falcon* 16
O *h's* ! the very letters seem to shake With cold,   ,,   447
Here, or else well in *H*, where all is well.   ,,   682
No other heart Of such magnificence in courtesy Beats—
out of *h*.   ,,   724
And so return—*H* help him !—to our son.   ,,   861
H hears you, Philip Edgar !   *Prom. of May* i 760
H curse him if he come not at your call !   ,,   i 764
The body !—*H's* ! I come !   ,,   ii 572
For all the blessed souls in *H*   ,,   iii 10
to be realised all at once, or altogether, or anywhere
but in *H* ?   ,,   iii 187
I pray *H* we may not have to take to the rushes.   *Foresters* i i 89
for the sake of the great blessed Mother in *h*,   ,,   i i 97
come as freely as *h's* air and mother's milk ?   ,,   i i 210
The high *H* guard thee from his wantonness,   ,,   i ii 121
while the lark flies up and touches *h* !   ,,   i ii 316
topmost tree, that shoots New buds to *h*,   ,,   i iii 26
that worship for me which *H* knows I ill deserve—   ,,   i iii 161
and the blessed Queen of *H*,   ,,   ii i 39
The groining hid the *h's* ;   ,,   ii i 62
Thou comest a very angel out of *h*.   ,,   ii i 105
Your *h* is vacant of your angel.   ,,   ii i 109
—the Sheriff, and by *h*, Prince John himself   ,,   ii i 173
Give it me, by *h*, Or I will force it from thee.   ,,   ii i 594
Thou seem'st a saintly splendour out from *h*,   ,,   ii i 607
forest lawns are all as bright As ways to *h*,   ,,   ii i 632
When *h* falls, I may light on such a lark !   ,,   iii 12
Those sweet tree-Cupids half-way up in *h*,   ,,   iii 36
Could live as happy as the larks in *h*,   ,,   iii 83
silent blessing of one honest man Is heard in *h*—   ,,   iii 322
Sweet *H's*, I could wish that all the land   ,,   iv 666
I breathe *H's* air, and *H* looks down on me,   ,,   iv 725
Heavenly   I know He knew not, but those *h* ears have
heard,   *Harold* iii i 258
Heavier   Is it so much *h* than thy Chancellor's robe ?   *Becket* i i 20
Not *h* than thine armour at Thoulouse ?   ,,   i i 25
Beware, Lord Legate, of a *h* crime Than heresy
is itself ;   *Queen Mary* iii iv 221
Heavy   Too *h* for me, this, off with it, Herbert !   *Becket* i i 18
h As thine own bolts that fall on crimeful heads   *Harold* v i 564
Hebrew   But here's some *H*.   *Queen Mary* ii i 125
Hedgar (*Edgar*)   What dost a knaw o' this Mr. *H* as
be a-lodgin' wi' ye ?   *Prom. of May* i 200
but if iver I cooms upo' Gentleman *H* ageän,   ,,   ii 137
Philip *H* o' Soomerset ! (repeat)   ,,   ii 586
whether thou be *H*, or *H's* business man,   ,,   ii 734
an' whether thou calls thysen *H* or Harold,   ,,   ii 737
Master *H*, Harold, or whativer They calls ye,   ,,   iii 726
Hedge   matched with my Harold is like a *h* thistle by
a garden rose.   ,,   iii 176
Hedged-in   This poor, flat, *h-i* field—no distance—   ,,   ii 344
Hedge-pig   besides *H-p's*, a savoury viand,   *Foresters* ii 193
Hedge-priest   He is but *h-p*, Sir King.   ,,   iv 930
Hedge-rose   like the wild *h-r* Of a soft winter,   *Queen Mary* iii vi 14
Heed (*See also* **Take heed**)   You *h* not how you soil her
maiden fame,   *Foresters* iv 479

Heed (*continued*)   I have had a year of prison-silence,
Robin, And *h* him not—   *Foresters* iv 925
Heel (*See also* **Under-heel**)   bursten at the toes, and
down at *h's*.   *Queen Mary* i i 53
Her cap would brush his *h's*.   ,,   iii i 14
become Hideously alive again from head to *h*,   ,,   iv iii 447
colt winced and whinnied and flung up her *h's* ;   *Becket, Pro.* 516
less loyalty in it than the backward scrape of the
clown's *h*—   ,,   iii iii 144
not yield To lay your neck beneath your citizen's *h*.   ,,   v i 32
my heart so down in my *h's* that if I stay, I can't
run.   *Foresters* ii i 347
Heerd (**heard**)   I *h* summat as summun towld summun
o' owld Bishop Gardiner's end ;   *Queen Mary* iv iii 501
Height (*See also* **Eagle-height**)   from that *h* something was
said to me   *Becket* ii i 59
Blared from the *h's* of all the thrones of her kings,   ,,   v ii 489
What breadth, *h*, strength—torrents of eddying bark !   *Foresters* iii 94
Heir   You, The *h* presumptive.   *Queen Mary* i iv 33
—after me Is *h* of England ;   ,,   i v 286
H of this England and the Netherlands !   ,,   i v 418
my father was the rightful *h* Of England,   ,,   ii ii 170
You must proclaim Elizabeth your *h*. (repeat)   ,,   v 191, 204
in happy state To give him an *h* male.   ,,   v ii 573
Mary hath acknowledged you her *h*.   ,,   v iii 31
She knew me, and acknowledged me her *h*,   ,,   v v 256
Pronounced his *h* of England.   *Harold* ii 195
I am *h* Of England by the promise of her king.   ,,   ii ii 124
Why then the *h* of England, who is he ?   ,,   ii 567
hath King Edward not pronounced his *h* ?   ,,   ii 576
leave the royalty of my crown Unlessen'd to
mine *h's*.   *Becket* ii i 108
citizen's *h* hath conquer'd me For the moment.   ,,   ii ii 60
left his *h*, Born, happily, with some sense of art,   *Prom. of May* i 496
And cursed me, as the last *h* of my race :   *Foresters* ii ii 109
Held   the boy she *h* Mimick'd and piped her ' Wyatt,'   *Queen Mary* ii ii 73
this day be *h* in after years More solemn   ,,   iii iii 89
I had *h* my head up then.   ,,   iii iii 246
were he wroth indeed, You *h* it less, or not at all.   ,,   iv i 107
That when I was Archbishop *h* with me.   ,,   iv ii 160
So *h* it till it all was burn'd,   ,,   iv iii 615
and *h* up by the hair ?   ,,   v ii 21
But *h* from you all papers sent by Rome,   ,,   v ii 45
nor as some have *h*, Because I love the Norman
better—   *Harold* i i 170
she *h* with Edward, At least methought she *h* with
holy Edward,   ,,   i ii 49
yet he *h* that Dane, Jute, Angle, Saxon,   ,,   iv i 75
He *h* with Morcar.—   ,,   iv i 43
were man's to have *h* The battle-axe by thee !   ,,   iv iii 12
whether that which *h* it Had weaken'd,   ,,   v i 105
Some *h* she was his wife in secret—   ,,   v ii 10
I *h* it with him in his English halls,   ,,   v ii 128
And that the false Northumbrian *h* aloof,   ,,   v ii 165
For Gilbert Foliot *h* himself the man.   *Becket* i i 43
I that *h* the orange blossom Dark as the yew ?   *Prom. of May* ii 629
True, I have *h* opinions, hold some still,   ,,   iii 622
I *h* for Richard, and I hated John.   *Foresters* i 52
I ever *h* that saying false That Love is blind,   ,,   ii i 642
who heads the movement, *h* him craven ?   ,,   ii i 701
Tho' you should queen me over all the realms *H* by
King Richard,   ,,   iv 709
but all those that *h* with him, Except I plead for them,   ,,   iv 748
Hell (*See also* **A-hell-fire**)   Look at the New World—a
paradise made *h* ;   *Queen Mary* ii i 208
Traced in the blackest text of *H*—' Thou shalt ! '   ,,   iii i 426
Into the deathless *h* which is their doom   ,,   iii ii 175
The unity of Universal *H*,   ,,   iii iii 232
He burns in Purgatory, not in *H*.   ,,   iv i 56
Or to be still in pain with devils in *h* ;   ,,   iv iii 222
find Heaven or else *h* ready to swallow me,   ,,   iv iii 224
There's nought but the vire of God's *h* ez can burn
out that.   ,,   iv iii 527
Adulterous to the very heart of *H*.   ,,   v v 163
like a spirit in *H* who skips and flies   *Harold* i i 11

Hell (*continued*)   is this pendent *h* in heaven A harm to
England ?   *Harold* i i 76
Is thy wrath *H*, that I should spare to cry,   „   v i 37
H take thy bishop then, and my kingship too !   *Becket, Pro.* 93
With a wanton in thy lodging—*H* requite 'em !   „   i i 9
I scatter all their cowls to all the *h*'s.   „   ii i 93
Fling not thy soul into the flames of *h* :   „   ii i 316
which *H*'s own heat So dwelt on that they rose   „   ii ii 204
I hear the yelping of the hounds of *h*.   „   iii ii 48
I would the Church were down in *h* !   „   v i 218
Too late on earth may be too soon in *h*.   „   v ii 528
She lies ! They are made in *H*.   *Prom. of May* iii 711
By all the devils in and out of *H* !   *Foresters* ii i 27
Devils, that make this blessed England *h*.   „   iii 128
yells of thief And rogue and liar echo down in *H*,   „   iii 324
Maid ?   *Friar.*   Paramour !   *Friar.*   *H* take her !   „   iii 403
Or, like the Devils they are, straight up from *H*.   „   iv 595
If anywhere, I shall find thee in *h*.   „   iv 803
Hellebore   madden Against his priest beyond all *h*.   *Becket* iv i 460
Hell-fire   and the soul of Eleanor from *h-f*.   „   *Pro.* 151
Hellstow   Into Godstow, into *H*, Devilstow !   „   v i 215
Helm (**armour for the head**)   Cowl, *h* ; and crozier,
battle-axe.   *Harold* v i 444
Helm (**as of a boat**)   Cranmer, as the helmsman at
the *h* Steers,   *Queen Mary* iv iii 578
Helm (**verb**)   wherefore not *H* the huge vessel of
your state,   „   v i 73
and no forsworn Archbishop Shall *h* the Church.   *Becket* i iii 598
Helmet   his hand Upon his *h*.   *Queen Mary* v v 31
Of the Northumbrian *h* on the heath ?   *Harold* v i 144
gonfanon of Holy Peter Floating above their *h*'s—   „   v i 550
Helmeted   not courtly to stand *h* Before the Queen.   *Queen Mary* v v 36
Helmsman   Cranmer, as the *h* at the helm Steers,   „   iv iii 578
Help (**s**)   thro' thine *h* we are come to London Bridge ;   „   ii iii 8
Then whither should I flee for any *h* ?   „   iv iii 126
Without the *h* of Spain.   „   v iii 78
England our own Thro' Harold's *h*,   *Harold* ii 79
all promises Made in our agony for *h* from heaven ?   „   iii i 288
No sacrifice to heaven, no *h* from heaven ;   „   iii i 350
pray, pray, pray—no *h* but prayer,   „   iii ii 195
but our *h* Is Harold, king of England.   „   iv i 10
old crown Were little *h* without our Saxon carles   „   iv i 35
Call not for *h* from me.   I knew him not.   „   v ii 54
butts him from his chair, Will need my *h*—   *Becket, Pro.* 218
Past *h* ! his paws are past *h*.   God help him !   „   i iv 110
Man's *h* ! but we, we have the Blessed Virgin   „   v ii 219
But for the slender *h* that I can give,   *Prom. of May* ii 421
Help (**verb**)   I cannot *h* it.   *Queen Mary* ii 60
I will *h* you, Madam, Even to the utmost.   „   i v 177
But *h* her in this exigency,   „   ii ii 18
The King of France will *h* to break it.   „   iii i 105
H it can I ? with my hands Milking the cow ?   „   iii v 101
H me : what think you, Is it life or death ?   „   iii i 192
I'll *h* you, if I may.   „   iii v 205
these burnings will not *h* The purpose of the faith ;   „   iv ii 184
May God *h* you Thro' that dark hour !   „   iv ii 195
are profitless to the burners, And *h* the other side.   „   iv ii 220
Heaven *h* that this re-action not re-act   „   iv iii 108
Not to *h* me ?   They hate *me* also for my love to you,   „   v i 94
many English in your ranks To *h* your battle.   „   v i 112
Will you not *h* me here ?   „   v i 161
You did but *h* King Philip's war with France,   „   v ii 313
God *h* me, but methinks I love her less   „   v ii 420
Drugs—but he knows they cannot *h* me—   „   v v 61
—*H* me hence.   „   v v 200
Would *h* thee from the trap.   *Harold* i i 383
H the good ship, showing the sunken rock,   „   ii i 100
Good, good, and thou wilt *h* me to the crown ?   „   ii ii 614
I ask thee, wilt thou *h* me to the crown ?   „   ii ii 627
Swear thou to *h* me to the crown of England.   „   ii ii 705
I swear to *h* thee to the crown of England . . .
(repeat)   *Harold* ii ii 712, 721
h to build a throne Out-towering hers of France . . .   *Harold* ii ii 763
To *h* us from their brethren yonder ?   „   iii i 221
Oh God ! I cannot *h* it, but at times They seem to me   „   iii ii 63

HH*

Help (**verb**) (*continued*)   God *h* me !   I know nothing—   *Harold* iii ii 193
To *h* the realm from scattering.   „   iv i 106
will ye upon oath, *H* us against the Norman ?   „   iv i 181
I cannot find his body.   O *h* me thou !   „   v ii 20
Forgive me thou, and *h* me here !   „   v ii 22
Not *h* me, nor forgive me ?   „   v ii 24
thou didst *h* me to my throne In Theobald's time,   *Becket, Pro.* 200
Shall I not *h* your lordship to your rest ?   „   i i 1
better than thyself That thou shouldst *h* me ?   „   i i 5
H me off, Herbert, with this—   „   i i 10
Past help ! his paws are past help.   God *h* him !   „   i iv 110
God *h* her, That she was sworn to silence.   „   iii i 77
Heaven *h* you ; get you hence in haste   „   iv ii 26
H ! *h* !   *Eleanor.*   They say that walls have ears ;   „   iv ii 78
God *h* thee !   „   v ii 296
laid mine own life down To *h* him from them,   „   iv ii 340
I cannot *h* the mould that I was cast in.   *The Cup* i iii 25
Employ us, heat us, quicken us, *h* us,   „   i iii 131
O *h* us from all that oppress us !   „   ii 5
Will hardly *h* to make him sane again.   *The Falcon* 83
Not quite recover'd your wound, the wine Might *h* you.   „   592
And so return—Heaven *h* him !—to our own.   „   861
We two together Will *h* to heal your son—   „   923
H me to move this bench for him into the sun.   *Prom. of May* i 80
Seem my good angel who may *h* me from it.   „   ii 388
How can I *h* him ?   „   ii 392
I trust I may be able by-and-by to *h* you in the
business of the farm ;   „   iii 222
and I asked her once more to *h* me,   „   iii 388
And I will follow thee, and God *h* us both.   *Foresters* i i 278
God's good Angel *H* him back hither,   „   i ii 11
I must pass overseas to one that I trust will *h* me.   „   i ii 153
I cannot *h* you in this exigency ;   „   i ii 273
A worthy messenger ! how should he *h* it ?   „   i iii 86
for, God *h* us, we lie by nature.   „   ii i 237
to *h* the old man When he was fighting.   „   ii i 541
balms and simples of the field To *h* a wound.   „   ii ii 13
Robin's an outlaw, but he *h*'s the poor.   While Richard
hath outlaw'd himself, and *h*'s Nor rich, nor poor.   „   iv 358
—God *h* the mark—   „   iv 714
Hail, knight, and *h* us.   „   iv 765
Help'd-helpt (*See also* **Holp, Holpen**)   Pole Will tell
you that the devil *helpt* them thro' it.   *Queen Mary* iv iii 352
some familiar spirit must have *help'd* him.   *Harold* ii ii 677
The Norseman's raid Hath *helpt* the Norman,   „   v 292
and his brother Tostig *helpt* ;   „   v 47
King Stephen gave Many of the crown lands to those
that *helpt* him,   *Becket* i iii 151
King Louis, Who *helpt* me when none else.   „   iii ii 249
frost That *help'd* to check the flowing of the blood.   *The Falcon* 645
Helping   as she was *h* to build the mound against the
city.   *Foresters* ii i 308
Helpless   the red man, that good *h* creature, starved,
maim'd, flogg'd,   *Queen Mary* ii i 209
And cruel at it, killing *h* flies ;   „   iii iv 65
our *h* folk Are wash'd away, wailing, in their own
blood—   *Harold* ii ii 470
Helpt   *See* **Help'd**
Heman (**a singer**)   sing, Asaph ! clash The cymbal, *H* !   „   iii i 188
Hen (*See also* **Sitting-hen**)   a fox may filch a *h* by
night,   *Queen Mary* iii v 157
Who stole the widow's sitting *h* o' Sunday,   *Becket* i iv 121
Sitting *h* ! Our Lord Becket's our great sitting-hen cock,   „   i iv 124
The *h* cluckt late by the white farm gate,   *Prom. of May* i 38
a fox from the glen ran away with the *h*,   „   i 52
Henceforward   none shall hold them in his house and
live, *H*.   *Queen Mary* iv i 98
Henry (**Bedingfield**) (*See also* **Henry Bedingfield**)   I woke
Sir *H*—and he's true to you—   „   iii v 60
Henry (**King of France**)   but we play with *H*, King of
France,   „   i iii 131
King *H* warms your traitors at his hearth.   „   v i 123
this *H* Stirs up your land against you   „   v i 130
Henry (**son of Henry II.**)   I will have My young son *H*
crown'd the King of England,   *Becket, Pro.* 224

Heretic (s) (*continued*) And there be many *h*'s in the
town,   *Queen Mary* IV ii 30
Did I call him *h*? A huge heresiarch!   ,,   IV iii 45
Ay, stop the *h*'s mouth! Hale him away!   ,,   IV iii 282
I know them *h*'s, but right English ones.   ,,   IV iii 344
I have seen *h*'s of the poorer sort,   ,,   IV iii 436
No faith with *h*'s, my Lord!   ,,   IV iii 458
Than *h* of these times;   ,,   IV iii 599
blood and sweat of *h*'s at the stake Is God's best dew   ,,   v i 101
But she's a *h*, and, when I am gone,   ,,   v i 200
So brands me in the stare of Christendom, A *h*!   ,,   v ii 63
all my lifelong labour to uphold The primacy—a *h*.   ,,   v ii 71
A *h*! He drew his shaft against me to the head,   ,,   v ii 79
have sent me Legate hither, Deeming me *h*?   ,,   v ii 89
I, a *h*? Your Highness knows that in pursuing heresy   ,,   v ii 95
the Pope Pointing at me with ' Pole, the *h*,   ,,   v ii 175
H and rebel Point at me and make merry.   ,,   v ii 316
Heretical Touch him upon his old *h* talk,   ,,   III iv 352
I will take Such order with all bad, *h* books   ,,   IV i 95
Hereward the Wake have loved Harold the Saxon, or *H t W*.   *Foresters* I i 228
our great Earl, the bravest English heart Since *H t W*,   ,,   II i 688
Heritage to the intent That you may lose your
English *h*.   *Queen Mary* v i 133
Yea, let a stranger spoil his *h*,   *Becket* II ii 259
Hern No bird? *Filippo*. Half a tit and a *h*'s bill.   *The Falcon* 131
Hern (hers) Our Daisy's butter's as good 'z *h*.   *Queen Mary* III iii 482
Herod since your *H*'s death, How oft hath Peter   ,,   III ii 61
Herod-Henry When *H-H* first Began to batter   ,,   III iv 184
Hero-like howsoever *h-l* the man Dies in the fire,   ,,   IV iii 324
Herring-pond liest as loud as the black *h-p* behind thee.   *Harold* II i 26
Herring-shoal here's a crowd as thick as *h-s*'s.   *Queen Mary* III i 182
Hers *See* **Hern**
Herse (horse) Blacksmith, thaw he niver shoes a *h* to
my likings;   *Prom. of May* I 448
Herse-pond (horse-pond) I'd like to drag 'im thruff the
h-p, and she to be a-lookin' at it.   ,,   II 593
Hew His sword shall *h* the heretic peoples down!   *Queen Mary* III ii 178
Hewn I'll have the drawbridge *h* into the Thames,   ,,   II ii 376
They had *h* the drawbridge down into the river.   ,,   II iii 18
Hid with his brother Odo The Bayeux bishop, and I *h*
myself.   *Harold* II ii 348
I was afraid of her, and I *h* myself.   *Prom. of May* I 551
She *h* this sister, told me she was dead—   ,,   III 689
The groining *h* the heavens;   *Foresters* I i 62
Hidden Then *h* in the street He watch'd her pass   *Becket* II iii 39
From all the *h* by-ways of the world   ,,   III iii 15
I hate *h* faces. (repeat)   *Foresters* I ii 245, 251
Hide (skin) then Hung out raw *h*'s along their walls,   *Harold* II iii 383
clench'd their pirate *h*'s To the bleak church doors,   ,,   IV iii 36
Hide (verb) and *h* himself and die;   *Queen Mary* I ii 142
To *h* the scar left by thy Parthian dart.   *Becket, Pro.* 377
Save me, father, *h* me—they follow me—   ,,   I i 181
and once he strove to *h* his face,   ,,   III iii 103
I will *h* my face, Blacken and gipsyfy it;   ,,   IV ii 98
But these arm'd men—will you not *h* yourself?   ,,   v ii 247
Pray you, *h* yourself.   ,,   v ii 257
The murderers, hark! Let us *h*! let us *h*!   ,,   v iii 47
Why wearest thou thy cowl to *h* thy face?   *Foresters* I ii 206
thou canst not *h* thyself From her who loves thee.   ,,   II ii 24
You *h* this damsel in your forest here,   ,,   IV 476
Hide and seek You play at *h* a *s*.   *Queen Mary* I v 305
Higgins (a farm labourer) *H*, Jackson, Luscombe, Nokes,   *Prom. of May* III 52
High Before our own *H* Court of Parliament,   *Queen Mary* II ii 234
There stands a man, once of so *h* degree,   ,,   IV iii 68
And bolts of thunder moulded in *h* heaven To serve the
Norman purpose,   *Harold* II ii 32
that thus baptized in blood Grew ever *h* and higher,   ,,   III i 148
let our *h* altar Stand where their standard fell . . .   ,,   v i 138
Then I saw Thy *h* black steed among the flaming furze,   *Becket* II i 55
And is the King's *if* too *h* a stile for your lordship to
overstep   ,,   III iii 281
But crowns must bow when mitres sit so *h*.   ,,   IV ii 298
The *h* Heaven guard thee from his wantonness,   *Foresters* I ii 121
Till Nature, *h* and low, and great and small Forgets
herself,   ,,   I ii 326

Highback'd The deer, the *h* polecat, the wild boar,   *Foresters* I iii 119
High-dropsy Or a *h-d*, as the doctors call it.   *Queen Mary* III ii 225
Higher I'll have my head set *h* in the state;   ,,   II i 250
eyes So bashful that you look'd no *h*?   ,,   III i 65
O *h*, holier, earlier, purer church,   ,,   IV ii 108
Grew ever high and *h*, beyond my seeing,   *Harold* III i 148
Your ladyship lives *h* in the sun.   *The Falcon* 583
strain to make ourselves Better and *h* than Nature,   *Prom. of May* I 604
Highest That all of you, the *h* as the lowest,   *Queen Mary* III iii 64
great Angel past along the *h* Crying   *Harold* II i 133
Angel rose And past again along the *h*   ,,   III i 156
Glory to God in the *H*! fallen, fallen!   ,,   v i 636
High-hearted Then the maid is not *h-h* enough.   *Foresters* I i 258
High-priest I have it . . . My lord Paramount, Our
great *H-p*,   *Becket* IV ii 357
High-set sitting here Between the two most *h-s*
thrones on earth,   *Queen Mary* III ii 106
Hildebrand (afterwards Pope Gregory VII.) and that Archdeacon *H* His master,   *Harold* III ii 144
Hill this land is like a *h* of fire,   *Queen Mary* II ii 521
signs on earth! Knowest thou Senlac *h*?   *Harold* III i 361
passing by that *h* three nights ago—   ,,   III i 366
And dreadful shadows strove upon the *h*,   ,,   III i 378
A *h*, a fort, a city—that reach'd a hand   ,,   IV i 44
another *h* Or fort, or city, took it,   ,,   IV i 49
had in it Wales, Her floods, her woods, her *h*'s: ,,   IV i 207
and yet I saw thee drive him up his *h*'s—   ,,   IV i 211
Scatter thy people home, descend the *h*,   ,,   v i 10
tell him we stand arm'd on Senlac *H*,   ,,   v i 60
Gurth, Leofwin, go once more about the *h*—   ,,   v i 183
To tell thee thou shalt die on Senlac *h*—   ,,   v i 242
He glitters on the crowning of the *h*.   ,,   v i 488
All the Norman foot Are storming up the *h*.   ,,   v i 523
axes lighten with a single flash About the summit of the *h*,   ,,   v i 539
their horse Swallow the *h* locust-like,   ,,   v i 560
The horse and horseman roll along the *h*,   ,,   v i 595
Look out upon the *h*—is Harold there?   ,,   v i 669
build a church to God Here on the *h* of battle;   ,,   v ii 138
open'd out The purple zone of *h* and heaven;   *The Cup* I i 408
whose breath Is balmy wind to robe our *h*'s with grass,   ,,   II 265
storm was drawing hither Across the *h*'s   ,,   II 320
there is Monna Giovanna coming down the *h* from the
castle.   *The Falcon* 161
out of the forest and over the *h*'s and away,   *Foresters* II ii 176
Old as the *h*'s.   ,,   IV 301
I see two figures crawling up the *h*.   ,,   IV 333
Hillo *H*, the stag! What, you are all unfurnish'd?   *The Cup* I i 205
H! *H*!   ,,   I 214
Hilt Look at the *h*. What excellent workmanship.   *Becket* IV ii 314
Himself *See* **'Issen**
Hinder I'd make a move myself to *h* that: *Queen Mary* III i 127
What *h*'s but that Spain and England join'd,   ,,   v iii 68
What *h*'s me to hold with mine own men?   *Harold* II i 102
yon huge keep that *h*'s half the heaven.   ,,   II ii 228
Hindering *See* **Burial-hindering**
Hinted Yet her—what her? he *h* of some her—   *Becket* III i 243
Hip Back and side and *h* and rib,   *Foresters* II ii 120
Hiss and *h* Against the blaze they cannot quench—   *Harold* III i 395
Hiss'd As we past, Some hail'd, some *h* us.   *Queen Mary* II ii 61
And *h* against the sun?   *Becket* v iii 45
Hissing Stab me in fancy, *h* Spain and Philip;   *Queen Mary* I v 150
Whose doings are a horror to the east, A *h* in the west!'   *Becket* IV ii 245
History how often in old *histories* have the great men   *Foresters* I i 242
Hit This is the likelier tale. We have *h* the place.   *Becket* III ii 43
This is no bow to *h* nightingales;   *Foresters* II i 391
H! Did I not tell you an old woman could shoot
better?   ,,   I 406
Hive So hated here! I watch'd a *h* of late;   *Queen Mary* III iii 46
bees, If any creeping life invade their *h*   ,,   III iii 54
when our good *h* Needs every sting to save it.   *Harold* IV i 17
Hoäm (home) *H* wi' it, then. *Haymaker*. Well, it
be the last loäd *h*.   *Prom. of May* II 143
as I beäk afoor, it be the last loäd *h*; do thou and
thy sweet'art sing us *h* to supper—   ,,   II 169
—' The Last Loäd *H*.' (repeat)   ,,   II 171, 172

Hoäm (home) (_continued_) At the end of the daäy,
For the last loäd h? (repeat) _Prom. of May_ II 184, 195
Till the end of the daäy And the last loäd h. „ II 209
Till the end o' the daäy An' the last loäd h.' „ II 239
To the end o' the daäy An' the last loäd h.' „ II 260
An' the last loäd h, Loäd h.' „ II 293
H? fro' the bottom o' the river? „ III 443

Hoäm-maäde (home-made) and Baäker, thaw I
sticks to h-m— „ I 449

Hoarse I have, my Lord, shouted till I am h. _Queen Mary_ III i 291

Hobnail'd Your rights and charters h into slush— „ II ii 278

Hodge H 'ud ha' been a-harrowin' o' white peasen i' the
outfield— „ IV iii 491

Hog The h hath tumbled himself into some corner, _Becket_ I i 369

Hoist But I would h the drawbridge, like thy master. _Foresters_ I i 318

Hold (s) (_See also_ **Holt**) hottest h in all the devil's den _Queen Mary_ V iv 15

Hold (verb) (_See also_ **'Owd**) Seek to possess our
person, h our Tower. „ II ii 158
I may be wrong, sir. This marriage will not h. „ III i 103
There's a brave man, if any. _Bagenhall._ Ay; if it h. „ III i 176
that no foreigner H office in the household, „ III iii 72
So then you h the Pope— _Gardiner._ I h the Pope!
What do I h him? what do I h the Pope? „ III iv 371
none shall h them in his house and live, „ IV i 96
could scarce meet his eye And h your own; „ IV i 105
I h by all I wrote within that book. „ IV iii 275
I do h The Catholic, if he have the greater right, „ IV iii 381
strike Their hearts, and h their babies up to it. _Harold_ I i 35
much ado To h mine own against old Gurth. „ I i 438
thine eyelids into sleep, Will h mine waking. „ I ii 141
H thine own, if thou canst! „ II i 79
my men H that the shipwreckt are accursed of God;—
What hinders me to h with mine own men? „ II i 100
We h our Saxon woodcock in the springe, „ II ii 1
Yet I h out against them, as I may, Yea—would h out, „ II ii 552
Better to be a liar's dog, and h My master honest, „ III ii 125
And Morcar h's with us. „ IV ii 46
must h The sequel had been other than his league „ IV iii 87
No power mine To h their force together . . . „ IV iii 213
This is the hottest of it: h, ash! h, willow! „ V i 628
The Church should h her baronies of me, _Becket, Pro._ 24
Thou hast not to h but thy hand. „ _Pro._ 412
And many a baron h's along with me— „ I ii 52
among you those that h Lands reft from Canterbury. „ I iii 140
And mean to h it, or— _Becket._ To have my life. „ I iii 162
Wilt thou h out for ever, Thomas Becket? „ I iii 265
h's his cross before him thro' the crowd, „ I iii 477
I h not by my signing. „ I iii 563
But we h Thou art forsworn; „ I iii 595
I h Nothing in fee and barony of the King. Whatever
the Church owns—she h's it in Free and perpetual alms, „ I iii 677
If the King h his purpose, I am myself a beggar. „ I iv 89
England scarce would h Young Henry king, „ II ii 31
We h by his defiance, not his defect. „ II ii 218
cursed those De Brocs That h our Saltwood Castle from
our see! „ II ii 269
Map scoffs at Rome. I all but h with Map. „ II ii 385
keep the figure moist and make it h water, „ III iii 166
the lady h's the cleric Lovelier than any soldier, „ V i 193
Who h With York, with York against me. „ V ii 62
De Morville, h her away. _De Morville._ I h her. „ V iii 173
See here—I stretch my hand out—h it there. _The Cup_ II 210
I am sinking—h me—Let me alone. „ II 478
I think I scarce could h my head up then. _Prom. of May_ I 689
True, I have held opinions, h some still, „ III 622
Lady Marian h's her nose when she steps across it. _Foresters_ I i 83
handle all womankind gently, and h them in all honour, „ I i 99
there is a lot of wild fellows in Sherwood Forest who h
by King Richard. „ I ii 73
last time When I shall h my birthday in this hall: „ I ii 89
How she looks up at him, how she h's her face! „ I ii 144
I fear you be of those who h more by John than Richard. „ I ii 198
good fellows there in merry Sherwood That h by Richard, „ I iii 100
They h by Richard—the wild wood! „ I iii 110
O h thy hand! this is our Marian. „ II ii 36

Hold (verb) (_continued_) but I h thee The husband of my heart, _Foresters_ III 139
You hope to h and keep her for yourself, „ IV 477
mate with one that h's no love is pure, „ IV 711
if you h us here Longer from our own venison. „ IV 941

Holdest thou, De Broc, that h Saltwood Castle— _Becket_ I iii 160
that h thine estates In fee and barony „ II 674

Hold-fast Such h-f claws that you perforce again „ II ii 86

Holding true To either function, h it; „ III 538

Hold'st Thou h with him? (repeat) _Foresters_ II i 526, 530

Hole skulk into corners Like rabbits to their h's. _Queen Mary_ II iv 56
creep down into some dark h Like a hurt beast, „ IV i 141
crawl down thine own black h To the lowest Hell. _The Cup_ II 495

Holiday a boon, my king, Respite, a h: _Harold_ I i 227

Holier O higher, h, earlier, purer church, _Queen Mary_ V ii 108
They are so much h than their harlot's son _Harold_ V ii 11
Foliot is the h man, perhaps the better. _Becket_ III iii 92

Holiest From all the h shrines in Normandy! _Harold_ II ii 735
The H of our H one should be This William's fellow-
tricksters; „ III ii 76
More, what the mightiest and the h Of all his predecessors _Becket_ II i 179

Holiness that you might not seem To disobey his H. _Queen Mary_ V ii 53
his politic H Hath all but climb'd the Roman perch _Becket_ II ii 45
His H, pushed one way by the Empire and another by
England, „ II ii 327
will not your H Vouchsafe a gracious answer „ IV ii 358

Holla'd (shouted) I h to him, but he didn't hear me: „ III ii 25

Holler (hollow) Dan Smith's cart hes runned ower a
laädy i' the h laäne, _Prom. of May_ II 569
Ye sees the h laäne be hallus sa dark i' the afternoon, „ III 92

Hollow (adj.) (_See also_ **Holler**) —no distance—this H
Pandora-box, „ II 346
when you lamed the lady in the h lane. „ III 90
Do you still suffer from your fall in the h lane. „ III 241
Scarlet hacking down A h ash, a bat flew out at him _Foresters_ II ii 96
though thou wert like a bottle full up to the cork, or
as h as a kex. „ II 211

Hollow (verb) voice of the deep as it h's the cliffs of the land. _Becket_ I i 4
tho' the drop may h out the dead stone, _Becket_ III iii 315

Hollow'd All h out with stinging heresies;— _Queen Mary_ III i 203

Hollow-hearted Some h-h from exceeding age— _Foresters_ III 96

Hollowness Bring not thy h On our full feast. _Harold_ IV iii 203

Holocaust wherein have been Such h's of heresy! _Queen Mary_ III iv 108

Holp (_See also_ **Help'd**) he h the King to break down our
castles, _Becket, Pro._ 446
I do believe he h Northumberland Against me. _Queen Mary_ I v 278

Holpen (_See also_ **Help'd**) Had h Richard's tottering
throne to stand, „ III i 114
Not so well h in our wars with France, „ III vi 188
All widows we have h pray for us, _Foresters_ IV 1078

Holt (hold) and tells un ez the vire has tuk h. _Queen Mary_ IV iii 512

Holy —hath sent for the h legate of the h father
the Pope, Cardinal Pole, to give us all that
absolution which— „ I iii 26
H absolution! h Inquisition! „ I iii 31
Son Courtenay, wilt thou see the h father Murdered „ I iii 64
No, by the h Virgin, being noble, But love me only: „ I v 70
H Virgin, Plead with thy blessed Son; „ I v 83
Makes me his mouth of h greeting. „ III ii 80
sent me here as Legate From our most H Father Julius,
Pope, „ III iii 126
Against the H Father's primacy, „ III iii 131
of all censures Of H Church that we be fall'n into, „ III iii 158
Unto the h see and reigning Pope Serve God „ III iii 212
Our Lord and H Father, Julius, God's Vicar „ III iv 248
or more Denied the H Father! „ III iv 359
I kept my head for use of H Church; „ III v 80
range Among the pleasant fields of H Writ „ III v 243
As once the H Father did with mine, „ III vi 33
Against the King, the Queen, the H Father, „ III vi 199
The H Virgin not have me yet Lose the sweet hope „ III vi 199
The H Father in a secular kingdom Is as the soul „ IV i 34
It is God's will, the H Father's will, „ IV i 184
and I Scraped from your finger-points the h oil; „ IV ii 132
As if he had been the H Father, sat And judged it. „ IV iii 44
For if our H Queen not pardon him, „ IV iii 61

Holy (*continued*) O *H* Ghost! proceeding from them
both,   *Queen Mary* IV iii 119
Who deems it a most just and *h* war.   ,,   v i 147
and of his *h* head—   ,,   v i 157
And yet I must obey the *H* Father,   ,,   v ii 38
We have made war upon the *H* Father All for your
sake: ,,   v ii 307
No, Madam, not against the *H* Father;   ,,   v ii 312
And done such mighty things by *H* Church,   ,,   v v 74
set up The *H* Office here—garner the wheat,   ,,   v v 113
H Father Has ta'en the legateship from our cousin
Pole—   ,,   v v 125
Our *h* Norman bishops down from all Their thrones
in England?   *Harold* I i 50
I have builded the great Church of *H* Peter: ,,   I i 180
And, *H* Mary! How Harold used to beat him!   ,,   I i 431
At least methought she held with *h* Edward,   ,,   I ii 51
'O blessed relics!' O *H* Peter!'   ,,   I ii 171
And that the *H* Saints of Normandy When thou·art
home in England,   ,,   II ii 727
The *h* bones of all the Canonised   ,,   II ii 734
I would I were As *h* and as passionless as he!   ,,   III i 43
H? ay, ay, forsooth, A conscience for his own soul,   ,,   III i 61
loftiest minster ever built To *H* Peter in our English isle!   ,,   III i 206
And all our just and wise and *h* men That shall be born
hereafter.   ,,   III i 209
Our *h* king Hath given his virgin lamb to *H* Church   ,,   III i 334
for the king Is *h*, and hath talk'd with God,   ,,   III i 355
loved within the pale forbidden By *H* Church: ,,   III ii 24
Kiss me—thou art not A *h* sister yet, my girl,   ,,   III ii 81
and have sent him back A *h* gonfanon,   ,,   III ii 148
Forward! Forward! Harold and *H* Cross!   ,,   IV i 269
H Father Hath given this realm of England to the Norman.   ,,   v i 12
H Father To do with England's choice of her own king?   ,,   v i 17
the *H* Rood had lean'd And bow'd above me;   ,,   v i 102
made too good an use of *H* Church To break her close!   ,,   v i 312
the *H* Rood That bow'd to me at Waltham—   ,,   v i 382
Harold and *H* Cross! (repeat)   *Harold* v i 439, 519, 662
What power, *h* father?   *Harold* v i 454
gonfanon of *H* Peter Floating above their helmets—   ,,   v i 549
His oath was broken—O *h* Norman Saints,   ,,   v i 616
The *H* Father strangled him with a hair Of Peter,   ,,   v ii 45
And but that *H* Peter fought for us,   ,,   v ii 164
to whom thou art bound By *H* Church.   *Becket, Pro.* 68
I, true son Of *H* Church—no croucher to the Gregories   ,,   Pro. 211
the *H* Father, while This Barbarossa butts him from
his chair,   ,,   Pro. 215
Name him; the *H* Father will confirm him.   ,,   Pro. 244
Our *h* mother Canterbury, who sits With tatter'd robes.   ,,   I i 156
O, *h* father, when thou seest him next,   ,,   I i 322
Knowing how much you reverence *H* Church,   ,,   I ii 48
Are not so much at feud with *H* Church   ,,   I ii 54
and lay My crozier in the *H* Father's hands,   ,,   I iii 125
Have I the orders of the *H* Father?   ,,   I iii 233
The secret whisper of the *H* Father.   ,,   I iii 236
The spire of *H* Church may prick the graves—   ,,   I iii 553
Becket shall be king, and the *H* Father shall be king,   ,,   I iv 270
The *H* Thomas! Brother, you have traffick'd Between
the Emperor and the Pope,   ,,   II ii 66
H Church May rock, but will not wreck,   ,,   II ii 102
thanks of *H* Church are due to those That went before
us   ,,   II ii 190
Thee, thou *h* Thomas! I would that thou hadst been
the *H* Father.   ,,   II ii 398
I would have done my most to keep Rome *h*,   ,,   II ii 401
Forgive me and absolve me, *h* father.   ,,   II ii 441
with the *H* Father astride of it down upon his own
head.   ,,   III iii 77
False oath on *h* cross—for thou must leave him To-day,   ,,   IV ii 209
God's Grace and *H* Church deliver'd us.   ,,   IV ii 309
sometimes I have overshot My duties to our *H* Mother
Church,   ,,   v i 38
crying On *H* Church to thunder out her rights   ,,   v ii 31
Nor make me traitor to my *h* office.   ,,   v ii 149
To assail our *H* Mother lest she brood Too long   ,,   v ii 251

Holy (*continued*) scare me from my loyalty To God and to
the *H* Father.   *Becket* v ii 483
Valour and *h* life should go together.   ,,   v ii 587
Thy *h* follower founded Canterbury—   ,,   v iii 5
and take this *h* cup To lodge it in the shrine of
Artemis,   *The Cup* I ii 434
To lodge this cup Within the *h* shrine of Artemis,   ,,   I iii 53
H mother! To breakfast! Oh sweet saints!   *The Falcon* 214
I keep it For *h* vows made to the blessed Saints   *Foresters* I ii 175
he is a *h* Palmer, bounden by a vow not to show his face,
till he join King Richard in the *H* Land. *Robin.*   ,,   I ii 236
Going to the *H* Land to Richard!   ,,   I ii 239
by this *H* Cross Which good King Richard gave me   ,,   I ii 309
For playing upside down with *H* Writ.   ,,   III 168
And you three *h* men,   ,,   III 382
In the sweat of thy brow, says *H* Writ, shalt thou eat
bread,   ,,   IV 201
The *H* Virgin Stand by the strongest.   ,,   IV 263
our friar is so *h* That he's a miracle-monger,   ,,   IV 280
he flung His life, heart, soul into those *h* wars   ,,   IV 407
Heading the *h* war against the Moslem,   ,,   IV 818
like the man In *H* Writ, who brought his talent back;   ,,   IV 981
And join'd my banner in the *H* Land,   ,,   IV 1000

Holy Ghost O *H G*! proceeding from them both,   *Queen Mary* IV iii 119
   ,,   v v 254

Homage Then here she stands! my *h*.   ,,   v v 254
all manner of *h*'s, and observances, and circumbendibuses.   *Foresters* I i 103

Home (*See also* **Hoäm**) Struck *h* and won.   *Queen Mary* I v 554
nearer *h*, the Netherlands, Sicily, Naples,   ,,   II i 212
A smile abroad is oft a scowl at *h*.   ,,   III i 213
bring it *H* to the leisure wisdom of his Queen,   ,,   III vi 23
thou art reclaim'd; He brings thee *h*:   ,,   IV iii 84
Albeit he think himself at *h* with God,   ,,   IV iii 192
When I should guide the Church in peace at *h*,   ,,   v ii 68
You had best go *h*. What are you?   ,,   v iv 43
Good night! Go *h*. Besides, you curse so loud, The
watch will hear you. Get you *h* at once.   ,,   v iv 61
Thy life at *h* Is easier than mine here.   *Harold* I i 164
I pray thee, let me hence and bring him *h*.   ,,   I i 242
I should let him *h* again, my lord.   ,,   II ii 63
Since thou hast promised Wulfnoth *h* with us, Be *h* again
with Wulfnoth.   ,,   II ii 167
poor lad! how sick and sad for *h*!   ,,   II ii 326
When thou art *h* in England, with thine own,   ,,   II ii 728
No footfall—no Fitzurse. We have seen her *h*.   *Becket* I i 368
We be a-going *h* after our supper in all humbleness,   ,,   I iv 206
thy true *h*—the heavens—cry out for thee   ,,   IV ii 132
Moon bring him *h*, bring him *h*   *The Cup* I ii 5
H, sweet moon, bring him *h*, *H* with the flock   ,,   I ii 7
A miracle that they let him *h* again,   ,,   I ii 270
Strange that the words at *h* with me so long   *The Falcon* 525
how long you have been away from *h*!   *Prom. of May* I 768
Close by that alder-island in your brook, 'The
Angler's *H*.'   ,,   II 536
Let bygones be bygones. Go *h*! Good-night!   ,,   III 157
'Go *h*;' but I hadn't the heart or face to do it.   ,,   III 389
Eva has come *h*. *Steer.* Hoäm?   ,,   III 442
So happy in herself and in her *h*—   ,,   III 756
we should have better battels at *h*.   *Foresters* I i 58
Cleave to him, father! he will come *h* at last.   ,,   I i 198
till King Richard come *h* again.   ,,   I ii 141
Now the King is *h* again, and nevermore to roam again,
Now the King is *h* again, the King will have his own
again, *H* again, *h* again, and each will have his own
again, All the birds in merry Sherwood sing and sing
him *h* again.   ,,   IV 1103

Homely You have but trifled with our *h* salad,   *The Falcon* 672

Home-made *See* **Hoäm-maäde**

Home-nest gaping bills in the *h-n* Piping for bread—   *Becket* II ii 300

Home-return God and his free wind grant your lordship
a happy *h-r*   ,,   III iii 328

Homeward prosper all thy wandering out And *h*.   *Harold* I i 266
and pray in thy behalf For happier *h* winds   ,,   II ii 198

Homo *H* sum. I love my dinner—   *Foresters* I ii 66
H sum, sed virgo sum,

Hoped *h* to fall Into the wide-spread arms of fealty, *Queen Mary* II ii 263
I *h* I had served God with all my might! „ v ii 296
it was *h* Your Highness was once more in happy state „ v ii 570
H, were he chosen archbishop, *Becket* I iii 442
I would not be bold, Yet *h* ere this you might— „ III i 65
made more happy than I *h* Ever to be again. *The Falcon* 770
I wish'd, I *h* To make, to make— *Prom. of May* III 782
Hopeful and leaves me As *h*. *Queen Mary* I v 532
Hopeless (*See also* **Wholly-hopeless**) Ho there! thy rest of
life is *h* prison, *Becket* v i 180
First, free thy captive from *her h* prison. „ v i 183
Hopt He had but one foot, he must have *h* away, *Harold* II ii 675
Horder (order) if tha can't keep thy one cow i' *h*, how
can tha keep all thy scholards i' *h*? *Prom. of May* I 197
Horizon past is like a trav…ll'd land now sunk Below
the *h*— *The Cup* II 231
Horn (*See also* **Forest-horn**, **ar-horn**) draw back your
heads and your *h's* *Queen Mary* I i 5
Pope has pushed his *h's* beyond his mitre— „ v i 152
Alva will but touch him on the *h's*, And he withdraws; „ v i 156
Had I been by, I would have spoil'd his *h*. *Harold* II ii 73
would make the hard earth rive To the very Devil's *h's*, „ II ii 741
A ghostly *h* Blowing continually, „ III i 372
How ghostly sounds that *h* in the black wood! *Becket* III iii 16
when the *h* sounds she comes out as a wolf. „ III ii 23
when that *h* sounds, a score of wolf-dogs are let loose „ III ii 38
Linger not till the third *h*. Fly! „ III ii 41
or you'd have heard his *h* before now. „ IV i 55
have forgotten my *h* that calls my men together. *Foresters* II i 185
Fifty leagues Of woodland hear and know my *h*, „ III 104
Wherever the *h* sound and the buck bound, „ III 345
Wherever the buck bound, and the *h* sound, „ III 355
When *h* and echo ring, „ III 428
Accept this *h*! if e'er thou be assail'd „ IV 423
Wait till he blow the *h*. „ IV 787
Why blowest thou not the *h*? „ IV 791
I blow the *h* against this rascal rout! „ IV 794
And catch the winding of a phantom *h*. „ IV 1092
Horologe always in suspense, like the tail of the *h*— *Becket* II i 366
Horrible scourge Of England! *Courtier*. H! *Harold* I i 6
From all the holiest shrines in Normandy! *Harold*. H! „ II ii 736
Harvestless autumns, *h* agues, plague— *Queen Mary* V ii 99
H! flaying, scourging, crucifying— *The Cup* I ii 235
Horror I read his honest *h* in his eyes. *Queen Mary* III v 61
carrion-nosing mongrel vomit With hate and *h*. „ IV iii 450
What with this flaming *h* overhead? *Harold* I i 232
hath talk'd with God, and seen A shadowing *h*; „ III i 357
Whose doings are a *h* to the east, A hissing in the west!' *Becket* IV ii 244
And make thee a world's *h*. „ IV ii 288
And blanch the crowd with *h*. *The Cup* II 154
Horse (*See also* **'Erse, Herse**) she met the Queen at
Wanstead with five hundred *h*, *Queen Mary* I i 78
with an ass's, not a *h's* head, „ I iii 169
that's a noble *h* of yours, my Lord. „ I iv 143
And broken bridge, or spavin'd *h*, „ I v 355
a pale *h* for Death and Gardiner for the Devil. „ III i 234
Your boots are from the *h's*. „ III v 180
I had *h's* On all the road from Dover, „ v ii 576
H's there, without! „ v iii 109
Why did you keep me prating? *H's*, there! „ v iii 113
Because I broke The *h's* leg— *Harold* II ii 110
Thousands of *h's*, like as many lions „ IV iii 196
No Norman *h* Can shatter England, „ v i 195
No *h*—thousands of *h's*—our shield wall— „ v i 231
range of knights Sit, each a statue on his *h*, „ v i 525
they fall behind the *h*—Their *h* are thronging „ v i 546
all their *h* Swallow the hill locust-like, „ v i 559
The *h* and horseman cannot meet the shield, The
blow that brains the horseman cleaves the *h*,
The *h* and horseman roll along the hill, „ v i 591
They turn on the pursuer, *h* against foot, „ v i 608
No, no, his *h*—he mounts another— „ v i 638
Three *h's* had I slain beneath me: „ v i 171
I could tear him asunder with wild *h's* *Becket* II i 267
Our *h's* grazing by us, when a troop, *The Falcon* 611

Horse (*continued*) A troop of *h*—— *Filippo*. Five
hundred! *The Falcon* 617
how long we strove before Our *h's* fell beneath us; „ 639
lanker than an old *h* turned out to die on the common. *Foresters* I i 51
our *h* and our little cart— „ II i 191
when the Sheriff took my little *h* for the King without
paying for it— „ II i 301
I left mine *h* and armour with a Squire, „ IV 414
A *h*! a *h*! I must away at once; „ IV 797
Horseback How should a baron love a beggar on *h*, *Becket*, Pro. 444
Horseman The horse and *h* cannot meet the shield, The
blow that brains the horse, The horse
and *h* roll along the hill, *Harold* v i 591
Horse-pond See **Herse-pond**
Horsiness To rose and lavender my *h*, *Queen Mary* III v 185
Hospitable and seeing the *h* lights in your castle, *Foresters* I ii 194
Hospital See **Spital**
Hospitality a graceless *h* To chain the free guest *Harold* II ii 192
knowing the fame of your *h*, we ventured in uninvited. *Foresters* I ii 196
Host (a consecrated wafer) Have I not heard them
mock the blessed H *Queen Mary* IV iii 366
Host (array of men) and send her *h's* Of injured Saints *Harold* II ii 744
And Edward would have sent a *h* against you, „ IV i 99
join our hands before the *h's*, That all may see. „ IV i 242
Host (entertainer of guests) He was thine *h* in England
when I went To visit Edward. „ II ii 4
I found him all a noble *h* should be. „ II ii 10
She hath follow'd with our *h*, and suffer'd all. „ IV i 29
A cleric violated The daughter of his *h*, *Becket* I iii 383
Hostage four of her poor Council too, my Lord, As *h's*. *Queen Mary* II ii 44
Is not my brother Wulfnoth *h* there *Harold* I i 239
Poor brother! still a *h*! „ II ii 329
They did thee wrong who made thee *h*; „ II ii 350
Remain a *h* for the loyalty Of Godwin's house.' „ III i 90
Hostis H in Angliam Ruit prædator, „ v i 506
H per Angliae Plagas bacchatur; „ v i 510
Hot and the H Gospellers will go mad upon it. *Queen Mary* I i 115
But you so bubbled over with *h* terms Of Satan, „ I ii 94
And *h* desire to imitate; „ III iv 171
There are H Gospellers even among our guards— „ v v 102
jerk'd out of the common rut Of Nature in the *h*
religious fool, *Harold* I i 139
H blood, ambition, pride So bloat and redden his
face— *The Cup* ii 168
Thou blowest *h* and cold. Where is she then? *Foresters* I i 490
Hot-blooded *H-b*! I have heard them say in Rome, *The Cup* I i 135
Hot-headed *H-h* fools—to burst the wall of shields! *Harold* v i 612
I can see further into a man than our *h-h* Henry, *Becket*, Pro. 463
Hottest This is the *h* of it: hold, ash! hold, willow! *Harold* v i 628
The *h* hold in all the devil's den Were but a sort
of winter; *Queen Mary* v iv 15
Hound with mine old *h* Couch'd at my hearth, „ III i 45
Sick for an idle week of hawk and *h* *Harold* I i 103
I hear the yelping of the *h's* of hell. *Becket* III ii 48
Huntsman, and *h*, and deer were all neck-broken! *The Cup* I ii 23
You saw my *h's* True to the scent; „ I ii 110
Hounded We never *h* on the State at home To spoil the
Church. *Becket* II ii 96
Hour Ay, that was in her *h* of joy; *Queen Mary* I i 84
some great doom when God's just *h* Peals— „ I iv 262
What do and say Your Council at this *h*? „ II ii 46
Who knows? the man is proven by the *h*. *White*.
The man should make the *h*, not this the man; „ II ii 364
An *h* will come When they will sweep her from the seas. „ III i 160
do triumph at this *h* In the reborn salvation „ III iii 181
tolerate the heretic, No, not an *h*. „ III iv 211
Their *h* is hard at hand, „ III iv 426
Ay, for an *h* in May. „ III v 10
It shall be all my study for one *h* „ III v 184
in strange *h's*, After the long brain-dazing colloquies, „ IV ii 91
May God help you Thro' that hard *h*! „ IV ii 196
Hooper burn'd Three-quarters of an *h*. „ IV ii 227
the *h* has come For utter truth and plainness; „ IV iii 272
Make us despise it at odd *h's*, my Lord. „ IV iii 386
Brook for an *h* such brute malignity? „ IV iii 544

Hour (continued) O would I were My father for an h! — Queen Mary v ii 294
And may not speak for h's. — " v ii 406
Sit down here: Tell me thine happiest h. — " v v 79
worse than that—not one h true to me! — " v v 159
A good entrenchment for a perilous h! — Harold iii i 363
among the goldenest h's Of Alfred, — " iv iii 51
O hapless Harold! King but for an h! — " v i 258
God of truth Fill all thine h's with peace!— — " v i 316
But the h is past, and our brother, Master Cook, — Becket i iv 59
I have but one h with thee— — " ii i 24
Let there not be one frown in this one h. — " ii i 44
out of the eclipse Narrowing my golden h! — " ii i 203
Come, come, mine h! I bargain for mine h. — " ii i 212
our mother 'ill sing me old songs by the h, — " iii i 185
We have had so many h's together, Thomas, So many happy h's — " iii iii 37
bound For that one h to stay with good King Louis, — " iii iii 247
thy life Was not one h's worth in England — " iii iii 251
Your Grace will never have one quiet h. — " v i 79
tho' it be their h, the power of darkness, But my h too, — " v iii 93
If I be not back in half an h, Come after me. — The Cup i ii 438
So falls the throne of an h. — " ii 486
Pride of his heart—the solace of his h's— — The Falcon 224
Ay, haäfe an h ago. She be in theer now. — Prom. of May i 14
Half an h late! why are you loitering here? — " ii 324
Who can tell What golden h's, with what full hands, — " ii 509
What feller wur it as 'a' been a-talkin' fur haäfe an h wi' my Dora? — " ii 576
niver 'a been talkin' haäfe an h wi' the divil 'at killed her oän sister, — " ii 603
may drop off any day, any h. You must see him at once. — " iii 407
the light Of these dark h's; — Foresters i ii 85
We make but one h's buzz, — " i ii 277
I am only merry for an h or two Upon a birthday: — " i iii 11
We will away in four-and-twenty h's, — " i iii 91
My lonely h! The king of day hath stept — " ii i 25
to carve One lone h from it, — " ii i 43
Why break you thus upon my lonely h? — " ii i 94
The ruler of an h, but lawful King, — " iv 47
Try me an h hence. — " iv 276
your free sports have swallow'd my free h. — " iv 340
No, not an h: the debt is due to-day. — " iv 447
are delivered here in the wild wood an h after noon. — " iv 509

Houris whose cheerless H after death Are Night and Silence, — Prom. of May i 249

House (See also Ale-house, Gate-house, Treasure-house)
So you would honour my poor h to-night, — Queen Mary i iii 118
To Ashridge, or some other country h. — " i iv 226
seek In that lone h, to practise on my life, — " i iv 284
my h hath been assaulted, — " i v 146
Spain in our ships, in our forts, in our h's, in our beds? — " ii i 180
Your h's fired—your gutters bubbling blood— — " ii ii 280
a plundering o' Bishop Winchester's h; — " ii iii 73
Here by this h was one; — " iii i 9
You are of the h? what will you do, Sir Ralph? — " iii i 435
there were those within the h Who would not have it. — " iii ii 66
also those without the h Who would not have it. — " iii ii 70
When will you that we summon both our h's — " iii ii 115
My lords of the upper h, And ye, my masters, of the lower h, — " iii iii 102
sole man in either h Who stood upright when both the h's fell. Bagenhall. The h's fell! Officer.
I mean the h's knelt — " iii iii 253
I am the one sole man in either h, — " iii iii 266
The h is all in movement. Hence, and see. — " iii v 83
play with fire as children do, And burn the h. — " iii vi 30
none shall hold them in his h and live, — " iv i 96
The stranger at his hearth, and all his h— — " iv i 164
The h half-ruin'd ere the lease be out; — " v i 66
When Wyatt sack'd the Chancellor's h in Southwark. — " v ii 505
light enough for Alfgar's h To strike thee down — Harold i i 307
powers of the h of Godwin Are not enframed in thee. — " i i 316

House (continued) running out at top To swamp the h. — Harold i i 379
Unwholesome talk For Godwin's h! — " i i 391
It means the lifting of the h of Alfgar. — " i i 473
all the sins of both The h's on mine head— — " i ii 206
see confusion fall On thee and on thine h. — " ii ii 490
Remain a hostage for the loyalty Of Godwin's h.' — " ii ii 91
I have built the Lord a h— (repeat) — Harold iii i 178, 181, 186
Fall, cloud, and fill the h— — Harold iii i 190
not his fault, if our two h's Be less than brothers. — " iv i 130
When will ye cease to plot against my h? — " iv i 162
Thou hast given it to an enemy of our h. — " iv ii 32
Thou hast no passion for the H of Godwin— — " iv ii 72
When I and thou were youths in Theobald's h, — Becket i iii 41
Not he That is not of the h, but from the street — " i iv 146
dawns darkly and drearily over the h of God— — " iii iii 60
Sudden change is a h on sand; — " iii iii 60
when he hears a door open in the h and thinks ' the master.' — " iii iii 99
I will be Sole master of my h. — " v i 151
and in thy name I pass'd From h to h. — " v ii 104
little fair-hair'd Norman maid Lived in my mother's h: — " v ii 261
yet threaten your Archbishop In his own h. — " v ii 506
dost thou know the h of Sinnatus? — The Cup i i 49
These grapes are for the h of Sinnatus— — " i i 51
this pious cup Is passport to their h, — " i i 83
They shall not harm My guest within my h. — " i ii 327
The child, a thread within the h of birth, — " ii 259
feud between our h's is the bar I cannot cross; — The Falcon 254
My comrade of the h, and of the field. — " 875
O this mortal h, Which we are born into, — Prom. of May ii 273
would fight for his rents, his leases, his h's, — Foresters i i 233
whose return Builds up our h again? — " iv 1009

House-breaker Beänt there h-b's down i' Littlechester, Dobson. — Prom. of May i 388
House-dog filch the linen from the hawthorn, poison the h-d, — Foresters iii 200
Household (adj.) The h dough was kneaded up with blood; — Becket iii 351
So rare the h honeymaking bee, — " v ii 217
to cast All threadbare h habit, — Foresters iii 112
Household (s) Your lavish h curb'd, — Queen Mary i v 113
no foreigner Hold office in the h, fleet, — " iii iii 72
No man without my leave shall excommunicate My tenants or my h. — Becket, Pro. 32
And when I was of Theobald's h, once— — " i i 60
you have put so many of the King's h out of communion. — " iii iii 311
Prince would have me of his—what? H? — Foresters iv 703
Houseless A h head beneath the sun and stars, — " ii i 64
House-side and there is a piece of beef like a h-s, — Prom. of May i 793
Hover At the park gate h's with our guards. — Queen Mary ii iv 15
Love will h round the flowers when they first awaken; — " v ii 370
That h's round your shoulder— — " v iii 52
sea-bird rouse himself and h Above the windy ripple, — Harold ii ii 335
How See 'Ow
Howard (Lord William, Lord High Admiral) (See also William, William Howard) had H spied me there And made them speak, — Queen Mary ii iii 32
This H, whom they fear, what was he saying? — " iii vi 54
And if he did I care not, my Lord H. — " iv i 129
Lord H, Sending an insolent shot that dash'd — " v i 56
H is all English! — " v i 61
Howiver (however) my rheumatizy be that bad h be I to win to the burnin'. — " iv iii 474
Howl if your wolf the while might h for more, — " i v 419
how those Roman wolfdogs h and bay him! — " iv iii 354
note Whereat the dog shall h and run, — Harold i ii 192
if it suit their purpose to h for the King, — Becket iii iii 324
They h for thee, to rend thee head from limb. — The Cup i ii 321
Howsoever See Howsomiver, S'iver
Howsomiver (howsoever) but a had to bide h, — Queen Mary iv iii 506
Hug thou wouldst h thy Cupid till his ribs cracked> — Becket, Pro. 504
Huge or else swam heavily Against the h corruptions of the Church, — Queen Mary iv iii 100
Did I call him heretic? A h heresiarch! — " iv iii 46
But wherefore not Helm the h vessel of your state, — " v i 73

Hurl *H's* his soil'd life against the pikes and dies. *Queen Mary* IV iii 311
  if his Northumbrians rise And *h* him from them,— *Harold* II ii 457
  And *h* the dread ban of the Church on those *Becket* III iii 210
  And *h's* the victor's column down with him *The Cup* II 295
Hurl'd and *h* our battles Into the heart of Spain ; *Queen Mary* III i 107
  sir, they *h* it back into the fire,   ,,   v iv 22
  and *h* it from him Three fields away, *Harold* III i 138
Hurrah *H* ! Vive le Roy ! *Becket* I iv 274
Hurry (s) I trod upon him even now, my lord, in my *h*,
  and broke him. *The Falcon* 410
Hurry (verb) Why do they *h* out there ? *Queen Mary* II ii 4
Hurt He can but creep down into some dark hole Like
  a *h* beast,   ,,   IV i 142
  H no man more Than you would harm   ,,   IV iii 187
  He had been *h*, And bled beneath his armour. *Foresters* II ii 4
  He hath been *h*, was growing whole again,   ,,   IV 451
Husband The traitor *h* dangled at the door, *Queen Mary* III i 10
  happily symboll'd by The King your *h*,   ,,   III ii 110
  Oh, Philip, *h* ! now thy love to mine Will cling   ,,   III ii 159
  Philip's no sudden alien—the Queen's *h*,   ,,   III iii 43
  parting of a *h* and a wife Is like the cleaving of a
  heart ;   ,,   III vi 194
  not were he ten times king, Ten times our *h*,   ,,   v i 64
  ' Your people hate you as your *h* hates you.'   ,,   v ii 337
  My *h* hates me, and desires my death.   ,,   v ii 347
  the child came not, and the *h* came not ;   ,,   v ii 581
  To marry and have no *h* Makes the wife fool. *Harold* II ii 309
  Who did discrown thine *h*, unqueen thee ? Didst
  thou not love thine *h* ?   ,,   IV i 193
  I had rather She would have loved her *h*.   ,,   IV i 224
  O Harold ! *h* ! Shall we meet again ?   ,,   v i 360
  because I love The *h* of another !   ,,   v i 649
  I have lost both crown And *h*.   ,,   v ii 410
  What was he like, this *h* ? like to thee ?   ,,   v ii 52
  I mean your goodman, your *h*, my lady, *Becket* III i 159
  for her *h*, King Louis—— *Rosamund.* Hush !   ,,   III i 170
  whom you call—fancy—my *h's* brother's wife.   ,,   III i 202
  Son, *h*, brother gash'd to death in vain, *The Cup* I ii 143
  To draw you and your *h* to your doom.   ,,   I ii 222
  And if you should betray me to your *h*—   ,,   I ii 243
  Still—I should tell My *h*.   ,,   I ii 304
  She may, perchance, to save this *h*.   ,,   I iii 33
  And for the sake of Sinnatus your *h*,   ,,   I iii 101
  So much of *h* in it still—that if   ,,   I ii 145
  Can't a girl when she loves her *h*, and he her, *Prom. of May* III 305
  but I hold thee The *h* of my heart, *Foresters* III 140
Husbanded nor yet so amorous That I must needs
  be *h* ; *Queen Mary* II ii 216
Husband-in-law *H-i-l*, our smooth-shorn suzerain, *Becket* II ii 40
Hush *H*—hear ! *Bourne.* —and so this unhappy
  land, *Queen Mary* I iii 19
  H ! *h* ! You wrong the Chancellor :   ,,   III iii 66
  H, father, *h* ! *Harold* III i 389
  for her husband, King Louis—— *Rosamund.* *H* ! *Becket* III i 171
  O *h* ! O peace ! This violence ill becomes *The Cup* II 214
Husk If we may judge the kernel by the *h*,   ,,   I 175
Hut we found a goat-herd's *h* and shared His fruits   ,,   I ii 427
  Here is the witch's *h*. *Foresters* II i 178
  They must have past. Here is a woodman's *h*.   ,,   II i 200
  Not in this *h* I take it.   ,,   II i 205
  There is but one old woman in the *h*.   ,,   II i 242
Hymen rather than so clip The flowery robe of *H*, *The Cup* II 436
Hymn (s) (*See also* **Battle-hymns, 'Ymn**) chants and *h's*
  In all the churches, *Becket* v ii 366
  standing up side by side with me, and singing the
  same *h* ? *Prom. of May* III 182
Hymn (verb) Hear thy priestesses *h* thy glory ! *The Cup* II 7
Hypocrisy never burn out the *h* that makes the
  water in her. *Queen Mary* IV iii 525
Hypocrite And yet I hate him for a *h*. *Becket* v i 232
  From whom he knows are *h's* and liars. *Foresters* IV 380

I

Ibyci And one an *uxor pauperis I*. *Becket* v ii 216
Iceberg To shove that stranded *i* off our shores, *Harold* IV iii 138
Ice-cold Stone-hard, *i-c*—no dash of daring in him. *Queen Mary* v i 331
  sat Stone-dead upon a heap of *i-c* eggs. *Becket* v ii 239
Iceland —Scotland, Ireland, *I*, Orkney, *Harold* III i 124
Icy white cells, beneath an *i* moon—   ,,   v i 325
Iden And he will prove an *I* to this Cade, *Queen Mary* II ii 369
Idiot This world of mud, on all its *i* gleams Of
  pleasure, *Prom. of May* III 722
Idiotcies What are all these ? *Harold.* Utopian *i*.   ,,   III 588
Idle But this is *i* of you. Well, sir, well, *Queen Mary* IV ii 75
  other things As *i* ; a weak Wyatt !   ,,   v i 292
  Sick for an *i* week of hawk and hound Beyond the seas— *Harold* I i 103
  Peace, friends ! what *i* brawl is this ? *Becket* I ii 2
Idol-worship one true faith, a loathsome *i-w* ? *Queen Mary* III iv 219
Idyll This Dobson of your *i* ? *Prom. of May* III 563
If Thine ' *i's* ' will sear thine eyes out—ay. *Harold* II ii 625
  He fenced his royal pomise with an *i*. *Becket* III iii 279
  is the King's *i* too high a stile for your lordship to
  overstep   ,,   III iii 280
  Ay, if this *i* be like the Devil's ' *i*   ,,   III iii 284
Ignorance Wyatt, who hath tamper'd with A public *i*, *Queen Mary* III i 182
  And I crying in the streets,   ,,   IV iii 377
  Spite, *i*, envy, Yea, honesty too, *Becket* II i 100
Ignorant She is *i* of all but that I love her.   ,,   *Pro.* 185
Ignorantly I am sure (Knowing the man, he wrought
  it *i*, *Queen Mary* III i 276
Ill The Queen is *i* advised : shall I turn traitor ?   ,,   I iv 5
  i counsel ! These let them keep at present ;   ,,   I v 405
  I am *i* disguised.   ,,   III i 33
  And fared so *i* in this disastrous world.   ,,   v ii 344
  My Lord Count, Her Highness is too *i* for colloquy.   ,,   v ii 613
  I news for guests, ha, Malet ! More ? What more ? *Harold* III i 302
  Harold served Tostig so *i*, he cannot serve for Tostig !   ,,   III i 162
  I news hath come ! Our hapless brother, Tostig—   ,,   III ii 120
  Madam, you do *i* to scorn wedded love. *Becket, Pro.* 353
  May God grant No *i* befall or him or thee when I
  Am gone.   ,,   II i 260
  Eleanor, Eleanor, have I Not heard *i* things of her
  in France ?   ,,   III i 231
  This violence *i* becomes The silence of our Temple. *The Cup* II 215
  but you turn right ugly when you're in an *i*
  temper ; *Prom. of May* I 160
  but the *i* success of the farm, and the debts,   ,,   II 68
  and so *i* in consequence all Monday,   ,,   III 80
  But *i* befitting such a festal day *Foresters* I iii 37
  Who hast that worship for me which Heaven knows
  I *i* deserve   ,,   I iii 162
Illa Their ' dies *I*,' which will test their sect. *Queen Mary* III iv 428
Ill-bested A maiden now Were *i-b* in these dark days
  of John, *Foresters* II ii 45
Illegitimate And mine a bitterer *i* hate, *Becket* I i 173
Ill-garrison'd Calais is but *i-g*, in Guisnes *Queen Mary* IV i 4
Illogically but unsymmetrically, preposterously, *i*, *Becket, Pro.* 336
Image beast might roar his claim To being in God's *i*, *Queen Mary* IV iii 369
  set up your broken *i's* ; Be comfortable to me.   ,,   v ii 300
  Who melts a waxen *i* by the fire, *Foresters* II i 671
Imagine And can you not *i* that the wreath, *The Falcon* 534
  I said you might *i* it was so.   ,,   545
Imitate And hot desire to *i* ; *Queen Mary* III iv 171
Imitative A Parliament of *i* apes !   ,,   III iii 235
Immanuel Goldsmiths *I G* was broke into o' Monday
  night, *Prom. of May* I 391
Immediate and they threaten The *i* thunder-blast of
  interdict : *Becket* III iii 26
Immemorial so violated the *i* usage of the Church,   ,,   III iii 72
Immortal Lovers hold True love *i*. *Foresters* II ii 616
  You seem, as it were, *I*, and we mortal.   ,,   IV 1060
  We have respect for man's *i* soul, *Harold* II ii 501

Imp	Venal *i* ! What say'st thou to the Chancellorship	*Becket* II i 224
Impair	or *i* in any way This royal state of England,	*Queen Mary* II ii 229
Imperial	What your *i* father said, my liege, To deal	
	with heresy gentlier.	„ III vi 56
	We cannot fight *i* Rome,	*The Cup* II 92
	let the new-made children Of our *i* mother see the show.	„ II 165
Implore	I thus *i* you, low upon my knees,	*Queen Mary* IV i 64
Import	It much *i's* me I should know her name.	*Becket* I i 192
	it may *i* her all as much Not to be known.	„ I i 197
Importance	policy in some matter Of small *i*	*Queen Mary* III vi 168
Impossible	*I* ; Except you put Spain down.	„ v iii 79
Impress	And she *i* her wrongs upon her Council,	„ III vi 183
Imprison	Degrade, *i* him—Not death for death.	*Becket* I iii 400
	Too politic for that. *I* me ?	„ IV ii 397
Imprison'd	I was but wounded by the enemy there And	
	then *i*.	*The Falcon* 389
Imprisonment	In your five years of *i*,	*Queen Mary* III iv 242
Impugn	Which might *i* or prejudice the same ;	„ III iii 133
Impute	it is the traitor that *i's* Treachery to his King !	*Becket* I iii 484
	Weak natures that *i* Themselves to their unlikes,	*Foresters* II i 691
Incalculable	Yea, even such as mine, *i*,	*Queen Mary* IV iii 147
Incapable	Old, miserable, diseased, *I* of children.	„ v v 179
Incarnate	Whose life was all one battle, *i* war,	*Harold* v i 397
Incavern'd	*See* **Deep-incavern'd**	
Incense	parch'd banks rolling *i*, as of old,	*Queen Mary* I v 91
	puffed out such an *i* of unctuosity into the nostrils of	
	our Gods of Church and State,	*Becket* III iii 115
Incenselike	All her breath should, *i*, Rise	*Queen Mary* III iii 164
Incest	As being born from *i* ;	„ I ii 69
Incestuous	Peter, I'll swear for him He *did* believe	
	the bond *i*.	„ I ii 77
Inch	Fire—*i* by *i* to die in agony !	„ IV ii 223
	If thou draw one *i* nearer,	*Foresters* I i 145
	being every *i* a man I honour every *i* of a woman.	„ III 63
	for old Much is every *i* a man,	„ IV 290
Incline	whether her Grace *i* to this splendid scion of	
	Plantagenet.	*Queen Mary* I i 134
Included	The *i* Danaë has escaped again Her tower,	*Becket* I i 395
Inconsistency	Nay, for bare shame of *i*,	*Queen Mary* I ii 39
Incurr'd	every bond and debt and obligation *I* as	
	Chancellor.	*Becket* I iii 712
Ind	His sceptre shall go forth from *I* to *I* !	*Queen Mary* III iv 340
Indeterminate	But a weak mouth, an *i*—ha ?	„ III iv 340
Indian	*I* shawl That Philip brought me in our happy	
	days !—	„ v ii 538
Indies	Spain would be England on her seas, and England	
	Mistress of the *I*.	„ v iii 74
	England Will be Mistress of the *I* yet,	„ v iii 77
Indifference	accuse you of *i* To all faiths, all religion ;	„ III iv 223
Indignation	begets An admiration and an *i*,	„ III iv 170
In-door	They are plagues enough *i-d*.	*Becket* II ii 91
Indraught	swoll'n and fed With *i's* and side-	
	currents,	*Queen Mary* II i 234
Indungeon'd	*I* from one whisper of the wind,	*Becket* IV ii 146
Infallible	of her most Royal, *I*, Papal Legate-	
	cousin.	*Queen Mary* III iv 433
Infamous	*I* wretch. Shall I tell her he is dead ?	*Prom. of May* III 336
Infamy	Fame of to-day is *i* to-morrow ; *I* of to-day	
	is fame to-morrow ;	*Becket* II i 103
Infant (adj.)	I had to cuff the rogue For *i* treason.	*Queen Mary* III iii 52
Infant (s)	blast your *i's*, dash The torch of war among	*Harold* II ii 747
Infatuated	—*i*—To sue you for his life ?	*Queen Mary* IV i 10
Infect	Thy fears *i* me beyond reason. Peace !	*Harold* II ii 451
Infinite	that it would please Him out of His *i* love to	
	break down all kingship and queenship,	*Queen Mary* IV iv 47
Infirmity	And *I*, that knew mine own *i*,	*Becket* I iii 696
	I pray God pardon mine *i*.	„ II ii 353
Ingratitude	*I*, Injustice, Evil-tongue, Labour-in-	
	vain.	*Queen Mary* v ii 156
	His heart so gall'd with thine *i*,	*Becket* I iii 44
Inhabitant	altho' the *i's* Seem semi-barbarous.	*Prom. of May* II 541
	not only love the country, But its *i's* too ;	„ II 546
	Then one at least of its *i's*	„ II 552
Inherit	Ay, sir ; *I* the Great Silence.	*Queen Mary* III iii 199
	Why then the throne is empty. Who *i's* ?	*Harold* III i 235
Inherit (continued)	Who *i's* ? Edgar the Atheling ?	*Harold* III i 239
	hand that next *I's* thee be but as true to thee	*Becket* I i 358
	Thou wilt *i* the land, And so wouldst sell	*Foresters* II i 534
Inherited	some will say because I have *i* my Uncle.	*Prom. of May* III 598
	True, and I have an *i* loathing of these black sheep	
	of the Papacy.	*Becket*, Pro. 460
Inheriting	which we *I* reap an easier harvest.	*Becket* II ii 194
Inheritor	That bright *i* of your eyes—your boy ?	*The Falcon* 306
Inhospitable	Friends, in that last *i* plunge Our boat	
	hath burst her ribs ;	*Harold* II i 1
Injure	That none should wrong or *i* your Archbishop.	*Becket* I iii 754
Injured	send her hosts Of *i* Saints to scatter sparks of	
	plague	*Harold* II ii 745
Injury	not be wanting Those that will urge her *i*—	*Queen Mary* III vi 176
Injustice	Ingratitude, *I*, Evil-tongue, Labour-in-vain.	„ v ii 156
	Shall *we* too work *i* ?	*Foresters* I iii 87
	we must at times have wrought Some great *i*,	„ III 156
	If the king and the law work *i*,	„ IV 229
	Do some *i*, if you hold us here Longer	„ IV 941
Ink	is written in invisible *i's* ' Lust, Prodigality,	*Prom. of May* II 283
Inland	we two Have track'd the King to this dark *i*	
	wood ;	*Becket* III ii 3
Inmost	weight of the very land itself, Down to the *i*	
	centre.	*Foresters* IV 1027
Inn	at the wayside *i* Close by that alder-island	*Prom. of May* II 534
Innocence	And witness to your Grace's *i*,	*Queen Mary* III v 50
	Life on the face, the brows—clear *i* !	*Becket* II i 195
	i's that will cry From all the hidden by-ways	„ III iii 14
	equal for pure *i* of nature, And loveliness of	
	feature.	*Prom. of May* II 372
	Except she could defend her *i*.	*Foresters* II i 47
Innocent (adj.)	and of the good Lady Jane as a poor *i*	
	child who had but obeyed her father ;	*Queen Mary* I i 94
	perchance A child more *i* than Lady Jane.	„ I v 502
	No, no ; her *i* blood had blinded me.	„ III i 345
	and when her *i* eyes were bound, She,	„ III i 405
	And love is joyful, *i*, beautiful, And jealousy is	
	wither'd, sour and ugly :	*Foresters* II ii 64
	and another—worse !—An *i* maid.	„ III 389
Innocent (s)	O God, how many an *i* Has left his bones	*Becket* II ii 408
Inquisition	Holy absolution ! holy *I* !	*Queen Mary* I iii 32
	cited me to Rome, for heresy, Before his *I*.	„ v ii 43
Insane	That palate is *i* which cannot tell	*Becket*, Pro. 104
Insolence	I hate him for his *i* to all. *De Tracy*. And	
	I for all his *i* to thee.	„ v i 226
Insolent	Sending an *i* shot that dash'd the seas Upon us,	*Queen Mary* v i 57
	I clown. Shall I smite him with the edge of the sword ?	*Becket* I v 223
Inspire	O Thou, that dost *i* the germ with life,	*The Cup* II 257
Inspired	Why should not Heaven have so *i* the King ?	*Becket* I i 130
Instant (adj.)	It craves an *i* answer, Ay or No. *Mary*.	
	An *i* Ay or No ! the Council sits. Give it me	
	quick.	*Queen Mary* I v 589
	and had my constant ' No ' For all but *i* battle.	*Harold* v i 7
Instant (s)	You are to come to Court on the *i* ;	*Queen Mary* III v 223
	Come, girl, thou shalt along with us on the *i*. *Friar*	
	Tuck. Then on the *i* I will break thy head.	*Foresters* IV 679
Instinct	following his own *i's* as his God,	*Prom. of May* I 588
Insured	I were *i*, Miss, an' I lost nowt by it.	„ II 57
Intent	to the *i* That you may lose your English	
	heritage.	*Queen Mary* v i 132
Intercept	did not Gardiner *i* A letter which	„ v ii 495
Intercession	That by your gracious means and *i*	„ III iii 121
	by your *i* May from the Apostolic see obtain,	„ III iii 146
Interdict	from the side of Rome, An *i* on England—	*Becket*, Pro. 223
	To blast my realms with excommunication And *i*.	„ II iii 53
	The immediate thunder-blast of *i* :	„ III iii 26
	bell-silencing, anti-marrying, burial-hindering *i*	„ III iii 56
	King at last is fairly scared by this cloud—this *i*.	„ III iii 64
	This Godstow-Becket *i* such	„ IV ii 457
Interpreter	is he thy mouthpiece, thine *i* ?	*Foresters* I iii 212
Interwoven	See here—an *i* H and E !	*Harold* I ii 57
Invade	bees, If any creeping life *i* their hive	*Queen Mary* III iii 54
Invader	May all *i's* perish like Hardrada !	*Harold* IV ii 77
Inverted	*I* Æsop—mountain out of mouse.	*Queen Mary* II i 67
Invisible	There, there, is written in *i* inks	*Prom. of May* II 283

Involve which hatred by and by *I's* the ruler   *Queen Mary* III iv 161
Inward Or am I slandering my most *i* friend,   " IV ii 105
Inwrought white satin his trunk-hose, *I* with silver,—   " III i 78
Ionian Artemis, Artemis, hear him, *I* Artemis !   *The Cup* II 277
Iræ Their hour is hard at hand, their ' dies *I*,'   *Queen Mary* III iv 426
Ireland —Scotland, *I*, Iceland, Orkney,   *Harold* III ii 124
Iron (adj.) The Duke Of Alva, an *i* soldier.   *Queen Mary* III i 194
   With golden deeds and *i* strokes that brought   *Harold* II ii 47
   A breath that fleets beyond this *i* world,   " II ii 197
   knowing that he *must* have Moved in the *i* grooves of Destiny ?   *Prom. of May* II 267
Iron (s) *I* on *i* clang,   *Harold* III iii 160
   With hands too limp to brandish *i*—   " v i 449
   flask or two Of that same vintage. There is *i* in it.   *The Falcon* 586
   I will fuse, and marble melt ;   *Prom. of May* II 505
Iron-mooded make yield this *i-m* Duke To let me go.   *Harold* II ii 339
Ironside or English *I* Who fought with Knut,   " III iii 53
Irregular This is *i* and the work of John. [' *I, i* !   *Foresters* I iii 71
Irresolute Fine eyes—but melancholy, *i*—   *Queen Mary* III iv 337
Irreverent St. Cupid, that is too *i*.   *Becket* I v 198
Irritable That *i* forelock which he rubs,   *Queen Mary* I iv 265
Iscariot Not red like *I's*.   " III i 217
Island (adj.) Yearns to set foot upon your *i* shore.   " I v 367
   and plunge His foreign fist into our *i* Church   " III iv 364
   Fair *i* star ! *Elizabeth.* I shine !   " I v 15
   And send thee back among thine *i* mists With laughter.   *Harold* II ii 181
   The spiritual giant with our *i* laws And customs,   *Becket* IV ii 444
Island (s) (*See also* **Alder-island, Spice-island**) or the stout old *i* will become A rotten limb   *Queen Mary* II i 104
   The *i's* call'd into the dawning church   " III iii 172
   We parted like the brook yonder about the alder *i*,   *Prom. of May* I 773
Island-Church would make Our *i-C* a schism from Christendom,   *Becket* I iii 116
Islander Because these *i's* are brutal beasts ?   *Queen Mary* III vi 153
Isle and rooted in far *i's* Beyond my seeing :   *Harold* III i 153
   To Holy Peter in our English *i* ?   " I i 207
   Keep him away from the lone little *i*.   *Becket* II i 16
   Row to the blessed *I's* ! the blessed *I's* !   *The Cup* II 525
   That ever blossom'd on this English *i*.   *Foresters* II i 124
Islip it be a var waay vor my owld legs up vro' *I*.   *Queen Mary* IV iii 473
   Dumble's the best milcher in *I*. (repeat)   " IV iii 478, 497
'Issen (himself) the owd man's coom'd ageän to '*i*,   *Prom. of May* II 703
Issue (s) Yea, were there *i* born to her,   *Queen Mary* I v 301
Issue (verb) he that lookt a fangless one, *I's* a venomous adder.   *Becket* I iii 453
Istis *Non defensoribus i*, Walter Map.   " II ii 346
Italian Catholic church as well Without as with the *I* ?   *Queen Mary* III iii 99
   He is all *I*, and he hates the Spaniard ;   " v ii 55
Italy I have seen A pine in *I* that cast   " III iv 136
   Tainted with Lutheranism in *I*.   " III iv 227
   In your soft *I* yonder !   " III iv 254
   To plump the leaner pouch of *I*.   " III iv 365
   You make your wars upon him down in *I* :—   " v i 142
   Your troops were never down in *I*.   " v ii 315
   and with him who died down in *I*.   " v ii 508
Itch (s) Crutches, and *i'es*, and leprosies, and ulcers,   *Becket* I iv 254
Itch (verb) Yet my fingers *i* to beat him into nothing.   " I iv 229
Iver (ever) I doänt believe he's *i* a 'eart under his waistcoat.   *Prom. of May* I 130
   but if *i* I cooms upo' Gentleman Hedgar ageän,   " II 136
   burnin' o' the owld archbishop 'll burn the Pwoap out o' this 'ere land vor *i* and *i*.   *Queen Mary* IV iii 536
Ivy Faster than *i*. Must I hack her arms off ?   *Harold* v ii 146
   Your names will cling like *i* to the wood.   *Foresters* IV 1085

J

Jachin (a brass pillar, entrance to Solomon's temple) lo ! my two pillars, *J* and Boaz !—   *Harold* III i 192
Jackson (labourer to Farmer Dobson) Higgins, *J*, Luscombe, Nokes,   *Prom. of May* III 53

Jacta *J tonitrua Deus bellator* !   *Harold* v i 569
Jade fellow that on a lame *j* came to court,   *Becket* v i 246
Jail whose bolts, That *j* you from free life,   *Queen Mary* III v 172
Jailor My *j*— *Bedingfield*. One, whose bolts,   " III v 170
   Hast thou such trustless *j's* in thy North ?   *Harold* II ii 685
Jalousies (jealousies) he be fit to bust hissen wi' spites and *j*.   *Prom. of May* II 165
James *J*, didst thou ever see a carrion crow   *Queen Mary* IV iii 5
James, St. *See* **St. James**
Jane (Lady Jane Grey) and of the good Lady *J* as a poor innocent child   " I i 94
   That gave her royal crown to Lady *J*.   " I ii 19
   saying of this Lady *J*, Now in the Tower ?   " I v 37
   Lady *J* stood up Stiff as the very backbone   " I v 42
   tell your Grace What Lady *J* replied.   " I v 50
   A child more innocent than Lady *J*.   " I v 502
   Or Lady *J* ? *Wyatt.* No, poor soul ; no.   " II i 241
   And Lady *J* had left us.   " II iv 139
   Lady *J* ? *Crowd.* God save their Graces !   " III i 341
   Cried no God-bless-her to the Lady *J*,   " III vi 45
Janus-faces But *J-f* looking diverse ways.   " III ii 75
Jar since the fondest pair of doves will *j*,   *Becket* IV ii 41
   that Dobbins, is it, With whom I used to *j* ?   *Prom. of May* II 613
Jarr'd but suddenly *J* on this rock.   *Becket* I iii 382
Jarring *See* **Ever-jarring**
Javelin Our *j's* Answer their arrows.   *Harold* v i 521
Jay Hawk, buzzard, *j*, the mavis and the merle,   *Foresters* I iii 115
Jealous (*See also* **Childlike-jealous**) and thou in thy way shouldst be *j* of the King,   *Becket, Pro.* 511
   will he not mock at me The *j* fool balk'd of her will—   " IV ii 423
   Art thou not *j* of her ?   *The Falcon* 6
   Ay, ruffle thyself—be *j* ! Thou shouldst be *j* of her.   22
   J of me with Eva ! Is it so ?   *Prom. of May* I 471
Jealousy (*See also* **Jalousies**) and *j* Hath in it an alchemic force   *Queen Mary* III vi 180
   Did you not tell me he was crazed with *j*,   *Prom. of May* III 566
   I am a man not prone to *jealousies*,   " III 626
   O Kate, true love and *j* are twins,   *Foresters* II ii 63
   And *j* is wither'd, sour and ugly :   " II ii 65
   J, *j* of the king.   " II ii 141
   Elf, with spiteful heart and eye, Talk of *j* ?   " II ii 173
Jean they were fishers of men, Father *J* says.   *Harold* II ii 35
Jeer heard One of your Council fleer and *j* at him.   *Queen Mary* II ii 393
   nursery-cocker'd child will *j* at aught   " II ii 395
   The statesman that shall *j* and fleer at men,   " II ii 397
   if he *j* not seeing the true man Behind his folly,   " II ii 400
   if he see the man and still will *j*,   " II ii 402
Jenny here's little Dickon, and little Robin, and little *J*—   " II iii 113
Jeopardy being in great *j* of his life, he hath made   *Becket* I iv 263
Jerk Let be thy jokes and thy *j's*, man !   *The Falcon* 133
Jerk'd Things that seem *j* out of the common rut   *Harold* I i 137
Jerusalem table steams, like a heathen altar ; nay, like the altar at *J*.   *Becket* I iv 70
   smell o' the mou'd 'ud ha' maäde ma live as long as *J*.   *Prom. of May* I 378
Jest (s) the tongue yet quiver'd with the *j*   *Queen Mary* I v 476
   a *j* In time of danger shows the pulses even.   " II ii 356
   And the Dutchman, Now laughing at some *j* ?   " III i 196
   nave and aisles all empty as a fool's *j* !   " IV iii 287
   Thy *j*—no more. Why—look—is this a sleeve   *Becket, Pro.* 249
   Then for thy barren *j* Take thou mine answer   " Pro. 281
   —That were a *j* indeed !   " Pro. 297
   There's no *j* on the brows of Herbert there.   " Pro. 390
   good old man would sometimes have his *j*—   " I i 62
   J or prophecy there ? *Herbert.* Both, Thomas, both.   " I i 67
   or any harm done to the people if my *j* be in defence of the Truth ?   " II ii 339
   if the *j* be so done that the people Delight   " II ii 341
   Bandy their own rude *j's* with them,   *The Cup* I ii 360
Jest (verb) Ha ! ha ! sir ; but you *j* ; I love it :   *Queen Mary* III iii 355
   Thou angerest me, man : I do not *j*.   *Becket, Pro.* 300
   We did but *j*.   " Pro. 389
   Why do you *j* with me, and try To fright me ?   *Prom. of May* I 664
Jester Thou art a *j* and a verse-maker.   *Becket* II ii 334

Jesting if you be not *j*, Neither the old world,   *Prom. of May* I 673
    They are *j* at us yonder, mocking us?   *Foresters* IV 676
Jesus Christ (*See also* **Christ, Christ Jesus**) save her
    thro' the blood Of *J C*   *Queen Mary* III i 388
                               ,,   III iii 191
Jetsam range with *j* and with offal thrown
Jew He calls us worse than *J's*, Moors, Saracens.   ,,   v i 150
    There is Antwerp and the *J's*.   ,,   v i 183
    Advanced thee at his instance by the *J's*,   *Becket* I iii 644
Jewel (adj.) Beetle's *j* armour crack'd, Queen.   *Foresters* II ii 160
Jewel (s) I left her with rich *j's* in her hand,   *Queen Mary* I iv 242
    I have the *j* of a loyal heart.   ,,   I iv 247
    left about Like loosely-scatter'd *j's*,   ,,   II i 28
    in whose crown our Kent is the fairest *j*.   ,,   II i 164
    How look'd the Queen? *Bagenhall*. No fairer
    for her *j's*.   ,,   III i 92
    To set that precious *j*, Roger of York.   *Becket, Pro.* 270
    God's eyes! what a lovely cross! what *j's*!   ,,   *Pro.* 371
    to people heaven in the great day When God makes
    up his *j's*.   ,,   v ii 497
    Behold the *j* of St. Pancratius   *Harold* II ii 700
    tho' I grudge the pretty *j*, that I Have worn,   *Prom. of May* I 473
    and *not* a heart like the *j* in it—   *The Falcon* 91
    Outvalues all the *j's* upon earth.   ,,   779
Jingling Has my simple song set you *j*?   *Becket, Pro.* 379
Joan (country wife) Pwoaps be pretty things, *J*,   *Queen Mary* IV iii 469
    Our Daisy's as good 'z her. *Tib.* Noä, *J*. *Joan.*
    Our Daisy's butter's as good 'z hern. *Tib.*
    Noä, *J*. *Joan.* Our Daisy's cheeses be better.
    Tib. Noä, *J*.   ,,   IV iii 480
    Ay, *J*, and my owld man wur up and awaay   ,,   IV iii 488
    Ay, *J*; and Queen Mary gwoes on a burnin'   ,,   IV iii 522
    but tek thou my word vor't, *J*,—   ,,   IV iii 533
Joan of Kent (Elizabeth Barton, executed 1534) 'twas
    you That sign'd the burning of poor *J o K*;   ,,   IV ii 206
Jocelyn (Bishop of Salisbury) (*See also* **Salisbury**) No
    saying of mine—*J* of Salisbury.   *Becket* II ii 372
John (Gospel of St.) They go like those old Pharisees
    in *J*   *Queen Mary* II ii 8
John (Little) *See* **Little John**
John (of Oxford, called the Swearer) (*See also* **John of**
    Oxford, John the Swearer) See if our pious—
    what shall I call him, *J*?—   *Becket* II ii 39
    J, Thou hast served me heretofore with Rome—   ,,   II ii 459
    Honest *J*! To Rome again! the storm begins again.   ,,   II ii 467
John (of Salisbury) (*See also* **John of Salisbury, Salisbury**)
    Our good *J* Must speed you to your bower   ,,   I i 290
    Dan *J* with a nun, That Map,   ,,   I i 305
    —*J*, and out of breath!   ,,   I i 388
    Why, *J*, my kingdom is not of this world.   ,,   v ii 18
    Dan *J*, how much we lose, we celibates,   ,,   v ii 197
    You hear them, brother *J*; Why do you stand so
    silent, brother *J*?   ,,   v ii 534
    Is it so, Dan *J*? well, what should I have done?   ,,   v ii 552
    My counsel is already taken, *J*.   ,,   v ii 561
    Methought they would have brain'd me with it, *J*.   ,,   v ii 613
John (Prince, afterwards King of England) and these are
    the days of Prince *J*:   *Foresters* I i 178
    A gallant Earl. I love him as I hate *J*.   ,,   I i 191
    in the service of our good king Richard against the
    party of *J*,   ,,   I i 195
    This *J*—this Norman tyranny—   ,,   I i 238
    I am old and forget. Was Prince *J* there? *Marian.*
    The Sheriff of Nottingham was there—not *J*. *Sir*
    Richard. Beware of *J* and the Sheriff of Nottingham.   ,,   I i 251
    he hath sold himself to that beast *J*—   ,,   I i 268
    Down with *J*! (repeat)   *Foresters* I i 4, 12, 16, 17, 30
    Perfect—who should know you for Prince *J*,   *Foresters* I ii 21
    ye did wrong in crying 'Down with *J*;' For be he
    dead, then *J* may be our King.   ,,   I ii 97
    But if it be so we must bear with *J*.   ,,   I ii 102
    I fear you be of those who hold more by *J* than
    Richard. *Sheriff.* True, for through *J* I had
    my sheriffship. I am *J's* till Richard come
    back again, and then I am Richard's.   ,,   I ii 199
    Beware of *J*! *Marian.* I hate him.   ,,   I ii 214

John (Prince, afterwards King of England) (*continued*) Bad
    me beware Of *J*: what maid but would beware of *J*?   *Foresters* I ii 256
    This is irregular and the work of *J*.   ,,   I iii 71
    How should we cope with *J*?   ,,   I iii 79
    I held for Richard, and I hated *J*.   ,,   II i 52
    Our vice-king *J*, True king of vice—   ,,   II i 82
    our *J* By his Norman arrogance and dissoluteness,   ,,   II i 84
    J—Shame on him!—Stole on her,   ,,   II i 110
    the Sheriff, and by heaven, Prince *J* himself   ,,   II i 173
    Prince *J*, the Sheriff, and a mercenary. *Sir Richard.*
    Prince *J* again. We are flying from this *J*.   ,,   II i 445
    be there wolves in Sherwood? *Marian.* The wolf, *J*!   ,,   II i 513
    this is Maid Marian Flying from *J*—disguised.   ,,   II i 680
    break, Far as he might, the power of *J*—   ,,   II i 696
    A maiden now Were ill-bested in these dark days of *J*,   ,,   II ii 46
    That *J* last week return'd to Nottingham,   ,,   III 147
    We robb'd the traitors that are leagued with *J*;   ,,   III 160
    My lord *J*, In wrath because you drove him from the
    forest,   ,,   III 449
    to 'scape The glance of *J*——   ,,   III 463
    The bee should buzz about the Court of *J*. No ribald
    J is Love, no wanton Prince,   ,,   IV 45
    Art thou for Richard, or allied to *J*? *Richard.* I am
    allied to *J*.   ,,   IV 136
    But being o' *J's* side we must have thy gold.   ,,   IV 157
    But I am more for Richard than for *J*.   ,,   IV 160
    or the head of a fool, or the heart of Prince *J*,   ,,   IV 213
    Break thine alliance with this faithless *J*,   ,,   IV 324
    Still I am more for Richard than for *J*.   ,,   IV 330
    for how canst thou be thus allied With *J*,   ,,   IV 351
    The Sheriff! the Sheriff, follow'd by Prince *J*   ,,   IV 588
    My liege, Prince *J*—— *Richard.* Say thou no word
    against my brother *J*.   ,,   IV 823
John (St.) *See* **John** (Gospel of St.), **St. John**
John of Oxford (*See also* **John, John the Swearer**) I, *J o O*,
    The President of this Council,   *Becket* I iii 74
    For *J o O* here to read to you.   ,,   I iii 417
    Cursed be *J o O*, Roger of York, And Gilbert Foliot!   ,,   II ii 265
John of Salisbury (*See also* **John, Salisbury**) We gave thee
    to the charge of *J o S*,   ,,   I i 247
    J o S Hath often laid a cold hand on my heats,   ,,   I i 383
    He watch'd her pass with *J o S*   ,,   I ii 40
    priest whom *J o S* trusted Hath sent another.   ,,   III i 69
    J o S committed The secret of the bower,   ,,   III iii 4
    I know him; our good *J o S*.   ,,   v ii 77
    make me not a woman, *J o S*,   ,,   v ii 148
John the Swearer (*See also* **John, John of Oxford**) They
    call thee *J t S*.   ,,   II ii 462
Join To *j* a voice, so potent with her Highness,   *Queen Mary* IV i 117
    May the great angels *j* their wings,   ,,   IV iv 6
    J hands, let brethren dwell in unity;   *Harold* I i 397
    j our hands before the hosts, That all may see.   ,,   IV 241
    And then thy King might *j* the Antipope,   *Becket* II ii 211
    every thread of thought Is broken ere it *j's*—   ,,   v ii 207
    I'll *j* with him: I may reap something from him—   *The Cup* I i 177
    tho' a stranger fain would be allow'd To *j* the hunt.   ,,   II 135
    And *j* your life this day with his,   *Prom. of May* I 797
    Well, my child, let us *j* them.   *Foresters* I ii 238
    till he *j* King Richard in the Holy Land.   ,,   III 84
    And *j* our feasts and all your forest games   ,,   III 417
    by St. Mary these beggars and these friars shall *j* you.   ,,   III 420
    J them and they are a true marriage.   ,,   IV 933
    Our rebel Abbot then shall *j* your hands,   ,,
Join'd What hinders but that Spain and England *j*,   *Queen Mary* v iii 69
    he *j* with thee To drive me outlaw'd   *Harold* IV ii 13
    a random guest Who *j* me in the hunt.   *The Cup* I ii 109
    And *j* my banner in the Holy Land,   *Foresters* II 1000
Joining Mary of England, *j* hands with Spain,   *Queen Mary* I v 298
Joke Let be thy *j's* and thy jerks, man!   *The Falcon* 132
Jolt Against the unpleasant *j's* of this rough road   *Prom. of May* I 228
Jonah that the fish had swallowed me, Like *J*,   *Harold* II i 38
    Rolf, what fish did swallow *J*? *Rolf.* A whale!   ,,   II ii 42
Jostle winds so cross and *j* among these towers.   ,,   II ii 155
Journey I am an old man wearied with my *j*,   *Queen Mary* III ii 128
    make ready for the *j*.   ,,   III v 278

Journey (*continued*) so much worse For last day's *j*.   *The Falcon* 834
Joy   Ay, that was in her hour of *j*;   *Queen Mary* I i 84
   wearied with my journey, Ev'n with my *j*.   ,, III ii 129
   An angel cry 'There is more *j* in Heaven,'—   ,, IV ii 10
   Either to live with Christ in Heaven with *j*,   ,, IV iii 221
   I wish you *j* o' the King's brother.   *Becket* III i 155
   O *j* for the promise of May, (repeat)   *Prom. of May* I 43, 44, 723, 725
   I reel beneath the weight of utter *j*—   *The Cup* II 450
   for who could embrace such an armful of *j*?   *Foresters* I ii 71
   Whate'er thy *j*'s, they vanish with the day;   ,, I iii 44
Joyful   And love is *j*, innocent, beautiful,   ,, II ii 64
Judas-lover   *J-l* of our passion-play Hath track'd us hither.   *Becket* IV ii 136
Judge (s)   *J*'s had pronounced That our young Edward   *Queen Mary* I ii 24
   if I'm any *j*, By God, you are as poor a poet,   ,, II i 112
   sat in mine own courts Judging my *j*'s,   *Becket* I iii 369
   Doubtless, like *j*'s of another bench,   *Foresters* II 153
Judge (verb)   I shall *j* with my own eyes   *Queen Mary* I i 133
   From thine own mouth I *j* thee;   ,, I iii 54
   You cannot *j* the liquor from the lees.   ,, IV iii 550
   Who but the bridegroom dares to *j* the bride.   *Becket* I iii 685
   If we may *j* the kernel by the husk,   *The Cup* I i 174
   Perhaps you *j* him With feeble charity :   ,, I ii 185
   Sit here, my queen, and *j* the world with me.   *Foresters* III 152
   But will the King, then, *j* us all unheard ?   ,, IV 897
Judged   As if he had been the Holy Father, sat And
   j it.   *Queen Mary* IV iii 45
   The Lord be *j* again by Pilate ?   No !   *Becket* I iii 97
   make my cry to the Pope, By whom I will be *j*;   ,, I iii 725
Judgement   what a day ! nigh upo' *j* daay loike.   *Queen Mary* IV iii 468
Judging   sat in mine own courts *J* my judges,   *Becket* I iii 369
Judgment (*See also* **Judgement**)
   accruing thereupon ;   *Queen Mary* III iii 219
   This was the cause, and hence the *j* on her.   ,, III iv 187
   For which God's righteous *j* fell upon you   ,, III iv 240
   and these *j*'s on the land—   ,, v i 96
   You must abide my *j*, and my father's,   ,, v i 145
   And our great lords will sit in *j* on him.   *Becket* I iii 549
   Sons sit in *j* on their father !—   ,, I iii 551
   decline The *j* of the King ?   ,, I iii 676
   Nay, but hear thy *j*.   The King and all his barons——
   Becket.   *J* !   Barons—   ,, I iii 682
   Ay, the princes sat in *j* against me,   ,, I iv 129
   yea, and in the day of *j* also,   ,, I iv 147
   there are men Of canker'd *j* everywhere—   ,, v ii 6
   by the *j* of the officers of the said lord king,   *Foresters* I iii 64
Judgment-seat   drag The cleric before the civil *j-s*,   *Becket* I iii 84
Juggle   What game, what *j*, what devilry are you playing ?   ,, v i 153
Juggled   She knew me from the first, she *j* with me,   *Prom. of May* III 687
Juggler   *J* and bastard—bastard—he hates that most—   *Harold* II ii 773
   And for *my* part therein—Back to that *j*,   ,, v i 54
Julius (the Third, Pope)   Legate From our most Holy
   Father *J*, Pope,   *Queen Mary* III iii 126
   Our Lord and Holy Father, *J*,   ,, III iii 212
   J the Third Was ever just, and mild, and father-like ;   ,, v ii 30
   reft me of that legatship Which *J* gave me,   ,, v ii 35
July   King closed with me last *J* That I should pass the
   censures of the Church   *Becket* v ii 389
Jumiéges   Did ye not outlaw your archbishop Robert, Robert
   of *J*—   *Harold* I i 57
   Robert the Archbishop !   Robert of *J*,   ,, II ii 530
Jumped   or the cow that *j* over the moon.   *Foresters* I i 435
Junction   Threaten our *j* with the Emperor—   *Becket* II ii 471
June   They did not last three *J*'s.   *Prom. of May* III 589
   How few *J*'s Will beat our pulses quicker !   *Foresters* III 1061
Juno   bust of *J* and the brows and eyes Of Venus ;   *The Cup* I i 120
Jupiter   O all ye Gods—*J* !—*J* !   ,, II 453
Just   O, *j* God !   Sweet mother, you had time and cause
   enough   *Queen Mary* I v 22
   His learning makes his burning the more *j*.   ,, IV i 160
   Who deems it a most *j* and holy war.   ,, v i 147
   Julius the Third Was ever *j*, and mild, and father-
   like ;   ,, v ii 31
   We have heard Of thy *j*, mild, and equal governance ;   *Harold* II ii 690
   And all our *j* and wise and holy men That shall be
   born hereafter.   ,, III i 209

Just (*continued*)   for it seem'd to me but *j* The Church should
   pay her scutage like the lords.   *Becket* I i 33
   All that you say is *j*.   I cannot answer it Till better times,   ,, III i 1
Justice   Your courts of *j* will determine that.   *Queen Mary* II iv 130
   By seeking *j* at a stranger's hand   IV i 20
   make his battle-axe keen As thine own sharp-dividing *j*,   *Harold* v i 564
   Ay, and the King of kings, Or *j* ;   *Becket* I i 33
   I trust I have not ;   Not mangled *j*.   ,, I i 356
   churl against the baron—yea, And did him *j*;   ,, I iii 367
   The King's will and God's will and *j*;   ,, I iii 420
   he's no respect for the Queen, or the parson, or the
   j o' peace, or owt.   *Prom. of May* I 133
   That were a wild *j* indeed.   ,, III 156
   how often *j* drowns Between the law and the letter of
   the law !   *Foresters* IV 512
   Was *j* dead because the King was dead ?   ,, IV 847
   We dealt in the wild *j* of the woods.   ,, IV 1072
Justiciary   Before the Prince and chief *J*,   *Becket* I iii 709
   I have sent to the Abbot and *j*   *Foresters* IV 88
   The Abbot of York and his *j*   ,, IV 335
   You, my lord Abbot, you *J*, I made you Abbot, you *J*:   ,, IV 842
Jute   Angle, *J*, Dane, Saxon, Norman,   *Harold* II ii 762
   yet he held that Dane, *J*, Angle, Saxon,   ,, IV i 77
Jutting   O thin-skinn'd hand and *j* veins,   *Queen Mary* IV ii 204
   But after rain o'erleaps a *j* rock And shoots three
   hundred feet.   *The Cup* I i 110

K

Kate (attendant on Marian)   You do well, Mistress *K*, to
   sing and to gather roses.   *Foresters* I i 23
   I would like to show you, Mistress *K*,   ,, I i 49
   O sweet *K*, my first love, the first kiss,   ,, I i 126
   I have played at the foils too with *K* :   ,, I i 218
   to stand between me and your woman, *K*.   ,, I i 305
   Speak to me, *K*, and say you pardon me !   ,, II ii 53
   O *K*, true love and jealousy are twins,   ,, II ii 62
   I have been a fool and I have lost my *K*.   ,, II ii 79
   O good *K*—If my man-Robin were but a bird-Robin,   ,, III 38
   call *K* when you will, for I am close at hand.   ,, III 50
   Why, where is *K* ?   *Marian*.   *K* !   ,, III 258
   Search them, *K*, and see if they have spoken truth.   ,, III 288
   Honour to thee, brave Marian, and thy *K*.   ,, III 300
   my lady, *K* and I have fallen out again,   ,, III 411
   come between me and my *K* and make us one again.   ,, III 422
   Embrace me, Marian, and thou, good *K*, Kiss and con-
   gratulate me, my good *K*.   ,, IV 1032
Katekin   I have lodged my pretty *K* in her bower.   ,, II 418
Keen   Take heed, take heed ! The blade is *k* as death.   *Queen Mary* v v 175
   make his battle-axe *k* As thine own sharp-dividing
   justice,   *Harold* v i 563
Keep (s)   he is here, And yonder is thy *k*.'   ,, II ii 359
Keep (verb)   Stand back, *k* a clear lane !   *Queen Mary* I i 1
   Have you, my Lord ?   Best *k* it for your own.   ,, I iv 133
   You've a bold heart ; *k* it so.   ,, I iv 269
   That I may *k* you thus, who am your friend   ,, I v 133
   These let them *k* at present ;   ,, I v 407
   To bind me first by oaths I could not *k*, And *k*   ,, I v 557
   To guard and *k* you whole and safe from all   ,, II i 246
   He *k*'s, they say, some secret that may cost   ,, III i 200
   Why do they *k* us here ?   ,, III v 15
   He is my good friend, and I would *k* him so ;   ,, v iii 91
   Why did you *k* me prating ?   Horses, there !   ,, v iii 113
   Pray'd me to pay her debts, and *k* the Faith ;   ,, v v 257
   and *k* me still In eyeshot.   *Harold* II ii 241
   arm'd men Ever *k* watch beside my chamber door,   ,, II ii 245
   He did not mean to *k* his vow.   ,, III i 248
   K that for Norman William !   ,, IV iii 169
   chart here mark'd ' *Her Bower*,' Take, *k* it, friend.   *Becket, Pro.* 161
   Wast thou not told to *k* thyself from sight ?   ,, I i 251
   And mean to *k* them, In spite of thee !   ,, I iii 142
   K him away from the lone little isle.   ,, II i 15

Keep (verb (*continued*)) That if they *k* him longer as their guest, *Becket* II i 91
You did your best or worse to *k* her Duchy. „ II ii 83
we make the time, we *k* the time, ay, and we serve the
   time; „ II ii 368
I would have done my most to *k* Rome holy, „ II ii 401
asked our mother if I could *k* a quiet tongue i' my head, „ III i 119
The King *k's* his forest head of game here, „ III ii 37
to *k* the figure moist and make it hold water, „ III iii 165
k her Indungeon'd from one whisper of the wind, „ IV ii 145
Rest you easy, For I am easy to *k*. „ V ii 513
That in the summer *k's* the mountain side, *The Cup* I i 108
Not one to *k* a woman's fealty when Assailed „ I i 176
k it, or you sell me To torment and to death. „ I i 214
k us From seeing all too near that urn, „ I iii 132
Then *k* your wreath, But you will find me *The Falcon* 772
I cannot *k* your diamonds, for the gift I ask for, „ 776
But he will *k* his love to you for ever ! „ 892
Owd Steer wur afeärd she wouldn't be back i' time
   to *k* his birthdaäy, *Prom. of May* I 17
I came back to *k* his birthday. *Dobson.* Well I
   be coomed to *k* his birthdaäy an' all. „ I 74
She *will* break fence. I can't *k* her in order. „ I 194
if tha can't *k* thy one cow i' horder, how can tha *k*
   all thy scholards i' horder ? „ I 196
Let him *k* awaäy, then ; but coom, „ I 424
if the child could *k* Her counsel. „ I 477
But *k* us lovers. „ I 639
K up your heart until we meet again. „ I 753
Noä, noä ! *K'* em. But I hed a word to saäy to ye. „ II 44
has promised to *k* our heads above water ; „ III 170
Come, come, *k* a good heart ! „ III 252
but I *k* a good heart and make the most of it, *Foresters* I i 28
Shall I *k* one little rose for Little John ? „ I i 112
so that you *k* the cowl down and speak not ? „ I ii 21
I *k* it For holy vows made to the blessed Saints „ I ii 174
but can *k* his followers true. „ II i 77
Why did ye *k* us at the door so long ? „ II i 223
I *k* it to kill nightingales. „ II i 380
He is old and almost mad to *k* the land. „ II i 528
I *k* it for her. *Robin.* Nay, she swore it never „ II i 591
You hope to hold and *k* her for yourself, „ IV 477
We all *k* watch. „ IV 608
And we shall *k* the land. „ IV 637
K silence, bully friar, before the King. „ IV 919
Keeper So less chance for false *k's*. *Harold* II ii 688
With Cain's answer, my lord. Am I his *k* ? *Becket* I iv 187
Keepest that thou *k* a record of his birthdays ? *Foresters* II ii 221
Keeping Might strengthen thee in *k* of thy word, *Harold* II ii 730
Is guiltier *k* this, than breaking it. „ II i 231
I have done wrong in *k* your secret ; *Prom. of May* III 399
Kennel if the city be sick, and I cannot call the *k* sweet, *Becket* II ii 349
Kent your worship the first man in *K* and Christendom, *Queen Mary* II i 64
Men of *K* ; England of England ! „ II i 157
in whose crown our *K* is the fairest jewel. „ II i 163
Or tamperers with that treason out of *K*. „ II ii 12
these rebels out of *K* Have made strong head „ II ii 145
The Queen of England or the rabble of *K* ? „ II ii 274
And strong to throw up Wyatts and all *K*. „ II iii 354
he was my neighbour once in *K*. „ II iii 86
A hundred here and hundreds hang'd in *K*. „ III i 2
'twas you That sign'd the burning of poor Joan of *K* ; „ IV ii 206
happy home-return and the King's kiss of peace in *K*. *Becket* III iii 329
Kentish The Queen of England—or the *K* Squire ? *Queen Mary* II ii 269
These *K* ploughmen cannot break the guards. „ II iv 17
Kept you that have *k* your old customs upright, „ II i 158
I *k* my head for use of Holy Church ; „ III iv 359
I had *k* My Robins and my cows in sweeter order „ III iv 269
thou hast sworn an oath Which, if not *k*, *Harold* II ii 739
Fain had I *k* thine earldom in thy hands „ V i 275
by thy wisdom Hast *k* it firm from shaking ? *Becket*, Pro. 204
she *k* the seventh commandment better than some I
   know on, „ III i 193
We never *k* a secret from each other ; *Prom. of May* I 552
you *k* your veil too close for that when they carried
   you in ; „ III 226

Kernel If we may judge the *k* by the husk, *The Cup* I i 174
Kex like a bottle full up to the cork, or as hollow as a *k*, *Foresters* IV 211
Key Give me thy *k's*. *Harold* II ii 681
See here this little *k* about my neck ! „ III i 10
Gave me the golden *k's* of Paradise. *Becket* I i 54
Kick if he did me the good grace to *k* me *Foresters* IV 364
Kick'd the cow *k*, and all her milk was spilt. *Queen Mary* III v 266
thou hast *k* down the board. I know thee of old. *Becket*, Pro. 315
slave that eat my bread has *k* his King ! „ V i 242
play'd at ball with And *k* it featureless— *The Cup* II 128
Kill We do not *k* the child for doing that *Queen Mary* I v 62
we know that ye be come to *k* the Queen, „ II iii 108
don't ye *k* the Queen here, Sir Thomas ; „ II iii 110
we pray you to *k* the Queen further off, „ II iii 114
I have not come to *k* the Queen Or here or there : „ II iii 117
We *k* the heretics that sting the soul— „ II iv 68
the shepherd doth not *k* The sheep that wander „ III iv 102
you must *k* him if you would have him rest— „ V v 69
If Hate can *k*, And Loathing wield a Saxon battle-axe— *Harold* IV i 413
k, *k* with knife or venom One of his slanderous harlots ? *Becket* IV ii 409
s'pose I *k's* my pig, and gi's it among 'em, *Prom. of May* I 147
' As flies to the Gods ; they *k* us for their sport.' „ I 264
It is Nature *k's*, And not for *her* sport either. „ I 272
That hold by Richard, tho' they *k* his deer. *Foresters* I iii 100
I keep it to *k* nightingales. „ II i 380
if we *k* a stag, our dogs have their paws cut off, „ IV 224
Kill'd Thy *k* but for their pleasure and the power *Queen Mary* III iv 74
and *k* away at once Out of the flutter. „ III v 163
O God, I have *k* my Philip ! „ V v 181
rose or no rose, has *k* the golden violet. *Becket*, Pro. 351
K half the crew, dungeon'd the other half „ V ii 444
a rumour then That you were *k* in battle. *The Falcon* 382
but we fought for it back, And *k*— „ 615
And we *k'* em by the score ! „ 620
mastiff, That all but *k* the beggar, *Prom. of May* I 559
niver 'a been talkin' haäfe an hour wi' the divil 'at
   k her oän sister, „ II 604
If it had *k* one of the Steers there the other day, „ III 249
K the sward where'er they sat, *Foresters* II ii 152
Killing And cruel at it, *k* helpless flies ; *Queen Mary* III iv 65
and the power They felt in *k*. „ III iv 76
Kin but follow'd the device of those Her nearest *k* : „ III i 380
Let kith and *k* stand close as our shield-wall, *Harold* I i 398
His *k*, all his belongings, overseas ; *Becket* II i 71
restore his *k*, Reseat him on his throne of Canterbury, „ II ii 117
Send back again those exiles of my *k* „ III iii 187
From whom, as being too *k*, you know, „ IV ii 307
I dare not brave my brother, Break with my *k*. *The Falcon* 257
Kind O, *k* and gentle master, the Queen's Officers, *Queen Mary* I ii 107
she had seen the Archbishop once, So mild, so *k*. *Becket* V ii 120
Weänt ye gi'e me a *k* answer at last ? *Prom. of May* II 63
saints were so *k* to both on us that he was dead
   before he was born. *Foresters* I i 372
Kindle He hath gone to *k* Norway against England, *Harold* III i 79
And *k* all our vales with myrtle-blossom, *The Cup* II 267
Kindled sparkles out as quick Almost as *k* ; *Queen Mary* I ii 74
and *k* with the palms Of Christ ! „ I v 93
you should know that whether A wind be warm or
   cold, it serves to fan A *k* fire. „ I v 621
after much smouldering and smoking, be *k* again
   upon your quarter. *Becket* II ii 313
the fire, when first *k*, said to the smoke, „ II ii 318
Kindlier The running down the chase is *k* sport „ IV ii 213
and will pray for you That *you* may thrive, but in
   some *k* trade. *Foresters* III 253
Kindliest The *k* man I ever knew ; *Queen Mary* IV iii 421
Kindly Be *k* to the Normans left among us, *Harold* III i 303
A *k* rendering Of ' Render unto Cæsar.' . . . „ III ii 167
Thou art too *k*. „ IV iii 32
Not *k* to them ? *Sinnatus.* *K* ? O the most *k* Prince
   in all the world ! *The Cup* I ii 354
Yet he seem'd *k*, And said he loathed the cruelties „ I ii 372
he always took you so *k*, he always took the world
   so *k*. *The Falcon* 187
made a wry mouth at it, but he took it so *k*, „ 191

Kindly (*continued*) he always took you so *k*—   *The Falcon* 195
And were my *k* father sound again,   *Foresters* III 81
Kindness beget A *k* from him, for his heart was rich, *Queen Mary* IV i 169
O Bonner, if I ever did you *k*—   „ IV ii 152
but smile As *k*, watching all,   *Harold* I i 367
King (*See also* Baby-king, Boy-king, Co-king, Father-king, Giant-king, Mock-king, Monk-king, Vice-king) and this wrought Upon the *k*;   *Queen Mary* I ii 71
You look'd a *k*.   „ I iii 103
but we play with Henry, *K* of France,   „ I iii 131
The *K* is skilful at it?   „ I iii 144
And so you well attend to the *k's* moves,   „ I iii 152
a *K* That with her own pawns plays against a Queen, Whose play is all to find herself a *K*.   „ I iii 161
make him *K* belike.   „ I iv 212
A *k* to be—is he not noble, girl?   „ I v 4
then the *K*—that traitor past forgiveness,   „ I v 28
What says the *K* your master?   „ I v 248
if this Philip be the titular *k* Of England,   „ I v 254
but your *k* stole her a babe from Scotland   „ I v 291
Thou speakest of the enemy of thy *k*.   „ I v 327
he will be *K*, *K* of England, my masters;   „ II i 173
and if Philip come to be *K*, O my God!   „ II i 199
to whom The *k*, my father, did commit his trust;   „ II ii 208
To be your *k*, ye would rejoice thereat,   „ II ii 224
Makes enemies for himself and for his *k*;   „ II ii 399
Their cry is, Philip never shall be *k*.   „ II iv 2
Left him and fled; and thou that would'st be *K*,   „ II iv 83
My foes are at my feet, and Philip *K*.   „ II iv 143
Nay, he is *K*, you know, the *K* of Naples. The father ceded Naples, that the son Being a *K*, might wed a Queen—   „ III i 72
The *K* of France will help to break it.   „ III i 105
The French *K* winks at it.   „ III i 160
Long live the *K* and Queen, Philip and Mary!   „ III i 208
There be both *K* and Queen, Philip and Mary. Shout!   „ III i 296
where you gave your hand To this great Catholic *K*.   „ III ii 92
happily symboll'd by The *K* your husband,   „ III ii 110
The *K* is here!—My star, my son!   „ III ii 183
He's here, and *k*, or will be—yet cocksbody!   „ III iii 44
The *K* and I, my Lords, now that all traitors   „ III iv 1
the *K* And you together our two suns in one;   „ III iv 18
bolster'd up The gross *K's* headship of the Church,   „ III iv 246
The Church's evil is not as the *K's*,   „ III iv 273
But not the force made them our mightiest *k's*.   „ III iv 336
Crown'd slave of slaves, and mitred *k* of *k's*.   „ III iv 381
'It is the *K's* wish, that you should wed Prince Philibert of Savoy.   „ III v 221
Why then the *K*! for I would have him bring it Against the *K*, the Queen, the Holy Father,   „ III vi 21
"The *K* hath wearied of his barren bride.'   „ III vi 140
K and Queen, To whom he owes his loyalty   „ IV i 21
Stood out against the *K* in your behalf,   „ IV i 126
And when the *K's* divorce was sued at Rome,   „ IV iii 41
Friend for so long time of a mighty *K*;   „ IV iii 73
Obey your *K* and Queen, and not for dread   „ IV iii 177
I conclude the *K* a beast; Verily a lion if you will—   „ IV iii 411
Here is the *K*.   „ V i 15
There is no *k*, not were he ten times *k*,   „ V i 62
The *K* of France the *K* of England too.   „ V i 198
Madam, I brought My *K's* congratulations;   „ V iii 570
My *K* would know if you be fairly served.   „ V iii 20
I take it that the *k* hath spoken to you;   „ V iii 85
Ay, tell the *K* that I will muse upon it;   „ V iii 89
But I am much beholden to your *K*.   „ V iii 99
I am much beholden to your *K*, your master.   „ V iii 111
the one *K*, the Christ, and all things in common, as in the day of the first church, when Christ Jesus was *K*.   „ V iv 53
fair a likeness As your great *K* in armour   „ V v 29
He can but read the *k's* face on his coins. *Stigand.* Ay, ay, young lord, *there* the *k's* face *is* power.   *Harold* I i 71
To sleek and supple himself to the *k's* hand.   „ I i 149
Too hardy with thy *k*!   „ I i 198
after those twelve years a boon, my *k*,   „ I i 226

King (*continued*) What lies upon the mind of our good *k*   *Harold* I i 269
Brother, the *k* is wiser than he seems; And Tostig knows it; Tostig loves the *k*. *Harold*. And love should know; and—be the *k* so wise,—   „ I i 272
The *k* hath made me Earl; make me not fool! Nor make the *K* a fool, who made me Earl!   „ I i 288
Who made the *K* who made thee, make thee Earl.   „ I i 294
Pray God the people choose their *k*!   „ I i 315
And thou art ever here about the *K*:   „ I i 321
To the good *k* who gave it—not to you—   „ I i 407
The *k*! the *k* is ever at his prayers.   „ I i 410
In all that handles matter of the state I am the *k*.   „ I i 413
thou hast taught the *k* to spoil him too;   „ I i 451
Farewell, my *k*. *Harold*. Not yet, but then—my queen.   „ I ii 137
If he were *K* of England, I his queen,   „ I ii 154
lest the *k* Should yield his ward to Harold's will.   „ I ii 158
'O thou more saint than *k*!'   „ I ii 168
Tostig, Edward hath made him Earl: he would be *k*:—   „ I ii 187
Harold Hear the *k's* music, all alone with him,   „ I ii 194
Who knows I may not dream myself their *k*!   „ I ii 252
a whale to a whelk we have swallowed the *K* of England.   „ II i 45
Who shall be *k's* of England. I am heir Of England by the promise of her *k*.   „ II ii 123
there the great Assembly choose their *k*,   „ II ii 127
I will be *k* of England by the laws,   „ II ii 130
More kinglike he than like to prove a *k*.   „ II ii 143
What said the *K*? 'I pray you do not   „ II ii 217
Yea, yea, he would be *k* of England.   „ II ii 369
And he our lazy-pious Norman *K*,   „ II ii 444
our good *K* Kneels mumbling some old bone—   „ II ii 468
The *k*, the lords, the people clear'd him of it.   „ II ii 522
and a child, Will England have him *k*?   „ II ii 573
promised that if ever he were *k* In England,   „ II ii 587
Ay . . . if the *k* have not revoked his promise.   „ II ii 609
Thou shalt be verily *k*—all but the name—   „ II ii 632
I, the Count—the *K*—Thy friend—   „ II ii 754
Then our great Council wait to crown thee *K*—   „ III i 4
sickness of our saintly *k*, for whom My prayers   „ III i 164
Nay—but the council, and the *k* himself,   „ III i 171
It lies beside thee, *k*, upon thy bed.   „ III i 195
Let me be buried there, and all our *k's*,   „ III i 208
It shall be granted him, my *k*;   „ III i 228
we be not bound by the *k's* voice In making of a *k*, yet the *k's* voice   „ III i 236
my lord, my *k*! He knew not whom he sware by.   „ III i 255
I did not dream then I should be *k*.—   „ III i 271
and dear son, swear When thou art *k*,   „ III i 306
but to please our dying *k*, and those Who make   „ III i 329
Our holy *k* Hath given his virgin lamb to Holy Church   „ III i 333
for the *K* Is holy, and hath talk'd with God,   „ III i 354
And our great Council wait to crown thee *K*.   „ III i 407
Crown'd, crown'd and lost, crown'd *K*—   „ III ii 2
Harold the *K*! *Harold*. Call me not *K*, but Harold. *Edith*. Nay, thou art *K*!   „ III ii 32
Thine, thine, or *K* or churl!   „ III ii 36
rather let me be *K* of the moment to thee,   „ III ii 41
than to reign *K* of the world without it.   „ III ii 45
thou be only *K* of the moment over England.   „ III ii 51
Tho' somewhat less a *k* to my true self   „ III ii 53
nor priestly *k* to cross Their billings ere they nest.   „ III ii 93
He, and the giant *K* of Norway,   „ III ii 122
The *K* hath cursed him, if he marry me;   „ III ii 189
Let not our great *k* Believe us sullen—only shamed to the quick Before the *k*—as having been so bruised By Harold, *k* of Norway; but our help Is Harold, *k* of England. Pardon us, thou! Our silence is our reverence for the *k*!   „ IV i 6
old Northumbrian crown, And *k's* of our own choosing.   „ IV i 33
Had in him kingly thoughts—a *k* of men,   „ IV i 83
Not made but born, like the great *k* of all,   „ IV i 85
bad the *k* Who doted on him,   „ IV i 102
K! thy brother, If one may dare to speak the truth,   „ IV i 107
good *k* would deign to lend an ear Not overscornful,   „ IV i 135
thence a *k* may rise Half-Godwin and half-Alfgar,   „ IV i 142
The *k* can scarcely dream that we,   „ IV i 163

King (*continued*) Who dares arraign us, *k*, of such a plot ? *Harold* IV i 168
   Yea, take the Sacrament upon it, *k*.   „ IV i 183
   The nimble, wild, red, wiry, savage *k*—   „ IV i 198
   Thou hast but cared to make thyself a *k*—   „ IV ii 75
   Every man about his *k* Fought like a *k* ; the *k* like his
     own man,   „ IV iii 56
   My lord the *K* ! William the Norman,   „ IV iii 180
   To do with England's choice of her own *k* ?   „ v i 20
   If the *k* fall, may not the kingdom fall ? But if I fall, I
     fall, and thou art *k* ; And, if I win, I win, and thou
     art *k* ;   „ v i 123
   How should the people fight When the *k* flies ?   „ v i 138
   How should the *K* of England waste the fields Of England, „ v i 140
   That scared the dying conscience of the *k*,   „ v i 212
   I thy *k*, who came before To tell thee   „ v i 235
   O hapless Harold ! *K* but for an hour !   „ v i 258
   The *k's* last word—' the arrow ! '   „ v i 266
   advise the *k* Against the race of Godwin.   „ v i 281
   Get thou into thy cloister as the *k* Will'd it :   „ v i 309
   I have not spoken to the *k* One word ;   „ v i 335
   The *k* commands thee, woman !   „ v i 340
   England Is but her *k*, and thou art Harold !   „ v i 376
   Edith, if I, the last English *K* of England—   „ v i 384
   all the monks of Peterboro' Strike for the *k* ;   „ v i 447
   k of England stands between his banners.   „ v i 486
   They have broken the commandment of the *k* !   „ v i 615
   With whom they play'd their game against the *k* !
     Aldwyth. The *k* is slain, the kingdom overthrown !   „ v ii 14
   being the true wife Of this dead *K*,   „ v ii 85
   And this dead *k's* Who, *k* or not,   „ v ii 123
   When all men counted Harold would be *k*,   „ v ii 133
   Every man about his *k* Fell where he stood.   „ v ii 181
   I am *K* of England, so they thwart me not,   „ v ii 196
   Look to your *k*.   *Becket,* Pro. 33
   my bishop Hath brought your *k* to a standstill.   „ Pro. 44
   Why, there then—down go bishop and *k* together.   „ Pro. 48
   to the statesman Who serves and loves his *k*, and whom
     the *k* Loves not as statesman,   „ Pro. 78
   That tread the *k's* their children under-heel—   „ Pro. 213
   My young son Henry crown'd the *K* of England,   „ Pro. 224
   K, Church, and State to him but foils wherein   „ Pro. 268
   God's favour and *k's* favour might so clash   „ Pro. 295
   Parthian shaft of a forlorn Cupid at the *K's* left breast,   „ Pro. 340
   and the *K* gave it to his Chancellor.   „ Pro. 431
   but because he had the love of the *K*.   „ Pro. 443
   retinue of three *k's* behind him, outroyalling royalty ?   „ Pro. 445
   he holp the *K* to break down our castles,   „ Pro. 446
   you could not see the *K* for the kinglings.   „ Pro. 453
   she, whom the *K* loves indeed, is a power in the State.   „ Pro. 482
   Rival !—ay, and when the *K* passes,   „ Pro. 484
   secret matter which would heat the *K* against thee   „ Pro. 488
   thou in thy way shouldst be jealous of the *K*,   „ Pro. 512
   then the *K* came honeying about her,   „ Pro. 516
   make her as hateful to herself and to the *K*,   „ Pro. 527
   wreak our spite on the rosefaced minion of the *K*, and
     bring her to the level of the dust, so that the *K*—   „ Pro. 530
   To please the *K* ! *Becket.* Ay, and the *K* of *k's*,   „ I i 31
   Shall I fall off—to please the *K* once more ?   „ I i 110
   Not fight—tho' somehow traitor to the *K*—   „ I i 113
   ' I mean to fight mine utmost for the Church, Against
     the *K* ' ? *Becket.* But dost thou think the *K* Forced
     mine election ? *Herbert.* I do think the *K* Was
     potent in the election, and why not ? Why should
     not Heaven have so inspired the *K* ?   „ I i 125
   The rift that runs between me and the *K*.   „ I i 141
   thro' The random gifts of careless *k's*,   „ I i 159
   here I gash myself asunder from the *K*,   „ I i 175
   What friend ! *Rosamund.* The *K*.   „ I i 326
   My friend, the *K* ! . . . O thou Great Seal of England,
     Given me by my dear friend the *K* of England—   „ I i 335
   To tell the *K*, my friend, I am against him.   „ I i 343
   O, my dear friend, the *K* ! O brother !—   „ I i 360
   Let the Great Seal be sent Back to the *K* to-morrow.   „ I i 376
   The *K* may rend the bearer limb from limb.   „ I i 378
   Of this wild Rosamund to please the *K*,   „ I i 393

King (*continued*) However *k's* and queens may frown on thee.   *Becket* I ii 18
   in your chancellorship you served The follies of the *K*.   „ I ii 31
   Priest Sits winking at the license of a *k*, Altho' we grant
     when *k's* are dangerous The Church must play into
     the hands of *k's* ;   „ I ii 66
   That *k's* are faithful to their marriage vow.   „ I ii 78
   Where I shall meet the Barons and my *K*.   „ I ii 85
   Stir up the *K*, the Lords !   „ I ii 88
   I will make thee hateful to thy *K*.   „ I ii 92
   Where is the *K* ? *Roger.* Gone hawking on the Nene.   „ I iii 1
   But by the *K's* command, are written down, And by the
     K's command I, John of Oxford,   „ I iii 72
   whether between laymen or clerics, shall be tried in the
     K's court.'   „ I iii 81
   he shall answer to the summons of the *K's* court to be
     tried therein.'   „ I iii 89
   the *K*, till another be appointed, shall receive the
     revenues thereof.'   „ I iii 100
   Is the *K's* treasury A fit place for the monies of the Church, „ I iii 104
   the *K* shall summon the chapter of that church to court, „ I iii 108
   with the consent of our lord the *K*, and by the advice   „ I iii 112
   Without the license of our lord the *K*.   „ I iii 130
   Are ye my masters, or my lord the *K* ?   „ I iii 135
   The *K* is quick to anger ;   „ I iii 164
   sheathe your swords, ye will displease the *K*.   „ I iii 180
   Save the *K's* honour here before his barons.   „ I iii 187
   He pray'd me to pray thee to pacify Thy *K* ; for if thou
     go against thy *K*, Then must he likewise go against
     thy *K*, And then thy *K* may join the Antipope,   „ I iii 207
   K swore to our cardinals He meant no harm   „ I iii 215
   He told me thou shouldst pacify the *K*,   „ I iii 225
   He heads the Church against the *K* with thee.   „ I iii 245
   I came, your *K* ! Nor dwelt alone,   „ I iii 357
   that found a *K* Who ranged confusions,   „ I iii 370
   The master of his master, the *K's k*.—God's eyes ! I
     had meant to make him all but *k*. Chancellor-
     Archbishop, he might well have sway'd All England
     under Henry, the young *K*,   „ I iii 462
   it is the traitor that imputes Treachery to his *K* !   „ I iii 485
   The *K* will not abide thee with thy cross.   „ I iii 488
   Make not thy *K* a traitorous murderer.   „ I iii 500
   Arm'd with thy cross, to come before the *K* ?   „ I iii 510
   Nay, nay, my lord, thou must not brave the *K*.   „ I iii 515
   Now as Archbishop goest against the *K* ;   „ I iii 531
   Ay, ay ! but art thou stronger than the *K* ?   „ I iii 535
   I promised The *K* to obey these customs,   „ I iii 557
   Tell what I say to the *K*.   „ I iii 564
   deliver Canterbury To our *K's* hands again,   „ I iii 581
   Fealty to the *k*, obedience to thyself ?   „ I iii 587
   But the *K* rages—most are with the *K* ;   „ I iii 591
   The *K's* ' God's eyes ! ' come now so thick and fast,   „ I iii 609
   the *K* demands three hundred marks,   „ I iii 626
   Tell the *K* I spent thrice that in fortifying his castles.   „ I iii 631
   the *K* demands seven hundred marks, Lent at the siege
     of Thoulouse by the *K*.   „ I iii 634
   the *K* demands five hundred marks,   „ I iii 641
   For which the *K* was bound security,   „ I iii 645
   K Demands a strict account of all those revenues   „ I iii 649
   my good lord Leicester, The *K* and I were brothers.
     All I had I lavish'd for the glory of the *K* ;   „ I iii 661
   The *K* and all his lords—— *Becket.* Son, first hear *me* !   „ I iii 671
   In fee and barony of the *K*, decline The judgment of
     the *K* ? *Becket.* The *K* ! I hold Nothing in fee
     and barony of the *K*.   „ I iii 675
   The *K* and all his barons—— *Becket.* Judgment !
     Barons !   „ I iii 683
   K would throne me in the great Archbishoprick :   „ I iii 693
   For the *K's* pleasure rather than God's cause   „ I iii 697
   God from me withdraws Himself, And the *K* too.   „ I iii 703
   Why thou, the *K*, the Pope, the Saints, the world,   „ I iii 705
   I refuse to stand By the *K's* censure,   „ I iii 723
   The *K*, these customs, all the Church,   „ I iii 726
   K commands you, upon pain of death,   „ I iii 752
   The *K* hath frowned upon me.   „ I iv 25
   there be those about our *K* who would have thy blood.'   „ I iv 55

Kiss (s) (*continued*)   She gave a weeping *k* to the Earl, And the maid a *k* to the man.   *Foresters* I i 20

She gave a weeping *k* to the Earl, The maid a *k* to the man.   „   I i 119

shall I give her the first *k*?   O sweet Kate, my first love, the first *k*, the first *k*!   „   I i 126

I came to give thee the first *k*, and thou hast given it me.   „   I i 132

does it matter so much if the maid give the first *k*? *Little John.* I cannot tell, but I had sooner have given thee the first *k*.   „   I i 136

now thou hast given me the man's *k*, let me give thee the maid's.   „   I i 143

may the maid give the first *k*?   „   I i 173

and is flustered by a girl's *k*.   „   I i 186

You shall give me the first *k*.   „   I ii 228

In *k'es*.   *Kate.* You, how dare you mention *k'es*?   „   III 126

Take thou this light *k* for thy clumsy word.   „   III 134

I Embrace thee with the *k'es* of the soul.   „   III 143

Kiss (verb)   *K* me would you? with my hands Milking the cow?   *Queen Mary* III v 87

Come, Robin, Robin, Come and *k* me now;   „   III v 100

Come behind and *k* me milking the cow!   „   III v 105

To *k* and cuff among the birds and flowers—   „   III v 258

K me—thou art not A holy sister yet,   *Harold* III ii 80

thy kiss—Sacred! I'll *k* it too.   *Becket* II i 185

K me, little one, Nobody near!   „   II i 100

Sinnatus, *k* me now.   *The Cup* I ii 419

and *k* me This beautiful May-morning.   *Prom. of May* I 564

I *k* it as a prelude to that privilege   „   II 528

Now if she *k* him, I will have his head.   *Foresters* I ii 146

Is it made up? Will you *k* me?   „   I ii 226

I thought I saw thee clasp and *k* a man   „   II ii 72

Thou see me clasp and *k* a man indeed.   „   II ii 76

Fancied he saw thee clasp and *k* a man.   „   III 23

K me again.   *Marian.* Robin, I will not *k* thee,   „   III 136

K him, Sir Richard—*k* him, my sweet Marian.   „   IV 1003

K and congratulate me, my good Kate.   „   IV 1033

I have seen thee clasp and *k* a man indeed,   „   IV 1035

Well then, who *k'es* first?   *Little John.*   *K* both together.   „   IV 1040

Kiss'd   *k* not her alone, but all the ladies   *Queen Mary* I i 80

you came and *k* me milking the cow. (repeat)   „   III v 91, 98

K me well I vow;   „   III v 93

You *k* me there For the first time.   *The Cup* I ii 417

should have told us how the man first *k* the maid.   *Foresters* I i 123

Kissin'   'er an' the owd man they fell a *k* o' one another   *Prom. of May* I 21

Kissing   *See* **A-bussin', Kissin'**

Kite (a toy)   You fly your thoughts like *k's*.   *Queen Mary* I v 390

Kite (bird)   And the stock-dove coo'd, till a *k* dropt down,   *Prom. of May* I 55

To the bleak church doors, like *k's* upon a barn.   *Harold* IV iii 37

Kith   Let *k* and kin stand close as our shield-wall,   „   I i 398

Knave   Shout, *k's*!   *Queen Mary* I i 9

Say for ten thousand ten—and pothouse *k's*,   „   II i 70

K, wilt thou wear thy cap before the Queen?   „   III i 236

Thy name, thou *k*?   *Man.* I am nobody, my Lord.   „   III i 246

God's passion! *k*, thy name?   „   III i 249

K, thou shalt lose thine ears and find thy tongue,   „   III i 255

God's passion! do you know the *k* that painted it?   „   III i 264

What hast thou shouted, *k*?   „   III i 293

K, there be two. There be both King and Queen,   „   III i 295

Must it be so, my Lord?   *Gardiner.* Ay, *k*.   „   III i 308

Where, *k*, where?   *Man.* Sign of the Talbot.   „   III i 318

The *k's* are easily cow'd.   „   III i 329

K, hast thou let thy prisoner scape?   *Harold* II ii 672

Woe *k* to thy familiar and to thee!   „   II ii 679

To be honest is to set all *k's* against thee.   *Becket* I iii 572

Come, you filthy *k's*, let us pass.   „   I iv 203

K, there is a lot of wild fellows in Sherwood Forest   *Foresters* I ii 72

Sit there, *k's*, till the captain call for you.   „   III 219

I know them arrant *k's* in Nottingham.   „   III 301

Louder, louder, ye *k's*.   „   III 396

mark'd if those two *k's* from York be coming?   „   IV 112

if these *k's* should know me for their King?   „   IV 133

Knaw (know   I *k's* nowt o' what foälks says, an' I caäres nowt neither.   Foälks doesn't hallus *k* thessens;   *Prom. of May* I 26

hallus a-fobbing ma off, tho' ye *k's* I love ye.   „   I 108

Squire Edgar as ha' coomed among us—the Lord *k's* how—   „   I 111

tha 'e *k's* I was hallus ageän heving schoolmaster i' the parish!   „   I 186

What dost a *k* o' this Mr. Hedgar as be a-lodgin' wi' ye?   „   I 199

and I *k's* what men be, and what masters be,   „   I 328

—ye all *k's* the ten-aäcre—   „   I 367

Noä; I *k's* a deäl better now.   „   II 26

doänt tha *k* he be sweet upo' Dora Steer,   „   II 160

k's the back on 'im—drest like a gentleman,   „   II 578

fur I haätes 'im afoor I *k's* what 'e be.   „   II 585

I'll maäke her *k*! (repeat)   „   II 608

dosta *k* this paäper? Ye dropt it upo' the road.   „   II 687

dosta *k* what tha meäns wi' by-and-by?   „   II 690

thou hesn't naw business 'ere wi' my Dora, as I *k's* on,   „   II 736

Knaw'd (knew)   *k* better nor to cast her sister's misfortin inter 'er teeth   „   II 126

Fur boäth on 'em *k* as well as mysen   „   II 313

she niver *k* 'is faäce when 'e wur 'ere afoor;   „   II 606

I *k* 'im when I seed 'im ageän an I telled feyther on 'im.   „   III 121

I beänt sa sewer o' that, fur Sally *k* 'im;   „   III 147

Knaw'd (known)   fur they be *k* as far as Littlechester.   „   I 213

Kneaded   household dough was *k* up with blood;   *Becket* I iii 351

Knee   (*See also* **Kneeä**)   fray'd i' the *k's*, and out at elbow,   *Queen Mary* I i 51

Cast myself down upon my *k's* before them,   „   I v 562

we'll pray for you all on our bended *k's*.   „   II iii 109

on our *k's*, we pray you to kill the Queen   „   II iii 114

pray for you on our bended *k's* till our lives' end.   „   II iii 122

round his *k*, misplaced, Our English Garter,   „   II i 82

gray rogue, Gardiner, Went on his *k's*,   „   III v 166

I thus implore you, low upon my *k's*,   „   IV i 64

I would dandle you upon my *k* At lisping-age.   „   V ii 142

With both her *k's* drawn upward to her chin.   „   V ii 391

bind a score All in one faggot, snap it over *k*,   *Harold* I i 58

This old Wulfnoth Would take me on his *k's*   „   IV i 72

—brave Gurth, one gash from brow to *k*!   „   V ii 71

been on my *k's* every day for these half-dozen years   *The Falcon* 184

I seed tha a-limpin' up just now wi' the roomatics i' tha *k*.   *Prom. of May* I 385

I laäme't my *k* last night running arter a thief.   „   I 387

look at our suits, out at *k*, out at elbow.   *Foresters* I i 33

I fall before thee, clasp Thy *k's*.   „   II i 600

Kneeä (knee)   fell ageän coalscuttle and my *k* gev waäy   *Prom. of May* I 404

Kneel   prelates *k* to you.   *Queen Mary* I iv 83

And worse than all, you had to *k* to *me*;   „   IV ii 134

good King *K's* mumbling some old bone—   *Harold* II ii 469

I *k* to thee—be friends with him again.   *Becket* I i 317

K to thy lord Fitzurse; Crouch even   „   IV i 221

I *k* once more to be forgiven.   *Foresters* II i 667

he *k's*! he has anger'd the foul witch,   „   II i 669

Kneeling   Behold thy father *k* to thee, Becket.   *Becket* I iii 252

Can I fancy him *k* with me, and uttering the same prayer;   *Prom. of May* III 180

Knelt   *k* And blubber'd like a lad,   *Queen Mary* III i 149

Then *k* and said the Miserere Mei—   „   III i 390

I mean the houses *k* Before the Legate—   „   III iii 257

Knew   (*See also* **Knaw'd**)   I *k* they would not do me any wrong,   „   I iii 100

if I either thought or *k* This marriage   „   II ii 226

Seventeen—and *k* eight languages—   „   III i 358

she thought they *k* the laws. But for herself, she *k* but little law.   „   III i 380

Who *k* it from the first.   „   III vi 114

O if I *k* you felt this parting, Philip, As I do!   „   III vi 251

if you *k* him As I do, ever gentle, and so gracious,   „   IV i 155

Against the truth I *k* within my heart,   „   IV iii 241

I *k* it would be so.   „   IV iii 252

The kindliest man I ever *k*;   „   IV iii 421

Knew (*continued*) I *k* it, cousin, But held from you all
  papers   *Queen Mary* v ii 44
What then, he *k* I was no Lutheran.   „ v ii 78
I thought you *k* me better.   „ v ii 186
Too young ! And never *k* a Philip.   „ v ii 361
She *k* me, and acknowledged me her heir,   „ v v 255
I *k* thy purpose ; he and Wulfnoth never Have met,   *Harold* II ii 84
I never *k* thee check thy will for ought   „ II ii 120
Far as he *k* in this poor world of ours—   „ II ii 363
He *k* not whom he sware by.   „ III i 256
I know He *k* not, but those heavenly ears have heard,   „ III i 258
Stigand believed he *k* not what he spake.   „ III i 61
I *k* him brave : he loved his land :   „ IV i 201
I smote him suddenly, I *k* not what I did.   „ IV ii 43
by whom I *k* not that I sware,—not for myself—   „ v 305
Call not for help from me. I *k* him not.   „ v ii 54
Since I *k* battle, And that was from my boyhood,   „ v ii 174
I *k* thy father ; he would be mine age Had he lived
  now ;   *Becket* I iii 249
Thought that I *k* him, err'd thro' love of him,   „ I iii 440
And I, that *k* mine own infirmity,   „ I iii 696
something was said to me I *k* not what.   „ II i 61
I never *k* an honest woman that could make songs,   „ III i 182
I never saw any such, Never *k* any such,   „ IV ii 127
Your Becket *k* the secret of your bower.   „ v i 177
I think our Abbess *k* it and allow'd it.   „ v ii 95
They *k* he loved me.   „ v ii 453
wrong'd Without there, *k* thee with Antonius.   *The Cup* I ii 320
One of the men there *k* him.   „ I ii 341
He *k* not at the moment who had fasten'd   „ I 49
but he *k* I meant to marry him.   *The Falcon* 51
if She *k* the giver ; but I bound the seller   „ 72
I *k* it would come to this. (repeat)   „ 156, 174
I always *k* it would come to this ! (repeat)   „ 158, 175
You *k* Eva, then ?   *Prom. of May* II 367
Surely I loved Eva More than I *k* !   „ 644
She *k* me from the first, she juggled with me,   „ III 687
Much, the miller's son, I *k* thy father :   *Foresters* I iii 146
So hollowly we *k* not which was which.   „ II i 260
far as we *k*, We never robb'd one friend   „ III 156

Knife   Hast thou a *k* ?   *Queen Mary* v v 164
callous with a constant stripe, Unwoundable. The *k* !   „ v v 173
Becket, beware of the *k* !   *Becket* I iv 133
As at this loveless *k* that stirs the riot,   „ IV ii 191
kill, with *k* or venom One of his slanderous harlots ?   „ IV iii 409
And my *k* there—and blast the king and me,   *The Cup* II 152
He drove his *k* into the heart of the deer,   *Foresters* IV 541

Knife-edge   crawl over *k-e* flint Barefoot,   *Becket* II 272

Knight   Call him a *K*, That, with an ass's,   *Queen Mary* I iii 168
They have taken away the toy thou gavest me, The
  Norman *k*.   *Harold* II ii 107
thou shalt have another Norman *k* !   „ II ii 114
range of *k's* Sit, each a statue on his horse,   „ v i 524
I led seven hundred *k's* and fought his wars.   *Becket* I iii 638
But I that threw the mightiest *k* of France,   „ I iii 746
K's, bishops, earls, this London spawn—   „ II ii 143
Monks, *k's*, five hundred, that were there and heard.   „ v ii 406
the *k's* are arming in the garden Beneath the sycamore.   „ v ii 569
A score of *k's* all arm'd with swords and axes—   „ v iii 71
O God, O noble *k's*, O sacrilege !   „ v iii 178
Did two *k's* pass ?   *Foresters* II i 230
Take thou mine arm. Who art thou, gallant *k* ?   „ II i 440
Seize on the *k* ! wrench his sword from him !   „ II i 676
we saw thee cowering to a *k* And thought thou wert
  bewitch'd.   „ II i 683
K, your good father had his draught of wine   „ II ii 1
No, no, false *k*, thou canst not hide thyself   „ II ii 23
Quick with thy sword ! the yeoman braves the *k*.   „ II ii 31
Art thou a *k* ?   „ IV 116
How much is it, Robin, for a *k* ?   „ IV 152
He hath got it from the bottle, noble *k*.   „ IV 237
Shall I undertake The *k* at quarterstaff,   „ IV 248
Thou seest, Sir *K*, our friar is so holy   „ IV 279
Hail, *k*, and help us.   „ IV 765

Knit   ere two souls be *k* for life and death,   *The Cup* II 359

Knock   *K* off his cap there, some of you about him !   *Queen Mary* III i 241
K, and it shall be open'd.   *Becket* v iii 64
it be i' *my* natur to *k* 'im o' the 'eäd now ;   *Prom. of May* I 288
K again ! *k* again !   *Foresters* II i 212

Knock'd   How oft hath Peter *k* at Mary's gate !   *Queen Mary* III ii 63

Knot   And here a *k* of ruffians all in rags,   „ II ii 66
thro' this common *k* and bond of love,   „ II ii 198

Know   (*See also* **Knaw**)   thou shouldst *k*, for thou art
  as white as three Christmasses.   „ I i 29
I *k* not if you *k*.   „ I i 101
child by child, you *k*, Were momentary sparkles   „ I i 72
I *k* it, my good Lord.   „ I i 92
and then, who *k's*—   „ I iv 25
Why do you ask ? you *k* it.   „ I iv 35
You *k* to flatter ladies.   „ I iv 98
You *k* your Latin—quiet as a dead body.   „ I iv 181
You do right well. I do not care to *k*   „ I iv 189
because they *k* him The last White Rose,   „ I iv 206
I do but bring the message, *k* no more.   „ I iv 229
I am of sovereign nature, that I *k*,   „ I iv 258
yet I *k* well, Your people, and I go with them so far,   „ I v 186
Ay, Simon Renard *k's* it.   „ I v 218
I *k* it a scandal.   „ I v 229
I *k* not wherefore—some mischance of flood,   „ I v 353
Yet I *k* the Prince,   „ I v 364
The text—Your Highness *k's* it,   „ I v 451
you should *k* that whether A wind be warm or cold,   „ I v 619
Song flies you *k* For ages.   „ II i 81
You *k* I *k* all this.   „ II i 120
Gardiner *k's*, but the Council are all at odds,   „ II i 138
I *k* Spain. I have been there with my father ;   „ II i 166
and the beds I *k*. I hate Spain.   „ II i 185
ye *k*, my masters, that wherever Spain hath ruled   „ II i 205
You *k* that after The Captain Brett,   „ II ii 25
K too what Wyatt said.   „ II ii 35
I *k* it. What do and say Your Council at this hour ?   „ II ii 45
waters of the fen they *k* not Which way to flow.   „ II ii 52
at once may *k* The wherefore of this coming,   „ II ii 137
To tell you what indeed ye see and *k*,   „ II ii 144
Now what I am ye *k* right well—your Queen ;   „ II ii 162
Ye *k* my father was the rightful heir   „ II ii 170
I *k* you loyal.   „ II ii 271
Who *k's* ? the man is proven by the hour.   „ II ii 363
' Who *k's* ? ' I am for England. But who *k's*, That *k's*   „ II ii 411
I *k* not my letters ; the old priests taught me nothing.   „ III ii 57
we *k* that ye be come to kill the Queen,   „ III iii 107
he is King, you *k*, the King of Naples.   „ III i 73
studded with great emeralds, Rubies, I *k* not what.   „ III i 86
I *k* some lusty fellows there in France.   „ III i 128
I *k* a set of exiles over there,   „ III i 155
God's passion ! do you *k* the knave that painted it ?   „ III i 264
there's the face coming on here of one Who *k's* me.   „ III i 472
I *k* that she was ever sweet to me.   „ III i 228
—all times for aught I *k*.   „ III iv 67
for you *k* Right well that you yourself   „ III iv 224
He *k's* not where he stands,   „ III iv 143
Nay, I *k* They hunt my blood.   „ III v 77
You *k* I never come till I be call'd.   „ III v 215
Best wisdom is to *k* the worst at once.   „ III v 220
I *k* that these are breeding A fierce resolve   „ III vi 30
Simon Renard *K's* me too well to speak   „ III vi 126
but, my Lord, you *k* what Virgil sings,   „ III vi 133
you *k* my father, Retiring into cloistral solitude   „ III vi 208
Not sued for that—he *k's* it were in vain.   „ IV i 13
I *k* not if he did ;   „ IV i 128
your Highness *k's* The saying, ' Martyr's blood—   „ IV i 145
You *k* that you recanted all you said   „ IV iii 261
Of recantation yield again, who *k's* ?   „ IV iii 315
I *k* them heretics, but right English ones.   „ IV iii 344
but I do *k* ez Pwoaps and vires be bad things ;   „ IV iii 500
Peters, you *k* me Catholic, but English.   „ IV iii 566
K's where he nested—ever comes again.   „ v i 26
and you *k* The crown is poor.   „ v i 169
Elizabeth—To Philibert of Savoy, as you *k*, We
  meant to wed her ;   „ v i 247

Know (*continued*) but I *k* it of old, he hates me too ;   *Queen Mary* v ii 60
   Your Highness *k's* that in pursuing heresy   "   v ii 96
   They *k* nothing ; They burn for nothing.   "   v ii 113
   who said that ?   I *k* not—true enough !   "   v ii 208
   Our drooping Queen should *k* !   "   v ii 457
   and you *k* me strong of arm ;   "   v ii 469
   light enough, God *k's*, And mixt with Wyatt's rising—   "   v ii 478
   And tell him that I *k* he comes no more.   Tell him at
     last I *k* his love is dead,   "   v ii 589
   My King would *k* if you be fairly served,   "   v ii 20
   Who *k* my right, and love me,   "   v iii 34
   God's death, forsooth—you do not *k* King Philip.   "   v iii 123
   Drugs—but he *k's* they cannot help me—   "   v v 60
   I took it, tho' I did not *k* I took it,   "   v v 97
   Who *k's* if Boleyn's daughter be my sister ?   "   v v 194
   Stigand should *k* the purposes of Heaven.   *Harold* i i 64
   I *k* it, son ; I am not thankless :   "   i i 215
   And Tostig *k's* it ; Tostig loves the king.   *Harold*.
     And love should *k* ; and—be the king so wise,—   "   i i 274
   He cannot guess who *k's*.   "   i ii 136
   Who *k's* I may not dream myself their king !   "   i ii 251
   we came to *k* Thy valour and thy value,   "   ii ii 201
   did Edward *k* of this ?   "   ii ii 304
   I *k* the Norman license—   "   ii ii 477
   Edward not pronounced his heir ?   *Harold.*   Not that I *k*.   "   ii ii 577
   None that I *k* . . . if that but hung   "   ii ii 599
   But hath he done it then ?   *Harold.*   Not that I *k*.   "   ii ii 612
   He is a liar who *k's* I am a liar,   "   ii ii 667
   I *k* your Norman cookery is so spiced,   "   ii ii 810
   Yea, I *k* He knew not, but those heavenly ears   "   iii i 257
   I *k* all Sussex ; A good entrenchment for a perilous
     hour !   "   iii i 362
   Do they ?   I did not *k* it.   "   iii ii 106
   God help me !   I *k* nothing—   "   iii ii 193
   Who *k's* what sows itself among the people ?   "   iv i 149
   who *k* His prowess in the mountains of the West,   "   iv i 164
   K what thou dost ; and we may find for thee,   "   iv ii 48
   They *k* King Edward's promise and thine — thine.
     Harold.   Should they not *k* free England crowns her-
     self ?   Nor *k* that he nor I had power to promise ?
   Not *k* that Edward cancell'd his own promise ?   "   v i 45
   blurt thy curse among our folk, I *k* not—   "   v i 90
   Whisper !   God's angels only *k* it.   Ha !   "   v ii 31
   I am grieved to *k* as much.   *Becket,* Pro. 4
   dost thou *k* I am not wedded to her.   *Becket.*   How
     should I *k* ?   "   Pro. 72
   I love thee and I *k* thee, I *k* thee,   "   Pro. 95
   How shouldst thou *k* that never hast loved one ?   "   Pro. 140
   God's eyes !   I *k* all that—   "   Pro. 148
   Nay—I *k* not, Thomas.   "   Pro. 197
   I *k* Some three or four good priests   "   Pro. 290
   thou hast kicked down the board.   I *k* thee of old.   "   Pro. 316
   The people *k* their Church a tower of strength,   "   i i 15
   It much imports me I should *k* her name.   "   i i 193
   let me pass, my lord, for I must *k*.   "   i i 206
   And *k* the ways of Nature.   "   i i 257
   Well—you *k*—the minion, Rosamund.   "   i ii 36
   Shame, wrath, I *k* not what.   "   i iii 322
   K that when made Archbishop I was freed,   "   i iii 707
   or in the land of France for aught I *k*.   "   i iv 197
   my fellows *k* that I am all one scale like a fish.   "   i iv 213
   cursed My friends at Veselay, I have let them *k*,   "   ii i 90
   —thine ! thine !   *Rosamund.*   I *k* it.   "   ii i 163
   Dost thou *k*, my boy, what it is to be Chancellor of
     England ?   "   ii i 231
   Thine enemy *k's* the secret of my bower.   "   ii i 264
   You are too cold to *k* the fashion of it.   "   ii ii 126
   I would have made Rome *k* she still is Rome—   "   ii ii 402
   Bee mustn't buzz, Whoop—but he *k's*. (repeat)   *Becket* iii i 99, 241
   what's an apple, you *k*, save to a child,   *Becket* iii i 141
   only you *k* the King's married, for King Louis—   "   iii i 166
   most on 'em *k* an honest woman and a lady when
     they see her,   "   iii i 179
   she kept the seventh commandment better than some
     I *k* on,   "   iii i 195

Know (*continued*) known Nothing but him—happy to *k* no
   more,   *Becket* iii i 224
   Whoop—but he *k's*, Whoop—but he *k's*.   "   iii i 263
   I *k* Thy meaning.   "   iii iii 18
   Hereford, you *k*, crown'd the first Henry.   "   iii iii 201
   Even now—Who *k's* ?—I might deliver all things   "   iii iii 269
   Why ?   *Geoffrey.*   Don't *k* why.   "   iv i 14
   but I don't *k* if I can find the way back again.   "   iv i 48
   K you not this bower is secret,   "   iv ii 21
   none shall *k* me ; The King shall never hear   "   iv ii 100
   Who *k's* but that thy lover May plead so pitifully,   "   iv ii 215
   we *k* you proud of your fine hand,   "   iv ii 260
   you *k* thro' all this quarrel I still have cleaved   "   v i 46
   I *k*—could swear—as long as Becket breathes,   "   v i 76
   and yet You *k* me easily anger'd,   "   v i 84
   Do you *k* this cross, my liege ?   "   v i 161
   I *k* him ; our good John of Salisbury.   "   v i 77
   Deal not with things you *k* not.   *Rosamund.*   I *k* him.   "   v ii 133
   I *k* not why You call these old things   "   v ii 269
   I marvel at you—Ye *k* what is between us.   "   v ii 500
   K you not You have spoken to the peril   "   v ii 515
   He *k's* the twists and turnings of the place.   "   v ii 576
   Hugh, I *k* well thou hast but half a heart   "   v iii 129
   Boy, dost thou *k* the house of Sinnatus ?   *The Cup* i i 49
   You *k* the waterfall That in the summer   "   i i 107
   She *k's* it ?   Ha !   "   i i 131
   Who are with him ?   I see no face that *k's* me.   "   i i 183
   k That we Galatians are both Greek and Gaul.   "   i i 202
   Scarce *k* what she has done.   "   i ii 135
   I *k* of no such wives in all Galatia.   "   i ii 191
   k myself am that Galatian Who sent the cup.   "   i ii 209
   I *k* they mean to torture him to death.   I dare not tell
     him how I came to *k* it ;   "   i ii 273
   I say it to you—you are wiser—Rome *k's* all, But you
     k not the savagery of Rome.   "   i ii 286
   is there danger ?   *Camma.*   Nay, None that I *k* :   "   i ii 442
   Will she come to me Now that she *k's* me Synorix ?   "   i iii 21
   I *k* that I am genial, I would be Happy,   "   i iii 28
   as you *k*, The camp is half a league without the city ;   "   i iii 183
   We will let her *k*.   "   ii 13
   the world may *k* You twain are reconciled,   "   ii 68
   It is old, I *k* not How many hundred years.   "   ii 342
   She not *k* ?   She *k's* There's none such other—   *The Falcon* 77
   He loves me, and he *k's* I he loves me !   "   245
   as your ladyship *k's*, his lordship's own foster-brother,   "   566
   You *k*, my lord, I told you I was troubled.   "   676
   you *k* the saying—' Better a man without riches,   "   749
   let me *k* the boon By granting which,   "   765
   You *k* that I can touch The ghittern   "   797
   You *k* sick people, More specially sick children,   "   815
   I don't *k* why I sing that song ; I don't love it.   *Prom. of May* i 61
   He's been arter Miss Eva, haän't he ?   *Dora.*   Not
     that I *k*.   "   i 123
   She *k's* nothing.   Man only *k's*,   "   i 273
   Who *k's* that he had ever dream'd of flying ?   "   i 654
   That's all nonsense, you *k*, such a baby as you are.   "   i 784
   Perhaps you *k* him ?   "   ii 439
   then you would *k* it is not So easy to forgive—   "   ii 484
   has suffer'd More than we *k*.   "   ii 502
   When you shall *k* me better.   "   ii 529
   who came to us three years after you were gone,
     how should she *k* you ?   "   iii 234
   was a mockery, you *k*, for he gave me no address,
     and there was no word of marriage ;   "   iii 331
   for you *k*, my dear, you were always his favourite—   "   iii 422
   Be he deäd ?   *Dora.*   Not that I *k*.   "   iii 434
   He will be sure to *k* you to-morrow.   "   iii 470
   I *k* more fully that *he* can What poor earthworms   "   iii 634
   You *k* her, Eva.   *Harold.*   Eva !   "   iii 663
   She—she *k's* me—now . . .   "   iii 686
   but now ye *k* why we live so stintedly,   *Foresters* i i 76
   I *k* not, but he may save the land,   "   i i 282
   but I *k* not if I will let thee go.   "   i i 311
   Him that is gone.   Who *k's* whither ?   "   i ii 9
   Perfect—who should *k* you for Prince John,   "   i ii 20

Know (*continued*) and more goes to make right than I
k of, *Foresters* I ii 50
Thou art the Earl's confessor and shouldst k. ,, I ii 55
I may not hate the King For aught I k, ,, I ii 116
that worship for me which Heaven k's I ill deserve— ,, I iii 161
Have past away, I k not where; ,, II i 120
My people are all scattered I k not where. ,, II i 176
what should you k o' the food o' the poor? ,, II i 282
If not with thee I k not where she is. ,, II i 494
What? do I not k mine own ring? ,, II i 589
Life, life. I k not death. ,, II i 622
I k not, can I trust myself With your brave band? ,, II i 703
We k all balms and simples of the field ,, II ii 11
I k I have done amiss, have been a fool. ,, II ii 51
Fifty leagues Of woodland hear and k my horn, ,, III 104
I k them arrant knaves in Nottingham. ,, III 301
Do me the service to tap it, and thou wilt k. ,, III 334
If not I have let them k Their lives unsafe ,, IV 92
if these knaves should k me for their King? ,, IV 134
but let him k our forest laws: ,, IV 199
Great woodland king, I k not quarterstaff. ,, IV 216
I k no quarterstaff. ,, IV 257
They k me. I must not as yet be known. ,, IV 336
From whom he k's are hypocrites and liars. ,, IV 380
Richard, again, is king over a realm He hardly k's, ,, IV 388
he falls And k's no more. ,, IV 527
Knowest Thou k we had to dodge, or duck, or die; *Queen Mary* III iv 357
Thou k I bad my chaplain, ,, III vi 73
Thou k never woman meant so well, ,, v ii 342
Thou k I soon go wild. *Harold* I i 297
K thou this? *Harold.* I learn it now. ,, II ii 589
Thou k I am his cousin, ,, II ii 592
And signs on earth! K thou Senlac hill? ,, III i 361
chances and all churches, And that thou k. ,, III ii 184
I doubt not but thou k Why thou art summon'd. ,, IV i 187
O Thou that k, let not my strong prayer ,, v i 646
K thou this other? ,, v ii 98
Thou k he was forced to fly to France; *Becket* I iii 204
in thy kingdom, as thou k, The spouse of the Great King, ,, III iii 174
Thou k that the Sheriff of Nottingham loves thee. *Foresters* I i 222
K thou not the Prince? ,, IV 683
Knowing (K the man) he wrought it ignorantly, *Queen Mary* II i 276
They say, his wife was k and abetting. *Harold* II ii 306
Canst thou love me, thou k where I love? ,, II v 226
K how much you reverence Holy Church, *Becket* I ii 48
K right well with what a tenderness He loved my son. ,, v 20
k the fame of your hospitality, we ventured in
uninvited. *Foresters* I ii 195
Have I the pleasure, friend, of k you? *Prom. of May* I 297
k that he *must* have Moved in the iron grooves ,, II 265
and k as I did That I had shot him thro' the heart, *Foresters* II i 122
Thou art tann'd almost beyond my k, brother. ,, IV 1016
Knowledge That k made him all the carefuller *Harold* III i 340
teach this Rome—from k of our people— *The Cup* II 96
Known (*See also* **Knaw'd**) but all things here At
court are k; *Queen Mary* I iv 58
The prince is k in Spain, in Flanders, ,, I v 207
(I have k a semi-madman in my time So fancy-ridd'n) ,, II i 9
it will be k that we have moved; ,, III i 198
—And I have k such women more than one— ,, III vi 178
never was it k That any man so writing, ,, IV iii 46
Council at this present deem it not Expedient to be k. ,, IV iii 57
The truth of God, which I had proven and k. ,, IV iii 150
men Have hardly k what to believe, ,, IV iii 405
Should make the mightiest empire earth has k. ,, v iii 71
than have k there were such devils. *Harold* II i 38
for thou Art k a speaker of the truth, ,, II ii 517
they follow me—and I must not be k. *Becket* I i 183
it may import her all as much Not to be k. ,, I i 199
'Tis k you are midwinter to all women, ,, I ii 27
and k Nothing but him—happy to know no more, ,, III i 223
you are k Thro' all the courts of Christendom ,, IV ii 324
for how slightly have I k myself. *Prom. of May* II 442
but I must not be k yet. ,, III 224
Shall I be k? is my disguise perfect? *Foresters* I ii 18

Known (*continued*) thee however mask'd I should have k. *Foresters* II i 650
I must not as yet be k. ,, IV 338
Know'st thou k my claim on England Thro' Edward's *Harold* II ii 12
And yet thou k how little of thy king! *Foresters* IV 401
Knut (**Canute, the Dane**) or English Ironside Who fought
with K, or K *Harold* IV iii 54
Knyvett (**adherent of Wyatt**) (*See also* **Antony, Antony
Knyvett**) Open the window, K; *Queen Mary* II i 154
I'll think upon it, K. ,, II i 240

L

La I would dance too. Fa, l, l, fa, l, l. *Foresters* I ii 59
Laäbourer (**labourer**) fur I wur nobbut a l, and now
I be a landlord— *Prom. of May* I 329
Laädy (**lady**) to turn out boäth my darters right down
fine *laädies.* ,, I 337
and you should sit i' your oän parlour quite like a l, ,, II 98
plaäy the pianner, if ye liked, all daäy long, like a l, ,, II 101
likes 'er all the better fur taäkin' me down, like a l, ,, II 134
Dan Smith's cart hes runned ower a l i' the holler
laäne, ,, II 568
'ow should I see to laäme the l, and meä coomin'
along pretty sharp an' all? ,, III 96
to saäy he's browt some of Miss Eva's roses for the
sick l to smell on. ,, III 347
Laäme't (**lamed**) I l my knee last night running arter a
thief. ,, I 386
Laäne (**lane**) Dan Smith's cart hes runned ower a laädy
i' the holler l, ,, II 569
the holler l be hallus sa dark i' the arternoon, ,, III 92
Laäy (**lay**) We l's out o' the waäy fur gentlefoälk
altogither— ,, I 210
and doänt l my cartwhip athurt 'is shou'ders, ,, II 138
Labour (s) And all my lifelong l to uphold The primacy
—a heretic. *Queen Mary* v ii 70
The more or less of daily l done— *Becket* II i 299
I fear me we have lost our l, then. *Foresters* II i 233
Labourer (*See also* **Laäbourer**) all that live By their own
hands, the l, the poor priest; ,, III 165
Labour-in-vain Ingratitude, Injustice, Evil-tongue,
L-i-v. . *Queen Mary* v ii 157
Labyrinthine after that This l brickwork maze in maze, *Becket, Pro.* 166
Lacerating If fast and prayer, and l scourge— ,, I iii 303
Lack (s) My liberality perforce is dead Thro' l of means of
giving. *The Falcon* 297
The man is able enough—no l of wit, *Foresters* I i 103
'Tis for no l of love to you, my lord, But l of happiness ,, I iii 130
thro' thy l of manhood hast betray'd Thy father ,, II i 568
Lack (verb) And tell this learned Legate he l's
zeal. *Queen Mary* III iv 272
Do I any money? ,, IV ii 40
I l a spiritual soldier, Thomas— *Becket, Pro.* 257
Lacking secular kingdom is but as the body L a soul; *Queen Mary* IV i 33
L the love of woman and of child. *Becket* v ii 199
Lacrymas Illorum in l Cruor fundatur! *Harold* v i 531
Lacrymation I should say rather, the l of a lamentation; *Becket* III iii 167
Lad knelt And blubber'd like a l, *Queen Mary* III i 150
but I hear she hath a dropsy, l, ,, III i 224
He stood upright, a l of twenty-one, ,, IV iii 335
Poor l's, they see not what the general sees, ,, v ii 447
poor l! how sick and sad for home! *Harold* II i 325
lied like a l That dreads the pendent scourge, ,, II ii 657
and the l's and lasses 'ull hev a dance. *Prom. of May* I 428
Eh l, if it be thou, I'll Philip tha! ,, II 590
l, dosta knaw this paäper?—Ye dropt it upo' the road. ,, II 686
Eh, l, dosta knaw what tha meäns wi' by-and-by? ,, II 690
Eh, l, but whether thou be Hedgar, ,, II 733
Laden a troop, L with booty and with a flag of ours *The Falcon* 612
Lady (*See also* **Laädy**) but all the *ladies* of her following. *Queen Mary* I i 81
Even so, fair l. ,, I iv 97
You know to flatter *ladies.* ,, I iv 98

Land (s) *(continued)* from the salt lips of the *l* we two Have
track'd   *Becket* III ii 2
lord of more *l* Than any crown in Europe,   ,,   v i 29
And wrought his worst against his native *l*,   *The Cup* I ii 178
past is like a travell'd *l* now sunk Below the horizon—   ,,   II 230
I never saw The *l* so rich in blossom as this year.   *The Falcon* 342
' The *l* belongs to the people ! '   *Prom. of May* I 140
s'pose my pig's the *l*, and you says it belongs to the
parish,   ,,   I 144
violated the whole Tradition of our *l*,   ,,   I 496
Who leaves me ɪ ll his *l* at Littlechester,   ,,   I 511
pacing my new *l's* at Littlechester,   ,,   II 647
We shall have to sell all the *l*,   ,,   III 165
The *l* belonged to the Steers i' the owd times,   ,,   III 450
I have heard the Steers Had *l* in Saxon times ;   ,,   III 608
I have *l* now And wealth, and lay both at your feet.   ,,   III 615
not with all your wealth, Your *l*, your life !   ,,   III 796
if they be not paid back at the end of the year, the
l goes to the Abbot.   *Foresters* I i 70
Sir Richard must scrape and scrape till he get to the *l* again.   ,,   I i 79
must be paid in a year and a month, or I lose the *l*.   ,,   I i 269
but he may save the *l*, (repeat)   ,,   I i 283
Well, thou shalt go, but O the *l* ! the *l* !   ,,   I i 328
and I shall lose my *l* also.   ,,   I i 339
Or I forfeit my *l* to the Abbot.   ,,   I i 151
pay My brother all his debt and save the *l*.   ,,   I ii 219
till he join King Richard in the Holy *L*.   *Robin*.
Going to the Holy *L* to Richard !   ,,   I ii 239
pay his mortgage to his brother, And save the *l*.   ,,   I ii 265
thou art dispossessed of all thy *l's*, goods, and chattels ;   ,,   I iii 60
There is no *l* like England (repeat)   *Foresters* II i 1, 5, 13, 17
thro' all the forest *l* North to the Tyne : being outlaw'd
in a *l* Where law lies dead,   *Foresters* II i 88
—if so the *l* may come To Marian, and they rate the
l fivefold The worth of the mortgage, and who
marries her Marries the *l*.   ,,   II i 147
and couldst never pay The mortgage on my *l*.   ,,   II i 454
but my father will not lose his *l*,   ,,   II i 523
He is old and almost mad to keep the *l*.   ,,   II i 529
what sort of man art thou For *l*, not love ? Thou
wilt inherit the *l*,   ,,   II i 534
betray'd Thy father to the losing of his *l*.   ,,   II i 570
Now he cries ' The *l* ! the *l* ! ' Come to him.   ,,   II ii 7
To a *l* where the fay,   ,,   II ii 180
thou seest the *l* has come between us,   ,,   IV 53
and I would thou wert the king of the *l*.   ,,   IV 233
if the *l* Were ruleable by tongue,   ,,   IV 398
if they were not repaid within a limited time your *l*
should be forfeit.   ,,   IV 468
The *l* ! the *l* ! (repeat)   *Foresters* IV 470, 491, 854
one thousand marks, Or else the *l*.   *Foresters* IV 475
old Sir Richard might redeem his *l*. He is all for
love, he cares not for the *l*.   ,,   IV 488
Out of our treasury to redeem the *l*.   ,,   IV 493
And Sir Richard cannot redeem his *l*.   ,,   IV 565
And we shall keep the *l*.   ,,   IV 637
It seems thy father's *l* is forfeited.   ,,   IV 640
He shall wed thee : The *l* shall still be mine.   ,,   IV 643
I could wish that all the *l* Were plunged   ,,   IV 667
Woe to that *l* shall own thee for her king !   ,,   IV 759
on the faith and honour of a king The *l* is his again.   ,,   IV 853
I am crazed no longer, So I have the *l*.   ,,   IV 856
The gold—my son—my gold, my son, the *l*—   ,,   IV 988
And join'd my banner in the Holy *L*,   ,,   IV 1000
weight of the very *l* itself, Down to the inmost centre.   ,,   IV 1025
Our Lady's blessed shrines throughout the *l*   ,,   IV 1080
Land (verb) So your king-parliament suffer him to *l*,   *Queen Mary* I v 366
Landed Are *l* North of Humber, and in a field   *Harold* III ii 126
William hath *l*, ha ? *Thane*. *L* at Pevensey—I am
from Pevensey—   ,,   IV iii 185
Landing Back'd by the power of France, and
l here,   *Queen Mary* III i 448
Landless Specially not this *l* Philibert Of Savoy ;   ,,   III v 240
Landlord fur I wur nobbut a laäbourer, and now I be
a *l*—   *Prom. of May* I 330

II

Land-surveyor and I taäked 'im fur soom sort of a *l-s*—
but a beänt.   *Prom. of May* I 204
Lane *(See also* **Laäne)** Stand back, keep a clear *l* !   *Queen Mary* I i 2
when you lamed the lady in the hollow *l*.   *Prom. of May* III 90
Do you still suffer from your fall in the hollow *l* ?   ,,   III 241
if met in a black *l* at midnight :   *Foresters* III 224
Language Seventeen—and knew eight *l's*—   *Queen Mary* III i 359
not half speaking The *l* of the land.   *Becket* II i 137
His wickedness is like my wretchedness—Beyond
all *l*.   *Prom. of May* III 748
Lanker I be *l* than an old horse turned out to die on the
common.   *Foresters* I i 51
Lap Milk ? *Filippo*. Three *l's* for a cat !   *The Falcon* 125
Lapse track of the true faith Your *l's* are far seen.   *Queen Mary* III iv 95
Lapwing ᴛʜe *l's* lies, says ' here ' when they are there.   ,,   III v 124
Larder Come, come, Filippo, what is there in the *l* ?   *The Falcon* 118
then there is anything in your lordship's *l* at your
lordship's service,   ,,   137
Large Hath he the *l* ability of the Emperor ?   *Queen Mary* I v 323
Hath he the *l* ability of his father ?   ,,   I v 438
They have brought it in *l* measure on themselves.   ,,   IV iii 363
thou thyself shalt have *L* lordship there of lands and
territory.   *Harold* II ii 83
they both have life In the *l* mouth of England,   ,,   IV iii 74
Without too *l* self-lauding I must hold The sequel   ,,   IV iii 87
Larger Will enter on the *l* golden age ;   *Prom. of May* I 590
The hope of *l* life hereafter, more Tenfold than under
roof.   *Foresters* II i 69
Largess Might cast my *l* of it to the crowd !   *The Cup* II 224
Lark Spit them like *l's* for aught I care.   *Queen Mary* I v 395
The *l* above, the nightingale below,   ,,   II i 52
the *l* sings, the sweet stars come and go,   *Harold* II ii 434
l first takes the sunlight on his wing,   *The Cup* I iii 43
thou that canst soar Beyond the morning *l*,   *The Falcon* 11
and the *l's* 'ud sing i' them daäys,   *Prom. of May* I 374
' O happy *l*, that warblest high Above thy lowly nest,   ,,   III 199
while the *l* flies up and touches heaven !   *Foresters* III ii 315
When heaven falls, I may light on such a *l* !   ,,   III 13
Could live as happy as the *l's* in heaven,   ,,   III 82
Larn (learn, teach) Wheer did they *l* ye that ? *Dora*.
In Cumberland, Mr. Dobson.   *Prom. of May* I 64
I'll git the book ageän, and *l* mysen the rest,   ,,   III 12
Them be what they *l's* the childer' at school,   ,,   III 39
Larned (learned, taught) 'at I ha' nobbut *l* mysen haäfe on it.   ,,   III 4
Lash (verb) If they prance, Rein in, not *l* them,   *Harold* I i 372
Lash (whip) with crimson rowel And streaming *l*.   *Queen Mary* III iv 184
    ,,   v iii 194
Lash'd *l* to death, or lie Famishing in black cells,   ,,   v iii 194
scorn'd the man, Or *l* his rascal back,   *Harold* II ii 507
now, perhaps, Fetter'd and *l*, a galley-slave,   *Foresters* II i 654
Lashing storm and shower *l* Her casement,   *Prom. of May* II 472
Lass Ay, *l*, but when thou be as owd as me   ,,   I 380
Why, *l*, what maäkes tha sa red ?   ,,   I 398
and the lads and *l'es* 'ull hev a dance.   ,,   I 428
Last Dear friend, for the *l* time ; farewell, and fly.   *Queen Mary* I ii 103
because they know him the *l* White Rose, the *l*
Plantagenet   ,,   I iv 207
L night I climb'd into the gate-house, Brett,   ,,   II iii 14
Did not his *l* breath Clear Courtenay and the Princess   ,,   III i 134
I have heard She would not take a *l* farewell of him,   ,,   III i 367
Laughs at the *l* red leaf, and Andrew's Day.   ,,   III iii 87
Thou *l* of all the Tudors, come away ! With us
is peace ! ' The *l* ? It was a dream ;   ,,   III v 151
A missive from the Queen : *l* time she wrote, I had
like to have lost my life :   ,,   III v 188
L night, I dream'd the faggots were alight,   ,,   IV ii 1
It is the *l*. *Cranmer*. Give it me, then.   ,,   IV ii 64
For death gives life's *l* word a power to live,   ,,   IV iii 161
forasmuch as I have come To the *l* end of life,   ,,   IV iii 218
This *l*—I dare not read it her.   ,,   v iii 183
and I say it For the *l* time perchance,   *Harold* I i 176
but *l* night An evil dream that ever came and went—   ,,   I ii 69
Friends, in that *l* inhospitable plunge Our boat hath
burst her ribs ;   ,,   II i 1
L night King Edward came to me in dreams—
(repeat)   *Harold* IV i 259, 265

Last (*continued*) Hear me again—for the *l* time. — *Harold* v i 8
Then for the *l* time, monk, I ask again — „ v i 15
Peace! The king's *l* word—'the arrow!' I shall die— — „ v i 266
wherefore now Obey my first and *l* commandment.
Go! — „ v i 359
Edith, if I, the *l* English King of England— — „ v i 384
but our sun in Aquitaine *l*'s longer. — *Becket, Pro.* 328
The *l* Parthian shaft of a forlorn Cupid at the King's
left breast, — „ *Pro.* 339
and his *l* words were a commendation of Thomas Becket — „ *Pro.* 400
L night I followed a woman in the city here. — „ *Pro.* 468
That rang Within my head *l* night, — „ I ii 71
at *l* tongue-free To blast my realms with excommuni-
cation — „ II ii 50
nigh at the end of our *l* crust, and that mouldy, — „ III i 114
He hath the Pope's *l* letters, and they threaten — „ III iii 24
Take thy one chance; Catch at the *l* straw. — „ IV ii 221
Let this be thy *l* trespass. — „ v ii 165
King closed with me *l* July That I should pass the
censures of the Church — „ v ii 388
Shall not Heaven be served Tho' earth's *l* earthquake
clash'd the minster-bells, — „ v iii 41
I need not fear the crowd that hunted me Across the
woods, *l* night. — *The Cup* I iii 17
He entreats you now For your *l* answer. — „ II 46
O would it were His third *l* apoplexy! — „ II 172
I had a touch of this *l* year—in—Rome. — „ II 446
crown'd victor of my will—On my *l* voyage— — „ II 521
came back *l* night with her son to the castle. — *The Falcon* 3
Thou art the *l* friend left me upon earth— — „ 31
And this *l* costly gift to mine own self, — „ 228
when he came *l* year To see me hawking, — „ 312
My *l* sight ere I swoon'd was one sweet face Crown'd — „ 647
so much weaker, so much worse For *l* day's journey. — „ 834
tha looks haäle anew to *l* to a hoonderd. *Steer.*
An' why shouldn't I *l* to a hoonderd? — *Prom. of May* I 355
Noä; I laäme't my knee *l* night running arter a
thief. — „ I 387
Oh, Philip, Father heard you *l* night. — „ I 557
but you must not be too sudden with it either, as
you were *l* year, — „ II 54
The *l* on it, eh? *Haymaker.* Yeas. — „ II 141
Well, it be the *l* loäd hoäm. — „ II 144
Well but, as I said afoor, it be the *l* loäd hoäm; — „ II 169
'The *L* Loäd Hoäm.' (repeat) — „ II 171
At the end of the daäy, For the *l* loäd hoäm? (repeat) — „ II 184, 195
Till the end of the daäy And the *l* loäd hoäm. — „ II 209
Till the end o' the daäy An' the *l* loäd
hoäm.' (repeat) — „ II 239, 293
To the end o' the daäy, An' the *l* loäd hoäm — „ II 260
Only *l* week at Littlechester, drove me From out
her memory. — „ II 404
Oh, *l* night, Tired, pacing my new lands at Littlechester, — „ II 645
spent all your *l* Saturday's wages at the ale-house; — „ III 78
It is almost the *l* of my bad days, I think. — „ III 471
They did not *l* three Junes. — „ III 589
But she there—her *l* word Forgave—and I forgive you. — „ III 810
Nay, this may be the *l* time When I shall hold my
birthday in this hall! — *Foresters* I ii 87
from their stillness in the grave By the *l* trumpet. — „ II i 48
and the old woman's blessing with them to the *l* fringe. — „ II i 196
We have him at *l* advantage. — „ II i 414
There came some evil fairy at my birth And cursed
me, as the *l* heir of my race: — *Harold* II ii 109
is it true?—That John *l* week return'd to Nottingham, — „ III 147
Lasting and the man has doubtless a good heart, and
a true and *l* love for me: — *Prom. of May* III 172
Late (adj. and adv.) my daughter said that when
there rose a talk of the *l* rebellion, — *Queen Mary* I i 92
I will go. I thank my God it is too *l* to fly. — „ I i 112
Her freaks and frolics with the *l* Lord Admiral? — „ I iv 20
My Lord, you *l* were loosed from out the Tower, — „ I iv 49
Who loathe you for your *l* return to Rome, — „ IV ii 32
in pursuing heresy I have gone beyond your *l* Lord
Chancellor,— — „ v ii 98

Late (adj. and adv.) (*continued*) Friend, tho' so *l*, it is
not safe to preach. — *Queen Mary* v iv 41
Am I too *l*? Cecil . . . God guide me lest I lose
the way. — „ v v 208
Ay, but what *l* guest, As haggard as a fast of forty
days, — *Harold* IV iii 175
Too *l*, my lord: you see they are signing there. — *Becket* I iii 288
The boy so *l*; pray God, he be not lost. — „ IV ii 1
Is it too *l* for me to save your soul? — „ v ii 524
Becket, it *is* too *l*. *Becket.* Is it too *l*? Too *l* on
earth may be too soon in hell. — „ v ii 526
Too *l*—thought myself wise—A woman's dupe. — *The Cup* II 480
—and better *l* than never— — *The Falcon* 200
I have heard That, thro' his *l* magnificence of living — „ 227
I am too *l* then with my quarterstaff! — *Foresters* II i 427
Late (s) There was one here of *l*—William the Silent — *Queen Mary* III ii 191
Later Sooner or *l* shamed of her among The ladies, — *Prom. of May* III 581
Lateran When had the *L* and the Holy Father — *Harold* v i 17
leave *L* and Vatican in one dust of gold— — *Becket* II ii 475
Latimer (Bishop of Worcester) Hooper, Ridley, *L* will
not fly. — *Queen Mary* I ii 14
Cranmer and Hooper, Ridley and *L*, — „ III iv 424
L Had a brief end—not Ridley. — „ IV ii 224
I saw the deaths of *L* and Ridley. — „ IV iii 295
And you saw *L* and Ridley die? *L* was eighty,
was he not? — „ IV iii 328
'not till I hears ez *L* and Ridley be a-vire;' — „ IV iii 508
When we had come where Ridley burnt with *L*, — „ IV iii 586
L! Sir, we are private with our women here— — „ v v 118
Latimer-sailor Our Ridley-soldiers and our *L-s's* — „ IV iii 348
Latin (adj.) for my verses if the *L* rhymes be rolled out
from a full mouth? — *Becket* II ii 337
That's a delicate *L* lay Of Walter Map: — „ v i 191
Latin (s) You know your *L*—quiet as a dead body. — *Queen Mary* IV i 181
Laugh And that's at *l* Lammas—never perhaps. — *Foresters* II i 86
Oh *L*'s at the last red leaf, and Andrew's Day. — *Queen Mary* III iii 87
Oh *l* not! . . . Strange and ghastly — *Harold* III i 157
Latter we could not but *l*, as by a royal necessity— — *Becket* III iii 158
Lauding *See* **Self-lauding**
Laugh'd William *l* and swore that might was right, — *Harold* II ii 361
The wicked sister clapt her hands and *l*; — „ v ii 49
part royal, for King and kingling both *l*, — *Becket* III iii 158
when we felt we had *l* too long and could not stay
ourselves— — „ III iii 160
such a comedy as our court of Provence Had *l* at. — „ v i 191
Laughing (*See also* **A-laughin'**) And the Dutchman,
Now *l* at some jest? — *Queen Mary* III i 196
Laughter (*See also* **Sea-laughter**) among thine island
mists With *l*. — *Harold* II ii 183
thunder-cloud That lours on England—*l*! — „ III ii 161
human in old Rome Before a Pope was born, — „ III ii 163
great motion of *l* among us, part real, part childlike, — *Becket* III iii 155
trumpets in the halls, Sobs, *l*, cries: — „ v ii 368
I Shall not be made the *l* of the village, — *Prom. of May* I 720
Lava-torrents Whose *l-t* blast and blacken a province — *The Cup* II 302
Lavender To rose and *l* my horsiness, — *Queen Mary* III v 185
Lavish Spare not thy tongue! be *l* with our coins, — *Becket* II ii 469
Your *l* household curb'd, and the remission — *Queen Mary* I v 113
Lavish'd All I had I *l* for the glory of the King; — *Becket* I iii 663
Law (s) the Queen, and the *l*'s, and the people, his
slaves. — *Queen Mary* II i 174
when I was wedded to the realm And the realm's *l*'s — „ II ii 165
seeks To bend the *l*'s to his own will, — „ II ii 184
But so I get the *l*'s against the heretic, — „ III i 323
she thought she knew the *l*'s. But for herself, she
knew but little *l*, — „ III i 381
Either in making *l*'s and ordinances — „ III iii 130
Of all such *l*'s and ordinances made; — „ III iii 142
I will be King of England by the *l*'s, — *Harold* II ii 131
For I shall rule according to your *l*'s, — „ II ii 759
I will rule according to their *l*'s. — „ v ii 198
Like other lords amenable to *l*. I'll have them written
down and made the *l*. — *Becket, Pro.* 25
sign'd These ancient *l*'s and customs of the realm. — „ I iii 7
to obey These ancient *l*'s and customs of the realm? — „ I iii 18

Law (s) (*continued*) and *l* From madness. *Becket* I iii 374
There wore his time studying the canon *l* ,, II ii 86
Co-kings we were, and made the *l's* together. ,, II ii 123
spiritual giant with our island *l's* And customs, ,, IV ii 444
it is the *l*, not he ; The customs of the realm. ,, V ii 126
—her main *l* Whereby she grows in beauty— *Prom. of May* I 282
according to the *l* and custom of the kingdom of England *Foresters* I iii 66
I have shelter'd some that broke the forest *l's*. ,, I iii 70
being outlaw'd in a land Where *l* lies dead, we make ourselves the *l*. ,, II i 91
An outlaw's bride may not be wife in *l*. ,, II ii 91
We robb'd the lawyer who went against the *l* ; ,, III 162
chief of these outlaws who break the *l* ? ,, IV 142
being out of the *l* how should we break the *l* ? if we broke into it we should break the *l*, ,, IV 144
Ay, ay, Robin, but let him know our forest *l's* : ,, IV 199
If the king and the *l* work injustice, is not he that goes against the king and the *l* the true king ,, IV 228
Church and *L*, halt and pay toll ! ,, IV 429
you see the bond and the letter of the *l*. ,, IV 505
Between the *l* and letter of the *l* ! O God, I would the letter of the *l* Were some strong fellow ,, IV 513
When the Church and the *l* have forgotten God's music, ,, IV 554
Sweet Marian, by the letter of the *l* ,, IV 639
You crost him with a quibble of your *l*. ,, IV 850
Hast broken all our Norman forest *l's*, ,, IV 886
That thou wilt break our forest *l's* again ,, IV 888
They break thy forest *l's*—nay, by the rood ,, IV 907
And have thy fees, and break the *l* no more. ,, IV 955

Law (inter.) (*See also* **Lor**) O *l*—yeäs, Sir ! I'll run fur 'im mysen. *Prom. of May* III 713

Law-bench Spain in the pulpit and on the *l-b* ; *Queen Mary* II i 178

Lawful Long live Queen Mary, the *l* and legitimate daughter Of Harry the Eighth ! ,, I i 8
with your *l* Prince Stand fast against our enemies and yours, ,, II ii 240
Your *l* Prince hath come to cast herself On loyal hearts and bosoms, ,, II ii 261
The ruler of an hour, but *l* King, *Foresters* IV 47
Were fighting underhand unholy wars Against your *l* king, ,, IV 822

Lawn forest *l's* are all as bright As ways to heaven, ,, II i 630
Thro' wood and *l* and ling, ,, III 425

Lawrence (**Saint**) The patience of St. *L* in the fire. *Queen Mary* IV iii 95

Lawyer leästwaäys, I should be wi' a *l*. *Prom. of May* III 34
We robb'd the *l* who went against the law ; *Foresters* III 161

Lay (s) That's a delicate Latin *l* Of Walter Map : *Becket* V i 192

Lay (verb, trans.) (*See also* **Laäy**) I love you, *L* my life in your hands *Queen Mary* I iv 105
God *l* the waves and strow the storms ,, I v 381
' Will you take it off Before I *l* me down ? ' ,, III i 403
I never *l* my head upon the pillow But that I think, ,, III v 131
See, I *l* it here, For I will come no nearer ,, III v 198
They will not *l* more taxes on a land ,, V i 167
to discourage and *l* lame The plots of France, ,, V i 188
L thou thy hand upon this golden pall ! *Harold* II ii 699
L hands of full allegiance in thy Lord's ,, V ii 11
l them both upon the waste sea-shore At Hastings, ,, V vii 159
l My crozier in the Holy Father's hands, *Becket* I iii 124
not yield To *l* your neck beneath your citizen's heel. ,, V ii 31
Where to *l* on her tribute—heavily here And lightly there. *The Cup* II 98
L down the Lydian carpets for the king. ,, II 187
strows our fruits, and *l's* Our golden grain, ,, II 286
But *l* them there for a moment ! *The Falcon* 763
I *l* them for the first time round your neck. ,, 907
l them there for the delicate-footed creature *Prom. of May* III 616

Lay (past tense [of **Lie**]) by God's providence a good stout staff *L* near me, *Queen Mary* V ii 469
And York *l* barren for a hundred years. *Becket* I iii 54
plow *L* rusting in the furrow's yellow weeds, ,, I iii 355
The town *l* still in the low sun-light, *Prom. of May* I 37
She *l* so long at the bottom of her well *Foresters* IV 242
The man *l* down—the delicate-footed creature ,, IV 535

Layest (intrans.) thou That *l* so long in heretic bonds with me ; *Queen Mary* III iv 280

Layest (trans.) but when thou *l* thy lip To this, *Becket* II i 306

Laying I saw the covers *l*. *Philip*. Let us have it. *Queen Mary* III vi 258

Layman whether between *laymen* or clerics, shall be tried in the King's court.' *Becket* I iii 80

Laymen-criminals be bound Behind the back like *l-c* ? ,, I iii 96

Lazar I marked a group of *l's* in the marketplace— ,, I iv 81

Lazarus Am I a prisoner ? *Leicester*. By St. *L*, no ! ,, I iii 730

Lazy We dally with our *l* moments here, *Queen Mary* V iii 108

Lazy-pious And he our *l-p* Norman King, *Harold* II ii 444

Lea I come here to see this daughter of Sir Richard of the *L* *Foresters* I ii 27
Robin, I am Sir Richard of the *L*. ,, II i 442
Where is this old Sir Richard of the *L* ? ,, IV 438
Where is this laggard Richard of the *L* ? ,, IV 450

Lea (**Sir Richard**) *See* **Richard, Richard Lea, Richard of the Lea**

Lea (**Walter**) *See* **Walter, Walter Lea**

Lead (**direction**) Follow my *l*, and I will make thee earl. *Morcar*. What *l* then ? *Harold* I ii 216

Lead (**metal**) My feet are tons of *l*, They will break in the earth— *The Cup* II 476

Lead (**verb**) we two will *l* The living waters of the Faith *Queen Mary* I v 87
l on ; ye loose me from my bonds. ,, IV ii 240
debonair to those That follow where he *l's*, *Harold* II ii 320
Thy voice will *l* the Witan—shall I have it ? ,, II ii 619
if thou wilt *l* me to thy mother. *Becket* IV i 41
Save by that way which *l's* thro' night to light. ,, V iii 88
and at last May *l* them on to victory— *The Cup* I ii 168
Give me your arm. *L* me back again. *Prom. of May* III 474
To *l* us thro' the windings of the wood. *Foresters* II i 634
O *l* me to my father ! (repeat) ,, II ii 22, 48
L us thou to some deep glen, ,, II ii 168

Leader the people Claim as their natural *l*— *Queen Mary* I iv 210
All arm'd, waiting a *l* ; ,, II i 108
and ye have called me to be your *l*. ,, II i 165
Northumberland, The *l* of our Reformation, ,, III i 149
After a riot We hang the *l's*, ,, IV i 74
I am no soldier, as he said—at least No *l*. *Becket* I iii 299
' Antonius *l* of the Roman Legion.' *The Cup* I i 167
I have heard of them. Have they no *l* ? *Foresters* I iii 104
Be thou their *l* and they will all of them ,, I iii 106
and their own want Of manhood to their *l* ! ,, II i 694

Leädin so ta'en up wi' *l* the owd man about all the blessed murnin' *Prom. of May* III 2

Leading (*See also* **Leädin'**) by God's grace, We'll follow Philip's *l*, *Queen Mary* V v 112

Leaf (*See also* **Lettuce-leaf**) Laughs at the last red *l*, and Andrew's Day. ,, III iii 87
Love will fly the fallen *l*, and not be overtaken ; ,, V iii 372
golden *leaves*, these earls and barons, that clung to me, *Becket* I iv 65
all the *l* of this New-wakening year. *The Falcon* 339
I tear away The *leaves* were darken'd by the battle— ,, 913
How happily would we lilt among the *leaves* *Foresters* III 41
When all the *leaves* are green ; (repeat) ,, III 426, 441
By all the *leaves* of spring, ,, III 439
I scent it in the green *leaves* of the wood. ,, IV 944
You see the darkness thro' the lighter *l*. ,, IV 976

Leaf-sky Pillaring a *l-s* on their monstrous boles, ,, III 100

League (**alliance**) may he not make A *l* with William, *Harold* II ii 461
sequel had been other than his *l* With Norway, ,, IV iii 88
We have had our *l's* of old with Eastern kings. *The Cup* II 101
There is my hand—if such a *l* there be. ,, I ii 103

League (**measure**) crawl over knife-edge flint Barefoot, a hundred *l's*, *Becket* I i 273
The camp is half a *l* without the city ; *The Cup* I iii 89
There—*l* on *l* of ever-shining shore ,, II 533
for Oberon flew away Twenty thousand *l's* to-day. *Foresters* II ii 143
Fifty *l's* Of woodland hear and know my horn, ,, III 103

League (**verb**) foes in Edward's hall To *l* against thy weal. *Harold* I ii 33
they are not like to *l* With Harold against *me*. ,, II ii 53

Leagued *l* together To bar me from my Philip. *Queen Mary* I iv 139
We robb'd the traitors that are *l* with John ; *Foresters* II 159

Leal Commands you to be dutiful and *l* To your young King *Becket* V ii 325

Lean (**adj.**) worse off than any of you, for I be *l* by nature, *Foresters* I i 45

Lean (adj.) (continued) I distrust thee. Thine is a half voice and a *l* assent.   *Queen Mary* III i 311

Lean (verb) He looks to and he *l*'s on as his God, ,, IV iii 306
I marvel why you never *l* On any man's *Becket* v ii 550

Lean'd the Holy Rood had *l* And bow'd above me; *Harold* v i 103

Leaner To plump the *l* pouch of Italy. *Queen Mary* III iv 365

Leaning A faint foot hither, *l* upon Tostig. *Harold* I i 144

Leap thro' the blood the wine *l*'s to the brain *Foresters* I iii 22
Nor care to *l* into each other's arms. ,, III 7

Leapt When the head *l*—so common! *Queen Mary* I v 477
That might have *l* upon us unawares. ,, II ii 295
Neighing and roaring as they *l* to land— *Harold* IV iii 197
Gurth hath *l* upon him And slain him: ,, v i 632

Lear (Shakespeare's play) 'What are we,' says the blind old man in *L*? *Prom. of May* I 263
Then the owd man i' *L* should be shaämed of hissen, ,, I 267

Learn (*See also* **Larn**) Your people have begun to *l* your worth. *Queen Mary* I v 109
You cannot *L* a man's nature from his natural foe. ,, I v 340
and so *l* Your royal will, and do it.— ,, II ii 138
to *l* That ev'n St. Peter in his time of fear ,, III iv 262
Will let you *l* in peace and privacy ,, III iv 326
May *l* there is no power against the Lord. ,, IV iii 66
Knowest thou this? *Harold.* I *l* it now. *Harold* II ii 591
Let me *l* at full The manner of his death, *Becket,* Pro. 425
I *l* but now that those poor Poitevins ,, II ii 427
Nor you, nor I Have now to *l*, my lord, ,, IV ii 274
Will he not fly from you if he *l* the story of my shame *Prom. of May* III 256
And *l* from her if she do love this Earl. *Foresters* I ii 187

Learned-Learn'd (adj.) but you still preferr'd Your *learned* leisure. ,, III iv 258
And tell this *learned* Legate he lacks zeal. ,, III iv 272
And I and *learned* friends among ourselves ,, v ii 74
I have done my best. I am not *learn'd*. *Becket* III i 25
Taught her the *learned* names, anatomized The flowers for her— *Prom. of May* II 302

Learned (verb) *See* **Larned**

Learning (part.) Or *l* witchcraft of your woodland witch, *Foresters* II i 500

Learning (s) and her *l* Beyond the churchmen; *Queen Mary* III i 361
The light of this new *l* wanes and dies: ,, III ii 172
New *l* as they call it; ,, IV i 78
ever gentle, and so gracious, With all his *l*— ,, IV i 157
His *l* makes his burning the more just. ,, IV i 159
Your *l*, and your stoutness, and your heresy, ,, IV ii 125
Brings the new *l* back. ,, v ii 204

Learnt Thou hast *learnt* Thy lesson, and I mine. *Queen Mary* v ii 584
He hath *learnt* to love our Tostig much of late.
Leofwin. And he hath *learnt*, despite the tiger in him, *Harold* I i 145
Thou hast not *learnt* thy quarters here. ,, II ii 153
When all the world hath *learnt* to speak the truth, ,, III i 68
' We have *learnt* to love him, let him a little longer ,, III i 88
but belike Thou hast not *learnt* his measure. ,, IV iii 118
Soon as she *learnt* I was a friend of thine, *Becket* v i 110
When man has surely *learnt* at last that all *Prom. of May* II 330

Lease The house half-ruin'd ere the *l* be out; *Queen Mary* IV vi 66
will give him, as they say, a new *l* of life. *Prom. of May* III 424
would fight for his rents, his *l*'s, his houses, *Foresters* I i 233

Least (adj.) out of which Looms the *l* chance of peril to our realm. *Queen Mary* II ii 238
even now You seem the *l* assassin of the four. *Becket* v ii 522
Anyhow we must Move in the line of *l* resistance *Prom. of May* II 670

Least (s) Ev'n to the *l* and meanest of my own, *Becket* II ii 181
Then one at *l* of its inhabitants *Prom. of May* II 552

Leather (beat) I'd like to *l* 'im black and blue, and she to be a-laughin' at it. ,, II 595
all on us, wi' your leave, we wants to *l* 'im. ,, III 137
Then you mun be his brother, an' we'll *l* 'im. ,, III 151

Leave (permission) By your Grace's *l* Your royal mother *Queen Mary* I v 15
thy *l* to set my feet On board, *Harold* I i 228
Harold, I will not yield thee *l* to go. ,, I i 257
No man without my *l* shall excommunicate *Becket,* Pro. 30

Leave (permission) (continued) No man without my *l* shall cross the seas *Becket* Pro. 34
can I send her hence Without his kingly *l*? ,, III i 220
By thy *l*, beauty. Ay, the same! ,, IV ii 203
—I have still thy *l* to speak. ,, v ii 44
mount with your lordship's *l* to her ladyship's castle, *The Falcon* 413
by your *l* if you would hear the rest, The writing. ,, 529

Leave (verb) I dare not *l* my post. *Queen Mary* I ii 55
You offend us; you may *l* us. ,, I v 210
we will *l* all this, sir, to our council. ,, I v 317
and *l*'s me As hopeful. ,, I v 531
that I should *l* Some fruit of mine own body ,, II ii 222
I *l* Lord William Howard in your city, ,, II ii 245
And *l* the people naked to the crown, ,, III i 119
Ay, rascal, if I *l* thee ears to hear. ,, III i 251
And shalt be thankful if I *l* thee that. ,, III i 257
I must *l* you. Fare you well, ,, III i 472
L me now, Will you, ,, III v 210
pass And *l* me, Philip, with my prayers for you. ,, III vi 228
I am vastly grieved to *l* your Majesty. ,, III vi 255
I have found thee and not *l* thee any more. ,, IV i 109
Tell me that, or I *l* All else untold. ,, IV iii 568
my Queen is like enough To *l* me by and by. *Feria.* To *l* you, sire? ,, v i 243
so my Queen Would *l* me—as—my wife. ,, v i 252
L me alone, brother, with my Northumbria: *Harold* I i 285
I *l* thee, brother. ,, I i 461
And *l* them for a year, and coming back ,, II i 89
I *l* thee to thy talk with him alone; ,, II ii 324
Better *l* undone Than do by halves— ,, II ii 495
L them! and thee too, Aldwyth, must I *l*— ,, IV iii 227
To *l* the Pope dominion in the West. ,, v i 23
but *l* this day to me. ,, v i 128
To *l* the foe no forage. ,, v i 133
L me. No more—Pardon on both sides—Go! ,, v i 353
L them. Let them be! ,, v ii 149
L me with Herbert, friend. *Becket* I i 9
I *l* that, Knowing how much you reverence Holy Church, ,, I i 47
My lord, permit us then to *l* thy service. ,, I iv 10
My Lord, we *l* thee not without tears. ,, I iv 16
I wrong the bird; she *l*'s only the nest she built, they *l* the builder. ,, I iv 45
I must *l* you to your banquet. ,, I iv 150
I mean to *l* the royalty of my crown Unlessen'd ,, II i 107
Not *l* these countryfolk at court. ,, II i 129
the Pope will not *l* them in suspense, ,, II ii 359
l Lateran and Vatican in one dust of gold— ,, II ii 474
—And to meet it I needs must *l* as suddenly. ,, III i 92
I am faint and sleepy. *L* me. ,, III i 208
And *l* you alone with the good fairy. ,, IV ii 60
I cannot *l* him yet. ,, IV ii 85
While this but *l*'s thee with a broken heart, ,, IV ii 173
sworn on this my cross a hundred times Never to *l* him— ,, IV ii 207
for thou must *l* him To-day, but not quite yet. ,, IV ii 210
L it, daughter; Come thou with me to Godstow nunnery, ,, IV ii 365
and *l* it A waste of rock and ruin, hear. *The Cup* II 306
And if he *l* me—all the rest of life— *The Falcon* 334
And thou too *l* us, my dear nurse, alone. ,, 700
Ay, the dear nurse will *l* you alone; ,, 703
An' how did ye *l* the owd uncle i' Coomberland? *Prom. of May* I 67
but *l*'s him A beast of prey in the dark, ,, I 503
Who *l*'s me all his land at Littlechester, ,, I 511
I must *l* you, love, to-day. *Eva.* *L* me, to-day! ,, I 624
that full feast That *l*'s but emptiness. ,, II 256
this, for the moment, Will *l* me a free field. ,, II 456
Tell him I cannot *l* the sick lady just yet. ,, III 352
Milly, my dear, how did you *l* Mr. Steer? ,, III 410
But shall we *l* our England? *Foresters* I iii 92
You see why We must *l* the wood and fly. ,, II ii 174
L it with him and add a gold mark thereto. ,, III 210
L them each what they say is theirs, ,, III 293
We *l* but happy memories to the forest. ,, IV 1070

Leaven the old *l* sticks to my tongue yet. *Queen Mary* I iii 48
so much of the anti-papal *l* Works in him yet, ,, IV i 15

Leaven (*continued*) be something Of this world's *l* in thee
too,   *Becket* v ii 29
Leaving But *l* light enough for Alfgar's house   *Harold* i i 307
L so many foes in Edward's hall   ,, i ii 31
Tho' *l* each, a wound ;   *Becket* i i 176
To steel myself against the *l* her ?   *Prom. of May* i 293
How could I think of *l* him ?   ,, ii 71
L your fair Marian alone here.   *Foresters* i ii 154
Led they *l* Processions, chanted litanies,   *Queen Mary* iii vi 94
I *l* seven hundred knights and fought his wars.   *Becket* i iii 638
S'iver we've *l* moäst on it.   *Prom. of May* ii 52
O Lord, I am easily *l* by words,   *Foresters* i ii 39
Ledge He met a stag there on so narrow a *l*—   ,, iv 532
Lees You cannot judge the liquor from the *l*.   *Queen Mary* iv iii 550
Left (adj.) The last Parthian shaft of a forlorn Cupid at
the King's *l* breast,   *Becket, Pro.* 340
On this *l* breast before so hard a heart,   ,, *Pro.* 375
Take the *l* leg for the love of God.   *Foresters* iv 577
Left (s) reels Now to the right, then as far to the *l*,   *Queen Mary* iv iii 396
Left (verb) I shall be *l* alone. No :   ,, i i 13
I *l* her with rich jewels in her hand,   ,, i iv 242
I scarce had *l* your Grace's presence   ,, i v 583
As tho' the nightmare never *l* her bed.   ,, i v 605
l about Like loosely-scatter'd jewels,   ,, ii i 27
flying to our side *L* his all bare,   ,, ii i 5
Their voice had *l* me none to tell you this.   ,, ii iii 36
Where is Pembroke ? *Courtenay.* I *l* him somewhere
in the thick of it. *Mary.* *L* him and fled ; and
thou that would'st be King,   ,, ii iv 80
And Lady Jane had *l* us.   ,, ii iv 139
L Mary a wife-widow here alone,   ,, iii i 462
Have you remain'd in the true Catholic faith I *l*
you in ?   ,, iv ii 19
When *l* alone in my despondency,   ,, iv ii 95
There is no hope of better *l* for him,   ,, iv iii 79
Her life, since Philip *l* her, and she lost   ,, iv iii 428
Methinks there is no manhood *l* among us.   ,, v ii 284
I *l* her lying still and beautiful,   ,, v v 261
Be kindly to the Normans *l* among us,   *Harold* iii i 303
Then *l* him for the meaner ! thee !—   ,, iv ii 71
I saw her even now : She hath not *l* us.   ,, v i 159
I *l* our England naked to the South To meet thee   ,, v i 289
I *l* him with peace on his face—   *Becket, Pro.* 395
Save for myself no Rome were *l* in England,   ,, ii ii 386
how many an innocent Has *l* his bones upon the way to
Rome   ,, ii ii 409
darkness of the gap *L* by that lack of love.   ,, iii i 61
Hath not thy father *l* us to ourselves ?   ,, iii i 271
And *l* all naked, I were lost indeed.   ,, iv ii 9
Well—well—too costly to be *l* or lost.   ,, iv ii 299
live what may be *l* thee of a life Saved   ,, v ii 367
I surely should have *l* That stroke to Rome.   *The Cup* i iii 159
Thou art the last friend *l* me upon earth—   *The Falcon* 31
and I *l* it privily At Florence, in her palace.   ,, 74
hasn't an eye *l* in his own tail to flourish   ,, 101
Ay, ay ! stare at it : it's all you have *l* us.   ,, 163
We may have *l* their fifty less by five.   ,, 625
They *l* us there for dead !   ,, 651
Ay, and I *l* two fingers there for dead.   ,, 653
I *l* him there for dead too !   ,, 659
had you *l* him free use of his wings,   *Prom. of May* i 652
Hesn't he *l* ye nowt ? *Dora.* No, Mr. Dobson.   ,, ii 7
Since I *l* her Here weeping, I have ranged the world,   ,, ii 251
L but one dreadful line to say,   ,, ii 411
Some of our workmen have *l* us,   ,, iii 28
—all still—and nothing *l* To live for.   ,, iii 681
I Was *l* alone, and knowing as I did   *Foresters* ii i 122
since the Sheriff *l* me naught but an empty belly,   ,, ii 278
He dozes. I have *l* her watching him.   ,, ii ii 80
I *l* mine horse and armour with a Squire,   ,, iv 414
Left-hand Absolve the *l-h* thief and damn the right ?   *Becket* ii ii 392
Left-handedness all *l-h* and under-handedness.   ,, *Pro.* 341
Leg about our *l*'s till we cannot move at all ;   *Queen Mary* ii i 204
it be a var waay vor my owld *l*'s up vro' Islip.   ,, iv iii 472
Haul like a great strong fellow at my *l*'s,   *Harold* ii i 11

Leg (*continued*) Because I broke The horse's *l*—   *Harold* ii ii 110
And may I break his *l*'s ?   ,, ii ii 116
this rag fro' the gangrene i' my *l*.   *Becket* i iv 237
On my *l*'s. *Eleanor.* And mighty pretty *l*'s too.   ,, iv i 5
and thy *l*'s, and thy heart, and thy liver,   *Foresters* iv 204
I have a swollen vein in my right *l*,   ,, iv 569
Take the left *l* for the love of God.   ,, iv 577
By my halidome I felt him at my *l* still.   ,, iv 628
Legacy My *l* of war against the Pope   *Harold* v i 328
Legate holy *l* of the holy father the Pope, Cardinal
Pole,   *Queen Mary* i iii 26
L's coming To bring us absolution from the Pope.   ,, iii i 431
Well said, Lord *L*.   ,, iii i 93
Lord Paget Waits to present our Council to the *L*.   ,, iii ii 98
No, my Lord *L*, the Lord Chancellor goes.   ,, iii ii 151
all one mind to supplicate The *L* here for pardon,   ,, iii iii 107
L From our most Holy Father Julius, Pope,   ,, iii iii 125
authority Apostolic Given unto us, his *L*,   ,, iii iii 211
I mean the houses knelt Before the *L*.   ,, iii iii 258
You brawl beyond the question ; speak, Lord *L* !   ,, iii iv 98
I am your *L* ; please you let me finish.   ,, iii iv 179
Beware, Lord *L*, of a heavier crime Than heresy   ,, iii iv 221
You, Lord *L* And Cardinal-Deacon,   ,, iii iv 260
And tell this learned *L* that he lacks zeal.   ,, iii iv 272
Your violence and much roughness to the *L*,   ,, iii iv 319
yet the *L* Is here as Pope and Master of the Church,   ,, iii iv 346
Our bashful *L*, saw'st not how he flush'd ?   ,, iii iv 350
So that you crave full pardon of the *L*.   ,, iii iv 392
the duty which as *L* He owes himself,   ,, iii iv 401
it would more become you, my Lord *L*,   ,, iv i 116
And how should he have sent me *L* hither,   ,, v ii 87
God curse her and her *L* !   ,, v ii 12
Legate-cousin Royal, Infallible, Papal *L-c*.   ,, iii iv 433
Legateship reft me of that *l* Which Julius gave me, and
the *l* Annex'd to Canterbury—   ,, v ii 34
Holy Father Has ta'en the *l* from our cousin Pole—   ,, v v 126
Legg'd *See* **Two-legg'd**
Legion 'A GALATIAN SERVING BY FORCE IN THE ROMAN
L.'   *The Cup* i i 48
'Antonius leader of the Roman *L*.'   ,, i i 167
'A GALATIAN SERVING BY FORCE IN THE ROMAN *L*.'   ,, i ii 76
Let him come—a *l* with him, if he will.   ,, ii 250
Legitimate Long live Queen Mary, the lawful and *l*
daughter of Harry the Eighth !   *Queen Mary* i i 8
That's a hard word, *l* ; what does it mean ?   ,, i i 12
Leicester (Lord) How much might that amount to, my
lord *L* ?   *Becket* i iii 656
my good lord *L*, The King and I were brothers.   ,, i iii 660
Cornwall's hand or *L*'s : they write marvellously alike.   ,, i iv 51
Was not my lord of *L* bidden to our supper ?   ,, i iv 56
Leicester (town) The Duke hath gone to *L* ;   *Queen Mary* ii i 4
Leisure (adj.) for I would have him bring it Home to
the *l* wisdom of his Queen,   ,, iii vi 23
Leisure (s) but you still prefer'd Your learned *l*.   ,, iii iv 258
Lend would deign to *l* an ear Not overscornful,   *Harold* iv i 136
Encumbered as we are, who would *l* us anything ?   *Prom. of May* iii 163
Length if you'd like to measure your own *l* upon the grass.   ,, i 466
Lenient I was too *l* to the Lutheran,   *Queen Mary* v ij 73
Lennox The Lady Suffolk and the Lady *L* ?—   ,, i iv 31
Lent *L* at the siege of Thoulouse by the King.   *Becket* i iii 636
Those two thousand marks *l* me by the Abbot   *Foresters* i 264
Leofric *L*, and all the monks of Peterboro'   *Harold* v i 446
Leofwin (Earl of Kent and Essex) Ask thou Lord *L* what he
thinks of this ! *Morcar.* Lord *L*, dost thou believe,
that these   ,, i i 40
as well as with mine earldom, *L*'s and Gurth's.   ,, i i 338
L, thou hast a tongue,   ,, i i 391
Vex him not, *L*.   ,, i i 403
L would often fight me, and I beat him.   ,, i i 434
Sign it, my good son Harold, Gurth, and *L*,   ,, iii i 200
Gurth, *L*, Morcar, Edwin !   ,, iv iii 220
And, *L*, art thou mad ?   ,, v i 138
Gurth, *L*, go once more about the hill—   ,, v i 182
And *L* is down !   ,, v i 644
And here is *L*. *Edith.* And here is *He* !   ,, v ii 72

Lie (verb) (*continued*)   that I think, ' Wilt thou *l* there
to-morrow ? '   *Queen Mary* III v 132
It *l's* there folded : is there venom in it ?   "   III v 216
lash'd to death, or *l* Famishing in black cells,   "   v ii 195
Come thou down.   *L* there.   "   v v 180
What *l's* upon the mind of our good king   *Harold* I i 268
That *l's* within the shadow of the chance.   "   II ii 463
Nay let them *l*.   Stand there and wait my will.   "   II ii 682
There *l's* a treasure buried down in Ely :   "   III i 11
It *l's* beside thee, king, upon thy bed.   "   III i 195
curse That *l's* on thee and England.   "   III i 279
Where *l* the Norsemen ? on the Derwent ?   "   IV i 253
He *l's* not here : not close beside the standard.   "   v ii 56
their standards fell . . . where these two *l*.   "   v ii 141
So then our good Archbishop Theobald *L's* dying.   *Becket, Pro.* 3
—there *l's* the secret of her whereabouts,   " *Pro.* 430
The daughter of Zion *l's* beside the way—   " III iii 177
All that *L's* with Antonius.   *The Cup* I ii 293
We *l* too deep down in the shadow here.   *The Falcon* 581
l down there together in the darkness which
would seem but for a moment,   *Prom. of May* III 194
I am very faint.   I must *l* down.   III 473
Where *l's* that cask of wine whereof   *Foresters* III 306
And *l* with us among the flowers, and drink—   " IV 965
Lied   To sit high Is to be *l* about.   *Queen Mary* v 430
Some said it was thy father's deed.   *Harold*.   They *l*.   *Harold* II ii 514
l like a lad That dreads the pendent scourge,   " II ii 656
Of all the lies that ever men have *l*,   " III i 99
Lief   we'd as *l* talk o' the Divil afoor ye as 'im,   *Prom. of May* III 130
Liefer   Far *l* had I in my country hall   *Queen Mary* III i 43
I had *l* that the fish had swallowed me,   *Harold* I 36
But I had *l* than this gold again—   *Foresters* IV 184
Liege   My *l's* and my lords, The thanks of Holy Church   *Becket* II i 189
Liege-lord   breathe one prayer for my *l-l* the King,   " v ii 191
Liest   thou *l* as loud as the black herring-pond   *Harold* II i 25
Norman, thou *l* ! liars all of you,   " IV i 104
Lieth   do you good to all As much as in you *l*.   *Queen Mary* IV iii 187
So he said who *l* here.   *Foresters* II ii 117
Lieu   some fresh device in *l* of it—   *Queen Mary* III i 268
Life (*See also* **After-life**, **Forest-life**)   Old Bourne to the *l* !   "   I iii 30
You've but a dull *l* in this maiden court, I fear, my
Lord ?   *Courtenay.*   A *l* of nods and yawns.   "   I iii 113
like a butterfly in a chrysalis, You spent your *l*;   "   I iv 52
I love you, Lay my *l* in your hands.   "   I iv 105
to practise on my *l*, By poison, fire, shot, stab—   "   I iv 284
I would his *l* Were half as goodly.   "   I v 201
If cold, his *l* is pure.   "   I v 333
A very wanton *l* indeed.   "   I v 336
Of a pure *l* ?   "   I v 448
And wastes more *l*.   "   I v 507
plain *l* and letter'd peace,   "   II i 49
and I warrant this fine fellow's *l*.   "   II iii 84
He has gambled for his *l*, and lost, he hangs.   "   II iii 91
pray for you on our bended knees till our *lives'* end.   "   II iii 122
La, to whistle out my *l*,   "   II iv 109
and save the *l* Of Devon : if I save him,   "   II iv 123
some secret that may cost Philip his *l*.   "   III i 202
you would fling your *lives* into the gulf.   "   III i 459
scarlet thread of Rahab saved his *l*;   "   III ii 39
bees, If any creeping *l* invade their hive   "   III iii 54
To take the *lives* of others that are loyal,   "   III iv 48
Paget, you are all for this poor *l* of ours, And care
but little for the *l* to be.   "   III iv 59
Watch'd children playing at *their l* to be,   "   III iv 63
the *lives* Of many among your churchmen   "   III iv 190
it is an age Of brief *l*, and brief purpose,   "   III iv 413
For there was *l*—And there was *l* in death—   "   III v 145
whose bolts, That jail you from free *l*,   "   III v 172
I had like to have lost my *l*:   "   III v 189
what think you, Is it *l* or death ?   "   III v 194
A right rough *l* and healthful.   "   III v 260
Is *l* and lungs to every rebel birth   "   III vi 51
Care more for our brief *l* in their wet land,   "   III vi 62
The sunshine sweeps across my *l* again.   "   III vi 250
To spare the *l* of Cranmer.   "   IV i 4

Life (*continued*)   To sue you for his *L* ?   *Mary.*   His *l* ?   *Queen Mary* IV i 11
Oh, no ;   "   IV i 47
Or into private *l* within the realm.   "   IV i 125
once he saved your Majesty's own *l*;   "   IV i 130
My *l* is not so happy, no such boon,   "   IV i 152
if he have to live so loath'd a *l*,   "   IV i 194
petition of the foreign exiles For Cranmer's *l*.   "   IV i 77
Exhort them to a pure and virtuous *l*;   "   IV iii 161
For death gives *l's* last word a power to live,   "   IV iii 218
as I have Come To the last end of *l*, and thereupon
Hangs all my past, and all my *l* to be,   "   IV iii 239
Or said or done in all my *l* by me ;   "   IV iii 242
Written for fear of death, to save my *l*,   "   IV iii 271
have borne a man loved plainness all my *l*;   "   IV iii 311
Hurls his soil'd *l* against the pikes and dies.   "   IV iii 330
his best Of *l* was over then.   "   IV iii 428
Her *l*, since Philip left her, and she lost
Philip is as warm in *l* As ever.   "   v ii 24
fast friend of your *l* Since mine began,   "   v ii 134
Your Majesty has lived so pure a *l*,   "   v v 73
see, he smiles and goes, Gentle as in *l*.   "   v v 147
More beautiful than in *l*.   "   v v 262
Her *l* was winter, for her spring was nipt :   "   v v 269
Thy *l* at home Is easier than mine here.   *Harold* I i 96
I have lived a *l* of utter purity: "   I i 178
A *l* of prayer and fasting well may see   "   I i 199
Love will stay for a whole *l* long.   "   I ii 17
praised The convent and lone *l*—within the pale—   "   I ii 47
then a fair *l* And bless the Queen of England.   "   I ii 206
We seldom take man's *l*, except in war;   "   II ii 502
Archbishop Robert hardly scaped with *l*.   "   II ii 527
Harold, I am thy friend, one *l* with thee,   "   II ii 650
Is naked truth actable in true *l* ?   "   III i 110
silent, cloister'd, solitary *l*, A *l* of life-long prayer   "   III i 277
' Love for a whole *l* long ' When was that sung ?   "   III ii 88
they both have *l* In the large mouth of England,   "   IV iii 73
Thou gavest thy voice against me in my *l*,   "   v 253
Whose *l* was all one battle, incarnate war,   "   v 397
that I fear the Queen would have her *l*.   *Becket, Pro.* 62
The *l* of Rosamund de Clifford more Than that   " *Pro.* 70
not my purveyor Of pleasures, but to save a *l*—her *l*;   " *Pro.* 150
And all the heap'd experiences of *l*,   "   I i 154
And mean to hold it, or——   *Becket.*   To have my *l*.   "   I iii 163
since your canon will not let you take *L* for a *l*,   "   I iii 391
being in great jeopardy of his *l*, he hath made   "   I iv 263
or can shatter a *l* till the *l* shall have fled ?   "   II i 12
Love that can lift up a *l* from the dead.   "   II i 14
O my *l's l*, not to smile Is all but death   "   II i 39
There may be crosses in my line of *l*.   "   II i 188
L on the hand is naked gipsy-stuff ; *L* on the face,   "   II i 193
He said thy *l* Was not one hour's worth   "   III iii 250
Thy *l* is worth the wrestle for it :   "   IV ii 194
fawn upon him For thy *l* and thy son's.   "   IV ii 225
to take a *l* which Henry bad me Guard   "   IV ii 268
rend away Eyesight and manhood, *l* itself,   "   IV ii 285
a *l* Saved by miracle alone with Him Who gave it.   "   IV ii 367
not *l* shot up in blood, But death drawn in ;—   "   IV ii 380
To take my *l* might lose him Aquitaine.   "   IV ii 396
thy rest of *l* is hopeless prison.   "   v i 180
Thanks in this *l*, and in the *l* to come.   "   v ii 161
drowning man, they say, remembers all The chances
of his *l*,   "   v ii 274
laid mine own *l* down To help him from them,   "   v ii 339
You have spoken to the peril of your *l* ?   "   v ii 516
Valour and holy *l* should go together.   "   v ii 587
Save him, he saved my *l*, he saved my child,   "   v iii 8
The power of *l* in death to make her free !   "   v iii 100
What would ye have of me ?   *Fitzurse.*   Your *l*. De
Tracy.   Your *l*.   "   v iii 117
But in this narrow breathing-time of *l*   *The Cup* I i 29
courtesans for aught I know Whose *l* is one dishonour.   "   I ii 194
However I thank thee ; thou hast saved my *l*.   "   I ii 333
loveliest *l* that ever drew the light From heaven   "   I iii 56
To warm the cold bounds of our dying *l*   "   I iii 129
He saved my *l* too.   Did he ?   "   I iii 160

Life (*continued*)   thou that art *l* to the wind, to the wave,   *The Cup* II 3
L yields to death and wisdom bows to Fate,   "   II 89
And join your *l* this day with his,   "   II 135
For all my truer *l* begins to-day.   "   II 229
that dost inspire the germ with *l*, The child,   "   II 258
ere two souls be knit for *l* and death,   "   II 359
came To plead to thee for Sinnatus's *l*,   "   II 392
Coming to visit my lord, for the first time in her *l* too !   *The Falcon* 171
And if he leave me—all the rest of *l*—   "   334
A colour, which has colour'd all my *l*,   "   364
I'd slääve out my *l* fur 'er.   *Prom. of May* I 178
And long *l* to boäth on 'em.   "   I 345
I have all my *l* before me—so has she—   "   I 482
heat and fire Of *l* will bring them out,   "   II 287
better death With our first wail than *l*—   "   II 291
not so much for Death As against *L* !   "   II 338
This beggarly *l*, This poor, flat, hedged-in field—   "   II 343
Colour Flows thro' my *l* again,   "   II 667
which Father, for a whole *l*, has been getting together,   "   III 165
O Love and *L*, how weary am I,   "   III 205
will give him, as they say, a new lease of *l*.   "   III 424
niver been surprised but once i' my *l*, and I went blind upon it.   "   III 440
Had threaten'd ev'n your *l*, and would say anything ?   "   III 567
'Twere best to make an end of my lost *l*.   "   III 786
not with all your wealth, Your land, your *l* !   "   III 796
whose whole *l* hath been folded like a blossom in the sheath,   *Foresters* I i 205
I saved his *l* once in battle.   "   I i 272
A question that every true man asks of a woman once in his *l*.   "   I ii 139
if this *l* of ours Be a good glad thing,   "   I iii 12
Sleep, happy soul ! all *l* will sleep at last.   "   I iii 48
mix with all The lusty *l* of wood and underwood,   "   I iii 114
The hope of larger *l* hereafter,   "   II i 69
I would give my *l* for thee,   "   II i 189
Ay, ay, the line o' *l* is marked enow ;   "   II i 352
Mislead us, and I will have thy *l* !   "   II i 377
L, *l*. I know not death.   "   II i 621
Our Robin beaten, pleading for his *l* !   "   II i 675
noblest light That ever flash'd across my *l*,   "   III 142
Whose writ will run thro' all the range of *l*.   "   IV 49
Their *lives* unsafe in any of these our woods,   "   IV 93
in the fear of thy *l* shalt thou eat the King's venison—   "   IV 205
Richard risks his *l* for a straw, So lies in prison—while our Robin's *l* Hangs by a thread,   "   IV 382
flung His *l*, heart, soul into those holy wars   "   IV 407
for by my *l*, you shall dance till he can.   "   IV 566
Thou hast risk'd thy *l* for mine : bind these two men.   "   IV 894
Our forest games are ended, our free *l*,   "   IV 1049

Life-giving   No sacrifice, but a *l-g* feast !   *Queen Mary* IV ii 112
Life-green   a thousand summers Robe you *l-g* again.   *Foresters* IV 1058
Life-long   To plunge thee into *l-l* prison here :—   *Harold* II ii 550
A life of *l-l* prayer against the curse   "   III i 278
she hath begun Her *l-l* prayer for thee.   "   I i 324
And all my *l* labour to uphold The primacy—a heretic.   *Queen Mary* V ii 70
I am a *l-l* lover of the chase,   *The Cup* I i 194
Lift   I cannot *l* my hands unto my head.   *Queen Mary* III i 240
L head, and flourish ;   "   III iv 24
Why do you *l* your eyebrow at me thus ?   "   III vi 102
I am ashamed to *l* my eyes to heaven,   "   IV iii 127
death is death, or else *L's* us beyond the lie.   *Harold* III ii 80
For, like a son, I *l* my hands to thee.   *Becket* I iii 264
Love that can *l* up a life from the dead.   "   II i 14
I pray you *l* me And make me walk awhile.   *The Cup* II 472
my hands are too sleepy To *l* it off.   "   II 531
Lifted   Then Cranmer *l* his left hand to heaven,   *Queen Mary* IV iii 608
☞ *L* our produce, driven our clerics out—   *Becket* V ii 432
Lifting   It means the *l* of the house of Alfgar.   *Harold* I i 472
Light (adj.)   My Lord of Devon—*l* enough, God knows,   *Queen Mary* V ii 477
Growing dark too—but *l* enough to row.   *The Cup* II 523
Take thou this *l* kiss for thy clumsy word.   *Foresters* III 134

Light (s)   By God's *l* a noble creature,   *Queen Mary* I i 68
The *l* of this new learning wanes and dies :   "   III ii 172
faith that seem'd to droop will feel your *l*,   "   III iv 23
yet not *l* alone, There must be heat—   "   III iv 24
springs to *l* That Centaur of a monstrous Commonweal,   "   III iv 162
White as the *l*, the spotless bride of Christ,   "   III iv 199
in a pale *l*, Rose hand in hand,   "   III v 147
Cool as the *l* in old decaying wood ;   "   IV ii 5
Unpardonable,—sin against the *l*,   "   IV iii 148
Is not yon *l* in the Queen's chamber ?   "   V iv 1
There's the Queen's *l*. I hear she cannot live.   "   V iv 10
in a closed room, with *l*, fire, physic, tendance ;   "   V iv 36
My grayhounds fleeting like a beam of *l*,   *Harold* I ii 130
dog, with thy lying *l's* Thou hast betray'd   "   II i 22
villains with their lying *l's* have wreck'd us !   "   II i 84
be as the shadow of a cloud Crossing your *l*.   "   II ii 178
dreadful *l's* crept up from out the marsh—   "   III i 379
Lost, lost, the *l* of day,   "   III ii 12
But a little *l* !—And on it falls the shadow   "   III ii 69
A *l* among the oxen.   "   IV i 87
Lower the *l*. He must be here.   "   V ii 63
the fire, the *l*, The spirit of On the twelve Apostles   *Becket* I i 49
moon Divides the whole long street with *l* and shade.   "   I i 365
As gold Outvalues dross, *l* darkness,   "   I iii 715
L again ! *l* again ! Margery ?   "   IV i 1
and went on and on till I found the *l* and the lady,   "   IV ii 18
Save by that way which leads thro' night to *l*.   "   V iii 89
I am not in the darkness but the *l*,   "   V iii 97
the dry *l* of Rome's straight-going policy,   *The Cup* I i 145
drew the *l* From heaven to brood upon her,   "   I iii 57
Lady, you bring your *l* into my cottage   *The Falcon* 283
her affections Will flower toward the *l* in some new face.   *Prom. of May* I 486
to be wakened again together by the *l* of the resurrection,   "   III 196
the *l* Of these dark hours ;   *Foresters* I ii 84
and seeing the hospitable *l's* in your castle,   "   I ii 194
I am but an angel by reflected *l*.   "   II i 108
Glide like a *l* across these woodland ways !   "   II i 159
l of the seas by the moon's long-silvering ray !   "   II ii 178
noblest *l* That ever flash'd across my life,   "   III 141
Robin, the sweet *l* of a mother's eye,   "   IV 2
Light (to come upon)   if thou *l* upon her—free me from her ?   *Becket, Pro.* 493
Light (to kindle)   then, who *l's* the faggot ? Not the full faith,   *Queen Mary* III iv 122
Thou *l* a torch that never will go out !   "   V v 122
Lighted (come upon)   and I have *l* On a new pleasure.   *Prom. of May* II 668
She may have *l* on your fairies here,   *Foresters* II i 496
Lighted (shone)   A twilight conscience *l* thro' a chink ;   *Harold* III i 65
Lighten (to brighten)   these lilies to *l* Sir Richard's black room,   *Foresters* I i 3
Lighten'd (to gleam)   Our axes *l* with a single flash   *Harold* V i 537
Lighten'd   gloom of Saul Was *l* by young David's harp.   *Queen Mary* V iii 359
l for me The weight of this poor crown,   *Harold* I ii 17
Lighter   Much *l* than a thousand marks in gold ;   *Foresters* IV 657
You see the darkness thro' the *l* leaf.   "   IV 975
Lightning   sword Of *l's*, wherewithal he cleft the tree   *Harold* I i 137
This *l* before death Plays on the word,—   "   III i 387
are sliver'd off and splinter'd by Their *l*—   "   II i 541
The *l's* that we think are only Heaven's Flash   *Becket* V ii 35
Lightning-like   swoops down upon him Eagle-like, *l-l*—   *The Falcon* 14
Like (adj. and adv.)   These princes are *l* children, must be physick'd,   *Queen Mary* I v 234
Is this *l* him ? *Renard.* Ay, somewhat ;   "   I v 442
Rascal !—this land is *l* a hill of fire,   "   II i 321
Much less shall others in *l* cause escape,   "   IV iii 62
How fair and royal—*l* a Queen, indeed ?   "   V i 235
methinks my Queen is *l* enough To leave me by and by.   "   V i 242
I mean not *l* to live. Elizabeth—   "   V i 245
There must be ladies many with hair *l* mine.   "   V iii 58
To draw him nearer with a charm *L* thine to thine.   *Harold* I ii 9
What was he *l*, this husband ? *l* to thee ?   "   V ii 52
have I fought men *L* Harold and his brethren,   "   V ii 179
A pretty lusty boy. *Rosamund.* So *l* to thee ; *L* to be liker.   *Becket* II i 248

II*

Little (continued)   *L*! we are Danes, Who conquer'd what
we walk on, our own field.   *Harold* IV i 37

He calls us *l*!   *Harold.*   The kingdoms of this world
began with *l*,   ,,   IV i 41

Keep him away from the lone *l* isle.   *Becket* II i 15

I'll call thee *l* Geoffrey.   ,,   II i 214

Look, look! if *l* Geoffrey have not tost His ball into the
brook!   ,,   II i 319

Kiss me, *l* one, Nobody near!   ,,   II i 100

Come to me, *l* one. How camest thou hither?   ,,   IV i 3

We can't all of us be as pretty as thou art—*l* bastard.   ,,   IV i 39

How fares thy pretty boy, the *l* Geoffrey?   ,,   V ii 167

There was a *l* fair-hair'd Norman maid   ,,   V ii 259

Nay, see, why she turns down the path through our *l*
vineyard,   *The Falcon* 168

When he was a *l* one, and I put the bitters on my
breast to wean him,   ,,   189

ye'll think more on 'is *l* finger than hall my hand at
the haltar.   *Prom. of May* I 112

How gracefully there she stands Weeping—the *l*
Niobe!   ,,   I 736

into nescience with as *l* pain As it is to fall asleep   ,,   II 341

The *l* 'ymn? Yeäs, Miss;   ,,   III 1

an' axed ma to be 'is *l* sweet-art,   ,,   III 120

Poor blind Father's *l* guide, Milly,   ,,   III 231

talk a *l* French like a lady; play a *l* like a lady?   ,,   III 303

Who said that? Taäke me awaäy, *l* gell.   ,,   III 465

Child, read a *l* history, you will find The common
brotherhood   ,,   III 542

and if you cram me crop-full I be *l* better than Famine
in the picture,   *Foresters* I i 46

and for the love of his own *l* mother on earth,   ,,   I i 98

O the sacred *l* thing! What a shape!   ,,   I i 108

Shall I keep one *l* rose for Little John? No.   ,,   I i 112

But he flutter'd his wings with a sweet *l* cry,   ,,   I i 154

But then your Sheriff, your *l* man,   ,,   I i 231

and our *l* Sheriff will ever swim with the stream!   ,,   I i 239

the Sheriff had taken all our goods for the King
without paying, and our horse and our *l* cart.   ,,   II i 192

for when the Sheriff took my *l* horse for the King
without paying for it—   ,,   II i 301

Littlechester (adj.)   and we dragg'd The *L* river all in
vain: *Prom. of May* II 414

Littlechester (s)   When theer wur a meeting o' farmers
at *L* t'other daäy,   ,,   I 137

fur they be knaw'd as far as *L*.   ,,   I 214

Beänt there house-breäkers down i' *L*, Dobson—   ,,   I 389

Who leaves me all his land at *L*,   ,,   I 511

afoor she went to school at *L*—   ,,   II 19

fur she tell'd me to taäke the cart to *L*.   ,,   II 323

Only last week at *L*, drove me From out her memory.   ,,   II 404

pacing my new lands at *L*,   ,,   II 647

Wasn't Miss Vavasour, our schoolmistress at *L*, a lady
born?   ,,   III 298

that dreadful night! that lonely walk to *L*,   ,,   III 367

Little John (a follower of Robin Hood)   She hath looked
well at one of 'em, *L J*.   *Foresters* I i 39

Shall I keep one little rose for *L J*? No.   ,,   I i 113

Wilt thou not give me rather the little rose for *L J*?   ,,   I i 148

thou hast ruffled my woman, *L J*.   ,,   I i 166

starched stiff creature, *L J*, the Earl's man.   ,,   I i 184

L J, Who hast that worship for me   ,,   I iii 159

Take him, good *L J*, and give him wine.   ,,   II i 469

thou That hast not made it up with *L J*! *Kate.* I
wait till *L J* makes up to *me*.   ,,   III 15

L J Fancied he saw thee clasp and kiss a man.   ,,   III 21

And let them warm thy heart to *L J*.   ,,   III 44

I *L J*, he Much the miller's son, and he Scarlet,   ,,   III 54

I *L J*, he, young Scarlet, and he, old Much, and all the
rest of us.   ,,   III 60

Search them, *L J*.   ,,   III 201

Shame on thee, *L J*, thou hast forgotten—   ,,   III 237

Play the air, *L J*.   ,,   III 418

Strike up our music, *L J*.   ,,   IV 559

You, good friar, You Much, you Scarlet, you dear *L J*,   ,,   IV 1083

Live   Long *l* Queen Mary, (repeat)   *Queen Mary* I i 7, 65

'Long *l* Elizabeth the Queen!'   ,,   I iii 7

we'll have no pope here while the Lady Elizabeth *l*'s.   ,,   I iii 44

But that with God's grace, I can *l* so still.   ,,   II ii 219

never Consent thereto, nor marry while I *l*;   ,,   II ii 231

Long *l* Queen Mary! Down with Wyatt! The Queen!   ,,   II ii 252

We have been glad together; let him *l*.   ,,   II iii 90

I *l* and die The true and faithful bride of Philip—   ,,   II iv 41

Long *l* the King and Queen, Philip and Mary!   ,,   III i 208

Long *l* Queen Mary!   ,,   III i 294

Where dost thou *l*? *Man.* In Cornhill.   ,,   III i 316

was not meet the heretic swine should *l* In Lambeth.   ,,   III ii 135

Let the dead letter *l*! Trace it in fire,   ,,   III iv 33

says she will *l* And die true maid—   ,,   III vi 45

none shall hold them in his house and *l*,   ,,   IV i 97

if he have to *l* so loath'd a life,   ,,   IV i 152

Ay—gentle as they call you—*l* or die!   ,,   IV i 162

set forth some saying that may *l* After his death
and better humankind; For death gives life's
last word a power to *l*,   ,,   IV iii 159

I pray you all to *l* together Like brethren;   ,,   IV iii 181

Either to *l* with Christ in Heaven with joy,   ,,   IV iii 220

That might I always in the sun's warm heart,   ,,   V i 22

I mean not like to *l*.   ,,   V i 245

Long *l* your Majesty! Shall Alice sing you   ,,   V ii 353

Make me full fain to *l* and die a maid.   ,,   V iii 98

There's the Queen's light. I hear she cannot *l*.   ,,   V iv 11

She hath but blood enough to *l*, not love.—   *Harold* I ii 161

We hear he hath not long to *l*,   ,,   II ii 565

Forgive me, brother, I will *l* here and die.   ,,   II ii 804

but happier lived, If happier be to *l*;   ,,   IV iii 73

l or die, I would I were among them!   ,,   V i 463

And if I *l*, No man without my leave   *Becket, Pro.* 29

For we would *l* and die for thee, my lord,   ,,   I i 16

And I shall *l* to trample on thy grave.   ,,   I ii 95

and the world shall *l* by the King's venison   ,,   I iv 271

one who *l*'s for thee Out there in France;   ,,   I i 309

Long *l* the good King Louis!   ,,   II ii 450

I *l* to die for it, I die to *l* for it.   ,,   III iii 335

They call her—But she *l*'s secret, you see.   ,,   IV i 12

Madam, let her *l*.   ,,   IV ii 157

And I what may be left thee of a life   ,,   IV ii 367

She *l*'s—but not for him; one point is gain'd.   ,,   IV ii 415

I will go *l* and die in Aquitaine. (repeat)   ,,   V i 109, 142

Here is the great Archbishop! He *l*'s! he *l*'s!   ,,   V iii 30

A woman I could *l* and die for.   *The Cup* I iii 65

Might I not *l* for that, And drown all poor self-passion   ,,   II 99

to *l* And die together.   ,,   II 443

as I *l*, there is Monna Giovanna coming down the hill
from the castle.   *The Falcon* 159

Your ladyship *l*'s higher in the sun.   ,,   583

For her sick son, if he were like to *l*,   ,,   854

What can a man, then, *l* for but sensations,   *Prom. of May* I 241

smell o' the mou'd 'ud ha' maäde ma *l* as long as
Jerusalem.   ,,   I 378

with some sense of art, to *l* By brush and pencil.   ,,   I 498

L with these honest folk—And play the fool!   ,,   I 744

if you cared To *l* some time among them.   ,,   II 550

For all the souls on earth that *l*   ,,   II 7

will be willing that you and Father should *l* with us;   ,,   III 261

in our spring-and-winter world If we *l* long enough!   ,,   III 512

—all still—and nothing left To *l* for.   ,,   III 682

She said 'all still. Nothing to *l* for.'   ,,   III 685

but now ye know why we *l* so stintedly,   *Foresters* I i 76

a Count in Brittany—he *l*'s near Quimper.   ,,   I i 272

Long *l* Richard, (repeat)   ,,   I ii 1, 3

Long *l* Robin, Robin and Richard! Long *l* Robin.   ,,   I ii 13

'Long *l* King Richard!'   ,,   I ii 25

O Lord, I will *l* and die for King Richard—   ,,   I ii 37

We will *l* and die with thee,   ,,   I iii 168

I believe there *l*'s No man who truly loves   ,,   II i 75

You gentles that *l* upo' manchet-bread and marchpane,   ,,   II i 281

Then I roast 'em, for I have nought else to *l* on.   ,,   II ii 388

Could *l* as happy as the larks in heaven,   ,,   III 82

L thou maiden! Thou art more my wife so feeling,   ,,   III 121

Look (verb) *(continued)* I wonder if I *l* as pale as she ?   *The Cup* II 322
Deigns to *l* in upon our barbarisms.   ,,   II 337
you *l* as beautiful this morning as the very Madonna   *The Falcon* 198
your ladyship were not Too proud to *l* upon the garland,   ,,   663
' Coomly to *l* at,' says she—but she said it spiteful-
like. To *l* at—yeas,   *Prom. of May* I 179
tha *l*'s haäle anew to last to a hoonderd.   ,,   I 354
and you *l* thin and pale. Is it for his absence ?   ,,   I 781
sweet upo' Dora Steer, and she weänt sa much as *l*
at 'im ?   ,,   II 162
How worn he *l*'s, poor man ! who is it, I wonder.   ,,   II 390
l to thysen, for, by the Lord, I'd think   ,,   II 695
L there—under the deaths.   ,,   II 710
I had to *l* over his letters.   ,,   II 720
could it *l* But half as lovely.   ,,   III 490
but, my flower, You *l* so weary and so worn !   ,,   III 499
L up ! One word, or do but smile !   ,,   III 675
Yes, deathlike ! Dead ? I dare not *l*: if dead,   ,,   III 717
How she *l*'s up at him, how she holds her face !   *Foresters* I ii 144
He often *l*'s in here by the moonshine.   ,,   II i 336
L, my lord, there goes one in the moonlight.   ,,   II i 394
O *l* ! before the shadow of these dark oaks   ,,   II i 604
L ! *l* ! he kneels ! he has anger'd the foul witch,   ,,   II i 669
L, there comes a deputation   ,,   II ii 144
warm thy heart to Little John.   *L* where he comes !   ,,   III 46
and *l*'s at once Maid Marian,   ,,   III 117
I *l* on the King's venison as my own.   ,,   IV 197
If a cat may *l* at a king, may not a friar speak to one ?   ,,   IV 921

Look'd-looked-lookt You *look'd* a king.   *Queen Mary* I iii 103
So that your sister were but *look'd* to closer.   ,,   I v 460
How *look'd* the city When you past it ? Quiet ?   ,,   II ii 57
and *look'd* As grim and grave as from a funeral.   ,,   II ii 64
And *look'd* as bloodless.   ,,   II ii 84
eyes So bashful that you *look'd* no higher ?   ,,   III i 65
How *look'd* the Queen ?   ,,   III i 91
then King Harry *look'd* from out a cloud,   ,,   IV ii 6
His eighty years *Look'd* somewhat crooked on him   ,,   IV iii 332
I do assure you, that it must be *look'd* too :   ,,   v i 2
It must be *look'd* to, If war should fall   ,,   v i 8
It shall be *look'd* to ;   ,,   v i 12
he *look'd* the Great Harry, You but his cockboat ;   ,,   v ii 145
In Hampton Court My window *look'd* upon the corridor ;   ,,   v i 459
I never *look'd* upon so fair a likeness   ,,   v v 28
L hard and sweet at me, and gave it me.   ,,   v v 95
but he that *lookt* a fangless one, Issues   *Becket* I iii 451
as to the young crownling himself, he *looked* so malapert
in the eyes,   ,,   III iii 109
yellow silk here and there, and it *looked* pretty like
a glowworm,   ,,   IV i 22
wine Ran down the marble and *lookt* like blood,   *The Cup* II 204
Glows thro' my veins since first I *look'd* on thee.   ,,   II 429
You never had *look'd* on me before,   *The Falcon* 865
for the past *Look'd* thro' the present,   *Prom. of May* II 641
She hath *looked* well at one of 'em, Little John.   *Foresters* I i 38

Lookest Why *l* thou so amazed ?   ,,   I i 130
Looketh ' Whosoever *L* after a woman,'   *Queen Mary* I v 453
Lookin' *(See also* **A-lookin'***)* I coom'd upon 'im
t'other daäy *l* at the coontry,   *Prom. of May* I 201
Looking *(part)* *(See also* **Lookin', Nobler - looking,**
Goodlier-looking, Simple-looking) But Janus-
faces *l* diverse ways.   *Queen Mary* III ii 75
ever *l* to the happy haven Where he shall rest at night, ,,   IV iii 579
Have you been *l* at the ' Dance of Death ' ?   *Becket* I iii 406
l thro' my reign, I found a hundred ghastly murders   ,,   VII 169
you should be in the hayfield *l* after your men ;   *Prom. of May* II 47
Looking (s) With *l* on the dead. Am I so white ?   *Harold* II ii 815
In *l* on a chill and changeless Past ?   *Prom. of May* II 504
Lookt *See* **Look'd**
Loom (s) heaven and earth are threads of the same *l*,   *Harold* I i 210
Loom (verb) out of which *L*'s the least chance of peril   *Queen Mary* II ii 238
blackness of my dungeon *l* Across their lamps   *Harold* II ii 406
Loon the brainless *l*'s That cannot spell   *Queen Mary* III i 280
Loop Philip ! quick ! *l* up my hair !   ,,   v i 534
Loose (adj.) a score of wolf-dogs are let *l* that will tear
thee piecemeal.   *Becket* III ii 39

Loose (verb) going now to the Tower to *l* the prisoners *Queen Mary* I i 109
lead on ; ye *l* me from my bonds.   ,,   IV ii 240
Loosed you late were *l* from out the Tower,   ,,   I iv 50
Loosely-scatter'd left about Like *l-s* jewels,   ,,   II i 28
Loove (love) And I would *l* tha moor nor ony
gentleman 'ud *l* tha.   *Prom. of May* II 104
Lor (inter.) *(See also* **Law)** Whoy, O *l*, Miss ! that
wur sa long back,   ,,   III 71
O *l*, Miss ! noä, noä, noä !   ,,   III 91
Lord *(See also* **Liege-lord, My-lord)** Gardiner for one,
who is to be made *L* Chancellor,   *Queen Mary* I i 87
Her freaks and frolics with the late *L* Admiral ?   ,,   I iv 20
She fears the *L*'s may side with you   ,,   I iv 158
The *L* Chancellor (I count it as a kind of virtue in him, ,,   I iv 191
Why, my *l* Bishop ? (repeat)   *Queen Mary* I iv 223, 227
Who waits, sir ? *Usher.* Madam, the *L* Chancellor. *Queen Mary* I v 96
that were hard upon you, my *L* Chancellor.   ,,   I v 159
The *L* Chancellor himself is on our side.   ,,   II i 193
Or—if the *L* God will it—on the stake.   ,,   II i 251
All hangs on her address, And upon you, *L* Mayor.   ,,   II ii 56
I, the *L* Mayor, and these our companies And guilds   ,,   II ii 127
I, *L* Mayor Of London, and our guilds and companies.   ,,   II ii 139
tho' my *L* Mayor here, By his own rule,   ,,   II ii 345
new *L*'s Are quieted with their sop of Abbeylands,   ,,   III i 141
No, my *L* Legate, the *L* Chancellor goes.   ,,   III ii 151
We, the *L*'s Spiritual and Temporal,   ,,   III iii 113
The *L* who hath redeem'd us With His own blood,   ,,   III iii 202
I am but of the laity, my *L* Bishop.   ,,   III iv 81
Yet my *L* Cardinal— *Pole.* I am your Legate ;   ,,   III iv 178
Till when, my *L*'s, I counsel tolerance.   ,,   III iv 203
Thou Christian Bishop, thou *L* Chancellor Of England !   ,,   III iv 300
My *L* Chancellor, You have an old trick of offending us ; ,,   III iv 313
O *L* ! your Grace, your Grace,   ,,   III v 248
I told my *L* He should not vex her Highness ;   ,,   III vi 65
And my *L* Paget and *L* William Howard,   ,,   IV i 6
Good morrow, my *L* Cardinal ;   ,,   IV i 42
My *L* of Ely, this. After a riot We hang the leaders,   ,,   IV i 72
And if he did I care not, my *L* Howard.   ,,   IV i 129
You are too politic for me, my *L* Paget.   ,,   IV i 150
May learn there is no power against the *L*.   ,,   IV iii 67
And be with Christ the *L* in Paradise.   ,,   IV iii 88
O *L* God, although my sins be great,   ,,   IV iii 135
And every syllable taught us by our *L*,   ,,   IV iii 231
No, here's *L* William Howard. What, my *L*,   ,,   IV iii 288
Thank the *L* therevore. (repeat)   *Queen Mary* IV iii 496, 520, 529
there wur an owld *l* a-cum to dine wi' un,   *Queen Mary* IV iii 504
' I wunt dine,' says my *L* Bishop,   ,,   IV iii 507
the owld *l* fell to 's meat wi' a will, God bless un !   ,,   IV iii 514
but when I came to wed your majesty, *L* Howard,   ,,   v i 56
I have gone beyond your late *L* Chancellor,—   ,,   v ii 98
cries continually with sweat and tears to the *L* God   ,,   v iv 46
Charles, the *l* of this low world, is gone ;   ,,   v v 54
Ask thou *L* Leofwin what he thinks of this !   *Harold* I i 40
L Leofwin, dost thou believe,   ,,   I i 42
Yea, I Harold.   ,,   I i 243
The king, the *l*'s, the people clear'd him of it,   ,,   II ii 522
many among our Norman *l*'s Hate thee for this,   ,,   II ii 545
I have built the *L* a house— (repeat)   *Harold* III i 178, 180, 186
the *L* hath dwelt In darkness.   *Harold* III i 178
The *L* was God and came as man—   ,,   III ii 172
Thou art one of those Who brake into *L* Tostig's
treasure-house   ,,   IV i 114
Lay hands of full allegiance in thy *L*'s   ,,   v ii 11
Like other *l*'s amenable to law.   *Becket, Pro.* 25
Church should pay her scutage like the *l*'s.   ,,   I i 35
And spake to the *L* God, and said ' O *L*, I have been
a lover of wines,   ,,   I i 74
And the *L* answer'd me, ' Thou art the man, (repeat)   ,,   I i 82, 98
' O *L* my God, Henry the King hath been my friend,   ,,   I i 86
Stir up the King, the *L*'s !   ,,   I ii 88
Is not the Church the visible *L* on earth ? Shall hands
that do create the *L* be bound   ,,   I iii 92
The *L* be judged again by Pilate ? No !   ,,   I iii 97
My *l* Archbishop, that we too should sign ?   ,,   I iii 272
Loyally and with good faith, my *l* Archbishop ?   ,,   I iii 279

Loud   And dazzled men and deafen'd by some bright
    L venture,   *Queen Mary* III i 453
    Not so *l* !   Our Clarence there Sees ever an aureole   ,,   v ii 411
    Not so *l*.   Lord Devon, girls !   ,,   v ii 484
    Go home.   Besides, you curse so *l*.   ,,   v iv 62
    So *l*, that, by St. Dunstan, old St. Thor—   *Harold* IV iii 146
    Why there—like some *l* beggar at thy gate—   *Becket* II i 180
    Wakening such brawls and *l* disturbances In England,   ,,   v ii 352
    L disturbances !   Oh, ay—the bells rang out even to
    deafening,   ,,   v ii 362
    Have our *l* pastimes driven them all away ?   *Foresters* II ii 105
Louder   *L* ! *l* !   Maid Marian, Queen o' the woods !   ,,   III 374
    L, *l*, ye knaves.   ,,   III 396
Loud-lung'd   Tho' all the *l-l* trumpets upon earth   *Becket* v II 487
Louis (**King of France**)   *L* of France loved me, and I
    dreamed that I loved *L* of France :   ,,   *Pro.* 355
    King *L* had no paramours, and I loved him   ,,   *Pro.* 474
    ' Fly at once to France, to King *L* of France :   ,,   I iv 53
    So that the fool King *L* feed them not.   ,,   II i 76
    brave The Pope, King *L*, and this turbulent priest.   ,,   II i 312
    O good son *L*, do not counsel me,   ,,   II ii 219
    My lord, I see this *L* Returning, ah !   ,,   II ii 417
    Long live the good King *L* !   ,,   II ii 451
    know the King's married for King *L*—— *Rosamund*.
    Married ! *Margery*.   Years and years, my lady,
    for her husband, King *L*—— *Rosamund*.   Hush !   ,,   III i 167
    bound For that one hour to stay with good King *L*,   ,,   III i 248
    He said so ?   *L*, did he ?   ,,   III iii 255
    When I was in mine anger with King *L*,   ,,   III iii 258
    my much constancy To the monk-king, *L*,   ,,   IV ii 305
    I, that thro' the Pope divorced King *L*,   ,,   IV ii 418
    You were but Aquitaine to *L*—no wife ;   ,,   v i 116
Lours   thunder-cloud That *l's* on England—laughter !   *Harold* III ii 161
Lousiest   Thou the lustiest and *l* of this Cain's brotherhood,
    answer.   *Becket* I iv 185
Lout   that all the *l's* to whom Their A B C is darkness,   *Queen Mary* III iv 34
    L, churl, clown !   *Prom. of May* III 739
Love (**adj.**)   What matters ?   State matters ? *l* matters ?   *Becket, Pro.* 320
Love (**s**)   O, my lord to be, My *l*, for thy sake only.   *Queen Mary* I v 67
    not with gold, But dearest links of *l*.   ,,   I v 539
    deem This *l* by you return'd as heartily ; And thro'
    this common knot and bond of *l*,   ,,   II ii 197
    A diamond, And Philip's gift, as proof of Philip's *l*,   ,,   III i 67
    She cast on him a vassal smile of *l*,   ,,   III i 98
    thy *l* to mine Will cling more close,   ,,   III ii 159
    make me shamed and tongue-tied in my *l*.   ,,   III ii 163
    Cranmer, Your more especial *l*,   ,,   III iv 418
    should her *l* when you are gone, my liege,   ,,   III vi 172
    should her *l*—And I have known such women   ,,   III vi 177
    to fuse Almost into one metal *l* and hate,—   ,,   III vi 182
    ' *L* of this world is hatred against God.'   ,,   IV iii 173
    They hate *me* also for my *l* to you, My Philip ;   ,,   v i 95
    Beauty passes like a breath and *l* is lost in loathing :   ,,   v ii 365
    L will hover round the flowers when they first awaken ;   ,,   v ii 370
    L will fly the fallen leaf, and not be overtaken ;   ,,   v ii 372
    Some say that Gardiner, out of *l* for him,   ,,   v ii 502
    he sends his veriest *l*, And says, he will come quickly.   ,,   v ii 564
    Tell him at last I know his *l* is dead,   ,,   v ii 590
    that it would please Him out of His infinite *l*   ,,   v iv 47
    And *l* should know ; and—be the king so wise,—   *Harold* I i 276
    Cling to their *l* ; for, now the sons of Godwin   ,,   I i 324
    Thy *l* ?   *Aldwyth*.   As much as I can give thee,   ,,   I i 478
    And thy *l* ?   *Aldwyth*.   As much as thou canst bear.   ,,   I i 483
    L is come with a song and a smile, Welcome *L* with a
    smile and a song : *L* can stay but a little while.   ,,   I ii 10
    L will stay for a whole life long.   ,,   I ii 17
    Sang out their *l's* so loud,   ,,   I ii 20
    And woo their *l's* and have forgotten thee ;   ,,   II ii 438
    Normans left among us, Who follow'd me for *l* !   ,,   III i 304
    The more the *l*, the mightier is the prayer ; The more
    the *l*, the more acceptable The sacrifice of both your
    l's to heaven.   ,,   III i 346
    ' *L*, I will guide thee.'   ,,   III ii 16
    ' *L* for a whole life long ' When was that sung ?   ,,   III ii 88
    Since Tostig came with Norway—fright not *l*.   ,,   IV i 174

Love (**s**) (*continued*)   Full hope have I that *l* will
    answer *l*.   *Harold* IV i 273
    —a sin against The truth of *l*.   ,,   v i 171
    With a *l* Passing thy *l* for Griffyth !   ,,   v i 356
    What matters ?   State matters ? love matters ?
    Henry.   My *l* for thee, and thine for me.   *Becket, Pro.* 321
    Madam, you do ill to scorn wedded *l*.   ,,   *Pro.* 354
    honeymoon is the gall of *l* ; he dies of his honeymoon.   ,,   *Pro.* 364
    Not for my *l* toward him, but because he had the *l*
    of the King.   ,,   *Pro.* 441
    thou shalt have our *l*, our silence, and our gold—   ,,   *Pro.* 492
    My Courts of *L* would have held thee guiltless of *l*—   ,,   *Pro.* 498
    worldly bond between us is dissolved, Not yet the *l* :   ,,   I i 348
    Ye make this clashing for no *l* o' the customs   ,,   I iii 136
    Thought that I knew him, err'd thro' *l* of him,   ,,   I iii 441
    Took it upon me—err'd thro' *l* of him.   ,,   I iii 699
    L that is born of the deep coming up with the sun
    from the sea. (repeat)   ,,   II i 9, 19
    L that can shape or can shatter a life   ,,   II i 11
    L that can lift up a life from the dead.   ,,   II i 13
    thou my golden dream of *L's* own bower,   ,,   II i 34
    A greater King Than thou art, *L*,   ,,   II i 116
    A bastard hate born of a former *l*.   ,,   II i 174
    Speak only of thy *l*.   ,,   II i 179
    boldness of this hand hath won it *L's* alms,   ,,   II i 184
    O by thy *l* for me, all mine for thee,   ,,   II i 314
    the gap Left by the lack of *l*.   *Henry*.   The lack of *l* !   ,,   III i 61
    bound me by his *l* to secrecy Till his own time.   ,,   III i 228
    stray'd From *l's* clear path into the common bush,   ,,   III i 247
    L is the only gold.   ,,   IV i 43
    I have heard of such that range from *l* to *l*, Like the
    wild beast—if you can call it *l*.   ,,   IV ii 120
    Come with me, *l*, And I will love thee . . .   ,,   IV ii 155
    King himself, for *l* of his own sons,   ,,   IV ii 344
    in aiming at your *l*, It may be sometimes   ,,   v i 36
    Would he were dead !   I have lost all *l* for him.   ,,   v i 92
    Lacking the *l* of woman and of child.   ,,   v ii 199
    how this *l*, this mother, runs thro' all   ,,   v ii 241
    But the fool-fire of *l* or lust,   *The Cup* I i 147
    woman's fealty when Assailed by Craft and *L*.   ,,   I i 177
    I love you—for your *l* to the great Goddess.   ,,   I i 218
    there You told your *l* ; and like the swaying vines—   ,,   I i 410
    —if I win her *l*, They too will cleave to me,   ,,   I iii 153
    all else Was *l* for you : he prays you to believe him.   ,,   II 55
    from maiden fears Or reverential *l* for him I loved,   ,,   II 197
    all drown'd in *l* And glittering at full tide—   ,,   II 233
    l I bear to thee Glow thro' thy veins ?   ,,   II 426
    The *l* I bear to thee Glows thro' my veins.   ,,   II 428
    But hath she yet return'd thy *l* ?   *The Falcon* 67
    I'll be bound to confess her *l* to him at last.   ,,   172
    Will he not pray me to return his *l*—   ,,   247
    Hath she return'd thy *l* ?   *Count*.   Not yet !   ,,   513
    For that would seem accepting of your *l*.   ,,   740
    It should be *l* that thus outvalues all.   You speak like
    l, and yet you love me not.   I have nothing in this
    world but *l* for you.   *Lady Giovanna*.   *L* ? it *is l*, *l*
    for my dying boy,   ,,   780
    —the *l* you said you bore   ,,   857
    But he will keep his *l* to you for ever !   ,,   892
    for the senses, *l*, are for the world ;   *Prom. of May* I 580
    if you *will* bind *l* to you for ever,   ,,   I 644
    That was only *true l* ; and I trusted—   ,,   I 712
    Have you fancied yourself in *l* with him ?   ,,   I 783
    all of them Loved her, and she was worthy of all *l*.   ,,   II 430
    the man has doubtless a good heart, and a true and
    lasting *l* for me :   ,,   III 172
    O *L* and Life, how weary am I,   ,,   III 205
    But the *l* of sister for sister can never be old-fashioned.   ,,   III 319
    A hundred times more worth a woman's *l*,   ,,   III 744
    for the *l* of his own little mother on earth,   *Foresters* I i 97
    come at their *l* with all manner of homages,   ,,   I i 102
    L flew in at the window As Wealth walk'd   ,,   I i 150
    as I am a true believer in true *l* myself,   ,,   I i 162
    and all her *l's* and hates Sink again into chaos.   ,,   I ii 328
    'Tis for no lack of *l* to you, my lord,   ,,   I iii 130

Love (s) (*continued*) The *l* of freedom, the desire of God, *Foresters* II i 68
Thou hast crost him in *l*, „ II i 343
what sort of man art thou For land, not *l*? „ II i 534
Mortal enough, If *l* for thee be mortal. Lovers
hold True *l* immortal. „ II i 614
ever held that saying false That *L* is blind, „ II i 644
Stay with us here, sweet *L*, Maid Marian, „ II ii 14
How should you love if you mistrust your *l*? *Little*
John. O Kate, true *l* and jealousy are twins,
And *l* is joyful, innocent, beautiful, „ II ii 61
Tit, for *l* and brevity, Not for *l* of levity. „ II ii 128
Fluting, and piping and luting ' *L*, *l*, *l* '— „ III 33
lilt among the leaves ' *L*, *l*, *l*, *l* '— „ III 42
take and wear this symbol of your *l*; „ III 80
L himself Seems but a ghost, „ III 111
Ha, brother. Toll, my dear? the toll of *l*. „ III 271
The *l* that children owe to both I give „ IV 7
No, sweetheart! out of tune with *L* and me. „ IV 31
No ribald John is *L*, no wanton Prince, „ IV 46
lips that never breathed *L's* falsehood to true maid
will seal *L's* truth „ IV 73
He is all for *l*, he cares not for the land. „ IV 489
mate with one that holds no *l* is pure, „ IV 711
Risk not the *l* I bear thee for a girl. „ IV 742
I am but the echo of the lips of *l*. „ IV 892
In this full tide of *l*, Wave heralds wave: „ IV 1043

Love (verb) up, son, and save him! They *l* thee, *Queen Mary* I iii 67
I *l* not to be called a butterfly: „ I iv 68
I *l* you, Lay my life in your hands. „ I iv 104
as a mastiff dog May *l* a puppy cur „ I iv 195
you are one Who *l* that men should smile upon you, „ I iv 274
by the holy Virgin, being noble, But *l* me only: „ I v 71
I pray God No woman ever *l* you, „ I v 602
If ye *l* your liberties or your skins, „ II i 216
cannot tell How mothers *l* their children ; yet, methinks,
A prince as naturally may *l* his people As these their
children : and be sure your Queen So *l's* you, „ II ii 190
Ha! ha! sir ; but you jest ; I *l* it : „ II ii 355
flying to our side Left his all bare, for which I *l* thee,
Brett. „ II iii 5
I do not *l* your Grace should call me coward. „ II iv 88
It was a sin to *l* her married, dead I cannot choose
but *l* her. „ III i 339
Perchance in England, *l's* her like a son. „ III iii 267
wholesome scripture, 'Little children, *L* one another.' „ III iv 86
To sing, *l*, marry, churn, brew, bake, and die, „ III v 111
Here by the side of her who *l's* you most ? „ v i 75
altho' you *l* her not, You must proclaim Elizabeth „ v i 189
I used to *l* the Queen with all my heart— „ v ii 418
I *l* her less For such a dotage upon such a man. „ v ii 420
And *l* to hear bad tales of Philip. „ v ii 429
and *l* me, as I *l* The people! whom God aid ! „ v iii 34
He never loved me—nay, he could not *l* me. „ v v 44
He hath learnt to *l* our Tostig much of late. *Harold* I i 145
Our Tostig *l's* the hand and not the man. „ I i 156
Because I *l* the Norman better—no, „ I i 171
England *l's* thee for it. „ I i 221
thyself wast wont To *l* the chase: „ I i 228
And Tostig knows it ; Tostig *l's* the king. „ I i 274
I *l* the man but not his phantasies. „ I i 279
Edward *l's* him, so Ye hate him. „ I i 427
I *l* thee for it—ay, but stay a moment ; „ I ii 3
Hate him ? I could *l* him More, „ I ii 142
I *l* him or think I *l* him. „ I ii 152
Nay, I do *l* him.— „ I ii 155
She hath but blood enough to live, not *l*.— „ I ii 162
not like Aldwyth . . . For which I strangely *l* him.
Should not England *L* Aldwyth, „ I ii 176
Art thou assured By this, that Harold *l's* but Edith ? „ I ii 210
that I—That Harold *l's* me—yea, „ I ii 222
I can but *l* this noble, honest Harold. *William.* L
him ! why not ? thine is a loving office. „ II ii 94
The Normans *l* thee not, nor thou the Normans, „ II ii 253
for my mother's sake I *l* your England, But for my
father I *l* Normandy. „ II ii 269

Love (verb) (*continued*) Harold, if thou *l* thine Edith,
ay. *Harold* II ii 622
' We have learnt to *l* him, let him a little longer „ III i 88
No, no, but Harold. I *l* him : he hath served me : „ III i 242
They *l* the white rose of virginity, „ III i 273
Son, there is one who *l's* thee : „ III i 289
Bless thou too That brother whom I *l* beyond the rest, „ III i 295
And let him pass unscathed ; he *l's* me, Harold ! „ III i 301
Care not for me who *l* thee. „ III ii 113
—but I *l* thee and thou me— „ III ii 180
and I *l* him now, for mine own father Was great, „ IV i 89
Canst thou *l* one Who did discrown thine husband,
unqueen thee ? Didst thou not *l* thine husband ? „ IV i 192
women Cling to the conquer'd, if they *l*, the more ; „ IV i 213
Canst thou *l* me, thou knowing where I *l*? „ IV i 226
Canst thou *l* one, who cannot *l* again ? „ IV i 235
save for Norway, Who *l's* not thee but war. „ IV ii 24
because I *l* The husband of another ! „ v i 648
I cannot *l* them, For they are Norman saints— „ v ii 8
Take them away, I do not *l* to see them. „ v ii 142
to the statesman Who serves and *l's* his king, and whom
the king *L's* not as statesman, *Becket, Pro.* 78
I *l* thee and I know thee, I know thee, „ Pro. 95
Well, who *l's* wine *l's* woman. „ Pro. 108
whom I *l* indeed As a woman should be loved— „ Pro. 132
how should he *l* A woman, as a woman should be
loved ? „ Pro. 138
She is ignorant of all but that I *l* her. „ Pro. 185
and tho' I *l* him heartily, I can spy already „ Pro. 233
but thou—dost thou *l* this Chancellor, „ Pro. 438
How should a baron *l* a beggar on horseback, „ Pro. 443
she, whom the King *l's* indeed, is a power in the State. „ Pro. 482
for the Archbishop *l's* humbleness, „ I iv 208
I *l* them More than the garden flowers, „ II i 132
I *l* them too, Yes. „ II i 137
something I had to say—I *l* thee none the less— „ II i 207
—the goodly way of women Who *l*, for which I *l* them. „ II i 258
Yet you both *l* God. „ II ii 376
and make Our waning Eleanor all but *l* me ! „ II ii 458
There is no woman that I *l* so well. „ III i 9
Of one we *l*. Nay, I would not be bold, „ III i 63
I do not *l* her. Must you go, my liege, „ III i 83
So that he loved me—and he *l's* me— „ III i 226
Wilt thou *l* me ? *Geoffrey.* No ; I only *l* mother. „ IV i 8
I *l* thy mother, my pretty boy. „ IV i 44
so, if you *l* him—Nay, if you *l* him, „ IV ii 92
there are those Who say you do not *l* him— „ IV ii 97
Come with me, love, And I will *l* thee . . . „ IV ii 156
if he *l* thee, Thy life is worth the wrestle „ IV ii 193
' None of such ? ' I *l* her none the more. „ IV ii 413
I am not so sure But that I *l* him still. „ IV ii 451
I think ye four have cause to *l* this Becket, „ v i 224
I do not *l* him, for he did his best To break the barons, „ v i 233
No man to *l* me, honour me, obey me ! „ v i 239
The people *l* thee, father. „ v ii 120
And *l* him next after my lord his father. „ v ii 342
L her, do you ? *The Cup* I i 127
I *l* you—for your love to the great Goddess. „ I ii 218
Camma for my bride—The people *l* her— „ I iii 153
And *l* thee and thou me, yet if Giovanna *The Falcon* 26
He *l's* me, and he knows I know he *l's* me ! „ 245
You speak like love, and yet you *l* me not. „ 782
O Federigo, Federigo, I *l* you ! „ 897
I will make Your brother *l* me. „ 912
I don't know why I sing that song ; I don't *l* it. *Prom. of May* I 62
hallus a-fobbing ma off, tho' ye knaws I *l* ye. „ I 108
that should make you happy, if you *l* her ! „ I 548
Oh, I *l* her so, I was afraid of her, „ I 550
Child, do you *l* me now ? „ I 640
Then you should wish us both to *l* for ever. „ I 643
they that *l* do not believe that death Will part them. „ I 662
I cannot *l* you ; nay, I think I never can be brought to
l any man. „ II 77
not only *l* the country, But its inhabitants too ; „ II 544
Well then, I must make her *L* Harold first, „ II 677

Love (verb) (*continued*)   and they both *l* me—I am
all in all to both; and he *l*'s me too,   *Prom. of May* III 212
and I *l* him so much—   *Eva.* Poor Dora!   „   III 284
Could I *l* him else?   „   III 291
Can't a girl when she *l*'s her husband, and he her,   „   III 304
for you have taught me To *l* you.   „   III 558
I *l* you and you me.   „   III 620
He is yours again—he will *l* *you* again;   „   III 673
Could *l* me, could be brought to *l* me   „   III 778
ask you all, did none of you *l* young Walter Lea?   *Foresters* I i 55
if a man and a maid *l* one another,   „   I i 172
A gallant Earl. I *l* him as I hate John.   „   I i 190
Dost thou *l* him indeed,   „   I i 220
Thou knowest that the Sheriff of Nottingham *l*'s thee.   „   I i 223
  Marian. The Sheriff dare to *l* me?   „   I i 223
I *l* him as a damsel of his day might have loved   „   I i 226
I *l* my dinner—but I can fast, I can fast;   „   I ii 63
I *l* thee much; and as I *am* thy friend,   „   I ii 181
And learn from her if she do *l* this Earl.   „   I ii 187
She took my ring. I trust she *l*'s me—yet   „   I iii 3
you *l* me, all of you, But I am outlaw'd,   „   I iii 162
No man who truly *l*'s and truly rules   „   II i 76
Come be thou My brother too. She *l*'s me.   „   II i 518
Do you doubt me when I say she *l*'s me, man?   „   II i 521
but abide with me who *l* thee.   „   II i 602
tho' I *l* thee, We cannot come together in this world.   „   II i 616
thou canst not hide thyself From her who *l*'s thee.   „   II ii 25
to mistrust the girl you say you *l* Is to mistrust your
own love for your girl! How should you *l* if you
mistrust your love?   „   II ii 58
'This boy will never wed the maid he *l*'s,   „   II ii 112
I could *l* you like a woman.   „   II ii 191
And you *l* her and she *l*'s you;   „   II ii 195
I *l* you all the same. Proceed.   „   III 438
Good, good, I *l* thee for that!   „   IV 173
Give me thy hand, Much; I *l* thee. At him, Scarlet!   „   IV 310
now I *l* thee mightily, thou tall fellow.   „   IV 321
And *l*'s and dotes on every dingle of it.   „   IV 390
I cannot *l* the Sheriff.   „   IV 662
And all I *l*, Robin, and all his men,   „   IV 722
He *l*'s the chivalry of his single arm.   „   IV 786

Loveable Is she less *l*, Less lovely, being wholly
mine?   *Prom. of May* I 740
Loved Whisper'd me, if I *l* him, not to yield   *Queen Mary* I ii 35
My brother rather hated me than *l*;   „   I v 82
I'd have you yet more *l*:   „   I v 119
I say your Grace is *l*.   „   I v 132
Queen Anne *l* him. All the women *l* him. I *l* him,   „   II i 34
he *l* the more His own gray towers,   „   II i 48
She is *l* by all of us.   „   II ii 112
We are not *l* here, and would be then   „   III vi 186
I have been a man *l* plainness all my life;   „   IV iii 270
I *l* the man, and needs must moan for him;   „   IV iii 635
I never *l* you more.   „   v i 219
Shut on him by the father whom he *l*,   „   v v 41
How he smiles As if he *l* me yet!   „   v v 43
He never *l* me—nay, he could not love me.   „   v v 43
I was walking with the man I *l*. I *l* him, but I
thought I was not *l*.   „   v v 88
she *l* much: pray God she be forgiven.   „   v v 271
Yet she *l* one so much—I needs must say—   „   v v 275
I conquer'd, and he *l* me none the less,   *Harold* I i 446
When he was here in Normandy, He *l* us   „   II ii 580
Father, we so *l*— *Aldred.* The more the love,   „   III i 345
they *l* within the pale forbidden By Holy Church: „   III ii 22
Then I, who *l* my brother, bad the king   „   IV i 101
I knew him brave: he *l* his land: „   IV i 201
I had rather She would have *l* her husband.   „   IV i 224
Take and slay me, For Edward *l* me.   „   IV ii 10
Because I *l* thee in my mortal day,   „   v i 240
To part me from the woman that I *l*!   „   v i 346
Alas, my lord, I *l* thee.   „   v i 355
Alas, my lord, she *l* thee.   „   v i 366
I *l* him as I hate This liar who made me liar.   „   v i 411
That he forsware himself for all he *l*,   „   v i 622

Loved (*continued*) They *l* him; and, pray God My Normans   *Harold* v ii 182
whom I love indeed As a woman should be *l*—   *Becket, Pro.* 133
how should he love A woman, as a woman should be
l? *Henry.* How shouldst thou know that never
hast *l* one?   „   *Pro.* 139
Louis of France *l* me, and I dreamed that I *l* Louis
of France: and I *l* Henry of England, and Henry
of England dreamed that he *l* me;   „   *Pro.* 356
King Louis had no paramours, and I *l* him none the
more. Henry had many, and I *l* him none the
less—   „   *Pro.* 475
Madam, I have *l* her in my time.   „   *Pro.* 495
I *l* according to the main purpose and intent of nature.   *Pro.* 501
So that he *l* me—and he loves me—   „   III 226
I am none such. I never *l* but one.   „   IV ii 118
with what a tenderness He *l* my son.   „   v 22
out with Henry in the days When Henry *l* me,   „   v ii 232
Reginald, all men know I *l* the Prince.   „   v ii 334
To help him from them, since indeed I *l* him,   „   v ii 341
They knew he *l* me.   „   v ii 453
worshipping in her Temple, and *l* you for it,   *The Cup* I i 40
beheld you afar off—*l* you—sends you this cup—   „   I ii 71
from maiden fears Or reverential love for him I *l*,   „   II 197
I that *l* her. *Camma.* I *l* him.   „   II 469
Her phantom call'd me by the name she *l*.   *Prom. of May* II 243
all of them *L* her, and she was worthy of all love.   „   II 429
Surely I *l* Eva More than I knew!   „   II 643
you are the first I ever have *l* truly.   „   III 649
So *l* by all the village people here,   „   III 755
could be brought to love me As I *l* you—   „   III 780
He *l* the Lady Anne; The lady *l* the master well, The
maid she *l* the man.   *Foresters* I i 7
have *l* Harold the Saxon, or Hereward the Wake.   „   I i 227
when I *l* A maid with all my heart to pass it down   „   I ii 296
Said I not, I *l* thee, man?   „   IV 740
Love-dream may not a girl's *l-d* have too much
romance in it   *Prom. of May* III 185
Love-goddess Like the *L-g*, with no bridal veil,   „   I 596
Loveless As at this *l* knife that stirs the riot,   *Becket* IV ii 191
I am as lone and *l* as thyself.   *The Falcon* 20
Lovelier the lady holds the cleric *L* than any soldier,   *Becket* v i 194
white In the sweet moon as with a *l* snow!   *The Cup* I ii 396
Loveliest This is the *l* day that ever smiled On
England   *Queen Mary* III i 161
The *l* life that ever drew the light From heaven   *The Cup* I iii 56
Loveliness but naked Nature In all her *l*.   *Prom. of May* I 600
Lovely Our bridemaids are not *l*—Disappointment,   *Queen Mary* v ii 154
God's eyes! what a *l* cross! what jewels!   *Becket, Pro.* 371
She saw it at a dance, upon a neck Less *l* than her own,   *The Falcon* 56
Is she less loveable, Less *l*, being wholly mine?   *Prom. of May* I 741
But you are young, and—pardon me—As *l* as your
sister.   „   II 508
could it look But half as *l*.   „   III 491
So *l* in the promise of her May,   „   III 753
What a shape! what *l* arms!   *Foresters* I i 109
Lover (*See also* **Judas-lover, Money-lover, Peace-lover**)
Two young *l*'s in winter weather,   *Harold* III ii 3
To which the *l* answers lovingly   „   III ii 13
not as statesman, but true *l* and friend.   *Becket, Pro.* 80
I have been a *l* of wines, and delicate meats,   „   I i 76
Who knows but that thy *l* May plead so pitifully,   „   IV ii 216
Ay, still a *l* of the beast and bird?   „   v ii 245
I am a life-long *l* of the chase,   *The Cup* I i 194
have a score of *l*'s and have not a heart for any of
them—   *The Falcon* 88
waiting To clasp their *l*'s by the golden gates.   *Prom. of May* I 248
But keep us *l*'s.   „   I 639
You tell me you have a *l*.   „   III 255
And this *l* of yours—this Mr. Harold—is a gentleman?   „   III 280
L's hold True love immortal.   *Foresters* II i 614
You never whisper close as *l*'s do,   „   III 6
You *l*'s are such clumsy summer-flies   „   IV 10
hundred *l*'s more To celebrate this advent of our King!   „   IV 1047
Love-sick Is to be *l-s* for a shadow   *Queen Mary* I v 535
so should all the *l-s* be sea-sick.   *Foresters* IV 673

Loving And as ye were most *l* unto him,   *Queen Mary* II ii 174
and so *l*, needs must deem This love by you return'd   „   II ii 195
And all our *l* subjects, most expedient.   „   II ii 211
And your so *l* sister ?   „   II iv 141
Your Grace hath a most chaste and *l* wife.   „   III vi 129
Hurt no man more Than you would harm your *l* natural brother   „   IV iii 189
Love him ! why not ? thine is a *l* office,   *Harold* II ii 97
Yet if she be a true and *l* wife She may,   *The Cup* I iii 32
Low You speak too *l*, my Lord ;   *Queen Mary* I iv 123
Wherefore now the Queen In this *l* pulse and palsy of the state,   „   II ii 103
you forget That long *l* minster where you gave your hand   „   III ii 90
and debased From councillor to caitiff—fallen so *l*,   „   IV iii 75
L, my lute ; speak *l*, my lute, but say the world is nothing—*L*, lute, *l* !   „   V ii 367
L, my lute ! oh *l*, my lute ! we fade and are forsaken —*L*, dear lute, *l* !   „   V ii 374
Take it away ! not *l* enough for me !   „   V ii 377
Your Grace hath a *l* voice.   „   V ii 378
A *l* voice Lost in a wilderness where none can hear !   „   V ii 380
A *l* voice from the dust and from the grave   „   V ii 385
There, am I *l* enough now ?   „   V ii 388
Does he think *L* stature is *l* nature, or all women's *L* as his own ?   „   V ii 434
It is the *l* man thinks the woman *l*;   „   V ii 439
And Charles, the lord of this *l* world, is gone ;   „   V v 54
Ay, raise his head, for thou hast laid it *l* !   *Harold* III i 163
Gentleness, *L* words best chime with this solemnity.   *The Cup* II 217
And when you came and dipt your sovereign head Thro' these *l* doors,   *The Falcon* 868
The town lay still in the *l* sun-light,   *Prom. of May* I 37
I sank so *l* that I went into service—   „   III 391
Till Nature, high and *l*, and great and small Forgets herself,   *Foresters* I ii 326
could I stoop so *l* As mate with one that holds no love is pure,   „   IV 710
Lower (adj.) And ye, my masters, of the *l* house,   *Queen Mary* III iii 102
you are even *l* and baser Than even I can well believe you. Go !   *Prom. of May* III 813
Lower (verb) made us *l* our kingly flag To yours of England.   *Queen Mary* V i 59
but must *l* his flag To that of England   „   V i 64
L the light. He must be here.   *Harold* V ii 63
Lowest (adj.) poor worm, crawl down thine own black hole To the *l* Hell.   *The Cup* II 496
Lowest (s) That all of you, the highest as the *l*,   *Queen Mary* IV iii 65
Lowliest beseech Your Highness to accept our *l* thanks   „   II ii 131
Lowly ' O happy lark, that warblest high Above thy *l* nest,   *Prom. of May* III 200
Low-moaning a sigh With these *l-m* heavens.   *Harold* V i 152
Low-spirited Your Grace is too *l-s*.   *Queen Mary* V i 605
Low-statured Than that you were *l-s*.   „   V ii 432
Loyal My Lord, I have the jewel of a *l* heart. *Gardiner*.
I doubt it not, Madam, most *l*.   „   I iv 247
is every morning's prayer Of your most *l* subject,   „   I v 104
But help her in this exigency, make Your city *l*,   „   II ii 19
on you, In your own city, as her right, my Lord, For you are *l*.   „   II ii 107
and we pray That we, your true and *l* citizens,   „   II ii 135
Your lawful Prince hath come to cast herself On *l* hearts and bosoms,   „   II ii 263
The Queen of England—or the Kentish Squire ? I know you *l*.   „   II ii 271
Your Highness hears This burst and bass of *l* harmony,   „   II ii 285
We thank your Lordship and your *l* city.   „   II ii 301
No, girl ; most brave and *l*, brave and *l*.   „   II iv 11
L and royal cousin, humblest thanks.   „   III ii 3
Yet there be some disloyal Catholics, And many heretics *l*;   „   III iv 44
To take the lives of others that are *l*.   „   III iv 48
Nay, Madam, there be *l* papers too,   „   V ii 221
Your England is as *l* as myself.   „   V ii 328
Said you not Many of these were *l* ?   „   V ii 331

Loyal (*continued*) and am in everything Most *l* and most grateful to the Queen.   *Queen Mary* V iii 25
and I do not then charm this secret out of our *l* Thomas, I am not Eleanor.   *Becket*, Pro. 467
for which our *l* service, And since we likewise swore to obey the customs,   „   v 52
I am all as *l* as thyself, but what a vow ! what a vow !   *Foresters* I i 293
Loyally *L* and with good faith, my lord Archbishop ?   *Becket* I iii 278
Loyalty To whom he owes his *l* after God,   *Queen Mary* IV i 23
less *l* in it than the backward scrape of the clown's heel—   *Becket* III iii 143
Comrades, I thank you for your *l*,   *Foresters* III 78
Lucullus that *L* or Apicius might have sniffed it in their Hades of heathenism,   *Becket* III iii 117
Ludgate I must set The guard at *L*.   *Queen Mary* II ii 409
If *L* can be reach'd by dawn to-morrow.   „   II iii 53
hath broken thro' the guards And gone to *L*.   „   II iv 21
brave Lord William Thrust him from *L*,   „   II iv 92
Lung Is life and *l*'s to every rebel birth   „   III vi 51
Lung'd *See* **Loud-lung'd**
Lunnun (London) but I taäkes 'im for a *L* swindler, and a burn fool.   *Prom. of May* I 309
seeäms to me the mark wur maäde by a *L* boot.   „   I 416
and I thinks ye weärs a *L* boot.   „   I 461
Lure (s) such a one As Harry Bolingbroke hath a *l* in it.   *Queen Mary* I iv 10
Lure (verb) I must *l* my game into the camp.   *The Cup* I iii 64
Lurk even while I speak There *l*'s a silent dagger,   *Queen Mary* V ii 216
Lurking Not the full faith, no, but the *l* doubt.   „   III iv 124
Luscombe *L*, Nokes, Oldham, Skipworth !   *Prom. of May* III 53
Lust (s) Which a young *l* had clapt upon the back,   *Queen Mary* IV iii 401
from the squint Of *l* and glare of malice.   *Becket* I i 313
But the fool-fire of love or *l*,   *The Cup* I i 147
He steep'd himself In all the *l* of Rome.   „   I i 369
fill all hearts with fatness and the *l* Of plenty—   „   II 273
' *L*, Prodigality, Covetousness, Craft,   *Prom. of May* II 284
Lust (verb) be those that *l* To burn each other ?   *Queen Mary* IV iii 197
Lustiest Thou the *l* and lousiest of this Cain's brotherhood, answer.   *Becket* I iv 184
Lusty I know some *l* fellows there in France.   *Queen Mary* II i 128
That was a *l* boy of twenty-seven ;   „   V v 48
A pretty *l* boy.   *Becket* I iv 247
mix with all The *l* life of wood and underwood,   *Foresters* I iii 114
L bracken beaten flat, Queen.   „   II ii 154
Lute Alice, my child, Bring us your *l*.   *Queen Mary* V ii 357
Give *me* the *l*. He hates me !   „   V ii 362
Low, my *l* ; speak low, my *l*, but say the world is nothing—Low, *l*, low !   „   V ii 367
Low, my *l* ! oh low, my *l* ! we fade and are forsaken —Low, dear *l*, low !   „   V ii 374
Luther (Martin) ghosts of *L* and Zuinglius fade Into the deathless hell   „   III ii 174
Ah, what an acrid wine has *L* brew'd,   „   IV iii 545
Lutheran possibly The *L* may be won to her again ;   „   III iv 202
I was too lenient to the *L*,   „   V ii 73
What then, he knew I was no *L*.   „   V ii 78
Seize him and burn him for a *L*.   „   V ii 245
Lutheranism Tainted with *L* in Italy.   „   III iv 227
Would freely canvass certain *L*'s.   „   V ii 76
Luting Fluting, and piping and *l* ' Love, love, love '—   *Foresters* III 33
Lydian Lay down the *L* carpets for the king.   *The Cup* II 187
Lying (adj. and part.) to take the guns From out the vessels *l* in the river.   *Queen Mary* II i 222
Shot off their *l* cannon, and her priests Have preach'd,   „   III vi 97
this Bonner or another Will in some *l* fashion mis-report His ending   „   IV iii 326
I left her *l* still and beautiful,   „   V v 261
dog, with thy *l* lights Thou hast betray'd us on these rocks of thine !   *Harold* II i 21
Thy villains with their *l* lights have wreck'd us !   „   II i 83
than believe that *l* And ruling men are fatal twins that cannot Move one without the other.   „   III i 126
A *l* devil hath haunted me—mine oath—my wife—   „   V i 316
Man, *l* here alone, Moody creature,   *Foresters* II ii 186

Madonna Come in, *M*, come in. — *The Falcon* 176
  you look as beautiful this morning as the very *M* — " 199
  No, no, not quite, *M*, not yet, not yet. — " 392
  This was penn'd, *M*, Close to the grating — " 440
  I bear with him no longer. *Count.* No, *M*! — " 886
Mad-woman O murderous *m-w*! I pray you lift — *The Cup* II 471
Magdalen (a character in "Queen Mary") Ah, *M*,
  sin is bold as well as dull. — *Queen Mary* v ii 442
Magdalen (St. Mary) Thanks to the blessed *M*, whose day
  it is. — *Becket* III iii 171
  All praise to Heaven, and sweet St. *M*! — " III iii 235
Maggot Foul *m*'s crawling in a fester'd vice! — *Queen Mary* v v 161
Magistrate all the *m*'s, all the nobles, and all the wealthy; — " v iv 50
Magnificence I have heard That, thro' his late *m* of living — *The Falcon* 227
  No other heart Of such *m* in courtesy Beats— — " 723
Magpie Peace, *m*! Give him the quarterstaff. — *Foresters* IV 249
Mahound by *M*, I had sooner have been born a
  Mussulman— — *Becket* II ii 144
  No God but one, and *M* is his prophet. — " II ii 225
  like *M*'s coffin hung between heaven and earth— — " II ii 361
  By *M* I could dine with Beelzebub! — *Foresters* IV 970
Maid says she will live And die true *m*— — *Queen Mary* III vi 46
  Make me full fain to live and die a *m*. — " v iii 98
  little fair-hair'd Norman *m* Lived in my mother's
  house: — *Becket* v ii 260
  The *m* to her dairy came in from the cow, — *Prom. of May* I 39
  The *m* she loved the man. — *Foresters* I i 9
  The *m* a rose to the man. (repeat) — *Foresters* I i 13, 106
  The *m* her hand to the man. (repeat) — " I i 17, 93
  the *m* a kiss to the man. (repeat) — " I i 21, 120
  should have told us how the man first kissed the *m*. — " I i 124
  if a man and a *m* care for one another, does it matter
  so much if the *m* give the first kiss? — " I i 134
  now thou hast given me the man's kiss, let me give
  thee the *m*'s. — " I i 144
  if a man and a *m* love one another, may the *m* give
  the first kiss? — " I i 172
  when they look at a *m* they blast her. — " I i 256
  Then the *m* is not high-hearted enough. — " I i 258
  Go now and ask the *m* to dance with thee, — " I ii 185
  what *m* but would beware of John? — " I ii 256
  when I loved A *m* with all my heart to pass it down — " I ii 297
  man and *m* be free To foil and spoil the tyrant — " II i 10
  There are no *m*'s like English *m*'s — " II i 19
  'This boy will never wed the *m* he loves,
  and another—worse!—An innocent *m*. — " II ii 111
  —to this *m*, this Queen o' the woods. — " III 388
  M! *Friar.* Paramour! *Friar.* Hell take her! — " III 394
  Air and word, my lady, are *m* and man. — " III 401
  lips that never breathed Love's falsehood to true *m* — " IV 73
  For so this *m* would wed our brother. — " IV 483
Maiden (adj.) You've but a dull life in this *m* court,
  I fear, my Lord? — *Queen Mary* I iii 114
  Would not for all the stars and *m* moon — " v ii 455
  whether from *m* fears Or reverential love for him
  I loved, — *The Cup* II 196
  Modest *m* lily abused, Queen. — *Foresters* II ii 158
  clothes itself In *m* flesh and blood, — " III 117
  Live thou *m*! Thou art more my wife so feeling, — " III 122
  You heed not how you soil her *m* fame, — " IV 479
Maiden (s) (See also **Bower-maiden**) My pretty *m*,
  tell me, did you ever Sigh for a beard? — *Queen Mary* I v 607
  my pretty *m*, A pretty man for such a pretty *m*. — " I v 612
  Then, pretty *m*, you should know that whether — " I v 618
  Peace, pretty *m*. I hear them stirring — " I v 627
  have thy conscience White as a *m*'s hand, — *Harold* II ii 284
  A *m* slowly moving on to music Among her *m*'s to this
  Temple— — *The Cup* I i 9
  When first he meets his *m* in a bower. — " I iii 41
  I am none of your delicate Norman *m*'s — *Foresters* I i 212
  A *m* now Were ill-bested in these dark days — " II ii 44
  and all your forest games As far as *m* might. — " III 86
  when Our English *m*'s are their prey, — " III 179
  and scare lonely *m*'s at the farmstead, — " III 200
  Save for this *m* and thy brother Abbot, — " IV 632

Maidenhood He that can pluck the flower of *m* — *Foresters* I ii 108
  Who art the fairest flower of *m* — " I ii 123
  Out upon all hard-hearted *m*! — " IV 50
Maiden-white Make blush the *m-w* of our tall cliffs, — *Harold* II ii 332
Maiden-wife O *m-w*, The oppression of our people — *Foresters* III 108
Maid Marian (daughter of Sir Richard Lea) (See also
  Marian) She has gone, *M M* to her Robin— — *Queen Mary* III v 156
  this is *M M* Flying from John—disguised. *Men.*
  M M? she? — *Foresters* II i 679
  Stay with us here, sweet love, *M M*, — " II ii 15
  and looks at once *M M*, — " II ii 119
  M M, Queen o' the woods! (repeat) — *Foresters* III 357, 374, 376, 397, 399
  M M. *Marian.* Yes, King Richard. — *Foresters* IV 859
Maidstone The bells are ringing at *M*. — *Queen Mary* II i 19
  and your worship's name heard into *M* market, — " II i 63
Mail I wear beneath my dress A shirt of *m*: — " I v 146
  And felt the sun of Antioch scald our *m*, — *Becket* II ii 93
  having lived For twenty days and nights in *m*, — *Foresters* IV 124
Mail'd *M* in the perfect panoply of faith, — *Becket* v ii 494
Maim when he springs And *m*'s himself against the
  bars, — *Queen Mary* v v 67
  It frights the traitor more to *m* and blind. — *Harold* II ii 503
Maim'd starved, *m*, flogg'd, flay'd, burn'd, — *Queen Mary* v v 209
  They have so *m* and murder'd all his face — *Harold* v iv 76
  And lamed and *m* to dislocation, — *Becket* IV ii 266
  Not caught, *m*, blinded him. — *The Cup* II ii 271
Main (adj.) Madam, I loved according to the *m* purpose
  and intent of nature. — *Becket, Pro.* 502
  Like sudden night in the *m* glare of day. — " I 57
  That I am his *m* paramour, his sultana. — " IV ii 39
  her *m* law Whereby she grows in beauty— — *Prom. of May* I 281
Main (s) Calais! Our one point on the *m*, — *Queen Mary* I v 125
  Had prosper'd in the *m*, but suddenly Jarr'd — *Becket* I iii 381
Mainland gateway to the *m* over which Our flag — *Queen Mary* v ii 260
Maintain we shall still *m* All former treaties — " I v 265
  I trust I still *m* my courtesy; — *The Falcon* 294
Maintain'd *M*, and entertain'd us royally! — *Harold* II ii 159
Majestic Be somewhat less—*m* to your Queen. — *Queen Mary* III vi 149
Majesty When will her *M* pass, sayst thou? — " I i 2
  Her *M* Hears you affect the Prince— — " I iv 81
  A happy morning to your *M*. — " I v 244
  maintain all former treaties with his *M*. — " I v 266
  Follow their *Majesties*. — " III i 331
  my wish Echoes your *M*'s. *Pole.* It shall be so. — " III iii 93
  Do make most humble suit unto your *Majesties*, — " III iii 119
  Whereon we humbly pray your *Majesties*, — " III iii 143
  Serve God and both your *Majesties*. — " III iii 159
  My Lords, you cannot see her *M*. — " III vi 20
  in all this, my Lord, her *M* Is flint of flint, — " III vi 37
  Your *M* shall go to Dover with me, — " III vi 218
  Then one day more to please her *M*. — " III vi 248
  I am vastly grieved to leave your *M*. — " III vi 255
  Long live your *M*! Shall Alice sing you — " v ii 354
  Your *M* has lived so pure a life, — " v v 72
Make (See also **Maäke**) *m* what noise you will with
  your tongues, — " I i 5
  didn't the Parliament *m* her a bastard? — " I i 16
  Parliament can *m* every true-born man of us a
  bastard. Old Nokes, can't it *m* thee a bastard? — " I i 27
  so they can't *m* me a bastard. — " I i 47
  if Parliament can *m* the Queen a bastard, why, it
  follows all the more that they can *m* thee one, — " I i 49
  To *m* me headless. — " I ii 41
  These beastly swine *m* such a grunting here, — " I iii 12
  That *m*'s for France. (repeat) — " I iii 89, 92, 94
  His Highness *m*'s his moves across the Channel, — " I iii 134
  m your boast that after all She means to wed you. — " I iv 87
  That you shall marry him, *m* him King belike. — " I iv 212
  she means to *m* A farewell present to your Grace. — " I iv 244
  M all tongues praise and all hearts beat for you. — " I v 117
  To *m* the crown of Scotland one with ours, — " I v 297
  Would *m* our England, France; — " I v 297
  I can *m* allowance for thee, — " I v 326
  M no allowance for the naked truth. — " I v 328
  Pope would have you *m* them render these; — " I v 403

Make (*continued*)   Your Highness is all trembling.

Mary.   *M* way. | Queen Mary | I v 595
Look ; can you *m* it English ? | ” | II i 127
m Your city loyal, and be the mightiest man | ” | II ii 18
To *m* free spoil and havock of your goods. | ” | II ii 186
Hear us now *m* oath To raise your Highness | ” | II ii 288
the half sight which *m*'s her look so stern, | ” | II ii 322
Courage, sir, *That m*'s a man or woman | ” | II ii 329
man should *m* the hour, not this the man ; | ” | II ii 365
M's enemies for himself and for his king ; | ” | II ii 399
Shall we *m* Those that we come to serve our sharpest
  foes ? | ” | II iii 76
you'll *m* the White Tower a black 'un | ” | II iii 100
cloth of gold, Could *m* it so. | ” | III i 55
I'd a move myself to hinder that : | ” | III i 127
You would but *m* us weaker, Thomas Stafford. | ” | III i 130
They *m* amends for the tails. | ” | III i 227
M themselves drunk and mad, | ” | III i 282
Will stir the living tongue and *m* the cry. | ” | III i 354
She could not *m* it white— | ” | III i 424
and *m* us A Spanish province ; | ” | III i 465
Seem'd as a happy miracle to *m* glide— | ” | III ii 29
I return As Peter, but to bless thee : *m* me well.' | ” | III ii 56
M's me his mouth of holy greeting. | ” | III ii 80
That *m* me shamed and tongue-tied in my love. | ” | III ii 162
news to the Both of us happy—ay, the Kingdom too. | ” | III ii 187
Do *m* most humble suit unto your Majesties, | ” | III iii 118
because to persecute *M*'s a faith hated, | ” | III iv 116
And *m* it look more seemly. | ” | III iv 152
m's the waverer pass Into more settled hatred | ” | III iv 157
These fields are only green, they *m* me gape. | ” | III v 7
One of those wicked wilfuls that men *m*, | ” | III v 76
And *m* a morning outcry in the yard ; | ” | III v 158
narrowness of the cage That *m*'s the captive testy ; | ” | III v 208
m ready for the journey. | ” | III v 277
Than any sea could *m* me passing hence, | ” | IV i 87
We *m* our humble prayer unto your Grace | ” | IV i 43
His learning *m*'s his burning the more just. | ” | IV i 159
M out the writ to-night. | ” | IV i 195
No man can *m* his Maker— | ” | IV ii 58
And *m* you simple Cranmer once again. | ” | IV ii 129
and *m*'s The fire seem even crueller than it is. | ” | IV ii 232
I wish some thunderbolt Would *m* this Cole a cinder, | ” | IV iii 11
M us despise it at odd hours, my Lord. | ” | IV iii 386
I cum behind tha, gall, and couldn't *m* tha hear. | ” | IV iii 466
never burn out the hypocrisy that *m*'s the water
  in her. | ” | IV iii 525
' *M* short ! *m* short ! ' and so they lit the wood. | ” | IV iii 606
You *m* your wars upon him down in Italy :— | ” | v 141
What *m*'s thy favour like the bloodless head | ” | v ii 19
wines, That ever *m* him fiercer. | ” | v ii 95
it was thought we two Might *m* one flesh, | ” | v ii 137
and *m* Musters in all the counties ; | ” | v ii 271
Heretic and rebel Point at me and *m* merry. | ” | v ii 318
Should *m* the mightiest empire earth has known. | ” | v iii 70
M me full fain to live and die a maid. | ” | v iii 98
And break your paces in, and *m* you tame ; | ” | v iii 121
and *m* Down for their heads to heaven ! | ” | v iv 7
Dead or alive you cannot *m* him happy. | ” | v v 71
I trust that God will *m* you happy yet. | ” | v v 76
if that May *m* your Grace forget yourself | ” | v v 81
—we will *m* England great. | Harold | I i 142
for heaven's credit *M*'s it on earth :
m me not fool ! Nor *m* the King a fool, who made
  me Earl ! *Harold.*   No, Tostig—lest I *m* myself
  a fool Who made the King who made thee, *m* thee
  Earl. | ” | I i 288
M not thou The nothing something. | ” | I i 362
the true *must* Shall *m* her strike as Power : | ” | I i 369
would but shame me, Rather than *m* me vain. | ” | I ii 117
Follow my lead, and I will *m* thee earl. | ” | I ii 217
Count-crab will *m* his nippers meet in thine heart ; | ” | II i 76
To *m* allowance for their rougher fashions, | ” | II ii 8
To marry and have no husband *M*'s the wife fool. | ” | II ii 310
M blush the maiden-white of our tall cliffs, | ” | II ii 332

Make (*continued*)   may he not *m* A league with William, | Harold | II ii 460
M thou not mention that I spake with thee. | ” | II ii 483
And I will *m* thee my great Earl of Earls, | ” | II ii 629
And *m*'s believe that he believes my word— | ” | II ii 668
would *m* the hard earth rive To the very Devil's horns, | ” | II ii 739
m your ever-jarring Earldoms move To music | ” | II ii 760
If thou canst *m* a wholesome use of these | ” | III i 20
as the libertine repents who cannot *M* done undone, | ” | III i 33
Not mean To *m* our England Norman, | ” | III i 250
and those Who *m* thy good their own— | ” | III i 330
which will *m* My kingship kinglier to me | ” | III ii 43
To *m* all England one, to close all feuds, | ” | IV i 141
Thou hast but cared to *m* thyself a king— | ” | IV ii 74
M not our Morcar sullen : it is not wise. | ” | IV ii 102
I am weary—go : *m* me not wroth with thee ! | ” | v i 31
there *m* strength to breast Whatever chance, | ” | v i 126
m their wall of shields Firm as thy cliffs, | ” | v i 478
m his battle-axe keen As thine own sharp-dividing
  justice, | ” | v i 562
M thou one man as three to roll them down ! | ” | v i 577
M them again one people—Norman, English ; | ” | v ii 188
A more awful one.   *M* me Archbishop ! | Becket, Pro. 289
m her as hateful to herself and to the King, | ” | Pro. 526
M an Archbishop of a soldier ? | ” | I i 41
we will *m* her whole ; Not one rood lost. | ” | I i 163
M it so hard to save a moth from the fire ? | ” | I i 283
if he follow thee, *M* him thy prisoner. | ” | I i 332
I will *m* thee hateful to thy King. | ” | I ii 91
Ye *m* this clashing for no love o' the customs | ” | I iii 136
I had meant to *m* him all but king. | ” | I iii 464
M not thy King a traitorous murderer. | ” | I iii 500
m it clear Under what Prince I fight. | ” | I iii 544
Serve my best friend and *m* him my worst foe ; | ” | I iii 568
m my cry to the Pope, By whom I will be judged ; | ” | I iii 723
he *m*'s moan that all be a-getting cold.   *Becket.*   And
  I *m* my moan along with him. | ” | I iv 61
We can *m* a black sin white. | ” | I iv 169
let him *m* it his own, let him reign in it— | ” | II i 17
who cares not for the word, *M*'s ' care not '— | ” | II i 118
m's after it too To find it. | ” | II i 321
mother Would *m* him play his kingship against mine. | ” | II ii 11
So we *m* our peace with him. | ” | II ii 62
we *m* the time, we keep the time, ay, and we serve
  the time ; | ” | II ii 367
and *m* Our waning Eleanor all but love me ! | ” | II ii 457
and to *m* me a woman of the world, | ” | III i 116
they say, she *m*'s songs, and that's against her, for I
  never knew an honest woman that could *m* songs, | ” | III i 181
tho' you *m* your butt too big, you overshoot it. | ” | III iii 121
keep the figure moist and *m* it hold water, | ” | III iii 166
I *m* thee full amends. | ” | III iii 219
How, do you *m* me a traitor ? | ” | III iii 240
Doth not the *fewness* of anything *m* the fulness of it
  in estimation ? | ” | III iii 302
she says she can *m* you sleep o' nights. | ” | IV ii 19
Give her to me to *m* my honeymoon. | ” | IV ii 142
m Thy body loathsome even to thy child ; | ” | IV ii 171
baseness as would *m* me Most worthy of it : | ” | IV ii 235
And *m* thee a world's horror. | ” | IV ii 288
But thou art like enough to *m* him thine. | ” | v i 132
m me not a woman, John of Salisbury, Nor *m* me traitor | ” | v ii 147
you would *m* his coronation void By cursing | ” | v ii 329
He *m*'s a King a traitor, me a liar. | ” | v ii 415
They seek—you *m*—occasion for your death. | ” | v ii 558
Ay, *m* him prisoner, do not harm the man. | ” | v iii 145
which well May *m* you lose yourself, | The Cup | I i 149
I would be Happy, and *m* all others happy so | ” | I iii 29
And I will *m* Galatia prosperous too, | ” | I iii 169
You will not easily *m* me credit that. | ” | II 25
—*m* me happy in my marriage ! | ” | II 274
To *m* my marriage prosper to my wish ! | ” | II 308
See first I *m* libation to the Goddess, | ” | II 377
Thou hast drunk deep enough to *m* me happy. | The Falcon 83
Will hardly help to *m* him sane again. | | 183
and tell her all about it and *m* her happy ? | ” |

Make (*continued*)   to give me his falcon, And that will *m* me well.'   *The Falcon* 243

I ha' heärd 'im a-gawin' on 'ud *m* your 'air—God bless it !—stan' on end.   *Prom. of May* I 134

you *m* The May and morning still more beautiful,   „ I 572

When the great Democracy *M's* a new world—   „ I 672

and *m* them happy in the long barn,   „ I 791

turn back at times, and *m* Courtesy to custom ?   „ II 634

I could *m* his age A comfort to him—   „ II 660

Well then, I must *m* her Love Harold first,   „ II 676

m herself anything he wishes her to be ?   „ III 305

I couldn't *m* it out. What was it ?   „ III 324

I mounted upon the parapet—— *Dora.* You *m* me shudder !   „ III 373

then what is it That *m's* you talk so dolefully ?   „ III 572

I doubt not I can *m* you happy. *Dora.* You *m* me Happy already.   „ III 641

M her happy, then, and I forgive you.   „ III 666

I wish'd, I hoped To *m*, to *m*—— *Dora. What* did you hope to *m* ? *Harold.* 'Twere best to *m* an end of my lost life. O Dora, Dora ! *Dora.* What did you hope to *m* ? *Harold. M, m !*   III 783

I keep a good heart and *m* the most of it,   *Foresters* I 29

What *m's* thee so down in the mouth ?   „ I ii 42

My Lady Marian you can *m* it so If you will deign   „ I ii 131

I promise thee to *m* this Marian thine.   „ I ii 183

We *m* but one hour's buzz,   „ I ii 277

m us merry Because a year of it is gone ?   „ I iii 14

Where law lies dead, we *m* ourselves the law.   „ II i 91

I came To eat him up and *m* an end of him.   „ II i 125

To *m* this Sherwood Eden o'er again,   „ II i 168

M for the cottage then !   „ II i 210

and *m* a ghostly wail ever and anon to scare 'em.   „ II i 215

let me go to *m* the mound :   „ II i 312

but *m* haste then, and be silent in the wood.   „ II i 364

Besides, tho' Friar Tuck might *m* us one,   „ II ii 88

What *m's* you seem so cold to Robin, lady ? *Marian.* What *m's* thee think I seem so cold to Robin ?   „ III 1

I wait till Little John 's up to me.   „ III 17

so you would *m* it two I should be grateful.   „ III 194

come between me and my Kate and *m* us one again.   „ III 423

and can *m* Five quarts pass into a thimble.   „ IV 282

M at him, all of you, a traitor coming   „ IV 780

m me The monkey that should roast   „ IV 804

Maker (God)   No man can make his *M*—   *Queen Mary* IV ii 58

Maker   *See* **Verse-maker**

Mak'st   Thou *m* me much ashamed   „ III iv 304

Making (part.)   (*See also* **A-makin', Maäkin'**) *M* libation to the Goddess.   *The Cup* II 364

m us feel guilty Of her own faults.   *Prom. of May* II 269

Making (s)   (*See also* **Bastard-making, Sonnet-making**) Either in *m* laws and ordinances   *Queen Mary* III iii 130

we be not bound by the king's voice In *m* of a king, yet the king's voice Is much toward his *m*.   *Harold* III i 237

spirit of the twelve Apostles enter'd Into thy *m*.   *Becket* I 51

the *m* of your butter, and the managing of your poultry ?   *Prom. of May* II 93

Malapert   as to the young crownling himself, he looked so *m* in the eyes,   *Becket* III iii 109

Male   it was hoped Your Highness was once more in happy state To give him an heir *m*.   *Queen Mary* V ii 573

Malet   Come *M*, let us hear !   *Harold* II ii 211

M, thy mother was an Englishwoman ;   „ II ii 264

How, *M*, if they be not honourable !   „ II ii 278

I should be there, *M*, I should be there !   „ II ii 293

Ill news for guests, ha, *M* !   „ II ii 302

M, I vow to build a church to God   „ V ii 137

Pluck the dead woman off the dead man, *M* !   „ V ii 145

Malice   he wrought it ignorantly, And not from any *m*.   *Queen Mary* III i 278

Wherewith they plotted in their treasonous *m*,   „ III iv 5

from the squint Of lust and glare of *m*.   *Becket* I i 313

Twice did thy *m* and thy calumnies Exile me   „ I iii 42

Malign   For whether men *m* thy name, or no,   *The Cup* I iii 84

Malignant   His face was not *m*, and he said   „ I ii 451

Malign'd   I am sure of being every way *m*.   *The Cup* I ii 241

I am much *m*. I thought to serve Galatia.   „ I ii 223

and he said That men *m* him.   „ I ii 452

Malignity   Brook for an hour such brute *m* ?   *Queen Mary* IV iii 544

War, waste, plague, famine, all *malignities*.   *Harold* I i 466

Malvoisie (a malmsey wine)   I marvel is it sack or *M* ?   *Foresters* III 332

The king's good health in ale and *M*.   „ IV 969

Man (*See also* **Farming-men, Goodman, Man-in-arms, Men-at-arms**), That was after, *m* ; that was after.   *Queen Mary* I i 19

Parliament can make every true-born *m* of us a bastard   „ I i 27

I was born true *m* at five in the forenoon   „ I i 45

was born of a true *m* and a ring'd wife,   „ I i 54

thinkest thou that anyone Suspected thee to be my *m* ?   „ I iii 176

wish before the word Is *m's* good Fairy—   „ I iv 240

Who love that *men* should smile upon you,   „ I iv 274

Men would murder me,   „ I v 155

He is every way a lesser *m* than Charles ;   „ I v 330

You cannot Learn a *m's* nature from his natural foe.   „ I v 340

And those hard *men* brake into woman-tears,   „ I v 564

A pretty *m* for such a pretty maiden. *Alice.* My Lord of Devon is a pretty *m*.   „ I v 613

no old news that all *men* hate it.   „ II i 17

ten thousand *men* on Penenden Heath all calling   „ II i 61

your worship the first *m* in Kent and Christendom,   „ II i 64

Men of Kent ; England of England ;   „ II i 157

If this *m* marry our Queen,   „ II i 170

the red *m*, that good helpless creature,   „ II i 208

I have striven in vain to raise a *m* for her.   „ II ii 17

and be the mightiest *m* This day in England.   „ II ii 19

had gone over to him With all his *men*,   „ II ii 29

To raise your Highness thirty thousand *men*,   „ II ii 291

As if to win the *m* by flattering him.   „ II ii 312

If not, there's no *m* safe. *White.* Yes, Thomas White. I am safe enough ; no *m* need flatter me. *Second Alderman.* Nay, no *m* need ; but did you mark our Queen ?   „ II ii 315

That makes or *m* or woman look their goodliest.   „ II ii 329

The *m* had children, and he whined for those. Methinks most *men* are but poor-hearted,   „ II ii 335

all *men* cry, She is queenly, she is goodly.   „ II ii 343

Who knows ? the *m* is proven by the hour. *White.* The *m* should make the hour, not this the *m* ;   „ II ii 363

gather your *men*—Myself must bustle.   „ II ii 373

The statesman that shall jeer and fleer at *men*,   „ II ii 398

if he jeer not seeing the true *m* Behind his folly, he is thrice the fool ; And if he see the *m* and still will jeer,   „ II ii 400

There, any *m* can read that.   „ II iii 68

Stafford, I am a sad *m* and a serious.   „ III i 41

We have no *men* among us.   „ III i 140

No *men* ? Did not Lord Suffolk die like a true *m* ? Is not Lord William Howard a true *m* ?   „ III i 163

And I, by God, believe myself a *m*. Ay, even in the church there is a *m*—Cranmer. Fly would he not when all *men* bad him fly.   „ III i 168

There's a brave *m*, if any.   „ III i 175

Thou art one of Wyatt's *men* ? *Man.* No, my Lord, no.   „ III i 244

The *m* shall paint a pair of gloves.   „ III i 274

(Knowing the *m*) he wrought it ignorantly,   „ III i 276

I say There is no *m*—there was one woman with us—   „ III i 337

dazzled *men* and deafen'd by some bright   „ III i 451

I am an old *m* wearied with my journey,   „ III ii 127

You were the one sole *m* in either house Who stood upright,   „ III iii 252

I say you were the one sole *m* who stood. *Bagenhall.* I am the one sole *m* in either house,   „ III iii 264

Well, you one *m*, because you stood upright,   „ III iii 268

If any *m* in any way would be The one *m*,   „ III iii 274

when *men* are tost On tides of strange opinion,   „ III iv 118

Lest *men* accuse you of indifference To all faiths,   „ III iv 223

Smiles that burn *men*.   „ III iv 404

Men now are bow'd and old, the doctors tell you,   „ III iv 408

One of those wicked wilfuls that *men* make,   „ III v 75

Manners   and those bleak *m* thaw,   *Queen Mary* III ii 161
like his cloak, his *m* want the nap And gloss of
court ;   „   III v 69
Am I to change my *m*, Simon Renard,   „   III vi 151
How beautiful His *m* are, and how unlike the
farmer's !   *Prom. of May* II 531
so that you do not copy his bad *m* ?   „   III 362
M be so corrupt, and these are the days of Prince John.   *Foresters* I i 176
Manor   since we would be lord of our own *m*,   *Becket* II ii 20
They slew my stags in mine own *m* here,   „   v ii 438
Man-Robin   If my *m-R* were but a bird-Robin,   *Foresters* III 39
Mansfield   I have heard 'em in the market at M.   „   III 407
Mantle   Flung by the golden *m* of the cloud,   „   II i 28
Many   Thro' *m* voices crying right and left,   *Queen Mary* I ii 48
The downfall of so *m* simple souls,   „   I ii 54
for the two were fellow-prisoners So *m* years in yon
accursed Tower—   „   I iv 200
there were *m* wolves among you Who dragg'd the
scatter'd limbs   „   I v 399
For tho' we touch'd at *m* pirate ports,   *Foresters* IV 983
Many-breasted   The *m-b* mother Artemis Emboss'd upon it. *The Cup* II 340
Map   (*See also* **Walter Map**)   That *M*, and these new railers
at the Church   *Becket* I i 306
M scoffs at Rome.   I all but hold with *M*.   „   II ii 384
M, tho' you make your butt too big, you overshoot it.   „   III iii 121
False figure, *M* would say.   „   III iii 346
Mar   as one That *m's* a cause with over-violence.   „   IV ii 327
Marah   this bitter world again—These wells of *M*.   „   v ii 82
Marble (adj.)   have you not mark'd Her eyes were ever on
the *m* floor ?   *The Cup* II 19
Marble (s)   Vein'd *m*—not a furrow yet—   *Becket* II i 197
wine Ran down the *m* and lookt like blood,   *The Cup* II 204
Iron will fuse, and *m* melt ;   *Prom. of May* II 505
This is mere *m*.   Old hag, how should thy one tooth   *Foresters* I i 275
March   may not those, who *m* Before their age,   *Prom. of May* II 632
Marchpane   You gentles that live upo' manchet-bread
and *m*,   *Foresters* II 282
Margery   I hear *M* : I'll go play with her.   *Becket* II i 274
M ? no, that's a finer thing there.   How it glitters !   „   IV i 1
I sent this *M*, and she comes not back ;   „   IV ii 3
You said you couldn't trust *M*,   „   IV ii 16
Maria   Ave *M*, gratia plena, Benedicta tu in mulieribus. *Queen Mary* III ii 1
Marian (daughter of Sir Richard Lea)   (*See also* **Maid Marian**)
These roses for my Lady *M* ;   *Foresters* I i 2
Sir Richard and my Lady *M* fare wellnigh as sparely as
their people.   „   I i 30
Lady *M* holds her nose when she steps across it.   „   I i 83
M !   *Marian*.   Father !   „   I i 179
Lady *M*, your woman so flustered me that I forgot   „   I i 295
My Lady *M* you can make it so If you will deign   „   I ii 130
Leaving your fair *M* alone here.   „   I ii 154
I promise thee to make this *M* thine.   „   I ii 183
Farewell, Sir Richard ; farewell, sweet *M*.   „   I ii 285
thou art the very woman who waits On my dear *M*.   „   II i 103
She struck him, my brave *M*, struck the Prince,   „   II i 134
Sheriff Would pay this cursed mortgage to his brother If
M would marry him ;   „   II i 146
—if so the land may come To *M*,   „   II i 149
Thou wilt not see My *M* more.   „   II i 456
Give me some news of my sweet *M*.   Where is she ?
Marian.   Thy sweet *M* ?   I believe She came with me   „   II i 481
O thou unworthy brother of my dear *M* !   „   II i 539
O my dear *M*, Is it thou, is it thou ?   „   II i 597
O hold thy hand ! this is our *M*.   „   II ii 37
You shall wed your *M*.   She is true, and you are true,   „   II ii 193
honouring all womankind, and more especially my lady *M*,   „   III 57
thou feel'st with me The ghost returns to *M*,   „   III 115
M, thou and thy woman, Why, where is Kate ?   „   III 257
Honour to thee, brave *M*, and thy Kate.   „   III 300
And they shall pledge thee, *M*,   „   III 316
M !   *Marian*.   Speak not.   „   IV 609
Sweet *M*, by the letter of the law It seems   „   IV 638
would clutch Our pretty *M* for his paramour,   „   IV 767
On those two here, Robin and *M*.   „   IV 929
Kiss him, Sir Richard—kiss him, my sweet *M*.   „   IV 1004

Marian (daughter of Sir Richard Lea) (*continued*)   Embrace
me, *M*, and thou, good Kate,   *Foresters* IV 1031
these old oaks will murmur thee *M* along with Robin.   „   IV 1095
Maries   in his scared prayers Heaven and earth's *M* ; *Queen Mary* II ii 88
Mark (an object)   (*See also* **Sea-marks**)   Wide of the
m ev'n for a madman's dream.   „   v iii 81
Mark (coin)   the King demands three hundred *m's*,   *Becket* I iii 627
the King demands seven hundred *m's*,   „   I iii 635
the King demands five hundred *m's*,   „   I iii 642
Some thirty—forty thousand silver *m's*.   „   I iii 658
What ! forty thousand *m's* !   „   I iii 704
Forty thousand *m's* ! forty thousand devils—   „   I iv 90
ransomed for two thousand *m's* in gold.   *Foresters* I i 65
Those two thousand *m's* lent me by the Abbot   „   I i 354
I ran into my debt to the Abbot, Two thousand *m's* in gold. „   II i 464
These two have forty gold *m's* between them, Robin.   „   III 203
Leave it with him and add a gold *m* thereto.   „   III 211
Take his penny and leave him his gold *m*.   „   III 218
I have one *m* in gold which a pious son of the Church   „   III 280
Well, as he said, one *m* in gold.   „   III 285
One *m* in gold.   „   III 287
they have each ten *m's* in gold.   „   III 292
take the twenty-seven *m's* to the captain's treasury.   „   III 295
How much is it, Robin, for a knight ?   *Robin*.   A *m*.   „   IV 153
I had one *m*.   *Robin*.   What more.   „   IV 165
Where he would pay us down his thousand *m's*.   „   IV 442
Lest he should fail to pay these thousand *m's*   „   IV 455
What more ? one thousand *m's*, Or else the land.   „   IV 474
Here be one thousand *m's* Out of our treasury   „   IV 492
Ay, ay, but there is use, four hundred *m's*.   *Robin*.
There then, four hundred *m's*.   „   IV 496
my tongue tript—five hundred *m's* for use.   „   IV 499
Would buy me for a thousand *m's* in gold—   „   IV 652
Much lighter than a thousand *m's* in gold ;   „   IV 657
Is weightier than a thousand *m's* in gold.   „   IV 660
Thou art worth thy weight in all those *m's* of gold,   „   IV 1024
Mark (impression)   Lord hath set his *m* upon him that no
man should murder him.   *Becket* I iv 192
but he left the *m* of 'is foot i' the flower-bed ;   *Prom. of May* I 408
I measured his foot wi' the *m* i' the bed, but it
wouldn't fit—seeäms to me the *m* wur maäde
by a Lunnun boot.   „   I 414
Mark (verb)   I'll have one *m* it And bring it me.   *Queen Mary* I v 372
no man need ; but did you *m* our Queen ?   „   II ii 320
I was too sorry for the *m* in the dress.   „   III i 59
said the Miserere Mei—But all in English, *m* you ;   „   III i 392
Nor *m* the sea-bird rouse himself and hover   *Harold* II ii 334
hereafter Shall *m* out Vice from Virtue   *Prom. of May* I 540
Mark'd   Had *m* her for my brother Edward's bride ;   *Queen Mary* I v 289
have *m* the haughtiness of their nobles ;   „   II ii 168
And *m* me ev'n as Cain.   „   II ii 55
I stood near—*M* him ?   „   IV iii 618
Hast thou not *m*—come closer to mine ear—   „   v 225
if your Grace hath *m* it, so have I.   *Philip*.   Hast
thou not likewise *m* Elizabeth,   „   v 231
That if your Grace hath *m* her, so have I.   „   v 239
m the sons of those Who made this Britain England,   *Harold* IV iii 152
M how the war-axe swang,   „   IV iii 156
M how the spear-head sprang,   „   IV iii 158
This chart here *m* ' Her Bower,'   *Becket*, Pro. 160
I *m* a group of lazars in the marketplace—   „   I iv 80
m Her eyes were ever on the marble floor ?   *The Cup* II 18
Ay, ay, the line o' life is *m* enow ;   *Foresters* I i 352
They are all *m* men.   „   III 290
What deer when I have *m* him ever yet Escaped
mine arrow ?   „   IV 63
m if those two knaves from York be coming ?   „   IV 112
Market   And your worship's name heard into
Maidstone *m*,   *Queen Mary* II i 63
men are at their *m's*, in their fields,   *Harold* II ii 436
have won Their value again—beyond all *m's*—   *The Falcon* 905
I have heard 'em in the *m* at Mansfield.   *Foresters* III 407
Marketplace   I marked a group of lazars in the *m*—   *Becket* I iv 81
Marriage (adj.)   While this same *m* question was being
argued,   *Queen Mary* II ii 37

Marriage (adj.) *(continued)* tore away My *m* ring, and rent
  my bridal veil ; — Harold I ii 80
I am his wife ! and she—For look, our *m* ring ! — „ v ii 108
herself should see That kings are faithful to their *m*
  vow. — Becket I ii 78
the *m* cup Wherefrom we make libation to the
  Goddess — The Cup II 198
Go on with the *m* rites. (repeat) — „ II 399, 421

Marriage (s) (*See also* **After-marriage, First-marriage**)
Have sworn this Spanish *m* shall not be. — Queen Mary I iv 115
side with you and him Against her *m* ; — „ I iv 160
Because they think me favourer of this *m*. — „ I v 157
Feigning to treat with him about her *m*— — „ II ii 34
this *m* is the least Of all their quarrel. — „ II ii 154
As to this *m*, ye shall understand — „ II ii 202
This *m* had the assent of those to whom — „ II ii 206
This *m* should bring loss or danger to you, — „ II ii 227
Moreover, if this *m* should not seem, — „ II ii 232
whether It beats hard at this *m*. — „ III i 39
I may be wrong, sir. This *m* will not hold. — „ III i 103
with all of us Against this foreign *m*, — „ III iii 7
forfeited her right to reign By *m* with an alien— — „ v i 291
My sister's *m*, and my father's *m*'s, — „ v iii 96
That *m* was half sin. — Harold I ii 53
a peace-offering, A scape-goat *m*— — „ I i 204
and our *m* and thy glory Been drunk together ! — „ IV iii 8
I fain Had made my *m* not a lie ; — „ v i 320
for *m*, rose or no rose, has killed the golden violet. — Becket, Pro. 350
it is the cup we use in our *m*'s. — The Cup I i 44
sends you this cup—the cup we use in our *m*'s— — „ I ii 73
Throne him—and then the *m*—ay and tell him — „ II 156
I have no fears at this my second *m*. — „ II 209
Entreats he may be present at our *m*. — „ II 249
—make me happy in my *m* ! — „ II 275
To make my *m* prosper to my wish ! — „ II 308
In honour of his gift and of our *m*, — „ II 351
Bring me The costly wines we use in *m*'s. — „ II 365
Drink and drink deep—our *m* will be fruitful. — „ II 380
they are made by the blessed saints—these *m*'s. *Lady*
  Giovanna. *M*'s ? I shall never marry again ! — The Falcon 203
She will urge *m* on me. I hate tears. *M* is but
  an old tradition. — Prom. of May I 489
M ! That fine, fat, hook-nosed uncle of mine, — „ I 508
oust me from his will, if I Made such a *m*. And *m*
  in itself— — „ I 515
traditions, customs, *m* One of the feeblest ! — „ I 520
I have no thought of *m*, my friend. — „ II 65
which is my dream of a true *m*. — „ III 179
I had once a vision of a pure and perfect *m*, — „ III 189
Has he offered you *m*, this gentleman ? — „ III 290
are you quite sure that after *m* — „ III 293
he gave me no address, and there was no word of *m* ; — „ III 333
If *m* ever brought a woman happiness — „ III 639
an' wants To hev a word wi' ye about the *m*. *Harold.*
  The what ? *Milly*. The *m*. *Harold*. The *m* ?
  Milly. Yeäs, the *m*. Granny says *m*'s be maäde
  i' 'eaven. — „ III 704
Robin, I will not kiss thee, For that belongs to *m* ; — Foresters III 138
Join them and they are a true *m* ; — „ IV 421
M if of the soul, not of the body. — „ IV 720

Marriage-banquet Answer them thou ! Is this our *m-b* ? — Harold IV iii 5
Marriage-garland the *m-g* withers ever with the putting
  on, — Becket, Pro. 359
Marriage-morn For so methought it was our *m-m*, — Harold I ii 76
Married *m* The mother of Elizabeth— — Queen Mary I v 31
Mary of Scotland, *m* to your Dauphin, — „ I v 295
It was a sin to love her *m*, — „ III i 339
Before my father *m* my good mother,— — „ III v 245
The Queen of Scots is *m* to the Dauphin, — „ v v 52
I *m* her for Morcar—a sin against The truth of love. — Harold v i 169
only you know the King's *m*, for King Louis——
  Rosamund. *M* ! — Becket III i 167
Do you believe that you are *m* to him ? (repeat) — „ IV ii 46, 54
Will you not say you are not *m* to him ? — „ IV ii 109
m Since—*m* Sinnatus, the Tetrarch here— — The Cup I i 15

Married (*continued*) I envied Sinnatus when he *m* her. — The Cup I i 130
cloudless heaven which we have found together In our
  three *m* years ! — „ I ii 417
In symbol of their *m* unity, — „ II 363
Why should I ? I am not to be *m*. — „ II 370
That was the very year before you *m*. *Lady Giovanna.*
  When I was *m* you were at the wars. — The Falcon 374
to go on together again, till one of us be *m*. — Prom. of May I 776
And your sweetheart—when are you and he to be
  m ? — „ III 111
I am sure that when we are *m* he will be willing — „ III 260
said that whenever I *m* he would give me away, — Foresters I i 288
Marrow And drains the heart and *m* from a man. — „ II i 672
Marry council and all her people wish her to *m*. — Queen Mary I i 113
some say, That you shall *m* him, — „ I iv 212
Would I *m* Prince Philip, if all England hate him ? — „ I v 138
Madam, take it bluntly ; *m* Philip, — „ I v 205
That you may *m* Philip, Prince of Spain— — „ I v 251
if we *m*, we shall still maintain All former treaties — „ I v 265
If this man *m* our Queen, — „ II i 170
never Consent thereto, nor *m* while I live ; — „ II ii 231
To sing, love, *m*, churn, brew, bake, and die, — „ III v 111
I think I will not *m* anyone, — „ III v 239
To *m* and have no husband Makes the wife fool. — Harold II ii 309
' *M*, the Saints must go along with us, — „ II ii 365
The King hath cursed him, if he *m* me ; The Pope
  hath cursed him, *m* me or no ! — „ III i 190
Wilt thou go with him ? he will *m* thee. — Becket I ii 162
arms of her first love, Fitzurse, Who swore to *m* her. — „ IV ii 336
Hath she made up her mind to *m* him ? *Priestess.*
  To *m* him who stabb'd her Sinnatus. — The Cup II 22
You will not *m* Synorix ? — „ II 27
I am the bride of Death, and only *M* the dead. — „ II 30
You mean to *m* him ? *Camma*. I mean to *m* him— — „ II 60
He wills you then this day to *m* him, — „ II 66
I am sure you will not *m* him. — „ II 105
but he knew I meant to *m* him. — The Falcon 51
Marriages ? I shall never *m* again ! — „ 205
To *m* him ?—I can never *m* him. — „ 248
but be sure That I shall never *m* again, — „ 742
he would *m* me to the richest man In Florence ; — „ 747
Philip, if you do not *m* me, — Prom. of May I 681
grant you what they call a license To *m*. — „ I 696
Thy feyther eddicated his darters to *m* gentlefoälk, — „ II 116
Farmer Dobson, were I to *m* him, has promised — „ III 169
and prattled to each other that we would *m* fine
  gentlemen, — „ III 277
I eddicated boäth on 'em to *m* gentlemen, — „ III 455
asking his consent—you wish'd me—That we
  should *m* ; — „ III 495
thou shouldst *m* one who will pay the mortgage. — Foresters I i 280
mortgage to his brother If Marian would *m* him ; — „ II i 146
and who *marries* her *Marries* the land. — „ II i 152
That such a brother—she *m* the Sheriff ! — „ II i 550
Thou shalt not *m* The Sheriff, but abide with me who
  love thee. — „ II i 601
She will not *m* till her father yield. — „ II ii 82
—and she will not *m* till Richard come, — „ II ii 84
Father, I cannot *m* till Richard comes. — „ IV 648
and she will not *m* till Richard come. — „ IV 773
Thou wouldst *m* This Sheriff when King Richard came — „ IV 861
If you would *m* me with a traitor sheriff, — „ IV 875
Marrying (*See also* **Anti-marrying**) your Scottish
  namesake *m* The Dauphin, — Queen Mary v i 134
from the sons of Alfgar By such a *m* ? — Harold I ii 182
Art thou—still bent—on *m* ? — The Cup II 324
Who thought to buy your *m* me with gold. — Foresters IV 718
if the King forbid thy *m* With Robin. — Harold III i 380
Marsh dreadful lights crept up from out the *m*— — „
Martyr (s) Old Rome, that first made *m*'s in the
  Church, — Queen Mary III iv 126
' *M*'s blood—seed of the Church.' — „ IV i 146
so past martyr-like—*M* I may not call him— — „ v iii 625
I am *m* in myself already.—Herbert ! — Becket I i 362
Who will be *m* when he might escape. — „ v ii 279

Master (*continued*) You, *M* Hedgar, Harold, or what-
    iver They calls ye,   *Prom. of May* III 726
The lady loved the *m* well,   *Foresters* I i 8
My *m*, Robin the Earl, is always a-telling us   „   I i 94
I would hoist the drawbridge, like thy *m*.   „   I i 319
I am a virgin, my *m's*, I am a virgin. *Much.* And
    a virgin, my *m's*, three yards about the waist   „   I ii 67
My *m's*, welcome gallant Walter Lea.   „   IV 1002
Strike up a stave, my *m's*, all is well.   „   IV 1101
Master'd old affection *m* you, You falter'd into tears.   *Becket* V ii 143
Mastiff (adj.) as a *m* dog May love a puppy cur for no
    more reason   *Queen Mary* I iv 194
Mastiff (s) Our savage *m*, That all but kill'd the
    beggar,   *Prom. of May* I 558
Match (an equal) Thou and thy woman are a *m* for three
    friars.   *Foresters* III 262
Match (marriage) But is Don Carlos such a goodly *m*?   *Queen Mary* V iii 86
That was, my lord, a *m* of policy.   *Harold* IV i 199
thy *m* shall follow mine.   *Foresters* IV 1044
Match (verb) If such a one as you should *m* with
    Spain,   *Queen Mary* V iii 66
Match'd You do misname me, *m* with any such,   *Becket* IV ii 128
    and *m* with my Harold is like a hedge thistle by
    a garden rose.   *Prom. of May* III 175
Mate (s) (*See also* **Co-mate, Maäte**) News, *m's*! a
    miracle, a miracle !   *Queen Mary* III ii 209
Mad for thy *m*, passionate nightingale . . .   *Harold* I ii 1
They are not so true, They change their *m's*.   „   III ii 105
he frown'd ' No *m* for her, if it should come to that '—   *Becket* III i 259
I would thou hadst a *m* !   *The Falcon* 17
Mate (verb) Let York bear his to *m* with Canterbury.   *Becket* I i 512
Not half *her* hand—no hand to *m* with *her*,   „   II i 190
As *m* with one that holds no love is pure,   *Foresters* IV 711
Mated *See* **Maäted**
Mater Salva patriam, Sancta *M*.   *Harold* V i 471
Matilda (or Maud, daughter of Henry I.) So did *M*, the
    King's mother.   *Becket* I iii 152
Matter (s) stir not yet This *m* of the Church lands.   *Queen Mary* I v 409
I scarce have heart to mingle in this *m*,   „   II i 114
These are forgiven—*m's* of the past—   „   III iii 190
might it not be policy in some *m* Of small importance   „   III vi 167
And if you be not secret in this *m*,   „   I 272
That were too small a *m* for a comet !   *Harold* I i 470
No *m* ! *Aldwyth.* How no *m*, Harold slain ?—   „   V ii 17
No *m* ! *Aldwyth.* Not help me,   „   V ii 23
my mind was set upon other *m's*. *Eleanor.* What
    m's ? State *m's* ? love *m's* ?   *Becket, Pro.* 318
and the *m* in the metre.   „   *Pro.* 384
that secret *m* which would heat the King against thee.   „   *Pro.* 487
And on a *m* wholly spiritual.   „   I iii 85
You have had the better of us In secular *m's*.   „   II ii 81
I have been more for the King than the Church in
    this *m*—   „   III iii 66
it was but the sacrifice of a kingdom to his son, a
    smaller *m* ;   „   III iii 107
This is no secret, but a public *m*.   „   xi 320
No *m* ! see your cloth be white as snow !   *The Falcon* 498
A moment for some *m* of no moment !   *Foresters* II i 474
Matter (verb) No, no ; what *m's* ? Forlorn I am,   *Queen Mary* V ii 237
What *m's* how I look ?   *Harold* I v 394
That doth not *m* either.   „   V ii 62
What *m's* ? Royal—I mean to leave the royalty   *Becket* I i 106
That's not. Take thou this cup and leave it   *The Cup* I i 66
Savage, is he ? What *m's* ?   *Prom. of May* I 563
Maurice (*See also* **Maurice Berkeley**) told Sir *M* there
    was one Cognisant of this,   *Queen Mary* II iv 99
Maurice Berkeley there by Sir *M B* Was taken
    prisoner.   „   II iv 94
Mavis Hawk, buzzard, jay, the *m* and the merle,   *Foresters* I iii 115
May Ay, for an hour in *M*. But court is always *M*,
    buds out in masques,   *Queen Mary* III v 10
which a breeze of *M* Took ever and anon,   *The Cup* I ii 406
Richer than all the wide world-wealth of *M*,   *The Falcon* 467
O joy for the promise of *M*, of *M*, O joy for the
    promise of *M*. (repeat)   *Prom. of May* I 43, 723

May (*continued*) O grief for the promise of *M*, of
    M, O grief for the promise of *M*. (repeat)   *Prom. of May* I 59, 750
most beautiful *M* we have had for many years !   „   I 567
Is the most beautiful morning of this *M*.   „   I 570
you make The *M* and morning still more beautiful,
    You, the most beautiful blossom of the *M*.   „   I 573
So lovely in the promise of her *M*,   „   III 753
Maybe *See* **Mebbe**
May-morning and kiss me This beautiful *M-m*.   *Prom. of May* I 565
Mayn't and she *m* be so fur out theer.   „   I 181
Mayor All hangs on her address, And upon you, Lord *M*.   *Queen Mary* II ii 56
I, the Lord *M*, and these our companies And guilds   „   II ii 127
I, Lord *M* Of London, and our guilds and companies.   „   II ii 139
tho' my Lord *M* here, By his own rule,   „   II ii 345
May-time It was *M-t*, And I was walking   „   V v 87
or a stump-tailed ox in *M-t*,   *Foresters* II i 435
Maze This labyrinthine brickwork *m* in *m*,   *Becket, Pro.* 166
Mazed *See* **Maäzed**
Meadow (*See also* **Midder, Mountain-meadow**) there
    stole into the city a breath Full of the *m's*,   *Becket* I i 263
With other beauties on a mountain *m*,   *The Falcon* 352
I have lost a cow from my *m*.   *Foresters* II i 326
Meadowsweet Forget-me-not, *m*, willow-herb.   *Prom. of May* II 299
Meal (ground corn) so dusted his back with the *m* in
    his sack,   *Becket* I iv 174
M enough, meat enough, well fed ;   *The Falcon* 165
Meal (repast) make Thy slender *m* out of those scraps
    and shreds   „   146
Mean That's a hard word, legitimate ; what does it
    m ? *Second Citizen.* It *m's* a bastard. *Third
    Citizen.* Nay, it *m's* true-born.   *Queen Mary* I i 12
I *m* the Lady Elizabeth.   „   I i 74
boast that after all She *m's* to wed you.   „   I iv 89
she *m's* to counsel your withdrawing To Ashridge,   „   I iv 224
she *m's* to make A farewell present to your Grace.   „   I iv 243
they *m* to pardon me.   „   IV ii 50
I *m* not like to live.   „   V i 245
Do you *m* to drive me mad ?   „   V ii 200
Gamel, son of Orm, What thinkest thou this *m's*?
    (repeat)   *Harold* I i 21, 464
m The doom of England and the wrath of Heaven ?   „   I i 45
And cannot answer sanely . . . What it *m's* ?   „   I i 89
It *m's* the fall of Tostig from his earldom.   „   I i 468
It *m's* the lifting of the house of Alfgar.   „   I i 472
What did he *m* ?   „   II ii 223
He did not *m* to keep his vow. *Harold.* Not *m*
    To make our England Norman.   „   III i 248
Morcar ! Edwin ! What do they *m* ?   „   IV i 134
Look you, we never *m* to part again.   „   V ii 80
I have heard him say He *m's* no more ;   *Becket* I iii 193
sworn upon his side, And ever *m* to do it.   „   III i 466
What is it you *m* ? *Margery.* I *m* your goodman,   „   III i 157
I *m* her whom you call—fancy—   „   III i 201
Meän'd (meant) I *m* they be as blue as violets.   *Prom. of May* I 103
Meaner Then left him for the *m* ! thee !—   *Harold* IV ii 71
Meanest Ev'n to the least and *m* of my own,   *Becket* II ii 181
Meaning might chance—perchance—To guess their *m*.
    Morcar. Thine own *m*, Harold, To make all
    England one,   *Harold* IV i 139
I know Thy *m*. Perish she, I, all,   *Becket* III iii 19
And smiles at my best *m's*,   *Foresters* IV 727
Means stakes high ? *Noailles.* But not beyond
    your *m*.   *Queen Mary* I iii 147
That by your gracious *m* and intercession   „   III iii 121
These are the *m* God works with,   „   III vi 68
My liberality perforce is dead Thro' lack of *m* of giving.   *The Falcon* 297
How hadst thou then the *m* to buy a cow ?   *Foresters* II i 303
Meant (*See also* **Meän'd**) I *m* True matters of the
    heart.   *Queen Mary* I iv 99
Elizabeth—To Philibert of Savoy, as you know,
    We *m* to wed her ;   „   V i 248
Thou knowest never woman *m* so well,   „   V ii 342
Said ' ay ' when I *m* ' no,' lied like a lad   *Harold* II ii 656
He *m* no harm nor damage to the Church.   *Becket* I iii 216
I had *m* to make him all but king.   „   I iii 464

Meant (*continued*) I never *m* you harm in any way.   *Becket* IV ii 106
Not if you *m* it, I am sure.   „ IV ii 184
I *m* thee to have follow'd—better thus.   *The Cup* II 498
but he knew I *m* to marry him.   *The Falcon* 51
Why? because I *m* it!—   *Prom. of May* III 365
Measure (s) (*See also* **Over-measure**) still All within
    m—nay,   *Queen Mary* I v 436
They have brought it in large *m* on themselves.   „ IV iii 363
And he is with you in a *m* still.   „ v v 27
but belike Thou hast not learnt his *m*.   *Harold* IV iii 118
I thinks I'd like to taäke the *m* o' your foot.   *Prom. of May* I 464
If you will deign to tread a *m* with me.   *Foresters* I ii 132
Measure (verb) if you'd like to *m* your own length
    upon the grass.   *Prom. of May* I 465
Measured an' I *m* his foot wi' the mark i' the bed,   „ I 413
Meat owld lord fell to 's *m* wi' a will, God bless un !   *Queen Mary* IV iii 514
I have been a lover of wines, and delicate *m's*,   *Becket* I i 77
King's *m* ! By the Lord,   „ I iv 140
And take a hunter's vengeance on the *m's*   *The Cup* I ii 44
Meal enough, *m* enough, well fed ;   *The Falcon* 165
each of 'em as full of *m* as an egg.   *Foresters* I i 42
Mebbe (maybe) the fault, *m*, wur as much mine as yours ;   *Prom. of May* I 325
and Parson *m*, thaw he niver mended that gap   „ I 445
Meddle I'll not *m* wi' 'im if he doänt *m* wi' meä.   „ I 173
I promised one of the Misses I wouldn't *m* wi' ye,   „ I 470
She telled me once not to *m* wi' 'im,   „ II 599
Medicine I have a wholesome *m* here Puts that belief
    asleep.   *Becket* IV ii 50
It has been much commended as a *m*.   *The Falcon* 588
Meditate so to *m* Upon my greater nearness   *Foresters* I i 43
Medway (river) green field Beside the brimming *M*,   *Queen Mary* II i 244
Meek yet so *m*, so modest, So wife-like humble   „ III i 362
Ah, weak and *m* old man,   „ v v 131
Meet When do you *m* ? *Noailles.* To-night.   „ I iii 154
these shall *m* upon St. Andrew's day.   „ III ii 125
It was not *m* heretic swine should live In Lambeth.   „ III ii 134
We *m* at Brussels.   „ III vi 214
why my friend Should *m* with a lesser mercy   „ IV i 70
you scarce could *m* his eye And hold your own ;   „ IV i 104
Count-crab will make his nippers *m* in thine heart ;   *Harold* I i 76
shall they *m* In private ?   „ II ii 87
fears that these may act On Harold when they *m*.
    William. Then let them *m* !   „ II ii 92
To *m* thee in the North.   „ v i 290
O Harold ! husband ! Shall we *m* again ?   „ v i 361
I have had it fashion'd, see, to *m* my hand.   „ v i 422
And no David To *m* him ?   „ v i 497
The horse and horseman cannot *m* the shield,   „ v i 591
Where I shall *m* the Barons and my King.   *Becket* I ii 84
—And to *m* it I needs must leave as suddenly.   „ III i 91
And so farewell until we *m* in England. *Becket.* I
    fear, my liege, we may not *m* in England.   „ III iii 237
Strike ! I challenge thee to *m* me before God.   „ IV ii 254
bow'd herself to *m* the wave Of humiliation,   „ IV ii 388
But he and he must never *m* again.   „ IV ii 425
I go to *m* my King ! *Grim.* To *m* the King ?   „ v ii 620
I will go out and *m* them.   „ v iii 52
shun To *m* her face to face at once !   *The Cup* I i 59
When first he *m's* his maiden in a bower.   „ I iii 41
walk with me we needs must *m* Antonius coming,   „ I iii 92
I will go To *m* him, crown'd !   „ II 519
Why comes he not to *m* ?   „ II 528
Still I am half-afraid to *m* her now.   *Prom. of May* I 488
Keep up your heart until we *m* again.   „ I 754
If that should break before we *m* again ?   „ I 756
and he trusted that some time we should *m* again,   „ III 329
If ever I *m* thee there, I will break thy sconce   *Foresters* I ii 74
they can *m* upon anything thro' a millstone.   „ II ii 280
I will not *m* him yet, I'll watch him   „ III 47
Thou told'st us we should *m* him in the forest,   „ IV 439
I cannot *m* his eyes.   „ IV 799
Meeting (part) Gardiner, coming with the Queen,
    And *m* Pembroke,   *Queen Mary* II ii 310
Meeting (s) When theer wur a *m* o' farmers at Little-
    chester t'other daäy,   *Prom. of May* I 137

Melancholy Fine eyes—but *m*, irresolute—   *Queen Mary* III iv 337
Mellow and as sleek and as round-about as a *m* codlin.   *Foresters* I i 43
Melt Till doomsday *m* it.   *Queen Mary* III v 51
may strike fire from her, Not hope to *m* her.   „ III vi 40
Iron will fuse, and marble *m* ;   *Prom. of May* II 505
Who *m's* a waxen image by the fire,   *Foresters* II i 671
Memorial wear it as *m* of a morning   *Queen Mary* I v 529
Memory This *m* to thee !—and this to England,   *Harold* v i 326
My *m* is as dead.   *The Falcon* 524
drove me From out her *m*.   *Prom. of May* II 405
We leave but happy *memories* to the forest.   *Foresters* IV 1070
Menace if Philip *m* me, I think that I will play   *Queen Mary* III vi 241
Menaced whereupon I *m* her with this,   *Becket* IV ii 348
Men-at-arms *m-a-a* Guard my poor dreams for
    England.   *Queen Mary* I v 152
I would set my *m-a-a* to oppose thee,   *Foresters* I i 323
and there be *m-a-a* to guard her.   „ I ii 158
Mended he niver *m* that gap i' the glebe fence as I
    tell'd 'im ;   *Prom. of May* I 446
Mene *M, M,* Tekel ! Is thy wrath Hell,   *Harold* v i 35
Mention (s) hang On the chance *m* of some fool   *Queen Mary* III v 43
Make thou not *m* that I spake with thee.   *Harold* II ii 483
Mention (verb) I never heard her *m* you.   *Prom. of May* II 395
An' we weänt *m* naw naämes,   „ III 129
You, how dare you *m* kisses ?   *Foresters* II i 127
Mentioned You haven't even *m* him in your last ?   *Prom. of May* I 778
you *m* her name too suddenly before my father.   „ II 23
And if she never *m* me,   „ II 400
Mercenary one of those *mercenaries* that suck the blood
    of England.   *Foresters* II i 174
Strike, Sheriff ! Strike, *m* !   „ II i 416
Prince John, the Sheriff, and a *m*.   „ II i 446
Is coming with a swarm of *mercenaries*   „ III 452
follow'd by Prince John And all his *mercenaries* !   „ IV 589
Merchant raise us loans and subsidies Among the *m's* ;   *Queen Mary* v i 180
To this son of a London *m*—   *Becket*, Pro. 434
Thomas, son Of Gilbert Becket, London *m*.   „ II ii 231
Mercians Earl of the *M* ! if the truth be gall,   *Harold* IV 14
Merciful It were more *m* to burn him now.   *Queen Mary* IV i 153
O God, For thou art *m*, refusing none   „ IV iii 131
Your Grace hath been More *m* to many a rebel head   „ v ii 5
Mercy Yet too much *m* is a want of *m*,   „ I v 505
He by His *m* absolve you !   „ III iii 208
to cast myself Upon the good Queen's *m* ;   „ III v 168
M, that herb-of-grace, Flowers now but seldom.   „ III vi 9
To reach the hand of *m* to my friend.   „ IV i 65
why my friend Should meet with lesser *m* than myself ?   „ IV i 70
God grant you ampler *m* at your call   „ IV i 189
Will they have *m* on me ? *Villa Garcia.* Have
    you good hopes of *m* ! So, farewell.   „ IV ii 84
Three persons and one God, have *m* on me,   „ IV iii 121
For thy great *m* have *m* !   „ IV iii 137
Thy *m* must be greater than all sin.   „ IV iii 151
Why then to heaven, and God ha' *m* on him.   „ IV iii 632
Have you found *m* there, Grant it me here :   „ v v 144
Ay, Madam, but o' God's *m*—   „ v v 166
allegiance in thy Lord's And crave his *m*,   *Harold* v i 12
Have *m* on us ! (repeat)   *Harold* v i 501, 611, 643, 645
The child . . . No . . . *m* ! No !   *Becket* IV ii 186
M, m, As you would hope for *m*.   „ v iii 175
When you have charm'd our general into *m*,   *The Cup* I ii 312
a Sister of *M*, come from the death-bed of a
    pauper.   *Prom. of May* III 376
Mere (adj.) *M* compliments and wishes.   *Queen Mary* v ii 596
The *m* wild-beast !   *Prom. of May* II 736
This is *m* marble.   *Foresters* II i 275
A shadow, a poetical fiction—did ye not call me king
    in your song ?—a *m* figure.   „ IV 221
Mere (s) The brows unwrinkled as a summer *m*.—   *Harold* III i 49
A summer *m* with sudden wreckful gusts   „ III i 50
Merit (s) Forgive me, Father, for no *m* of mine,   *Queen Mary* IV iii 152
Merit (verb) and that *m's* death—False oath on holy
    cross—   *Becket* IV ii 207
Merle Hawk, buzzard, jay, the mavis and the *m*,   *Foresters* I iii 116
Merriest beyond The *m* murmurs of their banquet clank   *Harold* II ii 408

Merriment   Breaks into feather'd *m's*,   *Queen Mary* III v 13
   in the end we flourished out into a *m*;   *Becket* III iii 138
Merry   Be *m*! yet, Sir Ralph, you look but sad.   *Queen Mary* II ii 358
   But then he looks so *m*.   ,,   III i 203
   Heretic and rebel Point at me and make *m*.   ,,   v ii 318
   It was never *m* world In England, since the Bible came among us.   ,,   v v 240
   It never will be *m* world in England,   ,,   v v 246
   Thou hast misread this *m* dream of thine,   *Harold* I ii 98
   To-night we will be *m*. (repeat)   *Harold* II ii 768, 771
   Feed, feast, and be *m*.   *Becket* I iv 152
   let us be *m* to-night at the banquet.   *Foresters* I i 344
   I am only *m* for an hour or two Upon a birthday: ,,   I iii 11
   why should we make us *m* Because a year of it is gone?   ,,   I iii 14
   There be good fellows there in *m* Sherwood That hold by Richard,   ,,   I iii 98
   'Love, love, love, love'—what *m* madness—listen!   ,,   III 42
   All the birds in *m* Sherwood sing and sing him home again.   ,,   IV 1109
Mesh   Tho' scarce at ease; for, save our *m'es* break,   *Harold* II ii 140
   The simple lobster-basket, and the *m*—   *Becket* II ii 298
Message   I do but bring the *m*, know no more.   *Queen Mary* I iv 228
   I will give your *m*.   ,,   III vi 41
   But shall I take some *m* from your Grace?   ,,   v ii 597
   we bring a *m* from the King Beyond the water;   *Becket* v iii 301
   Had you then No *m* with the cup?   *The Cup* I ii 68
   Well, Madam, I will give your *m* to him.   *The Falcon* 217
   that I forgot my *m* from the Earl.   *Foresters* I i 297
Messenger   and there are *m's* That go between us.   *Queen Mary* I iii 137
   I chanced upon the *m* Who brings that letter   ,,   I v 585
   Not thee, my son: some other *m*.   *Harold* I i 244
   —thou art but a *m* of William.   ,,   v 29
   I am the *m* of God, His Norman Daniel!   ,,   v 33
   The *m* from Synorix who waits Before the Temple?   *The Cup* II 37
   too rich a prize To trust with any *m*.   *The Falcon* 726
   It is a royal *m*, my lord: *Foresters* I i 52
   A worthy *m*! how should he help it?   ,,   I iii 85
Met   she *m* the Queen at Wanstead   *Queen Mary* I i 77
   hands Came from the crowd and *m* his own;   ,,   IV iii 583
   Thou hast rounded since we *m*.   *Harold* I i 95
   he and Wulfnoth never Have *m*, except in public;   ,,   II ii 86
   Look rather than all-royal as when first I *m* thee.   *Becket* I i 47
   I *m* a robber once, I told him I was bound   ,,   v ii 98
   'Tis long since we have *m*!   *The Falcon* 274
   never since have *m* Her equal for pure innocence   *Prom. of May* II 371
   I *m* her first at a farm in Cumberland—Her uncle's.   ,,   I 396
   he tells me that he *m* you once in the old times,   ,,   III 262
   I do believe I lost my heart to him the very first time we *m*,   ,,   III 284
   if *m* in a black lane at midnight: *Foresters* III 224
   He *m* a stag there on so narrow a ledge—   ,,   IV 531
Metal   to fuse Almost into one *m* love and hate,—   *Queen Mary* III vi 182
Meteor   These *m's* came and went before our day,   *Harold* I i 131
Methinks   and yet, *m*, I have seen goodlier.   *Queen Mary* I v 6
   Madam, *m* a cold face and a haughty.   ,,   I v 196
   m, A prince as naturally love his people   ,,   II ii 191
   M most men are but poor-hearted,   ,,   II ii 337
   M the good land heard me,   ,,   III ii 57
   M that under our Queen's regimen We might go   ,,   III iv 181
   And yet *m* he falters: ,,   III iv 398
   M that would you tarry one day more   ,,   III vi 232
   m my Queen is like enough To leave me by and by.   ,,   v i 241
   M there is no manhood left among us.   ,,   v ii 284
   m I love her less For such a dotage upon such a man.   ,,   v ii 420
   M I am all angel, that I bear it   ,,   v iii 3
   so *m*, my boy, Thy fears infect me beyond reason.   *Harold* II ii 450
   Better *m* have slain the man at once!   ,,   II ii 498
Methought   glance of some distaste, Or so *m*, return'd.   *Queen Mary* III i 101
Methusaleh   live as long as Jerusalem. *Eva. M*, father.   *Prom. of May* I 379
Metre   and the matter in the *m*.   *Becket, Pro.* 384
Metropolitan   He here, this heretic *m*,   *Queen Mary* IV iii 43
Mexico   The voices of Peru and *M*,   ,,   v i 47
Michaelmas   At *M*, Miss, please God.   *Prom. of May* III 112

Mid   strike, make his feathers Glance in *m* heaven.   *The Falcon* 16
Mid-battle   will you crown my foe My victor in *m-b*?   *Becket* v i 15G
Mid-day   Hang'd at *m-d*, their traitor of the dawn   *The Cup* II 123
Midder (meadow)   An' the *m's* all mow'd, an' the sky sa blue— (repeat)   *Prom. of May* II 176, 188, 200
Middle (adj.)   For, like a fool, thou knowest no *m* way.   *Becket* I iii 532
Middle (s)   in the *m* of that fierce fight At Stamfordbridge.   *Harold* IV iii 183
Midland   or wreck And dead beneath the *m* ocean,   *Foresters* II i 657
Midmost   As in the *m* heart of Paradise.   *The Cup* II 186
Midnight   I hardly gain'd The camp at *m*.   ,,   I iii 19
   dead *m* when I came upon the bridge;   *Prom. of May* III 368
   if met in a black lane at *m*:   *Foresters* III 224
Midriff-shaken   many *m-s* even to tears, as springs gush out after earthquakes.   *Becket* III iii 162
Mid-sea   whose quick flash splits The *m-s* mast,   *The Cup* II 293
Mid-summer   full *m-s* in those honest hearts.   *Becket* v ii 373
Midwinter   Yon gray old Gospeller, sour as *m*,   *Queen Mary* I iii 40
   'Tis known you are *m* to all women,   *Becket* I ii 27
   Save that it was *m-w* in the street,   ,,   v ii 372
Might (s)   'Thine is the right, for thine the *m*;   *Harold* II i 357
   William laugh'd and swore that *m* was right,   ,,   II ii 362
   Waste not thy *m* before the battle!   ,,   v i 415
Might (verb)   *See* **Mowt**
Mightier   but those of Normanland Are *m* than our own.   *Harold* III i 225
   The more the love, the *m* is the prayer;   ,,   III i 347
   that Tostig Conjured the *m* Harold from his North   ,,   IV ii 68
   Their giant-king, a *m* man-in-arms Than William.   ,,   v i 399
   But we must have a *m* man For his successor.   *Becket, Pro.* 6
   Thou art the man—be thou A *m* Anselm.   ,,   I i 134
   'Fore God, I am a *m* man than thou.   ,,   I i 223
   We find that it is *m* than it seems—   ,,   IV ii 263
   I think they will be *m* than the king.   *Foresters* I ii 119
Mightiest (adj.)   and be the *m* man This day in England.   *Queen Mary* II ii 19
   But not the force made them our *m* kings.   ,,   III iv 335
   You are the *m* monarch upon earth, I but a little Queen: ,,   v i 52
   Bride of the *m* sovereign upon earth?   ,,   v ii 544
   Should make the *m* empire earth has known.   ,,   v iii 70
   Thou art the *m* voice in England, man,   *Harold* II ii 617
   But I that threw the *m* knight of France,   *Becket* I iii 746
Mightiest (s)   More, what the *m* and the holiest Of all his predecessors   ,,   II ii 179
Mighty (adj. and adv.)   For I am *m* popular with them, Noailles.   *Queen Mary* I iii 101
   Ay, ay, but *m* doctors doubted there.   ,,   IV i 83
   Friend for so long time of a *m* King;   ,,   IV iii 73
   And done such *m* things by Holy Church,   ,,   v v 74
   Thou art a *m* man In thine own earldom!   *Harold* I i 92
   And *m* pretty legs too. Thou art the prettiest child I ever saw.   *Becket* IV i 6
   But my sister wrote that he was *m* pleasant,   *Prom. of May* I 116
   But he were *m* fond o' ye, warn't he?   ,,   II 9
   ready To make allowances, and *m* slow To feel offences.   ,,   II 629
Mighty (s)   How are the *m* fallen, Master Cranmer!   *Queen Mary* IV ii 146
Milan (town)   Granada, Naples, Sicily, and *M*,—   ,,   v i 44
Milcher (milch-cow)   Dumble's the best *m* in Islip. (repeat)   ,,   IV iii 478, 497
Mild   Your *m* Legate Pole Will tell you that the devil helpt them thro' it.   ,,   IV iii 351
   Julius the Third Was ever just, and *m*, and father-like;   ,,   v ii 31
   We have heard Of thy just, *m*, and equal governance;   *Harold* II ii 690
   she had seen the Archbishop once, So *m*, so kind.   *Becket* v ii 120
Milder   Ye govern *m* men. *Gurth.* We have made them *m* by just government.   *Harold* I i 339
Mile   seen your steps a *m* From me and Lambeth?   *Queen Mary* I ii 81
   I would not; but a hundred *m's* I rode,   ,,   I v 551
   we must round By Kingston Bridge. *Brett.* Ten *m's* about.   ,,   III iii 49
   brook across our field For twenty *m's*,   ,,   v v 84
   I ha' carried him ever so many *m's* in my arms,   *Becket* I iv 98
   What be he a-doing here ten *m* an' moor fro' a raäïl?   *Prom. of May* I 209
Militant   Thou hast roll'd over the Church *m*   *Foresters* IV 273

KK

Molochize   I think that they would *M* them too,   *Harold* I i 36

Moment   Quiet a *m*, my masters;   *Queen Mary* I iii 16

Queen would see your Grace upon the *m*.   ,, I iv 222

Or will be in a *m*.   ,, I iv 289

sonnet's a flying ant, Wing'd for a *m*.   ,, II i 85

Cries of the *m* and the street—   ,, II iv 128

Nay come with me—one *m* !   ,, III ii 189

That I was for a *m* wroth at thee.   ,, III iv 306

Yet, a *m* since, I wish'd myself the milkmaid   ,, III v 255

Whose colours in a *m* break and fly,   ,, IV iii 169

seeing in a *m*, I shall find Heaven or else hell   ,, IV iii 223

Whose colours in a *m* break and fly !'   ,, v ii 206

so your Grace would bide a *m* yet.   ,, v ii 547

We dally with our lazy *m*'s here, And hers are number'd.   ,, v iii 108

He had his gracious *m*, Altho' you'll not believe me.   ,, v v 38

And in a *m* I shall follow him.   ,, v v 57

but stay a *m* ; *He* can but stay a *m* :   *Harold* I ii 3

but rather let me be King of the *m* to thee,   ,, III ii 41

thou be only King of the *m* over England.   ,, III ii 51

There *was* a *m* When being forced aloof   ,, IV iii 14

A *m* ! thou didst help me to my throne   *Becket, Pro.* 200

citizen's heir hath conquer'd me For the *m*.   ,, II ii 62

They have made it up again—for the *m*.   ,, III iii 170

made me for the *m* proud Ev'n of that stale Church-bond   ,, IV ii 445

A *m* ! If you track this Sinnatus In any treason,   *The Cup* I i 161

And that sets her against me—for the *m*.   ,, I iii 164

He knew not at the *m* who had fasten'd   ,, II 49

Your arm—a *m*—It will pass.   ,, II 449

But lay them there for a *m* !   *The Falcon* 763

this, for the *m*, Will leave me a free field.   *Prom. of May* II 455

lie down there together in the darkness which would seem but for a *m*,   ,, III 195

The shelter of *your* roof—not for one *m*—   ,, III 801

Tho' in one *m* she should glance away,   *Foresters* II i 161

Young Walter, nay, I pray thee, stay a *m*. *Marian.* A *m* for some matter of no *m* ! Well—take and use your *m*, while you may.   ,, II i 473

That I might breathe for a *m* free of shield   ,, IV 128

We sighted 'em Only this *m*.   ,, IV 591

for the *m* strike the bonds From these three men,   ,, IV 961

Momentary   Were *m* sparkles out as quick Almost as kindled ;   *Queen Mary* I ii 73

are only like The rainbow of a *m* sun.   *Foresters* II i 279

Monarch (adj.)   his *m* mane Bristled about his quick ears—   *The Cup* I ii 120

Monarch (s)   You are the mightiest *m* upon earth,   *Queen Mary* v i 52

That never English *m* dying left England so little.   ,, v v 277

Monday (adj.)   Immanuel Goldsmiths was broke into o' *M* night,   *Prom. of May* I 393

Monday (s)   I'll hev it done o' *M*.   ,, III 45

you were stupid drunk all Sunday, and so ill in consequence all *M*,   ,, III 81

Money   Confiscate lands, goods, *m*—   *Queen Mary* II i 102

Is that it ? That's a big lot of *m*.   ,, II iii 63

Do you lack any *m* ?   ,, IV ii 40

A fit place for the *monies* of the Church,   *Becket* I iii 105

I had no heart to part with her for *m*. *Giovanna.* No, not for *m*.   *The Falcon* 326

and now, as far as *m* goäs, I be a gentleman,   *Prom. of May* I 331

Count the *m* and see if it's all right.   ,, III 64

sits and eats his heart for want of *m* to pay the Abbot.   *Foresters* I i 5

he borrowed the *monies* from the Abbot of York, the Sheriff's brother.   ,, I i 67

his *monies*, his oxen, his dinners, himself.   ,, I i 234

He has *monies*. I will go to him.   ,, I i 273

Must you have these *monies* before the year and the month end ?   ,, I ii 149

He has a friend there will advance the *monies*,   ,, II i 629

That baseness which for fear or *monies*,   ,, II i 706

how much *m* hast thou in thy purse ?   ,, III 273

How should poor friars have *m* ?   ,, III 276

and took His *monies*.   ,, III 363

it was agreed when you borrowed these *monies* from the Abbot   ,, IV 466

these *monies* should be paid in to the Abbot at York,   ,, IV 506

You have the *monies* and the use of them.   ,, IV 548

Money (continued)   Sir Richard paid his *monies* to the Abbot.   *Foresters* IV 849

Money-lover   No *m-l* he !   *Harold* II ii 216

Monger   *See* **Miracle-monger, Word-monger**

Mongering   *See* **Perjury-mongering**

Mongrel   Made even the carrion-nosing *m* vomit   *Queen Mary* IV iii 448

Monk   It was a wheedling *m* Set up the mass.   ,, I ii 90

M, Thou hast said thy say,   *Harold* v i 4

m, I ask again When had the Lateran and the Holy Father   ,, v i 15

Out, beast *m* ! I ever hated *m*'s.   ,, v i 75

Leofric, and all the *m*'s of Peterboro'   ,, v i 446

Mock me not. I am not even a *m*.   *Becket, Pro.* 248

Go like a *m*, cowling and clouding up   ,, I ii 311

as I hate the dirty gap in the face of a Cistercian *m*,   ,, II ii 382

A stranger *m* desires access to you.   ,, v ii 65

The *m*'s disguise thou gavest me for my bower :   ,, v ii 93

M's, knights, five hundred, that were there and heard.   ,, v ii 406

Robert, The apostate *m* that was with Randulf   ,, v ii 574

I cannot tell why *m*'s should all be cowards.   ,, v ii 581

Why should all *m*'s be cowards ?   ,, v ii 588

Ay, *m*'s, not men. *Grim.* I am a *m*, my lord.   ,, v ii 602

these are our own *m*'s who follow'd us !   ,, v iii 59

I and my friend, this *m*, were here belated,   *Foresters* I ii 193

What *m* of what convent art thou ?   ,, I ii 205

Sheriff, thy friend, this *m*, is but a statue.   ,, I ii 233

We spoil'd the prior, friar, abbot, *m*,   ,, III 167

Monkery   divorced King Louis, Scorning his *m*,—   *Becket* IV ii 419

Monkey   The *m* that should roast his chestnuts for him !   *Foresters* IV 806

Monk-king   good brother, They call you the *M-K*.   *Becket* II ii 73

I am proud of my ' *M-K*,'   ,, II ii 101

my much constancy To the *m-k*, Louis,   ,, IV ii 305

Monna Giovanna   (*See also* **Giovanna**)   Ah, *M G*, you here again !   *The Falcon* 85

and all along o' you, *M G*,   ,, 103

there is *M G* coming down the hill from the castle.   ,, 160

Monster   *M*'s of mistradition, old enough   *Queen Mary* IV ii 102

Monstrous   *M* ! blasphemous ! She ought to burn.   ,, I v 57

(thus there springs to light That Centaur of a *m* Commonweal, The traitor-heretic)   ,, III iv 163

Bark'd out at me such *m* charges,   *Becket* IV ii 342

She too—she too—the bride ! the Queen ! and I—*M* ! I that loved her.   *The Cup* II 469

and some Pillaring a leaf-sky on their *m* boles,   *Foresters* III 100

Month   for women To go twelve *m*'s in bearing   *Queen Mary* IV vi 91

Give her a *m* or two, and her affections   *Prom. of May* I 484

must be paid in a year and a *m*, or I lose the land.   *Foresters* I i 269

Must you have these monies before the year and the *m* end ?   ,, I ii 150

Give him another *m*, and he will pay it. *Justiciary.* We cannot give a *m*.   ,, IV 443

paid in to the Abbot of York, at the end of the *m* at noon,   ,, IV 508

Mood   I am in no *m* : I should be as the shadow   *Harold* II ii 176

to thwart them in their *m* May work them grievous harm   *The Falcon* 820

man not prone to jealousies, Caprices, humours, *m*'s ;   *Prom. of May* III 627

Mooded   *See* **Iron-mooded**

Moody   You, Scarlet, you are always *m* here.   *Foresters* I iii 128

Man, lying here alone, *M* creature,   ,, II ii 187

Moon   a star beside the *m* Is all but lost ;   *Queen Mary* v i 80

Would not for all the stars and maiden *m*   ,, v ii 456

Not must, but will. It is but for one *m*.   *Harold* II ii 30

In cold, white cells beneath an icy *m*—   ,, v i 325

the harvest *m* is the ripening of the harvest,   *Becket, Pro.* 363

m Divides the whole long street with light and shade.   ,, I i 364

Dark even from a side glance of the *m*,   ,, IV iii 149

No Sinnatus yet—and there the rising *m*. *M* on the field and the foam, *M* on the waste and the wold, *M* bring him home, bring him home   *The Cup* I ii 2

Home, sweet *m*, bring him home,   ,, I ii 7

In the sweet *m* as with a lovelier snow !   ,, I ii 396

but this new *m*, I fear, Is darkness   *Foresters* I i 85

or the cow that jumped over the *m*.   ,, II i 436

perchance Up yonder with the man i' the *m*.   ,, II i 507

Clothed with the mystic silver of her *m*.   ,, II i 609

Moon (*continued*) light of the seas by the *m*'s long-silvering ray !   *Foresters* II ii 179

Moonlight (adj.) And how her shadow crosses one by one The *m* casements   *Queen Mary* v v 9

Moonlight there goes one in the *m*. Shoot !   *Foresters* II i 395

What sparkles in the *m* on thy hand ?   „   II i 582

Moonshine He often looks in here by the *m*.   „   II i 337

Moor I remember it well. There on the *m*'s.   *Becket* II i 52

Moor (more) I warrants ye'll think *m* o' this young Squire Edgar as ha' coomed among us—   *Prom. of May* I 109

What be he a-doing here ten mile an' *m* fro' a raäil ?   „   I 209

I' mun ha' plowed it *m* nor a hoonderd times ;   „   I 368

And I would loove tha *m* nor ony gentleman 'ud loove tha.   „   II 104

I'd think na *m* o' maäkin' an end o' tha nor a carrion craw—   „   II 696

An' I thanks ye fur that, Miss, *m* nor fur the waäge.   „   III 117

Moorish or closed For ever in a *M* tower,   *Foresters* II i 656

Moors He calls us worse than Jews, *M*, Saracens.   *Queen Mary* v i 150

the boy was taken prisoner by the *M*.   *Foresters* I i 61

fell'st into the hands Of these same *M*   „   II i 564

Mooted whene'er your royal rights Are *m* in our councils—   *Becket* I i 431

Moraine I have seen it like the snow on the *m*.   *The Falcon* 506

Moral (adj.) Against the *m* excess No physical ache,   *Becket* I i 381

Moral (s) Nature's *m* Against excess.   „   I 373

His swaddling-bands, the *m*'s of the tribe,   *Prom. of May* I 586

Morcar (Earl of Northumbria) *M* ! Why creep'st thou like a timorous be st   *Harold* I ii 211

M and Edwin have ·tirr'd up the Thanes   „   II ii 288

have overthrown *M* and Edwin.   „   III ii 132

Tostig's banishment, and choice of *M*,   „   IV i 105

Again ! *M* ! Edwin ! What do they mean ?   „   IV i 133

M, it is all but duty in her To hate me ;   „   IV i 153

M and Edwin, When will ye cease to plot   „   IV i 160

M and Edwin, will ye, if I yield,   „   IV i 175

M and Edwin, will ye upon oath, Help us   „   IV i 179

We never—oh ! good *M*, speak for us,   „   IV i 216

M, collect thy men ; Edwin, my friend—   „   IV i 256

He held with *M*.—   „   IV ii 44

And *M* holds with us.   „   IV ii 46

Make not our *M* sullen : it is not wise.   „   IV iii 103

Gurth, Leofwin, *M*, Edwin !   „   IV iii 220

Nought of *M* then ?   „   v i 160

I married her for *M*—a sin against The truth of love.   „   v i 169

More *See* **Moor**

More (Sir Thomas, Lord Chancellor) Did not *M* die, and Fisher ? he must burn.   *Queen Mary* IV i 52

Moreing thou and thy youngsters are always muching and *m* me.   *Foresters* IV 296

Morn (*See also* **Marriage-morn**) Close to the grating on a winter *m*   *The Falcon* 441

Morning (adj.) Brain-dizzied with a draught of *m* ale.   *Queen Mary* II i 71

And make a *m* outcry in the yard ;   „   IV v 158

But you, twin sister of the *m* star,   *The Cup* I iii 45

Their shield-borne patriot of the *m* star   „   II 122

thou that canst soar Beyond the *m* lark,   *The Falcon* 11

Morning (s) (*See also* **May-morning, Murnin'**) Good *m*, Noailles.   *Queen Mary* I iii 159

Good *m*, my good Lord. *Gardiner.* That every *m* of your Majesty May be most good,   „   I v 98

Good *m*, Sir de Noailles. *Noailles.* A happy *m* to your Majesty. *Mary.* And I should some time have a happy *m* ;   „   I v 242

take And wear it as memorial of a *m*   „   I v 529

I am sure Her *m* wanted sunlight,   *Harold* I ii 45

on that *m* when I came To plead to thee   *The Cup* II 390

and I sneezed three times this *m*.   *The Falcon* 169

in hope that the saints would send us this blessed *m* ;   „   186

you look as beautiful this *m* as the very Madonna   „   198

Where have you lain in ambush all the *m* ?   *Prom. of May* I 545

Is the most beautiful *m* of this May.   „   I 569

you make The May and *m* still more beautiful,   „   I 573

seen us that wild *m* when we found Her bed unslept in,   „   II 469

and I wish you and your ladyship's father a most exceeding good *m*.   *Foresters* I i 309

Morning (s) (*continued*) Who breaks the stillness of the *m* thus ?   *Foresters* I iii 51

gave me this *m* on my setting forth.   III 282

Only this *m* in his agony   „   IV 453

Morrow Good *m*, my Lord Cardinal ;   *Queen Mary* IV i 42

Morsel (*See also* **Mossel**) Come, come, the *m* stuck—this Cardinal's fault—   „   III iv 375

Not a *m*, not one *m*. I have broken My fast already.   *The Falcon* 573

Mortal seeming not as brethren, But *m* foes !   *Queen Mary,* IV iii 186

Because I loved thee in my *m* day,   *Harold* v i 240

Is it possible That *m* men should bear their earthly heats   „   v i 283

how he fells The *m* copse of faces !   „   v i 589

but the Chancellor's and the Archbishop's Together more than *m* man can bear.   *Becket* I i 24

Who stands aghast at her eternal self And shakes at *m* kings—   „   II ii 405

I ask no leave of king, or *m* man,   „   v ii 458

Out, begone ! Henceforth I am thy *m* enemy.   *The Cup* I ii 330

And, lest we freeze in *m* apathy,   „   I iii 130

O this *m* house, Which we are born into,   *Prom. of May* II 273

'O man, forgive thy *m* foe,   „   III 5

But to show thou art *m*. *Marian.* *M* enough, If love for thee be *m*.   *Foresters* II i 612

Not *m* ! after death, if after death—   „   II i 619

would cower to any Of *m* build.   „   II i 690

You seem, as it were, Immortal, and we *m*.   „   IV 1060

Mortality As may be consonant with *m*.   *Queen Mary* IV iii 419

Mortally I am *m* afear'd o' thee, thou big man,   *Foresters* IV 316

Mortgage thou shouldst marry one who will pay the *m*.   „   I i 280

Himself would pay this *m* to his brother,   „   I ii 263

he would pay The *m* if she favour'd him.   „   I iii 7

Sheriff Would pay this cursed *m* to his brother   „   II i 144

rate the land fivefold The worth of the *m*,   „   II i 151

and couldst never pay The *m* on thy land.   „   II i 454

Mortgaged I am *m* as thyself.   „   I ii 280

Mortice Hath no more *m* than a tower of cards ;   *Queen Mary* II i 442

Mortify Fast, scourge thyself, and *m* thy flesh,   *Becket* I iii 539

Mortifying In scourgings, macerations, *m*'s, Fasts,   „   v i 41

Moslem like the *M* beauties waiting To clasp   *Prom. of May* I 246

I that have turn'd their *M* crescent pale—   *Foresters* IV 793

Heading the holy war against the *M*,   „   IV 818

And cleft the *M* turban at my side.   „   IV 1001

Mossel (morsel) avore a could taste a *m*,   *Queen Mary* IV iii 517

Most I do my *m* and best.   „   II ii 24

Mot blow upon it Three *m*'s, this fashion—listen !   *Foresters* IV 425

Moth Make it so hard to save a *m* from the fire ?   *Becket* I i 283

would not blur A *m*'s wing by the touching ;   *Prom. of May* II 492

Mother My *m* said, Go up ; and up I went.   *Queen Mary* I iii 98

my good *m* came (God rest her soul) Of Spain,   „   I v 11

Your royal *m* came of Spain,   „   I v 16

m, you had time and cause enough To sicken   „   I v 23

married The *m* of Elizabeth—a heretic   „   I v 32

Here was a young *m*, Her face on flame,   „   II ii 69

felt the faltering of his *m*'s heart,   „   II ii 82

I, that was never *m*, cannot tell How *m*'s   „   II ii 189

nay, his noble *m*'s, Head fell—   „   III iv 295

Before my father married my good *m*,—   „   III v 246

Her foul divorce—my sainted *m*—No !—   „   IV i 81

M of God, Thou knowest never woman meant so well,   „   v ii 340

and in her agony The *m* came upon her—   „   IV v 20

prattling to her *m* Of her betrothal   „   v v 232

Malet, thy *m* was an Englishwoman ;   *Harold* II ii 264

for my *m*'s sake I love your England,   „   II ii 268

Speak for thy *m*'s sake, and tell me true. *Malet.* Then for my *m*'s sake, and England's sake   „   II ii 271

And for our *M* England ?   „   II ii 425

for he Who vows a vow to strangle his own *m*   „   III i 230

My *m* is a Dane, and I am English ;   „   IV i 54

Trampling thy *m*'s bosom into blood ?   „   IV ii 26

A cleric lately poison'd his own *m*,   *Becket, Pro.* 11

My *m*, ere she bore me, Dream'd that twelve stars   „   I i 44

So did Matilda, the King's.   „   I iii 152

took back not only Stephen's gifts, But his own *m*'s,   „   I iii 155

Age, orphans, and babe-breasting *m*'s—   „   II i 73

Move (verb) (*continued*) ever-jarring Earldoms *m* To music
and in order— *Harold* II ii 761
Did the chest *m*? did it *m*? ,, II ii 799
twins that cannot *M* one without the other. ,, III i 129
Our Saints have moved the Church that *m*'s the world, ,, v i 42
Call when the Norman *m*'s— ,, v i 230
The Norman *m*'s! ,, v i 438
dead So piled about him he can hardly *m*. ,, v i 658
pray God My Normans may but *m* as true with me ,, v i 184
My liege, I *m* my bishop. *Becket, Pro.* 28
Well—will you *m*? ,, *Pro.* 38
Check—you *m* so wildly. ,, *Pro.* 40
and the walks Where I could *m* at pleasure, ,, i i 266
I would *m* this wanton from his sight ,, i ii 70
if he *m* at all, Heaven stay him, is fain to diagonalise. ,, II ii 329
you still *m* against him, you may have no less than to die ,, III iii 325
The crowd are scattering, let us *m* away! ,, III iii 357
I cannot think he *m*'s against my son, ,, v i 18
But Becket ever *m*'s against a king. ,, v i 25
Why do you *m* with such a stateliness? ,, v i 622
Would I could *m* him, Provoke him any way! *The Cup* I ii 136
love for my dying boy, *M*'s me to ask it of you. *The Falcon* 788
Help me to *m* this bench for him into the sun. *Prom. of May* I 80
—the crowd would call it conscience—*M*'s me ,, II 639
we must *M* in the line of least resistance ,, II 670
The oppression of our people *m*'s me so, *Foresters* III 109
M me no more! I am sick and faint with pain! ,, IV 598
Robin, shall we not *m*? ,, IV 782

Moved it will be known that we have *m*; *Queen Mary* II i 198
when the Duke of Norfolk *m* against us ,, II iii 2
I never saw your Highness *m* till now. ,, III vi 104
Where he shall rest at night, *m* to his death; ,, IV iii 580
Our Saints have *m* the Church that moves the world, *Harold* v i 41
Thomas, thou art *m* too much. *Becket* I i 172
state more cruelly trampled on Than had she never *m*. *The Cup* I ii 147
M in the iron grooves of Destiny? *Prom. of May* II 267
sometimes been *m* to tears by a chapter of fine
writing in a novel; ,, III 208
would she *m* beside me like my shadow! *Foresters* II i 164

Movement The house is all in *m*. Hence, and see. *Queen Mary* III v 83
There is a *m* there, A blind one— *Harold* I i 354
There is a *m* yonder in the crowd— *Becket* II ii 36
if the followers Of him, who heads the *m*, *Foresters* I i 701

Moving *m* side by side Beneath one canopy, *Queen Mary* III i 95
A maiden slowly *m* on to music *The Cup* I i 9

Mow'd An' the midders all *m*, an' the sky
sa blue— (repeat) *Prom. of May* II 176, 188, 200

Mowt (might) What we *m* saäy, and what we *m* do, *Prom. of May* II 191

Mr. (*See also* **Master, Mister**) I'm coming down, *M*
Dobson. ,, I 46
Wheer did they larn ye that? *Dora.* In
Cumberland, *M* Dobson. ,, I 66
Getting better, *M* Dobson. ,, I 69
The owd man be heighty to-daäy, beänt he? *Dora.*
Yes, *M* Dobson. , I 78
Where do they blow, *M* Dobson? ,, I 87
And your eyes be as blue as—— *Dora.* What,
M Dobson? ,, I 93
Very likely, *M* Dobson. She *will* break fence. ,, I 193
What dost a knaw o' this *M* Hedgar as be a-lodgin'
wi' ye? ,, I 199
Nor I either, *M* Dobson. ,, I 236
But I have, *M* Dobson. ,, I 257
You never find one for me, *M* Dobson. ,, I 306
Hev' ony o' ye seen Eva? *Dobson.* Noä, *M* Steer. ,, I 314
Wheer be *M* Edgar? about the premises? ,, I 432
Yeas, yeas! Three cheers for *M* Steer! ,, I 456
But where is this *M* Edgar whom you praised so
in your first letters? 1776
Yes, *M* Dobson, I've been attending on his death-
bed and his burial. ,, II 3
Hesn't he left ye nowt? *Dora.* No, *M* Dobson. ,, II 8
I thought *M* Edgar the best of men, and he has
proved himself the worst. ,, II 85
Cannot you understand plain words, *M* Dobson? ,, II 113

Mr. (*continued*) Sally Allen, you worked for *M*
Dobson, didn't you? *Prom. of May* III 102
Him as did the mischief here, five year' sin'. *Dora.*
M Edgar? ,, III 141
And this lover of yours—this *M* Harold—is a
gentleman? ,, III 281
Pleäse, Miss, *M* Dobson told me to saäy he's browt
some of Miss Eva's roses ,, III 345
Milly, my dear, how did you leave *M* Steer? ,, III 410
What is it? *Milly.* *M* 'Arold, Miss. ,, III 478

Much Madam, my master hears with *m* alarm, *Queen Mary* I v 250
He hath learnt to love our Tostig *m* of late. *Harold* I i 145
He hath as *m* of cat as tiger in him. ,, I i 154
Too *m*! What! we must use our battle-axe to-day. ,, v i 204
But wonder'd more at my *m* constancy To the monk-king, *Becket* IV ii 304
Madam, I am as *m* man as the King. ,, IV ii 432
Thou as *m* man! No more of that; ,, IV ii 451
Pray for me too: *m* need of prayer have I. ,, v ii 195
This friar is of *m* boldness, noble captain. *Foresters* IV 234
M would have more,' says the proverb; ,, IV 308

Much (**a companion of Robin Hood**) Thou *M*, miller's
son, hath not the Earl right? ,, I ii 46
M, the miller's son, I knew thy father; He was a
manly man, as thou art, *M*, And gray before his
time as thou art, *M*. ,, I iii 146
I can sing it. *Robin.* Not now, good *M*! ,, I iii 158
I Little John, he *M* the miller's son, and he Scarlet, ,, III 54
he, young Scarlet, and he, old *M*, and all the rest of us. ,, III 61
And I, old *M*, say as much, ,, III 62
Friend Scarlet, art thou less a man than *M*? ,, III 66
Up, good *M*. *Tuck.* And show thyself more of a
man than me. ,, IV 284
Ay, for old *M* is every inch a man. ,, IV 289
always so much more of a man than my youngsters old *M*. ,, IV 299
Well, we *M*'es be old. ,, IV 300
' Much would have more,' says the proverb; but *M*
hath had more ,, IV 308
Give me thy hand, *M*; I love thee. At him, Scarlet! ,, IV 310
You, good friar, You *M*, you Scarlet, you dear Little
John, ,, IV 1083

Muching thou and thy youngsters are always *m* and
moreing me. ,, IV 296

Mud (*See also* **Squad**) I'll have the scandal sounded
to the *m*. *Queen Mary* I v 228
drop The *m* I carried, like yon brook, *Becket* II i 159
I am snow to *m*. ,, IV ii 130
My curse on all This world of *m*, *Prom. of May* III 722

Mudded wolf *M* the brook and predetermined all. *Harold* v i 3

Muddled an' maäzed, an' maäted, an' *m* ma. *Prom. of May* II 729

Mule *See* **Sumpter-mule**

Mulieribus Ave Maria, gratia plena, Benedicta tu in *m*. *Queen Mary* III ii 2

Mumbling Catholic, *M* and mixing up in his scared
prayers ,, II ii 86
our good King Kneels *m* some old bone— *Harold* II ii 469

Mummy-saints over His gilded ark of *m*'s, ,, v i 304

Mun (must) There *m* be summat wrong theer, Wilson,
fur I doänt understan' it. *Prom. of May* I 233
S'iver I *m* git along back to the farm, ,, II 321
It *m* be him. Noä! ,, II 602
Naäy, but I *m* git out on 'is waäy now, ,, II 609
Deäd! It *m* be true, fur it wur i' print as black as owt. ,, II 730
Then yon *m* be his brother, an' we'll leather 'im. ,, III 150
If it be her ghoäst, we *m* abide it. ,, III 460

Murder (s) (*See also* **Self-murder**) No—*m* fathers *m*: *Queen Mary* III i 335
This was against her conscience—would be *m*! ,, III i 419
' Thou shalt do no *m*,' ,, III i 421
when *m* common As nature's death, *Becket* I iii 342
What doth hard *m* care For degradation? ,, I iii 393
I found a hundred ghastly *m*'s done By men, ,, I iii 407
Covetousness, Craft, Cowardice, *M*'— *Prom. of May* II 285
whenever a—*m* is to be done again she yells out i'
this way— *Foresters* II i 246
Ay, do you hear? There may be *m* done. ,, II i 340

Murder (verb) Men would *m* me, *Queen Mary* I v 155
some Papist ruffians hereabout Would *m* you. ,, III v 175

Murder (verb) (*continued*)   Robert of Jumiéges—well-nigh *m*
him too ?   *Harold* I i 57
The dead men made at thee to *m* thee,   „   I ii 85
It is the flash that *m's*, the poor thunder   „   I ii 231
but a voice Among you : *m*, martyr me if ye will—   „   v i 78
They *m* all that follow.   „   v i 610
for he would *m* his brother the State.   *Becket* I iv 190
Lord hath set his mark upon him that no man should
m him.   „   I iv 193
the wolves of England Must *m* her one shepherd,   „   III iii 344
They stood on Dover beach to *m* me,   „   v ii 436
Win me you cannot, *m* me you may,   *Foresters* IV 721
Murder'd   see the holy father *M* before thy face ?   *Queen Mary* I iii 65
You would not have him *m* as Becket was ?   „   III i 334
And I the race of *m* Buckingham—   „   III i 454
The little *m* princes, in a pale light,   „   III v 147
Hast *m* thine own guest, the son of Orm,   *Harold* IV ii 37
They have so maim'd and *m* all his face   „   IV ii 76
A cleric violated The daughter of his host, and *m* him.   *Becket* I iii 383
Say that a cleric *m* an archbishop,   „   I iii 399
Am I to be *m* to-night ?   „   I iv 47
M by that adulteress Eleanor,   „   IV ii 243
Dead ! you have *m* her, Found out her secret bower
and *m* her.   „   v i 173
What matters *m* here, or *m* there ?   „   v ii 630
Our gallant citizens *m* all in vain,   *The Cup* II 142
She was *m* here a hundred year ago,   *Foresters* II i 245
Murderer   Make not thy King a traitorous *m*.   *Becket* I iii 500
The *m's*, hark ! Let us hide !   „   v iii 46
Murderess   *M* !   *Eleanor.*   My lord, we know you proud   „   IV ii 259
Murderous   Were such *m* liars In Wessex—   *Harold* II i 94
The man that hath to foil a *m* aim May,   „   II ii 417
braced and brazen'd up with Christmas wines For any
m brawl.   *Becket* v ii 425
O *m* mad-woman ! I pray you lift me And make me
walk awhile.   *The Cup* II 471
Murmur (s)   there be *m's*, for thy brother breaks us   *Harold* I i 108
merriest *m's* of their banquet clank The shackles   „   II ii 408
Murmur (verb)   these old oaks will *m* thee Marian along
with Robin.   *Foresters* IV 1094
Murnin' (morning)   and he wur in a tew about it all
the *m* ;   *Prom. of May* I 19
they be two o' the purtiest gels ye can see of a
summer *m*.   „   I 31
Good *m*, neighbours, and the saäme to you, my
men.   „   I 317
sa ta'en up wi' leädin' the owd man about all the
blessed *m*   „   III 3
nine o'clock, upo' Tuesday *m*,   „   III 136
He wur sa bellows'd out wi' the wind this *m*,   „   III 432
Muse   I will not *m* upon it.   *Queen Mary* IV ii 230
tell the King that I will *m* upon it ;   „   v iii 90
that made me *m*, Being bounden by my coronation
oath   *Becket* I iii 395
Music   in *m* Peerless—her needle perfect,   *Queen Mary* III i 359
Thou art my *m* !   *Harold* I ii 25
Harold Hear the king's *m*, all alone with him,   „   I ii 194
ever-jarring Earldoms move To *m* and in order—   „   II ii 762
hand of one To whom thy voice is all her *m*,   *Becket* II i 177
A maiden slowly moving on to *m*   *The Cup* I i 9
And *m* there to greet my lord the king.   „   II 191
Repeat them to their *m*.   *Count.*   You can touch
No chord in me that would not answer you In *m*.   *The Falcon* 454
When the Church and the law have forgotten God's
m, they shall dance to the *m*   *Foresters* IV 555
Strike up our *m*, Little John.   „   IV 559
Musical   There goes a *m* score along with them,   *The Falcon* 452
Musically   That is *m* said.   „   458
Musing   What are you *m* on, my Lord of Devon ?   *Queen Mary* I iv 26
Well, I was *m* upon that ;   „   I iv 40
For I was *m* on an ancient saw,   *Becket* IV ii 537
Mussulman   I had sooner have been born a *M*—   „   II ii 145
and turn me *M* ! No God but one,   „   II ii 224
Almost as many as your true *M*—   „   IV ii 34
Must   *See* **Moänt, Mun**

Muster   and make *M's* in all the counties ;   *Queen Mary* v ii 272
Mutable   Woman is various and most *m*.   „   III vi 135
Mute   another, *m* as death, And white as her own milk ;   „   II ii 78
And when my voice Is martyr'd *m*, and this man
disappears,   *Becket* III iii 350
Why art thou *m* ? Dost thou not honour woman ?   *Foresters* III 67
Mutilated   *M*, poor brute, my sumpter-mule,   *Becket* IV ii 440
Mutter   What is that you *m* ?   *Queen Mary* I v 203
Muttering   And *m* to himself as heretofore.   „   II i 16
My-lord   Why do you so *m-l* me, Who am disgraced ?   „   IV ii 176
Myriad   sent his *m's* hither To seize upon the forts   „   III i 463
Myrtle   apricot, Vine, cypress, poplar, *m*,   *The Cup* II 267
Myrtle-blossom   And kindle all our vales with *m-b*,   „   II 267
Mysen (myself)   I niver thowt o' *m* i' that waäy ;   *Prom. of May* I 176
and, thaw I says it *m*, niver men 'ed a better master—   „   I 327
fur I 'ednt naw time to maäke *m* a scholard while I
wur maäkin' *m* a gentleman,   „   I 333
now theer be noän o' my men, thinks I to *m*,   „   I 410
fur I'd ha' done owt fur 'er *m* ;   „   II 33
Fur boäth on 'em knawed as well as *m*   „   II 314
'at I ha' nobbut larned an haäfe on it.   „   III 4
But I'll git the book ageän, and larn *m* the rest,   „   III 13
O law—yeäs, Sir ! I'll run fur 'im *m*.   „   III 714
Mystery   was the great *m* wrought ;   *Queen Mary* IV iii 141
see Deeper into the *mysteries* of heaven   *Harold* I i 200
The folds have fallen from the *m*,   *Becket* IV ii 8
Mystic   Clothed with the *m* silver of her moon.   *Foresters* II i 608

N

Naäiled (nailed)   I'll hev the winder *n* up, and put
Towser under it.   *Prom. of May* I 420
Naäme (name)   noän o' the parishes goäs by that *n*
'ereabouts.   „   I 268
then he called me a rude *n*, and I can't abide 'im.   „   II 159
Fanny be the *n* i' the song, but I swopt it fur *she*.   „   II 211
An' we weänt mention naw *n's*,   „   II 130
says the master goäs cleän off his 'eäd when he
'eärs the *n* on 'im ;   „   III 133
I warrants that ye goäs By haäfe a scoor o' *n's*—   „   III 729
Naämed (named)   Theer, Miss ! You ha' *n* 'im—not me.   „   III 142
Naäy (nay)   *N*, I knaws nowt o' what foälks says,   „   I 26
N then. I meän'd they be as blue as violets.   „   I 103
N, but I hev an owd woman as 'ud see to all that ;   „   II 95
N, but I mun git out on 'is waäy now,   „   II 609
Nail   tigress had unsheath'd her *n's* at last,   *Queen Mary* III i 3
But one that pares his *n's* ; to me ?   „   III v 65
There you strike in the *n*.   „   v ii 437
Nailed   *See* **Naäiled**
Naked   Make no allowance for the *n* truth.   *Queen Mary* I v 329
And leave the people *n* to the crown, And the
crown *n* to the people   „   III i 119
And tropes are good to clothe a *n* truth,   „   III iv 151
To ours in plea for Cranmer than to stand On *n*
self-assertion.   „   IV i 120
and then Cast on the dunghill *n*,   „   IV iii 446
Thy *n* word thy bond ! confirm it now   *Harold* II ii 693
I that so prized plain word and *n* truth Have sinn'd
against it—   „   III i 93
Is *n* truth actable in true life ?   „   III i 109
I thought that *n* Truth would shame the Devil The
Devil is so modest.   „   III i 118
I left our England *n* to the South To meet thee
in the North.   „   vi 289
They are stripping the dead bodies *n* yonder,   „   v ii 46
Life on the hand is *n* gipsy-stuff ;   *Becket* II i 193
she sits *n* by a great heap of gold in the middle of
the wood,   „   III ii 21
And left all *n*, I were lost indeed.   „   IV ii 9
but *n* Nature In all her loveliness.   *Prom. of May* I 598
Flung by the golden mantle of the cloud, And sets,
a *n* fire.   *Foresters* II i 29

Nakedly That, were a man of state *n* true, — *Harold* III i 113
Nakedness to spy my *n* In my poor North ! — „ I i 352
Name (s) (*See also* **Naäme**) your *n* Stands first of those who sign'd — *Queen Mary* I i 16
your worship's *n* heard into Maidstone market, — „ II i 62
The *n's* of Wyatt, Elizabeth, Courtenay, — „ II ii 94
Elizabeth—Her *n* is much abused — „ II ii 110
Speak ! in the *n* of God ! — „ II ii 271
Thy, *n*, thou knave ? *Man.* I am nobody, my Lord. — „ III i 246
God's passion ! knave, thy *n* ? — „ III i 249
Find out his *n* and bring it me. — „ III i 253
What is thy *n* ? *Man.* Sanders. — „ III i 312
In our own *n* and that of all the state, — „ III iii 120
How many *n's* in the long sweep of time — „ III v 39
But that Thy *n* by man be glorified, — „ IV iii 153
Ay, but they use his *n*. — „ v i 129
you will find written Two *n's*, Philip and Calais ; — „ v v 155
miracles will in my *n* be wrought Hereafter.— — *Harold* I i 183
Thou shalt be verily king—all but the *n*— — „ II ii 633
Why cry thy people on thy sister's *n* ? — „ IV i 21
in the *n* of the great God, so be it ! — „ IV i 239
no !—not once—in God's *n*, no ! — *Becket, Pro.* 126
It much imports me I should know her *n*. — „ I i 193
May plaister his clean *n* with scurrilous rhymes ! — „ I i 308
When Canterbury hardly bore a *n*. — „ I iii 60
I'll have the paper back—blot out my *n*. — „ I iii 287
Blessed is he that cometh in the *n* of the Lord ! — „ I iii 758
Shame fall on those who give it a dog's *n*— — „ II i 142
Son, I absolve thee in the *n* of God. — „ II ii 443
found thy *n* a charm to get me Food, roof, and rest. — „ v ii 96
in thy *n* I pass'd From house to house. — „ v ii 102
if Rosamund is The world's rose, as her *n* imports — „ v ii 263
in his *n* we charge you that ye keep This traitor — „ v ii 509
Save him, his blood would darken Henry's *n* ; — „ v iii 11
Your *n* ? *Synorix.* Strato, my *n*. *Sinnatus.* No Roman *n* ? *Synorix.* A Greek, my lord ; — *The Cup* I i 198
n's of those who fought and fell are like — „ I ii 164
For whether men malign thy *n*, or no, — „ I iii 84
in your lordship's and her ladyship's *n*, — *The Falcon* 415
mentioned her *n* too suddenly before my father. — *Prom. of May* II 23
Her phantom call'd me by the *n* she loved. — „ II 242
Taught her the learned *n's*, anatomized — „ II 302
Might I ask your *n* ? *Harold.* Harold. — „ II 393
five years' absence, and my change of *n*, — „ II 616
My *n* is Harold ! Good day, Dobbins ! — „ II 726
I spoke of your *n's*, Allen, — „ III 35
your own *n* Of Harold sounds so English — „ III 609
And *what* was Your *n* before ? — „ III 618
O yes ! In the *n* of the Regent. — *Foresters* I iii 55
Ay, ay, because I have a *n* for prowess. — „ II i 560
in the *n* of all our woodmen, present her with — „ III 57
a traitor coming In Richard's *n*— — „ IV 781
Your *n's* will cling like ivy to the wood. — „ IV 1085
Name (verb) *N* him ; the Holy Father will confirm him. — *Becket, Pro.* 244
My fault to *n* him ! — „ II i 175
when those, that *n* themselves Of the King's part, — „ v ii 428
Named (*See also* **Naämed**) proud of my ' Monk-King,' Whoever *n* me ; — „ II ii 102
Nameless Corpse-candles gliding over *n* graves— — *Harold* III i 381
Namesake your Scottish *n* marrying The Dauphin, — *Queen Mary* v i 134
which King Harold gave To his dead *n*, — *Harold* IV iii 110
Nap his manners want the *n* And gloss of court ; — *Queen Mary* III v 70
Napkin I will bind up his wounds with my *n*. — *Becket* I v 107
Naples the Netherlands, Sicily, *N*, Lombardy. — *Queen Mary* II i 212
he is King, you know, the King of *N*. The father ceded *N*, that the son Being a King, — „ III i 73
Granada, *N*, Sicily, and Milan,— — „ v i 44
The Pope would cast the Spaniard out of *N* : — „ v i 149
Napoleon make the soil For Cæsars, Cromwells, and *N's* — *Prom. of May* III 593
Nard *N*, Cinnamon, amomum, benzoin. — *The Cup* II 184
Narrow and the French fleet Rule in the *n* seas. — *Queen Mary* v i 7
but at times They seem to me too *n*, — *Harold* III ii 64
I send my voice across the *n* seas— — „ v i 246

Narrow (*continued*) And in a *n* path. A plover flew before thee. — *Becket* II i 53
But in this *n* breathing-time of life — *The Cup* I i 29
I hate Traditions, ever since my *n* father, — *Prom. of May* I 492
He met a stag there on so a *n* ledge— — *Foresters* IV 531
Narrowing Gone *n* down and darkening to a close. — *Queen Mary* IV iii 431
out of the eclipse *N* my golden hour ! — *Becket* II i 203
Narrowness It is the heat and *n* of the cage — *Queen Mary* III v 207
God's revenge upon this realm For *n* and coldness : — *Harold* I i 174
Nation comes a deputation From our finikin fairy *n*. — *Foresters* II ii 145
Native Feeling my *n* land beneath my foot, I said thereto : ' Ah, *n* land of mine, — *Queen Mary* III ii 47
And wrought his worst against his *n* land, — *The Cup* I ii 177
Natur (nature) *N* ! *N* ! Well, it be i' my *n* to knock — *Prom. of May* I 287
Natur' (nature) It's humbling—it smells o' human *n*. — *Becket* I iv 238
Natural the people Claim as their *n* leader— — *Queen Mary* IV i 210
You cannot Learn a man's nature from his *n* foe. — „ I v 340
Nay swears, it was no wicked wilfulness, Only a *n* chance. — „ III v 73
By seeking justice at a stranger's hand Against my *n* subject. — „ IV i 21
These are but *n* graces, my good Bishop, — „ IV i 176
Hurt no man more Than you would harm your loving *n* brother — „ IV iii 189
Gone beyond him and mine own *n* man (It was God's cause) ; — „ v ii 102
A sane and *n* loathing for a soul Purer, — *Becket* II i 171
all the foul fatalities That blast our *n* passions into pains ! — *Prom. of May* III 724
Naturally *N* enough ; for I am closely related — „ II 714
N again ; for as I used to transact all his business — „ II 718
Nature (*See also* **Natur**) I am of sovereign *n*, that I know, — *Queen Mary* I iv 258
You cannot Learn a man's *n* from his natural foe. — „ I v 340
Nor shame to call it *n*. — „ III v 77
craft that do divide The world of *n* ; — „ III v 121
For the pure honour of our common *n*, — „ IV iii 298
Why, *n's* licensed vagabond, the swallow, — „ v i 20
Does he think Low stature is low *n*, — „ v ii 434
Things that seem jerk'd out of the common rut Of *N* — *Harold* I i 139
I loved according to the main purpose and intent of *n*. — *Becket, Pro.* 502
And know the ways of *N*. — „ I i 257
N's moral Against excess. — „ I i 373
when murder common As *n's* death, — „ I iii 344
I doubt not from your nobleness of *n*, — *The Falcon* 804
my nobleness Of *n*, as you deign to call it, — „ 811
It is *N* kills, And not for *her* sport either. — *Prom. of May* I 272
—is not that the course of *N* too, — „ I 279
this poor *N* ! *Dobson.* Natur ! Natur ! — „ I 286
but naked *N* In all her loveliness. — „ I 599
strain to make ourselves Better and higher than *N*, — „ I 604
N a liar, making us feel guilty Of her own faults. — „ II 269
equal for pure innocence of *n*, And loveliness of feature. — „ II 372
Here crawling in this boundless *N*. — „ III 637
worse off than any of you, for I be lean by *n*, — *Foresters* I i 45
Till *N*, high and low, and great and small — „ I ii 326
for, God help us, we lie by *n*. — „ II i 238
Weak *n's* that impute Themselves to their unlikes, — „ II i 690
Of a *n* Stronger, sadder than my own, — „ II ii 188
yet in tune with *N* and the bees. — „ IV 32
Natured See **Hard-natured, Noblest-natured**
Naught (*See also* **Nought**) and since the Sheriff left me *n* but an empty belly, — *Foresters* II i 279
Nave *n* and aisles all empty as a fool's jest ! — *Queen Mary* IV iii 286
Navy and might have sunk a *n*— — *Becket* III iii 125
Naw (no) thaw I beänt *n* scholard, fur I 'ednt *n* time to maäke mysen a scholard — *Prom. of May* I 332
He 'ant *n* pride in 'im, and we'll git 'im to speechify for us arter dinner. — „ I 439
thou hesn't *n* business 'ere wi' my Dora, — „ II 735
we worked *n* wuss upo' the cowd tea ; — „ III 58
An' we weänt mention *n* naämes, — „ III 130
Nawbody (nobody) why there wudn't be a dinner for *n*, — „ I 149

Nawbody (nobody) (*continued*)　When ye thowt there
　were *n* watchin' o' you,　　*Prom. of May* II 179
Nay　*See* **Naäy**
Neap-tide　the realm is poor, The exchequer at *n-t* :　*Queen Mary* I v 121
Near　They call me *n*, for I am close to thee And
　England—　　*Harold* III i 6
Stay !—too *n* is death.　　*The Cup* I iii 104
Nearer　For I will come no *n* to your Grace ;　*Queen Mary* III v 200
No *n* to me ! back !　　*Foresters* IV 692
Nearest (adj.)　She had but follow'd the device of
　those Her *n* kin :　　*Queen Mary* III i 380
Nearest (s)　Who stands the *n* to her.　　" v ii 416
The Atheling is *n* to the throne.　　*Harold* II ii 569
Nearness　Upon my greater *n* to the birthday　*Foresters* III i 44
Necessity　Statesmen that are wise Shape a *n*,　*Queen Mary* III iii 33
　bound To that *n* which binds us down ;　*Harold* I i 108
so we could not but laugh, as by a royal *n*—　*Becket* III iii 159
Neck　on his *n* a collar, Gold, thick with diamonds ;　*Queen Mary* III i 78
and weight of all the world From off his *n* to mine.　" vi 214
rear and run And break both *n* and axle.　*Harold* I i 374
See here this little key about my *n* !　　" III i 10
swear nay to that by this cross on thy *n*.　*Becket*, Pro. 370
Has wheedled it off the King's *n* to her own.　" IV ii 201
not yield To lay your *n* beneath your citizen's heel.　" v i 31
upon a *n* Less lovely than her own,　　*The Falcon* 55
I wore the lady's chaplet round my *n* ;　　" 631
I lay them for the first time round your *n*.　　" 908
Swear to me by that relic on thy *n*.　*Prince John*. I
　swear then by this relic on my *n*—　*Foresters* I ii 170
twist it round thy *n* and hang thee by it.　" IV 688
Neck-broken　Huntsman, and hound, and deer were all
　n-b !　　*The Cup* I ii 24
Necklace　if we *will* buy diamond *n's* To please our lady,　*The Falcon* 44
She should return thy *n* then.　　" 70
Need (s)　Ask me for this at thy most *n*, son Harold, At
　thy most *n*.　　*Harold* III i 14
No *n* ! no *n* ! . . . There is a bench.　　*Becket* II i 123
Good Prince, art thou in *n* of any gold ?　*Foresters* II i 162
Need (verb)　I *n* thee not. Why dost thou follow me ?　*Harold* II ii 231
Needed　fly like bosom friends when *n* most.　*The Falcon* 527
Needle—in music Peerless—her *n* perfect,　*Queen Mary* III i 360
Negative　(*See also* **Positive-negative**)　Or answer'd them
　in smiling *n's* ;　　" IV iii 603
not a heart like a jewel in it—that's too *n* ;　*The Falcon* 92
Neighbour　he was my *n* once in Kent.　*Queen Mary* II iii 85
good *n*, There should be something fierier than
　fire　　" v iv 25
my foundation For men who serve the *n*,　*Harold* v i 98
Good murnin', *n's*, and the saäme to you, my men.　*Prom. of May* I 317
Neighing　*N* and roaring as they leapt to land—　*Harold* IV iii 197
Neither　No friendship sacred, values *n* man Nor woman
　save as tools—　　*Foresters* IV 713
Nene (river)　Gone hawking on the *N*,　　*Becket* I iii 3
Nescience　Back into *n* with as little pain　*Prom. of May* II 341
Nest (s)　(*See also* **Home-nest**)　then would find Her *n*
　within the cloister.　　*Harold* IV i 234
A *n* in a bush.　*Becket*.　And where, my liege ?　*Becket*, Pro. 155
And where is she ?　There in her English *n* ?　" Pro. 178
I wrong the bird ; she leaves only the *n* she built,　" I iv 46
came upon A wild-fowl sitting on her *n*,　" v ii 234
lark, that warblest high Above thy lowly *n*,　*Prom. of May* III 200
all in all to one another from the time when we
　first peeped into the bird's *n*,　　" III 274
When I and thou will rob the *n* of her.　*Foresters* I ii 161
So that myself alone may rob the *n*.　*Prince John*.
　Well, well then, thou shalt rob the *n* alone.　" I ii 166
Nest (verb)　nor priestly king to cross Their billings ere
　they *n*.　　*Harold* III ii 95
Nested　Knows where he *n*—ever comes again.　*Queen Mary* v i 26
Net (s)　We be fishermen ; I came to see after my *n's*.　*Harold* II i 27
thou hast them in thy *n*.　　*Becket* II i 287
No rushing on the game—the *n*,—the *n*.　*The Cup* I i 170
Net (verb)　How dense a fold of danger *n's* him round,　*Harold* II ii 17
Netherlands　Heir of this England and the *N* !　*Queen Mary* I v 418
nearer home, the *N*, Sicily, Naples, Lombardy.　" II i 212

Netherlands (*continued*)　Look to the *N*, wherein
　have been　　*Queen Mary* III iv 106
The voices of Franche-Comté, and the *N*,　" v i 46
Never　*See* **Niver**
Never-dawning　Shall mark out Vice from Virtue in
　the gulf Of *n-d* darkness ?　　*Prom. of May* I 542
New (adj.)　out you flutter Thro' the *n* world, go zigzag,　*Queen Mary* I iv 54
But hatch you some *n* treason in the woods.　" I v 465
None so *n*, Sir Thomas, and none so old, Sir Thomas.
　No *n* news that Philip comes to wed Mary, no old
　news that all men hate it.　　" II i 14
Look at the *N* World—a paradise made hell ;　" II i 207
The *n* Lords Are quieted with their sop of Abbey-
　lands,　　" III i 140
The light of this *n* learning wanes and dies :　" III ii 172
Well, Madam, this *n* happiness of mine ?　" III ii 208
N learning as they call it ;　　" IV i 78
in the Testaments, Both Old and *N*.　　" IV iii 234
But she's a heretic, and when I am gone, Brings
　the *n* learning back.　　" v i 202
But this *n* Pope Caraffa, Paul the Fourth,　" v ii 32
A *n* Northumberland, another Wyatt ?　" v v 188
That palate is insane which cannot tell A good dish
　from a bad, *n* wine from old.　　*Becket*, Pro. 106
I care not for thy *n* archbishoprick.　　" I i 217
Shall I forget my *n* archbishoprick And smite thee　" I i 220
It well befits thy *n* archbishoprick To take the vaga-
　bond woman　　" I i 225
That Map, and these *n* railers at the Church　" I i 306
What, this ! and this !—what ! *n* and old together !　" I iii 309
Die for a woman, what a faith is this ?　*The Cup* I iii 67
One ghost of all the ghosts—as yet so *n*,　" II 142
We cannot flaunt it in *n* feathers now :　*The Falcon* 42
and her affections Will flower toward the light in
　some *n* face.　　*Prom. of May* I 486
tide Of full democracy has overwhelm'd This Old
　World, from that flood will rise the *N*,　" I 595
When the great Democracy Makes a *n* world—　" I 672
Neither the old world, nor the *n*, nor father,　" I 674
Oh, last night, Tired, pacing my *n* lands at
　Littlechester,　　" II 647
and I have lighted On a *n* pleasure.　　" II 669
will give him, as they say, a *n* lease of life.　" III 424
but this *n* moon, I fear, Is darkness.　*Foresters* I ii 85
whereon the throstle rock'd Sings a *n* song to the
　n year—　　" I iii 28
We must fly from Robin Hood And this *n* queen
　of the wood.　　" II ii 139
Shall drink the health of our *n* woodland Queen.　" III 314
Drink to the health of our *n* Queen o' the woods.　" III 368
We drink the health of thy *n* Queen o' the woods.　" III 372
so thou fight at quarterstaff for thy dinner with
　our Robin, that will give thee a *n* zest for it,　" IV 209
or shall I call it by that *n* term Brought from the
　sacred East,　　" IV 704
New (adv.)　Ay, that am I, *n* converted, but the old
　leaven sticks to my tongue yet.　*Queen Mary* I iii 47
New-made　*n-m* children Of our imperial mother see the
　show.　　*The Cup* II 164
And I could see that as the *n-m* couple Came from
　the Minster,　　*Queen Mary* III i 93
News　*N* to me ! It then remains for your poor
　Gardiner,　　" I v 219
N abroad, William ?　　" II i 13
No new *n* that Philip comes to wed Mary, no old
　n that all men hate it.　　" II i 16
There *is n*, there *is n*,　　" II i 58
Good *n* have I to tell you, *n* to make　" III ii 186
N, mates ! a miracle, a miracle ! *n* !　" III ii 209
whether this flash of *n* be false or true,　" III ii 234
whether it bring you bitter *n* or sweet,　" III v 201
(The *n* was sudden) I could mould myself
　Reginald Pole, what *n* hath plagued thy heart ?　" v ii 17
Madam, he may bring you *n* from Philip.　" v ii 229
I bring your Majesty such grievous *n*　" v ii 240

Noä (no) *(continued)* N, fur thou be nobbut school-
  master ;   *Prom. of May* I 307
N, Mr. Steer.   „   I 314
N ; I laäme't my knee last night running arter a thief. „ I 386
N ; I knaws a deäl better now.   „   II 26
N, n ! Keep 'em.   „   II 44
N, not yet.   „   II 132
Philip Hedgar o' Soomerset !—N—yeas—   „   II 588
It mun be *him*. N !   „   II 602
n—thaw they hanged ma at 'Size fur it.   „   II 697
N, Miss ; we worked naw wuss upo' the cowd tea ; „   III 58
O lor, Miss ! n, n, n !   „   III 92
Noailles (French Ambassador) I am mighty popular
  with them, N.   *Queen Mary* I iii 102
Good morning, N.   „   I iii 159
King of France, N the Ambassador,   „   I iv 110
Good morning, Sir de N.   „   I v 242
A letter which the Count de N wrote   „   v ii 496
Noän (none) but n o' the parishes goäs by that name
  'ereabouts.   *Prom. of May* I 268
now theer be n o' my men, thinks I to mysen,   „   I 409
Miss Dora, that I ha' been n too sudden wi' you, „   II 60
Meä ? why, it be the Lord's doin', n o' mine ;   „   III 49
Nobbut (only) *(See also* **Nubbut**) Noä, fur thou be n
  schoolmaster ;   „   I 307
fur I wur n a laäbourer,   „   I 329
if I could ha' gone on wi' the plowin' n the smell o'
  the mou'd   „   I 376
and it seems to me n t'other day.   „   II 6
and if ye would n hev me,   „   II 73
'at I ha' n larned mysen haäfe on it.   „   III 4
Noble (adj.) By God's light a n creature, right royal ! *Queen Mary* I i 69
but to my mind the Lady Elizabeth is the more n
  and royal.   „   I i 72
Well, that's a n horse of yours, my Lord.   „   I iv 143
A king to be,—is he not n, girl ?   „   I v 4
No, by the holy Virgin, being n,   „   I v 70
Swear with me, n fellow-citizens, all,   „   II ii 296
And that this n realm thro' after years   „   III iii 156
do triumph at this hour In the reborn salvation of a
  land So n.   „   III iii 183
But this most n prince Plantagenet, Our good Queen's
  cousin—dallying over seas Even when his brother's,
  nay, his n mother's, Head fell—   „   III iv 291
Out, girl, you wrong a n gentleman.   „   III v 68
N as his young person and old shield.   „   v iii 513
Doth he not look n ? I had heard of him in battle
  over seas,   „   v v 32
Courage, n Aldwyth ! Let all thy people bless thee ! *Harold* I ii 182
I found him all a n host should be.   „   II ii 10
I can but love this n, honest Harold.   „   II ii 94
whereby we came to know Thy valour and thy value, n earl. „ II ii 202
Thou must swear absolutely, n Earl.   „   II ii 716
' If ye side with William Ye are not n.'   „   II ii 789
O n Harold, I would thou couldst have sworn.   „   III i 325
This is n ! That sounds of Godwin.   „   IV ii 57
N Gurth ! Best son of Godwin ! If I fall, I fall— „   v i 134
dashes it on Gurth, and Gurth, Our n Gurth, is down ! „ v i 642
for were all, my lord, as n as yourself, who would
  look up to you ?   *Becket* III iii 306
O God, O n knights, O sacrilege !   „   v iii 178
A n anger ! but Antonius To-morrow will demand your
  tribute—   *The Cup* I ii 95
A gallant boy, A n bird, each perfect of the breed. *The Falcon* 320
A n saying—and acted on would yield A nobler breed
  of men and women.   „   753
Nothing but my brave bird, my n falcon,   „   873
Why then the dying of my n bird Hath served me better
  than her living—   „   900
Ay, n Earl, and never part with it.   *Foresters* I ii 303
Not till she clean forget thee, n Earl.   „   I ii 306
Ay dear Robin ! ah n captain, friend of the poor ! „ II i 182
N Robin.   „   III 185
I thank you, n sir, the very blossom Of bandits. „   III 246
I thank you, n sir, and will pray for you   „   III 250

Noble (adj.) *(continued)* This friar is of much boldness,
  n captain. *Robin.* He hath got it from the bottle,
  n knight.   *Foresters* IV 235
Damsel, is this the truth ? *Marian.* Ay, n knight. „ IV 771
Noble (s) have marked the haughtiness of their n's ; *Queen Mary* II i 169
Spain moves, bribes our n's with her gold,   „   II i 202
Could Harry have foreseen that all our n's Would perish „ III i 117
We have given the church-lands back : The n's
  would not ;   „   v i 172
all the magistracy, all the n's, and all the wealthy ; „ v v 51
N's we dared not touch.   „   v v 104
he speaks to a n as tho' he were a churl, and to a churl
  as if he were a n.   *Becket*, Pro. 455
Nobleness I doubt not from your n of nature, *The Falcon* 803
Nobler Tell him the Saints are n than he dreams, Tell him
  that God is n than the Saints,   *Harold* v i 55
What n ? men must die.   „   v i 270
Go therefore like a friend slighted by one That hath
  climb'd up to n company.   *Becket* I i 351
A sane and natural loathing for a soul Purer, and truer
  and n than herself ;   „   II i 172
and acted on would yield A n breed of men and women. *The Falcon* 755
n The victim was, the more acceptable Might be the
  sacrifice.   „   879
if our true Robin Be not the n lion of the twain. *Foresters* IV 396
Nobler-looking Ay, but n-l.   *Queen Mary* I v 322
Noblest I am the n blood in Europe, Madam,   „   I iv 84
the n light That ever flash'd across my life, *Foresters* III 140
Noblest-natured scorns The n-n man alive, and I— *The Falcon* 259
Nobody *(See also* **Nawbody**) Thy name, thou knave ? *Queen Mary* III i 247
  Man. I am n, my Lord.   „   III i 247
Nod A life of n's and yawns.   *Becket* I iv 196
With Cain belike, in the land of N,   „   I iv 196
No-hows (unsatisfactorily) and so brought me n-h as I may
  say,   „   III i 129
Noise make what n you will with your tongues, *Queen Mary* I i 6
What n was that ? she told us of arm'd men *Becket* v ii 226
Nokes (a character in Queen Mary) Old N, can't it make
  thee a bastard ?   *Queen Mary* I i 28
No, old N. Old *Nokes.* It's Harry !   „   I i 33
Nokes (a farm hand) Luscombe, N, Oldham,
  Skipworth !   *Prom. of May* III 53
Nolo N *episcopari. Henry.* Ay, but N *Archiepiscopari,* *Becket*, Pro. 284
None See **Noän**
Nonsense That's all n, you know, such a baby as you
  are.   *Prom. of May* I 784
I am glad my n has made you smile !   „   III 314
Noon a bat flew out at him In the clear n, *Foresters* II ii 97
monies should be paid in to the Abbot of York, at the
  end of the month at n, and they are delivered here
  in the wild wood an hour after n.   „   IV 508
Norfolk (Duke of) when the Duke of N moved
  against us   *Queen Mary* II iii 2
Norman (adj.) *(See also* **Demi-Norman**) Did ye not cast
  with bestial violence Our holy N bishops down from
  all Their thrones   *Harold* I i 50
I have a N fever on me, son, And cannot answer sanely . . . „ I i 87
Is not the N Count thy friend and mine ?   „   I i 247
And bolts of thunder moulded in high heaven To serve
  the N purpose,   „   II ii 34
They have taken away the toy thou gavest me, The N
  knight.   „   II ii 107
Well, thou shalt have another N knight !   „   II ii 114
Stay—as yet Thou hast but seen how N hands can strike,
  But walk'd our N field,   „   II ii 171
And we will fill thee full of N sun,   „   II ii 180
And he our lazy-pious N King,   „   II ii 444
Then our modest women—I know the N license—thine
  own Edith—   „   II ii 477
if there sat within the N chair A ruler all for England— „ II ii 533
We could now move from Dover to the Humber Saving
  thro' N bishopricks—   „   II ii 538
Ay, ay, but many among our N lords Hate thee for this, „ II ii 544
confirm it now Before our gather'd N baronage,   „   II ii 695
I know your N cookery is so spiced, It masks all this. „ II ii 810

Norman (adj.) (continued) They have built their castles here;
Our priories are *N*; the *N* adder Hath bitten us; — *Harold* III i 37
To save thee from the wrath of *N* Saints. *Stigand.* — „ III i 217
N enough! — „ III i 250
Not mean To make our England *N*. — „ IV i 64
Or *N*? *Voices.* No! — „ IV i 81
Who shook the *N* scoundrels off the throne, — „ IV iii 169
Keep that for *N* William! — „ IV iii 181
William the *N*, for the wind had changed— — „ v i 35
His *N* Daniel! Mene, Mene, Tekel! — „ v i 194
No *N* horse Can shatter England, standing shield by shield; — „ v i 225
But by all Saints— *Leofwin.* Barring the *N*! — „ v i 483
The *N* arrow! — „ v i 522
All the *N* foot Are storming up the hill. — „ v i 553
The *N* Count is down. — „ v i 607
Truth! no; a lie, a trick, a *N* trick! — „ v i 617
His oath was broken—O holy *N* Saints, — „ v i 620
and see beyond Your *N* shrines, pardon it, pardon it, — „ v ii 9
I cannot love them, For they are *N* saints— — „ v ii 188
Make them again one people—*N*, English; And English, *N*; — *Becket* v ii 260
There was a little fair-hair'd *N* maid Lived in my mother's house: — „ v ii 355
that he calls you oversea To answer for it in his *N* courts. — *Foresters* I i 212
I am none of your delicate *N* maidens who can only broider — „ I i 238
This John—this *N* tyranny—the stream is bearing us all down, — „ II i 85
our John By his *N* arrogance and dissoluteness, — „ III 178
Dear, in these days of *N* license, when Our English maidens are their prey, if ever A *N* damsel fell into our hands, — „ III 308
Where lies that cask of wine whereof we plunder'd The *N* prelate? — „ IV 886
Earl, thou when we were hence Hast broken all our *N* forest laws,

Norman (s) rest of England bow'd theirs to the *N*, — *Queen Mary* II i 160
Our friends, the *N's*, help to shake his chair. I have a Norman fever on me, son, — *Harold* I i 85
it threatens us no more Than French or *N*. — „ I i 135
Because I love the *N* better—no, — „ I i 171
my father drove the *N's* out Of England?— — „ I i 252
N's up To fight for thee again! — „ II ii 58
Count of the *N's*, thou hast ransom'd us, — „ II ii 157
The *N's* love thee not, nor thou the *N's*, — „ II ii 253
And he our lazy-pious Norman King, With all his *N's* round him once again, — „ II ii 445
I have heard the *N's* Count upon this confusion— — „ II ii 458
Descends the ruthless *N*— — „ II ii 467
thou and he drove our good *N's* out From England, — „ II ii 525
Saving thro' Norman bishopricks—I say Ye would applaud that *N* who should drive — „ II ii 539
because we found him A *N* of the *N's*. — „ II ii 582
Angle, Jute, Dane, Saxon, *N*, — „ II ii 763
let earth rive, gulf in These cursed *N's*— — „ II ii 783
If e'er the *N* grow too hard for thee, — „ III i 12
wholesome use of these To chink against the *N*, — „ III i 22
Not mean To make our England Norman. *Edward.*
There spake Godwin, Who hated all the *N's*; — „ III i 252
Be kindly to the *N's* left among us, — „ III i 303
will ye upon oath, Help us against the *N*? — „ IV i 181
Holy Father Hath given this realm of England to the *N*. — „ v i 14
The *N*, What is he doing? — „ v i 217
Call when the *N* moves— — „ v i 230
The Norseman's raid Hath helpt the *N*, — „ v i 292
when I sware Falsely to him, the falser *N*, — „ v i 303
The *N* moves! — „ v i 438
and they fly—the *N* flies. — „ v i 541
They fly once more, they fly, the *N* flies! — „ v i 596
The *N* sends his arrows up to Heaven, — „ v i 666
N, thou liest! liars all of you, — „ v ii 104
My *N's* may but move as true with me — „ v ii 184
like his kingly sires, The *N*, striving still — *Becket* IV ii 442
both fought against the tyranny of the kings, the *N's*. — *Foresters* I i 230

Norman-blooded I say not this, as being Half *N-b*, — *Harold* I i 169
Normandy if it pass, Go not to *N*—go not to *N*. *Harold.*
And wherefore not, my king, to *N*? — „ I i 235
And why not me, my lord, to *N*? — „ I i 246
I pray thee, do not go to *N*. — „ I i 250
That he should harp this way on *N*? — „ I i 271
'I pray you do not go to *N*.' — „ II ii 218
But for my father I love *N*. — „ II ii 270
Go not to *N*— (repeat) — „ II ii 327
I am thy fastest friend in *N*. — „ II ii 556
When he was here in *N*, He loved us and we him, — „ II ii 579
Foremost in England and in *N*; — „ II ii 631
For I shall most sojourn in *N*; — „ II ii 634
And that the Holy Saints of *N* — „ II ii 727
From all the holiest shrines in *N*! — „ II ii 735
And Wulfnoth is alone in *N*. — „ III i 81
Praying for *N*; — „ v i 219
When I am out in *N* or Anjou. — *Becket, Pro.* 144
Barons of England and of *N*, — „ I iii 742
A hundred, too, from *N* and Anjou: — „ II ii 173
Normanism He hath clean repented of his *N*. — *Harold* III i 30
Normanize Plays on the word,—and *N's* too! — „ III i 388
Normanland in *N* God speaks thro' abler voices, — „ I i 165
but those of *N* Are mightier than our own. — „ III i 223
Norseland hugest wave from *N* ever yet Surged on us, — „ I i 62
Have we not broken Wales and *N*? — „ v i 395
Norseman Would ye be *Norsemen*? *Voices.* No! — „ I i 62
That these will follow thee against the *Norsemen*, — „ IV i 158
will ye, if I yield, Follow against the *N*? — „ IV i 177
Where lie the *Norsemen*? on the Derwent? — „ IV i 253
Why didst thou let so many *Norsemen* hence? — „ IV iii 33
The *N's* raid Hath helpt the Norman, — „ v i 290
North Stays longer here on our poor *n* than you:— — *Queen Mary* v i 24
Hath taken Scarboro' Castle, *n* of York; — „ v i 287
Is the *N* quiet, Gamel? — *Harold* I i 107
to spy my nakedness In my poor *N*! — „ I i 353
For if the *N* take fire, I should be back; — „ I ii 67
shake the *N* With earthquake and disruption— — „ I ii 199
And all the *N* of Humber is one storm. — „ II ii 291
Hast thou such trustless jailors in thy *N*? — „ II ii 685
N and South Thunder together, — „ III i 391
the truth Was lost in that fierce *N*, — „ III ii 26
Are landed *N* of Humber, and in a field — „ III ii 126
Well then, we will to the *N*. — „ III ii 139
Should care to plot against him in the *N*. — „ IV i 167
Conjured the mightier Harold from his *N* — „ IV ii 69
send the shatter'd *N* again to sea, — „ IV iii 140
Who made this Britain England, break the *N*: — „ IV iii 155
in South and *N* at once I could not be. — „ IV iii 218
To meet thee in the *N*. — „ v i 290
—your *n* chills me. — *Becket, Pro.* 330
thro' all the forest land *N* to the Tyne: — *Foresters* II ii 89
There was a man of ours Up in the *n*, — „ v 530
Northampton on a Tuesday did I fly Forth from *N*; — *Becket* v ii 287
North-east the *N-e* took and turned him South-west, then the South-west turned him South-*e*, — „ II ii 320
Northumberland (Northumbria) Thou art a great voice in *N*! — *Harold* I i 114
I heard from *N* to-day. — „ I i 350
Wash up that old crown of *N*. — „ v i 167
Northumberland (Earl of) and death to *N*! — *Queen Mary* I i 67
she spoke even of *N* pitifully, — „ I i 93
I do believe he holp *N* — „ I v 278
when you put *N* to death, — „ I v 485
never Like that poor heart, *N*, — „ II iii 333
Was not Lord Pembroke with *N*? — „ II iv 8
His breaking with *N* broke *N*. — „ II iv 13
False to *N*, is he false to me? — „ II iv 39
Why, ev'n the haughty prince, *N*, — „ III i 147
The stormy Wyatts and *N's*, — „ III ii 168
A new *N*, another Wyatt? — „ v v 188
Northumbria (ancient earldom) When didst thou hear from thy *N*? — *Harold* I i 281
Leave me alone, brother, with my *N*: — „ I i 286
I heard from my *N* yesterday. — „ I i 331
How goes it then with thy *N*? — „ I i 333

Northumbria (ancient earldom) (*continued*) fain had calcined
   all *N* To one black ash,   *Harold* III i 56
I come for mine own Earldom, my *N* ;   „   IV ii 30
N threw thee off, she will not have thee,   „   IV ii 33
Northumbrian (adj.) Among the good *N* folk,   „   I ii 220
Our old *N* crown, And kings of our own choosing.   „   IV i 31
Of the *N* helmet on the heath ?   „   v i 144
Northumbrian (s) if his *N's* rise And hurl him from them,—   „   II ii 455
Thou didst arouse the fierce *N's* !   „   v i 347
And that the false *N* held aloof,   „   v ii 165
Norway (country) and the giant King of *N*, Harold
   Hardrada—   „   III ii 122
   as having been so bruised By Harold, king of *N* ;   „   IV i 10
Norway (King) He hath gone to kindle *N* against England,   „   I ii 79
Since Tostig came with *N*—   „   IV i 173
I am foraging For *N's* army.   „   IV ii 6
Free thee or slay thee, *N* will have war ; No man
   would strike with Tostig, save for *N*.   „   IV ii 18
Thou art nothing in thine England, save for *N*,   „   IV ii 23
What for *N* then ?   He looks for land among us,   „   IV ii 52
sequel had been other than his league With *N*,   „   IV iii 89
Here by dead *N* without dream or dawn !   „   IV iii 122
Nose cackling of bastardy under the Queen's own *n* ?   *Queen Mary* I i 59
Who rub their fawning *n's* in the dust,   „   III iii 242
God hath blest or cursed me with a *n*—   „   III v 179
God hath given your Grace a *n*, or not,   „   III v 203
rose but pricks his *n* Against the thorn,   *Harold* I i 422
when I was a-getting o' bluebells for your ladyship's
   n to smell on—   *Becket* iii i 162
wait Till his *n* rises ; he will be very king.   „   v ii 184
Lady Marian holds her *n* when she steps across it.   *Foresters* I i 84
Nosing   *See* **Carrion-nosing**
Nostril   puffed out such an incense of unctuosity into
   the *n's* of our Gods of Church and State,   *Becket* iii iii 116
Note He never yet could brook the *n* of scorn.   „   v ii 299
play the *n* Whereat the dog shall howl   *Harold* I ii 191
Nothing (*See also* **Naught, Nought, Nowt, Something-
nothing**) *N* ? *Alice.* Never, your Grace.   *Queen Mary* I v 574
What such a one as Wyatt says is in :   „   III i 139
And *n* of the titles to the crown ;   „   III i 383
he is free enough in talk, But tells me *n*.   „   III ii 194
They know *n* ; They burn for *n*.   „   v iii 113
but say the world is *n*—   „   v iii 368
N, Madam, Save that methought I gather'd   „   v iii 101
N ; but ' come, come, come,' and all awry,   „   v v 15
quiet, ay, as yet—*N* as yet.   *Harold* I i 111
Make not thou The *n* something.   „   I i 363
On a sudden—at a something—for a *n*—   „   I i 443
Anything or *n* ?   *The Falcon* 133
he would answer *n*, I could make *n* of him ;   *Prom. of May* I 496
N from you ! (repeat)   „   II 802, 809
we be beggars, we come to ask o' you.   We ha' *n*.
   Second Beggar.   Rags, *n* but our rags.   *Foresters* III 190
Notice I have *n* from our partisans Within the city   *Queen Mary* II iii 51
A *n* from the priest,   *Becket* iii iii 3
Flutter'd or flatter'd by your *n* of her,   *The Falcon* 538
Nottingham Thou knowest that the Sheriff of *N* loves
   thee.   *Foresters* I i 223
The Sheriff of *N* was there—not John.   „   I i 252
Beware of John and the Sheriff of *N*.   „   I i 255
What art thou, man ?   Sheriff of *N* ?   „   I ii 191
in *N* they say There bides a foul witch   „   II i 202
if thou wilt show us the way back to *N*.   „   II i 361
is it true ?—That John last week return'd to *N*,   „   III 147
Part shall go to the almshouses at *N*,   „   III 206
That business which we have in *N*—   „   III 230
And may your business thrive in *N* !   „   III 245
I know them arrant knaves in *N*.   „   III 302
Black news, black news from *N* !   „   III 447
I go to *N*.   Sheriff, thou wilt find me at *N*.   „   IV 800
No, let him be.   Sheriff of *N*,   „   IV 815
Nought (nothing) There's *n* but the vire of God's
   hell   *Queen Mary* IV iii 526
Novel sometimes been moved to tears by a chapter
   of fine writing in a *n* ;   *Prom. of May* III 209

Noviciate Breaking already from thy *n*   *Becket* v ii 80
Small peace was mine in my *n*,   „   v ii 87
Noway and I *n* doubt But that with God's grace, I
   can live so still.   *Queen Mary* II ii 218
Nowt (nothing) I knaws *n* o' what foälks says,   *Prom. of May* I 27
N—what could he saäy ?   „   I 152
But if that be *n* to she, then it be *n* to me.   „   I 182
Hesn't he left ye *n* ?   *Dora.*   No, Mr. Dobson.   „   II 7
I were insured, Miss, an' I lost *n* by it.   „   II 58
Out o' the chaumber !   I'll mash tha into *n*.   „   III 735
Nubbut (only) (*See also* **Nobbut**) Owd Steer gi'es *n* cowd
   tea to 'is men, and owd Dobson gi'es beer.   „   II 224
Numb'd Has often *n* me into apathy Against the   „   I 227
Number'd We dally with our lazy moments here,
   And hers are *n*.   *Queen Mary* v iii 109
Nun Thou art *my n*, thy cloister in mine arms.   *Harold* I ii 63
saw thy willy-nilly *n* Vying a tress   „   v i 148
What shall it be ?   I'll go as a *n*.   *Becket.*   No.
   Rosamund.   What, not good enough Even to
   play at *n* ?   *Becket.*   Dan John with a *n*,
   That Map,   *Becket* i i 301
thy solitude among thy *n's*, May that save thee !   „   v ii 176
Nunnery Put her away into a *n* !   „   *Pro.* 65
Come thou with me to Godstow *n*,   „   IV ii 366
To put her into Godstow *n*. (repeat)   *Becket* v i 208, 210
He bad me put her into a *n*—   *Becket* v i 214
Get thee back to thy *n* with all haste ;   „   v ii 163
Nurse (s) The *n's* yawn'd, the cradle gaped,   *Queen Mary* III vi 93
My *n* would tell me of a molehill   *Harold* IV ii 128
My good old *n*, I had forgotten thou wast sitting
   there.   *The Falcon* 34
You can take it, *n* !   „   490
my *n* has broken The thread of my dead flowers,   „   521
I thank you, my good *n*.   „   560
And thou too leave us, my dear *n*, alone.   „   701
Ay, the dear *n* will leave you alone ;   „   702
I have anger'd your good *n* ;   „   707
Our old *n* crying as if for her own child,   *Prom. of May* II 479
Nursery (adj.) Then she got me a place as *n* governess,   „   III 385
Nursery (s) That may seem strange beyond his *n*.   *Queen Mary* II ii 396
Nursery-cocker'd The *n-c* child will jeer at aught   „   II ii 394
Nursery-tale That *n-t* Still read, then ?   *Prom. of May* III 525
Nut woodland squirrel sees the *n* Behind the shell,   *Foresters* II i 647
On *n's* and acorns, ha !   Or the King's deer ?   „   IV 882

O

Oaf *o's*, ghosts o' the mist, wills-o'-the-wisp ;   *Foresters* II i 263
Oak (*See also* **Shambles-oak**) Pine, beech and plane,
   o, walnut,   *The Cup* I i 1
whose storm-voice Unsockets the strong *o*,   „   II 283
Such hearts of *o* as they be.   *Foresters* II i 4
And these rough *o's* the palms of Paradise !   „   II i 169
Here's a pot o' wild honey from an old *o*,   „   II i 296
before the shadow of these dark *o's*   „   II i 605
hundreds of huge *o's*, Gnarl'd—   „   III 91
In that *o*, where twelve Can stand upright,   „   III 309
Our feast is yonder, spread beneath an *o*,   „   IV 190
Meanwhile, farewell Old friends, old patriarch *o's*.   „   IV 1054
yet I think these *o's* at dawn and even,   „   IV 1066
these old *o's* will murmur thee Marian along with Robin.   „   IV 1093
Oaken present her with this *o* chaplet as Queen of the wood,   „   III 59
Oak-tree Come from out That *o-t* !   „   IV 998
Oän (own) and he calls out among our *o* men, ' The
   land belongs to the people !'   *Prom. of May* I 140
fur I niver touched a drop of owt till my *o*
   wedding-daäy,   „   I 362
then back ageän, a-follering my *o* shadder—   „   I 371
an' them theer be soom of her *o* roses,   „   II 38
the Lord bless 'er—'er *o* sen ;   „   II 40
I would taäke the owd blind man to my *o* fireside.   „   II 74

Oän (own) (*continued*) and you should sit i' your *o*
  parlour quite like a laädy, ye should !   *Prom. of May* II 97
  Fur she'd niver 'a been talkin' haäfe an hour wi'
  the divil 'at killed her *o* sister,   ,, II 604
'Oäpe (hope) They can't be many, my dear, but I '*o's*
  they'll be 'appy.   ,, I 353
Oath To bind me first by *o's* I could not keep,   *Queen Mary* I v 557
  he freed himself By *o* and compurgation   *Harold* II ii 520
  he hath not bound me by an *o*—Is ' ay ' an *o* ? is
  ' ay ' strong as an *o* ?   ,, II ii 661
  same sin to break my word As break mine *o* ?   ,, II ii 665
  thou hast sworn an *o* Which, if not kept,   ,, II ii 738
  —am grateful for thine honest *o*,   ,, II ii 756
  Hast thou had absolution for thine *o* ?   ,, III i 212
  O son, when thou didst tell me of thine *o*,   ,, III i 268
  my son ! Are all *o's* to be broken then,   ,, III i 286
  lost Somewhat of upright stature thro' mine *o*,   ,, III i 57
  will ye upon *o*, Help us against the Norman ?   ,, IV i 180
  devil Hath haunted me—mine *o*—my wife—   ,, V i 318
  My fatal *o*—the dead Saints—the dark dreams—   ,, V i 380
  His o was broken—O holy Norman Saints,   ,, V i 616
  He that was false in *o* to me,   ,, V ii 151
  Being bounden by my coronation *o* To do men justice.   *Becket* I iii 396
  that merits death,—False *o* on holy cross—   ,, IV ii 209
Ob Wouldst thou call my Oberon *O* ?   *Foresters* II ii 131
  Never *O* before his face.   ,, II ii 133
Obedience promise full Allegiance and *o* to the
  death.   *Queen Mary* II ii 169
  in this unity and *o* Unto the holy see   ,, III iii 157
  His tractate upon True *O*,   ,, IV i 92
  serviceable In all *o*, as mine own hath been :   *Harold* I i 292
  by that canonical *o* Thou still hast owed   *Becket* I iii 275
  Fealty to the King, *o* to thyself ?   ,, I iii 587
Obedient —the world A most *o* beast and fool—   *Queen Mary* IV iii 414
Oberon And capering hand in hand with *O*.   *Foresters* II i 498
  Wouldst thou call my *O* Ob ?   ,, II ii 131
  for *O* fled away Twenty thousand leagues to-day.   ,, II ii 142
Obey Well, well, you must *o* ;   *Queen Mary* I iv 253
  I must *o* the Queen and Council, man.   ,, IV ii 164
  O your King and Queen, and not for dread   ,, IV iii 177
  Sire, I *o* you. Come quickly.   ,, V i 220
  And yet I must *o* the Holy Father,   ,, V ii 38
  O the Count's conditions, my good friend.   *Harold* II ii 276
  Seem to *o* them.   ,, II ii 280
  O him, speak him fair,   ,, II ii 317
  O my first and last commandment. Go !   ,, V i 359
  Didst thou not promise Henry to *o* These ancient laws   *Becket* I iii 17
  Sign and *o* !   ,, I iii 132
  Sign, and *o* the crown !   ,, I iii 144
  And swear to *o* the customs.   ,, I iii 270
  I promised The King to *o* these customs,   ,, I iii 557
  That thou *o*, not me, but God in me,   ,, I iii 721
  since we likewise swore to *o* the customs,   ,, V i 54
  No man to love me, honour me, *o* me !   ,, V i 240
  Still I must *o* them. Fare you well.   *The Cup* I i 158
  Up with you, all of you, out of it ! hear and *o*.   *Foresters* II ii 185
  You hear your Queen, *o* !   ,, III 464
Obeyed who had but *o* her father ;   *Queen Mary* I i 95
  the child *o* her father.   ,, I v 494
  crown Would cleave to me that but *o* the crown,   *Becket* V i 50
Obligation With bitter *o* to the Count—   *Harold* II ii 221
  every bond and debt and *o* Incurr'd as Chancellor.   *Becket* I iii 710
Obliged you worked well enough, and I am much *o*
  to all of you.   *Prom. of May* III 62
Observance all manner of homages, and *o's*, and circumbendibuses.   *Foresters* I i 103
Obtain by your intercession May from the Apostolic
  see *o*,   *Queen Mary* III iii 147
Occasion on a great *o* sure to wake As great a wrath in
  Becket—   *Becket* III i 87
  They seek—you make—*o* for your death.   ,, V ii 558
  two-legg'd dogs Among us who can smell a true *o*,   *The Cup* II ii 113
  but this day has brought A great *o*.   *The Falcon* 489
Occupy that anyone Should seize our person, *o* our
  state,   *Queen Mary* II ii 178

Ocean And roll the golden *o's* of our grain,   *The Cup* II 269
  or wreckt And dead beneath the midland *o*,   *Foresters* II i 657
Odd (adj.) Make us despise it at *o* hours, my Lord.   *Queen Mary* IV iii 386
  I have to pray you, some *o* time,   ,, V i 258
  But doth not the weight of the flesh at *o* times over-
  balance the weight of the church, ha friar ?   *Foresters* I i 61
Odd (s) They are all too much at *o's* to close at once   *Queen Mary* I v 632
  Gardiner knows, but the Council are all at *o's*,   ,, II i 139
  But seeing valour is one against all *o's*,   *Foresters* IV 318
Odo (Bishop of Bayeux) coming with his brother *O* The
  Bayeux bishop,   *Harold* II ii 347
  and *O* said, ' Thine is the right,   ,, II ii 356
Odour Let all the air reel into a mist of *o*,   *The Cup* II 185
O'erleap after rain *o's* a jutting rock And shoots   ,, I i 110
Offal with *o* thrown Into the blind sea of forget-
  fulness.   *Queen Mary* III iii 191
  scum And *o* of the city would not change   ,, III 77
  men, the scum and *o* of the Church ;   *Becket* I iii 408
Offence As persons undefiled with our *o*,   *Queen Mary* III iii 144
  and mighty slow To feel *o's*.   *Prom. of May* II 630
Offend You *o* us ; you may leave us.   *Queen Mary* I v 210
  You *o* us. *Gardiner*. These princes are like children,   ,, I v 232
  It is the crown *O's* him—   *The Cup* II 530
Offended I have *o* against heaven and earth   *Queen Mary* IV iii 124
  since my hand *o*, having written Against my heart,   ,, IV iii 247
  ' This hath *o*—this unworthy hand ! '   ,, IV iii 613
Offending You have an old trick of *o* us ;   ,, III iv 315
Offer a formal *o* of the hand Of Philip ?   ,, I v 349
  The formal *o* of Prince Philip's hand.   ,, I v 588
Offer'd has *o* her his son Philip, the Pope and the Devil.   ,, I i 105
  a hundred Gold pieces once were *o* by the Duke.   *The Falcon* 324
  Has he *o* you marriage, this gentleman ?   *Prom. of May* III 289
Offering *See* **Peace-offering**
Office I have lost mine *o*,   *Queen Mary* I v 236
  Spain in all the great *o's* of state ;   ,, II i 178
  no foreigner Hold *o* in the household,   ,, III iii 72
  set up The Holy *O* here—garner the wheat,   ,, V v 113
  tell the cooks to close The doors of all the *o's* below.   ,, V v 117
  Love him ! why not ? thine is a loving *o*,   *Harold* II ii 97
  fill'd All *o's*, all bishopricks with English—   *Becket* I iii 535
  I had been so true To Henry and mine *o*   ,, I iii 693
  both of us Too headlong for our *o*.   ,, II ii 290
  Nor make me traitor to my holy *o*.   ,, V ii 149
  You should attend the *o*, give them heart.   ,, V ii 598
  He said, ' Attend the *o*.' *Becket*. Attend the *o* ?   ,, V ii 608
  get you back ! go on with the *o*.   ,, V iii 33
  Back, I say ! Go on with the *o*.   ,, V iii 39
Officer the Queen's *O's* Are here in force   *Queen Mary* II i 108
  by the judgment of the *o's* of the said lord king,   *Foresters* I iii 65
Ofs King Hath divers *o* and ons, *o* and belongings,   *Becket* IV ii 32
Oftener But you were *o* there. I have none but you.   ,, II i 53
Oil I Scraped from your finger-points the holy *o* ;   *Queen Mary* IV ii 133
Olaf (a Norwegian king) St. *O*, not while I am by !   *Harold* I i 395
Old (adj.) (*See also* **Owd, Owld**) *O* Nokes, can't it make
  thee a bastard ?   *Queen Mary* I i 28
  No, *o* Nokes. It's Harry.   ,, I i 33
  Old Nokes. It's Harry.   ,,
  for thou was born i' the tail end of *o* Harry the Seventh.   ,, I i 42
  I was born true man at five in the forenoon i' the tail
  of *o* Harry,   ,, I i 46
  but I and my *o* woman 'ud burn upon it,   ,, I i 56
  Ay, but he's too *o*.   ,, I i 121
  O Bourne to the life !   ,, I iii 30
  Yon gray *o* Gospeller, sour as midwinter, Begin with him.   ,, I iii 40
  By the mass, *o* friend, we'll have no pope here   ,, I iii 42
  Ay, that am I, new converted, but the *o* leaven sticks
  to my tongue yet.   ,, I iii 48
  but this fierce *o* Gardiner—his big baldness,   ,, I iv 263
  or wave And wind at their *o* battle : he must have
  written.   ,, I v 357
  Not yet ; but your *o* Traitors of the Tower—   ,, I v 483
  Why comes that *o* fox-Fleming back again ?   ,, I v 581
  None so new, Sir Thomas, and none so *o*, Sir Thomas.
  No new news that Philip comes to wed Mary, no
  o news that all men hate it. *O* Sir Thomas would
  have hated it.   ,, II i 15

Old (adj.) (continued)   O Sir Thomas always granted the
 wine.   *Queen Mary* II i 41
Ay—sonnets—a fine courtier of the *o* court, *o* Sir
 Thomas.   ,, II i 46
Wake, or the stout *o* island will become A rotten
 limb of Spain.   ,, II i 104
you that have kept your *o* customs upright, ,, II i 158
I have been there with *o* Sir Thomas, and the beds
 I know.   ,, II i 184
Ay, gray *o* castle of Alington, green field Beside the
 brimming Medway,   ,, II i 243
They go like those *o* Pharisees in John Convicted
 by their conscience,   ,, II ii 8
And scared the gray *o* porter and his wife. ,, II iii 16
I know not my letters ; the *o* priest taught me nothing. .. II iii 57
Far liefer had I in my country hall Been reading
 some *o* book, with mine *o* hound Couch'd at my
 hearth, and mine *o* flask of wine Beside me, ,, III i 44
I am an *o* man wearied with my journey, Ev'n with
 my joy.   ,, III ii 127
and are well agreed That those *o* statutes touching
 Lollardism   ,, III iv 7
O Rome, that first made martyrs in the Church, ,, III iv 126
You have an *o* trick of offending us ; ,, III iv 315
Touch him upon his *o* heretical talk, ,, III iv 352
Men now are bow'd and *o*, the doctors tell you, ,, III iv 408
Our *o* friend Cranmer, Your more especial love, ,, III iv 416
there's An *o* world English adage to the point. ,, IV i 175
Cool as the light in *o* decaying wood ; ,, IV ii 5
Monsters of mistradition, *o* enough To scare me
 into dreaming,   ,, IV ii 102
Good day, *o* friend ; what, you look somewhat worn ; ,, IV ii 115
in the Testaments, Both *O* and New. ,, IV iii 234
Crying, ' Forward ! '—set our *o* church rocking, ,, IV iii 403
Hist ! there be two *o* gossips—gospellers. ,, IV iii 460
And the gray dawn Of an *o* age that never will be
 mine   ,, V ii 234
Probing an *o* state-secret—how it chanced That this
 young Earl   ,, V ii 487
Noble as his young person and *o* shield. ,, V ii 513
Ah, weak and meek *o* man, Seven-fold dishonour'd ,, V v 132
O, miserable, diseased,   ,, V v 178
I am a harm to England.   O uncanonical Stigand— *Harold* I i 81
Stand by him, mine *o* friend,   ,, I i 112
So says *o* Gurth, not I : yet hear ! thine earldom,
 Tostig, hath been a kingdom.   Their *o* crown Is
 yet a force among them,   ,, I i 302
and I beat him.   Even *o* Gurth would fight.   I had
 much ado To hold mine own against *o* Gurth.
 O Gurth,   ,, I i 436
I dug mine into My *o* fast friend the shore, ,, II i 7
Counts his *o* beads, and hath forgotten thee. ,, II ii 447
our good King Kneels mumbling some *o* bone— ,, II ii 469
I, *o* shrivell'd Stigand, I, Dry as an *o* wood-fungus
 on a dead tree,   ,, III i 7
I do believe My *o* crook'd spine would bud out two
 young wings   ,, III i 24
No, not strange This was *o* human laughter in *o* Rome ,, III ii 163
Our *o* Northumbrian crown, And kings of our own
 choosing.   ,, IV i 31
Your *o* crown Were little help without our Saxon
 carles   ,, IV i 34
There is a pleasant fable in *o* books, ,, IV i 56
This *o* Wulfnoth Would take me on his knees and
 tell me tales   ,, IV i 71
O man, Harold Hates nothing ; not *his* fault, ,, IV i 128
So loud, that, by St. Dunstan, *o* St. Thor— ,, IV iii 146
but our *o* Thor Heard his own thunder again, ,, IV iii 149
O dog, Thou art drunk, *o* dog ! ,, IV iii 163
Wash up that *o* crown of Northumberland. ,, V i 167
And chanting that *o* song of Brunanburg Where
 England conquer'd.   ,, V i 215
And our *o* songs are prayers for England too ! ,, V i 222
but I, *o* wretch, *o* Stigand, With hands too limp
 to brandish iron—   ,, V i 447

Old (adj.) (continued)   He is chanting some *o* warsong. *Harold* V i 495
War-woodman of *o* Woden, how he fells The mortal
 copse of faces !   ,, V i 588
and most amorous Of good *o* red sound liberal
 Gascon wine :   *Becket*, Pro. 100
believe thee The veriest Galahad of *o* Arthur's hall. ,, Pro. 129
Well, well, *o* men must die, or the world would grow
 mouldy,   .. Pro. 408
The good *o* man would sometimes have his jest— .. II i 61
You will do much To rake out all *o* dying heats, ,, II ii 114
I hate a split between *o* friendships as I hate the
 dirty gap   ,, II ii 380
And that *o* priest whom John of Salisbury trusted
 Hath sent another.   ,, III i 69
for to be sure it's no more than a week since our *o*
 Father Philip   ,, III i 110
tho' to be sure our mother 'ill sing me *o* songs .. III i 184
for the *o* King would act servitor and hand a dish
 to his son ;   ,, III iii 138
Mine *o* friend, Thomas, I would there were that
 perfect trust between us,   ,, III iii 262
You could not—*o* affection master'd you, ,, V ii 143
I know not why You call these *o* things back again, ,, V ii 270
The *o* King's present, carried off the casks, ,, V ii 442
And lose his head as *o* St. Denis did. ,, V ii 480
May they not say you dared not show yourself In
 your *o* place ?   ,, V ii 596
I am not mad, not sick, not *o* enough To doat on one
 alone.   *The Cup* I iii 69
It is *o*, I know not How many hundred years. ,, II 342
we would add Some golden fringe of gorgeousness
 beyond *O* use,   ,, II 439
Did not some *o* Greek Say death was the chief good ? ,, II 513
This *o* thing here they are but blue beads—my Piero, *The Falcon* 47
Ay, my lady, but won't you speak with the *o* woman first, ,, 182
And yet to speak white truth, my good *o* mother, ,, 504
It's the *o* Scripture text, ' Let us eat and drink,
 for to-morrow we die.'   *Prom. of May* I 258
' What are we,' says the blind *o* man in Lear ? ,, I 263
I hate tears.   Marriage is but an *o* tradition. ,, I 491
That fine, fat, hook-nosed uncle of mine, *o* Harold, ,, I 510
will each Bid their *o* bond farewell with smiles, not
 tears ;   ,, I 524
for when the tide Of full democracy has overwhelm'd
 This *O* world,   ,, I 594
Tut ! you talk *O* feudalism. ,, I 670
Neither the *o* world, nor the new, nor father, ,, I 674
And poor *o* father not die miserable. ,, I 722
Our *o* nurse crying as if for her own child, ,, II 479
I do not dare, like an *o* friend, to shake it. ,, II 526
I have always told Father that the huge *o* ashtree
 there would cause an accident some day ; ,, III 244
for, indeed, he tells me that he met you once in
 the *o* times,   ,, III 263
and when the children grew too *o* for me, ,, III 387
your Father must be now in extreme *o* age. ,, III 400
We Steers are of *o* blood, tho' we be fallen. ,, III 604
and your own name Of Harold sounds so English
 and so *o*   ,, III 610
I be lanker than an *o* horse turned out to die on the
 common.   *Foresters* I i 51
and your Ladyship hath sung the *o* proverb out of
 fashion.   ,, I i 164
And how often in *o* histories have the great men striven
 against the stream,   ,, I i 242
I am *o* and forget.   Was Prince John there ? ,, I i 250
o faces Press round us, and warm hands close with
 warm hands,   ,, I iii 18
Ay, ay, gown, coif, and petticoat, and the *o* woman's
 blessing with them to the last fringe. ,, II i 195
Except this *o* hag have been bribed to lie. *Robin.*
We *o* hags should be bribed to speak truth, ,, II i 234
There is but one *o* woman in the hut. ,, II i 241
There is yet another *o* woman. ,, II i 244
O hag, how should thy one tooth drill thro' this ? ,, II i 275

Old (adj.) (continued) There's for you, and there's for
　you—and the o woman's welcome.　　　　　*Foresters* II i 290
The o wretch is mad, and her bread is beyond me :　　　" II i 291
Here's a pot o' wild honey from an o oak,　　　　　" II i 296
And, o hag tho' I be, I can spell the hand.　　　　" II i 350
Why do you listen, man, to the o fool ?　　　　　" II i 358
All the sweet saints bless your worship for your alms
　to the o woman !　　　　　　　　　　　　　" II i 364
How should this o lamester guide us !　　　　　" II i 369
Why, an o woman can shoot closer than you two.　　" II i 400
and make thine o carcase a target for us three.　　" II i 404
Did I not tell you an o woman could shoot better ?　" II i 407
Thou art no o woman—thou art disguised—thou art
　one of the thieves.　　　　　　　　　　　" II i 410
O as I am, I will not brook to see Three upon two.　" II i 422
A brave o fellow but he angers me.　　　　　　" II i 471
He is o and almost mad to keep the land.　　　　" II i 528
thou wast by And never drewest sword to help the o
　man　　　　　　　　　　　　　　　　" II i 541
The o man dotes.　　　　　　　　　　　　" II ii 83
And I, o Much, say as much, for being every inch a
　man I honour every inch of a woman.　　　　" III 62
When the flower was wither'd and o.　　　　　" IV 22
at last I crawl'd like a sick crab from my o shell,　" IV 126
Ay, for o Much is every inch a man.　　　　　" IV 289
Because thou art always so much more of a man than
　my youngsters o Much.　*Much.* Well, we Muches
　be o. *Robin.* O as the hills. *Much.* O as the mill.　" IV 299
Where is this o Sir Richard of the Lea ?　　　　" IV 438
and thus This o Sir Richard might redeem his land.　" IV 487
By o St. Vitus Have you gone mad ?　　　　　" IV 614
And this o crazeling in the litter there.　　　　" IV 634
Child, thou shalt wed him, Or thine o father will
　go mad—he will,　　　　　　　　　　　" IV 645
Carry her off, and let the o man die.　　　　　" IV 677
Meanwhile, farewell O friends, o patriarch oaks.　" IV 1054
And surely these o oaks will murmur thee Marian
　along with Robin.　　　　　　　　　　　" IV 1093
Old (s) and watch The parch'd banks rolling incense,
　as of o,　　　　　　　　　　　*Queen Mary* I v 92
Should not this day be held in after years More
　solemn than of o ?　　　　　　　　　　" III iii 91
This hard coarse man of o hath crouch'd to me　" IV iii 169
but I know it of o, he hates me too ;　　　　　" v ii 60
Did not Heaven speak to men in dreams of o ?
　Harold. Ay—well—of o.　　　　　*Harold* I ii 95
What, this ! and this !—what ! new and o together !　*Becket* I iii 310
We have had our leagues of o with Eastern kings.　*The Cup* I ii 101
Perhaps I thought with those of o,　　　　*The Falcon* 878
Olden Is like a word that comes from o days,　*Queen Mary* III v 34
Let these decide on what was customary In o days,　*Becket* II ii 176
Older I am eleven years o than he is.　　*Queen Mary* I v 68
I am eleven years o than he, Poor boy !　　　　" v 46
oaks, Gnarl'd—o than the thrones of Europe—　*Foresters* III 92
Oldest *Becket*, I am the o of the Templars,　*Becket* I iii 247
I am the o of thy men, and thou and thy youngsters　*Foresters* IV 294
Old-fashioned I have heard that ' your Lordship,' and
　' your Ladyship,' and ' your Grace ' are all grow-
　ing o-f !　　　　　　　　　　　*Prom. of May* III 318
But the love of sister for sister can never be o-f.　" III 320
Oldham Luscombe, Nokes, O, Skipworth !　　" III 53
Old-world There was an o-w tomb beside my
　father's,　　　　　　　　　　*Queen Mary* v ii 393
these o-w servants Are all but flesh and blood　*The Falcon* 707
full democracy has overwhelm'd This O w,　*Prom. of May* I 594
learnt at last that all His o-w faith,　　　　" II 332
Olive-branch more of o-b and amnesty For foes at home—　*Becket* v ii 15
Ominous Not stagger'd by this o earth and heaven :　*Harold* I i 207
Ommost (almost) Seeäms I o knaws the back on 'im—*Prom. of May* II 577
One There is but o thing against them.　*Queen Mary* I i 100
and sever'd from the faith, will return into the o
　true fold,　　　　　　　　　　　　　" I iii 22
Calais ! Our o point on the main, the gate of France !　" I v 125
Spain and we, O crown, might rule the world.　　" I v 303
But Philip never writes me o poor word,　　　　" I v 360

One (continued) For Philip comes, o hand in mine,
　and o Steadying the tremulous pillars of the
　Church—　　　　　　　　　　　*Queen Mary* I v 515
They are all too much at odds to close at once In
　o full-throated No !　　　　　　　　　" I v 634
you stroke me on o cheek, Buffet the other.　　　" II i 117
So I say Your city is divided, and I fear O scruple,　" II ii 100
Am I Thomas White ? O word before she comes.　" II ii 109
And arm and strike as with o hand,　　　　　" II ii 202
moving side by side Beneath o canopy,　　　　" III i 97
They smile as if content with o another.　　　　" III i 211
O crater opens when another shuts.　　　　　" III i 322
but I say There is no man—there was o woman
　with us—　　　　　　　　　　　　　" III i 337
Nay come with me—o moment !　　　　　　" III ii 189
You were the o sole man in either house Who
　stood upright　　　　　　　　　　　" III iii 252
I say you were the o sole man who stood.　　　" III iii 263
I am the o sole man in either house,　　　　　" III iii 265
Well, you o man, because you stood upright,　　" III iii 268
If any man in any way would be The o man, he
　shall be so to his cost.　　　　　　　　" III iii 276
yet I found O day, a wholesome scripture,　　　" III iv 84
call they not The o true faith, a loathsome idol-
　worship ?　　　　　　　　　　　　　" III iv 219
there comes a missive from the Queen It shall
　be all my study for o hour　　　　　　　" III v 184
with free wing The world were all o Araby.　　" III v 210
o half Will flutter here, o there.　　　　　　" III vi 196
Methinks that would you tarry o day more (The
　news was sudden)　　　　　　　　　　" III vi 233
For o day more, so far as I can tell.　　　　　" III vi 246
Then o day more to please her Majesty.　　　" III vi 247
return'd To the o Catholic Universal Church,
　Repentant of his errors ?　　　　　　　" IV iii 21
Pray with o breath, o heart, o soul for me.　　" IV iii 104
What, not o day ?　　　　　　　　　　　" v i 209
and it was thought we two Might make o flesh,　" v i 137
No—we were not made O flesh in happiness, no
　happiness here ; But now we are made o flesh
　in misery ;　　　　　　　　　　　　" v ii 150
And there is o Death stands behind the Groom,
　And there is o Death stands behind the Bride—　" v ii 165
and to send us again, according to His promise,
　the o King, the Christ,　　　　　　　　" v iv 53
Ay, worse than that—not o hour true to me !　　" v v 159
Why then the wrath of Heaven hath three tails,
　The devil only o.　　　　　　　　*Harold* I i 62
But heaven and earth are threads of the same loom,
　Play into o another,　　　　　　　　　" I i 211
It is but for o moon.　　　　　　　　　　" I ii 30
And all the North of Humber is o storm.　　　" II ii 291
Harold, I am thy friend, o life with thee,　　　" II ii 649
Sir Count, He had but o foot, he must have hopt away,　" II ii 675
were or should be all O England, for this cow-herd, like
　my father,　　　　　　　　　　　　" IV i 79
Ye heard o witness even now.　　　　　　　" IV i 170
I have not spoken to the king O word ; and o I must.
　Farewell !　　　　　　　　　　　　" v i 336
Whose life was all o battle, incarnate war,　　　" v i 397
Make thou o man as three to roll them down !　" v i 577
No, o—brave Gurth, o gash from brow to knee !　" v ii 70
But o woman ! Look you, we never mean to part again.　" v ii 79
Death !—and enough of death for this o day,　　" v ii 120
Of o self-stock at first, Make them again o people—　" v ii 186
True, o rose will outblossom the rest, o rose in a
　bower.　　　　　　　　　　　*Becket*, Pro. 345
but I fear this o fancy hath taken root,　　　" Pro. 480
And goodly acres—we will make her whole ; Not o
　rood lost.　　　　　　　　　　　　" I i 165
So that you grant me o slight favour.　　　　" I ii 58
And some are reeds, that o time sway to the current,　" I iii 593
Grant me o day To ponder these demands.　　" I iii 668
she holds it in Free and perpetual alms, unsubject
　to O earthy sceptre.　　　　　　　　" I iii 681

Open'd this was *o*, and the dead were found Sitting,   *Queen Mary* v ii 395
   into thy mouth hadst thou but *o* it to thank him.   *Becket* iii iii 277
   Knock, and it shall be *o*.   „   v iii 64
   o out The purple zone of hill and heaven;   *The Cup* i ii 407
   The blossom had *o* on every bough;   *Prom. of May* i 42
Opening Beware of *o* out thy bosom to it,   *Becket* iii iii 30
   That beam of dawn upon the *o* flower,   *Foresters* iv 3
Opinion when men are tost On tides of strange *o*,   *Queen Mary* iii iv 119
   True, I have held *o*'s, hold some still,   *Prom. of May* iii 622
Opportunity our *o* When I and thou will rob the nest of
   her.   *Foresters* i ii 160
Oppose I would set my men-at-arms to *o* thee,   „   i i 323
Opposite we will climb The mountain *o* and watch the
   chase.   *The Cup* i i 117
Oppress The walls *o* me, And yon huge keep   *Harold* ii ii 227
   O help us from all that *o* us !   *The Cup* ii 6
Oppression The *o* of our people moves me so,   *Foresters* iii 109
Opulent *See* **Over-opulent**
Oracle this *o* of great Artemis Has no more power than
   other *o*'s   *The Cup* ii 33
Oran (in Algeria) Tunis, and *O*, and the Philippines,   *Queen Mary* v 48
Orange (plant) You lived among your vines and *o*'s,   „ iv 253
   I that held the *o* blossom Dark as the yew ?   *Prom. of May* ii 629
Orange (town) William of *O*, William the Silent.   *Queen Mary* iii i 197
Order (arrangement, etc.) Like loosely-scatter'd jewels,
   in fair *o*,   „ ii i 28
   my cows in sweeter *o* Had I been such.   „ iii v 271
   ever-jarring Earldoms move To music and in *o*—   *Harold* ii v 762
   She *will* break fence. I can't keep her in *o*.   *Prom. of May* i 195
Order (command, etc.) (*See also* **Horder**) To take such
   o with all heretics   *Queen Mary* i v 34
   If this be not your Grace's *o*,   „ ii iv 64
   Have I the *o*'s of the Holy Father ? *Philip de Eleemosyna*—
   O's, my lord—why, no ; for what am I?   *Becket* i iii 232
   I give you here an *o* To seize upon him.   *The Cup* i i 164
   Will *you* betray him by this *o* ?   „ i 245
   Is this your brother's *o* ?   *The Falcon* 745
Order (rank, etc.) Saving the honour of my *o*—ay.   *Becket* i iii 21
   Saving thine *o* !   „ i iii 26
   Saving thine *o*, Thomas, Is black and white   „ i iii 30
Ordered pity this poor world myself that it is no better *o*.   „ *Pro.* 367
Ordinance Either in making laws and *o*'s   *Queen Mary* iii iii 130
   Of all such laws and *o*'s made;   „ iii iii 142
   Against the solemn *o* from Rome,   *Becket* i iii 505
Ordinary She looks comelier than *o* to-day;   *Queen Mary* i i 71
Ordnance there is *o* On the White Tower and on the
   Devil's Tower,   „ ii iii 43
Organ *O* and pipe, and dulcimer, chants and hymns   *Becket* v ii 365
Original Cleaving to your *o* Adam-clay,   *Queen Mary* iv iii 418
Orkney —Scotland, Ireland, Iceland, *O*,   *Harold* iii i 125
Orm Gamel, son of *O*, What thinkest thou this means?
   (repeat)   „ i 20, 463
   Hail, Gamel, son of *O* !   „ i 92
   that was his guest, Gamel, the son of *O*:   „ ii ii 299
   murder'd thine own guest, the son of *O*, Gamel,   „ iv ii 38
Ornament The golden *o*'s are stolen from her—   *Becket* iii iii 180
Orphan (adj.) a widow And *o* child, whom one of thy wild
   barons—   „ *Pro.* 188
Orphan (s) Age, *o*'s, and babe-breasting mothers—   „ ii i 72
   Babes, *o*'s, mothers ! is that royal, Sire ?   „ ii i 80
Orthodoxy He'll burn a diocese to prove his *o*.   *Queen Mary* iii iv 353
Other (*See also* **T'other**) counsel your withdrawing
   To Ashridge, or some *o* country house.   „ i iv 226
   As Thirlby says, are profitless to the burners,
   And help the *o* side.   „ iv ii 220
   O reasons There be for this man's ending,   „ iv iii 53
   Might it not be the *o* side rejoicing In his brave
   end ?   „ iv iii 356
   o things As idle ; a weak Wyatt !   „ v 291
   Not thee, my son : some *o* messenger.   *Harold* i i 244
   And *o* bells on earth, which yet are heaven's;   „ i ii 133
   Like *o* lords amenable to law.   *Becket*, *Pro.* 25
   Than that of *o* paramours of thine ?   „ *Pro.* 71
   True enough, my mind was set upon *o* matters.   „ *Pro.* 318
   Ay, my lord, and divers *o* earls and barons.   „ i iv 59

Other (*continued*) look you, you shall have None *o* God but
   me—   *Becket* ii ii 229
   then the South-west turned him North-west, and so of
   the *o* winds;   „ ii ii 323
   Go, you shall tell me of her some *o* time.   „ iii i 191
   he hath pass'd out again, And on the *o* side.   „ iii ii 13
   Then speak ; this is my *o* self,   „ v ii 74
   dungeon'd the *o* half In Pevensey Castle—   „ v ii 444
   At times this oracle of great Artemis Has no more power
   than *o* oracles   *The Cup* ii 34
   With *o* beauties on a mountain meadow,   *The Falcon* 351
   And the *o* nine ? *Filippo*. Sold !   „ 411
   No *o* heart Of such magnificence in courtesy Beats—   „ 721
   Is there no *o* way ?   *Prom. of May* i 691
   If it had killed one of the Steers there the *o* day,   „ iii 250
   there is no *o* man that shall give me away.   *Foresters* i i 290
   That *o* thousand—shall I ever pay it ?   „ ii i 466
Other-world that sweet *o-w* smile, which will be reflected   *Becket*, *Pro.* 396
Otter And I would swim the moat, like an *o*.   *Foresters* i i 321
Oubliette but in our *o*'s Thou shalt or rot or ransom.   *Harold* ii i 107
   And deeper still the deep-down *o*,   „ ii ii 429
   from my ghastly *o* I send my voice   „ v i 245
Oublietted And *o* in the centre—No !   *Becket* iv ii 150
Ought (*See also* **Aught, Owt**) I am dead as Death this day
   to *o* of earth's   *Harold* v i 425
Ouphe *o*'s, oafs, ghosts o' the mist, wills-o'-the-wisp;   *Foresters* ii i 263
Oust Stir up thy people: *o* him !   *Harold* i i 482
   would *o* me from his will, if I Made such a marriage.   *Prom. of May* i 513
Ousted You have *o* the mock priest,   *Queen Mary* i v 180
   Ay, Lambeth has *o* Cranmer.   „ ii ii 132
Outblossom one rose will *o* the rest, one rose in a bower.   *Becket*, *Pro.* 345
Out-Bonner Bonner cannot *o-B* his own self—   *Queen Mary* iii vi 27
Outcry And make a morning *o* in the yard;   „ v 158
Outdoor One of much *o* bluster.   „ ii ii 380
Outdraught Felt the remorseless *o* of the deep   *Harold* ii i 9
Outfield (outlying field) Hodge 'ud ha' been a-
   harrowin' o' white peasen i' the *o*   *Queen Mary* iv iii 492
Out-Gardiners Gardiner *o-G* Gardiner in his heat,   „ vi 25
Outlander wrench this *o*'s ransom out of him—   *Harold* ii i 58
Outlaw (s) Thou art an *o*, and couldst never pay   *Foresters* ii i 452
   An *o*'s bride may not be wed in law.   „ ii i 90
   The chief of these *o*'s who break the law ?   „ iv 141
   and then we were no longer *o*'s.   „ iv 147
   Robin's an *o*, but he helps the poor.   „ iv 358
   my liege, these men are *o*'s, thieves,   „ iv 906
Outlaw (verb) Did ye not *o* your archbishop Robert,   *Harold* i 55
Outlaw'd he join'd with thee To drive me *o*.   „ iv ii 14
   I may be *o*, I have heard a rumour.   *Foresters* i ii 91
   Robin Hood Earl of Huntingdon is *o* and banished.   „ i iii 68
   I am *o*, and if caught, I die.   „ i iii 163
   Am I worse or better ? I am *o*.   „ ii i 50
   being *o* in a land Where law lies dead,   „ ii i 89
   While Richard hath *o* himself,   „ iv 360
Out-passion'd with our great Council against Tostig, *O-p*
   his !   *Harold* iii i 61
Outraged Wasted our diocese, *o* our tenants,   *Becket* v ii 431
Out-towering help to build a throne *O-t* hers of France ...   *Harold* ii ii 765
Outvalue As gold *O*'s dross, light darkness,   *Becket* i iii 715
   wreath That once you wore *o*'s twenty-fold   *The Falcon* 759
   O's all the jewels upon earth.   „ 779
   It should be love that thus *o*'s all.   „ 781
Outward To veil the fault of my most *o* foe—   *Queen Mary* iv ii 106
Outwoman She could not be unmann'd—no, nor *o*—   „ iii i 370
Over *See* **Ower**
Overbalance weight of the flesh at odd times *o* the weight
   of the church,   *Foresters* i ii 61
Overbold Thou art *o*. *Robin*. My king,   „ iv 890
Over-breathed I am *o-b*, Friar, by my two bouts at
   quarterstaff.   „ iv 265
Over-confident Brave—ay—too brave, too *o-c*,   *The Cup* i ii 262
Overdid must we follow All that they *o* or underdid ?   *Becket* ii ii 214
Overhead loud enough To fright the wild hawk passing *o*,   *Foresters* iii 318
Overleap There is a fence I cannot *o*, My father's will.   „ iii 9
Overlive O friends, I shall not *o* the day.   *Harold* iii i 232
Overlook would hardly care to *o* This same petition   *Queen Mary* iv i 192

Over-measure By St. Edmund I *o-m* him.   *Harold* IV iii 120
Overmuch Sir, this dead fruit was ripening *o*, *Queen Mary* III i 26
    Then without tropes, my Lord, An *o* severeness,   ,, III iv 156
Over-opulent if you cared To fee an *o-o* superstition, *Prom. of May* I 693
Overscornful would deign to lend an ear Not *o*, *Harold* IV i 137
Oversea And *o* they say this state of yours *Queen Mary* III i 441
    His kin, all his belongings, *o's*; *Becket* II i 71
    calls you *o* To answer for it in his Norman courts, ,, v ii 354
    one that should be grateful to me *o's*, a Count in Brittany— *Foresters* I i 271
    I must pass *o's* to one that I trust will help me. ,, I ii 152
    And I and he are passing *o's*: ,, II i 627
Overshoot you make your butt too big, you *o* it, *Becket* III iii 122
Overshot I have *o* My duties to our Holy Mother Church, ,, v i 37
Overstep is the King's *if* too high a stile for your lordship to *o* ,, III iii 281
Overtaken Love will fly the fallen leaf, and not be *o*; *Queen Mary* V ii 372
Over-taxing for thy brother breaks us With *o-t*— *Harold* I i 110
Overthrown Doubt not they will be speedily *o*. *Queen Mary* II ii 200
    have *o* Morcar and Edwin. *Harold* III ii 131
    The king is slain, the kingdom *o*! ,, v i 16
Overturn when they seek to *o* our rights, *Becket* v ii 456
Over-violence as one That mars a cause with *o-v*. ,, IV ii 327
Overwhelm'd We shall be *o*. Seize him and carry him! ,, v iii 141
    full democracy has *o* This Old world, *Prom. of May* I 593
'Ow (how) and *'o* should I see to laäme the laädy, ,, III 95
'Owd (hold) they'll hev' a fine cider-crop to-year if the blossom *'o's*. ,, I 317
Owd (old) Why, o' coorse, fur it be the *o* man's birthdaäy. ,, I 6
    O Steer wur afeärd she wouldn't be back i' time to keep his birthdaäy. ,, I 16
    and 'er an' the *o* man they fell a-kissin' o' one another ,, I 21
    An' how did ye leäve the *o* uncle i' Coomberland? ,, I 68
    An' how d'ye find the *o* man 'ere? ,, I 71
    The *o* man be heighty to-daäy, beänt he? ,, I 76
    An' I haätes boooks an' all, fur they puts foälk off the *o* waäys. ,, I 222
    Then the *o* man i' Lear should be shaämed of hissen, ,, I 266
    but when thou be as *o* as me thou'll put one word fur another as I does. ,, I 381
    So the *o* uncle i' Coomberland be deäd, Miss Dora, beänt he? ,, II 1
    I seed how the *o* man wur vext. ,, II 27
    I would taäke the *o* blind man to my oän fireside. ,, II 74
    Naäy, but I hev an *o* woman as 'ud see to all that: ,, II 95
    Yeas, an' *o* Dobson should be glad on it. ,, II 146
    Why, coom then, *o* feller, I'll tell it to you; ,, II 202
    Ye shall sing that ageän to-night, fur *o* Dobson 'll gi'e us a bit o' supper. *Sally.* I weänt goä to *o* Dobson; ,, II 216
    O Steer's gotten all his grass down and wants a hand, and I'll goä to him. ,, II 220
    O Steer gi'es nubbut cowd tea to 'is men, and *o* Dobson gi'es beer. *Sally.* But I'd like *o* Steer's cowd tea better nor Dobson's beer. Good-bye. ,, II 223
    when *o* Dobson coom'd upo' us? ,, II 232
    but I wur so ta'en up wi' leädin' the *o* man about all the blessed murnin' ,, III 2
    The Steers was all gentlefoälks i' the *o* times, ,, III 448
    The land belonged to the Steers i' the *o* times, ,, III 451
    He be saäyin' a word to the *o* man, but he'll coom up if ye lets 'im. ,, III 481
    The *o* man's coom'd ageän to 'issen, an' wants To hev a word wi' ye ,, III 702
Owe the duty which as Legate He *o's* himself, *Queen Mary* III iv 402
    To whom he *o's* his loyalty after God, ,, IV i 23
    unto him you *o* That Mary hath acknowledged ,, v iii 29
    you That *o* to me your power over me— *Becket* II i 152
    I *o* you thanks for ever. *The Cup* I ii 249
    love that children *o* to both I give To him alone. *Foresters* IV 7
Owed Thou still hast *o* thy father, Gilbert Foliot. *Becket* I iii 276
    more than one brave fellow *o* His death *The Falcon* 634
Ower (over) I should saäy 'twur *o* by now. *Queen Mary* IV iii 475
    and *o* a hoonderd pounds worth o' rings stolen. *Prom. of May* I 393

Ower (over) (*continued*) Dan Smith's cart hes runned *o* a laädy i' the holler laäne, *Prom. of May* II 568
    and my missus a-gittin' *o* 'er lyin'-in, ,, III 74
Owl (*See also* **Scritch-owl**) The wood is full of echoes, *o's*, elfs, *Foresters* II i 263
Owld (old) it be a var waay vor my *o* legs up vro' Islip. *Queen Mary* IV iii 472
    Eh, then ha' thy waay wi' me, Tib; ez thou hast wi' thy *o* man. ,, IV iii 487
    Ay, Joan, and my *o* man wur up and awaay betimes ,, IV iii 488
    I heerd summat as summun towld summun o' *o* Bishop Gardiner's end; ,, IV iii 503
    there wur an *o* lord a-cum to dine wi' un, and a wur so a couldn't bide vor his dinner, ,, IV iii 504
    and the *o* lord fell to 's meat wi' a will, ,, IV iii 514
    the burnin' o' the *o* archbishop 'll burn the Pwoap out o' this 'ere land vor iver and iver. ,, IV iii 535
Own (adj.) (*See also* **Oän**) What are you cackling of bastardy under the Queen's *o* nose? ,, I i 59
    I shall judge with my *o* eyes whether her Grace incline ,, I i 134
    Peace! hear him; let his *o* words damn the Papist. ,, I iii 53
    From thine *o* mouth I judge thee—tear him down! ,, I iii 162
    a King That with her *o* pawns plays against a Queen, ,, I iv 168
    But your *o* state is full of danger here. ,, I iv 232
    'Tis mine *o* wish fulfill'd before the word Was spoken, ,, I v 523
    Tho' Queen, I am not Queen Of mine *o* heart, ,, II i 49
    he loved the more His *o* gray towers, ,, II i 86
    Well, for mine *o* work, ,, II i 167
    I have seen them in their *o* land; ,, II ii 80
    mute as death, And white as her *o* milk; ,, II ii 106
    on you, In your *o* city, as her right, my Lord, For you are loyal. ,, II ii 136
    From your *o* royal lips, at once may know ,, II ii 142
    In mine *o* person am I come to you, ,, II ii 184
    seeks To bend the laws to his *o* will, ,, II ii 223
    that I should leave Some fruit of mine *o* body after me, ,, II ii 234
    Before our *o* High Court of Parliament, ,, II ii 347
    By his *o* rule, he hath been so bold to-day, ,, II ii 386
    his fault So thoroughly to believe in his *o* self. ,, II ii 388
    Yet thoroughly to believe in one's *o* self, So one's *o* self be thorough, ,, III i 23
    Well, the tree in Virgil, sir, That bears not its *o* apples. ,, III ii 112
    the Pope's Holiness By mine *o* self. ,, III iii 34
    Statesmen that are wise Shape a necessity, as a sculptor clay, To their *o* model. ,, III iii 120
    In our *o* name and that of all the state, ,, III iii 136
    As well for our *o* selves as all the realm, ,, III iii 203
    The Lord who hath redeem'd us With his *o* blood, ,, III iv 120
    and not sure Of their *o* selves, they are wroth with their *o* selves, ,, III iv 128
    Trembled for her *o* gods, for these were trembling— ,, III v 262
    But the wench Hath her *o* troubles; she is weeping now; ,, III vi 27
    Bonner cannot out-Bonner his *o* self— ,, IV i 18
    he hath pray'd me not to sully Mine *o* prerogative, ,, IV i 125
    Yet once he saved your Majesty's *o* life; Stood out against the King in your behalf, At his *o* peril. ,, IV ii 202
    By mine *o* self—by mine *o* hand! ,, IV iii 375
    The parson from his *o* spire swung out dead, ,, IV iii 381
    I say they have drawn the fire On their *o* heads: ,, v ii 12
    I could weep for them And her, and mine *o* self and all the world. ,, v ii 102
    Gone beyond him and mine *o* natural man (It was God's cause) ,, v ii 561
    That his *o* wife is no affair of his. ,, v iii 42
    Nay, but I speak from mine *o* self, not him; ,, v v 134
    Seven-fold dishonour'd even in the sight Of thine *o* sectaries— *Harold* I i 343
    Ay, ever give yourselves your *o* good word. ,, I ii 110
    I swear it, By mine *o* eyes—and these two sapphires— ,, II ii 711
    Swear thou to-day, to-morrow is thine *o*. *Becket, Pro.* 11
    A cleric lately poison'd his *o* mother, ,, *Pro.* 513
    what shall I call it, affect her thine *o* self.

P

Paäin (pain) I niver 'es sa much as one pin's prick of *p*; *Prom. of May* I 360
Paäper (paper) then a-scrattin upon a bit o' *p*, then a-lookin' ageän;   ,, I 203
   dosta knaw this *p*? Ye dropt it upo' the road. ,, II 687
Pace (s) break your *p*'s in, and make you tame; *Queen Mary* V iii 121
Pace (verb) king should *p* on purple to his bride, *The Cup* II 189
Pacify pray'd me to pray thee to *p* Thy King; *Becket* I iii 206
   He told me thou shouldst *p* the King, ,, I iii 224
Pacing *p* my new lands at Littlechester, *Prom. of May* I 647
   But I am weary *p* thro' the wood. *Foresters* II i 129
Packt So *p* with carnage that the dykes and brooks *Harold* III ii 128
Padua (city of Venetia) And died in P. *Queen Mary* V ii 516
Pagan The *p* temple of a *p* Rome! *Becket* I iii 61
Page who call'd the mind Of children a blank *p*, *Prom. of May* II 282
Pageant second actor in this *p* That brings him in; *Queen Mary* III v 14
   and flowers In silken *p*'s. ,, III v 15
Paget (Lord) *P* is for him—for to wed with Spain ,, I v 75
   P is ours. Gardiner perchance is ours; ,, I v 386
   Lord *P*'s ' Ay' is sure—who else? ,, I v 630
   Spite of Lord *P* and Lord William Howard, ,, III i 324
   Lord *P* Waits to present our Council to the Legate. ,, III ii 97
   If we could burn out heresy, my Lord *P*, ,, III iv 54
   P, you are all for this poor life of ours, ,, III iv 59
   Look to your Bible, *P*! we are fallen. ,, III iv 80
   P, You stand up here to fight for heresy, ,, III iv 91
   they are many, As my Lord *P* says. ,, III iv 177
   my Lord *P* and Lord William Howard, Crave, ,, IV i 6
   You are too politic for me, my Lord *P*. ,, IV i 151
   Ay, ay, *P*, They have brought it in large measure ,, IV iii 362
   yet, *P*, I do hold The Catholic, ,, IV iii 381
   O *P*, *P*! I have seen heretics of the poorer sort, ,, IV iii 435
   P, despite his fearful heresies, ,, IV iii 633
Paid he *p* his ransom back. *Harold* II ii 50
   I have once more *p* them all. *Prom. of May* III 158
   if they be not *p* back at the end of the year, the land goes to the Abbot. *Foresters* I i 69
   must be *p* in a year and a month, or I lose the land. ,, I i 268
   You shall wait for mine till Sir Richard has *p* the Abbot. ,, I ii 232
   I have *p* him half. That other thousand— ,, II i 465
   these monies should be *p* in to the Abbot at York, ,, IV 507
   The debt hath not been *p*. ,, IV 612
   Has it been *p*? *Abbot.* O yes. ,, IV 616
   Not *p* at York—the wood—prick me no more! ,, IV 623
   Sir Richard *p* his monies to the Abbot. ,, IV 849
Pain (See also **Paäin**) Judgment, and *p* accruing thereupon; *Queen Mary* III iii 219
   Or to be still in *p* with devils in hell; ,, IV iii 222
   he never uttered moan of *p*: ,, IV iii 619
   evilly used And put to *p*. *Becket* II ii 434
   Geoffrey, the *p* thou hast put me to! ,, IV ii 10
   This *p*—what is it?—again? *The Cup* II 445
   With cold, with *p* perhaps, poor prisoner! *The Falcon* 449
   And if my pleasure breed another's *p*, *Prom. of May* I 278
   with as little *p* As it is to fall asleep. ,, II 341
   to spare myself, And her too, *p*, *p*, *p*? ,, III 720
   That blast our natural passions into *p*'s! ,, III 725
   Move me no more! I am sick and faint with *p*! *Foresters* IV 599
Painful perhaps The *p* circumstances which I heard— *Prom. of May* II 402
Paint Tell him to *p* it out, *Queen Mary* III i 267
   The man shall *p* a pair of gloves. ,, III i 274
   honesty too, *p* her what way they will. *Becket* II i 101
Painted If you have falsely *p* your fine Prince; *Queen Mary* I v 598
   The conduit *p*—the nine worthies—ay! ,, III i 258
   God's passion! do you know the knave that *p* it? ,, III i 265
Pair But since the fondest *p* of doves will jar, *Becket* IV ii 40
   You are an honest *p*. I will come to your wedding. *Prom. of May* III 114
Pair'd Ay, if Wisdom *P* not with Good. *Harold* V i 178

Palace (adj.) Hark, there is battle at the *p* gates, *Queen Mary* II iv 47
   I found it fluttering at the *p* gates:— ,, III ii 218
Palace (s) Hast thou let fall those papers in the *p*? ,, I iii 2
   And unto no dead world; but Lambeth *p*, ,, III ii 154
   There was a paper thrown into the *p*, ,, III vi 139
   which I found Strewn in your *p*. ,, V ii 173
   I left it privily At Florence, in her *p*. *The Falcon* 75
   And welcome turns a cottage to a *p*. ,, 273
   Who never deign'd to shine into my *p*. ,, 286
   My *p* wanting you was but a cottage; My cottage, while you grace it, is a *p*. ,, 287
   In cottage or in *p*, being still Beyond your fortunes, ,, 290
Palate That *p* is insane which cannot tell *Becket*, Pro. 104
Pale (adj.) The word has turn'd your Highness *p*; *Queen Mary* I v 471
   How deathly *p*! a chair, your Highness. ,, I v 636
   a *p* horse for Death and Gardiner for the Devil. ,, III i 234
   Mary rubb'd out *p*— ,, III i 423
   fieriest partisans—are *p* Before my star! ,, III ii 170
   The little murder'd princes, in a *p* light, ,, III v 147
   Peters, how *p* you look! you bring the smoke ,, IV iii 560
   Brother! why so *p*? *Harold* I i 28
   God redden your *p* blood! *Becket* I iv 35
   I wonder if I look as *p* as she? *The Cup* II 322
   more blessed were the rags Of some *p* beggar-woman *The Falcon* 852
   and you look thin and *p*. Is it for his absence? *Prom. of May* I 782
   You are *p*, my Dora! but the ruddiest cheek ,, I 486
   I that have turn'd their Moslem crescent *p*— *Foresters* IV 793
   All those *p* mouths which we have fed will praise us— ,, IV 1076
Pale (s) praised The convent and lone life—within the *p*— *Harold* I ii 48
   loved within the *p* forbidden By Holy Church: ,, III ii 22
   Thou hast broken thro' the *p*'s Of privilege, *Becket* III ii 193
Paleness a *p*, Like the wan twilight after sunset, ,, I iii 325
Palisade The trenches dug, the *p*'s uprear'd *Harold* V i 189
   strengthen their *p*'s! ,, V i 481
   They fall on those within the *p*! ,, V i 668
Pall Lay thou thy hand upon this golden *p*! ,, II ii 699
   Foliot may claim the *p* For London too. *Becket* I iii 56
   The *P*! I go to meet my King! ,, V ii 619
Pallium Who had my *p* from an Antipope! *Harold* I i 82
   Because I had my Canterbury *p*, ,, I i 106
Palm and kindled with the *p*'s of Christ! *Queen Mary* I v 93
   P's, flowers, pomegranates, golden cherubim *Harold* III i 182
   And these rough oaks the *p*'s of Paradise! *Foresters* II i 169
Palmer he is a holy *P*, bounden by a vow not to show ,, I ii 236
Palsied while thy hands *p* here, *Harold* II ii 455
Palsy In this low pulse and *p* of the state, *Queen Mary* II ii 103
Palter My friend, thou hast gone too far to *p* now. *Harold* II ii 707
   Why do you *p* with the ceremony? *The Cup* II 419
Pan Swarm to thy voice like bees to the brass *p*. *Foresters* I iii 109
Pancratius (St. Pancras) jewel of St. *P* Woven into the gold. *Harold* II ii 700
Pander I am your subject, not your—— *Henry.* P. *Becket*, Pro. 147
   Profligate *p*! *Fitzurse.* Do you hear that? ,, V iii 160
Pandora-box this Hollow *P-b*, With all the pleasures flown, *Prom. of May* II 346
Pang in the front rank of the fight With scarce a *p*. *The Cup* I ii 155
Panoply Mail'd in the perfect *p* of faith, *Becket* V ii 494
Pant sure she hates thee, *P*'s for thy blood. *Harold* I ii 39
Panting And *p* for my blood as I go by. *Queen Mary* IV iii 219
Papacy We strove against the *p* from the first, ,, III iii 225
   God save the Crown! the *P* is no more. ,, V v 286
   inherited loathing of these black sheep of the *P*. *Becket*, Pro. 462
   that would shake the *P* as it stands. ,, I iii 213
Papal (See also **Anti-papal**) not to yield His Church of England to the *P* wolf And Mary, *Queen Mary* I ii 36
   And be regather'd to the *P* fold? ,, III ii 117
   Wanting the *P* mitre. ,, III iv 148
   of her most Royal, Infallible, *P* Legate-cousin. ,, IV iii 433
   That so the *P* bolt may pass by England, *Becket*, Pro. 226
Paper (See also **Paäper**) Hast thou let fall those *p*'s in the palace? *Queen Mary* I iii 2
   I've found this *p*; pray your worship read it; ,, II iii 56
   This *p*, Dickon. I found it fluttering at the palace gates:— ,, III ii 217
   There was a *p* thrown into the palace, ,, III vi 139

Part (verb) (continued) Ay, noble Earl, and never *p* with it. *Foresters* I i 304
  precious ring I promised Never to *p* with—   " II i 662
Partaken had they remained true to me whose bread they
  have *p*.   *Becket* I iv 150
Parted No, for we trust they *p* in the swine.   *Queen Mary* III ii 142
  Our Tostig *p* cursing me and England;   *Harold* I i 76
  We have *p* from our wife without reproach,   " v 154
  It seemed to me that we were *p* for ever.   *Prom. of May* I 770
  We *p* like the brook yonder about the alder island,   " I 772
  Who *p* from thee even now?   *Foresters* I i 181
  How came we to be *p* from our men?   " II i 254
Parthian *P* shaft of a forlorn Cupid at the King's left
  breast,   *Becket*, Pro. 339
  To hide the scar left by thy *P* dart.   " Pro. 377
Partic'lar Yeäs, Miss; and he wants to speak to ye *p*.   *Prom. of May* III 351
  but he says he wants to tell ye summut very *p*.   " III 355
Parting (*See also* A-parting) *p* of a husband and a
  wife Is like the cleaving of a heart;   *Queen Mary* III vi 194
  if I knew you felt this *p*, Philip, As I do!   " III vi 251
  Myself confused with *p* from the King.   *Becket* I ii 237
  and no more *p*'s for ever and for ever.   *Prom. of May* III 197
Partisan I have notice from our *p*'s Within the city   *Queen Mary* II iii 51
  And all her fieriest *p*'s—   " III ii 170
Party I should be still A *p* in the state;   " I iv 24
  a great *p* in the state Wills me to wed her.   " I iv 91
  as great a *p* in the state Will you to wed me?   " I iv 95
  My heart, my Lord, Is no great *p* in the state   " I iv 102
  Is it England, or a *p*? Now, your answer.   " I v 142
  and *p* thereunto, My Lord of Devon.   " II iv 100
  Princess Cognisant thereof, and *p* thereunto.   " II iv 113
  Stirr'd up a *p* there against your son—   *Becket* v i 6
  ' I am sorry that we could not attend your Grace's
  p on the 10th !'   *Prom. of May* III 313
Pass (s) All *p*'es block'd.   *Harold* II i 317
  Along the glades and *p*'es of the wood   *Foresters* III 457
Pass (verb) When will her Majesty *p*, sayst thou?   *Queen Mary* I i 3
  She cannot *p* her traitor council by,   " I ii 40
  as we *p*, And pour along the land,   " II i 231
  There yet is time, take boat and *p* to Windsor. *Mary.*
  I *p* to Windsor and I lose my crown. *Gardiner. P*,
  then, I pray your Highness, to the Tower.   " II iv 27
  makes the waverer *p* Into more settled hatred   " III iv 158
  if this *p*, We two shall have to teach him;   " III iv 421
  And *p*'es thro' the peoples: " III v 35
  and *p* And leave me, Philip,   " III vi 227
  Beauty *p*'es like a breath and love is lost in loathing: " v ii 365
  Well, when it *p*'es then. *Edward.* Ay if it *p*. Go not
  to Normandy—   *Harold* I i 233
  And let him *p* unscathed; he loves me, Harold !   " III i 301
  And *p* her to her secret bower in England.   *Becket*, Pro. 183
  That so the Papal bolt may *p* by England,   " Pro. 226
  when the King *p*'es, there may come a crash   " Pro. 484
  P in with Herbert there.   " I i 184
  let me *p*, my lord, for I must know.   " I i 206
  To *p* thee to thy secret bower to-morrow.   " I i 249
  He watch'd her *p* with John of Salisbury.   " I ii 40
  Come, you filthy knaves, let us *p*. *3rd Beggar.* Nay,
  my lord, let *us p*.   " I iv 204
  But it *p*'es away,   " II i 280
  ' *P* on,' he said, and in thy name I pass'd   " v ii 102
  I will but *p* to vespers, And breathe one prayer   " v ii 190
  That I should *p* the censures of the Church   " v ii 390
  And *p* at once perfect to Paradise.   " v iii 14
  Shall I too *p* to the choir,   " v iii 74
  He will *p* to-morrow In the gray dawn   *The Cup* I i 294
  Your arm—a moment—It will *p*.   " II 449
  Bird-babble for my falcon ! Let it *p*.   *The Falcon* 39
  If possible, here ! to crop the flower and *p*.   *Prom. of May* I 254
  I am half afraid to *p*.   " II 328
  Allow me, sir, to *p* you.   " II 355
  I cannot *p* that way.   " III 733
  on this cross I have sworn that till I myself *p* away,   *Foresters* I i 290
  I must *p* overseas to one that I trust will help me.   " I ii 152
  to *p* it down A finger of that hand   " I ii 297
  Did we not hear the two would *p* this way?   " II i 198

Pass (verb) (continued) Ghost ! did one in white *p*?   *Foresters* II i 228
  Did two knights *p*?   " II i 230
  Then let her *p* as an exception, Scarlet.   " III 71
  And if a woman *p*—   " III 176
  One half shall *p* into our treasury.   " III 305
  and can make Five quarts *p* into a thimble.   " IV 283
Passage that's the winder at the end o' the *p*, that
  goäs by thy chaumber.   *Prom. of May* I 397
Pass'd *See* Past
Passing (adj. and part.) (*See also* A-passing) she was
  p Some chapel down in Essex,   *Queen Mary* I v 39
  every tongue Alters it *p*,   " III v 36
  Than any sea could make me *p* hence,   " III vi 87
  And might assail you *p* through the street,   " IV ii 34
  A *p* bell toll'd in a dying ear—   " IV ii 41
  Who *p* by that hill three nights ago—   *Harold* III i 366
  With a love *P* thy love for Griffyth?   " v i 357
  And I and he are *p* overseas: *Foresters* II i 626
  To fright the wild hawk *p* overhead,   " III 318
Passing (s) In *p* to the Castle even now.   *Becket* I i 13
  should be stay'd From *p* onward.   *Foresters* III 242
Passion (*See also* Self-passion) and in that *p* Gave
  me my Crown.   *Queen Mary* I v 567
  God's *p* ! knave, thy name !   " III i 248
  God's *p* ! do you know the knave that painted it ?   " III i 264
  Nay, God's *p*, before me ! speak !   " III iv 285
  within the pale—Beyond the *p*.   *Harold* I ii 49
  thy patriot *p* Siding with our great Council   " I i 58
  Our living *p* for a dead man's dream;   " III ii 60
  Thou hast no *p* for the House of Godwin—   " IV ii 72
  illogically, out of *p*, without art—   *Becket*, Pro. 337
  with such true *p* As at this loveless knife   " IV ii 190
  I never felt such *p* for a woman.   *The Cup* I i 34
  So end all *p*'s. Then what use in *p*'s ?   " I iii 126
  The ghosts of the dead *p*'s of dead men ?   *Prom. of May* II 275
  may not be seized With some fierce *p*,   " II 336
  That blast our natural *p*'s into pains !   " II 724
  I have a sudden *p* for the wild wood.   *Foresters* I iii 122
  The hunter's *p* flash'd into the man,   " IV 539
Passionate no *p* faith—But—if let be—balance and
  compromise ;   *Queen Mary* v v 221
  He is *p* but honest.   *Harold* I i 118
  Mad for thy mate, *p* nightingale . . . I love thee for it—   " I ii 1
Passion'd *See* Out-passion'd
Passionless I would I were As holy and as *p* as he !   " III i 43
  P? How he flamed When Tostig's anger'd earldom,   " III i 52
Passion-play Judas-lover of our *p-p* Hath track'd us hither. *Becket* IV ii 137
Passover Dash'd red with that unhallow'd *p*;   " II i 348
Passport this pious cup Is *p* to their house,   *The Cup* I i 83
Past (s) These are forgiven—matters of the *p*—   *Queen Mary* III iii 190
  Hangs all my *p*, and all my life to be,   " IV iii 219
  see, see, I speak of him in the *p*.   " IV iii 422
  The *p* is like a travell'd land now sunk   *The Cup* II 230
  In looking on a chill and changeless *P*?   *Prom. of May* II 504
  the *P* Remains the *P*.   " II 505
  for the *p* Look'd thro' the present,   " II 640
  or is it but the *p* That brightens in retiring ?   " II 644
  Sleep, mournful heart, and let the *p* be past !   *Foresters* I iii 47
Past-Pass'd he's *past* your questioning.   *Queen Mary* I i 39
  The sentence having *past* upon them all,   " I v 487
  How look'd the city When now you *past* it ?   " II ii 58
  As we *past*, Some hail'd, some hiss'd us.   " II ii 60
  Before he go, that since these statutes *past*,   " III vi 24
  He *pass'd* out smiling, and he walk'd upright;   " IV iii 302
  You saw him how he *past* among the crowd   " IV iii 574
  —*past*—but whither ? *Paget.* To purgatory, man,   " IV iii 625
  And all his wars and wisdoms *past* away;   " v v 56
  Then claspt the cross, and *pass'd* away in peace.   " v v 259
  had *past* me by To hunt and hawk elsewhere,   *Harold* II ii 27
  Then a great Angel *past* along the highest   " III i 133
  great Angel rose And *past* again along the highest   " III i 156
  when I *past* by Waltham, my foundation For mèn   " v 96
  longed much to see your Grace and the Chancellor ere
  he *past*,   *Becket*, Pro. 400
  But the hour is *past*, and our brother, Master Cook,   " I iv 60

Past-Pass'd (continued)   Past help! his paws are past help.   *Becket* I iv 110
he hath *pass'd* out again, And on the other side.   "   III ii 12
a man *passed* in there to-day: I holla'd to him,   "   III ii 24
and in thy name I *pass'd* From house to house.   "   v ii 103
on a Tuesday *pass'd* From England into bitter banishment;   "   v ii 288
She *past* me here Three years ago when I was flying   *The Cup* I i 4
in a city thro' which he *past* with the Roman army: "   I i 43
in some city where Antonius *past*.   "   I ii 58
having *pass'd* unwounded from the field,   *The Falcon* 608
but they, the shadows of ourselves, Have *past* for ever.   *Prom. of May* I 272
You never told her, then, of what has *past* Between us.   "   I 729
Sleep, mournful heart, and let the past be *past*!   *Foresters* II i 47
She and Sir Richard Have *past* away,   "   II i 120
They must have *past*. Here is a woodman's hut.   "   II i 199
You see he is *past* himself. What would you more?   "   IV 471
Past the bank Of foxglove, then to left by that one yew.   "   IV 973
Pastime   While you can take your *p* in the woods.   *The Cup* I i 190
Cannot *he* take his *p* like the flies?   *Prom. of May* I 277
It is but *p*—nay, I will not harm thee.   *Foresters* II i 554
Have our loud *p*'s driven them all away?   "   II ii 105
Pastor   *P* fugatur Grex trucidatur—   *Harold* v i 513
Pastoral   The polish'd Damon of your *p* here,   *Prom. of May* III 562
Pat   gave me a great *p* o' the cheek for a pretty wench,   *Becket* II i 125
Patch   I must *p* up a peace—   "   II ii 53
Patent   your name Stands first of those who sign'd the Letters *P*   *Queen Mary* I ii 18
State secrets should be *p* to the statesman   *Becket, Pro.* 76
Pater   Salva patriam Sancte *P*,   *Harold* v i 467
Path   in a narrow *p*. A plover flew before thee.   *Becket* II i 53
I strike into my former *p* For England,   "   II i 455
stray'd From love's clear *p* into the common bush,   "   III i 247
so many alleys, crossings, *P*'s, avenues—   "   IV ii 7
she turns down the *p* through our little vineyard,   *The Falcon* 167
Pathway   A hundred *p*'s running everyway,   *Becket, Pro.* 163
—would have made my *p* flowers.   "   v ii 370
Patience   age Of brief life, and brief purpose, and brief *p*,   *Queen Mary* III iv 414
The *p* of St. Lawrence in the fire.   "   IV iii 95
Patient   with that sweet worn smile Among thy *p* wrinkles—   "   v v 200
till now, by the *p* Saints, she's as crabb'd as ever.   *Harold* II i 50
Patriam   Salva *p* Sancte Pater,   "   v i 466
Salva *p*, Sancta Mater.   "   v i 470
Patriarchal   And die upon the *P* throne Of all my predecessors?   *Becket* v iii 75
Patrimony   When I was ruler in the *p*,   *Queen Mary* v ii 72
That be the *p* of the poor?   *Becket* I iii 106
Patriot (adj.)   but that thy *p* passion Siding with our great Council against Tostig,   *Harold* III i 57
Patriot (s)   Their shield-borne *p* of the morning star   *The Cup* II i 121
Patriotism   you suspect This Sinnatus of playing *p*,   "   I i 78
Pattern'd   moonlight casements *p* on the wall,   *Queen Mary* v v 9
Paul (Saint)   (*See also* **St. Paul**)   what saith *P*? 'I would they were cut off   "   III iv 31
Paul the Fourth (Pope)   But this new Pope Caraffa, *P t F*,   "   v ii 32
Pauper   a Sister of Mercy, come from the death-bed of a *p*,   *Prom. of May* III 377
Pauper'd   Why then, my lord, we are *p* out and out.   *The Falcon* 268
Pauperes   *Sederunt principes, ederunt p*.   *Becket* I iv 132
Pauperis   And one an *uxor p Ibyci*.   "   v ii 216
Pauperism   Sunk in the deepest pit of *p*,   *Prom. of May* III 803
Pause (s)   so in this *p*, before The mine be fired,   *Queen Mary* II i 25
Pause (verb)   Wherefore *p* you—what?   "   v iii 39
Pavement   To bathe this sacred *p* with my blood.   *Becket* v iii 131
Paw   King's verdurer caught him a-hunting in the forest, and cut off his *p*'s.   "   I iv 96
Past help! his *p*'s are past help.   "   I iv 111
One downward plunge of his *p* would rend away   "   IV ii 283
if we kill a stag, our dogs have their *p*'s cut off,   *Foresters* IV 225
Pawn   a King That with her own *p*'s plays against a Queen,   *Queen Mary* I iii 162

Pawn (continued)   Courtenay seems Too princely for a *p*.   *Queen Mary* I iii 167
Pay   Your pious wish to *p* King Edward's debts,   "   I v 111
but to *p* them full in kind,   "   v iv 14
Pray'd me to *p* her debts, and keep the Faith;   "   v v 257
What conditions? *p* him back His ransom?   *Harold* II ii 213
Church should *p* her scutage like the lords.   *Becket* I i 34
and he *p*'s me regular every Saturday.   *Prom. of May* I 311
Why should I *p* you your full wages?   "   III 83
sits and eats his heart for want of money to *p* the Abbot.   *Foresters* I i 5
thou shouldst marry one who will *p* the mortgage.   "   I i 280
I would *p* My brother all his debt and save the land.   "   I ii 217
Himself would *p* this mortgage to his brother,   "   I ii 263
he would *p* The mortgage if she favour'd him.   "   I iii 6
Sheriff Would *p* this cursed mortgage to his brother   "   II i 144
and couldst never *p* The mortgage on my land.   "   II i 453
That other thousand—shall I ever *p* it?   "   II i 466
Take thou my bow and arrow and compel them to *p* toll.   "   III 263
he that *p*'s not for his dinner must fight for it.   "   IV 199
Church and Law, halt and *p* toll!   "   IV 430
Where he would *p* us down his thousand marks.   "   IV 441
Give him another month, and he will *p* it.   "   IV 444
Lest he should fail to *p* these thousand marks   "   IV 454
he Would *p* us all the debt at once,   "   IV 485
Payest   Thou *p* easily, like a good fellow,   "   IV 155
Paying   but the schoolmaster looked to the *p* you   *Prom. of May* III 22
Sheriff had taken all our goods for the King without *p*,   *Foresters* II i 191
when the Sheriff took my little horse for the King without *p* for it—   "   II i 302
Pea   *See* **Peasen**
Peace   be no *p* for Mary till Elizabeth lose her head.'   *Queen Mary* I iii 4
P! hear him! let his own words damn the Papist.   "   I iii 52
Ay, tho' you long for *p*;   "   I v 258
Some settled ground for *p* to stand upon.   "   I v 315
P, pretty maiden. I hear them stirring   "   I v 627
plain life and letter'd *p*,   "   II i 50
P. False to Northumberland, is he false to me?   "   II iv 38
The second Prince of *P*.   "   III ii 164
P—the Queen, Philip, and Pole.   "   III iii 83
' I come not to bring *p* but a sword'?   "   III iv 88
P, madman! Thou stirrest up a grief   "   III iv 297
Will let you learn in *p* and privacy   "   III iv 326
With us is *p*!' The last? It was a dream;   "   IV iii 152
P among you, there!   "   IV iii 199
When I should guide the Church in *p* at home,   "   v i 67
P, cousin, *p*! I am sad at heart myself.   "   v ii 159
It gilds the greatest wronger of her *p*,   "   v ii 415
sleeping after all she has done, in *p* and quietness,   "   v iv 35
Then claspt the cross, and pass'd away in *p*.   "   v v 260
P is with the dead.   "   v v 267
P with the dead, who never were at *p*!   "   v v 273
left me time And *p* for prayer to gain   *Harold* I i 220
Ay, ay and wise in *p* and great in war—   "   I i 313
Thy fears infect me beyond reason. *P*!   "   II ii 452
P be with him!   "   IV iii 89
p with them Likewise, if *they* can be at *p*   "   IV iii 98
A snatch of sleep were like the *p* of God.   "   v i 180
Come yet once more, from where I am at *p*,   "   v i 239
P! the king's last word—'the arrow!'   "   v i 265
God of truth Fill all thine hours with *p*!—   "   v i 316
P to his soul!   *Becket, Pro.* 394
I left him with *p* on his face—   "   Pro. 395
P, fools! *Becket*. *P*, friends!   "   I ii 1
P, *p*, my lords! these customs are no longer   "   I iii 68
none could sit By his own hearth in *p*;   "   I iii 342
To our King's hands again, and be at *p*.   "   I iii 582
I am confounded by thee. Go in *p*. *De Broc.* In *p* now—but after. Take that for earnest.   "   I iii 731
Ay, go in *p*, caitiff, caitiff!   "   I iii 735
P! *Beggar*. The black sheep baaed to the miller's ewe-lamb,   "   I iv 161
P! *Beggar*. 'Ewe lamb, ewe lamb,   "   I iv 170
the nightmare breaking on my *p* With 'Becket.'   "   II i 37
I must patch up a *p*—   "   II ii 53
So we make our *p* with him.   "   II ii 63

People (s) (*continued*) Rome Made war upon the *p's* not
⌣⌣' the Gods.   *The Cup* I ii 60
His own true *p* cast him from their doors   ,, I ii 351
Camma for my bride—The *p* love her—   ,, I iii 153
Hear thy *p* who praise thee!   ,, II 5
throned together in the sight Of all the *p*,   ,, II 68
teach this Rome—from knowledge of our *p*—   ,, II 97
all the fleeted wealth of kings And *p's*, hear.   ,, II 290
if my *p* must be thralls of Rome,   ,, II 500
Thou art one With thine own *p*, and though a Roman   ,, II 504
You know sick *p*, More specially sick children,   *The Falcon* 816
'The land belongs to the *p*!'   *Prom. of May* I i 141
So loved by all the village *p* here,   ,, III 755
Sir Richard and my Lady Marian fare wellnigh as
  sparely as their *p*.   *Foresters* I i 31
so true a friend of the *p* as Lord Robin of Huntingdon.   ,, I i 188
fights not for himself but for the *p* of England.   ,, I i 237
to save his country, and the liberties of his *p*!   ,, I i 247
My *p* are all scattered I know not where.   ,, II i 176
The oppression of our *p* moves me so,   ,, III 109
Robin, the *p's* friend, the King o' the woods!   ,, III 347
These be the lies the *p* tell of us,   ,, III 392

People (verb) to *p* heaven in the great day When God
  makes up his jewels.   *Becket* v ii 496
Perceive man *p's* that The lost gleam of an after-life   *Prom. of May* I i 502
Perch his politic Holiness Hath all but climb'd the Roman *p*   *Becket* II ii 46
Perch'd Him *p* up there? I wish some thunderbolt   *Queen Mary* IV iii 9
Pereant *P, p*, Anglia precatur.   *Harold* I i 533
Peregrine And hear my *p* and her bells in heaven;   ,, I ii 131
Perennial and his wealth A fountain of *p* alms—   *Queen Mary* I ii 385
Perfect No! the disguise was *p*. Let's away.   ,, I iii 178
her needle *p*, and her learning Beyond the churchmen;   ,, III i 360
and is furthermore No *p* witness of a *p* faith In him
  who persecutes: ,, III iv 117
Thou art manlike *p*.   *Becket* II i 253
My friend of Canterbury and myself Are now once
  more in *p* amity.   ,, III iii 229
I would there were that *p* trust between us,   ,, III iii 264
That *p* trust may come again between us,   ,, III iii 351
Mail'd in the *p* panoply of faith,   ,, v ii 494
Honour to thee! thou art *p* in all honour!   *Harold* I ii 691
But wherefore slur the *p* ceremony?   *The Cup* II 431
A gallant boy, A noble bird, each *p* of the breed.   *The Falcon* 320
And yet I had once a vision of a pure and *p*
  marriage,   *Prom. of May* III 188
Shall I be known? is my disguise *p*? *Sheriff.* P—
who should know you for Prince John,   *Foresters* I ii 19

Perhaps *See* **P'raps**
Peril Looms the least chance of *p* to our realm.   *Queen Mary* II ii 238
are you not in *p* here? *Stafford.* I think so.   ,, II i 34
in your behalf, At his own *p*.   ,, IV i 127
day of *p* that dawns darkly and drearily   *Becket* I iv 145
At their *p*, at their *p*—   ,, III iii 313
Thou hast saved my head at the *p* of thine own.   *Foresters* IV 796
Perilous Many points weather'd, many *p* ones,   *Queen Mary* v v 212
A good entrenchment for a *p* hour!   *Harold* III i 363
a *p* game For men to play with God.   *Becket* II ii 70
all these walks are Robin Hood's And sometimes *p*.   *Foresters* IV 121
Perish Would *p* on the civil slaughter-field,   *Queen Mary* III i 118
May all invaders *p* like Hardrada!   *Harold* IV iii 77
So *p* all the enemies of Harold!   ,, v i 550
So *p* all the enemies of England!   ,, v v 554
P she, I, all, before The Church should suffer wrong!   *Becket* III iii 20
Perjured And thou art *p*, and thou wilt not seal.   ,, I iii 526
And that too, *p* prelate—and that, turncoat shaveling!   ,, I iii 736
Perjury-mongering the *p-m* Count Hath made too good an
  use   *Harold* v i 310
Permission *P* of her Highness to retire To Ashridge,   *Queen Mary* I iv 236
Permit *P* me to withdraw To Lambeth?   ,, III ii 129
P me, my good lord, to bear it for thee,   *Becket* I iii 490
wilt thou *p* us—— *Becket.* To speak without
  stammering   ,, I iv 6
My lord, *p* us then to leave thy service.   ,, I iv 9
Perpendicular Your lordship affects the unwavering *p*;   ,, II ii 326
Perpetual Their wafer and *p* sacrifice: *Queen Mary* I ii 45

Perpetual (*continued*) she holds it in Free and *p* alms,   *Becket* I iii 680
the voice Of the *p* brook, these golden slopes   ,, III i 46
doth not the living skin thicken against *p* whippings?   ,, III iii 316
Close to the grating on a winter morn In the *p* twilight
  of a prison,   *The Falcon* 441
Persecute the worse is here To *p*, because to *p*   *Queen Mary* III iv 115
of a perfect faith In him who *p's*:   ,, III iv 118
Person demanded Possession of her *p* and the Tower.   ,, II ii 41
In mine own *p* am I come to you,   ,, II ii 142
Seek to possess our *p*, hold our Tower.   ,, II ii 158
that anyone Should seize our *p*, occupy our state,   ,, II ii 178
yield Full scope to *p's* rascal and forlorn,   ,, II ii 185
As *p's* undefiled with our offence,   ,, III iii 144
first In Council, second *p* in the realm,   ,, IV iii 72
Three *p's* and one God, have mercy on me,   ,, IV iii 121
Noble as his young *p* and old shield.   ,, v i 513
if our *p* be secured From traitor stabs—   ,, v v 280
Then fling mine own fair *p* in the gap A sacrifice   *Harold* I ii 202
I cannot bear a hand upon my *p*,   *Becket* v iii 20
I came In *p* to return them.   *The Falcon* 727
Persuaded She would have *p* me to come back here,   *Prom. of May* III 383
Pertest *P* of our flickering mob,   *Foresters* II ii 130
Peru The voices of *P* and Mexico,   *Queen Mary* v i 47
Peruse *P* it; is it not goodly, ay, and gentle?   ,, I v 195
wherefore dost thou so *p* it?   *Becket* II i 186
Pesteringly Unalterably and *p* fond!   *Queen Mary* v i 120
Pestilent Will no man free me from this *p* priest?   *Becket* I iii 262
Peter The Eternal *P* of the changeless chair,   *Queen Mary* III iv 380
Peter (Peter Martyr) *P*, I'll swear for him He *did* believe   ,, I i 76
Peter (Saint) (*See also* **St. Peter**) and I return As *P*,
  but to bless thee: ,, III ii 56
How oft hath *P* knock'd at Mary's gate!   ,, III ii 63
The Church on *P's* rock? never!   ,, III iv 134
I have builded the great church of Holy *P*:   *Harold* I i 180
'O blessed relics!' 'O Holy *P*!'   ,, I ii 171
loftiest minster ever built To Holy *P*   ,, III i 207
Like *P's* when he fell, and thou wilt have To wail for it
  like *P*.   ,, III ii 283
and a blessed hair Of *P*, and all France,   ,, III ii 149
gonfanon of Holy *P* Floating above their helmets—   ,, v i 549
Holy Father strangled him with a hair Of *P*,   ,, v ii 47
And but that Holy *P* fought for us,   ,, v ii 164
The customs of the Church are *P's* rock.   *Becket* I iii 24
Which even *P* had not dared?   ,, III iii 395
And as for the flesh at table, a whole *P's* sheet,   ,, III iii 129
Peterboro' Leofric, and all the monks of *P*   *Harold* v i 446
Peter Carew (*See also* **Carew**) Sir *P C* and Sir
  Thomas Wyatt,   *Queen Mary* I iii 123
Duke of Suffolk and Sir *P C*,   ,, I iv 112
'Sir *P C* fled to France!   ,, II i 135
Is *P C* fled? Is the Duke taken?   ,, II i 142
Peters (Gentleman of Lord Howard) *P*, my gentleman,
  an honest Catholic,   ,, IV iii 553
P, how pale you look! you bring the smoke   ,, IV iii 560
P, you know me Catholic, but English.   ,, IV iii 566
Ay, Master *P*, tell us.   ,, IV iii 573
Petition long *p* from the foreign exiles To spare   ,, IV i 3
This same *p* of the foreign exiles For Cranmer's life.   *Foresters* II i 195
Petticoat Ay, ay, gown, coif, and *p*,   *Queen Mary* III i 13
Petty To still the *p* treason therewithin,   *Becket* II ii 293
the sea-creek—the *p* rill That falls into it—   ,, I iii 65
Petulancy Thou goest beyond thyself in *p*!   ,, v ii 446
Pevensey dungeon'd the other half In *P* Castle—   ,, v ii 446
Landed at *P*—I am from *P*—Hath wasted all the land
  at *P*—   *Harold* IV iii 188
I have ridden night and day from *P*—   ,, IV iii 192
Phantasy Nay, pure *p*, your Grace.   *Queen Mary* v i 280
Not as from me, but as your *p*;   ,, v i 260
This coarseness is a want of *p*.   ,, v ii 438
I love the man but not his *phantasies*.   *Harold* I i 279
Phantom (adj.) The *p* cry! *You*—did *you* hear a cry?   *Prom. of May* III 651
And catch the winding of a *p* horn.   *Foresters* IV 1091
Phantom (s) to victory—I hope so—Like *p's* of the Gods.   *The Cup* II ii 170
Her *p* call'd me by the name she loved.   *Prom. of May* II 242
That I may feel thou art no *p*—   *Foresters* IV 1013

Philip Harold (Philip Edgar) Nay—now—not one, for I am P H. — *Prom. of May* II 451
Philip Hedgar (Edgar) P H o' Soomerset! (repeat) — „ II 586
Philippines Tunis, and Oran, and the P, — *Queen Mary* v i 48
Philosopher A poor p who call'd the mind — *Prom. of May* II 281
Phœbe P, that man from Synorix, who has been — *The Cup* II 9
Phrase Do not scrimp your p, — *Queen Mary* III iii 260
now I see That I was blind—suffer the p— — *Becket* II ii 438
If the p 'Return' displease you, we will say— — *The Falcon* 728
Phryne With P, Or Lais, or thy Rosamund, — *Becket, Pro.* 55
Physic in a closed room, with light, fire, p, tendance; — *Queen Mary* v iv 37
Physical Against the moral excess No p ache, — *Becket* I i 382
Physician Nay, dearest Lady, see your good p. — *Queen Mary* v v 59
Physick'd These princes are like children, must be p, — „ I v 234
Pianner (piano) plaäy the p, if ye liked, all daäy long, like a laädy, — *Prom. of May* II 100
Pick What should I say, I cannot p my words— — *Queen Mary* vi vi 147
Picture we prize The statue or the p all the more — *Prom. of May* III 514
poor Steer looks The very type of Age in a p, — „ III 514
More like the p Of Christian in my 'Pilgrim's Progress' — „ III 518
if you cram me crop-full I be little better than Famine in the p, — *Foresters* I i 47
Piece Henry broke the carcase of your church To p's, — *Queen Mary* I v 399
It lies there in six p's at your feet; — „ I 87
Give me a p of paper! — „ II iii 66
A p in this long-tugged-at, threadbare-worn Quarrel — *Becket* II ii 54
I dash myself to p's—I stay myself— — „ II ii 150
God's full curse Shatter you all to p's if ye harm — „ v iii 135
I tear it all to p's, never dream'd Of acting on it. — *The Cup* I ii 247
a hundred Gold p's once were offer'd by the Duke. — *The Falcon* 324
but one p of earthenware to serve the salad in to my lady, — „ 481
Towser'ill tear him all to p's. — *Prom. of May* I 423
and there is a p of beef like a house-side, — „ I 793
break it all to p's, as you would break the poor, — *Foresters* II i 285
Piecemeal And tear you p: so you have a guard. — *Queen Mary* I v 36
a score of wolf-dogs are let loose that will tear thee p. — *Becket* III ii 40
Pier Ran sunless down, and moan'd against the p's. — *Queen Mary* II iii 27
Pierced Tho' we have p thro' all her practices; — *Harold* v i 156
Piero they are but blue beads—my P, — *The Falcon* 48
Pig (See also **Hedge-pig**) s'pose I kills my p, and gi'es it among 'em, why there wudn't be a dinner for nawbody, and I should ha' lost the p. — *Prom. of May* I 147
Pigeon See **Carrier-pigeon**
Pike Hurls his soil'd life against the p's and dies. — *Queen Mary* IV iii 311
Pilate The Lord be judged again by P? No! — *Becket* I iii 97
Piled dead So p about him he can hardly move. — *Harold* v i 658
'Pilgrim's Progress' More like the picture Of Christian in my 'P P' — *Prom. of May* III 519
Pillage (s) The p of his vassals. — *Foresters* III 107
Richard sacks and wastes a town With random p, — „ IV 378
Pillage (verb) they p Spain already. — *Queen Mary* III i 158
Pillar Steadying the tremulous p's of the Church— — „ I v 517
Be limpets to this p, or we are torn — „ III i 184
stand behind the p here; — „ IV vii 462
But thou didst back thyself against a p, — *Harold* I ii 88
Taken the rifted p's of the wood — „ I ii 100
lo! my two p's, Jachin and Boaz!— — „ III i 191
Pillaring P a leaf-sky on their monstrous boles, — *Foresters* III 100
Pillow I never lay my head upon the p — *Queen Mary* III v 131
A gnat that vext thy p! — *Harold* II i 71
Pilot Saints P and prosper all thy wandering out — „ I i 265
Pincer fiends that utter them Tongue-torn with p's, — *Queen Mary* v ii 194
Pinch give me one sharp p upon the cheek — *Foresters* IV 1011
Pine (tree) I have seen A p in Italy that cast its shadow Athwart a cataract; firm stood the p— — *Queen Mary* IV iv 136
the p was Rome. You see, my Lords, — „ III iv 142
wind of the dawn that I hear in the p overhead? — *Becket* II i 2
P, beech and plane, oak, walnut, — *The Cup* I i 1
Beneath the shadow of our p's and planes! — „ II 227
Pine (verb) poor Pole p's of it, As I do, to the death. — *Queen Mary* v v 128
Pinfold I seed that one cow 'o thine i' the p ageän — *Prom. of May* I 191
Pinned What's here? a scroll P to the wreath. — *The Falcon* 425

Pious Your p wish to pay King Edward's debts, — *Queen Mary* I v 111
it were a p work To string my father's sonnets, — „ II i 26
Here a p Catholic, Mumbling and mixing up in his scared prayers — „ II ii 84
See if our p—what shall I call him, John?— — *Becket* II ii 38
now this p cup Is passport to their house, — *The Cup* I i 81
I have one mark in gold which a p son of the Church gave me this morning — *Foresters* III 281
Pipe Organ and p, and dulcimer, chants and hymns — *Becket* v ii 365
Piped boy she held Mimick'd and p her — *Queen Mary* II ii 74
Pipest thou, my bird, thou p Becket, Becket— — *Becket* I i 32
Piping gaping bills in the home-nest P for bread— — „ II ii 301
Fluting, and p and luting 'Love, love, love'— — *Foresters* III 33
Pirate Thy fierce forekings had clench'd their p hides To the bleak church doors, — *Harold* IV iii 36
For tho' we touch'd at many p ports, — *Foresters* IV 983
Pit plunge and fall Of heresy to the p: — *Queen Mary* III iv 142
Sunk in the deepest p of pauperism, — *Prom. of May* III 803
Pitchfork fur him as be handy wi' a book bean't but haäfe a hand at a p. — „ I 189
hunt him With p's off the farm, — „ II 427
Piteous perhaps the man himself, When hearing of that p death, — „ II 500
Pitiful Be somewhat p, after I have gone, — *Queen Mary* IV ii 157
P to this p heresy? — „ IV ii 163
Pitiless And by the churchman's p doom of fire, — „ III iv 49
Pity (s) Hate not one who felt Some p for thy hater! — *Harold* I i 44
the Pope our master, Have p on him, — *Becket* I iii 202
P, my lord, that you have quenched the warmth — „ II ii 310
said it was a p to blindfold such eyes as mine — „ III i 126
more the p then That thy true home— — „ IV ii 131
I have wasted p on her—not dead now— — *Prom. of May* III 691
Have you no p? must you see the man? — *Foresters* IV 457
Have you no p? — „ IV 519
What p have you for your game? — „ IV 521
P, my lord!—There was a man of ours Up in the north, — „ IV 528
I fear I had small p for that man.— — „ IV 547
But p for a father, it may be, — „ IV 659
Pity (verb) She said—pray pardon me, and p her— — *Queen Mary* v 53
I could p this poor world myself that it is no better ordered. — *Becket, Pro.* 365
and I have none—to p thee. — „ IV ii 81
Plaäy (play) And p the pianner, if ye liked, all daäy like a laädy, — *Prom. of May* II 100
Wi' the butterflies out, and the swallers at p, — „ II 199
Place (s) (See also **Pleace**, **Tomb-place**) Is bounden by his power and p to see — *Queen Mary* III iv 212
No p for worse. — „ IV iii 80
Gardener, and huntsman, in the parson's p, — „ IV iii 374
Is this a p To wail in, Madam? — „ v i 212
battle-axe Was out of p; it should have been the bow.— — *Harold* I ii 106
yea, and thou Chair'd in his p. — „ I ii 247
Then shalt thou step into my p and sign. — *Becket* I iii 15
A fit p for the monies of the Church, — „ I iii 105
This is the likelier tale. We have hit the p. — „ III ii 43
And weeps herself into the p of power; — „ v ii 214
He knows the twists and turnings of the p. — „ v ii 577
not show yourself In your old p? — „ v ii 596
Thou shouldst have ta'en his p, and fought for him. — *Foresters* v i 546
Place (verb) P and displace our councillors, — *Queen Mary* II ii 160
We therefore p ourselves Under the shield — *Becket* I i 599
let me p this chair for your ladyship. — *The Falcon* 178
Placed freed him from the Tower, p him at Court; — *Queen Mary* I v 163
And softly p the chaplet on her head. — *The Falcon* 362
will be p Beneath the window, Philip. — *Prom. of May* I 560
Plagas Hostis per Angliae P bacchatur; — *Harold* v i 511
Plague (s) so the p Of schism spreads; — *Queen Mary* III iv 171
Harvestless autumns, horrible agues, p— — „ v i 99
War, waste, p, famine, all malignities. — *Harold* I i 466
Saints to scatter sparks of p Thro' all your cities, — „ II ii 746
like Egypt's p, had fill'd All things with blood; — *Becket* I iii 344
They are p's enough in-door. — „ II ii 91
The p's That smite the city spare the solitudes — „ v ii 172
Whose arrow is the p—whose quick flash — *The Cup* II 291
Push'd from all doors as if we bore the p, — *Prom. of May* III 805

Please (continued) You are hard to p. *Queen Mary* III iv 154
Then one day more to p her Majesty. „ III vi 247
So p your Majesty, A long petition „ IV i 2
Might I not say—to p your wife, the Queen? „ v i 307
that it would p Him out of His infinite love „ v iv 46
to p our dying king, and those Who make *Harold* III i 328
Well, well, I swear, but not to p myself. *Becket, Pro.* 193
Doth it p you? Take it and wear it on that hard heart „ *Pro.* 372
To p the King? „ I i 31
Shall I fall off—to p the King once more? „ I i 110
Of this wild Rosamund to p the King, „ I i 392
whom it p's him To call his wives; „ IV i 35
if we *will* buy diamond necklaces To p our lady, *The Falcon* 45
I am glad it p's you; *Prom. of May* II 543
Nay, an p your Elfin Grace, *Foresters* II ii 132
Pleäse P, Miss, Mr. Dobson told me to saäy *Prom. of May* III 345
Pleased All p you so at first. *Becket* III i 50
and the master 'ud be straänge an' p if you'd step in fust, *Prom. of May* I 168
Pleasure Thou hast shouted for thy p, shout for mine ! *Queen Mary* I i 304
They kill'd but for their p and the power „ III iv 74
you will find in it P as well as duty, „ III iv 430
For thine own p? *Harold* III i 327
not my purveyor Of p's, but to save a life *Becket, Pro.* 150
and the walks Where I could move at p, „ I i 266
For the King's p rather than God's cause .. I iii 697
daily want supplied—The daily p to supply it. .. II iii 303
for I have p in the p of crowds, „ III iii 82
Here, Madam, at your p. *Eleanor.* My p is to have a man about me. „ IV iv 428
She would have robb'd me then of a great p. *The Falcon* 65
The p of his eyes—boast of his hand— „ 221
And if my p breed another's pain, *Prom. of May* I 278
Have I the p, friend, of knowing you? „ I 297
No p then taboo'd: for when the tide Of full democracy „ I 591
Hollow Pandora-box, With all the p's flown, „ II 347
and I have lighted On a new p. „ II 669
on all its idiot gleams Of p, „ III 723
Not p's, women's matters. *Foresters* I ii 176
Plebeian Pride of the p ! *Fitzurse.* And this p like to be Archbishop? *Becket, Pro.* 457
Pledge (s) I be ready to taäke the p. *Prom. of May* III 85
Pledge (verb) I p you, Strato. *Synorix.* And I you, my lord. *The Cup* I ii 49
I will p you. Wine ! Filippo, wine ! *The Falcon* 575
P the Plantagenet, Him that is gone. *Foresters* I ii 7
And they shall p thee, Marian, „ III 316
They p me, Robin ? „ III 320
Pleiads To the P, unseen ; they have lost a sister. *Queen Mary* I iv 293
Plenty will be p to sunder and unsister them again : „ I i 84
fill all hearts with fatness and the lust Of p— *The Cup* II 274
Plied Still p him with entreaty and reproach: *Queen Mary* IV iii 577
and still the friars P him, „ IV iii 601
Plot (s) Mix not yourself with any p I pray you; „ I iv 173
to discourage and lay lame The p's of France, „ v iii 992
the p's against him Had madden'd tamer men. *Harold* IV i 110
P's and feuds ! This is my ninetieth birthday. (repeat) „ IV i 120, 125
Who dares arraign us, king, of such a p ? „ IV i 169
Hath Sinnatus never told you of this p ? *Camma.* What p ? *The Cup* I ii 251
I am sure I told him that his p was folly. „ I ii 283
Plot (verb) When will ye cease to p against my house ? *Harold* IV i 161
Should care to p against him in the North. „ v i 166
Plotted Wherewith they p in their treasonous malice, *Queen Mary* IV i 39
Plotting They have been p here ! *Harold* IV i 40
If you had found him p against Rome, *The Cup* II 406
But had I found him p, I had counsell'd him „ II 412
Ploughman-Plowman These Kentish *ploughmen* cannot break the guards. *Queen Mary* IV ii 17
burn a *plowman*, and now, as far as money goäs, *Prom. of May* I 330
That ever charm'd the *plowman* of your wolds „ III 488
Plover in a narrow path. A p flew before thee. *Becket* I iv 54
Plow p Lay rusting in the furrow's yellow weeds, „ I iii 354
and I'd drive the p straäit as a line *Prom. of May* I 369

Plowed I ha' p the ten-aäcre—it be mine now— *Prom. of May* I 365
I mun ha' p it moor nor a hoonderd times ; „ I 367
Plowest steer wherewith thou p thy field is cursed, *Harold* v i 71
Plowin' if I could ha' gone on wi' the p *Prom. of May* I 376
Pluck P the dead woman off the dead man, Malet ! *Harold* v ii 144
King p's out their eyes Who anger him, *Becket* IV ii 405
He that can p the flower of maidenhood *Foresters* I ii 108
Pluck'd He all but p the bearer's eyes away. *Becket* I iii 11
Plumed My princess, of the cloud my p purveyor, *The Falcon* 7
Plump To p the leaner pouch of Italy. *Queen Mary* III iv 365
Plum-pudding and a p-p as big as the round haystack. *Prom. of May* I 794
Plunder they p—yea, ev'n bishops, Yea, even archbishops— *Foresters* IV 909
Plunder'd P the vessel full of Gascon wine, *Becket* v ii 441
cask of wine whereof we p The Norman prelate ? *Foresters* IV 307
Plundering a p o' Bishop Winchester's house ; *Queen Mary* II iii 73
Plunge (s) Our short-lived sun, before his winter p, „ III iii 86
headlong p and fall Of heresy to the pit: „ III iv 140
last inhospitable p Our boat hath burst her ribs ; *Harold* II i 2
One downward p of his paw would rend *Becket* IV ii 283
Plunge (verb) and p His foreign fist into our island Church *Queen Mary* III iv 363
Tear out his eyes, And p him into prison. *Harold* II ii 492
To p thee into life-long prison here:— „ II ii 550
To p into this bitter world again— *Becket* v ii 81
I might p And lose myself for ever. *Prom. of May* II 305
Plunged beast-body That God has p my soul in— *Becket* II i 150
Were p beneath the waters of the sea, *Foresters* IV 668
Pocket but he would p the purse. *Becket* II i 371
Pœna Illorum scelera P sequatur ! (repeat) *Harold* v i 518, 605
Poet you are as poor a p, Wyatt, As a good soldier. *Queen Mary* I i 113
There ! my lord, you are a p, *The Falcon* 533
Poetical A shadow, a p fiction—did ye not call me king in your song ? *Foresters* IV 219
Poinet (**John, Bishop of Winchester**) P, Barlow, Bale, Scory, Coverdale ; *Queen Mary* I ii 5
Point (s) (*See also* **Finger-point**) Calais ! Our one p on the main, „ I v 125
then to cede A p to her demand ? „ III vi 170
there's An old world English adage to the p. „ v i 175
Many p's weather'd, many perilous ones, „ v v 211
The p you aim'd at, and pray God she prove *Becket* II ii 77
She lives—but not for him ; one p is gain'd. „ IV ii 415
Point (verb) Heretic and rebel P at me and make merry. *Queen Mary* v ii 318
Shouts something—he p's onward— *Harold* v i 558
Pointed With fingers p like so many daggers, *Queen Mary* I v 149
And p full at Southwark ; „ III iii 46
How their p fingers Glared at me ! *Harold* II ii 789
rose From the foul flood and p toward the farm, *Prom. of May* II 653
Pointing the Pope P at me with ' Pole, the heretic, *Queen Mary* IV iii 175
Poison (s) practise on my life, By p, fire, shot, stab— „ I iv 285
Lest your whole body should madden with the p ? „ III iv 208
Give me the p ; set me free of him ! *Becket* IV ii 164
I have heard these p's May be walk'd down. *The Cup* II 474
Poison (verb) filch the linen from the hawthorn, p the house-dog, *Foresters* III 199
Poison'd to see His people be not p. *Queen Mary* III iv 213
the Norman adder hath bitten us ; we are p : *Harold* II i 39
A cleric lately p his own mother, *Becket, Pro.* 10
we shall all be p. Let us go. „ I iv 244
I am p. She—close the Temple door. *The Cup* II 459
He had my fate for it, P. „ II 517
Poisoning So p the Church, so long continuing, *Queen Mary* IV iii 48
Poitevins I learn but now that those poor P *Becket* II ii 427
Poitou and all France, all Burgundy, P, all Christendom *Harold* III ii 150
Have we not heard Raymond of P, thine own uncle— *Becket* IV ii 247
Pole (**Reginald, Cardinal and Papal Legate**) (*See also* **Reginald Pole**) holy legate of the holy father the Pope, Cardinal P, *Queen Mary* I iii 28
(Nay, there is Cardinal P, too), „ I iv 208
So would your cousin, Cardinal P ; „ I v 405
True, good cousin, P ; And there were also those „ III iii 68
Peace—the Queen, Philip, and P. „ III iii 84
Then must I play the vassal to this P „ III iii 112

Pole (Reginald, Cardinal and Papal Legate) (*continued*)
Our supplication be exhibited To the Lord Cardinal *P*, *Queen Mary* iii iii 124
Cousin *P*, You are fresh from brighter lands. „ iii iv 321
P has the Plantagenet face, „ iii iv 333
Doth *P* yield, sir, ha! „ iii iv 394
I am sorry for it If *P* be like to turn. „ iii iv 416
Write to him, then. *Pole.* I will. *Mary.* And sharply, *P*. „ iv i 39
P Will tell you that the devil helpt them thro' it. „ iv iii 351
Reginald *P*, what news hath plagued thy heart? „ v ii 17
the Pope Pointing at me with '*P*, the heretic, „ v ii 175
for the death Of our accursed Queen and Cardinal *P*.' „ v ii 182
let my cousin *P* Seize him and burn him „ v ii 244
Saving my confessor and my cousin *P*. „ v ii 527
They say she's dying. *First.* So is Cardinal *P*. „ v iv 5
Holy Father Has ta'en the legateship from our cousin *P*—Was that well done? and poor *P* pines of it, As I do, to the death. „ v v 127
'twas I and Bonner did it, And *P*; „ v v 143
Polecat The deer, the highback'd *p*, the wild boar, *Foresters* i iii 119
Policy (*See also* **Church-policy, State-policy**) Your Grace's *p* hath a farther flight *Queen Mary* i v 312
Mismatch'd with her for *p*! „ iii i 365
Were but a thankless *p* in the crown, „ iii iv 51
might it not be *p* in some matter „ iii vi 166
It was his father's *p* against France. „ v v 45
You will find Philip only, *p*, *p*,— „ v v 158
That was, my lord, a match of *p*. *Harold* iv i 199
A great and sound *p* that: I could embrace him for it: *Becket, Pro.* 451
A *p* of wise pardon Wins here as well as there. „ v ii 22
the dry light of Rome's straight-going *p*, *The Cup* i i 146
The One Who shifts his *p* suffers something, „ ii 113
And apt at arms and shrewd in *p*. *Foresters* i ii 104
Polish'd But you, my Lord, a *p* gentleman, *Queen Mary* iii iv 250
Politic You are too *p* for me, my Lord Paget. „ iv i 150
If this be *p*, And well for thee and England— *Harold* iii ii 110
his *p* Holiness Hath all but climb'd the Roman perch again, *Becket* ii ii 45
Too *p* for that. Imprison me? „ iv ii 397
Pomegranate Palms, flowers, *p's*, golden cherubim *Harold* iii i 182
Pompey *See* **Pumpy**
Pond *See* **Herring-pond, Herse-pond**
Ponder Grant me one day To *p* these demands. *Becket* i iii 669
Ponthieu (adj.) drave and crack'd His boat on *P* beach; *Harold* ii ii 36
Ponthieu (s) Guy, Count of *P*? „ ii i 81
winds than that which crack'd Thy bark at *P*,— „ ii ii 200
Pontigny He shelter'd in the Abbey of *P*. *Becket* ii i 84
On a Tuesday at *P* came to me The ghostly warning „ v ii 290
Pontus Have you alliances? Bithynia, *P*, Paphlagonia? *The Cup* i ii 100
Pooh *P*, *p*, my Lord! poor garrulous country-wives. *Queen Mary* iv iii 546
Pool stormless shipwreck in the *p's* Of sullen slumber, *Harold* v i 296
I only wish This *p* were deep enough, *Prom. of May* ii 304
Poor (adj.) and of the good Lady Jane as a *p* innocent child *Queen Mary* i i 94
So you would honour my *p* house to-night, „ i iii 118
the realm is *p*, The exchequer at neap-tide: „ i v 120
a hundred men-at-arms Guard my *p* dreams for England „ i v 154
It then remains for your *p* Gardiner, „ i v 220
But Philip never writes me one *p* word, „ i v 360
but, if I'm any judge, By God, you are as *p* a poet, Wyatt, As a good soldier. „ ii i 113
You as *p* a critic As an honest friend: „ ii i 115
No, *p* soul; no. „ ii i 242
And four of her *p* Council too, my Lord, As hostages. „ ii ii 42
he says he's a *p* gentleman. „ ii iii 74
He's *p* enough, has drunk and gambled out All that he had, „ ii iii 87
Take thy *p* gentleman! „ ii iii 94
She, with her *p* blind hands feeling—' where is it? „ iii i 407
Amplier than any field on our *p* earth Can render thanks „ iii iii 197
Paget, you are all for this *p* life of ours, „ iii iv 59
So they have sent *p* Courtenay over sea. „ iii v 1
and my *p* chronicle Is but of glass. „ iii v 46
Draw with your sails from our *p* land, „ iii vi 226

Poor (adj.) (*continued*) To the *p* flock—to women and to children— *Queen Mary* iv ii 158
but my *p* voice Against them is a whisper to the roar Of a spring-tide. „ iv ii 185
'twas you That sign'd the burning of *p* Joan of Kent; „ iv ii 206
Pooh, pooh, my Lord! *p* garrulous country-wives. „ iv iii 546
Stays longer here in our *p* north than you:— „ v i 24
and you know The crown is *p*. „ v i 170
I have play'd with this *p* rose so long I have broken off the head. „ v ii 2
And the *p* son turn'd out into the street To sleep, „ v ii 125
I still will do mine utmost with the Pope. *P* cousin! „ v ii 132
I had forgotten How these *p* libels trouble you. „ v ii 202
P lads, they see not what the general sees, „ v ii 447
this *p* throat of mine, Barer than I should wish a man to see it,— „ v ii 460
I would she could have wedded that *p* youth, „ v ii 476
There—up and down, *p* lady, up and down. „ v v 6
I am eleven years older than he, *P* boy! „ v v 47
P enough in God's grace! „ v v 50
and *p* Pole pines of it, As I do, to the death. „ v v 128
Why would you vex yourself, *P* sister? „ v v 264
lighten'd for me The weight of this *p* crown, *Harold* i i 218
From spies of thine to spy my nakedness In my *p* North! „ i i 353
Spite of this grisly star ye three must gall *P* Tostig. „ i i 420
the *p* thunder Never harm'd head. „ i ii 231
How wan, *p* lad! how sick and sad for home! „ ii ii 325
P brother! still a hostage! „ ii ii 329
Far as he knew in this *p* world of ours— „ ii ii 363
P Wulfnoth! do they not entreat thee well? „ ii ii 403
Alas! *p* man, *His* promise brought it on me. „ iii i 337
only grandson To Wulfnoth, a *p* cow-herd. „ iv i 70
For England, for thy *p* white dove, who flutters „ iv i 230
these *p* hands but sew, Spin, broider— „ iv iii 9
thy victories Over our own *p* Wales, „ iv iii 27
Tostig, *p* brother, Art *thou* so anger'd? „ v i 272
Praying perchance for this *p* soul of mine In cold, „ v i 323
I know Some three or four *p* priests a thousand times *Becket, Pro.* 291
I could pity this *p* world myself that it is no better ordered. „ *Pro.* 366
P bird of passage! so I was; but, father, „ i i 253
P soul! *p* soul! My friend, the King! . . . „ i i 334
p rogues (Heaven bless 'em) who never saw nor dreamed of such a banquet. „ i iv 82
My lord Archbishop, may I come in with my *p* friend, my dog? „ i iv 94
P beast! *p* beast! set him down. „ i iv 105
That my *p* heretic heart would excommunicate His excommunication, „ ii i 283
P man, beside himself—not wise. „ ii ii 235
I learn but now that those *p* Poitevins, „ ii ii 427
his fond excess of wine Springs from the loneliness of my *p* bower, „ iii i 40
I have lived, *p* bird, from cage to cage, „ iii i 222
In our *p* west We cannot do it so well. „ iv ii 316
his *p* tonsure A crown of Empire. „ v i 194
p mother, Soon as she learnt I was a friend of thine, „ v ii 109
Mutilated, *p* brute, my sumpter-mule, „ v ii 440
And drown all *p* self-passion in the sense Of public good? *The Cup* ii 101
Thy way? *p* worm, crawl down thine own black hole „ ii 494
Welcome to this *p* cottage, my dear lady. *The Falcon* 270
I will, I will. *P* fellow! „ 281
you have said so much Of this *p* wreath that I was bold enough „ 427
very letters seem to shake With cold, with pain perhaps, *p* prisoner! „ 449
P Federigo degli Alberighi Takes nothing in return „ 715
that her flies Must massacre each other? this *p* Nature! *Prom. of May* i 285
you have robb'd *p* father Of ten good apples. „ i 615
And *p* old father not die miserable. „ i 722
Fonder of *p* Eva—like everybody else. „ ii 11
Eva's saäke. Yeas. *P* gel, *p* gel! „ ii 31
P sister, I had it five years ago. „ ii 82

Porter And scared the gray old *p* and his wife. *Queen Mary* II iii 16
The *p*, please your Grace, hath shut the gates ,, II iv 60
Positive and the heart of a—that's too *p*! *The Falcon* 87
heart like the stone in it—that's *p* again— ,, 94
Positive-negative not a heart for any of them—that's *p-n*: ,, 89
Possess Seek to *p* our person, hold our Tower, *Queen Mary* II ii 158
Thou didst *p* thyself of Edward's ear *Harold* v i 345
Possession demanded *P* of her person and the Tower. *Queen Mary* II ii 41
Possible hedge-rose Of a soft winter, *p*, not probable, ,, vi 16
Is it *p* That mortal men should bear their earthly heats *Harold* v i 282
Pos t (messenger) there is a *p* from over seas With news for thee. *Harold* II ii 208
Post (position) I dare not leave my *p*. *Queen Mary* I ii 5ç
Post (post-haste) till his man cum in *p* vro' here, *Queen Mary* IV iii 511
Post *See* **Door-post**
Pot Here's a *p* o' wild honey from an old oak, *Foresters* II i 295
Potato *See* **Taäter**
Potent To join a voice, so *p* with her Highness, *Queen Mary* IV i 117
I do think the King Was *p* in the election, *Becket* I i 129
Pothouse next time you waste them at a *p* you get no more from me. *Prom. of May* III 99
Pouch To plump the leaner *p* of Italy. *Queen Mary* III iv 365
I have but one penny in *p*, *Foresters* III 194
Poultry making of your butter, and the managing of your *p*? *Prom. of May* II 94
Pounce *p* like a wild beast out of his cage *Queen Mary* I i 87
Pound shall have a hundred *p*'s for reward.' ,, II iii 61
Pour as we pass, And *p* along the land, ,, II i 232
P not water In the full vessel running out at top *Harold* I i 376
Poured and when ye shall hear it is *p* out upon earth, *Becket* I iv 37
Pout Nay, *p* out, cousin. *Queen Mary* I iv 134
Poverty I But add my *p* to thine. *The Falcon* 143
P crept thro' the door. *Foresters* I i 157
Powder Until the *p* suddenly blew him dead. *Queen Mary* IV iii 340
Power and God grant me *p* to burn! ,, I ii 99
Mine is the fleet and all the *p* at sea— ,, I iv 287
may fence round his *p* with restriction, ,, II i 172
Back'd by the *p* of France, and landing here, ,, III i 447
and the *p* They felt in killing. ,, III iv 75
Is bounden by his *p* and place to see ,, III iv 212
What would'st thou do hadst thou his *p*, ,, III iv 279
What *p* this cooler sun of England hath ,, III iv 327
P hath been given you to try faith by fire— ,, IV ii 153
May learn there is no *p* against the Lord. ,, IV iii 66
I am but a woman, I have no *p*.— ,, v v 131
ay, young lord, *there* the king's face is *p*. *Harold* I i 73
p's of the house of Godwin Are not enframed ,, I i 316
Crush it at once With all the *p* I have!— ,, I i 357
Wisdom when in *p* And wisest, should not frown as *P*, ,, I i 364
the true *must* Shall make her strike as *P*: ,, I i 369
Come hither, I have a *p*; ,, III i 5
wood-fungus on a dead tree, I have a *p*! ,, III i 9
when Tostig hath come back with *p*, ,, IV i 118
No *p* mine To hold their force together . . . ,, IV iii 212
Not know that he nor I had *p* to promise? ,, v i 49
p to balk Thy puissance in this fight ,, v i 117
I have a *p*—would Harold ask me for it—I have a *p*. ,, v i 451
What *p*, holy father? *Stigand.* *P* now from Harold to command thee hence ,, v i 454
she, whom the King loves indeed, is a *p* in the State. *Becket, Pro.* 483
you That owe to me your *p* over me— ,, II ii 152
The King had had no *p* except for Rome. ,, II ii 412
who am, or was, A sovereign *p*? ,, IV ii 405
And weeps herself into the place of *p*; ,, v ii 215
tho' it be their hour, the *p* of darkness, But my hour too, the *p* of light ,, v iii 93
The *p* of life in death to make her free! ,, v iii 100
At the right hand of *P*—*P* and great glory— ,, v iii 193
have you *p* with Rome? use it for him! *The Cup* I ii 289
Alas! I have no such *p* with Rome. ,, I ii 292
Has no more *p* than other oracles ,, II 34
happiest, Lady, in my *p* To make you happy. ,, II 240
and Napoleons To root their *p* in. *Prom. of May* II 594
Not her, the father's *p* upon her. *Foresters* I iii 9
break, Far as he might, the *p* of John— ,, II i 696

Power (continued) In this dark wood when all was in our *p* *Foresters* III 183
Practice Tho' we have pierced thro' all her *p*'s; *Harold* v i 156
Practise to *p* on my life, By poison, fire, shot, stab— *Queen Mary* I iv 284
I am tender enough. Why do you *p* on me? *Synorix.*
Why should I *p* on you? *The Cup* I ii 238
Præcipitatur Equus cum equite *P*. *Harold* v i 599
Prædator Hostis in Angliam Ruit *p*, ,, v i 507
Præpediatur Equus cum pedite *P*! ,, v i 530
Praise (s) in grateful *p* of Him Who now recalls *Queen Mary* III iii 165
Out of the mouths of babes and sucklings, *p*! *Becket* II ii 279
All *p* to Heaven, and sweet St. Magdalen! ,, III iii 234
Praise (verb) Make all tongues *p* and all hearts beat for you. *Queen Mary* I v 117
His friends would *p* him, I believed 'em, ,, v 623
P the Saints. It is over. No more blood! *Harold* v ii 194
gangrenes, and running sores, *p* ye the Lord, *Becket* I iv 256
Hear thy people who *p* thee! *The Cup* II 5
those pale mouths which we have fed will *p* us— *Foresters* IV 1077
Praised *P*, where you should have blamed him, *Queen Mary* I v 600
she so *p* The convent and lone life— *Harold* I ii 46
where is this Mr. Edgar whom you *p* so in your first letters? *Prom. of May* I 777
Prance If they *p*, Rein in, not lash them, *Harold* I i 371
P'raps (perhaps) And *p* ye hears 'at I soomtimes taäkes a drop too much; *Prom. of May* II 107
Prate Come, sirs, we *p*; hence all— *Queen Mary* II ii 372
P not of bonds, for never, oh, never again *Becket* v ii 356
yet they *p* Of mine, my brawls, when those, ,, vi 426
Prated fat fool! He drawl'd and *p* so, *Harold* IV ii 41
Prating Why did you keep me *p*? Horses, there! *Queen Mary* v iii 113
Prattled and *p* to each other that we would marry fine gentlemen, *Prom. of May* III 276
Prattling *p* to her mother Of her betrothal *Queen Mary* v v 231
Save for the *p* of thy little ones. *Harold* II ii 122
Pray *P*—consider— *Queen Mary* I iv 141
Mix not yourself with any plot I *p* you; ,, I iv 173
And so take heed I *p* you— ,, I iv 273
P God he do not be the first to break them, ,, I v 269
I *p* God No woman ever love you, ,, I v 601
and we *p* That we, your true and loyal citizens, ,, II ii 134
I've found this paper; *p* your worship read it; ,, II iii 56
Sir Thomas, *p* you go away, ,, II iii 99
we'll *p* for you all on our bended knees, ,, II iii 109
we *p* you to kill the Queen further off, ,, II iii 114
we'll *p* for you on our bended knees ,, II iii 121
Pass then, I *p* your Highness, to the Tower. ,, II iv 31
P you go on. (repeat) ,, III i 374, 389
Whereon we humbly *p* your Majesties, ,, III iii 143
And *p* Heaven That you may see according to our sight. ,, III iv 329
P God, we 'scape the sunstroke. ,, III v 279
P you write out this paper for me, Cranmer. ,, IV ii 60
You are to beg the people to *p* for you; ,, IV ii 76
So, so; this will I say—thus will I *p*. ,, IV ii 114
P you, remembering how yourself have changed, ,, IV ii 155
P for him. *Cranmer.* Ay, one and all, dear brothers, *p* for me; *P* with one breath, ,, IV iii 101
Again, I *p* you all that, next to God, ,, IV iii 175
I *p* you all to live together Like brethren; ,, IV iii 181
Go in, I *p* you. ,, v i 214
I have to *p* you, some odd time, ,, v i 257
I *p* you be not so disconsolate; ,, v ii 129
' We *p* continually for the death Of our accursed Queen ,, v ii 180
she loved much: *p* God she be forgiven. ,, v v 271
I *p* thee, let me hence and bring him home. *Harold* I i 241
I *p* thee, go to Normandy. ,, I i 249
Son Harold, I will in and *p* for thee. ,, I i 267
P God the people choose thee for their king! ,, I i 314
p in thy behalf For happier homeward winds ,, II ii 197
' I *p* you do not go to Normandy.' ,, II ii 218
can but *p* For Harold—*p*, *p*, *p*— ,, III ii 194
p God My Normans may but move as true with me —I *p* your pardon *Becket, Pro.* 36
My liege, I *p* thee let me hence: ,, *Pro.* 186
May we not *p* you, Madam, to spare us the hardness ,, *Pro.* 385
pray'd me to *p* thee to pacify Thy King; ,, I iii 206

LL

Promised letter which thine Emperor *p* Long since,   *Queen Mary* I v 348
Wyatt, but now you *p* me a boon.   „ II iii 81
Since thou hast *p* Wulfnoth home with us,   *Harold* II ii 167
He *p* that if ever he were king In England,   „ II ii 587
I *p* The King to obey these customs,   *Becket* I iii 556
Have I not *p* to restore her, Thomas,   „ III iii 182
Have I not *p*, man, to send them back ?   „ III iii 190
I *p* one of the Misses I wouldn't meddle wi' ye,   *Prom. of May* I 469
has *p* to keep our heads above water;   „ III 169
bit by bit—for she *p* secrecy—I told her all.   „ III 380
precious ring I *p* Never to part with—   *Foresters* II i 661
fair play Betwixt them and Sir Richard—*p* too,   „ IV 99
Promising By this our supplication *p*,   *Queen Mary* III iii 135
Prona Acies Acies, *P* sternatur !   *Harold* v i 582
Prone I cast me down *p*, praying,   „ v i 100
I am a man not *p* to jealousies,   *Prom. of May* III 626
Pronounce Thou shalt *p* the blessing of the Church   *Foresters* II i 927
Pronounced Judges had *p* That our young Edward   *Queen Mary* I ii 24
He is *p* anathema.   „ IV i 187
P his heir of England.   *Harold* I ii 195
hath King Edward not *p* his heir ?   „ II ii 576
Proof A diamond, And Philip's gift, as *p* of Philip's love,   *Queen Mary* III i 67
There was no *p* against him.   „ v ii 492
with full *p* Of Courtenay's treason ?   „ v ii 498
You have yet No *p* against him :   *The Cup* I i 81
—having *p* enough Against the man,   „ I iii 157
Prophecy Dream, Or *p*, that ?   *Becket* I i 56
Well, dream and *p* both.   „ I i 57
Jest or *p* there ? *Herbert.* Both, Thomas, both.   „ I i 67
Prophet (adj.) our hearts, our *p* hopes Let in the happy distance,   *The Cup* I ii 413
Prophet (s) His *p*'s, and apostles, in the Testaments,   *Queen Mary* IV iii 232
No God but one, and Mahound is his *p*.   *Becket* II ii 226
Thou art no *p*, Nor yet a *p*'s son.   „ II ii 421
And some of you were *p*'s that I might be   *Foresters* I ii 81
Prosper Saints Pilot and *p* all thy wandering out   *Harold* I i 265
If you *p*, Our Senate, wearied of their tetrarchies,   *The Cup* I i 88
To make my marriage *p* to my wish !   „ II 308
Prosper'd Had *p* in the main, but suddenly   *Becket* I iii 381
Prosperous And I will make Galatia *p* too,   *The Cup* I iii 169
Protect ' If any cleric be accused of felony, the Church shall not *p* him ;   *Becket* I iii 88
No : it must *p* me.   „ I iii 493
Protector Proclaims himself *p*, and affirms The Queen   *Queen Mary* II ii 289
Protest I *p* Your Grace's policy hath a farther flight   „ I v 311
we do *p* That our commission is to heal,   „ III iii 184
By St. James I do *p*,   „ VI vi 253
Proud But if this Philip, the *p* Catholic prince,   „ I iv 280
You are shy and *p* like Englishmen,   „ II ii 257
But this *p* Prince— *Bagenhall.* Nay, he is King, you know,   „ III i 71
As *p* as Becket.   „ III i 332
The *p* ambitions of Elizabeth, And all her fieriest partisans—   „ III ii 169
it is not fit for us To see the *p* Archbishop mutilated.   *Becket* I iii 614
I am *p* of my 'Monk-King,'   „ II ii 101
we know you *p* of your fine hand,   „ IV ii 261
But kinglike fought the *p* Archbishop,—kinglike   „ IV ii 438
p Ev'n of that stale Church-bond which link'd   „ IV ii 446
ladyship were not Too *p* to look upon the garland,   *The Falcon* 663
fur we was all on us *p* on 'er,   *Prom. of May* II 37
I am sure you must be *p* of it.   „ III 611
than if my wife And siding with these *p* priests,   *Foresters* III 125
Prove If but to *p* your Majesty's goodwill,   *Queen Mary* I v 260
And Thomas White will *p* this Thomas Wyatt, And he will *p* an Iden   „ II ii 367
He'll burn a diocese to *p* his orthodoxy.   „ III iv 353
More kinglike he than like to *p* a king.   *Harold* II ii 142
p me nothing of myself !   *Becket* I iii 292
and pray God she *p* True wife to you.   „ II ii 78
to *p* Bigger in our small world than thou art.   „ v i 127
I fear I might *p* traitor with the sheriff.   *Foresters* IV 872
Proved I thought Mr. Edgar the best of men, and he has *p* himself the worst.   *Prom. of May* II 86

Proven (adj.) And thou thyself a *p* wanton ?   *Becket* IV ii 115
Proven (verb) Who knows ? the man is *p* by the hour.   *Queen Mary* II ii 364
Much suspected, of me Nothing *p* can be.   „ III v 20
However you have *p* it.   „ III vi 17
The truth of God, which I had *p* and known.   „ IV iii 149
That Love is blind, but thou hast *p* it true.   *Foresters* II i 644
Provençal translated that hard heart into our *P* facilities,   *Becket, Pro.* 380
Provence Of *P* blew you to your English throne ;   „ v i 123
such a comedy as our court of *P* Had laugh'd at.   „ v i 189
Proverb your Ladyship hath sung the old *p* out of fashion.   *Foresters* I i 164
' Much would have more,' says the *p* ;   „ v 308
Provided perchance a happy one for thee, *P*—   *Harold* II ii 204
Providence by God's *p* a good stout staff Lay near me ;   *Queen Mary* v ii 468
Province and make us A Spanish *p* ;   „ III i 466
Sometime the viceroy of those *p*'s—   „ III ii 196
p's Are hard to rule and must be hardly ruled ;   „ III ii 200
beyond his mitre—Beyond his *p*.   „ v i 154
I am the Dean of the *p* : let me bear it.   *Becket* I iii 498
Out of thy *p* ?   „ I iii 506
With revenues, realms, and golden *p*'s   „ II i 346
you a Prince and Tetrarch in this *p*— *Sinnatus.* *P* !   *The Cup* I ii 90
they call it so in Rome. *Sinnatus.* *P* !   „ I ii 94
Whose lava-torrents blast and blacken a *p* To a cinder,   „ I iii 303
Proving all but *p* man An automatic series of sensations,   *Prom. of May* I 225
Provoke Would I could move him, *P* him any way !   *The Cup* I ii 137
Prow Our silver cross sparkled before the *p*,   *Queen Mary* III ii 9
Prowess who know His *p* in the mountains of the West,   *Harold* I v 165
Ay, ay, because I have a name for *p*.   *Foresters* II i 560
Prowling that our wolf-Queen Is *p* round the fold.   *Becket* III iii 8
Prune (s) and one plate of dried *p*'s be all-but-nothing,   *The Falcon* 136
Oh sweet saints ! one plate of *p*'s !   „ 216
p's, my lady, from the tree that my lord   „ 562
the *p*'s, my lady, from the tree that his lordship—   „ 684
But the *p*'s that your lordship—   „ 692
Prune (verb) Ay, *p* our company of thine own and go !   „ 695
Pruning-hook not Spear into *p-h*—   *Harold* v i 442
Psalm-singing Ay, the *p-s* weavers, cobblers, scum—   *Queen Mary* III iv 289
Psalter They scarce can read their *P* ;   *Harold* I i 163
Public (adj.) Wyatt, who hath tamper'd with A *p* ignorance,   *Queen Mary* II ii 182
The *p* form thereof.   „ IV vi 71
Is this a place To wail in, Madam ? what ! a *p* hall.   „ v i 213
O father, mock not at a *p* fear,   *Harold* I i 74
This is no secret, but a *p* matter.   *Becket* IV ii 319
And drown all poor self-passion in the sense Of *p* good ?   *The Cup* II 103
Public (s) he and Wulfnoth never Have met, except in *p* ;   *Harold* II ii 86
Publius *P* ! *Publius.* Here !   *The Cup* II i 1
P ! *P* ! No,   „ I iii 119
Pudding *See* **Plum-pudding**
Puddle I raised him from the *p* of the gutter,   *Becket* I iii 436
Puff (s) And that a *p* would do it—   *Queen Mary* III i 444
Puff (inter.) I stay myself—*P*—it is gone.   *Becket* II ii 151
Puffed *p* out such an incense of unctuosity into the nostrils of our Gods of Church and State,   „ III iii 114
Puissance And all the *p* of the warrior,   „ I i 152
Pull ' *P* him down ! Away with him ! '   *Queen Mary* IV iii 280
Pulled or rather *p* all the Church with the Holy Father   *Becket* III iii 76
Pulpit Spain in the *p* and on the law-bench ;   *Queen Mary* II ii 177
Would make this Cole a cinder, *p* and all.   „ IV iii 11
Pulpited *See* **Re-pulpited**
Pulse In this low *p* and palsy of the state,   „ II ii 103
a jest In time of danger shows the *p*'s even.   „ II ii 357
I came to feel the *p* of England,   „ III i 37
There somewhere beats an English *p* in thee !   *Harold* II ii 266
How few Junes Will heat our *p*'s quicker !   *Foresters* IV 1062
Pulsed blood That should have only *p* for Griffyth,   *Harold* I ii 150
Pumpy (Pompey, name of horse) Scizzars an' *P* was good uns to goä (repeat)   *Prom. of May* II 308, 318
Punish Not *p* of your own authority ?   *Becket* v ii 450
Punishment My *p* is more than I can bear.   *Harold* v ii 201
Pupil *See* **Fellow-pupil**
Puppy as a mastiff dog May love a *p* cur for no more reason   *Queen Mary* I iv 195
Purchase To *p* for Himself a stainless bride ;   „ III iii 205

Purchased   I stept between and *p* him,   *Harold* II ii 40
Pure   Your royal father (For so they say) was all *p* lily
    and rose   *Queen Mary* II v 20
    Nay, *p* phantasy, your Grace.   „   I v 280
    If cold, his life is *p*.   „   I v 333
    Of a *p* life ?   *Renard*.   As an angel among angels.   „   I v 448
    Exhort them to a *p* and virtuous life ;   „   IV ii 77
    For the *p* honour of our common nature,   „   IV iii 297
    Your Majesty has lived so *p* a life,   „   v v 73
    A gentle, gracious, *p* and saintly man !   *Harold* II ii 584
    the heavens—cry out for thee Who art too *p* for earth.   *Becket* IV ii 134
    never since have met Her equal for *p* innocence of
    nature,   *Prom. of May* II 372
    And yet I had once a vision of a *p* and perfect
    marriage,   „   III 188
    could I stoop so low As mate with one that holds no
    love is *p*,   *Foresters* IV 712
Purer   O higher, holier, earlier, *p* church,   *Queen Mary* IV ii 108
    A sane and natural loathing for a soul *P*, and truer   *Becket* II i 172
Purgatory   He burns in *P*, not in Hell.   *Queen Mary* IV i 56
    To *p*, man, to *p*.   *Peters*.   Nay, but, my Lord he
    denied *p*.   „   IV iii 627
    He miss the searching flame of *p*,   *Becket* V iii 13
Purge   that his fan may thoroughly *p* his floor.   *Queen Mary* III iv 369
Purging   you are art and part with us In *p* heresy,   „   IV iv 317
Purity   I have lived a life of utter *p*:   *Harold* I i 178
Purple   He slew not him alone who wore the *p*,   *Queen Mary* I v 500
    same chair, Or rather throne of *p*, on the deck.   „   III ii 8
    and open'd out The *p* zone of hill and heaven;   *The Cup* I ii 408
    The king should pace on *p* to his bride,   „   II 189
    Wrap them together in a *p* cloak And lay them both   *Harold* V ii 158
Purpose   it is an age Of brief life, and brief   *Queen Mary* III iv 413
    these burnings will not help The *p* of the faith;   „   IV ii 185
    Somewhat beyond your settled *p* ?   „   v 207
    Stigand should know the *p*'s of Heaven.   *Harold* I i 64
    thunder moulded in high heaven To serve the Norman *p*,   „   II ii 34
    I knew thy *p*; he and Wulfnoth never Have met,   „   II ii 84
    I loved according to the main *p* and intent of nature.   *Becket, Pro.* 502
    If the King hold his *p*, I am myself a beggar.   „   I iv 89
    if it suit their *p* to howl for the King,   „   III iii 324
    I see now Your *p* is to fright me—   „   IV iv 180
    can touch The ghittern to some *p*.   *The Falcon* 799
    The *p* of my being is accomplish'd,   „   926
Purse   Red gold—a hundred *p*'s—yea, and more !   *Harold* III i 18
    if you boxed the Pope's ears with a *p*, you might
    stagger him, but he would pocket the *p*.   *Becket* II ii 370
    how much money hast thou in thy *p* ?   *Foresters* III 274
Pursue   retire To Ashridge, and *p* my studies there.   *Queen Mary* I iv 237
Pursuer   only pulsed for Griffyth, beat For his *p*.   *Harold* I ii 152
    They turn on the *p*, horse against foot,   „   v i 608
Pursuing   Your Highness knows that in *p* heresy   *Queen Mary* IV v 96
    fled from his own church by night, No man *p*.   *Becket* II ii 158
Purtiest (prettiest)   they be two o' the *p* gels ye can see
    of a summer murnin'.   *Prom. of May* I 30
Purveyor   not my *p* Of pleasures, but to save a life—   *Becket, Pro.* 149
    My princess of the cloud, my plumed *p*,   *The Falcon* 8
Push   To shake my throne, to *p* into my chamber—   *Becket* I v 249
Push'd   *P* by the crowd beside—   *Queen Mary* IV iii 397
    Pope has *p* his horns beyond his mitre—   „   v 152
    like a thief, *p* in his royal hand ;   „   v ii 466
    And *p* our lances into Saracen hearts.   *Becket* II ii 94
    His Holiness, *p* one way by the Empire and another
    by England,   „   II ii 327
    Are *p* from out communion of the Church.   „   v i 58
    P from all doors as if we bore the plague,   *Prom. of May* III 804
Put   Not prettily *p* ?   I mean,   *Queen Mary* I v 611
    that these statutes may be *p* in force,   „   III iv 367
    p off the rags They had mock'd his misery with,   „   IV iii 589
    Ay, Renard, if you care to *p* it so.   „   v 309
    Had *p* off levity and *p* graveness on.   „   v ii 510
    And *p* it in my bosom, and all at once   „   v v 98
    P thou the comet and this blast together—   *Harold*.
    P thou thyself and mother-wit together.   *Harold* II i 15
    P her away, *p* her away, my liege !   *P* her away into a
    nunnery !   *Becket, Pro.* 63

Put (*continued*)   As one that *p*'s himself in sanctuary.   *Becket* I iii 479
    Our brother's anger *p*'s him, Poor man,   „   II ii 234
    evilly used And *p* to pain.   „   II ii 434
    when I shall *p* away——   *Rosamund*.   What will
    you *p* away ?   „   III i 3
    she was hard *p* to it, and to speak truth,   „   III i 113
    you have *p* so many of the King's household out of
    communion,   „   III iii 310
    Geoffrey, the pain thou hast *p* me to !   „   IV ii 10
    wholesome medicine here *P*'s that belief asleep.   „   IV ii 52
    To *p* her into Godstow nunnery. (repeat)   *Becket, Pro.* v 208, 209
    He bad me *p* her into a nunnery—   *Becket* v i 214
    I *p* the bitters on my breast to wean him,   *The Falcon* 189
    Was it there to take ?   *P* it there, my lord.   „   599
    I have *p* him off as often ; but to-day   „   831
    I could *p* all that o' one side eäsy anew.   *Prom. of May* II 111
    What is it Has *p* you out of heart ?   *Dora*.   It *p*'s
    me in heart Again to see you ; but indeed the
    state Of my poor father *p*'s me out of heart.   „   III 501
    they *p* it upon me because I have a bad wife.   *Foresters* III 437
Putrid   And *p* water, every drop a worm,   *Queen Mary* IV iii 444
    And I ha' nine darters i' the spital that be dead
    ten times o'er i' one day wi' the *p* fever ;   *Becket* I iv 251
Putting   *p* by his father's will.   *Queen Mary* I ii 28
Putting on   marriage-garland withers even with the
    p o,   *Becket, Pro.* 360
Pwoap (Pope)   *P*'s be pretty things, Joan,   *Queen Mary* IV iii 468
    but I do know ez *P*'s and vires be bad things ;   „   IV iii 500
    'll burn the *P* out o' this 'ere land vor iver and
    iver.   „   IV iii 536
Pyx   and the Lady Anne Bow'd to the *P* ;   „   I v 42

Q

Quack   Quash'd my frog that used to *q*   *Foresters* II ii 149
Quadruple   would treble and *q* it With revenues,   *Becket* v ii 345
Quail   some may *q*, Yet others are that dare   *Queen Mary* III iv 166
Quarrel (s)   this marriage is the least Of all their *q*.   „   II ii 155
    and there bide The upshot of my *q*,   „   II iv 86
    one to rule All England beyond question, beyond *q*.   *Harold* IV i 146
    Q of Crown and Church—to rend again.   *Becket* II i 56
    thro' all this *q* I still have cleaved to the crown,   „   v i 47
    Their *q*'s with themselves, their spites   *The Cup* I i 90
Quarrel (verb)   we will not *q* about the stag.   „   I ii 39
Quarry   and howsoe'er Thy *q* wind and wheel,   *The Falcon* 12
    Why didst thou miss thy *q* yester-even ?   „   151
Quart   To reign is restless fence, Tierce, *q*, and
    trickery.   *Queen Mary* v v 267
    and can make Five *q*'s pass into a thimble.   *Foresters* IV 283
Quarter   Thou hast not learnt thy *q*'s here.   *Harold* II ii 154
    after much smouldering and smoking, be kindled
    again upon your *q*.   *Becket* I ii 314
Quarterstaff   I will break thy sconce with my *q*.   *Foresters* I ii 76
    I am too late then with my *q* !   „   II i 428
    thou fight at *q* for thy dinner with our Robin,   „   IV 207
    Great woodland king, I know not *q*.   „   IV 216
    Shall I undertake The knight at *q*,   „   IV 248
    Give him the *q*.   „   IV 250
    I know no *q*.   „   IV 257
    I am overbreathed, Friar, by my two bouts at *q*.   „   IV 267
    That thou mightst beat him down at *q* !   „   IV 518
Quash   so you *q* rebellion too,   *Queen Mary* III iv 37
Quash'd   *Q* my frog that used to quack   *Foresters* II ii 149
Queen (s)   (*See also* **Wolf-queen**)   if Parliament can
    make the *Q* a bastard,   *Queen Mary* I i 49
    cackling of bastardy under the *Q*'s own nose ?   „   I i 59
    met the *Q* at Wanstead with five hundred horse,
    and the *Q*   „   I i 77
    setting up a mass at Canterbury To please the *Q*.   „   I ii 89
    Q's Officers Are here in force to take you to the Tower.   „   I ii 107
    'Long live Elizabeth the *Q* !'   „   I iii 8

Queen (s) (*continued*) our gracious Virgin *Q* hath——

Crowd. No pope ! no pope !	*Queen Mary* I iii 23
our Gracious *Q*, let me call her our second Virgin	
Mary,	,, I iii 57
Prince of Spain coming to wed our *Q* !	,, I iii 84
Arise against her and dethrone the *Q*—	,, I iii 91
does your gracious *Q* entreat you kinglike ?	,, I iii 110
with her own pawns plays against a *Q*,	,, I iii 163
The *Q* is ill advised :	,, I iv 5
my Lady *Q*, tho' by your age,	,, I iv 11
Has not the *Q*— *Elizabeth*. Done what, Sir ?	,, I iv 28
I am utterly submissive to the *Q*.	,, I iv 39
the *Q* Is both my foe and yours :	,, I iv 41
you have solicited The *Q*, and been rejected.	,, I iv 59
So royal that the *Q* forbad you wearing it.	,, I iv 76
Your ear ; You shall be *Q*.	,, I iv 122
He hath fallen out of favour with the *Q*.	,, I iv 157
Q would see your Grace upon the moment.	,, I iv 221
the *Q* is yours. I left her with rich jewels	,, I iv 240
Come, come, I will go with you to the *Q*.	,, I iv 298
I am English *Q*, not Roman Emperor.	,, I v 503
Tho' *Q*, I am not *Q* Of mine own heart,	,, I v 521
when I, their *Q*, Cast myself down upon my knees	,, I v 561
for the *Q's* down, and the world's up,	,, II i 65
but, for appearance sake, stay with the *Q*.	,, II i 138
and the *Q* hath no force for resistance.	,, II i 140
If this man marry our *Q*,	,, II i 170
the *Q*, and the laws, and the people, his slaves.	,, II i 174
must we levy war against the *Q's* Grace ?	,, II i 187
war for the *Q's* Grace—to save her	,, II i 189
I trust the *Q* comes hither with her guards.	,, II ii 1
Q in that distress Sent Cornwallis and Hastings	,, II ii 29
Nay the *Q's* right to reign—	,, II ii 96
now the *Q* In this low pulse and palsy	,, II ii 102
Q had written her word to come to court :	,, II ii 117
your *Q* ; To whom, when I was wedded to the realm	,, II ii 163
and be sure your *Q* So loves you,	,, II ii 194
Long live Queen Mary ! Down with Wyatt ! The *Q* !	,, II ii 252
The *Q* of England—or the Kentish Squire ?	,, II ii 269
The *Q* of England or the rabble of Kent ?	,, II ii 273
No ! No ! The *Q* ! the *Q* !	,, II ii 282
Gardiner, coming with the *Q*, And meeting Pembroke,	,, II ii 309
no man need ; but did you mark our *Q* ?	,, II ii 320
Q stands up, and speaks for her own self ;	,, II ii 341
That knows the *Q*, the Spaniard, and the Pope,	,, II ii 413
Whether I be for Wyatt, or the *Q* ?	,, II ii 415
we know that ye be come to kill the *Q*,	,, II iii 108
don't ye kill the *Q* here, Sir Thomas ;	,, II iii 111
we pray you to kill the *Q* further off, Sir Thomas.	
Wyatt. My friends, I have not come to kill the *Q*	,, II iii 115
The *Q* must to the Tower.	,, II iv 73
My foes are at my feet and I am *Q*.	,, II iv 119
that the son Being a King, might wed a *Q*—	,, III i 75
How look'd the *Q* ?	,, III i 91
before the *Q's* face Gardiner buys them	,, III i 143
Long live the King and *Q*, Philip and Mary !	,, III i 208
wilt thou wear thy cap before the *Q* ?	,, III i 237
There be both King and *Q*, Philip and Mary. Shout !	,, III i 296
The *Q* comes first, Mary and Philip.	,, III i 299
The *Q* hath felt the motion of her babe !	,, III ii 213
' The *Q* of England is delivered of a dead dog ! '	,, III ii 219
The *Q* would have him !	,, III iii 27
The *Q* would have it !	,, III iii 31
Philip's no sudden alien—the *Q's* husband,	,, III iii 42
if the *Q* should die without a child,	,, III iii 74
Peace—the *Q*, Philip, and Pole.	,, III iii 83
Her Grace the *Q* commands you to the Tower.	,, III iii 270
under our *Q's* regimen We might go softlier	,, III iv 181
I would not, were I *Q*, tolerate the heretic,	,, III iv 209
And done your best to bastardise our *Q*,	,, III iv 239
Our good *Q's* cousin—dallying over seas	,, III iv 292
Q, most wroth at first with you,	,, III iv 387
colours of our *Q* are green and white,	,, III v 5
to cast myself Upon the good *Q's* mercy ; ay, when,	
my Lord ? God save the *Q* !	,, III v 168

Queen (s) (*continued*)   When next there comes a

missive from the *Q*	*Queen Mary* III v 183
A missive from the *Q* :	,, III v 187
and think of this in your coming. ' MARY THE *Q*.'	,, III v 225
I think the *Q* may never bear a child ; I think that	
I may be some time the *Q*, Then, *Q* indeed :	,, III v 231
You cannot see the *Q*. Renard denied her,	,, III vi 1
Q hath been three days in tears For Philip's going—	,, III vi 12
bring it Home to the leisure wisdom of his *Q*,	,, III vi 23
Against the King, the *Q*, the Holy Father,	,, III vi 33
Would *she* had been the *Q* !	,, III vi 47
The *Q* of Philip should be chaste.	,, III vi 131
Be somewhat less—majestic to your *Q*.	,, III vi 150
King and *Q*, To whom he owes his loyalty after God,	,, IV i 22
Declare the *Q's* right to the throne.	,, IV ii 78
I must obey the *Q* and Council, man.	,, IV ii 164
causes Wherefore our *Q* and Council at this time	,, IV iii 36
which our *Q* And Council at this present	,, IV iii 55
For if our Holy *Q* not pardon him,	,, IV iii 61
Obey your King and *Q*, and not for dread	,, IV iii 177
Hard-natured *Q*, half-Spanish in herself,	,, IV iii 424
Done right against the promise of this *Q* Twice given.	,, IV iii 456
I but a little *Q* ; and, so indeed,	,, V i 53
A little *Q* ! but when I came to wed your majesty,	,, V i 55
Being *Q* of England, I have none other.	,, V i 69
She stands between you and the *Q* of Scots. *Mary*.	
The *Q* of Scots at least is Catholic.	,, V i 192
The *Q* in tears !	,, V i 223
How doubly aged this *Q* of ours hath grown	,, V i 227
Elizabeth, How fair and royal—like a *Q*, indeed ?	,, V i 235
methinks my *Q* is like enough To leave me	,, V i 242
so my *Q* Would leave me—as—my wife.	,, V i 251
and I shall urge his suit Upon the *Q*,	,, V i 267
affirms The *Q* has forfeited her right to reign	,, V i 290
Might I not say—to please your wife, the *Q* ?	,, V i 308
for the death Of our accursed *Q* and Cardinal Pole.'	,, V ii 181
Unhappiest Of *Q's* and wives and women !	,, V ii 408
Sees ever such an aureole round the *Q*,	,, V ii 418
I used to love the *Q* with all my heart—	,, V ii 418
Our drooping *Q* should know !	,, V ii 457
Most loyal and most grateful to the *Q*.	,, V iii 26
You will be *Q*, And, were I Philip—	,, V iii 37
gather'd from the *Q* That she would see your Grace	,, V iii 103
Is not yon light in the *Q's* chamber ?	,, V iv 1
There's the *Q's* light. I hear she cannot live.	,, V iv 10
not courtly to stand helmeted Before the *Q*.	,, V v 37
The *Q* of Scots is married to the Dauphin,	,, V v 52
How is the good *Q* now ?	,, V v 229
The *Q* is dying, or you dare not say it. *Elizabeth*.	
The *Q* is dead.	,, V v 250
I swear I have no heart To be your *Q*.	,, V v 265
God save Elizabeth, the *Q* of England !	,, V v 283
God save the *Q* !	,, V v 288
Thou art the *Q* ; ye are boy and girl no more :	*Harold* I i 455
Not yet, but then—my *q*.	,, I ii 138
If he were King of England, I his *q*,	,, I ii 154
And bless the *Q* of England.	,, I ii 207
Sign it, my *q* !	,, I ii 201
They shout as they would have her for a *q*.	,, IV i 27
The *Q* of Wales ! Why, Morcar,	,, IV i 152
Not true, my girl, here is the *Q* !	,, V ii 92
Wast thou his *Q* ? *Aldwyth*. I was the *Q* of Wales.	,, V ii 94
that I fear the *Q* would have her life.	*Becket*, Pro. 61
The *Q* should play his kingship against thine !	,, Pro. 236
Dead is he, my *Q* ?	,, Pro. 368
However kings and *q's* may frown on thee.	,, I i 18
Ay, Madam, and *q's* also. *Eleanor*. And *q's* also !	,, I ii 80
Remember the *Q* !	,, I iv 201
Vouchsafe a gracious answer to your *Q* ?	,, IV ii 360
shall not I, the *Q*, Tear out her heart—	,, IV ii 408
My liege, the *Q* of England. *Henry*. God's eyes !	,, V i 96
Of England ? Say of Aquitaine. I am no *Q* of England.	,, V i 101
I had dream'd I was the bride of England, and a *q*.	,, V i 103
He sends you This diadem of the first Galatian *Q*,	*The Cup* II 132
I wait him his crown'd *q*.	,, II 161

R

Read (*continued*) I sign it with my presence, if I *r* it. | *Queen Mary* IV ii 73
That Cranmer *r* all papers that he sign'd ? | ,, IV iii 318
This last—I dare not *r* it her— | ,, V ii 183
I never *r*, I tear them ; | ,, V ii 187
I may die Before I *r* it. Let me see him at once. | ,, V ii 550
to *r* the letter which you bring. | ,, V ii 555
what hath she written ? *r*. | ,, V v 2
I cannot *r* the face of heaven ; | *Harold* I i 66
He can but *r* the king's face on his coins, | ,, I i 70
They scarce can *r* their Psalter ; | ,, I i 163
on those Who *r* their doom and die. | ,, IV i 252
President of this Council, *r* them. *Becket*. R ! | *Becket* I iii 76
For John of Oxford here to *r* to you. | ,, I iii 417
I could but *r* a part to-day, because— | ,, I iii 422
and to *r* the faces of men at a great show. | ,, III iii 83
paper sign'd Antonius—will you take it, *r* it ? | *The Cup* II ii 226
Might I *r* ? *Count*. Ay, if you will. | *The Falcon* 433
Shall I Sit by him, *r* to him, tell him my tales, | ,, 795
Well, my man, it seems that you can *r*. | *Prom. of May* II 710
tho' you can't *r*, you could whitewash that cottage | ,, III 42
That nursery-tale Still *r*, then ? | ,, III 526
Child, *r* a little history, you will find | ,, III 542
Readier I am *r* to be slain, than thou to slay. | *Becket* V iii 128
Readiness Have him away ! I sicken of his *r*. | *Queen Mary* V ii 611
Reading (*See also* **A-reädin'**) Been *r* some old book, | ,, III i 44
Ready make *r* for the journey. Pray God, we 'scape the sunstroke. *R* at once. | ,, III v 277
Simon, is supper *r* ? | ,, III vi 256
We are *r* To take you to St. Mary's, Master Cranmer. | ,, IV ii 237
I be *r* to taäke the pledge. *Dora*. And as *r* to break it again. | *Prom. of May* III 84
but very *r* To make allowances, and mighty slow To feel offences. | ,, III 628
Real And you, that would not own the *R* Presence, Have found a *r* presence in the stake, | *Queen Mary* IV ii 140
there was a great motion of laughter among us, part *r*, part childlike, to be freed from the dulness— | *Becket* III iii 155
Real Hard Tillery (**Royal Artillery**) 'Listed for a soädger, Miss, i' the Queen's *R H T*. | *Prom. of May* III 109
Realised to be *r* all at once, or altogether, or anywhere but in Heaven ? | ,, III 186
Realm The *r* is poor, The exchequer at neap-tide : | *Queen Mary* I v 119
when I was wedded to the *r* And the *r's* laws | ,, II i 164
But for the wealth and glory of our *r*, | ,, II ii 210
To be of rich advantage to our *r*, | ,, II ii 235
Looms the least chance of peril to our *r*. | ,, II ii 239
From stirring hand or foot to wrong the *r*. | ,, III iii 61
Presenting the whole body of this *r* Of England, | ,, III iii 116
As well for our own selves as all the *r*, | ,, III iii 136
this noble *r* thro' after years May in this unity | ,, III iii 156
God to this *r* hath given A token | ,, III iii 168
all the *r* And its dominions from all heresy, | ,, III iii 215
I think they fain would have me from the *r* ; | ,, III v 230
a day may sink or save a *r*. | ,, III vi 239
and degrade the *r* By seeking justice | ,, IV i 19
I cannot be True to this *r* of England and the Pope | ,, IV i 27
Or into private life within the *r*. | ,, IV i 47
A shaker and confounder of the *r* ; | ,, IV iii 40
first In Council, second person in the *r*, | ,, IV iii 72
God's revenge upon this *r* For narrowness | *Harold* I i 173
A conscience for his own soul, not his *r* ; | ,, III i 64
And given thy *r* of England to the bastard. | ,, III i 154
To help the *r* from scattering. | ,, IV i 106
Holy Father Hath given this *r* of England to the Norman. | ,, V i 13
The *r* for which thou art forsworn is cursed, | ,, V i 63
But by the royal customs of our *r* | *Becket, Pro.* 23
For my *r's* sake, myself must be the wizard | ,, *Pro.* 206
sign'd These ancient laws and customs of the *r*. | ,, I iii 8
to obey These ancient laws and customs of the *r* ? | ,, I iii 19
Ringing their own death-knell thro' all the *r*. | ,, I iii 173
Barons and bishops of our *r* of England, | ,, I iii 336
Much corn, repeopled towns, and a *r* again. | ,, I iii 377
Then, glancing thro' the story of this *r*, | ,, I iii 411
To blast my *r's* with excommunication And interdict. | ,, II ii 52

Realm (*continued*) since he flouts the will of either *r*, | *Becket* II ii 256
Louis Returning, ah ! to drive thee from his *r*. | ,, II ii 419
Rest in our *r*, and be at peace with all. | ,, II ii 448
it is the law, not he ; The customs of the *r*. | ,, V ii 127
With revenues, *r's*, and golden provinces | ,, V ii 346
On those that crown'd young Henry in this *r*, | ,, V ii 393
Whose winter-cataracts find a *r* and leave it | *The Cup* II 305
Synorix, first King, Camma, first Queen o' the *R*, | *Foresters* II ii 134
Fairy *r* is breaking down | ,, IV 387
Richard, again, is king over a *r* He hardly knows, | ,, IV 403
What was this *r* of England, all the crowns | ,, IV 708
Tho' you should queen me over all the *r's* Held by King Richard, | ,, IV 820
thou and others in our kingless *r's* Were fighting | ,, IV 820
Reap which we Inheriting *r* an easier harvest. | *Becket* II ii 194
I may *r* something from him—come upon *her* | *The Cup* I i 179
Rear lest they *r* and run And break both | *Harold* I i 372
and *r's* his root Beyond his head, | *The Cup* II 283
Reason mastiff dog May love a puppy cur for no more *r* | *Queen Mary* I iv 195
Your Grace will hear her *r's* from herself. | ,, I iv 230
with right *r*, flies that prick the flesh. | ,, III iv 70
They had not reach'd right *r* ; little children ! | ,, III iv 73
What human *r* is there why my friend | ,, IV i 68
Other *r's* There be for this man's ending, | ,, III iii 53
Is there no *r* for the wrath of Heaven ? | *Harold* I i 59
Thy fears infect me beyond *r*. Peace ! | ,, II ii 451
Why, that is *r* ! Warrior thou art, | ,, II ii 542
And with good *r* too, | *Becket* I iii 58
ay, or himself In any *r*, | ,, II ii 170
For this *r*, That, being ever duteous to the King, | ,, II ii 463
I hate him for I hate him is my *r*, | ,, V i 231
Reave We fear that he may *r* thee of thine own. | ,, I iii 611
Rebel (**adj.**) that she breathes in England Is life and lungs to every *r* birth | *Queen Mary* III vi 51
Your Grace hath been More merciful to many a *r* head | ,, V ii 5
Our *r* Abbot then shall join your hands, | *Foresters* IV 933
Rebel (s) (*See also* **Co-rebels**) How traitorously these *r's* out of Kent | *Queen Mary* II ii 145
spoil and sackage aim'd at by these *r's*, | ,, II ii 249
Charing Cross ; the *r's* broke us there, | ,, II iv 76
Heretic and *r* Point at me and make merry. | ,, V ii 317
Rebel (**verb**) Will not thy body *r*, man, if thou flatter it ? | *Becket, Pro.* 102
Rebellion when there rose a talk of the late *r*, | *Queen Mary* I i 92
and all *r's* lie Dead bodies without voice. | ,, II i 79
let *R* Roar till throne rock, and crown fall. | ,, III i 144
fly out and flare Into *r's*. | ,, III i 284
so you quash *r* too, | ,, III iv 37
Reborn In the *r* salvation of a land So noble. | ,, III iii 182
Rebuilt Saints, I have *r* Your shrines, | ,, V ii 299
Rebuked And Herbert hath *r* me even now. | *Becket* I i 385
Recall Who now *r's* her to His ancient fold. | *Queen Mary* III iii 167
Recant It is against all precedent to burn One who *r's* ; | ,, IV ii 50
Recantation read your *r* Before the people in St. Mary's Church. | ,, IV ii 27
Repeat your *r* in the ears Of all men, | ,, IV ii 193
Well, they shall hear my *r* there. | ,, IV ii 199
another *r* Of Cranmer at the stake. | ,, IV iii 299
after all those papers Of *r* yield again, | ,, IV iii 315
Papers of *r* ! Think you then That Cranmer read | ,, IV iii 316
Recanted on the scaffold *R*, and resold himself to Rome. | ,, III i 152
He hath *r* all his heresies. | ,, IV i 49
He hath *r*, Madam. | ,, IV i 54
I have err'd with him ; with him I have *r*. | ,, IV i 67
And so you have *r* to the Pope. | ,, IV i 145
you *r* all you said Touching the sacrament | ,, IV iii 261
Recanting any one *r* thus at full, As Cranmer hath, | ,, IV i 59
but saved in heaven By your *r*. | ,, IV iii 180
Receive Thou shalt *r* the penitent thief's award, | ,, IV iii 86
the King, till another be appointed, shall *r* the revenues thereof. | *Becket* I iii 101
R it from one who cannot at present write | *The Cup* I i 44
Dare beg him to *r* his diamonds back— | *The Falcon* 262

Received His friends—as Angels I *r* 'em,	*Queen Mary* I v 625
again *r* into the bosom And unity of Universal	
Church;	„ III iii 154
Reck We *r* not tho' we lost this crown of England—	„ III iv 55
You *r* but little of the Roman here,	*The Cup* I i 189
Reckon I *r's* they'll hev' a fine cider-crop to-year if	
the blossom 'owds.	*Prom. of May* I 315
Reckoning people do say that this is bad beyond all *r*,	
and—— *Rosamund.* The people lie.	*Becket* III i 175
Reclaimed thou art *r*; He brings thee home:	*Queen Mary* IV iii 83
Recognise Now you, that would not *r* the Pope,	„ IV ii 138
Recommend I can *r* our Voltigeur.'	*Prom. of May* III 311
Reconcile We come not to condemn, but *r*;	*Queen Mary* III iii 186
Reconciled Is *r* the word? the Pope again?	„ III iii 3
the world may know You twain are *r*,	*The Cup* II 69
Record that thou keepest a *r* of his birthdays?	*Foresters* I i 221
Recover Stay with us in this wood, till he *r*.	„ II ii 10
Recover'd Methought I had *r* of the Becket,	*Becket* v i 136
I see you quite *r* of your wound.	*The Falcon* 391
if you be Not quite *r* of your wound,	„ 590
'I hope your Lordship is quite *r* of your gout?'	*Prom. of May* III 309
Recoverer but our *r* and upholder of customs hath	*Becket* III iii 69
Re-create And bid him *r-c* me, Gilbert Foliot.	„ I iii 126
Recrost Crost and *r*, a venomous spider's web—	„ II i 199
Recurring And thousand-times *r* argument Of those	
two friars	*Queen Mary* IV ii 93
Red (*See also* **Blood-red, Human-red, Stormy-red**) All	
r and white, the fashion of our land.	„ I v 10
but took To the English *r* and white.	„ I v 18
Her face on flame, her *r* hair all blown back,	„ II ii 70
as *r* as she In hair and cheek;	„ II ii 74
She wore *r* shoes! *Stafford.* R shoes!	„ III i 59
Not *r* like Iscariot's.	„ III ii 217
Laughs at the last *r* leaf, and Andrew's Day.	„ III iii 87
R gold—a hundred purses—yea, and more!	*Harold* III i 18
The nimble, wild, *r*, wiry, savage king—	„ IV i 197
He hath blown himself as *r* as fire with curses.	„ v i 87
and most amorous Of good old *r* sound liberal Gascon	
wine:	*Becket, Pro.* 100
This chart with the *r* line! her bower! whose bower?	„ *Pro.* 308
Fitzurse, that chart with the *r* line—thou sawest it—	
her bower.	„ *Pro.* 428
A sight of that same chart which Henry gave you	
With the *r* line—' her bower.'	„ I ii 62
Dash'd *r* with that unhallow'd passover;	„ I iii 348
coming up with a song in the flush of the glimmer-	
ing *r*?	„ II i 8
What! have I scared the *r* rose from your face Into	
your heart?	„ IV ii 73
hand *R* with the sacred blood of Sinnatus?	*The Cup* II 84
HE! . . . HE, with that *r* star between the ribs,	„ II 150
that the *r* wine Ran down the marble and lookt like blood,	„ II 202
and seen the *r* of the battle-field,	*The Falcon* 549
But a *r* fire woke in the heart of the town,	*Prom. of May* I 50
Why, lass, what maäkes tha sa *r*?	„ I 399
R with his own and enemy's blood—	*Foresters* I i 32
We had it i' the *R* King's time,	„ IV 303
Red-blooded And, when again *r-b*, speak again;	*Harold* IV iii 208
Red-cheek'd Right honest and *r-c*;	*Queen Mary* IV v 106
Redden God *r* your pale blood! But mine is human-red;	*Becket* I iv 35
How the good Archbishop *r's*!	„ v ii 298
ambition, pride So bloat and *r* his face—	*The Cup* II 170
Redden'd shown And *r* with his people's blood	*Harold* I ii 243
Redder Theer be *r* blossoms nor them, Miss Dora.	*Prom. of May* I 85
Redeem old Sir Richard might *r* his land.	*Foresters* I i 487
Out of our treasury to *r* the land.	„ IV 493
And Sir Richard cannot *r* his land.	„ IV 565
Redeem'd who hath *r* us With His own blood,	*Queen Mary* III iii 202
Redeemer O Son of God, R of the world!	„ IV iii 118
Red-faced ' Adulterous dog!' that *r-f* rage at me!	*The Cup* I iii 122
Redhats But the King hath bought half the College of R.	*Becket* II ii 374
Redress He shall absolve you . . . you shall have *r*.	„ v i 87
Reed some are *r's*, that one time sway to the current,	„ I iii 593
R I rock'd upon broken-back'd,	*Foresters* II i 162
Re-edify hath begun to *r-e* the true temple—	*Queen Mary* I iii 58

Reeking The *r* dungfork master of the mace!	*Queen Mary* II ii 275
Reel *r's* Now to the right, then as far to the left,	„ IV iii 395
Let all the air *r* into a mist of odour,	*The Cup* II 185
I *r* beneath the weight of utter joy—	„ II 450
Refer R my cause, my crown to Rome! . . .	*Harold* v i 1
r myself, The King, these customs,	*Becket* I iii 725
Re-flame Stamp out the fire, or this Will smoulder	
and *r-f*,	*Queen Mary* I v 509
Reflected will be *r* in the spiritual body among the angels.	*Becket, Pro.* 397
O my good lord, I am but an angel by *r* light.	*Foresters* II i 108
Reflection I shone from him, for him, his glory, his R :	*Becket* I iii 665
Reformation Northumberland, The leader of our R,	*Queen Mary* III i 149
Reformer disaffected, heretics, *r's*, Look to you	„ I iv 170
Refractory be we not in my lord's own *r*?	*Becket* I iv 170
Refrain We will *r*, and not alone from this,	*Queen Mary* II ii 236
Refreshment To find the sweet *r* of the Saints.	*Harold* I i 177
Reft Not only *r* me of that legateship	*Queen Mary* IV ii 34
Refuge And I can find no *r* upon earth.	„ IV iii 128
Take *r* in your own cathedral, (repeat)	*Becket* v ii 583, 590
Refuse and *r*, Reject him, and abhor him.	*Queen Mary* IV iii 278
I *r* to stand By the King's censure,	*Becket* I iii 722
Refused More than once You have *r* his hand.	*The Cup* II 43
Refusing *r* none That come to Thee for succour,	*Queen Mary* IV iii 193
Regal were as glowing-gay As *r* gardens;	„ III ii 14
face me out of all My *r* rights.	*Becket* II ii 166
Regard even drown you In the good *r* of Rome.	*The Cup* I i 151
Regarding and all men R her?	*Queen Mary* IV iii 379
Regather'd And be *r* to the Papal fold?	„ III ii 117
Regent O yes! In the name of the R.	*Foresters* I iii 56
Regimen Sir, no woman's *r* Can save us.	*Queen Mary* III i 122
under our Queen's *r* We might go softlier	„ III iv 181
Reginald (**Fitzurse, knight**) (*See also* **Fitzurse, Reginald**	
Fitzurse) Ay! what wouldst thou, R ?	*Becket* I i 186
R, all men know I loved the Prince.	„ v ii 333
I spake no word of treachery, R.	„ v ii 402
No, R, he is dead.	„ v iii 204
Reginald Fitzurse My lord, I follow'd R F.	„ I ii 126
R F! *Fitzurse.* Here, Madam, at your pleasure.	„ IV ii 426
Reginald Pole (**Cardinal and Papal Legate**) (*See also*	
Pole) again to her cousin R P, now Cardinal;	*Queen Mary* I i 123
R P, what news hath plagued thy heart?	„ v ii 17
Reg'lar and see that all be right and *r* fur 'em afoor	
he coöm.	*Prom. of May* I 169
Reign (**s**) Suffer not That my brief *r* in England	*Queen Mary* v ii 302
The *r* of the roses is done— (repeat)	*Becket, Pro.* 303, 304
A *r* which was no *r*,	„ I iii 340
looking thro' my *r*, I found a hundred ghastly murders	„ I iii 406
Reign (**verb**) Madam, when the Roman wish'd to *r*,	*Queen Mary* I v 498
Ay, for the Saints are come to *r* again.	„ II i 22
we will teach Queen Mary how to *r*.	„ II i 148
Nay the Queen's right to *r*—	„ II ii 96
forfeited her right to *r* By marriage with an alien—	„ v i 290
To *r* is restless fence, Tierce, quart, and trickery.	„ v v 265
The Christian manhood of the man who *r's* !	*Harold* III ii 105
than to *r* King of the world without it.	„ III ii 44
let him make it his own, let him *r* in it—	*Becket* I i 18
Reign'd when that which *r* Call'd itself God.—	*Harold* III ii 166
I have *r* one year in the wild wood.	*Foresters* III i 36
Reigning Unto the holy see and *r* Pope Serve God	*Queen Mary* III i 158
Rein (**s**) no more *r* upon thine anger Than any child!	„ IV iv 302
Rein (**verb**) If they prance, R in, not lash them,	*Harold* I i 372
Reject and refuse, R him, and abhor him.	*Queen Mary* IV iii 279
Rejected you have solicited The Queen, and been *r*.	„ I v 59
Rejoice To be your king, ye would *r* thereat,	„ II ii 224
blessed angels who *r* Over one saved	„ III iii 180
I shall *r* To find my stray sheep back	*Becket* III iii 354
Rejoicing Might it not be the other side *r* In his	
brave end?	*Queen Mary* IV iii 357
Relate some *r* that it was lost When Wyatt sack'd	„ v ii 503
Related for I am closely *r* to the dead man's family.	*Prom. of May* II 715
Release full *r* from danger of all censures	*Queen Mary* III iii 150
Relent O yet *r*. O, Madam, if you knew him	„ IV i 154
Relic 'O blessed *r's* !' 'O Holy Peter!'	*Harold* I ii 170
Swear to me by that *r* on thy neck. *Prince John.*	
I swear then by this *r* on my neck—	*Foresters* I ii 169

Respect   We have *r* for man's immortal soul,   *Harold* II ii 500
he's no *r* for the Queen, or the parson, or the
justice o' peace, or owt.   *Prom. of May* I 132
Respite   a boon, my king, R, a holiday :   *Harold* I i 227
Rest (remainder)   the *r* of England bow'd theirs to
the Norman,   *Queen Mary* II i 159
Should look more goodly than the *r* of us.   „   II ii 349
why should I be bolder than the *r*,   „   III i 438
Bless thou too That brother whom I love beyond
the *r*,   *Harold* III i 295
The *r* you see is colour'd green—   *Becket*, Pro. 171
Cursed Fitzurse, and all the *r* of them   „   II ii 271
Coom along then, all the *r* o' ye !   *Prom. of May* I 442
I'll git the book ageän, and larn mysen the *r*,   „   III 13
he, young Scarlet, and he, old Much, and all the *r*
of us.   *Foresters* III 61
Rest (repose)   says That *r* is all—tells me I must not
think—   *Queen Mary* V v 62
All is well then ; *r*—I will to *r* ; he said, I must
have *r*.   „   V v 186
Shall I not help your Lordship to your *r* ?   *Becket* I i 2
He hath retired to *r*, and being in great jeopardy   „   I iv 262
And how I long for *r*.'   *Prom. of May* III 206
Rest (verb)   my good mother came (God *r* her soul)   *Queen Mary* I v 11
the happy haven Where he shall *r* at night,   „   IV iii 580
That you might *r* among us, till the Pope,   „   V ii 47
Let dead things *r*.   „   V ii 506
That I must *r*—I shall *r* by and by.   „   V v 64
maims himself against the bars, say ' *r* ' : Why, you
must kill him if you would have him *r*—   „   V v 68
Nay, *r* a week or two,   *Harold* II ii 179
That I might *r* as calmly !   „   III i 44
I needs must *r*.   „   V i 229
To *r* upon thy bosom and forget him—   *Becket* I i 31
R in our realm, and be at peace with all.   „   II ii 448
Let me *r*. I'll call you by and by.   „   V i 89
R you easy, For I am easy to keep.   „   V ii 512
I had counsell'd him To *r* from vain resistance.   *The Cup* II 414
God *r* his honest soul, he bought 'em for me,   *The Falcon* 49
Show me some cave or cabin where I may *r*.   *Foresters* II i 131
Rested   some waxen doll Thy baby eyes have *r* on,   *Queen Mary* I v 9
Restless   To reign is *r* fence,   „   V v 265
Restore   we *r* you to the bosom And unity of Universal
Church.   „   III iii 220
and *r* his kin, Reseat him on his throne   *Becket* II ii 116
Have I not promised to *r* her, Thomas,   „   III iii 183
Restored   I shall have my tetrarchy *r* By Rome,   *The Cup* I i 20
Restriction   may fence round his power with *r*,   *Queen Mary* II i 172
Resurrection   to be wakened again together by the
light of the *r*,   *Prom. of May* III 197
Retinue   with the *r* of three kings behind him, out-
royalling royalty ?   *Becket*, Pro. 444
Retire   Permission of her Highness to *r* To Ashridge,   *Queen Mary* I iv 236
You are fresh from brighter lands. *R* with me.   „   III iv 322
Her Highness is unwell. I will *r*.   „   V ii 247
There was no room to advance or to *r*.   *Foresters* IV 534
Retired   He hath *r* to rest, and being in great jeopardy   *Becket* I iv 262
Retiring (part.)   *R* into cloistral solitude To yield   *Queen Mary* III vi 209
Retiring (s)   or is it but the past That brightens
in *r* ?   *Prom. of May* II 645
Retract   and *r* That Eucharistic doctrine in your
book.   *Queen Mary* IV ii 80
Return (s)   (*See also* **Home-return**)   Who loathe you
for your late *r* to Rome,   „   IV ii 32
Takes nothing in *r* from you except *R* of his
affection—   *The Falcon* 716
Many happy *r*'s of the day, father.   *Prom. of May* I 350
I trust that your *r*—for you know, my dear,   „   III 421
This is the gala-day of thy *r*.   *Foresters* IV 960
whose *r* Builds up our house again ?   „   IV 1008
Return (verb)   will *r* into the one true fold,   *Queen Mary* I iii 22
and I *r* As Peter, but to bless thee :   „   III ii 55
Yet will I be your swallow and *r*—   „   V i 91
R, And tell him that I know he comes no more.   „   V ii 588
R to Sens, where we will care for you.   *Becket* II ii 444

Return (verb) (*continued*)   And, being scratch'd, *r*'s to his
true rose,   *Becket* III i 249
His child and mine own soul, and so *r*.   „   V ii 194
I here *r* like Tarquin—for a crown.   *The Cup* I i 142
R's with this Antonius.   „   I ii 179
You, Strato, make good cheer till I *r*.   „   I ii 206
Or tell him, if you will, when you *r*,   „   I ii 310
R and tell him Synorix is not here.   „   I ii 334
Within the holy shrine of Artemis, And so *r*.   „   I iii 54
I trust she *will r*.   „   I iii 61
She should *r* thy necklace then.   *The Falcon* 69
Will he not pray me to *r* his love—   „   247
Was yet too bashful to *r* for it ?   „   540
My lord, I have a present to *r* you,   „   711
I came In person to *r* them.   „   727
If the phrase ' *R* ' displease you, we will say—   „   729
Shall I *r* to the castle with you ?   „   793
And so *r*—Heaven help him !—to our son.   „   861
And when will you *r* ? *Edgar.* I cannot tell
precisely ;   *Prom. of May* I 627
but call for Philip when you will, And he *r*'s.   „   I 759
Never to *r* again,   *Foresters* II ii 170
thou feel'st with me The ghost *r*'s to Marian,   „   III 115
When wilt thou *r* ? *Richard.* R, I ? when ? when
Richard will *r*.   „   IV 417
I trust We shall *r* to the wood.   „   IV 1052
Return'd   deem This love by you *r* as heartily ;   *Queen Mary* II 197
glance of some distaste, Or so methought, *r*.   „   III i 101
that hath *r* To the one Catholic Universal Church,   „   IV iii 20
Thomas, I would thou hadst *r* to England,   *Becket* V ii 12
On a Tuesday from mine exile I *r*,   „   V ii 293
But hath she yet *r* thy love ?   *The Falcon* 66
happy was the prodigal son, For he *r* to the rich father ;   „   142
Hath she *r* thy love ? *Count.* Not yet !   „   513
They say your sister, Dora, has *r*,   *Prom. of May* I 546
almost think she half *r* the pressure Of mine.   „   II 627
That John last week *r* to Nottingham,   *Foresters* II 147
Returning   Louis *R*, ah ! to drive thee from his realm.   *Becket* II ii 418
Revel (s)   loom Across their lamps of *r*,   *Harold* II 407
Reaction needs must follow *r*—yet—   *Prom. of May* II 264
Revel (verb)   It is our forest custom they should *r* Along
with Robin.   *Foresters* III 174
Reveller   *See* **Co-reveller**
Revelling   You see they have been *r*, and I fear   *Becket* V ii 421
Revelry   So the wine run, and there be *r*,   *Queen Mary* III ii 236
Thou and I will still their *revelries* presently.   *Foresters* I ii 24
Revenge   But dreading God's *r* upon this realm   *Harold* I i 172
Of this dead King, who never bore *r*.   „   V ii 85
I heard him swear *r*.   *Becket* I i 280
I follow out my hate and my *r*.   „   IV ii 151
You bad me take *r* another way—   „   IV ii 152
Revenged   Thus then thou art *r*—   *Harold* V i 288
Revenue   Meanwhile the *r*'s are mine.   *Becket*, Pro. 413
King, till another be appointed, shall receive the *r*'s
thereof.'   „   I iii 101
King Demands a strict account of all those *r*'s   „   I iii 651
With *r*'s, realms, and golden provinces   „   V ii 346
wasted his *r*'s in the service of our good king Richard   *Foresters* I i 193
Reverence (s)   Our silence is our *r* for the king !   *Harold* IV i 13
Who have that *r* for him that I scarce   *The Falcon* 260
honey from an old oak, saving your sweet *r*'s.   *Foresters* II i 297
Reverence (verb)   Knowing how much you *r* Holy
Church,   *Becket* I ii 48
I *r* all women, bad me, dying,   *Foresters* II i 40
Reverend   Thro' this most *r* Father, absolution,   *Queen Mary* III iii 148
For how should *r* prelate or throned prince Brook
for an hour   „   IV iii 542
Reverential   whether from maiden fears Or *r* love for
him I loved,   *The Cup* II 197
Reversed   Ye have *r* the attainder laid on us   *Queen Mary* III iii 194
R his doom, and that you might not seem   „   V ii 51
Revived   And others of our Parliament, *r*,   „   III i 326
Revoked   Ay . . . if the king have not *r* his promise.   *Harold* II ii 610
Revolt (s)   all of us abhor The venomous, bestial,
devilish *r* Of Thomas Wyatt.   *Queen Mary* II ii 287

Revolt (s) (*continued*)   A cry! What's that?
  Elizabeth? *r*?   *Queen Mary* v v 187
Revolt (verb)   Good, then, they will *r*:
                           "   i v 174
  would hold out, yea, tho' they should *r*—   *Harold* II ii 554
Reward   shall have a hundred pounds for *r*.'   *Queen Mary* II iii 61
  Have courage, your *r* is Heaven itself.   "   v ii 108
Rheumatics   *See* **Roomatics**
Rheumatizy (Rheumatism)   Eh, my *r* be that bad
  howiver   *Queen Mary* IV iii 475
Rhyme (s)   And head them with a lamer *r* of mine,
  A true *r*.   *Lady.*   Cut with a diamond;   "   II i 29
  I could so play about it with the *r*——   *Henry.*   That   "   III v 24
  the heart were lost in the *r*   *Becket,* Pro. 382
  May plaister his clean name with scurrilous *r's*!   "   i i 309
  for my verses if the Latin *r's* be rolled out from a full
  mouth?   "   II ii 337
  shall we say this wreath and your sweet *r's*?   *The Falcon* 735
  Your worship may find another *r* if you care   *Foresters* II ii 322
Rhyme (verb)   To read and *r* in solitary fields,   *Queen Mary* IV i 51
Rhyming   written scroll That seems to run in *r's*.   *The Falcon* 432
Rib   plunge Our boat hath burst her *r's*;   *Harold* II i 3
  thou wouldst hug thy Cupid till his *r's* cracked—   *Becket,* Pro. 504
  with that red star between the *r's*,   *The Cup* II 151
  how bare and spare I be on the *r*:   *Foresters* I i 50
  Spare me thy spare *r's*, I pray thee;   "   i i 53
  Back and side and hip and *r*,   "   II ii 120
Ribald   No *r* John is Love, no wanton Prince,   "   IV 46
Ribaldry   O drunken *r*!   Out, beast! out, bear!   *Becket* I i 230
Ribbon   I ask'd A *r* from her hair to bind it with;   *The Falcon* 359
  this faded *r* was the mode In Florence   "   422
Rich   I left her with *r* jewels in her hand,   *Queen Mary* I iv 242
  To be of *r* advantage to our realm,   "   II ii 235
  for his heart was *r*, Of such fine mould,   "   IV i 169
  'How hard it is For the *r* man to enter into Heaven;'
  Let all *r* men remember that hard word.   "   IV iii 205
  Till all men have their Bible, *r* and poor.   "   v v 248
  She *r* enough to have bought it for herself!   *The Falcon* 62
  happy was the prodigal son, For he return'd to the *r*
  father;   "   142
  And yet I never saw The land so *r* in blossom as this
  year.   "   342
  They seem'd too *r* a prize To trust with any messenger.   "   725
  I remember Her bright face beaming starlike down
  upon me Thro' that *r* cloud of blossom.   *Prom. of May* II 250
  I'll cleave to you *r* or poor.   *Foresters* I i 155
  green earth drink Her health along with us in this *r*
  draught,   "   III 351
  And this *r* Sheriff too has come between us;   "   IV 57
  While Richard hath outlaw'd himself, and helps Nor *r*,
  nor poor.   "   IV 362
**Richard (de Brito, knight of the household of King
  Henry II.)**   (*See also* **Brito, De Brito**)   *R*,
  if he be mine—I hope him mine.   *Becket* v i 130
Richard (Lea)   (*See also* **Richard Lea, Richard of the Lea**)
  these lilies to lighten Sir *R's* black room,   *Foresters* I i 3
  Sir *R* and my Lady Marian fare wellnigh as sparely
  as their people.   "   I i 30
  Sir *R* was told he might be ransomed   "   I i 63
  Sir *R* must scrape and scrape till he get to the land
  again.   "   I i 78
  My guests and friends, Sir *R*,   "   I ii 78
  the Earl and Sir *R* come this way.   "   I ii 148
  You shall wait for mine till Sir *R* has paid the Abbot.   "   I ii 232
  O good Sir *R*, I am sorry my exchequer   "   I ii 271
  Farewell, Sir *R*; farewell, sweet Marian.   "   I ii 284
  She and Sir *R* Have past away,   "   II i 119
  but see fair play Betwixt them and Sir *R*—   "   IV 99
  Sir *R*, it was agreed when you borrowed   "   IV 465
  and thus This old Sir *R* might redeem his land.   "   IV 487
  And Sir *R* cannot redeem his land.   "   IV 564
  Sir *R* paid his monies to the Abbot.   "   IV 849
  I thank thee, good Sir *R*.   "   IV 858
  O good Sir *R*, I am like the man In Holy Writ,   "   IV 980
  Sir *R*, let that wait till we have dined.   "   IV 991
  Kiss him, Sir *R*—kiss him, my sweet Marian.   "   IV 1003

Richard (the First, Cœur de Lion)   wasted his revenues
  in the service of our good king *R* against the party
  of John, as I have done, as I have done: and
  where is *R*?   *Foresters* I i 194
  I believed this Abbot of the party of King *R*,   "   I i 267
  This Robin, this Earl of Huntingdon—he is a friend
  of *R*—   "   I i 282
  Long live *R*, Robin and *R*!   Long live *R*!   "   I ii 1
  Love live Robin, Robin and *R*!   "   I ii 14
  ' Long live King *R*!'   "   I ii 25
  O Lord, I will live and die for King *R*—   "   I ii 38
  there is a lot of wild fellows in Sherwood Forest who
  hold by King *R*.   "   I ii 74
  but we have no news of *R* yet,   "   I ii 95
  not answer it, my lord, till King *R* come home again.   "   I ii 141
  you be of those who hold more by John than *R*.   "   I ii 199
  I am John's till *R* come back again, and then I
  am *R's*.   "   I ii 202
  I cannot answer thee till *R* come.   "   I ii 221
  till he join King *R* in the Holy Land.   *Robin.*
  Going to the Holy Land to *R*!   "   I ii 238
  by this Holy Cross Which good King *R* gave me   "   I ii 310
  good fellows there in merry Sherwood That hold by *R*,   "   I iii 100
  They hold by *R*—the wild wood!   "   I iii 110
  I held for *R*, and I hated John.   "   II i 52
  she will not marry till *R* come,   "   II ii 84
  Art thou for *R*, or allied to John?   "   IV 135
  But I am more for *R* than for John.   "   IV 160
  Still I am more for *R* than for John.   "   IV 329
  and serve King *R* save thou be A traitor or a goose?   "   IV 351
  For Robin is no scatterbrains like *R*, Robin's a wise
  man, *R* a wiseacre,   "   IV 356
  While *R* hath outlaw'd himself,   "   IV 360
  R's the king of courtesy,   "   IV 362
  R sacks and wastes a town With random pillage,   "   IV 376
  R risks his life for a straw, So lies in prison—   "   IV 382
  R, again, is king over a realm He hardly knows,   "   IV 387
  Again this *R* is the lion of Cyprus,   "   IV 391
  to *R* when he flung His life, heart,   "   IV 405
  Return, I? when? when *R* will return.   "   IV 419
  Father, I cannot marry till *R* comes.   "   IV 648
  save King *R*, when he comes, forbid me.   "   IV 664
  Tho' you should queen me over all the realms Held
  by King *R*,   "   IV 709
  When *R* comes he is soft enough to pardon   "   IV 746
  and she will not marry till *R* come.   "   IV 773
  a traitor coming In *R's* name—   "   IV 781
  Maid Marian.   *Marian.*   Yes, King *R*.   *King
  Richard.*   Thou wouldst marry This Sheriff
  when King *R* came   "   IV 860
  Give me that hand which fought for *R* there.   "   IV 1030
Richard (the Third)   Who's a-passing?   King Edward
  or King *R*?   *Queen Mary* I i 32
  Had holpen *R's* tottering throne to stand,   "   III i 114
Richard Lea   (*See also* **Richard, Richard of the Lea**)   We
  heard Sir *R L* was here with Robin.   *Foresters* IV 978
Richard of the Lea   (*See also* **Richard, Richard Lea**)   I come
  here to see this daughter of Sir *R o t L*   "   I ii 27
  Robin, I am Sir *R o t L*.   "   II i 441
  Where is this old Sir *R o t L*?   "   IV 438
  Where is this laggard *R o t L*?   "   IV 449
Richer   Was not the year when this was gather'd *r*?   *The Falcon* 345
  R than all the wide world-wealth of May,   "   466
  Our Lady's blessed shrines throughout the land Be
  all the *r* for us.   *Foresters* IV 1081
Riches   ' Better a man without *r*, than *r* without a man.'   *The Falcon* 751
Richest   Drew here the *r* lot from Fate, to live And die
  together.   *The Cup* II 442
  For he would marry me to the *r* man In Florence;   *The Falcon* 747
Rid   This last to *r* thee of a world of brawls!   *Becket* v iii 198
Ridden   (*See also* **Fancy-ridd'n**)   I have *r* night and day
  from Pevensey—   *Harold* IV iii 192
  tho' we have been a soldier, and *r* by his lordship's
  side,   *The Falcon* 548
Ride   To-morrow we will *r* with thee to Harfleur,   *Harold* II ii 195

Ride (*continued*) To-morrow will we *r* with thee to Harfleur.   *Harold* II ii 647

To-morrow will I *r* with thee to Harfleur.   „ II ii 769

He *r*'s abroad with armed followers,   *Becket* v i 2

'Will your Ladyship *r* to cover to-day?   *Prom. of May* III 310

mayhap *r* a-hawking with the help of the men.   *Foresters* I i 213

Ridley (**Bishop of London**) Hooper, *R*, Latimer will not fly.   *Queen Mary* I ii 14

Cranmer and Hooper, *R* and Latimer,   „ III iv 424

Latimer Had a brief end—not *R*.   „ IV ii 225

I saw the deaths of Latimer and *R*.   „ IV iii 295

And you saw Latimer and *R* die?   „ IV iii 328

R was longer burning; but he died As manfully   „ IV iii 342

'not till I hears ez Latimer and *R* be a-vire;'   „ IV iii 509

When we had come where *R* burnt with Latimer,   „ IV iii 585

Ridley-soldier Our *R*-*s*'s and our Latimer-sailors   „ IV iii 348

Rift (**s**) The *r* that runs between me and the King.   *Becket* I i 140

that the *r* he made May close between us,   „ II ii 131

Rift (**verb**) and *r*'s the tower to the rock,   *The Cup* II 293

Rifted Taken the *r* pillars of the wood For smooth stone columns of the sanctuary,   *Harold* I ii 100

Right (**adj. and adv.**) By God's light a noble creature, *r* royal !   *Queen Mary* I i 69

He says *r*; by the mass we'll have no mass here.   „ I iii 50

This dress was made me as the Earl of Devon To take my seat in; looks it not *r* royal?   „ I iv 74

You do *r* well—I do not care to know;   „ I iv 188

Now what I am ye know *r* well—your Queen;   „ II ii 162

R, your Grace. Paget, you are all for this poor life of ours,   „ III iv 58

They, with *r* reason, flies that prick the flesh.   „ III iv 70

They had not reach'd *r* reason; little children !   „ III iv 73

for you know *R* well that you yourself have been supposed   „ III iv 225

R honest and red cheek'd; Robin was violent,   „ III v 106

A *r* rough life and healthful.   „ III v 260

I know them heretics, but *r* English ones.   „ IV iii 344

Said I not *r*? For how should reverend prelate or throned prince   „ IV iii 541

there is the *r* hand still Beckons me hence.   „ v v 136

Knowing *r* well with what a tenderness He loved my son.   *Becket* v i 20

At the *r* hand of Power—Power and great glory—   „ v iii 193

R. Back again. How many of you are there?   *The Cup* I iii 11

having his *r* hand Lamed in the battle, wrote it with his left.   *The Falcon* 443

Ay, but you turn *r* ugly when you're in an ill temper;   *Prom. of May* I 159

and see that all be *r* and reg'lar fur 'em afoor he coöm.   „ I 169

and I'd drive the plow straäit as a line *r* i' the faäce o' the sun,   „ I 370

But now you will set all *r* again,   „ I 718

Come, you will set all *r* again, and father Will not die miserable.'   „ II 658

Count the money and see if it's all *r*.   „ III 65

Sister Agatha is *r*.   „ III 403

R as an Oxford scholar, but the boy was taken prisoner by the Moors.   *Foresters* I i 59

There, there ! You see I was *r*.   „ I i 115

Had I a bulrush now in this *r* hand For sceptre,   „ III 76

Rogue, I have a swollen vein in my *r* leg,   „ IV 569

Right (**s**) Nay the Queen's *r* to reign—   *Queen Mary* II ii 96

on you, In your own city, as her *r*, my Lord,   „ II ii 106

and his *r* came down to me,   „ II ii 171

Your *r*'s and charters hobnail'd into slush—   „ II ii 278

And let the Pope trample our *r*'s,   „ III iv 362

Declare the Queen's *r* to the throne;   „ IV ii 78

I do hold The Catholic, if he have the greater *r*,   „ IV iii 382

reels Now to the *r*, then as far to the left,   „ IV iii 396

And thrust his *r* into the bitter flame;   „ IV iii 610

Who know my *r*, and love me,   „ v iii 34

what *r* had he to get himself wrecked   *Harold* II i 59

Can have no *r* to the crown,' and Odo said, 'Thine is the *r*, for thine the might;   „ II ii 355

William laugh'd and swore that might was *r*,   „ II ii 362

Right (**s**) (*continued*) bad me seal against the *r*'s of the Church,   *Becket* I iii 312

whene'er your royal *r*'s Are mooted in our councils—   „ I iii 430

face me out of all My regal *r*'s.   „ II ii 166

And trampled on the *r*'s of Canterbury.   „ II v 394

when they seek to overturn our *r*'s,   „ v i 457

Thou art in the *r*. This blessing is for Synorix   *The Cup* II 375

I am easily led by words, but I think the Earl hath *r*.   *Foresters* I ii 41

Scarlet, hath not the Earl *r*?   „ I ii 47

Thou Much, miller's son, hath not the Earl *r*?   „ I ii 50

more goes to make *r* than I know of, but for all that I will swear the Earl hath *r*.

Righteous For which God's *r* judgment fell upon you   *Queen Mary* III iv 240

Rightful Ye know my father was the *r* heir Of England,   „ II ii 170

What *r* cause could grow to such a heat   *Foresters* I ii 698

Rill the sea-creek—the petty *r* That falls into it—   *Becket* II ii 294

Rind Most fruitful, yet, indeed, an empty *r*,   *Queen Mary* III ii 202

Ring (**s**) (*See also* **Fairy-ring**) spousal *r* whereof, Not even to be laid aside,   „ II ii 165

You have a gold *r* on your finger,   „ IV v 32

Take thou this *r*;   *Harold* II ii 58

tore away My marriage *r*, and rent my bridal veil;   „ I ii 80

but take back thy *r*. It burns my hand—   „ III iii 185

The *r* thou darest not wear,   „ v i 421

And thou art come to rob them of their *r*'s !   „ v ii 37

For look, our marriage *r* !   „ v ii 108

and ower a hoonderd pounds worth o' *r*'s stolen.   *Prom. of May* I 394

R, trinket of the Church,   „ I 598

This *r* my mother gave me: it was her own Betrothal *r*.   *Foresters* I ii 293

All gone !—my *r*—I am happy—should be happy. She took my *r*. I trust she loves me—yet   „ I iii 1

Thou hast robb'd my girl of her betrothal *r*.   „ II i 587

What ! do I not know mine own *r*?   „ II i 590

the precious *r* I promised Never to part with—   „ II i 660

What's here? a dead bat in the fairy—   „ II ii 94

All our *r*'s be trampled out.   „ II ii 167

The Sheriff ! This *r* cries out against thee. Say it again, And by this *r* the lips that never breathed Love's falsehood   „ IV 69

Ring (**verb**) The bells must *r*; Te Deums must be sung;   *Queen Mary* III ii 211

like the gravedigger's child I have heard of, trying to *r* the bell,   *Becket* III iii 74

Did not a man's voice *r* along the aisle,   „ v ii 150

When horn and echo *r*,   *Foresters* III 428

What shouts are these that *r* along the wood ?   „ IV 763

Ringdove *R*'s coo again, All things woo again.   *Queen Mary* III v 103

Ring'd I was born of a true man and a *r* wife,   „ I i 55

Ringed (**rang**) ye *r* fur that, Miss, didn't ye?   *Prom. of May* III 14

Ringing The bells are *r* at Maidstone.   *Queen Mary* II i 19

with all his rooftree *r* ' Harold,'   *Harold* v ii 129

R their own death-knell thro' all the realm.   *Becket* I iii 172

Riot After a *r*, We hang the leaders,   *Queen Mary* IV i 73

As at this loveless knife that stirs the *r*,   *Becket* II i 191

Ripen'd Who, waiting till the time had *r*,   *Queen Mary* III i 78

Ripening (**part**) this dead fruit was *r* overmuch,   „ III i 26

Ripening (**s**) harvest moon is the *r* of the harvest,   *Becket*, Pro. 363

Ripple The *r*'s twinkled at their diamond-dance,   *Queen Mary* III ii 10

and hover Above the windy *r*,   *Harold* II ii 336

Rise At his coming Your star will *r*.   *Queen Mary* I v 411

We are fallen, and as I think, Never to *r* again.   „ III i 125

He comes, and my star *r*'s.   „ III ii 167

R to the heavens in grateful praise   „ III iii 165

That should have fallen, and may *r* again.   „ v ii 6

let England as of old *R* lionlike,   „ v ii 267

if his Northumbrians *r* And hurl him from them,—   *Harold* IV i 456

thence a king may *r* Half-Godwin and half-Alfgar,   „ IV i 143

wait Till his nose *r*'s; he will be very king.   *Becket* v ii 184

I *r* to-morrow In the gray dawn,   *The Cup* I i 433

it would *r* HE ! . . . HE with that red star   „ II 149

R—I could almost think that the dead garland   *The Falcon* 917

Nay, nay, I pray you *r*.   „ 921

from that flood will *r* the New,   *Prom. of May* I 594

And darkness *r*'s from the fallen sun.   *Foresters* I iii 42

Risen And Mary would have *r* and let him in,   *Queen Mary* III ii 64

Rosamund (de Clifford) (*continued*) R hath not answer'd you one word ; *Becket* IV ii 361
if *R* is The world's rose, as her name imports " v ii 261
Rosamund de Clifford wherefore should she seek The life of R d C " *Pro.* 70
R d C ! Rosamund. Save me, father, " I i 180
R d C. Rosamund. Here am I. " I i 244
Rosary It served me for a blessed *r.* *The Falcon* 632
Rose (s) (*See also* **Hedge-rose, White Rose**) was all pure lily and *r* In his youth, *Queen Mary* I v 20
To sicken of his lilies and his *r's.* " I v 25
Seventeen—a *r* of grace ! Girl never breathed to rival such a *r* ; *R* never blew that equall'd such a bud. " III i 371
I have play'd with this poor *r* so long " v ii 2
He cannot smell a *r* but pricks his nose Against the thorn, and rails against the *r.* Queen. I am the only *r* of all the stock That never thorn'd him ; *Harold* I i 422
They love the white *r* of virginity, " III i 273
The reign of the *r's* is done— (repeat) *Becket, Pro.* 303, 325
Over and gone with the *r's*, (repeat) " *Pro.* 326, 333, 343
Not over and gone with the *r.* True, one *r* will outblossom the rest, one *r* in a bower. *Becket, Pro.* 344
r or no *r*, has killed the golden violet. " *Pro.* 351
The rosebud of my *r* !— " II i 68
But, my liege, I am sure, of all the *r's*— " II i 140
Thou *r* of the world ! Thou *r* of all the *r's* ! " II i 146
My brave-hearted *R* ! Hath he ever been to see thee ? " II i 287
Babble in bower Under the *r* ! " III i 97
And, being scratch'd, returns to his true *r*, " II i 250
scared the red *r* from your face Into your heart ? " IV ii 73
if Rosamund is The world's rose, as her name imports " v ii 263
I ha' browt these *r's* to ye—I forgits what they calls 'em, *Prom. of May* II 14
soom of her oän *r's*, an' she wur as sweet as ony on 'em— " II 38
but I thowt I'd bring tha them *r's* fust. " II 50
Wi' the wild white *r*, an' the woodbine sa gaäy, " II 174
matched with my Harold is like a hedge thistle by a garden *r.* " III 176
to saäy he's browt some of Miss Eva's *r's* for the sick laädy to smell on. " III 347
Might wish its *r* a lily, " III 490
These *r's* for my Lady Marian ; *Foresters* I i 2
The lady gave a *r* to the Earl, The maid a *r* to the man. (repeat) *Foresters* I i 12, 105
You do well, Mistress Kate, to sing and to gather *r's.* " I i 23
A *r* to the man ! Ay, the man had given her a *r* and she gave him another. *Kate.* Shall I keep one little *r* for Little John ? " I i 109
Wilt thou not give me rather the little *r* for Little John ? " I i 148
Rose (verb) To *r* and lavender my horsiness, *Queen Mary* III v 185
Rose (past tense) when there *r* a talk of the late rebellion, " I i 91
r again, And, when the headsman pray'd " III i 392
R hand in hand, and whisper'd ' come away ! " III v 148
a dead man *R* from behind the altar, *Harold* I ii 79
And then I *r* and ran. " II i 12
great Angel *r* And past again along the highest " III i 155
when I *r*, They told me that the Holy Rood " v i 101
So dwelt on that they *r* and darken'd Heaven. *Becket* II i 205
Most like the city *r* against Antonius. *The Cup* I ii 62
And presently all *r*, and so departed. *The Falcon* 367
Fell with her motion as she *r*, and she, " 536
She *r* From the foul flood and pointed *Prom. of May* II 652
Rosebud The *r* of my rose !— *Becket* II i 68
Rosefaced I and all would be glad to wreak our spite on the *r* minion of the King, " *Pro.* 529
Rosy The *r* face, and long down-silvering beard, *Harold* III i 46
The *r* face and long down-silvering beard— " IV i 261
Thank you. Look how full of *r* blossom it is. *Prom. of May* I 84
Rot in our oubliettes Thou shalt or *r* or ransom. *Harold* II i 108
Rotted Until they died of *r* limbs ; and then Cast on the dunghill naked, *Queen Mary* IV iii 445

Rotten (adj.) Wake, or the stout old island will become A *r* limb of Spain. *Queen Mary* II i 105
swirling under me in the lamplight, by the *r* wharfs— *Prom. of May* III 371
Rotten (s) cut out the *r* from your apple, *Queen Mary* II ii 5
Rou Ha *R* ! Ha *R* ! (repeat) *Harold* v i 437, 528, 631, 650, 661, 664
Rough Might it not Be the *r* preface of some closer bond ? *Queen Mary* I iv 48
Beheld our *r* forefathers break their Gods, " III i 120
A right *r* life and healthful. " III v 260
Ever a *r*, blunt, and uncourtly fellow— " v v 120
Like the *r* bear beneath the tree, good brother, *Harold* I i 327
If this war-storm in one of its *r* rolls " v i 165
He comes, a *r*, bluff, simple-looking fellow. *The Cup* I i 172
nor our Archbishop Stagger on the slope decks for any *r* sea *Becket* II ii 106
Against the unpleasant jolts of this *r* road *Prom. of May* I 228
Yeäs, Miss ; but he wur so *r* wi' ma, I couldn't abide 'im. *Dora.* Why should he be *r* with you ? " III 104
And these *r* oaks the palms of Paradise ! *Foresters* II i 169
Rougher To make allowance for their *r* fashions, *Harold* II ii 8
Roughness Your violence and much *r* to the Legate, *Queen Mary* III iv 318
" III iii 279
Round A *r* fine likelier. Your pardon.
and a plum-pudding as big as the *r* haystack. *Prom. of May* I 794
Round-about as sleek and as *r-a* as a mellow codlin. *Foresters* I i 43
Rounded Thou hast *r* since we met. *Harold* I i 95
Rouse Not so dead, But that a shock may *r* her. *Queen Mary* III i 30
sea-bird *r* himself and hover Above the windy ripple, *Harold* II i 334
R the dead altar-flame, fling in the spices, *The Cup* I i 182
Roused *R* by the clamour of the chase he woke, " I i 117
Rout (s) All our games be put to *r*, *Foresters* II ii 166
I blow the horn against this rascal *r* ! " IV 794
Row but light enough to *r*. *R* to the blessed Isles ! *The Cup* II 245
Row'd more than one *R* in that galley—Gardiner to wit, *Queen Mary* IV i 87
Rowel softlier than with crimson *r* And streaming lash. " III iv 183
Roy Hurrah ! Vive le *R* ! *Becket* I iv 274
Royal (*See also* **All-royal, Real Hard Tillery**) By God's light a noble creature, right *r* ! *Queen Mary* I i 69
but to my mind the Lady Elizabeth is the more noble and *r.* " I i 73
and among them Courtenay, to be made Earl of Devon, of *r* blood, " I i 111
That gave her *r* crown to Lady Jane. " I ii 19
This dress was made me as the Earl of Devon To take my seat in ; looks it not right *r* ? *Elizabeth.* So *r* that the Queen forbad you wearing it. " I iv 75
By your Grace's leave Your *r* mother came of Spain. " I v 16
Your *r* father (For so they say) was all pure lily and rose In his youth, " I v 19
Our *r* word for that ! and your good master, " I v 267
after me Is heir of England ; and my *r* father, " I v 286
God send her well ; Here comes her *R* Grace. " II ii 126
From your own *r* lips, at once may know The wherefore of this coming, and so learn Your *r* will, and do it.— " II ii 136
or impair in any way This *r* state of England, " II ii 230
And I sped hither with what haste I might To save my *r* cousin. " II iv 78
Elizabeth, Your *R* sister. " II iv 117
That *r* commonplace too, cloth of gold, Could make it so. " III i 54
Loyal and *r* cousin, humblest thanks. " III ii 3
We had your *r* barge, and that same chair, " III ii 6
now that all traitors Against our *r* state have lost the heads " III iv 3
He owes himself, and with such *r* smiles— " III iv 402
of her most *R*, Infallible, Papal Legate-cousin. " III iv 433
But I am *r*, tho' your prisoner. " III v 177
How fair and *r*—like a Queen, indeed ? " v i 235
And, like a thief, push'd in his *r* hand ; " v ii 466
Your *r* sister cannot last ; your hand Will be much coveted ! " v iii 43
Madam, your *r* sister comes to see you. " v v 191
' This Harold is not of the *r* blood, *Harold* II ii 354

Royal (*continued*)   But by the *r* customs of our realm The Church should hold   *Becket, Pro.* 23

No ; too *r* for me. And I'll have no more Anselms.   „   *Pro.* 274

And for these *R* customs, These ancient *R* customs— they are *R*, Not of the Church—   „   ɪ i 165

and the election shall be made in the Chapel *R*,   „   ɪ iii 111

Good *r* customs—had them written fair For John of Oxford here to read to you.   „   ɪ iii 415

As is his wont Too much of late whene'er your *r* rights   „   ɪ iii 429

Babes, orphans, mothers ! is that *r*, Sire ?   *Henry.*

And I have been as *r* with the Church.   „   ɪɪ i 81

And is that altogether *r* ?   „   ɪɪ i 95

A faithful traitress to thy *r* fame.   „   ɪɪ i 98

What matters ?   *R*—   „   ɪɪ i 106

Still—thy fame too : I say that should be *r*.   „   ɪɪ i 110

I bad them clear A *r* pleasaunce for thee, in the wood,   „   ɪɪ i 128

I here deliver all this controversy Into your *r* hands.   „   ɪɪ ii 137

part *r*, for King and kingling both laughed, and so we could not but laugh, as by a *r* necessity—   „   ɪɪɪ iii 157

when the full fruit of the *r* promise might have dropt into thy mouth hadst thou but opened it to thank him.   *Becket.*   He fenced his *r* promise with an *if*.   „   ɪɪɪ iii 275

We trust your *R* Grace, lord of more land Than any crown in Europe,   „   v i 28

My *r* liege, in aiming at your love,   „   v i 35

It is a *r* messenger, my lord :   *Foresters* ɪ iii 52

and he hath seized On half the *r* castles.   „   ɪ iii 83

Royal-cousin   their two Graces Do so dear-cousin and *r-c* him,   *Queen Mary* ɪɪɪ iv 400

Royalty   retinue of three kings behind him, outroyalling *r* ?   *Becket, Pro.* 446

leave the *r* of my crown Unlessen'd to mine heirs.   „   ɪ i 107

Rub   That irritable forelock which he *r*'s,   *Queen Mary* ɪ iv 265

Who *r* their fawning noses in the dust,   „   ɪɪɪ iii 242

what hath fluster'd Gardiner ? how he *r*'s His forelock !   „   ɪɪɪ iv 12

Rubb'd   Mary *r* out pale—   „   ɪɪɪ i 422

Ruby   emeralds, *Rubies*, I know not what.   „   ɪɪɪ i 86

eyes—and these two sapphires—these Twin *rubies*—   *Harold* ɪ ii 112

Rudder   such a one Was without *r*, anchor, compass—   *Prom. of May* ɪɪɪ 534

Ruddiest   You are pale, my Dora ! but the *r* cheek   „   ɪɪ 487

Rude   Bandy their own *r* jests with them,   *The Cup* ɪ ii 360

and then he call'd me a *r* naäme, and I can't abide 'im.   *Prom. of May* ɪɪ 159

he wur *r* to me i' tha hayfield, and he'll be *r* to me ageän to-night.   „   ɪɪ 219

Ruffian   And here a knot of *r*'s all in rags,   *Queen Mary* ɪɪ ii 66

some Papist *r*'s hereabout Would murder you.   „   ɪɪɪ v 174

your friends, those *r*'s, the De Brocs,   *Becket* v ii 434

Ruffle   Ay, *r* thyself—be jealous !   *The Falcon* 21

Ruffled   but thou hast *r* my woman, Little John.   *Foresters* ɪ i 165

Ruffler   too solemn and formal to be a *r*. Out upon thee !   *Little John.*   I am no *r*, my lady ;   „   ɪ i 169

Ruffling   that I bear it Without more *r*.   *Queen Mary* v iii 4

Ruin (s)   the general sees, A risk of utter *r*.   „   v ii 449

Delay is death to thee, *r* to England.   *Harold* ɪɪ ii 718

whether it symbol'd *r* Or glory, who shall tell ?   „   v i 110

and leave it A waste of rock and *r*, hear.   *The Cup* ɪɪ 307

But for the slender help that I can give, Fall into *r*.   *Prom. of May* ɪɪ 422

Whose ransom was our *r*,   *Foresters* ɪv 1007

Ruin (*verb*)   Too like to *r* himself, and you, and me !   *The Cup* ɪɪ 263

Ruin'd   (*See also* **Half-ruin'd**) and the race of Godwin Hath *r* Godwin   *Harold* v i 294

Rule (s)   my Lord Mayor here, By his own *r*,   *Queen Mary* ɪɪ ii 347

by this *r*, Foliot may claim the pall For London   *Becket* ɪ iii 55

not to speak one word, for that's the *r* o' the garden,   „   ɪɪɪ i 138

and so cannot suffer by the *r* of frequency.   „   ɪɪɪ iii 319

Rule (*verb*)   Spain and we, One crown, might *r* the world.   *Queen Mary* ɪ v 303

provinces Are hard to *r* and must be hardly ruled ;   „   ɪɪɪ ii 201

hatred of the doctrines Of those who *r*,   „   ɪɪɪ iv 160

So that she come to *r* us.   „   ɪv iii 390

and the French fleet *R* in the narrow seas.   „   v i 7

Rule (*verb*) (*continued*)   Thou art the man to *r* her !   *Harold* ɪ i 223

For I shall *r* according to your laws,   „   ɪɪ ii 759

he hath served me : none but he Can *r* all England.   „   ɪɪɪ i 244

one to *r* All England beyond question, beyond quarrel.   „   ɪv i 144

I will *r* according to their laws.   „   v ii 198

Rome is fated To *r* the world.   *The Cup* ɪɪ 416

when The stronger motive *r*'s.   *Prom. of May* ɪɪ 671

No man who truly loves and truly *r*'s   *Foresters* ɪɪ i 76

Ruleable   if the land Were *r* by tongue,   „   ɪv 399

Ruled   wherever Spain hath *r* she hath wither'd   *Queen Mary* ɪɪ i 206

provinces Are hard to rule and must be hardly *r* ;   „   ɪɪɪ ii 201

Ruler   which hatred by and by Involves the *r*   „   ɪɪɪ iv 161

The *r* of a land Is bounden by his power   „   ɪɪɪ iv 211

When I was *r* in the patrimony,   „   ɪv i 72

sat within the Norman chair A *r* all for England—   *Harold* ɪɪ ii 534

The *r* of an hour, but lawful King,   *Foresters* ɪv 47

Ruling   And *r* men are fatal twins that cannot Move   *Harold* ɪɪ i 127

Rumour   *r* that Charles, the master of the world,   *Queen Mary* ɪ i 104

I trust it is but a *r*.   „   ɪ i 107

I hear unhappy *r*'s—nay, I say not, I believe.   „   v i 35

a *r* then That you were kill'd in battle.   *The Falcon* 381

I may be outlaw'd, I have heard a *r*.   *Foresters* ɪ ii 92

Run   (*See also* **Runned**) So the wine *r*, and there be revelry,   *Queen Mary* ɪɪɪ ii 236

See how the tears *r* down his fatherly face.   „   ɪv iii 4

There *r*'s a shallow brook across our field   „   v v 83

lest they rear and *r* And break both neck and axle.   *Harold* ɪ i 373

play the note Whereat the dog shall howl and *r*,   „   ɪɪ i 192

R thou to Count Guy ; he is hard at hand.   „   ɪɪ i 54

That *r*'s thro' all the faiths of all the world.   „   ɪɪɪ i 352

r in upon her and devour her, one and all   *Becket, Pro.* 525

The rift that *r*'s between me and the King.   „   ɪ i 140

Among these happy dales, *r* clearer,   „   ɪɪ i 157

this love, this mother, *r*'s thro' all The world   „   ᴠɪ i 241

Why, whither *r*'s the boy ?   *The Cup* ɪ i 70

break of precipice that *r*'s Thro' all the wood,   „   ɪ ii 21

r my mind out to a random guest Who join'd me   „   ɪ i 107

my friends may spy him And slay him as he *r*'s.   „   ɪ i 392

r's to sea and makes it Foam over all the fleeted wealth   „   ɪɪ 287

a written scroll That seems to *r* in rhymings.   *The Falcon* 432

tho' the fire should *r* along the ground,   *Prom. of May* ɪ 703

O law—yeäs, Sir ! I'll *r* fur 'im mysen.   „   ɪɪɪ 714

I am sorry my exchequer *r*'s so low   *Foresters* ɪɪ 272

if I hadn't a sprig o' wickentree sewn into my dress, I should *r*.   „   ɪɪ i 251

my heart so down in my heels that if I stay, I can't *r*.   „   ɪɪ i 348

most beaten track *R*'s thro' the forest,   „   ɪɪɪ 90

And thou wouldst *r* more wine than blood.   „   ɪɪɪ 337

Whose writ will *r* thro' all the range of life.   „   ɪv 48

You *r* down your game, We ours.   „   ɪv 520

Runned (ran)   I *r* arter thief i' the dark,   *Prom. of May* ɪ 402

Runned (run)   Dan Smith's cart hes *r* ower a laädy i' the holler laäne,   „   ɪɪ 568

Running   In the full vessel *r* out at top   *Harold* ɪ 378

A hundred pathways *r* everyway,   *Becket, Pro.* 163

and leprosies, and ulcers, and gangrenes, and *r* sores,   „   ɪv 256

r down the chase is kindlier sport Ev'n than the death.   *The Foresters* ɪv ii 213

I laäme't my knee last night *r* arter a thief.   *Prom. of May* ɪ 387

Rush   Carry fresh *r*'es into the dining-hall,   *Foresters* ɪ 81

I pray Heaven we may not have to take to the *r*'es.   „   ɪ i 90

Rushing   No *r* on the game—the net,—the net.   *The Cup* ɪ i 170

Rust   link *r*'s with the breath of the first after-marriage kiss,   *Becket, Pro.* 361

Rustic   Is not this wood-witch of the *r*'s fear   „   ɪɪɪ ii 31

A lady that was beautiful as day Sat by me at a *r* festival   *The Falcon* 350

he, your *r* amourist, The polish'd Damon of your pastoral here,   *Prom. of May* ɪɪɪ 561

Rusting   plow Lay *r* in the furrow's yellow weeds,   *Becket* ɪ iii 355

Rut   Things that seem jerk'd out of the common *r* Of Nature   *Harold* ɪ i 138

Ruthless   And like a river in flood thro' a burst dam Descends the *r* Norman—   „   ɪɪ ii 467

S

Saäke (sake) fur 'er s an' fur my s an' all? — *Prom. of May* II 41
Saäme (same) a-pläayin' the s gaäme wi' my Dora—
  I'll Soomerset tha. — " II 591
Saäve (save) if she weänt listen to me when I be
  a-tryin' to s 'er— — " II 694
Saäy (say) I should s 'twur ower by now. — *Queen Mary* IV iii 475
  Nowt—what could he s? — *Prom. of May* I 152
  and I will s niver master 'ed better men: — " I 323
  But I hed a word to s to ye. — " II 45
  What did ye do, and what did ye s, — " II 173
  What did ye s, and what did ye s, (repeat) — " II 178, 196
  What did we do, and what did we s, — " II 185
  What we mowt s, and what we mowt do, — " II 191
  But what 'ud she s to that? — " II 598
  and s it to ye afoor dark; — " III 13
  to s he's browt some of Miss Eva's roses for the
    sick laädy to smell on. — " III 346
  she moänt coom here. What would her mother s? — " III 459
Saäyin' (saying) What hasta been s to my Dora? — " II 704
  He be s a word to the owd man, — " III 480
Sack (a wine) I marvel is it s or Malvoisie? — *Foresters* III 331
Sack (bag) so dusted his back with the meal in his s, — *Becket* I iv 175
  and the s's, and the taäters, and the mangles, — *Prom. of May* I 452
Sack (verb) Richard s's and wastes a town With random
  pillage, — *Foresters* IV 376
Sackage safe from all The spoil and s aim'd — *Queen Mary* II ii 248
Sack'd By him who s the house of God; — " III iii 195
  When Wyatt s the Chancellor's house in Southwark. — " v ii 504
Sacrament Touching the s in that same book — " IV iii 263
  Yea, take the S upon it, King. — *Harold* IV i 183
Sacred thy kiss—S! I'll kiss it too. — *Becket* II i 185
  More s than his forests for the chase? — " IV ii 24
  To bathe this s pavement with my blood. — " v iii 131
  A s cup saved from a blazing shrine Of our great
    Goddess, — *The Cup* I ii 54
  and the s shrine By chance was burnt along with it. — " I ii 64
  that you should clasp a hand Red with the s blood of
    Sinnatus? — " II 84
  Antonius. Here is another s to the Goddess, — " II 346
  O the s little thing. What a shape! — *Foresters* I i 107
  And coil'd himself about her s waist. — " II 138
  or shall I call it by that new term Brought from the s
    East, his harem? — " IV 705
  No friendship s, values neither man Nor woman save
    as tools— — " IV 713
Sacrifice Their wafer and perpetual s: — *Queen Mary* I ii 45
  A holy supper, not a s; — " IV ii 57
  No s, but a life-giving feast! — " IV ii 112
  A s to Harold, a peace-offering, — *Harold* I ii 203
  The more the love, the more acceptable The s of both
    your loves to heaven. No s to heaven, no help
    from heaven; — " III i 349
  And s there must be, for the king Is holy, — " III i 354
  it was but the s of a kingdom to his son, — *Becket* III iii 106
  nobler The victim was, the more acceptable Might be
    the s. — *The Falcon* 881
Sacrificed like the Greek king when his daughter was s, — *Becket* III iii 105
Sacrilege Take fees of tyranny, wink at s, — " II ii 394
  O God, O noble knights, O s! — " v iii 179
Sad Be merry! yet, Sir Ralph, you look but s. — *Queen Mary* II ii 359
  Stafford, I am a s man and a serious. — " II i 41
  Peace, cousin, peace! I am s at heart myself. — " v ii 159
  poor lad! how sick and s for home! — *Harold* II ii 325
  Why art thou s? — " IV iii 20
  but they were s, And somewhat sadden'd me. — " v i 112
Sadden'd but they were sad, And somewhat s me. — " v i 113
Sadder Of a nature Stronger, s than my own, — *Foresters* III ii 189
Saddle A ragged cloak for s—he, he, he, — *Becket* v i 248
Saddle-bow bent to his s-b, As if to win the man — *Queen Mary* II ii 311
Sadness There is a touch of s in it, my lord, — *Foresters* I iii 35
  I have a touch of s in myself. — " I iii 38

Safe They have given me a s conduct: — *Queen Mary* I ii 101
  and keep you whole and s from all The spoil — " II ii 246
  Is he so s to fight upon her side? — " II ii 313
  If not, there's no man s. — " II ii 315
  Yes, Thomas White. I am s enough; — " II ii 317
  Friend, tho' so late, it is not s to preach. — " v iv 42
  See him out s! (repeat) — *Harold* v i 85, 93
  into thy cloister as the king Will'd it: be s: — " v i 310
  Stigand will see thee s, And so—Farewell. — " v i 419
  And see thee s from Senlac. — " v i 457
  Look out upon the battle—is he s? (repeat) — " v i 485, 655
  S enough there from her to whom thou art bound — *Becket, Pro.* 66
  that is s with me as with thyself: — " *Pro.* 489
  It is not s for me to look upon him. — " I iii 486
  S from the dark and the cold, — *The Cup* I ii 6
  Home with the flock to the fold—S from the wolf— — " I ii 9
  S from the wolf to the fold— — " I ii 19
  charm'd our general into mercy, And all is s again. — " I ii 313
  Who causest the s earth to shudder and gape, — " II 298
Safe-conduct Rogue, we have thy captain's s-c; — *Foresters* IV 432
Safeguard Under the shield and s of the Pope, — *Becket* I iii 600
Safelier you had s have slain an archbishop than a she-goat: — " III iii 68
Safer I fear you come to carry it off my shoulders, And
  sonnet-making's s. — *Queen Mary* II i 93
Said my daughter s that when there rose — " I i 91
  she s that no one in her time should be burnt for
    heresy. — " I i 96
  Know too what Wyatt s. — " II ii 35
  What Wyatt s, or what they s he s, — " II iv 127
  He s it. *Gardiner.* Your courts of justice — " II iv 129
  s she was condemn'd to die for treason; — " III i 377
  Then knelt and s the Miserere Mei— — " III i 390
  Well s, Lord Legate. *Mary.* Nay, not well s; I
    thought of you, my liege, — " III ii 93
  Or s or done in all my life by me; — " IV iii 239
  you recanted all you s Touching the sacrament — " IV iii 262
  I have s. *Cries.* 'Pull him down! — " IV iii 269
  S I not right? For how should reverend prelate — " IV iii 541
  Have I not s? Madam, I came to sue Your Council — " v i 106
  Why, who s that? I know not—true enough! — " v ii 208
  What s you, my good Lord, that our brave English — " v ii 254
  S you not Many of these were loyal? — " v ii 329
  what you s When last you came to England? — " v ii 567
  you s more; You s he would come quickly. — " v ii 574
  Is it so fine? Troth, some have s so. — " v iii 54
  He s it was not courtly to stand helmeted — " v v 35
  He s (thou heardst him) that I must not hence Save on
    conditions. *Malet.* So in truth he s. — *Harold* II ii 260
  He s that he should see confusion fall — " II ii 489
  Some s it was thy father's deed. *Harold.* They lied. — " II ii 513
  S 'ay' when I meant 'no,' lied like a lad — " II ii 656
  The Devil is so modest. *Gurth.* He never s it! — " III i 121
  Since Griffyth's head was sent To Edward, she hath s it. — " IV i 222
  Monk, Thou hast s thy say, — " v i 5
  The manner of his death, and all he s. — *Becket, Pro.* 426
  And I have s no word of this to him: — " I i 97
  They s—her Grace's people—thou wast found— — " I ii 4
  And what s the black sheep, my masters? — " I iv 167
  from that height something was s to me I knew not what. — " II ii 420
  He s as much before. — " II ii 420
  from those, as I s before, there may come a conflagration— — " III iii 164
  He s so? Louis, did he? — " III iii 255
  You wrong the King: he meant what he s to-day. — " III iii 299
  You s you couldn't trust Margery, — " IV ii 15
  ready To tear himself for having s as much. — " IV ii 279
  I s it was the King's courts, not the King; — " v ii 114
  Why s you not as much to my brave Sinnatus? — *The Cup* I ii 259
  Not say as much? I all but s as much. — " II 281
  And s he loathed the cruelties that Rome — " I ii 373
  As I s before, you are still too early. — " I iii 80
  Do what I s; (repeat) — *The Falcon* 265, 269
  you have s so much Of this poor wreath — " 426
  That is musically s. — " 459
  I s you might imagine it was so. — " 545
  Master Dobson, did you hear what I s? — *Prom. of May* I 172

Salisbury (John of) (*continued*) John of *S* Hath often laid a
cold hand on my heats,   *Becket* I i 383
He watch'd her pass with John of *S*   ,, I ii 40
priest whom John of *S* trusted Hath sent another. ,, III i 69
John of *S* committed The secret of the bower, ,, III iii 4
I know him; our good John of *S*.   ,, v ii 77
make me not a woman, John of *S*,   ,, v ii 148

Sallied that our brave English Had *s* out from Calais *Queen Mary* v ii 256

Sally (Allen, servant to Farmer Dobson) (*See also*
Sally Allen) wheniver 'e sees two sweet'arts
togither like thou and me, *S*, *Prom. of May* II 164
And you an' your *S* was forkin' the haäy, ,, II 181
When me an' my *S* was forkin' the haäy, ,, II 192
For me an' my *S* we sweär'd to be true, ,, II 204
I can't let tha aloän if I would, *S*. ,, II 234
but us three, arter *S'*d tell'd us on 'im, ,, III 133
I beänt sa sewer o' that, fur *S* knaw'd 'im; ,, III 147
Some foolish mistake of *S's*; ,, III 154
as the good *S* says, ' I can't abide him '— ,, III 174

Sally Allen *S A*, you worked for Mr. Dobson, didn't you? ,, III 101

Salt (adj.) Up from the *s* lips of the land we two *Becket* III ii 1
like a barren shore That grew *s* weeds, *The Cup* II 232
And a *s* wind burnt the blossoming trees; *Prom. of May* I 57

Salt (s) Have I sown it in *s*? I trust not, *Becket* III iii 320

Saltwood (adj.) thou, De Broc, that holdest *S* Castle— ,, I iii 160
cursed those De Brocs That hold our *S* Castle ,, II ii 269
Perchance the fierce De Brocs from *S* Castle, ,, v ii 249

Saltwood (s) but an he come to *S*, By God's death, ,, I i 182

Salva *S* patriam Sancte Pater, *S* Fili, *S* Spiritus, *S*
patriam, *Harold* v i 466

Salvation In the reborn *s* of a land So noble. *Queen Mary* III iii 182
I promise thee on my *s* That thou wilt hear *Becket* I iii 254

Same (*See also* **Saäme**) While this *s* marriage
question was being argued, *Queen Mary* II ii 37
and that *s* tide Which, coming with our coming, ,, II iii 20
We had your royal barge, and that *s* chair, ,, III ii 7
the clauses added To that *s* treaty which the
emperor sent us ,, III iii 69
Crave, in the *s* cause, hearing of your Grace. ,, IV i 8
This *s* petition of the foreign exiles For Cranmer's life. ,, IV i 193
Hurt no man more Than you would harm your
loving natural brother Of the *s* roof, *s* breast. ,, IV iii 191
Touching the sacrament in that *s* book ,, IV iii 263
But heaven and earth are threads of the *s* loom, *Harold* I i 210
A sight of that *s* chart which Henry gave you *Becket* I ii 60
The bird that moults sings the *s* song again, ,, I iii 447
The *s* smile still. ,, III iii 44
And that *s* head they would have play'd at ball with *The Cup* II 126
Have I not drunk of the *s* cup with thee? ,, II 463
If I might send you down a flask or two Of that *s*
vintage? *The Falcon* 586
Giovanna, my dear lady, in this *s* battle We had been
beaten— ,, 602
crown you Again with the *s* crown my Queen of Beauty. ,, 915
But he'll never be the *s* man again. *Prom. of May* I 70
Can I fancy him kneeling with me, and uttering
the *s* prayer; standing up side by side with me,
and singing the *s* hymn? ,, III 181
I believe thou fell'st into the hands Of these *s* Moors *Foresters* II i 564
Prettier than that *s* widow which you wot of. ,, III 268
or by that *s* love of God we will hang *thee*, prince or
no prince, ,, IV 582

Sanction *s* your decree Of Tostig's banishment, *Harold* IV i 103
He s thee to excommunicate The prelates *Becket* v ii 398

Sanctuary For smooth stone columns of the *s*, *Harold* I ii 101
As one that puts himself in *s*. *Becket* I iii 479
Antonius would not suffer me to break Into the *s*. *The Cup* I iii 121

Sand sea may roll *S*, shingle, shore-weed, *Harold* I ii 119
from the liquid *s's* of Coesnon Haled ,, II ii 56
Sudden change is a house on *s*; *Becket* III iii 60

Sand-castle A child's *s-c* on the beach *The Cup* I ii 253

Sanders What is thy name? *Man. S.* *Queen Mary* III i 313

Sane Brave, wary, *s* to the heart of her— ,, v v 224
A *s* and natural loathing for a soul Purer, *Becket* II i 170
Will hardly help to make him *s* again. *The Falcon* 83

Sang *S* out their loves so loud, *Harold* I ii 20
Heard how the war-horn *s*, ,, III i 157

Sanguelac Senlac! *S*, The Lake of Blood! ,, III i 385
S! *S*! the arrow! the arrow! ,, III i 402
the dead man call it—*S*, The lake of blood? ,, v i 184
thou shalt die on Senlac hill—*S*! ,, v i 243
dear brother, nevermore—*S*! ,, v i 249
my voice against thee from the grave—*S*! ,, v i 256
S! *S*! The arrow! the arrow! ,, v i 262
S—S—the arrow— the arrow!—away! ,, v i 671

Sank I *s* so low that I went into service— *Prom. of May* III 391

Sap Like April *s* to the topmost tree, *Foresters* I iii 24

Sapphire eyes—and these two *s's*—these Twin rubies, *Harold* I ii 110

Saracen (adj.) And push'd our lances into *S* hearts. *Becket* II ii 94

Saracen (s) He calls us worse than Jews, Moors, *S's*. *Queen Mary* v i 151

Sarve (serve) if ye be goin' to *s* our Dora as ye served
our Eva— *Prom. of May* II 691

Sarved (served) fur I ha' *s* for ye well nigh as long as
the man *s* for 'is sweet'art i' Scriptur'. ,, II 61
if ye be goin' to sarve our Dora as ye *s* our Eva— ,, II 692

Sat As if he had been the Holy Father, *s* And
judged it, *Queen Mary* IV iii 44
if there *s* within the Norman chair A ruler *Harold* II ii 532
He *s* down there And dropt it in his hands, *Becket* I iii 323
s in mine own courts Judging my judges, ,, I iii 367
Ay, the princes *s* in judgment against me, ,, I iv 129
a son stone-blind *S* by his mother's hearth: ,, v ii 106
s Stone-dead upon a heap of ice-cold eggs. ,, v ii 238
S by me at a rustic festival *The Falcon* 350
and *s* Thro' every sensual course of that full feast *Prom. of May* II 253
while I *s* Among my thralls in my baronial hall *Foresters* I i 60
Kill'd the sward where'er they *s*, ,, II ii 152

Satan terms Of *S*, liars, blasphemy, Antichrist, *Queen Mary* I ii 95
A spice of *S*, ha! ,, III iv 79
betwixt thine Appeal, and Henry's anger, yield.
Becket. Hence, *S*! *Becket* I iv 624

Satin white *s* his trunk-hose, Inwrought with silver,— *Queen Mary* III i 76

Satisfaction we cannot yield thee an answer altogether to
thy *s*. *Becket* I iv 22

Satisfy Have I not writ enough to *s* you? *Queen Mary* IV ii 63

Saturday and he pays me regular every *S*. *Prom. of May* I 311
spent all your last *S's* wages at the ale-house; ,, II 78

Sauce-deviser A *s-d* for thy days of fish, *Becket, Pro.* 98

Saul (first Hebrew King) gloom of *S* Was lighten'd by
young David's harp. *Queen Mary* v ii 358

Savage The nimble, wild, red, wiry, *s* king— *Harold* IV i 197
I heard your *s* cry. *Becket* IV i 320
You have spoilt the farce. My *S* cry? ,, IV ii 338
Our *s* mastiff, That all but kill'd the beggar, *Prom. of May* I 557
S, is he? What matters? ,, I 562
' I go to fight in Scotland With many a *s* clan;' *Foresters* I i 15

Savagery hast thou never heard His *s* at Alençon,— *Harold* II ii 382
But you know not the *s* of Rome. *The Cup* I ii 287

Save (verb) (*See also* **Saäve**) up, son, and *s* him!
They love thee, *Queen Mary* I iii 66
To *s* your crown that it must come to this. ,, IV 479
no glory Like his who *s's* his country: ,, II i 110
to *s* her from herself and Philip— ,, II i 189
I come to *s* you all, And I'll go further off. ,, III iii 118
but we can *s* your Grace. The river still is free. ,, II iv 23
with what haste I might To *s* my royal cousin. ,, II iv 78
and *s* the life Of Devon: if I *s* him, ,, II iv 123
Sir, no woman's regimen Can *s* us. ,, III i 123
God *s* their Graces! (repeat) *Queen Mary* III i 177, 187, 342, 412
trusted God would *s* her thro' the blood Of Jesus
Christ *Queen Mary* III i 386
God *s* the Queen! ,, III v 170
a day may sink or *s* a realm. *Mary.* A day may
s a heart from breaking too. ,, III vi 239
Yet to *s* Cranmer were to serve the Church, ,, IV i 135
Written for fear of death, to *s* my life, ,, IV iii 242
Tell, tell me; *s* my credit with myself. ,, v v 452
God *s* Elizabeth, the Queen of England! ,, v v 283
God *s* the Queen! ,, v v 288
Their saver, save thou *s* him from himself. *Harold* II ii 61

Save (verb) *(continued)* I have commission'd thee to *s* the man : *Harold* II ii 98
For having lost myself to *s* myself,   „ II ii 654
To *s* thee from the wrath of Norman Saints.   „ II i 217
lamb to Holy Church To *s* thee from the curse.   „ III i 336
when our good hive Needs every sting to *s* it.   „ IV i 18
This brother comes to *s* Your land from waste ;   „ IV i 94
not my purveyor Of pleasures, but to *s* a life— *Becket, Pro.* 150
S me, father, hide me—they follow me—   „ I i 181
Make it so hard to *s* a moth from the fire ?   „ I i 283
S the King's honour here before his barons.   „ I iii 187
God *s* him from all sickness of the soul !   „ ' v ii 174
thy solitude among thy nuns, May that *s* thee !   „ v ii 177
Is it too late for me to *s* your soul ?   „ v ii 524
S that dear head which now is Canterbury, *S* him,
   he saved my life, he saved my child, *S* him, his
   blood would darken Henry's name ; *S* him till
   all as saintly as thyself   „ v iii 6
He is not here—Not yet, thank heaven.   O *s* him !   „ v iii 17
That way, or this ! *S* thyself either way.   „ v iii 85
And *s* her from herself, and be to Rome *The Cup* I i 101
She may, perchance, to *s* this husband,   „ I iii 33
but he may *s* the land, (repeat) *Foresters* I i 283
pay My brother all his debt and *s* the land.   „ I ii 218
pay this mortgage to his brother, And *s* the land.   „ I ii 265
God *s* the King !   „ IV 857

Save (quasi-prep. and conj.) *S* for my daily range
   Among the pleasant fields *Queen Mary* III v 78
s for the fate Which hunted *him* *Harold* II ii 28
Their saver, *s* thou save him from himself.   „ II ii 61
S for the prattling of thy little ones.   „ II ii 122
I must not hence *S* on conditions.   „ II ii 262
S for thy wild and violent will that wrench'd   „ v i 277
S for some once or twice, *Becket, Pro.* 122
S from the throne of thine archbishoprick ?   „ I i 119

Saved I trust this day, thro' God, I have *s* the
   crown. *Queen Mary* II ii 303
scarlet thread of Rahab *s* her life ;   „ III ii 39
blessed angels who rejoice Over one *s*   „ III iii 181
once he *s* your Majesty's own life ;   „ IV i 124
Who *s* it or not *s*.   „ IV i 133
but *s* in heaven By your recanting.   „ IV ii 178
I thank thee for having *s* thyself. *Harold* II ii 653
save Your land from waste ; I *s* it once before,   „ IV i 95
I have *s* many of 'em. *Becket* I i 285
for to-night ye have *s* our Archbishop !   „ I i 257
life *S* as by miracle alone with Him Who gave it.   „ IV i 368
but *s* From all that by our solitude.   „ v ii 170
all the souls we *s* and father'd here   „ v ii 223
Save him, he *s* my life, he *s* my child,   „ v iii 8
sacred cup *s* from a blazing shrine *The Cup* I ii 54
However I thank thee ; thou hast *s* my life.   „ I ii 333
He *s* my life too.   Did he ?   „ I iii 160
I *s* his life once in battle.   He has monies.   I will
   go to him.   I *s* him.   I will try him. *Foresters* I i 272
Thou hast *s* my head at the peril of thine own.   „ IV 795

Saver ' Hail, Daughter of God, and *s* of the faith. *Queen Mary* III iii 82
Their *s*, save thou save him from himself. *Harold* II ii 61

Saving to the *s* of their souls, Before your execution. *Queen Mary* IV i 194
S my confessor and my cousin Pole.   „ v ii 527
S thro' Norman bishopricks— *Harold* II ii 538
And even as I should bless thee *s* mine,   „ II ii 651
S the honour of my order—ay. *Becket* I iii 20
S thine order !   But King Henry sware That, *s* his
   King's kingship,   „ I iii 26
S thine order, Thomas, Is black and white at once,   „ I iii 30
Queen Mary v v 116

Savour Burn !—Fie, what a *s* ! *The Cup* I iii 86
It bears an evil *s* among women. *Foresters* IV 193

Savoury geese, beside Hedge-pigs, a *s* viand,

Savoy ' It is the King's wish, that you should wed
   Prince Philibert of *S*. *Queen Mary* III v 222
Specially not this landless Philibert Of *S* ;   „ III v 240
She will not have Prince Philibert of *S*,   „ III vi 43
Elizabeth—To Philibert of *S*, as you know,   „ v i 247
She will not have Prince Philibert of *S*.   „ v i 254
Becket v ii 538

Saw (maxim) For I was musing on an ancient *s*,

Saw (verb) *(See also* **Seed***)* and *s* They had hewn
   the drawbridge *Queen Mary* II iii 17
I *s* Lord William Howard By torchlight,   „ II iii 28
than have seen it : yet I *s* it.   „ III i 48
changed not colour when she *s* the block,   „ III i 399
I never *s* your Highness moved till now.   „ III vi 103
Ay, my liege, I *s* the covers laying.   „ III vi 258
I *s* the deaths of Latimer and Ridley.   „ IV iii 295
And you *s* Latimer and Ridley die ?   „ IV iii 328
You *s* him how he past among the crowd ;   „ III vi 574
s the church all fill'd With dead men *Harold* I ii 81
Griffyth when I *s* him flee, Chased deer-like   „ I ii 146
I *s* him over there.   „ I ii 46
I *s* him coming with his brother Odo   „ II ii 347
whose baby eye *S* them sufficient.   „ III ii 67
and yet I *s* thee drive him up his hills—   „ IV i 211
I *s* the hand of Tostig cover it.   „ IV iii 81
someone *s* thy willy-nilly nun Vying a tress   „ v i 148
I *s* her even now : She hath not left us.   „ v i 158
I *s* it in her eyes !   „ v i 368
I *s* that door Close even now upon the woman. *Becket* I i 201
who never *s* nor dreamed of such a banquet.   „ I iv 83
Then I *s* Thy high black steed among the flaming furze,   „ II i 54
bad me whatever I *s* not to speak one word,   „ II i 133
s your ladyship a-parting wi' him even now   „ III i 159
Thou art the prettiest child I ever *s*.   „ IV i 7
I *s* the ball you lost in the fork of the great willow   „ IV ii 56
I never *s* any such, Never knew any such,   „ IV ii 125
I *s* you there.   *Fitzurse.*   I was not.   „ v ii 411
You *s* my hounds True to the scent ; *The Cup* I ii 109
When last I *s* you, You all but yielded.   „ II 44
that ye *s* me crown myself withal.   „ II 159
She *s* it at a dance, upon a neck Less lovely *The Falcon* 54
I never *s* The land so rich in blossom as this year.   „ 341
Before I *s* you—all my nobleness Of nature,   „ 810
I *s* a man go in, my lord. *Foresters* II i 207
Captain, we *s* thee cowering to a knight   „ II i 682
I thought I *s* thee clasp and kiss a man   „ II ii 71
I never *s* them : yet I could believe   „ II ii 107

Saw *See also* **See-saw**

Saw'st Our bashful Legate, *s* not how he flush'd ? *Queen Mary* III iv 350
that chart with the red line—thou *s* it— *Becket, Pro.* 428

Saxon *(See also* **Un-Saxon, West Saxon***)* We hold our *S*
   woodcock in the springe, *Harold* II ii 1
Breathe the free wind from off our *S* downs,   „ II ii 186
Angle, Jute, Dane, *S*, Norman   „ II ii 763
little help without our *S* carles Against Hardrada.   „ IV i 35
yet he held that Dane, Jute, Angle, *S*,   „ IV i 77
And Loathing wield a *S* battle-axe—   „ v i 414
Ay, there springs a *S* on him,   „ v i 498
I have heard the Steers Had land in *S* times ; *Prom. of May* III 608
have loved Harold the *S*, or Hereward the Wake. *Foresters* I i 228
True soul of the *S* churl for whom song has no charm.   „ II i 385
Harold v i 5

Say (s) Monk, Thou hast said thy *s*,
Say all thy *s*, But blaze not out before the Frenchmen *Becket* III iii 220

Say (verb) *(See also* **Saäy***)* from their sees Or fled, they
   s, or flying— *Queen Mary* I i 5
hear what the shaveling has to *s* for himself.   „ I iii 17
He *s*'s right ; by the mass we'll have no mass   „ I iii 50
Perinde ac cadaver—as the priest *s*'s,   „ I iv 180
some *s*, That you shall marry him, make him King
   belike.   *Elizabeth.*   Do they *s* so, good uncle ?   „ I iv 211
But why *s* that ? what have you done to lose her ?   „ I iv 295
Your royal father (For so they *s*)   „ I v 20
I *s* your Grace is loved.   „ I v 131
What *s*'s the King your master ?   „ I v 247
No, I come.   I won by boldness once.   „ I v 547
S for ten thousand ten—and pothouse knaves,   „ II i 69
I *s* no more—only this, their lot is yours.   „ II i 213
What do and *s* Your Council at this hour ?   „ II ii 45
So I *s* Your city is divided,   „ II ii 98
I *s*, I, that was never mother, cannot tell   „ II iii 188
he *s*'s he's a poor gentleman.   „ II iii 74
Hang him, I *s*.   „ II iii 80
whom—whom did you *s* ? *Messenger.* Elizabeth,   „ II iv 115

Say (verb) (*continued*) What such a one as Wyatt

s's is nothing :	*Queen Mary* III i 139
He keeps, they *s*, some secret that may cost	„ III i 200
I *s* There is no man—there was one woman with us—	„ III i 336
oversea they *s* this state of yours Hath no more mortice	„ III i 441
What *s* you ? *Bagenhall.* We talk and talk.	„ III iii 37
But stretch it wider ; *s* when England fell.	„ III iii 261
I *s* you were the one sole man who stood.	„ III iii 263
yet I would not *s* Burn !	„ III iv 174
there are many, As my Lord Paget *s*'s.	„ III iv 177
beware, I *s*, Lest men accuse you of indifference	„ III iv 222
But truth, they *s*, will out,	„ III v 28
To *s* ' I did not ? ' and my rod's the block.	„ III v 130
she would *s* These are the means God works with,	„ III vi 67
What should I *s*, I cannot pick my words—	„ III vi 147
You *s* true, Madam.	„ III vi 198
I *s*, Your father had a will that beat men down ;	„ IV i 107
So, so ; this will I *s*—thus will I pray.	„ IV ii 113
I'll *s* something for you—so—good-bye.	„ IV ii 167
And first I *s* it is a grievous case,	„ IV iii 167
I *s*, I hold by all I wrote within that book.	„ IV iii 274
I *s* they have drawn the fire On their own heads :	„ IV iii 379
' Now,' *s*'s the Bishop, *s*'s he, ' we'll gwo to dinner ; '	„ IV iii 512
I hear unhappy rumours—nay, I *s* not, I believe.	„ V i 36
They *s* your wars are not the wars of England.	„ V i 165
S go ; but only *s* it lovingly.	„ V i 216
Might I not *s*—to please your wife, the Queen ?	„ V i 307
They *s* the gloom of Saul Was lighten'd	„ V ii 358
but *s* the world is nothing—	„ V ii 367
How dare you *s* it ?	„ V ii 379
And *s*'s, he will come quickly.	„ V ii 565
Then I may *s* your Grace will see your sister ?	„ V ii 603
They *s* she's dying. *First.* So is Cardinal Pole.	„ V iv 4
s's That rest is all—tells me I must not think—	„ V v 61
And who *s*'s that ? *Alice.* It is a saying among the Catholics.	„ V v 243
The Queen is dying, or you dare not *s* it.	„ V v 251
I needs must *s*—That never English monarch	„ V v 276
I *s* not this, as being Half Norman-blooded,	*Harold* I i 168
and I *s* it For the last time perchance,	„ I i 174
So *s*'s old Gurth, not I :	„ I i 302
I *s*, thou hast a tongue,	„ I i 400
What do they *s* ? did Edward know of this ? *Malet.* They *s*, his wife Is knowing and abetting. *Harold.* They *s*, his wife !—	„ II ii 304
I *s* Ye would applaud that Norman who should drive	„ II ii 538
send thy saints that I may *s* Ev'n to their faces,	„ II ii 786
forbidden By Holy Church : but who shall *s* ?	„ III ii 24
They *s* thou art to wed the Lady Aldwyth. *Harold.* They *s*, they *s*.	„ III ii 107
Never shall any man *s* that I, that Tostig	„ IV ii 66
He means the thing he *s*'s. See him out safe !	„ V i 84
I *s* it now, forgive me !	„ V ii 27
S, The Queen should play his kingship	*Becket, Pro.* 235
They *s* that you are wise in winged things,	„ I i 255
We are friends no more : he will *s* that, not I.	„ I i 345
I have heard him *s* He means no more ;	„ I iii 192
S that a cleric murder'd an archbishop,	„ I iii 399
What did the traitor *s* ?	„ I iii 471
Tell what I *s* to the King.	„ I iii 564
What is the bishops *s* ?	„ I iii 589
S that he blind thee and tear out thy tongue.	„ I iii 615
Wilt thou not *s*, ' God bless you,' ere we go ?	„ I iv 33
Call them in, I *s*.	„ I iv 85
and they do *s* the very breath catches.	„ I iv 222
And I *s*, I care not for thy saying. (repeat)	„ II i 111
I almost fear to *s* That my poor heretic heart	„ II i 282
I *s* that those Who went before us	„ II ii 201
All that you *s* is just. I cannot answer it	„ III i 1
and so brought me no-hows as I may *s*,	„ III i 130
people do *s* that his is bad beyond all reckoning, and— *Rosamund.* The people lie.	„ III i 174
that is to *s* in her time when she had the ' Crown.'	„ III i 197
S all thy say, But blaze not out before the Frenchmen	„ III iii 219
but I *s* no more . . . farewell, my lord.	„ III iii 271

Say (verb) (*continued*) base as—who shall I *s*—Fitzurse

and his following—	*Becket* III iii 308
False figure, Map would *s*.	„ III iii 347
she *s*'s she can make you sleep o' nights.	„ IV ii 19
They *s* that walls have ears ;	„ IV ii 79
there are those Who *s* you do not love him—	„ IV ii 97
See, I can *s* no more. *Eleanor.* Will you not *s* you are not married to him ? *Rosamund.* Ay, Madam, I can *s* it, if you will.	„ IV ii 107
And what would my own Aquitaine *s* to that ?	„ V i 182
York will *s* anything. What is he saying now ?	„ V ii 5
What *s* ye there of Becket ?	„ V ii 56
They *s* that Rome Sprang from a wolf.	*The Cup* I ii 12
Do not *s* so. I know of no such wives	„ I ii 190
I have much to *s*, no time to *s* it in.	„ I ii 207
Not *s* as much ? I all but said as much.	„ I ii 281
I *s* it to you—you are wiser—Rome knows all,	„ I ii 285
What did that villain Synorix *s* to you ?	„ I ii 336
What did he *s* ? *Camma.* What *should* he *s* ? *Sinnatus.* What *should* he *s*,	„ I ii 345
He should *s* this, that being Tetrarch once	„ I ii 349
What should he *s* ? He should *s* nothing	„ I ii 365
Lady, I *s* it with all gentleness,	„ I iii 99
How dare she *s* it ? I could hate her for it	„ II 177
some old Greek *S* death was the chief good ?	„ II 515
Call him back and *s* I come to breakfast with him.	*The Falcon* 212
for when I *s* What can I do—	„ 238
How long since do you *s* ?	„ 372
How can your lordship *s* so ?	„ 508
I did not *s*, my lord, that it was so ;	„ 544
shall we *s* this wreath and your sweet rhymes ?	„ 734
And what did *you* *s* to that ?	*Prom. of May* I 142
And what did he *s* to that ?	„ I 151
thaw I *s*'s it mysen, niver men 'ed a better master—	„ I 326
Shall I *s* it ?—fly with me to-day.	„ I 678
Didn't I *s* that we had forgiven you ?	„ III 75
S that the sick lady thanks him !	„ III 348
but he *s*'s he wants to tell ye summut	„ III 354
some will *s* because I have inherited my Uncle.	„ III 596
I *s* to it, Thou art mine, and it answers,	*Foresters* I i 335
What did he *s* to thee ?	„ I ii 254
Do you doubt me when I *s* she loves me, man ?	„ II i 520
Speak to me, Kate, and *s* you pardon me !	„ II ii 53
Leave them each what they *s* is theirs,	„ III 294
Out on it, I *s*, as out of tune and time !	„ IV 34
S it again, And by this ring the lips	„ IV 69
What did I *s* ? Nay, my tongue tript—	„ IV 498

Saying (part.) (*See also* **Saäyin**) I cannot catch what

Father Bourne is *s*.	*Queen Mary* I iii 15
What wast thou *s* of this Lady Jane ?	„ I v 37
This Howard, whom they fear, what was he *s* ?	„ II vi 55
hear that you are *s* behind his back what you see you are *s* afore his face ?	*The Falcon* 106

Saying (s) It is a *s* among the Catholics.

I have heard a *s* of thy father Godwin,	*Queen Mary* V v 244
And I say, I care not for thy *s*. (repeat)	*Harold* III i 111
No *s* of mine—Jocelyn of Salisbury.	*Becket* I ii 112
slopes Of Solomon-shaming flowers—that was your *s*,	„ II ii 372
I heard a *s* in Egypt, that ambition Is like the sea wave,	„ III i 49
you know the *s*—' Better a man without riches,	*The Cup* I iii 137
A noble *s*—and acted on would yield A nobler breed	*The Falcon* 750
	„ 753

Sayst Why (*smiling*), no, indeed. *Mary.* *S* thou ? *Queen Mary* I v 335

Scaäred (scared) I be a bit deaf, and I wur hallus *s* by a big word ! *Prom. of May* III 33

Scabbard Down *s*, and out sword ! *Queen Mary* II i 143

Scaffold on the *s* Recanted, and resold himself to

Rome.	„ III i 151
She came upon the *s*,	„ III i 376
You'll hear of me again. *Bagenhall.* Upon the *s*.	„ III i 475

Scald And felt the sun of Antioch *s* our mail, *Becket* II ii 93

Scale (for weighing) always in suspense, like the *s*, *Becket* II ii 363

But lest we turn the *s* of courtesy *Harold* II ii 164

Scale (of a fish) my fellows know that I am all one *s* like a fish. *Becket* I iv 213

Scourge (verb)   Threaten the child ; ' I'll *s* you if you did it : '   *Queen Mary* III v 126

Fast, *s* thyself, and mortify thy flesh,   *Becket* I iii 539

once I wish'd to *s* them to the bones.   *The Cup* I i 27

Scourging   In *s*'s, macerations, mortifyings, Fasts,   *Becket* v i 41

Horrible ! flaying, *s*, crucifying—   *The Cup* v i 235

Scout   Our *s*'s have heard the tinkle of their bells.   *Harold* v i 220

Scouted   I am glad that France hath *s* him at last :   *Becket* II ii 252

Scowl   A smile abroad is oft a *s* at home.   *Queen Mary* III i 213

Scowl'd   *S* that world-hated and world-hating beast,   ,, II ii 90

Scrape (s)   less loyalty in it than the backward *s* of the clown's heel—   *Becket* III iii 143

Scrape (verb)   Sir Richard must *s* and *s* till he get to the land again.   *Foresters* I i 78

Scraped   I *S* from your finger-points the holy oil ;   *Queen Mary* IV i 132

Scraps   make Thy slender meal out of those *s* and shreds   *The Falcon* 146

Scratch'd   And, being *s*, returns to his true rose,   *Becket* III i 249

Scratching   *See* **A-scrattin**

Scream   the *s* of some wild woodland thing.   *Foresters* II i 252

Scream'd   *S* as you did for water.   *Queen Mary* III v 58

Scrimp   Do not *s* your phrase,   ,, III iii 259

Scriptur'   as long as the man sarved for 'is sweet'art i' *S*.   *Prom. of May* II 63

Scripture (adj.)   It's the old *S* text, ' Let us eat and drink,   ,, I 258

Scripture (s)   (*See also* **Scriptur'**)   wholesome *s*, ' Little children Love one another.'   *Queen Mary* III iv 84

Did you find a *s*, ' I come not to bring peace   ,, III iv 87

Scritch-owl   Anger the *s-o*.   *Mercenary.* But, my lord, the *s-o* bodes death, my lord.   *Foresters* II i 331

Scroll   But then what's here ?   King Harry with a *s*.   *Queen Mary* III i 261

What's here ?   a *s* Pinned to the wreath.   *The Falcon* 424

a written *s* That seems to run in rhymings.   ,, 431

Scruple   and I fear One *s*, this or that way,   *Queen Mary* IV ii 100

Winnow and scatter all *s*'s to the wind,   *Becket* I i 150

Scruplest   And *s* not to flaunt it to our face   *Foresters* IV 887

Sculptor   as a *s* clay, To their own model.   *Queen Mary* III iii 33

Scum   the psalm-singing weavers, cobblers, *s*—   ,, III iv 290

s And offal of the city would not change Estates   ,, IV iii 76

men, the *s* and offal of the Church ;   *Becket* I i 408

Scurrilous   May plaister his clean name with *s* rhymes !   ,, I i 309

Scurrying   the *s* of a rat Affrighted me,   *Queen Mary* III v 143

Scutage   Church should pay her *s* like the lords.   *Becket* I i 34

Scuttle   *S* his cockle-shell ?   *Harold* IV iii 142

Scutum   Illorum, Domine, *S* scindatur !   ,, v i 509

Scythe   Your havings wasted by the *s* and spade—   *Queen Mary* II ii 276

Sea   (*See also* **Mid-sea**,)   I spy the rock beneath the smiling *s*.   ,, I iv 279

Mine is the fleet and all the power at *s*—   ,, I iv 288

God lay the waves and strow the storms at *s*,   ,, I v 382

When they will sweep her from the *s*'s.   ,, III i 162

Our voyage by *s* was all but miracle ;   ,, III ii 25

And here the river flowing from the *s*,   ,, III ii 26

offal thrown Into the blind *s* of forgetfulness.   ,, III iii 193

dallying over *s*'s Even when his brother's,   ,, III iv 293

So they have sent poor Courtenay over *s*.   ,, III v 2

I am sicker staying here Than any *s* could make me passing hence, Tho' I be ever deadly sick at *s*.   ,, III vi 87

and the French fleet Rule in the narrow *s*'s.   ,, v i 7

Sending an insolent shot that dash'd the *s*'s Upon us,   ,, v i 58

must lower his flag To that of England in the *s*'s   ,, v i 66

A voice of shipwreck on a shoreless *s* !   ,, v ii 384

Spain would be England on her *s*'s, and England Mistress of the Indies.   ,, v iii 72

I had heard of him in battle over *s*'s,   ,, v v 33

Beyond the *s*'s—a change !   *Harold* I i 104

and hunt and hawk beyond the *s*'s !   ,, I i 230

s shall roll me back To tumble at thy feet.   ,, I ii 114

The *s* may roll Sand, shingle, shore-weed,   ,, I ii 117

there is a post from over *s*'s With news for thee.   ,, II ii 209

I'll hack my way to the *s*.   ,, II ii 312

Our Duke is all between thee and the *s*,   ,, II ii 315

God and the *s* have given thee to our hands—   ,, II ii 548

a lake, A *s* of blood—we are drown'd in blood—   ,, III i 398

dumb'd his carrion croak From the gray *s* for ever.   ,, IV iii 67

Sea (*continued*)   send the shatter'd North again to *s*,   *Harold* IV iii 141

I send my voice across the narrow *s*'s—   ,, v i 246

Till the *s* wash her level with her shores,   ,, v i 331

The sign in heaven—the sudden blast at *s*—   ,, v i 379

Follow them, follow them, drive them to the *s* !   ,, v i 603

No man without my leave shall cross the *s*'s   *Becket*, Pro. 35

I mean to cross the *s* to France,   ,, I iii 124

Wilt not be suffer'd so to cross the *s*'s   ,, I iii 129

Love that is born of the deep coming up with the sun from the *s*. (repeat)   ,, II i 10, 20

for any rough *s* Blown by the breath of kings.   ,, II ii 107

Shall the waste voice of the bond-breaking *s*   ,, v ii 359

bays And havens filling with a blissful *s*.   *The Cup* II 236

runs to *s* and makes it Foam over all the fleeted wealth   ,, II 287

The sky ? or the *s* on a blue day ?   *Prom. of May* I 101

myself Would guide you thro' the forest to the *s*.   *Foresters* II i 639

light of the *s*'s by the moon's long-silvering ray !   ,, II ii 178

Were plunged beneath the waters of the *s*,   ,, IV 669

Sea-bird   Nor mark the *s-b* rouse himself and hover Above the windy ripple,   *Harold* II ii 334

Sea-creek   the *s-c*—the petty rill That falls into it—   *Becket* II ii 293

Seal (s)   Let the Great *S* be sent Back to the King to-morrow.   ,, I i 374

O thou Great *S* of England, Given me by my dear friend   ,, I i 336

Send the Great *S* by daybreak.   ,, I i 405

Thy sending back the Great *S* madden'd him,   ,, I iii 9

Flung the Great *S* of England in my face—   ,, I iii 318

Seal (verb)   except he *s* his faith In sight of all   *Queen Mary* IV iii 28

My lord Archbishop, thou hast yet to *s*.   *Becket* I iii 306

S ?   If a seraph shouted from the sun, And bad me *s*   ,, I iii 311

I will not *s*.   ,, I iii 315

He would not *s*.   ,, I iii 319

the man shall *s*, Or I will *s* his doom.   ,, I iii 330

And thou art perjured, and thou wilt not *s*.   ,, I iii 527

Sign ? *s* ?   I promised The King to obey these customs,   ,, I iii 555

will *s* Love's truth On those sweet lips   *Foresters* IV 73

Sea-laughter   and fill the sky With free *s-l*—   *Harold* II ii 337

Seal'd   Sign'd and not *s* !   How's that ?   *Queen Mary* v iii 84

Seaman   Perhaps ; but we have *seamen*.   *Harold* II i 97

Sea-marks   they should hang Cliff-gibbeted for *s-m* ;   ,, II i 97

Sea-mew   our *s-m* Winging their only wail !   ,, II ii 626

Sear   Thine ' ifs ' will *s* thine eyes out—ay.   *Foresters* III 201

Search   *S* them, Little John.   ,, III 207

S this other—   ,, III 288

S them, Kate, and see if they have spoken truth.   ,, IV 163

s him then.   How much hast thou about thee ?   ,, IV 178

S me then.   I should be hard beset with thy fourscore.   ,, IV 169

Search'd   But how then if I will not bide to be *s* ?   *Becket* I i 13

Searching   He miss the *s* flame of purgatory.   *Queen Mary* IV iii 385

Sea-saw   The miserable *s-s* of our child-world,   *Harold* v ii 159

Sea-shore   lay them both upon the waste *s-s* At Hastings,   *Foresters* II 673

Sea-sick   so should all the love-sick be *s-s*.   *Becket*, Pro. 350

Season   not in tune, a nightingale out of *s* ;   *Queen Mary* I iv 74

Seat   (*See also* **Judgment-seat**)   This dress was made me as the Earl of Devon To take my *s* in ;   ,, v ii 536

Throw cushions on that *s*, and make it throne-like.   *The Falcon* 610

Seated   Were *s* sadly at a fountain side,   *Harold* II i 20

Sea-will-o'-the-wisp   Wicked *s-w-o'-t-w* !   *Queen Mary* I iii 57

Second   let me call her our *s* Virgin Mary,   ,, III ii 164

The *s* Prince of Peace—   ,, III iii 13

Should play the *s* actor in this pageant That brings him in ;   ,, III v 52

Or a *s* fire, Like that which lately crackled underfoot   ,, IV iii 72

first In Council, *s* person in the realm,   *Harold* III ii 47

and the *s* curse Descend upon thine head,   *Becket* III ii 212

Who made the *s* mitre play the first, And acted me ?   ,, III iii 317

This is the *s* grain of good counsel I ever proffered thee,   ,, v ii 336

and I Became his *s* father :   *The Cup* II 209

I have no fears at this my *s* marriage.   *Prom. of May* III 772

It seem'd so ; only there was left A *s* daughter,   *The Cup* II 198

Second-sight   Or some strange *s-s*, the marriage cup   *Harold* v i 210

Second-sighted   Your *s-s* man That scared the dying   *Becket* III i 228

Secrecy   bound me by his love to *s* Till his own time.   *Queen Mary* II ii 121

Secret (adj.)   And fearing for her, sent a *s* missive,   ,, v i 271

And if you be not *s* in this matter,   *Becket*, Pro. 153

I have built a *s* bower in England, Thomas,

Secret (adj.) (continued) We take her from her s bower in
Anjou And pass her to her s bower in England. *Becket* Pro. 181
that s matter which would heat the King against thee „ Pro. 487
To pass thee to thy s bower to-morrow. „ i i 249
The s whisper of the Holy Father. „ i iii 236
And that old priest whom John of Salisbury trusted
Hath sent another. *Henry.* S? „ iii i 72
Henry. S, then? „ iii i 82
Know ye not this is s, „ iv ii 22
Found out her s bower and murder'd her. „ v i 175
Secret (s) (*See also* **State-secret**) some s that may
cost Philip his life. *Queen Mary* iii i 201
That is my s, Thomas. *Becket.* State s's should be
patent to the statesman *Becket,* Pro. 75
—there lies the s of her whereabouts. „ Pro. 430
I do not then charm this s out of our loyal Thomas, „ Pro. 466
Thine enemy knows the s of my bower. „ i i 265
Is our s ours? Have you had any alarm? „ iii i 27
John of Salisbury committed The s of the bower, „ iii iii 6
This is no s, but a public matter. „ v ii 319
That is my s: keep it, or you sell me *The Cup* i ii 214
We never kept a s from each other; *Prom. of May* i 552
I have done wrong in keeping your s; „ iii 399
Sect Their ' dies Illa,' which will test their s. *Queen Mary* iii iv 428
worthy Bonner,—To test their s. „ iii iv 431
Sectaries dishonour'd even in the sight Of thine
own s. „ v v 134
Secular A s kingdom is but as the body Lacking a
soul; and in itself a beast. The Holy Father
in a s kingdom Is as the soul descending out of
heaven Into a body generate. „ iv i 32
he was deliver'd To the s arm to burn; „ iv ii 214
I have been a lover of wines, and delicate meats,
And s splendours, *Becket* i i 78
You have had the better of us In s matters. „ iii ii 81
Secured if our person be s From traitor stabs— *Queen Mary* v v 280
Security Ay, ay, but what s, „ iii iii 81
Sederunt S *principes, ederunt pauperes.* *Becket* i iv 131
See (a bishoprick) And from the Apostolic s of
Rome; *Queen Mary* iii iii 127
by your intercession May from the Apostolic s obtain, „ iii iii 147
obedience Unto the holy s and reigning Pope „ iii iii 158
our Bishops from their s's Or fled, „ ii ii 4
From all the vacant s's and abbacies, *Becket* i i 652
That hold our Saltwood Castle from our s! „ ii ii 270
See (verb) fear, I s you, Dear friend, for the last time; *Queen Mary* i i 102
my Lord; I s you in the Tower again. „ i iv 80
S that you neither hear them nor repeat! „ i v 576
To tell you what indeed ye s and know, „ ii ii 144
And s the citizens arm'd. Good day; „ ii ii 378
if he s the man and still will jeer. „ ii ii 402
I could s that as the new-made couple „ iii i 93
Bagenhall, I s The Tudor green and white. „ iii i 179
S there be others that can use their hands. „ iii i 243
Did you s her die? „ iii i 344
No, cousin, happy—Happy to s you; „ iii ii 87
Ay; but s here! *First Page.* S what? „ iii ii 215
pray Heaven That you may s according to our sight. „ iii iv 331
You cannot s the Queen. Renard denied her, „ iii vi 1
My Lords, you cannot s her Majesty. „ iii vi 19
Can I not s him? *Renard.* Not now. „ iii vi 35
farewell; Until I s you in St. Mary's Church. „ iv ii 47
You have not gone to s the burning? „ iv iii 290
I could s that many silent hands Came from the crowd „ iv iii 582
Not to s me? *Philip.* Ay, Madam, to s you. „ v i 118
Count de Feria waits without, In hopes to s your
Highness. „ v ii 401
She neither s's nor hears, „ v ii 404
Our Clarence there S's ever such an aureole „ v ii 413
Sin is too dull to s beyond himself. „ v ii 441
they s not what the general s's, A risk of utter ruin. „ v ii 447
throat of mine, Barer than I should wish a man to
s it,— „ v ii 462
I will s no man hence for evermore, „ v ii 525
I may die Before I read it. Let me s him at once. „ v ii 550

See (verb) (*continued*) Then I may say your Grace
will s your sister? *Queen Mary* v ii 604
You s the lodging, sir, „ v iii 23
That she would s your Grace before she—died. „ v iii 104
Nay, dearest Lady, s your good physician. „ v v 59
your royal sister comes to s you. *Mary.* I will
not s her. „ v v 192
I will s none except the priest. Your arm. „ v v 196
For all the world s's it as well as England. *Harold* i i 129
I s the flashing of the gates of pearl „ i i 186
s Deeper into the mysteries of heaven „ i i 199
S's he into thine, That thou wouldst have „ i i 202
S here—an interwoven H and E ! „ i ii 57
thou shalt s My grayhounds fleeting „ i ii 128
I s the goal and half the way to it.— „ i ii 196
We be fishermen; I came to s after my nets. „ ii i 27
He came not to s me, had past me by To hunt „ ii ii 27
He's me not—and yet he dreams of me. „ ii ii 144
And s thee shipt, and pray in thy behalf „ ii ii 197
I Shall s the dewy kiss of dawn no more „ ii ii 331
I s the blackness of my dungeon loom „ ii ii 405
s confusion fall On thee and on thine house. „ ii ii 489
S here this little key about my neck! „ iii i 10
to s my solemn vow Accomplish'd. „ iii i 306
join our hands before the hosts, That all may s. „ iv i 243
cannot s the world but thro' their wines! „ iv iii 225
S him out safe! (repeat) „ v i 84, 93
S all be sound and whole. „ v i 194
I s it in thine. And not on thee— „ v i 369
Stigand will s thee safe, And so—Farewell. „ v i 418
And s thee safe from Senlac. „ v i 457
I can s it From where we stand; „ v i 462
I s the gonfanon of Holy Peter „ v i 549
and s beyond Your Norman shrines, „ v i 618
Our Harold—we shall never s him more. „ v ii 3
Take them away, I do not love to s them. „ v ii 142
s my bishop Hath brought your king to a standstill. *Becket,* Pro. 42
Ay! blood, perchance, except thou s to her. „ Pro. 176
Ay, ay, but swear to s to her in England. „ Pro. 190
longed much to s your Grace and the Chancellor ere he
past, „ Pro. 399
you could not s the King for the kinglings. „ Pro. 452
I can s further into a man than our hot-headed Henry, „ Pro. 462
I stand and s The rift that runs between me „ i i 139
herself should s That kings are faithful „ i ii 77
He will not s thy face till thou hast sign'd „ i iii 5
I s it, I s it. „ i iii 297
Foliot, let me s what I have sign'd. „ i iii 307
To s the proud Archbishop mutilated. „ i iii 614
and s it mounting to Heaven, my God bless you, „ i iv 37
s here, my fool, this rag fro' the gangrene i' my leg. „ i iv 236
My brave-hearted Rose ! Hath he ever been to s thee? „ ii i 288
S if our pious—what shall I call him, John?— „ ii ii 38
How should you s this rightly? „ ii ii 98
now I s That I was blind—suffer the phrase— „ ii ii 437
Bird mustn't tell, Whoop—he can s. (repeat) „ iii i 107, 256
I s—some confusion, Some strange mistake. „ iii i 233
S here ! *Herbert.* What's here? „ iii iii 1
Do you s, my lord, There is the King „ iii iii 21
Do you s that great black cloud „ iii iii 45
And s you yon side-beam that is forced from under it, „ iii iii 49
Ay, but some one comes to s her now and then. „ iv i 16
we shall s the silk here and there, and I want my supper. „ iv i 56
S, I can say no more. „ iv ii 107
what uncomely faces, could he s you ! „ v i 201
I told him I was bound to s the Archbishop, „ v ii 100
You s they have been revelling, and I fear „ v ii 421
Who are with him? I s no face that knows me. *The Cup* i i 183
Had you then No Message with the cup? *Camma.*
Why, yes, s here. „ i ii 69
a brave one Which you shall s to-morrow. „ i ii 432
S, s, my white bird stepping toward the snare. „ i iii 35
who has been So oft to s the Priestess, „ ii 11
Are you so sure? I pray you wait and s. „ ii 107
S here—I stretch my hand out—hold it there. „ ii 210

See (verb) (*continued*)   I am glad I shall not *s* it.   *The Cup* II 513
Beneath an ever-rising sun—I *s* him—   „   II 535
s, why she turns down the path through our little vineyard,   *The Falcon* 167
I *s* you quite recover'd of your wound.   „   391
I *s* There goes a musical score along with' them,   „   451
S, my lady !   *Giovanna.*   I *s*, Filippo !   „   654
and *s* that all be right and reg'lar fur 'em afoor he coöm.   *Prom. of May* I 168
S that you do not do so again !   „   II 24
And wheniver 'e *s*'s two sweet'arts togither like thou and me, Sally,   „   II 163
Which told us we should never *s* her more—   „   II 477
Letters !   Yeas, I *s*'s now.   „   III 38
Ye *s*'s the holler laäne be hallus so dark i' the arternoon,   „   III 92
I cannot and I will not *s* anybody.   „   III 340
may drop off any day, any hour. You must *s* him at once.   „   III 408
Tell him that I and the lady here wish to *s* him.   „   III 415
It puts me in heart Again to *s* you ;   „   III 503
I *s* it all now.   O she has fainted.   „   III 670
you *s* her there !   Only fifteen when first you came on her,   „   III 749
There, there !   You *s* I was right.   *Foresters* I i 114
She doesn't *s* me.   Shall I be bold ?   „   I i 124
I could *s* her for a moment Glide like a light   „   II i 157
You *s*, they are so fond o' their own voices   „   II i 382
I will not brook to *s* Three upon two.   „   II i 423
S whether there be more of 'em in the wood.   ,   II i 430
Thou wilt not *s* My Marian more.   „   II i 455
S, thou hast wrong'd my brother and myself.   „   II i 665
S then, I kneel once more to be forgiven.   „   II i 667
Thou *s* me clasp and kiss a man indeed,   „   II ii 76
that he may *s* The fashion of it.   „   IV 253
left mine horse and armour with a Squire, And I must *s* to 'em.   „   IV 416
You *s* he is past himself.   What would you more ?   .,   IV 471
S you not They are jesting at us yonder,   „   IV 675
S thou thwart me not, thou fool !   „   IV 744

Seeäms (seems)   *S* I ommost knaws the back on 'im—   *Prom. of May* II 577

Seed (s)   'Martyr's blood'—*s* of the Church.'   *Queen Mary* IV i 146
sow'd therein The *s* of Hate, it blossom'd Charity.   „   IV i 172
The *s* thou sowest in my field is cursed,   *Harold* VI 70

Seed (saw)   I *s* that one cow 'o thine i' the pinfold   *Prom. of May* I 190
I *s* tha a-limpin' up just now wi' the roomatics i' the knee.   „   I 384
I *s* how the owd man wur vext.   „   II 27
I knaw'd 'im when I *s* 'im ageän   „   III 121

Seed (seen)   Noä, Miss.   I ha'n't *s* 'er neither.   „   I 48

Seeing (part.)   *s* that our gracious Virgin Queen hath—   *Queen Mary* I iii 23
if he jeer not *s* the true man Behind his folly,   „   II ii 400
S there lie two ways to every end,   „   IV ii 113
s now The poor so many, and all food so dear.   „   IV iii 208
And, *s* in a moment, I shall find Heaven   „   IV iii 223
religious fool, Who, *s* war in heaven,   *Harold* I i 140
and *s* the hospitable lights in your castle,   *Foresters* I ii 194

Seeing (s)   Grew ever high and higher, beyond my *s*,   *Harold* III i 149
and rooted in far isles Beyond my *s* :   „   I 154
keep us From *s* all too near that urn,   *The Cup* I iii 133

Seek   *S* In that lone house, to practise on my life,   *Queen Mary* I v 283
You play at hide and *s*.   „   I v 305
We but *s* Some settled ground for peace   „   I v 314
S to possess our person, 'hold our Tower,   „   II ii 158
s's To bend the laws to his own will,   „   II ii 183
Or *s* to rescue me.   I thank the Council.   „   IV ii 38
I am not vext,—Altho' ye *s* to vex me,   *Harold* I i 405
wherefore should she *s* The life of Rosamund de Clifford   *Becket, Pro.* 69
where to *s* ?   I have been about the city.   „   I i 397
when they *s* to overturn our rights,   „   V ii 456
They *s*—you make—occasion for your death.   „   V ii 558
I am he ye *s*.   What would ye have of me ?   „   V iii 115
S not for me, or you may find me at the bottom of the river.—   *Prom. of May* II 87

Seek (*continued*)   why did you write ' *S* me at the bottom of the river ' ?   *Prom. of May* III 363
Because we *s* to curb their viciousness.   *Foresters* III 393

Seeking   By *s* justice at a stranger's hand   *Queen Mary* IV i 20
I am *s* one who wedded me in secret.   *Harold* V ii 29
I tell thee, girl, I am *s* my dead Harold.   „   V i 43
pale beggar-woman *s* alms For her sick son,   *The Falcon* 852

Seem (*See also* **Seeäms**)   it *s*'s that we shall fly These bald, blank fields,   *Queen Mary* III v 250
even now You *s* the least assassin of the four.   *Becket* V ii 522

Seem'd   *S* thro' that dim dilated world of hers,   *Queen Mary* II ii 324
s to smile And sparkle like our fortune   „   II iii 22
S as a happy miracle to make glide—   „   III ii 29
it *s* to me but just The Church should pay   *Becket* I i 33
It *s* to me that we were parted for ever.   *Prom. of May* I 769
It *s* so ; only there was left A second daughter,   „   III 770

Seeming   *s* not as brethren, But mortal foes !   *Queen Mary* IV iii 184
As *s* his, not mine, and fall abroad.   *Becket, Pro.* 228

Seen (*See also* **Seed**)   I have *s* enough for this day.   *Queen Mary* I i 130
should already have *s* your steps a mile   „   I ii 80
do not you Be *s* in corners with my Lord of Devon,   „   I iv 154
and yet, methinks, I have *s* goodlier.   „   I v 7
Have you *s* Philip ever ?   *Noailles.*   Only once.   „   I v 319
I have *s* them in their own land ;   „   II 167
I have never *s* her So queenly or so goodly.   „   II ii 326
flask of wine Beside me, than have *s* it : yet I saw it.   „   III i 48
track of the true faith Your lapses are far *s*.   „   III iv 95
I have *s* A pine in Italy that cast its shadow   „   III iv 135
when she once more is *s* White as the light,   „   III iv 198
Brief-sighted tho' they be, I have *s* them,   „   III vi 158
never *s* That any one recanting thus at full,   „   IV i 58
It will be *s* now, then.   „   IV i 62
Have I not *s* the gamekeeper, the groom,   „   IV iii 371
I have *s* heretics of the poorer sort,   „   IV iii 436
old age that never will be mine Is all the clearer *s*.   „   V ii 236
s the true men of Christ lying famine-dead by scores,   „   V iv 37
Thou hast but *s* how Norman hands can strike,   *Harold* II ii 171
I dare not well be *s* in talk with thee.   „   II ii 481
Edward wakes !—Dazed—he hath *s* a vision.   „   III i 131
hath talk'd with God, and *s* A shadowing horror ;   „   III i 356
Nor *s*, nor heard ; thine,   „   V i 161
I have *s* The trenches dug, the palisades uprear'd   „   V i 188
No footfall—no Fitzurse.   We have *s* her home.   *Becket* I i 367
The world had never *s* the like before.   „   II ii 125
and I ha' *s* what I ha' *s*,   *Becket* III i 109, 143, 151
and to be sure I ha' *s* great ones to-day—   *Becket* III i 136
and I ha' *s* the King once at Oxford,   „   III i 163
she had *s* the Archbishop once, So mild, so kind.   „   V iii 118
S by the Church in Heaven, the Church on earth—   „   V iii 98
S in the thicket at the bottom there   *The Cup* I i 113
—all *s*,—all calculated, All known by Rome.   „   II 255
It may be I had never *s* the wars.   *The Falcon* 379
I have *s* it like the snow on the moraine.   „   505
and *s* the red of the battle-field,   „   548
I haven't *s* Eva yet.   Is she anywhere in the garden ?   *Prom. of May* I 46
I can't tell, for I have never *s* him.   „   I 115
She would have *s* at once into my trouble,   „   I 553
if you Had *s* us that wild morning when we found   „   II 469
—had you been one of us And *s* all this,   „   II 484
I have *s* the world—And cheer his blindness   „   II 513
since then, no one has *s* you but myself.   „   III 228
I have *s* thee clasp and kiss a man indeed,   *Foresters* IV 1035

See-saw   The miserable *s*-*s* of our child-world,   *Queen Mary* IV iii 385

Seest   when thou *s* him next, Commend me to thy friend.   *Becket* I i 323
Thou *s*, Sir Knight, our friar is so holy   *Foresters* IV 279

Seethed   She *s* with such adulteries,   *Queen Mary* III iv 189

Seize   that anyone Should *s* our person,   „   II 178
To *s* upon the forts and fleet,   „   III i 464
S him and burn him for a Lutheran.   „   IV 245
Stumble not in the darkness, Lest they should *s* thee.   *Becket* V iii 80
We shall be overwhelm'd.   *S* him and carry him !   „   V iii 141
I give you here an order To *s* upon him.   *The Cup* I i 165
' You are to *s* on Sinnatus,—if——'   „   I ii 228

Seize (*continued*) to *s* On whomsover may be talking with
you,   *The Cup* I iii 6
For *my* sake—or they *s* on thee.   „   I iii 113
Why come we now ? Whom shall we *s* upon ?   „   I iii 178
S on the knight ? wrench his sword from him !   *Foresters* II i 676
S him and truss him up, and carry her off.   „   IV 690
S her and carry her off into my castle.   „   IV 738
Seized   may not be *s* With some fierce passion,   *Prom. of May* III 335
he hath *s* On half the royal castles.   *Foresters* I iii 82
Self   The Queen stands up, and speaks for her own *s*;   *Queen Mary* II ii 342
his fault So thoroughly to believe in his own *s*.   „   II ii 386
Yet thoroughly to believe in one's own *s*, So one's
own *s* be thorough,   „   II ii 388
the Pope's Holiness By mine own *s*.   „   III ii 112
As well for our own *selves* as all the realm,   „   III iii 136
and not sure Of their own *selves*, they are wroth
with their own *selves*,   „   III iv 120
Bonner cannot out-Bonner his own *s*—   „   III vi 27
By mine own *s*—by mine own hand !   „   IV ii 202
and mine own *s* and all the world.   „   v ii 12
but I speak from mine own *s*, not him ;   „   v iii 42
—yea and mine own *s*.   *Harold* II ii 784
Tho' somewhat less a king to my true *s*   „   III ii 53
where mine own *s* Takes part against myself !   „   v i 299
what shall I call it, affect her thine own *s*.   *Becket*, Pro. 513
Look to it, your own *selves* !   „   I iii 398
Strong—not in mine own *s*, but Heaven ;   „   I iii 537
Who stands aghast at her eternal *s*   „   II ii 404
on mine own *s* The King had had no power   „   II ii 411
kingly promise given To our own *s* of pardon,   „   II ii 433
' great honour,' says he, ' from the King's *s* to the
King's son.'   „   III iii 145
I am mine own *s* Of and belonging to the King.   „   IV ii 29
I'll swear to mine own *s* it was a feint.   „   IV ii 401
The soldier, when he lets his whole *s* go Lost in the
common good, the common wrong, Strikes truest
ev'n for his own *s*.   „   v ii 39
Then speak ; this is my other *s*,   „   v ii 74
as beautiful this morning as the very Madonna her
own *s*—   *The Falcon* 199
And this last costly gift to mine own *s*,   „   228
Vice and Virtue Are but two masks of *s* ;   *Prom. of May* I 538
I have found it once again In your own *s*.   „   II 377
—so be more at peace With mine own *s*.   „   II 663
till we be only bones our own *selves*.   *Foresters* I i 26
I remain Mistress of mine own *s* and mine own soul.   „   IV 729
Self-assertion   than to stand On naked *s-a*.   *Queen Mary* IV i 120
Self-blotted   he is effaced, *S-b* out ;   „   IV i 138
Self-disdain   for a spark Of *s-d* born in me when I sware   *Harold* v i 302
Self-exposure   Why will you court it By *s-e* ?   *Becket* I i 282
Self-lauding   Without too large *s-l* I must hold   *Harold* IV iii 87
Selfless   The simple, silent, *s* man Is worth a world of
tonguesters.   „   v i 81
Self-murder   lying were *s-m* by that state   „   III i 70
Self-passion   drown all poor *s-p* in the sense Of public
good ?   *The Cup* II 101
Self-stock   Of one *s-s* at first, Make them again   *Harold* v ii 186
Self-uncertain   and yet We are *s-u* creatures,   *Becket* v ii 48
Sell   *s* not thou Our living passion for a dead man's dream;   *Harold* III ii 58
keep it, or you *s* me To torment and to death.   *The Cup* I i 214
We shall have to *s* all the land,   *Prom. of May* III 164
And so wouldst *s* thy sister to the Sheriff,   *Foresters* I 536
' *S* all thou hast and give it to the poor ; '   „   III 169
S me again perchance for twice as much.   „   v 654
Seller   but I bound the *s* To silence,   *The Falcon* 73
Semi-barbarous   altho' the inhabitants Seem *s-b*.   *Prom. of May* II 542
Semi-madman   known a *s-m* in my time So fancy-ridd'n)   *Queen Mary* II 9
Senate   Our *S*, wearied of their tetrarchies,   *The Cup* I i 89
What filthy tools our *S* works with !   „   I i 156
Save for some slight report in her own *S*   „   I i 134
Roman *S*, For I have always play'd into their hands,   „   I iii 149
tell the *S* I have been most true to Rome—   „   II 482
Send   God *s* her well ; Here comes her Royal Grace.   *Queen Mary* II i 125
s's His careful dog to bring them to the fold.   „   III iv 104
S out : let England as of old Rise lionlike,   „   v ii 265

Send (*continued*)   *S* out, *s* out, and make Musters in
all the counties ;   *Queen Mary* v ii 270
S out ; I am too weak to stir abroad :   „   v ii 286
he *s*'s his veriest love, And says, he will come quickly.   „   v ii 563
and to *s* us again, according to His promise,   „   v iv 52
s thee back among thine island mists With laughter.   *Harold* II ii 181
s her hosts Of injured Saints to scatter sparks   „   II ii 743
and *s* thy saints that I may say Ev'n to their faces,   „   II ii 785
And *s* the shatter'd North again to sea,   „   IV iii 140
I *s* my voice across the narrow seas—   „   v i 246
The Norman *s*'s his arrows up to Heaven,   „   v i 666
I *s* thee as a common friend To tell the King,   *Becket* I i 341
S the Great Seal by daybreak.   „   I i 405
S for him back.   „   I iii 334
he *s*'s me to bid you this night pray for him   „   I iv 265
can I *s* her hence Without his kingly leave ?   „   III ii 218
And *s* thee back again to Canterbury ?   „   III iii 184
S back again those exiles of my kin   „   III iii 186
Have I not promised, man, to *s* them back ?   „   III iii 191
She *s*'s it back, as being dead to earth,   „   v i 170
and *s* Her whole heart's heat into it,   „   v ii 254
s's you this cup rescued from the burning   *The Cup* I i 41
I *s* it to the wife of Sinnatus,   „   I i 72
—*s*'s you this cup—the cup we use in our marriages—   „   I ii 72
He *s*'s you This diadem of the first Galatian Queen,   „   II 131
and *s* him forth The glory of his father—   „   II 261
in hope that the saints would *s* us this blessed morning ;   *The Falcon* 186
I might *s* you down a flask or two   „   584
if the farming-men be come for their wages, to *s*
them up to me.   *Prom. of May* III 16
Sending   Lord Howard, *S* an insolent shot that dash'd   *Queen Mary* v i 57
Thy *s* back the Great Seal madden'd him,   *Becket* I iii 9
Seneschal   and confer with my ladyship's *s*,   *The Falcon* 416
Senlac (*adj.*)   signs on earth ! Knowest thou *S* hill ?   *Harold* III i 361
tell him we stand arm'd on *S* Hill,   „   v i 59
To tell thee thou shalt die on *S* hill—   „   v i 241
Senlac (*s*)   over nameless graves— *Harold*. At *S* ?   *Aldred*. *S*.   „   III i 383
S ! Sanguelac, The Lake of Blood !   „   III i 385
And see thee safe from *S*.   „   v i 457
Sens (a French town)   Return to *S*, where we will care for
you.   *Becket* II ii 444
Sensation   all but proving man An automatic series
of *s*'s,   *Prom. of May* I 226
What can a man, then, live for but *s*'s,   „   I 242
if man be only A willy-nilly current of *s*'s—   „   I 263
Sense   thro' his dying *s* Shrills ' lost thro' thee.'   *Harold* III i 34
Which in your *s* is treason.   *The Cup* I i 79
for the *s*'s, love, are for the world ; That for the *s*'s.   *Prom. of May* I 580
Sensual   and sat Thro' every *s* course of that full feast   „   II 254
Sent   I stood out, till Edward *s* for me.   *Queen Mary* I ii 29
hath *s* for the holy legate of the holy father   „   I iii 26
God hath *s* me here To take such order   „   I v 33
You have *s* her from the court,   „   I v 462
S out my letters, call'd my friends together,   „   I v 552
S Cornwallis and Hastings to the traitor,   „   II ii 31
And fearing for her, *s* a secret missive,   „   II ii 121
But we *s* divers of our Council to them,   „   II ii 152
s his myriads hither To seize upon the forts   „   III i 463
which the emperor *s* us Were mainly Gardiner's :   „   III iii 70
s here as Legate From our most Holy Father   „   III iii 124
You were *s* for, You were appeal'd to,   „   III iv 255
I am *s* to fetch you.   „   III iv 393
So they have *s* poor Courtenay over sea.   „   III v 1
But held from you all papers *s* by Rome,   „   v ii 45
And how should he have *s* me Legatic hither,   „   v ii 87
this young Earl was *s* on foreign travel,   „   v ii 489
and have *s* him back A holy gonfanon,   *Harold* III ii 146
And Edward would have *s* a host against you,   „   IV i 99
Since Griffyth's head was *s* To Edward,   „   IV i 221
Have thy two brethren *s* their forces in ?   „   v i 342
arrow which the Saints Sharpen'd and *s* against him—   „   v i 169
Let the Great Seal be *s* Back to the King to-morrow.   *Becket* I i 375
s his folk, His kin, all his belongings,   „   II i 69
priest whom John of Salisbury trusted Hath *s* another.   „   III i 71

Sent (*continued*)   I *s* this Margery, and she comes not back;

    I *s* another, and she comes not back.   *Becket* IV ii 3

    A strange gift *s* to me to-day.   *The Cup* I ii 52

    know myself am that Galatian Who *s* the cup.   ,,   I ii 210

    The Romans *s* me here a spy upon you,   ,,   I ii 220

    I might have *s* him prisoner to Rome.   ,,   II 418

    and he *s* me wi' the gig to Littlechester to fetch 'er;   *Prom. of May* I 19

    cotched 'im once a-steälin' coäls an' I *s* fur 'im,   ,,   I 413

    and he *s* 'im awaäy to t'other end o' the field;   ,,   II 153

    but he *s* me an alphabetical list of those that remain,   ,,   III 28

    What hasta *s* fur me, then, fur?   ,,   III 435

    I have *s* to the Abbot and justiciary   *Foresters* IV 87

    I had despair'd of thee—that *s* me crazed,   ,,   IV 1022

Sentence   The *s* having past upon them all,   *Queen Mary* IV v 487

    Hear first thy *s*!   *Becket* I iii 670

Sequatur   Illorum scelera Pœna *s*! (*repeat*)   *Harold* v i 518, 605

Sequel   The *s* had been other than his league With Norway,   ,,   IV iii 88

Seraph   If a *s* shouted from the sun,   *Becket* I iii 311

Serf   All those poor *s*'s whom we have served will bless us,   *Foresters* IV 1074

Series   all but proving man An automatic *s* of sensations,   *Prom. of May* I 226

Serious   Stafford, I am a sad man and a *s*.   *Queen Mary* III i 42

Serjeant   *See* **Drill-serjeant**

Serpent   *s* that hath slough'd will slough again.   *Queen Mary* III iii 18

    Tut, then we all are *s*'s.   ,,   III iii 21

    Let her eat it like the *s*,   *Becket*, *Pro.* 533

    s that had crept into the garden And coil'd himself   *Foresters* II i 136

Servant   these old-world *s*'s Are all but flesh and blood   *The Falcon* 708

Serve   (*See also* **Sarve**)   it *s*'s to fan A kindled fire.   *Queen Mary* I v 620

    make Those that we come to *s* our sharpest foes?   ,,   II iii 77

    S God and both your Majesties.   ,,   III iii 159

    Yet to save Cranmer were to *s* the Church,   ,,   IV i 136

    but I am not sure She will not *s* me better—   ,,   v i 250

    May *s* to charm the tiger out of him.   *Harold* I i 153

    thunder moulded in high heaven To *s* the Norman purpose,   ..   II ii 34

    Let Harold *s* for Tostig!   Queen.   Harold served Tostig so ill, he cannot *s* for Tostig!   ,,   III i 160

    sight of Danish blood Might *s* an end not English—   ,,   IV iii 98

    my foundation For men who *s* the neighbour,   ,,   v i 98

    to the statesman Who *s*'s and loves his king,   *Becket*, *Pro.* 78

    I am his no more, and I must *s* the Church.   ,,   i 145

    S my best friend and make him my worst foe;   ,,   I iii 567

    Then there isn't a goodly wench to *s* him with it: ,,   I iv 159

    tongue lick him whole again To *s* your will?   ,,   II ii 26

    wriggle out of them like an eel When the time *s*'s.   ,,   II ii 188

    we make the time, we keep the time, ay, and we *s* the time;   ,,   II ii 368

    Well—I shall *s* Galatia taking it,   *The Cup* I i 100

    S by force?   No force Could make me *s* by force.   ,,   I ii 79

    Then that I *s* with Rome to *s* Galatia.   ,,   I ii 212

    my serving Rome To *s* Galatia.   ,,   I ii 279

    I am much malign'd.   I thought to *s* Galatia.   *Sinnatus.*

    S thyself first, villain!   They shall not harm   ,,   I ii 324

    Well used, they *s* us well.   ,,   I iii 136

    one piece of earthenware to *s* the salad in to my lady,   *The Falcon* 481

    servants Are all but flesh and blood with those they *s*.   ,,   710

    I ha' served the King living, says she, and let me *s* him dead,   *Foresters* II i 311

    and *s* King Richard save thou be A traitor or a goose?   ,,   IV 351

Served   (*See also* **Sarved**, **Well-served**)   I hoped I had *s* God with all my might!   *Queen Mary* v ii 296

    if you be fairly *s*, And lodged, and treated.   ,,   v iii 21

    For I have *s* thee long and honestly.   *Harold* I i 214

    Harold *s* Tostig so ill, he cannot serve for Tostig!   ,,   III i 161

    No, no, but Harold.   I love him: he hath *s* me.   ,,   III i 242

    I *s* our Theobald well when I was with him;   *Becket* I i 142

    I *s* King Henry well as Chancellor;   ,,   I ii 30

    in your chancellorship you *s* The follies of the King.   ,,   II ii 460

    Thou hast *s* me heretofore with Rome—

    Heaven be *s* Tho' earth's last earthquake   ,,   v iii 40

    It *s* me for a blessed rosary.   *The Falcon* 632

    Hath *s* me better than her living—   ,,   901

    I ha' *s* the King living, says she, and let me serve him dead,   *Foresters* II i 310

    those poor serfs whom we have *s* will bless us,   ,,   IV 1075

Service   (I have a daughter in her *s* who reported it)   *Queen Mary* I i 76

    This chains me to your *s*,   ,,   I v 537

    Twelve years of *s*!   *Harold* I i 221

    My lord, permit us then to leave thy *s*.   *Becket* I iv 10

    told me he would advance me to the *s* of a great lady,   ,,   III i 123

    which our loyal *s*, And since we likewise   ,,   v i 53

    For all his faithful *s*'s to Rome.   *The Cup* II 65

    then there is anything in your lordship's larder at your lordship's *s*,   *The Falcon* 138

    cold-manner'd friend may strangely do us The truest *s*,   ,,   644

    I sank so low that I went into *s*—   *Prom. of May* III 392

    wasted his revenues in the *s* of our good king Richard   *Foresters* I i 193

    All thanks for all your *s*;   ,,   I iii 165

    Do me the *s* to tap it, and thou wilt know.   ,,   III 333

    I would tap myself in thy *s*, Robin.   ,,   III 336

    And both at thy *s*, Robin.   ,,   III 339

Serviceable   so she be *s* In all obedience,   *Harold* III i 291

Serving (adj. and part.)   We be more like scarecrows in a field than decent *s* men;   *Foresters* I i 35

    'A GALATIAN *s* BY FORCE IN THE ROMAN LEGION.'   *The Cup* I i 47

    'A GALATIAN *s* BY FORCE IN THE ROMAN LEGION.'

    S by force!   ,,   I i 75

Serving (s)   my *s* Rome To serve Galatia: ,,   I ii 277

Servitor   King would act *s* and hand a dish to his son;   *Becket* III iii 139

Session   Your Council is in *S*, please your Majesty.   *Queen Mary* I v 543

Set (s)   I know a *s* of exiles over there,   ,,   III i 155

Set (sit)   they wunt *s* i' the Lord's cheer o' that daay.   ,,   IV iii 470

Set (verb)   was a wheedling monk *S* up the mass.   ,,   I ii 91

    s yourselves by hundreds against one?   ,,   I iii 72

    Yearns to *s* foot upon your island shore.   ,,   I v 367

    s it round with gold, with pearl, with diamond.   ,,   I v 375

    I'll have my head *s* higher in the state;   ,,   II i 250

    Few things have fail'd to which I *s* my will.   ,,   II ii 22

    s no foot theretoward unadvised Of all our Privy Council;   ,,   II ii 204

    I am not so *s* on wedlock as to choose   ,,   II ii 214

    I must *s* The guard at Ludgate.   ,,   II ii 408

    you'll *s* the Divil's Tower a-spitting,   ,,   II iii 102

    cry To have the gates *s* wide again,   ,,   II iv 65

    They are the flower of England; *s* the gates wide.   ,,   II iv 70

    S up a viceroy, sent his myriads hither To seize   ,,   II iv 463

    So to *s* forth this humble suit of ours   ,,   III iii 145

    Like dogs that *s* to watch their master's gate,   ,,   III iv 309

    Would fain *s* forth some saying that may live   ,,   IV iii 158

    For there be writings I have *s* abroad   ,,   IV iii 240

    Crying, 'Forward!'—*s* our old church rocking,   ,,   IV iii 403

    s up your broken images; Be comfortable to me.   ,,   v ii 300

    and *s* up The Holy office here—   ,,   v v 112

    thy leave to *s* my feet On board,   *Harold* I i 228

    a sun *s* But leaving light enough for Alfgar's house   ,,   I i 306

    and *s* her up again, till now,   ,,   II i 50

    And over thee the suns arise and *s*,   ,,   II ii 433

    sunder'd tree again, and *s* it Straight on the trunk,   ,,   III i 145

    S forth our golden Dragon,   ,,   IV 245

    shall cross the seas To *s* the Pope against me—   *Becket*, *Pro.* 36

    will *s* it trembling Only to base it deeper.   ,,   *Pro.* 208

    To *s* that precious jewel, Roger of York.   ,,   *Pro.* 270

    True enough, my mind was *s* upon other matters.   ,,   *Pro.* 318

    Has my simple song *s* you jingling?   ,,   *Pro.* 378

    He took his mitre off, and *s* it on me,   ,,   I i 63

    S all on fire against him!   ,,   I ii 89

    Strike, and ye *s* these customs by my death   ,,   I iii 170

    Fight for the Church, and *s* the Church against me!   Herbert.   To be honest is to *s* all knaves against thee.   ,,   I iii 569

    s the Church This day between the hammer and the anvil—   ,,   I iii 584

    Poor beast! poor beast! *s* him down.   ,,   I iv 106

    Lord hath *s* his mark upon him that no man should murder him.   ,,   I iv 192

    I brought them In from the wood, and *s* them here.   ,,   II i 131

    and *s*'s the church-tower over there all a-hell-fire as it were?   ,,   III iii 51

    Give me the poison; *s* me free of him!   ,,   IV ii 164

Set (verb) (*continued*) To *s* them straight again. | *Becket* v ii 459
Not *s* myself abroach And run my mind | *The Cup* I ii 106
Would *s* him in the front rank of the fight | ,, I ii 153
And that *s*'s her against me—for the moment. | ,, I iii 163
tho' Rome may *s* A free foot where she will, | ,, II 245
it is thou Hath *s* me this hard task, | *The Falcon* 237
S, as you say, so lightly on her head, | ,, 535
I had but emptiness to *s* before you, | ,, 870
But now you will *s* all right again, | *Prom. of May* I 718
she *s* the bush by my dairy winder afoor | ,, II 18
Come, you will *s* all right again, | ,, II 658
I be afeard I shall *s* him a-sweäring like onythink. | ,, III 359
I would *s* my men-at-arms to oppose thee, like the Lord of the Castle. | *Foresters* I i 322
whenever I *s* my own foot on it I say to it, | ,, I i 334
mantle of the cloud, And *s*'s, a naked ûre. | ,, II i 29
a price is *s* On this poor head; | ,, II i 73
Well, *s* them forth. I could eat anything. | ,, II i 273
you are sturdy rogues that should be *s* to work. | ,, III 197
See that men be *s* Along the glades | ,, III 456

Set *See* **High-set**

Setting slander'd you For *s* up a mass at Canterbury | ,, I ii 88
gave me this morning on my *s* forth. | *Foresters* III 282

Settle now would *s* Upon this flower, | *Queen Mary* I v 55
in the eternal distance To *s* on the Truth. | *Harold* III ii 103

Settled We but seek Some *s* ground for peace to stand upon. | *Queen Mary* I v 315
pass Into more *s* hatred of the doctrines Of those who rule, | ,, III iv 159
but you will stay your going Somewhat beyond your *s* purpose? | ,, v i 207

Seven (*See also* **Twenty-seven**) Some six or *s* Bishops, diamonds, pearls, | ,, III i 52
Not for the *s* devils to enter in? | ,, III ii 140
The *s* sleepers in the cave at Ephesus Have turn'd from right to left. | *Harold* I i 192
S feet of English land, or something more, Seeing he is a giant. | ,, IV ii 54
'*S* feet of English earth, or something more, Seeing he is a giant!' | ,, IV iii 112
My lord, the King demands *s* hundred marks, | *Becket* I iii 634
I led *s* hundred knights and fought his wars. | ,, I iii 638
Forgive him seventy times and *s*; | *Prom. of May* III 9

Seven-fold weak and meek old man, *S-f* dishonour'd | *Queen Mary* v 133
Seventeen *S*—and knew eight languages— | ,, III i 358
s—a rose of grace! | ,, III i 371
Seventh Lo! there once more—this is the *s* night! | *Harold* I i 2
only she kept the *s* commandment better than some I know on, | *Becket* III i 194
Seventy Forgive him *s* times and seven; | *Prom. of May* III 9
Seven-years' My *s-y* friend was with me, my young boy; | *Queen Mary* III iii 47
Several In *s* bills and declarations, Madam, | ,, IV i 48
Sever'd long divided in itself, and *s* from the faith, | ,, I iii 21
My arm is *s*. I can no more— | *Becket* v ii 188
Severeness An overmuch *s*, I repeat, | *Queen Mary* III iv 156
Sew these poor hands but *s*, Spin, broider— | *Harold* IV iii 10
Sewer (sure) Ay, to be *s*! Be thou? | *Prom. of May* I 3
but *s* I be, they be two o' the purtiest gels ye can see of a summer murnin'. | ,, I 29
and I feel *s*, Miss Dora, that I ha' been noän too sudden wi' you, | ,, II 59
I be Farmer Dobson, *s* anew; | ,, II 136
I beänt sa *s* o' that, fur Sally knaw'd im; Now then? | ,, III 146
Sewer In breathless dungeons over steaming *s*'s, | *Queen Mary* IV iii 441
Sewn if I hadn't a sprig o' wickentree *s* into my dress, | *Foresters* II i 250
Shaäky (shaky) The weather's well anew, but the glass be a bit *s*. | *Prom. of May* II 52
Shaämed (ashamed) Then the owd man i' Lear should be *s* of hissen, | ,, I 267
Shackle The *s*'s that will bind me to the wall. | *Harold* II ii 410
Shadder (shadow) then back ageän, a-follering my oän *s*— | *Prom. of May* I 372
Shade moon Divides the whole long street with light and *s*. | *Becket* I i 366

Shadow (*See also* **Shadder**) Is to be love-sick for a *s*. | *Queen Mary* I v 535
pine in Italy that cast its *s* Athwart a cataract; firm stood the pine—The cataract shook the *s*. | ,, III iv 136
It was the *s* of the Church that trembled; Your church was but the *s* of a church, | ,, III iv 144
And how her *s* crosses one by one | ,, v v 7
a Tudor School'd by the *s* of death— | ,, v v 226
s's of a hundred fat dead deer For dead men's ghosts. | *Harold* I ii 103
dog that snapt the *s*, dropt the bone.— | ,, I ii 188
be as the *s* of a cloud Crossing your light. | ,, II ii 177
That lies within the *s* of the chance. | ,, II ii 463
And dreadful *s*'s strove upon the hill, | ,, III i 377
And on it falls the *s* of the priest; | ,, III ii 70
Yet if a fear, Or *s* of a fear, | ,, v 115
Surely too young Even for this *s* of a crown; | *Becket, Pro.* 231
That were but as the *s* of an assent. | ,, III iii 195
cloud that hath come over the sun and cast us all into *s*? | ,, III iii 47
Your *s*. Synorix— | *The Cup* I ii 450
and enrich Earth with her *s*! | ,, I iii 60
Tell him there is one *s* among the *s*'s, | ,, II 139
Beneath the *s* of our pines and planes! | ,, II 227
We lie too deep down in the *s* here. | *The Falcon* 581
but they, the *s*'s of ourselves, Have past for ever. | *Prom. of May* I 271
would she moved beside me like my *s*! | *Foresters* II i 165
O look! before the *s* of these dark oaks | ,, II i 604
A *s*, a poetical fiction— | ,, IV 219
Shadowing hath talk'd with God, and seen A *s* horror; | *Harold* I i 357
And *s* of this double thunder-cloud | ,, III ii 159
Shaft He drew this *s* against me to the head, | *Queen Mary* v 80
Parthian *s* of a forlorn Cupid at the King's left breast, | *Becket, Pro.* 339
Shake Our friends, the Normans, help to *s* his chair. | *Harold* I i 85
to *s* the North With earthquake and disruption— | ,, I ii 198
Come, Harold, *s* the cloud off! | ,, III i 73
that would *s* the Papacy as it stands. | *Becket* I iii 213
When what ye *s* at doth but seem to fly, | ,, I iii 743
s's at mortal kings—her vacillation, Avarice, craft— | ,, II ii 405
To *s* my throne, to push into my chamber— | ,, v i 249
That this brave heart of mine should *s* me so, | *The Cup* I iii 39
the very letters seem to *s* With cold, | *The Falcon* 448
I do not dare it, like an old friend, to *s* it. | *Prom. of May* II 527
Shaken When he hath *s* off the Emperor, | *Becket* I iii 244
dead Are *s* from their stillness in the grave | *Foresters* II i 46
Shaker A *s* and confounder of the realm; | *Queen Mary* IV iii 40
Shakest thou *s*! Here, here—a cup of wine— | *Foresters* I iii 88
Shaking (*See also* **A-shaäkin'**, **Head-shaking**) by thy wisdom Hast kept it firm from *s*; | *Becket, Pro.* 204
Shaky *See* **Shaäky**
Shallow There runs a *s* brook across our field For twenty miles, | *Queen Mary* v v 83
But thou hast drain'd them *s* by thy tolls, | *Harold* I i 319
Shambles-oak or the *s-o*, or a weasel-sucked egg, | *Foresters* IV 211
Shame (s) Nay, for bare *s* of inconstancy, | *Queen Mary* I iii 39
S, *s*, my masters! are you English-born, | ,, I iii 69
A gracious guard Truly; *s* on them! | ,, II iv 58
S upon you, Robin, *S* upon you now! | ,, v 85
And bring us all to *s*? | *Becket* I iii 38
S, wrath, I know not what. | ,, I iii 322
and the more *s* to him after his promise, | ,, I iii 130
Will feel no *s* to give themselves the lie. | '*The Cup* II 117
S on him that she took it at thy hands, | *The Falcon* 60
it's all you have left us. *S* on you! | ,, 163
S on her then! | ,, 206
I scarce believe it! *Elisabetta*. *S* upon her then! | ,, 518
I shall go mad for utter *s* and die. | *Prom. of May* I 682
Will he not fly from you if he learn the story of my *s* | ,, III 257
Five years of *s* and suffering broke the heart | ,, III 761
John—*S* on him!—Stole on her, | *Foresters* II i 111
S on thee, Little John, thou hast forgotten— | ,, III 237
Shame (verb) Nor *s* to call it nature. | *Queen Mary* v 77
no need For Philip so to *s* himself again. | ,, v ii 587
That would but *s* me, Rather than make me vain. | *Harold* I ii 116
thought that naked Truth would *s* the Devil | ,, II ii 118
I *s* to quote 'em—caught, my lord, | *Becket* I ii 7
Shamed (*See also* **Half-shamed**) make me *s* and tongue-tied in my love. | *Queen Mary* III ii 162

Shamed (*continued*) only *s* to the quick Before the king—   *Harold* IV i 7

s of his poor farmer's daughter among the ladies in his drawing-room?   *Prom. of May* III 294

S of me in a drawing-room! (repeat)   „ III 296, 306

Sooner or later *s* of her among The ladies,   „ III 581

But—*s* of you, my Empress!   „ III 599

S a too trustful widow whom you heard In her confession;   *Foresters* III 385

Shaming See **Solemn-shaming**

Shape (*s*) struck a *s* from out the vague,   *Becket* I iii 373

my sleeping-draught May bloat thy beauty out of *s*,   „ IV ii 170

What a *s*! what lovely arms!   *Foresters* I i 108

Shape Statesmen that are wise *S* a necessity,   *Queen Mary* III iii 33

stay Yet for awhile, to *s* and guide the event.   „ v 303

Love that can *s* or can shatter a life   *Becket* II i 11

Shaped See **Well-shaped**

Share Come, come! thou hadst thy *s* on her.   „ I iv 124

S and *s* alike!   *Harold* II i 64

Shared and *s* His fruits and milk. Liar!   *The Cup* I ii 427

Sharp stake and fire—*S* work and short.   *Queen Mary* III i 329

Here—give me one *s* pinch upon the cheek   *Foresters* IV 1011

Sharp-dividing battle-axe keen As thine own *s-d* justice,   *Harold* v 564

Sharpen'd Renard and the Chancellor *s* them.   *Queen Mary* III i 5

arrow which the Saints *S* and sent against him—   *Harold* v ii 169

Sharper A *s* harm to England and to Rome, Than Calais taken.   *Queen Mary* v ii 29

Sharpest Shall we make Those that we come to serve our *s* foes?   „ II iii 77

Shatter Will front their cry and *s* them into dust.   „ II iv 5

No Norman horse Can *s* England,   *Harold* IV i 196

Love that can shape or can *s* a life   *Becket* II i 11

God's full curse *S* you all to pieces   „ v iii 135

Shatter'd or whether England Be *s* into fragments.   *Harold* II ii 286

have we *s* back The hugest wave from Norseland   „ IV iii 60

And send the *s* North again to sea,   „ IV iii 140

Shaveling hear what the *s* has to say for himself.   *Queen Mary* I iii 17

—and that, turncoat *s*!   *Becket* I iii 737

Shaven beard, which he had never *s* Since Henry's death,   *Queen Mary* IV iii 593

Shawl Indian *s* That Philip brought me in our happy days!—   „ v ii 539

Sheath Take up your dagger; put it in the *s*.   *Becket* IV ii 294

whose whole life hath been folded like a blossom in the *s*,   *Foresters* I 206

Sheathe *s* your swords, ye will displease the King.   *Becket* I iii 178

Shed True tears that year were *s* for you in Florence.   *The Falcon* 384

Sheep *S* at the gap which Gardiner takes,   *Queen Mary* III iii 236

doth not kill The *s* that wander from his flock,   „ III iv 103

inherited loathing of these black *s* of the Papacy.   *Becket, Pro.* 461

But thou the shepherd hast betray'd the *s*,   „ I iii 525

Swine, *s*, ox—here's a French supper.   „ I iv 112

black *s* baaed to the miller's ewe-lamb,   „ I iv 162

Black *s*, quoth she, too black a sin for me. And what said the black *s*, my masters?   „ I iv 165

That he made the black *s* white.   „ I iv 176

Out from among us; thou art our black *s*.   „ I iv 181

S, said he? And *s* without the shepherd, too.   „ I iv 182

Smite the shepherd and the *s* are scattered. Smite the *s* and the shepherd will excommunicate thee.   „ I iv 227

that the *s* May feed in peace.   „ III iii 345

To find my stray *s* back within the fold.   „ III iii 355

Sheet And as for the flesh at table, a whole Peter's *s*,   „ III iii 129

Sheeted when all the *s* dead Are shaken from their stillness in the grave   *Foresters* II i 45

She-goat you had safelier have slain an archbishop than a *s-g*:   *Becket* III iii 69

Shelf *Shelves* and hooks, *shelves* and hooks, and when I see the *shelves*   *The Falcon* 119

Shell (*See also* **Cockle-shell**) she that has eaten the yolk is scarce like to swallow the *s*.   „ 705

woodland squirrel sees the nut Behind the *s*,   *Foresters* II i 648

I crawl'd like a sick crab from my old *s*,   „ IV 127

Shelter (*s*) The *s* of *your* roof—not for one moment—   *Prom. of May* III 800

Shelter (**verb**) We *s* you no more.   *Becket* II ii 249

I will *s* here.   *Foresters* II i 180

Shelter'd Ah! much heresy *S* in Calais.   *Queen Mary* v ii 299

He *s* in the Abbey of Pontigny.   *Becket* II i 84

I have *s* some that broke the forest laws.   *Foresters* I iii 69

Shepherd re-pulpited The *s* of St. Peter,   *Queen Mary* I v 182

the *s* doth not kill The sheep that wander   „ III iv 101

The Good *S*! Take this, and render that.   *Harold* III iii 169

But thou the *s* hast betray'd the sheep,   *Becket* I iii 524

And sheep without the *s*, too.   „ I iv 183

Smite the *s* and the sheep are scattered. Smite the sheep and the *s* will excommunicate thee.   „ I iv 226

the wolves of England Must murder her one *s*,   „ III iii 344

This mountain *s* never dream'd of Rome.   *The Cup* I ii 17

our carters and our *s*'s find a comfort there.   *Prom. of May* III 527

Harold. Carters and *s*'s!

Sheriff Thou knewest that the *S* of Nottingham loves thee. *Marian.* The *S* dare to love me?   *Foresters* I i 223

But then your *S*, your little man,   „ I i 231

our little *S* will ever swim with the stream!   „ I i 240

The *S* of Nottingham was there—not John.   „ I i 252

Beware of John and the *S* of Nottingham.   „ I i 255

What art thou, man? *S* of Nottingham?   „ I ii 190

S, thy friend, this monk, is but a statue.   „ I ii 233

How close the *S* peered into thine eyes!   „ I ii 253

Did he say so, the *S*?   „ I ii 267

I heard this *S* tell her he would pay   „ I iii 5

after some slight speech about the *S*   „ II i 115

the *S* Would pay this cursed mortgage to his brother   „ II i 143

Most honourable *S*!   „ II i 154

the *S*, and by heaven, Prince John himself   „ II i 173

the *S* had taken all our goods for the King without paying,   „ II i 190

since the *S* left me naught but an empty belly,   „ II i 278

when the *S* took my little horse for the King without paying for it—   „ II i 300

Missed! There goes another. Shoot, *S*!   „ II i 397

Strike *S*! Strike, mercenary!   „ II i 416

Prince John, the *S*, and a mercenary.   „ II i 445

The *S*—I am grieved it was the *S*;   „ II i 449

Rather than that would wed her with the *S*.   „ II i 525

And so wouldst sell thy sister to the *S*,   „ II i 537

That such a brother—*she* marry the *S*!   „ II i 551

In that great heat to wed her to the *S*,   „ II i 585

Thou shalt not marry The *S*, but abide with me   „ II i 602

Then you will wed the *S*?   „ III 11

And this rich *S* too has come between us;   „ IV 57

The *S*! This ring cries out against thee.   „ IV 68

What wilt thou do with the *S*?   „ IV 107

We told the Prince and the *S* of our coming.   „ IV 576

we will hang *thee*, prince or no prince, *s* or no *s*.   „ IV 584

The *S* the *S*, follow'd by Prince John   „ IV 587

But, Sir, the *S*— *Sir Richard*. Let me be, I say! The *S* will be welcome!   „ IV 600

And then the *S*! *Marian*. Ay, the *S*, father,   „ IV 650

I cannot love the *S*.   „ IV 662

S, Who thought to buy your marrying me   „ IV 717

S, thou wilt find me at Nottingham.   „ IV 801

No, let him be. *S* of Nottingham,   „ IV 815

Thou wouldst marry This *S* when King Richard came   „ IV 862

If you would marry me with a traitor *s*, I fear I might prove traitor with the *s*.   „ IV 871

Here Abbot, *S*—no—no, Robin Hood.   „ IV 989

Sheriffship True, for through John I had my *s*.   „ I ii 201

Sherwood (**adj.**) there is a lot of wild fellows in *S* Forest who hold by King Richard.   „ I ii 73

In *S* Forest. I have heard of them.   „ I iii 102

Sherwood (**s**) good fellows there in merry *S* That hold by Richard,   „ I iii 99

To make this *S* Eden o'er again,   „ II i 168

Tut! be there wolves in *S*?   „ II i 512

Robin king of *S*, And loves and dotes   „ IV 389

Robin, the lion of *S*—   „ IV 392

All the birds in merry *S* sing and sing him home again.   „ IV 1109

Shield (**adj.**) our *s* wall—Wall—break it not—break not—   *Harold* v i 232

Shield (**s**) Noble as his young person and old *s*.   *Queen Mary* v ii 513

No Norman horse Can shatter England, standing *s* by *s*;   *Harold* v i 196

Shield (s) (continued) bit his s, and dash'd it on the ground, *Harold* v i 405
make their wall of s's Firm as thy cliffs, „ v i 479
The horse and horseman cannot meet the s, „ v i 592
Hot-headed fools—to burst the wall of s's! „ v i 613
Under the s and safeguard of the Pope, *Becket* i iii 600
See there our s. *Prom. of May* iii 606
That I might breathe for a moment free of s *Foresters* iv 129
Shield-borne Their s-b patriot of the morning star *The Cup* ii 121
Shielded You are doubly fenced and s sitting here *Queen Mary* iii ii 104
And grateful to the hand that s him, *Harold* ii ii 586
Shield-wall Let kith and kin stand close as our s-w, „ i i 399
Heard how the s-w rang, „ iv iii 159
Shift (s) a s, a trick Whereby to challenge, *Becket* ii ii 163
Shift (verb) Will s the yoke and weight of all the world *Queen Mary* iv ii 212
the currents So s and change, „ iv iii 409
there is barely room to s thy side, *Harold* ii ii 441
The One Who s his policy suffers something, *The Cup* ii 113
Shifting for how their lances snap and shiver Against the s
blaze of Harold's axe! *Harold* v i 587
Shine so the beams of both may s upon us, *Queen Mary* iv i 20
dance into the sun That s's on princes, „ iii v 254
you want the sun That s's at court; „ iii v 277
I s! What else, Sir Count? „ v iii 16
Our day beside the Derwent will not s Less than a star *Harold* iv iii 50
Could s away the darkness of that gap *Becket* iii i 59
What are you crying for, when the sun s's? „ ii i 270
Who never deign'd to s into my palace. *The Falcon* 285
how the sun 'ud s, and the larks 'ud sing *Prom. of May* i 373
Shingle sea may roll Sand, s, shore-weed, *Harold* i ii 119
Shining *See* **Ever-shining**
Ship Spain in our s's, in our forts, *Queen Mary* ii i 179
Help the good s, showing the sunken rock, *Harold* ii ii 100
A thousand s's—a hundred thousand men— „ iv iii 194
lest ye should draw together like two s's in a calm. *Becket* iii iii 298
Shipt And see thee s, and pray in thy behalf *Harold* ii ii 197
Shipwreck A voice of s on a shoreless sea! *Queen Mary* v ii 384
stormless s in the pools Of sullen slumber, *Harold* v i 296
Shipwreckt that the s are accursed of God;— „ ii i 100
Shire is not the cause of a county or a s, *Queen Mary* ii i 162
Shirt I wear beneath my dress A s of mail: „ i v 146
Shiver lances snap and s Against the shifting *Harold* v i 586
Shoal (*See also* **Herring-shoal**) No, but a s of wives upon
the heath, „ v i 146
His Holiness cannot steer straight thro' s's, *Becket* ii ii 59
Shock No so dead, But that a s may rouse her. *Queen Mary* iii v 30
To find one s upon the field when all The harvest has
been carried. *The Falcon* 301
Shock'd Hath s me back into the daylight truth *Queen Mary* iii v 135
Shoe (s) She wore red s's! *Stafford.* Red s's! „ iii i 59
Shoe (verb) Blacksmith, thaw he niver s's a herse to
my likings; *Prom. of May* i 448
Shone I s from him, for him, his glory, his Reflection: *Becket* i iii 664
Shook The cataract s the shadow. *Queen Mary* iii iv 138
but Cranmer only s his head, „ iv iii 601
He s so that he scarce could out with it— *Harold* iii i 368
Who s the Norman scoundrels off the throne, „ iv i 81
He sued my hand. I s at him. *Becket* i i 273
So s within my hand, that the red wine *The Cup* ii 202
Shoot By the hard root, which s's again; *Becket* ii i 209
o'erleaps a jutting rock And s's three hundred feet. *The Cup* i i 111
and I'd like to s tha like a rabbit an' all. *Prom. of May* ii 740
I can s almost as closely with the bow *Foresters* i i 216
that s's New buds to heaven, „ i iii 25
there goes one in the moonlight. S! *Prince John.*
Missed! There goes another. S, Sheriff! „ ii i 395
an old woman can s closer than you two. *Prince
John.* S then, and if thou miss I will fasten thee „ ii i 400
Did I not tell you an old woman could s better? „ ii i 407
Shore (*See also* **Sea-shore**) Yearns to set foot upon
your island s. *Queen Mary* i v 367
your s's Wore in mine eyes the green of Paradise. „ iii 17
I dug mine into My old fast friend the s, *Harold* ii i 7
Wolf of the s! dog, with thy lying lights „ ii 21
To shove that stranded iceberg off our s's, „ iv iii 139
Till the sea wash her level with her s's, „ v i 331

MM

Shore (continued) like a barren s That grew salt weeds, *The Cup* ii 231
There—league on league of ever-shining s „ ii 534
Shoreless A voice of shipwreck on a s sea! *Queen Mary* v ii 384
Shore-swallow'd s-s, armour'd Normans up To fight *Harold* ii ii 57
Shore-weed sea may roll Sand, shingle, s-w, „ i ii 119
Shorn (*See also* **Smooth-shorn**) lest the crown should be
S of ancestral splendour. *Becket* i iii 157
Gave his s smile the lie. *Harold* ii ii 226
Short stake and fire—Sharp work and s. *Queen Mary* i i 329
Hast not thou drawn the s straw? *Becket* i iv 3
Daughter, my time is s, I shall not do it. „ v ii 157
Then with one quick s stab—eternal peace. *The Cup* i iii 124
Short-lived Our s-l sun, before his winter plunge, *Queen Mary* iii iii 85
Shot (s) practise on my life, By poison, fire, s, stab— „ i iv 285
insolent s that dash'd the seas Upon us, „ v i 57
Shot (verb) clash'd their bells, S off their lying cannon, „ iii vi 97
s out sidelong boughs across the deep *Harold* i i 150
not life s up in blood, But death drawn in;— *Becket* iv ii 380
I have s her thro' the heart. *Kate.* He lies, my lord.
I have s *him* thro' the heart. *Foresters* ii i 97
That I had s him thro' the heart, „ ii i 123
Turk s her as she was helping to build the mound „ ii i 308
Shou'der (shoulder) and doänt laäy my cartwhip athurt
'is s's, *Prom. of May* ii 138
Shoulder (*See also* **Shou'der**) If you can carry your
head upon your s's. *Wyatt.* I fear you come
to carry it off my s's, *Queen Mary* ii i 90
over his bow'd s Scowl'd that world-hated „ ii i 89
and brush This Wyatt from our s's, „ ii ii 294
That hovers round your s— „ v iii 52
and the weight of the church to boot on my s's, *Foresters* ii i 58
Shout (s) Came with a sudden splendour, s, and show, *Queen Mary* iii i 449
s of Synorix and Camma sitting Upon one throne, *The Cup* ii 146
But s and echo play'd into each other *Foresters* ii i 258
We be scared with song and s. „ ii ii 164
What s's are these that ring along the wood? „ iv 762
Shout (verb) S, knaves! *Queen Mary* i i 9
And get the swine to s Elizabeth. „ i iii 39
Who are those that s below there? „ ii i 149
Stand staring at me! s, you gaping rogue! „ iii i 288
There be both King and Queen, Philip and Mary. S! „ iii i 297
S, Mary and Philip! „ iii i 300
Thou hast shouted for thy pleasure, s for mine! „ iii i 304
They s as they would have her for a queen. *Harold* iv i 26
S's something—he points onward— „ v i 558
Shouted (*See also* **Holla'd**) I have, my Lord, s till I
am hoarse. *Gardiner.* What hast thou s,
knave? *Queen Mary* iii i 290
Thou hast s for thy pleasure, shout for mine! „ iii i 304
But s in Queen Mary. „ iii iv 46
If a seraph s from the sun, *Becket* i iii 311
Most like it was the Roman soldier s. *The Cup* ii 120
We s, and *they* s, as I thought, *Foresters* ii i 256
Shouting Then followed the thunder of the captains and
the s, *Becket* iii iii 113
Shove To s that stranded iceberg off our shores, *Harold* iv iii 138
Show (s) Came with a sudden splendour, shout, and s, *Queen Mary* iii i 450
To stand at ease, and stare as at a s, „ iv iii 292
and to read the faces of men at a great s. *Becket* iii ii 83
new-made children Of our imperial mother see the s. *The Cup* ii 165
Show (verb) S me your faces! *Queen Mary* i v 307
Philip s Some of the bearing of your blue blood— „ i v 433
So doubtless will ye s yourselves to me. „ ii ii 175
a jest In time of danger s's the pulses even. „ ii ii 357
I will s fire on my side— „ iii i 327
They s their teeth upon it; „ v i 299
Too small! a comet would not s for that! *Harold* i i 475
S him by whom he hath sworn. „ ii ii 732
mine own, a grief To s the scar for ever— *Becket* i i 178
hath he sign'd? s me the papers! „ i iii 317
And wake with it, and s it to all the Saints. „ ii ii 303
S me where thou camest out of the wood. „ iv i 45
May they not *say* you dared not s yourself „ v ii 595
If he should ever s his face among us, *Prom. of May* ii 423
I would like to s you, Mistress Kate, *Foresters* i i 49

Show (verb) (*continued*) a tenderness toward me, but is
  too shy to *s* it.   *Foresters* I i 116
  bounden by a vow not to *s* his face.   „   I ii 237
  S me some cave or cabin where I may rest.   „   II i 130
  if thou wilt *s* us the way back to Nottingham.   „   II i 360
  But to *s* thou art mortal.   „   II i 612
  And *s* thyself more of a man than me.   „   IV 285
Show'd *s* his back Before I read his face.   *Queen Mary* II i 131
  s her The weakness and the dissonance   *The Cup* I i 22
Shower *s*'s of blood are blown Before a never ending blast,   *Harold* III i 393
  storm and *s* lashing Her casement,   *Prom. of May* II 471
Showing Help the good ship, *s* the sunken rock,   *Harold* II i 100
Shown and brief patience, As I have *s* to-day.   *Queen Mary* III iv 415
  I have but *s* a loathing face to you,   „   III vi 113
  Than you have *s* to Cranmer.   „   IV i 190
  have *s* And redden'd with his people's blood   *Harold* I ii 242
  Thou still hast *s* thy primate, Gilbert Foliot.   *Becket* I iii 282
  You have *s* me that, though fortune had born
     you   *Prom. of May* II 119
Shrank you perforce again *S* into France.   *Becket* II ii 88
Shreds make Thy slender meal out of those scraps and *s*   *The Falcon* 147
Shrew Is broken ere it joins—a *s* to boot,   *Becket* V ii 207
Shrewd I find you a *s* bargainer.   *The Falcon* 757
  But you will find me a *s* bargainer still.   „   774
  And apt at arms and *s* in policy.   *Foresters* I ii 104
Shriek And *s* to all the saints among the stars: *Becket* IV ii 239
  Who *s*'s by day at what she does by night,   *Prom. of May* I 532
Shrill thro' his dying sense *S*'s 'lost thro'' thee.'   *Harold* III i 35
Shrilling She s 'Wyatt,' while the boy she held   *Queen Mary* II i 72
Shrine Saints, I have rebuilt Your *s*'s,   „   V ii 300
  as He dwells In statelier *s*'s.   *Harold* I i 168
  From all the holiest *s*'s in Normandy !   „   II ii 735
  and see beyond Your Norman *s*'s,   „   V i 620
  rescued from the burning of one of her *s*'s   *The Cup* I i 42
  cup saved from a blazing *s* Of our great Goddess,   „   I ii 55
  sacred *s* By chance was burnt along with it.   „   I ii 65
  take this holy cup To lodge it in the *s* of Artemis   „   I ii 435
  To lodge this cup Within the holy *s* of Artemis   „   I iii 53
  part to the *s* of our Lady.   *Foresters* III 207
  Our Lady's blessed *s*'s throughout the land   „   IV 1079
Shrink And when he flash'd it *S* from me,   *Becket* II i 277
Shrivell'd I, old *s* Stigand, I, Dry as an old wood-fungus on
  a dead tree,   *Harold* III i 7
Shroud But after they had stript him to his *s*,   *Queen Mary* IV iii 334
  I'll have it with me in my *s*,   *Becket* II i 302
Shudder causest the safe earth to *s* and gape,   *The Cup* II 298
  I mounted upon the parapet—— *Dora.* You
    make me *s* !   *Prom. of May* III 373
Shun Who is he? let me *s* him.   *Queen Mary* II ii 405
  and now but *s*'s The semblance of defeat;   *Becket* I iii 190
  s To meet her face to face at once !   *The Cup* I i 58
Shut shame on them ! they have *s* the gates !   *Queen Mary* II iv 58
  hath *s* the gates On friend and foe.   „   II iv 61
  One crater opens when another *s*'s.   „   III i 322
  Have *s* you from our counsels.   „   III iv 320
  hath the door *S* on him by the father whom he
    loved,   „   V ii 122
  She to *s* up my blossom in the dark !   *Harold* I ii 62
  to *s* in A happier dream.   „   I ii 126
  S the hall-doors.   *Becket* V ii 532
  S the doors ! We will not have him slain   „   V iii 53
  Was not the great gate *s* ?   „   V iii 138
Shut-up There were citizens Stood each before his
  s-u booth.   *Queen Mary* II ii 63
Shy You are *s* and proud like Englishmen,   „   II i 257
  a tenderness toward me, but is too *s* to show it.   *Foresters* I i 116
Sicily the Netherlands, *S*, Naples, Lombardy.   *Queen Mary* II i 212
  Granada, Naples, *S*, and Milan.   „   V i 44
Sick (*See also* **Fancy-sick, Heart-sick, Love-sick, Sea-**
  sick) sent a secret missive, Which told her to
  be *s*. Happily or not, It found her *s* indeed.   „   II ii 122
  We heard that you were *s* in Flanders, cousin.   „   III ii 33
  Tho' I be ever deadly *s* at sea. So *s* am I   „   III vi 88
  didst thou ever see a carrion crow Stand watching
  a *s* beast before he dies ?   „   IV iii 7

Sick (*continued*) Art thou *s*, good Earl? *Harold. S* as
  an autumn swallow for a voyage, *S* for an idle
  week of hawk and hound   *Harold* I i 100
  poor lad ! how *s* and sad for home !   „   II ii 325
  'Wulfnoth is *s*,' he said ; 'he cannot follow ;'   „   III i 84
  so if the city be *s*, and I cannot call the kennel sweet,   *Becket* II ii 348
  'The King is *s* and almost unto death.'   „   V ii 152
  I am not mad, not *s*, not old enough   *The Cup* I iii 69
  O my *s* boy ! My daily fading Florio,   *The Falcon* 235
  S ! is it so? why, when he came last year   „   311
  I give it my *s* son, and if you be Not quite recover'd of
    your wound,   „   589
  My one child Florio lying still so *s*,   „   678
  You know *s* people, More specially *s* children, have
    strange fancies,   „   816
  How often has my *s* boy yearn'd for this !   „   829
  more blessed were the rags Of some pale beggar-woman
    seeking alms For her *s* son,   „   854
  The *s* lady here might have been asleep.   *Prom. of May* III 343
  Mr. Dobson told me to saäy he's browt some of
    Miss Eva's roses for the *s* laädy to smell on.
    Dora. Take them, dear. Say that the *s* lady
    thanks him !   „   III 347
  Tell him I cannot leave the *s* lady just yet.   „   III 353
  And my *s* father here has come between us   *Foresters* IV 55
  Being so *s* How should he, Robin ?   „   IV 82
  at last I crawl'd like a *s* crab from my old shell,   „   IV 126
  Move me no more ! I am *s* and faint with pain !   „   IV 599
Sicken To *s* of his lilies and his roses.   *Queen Mary* I v 25
  lest living Spain Should *s* at dead England.   „   III i 28
  Nay, you *s* me, To hear you.   „   IV vii 451
  Have him away ! I *s* of his readiness.   „   V ii 611
  they cried Sinnatus Not so long ago—they *s* me.   *The Cup* II 111
  And wake the Devil, and I may *s* by 'em.   *Foresters* II 325
Sickening *S* himself with sweets.   *Queen Mary* I v 172
Sicker I am *s* staying here Than any sea could make me   „   III vi 86
Sickly But *s*, slight, half-witted and a child,   *Harold* II ii 571
Sickness The *s* of our saintly king, for whom   „   III i 164
  I ha' three sisters a-dying at home o' the sweating *s*.   *Becket* I iv 247
  No fever, cough, croup, *s*?   „   V ii 169
  God save him from all *s* of the soul !   „   V ii 174
  he hath fallen Into a *s*, and it troubles me.   *The Falcon* 310
Side (adj.) Dark even from a *s* glance of the moon,   *Becket* IV ii 148
Side (s) The Council, the Court itself, is on our *s*.
  The Lord Chancellor himself is on our *s*.   *Queen Mary* II i 193
  Is he so safe to fight upon her *s* ?   „   II ii 313
  moving *s* by *s* Beneath one canopy,   „   III i 95
  I will show fire on my *s*—stake and fire—   „   III i 327
  are profitless to the burners, And help the other *s*.   „   IV ii 220
  Those of the wrong *s* will despise the man,   „   IV iii 24
  Might it not be the other *s* rejoicing In his brave end ?   „   IV vii 357
  Here by the *s* of her who loves you most?   „   V i 75
  there is barely room to shift thy *s*,   *Harold* II ii 442
  when at thy *s* He conquer'd with thee.   „   V viii 28
  we might take your *s* against the customs—   *Becket* I ii 56
  Two rivers gently flowing *s* by *s*—   „   I iii 445
  I evermore have sworn upon his *s*,   „   II ii 465
  he hath pass'd out again, And on the other *s*.   „   III ii 13
  That in the summer keeps the mountain *s*,   *The Cup* I i 109
  You on this *s* the altar. You on that.   „   II 254
  tho' we have been a soldier, and ridden by his lord-
    ship's *s*,   *The Falcon* 548
  Were seated sadly at a fountain *s*,   „   610
  I could put all that o' one *s* eäsy anew.   *Prom. of May* II 111
  meä and my sweet'art was a workin' along o' one
    s wi' one another,   „   II 153
  standing up *s* by *s* with me, and singing the same
    hymn?   „   III 181
  But being o' John's *s* we must have thy gold.   *Foresters* IV 157
  And cleft the Moslem turban at my *s*.   „   IV 1001
Side (verb) 'If ye *s* with William Ye are not noble.'   *Harold* II ii 787
  It is, my boy, to *s* with the King when Chancellor,   *Becket* I i 235
Side-beam see you yon *s-b* that is forced from under it,   „   III iii 49
Side-cousin —though she's but a *s-c*—   *Queen Mary* II iii 113
Side-current swoll'n and fed With indraughts and *s-c*'s,   „   II i 234

Side-gorge with sudden wreckful gusts From a *s-g.*   *Harold* III i 52
Sidelong And shot out *s* boughs across the deep   „   III i 150
Side-smile that hath squeezed out this *s-s* upon Canterbury,   *Becket* III iii 56
Sideway Lest thou be *s*'s guilty of the violence.   *Harold* II i 458
Siding *S* with our great Council against Tostig,   „   III i 59
Siege Lent at the *s* of Thoulouse by the King.   *Becket* I iii 636
Sigh (s) a *s* With these low-moaning heavens.   *Harold* v i 151
Sigh (verb) tell me, did you ever *S* for a beard?   *Queen Mary* I v 609
   Wherefore do you *s*?   *Count.*   I have lost a friend
     of late. *Lady Giovanna.* I could *s* with you For
     fear of losing more than friend,   *The Falcon* 328
Sight (*See also* **Second-sight**) the half *s* which makes
     her look so stern,   *Queen Mary* II ii 322
   Gamble thyself at once out of my *s,*   „   II ii 95
   pray Heaven That you may see according to our *s.*   „   III iv 331
   Behold him—— *People.* Oh, unhappy *s!*   „   IV iii 2
   dishonour'd even in the *s* Of thine own sectaries—   „   v v 133
   s of Danish blood Might serve an end not English—   *Harold* IV iii 96
   My *s* is eagle, but the strife so thick—   „   v i 627
   let not my strong prayer Be weaken'd in thy *s,*   „   v i 648
   Wast thou not told to keep thyself from *s*?   *Becket* I i 252
   A *s* of that same chart which Henry gave you   „   I ii 60
   I would move this wanton from his *s*   „   II i 71
   throned together in the *s* Of all the people,   *The Cup* II 67
   to the fullest in the *s* Of all the Gods.   „   II 433
   My last *s* ere I swoon'd was one sweet face   *The Falcon* 647
   and I haätes the very *s* on him.   *Prom. of May* I 154
   were I taken They would prick out my *s.*   *Foresters* II i 72
Sighted (*See also* **Brief-sighted, Second-sighted**) We *s* 'em
     Only this moment.   „   IV 589
Sign (s) if yon weird *s* Not blast us in our dreams.   *Harold* I i 121
   In heaven *s*'s!   *S*'s upon earth!   *s*'s everywhere!   „   I i 159
   there are *s*'s in heaven—   „   III i 357
   And *s*'s on earth!   Knowest thou Senlac hill?   „   III i 360
   The *s* in heaven—the sudden blast at sea—   „   v i 378
   Where, knave, where?   *Man.*   *S* of the Talbot.   *Queen Mary* III i 319
Sign (verb) Now *s.*   *Cranmer.*   I have sign'd enough,
     and I will *s* no more.   „   IV ii 66
   I *s* it with my presence, if I read it.   „   IV ii 73
   Will you not *s* it now?   *Cranmer.*   No, Villa
     Garcia, I *s* no more.   „   IV ii 82
   S, s at once—take, *s* it, Stigand, Aldred!   *S* it, my
     good son Harold, Gurth, and Leofwin, *S* it,   *Harold* III i 197
   Then shalt thou step into my place and *s.*   *Becket* I iii 15
   that I cannot *s*: for that would drag The cleric   „   I iii 82
   And that I cannot *s.* (repeat)   *Becket* I iii 91, 103, 114
   That, too, I cannot *s.*   *S* and obey!   *Becket* I iii 131
   S, and obey the crown!   „   I iii 144
   O my good lord, I do entreat thee—*s.*   „   I iii 186
   He hath sworn that thou shouldst *s,*   „   I iii 189
   so if thou *s,* my lord, That were but as the shadow   „   I iii 193
   Cannot the Pope absolve thee if thou *s*?   „   I iii 231
   Why—there then—there—I *s,*   „   II iii 269
   that we too should *s*?   „   I iii 273
   S? seal? I promised The King to obey these customs,   „   I iii 555
   order To seize upon him.   Let me *s* it.   *The Cup* I i 165
Sign'd first of those who *s* the Letters Patent   *Queen Mary* II i 17
   Those that are now her Privy Council, *s* Before me: „   I ii 23
   then I could no more—I *s.*   „   I ii 38
   'Thou shalt!'   And *s* it—Mary!   *Stafford.*   Philip
     and the Pope Must have *s* too.   „   III i 428
   I have *s* enough, and I will sign no more.   *Villa*
     Garcia. It is no more than what you have *s*
     already,   „   IV ii 67
   'twas you That *s* the burning of poor Joan of Kent;   „   IV ii 206
   papers by my hand *S* since my degradation—by
     this hand Written and *s*—   „   IV iii 244
   That Cranmer read all papers that he *s*?   Or *s* all
     those they tell us that he *s*?   „   IV iii 319
   We have *s* it.   *Harold* III i 202
   s These ancient laws and customs of the realm.   *Becket* I iii 6
   'Twould seem too like the substance, if I *s.*   „   I iii 197
   Foliot, let me see what I have *s.*   „   I iii 308
   hath he *s!* show me the papers!   *S* and not seal'd!   „   I iii 317
   when he *s,* his face was stormy-red—   „   I iii 320

Sign'd (*continued*) Hadst thou not *s,* I had gone along with
     thee;   *Becket* I iii 522
   true too, that when written I *s* them—   „   I iii 561
   This paper *s* Antonius—will you take it,   *The Cup* I i 225
   O Dora, he *s* himself 'Yours gratefully'!   *Prom. of May* III 334
Signing Smooth thou his pride—thy *s* is but form;   *Becket* I iii 218
   Too late, my lord: you see they are *s* there.   „   I iii 289
   I hold not by my *s.*   „   I iii 563
Sign of the Talbot Where, knave, where?   *Man.*
     S o t T.   *Queen Mary* III i 319
Silence (s) (*See also* **Prison-silence**) Ay, sir; Inherit
     the great *S.*   „   III ii 199
   They can but weep in *s.*   „   IV iii 361
   Our *s* is our reverence for the king!   *Harold* IV i 13
   thou shalt have our love, our *s,* and our gold—   *Becket, Pro.* 492
   ever spread into the man Here in our *s*?   „   III i 23
   God help her, That she was sworn to *s.*   „   III i 78
   This violence ill becomes The *s* of our Temple.   *The Cup* II 216
   whose cheerless Houris after death Are Night
     and *S,*   *Prom. of May* I 251
   Thou art alone in the *s* of the forest   *Foresters* IV 630
Silence (verb) may give that egg-bald head The tap that *s*'s.   *Harold* v i 92
Silenced Little doubt This buzz will soon be *s*;   *Queen Mary* v i 293
Silencing *See* **Bell-silencing**
Silent four guns gaped at me, Black, *s* mouths: *Queen Mary* II iii 32
   William of Orange, William the *S.*   „   III ii 199
   And I could see that many *s* hands Came from the crowd   „   IV iii 582
   even while I speak There lurks a *s* dagger,   „   v ii 216
   And both were *s,* letting the wild brook Speak for us—   „   v v 90
   The *s,* cloister'd, solitary life,   *Harold* v i 277
   The simple, *s,* selfless man Is worth a world of
     tonguesters.   „   v i 81
   Why do you stand so *s,* brother John?   *Becket* v ii 535
   All *s* there, Yes, deathlike!   Dead?   *Prom. of May* III 715
   I am a *s* man myself, and all the more wonder at our
     Earl.   *Foresters* I ii 34
   but make haste then, and be *s* in the wood.   Follow me.   „   II ii 365
   The *s* blessing of one honest man Is heard in heaven—   „   II 321
Silk There was a bit of yellow *s* here and there,   *Becket* IV i 22
   shall see the *s* here and there, and I want my supper.   „   IV i 56
Silken Breaks into feather'd merriments, and flowers
     In *s* pageants.   *Queen Mary* III v 15
Silking *See* **A-silking**
Silver (adj.) Our *s* cross sparkled before the prow,   *Queen Mary* III ii 9
   Some thirty—forty thousand *s* marks.   *Becket* I iii 658
   and we haven't never so much as a *s* one for the golden
     lips of her ladyship.   *Count.*   Have we not half a
     score of *s* spoons?   *The Falcon* 403
   I will give thee a *s* penny if thou wilt show us the
     way back to Nottingham.   *Foresters* II i 359
Silver (s) — white satin his trunkhose, Inwrought with
     s,—   *Queen Mary* III i 78
   Clothed with the mystic *s* of her moon.   *Foresters* II i 608
   if his backward-working alchemy Should change this
     gold to *s,* why, the *s* Were dear as gold,   „   IV 40
Silvering *See* **Down-silvering, Long-silvering**
Simon (**Renard, Spanish Ambassador**) (*See also*
     Renard, Simon Renard) *S,* is supper ready?   *Queen Mary* III vi 256
Simoniacal your Priests Gross, worldly, *s,* unlearn'd!   *Harold* I i 162
Simon Renard so that Gardiner And *S R* spy not out   *Queen Mary* I iii 173
   Ay, *S R* knows it.   „   I v 218
   trust him somewhat less Than *S R,*   „   I v 223
   Thou art ever welcome, *S R.*   „   I v 345
   S R!—This Howard, whom they fear,   „   III vi 53
   May *S R* speak a single word?   „   III vi 121
   S R Knows me too well to speak a single word   „   III vi 125
   Am I to change my manners, *S R,*   „   III vi 152
   Well, *S R,* shall we stop a day?   „   III vi 242
Simple The downfall of so many *s* souls,   „   I ii 54
   Then have my *s* headstone by the church,   „   III v 113
   And make you *s* Cranmer once again.   „   IV ii 129
   S! let fly the bird within the hand,   *Harold* II ii 65
   The *s,* silent, selfless man Is worth a world of tonguesters.   „   v i 81
   Has my *s* song set you jingling?   *Becket, Pro.* 378
   The *s* lobster-basket, and the mesh—   „   II ii 297

Simple (*continued*) This author, with his charm of *s* style And close dialectic, — *Prom. of May* I 224
And out upon all *s* batchelors ! — *Foresters* IV 52
Simple-looking He comes, a rough, bluff, *s-l* fellow. — *The Cup* I i 173
Sin It was a *s* to love her married, — *Queen Mary* III i 339
With His own blood, and wash'd us from our *s's*, — ,, III iii 204
O Lord God, although my *s's* be great, — ,, IV iii 135
not for little *s's* Didst thou yield up thy Son to human death ; But for the greatest *s* that can be sinn'd, — ,, IV iii 143
Unpardonable,—*s* against the light, — ,, IV iii 148
Thy mercy must be greater than all *s*. — ,, IV iii 151
what *s* Beyond all grace, all pardon ? — ,, v iii 339
S is too dull to see beyond himself. *Alice.* Ah, Magdalen, *s* is bold as well as dull. — ,, v i 441
That marriage was half *s*. — *Harold* I ii 53
s's of both The houses on mine head— — ,, I ii 204
Or is it the same *s* to break my word — ,, II ii 664
—a *s* against The truth of love. — ,, v i 170
Black sheep, quoth she, too black a *s* for me. — *Becket* I iv 165
We can make a black *s* white. — ,, I iv 169
Thou shalt confess all thy sweet *s's* to me. — ,, II i 292
Well, it's no *s* in a gentleman not to fish. — *Prom. of May* I 215
Bow'd to the dust beneath the burthen of *s*. *Harold.* *S* ! What *s* ? — ,, III 522
Veiling one *s* to act another. — ,, III 773
Sin' (*since*) It be five year *s* ye went afoor to him, — *Prom. of May* II 5
Him as did the mischief here, five year' *s*. — ,, III 140
Sing To *s*, love, marry, churn, brew, bake, and die, — *Queen Mary* III v 111
but, my Lord, you know what Virgil *s's*, — ,, II vi 134
Shall Alice *s* you One of her pleasant songs ? — ,, v ii 354
the lark *s's*, the sweet stars come and go, — *Harold* II ii 434
s, Asaph ! clash The cymbal, Heman ! — ,, III i 186
bird that moults *s's* the same song again, — *Becket* I iii 447
our mother 'ill *s* me old songs by the hour, — ,, I i 184
tell him my tales, *S* him my songs ? — *The Falcon* 797
I don't know why I *s* that song ; I don't love it. — *Prom. of May* I 61
and the larks 'ud *s* i' their daäys, — ,, I 374
do thou and thy sweet'art *s* us hoäm to supper— — ,, II 170
Ye shall *s* ageän to-night, — ,, II 215
You do well, Mistress Kate, to *s* and to gather roses. — *Foresters* I i 23
S's a new song to the new year— — ,, I iii 28
I have a touch of sadness in myself. *S*. — ,, I iii 40
I can *s* it. *Robin.* Not now, good Much ! — ,, I iii 157
To *s* the songs of England Beneath the greenwood tree. — ,, II i 23
S, and by St. Mary These beggars and these friars — ,, III 416
And all the birds that *s* — ,, III 440
Did I not *s* it in tune ? — ,, IV 29
Till thou thyself shall come to *s* it—in time. — ,, IV 37
Let the birds *s*, and do you dance to their song. — ,, IV 557
All the birds in merry Sherwood *s* and *s* him home again. — ,, IV 1109
Singing (*See also* **Psalm-singing**) I wish'd myself the milkmaid *s* here, — *Queen Mary* III v 256
standing up side by side with me, and *s* the same hymn ? — *Prom. of May* III 182
Single May Simon Renard speak a *s* word ? — *Queen Mary* III vi 121
Simon Renard Knows me too well to speak a *s* word That could not be forgiven. — ,, III vi 126
Our axes lighten with a *s* flash About the summit of the hill, — *Harold* v v 538
But dallied with a *s* lettuce-leaf ; — *The Falcon* 673
He loves the chivalry of his *s* arm. — *Foresters* IV 786
Sing-songing and you sit *S-s* here ; — *Queen Mary* II i 112
Sink a day may *s* or save a realm. — ,, III vi 238
Here's to him, *s* or swim ! *Thane.* God *s* him ! — *Harold* IV iii 133
and all her loves and hates *S* again into chaos. — *Foresters* II i 330
Perchance this day may *s* as gloriously, — ,, II i 31
Sinking I am *s*—hold me—Let me alone. — *The Cup* II 478
Sinnatus (a Tetrarch) married Since—married *S*, the Tetrarch — ,, I i 16
'To the admired Camma, wife of *S*, the Tetrarch, — ,, I i 37
Boy, dost thou know the house of *S* ? *Boy.* These grapes are from the house of *S*— — ,, I i 50
and this cup to Camma, The wife of *S*. *Boy.* Going or gone to-day To hunt with *S*. — ,, I i 63
I send it to the wife of *S*, — ,, I i 73

Sinnatus (a Tetrarch) (*continued*) you suspect This *S* of playing patriotism, — *The Cup* I i 78
I envied *S* when he married her. — ,, I i 129
Nor *S* either ? *Synorix.* No, nor *S*. — ,, I i 133
If you track this *S* In any treason, — ,, I i 162
No *S* yet—and there the rising moon. — ,, I ii 1
Lord *S*, I once was at the hunting of a lion. — ,, I ii 115
were he living And grown to man and *S* will'd it, — ,, I ii 151
'You are to seize on *S*,—if——' — ,, I ii 229
Hath *S* never told you of this plot ? — ,, I ii 250
No chance for *S*. — ,, I ii 258
Why said you not as much to my brave *S* ? — ,, I ii 260
S, you remember—yea, you must, — ,, I ii 400
S, kiss me now. — ,, I ii 419
Not if *S* Has told her all the truth about me. — ,, I iii 22
And for the sake of *S* your husband, — ,, I iii 100
body of that dead traitor *S*. Bear him away. — ,, I iii 180
To marry him who stabb'd her *S*. — ,, II 24
When he struck at *S*— — ,, II 47
hand Red with the sacred blood of *S* ? — ,, II 84
found All good in the true heart of *S*, — ,, II 87
So they cried *S* Not so long since— — ,, II 110
O how unlike our goodly *S*. — ,, II 173
A goodlier-looking man than *S*. — ,, II 176
Dost thou remember when I wedded *S* ? — ,, II 194
came To plead to thee for *S's* life, — ,, II 392
Would you have tortured *S* to death ? — ,, II 408
S ! Why comes he not to meet me ? — ,, II 527
' Camma, Camma ! ' *S*, *S* ! — ,, II 536
Sinn'd But for the greatest sin that can be *s*, — *Queen Mary* IV iii 146
Have *s* against it—all in vain. — *Harold* III i 95
Sinner Most miserable, *s*, wretched man. — *Queen Mary* IV iii 123
We are *s's* all, The best of all not all-prepared — *Becket* v i 563
Sire The *s* begets Not half his likeness — *Queen Mary* II i 53
like his kingly *s's*, The Normans, — *Becket* IV iii 441
Sister took her hand, call'd her sweet *s*, — *Queen Mary* I i 80
To the Pleiads, uncle ; they have lost a *s*. — ,, I iv 294
bastard sprout, My *s*, is far fairer than myself. — ,, I v 72
My *s* cowers and hates me. — ,, I v 83
—for I have not own'd My *s*, and I will not.— — ,, I v 285
So that your *s* were but look'd to closer. — ,, I v 460
whom did you say ? *Messenger.* Elizabeth, Your Royal *s*. — ,, II iv 117
And your *s* so loving ? *Mary.* She shall die. — ,, II iv 141
Our little *s* of the Song of Songs ! — ,, III ii 103
Then I may say your Grace will see your *s* ? — ,, v ii 604
Your royal *s* cannot last ; your hand Will be much coveted ! — ,, v iii 43
My *s's* marriage, and my father's marriages, — ,, v iii 96
Madam, your royal *s* comes to see you. — ,, v v 192
Who knows if Boleyn's daughter be my *s* ? — ,, v v 195
Why would you vex yourself, Poor *s* ? — ,, v v 264
Tostig, *s*, galls himself ; — *Harold* I i 421
Nay, my good *s*— — ,, I i 462
Our *s* hates us for his banishment ; — ,, III i 78
thou art not A holy *s* yet, my girl, — ,, III ii 82
And more than *s* in thine own. — ,, III ii 85
Why cry thy people on thy *s's* name ? — ,, IV i 21
Where is thy *s* ? — ,, IV i 184
For there was more than *s* in my kiss, — ,, v ii 5
wicked *s* clapt her hands and laugh'd ; — ,, v ii 48
Two *s's* gliding in an equal dance, — *Becket* I iii 444
I ha' three *s's* a-dying at home o' the sweating sickness. — ,, IV 246
twin *s* of the morning star, Forelead the sun. — *The Cup* I iii 45
my *s* wrote that he was mighty pleasant, and had no pride in him. — *Prom. of May* I 116
nor father, *S*, nor you, shall ever see me more. — ,, I 676
My *s* far away—and you, a gentleman, — ,, I 708
Speak not so loudly ; that must be your *s*. — ,, I 727
not only on my *s's* account, but the ill success of the farm, — ,, II 67
It seems to me that I hate men, ever since my *s* left us. — ,, II 80
Poor *s*, I had it five years ago. — ,, II 82
knaw'd better nor to cast her *s's* misfortin inter 'er teeth — ,, II 127
Are you—you are—that Dora, The *s*. — ,, II 364
you are young, and—pardon me—As lovely as your *s*. — ,, II 508

Sister (*continued*) niver 'a been talkin' haäfe an hour wi' the divil 'at killed her oän s, — *Prom. of May* II 604
But the love of s for s can never be old-fashioned. — " III 319
a S of Mercy, come from the death-bed of a pauper, — " III 376
S took me to her house, and bit by bit— — " III 379
I appealed to the S again, her answer— — " III 394
O she has fainted. S, Eva, s! — " III 672
She hid this s, told me she was dead— — " III 689
And so wouldst sell thy s to the Sheriff, — *Foresters* II i 536
But thou art fair as ever, my sweet s. — " IV 1018

Sit (*See also* **Set**) To s high Is to be lied about. — *Queen Mary* I v 428
burn the throne Where you should s with Philip: — " I v 511
Sir, let them s. I must have time to breathe. — " I v 545
An instant Ay or No! the Council s's. — " I v 591
and you s Sing-songing here; . — " II i 111
S down here, all; — " III ii 99
St. Andrew's day; s close, s close, we are friends. — " III iii 1
You s upon this fallen Cranmer's throne', — " IV i 114
S down here: Tell me thine happiest hour. — " V v 78
sons of Godwin S topmost in the field of England, — *Harold* I i 326
where he s's My ransom'd prisoner. — " II ii 44
S down, s down, and eat, — " IV iii 206
range of knights S, each a statue on his horse, — " v i 525
If I s, I grow fat. — *Becket*, Pro. 414
mother Canterbury, who s's With tatter'd robes. — " I i 156
Priest S's winking at the license of a king, — " I ii 66
none could s By his own hearth in peace; — " I iii 341
And our great lords will s in judgment on him. — " I iii 549
Sons s in judgment on their father!— — " I iii 551
There is a bench. Come, wilt thou s? — " II i 124
she s's naked by a great heap of gold in the middle of the wood, — " III ii 21
even among those Who s on thrones— — " IV ii 125
crowns must bow when mitres s so high. — " IV ii 297
S and eat, And take a hunter's vengeance — *The Cup* I i 41
Shall I S by him, read to him, tell him my tales, — *The Falcon* 795
and you should s i' your oän parlour quite like a laädy, — *Prom. of May* II 97
s's and eats his heart for want of money to pay the Abbot. — *Foresters* I i 4
S here by me, where the most beaten track — " III 88
S here, my queen, and judge the world with me. — " III 151
S there, knaves, till the captain call for you. — " III 219
S there till you be called for. — " III 295

Sitting (*See also* **A-sitting**) s here Between the two most high-set thrones — *Queen Mary* III ii 104
and the dead were found S, and in this fashion; — " v ii 397
Who stole the widow's one s hen o' Sunday, — *Becket* I iv 121
S hen! Our Lord Becket's our great sitting-hen cock, we shouldn't ha' been s here if the barons and bishops hadn't been a-sitting on the Archbishop. — " I iv 124
shout of Synorix and Camma s Upon one throne, — *The Cup* II 146
nurse, I had forgotten thou wast s there. — *The Falcon* 35

Sitting-hen (*See also* **Sitting**) Our Lord Becket's our great s-h cock, — *Becket* I iv 124
S'iver (**Howsoever**) S we've led moäst on it. — *Prom. of May* II 52
S I mun git along back to the farm. — " II 321
Six It lies there in s pieces at your feet; — *Queen Mary* II i 87
Some s or seven Bishops, diamonds, pearls, — " I i 52
Then for the bastard S feet and nothing more! — *Harold* IV iii 116
Yet this no wife—her s and thirty sail Of Provence — *Becket* v 122
She was there s years ago. — *Prom. of May* II 399
Dan Smith, they tell me that you—and you have s children—spent all your last Saturday's wages at the ale-house; — " III 77
Sixteen gather all From s years to sixty; — *Queen Mary* v ii 273
Sixty And Counts, and s Spanish cavaliers, — " III i 51
gather all From sixteen years to s; — " v ii 273
Sixty-fold Do here and now repay you s-f, — " III iii 199
'Size (**assize**) thaw they hanged ma at 'S fur it. — *Prom. of May* II 698
Sketching but I Take some delight in s, — " II 539
Skilful The King is s at it? — *Queen Mary* I iii 144
For all that, Most honest, brave, and s; — " II ii 383
Skill Upon the s and swiftness of the players. — " I iii 143

Skill (*continued*) with this s of fence! let go mine arm. — *Foresters* II ii 38
Skim Not while the swallow s's along the ground, — " I i 313
Skin If ye love your liberties or your s's, — *Queen Mary* II i 216
doth not the living s thicken against perpetual whippings? — *Becket* III iii 316
Skinn'd *See* **Thin-skinn'd**
Skip S's every way, from levity or from fear. — *Queen Mary* I iii 170
who s's and flies To right and left, — *Harold* I i 11
Skipping And now be s in their fairy-rings, — *Foresters* II i 497
Skipworth (a farm labourer) Luscombe, Nokes, Oldham, S! — *Prom. of May* III 54
Skulk S into corners Like rabbits to their holes. — *Queen Mary* III 54
Skull And smite thee with my crozier on the s? — *Becket* I i 222
Sky (*See also* **Leaf-sky**) So from a clear s falls the thunderbolt! — *Queen Mary* v iii 115
Look to the skies, then to the river, — *Harold* I i 34
and fill the s With free sea-laughter— — " II ii 336
the bright s cleave To the very feet of God, — " II ii 741
dash us down Our dinner from the skies. — *The Falcon* 154
The s? or the sea on a blue day? — *Prom. of May* I 101
An' the midders all mow'd, an' the s sa blue—(repeat) — *Prom. of May* II 176, 188, 200
O tower spiring to the s, — *Prom. of May* II 203
And the white cloud is roll'd along the s! — *Foresters* II ii 320
Slack O God! I have been too s, too s; — *Queen Mary* v v 100
Slain and there be more As villainously s. — *Harold* II ii 300
Better methinks have s the man at once! — " II ii 498
s, Whose life was all one battle, — " v i 396
Gurth hath leapt upon him And s him: — " v i 634
The king is s, the kingdom overthrown! — " v ii 15
Three horses had I s beneath me: — " v ii 171
you had safelier have s an archbishop than a she-goat: — *Becket* III iii 68
They fear you s; they dread they know not what. — " v i 600
We will not have him s before our face. — " v iii 54
And will you bolt them out, and have them s? — " v iii 61
I am readier to be slain, than thou to slay. — " v iii 128
Slander (s) heard S's against Prince Philip in our Court? *Alice.* What s's? — *Queen Mary* I v 570
Slander (verb) And let him go? To s thee again? — *Harold* I i 508
she question'd me. Did she not s him? — *Becket* III i 214
Slander'd when they s you For setting up a mass — *Queen Mary* I ii 86
Slandering Or am I s my most inward friend, — " IV i 105
Slanderous kill, kill with knife or venom One of his s harlots? — *Becket* IV i 411
Slaughter peril mine own soul By s of the body? — *Queen Mary* v v 169
Slaughter-field Would perish on the civil s-f, — " III i 118
Slave (*See also* **Galley-slave**) the Queen, and the laws, and the people, his s's. — " II i 175
Crown'd s of s's, and mitred king of kings, — " III iv 381
S, if he love thee, Thy life is worth the wrestle — *Becket* IV ii 192
The s that eat my bread has kick'd his King! — " v i 242
My bed, where ev'n the s is private— — " v i 251
Slay I could take and s thee. — *Harold* IV ii 7
Take and s me, For Edward loved me. — " IV ii 9
Take and s me, I say, Or I shall count thee fool. — " IV ii 14
Free thee or s thee, Norway will have war; — " IV ii 18
dash thyself against me that I may s thee! — *Becket* IV ii 196
I am readier to be slain, than thou to s. — " v iii 128
if he be conspirator, Rome will chain, Or s him. — *The Cup* I i 19
my friends may spy him And s him as he runs. — " I ii 392
true woodman's bow of the best yew-wood to s the deer. — *Foresters* II i 393
What! go to s his brother, and make me — " IV 804
O Thou that s the babe within the womb — *The Cup* II 278
Slayest or after s him As boy or man, — " II 280
Sleek To s and supple himself to the king's hand. — *Harold* I i 149
She beautiful: s as a miller's mouse! — *The Falcon* 164
as s and as round-about as a mellow codlin. — *Foresters* I i 42
Sleep (s) kiss that charms thine eyelids into s, — *Harold* I ii 140
Sound s to the man Here by dead Norway — " IV iii 120
A snatch of s were like the peace of God. — " v i 180
The Virgin, in a vision of my s, — *Becket* I i 53
All my brain is full of s. — *The Cup* I ii 446
He's been a-moänin' and a-groänin' in 'is s, — *Prom. of May* III 412

Sleep (s) (*continued*)   She must be crying out 'Edgar'
    in her *s*.   *Harold*.   Who must be crying out
    'Edgar' in her *s* ?   *Prom. of May* III 654
    'To *s* ! to *s* !' (repeat)   *Foresters* I iii 34, 41, 43, 46, 49
    Whate'er thy griefs, in *s* they fade away.   *Foresters* I iii 45
    Why so I said, *my* arrow.   Well, to *s*.   *The Cup* I ii 386
Sleep (verb)   when I *s*, a hundred men-at-arms   *Queen Mary* I v 152
    I couldn't *s* in Spain.   „   II i 36
    son turn'd out into the street To *s*, to die—   „   v ii 127
    The room she *s's* in—is not this the way ?   „   v v 205
    let them turn from left to right And *s* again.   *Harold* I i 197
    S, *s*, and thou shalt see My grayhounds   „   I ii 127
    the people stupid-sure *S* like their swine . . .   „   IV iii 217
    Go home, and *s* thy wine off, for thine eyes   *Becket* I i 212
    I sometimes think he *s's* When he would watch ;   „   III i 33
    can't *s* sound o' nights because of the bad fairies.   „   IV i 30
    she shall *s* sound enough if thou wilt take me to her.   „   IV i 33
    she says she can make you *s* o' nights.   „   IV ii 20
    I could not eat, *s*, pray ;   „   v ii 92
    S, mournful heart, and let the past be past !   *S*,
    happy soul ! all life will *s* at last.   *Foresters* I iii 47
    I cannot *s* o' nights by cause on 'em.   „   II i 383
Sleeper   seven *s's* in the cave at Ephesus Have turn'd   *Harold* I i 192
    like a careless *s* in the down ;   *Foresters* I i 207
Sleeping   *s* after all she has done, in peace and
    quietness,   *Queen Mary* A iv 34
    S or dying there ?   If this be death,   *Harold* III i 1
Sleeping-draught   I pray you then to take my *s-d* ;   *Becket* IV ii 69
    my *s-d* May bloat thy beauty out of shape,   „   IV i 168
Sleepy   I am faint and *s*.   Leave me.   „   III i 208
    and my hands are too *s* To lift it off.   *The Cup* II 530
Sleeve   look—is this a *s* For an archbishop ?   *Becket, Pro.* 250
Slender   Pray thee make Thy *s* meal out of those scraps
    and shreds   *The Falcon* 146
    But for the *s* help that I can give,   *Prom. of May* II 421
Slept   Our guardsmen have *s* well, since we came in ?
    Leofwin.   Ay, *s* and snored.   *Harold* v i 207
    when I *s* Methought I stood in Canterbury Minster,   *Becket* I i 72
Slew   *s* not him alone who wore the purple,   *Queen Mary* I v 499
    And *s* two hundred of his following,   *Harold* IV i 116
    They *s* my stags in mine own manor here,   *Becket* I i 438
    And he was scared and *s* it.   *Foresters* II ii 99
Sliced   He tore their eyes out, *s* their hands away,   *Harold* II ii 389
Slight (adj.)   Not for *s* faults alone, when thou becamest
    Man in the Flesh,   *Queen Mary* IV iii 139
    But sickly, *s*, half-witted and a child,   *Harold* II 571
    So that you grant me one *s* favour.   *Becket* I i 58
    then Save for some *s* report in her own Senate   *The Cup* I ii 133
    And after some *s* speech about the Sheriff He caught
    her round the waist,   *Foresters* II i 114
    He is stricken with a *s* paralysis.   „   IV 456
Slight (verb)   When the fairy *s's* the crown.   „   II ii 135
Slighted   like a friend *s* by one That hath climb'd up to
    nobler company.   Not *s*—all but moan'd for :
    thou must go.   *Becket* I i 350
Slimy   the river, black, *s*, swirling under me in the
    lamplight,   *Prom. of May* III 369
Slink   Why did you *s* away so like a cur ?   *Becket* IV ii 431
Sliver'd   are *s* off and splinter'd by Their lightning—   *Harold* v i 540
Slope (adj.)   nor our Archbishop Stagger on the *s* decks for
    any rough sea   *Becket* II ii 106
Slope (s)   I am half-way down the *s*—will no man stay me ?   „   II ii 148
    golden *s's* Of Solomon-shaming flowers—   „   I 47
Slouch   Dares the bear *s* into the lion's den ?   „   IV ii 282
Slough   serpent that hath slough'd will *s* again.   *Queen Mary* III iii 19
    snake that *s's* comes out a snake again.   *Becket* I iii 449
Slough'd   serpent that hath *s* will slough again.   *Queen Mary* III iii 18
Slow   The *s*, fat fool !   He drawl'd and prated so, I smote
    him suddenly,   *Harold* IV iv 40
    One *s*, fat, white, a burthen of the hearth ;   *Becket* v ii 211
    but very ready To make allowances, and mighty *s*
    To feel offences.   *Prom. of May* III 629
Sluggard   honour me, obey me !   *S's* and fools !   *Becket* v i 241
    S's and fools, why do you stand and stare ?   „   v i 256
Slum   even if I found it Dark with the soot of *s's*.   *Prom. of May* III 602

Slumber   stormless shipwreck in the pools Of sullen *s*,   *Harold* v i 297
Slur   But wherefore *s* the perfect ceremony ?   *The Cup* II 431
Slush   Your rights and charters hobnail'd into *s*—   *Queen Mary* II ii 279
    Thruf *s* an' squad When roäds was bad,   *Prom. of May* II 309
Slut   a *s* whose fairest linen seems Foul as her dust-cloth,   *Becket* v ii 202
Smack   kind of unction in it, a *s* of relish about it.   *Foresters* I i 187
Small   Are you so *s* a man ?   *Queen Mary* III v 192
    matter Of *s* importance now and then to cede A
    point to her demand ?   „   III vi 168
    Beyond his aim—but I am *s* and scandalous,   „   III v 427
    That were too *s* a matter for a comet !   *Harold* I i 470
    Too *s* ! a comet would not show for that !   *Aldwyth*.
    Not *s* for thee, if thou canst compass it.   „   I i 474
    Bigger in our *s* world than thou art.   *Becket* v i 128
    S peace was mine in my noviciate, father.   „   v ii 86
    And the *s* state more cruelly trampled on   *The Cup* I ii 145
    And I have *s* hope of the gentleman gout in my great
    toe.   *The Falcon* 656
    Dance ! *s* heart have I to dance.   *Prom. of May* I 429
    Till Nature, high and low, and great and *s* Forgets
    herself,   *Foresters* I i 327
    I fear I had *s* pity for that man.—   „   IV 547
Smaller   it was but the sacrifice of a kingdom to his son,
    a *s* matter ;   *Becket* III iii 107
Smash   (*See also* **Mash**)   he'll *s* all our bits o' things,
    worse than Philip o' Spain.   *Queen Mary* II iii 103
Smattering   I had some *s* of science then,   *Prom. of May* II 301
Smell (s)   Wilt thou smell it, my lord ? for the Archbishop
    likes the *s* on it, my lord ;   *Becket* I iv 240
    so that the *s* of their own roast had not come across it—   „   III iii 119
    and the *s* o' the mou'd an' all.   *Prom. of May* I i 375
    the *s* o' the mou'd 'ud ha' maäde ma live as long
    as Jerusalem.   „   I i 377
Smell (verb)   He cannot *s* a rose but pricks his nose   *Harold* I i 422
    It's humbling—it *s's* of human natur'.   Wilt thou *s* it,
    my lord ? for the Archbishop likes the smell on it,   *Becket* I iv 238
    Do but *s* !   „   II i 145
    when I was a-getting o' bluebells for your ladyship's
    nose to *s* on—   „   III i 163
    two-legg'd dogs Among us who can *s* a true occasion,   *The Cup* I ii 113
    Yes ; how sweet they *s* !   *Prom. of May* I 608
    to saäy he's browt some of Miss Eva's roses for the
    'sick laädy to *s* on   „   III 347
    so greasy, and *s* so vilely that my Lady Marian   *Foresters* I i 82
Smelt   Methought I *s* out Renard in the letter,   *Queen Mary* II ii 119
Smile (s)   (*See also* **Side-smile**)   She cast on him a
    vassal *s* of love,   „   III i 98
    A *s* abroad is oft a scowl at home.   „   III i 212
    and with such royal *s's*—   *Gardiner*.   *S's* that
    burn men.   „   III iv 403
    with a cheerful *s*, as one whose mind Is all made up,   „   IV iii 587
    sweet worn *s* Among thy patient wrinkles—   „   v v 199
    Love is come with a song and a *s*, Welcome Love with
    a *s* and a song :   *Harold* I ii 10
    Gave his shorn *s* the lie.   „   II ii 226
    Then with that friendly-fiendly *s* of his,   „   III i 226
    that sweet other-world *s*, which will be reflected   *Becket, Pro.* 396
    Still with a *s*.   „   III iii 36
    The same *s* still.   „   III iii 44
    Bid their old bond farewell with *s's*, not tears ;   *Prom. of May* I 524
Smile (verb)   love that men should *s* upon you, niece.
    They'd *s* you into treason—   *Queen Mary* I iv 274
    seem'd to *s* And sparkle like our fortune   „   II iii 23
    They *s* as if content with one another.   „   III i 210
    How he *s's* As if he loved me yet !   „   v v 40
    and see, he *s's* and goes, Gentle as in life.   „   v v 145
    but *s* As kindness, watching all,   *Harold* I i 366
    Why dost thou *s* So dolorously ?   *Becket, Pro.* 134
    not to *s* Is all but death to me.   „   II i 40
    Or scarce would *s* that fashion.   „   III iii 28
    that they began to *s* at it.   „   III iii 312
    and *s* At bygone things till that eternal peace.   *The Cup* I iii 171
    She *s's* at him—how hard the woman is !   *The Falcon* 660
    Nay, you must *s* upon me !   *Prom. of May* I 571
    I am glad my nonsense has made you *s* !   „   III 315

Smile (verb) *(continued)* One word, or do but *s*! *Prom. of May* III 677
but Hope *S*'s from the threshold of the year *Foresters* I iii 16
I could but sneak and *s* and call it courtesy, ,, IV 366
And *s* at my best meanings, ,, IV 727
Smiled loveliest day that ever *s* On England. *Queen Mary* III iii 162
Smiling I spy the rock beneath the *s* sea. ,, I iv 279
He pass'd out *s*, and he walk'd upright; ,, IV iii 302
Or answer'd them in *s* negatives; ,, IV iii 603
Down thirty feet below the *s* day— *Harold* II ii 430
Smite The sword Is in her Grace's hand to *s* with. *Queen Mary* III iv 90
I fell. Why fall? Why did He *s* me? *Becket* I i 109
And *s* thee with my crozier on the skull? ,, I i 221
Shall I *s* him with the edge of the sword? ,, I i 224
S the shepherd and the sheep are scattered. *S* the sheep and the shepherd will excommunicate thee. ,, I iv 226
plagues That *s* the city spare the solitudes. ,, v ii 173
Shall I not *s* him with his own cross-staff? ,, v ii 313
Smith (Dan) *See* **Dan Smith**
Smitten our good Gurth hath *s* him to the death. *Harold* v i 503
S-with fever in the open field, *Prom. of May* III 806
Smoke you bring the *s* Of Cranmer's burning with you. *Queen Mary* IV iii 561
s of Cranmer's burning wrapt me round. ,, IV iii 564
a candle in the sun Is all but *s*— ,, v i 79
Ay, if he do not end in *s* again. *Becket* II ii 316
said to the *s*, ' Go up, my son, straight to Heaven.' ,, II ii 318
And the *s* said, 'I go;' ,, II ii 318
while the *s* floats from the cottage roof, *Foresters* II ii 317
Smoking after much smouldering and *s*, be kindled again upon your quarter. *Becket* II ii 313
Smooth (adj.) Taken the rifted pillars of the wood For *s* stone columns of the sanctuary, *Harold* I ii 101
Cannot a *s* tongue lick him whole again To serve your will? *Becket* II ii 24
That all was planed and bevell'd *s* again, ,, v i 138
Smooth-Smoothe (verb) *Smooth* thou my way, before he clash with me; *Harold* II ii 69
Smoothe thou his pride—thy signing is but form; *Becket* I iii 218
Smooth-shorn Husband-in-law, our *s-s* suzerain, ,, II ii 40
Smote Methought some traitor *s* me on the head. *Queen Mary* v iii 252
I *s* him suddenly, I knew not what I did. *Harold* IV ii 41
And *s* me down upon the Minster floor. *Becket* I i 104
Smoulder or this Will *s* and re-flame, *Queen Mary* I v 509
Smouldering after much *s* and smoking, be kindled again upon your quarter. *Becket* II ii 313
Snaffle Then I and he will *s* your ' God's death,' *Queen Mary* III v 119
Snake A *s*—and if I touch it, it may sting. ,, III v 218
s that sloughs comes out a *s* again. *S*—ay, *Becket* I iii 449
Snake-like creeps *s-l* about our legs *Queen Mary* I ii 203
Snap bind a score All in one faggot, *s* it over knee, *Harold* IV i 58
S not the faggot-band then. ,, IV i 66
lances and shiver Against the shifting blaze ,, v i 586
Snapt dog that *s* the shadow, dropt the bone.— ,, I ii 188
Snare Before he fell into the *s* of Guy; ,, v ii 131
my white bird stepping toward the *s*. *The Cup* I iii 36
Snatch A *s* of sleep were like the peace of God. *Harold* v i 180
Sneak I could but *s* and smile and call it courtesy, *Foresters* I iii 366
Sneezed and I *s* three times this morning. *The Falcon* 168
Sniffed that Lucullus or Apicius might have *s* it in their Hades of heathenism, *Becket* III iii 118
Snore (s) Misheard their *s*'s for groans. *Harold* v i 213
Snore (verb) to *s* away his drunkenness Into the sober headache,— *Becket* I i 371
Nip him not, but let him *s*. *Foresters* II ii 122
Snored Ay, slept and *s*. *Harold* v i 209
Snow And winter again and the *s*'s. *Becket, Pro.* 334
I am *s* to mud. ,, IV vi 130
s had frozen round her, and she sat Stone-dead ,, v ii 237
In the sweet moon as with a lovelier *s*! *The Cup* I ii 397
see your cloth be white as *s*! *The Falcon* 499
as the *s* yonder on the very tip-top o' the mountain. ,, 501
I have seen it like the *s* on the moraine. ,, 505
Soä (so) An' *s* they be. *Man. S* they be! *s* they be! *Prom. of May* I 338
an' *s* I know'd 'im when I seed 'im ageän ,, III 121

Soädger (soldier) 'Listed for a *s*, Miss, i' the Queen's Real Hard Tillery. *Prom. of May* III 108
Soak'd he *s* the trunk with human blood, *Harold* III i 142
Soar thou that canst *s* Beyond the morning lark, *The Falcon* 10
Sob trumpets in the halls, *S*'s, laughter, cries: *Becket* v ii 368
Sober to snore away his drunkenness Into the *s* headache,— ,, I i 373
Socialist I that have been call'd a *S*, A Communist, *Prom. of May* III 584
Soft You lived among your vines and oranges, In your *s* Italy yonder ! *Queen Mary* III iv 254
What weapon hath the child, save his *s* tongue, ,, III v 129
like the wild hedge-rose Of a *s* winter, possible, ,, III vi 16
The *s* and tremulous coward in the flesh ? ,, IV ii 107
You have a gold ring on your finger, and *s* raiment about your body; ,, v iv 32
on a *s* bed, in a closed room, with light, fire, physic, tendance; ,, v iv 36
Except it be a *s* one, And undereaten to the fall. *Harold* I ii 122
Nor dwelt alone, like a *s* lord of the East, *Becket* I iii 358
When Richard comes he is *s* enough to pardon His brother; *Foresters* IV 746
Softlier We might go *s* than with crimson rowel And streaming lash. *Queen Mary* III iv 182
Soil (s) make the *s* For Cæsars, Cromwells, and Napoleons *Prom. of May* III 592
Soil (verb) You heed not how you *s* her maiden fame, *Foresters* IV 479
Soil'd and the man Hurls his *s* life against the pikes and dies. *Queen Mary* IV vii 311
Sojourn For I shall most *s* in Normandy ; *Harold* II ii 634
Solace Pride of his heart—the *s* of his hours— *The Falcon* 223
Sold Thou hast *s* me for a cry.— *Harold* IV i 76
And *s* thine own To buy it for her. *The Falcon* 76
And the other nine ? *Filippo. S*! ,, 412
and he hath *s* himself to that beast John— *Foresters* I i 267
Soldan I had it from an Arab *s*, who, *Becket* IV i 300
Solder *S*'s a race together—yea—tho' they fail, *The Cup* I i 162
Soldier (*See also* **Soädger**) you are as poor a poet, Wyatt, As a good *s*. *Queen Mary* II i 114
Wyatt was a good *s*, yet he fail'd, ,, III i 132
The Duke Of Alva, an iron *s*. ,, III i 194
His eye was like a *s*'s, ,, IV iii 304
Stupid *s*'s oft are bold. ,, v ii 445
A *s*'s, not a spiritual arm. *Henry.* I lack a spiritual *s*, Thomas. *Becket, Pro.* 255
as brave a *s* as Henry and a goodlier man : ,, *Pro.* 437
Make an Archbishop of a *s*? ,, I i 41
not the *s* As Foliot swears it.— ,, I i 387
I am no *s*, as he said—at least No leader. ,, I iii 298
the lady holds the cleric Lovelier than any *s*, ,, v i 194
The *s*, when he lets his whole self go ,, v ii 39
You come here with your *s*'s to enforce *The Cup* I i 75
Most like it was the Roman *s* shouted. ,, II 120
tho' we have been a *s*, and ridden by his lordship's side, *The Falcon* 547
Sole I say you were the one *s* man who stood. *Bagenhall.* I am the one *s* man in either house, *Queen Mary* III iii 263
I will be *S* master of my house. *Becket* v i 151
Solemn Should not this day be held in after years More *s* than of old ? *Queen Mary* III iii 91
swear When thou art king, to see my *s* vow Accomplish'd. *Harold* III i 306
Against the *s* ordinance from Rome, *Becket* I iii 505
I bound myself, and by a *s* vow, *The Falcon* 679
I believed thee to be too *s* and formal to be a ruffler. *Foresters* I i 168
Solemnity Low words best chime with this *s*. *The Cup* II 217
Solicited you have *s* The Queen, and been rejected. *Queen Mary* I iv 58
Solid Far from *s* foot of men, Never to return again, *Foresters* II 169
Solitary To read and rhyme in *s* fields, *Queen Mary* II i 51
The silent, cloister'd, *s* life, *Harold* III i 277
Solitude Retiring into cloistral *s* To yield *Queen Mary* III vi 209
but saved From all that by our *s*. The plagues That smite the city spare the *s*'s. *Becket* v ii 171
thy *s* among thy nuns, May that save thee ! ,, v ii 176
Solomon-shaming golden slopes Of *S-s* flowers— ,, III i 48

Some (*See also* **Soom**) Might it not Be the rough preface of *s* closer bond? *Queen Mary* I iv 48
counsel your withdrawing To Ashridge, or *s* other country house. ,, I iv 226
I have felt within me Stirrings of *s* great doom when God's just hour Peals— ,, I iv 261
Some one *See* **Summun**
Somerset-Somersetshire (*See also* **Soomerset**) He's a *Somersetshire* man, and a very civil-spoken gentleman. *Prom. of May* I 206
Philip Edgar of Toft Hall In *Somerset*. ,, II 439
One Philip Edgar of Toft Hall in *Somerset* Is lately dead. ,, II 445
I have been telling her of the death of one Philip Edgar of Toft Hall, *Somerset*. ,, II 707
Yes; it was in the *Somersetshire* papers. ,, III 148
Something (*See also* **Summat, Summut**) I miss *s*.
The tree that only bears dead fruit is gone. *Queen Mary* III i 18
I'll say *s* for you—so—good-bye. ,, IV i 167
and our Latimer-sailors Will teach her *s*. ,, IV iii 350
There should be *s* fierier than fire ,, V iv 26
Make not thou The nothing *s*. *Harold* I i 363
On a sudden—at a *s*—for a nothing— ,, I i 442
and I had to say—I love thee none the less—Which will so vex thee. *Rosamund*. *S* against *me*? *Becket* II i 206
We that are kings are *s* in this world, ,, II ii 245
S that would displease me. ,, III i 245
may there not be *s* Of this world's leaven in thee too, ,, V ii 28
Something-nothing Some daily *s-n*. ,, III i 80
Sometime (*See also* **Soomtimes**) It may be *s's* I have overshot My duties ,, V i 37
s's been moved to tears by a chapter of fine writing in a novel; *Prom. of May* III 208
Somewhat (*See also* **Summat, Summut**) trust him *s* less Than Simon Renard, *Queen Mary* I v 221
S beyond your settled purpose? ,, V i 207
Son has offer'd her his *s* Philip, the Pope and the Devil. ,, I i 106
S Courtenay, wilt thou see the holy father Murdered before thy face? up, *s*, and save him! They love thee, ,, I iii 63
Most goodly, Kinglike and an Emperor's *s*,— ,, I v 3
Holy Virgin, Plead with thy blessed *S*; ,, I v 85
And be stepmother of a score of *s's*! ,, I v 206
princely *s*, Heir of this England and the Netherlands! ,, I v 417
sire begets Not half his likeness in the *s*. ,, II i 55
that the *s* Being a King, might wed a Queen— ,, III i 74
The King is here!—My star, my *s*! ,, III ii 184
Perchance in England, loves her like a *s*. ,, III iii 267
O *S* of God, Redeemer of the world! ,, IV iii 118
O God the *S*, Not for slight faults alone, ,, IV iii 138
Didst thou yield up thy *S* to human death; ,, IV iii 144
And Thy most blessed *S's*, who died for man. ,, IV iii 154
For Alva is true *s* of the true church— ,, V i 159
Have done my best, and as a faithful *s*, ,, V ii 117
And the poor *s* turn'd out into the street ,, V ii 125
Gamel, *s* of Orm, What thinkest thou this means? (repeat) *Harold* I i 20, 463
I have a Norman fever on me, *s*, ,, I i 87
Hail, Gamel, *s* of Orm! ,, I i 92
War there, my *s*? is that the doom of England? ,, I i 125
Tostig says true; my *s*, thou art too hard, ,, I i 205
I know it, *s*; I am not thankless: ,, I i 215
Not thee, my *s*: some other messenger. ,, I i 243
now the *s's* of Godwin Sit topmost in the field ,, I i 324
feuds that part The *s's* of Godwin from the *s's* of Alfgar ,, I ii 180
that was his guest, Gamel, the *s* of Orm: ,, II ii 299
O *s*, when thou didst tell me of thine oath, ,, III i 267
My *s*, the Saints are virgins; ,, III i 271
O my *s*! Are all oaths to be broken then, ,, III i 285
S, there is one who loves thee: ,, III i 289
and dear *s*, swear When thou art king, ,, III i 304
O good *s*! That knowledge made him all the carefuller ,, III i 339
Come thou back, and be Once more a *s* of Godwin. ,, IV ii 60
Of Alfred, or of Edward his great *s*, ,, IV iii 52
mark'd the *s's* of those Who made this Britain England, ,, IV iii 152
Noble Gurth! Best *s* of Godwin! ,, V i 135

Son (*continued*) They are so much holier than their harlot's *s* *Harold* V ii 12
I, true *s* Of Holy Church—no croucher *Becket, Pro*. 210
To this *s* of a London merchant— ,, Pro. 433
Look on me as I were thy bodily *s*, For, like a *s*, ,, I iii 263
My burgher's *s*—Nay, if I cannot break him ,, I iii 332
S's sit in judgment on their father!— ,, I iii 551
S, first hear *me*! ,, I iii 672
Hear me, *s*. As gold Outvalues dross, ,, I iii 713
I thank you, *s's*; when kings but hold by crowns, ,, II ii 280
Thou art no prophet, Nor yet a prophet's *s*. ,, II ii 422
S, I absolve thee in the name of God. ,, II ii 442
it was but the sacrifice of a kingdom to his *s*, a smaller matter; ,, III iii 107
King would act servitor and hand a dish to his *s*; ,, III iii 140
'great honour,' says he, 'from the King's self to the King's.' ,, III iii 146
'Should not an earl's *s* wait on a king's *s*?' ,, III iii 151
crowning thy young *s* by York, London and Salisbury —not Canterbury. ,, III iii 194
fawn upon him For thy life and thy *s's*. *Rosamund*. I am a Clifford, My *s* a Clifford and Plantagenet. ,, IV ii 225
King himself, for love of his own *s's*, ,, IV ii 345
link'd me with him To bear him kingly *s's*. ,, IV ii 449
Stirr'd up a party there against your *s*— ,, V i 7
I cannot think he moves against my *s*, Knowing right well with what a tenderness He loved my *s*. ,, V i 19
that but obey'd the crown, Crowning your *s*; ,, V i 52
this no wife has born you four brave *s's*, ,, V i 126
In one a stone-blind Sat by his mother's hearth: ,, V ii 104
The prelates whom he chose to crown his *s*! ,, V ii 400
S, husband, brother gash'd to death in vain, *The Cup* I ii 143
came back last night with her *s* to the castle. *The Falcon* 3
How couldst thou do it, my *s*? ,, 52
happy was the prodigal *s*, For he return'd to the rich father; ,, 141
For fear of losing more than friend, a *s*; ,, 333
White? I warrant thee, my *s*, as the snow ,, 500
O my dear *s*, be not unkind to me. ,, 509
give my time To him that is a part of you, your *s*. ,, 792
I would you had a *s*! ,, 824
beggar-woman seeking alms For her sick *s*, ,, 854
We two together Will help to heal your *s*—your *s* ,, 923
After my frolic with his tenant's girl, Made younger elder *s*, *Prom. of May* I 494
I have lost my gold, I have lost my *s*, *Foresters* I i 338
Thou Much, miller's *s*, hath not the Earl right? ,, I ii 46
Much, the miller's *s*, I knew thy father: ,, I iii 146
And all their *s's* be free, ,, II i 22
and the *s* Is most like dead— ,, II i 146
This is my *s* but late escaped from prison, ,, II i 460
I Little John, he Much the miller's *s*, and he Scarlet, ,, III 55
which a pious *s* of the Church gave me this morning ,, III 281
Blown like a true *s* of the woods, ,, IV 427
I grieve to say it was thy father's *s*. ,, IV 811
We ever fail'd to light upon thy *s*. ,, IV 984
The gold—my *s*—my gold, my *s*, the land— ,, IV 987
Art thou my *s*? *Walter Lea*. I am, good father, ,, IV 1019
Song According to the *s*. *Queen Mary* I v 622
And answer them in *s*. ,, II i 53
S flies you know For ages. ,, II i 80
Our little sister of the *S* of *S's*! ,, III ii 103
mock the blessed Host In *s's* so lewd, ,, IV iii 367
Shall Alice sing you One of her pleasant *s's*? ,, V ii 355
Love is come with a *s* and a smile, Welcome Love with a smile and a *s*: *Harold* I ii 10
And chanting that old *s* of Brunanburg ,, V i 215
our old *s's* are prayers for England too! ,, V i 222
—like a *s* of the people. *Becket, Pro*. 338
Has my simple *s* set you jingling? ,, Pro. 378
bird that moults sings the same *s* again, ,, I iii 447
coming up with a *s* in the flush of the glimmering red? ,, II i 7
they say, she makes *s's*, and that's against her, for I never knew an honest woman that could make *s's*, tho' to be sure our mother 'ill sing me old *s's* by the hour, ,, III i 181

Song (*continued*)   none on 'em ever made *s*'s, and they were
all honest.   *Becket* III i 189
Whose evil *s* far on into the night   „   v ii 208
tell him my tales, Sing him my *s*'s?   *The Falcon* 797
I don't know why I sing that *s*; I don't love it.   *Prom. of May* I 61
Fanny be the naäme i' the *s*, but I swopt it fur *she*.   „   II 212
Sings a new *s* to the new year—and you Strike up a *s*,   *Foresters* I iii 28
There was a *s* he made to the turning wheel—   „   I iii 153
To sing the *s*'s of England Beneath the greenwood tree.   „   II i 23
True soul of the Saxon churl for whom *s* has no charm.   „   II i 386
We be scared with a shout.   „   II ii 164
we have made a *s* in your honour, so your ladyship care
to listen.   „   III 414
Out on thy *s*!   „   IV 28
did ye not call me king in your *s*?   „   IV 220
Let the birds sing, and do you dance to their *s*.   „   IV 557
Songing   *See* **Sing-songing**
Son-in-law   For, Robin, he must be my *s-i-l*.   *Foresters* II i 451
Sonnet   (*See also* **Sonnet-making**)   were a pious work
To string thy father's *s*'s,   *Queen Mary* II i 27
Hand me the casket with my father's *s*'s.   *William*.
Ay—*s*'s   „   II i 44
Tut, your *s*'s a flying ant,   „   II i 83
Write you as many *s*'s as you will.   „   II i 95
Sonneteer   Or would you have me turn a *s*,   „   III vi 154
Sonnet-making   and no call for sonnet-sorting now, nor
for *s-m* either,   „   II i 60
And *s-m*'s safer.   „   II i 93
Sonnet-sorting   and no call for *s-s* now, nor for sonnet-
making either,   „   II i 59
Sonnetting   Come, now, you're *s* again.   „   II i 247
Soom (*some*)   and I taäked 'im fur *s* sort of a land-
surveyor—   *Prom. of May* I 204
but I hallus gi'ed *s* on 'em to Miss Eva at this time
o' year.   „   II 15
so I allus browt soom on 'em to her;   „   II 20
an' them theer be *s* of her oän roses,   „   II 38
Soomerset (**Somerset**)   Philip Hedgar o' *S*! (repeat)   „   II 587
—I'll *S* tha.   „   II 592
' O' the 17th, Philip Edgar, o' Toft Hall, *S*.'   „   II 712
Soomtimes (**sometimes**)   And p'raps ye hears 'at I *s*
taäkes a drop too much;   „   II 108
Sooner   He'd *s* be, While this same marriage question   *Queen Mary* II ii 36
At thy most need—not *s*.   *Harold*.   So I will.   *Harold* I i 16
S or later shamed of her among The ladies,   *Prom. of May* III 581
No *s*? when will that be?   *Foresters* IV 420
Soot   even if I found it Dark with the *s* of slums.   *Prom. of May* III 602
Sop   new Lords Are quieted with their *s* of Abbey-
lands,   *Queen Mary* III i 142
Sore (adj.)   (*See also* **Half-sore**)   Remember that *s*
saying spoken once By Him   „   IV iii 202
Sore (s)   gangrenes, and running *s*'s, praise ye the Lord,   *Becket* I iv 256
Sorrier   thou canst not be *s* than I am.   „   II i 282
Sorrow   Grace to repent and *s* for their schism;   *Queen Mary* III iii 177
Following her like her *s*.   „   V v 11
Sorrow'd   I *s* for my random promise given   *Harold* I i 269
Have *s* for her all these years in vain.   *Prom. of May* II 415
Sorry   Good faith, I was too *s* for the woman To mark
the dress.   *Queen Mary* II i 57
I am *s* for it If Pole be like to turn.   „   III iv 415
I'm *s* for it, for, tho' he never comes to church,   *Prom. of May* I 260
I am *s* Mr. Steer still continues too unwell to attend to you,   „   III 21
though I can be *s* for him—as the good Sally says,   „   III 173
' I am *s* that we could not attend your Grace's party
on the 10th!'   „   III 312
I am *s* my exchequer runs so low   *Foresters* I ii 272
Here is thy gold again.   I am *s* for it.   „   IV 985
Sort   What *s* of brothers then be those that lust   *Queen Mary* IV iii 196
I have seen heretics of the poorer *s*,   „   IV iii 436
I think that in some *s* we may.   „   IV iii 551
Were but a *s* of winter;   „   V iv 16
As . . . in some *s* . . . I have been false to thee.   *Harold* V i 351
Yes, in some *s* I do.   *Foresters* II i 527
I tell thee, in some *s*.   *Robin*.   *S*! *s*! what *s*? what
s of man art thou For land,   „   II i 531

MM*

Sought   I *s* him and I could not find him.   *The Cup* II 396
That *s* to free the tomb-place of the King   *Foresters* IV 408
Soul   The downfall of so many simple *s*'s,   *Queen Mary* I ii 54
my good mother came (God rest her *s*)   „   I v 12
Or Lady Jane?   *Wyatt*.   No, poor *s*; no.   „   II i 242
We kill the heretics that sting the *s*—   „   III iv 69
And every *s* of man that breathes therein.   „   III iv 107
A secular kingdom is but as the body Lacking a *s*;   „   IV i 33
Is as the *s* descending out of heaven   „   IV i 35
to the saving of their *s*'s, Before your execution.   „   IV iii 194
for thy *s* shall masses here be sung   „   IV iii 100
Pray with one breath, one heart, one *s* for me.   „   IV iii 104
peril mine own *s* By slaughter of the body?   „   V i 168
Let the great Devil fish for your own *s*'s.   *Harold* II i 32
We have respect for man's immortal *s*,   „   II ii 501
A conscience for his own *s*, not his realm;   „   II i 63
But wing'd *s*'s flying Beyond all change   „   III ii 100
one for all, and all for one, One *s*!   „   IV iii 60
The *s* who fighteth on thy side is cursed,   „   V i 69
Praying perchance for this poor *s* of mine   „   V i 323
and the *s* of Eleanor from hell-fire.   *Becket, Pro.* 151
Peace to his *s*!   „   *Pro.* 394
Poor *s*! poor *s*! My friend, the King! . . .   „   I i 334
The *s* the body, and the Church the Throne,   „   I iii 717
loathing for a *s* Purer, and truer and nobler   „   II i 171
Fling not thy *s* into the flames of hell: „   II i 316
And break the *s* from earth.   „   V i 44
God save him from all sickness of the *s*!   „   V ii 175
His child and mine own *s*, and our future.   „   V ii 193
all the *s*'s we saved and father'd here Will greet us   „   V ii 223
Is it too late for me to save your *s*?   „   V ii 524
ere two *s* be knit for life and death,   *The Cup* I 359
God rest his honest *s*, he bought 'em for me,   *The Falcon* 49
For all the *s*'s on earth that live   *Prom. of May* III 7
For all the blessed *s*'s in Heaven   „   III 10
A *s* with no religion—My mother used to say   „   III 532
Sleep, happy *s*! all life will sleep at last.   *Foresters* I iii 48
The *s* of the woods hath stricken thro' my blood,   „   I i 66
True *s* of the Saxon churl for whom song has no charm.   „   II i 385
And that would quite *unman* him, heart and *s*.   „   III 30
I Embrace thee with the kisses of the *s*.   „   III 143
flung His life, heart, *s* into those holy wars   „   IV 407
Who hunger for the body, not the *s*—   „   IV 700
Marriage is of the *s*, not of the body.   „   IV 720
I remain Mistress of mine own self and mine own *s*.   „   IV 730
Sound (adj.)   *S* sleep to the man Here by dead Norway
without dream or dawn!   *Harold* IV iii 120
Go round once more; See all be *s* and whole.   „   V i 194
and most amorous Of good old red *s* liberal Gascon
wine: *Becket, Pro.* 100
A great and *s* policy that: I could embrace him for it: „   *Pro.* 451
And were my kindly father *s* again,   *Foresters* II 81
S at the core as we are.   „   III 102
Sound (s)   What is that whirring *s*? (repeat)   *Harold* V i 482, 665
Sound (verb)   To *s* the Princess carelessly on this;   *Queen Mary* V i 259
That is noble! That *s*'s of Godwin.   *Harold* IV i 58
How ghostly *s*'s that horn in the black wood!   *Becket* III ii 16
when the horn *s*, she comes out as a wolf.   „   III ii 23
when that horn *s*'s, a score of wolf-dogs are let loose   „   III ii 38
all that *s*'s so wicked and so strange;   *Prom. of May* I 656
name Of Harold's *s* so English and so old   „   III 610
Wherever the horn *s*, and the buck bound,   *Foresters* III 345
Wherever the buck bound, and the horn *s*,   „   III 356
Sounded   I'll have the scandal *s* to the mud.   *Queen Mary* I v 227
Sour   Yon gray old Gospeller, *s* as midwinter,   „   I iii 40
S milk and black bread.   *Foresters* II i 272
And jealousy is wither'd, *s* and ugly: „   II ii 65
South   North and *S* Thunder together,   *Harold* III i 392
The men that guarded England to the *S*   „   IV iii 210
in *S* and North at once I could not be.   „   IV iii 217
I left our England naked to the *S*   „   V i 289
Southern   The tan of *s* summers and the beard?   *Prom. of May* III 617
Southwark   Wyatt comes to *S*;   *Queen Mary* II ii 375
And pointed full at *S*;   „   II iii 46

Southwark (*continued*) When Wyatt sack'd the
Chancellor's house in *S*.   *Queen Mary* v ii 505
South-west North-east took and turned him *S-w*, then the
S-w turned him North-east,   *Becket* ii ii 321
Sovereign (adj.) I am of *s* nature, but I know, Not to
be quell'd;   *Queen Mary* i iv 258
Our *s* Lady by King Harry's will;   ,,   ii ii 268
Why should I swear, Eleanor, who am, or was, A *s*
power?   *Becket* iv ii 405
And when you came and dipt your *s* head Thro' these
low doors,   *The Falcon* 867
Sovereign (s) Bride of the mightiest *s* upon earth?   *Queen Mary* v ii 544
he and I are both Galatian-born, And tributary *s's*,   *The Cup* ii 95
The *s* of Galatia weds his Queen.   ,,   ii 432
Sow Who knows what *s's* itself among the people?   *Harold* iv i 149
That *s* this hate between my lord and me!   *Becket* ii ii 272
Sow'd if you *s* therein The seed of Hate,   *Queen Mary* iv i 170
Who *s* this fancy here among the people?   *Harold* iv i 147
Sowest The seed thou *s* in thy field is cursed,   ,,   v i 70
Sown Can render thanks in fruit for being *s*,   *Queen Mary* iii iii 198
Have I *s* it in salt? I trust not,   *Becket* iii iii 320
Space For a little *s*, farewell;   *Queen Mary* iv i 46
Spade Your havings wasted by the scythe and *s*—   ,,   ii ii 277
Spain Prince of *S* coming to wed our Queen!   ,,   i iii 83
my good mother came (God rest her soul) Of *S*,   ,,   i v 13
Your royal mother came of *S*,   ,,   i v 16
for to wed with *S* Would treble England—   ,,   i v 75
Stab me in fancy, hissing *S* and Philip;   ,,   i v 150
prince is known in *S*, in Flanders,   ,,   i v 207
That you may marry Philip, Prince of *S*—   ,,   i v 252
Mary of England, joining hands with *S*,   ,,   i v 299
S and we, One crown, might rule the world.   ,,   i v 301
Who waits? *Usher.* The Ambassador of *S*,   ,,   i v 342
would not graze The Prince of *S*.   ,,   i v 454
I was in *S* with him. I couldn't eat in *S*, I couldn't
sleep in *S*, Sir Thomas. *Wyatt.* But
thou could'st drink in *S* if I remember.   ,,   ii i 35
Philip and the black-faced swarms of *S*,   ,,   ii i 99
island will become A rotten limb of *S*.   ,,   ii i 105
I know *S*. I have been there with my father;   ,,   ii i 166
shall we have *S* on the throne and in the parliament;
S in the pulpit and on the law-bench; *S* in all
the great offices of state; *S* in our ships,   ,,   ii i 176
No! no! no *S*! *William.* No *S* in our beds—
and the beds I know. I hate *S*.   ,,   ii i 181
—war against *S*.   ,,   ii i 185
the world is with us—war against *S*!   ,,   ii i 190
If we move not now, *S* moves,   ,,   ii i 197
wherever *S* hath ruled she hath wither'd all   ,,   ii i 202
They would not have me wed the Prince of *S*;   ,,   ii ii 149
Who mouth and foam against the Prince of *S*.   ,,   ii ii 251
smash all our bits o' things worse than Philip o' *S*.
Second Woman. Don't ye now go to think that
we be for Philip o' *S*.   ,,   ii iii 104
lest living *S* Should sicken at dead England.   ,,   iii i 27
and hurl'd our battles Into the heart of *S*; but England
now Is but a ball chuck'd between France and *S*,
they pillage *S* already.   ,,   iii i 109
Looks very *S* of very *S*?   ,,   iii i 158
Philip had been one of those black devils of *S*,   ,,   iii i 192
How should he bear a bridegroom out of *S*?   ,,   iii i 216
married my good mother,—For fear of *S*.   ,,   iii iii 26
Than yours in happier *S*.   ,,   iii v 247
In hope to charm them from their hate of *S*. *Philip.*   ,,   iii vi 64
In hope to crush all heresy under *S*.   ,,   iii vi 83
If ever, as heaven grant, we clash with *S*,   ,,   iv iii 347
And grafted on the hard-grain'd stock of *S*—   ,,   iv iii 427
Into one sword to hack at *S* and me.   ,,   v i 138
I would we had you, Madam, in our warm *S*.   ,,   v ii 608
Count de Feria, from the King of *S*.   ,,   v iii 9
Were you in *S*, this fine fair gossamer gold—   ,,   v iii 48
If such a one as you should match with *S*, What
hinders but that *S* and England join'd,   ,,   v iii 67
S would be England on her seas, and England
Mistress of the Indies.   ,,   v iii 72

Spain (*continued*) Without the help of *S*. *Feria.*
Impossible; Except you put *S* down.   *Queen Mary* v iii 78
Spake (*See also* **Spoke**) That was their pretext—so
they *s* at first—   ,,   ii ii 150
and wherefore *s* you not before?   ,,   v iii 107
Make thou not mention that I *s* with thee.   *Harold* ii ii 483
There *s* Godwin, Who hated all the Normans;   ,,   iii i 251
Stigand believed he knew not what he *s*.   ,,   iii ii 62
And *s* to the Lord God, and said,   *Becket* i i 74
I *s* no word of treachery, Reginald.   ,,   v ii 401
Antonius—'Camma!' who *s*?   *The Cup* ii 401
I am all but sure that some one *s*.   ,,   ii 405
Spaniard (*See also* **Spaniel-Spaniard**) Stave off the
crowd upon the *S* there.   *Queen Mary* i iii 77
Will brook nor Pope nor *S* here   ,,   i v 189
That knows the Queen, the *S*, and the Pope,   ,,   ii ii 413
that every *S* carries a tail like a devil   ,,   iii i 223
Would I had been Born *S*!   ,,   iii iii 246
Upon the faith and honour of a *S*,   ,,   iii vi 254
Here swings a *S*—there an Englishman;   ,,   v i 87
The Pope would cast the *S* out of Naples: ,,   v i 148
He is all Italian, and he hates the *S*;   ,,   v ii 56
And more than all—no *S*.   ,,   v ii 483
Spaniel her poor *s* wailing for her,   *Prom. of May* ii 473
Spaniel-Spaniard These *s-S* English of the time,   *Queen Mary* iii iii 240
Spanish (*See also* **Half-Spanish**) sworn this *S*
marriage shall not be.   ,,   i iv 115
and I am *S* in myself,   ,,   i v 13
We'll dust him from a bag of *S* gold.   ,,   i v 421
And Counts, and sixty *S* cavaliers,   ,,   iii i 51
and English carrot's better than *S* licorice;   ,,   iii i 220
every *S* priest will tell you that   ,,   iii i 228
and make way a A *S* province;   ,,   iii i 466
as he walk'd the *S* friars Still plied   ,,   iv iii 576
Our *S* ladies have none such—   ,,   v iii 46
Spare (adj.) how bare and *s* I be on the rib: *Foresters* i i 50
Spare me thy *s* ribs, I pray thee;   ,,   i i 53
Spare (verb) To *s* the life of Cranmer.   *Queen Mary* iv i 4
That I should *s* to take a heretic priest's,   ,,   iv i 131
S and forbear him, Harold, if he comes!   *Harold* iii i 299
Edward bad me *s* thee.   ,,   iv ii 11
Is thy wrath Hell, that I should *s* to cry,   ,,   v i 37
to *s* us the hardness of your facility?   *Becket, Pro.* 385
S not thy tongue! be lavish with our coins,   ,,   iv ii 469
plead so pitifully, that I may *s* thee?   ,,   iv ii 217
S this defence, dear brother.   ,,   v iii 168
Let him—he never *s's* me to my face!   *The Falcon* 109
I never *s* your lordship to your lordship's face,   ,,   111
to *s* myself, And her too, pain, pain, pain?   *Prom. of May* iii 718
S me thy spare ribs, I pray thee;   *Foresters* i i 53
Spared *S* you the Duke of Suffolk, Guildford Dudley,   *Queen Mary* i v 489
Rome never yet hath *s* conspirator.   *The Cup* i ii 234
We *s* the craftsman, chapman,   *Foresters* iii 163
Spark Saints to scatter *s's* of plague Thro' all your cities,   *Harold* ii ii 745
for a *s* Of self-disdain born in me when I sware   ,,   v i 301
Sparkle *s* out as quick Almost as kindled;   *Queen Mary* ii i 73
seem'd to smile And *s* like our fortune   ,,   ii iii 24
What *s's* in the moonlight on thy hand?   *Foresters* ii i 582
Sparkled Our silver cross *s* before the prow,   *Queen Mary* iii ii 9
Spatter my battle-axe and him To *s* his brains!   *Harold* ii ii 781
Spavin'd And broken bridge, or *s* horse, or wave And
wind at their old battle;   *Queen Mary* i v 355
Spawn Knights, bishops, earls, this London *s*—   *Becket* ii ii 144
Speak You *s* too low, my Lord; I cannot hear you.   *Queen Mary* iv i 123
S not thereof—no, not to your best friend,   ,,   i iv 176
ever faithful counsellor, might I *s*?   ,,   i v 136
that will *s* When I and thou and all rebellious lie
fifty That followed me from Penenden Heath in
hope To hear you *s*.   ,,   ii i 78
The mine is fired, and I will *s* to them.   ,,   ii i 153
S at once—and all! For whom?   ,,   ii i 155
S! in the name of God!   ,,   ii ii 265
The Queen stands up, and *s's* for her own self;   ,,   ii ii 271
had Howard spied me there And made them *s*,   ,,   ii ii 341
S for yourself.   ,,   ii iii 34
   ,,   iii iii 22

Speak (*continued*)   You brawl beyond the question;
s, Lord Legate !   *Queen Mary* III iv 98
S, friend Bonner, And tell this learned Legate   „   III iv 270
Nay, God's passion, before me ! s !   „   III iv 286
till it spells and s's Quite other than at first.   „   III v 36
May Simon Renard s a single word ?   „   III vi 121
to s a single word That could not be forgiven.   „   III vi 126
Yourselves shall hear him s.   S, Master Cranmer,   „   IV iii 110
After the vanish'd voice, and s to men.   „   IV iii 164
see, see, I s of him in the past.   „   IV iii 422
even while I s There lurks a silent dagger,   „   V ii 215
Low, my lute ; s low, my lute,   „   V ii 367
And may not s for hours.   „   V ii 406
When he we s of drove the window back,   „   V vii 464
but I s from mine own self, not him ;   „   V iii 41
letting the wild brook S for us—   „   V v 92
—they cannot s—for awe ;   *Harold* I i 32
s him sweetly, he will hear thee.   „   I i 116
in Normanland God s's thro' abler voices,   „   I i 167
Did not Heaven s to men in dreams of old ?   „   II i 94
He'll s for himself ! Hold thine own, if thou canst !   „   II i 79
S for thy mother's sake, and tell me true.   „   II ii 271
Obey him, s him fair,   „   II ii 317
Is it not better still to s the truth ?   „   II ii 373
O s him fair, Harold, for thine own sake.   „   II ii 395
Oh no, no—s him fair !   „   II ii 413
thou be my vice-king in England. S.   „   II ii 636
When all the world hath learnt to s the truth,   „   II i 68
If one may dare to s the truth,   „   IV i 108
We never—oh ! good Morcar, s for us,   „   IV i 216
And, when again red-blooded, s again ;   „   IV iii 208
I s after my fancies, for I am a Troubadour,   *Becket*, Pro. 346
he s's to a noble as tho' he were a churl,   „   Pro. 454
And all that s for them anathema.   „   I i 171
Do thou s first.   „   I iv 1
To s without stammering and like a free man ?   „   I iv 7
Who misuses a dog would misuse a child—they
    cannot s for themselves—   „   I iv 110
S only of thy love.   „   II i 179
He s's As if it were a cake of gingerbread.   „   II i 229
and to s truth, night at the end of our last crust,   „   III i 113
and not s till I was spoke to,   „   III i 120
bad me whatever I saw not to s one word,   „   III i 133
not to s one word, for that's the rule o' the garden,   „   III i 137
tho' I shouldn't s one word,   „   III i 154
tho' I be sworn not to s a word, I can tell you all
    about her,   „   III i 205
That I would s with you once more alone.   „   III iii 40
Did the King S of the customs ?   „   III iii 333
You have wrong'd Fitzurse. I s not of myself.   „   IV i 328
—I have still thy leave to s.   „   V i 45
Can I s with you Alone, my father ?   „   V i 69
Then s ; this is my other self,   „   V ii 73
Better perhaps to s with them apart.   „   V ii 310
S with them privately on this hereafter.   „   V ii 419
As I shall s again.   „   V ii 517
I pray you for one moment stay and s.   „   V ii 525
Some friends of mine would s with me without.   *The Cup* I ii 203
no more power than other oracles To s directly.
    Phœbe.   Will you s to him, The messenger
    from Synorix   „   II 35
Did not this man S well ?   „   II 92
Nor s I now too mightily, being King And happy !   „   II 237
These are strange words to s to Artemis.   „   II 326
S freely, tho' to call a madman mad   *The Falcon* 81
Can I s with the Count ?   „   179
won't you s with the old woman first,   „   182
yet to s white truth, my good old mother,   „   503
Can I not s with you once more alone ?   „   688
You s like love, and yet you love me not.   „   782
No more, but s.   *Giovanna.*   I will.   „   814
And s for him after—you that are so clever !   *Prom. of May* I 619
S not so loudly ; that must be your sister.   „   I 726
Did you s, Philip ?   „   I 748
Is not this To s too pitilessly of the dead ?   „   II 461

Speak (*continued*)   will you not s with Father to-day ?   *Prom. of May* III 237
Can't I s like a lady ; pen a letter like a lady ;   „   III 501
and he wants to s to ye partic'lar.   „   III 351
What ails you ?   *Harold.*   S.   „   III 662
and s small to 'em, and not scare 'em   *Foresters* I i 100
I will s with her.   „   I i 306
so that you keep the cowl down and s not ?   „   I ii 22
nor to s word to anyone,   „   I ii 237
We old hags should be bribed to s truth,   „   II i 237
S straight out, crookback.   „   II i 270
I beseech you all to s lower.   „   II i 334
S but one word not only of forgiveness,   „   II ii 610
S to me, I am like a boy now going to be whipt ;   „   II ii 49
S to me, Kate, and say you pardon me ! *Kate.* I
    never will s word to thee again.   „   II ii 53
How much ? how much ?   S, or the arrow flies.   „   III 278
S not.   I wait upon a dying father.   „   IV 610
If a cat may look at a king, may not a friar s to one ?   „   IV 922
Speaker   It would have burnt both s's.   *Queen Mary* III vi 164
for thou Art known a s of the truth,   *Harold* II ii 517
Speakest   Thou s of the enemy of thy king.   *Queen Mary* I v 327
Thou s like a fool or a woman.   *Foresters* I i 203
Thou standest straight. Thou s manlike.   „   II 409
Speaking   I can forespeak your s.   *Queen Mary* I v 137
or by s aught Which might impugn or prejudice   „   III iii 132
not half s The language of the land.   *Becket* II i 136
I was s with Your father, asking   *Prom. of May* III 491
Spear   not S into pruning-hook—   *Harold* IV i 442
Spear-head   Mark'd how the s-h sprang,   „   IV iii 158
Sped   And I s hither with what haste   *Queen Mary* II iv 77
Speech   after some slight s about the Sheriff   *Foresters* I i 114
Speechify   and we'll git 'im to s for us arter dinner.   *Prom. of May* I 440
Speed   That sun may God s !   *Harold* III i 72
Must s you to your bower at once.   *Becket* I i 194
Speedwell   Bluebell, harebell, s, bluebottle,   *Prom. of May* I 97
Spell (s)   Eva's eyes thro' hers—A s upon me !   „   II 643
Weary—weary As tho' a s were on me.   *Foresters* I i 115
Spell (verb)   loons That cannot s Esaïas from St. Paul,   *Queen Mary* III i 281
till it s's and speaks Quite other than at first.   „   III v 36
old hag tho' I be, I can s the hand.   *Foresters* II i 351
Spend   For she shall s her honeymoon with me.   „   IV 757
Spent   like a butterfly in a chrysalis, You s your life ;   *Queen Mary* I iv 52
I s thrice that in fortifying his castles.   *Becket* I iii 632
s all your last Saturday's wages at the ale-house ;   *Prom. of May* III 78
Spice   Some s of wisdom in my telling you,   *Queen Mary* II iv 134
A s of Satan, ha !   „   III iv 77
fling in the s's, Nard, Cinnamon,   *The Cup* II 183
Spiced   I know your Norman cookery is so s,   *Harold* II ii 811
Spice-islands   And all the fair s-i's of the East.   *Queen Mary* V i 49
Spider   Crost and recrost, a venomous s's web—   *Becket* II i 199
Then I would drop from the casement, like a s.   *Foresters* I i 317
Spied   had Howard s me there And made them speak,   *Queen Mary* II iii 32
s my people's ways ;   *Becket* I iii 363
I never s in thee one gleam of grace.   „   V ii 474
Spilt   the cow kick'd, and all her milk was s.   *Queen Mary* III v 267
Spin   these poor hands but sew, S, broider—   *Harold* IV iii 11
Spine   My old crook'd s would bud out   „   III i 24
Spire   parson from his own s swung out dead,   *Queen Mary* IV iii 375
s of Holy Church may prick the graves—   *Becket* I iii 553
Spiring   O tower s to the sky,   *Prom. of May* III 203
Spirit   If Cranmer's s were a mocking one,   *Queen Mary* V vii 210
like a s in Hell who skips and flies   *Harold* I i 10
some familiar s must have help'd him.   „   II ii 677
s of the twelve Apostles enter'd Into thy making.   *Becket* I i 50
and mortify thy flesh, Not s—   „   I iii 541
talk not of cows.   You anger the s.   *Foresters* II i 330
Spiritual   We, the Lords S and Temporal,   *Queen Mary* III iii 113
A soldier's, not a s arm. *Henry.*   I lack a soldier,
    Thomas,   *Becket*, Pro. 255
that sweet other-world smile which will be reflected
    in the s body among the angels.   „   Pro. 397
And on a matter wholly s.   „   I iii 85
striving still to break or bind The s giant with our
    island laws And customs,   „   IV ii 444
Fasts, disciplines that clear the s eye,   „   V i 42

Steady How s it is ! *Phœbe.* S enough to stab him ! — *The Cup* II 212
Steadying S the tremulous pillars of the Church— — *Queen Mary* I v 517
Steal Friend Roger, s thou in among the crowd, — „ I iii 37
  fear creeps in at the front, honesty s's out at the back, — *Becket* III iii 62
  Were it best to s away, to spare myself, — *Prom. of May* III 718
Stealing (*See also* **A-steälin'**) my father and I forgave you s our coals. — „ III 69
Steam look how the table s's, like a heathen altar ; — *Becket* I iv 69
Steam'd S upward from the undescendible Abysm. — *Harold* I i 14
Steaming In breathless dungeons over s sewers, — *Queen Mary* IV iii 440
Steed Thy high black s among the flaming furze, — *Becket* II i 55
Steel To s myself against the leaving her ? — *Prom. of May* I 293
Steep'd He s himself In all the lust of Rome. — *The Cup* II 367
Steeple Let all the s's clash, — *Queen Mary* III ii 237
Steep-up And on the s-u track of the true faith — „ III iv 94
Steer (Dora) *See* **Dora, Dora Steer**
Steer (Farmer) Owd S wur afeärd she wouldn't be back i' time — *Prom. of May* I 16
  Why if S han't haxed schoolmaster to dinner, — „ I 184
  Hev' ony o' ye seen Eva ? *Dobson.* Noä, Mr. *S.* — „ I 314
  An' the saäme to you, Master S, likewise. — „ I 347
  But, S, thaw thou be haäle anew — „ I 383
  Yeas, yeas ! Three cheers for Mr. S ! — „ I 456
  an' ony o' S's men, an' ony o' my men — „ II 34
  Owd S's gotten all his grass down and wants a hand, — „ II 221
  Owd S gi'es nubbut cowd tea to 'is men, — „ II 223
  But I'd like owd S's cowd tea better — „ II 226
  I am sorry Mr. S still continues too unwell to attend — „ III 21
  Milly, my dear, how did you leave Mr. S ? — „ III 410
  poor S looks The Very type of Age in a picture, — „ III 512
Steer (verb) Cranmer, as the helmsman at the helm S's, — *Queen Mary* IV iii 579
  Let every craft that carries sail and gun S toward Calais. — „ v ii 276
  His Holiness cannot s straight thro' shoals, — *Becket* II ii 58
Steer (young ox) The s wherewith thou plowest thy field is cursed, — *Harold* v i 71
Steering therein Sunk rocks—they need fine s— — *Queen Mary* v v 214
Steers (family of) because one of the S's had planted it there in former times. — *Prom. of May* III 247
  If it had killed one of the S's there the other day, — „ III 250
  The S's was all gentlefoälks i' the owd times, — „ III 447
  The land belonged to the S's i' the owd times, an' it belongs to the S's ageän. — „ III 450
  We S's are of old blood, tho' we be fallen. — „ III 604
  I have heard the S's Had land in Saxon times ; — „ III 607
Step (s) S after s, Thro' many voices crying — *Queen Mary* I ii 47
  seen your s's a mile From me and Lambeth ? — „ I ii 80
  myself upon the s's. — „ v ii 238
  No, to the crypt ! Twenty s's down. — *Becket* v iii 78
  Not twenty s's, but one. — „ v iii 90
  one s in the dark beyond Our expectation, — *The Cup* I ii 212
  'tis but a s from here To the Temple. — „ I ii 442
  No, not one s with thee. Where is Antonius ? — „ I iii 96
Step (verb) Then shalt thou s into my place and sign. — *Becket* I iii 14
  the master 'ud be straänge an' pleased if you'd s in fust, — *Prom. of May* I 168
  Better s out of his road, then, for he's walking to us, — „ I 218
  Lady Marian holds her nose when she s's across it. — *Foresters* I i 84
Stephen (King of England) Church in the pell-mell of S's time — *Becket, Pro.* 19
  Him who crown'd S—King S's brother ! — „ Pro. 273
  may come a crash and embroilment as in S's time ; — „ Pro. 462
  That havock'd all the land in S's day. — „ I i 242
  King S gave Many of the crown lands — „ I iii 149
  Then he took back not only S's gifts, — „ I iii 154
  After the nineteen winters of King S— — „ I iii 339
Stephen Gardiner (Bishop of Winchester and Lord Chancellor) (*See also* **Gardiner**) is every morning's prayer Of your most loyal subject, S G. — *Queen Mary* I v 104
Stepmother And be s of a score of sons ! — „ I v 206
Stepping my white bird s toward the snare. — *The Cup* I iii 35
  delicate-footed creature Came s o'er him, — *Foresters* IV 537

Stept I s between and purchased him, — *Harold* II ii 40
  king of day hath s from off his throne, — *Foresters* II i 26
Stern half sight which makes her look so s, — *Queen Mary* II ii 323
Sternatur Acies, Acies Prona s ! — *Harold* v i 582
Stick (s) Ye take a s, and break it ; — „ I 57
  as when we threaten A yelper with a s. — *Becket* IV ii 350
Stick (verb) old leaven s's to my tongue yet. — *Queen Mary* I iii 48
  so 'z we was forced to s her, — „ IV iii 495
  By God's death, thou shalt s him like a calf ! — *Becket* I iii 183
  and Baäker, thaw I s's to hoäm-maäde— — *Prom. of May* I 449
  if thou s to she I'll s to thee—s to tha like a weasel — „ II 738
Stiff S as the very backbone of heresy. — *Queen Mary* I v 44
  That strange starched s creature, Little John, the — *Foresters* I i 183
Stigand (Archbishop of Canterbury) S should know the purposes of Heaven. — *Harold* I i 64
  Old uncanonical S—ask of me Who had my pallium — „ I i 81
  Well, father S—War there, my son ? — „ I i 123
  S shall give me absolution for it— — „ II ii 798
  I, old shrivell'd S, I, — „ III i 7
  one whom they dispoped ? *Harold.* No, S, no ! — „ III i 108
  Ay—S, unriddle This vision, canst thou ? — „ III i 173
  take, sign it, S, Alfred ! Sign it, — „ III i 198
  S hath given me absolution for it. *Edward.* S is not canonical enough To save thee — „ III i 213
  S believed he knew not what he spake. — „ III ii 61
  S will see thee safe, And so—Farewell. — „ v i 418
  old S, With hands too limp to brandish iron— — „ v i 448
  S, O father, have we won the day ? — „ v i 543
Stile is the King's if too high a s for your lordship to overstep — *Becket* III iii 281
Still To s the petty treason therewithin, — *Queen Mary* III i 13
  I left her lying s and beautiful, — „ v v 261
Still'd Nay, have we s him ? — *Becket* v iii 201
Stillness Who breaks the s of the morning thus ? — *Foresters* I iii 50
  dead Are shaken from their s in the grave — „ II i 46
Stilt And that would s up York to twice himself. — *Becket* II ii 34
Sting (s) an amphisbæna, Each end a s : — *Queen Mary* III iv 40
  when our good hive Needs every s to save it. — *Harold* v i 18
Sting (verb) We kill the heretics that s the soul— — *Queen Mary* III iv 69
  A snake—and if I touch it, it may s. — „ III v 218
Stinging All hollow'd out with s heresies ; — „ III ii 203
Stir s not yet This matter of the Church lands. — „ I v 407
  Carew is In Devon : — „ II i 5
  Will s the living tongue and make the cry. — „ III i 354
  He s's within the darkness ! — „ III ii 158
  this Henry S's up your land against you — „ v i 131
  Send out ; I am too weak to s abroad : — „ v ii 287
  S up thy people : oust him ! — *Harold* I i 482
  S up the King, the Lords ! — *Becket* I ii 88
  As at this loveless knife that s's the riot, — „ IV ii 191
  she did not s ; The snow had frozen round her, — „ v ii 236
Stirr'd never s or writhed, but, like a statue, — *Queen Mary* IV iii 620
  Morcar and Edwin have s up the Thanes — *Harold* II ii 288
  That in thy cause were s against King Henry, — *Becket* II ii 429
  S up a party there against your son— — „ v i 6
Stirrest Thou s up a grief thou canst not fathom. — *Queen Mary* III iv 298
Stirring S's of some great doom when God's — „ I iv 261
  I hear them s in the Council Chamber. — „ I v 628
  From s hand or foot to wrong the realm. — „ III iii 60
  S her baby-king against me ? ha ! — *Becket* I v 106
  What is this ? some one been s Against me ? — *Prom. of May* III 560
Stitch'd they be fine ; I never s none such. — *Queen Mary* III i 226
Stock (*See also* **Self-stock**) And grafted on the hard-grain'd s of Spain— — „ IV iii 426
  only rose of all the s That never thorn'd him ; — *Harold* I i 426
  I am but a stone and a dead s to thee. — *Foresters* II ii 69
Stock-dove The s-d coo'd at the fall of night, — *Prom. of May* I 41
  And the s-d coo'd, till a kite dropt down, — „ I 55
Stole there your king s her a babe from Scotland — *Queen Mary* v i 291
  there s into the city a breath Full of the meadows, — *Becket* I i 261
  Who s the widow's one sitting hen o' Sunday, — „ I iv 120
  S on her, then she was walking in the garden, — *Foresters* I i 112
Stolen The golden ornaments are s from her— — *Becket* III iii 180
  and ower a hoonderd pounds worth o' rings s. — *Prom. of May* I 394

Stolen (*continued*) For thou hast *s* my will, and made it
thine.   *Foresters* III 329
Stone (adj.) For smooth *s* columns of the sanctuary,   *Harold* I ii 101
Stone (s) into some more costly *s* Than ever blinded eye.   *Queen Mary* I v 370
why fling back the *s* he strikes me with ?   „   IV ii 150
Albeit no rolling *s*, my good friend Gamel,   *Harold* I i 93
tho' the drop may hollow out the dead *s*,   *Becket* III iii 315
a cheek like a peach and a heart like the *s* in it—   *The Falcon* 94
Hard as the *s's* of his abbey.   *Foresters* I ii 270
I am but a *s* and a dead stock to thee.   „   II ii 69
Stone (verb) Our men and boys would hoot him, *s*
him,   *Prom. of May* II 425
Stone-blind a son *s-b* Sat by his mother's hearth :   *Becket* V ii 105
Stone-cut And, like the *s-c* epitaph,   *Queen Mary* IV iii 163
Stone-dead sat *S-d* upon a heap of ice-cold eggs.   *Becket* V ii 239
Stone-hard *S-h*, ice-cold—no dash of daring in him.   *Queen Mary* I v 331
Stood I *s* out, till Edward sent for me.   „   I ii 29
Lady Jane *s* up Stiff as the very backbone   „   I v 42
citizens *S* each before his shut-up booth,   „   II ii 63
and almost elbowing her, So close they *s*,   „   II ii 78
In every London street a gibbet *s*.   „   III i 7
Who *s* upright when both the houses fell.   „   III iii 254
Well, you one man, because you *s* upright,   „   III iii 269
firm *s* the pine—The cataract shook   „   III iv 137
S out against the King in your behalf,   „   IV i 126
At your trial Never *s* up a bolder man than you ;   „   IV ii 122
He *s* upright, a lad of twenty-one,   „   IV iii 335
s More like an ancient father of the Church,   „   IV iii 597
I *s* near—Mark'd him—   „   IV iii 616
while we *s* together, a dead man Rose   *Harold* I ii 78
and at once He *s* beside me,   „   II i 136
Every man about his king Fell where he *s*.   „   v ii 182
Methought I *s* in Canterbury Minster,   *Becket* I i 73
as the case *s*, you had safelier have slain an archbishop
than a she-goat.'   „   III iii 67
They *s* on Dover beach to murder me,   „   v i 436
he *s* there Staring upon the hunter.   *The Cup* II i 121
How often have I *s* With Eva here !   *Prom. of May* II 296
O would she *s* before me as my queen,   *Foresters* I i 166
Stoop Might not your courtesy *s* to hand it me ?   *Becket* IV i 296
could I *s* so low As mate with one that holds   *Foresters* IV 709
Stoop'd he *s* and gather'd one From out a bed   *Queen Mary* V v 92
Stop Well, Simon Renard, shall we *s* a day ?   „   III vi 243
s the heretic's mouth ! Hale him away !   „   IV iii 282
S's and stares at our cottage.   *The Falcon* 161
But hallus ud *s* at the Vine-an'-the-Hop,   *Prom. of May* II 311
Storm (*See also* **War-storm**) and strow the *s's* at
sea,   *Queen Mary* I v 381
Wet, famine, ague, fever, *s*, wreck, wrath,—   „   v v 108
all the North of Europe in one *s*.   *Harold* III ii 292
To Rome again ! the *s* begins again.   *Becket* II ii 468
tho' I am none of those that would raise a *s* between you,   III iii 296
Can you not hear them yonder like a *s*,   „   IV i 625
the *s* was drawing hither Across the hills   *The Cup* II 319
The *s* is hard at hand will sweep away Thrones,   *Prom. of May* I 517
I will fly to you thro' the night, the *s*—   „   I 702
s and shower lashing Her casement,   „   II 471
Out in the fiercest *s* That ever made earth tremble—   „   III 797
Storming All the Norman foot Are *s* up the hill.   *Harold* V i 523
Stormless No—our waking thoughts Suffer a *s* shipwreck
in the pools   „   v i 296
Storm-voice whose *s-v* Unsockets the strong oak,   *The Cup* II 282
Stormy The *s* Wyatts and Northumberlands,   *Queen Mary* III ii 168
Stormy-red when he sign'd, his face was *s-r*—   *Becket* I iii 320
Story But truth of *s*, which I glanced at,   *Queen Mary* III v 33
Then, glancing thro' the *s* of this realm,   *Becket* I iii 410
The *s* of your battle and your wound.   *The Falcon* 594
Will he not fly from you if he learn the *s* of my
shame   *Prom. of May* III 257
Stout Wake, or the *s* old island will become A rotten
limb of Spain.   *Queen Mary* II i 104
But by God's providence a good *s* staff Lay near me ;   „   v ii 468
And Tostig is not *s* enough to bear it.   *Harold* I i 402
I have a *s* crabstick here, which longs to break itself
across their backs.   *Foresters* IV 917

Stoutness Your learning, and your *s*, and your
heresy,   *Queen Mary* IV ii 125
Straäit (straight) hallus hup at sunrise, and I'd drive
the plow *s* as a line right i' the faäce o' the sun,   *Prom. of May* I 370
Straänge (strange) and the master 'ud be *s* an' pleased
if you'd step in fust,   „   I 167
Straight (*See also* **Straäit**) and set it *S* on the trunk,   *Harold* III i 146
Speak *s* out, crookback.   *Foresters* II i 271
Straight-going the dry light of Rome's *s-g* policy,   *The Cup* I i 145
Strain (s) A *s* of hard and headstrong in him.   *Becket, Pro.* 234
Strain (verb) if we did not *s* to make ourselves Better   *Prom. of May* I 602
Strain'd I cannot cope with him : my wrist is *s*.   *Foresters* IV 313
Strand voice coming up with the voice of the deep
from the *s*,   *Becket* II i 6
Stranded To shove that *s* iceberg off our shores,   *Harold* IV iii 138
Strange (*See also* **Straänge**) *S* game of chess : a
King That with her own pawns plays against
a Queen,   *Queen Mary* I iii 160
S in a wooer !   „   I v 363
A *s* youth Suddenly thrust in on me, whisper'd,   „   II i 128
That may seem *s* beyond his nursery.   „   II ii 396
how *s*, That Gardiner, once so one with all of us
Against this foreign marriage, should have yielded
So utterly !—*s* !   „   III iii 5
when men are tost On tides of *s* opinion,   „   III iv 119
however, in *s* hours, After the long brain-dazing
colloquies,   „   IV ii 90
His Highness is so vex'd with *s* affairs—   „   v ii 560
What is the *s* thing happiness ? Sit down here :   „   V v 77
S and ghastly in the gloom And shadowing of this
double thunder-cloud   *Harold* III ii 157
No, not *s* This was old human laughter in old Rome   „   III ii 162
lest the *s* Saints By whom thou swarest,   „   v i 115
I see it—some confusion, Some *s* mistake.   *Becket* II i 235
A *s* gift sent to me to-day.   *The Cup* I ii 52
So mad, I fear some *s* and evil chance Coming upon
me, for by the Gods I seem *S* to myself.   „   I iii 74
So *s* among them—such an alien there,   „   II 143
Or some *s* second-sight, the marriage cup Wherefrom   „   II 198
Surely—yet These are *s* words to speak to Artemis.   „   II 326
S that the words at home with me so long Should fly   *The Falcon* 525
sick people, More specially sick children, have *s*
fancies, *S* longings ;   „   817
But all that sounds so wicked and so *s* ;   *Prom. of May* I 657
Come, come, my girl, enough Of this *s* talk.   „   III 620
That *s* starched stiff creature, Little John, the Earl's
man.   *Foresters* I i 183
Stranger (adj.) A *s* monk desires access to you   *Becket* V ii 65
Stranger (compar.) strange ! but *s* still that he, So
fierce against the Headship of the Pope,   *Queen Mary* III iii 9
Stranger (s) By seeking justice at a *s's* hand   „   IV i 20
The *s* at his hearth, and all his house—   „   IV i 163
Norman who should drive The *s* to the fiends !   *Harold* II ii 541
Yea, let a *s* spoil his heritage,   *Becket* II ii 258
Have you had any alarm ? no *s* ?   „   III i 28
tho' a *s* fain would be allow'd To join the hunt.   *The Cup* I i 196
And you, that seldom brook the *s* here,   „   I i 378
Strangle for he Who vows a vow to *s* his own mother   *Harold* III i 229
Such rampant weeds *S* each other,   *Prom. of May* II 591
Strangled Holy Father *S* him with a hair Of Peter,   *Harold* V ii 45
Strasburg To *S*, Antwerp, Frankfort, Zurich,   *Queen Mary* I ii 1
Strato Your name ? *Sinnatus*. *S*, my name.   *The Cup* I i 199
Who is our guest ? *Sinnatus*. *S* he calls himself.
Sinnatus. I pledge you, *S*. *Synorix*. And I
you, my lord.   „   I ii 48
You, *S*, make good cheer till I return.   „   I ii 205
Straw Hast not thou drawn the short *s* ?   *Becket* I iv 4
Take thy one chance ; Catch at the last *s*.   „   IV ii 221
Richard risks his life for a *s*, So lies in prison—   *Foresters* IV 383
Stray not here I shall rejoice To find my *s* sheep back
within the fold.   *Becket* III iii 355
Stray'd Hath he *s* From love's clear path into the
common bush,   „   III i 246
Stream foul *s* Thro' fever-breeding levels,—at her side,   „   II i 155
—the *s* is bearing us all down,   *Foresters* I i 238

Stream (*continued*) our little Sheriff will ever swim with
    the s !   *Foresters* I i 240
have the great men striven against the s,   „   I i 243
Streamer and dropt Their s's earthward,   *The Cup* I ii 405
Streaming We might go softlier than with crimson
    rowel And s lash.   *Queen Mary* III iv 184
And flung them s o'er the battlements   *Harold* II ii 391
Street Cries of the moment and the s—   *Queen Mary* II iv 128
In every London s a gibbet stood.   „   III i 7
And might assail you passing through the s,   „   IV ii 35
And Ignorance crying in the s's,   „   IV iii 377
son turn'd out into the s To sleep, to die—   „   VII 126
To take the vagabond woman of the s Into thine
    arms !   *Becket* I i 228
moon Divides the whole long s with light and shade.   „   I i 365
Then hidden in the s He watch'd her   „   I ii 39
from the s Stain'd with the mere thereof.   „   I iii 690
Call in the poor from the s's, and let them feast.   „   I iv 72
they were fighting for her to-day in the s.   „   I iv 160
Save that it was mid-winter in the s,   „   III iv 480
Strength I not doubt that God will give me s,   *Queen Mary* IV ii 235
Or give thee saintly s to undergo.   „   IV iii 99
s To shove that stranded iceberg off our shores,   *Harold* IV iii 137
there make s to breast Whatever chance,   „   v i 126
The people know their Church a tower of s,   *Becket* I i 16
Is s less strong when hand-in-hand with grace ?   „   v ii 540
Curse on your brutal s ! I cannot pass that way.   *Prom. of May* III 732
So—so—I have presumed Beyond my s.   *Foresters* II i 458
What breadth, height, s—torrents of eddying bark !   „   III 94
Strengthen Might s thee in keeping of thy word,   *Harold* II ii 730
s their palisades !   „   v i 480
Strengthen'd yet he fail'd, And s Philip.   *Queen Mary* III i 133
Stretch Do not scrimp your phrase, But s it wider ;   „   III iii 261
See here—I s my hand out—hold it there.   *The Cup* II 210
Strew *See* **Strow**
Strewn which I found S in your palace.   *Queen Mary* v ii 173
Stricken (*See also* **Famine-stricken**) My father s with
    his first paralysis.   *Prom. of May* II 481
soul of the woods hath s thro' my blood,   *Foresters* II i 66
I think I should have s him to the death.   „   III i 140
He is s with a slight paralysis.   „   IV 456
Strict The King Demands a s account of all those
    revenues   *Becket* I iii 650
Strife My sight is eagle, but the s so thick—   *Harold* v i 627
Strike And arm and s as with one hand,   *Queen Mary* II ii 292
Can I s Elizabeth ?—not now and save the life Of
    Devon :   „   II iv 122
he and his Are bound to me—may s hereafter.   „   II iv 125
you may s fire from her, Not hope to melt her.   „   III vi 38
To s too soon is oft to miss the blow.   „   III vi 72
why fling back the stone he s's me with ?   „   IV ii 150
He s's thro' me at Philip and yourself.   „   v ii 58
s hard and deep into The prey they are rending   „   v ii 267
There you s in the nail.   „   v ii 436
s Their hearts, and hold their babies up to it.   *Harold* I i 34
light enough for Alfgar's house To s thee down   „   I i 308
the true *must* Shall make her s as Power : but when to s—   „   I i 369
And s among them with thy battle-axe—   „   I ii 89
Thou hast but seen how Norman hands can s,   „   II ii 172
No man would s with Tostig, save for Norway.   „   IV ii 20
the childish fist That cannot s again.   „   IV iii 31
all the monks of Peterboro' S for the king ;   „   v i 447
We wait but the King's word to s thee dead.   *Becket.*
    S, and I die the death of martyrdom ; S, and ye set
    these customs by my death Ringing   *Becket* I iii 166
The man shall feel that I can s him yet.   „   II i 78
Why then I s into my former path For England,   „   II ii 455
S ! I challenge thee to meet me before God.   „   IV ii 253
S, then, at once, the King would have him—   „   v i 237
S's truest ev'n for his own self.   „   v ii 42
Do you hear that ? S, s.   „   v iii 162
S him, Tracy ! *Rosamund.* No, No, No, No !   „   v iii 169
S, I say.   „   v iii 177
S' our Archbishop in his own cathedral !   „   v iii 180
Answer not, but s.   „   v iii 186

Strike (*continued*) And I may s your game when you are
    gone.   *The Cup* I ii 36
Why did I s him?—having proof enough   „   I iii 157
s, make his feathers Glance in mid heaven.   *The Falcon* 14
Nor ever s him blow for blow ;   *Prom. of May* iii 6
you S up a song, my friends, and then to bed.   *Foresters* I iii 30
these will s for England And man and maid be free   „   II i 9
S, Sheriff ! S, mercenary !   „   II i 415
They s the deer at once to death—   „   IV 525
S up our music, Little John.   „   IV 558
s the bonds From these three men,   „   IV 961
S up a stave, my masters, all is well.   „   IV 1101
Striking And s at Hardrada and his madmen   *Harold* IV iii 17
I have heard of you. The likeness Is very s.   *Prom. of May* II 366
String were a pious work To s my father's sonnets,   *Queen Mary* II i 27
Strip A thousand winters Will s you bare as death,   *Foresters* IV 1056
Stripe callous with a constant s, Unwoundable.   *Queen Mary* v 172
Stripping They are s the dead bodies naked yonder,   *Harold* v ii 34
Stript But after they had s him to his shroud,   *Queen Mary* IV iii 334
Strive And in thy cause I s against him now.   *Becket* v i 16
great man s against it again to save his country,   *Foresters* I i 245
Striven I have s in vain to raise a man for her.   *Queen Mary* II i 17
have the great men s against the stream,   *Foresters* I i 243
Striving Not s still, however much in vain,   *Becket* III iii 232
s still to break or bind The spiritual giant   „   IV ii 442
Stroke (s) Toll of a bell, S of a clock,   *Queen Mary* III v 143
and iron s's that brought Thy war with Brittany   *Harold* II ii 47
But I heard say he had had a s,   *Becket* I iv 54
Guard from the s that dooms thee after death   „   IV ii 270
I surely should have left That s to Rome.   *The Cup* I ii 160
As scare his act :—a random s :   „   II 53
Stroke (verb) you s me on one cheek, Buffet the other.   *Queen Mary* II i 116
Stroking Cannot be heal'd by s.   „   III iv 274
Strong Would be too s for France.   „   I v 300
Have made s head against ourselves and you.   „   II ii 146
And s to throw ten Wyatts and all Kent.   „   II ii 353
or we are torn Down the s wave of brawlers.   „   III i 186
And their s torment bravely borne,   „   III iv 168
A drinker of black, s, volcanic wines,   „   v ii 93
I would I were as tall and s as you.   „   v ii 422
and you know me s of arm ;   „   v ii 469
Haul like a great s fellow at my legs,   *Harold* II i 11
Is 'ay' an oath ? is s 'ay' s as an oath ?   „   II ii 662
let not my s prayer Be weaken'd in thy sight,   „   v i 647
S—not in mine own self, but Heaven ;   *Becket* I iii 536
A s hate-philtre as may madden him—   „   IV ii 458
Is strength less s when hand-in-hand with grace ?   „   v ii 540
whose storm-voice Unsockets the s oak, and rears his
    root Beyond his head,   *The Cup* II 283
Were some s fellow here in the wild wood,   *Foresters* v 515
Stronger Ay, ay, but art thou s than the King ?   *Becket* I iii 534
and now the s motive, Misnamed free-will—   *Prom. of May* II 635
Anyhow we must Move in the line of least resist-
    ance when The s motive rules.   „   II 671
only differing as the s and the weaker,   „   III 190
Of a nature S, sadder than my own,   *Foresters* II i 189
Strongest Well, well, be it so, thou s thief of all,   „   III 327
The Holy Virgin Stand by the s.   „   IV 265
Strong-wing'd the best, s-w against the wind.   *Harold* II i 148
Strove We s against the papacy from the first,   *Queen Mary* III iii 224
And dreadful shadows s upon the hill,   *Harold* III i 377
and once he s to hide his face,   *Becket* III iii 103
s To work against her license for her good,   „   IV ii 339
In mine own cause I s against him there,   „   v 14
I cannot tell how long we s before   *The Falcon* 638
Strow and s the storms at sea,   *Queen Mary* I v 381
s's our fruits, and lays Our golden grain,   *The Cup* II 285
Struck S home and won.   *Queen Mary* I v 554
Gardiner wur s down like by the hand o' God   „   IV iii 516
And a shape from out the vague,   *Becket* I iii 373
Very bad. Somebody s him.   „   IV i 50
I tell thee, my good fellow, *My* arrow s the stag.   *The Cup* I ii 28
I am sure *I* s him. *Synorix.* And I am just as sure,
    my lord, I s him.   „   I ii 33
I warrant you now, he said, *he* s the stag.   „   I ii 382

Suffolk (Lady) The Lady *S* and the Lady Lennox ? *Queen Mary* I iv 31
Suit (courtship) and I shall urge his *s* Upon the Queen,   ,, v i 266
Suit (of clothes) And look at our *s*'s, out at knee, out at
   elbow.   *Foresters* I i 33
Suit (petition) Do make most humble *s* unto your
   Majesties,   *Queen Mary* III iii 118
   So to set forth this humble *s* of ours   ,, III iii 145
Suit (verb) if it *s* their purpose to howl for the King, *Becket* III iii 323
Sullen What ! are thy people *s* from defeat ? *Harold* IV i 1
   Let not our great king Believe us *s*—   ,, IV i 7
   Make not our Morcar *s* : it is not wise.   ,, IV iii 103
   our waking thoughts Suffer a stormless shipwreck in the
   pools Of *s* slumber,   ,, v i 297
Sully pray'd me not to *s* Mine own prerogative, *Queen Mary* IV i 17
Sulphur I was born with it, and *s* won't bring it out o' me. *Becket* I iv 232
Sultana That I am his main paramour, his *s*.   ,, IV ii 39
Summat (something) I heerd *s* as summun towld
   summun o' owld Bishop Gardiner's end ; *Queen Mary* IV iii 502
Summer (something) The brows unwrinkled as a *s* mere.—
   Stigand. A *s* mere with sudden wreckful gusts *Harold* III i 48
   they be two o' the purtiest gels ye can see of a *s*
   murnin'.   *Prom. of May* I 31
Summer (s) (*See also* **Mid-summer**) —That was many a *s*
   gone—   *Harold* I i 253
   Over ! the sweet *s* closes, (repeat) *Becket*, Pro. 302, 323, 331
   Bar the bird From following the fled *s*— *Becket* I i 259
   Cold after warm, winter after *s*,   ,, I iv 65
   belike it 'ud ha' been always *s*,   ,, III i 149
   That in the *s* keeps the mountain side, *The Cup* I i 403
   How long ago was that ? *Count.* Alas, ten *s*'s ! *The Falcon* 348
   The tan of southern *s*'s and the beard ? *Prom. of May* II 617
   Thy thirtieth *s* may be thirty-fold *Foresters* II i 128
   a thousand *s*'s Robe you life-green again.   ,, IV 1057
Summer-flies flash out at times Of festival like
   burnish'd *s-f*,   ,, I ii 276
   You lovers are such clumsy *s-f*   ,, IV 10
Summit flash About the *s* of the hill, *Harold* v i 539
   vast vine-bowers Ran to the *s* of the trees, *The Cup* I ii 403
Summon When will you that we *s* both our houses *Queen Mary* III ii 114
   the King shall *s* the chapter of that church to court, *Becket* I iii 109
   S your barons ; take their counsel :   ,, v i 74
Summon'd seems then I was *s* hither But to be
   mock'd *Queen Mary* III iv 269
   I doubt not but thou knowest Why thou art *s*. *Harold* IV i 188
Summons he shall answer to the *s* of the King's court
   to be tried therein.' *Becket* I iii 89
Summun (some one) I heerd summat as *s* towld *s* o'
   owld Bishop Gardiner's end ; *Queen Mary* IV iii 502
   why then I beänt Farmer Dobson, but *s* else— *Prom. of May* IV 140
   Minds ma o' *s*.   ,, II 583
Summut (something) There mun be *s* wrong theer,
   Wilson,   ,, I 234
   but he says he wants to tell ye *s* very partic'lar. ,, III 355
Sumpter-mule Mutilated, poor brute, my *s-m*, *Becket* v ii 440
Sun the most princelike Prince beneath the *s*. *Queen Mary* I v 446
   amazed To find as fair a *s* as might have flash'd ,, III ii 22
   Till the *s* dance, as upon Easter Day.   ,, III ii 238
   Our short-lived *s*, before his winter plunge, ,, III iii 85
   your Highness is our *s*, the King And you together
   our two *s*'s in one ;   ,, III iv 18
   What power this cooler *s* of England hath ,, III iv 327
   dance into the *s* That shines on princes.   ,, III v 253
   you want the *s* That shines at court ;   ,, III v 276
   That might live always in the *s*'s warm heart, ,, v i 22
   a candle in the *s* Is all but smoke—   ,, v i 78
   a *s* set But leaving light enough *Harold* I i 306
   And we will fill thee full of Norman *s*,   ,, II ii 180
   And over thee the *s*'s arise and set,   ,, II ii 433
   Thine by the *s* ; nay, by some *s* to be,   ,, III i 67
   That *s* may God speed !   ,, III i 72
   And over and gone with the *s*. Here ; but our *s* in
   Aquitaine lasts longer. *Becket*, Pro. 327
   If a seraph shouted from the *s*,   ,, I iii 311
   Love that is born of the deep coming up with the *s*
   from the sea. (repeat)   ,, II i 10, 20

Sun (*continued*) My *s*, no cloud ! Let there not be one frown *Becket* II i 41
   Out of the cloud, my *S*—out of the eclipse   ,, II i 202
   And felt the *s* of Antioch scald our mail,   ,, II ii 93
   The *s* himself, should he be changed to one, ,, III i 57
   What are you crying for, when the *s* shines ? ,, III i 270
   cloud that hath come over the *s* and cast us all into
   shadow ?   ,, III iii 46
   And hiss'd against the *s* ?   ,, v iii 45
   twin sister of the morning star, Forelead the *s*. *The Cup* I iii 47
   Beneath an ever-rising *s*—I see him—   ,, II 535
   Your ladyship lives higher in the *s*. *The Falcon* 583
   Help me to move this bench for him into the *s*. *Prom. of May* I 81
   plow straäit as a line right i' the faäce o' the *s*, ,, I 371
   —then hup ageän i' the faäce o' the *s*. Eh ! how
   the *s* 'ud shine,   ,, I 373
   like The rainbow of a momentary *s*. *Foresters* I ii 279
   And darkness rises from the fallen *s*.   ,, I iii 42
   A houseless head beneath the *s* and stars, ,, I i 64
Sunday Who stole the widow's one sitting hen o' *S*, *Becket* I iv 121
   you were stupid drunk all *S*, *Prom. of May* III 80
Sunder plenty to *s* and unsister them again : *Queen Mary* I 85
Sunder'd And brought the *s* tree again, and set it Straight
   on the trunk, *Harold* III i 144
Sung The bells must ring ; Te Deums must be *s* ; *Queen Mary* III ii 212
   shall masses here be *s* By every priest in Oxford. ,, IV iii 100
   'Love for a whole life long' When was that *s* ? *Harold* III ii 89
   Well *s* ! *James.* Fanny be the naäme i' the song, *Prom. of May* II 210
   your Ladyship hath *s* the old proverb out of fashion. *Foresters* I i 163
Sun-gilt Like *s-g* breathings on a frosty dawn— *Queen Mary* IV v 50
Sunk and might have a *s* navy— *Becket* III iii 125
   past is like a travell'd land now *s* Below the horizon— *The Cup* II 230
   S in the deepest pit of pauperism, *Prom. of May* III 803
   sudden touches For him, or him—*s* rocks ; *Queen Mary* v v 221
Sunken Help the good ship, showing the *s* rock, *Harold* II i 100
Sunless Ran *s* down, and moan'd against the piers. *Queen Mary* II iii 26
Sunlight I am sure Her morning wanted *s*, *Harold* I ii 45
   lark first takes the *s* on his wing, *The Cup* I iii 43
   The town lay still in the long *s-l*, *Prom. of May* I 37
Sunrise hallus up at *s*, and I'd drive the plow   ,, I 369
Sunrising which he Gainsays by next *s*— *Becket* IV ii 278
Sunset a paleness, Like the wan twilight after *s*, ,, I iii 326
Sunshine Like universal air and *s* ! *Queen Mary* III ii 182
   The *s* sweeps across my life again.   ,, III iv 249
   Air and *s*. I would we had you,   ,, v ii 606
   Winter *s* ! Beware of opening out thy bosom *Becket* III iii 29
Sunstroke Pray God, we 'scape the *s*. *Queen Mary* III v 279
Superstition letter you wrote against Their *s*   ,, I ii 86
   if you cared To fee an over-opulent *s*, *Prom. of May* I 693
Superstitious *S* fool, What brought me here ?   ,, II 350
Supper Simon, is *s* ready ? *Queen Mary* III vi 256
   A holy *s*, not a sacrifice ;   ,, IV i 57
   Was not my lord of Leicester bidden to our *s* ? *Becket* I iv 57
   Swine, sheep, ox—here's a French *s*.   ,, I iv 113
   Is the Archbishop a thief who gives thee thy *s* ? ,, I iv 116
   We be a-going home after our *s* in all humbleness, ,, I iv 207
   shall see the silk here and there, and I want my *s*. ,, IV i 57
   Cheese ? *Filippo.* A *s* for twelve mites. *The Falcon* 127
   do thou and thy sweet'art sing us hoäm to *s*— *Prom. of May* II 170
   fur owd Dobson 'll gi'e us a bit o' *s*.   ,, II 217
Supping *See* **A-supping**
Supple (adj.) You must be sweet and *s*, like a
   Frenchman. *Queen Mary* v i 275
Supple (verb) To sleek and *s* himself to the king's hand. *Harold* I i 149
Supplicate all one mind to *s* The Legate here for
   pardon, *Queen Mary* III iii 106
Supplication Our *s* be exhibited To the Lord
   Cardinal Pole,   ,, III iii 123
   By this our *s* promising.   ,, III iii 135
Supplied daily want *s*—The daily pleasure to supply it. *Becket* II ii 301
Supply daily want supplied—The daily pleasure to *s* it. ,, II ii 303
Supposed have been *s* Tainted with Lutheranism *Queen Mary* IV iv 226
Supposition But you, my Lord, beyond all *s*,   ,, III iv 229
Suppress to *s* God's honour for the sake Of any king *Becket* II ii 220
Sure (*See also* **Sewer, Stupid-sure**) Lord Paget's
   'Ay' is *s*—who else ? *Queen Mary* I v 630

Sure (*continued*)   I am *s* (Knowing the man) he
     wrought it   *Queen Mary* III i 275
I should fight then. *Stafford.* I am *s* of it.   „   III i 469
and not *s* Of their own selves,   „   III iv 119
Of this be *s*, he is whole worlds away.   „   IV iii 194
but I am not *s* She will not serve me better—   „   v i 249
Papacy is no more. *Paget.* Are we so *s* of that? „   v v 287
I am *s* she hates thee, Pants for thy blood.   *Harold* I ii 37
I his queen, I might be *s* of it.   „   I ii 155
I am *s* this body Is Alfwig, the king's uncle.   „   v ii 67
Art thou so *s* thou followedst anything?   *Becket* I i 210
But, my liege, I am *s*, of all the roses—   „   II i 139
for to be *s* it's no more than a week since our old Father
     Philip   „   III i 109
be *s* they be, but he blinded 'em for all that,   „   III i 128
and to be *s* I ha' seen great ones to-day—   „   III i 136
tho' to be *s* if I had been Eve i' the garden I shouldn't
     ha' minded the apple,   „   III i 139
to be *s* if I hadn't minded it we should all   „   III i 144
tho' to be *s* our mother 'ill sing me old songs by the hour,   „   III i 184
You had never used so many, Not if you meant it, I
     am *s*.   „   IV ii 184
And yet I am all but *s* my dagger was a feint Till the
     worm turn'd—   „   IV ii 379
I am not so *s* But that I love him still.   „   IV ii 450
I am *s* I struck him. *Synorix.* And I am just as *s*,
     my lord, *I* struck him.   *The Cup* I i 34
Wise I am *s* as she is beautiful,   „   I ii 139
I am *s* of being every way malign'd.   „   I ii 241
I am *s* I told him that his plot was folly.   „   I ii 283
Plead to him, I am *s* you will prevail.   „   I ii 302
I am *s* you will not marry him. *Camma.* Are you so *s*?   „   II 104
I am all but *s* that some one spake.   „   II 404
I am most *s* that some one call'd.   „   II 509
I am *s* that more than one brave fellow   *The Falcon* 633
but be *s* That I shall never marry again, my lord !
     Count. *S* ?   „   741
I am *s* I wish her happy.   *Prom. of May* I 478
But *s* am I that of your gentleness You will
     forgive him.   „   II 487
and that, I am *s*, would be the death of him.   „   III 167
and he loves me too, I am quite *s* of that.   „   III 214
I am *s* that when we are married he will be willing   „   III 259
are you quite *s* that after marriage this gentleman   „   III 292
He will be *s* to know you to-morrow.   „   III 470
But there I am *s* the ballad is at fault.   *Foresters* I i 122
I am all but *s* of him. I will go to him.   „   I i 275
Nay—that, my friend, I am *s* I did not say.   „   II i 489
Surgas *S* e tenebris, Sis vindicator !   *Harold* v i 571
Surged hugest wave from Norseland ever yet *S* on us,
                   „   IV iii 64
Surname He must deserve his *s* better.   *Queen Mary* III i 197
Surprise Well, Father, I have a *s* for you.   *Prom. of May* III 438
Surprised niver been *s* but once i' my life, and I went
     blind upon it.   „   III 439
Surrendering *s* God's honour to the pleasure of a man.   *Becket* II ii 439
Survey Not an eye to *s*,   *Foresters* II ii 181
Surveyor *See* **Land-surveyor**
Suspect Why still *s* your Grace ?   *Queen Mary* III v 17
     you *s* This Sinnatus of playing patriotism,   *The Cup* I i 77
Suspected anyone *S* thee to be my man ?   *Queen Mary* I iii 176
     Much *s*, of me Nothing proven can be.   „   III v 19
Suspend I will *s* myself from all my functions.   *Becket* I iii 301
     your lordship would *s* me from verse-writing,   „   II ii 349
     and tho' you *s* Foliot or another,   „   II ii 358
Suspended as you *s* yourself after sub-writing to the
     customs.   „   II ii 350
     tho' you *s* yourself, The Pope let you down again ;   „   II ii 356
Suspense the Pope will not leave them in *s*, for the Pope
     himself is always in *s*,   „   II ii 359
     —always in *s*, like the scales,   „   II ii 362
     always in *s*, like the tail of the horologe—   „   II ii 365
Sussex I know all *S* ; A good entrenchment   *Harold* III i 362
Suzerain Husband-in-law, our smooth-shorn *s*,   *Becket* II ii 40
Swaddling-band flings aside His *s-b's*,   *Prom. of May* I 586
Swale in the cruel river *S* A hundred years ago ;   *Harold* III ii 10

Swaller (**swallow**) Wi' the butterflies out, and the *s's*
     at plaäy,   *Prom. of May* II 198
Swallow (**s**) (*See also* **Swaller**) *S's* fly again, Cuckoos
     cry again,   *Queen Mary* III v 96
Why, nature's licensed vagabond, the *s*,   „   v i 21
Yet will I be your *s* and return—   „   v i 91
Sick as an autumn *s* for a voyage,   *Harold* I i 101
Farewell, friends ! farewell, *s's* !   *Becket* I iv 45
Not while the *s* skims along the ground,   *Foresters* I i 313
Swallow (**verb**) find Heaven or else hell ready to *s* me,   *Queen Mary* IV iii 224
Rolf, what fish did *s* Jonah ? *Rolf.* A whale !   *Harold* II i 41
all their horse *S* the hill locust-like,   „   v i 560
My one grain of good counsel which you will not *s*.   *Becket* II ii 379
that will *s* anything. Farewell.   „   II ii 382
Will the earth gape and *s* us ?   „   v iii 206
she that has eaten the yolk is scarce like to *s* the shell.   *The Falcon* 705
Swallowed (*See also* **Shore-swallow'd**) I had liefer that the
     fish had *s* me,   *Harold* II i 37
whale to a whelk we have *s* the King of England.   „   II i 45
glory of the Church Hath *s* up the glory of the King ;   *Becket* I iii 666
And *s* in the conqueror's chronicle.   *The Cup* I ii 158
your free sports have *s* my free hour.   *Foresters* IV 339
Swam or else *s* heavily Against the huge corruptions   *Queen Mary* IV ii 98
Swamp running out at top To *s* the house.   *Harold* I i 379
Swan flocks of *s's*, As fair and white as angels ;   *Queen Mary* III ii 15
Swang Mark'd how the war-axe *s*,   *Harold* IV iii 156
Swapped *See* **Swopt**
Sward Kill'd the *s* where'er they sat,   *Foresters* II ii 152
Sware (*See also* **Swore**) He knew not whom he *s* by.   *Harold* III i 256
     and I *s* To consecrate my virgin here   „   III i 275
born in me when I *s* Falsely to him,   „   v i 302
by whom I knew not that I *s*,—   „   v i 305
King Henry *s* That, saving his King's kingship,   *Becket* I iii 27
I *s* I would not give the kiss of peace,   „   III iii 259
Swarest Swearing thou *s* falsely by his Saints :   *Harold* III ii 142
     lest the strange Saints By whom thou *s*,   „   v i 117
Thou *s* falsely by our blessed bones,   „   v i 259
Swarm (**s**) Philip and the black-faced *s's* of Spain,   *Queen Mary* II i 98
Out crept a wasp, with half the *s* behind.   „   III iii 49
Is coming with a *s* of mercenaries To break   *Foresters* III 452
Swarm (**verb**) they *s* into the fire Like flies—for what ?
     no dogma.   *Queen Mary* v ii 110
S to thy voice like bees to the brass pan.   *Foresters* I iii 108
Swarming Swallow the hill locust-like, *s* up.   *Harold* v i 560
Sway Now the spoilt child *s's* both.   „   I i 453
that one time to the current, And to the wind
     another.   *Becket* I iii 593
And *s* the long grape-bunches of our vines,   *The Cup* II 270
Sway'd might well have *s* All England under Henry,   *Becket* I iii 467
Swaying And *s* his two-handed sword about him,   *Harold* v i 407
     and like the *s* vines—Yea, with our eyes,—   *The Cup* I ii 410
Swear (*See also* **Sweär**) He *s's* by the Rood. Whew !   *Queen Mary* I i 62
Peter, I'll *s* for him He *did* believe   „   I ii 76
S with me, noble fellow-citizens, all,   „   II ii 296
We *s* ! *Mary.* We thank your Lordship and your
     loyal city.   „   II ii 299
I *s* you do your country wrong, Sir Ralph.   „   III i 153
but of this fire he says, Nay *s's*,   „   III v 72
I *s* I have no heart To be your Queen.   „   v v 264
I *s* it, By mine own eyes—   *Harold* I ii 109
to *s* Vows that he dare not break.   „   II ii 76
S thou on this ! *Harold.* What should I *s* ? Why
     should I *s* on this ? *William.* *S* thou to help me
     to the crown of England.   „   II ii 701
S thou to-day, to-morrow is thine own.   „   II ii 709
I *s* to help thee to the crown of England . . .
     (repeat)   *Harold* II ii 712, 721
Thou must *s* absolutely, noble Earl.   „   II ii 715
S, dearest brother, I beseech thee, *s* !   „   II ii 719
I made thee *s*.—Show him by whom he hath sworn.   „   II ii 732
and dear son, *s* When thou art king,   „   III i 305
for I have sworn Not to *s* falsely twice. *Edward.*
     Thou wilt not *s* ? *Harold.* I cannot.   „   III i 311
For I can *s* to that, but cannot *s* That these will
     follow thee   „   IV i 156

Swear (*continued*) who made And heard thee *s*—   *Harold* v i 121
There is no man can *s* to him.   „   v ii 78
Ay, ay, but *s* to see to her in England.   *Becket.*   Well,
   well, I *s*, but not to please myself.   *Becket, Pro.* 190
s nay to that by this cross on thy neck.   „   *Pro.* 369
I heard him *s* revenge.   „   i i 280
not the soldier As Foliot *s*'s it.—   „   i i 388
And *s* to obey the customs.   „   i i 270
I, my liege, could *s*, To death for death.   „   i iii 404
I can easily *s* to these as being The King's will   „   i iii 419
Cross swords all of you ! *s* to follow him !   „   i iv 200
S and unswear, state and misstate thy best !   „   ii ii 476
But can I *s* to that, had she but given   „   iv ii 384
I'll *s* to mine own self it was a feint.   Why should I *s*,
   Eleanore, who am, or was,   „   iv ii 401
I know—could *s*—as long as Becket breathes,   „   v i 76
I will *s* by the head of the Earl.   *Foresters* i ii 45
but for all that I will *s* the Earl hath right.   „   i ii 51
S to me by that relic on thy neck.   „   i ii 169
I *s* then by this relic on my neck—No, no, I will not
   s by this ;   „   i ii 171
I have heard him *s* he will be even wi' thee.   „   ii i 344
Not any of these, I *s*.   *Men.*   No, no, we *s*.   „   ii i 710
Sweär Minds ma o' summun. I could *s* to that ;   *Prom. of May* ii 583
Swear'd (**swore**) For me an' my Sally we *s* to be true,   „   i 204
Swearer They call thee John the *S.*   *Becket* ii ii 462
Swearest that *s* by the mass ?   *Queen Mary* i iii 46
Swearing (*See also* **A-sweäring**) For *s* falsely by those
   blessed bones ;   *Harold* iii i 246
S thou swarest falsely by his Saints :   „   iii ii 142
Sweat (**s**) hand, Damp with the *s* of death,   *Queen Mary* ii i 33
blood and *s* of heretics at the stake   „   v i 100
cries continually with *s* and tears to the Lord God   „   v iv 45
In the *s* of thy brow, says Holy Writ, shalt thou eat
   bread, but in the *s* of thy brow   *Foresters* iv 201
Sweat (*verb*) he'll *s* it out of thee, (*repeat*)   *Harold* i 77
S out your gout, friend, for by my life,   *Foresters* iv 565
Sweating My lord, I ha' three sisters a-dying at home o'
   the *s* sickness.   *Becket* i iv 246
Sweep (**s**) How many names in the long *s* of time   *Queen Mary* iii v 40
in the long *s* of years to come must the great man   *Foresters* i i 244
Sweep (*verb*) When they will *s* her from the seas.   *Queen Mary* iii i 162
The sunshine *s*'s across my life again.   „   iii vi 249
storm is hard at hand will *s* away Thrones,   *Prom. of May* i 517
Sweeping *See* **Down-sweeping**
Sweet took her hand, call'd her *s* sister, and kiss'd not
   her alone,   *Queen Mary* i i 80
but you, cousin, are fresh and *s* As the first flower   „   i iv 62
I have a head to lose for your *s* sake.   „   i iv 131
S mother, you had time and cause enough To sicken   „   i v 23
More like a school-boy that hath broken bounds,
   Sickening himself with *s*'s.   „   i v 172
The bitter in the *s*.   „   i v 235
S cousin, you forget That long low minster where
   you gave your hand To this great Catholic
   King.   „   iii ii 89
I know that she was ever *s* to me.   „   iii ii 228
And she was crafty—a *s* violence, And a *s* craft.   „   iii ii 108
They are not *s*, The violence and the craft that do
   divide The world of nature ;   „   iii v 119
And, whether it bring you bitter news or *s*,   „   iii v 202
Lose the *s* hope that I may bear a prince.   „   iii vi 201
You must be *s* and supple, like a Frenchman.   „   v i 275
Your pardon, *S* cousin, and farewell !   „   v ii 204
Look'd hard and *s* at me, and gave it me.   „   v v 95
O Saint of Aragon, with that *s* worn smile   „   v v 198
before I go To find the *s* refreshment of the Saints.   *Harold* i i 177
And the lark sings, the *s* stars come and go,   „   ii i 434
All the *s* Saints bless him !   „   iii i 297
Their anthems of no church, how *s* they are !   „   iii ii 92
Over ! the *s* summer closes, (*repeat*)   *Becket, Pro.* 301, 323, 331
I left him with peace on his face—that *s* other-world
   smile,   *Becket, Pro.* 396
and it minded me Of the *s* woods of Clifford,   „   i i 264
Be *s* to her, she has many enemies.   „   i i 404

Sweet (*continued*) that seems *s* to you now, will blast and
   blind you like a curse.   *Becket* i iv 39
that seem at most *S* guests, or foreign cousins,   „   ii i 135
Thou shalt confess all thy *s* sins to me.   „   ii i 292
so if the city be sick, and I cannot call the kennel *s*,   „   ii ii 349
All praise to Heaven, and *s* St. Magdalen !   „   iii iii 235
And I will fly with my *s* boy to heaven,   „   iv ii 237
Home, *s* moon, bring him home,   *The Cup* ii ii 7
white In the *s* moon as with a lovelier snow !   „   i ii 396
and bless your *s* face, you look as beautiful this
   morning as the very Madonna her own self—   *The Falcon* 197
Oh *s* saints ! one plate of prunes !   „   215
My last sight ere I swoon'd was one *s* face Crown'd
   with the wreath.   „   648
Well, shall we say this wreath and your *s* rhymes ?   „   735
My *s* Eva, Where have you lain in ambush all the
   morning ?   *Prom. of May* i 543
we might be As happy as the bees there at their
   honey In these *s* blossoms.   *Eva.*   Yes ; how
   s they smell !   „   i 607
an' them theer be soom of her oän roses, an' she
   wur as *s* as ony on 'em—   „   ii 39
Why, lass, doänt tha knaw he be *s* upo' Dora Steer,   „   ii 161
Can tell me anything of our *s* Eva When in her
   brighter girlhood,   „   ii 520
Be not so cast down, my *s* Eva.   „   iii 468
O *s* Kate, my first love, the first kiss, the first kiss !   *Foresters* i i 126
But he flutter'd his wings with a *s* little cry,   „   i i 154
Farewell, Sir Richard ; farewell, *s* Marian.   „   i ii 285
Here's a pot o' wild honey from an old oak, saving
   your *s* reverences.   „   ii i 296
O *s* sir, talk not of cows. You anger the spirit.   „   ii i 329
All the *s* saints bless your worship for your alms to
   the old woman !   „   ii i 363
and if thou be as gentle Give me some news of my *s*
   Marian. Where is she ?   *Marian.*   Thy *s* Marian ?   „   ii i 481
Stay with us here, *s* love,   „   ii ii 14
Those *s* tree-Cupids half-way up in heaven,   „   iii 35
Robin, the *s* light of a mother's eye,   „   iv 2
On those *s* lips that dare to dally with it.   „   iv 75
S Marian, by the letter of the law It seems thy
   father's land is forfeited.   „   iv 638
S heavens, I could wish that all the land Were plunged   „   iv 666
Kiss him, Sir Richard—kiss him, my *s* Marian.   „   iv 1004
But thou art fair as ever, my *s* sister.   „   iv 1018
Sweet'art (**sweetheart**) kissin' o' one another like two *s*'s
   i' the poorch   *Prom. of May* i 22
as long as the man sarved for 'is *s* i' Scriptur'.   „   ii 62
meä and my *s* was a workin' along o' one side wi'
   one another,   „   ii 152
telled me 'at *s*'s niver worked well togither ; and I
   telled 'im 'at *s*'s allus worked best togither ;   „   ii 156
wheniver 'e sees two *s*'s togither like thou and me,   „   ii 163
do thou and thy *s* sing us hoäm to supper—   „   ii 170
an' axed ma to be 'is little *s*,   „   ii 120
Sweeten Hast thou anything to *s* this ?   *Foresters* ii i 294
Sweeter I had kept My Robins and my cows in *s*
   order Had I been such.   *Queen Mary* iii v 270
S than any violet of to-day,   *The Falcon* 465
Sweetest This wild one—nay, I shall not prick myself—Is *s*.   *Becket* ii i 145
And then the *s* flower of all the wolds,   *Prom. of May* i 751
Sweetheart (*See also* **Sweet'art**) How sayst thou, *s* ?   *Becket* iv ii 161
And your *s*—when are you and he to be married ?   *Prom. of May* iii 110
Wilt thou embrace thy *s* 'fore my face ?   *Foresters* ii i 28
No, *s* ! out of tune with Love and me.   „   iv 30
Sweetness Lilylike in her stateliness and *s* !   *Prom. of May* ii 621
Swept We have had it *s* and garnish'd after him.   *Queen Mary* iii ii 138
Swiftness Upon the skill and *s* of the players.   „   i iii 143
Swim Here's to him, sink or *s* !   *Thane.*   God sink
   him !   *Harold* iv iii 134
our little Sheriff will ever *s* with the stream !   *Foresters* i i 240
And I would *s* the moat, like an otter.   „   i i 320
Swimming hardly, save by boat, *s*, or wings.   *Queen Mary* ii iii 13
Swindler but I taäkes 'im for a Lunnun *s*, and a
   burn fool.   *Prom. of May* i 309

Tail (s) (*continued*)   that every Spaniard carries a *t*
like a devil   *Queen Mary* III i 223
They make amends for the *t*'s.   „   III i 227
tell you that all English heretics have *t*'s.   „   III i 230
wrath of Heaven hath three *t*'s, The devil only one.   *Harold* I i 61
always in suspense, like the *t* of the horologe—   *Becket* I ii 366
hasn't an eye left in his own *t* to flourish   *The Falcon* 102

Tailed   *See* **Stump-tailed**

Taint   I bring the *t* on it along wi' me, for the
Archbishop likes it,   *Becket* I iv 252

Tainted   *T* with Lutheranism in Italy.   *Queen Mary* III iv 227

Take   (*See also* **Taäke, Take care, Take heed, Tek**)
Officers Are here in force to *t* you to the Tower.   „   I ii 109
as the Earl of Devon To *t* my seat in ;   „   I iv 74
To *t* such order with all heretics   „   I v 34
Madam, *t* it bluntly ; marry Philip,   „   I v 204
t And wear it as memorial of a morning   „   I v 528
to *t* the guns From out the vessels lying in the river.   „   II i 220
T thy poor gentleman !   „   III iii 93
There yet is time, *t* boat and pass to Windsor.   „   II iv 27
heard She would not *t* a last farewell of him,   „   III i 367
' Will you *t* it off Before I lay me down ? '   „   III i 401
To *t* this absolution from your lips,   „   III ii 116
Statesmen that are wise *T* truth herself for model.   „   III iii 37
Sheep at the gap which Gardiner *t*'s,   „   III iii 236
To *t* the lives of others that are loyal,   „   III iv 48
it *t*'s my breath :   „   III v 189
I will *t* Such order with all bad,   „   IV i 94
That I should spare to *t* a heretic priest's,   „   IV i 131
My fancy *t*'s the burner's part,   „   IV ii 231
We are ready To *t* you to St. Mary's, Master Cranmer.   „   IV iii 238
T therefore, all, example by this man,   „   IV iii 59
there be two old gossips—gospellers, I *t* it ;   „   IV iii 462
And tell me how she *t*'s it.   „   v i 261
and your Grace, So you will *t* advice of mine,   „   v i 301
T it away ! not low enough for me !   „   v ii 377
But shall I *t* some message from your Grace ?   „   v iii 85
I *t* it that the King hath spoken to you ;   *Harold* I ii 58
T thou this ring ;   „   I ii 67
For if the North *t* fire, I should be back ;   „   II ii 207
So thou, fair friend, will *t* them easily,   „   II ii 502
We seldom *t* man's life, except in war ;   „   III i 114
Men would but *t* him for the craftier liar.   „   III i 197
t, sign it, Stigand, Aldred ! Sign it,   „   III ii 170
The Good Shepherd ! *T* this, and render that.   „   III ii 185
but *t* back thy ring. It burns my hand—   „   IV i 57
Ye *t* a stick, and break it ;   „   IV i 72
This old Wulfnoth Would *t* me on his knees   „   IV i 183
Yea, *t* the Sacrament upon it, king.   „   IV ii 7
I could *t* and slay thee.   „   IV ii 9
T and slay me, For Edward loved me.   *Harold.*
T and slay me, I say, Or I shall count thee fool.   *Harold.*
T thee, or free thee, Free thee or slay thee,   „   IV ii 14
where mine own self *T*'s part against myself !   „   v i 300
Thou art half English. *T* them away !   „   v ii 136
T them away, I do not love to see them.   „   v ii 142
Hell *t* thy bishop then, and my kingship too !   *Becket, Pro.* 93
Nay, then, I *t* thee at thy word—   „   Pro. 127
chart mark'd ' *Her Bower,*' *T,* keep it, friend.   „   Pro. 161
We *t* her from her secret bower in Anjou   „   Pro. 181
T thou mine answer in bare commonplace—   „   Pro. 282
chart is not mine, but Becket's : *t* it, Thomas.   „   Pro. 311
T it and wear it on that hard heart of yours !   „   Pro. 372
To *t* the vagabond woman of the street Into thine arms !   „   I i 227
Herbert, *t* out a score of armed men   „   I i 327
we might *t* your side against the customs—   „   I ii 56
And *t* the Church's danger on myself.   „   I ii 72
T it not that way—balk not the Pope's will.   „   I iii 242
since your canon will not let you *t* Life for a life,   „   I iii 390
In peace now—but after. *T* that for earnest.   „   I iii 733
I brought not ev'n my crucifix. *Henry.* *T* this.   „   II i 296
And let another *t* his bishoprick !   „   II ii 260
I pray you come and *t* it.   „   II ii 263
Nay, my lord, *t* heart ;   „   II ii 355
a good fairy to thy mother. *T* me to her.   „   IV i 26

Take (*continued*)   shall sleep sound enough if thou wilt *t* me
to her.   *Becket* IV i 33
I pray you then to *t* my sleeping-draught ;   „   IV ii 69
But if you should not care to *t* it—   „   IV ii 71
You bad me *t* revenge another way—   „   IV ii 152
T thy one chance ; Catch at the last straw.   „   IV ii 220
to *t* a life which Henry bad me Guard   „   IV ii 268
T up your dagger ; put it in the sheath.   „   IV ii 293
To *t* my life might lose him Aquitaine.   „   IV ii 396
T care o' thyself, O King.   „   v i 66
Summon your barons ; *t* their counsel :   „   v i 75
If God would *t* him in some sudden way—   „   v i 93
a man may *t* good counsel Ev'n from his foe.   „   v ii 3
T refuge in your own cathedral, (repeat)   *Becket* v ii 583, 590
T thou this letter and this cup to Camma,   *The Cup* I i 61
T thou this cup and leave it at her doors.   „   I i 67
While you can *t* your pastime in the woods.   „   I i 190
And *t* a hunter's vengeance on the meats.   „   I ii 43
paper sign'd Antonius—will you *t* it, read it ?   „   I ii 226
t this holy cup To lodge it in the shrine of Artemis.   „   I ii 434
lark first *t*'s the sunlight on his wing,   „   I iii 43
that I was bold enough To *t* it down,   *The Falcon* 429
You can *t* it, nurse ! *Elisabetta.* I did *t* it,   „   489
will you *t* the word out of your master's own mouth ?
   Filippo. Was it there to *t* ? Put it there, my lord.   „   597
T's nothing in return from you except   „   716
Then I require you to *t* back your diamonds—   „   720
Cannot *t* his pastime like the flies ?   *Prom. of May* I 277
Altho' at first he *t* his bonds for flowers,   „   I 645
I *t* them, then, for Eva's sake.   „   II 29
t to the milking of your cows, the fatting of your
calves,   „   II 91
but I *T* some delight in sketching,   „   II 539
you, I doubt not, Would *t* to them as kindly,   „   II 548
T them, dear. Say that the sick lady thanks him !   „   III 348
T it again, dear father, be not wroth   *Foresters* II i 341
Not in this hut I *t* it.   „   II i 205
T thou mine arm. Who art thou, gallant knight ?   „   II i 439
T him, good Little John, and give him wine.   „   II i 469
—*t* and use your moment, while you may.   „   II i 476
And *t* and wear this symbol of your love ;   „   III 79
T thou this light kiss for thy clumsy word.   „   III 134
T all they have and give it to thyself !   „   III 171
T this penny and leave him his gold mark.   „   III 217
T thou my bow and arrow and compel them to pay toll.   „   III 262
t the twenty-seven marks to the captain's treasury.   „   III 294
Maid ? *Friar. Paramour ! Friar.* Hell *t* her !   „   III 403
The flower said ' *T* it, my dear,   „   IV 16
T him and try him, friar.   „   IV 268
Robin *t*'s From whom he knows are hypocrites   „   IV 379
T the left leg for the love of God.   „   IV 577
T up the litter !   „   IV 597
I will *t* the rope from off thy waist   „   IV 686

Take care   *T* c, *t* c ! I dance—I will dance—   „   IV 585

Take heed   And so *t* h I pray you—   *Queen Mary* I iv 273
So thou and thine must be. *T* h !   „   III ii 232
T h, *t* h ! The blade is keen as death.   „   v v 174
T h, *t* h ; Thou art the Queen ;   *Harold* I i 453
My lord— *Malet.* *T* h now.   „   II ii 641
T h, lest he destroy thee utterly.   *Becket* I iii 13
T h he do not turn and rend you too :   „   III i 160
T h, *t* h ! in Nottingham they say There bides   *Foresters* II i 201

Taken   (*See also* **Taäen, Ta'en, Tuk**)   Hath *t* to this
Courtenay.   *Queen Mary* I iv 201
it is thought the Duke will be *t*.   „   II i 136
Is Peter Carew fled ? Is the Duke *t* ?   „   II i 142
there by Sir Maurice Berkeley Was *t* prisoner.   „   IV iv 96
Hath *t* Scarboro' Castle, north of York ;   „   v i 287
Is Calais *t* ?   „   v ii 27
sharper harm to England and to Rome, Than Calais *t*.   „   v ii 30
Madam, Calais is *t*.   „   v ii 242
Guisnes is not *t* yet ? (repeat)   „   v ii 277
T the rifted pillars of the wood   *Harold* I ii 100
They have *t* away the toy thou gavest me,   „   II ii 105
They have *t* York.   „   III ii 171

Taken (*continued*) York *t*? *Gurth.* Yea, Tostig hath
  t York !   *Harold* III ii 174
  Brother of France, you have *t*, cherish'd him   *Becket* II ii 154
  Ay, but he's *t* the rain with him.   ,,   III i 273
  gone to the King And *t* our anathema with him.   ,,   v ii 8
  You should have *t* counsel with your friends   ,,   v ii 555
  My counsel is already *t*, John.   ,,   v ii 560
  and was much *t* with you, my dear. *Eva. T*
    with me ;   *Prom. of May* III 263
  the boy was *t* prisoner by the Moors.   *Foresters* I i 60
  were I *t* They would prick out my sight.   ,,   II i 71
  Sheriff had *t* all our goods for the King without paying,   ,,   II i 190
Taker if giver And *t* be but honest !   *Harold* I i 346
Taking (*See also* **Taäkin'**) thou wast not happy *t* charge
  Of this wild Rosamund   *Becket* I i 391
  that *t* The Fiend's advantage of a throne,   ,,   II i 151
  Well—I shall serve Galatia *t* it,   *The Cup* I i 100
  made me A Quietist *t* all things easily.   *Prom. of May* I 232
  A Quietist *t* all things easily—   ,,   I 290
Talbot Where, knave, where ? *Man.* Sign of the *T.*   *Queen Mary* III i 319
Tale (*See also* **Nursery-tale**) And love to hear bad *t's*
  of Philip.   ,,   v ii 429
  tell me *t's* Of Alfred and of Athelstan the Great   *Harold* IV i 73
  This is the likelier *t*. We have hit the place.   *Becket* III ii 42
  tell him my *t's*, Sing him my songs?   *The Falcon* 796
  And cheer his blindness with a traveller's *t's* ?   *Prom. of May* II 516
Talent like the man In Holy Writ, who brought his *t*
  back ;   *Foresters* IV 981
Talk (s) when there rose a *t* of the late rebellion,   *Queen Mary* I i 92
  I am somewhat faint With our long *t*.   ,,   I v 521
  —he is free enough in *t*, But tells me nothing.   ,,   III i 193
  Touch him upon his old heretical *t*,   ,,   III iv 352
  Nor let Priests' *t*, or dream of worlds to be,   ,,   v v 217
  More *t* of this to-morrow, if yon weird sign   *Harold* I i 120
  Unwholesome *t* For Godwin's house !   ,,   I i 390
  I leave thee to thy *t* with him alone ;   ,,   II ii 324
  I dare not well be seen in *t* with thee.   ,,   II ii 482
  Ha, Becket ! thou rememberest our *t* !   *Becket, Pro.* 405
  The king, the crown ! their *t* in Rome ?   *The Cup* I i 99
  That must be *t*, not truth, but truth or *t*,   *The Falcon* 232
  Come, come, my girl, enough Of this strange *t*.   *Prom. of May* III 620
Talk (verb) when your Highness *t's* of Courtenay—   *Queen Mary* I v 198
  Why do they *t* so foully of your Prince,   ,,   I v 425
  We *t* and. *Member.* Ay, and what use to *t*?   ,,   III iii 39
  We *t* and Cranmer suffers.   ,,   IV iii 420
  I warrant you they *t* about the burning.   ,,   IV iii 463
  You *t* almost as if it.Might be the last.   *The Cup* I i 422
  Tut ! you *t* Old feudalism.   *Prom. of May* I 669
  we'd as lief *t* o' the Divil afoor ye as 'im,   ,,   III 130
  t a little French like a lady ;   ,,   III 302
  then what is it That makes you *t* so dolefully?   ,,   III 572
  Go with him. I will *t* with thee anon.   *Foresters* II i 132
  O sweet sir, *t* not of cows.   ,,   II i 329
  Elf, with spiteful heart and eye, *T* of jealousy ?   ,,   II ii 173
Talked They've almost *t* me into it: *Queen Mary* I iv 7
  When last we *t*, that Philip would not come   ,,   II iv 135
  Have *t* together, and are well agreed   ,,   III iv 6
  I *t* with her in vain—says she will live   ,,   III vi 44
  Council (I have *t* with some already) are for war.   ,,   v i 295
  I have often *t* with Wulfnoth,   *Harold* II ii 88
  for the king Is holy, and hath *t* with God,   ,,   III i 355
  Hath Henry told thee? hast thou *t* with him?   *Becket* I iii 258
  I could have *t* him out of His ten wives into one.   ,,   IV ii 311
Talkin' she'd niver 'a been *t* haäfe an hour wi' the
  divil 'at killed her oän sister,   *Prom. of May* II 603
Talking (*See also* **A-talkin'**, **Talkin'**) what's the good of
  my *t* to myself,   *Becket* III i 152
  There is the King *t* with Walter Map ?   ,,   III iii 22
  to seize On whomsoever may be *t* with you,   *The Cup* I iii 7
Tall I would I were as *t* and strong as you. *Lady*
  Magdalen. I seem half-shamed at times to
  be so *t*.   *Queen Mary* v ii 422
  Make blush the maiden-white of our *t* cliffs,   *Harold* II ii 332
  So *t* and bold as they be.   *Foresters* II i 8
  I can bring down Fourscore *t* fellows on thee.   ,,   IV 177

Tall (*continued*) Good, now I love thee mightily, thou
  t fellow.   *Foresters* IV 322
Tame (adj.) And break your paces in, and make
  you *t*;   *Queen Mary* v iii 122
Tame (verb) King hath many more wolves than he can *t*   *Becket* III iii 322
Tamer but the plots against him Had madden'd *t* men.   *Harold* IV i 112
Tamper'd Wyatt, who hath *t* with A public ignorance,   *Queen Mary* II ii 180
Tamperer Or *t's* with that treason out of Kent.   ,,   II ii 11
Tan The *t* of southern summers and the beard ?   *Prom. of May* II 617
Tann'd Thou art *t* almost beyond my knowing, brother.   *Foresters* IV 1015
Tanner and cried ' Work for the *t*.'   *Harold* II i 385
  William the *t's* bastard !   ,,   II ii 775
  The *t's* bastard !   ,,   IV iii 173
Tap (s) may give that egg-bald head The *t* that silences.   ,,   v i 92
Tap (verb) Do me the service to *t* it, and thou wilt know.
  Friar Tuck. I would *t* myself in thy service,
  Robin.   *Foresters* III 333
Tare burn the *t's* with unquenchable fire !   *Queen Mary* v v 114
Target and make thine old carcase a *t* for us three.   *Foresters* II i 404
Tarquin (**II., the seventh and last King of Rome**) violence
  to a woman, As Rome did *T.*   *The Cup* I i 140
  I here return like *T*—for a crown. *Antonius.* And
  may be foil'd like *T*, if you follow   ,,   I i 142
Tarry Methinks that would you *t* one day more   *Queen Mary* III vi 232
Task it is thou Hath set me this hard *t*,   *The Falcon* 237
Taste by the hand o' God avore a could *t* a
  mossel,   *Queen Mary* IV iii 517
  Not *t* his venison first ?   *Foresters* I 343
Tasted scarce touch'd or *t* The splendours of our Court.   *Harold* II ii 174
  This Almoner hath *t* Henry's gold.   *Becket* I iii 294
Tatter'd Our holy mother Canterbury, who sits With *t* robes.   ,,   I i 157
Taught (*See also* **Larned**) the old priests *t* me
  nothing.   *Queen Mary* II iii 58
  And every syllable *t* us by our Lord,   ,,   II iii 231
  thou hast *t* the king to spoil him too ;   *Harold* I i 451
  then I *t* him all our hawking-phrases.   *The Falcon* 314
  T her the learned names, anatomized   *Prom. of May* II 302
  for you have *t* me To love you.   ,,   III 557
Tawny The *t* squirrel vaulting thro' the boughs,   *Foresters* III 117
Tax They will not lay more *t'es* on a land   *Queen Mary* v i 167
Taxing *See* **Over-taxing**
Tea Owd Steer gi'es nubbut cowd *t* to '*is* men,   *Prom. of May* II 224
  But I'd like owd Steer's cowd *t* better nor
  Dobson's beer.   ,,   II 227
  worked at all the worse upon the cold *t* than you
  would have done upon the beer ?   ,,   III 56
  we worked naw wuss upo' the cowd *t*;   ,,   III 59
Teach (*See also* **Larn**) we will *t* Queen Mary how to
  reign.   *Queen Mary* II i 147
  if this pass, We two shall have to *t* him ;   ,,   III iv 422
  and our Latimer-sailors Will *t* her something.   ,,   IV iii 350
  he and I Might *t* this Rome—   *The Cup* II 96
Tear (s) (*See also* **Woman-tears**) Spite of her *t's* her
  father forced in on her.   *Queen Mary* I v 495
  those hard men brake into woman *t's*, Ev'n Gardiner,   ,,   I v 565
  Queen hath been three days in *t's*   ,,   III vi 13
  See how the *t's* run down his fatherly face.   ,,   IV iii 3
  The Queen in *t's* !   ,,   v i 223
  cries continually with sweat and *t's* to the Lord God   ,,   v iv 45
  And blotted by her *t's*. This cannot last.   ,,   v v 17
  My prayers go up as fast as my *t's* fall,   *Harold* III i 166
  Vying a *t* with our cold dews,   ,,   v i 150
  My heart is full of *t's*—I have no answer.   *Becket, Pro.* 406
  My lord, we leave thee not without *t's*. *Becket.* *T's* ?
  Why not stay with me then ?   I iv 17
  many midriff-shaken even to *t's*, as springs gush out
  after earthquakes—   ,,   III iii 162
  old affection master'd you, You falter'd into *t's*.   ,,   v ii 145
  True *t's* that year were shed for you in Florence.   *The Falcon* 384
  I hate *t's*. Marriage is but an old tradition.   *Prom. of May* I 490
  Bid their old bond farewell with smiles, not *t's*;   ,,   I 525
  That desolate letter, blotted with her *t's*,   ,,   II 476
  should walk hand in hand together down this valley
  of *t's*,   ,,   III 192
  T's ! I have sometimes been moved to *t's*   ,,   III 207

Tear (s) (*continued*) but what have I to do with *t's* now ? | *Prom. of May* III 210
And ever a *t* down ran. | *Foresters* I i 19
Tear (verb) From thine own mouth I judge thee—*t* him down ! | *Queen Mary* I iii 54
T up that woman's work there. | „ II i 75
And *t* you piecemeal : so you have a guard. | „ IV ii 36
I never read, I *t* them ; | „ V i 188
T out his tongue. *Officer.* He shall not rail again. | *Harold* II ii 487
T out his eyes, And plunge him into prison. | „ II ii 491
Say that he blind thee and *t* out thy tongue. | *Becket* I i 615
I could *t* him asunder with wild horses | „ II i 266
score of wolf-dogs are let loose that will *t* thee piecemeal. | „ III ii 39
ready To *t* himself for having said as much. | „ IV ii 279
shall not I, the Queen, *T* out her heart— | „ IV ii 409
I *t* it all to pieces, never dream'd Of acting on it. | *The Cup* I ii 247
I *t* away The leaves were darken'd by the battle— | *The Falcon* 912
Towser'll *t* him all to pieces. | *Prom. of May* I 423
Down with him, *t* his coat from his back. | *Foresters* I iii 73
if they come I will not *t* the bond, | „ IV 98
Te Deum *See* **Deum**
Tek (take) but *t* thou my word vor't, Joan,— | *Queen Mary* IV iii 533
Tekel Mene, Mene, *T* ! Is thy wrath Hell, | *Harold* I i 36
Tell might be forgiven. I *t* you, fly, my Lord. | *Queen Mary* I ii 43
I charge you, *T* Courtenay nothing. | „ I iv 191
t your Grace What Lady Jane replied. | „ I v 49
Come you to *t* me this, my Lord ? | „ I v 106
t me, did you ever Sigh for a beard ? | „ I v 607
Bad me to *t* you that she counts on you | „ II ii 104
To *t* you what indeed ye see and know, | „ II ii 144
cannot *t* How mothers love their children ; | „ II ii 189
Their voice had left me none to *t* you this. | „ II iii 36
I cannot *t* you why they call him so. | „ III i 204
will *t* you that all English heretics have tails. | „ III i 229
T him to paint it out, | „ III i 267
doubtless you can *t* me how she died ? | „ III i 356
Good news have I to *t* you, news to make | „ III ii 186
he is free enough in talk, But *t's* me nothing. | „ III ii 194
And *t* this learned Legate he lacks zeal. | „ III iv 272
mad brute Must have the cautery—*t* him— | „ III iv 276
I cannot *t* you, His bearing is so courtly-delicate ; | „ III iv 396
For one day more, so far as I can *t*. | „ III vi 246
Ay, *t* us that. | „ IV iii 23
More grievously than any tongue can *t*. | „ IV iii 125
Or sign'd all those they *t* us that he sign'd ? | „ IV iii 320
Pole Will *t* you that the devil helpt them thro' it. | „ IV iii 352
and *t's* un ez the vire has tuk holt. | „ IV iii 511
T me that, or leave All else untold. | „ IV iii 568
Then *t* me all. *Paget.* Ay Master Peters, *t* us. | „ IV iii 572
Sir Nicholas *t's* you true, | „ V i 16
And *t* me how she takes it. | „ V i 261
T my mind to the Council—to the Parliament : | „ V ii 288
T, *t* me ; save my credit with myself. | „ V ii 452
I might dare to *t* her that the Count— | „ V ii 523
And *t* him that I know he comes no more. *T* him at last I know his love is dead, | „ V ii 589
T her to come and close my dying eyes, | „ V ii 599
t the King that I will muse upon it ; | „ V iii 89
Have you aught else to *t* me ? | „ V iii 100
t's me I must not think—That I must rest— | „ V v 62
Sit down here : *T* me thine happiest hour. | „ V v 79
t the cooks to close The doors of all the offices below. | „ V v 116
But *t* us, is this pendent hell in heaven | *Harold* I i 76
he may *t* thee, *I* am a harm to England. | „ I i 79
I may *t* thee, Tostig, I heard from thy Northumberland | „ I i 349
and *t* him That where he was but worsted, | „ I i 448
I *t* thee what, my child ; Thou hast misread | „ I ii 96
T him what hath crept into our creel, | „ I ii 56
Fly thou to William ; *t* him we have Harold. | „ II i 110
I'll *t* them I have had my way with thee. | „ II ii 118
I cannot *t*. I have the Count's commands. | „ II ii 238
Speak for thy mother's sake, and *t* me true. | „ II ii 272
O son, when thou didst *t* me of thine oath, | „ III i 267
and *t* me tales Of Alfred and of Athelstan | „ IV i 72
Is there so great a need to *t* thee why ? | „ IV iii 40

Tell (*continued*) My nurse would *t* me of a molehill | *Harold* IV iii 128
T him the Saints are nobler than he dreams, *T* him that God is nobler than the Saints, And *t* him we stand arm'd on Senlac Hill, | „ V 55
whether it symbol'd ruin Or glory, who shall *t* ? | „ V 111
T that again to all. *Gurth.* I will, good brother. | „ V 198
To *t* thee thou shouldst win at Stamford-bridge, | „ V 236
To *t* thee thou shalt die on Senlac hill— | „ V 241
I *t* thee, girl, I am seeking my dead Harold. | „ V ii 42
and sent against him—who can *t* ?— | „ V ii 170
which cannot *t* A good dish from a bad, | *Becket, Pro.* 105
Then *t* me who and what she is. | „ I i 208
Back, man, I *t* thee ! | „ I i 218
He found me once alone. Nay—nay—I cannot *T* you : | „ I i 276
To *t* the King, my friend, I am against him. | „ I i 343
And I can *t* you, lords, ye are all as like | „ I iii 174
T what I say to the King. | „ I iii 564
T the King I spent thrice that in fortifying | „ I iii 631
I would be true—would *t* thee all— | „ II i 205
Bird mustn't *t*, Whoop—he can see. (repeat) | „ III i 106, 255
you shall *t* me of her some other time. *Margery.* |
There's none so much to *t* on her, my lady, | „ III i 190
tho' I be sworn not to speak a word, I can *t* you all about her, | „ III i 205
stay, fool, and *t* me why thou fliest. | „ III ii 34
Who is he ? *Geoffrey.* Can't *t*. | „ IV i 17
Can't *t*. But I heard say he had had a stroke, | „ IV i 53
Henry—Becket *t's* him this—To take my life | „ IV ii 394
Did she not *t* me I was playing in her presence ? | „ IV ii 399
I cannot *t* why monks should all be cowards. | „ V ii 581
No, I *t* you ! I cannot bear a hand | „ V iii 19
I *t* thee, my good fellow, My arrow struck the stag. | *The Cup* I ii 26
as you *t* me Tetrarch, there might be willing wives | „ I ii 186
I dare not *t* him how I came to know it ; | „ I ii 275
Still—I should *t* My husband. | „ I ii 303
Then do not *t* him. Or *t* him, if you will, | „ I ii 309
Return and *t* them Synorix is not here. | „ I ii 335
T him there is one shadow among the shadows, | „ II 139
t him That I accept the diadem of Galatia— | „ II 157
I wait him his crown'd queen. *Noble.* So will I *t* him. | „ II 162
t the Senate I have been most true to Rome— | „ II 481
and *t* her all about it and make her happy ? | *The Falcon* 183
I can *t* you True tears that year were shed | „ 383
Well, *T* me the words—or better— | „ 451
I can *t* you, my lady, I can *t* you. | „ 595
I cannot *t* how long we strove before | „ 637
t him my tales, Sing him my songs ? | „ 795
How shall I break it to him ? how shall I *t* him ? | „ 849
I can't *t*, for I have never seen him. | *Prom. of May* I 115
Will he ? How can I *t* ? | „ I 120
And I *t's* ye what, Miss Dora : he's no respect for the Queen, | „ I 131
I forgot to *t* you He wishes you to dine along with us, | „ I 616
And when will you return ? *Edgar.* I cannot *t* precisely ; | „ I 628
But you shall *t* me all about it. | „ I 785
They *t* me that yesterday you mentioned | „ II 22
I *t* you, it cannot be. | „ II 113
Do ye think I be gawin' to *t* it to you, | „ II 190
Why, coom then, owd feller, I'll *t* it to you ; | „ II 202
Who can *t* What golden hours, | „ II 508
but if you Can *t* me anything of our sweet Eva | „ II 520
I cannot *t*, tho' standing in her presence. | „ II 557
they *t* me that you—and you have six children— | „ III 76
You *t* me you have a lover. | „ III 255
he *t's* me that he met you once in the old times, | „ III 262
I dare not *t* him how much I love him. | „ III 287
Shall I *t* her he is dead ? No ; She is still too feeble. | „ III 337
T him I cannot leave the sick lady just yet. | „ III 352
says he wants to *t* ye summut very partic'lar. | „ III 355
T him that I and the lady here wish to see him. | „ III 414
T him, then, that I'm waiting for him. | „ III 483
Did you not *t* me he was crazed with jealousy, | „ III 565
I can *t* you, We Steers are of old blood, | „ III 603
T them to fly for a doctor. | „ III 712

Thank (continued) I t you, my good nurse. — *The Falcon* 559
I t you heartily for that—and you, — „ 801
My lord, we t you for your entertainment. — „ 859
scarce Will t me for your entertainment now. — „ 882
T you. Look how full of rosy blossom it is. — *Prom. of May* I 83
I t you for that, Miss Dora, onyhow. — „ I 157
saäme to you, Master Steer, likewise. *Steer.* T ye. — „ I 348
I t you. They tell me that yesterday — „ II 22
if the fever spread, the parish will have to t you for it. — „ III 47
But I t's ye all the saäme, Miss. — „ III 50
All right, Miss; and t ye kindly. — „ III 66
An' I t's ye fur that, Miss, moor nor fur the waäge. — „ III 116
Say that the sick lady t's him! — „ III 349
I t you, my lady, and I wish you — *Foresters* I i 307
We t you, and farewell. — „ I ii 248
Comrades, I t you for your loyalty, — „ III 78
I t thee. *Marian.* Scarlet told me— — „ III 144
I t you, my lord. — „ III 213
I t you, noble sir, the very blossom Of bandits. Curtsey
to him, wife, and t him. *Wife.* I t you, noble sir,
and will pray for you — „ III 246
There is our bond. *Robin.* I t thee. — „ IV 436
Here is my father's bond. *Robin.* I t thee, dear. — „ IV 464
I t thee, good Sir Richard. — „ IV 858
Thank'd She t her father sweetly for his book — *Queen Mary* V v 236
Thankful And shalt be t if I leave thee that. — „ III i 257
Thankless Were but a t policy in the crown, — „ III iv 51
I know it, son; I am not t: — *Harold* I i 216
Thanks I am all t To God and to your Grace: — *Queen Mary* I v 185
beseech Your Highness to accept our lowliest t — „ II ii 132
T, Sir Thomas, we be beholden to you, — „ II iii 120
Loyal and royal cousin, humblest t. — „ III ii 4
Can render t in fruit for being sown, — „ III iii 198
Madam, my t. — „ v 184
T, truthful Earl; I did not doubt thy word, — *Harold* II ii 723
Full t for your fair greeting of my bride! — „ IV iii 46
T, Gurth! The simple, silent, selfless man — „ v i 80
Our humblest t for your blessing. — *Becket* I iv 42
t of Holy Church are due to those That went — „ II ii 190
T to the blessed Magdalen, whose day it is. — „ III iii 171
T in this life, and in the life to come. — „ v ii 161
I owe you t for ever. — *The Cup* I ii 249
My t. But, look, how wasteful of the blossom — *Prom. of May* I 611
Yeäs; and t to ye. — „ III 26
T, my lady—inasmuch as I am a true believer — *Foresters* I i 161
All t for all your service; — „ I iii 164
Thaw and those bleak manners t, — *Queen Mary* III ii 161
cold corners of the King's mouth began to t, — *Becket* III iii 154
Thaw (though) t 'e knaws I was hallus ageän heving
schoolmaster i' the parish! — *Prom. of May* I 185
fur t I may ha' fallen out wi' ye sometimes, — „ I 324
and, t I says it mysen, niver men 'ed a better
master— — „ I 326
I be a gentleman, t I beänt naw scholard, — „ I 332
fur t I be heighty this very daäy, — „ I 358
But, Steer, t thou be haäle anew I seed tha a-limpin'
up just now — „ I 383
Churchwarden be a coomin', t me and 'im we niver
'grees about the tithe; and Parson mebbe, t he
niver mended that gap i' the glebe fence as I
telled 'im; and Blacksmith, t he niver shoes a
herse to my likings; and Baäker, t sticks to
hoäm-maäde— — „ I 443
Noä—yeas—t the feller's gone and maäde such a
litter of his faäce. — „ II 588
noä—t they hanged ma at 'Size fur it. — „ II 697
Themselves *See* **Thessens**
Theobald (Archbishop of Canterbury) So then our good
Archbishop T Lies dying. — *Becket, Pro.* 2
thou didst help me to my throne In T's time, — „ *Pro.* 202
when I was of T's household, once— — „ I i 59
I served our T well when I was with him; — „ I i 142
I and thou were youths in T's house, — „ I iii 40
Exile me from the face of T. — „ I iii 43
Even when you both were boys at T's. — „ v i 11

Therevore (therefore) Thank the Lord t.
(repeat) — *Queen Mary* IV iii 496, 520, 529
Therewithin To still the petty treason t, — *Queen Mary* III i 13
Thessens (themselves) Foälks doesn't hallus knaw t; — *Prom. of May* I 29
Thick (adj.) on his neck a collar, Gold, t with
diamonds; — *Queen Mary* III i 80
And here's a crowd as t as herring-shoals. — „ III i 182
till he stoop'd and gather'd one From out a bed of
t forget-me-nots, — „ v v 94
The people are as t as bees below, — *Harold* I i 31
And wattled t with ash and willow-wands; — „ v i 190
My sight is eagle, but the strife so t— — „ v i 627
The King's 'God's eyes!' come now so t and fast, — *Becket* I iii 610
Thick (s) I left him somewhere in the t of it. — *Queen Mary* II iv 81
Thicken doth not the living skin t against perpetual
whippings? — *Becket* III iii 316
Thicket Seen in the t at the bottom there — *The Cup* I i 113
Thief Gentleman! a t! Go hang him. — *Queen Mary* IV i 75
when the t is ev'n within the walls, — „ III iv 311
Thou shalt receive the penitent t's award, — „ IV iii 86
And, like a t, push'd in his royal hand; — „ v ii 466
When *thieves* fall out, honest men— — *Becket* I iv 113
Is the Archbishop a t who gives thee thy supper? — „ I iv 116
When honest men fall out, *thieves*— — „ I iv 119
Absolve the left-hand t and damn the right? — „ II ii 392
like a t at night when he hears a door open — „ III iii 97
I laäme't my knee last night running arter a t. — *Prom. of May* I 387
I runned arter t i' the dark, — „ I 402
I am a t, ay, and a king of *thieves*. — *Foresters* I i 53
By a t. *Sheriff.* Who, woman, who? — „ II i 317
Softly! softly! there may be a t in every bush. — „ II i 368
thou art disguised—thou art one of the *thieves*. — „ II i 411
It is the very captain of the *thieves*! — „ II i 413
These friars, *thieves*, and liars, Shall drink — „ III 312
yells of t And rogue and liar echo down in Hell, — „ III 323
Well, well, be it so, thou strongest t of all, — „ III 327
But Robin is a t of courtesy — „ IV 370
There—to be a t of courtesy— — „ IV 373
my liege, these men are outlaws, *thieves*, — „ IV 906
Thief-like Who t-l fled from his own church by night, — *Becket* II ii 156
Thimble and can make Five quarts pass into a t. — *Foresters* IV 283
Thimbleful I am misty with my t of ale. — „ IV 278
Thin He! too t, too t. — *Becket, Pro.* 261
Ay, child; and you look t and pale. — *Prom. of May* I 781
that wur sa long back, and the walls sa t, — „ III 72
It is but t and cold, Not like the vintage — *The Falcon* 578
Thing There is but one t against them. — *Queen Mary* I i 101
but all t's here At court are wrong; — „ I iv 56
I must needs wish all good t's for France. — „ I v 309
the t Was no such scarecrow in your father's time. — „ I v 472
Few t's have fail'd to which I set my will. — „ II i 22
were to do Great t's, my Lord. — „ II ii 390
smash all our bits o' t's worse than Philip o' Spain. — „ II iii 104
These are the t's that madden her. Fie upon it! — „ III ii 221
By bonds of beeswax, like your creeping t; — „ III iii 63
Nor yet to question t's already done; — „ III iii 189
Ringdoves coo again, All t's woo again. — „ IV v 104
all t's lived and ended honestly. — „ III v 115
Fancy-sick; these t's are done, — „ IV iii 453
Pwoaps be pretty t's, Joan, — „ IV iii 469
I do know ez Pwoaps and vires be bad t's; — „ IV iii 501
other t's As idle; a weak Wyatt! — „ v 291
Let dead t's rest. — „ v ii 506
the one King, the Christ, and all t's in common, — „ v iv 54
And done such mighty t's by Holy Church, — „ v v 74
What is the strange t happiness? — „ v v 219
dream of worlds to be, Miscolour t's about her— — „ v v 219
worst that follows T's that seem jerk'd — *Harold* I i 137
thou be a wild t Out of the waste, — „ I i 380
where *they* were lost, Where all good t's are lost, — „ III ii 28
I hate myself for all t's that I do. — „ IV ii 45
He means the t he says. See him out safe! — „ v 84
They say that you are wise in winged t's, — *Becket* I i 256
like Egypt's plague, had fill'd All t's with blood; — „ I iii 346
have I Not heard ill t's of her in France? — „ III i 231

Thing (*continued*) Some dreadful *t* is coming on me.   *Becket* III i 267
   all manner of game, and four-footed *t*'s, and fowls—   „   III iii 130
   And all manner of creeping *t*'s too?   „   III iii 133
   Yet one *t* more.   Thou hast broken thro' the pales   „   III iii 192
   I might deliver all *t*'s to thy hand—   „   III iii 270
   to overstep and come at all *t*'s in the next field?   „   III iii 282
   that's a finer *t* there.   How it glitters!   „   IV i 2
   Henry Says many a *t* in sudden heats,   „   IV ii 276
   Deal not with *t*'s you know not.   „   V ii 133
   I know not why You call these old *t*'s back   „   V ii 270
   and smile At bygone *t*'s till that eternal peace.   *The Cup* I iii 172
   This old *t* here they are but blue beads—   *The Falcon* 47
   My one *t* left of value in the world!   „   496
   and profess to be great in green *t*'s and in garden-stuff.   „   551
   made me A Quietist taking all *t*'s easily.   *Prom. of May* I 232
   A Quietist taking all *t*'s easily—   „   I 290
   O the sacred little *t*!   What a shape!   *Foresters* I i 108
   to whom all *t*'s, up to this present,   „   I i 209
   if this life of ours Be a good glad *t*,   „   I iii 13
   Because thou sayest such fine *t*'s of women,   „   I iii 137
   the scream of some wild woodland *t*.   „   II i 253
   criedst 'I yield' almost before the *t* was ask'd,   „   II i 566
   True, she is a goodly *t*.   „   II ii 140
   A woman's heart is but a little *t*,   „   IV 656

Think   I *t* she entreats me like a child.   *Queen Mary* I iii 111
   I *t* you may.   „   I iii 153
   I *t* she means to counsel your withdrawing   „   I iv 224
   I *t* my time will come.   „   I iv 256
   Because they *t* me favourer of this marriage.   „   I v 156
   I do *t* To save your crown that it must come to this.   „   I v 478
   And *t* not we shall be alone—   „   II i 191
   I'll *t* upon it, Knyvett.   „   II i 240
   Don't ye now go to *t* that we be for Philip o' Spain.   „   II iii 106
   are you not in peril here?   *Stafford*.   I *t* so.   „   III i 36
   I *t* with you.   The King of France will help   „   III i 104
   We are fallen, and as I *t*, Never to rise again.   „   III i 124
   I *t* I should fight then.   „   III i 468
   that I *t*, 'Wilt thou lie there to-morrow?'   „   III v 132
   Help me: what *t* you, Is it life or death?   „   III v 193
   and *t* of this in your coming.   'MARY THE QUEEN.'   „   III v 224
   T!   I have many thoughts; I *t* there may be birdlime here for me; I *t* they fain would have me from the realm; I *t* the Queen may never bear a child; I *t* that I may be some time the Queen,   „   III v 226
   I *t* I will not marry anyone,   „   III v 239
   I *t* that I will play with Philibert,—   „   III v 242
   Albeit he *t* himself at home with God,   „   IV iii 192
   T you then That Cranmer read all papers   „   IV iii 316
   I *t* that in some sort we may.   But see,   „   IV iii 551
   Does he *t* Low stature is low nature,   „   V ii 433
   It is the low man *t*'s the woman low;   „   V ii 439
   T you That I might dare to tell her that the Count—   „   V ii 522
   tells me I must not *t*—That I must rest—   „   V v 63
   I *t* that they would Molochize them too,   *Harold* I i 36
   Ask thou Lord Leofwin what he *t*'s of this!   „   I i 40
   I love him or I love him.   „   I ii 152
   As I *t* He was thine host in England   „   II ii 3
   I *t* it so, I *t* I am a fool To *t* it can be otherwise   „   III ii 102
   Some *t* they loved within the pale forbidden   „   III ii 22
   I *t* that this is Thurkill.   „   V ii 65
   I will not *t* so, Thomas.   *Becket, Pro.* 238
   dost thou *t* the king Forced mine election?   *Herbert*.
   I do *t* the King Was potent in the election,   „   I i 126
   T on it again.   „   I i 380
   t of me as thy father!   „   I iii 250
   I ask'd the way.   *Rosamund*.   I *t* so.   „   II i 63
   I sometimes *t* he sleeps When he should watch;   „   III i 32
   when he hears a door open in the house and *t*'s 'the master.'   „   III iii 99
   I *t*, time given, I could have talk'd   „   IV ii 311
   I cannot *t* he moves against my son,   „   V i 18
   I *t* ye four have cause to love this Becket.   „   V i 224
   lightnings that we *t* are only Heaven's Flash   „   V ii 35
   I *t* our Abbess knew it and allow'd it.   „   V ii 95

Think (*continued*) but *t* not of the King: farewell!   *Becket* V ii 185
   T,—torture,—death,—and come.   *The Cup* I ii 314
   I warrants ye'll *t* moor o' this young Squire Edgar   *Prom. of May* I 109
   ye'll *t* more on 'is little finger than hall my hand   „   I 111
   Dobbins, I *t*.   *Dobson*.   Dobbins, you *t*'s; and I *t*'s ye weärs   „   I 459
   I *t*'s I'd like to taäke the measure o' your foot.   „   I 463
   I can't abeär to *t* on 'er now,   „   II 32
   How could I *t* of leaving him?   „   II 71
   Do ye *t* I be gawin' to tell it to you,   „   II 190
   almost *t* she half return'd the pressure Of mine.   „   II 627
   I'd na moor o' maäkin' an end o' tha nor a carrion craw—   „   II 695
   d'ye *t* I'd gi'e 'em the fever?   „   III 49
   Do you *t* that I may?   No, not yet.   „   III 238
   her answer—I *t* I have it about me—yes, there it is!   „   III 395
   I *t* That I should break my heart,   „   III 555
   I am easily led by words, but I *t* the Earl hath right.   *Foresters* I i 40
   I *t* they will be mightier than the king.   „   I ii 119
   What makes thee *t* I seem so cold to Robin?   „   II 3
   That when I *t* of it hotly, Love himself Seems   „   III 111
   Robin—I crave pardon, I always *t* of you as my lord,   „   III 410

Thinkest   Roger, *t* thou that anyone Suspected thee   *Queen Mary* III 204
   Gamel, son of Orm, What *t* thou this means? (*repeat*)   *Harold* I i 21, 464
Thinking   —I was *t* of her when—O yes,   *Prom. of May* II 368
Thin-skinn'd   O *t*-s hand and jutting veins,   *Queen Mary* IV ii 204
Third   Linger not till the *t* horn.   Fly!   *Becket* III ii 40
   O would it were His *t* last apoplexy!   *The Cup* II 172
Thirlby (**Bishop of Ely**)   (*See also* **Ely**)   Bishop *T*, And my Lord Paget   *Queen Mary* IV i 5
   Weep not, good *T*.   „   IV ii 172
   Will they burn me, *T*?   „   IV ii 182
   And may God bless you, *T*!   „   IV ii 198
   these burnings, As *T* says, are profitless   „   IV ii 218
Thirst   which the more you drink, The more you *t*—   *The Cup* I iii 140
Thirtieth   To-day he hath accomplished his *t* birthday,   *Foresters* I i 298
   all of your Who deign to honour this my *t* year,   „   I ii 79
   pray Thy *t* summer may be thirty-fold As happy   „   I ii 128
Thirty   To raise your Highness *t* thousand men,   *Queen Mary* II ii 290
   Sailing from France, with *t* Englishmen,   „   VI 285
   Down *t* feet below the smiling day—   *Harold* II ii 430
   Some *t*—forty thousand silver marks.   *Becket* I iii 657
   her six and *t* sail Of Provence blew you to your English throne;   „   VI 122
Thirty-fold   Thy thirtieth summer may be *t-f*   *Foresters* I ii 128
This   *t* Gardiner for one, who is to be made Lord Chancellor,   *Queen Mary* I i 85
   My masters, yonder's fatter game for you Than *t* old gaping gurgoyle: „   I iii 81
   but *t* fine blue-blooded Courtenay seems Too princely for a pawn.   „   I iii 165
   now would settle Upon *t* flower, now that;   „   I iv 56
   T dress was made me as the Earl of Devon To take my seat in;   „   I iv 72
   Have sworn *t* Spanish marriage shall not be.   „   I iv 115
   And if *t* Prince of fluff and feather come To woo you, niece,   „   I iv 162
   He commends me now From out his grave to *t* archbishoprick.   *Becket, Pro.* 420
   and I do not then charm *t* secret out of our loyal Thomas,   „   Pro. 466
   Follow me *t* Rosamund day and night, whithersoever she goes;   „   Pro. 506
   and *t* Becket, her father's friend, like enough staved us from her.   „   Pro. 517
   And mine uplifter in *t* world, and chosen me For *t* thy great archbishoprick,   „   I i 89
   and I sneezed three times *t* morning.   *The Falcon* 169
   To make amends I come *t* day to break my fast with you.   „   276
Thistle   matched with my Harold is like a hedge *t* by a garden rose.   *Prom. of May* III 176
Thomas (**Becket, Chancellor of England, afterwards Archbishop of Canterbury**)   (*See also* **Becket, Thomas Becket, Thomas of Canterbury**)   That is my secret, *T*.   *Becket, Pro.* 75

Thousand (*continued*)   And think not we shall be alone—*t's*
will flock to us.   *Queen Mary* II i 191
To raise your Highness thirty *t* men,   „   II ii 290
A hundred, yea, a *t* thousand-fold,   „   III iii 300
A *t* ships—a hundred *t* men—*T's* of horses,   *Harold* IV iii 194
I know Some three or four poor priests a *t* times Fitter
for this grand function.   *Becket, Pro.* 291
Some thirty—forty *t* silver marks.   „   I iii 657
What ! forty *t* marks !   „   I iii 704
Forty *t* marks ! forty *t* devils—and these craven
bishops !   „   I iv 90
Spite of ten *t* brothers, Federigo.   *The Falcon* 898
I took it For some three *t* acres.   *Prom. of May* III 614
And Sir Richard was told he might be ransomed for two
t marks in gold.   *Foresters* I i 64
Those two *t* marks lent me by the Abbot   „   I i 264
they have trodden it for half a *t* years,   „   I i 334
Two *t* marks in gold. I have paid him half. That
other *t*—   „   II i 464
for Oberon fled away Twenty *t* leagues to-day.   „   II ii 143
Where he would pay us down his *t* marks.   „   IV 441
Lest he should fail to pay these *t* marks   „   IV 454
What more ? one *t* marks, Or else the land.   „   IV 473
Here be one *t* marks Out of our treasury to redeem the
land.   „   IV 492
Would buy me for a *t* marks in gold—   „   IV 652
Is weightier than a *t* marks in gold,   „   IV 660
A *t* winters Will strip you bare as death, a *t* summers
Robe you life-green again.   „   IV 1055
Thousand-fold   A hundred, yea, a thousand *t-f*,   *Queen Mary* III iii 200
The force of Rome a *t-f* our own.   *The Cup* I ii 85
Thousand-times   And *t-t* recurring argument Of those
two friars   *Queen Mary* IV ii 93
Thowt (**thought**)   Coomly, says she. I niver *t* o'
mysen i' that waäy ;   *Prom. of May* I 176
So I *t*, and I heärd the winder—   „   I 395
but I *t* I'd bring tha them roses fust.   „   II 50
When ye *t* there were nawbody watchin' o' you,   „   II 179
I should ha' *t* they'd hed anew o' gentlefoälk,   „   II 580
Thrall   if my people must be *t's* of Rome,   *The Cup* I ii
sat Among my *t's* in my baronial hall   *Foresters* II i 61
The scarlet *t* of Rahab saved her life ;   *Queen Mary* III ii 38
Thread   heaven and earth are *t's* of the same loom,   *Harold* I i 209
that every *t* of thought Is broken ere it joins—   *Becket* v 205
The child, a *t* within the house of birth,   *The Cup* I ii 259
my nurse has broken The *t* of my dead flowers,   *The Falcon* 522
while our Robin's life Hangs by a *t*,   *Foresters* IV 385
Threadbare   to cost All *t* household habit,   „   I iii 112
Threadbare-worn   long-tugged at, *t-w* Quarrel of Crown and
Church—   *Becket* II ii 54
Threat   *T's* ! *t's* ! ye hear him.   „   v ii 464
Threaten   *T* the child ; ' I'll scourge you if you did
it : '   *Queen Mary* III v 126
it *t's* us no more Than French or Norman.   *Harold* I i 133
and *t* us thence Unschool'd of Death ?   „   v i 285
Not in my chin, I hope ! That *t's* double.   *Becket* I i 251
T our junction with the Emperor—   „   II ii 471
they *t* The immediate thunder-blast of interdict :   „   III iii 25
as when we *t* A yelper with a stick.   „   IV ii 349
yet *t* your Archbishop In his own house.   „   v ii 504
Threaten'd   Had *t* ev'n your life, and would say any-
thing ?   *Prom. of May* III 567
Three   (*See also* **Dree**)   for thou art as white as *t*
Christmasses.   *Queen Mary* I i 30
T voices from our guilds and companies !   „   II 255
Because the Queen hath been *t* days in tears   „   III vi 12
God made the fierce fire seem To those *t* children
like a pleasant dew.   „   IV iii 91
T persons and one God, have mercy on me,   „   IV iii 121
that these *T* rods of blood-red fire up yonder mean   *Harold* I i 44
Why then the wrath of Heaven hath *t* tails, The devil
only one.   „   I i 61
and hurl'd it from him *T* fields away,   „   III i 140
There is one Who passing by that hill *t* nights ago—   „   III i 366
T horses had I slain beneath me :   „   v ii 171

Three (*continued*)   I know Some *t* or four poor priests a
thousand times   *Becket, Pro.* 291
with the retinue of *t* kings behind him, outroyalling
royalty ?   „   *Pro.* 445
My lord, the King demands *t* hundred marks,   „   I iii 626
My lord, I ha' *t* sisters a-dying at home   „   I iv 245
She past me here *T* years ago when I was flying from My
Tetrarchy to Rome.   *The Cup* I i 6
But after rain o'erleaps a jutting rock And shoots *t*
hundred feet.   „   I i 111
who has dwelt *t* years in Rome And wrought his worst
against his native land,   „   I ii 175
That there *t* years ago—the vast vine-bowers   „   I ii 401
cloudless heaven which we have found together In our *t*
married years,   „   I ii 417
T laps for a cat !   *The Falcon* 125
and I sneezed *t* times this morning.   „   169
Yeas, yeas ! *T* cheers for Mr. Steer !   *Prom. of May* I 455
Why, Miss Dora, meä and my maätes, us *t*, we
wants to hev *t* words wi' ye.   „   III 126
Milly, who came to us *t* years after you were gone,   „   III 232
They did not last *t* Junes.   „   III 589
I took it For some *t* thousand acres.   „   III 614
t yards about the waist is like to remain a virgin,   *Foresters* I ii 69
Here come *t* beggars.   „   III 187
Here come *t* friars.   „   III 256
Thou and thy woman are a match for *t* friars.   „   III 262
Here, you *t* rogues,   „   III 358
blow upon it *T* mots, this fashion—listen !   „   IV 425
for the moment strike the bonds From these *t* men,   „   IV 963
Three-score   the doctors tell you, At *t-s* years ;   *Queen Mary* III iv 410
Threshold   I'll fight it on the *t* of the grave.   „   v v 189
Hope Smiles from the *t* of the year to come   *Foresters* I iii 16
Threw   Northumbria *t* thee off, she will not have thee,   *Harold* IV ii 33
But I that *t* the mightiest knight of France,   *Becket* I iii 746
Thrill   *T's* to the topmost tile—no hope but death ;   „   v ii 209
Thrive   And may your business in *t* in Nottingham !   *Foresters* III 244
That *you* may *t*, but in some kindlier trade.   „   III 252
Throat   heretic *t's* Cried no God-bless-her   *Queen Mary* III iv 44
this poor *t* of mine, Barer than I should wish a
man to see it,—   „   v ii 460
I have my dagger here to still their *t's*.   *Becket* III ii 50
Madam, I saw your dagger at her *t* ;   „   IV ii 319
not at the moment who had fasten'd About his *t*—   *The Cup* II 51
t might gape before the tongue could cry who ?   *Foresters* III 225
Throated   *See* **Full-throated**
Throne (s)   Until your *t* had ceased to tremble.   *Queen Mary* I v 393
But his assessor in the *t*,   „   I v 501
burn the *t* Where you should sit with Philip :   „   I v 510
let Rebellion Roar till *t* rock, and crown fall.   „   II i 145
shall we have Spain on the *t* and in the parliament ;   „   II i 176
Had holpen Richard's tottering *t* to stand,   „   III i 114
same chair, Or rather *t* of purple, on the deck.   „   III ii 8
Between the two most high-set *t's* on earth,   „   III ii 106
no foreign prince or priest Should fill my *t*,   „   III v 237
You sit upon this fallen Cranmer's *t* ;   „   IV i 114
Declare the Queen's right to the *t*,   „   IV ii 78
floated downward from the *t* Of God Almighty.   *Harold* I i 18
bishops down from all Their *t's* in England ?   „   I i 51
The Ätheling is nearest to the *t*.   „   II ii 570
help to build a *t* Out-towering hers of France . . .   „   II ii 764
Why then the *t* is empty. Who inherits ?   „   III i 234
Who shook the Norman scoundrels off the *t*,   „   IV i 82
To thrust our Harold's *t* from under him ?   „   IV iii 126
Hath climb'd the *t* and almost clutch'd the crown ;   *Becket, Pro.* 21
thou didst help me to my *t* In Theobald's time,   „   *Pro.* 201
A bulwark against *T* and Baronage.   „   I i 17
weight down all free choice beneath the *t*.   „   I iii 119
The soul the body, and the Church the *T*,   „   I iii 718
I, that taking The Fiend's advantage of a *t*,   „   II i 152
Reseat him on his *t* of Canterbury,   „   III ii 118
yea, even among those Who sit on *t's*—   „   IV ii 125
Of Provence blew you to your English *t* ;   „   v i 124
Lest Becket thrust you even from your *t*.   „   v i 160
To shake my *t*, to push into my chamber—   „   v i 249

Throne (s) (*continued*) Blared from the heights of all the
t's of her kings,   *Becket* v ii 489
die upon the Patriarchal *t* Of all my predecessors?   „   v iii 75
and wear it Beside him on his *t*.   *The Cup* ii 137
shout of Synorix and Camma sitting Upon one *t*,   „   ii 148
He climbs the *t*. Hot blood,   „   ii 168
So falls the *t* of an hour. *Synorix*. *T*? is it thou?   „   ii 486
T's, churches, ranks, traditions, customs,   *Prom. of May* i 519
king of day hath stept from off his *t*,   *Foresters* ii 27
oaks, Gnarl'd—older than the *t*'s of Europe—   „   iii 92
Throne (*verb*) King Would *t* me in the great Archbishoprick: *Becket* i iii 694
and *t* One king above them all,   *The Cup* i 92
T him—and then the marriage—ay and tell him   „   ii 156
Throned For how should reverend prelate or *t* prince *Queen Mary* iv iii 543
And so be *t* together in the sight   *The Cup* ii 67
is it thou? the Fates are *t*, not we—   „   ii 488
Throne-like Throw cushions on that seat, and make
it *t-l*.   *Queen Mary* v ii 537
Thronging Their horse are *t* to the barricades;   *Harold* v i 547
They are *t* in to vespers—half the town.   *Becket* v iii 139
Throning Not to a Gregory of my *t*! No.   „   v i 34
Throstle New buds to heaven, whereon the *t* rock'd   *Foresters* i iii 27
Throttle say nothing to my wife if I Were by to *t* him!   *The Cup* i i 367
Throw strong to *t* ten Wyatts and all Kent.   *Queen Mary* ii ii 353
T cushions on that seat, and make it throne-like.   „   v ii 536
Why, I could *t* four o' ye;   *Prom. of May* i 468
Thrown offal *t* Into the blind sea of forgetfulness. *Queen Mary* iii iii 192
There was a paper *t* into the palace,   „   iii vi 139
dogs' food *t* upon thy head.   *Harold* ii ii 431
she had *t* my chaplet on the grass,   *The Falcon* 368
Had she not *t* my chaplet on the grass,   „   377
Thrush *See* **Mavis**
Thrust A strange youth Suddenly *t* it on me,   *Queen Mary* ii i 129
brave Lord William *T* him from Ludgate,   „   ii iv 92
invade their hive Too gross to be *t* out,   „   iii iii 55
And *t* his right into the bitter flame;   „   iv iii 610
To *t* our Harold's throne from under him?   *Harold* iv iii 126
Why do you *t* this Becket on me again?   *Becket* v i 155
Thumb A lesson worth Finger and *t*—thus   *Harold* i i 55
Thumbscrew the *t*, the stake, the fire.   *Queen Mary* ii i 200
Thunder (s) the poor *t* Never harm'd head.   *Harold* ii i 232
But it may bring down That which the flash   „   i ii 234
And bolts of *t* moulded in high heaven   „   ii ii 32
Wilt *thou* play with the *t*?   „   iii i 391
but our old Thor Heard his own *t* again,   „   iv vii 150
T! Ay, ay, the storm was drawing hither   *The Cup* ii 318
Thunder (verb) I will both flash And *t* for thee.   *Harold* i ii 229
North and South *T* together,   „   iii i 393
They *t* again upon the barricades,   „   v i 625
crying On Holy Church to *t* out her rights   *Becket* v ii 31
Thunder-blast The immediate *t-b* of interdict: „   iii iii 26
Thunderbolt I wish some *t* Would make this Cole a
cinder,   *Queen Mary* iv iii 10
So from a clear sky falls the *t*!   „   viii 116
with this black *t* of Rome Above him,   *The Cup* ii 265
Thunder-cloud shadowing of this double *t-c* That lours *Harold* iii ii 159
Thurkill I think that this is *T*.   „   v ii 65
Thwack But I shall have to *t* her if I stay.   *Foresters* i iii 139
Thwack'd I would have *t* the woman, but I did not,   „   iii 135
Thwart That shalt thou never be If I can *t* thee.   *Harold* i i 415
but tramples flat Whatever *t*'s him;   „   ii ii 380
Thysen (**thyself**) Why, Wilson, tha 'eärd 'im *t*—   *Prom. of May* i 302
Maäke it eäsy.   „   i 419
if she weänt—look to *t*,   „   ii 695
an' whether thou calls *t* Hedgar or Harold,   „   ii 737
Tib (country wife) Why, it be *T*!   *Queen Mary* iv iii 464
I must set down myself, *T*;   „   iv iii 471
Eh, then ha' thy waay wi' me, *T*;   „   iv iii 487
Thou's thy way wi' man and beast, *T*.   „   iv iii 499
Tick-tack like the tail of the horologe—to and fro—*t-t*— *Becket* ii ii 367
Tide same *t* Which, coming with our coming,   *Queen Mary* ii 21
(for they thought not of our *t*'s),   „   iii ii 28
when men are tost On *t*'s of strange opinion,   „   iii iv 119
William's or his own As wind blows, or *t* flows;   *Harold* v i 163
all drown'd in love And glittering at full *t*—   *The Cup* ii 234

Tide (*continued*) for when the *t* Of full democracy   *Prom. of May* i 592
In this full *t* of love, Wave heralds wave: *Foresters* iv 1043
Tidings My liege, I bring you goodly *t*.   *Queen Mary* v i 280
Tied (*See also* **Tongue-tied**) that the twain have been
t up together,   „   i iv 196
Tierce To reign is restless fence, *T*, quart, and trickery.   „   v v 267
Tiger And *he* hath learnt, despite the *t* in him,   *Harold* i i 148
May serve to charm the *t* out of him. *Leofwin*. He
hath as much of cat as *t* in him.   „   i i 153
Tigress *t* had unsheath'd her nails at last,   *Queen Mary* iii i 3
Tile Thrills to the topmost *t*—no hope but death;   *Becket* v ii 209
Till'd —our fallows *t*, Much corn,   „   i iii 376
Time (*See also* **Breathing-time, Thousand-times**) no
one in her *t* should be burnt for heresy.   *Queen Mary* i i 97
Well, sir, I look for happy *t*'s.   „   i i 99
am I trenching on the *t* That should already   „   i ii 79
fear, I see you, Dear friend, for the last *t*;   „   i ii 103
These birds of passage come before their *t*:   „   i iii 76
Have we not heard of her in Edward's *t*,   „   i iv 19
Your *t* will come. *Elizabeth*. I think my *t* will come.   „   i iv 255
you had *t* and cause enough To sicken   „   i v 23
I should some *t* have a happy morning;   „   i v 245
no such scarecrow in your father's *t*.   „   i v 474
let them sit. I must have *t* to breathe.   „   i v 546
known a semi-madman in my *t* So fancy-ridd'n)   „   ii i 10
I fear the mine is fired before the *t*.   „   ii i 123
a jest In *t* of danger shows the pulses even.   „   ii ii 357
There yet is *t*, take boat and pass to Windsor.   „   ii iv 27
Who, waiting till the *t* had ripen'd,   „   iii ii 78
This Gardiner turn'd his coat in Henry's *t*;   „   iii iii 17
In William's *t*, in our first Edward's *t*, And in my
master Henry's *t*;   „   iii iii 226
These spaniel-Spaniard English of the *t*,   „   iii iii 241
I have some *t*, for curiousness, my Lord,   „   iii iv 61
Such is our *t*—all *t*'s for aught I know.   „   iii iv 66
Did she not In Henry's *t* and Edward's?   „   iii iv 132
St. Peter in his *t* of fear Denied his Master,   „   iii iv 263
In those *t*'s, Thou knowest we had to dodge,   „   iii iv 356
For a *t*, for a *t*.   „   iii iv 366
Rogers and Ferrar, for their *t* is come,   „   iii v 425
How many names in the long sweep of *t*   „   iii v 40
last *t* she wrote, I had like to have lost my life: „   iii v 188
I think that I may be some *t* the Queen,   „   iv iii 233
Wherefore our Queen and Council at this *t*   „   iv iii 37
Friend for so long *t* of a mighty King;   „   iv iii 73
every man at *t* of death Would fain set forth   „   iv iii 156
I have not *t* for more: „   iv iii 207
Than heretic of these *t*'s;   „   iv iii 599
not were he ten *t*'s king, Ten *t*'s our husband,   „   v i 62
I have to pray you, some odd *t*,   „   v i 258
even now, when bow'd before my *t*,   „   v i 65
T that I were gone too!   „   v ii 320
I seem half-shamed at *t*'s to be so tall.   *Harold* i i 176
and I say it For the last *t* perchance,   „   i i 219
left me *t* And peace for prayer to gain a better one.   „   iii ii 63
but at *t*'s They seem to me too narrow,   „   iv i 151
A goodly flower at *t*'s.   „   v i 9
Hear me again—for the last *t*.   „   v i 15
Then for the last *t*, monk, I ask again   „   v i 175
Good for good hath borne at *t*'s   *Becket, Pro.* 20
Church in the pell-mell of Stephen's *t*   „   *Pro.* 220
—be facile to my hands. Now is my *t*.   „   *Pro.* 292
thousand *t*'s Fitter for this grand function.   „   *Pro.* 496
Madam, I have loved her in my *t*.   „   i iii 229
And Earth should get the better—for the *t*.   „   i iv 250
that be dead ten *t*'s o'er i' one day wi' the putrid fever;   „   ii ii 188
wriggle out of them like an eel When the *t* serves.   „   ii ii 367
we make the *t*, we keep the *t*, ay, and we serve the *t*;   „   iii i 3
I cannot answer it Till better *t*'s,   „   iii i 7
That which you ask me Till better *t*'s.   „   iii i 191
you shall tell me of her some other *t*.   „   iii i 198
that is to say in her *t* when she had the 'Crown.'   „   iii i 229
bound me by his love to secrecy Till his own *t*.   „   iv ii 206
sworn on this my cross a hundred *t*'s Never to leave him— „   v ii 157
Daughter, my *t* is short, I shall not do it.   „   v ii 157

Time (*continued*) I have much to say, no *t* to say it in.   *The Cup* I ii 208
  As I have many a *t* declared to you—   „   II 48
  and I sneezed three *t's* this morning. Coming to visit
    my lord, for the first *t* in her life too !   *The Falcon* 169
  fine fowl for my lady ; I had scant *t* to do him in.   „   556
  What ? my *t* ? Is it my *t* ? Well, I can give my *t*   „   789
  and they was all a-crying out at the bad *t's,*   *Prom. of May* I 139
  fur I 'ednt naw *t* to maäke mysen a scholard   „   I 333
  I mun ha' plowed it moor nor a hoonderd *t's* ;   „   I 368
  Forgive him seventy *t's* and seven ;   „   III 9
  next *t* you waste them at a pot-house you get no
    more from me.   „   III 99
  because one of the Steers had planted it there in
    former *t's.*   „   III 248
  he tells me that he met you once in the old *t's,*   „   III 263
  all in all to one another from the *t* when we first
    peeped   „   III 273
  and he trusted that some *t* we should meet again,   „   III 328
  The Steers was all gentlefoäks i' the owd *t's,*   „   III 448
  The land belonged to the Steers i' the owd *t's,*   „   III 451
  A hundred *t's* more worth a woman's love,   „   III 743
  weight of the flesh at odd *t's* overbalance the weight of
    the church,   *Foresters* I ii 61
  last *t* When I shall hold my birthday in his hall :   „   I ii 88
  Till better *t's.* *Robin.* But if the better *t's*   „   I ii 286
  And if the worst *t* come ?   „   I ii 290
  Why then I will be better than the *t.*   „   I ii 292
  we must at *t's* have wrought Some great injustice,   „   III 154
  Out in the *t,* I say, out of tune and *t* ! *Marian.* Till
    thou thyself shall come to sing it—in *t.* *Robin.*
    T ! if his backward-working alchemy   „   IV 35
  We had it i' the Red King's *t,*   „   IV 303
  if they were not repaid within a limited *t* your land
    should be forfeit.   „   IV 468
Timorous Why creep'st thou like a *t* beast of prey   *Harold* I ii 212
Tinkle Our scouts have heard the *t* of their bells.   „   V i 220
Tipsy —and I fear you were *t* then, too—   *Prom. of May* III 88
Tip-top snow yonder on the very *t-t* o' the mountain.   *The Falcon* 501
Tire would she were but his paramour, for men *t* of
  their fancies ;   *Becket, Pro.* 479
Tired last night, *T,* pacing my new lands   *Prom. of May* II 647
Tit Kiss in the bower, *T* on the tree !   *Becket* III i 105
  No bird ? *Filippo.* Half a *t* and a hern's bill.   *The Falcon* 131
  T, my queen, must it be so ?   *Foresters* II ii 124
  And you dare to call me *T.* *T,* for love and brevity,   „   II ii 127
Titania I *T* bid you flit,   „   II ii 126
Tit-bit You be fed with *t-b's,* you,   „   I i 24
  I am fed with *t-b's* no more than you are,   „   I i 27
Tithe thaw me and 'im we niver 'grees about the *t* ;   *Prom. of May* I 445
Title And nothing of the *t's* to the crown ;   *Queen Mary* III i 383
Titular That if this Philip be the *t* king Of England,   „   I v 254
Toad you that have *not* the head of a *t,*   *The Falcon* 91
Tod Like a *t* of wool from wagon into warehouse.   *Foresters* IV 274
To-daäy (to-day) The owd man be heighty *t-d,*
  beänt he ?   *Prom. of May* I 77
  as I telled 'er *t-d* when she fell foul upo' me.   „   II 581
To-day (*See also* **To-daäy**) She looks comelier than
  ordinary *t-d* ;   *Queen Mary* I i 71
  I trust that he will carry you well *t-d,*   „   I iv 145
  he hath been so bold *t-d,*   „   II ii 348'
  They are down *t-d.*   „   III i 8
  for *t-d* My heart beats twenty,   „   III i 57
  and brief patience, As I have shown *t-d.*   „   III iv 415
  into the daylight truth That it may fall *t-d* !   „   III v 137
  That you *t-d* should read your recantation   „   IV i 27
  t-d Thou shalt receive the penitent thief's award,   „   IV iii 85
  When camest thou hither ? *Gamel.* *T-d,* good Earl.   *Harold* I i 106
  I heard from thy Northumberland *t-d.*   „   I i 350
  Lady Aldwyth Was here *t-d,*   „   I ii 35
  Swear thou *t-d,* to-morrow is thine own.   „   II ii 710
  we must use our battle-axe *t-d.*   „   V i 205
  Thy death !—*t-d* ! Is it not thy birthday ?   „   V i 428
  that blighted vow Which God avenged *t-d.*   „   V ii 157
  I could but read a part *t-d,* because—   *Becket* I iii 422
  they were fighting for her *t-d* in the street.   „   I iv 160

To-day (*continued*) Fame of *t-d* is infamy to-morrow ;
  Infamy of *t-d* is fame to-morrow ;   *Becket* II i 103
  He warmed to you *t-d,* and you have chilled him again.   „   II i 375
  T-d I almost fear'd your kiss was colder—   „   III i 16
  and to be sure I ha' seen great ones *t-d*—   „   III i 136
  a man passed in there *t-d* : I holla'd to him,   „   III ii 25
  You wrong the King : he meant what he said *t-d.*   „   III iii 299
  for thou must leave him *T-d,* but not quite yet.   „   IV ii 211
  Going or gone *t-d* To hunt with Sinnatus.   *The Cup* I i 64
  come upon *her* Again, perhaps, *t-d*—her.   „   I i 181
  A strange gift sent to me *t-d.*   „   I ii 53
  Have let him hunt the stag with you *t-d.*   „   I ii 379
  T-d they are fixt and bright—they look straight out.   „   II 20
  T-d ? Too sudden. I will brood upon it.   „   II 72
  I would that every man made feast *t-d*   „   II 225
  For all my truer life begins *t-d.*   „   II 229
  T-d, my beauty, thou must dash us down   *The Falcon* 152
  Sweeter than any violet of *t-d,*   „   465
  but *t-d* I dared not—so much weaker,   „   831
  I must leave you, love, *t-d.* *Eva.* Leave me, *t-d* !   *Prom. of May* I 625
  Shall I say it ?—fly with me *t-d.*   „   I 678
  will you not speak with Father *t-d* ?   „   III 237
  ' Will your Ladyship ride to cover *t-d* ?   „   III 310
  but you seem somewhat better *t-d.*   „   III 322
  Not *t-d.* What are you staying for ?   „   III 356
  but is not *t-d* his birthday ?   *Foresters* I i 219
  T-d he hath accomplished his thirtieth birthday,   „   I i 297
  No, Sir Earl, I will not fight *t-d.*   „   II i 575
  for Oberon fled away Twenty thousand leagues *t-d.*   „   II ii 143
  thy father will not grace our feast With his white
    beard *t-d* ?   „   IV 81
  No, not an hour : the debt is due *t-d.*   „   IV 448
Toe bursten at the *t's,* and down at heels.   *Queen Mary* I i 53
  small hope of the gentleman gout in my great *t.*   *The Falcon* 657
Toft Hall Philip Edgar of *T H* In Somerset.   *Prom. of May* II 438
  One Philip Edgar of *T H* in Somerset Is lately dead.   „   II 445
  I have been telling her of the death of one Philip
    Edgar of *T H,* Somerset.   „   II 706
  ' O' the 17th, Philip Edgar, o' *T H,* Soomerset.'   „   II 712
Togither (together) Didn't I spy 'em a-sitting i' the
  woodbine harbour *t* ?   „   I 125
  he tell'd me 'at sweet'arts niver worked well *t* ; and
    I telled *'im* 'at sweet'arts allus worked best *t* ;   „   II 156
  And wheniver 'e sees two sweet'arts *t* like thou and
    me, Sally,   „   II 163
Toil we have him in the *t's.*   *Harold* II ii 14
Toil'd Our guardsman hath but *t* his hand and foot,   „   V i 201
Token given A *t* of His more especial Grace ;   *Queen Mary* III 170
  an' I be half dog already by this *t,*   *Becket* I iv 219
Told (*See also* **Telled, Towld**) Whether he *t* me
  anything or not,   *Queen Mary* I iv 184
  secret missive, Which *t* her to be sick.   „   II ii 122
  'Tis said he *t* Sir Maurice there was one Cognisant   „   II iv 98
  I *t* my Lord He should not vex her Highness ;   „   vi 64
  He *t* me I should conquer :—   *Harold* IV i 263
  And *t* me we should conquer.   „   IV i 267
  They *t* me that the Holy Rood had lean'd   „   V i 102
  how been made Archbishop hadst thou *t* him,   *Becket* I i 122
  Wast thou not *t* to keep thyself from sight ?   „   I i 251
  He *t* me thou shouldst pacify the King,   „   I iii 224
  Hath Henry *t* thee ? hast thou talk'd with him ?   „   I iii 258
  'Tis true What Becket *t* me, that the mother   „   II ii 9
  I *t* the Pope what manner of man he was.   „   II ii 253
  t me he would advance me to the service of a great lady,   „   III i 122
  you *t* me a great fib : it wasn't in the willow.   „   IV iii 370
  I *t* him I was bound to see the Archbishop ;   „   V ii 100
  she *t* us of arm'd men Here in the city.   „   V ii 226
  but I *t* them I would wait them here.   „   V ii 592
  I *t* thee that I should remember thee !   „   V iii 158
  Hath Sinnatus never *t* you of this plot ?   *The Cup* I ii 250
  I am sure I *t* him that his plot was folly.   „   I ii 283
  there You *t* your love ; and like the swaying vines—   „   I ii 410
  Do you remember what I *t* you ?   „   I iii 4
  Not if Sinnatus Has *t* her all the truth about me.   „   I iii 23
  She *t* thee as much ?   *The Falcon* 58

Told (continued) Do what I *t* thee. Must I do it myself ?   *The Falcon* 279
None has ever *t* me yet The story of your battle   „ 592
You know, my lord, I *t* you I was troubled.   „ 676
Eva *t* me that he was taking her likeness. He's an artist.   *Prom. of May* I 126
and you, a gentleman, *T* me to trust you :   „ I 710
You never *t* her, then, of what has past   „ I 728
I *t* her I should hear her from the grave.   „ II 244
She has disappear'd, They *t* me, from the farm—   „ II 407
Which *t* us we should never see her more—   „ II 477
always *t* Father that the huge old ashtree there would cause an accident some day ;   „ III 243
Have you *t* him I am here ? *Dora.* No ; do you wish it ?   „ III 266
bit by bit—for she promised secrecy—I *t* her all.   „ III 380
Is yours yet living ? *Harold.* No—I *t* you.   „ III 506
I *t* you—My father.   „ III 573
Can it be ? They *t* me so. Yes, yes !   „ III 670
She hid this sister, *t* me she was dead—   „ III 689
Sir Richard was *t* he might be ransomed   *Foresters* I i 63
It should have *t* us how the man first kissed the maid.   „ I i 123
Scarlet *t* me—is it true ?—   „ III 145
They have *t* but a tenth of the truth :   „ III 291
We *t* the Prince and the Sheriff of our coming.   „ IV 575
Told'st Thou *t* us we should meet him in the forest,   „ IV 439
Tolerance Till when, my Lords, I counsel *t*.   *Queen Mary* III iv 203
Tolerate I would not, were I Queen, *t* the heretic,   „ III iv 209
T them ! Why ? do they *t* you ?   „ III iv 213
Toll *T* of a bell, Stroke of a clock,   „ III v 141
thou hast drain'd them shallow by thy *t's*,   *Harold* I i 320
T ! *Beggar.* Eh ! we be beggars,   *Foresters* III 188
Take thou my bow and arrow and compel them to pay *t*. *Marian.* *T* !   „ III 264
Ha, brother. *T*, my dear ? the *t* of love.   „ III 270
Church and Law, halt and pay *t* !   „ IV 430
Toll'd A passing bell *t* in a dying ear—   *Queen Mary* V ii 41
Tomb There was an old-world *t* beside my father's,   „ V ii 393
Tomb-place free the *t-p* of the King Of all the world ?   *Foresters* IV 408
To-morrow If Ludgate can be reach'd by dawn *t-m*.   *Queen Mary* II iii 53
Come to me *t-m*.—   „ III i 320
that I think, ' Wilt thou lie there *t-m* ? '   „ III v 132
And goes *t-m*.   „ III vi 119
More talk of this *t-m*, if yon weird sign   *Harold* I i 120
No more now—   „ I i 487
T-m—first to Bosham, then to Flanders.   „ I ii 239
T-m we will ride with thee to Harfleur,   „ II ii 195
I will go with thee *t-m*—   „ II ii 204
T-m will we ride with thee to Harfleur,   „ II ii 647
Swear thou to-day, *t-m* is thine own.   „ II ii 710
T-m will I ride with thee to Harfleur.   „ II ii 769
To-night we will be merry—and *t-m*—   „ II ii 772
Come to me *t-m*.   *Becket, Pro.* 411
To pass thee to thy secret bower *t-m*.   „ I i 249
Let the Great Seal be sent Back to the King *t-m*.   „ I i 376
Fame of to-day is infamy *t-m* ; Infamy of to-day is fame *t-m* ;   „ II i 103
and crown Young Henry there *t-m*.   „ III ii 10
Who shall vouch for his *t-m's* ? One word further.   „ III iii 300
Antonius *T-m* will demand your tribute—   *The Cup* I ii 97
He will pass *t-m* In the gray dawn   „ I ii 294
—a brave one Which you shall see *t-m*. *Camma.* I rise *t-m* In the gray dawn   „ I ii 432
' Let us eat and drink, for *t-m* we die.'   *Prom. of May* I 259
He will be sure to know you *t-m*.   „ III iii 300
T-m then ? *Marian.* Well, I will fight *t-m*.   *Foresters* II i 576
Tongue (*See also* Evil-tongue) make what noise you will with your *t's*,   *Queen Mary* I i 6
old leaven sticks to my *t* yet.   „ I iii 48
Make all *t's* praise and all hearts beat for you.   „ I v 117
t yet quiver'd with the jest When the head leapt—   „ I v 475
thou shalt lose thine ears and find thy *t*,   „ III i 256
Will stir the living *t* and make the cry.   „ III i 354
every *t* Alters it passing, till it spells   „ III v 35
What weapon hath the child, save his soft *t*,   „ III v 129
More grievously than any *t* can tell.   „ IV iii 125

Tongue (continued) Fed with rank bread that crawl'd upon the *t*,   *Queen Mary* IV iii 443
the *t* on un cum a-lolluping out o' 'is mouth as black as a rat.   „ IV iii 518
Leofwin, thou hast a *t* !   *Harold* I i 392
I say, thou hast a *t*,   „ I i 401
Tear out his *t*. *Officer.* He shall not rail again.   „ II ii 487
Treble denial of the *t* of flesh,   „ III i 281
play The William with thine eyesight and thy *t*.   „ V i 28
Say that he blind thee and tear out thy *t*.   *Becket* I ii 616
Cannot a smooth *t* lick him whole again   „ II ii 25
Spare not thy *t* ! be lavish with our coins,   „ II ii 469
asked our mother if I could keep a quiet *t* i' my head,   „ III i 119
So charged with *t*, that every thread   „ V ii 205
Well, well, well ! I bite my *t*.   *The Falcon* 624
throat might gape before the *t* could cry who ?   *Foresters* III 225
if the land Were ruleable by *t*,   „ IV 399
Nay, my *t* tript—five hundred marks for use.   „ IV 499
Tongue-free Crow over Barbarossa—at last *t-f*   *Becket* II ii 50
Tongueless —*t* and eyeless, prison'd—   *Harold* II ii 496
Tonguester selfless man Is worth a world of *t's*.   „ V i 82
Tongue-tied make me shamed and *t-t* in my love.   *Queen Mary* III ii 162
Tongue-torn fiends that utter them *T-t* with pincers,   „ V ii 194
To-night you would honour my poor house *t-n*,   „ I ii 118
When do you meet ? *Noailles.* *T-n*.   „ I iii 155
Make out the writ *t-n*.   „ IV i 195
T-n we will be merry.   *Harold* II i 767
T-n we will be merry—and to-morrow—   „ II ii 771
Go with her—at once—*T-n*—   *Becket* I i 402
T-n. *Retainer.* *T-n*, my lord.   „ I iv 13
Am I to be murdered *t-n* ?   „ I iv 48
I must fly to France *t-n*.   „ I iv 154
The miller's away for *t-n*.   „ I iv 164
for *t-n* ye have saved our Archbishop !   „ I iv 257
not *t-n*—the night is falling. What can be done *t-n* ?   „ II ii 51
Ye shall sing that ageän *t-n*,   *Prom. of May* II 216
and he'll be rude to me ageän *t-n*,   „ II 220
prays your ladyship and your ladyship's father to be present at his banquet *t-n*.   *Foresters* I i 301
let us be merry *t-n* at the banquet.   „ I i 344
Tonitrua Jacta *t* Deus bellator !   *Harold* I v 569
Tonsure crept Up even to the *t*, and he groan'd,   *Becket* I iii 327
his poor *t* A crown of Empire.   „ V i 195
Tonsured Ye haled this *t* devil into your courts ;   „ I iii 387
Took (*See also* **Taäked**) *t* her hand, call'd her sweet sister,   *Queen Mary* I i 79
but *t* To the English red and white.   „ I v 17
For the wrong Robin *t* her at her word.   „ III v 264
I *t* it, tho' I did not know I *t* it,   „ V v 97
another hill Or fort, or city, *t* it,   *Harold* IV i 50
if I *t* and translated that hard heart   *Becket, Pro.* 379
He *t* his mitre off, and set it on me,   „ I i 63
Then he *t* back not only Stephen's gifts,   „ I iii 154
rather than God's cause *T* it upon me—   „ I iii 699
North-east *t* and turned him South-west,   „ II ii 321
t me ever so far away, and gave me a great pat   „ III i 124
which a breeze of May *T* ever and anon,   *The Cup* I ii 407
Shame on her that she *t* it at thy hands,   *The Falcon* 187
he always *t* you so kindly, he always *t* the world so kindly.   „ 191
he made a wry mouth at it, but he *t* it so kindly,   „ 194
he always *t* you so kindly—   *Prom. of May* III 379
the Sister *t* me to her house, and bit by bit—   „ III 613
I *t* it For some three thousand acres.   *Foresters* II i 3
She *t* my ring. I trust she loves me—   „ II i 300
when the Sheriff *t* my little horse for the King and *t* His monies.   „ III 362
O no, we *t* Advantage of the letter—   „ V 620
Tool What filthy *t's* our Senate works with !   *The Cup* I i 156
values neither man Nor woman save as *t's*—   *Foresters* IV 714
Tooth They show their *teeth* upon it ;   *Queen Mary* I i 299
His early follies cast into his *teeth*,   „ V i 124
the *teeth* That shall be broken by us—   *Harold* I ii 244
knaw'd better nor to cast her sister's misfortin inter 'er *teeth*   *Prom. of May* II 128
how should thy one *t* drill thro' this ?   *Foresters* II i 276

Tower (*continued*) you'll make the White *T* a black
'un   *Queen Mary* II iii 100
    you'll set the Divil's *T* a-spitting,   "   II iii 102
    Pass, then, I pray your Highness, to the *T*.   "   II iv 32
    I shall but be their prisoner in the *T*.   "   II iv 34
    The Queen must to the *T*.   "   II iv 73
    To the *T* with *him*! (repeat)   "   II iv 97, 102
    the *T*, the *T*, always the *T*, I shall grow into it—
    I shall be the *T*.   "   II iv 103
    To the *T* with *her*!   "   II iv 118
    Hath no more mortice than a *t* of cards ;   "   III i 442
    Her Grace the Queen commands you to the *T*.   "   III iii 271
    By the river to the *T*.   "   III iii 281
    damp, black, dead Nights in the *T* ;   "   III v 139
    For freeing my friend Bagenhall from the *T* ;   "   III vi 8
    winds so cross and jostle among these *t*'s.   *Harold* II ii 156
    The people know their Church a *t* of strength,   *Becket* I i 16
    Danaë has escaped again Her *t*, and her Acrisius—   "   I i 396
    and rifts the *t* to the rock,   *The Cup* II 293
    O *t* spiring to the sky,   *Prom. of May* III 203
    or closed For ever in a Moorish *t*,   *Foresters* II i 656

Towering   *See* **Out-towering**

Towld (told)   summun *t* summun o' owld Bishop
Gardiner's end ;   *Queen Mary* IV iii 502

Town   and we cannot burn whole *t*'s ; they are many,   "   III iv 175
    And there be many heretics in the *t*,   "   IV iv 31
    the *t* Hung out raw hides along their walls,   *Harold* II ii 382
    My lord, the *t* is quiet, and the moon Divides   *Becket* I i 364
    Much corn, repeopled *t*'s, a realm again.   "   I iii 377
    Close the great gate—ho, there—upon the *t*.   "   v 531
    They are thronging in to vespers—half the *t*.   "   v iii 140
    The *t* lay still in the low sun-light,   *Prom. of May* I 37
    a red fire woke in the heart of the *t*,   "   I 50
    Richard sacks and wastes a *t* With random pillage,   *Foresters* IV 377

Towser (a dog's name)   I'll hev the winder naäiled up,
and put *T* under it.   *Prom. of May* I 420
    T'll tear him all to pieces.   "   I 423

Toy   They have taken away the *t* thou gavest me,   *Harold* II ii 106
    I like to have my *t*'s, and break them too.   "   II ii 112

To-year (this year)   they'll hev' a fine cider-crop *t-y* if
the blossom 'owds.   *Prom. of May* I 316

Trace   Let the dead letter live !   *T* it in fire,   *Queen Mary* III iv 34
    who could *t* a hand So wild and staggering ?   *The Falcon* 438
    but can he *t* me Thro' five years' absence,   *Prom. of May* II 614

Traced   *T* in the blackest text of Hell—' Thou shalt !'   *Queen Mary* III i 426

Track (s)   most beaten *t* Runs thro' the forest,   *Foresters* III 89

Track (verb)   *t* her, if thou canst, even into the King's
lodging,   *Becket, Pro.* 507
    If you *t* this Sinnatus In any treason,   *The Cup* I i 162

Track'd   Have *t* the King to this dark inland wood ;   *Becket* III ii 3
    Judas-lover of our passion-play Hath *t* us hither.   "   IV ii 138

Tractate   His *t* upon True Obedience,   *Queen Mary* IV i 92

Tracy (Sir William de, knight of the household of King
Henry II.)   (*See also* **De Tracy**)   *T*, what dost
thou here ?   *Becket* I i 234
    France ! Ha ! De Morville, *T*, Brito—fled is he ?   "   I iv 199
    —on a Tuesday—*T* ! God help thee !   "   v ii 295
    Strike him, *T* !   *Rosamund*. No, No, No, No !   "   v iii 169
    Nay, nay, good *T*.   *Fitzurse*. Answer not,   "   v iii 185

Trade   With all your *t*'s, and guilds, and companies.   *Queen Mary* II ii 297
    That *you* may thrive, but in some kindlier *t*.   *Foresters* III 253
    There is a *t* of genius, there's glory !   "   IV 375

Tradition   Customs, *t*'s,—clouds that come and go ;   *Becket* I iii 22
    Marriage is but an old *t*. I hate *T*'s,   *Prom. of May* I 491
    violated the whole *T* of our land,   "   I 496
    Thrones, churches, ranks, *t*'s, customs,   "   I 519

Traffick'd   you have *t* Between the Emperor and the Pope,   *Becket* II ii 67

Tragedy   A comedy meant to seem a *t*—   "   IV ii 322

Tragic   You are too *t* : both of us are players   "   v i 187

Train   Captain Brett, who went with your *t* bands To
fight with Wyatt,   *Queen Mary* II ii 27

Train'd   (*See also* **Full-train'd**)   Good dogs, my liege, well *t*, *Becket, Pro.* 120

Traitor (adj.)   She cannot pass her *t* council by,   *Queen Mary* I ii 40
    The *t* husband dangled at the door, And when the *t*
wife came out for bread   "   III i 10

Traitor (adj.) (*continued*)   But with Cecil's aid And
others, if our person be secured From *t* stabs—   *Queen Mary* v v 281
    Traitors are rarely bred Save under *t* kings.   *Foresters* II i 81
    If you would marry me with a *t* sheriff,   "   IV 870

Traitor (s)   down with all *t*'s !   *Queen Mary* I i 66
    shall I turn *t* ?   "   I iv 6
    He cannot touch you save that you turn *t* ;   "   I v 272
    the King—that *t* past forgiveness,   "   I v 28
    being *t* Her head will fall :   "   I v 59
    but your old *T*'s of the Tower—   "   I v 484
    Sent Cornwallis and Hastings to the *t*,   "   II ii 32
    Her name is much abused among these *t*'s.   "   II ii 111
    a *t* so presumptuous As this same Wyatt,   "   II ii 179
    He is child and fool, and *t* to the State.   "   II ii 403
    ' Whosoever will apprehend the *t* Thomas Wyatt   "   III iii 60
    The *t* ! treason ! Pembroke !   "   II iv 35
    will do you right Against all *t*'s.   "   II iv 68
    and the *t* flying To Temple Bar,   "   II iv 92
    As *t*, or as heretic, or for what ?   "   III iii 272
    all *t*'s Against our royal state have lost the heads   "   III iv 2
    For heretic and *t* are all one :   "   IV iii 38
    He hath been a *t*,   "   IV iii 39
    Liar ! dissembler ! *t* ! to the fire !   "   IV iii 259
    King Henry warms your *t*'s at his hearth.   "   v i 123
    What *t* spoke ? Here, let my cousin Pole   "   v ii 243
    Methought some *t* smote me on the head.   "   v ii 252
    Noailles wrote To that dead *t*, Wyatt,   "   v ii 498
    It frights the *t* more to maim and blind.   *Harold* II ii 503
    All *t*'s fail like Tostig !   "   IV iii 79
    Not fight—tho' somehow *t* to the King—   *Becket* I i 112
    Let *t* be ; For how have fought thine utmost   "   I i 116
    What did the *t* say ?   "   I iii 470
    it is the *t* that imputes Treachery to his King !   "   I iii 483
    There, there, there ! *t*, *t*, *t* !   "   I iii 737
    How, do you make me a *t* ?   "   III iii 241
    Nor make me *t* to my holy office.   "   v ii 149
    He makes the King a *t*, me a liar.   "   v ii 416
    charge you that ye keep This *t* from escaping.   "   v ii 511
    Where is the *t* Becket ?   *Becket* v iii 103
    Where is this treble *t* to the King ?   "   v iii 108
    No *t* to the King, but Priest of God,   "   v iii 112
    The *t* 's dead, and will arise no more.   "   v iii 200
    Or man, or woman, as *t*'s unto Rome.   *The Cup* I iii 9
    Hang'd at mid-day, their *t* of the dawn   "   II 123
    T's are rarely bred Save under traitor kings.   *Foresters* II i 79
    We robb'd the *t*'s that are leagued with John ;   "   II 159
    serve King Richard save thou be A *t* or a goose ?   "   IV 353
    a *t* coming In Richard's name—   "   IV 780
    I never found one *t* in my band.   "   IV 836
    You both are utter *t*'s to your king.   "   IV 844
    If you would marry me with a traitor sheriff, I fear
I might prove *t* with the sheriff.   "   IV 872
    I can defend my cause against the *t*'s Who fain would
make me *t*.   "   IV 899

Traitor-brother   Our dear, dead, *t-b*, Tostig,   *Harold* IV iii 83

Traitor-heretic   So there be Some *t-h*,   *Queen Mary* III iv 47
    Centaur of a monstrous Commonweal, The *t-h*)   "   III iv 165

Traitorous   Make not thy King a *t* murderer.   *Becket* I iii 500

Traitress   *T* !   *Rosamund*. A faithful *t* to thy royal
fame.   "   II i 96

Tramp   You are those that *t* the country,   *Foresters* III 198

Trample   And let the Pope *t* our rights,   *Queen Mary* III iv 362
    but *t* flat Whatever thwarts him ;   *Harold* II ii 378
    And I shall live to *t* on thy grave.   *Becket* I ii 95
    From off the stalk and *t* it in the mire,   *Foresters* I ii 110

Trampled   And *t* on the rights of Canterbury.   *Becket* v ii 394
    state more cruelly *t* on Than had she never moved.   *The Cup* I ii 145
    Crush'd, hack'd at, *t* underfoot.   *The Falcon* 640
    And boast that he hath *t* it.   *Foresters* I ii 112
    All our rings be *t* out.   "   II ii 167

Trampling   *T* thy mother's bosom into blood ?   *Harold* IV ii 26

Trance   Wait he must—Her *t* again.   *Queen Mary* v ii 404

Transact   as I used to *t* all his business for him,   *Prom. of May* II 719

Translated   if I took and *t* that hard heart   *Becket, Pro.* 379

Translating   *T* his captivity from Guy   *Harold* II ii 42

Transparent his frail *t* hand, Damp with the sweat of death,   *Queen Mary* I ii 31
Trap Would help thee from the *t*.   *Harold* I i 383
Travel this young Earl was sent on foreign *t*,   *Queen Mary* V ii 490
Travell'd The past is like a *t* land now sunk Below the horizon—   *The Cup* II 230
Traveller And cheer his blindness with a *t's* tales ?   *Prom. of May* II 515
Treachery it is the traitor that imputes *T* to his King !   *Becket* I iii 485
   What ! dare you charge the King with *t* ?   ,,   v ii 397
Tread Ay, sir ; she needs must *t* upon them.   *Queen Mary* I iii 9
   That *t* the kings their children under-heel—   *Becket, Pro.*
   The priests of Baal *t* her underfoot—   ,,   III i 179
   If you will deign to *t* a measure with me.   *Foresters* I ii 132
Treason so it be not *t*.   *Queen Mary* I i 7
   They'd smile you into *t*—some of them.   ,,   I iv 276
   But hatch you some new *t* in the woods.   ,,   I v 465
   Or temperers with that *t* out of Kent.   ,,   II ii 11
   They have betrayed the *t* of their hearts :   ,,   II ii 156
   The traitor ! *t* ! Pembroke ! *Ladies.* *T* ! *t* !   ,,   II iv 35
   To still the petty *t* therewithin,   ,,   III i 13
   said she was condemn'd to die for *t* ;   ,,   III i 378
   I had to cuff the rogue For infant *t*.   ,,   III iii 52
   with full proof Of Courtenay's *t* ?   ,,   v ii 499
   you were burnt for heresy, not for *t*,   ,,   v v 140
   Which in your sense is *t*.   *The Cup* I i 79
   If you track this Sinnatus In any *t*,   ,,   I i 163
Treasonous Wherewith they plotted in their *t* malice,   *Queen Mary* III iv 4
Treasure There lies a *t* buried down in Ely :   *Harold* IV i 114
Treasure-house Who brake into Lord Tostig's *t-h*   ,,   IV i 114
Treasury Is the King's *t* A fit place for the monies   *Becket* I iii 104
   Cast them into our *t*, the beggars' mites.   *Foresters* III 204
   take the twenty-seven marks to the captain's *t*.   ,,   III 295
   One half shall pass into our *t*.   ,,   III 305
   Out of our *t* to redeem the land.   ,,   IV 493
Treat Feigning to *t* with him about her marriage—   *Queen Mary* II ii 33
Treated if you be fairly served, And lodged, and *t*.   ,,   v iii 22
Treaty fain have some fresh *t* drawn between you.   ,,   I v 261
   Why some fresh *t* ? wherefore should I do it ?   ,,   I v 263
   maintain All former *treaties* with his Majesty.   ,,   I v 266
   understand We made thereto no *t* of ourselves,   ,,   II ii 203
   clauses added To that same *t* which the emperor   ,,   III iii 69
   broken Your bond of peace, your *t* with the King—   *Becket* I iii 350
Treble —for to wed with Spain Would *t* England   *Queen Mary* I v 76
   would *t* and quadruple it With revenues,   *Becket* v ii 345
   Where is this *t* traitor to the King ?   ,,   v ii 108
   T denial of the tongue of flesh,   *Harold* III i 281
Treble-brandish'd Yon grimly-glaring, *t-b* scourge Of England !   ,,   I i 3
Tree *t* that only bears dead fruit is gone. *Stafford.* What *t*, sir ? *Bagenhall.* Well, the *t* in Virgil,   *Queen Mary* III i 19
   Like the rough bear beneath the *t*,   *Harold* I i 327
   Dry as an old wood-fungus on a dead *t*,   ,,   III i 8
   The green *t* ! Then a great Angel past   ,,   III i 132
   cleft the *t* From off the bearing trunk,   ,,   III i 137
   sunder'd *t* again, and set it Straight on the trunk,   ,,   III i 144
   Men are God's *t's*, and women are God's flowers ;   *Becket, Pro.* 111
   The *t's* are all the statelier, and the flowers   ,,   *Pro.* 115
   Kiss in the bower, Tit on the *t* !   ,,   III i 105
   By this *t* ; but I don't know if I can find   ,,   IV i 47
   vast vine-bowers Ran to the summit of the *t's*,   *The Cup* I ii 403
   t that my lord himself planted here   *The Falcon* 562
   prunes, my lady, from the *t* that his lordship—   ,,   685
   And a salt wind burnt the blossoming *t's* ;   *Prom. of May* I 58
   No, not that way—here, under the apple *t*.   ,,   I 83
   Like April sap to the topmost *t*,   *Foresters* II i 24
   Beneath the greenwood *t*. (repeat)   ,,   II i 12, 24
   I'll watch him from behind the *t's*,   ,,   III 48
Tree-Cupid Those sweet *t-C's* half-way up in heaven,   ,,   III 35
Tree-tower Yet these *t-t's*, Their long bird-echoing   *Becket* III i 43
Tremble Until your throne had ceased to *t*.   *Queen Mary* I v 393
   But when did our Rome *t* ?   ,,   III iv 130
   I have made her *t*.   *The Cup* I ii 272
   fiercest storm That ever made earth *t*—   *Prom. of May* III 798
Trembled *T* for her own gods, for these were trembling—   *Queen Mary* III iv 128

Trembled (*continued*) It was the shadow of the Church that *t* ;   *Queen Mary* III iv 145
Trembling Your Highness is all *t*. *Mary.* Make way.   ,,   I v 594
   Trembled for her own gods, for these were *t*—   ,,   III iv 129
   will set it *t* Only to base it deeper.   *Becket, Pro.* 209
   thy flock should catch An after ague-fit of *t*.   ,,   III iii 33
   But you are *t*.   *Prom. of May* II 573
Tremulous and one Steadying the *t* pillars of the Church—   *Queen Mary* I v 517
   The soft and *t* coward in the flesh ?   ,,   IV ii 107
Trench and driven back The Frenchmen from their *t'es* ?   ,,   IV ii 258
   The *t'es* dug, the palisades uprear'd   *Harold* v i 189
Trenching am I *t* on the time That should already   *Queen Mary* I ii 78
Trespass Let this be thy last *t*.   *Becket* v ii 165
Trespassed by force and arms hath *t* against the king in divers manners,   *Foresters* I iii 63
Tress nun Vying a *t* against our golden fern.   *Harold* v i 149
Trial At your *t* Never stood up a bolder man than you ;   *Queen Mary* IV ii 121
   If the King Condemn us without *t*,   *Foresters* IV 902
Tribe His swaddling-bands, the morals of the *t*,   *Prom. of May* I 587
Tributary This *t* crown may fall to you.   *The Cup* I i 97
   There then I rest, Rome's *t* king.   ,,   I iii 156
   And *t* sovereigns, he and I Might teach this Rome—   ,,   II 95
Tribute to enforce The long-withholden *t* :   ,,   I i 77
   Antonius To-morrow will demand your *t*—   ,,   I ii 97
   Where to lay on her *t*—heavily here And lightly there.   ,,   II 98
Trick I will be there ; the fellow's at his *t's*—   *Queen Mary* I iv 157
   You have an old *t* of offending us ;   ,,   III iv 315
   Ay, my girl, no *t's* in him—   *Harold* v i 401
   Truth ! no ; a lie ; a *t*, a Norman *t* !   ,,   v i 606
   a shift, a *t* Whereby to challenge,   *Becket* II ii 164
   It is the *t* of the family, my lord.   *Foresters* I iii 151
Trick'd Daughter, the world hath *t* thee.   *Becket* IV ii 364
   The world hath *t* her—that's the King ;   ,,   IV 375
Trickery To reign is restless fence, Tierce, quart, and *t*.   *Queen Mary* v v 267
Trickster *See* **Fellow-trickster**
Trie (Sir Engelram de) *See* **Engelram de Trie**
Tried If I *t* her and la—she's amorous.   *Queen Mary* I iv 171
   As the first flower no bee has ever *t*.   ,,   I iv 63
   whether between laymen or clerics, shall be *t* in the King's court.'   *Becket* I iii 80
   he shall answer to the summons of the King's court to be *t* therein.'   ,,   I iii 89
Trifled You have but *t* with our homely salad,   *The Falcon* 671
Trifling perchance were *t* royally With some fair dame   *Queen Mary* III vi 159
Trinket Ring, *t* of the Church,   *Prom. of May* I 598
Tripping We have our spies abroad to catch her *t*,   *Queen Mary* I v 468
   there's no Renard here to ' catch her *t*.'   ,,   III v 160
Tript my tongue *t*—five hundred marks for use.   *Foresters* IV 499
Triumph (s) The *t* of St. Andrew on his cross,   *Queen Mary* IV iii 94
Triumph (verb) do *t* at this hour In the reborn salvation   ,,   III iii 181
Trivial So wife-like humble to the *t* boy   ,,   I i 364
Trod I *t* upon him even now, my lord, in my hurry,   *The Falcon* 409
Trodden For thou hast *t* this wine-press alone.   *Becket* III iii 290
   Becket hath *t* on us like worms, my liege ; *T* one half dead ;   ,,   v i 61
   they have *t* it for half a thousand years,   *Foresters* I i 333
Troop when a *t*, Laden with booty and with a flag   *The Falcon* 611
   A *t* of horse—— *Filippo.* Five hundred !   ,,   617
Troops Your *t* were never down in Italy.   *Queen Mary* v ii 315
Trope Here be *t's*. *Pole.* And *t's* are good to clothe   ,,   III iv 149
   T's again ! *Pole.* You are hard to please. Then without *t's*, my Lord,   ,,   III iv 153
Troth they be both bastards by Act of Parliament   ,,   I i 23
   Is it so fine ? *T*, some have said so.   ,,   v iii 54
Troubadour for I am a *T*, you know,   *Becket, Pro.* 347
   —a *t*, You play with words.   ,,   IV vi 180
Trouble (s) all Your *t* to the dogstar and the devil.   *Queen Mary* I iv 292
   But the wench Hath her own *t's* ;   ,,   III v 262
   She would have seen at once into my *t*,   *Prom. of May* I 554
   I have been in *t*, but I am happy—   ,,   I 788
   Indeed, you seem'd in *t*, sir.   ,,   II 385
Trouble (verb) ' I would they were cut off That *t* you.'   *Queen Mary* III iv 33
   yet she must have him ; She *t's* England :   ,,   III vi 21

True (*continued*) A question that every *t* man asks of
a woman once in his life.   *Foresters* I ii 138
T, for through John I had my sheriffship.   ,,   I ii 200
That is no *t* man's hand. I hate hidden faces.   ,,   I ii 244
T, were I taken They would prick out my sight.   ,,   II i 71
there lives No man who truly loves and rules His
following, but can keep his followers *t*.   ,,   II i 78
T king of vice—*t* play on words—   ,,   II i 83
T soul of the Saxon churl for whom song has no charm.   ,,   II i 385
this is a *t* woodman's bow of the best yew-wood   ,,   II i 392
Lovers hold *T* love immortal.   ,,   II i 616
I ever held that saying false That Love is blind, but
thou hast proven it *t*.   ,,   II i 645
O Kate, *t* love and jealousy are twins,   ,,   II i 62
T, she is a goodly thing.   ,,   II ii 140
She is *t*, and you are *t*,   ,,   II ii 194
Scarlet told me—is it *t*?   ,,   III 146
We never robb'd one friend of the *t* King.   ,,   III 157
so His own *t* wife came with him,   ,,   III 240
Join them and they are a *t* marriage;   ,,   III 421
Love's falsehood to *t* maid will seal Love's truth   ,,   IV 73
is not he that goes against the king and the law the *t*
king in the sight of the King of kings?   ,,   IV 230
if our *t* Robin Be not the nobler lion of the twain.   ,,   IV 394
Blown like a *t* son of the woods. Farewell!   ,,   IV 427
Our bowmen are so *t* They strike the deer at once to death—   ,,   IV 524
Mine eye most *t* to one hair's-breadth of aim.   ,,   IV 694
The King forbad it. *T*, my liege.   ,,   IV 865
True-born Nay, it means *t-b*.   *Queen Mary* I i 14
Parliament can make every *t-b* man of us a bastard.   ,,   I i 27
Truer That's a *t* fear!   *Harold* I ii 66
Purer, and *t* and nobler than herself;   *Becket* II i 172
For all my *t* life begins to-day.   *The Cup* II 229
Truest Here fell the *t*, manliest hearts of England.   *Harold* V ii 58
As some cold-manner'd friend may strangely do us The
t service,   *The Falcon* 644
Trumpet Hark! the *t*'s.   *Queen Mary* I i 64
And after that, the *t* of the dead. Why, there are
t's blowing now: what is it?   ,,   IV i 12
Why are the *t*'s blowing, Father Cole?   ,,   IV ii 23
blow the *t*, priest!   *Harold* III i 188
Were the great *t* blowing doomsday dawn,   ,,   IV 227
t's in the halls, Sobs, laughter, cries: *Becket* V ii 367
Tho' all the loud-lung'd *t*'s upon earth   ,,   V ii 487
The *t*'s of the fight had echo'd down,   *The Falcon* 605
stillness in the grave By the last *t*.   *Foresters* II i 48
Trunk cleft the tree From off the bearing *t*,   *Harold* III i 138
he soak'd the *t* with human blood,   ,,   III i 142
sunder'd tree again, and set it Straight on the *t*,   ,,   III i 146
Trunk-hose white satin his *t-h*, Inwrought with silver,— *Queen Mary* III i 76
tail like a devil under his *t-h*. *Tailor*. Ay, but see
what *t-h's*!   ,,   III i 224
Truss Seize him and *t* him up, and carry her off.   *Foresters* IV 690
Trust (s) to whom The king, my father, did commit
his *t*;   *Queen Mary* II ii 208
I have lost all *t* in him.   *Becket* II ii 434
Thomas, I would there were that perfect *t* between us,   ,,   III iii 264
That perfect *t* may come again between us,   ,,   III iii 351
Trust (verb) I *t* it is but a rumour.   *Queen Mary* I i 107
Nay; not so long I *t*.   ,,   I iii 141
I *t* that he will carry you well to-day,   ,,   I iv 145
So you still care to *t* him somewhat less   ,,   I v 221
Farewell, and *t* me, Philip is yours.   ,,   I v 540
I *t* the Queen comes hither with her guards.   ,,   II ii 1
Trusted than *t*—the scoundrel—   ,,   II ii 39
I will *t* you. We fling ourselves on you,   ,,   II ii 47
And it would be your comfort, as I *t*;   ,,   II ii 225
And will not *t* your voices.   ,,   II ii 259
I *t* this day, thro' God, I have saved the crown.   ,,   II ii 302
I *t* by this your Highness will allow   ,,   II iv 132
I *t* that you would fight along with us.   ,,   III i 457
No, for we *t* they parted in the swine.   ,,   III ii 142
You will be, we *t*, Sometime the viceroy   ,,   III ii 195
I *t* your Grace is well.   ,,   V ii 551
I *t* that God will make you happy yet.   ,,   V v 76

Trust (verb) (*continued*) I *t* the kingly touch that cures
the evil   *Harold* I i 151
Nay, I *t* not, For I have served thee long   ,,   I i 213
I *t* he may do well, this Gamel.   ,,   I i 190
Were I Thomas, I wouldn't *t* it.   *Becket* III iii 59
Have I sown it in salt? I *t* not,   ,,   III iii 320
You said you couldn't *t* Margery,   ,,   IV ii 15
We *t* your Royal Grace, lord of more land   ,,   v i 28
I durst not *t* him with—my serving Rome   *The Cup* I ii 277
I *t*, my dear, we shall be always friends.   *Prom. of May* I 631
and you, a gentleman, Told me to *t* you: ,,   I 710
I *t* I shall forgive him—by-and-by—   ,,   II 465
I *t* I may be able by-and-by to help you in the
business of the farm;   ,,   III 222
I *t* he will, but if he do not I and thou   *Foresters* II 199
can I *t* myself With your brave band?   ,,   II i 703
I *t* We shall return to the wood.   ,,   IV 1051
never I *t* to roam So far again,   ,,   IV 1099
Trusted *T* than trust—the scoundrel—   *Queen Mary* II ii 39
And *t* God would save her thro' the blood   ,,   I 386
priest whom John of Salisbury *t* Hath sent another. *Becket* III i 70
That was the only *true* love; and I *t*— *Prom. of May* I 713
and be *t* that some time we should meet again,   ,,   III 328
Trustful A child, and all as *t* as a child?   ,,   III 759
one of you Shamed a too *t* widow whom you heard *Foresters* III 385
Trustless Hast thou such *t* jailors in thy North? *Harold* II ii 685
Trusty Your faithful friend and *t* councillor. *Queen Mary* IV v 89
Truth in *t* I had meant to crave Permission   ,,   I iv 234
Make no allowance for the naked *t*.   ,,   I v 329
Statesmen that are wise Take *t* herself for model.   ,,   III iii 37
tropes are good to clothe a naked *t*,   ,,   III iv 151
Cut with a diamond; so to last like *t*. *Elizabeth*.
Ay, if *t* last. *Lady*. But *t*, they say,   ,,   III v 26
T, a word! The very *t* and very Word are one.   ,,   III v 31
But *t* of story, which I glanced at, girl,   ,,   III v 33
into the daylight *t* That it may fall to-day!   ,,   III v 136
rage of one who hates a *t* He cannot but allow.   ,,   III vi 144
Then never read it. The *t* is here.   ,,   IV i 100
The *t* of God, which I had proven and known.   ,,   IV iii 149
saying spoken once By Him that was the *t*,   ,,   IV iii 203
Against the *t* I knew within my heart,   ,,   IV iii 241
hour has come For utter *t* and plainness;   ,,   IV iii 273
So in *t* he said.   *Harold* II ii 263
Is it not better still to speak the *t*?   ,,   II ii 374
Welshman says, 'The *T* against the World,' Much more
the *t* against myself.   ,,   II ii 398
for thou Art known a speaker of the *t*,   ,,   II ii 517
When all the world hath learnt to speak the *t*,   ,,   III i 69
I that so prized plain word and naked *t*   ,,   III i 94
By all the *t*'s that ever priest hath preach'd,   ,,   III i 97
Is naked *t* actable in true life?   ,,   III i 109
thought that naked *T* would shame the Devil   ,,   III i 118
the *t* Was lost in that fierce North,   ,,   III ii 25
in the eternal distance To settle on the *T*.   ,,   III ii 103
if the *t* be gall, Cram me not thou with honey,   ,,   IV i 15
If one may dare to speak the *t*,   ,,   IV i 108
—a sin against The *t* of love.   ,,   v i 171
the God of *t* hath heard my cry.   ,,   v i 600
T! no; a lie; a trick, a Norman trick!   ,,   v i 606
or any harm done to the people if my jest be in defence
of the *T*?   *Becket* II ii 340
Till *T* herself be shamed of her defender.   ,,   II ii 344
some dreadful *t* is breaking on me—   ,,   III i 266
Earth's falses are heaven's *t*'s.   ,,   III iii 348
But for the *t* of this I make appeal   ,,   v ii 403
Not if Sinnatus Has told her all the *t* about me. *The Cup* I iii 23
That must be talk, not *t*, but *t* or talk,   *The Falcon* 232
yet to speak white *t*, my good old mother,   ,,   503
and *t* to say, Sir Richard and my Lady Marian *Foresters* I i 29
We old hags should be bribed to speak *t*,   ,,   II i 237
They have told but a tenth of the *t*:   ,,   III 291
will seal Love's *t* On those sweet lips   ,,   IV 74
Boldness is in the blood, *T* in the bottle.   ,,   IV 240
Damsel, is this the *t*? *Marian*. Ay, noble knight.   ,,   IV 770
Even this brawler of harsh *t*'s—I trust Half *t*'s,   ,,   IV 948

Two (*continued*) and there you will find written *T*
  names, Philip and Calais; *Queen Mary* v v 155
By mine own eyes—and these *t* sapphires—these Twin
  rubies, *Harold* i ii 110
I do believe My old crook'd spine would bud out *t*
  young wings „ iii i 24
lo! my *t* pillars, Jachin and Boaz!— „ iii i 191
T young lovers in winter weather, „ iii ii 3
And slew *t* hundred of his following, „ iv i 116
if our *t* houses Be less than brothers. „ iv i 129
Have thy *t* brethren sent their forces in? „ v i 342
T deaths at every swing, ran in upon us And died so, „ v i 409
Gregory bid St. Austin here Found *t* archbishopricks,
  London, and York? *Becket* i iii 50
T sisters gliding in an equal dance, *T* rivers gently flowing
  side by side— „ i iii 444
who hath withstood *t* Kings to their faces for the honour
  of God. „ ii ii 276
He thought less of *t* kings than of one Roger the king of
  the occasion. „ iii iii 90
lest ye should draw together like *t* ships in a calm. „ iii iii 298
My *t* good friends, What matters murder'd here, or
  murder'd there? „ v ii 629
That ere *t* souls be knit for life and death, *The Cup* ii 359
Ay, and I left *t* fingers there for dead. *The Falcon* 653
they fell a kissin' o' one another like *t* sweet'arts i'
  the poorch *Prom. of May* i 22
and Vice and Virtue Are but *t* masks of self; „ i 538
And wheniver 'e sees *t* sweet'arts togither like thou
  and me, Sally, „ ii 163
And Sir Richard was told he might be ransomed for
  t thousand marks in gold. *Foresters* i i 64
Those *t* thousand marks lent me by the Abbot for the
  ransom of my son Walter— „ i i 263
Did *t* knights pass? „ ii i 230
For whom I ran into my debt to the Abbot, *T* thousand
  marks in gold. „ ii i 464
And mark'd if those *t* knaves from York be coming? „ iv i 112
Friar, by my *t* bouts at quarterstaff. „ iv i 267
at the far end of the glade I see *t* figures crawling up
  the hill. „ iv i 333
Thou hast risk'd thy life for mine: bind these *t* men. „ iv i 894
Two-handed And swaying his *t-h* sword about him, *Harold* v i 407
Two-legg'd *t-l* dogs Among us who can smell *The Cup* i ii 111
'Twur (it were, it was) I should saay '*t* ower by now. *Queen Mary* iv iii 475
Tyne (river) thro' all the forest land North to the *T*: *Foresters* i i 89
Type poor Steer looks The very *t* of Age in a picture, *Prom. of May* iii 514
Typed cataract *t* the headlong plunge and fall *Queen Mary* iii iv 140
Tyranny Take fees of *t*, wink at sacrilege, *Becket* ii i 394
  both fought against the *t* of the kings, the Normans. *Foresters* i i 230
  This John—this Norman— „ ii i 238
Tyrant brook nor Pope nor Spaniard here to play The *t*, *Queen Mary* iv i 191
Is this the face of one who plays the *t*? „ i v 194
you yourself have truckled to the *t*, „ iii iv 237
This Tostig is, or like to be, a *t*; *Harold* i i 481
This Synorix Was Tetrarch here, and *t* also— *The Cup* i ii 183
To foil and spoil the *t* Beneath the greenwood tree. *Foresters* i ii 11
maiden freedom which Would never brook the *t*. „ iii 121
men will call him An Eastern *t*, not an English king. „ iv 904

U

Ugly Ay, but you turn right *u* when you're in an ill
  temper; *Prom. of May* i 159
And jealousy is wither'd, sour and *u*: *Foresters* ii ii 65
Ulcer Crutches, and itches, and leprosies, and *u*'s, *Becket* i iv 255
Unadvised theretoward *u* Of all our Privy Council; *Queen Mary* ii ii 204
Unalterably *U* and pesteringly fond! „ v i 120
Unarmour'd And walkest here *U*? *Foresters* i 119
Unask'd She gave her hand, *u*, at the farm-gate; *Prom. of May* ii 625
Unaware That might have leapt upon us *u*'s. *Queen Mary* ii ii 295
Unbearded As helplessly as some *u* boy's *The Cup* i iii 40

Unborn The great *u* defender of the Faith, *Queen Mary* iii ii 165
Unbrotherlike O brother, most *u* to me, *Harold* v i 251
Uncanonical Old *u* Stigand—ask of *me* Who had my
  pallium from an Antipope! „ i i 81
Thou *u* fool, Wilt *thou* play with the thunder? „ iii i 390
Uncared upon the way to Rome Unwept, *u* for. *Becket* ii ii 410
Uncertain *See* **Self-uncertain**
Uncle Not very dangerous that way, my good *u*. *Queen Mary* i iv 167
I follow your good counsel, gracious *u*. „ i iv 186
Do they say so, good *u*? „ i iv 215
You should not play upon me. *Elizabeth*. No, good *u*. „ i iv 220
U, I am of sovereign nature, „ i iv 257
To the Pleiads, *u*; they have lost a sister. „ i iv 293
I am sure this body Is Alfwig, the king's *u*. *Harold* v ii 68
Have we not heard Raymond of Poitou, thine own *u*— *Becket* iv ii 247
An' how did ye leäve the owd *u* i' Coomberland? *Prom. of May* i 68
That fine, fat, hook-nosed *u* of mine, old Harold, „ i 509
So the owd *u* i' Coomberland be deäd, Miss Dora, „ ii 1
I met her first at a farm in Cumberland—Her *u*'s. „ ii 398
some will say because I have inherited my *U*. „ iii 598
Uncomely Nay, what *u* faces, could he see you! *Becket* v i 201
Uncourtly Ever a rough, blunt, and *u* fellow— *Queen Mary* v v 120
Uncouth and your churches, *U*, unhandsome, *Harold* i i 165
Unction that very word 'greasy' hath a kind of *u* in it, *Foresters* i i 87
Unctuosity puffed out such an incense of *u* into the nostrils
  of our Gods of Church and State, *Becket* iii iii 115
Undefiled As persons *u* with our offence, *Queen Mary* iii iii 144
Underdid must we follow All that they overdid or *u*? *Becket* ii ii 214
Underdone I hope he be not *u*, for we be undone in the
  doing of him. *The Falcon* 557
Undereaten Except it be a soft one, And *u* to the fall. *Harold* i ii 123
Underfoot the wild hawk passing overhead, The
  mouldwarp *u*. *Foresters* iii 319
crackled *u* And in this very chamber, *Queen Mary* iii v 53
and *u* An earthquake; „ iv iii 397
The priests of Baal tread her *u*— *Becket* iii iii 179
Crush'd, hack'd at, trampled *u*. *The Falcon* 640
Undergo Or give thee saintly strength to *u*. *Queen Mary* iv iii 99
men of old would *u* Unpleasant for the sake of
  pleasant ones Hereafter, *Prom. of May* i 243
Underground They must have sprung like Ghosts from *u*, *Foresters* iv 593
Underhand Were fighting *u* unholy wars Against your
  lawful king. „ iv 821
Under-handedness and all left-handedness and *u-h*. *Becket, Pro.* 341
Under-heel That tread the kings their children *u-h*— „ *Pro.* 213
Understan' summat wrong theer, Wilson, fur I doänt
  u it. *Prom. of May* i 235
An' thou doänt *u* it neither—and thou school-
  master an' all. „ i 239
Cannot you *u* plain words, Mr. Dobson? „ ii 112
Understand (*See also* **Understan'**) *u* We made thereto
  no treaty of ourselves, *Queen Mary* ii ii 202
U: Your lawful Prince hath come „ ii ii 259
because I am not certain: You *u*, Feria. „ v i 269
You *u* me there, too? „ v i 273
Undertake Shall I *u* The knight at quarterstaff, *Foresters* iv 247
Underwood mix with all The lusty life of wood and *u*, „ i iii 114
Undescendible Steam'd upward from the *u* Abysm. *Harold* i i 15
Undone I hope he be not underdone, for we be *u* in the
  doing of him. *The Falcon* 558
Undoubted and proclaim Your true *u* faith, that all
  may hear. *Queen Mary* iv iii 114
Unfamiliar marvell'd at Our *u* beauties of the west; *Becket* iv ii 303
Unfurnish'd you are all *u*? Give him a bow and arrows— *The Cup* i i 207
Unhallow'd Dash'd red with that *u* passover; *Becket* i iii 348
Unhandsome and your churches Uncouth, *u*, *Harold* i i 165
Unhappiest *U* Of Queens and wives and women! *Queen Mary* iv i 407
Unhappiness brooding Upon a great *u* when you spoke. *Prom. of May* ii 383
Unhappy and so this *u* land, long divided in itself, *Queen Mary* i iii 20
Behold him— *People*. Oh, *u* sight! „ iv iii 112
U land! Hard-natured Queen, half-Spanish in herself, „ iv iii 422
Voices—I hear *u* rumours—nay, I say not, I believe. „ v iii 141
O this *u* world! How shall I break it to him? *The Falcon* 846
I am most unlucky, most *u*. „ 864
Unheard But will the King, then, judge us all *u*? *Foresters* iv 897

Unholy Were fighting underhand *u* wars Against your
lawful king. *Foresters* IV 821

Uninvited knowing the fame of your hospitality, we
ventured in *u*.   „   I ii 196

Unity again received into the bosom And *u* of
Universal Church; *Queen Mary* III iii 155
in this *u* and obedience Unto the holy see   „   III iii 157
to the bosom And *u* of Universal Church.   „   III iii 221
but now, The *u* of Universal Church,   „   III iii 229
The *u* of Universal Hell,   „   III iii 232
Join hands, let brethren dwell in *u*; *Harold* I i 397
In symbol of their married *u*, *The Cup* II 363

Universal Like *u* air and sunshine! Open, *Queen Mary* III iii 182
Be once again received into the bosom And unity
of *U* Church;   „   III iii 155
And also we restore you to the bosom And unity
of *U* Church.   „   III iii 221
but now, The unity of *U* Church, Mary would
have it; and this Gardiner follows; The
unity of *U* Hell,   „   III iii 229
Yet wherefore should he die that hath return'd
To the one Catholic *U* Church,   „   IV iii 21

Unkind O my dear son, be not *u* to me. *The Falcon* 509
Unkingly *U* should I be, and most unknightly, *Becket* III iii 230
Unknightly Unkingly should I be, and most *u*,   „   III iii 230
Unlearn'd your Priests Gross, wordly, simoniacal, *u*! *Harold* I i 162
Unlike The peoples are *u* as their complexion; *Queen Mary* V i 89
O how *u* our goodly Sinnatus. *The Cup* II 173
Weak natures that impute Themselves to their *u*'s, *Foresters* II i 692
Unlord after that, We had to dis-archbishop and *u*, *Queen Mary* IV ii 128
Unlucky I am most *u*, most unhappy. *The Falcon* 864
Unman She fear'd it might *u* him for his end. *Queen Mary* III i 368
And that would quite *u* him, heart and soul. *Foresters* III 29
Unmann'd She could not be *u*—no, nor outwoman'd— *Queen Mary* III i 369
Unmatchable face and form *u*! *The Cup* I i 122
Unmoving *U* in the greatness of the flame, *Queen Mary* IV iii 622
Unpardonable Yea, even such as mine, incalculable,
U,,   „   IV iii 148
Unpleasant Against the *u* jolts of this rough road *Prom. of May* I 228
men of old would undergo *U* for the sake of pleasant
ones Hereafter,   „   I 245
Unprincely For some *u* violence to a woman, *The Cup* I i 139
God help the mark—To his own *u* ends. *Foresters* IV 716
Unqueen Who did discrown thine husband, *u* thee? *Harold* III i 193
Unquenchable And burn the tares with *u* fire! *Queen Mary* V v 114
Unquiet and the people so *u*—   „   III i 453
Unriddle Stigand, *u* This vision, canst thou? *Stigand*.
Dotage! *Harold* III i 174
Unsafe Their lives *u* in any of these our woods, *Foresters* IV 93
Un-Saxon Which hunted *him* when that *u-S* blast, *Harold* II ii 30
Unscathed And let him pass *u*; he loves me, Harold!   „   III i 301
Unschool'd and threaten us thence *U* of Death?   „   V i 287
Unsheath'd tigress had *u* her nails at last, *Queen Mary* III i 3
Unsister plenty to sunder and *u* them again: „   I i 85
Unslept seen us that wild morning when we found
Her bed *u* in, *Prom. of May* II 471
Unsocket whose storm-voice *U*'s the strong oak, *The Cup* II 283
Unsubject to One earthly sceptre. *Becket* I iii 680
Unswear Swear and *u*, state and misstate thy best!   „   II ii 476
Unsymmetrically but *u*, preposterously, illogically,   „   Pro. 336
Untold Tell me that, or leave All else *u*. *Queen Mary* IV iii 569
Unwavering Your lordship affects the *u* perpendicular; *Becket* iii 326
Unwell Ah, heaven! *Pole*. *U*, your Grace? *Queen Mary* III ii 85
Her Highness is *u*. I will retire.   „   V i 246
I am sorry Mr. Steer still continues too *u* to
attend to you, *Prom. of May* III 22
Unwept upon the way to Rome *U*, uncared for. *Becket* II ii 410
Unwholesome *U* talk For Godwin's house! *Harold* I i 390
Unwilling I have been *u* to trouble you with
questions, *Prom. of May* III 321
Unwillingness Foreseeing, with whate'er *u*, *Queen Mary* I v 253
Unworthy 'This hath offended—this *u* hand!'   „   IV iii 613
O thou *u* brother of my dear Marian! *Foresters* II i 538
Unwoundable callous with a constant stripe, *U*. *Queen Mary* V v 173
Unwounded having passed *u* from the field, *The Falcon* 608

Unwrinkled The brows *u* as a summer mere.— *Harold* III i 48
Up *See* **Hup, Oop, Shut-up, Steep-up**
Uphold all my lifelong labour to *u* The primacy—a
heretic. *Queen Mary* V ii 70
Wilt *thou u* my claim? *Harold* II ii 602
Upholder our recoverer and *u* of customs hath in this
crowning *Becket* III iii 70
Uplifter And mine *u* in this world,   „   I i 89
Upper My lords of the *u* house, *Queen Mary* III iii 101
Uprear'd The trenches dug, the palisades *u* *Harold* V i 189
Upright you that have kept your old customs *u*, *Queen Mary* II i 159
Well, you one man, because you stood *u*,   „   III iii 269
He pass'd out smiling, and he walk'd *u*;   „   IV iii 303
He stood *u*, a lad of twenty-one,   „   IV iii 335
and saw the church all fill'd With dead men *u* from their
graves, *Harold* I i 83
And thou art *u* in thy living grave,   „   II ii 440
for I have lost Somewhat of *u* stature thro' mine oath,   „   III ii 56
Uproar —made an *u*. *Henry*. And Becket had my
bosom *Becket* I iii 432
Upshot and there bide The *u* of my quarrel, *Queen Mary* II iv 86
Upwards *See* **Huppads**
Urge not be wanting Those that will *u* her injury— *Queen Mary* III vi 176
and I shall *u* his suit Upon the Queen,   „   V i 265
She will *u* marriage on me. *Prom. of May* I 489
Urn keep us From seeing all too near that *u*, *The Cup* I iii 133
Usage I came on certain wholesome *u*'s, *Becket* I iii 412
so violated the immemorial *u* of the Church,   „   III iii 72
Use (s) Ay, and what *u* to talk? *Queen Mary* III iii 40
I kept my head for *u* of Holy Church;   „   IV iii 359
wholesome *u* of these To chink against the Norman, *Harold* III i 20
made too good an *u* of Holy Church To break   „   V i 312
Not yet. Stay. *Edith*. To what *u*?   „   V i 339
fringe of gorgeousness beyond Old *u*, *The Cup* II 439
had you left him free *u* of his wings, *Prom. of May* I 652
but there is *u*, four hundred marks. *Foresters* IV 495
my tongue tript—five hundred marks for *u*.   „   IV 500
You have the monies and the *u* of them.   „   IV 548
Use (verb) Well, we shall *u* him somehow, *Queen Mary* I iii 171
and *u* Both us and them according as they will.   „   II ii 160
Ay, but they *u* his name.   „   V i 129
we must *u* our battle-axe to-day. *Harold* V i 205
King's courts would *u* thee worse than thy dog— *Becket* I iv 102
it is the cup we *u* in our marriages. *The Cup* I i 44
sends you this cup—the cup we *u* in our marriages—   „   I ii 72
have you power with Rome? *u* it for him!   „   I ii 290
we never *u* it For fear of breakage— *The Falcon* 486
—take and *u* your moment, while you may. *Foresters* II i 476
Used evilly *u* And put to pain. *Becket* II i 433
You had never *u* so many,   „   IV ii 183
Hath *u* the full authority of his Church   „   V i 207
Foul as her dust-cloth, if she *u* it—   „   V i 228
Well *u*, they serve us well. *The Cup* I iii 135
Used (was accustomed) I *u* to love the Queen with
all my heart— *Queen Mary* V ii 418
that Dobbins, is it, With whom I *u* to jar? *Prom. of May* II 613
as I *u* to transact all his business for him,   „   II 719
Useless But your moan is *u* now: *Queen Mary* IV iii 638
Using fears he might be crack'd in *u*,   „   II i 8
Usurper And thou, *u*, liar— *Harold*. Out, beast monk! *Harold* V i 74
Utmost I will help you, Madam, Even to the *u*. *Queen Mary* I i 178
To do to the *u* all that in us lies   „   III iii 140
Utopian What are all these? *Harold*. *U* idiotcies. *Prom. of May* III 588
Utter (adj.) but the hour has come For *u* truth and
plainness; *Queen Mary* IV iii 273
Poor lads, they see not what the general sees, A
risk of *u* ruin.   „   V ii 449
I have lived a life of *u* purity: *Harold* I i 178
I reel beneath the weight of *u* joy— *The Cup* IV 450
I shall go mad for *u* shame and die. *Prom. of May* I 682
You both are *u* traitors to your king. *Foresters* IV 844
Utter (verb) fiends that *u* them Tongue-torn with
pincers, *Queen Mary* V ii 192
I never heard him *u* worse of you Than that   „   V ii 431
Uttered he never *u* moan of pain: „   IV iii 618

Very (*continued*) Why there, now! that *v* word 'greasy'
hath a kind of unction in it,   *Foresters* I i 86
I am thine to the *v* heart of the earth—   „ I i 337
My God, thou art the *v* woman who waits On my dear
Marian.   „ II i 101
Thou comest a *v* angel out of heaven.   „ II i 105
and what doest thou with that who art more bow-bent
than the *v* bow thou carriest?   „ II i 378
It is the *v* captain of the thieves!   „ II i 412
I thank you, noble sir, the *v* blossom Of bandits.   „ III 247
It is not he—his face—tho' *v* like—No, no!   „ IV 777
Yea, and the weight of the *v* land itself,   „ IV 1025
Veselay But since he cursed My friends at *V*,   *Becket* II i 89
Vesper I will but pass to *v's*, And breathe one prayer   „ v ii 190
In your old place? and *v's* are beginning.   „ v ii 596
Come, then, with us to *v's*.   „ v iii 35
They are thronging in to *v's*—half the town.   „ v iii 139
Vessel guns From out the *v's* lying in the river.   *Queen Mary* II ii 222
wherefore not Helm the huge *v* of your state,   „ v i 73
In the full *v* running out at top   *Harold* I i 378
Plunder'd the *v* full of Gascon wine,   *Becket* v ii 441
Vex *V* him not, Leofwin. *Tostig.* I am not vext,—Altho'
ye seek to *v* me,   *Harold* I i 403
I told my Lord He should not *v* her Highness;   *Queen Mary* III vi 66
Why do you *v* me?   „ IV i 134
Why would you *v* yourself, Poor sister?   „ v v 263
Which will so *v* thee.   *Becket* II i 208
I will not *v* you by repeating them—   *Prom. of May* II ii 403
Why do you *v* me With raven-croaks   *Foresters* II i 623
Vex'd-Vext His Highness is so *vex'd* with strange
affairs—   *Queen Mary* v ii 559
No, I am not *vext*,—Altho' ye seek to vex me,   *Harold* I i 404
—I am not *vext* at all.   „ I i 409
A gnat that *vext* thy pillow!   „ II i 71
I seed how the owd man wur *vext*.   *Prom. of May* II 28
Viand besides Hedge-pigs, a savoury *v*,   *Foresters* IV 193
Vicar Julius, God's *v* and Vicegerent upon earth,   *Queen Mary* III ii 213
and adore This *V* of their *V*.   „ III iii 244
„ v v 162
Vice Foul maggots crawling in a fester'd *v*!
Would call this *v*; but one time's *v* may be The
virtue of another; and *V* and Virtue Are but
two masks of self; and what hereafter Shall
mark out *V* from Virtue   *Prom. of May* I 534
Our vice-king John,—True king of *v*—   *Foresters* II i 83
Vicegerent Julius, God's Vicar and *V* upon earth,   *Queen Mary* III iii 213
Vice-king And thou be my *v-k* in England.   *Harold* II i 635
Our *v-k* John, True king of vice—   *Foresters* II i 81
Viceroy Set up a *v*, sent his myriads   *Queen Mary* III i 463
Sometime the *v* of those provinces   „ III ii 196
Viciousness Because we seek to curb their *v*.   *Foresters* III 393
Victim nobler The *v* was, the more acceptable Might be
the sacrifice.   *The Falcon* 880
Or happy fallen a *v* to the wolf.   *Foresters* II i 509
Victor will you crown my foe My *v* in mid-battle?   *Becket* v i 150
crown'd *v* of my will—   *The Cup* II 519
Victory wines Of wedding had been dash'd into the cups
Of *v*,   *Harold* IV iii 8
thy *victories* Over our own poor Wales,   „ IV iii 26
I ever had my *victories* among women.   *The Cup* I i 153
at last May lead them on to *v*—   „ I i 168
Vile With that *v* Cranmer in the accursed lie Of
good Queen Catharine's divorce—   *Queen Mary* IV iv 231
Villa Garcia No man can make his Maker—*V G*.   „ IV ii 58
No, *V G*, I sign no more.   „ IV ii 83
Village (adj.) His *v* darling in some lewd caress   *Becket* IV ii 200
So loved by all the *v* people here,   *Prom. of May* III 755
Village (s) I Shall not be made the laughter of the *v*,   „ I 721
Villain *v's* with their lying lights have wreck'd us!   *Harold* I i 83
Serve thyself first, *v*! They shall not harm   *The Cup* I ii 325
that *v*, Edgar, If he should ever show   *Prom. of May* II 422
Vindicator Surgas e tenebris, Sis!   *Harold* v i 572
Vine You lived among your *v's* and oranges,   *Queen Mary* III iv 253
Perhaps our *v's* will grow the better for it.   *Harold* I i 68
apricot, *V*, cypress, poplar, myrtle,   *The Cup* I i 3
and like the swaying *v's*—Yea,—   „ I ii 411

Vine (*continued*) we will chirp among our *v's*, and smile   *The Cup* I iii 170
sway the long grape-bunches of our *v's*,   „ II 271
Vine-an'-the-Hop (inn sign) But hallus ud stop at
the *V-a-t-H*,   *Prom. of May* II 311
Vine-bower vast *v-b's* Ran to the summit of the trees,   *The Cup* I ii 402
Vineyard she turns down the path through our little *v*,   *The Falcon* 168
Vino *In v veritas*.   *Foresters* IV 247
Vintage Not like the *v* blowing round your castle.   *The Falcon* 579
send you down a flask or two Of that same *v*?   „ 586
Violate These Romans dare not *v* the Temple.   *The Cup* I iii 62
Violated A cleric *v* The daughter of his host,   *Becket* I iii 382
so *v* the immemorial usage of the Church,   „ III 72
v the whole Tradition of our land,   *Prom. of May* I 494
Violence (*See also* **Over-violence**) Your *v* and much
roughness to the Legate,   *Queen Mary* III iv 318
—a sweet *v*, And a sweet craft.   „ III v 108
v and the craft that do divide The world   „ III v 120
cast with bestial *v* Our holy Norman bishops   *Harold* I i 49
Side not with Tostig in any *v*,   „ I i 457
For some unprincely *v* to a woman,   *The Cup* I i 139
This *v* ill becomes The silence of our Temple.   „ II 215
Violent Robin was *v*, And she was crafty—   *Queen Mary* III v 107
Save for thy wild and *v* will that wrench'd All hearts of
freemen from thee.   *Harold* v i 277
Violet and won the *v* at Toulouse;   *Becket, Pro.* 348
rose or no rose, has killed the golden *v*.   „ *Pro.* 352
Sweeter than any *v* of to-day,   *The Falcon* 465
I meän'd they be as blue as *v's*.   *Prom. of May* I 104
Viper Two *v's* of one breed—an amphisbæna,   *Queen Mary* IV iv 39
Vire (fire) I do know ez Pwoaps and *v's* be bad things;   „ IV iii 501
and tells un ez the *v* has tuk holt.   „ IV iii 512
There's nought but the *v* of God's hell ez can burn
out that.   „ IV iii 527
Virgil Well. the tree in *V*, sir,   „ III i 22
but, my Lord, you know what *V* sings,   „ III vi 134
Virgin (adj.) seeing that our gracious *V* Queen hath—   „ I iii 23
Virgin (s) (*See also* **Mary**) let me call her our second *V* Mary,   „ I iii 57
V Mary! we'll have no virgins here—   „ I iii 60
we'll have no *v's* here—we'll have the Lady
Elizabeth!   „ I iii 61
by the holy *V*, being noble, But love me only: „ I v 70
Holy *V*, Plead with thy blessed Son!   „ I v 84
I thank God, I have lived a *v*,   „ II ii 218
Holy *V* will not have me yet Lose the sweet hope   „ III vi 199
My son, the Saints are *v's*;   *Harold* III i 272
I have been myself a *v*; and I sware To consecrate my
v here   „ III i 275
Yea, by the Blessed *V*!   *Becket, Pro.* 520
The *V*, in a vision of my sleep,   „ I i 53
we have the Blessed *V* For worship,   „ v ii 220
I do commend my cause to God, the *V*,   „ v iii 164
I am a *v*, my masters, I am a *v*. *Much.* And a *v*, my
masters, three yards about the waist is like to
remain a *v*,   *Foresters* I ii 67
And you three holy men, You worshippers of the *V*,   „ III 383
The Holy *V* Stand by the strongest.   „ IV 264
Our holy king Hath given his *v* lamb to Holy Church   *Harold* I i 334
Virginity They love the white rose of *v*,   „ III i 273
Virgo Homo sum, sed *v* sum,   *Foresters* I ii 66
Virtue (I count it as a kind of *v* in him,   *Queen Mary* I iv 193
Is not *v* prized mainly for its rarity   *Becket* III iii 303
one time's vice may be The *v* of another; and Vice
and *V* Are but two masks of self; and what here-
after Shall mark out Vice from *V*   *Prom. of May* I 536
Virtuous Exhort them to a pure and *v* life;   *Queen Mary* IV ii 77
Virtus *Gratior in pulchro corpore v*.   *Becket* v ii 542
Visible Is not the Church the *v* Lord on earth?   „ I iii 92
Vision I have had a *v*;   *Harold* I i 191
Edward wakes!—Dazed—he hath seen a *v*.   „ III i 131
Stigand, unriddle This *v*, canst thou? *Stigand.* Dotage!   „ III i 175
The Virgin, in a *v* of my sleep,   *Becket* I i 53
It will be so—my *v's* in the Lord: „ III iii 341
I had once a *v* of a pure and perfect marriage,   *Prom. of May* III 188
Shall I be happy? Happy *v*, stay.   *Foresters* II ii 199
Visionary And found it all a *v* flame,   *Queen Mary* IV iv 4

Visit thine host in England when I went To *v* Edward. *Harold* II ii 6
Coming to *v* my lord, for the first time in her life too ! *The Falcon* 170
Visited When I *v* England, Some held she was his wife *Harold* v ii 99
Vitus (Saint) By old St. *V* Have you gone mad ? *Foresters* IV 614
Vive le Roy Hurrah ! *V l R* ! *Becket* I iv 274
Voice (*See also* **Storm-voice**) Thro' many *v*'s crying
right and left, *Queen Mary* I ii 48
and all rebellions lie Dead bodies without *v.* „ II i 80
Three *v*'s from our guilds and companies ! „ II ii 255
And will not trust your *v*'s. „ II ii 259
Their *v* had left me none to tell you this. „ II iii 36
A sound Of feet and *v*'s thickening hither— „ II iv 45
Thine is a half *v* and a lean assent. „ III i 311
To join a *v*, so potent with her Highness, „ IV i 117
All your *v*'s Are waves on flint. „ IV i 121
my poor *v* Against them is a whisper to the roar „ IV ii 186
remain After the vanish'd, „ IV iii 164
crying, in his deep *v*, more than once, „ IV iii 611
Ay, ay ; but many *v*'s call me hence. *Mary.* *V*'s „ v i 32
—I hear unhappy rumours—nay, „ v i 36
What *v*'s call you Dearer than mine „ v i 36
Alas, my Lord ! what *v*'s and how many ? *Philip.*
The *v*'s of Castille and Aragon, „ v i 40
v's of Franche-Comté, and the Netherlands, The *v*'s
of Peru and Mexico, „ v i 45
if the fetid gutter had a *v* And cried „ v ii 323
Your Grace hath a low *v.* „ v ii 378
A low *v* Lost in a wilderness where none can hear !
A *v* of shipwreck on a shoreless sea ! A low *v*
from the dust and from the grave „ v ii 381
No, that way there are *v*'s. Am I too late ? „ v v 207
Thou art a great *v* in Northumberland ! *Harold* I i 114
in Normanland God speaks thro' abler *v*'s, „ I i 167
I want his *v* in England for the crown, I want thy *v* with
him to bring him round ! „ II ii 71
The choice of England is the *v* of England. *William.* I
will be king of England by the laws, The choice, and
v of England. „ II ii 128
v of any people is the sword That guards them, „ II ii 134
would give his kingly *v* To me as his successor. „ II ii 588
Thou art the mightiest *v* in England, man, Thy *v* will
lead „ II ii 617
we be not bound by the king's *v* In making of a king,
yet the king's *v* „ III i 236
The *v* of Gurth ! Good even, my good brother ! „ III i 115
Wessex dragon flies beyond the Humber, No *v* to greet it. „ IV i 5
Thou gavest thy *v* against me in the Council— „ IV ii 77
till *her v* Die with the world. „ IV iii 75
I am but a *v* Among you : murder, martyr me „ v i 77
I send my *v* across the narrow seas— „ v i 246
Thou gavest thy *v* against me in my life, I give my *v*
against thee from the grave— „ v i 252
We give our *v* against thee out of heaven ! „ v i 260
My battle-axe against your *v*'s. „ v i 265
my *v* is harsh here, not in tune, *Becket, Pro.* 349
v of the deep as it hollows the cliffs of the land, „ II i 3
a *v* coming up with the *v* of the deep from the strand, „ II i 5
hand of one To whom thy *v* is all her music, „ II i 177
the *v* Of the perpetual brook, „ III i 45
The brook's *v* is not yours, and no flower, „ III i 55
when my *v* Is martyr'd mute, and this man disappears, „ III iii 349
Did not a man's *v* ring along the aisle, „ v i 150
The King beyond the water, thro' our *v*'s, „ v ii 324
Shall the waste *v* of the bond-breaking sea „ v ii 358
Blessings on your pretty *v*, Miss Dora. *Prom. of May* I 64
arter she'd been a-reädin' me the letter wi' 'er *v*
a-shaäkin', „ II 129
And *her* charm Of *v* is also yours; „ II 381
I heard a *v*, ' Girl, what are you doing there ? ' „ III 375
Swarm to thy *v* like bees to the brass pan. *Foresters* I iii 108
they are so fond o' their own *v*'s „ II i 383
Thou art her brother, and her *v* is thine, „ II i 479
In the cold water that she lost her *v*, „ IV 243
Void you would make his coronation *v* By cursing those
who crown'd him. *Becket* v ii 330

Volcanic A drinker of black, strong, *v* wines, *Queen Mary* v ii 93
Volk (folk) and a-makin' o' *v* madder and madder ; „ IV iii 532
Voltigeur I can recommend our *V*.' *Prom. of May* III 311
Voluntary that thou hast sworn a *v* allegiance to him ? *Becket, Pro.* 439
Vomit Made even the carrion-nosing mongrel *v* *Queen Mary* IV iii 449
Vor (for) it be a var waay *v* my owld legs up vro' Islip. „ IV iii 472
the burnin' o' the owld archbishop 'll burn the
Pwoap out o' this 'ere land *v* iver and iver. „ IV iii 472
Vor't (for it) but tek thou my word *v*, Joan,— „ IV iii 533
Vouch Who shall *v* for his to-morrows ? One word further. *Becket* III iii 300
Vouchsafe *V* a gracious answer to your Queen ? „ IV iii 359
Vour (four) and so they bided on and on till *v* o' the
clock, *Queen Mary* IV iii 510
Vow (s) to swear *V*'s that he dare not break. *Harold* II ii 157
for he Who vows a *v* to strangle his own mother „ III i 229
He did not mean to keep his *v.* „ III i 248
to see my solemn *v* Accomplish'd. „ III i 307
that blighted *v* Which God avenged to-day. „ v ii 156
That kings are faithful to their marriage *v.* *Becket* I ii 78
I bound myself, and by a solemn *v*, *The Falcon* 679
but what a *v* ! what a *v* ! *Foresters* I i 294
For holy *v*'s made to the blessed Saints „ I ii 175
bounden by a *v* not to show his face, „ I ii 236
Vow (verb) Kiss'd me well I *v*; *Queen Mary* III v 93
for he Who *v*'s a vow to strangle his own mother *Harold* III i 229
I *v* to build a church to God Here on the hill of battle; „ v ii 137
Voyage Had you a pleasant *v* up the river ? *Queen Mary* III ii 5
Our *v* by sea was all but miracle ; „ III ii 25
Sick as an autumn swallow for a *v*, *Harold* I i 102
On my last *v*—but the wind has fail'd— *The Cup* II 521
Vro' (from) and it be a var waay vor my owld legs
up *v* Islip. *Queen Mary* IV iii 473
till his man cum in post *v* here, „ IV iii 511
Vying saw thy willy-nilly nun *V* a tress against our golden
fern. *Harold.* *V* a tear with our cold dews, *Harold* v i 149

W

Waage (wage) An' I thanks ye fur that, Miss, moor
nor fur the *w.* *Prom. of May* III 117
Waäist (waist) 'A cotched ma about the *w*, Miss, „ III 119
Waäy (way) it be a var *w* vor my owld legs up vro'
Islip. *Queen Mary* IV iii 472
Eh, then ha' thy *w* wi' me, Tib ; „ IV iii 486
I niver thowt o' mysen i' that *w* ; but if she'd
taäke to ma i' that *w*, or ony *w*, *Prom. of May* I 176
We laäys out o' the *w* fur gentlefoälk altogither— „ I 210
An' I haätes boooks an' all, fur they puts foälk off
the owd *w*'s. „ I 222
fell ageän coalscuttle and my kneeä gev *w* „ I 404
I mun git out on 'is *w* now, or I shall be the death
on 'im. „ II 609
Waded As if she had *w* in it. *Queen Mary* I i 63
w in the brook, ran after the butterflies, *Prom. of May* III 275
Wafer Their *w* and perpetual sacrifice: *Queen Mary* I ii 45
Waged Thou hast *w* God's war against the King ; *Becket* VI 46
Wages (*See also* **Waäge**) if the farming-men be come
for their *w*, to send them up to me. *Prom. of May* III 16
but the schoolmaster looked to the paying you
your *w* when I was away, „ III 24
spent all your last Saturday's *w* at the ale-house ; „ III 78
Why should I pay you your full *w* ? „ III 83
there are your *w* ; the next time you waste „ III 98
Wagon Like a tod of wool from *w* into warehouse. *Foresters* II 274
Wail (s) our sea-mew Winging their only *w* ! *Harold* II i 98
better death With our first *w* than life— *Prom. of May* II 291
—how she made her *w* as for the dead ! „ II 698
and make a ghostly *w* ever and anon to scare 'em. *Foresters* II i 216
Wail (verb) Is this a place To *w* in, Madam ? *Queen Mary* v i 213
thou wilt have To *w* for it like Peter. *Harold* III i 285
dooms thee after death To *w* in deathless flame. *Becket* IV ii 272

Waning and make Our *w* Eleanor all but love me!   *Becket* II ii 458

Wanstead she met the Queen at *W*   *Queen Mary* I i 77

Want (s)   Yet too much mercy is a *w* of mercy,   „ I v 506
This coarseness is a *w* of phantasy.   „ v ii 438
Thine absence well may seem a *w* of care.   *Harold* I i 322
That suffers in the daily *w* of thee,   „ II ii 275
daily *w* supplied—The daily pleasure to supply it.   *Becket* II ii 301
Yet if thro' any *w*— *Harold*. Of this religion? *Prom. of May* III 540
ever have happen'd thro' the *w* Of any or all of them.   „ III 547
If thro' the *w* of any—I mean the true one—   „ III 550
who never hast felt a *w*, to whom all things,   *Foresters* I i 208
and their own *w* Of manhood to their leader!   „ II 693

Want (verb)   his manners *w* the nap And gloss of court;   *Queen Mary* III v 70
you *w* the sun That shines at court;   „ III v 276
I *w* his voice in England for the crown, I *w* thy voice with him to bring him round;   *Harold* II ii 71
and I *w* to bite, I *w* to bite,   *Becket* I iv 221
shall see the silk here and there, and I *w* my supper.   „ IV i 57
Do you *w* them back again?   *Prom. of May* II 43
Owd Steer's gotten all his grass down and *w's* a hand,   „ II 222
Miss Dora, meä and my maätes, us three, we *w's* to hev three words wi' ye.   „ III 125
all on us, wi' your leave, we *w's* to leather 'im.   „ III 137
and he *w's* to speak to ye partic'lar.   „ III 350
says he *w's* to tell ye summut very partic'lar.   „ III 355
an *w's* To hev a word wi' ye about the marriage.   „ III 703

Wanted I am sure Her morning *w* sunlight,   *Harold* II i 45

Wanting *W* the Papal mitre.   *Queen Mary* III iv 148
not be *w* Those that will urge her injury—   „ III vi 175
My palace was but a cottage;   *The Falcon* 287

Wanton (adj.)   A very *w* life indeed.   *Queen Mary* I v 336
No ribald John is Love, no *w* Prince,   *Foresters* IV 46

Wanton (s)   With a *w* in thy lodging—Hell requite 'em!   *Becket* I ii 9
I would move this *w* from his sight   „ I i 70
And thou thyself a proven *w*?   „ IV ii 116
Lest thou shouldst play the *w* there again.   „ v i 112
This *w* here. De Morville, Hold her away.   „ v iii 171

Wantonness high Heaven guard thee from his *w*,   *Foresters* I ii 122

War and at *w* with him, your Grace And kingdom will be suck'd into the *w*,   *Queen Mary* I v 255
must we levy *w* against the Queen's Grace?
Wyatt. No, my friend; *w* for the Queen's Grace—to save her from herself and Philip —*w* against Spain.   „ II i 187
the world is with us—*w* against Spain!   „ II i 196
not mix us any way With his French *w's*—   „ III iii 79
The civil *w's* are gone for evermore: „ III v 150
Not so well holpen in our *w's* with France,   „ III vi 188
If *w* should fall between yourself and France;   „ v i 9
came to sue Your Council and yourself to declare *w*. (repeat)   „ v i 109, 116
soon or late you must have *w* with France;   „ v i 121
You make your *w's* upon him down in Italy:—   „ v i 141
Who deems it a most just and holy *w*.   „ v i 147
Alas! the Council will not hear of *w*. They say your *w's* are not the *w's* of England.   „ v i 164
There *will* be *w* with France, at last, my liege;   „ v i 282
the Council (I have talk'd with some already) are for *w*.   „ v i 296
He cannot dream that *I* advised the *w*;   „ v ii 57
We have made *w* upon the Holy Father All for your sake: „ v ii 307
You did but help King Philip's *w* with France,   „ v ii 313
Dear Madam, Philip is but at the *w's*;   „ v v 25
And all his *w's* and wisdoms past away;   „ v v 56
W, my dear lady!   *Harold* I i 22
W there, my son? is that the doom of England?   „ I i 124
W? the worst that follows Things that seem   „ I i 135
religious fool, Who, seeing *w* in heaven,   „ I i 140
Ay, ay and wise in peace and great in *w*—   „ I i 313
W, my dear lady, *W*, waste, plague,   „ I i 465
brought Thy *w* with Brittany to a goodlier close   „ II ii 49
We seldom take man's life, except in *w*;   „ II ii 502
dash The torch of *w* among your standing corn,   „ II ii 749

War (continued)   Eternal *w*, than that the Saints at peace   *Harold* III ii 75
Free thee or slay thee, Norway will have *w*;   „ IV ii 19
save for Norway, Who loves not thee but *w*.   „ IV ii 24
My legacy of *w* against the Pope   „ v 328
Whose life was all one battle, incarnate *w*,   „ v 398
I led seven hundred knights and fought his *w's*   *Becket* I iii 639
You will have *w*; and tho' we grant   „ II ii 241
Like some wise prince of this world from his *w's*,   „ v ii 14
Thou hast waged God's *w* against the King;   „ v ii 46
Rome Made *w* upon the peoples not the Gods.   *The Cup* I ii 60
you, Can you make *w*? Have you alliances?   „ I ii 99
submit at once Is better than a wholly-hopeless *w*,   „ I ii 141
Whereas in *w's* of freedom and defence   „ I ii 160
When I was married you were at the *w's*.   *The Falcon* 376
It may be I had never seen the *w's*.   „ 379
flung His life, heart, soul into those holy *w's*   *Foresters* IV 407
Heading the holy *w* against the Moslem,   „ IV 818
fighting underhand unholy *w's* Against your lawful king.   „ IV 821

War-axe Mark'd how the *w-a* swang,   *Harold* IV iii 156

Warble And *w* those brief-sighted eyes of hers?   *Queen Mary* III vi 155

Warblest 'O happy lark, that *w* high   *Prom. of May* III 199

War-club wields His *w-c*, dashes it on Gurth,   *Harold* V i 640

War-crash a *w-c*, and so hard, So loud, that,   „ IV iii 144

War-cry I do not hear our English *w-c*.   „ v i 652

Ward lest the king Should yield his *w* to Harold's will.   „ I ii 159

Warden When thou thereof wast *w*.   *Becket* I iii 630

Warder The *w* of the bower hath given himself   „ III i 30
Where's the *w*? *Geoffrey*. Very bad.   „ IV i 49

Warehouse Like a tod of wool from wagon into *w*.   *Foresters* IV 275

War-horn Heard how the *w-h* sang,   *Harold* IV iii 157

Warm (adj.)   know that whether A wind be *w* or cold,   *Queen Mary* V 620
That might live always in the sun's *w* heart,   „ v 22
Philip is as *w* in life As ever.   „ v ii 24
I would we had you, Madam, in our *w* Spain.   „ v ii 607
Cold after *w*, winter after summer,   *Becket* I iv 64
old faces Press round us, and *w* hands close with *w* hands,   *Foresters* I iii 20
so she glided up into the heart O' the bottle, the *w* wine,   „ IV 245

Warm (verb)   King Henry *w's* your traitors at his hearth.   *Queen Mary* v i 123
To *w* the cold bounds of our dying life   *The Cup* II i 128
And let them *w* thy heart to Little John.   *Foresters* III 44

Warmed He *w* to you to-day, and you have chilled him again.   *Becket* II ii 374

Warmth quenched the *w* of France toward you,   „ II ii 311

Warn To *w* us of his coming?   *Foresters* III 458

Warning (part.) Was *w* me that if a gentleman   *Prom. of May* III 578

Warning (s)   he must die, For *w* and example.   *Queen Mary* IV iii 52
Kind of the witch to give thee *w* thro'.   *Becket* III iii 30
The ghostly *w* of my martyrdom;   „ v ii 292

Warping You see thro' *w* glasses.   *Queen Mary* I v 212

Warrant but then she goes, I *w*,   „ I v 464
and I *w* this fine fellow's life.   „ III iii 83
I *w* you. *Cole*. Take, therefore,   „ IV iii 58
I *w* you they talk about the burning.   „ IV iii 463
I *w* thee! thou wouldst hug thy Cupid   *Becket, Pro.* 503
We'll baffle them, I *w*.   „ I i 299
I *w* you, or your own either.   „ I iv 23
So we will—so we will, I *w* thee.   „ I iv 269
Ay, and I *w* the customs.   „ III iii 331
Doth he remember me? *Rosamund*. I *w* him.   „ v i 179
there I *w* I worm thro' all their windings.   *The Cup* I i 86
I *w* you now, he said he struck the stag.   „ I ii 381
White? I *w* thee, my son, as the snow   *The Falcon* 500
I *w's* ye'll think moor o' this young Squire Edgar   *Prom. of May* I 109
I *w's* that ye goäs By haäfe a scoor o' naämes—   „ III 728
I *w* thee—thou canst not be sorrier   *Foresters* II i 281

Warring Wailing! not *w*? Boy, thou hast forgotten   *Harold* II ii 473

Warrior (adj.)   The *w* Earl of Allendale, He loved the Lady Anne;   *Foresters* I i 6
' Farewell, farewell, my *w* Earl!'   „ I i 18

Warrior (s)   And I would have my *w* all in arms.   *Queen Mary* v v 34
W thou art, and mighty wise withal!   *Harold* II ii 543
Advance our Standard of the *W*,   „ IV i 248

Way (*continued*) like a fool, thou knowest no middle *w*.   *Becket* I iii 533
I ask'd the *w*.   *Rosamund.*   I think so.   „   II i 62
the goodly *w* of women Who love,   „   II i 256
daughter of Zion lies beside the *w*—   „   III iii 178
Well, well, then—have thy *w*!   „   III iii 215
If God would take him in some sudden *w*—   „   v i 94
That *w*, or this! Save thyself either *w*.   *Becket.*   Oh,
   no, not either *w*, nor any *w* Save by that *w*   „   v iii 84
Slowly but surely—till I see my *w*.   *The Cup* I i 211
Thou—coming my *w* too—Camma — good-night.
   Camma. Thy *w*? poor worm, crawl down thine
   own black hole   „   II 492
No, not that *w*—here, under the apple tree.   *Prom. of May* I 82
yet that might be The best *w* out of it,   „   I 476
Is there no other *w*?   „   I 691
the rain beating in my face all the *w*,   „   III 368
I was dreaming of it all the *w* hither.   *Foresters* I i 139
Dream of it, then, all the *w* back,   „   I i 140
Glide like a light across these woodland *w's*!   „   II i 160
Did we not hear the two would pass this *w*?   „   II i 198
only they that be bred in it can find their *w* a-nights in it.   „   II i 265
forest lawns are all as bright As *w's* to heaven,   „   II i 632
Have ye glanced down thro' all the forest *w's*   „   IV 111
So now which *w* to the dinner?   „   IV 972

Wayside   Yes, at the *w* inn Close by that alder-island
   in your brook,   *Prom. of May* II 534

Weak   But a *w* mouth, an indeterminate—ha?
   Bonner.   Well, a *w* mouth, perchance.   *Queen Mary* III iv 340
what is *w* must lie;   „   III v 121
other things As idle; a *w* Wyatt!   „   v i 292
Send out; I am too *w* to stir abroad: „   v ii 286
Ah, *w* and meek old man,   „   v v 131
W natures that impute Themselves to their unlikes,   *Foresters* II i 690

Weaken'd   whether that which held it Had *w*,   *Harold* v i 106
let not my strong prayer Be *w* in thy sight,   „   v i 648

Weaker   You would but make us *w*, Thomas Stafford.   *Queen Mary* III i 130
so much *w*, so much worse For last day's journey.   *The Falcon* 832
where the man and the woman, only differing as
   the stronger and the *w*,   *Prom. of May* III 191

Weakness   was it boldness Or *w* that won there?   *Queen Mary* I v 560
The *w* and the dissonance of our clans,   *The Cup* I i 23

Weal   foes in Edward's hall To league against thy *w*.   *Harold* I ii 33
You scheme against her father's *w* and hers,   *Foresters* IV 481

Wealth   (*See also* **World-wealth**) He wrecks his health
   and *w* on courtesans,   *Queen Mary* I v 167
Which in his absence had been all my *w*.   „   I v 362
But for the *w* and glory of our realm,   „   II ii 210
his *w* A fountain of perennial alms—   „   II ii 384
to those that own exceeding *w*,   „   IV iii 201
The wine and *w* of all our France are yours;   *Becket* II ii 446
Foam over all the fleeted *w* of kings   *The Cup* I ii 289
Than all my childless *w*, if mine must die.   *The Falcon* 855
I have land now And *w*, and lay both at your feet.   *Prom. of May* III 616
not with all your *w*, Your land, your life!   „   III 795
As *W* walk'd in at the door. ' You have come for you
   saw *W* coming,'   *Foresters* I i 151
W dropt out of the window,   „   I i 156
' Well now you would fain follow *W*,'   „   I i 158
What a *w* of words—O Lord, I will live   „   I ii 36

Wealthy   all the magistracy, all the nobles, and all
   the *w*;   *Queen Mary* v iv 51

Wean   I put the bitters on my breast to *w* him,   *The Falcon* 190

Wean'd   She hath *w* me from it with such bitterness.   *Harold* IV ii 27

Weänt (will not)   Well, it be i' *my* natur to knock 'im
   o' the 'eäd now; but I *w*.   *Prom. of May* I 289
but I promised one of the Misses I wouldn't meddle
   wi' ye, and I *w*.   „   I 470
an' *w* ye taäke 'em now, Miss Dora,   „   II 40
But I *w* be too sudden wi' it;   „   II 58
W ye gi'e me a kind answer at last?   „   II 63
but that be all along o' you, Miss, because ye *w* hev me;   „   II 110
and she *w* sa much as look at 'im?   „   II 161
I *w* goä to owd Dobson;   „   II 218
then, by-and-by, if she *w* listen to me when I be
   a-tryin' to saäve 'er—if she *w*—   „   II 693

Weänt (will not) (*continued*)   An' we *w* mention
   naw naämes,   *Prom. of May* III 129

Weapon   What *w* hath the child, save his soft tongue,   *Queen Mary* IV v 128
I had wish'd for any *w*.   *Harold* IV iii 19

Wear   (*See also* **Weär**)   I *w* it then to spite her.   *Queen Mary* I iv 78
I *w* beneath my dress A shirt of mail: „   I v 144
Ev'n that young girl who dared to *w* your crown?   „   I v 491
w it as memorial of a morning Which found me   „   I v 529
I *w* Upon this finger), ye did promise full Allegiance   „   II ii 167
wilt thou *w* thy cap before the Queen?   „   III i 236
And *w* my crown, and dance upon my grave.   „   v ii 601
I dare not *w* it.   *Harold* III ii 187
The ring thou darest not *w*,   „   v i 421
Take it and *w* it on that hard heart of yours   *Becket, Pro.* 373
The Mitre!   *Salisbury.*   Will you *w* it?—   „   v ii 617
She will be glad at last to *w* my crown.   *The Cup* I iii 168
and *w* it Beside him on his throne.   „   II 136
The diamonds that you never deign'd to *w*.   *The Falcon* 762
I *w* it next my heart.   *Prom. of May* II 81
Will you have it?   Will you *w* it?   *Foresters* I i 302
And take and *w* this symbol of your love;   „   III 79

Weär   and I thinks ye *w's* a Lunnon boot.   *Prom. of May* I 461

Wearest   Why *w* thou thy cowl to hide thy face?   *Foresters* I ii 206

Wearied   I am an old man *w* with my journey,   *Queen Mary* III ii 127
King hath *w* of his barren bride.'   „   III vi 140
Thou art *w* out With this day's work,   *Becket* I i 6
Our Senate, *w* of their tetrarchies,   *The Cup* I i 89

Wearier   Yours must have been a *w*.   „   I ii 41

Wearing   So royal that the Queen forbad you *w* it.   *Queen Mary* I v 77

Weary   So *w* am I of this wet land of theirs,   „   III vi 105
I am *w*—go; make me not wroth with thee!   *Harold* v i 31
I have had a *w* day in watching you.   *The Cup* I ii 40
O Love and Life, how *w* am I,   *Prom. of May* III 205
but, my flower, You look so *w* and worn!   „   III 499
But I am *w* pacing thro' the wood.   *Foresters* II i 129
I am *w*. What's here?   „   II ii 92
W—*w* As tho' a spell were on me.   „   II ii 114

Weasel   stick to tha like a *w* to a rabbit, I will.   *Prom. of May* II 739

Weasel-sucked   or the shambles-oak, or a *w-s* egg,   *Foresters* IV 212

Weather   Two young lovers in winter *w*,   *Harold* III ii 3
you couldn't have more splendid *w*.   *Prom. of May* II 48
The *w's* well anew, but the glass be a bit shaäky.   „   II 51
the winders brokken, and the *w* sa cowd,   „   II 73

Weather'd   Many points *w*, many perilous ones,   *Queen Mary* v v 211

Weave   the web That may confound thee yet.   *Harold* I i 211

Weaver   the psalm-singing *w's*, cobblers, scum—   *Queen Mary* III iv 290

Web   weave the *w* That may confound thee yet.   *Harold* I i 211
Crost and recrost, a venomous spider's *w*—   *Becket* II i 200

Wed   ' Thou shalt not *w* thy brother's wife.'   *Queen Mary* I ii 63
Prince of Spain coming to *w* our Queen !   „   I iii 83
that after all She means to you.   „   I iv 89
great party in the state Wills me to *w* her.   „   I iv 93
as great a party in the state Will you to *w* me?   „   I iv 96
—for to *w* with Spain Would treble England—   „   I v 75
No new news that Philip comes to *w* Mary,   „   II i 16
Philip shall not *w* Mary;   „   II i 164
They would not have me *w* the Prince of Spain ;   „   II ii 148
that the son Being a King, might *w* a Queen—   „   III i 75
' It is the King's wish, that you should *w* Prince
   Philibert of Savoy.   „   III v 222
when I came to *w* your majesty, Lord Howard,   „   v i 56
as you know, We meant to *w* her;   „   v i 248
Why then, thou must not *w* him.   *Harold* III i 265
They say thou art to *w* the Lady Aldwyth.   „   III ii 107
The sovereign of Galatia *w's* his Queen.   *The Cup* II 432
if a gentleman Should *w* a farmer's daughter,   *Prom. of May* III 579
And these shall *w* with freemen,   *Foresters* II i 21
Rather than that would *w* her with the Sheriff.   „   II i 524
In that great heat to *w* her to the Sheriff   „   II i 584
till thou *w* what man thou wilt.   „   II ii 15
' This boy will never *w* the maid he loves,   „   II ii 111
You shall *w* your Marian. She is true, and you are
   true,   „   II ii 193
Then you will *w* the Sheriff?   „   III 11
For so this maid would *w* our brother,   „   IV 483

Wed (continued) He shall *w* thee : The land shall still be mine. Child, thou shalt *w* him, Or thine old father will go mad— *Foresters* IV 642

But thou wilt *w* him ?   "   IV 663

Wedded Were I in Devon with my *w* bride, *Queen Mary* I iv 119

when I was *w* to the realm And the realm's laws   "   II ii 164

I would she could have *w* that poor youth,   "   v ii 475

God bless thee, *w* daughter. *Harold* III i 293

I am seeking one who *w* me in secret.   "   v ii 29

How dost thou know I am not *w* to her? *Becket, Pro.* 73

Madam, you do ill to scorn *w* love.   "   Pro. 354

W ? *Rosamund.* Father !   "   i 318

I that *w* Henry, Honouring his manhood—   "   IV ii 419

I be wife to one That only *w* me for Aquitaine ?   "   v i 121

Dost thou remember when I *w* Sinnatus ? *The Cup* II 194

Wedding wines Of *w* had been dash'd into the cups Of victory, *Harold* IV iii 7

You are an honest pair. I will come to your *w*. *Prom. of May* III 115

Wedding-daäy (day) niver touched a drop of owt till my oän *w-d*,   "   I 362

Wedlock I am not so set on *w* as to choose *Queen Mary* II ii 214

Weed (*See also* **Shore-weed**) But on the heretic dunghill only *w's*.   "   IV i 180

Such *w's* make dunghills gracious.   "   IV i 181

plow Lay rusting in the furrow's yellow *w's*, *Becket* I iii 355

like a barren shore That grew salt *w's*, *The Cup* II 232

Such rampant *w's* Strangle each other, *Prom. of May* III 590

Week Sick for an idle *w* of hawk and hound *Harold* I i 103

Nay, rest a *w* or two,   "   II ii 179

I ha' been but a *w* here and I ha' seen *Becket* III i 108

What day of the *w* ? Tuesday ?   "   III i 281

Only last *w* at Littlechester, drove me *Prom. of May* II 404

That John last *w* return'd to Nottingham, *Foresters* III 147

Why then a *w*. *Justiciary.* No, not an hour: "   IV 446

Weep *W* not, good Thirlby. *Queen Mary* IV ii 172

Who would not *w* ?   "   IV 175

Behold him, brethren : he hath cause to *w* !—So have we all : *w* with him if ye will, Yet——   "   IV iii 14

They can but *w* in silence.   "   IV iii 361

I could *w* for them And her, and mine own self   "   v ii 11

And *w's* herself into the place of power ; *Becket* v ii 214

Weeping she is *w* now ; For the wrong Robin took her *Queen Mary* IV v 262

My girl, thou hast been *w* : *Harold* III ii 38

I was *w* for him ; He gave me his hand : *The Falcon* 834

How gracefully there she stands *W*— *Prom. of May* I 736

Since I left her Here *w*, I have ranged the world,   "   II 252

She gave a *w* kiss to the Earl, (repeat) *Foresters* I 20, 119

Weigh the cause that *w's* Upon my conscience *Queen Mary* IV iii 237

Which *w's* even on me. *Becket* III i 42

Weight (s) Will shift the yoke and *w* of all the world *Queen Mary* III vi 212

lighten'd for me The *w* of this poor crown, *Harold* I i 218

Charged with the *w* of heaven wherefrom they fall !   "   v i 567

dead man's dying wish should be of *w*. *Becket, Pro.* 423

till the *w* of Germany or the gold of England brings one of them down to the dust—   "   II ii 363

I reel beneath the *w* of utter joy— *The Cup* II 450

but that I am a man of *w*, and the *w* of the church to boot *Foresters* I ii 57

doth not the *w* of the flesh at odd times overbalance the *w* of the church,   "   I ii 60

Thou art worth thy *w* in all those marks of gold, Yea, and the *w* of the very land   "   IV 1023

Weight (verb) And *w* down all free choice beneath the throne. *Becket* I iii 118

Weightier Is *w* than a thousand marks in gold. *Foresters* IV 660

Weird if yon *w* sign Not blast us in our dreams.— *Harold* I i 120

Welcome (adj.) Thou art ever *w*, Simon Renard. *Queen Mary* I v 345

To whom the fire were *w*,   "   IV iii 438

but all on 'em *w*, all on 'em *w* ; *Prom. of May* I 450

You are *w*, though I fear you be of those *Foresters* I ii 197

Let me be, I say ! The Sheriff will be *w* !   "   IV 602

Welcome (inter.) *W* to England ! *Queen Mary* v iii 13

W to this poor cottage, my dear lady. *The Falcon* 270

Welcome (s) And *w* turns a cottage to a palace. *The Falcon* 272

Will bid you *w*, and will listen to you. *Prom. of May* II 522

Welcome (s) (continued) and there's for you—and the old woman's *w*. *Foresters* II i 290

Welcome (verb) let us *w* him, Love that can lift up *Becket* II i 13

My masters, *w* gallant Walter Lea. *Foresters* IV 1002

Weld he would *w* France, England, Scotland, *Queen Mary* v i 136

Welfare Believe it will be better for your *w*.   "   I iv 254

be curious About the *w* of their babes, *The Cup* I ii 362

Well (adj. and adv.) God send her *w* ; Here comes her Royal Grace. *Queen Mary* II ii 125

Now what I am ye know right *w*—your Queen ;   "   II ii 162

But all is *w* ; 'twas ev'n the will of God,   "   III ii 77

Can we not have the Catholic church as *w* Without as with the Italian ?   "   III iii 98

Philip, can that be *w* ?   "   v i 143

Thou knowest never woman meant so *w*,   "   v i 343

I trust your Grace is *w*.   "   v ii 551

I am not *w*, but it will better me,   "   v ii 553

All is *w* then ; rest—I will to rest ; he said, I must have rest.   "   v v 185

a Boleyn, too, Glancing across the Tudor—not so *w*.   "   v v 228

And it is *w* with me, tho' some of you Have scorn'd me *Harold* I i 187

w, *w*—a dream—no more !   "   I ii 92

Ay—*w*—of old. I tell thee what, my child ;   "   I ii 96

And it were *w*, if thou shouldst let him feel,   "   II ii 15

And *w* for thee and England—and for her—   "   III ii 111

Tho' we have pierced thro' all her practices ; And that is *w*.   "   v i 157

That is *w*. The Norman, What is he doing ?   "   v i 217

W ? *Fitzurse.* Nay, let me pass, my lord, for I must know. *Becket* I i 204

an' it 'ud be *w* for me in the end,   "   III i 134

W—*w*—away.   "   III ii 54

I mean to marry him—if that be *w*. *The Cup* I 62

Great Artemis ! O Camma, can it be *w*,   "   II 81

' Get the Count to give me his falcon, And that will make me *w*.' *The Falcon* 243

when he came last year To see me hawking, he was *w* enough: "   313

It might have been as *w* for me.   "   386

Here, or else *w* in Heaven, where all is *w*.   "   682

He gave me his hand : ' I should be *w* again If the good Count would give me——'   "   836

As *w* as ever. I came back to keep his birthday. *Prom. of May* I 73

The weather's *w* anew, but the glass be a bit shaäky.   "   II 51

Eh, but I be *w* to do ;   "   II 72

Courage, courage ! and all will go *w*.   "   III 215

Crown thee with flowers ; and he will soon be *w* : All will be *w*. *Foresters* II ii 20

Then all is *w*. In this full tide of love, Wave heralds wave :   "   IV 1042

Strike up a stave, my masters, all is *w*.   "   IV 1102

Well (s) The *w's* of Castaly are not wasted upon the desert. *Becket, Pro.* 387

this bitter world again—These *w's* of Marah.   "   v ii 82

We are almost at the bottom of the *w* : *Prom. of May* III 161

She lay so long at the bottom of her *w* *Foresters* IV 242

Well-beloved God bless our *w-b* Robin, Earl of Huntingdon.   "   I i 248

Wells Deans Of Christchurch, Durham, Exeter, and *W*— *Queen Mary* I i 10

Well-served I am *w-s*, and am in everything   "   v iii 24

Well-shaped I am as *w-s* as my lady here, *Becket* III i 150

Well to do but I be *w t d* ; and if ye would nobbut hev me, *Prom. of May* II 72

Welsh had I been his, I had been all *W*. *Aldwyth.* Oh, ay—all *W*—and yet I saw thee drive him up his hills— *Harold* IV i 209

   "   II ii 397

Welshman Your *W* says, ' The Truth against the World,' *Queen Mary* IV ii 261

Wench But the *w* Hath her own troubles ; *Becket* I iv 159

Then there isn't a goodly *w* to serve him with it :   "   III i 126

gave me a great pat o' the cheek for a pretty *w*, *Queen Mary* I iii 99

Went My mother said, Go up ; and up I *w*.   "   II ii 26

who *w* with your train bands To fight with Wyatt,   "   III v 166

gray rogue, Gardiner, *W* on his knees,   "   III v 198

all boots were ever made Since man *w* barefoot. *Harold* I i 131

These meteors came and *w* before our day,   "   I i 334

wouldst thou that it *w* aught else than well ?

Went (*continued*) I would it *w* as well as with mine earldom,   *Harold* I i 336
An evil dream that ever came and *w*—   ,,   I ii 70
thine host in England when I *w* To visit Edward.   ,,   II ii 5
Your comet came and *w*.   ,,   III i 359
w abroad Thro' all my counties,   *Becket* I iii 362
due to those That *w* before us for their work,   ,,   II ii 192
those Who *w* before us did not wholly clear   ,,   II ii 202
lost her and *w* on and on till I found the light and the lady,   ,,   IV ii 18
besides the wind *W* with *my* arrow.   *The Cup* I ii 32
It be five year sin' ye *w* afoot to him,   *Prom. of May* II 5
I sank so low that I *w* into service—   ,,   III 391
an' one on 'em *w* an' lost hersen i' the river.   ,,   III 456
As happy as any of those that *w* before.   *Foresters* II 129
Wept then all *w* but she, Who changed not colour   *Queen Mary* III i 397
That heaven *w* and earth blush'd.   ,,   III iv 193
under no ceiling but the cloud that *w* on them,   ,,   V v 40
Wessex (adj.) Our *W* dragon flies beyond the Humber,   *Harold* IV i 3
Wessex (s) (**kingdom of the West Saxons**) Harold, Earl of *W* !   ,,   II i 82
Art thou not Earl of *W* ?   ,,   II i 85
Were such murderous liars In *W*—   ,,   II i 95
West (adj.) we fun' 'im out a-walkin' i' *W* Field wi' a white 'at,   *Prom. of May* III 135
Yet Thou art but a *W* Saxon: *we* are Danes !   *Harold* IV i 53
West (s) (*See also* **South-west**) Tho' charged with all the wet of all the *w*.   ,,   II ii 189
who know His prowess in the mountains of the *W*,   ,,   IV i 165
To leave the Pope dominion in the *W*. He gave him all the kingdoms of the *W*.   ,,   V i 23
Whose doings are a horror to the east, A hissing in the *w* !'   *Becket* IV ii 245
marvell'd at Our unfamiliar beauties of the *w*;   ,,   IV ii 303
In our poor *w* We cannot do it so well.   ,,   IV ii 316
Westminster (**abbey and city**) Where is the charter of our *W* ?   *Harold* III i 194
Seeing he must to *W* and crown Young Henry   *Becket* III ii 9
Westminster (**Bishop**) Bishops—York, London, Chichester, *W*—   ,,   I iii 386
West Saxon Thou art but a *W S*: *we* are Danes !   *Harold* IV i 53
Wet (adj.) it would seem this people Care more for our brief life in their *w* land,   *Queen Mary* III vi 62
So weary am I of this *w* land of theirs,   ,,   III vi 105
Will my faggots Be *w* as his were ?   ,,   IV ii 229
Wet (s) Eh, the wind and the *w* !   ,,   IV iii 467
barrin' the *w*, Hodge 'ud ha' been a-harrowin'   ,,   IV iii 491
W, famine, ague, fever, storm, wreck, wrath,—   ,,   V v 108
Tho' charged with all the *w* of all the west.   *Harold* II ii 188
Whale Rolf, what fish did swallow Jonah ? *Rolf.* A *w* ! *Fisherman.* Then a *w* to a whelk we have swallowed the King of England.   ,,   II i 43
Wharf swirling under me in the lamplight, by the rotten *w*'s—   *Prom. of May* III 371
Wharton (**Lady Anne**) *See* **Anne, Anne Wharton**
Wheat garner the *w*, And burn the tares   *Queen Mary* V v 113
Wheedle I could not force or *w* to my will.   *The Cup* I iii 167
Wheedled Has *w* it off the King's neck to her own.   *Becket* IV iii 201
Wheedling It was a *w* monk Set up the mass.   *Queen Mary* I ii 90
Wheel (s) The *w* of Fate has roll'd me to the top.   *The Cup* II 221
There was a song he made to the turning *w*—   *Foresters* I iii 154
Wheel (verb) and howsoe'er Thy quarry wind and *w*,   *The Falcon* 12
Whelk whale to a *w* we have swallowed the King of England.   *Harold* II i 44
Whelmest corpse thou *w* with thine earth is cursed,   ,,   V i 67
When When did I hear aught but this ' *W* ' from thee ?   ,,   I i 284
Whew He swears by the Rood. *W* !   *Queen Mary* I i 63
Whine never *w* Like that poor heart, Northumberland,   ,,   II ii 332
Whined The man had children, and he *w* for those.   ,,   II ii 336
Whinnied colt winced and *w* and flung up her heels ;   *Becket, Pro.* 515
Whipping doth not the living skin thicken against perpetual *w*'s ?   ,,   III iii 317
Whipt for doing that His father *w* him into doing—   *Queen Mary* I v 63
I hope they *w* him. I would have hang'd him.   *Becket, Pro.* 15
I am like a boy now going to be *w*;   *Foresters* II i 50
Whirl in the *w* of change may come to be one.   *Queen Mary* I iii 106
Whirring What is that *w* sound ? (repeat)   *Harold* V i 482, 665

Whisking And *w* round a corner, show'd his back   *Queen Mary* II i 131
Whisper (s) voice Against them is a *w* to the roar   ,,   IV ii 187
The secret *w* of the Holy Father.   *Becket* I iii 236
Indungeon'd from one *w* of the wind,   ,,   IV ii 146
Thro' all closed doors a dreadful *w* crept   ,,   V ii 88
Whisper (verb) *W* ! God's angels only know it. Ha !   *Harold* V ii 31
You never *w* close as lovers do,   *Foresters* III 5
Will *w* evermore of Robin Hood.   ,,   IV 1069
Whisper'd *W* me, if I loved him, not to yield   *Queen Mary* I ii 35
w, 'Wyatt,' And whisking round a corner,   ,,   II i 129
Rose hand in hand, and *w*, 'come away !   ,,   III v 148
I *w*, Let me crown you Queen of Beauty,   *The Falcon* 360
Whispering *W*—leagued together To bar me   *Queen Mary* I iv 139
Lord Devon, girls ! what are you *w* here ?   ,,   V ii 485
year to come *W* 'it will be happier,'   *Foresters* III 5
Whistle La, to *w* out my life,   *Queen Mary* II iv 109
I *w* to the bird has broken cage, And all in vain.   ,,   V v 19
Arrows *w* all about.   *Foresters* II ii 165
White (*See also* **Maiden-white**) for thou art as *w* as three Christmasses.   *Queen Mary* I i 30
because they know him The last *W* Rose, the last Plantagenet   ,,   I iv 207
All red and *w*, the fashion of our land.   ,,   I v 10
but took To the English red and *w*.   ,,   I v 18
another, mute as death, And *w* as her own milk ;   ,,   II ii 80
there is ordnance On the *W* Tower and on the Devil's Tower,   ,,   II iii 44
or you'll make the *W* Tower a black 'un for us this blessed day.   ,,   II iii 100
w satin his trunkhose, Inwrought with silver,—   ,,   III i 76
Bagenhall, I see The Tudor green and *w*.   ,,   III i 180
Mary rubb'd out pale—She could not make it *w*—   ,,   III i 424
and your flocks of swans, As fair and *w* as angels ;   ,,   III ii 16
So after that when she once more is seen *W* as the light,   ,,   III iv 199
The colours of our Queen are green and *w*,   ,,   III v 6
Hodge 'ud ha' been a-harrowin' o' *w* peasen i' the outfield   ,,   IV iii 492
Charged him to do it—he is *w* as death.   ,,   IV iii 558
and all in *w*, His long *w* beard, which he had never shaven   ,,   IV iii 591
Choose therefore whether thou wilt have thy conscience *W* as a maiden's hand,   *Harold* II ii 284
My lord ! thou art *w* as death.   ,,   II ii 813
Am I so *w* ? Thy Duke will seem the darker. Hence, I follow.   ,,   II ii 816
They love the *w* rose of virginity, The cold, *w* lily blowing in her cell :   ,,   III i 273
For England, for thy poor *w* dove, who flutters Between thee and the porch,   ,,   IV i 325
In cold, *w* cells beneath an icy moon—   ,,   V i 325
A doter on *w* pheasant-flesh at feasts,   *Becket, Pro.* 97
Is black and *w* at once, and comes to nought.   ,,   I iii 32
We can make a black sin *w*.   ,,   I iv 169
That he made the black sheep *w*.   ,,   I iv 176
w In the sweet moon as with a lovelier snow !   *The Cup* I ii 395
See, see, my *w* bird stepping toward the snare.   ,,   I iii 35
No matter ! see your cloth be *w* as snow !   *The Falcon* 498
W ? I warrant thee, my son, as the snow yonder on the very tip-top o' the mountain.   ,,   500
And yet to speak *w* truth, my good old mother,   ,,   503
The hen cluckt late by the *w* farm gate,   *Prom. of May* I 38
Why, now, what maäkes tha sa *w* ?   ,,   I 417
Wi' the wild *w* rose, an' the woodbine sa gaäy,   ,,   II 174
And the *w* cloud is roll'd along the sky !   *Foresters* II ii 319
I found this *w* doe wandering thro' the wood,   ,,   II i 95
Ghost ! did one in *w* pass ?   ,,   II i 228
thy father will not grace our feast With his *w* beard to-day.   ,,   IV 81
White (**Sir Thomas**) *See* **Thomas White**
White Rose The last *W R*, the last Plantagenet   *Queen Mary* I iv 207
Whitethorn There's *w*, girl.   ,,   III v 9
Whitewash you could *w* that cottage of yours   *Prom. of May* III 43
Whizzing Will hear our arrows *w* overhead,   *Foresters* IV 1090
Whoä (**stop**) Gee oop ! *w* ! Gee oop ! *w* ! (repeat)   *Prom. of May* II 307, 317

Whole   Why, such a game, sir, were *w* years a playing. *Queen Mary* I iii 140
To guard and keep you *w* and safe from all The
spoil   ,,   II ii 246
Presenting the *w* body of this realm Of England,   ,,   III iii 116
and we cannot burn *w* towns; they are many,   ,,   III iv 175
Lest your *w* body should madden with the poison?   ,,   III iv 207
And not like thine To gorge a heretic *w*, roasted
or raw.   ,,   III iv 344
' what am I, Cranmer, against *w* ages? '   ,,   IV ii 104
Of this be sure, he is *w* worlds away.   ,,   IV iii 194
I were *w* devil if I wrong'd you, Madam.   *Harold* I ii 17
Love will stay for a *w* life long.   *Harold* I ii 17
but ours are *w*; I have but bark'd my hands.   ,,   II i 4
' Love for a *w* life long ' When was that sung?   ,,   III ii 88
Go round once more; See all be sound and *w*.   ,,   v i 194
Sire, the business Of thy *w* kingdom waits me: *Becket, Pro.* 278
And goodly acres—we will make her *w*;   ,,   I i 164
O rare, a *w* long day of open field.   ,,   I i 296
and the moon Divides the *w* long street with light and
shade.   ,,   I i 365
Cannot a smooth tongue lick him *w* again To serve
your will?   ,,   II ii 25
And as for the flesh at table, a *w* Peter's sheet,   ,,   III iii 129
The soldier, when he lets his *w* self go Lost in the
common good,   ,,   v ii 39
and send Her *w* heart's heat into it,   ,,   v ii 255
The Pope, the King, will curse you—the *w* world
Abhor you;   ,,   v iii 183
violated the *w* Tradition of our land,   *Prom. of May* I 495
We shall have to sell all the land, which Father,
for a *w* life, has been getting together,   ,,   III 165
Canst thou endure to be a beggar whose *w* life hath
been folded like a blossom in the sheath,   *Foresters* I i 205
I would ha' given my *w* body to the King had he
asked for it,   ,,   II i 306

Wholesome   yet I found One day, a *w* scripture,   *Queen Mary* IV ii 84
If thou canst make a *w* use of these   *Harold* III i 20
the *w* plow Lay rusting in the furrow's yellow weeds,   *Becket* I iii 354
I came on certain *w* usages,   ,,   I iii 412
Because I have a *w* medicine here Puts that belief
asleep.   ,,   IV ii 50

Wholly   not for myself—For England—yet not *w*—   *Harold* v i 307
Only that the rift he made May close between us, here
I am *w* king,   *Becket* II ii 132
those Who went before us did not *w* clear The deadly
growths of earth,   ,,   II ii 202

Wholly-hopeless   submit at once Is better than a *w-h*
war,   *The Cup* II i 141

Whoop   Bee musn't buzz, *W*—but he knows. (repeat)   *Becket* III i 99, 241
Grasshopper, grasshopper, *W*—you can hear.   ,,   III i 103
Bird mustn't tell, *W*—he can see. (repeat)   ,,   III i 107, 256
W—but he knows, *W*—but he knows.   ,,   III i 262

Whose   *W* play is all to find herself a King.   *Queen Mary* I iii 164
but of this England, in *w* crown our Kent is the
fairest jewel.   ,,   II i 163
One, *w* bolts, That jail you from free life,   ,,   III v 171
Deserts?   Amen to what?   *W* deserts?   Yours?   ,,   v iv 31

Whoy (why)   *W*, O lor, Miss! that wur sa long back,   *Prom. of May* III 70

Wicked   Nay swears, it was no *w* wilfulness, Only a
natural chance.   *Queen Mary* III v 72
A chance—perchance One of those *w* wilfuls that
men make,   ,,   III v 75
W sea-will-o'-the-wisp!   Wolf of the shore!   *Harold* II i 20
The *w* sister clapt her hands and laugh'd;   ,,   III ii 48
But all that sounds so *w* and so strange;   *Prom. of May* I 656

Wickedness   His *w* is like my wretchedness—   ,,   III 747

Wickentree   if I hadn't a sprig o' *w* sewn into my dress,   *Foresters* II i 250

Wide   cry To have the gates set *w* again,   *Queen Mary* II iv 65
They are the flower of England; set the gates *w*.   ,,   II iv 70
W of the mark ev'n for a madman's dream.   ,,   v iii 81
O God, that I were in some *w*, waste field   *Harold* II ii 777
Fling *w* the doors and let the new-made children   *The Cup* II 163
Richer than all the *w* world-wealth of May,   *The Falcon* 466

Wider   But stretch it *w*; say when England fell.   *Queen Mary* III iii 261

Wide-spread   Into the *w-s* arms of fealty,   ,,   II ii 264

Widow   (*See also* **Wife-widow**)   a *w* And orphan child,
whom one of thy wild barons—   *Becket, Pro.* 187
Who stole the *w's* one sitting hen o' Sunday,   ,,   I iv 120
The stately *w* has no heart for me.   *The Falcon* 30
Prettier than that same *w* which you wot of.   *Foresters* III 268
Shamed a too trustful *w* whom you heard In her
confession;   ,,   III 385
All *w's* we have holpen pray for us,   ,,   IV 1078

Widow'd   Back thro' their *w* channel here,   *Queen Mary* I v 89

Wield   And Loathing *w* a Saxon battle-axe—   *Harold* v i 414
w's His war-club, dashes it on Gurth,   ,,   v i 639

Wife   (*See also* **Country-wives, Heart-wife, Maiden-wife**)
was born of a true man and a ring'd *w*,   *Queen Mary* I i 55
' Thou shalt not wed thy brother's *w*.'   ,,   I ii 63
And scared the gray old porter and his *w*.   ,,   II iii 16
Your Grace hath a most chaste and loving *w*.   ,,   III vi 130
parting of a husband and a *w* Is like the cleaving of a
heart;   ,,   III vi 195
so my Queen Would leave me—as—my *w*.   ,,   v i 252
Might I not say—to please your *w*, the Queen?   ,,   v i 307
and cleave unto each other As man and *w*?   ,,   v ii 139
Unhappiest Of Queens and *wives* and women!   ,,   v ii 408
That his own *w* is no affair of his.   ,,   v ii 561
They say, his *w* was knowing and abetting. *Harold*.
They say, his *w*!—To marry and have no husband
Makes the *w* fool.   *Harold* II ii 306
And that my *w* descends from Alfred?   ,,   II ii 594
a *w*, What matters who, so she be serviceable   ,,   II i 290
Yea, am I not thy *w*?   ,,   IV iii 41
No, but a shoal of *wives* upon the heath,   ,,   v i 146
We have parted from our *w* without reproach,   ,,   v i 154
devil Hath haunted me—mine oath—my *w*—   ,,   v i 318
being the true *w* Of this dead King,   ,,   v ii 84
Ay, and what art thou?   *Edith*.   His *w*!   ,,   v ii 90
Some held she was his *w* in secret—   ,,   v ii 100
I am his *w*! and she—For look,   ,,   v ii 106
Thy *w* am I for ever and evermore.   ,,   v ii 118
it seems Was false to his own *w*.   ,,   v ii 152
Who calls me? she That was my *w*,   *Becket* II ii 75
and pray God she prove True *w* to you.   ,,   II ii 79
convene This conference but to babble of our *wives*?   ,,   II ii 90
whom you call—fancy—my husband's brother's *w*.   ,,   III i 202
whom it pleases him To call his *wives*;   ,,   IV ii 37
talk'd him out of His ten *wives* into me.   ,,   IV ii 313
You were but Aquitaine to Louis—no *w*; You are only
Aquitaine to me—no *w*.   ,,   v i 117
I be to one That only wedded me for Aquitaine? Yet
this no *w*—   ,,   v i 120
this no *w* has born you four brave sons,   ,,   v i 125
I am true *w*, and have my fears Lest Becket   ,,   v i 157
for of your *wives* you shall Find one a slut   ,,   v ii 201
' To the admired Camma, *w* of Sinnatus, the Tetrarch,   *The Cup* I i 36
and this cup to Camma, The *w* of Sinnatus.   ,,   I i 63
I send it to the *w* of Sinnatus,   ,,   I i 72
Well spoken, *w*. *Synorix*.   Madam, so well I yield.   ,,   I ii 171
—did Dishonour to our *wives*.   ,,   I ii 184
be willing *wives* enough To feel dishonour, honour.   ,,   I ii 187
I know of no such *wives* in all Galatia.   ,,   I ii 191
What follows is for no *w's* eyes.   ,,   I ii 231
What *should* he say, my *w*!   ,,   I ii 348
welfare of their babes, their *wives*, O ay—their *wives*—
their *wives*.   ,,   I ii 363
He should say nothing to my *w* if I Were by   ,,   I ii 366
if she be a true and loving *w* She may,   ,,   I ii 32
will he ever be of one faith with his *w*?   *Prom. of May* III 178
But lack of happiness in a blatant *w*.   *Foresters* I iii 132
There are no *wives* like English *wives*   ,,   II i 15
An outlaw's bride may not be *w* in law.   ,,   II i 90
Robin, I do, but I have a bad *w*.   ,,   III 70
Thou art more my *w* so feeling, than if my *w*   ,,   III 123
Here comes a citizen, and I think his *w*.   ,,   III 228
dear *w*, we have fallen into the hands Of Robin Hood.   ,,   III 232
no man, so His own true *w* came with him,   ,,   III 240
Curtsey to him, *w*, and thank him.   ,,   III 248
Away, away, *w*, wilt thou anger him?   ,,   III 254

Wife (*continued*)   they put it upon me because I have a
    bad w.   *Foresters* III 438
   then each man That owns a w or daughter,   ,,   III 460
   dishonour The daughters and the *wives* of your own
    faction—   ,,   IV 698
Wife-like   So w-l humble to the trivial boy Mismatch'd
    with her for policy !   *Queen Mary* III i 364
Wife-widow   Left Mary a w-w here alone,   ,,   III i 462
Wild   and will pounce like a w beast out of his cage to
    worry Cranmer.   ,,   I i 88
   You are w; what headache ?   ,,   I iv 147
   like the w hedge-rose Of a soft winter, possible,   ,,   III vi 14
   Catch the w cat, cage him, and when he springs   ,,   v v 65
   letting the w brook Speak for us—   ,,   v v 90
   Thou knowest I soon go w.   *Harold* I i 297
   Come, come ! as yet thou art not gone so w   ,,   I i 299
   Nor thou be a w thing Out of the waste,   ,,   I i 380
   Our w Tostig, Edward hath made him Earl: he would
    be king:—   ,,   I ii 185
   W as he, born so :   ,,   IV i 110
   The nimble, w, red, wiry, savage king—   ,,   IV i 197
   Save for thy w and violent will that wrench'd All hearts   ,,   v i 277
   I lost it, playing with it when I was w.   ,,   v ii 110
   a widow And orphan child, whom one of thy w
    barons—   *Becket, Pro.* 188
   Thomas, thou wast not happy taking charge Of this w
    Rosamund to please the King,   ,,   I i 392
   This w one—nay, I shall not prick myself—   ,,   II i 143
   And I could tear him asunder with w horses Before he
    would betray it.   ,,   II i 267
   Like the w beast—if you can call it love.   ,,   IV ii 121
   Nay, for who could trace a hand So w and staggering ?   *The Falcon* 439
   Wi' the w white rose, an' the woodbine sa gaäy,   *Prom. of May* II 174
   if you Had seen us that w morning when we found
    Her bed unslept in,   ,,   II 469
   That were a w justice indeed.   ,,   III 156
   Knave, there is a lot of w fellows in Sherwood Forest   *Foresters* I i 72
   They hold by Richard—the w wood !   ,,   I iii 111
   the highback'd polecat, the w boar, The burrowing
    badger—By St. Nicholas I have a sudden passion
    for the w wood—We shall be free as air in the w
    wood—   ,,   I iii 120
   I have reign'd one year in the w wood.   ,,   II i 36
   Tut ! tut ! the scream of some w woodland thing.   ,,   II i 253
   Here's a pot o' w honey from an old oak,   ,,   II i 295
   might Betray me to the w Prince.   ,,   II i 708
   loud enough To fright the w hawk passing overhead,   ,,   III 318
   Venison, and w boar, hare, geese, besides Hedge-pigs,   ,,   IV 191
   and they are delivered here in the w wood an hour
    after noon.   ,,   IV 509
   Were some strong fellow here in the w wood,   ,,   IV 515
   When the Church and the law have forgotten God's
    music, they shall dance to the music of the w wood.   ,,   IV 556
   Then will I live for ever in the w wood.   ,,   IV 879
   We dealt in the w justice of the woods.   ,,   IV 1072
Wild-beast   The mere w-b ! *Dobson.* Out o' the
    chaumber,   *Prom. of May* III 736
Wilderness   Lost in a w where none can hear !   *Queen Mary* v 382
   pray for him who hath fed you in the w.   *Becket* I iv 267
Wildest   The w of the random youth of Florence   *The Falcon* 808
Wild-flower   My bank Of w-f's. At thy feet !   *Becket* II i 126
Wild-fowl   we came upon A w-f sitting on her nest,   ,,   v ii 234
Wilful   One of those wicked w's that men make,   *Queen Mary* III v 75
   W, w.   Go—the Saints Pilot   *Harold* I i 263
Wilfulness   was no wicked w, Only a natural chance.   *Queen Mary* III v 72
Will (s)   (*See also* **Free-will**)   putting by his father's w.   ,,   I ii 28
   Few things have fail'd to which I set my w.   ,,   II ii 23
   and so learn Your royal w, and do it.   ,,   II ii 139
   seeks To bend the laws to his own w,   ,,   II ii 184
   Our sovereign Lady by King Harry's w;   ,,   II ii 268
   But all is well; 'twas ev'n the w of God,   ,,   III ii 77
   Your father had a w that beat men down;   ,,   IV i 108
   It is God's w, the Holy Father's w, And Philip's w,   ,,   IV i 184
   Stand there and wait my w.   *Harold* II i 683
   Help us against the Norman ? *Morcar.* With good w;   ,,   IV i 182

Will (s) (*continued*)   Take it not that way—balk not the
    Pope's w.   *Becket* I iii 243
   Is it thy w, My lord Archbishop,   ,,   I iii 271
   it is the w of God To break me,   ,,   I iii 290
   ' False to myself ! It is the w of God !' *Henry.* God's
    w be what it will,   ,,   I iii 328
   The King's w and God's w and justice;   ,,   I iii 420
   The w of God—why, then it is my w—   ,,   I iii 473
   tongue lick him whole again To serve your w? *Henry.*
    He hates my w, not me.   ,,   II ii 26
   since he flouts the w of either realm,   ,,   II ii 256
   My liege, your w and happiness are mine.   ,,   III iii 42
   God's w be done ! (repeat)   ,, v ii 565, 567
   It is God's w. Go on.   ,,   v ii 634
   Why do you force me thus against my w?   ,,   v iii 22
   I could not force or wheedle to my w.   *The Cup* I iii 167
   would oust me from his w, if I Made such a
    marriage.   *Prom. of May* I 513
   There is a fence I cannot overleap, My father's w.   *Foresters* III 10
   For thou hast stolen my w, and made it thine.   ,,   III 329
Will (verb)   Or—if the Lord God w it—on the stake.   *Queen Mary* II i 251
   and use Both us and them according as they w.   ,,   II ii 161
   As you w. *Fitzurse.* Nay, as *you* w. *Becket.* Nay, as
    you w.   *Becket* v ii 306
   I w, I w. And I w not betray you.   *The Cup* I ii 315
   I w, I w. Poor fellow !   *The Falcon* 281
Will'd   Get thou into thy cloister as the king W it:
    were he living And grown to man and Sinnatus   *Harold* v i 310
    w it,   *The Cup* I ii 151
Willer (willow)   Wi' the briar sa green, an' the w sa
    graäy,   *Prom. of May* II 186
William (Lord William Howard)   (*See also* **Howard,**
    William Howard)   News abroad, W ?   *Queen Mary* II i 13
   brave Lord W Thrust him from Ludgate,   ,,   II iv 91
William (the Conqueror)   (*See also* **William the First**)   Fly
    thou to W; tell him we have Harold.   *Harold* II i 110
   W laugh'd and swore that might was right,   ,,   II ii 361
   That had anger'd me Had I been W.   ,,   II ii 387
   may he not make A league with W,   ,,   II ii 461
   I will not hear thee—W comes.   ,,   II ii 480
   W the tanner's bastard !   ,,   II ii 775
   ' If ye side with W Ye are not noble.'   ,,   II ii 788
   when I rode with W down to Harfleur,   ,,   III i 82
   one should be This W's fellow-tricksters;—   ,,   III ii 77
   Against St. Valery And W.   ,,   III ii 137
   but worse news: this W sent to Rome,   ,,   III ii 141
   Keep that for Norman W ! *Thane.* Down with W !   ,,   IV iii 169
   W the Norman, for the wind had changed—   ,,   IV iii 181
   W hath landed, ha?   ,,   IV iii 185
   play The W with thine eyesight and thy tongue.   ,,   v i 27
   —thou art but a messenger of W.   ,,   v i 30
   W's or his own As wind blows, or tide flows :   ,,   v i 162
   hath borne at times A bastard false as W.   ,,   v i 176
   A lake that dips in W As well as Harold.   ,,   v i 186
   a mightier man-in-arms Than W.   ,,   v i 400
   Save W's death or mine.   ,,   v i 427
William (the First)   (*See also* **William the Conqueror**)
    In W's time, in our first Edward's time,   *Queen Mary* III iii 226
   There was no Canterbury in W's time.   *Becket* III iii 200
William Howard (Lord, Lord High Admiral)   (*See also*
    Howard, William)   I leave Lord W H in your
    city,   *Queen Mary* II ii 245
   I saw Lord W H By torchlight,   ,,   II iii 28
   Is not Lord W H a true man ?   ,,   III i 165
   Spite of Lord Paget and Lord W H,   ,,   III i 324
   my Lord Paget and Lord W H, Crave,   ,,   IV i 6
   No, here's Lord W H.   ,,   IV iii 288
William of Orange   W o O, William the Silent.   ,,   III i 197
Williams (Lord, of Thame)   Whereat Lord W gave a
    sudden cry:—   ,,   IV iii 604
William the Silent (William of Orange)   William of
    Orange, W t S.   ,,   III ii 198
   W t S They call him—   ,,   III ii 191
Willing   he will be w that you and Father should live
    with us;   *Prom. of May* III 260

Willing (*continued*) there might be *w* wives enough To
  feel dishonour, honour.   *The Cup* I ii 187
Willingly Full *w*, my lord.   *Foresters* I ii 134
Willingness With most exceeding *w*, I will ;   *Queen Mary* III v 214
Will not *See* **Weänt, Wunt**
Willow (*See also* **Willer**) This is the hottest of it: hold,
  ash ! hold, *w* !   *Harold* v 629
  saw the ball you lost in the fork of the great *w*   *Becket* IV ii 58
  you told me a great fib : it wasn't in the *w*.   ,, IV 371
Willow-herb Forget-me-not, meadowsweet, *w-h*.   *Prom. of May* II 299
Willow-wands And wattled thick with ash and *w-w* ;   *Harold* v 190
Wills-o'-the-wisp (*See also* **Wisp**) oafs, ghosts o' the
  mist, *w-o'-t-w* ;   *Foresters* II i 264
Willy-nilly if man be only A *w-n* current of sensations—   *Prom. of May* I 263
  And someone saw thy *w-n* nun Vying a tress   *Harold* v 148
  This other, *w-n*, for his bride.   *Foresters* IV 768
Wilson (a schoolmaster) Well, *W*. I seed that one
  cow o' thine   *Prom. of May* I 190
  summat wrong theer, *W*, fur I doänt understan' it.   ,, I 234
  Why, *W*, tha 'eärd 'im thysen—   ,, I 301
  —what's the newspaäper word, *W* ?—celebrate—   ,, I 320
Win I'm the first of players. I shall *w*.   *Queen Mary* I ii 149
  As if to *w* the man by flattering him.   ,, II ii 312
  W thro' this day with honour to yourself,   ,, IV ii 165
  And, if I *w*, I *w*, and thou art king ;   *Harold* v 157
  To tell thee thou shouldst *w* at Stamford-bridge,   ,, v 236
  and to *w* my own bread,   *Becket* III i 117
  A policy of wise pardon *W's* here as well as there.   *The Cup* I iii 153
  —if I *w* her love, They too will cleave to me,   *The Cup* I iii 153
  his falcon Ev'n *w's* his dinner for him in the field.   *The Falcon* 231
  W me you cannot, murder me you may,   *Foresters* IV 721
Win (reach) Eh, my rheumatizy be that bad how-
  iver be I to *w* to the burnin'.   *Queen Mary* IV iii 474
Winced colt *w* and whinnied and flung up her heels ;   *Becket*, Pro. 515
Winchester a plundering o' Bishop *W's* house ;   *Queen Mary* II iii 73
  same book You wrote against my Lord of *W* ;   ,, IV iii 265
  Henry of *W* ? *Henry*. Him who crown'd Stephen—   *Becket*, Pro. 272
Wind (s) or wave And *w* at their old battle :   *Queen Mary* I v 357
  know that whether A *w* be warm or cold,   ,, I v 620
  Eh, the *w* and the wet !   ,, IV iii 466
  but Dumble wur blow'd wi' the *w*,   ,, IV iii 477
  barrin' the *w*, Dumble wur blow'd wi' the *w*,   ,, IV iii 493
  Proclaim it to the *w's*.   ,, v ii 290
  As few as I may in a *w*,   *Harold* II i 68
  the best, strong-wing'd against the *w*.   ,, II ii 149
  The *w's* so cross and jostle among these towers.   ,, II ii 155
  Breathe the free *w* from off our Saxon downs,   ,, II ii 186
  For happier homeward *w's* than that which crack'd   ,, II ii 198
  But wherefore is the *w*,   ,, II ii 256
  The *w* is fair For England now . . .   ,, II ii 766
  Heard, heard— *Harold*. The *w* in his hair ?   ,, III i 371
  we must fight. How blows the *w* ?   ,, III ii 135
  William the Norman, for the *w* had changed—   ,, IV iii 181
  William's or his own As *w* blows, or tide flows :   ,, v 163
  Winnow and scatter all scruples to the *w*,   *Becket* I i 151
  that one time sway to the current, And to the *w* another.   ,, I i 595
  Is it the *w* of the dawn that I hear   ,, II i 1
  and so of the other *w's* ;   ,, II ii 323
  God and his free *w* grant your lordship a happy home-
  return   ,, III iii 327
  Indungeon'd from one whisper of the *w*,   ,, IV ii 147
  besides the *w* Went with *my* arrow.   *The Cup* I ii 31
  thou that art life to the *w*, to the wave,   ,, II 3
  Thou whose breath Is balmy *w* to robe   ,, II 265
  On my last voyage—but the *w* has fail'd—   ,, II 521
  My far-eyed queen of the *w's*—   *The Falcon* 9
  And a salt *w* burnt the blossoming trees ;   *Prom. of May* I 57
  day's bright blade a friend, but the *w* east like an enemy.   I 79
  He wur sa bellows'd out wi' the *w* this murnin',   ,, III 432
  To break our band and scatter us to the *w's*.   *Foresters* III 454
Wind (verb) and howsoe'er Thy quarry *w* and wheel,   *The Falcon* 12
  if I *w* This forest-horn of mine,   *Foresters* IV 174
Winder (window) and I heärd the *w*—that's the *w* at
  the end o' the passage,   *Prom. of May* I 396
  afoor I coomed up he got thruff the *w* ageän.   ,, I 406

Winder (window) (*continued*) I'll hev the *w* naäiled up,
  and put Towser under it.   *Prom. of May* I 420
  she set the bush by my dairy *w*   ,, II 18
  the walls sa thin, and the *w's* brokken,   ,, III 72
Winding I warrant I worm thro' all their *w's*.   *The Cup* I i 87
  To lead us thro' the *w's* of the wood.   *Foresters* II i 634
  And catch the *w* of a phantom horn.   ,, IV 1091
Window (*See also* **Winder**) Open the *w*, Knyvett ;   *Queen Mary* I i 154
  My *w* look'd upon the corridor ;   ,, v ii 459
  When he we speak of drove the *w* back,   ,, v ii 464
  Got thro' the *w* again ?   *Prom. of May* I 561
  will be placed Beneath the *w*, Philip.   I 561
  Love flew in at the *w*   *Foresters* I i 150
  Wealth dropt out of the *w*,   ,, I i 156
Windsor There yet is time, take boat and pass to *W*.
  Mary. I pass to *W* and I lose my crown.   *Queen Mary* II iv 28
Windy for in our *w* world What's up is faith,   *Harold* I i 83
  Nor mark the sea-bird rouse himself and hover Above
  the *w* ripple,   ,, II ii 336
Wine we may grant the *w*. Old Sir Thomas always
  granted the *w*.   *Queen Mary* II i 41
  and mine old flask of *w* Beside me,   ,, i 47
  So the *w* ran, and there be revelry,   ,, III ii 236
  what an acrid *w* has Luther brew'd,   ,, IV iii 545
  A drinker of black, strong, volcanic *w's*,   ,, iv 94
  Would the *w's* Of wedding had been dash'd   *Harold* IV iii 6
  cannot see the world but thro' their *w's* !   ,, IV iii 226
  Some *w* ! Too much !   ,, v i 203
  amorous Of good old red sound liberal Gascon *w*:   *Becket*, Pro. 101
  A good dish from a bad, new *w* from old. *Henry*.
  Well, who loves *w* loves woman.   ,, Pro. 106
  when the Gascon *w* mounts to my head,   ,, Pro. 113
  I have been a lover of *w's*, and delicate meats,   ,, I i 76
  Go home, and sleep thy *w* off, for thine eyes Glare
  stupid-wild with *w*.   ,, I i 212
  Well—if that isn't goodly *w*—   ,, I iv 157
  that tho' I can drink *w* I cannot bide water,   ,, I iv 220
  The *w* and wealth of all our France are yours ;   ,, II ii 446
  warder of the bower hath given himself Of late to *w*.   ,, III i 32
  his fond excess of *w* Springs from the loneliness   ,, III i 39
  Are braced and brazen'd up with Christmas *w's*   ,, v ii 424
  Plunder'd the vessel full of Gascon *w*,   ,, v ii 441
  —we have eaten—we are heated. *W* !   *The Cup* I ii 46
  red *w* Ran down the marble and lookt like blood,   ,, II 203
  Bring me The costly *w's* we use in marriages.   ,, II 365
  W ! Filippo, *w* ! *Count*. It is but thin and cold,   *The Falcon* 576
  Not quite recover'd of your wound, the *w* Might help
  you.   ,, 591
  thro' the blood the *w* leaps to the brain   *Foresters* I iii 22
  Here, here—a cup of *w*—drink and begone !   ,, I iii 89
  Give me a draught of *w*.   ,, II i 459
  A draught of *w*. *Robin*. Our cellar is hard by.   ,, II i 467
  Take him, good little John, and give him *w*   ,, II i 470
  your good father had his draught of *w*   ,, II ii 2
  Where lies that cask of *w* whereof   ,, III 306
  And thou wouldst run more *w* than blood.   ,, III 338
  the warm *w*, and found it again.   ,, IV 245
Wine-press For thou hast trodden this *w-p* alone.   *Becket* III iii 290
Wing on the deck and spread his *w's* for sail !   *Queen Mary* I v 379
  hardly, save by boat, swimming, or *w's*.   ,, II iii 13
  free *w* The world were all one Araby.   ,, III v 209
  May the great angels join their *w's*,   ,, v iv 6
  Would their *w's* were mine To follow thee   *Harold* I ii 26
  two young *w's* To fly to heaven straight with.   ,, II i 25
  cherubim With twenty-cubit *w's* from wall to wall—   ,, III i 184
  not so with us—No *w's* to come and go.   ,, III ii 99
  let him flap The *w's* that beat down Wales !   ,, IV i 247
  and our battle-axes broken The Raven's *w*,   ,, IV iii 65
  hear him presently with clapt *w* Crow over Barbarossa—   *Becket* II ii 49
  we pray you, draw yourself from under The *w's* of France.   ,, II ii 249
  lark first takes the sunlight on his *w*,   *The Cup* I iii 44
  had you left him the free use of his *w's*,   *Prom. of May* I 653
  would not blur A moth's *w* by the touching ;   ,, II 492
  he flutter'd his *w's* with a sweet little cry,   *Foresters* I i 154
  he flutter'd his *w's* as he gave me the lie,   ,, I i 159

Wing'd (*See also* **Strong-wing'd**) sonnet's a flying ant,
W for a moment. *Queen Mary* II i 85
But w souls flying Beyond all change *Harold* III ii 100
They say that you are wise in w things, *Becket* I i 255

Winging our sea-mew W their only wail ! *Harold* II i 98

Wingless and thus I dumb thee too, my w nightingale ! „ I ii 24

Wink The French King w's at it. *Queen Mary* III i 160
I must not dream, not w, but watch. „ III v 154
Take fees of tyranny, w at sacrilege, *Becket* I ii 394

Winking Priest Sits w at the license of a king, „ I ii 66

Winnow W and scatter all scruples to the wind, „ I i 150

Winsome So w in her grace and gaiety, *Prom. of May* III 754

Winter (adj.) (*See also* **Spring-and-winter**) Tho' all
the world should bay like w wolves, *Queen Mary* II i 361
Our short-lived sun, before his w plunge, „ III ii 86
Two young lovers in w weather, *Harold* III ii 3
They are but of spring, They fly the w change— „ III ii 97
W sunshine ! Beware of opening out thy bosom to it, *Becket* III iii 29
Close to the grating on a w morn *The Falcon* 441

Winter (s) (*See also* **Midwinter**) like the wild hedge-
rose Of a soft w, *Queen Mary* III vi 16
Hath, like a brief and bitter w's day, „ IV iii 430
Were but a sort of w ; „ V iv 16
Her life was w, for her spring was nipt : „ V v 269
And be thy hand as w on the field, *Harold* V i 132
And w again and the snows. *Becket, Pro.* 334
After the nineteen w's of King Stephen— „ I iii 338
Cold after warm, w after summer, „ I iv 64
And in the w I will fire their farms. *Foresters* IV 95
A thousand w's Will strip you bare as death, „ IV 1055

Winter-cataracts Whose w-c find a realm and leave it *The Cup* II 305

Wiry The nimble, wild, red, w, savage king— *Harold* IV i 197

Wisdom Some spice of w in my telling you, *Queen Mary* II iv 134
Best w is to know the worst at once. „ III v 220
bring it Home to the leisure w of his Queen, „ III vi 23
And all his wars and w's past away ; „ V v 56
Fool still ? or w there, *Harold* I i 359
W when in power And wisest, should not „ I i 363
Ay, if W Pair'd with Good. „ I i 177
by thy w Hast kept it firm from shaking ; *Becket, Pro.* 203
And all the w of the Chancellor, „ I i 153
Life yields to death and w bows to Fate, *The Cup* II 89

Wise (*See also* **Stupid-wise**) Statesmen that are w
Shape a necessity, *Queen Mary* III iii 32
Statesmen that are w Take truth herself for model. „ III iii 36
But your w bees that stung him first to death. „ III iii 64
And love should know ; and—be the king so w,— *Harold* I i 277
Ay, ay and w in peace and great in war— „ I i 313
Fool still ? or wisdom there, My w head-shaking Harold ? „ I i 361
Warrior thou art, and mighty w withal ! „ II i 543
And all our just and w and holy men „ III i 209
Fool and w, I fear This curse, and scorn it. „ III ii 67
Make not our Morcar sullen : it is not w. „ IV iii 104
but I am wiser now . . . I am too w . . . „ V i 113
And w, yea truthful, till that blighted vow „ V ii 155
They say that you are w in winged things, *Becket* I i 255
I will be w and wary, not the soldier „ I i 387
Poor man, beside himself—not w. „ II ii 235
Like some w prince of this world from his wars, „ V ii 13
A policy of w pardon Wins here as well as there. „ V ii 22
Camma, W I am sure as she is beautiful, *The Cup* I ii 139
Or good, or w, that you should clasp a hand „ II 82
W ! Life yields to death and wisdom „ II 88
Too late—thought myself w—A woman's dupe. „ II 480
However w, we must at times have wrought Some
great injustice. *Foresters* III 154
Robin's a w man, Richard a wiseacre, „ IV 357

Wiseacre Robin's a wise man, Richard a w, „ IV 357

Wisely Have I done w, then, in accepting him ? *Prom. of May* III 183

Wiser Brother, the king is w than he seems ; *Harold* I i 272
Then Tostig too were w than he seems. „ I i 278
but I am w now . . . I am too wise . . . „ V ii 111
The w choice, because my sleeping-draught *Becket* IV ii 168
Woman again !—but I am w now. *The Cup* I i 169
I say it to you—you are w—Rome knows all, „ I ii 285

Wisest But thou canst hear the best and w of us. *Harold* I i 300
Wisdom when in power And w, „ I i 365
choose A hundred of the w heads from England, *Becket* II ii 171
wisdom bows to Fate, Is w, doing so. *The Cup* II 91

Wish (s) mine own w fulfill'd before the word *Queen Mary* I iv 232
to have the w before the word Is man's „ I iv 238
Your pious w to pay King Edward's debts, „ I v 111
my w Echoes your Majesty's. *Pole.* It shall be so. „ III iii 92
' It is the King's w, that you should wed Prince
Philibert of Savoy. „ III v 221
Mere compliments and w's. „ V ii 596
Amen to all Your w, and further. „ V iv 29
dead man's dying w should be of weight. *Becket, Pro.* 422
To make my marriage prosper to my w ! *The Cup* II 309
smiles, not tears ; Good w's, not reproaches ; *Prom. of May* I 526

Wish (verb) council and all her people w her to
marry. *Queen Mary* I i 113
I must needs w all good things for France. „ I v 309
I w some thunderbolt Would make this Cole a
cinder, „ IV iii 10
I w you a good morning, good Sir Nicholas : „ V i 13
I w her Highness better. „ V ii 615
I w you joy o' the King's brother. *Becket* III i 155
I am sure I w her happy. *Prom. of May* I 478
He w's you to dine along with us, „ I 618
Then you should w us both to love for ever. „ I 642
Do you w it ? *Eva.* Do I w it ? „ I 696
I only w This pool were deep enough, „ II 303
Have you told him I am here ? *Dora.* No ; do
you w it ? „ III 267
make herself anything he w's her to be ? „ III 306
Tell him that I and the lady here w to see him. „ III 415
Might w its rose a lily, „ III 490
I w you and your ladyship's father a most
exceedingly good morning. *Foresters* I i 308
I could w that all the land Were plunged „ IV 666

Wish'd Madam, when the Roman w to reign, *Queen Mary* I v 498
sometime I have w That I were caught, „ III v 162
I w myself the milkmaid singing here, „ III v 256
I had w for any weapon. *Harold* IV iii 19
and she w The Church were king : *Becket* V ii 117
once I w to scourge them to the bones. *The Cup* I i 27
Oh, how often I have w for you ! *Prom. of May* I 769
asking his consent—you w me— „ I 494
I w, if you—— *Dora.* If I—— „ III 776
I w, I hoped To make, to make— „ III 782
I cannot break it, Robin, if I w. *Foresters* IV 328

Wisp (*See also* **Wills-o'-the-wisp**) No, by w and glowworm, no. „ II ii 136

Wit (*See also* **Mother-wit**) The man is able enough—no
lack of w, „ I ii 103

Witan Ay . . . if the W will consent to this. *Harold* II ii 615
Thy voice will lead the W— „ II ii 619

Witch (*See also* **Wood-witch**) But then she was a w. *Queen Mary* IV ii 208
what are you flying from ? *Countryman.* The w !
the w ! *Becket* III ii 20
he'll never out again, the w has got him. „ III ii 26
Kind of the w to give thee warning tho'. „ III ii 29
Here is the w's hut. The fool-people call her a w—a
good w to me ! *Foresters* II i 178
in Nottingham they say There bides a foul w „ II i 203
Half-witted and a w to boot ! „ II i 375
Or learning witchcraft of your woodland w, „ II i 501
he kneels ! he has anger'd the foul w, „ II i 670

Witchcraft Or learning w of your woodland witch, „ II i 500

Witch'd Our woodland Circe that hath w the King ? *Becket* III ii 32

Withdraw we might w Part of our garrison at Calais. *Queen Mary* I v 122
Permit me to w. To Lambeth ? „ III ii 129
That Cranmer may w to foreign parts, „ IV i 45
Alva will but touch him on the horns, And he w's ; „ V i 157
God from me w's Himself, And the King too. *Becket* I iii 701
Will you not w ? „ V ii 228
speak with them apart. Let us w. „ V ii 311

Withdrawing means to counsel your w To Ashridge, *Queen Mary* I iv 225

Withdrew thought I might be chosen Pope, But then
w it. „ V ii 84

Wither   heat enough To scorch and *w* heresy to the
   root. *Queen Mary* III iv 28
   marriage-garland *w's* even with the putting on, *Becket, Pro.* 360
Wither'd   wherever Spain hath ruled she hath *w* *Queen Mary* II i 206
   That *w* wreath were of more worth to me. *The Falcon* 335
   That *w* wreath is of more worth to me. „ 337
   And jealousy is *w*, sour and ugly : *Foresters* II ii 65
   When the flower was *w* and old. „ IV 22
Withholden   *See* **Long-withholden**
Within-door   They burn themselves *w-d*. *Becket* I i 289
Withstood   who hath *w* two Kings to their faces for the
   honour of God. „ II ii 275
Witness (s)   Bear *w*, Renard, that I live and die *Queen Mary* II iv 41
   No perfect *w* of a perfect faith In him who persecutes : „ III iv 117
   Let all men here bear *w* of our bond ! *Harold* II ii 698
   Ye heard one *w* even now. „ IV i 170
   Bear me true *w*—only for this once— „ IV i 115
Witness (verb)   And *w* to your Grace's innocence, *Queen Mary* III v 50
   you are gone, my liege, *W* these papers, „ III vi 174
   w the brawls, the gibbets. „ v i 85
Witted   *See* **Half-witted**
Wizard   myself must be the *w* To raise that tempest *Becket, Pro.* 207
Woden   *W*, all Our cancell'd warrior-gods, *Harold* III ii 72
   War-woodman of old *W*, how he fells „ v i 588
Woe   *W* knave to thy familiar and to thee ! „ II i 679
Woke   I *w* Sir Henry—and he's true to you— *Queen Mary* III v 60
   and *w* and came Among us again, *Harold* IV iii 150
   Roused by the clamour of the chase he *w*, *The Cup* I ii 118
   a red fire *w* in the heart of the town, *Prom. of May* I 50
Wold   Moon on the waste and the *w*, *The Cup* I ii 4
   That ever charm'd the plowman of your *w's* *Prom. of May* II 489
   then the sweetest flower of all the *w's*, „ III 752
Wolf   not to yield His Church of England to the
   Papal *w* And Mary ; *Queen Mary* I ii 36
   there were many *wolves* among you Who dragg'd „ I v 399
   black night, and hear the *w*. „ I v 414
   if your *w* the while should howl for more, „ I v 419
   Tho' all the world should bay like winter *wolves*. „ II ii 362
   W of the shore ! dog, with thy lying lights *Harold* II i 21
   The *w* ! the beast ! „ II ii 301
   God gave us to divide us from the *w* ! „ IV iii 101
   The *w* Mudded the brook and predetermined all. „ v i 2
   Mannerless *wolves* ! *Becket* I iii 739
   when the horn sounds she comes out as a *w*. „ III ii 23
   King hath many more *wolves* than he can tame „ III iii 322
   wolves of England Must murder her one shepherd, „ III iii 342
   with the flock to the fold—Safe from the *w*— *The Cup* I ii 9
   They say that Rome Sprang from a *w*. „ I ii 14
   With some conspiracy against the *w*. „ I ii 16
   Safe from the *w* to the fold— „ I ii 19
   Or haply fallen a victim to the *w*. *Foresters* II i 510
   be there *wolves* in Sherwood ? *Marian.* The *w*, John ! „ II i 511
Wolfdog   how those Roman *w's* howl and bay him ! *Queen Mary* IV iii 354
   a score of *w-d's* are let loose that will tear thee
   piecemeal. *Becket* III ii 39
Wolf-queen   that our *w-Q* Is prowling round the fold. „ III iii 6
Woman   (*See also* **Beggar-woman, Mad-woman, Yeo-**
   woman)   I and my old *w* 'ud burn upon it, *Queen Mary* I i 56
   ' Whosoever Looketh after a *w*,' „ I v 453
   ⸜ pray God No *w* ever love you, „ I v 602
   All the *women* loved him. „ II i 34
   Tear up that *w's* work there. „ II i 75
   That makes or man or *w* look their goodliest. „ II ii 329
   Away ! *Women* and children ! „ III iii 97
   I was too sorry for the *w* To mark the dress. „ III i 58
   Sir, no *w's* regimen Can save us. „ III i 122
   I say There is no man—there was one *w* with us— „ III i 337
   for *women* To go twelve months in bearing „ III vi 90
   W is various and most mutable. „ III vi 135
   —And I have known such *women* more than one— „ IV vi 178
   To the poor flock—to *women* and to children— „ IV ii 158
   Thou knowest never *w* meant so well, „ v ii 342
   Hapless doom of *w* happy in betrothing ! „ v ii 364
   Unhappiest Of Queens and wives and *women* ! „ v ii 408
   or all *women's* Low as his own ? „ v ii 434

Woman (*continued*)   It is the low man thinks the *w*
   low ; *Queen Mary* v ii 439
   in Guernsey, I watch'd a *w* burn ; „ v iv 18
   the *w* up yonder sleeping after all she has done, „ v iv 34
   burnt The heretic priest, workmen, and *women* and
   children. „ v v 106
   we are private with our *women* here— „ v v 119
   Women, the Holy Father Has ta'en the legateship „ v v 124
   I am but a *w*, I have no power.— „ v v 130
   Women, when I am dead, Open my heart, „ v v 152
   I have given her cause—I fear no *w*. *Harold* I ii 42
   Then our modest *women*— „ II ii 476
   and *women* Cling to the conquer'd, „ IV i 212
   I am no *w* to put faith in dreams. „ IV i 264
   The king commands thee, *w* ! „ v i 341
   To part me from the *w* that I loved ; „ v i 346
   no man can swear to him. *Edith.* But one *w* ! „ v i 79
   Who be these *w* ? And what body is this ? „ v ii 86
   Pluck the dead *w* off the dead man, Malet ! „ v ii 144
   Well, who loves wine loves *w*. *Becket, Pro.* 109
   Men are God's trees, and *women* are God's flowers ; „ Pro. 111
   whom I love indeed As a *w* should be loved— „ Pro. 133
   if a man Wastes himself among *women*, how should
   he love A *w*, as a *w* should be loved ? „ Pro. 137
   Last night I followed a *w* in the city here. „ Pro. 469
   The *w* that I follow'd hither. „ I i 195
   I saw that door Close even now upon the *w*. „ I i 203
   To take the vagabond *w* of the street Into thine arms ! „ I i 227
   'Tis known you are midwinter to all *women*, „ I ii 28
   so long Have wander'd among *women*— „ II i 154
   the goodly way of *women* Who love, „ II i 257
   There is no *w* that I love so well. *Rosamund.* No
   w but should be content with that— „ III i 9
   and to make me a *w* of the world, „ III i 117
   more a *w* o' the world than my lady here, „ III i 142
   most on 'em know an honest *w* and a lady when
   they see her, „ III i 179
   I never knew an honest *w* that could make songs, „ III i 183
   there were Abbots—but they did not bring their *women* ; „ III iii 136
   if he Had aught of man, or thou of *w* ; „ IV ii 232
   Are ye king's men ? I am king's *w*, I. „ v i 265
   make me not a *w*, John of Salisbury, „ v ii 147
   Lacking the love of *w* and of child. „ v ii 199
   I never felt such passion for a *w*. *The Cup* I i 34
   With all my range of *women* should yet shun „ I i 57
   For some unprincely violence to a *w*, „ I i 139
   I ever had my victories among *women*. „ I i 153
   W again !—but I am wiser now. „ I i 168
   Not one to keep a *w's* fealty when Assailed „ I i 176
   Antonius, So gracious toward *women*, never yet Flung
   back a *w's* prayer. „ I ii 299
   ' He never yet flung back a *w's* prayer '— „ I ii 455
   Or man, or *w*, as traitors unto Rome. „ I iii 9
   A *w* I could live and die for. What ! Die for a *w*,
   what new faith is this ? „ I iii 65
   It bears an evil savour among *women*. „ I iii 86
   It is not easy to disarm a *w* ? „ I iii 106
   The *women* of the Temple drag her in. „ I iii 118
   I never found the *w* I could not force „ I iii 166
   thought myself wise—A *w's* dupe. „ II 481
   O *women*, Ye will have Roman masters. „ II 510
   Ah, the *women*, the *women* ! *The Falcon* 84
   won't you speak with the old *w* first, „ 182
   She smiles at him—how hard the *w* is ! „ 661
   best heart that ever Beat for one *w*. „ 668
   Well, well ! the *women* ! „ 699
   A nobler breed of men and *women*. „ 755
   theer be a thousand i' the parish, taäkin' in the
   women and childer ; *Prom. of May* I 146
   Then the man, the *w*, Following their best affinities, „ I 522
   but I hev an owd *w* as 'ud see to all that ; „ II 96
   My grandfather—of him They say, that *women*— „ II 272
   where the man and the *w*, only differing as the
   stronger and the weaker, „ III 189
   If marriage ever brought a *w* happiness „ III 639

Woodland (adj.) (continued)   Tut ! tut ! the scream of
some wild w thing.   Foresters II i 253
Or learning witchcraft of your w witch,   ,,   II i 501
Why—even your w squirrel sees the nut Behind the
shell,   ,,   II i 646
Shall drink the health of our new w Queen.   ,,   III 314
Great w king, I know not quarterstaff.   ,,   IV 215
Then, if ye cannot breathe but w air,   ,,   IV 952
Woodland (s)   Fifty leagues Of w hear and know my horn,   ,,   III 104
Woodman (See also **War-woodman**)   They must have
past. Here is a w's hut.   ,,   II i 199
true w's bow of the best yew-wood to slay the deer.   ,,   II i 392
in the name of all our woodmen, present her with   ,,   III 58
You caught a lonely w of our band,   ,,   III 359
Woodstock   banish'd us to W and the fields.   Queen Mary III v 3
Wood-witch   Is not this w-w of the rustic's fear   Becket III ii 31
Wooer   Strange in a w !   Queen Mary I v 363
Wool   Like a tod of w from wagon into warehouse.   Foresters IV 274
Word   That's a hard w, legitimate ; what does it
mean ?   Queen Mary I i 11
let his own w's damn the Papist.   ,,   I iii 53
yet the w Affrights me somewhat :   ,,   I iv 8
'Tis mine own wish fulfill'd before the w Was spoken,   ,,   I iv 233
wish before the w Is man's good Fairy—   ,,   I iv 239
Our royal w for that !   ,,   I v 267
Philip never writes me one poor w,   ,,   I v 360
The w has turn'd your Highness pale ;   ,,   I v 471
One w before she comes.   ,,   II ii 109
Queen had written her w to come to court :   ,,   II ii 117
No, no, my w's my w.   ,,   II iii 93
Ha—Verbum Dei—verbum—w of God !   ,,   III i 262
W of God In English !   ,,   III i 279
Is reconciled the w ? the Pope again ?   ,,   III iii 3
I have changed a w with him In coming, and may
change a w again.   ,,   III iv 14
not like a w, That comes and goes in uttering.   ,,   III v 29
Truth, a w ! The very Truth and very W are one.   ,,   III v 31
Is like a w that comes from olden days,   ,,   III v 34
For the wrong Robin took her at her w.   ,,   III v 265
May Simon Renard speak a single w ?   ,,   III vi 122
to speak a single w That could not be forgiven.   ,,   III vi 126
What should I say, I cannot pick my w's—   ,,   III vi 148
For death gives life's last w a power to live,   ,,   IV iii 161
Let all rich men remember that hard w.   ,,   IV iii 206
but tek thou my w vor't, Joan,—   ,,   IV iii 533
ever give yourselves your own good w.   Harold I i 343
May, surely, play with w's. Harold. W's are the man.   ,,   II ii 418
at thy w, for thou Art known a speaker   ,,   II ii 516
For thou art truthful, and thy w thy bond.   ,,   II ii 645
Or is it the same sin to break my w As break mine
oath ? He call'd my w my bond !   ,,   II ii 664
And makes believe that he believes my w—   ,,   II ii 669
Thy naked w thy bond !   ,,   II ii 693
Thanks, truthful Earl ; I did not doubt thy w, But
that my barons might believe thy w,   ,,   II ii 724
Might strengthen thee in keeping of thy w,   ,,   II ii 731
I that so prized plain w and naked truth   ,,   III i 93
This lightning before death Plays on the w,—   ,,   III i 388
The king's last w—' the arrow ! '   ,,   v i 266
I have not spoken to the king One w ;   ,,   v i 336
Nay, then, I take thee at thy w—   Becket, Pro. 128
his last w's were a commendation of Thomas Becket   ,,   Pro. 400
And I have said no w of this to him :   ,,   I i 97
We wait but the King's w to strike thee dead.   ,,   I iii 166
who cares not for the w, Makes ' care not '—   ,,   II i 117
The w should come from him.   ,,   II ii 134
W's ! he will wriggle out of them   ,,   II ii 186
bad me whatever I saw not to speak one w,   ,,   II iii 133
not to speak one w, for that's the rule o' the garden,   ,,   III i 137
tho' I shouldn't speak one w,   ,,   III i 155
tho' I be sworn not to speak a w, I can tell you all
about her, if— Rosamund. No w now.   ,,   III i 205
not thorn enough to prick him for it, Ev'n with a w ?   ,,   III i 253
One w further. Doth not the fewness of anything   ,,   III iii 301
we had w's of late, And thereupon he call'd   ,,   IV ii 42

Word (continued)   —a troubadour You play with w's.   Becket IV ii 182
Rosamund hath not answer'd you one w ; Madam, I
will not answer you one w.   ,,   IV ii 362
I spake no w of treachery, Reginald.   ,,   v ii 401
Ready to fall at Henry's w or yours—   ,,   v ii 486
Low w's best chime with this solemnity.   The Cup II 217
These are strange w's to speak to Artemis.   ,,   II 326
W's are not always what they seem, my King.   ,,   II 328
My lord, a w with you.   The Falcon 394
Well, Tell me the w's—or better—   ,,   451
A w with you, my lord !   ,,   472
A w, my lord ! Count. ' Dead flowers ! ' Elisabetta.
A w, my lord !   ,,   475
one w more. Count. Good ! let it be but one.   ,,   510
Strange that the w's at home with me so long   ,,   525
will you take the w out of your master's own mouth ?   ,,   598
I will never change w with you again.   Prom. of May I 163
—what's the newspaäper w, Wilson ?—celebrate—   ,,   I 320
thou'll put one w fur another as I does.   ,,   I 381
' Till death us part '—those are the only w's,   ,,   I 659
But I hed a w to saäy to ye.   ,,   II 45
Cannot you understand plain w's, Mr Dobson ?   ,,   II 113
I be a bit deaf, and I wur hallus scaäred by a big w ;   ,,   III 33
Miss Dora, meä and my maätes, us three, we wants
to hev three w's wi' ye.   ,,   III 126
he gave me no address, and there was no w of marriage ;   ,,   III 333
He be saäyin' a w to the owd man,   ,,   III 481
One w, or do but smile !   ,,   III 677
and wants To hev a w wi' ye about the marriage.   ,,   III 704
Than this, this—but I waste no w's upon him :   ,,   III 745
I cannot find the w—forgive it—Amends.   ,,   III 790
—her last w Forgave—and I forgive you—   ,,   III 810
that very w ' greasy ' hath a kind of unction in it,   Foresters I i 86
What a wealth of w's—O Lord, I will live   ,,   I ii 36
O Lord, I am easily led by w's,   ,,   I ii 40
nor to speak w to anyone,   ,,   I ii 237
True king of vice—true play on w's—   ,,   I i 83
Speak but one w not only of forgiveness,   ,,   II i 610
I never will speak w to thee again.   ,,   II ii 55
Then I am yeo-woman. O the clumsy w ! Robin.
Take thou this light kiss for thy clumsy w.   ,,   III 133
Air and w, my lady, are maid and man.   ,,   III 419
though he be the chief of rogues, he hath never
broken his w.   ,,   IV 434
Say thou no w against my brother John.   ,,   IV 824
Why then, my liege, I have no w to say.   ,,   IV 827
Word-eating   what, a truckler ! a w-e coward !   ,,   IV 162
Word-monger   Diagonalise ! thou art a w-m.   Becket II ii 332
Wore   slew not him alone who w the purple,   Queen Mary I v 499
She w red shoes ! Stafford. Red shoes !   ,,   III i 59
your shores W in mine eyes the green   ,,   III 18
There w his time studying the canon law   Becket II 85
he answer'd me, As if he w the crown already—   ,,   II ii 7
I w the lady's chaplet round my neck ;   The Falcon 631
wreath That once you w outvalues twenty-fold   ,,   759
He w thy colours once at a tourney.   Foresters I i 249
Work (s)   were a pious w To string my father's
sonnets,   Queen Mary II i 26
Tear up that woman's w there.   ,,   II i 75
Well, for mine own w,   ,,   II i 86
Sharp w and short.   ,,   III i 329
Cranmer, be thou glad. This is the w of God.   ,,   IV iii 82
That all day long hath wrought his father's w,   ,,   v ii 119
and cried ' W for the tanner.'   Harold II ii 385
Thou art wearied out With this day's w,   Becket I i 7
due to those That went before us for their w,   ,,   II ii 192
The w of the farm will go on still, but for how
long ?   Prom. of May III 159
Work (verb)   Your master w's against me in the dark.   Queen Mary I v 277
These are the means God w's with,   ,,   III vi 68
so much of the anti-papal leaven W's in him yet,   ,,   v i 16
For Henry could not w a miracle   Becket I i 40
studying the canon law To w it against me.   ,,   II ii 87
strove To w against her license for her good,   ,,   IV ii 340
but pray you do not w upon me.   ,,   v i 81

Work (verb) (*continued*) What filthy tools our Senate *w's*
with !   *The Cup* I i 156
May *w* them grievous harm at times,   *The Falcon* 821
Shall *we* too *w* injustice ?   *Foresters* I iii 87
If the king and the law *w* injustice,   „ IV 228

Worked   telled me 'at sweet'arts niver *w* well
togither ; and I telled '*im* 'at sweet'arts
allus *w* best together ;   *Prom. of May* II 156
Did you find that you *w* at all the worse upon the
cold tea   „ III 55
we *w* naw wuss upo' the cowd tea ; but we'd ha' *w*
better upo' the beer.   „ III 58
you *w* well enough, and I am much obliged to all
of you.   „ III 61
Sally Allen, you *w* for Mr. Dobson, didn't you ?   „ III 101
an' I *w* early an' laäte to maäke 'em all gentlefoälks
ageän.   „ III 448

Workin'   meä and my sweet'art was a *w* along o' one
side wi' one another,   „ II 152

Working   *See* **Backward-working, Workin'**

Workman   burnt The heretic priest, *workmen*, and
women and children.   *Queen Mary* V v 106
Some of our *workmen* have left us,   *Prom. of May* III 27

Workmanship   Look at the hilt. What excellent *w*.   *Becket* IV iii 315

Work-wan   Look ! am I not *W-w*, flesh-fallen ?   *Harold* I i 99

World   (*See also* **Child-world, Old-world, Other-world**)
rumour that Charles, the master of the *w*,   *Queen Mary* I i 105
broken, out you flutter Thro' the new *w*,   „ I iv 54
Spain and we, One crown, might rule the *w*.   „ I v 303
for the Queen's down, and the *w's* up,   „ II i 66
hardest, cruellest people in the *w*,   „ II i 100
the *w* is with us—war against Spain !   „ II i 196
Look at the New *W*—a paradise made hell ;   „ II i 207
The *w* as yet, my friend, Is not half-waked ;   „ II i 226
thro' that dim dilated *w* of hers, To read our faces ;   „ II ii 324
Tho' all the *w* should bay like winter wolves.   „ II ii 361
unto no dead *w* ; but Lambeth palace,   „ III ii 153
His faith shall clothe the *w* that will be his,   „ III ii 180
craft that do divide The *w* of nature ;   „ III v 121
free wing The *w* were all one Araby.   „ III v 210
and weight of all the *w* From off his neck to mine.   „ III vi 213
O Son of God, Redeemer of the *w* !   „ IV iii 118
Many so dote upon this bubble *w*,   „ IV iii 168
' Love of this *w* is hatred against God.'   „ IV iii 173
Of this be sure, he is whole *w's* away.   „ IV iii 194
The *w's* mad. *Paget.* My Lord, the *w* is like   „ IV iii 391
—the *w* A most obedient beast and fool—   „ IV iii 413
Come out, my Lord, it is a *w* of fools.   „ IV iii 639
and mine own self and all the *w*.   „ V ii 13
' O bubble *w*, Whose colours in a moment break and fly ! '   „ V ii 205
And fared so ill in this disastrous *w*.   „ V ii 344
but say the *w* is nothing—   „ V ii 368
Charles, the lord of this low *w*, is gone ;   „ V v 54
Priests' talk, or dream of *w's* to be,   „ V v 217
never merry *w* In England, since the Bible came
among us.   „ V v 240
It never will be merry *w* in England,   „ V v 246
for in our windy *w* What's up is faith,   *Harold* I i 83
Why not the doom of all the *w* as well ? For all the
w sees it   „ I i 128
Thou art the quietest man in all the *w*—   „ I i 312
an honest *w* Will not believe them.   „ I i 347
Far as he knew in this poor *w* of ours—   „ II ii 363
Welshman says, ' The Truth against the *W*,'   „ II ii 398
When all the *w* hath learnt to speak the truth,   „ III i 68
That runs thro' all the faiths of all the *w*.   „ III i 353
than to reign King of the *w* without it.   „ III ii 45
all the faiths Of this grown *w* of ours,   „ III ii 65
A breath that fleets beyond this iron *w*,   „ III ii 197
kingdoms of this *w* began with little,   „ IV i 42
till *her* voice Die with the *w*.   „ IV iii 76
cannot see the *w* but thro' their wines !   „ IV iii 225
Our Saints have moved the Church that moves the *w*,   „ V i 42
selfless man Is worth a *w* of tonguesters.   „ V i 82
I cannot fall into a falser *w*—   „ V i 271

World (*continued*) bear their earthly heats Into yon bloodless *w*,   *Harold* V i 285
should have a hand To grasp the *w* with,   „ V ii 192
A man of this *w* and the next to boot.   *Becket, Pro.* 259
I could pity this poor *w* myself that it is no better
ordered.   „ *Pro.* 366
old men must die, or the *w* would grow mouldy,   „ *Pro.* 409
And mine uplifter in this *w*,   „ I i 89
Why thou, the King, the Pope, the Saints, the *w*,   „ I iii 706
and the *w* shall live by the King's venison   „ I iv 271
Thou rose of the *w* !   „ II i 146
and turn the *w* upside down.   „ II i 238
promise thee not to turn the *w* upside down.   „ II i 242
Here is a ball, my boy, thy *w*,   „ II i 244
The *w* had never seen the like before.   „ II ii 125
we grant the Church King over this *w's* kings, yet,
my good lord, We that are kings are something
in this *w*,   „ II ii 243
Is the *w* any the worse for my verses   „ II ii 336
cried out on him to put me forth in the *w* and to
make me a woman of the *w*,   „ III i 116
into a garden and not into the *w*,   „ III i 132
more a woman o' the *w* than my lady here,   „ III i 143
From all the hidden by-ways of the *w*   „ III iii 16
Who wander famine-wasted thro' the *w*.   „ III iii 189
beg my bread along the *w* With my young boy,   „ IV ii 103
Daughter, the *w* hath trick'd thee.   „ IV ii 364
The *w* hath trick'd her—that's the King ;   „ IV ii 375
all the *w* allows I fall no inch Behind this Becket,   „ V i 39
to prove Bigger in our small *w* than thou art.   „ V i 128
Like some wise prince of this *w* from his wars,   „ V ii 13
Why, John, my kingdom is not of this *w*. *John of
Salisbury.* If it were more of this *w* it might be
More of the next.   „ V ii 19
be something Of this *w's* leaven in thee too,   „ V ii 29
To plunge into this bitter *w* again—   „ V ii 81
this mother, runs thro' all The *w* God made—   „ V ii 243
brood Too long o'er this hard egg, the *w*,   „ V ii 253
If Rosamund is The *w's* rose, as her name imports
her—she Was the *w's* lily.   „ V ii 263
What ! will he excommunicate all the *w* ?   „ V ii 467
Blowing the *w* against me,   „ V ii 491
—the whole *w* Abhor you ;   „ V iii 183
This last to rid thee of a *w* of brawls !   „ V iii 199
O the most kindly Prince in all the *w* !   *The Cup* I ii 357
the *w* may know You twain are reconciled,   „ I 68
Rome is fated To rule the *w*.   „ II 416
by the Gods of Rome and all the *w*,   „ II 466
he always took the *w* so kindly.   *The Falcon* 188
and your ladyship has given him bitters enough in this *w*,   „ 193
My one thing left of value in the *w* !   „ 497
I have nothing in this *w* but love for you.   „ 784
O this unhappy *w* ! How shall I break it to him ?   „ 847
no fear Of the *w's* gossiping clamour.   *Prom. of May* I 528
all the *w* is beautiful If we were happy,   „ I 576
for the senses, love, are for the *w* ;   „ I 581
for whom the tide Of full democracy has overwhelm'd
This Old *w*,   „ I 594
When the great Democracy Makes a new *w*—   „ I 672
Neither the old *w*, nor the new,   „ I 674
Since I left her Here weeping, I have ranged the *w*,   „ II 252
She has disappear'd, poor darling, from the *w*—   „ II 410
this *w* Is brighter for his absence as that other Is
darker for his presence.   „ II 457
I have seen the *w*—And cheer his blindness   „ II 514
Must come to in our spring-and-winter *w*   „ III 511
My curse on all This *w* of mud,   „ III 722
We cannot come together in this *w*.   *Foresters* II i 618
And all the foolish *w* is pressing thither.   „ III 149
Sit here, my queen, and judge the *w* with me.   „ III 152
He hath spoken truth in a *w* of lies.   „ III 212
all the crowns Of all this *w*,   „ IV 405
free the tomb-place of the King Of all the *w* ?   „ IV 410
Tho' all the *w* should go about in boats.   „ IV 670

World-hated   Scowl'd that *w-h* and world-hating beast,   *Queen Mary* II ii 90

World-hating   Scowl'd that world-hated and *w-h* beast,   „ II ii 90

Wretch (*continued*) Infamous *w*! Shall I tell her he
　is dead? *Prom. of May* III 336
　The old *w* is mad, and her bread is beyond me: *Foresters* II i 291
Wretched Most miserable sinner, *w* man. *Queen Mary* IV iii 123
　on a land So hunger-nipt and *w*; 　　　,, *v* i 168
　W race! And once I wish'd to scourge them to the bones. *The Cup* I i 25
Wretchedness yet have heard Of all their *w*. *Queen Mary* IV iii 212
　His wickedness is like my *w*— *Prom. of May* III 747
Wriggle he will *w* out of them like an eel *Becket* II ii 187
Wring what we *w* from them we give the poor. *Foresters* II i 56
Wrinkle sweet worn smile Among thy patient *w*'s— *Queen Mary* v v 200
　silver Were dear as gold, the *w* as the dimple. *Foresters* IV 42
Wrist I cannot cope with him: my *w* is strain'd. 　,, IV 313
Writ (s) range Among the pleasant fields of Holy *W* *Queen Mary* IV i 67
　Make out the *w* to-night. 　　　　　,, IV i 195
　by virtue of this *w*, whereas Robin Hood Earl of
　　Huntingdon *Foresters* I iii 61
　For playing upside down with Holy *W*. 　,, III 168
　Whose *w* will run thro' all the range of life. 　,, IV 48
　In the sweat of thy brow, says Holy *W*, shalt thou eat
　　bread, 　　　　　　　　　　,, IV 201
　like the man In Holy *W*, who brought his talent back; 　,, IV 981
Writ (verb) (*See also* **Written**) *W* by himself and
　Bonner? *Queen Mary* IV i 93
　Have I not *w* enough to satisfy you? 　　,, IV i 62
Write Philip never *w*'s me one poor word, 　,, I v 359
　yet—to *w* it down. 　　　　　　　,, II i 56
　W you as many sonnets as you will. 　　,, II i 95
　W to him, then. *Pole.* I will. 　　　,, IV i 37
　Pray you *w* out this paper for me, Cranmer. 　,, IV ii 60
　hands that *w* them should be burnt clean off 　,, IV i 190
　Cornwall's hand or Leicester's: they *w* marvellously alike. *Becket* I iv 52
　cannot at present *w* himself other than *The Cup* I i 45
　cannot at present *w* himself other than 　,, I ii 73
　You will *w* to me? *Edgar.* I will. *Prom. of May* I 699
　Eva, why did you *w* 'Seek me at the bottom of the
　　river'? 　　　　　　　　　,, III 363
Writhed never stirr'd or *w*, but, like a statue, *Queen Mary* IV iii 620
Writing (part.) That any man so *w*, preaching so, 　,, IV iii 47
Writing (s) (*See also* **Sub-writing, Verse-writing**)
　For these be *w*'s I have set abroad 　　,, IV iii 240
　by your leave if you would hear the rest, The *w*. *The Falcon* 531
　sometimes been moved to tears by a chapter of
　　fine *w* in a novel; *Prom. of May* III 209
Written (*See also* **Writ**) Stand first it may, but it was
　w last: *Queen Mary* I ii 21
　'Tis *w*, 'They shall be childless.' 　　,, I ii 64
　he must have *w*. 　　　　　　　,, I v 358
　Queen had *w* her word to come to court: 　,, II ii 117
　'tis not *w* Half plain enough. 　　　,, III ii 65
　What hath your Highness *w*? 　　　,, III v 23
　Hath he not *w* himself—infatuated— 　　,, IV i 10
　You have *w* much, But you were never raised 　,, II ii 209
　W for fear of death, to save my life, 　　,, IV iii 242
　by this hand *W* and sign'd— 　　　,, IV iii 245
　since my hand offended, having *w* Against my heart, 　,, IV iii 248
　what hath she *w*? read. 　　　　　,, v v 2
　What hath she *w* now? 　　　　　,, v v 13
　you will find *w* Two names, Philip and Calais; 　,, v v 154
　I'll have them *w* down and made the law. *Becket, Pro.* 26
　But by the King's command are *w* down, 　,, I iii 72
　Good royal customs—had them *w* fair 　,, I iii 416
　not yet *w*, Saving mine order; true too, that when *w* I
　　sign'd them— 　　　　　　　,, I iii 558
　What have I *w* to her? *The Cup* I i 35
　and I find a *w* scroll That seems to run in rhymings. *The Falcon* 431
　is *w* in invisible inks 'Lust, Prodigality, *Prom. of May* II 283
Wrong (adj.) I may be *w*, sir. This marriage will
　not hold. *Queen Mary* III i 102
　For the *w* Robin took her at her word. 　,, III v 264
　Those of the *w* side will despite the man, 　,, IV iii 24
　—and I bean't *w* not twice i' ten year— 　,, IV iii 534
　summut *w* theer, Wilson, fur I doänt understan' it. *Prom. of May* I 234
Wrong (s) I knew they would not do me any *w*, *Queen Mary* I iii 100
　You did me *w*, I love not to be called 　,, I iv 67

Wrong (s) (*continued*) And she impress her *w*'s upon
　her Council, *Queen Mary* III vi 183
　To do him any *w* was to beget A kindness 　,, IV i 167
　Ye do him *w*, ye do him *w*; *Harold* I ii 16
　They did thee *w* who made thee hostage; 　,, II ii 349
　I have done no man *w*. 　　　　　,, v i 272
　We mean thee no *w*. *Becket* I iv 32
　wilt but look into The *w*'s you did him, 　,, II ii 116
　before The Church should suffer *w*! 　,, III iii 20
　if you love him, there is great *w* done Somehow; 　,, IV ii 94
　Holy Church to thunder out her rights And thine own *w* 　,, v ii 33
　Lost in the common good, the common *w*, 　,, v ii 41
　crowd May wreak my *w*'s upon my wrongers. *Prom. of May* I 507
　I have done *w* in keeping your secret; 　,, III 399
　ye did *w* in crying 'Down with John;' *Foresters* I ii 96
　to such a heat As burns a *w* to ashes, 　,, II i 700
Wrong (verb) From stirring hand or foot to *w* the
　realm. *Queen Mary* III iii 60
　Hush, hush! You *w* the Chancellor: 　,, III iii 67
　Out, girl! you *w* a noble gentleman. 　,, v 67
　Perchance that Harold *w*'s me; *Harold* I ii 225
　That none should *w* or injure your Archbishop. *Becket* I iii 754
　I *w* the bird; she leaves only the nest she built, 　,, I iv 45
　You *w* the King: he meant what he said to-day. 　,, III iii 298
　Perhaps, my lord, you *w* us. 　　　,, v ii 604
　Why should I practise on you? How you *w* me! *The Cup* I ii 240
　You *w* him surely; far as the face goes 　,, II 174
　You *w* me there! hear, hear me! *Prom. of May* III 775
　but we rob the robber, *w* the wronger, *Foresters* II i 54
Wrong'd There's half an angel *w* in your account; *Queen Mary* v iii 2
　I were whole devil if I *w* you, Madam. 　,, v iii 7
　That where he was but worsted, he was *w*. *Harold* I i 450
　If one may dare to speak the truth, was *w*. 　,, IV i 109
　believing that our brother Had *w* you; *Becket* II ii 239
　The by-things of the Lord Are the *w* innocences that
　　will cry 　　　　　　　　　,, III iii 14
　You have *w* Fitzurse. I speak not of myself. 　,, IV ii 328
　One whom thou hast *w* Without there, *The Cup* I ii 319
　W by the cruelties of his religions *Prom. of May* II 545
　One that has been much *w*, whose griefs are mine, 　,, III 576
　thou hast *w* my brother and myself. *Foresters* II i 665
　We never *w* a woman. 　　　　　,, III 184
　One half of this shall go to those they have *w*, 　,, III 304
Wronger It gilds the greatest *w* of her peace, *Queen Mary* v iii 415
　In the great day against the *w*. *Becket* III ii 17
　crowd May wreak my wrongs upon my *w*'s. *Prom. of May* I 507
　but we rob the robber, wrong the *w*, *Foresters* II i 55
Wrote letter you *w* against Their superstition *Queen Mary* I ii 85
　I *w* it, and God grant me power to burn! 　,, I ii 98
　And what a letter he *w* against the Pope! 　,, III i 173
　which God's hand *W* on her conscience, 　,, III i 422
　last time she *w*, I had like to have lost my life: 　,, III v 188
　when last he *w*, declared His comfort 　,, III vi 77
　same book You *w* against my Lord of Winchester; 　,, IV ii 265
　I hold by all I *w* within that book. 　,, IV iii 275
　To compass which I *w* myself to Rome, 　,, v ii 49
　letter which the Count de Noailles *w* 　,, v ii 497
　right hand Lamed in the battle, *w* it with his left. *The Falcon* 445
　my sister he *w* was mighty pleasant, and had no
　　pride in him. *Prom. of May* I 116
Wroth they are *w* with their own selves, *Queen Mary* III iv 120
　That I was for a moment *w* at thee. 　,, III iv 306
　The Queen, most *w* at first with you, 　,, III iv 387
　Except when *w*, you scarce could meet his eye
　　And hold your own; and were he *w* indeed,
　　You held it less, or not at all. 　　,, IV i 103
　Why should not Heaven be *w*? *Harold* I i 53
　I am weary—go: make me not *w* with thee! 　,, v i 31
　Yon heaven is *w* with *thee*? 　　　,, v i 39
　And so the saints were *w*. 　　　,, v ii 7
　be not *w* at the dumb parchment. *Foresters* I i 342
Wrought and this *w* Upon the king; *Queen Mary* I ii 70
　he it ignorantly, And not from any malice. 　,, III i 276
　was the great mystery *w*; 　　　,, IV iii 142
　That all day long hath *w* his father's work, 　,, v ii 118

York (*continued*) crowning thy young son by Y, London and Salisbury—not Canterbury. *Becket* III iii 195
Y crown'd the Conqueror—not Canterbury. „ III iii 197
Roger of Y, you always hated him, „ v i 8
Y and myself, and our good Salisbury here, „ v i 56
Y said so? *Salisbury.* Yes: a man may take good counsel „ v ii 1
Y will say anything. What is he saying now? „ v ii 5
Y! Can the King de-anathematise this Y? „ v ii 9
Who hold With Y, with Y against me. „ v ii 63
Y against Canterbury, Y against God! „ v ii 66
he borrowed the monies from the Abbot of Y, the Sheriff's brother. *Foresters* I i 68
mark'd if those two knaves from Y be coming? „ IV 113
The Abbot of Y and his justiciary. „ IV 334
Not paid at Y—the wood—prick me no more! „ IV 623

Young (*adj.*) Judges had pronounced That our y Edward might bequeath the crown Of England, *Queen Mary* I ii 26
But our y Earl of Devon— *Mary.* Earl of Devon? „ I v 160
Ev'n that y girl who dared to wear your crown? „ I v 491
Here was a y mother, Her face on flame, „ II ii 68
My seven-years' friend was with me, my y boy; „ III iii 48
my Lord, Under y Edward. „ III iv 244
Which a y lust had clapt upon the back, „ IV iii 401
They say the gloom of Saul Was lighten'd by y David's harp. *Mary.* Too y! And never knew a Philip. „ v ii 359
how it chanced That this y Earl was sent on foreign travel, „ v ii 489
Noble as his y person and old shield. „ v ii 513
Ay, ay, y lord, *there* the king's face is power. *Harold* I i 72
Yet in thine own land in thy father's day They blinded my y kinsman, Alfred— „ II ii 511
I do believe My old crook'd spine would bud out two y wings „ III i 25
Two y lovers in winter weather, „ III ii 3
I will have My y son Henry crown'd the King of England, *Becket, Pro.* 224
Surely too y Even for this shadow of a crown; „ *Pro.* 230
Ay, but thy y colt winced and whinnied and flung up her heels; „ *Pro.* 514
And said 'My y Archbishop—thou wouldst make A stately Archbishop!' „ I i 65
he might well have sway'd All England under Henry, the y King, „ I iii 468
Deal gently with the y man Absalom. „ I iii 756
Too scared—so y! „ II i 67
You have not crown'd y Henry yet, my liege? „ II ii 3
But England scarce would hold Y Henry king, if only crown'd by York, „ II ii 32
crown y Henry there, and make Our waning Eleanor all but love me! „ II ii 456
I go to have y Henry crown'd by York. „ II ii 478
Seeing he must to Westminster and crown Y Henry there to-morrow. „ III ii 10
hath in this crowning of y Henry by York and London so violated the immemorial usage of the Church, „ III iii 71

Young (*adj.*) (*continued*) but as to the y crownling himself, he looked so malapert in the eyes, *Becket* III iii 108
Did you hear the y King's quip? „ III iii 146
Thou hast broken thro' the pales Of privilege, crowning thy y son by York, „ III iii 194
I do beseech you—my child is so y, „ IV ii 84
But the child is so y. „ IV ii 89
let me go With my y boy, and I will hide my face, „ IV ii 98
But I will beg my bread along the world With my y boy, „ IV ii 104
till it break Into y angels. „ v ii 257
Commands you to be dutiful and leal To your y King on this side of the water, „ v ii 326
On those that crown'd y Henry in this realm, „ v ii 392
If this be so, complain to your y King, „ v ii 448
I warrants ye'll think moor o' this y Squire Edgar as ha' coomed among us— *Prom. of May* I 109
But you are y, and—pardon me—As lovely as your sister. „ II 506
Taäke one o' the y 'uns fust, Miss, fur I be a bit deaf, „ III 31
the poor y heart Broken at last—all still— „ III 680
but now I ask you all, did none of you love y Walter Lea? *Foresters* I i 55
No news of y Walter? „ I i 72
Y Walter, nay, I pray thee, stay a moment. „ II i 472
I Little John, he, y Scarlet, and he, old Much, and all the rest of us. „ III 60
This y warrior broke his prison And join'd my banner in the Holy Land, „ IV 998
Young (*s*) The lion needs but roar to guard his y; *Queen Mary* III v 123
Youngest I am the y of the Templars, *Becket* I iii 261
an' I can taäke my glass along wi' the y, *Prom. of May* I 361
Youngster thou and thy y's are always muching and moreing me. *Foresters* IV 295
always so much more of a man than my y's old Much. „ IV 298
Youth (*adolescence*) was all pure lily and rose In his y, *Queen Mary* I v 21
Not scorn him for the foibles of his y. *Becket* v ii 328
blossom of his y, Has faded, falling fruitless— *Prom. of May* III 333
Youth (*young man*) strange y Suddenly thrust it on me, *Queen Mary* II i 128
I would she could have wedded that poor y, My Lord of Devon— „ v ii 476
When I and thou were y's in Theobald's house, *Becket* I iii 40
The wildest of the random y of Florence *The Falcon* 808

Z

Zeal tell this learned Legate he lacks z. *Queen Mary* III iv 272
Zerubbabel What else? *Man.* Z. „ III i 315
Zest that will give thee a new z for it, *Foresters* IV 209
Zion The daughter of Z lies beside the way— *Becket* III iii 177
Zone open'd out The purple z of hill and heaven; *The Cup* II ii 408
Zuinglius (**Zwingli, the Swiss reformer**) The ghosts of Luther and Z fade *Queen Mary* III ii 174
Zurich To Strasburg, Antwerp, Frankfort, Z, „ I ii 2

A CONCORDANCE to the POEMS

CONTAINED IN THE LIFE OF

ALFRED, LORD TENNYSON.

A

Abyss The starr'd *a's* of the sky, *'Tis not alone* 2

Accept *A's* the song you gave, and he sends *Little Aubrey* 2
  A on this your golden bridal day *Remembering him* 3

Ache Till heart and sight and hearing *a* *How strange it is* 3

Act (s) Steersman, be not precipitate in thine *a* Of steering *Steersman* 1

Act (verb) *a* on Eternity To keep thee here *That is his portrait* 39

Admire *A* that stalwart shape, those ample brows, " 4

Æon In the vast Of the rolling of the *a's*, *Little Aubrey* 6

Aerial Whose trumpet-tongued, *a* melody *O God, make this age* 3

Affectation Let it cry an *a*, *Immeasurable sadness!* 6

Affection To thee with whom my true *a's* dwell, *To thee with whom* 1

Afraid Truth-seeking he and not *a*, *He was too good* 5

Age when your *a* had somewhat riper grown, *Hear you the sound* 54
  O God, make this *a* great that we may be *O God, make this age* 1
  O'er the bow'd shoulder of a bland old *A*, *That is his portrait* 36
  To hold the Spirit of the *A* Against the Spirit *They wrought, etc.* 47

Agony An energy, an *a*, A labour working to an end. *Youth, lapsing ii* 3

Aileth What *a* thee, O bird divine, *Full light aloft* 5

Aim So lived I without *a* or choice, *Youth, lapsing i* 37

Air (*See also* **Under-air**) gaily spring In that unwholesome *a*, *Far off in the dun* 10
  glooms were spread Around in the chilling *a*, " 102
  With pleasant hymns they soothe the *a* Of death, " 109
  there Hovering, thoughtful, poised in *a*. *Not to Silence* 12

Airy On her forehead undefiled I will print an *a* kiss: *Not a whisper* 12

Ait Streaming thro' his osier'd *a's*! *Vicar of this* 20

Akin Great spirits grow *a* to base. *They wrought, etc.* 16

Alarum May blow *a* loud to every wind, *O God, make this age* 4

Ale lifts The creaming horn of corny *a*! *Yon huddled cloud* 7
  Gives stouter *a* and riper port " 7

Alfred little *A* in the East *Little Aubrey* 1

All *A* things please you, nothing vex you, *Vicar of this* 9
  that give The difference of *a* things to the sense, *Why suffers* 10
  An orb repulsive of *a* hate, A will concentric with a fate, A life four-square to *a* the winds. *Young is the grief* 14
  And how *a* things become the past. *Youth, lapsing i* 28
  And the guard gasp'd out '*A's* right.' *Far off in the dun* 88
  A freedom vanish'd— *Rise, Britons, rise* 3

All-perfect but rather bless The *A-p* Framer, *That is his portrait* 48

Alma At the battle of *A*. *Frenchman, etc.* 4
  That rests by the *A* River. " 12

Aloft Full light *a* doth the laverock spring *Full light aloft* 1

Alone 'Tis not *a* the warbling woods, *'Tis not alone* 1

Along voice Cried in the future 'Come *a*.' *Youth, lapsing i* 40

Altar bind Falsehood beneath the *a* of great Truth: *O God, make this age* 8

Alternation With click-clack *a* to and fro, *Half after midnight!* 8

Ambrosial and make beneath *A* gloom. *Hear you the sound* 30

Amethyst Of beryl, and of *a* Was the spiritual frame. *Far off in the dun* 123

Ample Admire that stalwart shape, those *a* brows, *That is his portrait* 4

Anacaona happy as *A*, The beauty of Espagnola, (repeat) *A dark Indian maiden* 10, 22

Anacaona (*continued*) Indian queen, *A*, Dancing on the blossomy plain *A dark Indian maiden* 28
  Happy happy was *A*, The beauty of Espagnola, " 34
  Happy, happy *A*, The beauty of Espagnola, " 46
  they smiled on *A*, The beauty of Espagnola, " 58
  No more in Xaraguay Wander'd happy *A*, " 70

Anadyomené more fair to me Than aught of *A*! *Not to Silence* 16

Anana By the crimson-eyed *a*, *A dark Indian maiden* 4

Ancestor battlemented towers Of my old *a's*! *Hear you the sound* 13

Ancient (*See also* **Antient**) He cares, if *a* usage fade, *They wrought, etc.* 33

Anger victim, Broken in this *a* of Aphrodite, *Faded ev'ry violet* 3

Ankle floating snake Roll'd round her *a's*, *One was the Tishbite* 10

Anon 'Tis a clear night, they will be here *a*. *Hear you the sound* 6

Another Into a shape, born of the first, As beautiful, but yet *a* world. *That is his portrait* 29
  and I will show to you *A* countenance, one yet more dear, " 45

Antient (*See also* **Ancient**) And somewhat loftier *a* heights Touch'd with Heaven's latest lights. *Thy soul is like* 11

Apart Not with this age wherefrom ye stand *a*, *Therefore your Halls* 11

Ape (s) We come from *a's*—and are far removed— *How is it that men* 4

Ape (verb) And the voice that *a's* a nation— *Immeasurable sadness!* 5

Aphrodite victim, Broken in this anger of *A*, *Faded ev'ry violet* 3

Apparel For they were kingly in *a*, *A dark Indian maiden* 63

Approach what lights *a* With heavenly melodies? *Far off in the dun* 105

Arch (s) look you what an *a* the brain has built *That is his portrait* 10
  Beneath those double *a'es* lie Fair with green fields *Youth, lapsing ii* 35

Arch (verb) thick dark oaks, that *a* their arms above, *Hear you the sound* 11

Archangel And a bright *a* drove. *Far off in the dun* 116

Areyto moving To her *A's* mellow ditty, *A dark Indian maiden* 50

Aristocrat proud *a's* whose lordly shadows, *Hear you the sound* 21

Arm thick dark oaks, that arch their *a's* above, " 11
  With one *a* stretch'd out bare, *One was the Tishbite* 3
  this one smiled, that other waved his *a's*, *That is his portrait* 22

Armed A sound of blows on *a* breasts! And individual interests Becoming bands of *a* foes! *They wrought, etc.* 18

Array And though girt in glad *a*, *The lamps were bright* 23

Art for *Art's* sake! Hail, *Art for Art's sake!* 1
  I hate the trim-set plots of *a*!' *I keep no more* 14
  A, Science, Nature, everything is full, *Why suffers* 7

Artist Like some wise *a*, Nature gives, *'Tis not alone* 6

Ash by fits the lady *a* With twinkling finger *Townsmen, etc.* 9

Ask *a* you whether you would be A great man in your time, *Hear you the sound* 56

Asleep sound of the deep when the winds are *a*; *That the voice* 3

Asphaltus slime Which from *A* flows. *Far off in the dun* 40

Athwart as 'twere *a* a colour'd cloud, *That is his portrait* 35
  A the bloomy morn. *Full light aloft* 4

Atrophy And his name was *A*! *Far off in the dun* 56

Attire And rich was their *a*: " 126

Attitude Down to his slightest turns and *a's*— *That is his portrait* 24

Aubrey Little *A* in the West! little Alfred in the East *Little Aubrey* 1

Austral *Your* flag thro' *A* ice is borne, *The noblest men* 6

Bony   But the ricketty blast runs shrilly and fast
Thro' the *b* branches there.   *Far off in the dun* 12

Book   your golden bridal day The *B* of Prayer.   *Remembering him* 4
full God-bless-you with this *b* of song,   *Take, Lady,* 2
I give this faulty *b* to you,   *The noblest men* 9

Boot   And his *b*'s creak'd heavily.   *Far off in the dun* 76

Booth   The hubbub of the market and the *b*'s: *That is his portrait* 21

Bore   Because she *b* the iron name Of him—   *Because she bore* 1
And *b* the child away.   *The child was sitting* 7
the merry bridegroom *B* the bride away !   *The lamps were bright* 4

Born   This chamber she was *b* in !   *Along this glimmering* 3
All Nature is the womb whence Man is *b*.   *Hold thou, my friend* 2
Into another shape, *b* of the first,   *That is his portrait* 29

Borne   (*See also* **Wind-borne**)   merry bridegroom Hath
b the bride away— (repeat)   *The lamps were bright* 20, 26, 38, 44
a merry bridegroom Had *b* the bride away,   „   50
Your flag thro' Austral ice is *b*,   *The noblest men* 6
Than if the vine had *b* the bitter sloe.   *To thee with whom* 4

Bough   through The knotted *b*'s of this long avenue   *Hear you the sound* 10

Bound (limit)   transgressing the low *b* Of mortal hope,   *That is his portrait* 38
The river rose and burst his *b*,   *The child was sitting* 4

Bound (verb)   When corny Lammas *b* the sheaves: *Youth, lapsing i* 16

Bounded   leaders *b*, the guard's horn sounded: *Far off in the dun* 89

Boundless   And rushes o'er a *b* field.   *Youth, lapsing ii* 32
Through all that *b* depth of fires is heard   *Half after midnight!* 13

Bow   With all his groves he *b*'s, he nods,   *Youth, lapsing ii* 49

Bow'd   O'er the *b* shoulder of a bland old Age, The
face of placid Death.'   *That is his portrait* 36

Bower   Now idly in my natal *b*'s,   *Youth, lapsing i* 49

Box (driver's seat)   grim old coachee strode to the *b*,   *Far off in the dun* 87

Box (house)   snug brick *b* Of some sleek citizen.   *Hear you the sound* 19

Boy   And the laugh of their rose-lipp'd *b*'s.   *Far off in the dun* 68
Thou dost remember, Michael, How, when a *b*,   *Hear you the sound* 31
we jar like *b*'s: And in the hurry and the noise   *They wrought, etc.* 14

Brain   His heart throbs thick, his *b* reels sick: *Far off in the dun* 27
The *b* is moulded,' she began,   *From shape to shape* 2
Is thy mad *b* drunk with the merry, red wine,   *Full light aloft* 7
what an arch the *b* has built Above the ear !   *That is his portrait* 10
dark form glances quick Thro' her worn *b*,   *The lamps were bright* 28
With reason cloister'd in the *b*:   *Young is the grief* 4

Brake   How every *b* and flower spread and rose,   *That is his portrait* 26

Branch   Waving a palm *b*, wondering, loving,   *A dark Indian maiden* 51
Thro' the bony *b*'es there.   *Far off in the dun* 12
singing lustily Among the moss-grown *b*'es,   *Hear you the sound* 42

Brave   whole world shall not *b* us ! (repeat)   *They say, etc.* 6, 13, 20

Break (s)   Dancing at the *b* of day,   *A dark Indian maiden* 66
At the very *b* of light ?   *Full light aloft* 8

Break (verb)   would have call'd you down to *b* your
fast,   *Hear you the sound* 47
Lightly lisping, *b*'s away;   *Not to Silence* 32
To *b* the pride of Britain,   *They say, etc.* 2
To *b* the noble pride of the Mistress of the Seas.   „   4
Not he that *b*'s the dams, but he   *They wrought, etc.* 29
B thro' with the hammer of iron rhyme,   *Wherever evil* 2

Breast   Long as the heart beats life within her *b*,   *Long as the heart* 1
And veils a *b* more fair to me   *Not to Silence* 15
And that large table of the *b* dispread,   *That is his portrait* 5
A sound of blows on armed *b*'s !   *They wrought, etc.* 18
These only do not move the *b* ;   *'Tis not alone* 5
An idle hope was in my *b*,   *What rustles* 11

Breathe   The May begins to *b* and bud,   *Life of the Life* 3

Bred   The noblest men methinks are *b*   *The noblest men* 1

Breeze   *B*'s from the palm and canna   *A dark Indian maiden* 14

Brick   or the snug *b* box Of some sleek citizen.   *Hear you the sound* 19

Brickwork   Inextricable *b* maze in maze ?   *What rustles* 8

Bridal (adj.)   Accept on this your golden *b* day   *Remembering him* 3

Bridal (s)   bitter, bitter *b*, The bitter bridal-day.   *The lamps were bright* 53
A merry, merry *b*, a merry bridal-day ! (repeat)   „   5, 13

Bridal-day   lamps were bright and gay On the
merry *b-d*,   „   2
A merry, merry bridal, A merry *b-d* ! (repeat)   „   6, 14
the bitter, bitter bridal, The bitter *b-d*.   „   54

Bride   the merry bridegroom Bore the *b* away !   „   4
Why the *b* is white as clay, Although the
merry bridegroom Bears the *b* away,   „   10

Bride (*continued*)   the merry bridegroom
Hath borne the *b* away—(repeat)   *The lamps were bright* 20, 26, 38, 44
tho' the merry bridegroom Might lead the *b*
away,   *The lamps were bright* 32
he a merry bridegroom Had borne the *b* away,   „   50

Bridegroom   the merry *b* Bore the bride away !   „   3
Although the merry *b* Bears the bride away,   „   11
the merry *b* Hath borne the bride away—(repeat)   „   19, 25 37, 43
tho' the merry *b* Might lead the bride away,   „   31
he a merry *b* Had borne the bride away,   „   49

Bridge   I stepp'd upon the old mill *b* ?   *Remember you* 4

Brief   Or sleep thro' one *b* dream upon the grass,—   *Townsmen, etc.* 4

Bright   *B* is the moon on the deep, *B* are the cliffs in
her beam,   *Bright is the moon* 1
And a *b* archangel drove.   *Far off in the dun* 116
his forehead heavenly *b* From the clear marble   *One was the Tishbite* 6
lamps were *b* and gay On the merry bridal-day,   *The lamps were bright* 1
And Heaven is dark and *b* by turns.   *Youth, lapsing ii* 16
A mountain *b* with triple peaks: „   48

Brim   He *b*'s his beaker to the top,   *Yon huddled cloud* 13

Bring   Behold, ye cannot *b* but good,   *Are those the far-famed* 5
break the pride of Britain, and *b* her on her
knees,   *They say, etc.* 2

Bringing   *b* To happy Hayti the new-comer,   *A dark Indian maiden* 37

Brink   but ever drawn Under either grassy *b*   *Not to Silence* 25
Upon the *b* A solitary fortress burns,   *Youth, lapsing ii* 13

Britain   every man in *B* Says ' I am of Havelock's
blood ! '   *Bold Havelock* 15
To break the pride of *B*,   *They say, etc.* 2
you gleam reset In *B*'s lyric coronet.   *We lost you* 4

Briton   let an honest *B* sit at home at ease: *Far off in the dun* 9

Broad   below The highway, *b* and flat,   „   128

Broke   They *b* the ground with hoofs of fire   *Faded ev'ry violet* 3

Broken   victim, *B* in this anger of Aphrodite,   *Not to Silence* 29

Brook   Partly river, partly *b*,   *How is it that men* 5

Brother   But rejoice when a bigger *b* has proved   *A dark Indian maiden* 41

Brought   Then she *b* the guava fruit,   *Not a whisper* 1
She whose birth *b* on my bliss :   *Far off in the dun* 1

Brow   His *b* is clammy and pale.   „   84
the white fly leapt About his hairless *b*.   *Hear you the sound* 48
knit your baby *b*'s Into your father's frown,   „   64
high birth Had writ nobility upon my *b*.   *That is his portrait* 4
Admire that stalwart shape, those ample *b*'s,   „   23
These careful and those candid *b*'s,   „

Brush   *B*'es of fire, hazy gleams,   *Hither, when all* 6

Brush'd   As the quick wheels *b*,   *Far off in the dun* 91

Bud   May begins to breathe and *b*,   *Life of the Life* 3

Build   Not to Silence would I *b* a temple   *Not to Silence* 1

Built   (*See also* **Slight-built**)   That Inn was *b* at the
birth of Time :   *Far off in the dun* 37
what an arch the brain has *b* Above the ear !   *That is his portrait* 10

Burn   hearts that in them *b* With power   *Far off in the dun* 29
her black eyes *b* With a light so wild and stern ?'   *The lamps were bright* 15
Upon the brink A solitary fortress *b*,   *Youth, lapsing ii* 14

Burning   (*See also* **Ever-burning**)   Far off in the dun,   *Far off in the dun* 2
dark occident, Behind the *b* Sun :   „   39
Cemented with the *b* slime Which from Asphaltus flows.   „   122
With a silver sound the wheels went round, The
wheels of *b* flame,   *Half after midnight!* 6
Hard by the *b* throne of my great grandsire,   *Far off in the dun* 119

Burst (s)   With a solemn *b* of thrilling light,   *The child was sitting* 4

Burst (verb)   The river rose and *b* his bound,   *Why suffers* 2
I could *b* into a psalm of praise,   *Youth, lapsing ii* 33
Out *b*'s a rainbow in the sky—   „   47
from the golden vapour *b*'s A mountain bright   *i* 11

Butterfly   Before the first white *butterflies*,

C

Caesar   A *C* of a punier dynasty   *Here, I that stood* 5

Call   You were wont to *c* it Your throne.   *Hear you the sound* 35
C to the freshly-flower'd hill.   *Remember you* 12
C to its mate when nothing stirr'd   „   15

Call'd would have *c* you down to break your fast,   *Hear you the sound* 47
Calm Before his eyes so grim and *c*   *Far off in the dun* 77
Came And the host *c* forth, and stood alone   „ 49
    There *c* a gaunt man from the dark Inn door,   „ 73
    wind *c* singing lustily Among the moss-grown branches,   *Hear you the sound* 41
    I *c* And would have call'd you down   „ 46
Candid These careful and those *c* brows, how each—   *That is his portrait* 23
Canna Breezes from the palm and *c*   *A dark Indian maiden* 14
Cap Jauntily sat the Proctor's *c*   *Sweet Kitty Sandilands* 11
Capacious *C* both of Friendship and of Love.   *That is his portrait* 51
Care He *c's*, if ancient usage fade,   *They wrought, etc.* 33
Careful These *c* and those candid brows, how each—   *That is his portrait* 23
Carmel-steeps As when he stood on *C-s*   *One was the Tishbite* 2
Carol Following her wild *c* She led them   *A dark Indian maiden* 61
Carolling *C* ' Happy, happy Hayti ! '   „ 52
Carouse no revelling tones Of *c* were heard within: *Far off in the dun* 42
Carved forms Of the unfading marble *c* upon them,   *Hear you the sound* 26
    First shaped, and *c*, and set me in my place.   *Here, I that stood* 4
Casement The *c's* sparkle on the plain,   *Youth, lapsing ii* 39
Cast every line Wore the pale *c* of thought,   *Methought I saw* 2
Castle Up the street we took her As far as to the *C*,   *Sweet Kitty Sandilands* 10
Cataract This goes straight forward to the *c*:   *Steersman* 4
    But tho' the *c* seem the nearer way,   „ 6
Caterwaul If the wind *c*, lay harder upon her   *Wherever evil* 7
Cause great *c* of Freedom round and round.   *First drink a health* 60
Carven Wax-lighted chapels, and rich *c* screens   *Therefore your Halls* 4
Cease These voices did not *c* to cry   *Youth, lapsing i* 22
Ceasing Confused, and *c* from my quest,   „ 45
Cedar-wooded *c-w* paradise Of still Xaraguay: *A dark Indian maiden* 20
Cellar For he, whose *c* is his pride,   *Yon huddled cloud* 6
Cemented *C* with the burning slime   *Far off in the dun* 39
Century Which speak of us to other *centuries*,   *Hear you the sound* 27
Cessation There may be short *c* of their wails,   *Half after midnight!* 12
Chamber This *c* she was born in !   *Along this glimmering* 3
    tho' the faults be thick as dust In vacant *c's*,   *The noblest men* 11
Chance lest it by *c* should mark The life that haunts   *How strange it is* 6
    pleasant spot Where it was my *c* to marry,   *Vicar of this* 2
Change (s) of the *c's* of the suns ?   *Little Aubrey* 6
    Mature, harbour'd from *c*, contemplative,   *That is his portrait* 12
    overhaste Should fire the many wheels of *c* !   *They wrought, etc.* 24
    to repair With seasonable *c's* fair   „ 35
    When from *c* to *c*, Led silently by power divine,   *Thou may'st remember* 8
    Thro' every *c* that made thee what thou art ?   *To thee with whom* 14
Change (verb) A sound of words that *c* to blows !   *They wrought, etc.* 17
Changed when the winds Are fallen or *c*;   *Woman of noble* 10
Channel river here, my friend, Parts in two *c's*,   *Steersman* 3
    thro' the *c's* of the state Convoys   *They wrought, etc.* 30
Chant And *c's* in the golden wakening   *Full light aloft* 3
Chanted He *c* some old doleful rhyme.   *Youth, lapsing i* 36
Chapel *c's* vaulted gloom Was misted with perfume.   *The lamps were bright* 7
Charged *C* with his gallant few,   *Bold Havelock* 6
Charnel-place tomb And *c-p* of purpose dead,   *Thou may'st remember* 4
Chase Uncertain of ourselves we *c* The clap of hands ;   *They wrought, etc.* 13
Chatter That they chuckle and *c* and mock ?   *How is it that men* 3
Chattering The *c* of the fleshless jaws,   *Far off in the dun* 95
Cheek There was not a tinge on each high *c* bone,   „ 51
    Those thoughtful furrows in the swarthy *c*;   *That is his portrait* 3
    eyes Are swallow'd in his pamper'd *c's*.   *Yon huddled cloud* 12
Chequer'd *C* with moonlight's variation,   *Hear you the sound* 22
Chief This tavern is their *c* resort,   *Yon huddled cloud* 5
Child A *c* she loved to play ;   *Along this glimmering* 2
    Thy *c* will bless thee, guardian mother mild,   *Long as the heart* 22
    bless'd By children of the children of thy *c*.   „ 4
    In that cradle sleeps my *c*,   *Not a whisper* 9
    c was sitting on the bank Upon a stormy day,   *The child was sitting* 1
    Took the *c* from off the ground, And bore the *c* away.   „ 6
    O the *c* so meek and wise,   „ 8
Childhood All her loving *c* Breezes from the palm   *A dark Indian maiden* 13
Children memory will be bless'd By *c* of the *c*   *Long as the heart* 4
Chill The tingling blood grew *c*,   *Far off in the dun* 78

Chilling There lies a land of *c* storms,   *Far off in the dun* 5
    Vast wastes of starless glooms were spread Around in the *c* air,   „ 102
Chimney Moan'd in her *c's* and her eaves ;   *Youth, lapsing i* 30
Choice So lived I without aim or *c*,   „ 37
Chuckle That they *c* and chatter and mock ?   *How is it that men* 3
Cinchona Crown'd with garlands of *c*,   *A dark Indian maiden* 26
Citizen snug brick box Of some sleek *c*.   *Hear you the sound* 20
    Whence your own *c's*, for their own renown,   *Here, I that stood* 7
    he, the *c*, Deep-hearted, moderate, firm,   *They wrought, etc.* 9
Claim those whom Freedom *c's* As patriot-martyrs   *Not such were those* 1
Clammy His brow is *c* and pale.   *Far off in the dun* 28
Clap Uncertain of ourselves we chase The *c* of hands ;   *They wrought, etc.* 14
Clapperclaw Till she *c* no longer,   *Wherever evil* 7
Clasp I *c* her slender waist, We kiss,   *How glad am I* 5
Clay Why the bride is white as *c*,   *The lamps were bright* 10
Clear 'Tis a *c* night, they will be here anon.   *Hear you the sound* 6
    oak Which towers above the lake that ripples out In the *c* moonshine.   „ 34
    From the *c* marble pouring glorious scorn,   *One was the Tishbite* 7
    Remember you the *c* moonlight   *Remember you* 1
    Rang like a trumpet *c* and dry,   *Youth, lapsing i* 19
Clear-edged *C-e*, and showing every bend   *Thy soul is like* 5
Clearer A *c* day Than our poor twilight dawn on earth—   *Gone into darkness* 4
Cleave land of many days that *c's* In two great halves,   *They wrought, etc.* 26
Clever Shadows of statesmen, *c* men !   „ 12
Click-clack With *c-c* alternation to and fro,   *Half after midnight!* 8
Cliff Bright are the *c's* in her beam,   *Bright is the moon* 2
Cloak They mounted slow in their long black *c's*,   *Far off in the dun* 85
    his *c* wind-borne Behind,   *One was the Tishbite* 1
Clock There is a *c* in Pandemonium,   *Half after midnight!* 1
    What's the *c* ? Mich. Half way toward midnight.   *Hear you the sound* 33
Cloister'd With reason *c* in the brain :   *Young is the grief* 4
Clomb Shudder'd with silent stars, she *c*,   *Hither, when all* 2
Close I met in all the *c* green ways,   *I met in all* 1
Cloud *c's* are sunder'd toward the morning-rise ;   *O God, make this age* 9
    a colour'd *c*, O'er the bow'd shoulder of a bland old Age,   *That is his portrait* 35
    A momentary *c* upon me fell :   *To thee with whom* 6
    Yon huddled *c* his motion shifts,   *Yon huddled cloud* 1
    The *c's* unswathe them from the height,   *Youth, lapsing ii* 4
Cloudless With him you love, be *c* and be long !   *Take, Lady* 4
Cloudy things of past days with their horrible eyes Look out from the *c* vast.   *Far off in the dun* 20
    And the moaning wind before it drives Thick wreaths of *c* dew.   „ 24
    Fast by me flash the *c* streaks,   *Youth, lapsing ii* 46
Clue think a cunning hand has found the *c*—   *What rustles* 14
Cluster *C's* and beds of worlds,   *Hither, when all* 7
Coach there stood a dark *c* at an old Inn door   *Far off in the dun* 35
    As the *c* ran on, and the sallow lights shone   „ 99
    those are the lights of the Paradise *c*,   „ 107
Coachee (coachman) grim old *c* strode to the box,   „ 87
    O *C, C*, what lights approach With heavenly melodies ?   „ 105
Coat A dreadnought *c* had he :   „ 74
Cockroach As the *c* crept, and the white fly leapt   „ 83
Cocoa-shadow'd In the *c-s* coves,   *A dark Indian maiden* 8
Coeval *C* with the battlemented towers   *Hear you the sound* 36
Cold *C* words I spoke, yet loved thee warm and well.   *To thee with whom* 8
    Seem'd I so *c* ? what madness moved my blood   „ 10
Coldness My *c* was mistimed like summer-snow,   „ 7
Colour'd At the end, as 'twere athwart a *c* cloud,   *That is his portrait* 35
Come Father will *c* to thee soon,   *Bright is the moon* 9
    Father will *c* to his babe in the nest,   „ 11
    ' And thro' all phases of all thought I *c*   *From shape to shape* 3
    We *c* from apes—and are far removed—   *How is it that men* 4
    The crowd have *c* to see thy grave,   *I keep no more* 2
    The year, that *c's*, may *c* with shame,   *I, loving Freedom* 6
    mock'd and said, ' *C*, cry aloud, he sleeps.'   *One was the Tishbite* 4
    That would have *c* to woo her.   *Sweet Kitty Sandilands* 8
    Thro' spiritual dark we *c* Into the light   *Thou may'st remember* 5
    far off from England's shore, He *c's* no more.   *What rustles* 10
    voice Cried in the future ' *C* along.'   *Youth, lapsing i* 40

Day (*See also* **Bridal-day**) All *d* long with laugh-
  ing eyes, — *A dark Indian maiden* 17
  upon the shore Dancing at the break of *d*,   „ 66
  things of past *d's* with their horrible eyes   *Far off in the dun* 19
  Ere the *d* be well-nigh done ;   *Full light aloft* 10
  clearer *d* Than our poor twilight dawn on earth— *Gone into darkness* 4
  I see the world's renewed youth A long *d's*
    dawn, — *O God, make this age* 7
  Old ghosts whose *d* was done ere mine began, *Old ghosts* 1
  That none can truly write his single *d*,   „ 13
  Take thou the ' bend,' 'twill save thee many a *d*. *Steersman* 8
  child was sitting on the bank Upon a stormy *d*, *The child was sitting* 2
  In the hall, at close of *d*, — *The lamps were bright* 35
  A land of many *d's* that cleaves In two great
    halves, — *They wrought, etc.* 26
  D by *d* Watch your standard roses blowing, *Vicar of this* 11
  The image of the sun by *d*, *Youth, lapsing i* 7
  Down from the summit sweeps the *d*   „ ii 31
Dead (adj.) March'd and fought himself *d*. *Bold Havelock* 12
  They lifted their eyes to the *d*, pale skies, *Far off in the dun* 61
  and threw up the dust Of *d* men's pulverised bones. *I keep no more* 8
  ' The dead are *d* and let them be.'
  ' From the tomb And charnel-place of
    purpose *d*, *Thou may'st remember* 4
Dead (s) Then pledge we our glorious *d*, *Frenchman, etc.* 9
  and so many *d*, And him the last. *Gone into darkness* 10
  ' The *d* are dead and let them be.' *I keep no more* 8
Deal Not *d's* in threats, but works with hope, *They wrought, etc.* 39
Dear And God's best blessing on each *d* head *Frenchman, etc.* 11
  one yet more *d*, More *d*, for what is lost is made
    more *d* ; ' More *d* ' *That is his portrait* 45
  Was I so harsh ? Ah *d*, it could not be. *To thee with whom* 9
Dearest Speak to me, *d*, lest I die. *Speak to me* 4
Death That ride to *d* the griefs of men ? *Are those the far-famed* 2
  The *D* for which they mourn is Life.' *Early-wise* 8
  pleasant hymns they soothe the air Of *d*, *Far off in the dun* 110
  The face of a placid *D*. *That is his portrait* 37
  silent Guardians But true till *D* ; *Woman of noble* 7
Declined she seeming blithe *D* her head : *One was the Tishbite* 14
Deemed I *d* her one of stately frame *Because she bore* 3
Deep (adj.) In the *d* wood no more,—By the *d*
  sea no more,— *A dark Indian maiden* 67
  D glens I found, and sunless gulfs, *Deep glens I found* 1
  D dells of snow sunk on each side below The
    highway, *Far off in the dun* 97
  Full light aloft doth the laverock spring From under
    the *d*, sweet corn, *Full light aloft* 2
  Hither, when all the *d* unsounded skies *Hither, when all* 1
  Often *d* beyond the sight, *Not to Silence* 22
  Yet her own *d* soul says nay : *The lamps were bright* 24
  Then a scream of wild dismay Thro' the *d* hall
    forced its way,   „ 42
  ' Come ' and I come, the vale is *d*, *Youth, lapsing ii* 27
Deep (s) Bright is the moon on the *d*, *Bright is the moon* 1
  Father is over the *d*,   „ 8
  sound in her ears like the sound of the *d*, Like the
    sound of the *d*, *That the voice* 1
Deepening Crown'd with soft shade her *d* floods *Youth, lapsing i* 3
Deeper past, in sleep, away By night, into the *d*
  night ! The *d* night ? *Gone into darkness* 3
  But his was minted in a *d* mould, *That is his portrait* 17
  Lower and *d* evermore They grew, *Youth, lapsing i* 25
Deep-hearted citizen, *D-h*, moderate, firm, *They wrought, etc.* 10
Deep-mouth'd mutter of *d-m* thunderings *Far off in the dun* 15
Deer *d* Bleat as with human voices in the park. *What rustles* 3
Delicious Which in one *d* nook, *Not to Silence* 30
Delight Nor proved I such *d* as he, *That is his portrait* 19
Dell Deep *d's* of snow sunk on each side *Far off in the dun* 97
Demure how *d* a smile, How full of wisest humour *That is his portrait* 6
Depth Through all that boundless *d* of fires *Half after midnight !* 13
Deserve Yet grief *d's* a nobler name : *Young is the grief* 5
Desire And lights at length on his *d* : *They wrought, etc.* 40
  The sharp *d* of knowledge still with knowing ! *Why suffers* 6
Despair To preach the freedom of *d*, *He was too good* 10
Despising Contends, *d* party-rage, *They wrought, etc.* 46

Despot The *d's* over yonder, let 'em do whate'er *They say, etc.* 16
Devil and we, Poor *d's*, babble ' we shall last.' *Well, as to Fame* 8
  and the *d——l* take the parties ! *They say, etc.* 10
Dew wind before it drives Thick wreaths of cloudy *d*. *Far off in the dun* 24
  ' I love the daisy weeping ' *I keep no more* 13
Die Of him who doomed the king to *d*, *Because she bore* 2
  Speak to me, dearest, lest I *d*. *Speak to me* 4
  When I *d*, the GHOULS ! ! ! *While I live* 2
Died Bold Havelock *d*, Tender and great *Bold Havelock* 13
Difference The *d* of all things to the sense, And all the
  likeness in the *d*. *Why suffers* 10
Dignity It show'd the seeds of innate *d* *Hear you the sound* 52
Dim Wherefore should your eyes be *d* ? *Early-wise* 5
  D grief did wait upon her, *The lamps were bright* 33
Dimly sallow lights shone *D* and blurly *Far off in the dun* 100
Disappear I have seen the four great empires *d* ! *Here, I that stood* 9
Disarrange hands that *d* The social engine ! *They wrought, etc.* 21
Discourse owning more *D*, growing wiser wise.' *From shape to shape* 8
Dishonest There's a treaty, so they tell us, of some *d* fellows *They say, etc.* 3
Dismay Then a scream of wild *d* *The lamps were bright* 41
Disploding *D* globes of roaring fire. *Deep glens I found* 6
Dispread that large table of the breast *d*, *That is his portrait* 5
Dissipation Unto the *d* of this Earth. *Half after midnight !* 4
Dissolve *D* a world, condense a star, *Are those the far-famed* 14
Distant He sees his father in *d* lands, *Bright is the moon* 5
  low sweet voices mourn'd In *d* fields, ' Come back,
    come back.' *Youth, lapsing i* 44
Distress I keep no more a lone *d*, *I keep no more* 1
Ditty moving To her Areyto's mellow *d*, *A dark Indian maiden* 50
Divine What aileth thee, O bird *d*, *Full light aloft* 5
  Most eloquent, who spake of things *d*. *Methought I saw* 1
  When from change to change, Led silently by
    power *d*, *Thou may'st remember* 9
Dizzy Yet am I *d* in the track, *Youth, lapsing ii* 43
Doctor Kitty Sandilands, The daughter of the *d*, *Sweet Kitty Sandilands* 7
Doleful He chanted some old *d* rhyme. *Youth, lapsing i* 36
Dome her keen eyes Pierced thro' the mystic *d*, *Hither, when all* 4
Done Ere the day be well-nigh *d* ; *Full light aloft* 10
  And there is something greatly *d* : *Youth, lapsing ii* 12
Doomed Of him who *d* the king to die, *Because she bore* 2
Door there stood a dark coach at an old Inn *d* *Far off in the dun* 35
  There came a gaunt man from the dark Inn *d*,   „ 73
  Step thro' these *d's*, and I will show to you *That is his portrait* 44
  Beside my *d* at morning stood The tearful spirit *Youth, lapsing i* 33
Doorway stood alone And still in the dark *d* : *Far off in the dun* 50
Double Beneath those *d* arches lie Fair with green
  fields the realms of Love. *Youth, lapsing ii* 35
Doubt I knew him in his hour Of darkest *d*, and in his
  power, To fling his *d's* into the street. *He was too good* 3
  Unvext by *d's* I cannot solve, *Youth, lapsing i* 50
Doubtful Where the *d* shadows play, *Not to Silence* 31
Dragon on every side The *d's* curves melted, *One was the Tishbite* 15
Dragon-fly The *d-f* and scarlet crane, *A dark Indian maiden* 32
Drank and *d* The sweet sad tears of wisdom.' *Methought I saw* 5
Draw To *d* strange comfort from the earth, *Far off in the dun* 31
Drawn but ever *d* Under either grassy brink *Not to Silence* 24
Dreadnought A *d* coat had he : *Far off in the dun* 74
Dream (*See also* **Half-dream**) And kisses him there
  in a *d*, *Bright is the moon* 6
  See, she dreameth happy *d's*, *Not a whisper* 13
  sleep thro' one brief *d* upon the grass,— *Townsmen, etc.* 4
Dreameth See, she *d* happy dreams, *Not a whisper* 13
Dreaming In the *d* of past things : *The lamps were bright* 22
Dreamt And *d* not of the miller's daughter. *I met in all* 8
Drest We *d* her in the Proctor's bands, *Sweet Kitty Sandilands* 3
Drew sun *D* down the West his feeble lights ; *Deep glens I found* 6
  Thro' strange seas *d* me to your monster town. *Here, I that stood* 8
Drifted That mystic field of *d* light In mid Orion, *Hither, when all* 10
Drink Let us *d* to the health of thine and mine *Frenchman, etc.* 9
  It is not good to *d* strong wine *Full light aloft* 9
  Shall *d* the fulness of thy victory, *O God, make this age* 13
Dripping I grieved as woods in *d* rains *Youth, lapsing i* 31
Drive moaning wind before it *d's* Thick wreaths *Far off in the dun* 23
  To *d* them where he will.   „ 80
Drop And sometimes with a twinkling *d*, *Yon huddled cloud* 1

Drove   And a bright archangel *d*.   *Far off in the dun* 116
   D into lines and studs of light The image   *Youth, lapsing i* 6
Drown   shriek and shout to *d* the thrilling noise.   *Half after midnight!* 16
Drunk   Is thy mad brain *d* with the merry, red wine,   *Full light aloft* 7
   But thou hast *d* of the merry, sweet wine,   " 11
Dry   earth is *d*, tho' the pall of the sky   *Far off in the dun* 21
   Rang like a trumpet clear and *d*,   *Youth, lapsing i* 19
Dulcimer   With sackbut, and with *d*,   *Far off in the dun* 111
Dull   and *d* The sharp desire of knowledge still with knowing !   *Why suffers* 5
   And startle the *d* ears of human kind !   *O God, make this age* 5
Dumb   The thunder cannot make thee *d* ;   *Youth, lapsing ii* 26
Dun   Far off in the *d*, dark occident,   *Far off in the dun* 1
Dust   threw up the *d* Of dead men's pulverised bones.   " 91
   tho' the faults be thick as *d* In vacant chambers.   *The noblest men* 10
Dwell   To thee with whom my true affections *d*,   *To thee with whom* 1
   ever young the face that *d*'s With reason   *Young is the grief* 3
Dwelling   near the *d* of some noble race ;   *Hear you the sound* 17
Dynasty   A Caesar of a punier *d*   *Here, I that stood* 5

E

Each   There was not a tinge on *e* high cheek bone,   *Far off in the dun* 51
   They hear *e* household voice :   " 66
   Deep dells of snow sunk on *e* side below The highway,   " 97
   And God's best blessing on *e* dear head That rests by the Alma River.   *Frenchman, etc.* 11
   when *e* one leaves The middle road of sober thought !   *They wrought, etc.* 27
   and showing every bend Of *e* dark hill against the Heaven,   *Thy soul is like* 6
Eager   Tall, *e*, lean and strong, his cloak   *One was the Tishbite* 5
Ear   Piercing the wrung *e*'s of the damn'd   *Half after midnight!* 10
   startle the dull *e*'s of human kind !   *O God, make this age* 5
   what an arch the brain has built Above the *e* !   *That is his portrait* 11
   sound in her *e*'s like the sound of the deep,   *That the voice* 2
   We faint unless the wanton *e* Be tickled   *They wrought, etc.* 6
Earliest   That watch't with love thine *e* infancy,   *To thee with whom* 12
Early   Are pleasant from the *e* Spring to when,   *Townsmen, etc.* 7
   It is the *e* morning, Hark !   *Youth, lapsing ii* 6
   and all comes back Which in that *e* voice was sweet,   " ii 42
Early-wise   *E-w*, and pure, and true,   *Early-wise* 1
Earth   the *e* is dry, tho' the pall of the sky   *Far off in the dun* 21
   To draw strange comfort from the *e*,   " 31
   They saw the green verge of the pleasant *e*,   " 63
   Than our poor twilight dawn on *e*—   *Gone into darkness* 5
   Unto the dissipation of this *E*.   *Half after midnight!* 4
   But as *E* her orbit runs,   *Little Aubrey* 3
   If *e* be seen from your conjectured heaven,   *Old ghosts* 2
   And none can write it for him upon *e*.   " 14
   Well, as to Fame, who strides,the *e*   *Well, as to "Fame"* 1
Ease   will not let an honest Briton sit at home at *e* :   *They say, etc.* 9
East   little Alfred in the *E*   *Little Aubrey* 1
   So pausing 'twixt the *E* and West,   *Youth, lapsing i* 47
Eastern   Remember you the clear moonlight That whiten'd all the *e* ridge,   *Remember you* 2
Eaves   dark vine leaves round the rustling *e*,   *Far off in the dun* 71
   Moan'd in her chimneys and her *e* ;   *Youth, lapsing i* 30
Eclipse   Why suffers human life so soon *e* ?   *Why suffers* 1
Eddy   Her silver *eddies* in their play Drove into lines   *Youth, lapsing i* 5
Edged   *See* **Clear-edged**
Either   but ever drawn Under *e* grassy brink   *Not to Silence* 25
   Whate'er the crowd on *e* bank may say,   *Steersman* 7
   And floats in *e* golden Ind.   *The noblest men* 8
Eloquent   Become a tacit *e* reproach Unto the dissipation of this Earth.   *Half after midnight!* 3
   Most *e*, who spake of things divine.   *Methought I saw* 3
Embraced   When she and I are thus *e*,   *How glad am I* 7
Empire   I have seen the four great *e*'s disappear !   *Here, I that stood* 9
Emptiness   the *e* And horrors of the formless dark.   *How strange it is* 7
End   I see At the *e*, as 'twere athwart a colour'd cloud,   *That is his portrait* 35
   He, seeing far an *e* sublime,   *They wrought, etc.* 45
   A labour working to an *e*.   *Youth, lapsing ii* 4

End (*continued*)   Parts in two channels, moving to one *e*—   *Steersman* 3
Energy   An *e*, an agony,   *Youth, lapsing ii* 3
Engine   hands that disarrange The social *e* !   *They wrought, etc.* 22
England   far off from *E*'s shore, He comes no more.   *What rustles* 9
Engrav'n   I hold Mother's love *e* in gold.   *Helen's Tower* 4
Entertain   Young is the grief I *e*,   *Young is the grief* 1
Enthusiastic   but I glow With an *e* love of them.   *Hear you the sound* 15
Envelope   night's eternal wings *E*'s the gloomy whole,   *Far off in the dun* 14
Epigram   Little poet, hear the little poet's *e* !   *Little Aubrey* 1
Equal   His fame is *e* to his years :   *That is his portrait* 42
Espagnola   happy as Anacaona, The beauty of *E*, (repeat)   *A dark Indian maiden* 11, 23
   happy was Anacaona, The beauty of *E*,   " 35
   happy Anacaona, The beauty of *E*, (repeat)   " 47, 71
   they smiled on Anacaona, The beauty of *E*,   " 59
Essence   Evermore The simpler *e* lower lies,   *From shape to shape* 6
Eternal   When the shadow of night's *e* wings Envelopes   *Far off in the dun* 13
Eternity   act on *E* To keep thee here amongst us !   *That is his portrait* 39
Eustace   Long, *E*, long May my strong wish,   " 37
Eve   blow Melodious thunders thro' your vacant courts At noon and *e*,   *Therefore your Halls* 10
Even   With the first twilight of the *e*,   *Thy soul is like* 4
Ever-burning   (an inner spirit fed Their *e-b* fires,)   *Far off in the dun* 118
Every   Faded *e* violet, all the roses ;   *Faded ev'ry violet*, 1
   E mile a battle, *E* battle a victory.   *Bold Havelock* 3
   And *e* man in Britain Says 'I am of Havelock's blood ! '   " 15
   aerial melody May blow alarm loud to *e* wind,   *O God, make this age* 4
   ' Methought I saw a face whose *e* line   *Methought I saw* 1
   E heart is lain to rest,   *Not a whisper* 5
   on *e* side The dragon's curves melted,   *One was the Tishbite* 14
   How *e* brake and flower spread and rose,   *That is his portrait* 26
   Your name is blown on *e* wind,   *The noblest men* 5
   Clear-edged, and showing *e* bend Of each dark hill against the Heaven,   *Thy soul is like* 5
   Thro' *e* change that made thee what thou art ?   *To thee with whom* 14
Evil   Glancing off from all things *e*,   *Vicar of this* 17
   Wherever *e* customs thicken,   *Wherever evil* 1
Example   A pure *e* to the lands,   *They wrought, etc.* 2
Expectant   Am large in hope that these *e* eyes Shall drink   *O God, make this age* 12
Eye   All day long with laughing *e*'s,   *A dark Indian maiden* 17
   With fair blue *e*'s and winning sweet,   *Because she bore* 6
   Large as a human *e* the sun Drew down the West   *Deep glens I found* 5
   Wherefore should your *e*'s be dim ?   *Early-wise* 5
   things of past days with their horrible *e*'s   *Far off in the dun* 19
   fiery *e*'s glared fiercely thro' The windows   " 47
   They lifted their *e*'s to the dead, pale skies,   " 61
   Before his *e*'s so grim and calm   " 77
   That so gaily meet their *e*'s !   " 108
   her keen *e*'s Pierced thro' the mystic dome,   *Hither, when all* 3
   Light of the Light within mine *e*'s, (repeat)   *Life of the Life* 2, 8
   large in hope that these expectant *e*'s   *O God, make this age* 12
   light of hazel *e*'s, Observing all things.   *That is his portrait* 13
   once he spake : ' I lift the *e*'s of thought,   " 33
   why her black *e*'s burn With a light so wild   *The lamps were bright* 15
   With a laughing crazed *e*,   " 52
   The green that fills the *e*—   *'Tis not alone* 4
   his little *e*'s Are swallow'd in his pamper'd cheeks.   *Yon huddled cloud* 11
   Considering what mine *e*'s have seen,   *Young is the grief* 9
Eyed   *See* **Crimson-eyed**
Eyeless   His sockets were *e*, but in them slept   *Far off in the dun* 81

F

Face   Loftily stepping with fair *f*'s.   *A dark Indian maiden* 64
   A land of thin *f*'s and shadowy forms,   *Far off in the dun* 7
   But his *f* was a yellow gray.   " 52
   The miller with his mealy *f*,   *I met in all* 3
   Methought I saw a *f* whose every line Wore   *Methought I saw* 1
   The *f* of placid Death.'   *That is his portrait* 37
   ever young the *f* that dwells With reason cloister'd   *Young is the grief* 3

Face (continued) When to this sound my *f* I turn'd, *Youth, lapsing i 41*
Faced *See* **Fair-faced**
Faction Wed to no *f* in the state, *I, loving Freedom 3*
Fade He cares, if ancient usage *f*, *They wrought, etc. 33*
Faded *F* ev'ry violet, all the roses; *Faded ev'ry violet 1*
Fail His limbs beneath him *f*; *Far off in the dun 26*
'Tis shame to *f* so far, and still My failing *Young is the grief 7*
Failing still My *f* shall be less my shame: „ 8
Faint (adj.) Now one *f* line of light doth glow, *Youth, lapsing ii 9*
F shouts are heard across the glen, „ ii 22
Faint (verb) We *f* unless the wanton ear Be tickled with the loud ' hear, hear,' *They wrought, etc. 6*
Fair Loftily stepping with *f* faces. *A dark Indian maiden 64*
With *f* blue eyes and winning sweet, *Because she bore 6*
And the forests, *f* and free. *Far off in the dun 72*
The whisper'd love of the *f* young wives; „ 67
And from the heart of all things *f* *He was too good 11*
And veils a breast more *f* to me Than aught of Anadyomené ! *Not to Silence 15*
With seasonable changes *f* And innovation grade by grade! *They wrought, etc. 35*
The two *f* lilies growing at thy side Have slowly prosper'd *Woman of noble 11*
Youth, lapsing thro' *f* solitudes, *Youth, lapsing i 1*
F with green fields the realms of Love. „ ii 36
I took delight in this *f* strand and free. *Here often when a child 2*
Fair-faced For they were *f-f* and tall, They were more *f-f* and tall, *A dark Indian maiden 55*
Fairy Spurge with *f* crescent set, *Spurge with fairy 1*
Faith No, *f*, not I. *Hear you the sound 2*
Fall These whispers rise, and *f* away, *'Tis not alone 10*
Fallen when the winds Are *f* or changed; *Woman of noble 10*
I grieved as woods in dripping rains Sigh over all their *f* leaves; *Youth, lapsing i 32*
Falling when nothing stirr'd To left or right but *f* floods. *Remember you 16*
False My hope is *f*, my terror's true ! *What rustles 12*
Falsehood when Poesy shall bind *F* beneath *O God, make this age 8*
Fame Mix'd with the phantom of his coming *f*, *That is his portrait 32*
His *f* is equal to his years: „ 42
His name is pure, his *f* is free: *They wrought, etc. 32*
Well, as to *F*, who strides the earth *Well, as to Fame 1*
Famed *See* **Far-famed**
Fancy Or a *f* for a madness,— *Immeasurable sadness! 7*
My *f* was the more luxuriant, *That is his portrait 16*
Fann'd *F* this queen of the green wildwood, *A dark Indian maiden 15*
Far Variously from its *f* spring, *Not to Silence 27*
Fare Ill *f*'s a people passion-wrought, *They wrought, etc. 25*
Far-famed Are those the *f-f* Victor Hours *Are those the far-famed 1*
Farthing As each put a *f* into his palm, *Far off in the dun 79*
Fast would have call'd you down to break your *f*, *Hear you the sound 47*
All the house is *f* in sleep, *Not a whisper 6*
Fat (adj.) Mine host is *f*, and gray, and wise, *Yon huddled cloud 9*
Fat (s) lights shone Dimly and blurly with simmering *f*. *Far off in the dun 100*
Fate A will concentric with all *f*, *Young is the grief 15*
Father He sees his *f* in distant lands, *Bright is the moon 5*
F is over the deep, *F* will cóme to thee soon, „ 8
F will come to his babe in the nest, „ 11
Prince, whose *F* lived in you, *Early-wise 2*
knit your baby brows Into your *f*'s frown, *Hear you the sound 49*
Fault Seest thou my *f*'s and wilt not speak ? *Speak to me 7*
tho' the *f*'s be thick as dust In vacant chambers, *The noblest men 10*
Faulty I give this *f* book to you, „ 9
Fear (s) Naked, without *f*, moving To her Areyto's *A dark Indian maiden 49*
f's that waste The strength of men, *They wrought, etc. 22*
Fear (verb) I *f* not; if I fear'd them, *Are those the far-famed 3*
These *f* not the mists of unwholesome damps *Far off in the dun 113*
Fear'd I fear not; if I *f* them, *Are those the far-famed 3*
Fed (an inner spirit *f* Their ever-burning fires,) *Far off in the dun 117*
One was the Tishbite whom the raven *f*, *One was the Tishbite 1*
Feeble the sun Drew down the West his *f* lights; *Deep glens I found 6*
Fell A momentary cloud upon me *f*: *To thee with whom 6*
Fellow a treaty, so they tell us, of some dishonest *f*'s *They say, etc. 3*

Feud Parish *f*, or party strife, *Vicar of this 8*
Few Charged with his gallant *f*, *Bold Havelock 6*
Field That mystic *f* of drifted light In mid Orion, would I build A temple in her naked *f*; *Hither, when all 10*
For Love flew over grove and *f*, *Not to Silence 2*
Full *f*'s of barley shifting tearful lights *The night, etc. 4*
In distant *f*'s, ' Come back, come back.' *Townsmen, etc. 8*
And rushes o'er a boundless *f*. *Youth, lapsing i 44*
Fair with green *f*'s the realms of Love. „ ii 32
„ 36
Fiery Strange *f* eyes glared fiercely thro' The windows of shaven bone. *Far off in the dun 47*
Before them flow'd a *f* stream ; „ 127
Bathe with me in the *f* flood, *Life of the Life 5*
Fifty Flooded *f* leagues around, *The child was sitting 5*
Fight gird up thy loins for *f*, *O God, make this age 10*
Figure And there sit *f*'s as of Gods *Youth, lapsing ii 51*
Fill The green that *f*'s the eye— *'Tis not alone 4*
Filthiest *f* of all paintings painted well *Art for Art's sake! 5*
Finer But to one of *f* sense, *Not to Silence 5*
Finger weave your waxen *f*'s in these locks *Hear you the sound 58*
With twinkling *f* sweeps her yellow keys. *Townsmen, etc. 10*
Finger-lipt *F-l*, but with right hand Moving *Not to Silence 10*
Fire (s) Disploding globes of roaring *f*. *Deep glens I found 4*
(an inner spirit fed Their ever-burning *f*'s,) *Far off in the dun 4*
They broke the ground with hoofs of *f* „ 128
Through all that boundless depth of *f*'s is heard *Half after midnight! 13*
Brushes of *f*, hazy gleams, *Hither, when all 6*
Fire (verb) Should *f* the many wheels of change ! *They wrought, etc. 24*
Fireside They see the light of their blest *f*'s, *Far off in the dun 65*
Firm citizen, Deep-hearted, moderate, *f*, *They wrought, etc. 10*
First Into another shape, born of the *f*, *That is his portrait 29*
Most delicately overdrawn With the *f* twilight of the even, *Thy soul is like 4*
Sent thro' my blood a prophet voice Before the *f* white butterflies, *Youth, lapsing i 11*
Fishing While *f* in the milldam-water, *I met in all 6*
Fit by *f*'s the lady ash With twinkling finger *Townsmen, etc. 9*
Flag Our *f*'s have waved together ! *Frenchman, etc. 2*
Our *f*'s together furl'd, „ 5
Your *f* thro' Austral ice is borne, *The noblest men 6*
Flame The wheels of burning *f*, *Far off in the dun 122*
damn'd that writhe Upon their beds of *f*, *Half after midnight! 11*
Flash Fast by me *f* the cloudy streaks, *Youth, lapsing i 46*
Flat below The highway, broad and *f*, *Far off in the dun 98*
„ 95
Fleshless The chattering of the *f* jaws, *The night, etc. 4*
Flew For love *f* over grove and field, „
Flight Is this blind *f* the winged Powers. *Are those the far-famed 4*
Were idler than a *f* of rooks. „ 12
Fling To *f* his doubts into the street. *He was too good 4*
Float And *f*'s in either golden Ind. *The noblest men 8*
there *f*'s upward from the gulf A murmur *Youth, lapsing ii 18*
Floated *F* in the silent summer: *A dark Indian maiden 40*
Floating and threw back Your *f* hair. *Hear you the sound 43*
the *f* snake Roll'd round her ankles, *One was the Tishbite 9*
Flock With the *f* of the thunder-stricken. *Wherever evil 5*
Flood Bathe with me in the fiery *f*, *Life of the Life 5*
To left or right but falling *f*, *Remember you 16*
The silent hills, the stormy *f*'s, *'Tis not alone 3*
Crown'd with soft shade her deepening *f*'s *Youth, lapsing i 3*
Flooded *F* fifty leagues around, *The child was sitting 5*
Flourish ye still shall *f* In your high pomp of shade, *Hear you the sound 23*
Flow (s) beside the *f* Of sacred Nile, *Here, I that stood 1*
Flow (verb) slime Which from Asphaltus *f*'s. *Far off in the dun 6*
Sweetly, smoothly *f* your life. *Vicar of this 6*
Sweetly *f* your life with Kate's, „ 16
Flow'd Before them a *f* a fiery stream ; *Far off in the dun 127*
Flower Espagnola, The golden *f* of Hayti? (repeat) *A dark Indian maiden 12, 24, 36, 48, 60, 72*
Like the *f* of Mahomet. *Spurge with fairy 2*
How every brake and *f* spread and rose, *That is his portrait 26*
Have slowly prosper'd *f* into stately *f*'s. *Woman of noble 12*
I sit among the scentless *f*'s *Youth, lapsing i 51*
Flower'd *See* **Freshly-flower'd**
Flower-laden Stepping lightly *f-l*, *A dark Indian maiden 3*
Flush never overflows With *f* of rain, *Not to Silence 20*

Fly white *f* leapt About his hairless brow.		*Far off in the dun* 83
Foe Becoming bands of armed *f's*!		*They wrought, etc.* 20
Fold left hand holds Her up-gather'd garment *f's*,		*Not to Silence* 14
Folded Her hands are *f* quietly,		*Not a whisper* 14
round her waist Knotted, and *f* once about her neck,		*One was the Tishbite* 11
Follow Intent to *f* on the track,		*Youth, lapsing i* 42
I *f* to the morning sun,		" *ii* 10
Following *F* her wild carol She led them		*A dark Indian maiden* 61
Fond We kiss, we are so *f*,		*How glad am I* 6
Foot and lie A thousand summers at her *f*.		*Because she bore* 8
A light wind wafts me from my *feet*.		*Youth, lapsing ii* 44
Footfall A step? a *f*? What is that I hear?		*What rustles* 2
Force Ev'n then the *f* of nature and high birth		*Hear you the sound* 63
Forced Thro' the deep hall *f* its way,		*The lamps were bright* 42
Forehead On her *f* undefiled I will print		*Not a whisper* 11
his *f* heavenly bright From the clear marble		*One was the Tishbite* 6
Foreign They say some *f* powers have laid		*They say, etc.* 1
Forest (adj.) Steeple, and stream, and *f* lawn,		*Thy soul is like* 2
Forest (s) And the *f's*, fair and free.		*Far off in the dun* 72
Forethinking *F* its twinfold necessity,		*That is his portrait* 49
Forlorn O leave not thou thy son *f*;		*O leave not thou* 1
Form A land of thin faces and shadowy *f's*,		*Far off in the dun* 7
As the shrivell'd *f's* of the shadowy grooms		" 59
monuments, with *f's* Of the unfading marble		*Hear you the sound* 25
Regions of lucid matter taking *f's*,		*Hither, when all* 5
And much of that which is her *f*,		*I, loving Freedom* 2
A dark *f* glances quick Thro' her worn brain,		*The lamps were bright* 27
Millions of *f's*, and hues, and shades,		*Why suffers* 9
Woman of noble *f* and noble mind!		*Woman of noble* 1
Formless The life that haunts the emptiness And horrors of the *f* dark.		*How strange it is* 8
Fortress Upon the brink A solitary *f* burns,		*Youth, lapsing i* 14
Forward This goes straight *f* to the cataract:		*Steersman* 4
Go *f*! crumble down a throne,		*Are those the far-famed* 13
Fought Ten men *f* a thousand, Slew them and overthrew. *Bold Havelock* 7
March'd and thought and *f*, March'd and *f* himself dead.		" 11
Found till the very wrong itself Had *f* him out.		*A surface man* 8
But *f* a maiden tender, shy,		*Because she bore* 5
Deep glens I *f*, and sunless gulfs,		*Deep glens I found* 1
When a great man's *f* to be bad and base,		*How is it that men* 2
Her thoughts have *f* their wings		*The lamps were bright* 21
Then they *f* him where he lay		" 47
We *f* you, and you gleam reset In Britain's		*We lost you* 3
And think a cunning hand has *f* the clue—		*What rustles* 14
I *f* the Present where I stay:		*Youth, lapsing i* 48
Up hither have I *f* my way,		" *ii* 29
Four I have seen the *f* great empires disappear!		*Here, I that stood* 9
Four-square A life *f-s* to all the winds.		*Young is the grief* 16
Fragrant Said, 'Open, Rosebud, open, yield Thy *f* soul.'		*The night, etc.* 6
Frail Alas, my life is *f* and weak:		*Speak to me* 6
Frame I deemed her one of stately *f*		*Because she bore* 3
Of beryl, and of amethyst Was the spiritual *f*.		*Far off in the dun* 124
The *f*, the mind, the soul of man,		*They wrought, etc.* 43
Framer but rather bless The All-perfect *F*,		*That is his portrait* 48
Free And the forests, fair and *f*.		*Far off in the dun* 72
And *f* from taint of sin.		" 132
The happy maiden's tears are *f*		*I keep no more* 5
His name is pure, his fame is *f*:		*They wrought, etc.* 32
I took delight in this fair strand and *f*;		*Here often when a child* 2
Freedom To preach the *f* of despair,		*He was too good* 10
I, loving *F* for herself,		*I, loving Freedom* 1
those whom *F* claims As patriot-martyrs		*Not such were those* 1
They worship *F* for her sake,		*They wrought, etc.* 1
great cause of *F* round and round.		*First drink a health* 60
All *f* vanish'd—		*Rise, Britons, rise* 3
Frenchman *F*, a hand in thine!		*Frenchman, etc.* 1
Fresh Would I could pile *f* life on life,		*Why suffers* 5
Freshly-flower'd Call to the *f-f* hill.		*Remember you* 12
Friend Hold thou, my *f*, no lesser life in scorn,		*Hold thou my friend* 1
My *f*, thou speakest from the heart,		*I keep no more* 15
the river here, my *f*, Parts in two channels,		*Steersman* 2
Thy soul is like a landskip, *f*,		*Thy soul is like* 1
bearest from the threshold of thy *f's*		*Woman of noble* 3
Friendship Gone into darkness, that full light Of *f*!		*Gone into darkness* 2

Friendship (continued) His and my *f* have not suffer'd loss,		*That is his portrait* 41
Capacious both of *F* and of Love.		" 51
Frosty And shook the *f* winter stars.		*Youth, lapsing i* 20
Frown (s) knit your baby brows Into your father's *f*,		*Hear you the sound* 49
Frown (verb) And on me *F* not, old ghosts,		*Old ghosts* 9
Fruit Then she brought the guava *f*,		*A dark Indian Maiden* 41
Full *F* light aloft doth the laverock spring		*Full light aloft* 1
Gone into darkness, that *f* light Of friendship!		*Gone into darkness* 1
Their *f* God-bless-you with this book of song,		*Take, Lady* 2
and all between Valleys *f* of solemn sound,		*Thy soul is like* 9
F fields of barley shifting tearful lights On growing spears,		*Townsmen, etc.* 8
Art, Science, Nature, everything is *f*, As my own soul is *f*, to overflowing—		*Why suffers* 7
Fulness Shall drink the *f* of thy victory,		*O God, make this age* 13
Furl'd Our flags together *f*,		*Frenchman, etc.* 5
Furrow Those thoughtful *f's* in the swarthy cheek;		*That is his portrait* 3
Fuse And *f* the peoples into one.		*Are those the far-famed* 16
Future voice Cried in the *f* 'Come along.'		*Youth, lapsing i* 40

G

Gale The night *g* in those trees.		*Hear you the sound* 8
Gallant Bold Havelock march'd, Charged with his *g* few, *Bold Havelock* 6
Gallery Along this glimmering *g* A child		*Along this glimmering* 1
Garden That little *g* was her pride,		" 5
Your *g's*, myriad-volumed libraries,		*Therefore your Halls* 3
Garland Crown'd with *g's* of cinchona,		*A dark Indian maiden* 26
Garment Her *g* slips, the left hand holds Her up-gather'd *g* folds,		*Not to Silence* 13
Gasp'd the guard *g* out 'All's right.'		*Far off in the dun* 88
Gate Smooth as Thames below your *g's*,		*Vicar of this* 18
Gather'd (*See also* **Up-gather'd**) Around him youths were *g*,		*Methought I saw* 4
Gaunt There came a *g* man from the dark Inn door, *Far off in the dun* 73
Gave She *g* them the yuccaroot,		*A dark Indian maiden* 43
She *g* the white men welcome all,		" 53
Accepts the songs you *g*, and he sends		*Little Aubrey* 2
Gay orange groves Naked, and dark-limb'd, and *g*,		*A dark Indian maiden* 6
lamps were bright and *g* On the merry bridal-day,		*The lamps were bright* 1
Gaze Worn and wan was their *g*, I trow,		*Far off in the dun* 58
Genius Hail *G*, Master of the Moral Will!		*Art for Art's sake!* 2
Get And *g* thee forth to conquer.		*O God, make this age* 11
Ghost Old *g's* whose day was done ere mine began,		*Old ghosts*
And on me Frown not, old *g's*,		" 9
Ghostly common objects that would keep Our awful inner *g* sense Unroused,		*How strange it is* 5
Ghoul When I die, the *G'S*!!!!		*While I live* 2
Giant that we may be As *g's* in Thy praise!		*O God, make this age* 11
Gilding Where his *g* ray is never sent,		*Far off in the dun* 3
Gird *g* up thy loins for fight, And get thee forth		*O God, make this age* 10
Girdle Richly and darkly *g* these gray walls,—		*Hear you the sound* 23
Girt And though *g* in glad array,		*The lamps were bright* 23
Give And she will weep and *g* them way;		*I keep no more* 6
Take, Lady, what your loyal nurses *g*,		*Take, Lady* 1
I *g* this faulty book to you,		*The noblest men* 9
Like some wise artist, Nature *g's*,		*'Tis not alone* 6
G's stouter ale and riper port		*Yon huddled cloud* 7
g The difference of all things to the sense,		*Why suffers* 9
Given You have *g* me such a wife!		*Vicar of this* 10
Glad How *g* am I to walk With Susan on the shore!		
How *g* am I to talk! I kiss her o'er and o'er.		*How glad am I* 1
The low voice of the *g* New Year Call to the freshly-flower'd hill.		*Remember you* 11
And though girt in *g* array,		*The lamps were bright* 23
Glade Pour'd by long *g's* and meadow mounds,		*Youth, lapsing i* 2
Glance form *g's* quick Thro' her worn brain,		*The lamps were bright* 27
Glancing *G* off from all things evil,		*Vicar of this* 17
Glared eyes *g* fiercely thro' The windows		*Far off in the dun* 47

Glasses   as with optic *g* her keen eyes | *Hither, when all* 3
Gleam (s)   Brushes of fire, hazy *g's,* | 6
Gleam (verb)   and you *g* reset In Britain's lyric coronet. | *We lost you* 3
The towers *g* among the vines ; | *Youth, lapsing* ii 40
Glen   Deep *g's* I found, and sunless gulfs, | *Deep glens I found* 1
Faint shouts are heard across the *g,* | *Youth, lapsing* ii 22
Glide   We may *g* from room to room, | *Not a whisper* 3
Glimmer (s)   In the *g* of the moon : | "
Glimmer (verb)   And *g's* to the northern morn, . | *The noblest men* 7
Glimmering   Along this *g* gallery | *Along this glimmering* 1
' I lift the eyes of thought, I look thro' all my *g* life, | *That is his portrait* 34
Glitter   The whole land *g's* after rain, | *Youth, lapsing* ii 37
Glitter'd   They *g* with a stedfast light, | *Far off in the dun* 129
Globe   Disploding *g's* of roaring fire. | *Deep glens I found* 4
Gloom   Dimly the travellers look'd thro' the *g's,* | *Far off in the dun* 57
Vast wastes of starless *g's* were spread | " 101
and make beneath Ambrosial *g.* | *Hear you the sound* 30
Not a whisper stirs the *g,* | *Not a whisper* 4
chapel's vaulted *g* Was misted with perfume. | *The lamps were bright* 7
Gloomy   When the shadow of night's eternal wings Envelopes the *g* whole, | *Far off in the dun* 14
Glorious   Gone the *g* promise ; and the victim, | *Faded ev'ry violet* 2
Then pledge we our *g* dead, | *Frenchman, etc.* 9
From the clear marble pouring *g* scorn, | *One was the Tishbite* 7
Glory   In *g* and in honour. | *The lamps were bright* 34
Glossy   Look on those manly curls so *g* dark, | *That is his portrait* 2
Glow (s)   in them slept A red infernal *g ;* | *Far off in the dun* 82
Glow (verb)   I *g* With an enthusiastic love of them. | *Hear you the sound* 14
Now one faint line of light doth *g,* | *Youth, lapsing* ii 9
Go   *G* forward ! crumble down a throne, | *Are those the far-famed* 13
Sender and sent-to *g* to make up this, | *Old ghosts* 7
This *goes* straight forward to the cataract : | *Steersman* 4
But the revel still *goes* on. | *The lamps were bright* 40
and let them *g* in hope, Like birds of passage, | *Woman of noble* 7
God   *G's* best blessing on each dear head | *Frenchman, etc.* 11
To pluck the sanction of a *G.* | *He was too good* 12
How strange it is, O *G,* to wake, | *How strange it is* 1
O *G,* make this age great that we may | *O God, make this age* 1
G bless the little isle where a man may still be true ! |
G bless the noble isle that is Mistress of the Seas ! | *They say, etc.* 17
G walk'd the waters of thy soul, | *Thou may'st remember* 7
G be gracious to my soul ! | *What rustles* 15
I thank thee, *G,* that thou hast made me live. | *Why suffers* 12
And there sit figures as of *G's* | *Youth, lapsing* ii 51
God-bless-you   full *G-b-y* with this book of song, | *Take, Lady* 2
Goddess   She no *g* is of mine : | *Not to Silence* 4
Golden   The beauty of Espagnola, The *g* flower of Hayti ? | *A dark Indian maiden* 12, 24, 36, 48, 60, 72
And chants in the *g* wakening Athwart the bloomy morn, | *Full light aloft* 3
Remembering all the *g* hours Now silent, | *Gone into darkness* 9
Accept on this your *g* bridal day The Book of Prayer. | *Remembering him* 3
And floats in either g Ind. | *The noblest men* 8
And from the *g* vapours bursts A mountain bright with triple peaks : | *Youth, lapsing* ii 47
Gone   *G* the glorious promise ; | *Faded ev'ry violet* 2
G into darkness, that full light Of friendship ! | *Gone into darkness* 1
He from the dance hath *g* | *The lamps were bright* 39
To speak of what had *g* before, | *Youth, lapsing* i 27
Good   Behold, ye cannot bring but *g,* | *Are those the far-famed* 5
Beauty, *G* and Knowledge are three sisters . . . | *Beauty, Good, etc.* 1
Havelock died, Tender and great and *g,* | *Bold Havelock* 14
It is not *g* to drink strong wine | *Full light aloft* 9
He was too *g* and kind and sweet, | *He was too good* 1
That were within me ; did it not, *g* Michael ? | *Hear you the sound* 53
He look'd so jolly and so *g—* | *I met in all* 5
Wore the pale cast of thought, a *g* old man, | *Methought I saw* 2
He moan'd, ' I wander from my *g !* ' | *Youth, lapsing* i 35
Gorgeous   For all wreath'd with green bays were the *g* lamps, | *Far off in the dun* 115
Grace   How is it that men have so little *g,* | *How is it that men* 1
Slow-ripening to the *g* of womanhood, | *To thee with whom* 13
Gracious   God be *g* to my soul ! | *What rustles* 15
Grade   And innovation *g* by *g:* | *They wrought, etc.* 36

Grand   did scan His countenance so *g* and mild, | *Methought I saw* 5
Grandsire   Hard by the burning throne of my great *g,* | *Half after midnight !* 6
Grass   sleep thro' one brief dream upon the *g,—* | *Townsmen, etc.* 4
Grassy   but ever drawn Under either *g* brink | *Not to Silence* 25
Grave   Those holly-thickets only hide Her *g—* | *Along this glimmering* 8
The crowd have come to see thy *g,* | *I keep no more* 2
Gray (adj.)   Richly and darkly girdle these *g* walls,— | *Hear you the sound* 23
You'd weave your waxen fingers in these locks (They are *g* now) | " 59
Mine host is fat, and *g,* and wise, | *Yon huddled cloud* 9
Gray (s)   But his face was a yellow *g.* | *Far off in the dun* 52
Great   Bold Havelock died, Tender and *g* and good, | *Bold Havelock* 14
Hard by the burning throne of my *g* grandsire, | *Half after midnight !* 6
and ask you whether you would be A *g* man in your time, | *Hear you the sound* 57
and tell me you were *g* Already in your birth. | " 59
I have seen the four *g* empires disappear ! | *Here I that stood* 9
When a *g* man's found to be bad and base, | *How is it that men* 2
O *G,* make this age *g* that we may | *O God, make this age* 1
Falsehood beneath the altar of *g* Truth : | 8
Teach me, *g* Nature : make me live. | *O leave not thou* 2
And in the hurry and the noise *G* spirits grow akin to base. | *They wrought, etc.* 16
A land of many days that cleaves In two *g* halves, | " 27
but he That thro' the channels of the state Convoys the people's wish, is *g :* | " 31
g cause of Freedom round and round, | *First drink a health* 60
Green (adj.)   Fann'd this queen of the *g* wildwood, Lady of the *g* Savannah : | *A dark Indian maiden* 15
There never *g* thing will gaily spring | *Far off in the dun* 59
They saw the *g* verge of the pleasant earth, | " 63
For all wreath'd with *g* bays were the gorgeous lamps, | " 115
I met in all the close *g* ways, | *I met in all* 1
And hoary holts on uplands *g,* | *Thy soul is like* 10
And your triple terrace growing *G* and greener every May ! | *Vicar of this* 15
Fair with *g* fields the realms of Love. | *Youth, lapsing* ii 36
Green (s)   The *g* that fills the eye— | *'Tis not alone* 4
Greener   terrace growing Green and *g* every May ! | *Vicar of this* 15
Greet   And I *g* it, and I meet it, | *Immeasurable sadness !* 3
And I meet it, and I *g* it, | 9
Grew   The tingling blood *g* chill, | *Far off in the dun* 78
Lower and deeper evermore They *g,* | *Youth, lapsing* i 26
Grief   That ride to death the *g's* of men ? | *Are those the far-famed* 2
Dim *g* did wait upon her, | *The lamps were bright* 33
Young is the *g* I entertain, | *Young is the grief* 1
Yet *g* deserves a nobler name : | " 31
Grieved   I *g* as woods in dripping rains | *Youth, lapsing* i 31
Grim   Before his eyes so *g* and calm | *Far off in the dun* 77
The *g* old coachee strode to the box, | " 87
Groan   And in the pauses *g's* of men. | *Youth, lapsing* ii 24
Groom   forms of the shadowy *g's* Yoked | *Far off in the dun* 59
Ground   Whoever walks that bitter *g* | " 25
They broke the *g* with hoofs of fire | " 128
Took the child from off the *g,* | *The child was sitting* 6
Groundsel   With yellow *g* grown ! | *Along this glimmering* 6
Grove   Wantoning in orange *g's* Naked, | *A dark Indian maiden* 5
For Love flew over *g* and field, | *The night, etc.* 4
With all his *g's* he bows, he nods, | *Youth, lapsing* ii 49
Grow   Great spirits *g* akin to base. | *They wrought, etc.* 16
Growing   your triple terrace *g* Green and greener | *Vicar of this* 15
The two fair lilies *g* at thy side | *Woman of noble* 11
Full fields of barley shifting tearful lights On *g* spears, | *Townsmen, etc.* 9
Grown   (*See also* **Moss-grown**)   With yellow groundsel *g* ! | *Along this glimmering* 6
And when your age had somewhat riper *g,* | *Hear you the sound* 54
When I was somewhat older *g* These voices | *Youth, lapsing* i 21
Guard   the *g* gasp'd out ' All's right.' | *Far off in the dun* 88
leaders bounded, the *g's* horn sounded : | " 89
Guardian (adj.)   Thy child will bless thee, *g* mother mild, | *Long as the heart* 2
Guardian (s)   silent *G's* But true till Death ; | *Woman of noble* 6
Guava   Then she brought the *g* fruit, | *A dark Indian maiden* 41
Gulf   Deep glens I found, and sunless *g's,* | *Deep glens I found* 1
floats upward from the *g* A murmur of heroic song, | *Youth, lapsing* ii 18
Gun   *See* **Pop-gun**

H

I

J

Jar we *j* like boys : And in the hurry and the noise   *They wrought, etc.* 14
Jaw The chattering of the fleshless *j*'s,   *Far off in the dun* 95
Jesu The ' Mercy *J* ' in the rain !   *I keep no more* 11
Joint Unsocket all the *j*'s of war,   *Are those the far-famed* 15
Joke With *j*'s you never heard before,   *Yon huddled cloud* 14
Jolly He look'd so *j* and so good—   *I met in all* 5
   No *j* host was he ;   *Far off in the dun* 54
Joy No sound of *j*, no revelling tones   " 41
   There's not a *j* beyond.   *How glad am I* 8
   All this so stirr'd him in his hour of *j*,   *That is his portrait* 31
   My *j* was only less than thine.   *Thou may'st remember* 12
   One only *j* I know, the *j* of life.   *Why suffers* 14
Joy'd I *j* to place me on The hollow-stemm'd   *Hear you the sound* 31
Joyful *j* when The wanton wind came singing   " 40
Joyfully But did not sound so *j* :   *Youth, lapsing i* 24
Just Knowing those laws are *j* alone That contemplate a mighty plan,   *They wrought, etc.* 41

K

Kate Sweetly flow your life with *K*'s,   *Vicar of this* 16
Keen And as with optic glasses her *k* eyes Pierced thro' the mystic dome,   *Hither when all* 3
Keep objects that would *k* Our awful inner   *How strange it is* 4
   I *k* no more a lone distress,   *I keep no more* 1
   act on Eternity To *k* thee here amongst us !   *That is his portrait* 40
   voice of a satisfied people may *k* A sound in her ears   *That the voice* 1
Keys With twinkling finger sweeps her yellow *k*.   *Townsmen, etc.* 10
Kind (adj.) He was too good and *k* and sweet,   *He was too good* 2
   It is not *k* to be so still ;   *Speak to me* 3
   I can trust *Your woman's nature* k *and true.*   *The noblest men* 12
Kind (s) And startle the dull ears of human *k* !   *O God, make this age* 5
King Of him who doomed the *k* to die,   *Because she bore* 2
   Is it the *k* ; is it my love Coming along   *What rustles* 5
King-craft Till priest-craft and *k*-c sicken,   *Wherever evil* 3
Kingliest A Pharaoh, *k* of his kingly race,   *Here, I that stood* 3
Kingly For they were *k* in apparel,   *A dark Indian maiden* 63
   A Pharaoh, kingliest of his *k* race,   *Here, I that stood* 3
Kiss (s) And mingle *k*'es, tears, and sighs,   *Life of the Life* 6
   I will print an airy *k* :   *Not a whisper* 3
Kiss (verb) And longed to *k* her hand and lie   *Because she bore* 7
   And *k*'es him there in a dream,   *Bright is the moon* 6
   I *k* her o'er and o'er.   *How glad am I* 4
   We *k*, we are so fond,   " 6
Kitty Sandilands Sweet *K S*, The daughter of the doctor,   *Sweet Kitty Sandilands* 1
Knee was wont to dandle you upon My *k*,   *Hear you the sound* 56
   To break the pride of Britain, and bring her on her *k*'s,   *They say, etc.* 2
Knew Ev'n when I *k* him in his hour   *He was too good* 2
Knit *k* your baby brows Into your father's frown,   *Hear you the sound* 48
   You were he that *k* the knot !   *Vicar of this* 5
Knot my tongue runs twenty *k*'s an hour :   *Half after midnight !* 19
   You were he that knit the *k* !   *Vicar of this* 5
Knotted round her waist *K*,   *One was the Tishbite* 11
   The *k* boughs of this long avenue Of thick dark oaks,   *Hear you the sound* 10
Know And I *k* it as a poet,   *Immeasurable sadness !* 2
   But I *k* it as a poet,   " 8
   Ye *k* that History is half-dream—   *Old ghosts* 3
   whatsoever *k*'s us truly, *k*'s That none   " 12
   That I was harsh to thee, let no one *k* ;   *To thee with whom* 2
   I *k* a little of her worth,   *Well, as to Fame* 3
   And I will tell you what I *k*—   " 4
   One only joy I *k*, the joy of life.   *Why suffers* 14
   Yet well I *k* that nothing stays,   *Youth, lapsing i* 53
Knowing *K* those laws are just alone   *They wrought, etc.* 41
   sharp desire of knowledge still with *k* !   *Why suffers* 6
Knowledge Beauty, Good and *K* are three sisters . . .   *Beauty, Good, etc.* 1
   sharp desire of *k* still with knowing !   *Why suffers* 6

L

Labour A *l* working to an end.   *Youth, lapsing ii* 4
Laden *See* **Flower-laden**
Lady (adj.) by fits the *l* ash With twinkling finger sweeps her yellow keys.   *Townsmen, etc.* 9
Lady (s) *L* of the green Savannah :   *A dark Indian maiden* 16
   L over wood and highland,   " 27
   Take, *L*, what your loyal nurses give,   " *Take, Lady* 1
Laid foreign powers have *l* their heads together   *They say, etc.* 1
Lain Every heart is *l* to rest,   *Not a whisper* 5
Lake *l* that ripples out In the clear moonshine.   *Hear you the sound* 33
Lammas When corny *L* bound the sheaves :   *Youth, lapsing i* 16
Lamp wreath'd with green bays were the gorgeous *l*'s,   *Far off in the dun* 115
   l's were bright and gay On the merry bridal-day,   *The lamps were bright* 1
Land He sees his father in distant *l*'s,   *Bright is the moon* 1
   There lies a *l* of chilling storms,   *Far off in the dun* 5
   A *l* of thin faces and shadowy forms,   " 7
   A pure example to the *l*'s,   *They wrought, etc.* 2
   A *l* of many days that cleaves In two great halves,   *Youth, lapsing ii* 37
   The whole *l* glitters after rain,   *Thy soul is like* 1
Landskip Thy soul is like a *l*, friend,   *Thy soul is like* 1
Lapse Pointing to the unheeded *l* of hours,   *Half after midnight !* 2
Lapsing Youth, *l* thro' fair solitudes,   *Youth, lapsing i* 1
Large *L* as a human eye the sun Drew down the West his feeble lights ;   *Deep glens I found* 5
   Am *l* in hope that these expectant eyes   *O God, make this age* 12
   And that *l* table of the breast dispread,   *That is his portrait* 5
Larger Or, if the sense of most require A precedent Of *l* scope,   *They wrought, etc.* 38
Lark *See* **Laverock**
Lass The *l*'es and the little ones, Jack Tars,   *They say, etc.* 15
Last (s) so many dead, And him the *l*.   *Gone into darkness* 11
Last (verb) can they *l* In the vast Of the rolling of the æons,   *Little Aubrey* 4
   we, Poor devils, babble ' we shall *l*.'   *Well, as to Fame* 8
Later Sooner or *l* from the haze The second voice   *Youth, lapsing i* 55
Latest *L* of her worshippers,   *Not to Silence* 7
   loftier antient heights Touch'd with Heaven's *l* lights.   *Thy soul is like* 12
   The *l* thunder-peal hath peal'd,   *Youth, lapsing ii* 30
Laugh (s) And the *l* of their rose-lipp'd boys.   *Far off in the dun* 68
Laugh (verb) when he *l*'s, his little eyes   *Yon huddled cloud* 11
   I heard Spring *l* in hidden rills,   *Youth, lapsing i* 13
Laughable 'twas *l*, and yet It show'd   *Hear you the sound* 51
Laugh'd I *l* to see him as he stood,   *I met in all* 7
Laughing All day long with *l* eyes,   *A dark Indian maiden* 17
   And they saw *her* standing by, With a *l* crazed eye,   *The lamps were bright* 52
Lava The walls of *l* rose,   *Far off in the dun* 38
Laverock *l* spring From under the deep,   *Full light aloft* 1
Law Knowing those *l*'s are just alone   *They wrought, etc.* 41
Lawn Here and there about the *l* Wholly mute,   *Not to Silence* 23
   Steeple, and stream, and forest *l*,   *Thy soul is like* 2
Lay See, The cradle where she *l* !   *Along this glimmering* 4
   Then they found him where *l*   *The lamps were bright* 47
   l harder upon her Till she clapperclaw   *Wherever evil* 6
Lead Which *l* the noblest life.   *Frenchman, etc.* 8
   tho' the merry bridegroom Might *l* the bride away,   *The lamps were bright* 32
Leader The *l*'s bounded, the guard's horn sounded :   *Far off in the dun* 89
Leaf summer plains with their shining *leaves*,   " 69
   dark vine *leaves* round the rustling eaves,   " 71
   Summer thro' all her sleepy *leaves*   *Youth, lapsing i* 14
   Sigh over all their fallen *leaves* ;   " 32
Leafless The hollow-stemm'd and well-nigh *l* oak   *Hear you the sound* 32
Leafy The nightingale in *l* woods Call to its mate   *Remember you* 14
League Flooded fifty *l*'s around,   *The child was sitting* 5
Lean Tall, eager, *l* and strong, his cloak   *One was the Tishbite* 5
Leaping shapes without heads Went *l*   *Far off in the dun* 104
Leapt white fly *l* About his hairless brow.   " 83
Leave pall of the sky *L* never an inch of blue ;   " 22

Leave (*continued*) O *l* not thou thy son forlorn ;   *O leave not thou* 1
   each one *l's* The middle road of sober thought !   *They wrought, etc.* 27
Led (*See also* **Wisdom-led**) She *l* them down the pleasant places,   *A dark Indian maiden* 62
   L silently by power divine,   *Thou may'st remember* 9
Left To *l* or right but falling floods.   *Remember you* 16
   the *l* hand holds Her up-gather'd garment folds,   *Not to Silence* 13
Length And lights at *l* on his desire: *They wrought, etc.* 40
Lengthen'd Far away thro' the night ran the *l* tones :   *Far off in the dun* 90
Less But these shall see it none the *l.*   *I keep no more* 4
   My joy was only *l* than thine.   *Thou may'st remember* 12
Lesser Hold thou, my friend, no *l* life in scorn,   *Hold thou, my friend* 1
Letter Their lies the *l,* but it is not he   *Old ghosts* 5
   The man's life in the *l's* of the man.   " 4
Level Thames along the silent *l,*   *Vicar of this* 19
Liana Indian maiden, Warbling in the bloom'd *l,*   *A dark Indian maiden* 2
Lie on her threshold *l,* Howling   *Beauty, Good etc.* 4
   l A thousand summers at her feet.   *Because she bore* 7
   There *l's* a land of chilling storms,   *Far off in the dun* 5
   Evermore The simpler essence lower *l's,*   *From shape to shape* 6
   There *l's* the letter, but it is not he   *Old ghosts* 5
   Beneath those double arches *l*   *Youth, lapsing ii* 35
Life The Death for which you mourn is *L.'*   *Early-wise* 1
   Which lead the noblest *life.*   *Frenchman, etc.* 8
   What *l,* so maim'd by night, were worth   *Gone into darkness* 7
   my friend, no lesser *l* in scorn,   *Hold thou, my friend* 1
   mark The *l* that haunts the emptiness   *How strange it is* 7
   L of the *L* within my blood, (repeat)   *Life of the Life* 1, 7
   Long as the heart beats *l* within her breast,   *Long as the heart* 1
   The man's *l* in the letters of the man.   *Old ghosts* 4
   Alas, my *l* is frail and weak :   *Speak to me* 1
   may the *l,* which, heart in heart, you live   *Take, Lady* 3
   I look thro' all my glimmering *l,*   *That is his portrait* 34
   Thro' one whole *l* an overflowing urn,   " 50
   come Into the light of spiritual *l.*   *Thou may'st remember* 6
   Sweetly, smoothly flow your *l.*   *Vicar of this* 6
   Sweetly flow your *l* with Kate's,   " 16
   Why suffers human *l* so soon eclipse ?   *Why suffers* 1
   Would I could pile fresh *l* on *l,*   " 5
   One only joy I know, the joy of *l.*   " 14
   A *l* four-square to all the winds.   *Young is the grief* 16
   L, to this wind, turn'd all her vanes,   *Youth, lapsing i* 29
Lift he spake : 'I *l* the eyes of thought,   *That is his portrait* 33
   l's The creaming horn of corny ale !   *Yon huddled cloud* 3
Lifted They *l* their eyes to the dead, pale skies,   *Far off in the dun* 91
Light (adj.) A *l* wind wafts me from my feet.   *Youth, lapsing ii* 44
Light (adv.) Full *l* aloft doth the laverock spring   *Full light aloft* 1
Light (come upon) And *l's* at length on his desire: *They wrought, etc.* 40
Light (s) sun Drew down the West his feeble *l's* ;   *Deep glens I found* 6
   A region void of *l,*   *Far off in the dun* 6
   No taper's *l* look'd out on the night,   " 45
   They see the *l* of their blest firesides,   " 65
   sallow *l's* shone Dimly and blurry   " 99
   what *l's* approach With heavenly melodies ?   " 105
   those are the *l's* of the Paradise coach,   " 107
   With a solemn burst of thrilling *l,*   " 119
   They glitter'd with a stedfast *l,*   " 129
   At the very break of *l* ?   *Full light aloft* 8
   Gone into darkness, that full *l* Of friendship !   *Gone into darkness* 8
   That mystic field of drifted *l* In mid Orion,   *Hither when all* 10
   L of the *L* within mine eyes, (repeat)   *Life of the Life* 2, 8
   Often shallow, pierced with *l,*   *Not to Silence* 21
   Lit as with inner *l.*   *One was the Tishbite* 8
   peaceful *l* of hazel eyes, Observing all things.   *That is his portrait* 13
   eyes burn With a *l* so wild and stern ?'   *The lamps were bright* 16
   come Into the *l* of spiritual life.'   *Thou may'st remember* 6
   Touch'd with Heaven's latest *l's.*   *Thy soul is like* 12
   Full fields of barley shifting tearful *l's*   *Townsmen, etc.* 8
   Drove into lines and studs of *l*   *Youth, lapsing i* 6
   Now one faint line of *l* doth glow,   " ii 9
   Ray'd round with beams of living *l.*   " 52
Like (*See also* **Bee-like**) *L* to one of us she seems,   *Not a whisper* 15
Likeness And all the *l* in the difference.   *Why suffers* 11
Lily The two fair *lilies* growing at thy side   *Woman of noble* 11
Limb His *l's* beneath him fail ;   *Far off in the dun* 26

Limb (*continued*) woman's youthful pride Of rounded *l's*—   *One was the Tishbite* 17
Limb'd *See* **Dark-limb'd**
Line While walking with my rod and *l,*   *I met in all* 2
   a face whose every *l* Wore the pale cast   *Methought I saw* 1
   Drove into *l's* and studs of light   *Youth, lapsing i* 6
   Now one faint *l* of light doth glow,   " ii 9
Link In many a silver loop and *l*   *Not to Silence* 26
Lip with right hand Moving toward her *l,*   *Not to Silence* 19
   Her perfect *l's* to taste,   *One was the Tishbite* 12
   Sleeps round those quiet *l's* ; not quite a smile ;   *That is his portrait* 9
   E'en scorn looks beautiful on human *l's* !   *Why suffers* 4
   Because the *l's* of little children preach Against you,   *Therefore your Halls* 12
Lipp'd *See* **Finger-lipt, Rose-lipp'd**
Lisping Lightly *l,* breaks away ;   *Not to Silence* 32
Lit *L* as with inner light.   *One was the Tishbite* 8
Little That *l* garden was her pride,   *Along this glimmering* 5
   Sleep, my *l* one, sleep !   *Bright is the moon* 3
   How is it that men have so *l* grace,   *How is it that men* 1
   L Aubrey in the West ! *l* Alfred in the East   *Little Aubrey* 1
   L Homer, *l* Dante, *l* Shakespeare, can they last   " 4
   L poet, hear the *l* poet's epigram !   " 7
   The lasses and the *l* ones, Jack Tars, they look to you !   *They say, etc.* 15
   God bless the *l* isle where a man may still be true !   " 17
   when he laughs, his *l* eyes Are swallow'd in his pamper'd cheeks.   *Yon huddled cloud* 11
Live And he prays that you may *l.*   *Little Aubrey* 3
   Teach me, great Nature: make me *l.*   *O leave not thou* 2
   life, which heart in heart, you *l* With him you love,   *Take, Lady* 3
   Yet he *l's* ; His and my friendship   *That is his portrait* 40
   to each that *l's* A hint of somewhat unexprest.   *'Tis not alone* 1
   L and prosper ! Day by day Watch your standard roses   *Vicar of this* 11
   While I *l* !   *While I live* 1
   I thank thee, God, that thou hast made me *l:*   *Why suffers* 12
Lived Prince, whose Father *l* in you,   *Early-wise* 2
   So *l* I without aim or choice,   *Youth, lapsing i* 37
Liveliest Whose blood in its *l* course would not pause   *Far off in the dun* 93
Living were worth Our *l* out ?   *Gone into darkness* 8
   there sit figures as of gods Ray'd round with beams of *l* light.   *Youth, lapsing ii* 52
Lock fingers in these *l's* (They are gray now)   *Hear you the sound* 58
Loftier somewhat *l* antient heights Touch'd with Heaven's latest lights.   *Thy soul is like* 11
Loins gird up thy *l* for fight, And get thee forth   *O God, make this age* 10
Loiter'd I *l* in the middle way,   *Youth, lapsing i* 46
London I was when *L* was not !   *Here, I that stood* 10
   This *L* once was middle sea,   *Well, as to Fame* 5
Lone I keep no more a *l* distress,   *I keep no more* 1
Lonely I shudder in my *l* nest,   *What rustles, etc.* 13
Long The skin hung lax on his *l* thin hands ;   *Far off in the dun* 53
   They mounted slow in their *l* black cloaks,   " 85
   The knotted boughs of this *l* avenue Of thick dark oaks,   *Hear you the sound* 9
   L as the heart beats life within her breast,   *Long as the heart* 1
   With *l* tracts of murmuring, Partly river, partly brook,   *Not to Silence* 28
   Methinks I see the world's renewed youth A *l* day's dawn,   *O God, make this age* 7
   you live With him you love, be cloudless and be *l* !   *Take, Lady* 4
   who strides the earth With that *l* horn she loves to blow,   *Well, as to Fame* 2
   Pour'd by *l* glades and meadowy mounds,   *Youth, lapsing i* 2
Longed And *l* to kiss her hand and lie   *Because she bore* 7
   And *l* to take his hand in mine.   *I met in all* 4
Longer lay harder upon her Till she clapperclaw no *l,*   *Wherever evil* 7
Look (s) Ye must be wiser than your *l's,*   *Are those the far-famed* 9
   And *l's* to awe the standers by,   *Because she bore* 4
Look (verb) *L* he smiles, and opens his hands,   *Bright is the moon* 4
   L out from the cloudy vast.   *Far off in the dun* 20
   How beautifully *l's* the moonbeam   *Hear you the sound* 9
   I never *l* upon them but I glow   " 14
   You would *l* down and knit your baby brows   " 48
   But *l,* for these are nature too.   *I keep no more* 16
   L on those manly curls so glossy dark,   *That is his portrait* 2

Look (verb) (continued) *l* you what an arch the brain
  has built — *That is his portrait* 10
I *l* thro' all my glimmering life, — " 34
lasses and the little ones, Jack Tars, they *l* to you! — *They say, etc.* 15
E'en scorn *l*'s beautiful on human lips! — *Why suffers* 4
Look'd No taper's light *l* out on the night, — *Far off in the dun* 45
  Dimly the travellers *l* thro' the glooms, — " 57
  He *l* so jolly and so good— — *I met in all* 5
Looking *l* far away On the blue mountains, — *Hear you the sound* 39
Loom *l* or plough To weigh them as they — *He was too good* 7
Loop In many a silver *l* and link — *Not to Silence* 26
Lord Hail, truest *L* of Hell! — *Art for Art's sake!* 1
Lordly Ye proud aristocrats whose *l* shadows, — *Hear you the sound* 21
Loss Another whispers sick with *l*: — *I keep no more* 9
  His and my friendship have not suffer'd *l*, — *That is his portrait* 41
Lost for what is *l* is made more dear; — " 46
  We *l* you for how long a time, — *We lost you* 1
Lot happy be your *l* In the Vicarage — *Vicar of this* 3
Loud *l* the roar Of wind and mingled shower, — *Far off in the dun* 33
  The stream is *l*: I cannot hear!' — *Remember you* 8
  The wind is *l* in holt and hill, — *Speak to me* 2
  wanton ear Be tickled with the *l* 'hear, hear,' — *They wrought, etc.* 7
Love (s) Nor *L* that holds a constant mood. — *Are those the far-famed* 8
  he that shuts out *L*, in turn shall be Shut out
    from *L*, — *Beauty, Good, etc.* 3
  whisper'd *l* of the fair young wives; — *Far off in the dun* 67
  I glow With an enthusiastic *l* of them. — *Hear you the sound* 15
  I murmur'd 'Speak again, my *l*, — *Remember you* 7
  They are not want of *l* for thee. — *Speak to me* 4
  How full of wisest humour and of *l*, — *That is his portrait* 7
  Capacious both of Friendship and of *L*. — " 51
  For *L* flew over grove and field, — *The night, etc.* 4
  Something of pain—of bliss—of *L*, — *'Tis not alone* 11
  heart That watch't with *l* thine earliest infancy, — *To thee with whom* 12
  is it my *l* Coming along the secret ways? — *What rustles* 5
  Fair with green fields the realms of *L*. — *Youth, lapsing ii* 36
Love (v) 'I *l* the daisy weeping dew, — *I keep no more* 8
  cuckoo-voice that *l*'s To babble its own name. — *I, loving Freedom* 7
  heart in heart, you live With him you *l*, — *Take, Lady* 4
  With that long horn she *l*'s to blow, — *Well, as to Fame* 5
Loved A child she *l* to play; — *Along this glimmering* 2
  This is he I *l*, This is the man — *That is his portrait* 14
  He *l* the river's roaring sound; — *The child was sitting* 3
  Cold words I spoke, yet *l* thee warm and well. — *To thee with whom* 8
Loving All her *l* childhood Breezes from the palm — *A dark Indian maiden* 13
  wondering, *l*, Carolling 'Happy, — " 51
  I, *l* Freedom for herself, — *I, loving Freedom* 1
Low The *l* voice of the glad New Year Call to the
    freshly-flower'd hill. — *Remember you* 11
  And that large table of the breast dispread,
    Between *l* shoulders; — *That is his portrait* 6
  long May my strong wish, transgressing the *l* bound
    Of mortal hope, — " 38
  Again the *l* sweet voices mourn'd In distant fields, — *Youth, lapsing i* 43
Lower Evermore The simpler essence *l* lies, — *From shape to shape* 6
  L and deeper evermore They grew, — *Youth, lapsing i* 25
Loyal Take, Lady, what your *l* nurses give, — *Take, Lady* 4
Lucid Regions of *l* matter taking forms, — *Hither, when all* 5
Lured *L* by the cuckoo-voice that loves — *I, loving Freedom* 7
Lute-toned A *l-t* whisper, 'I am here!' — *Remember you* 4
Luxuriant My fancy was the more *l*, — *That is his portrait* 16
Lyre And a sound of stringéd *l*'s. — *Far off in the dun* 120
Lyric and you gleam reset In Britain's *l* coronet. — *We lost you* 4

M

Mad Is thy *m* brain drunk with the merry, red wine, — *Full light aloft* 7
Madam the noblest place, M, is yours, — *The noblest men* 4
Made I thank thee, God, that thou hast *m* me live: — *Why suffers* 12
  for what is lost is *m* more dear; — *That is his portrait* 46
  All-perfect Framer, Him, who *m* the heart, — " 48
  Thro' every change that *m* thee what thou art? — *To thee with whom* 14

Madness Or a fancy or a *m*,— — *Immeasurable sadness!* 7
  what *m* moved my blood To make me thus belie — *To thee with whom* 10
Mahomet Like the flower of M. — *Spurge with fairy* 2
Maiden A dark Indian *m*, Warbling in the bloom'd
    liana, — *A dark Indian maiden* 1
  With her *m*'s to the bay, — " 42
  But found a *m* tender, shy, — *Because she bore* 5
  The happy *m*'s tears are free — *I keep no more* 5
Maim'd What life, so *m* by night, were worth — *Gone into darkness* 7
Main That thou singest with *m* and with might? — *Full light aloft* 6
Maizebread M and the yuccaroot, — *A dark Indian maiden* 44
Make and *m* beneath Ambrosial gloom. — *Hear you the sound* 29
  Sender and sent-to go to *m* up this, — *Old ghosts* 7
  Who *m* you utter things you did not say, — " 10
  Teach me great Nature: *m* me live. — *O leave not thou* 2
  To *m* me thus belie my constant heart — *To thee with whom* 11
  The thunder cannot *m* thee dumb; — *Youth, lapsing ii* 26
Man The white *m*'s white sail, bringing — *A dark Indian maiden* 37
  She gave the white men welcome all, — " 53
  Than the men of Xaraguay, — " 57
  That ride to death the grief's of men? — *Are those the far-famed* 2
  A surface *m* of many theories, — *A surface man* 1
  Ten men fought a thousand, Slew them — *Bold Havelock* 7
  every *m* in Britain Says 'I am of Havelock's blood!' — " 15
  There came a gaunt *m* from the dark Inn door, — *Far off in the dun* 73
  threw up the dust Of dead men's pulverised bones. — " 92
  I come Unto the perfect *m*. — *From shape to shape* 4
  ask you whether you would be A great *m* — *Hear you the sound* 57
  The true men banish'd— — *Rise, Britons, rise* 4
  All Nature is the womb whence M is born. — *Hold thou, my friend* 2
  How is it that men have so little grace, When a
    great *m*'s found to be bad and base, — *How is it that men* 1
  a good old *m*, Most eloquent, who spake — *Methought I saw* 2
  The *m*'s life in the letters of the *m*. — *Old ghosts* 4
  All the men ran from her (repeat) — *Sweet Kitty Sandilands* 5, 7
  This is the *m* of whom you heard me speak. — *That is his portrait* 15
  The noblest men methinks are bred — *The noblest men* 1
  God bless the little isle where a *m* may still be true! — *They say, etc.* 17
  Shadows of statesmen, clever men! — *They wrought, etc.* 12
  fears that waste The strength of men, — " 23
  The frame, the mind, the soul of *m*, — " 43
  The *m* that round me wove Inextricable brickwork — *What rustles* 17
  And in the pauses groans of men. — *Youth, lapsing ii* 24
Manly Look on those *m* curls so glossy dark, — *That is his portrait* 2
Many lest overhaste Should fire the *m* wheels of change! — *They wrought, etc.* 24
  A voice like *m* voices cries, — *Youth, lapsing i* 7
  A moan of *m* waterfalls. — " ii 23
Mar mould you all awry and *m* your worth; — *Old ghosts* 11
Marble forms Of the unfading *m* carved upon them, — *Hear you the sound* 26
  From the clear *m* pouring glorious scorn, — *One was the Tishbite* 7
March'd Bold Havelock *m*, (repeat) — *Bold Havelock* 1, 5, 9
  M and thought and fought, — " 11
  M and fought himself dead. — " 12
Mark by chance should *m* The life that haunts — *How strange it is* 6
  to *m* The humours of the polling and the wake, — *That is his portrait* 19
Market The hubbub of the *m* and the booths: — " 21
Married That mystic field of drifted light In mid Orion,
    and the *m* stars. — *Hither, when all* 11
Marry spot Where it was my chance to *m*, — *Vicar of this* 2
Mars She saw the snowy poles and Moons of M, — *Hither, when all* 9
Martyr *See* Patriot-martyrs
Master (adj.) A *m* mind with *m* minds, — *Young is the grief* 13
Master (s) Genius, M of the Moral Will! — *Art for Art's sake* 2
Mate Call to its *m* when nothing stirr'd — *Remember you* 15
Matter Regions of lucid *m* taking forms, — *Hither, when all* 5
Mature and what a settled mind, M, — *That is his portrait* 12
May (hawthorn-bloom) The M begins to breathe and bud, — *Life of the Life* 3
May (month) terrace growing Green and greener every M! — *Vicar of this* 15
Maze Inextricable brickwork *m* in *m*? — *What rustles* 8
Meadow Warm beams across the *m* stole; — *The night, etc.* 3
Meadowy Pour'd by long glades and *m* mounds, — *Youth, lapsing i* 2
Mealy The miller with his *m* face, — *I met in all* 3
Meant whose whims were *m* For virtue's servants, — *A surface man* 2
Meat *See* Pap-meat-pamper
Mediterranean Thence haled me toward the M sea, — *Here, I that stood* 6

Moving   *m* To her Areyto's mellow ditty,   *A dark Indian maiden* 49
    but with right hand *M* toward her lip,   *Not to Silence* 11
    Parts in two channels, *m* to one end—   *Steersman* 3
Murmur   The *m*'s of the rivulet, Rippling   *Townsmen, etc.* 5
    floats upward from the gulf A *m* of heroic song,   *Youth, lapsing ii* 19
Murmur'd   I *m* 'Speak again, my love,   *Remember you* 7
    Summer thro' all her sleepy leaves *M* :   *Youth, lapsing i* 15
Murmuring   With long tracts of *m*,   *Not to Silence* 28
Music   The southern stars a *m* peal'd,   *The night, etc.* 2
Mute   there about the lawn Wholly *m*,   *Not to Silence* 24
    Half after midnight ! these *m* moralizers,   *Half after midnight!* 1
Mutter   the *m* of deep-mouth'd thunderings   *Far off in the dun* 15
Myriad-volumed   Your gardens, *m-v* libraries,   *Therefore your Halls* 3
Mystery   A rumour of a *m*,   *Youth, lapsing ii* 1
Mystic   And as with optic glasses her keen eyes Pierced
    thro' the *m* dome,   *Hither, when all* 4
    That *m* field of drifted light In mid Orion,   " 10

N

Naked   orange groves *N*, and dark-limb'd,   *A dark Indian maiden* 6
    N, without fear moving To her Areyto's mellow
    ditty,   " 49
    Not to Silence would I build A temple in her *n* field ;   *Not to Silence* 2
Name   she bore the iron *n* Of him who doomed   *Because she bore* 1
    And his *n* was Atrophy !   *Far off in the dun* 56
    cuckoo-voice that loves To babble its own *n*.   *I, loving Freedom* 8
    They were not slaves that *n*'s mislead, Nor
    traitors that mislead by *n*'s !   *Not such were those* 3
    Your *n* is blown on every wind,   *The noblest men* 5
    His *n* is pure, his fame is free :   *They wrought, etc.* 32
    Yet grief deserves a nobler *n*:   *Young is the grief* 5
Natal   Now idly in my *n* bowers,   *Youth, lapsing i* 49
Nation   And the voice that apes a *n*—   *Immeasurable sadness!* 5
Nature   All *n* widens upward.   *From shape to shape* 5
    Ev'n then the force of *n* and high birth   *Hear you the sound* 63
    All *N* is the womb whence Man is born.   *Hold thou, my friend* 2
    But look, for these are *n* too.   *I keep no more* 16
    Teach me, great *N* : make me live.   *O leave not thou* 2
    And took in more of *N* than mine own :   *That is his portrait* 18
    which he compell'd once more Thro' his own *n*,   " 28
    I can trust Your woman's *n* kind and true.   *The noblest men* 12
    Like some wise artist, *N* gives,   *'Tis not alone* 6
    Tho' I was harsh, my *n* is not so :   *To thee with whom* 5
    Art, Science, *N*, everything is full,   *Why suffers* 7
    as pure a heart As e'er beat time to *N*,   *Woman of noble* 5
Nearer   But tho' the cataract seem the *n* way,   *Steersman* 6
Necessity   Forethinking its twinfold *n*,   *That is his portrait* 49
Neck   and folded once about her *n*,   *One was the Tishbite* 11
Nest   Father will come to his babe in the *n*,   *Bright is the moon* 11
    I shudder in my lonely *n*,   *What rustles* 13
New   And ever *n* the tale she tells,   *Young is the grief* 2
    The low voice of the glad *N* Year   *Remember you* 11
New-comer   bringing To happy Hayti the *n-c*,   *A dark Indian maiden* 38
New Year   low voice of the glad *N Y*   *Remember you* 11
Night (adj.)   The *n* gale in those trees.   *Hear you the sound* 8
Night (s)   then a *n*, all moons, confused The shadows   *Deep glens I found* 7
    Of vapors, and mist, and *n*.   *Far off in the dun* 8
    When the shadow of *n*'s eternal wings   " 13
    Dark was the *n*, and loud the roar Of wind   " 33
    No taper's light look'd out on the *n*,   " 45
    Far away thro' the *n* ran the lengthen'd tones :   " 90
    away By *n*, into the deeper *n* ! The deeper *n* ?   *Gone into darkness* 3
    If *n*, what barren toil to be ! What life, so maim'd
    by *n*, were worth Our living out ?   " 6
    'Tis a clear *n*, they will be here anon.   *Hear you the sound* 6
    The *n* with sudden odour reel'd,   *The night, etc.* 1
    The *n* is black and still; the deer Bleat   *What rustles* 3
    The image of the moon by *n*   *Youth, lapsing i* 8
    A voice, when *n* had crept on high,   " 17
Nightingale   The *n* in leafy woods Call   *Remember you* 12
Nile   beside the flow Of sacred *N*,   *Here, I that stood* 4

Nobility   high birth Had writ *n* upon my brow.   *Hear you the sound* 64
Noble   But near the dwelling of some *n* race ;   " 17
    To break the *n* pride of the Mistress of the Seas.   *They say, etc.* 4
    God bless the *n* isle that is Mistress of the Seas !   " 18
    Woman of *n* form and *n* mind !   *Woman of noble* 1
Nobler   Yet grief deserves a *n* name :   *Young is the grief* 5
Noblest   Which lead the *n* life.   *Frenchman, etc.* 8
    The *n* men methinks are bred   *The noblest men* 1
Nod   With all his groves he bows, he *n*'s,   *Youth, lapsing ii* 49
Nodding   The thirsty horseman, *n*, lifts   *Yon huddled cloud* 3
Noise   And in the hurry and the *n* Great spirits   *They wrought, etc.* 15
    A *n* of hands that disarrange The social engine !   " 21
    A *n* of winds that meet and blend,   *Youth, lapsing ii* 2
Nook   Which in one delicious *n*,   *Not to Silence* 30
Noon   At *n* and eve, because your manner sorts   *Therefore your Halls* 10
Norman   *See Saxo-Norman*
Northern   *And glimmers to the* n *morn,*   *The noblest men* 7
Nurse   Take, Lady, what your loyal *n*'s give,   *Take, Lady* 1

O

Oak   (*See also* **Oak-tree**) this long avenue Of thick
    dark *o*'s,   *Hear you the sound* 11
    leafless *o* Which towers above the lake   " 32
Oak-tree   *o-t* never should be planted   " 16
Object   ache For common *o*'s that would keep   *How strange it is* 4
Observing   light of hazel eyes, *O* all things.   *That is his portrait* 14
Occident   Far off in the dun, dark *o*,   *Far off in the dun* 1
Odour   The night with sudden *o* reel'd,   *The night, etc.* 1
Office   I must unto mine *o*.   *Half after midnight!* 20
Offspring   I and my son's son and our *o*,   *Hear you the sound* 24
    Their *o* of this union.   *Old ghosts* 8
Old   When there stood a dark coach at an *o* Inn door   *Far off in the dun* 35
    The grim *o* coachee strode to the box,   " 87
    Coeval with the battlemented towers Of my *o*
    ancestors !   *Hear you the sound* 13
    Wore the pale cast of thought, a good *o* man,   *Methought I saw* 2
    O ghosts whose day was done ere mine began,   *Old ghosts* 1
    And on me Frown not, *o* ghosts,   " 9
    I stepp'd upon the *o* mill bridge ?   *Remember you* 4
    O'er the bow'd shoulder of a bland *o* Age, The
    face of placid Death.'   *That is his portrait* 36
    Townsmen, or of the hamlet, young or *o*,   *Townsmen, etc.* 1
    He chanted some *o* doleful rhyme.   *Youth, lapsing i* 38
    Still humming snatches of *o* song,   " 21
Older   When I was somewhat *o* grown   *One was the Tishbite* 9
Olympias   One was *O* : the floating snake
One (adj.)   As when he stood on Carmel-steeps With
    o arm stretch'd out bare,   " 3
    Parts in two channels, moving to *o* end—   *Steersman* 3
    Thro' *o* whole life an overflowing urn,   *That is his portrait* 50
    Or sleep thro' *o* brief dream upon the grass,—   *Townsmen, etc.* 4
    O only joy I know, the joy of life.   *Why suffers* 14
    Now *o* faint line of light doth glow,   *Youth, lapsing ii* 9
One (pron. and s)   Sleep, my little *o*, sleep !   *Bright is the moon* 3
    Sleep, my pretty *o*, sleep !   " 10
    O was the Tishbite whom the raven fed,   *One was the Tishbite* 1
    O was Olympias : the floating snake   " 9
    The lasses and the little *o*'s, Jack Tars,   *They say, etc.* 15
Only   One *o* joy I know, the joy of life.   *Why suffers* 14
Open   Look he smiles, and *o*'s his hands,   *Bright is the moon* 4
    Said, ' O, Rosebud, *o*, yield Thy fragrant soul.'   *The night, etc.* 5
Optic   And as with *o* glasses her keen eyes Pierced   *Hither, when all* 3
Orange   Wantoning in *o* groves Naked,   *A dark Indian maiden* 7
Orb   An *o* repulsive of all hate,   *Young is the grief* 14
Orbit   But as Earth her *o* runs,   *Little Aubrey* 3
Orion   field of drifted light In mid *O*,   *Hither, when all* 11
Osier   Streaming thro' his *o* aits !   *Vicar of this* 20
Other   Henceforward no *o* strife—   *Frenchman, etc.* 6
    Which speak of us to *o* centuries,   *Hear you the sound* 27
Outer   Howling in *o* darkness.   *Beauty, Good, etc.* 5
Overdealt   praise Is neither *o* nor idly won.   *That is his portrait* 43

Overdrawn delicately *o* With the first twilight   *Thy soul is like* 3
Overflow as never *o's* With flush of rain,   *Not to Silence* 19
Overflowing As my own soul is full, to *o*—   *Why suffers* 8
Overhaste lest *o* Should fire the many wheels   *That is his portrait* 50
Thro' one whole life an *o* urn,   *They wrought, etc.* 23
Overthrew Slew them and *o*.   *Bold Havelock* 8
Owl While I live, the *o's* !   *While I live* 1
Own Whence your *o* citizens, for their *o* renown,   *Here, I that stood* 7
Lured by the cuckoo-voice that loves To babble its *o* name.   *I, loving Freedom* 8
Yet her *o* deep soul says nay :   *The lamps were bright* 24
which he compell'd once more Thro' his *o* nature,   *That is his portrait* 28
When thine *o* spirit was at strife With thine *o* spirit.   *Thou may'st remember* 2
As my *o* soul is full, to overflowing—   *Why suffers* 8
Owning *o* more Discourse, more widely wise.'   *From shape to shape* 7

P

Pain Something of *p*—of bliss—of Love,   *'Tis not alone* 11
Painted filthiest of all paintings *p* well Is mightier than the purest *p* ill !' Yes, mightier than the purest *p* well,   *Art for Art's sake!* 3
That is his portrait *p* by himself.   *That is his portrait* 1
Painting filthiest of all *p's* painted well   *Art for Art's sake!* 3
Pale His brow is clammy and *p*.   *Far off in the dun* 28
They lifted their eyes to the dead, *p* skies,   " 61
Methought I saw a face whose every line Wore the *p* cast of thought,   *Methought I saw* 2
Pall the *p* of the sky Leave never an inch   *Far off in the dun* 21
Palm (a tree) Breezes from the *p* and canna   *A dark Indian maiden* 14
Waving a *p* branch, wondering,   " 51
Palm (of the hand) As each put a farthing into his *p*,   *Far off in the dun* 79
Palmy All day long with laughing eyes, Dancing by a *p* bay,   *A dark Indian maiden* 18
Pamper *See* **Pap-meat-pamper**
Pamper'd his little eyes Are swallow'd in his *p* cheeks.   *Yon huddled cloud* 12
Pandemonium There is a clock in *P*,   *Half after midnight!* 5
Papao Beneath the *p* tree !   *A dark Indian maiden* 33
Pap-meat-pamper But *p-m-p* not the time   *Wherever evil* 4
Paradise (adj.) those are the lights of the *P* coach,   *Far off in the dun* 107
Paradise (s) In the wooded *p*, The cedar-wooded *p*   *A dark Indian maiden* 8
Parish *P* feud, or party strife,   *Vicar of this* 8
Park deer Bleat as with human voices in the *p*.   *What rustles* 4
Part river here, my friend, *P's* in two channels,   *Steersman* 3
Party (adj.) Parish feud, or *p* strife,   *Vicar of this* 8
Party (s) and the d——l take the *parties* !   *They say, etc.* 10
Party-rage Contends, despising *p-r*,   *They wrought, etc.* 46
Pass'd *See* **Past**
Passion-wrought Ill fares a people *p-w*,   *They wrought, etc.* 25
Past (adj.) things of *p* days with their horrible eyes   *Far off in the dun* 19
Her thoughts have found their wings In the dreaming of *p* things :   *The lamps were bright* 22
Past (s) These hills were plains within the *p*,   *Well, as to Fame* 6
In thy beginnings in the *p*,   *Young is the grief* 11
And how all things become the *p*.   *Youth, lapsing i* 28
Past-Pass'd (verb) They *pass'd* (an inner spirit fed Their ever-burning fires,)   *Far off in the dun* 117
past, in sleep, away By night,   *Gone into darkness* 9
And *past* her for the Proctor.   *Sweet Kitty Sandilands* 4
Path who sees His *p* before him ?   *They wrought, etc.* 11
Patriot-martyrs Freedom claims As *p-m* of her creed :   *Not such were those* 2
Pause (s) And in the *p's* groans of men.   *Youth, lapsing ii* 24
Pause (verb) not *p* At the strife of the shadowy wheels,   *Far off in the dun* 93
brief dream upon the grass,—*P* here.   *Townsmen, etc.* 5
Pausing So *p* 'twixt the East and West,   *Youth, lapsing i* 47
Peaceful Tempers the *p* light of hazel eyes,   *That is his portrait* 13
Peak A mountain bright with triple *p's* :   *Youth, lapsing ii* 48
Peal (s) *See* **Thunder-peal**
Peal (verb) The second voice will *p* again.   *Youth, lapsing i* 56
Peal'd The southern stars a music *p*,   *The night, etc.* 2

Peal'd (continued) The latest thunder-peal hath *p*,   *Youth, lapsing ii* 30
Pearl True *P* of our poetic prime !   *We lost you* 2
Pendulum The slow vibrations of whose *p*,   *Half after midnight!* 7
People And fuse the *p's* into one.   *Are those the far-famed* 16
That the voice of a satisfied *p*   *That the voice* 1
Did the *p* dance and play,   *The lamps were bright* 36
Ill fares a *p* passion-wrought,   *They wrought, etc.* 25
Convoys the *p's* wish, is great ;   " 31
Perfect (*See also* **All-perfect**) ' And thro' all phases of all thought I come Unto the *p* man.   *From shape to shape* 4
More complex is more *p*, owning more Discourse,   " 7
Her *p* lips to taste,   *One was the Tishbite* 12
Perfume chapel's vaulted gloom Was misted with *p*.   *The lamps were bright* 8
Perish and our offspring, all Shall *p*,   *Hear you the sound* 25
speak of us to other centuries, Shall *p* also,   " 28
Perplex But questions that *p* us now—   *He was too good* 6
Never tithe unpaid *p* you,   *Vicar of this* 7
Phantom Mix'd with the *p* of his coming fame,   *That is his portrait* 32
Pharaoh A *P*, kingliest of his kingly race,   *Here, I that stood* 3
Phase thro' all *p's* of all thought I come   *From shape to shape* 3
Pierced eyes *P* thro' the mystic dome,   *Hither, when all* 4
Often shallow, *p* with light,   *Not to Silence* 21
Piercing *P* the wrung ears of the damn'd   *Half after midnight!* 10
Pile Would I could *p* fresh life on life,   *Why suffers* 5
Place (s) (*See also* **Charnel-place**) She led them down the pleasant *p's*,   *A dark Indian maiden* 62
shaped, and carved, and set me in my *p*.   *Here, I that stood* 4
And in the world the noblest *p*,   *The noblest men* 3
Place (verb) joy'd to *p* me on The hollow-stemm'd   *Hear you the sound* 31
Placid O'er the bow'd shoulder of a bland Old Age, The face of *p* Death.'   *That is his portrait* 37
Plain Anacaona, Dancing on the blossomy *p*   *A dark Indian maiden* 29
summer *p's* with their shining leaves,   *Far off in the dun* 69
These hills were *p's* within the past, There will be *p's* again, and we,   *Well, as to Fame* 6
And I must traverse yonder *p* :   *Youth, lapsing i* 54
The casements sparkle on the *p*,   " ii 39
Plan That contemplate a mighty *p*,   *They wrought, etc.* 42
Planted oak-tree never should be *p* But near   *Hear you the sound* 16
Play (s) And your three young things at *p*,   *Vicar of this* 13
Her silver eddies in their *p* Drove into lines   *Youth, lapsing i* 5
Play (verb) A child she loved to *p* ;   *Along this glimmering* 2
Where the doubtful shadows *p*;   *Not to Silence* 31
Did the people dance and *p*,   *The lamps were bright* 36
Playing *P* with the scarlet crane,   *A dark Indian maiden* 31
Pleasant She led them down the *p* places,   " 62
They saw the green verge of the *p* earth,   *Far off in the dun* 63
With *p* hymns they soothe the air Of death,   " 109
Are *p* from the early Spring to when,   *Townsmen, etc.* 7
Vicar of this *p* spot Where it was my chance to marry,   *Vicar of this* 1
Please The despots over yonder, let 'em do whate'er they *p* !   *They say, etc.* 16
All things *p* you, nothing vex you,   *Vicar of this* 9
Pledge Then *p* we our glorious dead,   *Frenchmen, etc.* 9
Plot (s) I hate the trim-set *p's* of art !'   *I keep no more* 14
Plot (verb) and they *p* against us yonder,   *They say, etc.* 8
Plough loom or *p* To weigh them as they should   *He was too good* 7
Pluck To *p* the sanction of a God.   " 12
Poesy when *P* shall bind Falsehood beneath   *O God, make this age* 7
Poet I know it as a *p*, (repeat)   *Immeasurable sadness!* 2, 8
Little *p*, hear the little *p's* epigram !   *Little Aubrey* 1
' You're no *P* '—the critics cried ! ' Why ? ' said the *P*. ' You're unpopular ! '   *Popular, Popular* 2
' You're no *P* !' ' Why ? '—' You're popular ! '   " 5
Poetic True Pearl of our *p* prime !   *We lost you* 2
Pointing *P* to the unheeded lapse of hours,   *Half after midnight!* 2
Poised there Hovering, thoughtful, *p* in air.   *Not to Silence* 12
Pole thunderings Shakes all the starless *p*,   *Far off in the dun* 16
She saw the snowy *p's* and Moons of Mars,   *Hither, when all* 9
Polling The humours of the *p* and the wake,   *That is his portrait* 20
Pomp ye still shall flourish In your high *p* of shade,   *Hear you the sound* 29
Poor A clearer day Than our *p* twilight dawn on earth—   *Gone into darkness* 5
P devils, babble ' we shall last.'   *Well, as to Fame* 8
Pop-gun *P-g*, Popular and Unpopular !   *Popular, Popular* 6

Second Sooner or later from the haze The *s* voice will peal again.   *Youth, lapsing i 56*

Secret is it my love Coming along the *s* ways?   *What rustles 6*
And where the *s* streams rejoice.   *Youth, lapsing i 12*

See *S*, The cradle where she lay !   *Along the glimmering 3*
And *s*, ye dare not touch the truth,   *Are those the far-famed 6*
He *s's* his father in distant lands,   *"Bright is the moon 5*
They *s* the light of their blest firesides   *Far off in the dun 65*
The summer hills they *s* ;   *" 70*
The crowd have come to *s* thy grave,   *I keep no more 2*
But these shall *s* it none the less.   *" 4*
I laugh'd to *s* him as he stood,   *I met in all 7*
S, she dreameth happy dreams,   *Not a whisper 13*
Methinks I *s* the world's renewed youth   *O God, make this age 6*
Speak to me, let me hear or *s* !   *Speak to me 5*
I *s* At the end, as 'twere athwart   *That is his portrait 34*
who *s's* His path before him ?   *They wrought, etc. 10*
Whate'er I *s*, where'er I move,   *'Tis not alone 9*
And *s* and hear the world revolve :   *Youth, lapsing i 52*

Seed It show'd the *s's* of innate dignity   *Hear you the sound 52*

Seeing *S* is far an end sublime,   *They wrought, etc. 45*
S the heart so wondrous in her ways,   *Why suffers 3*

Seeking *See* **Truth-seeking**

Seem ' I *s*, but am not, far away ;   *Early-wise 4*
Like to one of us she *s's*,   *Not a whisper 15*
But tho' the cataract *s* the nearer way,   *Steersman 6*

Seem'd I heard, as I have *s* to hear,   *Remember you 9*
S I so cold ? what madness moved my blood   *To the with whom 10*

Seen I have *s* the four great empires disappear !   *Here, I that stood 9*
If earth be *s* from your conjectured heaven,   *Old ghosts 2*
Considering what mine eyes have *s*,   *Young is the grief 9*

Seest *S* thou my faults and wilt not speak ?   *Speak to me 7*

Self-control range Of prospect up to *s-c*,   *Thou may'st remember 11*

Send and he *s's* you his Salaam ;   *Little Aubrey 2*

Sender *S* and sent-to go to make up this,   *Old ghosts 7*

Sense keep Our awful inner ghostly *s* Unroused,   *How strange it is 5*
But to one of finer *s*,   *Not to Silence 5*
Or, if the *s* of most require   *They wrought, etc. 37*
The difference of all things to the *s*,   *Why suffers 10*

Sent Where his gilding ray is never *s*,   *Far off in the dun 9*
S thro' my blood a prophet voice   *Youth, lapsing i 10*

Sent-to Sender and *s-t* go to make up this,   *Old ghosts 7*

Servant whose whims were meant For virtue's *s's*,   *A surface man 3*

Set (*See also* **Trim-set**) *S* round with many a toppling spire,   *Deep glens I found 2*
shaped, and carved, and *s* me in my place.   *Here, I that stood 4*
Spurge with fairy crescent *s*,   *Spurge with fairy 1*

Settle To shape, to *s*, to repair   *They wrought, etc. 4*

Settled and what a *s* mind, Mature,   *That is his portrait 11*

Shade ye still shall flourish In your high pomp of *s*,   *Hear you the sound 29*
Millions of forms, and hues, and *s's*,   *Why suffers 9*
Crown'd with soft *s* her deepening floods   *Youth, lapsing i 3*

Shadow confused The *s's* from the icy heights.   *Deep glens I found 8*
When the *s* of night's eternal wings   *Far off in the dun 13*
Ye proud aristocrats whose lordly *s's*,   *Hear you the sound 21*
Where the doubtful *s's* play,   *Not to Silence 31*
S's of statesmen, clever men !   *They wrought, etc. 12*
And *s's* strike and *s's* sink,   *Youth, lapsing ii 15*
Away with *s's* ! On they move !   *" 34*

Shadow'd *See* **Cocoa-shadow'd**

Shadowy A land of thin faces and *s* forms,   *Far off in the dun 7*
As the shrivell'd forms of the *s* grooms Yoked the skeleton horses to.   *" 59*
Whose blood in its liveliest course would not pause At the strife of the *s* wheels.   *" 94*

Shake thunderings *S's* all the starless pole,   *" 16*
To which the slight-built hustings *s* ;   *They wrought, etc. 9*

Shaken They were *s* from the dance.—   *The lamps were bright 46*

Shakespeare Little Homer, little Dante, little *S*,   *Little Aubrey 4*

Shallow Often *s*, pierced with light,   *Not to Silence 21*

Shame The year, that comes, may come with *s*,   *I, loving Freedom 6*
'Tis *s* to fail so far, and still My failing shall be less my *s* :   *Young is the grief 7*

Shank his *s's* were shrunken to willow wands   *Far off in the dun 55*

Shape (s) heads without bodies and *s's* without heads   *Far off in the dun 103*
From *s* to *s* at first within the womb   *From shape to shape 1*
Admire that stalwart *s*, those ample brows,   *That is his portrait 4*
Into another *s*, born of the first,   *" 29*

Shape (verb) To *s*, to settle, to repair   *They wrought, etc. 34*

Shaped *s*, and carved, and set me in my place.   *Here, I that stood 4*

Sharp and dull The *s* desire of knowledge still with knowing !   *Why suffers 6*

Sharper Till suddenly a *s* voice Cried in the future ' Come along.'   *Youth, lapsing i 39*

Shaven Strange fiery eyes glared fiercely thro' The windows of *s* bone.   *Far off in the dun 48*

Sheaf When corny Lammas bound the *sheaves* :   *Youth, lapsing i 16*

Shift Yon huddled cloud his motion *s's*,   *Yon huddled cloud 1*

Shifting Full fields of barley *s* tearful lights   *Townsmen, etc. 8*

Shine Thro' wooded isles the river *s's*,   *Youth, lapsing ii 38*

Shining The summer plains with their *s* leaves,   *Far off in the dun 69*

Shook And *s* the frosty winter stars.   *Youth, lapsing i 20*

Shone sallow lights *s* Dimly and blurly   *Far off in the dun 99*
As stars they *s*, in raiment white,   *" 131*

Shore never more upon the *s* Dancing   *A dark Indian maiden 65*
How glad am I to walk With Susan on the *s* !   *How glad am I 2*
far off from England's *s*, He comes no more.   *What rustles 9*
That wash'd her *s's* with blissful sounds :   *Youth, lapsing i 4*

Short Thick sobs and *s* shrill screams arise Along the sunless waste,   *Far off in the dun 17*
and whensoe'er There may be *s* cessation of their wails,   *Half after midnight! 12*

Shoulder Down from the *s* moved :   *One was the Tishbite 13*
breast dispread Between low *s's* ;   *That is his portrait 6*
O'er the bow'd *s* of a bland old Age,   *" 36*

Shout (s) Faint *s's* are heard across the glen,   *Youth, lapsing i 22*

Shout (verb) shriek and *s* to drown the thrilling noise.   *Half after midnight! 16*

Show I will *s* to you Another countenance,   *That is his portrait 44*

Show'd It *s* the seeds of innate dignity   *Hear you the sound 52*

Shower (s) loud the roar Of wind and mingled *s*,   *Far off in the dun 34*

Shower (verb) *S's* in a whisper o'er the world.   *Not to Silence 34*

Showing *s* every bend Of each dark hill   *Thy soul is like 5*

Shriek *s* and shout to drown the thrilling noise.   *Half after midnight! 16*

Shrill Thick sobs and short *s* screams arise Along the sunless waste,   *Far off in the dun 17*
is heard The *s* and solemn warning ' Ever, Never' :   *Half after midnight! 14*

Shrine (s) Not to her would raise a *s* :   *Not to Silence 3*
Near the *s*, but half in sun,   *" 17*

Shrine (verb) I would *s* her in my verse !   *" 8*

Shrivell'd As the *s* forms of the shadowy grooms Yoked the skeleton horses to.   *Far off in the dun 59*

Shrunken his shanks were *s* to willow wands   *" 55*

Shudder I *s* in my lonely nest,   *What rustles 13*

Shudder'd *S* with silent stars, she clomb,   *Hither, when all 2*

Shut he that *s's* out Love, in turn shall be *S* out from Love,   *Beauty, Good, etc. 3*

Shy But found a maiden tender, *s*,   *Because she bore 5*

Sick His heart throbs thick, his brain reels *s* :   *Far off in the dun 27*
Another whispers *s* with loss :   *I keep no more 9*
Thro' her worn brain, hot and *s*.'   *The lamps were bright 28*

Sicken Till priest-craft and king-craft *s*,   *Wherever evil 3*

Side Deep dells of snow sunk on each *s*   *Far off in the dun 97*
on every *s* The dragon's curves melted,   *One was the Tishbite 14*

Sigh (s) And mingle kisses, tears, and *s's*,   *Life of the Life 6*

Sigh (verb) *S* over all their fallen leaves ;   *Youth, lapsing i 32*

Sight The tears bedimm'd their *s* :   *Far off in the dun 86*
Till heart and *s* and hearing ache   *How strange it is 3*
Often deep beyond the *s*,   *Not to Silence 22*

Sign rusty *s* of a skull and cross-bones   *Far off in the dun 43*

Silence Not to *S* would I build A temple   *Not to Silence 1*
Not like *S* shall she stand,   *" 9*

Silent Floated in the *s* summer :   *A dark Indian maiden 40*
Remembering all the golden hours Now *s*,   *Gone into darkness 10*
Shudder'd with *s* stars, she clomb,   *Hither, when all 2*
The *s* hills, the stormy floods,   *'Tis not alone 3*
Thames along the *s* level,   *Vicar of this 19*

Silent (continued) take with thee Our warmest wishes, s Guardians But true till death ; — *Woman of noble* 6

Silver S sails all out of the West, Under the s moon, — *Bright is the moon* 12

With a s sound the wheels went round, — *Far off in the dun* 121

In many a s loop and link Variously from its far spring, — *Not to Silence* 26

Her s eddies in their play Drove into lines and studs of light — *Youth, lapsing* i 5

Simmering sallow lights shone Dimly and blurly with s fat. — *Far off in the dun* 100

Simple Those holly-thickets only hide Her grave— a s stone ! — *Along this glimmering* 8

' O let the s slab remain ! — *I keep no more* 10

Simpler Evermore The s essence lower lies, — *From shape to shape* 6

Sin And free from taint of s. — *Far off in the dun* 132

Singest That thou s with main and with might ? — *Full light aloft* 6

Singing The wanton wind came s lustily — *Hear you the sound* 41

Single knows That none can truly write his s day, — *Old ghosts* 13

Sink And shadows strike and shadows s, — *Youth, lapsing* ii 15

Sister Beauty, Good and Knowledge are three s's . . . — *Beauty, Good, etc.* 1

S's,I could almost weep ! — *Not a whisper* 8

Her half s, Reticence. — *Not to Silence* 6

Sit You'd s there From dawn till sunset — *Hear you the sound* 38

will not let an honest Briton s at home at ease : — *They say, etc.* 9

I s among the scentless flowers — *Youth, lapsing* i 51

And there s figures as of Gods — " ii 51

Sitting The child was s on the bank — *The child was sitting* 1

Skeleton As the shrivell'd forms of the shadowy grooms Yoked the s horses to. — *Far off in the dun* 60

Skin The s hung lax on his long thin hands ; — " 53

Skinny ' They revel as they may,' That s witch did say, — *The lamps were bright* 18

Skull and Cross-bones (Inn sign) rusty sign of a s a c-b — *Far off in the dun* 43

Sky the pall of the s Leave never an inch of blue ; — " 21

Strange beauties from the s. — " 32

lifted their eyes to the dead, pale skies, — " 61

when all the deep unsounded skies — *Hither, when all* 1

And softly blow the balmy skies ; — *Life of the Life* 4

Speak to me from the stormy s ! — *Speak to me* 1

The starr'd abysses of the s, — ' Tis not alone 2

Out bursts a rainbow in the s— — *Youth, lapsing* ii 33

Slab ' O let the simple s remain ! — *I keep no more* 10

Slave heart of his Hard, and the s of vice ; — *A surface man* 4

They were not s's that names mislead, — *Not such were those* 3

Slay Whom the wedded wife did s, — *The lamps were bright* 48

Sleek or the snug brick box Of some s citizen. — *Hear you the sound* 20

Sleep (s) past, in s, away By night, — *Gone into darkness* 2

All the house is fast in s, — *Not a whisper* 6

Sleep (verb) S, my little one, s ! — *Bright is the moon* 3

kisses him there in a dream, S, s ! — " 7

S, my pretty one, s ! — " 10

Under the silver moon, S, s ! — " 14

To watch and wake while others s, — *How strange it is* 2

In that cradle s's my child, — *Not a whisper* 9

mock'd and said, ' Come, cry aloud, he s's.' — *One was the Tishbite* 4

S's round those quiet lips ; not quite a smile ; — *That is his portrait* 9

Or s thro' one brief dream upon the grass,— — *Townsmen, etc.* 4

' Come ' and I come, no more I s : — *Youth, lapsing* ii 25

Sleepy Summer thro' all her s leaves Murmur'd : — " i 5

Slender I clasp her s waist, We kiss, we are so fond, — *How glad am I* 5

Slept in them s A red infernal glow ; — *Far off in the dun* 81

Slew S them and overthrew. — *Bold Havelock* 8

Slight-built To which the s-b hustings shake ; — *They wrought, etc.* 8

Slightest Down to his s turns and attitudes— — *That is his portrait* 24

Slime Cemented with the burning s — *Far off in the dun* 39

Slip Her garment s's, the left hand holds — *Not to Silence* 13

Sloe Than if the vine had borne the bitter s. — *To thee with whom* 4

Slow The s vibrations of whose pendulum, — *Half after midnight !* 7

Slow-ripening S-r to the grace of womanhood, — *To thee with whom* 13

Slumber S not now, gird up thy loins for fight, — *O God, make this age* 10

Slumbrous Bathing in the s coves, — *A dark Indian maiden* 7

Small S thanks or credit shall I have, — *I keep no more* 3

Smile (s) how demure a s, How full — *That is his portrait* 6

Smile (s) (continued) Sleeps round those quiet lips ; not quite a s ; — *That is his portrait* 9

Smile (verb) Look he s's, and opens his hands, — *Bright is the moon* 4

Smiled And they s on Anacaona, — *A dark Indian maiden* 58

this one s, that other waved his arms, — *That is his portrait* 22

Smooth S as Thames below your gates, — *Vicar of this* 18

Snake floating s Roll'd round her ankles, — *One was the Tishbite* 9

Snatch Still humming s'es of old song, — *Youth, lapsing* i 38

Snout monstrous rocks from craggy s's — *Deep glens I found* 3

Snow (See also **Summer-snow**) Deep dells of s sunk on each side — *Far off in the dun* 97

With flush of rain, or molten s's, — *Not to Silence* 20

Snowy She saw the s poles and Moons of Mars, — *Hither, when all* 9

To s crofts and winding scars, — *Youth, lapsing* i 18

Snug or the s brick box Of some sleek citizen. — *Hear you the sound* 19

Sob Thick s's and short shrill screams — *Far off in the dun* 17

Sober when each one leaves The middle road of s thought ! — *They wrought, etc.* 28

Social A noise of hands that disarrange The s engine ! — " 22

Socket His s's were eyeless, but in them slept A red infernal glow ; — *Far off in the dun* 81

Soft Crown'd with s shade her deepening floods — *Youth, lapsing* i 3

Solemn When there stood a dark coach at an old Inn door At the s midnight hour. — *Far off in the dun* 36

With a s burst of thrilling light, — " 119

is heard The shrill and s warning ' Ever, Never ' : — *Half after midnight !* 14

Stately and mild, and all between Valleys full of s sound, — *Thy soul is like* 9

Solitary Upon the brink A s fortress burns, — *Youth, lapsing* ii 14

Solitude Youth, lapsing thro' fair s's, — " i 1

Solve Unvext by doubts I cannot s, — " i 50

Sombre Nor wanting many a s mound. — *Thy soul is like* 7

Something Was s that another could not be, — *That is his portrait* 25

And there is s greatly done : — *Youth, lapsing* ii 12

Son I and my s's s's and our offspring, — *Hear you the sound* 24

O leave not thou thy s forlorn ; — *O leave not thou* 1

Song air Of death, with s's of pride : — *Far off in the dun* 110

Accepts the s's you gave, and he sends — *Little Aubrey* 2

full God-bless-you with this book of s, — *Take, Lady* 2

Still humming snatches of old song, — *Youth, lapsing* i 38

from the gulf A murmur of heroic s, — " ii 19

Sooner S or later from the haze — " i 55

Soothe With pleasant hymns they s the air — *Far off in the dun* 109

Sorrow Nor S beauteous in her youth, — *Are those the far-famed* 7

I reck not for the s or the strife : — *Why suffers* 13

The sacred s's of as pure a heart — *Woman of noble* 4

Soul Yet her own deep s says nay : — *The lamps were bright* 24

Rosebud, open, yield Thy fragrant s.' — *The night, etc.* 6

The frame, the mind, the s of man, — *They wrought, etc.* 43

God walk'd the waters of thy s, — *Thou may'st remember* 7

Thy s is like a landskip, friend, — *Thy soul is like* 1

God be gracious to my s ! — *What rustles* 15

As my own s is full, to overflowing— — *Why suffers* 8

Sound (s) No s of joy, no revelling tones — *Far off in the dun* 41

And a s of stringèd lyres, — " 120

With a silver s the wheels went round, — " 121

Hear you the s of wheels ? — *Hear you the sound* 1

may keep A s in her ears like the s of the deep, Like the s — *That the voice* 2

He loved the river's roaring s ; — *The child was sitting* 3

A s of words that change to blows ! — *They wrought, etc.* 17

A s of blows on armèd breasts ! — " 18

between Valleys full of solemn s, — *Thy soul is like* 9

That wash'd her shores with blissful s's : — *Youth, lapsing* i 4

When to this s my face I turn'd, — " 41

Sound (verb) S ' Ever, Never ' thro' the courts of Hell, — *Half after midnight !* 9

But did not s so joyfully : — *Youth, lapsing* i 24

Sounded leaders bounded, the guard's horn s : — *Far off in the dun* 89

Southern The s stars a music peal'd, — *The night, etc.* 2

Spake man, Most eloquent, who s of things — *Methought I saw* 3

he s : ' I lift the eyes of thought, — *That is his portrait* 33

Spanish My S blood ran proudly in my veins. — *Hear you the sound* 45

Sparkle   The casements s on the plain,   *Youth, lapsing* ii 39
Speak   If you could s, would you not say :   *Early-wise* 3
        Which s of us to other centuries,   *Hear you the sound* 27
        I murmur'd ' S again, my love,   *Remember you* 7
        S to me from the stormy sky !   *Speak to me* 1
        S to me, dearest, lest I die.   „   4
        S to me, let me hear or see !   „   5
        Seest thou my faults and wilt not s ?   „   7
        This is the man of whom you heard me s.   *That is his portrait* 15
        He strokes his beard before he s's ;   *Yon huddled cloud* 10
        To s of what had gone before,   *Youth, lapsing* i 27
Speakest   My friend, thou s from the heart,   *I keep no more* 15
Spear   On growing s's, by fits the lady ash   *Townsmen, etc.* 9
Spire   Set round with many a toppling s,   *Deep glens I found* 2
Spirit   an inner s fed Their ever-burning fires,)   *Far off in the dun* 117
        The happy s's within ;   „   130
        I mourn in s when I think The year,   *I, loving Freedom* 5
        Were I not a s blest,   *Not a whisper* 7
        Great s's grow akin to base.   *They wrought, etc.* 16
        To hold the S of the Age Against the S of the Time.   „   47
        When thine own s was at strife With thine own s.   *Thou may'st remember* 2
        stood The tearful s of the time ;   *Youth, lapsing* i 34
        Warm beats my blood, my s thirsts ;   „   ii 45
Spiritual   Of beryl, and of amethyst Was the s frame.   *Far off in the dun* 124
        Thro' s dark we come Into the light of s life.'   *Thou may'st remember* 5
Spoke   Cold words I s, yet loved thee warm and well.   *To thee with whom* 8
Spot   s Where it was my chance to marry,   *Vicar of this* 1
Spread   were s Around in the chilling air,   *Far off in the dun* 101
        How every brake and flower s and rose,   *That is his portrait* 26
Spring (fountain)   Variously from its far s,   *Not to Silence* 27
Spring (season)   Are pleasant from the early S to when,   *Townsmen, etc.* 7
        I heard S laugh in hidden rills,   *Youth, lapsing* i 13
Spring (verb)   never green thing will gaily s In that   *Far off in the dun* 9
        the laverock s From under the deep,   *Full light aloft* 1
        That he s's from the common stock.   *How is it that men* 6
Springing   Over the dark sea-marge s,   *A dark Indian maiden* 39
Spur   She s's an imitative will ;   *Young is the grief* 6
Spurge   S with fairy crescent set,   *Spurge with fairy* 1
Square   See Four-square
Stalwart   Admire that s shape, those ample brows,   *That is his portrait* 4
Stand   Wherefore s I here ?   *Half after midnight !* 18
        Not like Silence shall she s,   *Not to Silence* 9
        Not with this age wherefrom ye s apart,   *Therefore your Halls* 11
Standard   Day by day Watch your s roses blowing,   *Vicar of this* 12
Standers by   And looks to awe the s b,   *Because she bore* 4
Standing   And they saw *her* s by,   *The lamps were bright* 51
Star   Dissolve a world, condense a s,   *Are those the far-famed* 14
        As s's they shone, in raiment white,   *Far off in the dun* 131
        Shudder'd with silent s's, she clomb,   *Hither, when all* 2
        light In mid Orion, and the married s's.   „   11
        The southern s's a music peal'd,   *The night, etc.* 2
        And shook the frosty winter s's.   *Youth, lapsing* i 20
Staring   And, s as in trance,   *The lamps were bright* 45
Starless   mutter of deep-mouth'd thunderings Shakes all the s pole,   *Far off in the dun* 16
        Vast wastes of s glooms were spread Around   „   101
Starr'd   The s abysses of the sky,   *'Tis not alone* 2
Starry   and bee-like swarms Of suns, and s streams.   *Hither, when all* 8
Startle   s the dull ears of human kind !   *O God, make this age* 5
State   Wed to no faction in the s,   *I, loving Freedom* 3
        thro' the channels of the s Convoys   *They wrought, etc.* 30
Stately   I deemed her one of s frame   *Because she bore* 3
        S and mild, and all between Valleys full of solemn sound,   *Thy soul is like* 8
        two fair lilies growing at thy side Have slowly prosper'd into s flowers.   *Woman of noble* 12
Statesman   Shadows of *statesmen*, clever men !   *They wrought, etc.* 12
Stay   I found the Present where I s :   *Youth, lapsing* i 48
        Yet well I know that nothing s's,   „   53
Stedfast   They glitter'd with a s light,   *Far off in the dun* 129
Steed   And his hot s's never run :   „   4
        Their s's were strong exceedingly :   „   125
Steeple   S, and stream, and forest lawn,   *Thy soul is like* 2
Steering   be not precipitate in thine act Of s,   *Steersman* 2
Steersman   S, be not precipitate in thine act   „   1

Stemm'd   See Hollow-stemm'd
Step (s)   A s ? a footfall ?   What is that I hear ?   *What rustles* 2
Step (verb)   S thro' these doors, and I will show   *That is his portrait* 44
Stepp'd-Stept   as he *stept* thro' the crowd,   *Far off in the dun* 75
        I *stepp'd* upon the old mill bridge ?   *Remember you* 4
Stepping   S lightly flower-laden,   *A dark Indian maiden* 3
        Loftily s with fair faces.   „   64
Stept   See Stepp'd
Stern   burn With a light so wild and s ? '   *The lamps were bright* 16
Still   The night is black and s ;   the deer   *What rustles* 3
        The cedar-wooded paradise Of s Xaraguay :   *A dark Indian maiden* 21
Still'd   waters of thy soul, And s them.   *Thou may'st remember* 8
Stir   Not a whisper s's the gloom,   *Not a whisper* 1
Stirr'd   Call to its mate when nothing s   *Remember you* 15
        this so s him in his hour of joy,   *That is his portrait* 31
Stithy   Bang thy s stronger and stronger,   *Wherever evil* 8
Stock   That he springs from the common s.   *How is it that men* 6
Stole   Warm beams across the meadows s ;   *The night, etc.* 3
Stone   Her grave—a simple s !   *Along this glimmering* 8
Stood   there s a dark coach at an old Inn door   *Far off in the dun* 35
        s alone And still in the dark doorway :   „   49
        I that s in On beside the flow   *'Here, I that stood* 1
        I laugh'd to see him as he s,   *I met in all* 7
        As when he s on Carmel-steeps   *One was the Tishbite* 3
        s The tearful spirit of the time ;   *Youth, lapsing* i 33
Storm   There lies a land of chilling s's,   *Far off in the dun* 5
        A voice before the s,   *I, loving Freedom* 4
Stormy   Speak to me from the s sky !   *Speak to me* 1
        The child was sitting on the bank Upon a s day,   *The child was sitting* 2
        The silent hills, the s floods,   *'Tis not alone* 1
Stouter   Gives s ale and riper port Than any in the country-side.   *Yon huddled cloud* 7
Strand   I took delight in this fair s and free ;   *Here often when a child* 2
Strange   To draw s comfort from the earth, S beauties from the sky.   *Far off in the dun* 31
        S fiery eyes glared fiercely thro' The windows of shaven bone.   „   47
        Thro' s seas drew me to your monster town.   *Here, I that stood* 8
        How s it is, O God, to wake,   *How strange it is* 1
Stranger   It were, O Heaven, a s tale to tell   *To thee with whom* 3
Streak   Fast by me flash the cloudy s's,   *Youth, lapsing* ii 46
Stream (s)   Before them flow'd a fiery s ;   *Far off in the dun* 127
        swarms Of suns, and starry s's.   *Hither, when all* 8
        The s is loud : I cannot hear ! '   *Remember you* 8
        Steeple, and s, and forest lawn,   *Thy soul is like* 2
        And where the secret s rejoice.   *Youth, lapsing* i 12
Stream (verb)   That s's about the bend ;   *Steersman* 5
Streaming   S thro' his osier'd aits !   *Vicar of this* 20
Street   To fling his doubts into the s.   *He was too good* 4
        Up the s we took her As far as to the Castle,   *Sweet Kitty Sandilands* 9
Strength   fears that waste The s of men,   *They wrought, etc.* 23
        all the s thou wouldst have been :   *Young is the grief* 12
Stretch'd   With one arm s out bare,   *One was the Tishbite* 3
Stricken   See Thunder-stricken
Stride   as to Fame, who s the earth   *Well, as to Fame* 1
Strife   not pause At the s of the shadowy wheels,   *Far off in the dun* 94
        Henceforward no other s—   *Frenchman, etc.* 6
        When thine own spirit was at s   *Thou may'st remember* 2
        Parish feud, or party s,   *Vicar of this* 8
        I reck not for the sorrow or the s :   *Why suffers* 13
Strike   And shadows s and shadows sink,   *Youth, lapsing* ii 15
        A tempest s's the craggy walls,   „   21
Stringéd   And a sound of s lyres.   *Far off in the dun* 120
Strode   grim old coachee s to the box,   „   87
Stroke   He s's his beard before he speaks ;   *Yon huddled cloud* 10
Strong   Their steeds were s exceedingly :   *Far off in the dun* 125
        It is not good to drink s wine Ere the day be well-nigh done ;   *Full light aloft* 9
        Tall, eager, lean and s, his cloak wind-borne Behind,   *One was the Tishbite* 5
        Long, Eustace, long May my s wish, transgressing the low bound Of mortal hope,   *That is his portrait* 38
        ' Come ' and I come, the wind is s :   *Youth, lapsing* ii 17
Stronger   Bang thy stithy s and s,   *Wherever evil* 8
Stud   Drove into lines and s's of light   *Youth, lapsing* i 6

Sublime   He, seeing far an end *s,*   *They wrought, etc.* 45
Such   Nor proved I *s* delight as he, to mark The humours of the polling and the wake,   *That is his portrait* 19
Sudden   The night with *s* odour reel'd,   *The night, etc.* 1
Suffer   Why *s's* human life so soon eclipse ?   *Why suffers* 1
Suffer'd   His and my friendship have not *s* loss,   *That is his portrait* 41
Summer (adj.)   The *s* plains with their shining leaves,
   The *s* hills they see ;   *Far off in the dun* 69
   to return with thee Some happy *S* morning,   *Woman of noble* 9
Summer (s)   Floated in the silent *s* :   *A dark Indian maiden* 40
   and lie A thousand *s's* at her feet.   *Because she bore* 8
   S thro' all her sleepy leaves Murmur'd :   *Youth, lapsing i* 14
Summer-snow   My coldness was mistimed like *s-s,*   *To thee with whom* 7
Summit   Thence, across the *s* hurl'd,   *Not to Silence* 33
   Down from the *s* sweeps the day   *Youth, lapsing ii* 31
Sun   *s* Drew down the West his feeble lights ;   *Deep glens I found* 5
   Behind the burning *S* :   *Far off in the dun* 2
   At the rising of the *s.*   *Full light aloft* 12
   bee-like swarms Of *s's,* and starry streams.   *Hither, when all* 7
   of the changes of the *s's* ?   *Little Aubrey* 6
   Near the shrine, but half in *s,*   *Not to Silence* 17
   The image of the *s* by day,   *Youth, lapsing i* 7
   I follow to the morning *s,*   *„ ii* 10
Sunbright   cocoa-shadow'd coves, Of *s* Xaraguay,   *A dark Indian maiden* 9
Sunder'd   That never can be *s* without tears.   *Beauty, Good, etc.* 2
   clouds are *s* toward the morning-rise :   *O God, make this age* 9
Sunk   Deep dells of snow *s* on each side   *Far off in the dun* 97
Sunless   Deep glens I found, and *s* gulfs,   *Deep glens I found* 1
   Thick sobs and short shrill screams arise Along the *s* waste,   *Far off the dun* 18
Sunset   You'd sit there From dawn till *s*   *Hear you the sound* 39
Surface   A *s* man of many theories, And yet not true to one :   *A surface man* 1
Susan   to walk With *S* on the shore !   *How glad am I* 2
Swallow'd   eyes Are *s* in his pamper'd cheeks.   *Yon huddled cloud* 12
Swarm   bee-like *s's* Of suns, and starry streams.   *Hither, when all* 7
Swarthy   Those thoughtful furrows in the *s* cheek ;   *That is his portrait* 3
Swear   *S* to be one for ever,   *Frenchman, etc.* 10
Sweep   With twinkling finger *s's* her yellow keys.   *Townsmen, etc.* 10
   Down from the summit *s's* the day   *Youth, lapsing ii* 31
Sweet   Maizebread and the yuccaroot, Of *s* Xaraguay :   *A dark Indian maiden* 45
   With fair blue eyes and winning *s,*   *Because she bore* 6
   the laverock spring From under the deep, *s* corn,   *Full light aloft* 2
   But thou hast drunk of the merry, *s* wine,   *„* 11
   He was too good and kind and *s,*   *He was too good* 1
   and drank The *s* sad tears of wisdom.'   *Methought I saw* 6
   S Kitty Sandilands, The daughter of the doctor,   *Sweet Kitty Sandilands* 1
   These voices did not cease to cry Only they took a *s* tone,   *Youth, lapsing i* 23
   Again the low *s* voices murmur'd In distant fields,   *„ i* 43
   and all comes back Which in that early voice was *s,*   *„ ii* 42
Sweetness   the *s* which thou wast In thy beginnings   *Young is the grief* 10
Swung   *S* creaking before the Inn.   *Far off in the dun* 44

T

Table   that large *t* of the breast dispread,   *That is his portrait* 5
Tacit   Become a *t* eloquent reproach Unto the dissipation of this Earth.   *Half after midnight !* 3
Taint   And free from *t* of sin.   *Far off in the dun* 132
Take   And long'd to *t* his hand in mine.   *I met in all* 4
   T thou the ' bend,' 'twill save thee many a day.   *Steersman* 8
   T, Lady, what your loyal nurses give,   *Take, Lady* 1
   and the d——l *t* the parties !   *They say, etc.* 10
   t with thee Our warmest wishes,   *Woman of noble* 5
Taking   Regions of lucid matter *t* forms,   *Hither, when all* 5
Tale   At some sad *t* of wrong, and do the wrong   *A surface man* 6
   a stranger *t* to tell Than if the vine   *To thee with whom* 3
   And ever new the *t* she tells,   *Young is the grief* 2
Talk   How glad am I to *t* ! I kiss   *How glad am I* 3

Tall   For they were fair-faced and *t,* They were more fair-faced and *t,*   *A dark Indian maiden* 55
   T, eager, lean and strong, his cloak   *One was the Tishbite* 5
Taper   No *t's* light look'd out on the night,   *Far off in the dun* 45
Tar   Up, Jack *T's,* and save us ! (repeat)   *They say, etc.* 5, 12, 19
   Up, Jack *T's,* my hearties !   *„* 10
   The lasses and the little ones, Jack *T's,* they look to you !   *„* 15
Tarry   Methinks they *t* somewhat. What's the clock ?   *Hear you the sound* 3
Tasse   And from it hung the *t.*   *Sweet Kitty Sandilands* 3
Taste   Her perfect lips to *t,*   *One was the Tishbite* 12
   ' To those who will not *t* it more ! '   *Yon huddled cloud* 16
Taught   with thee, Mother, *t* us first to pray,   *Remembering him* 2
Tavern   by the *t* in the dale, The thirsty horseman,   *Yon huddled cloud* 2
   This *t* is their chief resort,   *„* 5
Teach   *T* me, great Nature : make me live.   *O leave not thou* 2
   And *t* us nothing, feeding not the heart.   *Therefore your Halls* 14
Tear   That never can be sunder'd without *t's.*   *Beauty, Good, etc.* 2
   The *t's* bedimm'd their sight :   *Far off in the dun* 86
   The happy maiden's *t's* are free   *I keep no more* 5
   And mingle kisses, *t's,* and sighs,   *Life of the Life* 6
   drank The sweet sad *t's* of wisdom.'   *Methought I saw* 6
   water'd by thy *t's,* The two fair lilies   *Woman of noble* 10
Tearful   Full fields of barley shifting *t* lights On growing spears,   *Townsmen, etc.* 8
   Beside my door at morning stood The *t* spirit of the time ;   *Youth, lapsing i* 34
Tell   *t* me you were great Already in your birth.   *Hear you the sound* 59
   ' Now, *t* me, mother, pray,   *The lamps were bright* 9
   There's a treaty, so they *t* us,   *They say, etc.* 3
   a stranger tale to *t* Than if the vine   *To thee with whom* 3
   And I will *t* you what I know—   *Well, as to Fame* 4
   And ever new the tale she *t's,*   *Young is the grief* 2
Temper   *T's* the peaceful light of hazel eyes,   *That is his portrait* 13
Tempest   A *t* strikes the craggy walls,   *Youth, lapsing ii* 12
Temple   build A *t* in her naked field ;   *Not to Silence* 2
Ten   *T* men fought a thousand, Slew them and overthrew.   *Bold Havelock* 7
Tender   But found a maiden *t,* shy,   *Because she bore* 5
   Havelock died, *T* and great and good,   *Bold Havelock* 14
Terrace   your triple *t* growing Green and greener   *Vicar of this* 14
Terror   My hope is false, my *t's* true !   *What rustles* 14
Thames   Smooth as *T* below your gates,   *Vicar of this* 18
   T along the silent level,   *„* 19
Thank   I *t* thee, God, that thou hast made me live :   *Why suffers* 12
Thanks   Small *t* or credit shall I have,   *I keep no more* 3
Thatch'd   For it were almost mockery to hang it O'er the *t* cottage,   *Hear you the sound* 19
Theory   A surface man of many *theories,*   *A surface man* 1
Thick   *T* sobs and short shrill screams arise   *Far off in the dun* 17
   And the moaning wind before it drives *T* wreaths of cloudy dew.   *„* 24
   His heart throbs *t,* his brain reels sick :   *„* 27
   The knotted boughs of this long avenue Of *t* dark oaks,   *Hear you the sound* 11
   For, tho' the faults be t *as dust In vacant chambers,*   *The noblest men* 10
Thicken   Wherever evil customs *t,*   *Wherever evil* 1
Thicket   *See* **Holly-thickets**
Thin   A land of *t* faces and shadowy forms,   *Far off in the dun* 7
   The skin hung lax on his long *t* hands ;   *„* 53
Thing   never green *t* will gaily spring   *„* 9
   t's of past days with their horrible eyes   *„* 19
   And from the heart of all *t's* fair   *He was too good* 11
   man, Most eloquent, who spake of *t's* divine.   *Methought I saw* 3
   Who make you utter *t's* you did not say,   *Old ghosts* 10
   light of hazel eyes, Observing all *t's.*   *That is his portrait* 14
   In the dreaming of past *t's* :   *The lamps were bright* 22
   All *t's* please you, nothing vex you,   *Vicar of this* 9
   And your three young *t's* at play,   *„* 13
   Glancing off from all *t's* evil,   *„* 17
   The difference of all *t's* to the sense,   *Why suffers* 10
   And how all *t's* become the past.   *Youth, lapsing i* 28
Think   when I *t* The year, that comes,   *I, loving Freedom* 5
   t a cunning hand has found the clue—   *What rustles* 14
Thirst   Warm beats my blood, my spirit *t's* ;   *Youth, lapsing ii* 45

U

World (*continued*) Clusters and beds of *w's*, *Hither, when all* 7
Showers in a whisper o'er the *w.* *Not to Silence* 34
I see the *w's* renewed youth A long day's dawn, *O God, make this age* 6
flower spread and rose, A various *w* ! *That is his portrait* 27
As beautiful, but yet another *w.* 30
And in the w *the noblest place,* *The noblest men* 3
The whole *w* shall not brave us ! (repeat) *They say, etc.* 6, 13, 20
If the *w* caterwaul, lay harder upon her *Wherever evil* 6
And see and hear the *w* revolve : *Youth, lapsing i* 52
Worn *W* and wan was their gaze, I trow, *Far off in the dun* 58
A dark form glances quick Thro' her *w* brain, *The lamps were bright* 28
Worshipper Latest of her *w's*, *Not to Silence* 7
Worship They *w* Freedom for her sake ; *They wrought, etc.* 5
Worth were *w* Our living out ? *Gone into darkness* 7
mould you all awry and mar your *w* ; *Old ghosts* 11
I know a little of her *w*, *Well, as to Fame* 3
Wove *w* Inextricable brickwork maze in maze ? *What rustles* 7
Wreath drives Thick *w's* of cloudy dew. *Far off in the dun* 24
Wreath'd *w* with green bays were the gorgeous lamps, „ 115
Writ high birth Had *w* nobility upon my brow. *Hear you the sound* 64
Write none can truly *w* his single day, And none can
w it for him upon earth. *Old ghosts* 13
Writhe the damn'd that *w* Upon their beds of
flame, *Half after midnight !* 10
Wrong some sad tale of *w*, and do the *w* He wept for,
till the very *w* itself Had found him out. *A surface man* 6
Wrought (*See also* **Passion-wrought**) *W* with his
hand and his head, *Bold Havelock* 10
They *w* a work which Time reveres, *They wrought, etc.* 1
Wrung Piercing the *w* ears of the damn'd that
writhe Upon their beds of flame, *Half after midnight !* 10

X

Xaraguay cocoa-shadow'd coves Of sunbright *X*, *A dark Indian maiden* 9
cedar-wooded paradise Of still *X* : „ 21
Maizebread and the yuccaroot Of sweet *X* : „ 45
Than the men of *X*, „ 57
No more in *X* Wander'd happy Anacaona, „ 69

Y

Year I think The *y*, that comes, may come with
shame, *I, loving Freedom* 6
Of sacred Nile, a thousand *y's* ago !— *Here, I that stood* 2
The low voice of the glad New *Y* *Remember you* 11
His fame is equal to his *y's* : *That is his portrait* 42
For ever into coming *y's* ; *They wrought, etc.* 4
Yellow With *y* groundsel grown ! *Along this glimmering* 6
But his face was a *y* gray. *Far off in the dun* 52
by fits the lady ash With twinkling finger sweeps
her *y* keys. *Townsmen, etc.* 10
Yield *Y's* to the victor. *Faded ev'ry violet* 4
Rosebud, open, *y* Thy fragrant soul.' *The night, etc.* 5
Yoked *Y* the skeleton horses to. *Far off in the dun* 60
Yon Behind *y* hill the trumpets blow, *Youth, lapsing ii* 11
Yonder We quarrel here at home, and they plot against
us *y*, *They say, etc.* 8
The despots over *y*, let 'em do whate'er they
please ! „ 16
And I must traverse *y* plain : *Youth, lapsing i* 54
Young The whisper'd love of the fair *y* wives ; *Far off in the dun* 67
Townsmen, or of the hamlet, *y* or old, *Townsmen, etc.* 1
And your three *y* things at play, *Vicar of this* 13
Y is the grief I entertain, *Young is the grief* 1
And ever *y* the face that dwells With reason „ 3
Youth (**adolescence**) Nor Sorrow beauteous in
her *y*, *Are those the far-famed* 7
I see the world's renewed *y* A long day's
dawn, *O God, make this age* 6
Y, lapsing thro' fair solitudes, *Youth, lapsing i* 1
Youth (**young man**) Around him *y's* were gather'd, *Methought I saw* 4
Youthful and mingled with The woman's *y* pride
Of rounded limbs— *One was the Tishbite* 16
Yuccaroot She gave them the *y*, Maizebread and
the *y*, *A dark Indian maiden* 43

A CONCORDANCE TO THE SUPPRESSED POEMS

OF

ALFRED, LORD TENNYSON

(1830-1868)

A

Abide   So swiftly, that they nowhere would *a*,   *Love and Sorrow* 15
in him light and joy and strength *a's*;   *Love* 42
We will *a* in the golden vale Of the Lotos-land,   *Lotos-Eaters* 26
Absorbed   torrent of quick thought *A* me   *Timbuctoo* 142
Abstraction   The still serene *a*;   *The Mystic* 5
Abyss   The blossoming *a'es* of your hills?   *Timbuctoo* 44
showering circular *a* Of radiance.   ,,   173
Accent   In *a's* of majestic melody,   ,,   192
Accident   All on-set of capricious *A*,   ,,   26
Accurate   I know not if I shape These things with *a* similitude   ,,   134
Aching   We beat upon our *a* hearts with rage;   *Love* 18
Acorn   on an oaken sprout A goodly *a* grew; But winds
from heaven shook the *a* out,   *Lost Hope* 6
Acropolis   retir'd At midnight, in the lone *A*.   *Timbuctoo* 32
Act (s)   Yours are the public *a's* of public men,   *Sugg. by Reading* 21
Act (verb)   she did *a* the step-dame to mine eyes,   *Lover's Tale* i 664
Adage   widow'd, like the cur In the child's *a*?   ,,   770
Adore   all men *a* thee; Heaven crieth after thee;   *Love* 25
Afresh   And being there they did break forth *a*   *Lover's Tale* i 731
Afric   whose rapid interval Parts *A* from green Europe,   *Timbuctoo* 18
cried 'Wide *A*, doth thy Sun Lighten,   ,,   58
Again   And yet *a*, *a* and evermore,   *The Mystic* 19
Should war's mad blast *a* be blown,   *Hands all Round* 41
Age   and old *a* Is but to know thee: *Love* 15
for your manner sorts Not with this *a*,   *Cambridge* 11
Agglomerated   *A* swiftness, I had lived   *Lover's Tale* i 621
Aggression   Nor seek to bridle His vile *a's*,   *Britons, guard* 53
Agony   Wake on, my soul, nor crouch to *a*:   *Though night* 5
serpent in his *agonies* Awestricken Indians;   *Love* 30
in mine *a*, Did I make bare of all   *Lover's Tale* ii 50
Ailment   whom woful *a's* Of unavailing tears   ,,   i 818
Air   ev'n as flame draws *a*;   *Timbuctoo* 18
As *a* is th' life of flame: ,,   20
Blown round with happy *a's* of odorous winds?   ,,   46
The indistinctest atom in deep *a*,   ,,   100
Pure without heat, into a larger *a* Upburning,   *The Mystic* 44
And as light as *a*;   *The Grasshopper* 25
globefilled arch that, cleaving *a*,   *Chorus* 25
Filled with a finer *a*:   *D. of F. Women* 8
happy *a* shall woo The wither'd leaf   *Lover's Tale* i 693
nor breathe What *a's* he pleased!   ,,   693
Airily   Keen-eyed Sisters, singing *a*   *Hesperides, Song* i 25
Airy   Vaulting on thine *a* feet.   *The Grasshopper* 10
Airy-fashioned   There be some hearts so *a-f*,   *Lover's Tale* i 848
Alarm   Weariness and wild *a*,   *Lotos-Eaters* 2
Albion   New-risen o'er awakened *A*—   *Cambridge* 7
Alchemy   And dross to gold with glorious *a*,   *Though night* 7

All   Shadows to which, despite *a* shocks of Change,   *Timbuctoo* 25
And circled with the glory of living light And alternations
of *a* hues,   ,,   76
Man is the measure of *a* truth Unto himself.   οἱ ῥέοντες 3
A things are not told to *a*,   *Hesperides, Song* iii 12
and ceasing from *A* contemplation of *a* forms,   *Lover's Tale* i 67
The centre of *a* splendours, *a* unworthy Of such a
shrine—   ,,   69
And *a* the quaint old scraps of ancient crones,   ,,   288
And throwing by *a* consciousness of self,   ,,   787
Yet hands *a* round!   *Hands all Round* 21
Alley   Thro' yonder poplar *a* Below,   *Check every outflash* 4
Allied   God keep their lands *a*,   *God bless our Prince* 2
Almeida   Weep not, *A*, that I said to thee   *Love and Sorrow* 3
A, if my heart were substanceless,   ,,   13
Aloft   and *a* Winnow the purple, bearing   *Timbuctoo* 153
a Upon his renown'd Eminence bore globes   ,,   170
Alone   why muse you here *a* Upon the Mountain,   ,,   77
A she is there: *I' the glooming light* 8
Ever *a* She maketh her moan: ,,   16
To fight thy mother here *a*,   *Hands all Round* 43
All *a* she sits and hears Echoes   *Home they brought him* 3
Altarthrone   Offered to Gods upon an *a*;   *To* —— 7
Altercating   Alas, Church writers, *a* tribes—   *Sugg. by Reading* 73
Alternate   Dappled with hollow and *a* rise Of inter-
penetrated arc,   *Timbuctoo* 130
Alternation   And *a's* of all hues, he stood.   ,,   76
Amiss   For my doubts and fears were all *a*,   *The Ringlet* 19
Anakim   Piled by the strong and sunborn *A*   *A fragment* 20
Anarchy   To shapes of wildest *a*,   *Chorus* 4
Ancient   *A* dream as frail as those of *a* Time?'   *Timbuctoo* 62
There standeth our *a* enemy; (repeat)   *English War Song* 23, 45
Hark! he shouteth—the *a* enemy!   ,,   24
For his *a* heart is drunk with overwatchings
night and day,   *Hesperides, Song* ii 12
And the *a* secret reveal'd.   ,,   iii 5
In the valley some, and some On the *a* heights divine;   *Lotos-Eaters* 17
THEREFORE your halls, your *a* colleges,   *Cambridge* 1
Our *a* boast is this—we reverence law.   *Sugg. by Reading* 34
And trust an *a* manhood and the cause Of England   ,,   39
And all the quaint old scraps of *a* crones,   *Lover's Tale* i 288
Anew   Evermore it is born *a*;   *Hesperides, Song* i 18
Angel (adj.)   *a* mind which look'd from out The starry
glowing   *Timbuctoo* 88
Angel (s)   *A's* have talked with him, and showed him thrones: *The Mystic* 1
Over heaven's parapets the *a's* lean.   *To a Lady Sleep.* 10
What an *a*! How clothed with beams!   *Lover's Tale* i 351
I became to her A tutelary *a*   ,,   388
the *a's*, The watchers at heaven's gate,   ,,   615

Anger must your noble *a* blaze out more   *Blow ye the trumpet* 9
   Horrible with the *a* and the heat   *Lover's Tale i* 681
Angry Flooding its *a* cheek with odorous tears.   „ *i* 565
Annoy Basing thy throne above the world's *a*.   *Though night* 8
Another He hath not *a* dart;   *Burial of Love* 10
Antelope SURE never yet was *A* Could skip   *Skipping-rope* 1
Anxious Beat like a far wave on my *a* ear.   *Timbuctoo* 114
Apart *a* In intellect and power and will,   *The Mystic* 37
Apathy Shall hollow-hearted *a*, The cruellest form   *Burial of Love* 17
Ape and our mirth *A*'s the happy vein,   *Every day, etc.* 13
Appeal I honour much, I say, this man's *a*.   *Sugg. by Reading* 9
Apple THE golden *a*, the golden *a*, the hallowed fruit,   *Hesperides, Song i* 1
   Guard the *a* night and day,   „ 28
   and the golden *a* be stol'n away,   „ *ii* 11
   If the golden *a* be taken The world   „ 21
   The golden *a* stol'n away,   „ *iii* 4
   Make the *a* holy and bright,   „ *iv* 10
   But the *a* of gold hangs over the sea,   „ „ 23
   The golden *a*, the golden *a*, the hallowed fruit,   „ 30
   Dear room, the *a* of my sight,   *O darling room* 2
April Young fishes, on an *A* morn,   *Rosalind* 21
   Green springtide, *A* promise, glad new year   *Lover's Tale i* 277
Arabian from his mother's eyes Flow over the *A* bay,   *A Fragment* 24
Arc alternate rise Of interpenetrated *a*,   *Timbuctoo* 131
Arch With triple *a* of everchanging bows,   „ 74
   globefilled *a* that, cleaving air,   *Chorus* 25
   in and out the woodbine's flowery *a*'es   *Check every outflash* 11
   Stays on the flowering *a* of the bough,   *Hesperides, Song iv* 18
Arch'd wheel in wheel, *A* the wan Sapphire.   *Timbuctoo* 111
Archetype To its *A* that waits Clad in light   *Germ of 'Maud'* 31
Arching *A* blue-glossèd necks beneath   *Dualisms* 13
   A the billow in his sleep;   *Hesperides, Song iv* 3
Arch-mock This was the very *a-m* And insolence   *Lover's Tale i* 687
Archway All night through *a*'s of the bridgèd pearl   *Though night* 3
Argent windeth through The *a* streets o' the City,   *Timbuctoo* 231
   Pleached with her hair, in mail of *a* light Shot into gold,   *Pallid thunderstricken* 12
   Parted on either side her *a* neck,   *Lover's Tale i* 740
Argosy broad-blown *Argosies* Drave into haven?   *A Fragment* 7
Aright And my eyes read, they read *a*, her heart Was Lionel's: *Lover's Tale i* 602
Arise *A*, brave Poles, the boldest of the bold;   *Blow ye the trumpet* 3
Arm I dare not fold My *a*'s about thee—   *Oh, Beauty* 6
Arms Than vanquish all the world in *a*.   *Hands all Round* 28
Arrested love too high to be express'd *A* in its sphere,   *Lover's Tale i* 66
Arrogant It looks too *a* jest—   *New Timon* 42
Arrow Love is dead; His last *a* sped;   *Burial of Love* 9
Arrowy borne Adown the sloping of an *a* stream,   *Timbuctoo* 144
Art WE know him, out of Shakespeare's *a*,   *New Timon* 1
   An artist, Sir, should rest in *a*,   „ 21
   Strung in the very negligence of *A*, Or in the *a* of Nature,   *Lover's Tale i* 562
Artist An *a*, Sir, should rest in art,   *New Timon* 21
Ashes I lay! White as quench'd *a*,   *Lover's Tale i* 620
Ask I only *a* to sit beside thy feet.   *Oh, Beauty* 3
Assimilated Perchance *a* all our tastes   *Lover's Tale i* 238
Assyrian Some vast *A* doom to burst upon our race.   *Sugg. by Reading* 42
Astonishment full of strange *A* and boundless change. (repeat)   *Chorus* 10, 20, 30
Atalantis Divinest *A*, whom the waves Have buried deep,   *Timbuctoo* 22
Atlantic-Atlantick That ran bloombright into the *Atlantic* blue,   *The Hesperides* 9
   O rise, our strong *Atlantic* sons,   *Hands all Round* 49
   when the Sun Had fall'n below th' *Atlantick*,   *Timbuctoo* 4
Atmosphere Thou foldest, like a golden *a*,   *Love* 5
   drew the happy *a* Of my unhappy sighs,   *Lover's Tale i* 673
Atom The indistinctest *a* in deep air,   *Timbuctoo* 100
Attain teach him to *a* By shadowing forth the Unattainable;   „ 196
Austrian The Russian whips and *A* rods—   *Hands all Round* 18
Author Refused to look his *a* in the face,   *Lover's Tale i* 697
Autocrat We must not dread in you the nameless *a*.   *Sugg. by Reading* 18
Autumn in red *A* when the winds are wild   *Timbuctoo* 202
   The troublous *a*'s sallow gloom,   *Chorus* 17
   bitter blasts the screaming *a* whirl,   *Though night* 2
Avail Shall not *a* you when the day-beam sports   *Cambridge* 6

Awake He often lying broad *a*,   *The Mystic* 36
Awakened when the day-beam sports New-risen o'er *a* Albion—   *Cambridge* 7
Awakening See **Earth-awakening**
Awestricken As on a serpent in his agonies *A* Indians;   *Love* 31
Awful Before the *a* Genius of the place Kneels the pale Priestess in deep faith,   *Timbuctoo* 33
   A with most invariable eyes.   *The Mystic* 24
   Hallowed in *a* chasms of wheeling gloom,   *Love* 22
   And in his writhings *a* hues begin To wander down his sable sheeny sides,   „ 38
   A Memnonian countenances calm Looking athwart the burning flats,   *A Fragment* 16
   Five and three (Let it not be preached abroad) make an *a* mystery.   *Hesperides, Song i* 16
   But grow upon them like *a* glorious vision Of unconceived and *a* happiness,   *Lover's Tale i* 798
Aye Merry England! England for *a*! (repeat)   *English War Song* 11, 22, 33, 44, 55

B

Balanced and swum with *b* wings To some tall mountain.   *Lover's Tale i* 304
Ball Till your *b*'s fly as their true shafts have flown.   *Britons, guard* 47
   Think you hearts are tennis *b*'s To play with,   *Rosalind* 32
Balloon As when a man, that sails in a *b*,   *D. of F. Women* 1
Balm Thy locks are dripping *b*;   *Hero to Leander* 20
Baltic on the *B* shore Boleslas drove the Pomeranian.   *Blow ye the trumpet* 13
Banbury '*B* Cross,' 'The Gander'   *Lover's Tale i* 286
Bandbox to take *his* name You *b*.   *New Timon* 44
Banded Although we fought the *b* world alone,   *Britons, guard* 59
Banished The true men *b*,   „ 10
Bank (*See also* **Brookbank**) Gray sand *b*'s and pale sunsets —dreary wind,   *Mablethorpe* 7
Banner On the ridge of the hill his *b*'s rise;   *English War Song* 25
Barbarian Low-built, mud-walled, *B* settlement,   *Timbuctoo* 248
Bare Her shoulders are *b*;   *I' the glooming light* 10
   The *b* word KISS hath made my inner soul To tremble   *Oh, Beauty* 12
Bark (of a tree) Creeping under the fragrant *b*,   *Hesperides, Song i* 23
Bark (vessel) winedark wave our weary *b* did carry.   *Lotos-Eaters* 9
Based See **Broad-based**
Basing *B* thy throne above the world's annoy.   *Though night* 8
Bathe *B*'s the cold hand with tears,   *Timbuctoo* 38
   Come *b* me with thy kisses,   *Hero to Leander* 19
Bathed I have *b* thee with the pleasant myrrh;   „ 19
Battailing *B* with the glooms of my dark will,   *Lover's Tale i* 782
Battle (s) gather from afar The hosts to *b*:   *Blow ye the trumpet* 2
   To blow the *b* from their oaken sides.   *Britons, guard* 38
   We won old *b*'s with our strength, the bow.   „ 44
Battle (verb) Will he dare to *b* with the free?   *English War Song* 46
Battled Or loyally disloyal *b* for our rights.   *Sugg. by Reading* 36
Battlement Illimitable range of *b* On *b*,   *Timbuctoo* 164
Bay Your flowering Capes and your gold-sanded *b*'s   „ 45
   from his mother's eyes Flow over the Arabian *b*,   *A Fragment* 24
   Past Thymiaterion, in calmèd *b*'s,   *The Hesperides* 4
   Through vineyards from an island *b*.   *Rosalind* 29
Bayard The *B* of the meadow.   *The Grasshopper* 21
Bayona In old *B*, nigh the Southern Sea—   *There are three things* 11
Beam (*See also* **Day-beam**) What an angel! How clothed with *b*'s!   *Lover's Tale i* 352
Bear *b* them upward through the trackless fields   *Timbuctoo* 159
   There must no man go back to *b* the tale: No man to *b* it—Swear it! We swear it!   *Britons, guard* 56
Bearded Her tears are mixed with the *b* dews.   *I' the glooming light* 11
Bearing *b* on both sides Double display   *Timbuctoo* 154
   As *b* no essential fruits of excellence.   *Lover's Tale i* 385
   So *b* on thro' Being limitless The triumph   „ 514
Beast wondrous tones Of man and *b*   *Chorus* 9
Beat *B* like a far wave on my anxious ear.   *Timbuctoo* 114
   Thy heart *b*'s through thy rosy limbs   *Hero to Leander* 16
   the brazen *b* Of their broad vans,   *Shall the hag* 7
   We *b* upon our aching hearts with rage;   *Love* 18
   B upon his father's shield—   *Home they brought him* 9
   heart *b* Twice to the melody of hers.   *Lover's Tale i* 73

Blue (adj.) The ocean with the morrow light Will be both *b* and calm; — *Hero to Leander* 26
all the day heaven gathers back her tears Into her own *b* eyes so clear and deep, — *Tears of Heaven* 7
black eyes, and brown and *b*; I hold them all most dear; — *There are three things* 6
That ran bloombright into the Atlantic *b*, — *The Hesperides* 9
Stream from beneath him in the broad *b* noon, — *D. of F. Women* 3

Blue (s) chasms of deep, deep *b* Slumber'd unfathomable, — *Timbuctoo*
With eyes dropt downward through the *b* serene, — *To a Lady Sleep.* 9

Blue-glossèd Arching *b-g* necks beneath — *Dualisms* 13

Blue-green Through yonder poplar alley Below, the *b-g* river windeth slowly; — *Check every outflash* 5

Blush'd Ringlet, She *b* a rosy red, — *The Ringlet* 36

Boast Our ancient *b* is this—we reverence law. — *Sugg. by Reading* 34

Boat And sailing on Pactolus in a *b*, — *Pallid thunderstricken* 3

Body and yet Remaining from the *b*, — *The Mystic* 37
You cannot let a *b* be: — *New Timon* 30
Crept like the drains of a marsh thro' all my *b*; — *Lover's Tale ii* 56
Unto the growth of *b* and of mind; — " 74

Bold no men like Englishmen, So tall and *b* as they be. — *National Song* 8
nothing seems to me so wild and *b*, — *Oh, Beauty* 7
Caucasus is *b* and strong. — *Hesperides, Song iii* 7
B, subtle, careless Rosalind, — *Rosalind* 2
Arise, brave Poles, the boldest of the *b*; — *Blow ye the trumpet* 3

Bolder child in our cradles is *b* than he; — *English War Song* 35

Boldest Arise, brave Poles, the *b* of the bold; — *Blow ye the trumpet* 3

Bole gnarlèd *b* of the charmèd tree, — *Hesperides, Song iv* 29

Boleslas on the Baltic shore *B* drove the Pomeranian. — *Blow ye the trumpet* 14

Bond Thy spirit fetter'd with the *b* of clay: — *Timbuctoo* 83

Bone they plunge their doubts among old rags and *b's*. — *Sugg. by Reading* 72
dead skin withering on the fretted *b*, — *Lover's Tale i* 678

Boot A dapper *b*—a little hand— — *New Timon* 35

Bore *b* globes Of wheeling suns, or stars, — *Timbuctoo* 171
waves, which *b* The reflex of my City — " 238
b downward with the wave. — *Lover's Tale i* 375

Born (*See also* **Sunborn**) We laugh, we cry, we are *b*, we die, — *The 'How' and the 'Why'* 8
Through whose dim brain the wingèd dreams are *b*, — *To a Lady Sleep.* 2
Far better, far better he never were *b* — *English War Song* 18
Evermore it is *b* anew; — *Hesperides, Song i* 18

Borne (*See also* **Blastborne**) *b* Adown the sloping of an arrowy stream, — *Timbuctoo* 143
Through dark and bright Wingèd hours are *b*; — *Every day, etc.* 4
b abroad By the loud winds, — *Love* 8

Bosom My heart is warmer surely than the *b* of the main. — *Hero to Leander* 9
each rose Doth faint upon the *b* — *Lover's Tale i* 564

Both So that with hasty motion I did veil My vision with *b* hands, — *Timbuctoo* 69
bearing on *b* sides Double display of starlit wings — " 154
Yet on *b* sides at once thou canst not shine! — *Love and Sorrow* 7

Bottom Creep down into the *b* of the flower. — *Lover's Tale i* 560

Bough great bird sits on the opposite *b*, — *The 'How' and the 'Why'* 28
Stays on the flowering arch of the *b*, — *Hesperides, Song iv* 16
And a titmarsh in the *b*. — *A gate and a field* 4
fall'n in the woods, or blasted Upon this *b*? — *Lover's Tale i* 623

Bought ruthless host is *b* with plunder'd gold, — *Britons, guard* 7
hosts to battle: be not *b* and sold. — *Blow ye the trumpet* 2
She that gave you 's *b* and sold, — *The Ringlet* 33

Bound (s) The herald lightning's starry *b*, — *Chorus* 14
verge and *b* alone Of full beatitude. — *Timbuctoo* 95

Bound (verb) spirit With supernatural excitation *b* Within me, — " 91
Carol clearly, *b* along. (repeat) — *The Grasshopper* 4, 30

Bound (past of **Bind**) With a silken cord I *b* it. — *Anacreontics* 8

Bound (part.) sisters three, *B* about the golden tree. — *Hesperides, Song ii* 25
B about All round about The gnarlèd bole — " iv 27
Half bursten from the shroud, in cere cloth *b*, — *Lover's Tale i* 677

Bounding The fierceness of the *b* element? — *Timbuctoo* 148

Boundless Through length of porch and lake and *b* hall, — " 180
Astonishment and *b* change. (repeat) — *Chorus* 10, 20, 30

Bow With triple arch of everchanging *b's*, — *Timbuctoo*
His *b* unstrung With the tears he hath shed, — *Burial of Love* 5
We won old battles with our strength, the *b*. — *Britons, guard* 44

Bow'd As towards the gracious light I *b*, — *What time I wasted* 4
lithe limbs *b* as with a heavy weight — *Lover's Tale i* 126

Bower the light of vernal *b's*, — *Could I outwear* 6

Bowing *B* the seeded summerflowers. — *The Grasshopper* 8

Bowman Now practise, yeomen, Like those bowmen, — *Britons, guard* 46

Boy Who killed the girls and thrill'd the *b's* — *New Timon* 9
The *b* began to leap and prance, — *Home they brought him* 7
Let them so love that men and *b's* may say, — *Lover's Tale i* 801

Brain hurried through The riv'n rapt *b*: — *Timbuctoo* 121
my human *b* Stagger'd beneath the vision, — " 185
Through whose dim *b* the wingèd dreams are born, — *To a Lady Sleep.*
b could keep afloat The subtle spirit. — *Oh, Beauty* 10
And a juggle of the *b*. — *Germ of 'Maud'* 8
On those first-moved fibres of the *b*. — *Lover's Tale i* 21
They flash across the darkness of my *b*, — " 53
All unawares, into the poet's *b*; — " 557

Bramble matted *b* and the shining gloss Of ivy-leaves, — " 373

Branching And *b* silvers of the central globe, — *Pallid thunderstricken* 8

Brassy between whose limbs Of *b* vastness broad-blown Argosies Drave into haven? — *A Fragment* 7

Brave Arise, *b* Poles, the boldest of the bold; — *Blow ye the trumpet* 3

Brazen Would shatter and o'erbear the *b* heat Of their broad vans, — *Shall the hag* 7

Bread He shall eat the *b* of common scorn; — *English War Song* 13

Breadth With moral *b* of temperament. — *New Timon* 28

Break spheres Which *b* upon each other, — *Timbuctoo* 126
world will not change, and her heart will not *b*. — *I' the glooming light* 22
deep salt wave *b's* in above — *Hero to Leander* 34
B through your iron shackles—fling them far. — *Blow ye the trumpet* 4
summer winds *b* their soft sleep with sighs, — *Lover's Tale i* 559
they did *b* forth afresh In a new birth, — " 731

Breast Zone of flashing gold beneath His *b*, — *Timbuctoo* 73

Breath lips so cruel dumb Should have so sweet a *b*! — *The lintwhite* 18
redolent *b* Of this warm seawind ripeneth, — *Hesperides, Song iv* 1
Which waste with the *b* that made 'em. — *Lover's Tale i* 475
blood, the *b*, the feeling and the motion, — " ii 75

Breath-Breathe Before the face of God didst *breath* and move, — *Love* 3
Breathe on thy wingèd throne, and it shall move — " 27
Breathes low into the charmèd ears of morn — *A Fragment* 25
nor *breathe* What airs he pleased! — *Lover's Tale i* 692

Breathèd the new year warm *b* on the earth, — *Love* 33
WITH roses musky *b*, — *Anacreontics* 1
Intense delight and rapture that I *b*, — *Lover's Tale i* 381
for which I lived and *b*: — " ii 73

Breathing And the low west wind, *b* afar, — *Hesperides, Song iv* 8

Brere They from the blosmy *b* Call — *The lintwhite* 4

Brethren (*See also* **Brother**) Over their crowned *b* ON and OPH? *A Fragment* 21

Bride I can shadow forth my *b* — *Germ of 'Maud'* 9
GOD bless our Prince and *B*! — *God bless our Prince* 1

Bridge Your *b's* and your busted libraries, — *Cambridge* 3
With shouts from off the *b*, — *Lover's Tale i* 369
Upon the tremulous *b*, that from beneath — " 406

Bridged All night through archways of the *b* pearl — *Though Night* 3

Bridle Nor seek to *b* His vile aggressions, — *Britons, guard* 52

Brief COULD I outwear my present state of woe With one *b* winter, — *Could I outwear* 2

Bright (*See also* **Bloombright**) The *b* descent Of a young Seraph! — *Timbuctoo* 64
Through dark and *b* Wingèd hours are borne; — *Every day, etc.* 4
There is no *b* form Doth not cast a shade— — " 9
Thine is the *b* side of my heart, and thine My heart's day, — *Love and Sorrow* 8
I am so dark, alas! and thou so *b*, — *Me my own fate* 13
Make the apple holy and *b*, Holy and *b*, round and full, *b* and blest, — *Hesperides, Song iv* 10
No little room so warm and *b* Wherein to read, — *O'darling room* 5
Not any room so warm and *b*, Wherein to read, — " 17

Brightness hearts of all on Earth Toward their *b*, — *Timbuctoo* 18
it was wonderful With its exceeding *b*, — " 87

Brilliance beneath Two doors of blinding *b*, — " 178

Brilliant soon yon *b* towers Shall darken with the waving of her wand; — " 244

Brine roaring *b* Will rend thy golden tresses; — *Hero to Leander* 23
melancholy home At the limit of the *b*, — *Lotos-Eaters* 21

Bring Hoarded wisdom *b's* delight. — *Hesperides, Song ii* 6
And careless what this hour may *b*, — *New Timon* 18

Bringeth Laughter *b* tears: — *Every day, etc.* 1

Briny   Crocodiles in *b* creeks Sleep and stir not: all is mute.   *Hesperides, Song i* 8

British   For art thou not of *B* blood?   *Hands all Round* 40

shall see The *B* Goddess,   *Sugg. by Reading* 54

Briton   RISE, *B's*, rise, if manhood be not dead;   *Britons, guard* 1

B's, guard your own. (repeat)   *Britons, guard* 6, 12, 18, 24, 30, 36

free speech that makes a *B* known.   „   29

Broad   He often lying *b* awake, and yet Remaining from the body,   *The Mystic* 36

Would shatter and o'erbear the brazen heat Of their *b* vans,   *Shall the hag* 8

Stream from beneath him in the *b* blue noon,   *D. of F. Women* 3

Broad-based   Pyramids *B-b* amid the fleeting sands,   *A Fragment* 10

Broad-blown   *b-b* Argosies Drave into haven?   „   7

Broadsides   But let thy *b* roar with ours.   *Hands all Round* 44

Broke   note Hath melted in the silence that it *b*.   *Oh, Beauty* 14

That, strongly loathing, greatly *b*.   *New Timon* 4

Broken   *B* by the highland-steep,   *Hesperides, Song iv* 5

A child with a *b* slate,   *A gate and a field* 3

Brood (s)   Hateful with hanging cheeks, a withered *b*,   *Shall the hag* 4

Brood (verb)   The silence of all hearts,   *Love* 13

Brooding   placid Sphinxes *b* o'er the Nile?   *A Fragment* 14

Brook (s)   rapid *b* Shot down his inner thunders,   *Lover's Tale i* 371

Brook (verb)   thou wilt not *b* eclipse;   *Love* 11

Brookbank   By a mossed *b* on a stone   *O sad no more!* 3

Brother   (*See also* **Brethren**) The bulrush nods unto his *b*   *The 'How' and the 'Why'* 10

Joy is sorrow's *b*;   *Every day, etc.* 24

Brought   HOME they *b* him slain with spears. They *b* him home at even-fall: *Home they brought him* 1

Brow   compass'd round about his *b* With   *Timbuctoo* 73

My eyelids and my *b*.   *Hero to Leander* 13

beneath Severe and youthful *b's*,   *The Mystic* 27

Smiles on the earth's worn *b* to win her if she may.   *Tears of Heaven* 9

from his *b's* a crown of living light   *Love* 43

Fair year, with *b's* of royal love   *The lintwhite* 19

A perfect Idol, with profulgent *b's*   *A Fragment* 3

Let it pass, the dreary *b*,   *Germ of 'Maud'* 22

rather had some loathly ghastful *b*,   *Lover's Tale i* 676

Brown   black eyes, and *b* and blue; I hold them all most dear;   *There are three things* 6

Brummel   pardon little would-be Popes And *B's*,   *New Timon* 20

Brush   That *b* thee with their silken tresses?   *The Grasshopper* 39

Did *b* my forehead in their to-and-fro: *Lover's Tale i* 736

Buildeth   *b* up Huge mounds whereby to stay   *Timbuctoo* 14

Built   (*See also* **Low-built**) Why a church with a steeple *b*;   *The 'How' and the 'Why'* 34

b above With matted bramble   *Lover's Tale i* 372

Bulrush   The *b* nods unto his brother   *The 'How' and the 'Why'* 10

Buoyancy   felt Unutterable *b* and strength   *Timbuctoo* 158

Buried   (*See also* **Low-buried**) whom the waves Have *b* deep,   „   23

recalls the dewy prime Of youth and *b* time?   *Who can say* 7

Burn   wings which *b* Fanlike and fibred,   *Timbuctoo* 155

B, you glossy heretic, *b*, *B*, *b*.   *The Ringlet* 53

Burning   The *b* belts, the mighty rings,   *Chorus* 23

Awful Memnonian countenances calm Looking athwart the *b* flats,   *A Fragment* 17

Burnish'd   Stood out a pillar'd front of *b* gold Interminably high,   *Timbuctoo* 175

Burst   Some vast Assyrian doom to *b* upon our race.   *Sugg. by Reading* 42

Bursten   *See* **Half-bursten**

Bursting   The vocal spring of *b* bloom,   *Chorus* 15

Burthen   needs must sell the *b* of their wills   *Sugg. by Reading* 69

Bury   *B* him in the cold, cold heart—   *Burial of Love* 12

Busted   Your bridges and your *b* libraries,   *Cambridge* 3

Busy   And notes of *b* life in distant worlds   *Timbuctoo* 113

With her to whom all outward fairest things Were by the *b* mind referr'd,   *Lover's Tale i* 384

Buzz   Both alike, they *b* together,   *Dualisms* 3

C

Call   *C's* to him by the fountain to uprise.   *Love* 35

C to the fleeting year,   *The lintwhite* 5

Fair year, fair year, thy children *c*,   „   10

Call (*continued*)   Wandering waters unto wandering waters *c*;   *Hesperides, Song iii* 8

springtime *c's* To the flooding waters cool,   *Rosalind* 19

I can *c* it to my side,   *Germ of 'Maud'* 16

'They *c* this man as good *as me*.'   *New Timon* 32

This man is France, the man they *c* her choice.   *Britons, guard* 20

C home your ships across Biscayan tides,   „   37

I *c* on you To make opinion warlike,   *Sugg. by Reading* 86

Call'd   hill of woe, so *c* Because the legend ran that,   *Lover's Tale i* 365

Calm (adj.)   light Will be both blue and *c*;   *Hero to Leander* 26

Where in a creeping cove the wave unshock'd Lay's itself *c* and wide,   *Dualisms* 7

Awful Memnonian countenances *c* Looking athwart the burning flats,   *A Fragment* 16

Calm (s)   level *c* Is rig'd with restless   *Timbuctoo* 124

And muse midway with philosophic *c*   „   146

Golden *c* and storm Mingle day by day.   *Every day, etc.* 7

One mighty countenance of perfect *c*,   *The Mystic* 23

There is no rest, no *c*, no pause,   οἱ ῥέοντες 9

In a stripe of grassgreen *c*,   *Lotos-Eaters* 5

Poor soul! behold her: what decorous *c*!   *Sugg. by Reading* 61

Calmèd   Past Thymiaterion, in *c* bays,   *The Hesperides* 4

Calpe   and I Was left alone on *C*,   *Timbuctoo* 252

Came   night *C* down upon my eyelids,   „   187

Pride *c* beneath and held a light.   *Love, Pride, etc.* 6

C voices, like the voices in a dream,   *The Hesperides* 12

When I learnt from whom it *c*,   *To C. North* 5

About sunset We *c* unto the hill of woe,   *Lover's Tale i* 365

Camel   Seen by the high-necked *c* on the verge   *A Fragment* 18

Camilla   Did I love *C*?   *Lover's Tale i* 770

he would make his wedded wife, *C*!   „   794

And as for me, *C*, as for me,   „   805

Canker   I feel the thousand *c's* of our State,   *Sugg. by Reading* 43

Canopy   Imperial height Of *C* o'ercanopied,   *Timbuctoo* 166

Cap-a-pie   Armed *c-a-p*, Full fair to see;   *The Grasshopper* 14

Cape   Your flowering *C's* and your gold-sanded bays   *Timbuctoo* 45

Capricious   All on-set of *c* Accident,   „   26

Captain   who are to you As *c* is to subaltern.   *New Timon* 16

Captive   Rome's dearest daughter now is *c* France,   *Britons, guard* 31

Careless   And *c* what this hour may bring,   *New Timon* 18

Bold, subtle, *c* Rosalind,   *Rosalind* 2

Caress'd   The Church *c* him;   *Britons, guard* 4

Carol   *C* clearly, bound along. (repeat)   *The Grasshopper* 4, 30

Clap thy shielded sides and *c*, *C* clearly, chirrup sweet   „   11

Carolling   Do woo each other, *c* together.   *Dualisms* 9

Carry   To *c* through the world those waves,   *Timbuctoo* 238

Go—*c* him to his dark deathbed;   *Burial of Love* 11

winedark wave our weary bark did *c*.   *Lotos-Eaters* 9

Carved   Wax-lighted chapels and rich *c* screens,   *Cambridge* 4

Casket   such a costly *c* in the grasp Of memory?   *Lover's Tale i* 101

Cast   There is no bright form Doth not *c* a shade—   *Every day, etc.* 10

You *c* to ground the hope which once   *Lost Hope* 1

Cathedralled   *C* caverns of thick-ribbèd gold   *Pallid thunderstricken* 7

Caucasus   *C* is bold and strong.   *Hesperides, Song iii* 7

Cause   The *c* is nowhere found in rhyme.   *Who can say* 8

God the tyrant's *c* confound! (repeat)   *Hands all Round* 22, 34, 46, 58

What power is yours to blast a *c* or bless!   *Sugg. by Reading* 8

And trust an ancient manhood and the *c*   „   39

Cavalier   A gallant *c Sans peur et sans reproche*,   *The Grasshopper* 18

Cave   But Hatred in a gold *c* sits below,   *Pallid thunderstricken* 11

Cavern   Cathedralled *c's* of thick-ribbèd gold   „   7

Caverthroats   blow back Their wild cries down their *c*,   *Shall the hag* 10

Ceasing   *c* from All contemplation of all forms,   *Lover's Tale i* 66

Cedarn   Where are your moonlight halls, your *c* glooms,   *Timbuctoo* 43

Cedarshade   and zoned below with *c*,   *The Hesperides* 11

Cell   Sweet Love was withered in his *c*;   *Love, Pride, etc.* 8

Thronging the *c's* of the diseased mind,   *Shall the hag* 3

Center'd   and thou wert then A *c* glory-circled Memory   *Timbuctoo* 21

Central   And branching silvers of the *c* globe,   *Pallid thunderstricken* 8

winds, while they uprend the sea, Even from his *c* deeps: *Love* 10

Centre   he in the *c* fixed, Saw far on each side   *The Mystic* 33

Each sun which from the *c* flings Grand music   *Chorus* 21

The *c* of the splendours, all unworthy   *Lover's Tale i* 69

unhappy spirits Imprison'd in her *c*,   „   614

Cere   Half-bursten from the shroud, in *c* cloth bound,   „   677

Dearest (*continued*) my Camilla, who was mine No
longer in the *d* use of mine— — *Lover's Tale* i 599
Death *D* standeth by; She will not die; — *I' the glooming light* 12
either gate of life, Both birth and *d*; — *The Mystic* 33
night and pain and ruin and *d* reign here. — *Love* 4
But thou art deaf as *d*; — *The lintwhite* 11
in *d* They sleep with staring eyes — *A Fragment* 28
From which may rude *D* never startle them, — *Lover's Tale* i 796
in the *d* of love, if e'er they loved, — „ 849
Deathbed Go—carry him to his dark *d*; — *Burial of Love* 11
Decay (s) And, trampled on, left to its own *d*. — *Lover's Tale* ii 81
Decay (verb) And all her stars *d*.' — *The Ringlet* 10
Decent Stands in her pew and hums her *d* psalm
With *d* dippings at the name of Christ! — *Sugg. by Reading* 64
Decline little isle of Ithaca, beneath the day's *d*. — *Lotos-Eaters* 22
Decorous Poor soul! behold her: what *d* calm! — *Sugg. by Reading* 61
Decree the while your harsh *d* deplore, — *Lost Hope* 2
Deep (adj.) Flowing Southward, and the chasms of
d, *d* blue Slumber'd unfathomable, — *Timbuctoo* 7
Before the awful Genius of the place Kneels the
pale Priestess in *d* faith, — „ 34
The indistinctest atom in *d* air, — „ 100
For she hath half delved her own *d* grave. — *I' the glooming light* 7
The *d* salt wave breaks in above Those marble
steps below. — *Hero & Leander* 34
all the day heaven gathers back her tears Into her
own blue eyes so clear and *d*, — *Tears of Heaven* 7
To have the *d* poetic heart Is more than all poetic fame. — *New Timon* 23
Thin dilletanti *d* in nature's plan, — *Sugg. by Reading* 80
Eye feeding upon eye with *d* intent; — *Lover's Tale* i 64
whom woful ailments Of unavailing tears and heart *d*
moans Feed and envenom, — „ i 819
But over the *d* graves of Hope and Fear, — „ ii 61
Deep (adv.) Low-buried fathom *d* beneath with thee, — *O sad no more!* 8
Deep (s) thro' the sapphire *d*'s In wayward strength, — *Chorus* 28
Why *d* is not high, and high is not *d*? — *The 'How' and the 'Why'* 16
uprend the sea, Even from his central *d*'s: — *Love* 10
Two streams upon the violet *d*: — *Hesperides, Song* iv 6
Deep-furrowed *d-f* thought with many a name — *D. of F. Women* 15
Deep-rooted *D-r* in the living soil of truth: — *Timbuctoo* 225
Definite would scan *D* round. — „ 132
Deity As with a sense of nigher *D*, — *Lover's Tale* i 382
Delicious Most loveliest, most *d* union? — „ i 275
Delight I thus hope my lost *d*'s renewing, — *Could I outwear* 9
D is with thee gone, Oh! stay. — *The lintwhite* 33
Hoarded wisdom brings *d*. — *Hesperides, Song* ii 6
a flash of frolic scorn And keen *d*, — *Rosalind* 16
O DARLING room, my heart's *d*, — *O darling room* 1
I took *d* in this locality! — *Mablethorpe* 2
Alas for her and all her small *d*'s! — *Sugg. by Reading* 55
yet to both of us It was *d*, not hindrance: unto
both *D* from hardship be to overcome, — *Lover's Tale* i 378
Intense *d* and rapture that I breathed, — „ 381
Delighted Else had the life of that *d* hour — „ 465
Delirious Like a dreamy Lotos-eater, a *d* Lotos-eater! — *Lotos-Eaters* 13
Delved she hath half *d* her own deep grave. — *I' the glooming light* 7
Den From wronged Poerio's noisome *d*, — *Hands all Round* 15
Dense Dim shores, *d* rains, and heavy clouded sea. — *Mablethorpe* 8
Deplore the while your harsh decree *d*, — *Lost Hope* 2
Deploring Matter enough for *d* But aught — *1865-1866* 8
Depth lowest *d*'s were, as with visible love, — *Timbuctoo* 49
undescended *d* Of her black hollows. — „ 104
an unimagin'd *d* And harmony of planet-girded Suns — „ 108
The reflex of my City in their *d*'s. — „ 239
Descendant as when in some large lake From pressure of *d*
crags, — „ 122
Descent The bright *d* Of a young Seraph! — „ 64
Desert Grew to this strength among his *d*'s cold; — *Blow ye the trumpet* 6
Desire (s) Unto their hearts' *d*, (repeat) — *National Song* 12, 30
Desire (verb) Peace-lovers we—sweet Peace we all *d*— — *Britons, guard* 13
Despite Shadows to which, *d* all shocks of Change, — *Timbuctoo* 25
Devil For the *d* a whit we heed 'em, (repeat) — *National Song* 10, 28
And the merry *d* drive 'em (repeat) — 13, 31
Dew Unvisited with *d* of vagrant cloud, — *Timbuctoo* 103
Her tears are mixed with the bearded *d*'s. — *I' the glooming light* 11

Dew (*continued*) And filled the cup with *d*. — *Lost Hope* 8
To him the honey *d*'s of orient hope. — *Lover's Tale* i 675
the *d*, the sun, the rain, Under the growth of body — „ ii 73
Dew-drop Or as the *d-d*'s on the petal hung, — „ i 558
Dewy recalls the *d* prime Of youth and buried time? — *Who can say* 6
Diamond Behind, In *d* light, upsprung the dazzling Cones
Of Pyramids, — *Timbuctoo* 168
Diamonded The day, the *d* light, — *Chorus* 11
Diamondeyed Summer's tanling *d*. — *Dualisms* 22
Die Men clung with yearning Hope which would not *d*. — *Timbuctoo* 27
We laugh, we cry, we are born, we *d*, — *The 'How' and the 'Why'* 8
Whether we sleep or whether we *d*? — „ 18
No! sooner she herself shall *d*. — *Burial of Love* 24
Death standeth by; She will not *d*; — *I' the glooming light* 13
SHALL the hag Evil *d* with the child of Good, — *Shall the hag* 1
WHO fears to *d*? Who fears to *d*? Is there
any here who fears to *d* — *English War Song* 1
none shall grieve For the man who fears to *d*: — „ 4
scorn of the many shall cleave To the man who
fears to *d*. — „ 6
black eyes, I live and *d*, and only *d* for you. — *There are three things* 8
Kingdoms lapse, and climates change, and
races *d*; — *Hesperides, Song* ii 4
many a name Whose glory will not *d*. — *D. of F. Women* 16
Or tell me how to *d*. — *Skipping-rope* 10
Till it fade and fail and *d*, — *Germ of 'Maud'* 30
Died What marvel that she *d*? — *Love, Pride, etc.* 14
So *d* the Old: here comes the New: — *New Timon* 5
what profits it To tell ye that her father *d*, — *Lover's Tale* i 291
when hope *d*, part of her eloquence *D* — „ 751
Dig Come along! we will *d* their graves. — *English War Song* 39
Dilletanti Thin *d* deep in nature's plan, — *Sugg. by Reading* 80
Dim They with *d* eyes Behold me darkling. — *Timbuctoo* 212
D shadows but unwaning presences Fourfaced to
four corners of the sky; — *The Mystic* 15
Through whose *d* brain the wingèd dreams are borne, *To a Lady Sleep.* 2
Making their day *d*, so we gaze on thee. — *Love* 23
D shores, dense rains, and heavy clouded sea. — *Mablethorpe* 8
Diminution By *d* made most glorious, — *Lover's Tale* i 71
Dimple *D*'s, roselips, and eyes of any hue. — *There are three things* 4
Din Anon he rusheth forth with merry *d*, — *Love* 41
Dip Above her head the weak lamp *d*'s and winks — *Timbuctoo* 35
Dipp'd low-hung tresses, *d* In the fierce stream, — *Lover's Tale* i 374
Dipping With decent *d*'s at the name of Christ! — *Sugg. by Reading* 64
Dirt If half the little soul is *d*? — *New Timon* 36
Discernment So lethargised *d* in the sense, — *Lover's Tale* i 663
Discovery render up this home To keen *D*: — *Timbuctoo* 244
Diseased Thronging the cells of the *d* mind, — *Shall the hag* 3
Disgrace There hang within the heavens a dark *d*, — *Sugg. by Reading* 41
Dishonour doth the fruit of her *d* reap. — *Tears of Heaven* 5
Disjointed descendant crags, which lapse *D*, — *Timbuctoo* 123
Disk mighty *d* of their majestic sun, — *Love* 21
Disloyal Or loyally *d* battled for our rights. — *Sugg. by Reading* 36
Dismal Let the *d* face go by, — *Germ of 'Maud'* 23
Display Double *d* of starlit wings — *Timbuctoo* 155
Dissenting Would, unrelenting, Kill all *d*, — *Britons, guard* 34
Dissolution Which, lapt in seeming *d*, — *Lover's Tale* i 507
Distance Most pale and clear and lovely *d*'s. — *The Mystic* 35
Distant And notes of busy life in *d* worlds — *Timbuctoo* 113
Distinct momentary flash of light Grew thrillingly
d and keen. — „ 98
D and vivid with sharp points of light — „ 107
Distress Misery Forgot herself in that extreme *d*, — *Lover's Tale* i 628
Divine lowest depths were, as with visible love,
Fill'd with *D* effulgence, — *Timbuctoo* 50
and some On the ancient heights *d*; — *Lotos-Eaters* 17
With stony smirks at all things human and *d*! — *Sugg. by Reading* 48
Divinely Daughters of time, *d* tall, beneath — *The Mystic* 26
Divinest *D* Atalantis, whom the waves Have buried deep, — *Timbuctoo* 22
If to love be life alone, *D* Juliet, — *To ——* 3
Doctor Your *d*'s and your proctors and your deans — *Cambridge* 1
Dome rampart upon rampart, *d* on *d*, — *Timbuctoo* 163
soft inversion of her tremulous *D*'s; — „ 232
Doom (s) all things creeping to a day of *d*. — *The Mystic* 40
Some vast Assyrian *d* to burst upon our race. — *Sugg. by Reading* 42

Doom (verb) Ringlet, I *d* you to the flame. *The Ringlet* 50
Doometh ME my own fate to lasting sorrow *d* : *Me my own fate* 1
Door and beneath Two *d's* of blinding brilliance, *Timbuctoo* 178
   hinge on which the *d* of Hope, Once turning, *Lover's Tale i* 297
Double bearing on both sides *D* display of starlit wings *Timbuctoo* 155
Double-sweet And were in union more than *d-s*. *Lover's Tale i* 567
Doubt they plunge their *d's* among old rags and bones. *Sugg. by Reading* 72
   For my *d's* and fears were all amiss, *The Ringlet* 19
   That a *d* will only come for a kiss,   „ 21
Down Sneering bedridden in the *d* of Peace *Sugg. by Reading* 46
Downlooking *D* sees the solid shining ground *D. of F. Women* 2
Down-roll'd from the golden threshold had *d-r* Their heaviest thunder, *Lover's Tale i* 617
Drag We *d* so deep in our commercial mire, *Sugg. by Reading* 50
Dragon underneath the star Named of the *D*— *A Fragment* 6
   Lest the redcombed *d* slumber *Hesperides, Song ii* 9
   Hesper, the *d*, and sisters three,   „ 24
   Hesper, the *d*, and sisters three,   „ *iv* 25
Drain-cut The *d-c* levels of the marshy lea,— *Mablethorpe* 6
Drave broad-blown Argosies *D* into haven ? *A Fragment* 8
Draw as flame *d's* air ; *Timbuctoo* 18
Drawn *d* the frozen rain From my cold eyes *Could I outwear* 13
   From the root *D* in the dark, *Hesperides, Song i* 21
   Half round the mantling night is *d*,   „ *iii* 13
Dread We must not *d* in you the nameless autocrat. *Sugg. by Reading* 18
Dream (s) A *d* as frail as those of ancient Time ?' *Timbuctoo* 62
   d's of old Which fill'd the Earth   „ 78
   Less vivid than a half-forgotten *d*,   „ 136
   Through whose dim brain the wingèd *d's* are borne, *To a Lady Sleep.* 2
   ALL thoughts, all creeds, all *d's* are true, *οἱ ῥέοντες* 1
   Came voices, like the voices in a *d*, *The Hesperides* 12
   As men do from a vague and horrid *d*, *Lover's Tale i* 786
   their long life a *d* of linked love,   „ 795
Dream (verb) all Have faith in that they *d* : *οἱ ῥέοντες* 6
   But if I *d* that all these are, They are to me for that I *d*,   „ 13
Dreamful Driven back the billow of the *d* dark. *To a Lady Sleep.* 6
Dreamy Like a *d* Lotos-eater, a delirious Lotos-eater ! *Lotos-Eaters* 13
Dreary Black specks amid a waste of *d* sand, *Timbuctoo* 247
   Let it pass, the *d* brow, *Germ of 'Maud'* 22
   Gray sand banks and pale sunsets—*d* wind, *Mablethorpe* 7
Drew who *d* the happy atmosphere *Lover's Tale i* 673
Dried The course of Hope is *d*,—   „ 808
Drifting Shadow'd and crimson'd with the *d* dust,   „ 139
Drink FIRST *d* a health, this solemn night, *Hands all Round* 1
   To Europe's better health we *d*,   „ 23
   To France, the wiser France, we *d*,   „ 35
   We *d* to thee across the flood,   „ 38
   And the merry devil *d* 'em (repeat) *National Song* 13, 31
Driven *D* back the billow of the dreamful dark. *To a Lady Sleep.* 6
Drizzle white clouds *d* : her hair falls loose ; *I' the glooming light* 9
Droop hold aloft the cloud Which *d's* low *The Mystic* 32
Drooping Backward *d* his graceful head. *Burial of Love* 7
   ringlets, *D* and beaten with the plaining wind, *Lover's Tale i* 735
   And *d* daffodilly, And silverleavèd lily, *Anacreontics* 2
Drop Thine eye in *d's* of gladness swims. *Hero to Leander* 18
   Lest his scalèd eyelid *d*, *Hesperides, Song ii* 15
Dropping *D* the eyelid over the eyes.   „ 20
Dropt eyes *d* downward through the blue serene, *To a Lady Sleep.* 9
Dross And *d* to gold with glorious alchemy, *Though night* 7
Drove (*See also* **Drave**) on the Baltic shore Boleslas *d* the Pomeranian. *Blow ye the trumpet* 14
   Being wafted on the wind, *d* in my sight, *Lover's Tale i* 730
   Which *d* them onward—made them sensible ;   „ *ii* 77
Drown *D* soul and sense, while wistfully *Pallid thunderstricken* 4
Drowned or how we found The *d* seaman on the shore ? *Lover's Tale i* 293
Drunk heart is *d* with overwatchings night and day, *Hesperides, Song ii* 12
Dug with the shock Half *d* their own graves), *Lover's Tale ii* 50
Dull Thy sense is clogg'd with *d* mortality, *Timbuctoo* 82
   My thoughts which long had grovell'd in the slime Of this *d* world,   „ 150
   The *d* wave mourns down the slope, *I' the glooming light* 21
   Alas ! that one so beautiful Should have so *d* an ear. *The lintwhite* 9
   By a *d* mechanic ghost And a juggle of the brain. *Germ of 'Maud'* 7
Dumb Alas ! that lips so cruel *d* Should have so sweet a breath ! *The lintwhite* 17

Dusky like *d* worms which house Beneath unshaken waters, *Timbuctoo* 150
Dust Shadow'd and crimson'd with the drifting *d*, *Lover's Tale i* 139
Dwell I would *d* with thee, Merry grasshopper, *The Grasshopper* 22
Dweller As *d's* in lone planets look upon *Love* 20

E

Each *E* failing sense As with a momentary flash of light *Timbuctoo* 96
   with restless and increasing spheres Which break upon *e* other,   „ 126
   The wheatears whisper to *e* other : *The 'How' and the 'Why'* 11
   Grief and sadness steal Symbols of *e* other ; *Every day, etc.* 26
   Saw far on *e* side through the grated gates *The Mystic* 34
   E sun which from the centre flings Grand music *Chorus* 21
   Or in the art of Nature, where *e* rose Doth faint *Lover's Tale i* 563
   If, as I knew, they two did love *e* other,   „ 766
   Lo ! how they love *e* other !   „ 802
Eager Rapidly levelling *e* eyes. *Hesperides, Song ii* 18
   In *e* haste I shook him by the hand ; *Lover's Tale i* 788
Ear Beat like a far wave on my anxious *e*. *Timbuctoo* 114
   and his *e's* With harmonies of wind and wave   „ 206
   one so beautiful Should have so dull an *e*. *The lintwhite* 9
   Breathes low into the charmed *e's* of morn *A Fragment* 25
   There was a ringing in my *e's*, *O sad no more !* 5
   In the *e*, from far and near, *Rosalind* 7
   It's always ringing in your *e's*, *New Timon* 31
   by our *e's*, the huge roots strain and creak), *Lover's Tale i* 63
Earlier Than *e*, when on the Baltic shore *Blow ye the trumpet* 13
Earliest With *e* Light of Spring, *Timbuctoo* 200
   (the innocent light Of *e* youth pierced through and through *The Mystic* 29
   Thy Memnon, when his peaceful lips are kissed With *e* rays, *A Fragment* 23
   (Huge splinters, which the sap of *e* showers, *Lover's Tale ii* 45
Early but overleap All the petty shocks and fears That trouble life in *e* years, *Rosalind* 14
   Fresh as the *e* seasmell blown Through vineyards from an inland bay.   „ 28
Earth pillars high Long time eras'd from *E* : *Timbuctoo* 200
   whilome won the hearts of all on *E*   „ 17
   Which fill'd the *E* with passing loveliness,   „ 79
   smallest grain that dappled the dark *E*,   „ 99
   E's As Heaven than *E* is fairer.   „ 169
   so kin to *e* Pleasaunce fathers pain— *Every day, etc.* 14
   THE varied *e*, the moving heaven, *Chorus* 1
   hoarhead winter paving *e* With sheeny white,   „ 18
   HEAVEN weeps above the *e* all night till morn, *Tears of Heaven* 1
   Because the *e* hath made her state forlorn   „ 3
   Smiles on the *e's* worn brow to win her if she may.   „ 9
   Heaven crieth after thee ; *e* waileth for thee : *Love* 26
   the new year warm breathèd on the *e*,   „ 33
   'Come along ! we alone of the *e* are free ; *English War Song* 34
   As round the rolling *e* night follows day : *Me my own Fate* 10
   I grant you one of the great Powers on *e*, *Sugg. by Reading* 23
   and my neck his arm upstay'd From *e*. *Lover's Tale i* 721
   Crush'd link on link into the beaten *e*,   „ 859
Earth-awakening Upon some *e-a* day of spring *Timbuctoo* 152
Earthly And shook its *e* socket, for we heard, *Lover's Tale i* 788
Earthquake-shattered link The *e-s* chasm,   „ 408
Ease I fain would shake their triple-folded *e*, *Sugg. by Reading* 44
East Lest one from the *E* come and take it away. *Hesperides, Song i* 6
   Look from west to *e* along :   „ *iii* 6
   Till midnoon the cool *e* light Is shut out   „ *iv* 15
   Was not the South, The *E*, the West, all open, *Lover's Tale i* 699
Eat He shall *e* the bread of common scorn ; *English War Song* 13
   We will *e* the Lotos, *Lotos-Eaters* 14
Eater *See* **Lotos-Eater**
Ebbing A curve of whitening, flashing, *e* light ! *Timbuctoo* 63
Echo The *e*, feeble child of sound, *Chorus* 12
   Hearing apart the *e'es* of his fame. *D. of F. Women* 4
   E'es in his empty hall, *Home they brought him* 4
Eclipse His eyes in *e*, Pale cold his lips, *Burial of Love* 1
   thou wilt not brook *e* ; *Love* 11

Eye (*continued*) Till it dazzle and blind his *e's*.   *English War Song* 28
    Alas ! that *e's* so full of light   *The Lintwhite* 26
    from his mother's *e's* Flow over the Arabian bay,   *A Fragment* 23
    They sleep with staring *e's* and gilded lips,   ,,   29
    both my *e's* gushed out with tears.   *O sad no more* 6
    Dimples, roselips, and *e's* of any hue.   *There are three things* 4
    For which I live—black *e's*, and brown and blue ;   ,,   6
    black *e's*, I live and die, and only die for you.   ,,   7
    Of late such *e's* looked at me—   ,,   9
    I saw no more only those *e's*—   ,,   13
    knowest I dare not look into thine *e's*,   *Oh, Beauty* 4
    Looking under silver hair with a silver *e*.   *Hesperides, Song ii* 2
    Rapidly levelling eager *e's*.   ,,   18
    Dropping the eyelid over the *e's*.   ,,   20
    In my inner *e's* again,   *Germ of 'Maud'* 4
    Can it overlive the *e* ?   ,,   27
    my skipping-rope Will hit you in the *e*.   *Skipping-rope* 4
    The dewy dawnings and the amber *e's*,   *Lover's Tale i* 55
    E feeding upon *e* with deep intent ;   ,,   64
    mine image in her *e's*,   ,,   70
    e's were moved With motions of the soul,   ,,   72
    My *e's*, fix'd upon hers,   ,,   352
    And my *e's* read, they read aright,   ,,   602
    she did act the step-dame to mine *e's*,   ,,   664
    By the shuddering moonlight, fix'd his *e's*   ,,   680
    e's, I saw, were full of tears in the morn,   ,,   728
Eyed   *See* **Diamondeyed, Keen-eyed**
Eyelid   Came down upon my *e's*, and I fell.   *Timbuctoo* 187
    My *e's* and my brow.   *Hero to Leander* 13
    Lest his scalèd *e* drop,   *Hesperides, Song ii* 15
    Dropping the *e* over the eyes.   ,,   20
Eyne   With points of blastborne hail their heated *e* !   ,,   *Shall the hag* 11

F

Fable   labyrinthine veins Of the great vine of *F*,   *Timbuctoo* 222
Face   and the streets with ghastly *f's* throng'd   ,,   29
    look'd into my *f* With his unutterable,   ,,   66
    I look'd, but not Upon his *f*,   ,,   86
    And stares in his *f* and shouts ' how ? how ? ' *The 'How' and the 'Why'* 29
    Before the *f* of God didst breath and move,   *Love* 3
    all *f's* turned to where Glows rubylike   *D. of F. Women* 6
    paint the beauteous *f* Of the maiden,   *Germ of 'Maud'* 2
    Let the dismal *f* go by,   ,,   23
    a familiar *f*: I *thought* we knew him :   *New Timon* 6
    Refused to look his author in the *f*,   *Lover's Tale i* 697
    Known when their *f's* are forgot in the land.   ,,   804
Faced   *See* **Fullfaced**
Fade   Seasons flower and *f* ;   *Every day, etc.* 6
    Till it *f* and fail and die,   *Germ of 'Maud'* 30
Faded   and mightily outgrow The wan dark coil of *f* suffering—   *Could I outwear* 4
Faery   The silent Heavens were blench'd with *f* light, Uncertain whether *f* light or cloud,   *Timbuctoo* 5
Fail   Lotos-land, till the Lotos *f*,   *Lotos-Eaters* 27
    Till it fade and *f* and die,   *Germ of 'Maud'* 30
Fail'd   tried the Muses too : You *f*, Sir :   *New Timon* 14
Failing   Each *f* sense As with a momentary flash of light   *Timbuctoo* 96
Fain   I *f* would shake their triple-folded ease,   *Sugg. by Reading* 44
Faint   each rose Doth *f* upon the bosom   *Lover's Tale i* 564
Fair   (*See also* **Starry-fair**)   Where are ye Thrones of the Western wave, *f* Islands green ?   *Timbuctoo* 42
    thy hills enfold a City as *f* As those which starr'd the night o' the Elder World ?   ,,   59
    How chang'd from this *f* City ! '   ,,   249
    Armed cap-a-pie, Full *f* to see ;   *The Grasshopper* 15
    There are no wives like English wives, So *f* and chaste as they be.   *National Song* 22
    F year, *f* year, thy children call,   *The lintwhite* 10
    F year, with brows of royal love Thou comest, as a King.   ,,   19
    (when I view *F* maiden forms moving like melodies),   *There are three things* 3
    I can shadow forth my bride As I knew her *f* and kind *Germ of 'Maud'* 10
    'Tis a phantom *f* and good I can call it to my side,   ,,   15
    I hear a thunder though the skies are *f*,   *Sugg. by Reading* 89

Fair (*continued*) *F* fall this hallow'd hour,   *God bless our Prince* 8
    Farewell, *f* rose of May !   ,,   11
    her cheek was pale, Oh ! very *f* and pale :   *Lover's Tale i* 725
Fairer   as far surpassing Earth's As Heaven than Earth is *f*.   *Timbuctoo* 170
Fairest   Thou art the *f* of thy feres,   *The lintwhite* 35
    her to whom all outward *f* things   *Lover's Tale i* 383
Fairy-like   How *f-l* you fly !   *Skipping-rope* 6
Faith   Kneels the pale Priestess in deep *f*,   *Timbuctoo* 34
    and all Have *f* in that they dream :   οἱ ῥέοντες 6
    Has given all my *f* a turn ?   *The Ringlet* 52
    I know not, *f*:   *Lover's Tale i* 695
Falcon   My happy *f*, Rosalind,   *Rosalind* 25
Falconhearted   My *f* Rosalind   ,,   9
Fall   Because no shadow on you *f's*,   ,,   31
    In the summerwoods when the sun *f's* low, *The 'How' and the 'Why'* 27
    For her the showers shall not *f*,   *Burial of Love* 25
    her hair *f's* loose ;   *I' the glooming light* 9
    thick snow *f's* on her flake by flake,   ,,   20
    (Shame *f* 'em they are deaf and blind)   *The Grasshopper* 6
    Let them clash together, foam and *f*.   *Hesperides, Song iii* 9
    that never *f's* Away from freshness,   *Rosalind* 16
    Self-poised, nor fears to *f*.   *D. of F. Women* 12
    You *f* on those who are to you   *New Timon* 15
    Take care thou dost not fear to *f* ! '   *What time I wasted* 9
    Fair *f* this hallow'd hour,   *God bless our Prince* 8
    Did *f* away into oblivion.   *Lover's Tale i* 630
Fall'n   when the Sun Had *f* below th' Atlantick,   *Timbuctoo* 1
    Moon Had *f* from the night,   ,,   253
    THE Northwind *f*, in the newstarrèd night   *The Hesperides* 1
    leaf *f* in the woods, or blasted Upon this bough ?   *Lover's Tale i* 622
    if he had *f* In love in twilight ?   ,,   699
Falling   In rising and in *f* with the tide,   ,,   62
    f, they fell too, Crush'd link on link   ,,   858
False   If ye sing not, if ye make *f* measure,   *Hesperides, Song i* 10
Falsehood   Prove their *f* and thy quarrel.   *The Grasshopper* 9
Falter'd   since that hour, My voice hath somewhat *f*—   *Lover's Tale i* 750
Fame   Hearing apart the echoes of his *f*.   *D. of F. Women* 13
    Is more than all poetic *f*.   *New Timon* 24
Familiar   Regard him : a *f* face :   ,,   6
Fancy   Rosalind, hath daring *fancies* of her own,   *Rosalind* 26
    assimilated all our tastes And future *fancies*.   *Lover's Tale i* 239
    my *f* So lethargised discernment in the sense,   ,,   662
Fanged   *See* **Subtle-fanged**
Fanlike   wings which burn *F* and fibred,   *Timbuctoo* 156
Far   Beat like a *f* wave on my anxious ear.   ,,   114
    through the trackless fields Of undefin'd existence *f* and free.   ,,   160
    Saw round her feet the country *f* away,   *Lover's Tale i* 390
Farewell   *F* our England's flower,   *God bless our Prince* 9
    F, fair rose of May !   ,,   11
Far-up   all faces turned to where Glows rubylike the *f-u* crimson globe,   *D. of F. Women* 7
Fashioned   *See* **Airy-fashioned**
Fate   ME my own *f* to lasting sorrow doometh :   *Me my own fate* 1
    And insolence of uncontrolled *F*,   *Lover's Tale i* 688
Father (s)   *F* Hesper, *F* Hesper, watch, watch, ever and aye,   *Hesperides, Song ii* 1
    F, twinkle not thy stedfast sight ;   ,,   3
    Look to him, *f*, lest he wink,   ,,   11
    F Hesper, *F* Hesper, watch, watch, night and day,   ,, *iii* 1
    F, old Himla weakens,   ,,   7
    Rode upon his *f's* lance, Beat upon his *f's* shield—   *Home they brought him* 8
    what profits it To tell ye that her *f* died,   *Lover's Tale i* 291
Father (*verb*)   so kin to earth Pleasaunce *f's* pain—   *Every day, etc.* 15
Fathom   Low-buried *f* deep beneath with thee,   *O sad no more !* 8
Fear (s)   when *f* men's hopes and *f's* take refuge in The fragrance   *Timbuctoo* 226
    Till the end of *f's* Cometh in the shroud,   *Every day, etc.* 20
    Unknowing *f*, Undreading loss,   *The Grasshopper* 16
    edicts of his *f* Are mellowed into music,   *Love* 7
    know no strife Of inward woe or outward *f* ;   *Rosalind* 4
    shocks and *f's* That trouble life in early years,   ,,   13
    what with spites and what with *f's*,   *New Timon* 29
    For my doubts and *f's* were all amiss,   *The Ringlet* 19
    And a *f* to be kissed away.'   ,,   22
    lead me tenderly, for *f* the mind   *Lover's Tale i* 23

Fear (verb) WHO *f's* to die? Who *f's* to die? Is there any here who *f's* to die He shall find what he *f's*, and none shall grieve For the man who *f's* to die: *English War Song* 1

scorn of the many shall cleave To the man who *f's* to die.   " 6

Self-poised, nor *f's* to fall.   *D. of F. Women* 12

Take care thou dost not *f* to fall!'   *What time I wasted* 9

I *f* for you, as for some youthful king,   *Sugg. by Reading* 9

An honest isolation need not *f* The Court,   " 15

Fearful weak lamp dips and winks Unto the *f* summoning without: *Timbuctoo* 36

With which the *f* springtide flecks the lea,   *Love and Sorrow* 2

And with a *f* self-impelling joy Saw round her feet   *Lover's Tale* i 389

Feather two birds of glancing *f* Do woo each other,   *Dualisms* 8

Fed Memory tho' *f* by Pride Did wax   *Love, Pride, etc.* 11

unhappy sighs, *f* with my tears,   *Lover's Tale* i 674

Feeble The echo, *f* child of sound,   *Chorus* 12

Feed heart deep moans *F* and envenom,   *Lover's Tale* i 820

When the shrill storm blast *f's* it from behind,   " ii 47

Feeding taught nothing, *f* on the soul.   *Cambridge* 14

Eye *f* upon eye with deep intent;   *Lover's Tale* i 64

Feel and to *f* My fullness;   *Timbuctoo* 214

I *f* there is something; but how and what?   *The 'How' and the 'Why'* 23

Severe and quick to *f* a civic sin,   *Sugg. by Reading* 4

I *f* the thousand cankers of our State,   " 43

I *f* Exception to be character'd in fire.   " 51

She *f's* not how the social frame is rack'd.   " 56

Feeling A little *f* is a want of tact.   " 58

blood, the breath, the *f* and the motion,   *Lover's Tale* ii 75

Feign No Tithon thou as poets *f*   *The Grasshopper* 5

Fell Came down upon my eyelids, and I *f*.   *Timbuctoo* 187

The Moslem myriads *f*, and fled before—   *Blow ye the trumpet* 11

falling, they *f* too, Crush'd link on link   *Lover's Tale* i 858

had shatter'd from The mountain, till they *f*,   " ii 49

Felt I *f* my soul grow mighty,   *Timbuctoo* 90

now *f* Unutterable buoyancy and strength   " 157

not *f* and known A higher than they see: " 211

hath *f* The vanities of after and before,   *The Mystic* 5

the year First *f* his youth and strength,   *Lover's Tale* i 306

Fere Thy art the fairest of thy *f's*,   *The lintwhite* 35

Fetter'd Thy spirit *f* with the bond of clay: *Timbuctoo* 83

Fibre On those first-moved *f's* of the brain.   *Lover's Tale* i 21

Fibred wings which burn Fanlike and *f*,   *Timbuctoo* 156

Fie O *f*, you golden nothing, *f* You golden lie.   *The Ringlet* 43

Field (*See also* **Sandfield**) *f's* Of undefin'd existence far and free.   *Timbuctoo* 159

A GATE and a *f* half ploughed,   *A gate and a field* 1

Sun peeped in from open *f*,   *Home they brought him* 6

Fierce The *f* old man—to take *his* name You bandbox.   *New Timon* 43

whose low-hung tresses, dipp'd In the *f* stream.   *Lover's Tale* i 375

Fierceness The *f* of the bounding element?   *Timbuctoo* 148

Fiery Part of a throne of *f* flame,   " 181

The linkèd woes of many a *f* change Had purified,   *The Mystic* 9

Fight (s) charge to the *f*: Charge! charge to the *f*!   *English War Song* 47

We still were loyal in our wildest *f's*,   *Sugg. by Reading* 35

Fight (verb) Till we were left to *f* for truth alone.   *Britons, guard* 35

To *f* thy mother here alone,   *Hands all Round* 43

For better so you *f* for public ends;   *Sugg. by Reading* 26

Fill THERE are three things that *f* my heart with sighs   *There are three things* 1

Fill'd (*See also* **Globefilled**) *F* with Divine effulgence, circumfus'd,   *Timbuctoo* 50

dreams of old Which *f* the Earth with passing loveliness,   " 79

f My eyes with irresistible sweet tears,   " 190

I have *f* thy lips with power.   " 215

And *f* the cup with dew.   *Lost Hope* 8

F with a finer air: *D. of F. Women* 8

Film'd *f* the margents of the recent wound.   *Lover's Tale* i 764

Find He shall *f* what he fears,   *English War Song* 3

f The drain-cut levels of the marshy *l*,—   *Mablethorpe* 5

Fine And those *f* curses which he spoke;   *New Timon* 2

Finer Filled with a *f* air: *D. of F. Women* 8

Fire Rapid as *f*, inextricably link'd,   *Timbuctoo* 117

Changed into *f*, and blown about with sighs.   *To* —— 9

PP*

Fire (continued) By secret *f* and midnight storms That wander   *Chorus* 5

flings Grand Music and redundant *f*,   " 22

They stream like *f* in the skies;   *English War Song* 26

Through the water and the *f*. (repeat)   *National Song* 14, 32

The world is wasted with *f* and sword,   *Hesperides, Song* iv 22

But *f*, to blast the hopes of men.   *Hands all Round* 30

I feel Exception to be character'd in *f*.   *Sugg. by Reading* 52

Firmament Seemed with a cobweb *f* to link   *Lover's Tale* i 407

First I have rais'd thee higher to the Spheres of Heaven, Man's *f*, last home: *Timbuctoo* 217

O MAIDEN, fresher than the *f* green leaf   *Love and Sorrow* 1

For the two *f* were not, but only seemed One shadow   *The Mystic* 20

First-moved begins to play On those *f-m* fibres of the brain.   *Lover's Tale* i 21

Fish Young *f'es*, on an April morn,   *Rosalind* 21

Five *F* links, a golden chain, are we,   *Hesperides, Song* ii 23

F links, a golden chain, are we,   " iv 24

Fixed he in the centre, Saw far on each side   *The Mystic* 33

My eyes, *f* upon hers,   *Lover's Tale* i 352

By the shuddering moonlight, *f* his eyes   " 680

Flag takes his *f's* and waves them to the mob   *D. of F. Women* 5

Flake thick snow falls on her *f* by *f*,   *I' the glooming light* 20

Flame (s) ev'n as *f* draws air; But had their being in the heart of Man As air is th' life of *f*:   *Timbuctoo* 18

Part of a throne of fiery *f*,   " 181

Love unreturn'd is like the fragrant *f*   *To* — 5

a region of white *f*, Pure without heat,   *The Mystic* 43

Ringlet, I doom you to the *f*.   *The Ringlet* 50

Flame (verb) To *f* and sparkle and stream as of old,   " 8

Flash (s) As with a momentary *f* of light   *Timbuctoo* 97

With a *f* of frolic scorn And keen delight,   *Rosalind* 15

Flash (verb) They *f* across the darkness of my brain,   *Lover's Tale* i 53

Flashing A curve of whitening, *f*, ebbing light!   *Timbuctoo* 63

Girt with a Zone of *f* gold beneath His breast,   " 72

Her frantic city's *f* heats But fire,   *Hands all Round* 29

Flat Looking athwart the burning *f's*,   *A Fragment* 17

Flattering melody *f* the crisped Nile By columned Thebes.   " 26

Fleck which the fearful springtide *f's* the lea,   *Love and Sorrow* 2

Flecked *See* **Silverflecked**

Fled The Moslem myriads fell, and *f* before—   *Blow ye the trumpet* 11

Fleet more *f* and strong Than its precursor,   *Timbuctoo* 127

Though thou art *f* of wing, Yet stay.   *The lintwhite* 24

Fleeting Could link his shallop to the *f* edge,   *Timbuctoo* 145

They from the blosmy brere Call to the *f* year,   *The lintwhite* 5

the great Pyramids Broad-based amid the *f* sands,   *A Fragment* 10

Fleetness nature of itself With its own *f*.   *Timbuctoo* 143

Fling from the centre *f's* Grand music   *Chorus* 21

Thy golden largess *f*,   *The lintwhite* 22

Break through your iron shackles—*f* them far.   *Blow ye the trumpet* 4

Flinging Then *f* myself down upon my knees   *Lover's Tale* i 789

Flit Lets the great world *f* from him,   *D. of F. Women* 10

Float Down an ideal stream they ever *f*,   *Pallid thunderstricken* 2

Floating Like a swol'n river's gushings in still night Mingled with *f* music,   *Timbuctoo* 194

Nor blot with *f* shades the solar light.   *Shall the hag* 14

And onward *f* in a full, dark wave,   *Lover's Tale* i 739

Flood We drink to thee across the *f*,   *Hands all Round* 38

Flooded stars Were *f* over with clear glory   *Timbuctoo* 9

Flooding freshflushing springtime calls To the *f* waters cool,   *Rosalind* 20

F its angry cheek with odorous tears.   *Lover's Tale* i 565

Flow Nor the rivers *f*, nor the sweet birds sing,   *Burial of Love* 29

How scorn and ruin, pain and hate could *f*:   *Pallid thunderstricken* 10

And all things *f* like a stream. (repeat)   οἱ 'ρέοντες 8, 16

from his mother's eyes *F* over the Arabian bay,   *A Fragment* 24

Flower (s) (*See also* **Summerflowers**) Moving his crest to all sweet plots of *f's*   *Could I outwear* 7

I smelt a wildweed *f* alone;   *O sad no more!* 4

From an old garden where no *f* bloometh,   *Me my own fate* 7

Every *f* and every fruit the redolent breath   *Hesperides, Song* iv 9

Farewell our England's *f*,   *God bless our Prince* 9

Creep down into the bottom of the *f*.   *Lover's Tale* i 560

Flower (verb) Seasons *f* and fade;   *Every day, etc.* 6

Flowerbell Two bees within a chrystal *f* rockèd   *Dualisms* 1

Flowerèd Pushing the thick roots aside Of the singing *f* grasses,   *The Grasshopper* 38

Through and through the *f* heather.   *Dualisms* 5

Fruit (*continued*) The golden apple, the golden apple, the
   hallowed *f*,   *Hesperides, Song* 30
   As bearing no essential *f*'s of excellence.   *Lover's Tale i* 385
Fruitage The luscious *f* clustereth mellowly,   *Hesperides, Song iv* 19
Fruit-tree How many the mystic *f-t* holds,   "   *ii* 8
Full Upon the outward verge and bound alone Of *f*
   beatitude.   *Timbuctoo* 96
   Till Love have his *f* revenge.   *Burial of Love* 30
   are *f* of strange Astonishment and boundless change.
   (repeat)   *Chorus* 9, 19, 29
   Alas ! that eyes so *f* of light Should be so wandering ! *The lintwhite* 26
   Thy locks are *f* of sunny sheen In rings of gold yronne,   "   28
   Holy and bright, round and *f*, bright and blest, *Hesperides, Song iv* 11
   Her eyes, I saw, were *f* of tears in the morn,   *Lover's Tale i* 728
   And onward floating in a *f*, dark wave,   "   739
   laden with mournful thanks, From my *f* heart :   "   749
   Solemn but splendid, *f* of shapes and sounds,   "   799
Fullfaced But when the *f* sunset yellowly Stays on
   the flowering arch of the bough,   *Hesperides, Song iv* 17
Fullness and to feel My *f*;   *Timbuctoo* 215
Fullsailed Rosalind *F* before a vigorous wind,   *Rosalind* 10
Full-voiced when *f-v* Winter roofs The headland   *Timbuctoo* 203
Fulminating To charm a lower sphere of *f* fools. *Sugg. by Reading* 30
Furrowed *See* **Deep-furrowed**
Fusty I could *not* forgive the praise, *F* Christopher.   *To C. North* 9
Future In eternity no *f*, In eternity no past. *The 'How' and the 'Why'* 6
   Perchance assimilated all our tastes And *f* fancies.   *Lover's Tale i* 239

G

Gain pallid thunderstricken sigh for *g*,   *Pallid thunderstricken* 1
Galaxy clear *G* Shorn of its hoary lustre,   *Timbuctoo* 105
Gall by a spell Did change them into *g* ;   *Love, Pride, etc.* 10
   Memory tho' by Pride Did wax so thin on *g*,   "   12
Gallant A *g* cavalier *Sans peur et sans reproche*,   *The Grasshopper* 18
Gambol (s) when the winds are wild With *g*'s,   *Timbuctoo* 203
   The summer midges wove their wanton *g*,   *Check every outflash* 12
Gambol (verb) As they *g*, lilygarlands ever stringing: *Dualisms* 15
Gander 'The *G*' and 'The man of Mitylene,'   *Lover's Tale i* 287
Garden Her *g*'s frequent with the stately Palm,   *Timbuctoo* 233
   From an old *g* where no flower bloometh,   *Me my own fate* 7
Garland (*See also* **Lilygarlands**) A *g* for Lenora.   *Anacreontics* 7
Garment The snowy skirting of a *g* hung,   *Timbuctoo* 182
Gate low hung on either *g* of life,   *The Mystic* 32
   Saw far on each side through the grated *g*'s   "   34
   Clad in light by golden *g*'s,   *Germ of 'Maud'* 32
   A *G* and a field half ploughed,   *A gate and a field* 1
   the angels, The watchers at heaven's *g*,   *Lover's Tale i* 616
Gather all the day heaven *g*'s back her tears   *Tears of Heaven* 6
   g from afar The hosts to battle: *Blow ye the trumpet* 1
Gathering from this impulse Continuing and *g* ever,   *Lover's Tale i* 494
Gave She that *g* you 's bought and sold,   *The Ringlet* 33
   Ringlet, She *g* you me, and said,   "   40
Gay *See* **Golden-gay**
Gaze (s) where no *g* Might rest, stood open,   *Timbuctoo* 178
   Methinks I could have sooner met that *g* !   *Lover's Tale i* 684
Gaze (verb) Of those that *g* upon the noonday Sun.   *Timbuctoo* 71
   Thou whose fringèd lids I *g* upon,   *To a Lady Sleep.* 1
   Albeit we *g* not on thy glories near,   *Love* 2
   Making their day dim, so we *g* on thee.   "   23
   And now—methinks I *g* upon thee now,   "   29
Gaz'd I *g* upon the sheeny coast beyond,   *Timbuctoo* 10
   So *g* I on the ruins of that thought   *Lover's Tale ii* 71
Gazeth *g* on Those eyes which wear no light   *Timbuctoo* 38
Gazing whose eyes are dim With *g* on the light   *Lover's Tale i* 486
Genius Before the awful *G* of the place   *Timbuctoo* 33
Gentleman Nor like a *g* at ease With moral breadth   *New Timon* 27
George *G* for England ! (repeat) *English War Song* 9, 20, 31, 42, 53
Get Go, *g* you gone, you muse and mope—   *Skipping-rope* 7
Ghastful Oh ! rather had some loathly *g* brow,   *Lover's Tale i* 676
Ghastly and the streets with *g* faces throng'd   *Timbuctoo* 29
   Tho' its *g* sister glide And be moved around me still *Germ of 'Maud'* 18
Ghost By a dull mechanic *g*   "   7

Giant where the *G* of old Time infixed   *Timbuctoo* 11
   WHERE is the *G* of the Sun,   *A Fragment* 1
Gigantic *G* daughter of the West,   *Hands all Round* 37
Gilded somewhere in death They sleep with staring eyes
   and *g* lips,   *A Fragment* 29
Gird such as *g* The unfading foreheads   *Timbuctoo* 53
Girded *See* **Planet-girded**
Girding The heavy thunder's *g* might,   *Chorus* 13
Girl Who killed the *g*'s and thrill'd the boys   *New Timon* 9
   And a lad may wink, and a *g* may hint,   *The Ringlet* 17
Girt *G* with a Zone of flashing gold   *Timbuctoo* 72
Give speak low, and *g* up wholly Thy spirit   *Check every outflash* 2
   If you will *g* me one, but one,   *The Ringlet* 3
Given I have *g thee* To understand my presence,   *Timbuctoo* 213
   Has *g* all my faith a turn ?   *The Ringlet* 52
   earth beneath me yawning *g* Sign of convulsion ; *Lover's Tale i* 611
Giveth It *g* out a constant melody That drowns   "   534
Glad Thou art so *g* and free,   *The Grasshopper* 24
   Green springtide, April promise, *g* new year Of
   Being,   *Lover's Tale i* 277
Gladness Thine eye in drops of *g* swims.   *Hero to Leander* 18
   self-upborne With such *g*, as,   *Rosalind* 18
Glancing Over a stream two birds of *g* feather   *Dualisms* 8
Glare The lawless comets as they *g*,   *Chorus* 27
Glazèd With *g* eye She looks at her grave: *I' the glooming light* 14
Glide Both alike, they *g* together Side by side :   *Dualisms* 10
   Tho' its ghastly sister *g*   *Germ of 'Maud'* 18
Glimpse And *g* of multitudes of multitudes   *Timbuctoo* 183
Glistering Weak eyes upon the *g* sands that robe
   The understream.   *Pallid thunderstricken* 5
Globe bore *g*'s Of wheeling suns, or stars,   *Timbuctoo* 171
   And branching silvers of the central *g*,   *Pallid thunderstricken* 8
   Glows rubylike the far-up crimson *g*,   *D. of F. Women* 7
Globefilled The *g* arch that, cleaving air,   *Chorus* 25
Gloom springing In and out the emerald *g*'s,   *The Grasshopper* 42
   your moonlight halls, your cedarn *g*'s,   *Timbuctoo* 43
   Do pass from *g* to glory,   "   153
   complicated *g*'s And cool impleachèd twilights.   "   227
   The troublous autumn's sallow *g*,   *Chorus* 17
   shalt thou pierce the woven *g*'s of truth ;   *Though night* 11
   Hallowed in awful chasms the wheeling *g*,   *Love* 22
Gloometh Alone my hopeless melancholy *g*,   *Me my own fate* 5
Glooming I' the *g* light Of middle night, *I' the glooming light* 1
Glorious When I must render up this *g* home To keen
   Discovery: *Timbuctoo* 243
   And dross to gold with *g* alchemy,   *Though night, etc.* 7
   And dazzled to the heart with *g* pain. *There are three things* 14
   By diminution made most *g*,   *Lover's Tale i* 71
   I well remember, It was a *g* morning,   "   301
   But grow upon them like a *g* vision   "   797
Glory stars Were flooded over with clear *g*   *Timbuctoo* 9
   round their emerald cones In coronals and *glories*,   "   53
   it was play'd about With its peculiar *g*.   "   57
   And circled with the *g* of living light   "   75
   Do pass from gloom to *g*,   "   153
   But the *g* of the place Stood out   "   174
   wrapt about with clouds Of *g* of Heaven.   "   200
   showering down the *g* of lightsome day,   *Tears of Heaven* 8
   Albeit we gaze not on thy *glories* near,   *Love* 2
   Our *g* is our freedom, (repeat)   *National Song* 15, 33
   In the midnoon the *g* of old Rhodes,   *A Fragment* 2
   Thy spirit, circled with a living *g*,   *Me my own fate* 3
   The *g* unsealèd,   *Hesperides, Song iii* 3
   with many a name Whose *g* will not die.   *D. of F. Women* 16
   I had merged In *g*,   *Lover's Tale i* 516
Glory-circled and thou wert then A center'd *g-c* Memory,   *Timbuctoo* 21
Gloss bramble and the shining *g* Of ivy-leaves,   *Lover's Tale i* 373
Glossed *See* **Blue-glossèd**
Glossy Burn, you *g* heretic, burn, Burn, burn.   *The Ringlet* 53
Glow (s) And in the *g* of sallow Summertide,   *Timbuctoo* 201
Glow (verb) *G*'s rubylike the far-up crimson globe,   *D. of F. Women* 7
Glowing light Of the great angel mind which look'd from
   out The starry *g* of his restless eyes.   *Timbuctoo* 89
   and the opal width Of her small *g* lakes,   "   102
   The naked summer's *g* birth,   *Chorus* 16

Gnarlèd   All round about The *g* bole of the charmèd
tree,   *Hesperides, Song iv* 29

Go   The world is somewhat; it *goes* on
somehow;   *The 'How' and the 'Why'* 21
Why the life *goes* when the blood is spilt?   „   32
G—carry him to his dark deathbed;   *Burial of Love* 11
OH *g* not yet, my love, (repeat)   *Hero to Leander* 1, 32
Leander! *g* not yet.   „   38
Oh! *g* not yet,   „   40
Let the dismal face *g* by,   *Germ of 'Maud'* 23
G, get you gone, you muse and mope—   *Skipping-rope* 7
There must no man *g* back to bear the tale :   *Britons, guard* 56
Lest you *g* wrong from power in excess.   *Sugg. by Reading* 10
G, frightful omens.   „   85

God   Offered to *G's* upon an altarthrone;   *To ——* 7
Before the face of *G* didst breath and move,   *Love* 3
The very throne of the eternal *G* :   „   6
Shout for *G* and our right !   *English War Song* 50
As for the French, *G* speed 'em (repeat)   *National Song* 11, 29
' *G* save the Queen ' is here a truer cry.   *G* save the
Nation, The toleration,   *Britons, guard* 26
Too much we make our Ledgers, *G's*.   *Hands all Round* 20
G the tyrant's cause confound ! (repeat)   „ 22, 34, 46, 58
O fools, we want a manlike *G* and Godlike men !   *Sugg. by Reading* 84
G bless our Prince and Bride !   *G* keep their
lands allied,   *God bless our Prince* 1
G save the Queen ! (repeat)   „ 3, 7, 10
G bless thy marriage-day, *G* bless the Queen.   „ 13
I pray'd aloud to *G* that he would hold   *Lover's Tale i* 791

Goddess   shall see The British *G*,   *Sugg. by Reading* 54

Godlike   Who looks for *G* greatness here   „ 53
O fools, we want a manlike God and *G* men !   „ 84
with shining eyes Smiling a *g* smile   *The Mystic* 28

Goest   Thou *g* and returnest to His Lips   *Love* 12

Going   Wanderers coming and *g*   *1865–1866* 7

Gold   Imperial Eldorado roof'd with *g* :   *Timbuctoo* 24
Zone of flashing *g* beneath His breast,   „ 72
front of burnish'd *g* Interminably high, if *g* it were   „ 175
And dross to *g* with glorious alchemy,   *Though night* 7
Cathedralled caverns of thick-ribbèd *g*   *Pallid thunderstricken* 7
But Hatred in a *g* cave sits below,   „ 11
in mail of argent light Shot into *g*,   „ 13
Liquid *g*, honeysweet thro' and thro'.   *Hesperides, Song i* 24
the apple of *g* hangs over the sea,   „ *iv* 23
ruthless host is bought with plunder'd *g*,   *Britons, guard* 7
Thy locks are full of sunny sheen In rings of *g* yronne,   *The lintwhite* 29
then shall I know it is all true *g*   *The Ringlet* 7
I that took you for true *g*,   „ 32

Golden   *G* calm and storm Mingle day by day.   *Every day, etc.* 7
To-night the roaring brine Will rend thy *g* tresses   *Hero to Leander* 24
Lighting on the *g* blooms ?   *The Grasshopper* 44
Thou foldest, like a *g* atmosphere,   *Love* 5
they roam together Under a summervault of *g* weather ;   *Dualisms* 18
Thy *g* largess fling,   *The lintwhite* 22
The *g* apple, the *g* apple, the hallowed fruit,   *Hesperides, Song i* 1
Look to him, father, lest he wink, and the *g* apple be
stol'n away.   „ *ii* 11
If the *g* apple be taken The world will be overwise.   „ 21
Five links, a *g* chain, are we, Hesper, the dragon, and
sisters three, Bound about the *g* tree   „ 23
The *g* apple stol'n away,   „ *iii* 4
Five links, a *g* chain, are we,   „ *iv* 24
The *g* apple, the *g* apple, the hallowed fruit,   „ 30
We will abide in the *g* vale Of the Lotos-land,   *Lotos-Eaters* 26
To its Archetype that waits Clad in light by *g* gates,   *Germ of 'Maud'* 32
O fie, you *g* nothing, fie You *g* lie.   *The Ringlet* 43
And from the *g* threshold had down-roll'd Their
heaviest thunder,   *Lover's Tale i* 617
May their days be *g* days,   „ 794
Erewhile close couch'd in *g* happiness,   „ *ii* 79

Golden-circled   A center'd *g-c* Memory,   *Timbuctoo* 21

Goldencored   fruitage clustereth mellowly, Golden-
kernalled, *g*,   *Hesperides, Song iv* 20

Golden-gay   ringlets, That look so *g-g*,   *The Ringlet* 2
' My ringlet, my ringlet, That art so *g-g*,   „ 14

Golden-gay (*continued*)   O Ringlet, You still are *g-g*,   *The Ringlet* 28

Goldenkernelled   fruitage clustereth mellowly, *G*,
goldencored,   *Hesperides, Song iv* 20

Goldenlockèd   Mid May's darling *g*,   *Dualisms* 21

Gold-sanded   Your flowering Capes and your *g-s* bays   *Timbuctoo* 45

Gone   Delight is with thee *g*, Oh ! stay.   *The lintwhite* 33
Old Memphis hath *g* down :   *A Fragment* 27
Surely all pleasant things had *g* before,   *O sad no more !* 7
Go, get you *g*, you muse and mope—   *Skipping-rope* 7

Good   SHALL the hag Evil die with the child of *G*,   *Shall the hag* 1
Nor *g* nor ill, nor light nor shade,   οἱ 'ρέοντες 10
O you, the Press ! what *g* from you might spring !   *Sugg. by Reading* 9
All *g* things are in the west,   *Hesperides, Song iv* 14
'Tis a phantom fair and *g* I can call it to my side,   *Germ of 'Maud'* 15
' They call this man as *g* as me.'   *New Timon* 32

Goodly   So on an oaken sprout A *g* acorn grew ;   *Lost Hope* 6

Gorgeous   are thine obelisks Graven with *g* emblems
undiscerned ?   *A Fragment* 13

Graceful   Backward drooping his *g* head.   *Burial of Love* 7

Gracious   As towards the *g* light I bow'd,   *What time I wasted* 4

Grain   I saw The smallest *g* that dappled   *Timbuctoo* 99

Grand   Each sun which from the centre flings *G* music and
redundant fire,   *Chorus* 22

Grant   I *g* you one of the great Powers on earth,   *Sugg. by Reading* 23

Grasp   costly casket in the *g* Of memory ?   *Lover's Tale i* 101

Grass   For her the green *g* shall not spring,   *Burial of Love* 28
Of the singing flowered *g'es*,   *The Grasshopper* 38
where the *g* was warm where I had lain,   *Lover's Tale i* 790

Grassgreen   tuskèd seahorse walloweth In a stripe of
g calm,   *Lotos-Eaters* 5

Grasshopper   I would dwell with thee, Merry *g*,   *The Grasshopper* 23

Grated   Saw far on each side through the *g* gates   *The Mystic* 34

Grave   she hath half delved her own deep *g*.   *I' the glooming light* 7
With glazed eye She looks at her *g* :   „ 15
Come along ! we will dig their *g*.   *English War Song* 9
Will it lead me to the *g* ?   *Germ of 'Maud'* 24
and with the shock Half dug their own *g's*),   *Lover's Tale ii* 50

Graven   obelisks *G* with gorgeous emblems   *A Fragment* 13

Gray   (*See also* **Silver-gray**)   *G* sand banks and pale sunsets
—dreary wind,   *Mablethorpe* 9

Great   As when in some *g* City where the walls Shake,   *Timbuctoo* 28
Wound thro' your *g* Elysian solitudes,   „ 48
and the light Of the *g* angel mind which look'd   „ 88
All th' intricate and labyrinthine veins Of the *g* vine of *Fable*,   „ 222
And the *g* bird sits on the opposite bough,   *The 'How' and the 'Why'* 28
but only seemed One shadow in the midst of a *g* light,   *The Mystic* 21
Of changeful cycles the *g* Pyramids   *A Fragment* 9
the poet at his will Lets the *g* world flit from him,   *D. of F. Women* 10
To this *g* cause of Freedom drink, my friends,   *Hands all Round* 11
And the *g* name of England round and round.
(repeat)   „ 24, 48, 60
To our *g* kinsmen of the West, my friends,   „ 47
With such a heat as lives in *g* creative rhymes.   *Sugg. by Reading* 6
I grant you one of the *g* Powers on earth,   „ 23
The hogs who can believe in nothing *g*,   „ 45

Greatness   We move so far from *g*, that I feel   „ 51
Who looks for Godlike *g* here shall see   „ 53

Grecian   And here the *G* ships did seem to be.   *Mablethorpe* 4

Green   (*See also* **Blue-green, Grassgreen**)   whose rapid interval
Parts Afric from *g* Europe,   *Timbuctoo* 3
Where are ye Thrones of the Western wave, fair Islands *g* ?   „ 42
For her the *g* grass shall not spring,   *Burial of Love* 28
O MAIDEN, fresher than the first *g* leaf   *Love and Sorrow* 1
And Oberwinter's vineyards *g*,   *O darling room* 8
G springtide, April promise, glad new year   *Lover's Tale i* 277
Think not thy tears will make my name grow *g*,—   „ 806

Greenness   And taken away the *g* of my life,   „ 625

Grew   my mental eye *g* large With such a vast circumference *Timbuctoo* 92
G thrillingly distinct and keen.   „ 98
So on an oaken sprout A goodly acorn *g* ;   *Lost Hope* 6
ere the Czar *G* to this strength among his deserts
cold ;   *Blow ye the trumpet* 6

Grief   *G* and sadness steal Symbols of each other ;   *Every day, etc.* 25
bitter *g* Doth hold the other half in sovranty.   *Love and Sorrow* 4
O *G* and Shame if while I preach of laws   *Sugg. by Reading* 37

H

Heart (*continued*)   My *h* is lighted at thine eyes,   *To——* 8
world will not change, and her *h* will not break. *I' the glooming light* 22
Grow closer to my *h*.   My *h* is warmer surely than
    the bosom of the main.   *Hero to Leander* 8
My *h* of *h's* art thou.   "   11
Thy *h* beats through thy rosy limbs   "   16
Albeit, his spirit and his secret *h*   *The Mystic* 7
ERE yet my *h* was sweet Love's tomb,   *Love, Pride, etc.* 1
My *h* the honey-comb.   "   4
My *h*, where Hope had been and was no more.   *Lost Hope* 4
I said to thee That thou hast half my *h*,   *Love and Sorrow* 4
Thou art my *h's* sun in love's crystalline: "   6
Thine is the bright side of my *h*, and thine My *h's*
    day, but the shadow of my *h*,   "   8
my *h's* night Thou canst not lighten even with *thy* light,   "   10
Almeida, if my *h* were substanceless,   "   13
Some vital heat as yet my *h* is wooing: *Could I outwear* 12
thou dost ever brood above The silence of all *h's*,   *Love* 14
We beat upon our aching *h's* with rage;   "   18
The hollow at *h* shall crouch forlorn, *English War Song* 12
For where is the *h* and strength of slaves?   "   36
There are no *h's* like English *h's*,   *National Song* 3
Unto their *h's* desire, (repeat)   "   12, 30
THERE are three things that fill my *h* with sighs *There are three things* 1
And dazzled to the *h* with glorious pain.   "   6
h is drunk with overwatchings night and day, *Hesperides, Song ii* 12
Think you *h's* are tennis balls To play with,   *Rosalind* 32
O DARLING room, my *h's* delight,   *O darling room* 1
Lest my *h* be overborne,   *Germ of 'Maud'* 5
The old Timon, with his noble *h*,   *New Timon* 3
To have the deep poetic *h*   "   23
We hate not France, but this man's *h* of stone. *Britons, guard* 17
as my *h* beat Twice to the melody of hers. *Lover's Tale i* 73
And my *e*yes read, they read aright, her *h* Was Lionel's: "   602
and *h* deep moans Feed and envenom,   "   819

Hearted   *See* **Hollow-hearted**
Hearth   But be not you the blatant traitors of the *h*. *Sugg. by Reading* 24
Heat (s)   region of white flame, Pure without *h*, *The Mystic* 44
In thy *h* of summerpride,   *The Grasshopper* 36
Some vital *h* as yet my heart is wooing: *Could I outwear* 12
wind which bloweth cold or *h* Would shatter   *Shall the hag* 6
Her frantic city's flashing *h's* had fire, *Hands all Round* 29
With such a *h* as lives in great creative rhymes. *Sugg. by Reading* 6
with the *h* Of their infolding element ; *Lover's Tale i* 614
the *h* Of the remorseful soul alive within,   "   681
Heat (verb)   But knowing all your power to *h* or cool, *Sugg. by Reading* 31
Heated   and slake With points of blastborne hail their
    h eyne !   *Shall the hag* 11
Heather   Through and through the flowered *h*.   *Dualisms* 5
Heave   'Gan rock and *h* upon that painted sea; *Lover's Tale ii* 199
Heaven   silent *H's* were blench'd with faery light, *Timbuctoo* 5
unfading foreheads of the Saints in *H* ?   "   54
Earth's As *H* than Earth is fairer.   "   170
landing-place is wrapt about with clouds Of glory of *H*.   "   200
I have rais'd thee higher to the Spheres of *H*,   "   216
Reacheth to every corner under *H*,   "   224
Larks in *h's* cope Sing :   *Every day, etc.* 28
The white moon is hid in her *h* above, *Hero to Leander* 3
THE varied earth, the moving *h*,   *Chorus* 1
But winds from *h* shook the acorn out,   *Lost Hope* 7
H weeps above the earth all night till morn, *Tears of Heaven* 1
And all the day *h* gathers back her tears   "   6
Over *h's* parapets the angels lean.   *To a Lady Sleep.* 10
H crieth after thee ; earth waileth for thee: *Love* 26
Till all the comets in *h* are cold,   *The Ringlet* 9
H guard them from her tyrants' jails ! *Hands all Round* 14
There hang within the *h's* a dark disgrace, *Sugg. by Reading* 41
had the angels, The watchers at *h's* gate, *Lover's Tale i* 616
from that *H* in whose light I bloom'd   "   624
Heavenward   Then parted *H* on the wing: *Timbuctoo* 251
Heaviest   And from the golden threshold had down-
    roll'd Their *h* thunder,   *Lover's Tale i* 618
Heavy   Why the *h* oak groans, and the white
    willows sigh ?   *The 'How' and the 'Why'* 15
The *h* thunder's girding might,   *Chorus* 13

Heavy (*continued*)   And t*h*e *h* melon sleeps On the level of the
    shore :   *Lotos-Eaters* 35
Dim shores, dense rains, and *h* clouded sea.   *Mablethorpe* 8
The lithe limbs bow'd as with a *h* weight *Lover's Tale i* 126
Heed   For the devil a whit we *h* 'em, (repeat) *National Song* 10, 28
Height   her silver *h's* Unvisited with dew of vagrant cloud, *Timbuctoo* 102
Imperial *h* Of Canopy o'ercanopied.   "   165
and some On the ancient *h's* divine ; *Lotos-Eaters* 17
When Love was worshipp'd upon every *h*, *Lover's Tale i* 323
Held   Pride came beneath and *h* a light. *Love, Pride, etc.* 6
Herald   The *h* lightning's starry bound,   *Chorus* 14
Herb   as the milky blood Of hateful *h's* *Lover's Tale i* 821
Heretic   Burn, you glossy *h*, burn,   *The Ringlet* 53
Hesper   Father *H*, Father *H*, watch, watch, ever
    and aye,   *Hesperides, Song ii* 1
H, the dragon, and sisters three,   "   24
Father *H*, Father *H*, watch, watch, night and day,   "   iii 1
H hateth Phosphor, evening hateth morn.   "   15
H, the dragon, and sisters three,   "   iv 25
Hewn   *See* **New-hewn, Rock-hewn**
Hid   white moon is *h* in her heaven above, *Hero to Leander* 3
H now and then with sliding cloud. *What time I wasted* 6
Hide   You *h* the hand that writes: *Sugg. by Reading* 8
High   pillars *h* Long time eras'd from Earth: *Timbuctoo* 12
glory of the place Stood out a pillar'd front of burnish'd
    gold Interminably *h*,   "   176
Why deep is not *h*, and is not deep ? *The 'How' and the 'Why'* 16
They seem'd *h* palaces and proud, *What time I wasted* 5
And mine, with love too *h* to be express'd *Lover's Tale i* 65
Higher   few there be So gross of heart who have not felt
    and known A *h* than they see :   *Timbuctoo* 212
I have rais'd thee *h* to the Spheres of Heaven,   "   216
H thro' secret splendours mounting still, *D. of F. Women* 11
Highest   THOUGH Night hath climbed her peak of *h* noon, *Though night* 1
Highland   a *h* leaning down a weight Of cliffs, *The Hesperides* 10
Highland-steep   Broken by the *h-s*, *Hesperides, Song iv* 5
High-necked   far off Seen by the *h-n* camel on the verge
    Journeying southward ?   *A Fragment* 18
Highness   His soldier-ridden *H* might incline *Britons, guard* 49
Hill   The blossoming abysses of your *h's* ?   *Timbuctoo* 44
thy *h's* enfold a City as fair As those   "   59
On the ridge of the *h* his banners rise ; *English War Song* 25
between The *h's* to Bingen have I been, *O darling room* 1
About sunset We came unto the *h* of woe, *Lover's Tale i* 365
With all her interchange of *h* and plain   "   694
Hillbrow   light Is shut out by the round of the
    tall *h* ;   *Hesperides, Song iv* 16
Himla   Father, old *H* weakens,   "   iii 7
Hindrance   to both of us It was delight, not *h*: *Lover's Tale i* 378
Hinge   Which was the *h* on which the door of Hope,   "   297
Hint   And a lad may wink, and a girl may *h*, *The Ringlet* 17
Hiss   Hark how the wild rain *h'es*, *Hero to Leander* 14
Hit   my skipping-rope Will *h* you in the eye. *Skipping-rope* 4
Hive   I was the *h* and Love the bee, *Love, Pride, etc.* 3
Hoar   On the loud *h* foam,   *Lotos-Eaters* 19
Hoarded   *H* wisdom brings delight. *Hesperides, Song ii* 6
Hoarhead   The *h* winter paving earth With sheeny white,   *Chorus* 18
Hoary   The clear Galaxy Shorn of its *h* lustre, *Timbuctoo* 106
Like a lone cypress, through the twilight *h*, *Me my own fate* 6
Zidonian Hanno, voyaging beyond The *h* promontory
    of Soloë Past Thymiaterion,   *The Hesperides* 3
Hog   *h's* who can believe in nothing great, *Sugg. by Reading* 45
Hold   ever *h* aloft the cloud Which droops low *The Mystic* 31
grief Doth *h* the other half in sovranty. *Love and Sorrow* 5
H up the lion of England on high (repeat) *English War Song* 27, 49
I *h* them all most dear; but oh ! black eyes, *There are three things* 7
How many the mystic fruit-tree *h's*, *Hesperides, Song ii* 8
But the thing I *h* in scorn,   *Germ of 'Maud'* 6
I pray'd aloud to God that he would *h* The hand of
    blessing over Lionel,   *Lover's Tale i* 791
Hollow (**adj.**)   In the *h* rosy vale to tarry, *Lotos-Eaters* 12
Hollow (**s**)   And the unsounded, undescended depth Of her
    black *h's*.   *Timbuctoo* 105
Dappled with *h* and alternate rise Of interpenetrated
    arc,   "   130

Hollow-hearted   Shall *h-h* apathy, The cruellest form of perfect scorn,   *Burial of Love* 17

Holy   And all the haunted place is dark and *h*.   *Check every outflash* 8
The end of day and beginning of night Make the apple *h* and bright, *H* and bright, round and full,   *Hesperides, Song iv* 10

Home   Heaven, Man's first, last *h*:   *Timbuctoo* 217
render up this glorious *h* To keen *Discovery* :   „ 243
To the melancholy *h* At the limit of the brine,   *Lotos-Eaters* 20
Call *h* your ships across Biscayan tides,   *Britons, guard* 37
H they brought him slain with spears. They brought him *h* at even-fall: *Home they brought him* 1

Honest   A health to Europe's *h* men !   *Hands all Round* 13
An *h* isolation need not fear The Court,   *Sugg. by Reading* 15

Honey (adj.)   To him the *h* dews of orient hope.   *Lover's Tale i* 675

Honey (s)   Love laboured *h* busily.   *Love, Pride, etc.* 2

Honey-comb   My heart the *h-c.*   „ 4
Lotos, sweet As the yellow *h*,   *Lotos-Eaters* 15

Honeysweet   Liquid gold, *h* thro' and thro'.   *Hesperides, Song i* 24

Honour   In *h* of the silverflecked morn :   *To a Lady Sleep.* 4
H comes with mystery;   *Hesperides, Song ii* 5

Honour (verb)   I *h* much, I say, this man's appeal.   *Sugg. by Reading* 49

Honourable   An *h* eld shall come upon thee.   *Though night* 14

Honour'd   The precious jewel of my *h* life,   *Lover's Tale ii* 78

Hope (s)   Men clung with yearning *H* which would not die.   *Timbuctoo* 27
men's *h*'s and fears take refuge in The fragrance   „ 226
The light of his *h*'s unfed,   *Burial of Love* 3
Let us weep in *h*—   *Every day, etc.* 32
You cast to ground the *h* which once was mine,   *Lost Hope* 1
My heart, where *H* had been and was no more.   „ 4
But men of long enduring *h*'s,   *New Timon* 17
But fire, to blast the *h*'s of men.   *Hands all Round* 30
hinge on which the door of *H*, Once turning,   *Lover's Tale i* 297
cold as were the *h*'s Of my lorn love !   „ 620
To him the honey dews of orient *h*.   „ 675
when *h* died, part of her eloquence Died with her ?   „ 751
I To stand within the level of their *h*'s,   „ 768
Because my *h* was widow'd,   „ 769
The course of *H* is dried,—   „ 808
For me all other *H*'s did sway from that   „ 857

Hope (verb)   For she will not *h*.   *I' the glooming light* 19
Could I thus *h* my lost delights renewing,   *Could I outwear* 9
Nay, dearest, teach me how to *h*,   *Skipping-rope* 9

Hopeless   Alone my *h* melancholy gloometh,   *Me my own fate* 5

Horizon   lights on my *h* shine Into my night   „ 11

Horn   Between the Southern and the Western *H*,   *The Hesperides* 5

Horned   Hark ! how sweet the *h* ewes bleat On the solitary steeps,   *Lotos-Eaters* 29

Horrible   *H* with the anger and the heat   *Lover's Tale i* 681

Horrid   and tho' *h* rifts Sent up the moaning of unhappy spirits   „ 612
As men do from a vague and *h* dream,   „ 786

Host   gather from afar The *h*'s to battle: *Blow ye the trumpet* 2
His ruthless *h* is bought with plunder'd gold,   *Britons, guard* 7

Hot   Strain the *h* spheres of his convulsèd eyes,   *Love* 37

Hour   (*See also* **Summerhours**)   Wingèd *h*'s are borne ;   *Every day, etc.* 4
For him the silent congregated *h*'s,   *The Mystic* 25
In thy *h* of love and revel,   *The Grasshopper* 35
So in thine *h* of dawn, the body's youth,   *Though night* 13
And careless what this *h* may bring,   *New Timon* 18
WHAT time I wasted youthful *h*'s   *What time I wasted* 1
Should he land here, and for one *h* prevail,   *Britons, guard* 55
Fair fall this hallow'd *h*,   *God bless our Prince* 8
Move with me to that *h*,   *Lover's Tale i* 296
since that *h*, My voice had somewhat falter'd—   „ 749

House (s)   And a *h* with a chimney-pot ?   *The 'How' and the 'Why'* 35

House (verb)   worms which *h* Beneath unshaken waters,   *Timbuctoo* 150

Household   But yours are not their *h* privacies.   *Sugg. by Reading* 22

How   Who will riddle me the *h* and the why? (repeat)   *The 'How' and the 'Why'* 9, 20
H you are you ? Why I am I?   „ 19
I feel there is something ; but *h* and what ?   „ 23
And stares in his face and shouts '*h*? *h*?'   „ 29
And chaunts '*h*? *h*?' the whole of the night.   „ 31
Who will riddle me the *h* and the what?   „ 36

Howling   Which flung strange music on the *h* winds,   *Timbuctoo* 80

Hue   And alternations of all *h*'s, he stood.   „ 76
an ether of black *h*, Investeth and ingirds   *The Mystic* 45
indue i' the spring *H*'s of fresh youth,   *Could I outwear* 3
in his writhings awful *h*'s begin To wander   *Love* 38
Dimples, roselips, and eyes of any *h*.   *There are three things* 4

Huge   even as the sea When weary of wild inroad buildeth up *H* mounds   *Timbuctoo* 15
Close by our ears, the *h* roots strain and creak),   *Lover's Tale i* 63
(*H* splinters, which the sap of earliest showers,   „ ii 45

Hum (s)   the *h* of men, Or other things talking   *Timbuctoo* 111

Hum (verb)   *H* a lovelay to the westwind at noontide.   *Dualisms* 2
Both alike, they *h* together   „ 4
Stands in her pew and *h*'s her decent psalm   *Sugg. by Reading* 63

Human   for my *h* brain Stagger'd beneath the vision,   *Timbuctoo* 185
With stony smirks at all things *h* and divine !   *Sugg. by Reading* 48

Hung   (*See also* **Low-hung**)   The snowy skirting of a garment *h*,   *Timbuctoo* 182
Pagods *h* with music of sweet bells: „ 234
low *h* on either gate of life,   *The Mystic* 32
earthquake-shattered chasm, *h* with shrubs,   *Lover's Tale i* 408
Or as the dew-drops on the petal *h*,   „ 558
Hopes did sway from that Which *h* the frailest: „ 858

Hurried   *h* through The riv'n rapt brain :   *Timbuctoo* 120

Hush   'Oh *h*, my joy, my sorrow.'   *Home they brought him* 10

Hut   Darken, and shrink and shiver into *h*'s,   *Timbuctoo* 246

I

I   How you are you ? Why *I* am I,   *The 'How' and the 'Why'* 19

Ideal   Down an *i* stream they ever float,   *Pallid thunderstricken* 2

Idle   Why waste they yonder Their *i* thunder ?   *Britons, guard* 40
Shall we stand *i*, Nor seek to bridle   „ 51

Idol   A perfect *I*, with profulgent brows   *A Fragment* 3
Thy shadowy *I*'s in the solitudes,   „ 15

Ilion   Here stood the infant *I* of the mind,   *Mablethorpe* 3

Ill   Nor good nor *i*, nor light nor shade,   *oἱ ῥέοντες* 10
So to guard my life from *i*,   *Germ of 'Maud'* 17
Alas, our Church ! alas, her growing *i*'s,   *Sugg. by Reading* 67

Illimitable   *I* range of battlement On battlement,   *Timbuctoo* 164
Listenest the lordly music flowing from Th' *i* years.   „ 219

Image   did pause To worship mine own *i*,   *Lover's Tale i* 68
mine *i* in her eyes,   „ 70

Imaging   *i* The soft inversion of her tremulous Domes ;   *Timbuctoo* 231

Imbue   presence of his eyes To *i* his lustre ;   *Lover's Tale i* 419

Immingled   In a new birth, *i* with my own,   „ 732

Immortality   No withered *i*,   *The Grasshopper* 28

Impelling   *See* **Self-impelling**

Imperial   and thou of later name *I* Eldorado roof'd with gold :   *Timbuctoo* 24
and the *I* height Of Canopy o'ercanopied.   „ 165

Imperishable   *I* presences serene,   *The Mystic* 13

Impleachèd   The fragrance of its complicated glooms And cool *i* twilights.   *Timbuctoo* 228

Imprison'd   unhappy spirits *I* in her centre,   *Lover's Tale i* 614

Impulse   The issue of strong *i*, hurried through   *Timbuctoo* 120
each th' effect Of separate *i*,   „ 127
from this *i* Continuing and gathering ever,   *Lover's Tale i* 493

Increasing   level calm Is ridg'd with restless and *i* spheres   *Timbuctoo* 125 „ 139

Indecision   entwine The *i* of my present mind   *Love* 31

Indian   serpent in his agonies Awestricken *I*'s ;   *Timbuctoo* 100

Indistinctest   The *i* atom in deep air,   *Could I outwear* 2

Indue   *i* i' the spring Hues of fresh youth,   *Timbuctoo* 189

Ineffable   Then with a mournful and *i* smile,   *Mablethorpe* 3

Infant   Here stood the *i* Ilion of the mind,   *Timbuctoo* 47

Infinite   Where are the *i* ways which, Seraphtrod,   „ 11

Infixed   Giant of old Time *i* The limits   *Lover's Tale i* 615

Infolding   with the heat Of their *i* element ;   *Timbuctoo* 40

Inform   wherewith Her phantasy *i*'s them.   *The Mystic* 46

Ingird   Investeth and *i*'s all other lives.   *Me my own fate* 8

Inland   One cypress on an *i* promontory.   *Rosalind* 29
Through vineyards from an *i* bay.

Inmost   The written secrets of her *i* soul Lay like an open scroll   *Lover's Tale i* 600

Inner Among the *i* columns far retir'd At midnight, *Timbuctoo* 31
The bare word KISS hath made my *i* soul To tremble *Oh, Beauty* 12
In my *i* eyes again, *Germ of 'Maud'* 4
Sheer thro' the black-walk'd cliff the rapid brook
Shot down his *i* thunders, *Lover's Tale* i 372
Innocent Thy pleasant wiles Forgotten, and thine *i* joy? *Burial of Love* 16
(the *i* light Of earliest youth pierced through and
through *The Mystic* 28
Inroad as the sea When weary of wild *i* *Timbuctoo* 14
Insect But an *i* lithe and strong, *The Grasshopper* 7
Insolence And *i* of uncontrolled Fate, *Lover's Tale* i 688
Intellect apart In *i* and power and will, *The Mystic* 38
Intense unto me I delight and rapture that I breathed, *Lover's Tale* i 381
I had lived That *i* moment thro' eternity. „ 496
Intensest starlit wings which burn Fanlike and fibred, with
i bloom: *Timbuctoo* 156
Intent Eye feeding upon eye with deep *i*; *Lover's Tale* i 64
Interchange With all her *i* of hill and plain „ 694
Interpenetrated Dappled with hollow and alternate rise Of *i*
arc, *Timbuctoo* 131
Interval whose rapid *i* Parts Afric from green Europe, „ 2
crumbling from their parent slope At slender *i*, „ 124
Intricate All th' *i* and labyrinthine veins Of that great vine
of *Fable*, „ 221
Invariable Awful with most *i* eyes. *The Mystic* 24
Inversion soft *i* of her tremulous Domes; *Timbuctoo* 232
Investeth I and ingirds all other lives. *The Mystic* 46
Inviolate The headland with *i* white snow, *Timbuctoo* 204
Involving thoughts I and embracing each with each „ 116
Inward Is one of those who know no strife Of *i* woe or outward
fear; *Rosalind* 4
Inwoven So each with each *i* lived with each, *Lover's Tale* i 566
Iron Break through your *i* shackles—fling them far. *Blow ye the trumpet* 4
From *i* limbs and tortured nails! *Hands all Round* 16
Irresistible Which but to look on for a moment fill'd My
eyes with *i* sweet tears, *Timbuctoo* 191
Island Thrones of the Western wave, fair *I*'s green? „ 42
Islander Oh! *i*'s of Ithaca, we will not wander more, *Lotos-Eaters* 37
Oh! *i*'s of Ithaca, we will return no more. „ 40
Isle little *i* of Ithaca, beneath the day's decline. „ 22
The public conscience of our noble *i*, *Sugg. by Reading* 3
Isolation *i* need not fear The Court, the Church, „ 15
Issue The *i* of strong impulse, hurried *Timbuctoo* 120
I of its own substance, *Love and Sorrow* 10
Issueth When thy light perisheth That from thee *i*, *The lintwhite* 14
Issuing translucent wave, Forth *i* from darkness, *Timbuctoo* 230
in the pride of beauty *i* A sheeny snake, *Could I outwear* 15
Ithaca Men of *I*, this is meeter, *Lotos-Eaters* 11
little isle of *I*, beneath the day's decline. „ 22
Oh! islanders of *I*, we will not wander more, „ 37
Oh! islanders of *I*, we will return no more. „ 40
Ivy (adj.) Until the pleached *i* tress had wound Round
my worn limbs, *Lover's Tale* i 637
Ivy (s) And *i* darkly-wreathed, *Anacreontics* 4
Ivy-leaves bramble and the shining gloss Of *i-l*, *Lover's Tale* i 374

J

Jail Heaven guard them from her tyrants' *j*'s! *Hands all Round* 14
Jest It looks too arrogant a *j*— *New Timon* 42
Jesuit The *J* laughs, and reckoning on his chance, *Britons, guard* 32
Jewel The precious *j* of my honour'd life, *Lover's Tale* ii 78
Journeying on the verge *J* southward? *A Fragment* 19
Joy wiles Forgotten, and thine innocent *j*? *Burial of Love* 16
J is sorrow's brother; *Every day, etc.* 24
O *j*! O bliss of blisses! *Hero to Leander* 10
J of the summerplain, *The Grasshopper* 2
Soon thy *j* is over, „ 31
Turn cloud to light, and bitterness to *j*, *Though night* 6
in him light and *j* and strength abides; *Love* 42
In summer still a summer *j* resumeth. *Me my own fate* 4
' Oh hush, my *j*, my sorrow.' *Home they brought him* 10

Joy (continued) And with a fearful self-impelling *j* *Lover's Tale* i 389
Juggle And a *j* of the brain. *Germ of 'Maud'* 8
Juliet SAINTED *J*! dearest name! *To ——* 1
Divinest *J*, I love thee, and live; „ 3

K

Keen Each failing sense As with a momentary flash of light
Grew thrillingly distinct and *k*. *Timbuctoo* 98
When I must render up this glorious home To *k* Discovery: „ 244
pierced through and through with all *K* knowledges of
low-embowed eld) *The Mystic* 30
With a flash of frolic scorn And *k* delight, *Rosalind* 16
Keen-eyed *K-e* Sisters, singing airily, *Hesperides, Song* i 25
Keep brain could *k* afloat The subtle spirit. *Oh, Beauty* 10
That wish to *k* their people fools; *Hands all Round* 54
To soothe a civic wound or *k* it raw, *Sugg. by Reading* 9
God *k* their lands allied, *God bless our Prince* 2
Keeping *K* unchanged The purport of their coinage. *Lover's Tale* i 733
Kept To that half-pagan harlot *k* by France! *Sugg. by Reading* 70
Kernelled See Goldenkernelled
Khan Than when Zamoysky smote the Tartar *K*, *Blow ye the trumpet* 12
Kill Would, unrelenting, *K* all dissenting, *Britons, guard* 34
Killed Who *k* the girls and thrill'd the boys *New Timon* 9
Kin so *k* to earth Pleasaunce fathers pain— *Every day, etc.* 14
Kind Or propagate again her loathèd *k*, *Shall the hag* 2
I can shadow forth my bride As I knew her fair and *k* *Germ of 'Maud'* 10
King Thou comest, as a *K*. *The lintwhite* 20
Your portals statued with old *k*'s and queens, *Cambridge* 4
We curse the crimes of Southern *k*'s, *Hands all Round* 17
They *can* be understood by *k*'s. „ 52
I fear for you, as for some youthful *k*, *Sugg. by Reading* 9
Like to the wild youth of an evil *k*, *Lover's Tale* i 344
Kingdom *K*'s lapse, and climates change, and races die; *Hesperides, Song* ii 4
Kinsman To our great *kinsmen* of the West, *Hands all Round* 47
To our dear *kinsmen* of the West, „ 59
Kiss (s) waters Betraying the close *k*'es of the wind— *Timbuctoo* 209
Lest thy *k* should be the last. *Hero to Leander* 6
Come bathe me with thy *k*'es, „ 12
I'll stay thee with my *k*'es. „ 22
billow will embrace thee with a *k* as soft as mine. „ 27
As with one *k* to touch thy blessèd cheek. *Oh, Beauty* 8
word *K* hath made my inner soul To tremble „ 12
That a doubt will only come for a *k*, *The Ringlet* 21
Kiss (verb) Oh! *k* me, *k* me, once again, *Hero to Leander* 5
Oh *k* me ere we part; „ 7
Might I but *k* thy hand! *Oh, Beauty* 5
Methinks if I should *k* thee, *The Ringlet* 4
To *k* it night and day, „ 23
' Then *k* it, love, and put it by: „ 23
' Come, *k* it, love, and put it by: „ 41
Kissed peaceful lips are *k* With earliest rays, *A Fragment* 22
And a fear to be *k* away.' *The Ringlet* 22
Ringlet, I *k* you night and day, „ 26
Knee Nathless she ever clasps the marble *k*'s, *Timbuctoo* 37
Then flinging myself down upon my *k*'s *Lover's Tale* i 789
Kneel *K*'s the pale Priestess in deep faith, *Timbuctoo* 34
Knew Ye *k* him not: he was not one of ye, *The Mystic* 2
never learnt to love who never *k* to weep. *Love and Sorrow* 18
my bride As I *k* her fair and kind *Germ of 'Maud'* 10
a familiar face: I *thought* we *k* him: *New Timon* 7
A sharper lesson than we ever *k*. *Sugg. by Reading* 12
as I *k*, they two did love each other, *Lover's Tale* i 766
Knoll Warbled from yonder *k* of solemn larches, *Check every outflash* 10
Know I *k* not if I shape These things *Timbuctoo* 133
I *k* there is somewhat; but what and why! *The 'How' and the 'Why'* 24
How could ye *k* him? *The Mystic* 41
To *k* thee who art wisdom, and old age Is but to *k* thee: *Love* 15
one of those who *k* no strife Of inward woe *Rosalind* 3
WE *k* him, out of Shakespeare's art, *New Timon* 1
We *k* thee most, we love thee best, *Hands all Round* 39
yet the 'not too much' is all the rule she *k*'s. *Sugg. by Reading* 60
And then shall I *k* it is all true gold *The Ringlet* 7

Know (*continued*) I *k* not, faith : — *Lover's Tale* i 695
Knowest *k* I dare not look into thine eyes, — *Oh, Beauty* 4
Knoweth *k* not Beyond the sound he lists : — *Lover's Tale* i 657
Knowing But *k* all your power to heat or cool, — *Sugg. by Reading* 31
   Have ye aught that is worth the *k* ? — *1865-1866* 5
   But aught that is worth the *k* ? ' — " 9
Knowledge Keen *k*'s of low-embowèd eld) — *The Mystic* 30
Known felt and *k* A higher than they see : — *Timbuctoo* 211
   the free speech that makes a Briton *k*: — *Britons, guard* 29
   K when their faces are forgot in the land. — *Lover's Tale* i 804

L

Labour He said, 'The *l* is not small ; — *What time I wasted* 7
   the shore Than *l* in the ocean, — *Lotos-Eaters* 39
Laboured Love *l* honey busily. — *Love, Pride, etc.* 2
Labyrinthine All th' intricate and *l* veins Of the great vine
   of *Fable*, — *Timbuctoo* 221
Lad And a *l* may wink, and a girl may hint, — *The Ringlet* 17
Laden Strove to uprise, *l* with mournful thanks, — *Lover's Tale* i 748
Laid Beside her are *l*, Her mattock and spade, — *I' the glooming light* 5
   what time *l* low And crushing the thick fragrant reeds — *Love* 31
Lain I had *l* as still, And blind and motionless — *Lover's Tale* i 618
   new-hewn sepulchre, Where man had never *l*, — " 714
   the grass was warm where I had *l*, — " 790
Lake opal width Of her small glowing *l*'s, — *Timbuctoo* 102
   large *l* From pressure of descendant crags, — " 121
   length of porch and *l* and boundless hall, — " 180
Lameness strangling sorrow weigh Mine utterances with *l*. — *Lover's Tale* i 25
Lamp Above her head the weak *l* dips and winks — *Timbuctoo* 35
Lance Rode upon his father's *l*, — *Home they brought him* 8
Land (s) (*See also* **Lotos-land**) In music and in light o'er *l* and sea. — *Love* 28
   There is no *l* like England (repeat) — *National Song* 1, 5, 19, 23
   Mellowed in a *l* of rest ; — *Hesperides, Song iv* 12
   God keep their *l*'s allied, — *God bless our Prince* 2
   Known when their faces are forgot in the *l*. — *Lover's Tale* i 804
Land (verb) Should he *l* here, and for one hour prevail, — *Britons, guard* 55
Landing-place *l-p* is wrapt about with clouds — *Timbuctoo* 199
Land-wind But the *l-w* wandereth, — *Hesperides, Song iv* 4
Languor With *l* of most hateful smiles, — *Burial of Love* 19
Lapse descendant crags, which *l* Disjointed, — *Timbuctoo* 122
   Kingdoms *l*, and climates change, and races die ; — *Hesperides, Song i* 507
Lapt Which, *l* in seeming dissolution, — *Lover's Tale* i 507
Larch Warbled from yonder knoll of solemn *l*'es, — *Check every outflash* 10
Large and my mental eye grew *l* With such a vast circum-
   ference of thought, — *Timbuctoo* 92
   as when in some *l* lake From pressure of descendant crags, — " 121
Larger Pure without heat, into a *l* air Upburning, — *The Mystic* 44
Largess Thy golden *l* fling, — *The lintwhite* 22
Lark *L*'s in heaven's cope Sing : — *Every day, etc.* 28
   Though long ago listening the poisèd *l*, — *To a Lady Sleep.* 8
Last (adj.) I have rais'd thee higher to the Spheres of
   Heaven, Man's first, *l* home : — *Timbuctoo* 217
   Love is dead ; His *l* arrow sped ; — *Burial of Love* 9
   The world's *l* tempest darkens overhead ; — *Britons, guard* 2
   Lest thy kiss should be the *l*. — *Hero to Leander* 6
Last (s) he had well nigh reached The *l*, — *The Mystic* 43
Lasting ME my own fate to *l* sorrow doometh : — *Me my own fate* 1
Later and thou of *l* name Imperial Eldorado roof'd with gold : — *Timbuctoo* 23
Latest Oh City ! Oh *l* Throne ! where I was rais'd To be a
   mystery of loveliness — " 240
Lattice From an half-open *l* looked at *me*. — *There are three things* 12
Laugh We *l*, we cry, we are born, we die, — *The 'How' and the 'Why'* 8
   When we *l*, and our mirth Apes the happy vein, — *Every day, etc.* 12
   L not loudly ; watch the treasure Of the wisdom — *Hesperides, Song i* 13
   Jesuit *l*'s, and reckoning on his chance, — *Britons, guard* 32
Laugheth Madness *l* loud : — *Every day, etc.* 9
Laughing *l* clearly A light and thrilling laughter, — *Anacreontics* 9
Laughter *L* bringeth tears : — *Every day, etc.* 18
   laughing clearly A light and thrilling *l*, — *Anacreontics* 10
Laved mine own image, *l* in light, — *Lover's Tale* i 68
Law wondrous *l*'s which regulate The fierceness — *Timbuctoo* 147

Law (*continued*) Nor essence nor eternal *l*'s : — οἱ ῥέοντες 11
   Our ancient boast is this—we reverence *l*. — *Sugg. by Reading* 34
   O Grief and Shame if while I preach of *l*'s — " 37
Lawless The *l* comets as they glare, — *Chorus* 27
Lay (s) (*See also* **Lovelay**) You did late review my *l*'s, — *To C. North* 1
Lay (verb) wave unshockèd *L*'s itself calm and wide, — *Dualisms* 7
   How often, when a child I *l* reclined, — *Mablethorpe* 1
   L like an open scroll before my view, — *Lover's Tale* i 601
   And blind and motionless as then I *l* ! — " 619
Lea which the fearful springtide flecks the *l*, — *Love and Sorrow* 2
   Two children lovelier than love, adown the *l* are singing, — *Dualisms* 14
   At noon-tide beneath the *l* ; — *Lotos-Eaters* 6
   The drain-cut levels of the marshy *l*,— — *Mablethorpe* 6
Lead turretstairs are wet That *l* into the sea. — *Hero to Leander* 37
   Will it *l* me to the grave ? — *Germ of 'Maud'* 24
   Oh ! *l* me tenderly, for fear the mind — *Lover's Tale* i 23
Leaf (*See also* **Ivy-leaves**) growth of shadowing *l* and
   clusters rare, — *Timbuctoo* 223
   O MAIDEN, fresher than the first green *l* — *Love and Sorrow* 1
   What happy air shall woo The wither'd *l* — *Lover's Tale* i 622
Lean Over heaven's parapets the angels *l*. — *To a Lady Sleep.* 10
Leander And when thou art dead, *L*, — *Hero to Leander* 30
   L ! go not yet. — " 38
Leaneth my wish *l* evermore Still to believe it— — *Lover's Tale* i 270
Leaning Beneath a highland *l* down a weight Of cliffs, — *The Hesperides* 10
Leap *L* the little waterfalls That sing — *Rosalind* 23
   And the merry lizard *l*'s, — *Lotos-Eaters* 31
   The boy began to *l* and prance, — *Home they brought him* 7
Leaping Ever *l*, ever singing, — *The Grasshopper* 43
Learn lest we *l* A sharper lesson than we ever knew. — *Sugg. by Reading* 88
   For what is this which now I *l*, — *The Ringlet* 51
Learnt-Learn'd They never *learnt* to love who never
   knew to weep. — *Love and Sorrow* 18
   When I *learnt* from whom it came, — *To C. North* 5
   Because she *learn'd* them with me. — *Lover's Tale* i 290
Leave If thou dost *l* the sun, — *The lintwhite* 32
Leaved *See* **Silverleaved**
Led By such men *l*, our press had ever been — *Sugg. by Reading* 2
Ledgers Too much we make our *L*, Gods. — *Hands all Round* 20
Left (hand) In any town, to *l* or right, — *O darling room* 14
Left (verb) and I Was *l* alone on Calpe, — *Timbuctoo* 252
   Till we were *l* to fight for truth alone. — *Britons, guard* 35
   Or moisture of the vapour, *l* in clinging, — *Lover's Tale* ii 46
   And, trampled on, *l* to its own decay. — " 81
Legend And much I mus'd on *l*'s quaint and old — *Timbuctoo* 16
   hill of woe, so call'd Because the *l* ran that, — *Lover's Tale* i 366
Length *l* of porch and lake and boundless hall, — *Timbuctoo* 180
Lenora A garland for *L*. — *Anacreontics* 7
   L, laughing clearly A light and thrilling laughter, — " 9
Lesson lest we learn A sharper *l* than we ever knew. — *Sugg. by Reading* 88
Lethargised So *l* discernment in the sense, — *Lover's Tale* i 663
Level (adj.) the *l* calm Is ridg'd with restless and increasing
   spheres — *Timbuctoo* 124
Level (s) melon sleeps On the *l* of the shore : — *Lotos-Eaters* 36
   The drain-cut *l*'s of the marshy lea,— — *Mablethorpe* 6
   I To stand within the *l* of their hopes, — *Lover's Tale* i 768
Levelling Rapidly *l* eager eyes. — *Hesperides, Song ii* 18
Liar Peace-lovers we—but who can trust a *l* ?— — *Britons, guard* 14
Libraries Your bridges and your busted *l*, — *Cambridge* 3
Libyan *See* **Lybian**
Lid THOU whose fringèd *l*'s I gaze upon, — *To a Lady Sleep.* 1
   commend the tears to creep From my charged *l*'s. — *Could I outwear* 11
Lie (s) fie You golden *l*. — *The Ringlet* 44
Lie (verb) What the life is ? where the soul
   may *l* ? — *The 'How' and the 'Why'* 33
   crushing the thick fragrant reeds he *l*'s, — *Love* 32
   For her there *l* in wait millions of foes, — *Sugg. by Reading* 59
Life The precious jewel of my honour'd *l*, — *Lover's Tale* ii 78
   As air is th' *l* of flame : — *Timbuctoo* 20
   notes of busy *l* in distant worlds Beat — " 113
   The permeating *l* which courseth through — " 220
   Some say this *l* is pleasant, — *The 'How' and the 'Why'* 3
   Why the *l* goes when the blood is spilt ? — " 32
   What the *l* is ? where the soul may lie ? — " 33
   If to love be *l* alone, — *To* —— 2

Lizard	And the merry *l* leaps,	*Lotos-Eaters* 31
Loathe	thinking men of England, *l* a tyranny.	*Sugg. by Reading* 12
Loathèd	Or propagate again her *l* kind,	*Shall the hag* 2
	And damn'd unto his *l* tenement.	*Lover's Tale i* 683
Loathing	That, strongly *l*, greatly broke.	*New Timon* 4
Loathly	Oh! rather had some *l* ghastful brow,	*Lover's Tale i* 676
Locality	I took delight in this *l*!	*Mablethorpe* 2
Lock	Thy *l*'s are dripping balm;	*Hero to Leander* 20
	Thy *l*'s are full of sunny sheen	*The lintwhite* 28
Locked	*See* **Goldenlocked**	
Lone	Among the inner columns far retir'd At midnight, in the *l* Acropolis.	*Timbuctoo* 32
	As dwellers in *l* planets look upon The mighty disk	*Love* 20
	Like a *l* cypress, through the twilight hoary,	*Me my own fate* 9
Lonely	But yet my *l* spirit follows thine,	"
Long	pillars high *L* time eras'd from Earth:	*Timbuctoo* 13
	The nightingale, with *l* and low preamble,	*Check every outflash* 9
	But men of *l* enduring hopes,	*New Timon* 17
	Because the legend ran that, *l* time since,	*Lover's Tale i* 366
	Her *l* ringlets, Drooping and beaten with the plaining wind,	" 734
	And their *l* life a dream of linked love,	" 795
Longer	No *l* in the dearest use of mine—	" 599
Look	to *l* on for a moment fill'd My eyes	*Timbuctoo* 190
	With glazed eye She *l*'s at her grave:	*I' the glooming light* 15
	dwellers in lone planets *l* upon The mighty disk	*Love* 20
	L's through the thickstemmed woods by day and night	" 44
	knowest I dare not *l* into thine eyes,	*Oh, Beauty* 4
	L to him, father, lest he wink,	*Hesperides, Song ii* 11
	L from west to east along:	" iii 6
	You never *l* but half content:	*New Timon* 26
	It *l*'s too arrogant a jest—	" 42
	No, nor the Press! and *l* you well to that—	*Sugg. by Reading* 17
	Who *l*'s for Godlike greatness here shall see	" 53
	your ringlets, That *l* so golden-gay,	*The Ringlet* 2
	Refused to *l* his author in the face,	*Lover's Tale i* 697
Look'd	*l* into my face With his unutterable,	*Timbuctoo* 66
	I *l*, but not Upon his face,	" 85
	angel mind which *l* from out The starry glowing	" 88
	Of late such eyes *l* at me—	*There are three things* 9
	From an half-open lattice *l* at me.	" 12
Looking	(*See also* **Downlooking**) *L* athwart the burning flats,	*A Fragment* 17
	L warily Every way,	*Hesperides, Song i* 26
	L under silver hair with a silver eye.	" ii 2
Lord	We *l* it o'er the sea; (*repeat*)	*National Song* 16, 34
Lordly	Listenest the *l* music flowing from Th' illimitable years.	*Timbuctoo* 218
Lorn	cold as were the hopes Of my *l* love!	*Lover's Tale i* 621
Lose	But *l* themselves in utter emptiness.	*Love and Sorrow* 16
	We shall *l* eternal pleasure,	*Hesperides, Song i* 11
	Then I *l* it: it will fly:	*Germ of 'Maud'* 25
Loss	Unknowing fear, Undreading *l*,	*The Grasshopper* 17
		Chorus 26
Lost	*L* in its effulgence sleeps,	*Germ of 'Maud'* 3
	beauteous face Of the maiden, that I *l*,	*Britons, guard* 19
	We hate not France, but France has *l* her voice	*Could I outwear* 9
	Could I thus hope my *l* delights renewing,	*Lotos-Eaters* 14
Lotos	We will eat the *L*,	" 27
	Lotos-land, till the *L* fail;	*Lotos-Eaters* 13
Lotos-eater	Like a dreamy *L-e*, a delirious *L-e*!	" 25
	With the blissful *L-e*'s pale	" 27
Lotos-land	We will abide in the golden vale Of the *L-l*,	*The Hesperides* 7
Lotusflute	Nor melody o' the Lybian *l*	*Hero to Leander* 7
Loud	And the *l* sea roars below.	*The Grasshopper* 32
	A summer of *l* song,	
	edicts of his fear Are mellowed into music, borne abroad By the *l* winds,	*Love* 9
	On the *l* hoar foam,	*Lotos-Eaters* 19
	The moanings in the forest, the *l* stream,	*Lover's Tale ii* 123
Love (s)	lowest depths were, as with visible *l*,	*Timbuctoo* 49
	L is dead; (*repeat*)	*Burial of Love* 8, 13
	Oh, truest *l*! art thou forlorn,	" 14
	Till *L* have his full revenge.	" 30
	L unreturned is like the fragrant frame	*To* —— 5
	OH go not yet, my *l*, (*repeat*)	*Hero to Leander* 1, 32
	In thine hour of *l* and revel,	*The Grasshopper* 35
	·ERE yet my heart was sweet *L*'s tomb, *L* laboured honey busily.	*Love, Pride, etc.* 1

Love (s) (*continued*)	I was the hive and *L* the bee,	*Love, Pride, etc.* 3
	Sweet *L* was withered in his cell; Pride took *L*'s sweets, and by a spell Did change	" 8
	Thou art my heart's sun in *l*'s crystalline:	*Love and Sorrow* 6
	THOU, from the first, unborn, undying *l*,	*Love* 1
	brood above The silence of all hearts, unutterable *L*.	" 14
	Come, thou of many crowns, white-robèd *l*,	" 24
	Two children lovelier than *l*, adown the lea	*Dualisms* 14
	Fair year, with brows of royal *l* Thou comest,	*The Lintwhite* 19
	When in this valley first I told my *l*.	*Check every outflash* 14
	'Then take it, *l*, and put it by;	*The Ringlet* 11
	'Then kiss it, *l*, and put it by:	" 23
	'Come, kiss it, *l*, and put it by:	" 41
	with *l* too high to be express'd Arrested in its sphere,	*Lover's Tale i* 65
	Where *L* was worshipp'd upon every height, Where *L* was worshipp'd under every tree—	" 323
	cold as were the hopes Of my lorn *l*!	" 620
	if he had fall'n In *l* in twilight?	" 700
	And why was I to darken their pure *l*,	" 765
	And their long life a dream of linked *l*,	" 795
	till their *l* Shall ripen to a proverb unto all,	" 802
	That in the death of *l*, if e'er they loved,	" 849
Love (verb)	If to *l* be life alone,	*To* —— 2
	I *l* thee, and live; and yet Love unreturned never learnt to *l* who never knew to weep.	" 4
	For her I *l* so dearly,	*Love and Sorrow* 18
	We know thee most, we *l* thee best,	*Anacreontics* 6
	How much I *l* this writer's manly style!	*Hands all Round* 39
	She *l*'s a little scandal which excites;	*Sugg. by Reading* 1
	as I knew, they two did *l* each other,	" 57
	Did I *l* Camilla?	*Lover's Tale i* 766
	Let them so *l* that men and boys may say, Lo! how they *l* each other!	" 770
		" 801
Loved	And *l* me ever after.	*Anacreontics* 12
	It was the man she *l*, even Lionel,	*Lover's Tale i* 671
	That in the death of Love, if e'er they *l*,	" 849
Lovelay	Hum a *l* to the westwind at noontide.	*Dualisms* 2
Lovelier	Two children *l* than love, adown the lea, This is *l* and sweeter,	" 14
		Lotos-Eaters 10
Loveliest	Most *l*, most delicious union?	*Lover's Tale i* 275
Loveliness	Which fill'd the Earth with passing *l*,	*Timbuctoo* 79
	a mystery of *l* Unto all eyes,	" 241
Lovely	Most pale and clear and *l* distances.	*The Mystic* 35
	She is *l* by my side In the silence of my life—	*Germ of 'Maud'* 12
Lover	*See* **Peace-lover**	
Low	E'en so my thoughts, erewhile so *l*, now felt	*Timbuctoo* 157
	Thy voice is sweet and *l*;	*Hero to Leander* 33
	The nightingale, with long and *l* preamble,	*Check every outflash* 9
	And the *l* west wind, breathing afar,	*Hesperides, Song iv* 8
	Unfrequent, *l*, as tho' it told its pulses;	*Lover's Tale ii* 58
Low-built	*L-b*, mud-walled, Barbarian settlement,	*Timbuctoo* 248
Low-buried	*L-b* fathom deep beneath with thee,	*O sad No more!* 8
Low-embowèd	Keen knowledges of *l-e* eld)	*The Mystic* 30
Lower	To charm a *l* sphere of fulminating fools.	*Sugg. by Reading* 30
Lowest	Whose *l* depths were, as with visible love,	*Timbuctoo* 49
Low-hung	*l-h* tresses, dipp'd In the fierce stream,	*Lover's Tale i* 374
Loyal	Be *l*, if you wish for wholesome rule:	*Sugg. by Reading* 33
	We still were *l* in our wildest fights,	" 35
Loyally	Or *l* disloyal battled for our rights.	" 36
Lurlei	vineyards green, Musical *L*;	*O darling room* 9
Luscious	The *l* fruitage clustereth mellowly,	*Hesperides, Song iv* 19
Lustre	clear Galaxy Shorn of its hoary *l*,	*Timbuctoo* 106
Lutestring	inner soul To tremble like a *l*,	*Oh, Beauty* 13
Lybian	Nor melody o' the *L* lotusflute	*The Hesperides* 7
Lying	He often *l* broad awake,	*The Mystic* 36
	By *l* priest's the peasant's votes controlled.	*Britons, guard* 8

M

Mad	Should war's *m* blast again be blown,	*Hands all Round* 41
Made	Had purified, and chastened, and *m* free.	*The Mystic* 10
	Because the earth hath *m* her state forlorn	*Tears of Heaven* 3
	For nothing is, but all is *m*,	*οἱ ῥέοντες* 12
	A Lion, you, that *m* a noise,	*New Timon* 11

Made (*continued*) By diminution *m* most glorious, *Lover's Tale* i 71
Which waste with the breath that *m* 'em. ,, 475
The very spirit of Paleness *m* still paler ,, 679
my refluent health *m* tender quest Unanswer'd, ,, 742
drove them onward—*m* them sensible ; • ,, ii 77
Madness *M* laugheth loud : *Every day, etc.* 17
Mahmoud Better wild *M's* war-cry once again ! *Sugg. by Reading* 83
Maid There are no *m's* like English *m's*, *National Song* 25
Maiden (adj.) (when I view Fair *m* forms moving like melodies), *There are three things* 3
Maiden (s) O *M*, fresher than the first green leaf *Love and Sorrow* 1
beauteous face Of the *m*, that I lost, *Germ of 'Maud'* 3
Mail in *m* of argent light Shot into gold, *Pallid thunderstricken* 12
Mailèd Thou art a *m* warrior in youth and strength complete ; *The Grasshopper* 13
Main My heart is warmer surely than the bosom of the *m*. *Hero to Leander* 9
Majestic In accents of *m* melody, *Timbuctoo* 192
The mighty disk of their *m* sun, *Love* 21
Make Why two and two *m* four ? *The 'How' and the 'Why'* 13
If ye sing not, if ye *m* false measure, *Hesperides, Song* i 10
Five and three (Let it not be preached abroad) *m* an awful mystery. ,, 16
M the apple holy and bright, ,, iv 10
the free speech that *m's* a Briton known. *Britons, guard* 29
M their cause your own. ,, 54
Too much we *m* our Ledgers, Gods. *Hands all Round* 20
Who *m* the emphatic One, by whom is all, *Sugg. by Reading* 81
I call on you To *m* opinion warlike, ,, 87
lake, that, flooding, *m's* Cushions of yellow sand ; *Lover's Tale* i 536
her whom he would *m* his wedded wife, Camilla ! ,, 793
Think not thy tears will *m* my name grow green,— ,, 806
Maketh Ever alone She *m* her moan : *I' the glooming light* 17
Making *M* their day dim, so we gaze on thee. *Love* 23
Man being in the heart of *M* As air is th' life of flame : *Timbuctoo* 19
Men clung with yearning Hope which would not die. ,, 27
' O child of *m*, why muse you here alone ,, 77
the hum of *men*, Or other things talking ,, 111
Spirit than I to sway The heart of *m* : ,, 196
Heaven, *M's* first, last home : ,, 217
men's hopes and fears take refuge in The fragrance ,, 226
Child of *M*, See'st thou yon river, ,, 228
I am any *m's* suitor, If any will be my tutor ; *The 'How' and the 'Why'* 1
wondrous tones Of *m* and beast are full of strange Astonishment *Chorus* 9
all *men* adore thee ; Heaven crieth after thee ; *Love* 25
none shall grieve For the *m* who fears to die : *English War Song* 4
scorn of the many shall cleave To the *m* who fears to die. ,, 6
There are no *men* like Englishmen, *National Song* 7
M is the measure of all truth Unto himself. *oi ρέοντες* 3
All *men* do walk in sleep, ,, 5
Men of Ithaca, this is meeter, *Lotos-Eaters* 11
As when a *m*, that sails in a balloon, *D. of F. Women* 1
The padded *m*—that wears the stays— *New Timon* 8
But *men* of long enduring hopes, ,, 17
' They call this *m* as good *as me*.' ,, 32
fierce old *m*—to take *his* name You bandbox. ,, 43
The true *men* banished, *Britons, guard* 10
We have not France, but this *m's* heart of stone. ,, 17
This *m* is France, the *m* they call her choice. ,, 20
There must no *m* go back to bear the tale : No *m* to bear it—Swear it ! We swear it ! ,, 56
A health to Europe's honest *men* ! *Hands all Round* 13
But fire, to blast the hopes of *men*. ,, 30
By such *men* led, our press had ever been *Sugg. by Reading* 2
The thinking *men* of England, loathe a tyranny. ,, 12
Yours are the public acts of public *men*, ,, 21
I honour much, I say, this *m's* appeal. ,, 49
An essence less concentred than a *m* ! ,, 82
we want a manlike God and Godlike *men* ! ,, 84
I turn To you that mould *men's* thoughts ; ,, 86
' The Gander ' and ' The *m* of Mitylene,' *Lover's Tale* i 287
A woful *m* had thrust his wife and child ,, 368

Man (*continued*) It was the *m* she loved, even Lionel, *Lover's Tale* i 671
new-hewn sepulchre Where *m* had never lain. ,, 714
As *men* do from a vague and horrid dream, ,, 786
Let them so love that *men* and boys may say, ,, 801
Mane And shook a *m* en papillotes. *New Timon* 12
Manhood RISE, Britons, rise, if *m* be not dead ; *Britons, guard* 1
And trust an ancient *m* and the cause *Sugg. by Reading* 39
Manlike we want a *m* God and Godlike men ! ,, 84
Manly How much I love this writer's *m* style ! ,, 1
Manner for your *m* sorts Not with this age, *Cambridge* 10
Mantling Half round the *m* night is drawn, *Hesperides, Song* iii 13
Many Come, thou of *m* crowns, white-robèd love, *Love* 24
The *m* pleasant days, the moonlit nights, *Lover's Tale* i 54
Marble Nathless she ever clasps the *m* knees, *Timbuctoo* 37
The deep salt wave breaks in above Those *m* steps below. *Hero to Leander* 35
Margent Had film'd the *m's* of the recent wound. *Lover's Tale* i 764
Mark old *m* of rouge upon your cheeks. *New Timon* 38
Marksman We were the best of *marksmen* long ago, *Britons, guard* 43
Marriage-day God bless thy *m-d*, *God bless our Prince* 1
Marshy The drain-cut levels of the *m* lea,— *Mablethorpe* 6
Martial if France be she Whom *m* progress only charms ? *Hands all Round* 26
Marvel (s) Ye could not read the *m* in his eye, *The Mystic* 4
What *m* that she died ? *Love, Pride, etc.* 14
Marvel (verb) Would *m* from so beautiful a sight *Pallid thunderstricken* 9
Matted built above With *m* bramble and the shining gloss Of ivy-leaves, *Lover's Tale* i 373
Matter *M* enough for deploring *1865-1866* 8
Mattock Beside her are laid Her *m* and spade, *I' the glooming light* 6
May Mid *M's* darling goldenlockèd, *Dualisms* 3
All in the bloomèd *M*. (repeat) *The lintwhite* 3, 12, 21, 30
Farewell, fair rose of *M* ! *God bless our Prince* 11
Maze of piercing, trackless, thrilling thoughts *Timbuctoo* 115
Mead Tilth, hamlet, *m* and mound : *D. of F. Women* 4
Meadow The Bayard of the *m*. *The Grasshopper* 21
Meaning But what is the *m* of *then* and now ! *The 'How' and the 'Why'* 22
where, alack, is Bewick To tell the *m* now ? *A gate and a field* 6
Measure Man is the *m* of all truth *oi ρέοντες* 3
If ye sing not, if ye *m* make false *m*, *Hesperides, Song* i 10
Meat Over their scrips and shares, their *m's* and wine, *Sugg. by Reading* 47
Mechanic By a dull *m* ghost And a juggle of the brain. *Germ of 'Maud'* 4
Meditation 'Tis a beautiful And pleasant *m*, *Lover's Tale* i 240
Meek shall the blessing of the *m* be on thee ; *Though night* 12
Meet When we two *m* there's never perfect light. *Me my own fate* 14
Yet never did there *m* my sight, *O darling room* 13
I said, ' O years that *m* in tears, *1865-1866* 4
Meeter Men of Ithaca, this is *m*, *Lotos-Eaters* 11
Melancholy (adj.) To the *m* home At the limit of the brine, ,, 20
Melancholy (s) Thy spirit to mild-minded *M* ; *Check every outflash* 3
Alone my hopeless *m* gloometh, *Me my own fate* 5
Mellow And the black owl scuds down the *m* twilight, *The 'How' and the 'Why'* 30
Mellowed edicts of his fear Are *m* into music, *Love* 8
M in a land of rest ; *Hesperides, Song* iv 12
Melodious *M* thunders through your vacant courts At morn and even ; *Cambridge* 9
Melody In accents of majestic *m*, *Timbuctoo* 192
Clear *m* flattering the crispèd Nile *A Fragment* 26
Fair maiden forms moving like *melodies*), *There are three things* 3
Nor *m* o' the Lybian lotusflute *The Hesperides* 7
as my heart beat Twice to the *m* of hers. *Lover's Tale* i 74
It giveth out a constant *m* That drowns ,, 534
heavy *m* sleeps On the level of the shore : *Lotos-Eaters* 35
Melted From my cold eyes and *m* it again. *Could I outwear* 14
note Hath *m* in the silence that it broke. *Oh, Beauty* 14
Memnon Thy *M*, when his peaceful lips are kissed *A Fragment* 22
Memnonian Awful *M* countenances calm ,, 16
Memory A center'd golden-circled *M*, *Timbuctoo* 21
m of that mental excellence Comes o'er me, ,, 137
M tho' fed by Pride Did wax so thin on gall, *Love, Pride, etc.* 11
While I spoke thus, the seedsman, *M*, *D. of F. Women* 14
a costly casket in the grasp Of *m* ? *Lover's Tale* i 102
m of that sound With mighty evocation, ,, 667
Memphis Old *M* hath gone down : *A Fragment* 27

Noonday   Of those that gaze upon the *n* Sun.   *Timbuctoo* 71
Noontide   Hum a lovelay to the westwind at *n*.   *Dualisms* 2
   At *n-t* beneath the lea ;   *Lotos-Eaters* 6
Northwind   *N* fall'n, in the newstarrèd night   *The Hesperides* 1
Note   And *n's* of busy life in distant worlds   *Timbuctoo* 113
   ere the *n* Hath melted in the silence that it broke.   *Oh, Beauty* 13
Nothing   For *n* is, but all is made,   *οἱ ῥέοντες* 12
   O fie, you golden *n*,   *The Ringlet* 43
Now   But what is the meaning of *then* and *n* ! *The ' How ' and the ' Why '* 22
Number   *N*, tell them over and *n*   *The Hesperides, Song ii* 7

O

Oak   Why the heavy *o* groans,   *The ' How ' and the ' Why '* 15
   Such hearts of *o* as they be.   *National Song* 4
Oaken   So on an *o* sprout A goodly acorn grew ;   *Lost Hope* 5
   To blow the battle from their *o* sides.   *Britons, guard* 38
Oar   We'll lift no more the shattered *o*,   *Lotos-Eaters* 23
   and rowing with the *o*,   " 39
Obelisk   Her *o's* of rangèd Chrysolite,   *Timbuctoo* 235
   Egypt, are thine *o's* Graven with gorgeous emblems   *A Fragment* 12
Oberwinter   And *O's* vineyards green,   *O darling room* 8
Object   From visible *o's*, for but dimly now,   *Timbuctoo* 135
Oblivion   Did fall away into *o*.   *Lover's Tale i* 630
Ocean   The *o* with the morrow light   *Hero to Leander* 25
   Tossing on the tossing *o*,   *Lotos-Eaters* 3
   the shore Than labour in the *o*,   " 39
Odorous   Blown round with happy airs of *o* winds ?   *Timbuctoo* 46
   Flooding its angry cheek with *o* tears.   *Lover's Tale i* 565
Odour   And *o's* rapt from remote Paradise ?   *Timbuctoo* 81
   No western *o's* wander On the black   *Hero to Leander* 28
O'erbear   Would shatter and *o* the brazen beat   *Shall the hag* 7
O'ercanopied   Imperial height Of Canopy *o*.   *Timbuctoo* 166
Offence   Whereby to guard our Freedom from *o*—   *Sugg. by Reading* 38
Offered   *O* to Gods upon an altarthrone ;   *To ——* 7
Old (adj.)   There where the Giant of *o* Time infixed   *Timbuctoo* 11
   And much I mus'd on legends quaint and *o*   " 19
   To know thee is all wisdom, and *o* age Is but to know thee :   *Love* 15
   which stood In the midnoon the glory of *o* Rhodes,   *A Fragment* 2
   O Memphis hath gone down ?   " 27
   Wrapped round with spiced cerements in *o* grots   " 30
   From an *o* garden where no flower bloometh,   *Me my own fate* 7
   underneath a shadowy plane In *o* Bayona, nigh
    the Southern Sea   *There are three things* 11
   Lest the *o* wound of the world be healèd,   *The Hesperides, Song iii* 2
   Father, *o* Himla weakens, Caucasus is bold and strong.   " 7
   Your portals statued with *o* kings and queens,   *Cambridge* 2
   The *o* Timon, with his noble heart,   *New Timon* 3
   why we see The *o* mark of rouge upon your cheeks.   " 38
   The fierce *o* man—to take *his* name You bandbox.   " 43
   We won *o* battles with our strength, the bow.   *Britons, guard* 44
   Headlong they plunge their doubts among *o* rags
    and bones.   *Sugg. by Reading* 72
   And New Year and *O* Year met,   *1865-1866* 2
   O Year roaring and blowing   " 12
   And all the quaint *o* scraps of ancient crones,   *Lover's Tale i* 288
Old (s)   So did the O : here comes the New :   *New Timon* 5
Older   For he is *o* than the world.   *The Hesperides, Song ii* 16
Old Year   And New Year and *O Y* met,   *1865-1866* 2
   O Y roaring and blowing   " 12
Omen   Go, frightful *o's*.   *Sugg. by Reading* 85
On   Over their crowned brethren O and OPH ?   *A Fragment* 21
One   but only seemed O shadow in the midst of a
   great light, O reflex from eternity on time, O mighty
   countenance of perfect calm,   *The Mystic* 21
   O very dark and chilly night Pride came beneath
   and held a light.   *Love, Pride, etc.* 5
   COULD I outwear my present state of woe With *o*
   brief winter,   *Could I outwear* 2
   O cypress on an inland promontory.   *Me my own fate* 8
   As with *o* kiss to touch thy blessèd cheek.   *Oh, Beauty* 8
   Should he land here, and for *o* hour prevail,   *Britons, guard* 55
   O rainy night, when every wind blew loud,   *Lover's Tale i* 367

One (continued)   And yet again, three shadows, fronting *o*,
   O forward, *o* respectant, three but *o* ;   *The Mystic* 17
   Who make the emphatic *O*, by whom is all,   *Sugg. by Reading* 81
On-set   All *o-s* of capricious Accident,   *Timbuctoo* 26
Onward   drove them *o*—made them sensible ;   *Lover's Tale ii* 77
Opal   *o* width Of her small glowing lakes,   *Timbuctoo* 101
Open (adj.)   (*See also* **Half-open**)   where no gaze Might rest,
    stood *o*,   " 179
   The Sun peeped in from *o* field,   *Home they brought him* 6
   The written secrets of her inmost soul Lay like an
    o scroll before my view,   *Lover's Tale i* 601
   Was not the South, The East, the West, all *o*,   " 699
Open (verb)   *O* thine eye and see.'   *Timbuctoo* 84
Open'd   *o* far into the outward, And never closed again.   *Lover's Tale i* 298
Oph   Over their crowned brethren On and *O* ?   *A Fragment* 21
Opinion   I call on you To make *o* warlike,   *Sugg. by Reading* 87
Opposite   And the great bird sits on the *o*
    bough,   *The ' How ' and the ' Why '* 28
Orb   With his unutterable, shining *o's*,   *Timbuctoo* 67
Organ-pipe   Nor yet your solemn *o-p's* that blow   *Cambridge* 8
Orient   To him the honey dews of *o* hope.   *Lover's Tale i* 675
Other   Or *o* things talking in unknown tongues,   *Timbuctoo* 112
   Investeth and ingirds all *o* lives.   *The Mystic* 46
   for bitter grief Doth hold the *o* half in sovranty.   *Love and Sorrow* 5
   Then might thy rays pass thro' to the *o* side,   " 14
   Continuous till he reached the *o* sea.   *The Hesperides* 13
   such as in *o* minds Had film'd the margents of
    the recent wound.   *Lover's Tale i* 763
   For me all *o* Hopes did sway from that Which
    hung the frailest :   " 857
Outflash   CHECK every *o*, every ruder sally   *Check every outflash* 1
Outgrow   *o* The wan dark coil of faded suffering—   *Could I outwear* 3
Outset   Oh, happy, happy *o* of my days !   *Lover's Tale i* 276
Outspread   *o* With growth of shadowing leaf   *Timbuctoo* 222
Outward (adj.)   I seem'd to stand Upon the *o* verge   " 95
   Is one of those who know no strife Of inward woe or *o* fear ;   *Rosalind* 4
   With her two *o* All *o* fairest things   *Lover's Tale i* 383
Outward (s)   open'd far into the *o*, And never closed again.   " 298
Outwear   COULD I *o* my present state of woe   *Could I outwear* 1
Overborne   Lest my heart be *o*,   *Germ of ' Maud '* 5
Overcome   unto both Delight from hardship to be *o*   *Lover's Tale i* 379
Overdoing   *o* of her part Did fall away into oblivion.   " 629
Overhead   world's last tempest darkens *o* ;   *Britons, guard* 3
Overlast   Can it *o* the nerves ?   *Germ of ' Maud '* 26
Overleap   but *o* All the petty shocks and fears   *Rosalind* 12
Overlive   Can it *o* the eye ?   *Germ of ' Maud '* 27
Overthrown   And murder was her freedom *o*.   *Britons, guard* 23
Overwatching   heart is drunk with *o's* night
    and day,   *The Hesperides, Song ii* 12
Overwise   The world will be *o*.   " 22
Owl   black *o* scuds down the mellow twilight, *The ' How ' and the ' Why '* 30
Own   Absorbed me from the nature of itself With
    its *o* fleetness.   *Timbuctoo* 143
   For she hath half delved her *o* deep grave,   *I' the glooming light* 7
   Into her *o* blue eyes so clear and deep,   *Tears of Heaven* 7
   Issue of its *o* substance, my heart's night   *Love and Sorrow* 10
   Shall be steeped in his *o* salt tear :   *English War Song* 15
   ME my *o* fate to lasting sorrow doometh :   *Me my own fate* 1
   did pause To worship mine *o* image, laved in light,   *Lover's Tale i* 68
   and with the shock Half dug their *o* graves),   " *ii* 50
   And, trampled on, left to its *o* decay.   " 81
   In a new birth, immingled with my *o*,   " *i* 732

P

Pactolus   And sailing on *P* in a boat,   *Pallid thunderstricken* 3
Padded   What, it's you The *p* man—that wear the stays—   *New Timon* 8
Pagan   *See* **Half-pagan**
Pagod   Her *P's* hung with music of sweet bells :   *Timbuctoo* 234
Pain   so kin to earth Pleasaunce fathers *p*—   *Every day, etc.* 15
   How scorn and ruin, *p* and hate could flow :   *Pallid thunderstricken* 10
   Though night and *p* and ruin and death reign here.   *Love* 4
   dazzled to the heart with glorious *p*.   *There are three things* 14

Poisèd (*See also* **Self-poised**) Though long ago listening
the *p* lark,   *To a Lady Sleep.* 8
Poles Arise, brave *P*, the boldest of the bold;   *Blow ye the trumpet* 3
Polish rolled The growing murmurs of the *P* war!   " 8
Polish'd Flowing between the clear and *p* stems,   *Timbuctoo* 51
Pomeranian on the Baltic shore Boleslas drove the *P*. *Blow ye the trumpet* 14
Pool waterfalls That sing into the pebbled *p*.   *Rosalind* 24
Poor *P* soul! behold her: what decorous calm!   *Sugg. by Reading* 61
Pope For the French the *P* may shrive 'em, (repeat) *National Song* 9, 27
pardon little would-be *P*'s And Brummels,   *New Timon* 19
The *P* has bless'd him;   *Britons, guard* 3
Poplar Through yonder *p* alley Below,   *Check every outflash* 4
Poppy So I wove Even the dull-blooded *p*,   *Lover's Tale i* 342
Porch length of *p* and lake and boundless hall,   *Timbuctoo* 180
Portal *p*'s of pure silver walks the moon.   *Though night* 4
Your *p*'s statued with old kings and queens,   *Cambridge* 2
Pour And the foam-white waters *p*;   *Lotos-Eaters* 32
Pouring Waves on the shingle *p*,   *1865-1866* 11
Power I have fill'd thy lips with *p*.   *Timbuctoo* 215
and apart In intellect and *p* and will,   *The Mystic* 38
One of the shining wingèd *p*'s,   *What time I wasted* 2
Permit not thou the tyrant *p*'s   *Hands all Round* 42
What *p* is yours to blast a cause or bless!   *Sugg. by Reading* 8
Lest you go wrong from *p* in excess.   " 10
I grant you one of the great *P*'s on earth,   " 23
But knowing all your *p* to heat or cool,   " 31
Powerful All *p* in beauty as thou art.   *Love and Sorrow* 12
Practise Now *p*, yeomen, Like those bowmen,   *Britons, guard* 45
Praise You did mingle blame and *p*,   *To C. North* 3
I could *not* forgive the *p*,   " 8
Prance The boy began to leap and *p*,   *Home they brought him* 7
Prate You *p* of nature! you are he That spilt his life *New Timon* 39
Pray *See* **Pri' thee**
Pray'd He worked for both: he *p* for both: *Lover's Tale i* 223
I *p* aloud to God that he would hold   " 791
Preach words of little children *p* Against you,— *Cambridge* 12
O Grief and Shame if while I *p* of laws   *Sugg. by Reading* 37
Preached Five and three (Let it not be *p* abroad) *The Hesperides, Song i* 16
Preamble nightingale, with long and low *p*, *Check every outflash* 9
Precious The *p* jewel of my honour'd life,   *Lover's Tale ii* 78
Precursor more fleet and strong Than its *p*, *Timbuctoo* 128
Pregnant *See* **Fountain pregnant**
Prepare loud and long, the warning-note: *P*! *Sugg. by Reading* 90
Presence I have given *thee* To understand my *p*, *Timbuctoo* 214
The imperishable *p*'s serene,   *The Mystic* 13
p's Fourfacèd to four corners of the sky;   " 15
Present (adj.) The indecision of my *p* mind With its past
clearness,   *Timbuctoo* 139
COULD I outwear my *p* state of woe   *Could I outwear* 1
Present (s) In time there is no *p*,   *The 'How' and the 'Why'* 5
Press *p* had ever been The public conscience   *Sugg. by Reading* 2
O you, the *P*! what good from you might spring!   " 7
nor the *P*! and look you well to that—   " 17
Pressure lake From *p* of descendant crags,   *Timbuctoo* 122
Prevail Should he land here, and for one hour *p*, *Britons, guard* 55
Pride (*See also* **Summerpride**) *P* came beneath and
held a light.   *Love, Pride, etc.* 6
P took Love's sweets, and by a spell   " 9
Memory tho' fed by *P* Did wax so thin on gall,   " 11
in the *p* of beauty issuing A sheeny snake, *Could I outwear* 5
Priest By lying *p*'s the peasant's votes controlled. *Britons, guard* 8
Priestess Kneels the pale *P* in deep faith,   *Timbuctoo* 34
Prime dewy *p* Of youth and buried time?   *Who can say* 6
Prince GOD bless our *P* and Bride!   *God bless our Prince* 1
Pri' thee We *p t* pass not, (repeat)   *The lintwhite* 31, 36
Privacy But yours are not their homestead *privacies*. *Sugg. by Reading* 22
" 11
Privilege Take heed of your wide *p*'s!   *Cambridge* 5
Proctor Your doctors and your *p*'s and your deans   " 13
Profess ye that did *p* to teach And have taught nothing *New Timon* 33
Profit What *p*'s now to understand   *Lover's Tale, i* 290
what *p*'s it To tell ye that her father died,   *A Fragment* 3
Profulgent A perfect Idol, with *p* brows   *Hands all Round* 8
Progress if France be she Whom martial *p* only charms? *Me my own fate* 8
Promontory One cypress on an inland *p*.   *The Hesperides* 3
voyaging beyond The hoary *p* of Soloë   "

Propagate Or *p* again her loathèd kind,   *Shall the hag* 2
Proud They seem'd high palaces and *p*,   *What time I wasted* 5
Prove *P* their falsehood and thy quarrel,   *The Grasshopper* 9
Proved Now *p* counterfeit, was shaken out,   *Lover's Tale ii* 80
Proverb till their love Shall ripen to a *p*   *i* 803
Prowess infixed The limits of his *p*,   *Timbuctoo* 12
Psalm Stands in her pew and hums her decent *p* *Sugg. by Reading* 63
Public The *p* conscience of our noble isle,   " 3
And you, dark Senate of the *P* pen,   " 19
Yours are the *p* acts of *p* men,   " 21
For better so you fight for *p* ends;   " 26
Pure *P* without heat, into a larger air Upburning, *The Mystic* 44
And portals of *p* silver walks the moon.   *Though night, etc.* 4
And why was I to darken their *p* love,   *Lover's Tale i* 765
Purest starr'd at slender intervals With blossom tufts
of *p* white;   " 400
Purified Had *p*, and chastened, and made free.   *The Mystic* 10
Purple Waiting to light him with his *p* skies,   *Love* 34
Arching blue-glossèd necks beneath the *p* weather. *Dualisms* 13
Far sheening down the *p* seas to those   *A Fragment* 4
Lest the redcombed dragon slumber Rolled
together in *p* folds.   *The Hesperides, Song ii* 10
Purplefringed *P* with even and dawn.   *iii* 14
Purport Keeping unchanged The *p* of their coinage. *Lover's Tale i* 734
Push'd watcher's at heaven's gate, *p* them apart,   " 616
Pushing *P* the thick roots aside   *The Grasshopper* 37
Put 'Then take it, love, and *p* it by;   *The Ringlet* 11
'Then kiss it, love, and *p* it by: " 23
'Come, kiss it, love, and *p* it by: " 41
Ringlet, You *p* me much to shame,   " 48
Pyramids upsprung the dazzling Cones Of *P*,   *Timbuctoo* 169
P Broad-based amid the fleeting sands,   *A Fragment* 9

Q

Quaint And much I mus'd on legends *q* and old   *Timbuctoo* 16
And all the *q* old scraps of ancient crones,   *Lover's Tale i* 288
Quarrel Prove their falsehood and thy *q*,   *The Grasshopper* 9
Queen Your portals statued with old kings and *q*'s, *Cambridge* 2
'God save the *Q*' is here a truer cry.   *Britons, guard* 26
You must not mix our *Q* with those   *Hands all Round* 53
God save the *Q*! (repeat)   *God bless our Prince* 3, 7, 10
God bless the *Q*.   " 14
Quench'd White as *q* ashes, cold as were the hopes Of
my lorn love!   *Lover's Tale i* 620
Quest my refluent health made tender *q*   " 742
Quick Severe and *q* to feel a civic sin,   *Sugg. by Reading* 4
As even then the torrent of *q* thought Absorbed me *Timbuctoo* 141

R

Race Kingdoms lapse, and climates change, and
r's die;   *The Hesperides, Song ii* 4
She comprehends the *r* she rules.   *Hands all Round* 56
Some vast Assyrian doom to burst upon our *r*. *Sugg. by Reading* 42
Rack'd She feels not how the social frame is *r*,   " 56
Radiance showering circular abyss Of *r*.   *Timbuctoo* 174
Rag they plunge their doubts among old *r*'s and bones. *Sugg. by Reading* 72
Rage We beat upon our aching hearts with *r*;   *Love* 18
Rain (s) Hark how the wild *r* hisses   *Hero to Leander* 14
hath drawn the frozen *r* From my cold eyes *Could I outwear* 2
Dim shores, dense *r*'s, and heavy clouded sea.   *Mablethorpe* 8
the dew, the sun, the *r*, Under the growth of body *Lover's Tale ii* 73
Rain (verb) for fear the mind *R* thro' my sight,   *i* 24
Rainy One *r* night, when every wind blew loud,   " 367
Raise To *r* the people and chastise the times   *Sugg. by Reading* 5
Rais'd I *r* My voice and cried 'Wide Afric,   *Timbuctoo* 57
With ministering hand he *r* me up;   " 188
I have *r* thee higher to the Spheres of Heaven,   " 216
I was *r* To be a mystery of loveliness   " 240
Rampart chrystal pile Of *r* upon *r*, dome on dome,   " 163
Ran That *r* bloombright into the Atlantic blue,   *The Hesperides* 9
legend *r* that, long time since, One rainy night, *Lover's Tale i* 366
Range *r* of battlement On battlement,   *Timbuctoo* 164
Rangèd Her obelisks of *r* Chrysolite,   " 235

Rock Why the *r*'s stand still,   *The 'How' and the 'Why'* 14
'Gan *r* and heave upon that painted sea;   *Lover's Tale ii* 199
Rockèd Two bees within a chrystal flowerbell *r*   *Dualisms* 1
Rock-hewn grots *R-h* and sealed for ever.   *A Fragment* 31
Rod The Russian whips and Austrian *r*'s—   *Hands all Round* 18
Rode *R* upon his father's lance,   *Home they brought him* 8
Roll nor with the thoughts that *r*,   *Cambridge* 11
Rolled (*See also* **Down-roll'd**) *R* together in
   purple folds.   *The Hesperides, Song ii* 10
   r The growing murmurs of the Polish war!   *Blow ye the trumpet* 7
Rolling The murmurous planets' *r* choir,   *Chorus* 24
   As round the *r* earth night follows day: *Me my own fate* 10
Rome *R*'s dearest daughter now is captive France,   *Britons, guard* 31
Roof (s) the *r* and crown Of all I hoped and fear'd?   *Lover's Tale i* 27
Roof (verb) Winter *r*'s The headland with inviolate   *Timbuctoo* 203
Roof'd Imperial Eldorado *r* with gold: " 24
Room O darling *r*, my heart's delight, Dear *r*, the
   apple of my sight,   *O darling room* 1
   There is no *r* so exquisite, No little *r* so warm and bright   " 4
   A little *r* so exquisite,   " 15
   Not any *r* so warm and bright,   " 17
Root Pushing the thick *r*'s aside   *The Grasshopper* 37
   Standing about the charmèd *r*.   *The Hesperides, Song i* 4
   From the *r* Drawn in the dark,   " 20
   Standing about the charmèd *r*.   " *iv* 34
   by our ears, the huge *r*'s strain and creak),   *Lover's Tale i* 63
Rooted *See* **Deep-rooted**
Rosalind My *R*, my *R*, Bold, subtle, careless *R*,   *Rosalind* 1
   My falconhearted *R* Fullsailed   " 9
   My happy falcon, *R*,   " 25
   My *R*, my *R*, Because no shadow on you falls,   " 30
   hearts are tennis balls To play with, wanton *R*?   " 33
Rose (s) With *r*'s musky breathed,   *Anacreontics* 1
   Farewell, fair *r* of May!   *God bless our Prince* 11
   each *r* Doth faint upon the bosom of the other,   *Lover's Tale i* 563
   a red *r* Should change into a white one   " 726
Rose (verb) A tutelary angel as she *r*,   " 388
Roselip Dimples, *r*'s, and eyes of any hue.   *There are three things* 4
Rosy Thy heart beats through thy *r* limbs   *Hero to Leander* 16
   In the hollow *r* vale to tarry,   *Lotos-Eaters* 12
   O Ringlet, O Ringlet, She blush'd a *r* red,   *The Ringlet* 36
Rouge old mark of *r* upon your cheeks.   *New Timon* 38
Round Nor the *r* sun that shineth to all;   *Burial of Love* 26
   Yet hands all *r*   *Hands all Round* 21
   And the great name of England *r* and *r* (repeat)   " 24, 48, 60
   Why *r* is not square?   *The 'How' and the 'Why'* 13
   R about all is mute,   *The Hesperides, Song i* 13
   Holy and bright, *r* and full, bright and blest,   " *iv* 11
Roving The rapid waste of *r* sea,   *Chorus* 2
Rowing Than labour in the ocean, and *r* with the oar,   *Lotos-Eaters* 19
Royal Fair year, with brows of *r* love Thou comest,   *The lintwhite* 19
Rubylike Glows *r* the far-up crimson globe,   *D. of F. Women* 7
Rude From which may *r* Death never startle them,   *Lover's Tale i* 796
Ruder every *r* sally Of thought and speech;   *Check every outflash* 1
Ruin How scorn and *r*, pain and hate could flow: *Pallid thunderstricken* 10
   So gazed I on the *r*'s of that thought   *Lover's Tale ii* 71
   night and pain and *r* and death reign here.   *Love* 4
Ruin'd The wreck of *r* life and shatter'd thought,   *Lover's Tale ii* 62
Rule (s) Be loyal, if you wish for wholesome *r*:   *Sugg. by Reading* 33
   yet the 'not too much' is all the *r* she knows.   " 60
Rule (verb) She comprehends the race she *r*'s.   *Hands all Round* 56
Rumour Or is the *r* of thy Timbuctoo   *Timbuctoo* 61
Rusheth Anon he *r* forth with merry din,   *Love* 41
Russian The *R* whips and Austrian rods—   *Hands all Round* 18
Rustling A *r* of white wings!   *Timbuctoo* 64
Rusty You did mingle blame and praise, *R* Christopher.   *To C. North* 4
Ruth storms of sorrow and *r* That roar beneath;   *Though night* 9
Ruthless His *r* host is bought with plunder'd gold,   *Britons, guard* 7

S

Sable To wander down his *s* sheeny sides,   *Love* 39
Sacrifice Folding the slaughter of the *s*   *To —* 6
Sad O *s No more*! O sweet *No more*!   *O sad No more!* 1
Sadness Grief and *s* steal Symbols of each other;   *Every day, etc.* 25

Said *s* to thee That thou hast half my heart,   *Love and Sorrow* 3
   As I *s*, with these She crown'd her forehead.   *Lover's Tale i* 348
Sail (s) No more unfurl the straining *s*;   *Lotos-Eaters* 24
Sail (verb) As when a man, that *s*'s in a balloon,   *D. of F. Women* 1
Sailed (*See also* **Fullsailed**) to those Who *s* from Mizraim   *A Fragment* 5
Sailing And *s* on Pactolus in a boat,   *Pallid thunderstricken* 3
Saint unfading foreheads of the *S*'s in Heaven?   *Timbuctoo* 54
Sainted *S* Juliet! dearest name!   *To —* 1
Salient Though hourly pastured on the *s* blood?   *Shall the hag* 5
Sallow And in the glow of *s* Summertide,   *Timbuctoo* 201
   The troublous autumn's *s* gloom,   *Chorus* 17
Sally every ruder *s* Of thought and speech;   *Check every outflash* 1
Salt The deep *s* wave breaks in above Those marble
   steps below.   *Hero to Leander* 34
   It shall be steeped in the *s*, *s* tear, Shall be
   steeped in his own *s* tear: *English War Song* 14
Same *See* **Self-same**
Sand (adj.) Gray *s* banks and pale sunsets—dreary wind,   *Mablethorpe* 7
Sand (s) he passeth by, And gulphs himself in *s*'s,   *Timbuctoo* 237
   Black specks amid a waste of dreary *s*,   " 247
   glistering *s*'s that robe The understream.   *Pallid thunderstricken* 5
   Pyramids Broad-based amid the fleeting *s*'s,   *A Fragment* 10
   lake, that, flooding, makes Cushions of yellow *s*;   *Lover's Tale i* 537
Sanded *See* **Gold-sanded**
Sandfield As the *s* at the mountain-foot.   *The Hesperides, Song i* 7
Sang close above us, *s* the wind-tost pine,   *Lover's Tale i* 60
Sap And the *s* to three-fold music floweth,   *The Hesperides, Song i* 19
   Huge splinters, which the *s* of earliest showers,   *Lover's Tale ii* 45
Sapphire wheel in wheel, Arch'd the wan *S*.   *Timbuctoo* 111
   And thunder thro' the *s* deeps In wayward strength,   *Chorus* 28
Sardinia To take *S*, Belgium, or the Rhine: *Britons, guard* 50
Save 'God *s* the Queen' is here a truer cry.   " 26
   God *s* the Nation, The toleration,   " 27
   God *s* the Queen! (repeat)   *God bless our Prince* 3, 7, 10
Saw *s* before me Such colour'd spots   *Timbuctoo* 69
   I *s* The smallest grain that dappled the dark Earth,   " 98
   within the South methought I *s* A wilderness of spires,   " 161
   if I *s* These things distinctly,   " 184
   S far on each side through the grated gates   *The Mystic* 34
   I *s* no more only those eyes—   *There are three things* 13
   S round her feet the country far away,   *Lover's Tale i* 390
   eyes, I *s*, were full of tears in the morn,   " 728
Say (s) And a fool may say his *s*;   *The Ringlet* 18
Say (verb) nothing visible, they *s*, had birth   *Timbuctoo* 55
   Some *s* this life is pleasant,   *The 'How' and the 'Why'* 3
   What is it they *s*? What do they there?   " 12
   Who can *s* Why To-day To-morrow will be yesterday?"   *Who can say* 1
   I honour much, I *s*, this man's appeal.   *Sugg. by Reading* 49
   Let both the peoples *s*,   *God bless our Prince* 12
   And a fool may *s* his say;   *The Ringlet* 18
   Let them so love that men and boys may *s*,   *Lover's Tale i* 801
Scale step by step to *s* that mighty stair   *Timbuctoo* 198
Scalèd Lest his *s* eyelid drop,   *The Hesperides, Song ii* 15
Scan would *s* Definite round.   *Timbuctoo* 131
   eye could *s* Through length of porch and lake   " 179
Scandal She loves a little *s* which excites;   *Sugg. by Reading* 57
Scatter feeds it from behind, And *s*'s it before,   *Lover's Tale ii* 48
Scene Rhene Curves towards Mentz, a woody *s*.   *O darling room* 4
Science '*S* enough and exploring   *1865-1866* 6
Scorn The cruellest form of perfect *s*,   *Burial of Love* 18
   Ye scorned him with an undiscerning *s*:   *The Mystic* 3
   How *s* and ruin, pain and hate could flow: *Pallid thunderstricken* 10
   withering *s* of the many shall cleave   *English War Song* 5
   He shall eat the bread of common *s*;   " 13
   With a flash of frolic *s* And keen delight,   *Rosalind* 15
   By the thing I hold in *s*,   *Germ of 'Maud'* 6
   And *s* of perilous seeming: *Lover's Tale i* 380
Scorned Ye *s* him with an undiscerning *s*:   *The Mystic* 3
Scrap all the quaint old *s*'s of ancient crones,   *Lover's Tale i* 288
      ii 212
Screaming *s*, from me flung The empty phantom: *Though night, etc.* 2
   And bitter blasts the *s* autumn whirl,   *Cambridge* 4
Screen Wax-lighted chapels and rich carved *s*'s,   *Sugg. by Reading* 75
Scribe Christ cried: Woe, woe, to Pharisees and *S*'s!   " 47
Scrip Over their *s*'s and shares, their meats and wine,   "
Scroll Lay like an open *s* before my view,   *Lover's Tale i* 601

Scud black owl *s's* down the mellow
　twilight,　　　　　　*The 'How' and the 'Why'* 30
Sea Mountain which o'erlooks The narrow *s's*,　*Timbuctoo* 2
　even as the *s* When weary of wild inroad　　　" 13
　And the loud *s* roars below.　　　*Hero to Leander* 15
　odours wander On the black and moaning *s*,　　" 29
　turretstairs are wet That lead into the *s*.　　" 37
　The rapid waste of roving *s*,　　　*Chorus* 2
　loud winds, though they uprend the *s*,　　*Love* 9
　In music and in light o'er land and *s*.　　" 28
　We lord it o'er the *s*; (repeat)　*National Song* 16, 34
　Far sheening down the purple *s's* to those　*A Fragment* 4
　In old Bayona, nigh the Southern *S*—　*There are three things* 11
　Continuous till he reached the other *s*.　　*The Hesperides* 13
　But the apple of gold hangs over the *s*,　*The Hesperides, Song iv* 23
　narwhale swalloweth His foamfountains in the *s*.　*Lotos-Eaters* 8
　Dim shores, dense rains, and heavy clouded *s*.　*Mablethorpe* 8
　S's at my feet were flowing Waves　　*1865-1866* 10
　dreadful murmur indistinct Of the confused *s's*,　*Lover's Tale i* 657
　'Gan rock and heave upon that painted *s*;　　" *ii* 199
Seahorse Where the tuskèd *s* walloweth　*Lotos-Eaters* 4
Sealed grots Rock-hewn and *s* for ever.　*A Fragment* 31
Seaman *Seamen*, guard your own.　*Britons, Guard* 42
　or how we found The drowned *s* on the shore?　*Lover's Tale i* 293
Seam'd brain, Now *s* and chink'd with years—　　" 131
Seasmell Fresh as the early *s* blown　*Rosalind* 28
Season *S's* flower and fade;　*Every day, etc.* 6
　morning, such a one As dawns but once a *s*.　*Lover's Tale i* 302
Seaward Blown *s* from the shore;　*The Hesperides* 9
Seawind redolent breath Of this warm *s* ripeneth,　*The Hesperides, Song iv* 2
Secret (adj.) Albeit, his spirit and his *s* heart　*The Mystic* 7
　By *s* fire and midnight storms　*Chorus* 5
　Comes the bliss of *s* smiles,　*The Hesperides, Song iii* 11
　Higher thro' *s* splendours mounting still,　*D. of F. Women* 9
Secret (s) And the ancient *s* revealèd.　*The Hesperides, Song iii* 5
　written *s's* of her inmost soul Lay like an open scroll　*Lover's Tale i* 600
See Open thine eye and *s*.'　*Timbuctoo* 84
　who have not felt and known A higher than they *s*:　" 212
　Armed cap-a-pie, Full fair to *s*;　*The Grasshopper* 15
　Downlooking *s's* the solid shining ground　*D. of F. Women* 2
　we *s* The old mark of rouge upon your cheeks.　*New Timon* 37
　here shall *s* The British Goddess,　*Sugg. by Reading* 53
　When I did *s* her weep so ruefully;　*Lover's Tale i* 816
Seeded Bowing the *s* summerflowers.　*The Grasshopper* 8
Seedsman While I spoke thus, the *s*, Memory,　*D. of F. Women* 14
Seeing Lets the great world flit from him, *s* all,　" 10
Seek Nor *s* to bridle His vile aggressions,　*Britons, guard* 52
Seem *s's* to me As even then the torrent　*Timbuctoo* 140
　For all things are as they *s* to all, (repeat)　*οἱ ῥέοντες* 7, 15
　And nothing *s's* to me so wild and bold,　*Oh, Beauty* 7
　And here the Grecian ships did *s* to be.　*Mablethorpe* 4
Seem'd I *s* to stand Upon the outward verge　*Timbuctoo* 94
　only *s* One shadow in the midst of a great light,　*The Mystic* 20
　They *s* high palaces and proud,　*What time I wasted* 5
　from beneath *S* with a cobweb firmament　*Lover's Tale i* 407
Seeming And scorn of perilous *s*:　" 380
　Which, lapt in *s* dissolution,　" 507
Seen *S* by the high-necked camel on the verge　*A Fragment* 18
　For I the Nonnenwerth have *s*,　*O darling room* 7
See'st *S* thou yon river, whose translucent wave,　*Timbuctoo* 229
Self-impelling with a fearful *s-i* joy　*Lover's Tale i* 389
Self-poised *S-p*, nor fears to fall.　*D. of F. Women* 12
Self-same And mine wove chaplets of the *s-s* flower,　*Lover's Tale i* 333
Self-upborne *s-u* With such gladness, as,　*Rosalind* 17
Selfwrought With *s* evils of unnumbered years,　*Tears of Heaven* 4
Sell needs must *s* the burthen of their wills　*Sugg. by Reading* 69
Semblance suns, or stars, or *s's* Of either,　*Timbuctoo* 172
Senate you, dark *S* of the public pen,　*Sugg. by Reading* 19
Sense Thy *s* is clogg'd with dull mortality,　*Timbuctoo* 82
　Each failing *s* As with a momentary flash　" 96
　And sound which struck the palpitating *s*,　" 119
　with ravish'd *s* Listenest the lordly music　" 217
　Colossal, without form, or *s*, or sound,　*The Mystic* 14
　sailing on Pactolus in a boat, Drown soul
　and *s*,　　*Pallid thunderstricken* 4

Sense (*continued*) As with a *s* of nigher Deity,　*Lover's Tale i* 382
　Glory in glory, without *s* of change.　　" 516
　So lethargised discernment in the *s*,　　" 663
Sensible drove them onward—made them *s*;　　" *ii* 77
Sent horrid rifts *S* up the moaning of unhappy spirits　" *i* 613
Separate each th' effect Of *s* impulse,　*Timbuctoo* 127
Sepulchre new-hewn *s*, Where man had never lain.　*Lover's Tale i* 713
Seraph (adj.) Even that this name to which her *s* lips　" 451
Seraph (s) The bright descent Of a young *S*!　*Timbuctoo* 65
Seraphtrod *S*, Wound thro' your great Elysian solitudes,　" 47
Serene The still *s* abstraction;　*The Mystic* 5
　The imperishable presences *s*,　" 13
　eyes dropt downward through the blue *s*,　*To a Lady Sleep.* 9
Serpent As on a *s* in his agonies Awestricken Indians;　*Love* 30
Set The pleasant stars have *s*!　*Hero to Leander* 8
Settlement Low-built, mud-walled, Barbarian *s*,　*Timbuctoo* 248
Severe *S* and quick to feel a civic sin,　*Sugg. by Reading* 4
　beneath *S* and youthful brows, with shining eyes　*The Mystic* 27
Shackle Break through your iron *s's*—fling them far.　*Blow ye the trumpet* 4
Shade Amid the wild unrest of swimming *s*　*Timbuctoo* 129
　There is no bright form Doth not cast a *s*—　*Every day, etc.* 10
　Nor blot with floating *s's* the solar light.　*Shall the hag* 14
　Nor good nor ill, nor light nor *s*,　*οἱ ῥέοντες* 10
Shadow (s) (*See also* **Half-shadow**) *S's* to which, despite all
　shocks of Change,　*Timbuctoo* 25
　Dim *s's* but unwaning presences　*The Mystic* 15
　And yet again, three *s's*, fronting one,　" 17
　One *s* in the midst of a great light,　" 21
　In sunlight and in *s*,　*The Grasshopper* 9
　My heart's day, but the *s* of my heart,　*Love and Sorrow* 9
　Because no *s* on you falls,　*Rosalind* 31
Shadow (verb) I can *s* forth my bride　*Germ of 'Maud'* 9
Shadow'd *S* and crimson'd with the drifting dust,　*Lover's Tale i* 139
Shadowing By *s* forth the Unattainable;　*Timbuctoo* 197
　outspread With growth of leaf and clusters rare,　" 223
　they were the types and *s's* Of hers—　*Lover's Tale i* 386
Shadowy Thy *s* Idols in the solitudes,　*A Fragment* 15
　At sunset, underneath a *s* plane In old
　Bayona,　*There are three things* 10
Shaft Till your balls fly as their true *s's* have flown.　*Britons, guard* 47
Shake some great City where the walls *S*,　*Timbuctoo* 29
Shaken Now proved counterfeit, was *s* out,　*Lover's Tale ii* 80
Shakespeare WE know him, out of *S's* art,　*New Timon* 1
Shallop Could link his *s* to the fleeting edge,　*Timbuctoo* 145
Shame (*S* fall 'em they are deaf and blind)　*The Grasshopper* 6
　A Timon! Nay, nay, for *s*—　*New Timon* 41
　O Grief and *S* if while I preach of laws　*Sugg. by Reading* 37
　Ringlet, You put me much to *s*,　*The Ringlet* 48
　Than to *s* merry England here.　*English War Song* 17
Shameless Peace-lovers, haters Of *s* traitors,　*Britons, guard* 16
Shape Solemn but splendid, full of *s's* and sounds,　*Lover's Tale i* 799
　I know not if I *s* These things with accurate similitude　*Timbuctoo* 133
Share Over their scrips and *s's*, their meats and wine,　*Sugg. by Reading* 47
Sharp Distinct and vivid with *s* points of light　*Timbuctoo* 107
Sharper lest we learn A *s* lesson than we ever knew.　*Sugg. by Reading* 88
Shatter Would *s* and o'erbear the brazen beat　*Shall the hag* 7
Shattered (*See also* **Earthquake-shattered**) beneath the
　day's decline, We'll lift no more the *s* oar,　*Lotos-Eaters* 23
　had *s* from The mountain, till they fell,　*Lover's Tale ii* 48
　The wreck of ruin'd life and *s* thought,　" 62
Shed With the tears he hath *s*,　*Burial of Love* 6
Sheen Thy locks are full of sunny *s*　*The lintwhite* 28
Sheening Far *s* down the purple seas to those　*A Fragment* 4
Sheeny I gaz'd upon the *s* coast beyond,　*Timbuctoo* 10
　The hoarhead winter paving earth With *s* white,　*Chorus* 19
　Forth in the pride of beauty issuing A *s* snake,　*Could I outwear* 1
　And in his writhings awful hues begin To wander down his
　sable *s* sides,　*Love* 39
Shield Beat upon his father's *s*—　*Home they brought him* 9
Shielded Clap thy *s* sides and carol,　*The Grasshopper* 11
Shine Yet on both sides at once thou canst not *s*:　*Love and Sorrow* 9
　thy lights on my horizon *s* Into my night　*Me my own fate* 11
Shineth Nor the round sun that *s* to all;　*Burial of Love* 26
Shingle Waves on the *s* pouring,　*1865-1866* 11
Shining and look'd into my face With his unutterable, *s* orbs, *Timbuctoo* 67

Shining (*continued*) with *s* eyes Smiling a godlike smile — *The Mystic* 27
Downlooking sees the solid *s* ground — *D. of F. Women* 2
One of the *s* wingèd powers, — *What time I wasted* 2
'built above With matted bramble and the *s* gloss Of ivy-leaves, — *Lover's Tale i* 373
Ship And here the Grecian *s's* did seem to be. — *Mablethorpe* 4
Call home your *s's* across Biscayan tides, — *Britons, guard* 37
Shirt The merits of a spotless *s*— — *New Timon* 34
Shiver Darken, and shrink and *s* into huts, — *Timbuctoo* 246
Shock Shadows to which, despite all *s's* of Change, — " 25
s's and fears That trouble life in early years, — *Rosalind* 13
fell, and with the *s* Half dug their own graves), — *Lover's Tale ii* 49
Shook winds from heaven *s* the acorn out, — *Lost Hope* 7
And *s* a mane en papillotes. — *New Timon* 12
And *s* its earthly socket, for we heard, — *Lover's Tale i* 61
In eager haste I *s* him by the hand; — " 788
Shoot That *s* across the soul in prayer, — " 355
Shooting *S*, singing, ever springing — *The Grasshopper* 41
Shore Blown seaward from the *s*; — *The Hesperides* 8
on the Baltic *s* Boleslas drove the Pomeranian. — *Blow ye the trumpet* 13
heavy melon sleeps On the level of the *s*: — *Lotos-Eaters* 36
the *s* Than labour in the ocean, — " 38
Dim *s's*, dense rains, and heavy clouded sea. — *Mablethorpe* 8
Shorn clear Galaxy *S* of its hoary lustre, — *Timbuctoo* 106
Short But a *s* youth sunny and free. — *The Grasshopper* 29
Shot in mail of argent light *S* into gold, — *Pallid thunderstricken* 13
rapid brook *S* down his inner thunders, — *Lover's Tale i* 372
Shoulder Her *s's* are bare; — *I' the glooming light* 10
Shout (s) With *s's* from off the bridge, — *Lover's Tale i* 369
Shout (verb) And stares in his face and *s's* 'how? how?' — *The 'How' and the 'Why'* 15
S for England! (repeat) — *English War Song* 7, 18, 29, 40, 51
S for God and our right! — " 50
and waves them to the mob That *s* below, — *D. of F. Women* 6
Shouteth Hark! he *s*—the ancient enemy! — *English War Song* 24
Show in the dark of mine *S* traced with flame. — *Lover's Tale i* 296
Showed ANGELS have talked with him, and *s* him thrones: — *The Mystic* 1
S me cliffs with crown of towers, — *What time I wasted* 3
Shower For her the *s's* shall not fall, — *Burial of Love* 25
(Huge splinters, which the sap of earliest *s's*, — *Lover's Tale ii* 45
Showering *s* circular abyss Of radiance. — *Timbuctoo* 173
s down the glory of lightsome day, — *Tears of Heaven* 8
Shrill But *s* you, loud and long, — *Sugg. by Reading* 90
When the *s* storm-blast feeds it from behind, — *Lover's Tale ii* 47
Shrine Embalming with sweet tears the vacant *s*, — *Lost Hope* 3
Unroof the *s's* of clearest vision, — *To a Lady Sleep.* 3
all unworthy Of such a *s*— — *Lover's Tale i* 70
Shrink Darken, and *s* and shiver into huts, — *Timbuctoo* 246
Shrive For the French the Pope may *s* 'em, (repeat) — *National Song* 9, 27
Shroud Till the end of fears Cometh in the *s*, — *Every day, etc.* 21
ghastful brow, Half-bursten from the *s*, — *Lover's Tale i* 677
Shrub earthquake-shattered chasm, hung with *s's*, — " 408
Shuddering The very spirit of Paleness made still paler By the *s* moonlight, — " 680
Shut light Is *s* out by the round of the tall hillbrow; — *The Hesperides, Song iv* 16
Side Saw far on each *s* through the grated gates — *The Mystic* 34
Clap thy shielded *s* and carol, — *The Grasshopper* 11
Yet on both *s's* at once thou canst not shine: — *Love and Sorrow* 7
Thine is the bright *s* of my heart, — " 8
might thy rays pass thro' to the other *s*, — " 14
To wander down his sable sheeny *s's*, — *Love* 39
Both alike, they glide together *S* by *s*; — *Dualisms* 11
Like, unlike, they sing together *S* by *s*; — " 20
She is lovely by my *s* — *Germ of 'Maud'* 12
I can call it to my *s*, — " 16
To blow the battle from their oaken *s's*. — *Britons, guard* 38
Parted on either *s* her argent neck, — *Lover's Tale i* 740
Sigh (s) Changed into fire, and blown about with *s's*. — *To —* 9
THERE are three things that fill my heart with *s's* — *There are three things* 1
How canst thou let me waste my youth in *s's*; — *Oh, Beauty* 2
I hate that silly *s*. — *Skipping-rope* 8
When summer winds break their soft sleep with *s's*, — *Lover's Tale i* 559
who drew the happy atmosphere Of my unhappy *s's*, — " 674
Sigh (verb) and the white willows *s*? — *The 'How' and the 'Why'* 15
THE pallid thunderstricken *s* for gain, — *Pallid thunderstricken* 1

Sight with every *s* And sound which struck — *Timbuctoo* 118
Would marvel from so beautiful a *s* — *Pallid thunderstricken* 9
Father, twinkle not thy stedfast *s*; — *The Hesperides, Song ii* 3
Dear room, the apple of my *s*, — *O darling room* 2
Yet never did there meet my *s*, — " 13
for fear the mind Rain thro' my *s*, — *Lover's Tale i* 24
Being wafted on the wind, drove in my *s*, — " 730
Sign earth beneath me yawning given *S* of convulsion; — " 612
Silence brood above The *s* of all hearts, — *Love* 14
note Hath melted in the *s* that it broke. — *Oh, Beauty* 14
In the *s* of my life— — *Germ of 'Maud'* 13
Silent and above The *s* Heavens were blench'd with faery light, — *Timbuctoo* 5
For him the *s* congregated hours, — *The Mystic* 25
Silk Both in blosmwhite *s* are frockèd: — *Dualisms* 16
Silken That brush thee with their *s* tresses? — *The Grasshopper* 39
With a *s* cord I bound it. — *Anacreontics* 8
Silly I hate that *s* sigh. — *Skipping-rope* 8
Silver (adj.) her *s* heights Unvisited with dew of vagrant cloud, — *Timbuctoo* 102
Looking under *s* hair with a *s* eye. — *The Hesperides, Song ii* 2
Silver (s) portals of pure *s* walks the moon. — *Though night* 4
And branching *s's* of the central globe, — *Pallid thunderstricken* 8
Silverflecked In honour of the *s* morn: — *To a Lady Sleep.* 4
Silver-gray touch of Time Will turn it *s-g*; — *The Ringlet* 6
chilling touch of Time Can turn thee *s-g*; — " 16
O Ringlet, You should be *s-g*: — " 30
Silverleaved And *s* lily, And ivy darkly-wreathèd, — *Anacreontics* 3
Similitude shape These things with accurate *s* — *Timbuctoo* 134
Sin Severe and quick to feel a civic *s*, — *Sugg. by Reading* 4
Sing Nor the rivers flow, nor the sweet birds *s*, — *Burial of Love* 29
Larks in heaven's cope *S*: — *Every day, etc.* 29
watered vallies where the young birds *s*; — *Could I outwear* 8
Both alike, they *s* together, — *Dualisms* 12
Like, unlike, they *s* together Side by side; — " 19
And longer hear us *s*; — *The lintwhite* 23
If ye *s* not, if ye make false measure, — *The Hesperides, Song i* 10
S away, *s* aloud and evermore in the wind, — " ii 14
waterfalls That *s* into the pebbled pool. — *Rosalind* 24
Singing Pushing the thick roots aside Of the *s* flowerèd grasses, — *The Grasshopper* 38
Shooting, *s*, ever springing In and out the emerald glooms, Ever leaping, ever *s*, — " 41
Two children lovelier than love, adown the lea are *s*, — *Dualisms* 14
S airily, Standing about the charmèd root. — *The Hesperides, Song i* 3
Keen-eyed Sisters, *s* airily, — " 25
S airily, Standing about the charmèd root. — " iv 33
Single The *s* voice may speak his mind aloud; — *Sugg. by Reading* 14
Sink vessel and your Church may *s* in storms. — " 74
Sister Keen-eyed *S's*, singing airily, — *The Hesperides, Song i* 25
Hesper, the dragon, and *s's* three, — " ii 24
Hesper, the dragon, and *s's* three, — " iv 25
Tho' its ghastly *s* glide And be moved — *Germ of 'Maud'* 18
Sit great bird *s's* on the opposite bough, — *The 'How' and the 'Why'* 28
Worn Sorrow *s's* by the moaning wave; — *I' the glooming light* 7
But Hatred in a gold cave *s* below, — *Pallid thunderstricken* 11
I only ask to *s* beside thy feet. — *Oh, Beauty* 3
All alone she *s's* and hears Echoes — *Home they brought him* 3
Skin (s) dead *s* withering on the fretted bone, — *Lover's Tale i* 678
Skin (verb) *s's* the colour from her trembling lips. — *Pallid thunderstricken* 14
Skip Could *s* so lightly by. — *Skipping-rope* 2
Skipping-rope my *s-r* Will hit you in the eye. — " 3
How lightly whirls the *s-r*! — " 5
take it, take my *s-r* And hang yourself — " 11
Skirting snowy *s* of a garment hung, — *Timbuctoo* 182
Sky presences Fourfaced to four corners of the *s*; — *The Mystic* 16
Waiting to light him with his purple *skies*, — *Love* 34
They stream like fire in the *skies*; — *English War Song* 26
three things beneath the blessed *skies* For which I live— — *There are three things* 5
Spirit waits To embrace me in the *s*. — *Germ of 'Maud'* 34
I hear a thunder though the *skies* are fair, — *Sugg. by Reading* 89
Slain HOME they brought him *s* with spears. — *Home they brought him* 1
Slake and *s* With points of blastborne hail — *Shall the hag* 10
Slate A child with a broken *s*, — *A gate and a field* 3
Slaughter Folding the *s* of the sacrifice — *To —* 6

Slave For where is the heart and strength of *s's*?
    Oh! where is the strength of *s's*?   *English War Song* 36
    He is weak! we are strong; he a *s*, we are free;   "   38
Sleek shall see The British Goddess, *s* Respectability. *Sugg. by Reading* 54
Sleep (s) All men do walk in *s*,   οἱ ῥέοντες 5
    Arching the billow in his *s*,   *The Hesperides, Song iv* 3
    summer winds break their soft *s* with sighs,   *Lover's Tale i* 559
Sleep (verb) Whether we wake or whether we *s*?
    Whether we *s* or whether we die?   *The 'How' and the 'Why'* 17
    she cannot *s*;   *I' the glooming light* 15
    cleaving air, Lost in its effulgence *s's*,   *Chorus* 26
    Half-light, half-shadow, let my spirit *s*   *Love and Sorrow* 17
    They *s* with staring eyes and gilded lips,   *A Fragment* 29
    Crocodiles in briny creeks *S* and stir not: *The Hesperides, Song i* 9
                                 " *ii* 19
    If he *s*, we *s*,   *Lotos-Eaters* 35
    heavy melon *s's* On the level of the shore: *Timbuctoo* 124
Slender crumbling from their parent slope At *s* interval,
    starr'd at *s* intervals With blossom tufts of purest
    white;   *Lover's Tale i* 399
Slept all the white-stemmed pinewood *s* above—   *Check every outflash* 13
Sliding Hid now and then with *s* cloud.   *What time I wasted* 6
Slime grovell'd in the *s* Of this dull world,   *Timbuctoo* 149
                                     123
Slope crumbling from their parent *s* At slender interval, "
    The dull wave mourns down the *s*,   *I' the glooming light* 21
    but from a *s* That ran bloombright   *The Hesperides* 8
    To whom the *s* and stream of life,   *Rosalind* 5
    The *s* into the current of my years,   *Lover's Tale ii* 76
Sloped and *s* Into the slumberous summer noon;   *A Fragment* 10
Sloping borne Adown the *s* of an arrowy stream,   *Timbuctoo* 144
Slumber (s) *s* is more sweet than toil,   *Lotos-Eaters* 38
Slumber (verb) And *s's* in the clover.   *The Grasshopper* 33
    redcombed dragon *s* Rolled together in purple
    folds.   *The Hesperides, Song ii* 9
Slumber'd chasms of deep, deep blue *S* unfathomable,   *Timbuctoo* 8
Slumberous and sloped Into the *s* summer noon;   *A Fragment* 11
Small and the opal width Of her *s* glowing lakes,   *Timbuctoo* 102
    He said, 'The labour is not *s*;   *What time I wasted* 7
    Alas for her and all her *s* delights!   *Sugg. by Reading* 55
    Alas, our youth, so clever yet so *s*,   " 79
Smallest I saw The *s* grain that dappled the dark Earth,   *Timbuctoo* 99
Smell (*See also* Seasmell) Who can tell Why to *s* The violet, Who can say 5
Smelt I *s* a wildweed flower alone;   *O sad No more!* 4
Smile (s) Then with a mournful and ineffable *s*,   *Timbuctoo* 189
    With languor and her most hateful *s's*,   *Burial of Love* 19
    with shining eyes Smiling a godlike *s*   *The Mystic* 28
    Comes the bliss of secret *s's*,   *The Hesperides, Song iii* 11
Smile (verb) *S's* on the earth's worn brow to win her
    if she may.   *Tears of Heaven* 9
Smiling with shining eyes *S* a godlike smile   *The Mystic* 28
    from his spring Moved *s* toward his summer.   *Lover's Tale i* 307
Smirk stony *s's* at all things human and divine!   *Sugg. by Reading* 48
Smooth And she has mov'd in that *s* way so long,   " 65
Smote Than when Zamoysky *s* the Tartar Khan,   *Blow ye the trumpet* 12
Snake in the pride of beauty issuing A sheeny *s*,   *Could I outwear* 6
    a *s* her forehead clips And skins the colour   *Pallid thunderstricken* 13
    blood Of hateful herbs a subtle-fanged *s*.   *Lover's Tale i* 821
Sneering *S* bedridden in the down of Peace   *Sugg. by Reading* 46
Snow Winter roofs The headland with inviolate white *s*,   *Timbuctoo* 204
    thick *s* falls on her flake by flake,   *I' the glooming light* 20
Snowfield As the *s* on the mountain-peaks,   *The Hesperides, Song i* 6
Snowy wherefrom The *s* skirting of a garment hung,   *Timbuctoo* 182
Sobieski (John III., King of Poland) Than when
    from *S*, clan by clan,   *Blow ye the trumpet* 10
Social She feels not how the *s* frame is rack'd.   *Sugg. by Reading* 56
Socket And shook its earthly *s*, for we heard,   *Lover's Tale i* 61
Soft imaging The *s* inversion of her tremulous Domes;   *Timbuctoo* 232
    And the billow will embrace thee with a kiss as *s*
    as mine.   *Hero to Leander* 27
    With thy two couches *s* and white,   *O darling room* 3
    With two such couches *s* and white;   " 16
    When summer winds break their *s* sleep with sighs,   *Lover's Tale i* 559
Soil Deep-rooted in the living *s* of truth: *Timbuctoo* 225
Solar Nor blot with floating shades the *s* light.   *Shall the hag* 14
Sold be not bought and *s*.   *Blow ye the trumpet* 2
    She that gave you 's bought and *s*, *S*, *s*.   *The Ringlet* 33

Soldier-ridden His *s-r* Highness might incline   *Britons, guard* 49
Solemn Warbled from yonder knoll of *s* larches,   *Check every outflash* 10
    Nor yet your *s* organ-pipes that blow   *Cambridge* 8
    FIRST drink a health, this *s* night,   *Hands all Round* 1
    S but splendid, full of shapes and sounds,   *Lover's Tale i* 799
Solid Downlooking sees the *s* shining ground   *D. of F. Women* 2
Solitary Hark! how sweet the horned ewes bleat On
    the *s* steeps,   *Lotos-Eaters* 30
    A GATE and a field half ploughed, A *s* cow,   *A gate and a field* 2
Solitude Seraphtrod, Wound thro' your great Elysian *s's*,   *Timbuctoo* 48
    and in the *s* Of middle space confound them,   *Shall the hag* 8
    Thy shadowy Idols in the *s's*,   *A Fragment* 15
Soloë voyaging beyond The hoary promontory of *S*   *The Hesperides* 3
Sombre But in the middle of the *s* valley   *Check every outflash* 9
Some and swum with balanced wings To *s* tall mountain. *Lover's Tale i* 305
    Oh! rather had *s* loathly ghastful brow,   " 676
Somehow The world is somewhat? it goes
    on *s*;   *The 'How' and the 'Why'* 21
Something I feel there is *s*; but how and what?   " 23
Somewhat The world is *s*; it goes on somehow;   " 21
    I know there is *s*; but what and why! I   " 24
    cannot tell if that *s* be I.
Son We are the *s's* of freedom, We are free. (repeat) *National Song* 17, 35
    O rise, our strong Atlantic *s's*,   *Hands all Round* 49
Song A summer of loud *s*,   *The Grasshopper* 32
Soothe To *s* a civic wound or keep it raw,   *Sugg. by Reading* 32
Sorrow (s) Worn *S* sits by the moaning wave;   *I' the glooming light* 4
    Joy is *s's* brother;   *Every day, etc.* 24
    Thou hast no *s* or tears,   *The Grasshopper* 26
    storms of *s* and ruth That roar beneath;   *Though night* 9
    ME my own fate to lasting *s* doometh: *Me my own fate* 1
    'Oh hush, my joy, my *s*.'   *Home they brought him* 10
    strangling *s* weigh Mine utterance with lameness.   *Lover's Tale i* 24
Sorrow (verb) I *s* when I read the things you write,   *Sugg. by Reading* 77
Sort for your manner *s's* Not with this age,   *Cambridge* 10
Soul I felt my *s* grow mighty,   *Timbuctoo* 90
    What the life is? where the *s* may lie? *The 'How' and the 'Why'* 33
    My *s* shall follow thee!   *Hero to Leander* 31
    Wake on, my *s*, nor crouch to agony: *Though night* 5
    sailing on Pactolus in a boat, Drown *s* and sense, *Pallid thunderstricken* 4
    And steep my *s* in laughter   *There are three things* 2
    my inner *s* To tremble like a lutestring,   *Oh, Beauty* 12
    teach And have taught nothing, feeding on the *s*.   *Cambridge* 14
    If half the little *s* is dirt?   *New Timon* 36
    Poor *s*! behold her: what decorous calm!   *Sugg. by Reading* 61
    eyes were moved With motions of the *s*,   *Lover's Tale i* 73
    The written secrets of her inmost *s*   " 600
    the heat Of the remorseful *s* alive within,   " 682
Sound *s* which struck the palpitating sense,   *Timbuctoo* 119
    Colossal, without form, or sense, or *s*,   *The Mystic* 14
    The echo, feeble child of *s*,   *Chorus* 12
    and knoweth not Beyond the *s* he lists: *Lover's Tale i* 658
    the memory of that *s* With mighty evocation,   " 667
    Solemn but splendid, full of shapes and *s's*,   " 799
Sounding *S* on the morrow.   *Home they brought him* 5
South first within the *S* methought I saw   *Timbuctoo* 161
    Was not the *S*, The East, the West, all open,   *Lover's Tale i* 698
Southern underneath a shadowy plane In old
    Bayona, nigh the *S* Sea—   *There are three things* 11
    Between the *S* and the *W* Horn,   *The Hesperides* 5
    We curse the crimes of *S* kings,   *Hands all Round* 17
Southward faery light or cloud, Flowing *S*,   *Timbuctoo* 7
    camel on the verge Journeying *s*?   *A Fragment* 19
Sovranty grief Doth hold the other half in *s*.   *Love and Sorrow* 5
Sowed Memory *S* my deep-furrowed thought   *D. of F. Women* 5
Space in the solitude Of middle *s* confound them,   *Shall the hag* 9
Spade Beside her are laid, Her mattock and *s*,   *I' the glooming light* 6
Sparkle To flame and *s* and stream as of old,   *The Ringlet* 5
Speak She cannot *s*; she can only weep;   *I' the glooming light* 18
    s low, and give up wholly Thy spirit   *Check every outflash* 4
    —scarcely dare to *s*.   *Oh, Beauty* 9
    O *s* to Europe thro' your guns!   *Hands all Round* 51
    The single voice may *s* his mind aloud;   *Sugg. by Reading* 14
Spear HOME they brought him slain with *s's*.   *Home they brought him* 1
Speck Black *s's* amid a waste of dreary sand,   *Timbuctoo* 247

Sped   Love is dead ; His last arrow *s* ;   *Burial of Love* 9
Speech   every ruder sally Of thought and *s* ;   *Check every outflash* 2
And the free *s* that makes a Briton known.   *Britons, guard* 29
by that name was wont to live in her *s*,   *Lover's Tale i* 571
Speed   As for the French, God *s* 'em (repeat)   *National Song* 11, 29
Speedeth   Some think it *s* fast :   *The ' How ' and the ' Why '* 4
Spell   by a *s* Did change them into gall ;   *Love, Pride, etc.* 9
increasing *s*'s Which break upon each other,   *Timbuctoo* 125
Sphere   rais'd thee higher to the *S*'s of Heaven,   " 216
Strain the hot *s*'s of his convulsèd eyes,   *Love* 37
To charm a lower *s* of fulminating fools.   *Sugg. by Reading* 30
love too high to be express'd Arrested in its *s*,   *Lover's Tale i* 66
Sphinxes   placid *S* brooding o'er the Nile ?   *A Fragment* 14
Spiced   Wrapped round with *s* cerements in old grots   " 30
Spilt   Why the life goes when the blood is *s* ?   *The ' How ' and the ' Why '* 32
you are he That *s* his life about the cliques.   *New Timon* 40
Spire   methought I saw A wilderness of *s*'s,   *Timbuctoo* 162
Spirit   Thy *s* fetter'd with the bond of clay :   " 83
my *s* With supernatural excitation bound Within me,   " 90
no mightier *S* than I to sway The heart of man :   " 195
I am the *S*, The permeating life   " 219
Thus far the *S* : Then parted Heavenward on the wing :   " 250
Albeit, his *s* and his secret heart   *The Mystic* 7
Half-light, half shadow, let my *s* sleep   *Love and Sorrow* 17
Thy *s* to mild-minded Melancholy ;   *Check every outflash* 3
Thy *s*, circled with a living glory,   *Me my own fate* 3
But yet my lonely *s* follows thine,   " 9
brain could keep afloat The subtle *s*.   *Oh, Beauty* 11
S waits To embrace me in the sky.   *Germ of ' Maud '* 33
Sent up the moaning of unhappy *s*'s   *Lover's Tale i* 613
The very *s* of Paleness made still paler   " 679
Spite   And what with *s*'s and what with fears,   *New Timon* 29
What unheroic pertness ! what un-Christian *s* !   *Sugg. by Reading* 78
Splendid   Solemn but *s*, full of shapes and sounds,   *Lover's Tale i* 799
Splendour   thro' secret *s*'s mounting still,   *D. of F. Women* 11
centre of the *s*'s, all unworthy Of such a shrine—   *Lover's Tale i* 69
Splinter   fragments of the living rock, (Huge *s*'s,   " ii 45
Spoke   while I *s*, The bare word KISS hath made   *Oh, Beauty* 11
While I *s* thus, the seedsman, Memory,   *D. of F. Women* 14
And those fine curses which he *s* ;   *New Timon* 3
room Within the summer-house of which I *s*,   *Lover's Tale ii* 174
Sport   Shall not avail you when the day-beam *s*'s   *Cambridge* 6
Spot   colour'd *s*'s as dance athwart the eyes   *Timbuctoo* 70
Spotless   What profits now to understand The merits of a *s* shirt—   *New Timon* 34
Spring (s)   Upon some earth-awakening day of *s*   *Timbuctoo* 152
With earliest Light of *S*,   " 200
The vocal *s* of bursting bloom,   *Chorus* 15
and indue i' the *s* Hues of fresh youth,   *Could I outwear* 2
from his *s* Moved smiling toward his summer.   *Lover's Tale i* 306
Spring (verb)   For her the green grass shall not *s*,   *Burial of Love* 28
When war against our freedom *s*'s !   *Hands all Round* 50
O you, the Press !—what good from you might *s* !   *Sugg. by Reading* 7
Springing   *s* In and out the emerald glooms,   *The Grasshopper* 41
Springtide   which the fearful *s* flecks the lea,   *Love and Sorrow* 2
Green *s*, April promise, glad new-year   *Lover's Tale i* 277
Springtime   *s* calls To the flooding waters cool,   *Rosalind* 19
Sprout   on an oaken *s* A goodly acorn grew ;   *Lost Hope* 5
Spur   *S* along ! *s* amain ! charge to the fight :   *English War Song* 47
Spy   An epitaph that all may *s* ?   *Burial of Love* 23
You may not, like yon tyrant, deal in *spies*.   *Sugg. by Reading* 20
Spying   By tricks and *s*,   *Britons, guard* 31
Square   Why round is not *s* ?   *The ' How ' and the ' Why '* 13
Stagger'd   my human brain *S* beneath the vision,   *Timbuctoo* 186
Stair   step by step to scale that mighty *s*   " 198
Stand   I seem'd to *s* Upon the outward verge   " 94
Why the rocks *s* still,   *The ' How ' and the ' Why '* 14
S off, or else my skipping-rope Will hit you   *Skipping-rope* 3
He triumphs ; maybe, we shall *s* alone : (repeat)   *Britons, guard* 5, 11
Shall we *s* idle, Nor seek to bridle His vile aggressions, till we *s* alone ?   " 51
S's in her pew and hums her decent psalm   *Sugg. by Reading* 63
I To *s* within the level of their hopes,   *Lover's Tale i* 768
Standeth   Death *s* by ; She will not die ;   *I' the glooming light* 12
There *s* our ancient enemy ; (repeat)   *English War Song* 23, 45

Standing   Singing airily, *S* about the charmèd root.   *The Hesperides, Song i* 4
Singing airily, *S* about the charmèd root.   " iv 34
Star   *s*'s Were flooded over with clear glory   *Timbuctoo* 8
bore globes Of wheeling suns, or *s*'s,   " 172
The pleasant *s*'s have set !   *Hero to Leander* 39
underneath the *s* Named of the Dragon—   *A Fragment* 5
For the western sun and the western *s*,   *The Hesperides, Song i* 7
But the other, like a *s*,   *Germ of ' Maud '* 28
And all her *s*'s decay.'   *The Ringlet* 10
Stare   And *s*'s in his face and shouts ' how ? how ? '   *The ' How ' and the ' Why '* 29
Staring   somewhere in death They sleep with *s* eyes and gilded lips,   *A Fragment* 29
Starlit   bearing on both sides Double display of *s* wings   *Timbuctoo* 155
Starr'd   (*See also* **Newstarred**) those which *s* the night o' the Elder World ?   " 60
s at slender intervals With blossom tufts   *Lover's Tale i* 399
Starry   great angel mind which look'd from out The *s* glowing of his restless eyes.   *Timbuctoo* 89
The herald lightning's *s* bound,   *Chorus* 14
Starry-fair   Her face Was *s-f*, not pale,   *Lover's Tale i* 75
Startle   may rude Death never *s* them,   " 796
State (commonwealth)   I feel the thousand cankers of our *S*,   *Sugg. by Reading* 43
State (condition)   earth hath made her *s* forlorn   *Tears of Heaven* 3
COULD I outwear my present *s* of woe   *Could I outwear* 1
Stately   Her gardens frequent with the *s* Palm,   *Timbuctoo* 233
Statued   Your portals *s* with old kings and queens,   *Cambridge* 2
Stay   Huge mounds whereby to *s* his yeasty waves.   *Timbuctoo* 15
I'll *s* thee with my kisses.   *Hero to Leander* 22
If that he would then hear And *s*.   *The lintwhite* 7
Our life evanisheth : Oh ! *s*.   " 16
Though thou art fleet of wing, Yet *s*.   " 25
Delight is with thee gone, Oh ! *s*.   " 34
S's on the flowering arch of the bough,   *The Hesperides, Song iv* 18
Why *s* they there to guard a foreign throne ?   *Britons, guard* 41
Stays (corsets)   The padded man—that wears the *s*'s—   *New Timon* 8
Steal   and sadness *s* Symbols of each other,   *Every day, etc.* 25
Stedfast   Father, twinkle not thy *s* sight ;   *The Hesperides, Song ii* 3
Steep (adj.)   The path was *s* and loosely strewn with crags   *Lover's Tale i* 376
Steep (s)   (*See also* **Highland-steep**) ewes bleat On the solitary *s*'s,   *Lotos-Eaters* 30
Steep (verb)   And *s* my soul in laughter   *There are three things* 2
Steeped   It shall be *s* in the salt, salt tear, Shall be *s* in his own salt tear :   *English War Song* 14
Steeple   Why a church is with a *s* built ;   *The ' How ' and the ' Why '* 34
Stem   Flowing between the clear and polish'd *s*'s,   *Timbuctoo* 51
Stemmed   *See* **Thickstemmed, White-stemmed**
Step   *s* by *s* to scale that mighty stair   *Timbuctoo* 198
breaks in above Those marble *s*'s below.   *Hero to Leander* 35
Step-dame   she did act the *s-d* to mine eyes,   *Lover's Tale i* 664
Stern   his spirit and his secret heart The *S* experiences of converse lives,   *The Mystic* 8
Still   Like a swol'n river's gushings in *s* night   *Timbuctoo* 193
Ye could not read the marvel in his eye, The *s* serene abstraction ;   *The Mystic* 5
I had lain as *s*, And blind and motionless as then I lay !   *Lover's Tale i* 618
Sting   Popes And Brummels, when they try to *s*.   *New Timon* 20
Stir   So gladly doth it *s* ;   *Hero to Leander* 17
Crocodiles in briny creeks Sleep and *s* not :   *The Hesperides, Song i* 9
Stol'n   and the golden apple be *s* away,   " ii 11
The golden apple *s* away,   " iii 4
rare pity had *s* The living bloom away,   *Lover's Tale i* 725
Stone   By a mossed brookbank on a *s*   *O sad No more !* 3
Stony   With *s* smirks at all things human and divine !   *Sugg. by Reading* 48
Stood   I *S* upon the Mountain which o'erlooks   *Timbuctoo* 1
and he *s* beside me There on the ridge,   " 65
And alternations of all hues, he *s*.   " 76
S out a pillar'd front of burnish'd gold   " 175
where no gaze Might rest, *s* open,   " 179
Always there *s* before him, night and day,   *The Mystic* 11
which *s* In the midnoon the glory of old Rhodes,   *A Fragment* 1
Here *s* the infant Ilion of the mind,   *Mablethorpe* 3
I *S* on a tower in the wet,   *1865-1866* 1

Stop sing aloud and evermore in the wind,
without s, *The Hesperides, Song ii* 14
Storm calm and s Mingle day by day. *Every day, etc.* 7
By secret fire and midnight s's *Chorus* 5
s's of sorrow and ruth That roar beneath ; *Though night* 9
vessel and your Church may sink in s's. *Sugg. by Reading* 74
Storm-blast the shrill s-b feeds it from behind, *Lover's Tale ii* 47
Strain s Weak eyes upon the glistering sands *Pallid thunderstricken* 4
S the hot spheres of his convulsèd eyes, *Love* 37
Close by our ears, the huge roots s and creak), *Lover's Tale i* 63
Straining No more unfurl the s sail ; *Lotos-Eaters* 24
Strange Which flung s music on the howling winds, *Timbuctoo* 80
are full of s Astonishment and boundless change.
(repeat) *Chorus* 9, 19, 29
All visions wild and s ; ol 'ρέοντες 2
O SAD *No more!* O sweet *No more!* O s *No more!* O sad *No more!* 2
Strangling s sorrow weigh Mine utterance with lameness. *Lover's Tale i* 24
Stream (s) (*See also* **Understream**) borne Adown the
sloping of an arrowy s, *Timbuctoo* 144
Down an ideal s they ever float, *Pallid thunderstricken* 2
Over a s two birds of glancing feather *Dualisms* 8
And all things flow like a s. (repeat) ol 'ρέοντες 8, 16
Two s's upon the violet deep : *The Hesperides, Song iv* 6
To whom the slope and s of life, *Rosalind* 5
low-hung tresses, dipp'd In the fierce s, *Lover's Tale i* 375
the chillness of the mountain s Smote on my brow, „ 652
the loud s, Awoke me not, but were a part of sleep ; „ ii 123
Stream (verb) They s like fire in the skies ; *English War Song* 26
solid shining ground S from beneath him *D. of F. Women* 3
To flame and sparkle and s as of old, *The Ringlet* 8
Street and the s's with ghastly faces throng'd *Timbuctoo* 29
windeth through The argent s's o' the City, „ 231
Why change the titles of your s's ? *Hands all Round* 31
Strength buoyancy and s To bear them upward *Timbuctoo* 158
mailèd warrior in youth and s complete ; *The Grasshopper* 13
thro' the sapphire deeps In wayward s, *Chorus* 29
in him light and joy and s abides ; *Love* 42
For where is the heart and s of slaves ? Oh !
where is the s of slaves ? *English War Song* 36
ere the Czar Grew to this s *Blow ye the trumpet* 6
We won old battles with our s, the bow. *Britons, guard* 44
On that day the year First felt his youth and s, *Lover's Tale i* 306
Strewn path was steep and loosely s with crags „ 376
Stricken *See* **Awestricken, Thunderstricken**
Strife know no s Of inward woe or outward fear ; *Rosalind* 3
Strike some you s can scarce return the blow ; *Sugg. by Reading* 27
String *See* **Lutestring**
Stringing As they gambol, lilygarlands ever s : *Dualisms* 15
Stripe In a s of grassgreen calm, *Lotos-Eaters* 5
Stroke a lightning s had come Even from that Heaven *Lover's Tale i* 623
Strong The issue of s impulse, hurried through The riv'n
rapt brain : *Timbuctoo* 120
more fleet and s Than its precursor, „ 127
But an insect lithe and s, *The Grasshopper* 7
Where are thy monuments Piled by the s and sunborn
Anakim *A Fragment* 20
He is weak ! we are s ; he a slave, we are free ; *English War Song* 38
O rise, our s Atlantic sons, *Hands all Round* 49
Caucasus is bold and s. *The Hesperides, Song iii* 7
Stronger May Freedom's oak for ever live With s life
from day to day ; *Hands all Round* 6
Strove S to uprise, laden with mournful thanks, *Lover's Tale i* 748
Struck sound which s the palpitating sense, *Timbuctoo* 119
Strung S in the very negligence of Art, *Lover's Tale i* 562
Style How much I love this writer's manly s ! *Sugg. by Reading* 1
Subaltern who are to you As captain is to s. *New Timon* 16
Subject Free s's of the kindliest of all thrones, *Sugg. by Reading* 71
Substance Issue of its own s, *Love and Sorrow* 10
Substanceless Almeida, if my heart were s, „ 13
Subterranean and the streets with ghastly faces throng'd
Do utter forth a s voice, *Timbuctoo* 30
Subtle The s life, the countless forms Of living things, *Chorus* 7
no control Within the thrilling brain could keep afloat
The s spirit. *Oh, Beauty* 11
Bold, s, careless Rosalind, *Rosalind* 2

Subtle-fanged blood Of hateful herbs a s-f snake. *Lover's Tale i* 821
Such There are no hearts like English hearts, S hearts
of oak as they be. *National Song* 4
Of late s eyes looked at me—while I mused At
sunset, *There are three things* 9
self-upborne With s gladness, as, *Rosalind* 18
With two s couches soft and white ; *O darling room* 16
The centre of the splendours, all unworthy Of s a
shrine— *Lover's Tale i* 70
I well remember, It was a glorious morning, s a one
As dawns but once a season. Mercury On s a
morning would have flung himself From cloud to cloud, „ 301
There was no s thing.— „ 670
Suffer She hardly can believe that she shall s wrong. *Sugg. by Reading* 66
Suffering wan dark coil of faded s— *Could I outwear* 4
Sufficed with her week-day worldliness s, *Sugg. by Reading* 62
Suitor I am any man's s, If any will be my
tutor : *The 'How' and the 'Why'* 1
Summer (adj.) and sloped Into the slumberous s noon ; *A Fragment* 11
The s midges wove their wanton gambol, *Check every outflash* 12
In summer still a s joy resumeth. *Me my own fate* 4
When s winds break their soft sleep with sighs, *Lover's Tale i* 559
Summer (s) A s of loud song, *The Grasshopper* 32
The naked s's glowing birth, *Chorus* 16
A s still a summer joy resumeth. *Me my own fate* 4
S's tanling diamondeyed. *Dualisms* 22
from his spring Moved smiling toward his s. *Lover's Tale i* 307
Summerflowers Bowing the seeded s. *The Grasshopper* 8
Summerhours Life of the s, „ 3
Summerplain Joy of the s, „ 2
Summerpride In thy heat of s, „ 36
Summertide And in the glow of sallow S, *Timbuctoo* 201
Summervault Under a s of golden weather ; *Dualisms* 18
Summerwind VOICE of the s, *The Grasshopper* 1
Summerwood In the s's when the sun falls
low, *The 'How' and the 'Why'* 27
Summoning Unto the fearful s without : *Timbuctoo* 36
Sun when the S Had fall'n below th' Atlantick, „ 3
'Wide Afric, doth thy S Lighten, „ 58
Of those that gaze upon the noonday S. „ 71
planet-girded S's And moon-encircled planets, „ 109
bore globes Of wheeling s's, or stars, „ 172
In the summerwoods when the s falls low, *The 'How' and the 'Why'* 27
Nor the round s that shineth to all ; *Burial of Love* 21
Each s which from the centre flings *Chorus* 21
Thou art my heart's s in love's crystalline : *Love and Sorrow* 6
The mighty disk of their majestic s, *Love* 21
If thou dost leave me s, *The lintwhite* 32
WHERE is the Giant of the S, *A Fragment* 1
For the western s and the western star, *The Hesperides, Song iv* 1
S peeped in from open field, *Home they brought him* 6
the dew, the s, the rain, Unto the growth *Lover's Tale ii* 73
Sunborn Where are thy monuments Piled by the strong
and s Anakim *A Fragment* 20
Sunlight In s and in shadow, *The Grasshopper* 20
Sunny But a short youth s and free. „ 29
Thy locks are full of s sheen *The lintwhite* 28
Sunset while I mused At s, underneath a shadowy
plane *There are three things* 10
fullfaced s yellowy Stays on the flowering arch *The Hesperides, Song iv* 17
S ripened, above on the tree, „ 21
Gray sand banks and pale s's—dreary wind, *Mablethorpe* 7
About s We came unto the hill of woe, *Lover's Tale i* 364
Supernatural and my spirit With s excitation bound
Within me, *Timbuctoo* 91
Surpassing s Earth's As Heaven than Earth „ 169
Swalloweth narwhale s His foamfountains in the sea. *Lotos-Eaters* 7
Sway no mightier Spirit than I to s The heart *Timbuctoo* 195
Hopes did s from that Which hung the frailest : *Lover's Tale i* 857
Swear No man to bear it—S it ! We s it ! *Britons, guard* 58
We s to guard our own. „ 60
And I s henceforth by this and this, *The Ringlet* 20
Sweet (*See also* **Double-sweet**) for a moment fill'd My eyes
with irresistible s tears, *Timbuctoo* 191
Her Pagods hung with music of s bells : „ 234

Sweet (continued) Nor the rivers flow, nor the s birds sing, *Burial of Love* 29
Thy voice is s and low ; *Hero to Leander* 33
ERE yet my heart was s Love's tomb, *Love, Pride, etc.* 1
S Love was withered in his cell ; " 8
Embalming with s tears the vacant shrine, *Lost Hope* 3
Moving his crest to all s plots of flowers *Could I outwear* 7
THE lintwhite and the throstlecock Have voices s and clear ; *The lintwhite* 2
Alas ! that lips so cruel dumb Should have so s a breath ! " 18
O SAD *No more* ! O s *No more* ! *O sad No more* ! 1
OH, Beauty, passing beauty ! sweetest S ! *Oh, Beauty* 1
We will eat the Lotos, s As the yellow honeycomb, *Lotos-Eaters* 14
Surely, surely, slumber is more s than toil, " 38
Peace-lovers we—s Peace we all desire— *Britons, guard* 13

Sweeter This is lovelier and s, *Lotos-Eaters* 10

Sweetest OH, Beauty, passing beauty ! s Sweet ! *Oh, Beauty* 1

Swift till they minister'd Unto her s conceits ? *Lover's Tale* i 666

Swiftness Agglomerated s, I had lived " 495

Swim Thine eye in drops of gladness s's. *Hero to Leander* 18

Swimming till the eyes in vain Amid the wild unrest of s shade *Timbuctoo* 129

Swol'n Like a s river's gushings in still night " 193

Sword world is wasted with fire and s, *The Hesperides, Song iv* 22

Swum s with balanced wings To some tall mountain. *Lover's Tale* i 304

Symbol and sadness steal S's of each other ; *Every day, etc.* 26

T

Tact A little feeling is a want of t. *Sugg. by Reading* 58

Take men's hopes and fears t refuge in The fragrance *Timbuctoo* 226
Lest one from the East come and t it away. *The Hesperides, Song i* 29
t's his flags and waves them to the mob *D. of F. Women* 5
t it, t my skipping-rope And hang yourself *Skipping-rope* 11
fierce old man—to t his name You bandbox. *New Timon* 43
T care thou dost not fear to fall ! ' *What time I wasted* 9
To t Sardinia, Belgium, or the Rhine : *Britons, guard* 50
T heed of your wide privileges ! *Sugg. by Reading* 11
' Then t it, love, and put it by ; *The Ringlet* 11

Taken If the golden apple be t The world *The Hesperides, Song ii* 21
And t away the greenness of my life, *Lover's Tale* i 625

Tale There must no man go back to bear the t: *Britons, guard* 56

Talk *You* t of tinsel ! why we see *New Timon* 37

Talked ANGELS have t with him, and showed him thrones: *The Mystic* 5

Talking other things t in unknown tongues, *Timbuctoo* 112

Tall Daughters of time, divinely t, *The Mystic* 26
There are no men like Englishmen, So t and bold as they be. *National Song* 8
Till midnoon the cool east light Is shut out by the round of the t hillbrow ; *The Hesperides, Song iv* 16
and swum with balanced wings To some t mountain. *Lover's Tale* i 305

Tanling Summer's t diamondeyed. *Dualisms* 22

Tarry In the hollow rosy vale to t, *Lotos-Eaters* 12
BUT she *tarries* in her place And I paint *Germ of ' Maud '* 1

Tartar Than when Zamoysky smote the T Khan, *Blow ye the trumpet* 32

Taste assimilated all our t's And future fancies. *Lover's Tale* i 238

Taught did profess to teach And have t nothing, *Cambridge* 14

Teach t him to attain By shadowing forth *Timbuctoo* 196
did profess to t And have taught nothing, *Cambridge* 13
Nay, dearest, t me how to hope, *Skipping-rope* 9

Tear Bathes the cold hand with t's, *Timbuctoo* 38
fill'd My eyes with irresistable sweet t's, "
With the t's he hath shed, *Burial of Love* 5
Her t's are mixed with the bearded dews. *I' the glooming light* 11
Laughter bringeth t's : *Every day, etc.* 18
Thou hast no sorrow or t's, *The Grasshopper* 26
Embalming with sweet t's the vacant shrine, *Lost Hope* 3
all the day heaven gathers back her t's *Tears of Heaven* 6
commend the t's to creep From my charged lids ; *Could I outwear* 10
It shall be steeped in the salt, salt t, Shall be steeped in his own salt t : *English War Song* 14
And both my eyes gushed out with t's. *O sad No more* ! 6
I said, ' O years that meet in t's, *1865–1866* 4
We passed with t's of rapture. *Lover's Tale* i 409
Flooding its angry cheek with odorous t's. " 565
my unhappy sighs, fed with my t's, " 674

Tear (continued) eyes, I saw, were full of t's in the morn, *Lover's Tale* i 728
Think not thy t's will make my name grow green,— " 806
woful ailments Of unavailing t's and heart deep moans " 819

Tearless For ever write In the weathered light Of the t eye *Burial of Love* 22

Tell —Of winds which t of waters, *Timbuctoo* 208
I cannot t if that somewhat be I. *The ' How ' and the ' Why '* 25
Number, t them over and number How many *The Hesperides, Song ii* 7
Who can t Why to smell The violet, *Who can say* 4
where, alack, is Bewick To t the meaning now ? *A gate and a field* 6
Or t me how to die. *Skipping-rope* 10
Yet t her—better to be free Than vanquish *Hands all Round* 27
what profits it To t ye that her father died, *Lover's Tale* i 291

Temperament With moral breadth of t. *New Timon* 28

Tempest world's last t darkens overhead ; *Britons, guard* 2

Tender After my refluent health made t quest Unanswer'd, *Lover's Tale* i 742

Tenderly Oh ! lead me t, for fear the mind Rain thro' my sight, " 23
Her face Was starry-fair, not pale, t flush'd " 75

Tenement And damn'd unto his loathed t. " 683

Tennis Think you hearts are t balls To play with, *Rosalind* 32

Thanks Strove to uprise, laden with mournful t, *Lover's Tale* i 748

That and ever since t hour, My voice hath somewhat falter'd— " 749

Thebes melody flattering the crisped Nile By columned T. *A Fragment* 27

Then But what is the meaning of t and now ! *The ' How ' and the ' Why '* 22

Thick and t night Came down upon my eyelids, and I fell. *Timbuctoo* 186
The t snow falls on her flake by flake, *I' the glooming light* 20
Pushing the t roots aside Of the singing flowerèd grasses, *Grasshopper* 37
And crushing the t fragrant reeds he lies, *Love* 32

Thick-ribbèd Cathedralled caverns of t-r gold *Pallid thunderstricken* 7

Thickstemmed Looks through the t woods by day and night *Love* 44

Thin And Memory tho' fed by Pride Did wax so t on gall, *Love, Pride, etc.* 12
T dilettanti deep in nature's plan, *Sugg. by Reading* 80

Thing other t's talking in unknown tongues, *Timbuctoo* 112
shape These t's with accurate similitude " 134
And all t's creeping to a day of doom. *The Mystic* 40
the countless forms Of living t's, *Chorus* 8
For all t's are as they seem to all, (repeat) οἱ ῥέοντες 7, 15
And all t's flow like a stream. (repeat) 8, 16
Surely all pleasant t's had gone before, *O sad No more* ! 7
THERE are three t's that fill my heart with sighs *There are three things* 1
There are three t's beneath the blessed skies " 5
All t's are not told to all, *The Hesperides, Song iii* 12
All good t's are in the west, " iv 14
By the t I hold in scorn, *Germ of ' Maud '* 6
We likewise have our evil t's ; *Hands all Round* 19
stony smirks at all t's human and divine ! *Sugg. by Reading* 48
I sorrow when I read the t's you write, " 77
These t's Unto the quiet daylight of your minds *Lover's Tale* i 293
With her to whom all outward fairest t's " 383
There was no such t.— " 670

Think Some t it speedeth fast: *The ' How ' and the ' Why '* 4
T you hearts are tennis balls To play with, *Rosalind* 32
T not thy tears will make my name grow green,— *Lover's Tale* i 806

Thinking we T men of England, loathe a tyranny. *Sugg. by Reading* 12

Thought (s) With such a vast circumference of t, *Timbuctoo* 93
thrilling t's Involving and embracing each " 115
the torrent of quick t Absorbed me " 141
My t's which long had grovell'd in the slime " 149
E'en so my t's, erewhile so low, " 157
ALL t's, all creeds, all dreams are true, οἱ ῥέοντες 1
every ruder sally Of t and speech ; *Check every outflash* 2
Sowed my deep-furrowed t with many a name *D. of F. Women* 15
nor with the t's that roll, *Cambridge* 11
I turn To you that mould men's t's ; *Sugg. by Reading* 86
The wreck of ruin'd life and shatter'd t, *Lover's Tale* ii 62
So gazed I on the ruins of that t " 71

Thought (verb) a familiar face : I t we knew him: *New Timon* 7

Thousand I play about his heart a t ways, *Timbuctoo* 205
I feel the t cankers of our State, *Sugg. by Reading* 43

Three And yet again, t shadows, fronting one, *The Mystic* 17
THERE are t things that fill my heart with sighs *There are three things* 1
There are t things beneath the blessed skies For which I live— " 5

QQ

Three (continued) Hesper, the dragon, and sisters *t*, *The Hesperides, Song ii* 24
     Hesper, the dragon, and sisters *t*, Daughters *t*,   "   *iv* 25
Three-fold For the blossom unto *t-f* music bloweth :   "   *i* 17
Threshold from the golden *t* had down-roll'd   *Lover's Tale i* 617
Thrill'd Who killed the girls and *t* the boys   *New Timon* 9
Thrilling *t* thoughts Involving and embracing each with
     each Rapid as fire,   *Timbuctoo* 115
   Lenora, laughing clearly A light and *t* laughter,   *Anacreontics* 10
   no control Within the *t* brain could keep afloat The
     subtle spirit.   *Oh, Beauty* 10
Throne *T*'s of the Western wave, fair Islands green ?   *Timbuctoo* 42
   Part of a *t* of fiery flame,   "   181
   Oh latest *T* ! where I was rais'd   "   240
   ANGELS have talked with him, and showed him *t*'s :   *The Mystic* 1
   Basing thy *t* above the world's annoy.   *Though night* 8
   The very *t* of the eternal God :   *Love* 6
   Breathe on thy wingèd *t*, and it shall move   "   27
   Why stay they there to guard a foreign *t* ?   *Britons, guard* 41
   Free subjects of the kindliest of all *t*'s,   *Sugg. by Reading* 71
Throng'd and the streets with ghastly faces *t*   *Timbuctoo* 29
Thronging *T* the cells of the diseased mind,   *Shall the hag* 3
Throstlecock THE lintwhite and the *t*   *The lintwhite* 1
Throwing And *t* by all consciousness of self,   *Lover's Tale i* 787
Thrown I had *t* me on the vast,   "   493
Thrust woful man had *t* his wife and child   "   368
Thunder (s) The heavy *t*'s girding might,   *Chorus* 13
   Melodious *t*'s through your vacant courts   *Cambridge* 9
   Why waste they yonder Their idle *t* ?   *Britons, guard* 40
   I hear a *t* though the skies are fair,   *Sugg. by Reading* 89
   rapid brook Shot down his inner *t*'s,   *Lover's Tale i* 372
   had down-roll'd Their heaviest *t*,   "   618
Thunder (verb) And *t* thro' the sapphire deeps   *Chorus* 28
Thunderstricken THE pallid *t* sigh for gain,   *Pallid thunderstricken* 1
Thymiaterion Past *T*, in calmèd bays,   *The Hesperides* 4
Tide (*See also* **Summertime**) Call home your ships across
     Biscayan *t*'s,   *Britons, guard* 37
   In rising and in falling with the *t*,   *Lover's Tale i* 62
Tilth *T*, hamlet, mead and mound :   *D. of F. Women* 4
Timbuctoo Or is the rumour of thy *T*   *Timbuctoo* 61
Time (*See also* **Summertime**) Giant of old *T* infixed
     The limits of his prowess, pillars high Long *t*
     eras'd from Earth :   "   11
   A dream as frail as those of ancient *T* ?'   "   62
   the *t* is well nigh come When I must render up   "   242
   In *t* there is no present,   *The ' How' and the ' Why'* 5
   One reflex from eternity on *t*,   *The Mystic* 22
   Daughters of *t*, divinely tall,   "   26
   T flowing in the middle of the night,   "   39
   what *t* laid low And crushing the thick fragrant reeds   *Love* 31
   dewy prime Of youth and buried *t* ?   *Who can say* 7
   WHAT *t* I wasted youthful hours   *What time I wasted* 1
   To raise the people and chastise the *t*'s   *Sugg. by Reading* 5
   touch of *T* Will turn it silver-gray ;   *The Ringlet* 5
   touch of *T* Can turn thee silver-gray ;   "   15
   legend ran that, long *t* since, One rainy night,   *Lover's Tale i* 366
   Planting my feet against this mound of *t*   "   492
Timon The old *T*, with his noble heart,   *New Timon* 3
   A *T* you ! Nay, nay, for shame :   "   41
Tinsel *You* talk of *t* ! why we see The old mark   "   37
Tithon No *T* thou as poets feign   *The Grasshopper* 5
Title Why change the *t*'s of your streets ?   *Hands all Round* 31
Titmarsh And a *t* in the bough.   *A gate and a field* 4
To-and-fro Did brush my forehead in their *t-a-f* :   *Lover's Tale i* 736
To-day WHO can say Why *T-d*   *Who can say* 2
Toil slumber is more sweet than *t*,   *Lotos-Eaters* 38
Told When in this valley first I *t* my love.   *Check every outflash* 14
   All things are not *t* to all,   *The Hesperides, Song iii* 12
   For what is this which now I'm *t*,   *The Ringlet* 31
Tolerance And those who tolerate not her *t*,   *Sugg. by Reading* 68
Tolerate And those who *t* not her tolerance,   "   68
Toleration God save the Nation, The *t*,   *Britons, guard* 28
Tomb ERE yet my heart was sweet Love's *t*,   *Love, Pride, etc.* 1
   we deem the world thy *t*.   *Love* 19
To-morrow *T-m* will be yesterday ?   *Who can say* 3
Tone wondrous *t*'s Of man and beast   *Chorus* 8

Tongue other things talking in unknown *t*'s,   *Timbuctoo* 112
   Mute his *t*,   *Burial of Love* 4
To-night Thou shalt not wander hence *t-n*,   *Hero to Leander* 21
   T-n the roaring brine Will rend thy golden tresses ;   "   23
Took I *t* delight in this locality !   *Mablethorpe* 2
   I that *t* you for true gold,   *The Ringlet* 32
Tool Be noble, you ! nor work with faction's *t*'s   *Sugg. by Reading* 29
Torrent the *t* of quick thought Absorbed me   *Timbuctoo* 141
Tortured From iron limbs and *t* nails !   *Hands all Round* 16
Tossing *T* on the *t* ocean,   *Lotos-Eaters* 3
Tost *See* **Wind-tost**
Touch (s) chilling *t* of Time Will turn it silver-gray ;   *The Ringlet* 5
   chilling *t* of Time Can turn thee silver-gray ;   "   15
Touch (verb) As with one kiss to *t* thy blessèd cheek.   *Oh, Beauty* 8
Toucheth and sometimes *t* but one string,   *Lover's Tale i* 11
Tower rangèd Chrysolite, Minarets and *t*'s ?   *Timbuctoo* 236
   soon yon brilliant *t*'s Shall darken   "   244
   Show'd me vast cliffs with crown of *t*'s,   *What time I wasted* 3
   I STOOD on a *t* in the wet,   *1865-1866* 1
Town In any *t*, to left or right,   *O darling room* 14
Trackless A maze of piercing *t*, thrilling thoughts   *Timbuctoo* 115
   and strength To bear them upward through the *t* fields   "   159
Traitor But be not you the blatant *t*'s of the hearth.   *Sugg. by Reading* 24
   Peace-lovers, haters Of shameless *t*'s,   *Britons, guard* 16
Trampled And, *t* on, left to its own decay.   *Lover's Tale ii* 81
Transitory Thy woes are birds of passage, *t* :   *Me my own fate* 1
Translucent Child of Man, See'st thou yon river, whose *t*
     wave,   *Timbuctoo* 229
Treasure watch the *t* Of the wisdom of the West. *The Hesperides, Song i* 3
Tree (*See also* **Fruit-tree**) Round about the
     hallowed fruit *t* curled—   "   *ii* 13
   Bound about the golden *t*   "   25
   Sunset ripened, above on the *t*,   "   *iv* 21
   The gnarlèd bole of the charmed *t*,   "   29
   Where Love was worshipp'd under every *t*—   *Lover's Tale i* 324
Tremble inner soul To *t* like a lutestring,   *Oh, Beauty* 13
Trembling a snake her forehead clips And skins
     the colour from her *t* lips.   *Pallid thunderstricken* 14
Tremulous imaging The soft inversion of her *t* Domes ;   *Timbuctoo* 232
   At length, Upon the *t* bridge,   *Lover's Tale i* 406
Tress roaring brine Will rend thy golden *t*es ;   *Hero to Leander* 24
   That brush thee with their silken *t*es ?   *The Grasshopper* 39
   low-hung *t*es, dipp'd In the fierce stream,   *Lover's Tale i* 374
Tribe Alas, Church writers, altercating *t*'s—   *Sugg. by Reading* 73
Trick By *t*'s and spying,   *Britons, guard* 21
Tried And once you *t* the Muses too :   *New Timon* 13
Triple With *t* arch of everchanging bows,   *Timbuctoo* 74
Triple-folded I fain would shake their *t-f* ease,   *Sugg. by Reading* 44
Triumph (s) The *t* of this foretaste,   *Lover's Tale i* 515
Triumph (verb) He *t*'s ; maybe, we shall stand alone :
     (repeat)   *Britons, guard* 5, 11
Trod *See* **Seraphtrod**
Troubled Like light on *t* waters :   *Love* 40
Troublous The *t* autumn's sallow gloom,   *Chorus* 17
True ALL thoughts, all creeds, all dreams are *t*,   οἱ ῥέοντες 1
   The *t* men banished,   *Britons, guard* 10
   Till your balls fly as their *t* shafts have flown.   "   47
   And then shall I know it is all *t* gold   *The Ringlet* 7
   I that took you for *t* gold,   "   32
Truer ' God save the Queen' is here a *t* cry.   *Britons, guard* 14
Truest Oh, *t* love ! art thou forlorn,   *Burial of Love* 14
Trumpet BLOW ye the *t*, gather from afar   *Blow ye the trumpet* 1
Trust Peace-lovers we—but who can *t* a liar ?—   *Britons, guard* 14
   And *t* an ancient manhood and the cause   *Sugg. by Reading* 39
Truth Deep-rooted in the living soil of *t* :   *Timbuctoo* 225
   shalt thou pierce the woven glooms of *t* ;   *Though night* 11
   Man is the measure of all *t* Unto himself. All *t* is change : οἱ ῥέοντες 3
   Till we were left to fight for *t* alone.   *Britons, guard* 35
   Like them, you bicker less for *t* than forms.   *Sugg. by Reading* 76
Try when they *t* to sting.   *New Timon* 20
Turn (s) Has given all my faith a *t* ?   *The Ringlet* 58
Turn (verb) *T* cloud to light, and bitterness to joy,   *Though night* 6
   once more I *t* To you that mould men's thoughts ; *Sugg. by Reading* 85
   therefore now you *t*,   *New Timon* 14
   touch of Time Will *t* it silver-gray ;   *The Ringlet* 6

Turn (verb) (*continued*) touch of Time Can *t* thee silver-gray ;   *The Ringlet* 16
Turned all faces *t* to where Glows rubylike   *D. of F. Women* 6
Turning hinge on which the door of Hope, Once *t*,   *Lover's Tale i* 298
Turretstairs *t* are wet That lead into the sea.   *Hero to Leander* 36
Tuskèd Where the *t* seahorse walloweth   *Lotos-Eaters* 4
Tutelary I became to her A *t* angel   *Lover's Tale i* 388
Tutor I am any man's suitor, If any will be my *t* :   *The 'How' and the 'Why'* 2
Twenty *See* **Four-and-twenty**
Twilight glooms And cool impleachèd *t*'s.   *Timbuctoo* 228
   the back owl scuds down the mellow *t*,   *The 'How' and the 'Why'* 30
   Like a lone cypress, through the *t* hoary,   *Me my own fate* 6
   if he had fall'n In love in *t* ?   *Lover's Tale i* 700
Twinkle Father, *t* not thy stedfast sight ;   *The Hesperides, Song* iii 3
Two and beneath *T* doors of blinding brilliance,   *Timbuctoo* 178
   Why *t* and *t* make four ? Why round is not square ?   *The 'How' and the 'Why'* 13
   For the *t* first were not, but only seemed One shadow   *The Mystic* 20
   T bees within a chrystal flowerbell rockèd   *Dualisms* 1
   Over a stream *t* birds of glancing feather Do woo each other,   " 14
   T children lovelier than love, adown the lea are singing,   *The Hesperides, Song* iv 9
   T streams upon the violet deep :   *O darling room* 3
   With thy *t* couches soft and white,   " 16
   With *t* such couches soft and white ;   *Lover's Tale i* 386
Type they were the *t*'s and shadowings   *Sugg. by Reading* 12
Tyranny thinking men of England, loathe a *t*.   *Hands all Round* 42
Tyrant (adj.) Permit not thou the *t* powers To fight   " 14
Tyrant (s) Heaven guard them from her *t*s' jails !   *Hands all round* 10, 22, 34, 46, 58
   God the *t*'s cause confound ! (repeat)   *Sugg. by Reading* 20
   You may not, like yon *t*, deal in spies.

U

Unattainable By shadowing forth the *U* ;   *Timbuctoo* 197
Unavailing whom woful ailments Of *u* tears   *Lover's Tale i* 819
Unaware All *u*'s, into the poet's brain ;   " 557
Unborn Thou, from the first, *u*, undying love,   *Love* 1
Unchanged Keeping *u* The purport of their coinage.   *Lover's Tale i* 733
Un-Christian What unheroic pertness ! what *u-C* spite !   *Sugg. by Reading* 78
Unconceived vision Of *u* and awful happiness,   *Lover's Tale i* 798
Uncontrolled This was the very arch-mock And insolence of *u* Fate,   " 688
Undefin'd through the trackless fields Of *u* existence far and free.   *Timbuctoo* 160
Understand I have given *thee* To *u* my presence,   " 214
   What profits now to *u* The merits of a spotless shirt—   *New Timon* 33
Understood They *can* be *u* by kings.   *Hands all Round* 52
Understream glistering sands that robe The *u*.   *Pallid thunderstricken* 6
Undescended unsounded, *u* depth Of her black hollows.   *Timbuctoo* 104
Undiscerned obelisks Graven with gorgeous emblems *u* ?   *A Fragment* 1
Undiscerning Ye scorned him with an *u* scorn :   *The Mystic* 3
Undreading Unknowing fear, *U* loss,   *The Grasshopper* 17
Undying Thou, from the first, unborn, *u*, love,   *Love* 1
Unfading such as gird The *u* foreheads of the Saints in Heaven ?   *Timbuctoo* 54
Unfathomable chasms of deep, deep blue Slumber'd *u*,   " 8
Unfed. The light of his hopes *u*,   *Burial of Love* 3
Unfrequent *U*, low, as tho' it told its pulses ;   *Lover's Tale ii* 58
Unfurl No more *u* the straining sail ;   *Lotos-Eaters* 24
Unhappy and tho' horrid rifts Sent up the moaning of *u* spirits Imprison'd in her centre,   *Lover's Tale i* 613
   All joy ; who drew the happy atmosphere Of my *u* sighs,   " 674
Unheroic What *u* pertness ! what un-Christian spite !   *Sugg. by Reading* 78
Unicorn Those rhymes, 'The Lion and the *U*'   *Lover's Tale i* 285
Unimagin'd an *u* depth And harmony of planet-girded Suns   *Timbuctoo* 108
Union Most loveliest, most delicious *u* ?   *Lover's Tale i* 275
   And were in *u* more than double-sweet.   " 567
Unknowing *U* fear, Undreading loss,   *The Grasshopper* 16
Unknown Or other things talking in *u* tongues,   *Timbuctoo* 112
Unlike Like, *u*, they roam together Under a summer-vault of golden weather,   *Dualisms* 19
Unnumbered With selfwrought evils of *u* years,   *Tears of Heaven* 4

QQ*

Unrelenting Would, *u*, Kill all dissenting,   *Britons, guard* 33
Unrest Amid the wild *u* of swimming shade   *Timbuctoo* 129
Unreturned Love *u* is like the fragrant flame   *To* —— 5
Unrevenged love ! art thou forlorn, And *u* ?   *Burial of Love* 15
Unroof *U* the shrines of clearest vision,   *To a Lady Sleep.* 3
Unscathed Yet endure *u* Of changeful cycles   *A Fragment* 8
Unsealèd The glory *u*,   *The Hesperides, Song* iii 3
Unshaken like dusky worms which house Beneath *u* waters,   *Timbuctoo* 151
   u peace hath won thee :   *Though night* 10
Unshockèd wave *u* Lays itself calm and wide,   *Dualisms* 6
Unsounded the *u*, undescended depth Of her black hollows.   *Timbuctoo* 104
Unstrung His bow *u* With the tears he hath shed,   *Burial of Love* 5
Unutterable and look'd into my face With his *u*, shining orbs,   *Timbuctoo* 67
   erewhile so low, now felt *U* buoyancy and strength   " 158
   The silence of all hearts, *u* Love.   *Love* 14
Unvisited her silver heights *U* with dew   *Timbuctoo* 103
Unwaning Dim shadows but *u* presences Fourfacèd   *The Mystic* 15
Unworthy The centre of all splendours, all *u* Of such a shrine—   *Lover's Tale i* 69
Up *See* **Far-up**
Upborne *See* **Self-upborne**
Upburning without heat, into a larger air *U*,   *The Mystic* 45
Updrawn *U* in expectation of her change—   *Lover's Tale i* 597
   With mighty evocation, had *u*   " 668
Upheld *U*, and ever hold aloft the cloud   *The Mystic* 31
Uprend though they *u* the sea,   *Love* 9
Uprise Calls to him by the fountain to *u*.   " 35
   Strove to *u*, laden with mournful thanks,   *Lover's Tale i* 748
Upsprung *u* the dazzling Cones Of Pyramids,   *Timbuctoo* 168
Use No longer in the dearest *u* of mine—   *Lover's Tale i* 599
Utter Do *u* forth a subterranean voice,   *Timbuctoo* 30
   But lose themselves in *u* emptiness.   *Love and Sorrow* 16
Utterance strangling sorrow weigh Mine *u* with lameness.   *Lover's Tale i* 25

V

Vacant Embalming with sweet tears the *v* shrine,   *Lost Hope* 3
   Melodious thunders through your *v* courts At morn and even ;   *Cambridge* 9
Vagrant her silver heights Unvisited with dew of *v* cloud,   *Timbuctoo* 103
Vague As men do from a *v* and horrid dream,   *Lover's Tale i* 786
Vale In the hollow rosy *v* to tarry,   *Lotos-Eaters* 12
   We will abide in the golden *v* Of the Lotos-land,   " 26
Valley In the *v* some, and some On the ancient heights watered *vallies* where the young birds sing ;   *Could I outwear* 8
   But in the middle of the sombre *v*   *Check every outflash* 6
   When in this *v* first I told my love.   " 14
   Have hallowed out a *v* and a gulf   *Lover's Tale i* 26
Van the brazen beat Of their broad *v*'s,   *Shall the hag* 8
Vanish'd All freedom *v*,   *Britons, guard* 9
Vanity in my *v* I seem'd to stand Upon   *Timbuctoo* 94
   hath felt The *vanities* of after and before ;   *The Mystic* 6
Vanquish Than *v* all the world in arms.   *Hands all Round* 28
Vapour The cruel *v*'s went through all,   *Love, Pride, etc.* 7
   Or moisture of the *v*, left in clinging,   *Lover's Tale ii* 46
Varicoloured *See* **Vary**
Varied The *v* earth, the moving heaven,   *Chorus* 1
Vary Of wayward *v* coloured circumstance,   *The Mystic* 12
Vast (adj.) With such a *v* circumference of thought,   *Timbuctoo* 93
   Show'd me *v* cliffs with crown of towers,   *What time I wasted* 3
   Some *v* Assyrian doom to burst upon our race.   *Sugg. by Reading* 42
   The night is dark and *v* ;   *Hero to Leander* 2
Vast (s) I had thrown me on the *v*,   *Lover's Tale i* 493
Vastness between whose limbs Of brassy *v*   *A Fragment* 7
Vault *See* **Summervault**
Vaulting *V* on thine airy feet.   *The Grasshopper* 10
Veil (s) Athwart the *v*'s of evil which enfold thee   *Love* 17
   Oh ! rend the *v* in twain :   " 25
Veil (verb) I did *v* My vision with both hands,   *Timbuctoo* 68

Wild (*continued*) Hark how the *w* rain hisses, — *Hero to Leander* 14

and blow back Their *w* cries down their cavernthroats, — *Shall the hag* 10

All visions *w* and strange ; — οἱ 'ρέοντες 2

And nothing seems to me so *w* and bold, — *Oh, Beauty* 7

WE have had enough of motion, Weariness and *w* alarm, — *Lotos-Eaters* 2

Better *w* Mahmoud's war-cry once again ! — *Sugg. by Reading* 83

Her words were like a coronal of *w* blooms — *Lover's Tale i* 561

Wilderness methought I saw A *w* of spies, — *Timbuctoo* 162

Wildest The fountainpregnant mountains riven To shapes of *w* anarchy, — *Chorus* 4

We still were loyal in our *w* fights, — *Sugg. by Reading* 35

Wildweed I smelt a *w* flower alone ; — *O sad No more !* 4

Wile Thy pleasant *w*'s Forgotten, — *Burial of Love* 15

Out of watchings, out of *w*'s, — *The Hesperides, Song iii* 10

Will apart In intellect and power and *w*, — *The Mystic* 38

Willow and the white *w*'s sigh ? — *The 'How' and the 'Why'* 15

Win And *w* him unto me : — *Timbuctoo* 210

Smiles on the earth's worn brow to *w* her if she may. — *Tears of Heaven* 9

Wind (s) (*See also* **Land-wind, Northwind, Seawind, Summer-wind, Westwind**) Blown round with happy airs of odorous *w*'s ? — *Timbuctoo* 46

Which flung strange music on the howling *w*'s, — " 80

in red Autumn when the *w*'s are wild With gambols, — " 202

With harmonies of *w* and wave and wood — " 207

—Of *w*'s which tell of waters, and of waters Betraying the close kisses of the *w*— — " 208

But *w*'s from heaven shook the acorn out, — *Lost Hope* 7

the *w* which bloweth cold or heat Would shatter — *Shall the hag* 6

borne abroad By the loud *w*'s, — *Love* 9

sing aloud and evermore in the *w*, without stop, — *The Hesperides, Song ii* 14

And the low west *w*, breathing afar, — " *iv* 8

Rosalind Fullsailed before a vigorous *w*, — *Rosalind* 10

Gray sand banks and pale sunsets—dreary *w*, — *Mablethorpe* 3

And *w*'s were roaring and blowing ; — *1865-1866* 3

One rainy night, when every *w* blew loud, — *Lover's Tale i* 367

summer *w*'s break their soft sleep with sighs, — " 559

Being wafted on the *w*, drove in my sight, — " 730

ringlets, Drooping and beaten with the plaining *w*, — " 735

Wind (verb) Yet *w*'s the pathway free to all :— — *What time I wasted* 8

Windeth *w* through The argent streets o' the City, — *Timbuctoo* 230

the blue-green river *w* slowly ; — *Check every outflash* 5

channel *w* far Till it fade and fail and die, — *Germ of 'Maud'* 29

Wind-tost And close above us, sang the *w-t* pine, — *Lover's Tale i* 60

Windy By secret fire and midnight storms That wander round their *w* cones, — *Chorus* 6

Wine Over their scrips and shares, their meats and *w*, *Sugg. by Reading* 47

Winedark Long enough the *w* wave our weary bark did carry. — *Lotos-Eaters* 9

Wing A rustling of white *w*'s ! — *Timbuctoo* 64

starlit *w*'s which burn Fanlike and fibred, — " 155

Though thou art fleet of *w*, Yet stay. — *The lintwhite* 24

swum with balanced *w*'s To some tall mountain. *Lover's Tale i* 304

Wingèd Through dark and bright *W* hours are borne ; *Every day, etc.* 4

Through whose dim brain the *w* dreams are born *To a Lady Sleep.* 2

Breathe on thy *w* throne, and it shall move In music *Love* 27

One of the shining *w* powers, — *What time I wasted* 2

Wink Above her head the weak lamp dips and *w*'s *Timbuctoo* 35

Look to him, father, lest he *w*, — *The Hesperides, Song ii* 11

And a lady may *w*, and a girl may hint, — *The Ringlet* 17

Winnow *W* the purple, bearing on both sides *Timbuctoo* 154

Winter *W* roofs The headland with inviolate white snow, — " 203

hoarhead *w* paving earth With sheeny white, — *Chorus* 18

state of woe With one brief *w*, — *Could I outwear* 2

Wisdom To know thee is all *w*, — *Love* 15

watch the treasure Of the *w* of the West. *The Hesperides, Song i* 14

In a corner *w* whispers. — " 15

Hoarded *w* brings delight. — " *ii* 6

Wise The *w* could he behold Cathedralled caverns *Pallid thunderstricken* 6

Wiser To France, the *w* France, we drink, my friends, — *Hands all Round* 35

Wish That *w* to keep their people fools ; — " 54

Be loyal, if you *w* for wholesome rule : — *Sugg. by Reading* 33

Withered No *w* immortality, — *The Grasshopper* 28

Hateful with hanging cheeks, a *w* brood, — *Shall the hag* 4

What happy air shall woo The *w* leaf fall'n in the woods, — *Lover's Tale i* 622

Withered Sweet Love was *w* in his cell ; — *Love, Pride, etc.* 8

Withering dead skin *w* on the fretted bone, — *Lover's Tale i* 678

But the *w* scorn of the many shall cleave — *English War Song* 5

Woe All is change, *w* or weal ; — *Every day, etc.* 23

The linkèd *w*'s of many a fiery change — *The Mystic* 9

COULD I outwear my present state of *w* — *Could I outwear* 1

Thy *w*'s are birds of passage, transitory : — *Me my own fate* 2

know no strife Of inward *w* or outward fear ; — *Rosalind* 4

one of those who cannot weep For others' *w*'s, — " 12

About sunset We came to the hill of *w*, — *Lover's Tale i* 365

Christ cried : *W*, *w*, to Pharisees and Scribes ! — *Sugg. by Reading* 75

Woful A *w* man had thrust his wife and child — *Lover's Tale i* 368

whom *w* ailments Of unavailing tears — " 818

Won whilome *w* the hearts of all on Earth — *Timbuctoo* 17

unshaken peace hath *w* thee : — *Though night* 10

We *w* old battles with our strength, the bow. — *Britons, guard* 44

Wonder and what *w* That when hope died, — *Lover's Tale i* 750

Wonderful it was *w* With its exceeding brightness, — *Timbuctoo* 86

Galaxy Shorn of its hoary lustre, *w*, — " 106

Wondrous Upon the *w* laws which regulate The fierceness — " 147

the *w* tones Of man and beast are full of strange Astonishment — *Chorus* 8

Woo Do *w* each other, carolling together. — *Dualisms* 9

happy air shall *w* The wither'd leaf — *Lover's Tale i* 621

Wood (*See also* **Pinewood, Summerwood**) With harmonies of wind and wave and *w* — *Timbuctoo* 207

Looks through the thickstemmed *w*'s by day and night — *Love* 44

fall'n in the *w*'s, or blasted Upon this bough ? — *Lover's Tale i* 622

Woodbine in and out the *w*'s flowery arches — *Check every outflash* 11

Woody where the Rhene Curves towards Mentz, a *w* scene. — *O darling room* 12

Woo'd As I *w* her for my wife ; — *Germ of 'Maud'* 11

Wooing vital heat as yet my heart is *w* : — *Could I outwear* 12

Word bare *w* KISS hath made my inner soul — *Oh, Beauty* 12

Because the *w*'s of little children — *Cambridge* 12

w's were like a coronal of wild blooms — *Lover's Tale i* 561

Work Be noble, you ! nor *w* with faction's tools — *Sugg. by Reading* 29

Worked He *w* for both : he pray'd for both — *Lover's Tale i* 223

Working On that day, Love *w* shook his wings — " 308

World notes of busy life in distant *w*'s — *Timbuctoo* 113

grovell'd in the slime Of this dull *w*, — " 150

To carry through the *w* those waves, — " 238

The *w* is somewhat ; it goes on somehow ; *The 'How' and the 'Why'* 21

w will not change, and her heart will not break. *I' the glooming light* 22

Basing thy throne above the *w*'s annoy — *Though night* 8

For he is older than the *w*. — *The Hesperides, Song ii* 16

The *w* will be overwise. — " 22

Lest the old wound of the *w* be healèd, — " *iii* 4

The *w* is wasted with fire and sword, — " *iv* 22

Lets the great *w* flit from him, — *D. of F. Women* 10

The *w*'s last tempest darkens overhead ; — *Britons, guard* 2

Although we fought the banded *w* alone, — *Hands all Round* 28

Than vanquish all the *w* in arms. — *Lover's Tale i* 693

Was not the wide *w* free, — " 693

Worldliness with her week-day *w* sufficed, — *Sugg. by Reading* 62

Worm like dusky *w*'s which house Beneath unshaken waters, — *Timbuctoo* 150

Worn *W* Sorrow sits by the moaning wave ; — *I' the glooming light* 4

Smiles on the earth's *w* brow to win her if she may. *Tears of Heaven* 9

Eyes are *w* away Till the end of fears — *Every day, etc.* 19

Worship did pause To *w* mine own image, — *Lover's Tale i* 68

Worshipp'd Where Love was *w* upon every height, — " 323

Where Love was *w* under every tree— — " 324

Worth (adj.) *W* eternal want of rest. *The Hesperides, Song i* 12

Have ye aught that is *w* the knowing ? — *1865-1866* 5

But aught that is *w* the knowing ? — " 9

Worth (s) Lest the old of the world be healèd, *The Hesperides, Song iii* 4

Wound (s) To soothe a civic *w* or keep it raw, — *Sugg. by Reading* 32

Had film'd the margents of the recent *w*. — *Lover's Tale i* 764

Wound (verb) Seraphtrod, *W* thro' your great Elysian solitudes, — *Timbuctoo* 48

Wound (verb) (*continued*)   About her forehead *w* it,   *Anacreontics* 11
Wove   I *w* a crown before her,   *Anacreontics* 5
   summer midges *w* their wanton gambol,   *Check every outflash* 12
   mine *w* chaplets of the self-same flower,   *Lover's Tale* i 333
Woven   So shalt thou pierce the *w* glooms of truth ;   *Though night* 11
Wrapped-wrapt   *Wrapped* round with spiced cerements   *A Fragment* 30
   landing-place is *wrapt* about with clouds   *Timbuctoo* 199
Wreathed   *See* **Darkly-wreathed**
Wreck   The *w* of ruin'd life and shatter'd thought,   *Lover's Tale* ii 62
Write   For ever *w* In the weathered light   *Burial of Love* 20
   Wherein to read, wherein to *w*. (repeat)   *O darling room* 6, 18
   You hide the hand that *w's* :   *Sugg. by Reading* 25
   I sorrow when I read the things you *w*,   ,, 77
Writer   How much I love this *w's* manly style !   ,, 1
   Alas, Church *w's*, altercating tribes—   ,, 73
Written   The *w* secrets of her inmost soul   *Lover's Tale* i 600
Wrong   Lest you go *w* from power in excess.   *Sugg. by Reading* 10
Wronged   From *w* Poerio's noisome den,   *Hands all Round* 15
Wrote   With dandy pathos when you *w*,   *New Timon* 10
Wrought   *See* **Selfwrought**

Y

Year   music flowing from Th' illimitable *y's*.   *Timbuctoo* 219
   Thou hast no compt of *y's*,   *The Grasshopper* 27
   With selfwrought evils of unnumbered *y's*,   *Tears of Heaven* 4
   Call to the fleeting *y*,   *The lintwhite* 5
   Fair *y*, fair *y*, thy children call,   ,, 10
   Fair *y*, with brows of royal love Thou comest,   ,, 19
   That trouble life in early *y's*,   *Rosalind* 14
   And New *Y* and Old *Y* met,   *1865-1866* 2
   I said, ' O *y's* that meet in tears,   ,, 4
   Old *Y* roaring and blowing And New *Y* blowing
     and roaring.   ,, 12
   brain, Now seam'd and clink'd with *y's*—   *Lover's Tale* i 131
   the *y* First felt his youth and strength,   ,, 305
   The slope into the current of my *y's*,   ,, ii 76
Yearning   Men clung with *y* Hope which would not die.   *Timbuctoo* 27
Yeasty   Huge mounds whereby to stay his *y* waves.   ,, 15

Yellow   We will eat the Lotos, sweet As the *y* honeycomb,   *Lotos-Eaters* 15
   Lower down Spreads out a little lake, that, flooding,
     makes Cushions of *y* sand ;   *Lover's Tale* i 537
Yeoman   Now practise, *yeomen*, Like those bowmen,   *Britons, guard* 45
   Yeomen, guard your own.   ,, 48
Yesterday   To-morrow will be *y* ?   *Who can say* 3
Yon   Child of Man, See'st thou *y* river, whose translucent
     wave,   *Timbuctoo* 229
   soon *y* brilliant towers Shall darken with the waving
     of her wand ;   ,, 244
   You may not, like *y* tyrant, deal in spies.   *Sugg. by Reading* 20
Yonder   Through *y* poplar alley Below, the blue-green
     river windeth slowly ;   *Check every outflash* 4
   Warbled from *y* knoll of solemn larches,   ,, 10
You   How *y* are *y* ? Why I am I ?   *The ' How ' and the ' Why '* 19
Young   The bright descent Of a *y* Seraph !   *Timbuctoo* 65
   And watered vallies where the *y* birds sing ;   *Could I outwear* 8
   Y fishes, on an Arpil morn,   *Rosalind* 21
Youth   light Of earliest *y* pierced through and through   *The Mystic* 29
   mailed warrior in *y* and strength complete ;   *The Grasshopper* 13
   But a short *y* sunny and free.   ,, 29
   indue i' the spring Hues of fresh *y*,   *Could I outwear* 3
   So in thine hour of dawn, the body's *y*,   *Though night* 13
   How canst thou let me waste my *y* in sighs ;   *Oh, Beauty* 2
   the dewy prime Of *y* and buried time ?   *Who can say* 7
   Alas, our *y*, so clever yet so small,   *Sugg. by Reading* 79
   the year First felt his *y* and strength,   *Lover's Tale* i 306
   that thought Which was the playmate of my *y*—   ,, ii 72
Youthful   beneath Severe and *y* brows, with shining eyes   *The Mystic* 27
   WHAT time I wasted *y* hours   *What time I wasted* 1
   I fear for you, as for some *y* king,   *Sugg. by Reading* 9
Yronne   In rings of gold *y*,   *The lintwhite* 29

Z

Zamoysky   Than when *Z* smote the Tartar Khan,   *Blow ye the trumpet* 12
Zidonian   *Z* Hanno, voyaging beyond The hoary
     promontory of Soloë   *The Hesperides* 2
Zone   Girt with a *Z* of flashing gold   *Timbuctoo* 72
Zoned   and *z* below with cedarshade,   *The Hesperides* 11

ADDENDA

A

Askew   Then glanced *a* at those three knights of hers,   *Pelleas and E.* 134
'Asta (hast thou)   Wheer '*a* been?   *Prom. of May* I 349
Athurt (athwart)   and doänt laäy my cartwhip *a* 'is
shou'ders,   „   II 138
and wheere the big eshtree cuts *a* it,   „   III 94
Athwart   (*See also* **Athurt**)   mind Lies folded, often
sweeps *a* in storm—   *Lover's Tale* i 50
A pine in Italy that cast its shadow *A* a
cataract;   *Queen Mary* III iv 137
Atwain   cuts *a* The knots that tangle human creeds,   *Clear-headed friend* 2
Atween (between)   Fur *a* 'is reädin' an' writin' 'e snifft up
a box in a däay,   *Village Wife* 40
Aught   The nursery-cocker'd child will jeer at *a*   *Queen Mary* II ii 395
Av (if)   An', afther, I thried her meself *a* the bird 'ud come
to me call,   *Tomorrow* 45
Avore (before)   I'd ha' been here *a*,   *Queen Mary* IV iii 476
Gardiner wur struck down like by the hand o'
God *a* a could taste a mossel,   „   IV iii 517
Awkward   *See* **Hawkard**, p. 305

B

Back (adv.)   nor to round about and *b* to your lordship's
face again,   *The Falcon* 115
Back'd   *See* **Highback'd**, p. 955
Bakkuds (backwards)   But Billy fell *b* o' Charlie,   *Village Wife* 85
Bara   '*B!* ' what use?   *Sir J. Oldcastle* 19
Beänt (am not, are not, is not)   *B* Miss Eva gone off a
bit of 'er good looks o' laäte?   *Prom. of May* I 32
The owd man be heighty to-daäy, *b* he?   „   I 77
I taäked 'im fur soom sort of a land-surveyor—but
a *b*.   „   I 205
I be a gentleman, thaw I *b* naw scholard,   „   I 332
B there house-breäkers down i' Littlechester, Dobson—   „   I 388
So the owd uncle i' Coomberland be deäd, Miss Dora,
b he?   „   II 2
why then I *b* Farmer Dobson, but summun else—
blaäme't if I *b*!   „   II 139
or she *b* Dora Steer.   „   II 605
Dobbins, I think!   *Dobson.*   I *b* Dobbins.   „   II 700
I *b* sa sewer o' that, fur Sally knaw'd 'im;   „   III 146
Bean't (am not, is not)   —and I *b* wrong not twice
i' ten year—   *Queen Mary* IV iii 534
fur him as be handy wi' a book *b* but haäfe a
hand at a pitchfork.   *Prom. of May* I 188
Before   *See* **Afoor, Afore, Avore, 'Fore**
Bellows'd (out of breath)   He wur sa *b* out wi' the
wind this murnin',   *Prom. of May* III 432
Beslings-puddin'   Baäcon an' taätes, an' a *b-p*   *North Cobbler* 112
Bestial   and since his ways are sweet, And theirs
are *b*,   *Com. of Arthur* 181
Between   *See* **Atween**
Blackbird   (p. 846)   *See* **Merle**, p. 1006
Blazon'd   By two sphere lamps *b* like Heaven and Earth   *Princess* i 223
Blossomy   Creeping thro' *b* rushes and bowers of rose-
blowing bushes,   *Leonine Eleg.* 3
Blurly   sallow lights shone Dimly and *b* with simmer-
ing fat.   *Far off in the dun* 100
Boäth (both)   The Lord bless *b* on 'em!   *Prom. of May* I 342
And long life to *b* on 'em.   „   I 346
Fur *b* on 'em knawed as well as mysen   „   III 313
I eddicated *b* on 'em to marry gentlemen,   „   III 455
Bob (to curtsey)   little gells *b*'s to ma hoffens es I be
abroad i' the laänes,   *Spinster's S's.* 107
Born   *See* **Burn**
Both   *See* **Boäth**
Broad-imbased   rib and fret The *b-i* beach,   *Supp. Confessions* 127
Burn (born)   *B* i' traäde.   *Church-warden, etc.* 18
Buss (kiss)   Gi'e us a *b* fust, lass.   *Prom. of May* II 228

C

Caäre (care)   an' I *c*'s nowt neither.   *Prom. of May* I 27
Care   *See* **Caäre**
Casselty (unsettled)   Nasty, *c* weather!   *Church-warden, etc.* 2
Casualty   *See* **Casselty**
'Cep' (except)   'ud ha' done it '*c* it were Dan Smith,   *Prom. of May* I 411
Certain   *See* **Sartan**
Clock   (p. 101)   *See* **O'clock**, p. 506
Coarser   When did a frog *c* croak upon our Helicon?   *Trans. of Homer* 4
Confused   (p. 873)   *See* **Maäted**, p. 995
Coorse (course)   Why, o' *c*, fur it be the owd man's
birthdaäy.   *Prom. of May* I 5
Cum (come)   *See* **A-cum**
Current   (p. 125)   *See also* **Undercurrent**, p. 753
Curtsey   *See* **Bob**
Cycled   sons of flesh Shall gather in the *c* times   *In Mem. lxxxv* 28

D

Dewy   days Of *d* dawning,   *Lover's Tale* i 52
blight Lives in the *d* touch of pity   „   696
Divided   (p. 152)   *See* **Twelve-divided**, p. 751
Doänt (don't)   I *d* believe he's iver a 'eart under his
waistcoat.   *Prom. of May* I 129
I'll not meddle wi' 'im if he *d* meddle wi' meä.   „   I 174
But 'e *d* fish neither.   „   I 214
There mun be summut wrong theer, Wilson, fur I *d*
understan' it.   „   I 234
An' thou *d* understan' it neither—   „   I 238
Beänt there house-breäkers down in Littlechester,
Dobson—*d* ye hear of ony?   „   I 389
and *d* laäy my cartwhip athurt 'is shou'ders,   „   II 137
Why, lass, *d* tha knaw he be sweet upo' Dora Steer,   „   II 160
Dosta (do you)   By-and-by—eh, lad, *d* knaw this
paäper?   „   II 686
Eh, lad, *d* knaw what tha meäns wi' by-and-by?   „   II 690
Downward   And like a *d* smoke, the slender stream   *Lotos-Eaters* 8
some, like a *d* smoke, Slow-dropping veils of thinnest lawn,   „   10
How sweet it were, hearing the *d* stream,   „ *C. S.* 54
Duer   for song Is *d* unto freedom,   *Princess* iv 141
Dully   Far off she seem'd to hear the *d* sound Of human
footsteps fall.   *Palace of Art* 275
Dusk (adj.)   that making slide apart Their *d* wing-
cases,   *Gareth and L.* 687

E

Each   *See* **Aich**
Earned   *See* **Arn'd**
'Edn't (had not)   fur I '*e* naw time to maäke mysen a
scholard   *Prom. of May* I 333
Eighty   *See* **Heighty**
Enew (enough)   (*See also* **Enow**)   Warm *e* theere sewer-ly,   *Owd Roä* 111
Enough   *See* **Anew, Enew, Enow**
Enow (enough)   (*See also* **Enew**)   Tut: he was tame
and meek *e* with me,   *Gareth and L.* 718
' Ay,' thought Gawain, ' and you be fair *e*:   *Pelleas and E.* 388
Enter'd   *See* **Inter'd**
'Ereabouts (hereabouts)   but noän o' the parishes goäs
by that naäme '*e*.   *Prom. of May* I 269
Except   *See* **'Cep'**

N

Near *See* **Anear**
Niced (nice) Thaw thou was es soäber es daäy, wi' a *n* red faäce,   *Spinster's S's.* 75
Night *See* **Anight**
No *N* is trouble and cloud and storm,   *Window, No Answer* 8
Noän (none) wi' *n* to lend 'im a shuvv,   *N. Farmer, N. S.* 31
Nobbut (only) an' I Seeäd *n* the smile o' the sun   *North. Cobbler* 50
None *See* **Noän, Nöne**
Nöne (none) An' I didn't know him meself, an' *n* of the parish knew.   *Tomorrow* 76

O

Offens (often) An' sarvints runn'd in an' out, an' *o* we hed 'em to tea.   *Village Wife* 56
But Moother was free of 'er tongue, as I *o* 'ev tell'd 'er mysen,   *Owd Roä* 73
Often *See* **Hoffen, Offens**
Only *See* **Nobbut**
Onward sharp fancies, by down-lapsing thought Stream'd *o*,   *D. of F. Women* 50
Ourselves *See* **Wersens**
Outright Maim'd me and maul'd, and would *o* have slain,   *Last Tournament* 75
Outward (s) For Thought into the *o* springs,   *Mechanophilus* 11

P

Peak'd (adj.) And *p* wings pointed to the Northern Star.   *Holy Grail* 240

R

Re-frain Or Trade *r-f* the Powers From war with kindly links of gold,   *Epilogue* 15

S

Sanely Of saner worship *s* proud ;   *Freedom* 30
Sartan (certain) 'E reäds of a sewer an' *s* 'oäp o' the tother side ;   *Village Wife* 92

Say (sea) 'Your Danny,' they says, 'niver crasst over *s* to the Sassenach whate ;   *Tomorrow* 48
Scantly And there is *s* time for half the work.   *Marr. of Geraint* 288
Sea *See* **Say**
Set And he sung not alone of an old sun *s*,   *Dead Prophet* 41
Sewer (sure) 'E reäds of a *s* an' sartan 'oäp o' the tother side ;   *Village Wife* 92
Sewer-ly (surely) Warm enew theere *s-l*, but the barn was as cowd as owt,   *Owd Roä* 111
'Siver (howsoever) '*S*, I kep 'um, my lass   *N. Farmer, O. S.* 23
Snifft Fur atween 'is reädin' an' writin' 'e *s* up a box in a daäy,   *Village Wife* 40
Sorra (sorrow ; an expletive) An' *s* the bog that's in Hiven   *Tomorrow* 67
S the dhry eye thin but was wet for the frinds that was gone !   „   83
Sorrow (p. 661) *See* **Sorra**
Spent (p. 669) *See* **Weär'd**, p. 783
Sure *See* **Sewer**
Surely *See* **Sewer-ly**

T

Thereamong Three knights were *t* ; and they too smiled, *Pelleas and E.* 96
Thereat *T* once more he moved about,   *Pass. of Arthur* 462
Therebefore And *t* the lawless warrior paced Unarm'd,   *Gareth and L.* 914
Therebeside and *t*, Half-naked as if caught at once from bed   *Princess iv* 284
And *t* a horn, inflamed the knights At that dishonour done   *Last Tournament* 434
Theretoward set no foot *t* unadvised Of all our Privy Council ;   *Queen Mary* II ii 204
Thereunder From out *t* came an ancient man,   *Gareth and L.* 240
Therewithin a sign That *t* a guest may make True cheer   *Pro. to Gen. Hamley* 15
Through *See* **Thruf**
Thruf (through) Steevie be right good manners bang *t* to the tip o' the taäil.   *Spinster's S's.* 66

W

Wersens (ourselves) an' happt *w* oop as we mowt.   *Owd Roä* 112